CIVIL PROCEDURE

2006

CIVIL PROCEDURE

Volume 2

The Civil Procedure Rules and Practice Directions contained in this
volume are up-to-date to April 1, 2006. For further updates, see
http://www.sweetandmaxwell.co.uk/whitebook/

LONDON

SWEET & MAXWELL

2006

Published in 2006 by Sweet & Maxwell Limited of
100 Avenue Road, London NW3 3PF.
European, International, Practice Directions and Rules reference tables typeset by
Hobbs the Printers Ltd, Totton, Hampshire. All other typesetting by Sweet &
Maxwell electronic publishing system
Printed in England by Bath Press, UK

*No natural forests were destroyed to make this product; only farmed timber was used
and replanted.*

British Library Cataloguing in Publication Data
A catalogue record for this book is available from the British Library

ISBN 0 421 950803
978 0 421 95080 1

©
Sweet & Maxwell Limited
2006

SERVICE INFORMATION

The White Book Service 2006

During 2005 we again undertook a range of research with subscribers in order help steer the development of *The White Book Service*. We received an overwhelming response to a subscriber survey during the summer, and, in October, we held the first White Book focus group. Thank you to all who participated.

The 2006 edition sees several developments which stem from this subscriber input.

We have taken the opportunity to develop the commentary to several Parts, including Parts 3, 6, 34, 54, and RSC Order 115. The development of Volume 2 of the Service continues, with further commentary and materials added to Personal Injury and Proceedings under the Human Rights Act. Residential Tenancies has been renamed Housing and also includes new material. The Procedural Guides in Section D of Volume 1 have been reformatted to allow easier and faster reference and we have taken the opportunity to add in new ones.

We have removed some of the tables from the front of Volume 1, including Practice Directions and the Civil Procedure Rules – but leaving Cases and Statutes – as it was clear that these were taking up space but not being used frequently.

We have responded to requests concerning the automatic inclusion of the Forms Volume in *The White Book Service* (for new subscribers). New subscribers may now order the Forms Volume separately. However, all subscribers will continue to be updated with the latest forms by way of receiving the Forms Release. We do ask that you keep your Forms Volume from one year to the next and update by way of filing the releases supplied (published three times a year).

Of course, you may wish to sign up to receive our Forms email alerter service. An email notice is sent to you when new court forms are published by the Court Service. You can also download forms from our website: **www.sweetandmaxwell.co.uk/whitebook**. You will need to enter the password: **WB2006**.

You may also wish to sign up to receive our email alerter service to notify you of changes to the Civil Procedure Rules as they are introduced by Statutory Instrument and as the changes come into force. This service is also available on **www.sweetandmaxwell.co.uk/whitebook**.

Rapidforms, our electronic forms service powered by Rapidocs introduced in 2005, continues to be developed. This year sees around 100 forms converted, with more being added throughout the year, as well as new functionality.

If you have any comments about *The White Book Service 2006* we would like to hear them. Please write to *The Publishing Editor, The White Book Service, Sweet and Maxwell, 100 Avenue Road, London, NW3*

3PF or email *whitebook@sweetandmaxwell.co.uk*.

Up-to-date to April 1, 2006

Civil Procedure published on April 20, 2006. The Rules and Practice Directions have been updated to include changes introduced by the Civil Procedure (Amendment No. 4) Rules (S.I 2005 No. 3515) and the TSO CPR Update 41, which came into force on April 6, 2006. Amendments announced after April 1 will be published in the updating supplements in July and December. Notes have been included to indicate the in-force date of changes where necessary.

For further updates see **www.sweetandmaxwell.co.uk/whitebook**. You will need to enter your subscriber password: **WB2006**. This site contains the latest Civil Procedure Rules and Practice Directions. Changes which have been introduced since *The White Book* published in April are highlighted in red.

Every effort has been made to ensure that the commentary and case law is as stated at April 1, 2006. *Civil Procedure News* and the two updating supplements will keep you abreast of developments through the subscription year.

Civil Procedure Forms

Your 2006 subscription includes a CD-Rom containing all the forms provided in the Civil Procedure Forms Volume. We have converted many of these forms into Word documents and we have converted around 100 of the most regularly used forms into *Rapidforms*. See the accompanying Quick Reference Card for full details of this new service.

A reminder to register for the Forms Email Alerter Service – go to **www.sweetandmaxwell.co.uk/whitebook** to register to receive an email notice when new court forms are published by the Court Service. You can also download the forms from our website. You will need to enter the password: **WB2006**.

If you were a subscriber to *The White Book Service* in 2005, please remember to retain your *White Book Forms Volume*. This will continue to be updated during the 2006 subscription year. The thirteenth forms release is included with this new edition.

How to use Civil Procedure 2006

As ever, we have endeavoured to ensure that the content of *The White Book* is presented logically. The Civil Procedure Rules are now reproduced in bold type to ensure they are easily distinguished from editorial comment and Practice Directions. History notes have been added to provide a full record of the changes to the Civil Procedure Rules.

Please refer to your User Guide which walks you through the navigational features and various components of *The White Book Service*.

Volume One

The Civil Procedure Rules and Practice Directions (including Schedules 1 and 2 containing those RSC and CCR still in force) are contained in Volume 1 with the following exceptions:

- *CPR on Specialist lists* - CPR Parts 58 - 63 (dealing with the Commercial Court, the Mercantile Courts, the Technology and Construction Court, Admiralty Claims and Arbitrations, and Patents and Other Intellectual Property Claims) are set out in Volume 2, Section 2.

- *CPR Part 49 - Specialist proceedings* - the proceedings dealt with under the Practice Direction to Part 49 (Proceedings under the Companies Acts) are set out in Volume 2, Section 2.

Miscellaneous Practice Directions, Pre-Action Protocols, procedural guides and a guide to time limits are also reproduced in Volume One.

Volume Two

The main elements of Volume Two are the specialist areas of practice and procedure: the specialists lists dealt with by CPR Parts 58 - 63 and the specialist proceedings under CPR Part 49, other specialist proceedings (*e.g.* Housing and Consumer) and procedural legislation.

A quick guide to finding key materials is set out below. See the separate User Guide for further information.

How to find ...

... *CPR Rules and Supplementary Practice Directions (Vol. 1, Section A)*
The Civil Procedure Rules and Practice Directions are contained in Section A, which adopts the following paragraph system.

Part 3, r.1	Para. **3.1**
Commentary to Part 3, r.1	Para. 3.1.**1**, (3.1.**2** etc.)
Practice Direction supplementing Part 3	Para. 3**PD**.1
Second Practice Direction supplementing Part 3	Para. 3**BPD**.1

The paragraph numbers appear at the top outside corner of each page.

... *Rules of the Supreme Court, County Court Rules and Supplementary Practice Directions*
Section A also contains the re-enacted Rules of the Supreme Court and County Court Rules, with all supplementary Practice Directions. The following paragraph system is used:

RSC Order 52, r.1	Para. **sc**52.1
Commentary to RSC Order 52.1	Para. sc52.1.**1** (sc52.1.**2** etc.)
Practice Direction supplementing Order 52	Para. sc**pd**52.1
CCR Order 1, r.6	Para. **cc**1.6
Commentary to CCR Order 1, r.6	Para. cc1.6.**1**

... *Miscellaneous Practice Direction (Vol. 1, Section B)*
Practice Directions which are not supplementary to a rule (*e.g.* the Practice Direction on Insolvency Proceedings) are contained in Section B, which adopts the following paragraph system.

Practice Direction Insolvency Proceedings, etc.	Para. B1-001

... Pre-Action Protocols (Vol. 1, Section C)

The Pre-Action Protocols are contained in Section C, which adopts the following paragraph system:

Practice Direction—Protocols	Para. C0–001
Pre-Action Protocol for Personal Injury Claims	Para. C1-001

... Chancery Guide

The Chancery Guide Appears in Section 1 of Volume 2 and is numbered para. 1-1 onwards.

... Specialist Practice Directions under CPR Parts 58-63 and Specialist Court Guides, Applications under the Companies Act

Specialist Proceedings under CPR Parts 58-63 and Specialist Court Guides, Applications under the Companies Act appear in Section 2 of Volume 2 as follows:

CPR 58	Commercial Court
CPR 59	Mercantile Courts
CPR 60	Technology and Construction Courts
CPR 61	Admiralty Claims
CPR 62	Arbitration Claims
CPR 63	Patents and other Intellectual Property Claims
Practice Direction to CPR 49	Applications Under the Companies Act

... Forms

The forms are located in the Civil Procedure Forms Volume and on the Forms CD.

Service Elements

The White Book Service allows you to choose a customised product to suit your requirements.
Civil Procedure Volumes 1 & 2
Annual subscription includes:
Civil Procedure 2006 Volume 1
Civil Procedure 2006 Volume 2
Civil Procedure Forms Volume (on request to new subscribers)
Civil Procedure Forms Updates
Civil Procedure Forms CD
Two supplements
Civil Procedure News
Internet-based primary law updating
Forms E-mail Alerter Service
Rules E-mail Alerter Service
Subscription price: £349 plus VAT

Civil Procedure 2006 Volume 1
Annual subscription includes:
Civil Procedure 2006 Volume 1
Civil Procedure Forms Volume (on request to new subscribers)
Civil Procedure Forms Updates

Civil Procedure Forms CD
Two supplements
Civil Procedure News
Internet-based primary law updating
Forms E-mail Alerter Service
Rules E-mail Alerter Service
Subscription price: £239 plus VAT

Civil Procedure CD and Print Service
Annual subscription includes:
All materials in Volumes 1 and 2 and the Forms Volume on one CD
(plus 2 replacement CDs throughout the year)
Civil Procedure 2006 Volume 1
Civil Procedure 2006 Volume 2
Civil Procedure Forms Volume (on request to new subscribers)
Civil Procedure Forms Updates
Two paper supplements
Civil Procedure News
Internet-based primary law updating
Forms E-mail Alerter Service
Rules E-mail Alerter Service
Subscription price: £399 plus VAT

Premium Online Service

Please contact our WestlawUK helpdesk for further information on 0800 028 2200.

Customer Services

If you have a query relating to your subscription or you wish to purchase extra copies of Civil Procedure 2006, please call our Customer Services team on:

   UK direct customers: (020) 7449 1111

   UK trade customers: 0845 082 1032

   International customers: +44 1264 342906

Or you can write to:

   Customer Services
   Sweet & Maxwell Limited
   100 Avenue Road
   London
   England NW3 3PF
   DX: 38861 Swiss Cottage
   Website: http://www.sweetandmaxwell.thomson.com

Comments and feedback

We are always pleased to receive comments and suggestions from customers. Address correspondence to: Publishing Editor, The White Book Service, Sweet & Maxwell, 100 Avenue Road, London, NW3 3PF or e-mail to *whitebook@sweetandmaxwell.co.uk*

The White Book Team
March 2006

CONTENTS

CONTENTS

CONTENTS

CIVIL PROCEDURE RULES

SECTION 1

PRACTICE GUIDES

1A CHANCERY GUIDE

Editorial Introduction

Litigants in the Chancery Division and in Chancery District Registries will need to **1A–0** make careful reference to the Chancery Guide. Particular attention is directed in the Guide to administrative matters; separate parts deal with hearings before High Court Judges, Masters and Registrars and the preparation for such hearings, including time limits for filing bundles and skeleton arguments. Careful attention should be paid to the need for accurate time estimates for hearings and the likely costs consequences of inaccurate estimates.

An email protocol which is one of the appendices of the Guide was signed by the Chancellor in April 2005. It permits the filing of skeleton arguments, chronologies and draft orders by email but not authorities.

A new edition of the Guide was published in November 2005. As with previous editions it was issued after detailed consideration the Judges, Masters and Registrars of the Division.

Chancery Guide

October, 2005

Abbreviations used in this Guide: **1A–1**

Civil Procedure Rules	CPR
HM Courts Service	HMCS
Practice Direction supplementing a Civil Procedure Rule	PD
Rules of the Supreme Court 1965	RSC
Pre-trial review	PTR

Part 1 means CPR Part 1

rule 1.1 means CPR Part 1 rule 1.1

PD 52 means the PD supplementing CPR Part 52

The Civil Procedure Rules (comprising Rules, Practice Directions, Pre-Action Protocols and Forms) are published by the Stationery Office. They are also published on the Department of Constitutional Affairs' website: www.dca.gov.uk. This Guide will also be found on the Chancery Division section of the Courts Service website: www.hmcourts-service.gov.uk.

As from October 2005, the effective head of the Chancery Division is the Chancellor of the High Court, formerly the Vice-Chancellor.

Preface

This is the fifth edition of the Chancery Guide. It is published ten years after the publication of the first. The changes made in the conduct of civil proceedings generally and in the Chancery Division in particular in the intervening period have been profound. The substitution of the old Rules of the Supreme Court with the Civil Procedure Rules is now virtually complete and amendments to the first editions of the Civil Procedure Rules are coming through.

As I wrote in the Preface to the fourth edition, the Chancery Guide is no substitute for the Civil Procedure Rules and associated Practice Directions. It seeks to give practical guidance on the conduct of cases in the Chancery Division within the framework of those rules and practice directions.

This edition has been produced under the supervision of Sir Lawrence Collins. I am very grateful to him for undertaking the task. The amount of work involved is considerable. It is additional to the normal workload of a judge of the Chancery Division and, in his case, to the editorial responsibility for Dicey and Morris on the Conflict of Laws. He has been assisted with regard to various topics by many others to whom I send my thanks too. It is always dangerous to mention them by name lest someone is inadvertently omitted; nevertheless I would like to pay particular tribute to: Chief Master Winegarten; Master Bragge; Registrar Derrett; Mrs V C Bell; Mr A D Parkinson; Miss R Warner; Mr J Smethurst; Mr S Adamyk.

The pattern of the last ten years has been for a new edition to appear every two to three years. The proposals for changes to civil litigation now under consideration suggest that this pattern, at least, will continue in the future. In the meantime I hope and believe that this edition will be of considerable use to all those who, in whatever capacity, have occasion to participate in litigation in the Chancery Division.

Andrew Morritt
Chancellor of the High Court
October 2005

CHAPTER 1

INTRODUCTORY

The overriding objective

1A–2 1.1 The aim of the Civil Procedure Rules and the Practice Directions which supplement them is to remove excessive delay and expense, and to improve access to justice through quicker, cheaper and more proportionate justice. As an integral part of the process, cases are closely monitored through to trial by the judiciary.

1.2 To achieve these aims, all procedural decisions under the CPR are guided by the overriding objective stated in rule 1.1. The court must deal with cases justly; dealing justly with a case includes, so far as practicable, ensuring that the parties are on an equal footing, saving expense, dealing with the case in ways which are proportionate to the sum at stake, to the importance of the case, to its complexity and to each party's financial position, ensuring expedition and fairness and allotting to each case an appropriate share of the court's resources.

About the Chancery Division

1A–3 1.3 The Chancery Division is one of the three parts, or Divisions, of the High Court of Justice, the other two being the Queen's Bench Division and the Family Division. The effective head of the Chancery Division is the Chancellor of the High Court ("the Chancellor"). There are currently seventeen High Court judges attached to the Division. In addition, in the Royal Courts of Justice in London, there are six judges who are referred to as Masters (one of whom is the Chief Master), and six judges who are referred to as Bankruptcy Registrars (one of whom is the Chief Registrar). In the District Registries (see Chapter 12) the work done by Masters in London is performed by District Judges. References in this Guide to a Master include, in the case of proceedings in a District Registry, references to a District Judge. Deputies sit on a regular basis for both judges and Masters. Any reference to a judge or Master in the Guide includes a reference to a person sitting as a deputy.

1.4 In general, trials of claims are heard by the judges, as are interim applications involving injunctions (including applications for freezing and search orders), while the majority of other work, including most procedural work and most post-trial work (eg accounts and inquiries) is conducted by the Masters. Masters may, however, direct that a matter be listed before a judge although they have jurisdiction, for example in the case of lengthy inquiries as to damages (see paragraphs 3.2 and 9.20 below).

1.5 The Chancery Division undertakes civil work of many kinds, including specialist work such as companies, patents and contentious probate. The range of cases heard in the Chancery Division is wide and varied. The major part of the case-load today involves business disputes of one kind or another. Often these are complex and involve substantial sums of money.

1.6 In many types of case (e.g. claims for professional negligence against solicitors, accountants, valuers or other professionals) the claimant has a choice whether to bring the claim in the Chancery Division or elsewhere in the High Court. But there are other types of case which, in the High Court, must be brought in the Chancery Division including claims (other than claims in the Commercial Court) relating to the application of Articles 81 and 82 of the EC Treaty and the equivalent provisions in the Competition Act 1998. The specialist work of the Chancery Division is dealt with in Section B of this Guide. There are also certain claims which must be started in the

Chancery Division either in the High Court or in a District Registry where there is a Chancery District Registry or in the Central London Trial Centre (Chancery List).

About this Guide

1.7 The aim of this Guide is to provide additional practical information not already **1A–4** contained in the CPR or the Practice Directions supplementing them. Litigants and their advisers are expected to be familiar with the CPR. It is not the function of this Guide to summarise the CPR, nor should it be regarded as a substitute for them.

1.8 This Guide is published as part of a series of Guides to various civil courts. Where information is more readily available in another guide, this Guide may simply refer to it. A separate book contains Practice Forms for use in the Chancery Division and in the Queen's Bench Division. Some of the forms most commonly used in the Chancery Division are found in the Appendices to this Guide. Forms may also be downloaded from the HMCS website and may be found in the main procedural reference books.

1.9 Section A of this Guide is concerned with general civil work. Section B deals with specialist work. Some subjects are covered in more detail in the Appendices, and Appendix 1 sets out some contact details which may be useful.

1.10 Material which used to be contained in the Chancery Division Practice Directions and which remains relevant has been incorporated into either Section A or Section B of this Guide, as appropriate.

1.11 A reference in this Guide to a Part is to that Part of the CPR, to a rule is to the relevant rule in the CPR, unless otherwise stated, and to PD [number] is to the PD supplementing the Part so numbered, the title being given if necessary to distinguish one from another. The PD about costs, supplementing Parts 43 to 48, is called the Costs PD.

1.12 This Guide states the position as at September 2005. During the currency of the Guide, and even in some cases before publication, there are likely to be changes in matters covered in the text, including room numbers and other contact details; these should be checked as necessary. The Guide will be kept under review in the light of practical experience and of changes to the rules and practice directions. Any comments on the text of the Guide are welcome and should be addressed to the clerk to the Chancellor.

1.13 The text of the Guide is also to be found, together with other Court Guides and other useful information concerning the administration of justice in the Chancery Division and elsewhere, on the HMCS website. Amendments will appear on the Guide on the website as appropriate: *www.hmcourtsservice.gov.uk*. The Guide is also printed in the main procedural reference books.

SECTION A GENERAL CIVIL WORK

CHAPTER 2

STARTING PROCEEDINGS, SERVICE, ALLOCATION AND STATEMENTS OF CASE
Key Rules: CPR Parts 6, 7, 8, 9, 10, 15, 16, 18, 20 and 26 and CPR Schedule 1

How to start a claim

2.1 Claims are issued out of the High Court of Justice, Chancery Division, either in **1A–5** the Royal Courts of Justice (Chancery Chambers) or in a District Registry. There is no Production Centre for Chancery claims.

2.2 The claim form must be issued either as a Part 7 claim under Part 7, or as a Part 8 claim under the alternative procedure for claims in Part 8.

2.3 When issuing proceedings, the general rule is that the title of the claim should contain only the names of the parties to the proceedings. To this there are four exceptions: (a) proceedings relating to the administration of an estate, which should be entitled "In the estate of AB deceased" (some cases relating to the estates of deceased Lloyd's names require additional wording: see paragraph 26.53 below); (b) contentious probate proceedings, which should be entitled "In the estate of AB deceased (probate)"; (c) proceedings under the Inheritance (Provision for Family and Dependants) Act 1975, which should be entitled "In the Matter of the Inheritance (Provision for Family and Dependants) Act 1975"; and (d) proceedings relating to pension schemes, which may be entitled "In the Matter of the [] Pension Scheme". In addition, proceedings in the Companies Court are entitled in the matter of the relevant company or other person and of the relevant legislation: see paragraph 20.5.

Service

1A–6 2.4 Part 6 applies to the service of documents, including claim forms. Unless the claimant notifies the court that he or she wishes to serve the claim form, or the court directs otherwise, it will be served by the court. Many solicitors, however, will prefer to serve the claim form themselves and will notify the court that they wish to do so.

Allocation

1A–7 2.5 The vast majority of claims issued, and all those retained, in the Chancery Division will be either expressly allocated to the multi-track or in the case of Part 8 claims, deemed allocated to that track. Chapter 13 deals with transfer to county courts.

Statements of case

1A–8 2.6 In addition to the matters which PD 16 requires to be set out specifically in the particulars of claim, a party must set out in any statement of case:

> (1) full particulars of any allegation of fraud, dishonesty, malice or illegality;
>
> (2) where any inference of fraud or dishonesty is alleged, the facts on the basis of which the inference is alleged.

2.7 A party should not set out allegations of fraud or dishonesty unless there is material admissible in evidence to support the contentions made. Setting out such matters without such material being available may result in the particular allegations being struck out and may result in wasted costs orders being made against the legal advisers responsible.

2.8 Points of law may be set out in any statement of case, and any point to be taken under the Human Rights Act 1998 must be so set out.

2.9 In the preparation of statements of case, the guidelines in Appendix 2 should be followed.

2.10 The guidelines apply to: the claim form (unless no particulars are given in it); particulars of claim; defence; Part 20 claim; reply to a defence; and a response to a request for further information under Part 18.

2.11 Parties should not attach copies of documents or any expert's report to their statement of case if they are bulky.

2.12 Notwithstanding rule 15.8, claimants should if possible serve any reply before they file their allocation questionnaire. This will enable other parties to consider the reply before they file their allocation questionnaire.

Part 8 claims

1A–9 2.13 This procedure is appropriate in particular where there is no substantial dispute of fact, such as where the case raises only questions of the construction of a document or a statute. Additionally, however, a large number of particular claims must be brought under Part 8 pursuant to PD 8. Of particular relevance will be applications to enforce charging orders by sale, contested applications with respect to funds in court, contentious probate claims and proceedings relating to solicitors. Subject to jurisdiction, applications to enforce charging orders are now issued in the court in which the charging order was made. Proceedings to enforce charging orders made in any division of the High Court and the Court of Appeal are issued in the Chancery Division.

2.14 Provision is also made in Part 8 for a claim form to be issued without naming a defendant with the permission of the court. No separate application for permission is required where personal representatives seek permission to distribute the estate of a deceased Lloyd's name nor for applications under section 48 of the Administration of Justice Act 1985 (see further Chapter 26 - Trusts). Where permission is needed, it is to be sought by application notice under Part 23.

2.15 Part 8 claims will generally be disposed of on written evidence. The features of the Part 8 procedure are:

    (1) no particulars of claim

    (2) no defence

    (3) no allocation questionnaire

    (4) no judgment in default

    (5) normally no oral evidence.

2.16 Defendants who wish to contest a Part 8 claim or to take part in the proceedings should complete and file the acknowledgment of service in form N210 which accompanies the claim form. Alternatively the information required to be contained in the acknowledgment of service can be provided by letter. A party who does not wish to contest a claim should indicate that fact on the form acknowledging service or by letter.

2.17 Claimants must file the written evidence, namely evidence by witness statement, on which they intend to rely with the claim form. Defendants are required to file and serve their evidence when they file their acknowledgment of service, namely within 14 days after service of the claim form (rule 8.5(3)). By paragraph 5.6 of PD 8, Alternative Procedure for Claims, a defendant's time for filing evidence may be extended by agreement for not more than 14 days from the filing of the acknowledgment of service. Any such agreement must be filed with the court by the defendant at the same time as he or she files an acknowledgment of service. The claimant has 14 days for filing evidence in reply but this period may be extended by agreement for not more than 28 days from service of the defendant's evidence. Again, any such agreement must be filed with the court. Any longer extension either for the defendant or the claimant requires an application to the court. It is recognised that in substantial matters the provisions in Part 8 may be burdensome upon defendants and in such matters the court will readily grant an extension. If the parties are in agreement that such an extension should be granted the application should be made in writing by letter. The parties should at all times act cooperatively.

2.18 Defendants who acknowledge service but do not intend to file evidence should notify the court in writing when they file their acknowledgment of service that they do not intend to file evidence. This enables the court to know what each defendant's intention is when it considers the file.

2.19 The general rule (exceptions include, for example, some claims under the Variation of Trusts Act 1958 or where a party has made a Part 24 application) is that the court file will be considered by the court after the time for acknowledgment of service has expired, or, if the time for serving the defendant's evidence has been extended, after the expiry of that period.

2.20 In some cases if the papers are in order the court will not require any oral hearing, but will be able to deal with the matter on paper by making a final order. In other cases the court will direct that the Part 8 claim is listed either for a disposal hearing or for a case management conference.

CHAPTER 3

THE COURT'S CASE MANAGEMENT POWERS
Key Rules: CPR rule 1.4, and Parts 3, 18, 19, 26, 29, 31, 39

1A-10 3.1 A key feature of the CPR is that cases are closely monitored by the court. Case management by the court includes: identifying disputed issues at an early stage; fixing timetables; dealing with as many aspects of the case as possible on the same occasion; controlling costs; disposing of cases summarily where they disclose no case or defence; dealing with the case without the parties having to attend court; and giving directions to ensure that the trial of a case proceeds quickly and efficiently. The court will expect the parties to co-operate with each other. Where appropriate the court will encourage the parties to use alternative dispute resolution (on which see Chapter 17) or otherwise help them settle the case. In particular, the court will readily grant a short stay at allocation or at any other stage to accommodate mediation or any other form of settlement negotiations. The court will not, however, normally, grant an open-ended stay for such purposes and if, for any reason, a lengthy stay is granted it will be on terms that the parties report to the court on a regular basis in respect of their negotiations.

3.2 In the Chancery Division case management is normally carried out by the Masters, but a judge may be nominated by the Chancellor to hear the case and to deal with the case management where it is appropriate due to the size or complexity of the case or for other reasons. A request by any or all parties for such a nomination should be addressed to the Chancellor.

Directions

1A-11 3.3 It is expected that parties and their advisers will endeavour to agree proposals for management of the case at the allocation stage in accordance with rule 29.4 and paragraphs 4.6 to 4.8 of PD 29. In particular, the parties should act co-operatively and seek to agree directions and a list of the issues to be tried. The court will approve the parties' proposals, if they are suitable, and give directions accordingly without a hearing. If it does not approve the agreed directions it may give modified directions or its own directions or, more usually, direct a case management conference. If the parties cannot agree directions then each party should put forward its own proposals for the future management of the case for consideration by the court. Draft orders commonly made by the Masters on allocation and at case management conferences are set out at Appendix 3, and parties drafting proposed directions for submission to a Master on allocation or at a case management conference should have regard to and make use, as appropriate, of those draft orders.

3.4 If parties do not, at the allocation stage, agree or attempt to agree directions and if, in consequence, the court is unable to give directions without ordering a case management conference, the parties should not expect to recover any costs in respect of such a case management conference.

3.5 In many claims the court will give directions without holding a case management conference.

3.6 Any party who considers that a case management conference should be held before any directions are given should so state in his or her allocation questionnaire (or, in the case of a Part 8 claim, inform the court in writing) and give reasons why he or she considers that a case management conference is required. The court when sending out allocation questionnaires will also send out a questionnaire inviting the parties to give their time estimate for any case management conference and to specify any dates or times inconvenient for the holding of a case management conference.

3.7 Wherever possible, the advocate(s) instructed or expected to be instructed to appear at the trial should attend any hearing at which case management directions are likely to be given. To this end the court when ordering a case management conference, otherwise than upon allocation, will normally send out questionnaires to the parties in respect of their availability. Parties must not, however, expect that a case management conference will be held in abeyance for a substantial length of time in order to accommodate the advocates' convenience.

3.8 Case management conferences are intended to deal with the general management of the case. They are not an opportunity to make controversial interim applications without appropriate notice to the opposing party. Accordingly, as provided by paragraph 5.8(1) of PD 29, where a party wishes to obtain an order not routinely made at a case management conference (such as an order for specific disclosure or summary disposal) such application should be made by separate Part 23 application to be heard at the case management conference and the case management conference should be listed for a sufficient period of time to allow the application to be heard. Where parties fail to comply with this paragraph it is highly unlikely that the court will entertain, other than by consent, an application which is not of a routine nature. It is the obligation of the parties to ensure that a realistic time estimate for hearings is given to the court.

3.9 Even where routine orders are sought (i.e. orders falling within the topics set out in paragraph 5.3 of PD 29) care should be taken to ensure that the opposing party is given notice of the orders intended to be sought.

Applications for information and disclosure

3.10 Before a party applies to the court for an order that another party provides him **1A–12** or her with any further information or specific disclosure of documents he or she must communicate directly with the other party in an attempt to reach agreement or narrow the issues before the matter is raised with the court. If not satisfied that the parties have taken steps to reach agreement or narrow the issues, the court will normally require such steps to be taken before hearing the application.

Preliminary issues

3.11 Costs can sometimes be saved by identifying decisive issues, or potentially **1A–13** decisive issues, and ordering that they are tried first. The decision of one issue, although not itself decisive in law of the whole case, may enable the parties to settle the remainder of the dispute. In such cases a preliminary issue may be appropriate.

3.12 At the allocation stage, at any case management conference and again at any PTR, consideration will be given to the possibility of the trial of preliminary issues the resolution of which is likely to shorten proceedings. The court may suggest the trial of a preliminary issue, but it will rarely make an order without the concurrence of at least one of the parties.

Group Litigation Orders

3.13 Under rule 19.11, where there are likely to be a number of claims giving rise to **1A–14** common or related issues of fact, the court may make a Group Litigation Order ("GLO") for their case management. Such orders may be appropriate in chancery proceedings and there are a number in existence. A list of GLOs is published on the HMCS website. An application for a GLO is made under Part 23. The procedure is set out in PD 19 Group Litigation, which provides that the application should be made to the Chief Master, except for claims in a specialist list (such as the business of the Patents Court), when the application should be made to the senior judge of that list.

3.14 Claimants wishing to join in group litigation should issue proceedings in the normal way and should then apply (by letter) to be entered on the Group Register set up by a GLO. The details required for entry will be specified in the GLO. In the Chancery Division the Register is usually kept by the management court and is maintained either by the court or by the lead solicitors, as specified in the GLO. Where the Register is kept in the Chancery Division at the Royal Courts of Justice, it is kept by Mrs VC Bell, Chancery Lawyer (Room TM5.06, tel. 020 7947 6080). Any initial enquiries regarding GLOs may be addressed to her.

Trial timetable

3.15 The judge at trial, or sometimes at the PTR, may determine the timetable for **1A–15** the trial. The advocates for the parties should be ready to assist the court in this respect if so required. The time estimate given for the trial should have been based on an approximate forecast of the trial timetable, and must be reviewed by each party at the stage of the PTR and as preparation for trial proceeds thereafter. If that review requires a change in the estimate the other parties' advocates and the court must be informed.

3.16 When a trial timetable is set by the court, it will ordinarily fix the time for the oral submissions and factual and expert evidence, and it may do so in greater or lesser detail. Trial timetables are always subject to any further order by the trial judge.

Pre-Trial Review

1A–16 3.17 In cases estimated to take more than 10 days and in other cases where the circumstances warrant it, the court may direct that a PTR be held (see rule 29.7).

3.18 Such a PTR will normally be heard by a judge. The date and time should be fixed with the Chancery Judges' Listing Officer. If the trial judge has already been nominated, the application will if possible be heard by that judge. The advocates' clerks must attend the Chancery Judges' Listing Officer in sufficient time so that the PTR can be fixed between four and eight weeks before the trial date.

3.19 A PTR should be attended by advocates who are to represent the parties at the trial.

3.20 Not less than 7 days before the date fixed for the PTR the claimant, or another party if so directed by the court, must circulate a list of matters to be considered at the PTR, including proposals as to how the case should be tried, to the other parties, who must respond with their comments at least 2 days before the PTR.

3.21 The claimant, or another party if so directed by the court, should deliver a bundle containing the lists of matters to be considered and proposals served by the parties on each other and the trial timetable, together with the results of the discussions between the parties as to those matters, and any other documents the court is likely to need in order to deal with the PTR, to the Chancery Judges' Listing Office by 10am on the day before the day fixed for the hearing of the PTR.

3.22 At the PTR the court will review the state of preparation of the case, and deal with outstanding procedural matters, not limited to those apparent from the lists of matters lodged by the parties. The court may give directions as to how the case is to be tried, including directions as to the order in which witnesses are to be called (for example all witnesses of fact before all expert witnesses) or as to the time to be allowed for particular stages in the trial.

CHAPTER 4
DISCLOSURE OF DOCUMENTS AND EXPERT EVIDENCE
Key Rules: CPR Parts 18, 29, 31 and 35; PDs supplementing Parts 31 and 35

1A–17 4.1 As part of its management of a case, the court will give directions about the disclosure of documents and any expert evidence. Attention is drawn to paragraphs 3.8 to 3.10 above. An application for specific disclosure should be made by a specific Part 3 application and is not to be regarded as a matter routinely dealt with at a case management conference.

Disclosure of Documents

1A–18 4.2 Under the CPR, the normal order for disclosure is an order for standard disclosure, which requires disclosure of:

(1) *a party's own documents* - that is, the documents on which a party relies;

(2) *adverse documents* - that is, documents which adversely affect his or her own or another party's case or support another party's case; and

(3) *required documents* - that is, documents which a practice direction requires him or her to disclose.

4.3 The court may make an order for specific disclosure going beyond the limits of standard disclosure if it is satisfied that standard disclosure is inadequate.

4.4 The court will not make such an order readily. One of the clear principles underlying the CPR is that the burden and cost of disclosure should be reduced. The court will, therefore, seek to ensure that any specific disclosure ordered is proportionate in the sense that the cost of such disclosure does not outweigh the benefits to be obtained from such disclosure. The court will, accordingly, seek to tailor the order for disclosure to the requirements of the particular case. The financial position of the parties, the importance of the case and the complexity of the issues will be taken into account when considering whether more than standard disclosure should be ordered.

4.5 If specific disclosure is sought, the parties should give careful thought to the ways in which such disclosure can be limited, for example by requiring disclosure in stages or by requiring disclosure simply of sufficient documents to show a specified matter and so on. They should also consider whether the need for disclosure could be avoided by requiring a party to provide information under Part 18.

Expert Evidence

General

4.6 Part 35 contains particular provisions designed to limit the amount of expert **1A–19** evidence to be placed before the court and to reinforce the obligation of impartiality which is imposed upon an expert witness. The key question now in relation to expert evidence is the question as to what added value such evidence will provide to the court in its determination of a given case.

4.7 Fundamentally, Part 35 states that expert evidence must be restricted to what is reasonably required to resolve the proceedings and makes provision for the court to direct that expert evidence is given by a single joint expert. The parties should consider from the outset of the proceedings whether appointment of a single joint expert is appropriate.

Duties of an expert

4.8 It is the duty of an expert to help the court on the matters within his or her **1A–20** expertise; this duty overrides any obligation to the person from whom the expert has received instructions or by whom he or she is paid (rule 35.3). Attention is drawn to PD 35.

4.9 In fulfilment of this duty, an expert must for instance make it clear if a particular question or issue falls outside his or her expertise or he or she considers that insufficient data are available on which to express an opinion. Any material change of view by an expert should be communicated in writing (through legal representatives) to the other parties without delay, and when appropriate to the court.

Single joint expert

4.10 The introduction to PD 35 states that, where possible, matters requiring expert **1A–21** evidence should be dealt with by a single expert.

4.11 In very many cases it is possible for the question of expert evidence to be dealt with by a single expert. Single experts are, for example, often appropriate to deal with questions of quantum in cases where the primary issues are as to liability. Likewise, where expert evidence is required in order to acquaint the court with matters of expert fact, as opposed to opinion, a single expert will usually be appropriate. There remains, however, a substantial body of cases where liability will turn upon expert opinion evidence or where quantum is a primary issue and where it will be appropriate for the parties to instruct their own experts. For example, in cases where the issue for determination is as to whether a party acted in accordance with proper professional standards, it will often be of value to the court to hear the opinions of more than one expert as to the proper standard in order that the court becomes acquainted with the range of views existing upon the question and in order that the evidence can be tested in cross-examination.

4.12 It is not necessarily a sufficient objection to the making by the court of an order for a single joint expert that the parties have already appointed their own experts.

An order for a single joint expert does not prevent a party from having his or her own expert to advise him or her, but he or she may well be unable to recover the cost of employing his or her own expert from the other party. The duty of an expert who is called to give evidence is to help the court.

4.13 When the use of a single joint expert is contemplated the court will expect the parties to co-operate in developing, and agreeing to the greatest possible extent, terms of reference for the expert. In most cases the terms of reference will (in particular) detail what the expert is asked to do, identify any documentary material he or she is asked to consider and specify any assumptions he or she is asked to make.

More than one expert - exchange of reports

1A-22 4.14 In an appropriate case the court will direct that experts' reports are delivered sequentially. Sequential reports may, for example, be appropriate if the service of the first expert's report would help to define and limit the issues on which such evidence may be relevant.

Discussion between experts

1A-23 4.15 The court will normally direct discussion between experts before trial. Sometimes it may be useful for there to be further discussions during the trial itself. The purpose of these discussions is to give the experts the opportunity:

> (1) to discuss the expert issues; and
>
> (2) to identify the expert issues on which they share the same opinion and those on which there remains a difference of opinion between them (and what that difference is).

4.16 Unless the court otherwise directs, the procedure to be adopted at these discussions is a matter for the experts. It may be sufficient if the discussion takes place by telephone.

4.17 Parties must not seek to restrict their expert's participation in any discussion directed by the court, but they are not bound by any agreement on any issue reached by their expert unless they expressly so agree.

Written questions to experts

1A-24 4.18 It is emphasised that this procedure is only for the purpose (generally) of seeking clarification of an expert's report where the other party is unable to understand it. Written questions going beyond this can only be put with the agreement of the parties or with the permission of the court. The procedure of putting written questions to experts is not intended to interfere with the procedure for an exchange of professional opinion in discussions between experts or to inhibit that exchange of professional opinion. If questions that are oppressive in number or content are put or questions are put without permission for any purpose other than clarification of an expert's report, the court will not hesitate to disallow the questions and to make an appropriate order for costs against the party putting them.

Request by an expert to the court for directions

1A-25 4.19 An expert may file with the court a written request for directions to assist him or her in carrying out his or her function as expert: rule 35.14. Copies of any such request must be provided to the parties in accordance with rule 35.14(2) save where the court orders otherwise. The expert should guard against accidentally informing the court about, or about matters connected with, communications or potential communications between the parties that are without prejudice or privileged. The expert may properly be privy to the content of these communications because he or she has been asked to assist the party instructing him or her to evaluate them.

Assessors

1A-26 4.20 Under rule 35.15 the court may appoint an assessor to assist it in relation to any matter in which the assessor has skill and experience. The report of the assessor is made available to the parties. The remuneration of the assessor is determined by the court and forms part of the costs of the proceedings.

CHAPTER 5

APPLICATIONS

Key Rules: CPR Parts 23 and 25, PDs 23 and 25

5.1 This Chapter deals with applications to a judge, including applications for interim remedies, and applications to a Master. As regards the practical arrangements for making, listing and adjourning applications, the Chapter is primarily concerned with hearings at the Royal Courts of Justice. Hearings before Chancery judges outside London are dealt with in Chapter 12. **1A–27**

5.2 It is most important that applications which need to be heard by a judge (e.g. most applications for an injunction) should be made to a judge. Any procedural application (e.g. for directions) should be made to a Master unless there is some special reason for making it to a judge. Otherwise the application may be dismissed with costs. If an application is to be made to a judge, the application notice should state that it is a judge's application.

5.3 Part 23 contains rules as to how an application may be made. In some circumstances it may be dealt with without a hearing, or by a telephone hearing.

Applications without notice

5.4 Generally it is wrong to make an application without giving prior notice to the respondent. There are, however, two classes of exceptions. **1A–28**

(1) First, there are cases where the giving of notice might frustrate the order (e.g. a search order) or where there is such urgency that there has not been time to give notice. Even in an urgent case, however, the applicant should notify the respondent informally of the application if possible, unless secrecy is essential.

(2) Secondly, there are in the Chancery Division some procedural applications normally made without notice relating to such matters as service out of the jurisdiction, service, extension of the validity of claim forms, permission to issue writs of possession etc. All of these are properly made without notice but will be subjected by the rules to an express provision in any order made that the absent party will be entitled to apply to set aside or vary the order provided that application is so made within a given number of days of service of the order.

(3) Thirdly, there are cases in which the defendant can only be identified by description and not by name: *Bloomsbury Publishing Group Ltd v News Group Newspapers Ltd* [2003] EWHC 1205 (Ch), [2003] 3 All ER 736. An application made without giving notice which does not fall within the classes of cases where absence of notice is justified may be dismissed or adjourned until proper notice has been given.

Applications without a hearing

5.5 Part 23 makes provision for applications to be dealt with without a hearing. This is a useful provision in cases where the parties consent to the terms of the order sought or agree that a hearing is not necessary (often putting in written representations by letter or otherwise). It is also a useful provision in cases where, although the parties have not agreed to dispense with a hearing and the order is not consented to, the order sought by the application is, essentially, non-contentious. In such circumstances, the order made will, in any event, be treated as being made on the court's own initiative and will set out the right of any party affected by the application who has not been heard to apply to vary or set aside the order. **1A–29**

5.6 These provisions should not be used to deal with contentious matters without notice to the opposing party and without a hearing. Usually, this will result in delay since the court will simply order a hearing. It may also give rise to adverse costs orders. It will normally be wrong to seek an order which imposes sanctions in the event of non-compliance without notice and without a hearing. An application seeking such an order may well be dismissed.

Applications to a judge

1A–30   5.7 If an application is made to a judge in existing proceedings, e.g. for an injunction, it should be made by application notice. This is called an Interim Application. Normally three clear days' notice to the other party is required but in an emergency or for other good reason the application can be made without giving notice, or the full 3 days' notice, to the other side. Permission to serve on short notice may be obtained on application without notice to the Interim Applications judge. Such permission will not be given by the Master. Except in an emergency a party notifies the court of his or her wish to bring an application by delivering the requisite documents to the Chancery Judges' Listing Office (Room WG4) and paying the appropriate fee. He or she should at the same time deliver a completed "Judge's Application Information Form" in the form set out in Part 1 of Appendix 4. An application will only be listed if (1) two copies of the claim form and (2) two copies of the application notice (one stamped with the appropriate fee) are lodged in the Chancery Judges' Listing Office before 12 noon on the working day before the date for which notice of the application has been given.

5.8 The current practice is that one judge combines the functions of Interim Applications judge and Companies judge. His or her name will be found in the Daily Cause List and also in the Chancery Division Term List.

5.9 The Interim Applications judge is available to hear applications each day in term and an application notice can be served for any day in term except the last. If the volume of applications requires it, any other judge who is available to assist with Interim Applications will hear such applications as the Interim Applications judge may direct. Special arrangements are made for hearing applications out of hours and in vacation, for which see paragraphs 5.28 to 5.34 below.

5.10 At the beginning of each day's hearing the Interim Applications judge calls on each of the applications to be made that day in turn. This enables him or her to establish the identity of the parties, their state of readiness, their estimates of the duration of the hearing, and where relevant the degree of urgency of the case. On completion of this process, the judge decides the order in which he or she will hear applications and gives any other directions that may be necessary. Sometimes cases are released to other judges at this point. If cases are likely to take 2 hours or more (including pre-reading and oral delivery of judgment), the judge may order that they are given a subsequent fixed date for hearing (they are then called "Interim Applications by Order") and hears any application for a court order to last until the application is heard fully. Where on or before the day preceding the hearing it becomes likely that the time required for the application (including pre-reading and oral delivery of judgment) will exceed 2 hours, the Chancery Judges' Listing Officer (or, in appropriate cases, the clerk to the Applications Judge) must be notified immediately.

5.11 In such a case the solicitors or the clerks to counsel concerned should apply to the Chancery Judges' Listing Officer for a date for the hearing. Before so doing there must be lodged with the Chancery Judges' Listing Office a certificate signed by the advocate stating the estimated length of the hearing. Applications by order may be entered in the Interim Hearings List and, if not fixed by arrangement with the Chancery Judges' Listing Officer, will be liable to be listed for hearing in accordance with the timetable fixed by the judge.

5.12 Parties and their representatives should arrive at least ten minutes before the court sits. This will assist the usher to take a note of the names of those proposing to address the court and of their estimate of the hearing time. This information is given to the judge before he or she sits. Parties should also allow time before the court sits to agree any form of order with any other party if this has not already been done. If the form of the order is not agreed before the court sits, the parties may have to wait until there is a convenient break in the list before they can ask the court to make any agreed order. If an application, not being an Interim Application by Order, is adjourned the Associate in attendance will notify the Chancery Judges' Listing Office of the date to which it has been adjourned so that it may be relisted for the new date.

Agreed Adjournment of Interim Applications

5.13 If all parties to an Interim Application agree, it can be adjourned for not more than 14 days by counsel or solicitors attending the Chancery Judges' Listing Officer in Room WG4 at any time before 4pm on the day before the hearing of the application and producing consents signed by solicitors or counsel for all parties agreeing to the adjournment. A litigant in person must attend before the Chancery Judges' Listing Officer as well as signing a consent. This procedure may not be used for more than three successive adjournments and no adjournment may be made by this procedure to the last two days of any sitting. **1A–31**

Interim Applications by Order by agreement

5.14 This procedure should also be used where the parties agree that the application will take two hours or more and that, in consequence, the application should be adjourned to be heard as an Interim Application by Order. In that event, the consents set out above should also contain an agreed timetable for the filing of evidence or confirmation that no further evidence is to be filed. Any application arising from the failure of a party to abide by the timetable and any application to extend the timetable must be made to the judge. Interim Applications by Order will, initially at least, enter the Interim Hearings warned list on the first Monday after close of evidence. **1A–32**

5.15 Undertakings given to the court may be continued unchanged over any adjournment. If, however, on an adjournment an undertaking is to be varied or a new undertaking given then that must be dealt with by the court.

The duty of disclosure

5.16 On all applications made in the absence of the respondent the applicant and his or her legal representatives owe a duty to the court to disclose fully all matters relevant to the application, including matters, whether of fact or law, which are, or may be, adverse to it. If there is a failure to comply with this duty and an order is made, the court may subsequently set aside the order on that ground alone. The disclosure, if made orally, must be confirmed by witness statement or affidavit. The representatives for the applicant must specifically direct the court to passages in the evidence which disclose matters adverse to the application. **1A–33**

5.17 A party wishing to apply urgently to a judge for remedies without notice to the Respondent must notify the clerk to the Interim Applications judge by telephone (the number will be set out in the Daily Cause List). Where such an urgent application is made, two copies of the order sought and an electronic copy on disk (in Word for Windows) and a completed judge's Application Information Form in the form in Part 1 of Appendix 4 should, where possible, be included with the papers handed to the judge's clerk. Where an application is very urgent and the Interim Applications judge is unable to hear it promptly, it may be heard by any judge who is available, though the request for this must be made to the clerk to the Interim Applications judge, or, in default, to the Chancery Judges' Listing Officer. Every effort should be made to issue the claim form before the application is made. If this is not practicable, the party making the application must give an undertaking to the court to issue the claim form forthwith even if the court makes no order, unless the court orders otherwise. A party making an urgent application must ensure that all necessary fees are paid.

Freezing Injunctions and Search Orders

5.18 The grant of freezing injunctions (both domestic and world-wide) and search orders is a staple feature of the work of the Interim Applications judge. Applications for such orders are invariably made without notice in the first instance; and in a proper case the court will sit in private in order to hear them. Where such an **1A–34** application is to be listed, two copies of the order sought, together with the application notice, should be lodged with the Chancery Judges' Listing Office. If the application is to be made in private, it will be listed as 'Application without notice' without naming the parties. The judge will consider, in each case, whether publicity might defeat the object of the hearing and, if so, may hear the application in private.

5.19 Freezing injunctions and search orders are never granted as a matter of course. A strong case must be made out, and applications need to be prepared with great care. The application should always be accompanied by a draft of the order which the court is to be invited to make.

Period for which an injunction or an order appointing a receiver is granted if the application was without notice

1A–35 5.20 When an application for an injunction is heard without notice, and the judge decides that an injunction should be granted, it will normally be granted for a limited period only — usually not more than seven days. The same applies to an interim order appointing a receiver. The applicant will be required to give the respondent notice of his or her intention to apply to the court at the expiration of that period for the order to be continued. In the meantime the respondent will be entitled to apply, though generally only after giving notice to the applicant, for the order to be varied or discharged.

Opposed applications without notice

1A–36 5.21 These are applications of which proper notice has not been given to the respondents but which are made in the presence of both parties in advance of a full hearing of the application. The judge may impose time limits on the parties if, having regard to the pressure of business or for any other reason, he or she considers it appropriate to do so. On these applications, the judge may, in an appropriate case, make an order which will have effect until trial or further order as if proper notice had been given.

Implied cross-undertakings in damages where undertakings are given to the court

1A–37 5.22 Often the party against whom an injunction is sought gives to the court an undertaking which avoids the need for the court to grant the injunction. In these cases, there is an implied undertaking in damages by the party applying for the injunction in favour of the other. The position is less clear where the party applying for the injunction also gives an undertaking to the court. The parties should consider and, if necessary, raise with the judge whether the party in whose favour the undertaking is given must give a cross-undertaking in damages in those circumstances.

Orders on applications

1A–38 5.23 The judge may direct the parties to agree, sign and deliver to the court a statement of the terms of the order made by the court (commonly still referred to as a minute of order), particularly where complex undertakings are given.

Consents by parties not attending hearing

1A–39 5.24 It is commonly the case that on an interim application the respondent does not appear either in person or by solicitors or counsel but the applicant seeks a consent order based upon a letter of consent from the respondent or his or her solicitors or a draft statement of agreed terms signed by the respondent's solicitors. This causes no difficulty where the agreed relief falls wholly within the relief claimed in the application notice.

5.25 If, however, the agreed relief goes outside that which is claimed in the application notice or even in the claim form or when undertakings are offered then difficulties can arise. A procedure has been established for this purpose to be applied to all applications in the Chancery Division.

1A–40 5.26 Subject always to the discretion of the court, no order will be made in such cases unless a consent signed by or on behalf of the respondent to an application is put before the court in accordance with the following provisions:

(1) Where there are solicitors on the record for the respondent the court will normally accept as sufficient a written consent signed by those solicitors on their headed notepaper.

(2) Where there are solicitors for the respondent who are not on the record, the court will normally accept as sufficient a written consent signed by those solicitors on their headed notepaper only if in the consent (or some other document) the solicitors certify that they have fully explained to the respondent the effect of the order and that the respondent appeared to have understood the explanation.

(3) Where there is a written consent signed by a respondent acting in person the court will not normally accept it as sufficient unless the court is satisfied that the respondent understands the effect of the order either by reason of the circumstances (for example the respondent is himself a solicitor or barrister) or by means of other material (for example, the respondent's consent is given in reply to a letter explaining in simple terms the effect of the order).

(4) Where the respondent offers any undertaking to the court (a) the document containing the undertaking must be signed by the respondent personally, (b) solicitors must certify on their headed notepaper that the signature is that of the respondent and (c) if the case falls within (2) or (3) above, solicitors must certify that they have explained to the respondent the consequences of giving the undertaking and that the respondent appeared to understand the explanation.

Bundles and Skeleton Arguments

5.27 See Chapter 7 below.   **1A–41**

Out of hours emergency arrangements

5.28 An application should not be made out of hours unless it is essential. An   **1A–42** explanation will be required as to why it was not made or could not be made during normal court hours. Applications made during legal vacations must also constitute vacation business.

5.29 There is always a Duty Chancery Judge available to hear urgent out of hours applications. The following is a summary of the procedure:

(1) All requests for the Duty Chancery Judge to hear urgent matters are to be made through the judge's clerk. There may be occasions when the Duty Chancery Judge is not immediately available. The clerk will be able to inform the applicant of the judge's likely availability.

(2) Initial contact should be through the Security Office at the Royal Courts of Justice (tel: 020 7947 6260), who should be requested to contact the Duty Chancery Judge's clerk. The applicant must give a telephone number for the return call.

(3) When the clerk contacts the applicant, he or she will need to know:
  (a) the name of the party on whose behalf the application is to be made;
  (b) the name of the person who is to make the application and his or her status (counsel or solicitor);
  (c) the nature of the application;
  (d) the degree of urgency;
  (e) the contact telephone numbers.

(4) The Duty Judge will indicate to his or her clerk whether he or she is prepared to deal with the matter by telephone or whether it will be necessary for the matter to be dealt with by a hearing, in court or elsewhere. The clerk will inform the applicant and make the necessary arrangements.

(5) Applications for interim remedies will (normally) be heard by telephone only where the applicant is represented by counsel or solicitors (PD 25, Interim Injunctions, paragraph 4.5). If, however, an applicant not so represented indicates reasons why, exceptionally, the application should be heard by telephone, the judge may require that the applicant be attended by a responsible person who can confirm the identity of the applicant and the ac-

curacy of what is said: see PD 23 paragraphs 6.3 and 8 . If satisfied that it is really necessary, the judge may grant an injunction on such an application, but it is likely to be granted for as short a time as possible pending a hearing on notice to the respondent.

5.30 Which judge will, in appropriate cases, hear an out of hours application varies according to when the application is made.

> (1) Weekdays. Out of hours duty, during term time, is the responsibility of the Applications Judge. He or she is normally available from 4.15pm until 10.15am Monday to Thursday.
>
> (2) Weekends. A Duty Chancery Judge is nominated by rota for weekends, commencing 4.15pm Friday until 10.15am Monday.
>
> (3) Vacation. The Vacation Judge also undertakes out of hours applications.

5.31 Sealing orders out of hours. In normal circumstances it is not possible to issue a sealed order out of hours. The judge may direct the applicant to lodge a draft of the order made at Chancery Chambers Registry by 10am on the following working day.

5.32 County court matters. Similar arrangements exist for making urgent applications out of hours in county court matters in certain parts of England and Wales. Contact with the Circuit judge on duty for the London County Courts can be made through the Security Office of the Royal Courts of Justice.

Vacation arrangements

1A–43 5.33 There is a Chancery judge available to hear applications in vacation. Applications must generally constitute vacation business in that, in particular, they require to be immediately or promptly heard. Special arrangements exist, however, in the Companies Court for certain schemes of arrangement and reductions of capital to be heard in the Long Vacation (see paragraph 8 of PD 49—Applications under the Companies Act 1985).

5.34 In the Long Vacation, the Vacation judge sits each day to hear vacation business. In other vacations there are no regular sittings. Mondays and Thursdays are made available for urgent Interim Applications on notice. The judge is available on the remaining days for urgent business.

Applications to a Master

1A–44 5.35 Applications to a Master should be made by application notice. Application notices are issued by the Masters' Appointments section in Room TM7.09. If the Master has already directed a case management conference the parties should ensure that all applications in the proceedings are properly issued and listed to be heard at the case management conference. If the available listed time is likely to be insufficient to give directions and hear any application the parties should co-operate and invite the court to arrange a longer appointment. It is the duty of the parties to seek to agree directions if possible and to provide a draft of the order for consideration by the Master.

5.36 Applications to a Master estimated to last in excess of two hours will require serious co-operation between the parties and will require the Master's directions before they are listed. The Master will normally give his permission to list such an application on condition that there is compliance with directions given by the Master.

5.37 Those directions are likely to require:

> (1) that the applicant agrees the time estimate (see below) with his opponent;
>
> (2) that, if the time allowed subsequently becomes insufficient, the court is informed and a new and longer appointment given;
>
> (3) that the parties agree an appropriate timetable for filing evidence such that the hearing will be effective on the date listed;
>
> (4) that positive confirmation is to be given to the Master five working days before the hearing date that the hearing remains effective; and

(5) that, in the event of settlement, the Master be informed of that fact.

5.38 The agreed time estimate must take into account not only the hearing time of the application but the time for the Master to give any judgment at the conclusion of the hearing. It should also take into account any further time that may be required for the Master to assess costs, and for any application for permission to appeal.

5.39 Failure to comply with the Master's directions given in respect of the listing of an appointment in excess of two hours may result, depending upon the circumstances, in the application not being heard or in adverse costs orders being made.

5.40 On any matter of substance, the Master is likely to require a bundle and skeleton arguments to be provided before the hearing, as detailed in paragraphs 7.40 to 7.50 below. Where directions are given in respect of an application to which paragraph 5.36 applies, the provision of a bundle and skeleton arguments should form part of the agreed timetable.

5.41 The Masters may also allow applications to be made to them informally. The Masters are normally listed to hear oral applications without notice between 2.15pm and 2.45pm (see paragraph 6.32 below). Such applications should not be used in place of a Part 23 application and care must be taken to notify in appropriate cases parties likely to be affected by any order made on the application. Letters should not be used in place of a Part 23 application, and parties should be particularly careful to keep any correspondence with the Masters to a minimum and to ensure that opposing parties receive copies of any correspondence. Failure in this regard will mean that the Master will refuse to deal with the correspondence. Correspondence should state that it has been copied to the other parties (or should state why it has not been copied). Unless the matter is one of urgency correspondence and any other documents should be sent by post. If, in a case of real urgency, a letter is sent by fax, it should not be followed by a hard copy, unless it contains an original document which needs to be filed. Further guidance is set out in the Chief Master's Practice Note reproduced at Appendix 5.

5.42 There is no distinction between term time and vacation so far as business before the Chancery Masters is concerned. They will deal with all types of business throughout the year. When a Master is on holiday, his or her list will normally be taken by a deputy Master.

Applications for payment out of court

5.43 Applications for payment out of money held in court under paragraph 4.2 of **1A–45** PD 37 (for example, where money has been paid into court following compulsory purchase or repossession of property) must be made by Part 23 Application Notice (Form N244). The required documents should be sent to Room TM5.04. The following must be included:

(1) the reasons why the payment should be made (in Part C of the application notice)

(2) any relevant documents such as birth, marriage or death certificate, title deeds etc. (exhibited to the application notice)

(3) a statement whether or not anyone else has any claim to the money (in the Statement of Truth)

(4) bank details, ie the name and address of the relevant bank/building society branch, its Sort Code, and the Account Title and Number

(5) the Court fee of £50.

5.44 If there is a dispute as to entitlement to money in court, the Master may order the matter to proceed by Part 8 claim (see paragraph 2.13 above). In all other cases the Master will consider the file without a hearing and make an order for payment.

CHAPTER 6

LISTING ARRANGEMENTS

Key Rules: CPR Parts 29 and 39

1A–46 6.1 This Chapter deals with listing arrangements for hearings before judges and Masters in the Royal Courts of Justice.

Hearings before Judges

Responsibility for listing

1A–47 6.2 Subject to the direction of the Chancellor the Clerk of the Lists (Room WG3, Royal Courts of Justice) has overall responsibility for listing. Day by day management of Chancery listing is dealt with by the Chancery Judges' Listing Officer (Room WG4). All applications relating to listing should, in the first instance, be made to the Chancery Judges' Listing Officer, who will refer matters, as necessary, to the Clerk of the Lists. Any party dissatisfied with any decision of the Clerk of the Lists may, on one clear day's notice to all other parties, apply to the judge in charge of the list. Any such application should be made within seven days of the decision of the Clerk of the Lists and be arranged through the Chancery Judges' Listing Office.

6.3 There are three main lists in the Chancery Division: the Trial List, the General List and the Interim Hearings List. In addition there is a separate Patents List which is also controlled on a day-to-day basis by the Chancery Judges' Listing Officer in Room WG4 (see Chapter 23).

The Trial List

1A–48 6.4 This comprises a list of all trials to be heard with witnesses.

The Interim Hearings List

1A–49 6.5 This list comprises interim applications and appeals from Masters.

The General List

1A–50 6.6 This list comprises other matters including revenue, bankruptcy and pension appeals, Part 8 proceedings, applications for judgment and all company matters.

6.7 The procedure for listing Chancery cases to be heard in the Royal Courts of Justice and listed in the Trial List is that at an early stage in the claim the court will give directions with a view to fixing the period during which the case will be heard. In a Part 7 claim that period (the Trial Window) will be determined by the court either when the case is allocated or subsequently at any case management conference or other directions hearing. In a Part 8 claim covered by this procedure, that is to say a Part 8 claim to be heard with witnesses, similar directions will be given when the Part 8 claim is listed for preliminary directions or for a case management conference. It is only in a small minority of Part 8 claims that the claim is tried by a judge in the Trial List and the Trial Window procedure applies. The bulk of Part 8 claims are heard on written evidence either by the Master or by the judge. Additionally, many Part 8 claims, even where oral evidence is to be called, will be heard by the Master pursuant to the jurisdiction set out in paragraph 4.1 of PD 2B — Allocation of Cases to Levels of Judiciary.

Allocation of Cases to Levels of Judiciary

1A–51 6.8 In determining the Trial Window the court will have regard to the listing constraints created by the existing court list and will determine a Trial Window which provides the parties with enough time to complete their preparations for trial. A Trial Window, once fixed, will not readily be altered. A list of current trial windows is published on the HMCS website. When determining the Trial Window the court will direct that one party, normally the claimant, makes an appointment to attend on the Chancery Judges' Listing Officer (Room WG4) to fix a trial date within the Trial Window, by such date as may be specified in the order and gives notice of that appointment to all other parties. It is to be understood that an order to attend on the Chancery Judges' Listing Officer imposes a strict obligation of compliance, without which the Trial Window that has been given will be lost.

6.9 At the listing appointment, the Chancery Judges' Listing Officer will take account, insofar as it is practical to do so, of any difficulties the parties may have as to the availability of counsel, experts and witnesses. The Chancery Judges' Listing Officer will, nevertheless, try to ensure the speedy disposal of the trial by arranging a firm trial date as soon as possible within the Trial Window. If a Case Summary has been prepared (see PD 29 paragraphs 5.6 and 5.7) the claimant must produce a copy at the listing appointment together with a copy of the particulars of claim and any orders relevant to the fixing of the trial date. If, exceptionally, at the listing appointment, it appears to the Chancery Judges' Listing Officer that a trial date cannot be provided by the court within the trial window, he may fix the trial date outside the trial window at the first available date.

6.10 A party wishing to appeal a date allocated by the Chancery Judge's Listing Officer must, within 7 days of the allocation, make an application to the judge nominated to hear such applications. The application notice should be filed in the Chancery Judges' Listing Office and served, giving one clear day's notice to the other parties.

6.11 A trial date once fixed will, like a Trial Window, only rarely be altered or vacated. An application to adjourn a trial date will normally be made to the judge nominated to hear such applications (see further paragraph 7.38). Such an application will however be entertained by the Master if, for example, on the hearing of an interim application or case management conference it becomes clear that the trial date cannot stand without injustice to one or both parties.

Warned List—General and Interim Hearings Lists

6.12 On each Friday of term and on such other days as may be appropriate, the **1A–52** Chancery Judges' Listing Officer will publish a Warned List, showing the matters that are liable to be heard in the following week. Any matters for which no date has been arranged will be liable to appear in the list for hearing with no warning save that given by the next day's list of cases, posted each afternoon outside Room WG4. Where a case is listed in the Warned List, the parties may agree to offer the case for a specified date, in accordance with the statement of Chancery Judges' Listing Office practice on offering cases issued by the Clerk of the Lists.

Estimate of duration

6.13 If after a case is listed the estimated length of the hearing is varied, or if the case **1A–53** is settled, withdrawn or discontinued, the solicitors for the parties must forthwith inform the Chancery Judges Listing Officer in writing. Failure so to do may result in an adverse costs order being made. If the case is settled but the parties wish the Master to make a consent order, the solicitor must notify the Chancery Judges' Listing Officer in writing, whereupon he or she will take the case out of the list and notify the Master. The Master may then make the consent order.

6.14 Seven days before the date for the hearing, the claimant's solicitors must inform the Chancery Judges' Listing Officer whether there is any variation in the estimate of duration, and, in particular, whether the case is likely to be disposed of in some summary way. If the claimant is a litigant in person, this must be done by the solicitor for the first-named defendant who has instructed a solicitor. If a summary disposal is likely, the solicitor must keep the Chancery Listing Officer informed of any developments as soon as they occur.

Applications after listing

6.15 Where a case has been listed for hearing and because of the timing of the **1A–54** hearing an application is urgent, any application in the case may be made to the Interim Applications judge if the application cannot be heard by a Master without the hearing being delayed. Parties should not however list an application before the Interim Applications judge without first consulting the Masters' clerks (Room TM7.09) as to the availability of the assigned Master or, in an appropriate case, applying to the Master himself. Provision can be made for urgent applications to be dealt with by the Chief Master or a deputy (see further paragraph 6.29).

Appeals

6.16 All appeals for hearing by High Court judges in the Division are issued by the **1A–55**

Clerk of the Lists, High Court Appeals Office (Room WG8). Enquiries relating to such appeals are to be made in the first instance to that office, except as provided by paragraph 6.18 below.

Daily list of cases

1A–56 6.17 This list, known as the Daily Cause List, is available on the Courts Service website: *www.hmcourts-service.gov.uk.*

Listing of Particular Business

1A–57 6.18 **Appeals from Masters**

(1) Appeals from Masters, where permission has been given, will appear in the Appeals Warned List. Such appeals (stamped with the appropriate fee) must be filed with the Clerk of the Lists' Office in Room WG7. When an appeal is filed an appeal number will be allocated and any future order will bear both the original claim number and the appeal number. On being satisfied that the case has been placed in the Warned List, solicitors should forthwith inform the Chancery Judges' Listing Officer whether they intend to instruct counsel and, if so, the name or names of counsel.

(2) Any order made on appeal from a Master will be placed on the court file. However, practitioners should co-operate by ensuring that a copy of any relevant order is available to the Master at any subsequent hearing.

6.19 **Applications for permission to appeal from Masters**

Applications for permission to appeal from a decision of a Master (stamped with the appropriate fee) must be lodged in the clerk of the Lists' Office in Room WG7. If permission to appeal is granted the appeal will appear in the Interim Hearings List and the procedure set out above will apply.

6.20 **Bankruptcy Appeals**

Notice of appeal from the decision of a Registrar or of a county court should be lodged in the Clerk of the Lists' Office, Room WG7. The appeal will be entered in the Appeals Warned List, usually with a fixed date. The date of the hearing will be fixed by the Chancery Judges' Listing Officer in the usual way.

6.21 **Bankruptcy Applications**

All originating applications to the judge should be lodged with the Deputy Court Manager in Bankruptcy. Urgent applications without notice for (i) the committal of any person to prison for contempt or (ii) injunctions or the modification or discharge of injunctions will be passed directly to the clerk to the Interim Applications judge for hearing by that judge. All applications on notice for (i) and (ii) above, and applications referred to the judge by the Registrar, will be listed by the Chancery Judges' Listing Officer. Applications estimated not to exceed two hours will be heard by the Interim Applications judge. The Chancery Judges' Listing Officer is to give at least three clear days' notice of the hearing to the applicant and to any respondent who attended before the Registrar. Applications over two hours will be placed in the General List and listed accordingly.

6.22 **Companies Court**

Matters for hearing before the Companies judge, such as petitions for an administration order, petitions for approval by the court of schemes of arrangement and applications for the appointment of provisional liquidators, may be issued for hearing on any day of the week in term time (other than the last day of each term) and will be dealt with by the Interim Applications judge as Companies judge. Applications or petitions which are estimated to exceed two hours are liable to be stood over to a date to be fixed by the Chancery Judges' Listing Officer. Urgent applications will also be dealt with by the Interim Applications judge. Applications and petitions referred to the judge by the Registrar will be placed in the General List and listed accordingly.

24

6.23 Applications referred to the judge

Applications referred by the Master to the judge will be added to the Interim Hearings List. The power to refer applications made to the Master and in respect of which the Master has jurisdiction is now very sparingly exercised. The proper use of judicial resources dictates that where the Master has jurisdiction in respect of an interlocutory matter he should ordinarily exercise that jurisdiction.

6.24 Judge's Applications

Reference should be made to Chapter 5.

6.25 Revenue Appeals

Appeals will be entered in the Appeals Warned List, usually with fixed dates, and will be heard by such judges as are available. The dates for hearing are settled in the usual way on application to the Chancery Judges' Listing Officer. Where it would assist counsel and solicitor with their other commitments, the Chancery Listing Officer, if requested, will endeavour to fix two or more revenue appeals so that they will come on consecutively.

6.26 Short Applications

An application for judgment in default made to a judge (because the Master has no jurisdiction) should be made to the Interim Applications judge.

6.27 Summary Judgment

Where an application for summary judgment includes an application for an injunction, it usually has to be made to a judge because in most cases the Master cannot grant an injunction save in terms agreed by the parties. In such cases the application should be made returnable before the judge instead of the Master and will be listed in the General List. The return date to be inserted in the application notice should be a Monday at least 14 clear days after the application notice has been served. The application notice should be issued in the Chancery Judges' Listing Office (Room WG4) when there must be lodged two copies of the application notice and the witness statements or affidavits in support together with their exhibits. On the return date the application will normally be adjourned to a date to be fixed if the hearing is likely to take longer than thirty minutes. The adjourned date will be fixed in the usual way through the Chancery Judges' Listing Officer, and a certificate signed by an advocate as to the estimated length of the hearing must be lodged with the Chancery Judges' Listing Officer.

If the applicant informs the Chancery Judges' Listing Officer at the time of issue of an application notice for summary judgment returnable before a judge that directions have been agreed, or are not necessary, the application will be listed for a substantive hearing without being listed for directions.

If, subsequent to issue, the parties agree directions the Chancery Judges' Listing Officer will, on application, re-list the application for a substantive hearing and any directions hearing will be vacated. Time estimates should be agreed.

6.28 Variation of Trusts: Application to a judge

Applications under the Variation of Trusts Act 1958 for a hearing before the judge may be listed for hearing in the General List without any direction by a Master on the lodgment in Room WG4 of a certificate signed by advocates for all the parties, stating (i) that the evidence is complete and has been filed; (ii) that the application is ready for hearing; and (iii) the estimated length of the hearing.

Hearings before Masters

Assignment of cases before Masters

6.29 The general rule is that cases are assigned to the Masters in accordance with the **1A–58** last digit of the claim number. At present cases are allocated as follows:

25

0 and 1 Master Bragge
2 and 3 Master Teverson
4 and 5 Master Bowles
6 and 7 Master Price
8 and 9 Master Moncaster

In view of administrative responsibilities, the Chief Master does not have assigned cases. He will take individual cases or classes of case in his own discretion and arrangements will be made accordingly through the Court Manager. Where an application is required to be heard at short notice or is urgent but the assigned Master's list cannot accommodate an early date for the length of hearing necessary, arrangements can often be made for it to be listed before the Chief Master. Application should first be made to the assigned Master, who will determine whether the case is one which it is appropriate to release to the Chief Master. In that event arrangements are made by the Court Manager (Room TM6.06)

Applications by the Official Solicitor under rule 21.12 to be appointed a guardian of a minor's estate are normally dealt with by the Chief Master. All applications for a Group Litigation Order in the Chancery Division have to be made to the Chief Master: see paragraph 3.13.

6.30 An important exception to the general rule is that all registered trade mark claims are assigned to Master Bragge. Practitioners must, therefore, ensure, both at the date of issue of proceedings and when any application is to be made, that the court staff are aware that the claim is a registered trade mark claim and that, irrespective of the claim number, the claim and any application in the claim is assigned to and should be listed before Master Bragge. Each month in term time a day or more is usually set aside in Master Bragge's list specifically for trade mark applications and practitioners should, if possible, seek to have applications listed on that day. If the provisions of this paragraph are ignored and an application in a registered trade mark claim is listed other than before Master Bragge, it is likely that the Master before whom it is listed will refuse to hear it. If Master Bragge is away it is to be expected that the claim will be heard by the Deputy sitting for him.

6.31 In addition, from time to time, the Chief Master assigns particular classes of case to particular Masters. This will normally relate to managed litigation where the particular parties will be aware that their cases have been specifically assigned.

Oral applications without notice to the Masters

1A–59 6.32 Masters are normally available to hear short oral applications without notice at Applications without Notice time between 2.15pm and 2.45pm on working days. Notice should be given to the Master's Appointments section in Room TM7.09, or by telephone or fax, by 4.30pm on the previous working day (except in cases of real emergency when notice may be given at any time) so that the file will be before the Master. If this procedure is not followed the Master will be likely to refuse to deal with the application. The Master will expect notice of such an application to have been given in an appropriate case to the other party. Applications without Notice time must not be used as a substitute for cases where the issue and service of an Application Notice is appropriate. (See paragraph 5.41 above).

6.33 If the assigned Master is not available on any particular day, the applicant will be informed and (except in cases of emergency) asked to come when the assigned Master is next available. Applications will only be heard by another Master in cases of emergency or when the assigned Master is on vacation.

6.34 See also Chapter 5, paragraphs 5.35 to 42 (Applications to Masters).

CHAPTER 7

PREPARATION FOR HEARINGS

Key Rules: CPR Parts 29 and 39

1A–60 7.1 This Chapter contains guidance on the preparation of cases for hearings before judges and Masters. Guidelines about the conduct of trials are given in Chapter 8 of this Guide. When an affidavit or witness statement (or other document) is filed in Chancery Chambers in preparation for a hearing or for any other purpose, it should be accompanied by a written evidence lodgment form as set out in Part 2 of Appendix 4, unless it accompanies an application notice. The preparation of witness statements is covered in Chapter 8.

Hearings before Judges

7.2 To ensure court time is used efficiently there must be adequate preparation of cases prior to the hearing. This covers, among other things, the preparation and exchange of skeleton arguments, compiling bundles of documents and dealing out of court with queries which need not concern the court. The parties should also use their best endeavours to agree before any hearing what are the issues or the main issues. **1A–61**

Estimates

7.3 Realistic estimates of the length of time a hearing is expected to take must be given. **1A–62**

7.4 In estimating the length of a hearing, sufficient time must be allowed for reading any documents required to be read, the length of the speeches, the time required to examine witnesses (if any), and, if appropriate, an immediate judgment, together with the summary assessment of costs, in cases where that may arise, and any application for permission to appeal.

7.5 Except as mentioned below, a written estimate signed by the advocates for all the parties is required in the case of any hearing before a judge. This should be delivered to the Chancery Judges' Listing Officer:

    (1) in the case of a trial, on the application to fix the trial date; and

    (2) in any other case, as soon as possible after the application notice or case papers have been lodged withh the Chancery Judges' Listin Office.

7.6 If the estimate given in the application notice for an application to the Interim Applications judge (other than applications by order) or for an application listed before the Companies judge requires to be revised, the revised estimate should be given to the court orally when the application is called on.

Changes in Estimate

7.7 The parties must inform the court immediately of any material change in a time estimate. They should keep each other informed of any such change. In any event a further time estimate signed by the advocates to the parties must be lodged when bundles are lodged (see paragraph 7.17 below). **1A–63**

Inaccurate estimates

7.8 Where estimates prove inaccurate, a hearing may have to be adjourned to a later date and the party responsible for the adjournment is likely to be ordered to pay the costs thrown away. **1A–64**

Bundles

7.9 Bundles of documents for use in court will generally be required for all hearings if more than 25 pages are involved (and may be appropriate even if fewer pages are involved). The efficient preparation of bundles of documents is very important. Where bundles have been properly prepared, the case will be easier to understand and present, and time and costs are likely to be saved. Where documents are copied unnecessarily or bundled incompetently the cost may be disallowed. **1A–65**

7.10 Where the provisions of this Guide as to the preparation or delivery of bundles are not followed, the bundle may be rejected by the court or be made the subject of a special costs order.

7.11 The claimant or applicant (as the case may be) should begin his or her preparation of the bundles in sufficient time to enable:

(1) the bundles to be agreed with the other parties (so far as possible);

(2) references to the bundles to be used in skeleton arguments; and

(3) the bundles to be delivered to the court at the required time.

7.12 The representatives for all parties involved must co-operate in agreeing bundles for use in court. The court and the advocates should all have exactly the same bundles.

7.13 When agreeing bundles for trial, the parties should establish through their legal representatives, and record in correspondence, whether the agreement of bundles:

(1) extends no further than agreement of the composition and preparation of the bundles; or

(2) includes agreement that the documents in the bundles are authentic (see rule 32.19); or

(3) includes agreement that the documents may be treated as evidence of the facts stated in them.

The court will normally expect parties to agree that the documents, or at any rate the great majority of them, may be treated as evidence of the facts stated in them. A party not willing to agree should, when the trial bundles are lodged, write a letter to the court (with a copy to all other parties) stating that it is not willing to agree, and explaining why.

7.14 Documents disclosed are in general deemed to be admitted to be authentic under rule 32.19.

7.15 Detailed guidelines on the preparation of bundles are set out in Appendix 6, in addition to those in PD 39, Miscellaneous Provisions relating to Hearings, paragraph 3. These should always be followed unless there is good reason not to do so. Particular attention is drawn to the need to consider the preparation of a core bundle.

7.16 The general rule is that the claimant/applicant must ensure that one copy of a properly prepared bundle is delivered at the Chancery Judges' Listing Office not less than two clear days (and not more than seven days) before a trial or application by order. However, the court may direct the delivery of bundles earlier than this. Where oral evidence is to be given a second copy of the bundle must be available in court for the use of the witnesses. In the case of bundles to be used on judge's Applications (other than applications by order) the bundles must be delivered to the clerk to the Interim Applications judge by 10am on the morning preceding the day of the hearing unless the court directs otherwise. A bundle delivered to the court should always be in final form and parties should not make a request to alter the bundle after it has been delivered to the court save for good reason.

7.17 When lodging the agreed bundles there should also be lodged a further agreed time estimate, together with an agreed reading list and an agreed time estimate in respect of that reading list. The time estimates and reading list must be signed by the advocates for the parties. Failing agreement as to the time estimates or reading list then separate reading lists and time estimates must be submitted signed by the appropriate advocate. See Appendix 7 as to reading lists.

7.18 If the case is one which does not require the preparation of a bundle, the advocate should check before the hearing starts that all the documents to which he or she wishes to refer and which ought to have been filed have been filed, and, if possible, indicate to the associate which they are.

7.19 Bundles provided for the use of the court should be removed promptly after the conclusion of the hearing unless the court directs otherwise.

Skeleton Arguments

1A–66 7.20 The general rule is that for the purpose of all hearings before a judge skeleton arguments should be prepared. The exceptions to this general rule are where the application does not warrant one, for example because it is likely to be short, or where the application is so urgent that preparation of a skeleton argument is impracticable or where an application is ineffective and the order is agreed by all parties (see also paragraphs 26.26 and 26.33).

Time for delivery of skeleton arguments

7.21 **In the more substantial matters (e.g. trials and applications by order)**— not **1A–67** less than two clear days before the date or first date on which the application or trial is due to come on for hearing.

7.22 **On judge's applications without notice**— with the papers which the judge is asked to read on the application.

7.23 **On all other applications to a judge, including interim applications**— as soon as possible and not later than 10am on the day preceding the hearing.

7.24 Where a case is liable to be placed in the Warned List, consideration should be given to the preparation of skeleton arguments as soon as the case is placed in the Warned List, so that the skeleton arguments are ready to be delivered to the court on time. Preparation of skeleton arguments should not be left until notice is given that the case is to be heard. Notice may be given that the case is to be heard the next day.

Place to which skeleton arguments should be delivered

7.25 If the name of the judge is not known, or the judge is a Deputy Judge, skeleton **1A–68** arguments should be delivered to the Chancery Judges' Listing Office (Room WG4).

7.26 If the name of the judge (other than a Deputy Judge) is known, skeleton arguments should be delivered to the judge's clerk.

Content of skeleton arguments

7.27 Appendix 7 contains guidelines which should be followed on the content of **1A–69** skeleton arguments and chronologies, as well as indices and reading lists.

7.28 In most cases before a judge, a list of the persons involved in the facts of the case, a chronology and a list of issues will also be required. The chronology and list of issues should be agreed where possible. The claimant/applicant is responsible for preparing the list of persons involved and the chronology, and he or she should deliver these and his or her list of issues (if required) to the court with his or her skeleton argument.

7.29 Unless the court gives any other direction, the parties shall, as between themselves, arrange for the delivery, exchange, or sequential service of skeleton arguments and any list of persons involved, list of issues or chronology. Where there are no such arrangements, all such documents should, where possible, be given to the other parties (if any) in sufficient time before the hearing to enable them properly to consider them.

Failure to lodge bundles or skeleton arguments on time

7.30 Failure to lodge skeleton arguments and bundles in accordance with this Guide **1A–70** may result in:

    (1) the matter not being heard on the date in question;

    (2) the costs of preparation being disallowed; and

    (3) an adverse costs order being made.

7.31 In the Royal Courts of Justice, a log will be maintained of all late skeletons and bundles. The log will regularly be inspected by the Chancellor who will consider such further action as appropriate in relation to any recurrent failure by any chambers, barrister, or solicitors firm to comply with the requirements of the CPR and the Guide.

Authorities

1A–71 7.32 Unless photocopies of authorities are provided, lists of authorities should be supplied to the usher by 9am on the first day of the hearing. Delivery of skeleton arguments does not relieve a party of his or her duty to deliver his or her list of authorities to the usher by the time stated.

7.33 Advocates should exchange lists of authorities by 4pm on the day before the hearing. Any failure in this regard which has the effect of increasing the length of a hearing or of giving rise to delay in the hearing of an application may give rise to an adverse costs order.

7.34 Excessive citation of authority should be avoided and practitioners must have full regard to the matters contained in *Practice Note (citation of cases: restrictions and rules)* [2001] I WLR 1001. In particular, the citation of authority should be restricted to the expression of legal principle rather than the application of such principle to particular facts. Practitioners must also, when citing authority, seek to ensure that their citations comply with *Practice Direction (Judgments: Neutral Citations)* [2002] 1 WLR 346.

Oral Argument

1A–72 7.35 The court may indicate the issues on which it wishes to be addressed and those on which it wishes to be addressed only briefly.

Documents and Authorities

1A–73 7.36 Only the key part of any document or authority should be read aloud in court.

7.37 At any hearing, handing in written material designed to reduce or remove the need for the court to take a manuscript note will assist the court and save time.

Adjournments

1A–74 7.38 As a timetable for the case will have been fixed at an early stage, applications for adjournment of a trial should only be necessary where there has been a change of circumstances not known when the timetable was fixed.

When to apply
    (1) A party who seeks to have a hearing before a judge adjourned must inform the Chancery Judges' Listing Officer of his or her application as soon as possible.
    (2) Applications for an adjournment immediately before a hearing begins should be avoided as they take up valuable time which could be used for dealing with effective business and, if successful, they may result in a loss of court time altogether.

How to apply
    (3) If the application is agreed, the parties should, in writing, apply to the Chancery Judges' Listing Officer. The Officer will consult the judge nominated for such matters. The judge may grant the application on conditions and give directions as to a new hearing date. But the judge may direct that the application be listed for a hearing and that all parties attend.
    (4) If the adjournment is opposed the party asking for it should apply to the judge nominated for such matters or to the judge to whom the matter has been allocated. A hearing should be arranged, at the first opportunity, through the Chancery Judges' Listing Office.
    (5) A short summary of the reasons for the adjournment should be delivered to the Chancery Judges' Listing Office, where possible by 12 noon on the day before the application is made. A witness statement or affidavit is not generally required.
    (6) The party requesting an adjournment will, in general, be expected to show that he or she has conducted his or her own case diligently. Parties should

take all reasonable steps to ensure that their cases are adequately prepared in sufficient time to enable a hearing before the court to proceed. Likewise, they should take reasonable steps to prepare and serve any document (including any written evidence) required to be served on any other party in sufficient time to enable the other party similarly to be adequately prepared.

(7) If a failure to take reasonable steps necessitates an adjournment, the court may disallow costs as between solicitor and client, or order the person responsible to pay the costs under rule 48.7, or dismiss the application, or make any other order (including an order for the payment of costs on an indemnity basis).

(8) A trial date may, on occasion, also be vacated by the Master in the circumstances envisaged in paragraph 6.11.

Hearings before Masters and Registrars

7.39 As in the case of hearings before judges, there must be adequate preparation of **1A–75** cases prior to a hearing before the Masters and Registrars. Parties must ensure when issuing applications to be heard by the Masters and Registrars that time estimates are realistic and make proper allowance for the time taken to read any documents required to be read, give judgment and deal with the summary assessment of costs and any application for permission to appeal. The parties must inform the court and all other parties immediately of any material change in a time estimate. Where estimates prove inaccurate, the hearing may have to be adjourned to a later date and the party responsible for the adjournment is likely to be ordered to pay the costs thrown away.

7.40 In the case of a hearing before a Master or Registrar which is listed for one hour or more and in any other hearing before a Master or Registrar such as a case management conference, where a bundle would assist, a bundle should be provided.

7.41 Bundles must be provided for a trial or equivalent hearing (such as an account or inquiry or a Part 8 claim with oral evidence) which is listed before a Master or a Registrar. Such bundles must comply with Appendix 6 and contain or be accompanied by a reading list and an estimate of reading time as set out in paragraph 7.17 above.

7.42 Bundles provided for the use of the Master and Registrars should be removed promptly after the conclusion of the hearing unless the Master or Registrar directs otherwise.

7.43 *Delivery of Bundles for hearings before Masters*

(1) Bundles should be delivered to Masters' Appointments, Room TM7.09, not less than 2 (and not more than 7) clear working days before the hearing. They should be clearly marked "For hearing on....*[date]* before Master..........." They must not be taken to the Registry (Room TM5.04) or the Chancery Judges' Listing Office, and no document required for any hearing must be taken to the RCJ post room. Documents delivered to the wrong place are unlikely to reach the Master in time for the hearing, resulting in probable postponement and the party responsible for the adjournment is likely to be ordered to pay the costs thrown away.

(2) Detailed guidance on where to deliver documents in Chancery Chambers is at Appendix 8.

(3) Where no bundle is provided for the use of the Master, but a party intends to rely on the exhibits to a witness statement or affidavit, that party must ensure that those documents are filed with the court in sufficient time to be available to be read by the Master in advance of the hearing. Documents filed less than 10 days before a hearing must be taken to Masters' Appointments, Room TM7.09, for filing and marked "For hearing on....*[date]*before Master....." (Documents filed before that time should be filed in the Registry, Room TM5.04, in the normal way). Exhibits should not be placed in lever arch files but should be fastened securely, for example by treasury tags.

7.44 *Delivery of bundles for hearings before Bankruptcy Registrars*

Bundles should be delivered to Room TM1.10 not less than 2 (and not more than 7) clear working days before the hearing. The should be clearly marked "For hearing on....*[date]* before Registrar..........."

7.45 *Delivery of bundles for hearings before Companies Court Registrars*

Bundles should be delivered to Room TM4.04 not less than 2 (and not more than 7) clear working days before the hearing. They should be clearly marked "For hearing on....*[date]* before Registrar..........."

7.46 *Late delivery of bundles for hearings before Masters and Registrars*

Parties delivering bundles should note that a log will be kept recording the time of their delivery to Rooms TM1.10, TM4.04 and TM7.09. Any failure to comply with these requirements which results in the postponement of a hearing may render that party liable to pay the costs occasioned by the adjournment.

Note: Bundles for hearings before a Chancery judge must be delivered to the Chancery Judges' Listing Office (Room WG4).

Skeleton arguments

1A-76 **7.47** Skeleton arguments should normally be prepared in respect of any application before the Master or Registrar of one or more hours' duration and certainly for any trial or similar hearing. They are to be delivered to the same place and at the same time as bundles. The contents of the skeleton argument should be in accordance with Appendix 7.

7.48 Where a skeleton argument is required, photocopies of any authorities to be relied upon should be attached to the skeleton argument.

7.49 If pursuant to the e-mail protocol for communications with the Chancery Division (paragraph 14.8 below), a skeleton argument is sent electronically, then the provisions of the protocol as well as the time limits set out above must be followed. In particular, any authorities relied on should be delivered in hard form and, where it would assist, be accompanied by a copy of the skeleton argument in hard form.

7.50 Failure to deliver skeleton arguments or bundles in accordance with this Guide is likely to result in the matter not being heard on the date fixed, the costs of preparation being disallowed and an adverse costs order being made.

Compromise or settlement of hearings

1A-77 **7.51** When hearings before Masters are compromised or settled, Masters' Appointments (Room TM7.09) should be informed in writing immediately and in any event no later than 4pm on the day preceding the hearing. In the case of substantial hearings involving pre-reading Masters' Appointments should be informed immediately if it appears likely that a hearing will be ineffective, with a request that the Master is immediately notified. Written notification must be given to Room TM1.10 for Bankruptcy hearings and Room TM4.04 for Companies hearings. Failure to notify and consequent waste of court time may result in an adverse costs order being made.

CHAPTER 8

CONDUCT OF A TRIAL

Key Rules: CPR Parts 32 and 39

1A-78 **8.1** An important aim of all concerned must be to ensure that at trial court time is used as efficiently as possible. Thorough preparation of the case prior to trial is the key to this.

8.2 Chapter 7 of this Guide applies to preparation for a trial as well as for other hearings in court. This Chapter contains matters which principally affect trials.

Time limits

8.3 The court may, either at the outset of the trial or at any time thereafter, fix time **1A–79**
limits for oral submissions, and the examination and cross-examination of witnesses.
(See paragraphs 3.15 – 16.)

Oral submissions

8.4 In general, and subject to any direction to the contrary by the trial judge, there **1A–80**
should be a short opening statement on behalf of the claimant, at the conclusion of
which the judge will invite short opening statements on behalf of the other parties.

8.5 Unless notified otherwise, advocates should assume that the judge will have read
their skeleton arguments and the principal documents referred to in the reading list
lodged in advance of the hearing (see paragraph 7.17). The judge will state at an
early stage how much he or she has read and what arrangements are to be made
about reading any documents not already read, for which an adjournment of the trial
after opening speeches may be appropriate. If the judge needs to read any
documents additional to those mentioned in the reading list lodged in advance of the
hearing, a list should be provided during the opening.

8.6 It is normally convenient for any outstanding procedural matters to be dealt with
in the course of, or immediately after, the opening statements.

8.7 After the evidence is concluded, and subject to any direction to the contrary by
the trial judge, oral closing submissions will be made on behalf of the claimant first,
followed by the defendant(s) in the order in which they appear on the claim form,
followed by a reply on behalf of the claimant. In a lengthy and complex case each
party should provide written summaries of their closing submissions.

8.8 The court may require the written summaries to set out the principal findings of
fact for which a party contends.

Witness Statements

8.9 In the preparation of witness statements for use at trial, the guidelines in **1A–81**
Appendix 9 should be followed.

8.10 Unless the court orders otherwise, a witness statement will stand as the witness'
evidence in chief if he or she is called and confirms that he or she believes the facts
stated in the statement are true: rule 32.5.

8.11 A witness may be allowed to supplement his or her witness statement orally at
the trial before submitting to cross-examination, for example to deal with events
occurring, or matters discovered, after his or her statement was served, or in
response to matters dealt with by another party's witness, but a party seeking to
examine in chief a witness who has provided a witness statement must satisfy the
judge that there is good reason not to confine the evidence to the contents of his or
her witness statement: see rule 32.5(3) and (4). Where practicable a supplementary
witness statement should be prepared and served on the other parties, as soon as
possible, to deal with matters not dealt with in the original witness statement.
Permission is required to adduce a supplementary witness statement at trial if any
other party objects to it. This need not be sought prior to service; it can be sought at
a case management conference if convenient or, if need be, at trial.

8.12 Witnesses are expected to have re-read their witness statements shortly before
they are called to give evidence.

8.13 Where a party decides not to call a witness whose witness statement has been
served to give oral evidence at trial, prompt notice of this decision should be given to
all other parties. The party should make plain when he or she gives this notice
whether he or she proposes to put, or seek to put, the witness statement in as
hearsay evidence. If he or she does not put the witness statement in as hearsay
evidence, rule 32.5(5) allows any other party to put it in as hearsay evidence.

8.14 Facilities may be available to assist parties or witnesses with special needs, whether as regards access to the court, or audibility in court, or otherwise. The Chancery Judges' Listing Office should be notified of any such needs prior to the hearing. The Customer Service Officer (tel 020 7947 7731) can also assist with parking, access etc.

Cross-examination

1A–82 8.15 The party cross-examining is not necessarily obliged to put his or her case to each witness even if they deal in chief with the same point. It may be sufficient if he or she puts it to one of the other side's witnesses. If that witness makes any admission or expresses any opinion or otherwise adds a qualification to his or her evidence, the party cross-examining can rely on it in argument but he or she cannot assume that other witnesses would have made the same admission or qualification and expressed the same opinion: see *Re Yarn Spinners' Agreement* [1959] 1 All ER 299 at 309 per Devlin J.

Expert Evidence

1A–83 8.16 The trial judge may disallow expert evidence which either is not relevant for any reason, or which he or she regards as excessive and disproportionate in all the circumstances, even though permission for the evidence has been given.

8.17 The evidence of experts (or of the experts on a particular topic) is commonly taken together at the same time and after the factual evidence has been given. If this is to be done it should be agreed by the parties before the trial and should be raised with the judge at the PTR, if there is one, or otherwise at the start of the trial. Expert evidence should as far as possible be given by reference to the reports exchanged.

8.18 The evidence of experts must be impartial, complying with rule 35.3. If it is not it may be disregarded.

Physical exhibits

1A–84 8.19 Some cases involve a number of physical exhibits. The parties should endeavour to agree the exhibits in advance and their system of labelling. Where it would be desirable, a scheme of display should be agreed (e.g. on a board with labels readable from a distance). Where witness statements refer to these, a note in the margin (which can be handwritten) of the exhibit number should be added.

CHAPTER 9

JUDGMENTS, ORDERS AND PROCEEDINGS AFTER JUDGMENT
Key Rules: CPR Part 40, and PDs 40, 40B and 40D

Judgments

1A–85 9.1 Where judgment is reserved, the judge will normally deliver his or her judgment by handing down the written text without reading it out in open court. Where this course is adopted, the advocates will be supplied with the full text of the judgment in advance of delivery. In such cases, the advocates should familiarise themselves with the text of the judgment and be ready to deal with any points which may arise when judgment is delivered.

9.2 The text may be shown, in confidence, to the parties, but only for the purpose of obtaining instructions and on the strict understanding that the judgment, or its effect, is not to be disclosed to any other person, or used in the public domain, and that no action is taken (other than internally) in response to the judgment. Advocates should notify the judge's clerk of any obvious errors or omissions.

9.3 The judgment does not take effect until formally delivered in court, when, if requested and so far as practicable, it will be made available to the law reporters and the press. The judge will normally direct that the written judgment may be used for all purposes as the text of the judgment, and that no transcript of the judgment need be made. Where such a direction is made, copies of the judgment may be obtained from the Mechanical Recording Department.

Orders

9.4 It may often be possible for the court to prepare and seal an order more quickly **1A–86** if a draft of the order is handed in. Speed may be particularly important where the order involves the grant of an interim injunction or the appointment of a receiver without notice. In all but the most simple cases a draft order should be prepared and brought to the hearing.

9.5 The court may in any case direct the parties to agree and sign a statement of the terms of the order made by the court (still commonly called a minute of order). Where the proceedings are in the Royal Courts of Justice, the statement should, when agreed and signed, be delivered to Chancery Chambers Registry and Issue Section (Room TM5.04) unless otherwise requested. The statement must, under PD 40B, be filed no later than 7 days from the date of the order, unless the court directs otherwise. In the case of any dispute or difficulty as to the contents of the order, the parties should mention the matter to the judge or Master who heard the application.

9.6 Where a draft or an agreed statement of the terms of an order exists in electronic form, it is often helpful if the draft or agreed statement is provided to the court by e-mail or on disk as well as in hard copy, particularly if the order needs to be drawn quickly. Any disk supplied for this purpose must be new and newly-formatted before writing the material on it so as to minimise the risk of transferring a computer virus. The current word processing system used by the Chancery Associates is Word for Windows 2000. Enquiries regarding the provision of disks should be made of the associate responsible for drawing the order in question.

Drafting and Service of Orders

9.7 Where a judge or Master directs that a statement of the terms of an order be **1A–87** agreed and signed, the agreed statement should be filed in Room TM5.04 as set out in paragraph 9.5 above. Agreed statements will normally be adopted as the order of the court.

9.8 Orders will be drawn up by the court, unless the judge or Master directs that no order be drawn. Unless a contrary order is made, or the party concerned has asked to serve the order, a sealed order will be sent by the court to each party.

9.9 Where a particular order is required to be served personally, the party concerned (see above) will be responsible for service.

9.10 If the order is to be drawn up by a party, three engrossments of the order proposed should be delivered or posted to:
Chancery Chambers Registry
Room TM5.04
Thomas More Building
Royal Courts of Justice
Strand
London WC2A 2LL

Forms of Order

9.11 Recitals will be kept to a minimum and the body of the order will be confined to **1A–88** setting out the decision of the court and the directions required to give effect to it. If upon receipt of an order any party is of the view that it is not drawn up in such a way as to give effect to the decision of the court, prompt notice must be given to the Chancery Chambers Registry in Room TM5.04 and to all other parties setting out the reasons for dissatisfaction. If the differences cannot be resolved, the objecting party may apply on notice for the order to be amended and should do so promptly

Copies of Orders

9.12 Copies of orders may be obtained from Room TM5.04 upon payment of the **1A–89** appropriate fee.

Consent Orders

1A–90 9.13 All consent orders filed in Chancery Chambers and in respect of which a fee has been paid are referred to the Master for approval before the order is sealed.

Consent Orders under the Inheritance (Provision for Family and Dependants) Act 1975

1A–91 9.14 Every final order embodying terms of compromise made in proceedings in the Chancery Division under the 1975 Act must under paragraph 18.2 of PD 57 contain a direction that a memorandum of the order shall be endorsed on or permanently annexed to the grant and a copy of the order shall be sent to the Principal Registry of the Family Division with the relevant grant of probate or letters of administration for endorsement notwithstanding that any particular order may not, strictly speaking, be an order under the 1975 Act.

Consents by parties not attending the hearing

1A–92 9.15 This is covered in paragraphs 5.24–26 above.

Tomlin Orders

1A–93 9.16 Where proceedings are to be stayed on agreed terms to be scheduled to the order, the draft order should be drawn so as to read, with any appropriate provision in respect of costs, as follows:

"And the parties having agreed to the terms set out in the attached schedule
IT IS BY CONSENT ORDERED
That all further proceedings in this claim be stayed except for the purpose of carrying such terms into effect
AND for that purpose the parties have permission to apply".

This form of order is called a "Tomlin Order".

Proceedings after judgment

1A–94 9.17 Proceedings under judgments and orders in the Chancery Division are now regulated by PD 40 Accounts, Inquiries etc., PD 40B Judgments and Orders, and PD 40D Court's Powers in Relation to Land etc.

Directions

1A–95 9.18 Where a judgment or order directs further proceedings or steps, such as accounts or inquiries, it will often give directions as to how the accounts and inquiries are to be conducted, for example:

for accounts

    (1) who is to lodge the account and within what period;

    (2) within what period objection is to be made; and

    (3) arrangements for inspection of vouchers or other relevant documents;

for inquiries

    (4) whether the inquiry is to proceed on written evidence or with statements of case;

    (5) directions for service of such evidence or statements; and

    (6) directions as to disclosure.

9.19 If directions are not given in the judgment or order an application should be made to the assigned Master as soon as possible asking for such directions. The application notice should specify the directions sought. Before making the application, applicants should write to the other parties setting out the directions they seek and inviting their response within 14 days. The application to the court should not be made until after the expiry of that period unless there is some special urgency. The application must state that the other parties have been consulted and have attached to it copies of the applicant's letter to the other parties and of any response from them. The Master will then consider what directions are appropriate. In complex cases he or she may direct a case management conference.

9.20 If any inquiry is estimated to last more than two days and involves very large sums of money or strongly contested issues of fact or difficult points of law, the Master may direct that it be heard by a judge. The parties are under an obligation to consider whether in any particular case the inquiry is more suitable to be heard by a judge and should assist the Master in this. Accounts, however long they are estimated to take, will normally be heard by the Master. The Master is likely to want to give detailed directions in connection with the account and the form of it.

CHAPTER 10

APPEALS

Key Rules: CPR Part 52 and PD 52; PD Insolvency Proceedings, Part 4, paragraph 17: Appeals

General

10.1 This Chapter is concerned with the following appeals affecting the Chancery **1A–96** Division:

(1) Appeals within the ordinary work of the Division, from Masters to High Court judges;

(2) Insolvency appeals from High Court Registrars and from county courts to High Court judges;

(3) Appeals to High Court judges in the Chancery Division from orders in claims proceeding in a county court;

(4) Statutory appeals from tribunals and others to the Chancery Division.

Proceedings under the Companies Acts are specialist proceedings for the purposes of rule 49(2) and therefore as regards the destination of appeals. In those cases appeals from final decisions by a Registrar of the Companies Court go direct to the Court of Appeal. Such appeals are not covered in this Chapter.

10.2 This Chapter does not deal with appeals from High Court judges of the Division, except as regards permission to appeal, and as to giving notice to the court of an appeal in a contempt case. It does not deal with appeals in the course of the detailed assessment of costs.

10.3 The detailed procedure for appeals is set out in Part 52 and in PD 52, and in the PD relating to Insolvency Proceedings, to which reference should be made. This Chapter only refers to some of the salient points.

Permission to appeal

10.4 Permission to appeal is required in all cases except: (a) appeals against committal **1A–97** orders, (b) certain insolvency appeals and (c) certain statutory appeals. Permission to appeal will only be given where the court considers that the appeal would have a real prospect of success or there is some other compelling reason why the appeal should be heard (rule 52.3(6)).

10.5 An application for permission may be made to the lower court, but only if it is made at the hearing at which the decision to be appealed was made (rule 52.3(2)(a)). Permission may be granted, or refused, or granted in part (whether as to a part of the order, a ground of appeal or an issue) and refused as to the rest. It may be granted conditionally.

10.6 If the lower court refuses permission, or if permission is not applied for to the lower court at the original hearing, an application for permission may be made to the appeal court, by appeal notice.

10.7 An application to the appeal court for permission may be dealt with without a hearing, but if refused without a hearing the applicant may request that it be reconsidered at a hearing. Notice of the hearing is often given to the respondent; the respondent may submit written representations or attend the hearing but will not necessarily be awarded any costs of so doing even if permission to appeal is refused.

10.8 Guidance for litigants in relation to appeals to the High Court is available by way of a Practice Statement which may be obtained from the High Court Appeals Office at the Royal Courts of Justice (Room WG4).

10.9 If a party who wishes to appeal cannot lodge all the documents which are required at the time when the appellant's notice is issued, the Appeals Office is able to allow some further time by way of an extension, but beyond this any further extension has to be allowed by a judge, who will consider the case on paper. If there is a delay in obtaining a transcript of the judgment to be appealed, the appellant should endeavour to obtain a note of the judgment, which the lawyers representing any party at the hearing below ought to be able to provide, at least as an interim measure before a transcript is obtained.

10.10 If the documents required for consideration of an application for permission to appeal have not been lodged, despite any extension which has been allowed, the case may be listed for oral hearing in the Dismissal List, for the appellant to show cause why the case should not be dismissed. The respondent will not normally be notified of such a hearing.

Time for appealing

1A–98 10.11 The time limit for an appeal notice to be filed at the appeal court is 14 days after the decision of the lower court to be appealed, unless the lower court fixes some other period, which may be longer or shorter. The lower court can only fix a different period if it does so at the time it makes the order to be appealed from. Otherwise only the appeal court can alter the time limits.

Stay

1A–99 10.12 Unless the lower court or the appeal court orders otherwise, an appeal does not operate as a stay of any order or decision of the lower court. A stay of execution may be applied for in the appellant's notice. If it is, it may be dealt with on paper. If the stay is required as a matter of great urgency, or before the appellant's notice can be filed, an application should be made to the Applications judge.

Appeals from Masters in cases proceeding in the Chancery Division

1A–100 10.13 If permitted, an appeal from a decision of a Master in a case proceeding in the Chancery Division usually lies to a High Court judge of the Division. An appeal from a final decision of a Master in a claim allocated to the multi-track lies direct to the Court of Appeal.

10.14 The appeal to the judge is limited to a review of the decision of the lower court, unless the court considers that, in the circumstances of the individual appeal, it would be in the interests of justice to hold a re-hearing. This principle applies to all appeals dealt with in this Chapter except where some other provision is made, as mentioned below. Unless the court does decide, exceptionally, to hold a re-hearing, the appeal will be allowed if the decision of the lower court was wrong or if it was unjust because of a serious procedural or other irregularity in the proceedings in the lower court.

Insolvency appeals

1A–101 10.15 An appeal lies from a county court (Circuit or District Judge) or a High Court Registrar in bankruptcy or company insolvency matters to a High Court judge of the Chancery Division, for which permission is not required.

10.16 Appeals in proceedings under the Company Directors Disqualification Act 1986 are treated as being in insolvency proceedings.

10.17 The time limit for such an appeal is the same as for ordinary Chancery appeals. An appeal is limited to a review of the decision of the lower court.

Appeals from orders made in county court claims

10.18 An appeal against a decision of a circuit judge in a claim proceeding in a **1A–102** county court lies to the High Court, unless, either, the decision is a final decision in a claim allocated to the multi-track or in specialist proceedings to which rule 49(2) applies, or the decision is itself on an appeal; in either of these cases the appeal lies direct to the Court of Appeal. This does not apply, however, where the allocation to the multi-track is deemed, rather than the result of a specific order, so that in cases begun by a Part 8 claim form, even though they are deemed to be so allocated, appeals lie to the High Court. The general rules as to the requirement for permission described above apply to these appeals.

Statutory appeals

10.19 The Chancery Division hears a variety of appeals and cases stated under statute **1A–103** from decisions of tribunals and other persons. Some of these are listed or referred to in PD 52, but this is not exhaustive. Particular cases include appeals under the Taxes Management Act 1970 and the Inheritance Tax Act 1984, appeals from the Value Added Tax and Duties Tribunal, from the Pensions Ombudsman and the Occupational Pensions Regulatory Authority, from the Comptroller-General of Patents, Designs and Trade Marks, from the Chief Land Registrar, from the Commons Commissioners, and from the Charity Commissioners under the Charities Act 1993.

10.20 Tax and VAT appeals are dealt with in Chapter 25 below, and appeals in patent, design and trade mark matters in Chapter 23. For other appeals reference should be made to the relevant statute and to PD 52.

Appeals to the Court of Appeal: permission to appeal

10.21 An appeal lies from a judgment of a High Court judge of the Division to the **1A–104** Court of Appeal (unless an enactment makes it final and unappealable), but permission is required in all cases except where the order is for committal. Permission may be granted by the High Court judge, if applied to at the hearing at which the decision to be appealed was made, unless the order of the High Court judge was itself on an appeal, in which case permission may only be granted by the Court of Appeal.

Appeals in cases of contempt of court

10.22 Appellant's notices which by paragraph 21.4 of PD 52 are required to be **1A–105** served on "the court from whose order or decision the appeal is brought" may be served, in the case of appeals from the Chancery Division, on the Chief Master of the Chancery Division; service may be effected by leaving a copy of the notice of appeal with the clerk of the Lists in Room WG4, Royal Courts of Justice, Strand, London WC2A 2LL.

Dismissal by consent

10.23 The practice is as set out in paragraph 12 of PD 52, for all appeals except first **1A–106** appeals in insolvency matters. A document signed by solicitors for all parties must be lodged with the High Court Appeals Office (Room WG7), Royal Courts of Justice, Strand, London WC2A 2LL, requesting dismissal of the appeal. The appeal can be dismissed without any hearing by an order made in the name of the Chancellor. Any orders with directions as to costs will be drawn by the Chancery Associates. In the case of a first appeal in an insolvency matter, reference should be made to paragraph 17.22(8) of the PD Insolvency Proceedings.

CHAPTER 11

COSTS

Key Rules: CPR Parts 43 to 48 *and the PD supplementing them*

1A–107 11.1 This Chapter does not set out to do more than refer to some salient points on costs relevant to proceedings in the Chancery Division. In particular it does not deal with the processes of detailed assessment or appeals in relation to such assessments.

11.2 A number of provisions in respect of costs in the CPR and in the PD supplementing Parts 43 to 48 (Costs PD) are likely to be relevant to Chancery proceedings:

(1) *Informing the client of costs orders:* Solicitors have a duty to tell their clients, within 7 days, if an order for costs is made against them and they were not present at the hearing. Solicitors must also tell anyone else who has instructed them to act on the case or who is liable to pay their fees. They must inform these persons how the order came to be made (rule 44.2; Costs PD, paragraph 7.1).

(2) *Providing the court with estimates of costs:* The court can order a party to file an estimate of costs and to serve it on the other parties. (Costs PD, paragraph 6.3). This is to assist the court in deciding what case management orders to make and also to inform other parties as to their potential liability for costs. In addition parties must file estimates of costs when they file their allocation questionnaire or any listing questionnaire (Costs PD, paragraph 6.4).

(3) *Summary assessment of costs:* An outline of these provisions is given below. Their effect is that in the majority of contested hearings lasting no more than a day the court will decide, at the end of the hearing, not only who is to pay the costs but also how much those costs should be, and will order them to be paid, usually within 14 days. As a result the paying party will have to pay the costs at a much earlier stage than before.

(4) *Interim orders for costs:* Where the court decides immediately who is to pay particular costs, but does not assess the costs summarily, for example after a trial lasting more than a day, so that the final amount of costs payable has to be fixed by a detailed assessment, the court may order the paying party to pay a sum or sums on account of the ultimate liability for costs.

(5) *Interest on costs:* The court has power to award interest on costs from a date before the date of the order, so compensating the receiving party for the delay between incurring the costs and receiving a payment in respect of them from the paying party.

Summary Assessment

1A–108 11.3 The court will generally make a summary assessment of costs whenever the hearing lasts for less than one day. The judge or Master who heard the application or other hearing (which will include a trial, or the hearing of a Part 8 Claim, lasting less than a day) carries out the summary assessment. The court may decide not to assess costs summarily either because it orders the costs to be "costs in the case" or because it considers the case to be otherwise inappropriate for summary assessment, typically because substantial issues arise as to the amount of the costs claimed. Costs payable to a party funded by the Legal Services Commission cannot be assessed summarily.

11.4 In order that the court can assess costs summarily at the end of the hearing each party who intends to claim costs must, no later than 24 hours before the time fixed for the hearing, serve on the other party, and file with the court, his or her statement of costs. Paragraph 13.5 of the Costs PD contains requirements about the information to be included in this statement, and the form of the statement. Failure by a party to file and serve his or her statement of costs as required by paragraph 13.5 of the Costs PD will be taken into account by the court in deciding what order to make about costs and could result in a reduced assessment, in no order being made as to costs, or in the party being penalised in respect of the costs of any further hearing or detailed assessment hearing which may be required as a result of the party's failure.

11.5 Where the receiving party (the party to whom the costs are to be paid) is funded by the Legal Services Commission the court cannot assess costs summarily. It is not, however, prevented from assessing costs summarily by the fact that the paying party (the party by whom the costs are to be paid) is so funded. A summary assessment of costs payable by a person funded by the Legal Services Commission is not by itself a determination of the amount of those costs which the funded party is to pay (as to which see section 11 of the Access to Justice Act 1999 and regulation 10 of the Community Legal Services (Costs) Regulations 2000). Ordinarily, where costs are summarily assessed and ordered to be paid by a funded person the order will provide that the determination of any amount which the person who is or was in receipt of services funded by the Legal Services Commission is to pay shall be dealt with in accordance with regulation 10 of the Regulations.

11.6 The amount of costs to be paid by one person to another can be determined on the standard basis or the indemnity basis. The basis to be used is determined when the court decides that a person should pay the costs of another. The usual basis is the standard basis and this is the basis that will apply if the order does not specify the basis of assessment. Costs that are unreasonably incurred or are unreasonable in amount are not allowed on either basis.

11.7 On the standard basis the court only allows costs which are proportionate to the matters in issue. If it has any doubt as to whether the costs were reasonably incurred or reasonable and proportionate in amount, it resolves the doubt in favour of the paying party. The concept of proportionality will always require the court to consider whether the costs which have been incurred were warranted having regard to the issues involved. A successful party who incurs costs which are disproportionate to the issues involved and upon which he or she has succeeded will only recover an amount of costs which the court considers to have been proportionate to those issues.

11.8 On the indemnity basis the court resolves any doubt it may have as to whether the costs were reasonably incurred or were reasonable in amount in favour of the receiving party.

11.9 The court must take into account all the circumstances, including the parties' conduct and the other matters mentioned in rule 44.5. Indemnity costs are not confined to cases of improper or reprehensible conduct. They will not, however, usually be awarded unless there has been conduct by the paying party which the court regards as unreasonable or unless the case falls within rule 48.4 (see paragraph 11.13 below).

11.10 A party must normally pay costs which are awarded against him or her and summarily assessed within 14 days of the assessment. But the court can extend that time (rules 44.8, 3.1(2)(a)). The court may therefore direct payment by instalments, or defer the liability to pay costs until the end of the proceedings so that the costs can then be set against any costs or judgment to which the paying party then becomes entitled.

11.11 If the parties have agreed the amount of costs, they do not need to file a statement of the costs, and summary assessment is unnecessary. If the parties to an application are able to agree an order by consent without the parties attending they should also agree a figure for costs to be inserted in the order or agree that there should be no order as to costs. If the costs position cannot be agreed then the parties will have to attend on the appointment but unless good reason can be shown for the failure of the parties to deal with costs as set out above no costs will be allowed for that attendance. The court finds it most unsatisfactory if parties agree the terms of a consent order but not the provision for costs. Depending on the facts and circumstances, the court may not be able to decide on the question of costs without hearing the application fully, but it is not likely to be consistent with the overriding objective to allow the necessary amount of court time to the dispute on costs in such a case. The court may then have to decide the costs issue on a broad brush approach, making an order against one party or the other only if it is clear, without spending too much time on it, that such an order would be appropriate, and otherwise making no order as to the costs.

Conditional fee agreements

11.12 The court should be informed, on any application for the payment of costs, if **1A–109** any party has entered into a conditional fee agreement. The court can then consider whether, in the light of that agreement, to stay the payment of any costs which have been summarily assessed until the end of the action, or to decline to order the payment of costs on account under rule 44.3(8).

Other provisions

1A–110 11.13 Parts 45 to 48, and the Costs PD, contain provisions regarding:

(1) special cases in which costs are payable;

(2) wasted costs;

(3) fixed costs (these are payable for instance if judgment for a sum of money is given in default); and

(d) detailed assessment.

In the context of Chancery litigation attention is drawn to rule 48.2 (Costs orders in favour of or against non-parties); rule 48.3 (Amount of costs where costs are payable pursuant to a contract) (see further Costs PD paragraph 50 and see also Chapter 21—Mortgage Claims); and rule 48.4 and Costs PD paragraph 50A (Limitations on court's power to award costs in favour of trustee or personal representative). Reference may also be made to Chapter 26 as regards costs orders in trust litigation.

Chapter 12

District Registries

General

1A–111 12.1 Many Chancery cases are heard outside London. There are eight Chancery District Registries: Birmingham, Bristol, Cardiff, Leeds, Liverpool, Manchester, Newcastle-upon-Tyne, and Preston. High Court or Circuit Chancery judges sit regularly at all of these centres.

12.2 Outside London, county courts have exclusive jurisdiction in bankruptcy, and proceedings in bankruptcy must therefore be brought in the relevant county court which has bankruptcy jurisdiction rather than in the District Registries.

Judges

1A–112 12.3 Two Chancery judges supervise the arrangements for the hearing of Chancery cases out of London. Mr Justice Hart is the Chancery Supervising judge for the Western, Wales and Chester, and Midland Circuits. Mr Justice Patten, as Vice-Chancellor of the County Palatine of Lancaster, is concerned with Chancery hearings on the Northern and North Eastern Circuits. Both these judges regularly take substantial Chancery matters for hearing outside London. Mr Justice Hart sits regularly in Birmingham, Bristol and Cardiff, but if appropriate will sit elsewhere on the relevant circuit, for example in Chester. Mr Justice Patten sits regularly in Manchester, Liverpool, Leeds and Newcastle, and may sit in Preston or in other court centres on either circuit (e.g. Carlisle or Sheffield) if business so requires.

12.4 There are also Specialist Circuit judges who have the authority to exercise the powers of a judge of the Chancery Division (under section 9 of the Supreme Court Act 1981, therefore known as section 9 judges) and who normally sit out of London. They exercise a general Chancery jurisdiction, subject to exceptions. Those exceptions are proceedings directly concerning revenue, and proceedings before the Patents Court constituted as part of the Chancery Division under section 96 of the Patents Act 1977.

12.5 Currently the Circuit judges who sit regularly in Chancery matters out of London are:

Judge Weeks QC (Bristol)
Judge Norris QC (Birmingham)
Judge Wyn Williams QC (Cardiff)
Judge Howarth (Manchester, Liverpool and Preston)

Judge Behrens (Leeds and Newcastle)
Judge Kaye QC (Leeds and Newcastle)
Judge Hodge QC (Manchester, Liverpool and Preston)
Judge Gilliland QC (who normally sits in Salford hearing Technology and Construction cases), Judges Kershaw QC and Hegarty QC (who are the local Mercantile judges based in Manchester and Liverpool) and Judge Raynor QC also assist in the disposal of Chancery business on the Northern Circuit. So also, on the North-Eastern Circuit, does Judge Langan QC who is the Mercantile judge for Leeds and Newcastle. The Chancery, Mercantile and TCC judges assist each other in Birmingham, Bristol and Cardiff as well.

12.6 In addition certain other Circuit judges and some Queen's Counsel are authorised to take Chancery cases on the same basis.

Trials

12.7 If a Chancery case is proceeding in any District Registry other than a Chancery **1A–113** District Registry, the case should normally be transferred to the appropriate Chancery District Registry upon the first occasion the case comes before the court.

12.8 The venue of a Chancery trial out of London will normally be one of the centres mentioned above. However in appropriate circumstances (e.g. because of the number or age of local witnesses, the need for a site visit, or travel problems) arrangements can be made for a Chancery judge to sit elsewhere.

12.9 In cases of great difficulty or importance the trial may be by a High Court judge. Arrangements can also be made in exceptional circumstances for a High Court judge to deal with any of the matters excepted from the jurisdiction of an authorised Circuit judge. Such a judge may be one of the Chancery judges other than Hart or Patten JJ.

12.10 Where it is desired that a case be heard by a specialist Chancery judge outside one of the normal Chancery Centres, or be taken by a High Court judge, inquiries should normally be made in the first instance to the Listing Officer for the nearest Chancery District Registry on the relevant circuit . If the need arises, inquiries can also be made to the clerk to Mr Justice Hart or the clerk to Mr Justice Patten, as the case may be. If no relevant clerk is available, inquiries should be made to the Chancery Listing Officer at the Royal Courts of Justice in London. The clerks' contact numbers are in Appendix 1.

Applications

12.11 Subject to the following paragraphs any application should normally be made **1A–114** to a District Judge (unless it relates to a matter which a District Judge does not have power to hear).

12.12 A District Judge may of his or her own initiative (for instance because of the **1A–115** complexity of the matter or the need for specialist attention) direct that an application be referred to a High Court judge or an authorised Circuit Judge.

12.13 If all or any of the parties consider that the matter should be dealt with by a **1A–116** judge (High Court or Circuit), the parties or any of them may arrange that the matter be listed on one of the ordinary application days (see paragraph 12.14 below). The District Judges, who will consult where necessary with one of the Chancery judges (High Court or Circuit), are usually available by post or telephone to give guidance on procedural matters, for example the court before which the matter should come or whether the matter may be dealt with in writing.

Application Days before a judge

12.14 Applications days are listed regularly before a judge, when applications and **1A–117** short appeals, including all interim matters are heard. Normally all matters will be called into court at the commencement of the day in order to work out a running order. Matters will be heard without the court going into private session unless good reason is shown. Rights of audience are unaffected. Applications days in Newcastle are subject to the Newcastle telephone application pilot scheme (see PD 23B), and many applications there are dealt with by telephone hearings.

12.15 Applications days are: Monday in Birmingham, Thursday in Bristol and Friday in Cardiff. In Manchester and Liverpool application days are on Friday of each week alternating between Manchester and Liverpool. In Leeds and Newcastle Chancery and Mercantile application days are combined. In Leeds applications are heard most Fridays. In Newcastle there is at least one application day each month, on a Friday. An application which needs to be heard urgently may be made, by telephone or in person, on a day other than the regular applications day: the Listing Officer for the relevant centre should be approached as soon as possible when the need for an urgent hearing arises.

Applications out of hours and telephone applications

1A–118 12.16 These are governed by the general rules, save that in the case of applications out of hours, the party applying should contact the relevant court office. The main relevant contact numbers are set out in Appendix 1. In case of difficulty, contact the Royal Courts of Justice, on the number given in Appendix 1.

Agreed interim orders

1A–119 12.17 Normally a hearing will not be necessary. The procedure is as in the general rules.

12.18 A judge is unlikely to agree to more than two consent adjournments of an interim application. Applications to vacate a trial date will require substantial justification and a hearing, normally before the trial judge.

Local Listing Arrangements

1A–120 12.19 Listing arrangements may vary at different centres, depending on availability of judges and courtrooms. The current details are described below.

Birmingham: Shared Listing

1A–121 12.20 The Shared List

The shared list is primarily for use by the three specialised lists of the Birmingham District Registry - those operated by the Chancery, Mercantile and Technology and Construction Courts.

The shared list is in addition to the normal lists of those courts and allows better use to be made of judicial time. Given the settlement rate of trials in the three divisions, two additional cases, the fourth and fifth fixtures, will be listed at any one time, in addition to the three cases listed before the three specialist courts. Those two additional cases will be taken by any of the section 9 judges who become available. Cases are only entered into the shared list if there is a very strong expectation that they will be heard on the day fixed.

In order, therefore, for a case to enter the shared list it must be suitable for hearing before any of the section 9 specialist judges.

Suitability for listing a case in the shared list may be suggested by the District Judge at directions stage, or by the parties when applying for the case to be listed. It is likely that 4th and 5th fixtures will be allocated an earlier trial date than a case which has to be heard by the appropriate specialist judge.

The final decision to list a case in the shared list will lie with Judge Norris QC for Chancery cases, Judge Alton for Mercantile cases, and Judge Kirkham for Technology and Construction cases.

Bristol: Reserve Listing

1A–122 12.21 In order to make available earlier hearing dates than would otherwise be possible, a reserve list is operated for Chancery cases listed to be heard in the Bristol

District Registry. Cases in the reserve list are given a fixed date, usually as a second fixture. A second fixture will only be given when there is a very strong expectation of the case being heard on that date. Other judges are called upon in the event of both first and second fixtures being effective.

Cardiff: Reserve Listing

12.22 Judge Wyn Williams QC sits both as a Chancery judge and a judge of the Technology and Construction Court. His list contains both categories of case. All cases are allocated a fixed starting date but some are first and some reserve fixtures. Other judges are called upon in the event of both first and reserve fixtures being effective. All the judges who sit at the Cardiff Civil Justice Centre (Judges Price QC, Masterman, Chambers QC and Hickinbottom) are authorised to sit as Chancery judges. Any discussions concerning listing should be with the Chancery Listing clerk in Cardiff. **1A–123**

Manchester, Liverpool and Preston

12.23 The Shared List **1A–124**

When sitting at the same court centre, Judge Howarth and Judge Hodge QC will assist each other in the disposal of their respective daily lists. If necessary and if they are available at the relevant court centre, Judge Kershaw QC and Judge Hegarty QC (who are the local Mercantile judges), and other circuit judges will assist in the disposal of business. Listing for all Chancery matters in Manchester, Liverpool and Preston is dealt with from Manchester.

Second Fixtures

Given the very high settlement rate, most cases will be given a second fixture date as well as a first fixture date. Parties to second fixtures are notified in advance of the hearing date if the case will not be reached on that date. The amount of notice depends on the circumstances of the case. In some cases it may not be until the previous working day but it is usually farther ahead, and longer may be guaranteed in the case of particular difficulties.

Leeds and Newcastle

12.24 When sitting at the same time in Leeds or Newcastle Judge Behrens, Judge Langan QC and Judge Kaye QC will assist each other in the disposal of their respective daily lists. The Chancery and Mercantile Court lists are run on a shared basis in both Leeds and Newcastle. Second fixtures are used in the same way as on the Northern Circuit, and on the same basis. **1A–125**

CHAPTER 13

COUNTY COURTS

Key Rules: CPR Part 30; PD 7, paragraph 2

Unified procedure

13.1 A key feature of the civil justice reforms is the introduction of a unified procedure for the High Court and for county courts. The procedure to be followed in both courts is therefore the same. **1A–126**

Chancery cases brought in the county court

13.2 Any county court has jurisdiction to hear a Chancery case, subject to two principal exceptions: (1) a probate claim in a county court must be brought in a county court where there is a Chancery District Registry: CPR part 57.2(3); (2) an intellectual property claim must be brought in any such county court or in the Patents County Court: CPR Part 63.13 and PD 63 paragraph 18. **1A–127**

13.3 If a case of a Chancery nature is brought in any county court, the claim form should be marked "Chancery business" in the top left hand corner: CPR Part 7, PD 2.5.

13.4 If a Chancery case is brought in a county court which does not coincide with a Chancery District Registry, consideration ought to be given at an early stage to whether it needs to have specialist case management or a specialist trial judge, because of the nature of the issues. If it needs either, then it may be necessary to transfer the case to a county court at a Chancery District Registry. If there are good reasons against such a transfer, for example because of the distance involved and the convenience of parties or witnesses, then it may be possible, with enough notice, to arrange that the trial is heard by a recorder with Chancery experience or even by a Chancery circuit judge. Guidance has been given to District Judges by the Chancery supervising judges as to the circumstances and types of case in respect of which either a transfer or a special arrangement for trial by a judge or recorder with specialist experience may be appropriate.

Transfer to a county court

1A–128 13.5 Any Chancery case which does not require to be heard by a High Court judge, and falls within the jurisdiction of the county courts, may be transferred to a county court. Where a case has been so transferred, the papers must be marked "Chancery Business" so as to ensure, so far as possible, suitable listing.

13.6 The jurisdiction of county courts is set out in the High Court and County Court Jurisdiction Order 1991 as amended, and in enactments amended by that Order.

13.7 The jurisdiction of the High Court to transfer cases to a county court is contained in the County Courts Act 1984, section 40, as substituted by the Courts and Legal Services Act 1990, section 2(1). Under that section, the court has jurisdiction in certain circumstances to strike out actions which ought to have been begun in a county court.

13.8 A claim with an estimated value of less than £50,000 will generally be transferred to a county court, if the county court has jurisdiction, unless it is either within a specialist list or is within the criteria in rule 30.3(2).

13.9 If the case is one of a specifically Chancery nature a transfer from the High Court will ordinarily be to the Central London County Court (Chancery List) ("the CLCC") where cases are heard by specialist Chancery Circuit judges or recorders and a continuous Chancery List is maintained, unless the parties prefer a transfer to a local county court.

13.10 Even where the estimated value of the claim is more than £50,000 transfer to the CLCC may still be ordered if the criteria in rule 30.3(2) point in that direction, in particular having regard to the criteria in rule 30.3(2)(d), namely the complexity of the facts, legal issues, remedies or procedures involved.

13.11 If a claim is transferred to a county court at the allocation stage no other directions will usually be given and all case management will be left to the county court.

13.12 The Chancery List at the CLCC is managed by the Business Chancery and Patents Section at 26 Park Crescent, London W1 4HT. The telephone number of the section manager is set out in Appendix 1. A guide to the Chancery List may be obtained from the section manager.

13.13 As an alternative to starting the case in the Chancery Division and transferring to the CLCC a case (if appropriate to be started there) may be started at the CLCC and a request made there for it to be transferred to the Chancery List. The request will receive judicial consideration and a transfer will be made if appropriate.

13.14 It should be noted that only in very limited circumstances may freezing orders or search orders be granted in the county court. If necessary, an application may be made in the High Court in aid of the county court proceedings if such an order is to be sought in a case where it cannot be granted in the county court.

13.15 Practitioners should continue to take care that Chancery cases requiring chancery expertise are dealt with in a county court with a Chancery District Registry.

Patents County Court

13.16 See Chapter 23 below.

1A–129

CHAPTER 14

USE OF INFORMATION TECHNOLOGY

Key Rules: CPR rule 1.4, Part 6;PD 6, PD 32, Annex 3

General

14.1 The CPR contain certain provisions about the use of information technology in the conduct of cases. Apart from these provisions, no standard practice has evolved or been prescribed for the use of information technology in civil cases, but it is possible to identify certain areas in which electronic techniques may be used which should encourage the efficient and economical conduct of litigation.

1A–130

14.2 It must be remembered, however, that it is unlikely that the number of litigants in person will diminish, and the number may well increase, in the future and that not all solicitors have available sophisticated IT facilities. Use of IT is acceptable only if no party to the case will be unfairly prejudiced and its use will save time or money.

14.3 A number of specific applications of information technology have been well developed in recent years. The use of fax, the provision of skeleton arguments on disk, and daily transcripts on disk (with or withou appropriate software) have become commonplace. Short applications may be economically heard by a conference telephone call, provided that the parties ensure that the judge or Master has the relevant documents and a draft order. Taking evidence by video link has become more common, and the available technology has improved considerably. There is still little experience of the intensive use of information technology in the ordinary course of the trial by, for example, providing documents as images to be displayed.

14.4 In any case in which it is proposed to use information technology in the preparation, management and presentation of a case in a manner which is not provided for by the CPR, it may be necessary for directions to be given by the judge who is to hear the case. It is unlikely to be satisfactory for parties and their solicitors to agree to a particular application of information technology (for example, using imaging techniques to deal either with disclosure or with the preparation of documents for use in court, in effect by way of electronic bundles) without the agreement of the judge. Accordingly it is likely, particularly in heavy cases, that it will be desirable for a judge to be nominated to conduct the case. Where a nomination is desired, application should be made to the Chancellor in writing by letter addressed to his clerk for a judge to be nominated.

14.5 In every case in which it is proposed to use information technology, the first step will be for the solicitors for all parties to determine whether it is possible to establish a common protocol for the electronic exchange and management of information. It is recommended that the protocol provided by the Technology and Construction Solicitors' Association ("TeCSA") be used. The TeCSA protocol has enjoyed success and is available from TeCSA's website at *http://www.tecsa.org.uk/protocol/protocol.htm*. The CPR's underlying policy of co-operation and collaboration is particularly important in this context. In a large case the parties must facilitate the task of the judge by providing any additional help and IT know-how, including, for example, demonstrations, which he or she requires in order to control the case properly.

14.6 The judges of the Chancery Division and their clerks are equipped with IBM compatible computers running Windows (usually NT 4.0 but in some cases another version) and MS Office 97 or 2000. To avoid compatibility problems it is preferable that text files to be provided for use by a judge or clerk be provided in Rich Text Format (RTF).

Provision of information on disk: Skeleton arguments etc

1A–131 14.7 Skeleton arguments, chronologies, witness statements, experts' reports and other documents (if available in electronic form) should be provided on disk (or by e-mail) if the judge requests it. Enquiry should be made of the judge's clerk for this purpose. Where the complexity of the case justifies it, attention must be given to providing the judge with versions of the documents containing links to enable cross-references to be followed up in a convenient manner. Disks provided to judges must be checked for virus contamination and be clean.

E-mail communications with the Chancery Division

1A–132 14.8 A protocol for e-mail communications with the Chancery Division sets out how parties may communicate by e-mail on certain matters, and can be found at www.hmcourts-service.gov.uk. The protocol applies PD 5B on electronic communication and filing of documents in respect of specified documents: skeleton arguments, chronologies, reading lists, lists of issues, lists of authorities (but not the authorities themselves) and lists of *dramatis personae* sent in advance of a hearing. The protocol sets out the relevant email addresses, which are also to be found in Appendix 1. The clerk to the judge concerned should be contacted to find out whether the judge will accept other documents by e-mail and whether documents should be sent by e-mail direct to the judge's clerk's e-mail address.

Transcripts

1A–133 14.9 The various shorthand writers provide a number of different transcript services. These range from an immediately displayed transcript which follows the evidence as it is given (usually with about 10 seconds delay) to provision of transcripts of a day's proceedings one or two days in arrears. The use of transcripts is always of assistance if they can be justified on the ground of cost and in long cases they are a considerable advantage. If an instantaneous service is proposed, inquiries should be made of the judge's clerk, and sufficient time for the installation of the equipment necessary and for any familiarisation on the part of the judge with the system should be found. If special transcript-handling software is to be used by the parties, consideration should be given to making the software available to the judge.

14.10 If the shorthand writers make disks available (and nearly all do) the judge should be provided with disks as they appear if he or she requires them.

Fax communications

1A–134 14.11 The use of fax in the service of documents is now authorised by rule 6.2(1) and PD 6.

14.12 Each of the judges sitting in the Chancery Division may be reached by fax if the occasion warrants it. The respective judges' clerks' telephone and fax numbers are set out in Appendix 1. Where the name of the judge is not known, short documents may be sent to the Chancery Judges' Listing Office, whose fax number is also given in Appendix 1. Written evidence should not be sent by fax to this number. All fax messages should have a cover sheet setting out the name of the case, the case number and the judge's name, if known.

Telephone hearings

1A–135 14.13 Applications may be heard by telephone, if the court so orders, but normally only if all parties entitled to be given notice agree, and none of them intends to be present in person. Special provisions apply where the applicant or another party is in person: see paragraph 6.3 of PD 23. Guidance on other aspects of telephone hearings, and in particular how to set them up, is contained in paragraph 6.5 of PD 23. When putting that guidance into practice once an order has been made for a hearing to take place by a telephone conference call, the following points may be useful:

> (1) A telephone hearing may be set up by calling the BT Legal Call Centre on 0800 028 4194. The caller's name and EB account number will have to be

given. Other telecommunications providers may also be able to offer the same facility.

(2) The names and telephone numbers of the participants in the hearing including the judge must be provided.

(3) The co-ordinator should be told the date, time and likely approximate duration of the hearing.

(4) The name and address of the court and the court case reference should be given, for delivery of the tape of the hearing.

(5) Then tell the court that the hearing has been arranged.

It is necessary to ensure that all participants in the hearing have all documents that it may be necessary for any of them to refer to by the time the hearing begins.

Video-conferencing

14.14 The court may allow evidence to be taken using video-conferencing facilities: **1A–136** rule 32.3. Experience has shown that normally taking evidence by this means is comparatively straightforward, but its suitability may depend on the particular witness, and the case, and on such matters as the volume and nature of documents which need to be referred to in the course of the evidence.

14.15 A video-link may also be used for an application, or otherwise in the course of any hearing.

14.16 Annex 3 to PD 32 (Video Conferencing Guidance) provides further detail on the manner in which video conferencing facilities are to be used in civil proceedings.

14.17 Video conferencing facilities are available at the Royal Courts of Justice in Court 38. It is convenient that these facilities should be used if at all possible in relation to proceedings which are under way in the Royal Courts of Justice. Attention is drawn to the following matters:

(1) Permission to use video conferencing during a hearing should be obtained as early as possible in the proceedings. If all parties are agreed that the use of video conferencing is appropriate, then a hearing may not be necessary to obtain such permission.

(2) Before an order fixing the appointment for the use of the facilities at the Royal Courts of Justice is obtained their availability must be ascertained from the video managers (Roger Little / Norman Muller, tel. 020 7947 7609, fax 020 7947 6357). When the order is made the video managers must be informed immediately so as to ensure that all necessary arrangements can be made well in advance of the hearing.

(3) If it is necessary for other facilities to be used, whether because the Royal Courts of Justice facilities are unavailable or for any other reason, consideration should be given to using the facilities available at the Bar Council or the Law Society. The party seeking to use the facilities will be responsible for making all the necessary arrangements.

(4) If the use of facilities other than those at the Royal Courts of Justice, the Bar Council or the Law Society is proposed, approval must first be obtained to the use of the particular facilities even if the parties are agreed.

CHAPTER 15

MISCELLANEOUS MATTERS

Key Rules: CPR Part 39; PD — Miscellaneous Provisions relating to Hearings supplementing CPR Part 39

Litigants in person

15.1 The provisions of this Guide in general apply to litigants in person. Thus, for **1A–137** example, litigants in person should:

(1) prepare a written summary of their argument in the same circumstances as

those in which a represented party is required to produce a skeleton argument;

(2) prepare a bundle of documents in the same way that a represented party is required to produce a bundle of documents; and

(3) be prepared to put forward their argument within a limited time if they are directed to do so by the court.

15.2 This means that litigants in person should identify in advance of the hearing those points which they consider to be their strongest points, and that they should put those points at the forefront of their oral and written submissions to the court.

15.3 It is not the function of court officials to give legal advice. However, subject to that, they will do their best to assist any litigant. Litigants in person who need further assistance should contact the Community Legal Service (CLS) through their Information Points. The CLS is developing local networks of people giving legal assistance such as law centres, local solicitors or the Citizens' Advice Bureaux. CLS Information Points are being set up in libraries and other public places. Litigants can telephone the CLS to find their nearest CLS Information Point on 0845 608 1122 or can log on to the CLS website at *www.justask.org.uk* for the CLS directory and for legal information.

15.4 The Royal Courts of Justice Advice Bureau off the Main Hall at the Royal Courts of Justice is open from Monday to Friday from 10am to 1pm and from 2pm to 5pm. The Bureau is run by lawyers in conjunction with the Citizens' Advice Bureau and is independent of the court. The Bureau operates on a "first come first served" basis, or telephone advice is available on 0845 120 3715 (or 020 7947 6880) from Monday to Friday between 11am and 12 noon and between 3 and 4pm. The Bureau also operates a Bankruptcy Court Advice Desk on Monday and Wednesday mornings (10am — 1pm) in the Consultation Room, 1st Floor, Thomas More Building.

15.5 Where a litigant in person is the applicant, the court may ask one of the represented parties to open the matter briefly and impartially, and to summarise the issues.

15.6 It is the duty of an advocate to ensure that the court is informed of all relevant decisions and enactments of which the advocate is aware (whether favourable or not to his or her case) and to draw the court's attention to any material irregularity.

15.7 Representatives for other parties must treat litigants in person with consideration. They should where possible be given photocopies of any authorities which are to be cited before the case starts in addition to the skeleton argument. They should be asked to give their names to the usher if they have not already done so. Representatives for other parties should explain the court's order after the hearing if the litigant in person does not appear to understand it.

15.8 If a litigant in person wishes to give oral evidence he or she will generally be required to do so from the witness box in the same manner as any other witness of fact.

15.9 A litigant in person must give an address for service in England or Wales. If he or she is a claimant, the address will be in the claim form or other document by which the proceedings are brought. If he or she is a defendant, it will be in the acknowledgment of service form which he or she must send to the court on being served with the proceedings. It is essential that any change of address should be notified in writing to Chancery Chambers and to all other parties to the case.

15.10 Notice of hearing dates will be given by post to litigants at the address shown in the court file. A litigant in person will generally be given a fixed date for trial on application. A litigant in person who wishes to apply for a fixed date should ask the Chancery Judges' Listing Office for a copy of its Guidance Notes for Litigants in Person.

Assistance to litigants in person

1A–138 15.11 A litigant who is acting in person may be assisted at a hearing by another person, often referred to as a McKenzie friend (see *McKenzie v. McKenzie* [1971] P 33). The litigant must be present at the hearing. If the hearing is in private, it is a matter of discretion for the court whether such an assistant is allowed to attend the hearing. That may depend, among other things, on the nature of the proceedings.

15.12 The McKenzie friend is allowed to help by taking notes, quietly prompting the litigant and offering advice and suggestions to the litigant. The court can, and sometimes does, permit the McKenzie friend to address the court on behalf of the litigant, by making an order to that effect under section 27(2)(c) of the Courts and Legal Services Act 1990 (by reference to sections 17 and 18 of that Act), but this is an exceptional course. Some factors which may be relevant to whether this should be permitted have been discussed in reported judgments, including *Izzo v. Philip Ross* [2002] BIPR 310 and *Paragon Finance v. Noueiri (Practice Note)* [2001] EWCA Civ 1402, [2001] 1 W.L.R. 2357.

15.13 The Personal Support Unit (Room M104) offers personal support for litigants in person, witnesses and others. The PSU will sometimes be able to accompany litigants into court to provide emotional support and give other guidance, but it does not give legal advice.

Representation on behalf of companies

15.14 Rule 39.6 allows a company or other corporation to be represented at trial by **1A–139** an employee if the employee has been authorised by the company or corporation to appear on its behalf and the court gives permission. Paragraph 5 of PD 39 describes what is needed to obtain permission from the court for this purpose and mentions some of the considerations relevant to the grant or refusal of permission.

Robed and unrobed hearings

15.15 Advocates (and judges) wear robes at hearings by High Court judges of trials **1A–140** (including preliminary issues) and statutory appeals or cases stated. Robes are not worn for other hearings, including appeals from Masters, Bankruptcy Registrars and county courts. The Daily Cause List states, in relation to each judge's list, whether the matter is to be heard robed or unrobed. Robes are not worn at hearings before Masters. Robes are worn at the following hearings before Bankruptcy and Companies Court Registrars: public examinations of bankrupts and of directors or other officers of companies; applications for discharge from bankruptcy or for suspension of such discharge; all proceedings under the Company Directors Disqualification Act 1986; petitions to wind up companies; final hearings of petitions for the reduction of capital of companies.

Solicitors' rights of audience

15.16 At hearings in chambers before 26 April 1999 solicitors had general rights of **1A–141** audience. The fact that a matter which would then have been heard in chambers is now heard in public under Part 39 does not affect rights of audience, so in such matters as would have been heard in chambers previously, the general right of audience for solicitors continues to apply. Such cases included appeals from Masters, applications for summary judgment, and those concerned with pleadings, security for costs and the like, pre-trial reviews, and applications concerned with the administration of a deceased person's estate, a trust or a charity. They did not include applications in what is now the Interim Applications List or the Companies Court, nor appeals from county courts or insolvency appeals. Solicitors do, however, have general rights of audience in personal insolvency matters; this is not affected by whether the hearing is in public or private.

15.17 If a solicitor who does not have the appropriate special right of audience wishes to be heard in a case which is not one which, before 26 April 1999, would have been heard in chambers nor a personal insolvency case, an application may be made for the grant of a special right of audience before the particular court and for the particular proceedings under the Courts and Legal Services Act 1990, section 27(2)(c).

Recording at hearings

15.18 In the Royal Courts of Justice it is normal to record all oral evidence and any **1A–142** judgment delivered during a hearing before a judge. If any party wishes a recording to be made of any other part of the proceedings, this should be mentioned in advance or at the time of the hearing.

15.19 At hearings before Masters, it is not normally practicable to record anything other than any oral evidence and the judgment, but these will be recorded. No party or member of the public may use recording equipment without the court's permission.

Chapter 16

Suggestions for Improvement and Court Users' Committees

16.1 Suggestions for improvements in this Guide or in the practice or procedure of the Chancery Division are welcome. Unless they fall within the remit of the committees mentioned at paras. 16.3 to 16.7 below, they should be sent to the clerk to the Chancellor.

Chancery Division Court Users' Committee

1A–143 16.2 The Chancery Division Court Users' Committee's function is to review, as may from time to time be required, the practice and procedure of all courts forming part of the Chancery Division, to ensure that they continue to provide a just, economical and expeditious system for the resolution of disputes. The Chancellor is the chairman. Its membership includes judges, a Master, barristers, solicitors and other representatives of court staff and users. Meetings are held three times a year, and more often if necessary. Suggestions for points to be considered by the Committee should be sent to the clerk to the Chancellor.

Insolvency Court Users' Committee

1A–144 16.3 Proposals for change in insolvency matters fall within the remit of the Insolvency Court Users' Committee unless they relate to the Insolvency Rules 1986. The members of the Insolvency Court Users' Committee include members of the Bar, the Law Society, the Insolvency Service and the Society of Practitioners of Insolvency. Meetings are held three times a year, and more often if necessary. Suggestions for points to be considered by the Committee should be sent to the clerk to the Chancellor.

Insolvency Rules Committee

1A–145 16.4 The Insolvency Rules Committee must be consulted before any changes to the Insolvency Rules 1986 are made. The Chairman of the Insolvency Rules Committee is Mr Justice David Richards. Proposals for changes in the Rules should be sent to The Insolvency Service, Room 502, PO Box 203, 21 Bloomsbury Street, London WC1B 3QW, with a copy to the clerk to Mr Justice David Richards.

Intellectual Property Court Users' Committee

1A–146 16.5 This considers the problems and concerns of intellectual property litigation generally. Membership of the committee includes the principal Patent judges, a Master, a representative of each of the Patent Bar Association, the Intellectual Property Lawyers Association, the Chartered Institute of Patent Agents, the Institute of Trade Mark Agents and the Trade Marks Designs and Patents Federation. It will also include one or more other Chancery judges. The Chairman is Mr Justice Pumfrey. Anyone having views concerning the improvement of intellectual property litigation is invited to make his or her views known to the committee, preferably through the relevant professional representative on the committee.

Pension Litigation Court Users' Committee

1A–147 16.6 This consists of a judge and a Master, two barristers and two solicitors. Its Chairman is Mr Justice Etherton. Any suggestions for consideration by the committee should be sent to the clerk to Mr Justice Etherton.

Court Users' Committees outside London

16.7 There are several Court Users' Committees relating to Chancery work on **1A–148** circuit. They are as follows:

(1) *The Northern Circuit and the North-Eastern Circuit Court Users Committees*: the Northern Circuit Chancery Court Users' Committee, which meets in Manchester; the Leeds Chancery and Mercantile Court Users' Committee; and the Newcastle Joint Chancery Mercantile and TCC Court Users' Committee. Each of these meets two or three times a year, and has a membership including judges, court staff, barristers and solicitors. The Vice-Chancellor of the County Palatine of Lancaster chairs these three Committees, and the Vice-Chancellor's clerk acts as secretary to each Committee. All communications should be to the clerk.

(2) *The Western Circuit, Wales & Chester and Midland Circuits Court User Committees*: the circuit committees normally meet three or four times per year. They have a membership including judges, court staff, barristers and solicitors.

    (a) *Western Circuit*: Judge Weeks chairs the committee in Bristol (or Mr Justice Hart when there), Mrs Liz Bodman acts as secretary. All communications should be addressed to her at Chancery Listing Section, Bristol Crown Court, Small Street, Bristol.

    (b) *Wales & Chester Circuit*: Judge Williams chairs the committee in Cardiff (or Mr Justice Hart when there), the Diary Manager, Annette Parsons acts as secretary. All communications should be addressed to her at Cardiff Civil Justice Centre, 2 Park Street, Cardiff.

    (c) *Midland Circuit*: Judge Norris chairs the committee in Birmingham (or Mr Justice Hart when there), the Chancery Listing Officer, Amanda Lee acts as secretary. All communications should be addressed to her at Chancery Listing Section, Birmingham Civil Justice Centre, 33 Bull Street, Birmingham.

CHAPTER 17

ALTERNATIVE DISPUTE RESOLUTION
Key Rules: CPR rules 3.1 and 26.4

17.1 While emphasising the primary role of the court as a forum for deciding cases, **1A–149** the court encourages parties to consider the use of ADR (such as, but not confined to, mediation and conciliation) as a possible means of resolving disputes or particular issues.

17.2 The settlement of disputes by means of ADR can:

(1) significantly help litigants to save costs;

(2) save litigants the delay of litigation in reaching finality in their disputes;

(3) enable litigants to achieve settlement of their disputes while preserving their existing commercial relationships and market reputation;

(4) provide litigants with a wider range of solutions than those offered by litigation; and

(5) make a substantial contribution to the more efficient use of judicial resources.

17.3 The court will in an appropriate case invite the parties to consider whether their dispute, or particular issues in it, could be resolved through ADR. In particular, it is to be expected that the judge or Master at any case management conference will inquire what steps can usefully be taken to resolve the dispute by settlement discussion, alternative dispute resolution or other means. The parties should be in a position to tell the court what steps have been taken or are proposed to be taken. The court may also adjourn the case for a specified period of time to encourage and enable the parties to use ADR and for this purpose extend the time for compliance by the parties or any of them with any requirement under the CPR or this Guide or any order of the court. The court may make such order as to the costs that the parties may incur by reason of the adjournment or their using or attempting to use ADR as may in all the circumstances seem appropriate.

17.4 Legal representatives in all cases should consider with their clients and the other parties concerned the possibility of attempting to resolve the dispute or particular issues by ADR and they should ensure that their clients are fully informed as to the most cost effective means of resolving their dispute.

17.5 Parties who consider that ADR might be an appropriate means of resolving their dispute, or particular issues in the dispute, may apply for directions at any stage.

17.6 The clerk to the Commercial Court keeps some published information as to individuals and bodies that offer ADR services. (The list also includes individuals and bodies that offer arbitration services.) If the parties are unable to agree upon a neutral individual, or panel of individuals, for ADR, they may refer to the judge for assistance, though the court will not recommend any particular body or individual to act as mediator or arbitrator.

SECTION B SPECIALIST WORK

CHAPTER 18

INTRODUCTION TO THE SPECIALIST WORK OF THE CHANCERY DIVISION

1A–150 18.1 As explained in Chapter 1 of this Guide, some proceedings in the High Court must be brought in the Chancery Division. These matters include:

(1) claims for the sale, exchange or partition of land, or the raising of charges on land;

(2) mortgage claims;

(3) claims relating to the execution of trusts;

(4) claims relating to the administration of the estates of deceased persons;

(5) bankruptcy matters;

(6) claims for the dissolution of partnerships or the taking of partnership or other accounts;

(7) claims for the rectification, setting aside or cancellation of deeds or other instruments in writing;

(8) contentious probate business;

(9) claims relating to patents, trade marks, registered designs, copyright or design right;

(10) claims for the appointment of a guardian of a minor's estate;

(11) jurisdiction under the Companies Acts 1985 and the Insolvency Act 1986 relating to companies;

(12) some revenue matters;

(13) claims relating to charities;

(14) some proceedings under the Solicitors Act 1974;

(15) proceedings under the Landlord and Tenant Acts 1927 (Part I), 1954 (Part II) and 1987 and the Leasehold Reform Act 1967;

(16) proceedings (other than those in the Commercial Court) relating to the application of Articles 81 and 82 of the EC Treaty and the equivalent provisions of the Competition Act 1998.

(17) proceedings under other miscellaneous statutory jurisdictions.

18.2 There is concurrent jurisdiction with the Family Division under the Inheritance (Provision for Family and Dependants) Act 1975.

18.3 Certain appeals lie to the Chancery Division under statute. These are dealt with in paragraph 10.19. Intellectual property appeals and revenue appeals are also covered in Chapters 23 and 25 respectively.

18.4 The Chancery judges are the nominated judges of the Court of Protection but this Guide does not deal with the Court of Protection.

CHAPTER 19

THE BANKRUPTCY COURT

1A–151 *Key Rules: PD—Insolvency Proceedings; Insolvency Rules 1986*

19.1 The Bankruptcy Court is part of the Chancery Division and disposes of **1A–152** proceedings relating to insolvent individuals arising under Parts VIII to XI of the Insolvency Act 1986 and related legislation. These include applications for interim orders to support an individual voluntary arrangement, applications to set aside a statutory demand, bankruptcy petitions and various applications concerned with the realisation and distribution of the assets of individuals who have been adjudged bankrupt, as well as proceedings concerning the administration in bankruptcy of the insolvent estate of a deceased person. The procedure in the Bankruptcy Court is governed by the Insolvency Rules and the PD—Insolvency Proceedings. Appeals in bankruptcy matters are covered in Chapter 10.

19.2 Proceedings in the Bankruptcy Court are issued in the Bankruptcy Issue and Search Room and are dealt with by the Registrars in Bankruptcy, not the Masters. Proceedings under Parts VIII to XI of the Insolvency Act 1986 should be entitled "IN BANKRUPTCY".

19.3 Certain matters, such as applications for injunctions or for committal for contempt, are heard by a judge. A judge is available to hear such matters each day in term time and applications may be listed for any such day. The judge will normally also be hearing the interim applications list for the day, but one or more other judges may be available to assist if necessary.

19.4 The Registrar may refer or adjourn proceedings to the judge, having regard to such matters as the complexity of the proceedings, whether the proceedings raise new or controversial points of law, the likely date and length of the hearing, public interest in the proceedings, and the availability of relevant specialist expertise. When proceedings have been referred or adjourned to the judge, interim applications and applications for directions or case management will be listed before a judge, except where liberty to apply to the Registrar has been given.

19.5 There are prescribed forms for use in connection with all types of statutory demand and of petitions for bankruptcy orders. Every other type of application is either an originating application in Form 7.1 (meaning an application to the court which is not an application in pending proceedings before the court) or an ordinary application in Form 7.2 (meaning any other application to the court).

Statutory demands

19.6 All applications to set aside a statutory demand are referred initially to a **1A–153** Registrar. The application may be dismissed by the court without a hearing if it fails to disclose sufficient grounds (see paragraph 12.4 of PD—Insolvency Proceedings and Insolvency Rules, r. 6.5(4). If it is not dismissed summarily, it will be allocated a hearing date when the Registrar may either dispose of it summarily or give directions for its disposal at a later date. Such directions will commonly include an order for the filing and service of written evidence and a listing certificate of compliance (see paragraph 19.13 below).

Bankruptcy petitions

19.7 The court will not normally allow more than one bankruptcy petition to be **1A–154** presented against an individual at any one time.

19.8 In cases where the statutory demand relied on has not been personally served on the debtor or where execution of the debt has been returned unsatisfied in whole or in part, the permission of the Registrar is required before a petition may be presented to the court. For service of statutory demands see paragraphs 10–11 and 13 of PD—Insolvency Proceedings.

19.9 On presentation to the court a bankruptcy petition is given a distinctive number. The details of the name and address of the petitioner, of his solicitors and of the debtor are entered on a computerised record which may be searched by attendance at the Issue and Search Room. It will also be endorsed with a hearing date which may be extended on application without notice if the petitioner has been unable to serve the petition on the debtor before the hearing date (see paragraph 14 of PD—Insolvency Proceedings).

19.10 A debtor who intends to oppose the making of a bankruptcy order should file and serve a written notice in the prescribed form stating his grounds for opposing the petition not less than seven days before the hearing date. The court may give such further directions as to the filing of evidence and of listing certificates (see paragraph 19.13 below) as it considers appropriate to the disposal of the petition.

Other applications

1A–155 19.11 Many different types of application may be made to the court for the purpose of the administration of the estate and affairs of a bankrupt individual or insolvent person who is subject to an individual voluntary arrangement (IVA). These may involve such matters as the examination of the bankrupt or of persons having knowledge of his affairs, the realisation of assets in his estate and the determination of disputes regarding the validity of a creditor's claim to dividend or entitlement to vote at a creditors' meeting. Such applications will be given a hearing date when the Registrar will give such directions as are appropriate to the type of case, which may include directions for the filing and service of written evidence, for the cross-examination of witnesses and for the filing of certificates of compliance (see paragraph 19.13 below).

Orders without attendance

1A–156 19.12 In suitable cases the court will normally be prepared to make orders under Part VIII of the Act (interim orders for IVAs) and consent orders without attendance by the parties. Details of these types of order are set out in paragraph 16 of the PD—Insolvency Proceedings.

Listing certificates

1A–157 19.13 In order to prevent waste of the court's time each party to insolvency proceedings may be required by the court to file a listing certificate in which he will be required to certify whether the directions previously given by the court have been complied with, whether and by whom he will be represented at the final hearing, his estimate of the time required for such hearing and his and his representative's dates to avoid. On the filing of the certificates in any particular case the court will fix a date for the final hearing of the case and notify the parties.

Preparation for hearings before the Registrars

1A–158 19.14 Paragraphs 7.39 to 7.50 apply to hearings before the Bankruptcy Registrars. Skeleton arguments and bundles should be delivered to the Bankruptcy Registry.

General information

1A–159 19.15 Inspection of the court's record and court file in any insolvency proceedings is governed by Insolvency Rules, rr. 7.28 and 7.31.

19.16 The following publications regarding practice and procedure in the Bankruptcy Court are available free from the Bankruptcy Issue and Search Room and from Room TM1.10 Thomas More Building, Royal Courts of Justice:

    (1) Current Practice Direction and Practice Notes

    (2) A concise Guide to procedure in the Bankruptcy Court

    (3) *"I want to set aside my statutory demand—what do I do?"*

    (4) *"I have a petition against me—what do I do?"*

    (5) *"I want to appeal an order made by a District Judge or an order made by a Bankruptcy Registrar of the High Court—what can I do?"*

    (6) *"I wish to apply for my Certificate of Discharge from Bankruptcy—what do I do?"*

    (7) Dealing with debt—how to make someone bankrupt

    (8) Dealing with debt—how to petition for your own bankruptcy.

CHAPTER 20

THE COMPANIES COURT

Key Rules: PD 49—Applications under the Companies Act; PD—Insolvency; Insolvency Rules 1986; Insolvent Companies (Disqualifica-

tion of Unfit Directors) Proceedings Rules 1987;PD—Directors Disqualification Proceedings

20.1 The Companies Court is a part of the Chancery Division. Applications in the **1A–160** High Court under the Companies Act 1985, the Insurance Companies Act 1982, the Financial Services and Markets Act 2002, the Insolvency Act 1986 in relation to companies registered in England and Wales, and the Company Directors Disqualification Act 1986, must be commenced in the Companies Court. Proceedings concerning insolvent partnerships, under the Insolvent Partnerships Order 1994, are also brought in the Companies Court (unlike proceedings against partners separately, which, if the partner is an individual, are brought in bankruptcy). Many other kinds of application are brought in the Companies Court. Appeals in Companies Court matters are dealt with in Chapter 10.

20.2 Applications, other than in insolvency, are governed by the Civil Procedure Rules and PD 49—Applications under the Companies Act 1985.

20.3 Applications in insolvency relating to companies (and to insolvent partnerships) are governed by the Insolvency Rules and PD—Insolvency Proceedings.

20.4 Proceedings under the Company Directors Disqualification Act 1986 are governed by the Insolvent Companies (Disqualification of Unfit Directors) Proceedings Rules 1987 and the PD—Directors Disqualification Proceedings.

20.5 Proceedings in the Companies Court under a particular statute should be entitled accordingly, thus:
"In the matter of [name and registration number of the company] And in the matter of the Companies Act 1985 [and of any other statute as appropriate]"
"In the matter of [name of the relevant company] And in the matter of the Company Directors Disqualification Act 1986"
"In the matter of [name of the debtor] And in the matter of the Insolvency Act 1986 [and of any appropriate order, such as the Insolvent Partnerships Order 1994]"

20.6 The Companies Court has a separate administrative procedure. Proceedings are issued in the Companies Court General Office, and they are dealt with by the Registrars.

20.7 Petitions for winding up, petitions for confirmation by the court of reduction of capital, and interim applications for directions in proceedings by shareholders are among the principal matters heard by the Registrars. A Registrar may direct that any case be heard by a judge even if it is a kind of application which would normally be heard by a Registrar.

20.8 Certain matters such as applications for an administration order under Part II of the Insolvency Act 1986, petitions for approval by the court of schemes of arrangement and applications for the appointment of provisional liquidators are heard by a judge. A judge is available to hear companies matters each day in term time, and applications to be heard by that judge may be listed for any such day. The judge will normally also be hearing the Interim Applications List for the day, but one or more other judges may be available to assist if necessary. The Registrar may refer or adjourn proceedings to the judge in accordance with the criteria set out in paragraph 19.4 above.

Preparation for hearings before the Registrars

20.9 Paragraphs 7.39 to 7.50 apply to hearings before the Registrars of the **1A–161** Companies Court. Skeleton arguments and bundles should be delivered to the Companies Court Issue Section.

Administration Orders

20.10 The statutory regime for administrations commencing on or after 15 **1A–162**

57

September 2003, with certain exceptions, is found in the Insolvency Act 1986, schedule B1, which should be read with the new Part 2 of the Insolvency Rules 1986. Administrations commenced before 15 September 2003 and administrations of certain bodies (building societies, insolvent partnerships, limited liability partnerships, certain insurers, and public utility companies listed in section 249(1)(a)–(d) of the Enterprise Act 2002) continue to be governed by Part II of the Insolvency Act 1986 (or enacted before the introduction of Schedule B1) and the former Part 2 of the Insolvency Rules 1986. Administration creates a statutory moratorium and allows the affairs, business and property of the company to be managed by an administrator.

20.11 Administrators may be appointed by the court or out of court. By paragraph 3(i) of Schedule B1 the administrator must perform his duties with the objective of:

(1) rescuing the company as a going concern, or

(2) achieving a better result for the company's creditors as a whole than would be likely if the company were wound up (without first being in administration), or

(3) realising property in order to make a distribution to one or more secured or preferential creditors.

Court Order

1A–163   20.12 An application to the court must be commenced by the prescribed form of application (Form 2.1B under the new regime) and must be supported by an affidavit. The Act and Rules specify the information which must be included in the affidavit. The application may be made by the company, its directors, one or more creditors, the justices' chief executive for a magistrates' court (in relation to a fine) or any combination of the above. The application will be listed before a judge.

20.13 To make the order the court must be satisfied that the company is or is likely to become unable to pay its debts and that the administration order is likely to achieve the purpose of the administration.

Out of court

1A–164   20.14 Under the new regime, the holder of a qualifying floating charge, the company or its directors, may appoint an administrator without going through the court process. The appointment becomes effective when a notice of appointment in the prescribed form accompanied by the dministrators' consent to act and a statement by him that in his opinion the purpose of the administration is likely to be achieved has been filed with the court. Rule 2.19 makes special provision for filing notice of appointment by fax out of business hours. (Form 2.7B). The fax number for filing notice in the Royal Courts of Justice is 020 7947 6607.

Schemes of arrangement

1A–165   20.15 A scheme under section 425 of the Companies Act 1985 can be proposed whether or not a company is in liquidation. It is necessary to obtain the sanction of the court to a scheme which has been approved by the requisite majority of members or creditors of each class at separately convened meetings directed by the court. If the company is insolvent the objective of the scheme may be more simply and economically achieved by a company voluntary arrangement under Part I of the Act. However, a scheme under section 425 has the advantage that the court may approve the distribution of assets otherwise than in accordance with creditors' strict legal rights.

20.16 The application for an order to convene meetings of members or creditors under section 425(1) is made by a CPR Part 8 claim form. The application will usually be heard by a Registrar, unless it is thought that issues of difficulty may arise, in which case it can be heard by a judge. The relevant practice is set out in *Practice Statement (Companies: Schemes of Arrangements)* [2002] 1 WLR 1345.

20.17 The application to sanction a scheme of arrangement, once approved by members or creditors by the statutory majority, is made by petition. The hearing of the petition at which the sanction of the court is sought will be before a judge. If the petition also seeks confirmation of a reduction of capital, there will first be an application to the Registrar for directions. In other cases the petition will go straight to a judge.

Winding up petitions

20.18 Proceedings to wind up a company are commenced by presenting a petition to the court. The presentation of a winding up petition can cause substantial damage to a company. A winding up petition should not be presented when it is known that there is a real dispute about the debt. Practitioners should make reasonable enquiries from their client as to the existence of any such dispute. The court may order a petitioner to pay the company's costs of a petition based on a disputed debt on the indemnity basis.

1A–166

20.19 When a winding up petition is presented to either the Companies Court, a Chancery District Registry or a county court having jurisdiction, particulars including the name of the company and the petitioner's solicitors are entered in a computerised register. This is called the Central Registry of Winding Up Petitions. It may be searched by personal attendance at the Companies Court General Office, or by telephone on 020 7947 7328.

20.20 The requirement to advertise the petition (Insolvency Rules, r. 4.11(2)(b)) is mandatory, and designed to ensure that the class remedy of winding up by the court is made available to all creditors, and is not used simply as a means of putting pressure on the company to pay the petitioner's debt. Failure to comply with the rule, without good reason accepted by the court, may lead to the summary dismissal of the petition on the return date (Insolvency Rules, r. 4.11(5)). If the court, in its discretion, grants an adjournment, this will be on condition that the petition is advertised in due time for the adjourned hearing. No further adjournment for the purpose of advertisement will normally be granted.

20.21 If an order is made restraining advertisement while an application is made to the court to stop the proceedings, the case is listed in the Daily Cause List by number only so that the name of the company is not given.

Proceedings for relief from unfairly prejudicial conduct under the Companies Act 1985, section 459

20.22 Petitions under the Companies Act 1985, section 459, are liable to involve extensive factual enquiry and many of the measures summarised in Section A of this Guide which are designed to avoid unnecessary cost and delay are particularly relevant to them. Procedure is governed by the Companies (Unfair Prejudice Applications) Proceedings Rules 1986 (SI 1986/2000).

1A–167

20.23 Where applications are brought in the Companies Court and in a related case in the Chancery Division at the same time, special arrangements can be made on request to the Chancery Judges' Listing Officer for the applications to be heard by the same judge.

Applications for leave to act as director of a company with a prohibited name

20.24 Section 216 of the Insolvency Act 1986 restricts the use of a company name by any person who was a director or shadow director of the company in the 12 month period ending with the day upon which it went into insolvent liquidation—except with the leave of the court: section 216(3).

1A–168

20.25 The application for leave is governed by the Insolvency Rules 1986, rr. 4.226 to 4.230. These rules provide for certain exceptions to the prohibition. The application for leave is by originating application supported by written evidence.

20.26 By r. 4.227 the court may call upon the liquidator for a report of the circumstances in which the company became insolvent and the extent of the applicant's apparent responsibility. However if the liquidator consents to the application it is helpful if his views are put before the court at the outset. The Registrar who then hears the application may be prepared to grant it at the first hearing.

20.27 Notice should be given to the Secretary of State and/or the Official Receiver.

General

1A-169 20.28 Inspection of the court's records and the court file in any insolvency proceedings is governed by Insolvency Rules, rr. 7.28 and 7.31.

20.29 The following leaflets are available from the Companies Court General Office:

(1) Current Practice Directions and Practice Notes

(2) *"I want to wind up a company which owes me money: what do I do?"*

(3) Treasury Solicitors'—A Guide to company restoration

(4) *"I want to apply to extend time for registration of a charge or to rectify a mis-statement or omission (in the registered particulars of a charge or of a memorandum of satisfaction): what do I do?"*

(5) Dealing with debt. How to wind up your own company

CHAPTER 21

MORTGAGE CLAIMS

Key Rules: CPR Parts 55 and 73 and the PDs supplementing them

1A-170 21.1 Under Part 55 mortgage possession claims commenced since 15 October 2001, whether in respect of residential or commercial property, are generally heard in the county courts. The only exceptions to this are (a) a relatively small number of cases where either the county court has no jurisdiction or where the claimant can certify, verified by a statement of truth, the reasons for bringing the claim in the High Court and (b) any remaining transitional cases, i.e. mortgage possession claims commenced before 15 October 2001, and proceedings to enforce charging orders commenced prior to 25 March 2002, as to which directions should be sought from the assigned Master.

21.2 PD 55 emphasises that High Court claims are to be regarded as exceptional and that while the value of the property and the size of the claim may well be relevant circumstances they will not, taken alone, normally justify the issue of proceedings in the High Court. High Court proceedings may, however, be justified where there are complicated disputes of fact or where a claim gives rise to points of law of general importance. Where a mortgage possession claim is issued in the High Court it is assigned to the Chancery Division. The provisions of Part 55 will apply to it.

21.3 The most common instance where, notwithstanding Part 55, the Chancery Division will retain jurisdiction in a mortgage possession case is where proceedings are brought seeking an order for sale under an equitable charge, ordinarily that created by a charging order, but where part of the relief claimed ancillary to the order for sale is an order for possession. Although rule 73.10 now provides that proceedings to enforce charging orders by sale should be made in the court in which the charging order was made, that provision is expressly subject to that court having jurisdiction. The jurisdiction of a county court to enforce a charge is confined to those cases where the amount secured by the charge falls within the relevant county court limit (currently £30,000) and it follows that in many cases where judgments have been obtained in county courts and charging orders made enforcement will nonetheless require proceedings in the High Court.

21.4 Such proceedings, as well as proceedings to enforce charging orders made in other divisions of the High Court, are assigned to the Chancery Division. The evidence required in support of such proceedings is that set out in paragraph 4.3 of PD 73.

21.5 There remains in the Chancery Division a number of mortgage possession proceedings issued prior to Part 55 coming into force (on 15 October 2001). Of those proceedings, some may never have been adjudicated upon and many will have given rise to suspended possession orders, in respect of which applications to issue execution may arise in reducing numbers.

21.6 Practitioners should also have regard to the fact that 'old' proceedings which have not been adjudicated upon and which were issued prior to 26 April 1999 will fall within the 'automatic stay' provisions of paragraph 19 of PD 51 so that a claimant wishing to proceed with such a claim will have to apply to lift the stay. Such an application may be made at the same time as the application for possession but the court will require sufficient evidence to allow it to determine properly whether it is appropriate to lift the stay. The application to lift the automatic stay should form one of the heads of relief in the Application Notice seeking possession. If the evidence in support exhibits a mortgage account sufficient to show what has happened on the account since the last time the claim was before the court (ex hypothesi from before 26 April 1999) no additional evidence will be likely to be necessary in support of the stay application.

21.7 The Chancery Division retains its jurisdiction in respect of redemption and foreclosure of mortgages and kindred matters.

21.8 Rule 48.3 and paragraph 50 of the Costs PD (Amount of costs where costs are payable under a contract) are of particular relevance to mortgage claims.

21.9 In summary, where under a mortgage a mortgagee has a contractual right to his or her costs, the court's discretion in respect of costs under section 51 of the Supreme Court Act 1981 should be exercised so as to reflect that contractual right. The power of the court to disallow a mortgagee's costs sought to be added to the security stems not from section 51 but from the power of the courts of equity to fix the terms upon which redemption will be allowed. A decision by the court to refuse costs to a mortgagee litigant may be a decision in the exercise of the court's discretion under section 51, or pursuant to its power to fix the terms upon which redemption will be allowed, or a decision as to the extent of the mortgagee's contractual right, in a given case, to add costs to his or her security, or any combination of these three things. A mortgagee is not to be deprived of a contractual or equitable right to add costs to his or her security without reference to the mortgagee's contractual or equitable rights to such costs and without a proper adjudication as to whether or not the mortgagee should be deprived of his or her costs.

CHAPTER 22

PARTNERSHIP CLAIMS AND RECEIVERS
Key Rules: RSC O.81 (in CPR, schedule 1); CPR Part 69, PDs 24 and 40

Partnership Claims

22.1 In claims for or arising out of the dissolution of a partnership often the only matters in dispute between the partners are matters of accounting. In such cases there will be no trial. The court will, if appropriate, make a summary order under paragraph 6 of PD 24 for the taking of an account. This will be taken before the Master.

22.2 Only if there is a dispute as to the existence of a partnership (whether it is claimed that there never was a partnership or that the partnership is still continuing and has not been dissolved) or if there is a material dispute as to the terms of the partnership (e.g. as to the profit sharing ratios) will there be a trial, at which the judge will decide those issues. In such cases there will be a two stage procedure with the judge deciding these issues at the trial and ordering the winding up of the partnership which will involve the taking of the partnership accounts by the Master (see PD 40 Accounts, Inquiries etc.).

22.3 In some cases and in order to reduce costs, it may be appropriate for the parties

1A–171

to invite the Master to determine factual issues as a preliminary to the account, eg issues as to terms of the partnership or assets comprised in it. At any case management conference it will be particularly important to identify issues to be determined before an effective account or inquiry can be made. The court will not simply order accounts and inquiries without identifying the issues.

22.4 The expense of taking an account in court is usually wholly disproportionate to the amount at stake. Parties are strongly encouraged to refer disputes on accounts to a jointly instructed accountant for determination or mediation.

22.5 The functions of a receiver in a partnership action are limited. It is not his or her duty to wind up the partnership, like the liquidator of a company. His or her primary function is to get in the debts and preserve the assets pending winding up by the court and he or she has no power of sale without the permission of the court.

Receivers

1A–172 22.6 The procedure for the appointment of receivers by the court is comprehensively governed by Part 69 and its PD. A new Guide for receivers in the Chancery Division is available. Copies of the Guide can be obtained from an associate or from the Court Manager, Chancery Chambers. The Guide is also reproduced at Appendix 10. Particular attention should be paid to remuneration and the fact that it must be authorised on the basis specified in an order of the court.

CHAPTER 23

THE PATENTS COURT AND TRADE MARKS ETC.

Key Rules: CPR Part 63 and PD 63—Patents, etc

1A–173 23.1 The matters assigned to the Patents Court are essentially all those concerned with patents or registered designs. CPR Part 63 and PD 63 deal with its particular procedures. Appeals in patent, design and trade mark cases are governed by Part 52 (see CPR 63.17); reference should be made to Chapter 10 for the general procedure as regards such appeals.

23.2 The principal Patent judges are Mr Justice Pumfrey and Mr Justice Kitchin. The other assigned Patents judges currently nominated are:

Mr Justice Patten
Mr Justice Lewison
Mr Justice Mann

Several senior practitioners have also been appointed to sit as Deputy High Court judges to hear Patent Court matters.

23.3 Mr Justice Pumfrey is the judge in charge of the Patents List.

23.4 In cases of great urgency, when a nominated judge or Deputy Judge is not available an application can be made to any other judge of the High Court, preferably a judge of the Chancery Division.

23.5 The procedure of the Patents Court is broadly that of the Chancery Division as a whole, but there are important differences.

23.6 The Patents Court has its own Court Guide which is available on the Patents Court website (*www.hmcourts-service.gov.uk*) and can also be found in Section 2F-111 of Volume 2 of the White Book. That Guide must be consulted for guidance as to the procedure in the Patents Court.

23.7 The Court's diary can be accessed on its website. The Patents Court will endeavour, if the parties so desire and the case is urgent, to sit in September.

Patents County Court

1A–174 23.8 Special provisions relate to the transfer of cases between the Patents Court and the Patents County Court. The Patents Court has no power to order the transfer to it of cases commenced in the Patents County Court which fall within the latter court's special jurisdiction (i.e. matters relating to patents and designs). On the other hand it does have the power to transfer cases commenced in the High Court to the Patents County Court.

Registered trademarks and other intellectual property rights

23.9 CPR 63.13 to 63.15 and paragraphs 18 to 27 of PD 63 apply to claims relating **1A–175** to matters arising out of the Trade Marks Act 1994 and other intellectual property rights (such as copyright, passing off, design rights, etc.) as set out in paragraph 18 of PD 63. Claims under the Trade Marks Act 1994 must be brought in the Chancery Division. Among the Chancery Masters trade mark cases are assigned to Master Bragge.

23.10 Appeals from decisions of the Registrar of Trade Marks are brought to the Chancery Division as a whole, not the Patents Court. Permission to appeal is not required.

CHAPTER 24

PROBATE AND INHERITANCE CLAIMS

Key Rules: CPR Part 57 and PD 57

Probate

24.1 In general, contentious probate proceedings follow the same pattern as an **1A–176** ordinary claim but there are important differences and Part 57 and PD 57 should be carefully studied. All probate claims are allocated to the multitrack. Particular regard should be had to the following:

(1) The claim form must be issued out of Chancery Chambers or out of the Chancery District Registries, or if the claim is suitable to be heard in the county court, a county court where there is also a Chancery District Registry, or the Central London County Court.

(2) A defendant must file an acknowledgment of service. An additional 14 days is provided for doing so.

(3) Save where the court orders otherwise, the parties must at the outset of proceedings lodge all testamentary documents in their possession and control with the court. At the same time parties must file written evidence describing any testamentary document of the deceased of which they have knowledge, stating, if any such document is not in the party's possession or control, the name and address, if known, of the person in whose possession or under whose control the document is. In the case of a claimant, these materials must be lodged at the time when the claim form is issued. In the case of a defendant, these materials must be lodged when service is acknowledged. If these requirements are not complied with it is likely that the claim will not be issued and, correspondingly, that the acknowledgment of service will not be permitted to be lodged.

(4) The court will generally ensure that all persons with any potential interest in the proceedings are joined as parties or served with notice under Part 19.8A.

(5) A default judgment cannot be obtained in a probate claim. Where, however, no defendant acknowledges service or files a defence, the claimant may apply for an order that the claim proceed to trial and seek a direction that the claim be tried on written evidence.

(6) If an order pronouncing for a will in solemn form is sought under Part 24, the evidence in support must include written evidence proving due execution of the will. In such a case, if a defendant has given notice under rule 57.7(5) that he raises no positive case but requires that the will be proved in solemn form and that, to that end, he wishes to cross examine the attesting witnesses, then the claimant's application for summary judgment is subject to the right of such a defendant to require the attesting witnesses to attend for cross examination.

(7) A defendant who wishes to do more than test the validity of the will by cross examining the attesting witnesses must set up by counterclaim his positive case in order to enable the court to make an appropriate finding or declaration as to which is the valid will, or whether a person died intestate or as the case may be.

(8) The proceedings may not be discontinued without permission. Even if they are compromised, it will usually be necessary to have an order stating to whom the grant is to be made, either under rule 57.11 (leading to a grant in common form), or after a trial on written evidence under paragraph 6.1(1) of PD 57 (leading to a grant in solemn form) or under section 49 of the Administration of Justice Act 1985 and paragraph 6.1(3) of PD 57 (again leading to a grant in solemn form). Practitioners should refer to PF38CH and adapt as appropriate.

24.2 When the court orders trial of a contentious probate claim on written evidence, or where the court is asked to pronounce in solemn form under Part 24, it is normally necessary for an attesting witness to sign a witness statement or swear an affidavit of due execution of any will or codicil sought to be admitted to probate. The will or codicil is at that stage in the court's possession and cannot be handed out of court for use as an exhibit to the witness statement or affidavit, so that the attesting witness has to attend at the Royal Courts of Justice.

24.3 Where an attesting witness is unable to attend the Royal Courts of Justice in order to sign his or her witness statement or swear his or her affidavit in the presence of an officer of the court, the solicitor concerned may request from Room TM7.09, a photographic copy of the will or codicil in question. This will be certified as authentic by the court and may be exhibited to the witness statement or affidavit of due execution in lieu of the original. The witness statement or affidavit must in that case state that the exhibited document is an authenticated copy of the document signed in the witness' presence.

24.4 When a probate claim is listed for trial outside London, the solicitor for the party responsible for preparing the court bundle must write to Room TM7.09 and request that the testamentary documents be forwarded to the appropriate District Registry.

Inheritance (Provision For Family And Dependants) Act 1975

1A–177 24.5 Claims under the Inheritance (Provision for Family and Dependants) Act 1975 in the Chancery Division will be allocated to the Multi-Track and are issued by way of a Part 8 claim. Ordinarily they will be tried by the Master unless an order is made transferring the claim to a county court for trial. They are governed by Part 57 and PD 57.

24.6 The written evidence filed by the claimant with the claim form must exhibit an official copy of the grant of probate or letters of administration together with every testamentary document in respect of which probate or letters of administration was granted.

24.7 A defendant must file and serve acknowledgment of service not later than 21 days after service of the Part 8 claim form. Any written evidence (subject to any extension agreed or directed) must likewise be served and filed no later than 21 days after service.

24.8 The personal representatives of the deceased are necessary defendants to a claim under the 1975 Act and the written evidence filed by a defendant who is a personal representative must comply with paragraph 16 of PD 57.

24.9 On the hearing of a claim under the 1975 Act, the personal representatives must produce the original grant of representation to the deceased's estate. If the court makes an order under the Act, the original grant together with a sealed copy of the order must, under paragraph 18.2 of PD 57, be sent to the Principal Registry of the Family Division, First Avenue House, 42–49 High Holborn, London WC1V 6NP for a memorandum of the order to be endorsed on or permanently annexed to the grant.

24.10 Where claims under the 1975 Act are compromised the consent order filed must comply with paragraph 9.14 of this Guide.

CHAPTER 25

REVENUE PROCEEDINGS

Key Rules: CPR Part 52, PD 52, paragraphs 23.2(11) to (16), 23.3 to 23.5, 23.8

25.1 Several kinds of revenue proceedings are heard in the Chancery Division. **1A–178** Usually the parties are HM Revenue and Customs on one side and a taxpayer on the other. The main examples are described below. Almost all of them are appeals against decisions made by lower level tribunals at first instance. The appeals are governed by Part 52. Reference should be made to Chapter 10 for the general procedure relating to such appeals.

Appeals from decisions of the General Commissioners relating to income tax, corporation tax or capital gains tax

25.2 The General Commissioners are a first instance appeal tribunal for cases **1A–179** concerning these three taxes. Appeals from their decisions, whether by the Revenue or by a taxpayer, are conducted on the basis of a case stated, drawn up by the General Commissioners, which sets out the facts, the arguments, and the General Commissioners' decision. The case stated is usually backed up by whatever documents were before the Commissioners. These appeals are limited to questions of law. The judge never hears evidence, and the appeal will almost certainly fail if the appellant's real complaint is that the General Commissioners got the facts wrong. The judge does have power to remit a case to the General Commissioners for them to hear further evidence and find further facts, but this is only rarely done.

25.3 The rules provide that, when the party who is appealing from the General Commissioners receives the case stated in its final form from the General Commissioners' clerk, the party has to transmit it to the High Court within 30 days. The court has no power to extend this time limit, which must be strictly observed if the court is to be able to hear the appeal: *New World Medical Ltd v Cormack* [2002] EWHC 124 5 (Ch), [2002] STC 1245.

Appeals from decisions of the Special Commissioners relating to income tax, corporation tax, capital gains tax or inheritance tax

25.4 The Special Commissioners are the other first instance appeal tribunal for tax **1A–180** purposes, and hear cases relating to all four taxes mentioned above, known as the direct taxes. Appeals from their decisions, whether by the Revenue or by a taxpayer, are conducted, not on the basis of a case stated, but on the basis of the Special Commissioners' decision and the papers which they had before them. Those papers may include a transcript of the evidence or the Special Commissioners' notes of the evidence, but, as with appeals from General Commissioners, appeals to the Chancery Division are limited to questions of law. The judge never hears evidence. Again as with the General Commissioners, the judge has power to remit a case to the Special Commissioners for them to hear further evidence and find further facts, but this is only rarely done. There are time limits for filing an Appellant's Notice for an appeal from a decision of the Special Commissioners. In most cases the limit is 56 days from the date of the Commissioners' decision, but in some cases it is shorter. For details reference should be made to paragraph 23.5 of PD 52.

25.5 Exceptionally, appeals from the Special Commissioners in relation to the direct taxes may go directly to the Court of Appeal, so leapfrogging the Chancery Division.

25.6 Some inheritance tax appeals are exceptions to the normal procedure and do not start before the Special Commissioners, so that the Chancery Division is the court of first instance. These are limited to cases where the issues to be decided are wholly or mainly issues of law and there is no substantial dispute about the facts. Detailed procedural rules about appeals of this nature are to be found in paragraph 23.3 of PD 52.

Stamp duty appeals

1A–181   25.7 These are heard in the Chancery Division, and are conducted on the basis of a case stated drawn up by HM Revenue and Customs. Usually there is no oral evidence, but it has occasionally been heard.

25.8 Appeals relating to stamp duty reserve tax are also heard in the Chancery Division. Rules relating to such appeals have been made, but no such appeal has yet arisen.

Appeals from the Value Added Tax and Duties Tribunal

1A–182   25.9 Most of these appeals relate to VAT, but occasionally appeals on other duties, such as excise duty, arise. An appeal may be brought either by HM Revenue and Customs or by the taxpayer. As with appeals from the Special Commissioners relating to the direct taxes, exceptionally leapfrog appeals may lie direct to the Court of Appeal, but normally the appeal will be to the Chancery Division.

25.10 As with appeals from the Special Commissioners, VAT appeals are based on the Tribunal's decision and the documents in the case. The judge never hears evidence. The documents usually include a transcript of the evidence before the Tribunal or the Tribunal's notes of the evidence. Nevertheless, like appeals from the Special Commissioners concerning the direct taxes, an appeal lies only on a point of law. Usually the time limit for filing the appellant's notice is 56 days from the decision of the Tribunal.

CHAPTER 26

TRUSTS

Key Rules: CPR Part 8; Part 19; Part 64 and PD 64

Introduction

1A–183   26.1 This Chapter contains material about a number of aspects of proceedings concerning trusts, the estates of deceased persons (other than probate claims) and charities.

26.2 The topics covered in this Chapter are (a) applications by trustees for directions and related matters; (b) the Variation of Trusts Act 1958; (c) section 48 of the Administration of Justice Act 1985; (d) vesting orders as regards property in Scotland; (e) trustees under a disability; (f) lodgment of funds; (g) the estates of deceased Lloyd's Names; and (h) judicial trustees.

Trustees' applications for directions

1A–184   26.3 Applications to the court by trustees for directions in relation to the administration of a trust or charity, or by personal representatives in relation to a deceased person's estate, are to be brought by Part 8 claim form, and are governed by Part 64, and its PDs; rule 8.2A is also relevant.

26.4 If confidentiality of the directions sought is important (for example, where the directions relate to actual or proposed litigation with a third party who could find out what directions the claimants are seeking through access to the claim form under rule 5.4) the statement of the remedy sought, for the purposes of rule 8.2(b), may be expressed in general terms. The trustees must, in that case, state specifically in the evidence what it is that they seek to be allowed to do.

26.5 The proceedings will normally be listed and heard in private: rule 39.2(3)(f) and paragraph 1.5 of PD 39. Accordingly the order made, and the other documents among the court records (apart from a claim form which has been served), will not be open to inspection by third parties without the court's permission: rule 5.4(2). If the matter is disposed of without a hearing, the order made will be expressed to have been made in private.

26.6 Part 64 deals with the joining of beneficiaries as defendants. Often, especially in the case of a private trust, it will be clear that some, and which, beneficiaries need to be joined as defendants. Sometimes, if there are only two views as to the appropriate course, and one is advocated by one beneficiary who will be joined, it may not be necessary for other beneficiaries to be joined since the trustees may be able to present the other arguments. Equally, in the case of a pension trust, it may not be necessary for a member of every possible different class of beneficiaries to be joined.

26.7 In some cases, it may be that the court will or might be able to assess whether or not to give the directions sought, or what directions to give, without hearing from any party other than the trustees. If the trustees consider that their case is in that category they may apply to the court under rule 8.2A for permission to issue the claim form without naming any defendants. They must apply to the court before the claim form is issued, and include a copy of the claim form that they propose to issue. Practitioners should note that this procedure may enable directions to be obtained about matters concerning the administration of a trust or estate in circumstances which would fall outside the relatively narrow confines of section 48 of the Administration of Justice Act 1985 where the expense and delay associated with an application naming defendants may not be in the interests of beneficiaries.

26.8 In other cases the trustees may know that beneficiaries need to be joined as defendants, or to be given notice, but may be in doubt as to which. Examples could include a case concerning a pension scheme with many beneficiaries and a number of different categories of interest, especially if they may be differently affected by the action for which directions are sought, or a private trust with a large class of discretionary beneficiaries. In those cases the trustees may apply for permission to issue the claim form without naming any defendants under rule 8.2A. The application may be combined with an application for directions as to which persons to join as parties or to give notice to under rule 19.8A.

26.9 In the case of a charitable trust the Attorney-General is always the appropriate defendant, and almost always the only one.

26.10 Applications for directions whether or not to take or defend or pursue litigation (see *Re Beddoe* [1893] 1 Ch 547) must be made by Part 8 claim, independently of the main litigation, to a Master not involved with the main case. They should be supported by evidence including the advice of an appropriately qualified lawyer as to the prospects of success and other matters relevant to be taken into account, including a cost estimate for the proceedings and any known facts concerning the means of the opposite party to the proceedings, and a draft of any proposed statement of case. There are cases in which it is likely to be so clear that the trustees ought to proceed as they wish that the costs of making the application, even on a simplified procedure without a hearing and perhaps without defendants, are not justified in comparison with the size of the fund or the matters at issue.

26.11 References to an appropriately qualified lawyer mean one whose qualifications and experience are appropriate to the circumstances of the case. The qualifications should be stated. If the advice is given on formal instructions, the instructions should always be put in evidence as well, so that the court can see the basis on which the advice was given. If it is not, the advice must state fully the basis on which it is given. If a hearing is necessary the lawyer whose opinion is relied on should if possible be the advocate at the hearing.

26.12 All applications for directions should be supported by evidence showing the value of the trust assets, the significance of the proposed litigation or other course of action for the trust, and why the court's directions are needed. In the case of a pension trust the evidence should include the latest actuarial valuation, and should describe the membership profile and, if a deficit on winding up is likely, the priority provisions and their likely effect.

26.13 On an application for directions about actual or possible litigation, the evidence should also state (i) whether any relevant Pre-Action Protocol has been followed, and (ii) whether the trustees have proposed or undertaken, or intend to propose, ADR, and (in each case) if not why not.

26.14 If a beneficiary of the trust is a party to the litigation about which directions are sought, with an interest opposed to that of the trustees, that beneficiary should be a defendant to the trustees' application, but any material which would be privileged as regards that beneficiary in the litigation should be put in evidence as exhibits to the trustees' witness statement, and should not be served on the beneficiary. However, if the claimant's representatives consider that no harm would be done by the disclosure of all or some part of the material then that material should be served on that defendant. That defendant may also be excluded from part of the hearing, including that which is devoted to discussion of the material withheld: see *Re Moritz* [1960] Ch 251; *Re Eaton* [1964] 1 W.L.R. 1269.

Case management directions

1A–185 26.15 The claim will be referred to the Master once a defendant has acknowledged service, or otherwise on expiry of the period for acknowledgment of service, (or, if no defendant is named, as soon as the claimant's evidence has been filed) to consider directions for the management of the case. Such directions may be given without a hearing in some cases; these might include directions as to parties or as to notice of proceedings, as mentioned in paragraph 26.8 above.

26.16 Case management directions will be given where the court grants an application to issue the claim form without naming a defendant under rule8.2A.

Proceeding without a hearing

1A–186 26.17 The court will always consider whether it is possible to deal with the application on paper without a hearing. The trustees must always consider whether a hearing is needed for any reason. If they consider that it is they should say so and explain why in their evidence. If a defendant considers that a hearing is needed, this should be stated, and the reasons explained, in his evidence, if any, or otherwise in a letter to the court.

26.18 If the court would be minded to refuse to give the directions asked for on a consideration of the papers alone, the parties will be notified and given the opportunity, within a stated time, to ask for a hearing.

26.19 In charity cases, the Master may deal with the case without a hearing on the basis of a letter from or on behalf of the Attorney-General setting out his attitude to the application.

26.20 Cases in which the directions can be given without a hearing include those where personal representatives apply to be allowed to distribute the estate of a deceased Lloyd's name, following the decision in *Re Yorke* (deceased) [1997] 4 All ER 907 (see paragraphs 26.50–55 below), as well as applications under section 48 of the Administration of Justice Act 1985 (see paragraphs 26.37–42 below).

Evidence

1A–187 26.21 The trustees' evidence should be given by witness statement. In order to ensure that, if directions are given, the trustees are properly protected by the order, they must ensure full disclosure of relevant matters, even if the case is to proceed with the participation of beneficiaries as defendants.

Consultation with beneficiaries

1A–188 26.22 The evidence must explain what, if any, consultation there has been with beneficiaries, and with what result. In preparation for an application for directions in respect of litigation, the following guidance is to be followed.

    (1) If the trust is a private trust where the beneficiaries principally concerned

are not numerous and are all or mainly adult, identified and traceable, the trustees will be expected to have canvassed with all the adult beneficiaries the proposed or possible courses of action before applying for directions.

(2) If it is a private trust with a larger number of beneficiaries, including those not yet born or identified, or children, it is likely that there will nevertheless be some adult beneficiaries principally concerned, with whom the trustees must consult.

(3) In relation to a charitable trust the trustees must have consulted the Attorney-General, through the Treasury Solicitor, as well as the Charity Commissioners, whose consent to the application will have been needed under section 33 of the Charities Act 1993.

(4) In relation to a pension trust, unless the members are very few in number, no particular steps by way of consultation with beneficiaries (including, where relevant, employers) or their representatives are required in preparation for the application, though the trustees' evidence should describe any consultation that has in fact taken place. If no consultation has taken place, the court could in some cases direct that meetings of one or more classes of beneficiaries be held to consider the subject-matter of the application, possibly as a preliminary to deciding whether a member of a particular class ought to be joined as a defendant, though in a case concerning actual or proposed litigation, steps would need to be considered to protect privileged material from too wide disclosure.

26.23 If the court gives directions allowing the claimant to take, defend or pursue litigation it may do so up to a particular stage in the litigation, requiring the trustees, before they carry on beyond that point, to renew their application to the court. What stage that should be will depend on the likely management of the litigation under the CPR. If the application is to be renewed after disclosure of documents, and disclosed documents need to be shown to the court, it may be necessary to obtain permission to do this from the court in which the other litigation is proceeding. However, the implied undertaking limiting the use of documents disclosed by another party to the litigation does not preclude their use on an application by trustee parties for directions, since that is use for the purposes of the litigation: *White v. Biddulph*, Hart J, unreported, 22 May 1998.

26.24 In such a case the court may sometimes direct that the case be dealt with at that stage without a hearing if the beneficiaries obtain and lodge an opinion of an appropriately qualified lawyer supporting the continuation of the directions. Any such opinion will be considered by the court and, if thought fit, the trustees will be given a direction allowing them to continue pursuing the proceedings without a hearing.

26.25 In a case of urgency, such as where a limitation period or period for service of proceedings is about to expire, the court may give directions on a summary consideration of the evidence to cover the steps which need to be taken urgently, but limiting those directions so that the application needs to be renewed for fuller consideration at an early stage.

26.26 On any application for directions where a child is a defendant, the court will expect to have put before it the instructions to and advice of an appropriately qualified lawyer as to the benefits and disadvantages of the proposed, and any other relevant, course of action from the point of view of the child beneficiary. Where the matters to be drawn to the attention of the court are fully covered in the instructions and written opinion, it should not be necessary for a separate skeleton argument to be lodged, but the court needs to be informed that this is the case. The opinion should be given by the lawyer who is to be the advocate at the hearing.

Hearing

26.27 The Master may give the directions sought though, if the directions relate to **1A–189** actual or proposed litigation, only if it is a plain case, and the Master may be prepared to proceed without a hearing: see PD 2 Allocation of Cases to Levels of Judiciary, paragraph 4.1 and paragraph 5.1(e), and see also paragraphs 26.17 to 26.20 above. Otherwise the case will be referred to the judge.

Representation Orders

1A–190   26.28 It is not necessary to make representation orders under rule 19.7 on an application for directions, and sometimes it would not be possible, for lack of separate representatives among the parties of all relevant classes of beneficiaries, but such orders can be useful in an appropriate case and they are sometimes made.

Costs

1A–191   26.29 Normally the trustees' costs of a proper application will be allowed out of the trust fund, on an indemnity basis, as will the assessed (or agreed) costs of beneficiaries joined as defendants, subject to their conduct of the proceedings having been proper and reasonable.

Prospective costs orders

1A–192   26.30 In proceedings brought by one or more beneficiaries against trustees, the court has power to direct that the beneficiaries be indemnified out of the trust fund in any event for any costs incurred by them and any costs which they may be ordered to pay to any other party, known as a prospective costs order: see *McDonald v. Horn* [1995] 1 All ER 961. Such an order may provide for payments out of the trust fund from time to time on account of the indemnity so that the beneficiaries' costs may be paid on an interim basis. Applications for prospective costs orders should be made on notice to the trustees. The court will require to be satisfied that there are matters which need to be investigated. How far the court will wish to go into that question, and in what way it should be done, will depend on the circumstances of the particular case. The order may be expressed to cover costs incurred only up to a particular stage in the proceedings, so that the application has to be renewed, if necessary, in the light of what has occurred in the proceedings in the meantime. See para. 6 of PD 64, to which is annexed a model form of order.

Charity trustees' applications for permission to bring proceedings

1A–193   26.31 In the case of a charitable trust, if the Charity Commissioners refuse their consent to the trustees applying to the court for directions, under Charities Act 1993 section 33(2), and also refuse to give the trustees the directions under their own powers, under sections 26 or 29, the trustees may apply to the court under section 33(5). On such an application, which may be dealt with on paper, the judge may call for a statement from the Charity Commissioners of their reasons for refusing permission, if not already apparent from the papers. The court may require the trustees to attend before deciding whether to grant permission for the proceedings. It is possible to require notice of the hearing to be given to the Attorney- General, but this would not normally be appropriate.

Variation of Trusts Act 1958

1A–194   26.32 An application under the Variation of Trusts Act 1958 should be made by a Part 8 claim form. As to listing of such applications see paragraph 6.27. The Master will not consider the file without an application.

26.33 Where any children or unborn beneficiaries will be affected by an arrangement under the Variation of Trusts Act 1958, evidence must normally be before the court which shows that their litigation friends or the trustees support the arrangements as being in the interests of the children or unborn beneficiaries, and exhibits a written opinion to this effect. In complicated cases a written opinion is usually essential to the understanding of the litigation friends and the trustees, and to the consideration by the court of the merits and fiscal consequences of the arrangement. If the written opinion was given on formal instructions, those instructions must be exhibited. Otherwise the opinion must state fully the basis on which it was given. The opinion must be given by the advocate who will appear on the hearing of the application. A skeleton argument may not be needed where a written opinion has been put in evidence and no matters not appearing from the instructions or the opinion are to be relied on: see paragraph 26.26 above.

26.34 Where the interests of two or more children, or two or more of the children and unborn beneficiaries, are similar, a single written opinion will suffice; and no written opinion is required in respect of those who fall within the proviso to section 1(1) of the Act (discretionary interests under protective trusts). Further, in proper cases the requirement of a written opinion may at any stage be dispensed with by the Master or the judge.

Stamp Duty

26.35 An undertaking by solicitors with regard to stamping is not required to be **1A–195** included in an order under the Variation of Trusts Act 1958 whether made by a judge or Master.

26.36 The Commissioners of Inland Revenue consider that the stamp duty position of duplicate orders is as follows:

(1) Orders confined to the lifting of protective trusts. These orders are not liable for duty at all and should not be presented to a stamp office.

(2) Orders effecting voluntary dispositions inter vivos. These orders may be certified under the Stamp Duty (Exempt Instruments) Regulations 1987 (S.I. 1987 No. 516), as within category L in the schedule to those regulations, in which case they should not be presented to a stamp office. Without such a certificate they attract 50p duty under the head "Conveyance or transfer of any kind not hereinbefore described."

(3) Orders outside those described at paragraphs (1) and (2) above that contain declarations of the trust, i.e. that effect no disposition of trust property. These orders attract 50p fixed duty under the head "Declaration of trust." They may be presented for stamping at any stamp office in the usual way, or sent for adjudication if preferred.

Applications under section 48 of the Administration of Justice Act 1985

26.37 Applications under section 48 of the Administration of Justice Act 1985should **1A–196** be made by Part 8 Claim Form without naming a defendant, under rule 8.2A. No separate application for permission under rule 8.2A need be made. The claim should be supported by a witness statement or affidavit to which are exhibited: (a) copies of all relevant documents; (b) instructions to a person with a 10-year High Court qualification within the meaning of the Courts and Legal Services Act 1990 ("the qualified person"); (c) the qualified person's opinion; and (d) draft terms of the desired order.

26.38 The witness statement or affidavit (or exhibits thereto) should state: (a) the names of all persons who are, or may be, affected by the order sought; (b) all surrounding circumstances admissible and relevant in construing the document; (c) the date of qualification of the qualified person and his or her experience in the construction of trust documents; (d) the approximate value of the fund or property in question; and (e) whether it is known to the applicant that a dispute exists and, if so, details of such dispute.

26.39 When the file is placed before the Master he will consider whether the evidence is complete and if it is send the file to the judge.

26.40 The judge will consider the papers and, if necessary, direct service of notices under rule 19.8A or request such further information as he or she may desire. If the judge is satisfied that the order sought is appropriate, the order will be made and sent to the claimant.

26.41 If following service of notices under rule 19.8A any acknowledgment of service is received, the claimant must apply to the Master (on notice to the parties who have so acknowledged service) for directions. If the claimant desires to pursue the application to the court, in the ordinary case the Master will direct that the case proceeds as a Part 8 claim.

26.42 If on the hearing of the claim the judge is of the opinion that any party who entered an acknowledgment of service has no reasonably tenable argument contrary to the qualified person's opinion, in the exercise of his or her discretion he or she may order such party to pay any costs thrown away, or part thereof.

Vesting orders — property in Scotland

1A–197 26.43 In applications for vesting orders under the Trustee Act 1925 any investments or property situate in Scotland should be set out in a separate schedule to the claim form, and the claim form should ask that the trustees may have permission to apply for a vesting order in Scotland in respect thereto.

26.44 The form of the order to be made in such cases will (with any necessary variation) be as follows:

"It is ordered that the   [   ] as   Trustees   have permission to take all steps that may be necessary to obtain a vesting order in Scotland relating to [the securities] specified in the schedule herein."

Disability of Trustee

1A–198 26.45 There must be medical evidence showing incapacity to act as a trustee at the date of issue of the claim form and that the incapacity is continuing at the date of signing the witness statement or swearing the affidavit. The witness statement or affidavit should also show incapacity to execute transfers, where a vesting order of stocks and shares is asked for.

26.46 The trustee under disability should be made a defendant to the claim but need not be served unless he or she is sole trustee or has a beneficial interest.

Lodgment of Funds

1A–199 26.47 Lodgment into the High Court of amounts of cash or securities of less than £500 under section 63 of the Trustee Act 1925, and rule 14(1) of the Court Funds Rules 1987 will not be accepted by the Accountant-General unless the Chief Master so signifies in writing.

26.48 The Accountant-General will refer the applicant to the Chief Master who will consider whether there is a more economical method of preserving the fund than lodging it in the High Court or, failing that, may suggest that the money be lodged in a county court (which has power to accept sums of up to £30,000 lodged under section 63 of the Trustee Act 1925).

26.49 If the Chief Master decides that a particular lodgment should be made in the High Court, he will so signify on the back of the request (in respect of applications under rule 14(1)(ii)(a)) or the office copy schedule to the affidavit (in respect of applications under rule 14(1)(ii)(b)).

Estates of Deceased Lloyd's Names

1A–200 26.50 The procedure concerning the estates of deceased Lloyd's names is governed by a *Practice Statement* [2001] 3 All ER 765.

26.51 Personal representatives who wish to apply to the court for permission to distribute the estate of a deceased Lloyd's Name following *Re Yorke* (deceased) [1997] 4 All ER 907, or trustees who wish to administer any will trusts arising in such an estate, may, until further notice and if appropriate in the particular estate, adopt the following procedure.

26.52 The procedure will be appropriate where:

(1) the only, or only substantial, reason for delaying distribution of the estate is the possibility of personal liability to Lloyd's creditors; and

(2) all liabilities of the estate in respect of syndicates of which the Name was a member have for the years 1992 and earlier (if any) been reinsured (whether directly or indirectly) into the Equitas group; and

(3) all liabilities of the estate in respect of syndicates of which the Name was a member have for the years 1993 and later (if any) arise in respect of syndicates which have closed by reinsurance in the usual way or are protected by the terms of an Estate Protection Plan issued by Centrewrite Limited or

are protected by the terms of EXEAT insurance cover provided by Centre-write Limited.

26.53 In these circumstances personal representatives (and, if applicable, trustees) may apply by a Part 8 Claim Form headed "In the Matter of the Estate of [..........] deceased (a Lloyd's Estate) and In the Matter of the Practice Direction dated May 25 2001" for permission to distribute the estate (and, if applicable, to administer the will trusts) on the footing that no or no further provision need be made for Lloyd's creditors. Ordinarily, the claim form need not name any other party. It may be issued in this form without a separate application for permission under rule 8.2A.

26.54 The claim should be supported by a witness statement or an affidavit substantially in the form set out in Appendix 11 adapted as necessary to the particular circumstances and accompanied by a draft of the desired order substantially in the form also set out in Appendix 11. If the amount of costs has been agreed with the residuary beneficiaries (or, if the costs are not to be taken from residue, with the beneficiaries affected) their signed consent to those costs should also be submitted. If the Claimants are inviting the court to make a summary assessment they should submit a statement of costs in the form specified in the Costs PD. If in his discretion the Master (or outside London the District Judge) thinks fit, he will summarily assess the costs but with permission for the paying party to apply within 14 days of service of the order on him to vary or discharge the summary assessment. Subject to the foregoing, the order will provide for a detailed assessment unless subsequently agreed.

26.55 The application will be considered in the first instance by the Master who, if satisfied that the order should be made, may make the order without requiring the attendance of the applicants, and the court will send it to them. If not so satisfied, the Master may give directions for the further disposal of the application.

Judicial Trustees

26.56 Judicial trustees are appointed by the court under the Judicial Trustees Act **1A–201** 1896, in accordance with the Judicial Trustee Rules 1983. An application for the appointment of a judicial trustee should be made by Part 8 claim (or, if in an existing claim, by an application notice in that claim) which must be served (subject to any directions by the court) on every existing trustee who is not an applicant and on such of the beneficiaries as the applicant thinks fit. Once appointed, a judicial trustee may obtain non-contentious directions from the assigned Master informally by letter, without the need for a Part 23 application (unless the court directs otherwise). Applications for directions can be sought from the court as to the trust or its administration by rule 8 of the Judicial Trustee Rules.

26.57 Where it is proposed to appoint the Official Solicitor as judicial trustee, inquiries must first be made to his office for confirmation that he is prepared to act if appointed. The Official Solicitor will not be required to give security.

26.58 A judicial trustee is entitled under rule 11 of the 1983 rules to such remuneration as is reasonable in respect of work reasonably performed. Applications for payment by the trustee must be by letter to the court, submitted with the accounts. A Practice Note issued by the Chief Chancery Master, with the authority of the Vice-Chancellor, on 1 July 2003 sets out the best practice to be followed in determining the amount of remuneration. The Practice Note mirrors the position regarding receivers' remuneration under CPR rule 69.7 and is reproduced at Appendix 12.

Appendices

APPENDIX 1

ADDRESSES AND OTHER CONTACT DETAILS

1.

1A–202 Clerks to the Chancery Judges

(all numbers to be preceded by 020 7947)

Clerk to:	telephone	fax
The Chancellor	6412	6572
Mr Justice Lindsay	6253	7185
Mr Justice Evans-Lombe	6657	6719
Mr Justice Blackburne	6589	7379
Mr Justice Lightman	6671	6291
Mr Justice Rimer	6418	6649
Mr Justice Park	6741	6196
Mr Justice Pumfrey	7482	6593
Mr Justice Hart	6419	6062
Mr Justice Lawrence Collins	7467	7298
Mr Justice Patten	7617	6650
Mr Justice Etherton	6116	6165
Mr Justice Peter Smith	6183	6133
Mr Justice Lewison	6039	6894
Mr Justice David Richards	7419	6743
Mr Justice Mann	7964	6739
Mr Justice Warren	7260	7740
Mr Justice Kitchin	6518	6439

2.

1A–203 E-Mail Communications

The e-mail protocol sets out how parties may communicate by e-mail on certain matters with the Chancery Division, and can be found at: *www.hmcourtsservice.gov.uk*

The relevant e-mail addresses are:

(a) For skeleton arguments, chronologies, reading lists, list of issues, lists of authorities (but not the authorities themselves) and lists of the persons involved in the facts of the case sent in advance of a hearing:

Judge:
rcjchancery.judgeslisting@hmcourts-service.gsi.gov.uk

[Note: The clerk to the judge concerned should be contacted to find out whether other documents will be accepted by e-mail, and whether documents should be sent direct to the judge's clerk's e-mail address.]

Chancery Master:
rcjchancery.mastersappointments@hmcourts-service.gsi.gov.uk

Bankruptcy Registrar:
rcjbankruptcy.registrarshearings@hmcourts-service.gsi.gov.uk

Companies Court Registrar:
rcjcompanies.orders@hmcourts-service.gsi.gov.uk

(b) For the agreed terms of an Order which is ready to be sealed following the conclusion of a hearing:

Judge:
rcjchancery.ordersandaccounts@hmcourts-service.gsi.gov.uk

Chancery Master:

rcjchancery.ordersandaccounts@hmcourts-service.gsi.gov.uk
Bankruptcy Registrar:
rcjbankruptcy.registrarshearings@hmcourts-service.gsi.gov.uk
Companies Court Registrar:
rcjcompanies.orders@hmcourts-service.gsi.gov.uk

3.

At the Royal Courts of Justice, Thomas More Building   1A–204

(All telephone extension numbers and fax numbers should be prefixed by 020 7947 unless otherwise specified)

<u>1ST FLOOR</u>

TM1.10	Bankruptcy Registrars' Clerks, applications without notice, Registrars' hearings and orders (6444) Bankruptcy Registrars' Chambers (6444/7387) Bankruptcy Court fax number (6378)

<u>2ND FLOOR</u>

TM2.04	Deputy Court Manager (6812)
TM2.07	Court Manager, Companies, Bankruptcy Courts (6870).
TM2.09	Companies Court General Office: issue of all winding-up petitions and all other Companies Court applications; filing of documents (6294); Central Index (7328)
TM2.11	Bankruptcy Issue and Search Room; issue of all petitions presented by creditors and debtors and applications to set aside statutory demand and applications for interim orders; search room (6448); setting down appeals from Registrars and District and Circuit Judges (6863); Companies Court Fax number (6958)

<u>3RD FLOOR</u>

TM3.08	Bankruptcy and Companies Registry. Filing affidavits, witness statements and documents and requesting bankruptcy and company files for applications without notice to be made in Chambers; requests for office copies, lodging applications for certificates of discharge in bankruptcy (6441)

<u>4TH FLOOR</u>

TM4.04	Companies Schemes and reductions of capital (6727
TM4.05	Companies Orders Section: Winding up Court (6780); Registrars' Orders and disqualification of directors (6822)

<u>5TH FLOOR</u>

TM5.04	Chancery Chambers Registry and Issue Section: issue and amendment of all Chancery process, filing affidavits and witness statements (save those lodged within two days of a hearing before a Master which are to be filed in Room TM7.09); filing acknowledgements of service, searches of cause book; applications for office copy documents, including orders; transfers in and out (6148/6167)
TM5.05	Deputy Court Manager, Chancery Chambers. Certification of documents for use abroad (6754)
TM5.06	Lawyer, Chancery Chambers (6080).
TM5.07	Orders and Accounts Section. Associates: preparation of all Chancery Orders and Companies and Bankruptcy Court Orders; small payments; bills of costs for assessment; settlement of payment and lodgment schedules; accounts of receivers, judicial trustees, guardians and administrators; applications relating to security set by the court; matters arising out of accounts and inquiries ordered by the court (6855); Chancery Orders and Accounts Fax number: (7049)

<u>6TH FLOOR</u>

TM6.04	Chancery Masters' Library

75

TM6.05	Master Price
TM6.06	Court Manager, Chancery Chambers (6075)
TM6.07	Master Bowles
TM6.08	Secretary to Masters (6777)
TM6.09	Master Bragge

7TH FLOOR

TM7.05	Mater Teverson
TM7.06	Master Moncaster
TM7.08	Chief Master Winegarten
TM7.09	Masters' Appointments. Issue of Masters' applications, including applications without notice to Masters; filing affidavits and witness statements in proceedings before Masters (only if filed within two working days of hearing before the Master); applications to serve out of jurisdiction; filing stop notices; filing testamentary documents in contested probate cases; filing grants lodged under Part57; filing affidavits relating to funds paid into court under the Trustee Act 1925, Compulsory Purchase Act 1965 and the Lands Clauses Consolidation Act 1845. Manager (6095); Clerks to Chancery Masters (6702/7391); Masters' Appointments Fax no: (7422)

4.

1A-205 **At the Royal Courts of Justice but Outside Thomas More Building**

(Prefaced by 020 7947 unless otherwise specified).

RCJ Switchboard (6000)

RCJ Security Office (6260)

Fees Office (Room E01) (6527)

Clerk of the Lists, Room WG3 (6318)

Chancery Judges' Listing Office, Room WG4 (6778/6690)

High Court Appeals Office, Room WG7 (7518)

Chancery Judges' Listing Office Fax number*: (7345) (*See paragraph 14.12)

Officer in charge of mechanical recording (Room WB.14) (6154)

Head Usher (6356, fax 6668)

Customer Service Officer (7731)

Video-conferencing managers (6581, fax 6613)

RCJ Advice Bureau (0845 120 3715, or 020 7947 6880, fax 020 7947 7167)

Personal Support Unit (Room M104). (7701/7703 fax 7702)

5.

1A-206 **London, Outside the Royal Courts of Justice**

Central London County Court

Civil Trial Centre, Chancery List, 26-29 Park Crescent, London W1N 4HT DX 97325 Regents Park 2

Business Chancery and Patents section (020 7917 7821/7887)

Fax 0207 917 7935/7940

6.

Outside London

The following are the Court addresses, telephone and fax numbers for the courts at which there are regular Chancery sittings outside London:

Birmingham: The Priory Courts, 33 Bull Street, Birmingham B4 6DS.
Telephone: 0121-681-3033. Fax: 0121-681-3121

Bristol: The Law Courts, Small Street, Bristol BS1 1DA.
Telephone: 0117-976-3098. Fax: 0117-976-3074

Cardiff: The Civil Justice Centre, 2 Park Street, Cardiff CF1 1ET.
Telephone: 01222-376402. Fax: 01222-376470

Leeds: The Court House, 1 Oxford Row, Leeds LS1 3BG.
Telephone: 0113-283-0040. Fax: 0113-244-8507.

Liverpool: Queen Elizabeth II Law Courts, Derby Square, Liverpool L2 1XA.
Telephone: 0151-473-7373. Fax: 0151-227-2806

Manchester: The Courts of Justice, Crown Square, Manchester M3 3FL.
Telephone: 0161-954-1800. Fax: 0161-832-5179

Newcastle: The Law Courts, Quayside, Newcastle-upon-Tyne NE1 3LB.
Telephone: 0191-201-2000. Fax: 0191-201-2001

Preston: The Law Courts, Openshaw Place, Ringway, Preston PR1 2LL.
Telephone: 01772-832300. Fax: 01772-832476.

In some centres resources do not permit the listing telephone numbers to be attended personally at all times. In cases of urgency, solicitors, counsel and counsel's clerks may come into the Chancery Court and leave messages with the member of staff sitting in Court.

Urgent Court business officer pager numbers for out of hours applications:

Birmingham (Midland Circuit):

	West Side:	07699-618079
	East Side:	07699-618078
Bristol:		07699-618088
Cardiff:		07699-618086
Manchester and Liverpool:		07699-618080
Preston		07699-618081
Newcastle		01399-618083
Leeds and Bradford		01399-618082

In case of difficulty out of hours, contact the Royal Courts of Justice on 020 7947 6260.

APPENDIX 2

GUIDELINES ON STATEMENTS OF CASE

1. The document must be as brief and concise as possible.

2. The document must be set out in separate consecutively numbered paragraphs and sub-paragraphs.

3. So far as possible each paragraph or sub-paragraph should contain no more than one allegation.

4. The document should deal with the case on a point by point basis, to allow a point by point response.

5. Where the CPR require a party to give particulars of an allegation or reasons for a denial (see rule 16.5(2)), the allegation or denial should be stated first and then the particulars or reasons listed one by one in separate numbered sub-paragraphs.

6. A party wishing to advance a positive case must identify that case in the document; a simple denial is not sufficient.

7. Any matter which if not stated might take another party by surprise should be stated.

8. Where they will assist, headings, abbreviatiions and definitions should b used and a glossary annexed.

9. Contentious headings, abbreviations, paraphrasing and definitions should not be used; every effort should be made to ensure that headings, abbreviations and definitions are in a form that will enable them to be adopted without issue by the other parties.

10. Particulars of primary allegations should be stated as particulars and not as primary allegations.

11. Schedules or appendices should be used if this would be helpful, for example where lengthy particulars are necessary.

12. The names of any witness to be called may be given, and necessary documents (including an expert's report) can be attached or served contemporaneously if not bulky (PD 16; Guide paragraph 2.11). Otherwise evidence should not be included.

13. A response to particulars stated in a schedule should be stated in a corresponding schedule.

14. A party should not set out lengthy extracts from a document in his or her statement of case. If an extract has to be included, it should be placed in a schedule.

15. The document must be signed by the individual person or persons who drafted it not, in the case of a solicitor, in the name of the firm only. It must be accompanied by a Statement of Truth.

APPENDIX 3

CASE MANAGEMENT DIRECTIONS

1A–209 DRAFT ORDERS FOR USE ON ALLOCATION OR AT CASE MANAGEMENT CONFERENCES

Claim No.

IT IS ORDERED
1. Allocation to multi-track
   (   ) that this claim is allocated to the multi-track.
2. Transfer of claims, including transfer from Part 8
   (   ) that the claim be transferred to:
   (a) the   Division of the High Court;
   (b) the   District Registry;
   (c) the   [Central London] County Court [Chancery List].
   (   ) that the issue(s)   (*define issue(s)*) be transferred
to   (*one of (a) to (c) above*) for determination.
   (   ) that the   (*party*) apply by   (*date*) to a Judge of the Technology and Construction Court [*or other Specialist List*] for an Order to transfer the claim to that Court.
   (   ) that the claim   (*title and claim number*) commenced in
[the   County Court][the District Registry of], be transferred from that Court to the Chancery Division of the High Court.

(   ) that this claim shall continue as if commenced under Part 7 and shall be allocated to the multi-track.

3. Alternative dispute resolution

This claim be stayed until   [*one month*] for the parties to try to settle the dispute by alternative dispute resolution or other means. The parties shall notify the Court in writing at the end of that period whether settlement has been reached. The parties shall at the same time lodge *either*:

    (a) (if a settlement has been reached) a draft consent Order signed by all parties; or

    (b) (if no settlement has been reached) a statement of agreed directions signed by all parties or (in the absence of agreed directions) statements of the parties' respective proposed directions.

4. Probate cases only

(   ) that the   [*party*] file [his][her] witness statement or affidavit of testamentary scripts and lodge any testamentary script at Room TM7.09, Thomas More Building, Royal Courts of Justice, Strand, London WC2A 2LL [District Registry] by   (*date*).

5. Case summary

(   ) that [each party][the   (*party*)] by   (*date*) prepare and serve a case summary [not exceeding   words] on all other parties, to be agreed by   (*date*) and filed by   (*date*) and if it is not agreed by that date the parties shall file their own case summaries.

6. Trial date

(   ) that the trial of the claim/issue(s) take place between   (*date*) and (*date*) ('the trial window').

(   ) that the   (*party*) shall make an appointment to attend on the Listing Officer (Room WG4, Royal Courts of Justice, Strand, London WC2A 2LL; Tel. 020 7947 6816; Fax No. 020 7947 7352) to fix a trial date within the trial window, such appointment to be not later than   (*date*) and give notice of the appointment to all other parties.

(   ) that

    (i) the claim be entered in the [Trial List][General List], with a listing category of   [A][B][C] (*to be decided by the Master with reference to the substance and difficulty of the case*), with a time estimate of   days/weeks

    (ii) the trial take place in London (*or identify venue*).

7. Pre Trial Review

(   ) [the trial being estimated to last more than 10 days] that there be a Pre Trial Review on a date to be arranged by the Listing Officer [in conjunction with the parties] [to take place shortly before the trial and, if possible, in front of the Judge who will be conducting the trial] at which, except for urgent matters in the meantime, the Court will hear any further applications for Orders.

8. All directions agreed.

(   ) The parties having agreed directions it is by consent ordered:—

    [Set out all the directions by reference to parties' draft Order on file].

9. Some directions agreed

(   ) The parties having agreed the following directions it is by consent ordered:

    [Set out the agreed directions by reference to parties' draft Order on file as above,   and any further directions to be given at this stage].

10. Case management conference etc.

(   ) that there be a [further] case management conference before the Master in Room TM ..., Thomas More Building, Royal Courts of Justice, Strand, London WC2A 2LL on   (*date*) at   o'clock (of   hours/minutes duration).

(   ) that there shall be a case management conference (of   hours/minutes duration). In order for the Court to fix a date the parties are to complete the accompanying questionnaire and file it by   (*date*).

(   ) that the   (*party*) apply for an appointment for a [further] case management conference by   (*date*).

(   ) At the case management conference, except for urgent matters in the meantime, the Court will hear any further applications for Orders and any party must file an Application Notice for any such Orders and serve it and supporting evidence (if any) by   (*date*).

11. Failure to file allocation questionnaire

(   ) that, ***no allocation questionnaire having been received from [the Claimant]/[the Defendant]***, if [the Claimant][the Defendant] [does not file [his][her] allocation questionnaire within 3 days after service of this Order upon [him][her], the [claim] [counterclaim] shall be struck out without further Order [*or as the case may be*].

[Add Order as to costs].

12. Amendments to statement of case

(   ) that the   (*party*) has permission to amend [his][her] statement of case as in the copy on the Court file [initialled by the Master].

(   ) that the amended statement of case be verified by a statement of truth.

(   ) that the amended statement of case be filed by   (*date*).

(   ) that [the amended statement of case be served by   (*date*).] [service of the amended statement of case be dispensed with].

(   ) that any consequential amendments to other statements of case be filed and served by   (*date*)

(   ) that the costs of and consequential to the amendment to the statement of case [shall be paid by   (*party*) in any event] [are assessed in the sum of £ and are to be paid by   (*party*)][within   (*time*)].

13. Addition of parties etc.

(   ) that the   (*party*) has permission:

(a) to [add][substitute][remove]   (*name of party*) as a   (*party*) and

(b) to amend [his][her] statement of case in accordance with the copy on the Court file [initialled by the Master].

and that the amended statement of case be verified by a statement of truth.

(   ) that the amended statement of case be:

(a) filed by   (*date*);

(b) served on   (*new party, existing parties or removed party, as appropriate*), by   (*date*).

(   ) that a copy of this Order be served on   (*new party, existing parties or removed party, as appropriate*), by   (*date*).

(   ) that any consequential amendments to other statements of case be filed and served by   (*date*).

(   ) that the costs of and consequential to the amendment to the statement of case [shall be paid by the   (*party*) in any event] [are assessed in the sum of £   and are to be paid by the   (*party*)].

14. Consolidation

(   ) that this claim be consolidated with claim number   (*number and title of claim*), the lead claim to be claim number   . [The title to the consolidated case shall be as set out in the Schedule to this Order].

15. Trial of issue

(   ) that the issue of   (*define issue*) be tried as-follows:

(a) with the consent of the parties, before a Master

(i) on   (*date*) in Room TM   Thomas More Building, Royal Courts of Justice, Strand, London WC2A 2LL;

(ii) with a time estimate of   (hours),

(iii) with the filing of listing questionnaires dispensed with, *or*

(b) before a Judge

(i) with the trial of the issue to take place between   (*date*) and-(*date*) ('the trial window')

(ii) with the   (*party*) to make an appointment to attend on the Listing Officer (Room WG4, Royal Courts of Justice, Strand, London WC2A 2LL; Tel. 020 7947 6778/6690; Fax No. 020 7947 7345) to fix a trial date within the trial window, such appointment to be not later than   (*date*) and to give notice of the appointment to all other parties.

    (iii) with the issue to be entered in the [Trial List][General List],
with a listing category of [A][B][C] *(to be decided by the Master with reference to the substance and difficulty of the case*, and a time estimate of   days/weeks and to take place in London (*or identify venue*).

16. Further information

(   ) that the   *(party)* provide by   *(date)* the [further information][clarification] sought in the request dated- *(date)* [initialled by the Master].

(   ) that any request for [further information][clarification] shall be served by   [*date*].

17. Disclosure of documents

(   ) that each party give by   *(date)* standard disclosure to every other party by list [by categories].

(   ) that the   *(party/parties)* give specific disclosure of documents [limited to the issues of   ] described in the Schedule to this Order [initialled by the Master] by list [by categories] by   *(date)*.

(   ) that the   *(party)* give by   *(date)* standard disclosure by list [by categories] to   *(party)* of documents limited to the issue(s) of   *(define issues)* by list.

18. Inspection of documents

(   ) that any requests for inspection or copies of disclosed documents shall be made   within days after service of the list.

19. Preservation of property

(   ) that the   *(party)* preserve   *(give details of relevant property)* until trial of the claim or further Order *or other remedy under* rule 25.1(1).

20. Witness statements

(   ) that each party serve on every other party the witness statement of the oral evidence which the party serving the statement intends to rely on in relation to [any issues of fact][the following issues of fact   *(define issues)*] to be decided at the trial, those statements [and any notices of intention to rely on hearsay evidence] to be

    (a) exchanged by   *(date)* or

    (b) served by   *(party)* by   *(date)* and by- *(party)* by   *(date)*   provided that before exchange the parties shall liaise with a view to agreeing a   method of identification of any documents referred to in any such witness statement.

(   ) that the   *(party)* has permission to serve a witness summary relating to the evidence of   *(name)* of   *(address)* [on every other party by][to be served on   *(party)*/exchanged at the same time as exchange of witness statements].

21. No expert evidence

(   ) no expert evidence being necessary, that [no party has permission to call or rely on expert evidence][permission to call or rely on expert evidence is refused].

22. Single expert

(   ) that evidence be given by the report of a single expert in the field of- *(define field)* instructed jointly by the parties, on the issue of- *(define issue)* [and [his][her] fees shall be limited to £   ].

(   ) that if the parties are unable to agree [by   *(date)*] who that expert is to be and about the payment of [his][her] fees any party may apply for further   directions.

(   ) that unless the parties agree in writing or the Court orders otherwise, the fees and expenses of the single expert shall be paid to [him][her] by the parties equally.

(   ) that each party give [his][her] instructions to the single expert by   *(date)*.

(   ) that the report of the single expert be filed and served by [him][her] on the parties by   *(date)*.

(   ) that no party may recover from another party more than £   for the fees and expenses of the expert.

(   ) that the evidence of the expert be given at the trial by [written report][oral   evidence] of the expert.

23. Separate Experts

(   ) that each party has permission to adduce [oral] expert evidence in the field of   (*specify*) [limited to   expert(s) [per party][on each side].

(   ) that the experts' reports shall be exchanged by   (*date*).

(   ) that the experts shall hold a discussion for the purpose of:

(a) identifying the issues, if any, between them; and

(b) where possible, reaching agreement on those issues.

(   ) that the experts shall by   [*specify date after discussion*] prepare and file a statement for the Court showing:

(a) those issues on which they are agreed; and

(b) those issues on which they disagree and a summary of their reasons for disagreeing.

(   ) No party shall be entitled to recover by way of costs from any other party more than £   for the fees or expenses of an expert.

24. Definition and reduction of issues.

(   ) that by   (*date*) the parties list and discuss the issues in the claim-   [including the experts' reports and statements] and attempt to define and narrow the   issues [including those issues the subject of discussion by the experts].

25. Trial bundle and skeleton arguments.

(   ) that not earlier than 7 days or later than 3 days before the date fixed for trial or of the claim entering the Warned List the Claimant shall file with the Chancery Listing Office a trial bundle for the use of the Judge in accordance with Appendix 6 of the Chancery Guide.

(   ) that skeleton arguments and chronologies shall be filed not less than 2 clear days before the date fixed for trial or of the claim entering the Warned List, in accordance with Appendix 7 of the Chancery Guide.

26. Settlement

(   ) that if the claim or part of the claim is settled the parties must immediately inform the Court, whether or not it is then possible to file a draft Consent Order to give   effect to the settlement.

27. Compliance with Directions

(   ) that the parties shall by   (*date*) notify the Court in writing that they have fully complied with all directions or state:

(a) with which directions they have not complied;

(b) why they have not complied; and

(c) what steps they are taking to comply with the outstanding directions in time for the trial.

If the Court does not receive such notification or if the steps proposed to comply   with outstanding directions are considered by the Court unsatisfactory, the Court   may order a hearing (and may make appropriate orders as to costs against a party in   default).

28. Costs

(   ) that the costs of this application be:

(a) costs in the case;

(b) summarily assessed at £   and paid by   (*party*); *or*

(c) the [party/parties]'[s] in any event, to be subject to detailed assessment.

NOTE 1

The attention of the parties is drawn to the importance of seeking to agree at an early stage directions for the management of the case as emphasised in the Practice Direction to Part 29 of the Civil Procedure Rules.

NOTE 2

The parties may, subject to any agreement being in accordance with the provisions of the Civil Procedure Rules, agree to extend the time periods given in the directions above provided this does not affect the date given for any case management conference or pre-trial review or the date of the trial or trial period.

NOTE 3

If you fail to attend a hearing that has been ordered, the Court may order you to pay the costs of the other party, or parties, that do attend. Failure to pay those costs within the time stated may lead to your statement of case (claim or defence) being struck out.

NOTE 4

If you do not comply with these directions, any other party to the claim will be entitled to apply to the Court for an order that your statement of case (claim or defence) be struck out.

APPENDIX 4

Part 1: Judge's Application Information Form

1A–210

Title as in claim form

Application Information

1.   [DATE APPLICATION TO BE HEARD]

2.   DETAILS OF SOLICITOR/PARTY LODGING THE APPLICATION

    a.   [Name]

    b.   [Address]

    c.   [Telephone No.]

    d.   [Reference]

    e.   [Acting for Claimant(s)/Defendant(s)]

3.   DETAILS OF COUNSEL/OR OTHER ADVOCATE

    a.   [Name]

    b.   [Address of Chambers/Firm]

    c.   [Telephone No.]

4.   DETAILS OF OTHER PART(Y'S)(IES') SOLICITORS

    a.   [Name]

    b.   [Address]

    c.   [Telephone No.]

    d.   [Reference]

[Acting for Claimant(s)/Defendant(s)]

Part 2: Written Evidence Lodgment Form

CHANCERY CHAMBERS

1A–211

TO FILING SECTION—ROOM TM5.04

CLAIM NO:

SHORT TITLE:

Herewith Affidavit or witness statement of.........

/or if other document specify...................

filed in respect of:—

	Tick
1. Application before Judge on...........................	
2. Application before Master on	
3. Charging Order	
4. Garnishee Order	
5. Permission to issue claim for possession	
6. Service by alternative method	
7. Service out of Jurisdiction	
8. Evidence	
9. Oral examination of debtor	
10. To enable a Master's order to be drawn	
11. Other (Specify)	

Signed

Solicitors for Claimant/Defendant

other (please specify)

Telephone No:

Ref:

APPENDIX 5

CORRESPONDENCE WITH CHANCERY MASTERS—PRACTICE NOTE

1A–212 1. One of the consequences of the new Rules and Practice Directions has been a significant increase in letters to the Court from parties and their solicitors. This imposes a heavy extra burden on the staff and Masters. It also means that court files have to be moved more often, which itself gives rise to problems. It would therefore be greatly appreciated if parties and solicitors involved in litigation before the Chancery Masters had regard to the following points.

2. When corresponding, please consider carefully (a) whether your letter is really necessary and (b) if it is who the correct addressee should be. Only address letters to the Master if the letter needs to be seen by him. If not address the letter to his clerk.

3. Letters and other documents should only be sent by fax if there is a real urgency, and should not be followed up with a hard copy. (If, exceptionally, a fax has contained a document the original of which needs to go on the court file, then the hard copy enclosing the original should be marked clearly "confirmation of fax".

4. As a general rule all correspondence, whether letter or fax, must be copied to the other parties. Correspondence should therefore state that it has been copied to the other parties (or else it should state that it has not and explain why).

5. Correspondence should not be used in place of a Part 23 application (which requires payment of a fee, a draft order and a statement of truth).

J Winegarten

Chief Chancery Master

July 2001

APPENDIX 6

GUIDELINES ON BUNDLES

1A–213 Bundles of documents must comply with paragraph 3 of PD 39 Miscellaneous Provisions relating to Hearings. These guidelines are additional to those requirements, and they should be followed wherever possible.

1A–214 1. The preparation of bundles requires co-operation between the legal representatives for all parties, and in many cases a high level of cooperation. It is the duty of all legal representatives to co-operate to the necessary level. Where a party is acting in person it is also that party's duty to co-operate as necessary with the other parties' legal representatives.

2. Bundles should be prepared in accordance with the following guidance.

Avoidance of duplication

1A–215 3. No more than one copy of any one document should be included, unless there is good reason for doing otherwise. One such reason may be the use of a separate core bundle.

4. If the same document is included in the chronological bundles and is also an exhibit to an affidavit or witness statement, it should be included in the chronological bundle and where it would otherwise appear as an exhibit a sheet should instead be inserted. This sheet should state the page and bundle number in the chronological bundles where the document can be found.

5. Where the court considers that costs have been wasted by copying unnecessary documents, a special costs order may be made against the relevant person. In no circumstances should rival bundles be presented to the court.

84

Chronological order and organisation

6. In general documents should be arranged in date order starting with the earliest document. **1A–216**

7. If a contract or other transactional document is central to the case it may be included in a separate place provided that a page is inserted in the chronological run of documents to indicate where it would have appeared chronologically and where it is to be found instead. Alternatively transactional documents may be placed in a separate bundle as a category.

Pagination

8. This is covered by paragraph 3 of the PD, but it is permissible, instead of numbering the whole bundle, to number documents separately within tabs. An exception to consecutive page numbering arises in the case of the core bundle. For this it may be preferable to retain the original numbering with each bundle represented by a separate divider. **1A–217**

9. Page numbers should be inserted in bold figures, at the bottom of the page and in a form that can clearly be distinguished from any other pagination on the document.

Format and presentation

10. Where possible, the documents should be in A4 format. Where a document has to be read across rather than down the page, it should so be placed in the bundle as to ensure that the top of the text starts nearest the spine. **1A–218**

11. Where any marking or writing in colour on a document is important, for example on a conveyancing plan, the document must be copied in colour or marked up correctly in colour.

12. Documents in manuscript, or not easily legible, should be transcribed; the transcription should be marked and placed adjacent to the document transcribed.

13. Documents in a foreign language should be translated; the translation should be marked and placed adjacent to the document translated; the translation should be agreed or, if it cannot be agreed, each party's proposed translation should be included.

14. The size of any bundle should be tailored to its contents. There is no point having a large lever-arch file with just a few pages inside. On the other hand bundles should not be overloaded as they tend to break. **No bundle should contain more than 300 pages.**

15. Binders and files must be strong enough to withstand heavy use.

16. Large documents, such as plans, should be placed in an easily accessible file. If they will need to be opened up often, it may be sensible for the file to be larger than A4 size.

Indices and labels

17. Indices should, if possible, be on a single sheet. It is not necessary to waste space with the full heading of the action. Documents should be identified briefly but properly, e.g. "AGS3—Defendants Accounts". **1A–219**

18. Outer labels should use large lettering, e.g. "A. Pleadings." The full title of the action and solicitors' names and addresses should be omitted. A label should be used on the front as well as on the spine.

19. A label should also be stuck on to the front inside cover of a file at the top left, in such a way that it can be seen even when the file is open.

Staples etc.

20. All staples, heavy metal clips etc. should be removed. **1A–220**

Statements of case

1A–221 21. Statements of case should be assembled in 'chapter' form, i.e. claim form followed by particulars of claim, followed by further information, irrespective of date.

22. Redundant documents, e.g. particulars of claim overtaken by amendments, requests for further information recited in the answers given, should generally be excluded. Backsheets to statements of case should also be omitted.

Witness statements, affidavits and expert reports

1A–222 23. Where there are witness statements, affidavits and/or expert reports from two or more parties, each party's witness statements etc. should, in large cases, be contained in separate bundles.

24. The copies of the witness statements, affidavits and expert reports in the bundles should have written on them, next to the reference to any document, the reference to that document in the bundles. This can be done in manuscript.

25. Documents referred to in, or exhibited to, witness statements, affidavits and expert reports should be put in a separate bundle and not placed behind the statement concerned, so that the reader can see both the text of the statement and the document referred to at the same time.

26. Backsheets to affidavits and witness statements should be omitted.

New Documents

1A–223 27. Before a new document is introduced into bundles which have already been delivered to the court—indeed before it is copied—steps should be taken to ensure that it carries an appropriate bundle/page number, so that it can be added to the court documents. It should not be stapled, and it should be prepared with punch holes for immediate inclusion in the binders in use.

28. If it is expected that a large number of miscellaneous new documents will from time to time be introduced, there should be a special tabbed empty loose-leaf file for that purpose. An index should be produced for this file, updated as necessary.

Inter-Solicitor Correspondence

1A–224 29. It is seldom that all inter-solicitor correspondence is required. Only those letters which are likely to be referred to should be copied. They should normally be placed in a separate bundle.

Core bundle

1A–225 30. Where the volume of documents needed to be included in the bundles, and the nature of the case, makes it sensible, a separate core bundle should be prepared for the trial, containing those documents likely to be referred to most frequently.

Basis of agreement of bundles

1A–226 31. See Chapter 7, paragraph 13.

Photocopy authorities

1A–227 32. If authorities, extracts from text-books etc. are photocopied for convenience for use in court, the photocopies should be placed in a separate bundle with an index and dividers. Reduced size copies (i.e. 2 pages of original to each A4 sheet) should not be used. Where only a short passage from a long case is needed, the headnote and key pages only should be copied and the usher should be asked to have the full volume in court. Whenever possible the parties' advocates should liaise about these bundles in order to avoid duplication of copies.

APPENDIX 7

GUIDELINES ON SKELETON ARGUMENTS, CHRONOLOGIES, INDICES AND READING LISTS

Skeleton arguments

1A–228 1. A skeleton argument is intended to identify both for the parties and the court those points which are, and those that are not, in issue, and the nature of the argument in relation to those points which are in issue. It is not a substitute for oral argument.

2. Every skeleton argument should therefore:

    (1) identify concisely:

        (a) the nature of the case generally, and the background facts insofar as they are relevant to the matter before the court;

        (b) the propositions of law relied on with references to the relevant authorities;

        (c) the submissions of fact to be made with reference to the evidence;

    (2) be as brief as the nature of the issues allows—it should not normally exceed 20 pages of double-spaced A4 paper and in many cases it should be much shorter than this;

    (3) be in numbered paragraphs and state the name (and contact details) of the advocate(s) who prepared it;

    (4) avoid arguing the case at length;

    (5) avoid formality and make use of abbreviations, e.g. C for Claimant, A/345 for bundle A page 345, 1.1.95 for 1st January 1995 etc.

3. Paragraph 1 also applies to written summaries of opening speeches and final speeches. Even though in a large case these may necessarily be longer, they should still be as brief as the case allows.

Reading lists

4. The documents which the Judge should if possible read before the hearing may be identified in a skeleton argument, but must in any event be listed in a separate reading list, if possible agreed between the advocates, which must be lodged with the agreed bundles, together with an estimate, if possible agreed, of the time required for the reading. **1A–229**

Chronologies and indices

5. Chronologies and indices should be non-contentious and agreed with the other parties if possible. If there is a material dispute about any event stated in the chronology, that should be stated in neutral terms and the competing versions shortly stated. **1A–230**

6. If time and circumstances allow its preparation, a chronology or index to which all parties have contributed and agreed can be invaluable.

7. Chronologies and indices once prepared can be easily updated and may be of continuing usefulness throughout the case.

APPENDIX 8

DELIVERY OF DOCUMENTS IN CHANCERY CHAMBERS

1.

Deliver of documents for Master's hearings

    (a) Deliver bundles and skeletons (if required) to Masters' Appointments, Room TM7.09, 2 clear working days (not more than 7) before the hearing. **1A–231**

    (b) Mark clearly "for hearing on..........*(date)* before Master ....

    (c) Insert a reading list and estimate of reading time if appropriate.

    (d) Bundles may be presented in ring binders or lever arch files, or as appropriate.

    (e) Documents for Masters' hearings should not be taken direct to the Master's room unless in any particular case the Master has directed otherwise.

    (f) Documents required for Masters' hearings should never be taken to (i) the Registry (Room TM5.04); (ii) the Chancery Judges' Listing Office (Room WG

4) or (iii) the RCJ Post Room) — if they are they may well not reach the Master in time.

Note:

Documents required for hearings before a Chancery judge must not be delivered to Chancery Chambers. They must be delivered to the Chancery Judges' Listing Office (Room WG 4).

2.

Filing of documents

1A–232

(a) Take or send documents required to be filed (i.e. placed on the Court file, either under the CPR or under an Order of the Court (e.g. statements of case, defences, allocation questionnaires, some witness statements)) to the Chancery Registry, Room TM5.04 for filing.

(b) But documents (e.g. witness statements, exhibits) required to be filed which are needed for a Masters' hearing within 10 working days must be delivered for filing to Masters' Appointments, Room 7.09 not the Registry.

(c) If bulky, use treasury tags, not files or ring binders.

APPENDIX 9

GUIDELINES ON WITNESS STATEMENTS

1A–233
1. The function of a witness statement is to set out in writing the evidence in chief of the maker of the statement. Accordingly witness statements should, so far as possible, be expressed in the witness's own words. This guideline applies unless the perception or recollection of the witness of the events in question is not in issue.

2. Witness statements should be as concise as the circumstances of the case allow. They should be written in consecutively numbered paragraphs. They should present the evidence in an orderly and readily comprehensible manner. They must be signed by the witness, and contain a statement that he or she believes that the facts stated in his or her witness statement are true. They must indicate which of the statements made are made from the witness' own knowledge and which are made on information and belief, giving the source of the information or basis for the belief.

3. Inadmissible material should not be included. Irrelevant material should likewise not be included.

4. Any party on whom a witness statement is served who objects to the relevance or admissibility of material contained in a witness statement should notify the other party of his or her objection within 28 days after service of the witness statement in question and the parties concerned should attempt to resolve the matter as soon as possible. If it is not possible to resolve the matter, the party who objects should make an appropriate application, normally at the PTR, if there is one, or otherwise at trial.

5. It is incumbent on solicitors and counsel not to allow the costs of preparation of witness statements to be unnecessarily increased by overelaboration of the statements. Any unnecessary elaboration may be the subject of a special order as to costs.

6. Witness statements must contain the truth, the whole truth and nothing but the truth on the issues covered. Great care must be taken in the preparation of witness statements. No pressure of any kind should be placed on a witness to give other than a true and complete account of his or her evidence. It is improper to serve a witness statement which is known to be false or which the maker does not in all respects actually believe to be true. In addition, a professional adviser may be under an obligation to check where practicable the truth of facts stated in a witness statement if he or she is put on enquiry as to their truth. If a party discovers that a witness statement which he or she has served is incorrect he or she must inform the other parties immediately.

7. A witness statement should simply cover those issues, but only those issues, on

which the party serving the statement wishes that witness to give evidence in chief. Thus it is not, for example, the function of a witness statement to provide a commentary on the documents in the trial bundle, nor to set out quotations from such documents, nor to engage in matters of argument. Witness statements should not deal with other matters merely because they may arise in the course of the trial.

8. Witness statements very often refer to documents. If there could be any doubt as to what document is being referred to, or if the document has not previously been made available on disclosure, it may be helpful for the document to be exhibited to the witness statement. If, to assist reference to the documents, the documents referred to are exhibited to the witness statement, they should nevertheless not be included in trial bundles in that form: see Appendix 6, paragraph 4. If (as is normally preferable) the documents referred to in the witness statement are not exhibited, care should be taken in identifying them, for example by reference to the lists of documents exchanged on disclosure. In preparation for trial, it will be necessary to insert cross-references to the trial bundles so as to identify the documents: see Appendix 6, paragraph 24.

9. If a witness is not sufficiently fluent in English to give his evidence in English, the witness statement should be in the witness' own language and a translation provided. If a witness is not fluent in English but can make himself understood in broken English and can understand written English, the statement need not be in his own words provided that these matters are indicated in the statement itself. It must however be written so as to express as accurately as possible the substance of his evidence.

APPENDIX 10

A GUIDE FOR RECEIVERS IN THE CHANCERY DIVISION

1. This guide sets out brief notes on the procedure to be followed after an order has been made appointing a receiver in the Chancery Division. The procedure is now governed by CPR Part 69 and its PD. **1A–234**

2. Appendix C contains notes on the main powers and duties of a receiver and a copy should be passed to the receiver.

Action on the Appointment of a Receiver (Rule 69.6; PD 6&8)

3. Where an order has been made appointing a receiver, it is generally necessary to apply for directions, by application notice under Part 23. Part 69 PD 6 lists the matters on which directions will usually be given. A draft order should normally be submitted with the Application Notice. **1A–235**

4. The application for directions should normally be made immediately after the making of the order appointing the receiver, especially where security has to be given within a limited time (see below). Only if the order appointing the receiver appoints him or her by name and gives full directions as to accounts and security will an application for directions not be necessary.

5. The receiver may of course apply to the Master at any time for other directions as necessary. Where the directions are unlikely to be contentious or important to the parties this may be done by letter (see Part 69 PD 8). *Giving Security* (Rule 69.5; PD 7).

Giving Security (Rule 69.5; PD 7).

6. The order appointing a receiver will normally include directions in relation to security, and will specify the date by which security is to be given. It is therefore important to obtain an early date for the directions hearing. If security is not completed within the time specified the receivership may be terminated and it will then be necessary for an application to be made to renew it. To avoid this, if it seems likely that security will not be given in time an application should be made at the directions hearing for an extension of time to give security. **1A–236**

7. When the amount of the security has been settled, a guarantee in Form PF 30 CH (Appendix A) must (unless the receiver is a licensed insolvency practitioner covered by bond, which has been extended to cover the appointment) be prepared and entered into with one of the four main clearing banks or the insurance company listed in Appendix B.

8. The guarantee must then be engrossed and executed, i.e. signed by the receiver and signed and sealed by the bank or insurance company. It should then be lodged in Chancery Chambers, Room TM7.09, Royal Courts of Justice, Strand London WC2A 2LL. It will then be signed by the Master and endorsed with a certificate of completion of security and placed on the court file. Where security is given by bond, written evidence of the extended bond and the sufficiency of its cover must be filed in Room 7.09 in accordance with the requirements of Part 69 PD 7.3(1).

9. If the amount of the security given is subsequently increased or decreased, an endorsement is made to the original guarantee.

Receiver's Remuneration (Rule 69.7; PD9)

1A–237   10. A receiver may only charge for his services if the court permits it and specifies the basis on which the receiver is to be remunerated. Unless the court directs the remuneration to be fixed by reference to some fixed scale, or percentage of rents collected, it will determine the amount in accordance with the criteria set out in rule 69.7(4).

Receiver's Accounts (Rule 69.8; PD 10).

1A–238   11. If directions as to the receiver's accounts have not been given in the order appointing the receiver, such directions must be obtained at the directions hearing.

12. Normally accounts are prepared half-yearly and must be delivered within a month of the end of the accounting period.

13. Generally accounts need only be presented to the court if any party receiving them serves notice on the receiver, under rule 69.8(3), that he objects to any item in the accounts.

Discharge of Receiver and Cancellation of Security (Rule 69.10&11)

1A–239   14. When a receiver has completed his duties, the receiver or any party should apply for an order discharging the receiver and cancelling the security.

15. When an order for cancellation of a receiver's security has been made, any guarantee and the duplicate order appointing the receiver are endorsed to that effect.

16. The endorsed guarantee and duplicate order should then be taken to the bank or insurance company by the solicitors for cancellation and return of any outstanding premium.

Appendix A to Guide for Receivers

Guarantee for receiver's acts and defaults[1]

IN THE HIGH COURT OF JUSTICE

CHANCERY DIVISION

[TITLE]

I,....(*Name*). of....(*address*), the Receiver [and manager] appointed by Order dated....(*date*) (*or* proposed to be appointed) in this claim hereby undertake to the

---

[1] Adapted from Form PF 30CH.

CH GUIDE

Court duly to account for all money and property received by me as such Receiver [and manager] at such times and in such manner in all respects as the Court directs.

And we....*(name (s) of surety or sureties)* hereby [jointly and severally[1]] undertake with the Court and guarantee to be answerable for any default by....*(name)* as such Receiver [and manager] and upon such default to pay to any person or persons or otherwise as the Court directs any sum or sums not exceeding £....in total that may from time to time be certified by [a Master of the Supreme Court][a District Judge] to be due from..........*(name)* as Receiver [and manager] and we submit to the jurisdiction of the Court in this action to determine any claim made under this undertaking.

DATED this..........day of..........20....

Signed sealed and delivered by the above named..........in the presence of

or

The Common Seal of..........was hereunto affixed in the presence of:—

(Signature of receiver)

(Seal of surety with appropriate signature or signatures)

Appendix B to Guide for Receivers

Guarantees for Personal Applicants

The insurance company detailed below is willing to act as surety

Name of company	Address to be shown on and for correspondence
Zurich GSG Limited	
	Hawthorn Hall
	Hall Road
	Wilmslow
	Cheshire SK9 5BZ

Appendix C to Guide for Receivers

The Powers and Duties of a Receiver

1. The main function of a receiver appointed by the court is to protect the assets received by him pending the court proceedings. The following notes set out some of the more important powers and duties a receiver should be aware of.

2. A receiver must obtain the permission of the court (which may be contained in the order appointing him) before he can:

    (a) bring, defend or compromise legal proceedings

    (b) *pay a debt (other than in a partnership claim)*

    (c) compromise a claim

    (d) purchase or sell assets other than in the normal course of business

    (e) grant obtain or surrender a lease or purchase or sell real property (even in the course of managing a business); since the appointment of a receiver is an equitable remedy it does not confer on him any title to land: unless the legal owner is prepared to join in the conveyance or lease the receiver would in any case have to obtain a vesting order under section 47 or section 50 of the Trustee Act 1925.

---

[1] Omit these words in the case of a guarantee or other company.

(f) borrow money

(h) carry on or close down or sell a business

(i) employ additional staff in the course of managing a business

(j) carry out repairs to property costing more than £1000 in any one accounting year

3. Receivers should ensure that they have insurance (if any) transferred into their own names and should consider the adequacy of the insurance cover.

4. Receivers are not entitled to instruct their own solicitors without the express permission of the court.

5. Receivers should seek the court's directions on any question of doubt which arises in the course of the receivership.

6. Receivers should bear in mind that their function as receiver does not include the preparation of partnership accounts and they cannot include fees for such work in their remuneration as receiver.

7. Unless expressly authorised by the court (whether in the Order appointing him or otherwise) the receiver must not part with assets in his hands, whether to the person appointing him or otherwise. If he has completed his functions as receiver before the disputes between the parties have been resolved in the proceedings, the receiver should normally apply to be discharged on lodging into court the money he is holding.

Appendix 11

Lloyd's Names' Estate Applications: Forms

Form of Witness Statement

1A-240
[Heading as in claim form]

1A-241
1. We are the personal representatives of the estate of the above-named Deceased ("the Deceased") who died on [   ]. We obtained [a grant of probate][letters of administration] out of the [   ] Registry on [   ] and a copy of the grant [and the Deceased's will dated [   ]] is now produced and shown to us marked "   . 1". We make this witness statement in support of our application for permission to distribute the Deceased's estate [and to administer the will trusts of which we will be the Trustees following administration.]. This witness statement contains facts and matters which, unless otherwise stated, are within our own knowledge obtained in acting in the administration of the estate. We believe them to be true.

2. The Deceased was before his death an underwriting member of Lloyd's of London whose underwriting activities are treated as having ceased on [   ]. The estate was sworn for probate purposes at £[   ]. We are now in a position to complete the administration of the estate and to distribute it to the beneficiaries but we do not wish to do so [or to constitute the will trusts] without the authority of the Court because of the existence of possible contingent claims arising out of the Deceased's underwriting liabilities for which we might be liable.

3. The position concerning the Deceased's Lloyd's liabilities is as follows:

[3.1 The Deceased's liabilities in respect of the years of account 1992 and earlier were reinsured into Equitas as part of the Lloyd's settlement. There is now produced and shown to us marked "   .2" a copy of the certificate or statement of rein-surance into Equitas].

3.2 [The syndicates in which the Deceased participated in the years of account 1993 and later have [closed by reinsurance in the usual way] [are the subject of an Estate Protection Plan issued to the Deceased by Centrewrite Limited][are protected by an EXEAT policy obtained by the Claimants from Centrewrite Limited].

4. There is now produced and shown to us marked "   .3" a copy of a letter

dated [   ] from the estate's Lloyd's agents confirming that [all] the syndicates have been reinsured to close [with the exception of [   ] which syndicate is protected by [the Estate Protection Plan][the EXEAT policy]] and confirming that in the case of failure of a reinsuring syndicate to honour its obligations, the primary liability to a creditor will fall on Lloyd's Central Fund. [A copy of the [Estate Protection Plan and Annual Certificate] [EXEAT policy] is now produced and shown to us marked "   .4".]

5. The Claimants believe that the interests of any Lloyd's claimant are reasonably secured by virtue of the fact that all the Lloyd's syndicates in which the Deceased participated have either been closed ultimately by reinsurance to close (in respect of any open years prior to 1992 into the Equitas group) or, in respect of subsequent years [have all closed by reinsurance] [are protected by the Estate Protection Plan][are protected by the EXEAT policy.] Equitas remains licensed to conduct insurance business and there is presently no reason to doubt its solvency. A copy of the latest report and accounts of Equitas Holdings Limited is now produced and shown to us marked "   .5". [The [Estate Protection Plan] [EXEAT policy] is provided by Centrewrite Limited which is a wholly-owned subsidiary of Lloyd's and the beneficiary of an undertaking by Lloyd's to maintain its solvency. We have no reason to doubt the solvency of Centrewrite. A copy of the latest report and accounts of Centrewrite Limited is now produced and shown to us marked "   . 6".]

6. As appears from the schedule now produced and shown to us marked ".7" in which we summarise the assets and liabilities of the estate, we have paid all the debts of the Deceased known to us (apart from the costs and expenses associated with the final administration of the estate) and we have also advertised for and dealt with all claimants in accordance with s.27 of the Trustee Act 1925 [or if not explain why].

7. We know of no special reason or circumstance which might give rise to doubt whether the provision described above can reasonably be regarded as adequate provision for potential claims against the estate and we ask for permission to distribute accordingly.

Form of Order

[Heading as in claim form]

1A–242

ON THE APPLICATION of the Claimants by Part 8 Claim Form dated [   ]
UPON READING the documents recorded on the Court file as having been read
IT IS ORDERED THAT:

1. the Claimants as [the personal representatives of the estate ("the Estate") of the above named deceased ("the Deceased")] [and] [the trustees of the trusts of the Deceased's will dated [   ]("the Will")] have permission to [distribute the Estate] [and] [administer the trusts of the Will and distribute capital and income in accordance with such trusts] without making any retention or further provision in respect of any contract of insurance or reinsurance under-written by the Deceased in the course of his business as an underwriting member of Lloyd's of London

2. the costs of the Claimants of this application [either in the agreed sum of £] [or summarily assessed in the sum of £[assessed in the sum of £....] (with permission to [the residuary beneficiaries][name beneficiaries] to apply within 14 days after service of this order on them for the variation or discharge of this summary assessment] [or subject to detailed assessment on the indemnity basis if not agreed by or on behalf of   [the residuary beneficiaries] name beneficiaries]] be raised and paid or retained out of the Estate in due course of administration.

APPENDIX 12

PRACTICE NOTE: REMUNERATION OF JUDICIAL TRUSTEES

1. When dealing with the assignment of remuneration to a judicial trustee under **1A–243** section 1(5) of the Judicial Trustees Act 1896 and rule 11 of the Judicial Trustee Rules 1983 the court will consider directions as to remuneration based on the common form of order set out below, subject to such modifications as may be required in any particular case.

2. In general the court when considering reasonable remuneration for the purposes of rule 11(1)(a) will need to be satisfied as to the basis upon which the remuneration is claimed, that it is justified and that the amount is reasonable and proportionate and within the limit of 15% of the capital value of the trust property specified in the rule.

3. The court may, before determining the amount of remuneration, require the judicial trustee to provide further information, alternatively refer the matter to a costs judge for him to assess remuneration.

4. When an application is made to the court for the appointment of a judicial trustee or when the court gives directions under rule 8 practitioners should produce to the court a draft order which should take account of the common form of order

Draft Paragraphs of Order

1A–244   [IT IS ORDERED]

..........that the remuneration of the Judicial Trustee shall be in such amount as may be approved from time to time by this court upon application for payment on examination of his accounts

..........that the Judicial Trustees accounts shall be endorsed by him with a certificate of the approximate capital value of the trust property at the commencement of the year of account

..........that every application for payment by the Judicial Trustee shall be in the form of a letter to the court (with a copy to the beneficiaries) which shall (a) set out the basis of the claim to remuneration, the scales or rates of any professional charges, the work done and time spent, any information concerning the complexity of the trusteeship that may be relied on and any other matters which the court shall be invited by the Judicial Trustee to take into account and (b) certify that he considers that the claim for remuneration is reasonable and proportionate

J. Winegarten
Chief Chancery Master

1st July
2003

With the authority of the Vice-Chancellor

94

1B QUEEN'S BENCH GUIDE

Editorial Note

The coming into force of the Civil Procedure Rules 1998 highlighted the need for a **1B–1** Guide which would clarify the complexities of proceedings in the High Court in accordance with the new Rules. Here then is the first Queen's Bench Guide.

The Guide is intended to assist a litigant who wishes to bring a claim in the Queen's Bench Division at the Royal Court's of Justice by drawing his attention to the relevant Rules and Practice Directions, together with the procedures of the various offices within the Central office and of other related areas such as Listing.

The Guide will be updated at regular intervals as the need arises.

May 2000

1.
INTRODUCTION

1.1 The Guide

1.1.1 This Guide has been prepared by the Senior Master, acting under the authority **1B–2** of the Lord Chief Justice, and provides a general explanation of the work and practice of the Queen's Bench Division with particular regard to proceedings started in the Central Office, and is designed to make it easier for parties to use and proceed in the Queen's Bench Division.

1.1.2 The Guide must be read with the Civil Procedure Rules ("the CPR") and the supporting Practice Directions. Litigants and their advisers are responsible for acquainting themselves with the CPR; it is not the task of this Guide to summarise the CPR, nor should anyone regard it as a substitute for the CPR. It is intended to bring the Guide up to date at regular intervals as necessary.

1.1.3 The Guide does not have the force of law, but parties using the Queen's Bench Division will be expected to act in accordance with this Guide. Further guidance as to the practice of the Queen's Bench Division may be obtained from the Practice Master (see paragraph 6.1 below).

1.1.4 It is assumed throughout the Guide that the litigant intends to proceed in the Royal Courts of Justice. For all essential purposes, though, the Guide is equally applicable to the work of the District Registries, which deal with the work of the Queen's Bench Division outside London, but it should be borne in mind that there are some differences.

1.1.5 The telephone numbers and room numbers quoted in the Guide are correct at the time of going to press. However, the room numbers quoted for the Clerk of the Lists and the Listing Office are effective as from 2nd October 2000.

1.2 The Civil Procedure Rules

1.2.1 The Overriding Objective set out in Part 1 of the CPR is central to the new **1B–3** culture which enables the court to deal with cases justly. To further this aim the work is allocated to one of three tracks—the small claims track, the fast track and the multi-track—so as to dispose of the work in the most appropriate and effective way combined with active case management by the court.

1.2.2 The CPR are divided into Parts. A particular Part is referred to in the Guide as Part 7, etc., as the case may be. Any particular rule within a Part is referred to as Rule 6.4(2), and so on.

1.3 The Practice Directions

1.3.1 Each Part—or almost each Part—has an accompanying Practice Direction or **1B–4** Directions, and other Practice Directions deal with matters such as the Pre-Action Protocols and the former Rules of the Supreme Court and the County Court Rules which are scheduled to Part 50.

1.3.2 The Practice Directions are made pursuant to statute, and have the same authority as do the CPR themselves[1]. However, in case of any conflict between a Rule and a Practice Direction, the Rule will prevail[2]. Each Practice Direction is referred to in the Guide with the number of any Part that it supplements preceding it; for example, the Practice Direction supplementing Part 6 is referred to as the Part 6 Practice Direction. But where there is more than one Practice Direction supplementing a Part it will also be described either by topic, for example, Part 25 Practice Direction—Interim Payments, or where appropriate, the Part 40B Practice Direction.

[THE NEXT PARAGRAPH IS 1B–7.]

1.4 The Forms

1B–7 1.4.1 The Practice Direction supplementing Part 4 (Forms) lists the practice forms that are required by or referred to in the CPR, and also those referred to in such of the Rules of the Supreme Court and the County Court Rules as are still in force (see Part 50 of the CPR; Schedules 1 and 2).

1.4.2 Those listed in Table 1 with a number prefixed by the letter N are new forms, a number of these forms have been published with the CPR. Those listed in Table 2 are forms still in use in the High Court but altered so as to conform to the CPR. They may be used as precedents and are set out in a separate Appendix to this Guide and include:

    (1) Forms that were previously prescribed forms; these are listed under the same numbers that previously identified them.

    (2) Former practice forms common to both the Chancery and Queen's Bench Divisions; these forms have been given numbers starting with the letters PF.

    (3) Former practice forms used mainly in the Queen's Bench Division; these forms have been given numbers ending with the letters QB.

    (4) Former practice forms used mainly in the Chancery Division; these forms have been given numbers ending with the letters CH.

1.4.3 The forms may be modified as circumstances in individual cases require[3], but it is essential that a modified form contains at least as full information or guidance as would have been given if the original form had been used.

1.4.4 Where the Royal Arms appears on any listed form it must appear on any modification of that form. The same format for the Royal Arms as is used on the listed forms need not be used. All that is necessary is that there is a complete Royal Arms.

1.5 The Queen's Bench Division

1B–8 1.5.1 The Queen's Bench Division is one of the three divisions of the High Court, together with the Chancery Division and Family Division. The Lord Chief Justice is President of the Queen's Bench Division, and certain High Court Judges and Masters are assigned to it. A Lord Justice of Appeal (currently Lord Justice Kennedy) has been appointed by the Lord Chief Justice to be the Vice-President of the Division; a High Court Judge is appointed as Judge in charge of the Jury List (currently Mr Justice Moreland); another is appointed as Judge in charge of the Trial List (currently Mr Justice Buckley).

1.5.2 Outside London, the work of the Queen's Bench Division is administered in provincial offices known as district registries. In London, the work is administered in the Central Office at the Royal Courts of Justice. The work in the Central Office of the Queen's Bench Division is the responsibility of the Senior Master, acting under the authority of the Lord Chief Justice.

---

[1] Civil Procedure Act 1997, ss.1 and 5, and Sched.1, paras 3 and 6
[2] There is one exception: Part 8
[3] See rule 4.3

1.5.3 The work of the Queen's Bench Division is (with certain exceptions) governed by the CPR. The Divisional Court, the Admiralty Court, the Commercial Court and the Technology and Construction Court are all part of the Queen's Bench Division. However, each does specialised work requiring a distinct procedure that to some extent modifies the CPR. For that reason each publishes its own Guide or Practice Direction, to which reference should be made by parties wishing to proceed in the specialist courts.

1.5.4 The work of the Queen's Bench Division consists mainly of claims for;
- (1) damages in respect of
    - (a) personal injury,
    - (b) negligence,
    - (c) breach of contract, and
    - (d) libel and slander (defamation),
- (2) non-payment of a debt, and
- (3) possession of land or property.

Proceedings retained to be dealt with in the Central Office of the Queen's Bench Division will almost invariably be multi-track claims.

1.5.5 In many types of claim—for example claims in respect of negligence by solicitors, accountants, etc. or claims for possession of land—the claimant has a choice whether to bring the claim in the Queen's Bench Division or in the Chancery Division. However, there are certain claims that may be brought only in the Queen's Bench Division, namely:
- (1) sheriff's interpleader proceedings,
- (2) enrolment of deeds,
- (3) registration of foreign judgments under the Civil Jurisdictions and Judgments Act 1982,
- (4) applications for bail in criminal proceedings,
- (5) applications under the Administration of Justice Act 1920 and the Foreign Judgments (Reciprocal Enforcement) Act 1933,
- (6) registration and satisfaction of Bills of Sale,
- (7) Election Petitions,
- (8) obtaining evidence for foreign courts.

1.6 The Central Office

1.6.1 The information in this and the following paragraph is to be found in the Part 2 Practice Direction at paragraph 2; it is reproduced here for the convenience of litigants. The Central Office is open for business from 10 a.m. to 4.30 p.m. (except during August when it is open from 10 a.m. to 2.30 p.m.) on every day of the year except;
- (1) Saturdays and Sundays,
- (2) Good Friday and the day after Easter Monday,
- (3) Christmas Day and, if that day is a Friday or Saturday, then 28th December,
- (4) Bank Holidays in England and Wales (under the Banking and Financial Dealings Act 1971), and
- (5) such other days as the Lord Chancellor, with the concurrence or the Lord Chief Justice, the Master of the Rolls, the President of the Family Division and the Vice-Chancellor, may direct.

1.6.2 One of the Masters of the Queen's Bench Division is present at the Central Office on every day on which the office is open for the purpose of superintending the business administered there and giving any directions that may be required on questions of practice and procedure. He is normally referred to as the "Practice Master". (See paragraph 6.1 below for information about the Practice Master and Masters in general.)

1.6.3 The Central Office consists of the Action Department, the Masters' Secretary's Department, the Queen's Bench Associates' Department, the Clerk of the Lists, the

Registry of the Technology and Construction Court and the Admiralty and Commercial Registry.

1.6.4 The Action Department deals with the issue of claims, responses to claims, admissions, undefended and summary judgments, enforcement, drawing up certain orders, public searches, provision of copies of court documents, enrolment of deeds, submission of references to the Court of Justice of the European Communities and registration of foreign judgments.

1.6.5 The Masters' Secretary's Department covers three discrete areas of work;
>   (1) the Masters' Support Unit which provides support (a) to the Masters, including assisting with case-management, and (b) to the Senior Master,
>   (2) Foreign Process, and
>   (3) Investment of Children's Funds.

1.6.6 The Queen's Bench Associates sit in court with the Judges during trials and certain interim hearings. The Chief Associate manages the Queen's Bench Associates and also provides support to the Senior Master as the Queen's Remembrancer and as the Prescribed Officer for Election Petitions. The Associates draw up the orders made in court at trial and those interim orders that the parties do not wish to draw up themselves.

1.6.7 The Clerk of the Lists lists all trials and matters before the Judges (see paragraph 8 below).

1.6.8 The Technology and Construction Court deals with claims which involve issues or questions which are technically complex or for which a trial by a Judge of that court is for any other reason desirable (see the Part 49C Practice Direction—Technology and Construction Court).

1.6.9 The Admiralty and Commercial Court deals mainly with shipping collision claims and claims concerning charters and insurance, and commercial arbitrations. See the Commercial Court Guide and the Part 49D Practice Direction—Commercial Court, the Part 49F Practice Direction—Admiralty and the Part 49G Practice Direction—Arbitrations.

1.7 The Judiciary

1B–10 1.7.1 The judiciary in the Queen's Bench Division consist of the High Court Judges (The Honourable Mr/Mrs Justice .... and addressed in court as my Lord/my Lady) and in the Royal Courts of Justice the Masters (Master ....); in the District Registries the work of the Masters is conducted by District Judges.

1.7.2 Trial normally takes place before a High Court Judge (or Deputy High Court Judge[1])who may also hear pre-trial reviews and other interim applications. Wherever possible the judge before whom a trial has been fixed will hear any pre-trial review. A High Court Judge will hear applications to commit for contempt of court, applications for injunctions[2] and most appeals from Masters' orders. (See the Practice Direction to Part 2B Allocation of cases to levels of Judiciary, and see paragraphs 7.11 and 7.12 below for more information on hearings and applications.)

1.7.3 The Masters deal with interim and some pre-action applications, and manage the claims so that they proceed without delay. The Masters' rooms are situated in the East Block of the Royal Courts of Justice. Hearings take place in these rooms or (short hearings only) in the Bear Garden.

1.7.4 Cases are assigned on issue by a court officer in the Action Department to Masters on a random basis, and that Master is then known as the assigned Master in

---

[1] A Deputy High Court Judge may be a Circuit Judge or a Queen's Counsel. A retired High Court Judge may also sit as a High Court Judge
[2] See Part 25 and the practice direction which supplements it for more information about injunctions and who may hear them, and interim remedies in general

relation to that case. (See paragraphs 6.2 and 6.3 below for more information about assignment and the Masters' lists.)

1.7.5 General enquiries about the business dealt with by the Masters should initially be made in writing to the Masters' Support Unit in Room E14.

2.

GENERAL

2.1 Essential matters

2.1.1 Before bringing any proceedings, the intending claimant should think carefully **1B–11** about the implications of so doing. (See paragraph 3 below about steps to be taken before issuing a claim form.)

2.1.2 A litigant who is acting in person faces a heavier burden in terms of time and effort than does a litigant who is legally represented, but all litigation calls for a high level of commitment from the parties. No intending claimant should underestimate this.

2.1.3 The Overriding Objective of the CPR is to deal with cases justly, which means dealing with the claim in a way which is proportionate (amongst other things) to the amount of money involved[1]. However, in all proceedings there are winners and losers; the loser is generally ordered to pay the costs of the winner and the costs of litigation can still be large. The risk of large costs is particularly acute in cases involving expert witnesses, barristers and solicitors. Also, the costs of an interim hearing are almost always summarily assessed and made payable by the unsuccessful party within 14 days after the order for costs is made[2]. There may be a number of interim hearings before the trial itself is reached, so the costs must be paid as the claim progresses. (See also paragraph 2.5 Costs below.)

2.1.4 The intending claimant should also keep in mind that every claim must be proved, unless of course the defendant admits the allegations. There is little point in incurring the risks and expense of litigating if the claim cannot be proved. An intending claimant should therefore be taking steps to obtain statements from his prospective witnesses before starting the claim; if he delays until later, it may turn out that he is in fact unable to obtain the evidence that he needs to prove his claim. A defendant faces a similar task.

2.1.5 Any party may, if he is to succeed, need an opinion from one or more expert witnesses, such as medical practitioners, engineers, accountants, or as the case may be. However he must remember that no expert evidence may be given at trial without the permission of the court. If the claim is for compensation for personal injuries, the claimant must produce a medical report with his particulars of claim.

2.1.6 The services of such experts are in great demand, especially as in some fields of expertise there are few of them. It may take many months to obtain an opinion, and the cost may be high. (See paragraph 7.9 below for information about experts' evidence.) The claimant must remember also not to allow the time limit for starting his claim to pass (see paragraph 2.3 below for information about time limits).

2.1.7 Any intending claimant should also have in mind that he will usually be required to give standard disclosure of the documents on which he relies. Although Rule 31.3(2) makes provision for a party not to be required to disclose documents if disclosure would be disproportionate to the value of the claim, in complex cases it may still be necessary to disclose relatively large quantities of documents, and this invariably involves much time, effort and expense. (See paragraph 7.8 below for information about disclosure.)

2.1.8 In many cases the parties will need legal assistance, whether by way of advice, drafting, representation at hearings or otherwise. It is not the function of court staff

[1] See rule 1.1
[2] See rule 44.8

to give legal advice, however, subject to that, they will do their best to assist any litigant. Litigants in person who need assistance or funding should contact the Community Legal Service through their Information Points. The CLS are developing local networks of people giving legal assistance such as law centres, local solicitors or the Citizens Advice Bureaux. CLS Information Points are being set up in libraries and other public places. Litigants can telephone the CLS to find their nearest CLS Information Point on 0845 608 1122 or can log on to the CLS website at www.justask.org.uk for the CLS directory and for legal information.

2.1.9 The RCJ Advice Bureau off the Main Hall at the Royal Courts of Justice is open Monday to Friday from 10.00 a.m. to 1.00 p.m. and from 2.00 p.m. to 5.00 p.m. The Bureau is run by lawyers in conjunction with the Citizens Advice Bureau and is independent of the court. The Bureau operates on a "first come first served" basis, or telephone advice is available on 020 7947 7604 Monday to Friday from 11.00 a.m. to 12.00 p.m. and from 3.00 p.m. to 4.00 p.m.

2.2 Inspection and Copies of Documents

1B–12 2.2.1 Intending claimants must not expect to be able to keep the details of a claim away from public scrutiny. In addition to the right of a party to obtain copies of documents in the proceedings to which he is a party from the court record (on payment of the prescribed fee), a claim form when it has been served, and the particulars of claim where they are included in or served with the claim form, may be inspected by anyone simply on payment of the fee. Any judgment or order made in public may also be inspected on payment of the fee. Additionally, other documents may be inspected with the permission of the court[1].

2.2.2 Witness statements[2] used at trial are open to inspection unless the court directs otherwise[3]. Considerations of publicity are often particularly important in deciding whether to commence proceedings in respect of an alleged libel or slander; such a claim may by its attendant publicity do more damage than was ever inflicted by the original publication. In such proceedings the claimant may decide to serve his particulars of claim separately from the claim form[4].

2.3 Time Limits

1B–12.1 2.3.1 There are strict time limits that apply to every claim. First, there are time limits fixed by the Limitation Act 1980 within which proceedings must be brought. There are circumstances in which the court may extend those time limits, but this should be regarded as exceptional. In all other cases, once the relevant time limit has expired, it is rarely possible to start a claim.

2.3.2 Secondly, in order to try and bring the proceedings to an early trial date, a timetable will be set with which all parties must comply. Unless the CPR or a Practice Direction provide otherwise, or the court orders otherwise, the timetable may be varied by the written agreement of the parties[5]. However, there are certain "milestone" events in the timetable in which the time limits may not be varied by the parties. Examples of these are;

    (1) return of the allocation questionnaire
    (2) date for the case management conference
    (3) return of the listing questionnaire
    (4) date fixed for trial.

Where parties have extended a time limit by agreement, the party for whom the time has been extended must advise the Masters' Support Unit in writing of the event in

---

[1] See rule 5.4 and the practice direction supplementing Part 5
[2] See paragraph 7.10 below about evidence
[3] See rule 32.13
[4] See paragraph 8.1 of the Part 16 practice direction for matters to be included in the claim form in a defamation claim where the particulars of claim are served separately
[5] See rule 2.11

the proceedings for which the time has been extended and the new date by which it must be done. For example, if an extension is agreed for the filing of the defence, it is for the defendant to inform the Masters' Support Unit.

2.3.3 The court has power to penalise any party who fails to comply with a time limit. If the court considers that a prior warning should be given before a penalty is imposed, it will make an 'unless' order; in other words, the court will order that, unless that party performs his obligation by the time specified, he will be penalised in the manner set out in the order. This may involve the party in default having his claim or statement of case struck out and judgment given against him.

2.4 Legal Representation

2.4.1 A party may act in person or be represented by a lawyer. A party who is acting **1B–13** in person may be assisted at any hearing by another person (often referred to as a McKenzie friend) subject to the discretion of the Court. The McKenzie friend is allowed to help by taking notes, quietly prompting the litigant and offering advice and suggestions. The litigant however, must conduct his own case; the McKenzie friend may not represent him and may only in very exceptional circumstances be allowed to address the court on behalf of the litigant under s.27(2)(c) of the Courts and Legal Services Act 1990.

2.4.2 A written statement should be provided to the court at any hearing concerning the representation of the parties in accordance with paragraph 5.1 of the Part 39 Practice Direction.

2.4.3 At a trial, a company or corporation may be represented by an employee if the company or corporation authorise him to do so and the court gives permission. Where this is to be the case, the permission of the Judge who is to hear the case may be sought informally; paragraph 5 of the Part 39 Practice Direction describes what is needed to obtain permission from the court for this purpose and mentions some of the considerations relevant to the grant or refusal of permission. A further statement concerning representation should be provided in accordance with paragraph 5.2 of the Part 39 Practice Direction.

2.4.4 The practice of allowing experienced outdoor clerks to appear before the Masters will continue.

2.5 Costs

2.5.1 Costs are dealt with in Parts 43 to 48. There are important new provisions in **1B–14** the costs rules, particularly with respect to;
  (1) informing the client of costs orders,
  (2) providing the court with estimates of costs, and
  (3) summary assessment of costs,
  (4) interim orders for costs, and
  (5) interest on costs.

2.5.2 Solicitors now have a duty under Rule 44.2 to notify their client within 7 days if an order for costs is made against him in his absence. Solicitors must also notify any other person who has instructed them to act in the proceedings or who is liable to pay their fees (such as an insurer, trade union or the Legal Services Commission (LSC)).They must also inform these persons how the order came to be made (paragraphs 7.1 and 7.2 of the Costs Practice Direction).

2.5.3 The court may at any stage order any party to file an estimate of base costs (substantially in the form of Precedent H in the Schedule of Costs Precedents annexed to the Costs Practice Direction) and serve copies on all the other parties (paragraph 6.3 of the Costs Practice Direction). This will both assist the court in deciding what case management directions to make and inform the other parties as to their potential liability for payment of costs.

2.5.4 If a party seeks an order for his costs, in order to assist the court in making a summary assessment, he must prepare a written statement of the costs he intends to claim in accordance with paragraph 13.5 of the Costs Practice Direction, following as closely as possible Form N260. In addition, when an Allocation Questionnaire or a Listing Questionnaire is filed, the party filing it must file and serve an estimate of costs on all the other parties.

2.5.5 If the parties have agreed the amount of costs, they do not need to file a statement of the costs, and summary assessment is unnecessary. Or, where the parties agree a consent order without any party attending on the application, the parties should insert either an agreed figure for costs or that there should be no order for costs in the order (paragraph 13.4 of the Costs Practice Direction).

2.5.6 Unless the court decides not to order an assessment of costs where, for example, it orders costs to be "costs in the case"[1], it may either make a summary assessment of costs or order a detailed assessment to take place[2]. The court will generally make a summary assessment of costs at any hearing which lasts for less than one day;

    (1) "summary assessment" is where the court, when making an order for costs, assesses those costs and orders payment of a sum of money in respect of them[3], and

    (2) "detailed assessment" is the procedure by which the amount of costs is decided by a costs officer at a later date in accordance with Part 47.

The provision of summary assessment means that the paying party is likely to be paying the costs at an earlier stage than he would have done under the previous rules (and see paragraph 2.5.15 below).

2.5.7 The court will not make a summary assessment of the costs of a receiving party (the party to whom the costs are to be paid) where he is;

    (1) a child or patient within the meaning of Part 21 unless the solicitor acting for the child or patient has waived the right to further costs[4], or

    (2) an assisted person or a person in receipt of funded services under sections 4-11 of the Access to Justice Act 1999.

The costs payable by a party who is a person in receipt of funded services may be summarily assessed as the assessment is not by itself a determination of the assisted person's liability to pay those costs[5].

2.5.8 Rule 44.3A prevents the court from assessing an additional liability in respect of a funding agreement before the conclusion of the proceedings. At an interim hearing therefore, the court will assess only the base costs. (See paragraph 14.9 of the Costs Practice Direction for assessing an additional liability and Section 19 for information about funding arrangements.)

2.5.9 Interim orders for costs; where the court decides immediately who is to pay particular costs, but does not assess the costs summarily, for example after a trial lasting more than a day, so that the final amount of costs payable has to be fixed by a detailed assessment, the court may order the paying party to pay a sum or sums on account of the ultimate liability for costs.

2.5.10 Interest on costs; the court has power to award interest on costs from a date before the date of the order, so compensating the receiving party for the delay between incurring costs and receiving a payment in respect of them.

---

  [1] See the table in para.8.5 of the Costs Practice Direction for some of the most common costs orders the court may make
  [2] See rule 44.7 and section 12 of the Costs Practice Direction
  [3] See the sections 12 and 13 of the Costs Practice Direction
  [4] See the Costs Practice Direction paras 13.11 and 51.1
  [5] See the Costs Practice Direction para.13.10

2.5.11 Parties should note that where the court makes an order which does not mention costs, no party is entitled to costs in relation to that order[1].

2.5.12 Rule 44.3 describes the court's discretion as to costs and the circumstances to be taken into account when exercising its discretion. Rules 44.4 and 44.5 set out the basis of assessment and the factors to be taken into account in deciding the amount of costs.

2.5.13 The amount of costs to be paid by one party to another can be assessed on the standard basis or on the indemnity basis. The basis to be used is decided when the court decides that a party should pay the costs of another. Costs that are unreasonably incurred or are unreasonable in amount are not allowed on either basis.

2.5.14 The standard basis is the usual basis for assessment, where only costs which are proportionate to the matters in issue are allowed, and any doubt as to whether the costs were reasonably incurred or reasonable and proportionate in amount is resolved in favour of the paying party. On the indemnity basis, any such doubts are resolved in favour of the receiving party.

2.5.15 A party must normally pay summarily assessed costs awarded against him within 14 days of the assessment, but the court can extend that time, direct payment by instalments, or defer the liability to pay the costs until the end of the proceedings so that they can then be set off against any costs or judgment to which the paying party becomes entitled.

2.5.16 Fixed costs relating to default judgments, certain judgments on admissions and summary judgments etc. are set out in Part 45. Part 46 relates to fast track costs.

2.5.17 Part 47 and Sections 28 to 49 of the Costs Practice Direction contain the procedure for detailed assessment together with the default provisions. Precedents A,B,C and D set out in the Schedule of Costs Precedents annexed to the Costs Practice Direction are model forms of bills of costs for detailed assessment. Section 43 deals with costs payable out of the Community Legal Service fund, Section 44 deals with costs payable out of a fund other than the CLS fund and Section 49 deals with costs payable by the LSC. Part 48 and Sections 50 to 56 of the Costs Practice Direction deal with Special Cases, in particular;
- (1) costs payable by or to a child or patient,
- (2) litigants in person, and
- (3) wasted costs orders– personal liability of the legal representative.

2.5.18 Costs only proceedings are dealt with in Rule 44.12A and Section 17 of the Costs Practice Direction. They may be brought in the High Court only where the dispute was of such a value or type that had proceedings been brought they would have been commenced in the High Court. Proceedings are brought under Part 8 by the issue of a Claim Form in the Supreme Court Costs Office at Clifford's Inn, Fetter Lane, London EC4A 1DQ. (See also paragraphs 4.1.16 and 6.8.13 below.)

2.6 Court Fees

2.6.1 The fees payable in the High Court are set out in Schedule 1 to the Supreme **1B–15** Court Fees Order 1999. Fees (as amended on 25th April 2000 and 2nd May 2000) relating to the Queen's Bench Division are listed in Annex 1 to the Guide.

2.6.2 In the Royal Courts of Justice fees are paid in the Fees Room E01 and are usually stamped on the document to which they relate.

2.7 Information Technology

2.7.1 To support the work of the Central Office in operating the provisions of the **1B–16** CPR, and to facilitate effective case management, a computerised system will be

---

[1] See Rule 44.13(1)

introduced to provide a record of proceedings and a search facility, and to produce court forms and orders. The full system is not yet available, but an interim system has been in use since 26th April 1999.

2.7.2 A number of specific applications of information technology have been well developed in recent years; the use of fax, the provision of skeleton arguments on disk and daily transcripts on disk have become commonplace. Short applications may be dealt with more economically by a conference telephone call, and taking evidence by video link has become more common and the available technology has improved considerably. The CPR contains certain provisions about the use of information technology, for example, Part 6 and the Part 6 Practice Direction deal with service of documents by Fax or other electronic means, the Part 23 Practice Direction refers to telephone hearings and video conferencing, Rule 32.3 allows the use of evidence given by video link and the Part 5 Practice Direction refers to the filing of documents at court by Fax.

2.7.3 Parties may agree to use information technology in the preparation, management and presentation of a case, however the agreement of the Judge or Master should be sought before providing the court with material in electronic form. Where permission has been given, the material for use at a hearing or in support of an application can be provided on a floppy disk. The parties should check with the court which word-processing format should be used. This will normally be Word 6 for Windows or WordPerfect for DOS 5.1.

2.7.4 A protocol has been prepared as a guide to all persons who are involved in the use of video conferencing equipment in civil proceedings in the High Court. It covers its use in courtrooms where the equipment may be installed, and also the situation where the court assembles in a commercial studio or conference room containing video conferencing equipment. Copies of the Video- conferencing Protocol may be obtained from the Bar Council at a charge of £2.50 to cover expenses. A room has now been made available as an audio/video conferencing courtroom for applications to Masters, as a pilot measure. More information may be obtained from the Senior Master through the Masters' Secretary's Department.

3.
STEPS BEFORE ISSUE OF A CLAIM FORM

3.1 Settlement

1B–17 3.1.1 So far as reasonably possible, a claimant should try to resolve his claim without litigation. The court is increasingly taking the view that litigation should be a last resort and parties may wish to consider the use of Alternative Dispute Resolution ("ADR"). (See paragraph 6.6 below.)

3.1.2 There are codes of practice for preliminary negotiations in certain types of claim. These codes of practice are called "Protocols" and are set out in a schedule to the Protocols Practice Direction to the CPR. At present there are protocols covering only the areas of personal injury and clinical negligence. Even if there is no protocol that applies to the claim, the parties will nonetheless be expected to comply with the spirit of the Overriding Objective[1].

3.1.3 An offer to settle a claim may be made by either party[2] whether before or after a claim is brought. The court will take account of any offer to settle made before proceedings are started when making any order as to costs after proceedings have started[3].

---

[1] See the Protocols practice direction paragraph 4
[2] See paragraph 3.21 of the Personal Injury protocol and paragraphs 3.22 and 3.26 of the Clinical Negligence protocol
[3] See rule 36.10 and rule 44.3(4)(c)

3.2 Disclosure Before Proceedings Are Started

3.2.1 An intending claimant may need documents to which he does not yet have **1B–18**
access. Rule 31.16 sets out the provisions for making an application for disclosure of
documents before proceedings have started.

3.2.2 Essentially, the court must be satisfied that the applicant and respondent to the
application are likely to be parties when proceedings are brought, that the required
documents are those that the respondent would be required to disclose under Rule
31.6 when proceedings are brought and that their early disclosure might dispose of
or assist the disposal of anticipated proceedings or save costs.

3.3 Defamation proceedings

3.3.1 Application may be made to the court before a claim is brought for the court's **1B–19**
assistance in accepting an offer of amends under section 3 of the Defamation Act
1996. The application is made by Part 8 Claim Form. For more information see
paragraph 4.1.15 Part 8 procedure and paragraph 12.7 defamation below.

4.

STARTING PROCEEDINGS IN THE CENTRAL OFFICE

4.1 Issuing The Claim Form

4.1.1 All claims must be started by issuing a Claim Form. The great majority of claims **1B–20**
involve a dispute of fact, and the Claim Form should be issued in accordance with
Part 7 of the CPR. The Part 8 procedure may be followed in the types of claim
described in paragraphs 4.1.14 to 4.1.16 below.

4.1.2 The requirements for issuing a Claim Form are set out in Part 7 and the Part 7
Practice Direction, the main points of which are summarised in the following
paragraphs.

4.1.3 The Practice Direction at paragraphs 2, 3 and 4 provides information as to;
  (1) where a claim should be started,
  (2) certain matters that must be included in the Claim Form, and
  (3) how the heading of the claim should be set out on the Claim Form.

In defamation cases see Part 53 and the Part 53 Practice Direction for matters that
should be included in the Claim Form and particulars of claim. See also paragraph
12.7 below.

4.1.4 Proceedings are started when the court issues a Claim Form, and a Claim Form
is issued on the date entered on the Claim Form by the court[1]. However, where a
Claim Form is received in the court office on an earlier date than the date of issue,
then, for the purposes of the Limitation Act 1980, the claim is brought on the earlier
date (see paragraphs 5.1 to 5.4 of the Part 7 Practice Direction).

4.1.5 To start proceedings in the Central Office, a claimant must use form N1 or
form N208 for a Part 8 claim (or a form suitably modified as permitted by Part 4),
and should take or send the Claim Form to Room E17, Action Department, Central
Office, Royal Courts of Justice, Strand, London WC2A 2LL. If the court is to serve
the Claim Form, the claimant must provide sufficient copies for each defendant. A
claimant who wishes to retain on his file a copy of the Claim Form as issued should
provide a further copy of the Claim Form which the court will seal and return it to
him marked "claimant's copy". This copy will bear any amendments which have been
made to the court's copy and the copies for service. Copies of practice forms relevant
to the work of the Action Department (including the Claim Form and Response Pack)
are available from that office. Alternatively, claimants may produce their own forms,
which may be modified as the circumstances require, provided that all essential
information, especially any information or guidance that the form gives to the
recipient, is included.

---

[1] See rule 7.2.

4.1.6 On issuing the Claim Form, the court will give or send the claimant a notice of issue endorsed with the date of issue of the Claim Form. If the claimant requires the court to serve the Claim Form, the date of posting and deemed date of service will also be endorsed on the notice of issue. Claimants, especially solicitors who have been accustomed to using the Action Department, are encouraged to continue to serve their own documents but must inform the court when service has been effected (see paragraph 4.2.4 in relation to service by the claimant and the certificate of service). For certain types of claims, the notice of issue contains the request for judgment. (See paragraph 5 below for information about default judgments.)

4.1.7 A Claim Form must be served within 4 months after the date of issue (Rule 7.5) unless it is to be served out of the jurisdiction, when the period is 6 months; and Rule 7.6 and paragraph 7 of the Practice Direction set out how an extension of time for service of the Claim Form may be sought. (See paragraph 4.2 below about service.)

4.1.8 The particulars of claim may be;
  (1) included in the Claim Form,
  (2) in a separate document served with the Claim Form, or
  (3) in a separate document served within 14 days of service of the Claim Form provided that the particulars of claim are served within the latest time for serving the Claim Form[1].

4.1.9 A Claim Form that does not include particulars of claim must nonetheless contain a concise statement of the nature of the claim[2]. Any Claim Form that;
  (1) does not comply with the requirements of rule 16.2, or
  (2) is garbled or abusive,

will be referred to a Master and is likely to be struck out by the court[3].

4.1.10 Where the particulars of claim are neither included in or served with the Claim Form;
  (1) the Claim Form must contain a statement that particulars of claim will follow, and
  (2) the particulars of claim must be served by the claimant[4].

However, where a Claim Form is to be served out of the jurisdiction[5], the particulars of claim must accompany the Claim Form. (See paragraph 4.2.13 below.)

4.1.11 Certain forms must accompany the particulars of claim when they are served on the defendant. These forms are listed in Rule 7.8 and are included in a Response Pack, which is available from the Action Department.

4.1.12 A party who has entered into a funding arrangement and who wishes to claim an additional liability must give the Court and any other party information about that claim if he is to recover the additional liability. Where the funding arrangement has been entered into before proceedings are commenced, the claimant should file a notice of funding in form N251 when the Claim Form is issued.

4.1.13 Part 22 requires the particulars of claim, and where they are not included in the Claim Form itself, the Claim Form to be verified by a statement of truth; see paragraph 6 of the Part 7 Practice Direction, and the Part 22 Practice Direction.

4.1.14 Part 16 and the Part 16 Practice Direction deal with statements of case, and in particular the contents of the Claim Form and the particulars of claim. Part 16 does

---

[1] See rule 7.4
[2] See rule 16.2(1), and paragraph 8 of the Part 16 practice direction in respect of defamation claims
[3] See rule 3.2
[4] See rule 7.4(1)(b)
[5] See rule 2.3 for the definition of "jurisdiction"

not apply to claims in respect of which the Part 8 alternative procedure for claims is being used. See paragraph 5.6 below for more about statements of case.

4.1.15 A claimant may use the Part 8 procedure where;

(1) he seeks the court's decision on a question that is unlikely to involve a substantial dispute of fact, or

(2) a rule or Practice Direction requires or permits the use of the Part 8 procedure[1],

however, the court may at any stage order the claim to continue as if the claimant had not used the Part 8 procedure[2].

4.1.16 Certain matters that must be included on the Claim Form when the Part 8 procedure is being used are set out in Rule 8.2. The types of claim for which the Part 8 procedure may be used include[3];

(1) a claim by or against a child or patient that has been settled before the commencement of proceedings, the sole purpose of the claim being to obtain the approval of the court to the settlement,

(2) provided there is unlikely to be a substantial dispute of fact, a claim for a summary order for possession against named or unnamed defendants occupying land or premises without the licence or consent of the person claiming possession (Schedule 1- RSC O.113),

(3) a claim for provisional damages that has been settled before the commencement of proceedings, the sole purpose of the claim being to obtain a judgment by consent,

(4) a claim under s.3 of the Defamation Act 1996 (made other than in existing proceedings) and

(5) a claim under Rule 44.12A where the parties have agreed all issues before the commencement of proceedings except the amount of costs and an order for costs is required.

4.1.17 In addition to the provisions of Rule 8.1, attention is drawn also to the Part 8(B) Practice Direction which deals with proceedings brought under "the Schedule Rules"[4].

See Paragraph 6.7 below for more information regarding the Part 8 procedure.

4.2 Service

4.2.1 Service of documents is dealt with in Part 6; Section I (Rules 6.1 to 6.11) **1B–21** contains provisions relating to service generally and Section II (Rules 6.12 to 6.16) contains special provisions relating to service of the Claim Form. Section III (Rules 6.17 to 6.31) deals with service out of the jurisdiction. Some of the more important provisions are described below.

Within the Jurisdiction

4.2.2 The methods by which a document may be served are to be found in Rule 6.2. **1B–22** The court will serve a document that it has issued or prepared unless;

(1) the party on whose behalf it is to be served notifies the court that he wishes to serve it himself,

(2) the court orders otherwise, or

(3) a Rule or Practice Direction provides otherwise[5].

It is anticipated that practitioners familiar with Central Office procedures will wish to continue to serve their own documents.

---

[1] See rule 8.1
[2] See rule 8.1(3)
[3] See paragraph 1.4 of the Part 8 practice direction
[4] See paragraph 1.1 of the Part 8B practice direction
[5] See rule 6.3

4.2.3 Where a party has entered into a funding agreement the notice of funding (form N251) must be served on all the other parties. If a claimant files his notice of funding when his Claim Form is issued, the Court will serve it on the other parties provided sufficient copies are provided. Otherwise the claimant must serve the notice of funding with the Claim Form. A defendant should file his notice of funding with his first document, *i.e.* his defence or acknowledgement of service etc. Sufficient copies of the notice should be provided for the Court to serve.

4.2.4 In all other circumstances a party must serve a notice of funding within 7 days of entering into the funding agreement.

4.2.5 Where the court has tried to serve a document but has been unable to serve it, the court will send a notice of non-service to the party on whose behalf it was to be served stating the method attempted[1]. On receipt of this notice, the party should take steps to serve the document himself, as the court is under no further duty to effect service. The method of service used by the court will normally be first-class post.

4.2.6 Where a claimant has served a Claim Form, he must file a certificate of service that complies with the provisions of Rule 6.10. The certificate of service must be filed within 7 days of service of the Claim Form, and the claimant may not obtain judgment in default if it has not been filed [2].

4.2.7 Information as to how personal service is to be effected and as to service by electronic means is to be found in the Part 6 Practice Direction. Rule 6.6 deals with service on a child or patient.

4.2.8 A party must give an address for service within the jurisdiction. Rule 6.5 contains information as to the address for service.

4.2.9 A party may make an application for permission to serve a document by an alternative method[3] to those set out in Rule 6.2. The application may be made without notice, and paragraph 9.1 of the Practice Direction sets out the evidence that will be required in support of the application. (Paragraph 7.12 below contains information in relation to applications.)

Out of the Jurisdiction

1B–23 4.2.10 The provisions for service out of the jurisdiction are contained in Rules 6.17 to 6.31. Rule 6.19 sets out the provisions whereby a Claim Form may be served out of the jurisdiction without the permission of the court, and Rule 6.20 sets out the circumstances where the court's permission is required. Parties should also see the Practice Direction on service out of the jurisdiction.

4.2.11 A claimant may issue a Claim Form against defendants, one or some of whom appear to be out of the jurisdiction, without first having obtained permission for service out of the jurisdiction, provided that where the Claim Form is not one which may be served without the permission of the court under Rule 6.19, the Claim Form is endorsed by the court that it is "not for service out of jurisdiction".

4.2.12 Where a Claim Form is to be served in accordance with Rule 6.19 it must contain a statement of the grounds on which the claimant is entitled to serve it out of the jurisdiction. The statement should be as follows:
  (1) "I, (*name*) state that the High Court of England and Wales has power under the Civil Jurisdiction and Judgments Act 1982 to hear this claim and that no proceedings are pending between the parties in Scotland, Northern Ireland or another Convention territory of any contracting state as defined by section 1(3) of the Act.", or
  (2) where the proceedings are those to which Article 16 of Schedule 1, 3C or 4 to the Act refers,

---

[1] See rule 6.11
[2] See rule 6.14(2)(b).
[3] See rule 6.8

"I, (*name*) state that the High Court of England and Wales has power under the Civil Jurisdiction and Judgements Act 1982, the claim having as its object rights in rem in immovable property or tenancies in immovable property (or otherwise in accordance with the provisions of Article 16 of Schedule 1, 3C or 4 to that Act) to which Article 16 of Schedule 1, 3C or 4 to that Act applies, to hear the claim and that no proceedings are pending between the parties in Scotland, Northern Ireland or another Convention territory of any contracting state as defined by section 1(3) of the Act.", or

(3) where the defendant is party to an agreement conferring jurisdiction to which Article 17 of Schedule 1, 3C or 4 to that Act applies,

"I, (*name*) state that the High Court of England and Wales has power under the Civil Jurisdiction and Judgments Act 1982, the defendant being a party to an agreement conferring jurisdiction to which Article 17 of Schedule 1, 3C or 4 to that Act applies, to hear the claim and that no proceedings are pending between the parties in Scotland, Northern Ireland or another Convention territory of any contracting state as defined by section 1(3) of the Act.".

4.2.13 The above statement should be signed and have set out the full name of the signatory. If a Claim Form as specified in paragraph 4.2.10 above does not bear the above statement, the Claim Form will be endorsed "not for service out of the jurisdiction".

4.2.14 An application for an order for permission to issue a Claim Form for service out of the jurisdiction or to serve the Claim Form out of the jurisdiction should be made in accordance with Part 23 (form PF 6(A) may be used). The application must be supported by written evidence, and may be made without notice. The written evidence should state the requirements set out in Rule 6.21(1) and (2).

4.2.15 An order giving permission for service out of the jurisdiction will be drawn up by the court (in form PF 6(B)), unless a party wishes to do so, and will;

(1) specify the country in which, or place at which, service is to be effected, and

(2) specify the number of days within which the defendant may either

    (a) file an acknowledgement of service,

    (b) file or serve an admission, or

    (c) file a defence to
    the claim, and where an acknowledgement of service is filed, specify a further 14 days within which the defendant may file a defence.

4.2.16 Where service is to be effected in a country which requires a translation of the documents to be served[1], it is the claimant's responsibility to provide the translation of all the documents for each defendant. In every case, it is the claimant's duty to ensure that the Response Pack clearly states the appropriate period for responding to the Claim Form, and form N9, form N1C and other relevant forms must be modified accordingly. Every translation must be accompanied by a statement by the person making it;

(1) that it is a correct translation, and

(2) including the person's name, address and qualifications for making the translation[2].

4.2.17 The periods for acknowledging service of a Claim Form served out of the jurisdiction are set out in Rule 6.22 and in the Table contained in the Part 6 Section III Practice Direction, and the periods for serving a defence to a Claim Form served out of the jurisdiction are set out in Rule 6.23 and in the Table in the Practice Direction. Rule 6.24 describes the methods of service.

4.2.18 Where the Claim Form is to be served through;

(1) the judicial authorities of the country where the Claim Form is to be served,

---

[1] See rule 6.28
[2] Rule 6.28(3)

(2) a British Consular authority in that country,

(3) the authority designated under the Hague Convention in respect of that country, or

(4) the government of that country, or

(5) where the court permits service on a State, the Foreign and Commonwealth Office,

the claimant should provide the Senior Master with the following documents by forwarding them to the Foreign Process section, Room E 02;

(1) a request for service by the chosen method (in form **PF 7**),

(2) a sealed copy and a duplicate copy of the Claim Form,

(3) the Response Pack as referred to in paragraph 4.2.14,

(4) a translation in duplicate, and the statement referred to in paragraph 4.2.13, and

(5) any other relevant documents.

4.2.19 Where service has been requested in accordance with paragraph 4.2.16, the particulars of claim, if not included in the Claim Form, must accompany the Claim Form (in duplicate). Where the claimant is effecting service of the Claim Form direct (and not as in paragraph 4.2.16) and the Claim Form states that particulars of claim are to follow, the permission of the court is not required to serve the particulars of claim out of the jurisdiction.

4.2.20 Where an official certificate of service[1] is received in a foreign language, it is the responsibility of the claimant to obtain a translation of the certificate. Where a defendant served out of the jurisdiction fails to attend a hearing, the official certificate of service is evidence of service. Otherwise the claimant may take no further steps against the defendant until written evidence showing that the Claim Form has been duly served is filed[2].

4.2.21 Further advice on service out of the jurisdiction may be obtained from the Foreign Process section, Room E 02.

5.

RESPONSE TO A PART 7 CLAIM

5.1 General

1B–24 5.1.1 Responding to particulars of claim is dealt with in Part 9. A defendant may respond to the service of particulars of claim by[3];

(1) filing or serving an admission in accordance with Part 14,

(2) filing a defence in accordance with Part 15,

(3) doing both if part only of the claim is admitted, or

(4) filing an acknowledgement of service in accordance with Part 10.

5.1.2 Where a defendant receives a Claim Form that states that particulars of claim are to follow, he need not respond to the claim until the particulars of claim have been served on him[4].

5.1.3 If a defendant fails to;

(1) file an acknowledgement of service within the time specified in rule 10.3, and

(2) file a defence within the time specified in Rule 15.4, or

(3) file or serve an admission in accordance with Part 14

---

[1] See rules 6.26(5) and 6.27(4)
[2] Rule 6.31
[3] See rule 9.2.
[4] See rule 9.1(2)

the claimant may obtain default judgment if Part 12 allows it[1]. (See paragraph 5.5 below for information about default judgments.)

5.2 Acknowledgement of Service

5.2.1 Acknowledgements of service are dealt with in Part 10. A defendant may file an acknowledgement of service if;   **1B–25**
    (1) he is unable to file a defence within the period specified in Rule 15.4, or
    (2) he wishes to dispute the court's jurisdiction[2].

Filing an acknowledgement of service extends the time for filing the defence by 14 days.

5.2.2 A defendant who wishes to acknowledge service of a Claim Form should do so by using form **N9**. Rule 10.5 states that the acknowledgement of service must;
    (1) be signed by the defendant or his legal representative, and
    (2) include the defendant's address for service.

The Part 10 Practice Direction contains information relating to the acknowledgement of service and how it may be signed.

5.3 Admissions

5.3.1 The manner in which a defendant may make an admission of a claim or part of a claim is set out in Rules 14.1 and 14.2, and Rules 14.3 to 14.7 set out how judgment may be obtained on a written admission.   **1B–26**

5.3.2 Included in the Response Pack that will accompany the particulars of claim when they are served on the defendant is an admission form (form N9A for a specified amount and form N9C for an unspecified amount). If the defendant makes an admission and requests time to pay, he should complete as fully as possible the statement of means contained in the admission form, or otherwise give in writing the same details of his means as could have been given in the admission form.

5.3.3 Where the defendant has;
    (1) made an admission in respect of a specified sum and requested time to pay, or
    (2) made an admission in respect of an unspecified sum, offered a sum in satisfaction (which is accepted) and requested time to pay,

and the claimant has not accepted the request for time to pay, on receipt of the claimant's notice the court will enter judgment for the amount admitted or offered (less any payments made) to be paid at the time and rate of payment determined by the court[3].

5.3.4 Where the defendant has;
    (1) made an admission for an unspecified amount, or
    (2) made an admission for an unspecified amount and offered in satisfaction a sum that the claimant has not accepted,

on receipt of the claimant's request for judgment the court will enter judgment for an amount to be decided by the court and costs[4].

5.3.5 The matters that the court will take into account when determining the time and rate of payment are set out in paragraph 5.1 of the Part 14 Practice Direction.

5.3.6 The court may determine the time and rate of payment with or without a hearing, but, where a hearing is to take place, the proceedings must, where the provisions of Rule 14.12(2) apply, be transferred to the defendant's home court.

---

[1] See rule 10.2.
[2] See rule 10.1(3)
[3] See rule 10.1(3)
[4] See rules 14.6(7) and 14.7(10)

Where the Claim Form was issued in the Royal Courts of Justice the defendant's home court will be the district registry for the district in which the defendant's address given in the admission form is situated. If there is no such district registry the proceedings will remain in the Royal Courts of Justice[1].

5.3.7 The procedure for an application for re-determination of a decision determining the time and rate of payment is to be found in Rule 14.13 and paragraphs 5.3 to 5.6 of the Practice Direction.

5.3.8 Where judgment has been entered for an amount to be decided by the court and costs, the court will give any directions that it considers appropriate, which may include allocating the case to a track[2]. (See paragraph 6.5 below about allocation.)

5.3.9 Judgment will not be entered on an admission where;
  (1) the defendant is a child or patient, or
  (2) the claimant is a child or patient and the admission is made in respect of
     (a) a specified amount of money, or
     (b) a sum offered in satisfaction of a claim for an unspecified amount of money.

See Part 21 and the Part 21 Practice Direction, and in particular Rule 21.10 which provides that, where a claim is made by or on behalf of a child or patient or against a child or patient, no settlement, compromise or payment shall be valid, so far as it relates to that person's claim, without the approval of the court.

5.4 Defence

1B–27 5.4.1 A defendant who wishes to defend all or part of a claim must file a defence, and if he fails to do so, the claimant may obtain default judgment if Part 12 allows it[3].The time for filing a defence is set out in Rule 15.4.

5.4.2 A form for defending the claim[4] is included in the Response Pack. The form for defending the claim also contains provision for making a counterclaim[5]. Part 22 requires a defence to be verified by a statement of truth (see the Part 15 Practice Direction, paragraph 2; and see also Part 22 and the Part 22 Practice Direction).

5.4.3 The parties may, by agreement, extend the period specified in Rule 15.4 for filing a defence by up to 28 days[6]. If the parties do so, the defendant must notify the court in writing of the date by which the defence must be filed.

5.5 Default judgment

1B–28 5.5.1 A party may obtain default judgment under Part 12 except in the circumstances set out in Rule 12.2 and paragraphs 1.2 and 1.3 of the Part 12 Practice Direction, which list the circumstances where default judgment may not be obtained.

5.5.2 To obtain default judgment under the circumstances set out in Rules 12.4(1) and 12.9(1), a party may do so by filing a request[7] . A request is dealt with by a court officer and provided he is satisfied that the provisions of paragraph 4.1 of the Part 12 Practice Direction have been complied with, he will enter the default judgment.

5.5.3 Default judgment in respect of claims specified in Rules 12.4(2)(a), 12.9 and 12.10 must be obtained by making an application to a Master. The following are some of the types of claim which require an application for default judgment;
  (1) against children and patients,

---

[1] Derived from rule 2.3
[2] See rule 14.8
[3] See rule 15.2 and 15.3
[4] Forms N9B and N9D
[5] See Part 20
[6] See Rule 15.5
[7] Practice forms N205A, N255, N225B or N227

(2) for costs (other than fixed costs) only,

(3) by one spouse against the other on a claim in tort,

(4) for delivery up of goods where the defendant is not allowed the alternative of paying their value,

(5) against the Crown, and

(6) against persons or organisations who enjoy immunity from civil jurisdiction under the provisions of the International Organisations Acts 1968 and 1981.

Paragraph 4 of the Practice Direction provides information about the evidence required in support of an application for default judgment.

5.5.4 Where default judgment has been obtained for an amount to be decided by the court, the matter will be referred to a Master for directions to be given concerning the management of the case and any date to be fixed for a hearing.

5.6 Statements of case

5.6.1 Statements of case comprise the particulars of claim and defence in the main proceedings and also in any Part 20 proceedings, and are dealt with in Part 16. (Part 16 does not apply to claims proceeding under Part 8.) **1B–29**

5.6.2 The particulars of claim, whether contained in the Claim Form or served separately, should set out the claimant's claim clearly and fully. The same principle applies to the defence.

5.6.3 Part 16 sets out certain matters which must be included in a statement of case. Paragraphs 8 and 9 of the Part 16 Practice Direction contain matters which should be included in the particulars of claim in specific types of claim, and paragraph 10 lists matters which must be set out in the particulars of claim if relied on. In addition to the matters listed in paragraph 10, full particulars of any allegation of dishonesty or malice and, where any inference of fraud or dishonesty is alleged, the basis on which the inference is alleged should also be included. Points of law may be set out in any statement of case. For information in respect of statements of case in defamation claims see the Part 53 Practice Direction.

5.6.4 In addition to the information contained in Part 16 and the Part 16 Practice Direction, the following guidelines on preparing a statement of case should be followed;

(1) a statement of case must be as brief and concise as possible,

(2) a statement of case should be set out in separate consecutively numbered paragraphs and sub-paragraphs,

(3) so far as possible each paragraph or sub-paragraph should contain no more than one allegation,

(4) the facts and other matters alleged should be set out as far as reasonably possible in chronological order,

(5) the statement of case should deal with the claim on a point by point basis, to allow a point by point response,

(6) where a party is required to give reasons[1], the allegation should be stated first and then the reasons listed one by one in separate numbered sub-paragraphs,

(7) a party wishing to advance a positive claim must identify that claim in the statement of case,

(8) any matter which if not stated might take another party by surprise should be stated,

(9) where they will assist, headings, abbreviations and definitions should be used and a glossary annexed; contentious headings, abbreviations, paraphrasing and definitions should not be used and every effort should be made to ensure that they are in a form acceptable to the other parties,

(10) particulars of primary allegations should be stated as particulars and not as primary allegations,

---

[1] See rule 16.5(2)

(11) schedules or appendices should be used if this would be helpful, for example where lengthy particulars are necessary, and any response should also be stated in a schedule or appendix,

(12) any lengthy extracts from documents should be placed in a schedule.

5.6.5 A statement of case should be verified by a statement of truth[1]. If a party fails to verify his statement of case, it will remain effective unless struck out, but that party may not rely on the statement of case as evidence of any of the matters contained in it[2]. Any party may apply to the court for an order to strike out a statement of case which has not been verified[3].

6.

PRELIMINARY CASE MANAGEMENT

6.1 The Practice Master

1B–30 6.1.1 On every working day, the Practice Master is available from 10.30a.m. to 1.00p.m. and from 2.00p.m. to 4.30p.m. to answer questions about the practice of the Queen's Bench Division. Usually, one Master takes the Morning Practice, and another Master takes the Afternoon Practice. This will be shown on the case-lists for the day and on the notice boards in the Masters' corridors. Also, a board is placed on the door of the Master who is sitting as Practice Master.

6.1.2 The Practice Master cannot give advice, whether about a given case or about the law generally. He is there simply to answer general questions about the CPR and practice governing the work of the Queen's Bench Division, and can deal with any consent order, notwithstanding that the claim in which it is to be made has been assigned to another Master. The Practice Master may grant stays of execution and deal with urgent applications which do not require notice to be given to the respondent. It is unnecessary to make an appointment to see the Practice Master, litigants are generally seen in order of arrival.

6.2 Assignment to Masters

1B–31 6.2.1 A claim issued in the Central Office will normally be assigned at the issue stage to a particular Master as the procedural judge responsible for managing the claim. The Action Department will endorse the name of the Assigned Master on the Claim form. However, assignment may be triggered at an earlier stage, for example, by one of the following events;

(1) an application for pre-action disclosure under Rule 31.16,

(2) an application for an interim remedy before the commencement of a claim or where there is no relevant claim (Part 25).

It occasionally happens that a claim is assigned to a Master who may have an "interest" in the claim. In such cases the Senior Master will re-assign the claim to another Master.

6.2.2. Where either an application notice or Part 8 Claim Form is issued which requires a hearing date to be given immediately, the Masters' Support Unit will give a hearing date and assign it to the Master who has the next available date for the hearing. The Masters' Support Unit will endorse the name of that Master on the application notice or Part 8 Claim Form at the time of entering it in the list for hearing.

6.2.3 The Senior Master may assign a particular Master to a class/group of claims or may re-assign work generally. At present clinical negligence claims are assigned to Master Murray and Master Ungley. In the event of an assigned Master being on leave or for any other reason temporarily absent from the Royal Courts of Justice

---

[1] See rule 22.1
[2] See rule 22.2(1)
[3] See rule 22.2(2) and (3)

then the Masters' Support Unit may endorse on the appropriate document the name of another Master.

6.2.4 A court file will normally be opened when a defence is filed, provided that the claim is not one that will automatically be transferred (see paragraph 6.4 below). The court file will be endorsed with the name of the assigned Master. Any application notice in an assigned claim for hearing before a Master should have the name of the assigned Master entered on it by the solicitors making the application.

6.3 Listing before Masters

6.3.1 The Masters' lists consist of;   **1B–32**
    (1) the ordinary list—short applications in Rooms E102 and E110 ("the Bear Garden lists"),
    (2) the Floating list,
    (3) private room appointments[1], and
    (4) the Sheriff's first return applications.

6.3.2 Parties attending on all applications before the Masters are requested to complete the Court Record Sheet (form PF 48) which will be used to record details of the claim, representation and the nature of the application, and will be used by the Master for his notes. Copies of this form may be found in the writing desks in the Masters' corridors and the Bear Garden.

6.3.3 Masters will sit each day at 10.30am in the Bear Garden to hear applications in the Bear Garden lists. Applications of up to 20 minutes duration are listed at 10.30am, 11.00am, 11.30am and 12 noon. Solicitors and Counsel may attend any application in these lists although the costs of being represented by Counsel may be disallowed if not fully justified. If an application is estimated to take longer than 20 minutes the applicant must request a private room appointment. To do so the applicant must complete the PRA form giving details of the parties' availability as fully as possible. Failure to do so may result in the request form being returned for further information thereby delaying the hearing date.

6.3.4 Hearing dates for the Bear Garden lists are given by the Masters' Support Unit. Hearing dates for private room appointments are given by the assigned Master personally. The parties or their legal representatives must inform the Masters' Support Unit of any settlements as soon as possible. All time estimates must be updated as necessary.

6.3.5 Applications in the Bear Garden list may, by agreement or where the application notice has not been served, be transferred (in the case of a 10 minute application) to the next available 12 noon list or (in either case) for a private room appointment on a date to be specified by the Master. In all other cases an application for a postponement of the hearing date must be made to the Master to whom the claim has been assigned. An application may be re-listed in the Bear Garden list without permission of a Master if for any reason the application has not been heard or has not been fully disposed of.

6.3.6 When an application in the Bear Garden list is adjourned by a Master he will specify the date to which it is adjourned. An application for the adjournment of a private room appointment must be made to the Master who gave the appointment unless the application is by agreement of all parties and the Master approves. The Master will usually require details of parties' availability. Any adjournment will normally now be to a new hearing date.

6.3.7 Where an application for which a Master has given a private room appointment has been settled, it is the duty of the parties or their legal representatives, particularly those who obtained that appointment, to notify the Master immediately.

---

[1] A private room appointment is given where the hearing will be more than 20 minutes and takes place in the Master's private room rather than a Bear Garden room. The appointment must be made by the Master personally

6.3.8 If the Master hearing an application considers that the result might affect the date fixed for a trial, he may refer the application to the Judge in charge of the List. This possibility should be considered when making an application and a request should be included in the application notice asking the Master to refer the application to the Judge.

6.3.9 If the Master considers that an application should more properly be heard by a Judge, he may either during the hearing or before it takes place refer the application to the Interim Applications Judge. Among the circumstances that may make this appropriate are;

    (1) that the time required for the hearing is longer than a Master could ordinarily make available,

    (2) that, whatever the Master's decision on the application, an appeal to the Judge is considered inevitable,

    (3) that the application raises issues of unusual difficulty or importance, etc. or

    (4) that the outcome is likely to affect the trial date or window.

However, it is emphasised that no single factor or combination of factors is necessarily decisive, and the Master has a complete discretion.

6.3.10 The Sheriff's first return applications are interpleader applications (under RSC O.17 as set out in Schedule 1 to the CPR) and are listed at monthly intervals.

6.3.11 The Floating List is run by the Masters' Support Unit. Applications in this list will usually have a time estimate of not more than 30 minutes and are released by the assigned Master, if he considers them suitable, when the request for a private room appointment is made. Dates and times of hearings are allocated by staff in Room E14. The parties should assemble at Room E14 well before the appointed time in order to facilitate the allocation of the application to a Master or deputy who is free.

Automatic transfer

1B–33 6.4.1 Part 26 requires certain claims to be transferred automatically[1]. Where;

    (1) the claim is for a specified amount of money,

    (2) the claim has not been issued in a specialist list[2],

    (3) the defendant, or one of the defendants is an individual,

    (4) the claim has not been issued in the individual defendant's home court, and

    (5) the claim has not already been transferred to another individual defendant's home court,

the claim will, on receipt of the defence, be transferred to the individual defendant's home court.

6.4.2 Where the Claim Form was issued in the Royal Courts of Justice the defendant's home court will be the district registry for the district in which the defendant's address for service as shown on the defence is situated. If there is no such district registry the proceedings will remain in the Royal Courts of Justice[3]. If the claim is against more than one individual defendant, the claim will be transferred to the home court of the defendant who first files his defence. (See paragraph 6.9 below about transfer following an order.)

6.5 Allocation

1B–34 6.5.1 When a defence to a claim is received in the Central Office from all the defendants, or from one or more of the defendants and the time for filing a defence has expired, the Action Department Registry will send an Allocation Questionnaire to those defendants who have filed a defence[4], unless it has been dispensed with.

---

[1] See rules 26.1 and 2
[2] See Part 49
[3] See rule 2.3(1)(b)
[4] See Part 26 and the Part 26 Practice Direction

116

6.5.2 The Allocation Questionnaire to be used in accordance with Part 26 is form N150. The Allocation Questionnaire will state the time within which it must be filed, which will normally be at least 14 days after the day on which it is deemed served. Where proceedings are automatically transferred to a defendant's home court, notwithstanding that the issuing court will send out the Allocation Questionnaire before transfer, the Allocation Questionnaire should nevertheless be returned to the receiving court.

6.5.3 Each party should state in his Allocation Questionnaire if there is any reason why the claim should be managed and tried at a court other than the Royal Courts of Justice or the trial centre for a particular district registry. Paragraph 2.6 of the Part 29 Practice Direction sets out certain types of claim which are suitable for trial in the Royal Courts of Justice. Form PF 49 will be sent out to parties with the Allocation Questionnaire requesting the parties to state convenient dates for a case management conference, if one should be ordered, or for other hearings. Parties are encouraged to agree directions for the management of the claim.

6.5.4 Where a party fails to file his Allocation Questionnaire within the specified time the court officer will refer the proceedings to the Master for his directions. The Master's directions may include "the standard unless order", that is that unless the defaulting party files his Allocation Questionnaire within 3 days, his statement of case will be struck out[1].

6.5.5 Where one but not all of the parties has filed an Allocation Questionnaire the Master may allocate the claim to the multi-track where he considers that he has sufficient information to do so. Alternatively, the Master may order that an allocation hearing take place and that all or any particular parties must attend. The court officer will then send out a Notice of Allocation Hearing (form N153) giving reasons for the hearing and any other directions.

6.5.6 Parties requesting a stay to settle the proceedings should do so in their Allocation Questionnaire or otherwise in writing. The court encourages parties to consider the use of ADR (see paragraph 6.6 below). The Master will normally direct the proceedings to be stayed for one month, but parties may by agreement seek an extension of the stay. Paragraph 3 of the Part 26 Practice Direction sets out the procedure for seeking an extension.

6.5.7 Parties are reminded that an estimate of costs should be filed and served when the Allocation Questionnaire is filed (see paragraph 6.4 of the Costs Practice Direction).

6.5.8 On receipt of the Allocation Questionnaires or on an allocation hearing the Master will allocate the claim to the multi-track or transfer the claim to the appropriate county court[2]. Rule 26.6 sets out the scope of each track. Claims proceeding in the Royal Courts of Justice must be allocated to the multi-track.

6.6 Alternative Dispute Resolution ("ADR"):

6.6.1 Parties are encouraged to use ADR (such as, but not confined to, mediation and **1B–35** conciliation) to try to resolve their disputes or particular issues. Legal representatives should consider with their clients and the other parties the possibility of attempting to resolve the dispute or particular issues by ADR and they should ensure that their clients are fully informed as to the most cost effective means of resolving their dispute.

6.6.2 The settlement of disputes by ADR can;
   (1) significantly reduce parties' costs,
   (2) save parties the delay of litigation in resolving their disputes,
   (3) assist parties to preserve their existing commercial relationships while resolving their disputes, and

---

[1] See paragraph 2.5 of the Part 26 practice direction
[2] County Courts Act 1984, ss.40-2 and Part 30.

(4) provide a wider range of remedies than those available through litigation.

The Master will in an appropriate case invite the parties to consider whether their dispute, or particular issues in it, could be resolved by ADR. The Master may also either adjourn proceedings for a specified period of time or extend the time for compliance with an order, a Rule or Practice Direction to encourage and enable the parties to use ADR. Parties may apply for directions seeking a stay for ADR at any time.

6.6.3 Information concerning ADR may be obtained from the Admiralty and Commercial Court Registry.

6.7 Part 8—Alternative procedure for claims:

1B–36   6.7.1 Paragraphs 4.1.14 to 4.1.16 above deal with issuing a Part 8 Claim Form. The alternative procedure set out in Part 8 ("the Part 8 procedure") may not be used if a Practice Direction disapplies it in respect of a particular type of claim. A Practice Direction may require or permit the Part 8 procedure and may disapply or modify any of the rules contained in Part 8. The Part 8B Practice Direction deals with commencement of proceedings under the Rules of the Supreme Court and the County Court Rules the provisions of which remain in force in Schedules 1 and 2 to the CPR ("the Schedule rules"). The Schedule rules and the Practice Directions supporting them may require certain proceedings to be commenced by the issue of a Part 8 Claim Form with appropriate modifications to the Part 8 procedure.

6.7.2 The main features of the Part 8 procedure are;
   (1) Part 16 (statements of case) does not apply,
   (2) Part 15 (defence and reply) does not apply,
   (3) judgment in default may not be obtained (Rule 12.2),
   (4) Rules 14.4 to 14.7 (judgment by request on an admission) do not apply,
   (5) a Part 8 claim shall be treated as being allocated to the multi-track[1].

6.7.3 A Master may give directions for managing the claim as soon as the Part 8 Claim Form is issued. In certain circumstances this may include fixing a hearing date. Where a hearing date is fixed, notice of the hearing date must be served with the Claim Form[2]. Where the Master does not fix a hearing date when the Claim Form is issued he will give directions for the disposal of the claim as soon as practicable after the receipt of the acknowledgement of service or as the case may be, the expiry of the period for acknowledging service.

6.7.4 Where a Part 8 Claim Form has been issued for the purpose of giving effect to a consent order for an award of damages to a child or patient or an award of provisional damages as in paragraph 4.1.15 (1) and (2) above, a draft of the order sought should be attached to the claim form. For more information see paragraphs 6.8.1 to 6.8.8 and 9.3.8 to 9.3.10 below about children and patients, and paragraphs 6.8.12, 9.3.11 and 9.3.12 below about provisional damages.

6.7.5 A defendant who wishes to respond to a Part 8 Claim Form should acknowledge service of it and may do so either by using form N210 or otherwise in writing giving the following information;
   (1) whether he contests the claim, and
   (2) where he is seeking a different remedy from that set out in the Claim Form, what that remedy is.

If a defendant does not acknowledge service of the Claim Form within the specified time, he may attend the hearing of the claim but may not take part in the hearing unless the court gives permission[3].

---

[1] Rule 8.9
[2] See paragraph 4 of the Part 8 practice direction (alternative procedure) about managing the claim
[3] See rule 8.4

6.7.6 Rules 8.5 and 8.6 and paragraph 5 of the Part 8 Practice Direction (alternative procedure) deal with evidence to be relied on in Part 8 proceedings; the claimant's evidence must be filed and served with the Claim Form, and the defendant's evidence (if any) must be filed with his acknowledgement of service. If the defendant files written evidence he must at the same time serve it on the other parties. It is helpful to the court if, where the defendant does not intend to rely on written evidence, he notifies the court in writing to that effect.

6.7.7 Where a defendant contends that the Part 8 procedure should not be used, he should state the reasons for his contention on his acknowledgement of service. On receipt of the acknowledgement of service, the Master will give appropriate directions for the future management of the claim.

6.8 Specific matters which may be dealt with under the Part 8 procedure

Settlements on behalf of children and patients

6.8.1 Part 21 and the Part 21 Practice Direction set out the requirements for litigation by or against children and patients. References in Part 21, the Part 21 Practice Direction and in this guide to;

    (1) "child" means a person under 18, and

    (2) "patient" means a person who by reason of mental disorder within the meaning of the Mental Health Act 1983 is incapable of managing and administering his own affairs[1].

1B–37

No settlement or compromise of a claim by or against a child or patient will be binding unless and until it has been approved by the court. In addition, a party may not obtain a default judgment against a child or patient without the permission of the court, and may not enter judgment on an admission against a child or patient.

6.8.2 A patient must have a litigation friend to conduct proceedings on his behalf, and so must a child unless the court makes an order permitting the child to act on his own behalf. A litigation friend is someone who can fairly and competently conduct proceedings on behalf of the child or patient. He must have no interest in the proceedings adverse to that of the child or patient, and all steps he takes in the proceedings must be taken for the benefit of the child or patient. Rules 21.5 to 21.8 and paragraphs 2 and 3 of the Practice Direction set out how a person may become a litigation friend.

6.8.3 Applications for the approval of settlements or compromises of claims by or against a child or patient proceeding in the Central Office are heard by a Master. If the purpose of starting the claim is for the approval of a settlement, a Part 8 Claim Form should be issued in accordance with form PF 170(A) which must contain a request for approval of the settlement (or compromise) and, in addition to the details of the claim, must set out the terms of the settlement (or compromise) or must have attached to it a draft consent order. The draft consent order should be in form N292. See paragraph 6 of the Practice Direction for further information which the Master will require.

6.8.4 Where parties reach a settlement (or compromise) in proceedings started by the issue of a Part 7 Claim Form (where the trial has not started) an application may be made to the Master in accordance with Part 23 for the approval of the settlement. The application notice should be in form PF 170(B) and should have attached to it a draft consent order in form N292. The application notice should be filed in Room E16. (See paragraph 7.12 below for information about applications.) However, where the trial hearing has been listed, the application notice should be filed in Room WG5. If the trial has started, oral application may be made to the trial judge. Applications for approval of a settlement on behalf of a child or patient will normally be heard in public unless the Judge or Master orders otherwise[2]. If a settlement is approved in private, the terms of settlement can be announced in public.

---

[1] See rule 21.1(2)
[2] See rule 39.2

6.8.5 Paragraph 8 of the Practice Direction gives information about control of money recovered by or on behalf of a child or patient. Paragraph 10 deals with investment of money on behalf of a child and paragraph 11 deals with investment on behalf of a patient. Enquiries concerning investment for a child are dealt with in Room E13.

6.8.6 In respect of investment on behalf of a child, the litigation friend or his legal representative should provide the Master with form PF 172 (request for investment) for completion by the Master. The child's birth certificate should also be provided. The PF 172 will then be forwarded to the Court Funds Office for their investment managers to make the appropriate investment. The Court of Protection is responsible for the administration of patients' funds (unless they are small). Paragraph 11 of the Practice Direction gives full information about procedure for investment by the Court of Protection. These procedures may also be used for investment of money on behalf of a child or patient following an award of damages at trial.

6.8.7 Damages may also be paid to a child or patient by way of a structured settlement. A structured settlement on behalf of a child or patient must be approved by a Judge or Master. A structured settlement on behalf of a patient must also be approved by the Court of Protection. (For more information about structured settlements see the Part 40C Practice Direction—Structured Settlements.)

6.8.8 Control of a child's fund, provided he is not also a patient, passes to him when he reaches the age of 18 (see paragraph 12.2 of the Practice Direction).

Summary order for possession

6.8.9 Where there is unlikely to be a substantial dispute of fact, a claim for a summary order for possession against named or unnamed defendants occupying land or premises without the licence or consent of the person claiming possession under RSC O.113 (Schedule 1 to the CPR) may be started by the issue of a Part 8 Claim Form.

6.8.10 When the Claim Form has been issued in the Action Department it will be passed to the Masters' Support Unit who will assign a Master to the claim and fix a hearing date. Parties should check that they have sufficient time for service.

6.8.11 At the hearing the Master may make the order sought or such other order as appropriate including directions for the management of the claim.

Settlement of a provisional damages claim

6.8.12 A claim for provisional damages may proceed under Part 8 where the Claim Form is issued solely for the purpose of obtaining a consent judgment[1]. The claimant must state in his Claim Form in addition to the matters set out in paragraph 4.4 of the Part 16 Practice Direction that the parties have reached agreement and request a consent judgment. A draft order in accordance with paragraph 4.2 of the Part 41 Practice Direction should be attached to the Claim Form. The claimant or his legal representative must lodge the case file documents (set out in the draft order) in Room E14 for the case file to be compiled and preserved by the court. For more information about provisional damages claims and orders see Part 41 and the Part 41 Practice Direction, and paragraph 9.3 below.

Costs only proceedings

6.8.13 Proceedings may be brought under Part 8 where the parties to a dispute have reached a written agreement before proceedings have been started but have been unable to agree an amount of costs. The costs only proceedings may be started by the issue of a Claim Form in the Supreme Court Costs Office at Clifford's Inn, Fetter Lane, London EC4A 1DQ. The Costs Practice Direction at Section 17 sets out in detail the provisions for issue and proceeding with the claim.

---

[1] See paragraph 1.4(2) of the Part 8 practice direction

6.9 Transfer

6.9.1 Part 30 and the Part 30 Practice Direction deal with transfer of proceedings, **1B–38** within the High Court, and between county courts.The jurisdiction of the High Court to transfer proceedings to the county courts is contained in s.40 of the County Courts Act 1984 as substituted by s.2(1) of the Courts and Legal Services Act 1990. Under that section the court has jurisdiction in certain circumstances to strike out claims which should have been started in a county court.

6.9.2 Rule 30.2 sets out the provisions for the transfer of proceedings between;
(1) county courts,
(2) the Royal Courts of Justice and a district registry of the High Court, and
(3) between district registries.

Rule 30.3 sets out the criteria to which the court will have regard when making an order for transfer. The High Court may order proceedings in any Division of the High Court to be transferred to another Division or to or from a specialist list. An application for the transfer of proceedings to or from a specialist list must be made to a Judge dealing with claims in that list[1]. (See paragraph 6.4 above about automatic transfer.)

6.9.3 A claim with an estimated value of less than £50,000 will generally be transferred to a county court, if the county court has jurisdiction, unless it is to proceed in the High Court under an enactment or in a specialist list

6.9.4 An order for transfer takes effect from the date it is made[2]. When an order for transfer is made the court officer will immediately send notice of the transfer to the receiving court. The notice will contain the title of the proceedings and the claim number. At the same time, the court officer will also notify all parties of the transfer.

6.9.5 Paragraph 5 of the Practice Direction sets out the procedure for appealing an order for transfer. Where an order for transfer is made in the absence of a party, that party may apply to the court which made the order to have it set aside[3]. The transferring court will normally retain the court file until the time for appealing the order or applying to set it aside has expired, whereupon the court officer will send the court file to the Court Manager of the receiving court. If, at the time an order for transfer is made a court file has not been compiled, the court officer will send to the receiving court those documents which have been filed at that time.

6.9.6 Where money has been paid into court before an order for transfer is made, the court may direct transfer of the money to the control of the receiving court.

6.10 Part 20 proceedings:

6.10.1 Part 20 deals with (a) counterclaims and (b) other additional claims, being **1B–39** claims for contribution or indemnity and what were formerly called "third party" claims. A Part 20 claim is treated as a claim for the purpose of the CPR with certain exceptions, for which see Rule 20.3.

6.10.2 A defendant may make a counterclaim by completing the defence and counterclaim form provided in the Response Pack. If the counterclaim is not filed with the defence, the permission of the court is required[4]. Where a counterclaim brings in a new party, the defendant (Part 20 claimant) must apply to the court for an order in form PF 21A adding the new party as defendant[5].

6.10.3 A defendant claiming contribution or indemnity from another defendant may do so by filing a notice, in form PF 22, containing a statement of the nature and grounds of his claim and serving the notice on the other defendant[6].

---

[1] See rule 30.5
[2] See paragraph 3 of the Part 30 practice direction
[3] See paragraph 6 of the practice direction
[4] Rule 20.4
[5] Rule 20.5
[6] Rule 20.6

6.10.4 Any other additional claim may be brought by the issue of a Part 20 Claim Form, N211. If the Part 20 Claim Form is issued at a time other than when the defence is filed, the permission of the court is required. Rule 20.8 deals with service of a Part 20 Claim Form and Rule 20.12 sets out the forms which must accompany the Part 20 Claim Form.

6.11 Summary judgment

1B–40   6.11.1 The court may give summary judgment under Part 24 against a claimant or defendant;

> (1) if it considers that
>
> > (a) the claimant has no real prospect of succeeding on the claim or issue, or
> >
> > (b) the defendant has no real prospect of successfully defending the claim, and
>
> (2) there is no other reason why the claim or issue should be disposed of at a trial.

6.11.2 The court may give summary judgment against a claimant in any type of proceedings, and against a defendant in any type of proceedings except (a) proceedings for possession of residential premises against a mortgagor, or a tenant or person holding over after the end of his tenancy where occupancy is protected within the meaning of the Rent Act 1977 or the Housing Act 1988, (b) proceedings for an Admiralty claim in Rem, and (c) contentious probate proceedings[1]. For information about summary disposal of defamation claims see Part 53, the Part 53 Practice Direction and paragraph 12 7 below.

6.11.3 An application for summary judgment should be made in accordance with Part 23 and the application notice should contain the information set out in paragraph 2 of the Part 24 Practice Direction (parties may use forms PF 11 and PF 12 as precedents). The application notice should be filed and served on the respondent giving at least 14 days notice of the date fixed for the hearing and the issues to be decided at the hearing. Unless the application notice contains all the evidence on which the applicant relies, the application notice should identify that evidence. In claims which include a claim for;

> (1) specific performance of an agreement,
>
> (2) rescission of such an agreement, or
>
> (3) forfeiture or return of a deposit made under such an agreement,

the application notice and any evidence in support must be served on the defendant not less than 4 days before the hearing[2].

6.11.4 The application will normally be listed before a Master unless for example, an injunction is also sought. In that case the application notice should state that the application is intended to be made to a Judge.

6.11.5 Where an order made on an application for summary judgment does not dispose of the claim or issue, the court will give case management directions in respect of the claim or issue.

6.12 Offers to settle and payments into and out of court:

1B–41   6.12.1 A party may offer to settle a claim at any time. Part 36 deals with offers to settle and payments into court. An offer to settle made in accordance with Part 36 will have the costs and other consequences specified in that Part and may be made at any time after proceedings have started. Paragraph 1 of the Part 36 Practice Direction defines an offer made in accordance with Part 36. See also paragraph 5 of the Part 36 Practice Direction which contains general provisions concerning Part 36 offers and Part 36 payments.

6.12.2 A Part 36 offer may be made by any party, but to comply with Part 36 a

---

[1] See rule 24.3 but see also Schedule 1 RSC O.77 r.7(1).
[2] See the Part 24 practice direction paragraph 7.

defendant who makes an offer to settle for a specified sum must do so by way of a Part 36 payment into court. Paragraph 4.1(2) of the Part 36 Practice Direction sets out the requirements for making a Part 36 payment in respect of a claim proceeding in the Royal Courts of Justice. If a defendant has made a pre-action offer to settle and proceedings are then started, in order for the court to take account of his offer he must make a Part 36 payment of not less than the amount offered within 14 days of service of the Claim Form. See also paragraph 10 of the Part 36 Practice Direction which deals with compensation recovery in respect of Part 36 payments.

6.12.3 The times for accepting a Part 36 offer or Part 36 payment are set out in Rules 36.11 and 36.12; the general rule is that a Part 36 offer or Part 36 payment made more than 21 days before the start of the trial may be accepted without the permission of the court, within 21 days after it was made. Otherwise, the permission of the court must be obtained. A Part 36 offer is made when received by the offeree. A Part 36 payment is made when the Part 36 payment notice (form N242A) is served on the claimant.

6.12.4 A party may accept a Part 36 offer or Part 36 payment by serving on the offeror a notice of acceptance (form N243 may be used to accept a Part 36 payment) within the times set out in Rules 36.11 and 36.12. When a Part 36 offer or Part 36 payment is accepted within those times, the general rule is that the claimant will be entitled to his costs up to the date of service of the notice of acceptance.

6.12.5 To obtain money out of court on acceptance of a Part 36 payment, the claimant should file a request for payment (form N243) in the Action Department of the Central Office, and file a completed Court Funds Office form 201 in the Court Funds Office. See paragraph 8 of the Part 36 Practice Direction for more information about obtaining payment out of court.

6.12.6 The court's permission is required for acceptance of a Part 36 offer or Part 36 payment;
   (1) which is not made or accepted within the times set out in Rules 36.11 and 36.12,
   (2) where acceptance is by or on behalf of a child or patient[1], or
   (3) where a defence of tender has been put forward, or
   (4) otherwise as mentioned in Rule 36.17.

6.12.7 Where a Part 36 offer or Part 36 payment is not accepted and a trial of the claim takes place, Rule 36.20 sets out the costs consequences where a claimant fails to do better than the Part 36 offer or Part 36 payment, and Rule 36.21 sets out the costs and other consequences where a claimant does better than he proposed in his Part 36 offer.

7.

CASE MANAGEMENT AND INTERIM REMEDIES

7.1 Case management—general:

7.1.1 The CPR require the court to provide a high degree of case management. Case management includes; identifying disputed issues at an early stage; fixing timetables; dealing with as many aspects of the claim as possible on the same occasion; controlling costs; disposing of proceedings summarily where appropriate; dealing with the applications without a hearing where appropriate; and giving directions to ensure that the trial of a claim proceeds quickly and efficiently. The court will expect the parties to co-operate with each other, and where appropriate, will encourage the parties to use ADR or otherwise help them settle the case.

7.1.2 Parties and their legal representatives will be expected to do all that they can to agree proposals for the management of the claim in accordance with Rule 29.4 and

1B–42

---

[1] See rule 21.10.

paragraphs 4.6 to 4.8 of the Part 29 Practice Direction. There is provision in the Allocation Questionnaire for proposing certain directions to be made, otherwise parties may use form PF 50 for making the application (attaching to it the draft form of order in form PF 52) and file it for the Master's approval. If the Master approves the proposals he will give directions accordingly.

7.1.3 Parties should consider whether a case summary would assist the Master in dealing with the issues before him. Paragraph 5.7 of the Part 29 Practice Direction sets out the provisions for preparation of a case summary.

7.2 The Case Management Conference:

1B–43 7.2.1 Parties who are unable to agree proposals for the management of the case, should notify the Court of the matters which they are unable to agree.

7.2.2 Where;
    (1) the parties proposed directions are not approved, or
    (2) parties are unable to agree proposed directions, or
    (3) the Master wishes to make further directions,

the Master will generally either consult the parties or direct that a case management conference be held.

7.2.3 In relatively straightforward claims, the Court will give directions without holding a case management conference.

7.2.4 Any party who considers that a case management conference should be held before any directions are given should so state in his Allocation Questionnaire, (or in a Part 8 claim should notify the Master in writing), giving his reasons and supplying a realistic time estimate for the case management conference, with a list of any dates or times convenient to all parties, or most of them, in form PF 49.

7.2.5 Where a case management conference has been fixed, parties should ensure that any other applications are listed or made at that hearing. A party applying for directions at the case management conference should use form PF 50 for making their application and attach to it the draft order for directions (form PF 52).

7.2.6 The advocates instructed or expected to be instructed to appear at the trial should attend any hearing at which case management directions are likely to be given. In any event, the legal representatives who attend the case management conference must be familiar with the case and have sufficient authority to deal with any issues which may arise. Where necessary, the court may order the attendance of a party[1].

7.3 Preliminary issues:

1B–44 7.3.1 Costs can sometimes be saved by identifying decisive issues, or potentially decisive issues, and by the Court ordering that they be tried first. The decision of one issue, although not necessarily itself decisive of the claim as a whole, may enable the parties to settle the remainder of the dispute. In such a case, the trial of a preliminary issue may be appropriate.

7.3.2 At the allocation stage, at any case management conference and again at any pre-trial review, the court will consider whether the trial of a preliminary issue may be helpful. Where such an order is made, the parties and the court should consider whether the costs of the issue should be in the issue or in the claim as a whole.

7.3.3 Where there is an application for summary judgment, and issues of law or construction may be determined in the respondent's favour, it will usually be in the interests of the parties for such issues to be determined conclusively, rather than that the application should simply be dismissed.

---

[1] See rule 3.1(c).

7.4 Trial timetable:

7.4.1 To assist the court to set a trial timetable,[1] a draft timetable should be prepared **1B–45** by the claimant's advocate(s) after consulting the other parties advocates. If there are differing views, those differences should be clearly indicated in the timetable. The draft timetable should be filed with the trial bundle.

7.4.2 The trial timetable will normally include times for giving evidence (whether of fact or opinion) and for oral submissions during the trial.

7.4.3 The trial timetable may be fixed at the case management conference, at any pre-trial review or at the beginning of the trial itself.

7.5 Listing Questionnaire:

7.5.1 The court may send out a Listing Questionnaire (N170) to all parties for **1B–46** completion, specifying the date by which it must be returned. The Master will then fix the trial date or period ("the trial window"). It is likely however, that the Master will already have sufficient information to enable him to fix a trial window, and will dispense with the need for a Listing Questionnaire subject to any requirement of the Clerk of the Lists for one to be filed. Instead, the Master will direct the parties within a specified time to attend before the Clerk of the Lists to fix a trial date within that window.

7.5.2 Paragraph 6.4 of the Costs Practice Direction requires an estimate of costs to be filed with the Listing Questionnaire. If the filing of a Listing Questionnaire has been dispensed with, the estimate of costs should be filed on attendance before the Clerk of the Lists.

7.6 Pre-trial review:

7.6.1 Where the trial of a claim is estimated to last more than 10 days, or where the **1B–47** circumstances require it, the Master may direct that a pre-trial review ("PTR") should be held[2]. The PTR may be heard by a Master, but more usually is heard by a Judge.

7.6.2 Application should normally be made to the Clerk of the Lists for the PTR to be heard by the trial judge (if known), and the applicant should do all that he can to ensure that it is heard between 8 and 4 weeks before the trial date, and in any event long enough before the trial date to allow a realistic time in which to complete any outstanding matters.

7.6.3 The PTR should be attended by the advocates who are to represent the parties at the trial.

7.6.4 At least 7 days before the date fixed for the PTR, the applicant must serve the other parties with a list of matters to be considered at the PTR, and those other parties must serve their responses at least 2 days before the PTR. Account must be taken of the answers in any listing questionnaires filed. Realistic proposals must be put forward and if possible agreed as to the time likely to be required for each stage of the trial and as to the order in which witnesses are to be called.

7.6.5 The applicant should lodge a properly indexed bundle containing the listing questionnaires (if directed to be filed) and the lists of matters and the proposals, together with the results of discussions between the parties, and any other relevant material, in the Listing Office, Room WG5, by no later than 10.00am on the day before the day fixed for the hearing of the PTR. If the PTR is to take place before a Master and he asks for the bundle in advance, it should be lodged in the Masters' Support Unit, Room E14. Otherwise it should be lodged at the hearing.

7.6.6 At the PTR, the court will review the parties' state of preparation, deal with any

---

[1] See rules 29.8 and 39.4
[2] See rule 29.7

outstanding matters, and give any directions or further directions that may be necessary.

7.7 Requests for further information:

1B–48 7.7.1 A party seeking further information or clarification under Part 18 should serve a written request on the party from whom the information is sought before making an application to the court. Paragraph 1 of the Part 18 Practice Direction deals with how the request should be made, and paragraph 2 deals with the response. A response should be verified by a statement of truth[1]. Parties may use form PF 56 for a combined request and reply, if they so wish.

7.7.2 If a party who has been asked to provide further information or clarification objects or is unable to do so, he must notify the party making the request in writing[2].

7.7.3 Where it is necessary to apply for an order for further information or clarification the party making the application should set out in or have attached to his application notice;

(1) the text of the order sought specifying the matters on which further information or clarification is sought, and

(2) whether a request has been made and, if so, the result of that request[3].

Applicants may use form PF 57 for their application notice.

7.8 Disclosure:

1B–49 7.8.1 Under Part 31, there is no longer any general duty to disclose documents. Instead, a party is prevented from relying on any document that he has not disclosed, and is required to give inspection of any document to which he refers in his statement of case or in any witness statement, etc.[4] The intention is that disclosure should be proportionate to the value of the claim.

7.8.2 If an order for disclosure is made, unless the contrary is stated, the Court will order standard disclosure, namely disclosure of only;

(1) the documents on which a party relies,

(2) the documents that adversely affect his own or another party's case,

(3) the documents that support another party's case, and

(4) the documents required to be disclosed by a relevant practice direction.

Parties should give standard disclosure by completing form N265 but may also list documents by category[5].

7.8.3 The court may either limit or dispense with disclosure (and the parties may agree to do likewise). The court may also order disclosure of specified documents or specified classes of documents. In deciding whether to make any such order for specific disclosure, the court will want to be satisfied that the disclosure is necessary, that the cost of disclosure will not outweigh the benefits of disclosure and that a party's ability to continue the litigation would not be impaired by any such order.

7.8.4 The court will therefore seek to ensure that any specific disclosure ordered is appropriate to the particular case, taking into account the financial position of the parties, the importance of the case and the complexity of the issues.

7.8.5 If specific disclosure is sought, a separate application for specific disclosure should be made in accordance with Part 23; it is not a matter that would be routinely dealt with at the CMC. The parties should give careful thought to ways of limiting the burdens of such disclosure, whether by giving disclosure in stages, by dispensing

---

[1] See Part 22
[2] See paragraph 4 of the Part 18 practice direction
[3] See paragraph 5 of the Part 18 practice direction
[4] Rule 31.14 and 31.21.
[5] See paragraph 3.2 of the Part 31 practice direction.

with the need to produce copies of the same document, by requiring disclosure of documents sufficient merely for a limited purpose, or otherwise. They should also consider whether the need for disclosure could be reduced or eliminated by a request for further information.

7.8.6 A party who has the right to inspect a document[1] should give written notice of his wish to inspect to the party disclosing the document. That party must permit inspection not more than 7 days after receipt of the notice.

7.9 Experts and Assessors:

7.9.1 The parties in a claim must bear in mind that under Part 35 no party may call an expert or put in evidence an expert's report without the court's express permission, and the court is under a duty to restrict such evidence to what is reasonably required.

1B–50

7.9.2 The duty of an expert called to give evidence is to assist the court. This duty overrides any obligation to the party instructing him or by whom he is being paid (see the Part 35 Practice Direction). In fulfilment of this duty, an expert must for instance make it clear if a particular question or issue falls outside his expertise or if he considers that insufficient information is available on which to express an opinion.

7.9.3 Before the Master gives permission, he must be told the field of expertise of the expert on whose evidence a party wishes to rely and where practicable the identity of the expert. Even then, he may, before giving permission, impose a limit on the extent to which the cost of such evidence may be recovered from the other parties in the claim[2].

7.9.4 Parties should always consider whether a single expert could be appointed in a particular claim or to deal with a particular issue. Before giving permission for the parties to call separate experts, the Master will always consider whether a single joint expert ought to be used, whether in relation to the issues as a whole or to a particular issue[3].

7.9.5 In very many cases it is possible for the question of expert evidence to be dealt with by a single expert. Single experts are, for example, often appropriate to deal with questions of quantum in cases where primary issues are as to liability. Likewise, where expert evidence is required in order to acquaint the court with matters of expert fact, as opposed to opinion, a single expert will usually be appropriate. There remain, however, a body of cases where liability will turn upon expert opinion evidence and where it will be appropriate for the parties to instruct their own experts. For example, in cases where the issue for determination is as to whether a party acted in accordance with proper professional standards, it will often be of value to the court to hear the opinions of more than one expert as to the proper standard in order that the court becomes acquainted with the range of views existing upon the question and in order that the evidence can be tested in cross-examination.

7.9.6 It will not be a sufficient ground for objecting to an order for a single joint expert that the parties have already chosen their own experts. An order for a single joint expert does not prevent a party from having his own expert to advise him, though that is likely to be at his own cost, regardless of the outcome.

7.9.7 When the use of a single joint expert is being considered, the Master will expect the parties to co-operate in agreeing terms of reference for the expert. In most cases, such terms of reference will include a statement of what the expert is asked to do, will identify any documents that he will be asked to consider and will specify any assumptions that he is asked to make.

7.9.8 The court will generally also order that experts in the same field confer on a

---

[1] See rules 31.3 and 31.15
[2] Rule 35.4
[3] Rule 35.7

'without prejudice' basis, and then report in writing to the parties and the court on the extent of any agreement, giving reasons at least in summary for any continuing disagreement. A direction to 'confer' gives the experts the choice of discussing the matter by telephone or in any other convenient way, as an alternative to attending an actual meeting. Any material change of view of an expert should be communicated in writing to the other parties through their legal representatives, and when appropriate, to the court.

7.9.9 Written questions may be put to an expert within 28 days after service of his report, but are for purposes of clarification of the expert's report when the other party does not understand it. Questions going beyond this can only be put with the agreement of the parties or the Master's permission. The procedure of putting written questions to experts is not intended to interfere with the procedure for an exchange of professional opinion in discussions between experts or to inhibit that exchange of professional opinion. If questions that are oppressive in number or content are put, or questions are put without permission for any purpose other than clarification of the expert's report, the court is likely to disallow the questions and make an appropriate order for costs against the party putting them. (See paragraph 4.3 of the Part 35 Practice Direction with respect to payment of an expert's fees for answering questions under Rule 35.6.)

7.9.10 An expert may file with the court a written request for directions to assist him in carrying out his function as an expert[1]. The expert should guard against accidentally informing the court about, or about matters connected with, communications or potential communications between the parties that are without prejudice or privileged. The expert may properly be asked to be privy to the content of these communications because he has been asked to assist the party instructing him to evaluate them.

7.9.11 Under Rule 35.15 the court may appoint an assessor to assist it in relation to any matter in which the assessor has skill and experience. The report of the assessor is made available to the parties. The remuneration of the assessor is decided by the court and forms part of the costs of the proceedings.

7.10 Evidence:

1B–51 7.10.1 Evidence is dealt with in the CPR in Parts 32, 33 and 34.

7.10.2 The most common form of written evidence is a witness statement. The Part 32 Practice Direction at paragraphs 17, 18 and 19 contains information about the heading, body (what it must contain) and format of a witness statement. The witness must sign a statement of truth to verify the witness statement; the wording of the statement of truth is set out in paragraph 20.2 of the Practice Direction.

7.10.3 A witness statement may be used as evidence in support of an interim application and, where it has been served on any other party to a claim, it may be relied on as a statement of the oral evidence of the witness at the trial. Part 33 contains provisions relating to the use of hearsay evidence in a witness statement.

7.10.4 In addition to the information and provisions for making a witness statement mentioned in paragraph 7.10.2, the following matters should be borne in mind;
  (1) a witness statement must contain the truth, the whole truth and nothing but the truth on the issues it covers,
  (2) those issues should consist only of the issues on which the party serving the witness statement wishes that witness to give evidence in chief and should not include commentary on the trial bundle or other matters which may arise during the trial,
  (3) a witness statement should be as concise as the circumstances allow, inadmissible or irrelevant material should not be included,
  (4) the cost of preparation of an over-elaborate witness statement may not be allowed,

---

[1] See rule 35.14

(5) Rule 32.14 states that proceedings for contempt of court may be brought against a person if he makes, or causes to be made, a false statement in a document verified by a statement of truth without an honest belief in its truth,

(6) if a party discovers that a witness statement which they have served is incorrect they must inform the other parties immediately.

7.10.5 Evidence may also be given by affidavit[1] but unless an affidavit is specifically required either in compliance with a court order, a Rule or Practice Direction, or an enactment, the party putting forward the affidavit may not recover from another party the cost of making an affidavit unless the court so orders[2].

7.10.6 The Part 32 Practice Direction at paragraphs 3 to 6 contains information about the heading, body, jurat (the sworn statement which authenticates the affidavit) and the format of an affidavit. The court will normally give directions as to whether a witness statement or, where appropriate, an affidavit is to be filed[3].

7.10.7 A statement of case which has been verified by a statement of truth and an application notice containing facts which have been verified by a statement of truth may also stand as evidence other than at the trial.

7.10.8 Evidence by deposition is dealt with in Part 34. A party may apply to a Master for an order for a person to be examined before a hearing takes place (Rule 34.8). Evidence obtained on an examination under that Rule is referred to as a deposition. The Master may order the person to be examined before either a Judge, an examiner of the court or such other person as the court appoints. The Part 34 Practice Direction at paragraph 4 sets out in detail how the examination should take place.

7.10.9 Provisions relating to applications for evidence by deposition to be taken either;
(1) in this country for use in a foreign court[4], or
(2) abroad for use in proceedings within the jurisdiction[5]

are set out in detail in the Part 34 Practice Direction at paragraphs 5 and 6.

7.10.10 The procedure for issuing a witness summons is also dealt with in Part 34 and the Practice Direction. A witness summons may require a witness to;
(1) attend court,
(2) produce documents to the court, or
(3) both,

on either a date fixed for the hearing or another date as the court may direct[6] (but see also Rule 31.17 which may be used when there are areas of contention).

7.10.11 The court may also issue a witness summons in aid of a court or tribunal which does not have the power to issue a witness summons in relation to the proceedings before it (and see the Part 34 Practice Direction at paragraphs 1, 2 and 3).

7.10.12 To issue a witness summons, two copies should be filed in the Action Department, Room E14 for sealing; one copy will be retained on the court file.

7.11 Hearings:

Hearings generally

7.11.1 All hearings are in principle open to the public, even though in practice most of the hearings until the trial itself will be attended only by the parties and their **1B–52**

---

[1] See rule 32.15(2)
[2] See rule 32.15(1) and (2)
[3] See rule 32.4(3)(b)
[4] See RSC O.70 (Schedule 1 to Part 50)
[5] See rule 34.13
[6] See rule 34.2(4)

representatives. However, in an appropriate case the court may decide to hold a hearing in private. Rule 39.2 lists the circumstances where it may be appropriate to hold a hearing in private. In addition, paragraph 1.5 of the Part 39 Practice Direction sets out certain types of hearings which may be listed in private.

7.11.2 The court also has the power under section 11 of the Contempt of Court Act 1981 to make an order forbidding publication of any details that might identify one or more of the parties. Such orders are granted only in exceptional cases.

7.11.3 References in the CPR and Practice Directions to hearings being in public or private do not restrict any existing rights of audience or confer any new rights of audience in respect of applications or proceedings which under the rules previously in force would have been heard in court or chambers respectively[1]. Advocates (and judges) do not wear robes at interim hearings before High Court Judges, including appeals from Masters, District Judges and the county courts. Robes are worn for trials and certain other proceedings such as preliminary issues, committals etc. It is not intended that the new routes of appeal should restrict the advocate's right of audience, in that, a solicitor who appeared in a county court matter which is the subject of an appeal to a High Court Judge would normally be allowed to appear at the appeal hearing.

7.11.4 Parties are reminded that they are expected to act with courtesy and respect for the other parties present and for the proceedings of the court. Punctuality is particularly important; being late for hearings is unfair to the other parties and other court users, as well as being discourteous to them and to the court.

Preparation for hearings

7.11.5 To ensure court time is used efficiently there must be adequate preparation prior to the hearing. This includes the preparation and exchange of skeleton arguments, the compilation of bundles of documents and giving realistic time estimates. Where estimates prove inaccurate, a hearing may have to be adjourned to a later date, and the party responsible for the adjournment is likely to be ordered to pay the costs thrown away.

7.11.6 The parties should use their best endeavours to agree beforehand the issues, or main issues between them, and must co-operate with the court and each other to enable the court to deal with claims justly; parties may expect to be penalised for failing to do so.

7.11.7 A bundle of documents must be compiled for the court's use at the trial, and also for hearings before the Interim Applications Judge or a Master where the documents to be referred to total 25 pages or more. The party lodging a trial bundle should supply identical bundles to all parties and for the use of witnesses. The efficient preparation of bundles is very important. Where bundles have been properly prepared, the claim will be easier to understand and present, and time and costs are likely to be saved. Where documents are copied unnecessarily or bundled incompetently, the costs may be disallowed. Paragraph 3 of the Part 39 Practice Direction sets out in full the requirements for compiling bundles of documents for hearings or trial.

7.11.8 The trial bundle must be filed not more than 7 and not less than 3 days before the start of the trial. Bundles for a Master's hearing should be brought to the hearing unless the Master directs otherwise. The contents of the trial bundle should be agreed where possible, and it should be made clear whether in addition, they are agreeing that the documents in the bundle are authentic even if not previously disclosed and are evidence of the facts stated in them even if a notice under the Civil Evidence Act 1995 has not been served.

7.11.9 Lists of authorities for use at trial or at substantial hearings before a Judge should be provided to the usher by 9.00am on the first day of the hearing. For other

---

[1] See paragraph 1.14 of the Part 39 practice direction

applications before a Judge, or applications before a Master, copies of the authorities should be included in the bundle.

7.11.10 For trial and most hearings before a Judge, and substantial hearings before a Master, a chronology, a list of the persons involved and a list of the issues should be prepared and filed with the skeleton argument. A chronology should be non-contentious and agreed with the other parties if possible. If there is a material dispute about any event stated in the chronology, that should be stated.

7.11.11 Skeleton arguments should be prepared and filed;
- (1) for trials, not less than 2 days before the trial in the Listing Office, and
- (2) for substantial applications or appeals, not later than 1 day before the hearing in the Listing Office and, where the Master has requested papers in advance of the hearing, in the Masters' Support Unit Room E16.

7.11.12 A skeleton argument should;
- (1) concisely summarise the party's submissions in relation to each of the issues,
- (2) cite the main authorities relied on, which may be attached,
- (3) contain a reading list and an estimate of the time it will take the Judge to read,
- (4) be as brief as the issues allow and not normally be longer than 20 pages of double-spaced A4 paper,
- (5) be divided into numbered paragraphs and paged consecutively,
- (6) avoid formality and use understandable abbreviations, and
- (7) identify any core documents which it would be helpful to read beforehand.

7.11.13 Where a party decides not to call a witness whose witness statement has been served, to give oral evidence at trial, prompt notice of this decision should be given to all other parties. The party should also indicate whether he proposes to put, or seek to put, the witness statement in as hearsay evidence. If he does not, any other party may do so[1].

Recording of proceedings

7.11.14 At any hearing, including the trial, any oral evidence, the judgment or decision (including reasons) and any summing up to a jury will be recorded. At hearings before Masters, it is not normally practicable to record anything other than oral evidence and any judgment, but these will be recorded. A party to the proceedings may obtain a transcript of the proceedings on payment of the appropriate charge, from the Mechanical Recording Department, Room WB 14. A person who is not a party to the proceedings may not obtain a transcript of a hearing which took place in private without the permission of the court.

7.11.15 No person or party may use unofficial recording equipment at a hearing without the permission of the court; to do so constitutes a contempt of court[2].

7.12 Applications:

7.12.1 Applications for court orders are governed by Part 23 and the Part 23 Practice Direction. Rule 23.6 and paragraph 2 of the Part 23 Practice Direction set out the matters an application notice must include. The Part 23 Practice Direction states that form N244 may be used, however, parties may prefer to use form PF 244 which is available for use in the Royal Courts of Justice only. To make an application the applicant must file an application notice unless a Rule or Practice Direction permits otherwise or the court dispenses with the requirement for an application notice[3]. Except in cases of extreme urgency, or where giving notice might frustrate the order (as with a search order), an application notice must be served on every party unless a Rule or Practice Direction or a court order dispenses with service[4] (see paragraph 7.12.3 below).

1B–53

---

[1] Rule 32.5(5)
[2] S.9 Contempt of Court Act 1981
[3] See rule 23.3
[4] See rule 23.4

7.12.2 Applications for remedies which a Master has jurisdiction to grant should ordinarily be made to a Master. The Part 2 Practice Direction (Allocation of cases to levels of Judiciary) contains information about the types of applications which may be dealt with by Masters and Judges. An application notice for hearing by;

    (1) a Judge should be issued in the Listing Office, Room WG5, and

    (2) a Master should be issued in the Masters' Support Unit, Room E16,

and wherever possible should be accompanied by a draft in double spacing of the order sought.

7.12.3 The following are examples of applications which may be heard by a Master where service of the application notice is not required;

    (1) service by an alternative method (Rule 6.8),

    (2) service of a claim form out of the jurisdiction (section III of Part 6),

    (3) default judgment under Rule 12.11(4) or (5),

    (4) substituting a party under Rule 19.1(4),

    (5) permission to issue a witness summons under Rule 34.3(2),

    (6) deposition for use in a foreign court (Schedule 1 to the CPR— RSC O.70),

    (7) charging order to show cause (Schedule 1 to the CPR— RSC O.50 r.1(2)), and

    (8) garnishee order to show cause (Schedule 1 to the CPR— RSC O.49 r.2(1).

7.12.4 Paragraph 3 of the Part 23 Practice Direction states in addition that an application may be made without serving an application notice;

    (1) where there is exceptional urgency,

    (2) where the overriding objective is best furthered by doing so,

    (3) by consent of all parties, and

    (4) where a date for a hearing has been fixed and a party wishes to make an application at that hearing but does not have sufficient time to serve an application notice[1].

With the court's permission an application may also be made without serving an application notice where secrecy is essential.

7.12.5 Where an application is heard in the absence of one or more of the parties, it is the duty of the party attending to disclose fully all matters relevant to the application, even those matters adverse to the applicant. Failure to do so may result in the order being set aside. Any party who does not attend a hearing may apply to have the order set aside[2].

7.12.6 Where notice of an application is to be given, the application notice should be served as soon as practicable after issue and, if there is a hearing, at least 3 clear days before the hearing date[3]. Where there is insufficient time to serve an application notice, informal notice of the application should be given unless the circumstances of the application require secrecy.

7.12.7 The court may deal with an application without a hearing if;

    (1) the parties agree the terms of the order sought,

    (2) the parties agree that the application should be dealt with without a hearing, or

    (3) the court does not consider that a hearing would be appropriate[4].

7.12.8 The court may deal with an application or part of an application by telephone where it is convenient to do so or in matters of extreme urgency. See paragraph 6 of the Part 23 Practice Direction and paragraph 4.5 of the Part 25 Practice Direction (Interim Injunctions).

7.12.9 Applications of extreme urgency may be made out of hours and will be dealt

---

[1] See paragraph 2.10 of the Part 23 practice direction
[2] See rule 23.11
[3] See rule 23.7(1)(b)
[4] See rule 23.8

with by the duty judge. An explanation will be required as to why it was not made or could not be made during normal court hours.

7.12.10 Initial contact should be made through the Security Office on 020 7947 6260 who will require the applicants phone number. The clerk to the duty judge will then contact the applicant and will require the following information;
  (1) the name of the party on whose behalf the application is to be made,
  (2) the name and status of the person making the application,
  (3) the nature of the application,
  (4) the degree of urgency, and
  (5) the contact telephone number(s).

7.12.11 The duty judge will indicate to his clerk if he thinks it appropriate for the application to be dealt with by telephone or in court. The clerk will inform the applicant and make the necessary arrangements. Where the duty judge decides to deal with the application by telephone, and the facility is available, it is likely that the judge will require a draft order to be faxed to him. An application for an injunction will be dealt with by telephone only where the applicant is represented by counsel or solicitors.

7.12.12 It is not normally possible to seal an order out of hours. The judge is likely to order the applicant to file the application notice and evidence in support on the same or next working day, together with two copies of the order for sealing.

7.13 Interim remedies:

7.13.1 Interim remedies which the court may grant are listed in Rule 25.1. An order **1B–54** for an interim remedy may be made at any time including before proceedings are started and after judgment has been given[1]. Some of the most commonly sought remedies are injunctions, most of which are heard by the Interim Applications Judge.

7.13.2 An application notice for an injunction should be filed in the Listing Office, Room W11, and may be made without giving notice to the other parties in the first instance. This is most likely to be appropriate in applications for search orders and freezing injunctions which may also be heard in private if the judge thinks it appropriate to do so. Where the injunction is granted without the other party being present it will normally be for a limited period, seldom more than 7 days. The Part 25 (Interim Injunctions) Practice Direction at paragraph 4 deals fully with making urgent applications and those without notice, and paragraphs 6, 7 and 8 deal specifically with search orders and freezing injunctions, examples of which are annexed to the Practice Direction.

7.13.3 Applications for interim payments are heard by a Master. The application notice should be filed in the Masters' Support Unit, Room E13. The requirements for obtaining an order for an interim payment are fully dealt with in the Part 25 (Interim Payments) Practice Direction.

8.

LISTING BEFORE JUDGES

8.1 Responsibility for Listing:

8.1.1 The Clerk of the Lists (Room WG3, Royal Courts of Justice) is in general **1B–55** responsible for listing. All applications relating to listing should in the first instance be made to him. Any party dissatisfied with any decision of the Clerk of the Lists may, on one day's notice to all other parties, apply to the Judge in charge of the List.

8.1.2 The application should be made within 7 days of the decision of the Clerk of the Lists and should be arranged through the Queen's Bench Listing Office, Room WG5.

---

[1] See rule 25.2(1)

8.2 The Lists:

1B–56 8.2 There are three Lists, namely;
  (1) the Jury List
  (2) the Trial List, and
  (3) the Interim Hearings List.

The Lists are described below.

8.3 The Jury List:

1B–57 8.3.1 Claims for damages for libel and slander (defamation), fraud, malicious prosecution and false imprisonment will be tried by a Judge and jury unless the court orders trial by a Judge alone.

8.3.2 Where a claim is being tried by a Judge and jury it is vitally important that the jury should not suffer hardship and inconvenience by having been misled by an incorrect time estimate. It is therefore essential that time estimates given to the court are accurate and realistic.

8.3.3 Dates for the trial of substantial claims will be fixed by the Listing Office after consideration of the parties' views. In such cases the Listing Office may, in addition, impose an alternative reserve date several weeks or months in advance of the trial date, in an endeavour to dispose of claims more quickly and to fill gaps in the List created by frequent settlements. When a reserve date is so allocated a "cut off" date will be stated by the Clerk of the Lists again, after consideration of any views expressed by the parties and having regard to the complexity of the claim and the commitments of counsel and expert witnesses. On the cut off date a decision will be made by the Clerk of the Lists to break or confirm the reserved date for trial.

8.3.4 If a party considers that he will suffer significant prejudice as the result of the decision of the Clerk of the Lists relating to either a reserved date or the cut off date he may apply to the Judge in charge of the Jury List for reversal or variation of the decision, as set out in paragraph 8.1.1 above.

8.3.5 Jury applications will enter the Interim Warned List not less than two weeks from the date the application notice is filed. Parties may "offer" a date for hearing the application within the week for which they are warned. Subject to court availability, the application will be listed on the offered date. Any application not reached on the offered date will return to the current Warned List and will be taken from that List as and when required.

8.3.6 Applications in defamation claims in respect of "meaning" (for an explanation of "meaning" see paragraph 4.1 of the Part 53 Practice Direction) may be listed in private on a specific day allocated for such matters.

8.3.7 Jury applications of length and/or complexity may be fixed by the same manner as set out in paragraph 8.3.6 above. (See the section below on The Trial List for general information about fixing trials).

8.3.8 Applications for directions and other applications within the Master's jurisdiction should firstly be made to a Master unless;
  (1) a direction has been given for the arranging of a trial date, or
  (2) a date has been fixed or a window given for the trial.

Interim applications made after (1) or (2) above should be made to the Judge. The Master will use his discretion to refer a matter to the Judge if he thinks it right to do so.

8.3.9 If a party believes that the Master is very likely to refer the application to the Judge, for example where there is a substantial application to strike out, the matter should first be referred to the Master or Practice Master on notice to the other parties without waiting for a private room appointment. The Master will then decide whether the application should be referred to the Judge.

8.4 The Trial List:

8.4.1 This List consists of trials (other than Jury trials), preliminary questions or **1B–58** issues ordered to be tried and proceedings to commit for contempt of court.

8.4.2 The Royal Courts of Justice presents unique problems in terms of fixing trial dates. The number of Judges and Masters involved and their geographical location has caused, for the time being at least, a different approach to the fixing of trials in the Chancery and Queen's Bench Divisions.

8.4.3 The requirement of Judges to go on Circuit, sit in the Criminal Division of the Court of Appeal, deal with cases in the Crown Office and other lists make it difficult to fix dates for trials before particular Judges. Accordingly the following will only apply to the Listing Offices in the Royal Courts of Justice.

8.4.4 At as early an interim stage as practicable, the court will give directions with a view to fixing the trial date or period within which the trial is to begin (the trial window).

8.4.5 For that purpose the court may;
   (1) direct that the trial do not begin earlier than a specified date calculated to provide enough time for the parties to complete any necessary preparations for trial, and/or
   (2) direct that the trial date be within a specified period, and/or
   (3) specify the trial date or window.

8.4.6 If directions under 8.4.5(1) or (2) are given the court will direct the parties to attend upon the Clerk of the Lists in Room W11 at such time and place as may be specified in order to fix the trial date or trial window.

8.4.7 The claimant must, unless some other party agrees to do so, take out an appointment with the Clerk of the Lists within 7 days of obtaining the direction in paragraph 8.4.6 above and give notice of the appointment to all other parties. If an appointment is not taken out within the 7 days, the Listing Office will appoint a date for a listing hearing and give notice of the date to all parties.

8.4.8 At the listing hearing the Clerk of the Lists will take account, in so far as it is practical to do so, of any difficulties the parties may have as to availability of counsel, experts and witnesses. The Clerk of the Lists will, nevertheless, try to ensure the speedy disposal of the trial by arranging a firm trial date as soon as possible within the trial period or, as the case may be, after the "not before" date directed by the court under paragraph 8.4.5 above. If exceptionally it appears to the Clerk of the Lists at the listing hearing that a trial date cannot be provided within a trial window, he may fix the trial date outside the trial period at the first available date. (If a case summary has been prepared (see the Part 29 Practice Direction The Multi-track, paragraphs 5.6 and 5.7) the claimant must produce a copy at the listing hearing together with a copy of particulars of claim and any orders relevant to the fixing of the trial date.)

8.4.9 The Listing Office will notify the Masters' Support Unit of any trial date or trial window given. In accordance with Rule 29.2(3) notice will also be given to all the parties.

8.4.10 A party who wishes to appeal a date or window allocated by the Listing Officer must, within 7 days of the notification, make an application to the Judge nominated by each Division to hear such applications. The application notice should be filed in the Listing Office and served, giving one days notice, on the other parties.

8.5 The Interim Hearings List:

8.5.1 This List consists of interim applications, appeals and applications for judgment. **1B–59**

8.5.2 On each Thursday of Term and on such other days as may be appropriate, the Clerk of the Lists will publish a Warned List showing the matters in the Interim

Hearings List that are liable to be heard in the following week. Any matters for which no date has been arranged will be liable to appear in the List for hearing with no warning save that given by the Cause List for the following day, posted each afternoon outside Room WG5.

8.5.3 Fixtures will only be given in exceptional circumstances. The parties may by agreement "offer" preferred dates for their matter to be heard, to be taken from the List on designated days, within the week following entry into the Warned List in accordance with Listing Office practice. Matters lasting less than a day are usually offered for two preferred consecutive days and matters lasting more than a day are usually offered for three preferred consecutive days.

8.6 General:

1B–60 8.6.1 In addition to the matters listed to be heard by individual Judges, the Daily Cause List for each day may list "unassigned cases". These are matters from the two Lists to be heard that day but not assigned to a particular Judge. If on any day a matter assigned to a particular Judge proves to be ineffective, he will hear an unassigned case. It is hoped that the great majority of unassigned cases will be heard on the day that they are listed but this cannot be absolutely guaranteed. Parties engaged in matters listed as unassigned should attend outside the court where the matter is listed. The Clerk of the Lists will notify them as soon as possible which Judge is to hear the matter. It is not the practice to list cases as unassigned unless the parties consent and there are no witnesses.

8.6.2 Appeals from Masters' decisions will appear in the Interim Hearings List. The notices of appeal (stamped with the appropriate fee) must be filed in Room WG7. On being notified that the appeal has been set down the solicitors should immediately inform the Clerk of the Lists whether they intend to instruct counsel and, if so, the names of counsel.

8.7 Listing before the Interim Applications Judge:

1B–61 8.7.1 All interim applications on notice to the Interim Applications Judge will initially be entered in a List for hearing. They will be listed for hearing in Room E101 or some other nominated venue on any day of the week. Any matter which cannot be disposed of with within one hour will not be taken on the date given for the listed hearing.

8.7.2 If the parties agree that a matter cannot be disposed of within one hour, the applicant/appellant;
> (1) may, on filing the application notice/notice of appeal, seek to have the matter placed directly into the Interim Hearings Warned List, or
> (2) must as soon as practicable and in any event not later than 24 hours before the hearing date transfer the matter into the Interim Hearings List.

If the parties do not so agree, or agree less than 24 hours before the hearing date, the parties must attend on that date.

8.7.3 Matters in the Interim Hearings List will be listed by the Clerk of the Lists in Room WG3, and the parties will be notified by the Listing Office (Room WG5) of the date on which the matter will enter the Warned List. Matters in the Warned List may be listed for hearing at any time on or after that date.

8.7.4 In order to ensure that a complete set of papers in proper order is available for the Judge to read before the hearing, the parties must in advance of the hearing lodge in room WG4 a bundle, properly paginated in date order, and indexed, containing copies of the following documents;
> (1) the application notice or notice of appeal,
> (2) any statements of case,
> (3) copies of all written evidence (together with copy exhibits) on which any party intends to rely, and
> (4) any relevant order made in the proceedings.

8.7.5 The bundle should be agreed if possible. In all but simple cases a skeleton argument and, where that would be helpful, a chronology should also be lodged. (See paragraph 8.9.1 and 8.9.2 below in respect of skeleton arguments.)

8.7.6 Where a date for the hearing has been arranged the bundle must be lodged not later than 3 clear days before the fixed date. For application or appeals where there is no fixed date for hearing, the bundle must be lodged not later than 48 hours after the parties have been notified that the matter is to appear in the Warned List. (For information concerning trial bundles see the Part 39 Practice Direction.)

8.7.7 Except with the permission of the Judge no document may be used in evidence or relied on unless a copy of it has been included in the bundle referred to in paragraph 8.7.6 above. If any party seeks to rely on written evidence which has not been included in the bundle, that party should lodge the original (with copy exhibits) in Room WG5 in advance of the hearing, or otherwise with the Court Associate before the hearing commences.

8.7.8 In appeals from District Judges the provisions of paragraphs 8.7.4, 8.7.5, 8.7.6 and 8.7.7 should be complied with. In addition, the notes (if any) of reasons given by the District Judge, prepared by the District Judge, counsel or solicitors should be lodged.

8.7.9 Subject to the discretion of the Judge, any application or appeal normally made to the Interim Applications Judge may be made in the month of September. In the month of August, except with the permission of a Judge, only appeals in respect of orders;

    (1) to set aside a claim form, or service of a claim form,
    (2) to set aside judgment,
    (3) for stay of execution,
    (4) for any order by consent,
    (5) for permission to enter judgment,
    (6) for approval of settlements or for interim payment,
    (7) for relief from forfeiture,
    (8) for a charging order,
    (9) for a garnishee order,
    (10) for appointment or discharge of a receiver,
    (11) for relief by way of sheriff's interpleader,
    (12) for transfer to a county court or for trial by Master, or
    (13) for time where time is running in the month of August,

may be heard, and only applications of real urgency will be dealt with, for example, urgent applications in respect of injunctions, or for possession (under RSC O.113 in Schedule 1 to Part 50).

8.7.10 It is desirable, where this is practical, that application notices or notices of appeal are submitted to the Practice Master or a Judge prior to the hearing of the application or appeal so that they can be marked "fit for August" or "fit for vacation". If they are so marked, then normally the Judge will be prepared to hear the application or appeal in August, if marked "fit for August" or in September if marked "fit for vacation". The application to a Judge to have the papers so marked should normally be made in writing, the application shortly setting out the nature of the application or appeal and the reasons why it should be dealt with in August or in September, as the case may be.

8.8 The Lists generally:

8.8.1 Where a fixed date has been given it is the duty of the parties to keep the Clerk **1B–62** of the Lists fully informed as to the current position of the matter with regard to negotiations for settlement, whether all aspects of the claim are being proceeded with, an estimate of the length of the hearing, and so on.

8.8.2 Applications for adjournments will not be granted except for the most cogent reasons. If an application is made because solicitors were unaware of the state of the List they may be ordered personally to pay the costs of the application.

8.8.3 A party who seeks to have a hearing before a Judge adjourned must inform the Clerk of the Lists of his application as soon as possible. Applications for an adjournment immediately before a hearing begins should be avoided as they take up valuable time which could be used for dealing with effective matters and, if successful, may result in court time being wasted.

8.8.4 If the application is made by agreement, the parties should, in writing, apply to the Clerk of the Lists who will consult the Judge nominated to deal with such matters. The Judge may grant the application on conditions which may include giving directions for a new hearing date.

8.8.5 If the application is opposed the applicant should apply to either the nominated Judge or the Judge to whom the matter has been allocated. A hearing should then be arranged through the Clerk of the Lists. A short summary of the reasons for the adjournment should be lodged with the Listing Office where possible by 10.30am on the day before the application is to be made. Formal written evidence is not normally required.

8.8.6 The applicant will be expected to show that he has conducted his own case diligently. Any party should take all reasonable steps;
    (1) to ensure his case is adequately prepared in sufficient time to enable the hearing to proceed, and
    (2) to prepare and serve any document (including any evidence) required to be served on any other party in sufficient time to enable that party also to be prepared.

8.8.7 If a party or his solicitor's failure to take reasonable steps necessitates an adjournment, the court may dismiss the application or make any other order including an order penalising the defaulting party in costs.

8.9 Listing Office—general matters:

1B–63 8.9.1 To facilitate the efficient listing of proceedings, parties are reminded that skeleton arguments concisely summarising each party's submissions must be prepared and filed with the Listing Office;
    (1) for trials, not less than 3 days before the trial, and
    (2) for substantial applications or appeals, not later than 1 day before the hearing.

8.9.2 If it is anticipated that a Skeleton Argument will be filed late, a letter of explanation should accompany it which will be shown to the Judge before whom the trial or hearing is to take place.

8.9.3 For parties' information, the following targets for the disposal of matters in the Lists have been agreed as set out below:

Interim Hearings Warned List	within 4 weeks
From date of fixing;	
Trials under 5 days	with 4 months
Trials over 5 but under 10 days	with 6 months
Trials over 10 but under 20 days	within 9 months
Trials over 20 days	within 12 months

9.

TRIAL, JUDGMENTS AND ORDERS

9.1 General:

1B–64 9.1.1 The trial of a claim in the Royal Courts of Justice normally takes place before a High Court Judge or a Deputy sitting as a High Court Judge. A Master may assess the damages or sum due to a party under a judgment and, subject to any Practice Direction, may try a claim which is

(1) treated as being allocated to the multi-track because it is proceeding under Part 8, or

(2) with the consent of the parties, allocated to the multi-track under Part 26[1].

9.1.2 Claims for defamation, malicious prosecution or false imprisonment will be tried by a Judge sitting with a Jury unless the court orders otherwise.

9.2 The Trial:

9.2.1 See paragraphs 2.4.2 and 2.4.3 above about representation at the trial, and paragraphs 7.11.14 and 7.11.15 above about recording of proceedings. **1B–65**

9.2.2 Rule 39.3 sets out the consequences of a party's failure to attend the trial and see also paragraph 2 of the Part 39 Practice Direction.

9.2.3 The Judge may fix a timetable for evidence and submissions if it has not already been fixed. The claimant's advocate will normally begin the trial with a short opening speech, and the Judge may then allow the other party to make a short speech. Each party should provide written summaries of their opening speeches if the points are not covered in their skeleton arguments.

9.2.4 It is normally convenient for any outstanding procedural matters or applications to be dealt with in the course of, or immediately after, the opening speech. In a jury trial such matters would normally be dealt with before the jury is sworn in.

9.2.5 Unless the court orders otherwise, a witness statement will stand as the evidence in chief of the witness, provided he is called to give oral evidence. With the court's permission, a witness may amplify his witness statement or give evidence in relation to new matters which have arisen since the witness statement was served on the other parties[2].

9.2.6 The Court Associate will be responsible for any exhibits produced as evidence during the trial. After the trial, the exhibits are the responsibility of the party who produced them. Where a number of physical exhibits are involved, it is desirable, if possible, for the parties to agree a system of labelling and the manner of display, beforehand. The Associate will normally draw the Judgment or order made at the trial.

9.2.7 At a jury trial, it is the parties' responsibility to provide sufficient bundles of documents for the use of the jury.

9.2.8 Facilities are available to assist parties or witnesses with special needs. The Listing Office should be notified of any needs or requirements prior to the trial.

9.3 Judgments and orders:

9.3.1 Part 40 deals with judgments and orders. Rule 40.2 contains the standard requirements of a judgment or order and Rule 40.3 contains provisions about drawing them up, see also paragraph 1 of the Part 40B Practice Direction for more information. **1B–66**

9.3.2 Provisions concerning consent orders are contained in Rule 40.6 which sets out in paragraph (3) the types of consent judgments and orders that may be sealed and entered by a court officer, provided;

(1) that none of the parties is a litigant in person, and

(2) the approval of the court is not required by a Rule, a Practice Direction or an enactment.

---

[1] See paragraph 4 of the Part 2B practice direction
[2] Rule 32.5

Other types of consent order require an application to be made to a Master or Judge for approval. It is common for a respondent to a consent order not to attend the hearing but to provide a written consent. The consent may either be written on the document or contained in a letter, and must be signed by the respondent, or where there are solicitors on record as acting for him, by his solicitors. Paragraph 3 of the Part 40B Practice Direction contains further information about consent orders.

9.3.3 Rule 40.11 sets out the time for complying with a judgment or order, which is 14 days unless the judgment or order specifies otherwise (for example by instalments), or a Rule specifies a different time, or the judgment or proceedings have been stayed.

9.3.4 The Part 40B Practice Direction contains further information about the effect of non-compliance with a judgment or order (and sets out the penal notice), adjustment of the final judgment sum in respect of interim payments and compensation recovery, and refers to various precedents for types of judgments and orders. See also;

(1) the Part 40 Practice Direction- Accounts and Enquiries, and

(2) the Part 40C Practice Direction- Structured Settlements which sets out the procedure to be followed both on settlement and after trial. Precedents for structured settlement orders, Parts 1 and 2, are annexed to the Practice Direction.

9.3.5 Where judgment is reserved, the Judge may deliver his judgment by handing down the written text without reading it out in open court. Where this is the case, the advocates will be supplied with the full text of the judgment in advance of delivery. The advocates should then familiarise themselves with the contents and be ready to deal with any points which may arise when the judgment is delivered. Any direction or requirement as to confidentiality must be complied with.

9.3.6 The judgment does not take effect until formally delivered in court. If the judgment is to be handed down in writing copies will then be made available to the parties and, if requested and so far as practicable, to the law reporters and the press.

9.3.7 The Judge will usually direct that the written judgment may be used for all purposes as the text of the judgment, and that no transcript need be made. Where such a direction is made, a copy will be provided to the Mechanical Recording Department from where further copies may be obtained (and see paragraph 7.11.14 above).

Judgment or order for payment of money on behalf of a child or patient

9.3.8 The usual order made at trial will make provision for any immediate payment to the litigation friend or his legal representative and for the balance of the award to be placed to a special investment account pending application to a Master or District Judge (in the case of a child) or the Court of Protection (in the case of a patient) for investment directions. The order will specify the time within which the application should be made.

9.3.9 The litigation friend or his legal representative should then write to or make an appointment with;

(1) in the case of a child, the Master or District Judge in accordance with paragraph 6.8.6 above and the Part 21 Practice Direction, or

(2) in the case of a patient, the Court of Protection in accordance with paragraph 11 of the Part 21 Practice Direction.

9.3.10 Where after trial the Judge has found in favour of a child or patient, instead of judgment being given, the proposed award of damages may be paid by way of a structured settlement. The structure must be approved by the Judge, and in the case of a patient must also be approved by the Court of Protection. (See also the Part 40C Practice Direction – Structured Settlements.)

Provisional damages

9.3.11 Rule 41.1 defines an award of provisional damages. Where there is a chance that a claimant may in the future develop a particular disease or deterioration as a result of the event giving rise to the claim, he can seek an award of damages for personal injury on the assumption that he will not develop the disease or deterioration, with provision for him to make a further application within the time specified in the order, if he does so develop the disease or deterioration.

9.3.12 The Part 41 Practice Direction gives further information about provisional damages awards and, in particular, about the preservation of the case file for the time specified in the order for making a further application, and the documents to be included in the case file. A precedent for a provisional damages judgment is annexed to the Practice Direction.

10.

APPEALS

10.1 General:

10.1.1 Appeals are governed by Part 52 and the Part 52 Practice Direction. The **1B–67** contents of Part 52 are divided into two sections; General Rules about Appeals and Special Provisions applying to the Court of Appeal. The Practice Direction is divided into three sections; General Provisions about Appeals, General Provisions about Statutory Appeals and Appeals by way of Case Stated, and Provisions about Specific Appeals. The following paragraphs apply to orders made after 2nd May 2000 and are intended only to draw parties' attention to the basic provisions for making an appeal in or from the Queen's Bench Division. For further information about these procedures and about other specific types of appeal, parties should refer to the Part 52 Practice Direction and the Civil Appeals Guide.

10.1.2 In the Queen's Bench Division an appeal from a Master will lie to a High Court Judge unless it is a final decision in a claim allocated to the multi-track or in specialist proceedings referred to in Part 49 in which case the appeal will lie to the Court of Appeal. An appeal from a High Court Judge will lie to the Court of Appeal.

10.1.3 Unless the lower court or the appeal court orders otherwise, an appeal does not operate as a stay of any order or decisions of the lower court.

10.2 Permission to appeal:

10.2.1 Permission is required to appeal from a decision of a Judge in a county court **1B–68** or the High Court, except where the appeal is in respect of;
    (1) a committal order,
    (2) a refusal to grant habeas corpus,
    (3) certain insolvency appeals, and
    (4) certain statutory appeals.

For the purposes of Part 52 and the Part 52 Practice Direction, the term "Judge" includes a Master or District Judge.

(For more information see Rule 52.3).

10.2.2 Permission should be sought at the hearing at which the decision to be appealed against is made. If it is not, or if it is sought and refused, permission should be sought from the court appealed to ("the appeal court"). Where permission is sought from the appeal court it must be requested in the appellant's or respondent's notice. Permission may be granted, or refused, or granted in part (whether as to a part of the order, a ground of appeal or an issue) and refused as to the rest. Paragraphs 4.1 to 4.12 of the Practice Direction deal with permission to appeal including the matters to be stated in the notice and the documents to be filed with it.

10.2.3 An application to the appeal court for permission may be dealt with without a hearing, but if refused without a hearing the applicant may request that it be reconsidered at a hearing; the court need not require that notice of the hearing be given to the respondent.

10.3 Notices:

1B–69　10.3.1 Rule 52.4 and paragraph 5 of the Practice Direction deal with the appellant's notice. The appellant must file his notice at the appeal court either within a period specified by the court appealed from ("the lower court") or, if no such period is specified, within 14 days of the date of the decision appealed from. The notice must be served on each respondent as soon as practicable and in any event not later than 7 days after it is filed.

10.3.2 A respondent must file a notice where;
- (1) he also wishes to appeal the lower court's decision,
- (2) he wishes to uphold the decision of the lower court for different or additional reasons to those given by the lower court, or
- (3) he is seeking permission to appeal from the appeal court.

10.3.3 The respondent's notice must be filed either within a period specified by the lower court or, if no such period is specified, within 14 days of;
- (1) the date the respondent is served with the appellant's notice where
  - (a) permission to appeal was given by the lower court or
  - (b) permission to appeal is not required,
- (2) the date the respondent is served with notification that the appeal court has given the appellant permission to appeal, or
- (3) the date the respondent is served with notification that the application for permission to appeal and the appeal itself are to be heard together.

(Paragraph 7 of the Practice Direction deals with the respondent's notice of appeal.)

10.3.4 The notices to be used are as follows;
- (1) the Appellant's Notice is form N161, and
- (2) the Respondent's Notice is form N162.

There is a leaflet available from the Listing Office, Room WG5 entitled "I want to appeal", which provides information about appealing other than to the Court of Appeal.

10.4 Appeals in cases of contempt of court:

1B–70　10.4.1 Appellant's notices which by paragraph 21.4 of the Part 52 Practice Direction are required to be served on "the court from whose order or decision the appeal is brought" may be served, in the case of appeals from the Queen's Bench Division, on the Senior Master of the Queen's Bench Division; service may be effected by leaving a copy of the notice of appeal with the Clerk of the Lists in Room WG5, Royal Courts of Justice, Strand, London WC2A 2LL.

11.

ENFORCEMENT

11.1 General:

1B–71　11.1.1 Enforcement in the High Court is still governed by RSC Orders 17, 45 to 52 and 71 as in Schedule 1 to the CPR.

11.1.2 RSC O. 45 deals with enforcement generally. A judgment or order for payment of money (other than into court) may be enforced by a writ of fieri facias, garnishee proceedings, a charging order or the appointment of a receiver[1]. A judgment or order to do or abstain from doing an act may be enforced by a writ of sequestration (with the permission of the court) or an order of committal[2]. A

---

[1] RSC O.45 r.1
[2] RSC O.45 r.5

judgment or order for possession of land may be enforced by a writ of possession[1], and a judgment or order for delivery of goods without the alternative of paying their value by a writ of specific delivery[2]. In each case, where RSC O.45 r.5 applies enforcement may also be by a writ of sequestration or an order of committal.

11.2 Writs of execution:

11.2.1 RSC O.46 deals with writs of execution generally. Rules 2 and 3 set out the **1B–72** circumstances when permission to issue a writ is necessary[3]. Rule 4 contains provisions for making an application for permission. Rule 5 deals with applications for permission to issue a writ of sequestration. RSC O. 47 contains provisions concerning writs of fieri facias. Forms of writs of execution may be used as follows:

(1) writs of fieri facias in form No 53 to No 63,
(2) writs of delivery in form No 64 and No 65,
(3) writs of possession in form No 66 and No 66A,
(4) writ of sequestration in form No 67,
(5) writ of restitution in form No 68,
(6) writ of assistance in form No 69.

11.2.2 With certain exceptions, writs of execution issued in the Royal Courts of Justice are executed by the Sheriff of the County in which the debtor has assets, or his officer. RSC O.46 r.6 sets out the provisions for issue of writs of execution. In the Queen's Bench Division writs of execution are issued in the Central Office in Room E17. Before the Writ can be sealed for issue, a signed praecipe for its issue must be filed[4] in one of forms PF 86 to 90, as appropriate, stamped with the appropriate fee. A copy of the judgment or order requiring enforcement should also be provided.

11.2.3 On an application for permission to issue a writ of possession under RSC O.45 r.3(2), if the property consists of a house of which various parts are sublet to, or in the occupation of, different persons, the evidence in support should show the nature and length of the notice which has been given to the various occupiers. Where the defendant or any other persons are in actual possession of the premises of which possession is sought, the evidence must contain the following information:

(1) whether the premises or any part of it is residential,
(2) if so,
    (a) what is the rateable value of the residential premises, and
    (b) whether it is let furnished or unfurnished and, if furnished, the amount of furniture it contains, and
(3) any other matters that will assist the Master in deciding whether any occupier is protected by the Rent Acts.

11.2.4 Where a party wishes to enforce a judgment or order expressed in a foreign currency by the issue of a writ of fieri facias, the praecipe must be endorsed with the following certificate:

"I/We certify that the rate current in London for the purchase of (*state the unit of foreign currency in which the judgment is expressed*) at the close of business on (*state the nearest preceding date to the date of issue of the writ of fieri facias*) was (   ) to the £ sterling and at this rate the sum of (*state amount of the judgment debt in the foreign currency*) amounts to £   ."

The schedule to the writ of fieri facias should be amended;

(1) showing the amount of the judgment or order in the foreign currency at paragraph 1.
(2) inserting a new paragraph 2. as follows: "2. Amount of the sterling equivalent as appears from the certificate endorsed on the praecipe for issue of the writ   £   "

---

[1] RSC O.45, r.3
[2] RSC O.45, r.4
[3] See also RSC O.45, r.3
[4] RSC O.46 r.6(3)

(3) renumbering the remaining paragraphs accordingly.

11.2.5 County court judgments or orders to which Article 8(1) of the High Court and County Courts Jurisdiction Order 1991 applies may be enforced in the High Court, and since 26th April 1999, any county court judgment for over £600 may be transferred to the High Court Sheriff for enforcement (except where it is a judgment arising from a regulated agreement under the Consumer Credit Act).

11.2.6 The party seeking enforcement should obtain from the appropriate county court a certificate of judgment of the county court in compliance with CCR O. 22 r.8(1A) (in Schedule 2 to the CPR), setting out details of the judgment or order to be enforced, sealed with the seal of that court and dated and signed by an officer of that court and stating on its face that it is granted for the purpose of enforcing the judgment or order by execution against goods in the High Court. Form N293A is a "Combined Certificate of Judgment and Request for Writ of Fieri Facias" and should be used.

11.2.7 A correctly completed form N293A together with a copy should be filed in Room E17 where the court officer will;

(1) allocate a reference number,

(2) date seal the Certificate and copy, returning the original to the party and retaining the copy, and

(3) enter the proceedings in a register kept for that purpose.

The certificate shall be treated for enforcement purposes as a High Court judgment and interest at the appropriate rate shall run from the date of the Certificate.

11.2.8 The title of all subsequent documents shall be set out as follows:

"
IN THE HIGH COURT OF JUSTICE
QUEEN'S BENCH DIVISION
High Court Claim No.
County Court Claim No.

(Sent from the [   ] County Court by Certificate dated (*date*))

Claimant

Defendant   "

When the writ of fieri facias is issued, the Certificate of judgment retained by the party shall be date sealed by the court officer on the bottom left hand corner and endorsed with the designation of the Sheriff to whom the writ is directed.

11.2.9 The Sheriffs Lodgment Centre at 2 Serjeant's Inn, Fleet Street. London EC4Y 1NX provides a service for arranging transfer up of county court judgments, and will complete the required forms and take all the above steps on behalf of the judgment creditor. (A helpline is provided on 020 7353 3640.)

11.2.10 It is important to remember in these cases that although any application for a stay of execution may be made to a Master in the High Court by application notice filed in accordance with Part 23, all other applications for enforcement or other relief must be made to the issuing county court. This practice is followed in the district registries with such variations as circumstances require.

11.2.11 When a writ of execution has been issued in the Royal Courts of Justice it may then be delivered to the Sheriff Lodgment Centre. Value Added Tax is payable in addition to the Sheriff's fee on the services for which the fee is payable, and must be paid at the time of delivery. If the goods, chattels and property to be seized in execution are not within Greater London, the Sheriff will direct the writ to the Sheriff of the appropriate county. Goods which may not be seized in execution of a writ are set out in s.138(3A) of the Supreme Court Act 1981 as follows:

(1) such tools, books, vehicles and other items of equipment as are necessary to that person for use personally by him in his employment, business or vocation,

(2) such clothing, bedding, furniture, household equipment and provisions as are necessary for satisfying the basic domestic needs of that person and his family,

(3) any money, bank notes, bills of exchange, promissory notes, bonds, specialties or securities for money belonging to that person.

11.2.12 When first executing a writ of fieri facias the Sheriff will deliver to the debtor or leave at each place where execution is levied a notice of seizure in form No 55[1]. This is commonly known as "walking possession" and the notice explains to the debtor the situation with regard to the goods seized and what he then has to do.

11.2.13 After execution of a writ of execution, the Sheriff will endorse on the writ a statement of the manner in which he has executed it and will send a copy of the statement to the party issuing the writ.

11.3 Interpleader proceedings (RSC O.17):

11.3.1 Where a person is under liability in respect of a debt or property and has **1B–73** been, or expects to be claimed against by two or more persons claiming the same debt or property, if the person under liability does not dispute the debt or claim the property, he may apply to the court for relief by way of interpleader, *i.e.* for the

---

[1] RSC O.45 r.2

entitlement of the persons claiming the same debt or property to be established in separate proceedings between them.

11.3.2 Where the Sheriff has seized goods in execution and a person other than the person against whom the writ of execution was issued wishes to claim the goods seized, he must give notice of his claim to the Sheriff, including in his notice a statement of his address which will be his address for service. The Sheriff will then give notice of that claim to the claimant on whose behalf the goods were seized in form PF 23. The notice requires the claimant to state whether he admits or disputes the claim. The claimant must do so within 7 days of receipt of the Sheriff's notice and may use form PF 24 to do so.

11.3.3 Where the claimant admits the claim, the Sheriff will withdraw from possession of the goods and may apply under RSC O.17 r.2(4) for an order to restrain a claim being brought against him for having taken possession of the goods. Where the claimant disputes the claim, the Sheriff may apply for interpleader relief. An application for interpleader relief if made in existing proceedings is made by an application in accordance with Part 23, otherwise it is made by the issue of a Part 8 claim form.

11.3.4 The Master may deal with the claims summarily, or may direct an issue to be tried between the parties in dispute (see RSC O.17 r.5) or make such other order as is appropriate.

11.4 Examination of judgment debtor (RSC O.48):

1B–74   11.4.1 Where a person ("the judgment creditor") has obtained a judgment or order for payment of a sum of money against a person ("the judgment debtor"), the judgment creditor may apply for an order requiring the judgment debtor to attend to be orally examined concerning his assets and means[1]. If the judgment debtor is a company or corporation, the court will order an officer of the company or corporation to attend for examination. In the case of a judgment or order which is not for payment of a sum of money, the court may make an order for the attendance of the party liable for his examination on such questions as may be specified in the order.

11.4.2 An application for an order under RSC O.48 r.1 should be made in accordance with Part 23 without notice to any other party. The application must be supported by evidence giving details of the judgment or order, including the amount still owing, and showing that the judgment creditor is entitled to enforce the judgment or order. Where the judgment debtor is a company or corporation the evidence must give details of the officer to be examined. Form PF 98 may be used as a precedent for the evidence in support. Where a judgment creditor has obtained judgments in several different proceedings against the same judgment debtor, only one application need be made, setting out in the body of the application details of all the judgments on which examination is sought.

11.4.3 The examination will take place before a Master, Registrar, district judge or nominated officer, as may be ordered, and will normally be at the court where the least expense will be incurred, usually the county court for the area where the judgment debtor lives. If a different court is requested the reason why should be given.

11.4.4 The application notice/evidence should be filed in the Masters' Support Unit Room E16 for consideration by a Master who will, if satisfied, make the order sought. Where the examination is to take place in a county court, the judgment creditor should lodge a copy of the order with the county court and obtain an appointment for the examination. If the examination is to take place in the Royal Courts of Justice, the order should be taken to Room E17 where the appointment will be endorsed on the order. In the Central Office the nominated officer is nominated at the discretion of the Senior Master and their names may be obtained from Room E17.

---

[1] RSC O.48 r.1

11.4.5 The order (endorsed with the penal notice as set out in paragraph 9.1 of the Part 40B Practice Direction) together with details of the appointment must be served personally on the judgment debtor or on the officer of the judgment debtor company or corporation to be examined. A judgment debtor should be offered his conduct money, *i.e.* expenses of travelling to and from the examination and of attending to give evidence.

11.4.6 The officer conducting the examination will take down, or arrange to have taken down in writing the judgment debtor's statement. The officer will read the statement to the judgment debtor and will ask him to sign it. If he refuses to do so the officer will sign the statement. If the judgment debtor refuses to answer any question or if any other difficulties arise, the matter will be referred to the Senior Master or the Practice Master who will give such direction as he thinks fit.

11.5 Garnishee proceedings (RSC O.49):

11.5.1 Where a judgment creditor has obtained a judgment or order for payment of a sum of money of at least £50 against a judgment debtor, and another person ("the garnishee") is indebted to the judgment debtor, the judgment creditor may apply to the Master for an order that the garnishee pays to the judgment creditor the amount of the debt due to the judgment debtor, or sufficient of it to satisfy the judgment debt.   **1B–75**

11.5.2 The application should be made in accordance with Part 23 but the application notice need not be served on the judgment debtor. The application will normally be dealt with without a hearing and must be supported by evidence as set out in RSC O.49 r.2. Parties may use form PF 100 for their evidence in support. If the Master is satisfied that such an order is appropriate, he will make an order in form No 72 specifying the debt attached and appointing a time for the garnishee to attend and show cause why the order should not be made absolute.

11.5.3 The garnishee order to show cause must be served personally on the garnishee, and served on the judgment debtor, in accordance with RSC O.49 r.3. Where the garnishee fails to attend the hearing or attends but does not dispute the debt, the Master may make a garnishee order absolute against the garnishee under RSC O.49 r.1. The order absolute may be enforced in the same manner as any other order for the payment of money[1]. Where the garnishee disputes the debt, the Master may dispose of the matter as set out in RSC O.49 r.5.

11.5.4 Where the judgment creditor seeks to enforce a judgment expressed in a foreign currency by garnishee proceedings, the evidence in support of the application must contain words to the following effect:
> "The rate current in London for the purchase of (*state the unit of foreign currency in which the judgment is expressed*) at the close of business on (*state the nearest preceding date to the date of verifying the evidence*) was ( ) to the £ sterling, and at this rate the sum of (*state the amount of the judgment debt in the foreign currency*) amounts to £ . I have obtained this information from (*state source*) and believe it to be true."

11.6 Charging Orders (RSC O.50):

11.6.1 A judgment creditor may apply for a charging order on the property or assets of the judgment debtor, which will have the effect of providing him with security over the property of the judgment debtor. The High Court has jurisdiction to impose a charging order in the following cases: **1B–76**
  (1) where the property is a fund lodged in the High Court,
  (2) where the order to be enforced is a maintenance order[2] of the High Court, and

---

[1] RSC O.49 r.4(2)
[2] See s.2(a) Attachment of Earnings Act 1971

(3) where the judgment or order is made in the High Court and exceeds £5000[1].

The property and assets of the judgment debtor on which a charge may be imposed by a charging order are specified by s.2 of the Charging Orders Act 1979.

11.6.2 A charging order to show cause imposing a charge on land will be drawn in respect of the judgment debtors interest in the land and not the land itself, unless the court orders otherwise. If a charging order to show cause is made on stocks or shares in more than one company, a separate order must be drawn in respect of each company. If the judgment debt is expressed in a foreign currency, the evidence in support of any application for a charging order should contain a similar provision to that set out in paragraph 11.5.4 above.

11.6.3 The application for a charging order is made to a Master and should be made in accordance with Part 23 but the application is made without being served on the judgment debtor. The application will normally be dealt with without a hearing and must be supported by evidence as set out in RSC O.50 r.3. Parties may use form PF 101 for their evidence in support. If the Master is satisfied that such an order is appropriate, he will make an order in form No 75 appointing a time for the judgment debtor to attend and show cause why the order should not be made absolute.

11.6.4 The order to show cause and the evidence in support should be served in accordance with RSC O.50 r.2, or otherwise as directed by the Master. After further consideration at the hearing the Master will either make the order absolute (with or without modifications) as in form No 76, or discharge it. Where the order is discharged, the order of discharge must be served in accordance with RSC O.50 r.7.

11.6.5 See RSC O.50 r.4 for provisions concerning imposing a charge on an interest held by a trustee. RSC O.50 r.5 deals with the effects of a charging order in relation to securities out of court, and RSC O.50 r.6 with funds in court. Proceedings for the enforcement of a charging order by sale of the property charged must be begun by a Part 8[2] Claim Form issued out of Chancery Chambers or a Chancery district registry (RSC O.50 r.9A).

11.7 Receivers; equitable execution (RSC O.51):

1B–77   11.7.1 Equitable execution is a process which enables a judgment creditor to obtain payment of the judgment debt where the interest of the judgment debtor in property cannot be reached by ordinary execution.

11.7.2 An application for appointment of a receiver by way of equitable execution may be made to a Master, who also has jurisdiction to grant an injunction if, and only so far as, the injunction is ancillary or incidental to the order. The procedure follows that set out in RSC O.30 rr.1 to 6, and the application should be made in accordance with Part 23 and the Part 23 Practice Direction as described in the following paragraphs.

11.7.3 If the judgment creditor seeks an injunction (as in 11.7.2 above) he should file his application notice based on form No 82 but setting out in addition the injunction sought, together with a witness statement or affidavit in support stating:
   (1) the date and particulars of the judgment, and that it remains wholly unsatisfied, or to what extent it remains unsatisfied,
   (2) the particulars and result of any execution which has been issued, and the nature of the sheriff's return (if any),
   (3) that the judgment debtor has no property which can be taken by the ordinary process of execution, (*if he has, give reasons showing that legal execution would be futile*),
   (4) particulars of the property in respect of which it is proposed to appoint a receiver,

---

[1] In the case of subparas (2) and (3) the county court also has jurisdiction
[2] See Table 1, Part 8B Practice Direction

(5) the name and address of the receiver proposed to be appointed, and that in the deponent's judgment he is a fit and proper person to be appointed receiver, and

(6) that the judgment debtor is in financial difficulties [that the immediate appointment of a receiver without the delay of giving security is of great importance] and that the deponent believes that the judgment debtor may assign or dispose of his estate or interest in (*give details of property*) unless restrained from doing so by the order and injunction of the court.

11.7.4 The judgment creditor need not give notice of this application which will normally be dealt with without a hearing. If the Master is satisfied with the evidence he will make an order in form No 83 for a hearing to take place in respect of the application for the appointment of the receiver and granting an injunction meanwhile.

11.7.5 If the judgment creditor does not seek an injunction, the application notice should be filed and served together with the evidence in support (as in paragraph 11.7.3 above but without paragraph (6)).

11.7.6 At the hearing of the application to appoint the receiver, the Master will, if he thinks fit, make an order in form No 84. A copy of the order appointing the receiver shall be served by the judgment creditor on the receiver and all other parties to the proceedings[1].

11.7.7 Where a receiver has been ordered to give security under RSC O.30 r.2, the judgment creditor should obtain an appointment before the Master who made the order appointing the receiver, to settle the form and amount of the security. Unless otherwise ordered, the security will be in the form of a guarantee. The judgment creditor should have prepared a draft form of guarantee for the Master to approve at the appointment. Form PF 30CH may be used as a precedent for the guarantee.

11.7.8 RSC O.30 r.3 deals with the remuneration of the receiver which may either be assessed by the Master or referred to a costs judge. RSC O.30 r.5 contains the provisions for submitting the receiver's accounts.

11.8 Committals, etc. (RSC O.52):

11.8.1 The court has power to punish contempt of court by an order of committal to prison or by other means. These may be by ordering the payment of a fine, by the issue of a writ of sequestration, or by making a hospital or guardianship order under certain provisions of the Mental Health Act 1983. Committal applications under RSC O.52 r.4 are always dealt with by a High Court Judge. The following provisions apply to applications made under RSC O.52 r.4.

1B–78

11.8.2 The application should be made in existing proceedings by filing an application notice. If not in existing proceedings, a Part 8 Claim Form should be issued[2] (see paragraphs 2.1 and 2.2 of the Practice Direction—Committal Applications). Evidence in support of a committal application must be by affidavit[3] and, together with the Part 8 Claim Form or application notice, must be served personally on the person sought to be committed. A date for the hearing must be obtained from the Listing Office, Room WG5 and endorsed on or served with the Claim Form or application notice.

11.8.3 Paragraphs 2.5, 2.6 and 3.1 to 3.4 of the Practice Direction deal with the content of the evidence, and serving and filing, and paragraph 4 deals with the hearing date and management of the proceedings.

11.8.4 Committal proceedings will normally be heard in public, but see RSC O.52 r.6 which sets out certain types of cases which may be heard in private, and see paragraph 9 of the Practice Direction.

---

[1] RSC O.30 r.4
[2] See the Part 8B practice direction, Table 1
[3] RSC O.52 r.4(2)

11.8.5 Where the court makes a finding of contempt, details of the contempt and of the order or undertaking breached (where appropriate) must be set out in the order. The term of any period of committal must be stated in the order and must not exceed two years[1]. A fine must be expressed as payable to Her Majesty the Queen and the order must state the amount of the fine and the date and time within which it must be paid. A contemnor and his solicitors will be notified separately as to how the fine should be paid. A precedent of the order is in form No 85 and will normally be drawn by the court.

11.8.6 When an order for committal to prison is made, the court will issue a warrant to the Tipstaff authorising him to convey the contemnor to the appropriate prison. A copy of the order should be served on the prison governor. RSC O.52 r.8 deals with the discharge of a person committed.

11.9 Execution against property of Foreign or Commonwealth States:

1B–79 11.9.1 In cases where judgment has been obtained against a foreign or Commonwealth State and it is sought to execute the judgment by a writ of fieri facias, a charging order or a garnishee order, the following provisions apply:

(1) Before the writ of fieri facias is issued, the Master must be informed in writing and his direction sought. In cases where an application is to be made for a charging order to show cause or a garnishee order to show cause, the evidence in support of the application must include a statement that the execution sought is against a foreign or Commonwealth State.

(2) The Master, having been so informed will, as soon as practicable, inform the Foreign and Commonwealth Office ("FCO") of the application and will not permit the issue of a writ of fieri facias, nor grant an order to show cause until the FCO has been so informed. The Privileges and Immunities Section of the Protocol Department of the FCO may be contacted by telephone on 020 7210 4053 or by Fax on 020 7270 4126.

(3) Having regard to all the circumstances of the case, the Master may postpone the decision whether to issue the writ or grant the order to show cause for so long as he considers reasonable for the purpose of enabling the FCO to furnish further information relevant to his decision, but not for longer than 3 days from the time of his contacting the FCO. In the event that no further information is received from the FCO within 24 hours of its being informed, then the writ of fieri facias may be issued or the order to show cause may be sealed without further delay.

11.10 Recovery of enforcement costs:

1B–80 11.10.1 Subsection (3) of section 15 of the Courts and Legal Services Act 1990 enables a person taking steps to enforce a money judgment in the High Court to recover the costs of any previous attempt to enforce that judgment. Subsection (4) of section 15 excludes costs that the court considers to have been unreasonably incurred.

11.10.2 The application for an enforcement costs order is made to a Master and should be made in accordance with Part 23 but the application notice need not be served on the judgment debtor. The application will normally be dealt with without a hearing and must be supported by evidence substantially as set out in form PF 205. The deponent should exhibit sufficient vouchers, receipts or other documents as are reasonably necessary to verify the amount of the costs of previous attempts to enforce the judgment.

11.10.3 If the Master is satisfied that such an order is appropriate, he will make an order for payment of the amount of such costs as he considers may be recoverable under subsection (3) of section 15. If the amount of such costs is less than that claimed by the judgment creditor, the Master may either disallow the balance or give directions for a detailed assessment or other determination of the balance. If after assessment or other determination it appears that the judgment creditor is entitled to

---

[1] Contempt of Court Act 1981, s.14

further costs beyond those originally allowed, he may issue a further writ of fieri facias or take other lawful steps to enforce those costs. Interest on the costs runs either from the date the Master made the enforcement costs order or from the date of the costs certificate.

11.11 Enforcement of Magistrates' Courts' orders:

11.11.1 The Magistrates' Courts Act 1980, s.87 provides that payment of a sum **1B–81** ordered to be paid on a conviction of a magistrates' court may be enforced by the High Court or a county court (otherwise than by the issue of a writ of fieri facias or other process against goods or by imprisonment or attachment of earnings) as if the sum were due to the clerk of the magistrates' court under a judgment of the High Court or county court, as the case may be.

11.11.2 In the Central Office, the application is made to a Master and should be made in accordance with Part 23. Where enforcement is sought by a garnishee or charging order to show cause, the application will normally be dealt with without a hearing. Otherwise the application notice and evidence in support should be served on the defendant.

11.11.3 The application must be supported by a witness statement or affidavit in a form appropriate to the type of execution sought and must have exhibited to it the authority of the magistrates' court to take the proceedings which will recite the conviction, the amount outstanding and the nature of the proceedings authorised to be taken (Magistrates Courts Forms Rules 1981, Form 63).

11.11.4 The application notice and evidence in support together with an additional copy of the exhibit should be filed in Room E15 where it will be assigned a reference number from the register kept for that purpose. The matter will then be dealt with by the Master according to the type of enforcement sought.

11.11.5 This practice will also be followed in the District Registries with such variations as circumstances may render necessary.

11.12 Reciprocal enforcement of judgments and enforcement of European Community judgments and recommendations etc. under the Merchant Shipping (Liner Conferences) Act 1982 (RSC O.71):

Reciprocal enforcement; the Administration of Justice Act 1920 and the Foreign Judgments (Reciprocal Enforcement) Act 1933

11.12.1 RSC O.71 r.2 sets out how an application under s.9 of the Act of 1920 or **1B–82** under s.2 of the Act of 1933 for registration of a foreign judgment in the High Court may be made. The application should be made without notice being served on any other party, but the Master may direct that a Part 8 Claim Form should be issued and served.

11.12.2 RSC O.71 r.3 sets out what the evidence in support of the application should contain or have exhibited to it. The title of the witness statement or affidavit should;
  (1) expressly state whether it is made "In the matter of the Administration of Justice Act 1920" or "In the matter of the Foreign Judgments (Reciprocal Enforcement) Act 1933", and
  (2) identify the judgment by reference to the Court in which it was obtained and the date it was given.

The foreign judgment will be registered in the foreign currency in which it is expressed and must not be converted into Sterling in the evidence in support. When it comes to enforcing the foreign judgment, the amount should then be converted in accordance with the instructions set out above in paragraph 11 in respect of the type of enforcement sought.

11.12.3 The order giving permission to register the judgment must be drawn up by, or on behalf of the judgment creditor (form PF 154 may be used as a precedent) and will be entered in the Register of Judgments kept in the Central Office for that purpose[1]. The order will usually contain a direction that the costs of and caused by the application and the registration be assessed and added to the judgment as registered. Notice of registration of the judgment must state the matters set out in RSC O.71 r.7(3) including the right of the judgment debtor to apply, and the time within he may do so, to have the registration set aside. The notice must be served on the judgment debtor in accordance with RSC O.71, r.7(1).

11.12.4 An application to set aside the registration of a judgment under RSC O.71 r.9 must be made in accordance with Part 23 and be supported by a witness statement or affidavit.

11.12.5 An application for a certified copy of a judgment entered in the High Court must be made without notice by witness statement or affidavit in accordance with RSC O.71 r.13. The certified copy will be endorsed with a certificate signed by the Master in accordance with RSC O.71 r.13(4). Where the application was made under s.10 of the Act of 1933, an additional certificate will be issued and signed by the Master as in form PF 155. Judgment creditors who intend to seek enforcement abroad should ensure that their judgment is endorsed as follows:

"This judgment carries interest from (*date*) at the rate of £80 per annum in accordance with the provisions of the Judgments Act 1838."

Enforcement of European Community judgments

11.12.6 RSC O.71 rr. 15 to 24 contains provisions concerning applications for enforcement of Community judgments and Euratom inspection orders under the European Communities (Enforcement of Community Judgments) Order 1972 and for their enforcement. The application for registration may be made without notice being served on any other party and must be supported by a witness statement or affidavit containing or having exhibited to it the matters referred to in RSC O.71 r.18. Form PF 156 may be used as a precedent.

11.12.7 The order for registration (form PF 157) will be entered in the register of the Community judgments and Euratom inspection orders kept in the Central Office for that purpose. The court will serve notice of the registration in form PF 158 in accordance with RSC O.71 r.20.

11.12.8 An application to vary or cancel a registration under the provisions of RSC O.71 r.22 shall be made by application notice in accordance with Part 23, supported by a witness statement or an affidavit.

Reciprocal enforcement; the Civil Jurisdiction and Judgments Act 1982

Applications under s.4 of the Act of 1982

11.12.9 The provisions concerning applications for registration of judgments of another Contracting State under s.4 of the Act of 1982 are set out in RSC O.71 rr. 25 to 35. The application is made without notice being served on any other party and must be supported by evidence as set out in RSC O.71 r.28. Form PF 159 may be used as a precedent.

11.12.10 The order for registration (form PF 160) will be entered in the register of judgments ordered to be registered under s.4 of the Act of 1982 kept in the Central Office for that purpose. The notice of registration in form PF 161 should be served in accordance with RSC O.71 r.32.

11.12.11 An appeal against registration must be made to a Judge under the provisions of RSC O.71 r.33(2) by application notice in accordance with Part 23, and should be served in accordance with RSC O.71 r.33(2)(a) and (b).

Applications under s.12 of the Act of 1982

11.12.12 RSC O.71 r.36 deals with applications for enforcement of High Court judgments in other Contracting States under s.12 of the Act of 1982. The application

---

[1] RSC O.71 rr. 5 and 6

for a certified copy of the judgment entered in the High Court must be made without notice being served on any other party and must be supported by evidence as set out in RSC O.71 r.36(2). Form PF 163 may be used as a precedent.

11.12.13 The court will issue a certified copy of the judgment together with a Certificate in form PF 110 signed by the Master, and having annexed to it a copy of the claim form by which the proceedings were begun.

Applications under s.18 of the Act of 1982; judgment containing money provisions

11.12.14 RSC O.71 r.37 deals with applications for registration in the High Court of a certificate in respect of any money provisions contained in a judgment given in another part of the United Kingdom. The certificate may be obtained by filing a draft certificate in form No 111 together with a witness statement or affidavit in accordance with RSC O.71 r.37(3). Form PF 164 may be used as a precedent.

11.12.15 The certificate must be filed for registration in Room E13 in the Central Office within 6 months from the date of its issue. Under paragraph 9 of schedule 6 to the Act of 1982 an application may be made to stay the enforcement of the certificate. The application may be made without notice being served on any other party supported by a witness statement or affidavit stating that the applicant is entitled and intends to apply to the judgment court to set aside or stay the judgment.

Applications under s.18 of the Act of 1982; judgment containing non-money provisions

11.12.16 RSC O.71 r.38 deals with applications for registration in the High Court of a judgment which contains non-money provisions, given in another part of the United Kingdom. The application should be made broadly in accordance with paragraphs 11.12.11 and 11.12.12 above, without notice being served on any other party, but the Master may direct that a Part 8 Claim Form should be issued and served.

11.12.17 The application should be accompanied by a draft certificate in form No 112 and must be supported by a witness statement or affidavit in accordance with RSC O.71 r.37(3) (with the necessary modifications). Form PF 165 may be used as a precedent. An application to set aside registration of a judgment under schedule 7 to the Act of 1982 may be made in accordance with RSC O.71 r.9 (1) and (2).

11.12.18 The certificates will be entered in the register of certificates in respect of judgments ordered to be registered under Schedules 6 or 7 of the Act of 1982 kept in the Central Office for that purpose.

Enforcement of recommendations etc. under the Merchant Shipping (Liner Conferences) Act 1982

11.12.19 Applications under s.9 of the Act of 1982 for registration of a recommendation, determination or award, are dealt with by a Commercial Judge and shall be made by the issue of a Part 8 Claim Form[1]. The application should be supported by evidence in accordance with RSC O.71 r.42.

11.12.20 The order giving permission to register the recommendation, determination or award must be drawn up by or on behalf of the party making the application, and entered in the register of the recommendations, determinations and awards ordered to be registered under s.9 of the Act of 1982, directed by the Senior Master to be kept in the Admiralty and Commercial Registry.

12.

MISCELLANEOUS

12.1 Service of foreign process (RSC O.69):

---

[1] RSC O.71 r.41 and the Part 8B Practice Direction, Table 1

1B–83 12.1.1 RSC O.69 applies to the service on a person in England or Wales of any process in connection with civil or commercial proceedings in a foreign court or tribunal. A request for service is made to either the Senior Master from either Her Majesty's Principal Secretary of State for Foreign and Commonwealth Affairs, or where the foreign court or tribunal is in a convention country[1], from a consular or other authority of that country.

12.1.2 Where the foreign court or tribunal certifies that the person to be served understands the language of the process, it is not necessary to provide a translation. RSC O.69 r.3 deals with the manner of service; the process may be served through the machinery of the county court and the usual practice is for the Senior Master to provide a certificate for the bailiff or county court officer to use. The Senior Master may make an order for service by an alternative method based on the bailiff's certificate.

12.1.3 When service has been effected, the Senior Master will send a certificate, together with a copy of the process served, to the authority who requested service, stating how service was effected, or why service could not be effected. There is a discretion to charge for the costs of service or attempted service, but recovery is usually sought only where the country requesting service does not provide a reciprocal free service.

12.2 Rectification of register of deeds of arrangement (RSC O.94 r.4):

1B–84 12.2.1 Deeds of arrangement must be registered[2]. The registration office is at the Department of Trade.

12.2.2 An application for an order as set out in RSC O.94 r.4(1)(a) or (b) must be made to a Master of the Queen's Bench Division. Notice need not be served on any other party and the application must be supported by a witness statement or affidavit as described in rule 4(2).

12.3 Exercise of jurisdiction under the Representation of the People Acts (RSC O.94 r.5):

1B–85 12.3.1 RSC O.94 r.5 describes the jurisdiction of the High Court under the above Acts. The practice is governed by the Election Petition Rules 1960 (as amended).

12.3.2 Under Part III of the Representation of the People Act 1983, the result of a parliamentary or local government election may be questioned on the grounds of some irregularity either before or during the election. The provisions of Part III have also been applied to European Parliamentary elections.

12.3.3 The challenge is made by the issue of an election petition
    (1) in respect of a Parliamentary election by one or more electors or
    (2) in respect of a local government election by four or more electors,

or by an unsuccessful or alleged candidate. The member/councillor whose election is complained of is a respondent to the petition as is the Returning Officer if his conduct is complained of. The petition is issued in the Election Petitions Office, Room E218, normally within 21 days of the election, although this may be extended in certain circumstances.

12.3.4 The petition is tried by two High Court Judges of the Queen's Bench Division in respect of parliamentary elections or by a Commissioner in respect of local government elections. The Commissioner must be a lawyer of not less than 10 years standing who neither resides nor practices in the area concerned. The trial usually takes place in the constituency/local government area although preliminary matters are dealt with at the Royal Courts of Justice.

---

[1] For definition of "convention country" see RSC O.69 r.1
[2] Deeds of Arrangement Act 1914, as amended by the Administration of Justice Act 1925, s.22

12.3.5 The election court may confirm the result of the election, or substitute another candidate as the member/councillor, or may order the election to be re-run.

12.3.6 Applications for remedies under various sections of the Representation of the People Act 1983 are also issued in the Election Petitions Office, and are usually heard by an Election Rota Judge.

12.3.7 Outside the court offices' opening times, but while the building is still open to the public, election petitions and applications may be left in the letter box fixed to the door of Room E218. When the building is closed, election petitions and applications may be left with Security at the Main Entrance, up until midnight.

12.4 Bills of Sale Acts 1878 and 1882 and the Industrial and Provident Societies Act 1967 (RSC O.95):

12.4.1 Every bill of sale and absolute bill of sale to which the Act of 1878 applies must **1B–86** be registered under s.8 of that Act, within 7 clear days of its making, and, under s.11 of the Act of 1878, the registration of a bill of sale must be renewed at least once every 5 years. The register for the purpose of the Bills of Sale Acts contains the particulars of registered bills of sale and an alphabetical index of the names of the grantors, and is kept in the Action Department in Room E10.

12.4.2 An application to register a bill of sale which is made within the prescribed time should be made by filing in Room E17 the original bill of sale and any document annexed to it together with a witness statement or affidavit in form PF 179 or PF 180. An application to re-register a bill of sale which is made within the prescribed time should be made by filing in Room E17 a witness statement or affidavit in form PF 181.

12.4.3 An application to rectify;
   (1) an omission to register, by extending the time for registration, or
   (2) an omission or mis-statement of the name, residence or occupation of a person in the register, by correcting the registration,

must be made by witness statement or affidavit to a Master of the Queen's Bench Division. In addition to the matters set out in forms PF 179 or PF 180, the evidence in support must also set out the particulars of the omission and state the grounds on which the application is made.

12.4.4 Where the residence of the grantor of the bill of sale or the person against whom the process is issued is outside the London bankruptcy district, or where the bill of sale describes the goods as being in a place outside that district, the Central Office will send copies of the bill of sale to the appropriate county court district judge[1].

12.4.5 The Master, on being satisfied that the omission or mis-statement of name, residence or occupation of a person in the register was accidental or due to inadvertence, may order the omission or mis-statement to be rectified by the insertion in the register of the correct name, residence or occupation of the person.

12.4.6 Where the Master is satisfied that the omission to register a bill of sale or a witness statement or affidavit of renewal within the prescribed time was accidental or due to inadvertence, he may extend the time for registration on such terms as he thinks fit. In order to protect any creditors who have accrued rights of property in the assets in respect of which the bill of sale was granted between the date of the bill and its actual registration, any order to extend the time for registration will normally be made "without prejudice" to those creditors. The order will be drawn up in form PF 182.

12.4.7 An application for an order that a memorandum of satisfaction be written on a registered copy of a bill of sale, made without the consent of the person entitled to

---

[1] s.11, Bills of Sale Act 1882 and the Bills of Sale (Local Registration) Rules 1960

the benefit of the bill of sale, must be made by the issue of a Part 8 Claim Form. Where the consent of the person entitled to the benefit of the bill of sale has been obtained, the application may be made by a witness statement or affidavit[1] containing that consent and verifying the signature on it. Form PF 183 contains precedents for the evidence and forms of consent. Where the application is made with consent, the evidence need not be served on any other person. If the Master is satisfied on the evidence, he will endorse his approval on the witness statement or affidavit (an order is not normally drawn up) and send it to Room E17 for satisfaction to be entered. If a copy of the bill of sale has been sent to a county court district judge, a notice of satisfaction will be sent to that district judge.

12.4.8 Where the consent has not been obtained, the Claim Form must be served on the person entitled to the benefit of the bill of sale and must be supported by evidence that the debt (if any) for which the bill of sale was made has been satisfied or discharged.

12.4.9 An application to restrain removal on sale of goods seized in accordance with RSC O.95 r.3 and under the proviso to s.7 of the Bills of Sale Act (1878) Amendment Act 1882 must be made by the issue of a Part 8 Claim Form for hearing before the Interim Applications Judge.

12.4.10 Under the Industrial and Provident Societies Act 1967 an application to record an instrument creating a fixed or floating charge on the assets of a registered society or to rectify any omission or mis-statement in it must be made within 14 days beginning with the date of its execution.

12.4.11 Under RSC O.95 r.5 and in accordance with s.1(5) of the Act of 1967 the court may order;
    (1) that the period for making an application for recording a charge be extended, or
    (2) an omission or mis-statement in such an application be rectified.

The procedure for obtaining an order as in (1) or (2) above is similar to that under s.14 of the Bills of Sale Act 1878 and must be made by witness statement or affidavit to a Master of the Queen's Bench Division as in paragraph 12.4.3 above and must exhibit a copy of the instrument duly authenticated in the prescribed manner together with any other particulars relating to the charge.

12.4.12 RSC O.95 r.3 refers to the assignment of book debts; the register of assignments of book debts is kept in Room E10 in the Central Office. An application for registration under s.344 of the Insolvency Act 1986 should be made in accordance with RSC O.95 r.6(2). Parties may use form PF 186 for their evidence in support. It is helpful if the original assignment is also produced.

12.5 Enrolment of deeds and other documents:

1B–87 12.5.1 Any deed or document which by virtue of any enactment is required or authorised to be enrolled in the Supreme Court may be enrolled in the Central Office. See the Part 5 Practice Direction at paragraph 6 which fully sets out the procedure for enrolment and contains in an appendix the Enrolment of Deeds (Change of Name) Regulations 1994.

12.6 Bail (RSC O.79 r.9):

1B–88 12.6.1 Under the provisions of subsections (1) and (2) of section 22 of the Criminal Justice Act 1967 (as amended by Schedule 2 to the Bail Act 1976) the High Court may grant bail in criminal proceedings to a defendant in custody who has been refused bail, or vary the arrangements for bail of an inferior court.

12.6.2 The application must be made to the Interim Applications Judge by the issue of a Part 8 Claim Form in form No 97 or No 97A, and supported by a witness

---

[1] See the Practice Direction—Bills of Sale

statement or affidavit in accordance with RSC O.79 r.9 (1) to (3). The Claim Form should be issued in the Listing Office, Room WG5, and will be given a bail number from the register kept there for recording bail applications.

12.6.3 If a defendant wishing to apply for bail is unable to instruct a solicitor to act for him through lack of means, he may write to the Interim Applications Judge to that effect and requesting that the Official Solicitor act for him. The letter should be addressed to the Listing Office, Room WG5, marked for the attention of the Interim Applications Judge. Where the Judge assigns the Official Solicitor to act for the defendant, he may dispense with the issue of a claim form and a witness statement or affidavit in support.

12.6.4 Where the Judge grants bail, the order will be drawn up in form No 98 which provides for the conditions to be complied with both before release, including the provision of sureties, and after release. An order varying the arrangements for bail will be drawn up in form No 98A. Copies of those orders must be sent to the appropriate officer of the Crown Court or of the court which committed the defendant.

12.7 Defamation:

12.7.1 Defamation claims are governed by Part 53 and the Part 53 Practice Direction. **1B–89** Paragraph 2 of the Practice Direction sets out the information which should be included in a statement of case.

Offer to make amends

12.7.2 Under section 2 of the Defamation Act 1996 a person who has published a statement alleged to be defamatory of another may offer to make amends ("a section 2 offer"). The section 2 offer must;
   (1) be in writing,
   (2) be expressed to be an offer to make amends under section 2 of the Act, and
   (3) state whether it is a qualified offer, and if so, set out the defamatory meaning in relation to which it is made.

A section 2 offer is an offer;
   (1) to make a suitable correction of the statement complained of and sufficient apology,
   (2) to publish the correction and apology in a manner that is reasonable and practicable in the circumstances, and
   (3) to pay to the aggrieved party compensation (if any) and costs as may be agreed or determined to be payable.

12.7.3 Where a section 2 offer is accepted by an aggrieved person he may not bring or continue defamation proceedings against the person making the offer, but he may apply to the court under section 3 of the Act for an order that the other party fulfil his offer by taking the agreed steps. If the parties are unable to agree the amount of compensation or costs, the aggrieved party may apply to the court for the amount to be decided.

12.7.4 In the event that the parties are unable to agree on the steps to be taken, the person making the offer may take such steps as he thinks appropriate, including making an application for the court's approval of the terms of a statement to be read in Court containing a correction and apology. He may also give an undertaking to the court as to the manner of their publication.

12.7.5 In existing proceedings the above applications may be made in accordance with Part 23, otherwise a Part 8 Claim Form should be issued. The application or claim must be supported by written evidence as set out in the Part 53 Practice Direction at paragraph 3.3, and should be made to a Master. If the application or claim involves the court's approval for a statement to be read in Court, it should be made to the Senior Master. The Claim Form or application notice should be issued or filed in the Masters' Support Unit, Room E17.

Ruling on meaning

12.7.6 An application for an order determining whether or not a statement complained of is capable of;

    (1) having any meaning or meanings attributed to it in a statement of case,

    (2) being defamatory of the claimant, or

    (3) bearing any other meaning defamatory of the claimant,

should be made in accordance with Part 23 and may be made at any time after service of the particulars of claim. Paragraphs 4.3 and 4.4 or the Practice Direction state the information which must be included in the application notice and evidence in support.

12.7.7 The application notice should be filed in the Listing Office, Room WG5, for hearing by the Judge in charge of the Jury list, or another designated Judge.

Summary disposal

12.7.8 Section 8 of the Act gives the court power to dispose summarily of the claimant's claim. The court may;

    (1) dismiss the claim if it appears that it has no realistic prospect of success and there is no reason why it should be tried, or

    (2) give judgment for the claimant and grant him summary relief.

12.7.9 Summary relief includes the following;

    (1) a declaration that the statement was false and defamatory of the claimant,

    (2) an order that the defendant publish or cause to be published a suitable correction and apology,

    (3) damages not exceeding £10,000,

    (4) an order restraining the defendant from publishing or further publishing the matter complained of.

12.7.10 Applications for summary disposal are dealt with in Rule 53.2 and paragraphs 5.1 to 5.3 of the Part 53 Practice Direction. Substantial claims and those involving the Police authorities or the Media or those seeking an order restraining publication will be dealt with by the Judge in charge of the Jury list or another designated Judge, and the application notice should be filed in the Listing Office, Room WG5. Applications for summary disposal in other defamation claims may be made at first instance to a Master.

12.7.11 An application notice for summary disposal must state;

    (1) that it is an application for summary disposal made in accordance with section 8 of the Act,

    (2) the matters set out in paragraph 2(3) of the Part 24 Practice Direction, and

    (3) whether or not the defendant has made an offer to make amends under section 2 of the Act, and whether or not it has been withdrawn.

The application may be made at any time after service of the particulars of claim and the provisions of Rule 24.4(1)(a) and (b) do not apply.

12.7.12 Where the court has made an order for summary relief as in 12.7.9(2) above (specifying the date by which the parties should agree the content, time, manner, form and place of publication of the correction and apology) and the parties are unable to comply within the specified time, the claimant must prepare a summary of the court's judgment and serve it on the other parties within 3 days following the date specified in the order for the content to be agreed by the parties[1].

12.7.13 If the parties are unable to agree the summary, they must within 3 days of its receipt, apply to the court by;

---

[1] Para. 5.3 of the Part 53 practice direction

(1) filing an application notice, and

(2) filing and serving on all the other parties a copy of the summary showing the revisions they wish to make to it.

The court (normally the Judge who delivered the judgment) will then settle the summary.

Statements read in Court

12.7.14 Paragraph 6 of the Practice Direction only applies where a party wishes to accept a Part 36 offer, Part 36 payment or other offer of settlement.

12.7.15 An application for permission to make the statement before a Judge in Court may be made before or after acceptance of the Part 36 offer, Part 36 payment or other offer to settle, and should be made in accordance with Part 23 to the Senior Master, or if he is not available, to the Practice Master. The application notice, together with a copy of the statement, should be filed in the Masters' Support Unit, Room E17.

12.7.16 Where permission has been given, the parties may take a copy of the order to the Listing Office, Room WG5 for the matter will be listed before the Judge in charge of the Jury List for mention. Otherwise, the Action Department will send the court file to the Listing Office for the matter to be listed.

12.8 References to the Court of Justice of the European Communities:

12.8.1 A party wishing to apply for an order[1] under RSC O.114 (Schedule 1 to the **1B–90** CPR) may do so by application before or at the trial or hearing. An application made before the trial or hearing should be made in accordance with Part 23.

12.8.2 Before making an order for reference, the Court will pay close attention to the terms of the appropriate article, to RSC O.114, to form PF 109 and to the "Guidance of the Court of Justice of the European Communities on References by National Courts for Preliminary Rulings" which may be found in the *Practice Direction (ECJ References: Procedure)* [1999] 1 W.L.R. 260.

12.8.3 It is the responsibility of the Court, rather than the parties, to settle the terms of the reference. This should identify as clearly, succinctly and simply as the nature of the case permits the question to which the British court seeks an answer and it is very desirable that language should be used which lends itself readily to translation.

12.8.4 The referring court should, in a single document scheduled to the order (in form PF 109);

(1) identify the parties and summarise the nature and history of the proceedings,

(2) summarise the salient facts, indicating whether these are proved or admitted or assumed,

(3) make reference to the rules of national law (substantive and procedural) relevant to the dispute,

(4) summarise the contentions of the parties as far as relevant,

(5) explain why a ruling of the European Court is sought, identifying the EC provisions whose effect is in issue, and

(6) formulate, without avoidable complexity, the question(s) to which an answer is requested.

12.8.5 Where the document is in the form of a judgment, passages which are not relevant to the reference should be omitted from the text scheduled to the order.

---

[1] An "order" means an order referring a question to the European Court for a preliminary ruling under article 234 (formerly article 177) of the Treaty establishing the European Community, article 150 of the Treaty establishing the European Atomic Energy Community or article 41 of the Treaty establishing the European Coal and Steel Community, or for a ruling on the interpretation of any of the Brussels Conventions (within the meaning of s. 1(1) of the Civil Jurisdiction and Judgments Act 1982) or any of the instruments referred to in s.1 of the Contracts (Applicable Law) Act 1990.

Incorporation of appendices, annexes or enclosures as part of the document should be avoided, unless the relevant passages lend themselves readily to translation and are clearly identified.

12.8.6 When the order of reference has been approved by the Judge and sealed by the court, the order, together with any other necessary documents should be promptly passed to Room E.13 for the attention of the Senior Master of the Queen's Bench Division, for transmission to Luxembourg without avoidable delay.

12.9 Group Litigation Orders "GLOs":

1B–91 12.9.1 Section III of Part 19 and the Practice Direction—Group Litigation deal with claims where multiple parties are claimants.

12.9.2 When considering applying for a GLO, the applicant should contact the Law Society at 113 Chancery Lane, London WC2A 1PL, who may be able to assist in putting the applicant in contact with other parties who may also be interested in applying for a GLO in the same matter.

12.9.3 The consent of either the Lord Chief Justice or the Vice-Chancellor to the GLO is required. In the Queen's Bench Division the application should be made to the Senior Master in accordance with Part 23. If the Senior Master is minded to make the GLO he will forward a copy of the application notice and any written evidence to the Lord Chief Justice. The application notice should include the information set out in paragraph 3.2 of the Practice Direction.

12.9.4 A group register will be set up and maintained in the court of all the parties to the group of claims to be managed under the GLO. In order to publicise the GLO when it has been made, a copy should be supplied to the Law Society and to the Senior Master. A record of each GLO made will be maintained in the Central Office.

12.9.5 The Practice Direction sets out how the group litigation will be managed. In particular, a managing judge will be appointed. The case management directions are likely to direct;
- (1) that a "Group Particulars of Claim" containing the various claims of the claimants on the group register are served,
- (2) that one claim proceed as a "test" claim, and
- (3) a cut-off date after which no additions may be made to the group register.

ANNEX 1

FEES TO BE TAKEN

1B–92 | *Column 1* | *Column 2* |
| --- | --- |
| Number and description of fee | Amount of fee |

Section 1. Fees payable in the High Court only

1. Commencement of proceedings

1.1 On the commencement of originating proceedings (including originating proceedings issued after leave to issue is granted) to recover a sum of money, where the sum claimed:	
(a) does not exceed £50,000	£400
(b) exceeds £50,000 but does not exceed £100,000	£600
(c) exceeds £100,000 but does not exceed £150,000	£700

Column 1	Column 2	**1B–92**
Number and description of fee	Amount of fee	

Column 1	Column 2
(d) exceeds £150,000 or is not limited	£800
1.2 On the commencement of originating proceedings for any other remedy or relief (including originating proceedings issued after leave to issue is granted)	£180

Fees 1.1 and 1.2 Recovery of land or goods
Where a claim for money is additional or alternative to a claim for recovery of land or goods, only fee 1.2 shall be payable.

Fees 1.1 and 1.2 Claims other than recovery of land or goods
Where a claim for money is additional to a non money claim (other than a claim for recovery of land or goods) then fee 1.1 shall be payable in addition to fee 1.2. Where a claim for money is alternative to a non money claim (other than a claim for recovery of land or goods), only fee 1.1 shall be payable.

Fees 1.1 and 1.2 Generally
Where more than one non money claim is made in the same proceedings, fee 1.2 shall be payable once only, in addition to any fee which may be payable under fee 1.1.

Fees 1.1 and 1.2 shall not be payable where fee 1.5(b), fee 4.1 or fee 6 apply.

Fees 1.1 and 1.2 Amendment of claim or counterclaim
Where the claim or counterclaim is amended, and the fee paid before amendment is less than that which would have been payable if the document, as amended, had been so drawn in the first instance, the party amending the document shall pay the difference.

Column 1	Column 2
1.3 On the filing of proceedings against a party or parties not named in the originating proceedings	£30

Fee 1.3 shall be payable by a defendant who adds or substitutes a party or parties to the proceedings or by a claimant who adds or substitutes a defendant or defendants.

Column 1	Column 2
1.4 On the filing of a counterclaim	The same fee as if the relief or remedy sought were the subject of separate proceedings

1B–92

Column 1 Number and description of fee	*Column 2* Amount of fee
1.5 (a) On an application for leave to issue originating proceedings	£30
(b) On an application for an order under Part III of the Solicitors Act 1974 for the assessment of costs payable to a solicitor by his client or on the commencement of costs-only proceedings.	£30

2. General Fees

2.1 On the claimant filing an allocation questionnaire; or	£120

- where the court dispenses with the need for an allocation questionnaire, within 14 days of the date of despatch of the notice of allocation to track; or
- where the CPR or a Practice Direction provide for automatic allocation or provide that the rules on allocation shall not apply, within 28 days of the filing of the defence (or the filing of the last defence if there is more than one defendant), or within 28 days of the expiry of the time permitted for filing all defences if sooner

Fee 2.1 shall be payable by the claimant except where the action is proceeding on the counterclaim alone, when it shall be payable by the defendant -

- on the defendant filing an allocation questionnaire; or
- where the court dispenses with the need for an allocation questionnaire, within 14 days of the date of despatch of the notice of allocation to track; or
- where the CPR or a Practice Direction provide for automatic allocation or provide that the rules on allocation shall not apply, within 28 days of the filing of the defence to the counterclaim (or the filing of the last defence to the counterclaim if there is more than one party entitled to file a defence to a counterclaim), or within 28 days of the expiry of the time permitted for filing all defences to the counterclaim if sooner

Column 1	*Column 2*	**1B-92**
Number and description of fee	Amount of fee	

2.2 On the claimant filing a listing questionnaire; or
- where the court fixes the trial date or trial week without the need for a listing question-naire, within 14 days of the date of despatch of the notice (or the date when oral notice is given if no written notice is given) of the trial week or the trial date if no trial week is fixed

£600

Fee 2.2 shall be payable by the claimant except where the action is proceeding on the counterclaim alone, when it shall be payable by the defendant -
- on the defendant filing a listing question-naire; or
- where the court fixes the trial date or trial week without the need for a listing question-naire, within 14 days of the date of despatch of the notice (or the date when oral notice is given if no written notice is given) of the trial week or the trial date if no trial week is fixed

Where the court receives notice in writing -
- before the trial date has been fixed; or
- where a trial date has been fixed, at least 7 days before the trial date

from the party who paid fee 2.2 that the case is settled or discontinued, fee 2.2 shall be refunded.

Fees 2.1 and 2.2 Generally
Fees 2.1 and 2.2 shall be payable as appropriate where the court allocates a case to a track for a trial of the assessment of damages.
Fees 2.1 and 2.2 shall not be payable in relation to claims managed under a GLO after that GlO is made.
Fees 2.1 and 2.2 shall be payable once only in the same proceedings.
Fees 2.1 and 2.2 shall be payable where the pro-cedure in Part 8 of the CPR is used.

1B–92

Column 1 Number and description of fee	*Column 2* Amount of fee
2.3(a) Where permission to appeal is not required or has been granted by the lower court - • on filing an appellant's notice; or • on filing a respondent's notice where the respondent is appealing or wishes to ask the appeal court to uphold the order of the lower court for reasons different from or additional to those given by the lower court.	£100
2.3(b) Where in an appeal notice permission to appeal or an extension of timefor appealing is applied for (or both are applied for) - on filing an appellant's notice, or where the respondent is appealing, on filing a respondent's notice.	£150

Where fee 2.3(b) has been paid and permission to appeal (or extension of time) is not granted, £100 shall be refunded to the party who paid fee 2.3(b).

Fees 2.3(a) and (b)
Fees 2.3(a) and (b) do not apply on appeals against a decision made in detailed assessment proceedings.

2.4 On an application on notice where no other fee is specified	£60
2.5 On an application by consent or without notice for a judgment or order where no other fee is specified	£30

For the purpose of fee 2.5 a request for a judgment or order on admission or in default shall not constitute an application and no fee shall be payable.

Fees 2.4 and 2.5
Fees 2.4 and 2.5 shall not be payable when an application is made in an appeal notice or is filed at the same time as an appeal notice

2.6 On an application for a summons or order for a witness to attend court to be examined on oath, other than an application for which fee 3.2 is payable	£30
2.7 On an application to vary a judgment or suspend enforcement (where more than one remedy is sought in the same application only one fee shall be payable)	£30

3. Enforcement

3.1 On sealing a writ of execution/possession/delivery	£20

Column 1	Column 2	**1B–92**
Number and description of fee	Amount of fee	

Where the recovery of a sum of money is sought in addition to a writ of possession and delivery, no further fee is payable.

3.2 On an application to question a judgment debtor or other person on oath in connection with enforcement of a judgment	£40
3.3 On an application for a garnishee order nisi (to show cause)or a charging order nisi (to show cause), or the appointment of a receiver by way of equitable execution	£50

Fee 3.3 shall be payable in respect of each party against whom the order is sought.

3.4 On an application for a judgment summons	£90
3.5 On a request or application to register a judgment or order, or for leave to enforce an arbitration award, or for a certified copy of a judgment or order for use abroad	£30

4. Miscellaneous proceedings or matters
Bills of Sale

4.1 On filing any document under the Bills of Sale Acts 1878 and 1882 or an an application under Section 15 of the Bills of Sale Act 1878 for an order that a memorandum of satisfaction be written on a registered copy of the bill	£10

Searches

4.2 For an official certificate of the result of a search for each name, in any register or index held by the court; or in the Court Funds Office, for an official certificate of the result of a search of unclaimed balances for a specified period of up to 50 years	£5
4.3 On a search in person of the bankruptcy and companies records, including inspection, for each 15 minutes or part of 15 minutes	£5

Judge sitting as arbitrator
4.4 On the appointment of -

(a) a judge of the Commercial Court as an arbitrator or umpire under section 93 of the Arbitration Act 1996; or	£1,800

1B–92   *Column 1*   *Column 2*

Number and description of fee   Amount of
                                                      fee

(b) a judge of the Technology and Construction   £1,400
Court as an arbitrator or umpire under section
93 of the Arbitration Act 1996

Where fee 4.4 has been paid on the appointment
of a judge of the Commercial Court or a judge
of the Technology and Construction Court as an
arbitrator or umpire but the arbitration does not
proceed to a hearing or an award, the fee shall
be refunded.

4.5 For every day or part of a day (after the first
day) of the hearing before -

(a) a judge of the Commercial Court; or   £1,800

(b) a judge of the Technology and Construction   £1,400
Court

so appointed as arbitrator or umpire

Section 2. Fees payable in both the High Court
and in the Court of Appeal

7. Copy Documents

7.1 On a request for a copy of any document
(other than where fee 7.2 applies):

(a) for the first page (except the first page of a   £1
subsequent copy of the same document supplied
at the same time)

(b) per page in any other case   20p

Fee 7.1 shall be payable for a faxed copy or for
examining a plain copy and marking it as an
examined copy.

Fee 7.1 shall be payable whether or not the copy
is issued as an office copy.

7.2 On a request for a copy of a document   20p
required in connection with proceedings and
supplied by the party making the request at the
time of copying, for each page

7.3 On a request for a copy of a document on a   £3
computer disk or in other electronic form, for
each such copy

8. Affidavits

8.1 On taking an affidavit or an affirmation or
attestation upon honour in lieu of an affidavit or
a declaration except for the purpose of receipt of
dividends from the Accountant General and for
a declaration by a shorthand writer appointed in
insolvency proceedings

- for each person making any of the above   £5

8.2 For each exhibit referred to in an affidavit,   £2
affirmation, attestation or declaration for which
fee 8.1 is payable

Column 1	Column 2
Number and description of fee	Amount of fee

Section 3. Fees payable in the Court of Appeal only

9.1(a) Where in an appeal notice permission to appeal or an extension of time for appealing is applied for (or both are applied for) -
- on filing an appellant's notice; or
- where the respondent is appealing, on filing a respondent's notice

£100

9.1(b) Where permission to appeal is not required or has been granted by the lower court -

- on filing an appellant's notice; or
- on filing a respondent's notice where the respondent is appealing

£200

9.1(c) On the appellant filing an appeal questionnaire (unless the appellant has paid fee 9.1(b)), or on the respondent filing an appeal questionnaire (unless the respondent has paid fee 9.1(b))

£200

9.2 On filing a respondent's notice where the respondent wishes to ask the appeal court to uphold the order of the lower court for reasons different from or additional to those given by the lower court

£100

9.3 On filing an application notice Fee 9.3 shall not be payable for an application made in an appeal notice

£100

Section 4. Fees payable on the determination of costs

10. Determination of costs

Transitional Provision

Where a bill of costs or a request for detailed assessment or a request for a detailed assessment hearing is filed pursuant to an order made by the court before the coming into operation of this Order, or an application is made to review a taxing officer's decision made before the coming into operation of this Order, the fees payable shall be those which applied immediately before this Order came into force.

10.1 On the filing of a request for detailed assessment where the party filing the request is legally aided or is funded by the LSC and no other party is ordered to pay the costs of the proceedings

£120

1B–92

Column 1 Number and description of fee	*Column 2* Amount of fee
10.2 On the filing of a request for a detailed assessment hearing in any case where fee 10.1 does not apply; or on the filing of a request for a hearing date for the assessment of costs payable to a solicitor by his client pursuant to an order under Part III of the Solicitors Act 1974 Where there is a combined party and party and legal aid, or a combined party and party and LSC, or a combined party and party, legal aid and LSC determination of costs, fee 10.2 shall be attributed proportionately to the party and party, legal aid, or LSC (as the case may be) portions of the bill on the basis of the amount allowed.	£250
10.3 On a request for the issue of a default costs certificate	£40
10.4 On an appeal against a decision made in detailed assessment proceedings or on a request or an application to set aside a default costs certificate	£100
10.5 On applying for the court's approval of a certificate of costs payable from the Community Legal Service Fund	£30

Fee 10.5 is payable at the time of applying for the court's approval and is recoverable only against the Community Legal Service Fund.

ANNEX 2

1B–93 The following is a list of the abbreviations commonly used by Masters on endorsements of orders, though there may be some variation as between individual Masters.

A.D.R	Alternative Dispute Resolution
Aff.	Affidavit
A.M-T	Allocate to multi-track
A.N.	Appointment Notice
App.	Application
A.Q.	Allocation Questionnaire
A.S.	Assessed summarily
B.N.L.T.	By no later than
C.C.	County Court
C.I.A.	Costs in the application
C.I.A.E.	Costs in any event
C.I.C.	Costs in the case

Cl.	Claimant
Col.	Certificate for Counsel
C.M.C.	Case Management Conference
C.O.A.	Charging order absolute
C.O.C.B.	Costs of and caused by
C.O.S.C.	Charging order to show cause
C.R.	Costs reserved
C.T.R.	Costs of today reserved
D./Def	Defendant/Defence
D.A.I/N.A.	Detailed assessment if not agreed
Disc.	Disclosure
Dism.	Dismissed
Disp. C/S.	Dispense with requirement of certificate of service
F.C.	Fixed costs
F.I.	Further information
F.O.	Further order
F.O.D.	First open date
G.O.A.	Garnishee order absolute
G.O.S.C.	Garnishee order to show cause
I.A.E.	In any event
I.B.	Indemnity basis
Insp.	Inspection
J.	Judgment (as in Part 24 applications)
L.A.	Legal Aid
L.A.A.	Legal Aid assessment
L.Q.	Listing Questionnaire
O.	Order
On C.Serv.	On producing certificate of service
O. Exam.	Oral examination
P/C	Particulars of claim
P.D.	Practice direction
Pm.	Permission
Pm. A.	Permission to apply
Pm. R.	Permission to restore
Pm. R.F.D.	Permission to restore for further directions
Pt.	Part
P.R.A.	Private room appointment
R.	Rule
S.A.	Set aside/Special allowance
S.O.J.	Service out of the jurisdiction
S/C	Statement of Case
S.B.	Standard basis
S/T	Statement of truth

Tfr.	Transfer
W.N.	Without notice
W.C.O.	Wasted Costs Order
W.S.	Witness statement

SECTION 2

SPECIALIST PROCEEDINGS UNDER PART 49 OF THE CIVIL PROCEDURE RULES

2A COMMERCIAL COURTS

PART 58—COMMERCIAL COURT

Contents

Editorial introduction

Part 58 is added to the CPR by Civil Procedure (Amendment No. 5) Rules 2001 **2A–1**
(S.I. 2001 No. 4015), and came into force on March 25, 2002.

Related Sources

- Part 62—Arbitration Claims (see para. 2E–5 *et seq.*) **2A–2**
- The Admiralty and Commercial Courts Guide (see para. 2A–37 *et seq.*)
- Practice Direction—Arbitrations (see para. 2E–41 *et seq.* above)
- Arbitration Act 1950, Pt II (see para. 2E–51 *et seq.* above)
- Arbitration Act 1996 (see para. 2E–76 *et seq.* above)
- Civil Procedure Rules including CPR 1, 2, 6, 7, 8, 9, 10, 11, 12, 14, 15, 16, 17, 18, 20, 22, 23, 24, 25, 32, 34, 35, 43–48, 70, 71,72, 73 and 74.

Forms

- N1(CC) Claim form **2A–3**
- N1C(CC) Notes for defendant
- N9(CC) Acknowledgment of service
- N208(CC) Claim form (Part 8)
- N208C(CC) Notes for defendant
- N210(CC) Acknowledgment of service (Part 8)
- N211(CC) Claim form (Part 20)
- N211C(CC) Notes for Part 20 defendant
- N213(CC) Acknowledgment of service (Part 20)
- N244(CC) Application Notice
- N265(CC) List of documents: standard disclosure

[THE NEXT PARAGRAPH IS 2A–5.]

Scopeof this Part and interpretation[1]

2A-5   58.1—(1) **This Part applies to claims in the Commercial Court of the Queen's Bench Division.**

(2) **In this Part and its practice direction, "commercial claim" means any claim arising out of the transaction of trade and commerce and includes any claim relating to—**

    (a) **a business document or contract;**

    (b) **the export or import of goods;**

    (c) **the carriage of goods by land, sea, air or pipeline;**

    (d) **the exploitation of oil and gas reserves or other natural resources;**

    (e) **insurance and re-insurance;**

    (f) **banking and financial services;**

    (g) **the operation of markets and exchanges;**

    (h) **the purchase and sale of commodities;**

    (i) **the construction of ships;**

    (j) **business agency; and**

    (k) **arbitration.**

2A-6   *Note* —The Commercial Court may continue to hear a banking case notwithstanding that the debt is secured by a mortgage and that High Court claims for possession of land subject to mortgage are assigned to the Chancery Division by Practice Direction – Possession Claims, supplementing CPR 55 (*Midland Bank Ltd v. Stamp* [1978] 1 W.L.R. 627; [1978] 3 All E.R. 1, a case under the pre-October 1, 2001 law).

Specialist list[2]

2A-7   58.2—(1) **The commercial list is a specialist list for claims proceeding in the Commercial Court.**

(2) **One of the judges of the Commercial Court shall be in charge of the commercial list.**

Application of the Civil Procedure Rules[3]

2A-8   58.3 **These Rules and their practice directions apply to claims in the commercial list unless this Part or a practice direction provides otherwise.**

Proceedings in the commercial list[4]

2A-9   58.4—(1) **A commercial claim may be started in the commercial list.**

(2) **Rule 30.5 applies to claims in the commercial list, except**

---

[1] Introduced by Civil Procedure (Amendment No. 5) Rules 2001 (S.I. 2001 No. 4015).
[2] Introduced by Civil Procedure (Amendment No. 5) Rules 2001 (S.I. 2001 No. 4015).
[3] Introduced by Civil Procedure (Amendment No. 5) Rules 2001 (S.I. 2001 No. 4015).
[4] Introduced by Civil Procedure (Amendment No. 5) Rules 2001 (S.I. 2001 No. 4015) and amended by Civil Procedure (Amendment No. 4) Rules 2005 (S.I. 2005 No. 3515).

that a Commercial Court judge may order a claim to be transferred to any other specialist list.

(Rule 30.5(3) provides that an application for the transfer of proceedings to or from a specialist list must be made to a judge dealing with claims in that list).

Claim form and particulars of claim[1]

58.5—(1) If, in a Part 7 claim, particulars of claim are not   2A–10
contained in or served with the claim form—

  (a) the claim form must state that, if an acknowledgment of service is filed which indicates an intention to defend the claim, particulars of claim will follow;

  (b) when the claim form is served, it must be accompanied by the documents specified in rule 7.8(1);

  (c) the claimant must serve particulars of claim within 28 days of the filing of an acknowledgment of service which indicates an intention to defend; and

  (d) rule 7.4(2) does not apply.

(2) A statement of value is not required to be included in the claim form.

(3) If the claimant is claiming interest, he must—

  (a) include a statement to that effect; and

  (b) give the details set out in rule 16.4(2),

in both the claim form and the particulars of claim.

Acknowledgment of service[2]

58.6—(1) A defendant must file an acknowledgment of service in   2A–11
every case.

(2) Unless paragraph (3) applies, the period for filing an acknowledgment of service is 14 days after service of the claim form.

(3) Where the claim form is served out of the jurisdiction, or on the agent of a defendant who is overseas, the time periods provided by rules 6.16(4) , 6.21(4) and 6.22 apply after service of the claim form.

Disputing the court's jurisdiction[3]

58.7—(1) Part 11 applies to claims in the commercial list with   2A–12
the modifications set out in this rule.

(2) An application under rule 11(1) must be made within 28 days after filing an acknowledgment of service.

(3) If the defendant files an acknowledgment of service indicat-

---

[1] Introduced by Civil Procedure (Amendment No. 5) Rules 2001 (S.I. 2001 No. 4015).
[2] Introduced by Civil Procedure (Amendment No. 5) Rules 2001 (S.I. 2001 No. 4015).
[3] Introduced by Civil Procedure (Amendment No. 5) Rules 2001 (S.I. 2001 No. 4015).

ing an intention to dispute the court's jurisdiction, the claimant need not serve particulars of claim before the hearing of the application.

Default judgment[1]

2A-13   **58.8**—(1) If, in a Part 7 claim in the commercial list, a defendant fails to file an acknowledgment of service, the claimant need not serve particulars of claim before he may obtain or apply for default judgment in accordance with Part 12.

(2) Rule 12.6(1) applies with the modification that paragraph (a) shall be read as if it referred to the claim form instead of the particulars of claim.

Admissions[2]

2A-14   **58.9**—(1) Rule 14.5 does not apply to claims in the commercial list.

(2) If the defendant admits part of a claim for a specified amount of money, the claimant may apply under rule 14.3 for judgment on the admission.

(3) Rule 14.14(1) applies with the modification that paragraph (a) shall be read as if it referred to the claim form instead of the particulars of claim.

Defence and Reply[3]

2A-15   **58.10**—(1) Part 15 (defence and reply) applies to claims in the commercial list with the modification to rule 15.8 that the claimant must—

(a) **file any reply to a defence; and**
(b) **serve it on all other parties,**
within 21 days after service of the defence.

(2) Rule 6.23 (period for filing a defence where the claim form is served out of the jurisdiction) applies to claims in the commercial list, except that if the particulars of claim are served after the defendant has filed an acknowledgment of service the period for filing a defence is 28 days from service of the particulars of claim.

Statements of case[4]

2A-16   **58.11** The court may at any time before or after the issue of the claim form order a claim in the commercial list to proceed without the filing or service of statements of case.

---

[1] Introduced by Civil Procedure (Amendment No. 5) Rules 2001 (S.I. 2001 No. 4015).
[2] Introduced by Civil Procedure (Amendment No. 5) Rules 2001 (S.I. 2001 No. 4015).
[3] Introduced by Civil Procedure (Amendment No. 5) Rules 2001 (S.I. 2001 No. 4015).
[4] Introduced by Civil Procedure (Amendment No. 5) Rules 2001 (S.I. 2001 No. 4015).

Part 8 claims[1]

58.12 Part 8 applies to claims in the commercial list, with the modification that a defendant to a Part 8 claim who wishes to rely on written evidence must file and serve it within 28 days after filing an acknowledgment of service.   **2A–17**

Case management[2]

58.13—(1) All proceedings in the commercial list are treated as being allocated to the multi-track and Part 26 does not apply.   **2A–18**

(2) The following parts only of Part 29 apply—
  (a) rule 29.3(2) (legal representative to attend case management conferences and pre-trial reviews);
  (b) rule 29.5 (variation of case management timetable) with the exception of rule 29.5(1)(c).

(3) As soon as practicable the court will hold a case management conference which must be fixed in accordance with the practice direction.

(4) At the case management conference or at any hearing at which the parties are represented the court may give such directions for the management of the case as it considers appropriate.

Disclosure—ships papers[3]

58.14—(1) If, in proceedings relating to a marine insurance policy, the underwriters apply for specific disclosure under rule 31.12, the court may—   **2A–19**
  (a) order a party to produce all the ships papers; and
  (b) require that party to use his best endeavours to obtain and disclose documents which are not or have not been in his control.

(2) An order under this rule may be made at any stage of the proceedings and on such terms, if any, as to staying the proceedings or otherwise, as the court thinks fit.

The Order

(a) Although the insurer applying for an order is usually the defendant, the procedure is available to an insurer who is suing as claimant, *e.g.* to recover overpayments inducted by deception or mistake (*Boulton v. Houlder Bros.* [1904] 1 K.B. 784, CA).   **2A–20**

(b) *Persons to whom the order is directed.* The order is usually directed to the claimant himself and to all persons interested in the proceeding and in the insurance (*China Steamship Co v. Commercial Union Assurance Co* (1881) 8 QBD 142); "persons interested" means those interested on the claimant's side, not the underwriters themselves (*ibid.*). See also, as to the person to whom the order is to be directed, *China Traders Co v. Royal Exchange Assurance* [1898] 2 Q.B. 187 at 189; *London Insurance Co v. Chambers* (1900) 5 Com.Cas. 241. The affidavit or witness statement in answer must show the interest of the deponent or may be rejected as defective (*Avon v. Miall* (unrep.) November 27, 1925, Branson J. in Chambers) and must account for all documents in

---

[1] Introduced by Civil Procedure (Amendment No. 5) Rules 2001 (S.I. 2001 No. 4015).
[2] Introduced by Civil Procedure (Amendment No. 5) Rules 2001 (S.I. 2001 No. 4015).
[3] Introduced by Civil Procedure (Amendment No. 5) Rules 2001 (S.I. 2001 No. 4015).

COMMERCIAL COURT

the possession and control of those to whom the order is addressed (*Graham etc., Co v. Motor Union Co* [1922] 1 K.B. 563); if a particular "interested person" is thought to have relevant documents the order may expressly require an affidavit from him (*ibid.*).

(c) *Documents to be disclosed.* All material documents may be ordered to be disclosed and it is not a reason for refusing to make disclosure that they are not in the possession of the person to whom the order is directed: he must, in such a case, use all reasonable endeavors to obtain the documents and will only be excused on showing that these have been unavailing; thus a mortgagee must, if he can, obtain disclosure of the documents in possession of the mortgagor who operated the ship (*West of England Bank v. Canton Insurance Co* (1877) 2 Ex.D. 472) and cargo owners suing as claimants must, if they can, obtain disclosure of the papers in possession of the shipowners or their servants (*Teneria Moderna Franco Espanola v. New Zealand Insurance Co* [1924] 1 K.B. 79, CA).

(d) *Order staying proceedings.* The purpose of a stay may be to postpone the time for delivery of a defence or to ensure compliance with the order. It is a matter of discretion whether, and at what stage, a stay will be granted (*Probatina Shipping Co v. Sun Insurance Office* [1974] Q.B. 635; [1974] 2 All E.R. 478; [1974] 2 All E.R. 478, CA). It will be removed on compliance with the order or on showing to the Court that all reasonable endeavours have been made to comply (see cases cited in sub-paragraphs (b) and (c)).

A stay does not preclude the defendant from applying for a further and better information (*Abdela v. Mutual Property Investment Ltd* [1921] W.N. 23, CA) nor prevent a party from recovering costs for the reasonable preparation of his case while the stay is in force (*Pecheries Ostendaises v. Merchants' Marine Insurance Co* [1928] 1 K.B. 750, CA).

Judgments and orders[1]

2A–21   **58.15—(1) Except for orders made by the court on its own initiative and unless the court orders otherwise, every judgment or order will be drawn up by the parties, and rule 40.3 is modified accordingly.**

(2) An application for a consent order must include a draft of the proposed order signed on behalf of all the parties to whom it relates.

(3) Rule 40.6 (consent judgments and orders) does not apply.

---

[1] Introduced by Civil Procedure (Amendment No. 5) Rules 2001 (S.I. 2001 No. 4015).

PRACTICE DIRECTION—COMMERCIAL COURT

This Practice Direction supplements CPR Part 58

General

1.1 This practice direction applies to commercial claims proceed-   **2A–22**
ing in the commercial list of the Queen's Bench Division. It
supersedes all previous practice directions and practice statements in
the Commercial Court.

1.2 All proceedings in the commercial list, including any appeal
from a judgment, order or decision of a master or district judge
before the proceedings were transferred to the Commercial Court,
will be heard or determined by a Commercial Court judge, except
that—

(1)   another judge of the Queen's Bench Division or Chancery
      Division may hear urgent applications if no Commercial
      Court judge is available; and

(2)   unless the court otherwise orders, any application relating
      to the enforcement of a Commercial Court judgment or or-
      der for the payment of money will be dealt with by a master
      of the Queen's Bench Division or a district judge.

1.3 Provisions in other practice directions which refer to a master
or district judge are to be read, in relation to claims in the commercial list, as if they referred to a Commercial Court judge.

1.4 The Admiralty and Commercial Registry in the Royal Courts
of Justice is the administrative office of the court for all proceedings
in the commercial list.

Starting proceedings in the Commercial Court

2.1 Claims in the Commercial Court must be issued in the   **2A–23**
Admiralty and Commercial Registry.

2.2 When the Registry is closed, a request to issue a claim form
may be made by fax, using the procedure set out in Appendix A to
this practice direction. If a request is made which complies with that
procedure, the claim form is issued when the fax is received by the
Registry.

2.3 The claim form must be marked in the top right hand corner
"Queen's Bench Division, Commercial Court".

2.4 A claimant starting proceedings in the commercial list, other
than an arbitration claim, must use practice form **N1(CC)** for Part 7
claims or practice form **N208(CC)** for Part 8 claims.

Applications before proceedings are issued

3.1 A party who intends to bring a claim in the commercial list   **2A–24**
must make any application before the claim form is issued to a Commercial Court judge.

3.2 The written evidence in support of such an application must
state that the claimant intends to bring proceedings in the commercial list.

3.3 If the Commercial Court judge hearing the application considers that the proceedings should not be brought in the commercial
list, he may adjourn the application to be heard by a master or by a
judge who is not a Commercial Court judge.

Transferring proceedings to or from the Commercial Court

2A–25　**4.1** If an application is made to a court other than the Commercial Court to transfer proceedings to the commercial list, the other court may—

    (1)　adjourn the application to be heard by a Commercial Court judge; or

    (2)　dismiss the application.

4.2 If the Commercial Court orders proceedings to be transferred to the commercial list—

    (1)　it will order them to be transferred to the Royal Courts of Justice; and

    (2)　it may give case management directions.

4.3 An application by a defendant, including a Part 20 defendant, for an order transferring proceedings from the commercial list should be made promptly and normally not later than the first case management conference.

4.4 A party applying to the Commercial Court to transfer a claim to the commercial list must give notice of the application to the court in which the claim is proceeding, and the Commercial Court will not make an order for transfer until it is satisfied that such notice has been given.

Acknowledgment of service

2A–26　**5.1** For Part 7 claims, a defendant must file an acknowledgment of service using practice form **N9(CC)**.

5.2 For Part 8 claims, a defendant must file an acknowledgment of service using practice form **N210(CC)**.

Default judgment and admissions

2A–27　<u>**6.** The practice directions supplementing Parts 12 and 14 apply</u> with the following modifications—

    <u>(1)　paragraph 4.1(1) of the practice direction supplementing</u> Part 12 is to be read as referring to the service of the claim form; and

    (2)　the references to "particulars of claim" in paragraphs 2.1, 3.1 and 3.2 of the practice direction supplementing Part 14 are to be read as referring to the claim form.

Variation of time limits

2A–28　<u>**7.1** If the parties, in accordance with rule 2.11, agree in writing to</u> <u>vary a time limit, the claimant must notify the court in writing,</u> giving brief written reasons for the agreed variation.

7.2 The court may make an order overriding an agreement by the parties varying a time limit.

Amendments

2A–29　**8.** Paragraph 2.2 of the practice direction supplementing Part 17 is modified so that amendments to a statement of case must show the original text, unless the court orders otherwise.

Service of documents

2A–30　**9.** Unless the court orders otherwise, the Commercial Court will not serve documents or orders and service must be effected by the parties.

Case management

10.1 The following parts only of the practice direction supplement-   **2A–31**
ing Part 29 apply—

    (1)   paragraph 5 (case management conferences), excluding paragraph 5.9 and modified so far as is made necessary by other specific provisions of this practice direction; and

    (2)   paragraph 7 (failure to comply with case management directions).

10.2 If the proceedings are started in the commercial list, the claimant must apply for a case management conference—

    (a)   for a Part 7 claim, within 14 days of the date when all defendants who intend to file and serve a defence have done so; and

    (b)   for a Part 8 claim, within 14 days of the date when all defendants who intend to serve evidence have done so.

10.3 If the proceedings are transferred to the commercial list, the claimant must apply for a case management conference within 14 days of the date of the order transferring them, unless the judge held, or gave directions for, a case management conference when he made the order transferring the proceedings.

10.4 Any party may, at a time earlier than that provided in paragraphs 10.2 or 10.3, apply in writing to the court to fix a case management conference.

10.5 If the claimant does not make an application in accordance with paragraphs 10.2 or 10.3, any other party may apply for a case management conference.

10.6 The court may fix a case management conference at any time on its own initiative. If it does so, the court will give at least 7 days notice to the parties, unless there are compelling reasons for a shorter period of notice.

10.7 Not less than 7 days before a case management conference, each party must file and serve—

    (1)   a completed case management information sheet; and

    (2)   an application notice for any order which that party intends to seek at the case management conference, other than directions referred to in the case management information sheet.

10.8 Unless the court orders otherwise, the claimant, in consultation with the other parties, must prepare—

    (1)   a case memorandum, containing a short and uncontroversial summary of what the case is about and of its material case history;

    (2)   a list of issues, with a section listing important matters which are not in dispute; and

    (3)   a case management bundle containing—

        (a) the claim form;

        (b) all statements of case (excluding schedules), except that, if a summary of a statement of case has been filed, the bundle should contain the summary, and not the full statement of case;

   (c) the case memorandum;

   (d) the list of issues;

   (e) the case management information sheets and, if a pre-trial timetable has been agreed or ordered, that timetable;

   (f) the principal orders of the court; and

   (g) any agreement in writing made by the parties as to disclosure,

and provide copies of the case management bundle for the court and the other parties at least 7 days before the first case management conference or any earlier hearing at which the court may give case management directions.

10.9 The claimant, in consultation with the other parties, must revise and update the documents referred to in paragraph 10.8 appropriately as the case proceeds. This must include making all necessary revisions and additions at least 7 days before any subsequent hearing at which the court may give case management directions.

Pre-trial review

2A–32   **11.1** At any pre-trial review or case management hearing, the court will ensure that case management directions have been complied with and give any further directions for the trial that are necessary.

11.2 Advocates who are to represent the parties at the trial should represent them at the pre-trial review and any case management hearing at which arrangements for the trial are to be discussed.

11.3 Before the pre-trial review, the parties must discuss and, if possible, agree a draft written timetable for the trial.

11.4 The claimant must file a copy of the draft timetable for the trial at least two days before the hearing of the pre-trial review. Any parts of the timetable which are not agreed must be identified and short explanations of the disagreement must be given.

11.5 At the pre-trial review, the court will set a timetable for the trial, unless a timetable has already been fixed or the court considers that it would be inappropriate to do so or appropriate to do so at a later time.

Case management where there is a Part 20 claim

2A–33   **12.** Paragraph 5 of the practice direction supplementing Part 20 applies, except that, unless the court otherwise orders, the court will give case management directions for Part 20 claims at the same case management conferences as it gives directions for the main claim.

Evidence for applications

2A–34   **13.1** The general requirement is that, unless the court orders otherwise—

   (1)   evidence in support of an application must be filed and served with the application (see rule 23.7(3));

   (2)   evidence in answer must be filed and served within 14 days after the application is served; and

(3) evidence in reply must be filed and served within 7 days of the service of evidence in answer.

13.2 In any case in which the application is likely to require an oral hearing of more than half a day the periods set out in paragraphs 13.1 (2) and (3) will be 28 days and 14 days respectively.

13.3 If the date fixed for the hearing of an application means that the times in paragraphs 13.1(2) and (3) cannot both be achieved, the evidence must be filed and served—

(1) as soon as possible; and

(2) in sufficient time to ensure that the application may fairly proceed on the date fixed.

13.4 The parties may, in accordance with rule 2.11, agree different periods from those in paragraphs 13.1(2) and (3) provided that the agreement does not affect the date fixed for the hearing of the application.

Judgments and orders

14.1 An application for a consent order must include a draft of the proposed order signed on behalf of all parties to whom it relates (see paragraph 10.4 of the practice direction supplementing Part 23). **2A–35**

14.2 Judgments and orders are generally drawn up by the parties (see rule 58.15). The parties are not therefore required to supply draft orders on disk (see paragraph 12.1 of the practice direction supplementing Part 23).

APPENDIX A

Procedure for issue of claim form when Registry is closed—paragraph 2.2

1. A request to issue a claim form may be made by fax when the Registry is closed, provided that— **2A–36**

(a) the claim form is signed by a solicitor acting on behalf of the claimant; and

(b) it does not require the permission of the court for its issue (unless such permission has already been given).

2. The solicitor requesting the issue of the claim form ("the issuing solicitor") must—

(a) endorse on the claim form and sign the endorsement set out below;

(b) send a copy of the claim form so endorsed to the Registry by fax for issue under paragraph 2.2 of this practice direction; and

(c) complete and sign a certificate in the form set out below, certifying that he has received a transmission report confirming that the fax has been transmitted in full, and stating the time and date of transmission.

3. When the Registry is next open to the public after the issue of a claim form in accordance with this procedure, the issuing solicitor or his agent must attend and deliver to the Registry—

(a) the original of the claim form which was sent by fax (including the endorsement and the certificate) or, if the claim form has been served, a true and certified copy of it;

(b) as many copies of the claim form as the Registry requires; and

(c) the transmission report.

4. When a court officer at the Registry has checked that—

(a) the claim form delivered under paragraph 3 matches the claim form received by fax; and

(b) the correct issue fee has been paid,

he will allocate a number to the case, and seal, mark as "original" and date the claim form with the date of issue (being the date when the fax is recorded at the Registry as having been received).

5. If the issuing solicitor has served the unsealed claim form on any person, he must as soon as practicable—

(a) inform that person of the case number; and

(b) if requested, serve him with a copy of the sealed and dated claim form at any address in England and Wales.

6. Any person served with a claim form issued under this procedure may, without paying a fee, inspect and take copies of the documents lodged at the Registry under paragraphs 2 and 3 above.

7. The issue of a claim form in accordance with this procedure takes place when the fax is recorded at the Registry as having been received, and the claim form has the same effect for all purposes as a claim form issued under Part 7 or 8. Unless the court otherwise orders, the sealed version of the claim form retained by the Registry is conclusive proof that the claim form was issued at the time and on the date stated.

8. If the procedure set out in this Appendix is not complied with, the court may declare that a claim form shall be treated as not having been issued.

Endorsement

2A–37 A claim form issued pursuant to a request by fax must be endorsed as follows:

"1. This claim form is issued under paragraph 2.2 of the Commercial Court practice direction and may be served notwithstanding that it does not bear the seal of the Court.

2. A true copy of this claim form and endorsement has been sent to the Admiralty and Commercial Registry, Royal Courts of Justice, Strand, London WC2A 2LL, at the time and date certified below by the solicitor whose name appears below ("the issuing solicitor").

3. It is the duty of the issuing solicitor or his agent to attend at the Registry when it is next open to the public for the claim form to be sealed.

4. Any person served with this unsealed claim form—

(a) will be notified by the issuing solicitor of the case number;

(b) may require the issuing solicitor to serve him with a copy of the sealed claim form at an address in England and Wales; and

(c) may inspect without charge the documents lodged at the Registry by the issuing solicitor.

5. I, the issuing solicitor, undertake [to the Court, to the defendants named in this claim form, and to any other person served with this claim form]—

(a) that the statement in paragraph 2 above is correct;

(b) that the time and date given in the certificate with this endorsement are correct;

(c) that this claim form is a claim form which may be issued under paragraph 2.2 and Appendix A of the Commercial Court practice direction;

(d) that I will comply in all respects with the requirements of Appendix A of the Commercial Court practice direction; and

(e) that I will indemnify any person served with the claim form before it is sealed against any loss suffered as a result of the claim form being or becoming invalid as a result of any failure to comply with Appendix A of the Commercial Court practice direction.

(Signed)

Solicitor for the claimant"

[**Note**: the endorsement may be signed in the name of the firm of solicitors rather than an individual solicitor, or by solicitors' agents in their capacity as agents acting on behalf of their professional clients.]

Certificate

The issuing solicitor must sign a certificate in the following form— **2A–38**

"I certify that I have received a transmission report confirming that the transmission of a copy of this claim form to the Registry by fax was fully completed and that the time and date of transmission to the Registry were *[enter the time and date shown on the transmission report]*.

Dated

(Signed)

Solicitor for the claimant"

[**Note**: the certificate be signed in the name of the firm of solicitors rather than an individual solicitor, or by solicitors' agents in their capacity as agents acting on behalf of their professional clients.]

THE ADMIRALTY AND COMMERCIAL COURTS GUIDE

Section A	Preliminary
1	The procedural framework
2	The Admiralty and Commercial Registry
3	The Commercial Court Committee
4	Specialist Associations
Section B	**Commencement, Transfer and Removal**
1	Commercial cases
2	Starting a case in the Commercial Court
3	Part 7 claims

COMMERCIAL COURT

COMMERCIAL COURT

Introduction

This edition of the Admiralty & Commercial Courts Guide is published to coincide **2A–39** with the introduction of Parts 58, 61 and 62 of the Civil Procedure Rules dealing with Commercial and Admiralty proceedings and proceedings relating to arbitrations respectively. Most of the provisions which have hitherto been contained in the practice directions made under Part 49 and the 5th edition of the Commercial Court Guide are now to be found in these new rules and their associated practice directions, although the Guide still contains a number of additional provisions which are necessary to ensure the efficient conduct of business in the Admiralty and Commercial Courts.

For some time now the administration of the Admiralty and Commercial Courts has been undertaken by a single Registry and Listing Office and the two Courts have shared many common procedures. It seemed only natural, therefore, that this edition of the Guide should reflect that fact, both in its title and in the inclusion of a separate section dealing with admiralty proceedings.

This edition of the Guide draws heavily on its predecessor, but the introduction of the new rules has necessitated a substantial revision of the text. Moreover, the need to describe in detail various respects in which the procedure applicable to commercial proceedings diverges from that generally applicable under the Civil Procedure Rules, has diminished in importance as practitioners have become familiar both with the operation of the Rules themselves and with the procedures applicable in the Commercial and Admiralty Courts. We have therefore taken the opportunity to remove much of the explanatory material which we consider no longer serves a useful purpose in an attempt to produce a concise manual which meets the day to day needs of those who use the Courts. We have also taken the opportunity to review the Courts' procedures as a whole. This has resulted in the removal of some provisions which seemed to be otiose or to have outlived their usefulness and the introduction of others which we consider will enable the Courts to function more efficiently.

The fact that some provisions to be found in the 5th edition do not reappear in this edition should not necessarily be taken as an indication that they are no longer regarded as reflecting approved practice. In the interests of brevity we have not thought it necessary to reproduce all those provisions which were essentially matters of common sense or good practice, preferring in many cases to rely on the good sense and judgment of those who use the Courts. The Guide is not intended to be a blueprint to which all litigation must unthinkingly conform: as in the past, it seeks to provide a modern and flexible framework within which litigation can be conducted efficiently and in the interests of justice. We would emphasise that there has been no change in the Courts' approach to the business which comes before them or in their expectation that those who use the Courts will display the highest professional standards.

This Guide has been produced in order to set out in a convenient manner the practice which applies in the Admiralty and Commercial Courts. It should be read in conjunction with the Civil Procedure Rules and Practice Directions. For ease of reference we have included wherever possible references to the relevant rules and practice directions to which the reader should refer as necessary. In the interests of brevity references to the Practice Directions take the form "PD[rule number] § [paragraph number]". Accordingly, PD32 should be understood as meaning "the Practice Direction supplementing Part 32" and PD58 § 15 as meaning "paragraph 15 of the Practice Direction supplementing Part 58".

The Hon. Mr. Justice David Steel   The Hon. Mr. Justice Moore-Bick
Admiralty Judge   Judge in Charge of the Commercial List

February 2002

A. Preliminary

A1 The procedural framework

2A–40 A1.1 Proceedings in the Commercial Court are governed by the Civil Procedure Rules ("CPR") and Practice Directions. CPR Part 58 and its associated practice direction deal specifically with the Commercial Court. Part 61 deals with the Admiralty Court and Part 62 deals with arbitration applications. Parts 58 and 61 and their associated practice directions are set out in Appendix 1; Rule 62 and its associated practice direction is set out in Appendix 2.

A1.2 The Admiralty & Commercial Courts Guide is published with the approval of the Lord Chief Justice and the Head of Civil Justice in consultation with the Judges of the Admiralty and Commercial Courts and with the advice and support of the Admiralty Court and Commercial Court Committees. It is intended to provide guidance about the conduct of proceedings in the Admiralty and Commercial Courts and, within the framework of the Civil Procedure Rules and Practice Directions, to establish the practice to be followed in those courts.

A1.3 In matters for which specific provision is not made by the Guide, the parties, their solicitors and counsel will be expected to act reasonably and in accordance with the spirit of the Guide.

A1.4 The requirements of the Guide are designed to ensure effective management of proceedings in the Admiralty and Commercial Courts. If parties fail to comply with these requirements the court may impose sanctions including orders for costs and (where appropriate) wasted costs orders.

A1.5 Pre-trial matters in the Admiralty and Commercial Courts are dealt with by the judges of those Courts: **58PD § 1.2**.

A1.6 The Court expects a high level of co-operation and realism from the legal representatives of the parties. This applies to dealings (including correspondence) between legal representatives as well as to dealings with the Court.

A1.7 In order to avoid excessive repetition, the Guide has been written by reference to proceedings in the Commercial Court. Practitioners should treat the guidance as applicable to proceedings in the Admiralty Court unless the content of Part 61 or Section N of this Guide ("Admiralty") specifically requires otherwise.

A2 The Admiralty & Commercial Registry; the Commercial Court Listing Office

2A–41 A2.1 The administrative office for the Admiralty Court and the Commercial Court is the Admiralty & Commercial Registry ("the Registry") which is located at Room E200 in the Royal Courts of Justice, Strand, London WC2A 2LL. The Commercial Court Listing Office ("the Listing Office") is located at Room E201 in the Royal Courts of Justice, Strand, London WC2A 2LL.

A2.2 It is important that there is close liaison between legal representatives of the parties and both the Registry and the Listing Office.

A3 The Commercial Court Committee

2A–42 A3.1 The success of the Court's ability to meet the special problems and continually changing needs of the commercial community depends in part upon a steady flow of information and constructive suggestions between the Court, litigants and professional advisers.

A3.2 The Commercial Court Committee has assisted in this process for many years. It is expected to play an important part in helping to ensure that the procedures of the Court enable the achievement of the "overriding objective". All concerned with the Court are encouraged to make the fullest use of this important channel of communication. Correspondence raising matters for the consideration of the Committee should be addressed to the Clerk to the Commercial Court, Royal Courts of Justice, Strand, London WC2A 2LL.

A4 Specialist associations

2A–43 A4.1 There are a number of associations of legal representatives which liaise closely with the Commercial Court. These will also play an important part in helping to ensure that the Court remains responsive to the "overriding objective".

A4.2 The associations include the Commercial Bar Association ("COMBAR"), the London Common Law and Commercial Bar Association ("LCLCBA"), the City of London Law Society, the London Solicitors Litigation Association and the Admiralty Solicitors Group.

B. Commencement, Transfer and Removal

B1 Commercial cases

B1.1 Rule 58.1(2) describes a "commercial claim" as follows: **2A–44**

"any claim arising out of the transaction of trade and commerce and includes any claim relating to—

(a) a business document or contract;
(b) the export or import of goods;
(c) the carriage of goods by land, sea, air or pipeline;
(d) the exploitation of oil and gas reserves or other natural resources;
(e) insurance and re-insurance;
(f) banking and financial services;
(g) the operation of markets and exchanges;
(h) the purchase and sale of commodities;
(i) the construction of ships;
(j) business agency; and
(k) arbitration."

B2 Starting a case in the Commercial Court

B2.1 Except for arbitration applications which are governed by the provisions of CPR   **2A–45**
Part 62 and section O of the Guide, the case will be begun by a claim form under Part 7 or Part 8.

B2.2 Save where otherwise specified, references in this Guide to a claim form are to a Part 7 claim form.

B2.3 The Commercial Court may give a fixed date for trial (see section D16), but it does not give a fixed date for a hearing when it issues a claim. Rules 7.9 and 7.10 and their associated practice directions do not apply to the Commercial Court.

B3 Part 7 claims

The form

B3.1 A claimant starting proceedings in the Commercial Court must use practice   **2A–46**
form **N1(CC)** for Part 7 claims: **PD58 § 2.4.** A copy of this practice form is included at the end of the Guide.

Marking

B3.2 In accordance with PD58 § 2.3 the claim form should be marked in the top right hand corner with the words "Queen's Bench Division, Commercial Court", and on the issue of the claim form out of the Registry the case will be entered in the Commercial List. Marking the claim form in this way complies sufficiently with PD7 § 3.6(3).

Statement of value

B3.3 Rule 16.3, which provides for a statement of value to be included in the claim form, does not apply in the Commercial Court: rule 58.5(2).

Particulars of claim and the claim form

B3.4 Although particulars of claim may be served with the claim form, this is not a requirement in the Commercial Court. However, if the particulars of claim are not contained in or served with the claim form, the claim form must contain a statement that if an acknowledgment of service is filed indicating an intention to defend the claim, particulars of claim will follow: rule 58.5(1)(a).

B3.5 If particulars of claim do not accompany the claim form they must be served within 28 days after the defendant has filed an acknowledgment of service indicating an intention to defend the claim: rule 58.5(1)(c).

B3.6 The three forms specified in rule 7.8(1) must be served with the claim form. One of these is a form for acknowledging service: rule 58.5(1)(b).

Statement of truth

B3.7

(a) A claim form must be verified by a statement of truth: rule 22.1. Unless the court otherwise orders, any amendment to a claim form must also be verified: rule 22.1(2).

(b) The required form of statement of truth is set out at **PD7 § 7.2**.

(c) A claim form will remain effective even where not verified by a statement of truth, unless it is struck out: **PD22 § 4.1**.

(d) In certain cases the statement of truth may be signed by a person other than the party on whose behalf it is served or its legal representative: section C1.8–1.9.

Trial without service of particulars of claim or a defence

B3.8 The attention of the parties and their legal representatives is drawn to rule 58.11 which allows the court to order (before or after the issue of a claim form) that the case shall proceed without the filing or service of particulars of claim or defence or of any other statement of case.

Interest

B3.9 The claim form (and not only the particulars of claim) must comply with the requirements of rules 16.4(1)(b) and 16.4(2) concerning interest: rule 58.5(3).

B3.10 References to particulars of claim in rule 12.6(1)(a) (referring to claims for interest where there is a default judgment) and rule 14.14(1)(a) (referring to claims for interest where there is a judgment on admissions) may be treated as references to the claim form: rules 58.8(2) and 58.9(3).

Issue of a claim form when the Registry is closed

B3.11 A request for the issue of a Part 7 claim form may be made by fax at certain times when the Registry is closed to the public: **PD58 § 2.2**. The procedure is set out in Appendix 3. Any further details may be obtained from the Registry. The fax number is 020 7947 6667.

B4 Part 8 claims

Form

2A–47 B4.1 A claimant who wishes to commence a claim under CPR Part 8 must use practice form **N208(CC)**: **PD58 § 2.4**. A copy of this practice form is included at the end of this Guide.

B4.2 Attention is drawn to the requirement in rule 8.2(a) that where a claimant uses the Part 8 procedure his claim form must state that Part 8 applies. Similarly, PD7 § 3.3 requires that the claim form state (if it be the case) that the claimant wishes his claim to proceed under Part 8 or that the claim is required to proceed under Part 8.

Marking and statement of truth

B4.3 Sections B3.2 (marking) and B3.7 (statement of truth) also apply to a claim form issued under Part 8.

Issue of a claim form when the Registry is closed

B4.4 A request for the issue of a Part 8 claim form may be made by fax at certain times when the Registry is closed to the public: **PD58 § 2.2**. The procedure is set out in Appendix 3.

Time for filing evidence in opposition to a Part 8 claim

B4.5 A defendant to a Part 8 claim who wishes to rely on written evidence must file and serve it within 28 days after filing an acknowledgment of service: rule 58.12.

B5 Part 20 claims

Form

B5.1 Adapted versions of the Part 20 claim form and acknowledgment of service (Practice Forms no. **N211** and **N213**) and of the related Notes to Part 20 claimant and Part 20 defendant have been approved for use in the Commercial Court. Copies of the practice forms are included at the end of the Guide. **2A–48**

B6 Service of the claim form

Service by the parties

B6.1 Claim forms issued in the Commercial List are to be served by the parties, not by the Registry: **PD58 § 9.** **2A–49**

Methods of service

B6.2 Methods of service are set out in CPR Part 6, which is supplemented by a Practice Direction.

B6.3 PD6 §§ 2.1 and 3.1 concern service by document exchange and by fax. Service of the claim form on the legal representative of the defendant by document exchange or fax will not be effective unless that legal representative has authority to accept service. It is desirable to obtain confirmation from the legal representative in writing that he has instructions to accept service of a claim form on behalf of the defendant.

Applications for extension of time

B6.4 Applications for an extension of time in which to serve a claim form are governed by rule 7.6. Rule 7.6(3)(a), which refers to service of the claim form by the court, does not apply in the Commercial Court.

B6.5 The evidence required on an application for an extension of time is set out in PD7 § 8.2.

Certificate of service

B6.6 When the claimant has served the claim form he must file a certificate of service: rule 6.14(2). Satisfaction of this requirement is relevant, in particular, to the claimant's ability to obtain judgment in default (see Part 12) and to the right of a non-party to search for, inspect and take a copy of the claim form under rule 5.4(2)(a).

B7 Service of the claim form out of the jurisdiction

B7.1 Applications for permission to serve a claim form out of the jurisdiction are governed by rules 6.19 to 6.31. A guide to the appropriate practice is set out in Appendix 15. **2A–50**

B7.2 Service of process in some foreign countries may take a long time to complete; it is therefore important that solicitors take prompt steps to effect service.

COMMERCIAL COURT

B8 Acknowledgment of service

2A–51 *Part 7 claims*

B8.1

(a) A defendant must file an acknowledgment of service in every case: rule 58.6(1). An adapted version of practice form **N9** (which includes the acknowledgment of service) has been approved for use in the Commercial Court. A copy of this practice form (Form **N9(CC)**) is included at the end of the Guide, together with adapted versions of the notes for claimants and defendants on completing and replying to a Part 7 claim form.

(b) The period for filing an acknowledgment of service is calculated from the service of the claim form, whether or not particulars of claim are contained in or accompany the claim form or are to follow service of the claim form. Rule 9.1(2), which provides that in certain circumstances the defendant need not respond to the claim until particulars of claim have been served on him, does not apply: rule 58.6(1).

Part 8 claims

B8.2

(a) A defendant must file an acknowledgment of service in every case: rule 58.6(1). An adapted version of practice form **N210** (acknowledgment of service of a Part 8 claim form) has been approved for use in the Commercial Court. A copy of this practice form (Form **N210(CC)**) is included at the end of the Guide, together with adapted versions of the notes for claimants and defendants on completing and replying to a Part 8 claim form.

(b) The time for filing an acknowledgment of service is calculated from the service of the claim form.

Acknowledgment of service in a claim against a firm

B8.3

(a) PD10 § 4.4 allows an acknowledgment of service to be signed on behalf of a partnership by any of the partners or a person having the control or management of the partnership business, whether he be a partner or not.

(b) However, attention is drawn to Schedule 1 to the CPR which includes, with modifications, provisions previously contained in RSC Order 81 concerning acknowledgment of service by a person served as a partner who denies his liability as such. (see also the note at the end of CPR Part 10).

Time for filing acknowledgment of service

B8.4

(a) Except in the circumstances described in section B8.4(b) and B8.4(c), or is otherwise ordered by the court, the period for filing an acknowledgment of service is 14 days after service of the claim form.

(b) If the claim form has been served out of the jurisdiction without the permission of the court under rule 6.19, the time for filing an acknowledgment of service is governed by rule 6.22, save that in all cases time runs from the service of the claim form: rule 58.6(3).

(c) If the claim form has been served out of the jurisdiction with the permission of the court under rule 6.20 the time for filing an acknowledgment of service is governed by rule 6.21(4)(a), the second practice direction supplementing rule 6 and the table to which it refers, save that in all cases time runs from the service of the claim form: rule 58.6(3).

B9 Disputing the court's jurisdiction

2A–52 *Part 7 claims*

B9.1

(a) If the defendant intends to dispute the court's jurisdiction or contend that the court should not exercise its jurisdiction he must

    (i) file an acknowledgment of service — rule 11(2); and

    (ii) issue an application notice seeking the appropriate relief.

(b) An application to dispute the court's jurisdiction must be made within 28 days of filing an acknowledgment of service: rule 58.7(2).

(c) if the defendant wishes to rely on written evidence in support of that application, he must file and serve that evidence when he issues the application.

(d) If the defendant makes an application under rule 11(1), the claimant is not bound to serve particulars of claim until that application has been disposed of: rule 58.7(3).

Part 8 claims

B9.2

(a) The provisions of section B9.1(a)–(c) also apply in the case of Part 8 claims.

(b) If the defendant makes an application under rule 11(1), he is not bound to serve any written evidence on which he wishes to rely in opposition to the substantive claim until that application has been disposed of: rule 11.9.

Effect of an application challenging the jurisdiction

B9.3 An acknowledgment of service of a Part 7 or Part 8 claim form which is followed by an application challenging the jurisdiction under Part 11 does not constitute a submission by the defendant to the jurisdiction: rules 11(3) and 11(7).

B9.4 If an application under Part 11 is unsuccessful, and the court then considers giving directions for filing and serving statements of case (in the case of a Part 7 claim) or evidence (in the case of a Part 8 claim), a defendant does not submit to the jurisdiction merely by asking for time to serve and file his statement of case or evidence, as the case may be.

B10 Default judgment

B10 Default judgment is governed by Part 12 and PD12. However, because in the Commercial Court the period for filing the acknowledgment of service is calculated from service of the claim form, the reference to "particulars of claim" in PD12 § 4.1(1) should be read as referring to the claim form: **PD58 § 6(1)**. **2A–53**

B11 Admissions **2A–54**

B11

(a) Admissions are governed by CPR Part 14, and PD14, except that the references to "particulars of claim" in PD14 § § 2.1, 3.1 and 3.2 should be read as referring to the claim form: **PD58 § 6(2)**.

(b) Adapted versions of the practice forms of admission (practice forms no. **N9A** and no. **N9C**) have been approved for use in the Commercial Court. Copies of these practice forms (Forms **N9A(CC)** and **N9C(CC)**) are included at the end of the Guide.

B12 Transfer of cases into and out of the Commercial List

B12.1 The procedure for transfer and removal is set out in **PD58 § 4**. All such applications must be made to the Commercial Court: rule 30.5(3). **2A–55**

B12.2 Although an order to transfer a case to the Commercial List may be made at any stage, any application for such an order should normally be made at an early stage in the proceedings.

B12.3 Transfer to the Commercial List may be ordered for limited purposes only, but a transferred case will normally remain in the Commercial List until its conclusion.

B12.4 An order transferring a case out of the Commercial List may be made at any stage, but will not usually be made after a pre-trial timetable has been fixed at the case management conference (see section D8).

B12.5 Some commercial cases may more suitably, or as suitably, be dealt with in one of the Mercantile Courts. Parties should consider whether it would be more appropriate to begin proceedings in one of those courts and the Commercial Judge may on his own initiative order the case to be transferred there.

C. Particulars of Claim, Defence and Reply

2A–56 C1 Form, content, serving and filing

C1.1

(a) Particulars of claim, the defence and any reply must be set out in separate consecutively numbered paragraphs and be as brief and concise as possible.

(b) If it is necessary for the proper understanding of the statement of case to include substantial parts of a lengthy document the passages in question should be set out in a schedule rather than in the body of the case.

(c) The document must be signed by the individual person or persons who drafted it, not, in the case of a solicitor, in the name of the firm alone.

C1.2

(a) Particulars of claim, the defence and also any reply must comply with the provisions of rules 16.4 and 16.5, save that rules 16.5(6) and 16.5(8) do not apply.

(b) The requirements of PD16 § 8.4–9.1 (which relate to claims based upon oral agreements, agreements by conduct and Consumer Credit Agreements and to reliance upon evidence of certain matters under the Civil Evidence Act 1968) should be treated as applying to the defence and reply as well as to the particulars of claim.

    (i) full and specific details must be given of any allegation of fraud, dishonesty, malice or illegality; and

    (ii) where an inference of fraud or dishonesty is alleged, the facts on the basis of which the inference is alleged must be fully set out.

(d) Any legislative provision upon which an allegation is based must be clearly identified and the basis of its application explained.

(e) Any provision of The Human Rights Act 1998 (including the Convention) on which a party relies in support of its case must be clearly identified and the basis of its application explained.

(f) Any principle of foreign law or foreign legislative provision upon which a party's case is based must be clearly identified and the basis of its application explained.

C1.3

(a) PD16 § 7.3 relating to a claim based upon a written agreement should be treated as also applying to the defence, unless the claim and the defence are based on the same agreement.

(b) In most cases attaching documents to or serving documents with a statement of case does not promote the efficient conduct of the proceedings and should be avoided.

(c) If documents are to be served at the same time as a statement of case they should normally be served separately from rather than attached to the statement of case.

(d) Only those documents which are obviously of critical importance and necessary for a proper understanding of the statement of case should be attached to or served with it. The statement of case must itself refer to the fact that documents are attached to or served with it.

(e) An expert's report should not be attached to the statement of case and should not be filed with the statement of case at the Registry. A party must obtain permission from the court in order to adduce expert evidence at trial and therefore any party which serves an expert's report without obtaining such permission does so at his own risk as to costs.

(f) Notwithstanding PD16 § 7.3(1), a true copy of the complete written agreement may be made available at any hearing unless the court orders otherwise.

Adapted versions of the practice forms of defence and counterclaim have been approved for use in the Commercial Court. Copies of these practice forms are included at the end of this Guide.

Summaries

C1.4 If a statement of case exceeds 25 pages (excluding schedules), a summary, not exceeding 4 pages, must also be filed and served. The summary should cross-refer to the paragraph numbering of the full statement of case. The summary is to be included in the case management bundle: **section D7.2(ii)**.

Length

C1.5 Parties serving statements of case should bear in mind that the court will take into account the length of the document served when considering any application by another party for further time within which to respond.

Statement of truth

C1.6 Particulars of claim, a defence and any reply must be verified by a statement of truth: rule 22.1. So too must any amendment, unless the court otherwise orders: rule 22.1(2); see also **section C5.4**.

C1.7 The required form of statement of truth is as follows:
    (i) for particulars of claim, as set out in **PD7 § 7.2** or **PD16 § 3.4**;
    (ii) for a defence, as set out in **PD15 § 2.2** or **PD16 § 12.2**;
    (iii) for a reply the statement of truth should follow the form for the particulars of claim, but substituting the word "reply" for the words "particulars of claim" (see **PD22 § 2.1**).

C1.8

(a) A party may apply to the court for permission that a statement of truth be signed by a person other than one of those required by rule 22.1(6) or rule 58.8(1).
(b) Such an application may be made, for example, in a case where insurers are subrogated to the rights of the party in respect of the claim. The application may be made even after the issue of a claim form.

C1.9 If insurers are conducting proceedings on behalf of many claimants or defendants a statement of truth may be signed by a senior person responsible for the case at a lead insurer, but
    (i) the person signing must specify the capacity in which he signs;
    (ii) the statement of truth must be a statement that the lead insurer believes that the facts stated in the document are true; and
    (iii) the court may order that a statement of truth also be signed by one or more of the parties.

C1.10 A statement of case remains effective (although it may not be relied on as evidence) even where it is not verified by a statement of truth, unless it is struck out: **PD22 § § 4.1–4.3**.

Service

C1.11 All statements of case are served by the parties, not by the court: **PD58 § 9**.

Filing

C1.12 The statements of case filed with the court form part of the permanent record of the court.

C2 Serving and filing particulars of claim

2A–57 C2.1 Subject to any contrary order of the court and unless particulars of claim are contained in or accompany the claim form

(i) the period for serving particulars of claim is 28 days after filing an acknowledgment of service: rule 58.5(1)(c);

(ii) the parties may agree extensions of the period for serving the particulars of claim. However, any such agreement must be evidenced in writing and notified to the court, addressed to the Case Management Unit: **PD58 § 7.1**;

(iii) any notification of an agreed extension exceeding 6 weeks, or which when taken together with preceding extensions exceeds 6 weeks in total, must be accompanied by a brief statement of the reasons for the extension.

C2.2 The court may make an order overriding any agreement by the parties varying a time limit: **PD58 § 7.2**.

C2.3 The claimant must serve the particulars of claim on all other parties. A copy of the claim form will be filed at the Registry on issue. If the claimant serves particulars of claim separately from the claim form he must file a copy within 7 days of service together with a certificate of service: rule 7.4(3).

C3 Serving and filing a defence

2A–58 C3.1 The defendant must serve the defence on all other parties and must at the same time file a copy with the court.

C3.2

(a) If the defendant files an acknowledgment of service which indicates an intention to defend the period for serving and filing a defence is 28 days after service of the particulars of claim, subject to the provisions of rule 15.4(2). (See also Appendix 15 fr cases where the claim form has been served out of the jurisdiction.)

(b) The defendant and the claimant may agree that the period for serving and filing a defence shall be extended by up to 28 days: rule 15.5(1).

(c) An application to the court is required for any further extension. If the parties are able to agree that a further extension should be granted, a draft consent order should be provided together with a brief explanation of the reasons for the extension.

C3.3 The general power to agree variations to time limits contained in rule 2.11 and PD58 § 7.1 enables parties to agree extensions of the period for serving and filing a defence that exceed 28 days. The length of extension must in all cases be specified. Any such agreement must be evidenced in writing and comply with the requirements of section C2.1.

C3.4

(a) Where an extension is agreed the defendant must, in accordance with rule 15.5(2), notify the court in writing; the notification should be addressed to the Case Management Unit.

(b) Any notification of an agreed extension exceeding 6 weeks, or which when taken together with preceding extensions exceeds 6 weeks in total, must be accompanied by a brief statement (agreed by the claimant and the defendant) of the reasons for the extension. The reasons will be brought to the attention of the Judge in Charge of the Commercial List.

C3.5 The claimant must notify the Case Management Unit by letter when all defendants who intend to serve a defence have done so. This information is material to the fixing of the case management conference (see section D3.1).

C4 Serving and filing a reply

2A–59 C4.1 Subject to section C4.3, the period for serving and filing a reply is 21 days after service of the defence: rule 58.10(1).

C4.2

(a) A reply must be filed at the same time as it is served: rule 15.8(b); rule 15.8(a) does not apply in proceedings in the Commercial List.

(b) The reply should be served before case management information sheets are provided to the court (see section D8.5). In the normal case, this will allow the parties to consider any reply before completing the case management information sheet, and allow time for the preparation of the case memorandum and the list of issues each of which is required for the case management conference (see sections D4–D7).

C4.3 In some cases, more than 21 days may be needed for the preparation, service and filing of a reply. In such cases an application should be made on paper for an extension of time and for a postponement of the case management conference. The procedure to be followed when making an application on paper is set out in section F4.

C4.4 Any reply must be served by the claimant on all other parties: rule 58.10(1).

C5 Amendment

2A–60

C5.1

(a) Amendments to a statement of case must show the original text, unless the court orders otherwise: **PD58 § 8**.

(b) Amendments may be shown by using footnotes or marginal notes, provided they identify precisely where and when an amendment has been made.

(c) Unless the court so orders, there is no need to show amendments by colour-coding.

(d) If there have been extensive amendments it may be desirable to prepare a fresh copy of the statement of case. However, a copy of the statement of case showing where and when amendments have been made must also be made available.

C5.2 All amendments to any statement of case must be verified by a statement of truth unless the court orders otherwise: rule 22.1(2).

C5.3 Questions of amendment, and consequential amendment, should wherever possible be dealt with by consent. A party should consent to a proposed amendment unless he has substantial grounds for objecting to it.

C5.4 Late amendments should be avoided and may be disallowed.

D. Case Management in the Commercial Court

D1 Generally

D1.1 All proceedings in the Commercial List will be subject to management by the court.

2A–61

D1.2 All proceedings in the Commercial List are automatically allocated to the multi-track and consequently Part 26 and the rules relating to allocation do not apply: rule 58.13(1).

D1.3 Except for rule 29.3(2) (legal representatives to attend case management conferences and pre-trial reviews) and rule 29.5 (variation of case management timetable), Part 29 does not apply to proceedings in the Commercial List: rule 58.13(2).

D2 Key features of case management in the Commercial Court

D2 Case management is governed by rule 58.13 and PD58 § 10. In a normal commercial case commenced by a Part 7 claim form, case management will include the following 10 key features:

2A–62

(1) statements of case will be exchanged within fixed or monitored time periods;

(2) a case memorandum, a list of issues and a case management bundle will be produced at an early point in the case;

(3) the case memorandum, list of issues and case management bundle will be amended and updated or revised on a running basis throughout the life of the case and will be used by the court at every stage of the case;

(4) a mandatory case management conference will be held shortly after statements of case have been served, if not before (and preceded by the parties lodging case management information sheets identifying their views on the requirements of the case);

(5) at the case management conference the court will (as necessary) discuss the issues in the case and the requirements of the case with the advocates retained in the case. The court will set a pre-trial timetable and give any other directions as may be appropriate;

(6) before the progress monitoring date the parties will report to the court, using a progress monitoring information sheet, the extent of their compliance with the pre-trial timetable;

(7) on or shortly after the progress monitoring date a judge will (without a hearing) consider progress and give such further directions as he thinks appropriate;

(8) if at the progress monitoring date all parties have indicated that they will be ready for trial, all parties will complete a pre-trial checklist;

(9) in many cases there will be a pre-trial review; in such cases the parties will be required to prepare a trial timetable for consideration by the court;

(10) throughout the case there will be regular reviews of the estimated length of trial.

D3 Fixing a case management conference

2A–63 D3.1 A mandatory case management conference will normally take place on the first available date 6 weeks after all defendants who intend to serve a defence have done so. This will normally allow time for the preparation and service of any reply (see section C4).

D3.2

(a) If proceedings have been started by service of a Part 7 claim form, the claimant must take steps to fix the date for the case management conference with the Listing Office in co-operation with the other parties within 14 days of the date when all defendants who intend to file and serve a defence have done so: **PD58 § 10.2(a)**. The parties should bear in mind the need to allow time for the preparation and service of any reply.

(b) If proceedings have been begun by service of a Part 8 claim form, the claimant must take steps to fix a date for the case management conference with the Listing Office in co-operation with the other parties within 14 days of the date when all defendants who wish to serve evidence have done so: **PD58 § 10.2(b)**.

D3.3

(a) In accordance with section C3 the Registry will expect a defence to be served and filed by the latest of

(i) 28 days after service of particulars of claim (as certified by the certificate of service); or

(ii) any extended date for serving and filing a defence as notified to the court in writing following agreement between the parties; or

(iii) any extended date for serving and filing a defence as ordered by the court on an application.

(b) If within 28 days after the latest of these dates has passed for each defendant, the parties have not taken steps to fix the date for the case management conference, the Case Management Unit will inform the Judge in Charge of the List, and at his direction will take steps to fix a date for the case management conference without further reference to the parties.

D3.4 If the proceedings have been transferred to the Commercial List, the claimant must apply for a case management conference within 14 days of the date of the order transferring them, unless the judge held, or gave directions for, a case management conference when he made the order transferring the proceedings: **PD58 § 10.3**.

D3.5 If the claimant fails to make an application as required by the rules, any other party may apply for a case management conference: **PD58 § 10.5**.

D3.6

(a) In some cases it may be appropriate for a case management conference to take place at an earlier date.

(b) Any party may apply to the court in writing at an earlier time for a case management conference: **PD58 § 10.4**. A request by any party for an early case management conference should be made in writing to the Judge in Charge of the List, on notice to all other parties, at the earliest possible opportunity.

D3.7 If before the date on which the case management conference would be held in accordance with section D3 there is a hearing in the case at which the parties are represented, the business of the case management conference will normally be transacted at that hearing and there will be no separate case management conference.

D3.8 The court may fix a case management conference at any time on its own initiative. If it does so, the court will normally give at least 7 days notice to the parties: **PD58 § 10.6**.

D3.9 A case management conference may not be postponed or adjourned without an order of the court.

D4 Two-Judge team system   2A–64

D4.1

(a) Cases which are exceptional in size or complexity or in having a propensity to give rise to numerous pre-trial applications may be allocated to a management team of two designated judges.

(b) An application for the appointment of a two-judge management team should be made in writing to the Judge in Charge of the List at the time of fixing the case management conference.

(c) If an order is made for allocation to a two-judge team, one of the designated judges will preside at the case management conference.

D4.2 Except for an application for an interim payment, all applications in the case, and the trial itself, will be heard by one or other of the designated judges.

D5 Case memorandum

D5.1 In order that the judge conducting the case management conference may be   2A–65
informed of the general nature of the case and the issues which are expected to arise, after service of the defence and any reply the solicitors and counsel for each party shall draft an agreed case memorandum.

D5.2 The case memorandum should contain:

   (i) a short and uncontroversial description of what the case is about; and

   (ii) a very short and uncontroversial summary of the material procedural history of the case.

D5.3 Unless otherwise ordered, the solicitors for the claimant are to be responsible for producing and filing the case memorandum.

D5.4 The case memorandum should not refer to any application for an interim payment, to any order for an interim payment, to any voluntary interim payment, or to any payment or offer under CPR Part 36 or Part 37.

D5.5

(a) It should be clearly understood that the only purpose of the case memorandum is to help the judge understand broadly what the case is about. The case memorandum does not play any part in the trial. It is unnecessary, therefore, for parties to be unduly concerned about the precise terms in which it is drafted, provided it contains a reasonably fair and balanced description of the case.

(b) Accordingly, in all but the most exceptional cases it should be possible for the parties to draft an agreed case memorandum. However, if it proves impossible to do so, the claimant must draft the case memorandum and send a copy to the defendant. The defendant may provide its comments to the court (with a copy to the claimant) separately.

(c) The failure of the parties to agree a case memorandum is a matter which the court may wish to take into account when dealing with the costs of the case management conference.

D6 List of issues

2A–66 D6.1 After service of the defence (and any reply), the solicitors and counsel for each party shall produce an agreed list of the important issues in the case. The list should include both issues of fact and issue of law. A separate section of the document should list what is common ground between the parties (or any of them, specifying which).

D6.2 Unless otherwise ordered, the solicitors and counsel for the claimant are to have responsibility for the production and revision of the list of issues.

D7 Case management bundle

Preparation

2A–67 D7.1 Before the case management conference (see sections D3 and D8), a case management bundle should be prepared by the solicitors for the claimant: **PD58 § 10.8.**

Contents

D7.2 The case management bundle should only contain the documents listed below (where the documents have been created by the relevant time):

    (i) the claim form;

    (ii) all statements of case (excluding schedules), except that, if a summary has been prepared, the bundle should contain the summary, not the full statement of case;

    (iii) the case memorandum (see section D5);

    (iv) the list of issues (see section D6);

    (v) the case management information sheets and the pre-trial timetable if one has already been established (see sections D8.5 and D8.9);

    (vi) the principal orders in the case; and

    (vii) any agreement in writing made by the parties to disclose documents without making a list or any agreement in writing that disclosure (or inspection or both) shall take place in stages.

See generally **PD58 § 10.8.**

D7.3 The case management bundle must not include a copy of any order for an interim payment.

Lodging the case management bundle

D7.4 The case management bundle should be lodged with the Listing Office at least 7 days before the (first) case management conference (or earlier hearing at which the parties are represented and at which the business of the case management conference may be transacted: see section D3.7).

Preparation and upkeep

D7.5 The claimant (or other party responsible for the preparation and upkeep of the case management bundle), in consultation with the other parties, must revise and update the case management bundle as the case proceeds: **PD58 § 10.9**. The claimant should attend at the Case Management Unit for this purpose at the following stages:

(i) within 10 days of the case management conference, in order to add the pre-trial timetable (or any other order made at the case management conference) and an updated case memorandum;

(ii) within 10 days of an order being made on an application, if in the light of the order or the application it is necessary to add a copy of the order made (as a principal order in the case) or an updated case memorandum;

(iii) within 14 days of the service of any amended statement of case (or summary), in order to substitute a copy of the amended statement of case (or summary) for that which it replaces and to incorporate an updated case memorandum and (if appropriate) a revised list of issues;

(iv) within 10 days of any other revision to the case memorandum or list of issues, in order to incorporate the revised document.

D8 Case Management Conference

Application to postpone the case management conference

2A–68

D8.1

(a) An application to postpone the case management conference must be made within 21 days after all defendants who intend to serve a defence have done so.

(b) The application will be dealt with on paper unless the court considers it appropriate to direct an oral hearing.

Attendance at the case management conference

D8.2 Clients need not attend a case management conference unless the court otherwise orders. A representative who has conduct of the case must attend from each firm of solicitors instructed in the case. At least one of the advocates retained in the case on behalf of each party should also attend.

D8.3 The case management conference is a very significant stage in the case. It is not simply a substitute for the summons for directions under the former Rules of the Supreme Court and although parties are encouraged to agree proposals for directions for the consideration of the court, directions will not normally be made by consent without the need for attendance.

Applications

D8.4

(a) If by the time of the case management conference a party wishes to apply for an order in respect of a matter not covered by Questions (1)–(16) in the case management information sheet, he should make that application at the case management conference.

(b) In some cases notice of such an application may be given in the case management information sheet itself: see section D8.5(c).

(c) In all other cases the applicant should ensure that an application notice and any supporting evidence is filed and served in time to enable the application to be heard at the case management conference.

Materials: case management information sheet and case management bundle

D8.5

(a) All parties attending a case management conference must complete a case management information sheet: **PD58 § 10.7**. A standard form of case management information sheet is set out in Appendix 6. The information sheet is intended to include reference to all applications which the parties would wish to make at a case management conference.

(b) A completed case management information sheet must be provided by each party to the court (and copied to all other parties) at least 7 days before the case management conference.

(c) Applications not covered by the standard questions raised in the case management information sheet should be entered under Question (17). No other application notice is necessary if written evidence will not be involved and the 7 day notice given by entering the application on the information sheet will in all the circumstances be sufficient to enable all other parties to deal with the application.

D8.6 The case management bundle must be provided to the court at least 7 days before the case management conference: **PD58 § 10.8**. Only where it is essential for the court on the case management conference to see the full version of a statement of case that has been summarised in accordance with section C1.4 above should a copy of that statement of case be lodged for the case management conference.

The hearing

D8.7 The court's power to give directions at the case management conference is to be found in rules 3.1 and 58.13(4). At the case management conference the judge will:

(i) discuss the issues in the case, and the requirements of the case, with the advocates retained in the case;

(ii) fix the entire pre-trial timetable, or, if that is not practicable, fix as much of the pre-trial timetable as possible; and

(iii) in appropriate cases make an ADR order.

D8.8

(a) Rules 3.1(2) and 58.13(4) enable the court at the case management conference to stay the proceedings while the parties try to settle the case by alternative means. The case management information sheet requires the parties to indicate whether a stay for such purposes is sought.

(b) In an appropriate case an ADR order may be made without a stay of proceedings. The parties should consider carefully whether it may be possible to provide for ADR in the pre-trial timetable without affecting the date of trial.

(c) Where a stay has been granted for a fixed period for the purposes of ADR the court has power to extend it. If an extension of the stay is desired by all parties, a judge will normally be prepared to deal with an application for such an extension if it is made before the expiry of the stay by letter from the legal representatives of one of the parties. The letter should confirm that all parties consent to the application.

(d) An extension will not normally be granted for more than four weeks unless clear reasons are given to justify a longer period, but more than one extension may be granted.

The pre-trial timetable

D8.9 The pre-trial timetable will normally include:

(i) a progress monitoring date (see section D12 below); and

(ii) a direction that the parties attend upon the Clerk to the Commercial Court to obtain a fixed date for trial.

Variations to the pre-trial timetable

D8.10 The parties may agree minor variations to the time periods set out in the pre-trial timetable without the case needing to be brought back to the court provided that the variation

(i) will not jeopardise the date fixed for trial;

(ii) does not relate to the progress monitoring date; and

(iii) does not provide for the completion after the progress monitoring date of any step which was previously scheduled to have been completed by that date.

D8.11 If in any case it becomes apparent that variations to the pre-trial timetable are required which do not fall within section D8.10 above, the parties should apply to have the case management conference reconvened immediately. The parties should not wait until the progress monitoring date.

D9 Case management conference: Part 8 claims

D9 In a case commenced by the issue of a Part 8 claim form, a case management conference will normally take place on the first available date 6 weeks after service and filing of the defendant's evidence. At that case management conference the Court will make such pre-trial directions as are necessary, adapting (where useful in the context of the particular claim) those of the case management procedures used for a claim commenced by the issue of a Part 7 claim form. **2A–69**

D10 Case management conference: Part 20 claims

D10.1 Wherever possible, any party who intends to make a Part 20 claim should do so before the hearing of the case management conference dealing with the main claim. **2A–70**

D10.2 Where permission to make a Part 20 claim is required it should be sought at the case management conference in the main claim.

D10.3 If the Part 20 claim is a counterclaim by a defendant against a claimant alone, the court will give directions in the Part 20 claim at the case management conference in the main claim.

D10.4 If the Part 20 claim is not a counterclaim by a defendant against a claimant alone, the case management conference in the main claim will be reconvened on the first available date 6 weeks after service of the defence to the Part 20 claim.

D10.5 All parties to the proceedings (i.e. the parties to the main claim and the parties to the Part 20 claim) must attend the reconvened case management conference. There will not be a separate case management conference for the Part 20 claim alone.

D10.6 In any case involving a Part 20 claim the court will give case management directions at the same case management conferences as it gives directions for the main claim: **PD58 § 12**. The court will therefore normally only give case management directions at hearings attended by all parties to the proceedings.

D11 Management throughout the case

D11 The court will continue to take an active role in the management of the case throughout its progress to trial. Parties should be ready at all times to provide the court with such information and assistance as it may require for that purpose. **2A–71**

D12 Progress monitoring

Fixing the progress monitoring date

D12.1 The progress monitoring date will be fixed at the case management conference and will normally be after the date in the pre-trial timetable for exchange of witness statements and expert reports. **2A–72**

Progress monitoring information sheet

D12.2 At least 3 days (*i.e.* three clear days) before the progress monitoring date the parties must each send to the Case Management Unit (with a copy to all other parties) a progress monitoring information sheet to inform the court:

    (i) whether they have complied with the pre-trial timetable, and if they have not, the respects in which they have not; and

    (ii) whether they will be ready for a trial commencing on the fixed date specified in the pre-trial timetable, and if they will not be ready, why they will not be ready.

D12.3 A standard form of progress monitoring information sheet is set out in Appendix 12.

D13 Reconvening the case management conference

2A–73 D13.1 If in the view of the court the information given in the progress monitoring sheets justifies this course, the court may direct that the case management conference be reconvened.

D13.2 At a reconvened hearing of the case management conference the court may make such orders and give such directions as it considers appropriate.

D14 Pre-trial checklist

2A–74 D14 Not later than three weeks before the date fixed for trial each party must send to the Listing Office (with a copy to all other parties) a completed checklist confirming final details for trial (a "pre-trial checklist") in the form set out in Appendix 13.

2A–75 D15 Further information

D15.1

(a) If a party declines to provide further information requested under Part 18, the solicitors or counsel for the parties concerned must communicate directly with each other in an attempt to reach agreement before any application is made to the court.

(b) No application for an order that a party provide further information will normally be listed for hearing without prior written confirmation from the applicant that the requirements of this section D15.1(a) have been complied with.

D15.2 Because it falls within the definition of a statement of case (see rule 2.3(1)) a response providing further information under CPR Part 18 must be verified by a statement of truth.

D16 Fixed trial dates

2A–76 D16.1 Most cases will be given fixed trial dates immediately after the pre-trial timetable has been set at the case management conference.

D16.2 A fixed date for trial is given on the understanding that if previous fixtures have been substantially underestimated or other urgent matters need to be heard, the trial may be delayed. Where such delay might cause particular inconvenience to witnesses or others involved in the trial, the Clerk to the Commercial Court should be informed well in advance of the fixed date.

D17 Estimates of length of trial

2A–77 D17.1 At the case management conference an estimate will be made of the minimum and maximum lengths of the trial. The estimate will appear in the pre-trial timetable and will be the basis on which a date for trial will be fixed.

D17.2 If a party subsequently instructs new advocate(s) to appear on its behalf at the trial, the Listing Office should be notified of that fact within 14 days. Advocates newly instructed should review the estimate of the minimum and maximum lengths of the trial, and submit to the Listing Office a signed note revising or confirming the estimate as appropriate.

D17.3 A confirmed estimate of the minimum and maximum lengths of the trial, signed by the advocates who are to appear at the trial, should be attached to the pre-trial checklist.

D17.4 It is the duty of all advocates who are to appear at the trial to seek agreement, if possible, on the estimated minimum and maximum lengths of trial.

D17.5 The provisional estimate and (after it is given) the confirmed estimate must be kept under review by the advocates who are to appear at the trial. If at any stage an estimate needs to be revised, a signed revised estimate (whether agreed or not) must be submitted by the advocates to the Clerk to the Commercial Court.

D17.6 Accurate estimation of trial length is of great importance to the efficient functioning of the court. The court will be guided by, but will not necessarily accept, the estimates given by the parties

D18 Pre-Trial Review and trial timetable

D18.1 The court will order a pre-trial review in any case in which it considers it appropriate to do so. **2A–78**

D18.2 A pre-trial review will normally take place between 8 and 4 weeks before the date fixed for trial.

D18.3 Whenever possible the pre-trial review will be conducted by the trial judge. It should be attended by the advocates who are to appear at the trial: **PD58 § 11.2**.

D18.4 Before the pre-trial review the parties must attempt to agree a timetable for the trial providing for oral submissions, witnesses of fact and expert evidence: **PD58 § 11.3**. The claimant must file a copy of the draft timetable at least two days before the date fixed for the pre-trial review; any differences of view should be clearly identified: **PD58 § 11.4**. At the pre-trial review the judge may set a timetable for the trial and give such other directions for the conduct of the trial as he considers appropriate.

D19 Orders
2A–79

D19.1

(a) Except for orders made by the court on its own initiative under rule 3.3, and unless the court otherwise orders, every judgment or order will be drawn up by the parties and rule 40.3 is modified accordingly: rule 58.15(1).

(b) Consent orders are to be drawn up in accordance with the procedure described in section F9.

(c) All other orders are to be drawn up in draft by the parties and dated in the draft with the date of the judge's decision. The claimant is to have responsibility for drafting the order, unless it was made on the application of another party in which case that other party is to have the responsibility.

(d) Two copies of the draft, signed by the parties themselves, or by their solicitors or counsel, must be lodged with the Registry **within five days** of the decision of the court reflected in the draft.

D19.2 If the court orders that an act be done by a certain date without specifying a time for compliance, the latest time for compliance is 4.30 p.m. on the day in question.

D19.3 Orders that are required to be served must be served by the parties, unless the court otherwise directs.

E. Disclosure

E1 Generally

E1.1 The court will seek to ensure that disclosure is no wider than appropriate. Anything wider than standard disclosure (see section E3) will need to be justified. **2A–80**

E2 Procedure

E2.1 At the case management conference the court will normally wish to consider one or more of the following: **2A–81**

    (i) ordering standard disclosure: rule 31.5(1);

    (ii) dispensing with or limiting standard disclosure: rule 31.5(2);

    (iii) ordering sample disclosure;

    (iv) ordering disclosure in stages;

(v) ordering disclosure otherwise than by service of a list of documents, for example, by service of copy documents; and

(vi) ordering specific disclosure: rule 31.12.

E2.2 The obligations imposed by an order for disclosure continue until the proceedings come to an end. If, after a list of documents has been prepared and served, the existence (present or past) of further documents to which the order applies comes to the attention of the disclosing party, that party must prepare and serve a supplemental list.

E3 Standard disclosure

2A-82 E3.1 Standard disclosure is defined by rule 31.6. Where standard disclosure is ordered a party is required to disclose only:

(i) the documents on which he relies; and

(ii) documents which—
— adversely affect his own case;
— adversely affect another party's case; or
— support another party's case; and

(iii) documents which he is required to disclose by any relevant practice direction.

E3.1A All parties should have regard to issues which may specifically arise concerning electronic data and documents:

(1) Rule 31.4 contains a broad definition of a document. This extends to electronic documents, including e-mail and other electronic communications, word processed documents and databases. In addition to documents that are readily accessible from computer systems and other electronic devices and media, the definition covers those documents that are stored on servers and back-up systems and electronic documents that have been "deleted". It also extends to additional information stored and associated with electronic documents known as metadata. In most cases metadata is unlikely to be relevant.

(2) The parties should, prior to the first Case Management Conference, discuss any issues that may arise regarding searches for and the preservation of electronic documents. This may involve the parties providing information about the categories of electronic documents within their control, the computer systems, electronic devices and mediaon which any relevant documents may be held, the storage systems maintained by the parties and their document retention policies. In the case of difficulty or disagreement, the matter should be referred to a judge for directions at the earliest practical date, if possible at the first Case Management Conference.

(3) The parties should co-operate at an early stage as to the format in which electronic copy documents are to be provided on inspection. In the case of difficulty or disagreement, the matter should be referred to a Judge for directions at the earliest practical date, if possible at the first Case Management Conference.

(4) The existence of electronic documents impacts upon the extent of the reasonable search required by Rule 31.7 for the purposes of standard disclosure. The factors that may be relevant in deciding the reasonableness of a search for electronic documents include (but are not limited to) the following—

(a) The number of documents involved.

(b) The nature and complexity of the procedings.

(c) The ease and expense of retrieval of any particular document.
This includes:
(i) The accessibility of electronic documents or data including email communications on computer systems, servers, back-up systems and other electronic devices or media that may contain such documents taking into account alterations or developments in hardware or software systems used by the disclosing party and/or available to enable access to such documents.
(ii) The location of relevant electronic documents, data, computer systems, servers, back-up systems and other electronic devices or media that may contain such documents.

(iii) The likelihood of locating relevant data.

(iv) The cost of recovering any electronic documents.

(v) The cost of disclosing and providing inspection of any relevant electronic documents.

(vi) The likelihood that electronic documents will be materially altered in the course of recovery, disclosure or inspection.

(d) The significance of any document which is likely to be located during the search.

It may be reasonable to search some or all of the parties' electronic storage systems. In some circumstances, it may be reasonable to search for electronic documents by means of keyword searches (agreed as far as possible between the parties) even where a full review of each and every document would be unreasonable. There may be other forms of electronic search that may be appropriate in particular circumstances.

E3.2 A party who contends that to search for a category or class of document under rule 31.6(b) would be unreasonable must indicate this in his case management information sheet (see Appendix 6).

E3.3 In order to comply with rule 31.10(3) (which requires the list to identify the documents in a convenient order and manner and as concisely as possible) it will normally be necessary to list the documents in date order, to number them consecutively and to give each a concise description. However, where there is a large number of documents all falling within a particular category the disclosing party may (unless otherwise ordered) list those documents as a category rather than individually.

E3.4 Each party to the proceedings must serve a separate list of documents. This applies even if two or more parties are represented by the same firm of solicitors.

E3.5 If the physical structure of a file may be of evidential value (*e.g.* a placing or chartering file) solicitors should make one complete copy of the file in the form in which they received it before any documents are removed for the purpose of giving disclosure or inspection.

E3.6 Unless the Court directs otherwise, the disclosure statement must comply with the requirements of rules 31.7(3) and 31.10(6). In particular, it should

(i) expressly state that the disclosing party believes the extent of the search to have been reasonable in all the circumstances; and

(ii) draw attention to any particular limitations on the extent of the search adopted for reasons of proportionality and give the reasons why they were adopted.

E3.7 The disclosure statement for standard disclosure should begin with the following words:

"[I/we], [name(s)] state that [I/we] have carried out a reasonable and proportionate search to locate all the documents which [I am/*here name the party* is] required to disclose under [the order made by the Court or the agreement in writing made between the parties] on the [] day of [] 20[]."

E3.8 The disclosure statement for standard disclosure should end with the following certificate:

"[I/we] certify that [I/we] understand the duty of disclosure and to the best of [my/our] knowledge [I have/*here name the party* has] carried out that duty. [I/we] certify that the list above is a complete list of all documents which are or have been in [my/*here name the party's*] control and which [I am/*here name the party* is] obliged under [the said order or the said agreement in writing] to disclose."

E3.9 An adapted version of practice form **N265** (list of documents: standard disclosure) has been approved for use in the Commercial Court. A copy of this practice form (Form **N265(CC)**) is included at the end of the Guide. The court may at any stage order that a disclosure statement be verified by affidavit.

E3.10

(a) For the purposes of PD31 § 4.3 the court will normally regard as an appropriate person any person who is in a position responsibly and authoritatively to search for the documents required to be disclosed by that party and to make the statements contained in the disclosure statement concerning the documents which must be disclosed by that party

(b) A legal representative may in certain cases be an appropriate person.

(c) An explanation why the person is considered an appropriate person must still be given in the disclosure statement.

(d) A person holding an office or position in the disclosing party but who is not in a position responsibly and authoritatively to make the statements contained in the disclosure statement will not be regarded as an appropriate person to make the disclosure statement of the party.

(e) The court may of its own initiative or on application require that a disclosure statement also be signed by another appropriate person.

E4 Specific disclosure

2A–83 E4.1 Specific disclosure is defined by rule 31.12(2).

E4.2 An order for specific disclosure under rule 31.12 may in an appropriate case direct a party to carry out a thorough search for any documents which it is reasonable to suppose may adversely affect his own case or support the case of the party applying for disclosure or which may lead to a train of enquiry which has either of these consequences and to disclose any documents located as a result of that search: PD31 § 5.5.

E4.2A Where an application is made for specific disclosure the party from whom disclosure is sought should provide to the applicant and to the Court information as to the factors listed in E3.1A(4) above and its documents retention policy, to the extent such information is relevant to the application. At the hearing of the application, the Court may take into account the factors listed in E3.1A(4) as well as the width of the request and the conduct of the parties.

E4.3 The court may at any stage order that specific disclosure be verified by affidavit or witness statement.

E4.4 Applications for ship's papers are provided for in rule 58.14.

F. Applications

2A–84 F1 Generally

F1.1 ...

(a) Applications are governed by CPR Part 23 and PD23 as modified by rule 58 and PD58. As a result

 (i) PD23 § § 1 and 2.3–2.6 do not apply;

 (ii) PD23 § § 2.8 and 2.10 apply only if the proposed (additional) application will not increase the time estimate already given for the hearing for which a date has been fixed; and

 (iii) PD23 § 3 is subject in all cases to the judge's agreeing that the application may proceed without an application notice being served.

(b) An adapted version of practice form **N244** (application notice) has been approved for use in the Commercial Court. A copy of this practice form (Form **N244(CC)**) is included at the end of the Guide.

F1.2 An application for a consent order must include a draft of the proposed order signed on behalf of all parties to whom it relates: **PD58 § 14.1.**

F1.3 The requirement in PD23 § 12.1 that a draft order be supplied on disk does not apply in the Commercial Court since orders are generally drawn up by the parties: **PD58 § 14.2.**

Service

F1.4 Application notices are served by the parties, not by the court: **PD58 § 9**.

Evidence

F1.5

(a) Particular attention is drawn to PD23 § 9.1 which points out that even where no specific requirement for evidence is set out in the Rules or Practice Directions the court will in practice often need to be satisfied by evidence of the facts that are relied on in support of, or in opposition to, the application.

(b) Where convenient the written evidence relied on in support of an application may be included in the application notice, which may be lengthened for this purpose.

Time for service of evidence

F1.6 The time allowed for the service of evidence in relation to applications is governed by PD58 § 13.

Hearings

F1.7

(a) Applications (other than arbitration applications) will be heard in public in accordance with rule 39.2, save where otherwise ordered.

(b) With certain exceptions, arbitration applications will normally be heard in private: rule 62.10(3). See section O.

(c) An application without notice for a freezing order or a search order will normally be heard in private.

F1.8 Parties should pay particular attention to PD23 § 2.9 which warns of the need to anticipate the court's wish to review the conduct of the case and give further management directions. The parties should be ready to give the court their assistance and should be able to answer any questions that the court may ask for this purpose.

F1.9 PD23 § § 6.1–6.5 and § 7 deal with the hearing of applications by telephone (other than an urgent applications out of court hours) and the hearing of applications using video-conferencing facilities. These methods may be considered when an application needs to be made before a particular Commercial Judge who is currently on circuit. In most other cases applications are more conveniently dealt with in person.

F2 Applications without notice

F2.1 All applications should be made on notice, even if that notice has to be short, **2A–85** unless

(i) any rule or Practice Direction provides that the application may be made without notice; or

(ii) there are good reasons for making the application without notice, for example, because notice would or might defeat the object of the application.

F2.2 Where an application without notice does not involve the giving of undertakings to the court, it will normally be made and dealt with on paper, as, for example, applications for permission to serve a claim form out of the jurisdiction, and applications for an extension of time in which to serve a claim form.

F2.3 Any application for an interim injunction or similar remedy will require an oral hearing.

F2.4

(a) A party wishing to make an application without notice which requires an oral

211

hearing before a judge should contact the Clerk to the Commercial Court at the earliest opportunity.

(b) If a party wishes to make an application without notice at a time when no commercial judge is available he should apply to the Queen's Bench Judge in Chambers (see section P1.1).

F2.5 On all applications without notice it is the duty of the applicant and those representing him to make full and frank disclosure of all matters relevant to the application.

F2.6 The papers lodged for the application should include two copies of a draft of the order sought. Save in exceptional circumstances where time does not permit, all the evidence relied upon in support of the application and any other relevant documents must be lodged in advance with the Clerk to the Commercial Court. If the application is urgent, the Clerk to the Commercial Court should be informed of the fact and of the reasons for the urgency.

F3 Expedited applications

2A–86 F3.1 The Court will expedite the hearing of an application on notice in cases of sufficient urgency and importance.

F3.2 Where a party wishes to make an expedited application a request should be made to the Clerk to the Commercial Court on notice to all other parties.

2A–87 ### F4 Paper applications

F4.1

(a) Although contested applications are usually best determined at an oral hearing, some applications may be suitable for determination on paper.

(b) Attention is drawn to the provisions of rule 23.8 and PD23 § 11. If the applicant considers that the application is suitable for determination on paper, he should ensure before lodging the papers with the court

    (i) that the application notice together with any supporting evidence has been served on the respondent;

    (ii) that the respondent has been allowed the appropriate period of time in which to serve evidence in opposition;

    (iii) that any evidence in reply has been served on the respondent; and

    (iv) that there is included in the papers

        (A) the written consent of the respondent to the disposal of the application without a hearing; or

        (B) a statement by the applicant of the grounds on which he seeks to have the application disposed of without a hearing, together with confirmation that a copy has been served on the respondent.

(c) Only in exceptional cases will the court dispose of an application without a hearing in the absence of the respondent's consent.

F4.2

(a) Certain applications relating to the management of proceedings may conveniently be made in correspondence without issuing an application notice.

(b) It must be clearly understood that such applications are not applications without notice and the applicant must therefore ensure that a copy of the letter making the application is sent to all other parties to the proceedings.

(c) Accordingly, the following procedure should be followed when making an application of this kind:

    (i) the applicant should first ascertain whether the application is opposed by the other parties;

    (ii) if it is, the applicant should apply to the court by letter stating the nature of the order which it seeks and the grounds on which the application is made;

    (iii) a copy the letter should be sent (by fax, where possible) to all other parties at the same time as it is sent to the court;

    (iv) any other party wishing to make representations should do so by letter within two days (*i.e.* two clear days) of the date of the applicant's letter of application. The representations should be sent (by fax, where possible) to the applicant and all other parties at the same time as they are sent to the court;

    (v) the court will advise its decision by letter to the applicant. The applicant must forthwith copy the court's letter to all other parties, by fax where possible.

F5 Ordinary applications

F5.1 Applications likely to require an oral hearing lasting half a day or less are regarded as "ordinary" applications.

2A–88

F5.2 Ordinary applications will generally be heard on Fridays, but may be heard on other days. Where possible, the Listing Office will have regard to the availability of advocates when fixing hearing dates.

F5.3 Many ordinary applications, especially those in the non-Counsel list on Fridays, are very short indeed (e.g. applications to extend time). As in the past, it is likely that many, if not most, of such applications can be heard without evidence and on short (i.e. a few days) notice. The parties should however have in mind what is said in section F1.5(a) above.

F5.4

(a) The timetable for ordinary applications is set out in PD58 § 13.1 and is as follows:
    (i) evidence in support must be filed and served with the application;
    (ii) evidence in answer must be filed and served within 14 days thereafter;
    (iii) evidence in reply (if any) must be filed and served within 7 days thereafter.
(b) This timetable may be abridged or extended by agreement between the parties provided that any date fixed for the hearing of the application is not affected: **PD58 § 13.4**. In appropriate cases, this timetable may be abridged by the Court.

F5.5 An application bundle (see section F11) must be lodged with the Listing Office by 1 p.m. one clear day before the date fixed for the hearing. The case management bundle will also be required on the hearing; this file will be passed by the Listing Office to the judge. Only where it is essential for the court on the hearing of the ordinary application to see the full version of a statement of case that has been summarised in accordance with section C1.4 above should a copy of that statement of case be lodged for the ordinary application.

F5.6 Save in very short and simple cases, skeleton arguments must be provided by all parties. These must be lodged with the Listing Office and served on the advocates for all other parties to the application by 1 p.m. on the day before the date fixed for the hearing (i.e. the immediately preceding day). Guidelines on the preparation of skeleton arguments are set out in Part 1 of Appendix 9.

F5.7 Thus, for an application estimated for a half day or less and due to be heard on a Friday:
    (i) the application bundle must be lodged by 1 p.m. on Wednesday; and
    (ii) skeleton arguments must be lodged by 1 p.m. on Thursday.

F5.8 The applicant should, as a matter of course, provide all other parties to the application with a copy of the application bundle at the cost of the receiving party. Further copies should be supplied on request, again at the cost of the receiving party.

F5.9 Problems with the lodging of bundles or skeleton arguments should be notified to the Clerk to the Commercial Court as far in advance as possible. **If the application bundle or skeleton argument is not lodged by the time specified, the application may be stood out of the list without further warning**.

COMMERCIAL COURT

F6 Heavy applications

2A–89 F6.1 Applications likely to require an oral hearing lasting more than half a day are regarded as "heavy" applications.

F6.2 Heavy applications normally involve a greater volume of evidence and other documents and more extensive issues. They accordingly require a longer lead-time for preparation and exchange of evidence. Where possible the Listing Office will have regard to the availability of advocates when fixing hearing dates.

F6.3 The timetable for heavy applications is set out in PD58 § 13.2 and is as follows:
(i) evidence in support must be filed and served with the application;
(ii) evidence in answer must be filed and served within 28 days thereafter;
(iii) evidence in reply (if any) must be filed and served as soon as possible, and in any event within 14 days of service of the evidence in answer.

F6.4

(a) An application bundle (see section F11 must be lodged with the Listing Office by 4 p.m. two days (*i.e.* two clear days) before the date fixed for the hearing. The case management bundle will also be required on the hearing; this file will be passed by the Listing Office to the judge.

(b) Only where it is essential for the court on the hearing of the application to see the full version of a statement of case that has been summarised in accordance with section C1.4 above should a copy of that statement of case be lodged for the application.

F6.5 Skeleton arguments must be lodged with the Listing Office and served on the advocates for all other parties to the application as follows:–
(i) applicant's skeleton argument (with chronology unless one is unnecessary, and with a dramatis personae if one is warranted), by 4 p.m. two days (*i.e.* two clear days) before the hearing;
(ii) respondent's skeleton argument, by 4 p.m. one day (*i.e.* one clear day) before the hearing.

Guidelines on the preparation of skeleton arguments are set out in Part 1 of Appendix 9.

F6.6 Thus, for an application estimated for more than half a day and due to be heard on a Thursday:
(i) the application bundle and the applicant's skeleton argument must be lodged by 4 p.m. on Monday;
(ii) the respondent's skeleton argument must be lodged by 4 p.m. on Tuesday.

F6.7 The applicant must, as a matter of course, provide all other parties to the application with a copy of the application bundle at the cost of the receiving party. Further copies must be supplied on request, again at the cost of the receiving party.

F6.8 Problems with the lodging of bundles or skeleton arguments should be notified to the Clerk to the Commercial Court as far in advance as possible. **If the application bundle or skeleton argument is not lodged by the time specified, the application may be stood out of the list without further warning.**

F7 Evidence

2A–90 F7.1 Although evidence may be given by affidavit, it should generally be given by witness statement, except where PD32 requires evidence to be given on affidavit (as, for example, in the case of an application for a freezing order or a search order: **PD32 § 1.4**). In other cases the Court may order that evidence be given by affidavit: **PD32 § 1.4(1) and 1.6.**

F7.2 Witness statements and affidavits must comply with the requirements of PD32, save that photocopy documents should be used unless the court orders otherwise.

F7.3

(a) Witness statements must be verified by a statement of truth signed by the maker of the statement: rule 22.1.

(b) At hearings other than trial an applicant may rely on the application notice itself, and a party may rely on his statement of case, if the application notice or statement of case (as the case may be) is verified by a statement of truth: rule 32.6(2).

(c) A statement of truth in an application notice may also be signed as indicated in sections C1.8 and C1.9 above.

F7.4 Proceedings for contempt of court may be brought against a person who makes, or causes to be made, a false statement in a witness statement (or any other document verified by a statement of truth) without an honest belief in its truth: rule 32.14(1).

F8 Reading time   2A–91

F8

(a) It is essential for the efficient conduct of the court's business that the parties inform the court of the reading required in order to enable the judge to dispose of the application within the time allowed for the hearing and of the time likely to be required for that purpose. Accordingly

   (i) each party must lodge with the Listing Office by 1 p.m. on the day before the date fixed for the hearing of an application (*i.e.* the immediately preceding day) a reading list with an estimate of the time required to complete the reading;

   (ii) each party's reading list should identify the material **on both sides** which the court needs to read; and

   (iii) if any advocate considers that the time required for reading is likely to exceed 2¹/₂ hours, the Listing Office must be warned of that fact **not later than 4.00 p.m. one clear day before the hearing of the application**.

(b) **Failure to comply with these requirements may result in the adjournment of the hearing.**

F9 Applications disposed of by consent   2A–92

F9.1

(a) Consent orders may be submitted to the court in draft for approval and initialling without the need for attendance.

(b) Two copies of the draft, one of which (or a counterpart) must be signed on behalf of all parties to whom it relates, should be lodged at the Registry. The copies should be undated. The order will be dated with the date on which the judge initials it, but that does not prevent the parties acting on their agreement immediately if they wish.

(c) The parties should act promptly in lodging the copies at the Registry. If it is important that the orders are made by a particular date, that fact (and the reasons for it) should be notified in writing to the Registry.

F9.2 For the avoidance of doubt, this procedure is not normally available in relation to a case management conference or a pre-trial review. Whether or not the parties are agreed as between themselves on the directions that the court should be asked to consider giving at a case management conference or a pre-trial review, attendance will normally be required. See section D8.3.

F9.3 Where an order provides a time by which something is to be done the order should wherever possible state the particular date by which the thing is to be done rather than specify a period of time from a particular date or event: rule 2.9.

F10 Hearing dates, time estimates and time limits

F10.1 Dates for the hearing of applications to be attended by advocates are normally **2A–93** fixed after discussion with the counsel's clerks or with the solicitor concerned.

F10.2 The efficient working of the court depends on accurate estimates of the time needed for the oral hearing of an application. Over-estimating can be as wasteful as under-estimating.

F10.3 Subject to section F10.4, the Clerk to the Commercial Court will not accept or act on time estimates for the oral hearing of applications where those estimates exceed the following maxima:

Application to set aside service:	4 hours
Application for summary judgment:	4 hours
Application to set aside or vary interim remedy:	4 hours
Application to set aside or vary default judgment:	2 hours
Application to amend statement of case:	1 hour
Application for specific disclosure:	1 hour
Application for security for costs:	1 hour

F10.4 A longer listing time will only be granted upon application in writing specifying the additional time required and giving reasons why it is required. A copy of the written application should be sent to the advocates for all other parties in the case at the same time as it is sent to the Listing Office.

F10.5

(a) Not later than five days before the date fixed for the hearing the applicant must provide the Listing Office with his current estimate of the time required to dispose of the application.

(b) If at any time either party considers that there is a material risk that the hearing of the application will exceed the time currently allowed it must inform the Listing Office immediately.

F10.6

(a) All time estimates should be given on the assumption that the judge will have read in advance the skeleton arguments and the documents identified in the reading list. In this connection attention is drawn to section F8.

(b) A time estimate for an ordinary application should allow time for judgment and consequential matters; a time estimate for a heavy application should not.

F10.7 Save in the situation referred to at section F10.8, a separate estimate must be given for each application, including any application issued after, but to be heard at the same time as, another application.

F10.8 A separate estimate need not be given for any application issued after, but to be heard at the same time as, another application where the advocate in the case certifies in writing that

(i) the determination of the application first issued will necessarily determine the application issued subsequently; or

(ii) the matters raised in the application issued subsequently are not contested.

F10.9 If it is found at the hearing that the time required for the hearing has been significantly underestimated, the judge hearing the application may adjourn the matter and may make any special costs orders (including orders for the immediate payment of costs and wasted costs orders) as may be appropriate.

F10.10 Failure to comply with the requirements for lodging bundles for the application will normally result in the application not being heard on the date fixed at the expense of the party in default (see further sections F5.9 and F6.8 above). An order for immediate payment of costs may be made.

2A–94 F11 Application bundles

F11.1

216

(a) Bundles for use on applications may be compiled in any convenient manner but must contain the following documents (preferably in separate sections in the following order):

  (i) a copy of the application notice;

  (ii) a draft of the order which the applicant seeks;

  (iii) a copy of the statements of case;

  (iv) copies of any previous orders which are relevant to the application;

  (v) copies of the witness statements and affidavits filed in support of, or in op-position to, the application, together with any exhibits.

(b) Copies of the statements of case and of previous orders in the action should be provided in a separate section of the bundle. They should not be exhibited to witness statements.

(c) Witness statements and affidavits previously filed in the same proceedings should be included in the bundle at a convenient location. They should not be exhibited to witness statements.

F12 Chronologies, indices and dramatis personae

F12.1 For most applications it is of assistance for the applicant to provide a chronology. Dramatis personae are often useful as well.

2A–95

F12.2 Guidelines on the preparation of chronologies and indices are set out in Part 2 of Appendix 9.

F13 Authorities

F13.1 On some applications there will be key authorities that it would be useful for the judge to read before the oral hearing of the application. Copies of these authorities should be provided with the skeleton arguments.

2A–96

F13.2 It is also desirable for bundles of the authorities on which the parties wish to rely to be provided to the judge hearing the application as soon as possible after skeleton arguments have been exchanged.

F13.3 Unreported cases should only be cited where the advocate is ready to give an assurance that the transcript contains a statement of some principle of law, relevant to an issue on the application, of which the substance, as distinct from some mere choice of phraseology, is not to be found in any judgment that has appeared in one of the recognised series of law reports.

F14 Costs

F14.1 Costs are dealt with generally at section J13.

2A–97

F14.2 Reference should be also be made to the rules governng the summary assessment of costs for shorter hearings contained in Parts 43 and 44.

F14.3 In carrying out a summary assessment of costs, the court may have regard amongst other matters to:

  (i) advice from a Commercial Costs Judge or from the Chief Costs Judge on costs of specialist solicitors and counsel;

  (ii) any survey published by the London Solicitors Litigation Association showing the average hourly expense rate for solicitors in London;

  (iii) any information provided to the court at its request by one or more of the specialist associations (referred to at section A4.2) on average charges by specialist solicitors and counsel.

F15 Interim injunctions

Generally

2A–98

F15.1

(a) Applications for interim injunctions are governed by CPR Part 25.

(b) Applications must be made on notice in accordance with the procedure set out in CPR Part 23 unless there are good reasons for proceeding without notice.

F15.2 A party who wishes to make an application for an interim injunction must give the Clerk to the Commercial Court as much notice as possible.

F15.3

(a) Except when the application is so urgent that there has not been any opportunity to do so, the applicant must issue his claim form and obtain the evidence on which he wishes to rely in support of the application before making the application.

(b) On applications of any weight, and unless the urgency means that this is not possible, the applicant should provide the court at the earliest opportunity with a skeleton argument.

(c) An affidavit, and not a witness statement, is required on an application for a freezing order or a search order: **PD25 § 3.1**.

Fortification of undertakings

F15.4

(a) Where the applicant for an interim remedy is not able to show sufficient assets within the jurisdiction of the Court to provide substance to the undertakings given, particularly the undertaking in damages, he may be required to reinforce his undertakings by providing security.

(b) Security will be ordered in such form as the judge decides is appropriate but may, for example, take the form of a payment into court, a bond issued by an insurance company or a first demand guarantee or standby credit issued by a first-class bank.

(c) In an appropriate case the judge may order a payment to be made to the applicant's solicitors to be held by them as officers of the court pending further order. Sometimes the undertaking of a parent company may be acceptable.

Form of order

F15.5 Standard forms of wording for orders for freezing orders and search orders are set out in Appendix 5. The forms should be used save to the extent that the judge hearing a particular application considers there is good reason for adopting a different form.

F15.6 A phrase indicating that an interim remedy is to remain in force until judgment or further order means that it remains in force until the delivery of a final judgment. If an interim remedy continuing after judgment is required, say until judgment has been satisfied, an application to that effect must be made (see further section K1).

F15.7 It is good practice to draft an order for an interim remedy so that it includes a proviso which permits acts which would otherwise be a breach of the order to be done with the written consent of the claimant's solicitors. This enables the parties to agree in effect to variations (or the discharge) of the order without the necessity of coming back to the court.

Freezing orders

F15.8

(a) Freezing orders made on an application without notice will provide for a return date, unless the judge otherwise orders: **PD25 § 5.1(3)**. In the usual course, the return date given will be a Friday (unless a date for a case management conference has already been fixed, in which event the return date given will in the usual course be that date).

(b) If, after service or notification of the injunction, one or more of the parties considers that more than 15 minutes will be required to deal with the matter on the return date the Listing Office should be informed forthwith and in any event no later than 4 p.m. on the Wednesday before the Friday fixed as the return date.

(c) If the parties agree, the return date may be postponed to a later date on which all parties will be ready to deal with any substantive issues. In this event, an agreed form of order continuing the injunction to the postponed return date should be submitted for consideration by a judge and if the order is made in the terms submitted there will be no need for the parties to attend on the day originally fixed as the return date.

(d) In such a case the defendant and any other interested party will continue to have liberty to apply to vary or set aside the order.

F15.9 A provision for the defendant to give notice of any application to discharge or vary the order is usually included as a matter of convenience but it is not proper to attempt to fetter the right of the defendant to apply without notice or on short notice if need be.

F15.10 As regards freezing orders in respect of assets outside the jurisdiction, the standard wording in relation to effects on third parties should normally incorporate wording to enable overseas branches of banks or similar institutions which have offices within the jurisdiction to comply with what they reasonably believe to be their obligations under the laws of the country where the assets are located or under the proper law of the relevant banking or other contract relating to such assets.

F15.11 Any bank or third party served with, notified of or affected by a freezing order may apply to the court without notice to any party for directions, or notify the court in writing without notice to any party, in the event that the order affects or may affect the position of the bank or third party under legislation, regulations or procedures aimed to prevent money laundering.

Search orders

F15.12 Attention is drawn to the detailed requirements in respect of search orders set out in PD25 § § 7.1–8.3. The applicant for the search order will normally be required to undertake not to inform any third party of the search order or of the case until after a specified date.

Applications to discharge or vary freezing orders and search orders

F15.13 Applications to discharge or vary freezing orders and search orders are treated as matters of urgency for listing purposes. Those representing applicants for discharge or variation should ascertain before a date is fixed for the hearing whether, having regard to the evidence which they wish to adduce, the claimant would wish to adduce further evidence in opposition. If so, all reasonable steps must be taken by all parties to agree upon the earliest practicable date at which they can be ready for the hearing, so as to avoid the last minute need to vacate a fixed date. In cases of difficulty the matter should be referred to a judge who may be able to suggest temporary solutions pending the hearing.

F15.14 If a freezing order or a search order is discharged on an application to discharge or vary, or on the return date, the judge will consider whether it is appropriate that he should assess damages at once and direct immediate payment by the applicant.

Applications under section 25 of the Civil Jurisdiction and Judgments Act 1982

F15.15 A Part 8 claim form (rather than an application notice: cf. rule 25.4(2)) must be used for an application under section 25 of the Civil Jurisdiction and Judgments Act 1982 ("Interim relief in England and Wales and Northern Ireland in the absence of substantive proceedings"). The modified Part 8 procedure used in the Commercial Court is referred to at section B4 above.

F16 Security for costs

F16.1 Applications for security for costs are governed by rules 25.12–14.

2A–99

F16.2 The applicable practice is set out in Appendix 16.

G. Alternative Dispute Resolution ("ADR")

G1 Generally

2A-100 G1.1 While emphasising its primary role as a forum for deciding commercial cases, the Commercial Court encourages parties to consider the use of ADR (such as, but not confined to, mediation and conciliation) as an alternative means of resolving disputes or particular issues.

G1.2 Whilst the Commercial Court remains an entirely appropriate forum for resolving most of the disputes which are entered in the Commercial List, the view of the Commercial Court is that the settlement of disputes by means of ADR:

(i) significantly helps parties to save costs;

(ii) saves parties the delay of litigation in reaching finality in their disputes;

(iii) enables parties to achieve settlement of their disputes while preserving their existing commercial relationships and market reputation;

(iv) provides parties with a wider range of solutions than those offered by litigation; and

(v) is likely to make a substantial contribution to the more efficient use of judicial resources.

G1.3 The Commercial Judges will in appropriate cases invite the parties to consider whether their dispute, or particular issues in it, could be resolved through ADR.

G1.4 Legal representatives in all cases should consider with their clients and the other parties concerned the possibility of attempting to resolve the dispute or particular issues by ADR and should ensure that their clients are fully informed as to the most cost effective means of resolving their dispute.

G1.5 Parties who consider that ADR might be an appropriate means of resolving the dispute or particular issues in the dispute may apply for directions at any stage, including before service of the defence and before the case management conference.

G1.6 At the case management conference if it should appear to the judge that the case before him or any of the issues arising in it are particularly appropriate for an attempt at settlement by means of ADR but that the parties have not previously attempted settlement by such means, he may invite the parties to use ADR.

G1.7 The judge may, if he considers it appropriate, adjourn the case for a specified period of time to encourage and enable the parties to use ADR. He may for this purpose extend the time for compliance by the parties or any of them with any requirement under the rules, the Guide or any order of the Court.

G1.8 The Judge may further consider in an appropriate case making an ADR Order in the terms set out in Appendix 7.

G1.9

(a) The Clerk to the Commercial Court keeps some published information on individuals and bodies that offer ADR and arbitration services. If the parties are unable to agree upon a neutral individual or panel of individuals to act as a mediator, they may by consent refer to the judge for assistance in reaching such agreement.

(b) The court will not recommend any individual or body to act as a mediator or arbitrator.

G1.10 At the case management conference or at any other hearing in the course of which the judge makes an order providing for ADR he may make such order as to the costs that the parties may incur by reason of their using or attempting to use ADR as may in all the circumstances seem appropriate.

220

G2 Early neutral evaluation

G2.1 In appropriate cases and with the agreement of all parties the court will provide a without-prejudice, non-binding, early neutral evaluation ("ENE") of a dispute or of particular issues. **2A–101**

G2.2 The approval of the Judge in Charge of the List must be obtained before any ENE is undertaken.

G2.3 If, after discussion with the advocates representing the parties, it appears to a judge that an ENE is likely to assist in the resolution of the dispute or of particular issues, he will, with the agreement of the parties, refer the matter to the Judge in Charge of the List.

G2.4

(a) The Judge in Charge of the List will nominate a judge to conduct the ENE.
(b) The judge who is to conduct the ENE will give such directions for its preparation and conduct as he considers appropriate.

G2.5 The judge who conducts the ENE will take no further part in the case, either for the purpose of the hearing of applications or as the judge at trial, unless the parties agree otherwise.

H. Evidence for Trial

H1 Witnesses of fact

Preparation and form of witness statements

H1.1 Witness statements must comply with the requirements of PD32. The following points are also emphasised: **2A–102**

(i) the function of a witness statement is to set out in writing the evidence in chief of the witness; as far as possible, therefore, the statement should be in the witness's own words;

(ii) it should be as concise as the circumstances of the case allow without omitting any significant matters;

(iii) it should not contain lengthy quotations from documents;

(iv) it should not engage in argument;

(v) it must indicate which of the statements made in it are made from the witness's own knowledge and which are made on information or belief, giving the source for any statement made on information or belief;

(vi) it must contain a statement by the witness that he believes the matters stated in it are true; proceedings for contempt of court may be brought against a person if he makes, or causes to be made, a false statement in a witness statement without an honest belief in its truth: rule 32.14(1).

H1.2 It is improper to put pressure of any kind on a witness to give anything other than his own account of the matters with which his statement deals. It is also improper to serve a witness statement which is known to be false or which it is known the maker does not in all respects actually believe to be true.

Fluency of witnesses

H1.3 If a witness is not sufficiently fluent in English to give his evidence in English, the witness statement should be in the witness's own language and a translation provided.

H1.4 If a witness is not fluent in English but can make himself understood in broken English and can understand written English, the statement need not be in his own words provided that these matters are indicated in the statement itself. It must however be written so as to express as accurately as possible the substance of his evidence.

Witness statement as evidence in chief

H1.5

(a) Where a witness is called to give oral evidence, his witness statement is to stand as his evidence in chief unless the Court orders otherwise: rule 32.5(2).

(b) In an appropriate case the trial judge may direct that the whole or any part of a witness's evidence in chief is to be given orally. Any application for such an order should be made at the beginning of the trial.

Additional evidence from a witness

H1.6

(a) A witness giving oral evidence at trial may with the permission of the court amplify his witness statement and give evidence in relation to new matters which have arisen since the witness statement was served: rule 32.5(3). Permission will be given only if the Court considers that there is good reason not to confine the evidence of the witness to the contents of his witness statement: rule 32.5(4).

(b) A supplemental witness statement should normally be served where the witness proposes materially to add to, alter, correct or retract from what is in his original statement. Permission will be required for the service of a supplemental statement.

Notice of decision not to call a witness

H1.7

(a) A party who has decided not to call to give oral evidence at trial a witness whose statement has been served must give prompt notice of this decision to all other parties. He must at the same time state whether he proposes to put the statement in as hearsay evidence.

(b) If the party who has served the statement does not put it in as hearsay evidence, any other party may do so: rule 32.5(5).

Witness summonses

H1.8

(a) Rules 34.2–34.8 deal with witness summonses, including a summons for a witness to attend court or to produce documents in advance of the date fixed for trial.

(b) Witness summonses are served by the parties, not the court.

H2 Expert witnesses

Application for permission to call an expert witness

2A–103 H2.1 Any application for permission to call an expert witness or serve an expert's report should normally be made at the case management conference.

H2.2 Parties should bear in mind that expert evidence can lead to unnecessary expense and they should be prepared to consider the use of single joint experts in appropriate cases. In many cases the use of single joint experts is not appropriate and each party will generally be given permission to call one expert in each field requiring expert evidence. These are referred to in the Guide as "separate experts".

H2.3 When the use of a single joint expert is contemplated, the court will expect the parties to co-operate in developing, and agreeing to the greatest possible extent, terms of reference for that expert. In most cases the terms of reference will (in particular) identify in detail what the expert is asked to do, identify any documentary materials he is asked to consider and specify any assumptions he is asked to make.

Provisions of general application in relation to expert evidence

H2.4 The provisions set out in Appendix 11 to the Guide apply to all aspects of expert evidence (including expert reports, meetings of experts and expert evidence given orally) unless the court orders otherwise. Parties should ensure that they are drawn to the attention of any experts they instruct at the earliest opportunity.

Form and content of expert's reports

H2.5 Expert's reports must comply with the requirements of PD35 § § 1 and 2.

H2.6

(a) In stating the substance of all material instructions on the basis of which his report is written as required by rule 35.10(3) and PD35 § 1.2(8) an expert witness should state the facts or assumptions upon which his opinion is based.
(b) The expert must make it clear which, if any, of the facts stated are within his own direct knowledge.
(c) If a stated assumption is, in the opinion of the expert witness, unreasonable or unlikely he should state that clearly.

H2.7 It is useful if a report contains a glossary of significant technical terms.

Statement of truth

H2.8

(a) The report must be signed by the expert and must contain a statement of truth in accordance with Part 35.
(b) Proceedings for contempt of court may be brought against a person if he makes, or causes to be made, without an honest belief in its truth, a false statement in an expert's report verified in the manner set out in this section.

Request by an expert to the court for directions

H2.9 An expert may file with the court a written request for directions to assist him in carrying out his function as expert, but
 (i) at least 7 days before he does so (or such shorter period as the court may direct) he should provide a copy of his proposed request to the party instructing him; and
 (ii) at least 4 days before he does so (or such shorter period as the court may direct) he should provide a copy of his proposed request to all other parties.

Exchange of reports

H2.10 In appropriate cases the court will direct that the reports of expert witnesses be exchanged sequentially rather than simultaneously. This is an issue that the court will normally wish to consider at the case management conference.

Meetings of expert witnesses

H2.11 The court will normally direct a meeting or meetings of expert witnesses before trial. Sometimes it may be useful for there to be further meetings during the trial itself.

H2.12 The purposes of a meeting of experts are to give the experts the opportunity
 (i) to discuss the expert issues;
 (ii) to decide, with the benefit of that discussion, on which expert issues they share or can come to share the same expert opinion and on which expert issues there remains a difference of expert opinion between them (and what that difference is).

H2.13 Subject to section H2.16 below, the content of the discussion between the experts at or in connection with a meeting is without prejudice and shall not be referred to at the trial unless the parties so agree: rule 35.12(4).

H2.14 Subject to any directions of the court, the procedure to be adopted at a meeting of experts is a matter for the experts themselves, not the parties or their legal representatives.

H2.15 Neither the parties nor their legal representatives should seek to restrict the freedom of experts to identify and acknowledge the expert issues on which they agree at, or following further consideration after, meetings of experts.

H2.16 Unless the court orders otherwise, at or following any meeting the experts should prepare a joint memorandum for the court recording:
  (i) the fact that they have met and discussed the expert issues;
  (ii) the issues on which they agree;
  (iii) the issues on which they disagree; and
  (iv) a brief summary of the reasons for their disagreement.

H2.17 If experts reach agreement on an issue that agreement shall not bind the parties unless they expressly agree to be bound by it.

Written questions to experts

H2.18

(a) Under rule 35.6 a party may, without the permission of the court, put written questions to an expert instructed by another party (or to a single joint expert) about his report. Unless the court gives permission or the other party agrees, such questions must be for the purpose only of clarifying the report.
(b) The court will pay close attention to the use of this procedure (especially where separate experts are instructed) to ensure that it remains an instrument for the helpful exchange of information. The court will not allow it to interfere with the procedure for an exchange of professional opinion at a meeting of experts, or to inhibit that exchange of professional opinion. In cases where (for example) questions that are oppressive in number or content are put, or questions are put for any purpose other than clarification of the report, the court will not hesitate to disallow the questions and to make an appropriate order for costs against the party putting them.

Documents referred to in experts' reports

H2.19 Unless they have already been provided on inspection of documents at the stage of disclosure, copies of any photographs, plans, analyses, measurements, survey reports or other similar documents relied on by an expert witness as well as copies of any unpublished sources must be provided to all parties at the same time as his report.

H2.20

(a) Rule 31.14(e) provides that (subject to rule 35.10(4)) a party may inspect a document mentioned in an expert's report. In a commercial case an expert's report will frequently, and helpfully, list all or many of the relevant previous papers (published or unpublished) or books written by the expert or to which the expert has contributed. Requiring inspection of this material may often be unrealistic, and the collating and copying burden could be huge.
(b) Accordingly, a party wishing to inspect a document in an expert report should (failing agreement) make an application to the court. The court will not permit inspection unless it is satisfied that it is necessary for the just disposal of the case and that the document is not reasonably available to the party making the application from an alternative source.

Trial

H2.21 At trial the evidence of expert witnesses is usually taken as a block, after the evidence of witnesses of fact has been given.

H3 Evidence by video link

2A–104 H3.1 In an appropriate case permission may be given for the evidence of a witness to be given by video link. If permission is given the court will give directions for the conduct of this part of the trial.

H3.2 The party seeking permission to call evidence by video link should prepare and serve on all parties and lodge with the Court a memorandum dealing with the matters outlined in the Video-conferencing Protocol (Appendix 14) and setting out precisely what arrangements are proposed. Where the proposal involves transmission from a location with no existing video-link facility, experience shows that questions of feasibility, timing and cost will require particularly close investigation.

H3.3 An application for permission to call evidence by video link should be made, if possible, at the case management conference or, at the latest, at any pre-trial review. However, an application may be made at an even later stage if necessary.

H3.4 In considering whether to give permission for evidence to be given in this way the court will be concerned in particular to balance any potential savings of costs against the inability to observe the witness at first hand when giving evidence.

H4 Taking evidence abroad

H4.1 In an appropriate case permission may be given for the evidence of a witness to be taken abroad. CPR Part 34 contains provisions for the taking of evidence by deposition, and the issue of letters of request. **2A–105**

H4.2 In a very exceptional case, and subject in particular to all necessary approvals being obtained and diplomatic requirements being satisfied, the court may be willing to conduct part of the proceedings abroad. However, if there is any reasonable opportunity for the witness to give evidence by video link, the court is unlikely to take that course.

J. Trial

J1 Expedited trial

J1.1 The Commercial Court is able to provide an expedited trial in cases of sufficient urgency and importance. **2A–106**

J1.2 A party seeking an expedited trial should apply to the Judge in Charge of the Commercial List on notice to all parties at the earliest possible opportunity. The application should normally be made after issue and service of the claim form but before service of particulars of claim.

J2 Split trials

J2.1 It will sometimes be advantageous to try liability first. Assessment of damages can be referred to a judge of the Technology and Construction Court or to a Master, or the parties may choose to ask an arbitrator to decide them. The same approach can be applied to other factual questions. **2A–107**

J3 Documents for trial

J3.1 Bundles of documents for the trial must be prepared in accordance with Appendix 10. **2A–108**

J3.2 The number, content and organisation of the trial bundles must be approved by the advocates with the conduct of the trial.

J3.3 Consideration must always be given to what documents are and are not relevant and necessary. Where the court is of the opinion that costs have been wasted by the copying of unnecessary documents it will have no hesitation in making a special order for costs against the person responsible.

J3.4 The number content and organisation of the trial bundles should be agreed in accordance with the following procedure:

(i) the claimant must submit proposals to all other parties at least 6 weeks before the date fixed for trial; and

(ii) the other parties must submit details of additions they require and any suggestions for revision of the claimant's proposals to the claimant at least 4 weeks before the date fixed for trial.

This information must be supplied in a form that will be most convenient for the recipient to understand and respond to. The form to be used should be discussed between the parties before the details are supplied.

J3.5

(a) It is the claimant's responsibility to prepare and lodge the agreed trial bundles.

(b) If another party wishes to put before the court a bundle that the claimant regards as unnecessary he must prepare and lodge it himself.

J3.6

(a) Preparation of the trial bundles must be completed not later than 2 weeks before the date fixed for trial unless the court orders otherwise.

(b) Any party preparing a trial bundle should, as a matter of course, provide all other parties who are to take part in the trial with a copy, at the cost of the receiving party. Further copies should be supplied on request, again at the cost of the receiving party.

J3.7 Unless the court orders otherwise, a full set of the trial bundles must be lodged with the Listing Office at least 7 days before the date fixed for trial.

J3.8 Failure to comply with the requirements for lodging bundles for the trial may result in the trial not commencing on the date fixed, at the expense of the party in default. An order for immediate payment of costs may be made.

J3.9 If oral evidence is to be given at trial, the claimant must provide a clean unmarked set of all relevant trial bundles for use in the witness box. The claimant is responsible for ensuring that these bundles are kept up to date throughout the trial.

J4 Information technology at trial

2A–109 J4.1 The use of information technology at trial is encouraged where it is likely substantially to save time and cost or to increase accuracy.

J4.2 If any party considers that it might be advantageous to make use of information technology in preparation for, or at, trial, the matter should be raised at the case management conference. This is particularly important if it is considered that document handling systems would assist disclosure and inspection of documents or the use of documents at trial.

J4.3 Where information technology is to be used for the purposes of presenting the case at trial the same system must be used by all parties and must be made available to the court.

J5 Reading lists, authorities and trial timetable

2A–110 J5.1 Unless the court orders otherwise, a single reading list approved by all advocates must be lodged with the Listing Office not later than 1 p.m. two days (i.e. two clear days) before the date fixed for trial together with an estimate of the time required for reading.

J5.2

(a) If any party objects to the judge reading any document in advance of the trial, the objection and its grounds should be clearly stated in a letter accompanying the trial bundles and in the skeleton argument of that party.

(b) Parties should consider in particular whether they have any objection to the judge's reading the witness statements before the trial.

(c) In the absence of objection, the judge will be free to read the witness statements and documents in advance.

J5.3

(a) A composite bundle of the authorities referred to in the skeleton arguments should be lodged with the Listing Office as soon as possible after skeleton arguments have been exchanged.

(b) Unless otherwise agreed, the preparation of the bundle of authorities is the responsibility of the claimant, who should provide copies to all other parties. Advocates should liaise in relation to the production of bundles of authorities to ensure that the same authority does not appear in more than one bundle.

J5.4 Unreported cases should normally only be cited where the advocate is ready to give an assurance that the transcript contains a statement of some relevant principle of law of which the substance, as distinct from some mere choice of phraseology, is not to be found in any judgment that has appeared in one of the general or specialised series of law reports.

J5.5

(a) When lodging the reading list the claimant should also lodge a trial timetable.

(b) A trial timetable may have been fixed by the judge at the pre-trial review (section D18.4 above). If it has not, a trial timetable should be prepared by the advocate(s) for the claimant after consultation with the advocate(s) for all other parties.

(c) If there are differences of view between the advocate(s) for the claimant and the advocate(s) for other parties, these should be shown.

(d) The trial timetable will provide for oral submissions, witness evidence and expert evidence over the course of the trial. On the first day of the trial the judge may fix the trial timetable, subject to any further order.

J6 Skeleton arguments etc. at trial

J6.1 Written skeleton arguments should be prepared by each party. Guidelines on the preparation of skeleton arguments are set out in Part 1 of Appendix 9.　　**2A–111**

J6.2 Unless otherwise ordered, the skeleton arguments should be served on all other parties and lodged with the court as follows:

    (i) by the claimant, not later than 1 p.m. two days (*i.e.* two clear days) before the start of the trial;

    (ii) by each of the defendants, not later than 1 p.m. one day (*i.e.* one clear day) before the start of the trial.

J6.3 In heavier cases it will often be appropriate for skeleton arguments to be served and lodged at earlier times than indicated at section J6.2. The timetable should be discussed between the advocates and may be the subject of a direction in the pre-trial timetable or at any pre-trial review.

J6.4 The claimant should provide a chronology with his skeleton argument. Indices (i.e. documents that collate key references on particular points, or a substantive list of the contents of a particular bundle or bundles) and dramatics personae should also be provided where these are likely to be useful. Guidelines on the preparation of chronologies and indices are set out in Part 2 of Appendix 9.

J7 Trial sitting days and hearing trials in public

J7.1 Trial sitting days will not normally include Fridays.　　**2A–112**

J7.2 Where it is necessary in order to accommodate hearing evidence from certain witnesses or types of witness, the court may agree to sit outside normal hours.

J7.3 The general rule is that a hearing is to be in public: rule 39.2(1).

J8 Oral opening statements at trial

J8.1 Oral opening statements should as far as possible be uncontroversial and in any　　**2A–113**

COMMERCIAL COURT

event no longer than the circumstances require. Even in a very heavy case, oral opening statements may be very short.

J8.2 At the conclusion of the opening statement for the claimant the advocates for each of the other parties will usually each be invited to make a short opening statement.

J9 Applications in the course of trial

2A–114 J9.1 It will not normally be necessary for an application notice to be issued for an application which is to be made during the course of the trial, but all other parties should be given adequate notice of the intention to apply.

J9.2 Unless the judge directs otherwise the parties should prepare skeleton arguments for the hearing of the application

J10 Oral closing submissions at trial

2A–115 J10.1 All parties will be expected to make oral closing submissions, whether or not closing submissions have been made in writing. It is a matter for the advocate to consider how in all the circumstances these oral submissions should be presented.

J10.2 Unless the trial judge directs otherwise, the claimant will make his oral closing submissions first, followed by the defendant(s) in the order in which they appear on the claim form with the claimant having a right of reply.

2A–116 ### J11 Written closing submissions at trial

J11.1

(a) In a more substantial trial, the court will normally also require closing submissions in writing before oral closing submissions.

(b) In such a case the court will normally allow an appropriate period of time after the conclusion of the evidence to allow the preparation of these submissions.

(c) Even in a less substantial trial the court will normally require a skeleton argument on matters of law.

2A–117 ### J12 Judgment

J12.1

(a) When judgment is reserved the judge may deliver judgment orally or by handing down a written judgment.

(b) If the judge intends to hand down a written judgment a copy of the draft text marked

"Unapproved Judgment. No permission is granted to copy or use in Court"

and bearing the rubric

"Confidential to Counsel and Solicitors, but the substance may be communicated to clients not more than one hour before the giving of judgment".

will normally be supplied to the advocates one clear day before the judgment is to be delivered.

(c) Advocates should inform the judge's clerk not later than noon on the day before judgment is to be handed down of any typographical or other errors of a similar nature which the judge might wish to correct.

(d) The requirement to treat the text as confidential must be strictly observed. Failure to do so amounts to a contempt of court.

J12.2

(a) Judgment is not delivered until it is formally pronounced in open court.

(b) Copies of the approved judgment will be made available to the parties, to law reporters and to any other person wanting a copy.

(c) The judge may direct that the written judgment stand as the definitive record and that no transcript need be made. Any editorial corrections made at the time of handing down will be incorporated in an approved official text as soon as possible, and the approved official text, so marked, will be available from the Mechanical Recording Department.

J13 Costs

J13.1 The rules governing the award and assessment of costs are contained in CPR Parts 43 to 48. **2A–118**

J13.2 The summary assessment procedure provided for in Parts 43 and 44 also applies to trials lasting one day or less.

K. After Trial

K1 Continuation, variation and discharge of interim remedies and undertakings **2A–119**

K1.1

(a) Applications to continue, vary or discharge interim remedies or undertakings should be made to a Commercial Judge, even after trial.
(b) If a party wishes to continue a freezing order after trial or judgment, care should be taken to ensure that the application is made before the existing freezing order has expired.

K2 Accounts and enquiries

K2.1 The court may order that accounts and inquiries be referred to a judge of the Technology and Construction Court or to a Master. Alternatively, the parties may choose to refer the matter to arbitration. **2A–120**

K3 Enforcement

K3.1 Unless the court orders otherwise, all proceedings for the enforcement of any judgment or order for the payment of money given or made in the Commercial Court will be referred automatically to a master of the Queen's Bench Division or a district judge: **PD58 § 1.2(2)**. **2A–121**

K3.2 Applications in connection with the enforcement of a judgment or order for the payment of money should accordingly be directed to the Registry which will allocate them to the Admiralty Registrar or to one of the Queen's Bench masters as appropriate.

K4 Assessment of damages or interest after a default judgment

K4.1 Unless the court orders otherwise, the assessment of damages or interest following the entry of a default judgment for damages or interest to be assessed will be carried out by the Admiralty Registrar or one of the Queen's Bench masters to whom the case is allocated by the Registry. **2A–122**

L. Multi-party Disputes

L1 Early consideration

L1.1 Cases which involve, or are expected to involve, a large number of claimants or defendants require close case management from the earliest point. The same is true where there are, or are likely to be, a large number of separate cases involving the same or similar issues. Both classes of case are referred to as "multi-party" disputes. **2A–123**

L1.2

(a) The Judge in Charge of the List should be informed as soon as it becomes apparent that a multi-party dispute exists or is likely to exist and an early application for directions should be made.

(b) In an appropriate case an application for directions may be made before issue of a claim form. In some cases it may be appropriate for an application to be made without notice in the first instance.

L2 Available procedures

2A–124 L2.1 In some cases it may be appropriate for the court to make a Group Litigation Order under Part 19 of the Rules. In other cases it may be more convenient for the court to exercise its general powers of management. These include powers

(i) to dispense with statements of case;

(ii) to direct parties to serve outline statements of case;

(iii) to direct that cases be consolidated or managed and tried together;

(iv) to direct that certain cases or issues be determined before others and to stay other proceedings in the meantime;

(v) to advance or put back the usual time for pre-trial steps to be taken (for example the disclosure of documents by one or more parties or a payment into court).

L2.2 Attention is drawn to the provisions of Section III of Part 19, rules 19.10–19.15 and the practice direction supplementing Section III of Part 19. Practitioners should note that the provisions of Section III of Part 19 give the court additional powers to manage disputes involving multiple claimants or defendants. They should also note that a Group Litigation Order may not be made without the consent of the Lord Chief Justice: **PD19B § 3.3(1)**.

L2.3 An application for a Group Litigation Order should be made in the first instance to the Judge in Charge of the List: **PD19B § 3.5**.

M. Litigants in Person

M1 The litigant in person

2A–125 M1.1 Litigants in person appear less often in the Commercial Court than in some other courts. Their position requires special consideration.

M2 Represented parties

2A–126 M2.1 Where a litigant in person is involved in a case the court will expect solicitors and counsel for other parties to do what they reasonably can to ensure that he has a fair opportunity to prepare and put his case.

M2.2 The duty of an advocate to ensure that the court is informed of all relevant decisions and legislative provisions of which he is aware (whether favourable to his case or not) and to bring any procedural irregularity to the attention of the court during the hearing is of particular importance in a case where a litigant in person is involved.

M2.3 Further, the court will expect solicitors and counsel appearing for other parties to ensure that the case memorandum, the list of issues and all necessary bundles are prepared and provided to the court in accordance with the Guide, even where the litigant in person is unwilling or unable to participate.

M2.4 If the claimant is a litigant in person the judge at the case management conference will normally direct which of the parties is to have responsibility for the preparation and upkeep of the case management bundle.

M2.5 At the case management conference the court may give directions relating to the costs of providing application bundles and trial bundles to the litigant in person.

M3 Companies without representation

2A–127 M3.1 Although rule 39.6 allows a company or other corporation with the permission of the court to be represented at trial by an employee, the complexity of most cases in the Commercial Court makes that unsuitable. Accordingly, permission is likely to be given only in unusual circumstances.

N. Admiralty

N1 General

N1.1 Proceedings in the Admiralty Court are dealt with in Part 61 and its associated **2A–128** practice direction.

N1.2 The Admiralty & Commercial Courts Guide has been prepared in consultation with the Admiralty Judge. It has been adopted to provide guidance about the conduct of proceedings in the Admiralty Court. The Guide must be followed in the Admiralty Court unless the content of Part 61, its associated practice direction or the terms of this section N require otherwise.

N1.3 One significant area of difference between practice in the Commercial Court and practice in the Admiralty Court is that many interlocutory applications are heard by the Admiralty Registrar who has all the powers of the Admiralty judge save as provided otherwise: rule 61.1(4).

N2 The Admiralty Court Committee

N2.1 The Admiralty Court Committee provides a specific forum for contact and **2A–129** consultation between the Admiralty Court and its users. Any correspondence should be addressed to the Deputy Admiralty Marshal, Royal Courts of Justice, Strand, WC2A 2LL.

N3 Commencement of proceedings, service of Statements of Case and associated matters

N3.1 Sections B and C of this guide apply to all Admiralty claims except: **2A–130**
    (i) a claim in rem;
    (ii) a collision claim; and
    (iii) a limitation claim.

N4 Commencement and early stages of a claim in rem

N4.1 The early stages of an in rem claim differ from those of other claims. **2A–131**

The procedure is governed generally by rule 61.3 and PD61 § § 3.1–3.11.

N4.2 In addition, the following sections of the Guide apply to claims in rem: B3.3, B3.7–B3.11, B6.4–B6.6, C1.1–C1.9, C1.11 and C2.1 (ii)–C5.4.

N4.3 Subject to PD61 § 3.7, section C1.10 of the Guide also applies to claims in rem.

N4.4 After an acknowledgement of service has been filed a claim in rem follows the procedure applicable to a claim proceeding in the Commercial List, save that the Claimant is allowed 75 days in which to serve his particulars of claim: **PD61 § 3.10**.

N5 The early stages of a Collision Claim

N5.1 Where a collision claim is commenced in rem, the general procedure applicable **2A–132** to claims in rem applies subject to rule 61.4 and PD61 § § 4.1–4.5.

N5.2 Where a collision claim is not commenced in rem the general procedure applicable to claims proceeding in the Commercial List applies subject to rule 61.4 and PD61 § § 4.1–4.5.

N5.3 Service of a claim form out of the jurisdiction in a collision claim (other than a claim in rem) is permitted in the circumstances identified in rule 61.4(7) only and the procedure set out in Appendix 15 of the Guide should be adapted accordingly.

N5.4 One particular feature of a collision action is that the parties must prepare and file a Collision Statement of Case. Prior to the coming into force of Part 61, a

Collision Statement of Case was known as a Preliminary Act and the law relating to Preliminary Acts continues to apply to Collision Statements of Case: **PD61 § 4.5**.

N5.5 The provisions of Appendix 4 apply to part 2 of a Collision Statement of Case (but not to part 1).

N5.6 Every party is required, so far as it is able, to provide full and complete answers to the questions contained in part 1 of the Collision Statement of Case. The answers should descend to a reasonable level of particularity.

N5.7 The answers to the questions contained in part 1 are treated as admissions made by the party answering the questions and leave to amend such answers will be granted only in exceptional circumstances.

N6 The early stages of a Limitation Claim

2A–133 N6.1 The procedure governing the early stages of a limitation claim differs significantly from the procedure relating to other claims and is contained in rule 61.11 and PD61 § 10.1.

N6.2 Service of a limitation claim form out of the jurisdiction is permitted in the circumstances identified in rule 61.11 (5) only and the procedure set out in Appendix 15 of the Guide should be adapted accordingly.

N7 Issue of documents when the Registry is closed.

2A–134 N7.1 When the Registry is closed (and only when it is closed) an Admiralty claim form may be issued on the following designated fax machine: 020 7947 6667 and only on that machine.

N7.2 The procedure to be followed is set out in Appendix 3 of the Guide.

N7.3 The issue of an Admiralty claim form in accordance with the procedure set out in Appendix 3 shall have the same effect for all purposes as a claim form issued in accordance with the relevant provisions of rule 61 and PD61.

N7.4 When the Registry is closed (and only when it is closed) a notice requesting a caution against release may be filed on the following designated fax machine: 020 7947 6056 and only on that machine. This machine is manned 24 hours a day by court security staff (telephone 020 7947 6260).

N7.5 The notice requesting the caution should be transmitted with a note in the following form for ease of identification by security staff:
"CAUTION AGAINST RELEASE
Please find notice requesting caution against release of the ... (*name ship/identify cargo*) ... for filing in the Admiralty & Commercial Registry."

N7.6 The notice must be in Admiralty Form No. **ADM11** and signed by a solicitor acting on behalf of the applicant.

N7.7 Subject to the provisions of sections N7.9 and N7.10 below, the filing of the notice takes place when the fax is recorded as having been received.

N7.8 When the Registry is next open to the public, the filing solicitor or his agent shall attend and deliver to the Registry the document which was transmitted by fax together with the transmission report. Upon satisfying himself that the document delivered fully accords with the document received by the Registry, the court officer shall stamp the document delivered with the time and date on which the notice was received, enter the same in the caution register and retain the same with the faxed copy.

N7.9 Unless otherwise ordered by the court, the stamped notice shall be conclusive proof that the notice was filed at the time and on the date stated.

N7.10 If the filing solicitor does not comply with the foregoing procedure, or if the notice is not stamped, the notice shall be deemed never to have been filed.

N8 Case Management

N8.1 The case management provisions of the Guide apply to Admiralty claims save **2A–135** that:

(i) In Admiralty claims the case management provisions of the Guide are supplemented by PD61 § § 2.1–2.3 which make provision for the early classification and streaming of cases;

(ii) In a collision case the claimant should apply for a case management conference within 7 days after the last Collision Statement of Case is filed;

(iii) In a limitation claim where the right to limit is not admitted and the claimant seeks a general limitation decree, the claimant must, within 7 days after the date of the filing of the defence of the defendant last served or the expiry of the time for doing so, apply to the Admiralty Registrar for a case management conference: **PD61 § 10.7**;

(iv) In a collision claim or a limitation claim a mandatory case management conference will normally take place on the first available date 5 weeks after the date when the claimant is required to take steps to fix a date for the case management conference;

(v) In a limitation claim, case management directions are initially given by the Registrar: **PD61 § 10.8**;

(vi) In the Admiralty Court, the Case Management Information Sheet should be in the form in Appendix 6 of this Guide but should also include the following questions:–

1. Do any of the issues contained in the List of Issues involve questions of navigation or other particular matters of an essentially Admiralty nature which require the trial to be before the Admiralty Judge?

2. Is the case suitable to be tried before a Deputy Judge nominated by the Admiralty Judge?

3. Do you consider that the court should sit with nautical or other assessors? If you intend to ask that the court sit with one or more assessors who is not a Trinity Master, please state the reasons for such an application.

N8.2 The two judge team system referred to in section D.4 of the Guide does not apply to Admiralty claims.

N9 Evidence

N9.1 In collision claims, section H1.5 and Appendix 8 are subject to the proviso that **2A–136** experience has shown that it is usually desirable for the main elements of a witness' evidence in chief to be adduced orally.

Authenticity

N9.2 Where:

(i) the authenticity of any document or entry in any document is challenged;

(ii) it will be suggested at trial that a document or entry in a document was not made at the time or by the person stated; or

(iii) a document or entry in a document will be in any other way challenged in a manner which may require a witness to be produced at trial to support the document or entry in a document;

such challenge—

(i) must be raised in good time in advance of the trial to enable any such witness to be produced; and

(ii) must be contained in the skeleton argument.

Skeleton arguments in Collision Claims

N9.3 In collision claims the skeleton argument of each party must be accompanied by a plot or plots of that party's case or alternative cases as to the navigation of vessels during and leading to the collision. All plots must contain a sufficient indication of the assumptions used in the preparation of the plot.

COMMERCIAL COURT

N10 Split trials, accounts, enquiries and enforcement

2A-137 N10.1 In collision claims it is usual for liability to be tried first and for the assessment of damages and interest to be referred to the Admiralty Registrar.

N10.2 Where the Admiralty Court refers an account, enquiry or enforcement, it will usually refer the matter to the Admiralty Registrar.

N11 Release of vessels out of hours

2A-138 N11.1 This section makes provision for release from arrest when the Registry is closed.

N11.2 An application for release under rule 61.8(4)(c) or (d) may, when the Registry is closed, be made in, and only in, the following manner:

(i) The solicitor for the arrestor or the other party applying must telephone the security staff at the Royal Courts of Justice (020 7947 6260) and ask to be contacted by the Admiralty Marshal, who will then respond as soon as practicably possible;

(ii) Upon being contacted by the Admiralty Marshal the solicitor must give oral instructions for the release and an oral undertaking to pay the fees and expenses of the Admiralty Marshal as required in Form No. **ADM12**;

(iii) The arrestor or other party applying must then send a written request and undertaking on Form No. **ADM12** by fax to a number given by the Admiralty Marshal;

(iv) The solicitor must provide written consent to the release from all persons who have entered cautions against release (and from the arrestor if the arrestor is not the party applying) by sending such consents by fax to the number supplied by the Admiralty Marshal;

(v) Upon the Admiralty Marshal being satisfied that no cautions against release are in force, or that all persons who have entered cautions against release, and if necessary the arrestor, have given their written consent to the release, the Admiralty Marshal shall effect the release as soon as practicable.

N11.3 Practitioners should note that the Admiralty Marshal is not formally on call and therefore at times may not be available to assist. Similarly the practicalities of releasing a ship in some localities may involve the services of others who may not be available outside court hours.

N11.4 This service is offered to practitioners for use during reasonable hours and on the basis that if the Admiralty Marshal is available and can be contacted he will use his best endeavours to effect instructions to release but without guarantee as to their success.

N12 Use of postal facilities in the Registry

2A-139 N12.1 Applications together with the requisite documents may be posted to:

The Admiralty and Commercial Registry,
Room E200,
Royal Courts of Justice,
Strand,
London WC2A 2LL.

N12.2 In addition to the classes of business for which the use of postal facilities is permitted by the CPR or the Commercial Court Guide, the filing of the following classes of documents is also permitted in Admiralty matters:

(i) Requests for cautions;
(ii) Collision Statements of Case.

N12.3

(a) Documents sent by post for filing must be accompanied by two copies of a list of the documents sent and an envelope properly addressed to the sender.

(b) On receipt of the documents in the Registry, the court officer will, if the circumstances are such that had the documents been presented personally they would have been filed, cause them to be filed and will, by post, notify the sender that this has been done. If the documents would not have been accepted if presented personally the court officer will not file them but will retain them in the Registry for collection by the sender and will, by post, so inform the sender.

(c) When documents received through the post are filed by the court officer they will be sealed and entered as filed on the date on which they were received in the Registry.

N13 Insurance of arrested property

N13.1 The Marshal will not insure any arrested property for the benefit of parties at any time during the period of arrest (whether before or after the lodging of an application for sale, if any). **2A–140**

N13.2 The Marshal will use his best endeavours (but without any legal liability for failure to do so) to advise all parties known to him as being on the record in actions in rem against the arrested property, including those who have filed cautions against release of that property, before any such property moves or is moved beyond the area covered by the usual port risks policy.

N13.3 In these circumstances, practitioners' attention is drawn to the necessity of considering the questions of insuring against port risks for the amount of their clients' interest in any property arrested in an Admiralty action and the inclusion in any policy of a "Held Covered" clause in case the ship moves or is moved outside the area covered by the usual port risks policy. The usual port risks policy provides, among other things, for a ship to be moved or towed from one berth to another up to a distance of five miles within the port where she is lying.

N14 Assessors

14.1 In collision claims and other cases involving issues of navigation and seamanship, the Admiralty Court usually sits with assessors. The parties are not permitted to call expert evidence on such matters without the leave of the court: rule 61.13. **2A–141**

14.2 Provision is made in rule 35.15 for assessors' remuneration. The usual practice is for the court to seek an undertaking from the claimant to pay the remuneration on demand after the case has concluded.

O. Arbitration

O1 Arbitration claims
2A–142

O1.1

(a) Applications to the court under the Arbitration Acts 1950–1996 and other applications relating to arbitrations are known as "arbitration claims".

(b) The procedure applicable to arbitration claims is to be found in Part 62 and its associated practice direction. Separate provision is made

- (i) by Section I for claims relating to arbitrations to which the Arbitration Act 1996 applies;
- (ii) by Section II for claims relating to arbitrations to which the Arbitration Acts 1950–1979 ("the old law") apply; and
- (iii) by Section III for enforcement proceedings.

(c) For a full definition of the expression "arbitration claim" see rule 62.2(1) (claims under the 1996 Act) and rule 62.11(2) (claims under the old law).

(d) Part 58 applies to arbitration claims in the Commercial Court insofar as no specific provision is made by Part 62: rule 62.1(3).

Claims under the Arbitration Act 1996

O2 Starting an arbitration claim

O2.1 Subject to section O2.3 an arbitration claim must be started by the issue of an arbitration claim form in accordance with the Part 8 procedure: rule 62.3(1). **2A–143**

O2.2 The claim form must be substantially in the form set out in Appendix A to practice direction 62: **PD62 § 2.2**.

O2.3 An application to stay proceedings under section 9 of the Arbitration Act 1996 must be made by application notice in the proceedings: rule 62.3(2).

O3 The arbitration claim form

O3.1 The arbitration claim form must contain, among other things, a concise statement of the remedy claimed and, if an award is challenged, the grounds for that challenge: rule 62.4(1).

O3.2 Reference in the arbitration claim form to a witness statement or affidavit filed in support of the claim is not sufficient to comply with the requirements of rule 62.4(1).

O4 Service of the arbitration claim form

O4.1 An arbitration claim form issued in the Admiralty & Commercial Registry must be served by the claimant.

O4.2

(a) The rules governing service of the claim form are set out in Part 6 of the Civil Procedure Rules.

(b) Unless the court orders otherwise an arbitration claim form must be served on the defendant within 1 month from the date of issue: rule 62.4(2).

O4.3

(a) An arbitration claim form may be served out of the jurisdiction with the permission of the court: rule 62.5(1).

(b) Rules 6.24–6.29 apply to the service of an arbitration claim form out of the jurisdiction: rule 62.5(3).

O4.4 The court may exercise its powers under rule 6.8 to permit service of an arbitration claim form on a party at the address of the solicitor or other representative acting for him in the arbitration: **PD62 § 3.1**.

O4.5 The claimant must file a certificate of service within 7 days of serving the arbitration claim form: **PD62 § 3.2**.

O5 Acknowledgment of service

O5.1

(a) A defendant must file an acknowledgment of service of the arbitration claim form in every case: rule 58.6(1).

(b) An adapted version of practice form **N210** (acknowledgment of service of a Part 8 claim form) has been approved for use in the Commercial Court. A copy of this practice form (Form **N210(CC)**) is included at the end of the Guide, together with adapted versions of the notes for claimants and defendants on completing and replying to an arbitration claim form.

O5.2 The time for filing an acknowledgment of service is calculated from the service of the arbitration claim form.

O6 Standard directions

O6.1 The directions set out in **PD62 § 6.2–6.7** apply unless the court orders otherwise.

O6.2 The claimant should apply for a hearing date as soon as possible after issuing an arbitration claim form or (in the case of an appeal) obtaining permission to appeal.

O6.3 A defendant who wishes to rely on evidence in opposition to the claim must file and serve his evidence within 21 days after the date by which he was required to acknowledge service: **PD62 § 6.2**.

O6.4 A claimant who wishes to rely on evidence in response to evidence served by the defendant must file and serve his evidence within 7 days after the service of the defendant's evidence: **PD62 § 6.3**.

O6.5 An application for directions in a pending arbitration claim should be made by application notice under Part 23.

O7 Interim remedies

O7.1 An application for an interim remedy under section 44 of the Arbitration Act 1996 must be made in an arbitration claim form: **PD62 § 8.1**.

O8 Challenging the award

Challenge by way of appeal

O8.1 A party wishing to appeal against the award of an arbitrator or umpire must set **2A–144** out in the arbitration claim form

    (i) the question of law on which the appeal is based; and

    (ii) a succinct statement of the grounds of appeal,

identifying the relevant part(s) of the award and reasons.

O8.2 If the appeal is brought with the agreement of the other parties to the proceedings, a copy of their agreement in writing must be filed with the arbitration claim form.

O8.3 A party seeking permission to appeal must

    (i) state in his arbitration claim form the grounds on which he contends that permission to appeal should be given **PD62 § 12.1**; and

    (ii) file and serve with the arbitration claim form any written evidence on which he wishes to rely for the purposes of satisfying the court of the matters referred to in section 69(3) of the 1996 Act: **PD62 § 12.2**.

O8.4

(a) If the defendant wishes to oppose the claimant's application for permission to appeal he must file a witness statement setting out

    (i) the grounds on which he opposes the grant of permission; and

    (ii) any evidence on which he relies in relation to the matters mentioned in section 69(3) of the 1996 Act: **PD62 § § 12.3(1) & (2)**.

(b) If the defendant wishes to contend that the award should be upheld for reasons other than those expressed in the award, he must set out those reasons in his witness statement: **PD62 § 12.3(3)**.

O8.5 The court will normally determine applications for permission to appeal without an oral hearing. If the court considers that an oral hearing is required, it will give further directions as appropriate.

Challenging an award for serious irregularity

O8.6

(a) An arbitration claim challenging an award on the ground of serious irregularity under section 68 of the 1996 Act is appropriate only in cases where there are grounds for thinking

(i) that an irregularity has occurred which

(ii) has caused or will cause **substantial** injustice to the party making the challenge.

(b) An application challenging an award on the ground of serious irregularity should therefore not be regarded as an alternative to, or a means of supporting, an application for permission to appeal.

O8.7 The challenge to the award must be supported by evidence of the circumstances on which the claimant relies as giving rise to the irregularity complained of and the nature of the injustice which has been or will be caused to him.

O8.8 If the nature of the challenge itself or the evidence filed in support of it leads the court to consider that the claim has no real prospect of success, the court may exercise its powers under rule 3.3(4) to dismiss the application summarily. In such cases the applicant will have the right to apply to the court to set aside the order and to seek directions for the hearing of the application.

Multiple claims

O8.9 If the arbitration claim form includes both a challenge to an award by way of appeal and a challenge on the ground of serious irregularity, the applications should be set out in separate sections of the arbitration claim form and the grounds on which they are made separately identified.

O8.10 In such cases the papers will be placed before a judge to consider how the applications may most appropriately be disposed of. It is usually more appropriate to dispose of the application to set aside or remit the award before considering the application for permission to appeal.

O9 Time limits

2A–145 O9.1 An application to challenge an award under sections 67 or 68 of the 1996 Act or to appeal under section 69 of the Act must be brought within 28 days of the date of the award: **see** section 70(3).

O9.2 The court has power to vary the period of 28 days fixed by section 70(3) of the 1996 Act: rule 62.9(1). However, it is important that any challenge to an award be pursued without delay and the court will require cogent reasons for extending time.

O9.3 An application to extend time made **before** the expiry of the period of 28 days must be made in a Part 23 application notice, but the application notice need not be served on any other party: rule 62.9(2) and **PD62 § 11.1(1)**.

O9.4 An application to extend time made **after** the expiry of the period of 28 days must be made in the arbitration claim form in which the applicant is seeking substantive relief: rule 62.9(3)(a).

O9.5 An application to vary the period of 28 days will normally be determined without a hearing and prior to the consideration of the substantive application: **PD62 § 10.2.**

Claims under the Arbitration Acts 1950–1979

O10 Starting an arbitration claim

2A–146 O10.1 Subject to section O10.2 an arbitration claim must be started by the issue of an arbitration claim form in accordance with the Part 8 procedure: rule 62.13(1).

O10.2 The claim form must be substantially in the form set out in Appendix A to PD62 § 2.2.

O10.3 An application to stay proceedings on the grounds of an arbitration agreement must be made by application notice in the proceedings: rule 62.13(2).

O11 *The arbitration claim form*

O11.1 An arbitration claim form must state the grounds of the claim or appeal: rule 62.15(5)(a).

O11.2 Reference in the arbitration claim form to the witness statement or affidavit filed in support of the claim is not sufficient to comply with the requirements of rule 62.15(5)(a).

O12 *Service of the arbitration claim form*

O12.1 An arbitration claim form issued in the Admiralty & Commercial Registry must be served by the claimant.

O12.2 The rules governing service of the claim form are set out in Part 6 of the Civil Procedure Rules.

O12.3

(a) An arbitration claim form may be served out of the jurisdiction with the permission of the court: rule 62.16(1).
(b) Rules 6.24–6.29 apply to the service of an arbitration claim form out of the jurisdiction: rule 62.16(4).

O12.4 Although not expressly covered by PD62, the court may in an appropriate case exercise its powers under rule 6.8 to permit service of an arbitration claim form on a party at the address of the solicitor or other representative acting for him in the arbitration.

O12.5 The claimant must file a certificate of service within 7 days of serving the claim form.

Acknowledgment of service

2A–147

O13.1

(a) A defendant must file an acknowledgment of service in every case: rule 58.6(1).
(b) An adapted version of practice form **N210** (acknowledgment of service of a Part 8 claim form) has been approved for use in the Commercial Court. A copy of this practice form (Form **N210(CC)**) is included at the end of the Guide, together with adapted versions of the notes for claimants and defendants on completing and replying to an arbitration claim form.

O13.2 The time for filing an acknowledgment of service is calculated from the service of the arbitration claim form.

O14 *Standard directions*

O14.1 Where the claim or appeal is based on written evidence, a copy of that evidence must be served with the arbitration claim form: rule 62.15(5)(b).

O14.2 Where the claim or appeal is made with the consent of the arbitrator or umpire or other parties, a copy of every written consent must be served with the arbitration claim form: rule 62.15(5)(c).

O14.3 An application for directions in a pending arbitration claim should be made by application notice under Part 23.

O15 *Interim remedies*

O15.1 An application for an interim remedy under section 12(6) of the 1950 Act must be made in accordance with Part 25.

O15.2 The application must be made by arbitration claim form.

COMMERCIAL COURT

O15.3 A claim under section 12(4) of the 1950 Act for an order for the issue of a witness summons to compel the attendance of a witness before an arbitrator or umpire where the attendance of the witness is required within the district of a District Registry may be started in that Registry: rule 62.14.

O16 Challenging the award

Challenge by way of appeal

2A–148 O16.1 A party wishing to appeal against the award of an arbitrator or umpire must file and serve with the arbitration claim form a statement of the grounds for the appeal, specifying the relevant part(s) of the award and reasons: rule 62.15(6).

O16.2 A party seeking permission to appeal must also file and serve with the arbitration claim form any written evidence in support of the contention that the question of law concerns a term of the contract or an event which is not "one off": rule 62.15(6).

O16.3 Any written evidence in reply must be filed and served not less than 2 days before the hearing of the application for permission to appeal: rule 62.15(7).

O16.4 A party who wishes to contend that the award should be upheld for reasons other than those set out in the award and reasons must file and serve on the claimant a notice specifying the grounds of his contention not less than 2 days before the hearing of the application for permission to appeal: rule 62.15(8).

O16.5 Applications for permission to appeal will be heard orally, but will not normally be listed for longer than half an hour. Skeleton arguments should be lodged.

Claims to set aside or remit the award

O16.6 A claim to set aside or remit an award on the grounds of misconduct should not be regarded as an alternative to, or a means of supporting, an application for permission to appeal.

O16.7 The directions set out in PD62 § § 6.2–6.7 should be followed unless the court orders otherwise.

Multiple claims

O16.8 If the arbitration claim form includes both an appeal and an application to set aside or remit the award, the applications should be set out in separate sections of the arbitration claim form and the grounds on which they are made separately identified.

O16.9 The court may direct that one application be heard before the other or may direct that they be heard together, as may be appropriate. It is usually more appropriate to dispose of the application to set aside or remit the award before considering the application for permission to appeal.

2A–149 ### O17 Time limits

O17.1

(a) Time limits governing claims under the 1950 and 1979 Acts are set out in rule 62.15.

(b) Different time limits apply to different claims. **It is important to consult** rule 62.15 **to ensure that applications are made within the time prescribed.**

(c) The court has power under rule 3.1(2) to vary the time limits prescribed by rule 62.15, but will require cogent reasons for doing so.

Provisions applicable to all arbitrations

Enforcement of awards

2A–150 O18.1 All applications for permission to enforce awards are governed by Section III of Part 62, rule 62.17.

O18.2 An application for permission to enforce an award in the same manner as a judgment may be made without notice, but the court may direct that the arbitration claim form be served, in which case the application will continue as an arbitration claim in accordance with the procedure set out in Section I: rule 62.18(1)–(3).

O18.3 An application for permission to enforce an award in the same manner as a judgment must be supported written evidence in accordance with rule 62.18(6).

O18.4

(a) Two copies of the draft order must accompany the application.

(b) If the claimant wishes to enter judgment, the form of the judgment must correspond to the terms of the award.

(c) The defendant has the right to apply to the court to set aside an order made without notice giving permission to enforce the award and the order itself must state in terms

  (i) that the defendant may apply to set it aside within 14 days after service of the order or, if the order is to be served out of the jurisdiction, within such other period as the court may set; and

  (ii) that it may not be enforced until after the end of that period or any application by the defendant to set it aside has been finally disposed of: rule 62.18(9) & (10).

Matters of general application

O19 Transfer of arbitration claims

O19.1 An arbitration claim which raises no significant point of arbitration law or **2A–151** practice will normally be transferred

  (i) if a rent-review arbitration, to the Chancery Division;

  (ii) if a construction or engineering arbitration, to the Technology and Construction Court;

  (iii) if an employment arbitration, to the Central London County Court Mercantile List.

O19.2 Salvage arbitrations will normally be transferred to the Admiralty Court.

O20 Appointment of a Commercial Judge as sole arbitrator or umpire

O20.1 Section 93 of the Arbitration Act 1996 provides for the appointment of a Commercial Judge as sole arbitrator or umpire. The Act limits the circumstances in which a Judge may accept such an appointment.

O20.2 Enquiries should be directed to the Judge in charge of the Commercial List or the Clerk to the Commercial Court.

P. Miscellaneous

P1 Out of hours emergency arrangements

2A–152

P1.1

(a) When the Listing Office is closed, solicitors or counsel's clerks should in an emergency contact the Clerk to the Queen's Bench Judge in Chambers by telephone through the security desk at the Royal Courts of Justice: **PD58 § 2.2**.

(b) The telephone number of the security desk is included in the list of addresses and contact details at the end of the Guide.

P1.2 When the Listing Office is closed an urgent hearing will initially be dealt with by the Queen's Bench Judge in Chambers who may dispose of the application himself or make orders allowing the matter to come before a Commercial Judge at the first available opportunity.

P2 Index of unreported decisions

2A–153 P2.1 An Index has been prepared on a subject-matter basis of unreported Commercial Court and Admiralty Court judgments from 1995 onwards. The Index is updated regularly.

P2.2 The Index is provided as a service to litigants and to the legal profession, and to assist the Commercial Court and the Admiralty Court to maintain reasonable consistency of approach in those areas of law and procedure most frequently before them.

P2.3 The Index is available on disk to counsel and solicitors from the Listing Office, free of charge, in exchange for new unused 1.44 MB disks. Except in special circumstances no more than one disk will be issued to each set of chambers or firm of solicitors. Copies of the disk should not be made except for copies that are to be made available to members of the set of chambers or firm of solicitors to which it has been issued.

P2.4 The judgments referred to in the Index are kept in the Registry. They may be consulted there.

P2.5 Copies of the judgments referred to in the Index may be obtained from the Registry (or where there is difficulty, from the clerk to the judge) unless the judgment is in the form of a transcript, in which case copies should be obtained from the shorthand writers or other transcript agency.

Appendix 1

2A–154
Part 58 (Commercial Court)—reproduced at para. 2A–5 *et seq.*
Part 61 (Admiralty Court)—reproduced at para. 2D–4 *et seq.*
Practice Direction to Part 58—reproduced at para. 2A–22 *et seq.*
Practice Direction to Part 61—reproduced at para. 2D–82 *et seq.*

Appendix 2

2A–155
Part 62 (Arbitration)—reproduced at para. 2E–5 *et seq.*
Practice Direction to Part 62—reproduced at para. 2E–41 *et seq.*

Appendix 3

Procedure for issue of claim form when Registry closed

2A–156 (See generally sections B3.11 and B4.4 of the Guide.)

Procedure

The procedure is as follows:

1. The claim form must be signed by a solicitor acting on behalf of the claimant, and must not require the permission of the Court for its issue (unless such permission has already been given).

2. The solicitor causing the claim form to be issued ("the issuing solicitor") must

(i) endorse on the claim form the endorsement shown below and sign that endorsement;

(ii) send a copy of the claim form so endorsed to the Registry by fax for issue under this section; and

(iii) when he has received a transmission report stating that the transmission of the claim form to the Registry was completed in full and the time and the date of the transmission, complete and sign the certificate shown below.

3. When the Registry is next open to the public after the issue of a claim form in accordance with this procedure the issuing solicitor or his agent shall attend and deliver to the Registry the document which was transmitted by fax (including the endorsement and the certificate), or if that document has been served, a true and certified copy of it, together with as many copies as the Registry shall require and the transmission report.

4. When the proper officer at the Registry has checked and is satisfied that the document delivered under paragraph 3 fully accords with the document received under paragraph 2, and that all proper fees for issue have been paid, he shall allocate a number to the case, and seal, mark as "original" and date the claim form with the date on which it was issued (being, as indicated below, the date when the fax is recorded at the Registry as having been received).

5. As soon as practicable thereafter the issuing solicitor shall inform any person served with the unsealed claim form of the case number, and (on request) shall serve any such person with a copy of the claim form sealed and dated under paragraph 4 above (at such address in England and Wales as the person may request) and the person may, without paying a fee, inspect and take copies of the documents lodged at the Registry under paragraphs 2 and 3 above.

Effect of issue following request by fax.

The issue of a claim form in accordance with this procedure takes place when the fax is recorded at the Registry as having been received, and the claim form bearing the endorsement shall have the same effect for all purposes as a claim form issued under CPR Part 7 [or 8, as the case may be]. Unless otherwise ordered the sealed version of the claim form retained by the Registry shall be conclusive proof that the claim form was issued at the time and on the date stated. If the procedure set out in this Appendix is not complied with, the court may declare (on its own initiative or on application) that the claim form shall be treated as not having been issued.

2A–157

Endorsement

A claim form issued pursuant to a request by fax must be endorsed as follows:

2A–158

"1. This claim form is issued under section B3.11/B4.4 of the Commercial Court Guide and may be served notwithstanding that it does not bear the seal of the Court.

2. A true copy of this claim form and endorsement has been transmitted to the Admiralty and Commercial Registry, Royal Courts of Justice, Strand, London WC2A 2LL, at the time and date certified below by the undersigned solicitor.

3. It is the duty of the undersigned solicitor or his agent to attend at the Registry when it is next open to the public for the claim form to be sealed.

4. Any person upon whom this unsealed claim form is served will be notified by the undersigned solicitor of the number of the case and may require the undersigned solicitor to serve a copy of the sealed claim form at an address in England and Wales and may inspect without charge the documents which have been lodged at the Registry by the undersigned solicitor.

5. I, the undersigned solicitor, undertake to the Court, to the defendants named in this claim form, and to any other person upon whom this claim form may be served:

(i) that the statement in paragraph 2 above is correct;

(ii) that the time and date given in the certificate at the foot of this endorsement are correct;

(iii) that this claim form is a claim form which may be issued under section B3.11 (or B4.4, as the case may be) of the Commercial Court Guide;

(iv) that I will comply in all respects with the requirements of section B3.11/B4.4 of the Commercial Court Guide;

(v) that I will indemnify any person served with the claim form before it is sealed against any loss suffered as a result of the claim form being or becoming invalid in accordance with section B3.11/B4.4 of the Commercial Court Guide.

(Signed)

Solicitor for the claimant"

[**Note**: the endorsement may be signed in the name of the firm of solicitors rather than an individual solicitor, or by solicitors' agents in their capacity as agents acting on behalf of their professional clients.]

Certificate

2A–159   A solicitor who causes a claim form to be issued pursuant to a request sent by fax must sign a certificate in the following form:

> "I, the undersigned solicitor, certify that I have received a transmission report confirming that the transmission of a copy of this claim form to the Registry by fax was fully completed and that the time and date of transmission to the Registry were *[enter the time and date shown on the transmission report]*.
>
> Dated
>
> *(Signed)*
>
> Solicitor for the claimant."

[**Note**: the certificate may be signed in the name of the firm of solicitors rather than an individual solicitor, or by solicitors' agents in their capacity as agents acting on behalf of their professional clients]

Appendix 4

Statements of Case

2A–160   The following principles apply to all statements of case and should, as far as possible, also be observed when drafting a Part 8 claim form, which will not contain, or be followed by, particulars of claim:

1. The document must be as brief and concise as possible.

2. The document must be set out in separate consecutively numbered paragraphs and sub-paragraphs.

3. So far as possible each paragraph or sub-paragraph should contain no more than one allegation.

4. The document must deal with the case on a point by point basis to allow a point by point response.

5. Where particulars are given of any allegation or reasons given for a denial, the allegation or denial should be stated first and the particulars or reasons for it listed one by one in separate numbered sub-paragraphs.

6. A party wishing to advance a positive case should set that case out in the document; a simple denial is not sufficient.

7. Any matter which, if not stated, might take another party by surprise should be stated.

8. Where they will assist:
   (i) headings should be used; and
   (ii) abbreviations and definitions should be established and used, and a glossary annexed.

9. Contentious headings, abbreviations and definitions should not be used. Every effort should be made to ensure that headings, abbreviations and definitions are in a form that will enable them to be adopted without issue by the other parties.

10. Particulars of primary allegations should be stated as particulars and not as primary allegations.

11. If it is necessary to rely upon a substantial amount of detailed factual information or lengthy particulars in support of an allegation, these should be set out in schedules or appendices.

12. Particular care should be taken to set out only those factual allegations which are necessary to support the case. Evidence should not be included.

13. A response to particulars set out in a schedule should be set out in a corresponding schedule.

14. If it is necessary for the proper understanding of the statement of case to include substantial parts of a lengthy document the passages in question should be set out in a schedule rather than in the body of the case.

15. Contentious paraphrasing should be avoided.

16. The document must be signed by the individual person or persons who drafted it, not, in the case of a solicitor, in the name of the firm alone.

Appendix 5

Forms of Search Order and Freezing Injunction

2A–161

SEARCH ORDER

IN THE HIGH COURT OF JUSTICE

QUEEN'S BENCH DIVISION

COMMERCIAL COURT

Before The Honourable Mr Justice [   ]

Claim No.

BETWEEN

Claimant(s)

– and –

Defendant(s)

_____

Applicant(s)

Respondent(s)

PENAL NOTICE

If you [   ]¹ disobey this order you may be held to be in contempt of court and may be imprisoned, fined or have your assets seized.

Any other person who knows of this Order and does anything which helps or permits the Respondent to breach the terms of this Order may also be held to be in contempt of court and may be imprisoned, fined or have their assets seized.

THIS ORDER

1.   This is a Search Order made against [
] ("the Respondent") on [   ] by Mr Justice [
] on the application of [   ]   ("the Applicant"). The Judge read the Affidavits listed in Schedule F and accepted the undertakings set out in Schedules C, D and E at the end of this order.

2.   This order was made at a hearing without notice to the Respondent. The Respondent has a right to apply to the court to vary or discharge the order – see paragraph 27 below.

3   There will be a further hearing in respect of this order on [
] ("the return date").

4.   If there is more than one Respondent-
   (a)   unless otherwise stated, references in this order to "the Respondent" mean both or all of them; and
   (b)   this order is effective against any Respondent on whom it is served or who is given notice of it.

5.   This order must be complied with by-
   (a)   the Respondent;
   (b)   any director, officer, partner or responsible employee of the Respondent; and
   (c)   if the Respondent is an individual, any other person having responsible control of the premises to be searched.

THE SEARCH

6.   **The Respondent must permit the following persons²-**

---

¹ Insert name of Respondent.
² Where the premises are likely to be occupied by an unaccompanied woman and the Supervising Solicitor is a man, at least one of the persons accompanying him should be a woman.

(a)   [   ] ('the Supervising Solicitor);

(b)   [   ], a solicitor in the firm of [
                      ], the Applicant's solicitors; and

(c)   up to [   ] other persons[3] being [*their identity or capacity*] accompanying them,

(together "the search party"), to enter the premises mentioned in Schedule A to this order and any other premises of the Respondent disclosed under paragraph 18 below and any vehicles under the Respondent's control on or around the premises ("the premises") so that they can search for, inspect, photograph or photocopy, and deliver into the safekeeping of the Applicant's solicitors all the documents and articles which are listed in Schedule B to this order ("the listed items").

7.   Having permitted the search party to enter the premises, the Respondent must allow the search party to remain on the premises until the search is complete. In the event that it becomes necessary for any of those persons to leave the premises before the search is complete, the Respondent must allow them to re-enter the premises immediately upon their seeking re-entry on the same or the following day in order to complete the search.

RESTRICTIONS ON SEARCH

8.   This order may not be carried out at the same time as a police search warrant.

9.   Before the Respondent allows anybody onto the premises to carry out this order, he is entitled to have the Supervising Solicitor explain to him what it means in everyday language.

10.   The Respondent is entitled to seek legal advice and to ask the court to vary or discharge this order. Whilst doing so, he may ask the Supervising Solicitor to delay starting the search for up to 2 hours or such other longer period as the Supervising Solicitor may permit. However, the Respondent must-

(a)   comply with the terms of paragraph 27 below;

(b)   not disturb or remove any listed items; and

(c)   permit the Supervising Solicitor to enter, but not start to search.

11.   Before permitting entry to the premises by any person other than the Supervising Solicitor, the Respondent may, for a short time (not to exceed two hours, unless the Supervising Solicitor agrees to a longer period), gather together any documents he

---

[3] None of these persons should be people who could gain personally or commercially from anything they might read or see on the premises, unless their presence is essential.

believes may be [incriminating or][4] privileged and hand them to the Supervising Solicitor for him to assess whether they are [incriminating or] privileged as claimed. If the Supervising Solicitor decides that any of the documents may be [incriminating or] privileged or is in any doubt as to their status, he will exclude them from the search and retain them in his possession pending further order of the court.

12. If the Respondent wishes to take legal advice and gather documents as permitted, he must first inform the Supervising Solicitor and keep him informed of the steps being taken.

13. No item may be removed from the premises until a lst of the items to be removed has been prepared, and a copy of the list has been supplied to the Respondent, and he has been given a reasonable opportunity to check the list.

14. The premises must not be searched, and items must not be removed from them, except in the presence of the Respondent.

15. If the Supervising Solicitor is satisfied that full compliance with paragraphs 13 or 14 is not practicable, he may permit the search to proceed and items to be removed without fully complying with them.

DELIVERY UP OF ARTICLES/DOCUMENTS

16. The Respondent must immediately hand over to the Applicant's solicitors any of the listed items, which are in his possession or under his control, save for any computer or hard disk integral to any computer. Any items the subject of a dispute as to whether they are listed items must immediately be handed over to the Supervising Solicitor for safe keeping pending resolution of the dispute or further order of the court.

17. The Respondent must immediately give the search party effective access to the computers on the premises, with all necessary passwords, to enable the computers to be searched. If they contain any listed items the Respondent must cause the listed items to be displayed so that they can be read and copied.[5] The Respondent must provide the Applicant's Solicitors with copies of all listed items contained in the computers. All reasonable steps shall be taken by the Applicant

---

[4] References to incriminating documents should be omitted from orders made in intellectual property proceedings, where the privilege against self-incrimination does not apply – see paragraph 8.4 of the practice direction.
[5] If it is envisaged that the Respondent's computers are to be imaged (i.e. the hard drives are to be copied wholesale, thereby reproducing listed items and other items indiscriminately), special provision needs to be made and independent computer specialists need to be appointed, who should be required to give undertakings to the court.

and the Applicant's solicitors to ensure that no damage is done to any computer or data. The Applicant and his representatives may not themselves search the Respondent's computers unless they have sufficient expertise to do so without damaging the Respondent's system.

PROVISION OF INFORMATION

18. The Respondent must immediately inform the Applicant's Solicitors (in the presence of the Supervising Solicitor) so far as he is aware—
    (a)   where all the listed items are;
    (b)   the name and address of everyone who has supplied him, or offered to supply him, with listed items;
    (c)   the name and address of everyone to whom he has supplied, or offered to supply, listed items; and
    (d)   full details of the dates and quantities of every such supply and offer.

19. Within [   ] working days after being served with this order the Respondent must swear and serve an affidavit setting out the above information.[6]

PROHIBITED ACTS

20. Except for the purpose of obtaining legal advice, the Respondent must not directly or indirectly inform anyone of these proceedings or of the contents of this order, or warn anyone that proceedings have been or may be brought against him by the Applicant until 4.30 p.m. on the return date or further order of the court.

21. Until 4.30 p.m. on the return date the Respondent must not destroy, tamper with, cancel or part with possession, power, custody or control of the listed items otherwise than in accordance with the terms of this order.

22. [Insert any negative injunctions.]

23. [Insert any further order]

COSTS

---

[6] The period should ordinarily be longer than the period in paragraph (2) of Schedule D, if any of the information is likely to be included in listed items taken away of which the Respondent does not have copies.

24. The costs of this application are reserved to the judge hearing the application on the return date.

RESTRICTIONS ON SERVICE

25. This order may only be served between [   ] a.m./p.m. and [   ] a.m./p.m. [and on a weekday].[7]

26. This order must be served by the Supervising Solicitor, and paragraph 6 of the order must be carried out in his presence and under his supervision.

VARIATION AND DISCHARGE OF THIS ORDER

27. Anyone served with or notified of this order may apply to the court at any time to vary or discharge this order (or so much of it as affects that person), but they must first inform the Applicant's solicitors. If any evidence is to be relied upon in support of the application, the substance of it must be communicated in writing to the Applicant's solicitors in advance.

INTERPRETATION OF THIS ORDER

28. Any requirement that something shall be done to or in the presence of the Respondent means-
    (a) if there is more than one Respondent, to or in the presence of any one of them; and
    (b) if a Respondent is not an individual, to or in the presence of a director, officer, partner or responsible employee.

29. A Respondent who is an individual who is ordered not to do something must not do it himself or in any other way. He must not do it through others acting on his behalf or on his instructions or with his encouragement.

30. A Respondent which is not an individual which is ordered not to do something must not do it itself or by its directors, officers, partners, employees or agents or in any other way.

COMMUNICATIONS WITH THE COURT

---

[7] Normally, the order should be served in the morning (not before 9.30 a.m.) and on a weekday to enable the Respondent more readily to obtain legal advice.

All communications to the court about this order should be sent to Room E201, Royal Courts of Justice, Strand, London WC2A 2LL quoting the case number. The telephone number is 020 7947 6826.

The offices are open between 10 a.m. and 4.30 p.m. Monday to Friday.

SCHEDULE A

THE PREMISES

SCHEDULE B

THE LISTED ITEMS

SCHEDULE C

UNDERTAKINGS GIVEN TO THE COURT BY THE APPLICANT

(1) If the court later finds that this order or carrying it out has caused loss to the Respondent, and decides that the Respondent should be compensated for that loss, the Applicant will comply with any order the court may make. Further if the carrying out of this order has been in breach of the terms of this order or otherwise in a manner inconsistent with the Applicant's solicitors' duties as officers of the court, the Applicant will comply with any order for damages the court may make.

[(2) As soon as practicable the Applicant will issue a claim form [in the form of the draft produced to the court] [claiming the appropriate relief].]

(3) The Applicant will [swear and file an affidavit] [cause an affidavit to be sworn and filed] [substantially in the terms of the

draft affidavit produced to the court] [confirming the substance of what was said to the court by the Applicant's counsel/solicitors].

(4)   The Applicant will not, without the permission of the court use any information or documents obtained as a result of carrying out this order nor inform anyone else of these proceedings except for the purposes of these proceedings (including adding further Respondents) or commencing civil proceedings in relation to the same or related subject matter to these proceedings until after the return date.

[(5)   The Applicant will maintain pending further order the sum of £ [
                                   ] in an account controlled by the Applicant's solicitors.]

[(6)   The Applicant will insure the items removed from the premises.]

SCHEDULE D

UNDERTAKINGS GIVEN BY THE APPLICANT'S SOLICITORS

(1)   The Applicant's solicitors will provide to the Supervising Solicitor for service on the Respondent-
   (i)   a service copy of this order;
   (ii)   the claim form (with defendant's response pack) or, if not issued, the draft produced to the court;
   (iii) an application for hearing on the return date;
   (iv)   copies of the affidavits *[or draft affidavits]* and exhibits capable of being copied containing the evidence relied upon by the applicant;
   (v)   a note of any allegation of fact made orally to the court where such allegation is not contained in the affidavits or draft affidavits read by the judge; and
   (vi)   a copy of the skeleton argument produced to the court by the Applicant's [counsel/solicitors].

(2)   The Applicants' solicitors will answer at once to the best of their ability any question whether a particular item is a listed item.

(3)   Subject as provided below the Applicant's solicitors will retain in their own safe keeping all items obtained as a result of this order until the court directs otherwise.

(4)   The Applicant's solicitors will return the originals of all documents obtained as a result of this order (except original

documents which belong to the Applicant) as soon as possible and in any event within [two] working days of their removal.

SCHEDULE E

UNDERTAKINGS GIVEN BY THE SUPERVISING SOLICITOR

(1)   The Supervising Solicitor will use his best endeavours to serve this order upon the Respondent and at the same time to serve upon the Respondent the other documents required to be served and referred to in paragraph (1) of Schedule D.

(2)   The Supervising Solicitor will offer to explain to the person served with the order its meaning and effect fairly and in everyday language, and to inform him of his right to take legal advice (such advice to include an explanation that the Respondent may be entitled to avail himself of [the privilege against self-incrimination or] [legal professional privilege]) and to apply to vary or discharge this order as mentioned in paragraph 27 above.

(3)   The Supervising Solicitor will retain in the safe keeping of his firm all items retained by him as a result of this order until the court directs otherwise.

(4)   Within [48] hours of completion of the search the Supervising Solicitor will make and provide to the Applicant's solicitors, the Respondent or his solicitors and to the judge who made this order (for the purposes of the court file) a written report on the carrying out of the order.

SCHEDULE F

AFFIDAVITS

The Applicant relied on the following affidavits-

[name]   [number of affidavit]   [date sworn]   [filed   on behalf of]

(1)
(2)

NAME AND ADDRESS OF APPLICANT'S SOLICITORS

The Applicant's solicitors are—
[Name, address, reference, fax and telephone numbers both in and out of office hours.]

COMMERCIAL COURT

Before The Honourable Mr Justice [   ]

Claim No.

BETWEEN

Claimant(s)

– and –

Defendant(s)

Applicant(s)

Respondent(s)

PENAL NOTICE

If you [   ]⁸ disobey this order you may be held to be in contempt of court and may be imprisoned, fined or have your assets seized.

Any other person who knows of this order and does anything which helps or permits the Respondent to breach the terms of this order may also be held to be in contempt of court and may be imprisoned, fined or have their assets seized.

THIS ORDER

---

⁸ Insert name of Respondent(s).

Appendix 6

Case Management Information Sheet

Party lodging information sheet:
Name of solicitors:

2A–162

Name(s) of advocates for trial:

[Note: This Sheet should normally be completed with the involvement of the advocate(s) instructed for trial. If the claimant is a litigant in person this fact should be noted at the foot of the sheet and proposals made as to which party is to have responsibility for the preparation and upkeep of the case management bundle.]

(1) By what date can you give standard disclosure?

(2) In relation to standard disclosure, do you contend in relation to any category or class of document under rule 31.6(b) that to search for that category or class would be unreasonable? If so, what is the category or class and on what grounds do you so contend?

(3) Is specific disclosure required on any issue? If so, please specify.

(4) By what dates can you (a) give specific disclosure or (b) comply with a special disclosure order?

(5) May the time periods for inspection at rule 31.15 require adjustment, and if so by how much?

(6) Are amendments to or is information about any statement of case required? If yes, please give brief details of what is required.

(7) Can you make any additional admissions? If yes, please give brief details of the additional admissions.

(8) Are any of the issues in the case suitable for trial as preliminary issues?

(9) (a) On the evidence of how many witnesses of fact do you intend to rely at trial (subject to the directions of the Court)? Please give their names, or explain why this is not being done.

(b) By what date can you serve signed witness statements?

(c) How many of these witnesses of fact do you intend to call to give oral evidence at trial (subject to the directions of the Court)? Please give their names, or explain why this is not being done.

(d) Will interpreters be required for any witness?

(e) Do you wish any witness to give oral evidence by video link? Please give his or her name, or explain why this is not being done. Please state the country and city from which the witness will be asked to give evidence by video link.

(10) (a) On what issues may expert evidence be required?

(b) Is this a case in which the use of a single joint expert might be suitable (see rule 35.7)?

(c) On the evidence of how many expert witnesses do you intend to rely at trial (subject to the directions of the Court)? Please give their names, or explain why this is not being done. Please identify each expert's field of expertise.

(d) By what date can you serve signed expert reports?

(e) When will the experts be available for a meeting or meetings of experts?

(f) How many of these expert witnesses do you intend to call to give oral evidence at trial (subject to the directions of the Court)? Please give their names, or explain why this is not being done.

(g) Will interpreters be required for any expert witness?

(h) Do you wish any expert witness to give oral evidence by video link? Please give his or her name, or explain why this is not being done. Please state the country and city from which the witness will be asked to give evidence by video link.

(11) What are the advocates' present provisional estimates of the minimum and maximum lengths of the trial?

(12) What is the earliest date by which you believe you can be ready for trial?

(13) Is this a case in which a pre-trial review is likely to be useful?

(14) Is there any way in which the Court can assist the parties to resolve their dispute or particular issues in it without the need for a trial or a full trial?

(15) (a) Might some form of Alternative Dispute Resolution procedure assist to resolve or narrow the dispute or particular issues in it?

(b) Has the question at (a) been considered between the client and legal representatives (including the advocate(s) retained)?

(c) Has the question at (a) been explored with the other parties in the case?

(d) Do you request that the case is adjourned while the parties try to settle the case by Alternative Dispute Resolution or other means?

(e) Would an ADR order in the form of Appendix 7 to the Commercial Court Guide be appropriate?

(f) Are any other special directions needed to allow for Alternative Dispute Resolution?

(16) What other applications will you wish to make at the Case Management Conference?

(17) Does provision need to be made in the pre-trial timetable for any application or procedural step not otherwise dealt with above? If yes, please specify the application or procedural step.

(18) Are there, or are there likely in due course to be, any related proceedings (e.g. a Part 20 claim)? Please give brief details.

[Signature of solicitors]

Note: This information sheet must be lodged with the Clerk to the Commercial Court at least 7 days before the Case Management Conference (with a copy to all other parties): see section D8.5 of the Commercial Court Guide.

Appendix 7

Draft ADR Order

1. On or before [*] the parties shall exchange lists of 3 neutral individuals who are available to conduct ADR procedures in this case prior to [*]. Each party may [in addition] [in the alternative] provide a list identifying the constitution of one or more panels of neutral individuals who are available to conduct ADR procedures in this case prior to [*]. **2A–163**

2. On or before [*] the parties shall in good faith endeavour to agree a neutral individual or panel from the lists so exchanged and provided.

3. Failing such agreement by [*] the Case Management Conference will be restored to enable the Court to facilitate agreement on a neutral individual or panel:

4. The parties shall take such serious steps as they may be advised to resolve their disputes by ADR procedures before the neutral individual or panel so chosen by no later than [*].

5. If the case is not finally settled, the parties shall inform the Court by letter prior to [disclosure of documents/exchange of witness statements/exchange of experts' reports] what steps towards ADR have been taken and (without prejudice to matters of privilege) why such steps have failed. If the parties have failed to initiate ADR procedures the Case Management Conference is to be restored for further consideration of the case.

6. [Costs].

Note: The term "ADR procedures" is deliberately used in the draft ADR order. This is in order to emphasise that (save where otherwise provided) the parties are free to use the ADR procedure that they regard as most suitable, be it mediation, early neutral evaluation, non-binding arbitration etc.

Appendix 8

Standard Pre-Trial Timetable

1. [Standard disclosure is to be made by [*], with inspection [*] days after notice.] **2A–164**

2. Signed statements of witnesses of fact, and hearsay notices where required by rule 33.2, are to be exchanged not later than [*].

COMMERCIAL COURT

3. Unless otherwise ordered, witness statements are to stand as the evidence in chief of the witness at trial.

4. Signed reports of experts
   (i) are to be confined to one expert for each party from each of the following fields of expertise: [*];
   (ii) are to be confined to the following issues: [*];
   (iii) are to be exchanged [sequentially/simultaneously];
   (iv) are to be exchanged not later than [date or dates for each report in each field of expertise].

5. Meeting of experts
   (i) The meeting of experts is to be by [*];
   (ii) The joint memorandum of the experts is to be completed by [*];
   (iii) Any short supplemental expert reports are to be exchanged [sequentially/simultaneously] by not later than [date or dates for each supplemental report].

6. [If the experts' reports cannot be agreed, the parties are to be at liberty to call expert witnesses at the trial, limited to those experts whose reports have been exchanged pursuant to 4. above.]

[Or: The parties are to be at liberty to apply to call as expert witnesses at the trial those experts whose reports they have exchanged pursuant to 4. above, such application to be made not earlier than [*] and not later than [*].]

7. Preparation of trial bundles to be completed in accordance with Appendix 10 to the Commercial Court Guide by not later than [*].

8. The provisional estimated length of the trial is [*].

9. Within [*] days the parties are to attend on the Clerk to the Commercial Court to fix the date for trial which shall be not before [*].

10. The progress monitoring date is [*]. Each party is to lodge a completed progress monitoring information sheet with the Clerk to the Commercial Court at least 3 days before the progress monitoring date (with a copy to all other parties).

11. Each party is to lodge a completed pre-trial checklist not later than 3 weeks before the date fixed for trial.

12. [There is to be a pre-trial review not earlier than [*] and not later than [*]].

13. Save as varied by this order or further order, the practice and procedures set out in the Admiralty & Commercial Courts Guide are to be followed.

14. Costs in the case.

15. Liberty to restore the Case Management Conference.

Appendix 9

Skeleton Arguments, Chronologies and Indices

Part 1 Skeleton arguments

2A–165 1. A skeleton argument is intended to identify both for the parties and the court those points which are, and are not, in issue and the nature of the argument in relation to those points that are in issue. It is not a substitute for oral argument.

2. Skeleton arguments must therefore
   (a) identify concisely:

(i) the nature of the case generally and the background facts insofar as they are relevant to the matter before the court;

(ii) the propositions of law relied on with references to the relevant authorities;

(iii) the submissions of fact to be made with references to the evidence;

(b) be in numbered paragraphs and state the name of the advocate(s) who prepared them; and

(c) should avoid arguing the case at length.

Part 2 Chronologies and indices

3. As far as possible chronologies and indices should not be prepared in a tendentious form. The ideal is that the court and the parties should have a single point of reference that all find useful and are happy to work with. **2A–166**

4. Where there is disagreement about a particular event or description, it is useful if that fact is indicated in neutral terms and the competing versions shortly stated.

5. If time and circumstances allow its preparation, a chronology or index to which all parties have contributed and agreed can be invaluable.

6. Chronologies and indices once prepared can be easily updated and are of continuing usefulness throughout the life of the case.

Appendix 10

Preparation of Bundles

1. The preparation of bundles requires a high level of co-operation between legal representatives for all parties. It is the duty of all legal representatives to co-operate to this high level. **2A–167**

2. Bundles should be prepared as follows:

(i) No more than one copy of any one document should be included, unless there is good reason for doing otherwise;

(ii) Contemporaneous documents, and correspondence, should be included in chronological order;

(iii) Where a contract or similar document is central to the case it may be included in a separate place provided that a page is inserted in the chronological run of documents to indicate

(A) the place the contract or similar document would have appeared had it appeared chronologically and

(B) where it may be found instead;

(iv) Documents in manuscript, or not fully legible, should be transcribed; the transcription should be marked and placed adjacent to the document transcribed;

(v) Documents in a foreign language should be translated; the translation should be marked and placed adjacent to the document transcribed; the translation should be agreed, or, if it cannot be agreed, each party's proposed translation should be included;

(vi) If a document has to be read across rather than down the page, it should be so placed in the bundle as to ensure that the top of the text is nearest the spine;

(vii) **No bundle should contain more than 300 pages;**

(viii) Bundles should not be overfilled, and should allow sufficient room for later insertions. Subject to this, the size of file used should not be a size that is larger than necessary for the present and anticipated contents;

(ix) Bundles should be paginated, in the bottom right hand corner and in a form that can clearly be distinguished from any existing pagination on the document;

(x) Bundles should be indexed, save that a chronological bundle of contemporaneous documents need not be indexed if an index is unlikely to be useful;

(xi) Bundles should be numbered and named on the outside and on the inside front cover, the label to include the short title of the case, and a description of the bundle (including its number, where relevant).

3. Documents within bundles should be marked as follows:

(i) When copy documents from exhibits have been included in the bundle(s), then unless clearly unnecessary, the copy of the affidavit or witness statement to which the documents were exhibited should be marked in the right hand margin (in manuscript if need be) to show where the document referred to may be found in the bundle(s).

(ii) Unless clearly unnecessary, where copy documents in a bundle are taken from the disclosure of more than one party the documents should be marked in the top right hand corner (in manuscript if need be) to show from which party's disclosure the copy document has been taken;

(iii) Where there is a reference in a statement of case or witness statement to a document which is contained in the trial bundles a note should be made in the margin (if necessary in manuscript) identifying the place where that document is to be found. Unless otherwise agreed this is the responsibility of the party tendering the statement of case or witness statement.

4. For the trial a handy-sized core bundle should normally be provided containing the really important documents in the case. The documents in this bundle should be paginated, but each page should also bear its bundle and page number reference in the main bundles. It is particularly important to allow sufficient room for later insertions (see paragraph 2(viii) above).

5. Large documents, such as plans, should be placed in an easily accessible file.

6.

(a) When agreeing bundles for trial, the parties should also establish through their legal representatives, and record in correspondence, whether the agreement of bundles:

    (i) extends no further than agreement of the composition and preparation of the bundles; or

    (ii) includes agreement that the documents in the bundles are authentic (see further rule 32.19); or

    (iii) includes agreement that the documents may be treated as evidence of the facts stated in them.

(b) The Court will normally expect parties to agree that the documents or at any rate the great majority of them may be treated as evidence of the facts stated in them. A party not willing so to agree should, when the trial bundles are lodged, write a letter to the Court (with a copy to all other parties) stating that it is not willing so to agree, and explaining why that is so.

Appendix 11

Expert Evidence—Requirements of General Application

2A–168 1. It is the duty of an expert to help the court on the matters within his expertise: rule 35.3(1). This duty is paramount and overrides any obligation to the person from whom the expert has received instructions or by whom he is paid: rule 35.3(2).

2. Expert evidence presented to the court should be, and should be seen to be, the independent product of the expert uninfluenced by the pressures of litigation.

3. An expert witness should provide independent assistance to the court by way of objective unbiased opinion in relation to matters within his expertise. An expert witness should never assume the role of an advocate.

4. An expert witness should not omit to consider material facts which could detract from his concluded opinion.

5. An expert witness should make it clear when a particular question or issue falls outside his expertise.

6. If an expert's opinion is not properly researched because he considers that insufficient data is available, this must be stated in his report with an indication that the opinion is no more than a provisional one.

7. In a case where an expert witness who has prepared a report is unable to confirm that the report contains the truth, the whole truth and nothing but the truth without some qualification, that qualification must be stated in the report.

8. If, after exchange of reports, an expert witness changes his view on a material matter having read another expert's report or for any other reason, such change of view should be communicated in writing (through the party's legal representatives) to the other side without delay, and when appropriate to the court.

Appendix 12

Progress Monitoring Information Sheet

[SHORT TITLE OF CASE and FOLIO NUMBER]   2A–169
Fixed trial date/provisional range of dates for trial specified in the pre-trial timetable:
Party lodging information sheet:
Name of solicitors:
Name(s) of advocates for trial:
[Note: this information sheet should normally be completed with the involvement of the advocate(s) instructed for trial]
(1) Have you complied with the pre-trial timetable in all respects?
(2) If you have not complied, in what respects have you not complied?
(3) Will you be ready for a trial commencing on the fixed date (or, where applicable, within the provisional range of dates) specified in the pre-trial timetable?
(4) If you will not be ready, why will you not be ready?
[*Signature of solicitors*]
Note: This information sheet must be lodged with the Case Management Unit at least 3 days before the progress monitoring date (with a copy to all other parties): see section D12.2 of the Guide.

Appendix 13

Pre-Trial Checklist

[SHORT TITLE OF CASE and FOLIO NUMBER]   2A–170
a. Trial date:
b. Party lodging checklist:
c. Name of solicitors:
d. Name(s) of advocates for trial:
[**Note**: this checklist should normally be completed with the involvement of the advocate(s) instructed for trial]

1. Have you completed preparation of trial bundles in accordance with Appendix 10 to the Commercial Court Guide?
2. If not, when will the preparation of the trial bundles be completed?
3. Which witnesses of fact do you intend to call?
4. Which expert witness(es) do you intend to call (if directions for expert evidence have been given)?
5. Will an interpreter be required for any witness and if so, have any necessary directions already been given?

6. Have directions been given for any witness to give evidence by video link? If so, have all necessary arrangements been made?

7. What are the advocates' confirmed estimates of the minimum and maximum lengths of the trial? (A confirmed estimate of length signed by the advocates should be attached).

8. What is your estimate of costs already incurred and to be incurred at trial for the purposes of section 46 of the Practice Direction supplementing CPR Part 43? (If the trial is not expected to last more than **one day** the estimate should be substantially in the form of a statement of costs as illustrated in Form H of the Schedule of Costs Forms annexed to the Practice Direction).

[Signature of solicitors]

Appendix 14

Video-conferencing Protocol

2A–171 This protocol is for the use of video conferencing (VCF) in civil proceedings. It is in part based, with permission, upon the protocol of the Federal Court of Australia. It is intended to provide a guide to all persons involved in the use of VCF, although it does not attempt to cover all the practical questions which might arise.

Video conferencing generally

1. The protocol covers the use of VCF equipment both (a) in a courtroom, whether via equipment which is permanently placed there or via a mobile unit, and (b) in a separate studio or conference room. In either case, the location at which the judge sits is referred to as the "local site". The other site or sites to and from which transmission is made are referred to as "the remote site" and in any particular case any such site may be another courtroom. The protocol applies to cases where VCF is used for the taking of evidence and also to its use for other parts of any legal proceeding (for example, interim applications, case management conferences, pre-trial reviews).

2. VCF may be a convenient way of dealing with any part of proceedings: it can involve considerable savings in time and cost. Its use for the taking of evidence from overseas witnesses will, in particular, be likely to achieve a material saving of costs, and such savings may also be achieved by its use for taking domestic evidence. It is, however, inevitably not as ideal as having the witness physically present in court. Its convenience should not therefore be allowed to dictate its use. A judgment must be made in every case in which the use of VCF is being considered not only as to whether it will achieve an overall cost saving but as to whether its use will be likely to be beneficial to the efficient, fair and economic disposal of the litigation. In particular, it needs to be recognised that the degree of control a court can exercise over a witness at the remote site is or may be more limited than it can exercise over a witness physically before it.

3. When used for the taking of evidence, the objective should be to make the VCF setting as close as possible to the usual practice in a trial court where evidence is taken in open court. To gain the maximum benefit, several differences have to be taken into account. Some matters, which are taken for granted when evidence is taken in the conventional way, take on a different dimension when it is taken by VCF: for example, the administration of the oath, ensuring that the witness understands who is at the local site and what their various roles are, the raising of any objections to the evidence and the use of documents.

4. It should not be presumed that all foreign governments are willing to allow their nationals or others within their jurisdiction to be examined before a court in England or Wales by means of VCF. If there is any doubt about this, enquiries should be directed to the Foreign and Commonwealth Office with a view to ensuring that the country from which the evidence is to be taken raises no objection to it at diplomatic level. The party who is directed to be responsible for arranging the VCF (see

262

paragraph 8 below) will be required to make all necessary inquiries about this well in advance of the VCF and must be able to inform the court what those inquiries were and of their outcome.

5. Time zone differences need to be considered when a witness abroad is to be examined in England or Wales by VCF. The convenience of the witness, the parties, their representatives and the court must all be taken into account. The cost of the use of a commercial studio is usually greater outside normal business hours.

6. Those involved with VCF need to be aware that, even with the most advanced systems currently available, there are the briefest of delays between the receipt of the picture and that of the accompanying sound. If due allowance is not made for this, there will be a tendency to "speak over" the witness, whose voice will continue to be heard for a millisecond or so after he or she appears on the screen to have finished speaking.

7. With current technology, picture quality is good, but not as good as a television picture. The quality of the picture is enhanced if those appearing on VCF monitors keep their movements to a minimum.

Preliminary arrangements

8. The court's permission is required for any part of any proceedings to be dealt with **2A–172** by means of VCF. Before seeking a direction, the applicant should notify the listing officer, diary manager or other appropriate court officer of the intention to seek it, and should enquire as to the availability of court VCF equipment for the day or days of the proposed VCF. The application for a direction should be made to the Master, District Judge or Judge, as may be appropriate. If all parties consent, permission can be sought by letter, fax or e-mail, although the court may still require an oral hearing. All parties are entitled to be heard on whether or not such a direction should be given and as to its terms. If a witness at a remote site is to give evidence by an interpreter, consideration should be given at this stage as to whether the interpreter should be at the local site or the remote site. If a VCF direction is given, arrangements for the transmission will then need to be made. The court will ordinarily direct that the party seeking permission to use VCF is to be responsible for this. That party is hereafter referred to as "the VCF arranging party".

9. Subject to any order to the contrary, all costs of the transmission, including the costs of hiring equipment and technical personnel to operate it, will initially be the responsibility of, and must be met by, the VCF arranging party. All reasonable efforts should be made to keep the transmission to a minimum and so keep the costs down. All such costs will be considered to be part of the costs of the proceedings and the court will determine at such subsequent time as is convenient or appropriate who, as between the parties, should be responsible for them and (if appropriate) in what proportions.

10. The local site will, if practicable, be a courtroom but it may instead be an appropriate studio or conference room. The VCF arranging party must contact the listing officer, diary manager or other appropriate officer of the court which made the VCF direction and make arrangements for the VCF transmission. Details of the remote site, and of the equipment to be used both at the local site (if not being supplied by the court) and the remote site (including the number of ISDN lines and connection speed), together with all necessary contact names and telephone numbers, will have to be provided to the listing officer, diary manager or other court officer. The court will need to be satisfied that any equipment provided by the parties for use at the local site and also that at the remote site is of sufficient quality for a satisfactory transmission. The VCF arranging party must ensure that a technical assistant will be present at the local site to supervise the operation of the VCF throughout the transmission in order to deal with any technical problems. That party must also arrange for a technical assistant to be similarly present at the remote site for like purposes.

11. It is recommended that the judge, practitioners and witness should arrive at their respective VCF sites about 20 minutes prior to the scheduled commencement of the transmission.

12. If the local site is not a courtroom, but a conference room or studio, the judge will need to determine who is to sit where. The VCF arranging party must take care to ensure that the number of microphones is adequate for the speakers and that the panning of the camera for the practitioners' table encompasses all legal representatives so that the viewer can see everyone seated there.

13. The proceedings, wherever they may take place, form part of a trial to which the public is entitled to have access (unless only the court has determined that they should be heard in private). If the local site is to be a studio or conference room, the VCF arranging party must ensure that it provides sufficient accommodation to enable a reasonable number of members of the public to attend.

14. In cases where the local site is a studio or conference room, the VCF arranging party should make arrangements, if practicable, for the royal coat of arms to be placed above the judge's seat.

15. In cases in which the VCF is to be used for the taking of evidence, the VCF arranging party must arrange for recording equipment to be provided by the court which made the VCF direction so that the evidence can be recorded. An associate will normally be present to operate the recording equipment when the local site is a courtroom. The VCF arranging party should take steps to ensure that an associate is present to do likewise when it is a studio or conference room. The equipment should be set up and tested before the VCF transmission. It will often be a valuable safeguard for the arranging party also to arrange for the provision of recording equipment at the remote site. This will provide a useful back-up if there is any reduction in sound quality during the transmission. A direction from the court for the making of such a back-up recording must, however, be obtained first. This is because the proceedings are court proceedings and, save as directed by the court, no other recording of them must be made.

16. Some countries may require that any oath or affirmation to be taken by a witness accord with local custom rather than the usual form of oath or affirmation used in England and Wales. The VCF arranging party must make all appropriate prior inquiries and put in place all arrangements necessary to enable the oath or affirmation to be taken in accordance with any local custom. That party must be in a position to inform the court what those inquiries were, what their outcome was and what arrangements have been made. If the oath or affirmation can be administered in the manner normal in England and Wales, the VCF arranging party must arrange in advance to have the appropriate holy book at the remote site. The associate will normally administer the oath.

17. Consideration will need to be given in advance to the documents to which the witness is likely to be referred. The parties should endeavour to agree on this. It will usually be most convenient for a bundle of the copy documents to be prepared in advance, which the VCF arranging party should then send to the remote site.

18. Additional documents are sometimes quite properly introduced during the course of a witness's evidence. To cater for this, the VCF arranging party should ensure that equipment is available to enable documents to be transmitted between sites during the course of the VCF transmission. Consideration should be given to whether to use a document camera. If it is decided to use one, arrangements for its use will need to be established in advance. The panel operator will need to know the number and size of documents or objects if their images are to be sent by document camera. In many cases, a simpler and sufficient alternative will be to ensure that there are fax transmission and reception facilities at the participating sites.

The hearing

2A–173 19. The procedure for conducting the transmission will be determined by the judge. He will determine who is to control the cameras. In cases where the VCF is being used for an application in the course of the proceedings, the judge will ordinarily not enter the local site until both sites are on line. Similarly, at the conclusion of the hearing, he will ordinarily leave the local site while both sites are still on line. The following paragraphs apply primarily to cases where the VCF is being used for the taking of the evidence of a witness at a remote site. In all cases, the judge will need to decide whether court dress is appropriate when using VCF facilities. It might be appropriate when transmitting from courtroom to courtroom. It might not be when a commercial facility is being used.

20. At the beginning of the transmission, the judge will probably wish to introduce himself and the advocates to the witness. He will probably want to know who is at the remote site and will invite the witness to introduce himself and anyone else who is with him. He may wish to give directions as to the seating arrangements at the remote site so that those present are visible at the local site during the taking of the evidence. He will probably wish to explain to the witness the method of taking the oath or of affirming, the manner in which the evidence will be taken, and who will be conducting the examination and cross-examination. He will probably also wish to inform the witness of the matters referred to in paragraphs 6 and 7 above (co-ordination of picture with sound, and picture quality).

21. The examination of the witness at the remote site should follow as closely as possible the practice adopted when a witness is in the courtroom. During examination, cross-examination and re-examination, the witness must be able to see the legal representative asking the question and also any other person (whether another legal representative or the judge) making any statements in regard to the witness's evidence. It will in practice be most convenient if everyone remains seated throughout the transmission.

Appendix 15

Service Out of the Jurisdiction: Related Practice

Service out of the jurisdiction without permission

1. Before issuing a claim form or seeking permission to serve out of the jurisdiction, **2A–174** it is necessary to consider whether the jurisdiction of the English courts is affected by the Civil Jurisdiction and Judgments Act 1982. Where each claim in the claim form is a claim which the Court has by virtue of the Civil Jurisdiction and Judgments Act 1982 power to hear and determine, service of the claim form out of the jurisdiction may be effected without permission provided that the requirements of rule 6.19 are satisfied and the claim form is endorsed before issue with a statement that the court has power under the Act to hear and determine the claim against the defendant, and that no proceedings involving the same claim are pending between the parties in Scotland, Northern Ireland or another convention country. Care must be taken to see that the endorsement is not made unless the statement is accurate.

Application for permission: affidavit or witness statement   **2A–175**

2.

(a) On applications for permission under rule 6.20 the written evidence must, amongst other things:

    (i) identify the paragraph or paragraphs of rule 6.20 relied on as giving the court jurisdiction to order service out, together with a summary of the facts relied on as bringing the case within each such paragraph;

    (ii) state the belief of the deponent that there is a good claim and state in what place or country the defendant is or probably may be found;

    (iii) summarise the considerations relied upon as showing that the case is a proper one in which to subject a party outside the jurisdiction to proceedings within it;

    (iv) draw attention to any features which might reasonably be thought to weigh against the making of the order sought;

    (v) state the deponent's grounds of belief and sources of information;

    (vi) exhibit copies of the documents referred to and any other significant documents.

(b) Where convenient the written evidence should be included in the form of application notice, rather than in a separate witness statement. The form of application notice may be extended for this purpose.

Application for permission: copies of draft order

2A–176 3. The documents submitted with the application must include two copies of a draft of the order sought which must state the time allowed for acknowledgment of service in accordance with any applicable practice direction and paragraphs 6 and 7 below.

Application for permission: copy or draft of claim form

2A–177 4. A copy or draft of the claim form which the applicant intends to issue and serve must be provided for the judge to initial. If the endorsement to the claim form includes causes of action or claims not covered by the grounds on which permission to serve out of the jurisdiction can properly be granted, permission will be refused unless the draft is amended to restrict it to proper claims. Where the application is for the issue of a concurrent claim form, the documents submitted must also include a copy of the original claim form.

Arbitration matters

2A–178 5. Service out of the jurisdiction in arbitration matters is governed by Part 62. As to the 1968 Convention on Jurisdiction in the context of arbitration, see Article 1(4).

2A–179 **Practice under rules 6.19 and 6.20**

6.

(a) Although a Part 7 claim form may contain or be accompanied by particulars of claim, there is no need for it to do so and in many cases particulars of claim will be served after the claim form: rule 58.5.

(b) A defendant should acknowledge service in every case: rule 58.6(1).

(c) The period for filing acknowledgment of service will be calculated from the service of the claim form, whether or not particulars of claim are to follow: rule 58.6.

(d) The period for serving, and filing, particulars of claim (where they were not contained in the claim form and did not accompany the claim form) will be calculated from acknowledgment of service: rule 58.5(1)(c).

(e) The period for serving and filing the defence will be calculated from service of the particulars of claim: rule 58.10(2).

7. Time for serving and filing a defence is calculated as follows:

(i) where particulars of claim were included in or accompanied the claim form the period for serving and filing a defence is 21 or 31 days as prescribed by rule 6.23, or the number of days shown in the table in practice direction 6BPD, in either case plus an additional 14 days;

(ii) where particulars of claim were not included in and did not accompany the claim form, the period for serving and filing a defence is 28 days from the service of the particulars of claim.

Appendix 16

Security for Costs: Related Practice

First applications

2A–180 1. First applications for security for costs should not be made later than at the Case Management Conference and in any event any application should not be left until close to the trial date. Delay to the prejudice of the other party or the administration of justice will probably cause the application to fail, as will any use of the application to harass the other party. Where it is intended to make an application for security at the Case Management Conference the procedure, and timetable for evidence, for an ordinary application must be followed (see section F5 of the Guide).

Successive applications

2. Successive applications for security can be granted where the circumstances warrant. If a claimant wishes to seek to preclude any further application it is incumbent on him to make that clear. **2A–181**

Evidence

3. An affidavit or witness statement in support of an application for security for costs should deal not only with the residence of the claimant (or other respondent to the application) and the location of his assets but also with the practical difficulties (if any) of enforcing an order for costs against him. **2A–182**

Investigation of the merits of the case

4. Investigation of the merits of the case on an application for security is strongly discouraged. Only in those cases where it can be shown without detailed investigation of evidence or law that the claim is certain or almost certain to succeed or fail will the merits be taken into consideration. **2A–183**

Undertaking by the applicant

5. In appropriate cases an order for security for costs may only be made on terms that the applicant gives an undertaking to comply with any order that the court may make if the court later finds that the order for security for costs has caused loss to the claimant and that the claimant should be compensated for such loss. Such undertakings are intended to compensate claimants in cases where no order for costs is ultimately made in favour of the applicant. **2A–184**

Stay of proceedings

6. It is not usually convenient or appropriate to order an automatic stay of the proceedings pending the provision of the security. It leads to delay and may disrupt the preparation of the case for trial, or other hearing. Experience has shown that it is usually better to give the claimant (or other relevant party) a reasonable time within which to provide the security and the other party liberty to apply to the court in the event of default. This enables the court to put the claimant to his election and then, if appropriate, to dismiss the case. **2A–185**

Amount of security

7. Where the dispute on an application for security for costs relates to the correct evaluation of the amount of costs likely to be allowed to a successful defendant on an assessment of costs, parties should consider whether it would be advantageous for the judge hearing the application to sit with a Costs Judge as an informal assessor. The judge himself may take such an initiative. **2A–186**

ADDRESSES AND CONTACT DETAILS

The Admiralty Marshal:
 Room E203,
 Royal Courts of Justice,
 Strand,
 London WC2A 2LL
 Tel: 020 7947 6111
 Fax: 020 7947 7671
The Admiralty & Commercial Registry:
 Room E200,

Royal Courts of Justice,
Strand,
London WC2A 2LL
Tel: 020 7947 6112
Fax: 020 7947 6245
DX 44450 STRAND

The Admiralty & Commercial Court Listing Office:

Room E201,
Royal Courts of Justice,
Strand,
London WC2A 2LL
Tel: 020 7947 6826
Fax: 020 7947 7670
DX 44450 STRAND

The Admiralty & Commercial Case Management Unit:

Room E206,
Royal Courts of Justice,
Strand,
London WC2A 2LL
Tel: 020 7947 6256
Fax: 020 7947 7672

The Secretary to the Commercial Court Committee:

Mrs Angela Hodgson
Room E201
Royal Courts of Justice
Strand
London WC2A 2LL
Tel: 020 7947 6826
Fax: 020 7947 7670
DX 44450 STRAND

Out of hours emergency number:

(Security Office at Royal Courts of Justice): 020 7947 6000

Fax number for the procedure under sections B3.11 and B4.4 of the Guide for the issue of claim forms when the Registry is closed: 020 7947 6667.

THE COMMERCIAL AND ADMIRALTY COURTS

E-MAIL COMMUNICATIONS WITH THE COURT

GUIDANCE

Introduction

2A-187   1. This guidance sets out how parties may communicate by e-mail with the Commercial and Admiralty Courts on certain matters with effect from **17 March 2003**.

Initial period of application

2A-188   2. This guidance will apply for an initial period of 6 months. Towards the end of that period, the guidance will be reviewed in the light of the experience gained. It may then be revised as necessary. [Ed.: Since extended for an indefinite period.]

Documents for which e-mail may be used

2A-189   3. E-mail may only be used:

268

(a) to communicate with the Case Management Unit, including the lodging of progress monitoring information sheets;

(b) to communicate with the Registry in relation to the approval by the Judge of draft Order following a hearing before that Judge, queries on Orders made, requests to transfer a case into or out of the Commercial Court and general correspondence, including questions on practice;

Note: Orders submitted for sealing must be submitted on paper.

(c) to communicate with the Listing Office in matters relating to listing (including the lodging of pre-trial checklists) and to lodge skeleton arguments with the listing office;

(d) to communicate with the Admiralty Marshal (except for out of hours business).

Note: The Court cannot accept any other documents by e-mail at present. In particular e-mail cannot be used to lodge pleadings, affidavits, witness statements, case memoranda and lists of issues.

Restrictions

4. A party should not use e-mail to take any step in a claim which requires a fee to be paid for that step. If a party sends by e-mail a document for which a fee is payable upon filing, the document will be treated as not having been filed. **2A–190**

5. Where a party sends or lodges a document by e-mail he should still comply with any rule or practice direction requiring the document to be served on any other person.

6. Nothing in this guidance requires any person to accept service of a document by e-mail.

Sending e-mails to the Court: addresses

7. For Listing matters, the e-mail addresses are: **2A–191**

(a) For all matters relating to listing (except Friday applications), for the lodging of pre-trial check lists and for all skeleton arguments: ComCt.Listing@courtservice.gsi.gov.uk

(b) For matters relating to Friday applications (except skeleton arguments): ComCt.Friday@courtservice.gsi.gov.uk

8. For matters relating to case management and the Case Management Unit (including the lodging of progress monitoring sheets), the address is: ComCt.CMU@courtservice.gsi.gov.uk

9. For all correspondence for the Registry the address is: ComCt.Registry@courtservice.gsi.gov.uk

10. For all matters for the Admiralty Marshal or the business of the Admiralty Marshal, the address is: Admiralty.bus@courtservice.gsi.gov.uk

The subject line

11. The subject line of the e-mail should contain only the following information which should be in the following order: **2A–192**

(a) **First**, the proper title of the claim (abbreviated as necessary) with the claimant named first and the defendant named second; unless the action is an Admiralty action, the name of the ship should not be used:

(b) **Second**, the claim number.

Form and content of the e-mail

12. Correspondence and documents may be sent either as text or attachments, except that documents required to be in a practice form should be sent in that form as attachments using one of the formats specified in paragraph 17. **2A–193**

13. Parties must not use e-mail to send any document which exceeds 40 pages in the aggregate of normal typescript in length or 2 MB whichever is the smaller. Documents may not be subdivided to comply with this requirement.

14. Where a party files a document by e-mail, he should not send a hard copy in addition, unless there are good reasons for so doing or the Court requires.

15. Parties are advised to bear in mind when sending correspondence or documents of a confidential or sensitive nature that the security of e-mails cannot be guaranteed.

16. Where a time limit applies, it remains the responsibility of the party to ensure

that the document is filed in time. Parties are advised to allow for delays or downtime on their server or the servers used by the Court.

Attachments

2A–194 17. Attachments should be in one of the following formats:

(a) Microsoft Word viewer/reader (.doc) in Word 1997 or later format

(b) Rich Text Format as (.rtf) files

(c) Plain/Formatted Text as (.txt) files

(d) Hypertext documents as (.htm) files

(e) Adobe Acrobat as (.pdf) files minimum viewer version 4

Receipt of e-mail by the Court

2A–195 18. A document is not filed until the e-mail is received by the court at the addressee's computer terminal, whatever time it is shown to have been sent.

19. The time of receipt of an e-mail at the addressee's computer terminal will be recorded.

20. If an e-mail is received after 4 p.m. it will be treated as having been received on the next day the court office is open.

21. No automatic acknowledgment of the receipt of an e-mail will be sent; the subject matter of the e-mail will be considered in the ordinary way. If a response to the subject matter of the e-mail is not received within a reasonable period, the sender should assume that the court has not received it and should send the e-mail again, or file the document by another means.

22. Parties should not telephone to enquire as to the receipt of an e-mail. They should observe the procedure set out in paragraph 21.

Replies to e-mails sent to the court

2A–196 23. The court will normally send any reply by e-mail to documents or correspondence sent by e-mail.

(a) All replies will be sent to the e-mail address from which the e-mail has been sent. If the sender wishes the reply to be copied to other parties or to another e-mail address used by the sender of the message, such e-mail addresses must be specified in the copy line.

(b) The Court will not send copies to clients or others not on the record; the copy line must therefore not contain the addresses of such persons.

(c) The e-mail should also contain in the body of the e-mail the name and telephone number of the sender.

Note: It is important that each firm or set of chambers considers putting in place a system to deal with the absence of the individual who has sent the e-mail and to whom the Court will ordinarily reply. Two possible solutions are:

(a) A central mail box within each firm, either from which the e-mail is sent to the Court (and which will therefore receive the reply) or to which it is copied by the individual sender who sends it direct to the Court (and who will receive a copy of the reply);

(b) a second individual e-mail address within the firm to which the reply will be copied so that any reply can be monitored.

It must be for each firm and set of chambers to devise its own system.

Communication with the Clerk to a Commercial Judge

2A–197 24. No documents or correspondence should be sent by e-mail to the Clerk to a Commercial Judge dealing with a case, unless:

(a) an arrangement is made with the Clerk in each specific instance in which e-mail is to be used;

(b) if such an arrangement is made, the e-mail must be copied to the appropriate Listing Office Address, the Case Management Unit Address, The Registry Address, or the Admiralty Marshal Address, as the case may be.

Note: Draft Orders for the approval of the Judge must be submitted through the Registry.

11 March 2003

2B MERCANTILE COURTS

PART 59—MERCANTILE COURTS

Contents

Editorial introduction

Part 59 is added to the CPR by Civil Procedure (Amendment No. 5) Rules 2001   **2B–1**
(S.I. 2001 No. 4015), and came into force on March 25, 2002.

Scope of this Part and interpretation[1]

59.1—**(1) This Part applies to claims in Mercantile Courts.**   **2B–2**

(2) A claim may only be started in a Mercantile Court if it—

(a) **relates to a commercial or business matter in a broad sense; and**

(b) **is not required to proceed in the Chancery Division or in another specialist list.**

(3) **In this Part and its practice direction—**

(a) **"Mercantile Court" means a specialist list established within—**

(i) **the district registries listed in the practice direction; and**

(ii) **the Central London County Court, to hear mercantile claims;**

(b) **"mercantile claim" means a claim proceeding in a Mercantile Court; and**

(c) **"Mercantile judge" means a judge authorised to sit in a Mercantile Court.**

Application of the Civil Procedure Rules[2]

59.2 These Rules and their practice directions apply to mercan-   **2B–3**

---

[1] Introduced by Civil Procedure (Amendment No. 5) Rules 2001 (S.I. 2001 No. 4015).

[2] Introduced by Civil Procedure (Amendment No. 5) Rules 2001 (S.I. 2001 No. 4015).

tile claims unless this Part or a practice direction provides otherwise.

Transfer of proceedings[1]

2B–4   59.3 Rule 30.5 applies with the modifications that—

(a) a Mercantile judge may transfer a mercantile claim to another Mercantile Court; and

(b) a Commercial Court judge may transfer a claim from the Commercial Court to a Mercantile Court.

(Rule 30.5(3) provides that an application for the transfer of proceedings to or from a specialist list must be made to a judge dealing with claims in that list).

Claim form and particulars of claim[2]

2B–5   59.4—(1) If particulars of claim are not contained in or served with the claim form—

(a) the claim form must state that, if an acknowledgment of service is filed which indicates an intention to defend the claim, particulars of claim will follow;

(b) when the claim form is served, it must be accompanied by the documents specified in rule 7.8(1);

(c) the claimant must serve particulars of claim within 28 days of the filing of an acknowledgment of service which indicates an intention to defend; and

(d) rule 7.4(2) does not apply.

(2) If the claimant is claiming interest, he must—

(a) include a statement to that effect; and

(b) give the details set out in rule 16.4(2),

in both the claim form and the particulars of claim.

(3) Rules 12.6(1)(a) and 14.14(1)(a) apply with the modification that references to the particulars of claim shall be read as if they referred to the claim form.

Acknowledgment of service[3]

2B–6   59.5—(1) A defendant must file an acknowledgment of service in every case.

(2) Unless paragraph (3) applies, the period for filing an acknowledgment of service is 14 days after service of the claim form.

(3) Where the claim form is served out of the jurisdiction, or on the agent of a defendant who is overseas, the time periods provided

---

[1] Introduced by Civil Procedure (Amendment No. 5) Rules 2001 (S.I. 2001 No. 4015) and amended by Civil Procedure (Amendment No. 4) Rules 2005 (S.I. 2005 No. 3515).

[2] Introduced by Civil Procedure (Amendment No. 5) Rules 2001 (S.I. 2001 No. 4015).

[3] Introduced by Civil Procedure (Amendment No. 5) Rules 2001 (S.I. 2001 No. 4015).

by rules 6.16(4), 6.21(4) and 6.22 apply after service of the claim form.

Disputing the court's jurisdiction[1]

59.6—(1) Part 11 applies to mercantile claims with the modifica- 2B–7
tions set out in this rule.

(2) An application under rule 11(1) must be made within 28 days after filing an acknowledgment of service.

(3) If the defendant files an acknowledgment of service indicating an intention to dispute the court's jurisdiction, the claimant need not serve particulars of claim before the hearing of the application.

Default judgment[2]

59.7—(1) Part 12 applies to mercantile claims, except that rules 2B–8
12.10 and 12.11 apply as modified by paragraphs (2) and (3) of this rule.

(2) If, in am Part 7 claim—
  (a) the claim form has been served but no particulars of claim have been served; and
  (b) the defendant has failed to file an acknowledgment of service,
the claimant must make an application if he wishes to obtain a default judgment.

(3) The application may be made without notice, but the court may direct it to be served on the defendant.

Rule 59.8—Admissions

Admissions[3]

59.8—(1) Rule 14.5 does not apply to mercantile claims. 2B–9

(2) If the defendant admits part of a claim for a specified amount of money, the claimant may apply under rule 14.3 for judgment on the admission.

Rule 59.9—Defence and Reply

Defence and Reply[4]

59.9—(1) Part 15 (Defence and Reply) applies to mercantile 2B–10
claims with the modification to rule 15.8 that the claimant must—
  (a) file any reply to a defence; and

---

[1] Introduced by Civil Procedure (Amendment No. 5) Rules 2001 (S.I. 2001 No. 4015).
[2] Introduced by Civil Procedure (Amendment No. 5) Rules 2001 (S.I. 2001 No. 4015).
[3] Introduced by Civil Procedure (Amendment No. 5) Rules 2001 (S.I. 2001 No. 4015).
[4] Introduced by Civil Procedure (Amendment No. 5) Rules 2001 (S.I. 2001 No. 4015).

(b) **serve it on all other parties,** within 21 days after service of the defence.

(2) **Rule 6.23 (period for filing a defence where the claim form is served out of the jurisdiction) applies to mercantile claims, except that if the particulars of claim are served after the defendant has filed an acknowledgment of service the period for filing a defence is 28 days from service of the particulars of claim.**

Rule 59.10—Statements of case

Statements of case[1]

2B–11   **59.10 The court may at any time before or after issue of the claim form order a mercantile claim to proceed without the filing or service of statements of case.**

Rule 59.11—Case management

Case management[2]

2B–12   **59.11—(1) All mercantile claims are treated as being allocated to the multi-track, and Part 26 does not apply.**

(2) **The following parts only of Part 29 apply—**
    (a) **rule 29.3(2) (appropriate legal representative to attend case management conferences and pre-trial reviews); and**
    (b) **rule 29.5 (variation of case management timetable) with the exception of rule 29.5(1)(c).**

(3) **As soon as practicable the court will hold a case management conference which must be fixed in accordance with the practice direction.**

(4) **At the case management conference or at any hearing at which the parties are represented the court may give such directions for the management of the case as it considers appropriate.**

Rule 59.12—Judgments and orders

Judgments and orders[3]

2B–13   **59.12—(1) Except for orders made by the court of its own initiative and unless the court otherwise orders every judgment or order will be drawn up by the parties, and rule 40.3 is modified accordingly.**

(2) **An application for a consent order must include a draft of the proposed order signed on behalf of all the parties to whom it relates.**

(3) **Rule 40.6 (consent judgments and orders) does not apply.**

---

[1] Introduced by Civil Procedure (Amendment No. 5) Rules 2001 (S.I. 2001 No. 4015).
[2] Introduced by Civil Procedure (Amendment No. 5) Rules 2001 (S.I. 2001 No. 4015).
[3] Introduced by Civil Procedure (Amendment No. 5) Rules 2001 (S.I. 2001 No. 4015).

PRACTICE DIRECTION—MERCANTILE COURTS
This Practice Direction supplements Part 59

General

1.1 This practice direction applies to mercantile claims.

1.2 Mercantile Courts are established in—

  (1)   the following district registries of the High Court—Birmingham, Bristol, Cardiff, Chester, Leeds, Liverpool, Manchester and Newcastle; and

  (2)   the Central London County Court (previously called the Business List and now called the Mercantile List).

1.3 All mercantile claims will be heard or determined by a Mercantile judge, except that—

  (1)   an application may be heard and determined by any other judge who, if the claim were not a mercantile claim, would have jurisdiction to determine it, if—

     (a) the application is urgent and no Mercantile judge is available to hear it; or

     (b) a Mercantile judge directs it to be heard by another judge; and

  (2)   unless the court otherwise orders, all proceedings for the enforcement of a Mercantile Court judgment or order for the payment of money will be dealt with by a district judge.

1.4 Provisions in other practice directions which refer to a master or district judge are to be read, in relation to mercantile claims, as if they referred to a Mercantile judge.

Starting proceedings in a Mercantile Court

2.1 A claim should only be started in a Mercantile Court if it will benefit from the expertise of a Mercantile judge.

2.2 The claim form must be marked in the top right hand corner "Queen's Bench Division, ...District Registry, Mercantile Court" or "Central London County Court, Mercantile List" as appropriate.

2.3 A claim having a value less than £15,000 may not be issued in the Mercantile List at the Central London County Court without permission of the court.

2.4 A claim may be issued in the Mercantile List at the Central London County Court provided it has some connection with the South Eastern Circuit, for example, because—

  (1)   it is convenient for the claim to be dealt with in that court;

  (2)   the claim arises out of a transaction which took place within that circuit; or

  (3)   one of the parties resides or carries on business within that circuit.

Applications before proceedings are issued

3.1 A party who intends to bring a claim in a Mercantile Court must make any application before the claim form is issued to a judge of that court.

3.2 The written evidence in support of such an application should show why the claim is suitable to proceed as a mercantile claim.

2B–14

MERCANTILE COURT

Transfer of proceedings to or from a Mercantile Court

4.1 If a claim which has not been issued in a Mercantile Court is suitable to continue as a mercantile claim—

   (1)   any party wishing the claim to be transferred to a Mercantile Court may make an application for transfer to the court to which transfer is sought;

   (2)   if all parties consent to the transfer, the application may be made by letter to the mercantile listing officer of the court to which transfer is sought, stating why the case is suitable to be transferred to that court and enclosing the written consents of the parties, the claim form and statements of case.

4.2 If an application for transfer is made to a court which does not have power to make the order, that court may—

   (1)   adjourn the application to be heard by a Mercantile judge; or

   (2)   dismiss the application.

4.3 A Mercantile judge may make an order under rule 59.3 of his own initiative.

Default judgment and admissions

5. The practice directions supplementing Parts 12 and 14 apply with the following modifications—

   (1)   paragraph 4.1(1) of the practice direction supplementing Part 12 is to be read as referring to the service of the claim form; and

   (2)   the references to "particulars of claim" in paragraphs 2.1, 3.1 and 3.2 of the practice direction supplementing Part 14 are to be read as referring to the claim form.

Variation of time limits by agreement

6.1 If the parties, in accordance with rule 2.11, agree in writing to vary a time limit, the claimant must notify the court in writing, giving brief written reasons for the agreed variation.

6.2 The court may make an order overriding an agreement by the parties varying a time limit.

Case management

7.1 The following parts only of the practice direction supplementing Part 29 apply—

   (1)   paragraph 5 (case management conferences), excluding paragraph 5.9 and modified so far as is made necessary by other specific provisions of this practice direction; and

   (2)   paragraph 7 (failure to comply with case management directions).

7.2 If proceedings are started in a Mercantile Court, the claimant must apply for a case management conference—

   (1)   for a Part 7 claim, within 14 days of the date when all defendants who intend to file and serve a defence have done so; and

   (2)   for a Part 8 claim, within 14 days of the date when all defendants who intend to serve evidence have done so.

7.3 If proceedings are transferred to a Mercantile Court, the claimant must apply for a case management conference within 14 days of receiving an acknowledgment of the transfer from the receiving court, unless the judge held, or gave directions for, a case management conference when he made the order transferring the proceedings.

7.4 Any party may, at a time earlier than that provided in paragraphs 7.2 or 7.3, apply in writing to the court to fix a case management conference.

7.5 If the claimant does not make an application in accordance with paragraphs 7.2 or 7.3, any other party may apply for a case management conference.

7.6 The court may fix a case management conference at any time on its own initiative. If it does so, the court will give at least seven days' notice to the parties, unless there are compelling reasons for a shorter period of notice.

7.7 Not less than seven days before a case management conference—

   (1)   each party shall file and serve—

      (a) a case management information sheet substantially in the form set out at Appendix A to this practice direction; and

      (b) an application notice for any order which that party intends to seek at the case management conference, other than directions referred to in the case management information sheet; and

   (2)   the claimant (or other party applying for the conference) shall in addition file and serve—

      (a) a case management file containing—

      - the claim form;

      - the statements of case (excluding schedules of more than 15 pages);

      - any orders already made;

      - the case management information sheets; and

      - a short list of the principal issues to be prepared by the claimant; and

      (b) a draft order substantially in the form set out at Appendix B to this practice direction, setting out the directions which that party thinks appropriate.

7.8 In appropriate cases—

   (1)   the parties may, not less than 7 days before the date fixed for the case management conference, submit agreed directions for the approval of the judge;

   (2)   the judge will then either—

      (a) make the directions proposed; or

      (b) make them with alterations; or

      (c) require the case management conference to proceed; but

   (3)   the parties must assume that the conference will proceed until informed to the contrary.

MERCANTILE COURT

7.9 If the parties submit agreed directions and the judge makes them with alterations, any party objecting to the alterations may, within 7 days of receiving the order containing the directions, apply to the court for the directions to be varied.

7.10 The directions given at the case management conference—

(1) will normally cover all steps in the case through to trial, including the fixing of a trial date or window, or directions for the taking of steps to fix the trial date or window; and

(2) may include the fixing of a progress monitoring date or dates, and make provision for the court to be informed as to the progress of the case at the date or dates fixed.

7.11 If the court fixes a progress monitoring date, it may after that date fix a further case management conference or a pre-trial review on its own initiative if—

(1) no or insufficient information is provided by the parties; or

(2) it is appropriate in view of the information provided.

Pre-trial review and questionnaire

8.1 The court may order a pre-trial review at any time.

8.2 Each party must file and serve a completed pre-trial check list substantially in the form set out in Appendix C to this practice direction—

(1) if a pre-trial review has been ordered, not less than 7 days before the date of the review; or

(2) if no pre-trial review has been ordered, not less than 6 weeks before the trial date.

8.3 When pre-trial check lists are filed under paragraph 8.2(2)–

(1) the judge will consider them and decide whether to order a pre-trial review; and

(2) if he does not order a pre-trial review, he may on his own initiative give directions for the further preparation of the case or as to the conduct of the trial.

8.4 At a pre-trial review—

(1) the parties should if possible be represented by the advocates who will be appearing at the trial;

(2) any representatives appearing must be fully informed and authorised for the purposes of the review; and

(3) the court will give such directions for the conduct of the trial as it sees fit.

Evidence for applications

9.1 The general requirement is that, unless the court orders otherwise—

(1) evidence in support of an application must be filed and served with the application: see rule 23.7(3);

(2) evidence in answer must be filed and served within 14 days after the application is served;

(3) evidence in reply must be filed and served within 7 days of the service of the evidence in answer.

9.2 In any case in which the application is likely to require an oral hearing of more than half a day the periods set out in paragraphs 9.1 (2) and (3) will be 28 days and 14 days respectively.

9.3 If the date fixed for the hearing of the application means that the times in paragraphs 9.1 (2) and (3) cannot both be achieved, the evidence must be filed and served—

(1)   as soon as possible; and

(2)   in sufficient time to ensure that the application may fairly proceed on the date fixed.

9.3 The parties may, in accordance with rule 2.11, agree different periods from those provided above, provided that the agreement does not affect the ability to proceed on the date fixed for the hearing of the application.

Files for applications

10. Before the hearing of any application, the applicant must—

(1)   provide to the court and each other party an appropriate indexed file for the application with consecutively numbered pages; and

(2)   attach to the file an estimate of the reading time required by the judge.

Judgments and orders

11.1 After any hearing the claimant must draw up a draft order, unless the decision was made on the application of another party in which case that party must do so.

11.2 A draft order must be submitted by the party responsible for drawing it up within 3 clear days of the decision, with sufficient copies for each party and for one to be retained by the court.

11.3 The sealed orders will be returned to the party submitting them, who will be responsible for serving the order on the other parties.

11.4 Orders must be dated with the date of the decision, except for consent orders submitted for approval, which must be left undated.

MERCANTILE COURT

Annex A(1)

2B–15

CASE MANAGEMENT INFORMATION SHEET
MERCANTILE COURTS

[Title of Case]

**[This information sheet must be lodged with Mercantile Listing at least
7 days before the Case Management Conference, and copies supplied to
all other parties: see paragraph 4.6 of the Mercantile Courts Guide.]**

Party lodging:
Solicitors:
Advocate(s) for trial:
Date:

Substance of case
1. What in about 20 words maximum is the case about?
Please provide a separate concise list of issues in a complex case.

Parties
2. Are all parties still effective?
3. Do you intend to add any further party?

Statements of Case
4. Do you intend to amend your statement of case?
5. Do you require any 'further information' – CPR 18?

Disclosure
6. By what date can you give standard disclosure?
7. Do you contend that to search for any type of document falling within CPR 32.6(b) would
be unreasonable within CPR 31.7(2); if so, what type and on what grounds?
8. Is any specific disclosure required – CPR 31.12?
9. Is a full disclosure order appropriate?
10. By what date could you give
    (1) any specific disclosure referred to at 3
    (2) give full disclosure?
11. Is a full disclosure order appropriate?
12. By what date could you give full disclosure?

Admissions
13. Can you make any additional admissions?

Preliminary issues
14. Are any issues suitable for trial as preliminary issues? If yes, which?

Witnesses of fact

15. On how many witnesses of fact do you intend to rely at the trial (subject to the court's direction)?

16. Please name them, or explain why you do not.

17. Which of them will be called to give oral evidence?

18. When can you serve their witness statements?

19. Will any require an interpreter?

Expert evidence

20. Are there issues requiring expert evidence?

21. If yes, what issues?

22. Might a joint single expert be suitable on an issue (see CPR 35.7)?

23. What experts do you intend (subject to the court's direction) to call? Please give the number, their names and expertise.

24. By what date can you serve signed expert reports?

25. Should there be meetings of expertsof like disciplines, of all disciplines? By when?

26. Which experts, if any, do you intend not to call at the trial?

27. Will any require an interpreter?

Trial

28. What are the advocates' present estimates of the length of the trial?

29. What is the earliest date that you think the case can be ready for trial?

30. Where should the trial be held?

31. Is a Pre-Trial Review advisable?

A.D.R.

32. Might some form of Alternative Dispute Resolution assist to resolve the dispute or some part of it?

33. Has this been considered with the client?

34. Has this been considered with the other parties?

35. Do you want the case to be stayed pending A.D.R. or other means of settlement – see CPR 26.4; or any other directions relating to A.D.R.?

Other applications

36. What applications, if any, not covered above, will you be making at the conference?

Costs

37. What, do you estimate, are your costs to date?

38. What, do you estimate, will be your costs to end of trial?

[Signature of party/solicitor]

Annex A(2)

2B–16

Standard Directions in Mercantile Courts

[Title of case with Judge's name]

Order for Directions
made on [   ]

1. Standard disclosure is to be made by [   ].
   Inspection on 48 hours notice to be completed by [   ].

2. Signed statements of witnesses of fact, and hearsay notices when required by CPR 33.2, are to be exchanged not later than [   ].

   Unless otherwise ordered, the witness statements are to stand as the evidence in chief of the witnesses at trial.

3. Each party has permission to call at the trial expert witnesses as follows:

   Number   Expertise   Issue(s) to be covered

   whose reports are to be exchanged by [   ].

4. Experts of like disciplines are to:

   (i)   meet without prejudice by [   ] to identify the issues between them and to attempt to reach agreement on such issues, and

   (ii)   prepare a joint statement pursuant to CPR 35.12(3), by [   ].

or

3. Expert evidence in the following field(s) of expertise is limited to a written report by a single expert jointly instructed by the parties:

   Expertise   Issue(s) to be covered

4. (i)   The report of the single joint expert is to be produced by [   ].

   (ii)   Any questions to the expert are to be presented to him by [   ] and answered by [   ].

   (iii)   Any party may apply not later than [   ] for an order that the expert witness shall give oral evidence at the trial.

5. The case will be tried in [   ] by judge alone, estimated length of trial [   ] days, [commencing on   ] [not before   ].
   [The claimant is to apply to the mercantile listing officer to fix a date for the trial, not later than [   ], specifying dates which any party wishes to avoid.]

[6 .   The progress monitoring date is [   ]. Each party is to notify the court in writing
       by that date (with a copy to all other parties) of the progress of the case, including -

       (i)   whether the directions have been complied with in all respects;

       (ii)   if any directions are outstanding, which of them and why; and

       (iii)   whether a further case management conference or a pre-trial review is required.]

7.   There will be a pre-trial review on [   ].
       [In the event of both parties notifying the court in writing not less than [   ] days before the
       pre-trial review that it is not required, then it will be vacated.]

8.   Signed pre-trial check lists are to be filed and served by [   ] [not less than 7 days
       before the pre-trial review] [not less than 6 weeks before the trial date].

9.   Trial bundles must be agreed, prepared and delivered to counsel not less than [   ]
       days before the trial date, and to the court not less than [   ] days before the trial
       date.

10.   Costs in the case.

DATED

Annex A(3)

2B–17

PRE-TRIAL CHECK LIST
MERCANTILE COURTS

[Title of Action]

Where a Pre-Trial Review has been ordered, this check list must be lodged with Mercantile Listing at least 7 days before the Pre-Trial Review, and copies supplied to all other parties.
Where a Pre-Trial Review has not been ordered, it must be lodged not less than 6 weeks the trial date and copies supplied to all other parties.
See paragraphs 5.5(2) and 5.6 of the Mercantile Courts Practice Direction.

a. Trial Date:
b. Whether Pre-trial Review ordered:
c. Date of Review:
d. Party lodging:
e. Solicitors:
f. Advocate(s) for trial:
g. Date lodged:

[Note: this checklist should normally be completed with the involvement of the advocate(s) instructed for trial.]

1. Have all the directions made to date been carried out?

2. If not, what remains to be carried out? When will it be carried out?

3. Do you intend to take any further steps regarding:
a. statements of case?
b. disclosure?
c. witnesses and witness statements?
d. experts and expert reports?
   If yes in any case, what and by when?

4. Will the preparation of trial bundles be completed not later than 3 weeks before the date fixed for trial?

   If not, what is the position?

5. What witnesses of fact do you intend to call?

6. (Where directions for expert evidence have been given) what experts do you intend to call?

7. Is any interpreter needed; for whom?

8. If a Pre-Trial Review has not been ordered, do you think one would be useful?

9. What are the advocate(s)' confirmed estimates of the minimum and maximum lengths of the trial? A confirmed estimate signed by the advocate(s) and dated must be attached.

10. a. Might some form of alternative dispute resolution now assist?
b. Has the question been considered with the client?
c. Has the question been explored with the other parties to the case?

[Signature of party/solicitor]

Note

   Each of the Mercantile Courts now has its own guide, and these are available on the **2B–18** Court Service website or in hard copy from the individual courts concerned. For more information see www.courtservice.gov.uk.

MERCANTILE COURT

2C PROCEEDINGS IN THE TECHNOLOGY & CONSTRUCTION COURT

PART 60—TECHNOLOGY AND CONSTRUCTION COURT CLAIMS

Contents

Editorial introduction

Part 60 is added to the CPR by Civil Procedure (Amendment No. 5) Rules 2001 **2C-1** (S.I. 2001 No. 4015), and comes into force on March 25, 2002.

The Technology and Construction Court

This court is the successor in title to the Official Referees Courts. The first Official **2C-2** Referees of the Supreme Court of Justice were appointed in 1876 under the Judicature Acts 1873-75. Any question could be referred for trial with or without consent of the parties if it involved the prolonged investigation of documents or accounts or of any scientific or local investigation. The report of an Official Referee on a trial had to be accepted as if it were the verdict of a jury but he could not give judgment or make any order as to costs. By the Judicature Act 1884 power was given for an Official Referee to give a judgment, make orders for costs and exercise the powers of a High Court judge in a case referred to him. The Arbitration Act of 1889 enabled parties to an arbitration agreement to require an Official Referee to sit as an arbitrator. From the outset much of the Official Referee's work was concerned with the construction industry in all its aspects. The Courts Act 1971 provided that in future "Official Referees business" should be dealt with by such Circuit Judges as the Lord Chancellor should determine. Although the title "Official Referee" was not legally preserved it continued to be used universally. By 1998 references were a rarity and most of the work tried in the court was commenced in the Official Referees Registry or transferred from the Chancery Division or the Queen's Bench Division. The description of the court was considered to be inaccurate and anachronistic and in October of 1998 the Lord Chancellor with the concurrence of the Lord Chief Justice directed that the court should be renamed the Technology andConstruction Court of the High Court of Justice. The Technology and Construction Court (TCC) was opened by the Lord Chancellor on October 9, 1998. From that time the mode of address of all judges has been "my Lord". On April 26, 1999 the Civil Procedure Rules came into force incorporating many of the case management practices pioneered by the Official Referees during the 1980s and 1990s and reflecting the interventionist ethos of the court.

The Technology and Construction Courts in London —There are eight courts situated on the 2nd to 6th floors of St Dunstans House, 133-137 Fetter Lane, London EC4A 1HD. The Registry is on the 3rd floor.

The constitution of the Courts in London and elsewhere and assignment of cases is described in the Technology and Construction Court Guide, 2nd edition (see para. 2C-32 below), and the Technology and Construction Court: Statement by the Lord Chief Justice of England & Wales, June 7, 2005 (LCJ Statement), (see para. 2C-31) which deals with the interim arrangements pending a final determination as to the future of the TCC (para. 5 of the LCJ Statement).

General[1]

2C-3 60.1—(1) This Part applies to Technology and Construction Court claims ("TCC claims").

(2) In this Part and its practice direction—

(a) "TCC claim" means a claim which—

(i) satisfies the requirements of paragraph (3); and

(ii) has been issued in or transferred into the specialist list for such claims;

(b) "Technology and Construction Court" means any court in which TCC claims are dealt with in accordance with this Part or its practice direction; and

(c) "TCC judge" means any judge authorised to hear TCC claims.

(3) A claim may be brought as a TCC claim if—

(a) it involves issues or questions which are technically complex; or

(b) a trial by a TCC judge is desirable.

(The practice direction gives examples of types of claims which it may be appropriate to bring as TCC claims).

(4) TCC claims include all official referees' business referred to in section 68(1)(a) of the Supreme Court Act 1981[2].

(5) TCC claims will be dealt with—

(a) in a Technology and Construction Court; and

(b) by a TCC judge, unless—

(i) this Part or its practice direction permits otherwise; or

(ii) a TCC judge directs otherwise.

Specialist list[3]

2C-4 60.2—(1) TCC claims form a specialist list.

(2) A judge will be appointed to be the judge in charge of the TCC specialist list.

Application of the Civil Procedure Rules[4]

2C-5 60.3 These Rules and their practice directions apply to TCC claims unless this Part or a practice direction provides otherwise.

Issuing a TCC claim[5]

2C-6 60.4 A TCC claim must be issued in—

(a) the High Court in London;

---

[1] Introduced by Civil Procedure (Amendment No. 5) Rules 2001 (S.I. 2001 No. 4015).

[2] 1981 c. 54.

[3] Introduced by Civil Procedure (Amendment No. 5) Rules 2001 (S.I. 2001 No. 4015).

[4] Introduced by Civil Procedure (Amendment No. 5) Rules 2001 (S.I. 2001 No. 4015).

[5] Introduced by Civil Procedure (Amendment No. 5) Rules 2001 (S.I. 2001 No. 4015).

(b) a district registry of the High Court; or

(c) a county court specified in the practice direction.

Reply[1]

60.5 Part 15 (Defence and Reply) applies to TCC claims with the modification to rule 15.8 that the claimant must— 2C-7

(a) file any reply to a defence; and

(b) serve it on all other parties,

within 21 days after service of the defence.

Case management[2]

60.6—(1) All TCC claims are treated as being allocated to the multi-track and Part 26 does not apply. 2C-8

(2) Part 29 and its practice direction apply to the case management of TCC claims, except where they are varied by or inconsistent with the practice direction to this Part.

Judgments and Orders

60.7—(1) Except for orders made by the court of its own initiative and unless the court otherwise orders, every judgment or order made in claims proceeding in the Technology and Construction Court will be drawn up by the parties, and rule 40.3 is modified accordingly. 2C-8.1

(2) An application for a consent order must include a draft of the proposed order signed on behalf of all the parties to whom it relates.

(3) Rule 40.6 (consent judgments and orders) does not apply.

TCC

---

[1] Introduced by Civil Procedure (Amendment No. 5) Rules 2001 (S.I. 2001 No. 4015).

[2] Introduced by Civil Procedure (Amendment No. 5) Rules 2001 (S.I. 2001 No. 4015).

PRACTICE DIRECTION—TECHNOLOGY AND CONSTRUCTION COURT CLAIMS

2C–9   *This Practice Direction supplements CPR Part 60*

General

1. This practice direction applies to Technology and Construction Court claims ('TCC claims').

TCC Claims

2C–10   **2.1** The following are examples of the types of claim which it may be appropriate to bring as TCC claims–

(a)   building or other construction disputes, including claims for the enforcement of the decisions of adjudicators under the Housing Grants, Construction and Regeneration Act 1996;

(b)   engineering disputes;

(c)   claims by and against engineers, architects, surveyors, accountants and other specialised advisers relating to the services they provide;

(d)   claims by and against local authorities relating to their statutory duties concerning the development of land or the construction of buildings;

(e)   claims relating to the design, supply and installation of computers, computer software and related network systems;

(f)   claims relating to the quality of goods sold or hired, and work done, materials supplied or services rendered;

(g)   claims between landlord and tenant for breach of a repairing covenant;

(h)   claims between neighbours, owners and occupiers of land in trespass, nuisance etc.;

(i)   claims relating to the environment (for example, pollution cases);

(j)   claims arising out of fires;

(k)   claims involving taking of accounts where these are complicated; and

(l)   challenges to decisions of arbitrators in construction and engineering disputes including applications for permission to appeal and appeals.

2.2 A claim given as an example in paragraph 2.1 will not be suitable for this specialist list unless it demonstrates the characteristics in rule 60.1(3). Similarly, the examples are not exhaustive and other types of claim may be appropriate to this specialist list.

Comment

2C–11   A TCC claim in rule 60.1(3) is one which involves issues or questions which are technically complex or for which a trial by a judge of a TCC is for any other reason desirable. The effect of the rule is that a TCC judge may try any case within the business of the Chancery and Queens Bench divisions. The new rule is widely framed because the court has historically adapted itself to deal with new problems arising out of technical advances and customarily deals with cases involving multi-parties and cases which may occupy a great deal of time. See also section 1.3.1 of the TCC Guide, 2nd edition (see para. 2C–35 below).

How to start a TCC claim

2C–12   **3.1** TCC claims must be issued in the High Court or in a county court specified in this practice direction.

3.2 The claim form must be marked in the top right-hand corner 'Technology and Construction Court' below the words 'The High Court, Queen's Bench Division' or 'The _____ County Court'.

3.3 TCC claims brought in the High Court outside London may be issued in any District Registry, but it is preferable that wherever possible they should be issued in one of the following District Registries, in which a TCC judge will usually be available – Birmingham, Bristol, Cardiff, Chester, Exeter, Leeds, Liverpool, Newcastle, Nottingham and Salford.

3.4 The county courts in which a TCC claim may be issued are the following – Birmingham, Bristol, Cardiff, Central London, Chester, Exeter, Leeds, Liverpool, Newcastle, Nottingham and Salford.

Comment

    TCC claims may be dealt with in the High Court or County Court. Hitherto TCC **2C–13** business (formerly O.R. business) fell only within the jurisdiction of the High Court. A claim with a value under the County Court limit can be issued in any of the County Courts named in 3.4.

    A case of complexity or involving matters of public importance may be considered appropriate for transfer to the London Technology and Construction Court by way of example where a point on a contract is involved which may effect similar contracts commonly used in the construction industry. Otherwise such a case would proceed to trial in the appropriate County Court.

Applications before proceedings are issued

4.1 A party who intends to issue a TCC claim must make any ap- **2C–14** plication before the claim form is issued to a TCC judge.

4.2 The written evidence in support of such an application must state that the proposed claim is a TCC claim.

Transfer of proceedings

5.1 Where no TCC judge is available to deal with a claim which **2C–15** has been issued in a High Court District Registry or one of the county courts listed in paragraph 3.4 above, the claim may be transferred –

    (1)   if it has been issued in a District Registry, to another District Registry or to the High Court in London; or

    (2)   if it has been issued in a county court, to another county court where a TCC judge would be available.

5.2 Paragraph 5.1 is without prejudice to the court's general powers to transfer proceedings under Part 30.

    (Rule 30.5(3) provides that an application for the transfer of proceedings to or from a special list must be made to a judge dealing with claims in that list).

5.3 A party applying to a TCC judge to transfer a claim to the TCC specialist list must give notice of the application to the court in which the claim is proceeding, and a TCC judge will not make an order for transfer until he is satisfied that such notice has been given.

Assignment of claim to a TCC judge

6.1 When a TCC claim is issued or an order is made transferring a **2C–16** claim to the TCC specialist list, the court will assign the claim to a named TCC judge ('the assigned TCC judge') who will have the primary responsibility for the case management of that claim.

6.2 All documents relating to the claim must be marked in similar manner to the claim form with the words 'Technology and Construction Court' and the name of the assigned TCC judge.

Comment

2C–17   6.1 As to assignment see section 3.7 of the TCC Guide, 2nd edition (see para. 2C–51 below), and LCJ Statement (para. 2C–31).

Applications

2C–18   **7.1** An application should normally be made to the assigned TCC judge. If the assigned TCC judge is not available, or the court gives permission, the application may be made to another TCC judge

7.2 If an application is urgent and there is no TCC judge available to deal with it, the application may be made to any judge who, if the claim were not a TCC claim, would be authorised to deal with the application.

Comment

2C–19   In all vacations a TCC judge sits as a vacation judge on Wednesdays to deal with interlocutory matters of all kinds and at other times by arrangement with his clerk or the registry, to deal with applications for injunctions, charging applications and any other urgent matter.

Case management conference

2C–20   **8.1** The court will fix a case management conference within 14 days of the earliest of these events–

(1)   the filing of an acknowledgment of service;

(2)   the filing of a defence; or

(3)   the date of an order transferring the claim to a TCC.

8.2 When the court notifies the parties of the date and time of the case management conference, it will at the same time send each party a case management information sheet and a case management directions form.

(The case management information sheet and the case management directions form are in the form set out in Appendixes A and B to this practice direction).

8.3 Not less than two days before the case management conference, each party must file and serve on all other parties–

(1)   completed copies of the case management information sheet and case management directions form; and

(2)   an application notice for any order which that party intends to seek at the case management conference, other than directions referred to in the case management directions form.

8.4 The parties are encouraged to agree directions to propose to the court by reference to the case management directions form.

8.5 If any party fails to file or serve the case management information sheet and the case management directions form by the date specified, the court may–

(1)   impose such sanction as it sees fit; and

(2)   either proceed with or adjourn the case management conference.

8.6 The directions given at the case management conference will normally include the fixing of dates for—

(1)   any further case management conferences;

(2)   a pre-trial review;

(3)   the trial of any preliminary issues that it orders to be tried; and

(4)   the trial.

Comment

Note that 8.3 gives a minimum time for exchange and return of the case manage-   **2C–21** ment questionnaire and case management directions form. In substantial and complex cases it is desirable to exchange and serve at least four clear days before the hearing to assist the judge. An early exchange and return also gives the parties further opportunity to consider each other's proposals and agree matters before the hearing. 8.5 provides for sanctions and underlines the philosophy behind the rules and reflected in 4.3 (*supra*) there should be no slippage and the time and resource of the court should not be wasted.

Paragraph 8.6—The Agenda for the first case conference will be based upon the form at Appendix of the Practice Direction. Each case coming before the TCC varies as to its length, complexity and parties, and tailor made directions may be given or agreed to suit the case. For example, where a view is appropriate the timing of the view having regard to the changing state of the matter in dispute as when remedial work is being carried out. Directions may be given that a building or structure must not be altered before experts have had the proper opportunity to examine it fully; for the joint making of trial pits, bore holes, laboratory tests, or analyses; where a Scott schedule has been ordered, that the parties should select representative items for trial; arrangements for video displays, demonstrations and the like. It is at this stage that the court may consider whether an ADR direction may be given (see Pt 1.4(2)(E)) and whether it is necessary to extend time compliance requirements of the CPR to enable the parties to investigate ADR. Consideration may also be given at this stage as to whether an early neutral evaluation (ENE) would be appropriate by a judge of the court. In relation to resolution by trial, consideration will be given to the trial of an issue, or split trials of liability/damages.

Paragraph 8.6 contains provision that at the first case management conference, the court will usually fix the date for the trial of the case. This is so, but the direction will normally be in the following form:

Trial: Week beginning …	*For fees' purposes only this is not notice by the court of the trial date.*
Estimated length … days	(see Supreme Court Fees Order 1999, para. 2.2, Schedule 1, column 2).

See also the guidance given in section 5 of the TCC Guide, 2nd edition (see para. 2C–59 below). Paragraph 8.6(3) preliminary issues, see section 8 of the TCC Guide, 2nd edition (see para. 2C–83 below).

Pre-trial review

9.1 When the court fixes the date for a pre-trial review it will send   **2C–22** each party a pre-trial review questionnaire .

(The pre-trial review questionnaire is in the form set out in Appendix C to this practice direction).

9.2 Each party must file and serve on all other parties completed copies of the questionnaire not less than two days before the date fixed for the pre-trial review.

9.3 The parties are encouraged to agree directions to propose to the court .

9.4 If any party fails to return or exchange the questionnaire by the date specified the court may–

(1)   impose such sanction as it sees fit; and

(2)   either proceed with or adjourn the pre-trial review.

9.5 At the pre-trial review, the court will give such directions for the conduct of the trial as it sees fit.

Comment

2C–23   The parties will be reminded by a letter from the court of the date and time of the pre-trial review. That letter will contain the following text.

"For the purposes of the fees order notice is now given that the trial has been fixed for (date) accordingly a fee of £600 must be paid within 14 days of the date of this notice, *i.e.* by (date 14 days from the date of dispatch of the letter) by the claimant or claimants, if the action is proceeding on the counter claim alone by the defendant. Payment is to be made (preferably by cheque) at the Registry of this Court or to the Fees Room in the Main Building (*i.e.* at the Royal Courts of Justice). The PTR questionnaire (see below) must be presented when payment is made as the receipt of payment of the fee is stamped on it.

If the fee is not paid by the date specified rule 3.7(4) states that the claim (or counterclaim) will be struck out automatically and that the claimant (or the defendant, as the case may be) will be liable for the costs incurred by the other party(ies) unless the Court orders otherwise.

You are reminded that as well as the completed Pre-Trial Reviews Questionnaires all proposed directions (which should be agreed wherever possible) be lodged by all parties with me not later than two clear days before the date of the PTR. Copies of the Questionnaire and the PTR Direction Form are obtainable from the Registry. Any questions relating to the fee should be addressed to the Registry but all other questions about the PTR must be addressed to me. Signed Clerk to the Judge."

Paragraph 9.2—See note to 8.3 *supra.*

Paragraph 9.5—The court will take stock and ensure that there has been no unjustifiable slippage of the timetable. Where there has, directions will be given to ensure timely compliance. Since witness statements and experts may well have been exchanged this may be an appropriate time for parties to further consider ADR. In relation to conduct of the trial, further directions may be given to ensure that the proper issues are tried. The parties in the light of the pleadings, expert reports exchanged and witness statements served, may well have been required to provide a list of issues for trial to be considered at the PTR. If not already given, leave to call expert witnesses may be considered in the light of the exchange of expert reports and the identification of issues on which they are or are not agreed (see Pt 35.12(3)). Consideration will be given as to the necessity of supplemental witness/expert reports, and leave may be given. A trial timetable should be agreed by the parties and, failing such agreement, will be determined by the trial judge. Consideration will be given to such matters as the order of witnesses, *e.g.* the hearing of all witnesses' fact on both sides followed by the expert evidence, and to the organisation of trial bundles, *i.e.* indexing, time and service of index and proposed bundles, and the preparation of a core bundle(s) with cross references to the full trial bundles, where appropriate. Directions may be given at this as to whether the pleadings the claimant or defendant will open the trial and as to the service of written openings for the court/opposing party(ies) and written responses, if appropriate, and the provision of a chronology and cast list. A direction may be given as to the filing of disks (if obtainable) of the statements of case, witness statements, experts' reports, trial bundles and opening notes.

See also section 14 of the TCC Guide, 2nd edition (see para. 2C–115).

Listing

2C–24   **10** The provisions about listing questionnaires and listing in Part 29 and its practice direction do not apply to TCC claims.

Trial

2C–25   **11.1** Whenever possible the trial of a claim will be heard by the assigned TCC judge.

11.2 A TCC claim may be tried at any place where there is a TCC judge available to try the claim.

[THE NEXT PARAGRAPH IS 2C–27.]

Appendices

Appendix A

2C–27

Case management information sheet

`Click here to reset form`

To be completed by, or on behalf of,

who is [1ˢᵗ][2ⁿᵈ][3ʳᵈ][   ][Claimant][Defendant] [Part 20 claimant] in this claim

In the	County Court
High Court of Justice	
Queen's Bench Division	
Technology and Construction Court	

Claim No.	
Last date for filing with court office	
Assigned judge	

> Please read the notes on page five before completing this form.
>
> You should note the date by which it must be returned and the name of the court it should be returned to since this may be different from the court where the proceedings were issued.
>
> If you have settled this claim (or if you settle it on a future date) and do not need to have it heard or tried, you must let the court know immediately.

A   Settlement

Do you wish there to be a one month stay to attempt to settle the claim, either by informal discussion or by alternative dispute resolution?   ☐ Yes   ☐ No

B   Location of trial

Is there any reason why your claim needs to be heard at a particular court?   ☐ Yes   ☐ No

If Yes, say which court and why?

C   Pre-action protocols

The Construction and Engineering Disputes protocol applies to this claim.

Have you complied with it?   ☐ Yes   ☐ No

If No, please explain the reasons why on a separate sheet and attach it to this form.

D   Case management information

What amount of the claim is in dispute?   £

Is there a counterclaim to this claim?   ☐ Yes   ☐ No

If Yes, state value of counterclaim   £

TCC/CM1 Case management information sheet (03.02)   I

TCC

Applications

Have you made any application(s) in this claim? ☐ Yes ☐ No

If Yes, what for? [   ]   For hearing on [   ]
(e.g. summary judgment, add another party)

Witnesses

So far as you know at this stage, what witnesses of fact do you intend to call at the trial or final hearing including, if appropriate, yourself?

Witness name	Witness to which facts

Experts

Do you wish to use expert evidence at the trial or final hearing? ☐ Yes ☐ No

Have you already copied any experts' report(s) to the other party(ies)? ☐ None yet obtained ☐ Yes ☐ No

Do you consider the case suitable for a single joint expert in any field? ☐ Yes ☐ No

Please list any single joint experts you propose to use and any other experts you wish to rely on. Identify single joint experts with the initials 'SJ' after their name(s).

Expert's name	Field of expertise (eg. orthopaedic surgeon, surveyor, engineer)

Do you want your expert(s) to give evidence orally at the trial or final hearing? ☐ Yes ☐ No

If Yes, give the reasons why you think oral evidence is necessary:

[   ]

Disclosure

Are there any special considerations concerning disclosure of any documents that should be brought to the attention of the judge? ☐ Yes ☐ No

If Yes, please give details on a separate sheet and attach it to this form.

2

continue over ⮕

Transfer

If you think your case is suitable for a transfer to another court or track, say which:

> Court: Chancery Division/Queen's Bench Division/another TCC court/Commercial Court/ County Court
>
> Track: Small claims/Fast track

Please give brief reasons for your choice:

E   Trial or final hearing

How long do you estimate the trial or final hearing will take? | days | hours | minutes |

Are there any days when you, an expert or an essential witness will not be able to attend court for the trial or final hearing? ☐ Yes   ☐ No

If Yes, please give details

Name	Dates not available

F   Proposed directions *(Parties should agree directions wherever possible)*

See CPR Part 60 Practice Direction paras 8.4 and 8.6 and The Technology and Construction Court Guide

Have you attached a list of the directions you think appropriate for the management of the claim? ☐ Yes   ☐ No

If Yes, have they been agreed with the other party(ies)? ☐ Yes   ☐ No

G   Costs

*Do **not** complete this section if you have suggested your case is suitable for the small claims track **or** you have suggested one of the other tracks and you do not have a solicitor acting for you.*

What is your estimate of your costs incurred to date? £

What do you estimate your overall costs are likely to be? £

In substantial cases these questions should be answered in compliance with CPR Part 43

3

TCC

H Other information

Have you attached documents to this form? ☐ Yes ☐ No

Have you sent these documents to the other party(ies)? ☐ Yes ☐ No

If Yes, when did they receive them?

Do you intend to make any applications in the immediate future? ☐ Yes ☐ No

If Yes, what for?

Are video link facilities required? ☐ Yes ☐ No

In the space below, set out any other information you consider will help the judge to manage the claim, including any details about IT being used before or at trial

Signed _____   Date _____

[Counsel][Solicitor][for the][1st][2nd][3rd][   ]
[Claimant][Defendant][Part 20 claimant]

Please enter your firm's name, reference number and full postal address including (if appropriate) details of DX, fax or e-mail

	if applicable	
	fax no.	
	DX no.	
Tel. no. Postcode	e-mail	
Your reference no.		

4

Notes for completing a case management information sheet

- If you fail to return the form by the date given, the judge may give directions or make any order he thinks fit.
- Use a separate sheet if you need more space for your answers marking clearly which section the information refers to. You should write the claim number and the name of the assigned judge on it, and on any other documents you send with the form. Please ensure they are firmly attached to it.

A Settlement

If you think that you and the other party may be able to negotiate a settlement you should tick the 'Yes' box. The court may order a stay, whether or not all the other parties to the claim agree. You should still complete the rest of the form, even if you are requesting a stay. Where a stay is granted it will be for an initial period of one month. You may settle the claim either by informal discussion with the other party or by alternative dispute resolution (ADR). ADR covers a range of different processes which can help settle disputes. More information is available in the Legal Services Commission leaflet 'Alternatives to Court' free from the LSC leaflet line Phone: 0845 3000 343

B Location of trial

Whenever possible the trial of a claim will be heard by the assigned TCC judge. A TCC claim may be tried at any place where there is a TCC judge available to try the claim.

C Pre-action protocols

Before any claim is started, the court expects you to have exchanged information and documents relevant to the claim to assist in settling it, and to have complied with the construction and engineering disputes protocol

D Case management information

Applications

It is important for the court to know if you have already made any applications in the claim, what they are for and when they will be heard. The outcome of the applications may affect the case management directions the court gives.

Witnesses

Remember to include yourself as a witness of fact, if you will be giving evidence.

Experts

Oral or written expert evidence will only be allowed at the trial or final hearing with the court's permission. The judge will decide what permission it seems appropriate to give when the claim is allocated to track. Permission in small claims track cases will only be given exceptionally.

E Trial or final hearing

You should enter only those dates when you, your expert(s) or essential witness(es) will not be able to attend court because of holiday or other committments.

F Proposed directions

Attach the list of directions, if any, you believe will be appropriate to be given for the management of the claim. Agreed directions on fast and multi-track cases should be based on the forms of standard directions set out in the practice direction to CPR Part 28 and form PF52.

G Costs

Only complete this section if you are a solicitor and have suggested the claim is suitable for allocation to the fast or multi-track.

H Other Information

Answer the questions in this section. Decide if there is any other information you consider will help the judge to manage the claim. Give details in the space provided referring to any documents you have attached to support what you are saying.

5

Appendix B

Case Management Directions Form

Action no   HT-..........   2C–28

Delete or amend the following directions, as appropriate to the circumstances of the case.

1. Trial date .... For the purposes of payment of the trial fee, but for no other purposes, this date is provisional. This date will cease to be provisional and the trial fee will become payable on .... [usually be 2 months before the trial date].

2. Estimated length of trial ....

3. Directions, if appropriate, (a) for the trial of any preliminary issues or (b) for the trial to be divided into stages

....

4. This action is to be [consolidated] [managed and tried with] action no .... The lead action shall be .... All directions given in the lead action shall apply to both actions, unless otherwise stated.

5. Further statements of case shall be filed and served as follows:
- Defence and any counterclaim by 4 p.m. on ....
- Reply (if any) and defence to counterclaim (if any) by 4 p.m. on ....

6. Permission to make the following amendments ....

7. Disclosure of documents by 5 p.m. on .... [Standard disclosure dispensed with/ limited/ varied as follows ....]. Specific directions in respect of electronic disclosure ....

8. There shall be a Scott Schedule in respect of defects/ items of damage/ other ....
- The column headings shall be as follows ....
- Claimant/ defendant to serve Scott Schedule by 5 p.m. on ....
- Defendant/ claimant to respond to Scott Schedule by 5 p.m. on ....

9. Signed statements of witnesses of fact to be served by 5 p.m. on ....

[Supplementary statements of witnesses of fact to be served by 5 p.m. on ....]

10. The parties have permission to call the following expert witnesses in respect of the following issues:
- ....
- ....
- ....

11. In respect of any expert evidence permitted under paragraph 10:
- Directions for carrying out inspections/ taking samples/ conducting experiments/ performance of calculations shall be ....
- Experts in like fields to hold discussions in accordance with rule 35.12 by ....
- Experts' statements rule 35.12 (3) to be prepared and filed by 5 p.m. on ....
- Experts' reports to be served by 5 p.m. on ....

12. A single joint expert shall be appointed by the parties to report on the following issue(s) .... The following directions shall govern the appointment of the single joint expert:
- ....
- ....

13. The following documents shall be provided to the court electronically or in computer readable form, as well as in hard copy ....

14. A review case management conference shall be held on .... at ....a.m./p.m. Time allowed ....

15. The pre-trial review shall be held on .... at ....a.m./p.m. Time allowed....

16. The above dates and time limits may be extended by agreement between the parties. Nevertheless:
   - The dates and time limits specified in paragraphs .... may not be extended by more than .... days without the permission of the court.
   - The dates specified in paragraph 1 (trial) and paragraph 15 (pre-trial review) cannot be varied without the permission of the court.

16. Liberty to restore.

17. Costs in the case.

18. Claimant's solicitors to draw up this order by .... [Delete if order is to be drawn up by the court.]

Appendix C

2C–29

Pre-trial review questionnaire

Click here to clear text after printing

To be completed by, or on behalf of,

who is [1st][2nd][3rd][ ] [Claimant] [Defendant]
[Part 20 claimant] in this claim

In the	County Court
High Court of Justice	
Queen's Bench Division	
Technology and Construction Court	
Claim No.	
Last date for filing with court office	
Assigned judge	

- The judge will use the information which you and the other party(ies) provide to conduct a pre-trial review

- If you do not complete and return the questionnaire the judge may
    - make an order which leads to your statement of case (claim or defence) being struck out.
    - conduct the pre-trial review without it. You may be ordered to pay (immediately) the other parties' costs of attending.

A Directions complied with

1. Have you complied with all the previous directions given by the court? ☐ Yes   ☐ No

2. If no, please explain which directions are outstanding and why

Directions outstanding	Reasons directions outstanding

3. Are any further directions required to prepare the case for trial? ☐ Yes   ☐ No

(If no go to section B)

4. If yes, please explain directions required and give reasons

Directions required	Reasons required

TCC/PTR1 Pre-trial review questionnaire (03.02)

B Experts

1. Has the court already given permission for you to use written expert evidence? ☐ Yes ☐ No
(If no go to section C)

2. If yes, please give name and field of expertise.

Name of expert	Whether joint expert *(please tick, if appropriate)*	Field of expertise

3. Have the experts held discussions as directed? ☐ Yes ☐ No

4. Have they filed statements as directed following those discussions? ☐ Yes ☐ No

5. Have the expert(s') report(s) been served and filed as ordered? ☐ Yes ☐ No

6. Has the court already given permission for the expert(s) to give oral evidence at the trial? *(If yes go to Section C)* ☐ Yes ☐ No

7. If no, are you seeking that permission? ☐ Yes ☐ No
(If no go to section C)

8. If yes, give your reasons for seeking permission.

9. If yes, what are the names, addresses and fields of expertise of your experts?

Expert 1	Expert 2	Expert 3	Expert 4

10. Please give details of any dates within the trial period when your expert(s) will not be available.

Name of expert	Dates not available

C Other witnesses

(If you are not calling other witnesses go to section D)

1. How many other witnesses (including yourself) will be giving evidence on your behalf at the trial? *(do not include experts - see section B above)*

(Give number)

2. What are the names and addresses of your witnesses?

Witness 1	Witness 2	Witness 3	Witness 4

3. Please give details of any dates within the trial period when you or your witnesses will not be available?

Name of witness	Dates not available

4. Are any of the witness statements agreed? ☐ Yes ☐ No

(If no go to question C6)

5. If yes, give the name of the witness and the date of his or her statement

Name of witness	Date of statement

6. Do you or any of your witnesses need any special facilities? ☐ Yes ☐ No

(If no go to question C8)

7. If yes, what are they?

8. Will any of your witnesses be provided with an interpreter? ☐ Yes ☐ No

(If no go to section D)

9. If yes, say what type of interpreter e.g. language (stating which), deaf/blind etc.

D Legal representation

1. Who will be presenting your case at the hearing or trial? ☐ You ☐ Solicitor ☐ Counsel

2. Please give details of any dates within the trial period when the person presenting your case will not be available.

Name	Dates not available

E Other matters

1. How long do you estimate the whole trial will take, excluding judgment?

Minutes	Hours	Days

2. What is the estimated number of pages of evidence to be included in the trial bundle?

(please give number)

3. Please provide a case summary and proposals (agreed if possible) for directions to be given, by reference to the pre-trial review directions form.

Signed

Claimant/defendant or Counsel/Solicitor for the claimant/defendant

Dated

[THE NEXT PARAGRAPH IS 2C–31.]

TECHNOLOGY AND CONSTRUCTION COURT: STATEMENT BY THE LORD CHIEF JUSTICE OF ENGLAND & WALES

2C–31   **1.** This announcement is made on behalf of myself and the Lord Chancellor. It reflects the importance which both the Lord Chancellor and I attach to the work of the Technology and Construction Court ("TCC").

2. The TCC is a specialist court, which operates at eleven court centres across the country. It comprises one High Court judge (who devotes about half of his working time to the business of the TCC) and 41 senior circuit and circuit judges. Of these circuit judges eight are full time TCC judges and the remainder spend only part of their time hearing TCC cases. Of the eight full time TCC judges, five are based at St Dunstan's House in London ("the London TCC"), one in Birmingham, one in Manchester and one in Liverpool. There are also 23 recorders who, because of their experience of the relevant classes of work, are specifically authorised to hear TCC cases when required. Most of the full time TCC judges (and all of those at the London TCC) are senior circuit judges.

3. The construction sector accounts for about 10% of the UK's GDP. The IT sector also accounts for a significant and growing proportion of GDP. Disputes within these industries or between providers and end users are often of considerable complexity. The sums at issue are huge. Some of the disputes arise from construction projects overseas or involve international parties. These disputes are of comparable size and importance to general commercial litigation. TCC judges try some of the most arduous and complex cases which come before the civil courts.

4. The existing TCC judges have a high degree of expertise in the management and trial of complex construction and IT cases. I pay tribute to the excellent work, which those judges are doing and have done for many years. Nevertheless the lack of involvement of High Court judges in the work of the TCC has been a source of concern within the IT and construction industries and within the profession. Hitherto the TCC has only had the services of one High Court judge for approximately half of his working time. It is now desirable for High Court judges to play a larger role in the management and trial of IT and construction litigation.

5. Arrangements for the longer term future of the TCC are currently under consideration by the Lord Chancellor, the Lord Chief Justice and the Master of the Rolls. In the meantime, however, we have decided that interim arrangements must be put in place, in order to ensure that all TCC cases are tried by appropriate judges. The interim arrangements, which will come into effect today, are as follows:

(i) The High Court judge in charge of the TCC (currently Jackson J) will no longer be required to spend half of each term away from the TCC. Instead he will be principally based at the TCC and will only sit in other courts when there is no TCC work requiring the immediate involvement of a High Court judge.

(ii) The judge in charge of the TCC will (with the assistance

306

of the registry manager) consider every new case which is started in or transferred into the London TCC. He will classify each new case as "HCJ" or "SCJ". The most complex and heavy cases will be classified "HCJ". These will be managed and tried either by the judge in charge of the TCC or by another suitable High Court judge. The majority of cases, however, will be classified as "SCJ". These cases may be allocated to a named senior circuit judge by the judge in charge of the TCC; alternatively, they will be so allocated by operation of the rota.

(iii) It is neither practicable nor necessary for the judge in charge of the TCC to consider TCC cases which are commenced in, or transferred to, court centres outside London. Nevertheless, if any TCC case started outside London appears to require management and trial by a High Court judge, then the full time or principal TCC judge at that court centre should refer the case to the judge in charge of the TCC for a decision as to its future management and trial.

(iv) When proceedings are commenced in, or transferred to, the London TCC, any party to those proceedings may make brief representations by letter as to the appropriate classification.

6. Work is currently in progress on the preparation of a new edition of the TCC Guide. There has been widespread consultation with judges, court users and the profession about the contents of the Guide. The new edition of the Guide will set out the criteria which the judge in charge of the TCC will apply, when allocating cases to the appropriate level of judge. It will also provide that the judge in charge may change the classification of cases from "HCJ" to "SCJ", or vice versa, as appropriate.

7. I am confident that the TCC will continue, as it has done in the past, constantly seeking to improve the service which it provides to court users.

The Right Honourable The Lord Woolf
Lord Chief Justice of England and Wales
7th June 2005

Comment —The 2nd edition of the Technology and Construction Court Guide is set out below. As to allocation of cases in the London TCC, see Guide at paras 3.7.1 – 3.7.4 inclusive – see para. 2C–51.

Technology and Construction Court Guide

Second Edition

(with effect 3 October 2005)

2C–32

TCC

2C–33

SECTION 1.

INTRODUCTION

1.1 Purpose of Guide

1.1.1 This new edition of the Technology and Construction Court ("TCC") Guide is intended to provide straightforward, practical guidance to the conduct of litigation in the TCC. Whilst it is intended to be comprehensive, it naturally concentrates on the most important aspects of such litigation. It therefore cannot cover all the procedural points that may arise. It does, however, describe the main elements of the practice that is likely to be followed in most TCC cases.

1.1.2 The Guide reflects the flexible framework within which litigation in the TCC is habitually conducted. The requirements set out in the Guide are designed to ensure effective management of proceedings in the TCC. It must always be remembered that, if parties fail to comply with these requirements, the court may impose sanctions including orders for costs.

1.1.3 In respect of those procedural areas for which specific provision is not made in this Guide, the parties, together with their advisors, will be expected to act reasonably and in accordance with both the spirit of the Guide and the overriding objective at CPR Rule 1.1

1.1.4 It is not the function of the Guide to summarise the Civil Procedure Rules ("the CPR"), and it should not be regarded as a substitute for the CPR. The parties and their advisors are expected to familiarise themselves with the CPR and, in particular, to understand the importance of the "overriding objective" of the CPR. The TCC endeavours to ensure that all its cases are dealt with justly and with proper proportionality. This includes ensuring that the parties are on an equal footing; taking all practicable steps to save expenditure; dealing with the dispute in ways which are proportionate to the size of the claim and cross-claim and the importance of the case to the parties; and managing the case throughout in a way that takes proper account of its complexity and the different financial positions of the parties. The court will also endeavour to ensure expedition, and to allot to each case an appropriate share of the court's resources.

1.1.5 This new edition of the TCC Guide has been prepared in consultation with the judges of the TCC in London, Cardiff, Birmingham, Manchester and Leeds, and with the advice and support of TECBAR, TeCSA, the Society for Computers and Law and the TCC Users' Committees in London, Cardiff, Birmingham, Manchester, Liverpool and Leeds. The TCC Guide is published with the approval of the Head of Civil Justice and the deputy Head of Civil Justice.

1.2 The CPR

1.2.1 Proceedings in the TCC are governed by the CPR and the supplementary **2C–34** Practice Directions. CPR Part 60 and its associated Practice Direction deal specifically with the practice and procedure of the TCC.

1.2.2 Other parts of the CPR that frequently arise in TCC cases include Part 8 (Alternative Procedure for Claims); Parts 12 and 13 (Default Judgment and Setting Aside); Part 17 (Amendments); Part 20 (Counterclaims and Other Additional Claims); Part 24 (Summary Judgment); Part 25 (Interim Remedies and Security for Costs); Part 26 (Case Management); Part 32 (Evidence); Part 35 (Experts and Assessors) and Part 62 (Arbitration Claims).

1.3 The TCC

1.3.1 <u>What are TCC Claims?</u> CPR Rules 60.1 (2) and (3) provide that a TCC claim is **2C–35** a claim which (i) involves technically complex issues or questions (or for which trial by a TCC judge is desirable) and (ii) has been issued in or transferred into the TCC specialist list. Paragraph 2.1 of the TCC Practice Direction identifies the following as examples of the types of claim which it may be appropriate to bring as TCC claims—

    (a) building or other construction disputes, including claims for the enforcement of the decisions of adjudicators under the Housing Grants, Construction and Regeneration Act 1996;
    (b) engineering disputes;
    (c) claims by and against engineers, architects, surveyors, accountants and other specialised advisors relating to the services they provide;
    (d) claims by and against local authorities relating to their statutory duties concerning the development of land or the construction of buildings;
    (e) claims relating to the design, supply and installation of computers, computer software and related network systems;
    (f) claims relating to the quality of goods sold or hired, and work done, materials supplied or services rendered;
    (g) claims between landlord and tenant for breach of a repairing covenant;
    (h) claims between neighbours, owners and occupiers of land in trespass, nuisance, etc.
    (i) claims relating to the environment (for example, pollution cases);
    (j) claims arising out of fires;
    (k) claims involving taking of accounts where these are complicated; and
    (l) challenges to decisions of arbitrators in construction and engineering disputes including applications for permission to appeal and appeals.

It should be noted that this list is not exhaustive and other types of claim may well be appropriate for the TCC.

1.3.2 <u>The Court.</u> Both the High Court and the county courts deal with TCC business. Circuit judges and recorders only have jurisdiction to manage and try TCC cases if they have been nominated by the Lord Chancellor pursuant to section 68 (1) (a) of the Supreme Court Act 1981. It should be noted that those circuit judges who have been nominated pursuant to section 68(1) of the Supreme Court Act 1981 fall into

TCC

two categories: "full time" TCC judges and "part time" TCC judges. "Full time" TCC judges spend most of their time dealing with TCC business, although they will do other work when there is no TCC business requiring their immediate attention. "Part time" TCC judges are circuit judges who are only available to sit in the TCC for part of their time. They have substantial responsibilities outside the TCC.

In respect of a court centre where there is no full time TCC judge, the term "principal TCC judge" is used in this Guide to denote the circuit judge who has principal responsibility for TCC work.

The phrase "Technology and Construction Court" or "TCC" or "the court" is used in this Guide to denote any court which deals with TCC claims. All of the courts which deal with TCC claims form a composite group of courts. When those courts are dealing with TCC business, CPR Part 60, its accompanying Practice Direction and this Guide govern the procedures of those courts. The High Court judge in charge of the TCC ("the Judge in Charge"), although based principally in London, has overall responsibility for the judicial supervision of TCC business in those courts.

1.3.3 The TCC in London. The principal centre for TCC work is the High Court in London at St Dunstan's House, 133-137 Fetter Lane, London, EC4A 1HD. The Judge in Charge of the TCC sits principally at St Dunstan's House together with five full time TCC judges. Subject to paragraph 3.7.1 below, any communication or enquiry concerning a TCC case, which is proceeding at St Dunstan's House, should be directed to the clerk of the judge who is assigned to that case. The various contact details for the judges' clerks are set out in **Appendix D**.

The TCC judges who are based at St Dunstan's House will, when appropriate, sit at court centres outside London.

TCC county court cases in London are brought in (or transferred to) the Central London Civil Justice Centre, 13-14 Park Crescent, London W1N 4HT.

1.3.4 District Registries. TCC claims can be brought in the High Court outside London in any District Registry, although the Practice Direction states that it is preferable that, wherever possible, such claims should be issued in one of the following District Registries: Birmingham, Bristol, Cardiff, Chester, Exeter, Leeds, Liverpool, Newcastle, Nottingham and Salford (Manchester). There are full-time TCC Judges in Birmingham, Liverpool and Salford (Manchester). Contact details are again set out in **Appendix D**. There are part time TCC judges and/or recorders nominated to deal with TCC business available at most court centres throughout England and Wales.

In a number of regions a "TCC liaison district judge" has been appointed. It is the function of the TCC liaison district judge:

(a) To keep other district judges in that region well informed about the role and remit of the TCC (in order that appropriate cases may be transferred to the TCC at an early, rather than late, stage).

(b) To deal with any queries from colleagues concerning the TCC or cases which might merit transfer to the TCC.

(c) To deal with any subsidiary matter which a TCC judge directs should be determined by a district judge pursuant to rule 60.1(5)(b)(ii).

(d) To deal with urgent applications in TCC cases pursuant to paragraph 7.2 of the Practice Direction (i.e. no TCC judge is available and the matter is of a kind that falls within the district judge's jurisdiction).

1.3.5 County Courts outside London. TCC claims may also be brought in those county courts which are specified in the Part 60 **Practice Direction**. The specified county courts are: Birmingham, Bristol, Cardiff, Chester, Exeter, Leeds, Liverpool, Newcastle, Nottingham and Salford (Manchester). Contact details are again set out in **Appendix D**.

Where TCC proceedings are brought in a county court, statements of case and applications should be headed:

"In the ... County Court
Technology and Construction Court"

This heading is important because in TCC cases (subject to the limited exceptions mentioned in paragraph 1.3.4 above) district judges do not have jurisdiction to hear applications or make orders.

1.3.6 The division between High Court and county court TCC cases. As a general rule TCC claims for more than £50,000 are brought in the High Court, whilst claims for lower sums are brought in the county court. However, this is not a rigid dividing line. The monetary threshold for High Court TCC claims tends to be higher in London than in the regions. Regard must also be had to the complexity of the case and all other circumstances. Arbitration claims and claims to enforce or challenge adjudicators' awards are generally (but not invariably) brought in the High Court. The scale of fees differs in the High Court and the county court. This is a factor which should be borne in mind in borderline cases.

1.4 The TCC Users' Committees

1.4.1 The continuing ability of the TCC to meet the changing needs of all those involved in TCC litigation depends in large part upon a close working relationship between the TCC and its users. **2C–36**

1.4.2 London. The Judge in Charge chairs two meetings a year of the London TCC Users' Committee. The judge's clerk acts as secretary to the Committee and takes the minutes of meetings. That Committee is made up of representatives of the London TCC judges, the barristers and solicitors who regularly use the Court, the professional bodies, such as architects, engineers and arbitrators, whose members are affected by the decisions of the Court, and representatives of both employers and contractors' groups.

1.4.3 Outside London. There are similar meetings of TCC Users' Committees in Birmingham, Salford (Manchester), Liverpool, Cardiff and Leeds. Each Users' Committee is chaired by the full time TCC judge or the principal TCC judge in that location.

1.4.4 The TCC regards these channels of communication as extremely important and all those who are concerned with the work of the Court are encouraged to make full use of these meetings. Any suggestions or other correspondence raising matters for consideration by the Users' Committee should, in the first instance, be addressed to the clerk to the Judge in Charge at St. Dunstan's House or to the clerk to the appropriate TCC judge outside London.

1.5 Specialist Associations

1.5.1 There are a number of associations of legal representatives which are represented on the Users' Committees and which also liaise closely with the Court. These contacts ensure that the Court remains responsive to the opinions and requirements of the professional users of the Court. **2C–37**

1.5.2 The relevant professional organisations are the TCC Bar Association ("TECBAR") and the TCC Solicitors Association ("TeCSA"). Details of the relevant contacts at these organisations are set out on their respective websites, namely www.tecbar.org and www.tecsa.org.

SECTION 2.

PRE-ACTION PROTOCOL

2.1 Introduction

2.1.1 There is a Pre-Action Protocol for Construction and Engineering Disputes. Where the dispute involves a claim against architects, engineers or quantity **2C–38**

TCC

surveyors, this Protocol prevails over the Professional Negligence Pre-Action Protocol: see paragraph 1.1 of the Protocol for Construction and Engineering Disputes and paragraph A.1 of the Professional Negligence Pre-Action Protocol. The current version of the Construction and Engineering Pre-Action Protocol ("the Protocol") is set out in volume 1 of the White Book at section C.

2.1.2 The purpose of the Protocol is to encourage the frank and early exchange of information about the prospective claim and any defence to it; to enable parties to avoid litigation by agreeing a settlement of the claim before the commencement of proceedings; and to support the efficient management of proceedings where litigation cannot be avoided.

2.1.3 _Proportionality._ The overriding objective (CPR rule 1.1) applies to the pre-action period. The Protocol must not be used as a tactical device to secure advantage for one party or to generate unnecessary costs. In small TCC claims (such as those likely to proceed in the county court), the letter of claim and the response should be simple and the costs of both sides should be kept to a modest level. In all cases the costs incurred at the Protocol stage should be proportionate to the complexity of the case and the amount of money which is at stake. The Protocol does not impose a requirement on the parties to marshal and disclose all the supporting details and evidence that may ultimately be required if the case proceeds to litigation.

2.2 To Which Claims Does The Protocol Apply?

2C–39 2.2.1 The court will expect all parties to have complied in substance with the provisions of the Protocol in all construction and engineering disputes. The only exceptions to this are identified in paragraph 2.3 below.

2.2.2 The court regards the Protocol as setting out normal and reasonable pre-action conduct. Accordingly, whilst the Protocol is not mandatory for a number of the claims noted by way of example in paragraph 1.3.1 above, such as computer cases or dilapidations claims, the court would, in the absence of a specific reason to the contrary, expect the Protocol generally to be followed in such cases prior to the commencement of proceedings in the TCC.

2.3 What Are The Exceptions?

2C–40 2.3.1 A claimant does not have to comply with the Protocol if his claim:
    (a) is to enforce the decision of an adjudicator;
    (b) includes a claim for interim injunctive relief;
    (c) will be the subject of a claim for summary judgment pursuant to Part 24 of the CPR; or
    (d) relates to the same or substantially the same issues as have been the subject of a recent adjudication or some other formal alternative dispute resolution procedure.

2.3.2 In addition, a claimant need not comply with any part of the Protocol if, by so doing, his claim may become time-barred under the Limitation Act 1980. In those circumstances, a claimant should commence proceedings without complying with the Protocol and must, at the same time, apply for specific directions as to the timetable and form of procedure to be adopted. The court may order a stay of those proceedings pending completion of the steps set out in the Protocol.

2.4 What Are The Essential Ingredients Of The Protocol?

2C–41 2.4.1 _The Letter of Claim._ The letter of claim must comply with Section 3 of the Protocol. Amongst other things, it must contain a clear summary of the facts on which each claim is based; the basis on which each claim is made; and details of the relief claimed, including a breakdown showing how any damages have been quantified. The claimant must also provide the names of experts already instructed and on whom he intends to rely.

2.4.2 _The Defendant's Response._ The defendant has 14 days to acknowledge the letter of claim and 28 days (from receipt of the letter of claim) either to take any jurisdiction objection or to respond in substance to the letter of claim. Paragraph 4.3.1 of the Protocol enables the parties to agree an extension of the 28 day period up to a maximum of 4 months. In any case of substance it is quite usual for an extension of time to be agreed for the defendant's response. The letter of response must comply with section 4 of the Protocol. Amongst other things, it must state which claims are accepted, which claims are rejected and on what basis. It must set out any counterclaim to be advanced by the defendant. The defendant should also provide the names of experts who have been instructed and on whom he intends to rely. If the defendant fails either to acknowledge or to respond to the letter of claim in time, the claimant is entitled to commence proceedings.

2.4.3 Pre-action Meeting. The Construction and Engineering Protocol is the only Protocol under the CPR that generally requires the parties to meet, without prejudice, at least once, in order to identify the main issues and the root causes of their disagreement on those issues. The purpose of the meeting is to see whether, and if so how, those issues might be resolved without recourse to litigation or, if litigation is unavoidable, what steps should be taken to ensure that it is conducted in accordance with the overriding objective. At or as a result of the meeting, the parties should consider whether some form of alternative dispute resolution ("ADR") would be more suitable than litigation and if so, they should endeavour to agree which form of ADR to adopt. Although the meeting is "without prejudice", any party who attended the meeting is at liberty to disclose to the Court at a later stage that the meeting took place; who attended and who refused to attend, together with the grounds for their refusal; and any agreements concluded between the parties.

2.5 What Happens To The Material Generated By The Protocol?

2.5.1 The letter of claim, the defendant's response, and the information relating to attendance (or otherwise) at the meeting are not confidential or 'without prejudice' and can therefore be referred to by the parties in any subsequent litigation. The detail of any discussion at the meeting(s) and/or any note of the meeting cannot be referred to the court unless all parties agree.   **2C–42**

2.5.2 Normally the parties should include in the bundle for the first case management conference: (a) the letter of claim, (b) the response, and (c) any agreed note of the pre-action meeting: see Section 5 below. The documents attached to or enclosed with the letter and the response should not be included in the bundle.

2.6 What If One Party Has Not Complied With The Protocol?

2.6.1 There can often be a complaint that one or other party has not complied with the Protocol. The court will consider any such complaints once proceedings have been commenced. If the court finds that the claimant has not complied with one part of the Protocol, then the court may stay the proceedings until the steps set out in the Protocol have been taken.   **2C–43**

2.6.2 Paragraph 2.3 of the Practice Direction in respect of Protocols (section C of volume 1 of the White Book) makes plain that the court may make adverse costs orders against a party who has failed to comply with the Protocol. The court will exercise any sanctions available with the object of placing the innocent party in no worse a position than he would have been if the Protocol had been complied with.

2.6.3 The court is unlikely to be concerned with minor infringements of the Protocol or to engage in lengthy debates as to the precise quality of the information provided by one party to the other during the Protocol stages. The court will principally be concerned to ensure that, as a result of the Protocol stage, each party to any subsequent litigation has a clear understanding of the nature of the case that it has to meet at the commencement of those proceedings.

2.7 Costs of compliance with the Protocol

2.7.1 If compliance with the Protocol results in settlement, the costs incurred will not be recoverable from the paying party, unless this is specifically agreed.   **2C–44**

TCC

2.7.2 If compliance with the Protocol does not result in settlement, then the costs of the exercise cannot be recovered as costs, unless:

- those costs fall within the principles stated by Sir Robert Megarry V-C in *Re Gibson's Settlement Trusts* [1981] Ch 179; or
- the steps taken in compliance with the Protocol can properly be attributable to the conduct of the action.

SECTION 3.

COMMENCEMENT AND TRANSFER

3.1 Claim Forms

2C–45 3.1.1 All proceedings must be started using a claim form under CPR Part 7 or CPR Part 8. All claims allocated to the TCC are assigned to the Multi-Track: see CPR Rule 60.6(1).

3.2 Part 7 Claims

2C–46 3.2.1 The Part 7 claim form must be marked "Technology and Construction Court" in the appropriate place on the form.

3.2.2. Particulars of Claim may be served with the claim form, but this is not a mandatory requirement. If the Particulars of Claim are not contained in or served with the claim form, they must be served within **14 days** after service of the claim form.

3.2.3 A claim form must be verified by a statement of truth, and this includes any amendment to a claim form, unless the court otherwise orders.

3.3 Part 8 Claims

2C–47 3.3.1 The Part 8 claim form must be marked "Technology and Construction Court" in the appropriate place on the form.

3.3.2 A Part 8 claim form will normally be used where there is no substantial dispute of fact, such as the situation where the dispute turns on the construction of the contract or the interpretation of statute. For example, claims challenging the jurisdiction of an adjudicator or the validity of his decision are sometimes brought under Part 8. In those cases the relevant primary facts are often not in dispute. Part 8 claims will generally be disposed of on written evidence and oral submissions.

3.3.3 It is important that, where a claimant uses the Part 8 procedure, his claim form states that Part 8 applies and that the claimant wishes the claim to proceed under Part 8.

3.3.4 A statement of truth is again required on a Part 8 claim form.

3.4 Service

2C–48 3.4.1 Claim forms issued in the TCC at St Dunstan's House in London are to be served by the claimant, not by the Registry. In some other court centres claim forms are served by the court, unless the claimant specifically requests otherwise.

3.4.2 The different methods of service are set out in CPR Part 6 and the accompanying Practice Direction.

3.4.3 Applications for an extension of time in which to serve a claim form are governed by CPR Rule 7.6. The evidence required on an application for an extension of time is set out in paragraph 8.2 of Practice Direction A supplementing CPR Part 7.

3.4.4 When the claimant has served the claim form, he must file a certificate of service: Rule 6.14(2). This is necessary if, for instance, the claimant wishes to obtain judgment in default (CPR Part 12).

3.4.5 Applications for permission to serve a claim form out of the jurisdiction are subject to Rules 6.19–6.31 inclusive.

3.5 Acknowledgement of Service

3.5.1 A defendant must file an acknowledgment of service in response to both Part 7 **2C–49** and Part 8 claims. Save in the special circumstances that arise when the claim form has been served out of the jurisdiction, the period for filing an acknowledgment of service is **14 days** after service of the claim form.

3.6 Transfer

3.6.1 Proceedings may be transferred from any Division of the High Court or from **2C–50** any specialist list to the TCC pursuant to CPR rule 30.5. The order made by the transferring court should be expressed as being subject to the approval of a TCC judge. The decision whether to accept such a transfer must be made by a TCC judge: see rule 30.5(3). Many of these applications are uncontested, and may conveniently be dealt with on paper. Transfers from the TCC to other Divisions of the High Court or other specialist lists are also governed by CPR rule 30.5. In London there are quite often transfers between the Commercial Court and the TCC, in order to ensure that cases are dealt with by the most appropriate judge. Outside London there are quite often transfers between the TCC and the mercantile courts.

3.6.2 A TCC claim may be transferred from the High Court to one of the county courts noted above, and from any county court to the High Court, if the criteria stated in CPR Rule 30.3 are satisfied. In ordinary circumstances, proceedings will be transferred from the TCC in the High Court to the TCC in an appropriate county court if the amount of the claim does not exceed £50,000.

3.6.3 Where no TCC judge is available to deal with a TCC claim which has been issued in a district registry or one of the county courts noted above, the claim may be transferred to another district registry or county court or to the High Court TCC in London (depending upon which court is appropriate).

3.7 Assignment

3.7.1 Where a claim has been issued at or transferred to the TCC at St Dunstan's **2C–51** House in London, the Judge in Charge of the TCC ("the Judge in Charge") shall with the assistance of court staff classify the case either "HCJ" or "SCJ".
- (i) If the case is classified "HCJ", it shall be managed and tried either by the Judge in Charge or by another High Court judge, who will be identified after consultation between the Judge in Charge and the Vice-President of the Queen's Bench Division. The clerical administration of "HCJ" cases will be carried out by the Case Administration Unit ("CAU") of the TCC at St Dunstan's House. The CAU will also deal with the listing of all applications and trials in such cases.
- (ii) If the case is classified "SCJ", it shall be managed and tried by one of the senior circuit judges, who is a full time TCC judge in London. Cases in the latter category will either (a) be assigned by the Judge in Charge to a specific senior circuit judge or (b) be assigned to a senior circuit judge by operation of the rota. The assigned judge will have primary responsibility for the management of that case.
- (iii) Although continuity of judge is regarded as important, it will sometimes be necessary for there to be a change of assigned judge. If no judge is available during the period fixed for trial, then the case may be tried by one of the deputy judges or recorders who has been nominated by the Lord Chancellor under section 68(1)(a) of the Supreme Court Act 1981.

3.7.2 When classifying a case "HCJ" or "SCJ", the Judge in Charge will take into account the following matters, as well as all the circumstances of the case:
1. The size and complexity of the case.
2. The nature and importance of any points of law arising.
3. The amount of money which is at stake.

TCC

4. Whether the case is one of public importance.
5. Whether the case has an international element or involves overseas parties.
6. The limited number of High Court judges and the needs of other court users, both civil and criminal.

Most TCC cases in London will be classified "SCJ". The Judge in Charge may change the classification of any case from "HCJ" to "SCJ" or from "SCJ" to "HCJ", if it becomes appropriate to do so. There will be a band of cases near the borderline between "HCJ" and "SCJ", where the classification will be liable to change depending upon the settlement rate of other cases and the availability of judges.

3.7.3 When proceedings are commenced in, or transferred to, the TCC at St Dunstan's House in London, any party to those proceedings may write to the court setting out matters relevant to classification. Any such letter must be clear and concise. It will seldom need to exceed one page and must never exceed two pages.

3.7.4 When a case has been assigned to a named senior circuit judge in the TCC at St Dunstan's House, all communications to the court about the case (save for communications in respect of fees) shall be made to that judge's clerk. When a TCC case has been assigned to a named High Court judge, all such communications shall be made to the CAU or to the judge's clerk as appropriate. All communications in respect of fees, however, should be sent to the Registry. All statements of case and applications should be marked with the name of the assigned judge.

3.7.5 There are full time TCC judges at Birmingham, Liverpool and Salford (Manchester). There are principal TCC judges at other court centres outside London. TCC cases at these court centres are assigned to judges either (a) by direction of the full time or principal TCC judge or (b) by operation of a rota. It will not generally be appropriate for the Judge in Charge (who is based in London) to consider TCC cases which are commenced in, or transferred to, court centres outside London. Nevertheless, if any TCC case brought in a court centre outside London appears to require management and trial by a High Court judge, then the full time or principal TCC judge at that court centre should refer the case to the Judge in Charge for a decision as to its future management and trial.

3.7.6 When a TCC case has been assigned to a named circuit judge at a court centre other than St Dunstan's House, all communications to the court about the case (save for communications in respect of fees) shall be made to that judge's clerk. All communications in respect of fees should be sent to the relevant registry. All statements of case and applications should be marked with the name of the assigned judge.

SECTION 4.

ACCESS TO THE COURT

4.1 General Approach

2C–52   4.1.1 There may be a number of stages during the case management phase when the parties will make applications to the court for particular orders: see Section 6 below. There will also be the need for the court to give or vary directions, so as to enable the case to progress to trial.

4.1.2 The court is acutely aware of the costs that may be incurred when both parties prepare for an oral hearing in respect of such interlocutory matters and is always prepared to consider alternative, and less expensive, ways in which the parties may seek the court's assistance.

4.1.3 There are certain stages in the case management phase when it will generally be better for the parties to appear before the assigned judge. Those are identified at Section 4.2 below. But there are other stages, and/or particular applications which a party may wish to make, which could conveniently be dealt with by way of a telephone hearing (Section 4.3 below) or by way of a paper application (Section 4.4 below).

4.2 Hearings in Court

4.2.1 <u>First Case Management Conference</u>. The court will normally require the parties to attend an oral hearing for the purposes of the first Case Management Conference. This is because there may be matters which the judge would wish to raise with the parties arising out of the answers to the case management information sheets and the parties' proposed directions: see section 5.4 below. Even in circumstances where the directions and the case management timetable may be capable of being agreed by the parties and the court, the assigned judge may still wish to consider a range of case management matters face-to-face with the parties, including the possibility of ADR. See paragraphs 7.2.3, 7.3.2, 8.1.3, 11.1, 13.3, 13.4 and 16.3.2 below. **2C–53**

4.2.2 Whilst the previous paragraph sets out the ideal position, it is recognised that in low value cases the benefits of personal attendance might be outweighed by the costs involved. This is particularly so at court centres outside London, where the parties may have to travel substantial distances to court. Ultimately, the question whether personal attendance should be dispensed with at any particular case management conference must be decided by the judge, after considering any representations made and the circumstances of that particular case.

4.2.3 <u>Pre-trial Review</u>. It will normally be helpful for the parties to attend before the judge on a Pre-trial Review ("PTR"). It is always preferable for Counsel or other advocates who will be appearing at the trial to attend the PTR. Again, even if the parties can agree beforehand any outstanding directions and the detailed requirements for the management of the trial, it is still of assistance for the judge to raise matters of detailed trial management with the parties at an oral hearing. In appropriate cases, e.g. where the amount in issue is disproportionate to the costs of a full trial, the judge may wish to consider with the parties whether there are other ways in which the dispute might be resolved.

4.2.4 Whether or not other interlocutory applications require to be determined at an oral hearing will depend on the nature and effect of the application being made. Disputed applications for interim payments, summary judgment and security for costs will almost always require an oral hearing. Likewise, the resolution of a contested application to enforce an adjudicator's decision will normally be heard orally. At the other end of the scale, applications for extensions of time for the service of pleadings or to comply with other orders of the court can almost always be dealt with by way of a telephone hearing or in writing.

4.3 Telephone Hearings

4.3.1 Depending on the nature of the application and the extent of any dispute between the parties, the Court is content to deal with many case management matters and other interlocutory applications by way of a telephone conference. **2C–54**

4.3.2 Whilst it is not possible to lay down mandatory rules as to what applications should be dealt with in this way (rather than by way of an oral hearing in court), it may be helpful to identify certain situations which commonly arise and which can conveniently be dealt with by way of a telephone conference.

   (a) If the location of the court is inconvenient for one or more of the parties, or the value of the claim is low, then the CMC and the PTR could, in the alternative to the procedure set out in Section 4.2 above, take place by way of a telephone conference. The judge's permission for such a procedure would have to be sought in advance.

   (b) If the parties are broadly agreed on the orders to be made by the court, but they are in dispute in respect of one or two particular matters, then a telephone hearing is a convenient way in which those outstanding matters can be dealt with by the parties and the assigned judge.

   (c) Similarly, specific arguments about costs, once a substantive application has been disposed of, or arguments consequential on a particular judgment or or-

TCC

der having been handed down, may also conveniently be dealt with by way of telephone hearing.

(d) Other applications which, depending on their size and importance, may conveniently be dealt with by way of a telephone hearing include limited applications in respect of disclosure and specific applications as to the scope and content of factual or expert evidence exchanged by the parties.

4.3.3 Telephone hearings are not generally suitable for matters which are likely to last for more than an hour, although the judge may be prepared, in an appropriate case, to list a longer application for a telephone hearing.

4.3.4 _Practical matters._ Telephone hearings can be listed at any time between 8.30 a.m. and 5.30 p.m., subject to the convenience of the parties and the availability of the judge. Any party, who wishes to have an application dealt with by telephone, should make such request by letter or e-mail to the judge's clerk, sending copies to all other parties. Except in cases of urgency, the judge will allow a period of three days for the other parties to comment upon that request before deciding whether to deal with the application by telephone.

4.3.5 If permission is given for a telephone hearing, the court will normally indicate which party is to make all the necessary arrangements. In most cases, it will be the applicant. The procedure to be followed in setting up and holding a telephone hearing is that set out in section 6 of the Practice Direction supplementing CPR Part 23. The party making arrangements for the telephone hearing must ensure that all parties and the judge have a bundle for that hearing with identical pagination.

It is vital that the judge has all the necessary papers, in good time before the telephone conference, in order that it can be conducted efficiently and effectively.

4.4 Paper Applications

2C-55 4.4.1 CPR rule 23.8 and section 11 of the accompanying Practice Direction enable certain applications to be dealt with in writing. Parties in a TCC case are encouraged to deal with applications in writing, whenever practicable. Applications for both abridgments of time and extensions of time can generally be dealt with in writing, as well as all other variations to existing directions which are wholly or largely agreed. Disputes over particular aspects of disclosure and evidence may also be capable of being resolved in this way.

4.4.2 If a party wishes to make an application to the court, it should ask itself the question: "Can this application be conveniently dealt with in writing?" If it can, then the party should issue the application and make its (short) written submissions both in support of its application and why it should be dealt with on paper. The application, any supporting evidence and the written submissions should be provided to all parties, as well as the court. These must include a draft of the precise order sought.

4.4.3 The party against whom the application is made, and any other interested party, should respond within **3 days** dealing both with the substantive application and the request for it to be dealt with in writing.

4.4.4 The court can then decide whether or not to deal with the application in writing. If the parties are agreed that the court should deal with it in writing, it will be rare for the court to take a different view. If the parties disagree as to whether or not the application should be dealt with in writing, the court can decide that issue and, if it decides to deal with it in writing can go on to resolve the substantive point on the basis of the parties' written submissions.

4.4.5 Further guidance in respect of paper applications is set out in Section 6.7 below.

4.4.6 It is important for the parties to ensure that all documents provided to the court are also provided to all the other parties, so as to ensure that both the court and the parties are working on the basis of the same documentation. The pagination of any bundle which is provided to the court and the parties must be identical.

4.5 E-mail Communications

4.5.1 The general rules relating to communication and filing of documents by e-mail **2C–56** are set out in CPR Part 5, Practice Direction B.

4.5.2 The judges' clerks all have e-mail addresses identified in **Appendix D**. They welcome communication from the parties electronically. By agreement with the judge's clerk, it may also be possible to provide documents to the Court in this way. However, it should be noted that HM Court Service has imposed a blanket restriction of 2MB on the length of any e-mail, including its attachments. This equates to approximately 40 pages of normal typescript.

4.5.3 Depending on the particular circumstances of an individual trial, the assigned judge may ask for an e-mail contact address for each of the parties and may send e-mail communications to that address. In addition, the judge may provide a direct contact email address so that the parties can communicate directly with him out of court hours. In such circumstances, the judge and the parties should agree the times at which the respective e-mail addresses can be used.

4.5.4 Every e-mail communication to and from the judge must be simultaneously copied to all the other parties.

4.5.5 The procedure for e-mail communication with the court and for filing documents by email is described in the "E-mail Court User Guidance". This is available on a website maintained by HM Court Service at: www.hmcourtsservice.gov.uk/infoabout/email__guidance/index.htm.

4.6 Video Conferencing

4.6.1 In appropriate cases, particularly where there are important matters in dispute **2C–57** and the parties' representatives are a long distance from one another and/or the court, the hearing may be conducted by way of a Video Conference ("VC"). Prior arrangements will be necessary for any such hearing.

4.6.2 In London, a VC can be arranged through the VC suite at the Royal Courts of Justice. However, this facility is popular and will need to be booked well in advance of the hearing. Alternatively, there are a number of other VC suites in the Strand/Fleet Street area which would be suitable. Details of these facilities are available from the judges' clerks.

4.6.3 Outside London, a VC can be arranged at the following TCC courts with the requisite facilities: Birmingham, Bristol, Cardiff, Central London, Chester, Exeter, Leeds, Liverpool, Newcastle-upon-Tyne, Nottingham and Salford (Manchester).

4.7 Contacting the court out of hours

4.7.1 Occasionally it is necessary to contact a TCC judge out of hours. For example, it **2C–58** may be necessary to apply for an injunction to prevent the commencement of building works which will damage adjoining property; or for an order to preserve evidence. A case may have settled and it may be necessary to inform the judge, before he/she spends an evening or a weekend reading the papers.

4.7.2 <u>At St Dunstan's House.</u> RCJ Security has been provided with the telephone numbers and other contact information of all the TCC judges based at St Dunstan's House and of the court manager. If contact is required with a judge out of hours, the initial approach should be to RCJ Security on 0207-947-6000. Security will then contact the judge and/or the court manager and pass on the message or other information. If direct contact with the judge or court manager is required, RCJ Security must be provided with an appropriate contact number. This number will then be passed to the judge and/or the court manager, who will decide whether it is appropriate for him or her to speak directly to the contacting party.

4.7.3 <u>At other court centres.</u> At the Central London Civil Justice Centre and at all court centres outside London there is a court officer who deals with out of hours applications.

TCC

Section 5.

Case Management and the First CMC

5.1 General

2C–59 5.1.1 The general approach of the TCC to case management is to give directions at the outset and then throughout the proceedings to serve the overriding objective of dealing with cases justly. The judge to whom the case has been assigned has wide case management powers, which will be exercised to ensure that:

- the real issues are identified early on and remain the focus of the ongoing proceedings;
- a realistic timetable is ordered which will allow for the fair and prompt resolution of the action;
- costs are properly controlled and reflect the value of the issues to the parties and their respective financial positions.

5.1.2 In order to assist the judge in the exercise of his case management functions, the parties will be expected to co-operate with one another at all times. See CPR rule 1.3. Costs sanctions may be applied, if the judge concludes that one party is not reasonably co-operating with the other parties.

5.1.3 A hearing at which the judge gives general procedural directions is a case management conference ("CMC"). CMCs are relatively informal and business-like occasions. Counsel are not robed. Representatives sit when addressing the judge.

5.1.4 The following procedures apply in order to facilitate effective case management:

- Upon commencement of a case in the TCC, it is allocated automatically to the multitrack. The provisions of CPR Part 29 apply to all TCC cases.
- The TCC encourages a structured exchange of proposals and submissions for CMCs in advance of the hearing, so as to enable the parties to respond on an informed basis to proposals made.
- The judges of the TCC operate pro-active case management. In order to avoid the parties being taken by surprise by any judicial initiative, the judge will consider giving prior notification of specific or unusual case management proposals to be raised at a case management conference.

5.1.5 The TCC's aim is to ensure that the trial of each case takes place before the judge who has managed the case since the first CMC. Whilst continuity of judge is not always possible, because of the need to double- or triple-book judges, or because cases can sometimes overrun their estimated length through no fault of the parties, this remains an aspiration of case management within the TCC.

5.2 The Fixing of the First CMC

2C–60 5.2.1 Where a claim has been started in the TCC, or where it has been transferred into the TCC, paragraph 8.1 of the Part 60 Practice Direction requires the court to fix the first CMC within **14 days** of the earliest of

- the filing by the defendant of an acknowledgement of service or
- the filing by the defendant of the defence or
- the date of the order transferring the case to the TCC.

5.2.2 This means that the first CMC takes place relatively early, sometimes before the defendant has filed a defence. However, if, as will usually be the case, the parties have complied with the protocol (Section 2 above) they will have a good idea of each other's respective positions, and an effective CMC can take place. If, on the other hand, there has been a failure to comply with the protocol, or there are other reasons why the issues are not clearly defined at the outset, then it may be important for the judge to be involved at an early stage.

5.2.3 Despite the foregoing considerations, it is sometimes apparent to the parties that it will be more cost effective to postpone the first CMC until after service of the defence or the defences. If any of the parties wishes to delay the first CMC until then, they can write to the judge's clerk explaining why a delayed CMC is appropriate. If such a request is agreed by the other party or parties, it is likely that the judge will grant the request.

5.3 The Case Management Information Sheet and Other Documents

5.3.1 All parties are expected to complete a detailed response to the case **2C–61** management information sheet sent out by the Registry when the case is commenced/transferred. A copy of a blank case management information sheet is attached as **Appendix A**. It is important that all parts of the form are completed, particularly those sections (e.g. concerned with estimated costs) that enable the judge to give directions in accordance with the overriding objective.

5.3.2 The Registry will also send out a blank standard directions form to each party. A copy is attached at **Appendix B**. This sets out the usual directions made on the first CMC. The parties should fill them in, indicating the directions and timetable sought. The parties should return both the questionnaire and the directions form to the court, so that the areas (if any) of potential debate at the CMC can be identified. The parties are encouraged to exchange proposals for directions and the timetable sought, with a view to agreeing the same before the CMC for consideration by the court.

5.3.3 If the case is large or complex, it is helpful for the advocates to prepare a Note to be provided to the judge the day before the CMC which can address the issues in the case, the suggested directions, and the principal areas of dispute between the parties. If such a Note is provided, it is unnecessary for the claimant also to prepare a Case Summary as well.

5.3.4 In smaller cases, a Case Summary for the CMC, explaining briefly the likely issues, can be helpful. Such Case Summaries should be non-contentious and should (if this is possible without incurring disproportionate cost) be agreed between the parties in advance of the hearing.

5.4 Checklist of Matters likely to be considered at the first CMC

5.4.1 The following checklist identifies the matters which the judge is likely to want to **2C–62** consider at the first CMC, although it is not exhaustive:

- The need for, and content of, any further pleadings. This is dealt with in Section 5.5 below.
- The outcome of the Protocol process, and the possible further need for ADR. ADR is dealt with in Section 7 below.
- The desirability of dealing with particular disputes by way of a Preliminary Issue hearing. This is dealt with in Section 8 below.
- Whether the trial should be in stages (e.g. stage 1 liability and causation, stage 2 quantum). In very heavy cases this may be necessary in order to make the trial manageable. In more modest cases, where the quantum evidence will be extensive, a staged trial may be in the interest of all parties.
- The appropriate orders in respect of the disclosure of documents. This is dealt with in Section 11 below.
- The appropriate orders as to the exchange of written witness statements. This is dealt with in Section 12 below. It should be noted that, although it is normal for evidence-in-chief to be given by way of the written statements in the TCC, the judge may direct that evidence about particular disputes (such as what was said at an important meeting) should be given orally without reference to such statements.
- Whether it is appropriate for the parties to rely on expert evidence and, if so, what disciplines of experts should give evidence, and on what issues. This may be coupled with an order relating to the carrying out of inspections, the obtaining of samples, the conducting of experiments, or the performance of calculations. Considerations relating to expert evidence are dealt with in Section 13 below. The parties must be aware that, in accordance with the overrid-

ing objective, the judge will only give the parties permission to rely on expert evidence if it is both necessary and appropriate, and, even then, will wish to ensure that the scope of any such evidence is limited as far as possible.

● In certain cases the possibility of making a costs cap order. See section 16.3 below.

● The appropriate timetable for the taking of the various interlocutory steps noted above, and the fixing of dates for both the PTR and the trial itself (subject to paragraph 5.4.2 below). The parties will therefore need to provide the judge with an estimate for the length of the trial, assuming all issues remain in dispute. Unless there is good reason not to, the trial date will generally be fixed at the first CMC (although this may be more difficult at court centres with only one TCC judge). Therefore, to the extent that there are any relevant concerns as to availability of either witnesses or legal representatives, they need to be brought to the attention of the court on that occasion. The length of time fixed for the trial will depend on the parties' estimates, and also the judge's own view.

If the parties' estimate of trial length subsequently changes, they should inform the clerk of the assigned judge immediately.

5.4.2 The fixing of the trial date at the CMC is usually as a provisional fixture. Therefore no trial fee is payable at this stage. The court should at the same time specify a date upon which the fixture will cease to be "provisional" and, therefore, the trial fee will become payable. This should ordinarily be two months before the trial date. It should be noted that:

● if the trial fee is not paid within 14 days of the due date, then the whole claim will be struck out: see CPR rule 3.7(1)(a) and (4);

● if the court is notified at least 14 days before the trial date that the case is settled or discontinued, then the trial fee, which has been paid, shall be refunded: see **fee 2.2** in Schedule 1 to the Civil Proceedings Fees Order 2004.

For all other purposes other than payment of the trial fee, the provisional date fixed at the CMC shall be regarded as a firm date.

5.4.3 Essentially, the judge's aim at the first CMC is to set down a detailed timetable which, in the majority of cases, will ensure that the parties need not return to court until the PTR.

5.5 Further Pleadings

2C–63 5.5.1 Defence. If no defence has been served prior to the first CMC, then (except in cases where judgment in default is appropriate) the court will usually make an order for service of the defence within a specified period. The defendant must plead its positive case. Bare denials and non-admissions are, save in exceptional circumstances, unacceptable.

5.5.2 Further Information. If the defendant wants to request further information of the Particulars of Claim, the request should, if possible, be formulated prior to the first CMC, so that it can be considered on that occasion. All requests for further information should be kept within reasonable limits, and concentrate on the important parts of the case.

5.5.3 Reply. A reply to the defence is not always necessary. However, where the defendant has raised a positive defence on a particular issue, it may be appropriate for the claimant to set out in a reply how it answers such a defence. If the defendant makes a counterclaim, the claimant's defence to counterclaim and its reply (if any) should be in the same document.

5.5.4 Part 20 Claims. The defendant should, at the first CMC, indicate (so far as possible) any Part 20 claims that it is proposing to make, whether against the claimant or any other party. Part 20 claims are required to be pleaded in the same detail as the original claim. They are a very common feature of TCC cases, because the widespread use of sub-contractors in the UK construction industry often makes it necessary to pass claims down a contractual chain. Defendants are encouraged to start any necessary Part 20 proceedings as soon as possible. It is undesirable for applications to join Part 20 defendants, to be made late in the proceedings.

5.6 Scott Schedules

5.6.1 It can sometimes be appropriate for elements of the claim, or any Part 20 claim, **2C–64** to be set out by way of a Scott Schedule. For example, claims involving a final account or numerous alleged defects or items of disrepair, may be best formulated in this way, which then allows for a detailed response from the defendant. Sometimes, even where all the damage has been caused by one event, such as a fire, it can be helpful for the individual items of loss and damage to be set out in a Scott Schedule. The secret of an effective Scott Schedule lies in the information that is to be provided. This is defined by the column headings. The judge may give directions for the relevant column headings for any Schedule ordered by the court. It is important that the defendant's responses to any such Schedule are as detailed as possible. Each party's entries on a Scott Schedule should be supported by a statement of truth.

5.6.2 Nevertheless, before any order is made or agreement is reached for the preparation of a Scott Schedule, both the parties and the court should consider whether this course (a) will genuinely lead to a saving of cost and time or (b) will lead to a wastage of costs and effort (because the Scott Schedule will simply duplicating earlier schedules, pleadings or expert reports). A Scott Schedule should only be ordered by the court, or agreed by the parties, in those cases where it is appropriate and proportionate.

5.6.3 When a Scott Schedule is ordered by the court or agreed by the parties, the format must always be specified. The parties must co-operate in the physical task of preparation. Electronic transfer between the parties of their respective entries in the columns will enable a clear and user-friendly Scott Schedule to be prepared, for the benefit of all involved in the trial.

5.7 Agreement Between the Parties

5.7.1 Many, perhaps most, of the required directions at the first CMC may be agreed **2C–65** by the parties. If so, the judge will endeavour to make orders in the terms which have been agreed, unless he considers that the agreed terms fail to take into account important features of the case as a whole, or the principles of the CPR. The agreed terms will always, at the very least, form the starting-point of the judge's consideration of the orders to be made at the CMC.

5.7.2 The approach outlined in paragraph 5.7.1 above is equally applicable to all other occasions when the parties come before the court with a draft order that is wholly or partly agreed.

5.8 Drawing Up of Orders

5.8.1 Unless the court itself draws up the order, it will direct one party (usually the **2C–66** claimant or applicant) to do so within a specified time. That party must draw up the order and lodge it with the court for approval. Once approved, the order will be stamped by the court and returned to that party for service upon all other parties.

5.9 Further CMC

5.9.1 In an appropriate case, the judge will fix a review CMC, to take place part way **2C–67** through the timetable that has been set down, in order to allow the court to review progress, and to allow the parties to raise any matters arising out of the steps that have been taken up to that point. This will not, however, be ordered automatically.

5.9.2 Each party will be required to give notice in writing to the other parties and the court of any order which it will be seeking at the review CMC, two days in advance of the hearing..

TCC

5.10 The Permanent Case Management Bundle

2C–68 5.10.1 In conjunction with the judge's clerk, the claimant's solicitor is responsible for ensuring that, for the first CMC and at all times thereafter, there is a permanent bundle of copy documents available to the judge, which contains:

- any relevant documents resulting from the Pre-Action Protocol;
- the claim form and all statements of case;
- all orders;
- all completed case management information sheets.

5.10.2 The permanent case management bundle can then be supplemented by the specific documents relevant to any particular application that may be made. Whether these supplementary documents should (a) become a permanent addition to the case management bundle or (b) be set on one side, will depend upon their nature. The permanent case management bundle may remain at court and be marked up by the judge; alternatively, the judge may direct that the permanent case management bundle be maintained at the offices of the claimant's solicitors and provided to the court when required.

SECTION 6.

APPLICATIONS AFTER THE FIRST CMC

6.1 Relevant parts of the CPR

2C–69 6.1.1 The basic rules relating to all applications that any party may wish to make are set out in CPR Part 23 and its accompanying Practice Directions.

6.1.2 Part 7 of the Practice Direction accompanying CPR Part 60 is also of particular relevance.

6.2 Application Notice

2C–70 6.2.1 As a general rule, any party to proceedings in the TCC wishing to make an application of any sort must file an application notice (rule 23.3) and serve that application notice on all relevant parties as soon as practicable after it has been filed (rule 23.4). Application notices should be served by the parties, unless (as happens in some court centres outside London) service is undertaken by the court.

6.2.2 The application notice must set out in clear terms what order is sought and, more briefly, the reasons for seeking that order: see rule 23.6.

6.2.3 The application notice must be served at least **3 days** before the hearing at which the Court deals with the application: rule 23.7 (1). Such a short notice period is only appropriate for the most straight-forward type of application.

6.2.4 Most applications, in particular applications for summary judgment under CPR Part 24 or to strike out a statement of case under CPR rule 3.4, will necessitate a much longer notice period than **3 days**. In such cases, it is imperative that the applicant obtain a suitable date and time for the hearing of the application from the assigned judge's clerk before the application notice is issued. The applicant must then serve his application notice and evidence in support sufficiently far ahead of the date fixed for the hearing of the application for there to be time to enable the respondent to serve evidence in response. Save in exceptional circumstances, there should be a minimum period of **10 working days** between the service of the notice (and supporting evidence) and the hearing date. If any party considers that there is insufficient time before the hearing of the application or if the time estimate for the application itself is too short, that party must notify the Judge's clerk and the hearing may then be refixed by agreement.

6.2.5 When considering the application notice, the judge may give directions in writing as to the dates for the provision or exchange of evidence and any written submissions or skeleton arguments for the hearing.

6.3 Evidence in Support

6.3.1 The application notice when it is served must be accompanied by all evidence in support: rule 23.7 (2). **2C–71**

6.3.2 Unless the CPR expressly requires otherwise, evidence will be given by way of witness statements. Such statements must be verified by a statement of truth signed by the maker of the statement: rule 22.1.

6.4 Evidence in opposition and Evidence in reply

6.4.1 Likewise, any evidence in opposition to the application should, unless the rules expressly provide otherwise, be given by way of witness statement verified by a statement of truth. **2C–72**

6.4.2 It is important to ensure that the evidence in opposition to the application is served in good time before the hearing so as to enable:
- the court to read and note up the evidence;
- the applicant to put in any further evidence in reply that may be considered necessary.

Such evidence should be served at least **5 working days** before the hearing.

6.4.3 Any evidence in reply should be served not less than **3 working days** before the hearing. Again, if there are disputes as to the time taken or to be taken for the preparation of evidence prior to a hearing, or any other matters in respect of a suitable timetable for that hearing, the court will consider the written positions of both parties and decide such disputes on paper. It will not normally be necessary for either a separate application to be issued or a hearing to be held for such a purpose.

6.4.4 If the hearing of an application has to be adjourned because of delays by one or other of the parties in serving evidence, the court is likely to order that party to pay the costs straight away, and to make a summary assessment of those costs.

6.5 Application Bundle

6.5.1 The bundle for the hearing of anything other than the most simple and straightforward application should consist of: **2C–73**
- the permanent case management bundle (see Section 5.8 above);
- the witness statements provided in support of the application, together with any exhibits;
- the witness statements provided in opposition to the application together with exhibits;
- any witness statements in reply, together with exhibits.

6.5.2 The permanent case management bundle will either be with the court or with the claimant's solicitors, depending on the order made at the first CMC: see paragraph 5.9 above. If it is with the claimant's solicitors, it should be provided to the court not less than **2 working days** before the hearing. In any event, a paginated bundle (see paragraph 6.5.4 below) containing any material specific to the application should also be provided to the court not less than **2 working days** before the hearing, unless otherwise directed by the judge. A failure to comply with this deadline may result in the adjournment of the hearing, and the costs thrown away being paid by the defaulting party.

6.5.3 In all but the simplest applications, the court will expect the parties to provide skeleton arguments and copies of any authorities to be relied on. The form and content of the skeleton argument is principally a matter for the author, although the judge will expect it to identify the issues that arise on the application, the important parts of the evidence relied on, and the applicable legal principles. For detailed guidance as to the form, content and length of skeleton arguments, please see paragraph 7.11.12 of the Queen's Bench Guide; Appendix 3 of the Chancery Guide; and Appendix 9 of the Commercial Court Guide.

6.5.4 For an application that is estimated to last ½ day or less, the skeleton should be provided no later than **1 pm on the last working day before the hearing**. It should be accompanied by photocopies of the authorities relied on.

6.5.5 For an application that is estimated to last more than $1/2$ day, the skeleton should be provided no later than **4 pm one clear working day before the hearing**. It should be accompanied by photocopies of the authorities relied on.

6.5.6 The time limits at paragraphs 6.5.4 and 6.5.5 above will be regarded as the latest times by which such skeletons should be provided to the court. Save in exceptional circumstances, no extension to these periods will be permitted.

6.5.7 Pagination. It is generally necessary for there to be a paginated bundle for the hearing. Where the parties have produced skeleton arguments, these should be crossreferred to the bundle page numbers.

6.6 Hearings

2C–74   6.6.1 Arbitration applications may be heard in private: see CPR rule 62.10. All other applications will be heard in public in accordance with CPR rule 39.2, save where otherwise ordered.

6.6.2 Provided that the application bundle and the skeletons have been lodged in accordance with the time limits set out above, the parties can assume that the court will have a good understanding of the points in issue. However, the court will expect to be taken to particular documents relied on by the parties and will also expect to be addressed on any important legal principles that arise.

6.6.3 It is important that the parties ensure that every application is dealt with in the estimated time period. Since many applications are dealt with on Fridays, it causes major disruption if application hearings are not disposed of within the estimated period. If the parties take too long in making their submissions, the application may be adjourned, part heard, and the Court may impose appropriate costs sanctions.

6.6.4 At the conclusion of the hearing, unless the court itself draws up the order, it will direct the applicant's solicitor to do so within a specified period.

6.7 Paper Applications

2C–75   6.7.1 Contested applications are usually best disposed of at an oral hearing (either in court or by telephone). However, as noted in Section 4 above, some applications may be suitable for determination on paper. The procedure for dealing with paper applications is outlined in paragraph 4.4 above.

6.7.2 In addition, certain simple applications (particularly in lower value cases) arising out of the management of the proceedings may be capable of being dealt with by correspondence without the need for any formal application or order of the court. This is particularly true of applications to vary procedural orders, which variations are wholly or largely agreed, or proposals to vary the estimated length of the trial. In such cases, the applicant should write to the other parties indicating the nature of its application and to seek their agreement to it. If, however, it emerges that there is an issue to be resolved by the court, then a formal application must be issued and dealt with in the normal manner.

6.8 Consent Orders

2C–76   6.8.1 Consent Orders may be submitted to the Court in draft for approval and initialling without the need for attendance.

6.8.2 Two copies of the draft order should be lodged, at least one of which should be signed. The copies should be undated.

6.8.3 As noted above, whilst the parties can agree between themselves the orders to be made either at the Case Management Conference or the Pre-Trial Review, it is normally necessary for the Court to consider the case with the parties (either at an oral hearing or by way of a telephone conference) on those occasions in any event.

6.8.4 Generally, when giving directions, the court will endeavour to identify the date by which the relevant step must be taken, and will not simply provide a period during which that task should be performed. The parties should therefore ensure that any proposed consent order also identifies particular dates, rather then periods, by which the relevant steps must be taken.

6.9 Costs

6.9.1 Costs are dealt with generally at Section 16 below.   **2C–77**

6.9.2 The costs of any application which took a day or less to be heard and disposed of will be dealt with summarily, unless there is a good reason for the court not to exercise its powers as to the summary assessment of costs.

6.9.3 Accordingly, it is necessary for parties to provide to the court and to one another their draft statements of costs no later than **24 hours** before the start of the application hearing. Any costs which are incurred after these draft statements have been prepared, but which have not been allowed for (e.g. because the hearing has exceeded its anticipated length), can be mentioned at the hearing.

SECTION 7.

ADR

7.1 General

7.1.1 The court will provide encouragement to the parties to use alternative dispute **2C–78**
resolution ("ADR") and will, whenever appropriate, facilitate the use of such a procedure. In this Guide, ADR is taken to mean any process through which the parties attempt to resolve their dispute, which is voluntary. In most cases, ADR takes the form of mediation conducted by a neutral mediator. Alternative forms of ADR include formal inter-party negotiations or (occasionally) early neutral evaluations. In an early neutral evaluation either a judge or some other neutral person receives a concise presentation from each party and then states his own evaluation of the case.

7.1.2 Although the TCC is an appropriate forum for the resolution of all IT and construction/engineering disputes, the use of ADR can lead to a significant saving of costs and may result in a settlement which is satisfactory to all parties.

7.1.3 Legal representatives in all TCC cases should ensure that their clients are fully aware of the benefits of ADR and that the use of ADR has been carefully considered prior to the first CMC.

7.2 Timing

7.2.1 ADR may be appropriate before the proceedings have begun or at any **2C–79**
subsequent stage.

7.2.2 The TCC Pre-Action Protocol (Section 2 above) itself provides for a type of ADR, because it requires there to be at least one face-to-face meeting between the parties before the commencement of proceedings. At this meeting, there should be sufficient time to discuss and resolve the dispute. As a result of this procedure having taken place, the court will not necessarily grant a stay of proceedings upon demand and it will always need to be satisfied that an adjournment is actually necessary to enable ADR to take place.

7.2.3 However, at the first CMC, the court will want to be addressed on the parties' views as to the likely efficacy of ADR, the appropriate timing of ADR, and the advantages and disadvantages of a short stay of proceedings to allow ADR to take place. Having considered the representations of the parties, the court may order a short stay to facilitate ADR at that stage. Alternatively, the court may simply encourage the parties to seek ADR and allow for it to occur within the timetable for the resolution of the proceedings set down by the court.

TCC

7.2.4 At any stage after the first CMC and prior to the commencement of the trial, the court, will, either on its own initiative or if requested to do so by one or both of the parties, consider afresh the likely efficacy of ADR and whether or not a short stay of the proceedings should be granted, in order to facilitate ADR.

7.3 Procedure

2C–80 7.3.1 In an appropriate case, the court may indicate the type of ADR that it considers suitable, but the decision in this regard must be made by the parties. In most cases, the appropriate ADR procedure will be mediation.

7.3.2 If at any stage in the proceedings the court considers it appropriate, an ADR order in the terms of **Appendix E** may be made. If such an order is made at the first CMC, the court may go on to give directions for the conduct of the action up to trial (in the event that the ADR fails). Such directions may include provision for a review CMC.

7.3.3 The court will not ordinarily recommend any individual or body to act as mediator or to perform any other ADR procedure. In the event that the parties fail to agree the identity of a mediator or other neutral person pursuant to an order in the terms of **Appendix E**, the court may select such a person from the lists provided by the parties. To facilitate this process, the court would also need to be furnished with the C.V's of each of the individuals on the lists.

7.3.4 Information as to the types of ADR procedures available and the individuals able to undertake such procedures is available from TeCSA, TECBAR, the Civil Mediation Council, and from some TCC court centres outside London.

7.4 Non-Cooperation

2C–81 7.4.1 Generally. At the end of the trial, there may be costs arguments on the basis that one or more parties unreasonably refused to take part in ADR. The court will determine such issues having regard to all the circumstances of the particular case. In *Halsey v Milton Keynes General NHS Trust* [2004] EWCA Civ 576; [2004] 1 WLR 3002, the Court of Appeal identified six factors that may be relevant to any such consideration:
a) the nature of the dispute;
b) the merits of the case;
c) the extent to which other settlement methods have been attempted;
d) whether the costs of the ADR would be disproportionately high;
e) whether any delay in setting up and attending the ADR would have been prejudicial;
f) whether the ADR had a reasonable prospect of success.

7.4.2 If an ADR Order Has Been Made. The court will expect each party to co-operate fully with anyADR which takes place following an order of the court. If any other party considers that there has not been proper co-operation in relation to arrangements for the mediation, the complaint will be considered by the court and cost orders and/or other sanctions may be ordered against the defaulting party in consequence. However, nothing in this paragraph should be understood as modifying the rights of all parties to a mediation to keep confidential all that is said or done in the course of that mediation.

7.5 Early Neutral Evaluation

2C–82 7.5.1 An early neutral evaluation ("ENE") may be carried out by any appropriately qualified person, whose opinion is likely to be respected by the parties. In an appropriate case, and with the consent of all parties, a TCC judge may provide an early neutral evaluation either in respect of the full case or of particular issues arising within it. Such an ENE will not, save with the agreement of the parties, be binding on the parties.

7.5.2 If the parties would like an ENE to be carried out by the court, then they can

328

seek an appropriate order from the assigned judge either at the first CMC or at any time prior to the commencement of the trial.

7.5.3 The assigned judge may choose to do the ENE himself. In such instance, the judge will take no further part in the proceedings once he has produced the ENE, unless the parties expressly agree otherwise. Alternatively, the assigned judge will select another available TCC judge to undertake the ENE.

7.5.4 The judge undertaking the ENE will give appropriate directions for the preparation and conduct of the ENE. This may include a stay of the substantive proceedings whilst the ENE is carried out. The ENE may be carried out entirely on paper. Alternatively, there may be an oral hearing (either with or without evidence). The parties should agree whether the entire ENE procedure is to be without prejudice, or whether it can be referred to at any subsequent trial or hearing.

SECTION 8.

PRELIMINARY ISSUES

8.1 General

8.1.1 The hearing of Preliminary Issues ("PI"), at which the court considers and **2C–83** delivers a binding judgment on particular issues in advance of the main trial, can be an extremely cost-effective and efficient way of narrowing the issues between the parties and, in certain cases, of resolving disputes altogether.

8.1.2 Some cases listed in the TCC lend themselves particularly well to this procedure. A PI hearing can address particular points which may be decisive of the whole proceedings; even if that is not the position, it is often possible for a PI hearing to cut down significantly on the scope (and therefore the costs) of the main trial.

8.1.3 At the first CMC the court will expect to be addressed on whether or not there are matters which should be taken by way of Preliminary Issues in advance of the main trial. Subject to paragraph 8.5 below, it is not generally appropriate for the court to make an order for the trial of preliminary issues until after the defence has been served. After the first CMC, and at any time during the litigation, any party is at liberty to raise with any other party the possibility of a PI hearing and the court will consider any application for the hearing of such Preliminary Issues. In many cases, although not invariably, a PI order will be made with the support of all parties.

8.1.4 Whilst, for obvious reasons, it is not possible to set out hard and fast rules for what is and what is not suitable for a PI hearing, the criteria set out in Section 8.2 below should assist the parties in deciding whether or not some or all of the disputes between them will be suitable for a PI hearing.

8.1.5 Drawbacks of preliminary issues in inappropriate cases. If preliminary issues are ordered inappropriately, they can have adverse effect. Evidence may be duplicated. The same witnesses may give evidence before different judges, in the event that there is a switch of assigned judge. Findings may be made at the PI hearing, which are affected by evidence called at the main hearing. The prospect of a PI hearing may delay the commencement of ADR or settlement negotiations. Also two trials are more expensive than one. For all these reasons, any proposal for preliminary issues needs to be examined carefully, so that the benefits and drawbacks can be evaluated. Also the court should give due weight to the views of the parties when deciding whether a PI hearing would be beneficial.

8.1.6 Staged trials. The breaking down of a long trial into stages should be differentiated from the trial of preliminary issues. Sometimes it is sensible for liability (including causation) to be tried before quantum of damages. Occasionally the subject matter of the litigation is so extensive that for reasons of case management the trial needs to be broken down into separate stages.

8.2 Guidelines

2C–84 8.2.1 The Significance of the Preliminary Issues. The court would expect that any issue proposed as a suitable PI would, if decided in a particular way, be capable of:

- resolving the whole proceedings or a significant element of the proceedings; or
- significantly reducing the scope, and therefore the costs, of the main trial; or
- significantly improving the possibility of a settlement of the whole proceedings.

8.2.2 Oral Evidence. The court would ordinarily expect that, if issues are to be dealt with by way of a PI hearing, there would be either no or relatively limited oral evidence. If extensive oral evidence was required on any proposed PI, then it may not be suitable for a PI hearing. Although it is difficult to give specific guidance on this point, it is generally considered that a PI hearing in a smaller case should not take more than about 2 days, and in a larger and more complex case, should not take more than about 4 days.

8.3 Common Types of Preliminary Issue

2C–85 The following are commonly resolved by way of a PI hearing:

- (a) Disputes as to whether or not there was a binding contract between the parties.
- (b) Disputes as to what documents make up or are incorporated within the contract between the parties and disputes as to the contents or relevance of any conversations relied on as having contractual status or effect.
- (c) Disputes as to the proper construction of the contract documents or the effect of an exclusion or similar clause.
- (d) Disputes as to the correct application of a statute or binding authority to a situation where there is little or no factual dispute.
- (e) Disputes as to the existence and/or scope of a statutory duty .
- (f) Disputes as to the existence and/or scope of a duty of care at common law in circumstances where there is no or little dispute about the relevant facts.

8.4 Other Possible Preliminary Issues

2C–86 The following can sometimes be resolved by way of a preliminary issue hearing, although a decision as to whether or not to have such a hearing will always depend on the facts of the individual case:

8.4.1 A Limitation Defence. It is often tempting to have limitation issues resolved in advance of the main trial. This can be a good idea because, if a complex claim is statutebarred, a decision to that effect will lead to a significant saving of costs. However, there is also a risk that extensive evidence relevant to the limitation defence (relating to matters such as when the damage occurred or whether or not there has been deliberate concealment) may also be relevant to the liability issues within the main trial. In such a case, a preliminary issue hearing may lead to a) extensive duplication of evidence and therefore costs and b) give rise to difficulty if the main trial is heard by a different judge.

8.4.2 Causation and 'No Loss' Points. Causation and 'No Loss' points may be suitable for a PI hearing, but again their suitability will diminish if it is necessary for the court to resolve numerous factual disputes as part of the proposed PI hearing. The most appropriate disputes of this type for a PI hearing are those where the defendant contends that, even accepting all the facts alleged by the claimant, the claim must fail by reason of causation or the absence of recoverable loss.

8.4.3 'One-Off' Issues. Issues which do not fall into any obvious category, like economic duress, or misrepresentation, may be suitable for resolution by way of a PI hearing, particularly if the whole case can be shown to turn on them.

8.5 Use of PI as an adjunct to ADR

2C–87 8.5.1 Sometimes parties wish to resolve their dispute by ADR, but there is one major issue which is a sticking point in any negotiation or mediation. The parties may wish to obtain the court's decision on that single issue, in the expectation that after that they can resolve their differences without further litigation.

8.5.2 In such a situation the parties may wish to bring proceedings under CPR Part 8, in order to obtain the court's decision on that issue. Such proceedings can be rapidly progressed. Alternatively, if the issue is not suitable for Part 8 proceedings, the parties may bring proceedings under Part 7 and then seek determination of the critical question as a preliminary issue. At the first CMC the position can be explained and the judge can be asked to order early trial of the proposed preliminary issue, possibly without the need for a defence or any further pleadings.

8.6 Precise Wording of PI

8.6.1 If a party wishes to seek a PI hearing, either at the first CMC or thereafter, that **2C–88** party must circulate a precise draft of the proposed preliminary issues to the other parties and to the court well in advance of the relevant hearing.

8.6.2 If the court orders a PI hearing, it is likely to make such an order only by reference to specific and formulated issues, in order to avoid later debate as to the precise scope of the issues that have been ordered. Of course, the parties are at liberty to propose amendments to the issues before the PI hearing itself, but if such later amendments are not agreed by all parties, they are unlikely to be ordered.

8.7 Appeals

8.7.1 When considering whether or not to order a PI hearing, the court will take into **2C–89** account the effect of any possible appeal against the PI judgment, and the concomitant delay caused.

8.7.2 At the time of ordering preliminary issues, both the parties and the court should specifically consider whether, in the event of an appeal against the PI judgment, it is desirable that the trial of the main action should (a) precede or (b) follow such appeal. It should be noted, however, that the first instance court has no power to control the timetable for an appeal. A first instance court's power to extend time under CPR rule 52.4(2)(a) for filing an appellant's notice is effectively limited to 14 days (see paragraph 5.19 of the Practice direction supplementing Part 52). The question whether an appeal should be (a) expedited or (b) stayed is entirely a matter for the Court of Appeal. Nevertheless, the Court of Appeal will take notice of any "indication" given by the lower court in this regard.

SECTION 9.

ADJUDICATION BUSINESS

9.1 Introduction

9.1.1 The TCC is ordinarily the court in which the enforcement of an adjudicator's **2C–90** decision and any other business connected with adjudication is undertaken. Adjudicators' decisions predominantly arise out of adjudications which are governed by the mandatory provisions of the Housing Grants, Construction and Regeneration Act 1996 ("HGCRA"). These provisions apply automatically to any construction contract as defined in the legislation. Some Adjudicators' decisions arise out of standard form contracts which contain adjudication provisions, and others arise from ad-hoc agreements to adjudicate. The TCC enforcement procedure is the same for all three kinds of adjudication.

9.1.2 In addition to enforcement applications, declaratory relief is sometimes sought in the TCC at the outset of an adjudication in respect of matters such as the jurisdiction of the adjudicator or the validity of the adjudication. This kind of application is dealt with in Paragraph 9.4 below.

9.1.3 The HGCRA provides for a mandatory 28-day period within which the entire adjudication process must be completed, unless a) the referring party agrees to an additional 14 days, or b) both parties agree to a longer period. In consequence, the TCC has moulded a rapid procedure for enforcing an adjudication decision that has not been honoured. Other adjudication proceedings are ordinarily subject to similar rapidity.

9.2 Procedure In Enforcement Proceedings

2C–91 9.2.1 Unlike arbitration business, there is neither a practice direction nor a claim form concerned with adjudication business. The enforcement proceedings normally seek a monetary judgment so that CPR Part 7 proceedings are usually appropriate. However, if the enforcement proceedings are known to raise a question which is unlikely to involve a substantial dispute of fact and no monetary judgment is sought, CPR Part 8 proceedings may be used instead.

9.2.2 The TCC has fashioned a procedure whereby enforcement applications are dealt with promptly. The details of this procedure are set out below.

9.2.3 The claim form should identify the construction contract, the jurisdiction of the adjudicator, the procedural rules under which the adjudication was conducted, the adjudicator's decision, the relief sought and the grounds for seeking that relief.

9.2.4 The claim form should be accompanied by an application notice that sets out the procedural directions that are sought. Commonly, the claimant's application will seek an abridgement of time for the various procedural steps, and summary judgment under CPR Part 24. The claim form and the application should be accompanied by a witness statement or statements setting out the evidence relied on in support of both the adjudication enforcement claim and the associated procedural application. This evidence should ordinarily include a copy of the adjudicator's decision.

9.2.5 The claim form, application notice and accompanying documents should be lodged in the appropriate registry or court centre clearly marked as being a "paper without notice adjudication enforcement claim and application for the urgent attention of a TCC judge". The parties will be informed that the enforcement proceedings will be assigned to a named judge. That judge will then manage the proceedings up to and including any hearing. He will ordinarily provide his directions made in connection with the procedural application within **3 working days** of the receipt of the application notice at the courts.

9.2.6 The procedural application is dealt with by a TCC judge on paper, without notice. The paper application and the consequent directions should deal with:
  (a) the abridged period of time in which the defendant is to file an acknowledgement of service;
  (b) the time for service by the defendant of any witness statement in opposition to the relief being sought;
  (c) an early return date for the hearing of the summary judgment application and a note of the time required or allowed for that hearing; and
  (d) identification of the judgment, order or other relief being sought at the hearing of the adjudication claim.

The order made at this stage will always give the defendant liberty to apply.

9.2.7 A direction providing for a date by which the claim form, supporting evidence and court order providing for the hearing are to be served on the defendant should ordinarily also be given when the judge deals with the paper procedural application.

9.2.8 The directions will ordinarily provide for an enforcement hearing within **28 days** of the directions being made and for the defendant to be given at least **14 days** from the date of service for the serving of any evidence in opposition to the adjudication application. In more straightforward cases, the abridged periods may be less.

9.2.9 Draft standard directions of the kind commonly made by the court on a procedural application by the claimant in an action to enforce the decision of an adjudicator are attached as **Appendix F**.

9.2.10 The claimant should, with the application, provide an estimate of the time needed for the hearing of the application. This estimate will be taken into account by the judge when fixing the date and length of the hearing. The parties should, if possible jointly, communicate any revised time estimate to the court promptly and the judge to whom the case has been allocated will consider whether to refix the hearing date or alter the time period that has been allocated for the hearing.

9.2.11 If the parties cannot agree on the date or time fixed for the hearing, a paper application must be made to the judge to whom the hearing has been allocated for directions.

9.3 The Enforcement Hearing

9.3.1 Where there is any dispute to be resolved at the hearing, the judge should be provided with copies of the relevant sections of the HGCRA, the adjudication procedural rules under which the adjudication was conducted, the adjudicator's decision and copies of any adjudication provisions in the contract underlying the adjudication. **2C–92**

9.3.2 The parties should lodge, **24 hours** before the hearing, a bundle containing the documents that will be required at the hearing, copies of any authorities which are to be relied on and short skeletons summarising their respective contentions as to why the adjudicator's decision is or is not enforceable or as to any other relief being sought.

9.3.3 The parties should be ready to address the court on the limited grounds on which a defendant may resist an application seeking to enforce an adjudicator's decision or on which a court may provide any other relief to any party in relation to an adjudication or an adjudicator's decision.

9.4 Other Proceedings Arising Out Of Adjudication

9.4.1 As noted above, the TCC will also hear any applications for declaratory relief arising out of the commencement of a disputed adjudication. Commonly, these will concern: **2C–93**

    a) Disputes over the jurisdiction of an adjudicator. It can sometimes be appropriate to seek a declaration as to jurisdiction at the outset of an adjudication, rather than both parties incurring considerable costs in the adjudication itself, only for the jurisdiction point to emerge again at the enforcement hearing.

    b) Disputes over whether there is a written contract between the parties or, in appropriate cases, whether there is a construction contract within the meaning of the Act.

    c) Disputes over the permissible scope of the adjudication, and, in particular, whether the matters which the claimant seeks to raise in the adjudication are the subject of a pre-existing dispute between the parties.

9.4.2 Any such application will be immediately assigned to a named judge. In such circumstances, given the probable urgency of the application, the judge will usually require the parties to attend a CMC **within 2 working days** of the assignment of the case to him, and he will then give the necessary directions to ensure the speedy resolution of the dispute.

9.4.3 It sometimes happens that one party to an adjudication commences enforcement proceedings, whilst the other commences proceedings under Part 8, in order to challenge the validity of the adjudicator's award. This duplication of effort is unnecessary and it involves the parties in extra costs, especially if the two actions are commenced at different court centres. Accordingly there should be sensible discussions between the parties or their lawyers, in order to agree the appropriate venue and also to agree who shall be claimant and who defendant. All the issues raised by each party can and should be raised in a single action.

SECTION 10.

ARBITRATION

10.1 Arbitration Claims in the TCC

10.1.1 "Arbitration claims" are any application to the court under the Arbitration Act 1996 and any other claim concerned with an arbitration that is referred to in CPR **2C–94**

62.2(1). Common examples of arbitration claims are challenges to an award on grounds of jurisdiction under section 67, challenges to an award for serious irregularity under section 68 or appeals on points of law under section 69 of the Arbitration Act 1996. Arbitration claims may be started in the TCC, as is provided for in paragraph 2.3 of the Practice Direction—Arbitration which supplements CPR Part 62.

10.1.2 In practice, arbitration claims arising out of or connected with a construction or engineering arbitration (or any other arbitration where the subject matter involved one or more of the categories of work set out in paragraph 1.3.1 above) should be started in the TCC. The only arbitration claims that must be started in the Commercial Court are those (increasingly rare) claims to which the old law (i.e. the pre-1996 Act provisions) apply: see CPR rule 62.12.

10.1.3 The TCC follows the practice and procedure for arbitration claims established by CPR Part 62 and (broadly) the practice of the Commercial Court as summarised by Section O of the *Admiralty and Commercial Courts Guide*. In the absence of any specific directions given by the court, the automatic directions set out in section 6 of the Practice Direction supplementing CPR Part 62 govern the procedures to be followed in any arbitration claim from the date of service up to the substantive hearing.

10.2 Leave to appeal

2C-95 10.2.1 Where a party is seeking to appeal a question of law arising out of an award pursuant to section 69 of the Arbitration Act 1996 and the parties have not in their underlying contract agreed that such an appeal may be brought, the party seeking to appeal must apply for leave to appeal pursuant to sections 69(2), 69(3) and 69(4) of that Act. That application must be included in the arbitration claim form as explained in paragraph 12 of the Practice Direction.

10.2.2 In conformity with the practice of the Commercial Court, the TCC will normally consider any application for permission to appeal on paper after the defendant has had an appropriate opportunity to answer in writing the application being raised.

10.2.3 The claimant must include within the claim form an application for permission to appeal . No separate application notice is required.

10.2.4 The claim form and supporting documents must be served on the defendant. The judge will not consider the application for permission to appeal until (a) a certificate of service has been filed at the appropriate TCC registry or court centre and (b) a further **28 days** have elapsed, so as to enable the defendant to file written evidence in opposition. Save in exceptional circumstances, the only material admissible on an application for permission to appeal is (a) the award itself and any documents annexed to the award and (b) evidence relevant to the issue whether any identified question of law is of general public importance.

10.2.5 If necessary, the judge dealing with the application will direct an oral hearing with a date for the hearing. That hearing will, ordinarily, consist of brief submissions by each party. The judge dealing with the application will announce his decision in writing or, if a hearing has been directed, at the conclusion of the hearing with brief reasons if the application is refused.

10.2.6 Where the permission has been allowed in part and refused in part:
(a) Only those questions for which permission has been granted may be raised at the hearing of the appeal.
(b) Brief reasons will be given for refusing permission in respect of the other questions.

10.2.7 If the application is granted, the judge will fix the date for the appeal, and direct whether the same judge or a different judge shall hear the appeal.

10.3 Appeals where leave to appeal is not required

10.3.1 Parties to a construction contract should check whether they have agreed in the underlying contract that an appeal may be brought without leave, since some construction and engineering standard forms of contract so provide. If that is the case, the appeal may be set down for a substantive hearing without leave being sought. The arbitration claim form should set out the clause or provision which it is contended provides for such agreement and the claim form should be marked "Arbitration Appeal—Leave not required".

2C–96

10.3.2 Where leave is not required, the claimant should identify each question of law that it is contended arises out of the award and which it seeks to raise in an appeal under section 69. If the defendant does not accept that the questions thus identified are questions of law or maintains that they do not arise out of the award or that the appeal on those questions may not be brought for any other reason, then the defendant should notify the claimant and the court of its contentions and apply for a directions hearing before the judge nominated to hear the appeal on a date prior to the date fixed for the hearing of the appeal. Unless the judge hearing the appeal otherwise directs, the appeal will be confined to the questions of law identified in the arbitration claim form.

10.3.3 In an appropriate case, the judge may direct that the question of law to be raised and decided on the appeal should be reworded, so as to identify more accurately the real legal issue between the parties.

10.4 The hearing of the appeal

10.4.1 Parties should ensure that the court is provided only with material that is relevant and admissible to the point of law. Again, save in exceptional circumstances, this will be limited to the award and any documents annexed to the award: see *Hok Sport Ltd v Aintree Racecourse Ltd* [2003] BLR 155 at 160.

2C–97

10.4.2 On receiving notice of permission being granted, or on issuing an arbitration claim form in a case where leave to appeal is not required, the parties should notify the court of their joint estimate or differing estimates of the time needed for the hearing of the appeal.

10.4.3 The hearing of the appeal is to be in open court unless an application (with notice) has previously been made that the hearing should be wholly or in part held in private and the court has directed that this course should be followed.

10.5 Section 68 applications—Serious Irregularity

10.5.1 In some arbitration claims arising out of construction and engineering arbitrations, a party will seek to appeal a question of law and, at the same time, seek to challenge the award under section 68 of the Arbitration Act 1996 on the grounds of serious irregularity. This raises questions of procedure, since material may be admissible in a section 68 application which is inadmissible on an application or appeal under section 69. Similarly, it may not be appropriate for all applications to be heard together. A decision is needed as to the order in which the applications should be heard, whether there should be one or more separate hearings to deal with them and whether or not the same judge should deal with all applications. Where a party intends to raise applications under both sections of the Arbitration Act 1996, they should be issued in the same arbitration claim form or in separate claim forms issued together. The court should be informed that separate applications are intended and asked for directions as to how to proceed.

2C–98

10.5.2 The court will give directions as to how the section 68 and section 69 applications will be dealt with before hearing or determining any application. These directions will normally be given in writing but, where necessary or if such is applied for by a party, the court will hold a directions hearing at which directions will be given. The directions will be given following the service of any documentation by the defendant in answer to all applications raised by the claimant.

10.6 Successive awards and successive applications

10.6.1 Some construction and engineering arbitrations give rise to two or more separate awards issued at different times. Where arbitration applications arise under

2C–99

more than one of these awards, any second or subsequent application, whether arising from the same or a different award, should be referred to the same judge who has heard previous applications. Where more than one judge has heard previous applications, the court should be asked to direct to which judge any subsequent application is to be referred.

10.7 Other applications and Enforcement

2C–100 10.7.1 All other arbitration claims, and any other matter arising in an appeal or an application concerning alleged serious irregularity, will be dealt with by the TCC in the same manner as is provided for in CPR Part 62, Practice Direction—Arbitration and Section O of *The Admiralty and Commercial Courts Guide*.

10.7.2 All applications for permission to enforce arbitration awards are governed by Section III of Part 62 (rules 62.17–62.19).

10.7.3 An application for permission to enforce an award in the same manner as a judgment or order of the court may be made in an arbitration claim form without notice and must be supported by written evidence in accordance with rule 62.18(6). Two copies of the draft order must accompany the application, and the form of the order sought must correspond to the terms of the award.

10.7.4 An order made without notice giving permission to enforce the award:

    (a) must give the defendant 14 days after service of the order (or longer, if the order is to be served outside the jurisdiction) to apply to set it aside;

    (b) must state that it may not be enforced until after the expiry of the 14 days (or any longer period specified) or until any application to set aside the order has been finally disposed of: rule 62.18(9) and (10).

10.7.5 On considering an application to enforce without notice, the judge may direct that, instead, the arbitration claim form must be served on specified parties, with the result that the application will then continue as an arbitration claim in accordance with the procedure set out in Section I of Part 62: see rule 62.18(1)–(3).

SECTION 11.
DISCLOSURE

11.1 Standard Disclosure

2C–101 11.1.1 The appropriate disclosure and inspection orders to be made will normally be considered and made at the first case management conference. This is governed by CPR Part 31 and the Practice Direction supplementing it. This procedure provides for standard disclosure, being disclosure and inspection in accordance with CPR Part 31 of:

    (a) the documents upon which a party relies;

    (b) the documents which adversely affect his or another party's case or support another party's case; and

    (c) the documents which a party is required to disclose by any relevant practice direction.

11.2 Limiting disclosure and the cost of disclosure

2C–102 11.2.1 In many cases being conducted in the TCC, standard disclosure will not be appropriate. This may for any one or more of the following reasons:

    (a) The amount of documentation may be considerable, given the complexity of the dispute and the underlying contract or contracts, and the process of giving standard disclosure may consequently be disproportionate to the issues and sums in dispute.

    (b) The parties may have many of the documents in common from their previous dealings so that disclosure is not necessary or desirable.

    (c) The parties may have provided informal disclosure and inspection of the majority of these documents, for example when complying with the pre-action Protocol.

(d) The cost of providing standard disclosure may be disproportionate.

In such cases, the parties should seek to agree upon a more limited form of disclosure or to dispense with formal disclosure altogether. Such an agreement could limit disclosure to specified categories of documents or to such documents as may be specifically applied for.

11.2.2 Where disclosure is to be provided, the parties should consider whether it is necessary for lists of documents to be prepared or whether special arrangements should be agreed as to the form of listing and identifying disclosable documents, the method, timing and location of inspection and the manner of copying or providing copies of documents. Where documents are scattered over several locations, or are located overseas or are in a foreign language, special arrangements will also need to be considered. Thought should also be given to providing disclosure in stages or to reducing the scope of disclosure by providing the relevant material in other forms.

11.2.3 Electronic data and documents give rise to particular problems as to searching, preserving, listing, inspecting and other aspects of discovery and inspection. These problems should be considered and, if necessary made the subject of special directions. Furthermore, in appropriate cases, disclosure, inspection and the provision of copies of hard copies may be undertaken using information technology. Attention is drawn to the relevant provisions in CPR Part 31, to *the Admiralty and Commercial Courts Guide* concerned with Electronic Disclosure, and to the TeCSA IT Protocol which provide guidance in relation to these matters. In appropriate cases the TCC will order that the provisions concerning electronic disclosure contained in section E of *the Admiralty and Commercial Courts Guide* shall apply.

11.2.4 All these matters should be agreed between the parties. If it is necessary to raise any of these matters with the court they should be raised, if possible, at the first CMC. If points arise on disclosure after the first CMC, they may well be capable of being dealt with by the court on paper.

11.3 Service using information technology

11.3.1 The parties should consult with each other before the first CMC with a view to **2C–103** arranging the service and (where required) filing of pleadings, schedules, witness statements, experts' reports, disclosure lists and other documents in computer readable form as well as in hard copy. The parties should also consider whether to maintain a common running index, so that every document which has been exchanged between the parties has a unique reference number. Any agreement reached on these matters should be recorded and made the subject of an order for directions. Where agreement is not possible, the parties should raise these matters for decision at a CMC.

SECTION 12.

WITNESS STATEMENTS AND FACTUAL EVIDENCE FOR USE AT TRIAL

12.1 Witness statements

12.1.1 Witness statements should be prepared generally in accordance with CPR Part **2C–104** 22.1 (documents verified by a statement of truth) and CPR Part 32 (provisions governing the evidence of witnesses) and their practice directions, particularly paragraphs 17 to 22 of the Practice Direction supplementing CPR Part 32.

12.1.2 Unless otherwise directed by the court, witness statements should <u>not</u> have annexed to them copies of other documents and should <u>not</u> reproduce or paraphrase at length passages from other documents. The only exception arises where a specific document needs to be annexed to the statement in order to make that statement reasonably intelligible.

12.1.3 When preparing witness statements, attention should be paid to the following matters:

(a) Even when prepared by a legal representative or other professional, the witness statement should be, so far as practicable, in the witness's own words.

(b) The witness statement should indicate which matters are within the witness's own knowledge and which are matters of information and belief. Where the witness is stating matters of hearsay or of either information or belief, the source of that evidence should also be stated.

(c) The witness statement must include a statement by the witness that he believes the facts stated to be true.

(d) A witness statement should be no longer than necessary and should not be argumentative.

12.2 Other matters concerned with witness statements

2C–105
12.2.1 Foreign language. If a witness is not sufficiently fluent in English to give his evidence in English, the witness statement should be in his or her own language and an authenticated translation provided. Where the witness has a broken command of English, the statement may be drafted by others so as to express the witness's evidence as accurately as possible. In that situation, however, the witness statement should indicate that this process of interpolation has occurred and also should explain the extent of the witness's command of English and how and to what parts of the witness statement the process of interpolation has occurred.

12.2.2 Reluctant witness. Sometimes a witness is unwilling or not permitted or is unavailable to provide a witness statement before the trial. The party seeking to adduce this evidence should comply with the provisions of CPR rule 32.9 concerned with the provision of witness summaries.

12.2.3 Hearsay. Parties should keep in mind the need to give appropriate notice of their intention to rely on hearsay evidence or the contents of documents without serving a witness statement from their maker or from the originator of the evidence contained in those documents. The appropriate procedure is contained in CPR rules 33.1–33.5.

12.3 Cross-referencing

2C–106
12.3.1 Where a substantial number of documents will be adduced in evidence or contained in the trial bundles, it is of considerable assistance to the court and to all concerned if the relevant page references are annotated in the margins of the copy witness statements. It is accepted that this is a time-consuming exercise, the need for which will be considered at the PTR, and it will only be ordered where it is both appropriate and proportionate to do so. See further paragraphs 14.5.1 and 15.2.3 below.

12.4 Video link

2C–107
12.4.1 If any witness (whose witness statement has been served and who is required to give oral evidence) is located outside England and Wales or would find a journey to court inconvenient or impracticable, his evidence might be given via a video link. Thought should be given before the PTR to the question whether this course would be appropriate and proportionate. Such evidence is regularly received by the TCC and facilities for its reception, whether in appropriate court premises or at a convenient venue outside the court building, are now readily available.

12.4.2 Any application for a video link direction and any question relating to the manner in which such evidence is to be given should be dealt with at the PTR. Attention is drawn to the Video-conferencing Protocol set out at Annex 3 to the Practice Direction—Witness Evidence. The procedure described in Annex 3 is followed by the TCC.

SECTION 13.

EXPERT EVIDENCE

13.1 Nature of expert evidence

13.1.1 Expert evidence is evidence as to matters of a technical or scientific nature and **2C–108** will generally include the opinions of the expert. The quality and reliability of expert evidence will depend upon (a) the experience and the technical or scientific qualifications of the expert and (b) the accuracy of the factual material that is used by the expert for his assessment. Expert evidence is dealt with in detail in CPR Part 35 ("Experts and Assessors") and in the Practice Direction supplementing Part 35. Particular attention should be paid to all these provisions, given the detailed reliance on expert evidence in most TCC actions. Particular attention should also be paid to the "Protocol for the instruction of experts to give evidence in civil claims" published by the Civil Justice Council in June 2005. This protocol has been approved by the Master of the Rolls.

13.1.2 The provisions in CPR Part 35 are concerned with the terms upon which the court may receive expert evidence. These provisions are principally applicable to independently instructed expert witnesses. In cases where a party is a professional or a professional has played a significant part in the subject matter of the action, opinion evidence will almost inevitably be included in the witness statements. Any points arising from such evidence (if they cannot be resolved by agreement) can be dealt with by the judge on an application or at the PTR.

13.2 Control of expert evidence

13.2.1 Expert evidence is frequently needed and used in TCC cases. Experts are **2C–109** often appointed at an early stage. Most types of case heard in the TCC involve more than one expertise and some, even when the dispute is concerned with relatively small sums, involve several different experts. Such disputes include those concerned with building failures and defects, delay and disruption, dilapidations, subsidence caused by tree roots and the supply of software systems. However, given the cost of preparing such evidence, the parties and the court must, from the earliest pre-action phase of a dispute until the conclusion of the trial, seek to make effective and proportionate use of experts. The scope of any expert evidence must be limited to what is necessary for the requirements of the particular case.

13.2.2 At the first CMC, or thereafter, the court may be asked to determine whether the cost of instructing experts is proportionate to the amount at issue in the proceedings, and the importance of the case to the parties. In dealing with any issues of proportionality, the court should be provided with estimates of the experts' costs.

13.2.3 The parties should also be aware that the court has the power to limit the amount of the expert's fees that a party may recover pursuant to CPR 35.4(4).

13.3 Prior to and at the first CMC

13.3.1 There is an unresolved tension arising from the need for parties to instruct **2C–110** and rely on expert opinions from an early pre-action stage and the need for the court to seek, wherever possible, to reduce the cost of expert evidence by dispensing with it altogether or by encouraging the appointment of jointly instructed experts. This tension arises because the court can only consider directing joint appointments or limiting expert evidence long after a party may have incurred the cost of obtaining expert evidence and have already relied on it. Parties should be aware of this tension. So far as possible, the parties should avoid incurring the costs of expert evidence on uncontroversial matters or matters of the kind referred to in paragraph 13.4.3 below, before the first CMC has been held.

13.3.2 In cases where it is not appropriate for the court to order a single joint expert, it is imperative that, wherever possible, the parties' experts co-operate fully with one another. This is particularly important where tests, surveys, investigations, sample gathering or other technical methods of obtaining primary factual evidence are needed. It is often critical to ensure that any laboratory testing or experiments are carried out by the experts together, pursuant to an agreed procedure. Alternatively, the respective experts may agree that a particular firm or laboratory shall carry out specified tests or analyses on behalf of all parties.

13.3.3 Parties should, where possible, disclose initial or preliminary reports to

TCC

opposing parties prior to any pre-action protocol meeting, if only on a without prejudice basis. Such early disclosure will assist in early settlement or mediation discussions and in helping the parties to define and confine the issues in dispute with a corresponding saving in costs.

13.3.4 Before and at the first CMC and at each subsequent pre-trial stage of the action, the parties should give careful thought to the following matters:

(a) The number, disciplines and identity of the expert witnesses they are considering instructing as their own experts or as single joint experts.

(b) The precise issues which each expert is to address in his/her reports, to discuss without prejudice with opposing parties' experts and give evidence about at the trial.

(c) The timing of any meeting, agreed statement or report.

(d) Any appropriate or necessary tests, inspections, sampling or investigations that could be undertaken jointly or in collaboration with other experts. Any such measures should be preceded by a meeting of relevant experts at which an appropriate testing or other protocol is devised. This would cover (i) all matters connected with the process in question and its recording and (ii) the sharing and agreement of any resulting data or evidence.

(e) Any common method of analysis, investigation or reporting where it is appropriate or proportionate that such should be adopted by all relevant experts. An example of this would be an agreement as to the method to be used to analyse the cause and extent of any relevant period of delay in a construction project, where such is in issue in the case.

(f) The availability and length of time that experts will realistically require to complete the tasks assigned to them.

13.3.5 In so far as the matters set out in the previous paragraph cannot be agreed, the court will give appropriate directions. In giving permission for the reception of any expert evidence, the court will ordinarily order the exchange of such evidence, with a definition of the expert's area of expertise and a clear description of the issues about which that expert is permitted to give evidence. It is preferable that, at the first CMC or as soon as possible thereafter, the parties should provide the court with the name(s) of their expert(s).

13.4 Single joint experts

2C–111 13.4.1 An order may be made, at the first CMC or thereafter, that a single joint expert should address particular issues between the parties. Such an order would be made pursuant to CPR Parts 35.7 and 35.8.

13.4.2 Single joint experts are not usually appropriate for the principal liability disputes in a large case, or in a case where considerable sums have been spent on an expert in the pre-action stage. They are generally inappropriate where the issue involves questions of risk assessment or professional competence.

13.4.3 On the other hand, single joint experts can often be appropriate:

(a) in low value cases, where technical evidence is required but the cost of adversarial expert evidence may be prohibitive;

(b) where the topic with which the single joint expert's report deals is a separate and self-contained part of the case, such as the valuation of particular heads of claim;

(c) where there is a subsidiary issue, which requires particular expertise of a relatively uncontroversial nature to resolve;

(d) where testing or analysis is required, and this can conveniently be done by one laboratory or firm on behalf of all parties.

13.4.4 Where a single joint expert is to be appointed or is to be directed by the court, the parties should attempt to devise a protocol covering all relevant aspects of the appointment (save for those matters specifically provided for by CPR rules 35.6, 35.7 and 35.8).

13.4.5 The matters to be considered should include: any ceiling on fees and disbursements that are to be charged and payable by the parties; how, when and by whom fees will be paid to the expert on an interim basis pending any costs order in the proceedings; how the expert's fees will be secured; how the terms of reference are to be agreed; what is to happen if terms of reference cannot be agreed; how and to whom the jointly appointed expert may address further enquiries and from whom he should seek further information and documents; the timetable for preparing any report or for undertaking any other preparatory step; the possible effect on such timetable of any supplementary or further instructions. Where these matters cannot be agreed, an application to the court, which may often be capable of being dealt with as a paper application, will be necessary.

13.4.6 The usual procedure for a single joint expert will involve:

(a) The preparation of the expert's instructions. These instructions should clearly identify those issues or matters where the parties are in conflict, whether on the facts or on matters of opinion. If the parties can agree joint instructions, then a single set of instructions should be delivered to the expert. However, rule 35.8 expressly permits separate instructions and these are necessary where joint instructions cannot be agreed

(b) The preparation of the agreed bundle, which is to be provided to the expert. This bundle must include CPR Part 35, the Practice Direction supplementing Part 35 and the section 13 of the TCC Guide.

(c) The preparation and production of the expert's report.

(d) The provision to the expert of any written questions from the parties, which the expert must answer in writing.

13.4.7 In most cases the single joint expert's report, supplemented by any written answers to questions from the parties, will be sufficient for the purposes of the trial. Sometimes, however, it is necessary for a single joint expert to be called to give oral evidence. In those circumstances, the usual practice is for the judge to call the expert and then allow each party the opportunity to cross-examine. Such cross-examination should be conducted with appropriate restraint, since the witness has been instructed by the parties. Where the expert's report is strongly in favour of one party's position, it may be appropriate to allow only the other party to cross-examine.

13.5 Meetings of experts

13.5.1 The desirability of holding without prejudice meetings between experts at all **2C–112** stages of the pre-trial preparation should be kept in mind. The desired outcome of such meetings is to produce a document whose contents are agreed and which defines common positions or each expert's differing position. The purpose of such meetings includes the following:

(a) to define a party's technical case and to inform opposing parties of the details of that case;

(b) to clear up confusion and to remedy any lack of information or understanding of a party's technical case in the minds of opposing experts;

(c) to identify the issues about which any expert is to give evidence;

(d) to narrow differences and to reach agreement on as many "expert" issues as possible; and

(e) to assist in providing an agenda for the trial and for cross examination of expert witnesses, and to limit the scope and length of the trial as much as possible.

13.5.2 In many cases it will be helpful for the parties' respective legal advisors to provide assistance as to the agenda and topics to be discussed at an experts' meeting. However, (save in exceptional circumstances and with the permission of the judge) the legal advisors must not attend the meeting. They must not attempt to dictate what the experts say at the meeting.

13.5.3 Experts' meetings can sometimes usefully take place at the site of the dispute. Thought is needed as to who is to make the necessary arrangements for access, particularly where the site is occupied or in the control of a non-party. Expert meetings are often more productive, if (a) the expert of one party (usually the claimant) is appointed as chairman and (b) the experts exchange in advance agendas listing the topics each wishes to raise and identifying any relevant material which they intend to introduce or rely on during the meeting.

TCC

13.5.4 It is generally sensible for the experts to meet at least once before they exchange their reports.

13.6 Experts' Joint Statements

2C–113 13.6.1 Following the experts' meetings, and pursuant to CPR 35.12 (3), the judge will almost always require the experts to produce a signed statement setting out the issues which have been agreed, and those issues which have not been agreed, together with a short summary of the reasons for their disagreement. In any TCC case in which expert evidence has an important role to play, this statement is a critical document and it must be as clear as possible.

13.6.2 It should be noted that, even where experts have been unable to agree very much, it is of considerable importance that the statement sets out their disagreements and the reasons for them. Such disagreements as formulated in the joint statement are likely to form an important element of the agenda for the trial of the action.

13.6.3 Whilst the parties' legal advisors may assist in identifying issues which the statement should address, those legal advisors must not be involved in either negotiating or drafting the experts' joint statement.

13.7 Experts' Reports

2C–114 13.7.1 It is the duty of an expert to help the court on matters within his expertise. This duty overrides any duty to his client: CPR rule 35.3. Each expert's report must be independent and unbiased.

13.7.2 The parties must identify the issues with which each expert should deal in his report. Thereafter, it is for the expert to draft and decide upon the detailed contents and format of his report, so as to conform with section 2 of the Part 35 Practice Direction. It is appropriate, however, for the party instructing an expert to indicate that the report (a) should be as short as is reasonably possible; (b) should not set out copious extracts from other documents; (c) should identify the source of any opinion or data relied upon; and (d) should not annex or exhibit more than is reasonably necessary to support the opinions expressed in the report.

Section 14.
The Pre-Trial Review

14.1 Timing and Attendance

2C–115 14.1.1 The Pre-Trial Review ("PTR") will usually be fixed for a date that is 4–6 weeks in advance of the commencement of the trial itself. It is vital that the advocates, who are going to conduct the trial, should attend the PTR and every effort should be made to achieve this. It is usually appropriate for the PTR to be conducted by way of an oral hearing or, at the very least, a telephone conference.

14.2 Documents

2C–116 14.2.1 The parties must complete the PTR Questionnaire (a copy of which is at **Appendix C** attached) and return it in good time to the court. In addition, the judge may order the parties to provide other documents for the particular purposes of the PTR.

14.2.2 In an appropriate case, the advocates for each party should prepare a Note for the PTR, which addresses:

- any outstanding directions or interlocutory steps still to be taken;
- the issues for determination at the trial;
- the most efficient way in which those issues might be dealt with at the trial, including all questions of timetabling of witnesses.

These Notes should be provided to the court **by 4 p.m. one clear day before the PTR.**

14.2.3 The parties should also ensure that, for the PTR, the court has an up-to-date permanent case management bundle, together with a bundle of the evidence (factual and expert) that has been exchanged. This Bundle should also be made available to the court **by 4 p.m. one clear day before the PTR**.

14.3 Outstanding Directions

14.3.1 It can sometimes be the case that there are still outstanding interlocutory steps **2C–117** to be taken at the time of the PTR. That will usually mean that one, or more, of the parties has not complied with an earlier direction of the court. In that event, the court is likely to require prompt compliance, and may make costs orders to reflect the delays.

14.3.2 Sometimes a party will wish to make an application to be heard at the same time as the PTR. Such a practice is unsatisfactory, because it uses up time allocated for the PTR, and it gives rise to potential uncertainty close to the trial date. It is always better for a party, if it possibly can, to make all necessary applications well in advance of the PTR. If that is not practicable, the court should be asked to allocate additional time for the PTR, in order to accommodate specific applications. If additional time is not available, such applications will not generally be entertained.

14.4 Issues

14.4.1 The parties should, if possible, provide the judge at the PTR with an agreed **2C–118** list of the Issues for the forthcoming trial (including, where appropriate, a separate list of technical issues to be covered by the experts).

14.4.2 If the parties are unable to agree the precise formulation of the issues, they should provide to the court their respective contentions as to what the issues are, and why.

14.4.3 In order to determine the best way to deal with the trial, it is necessary for the issues to be identified. If the precise formulation of the issues is a matter of dispute between the parties, the judge will note the parties' respective contentions, but is unlikely to give a ruling on this matter at the PTR.

14.5 Timetabling and Trial Logistics

14.5.1 Much of the PTR will be devoted to a consideration of the appropriate **2C–119** timetable for the trial, and other logistical matters. These will commonly include:
- Directions in respect of oral and written openings.
- Sequence of oral evidence; for example, whether all the factual evidence should be called before the expert evidence.
- Timetabling of oral evidence. (To facilitate this exercise, the advocates should tell the judge which witnesses need to be cross-examined and which evidence can be agreed.)
- Whether any form of time limits should be imposed. (Since the purpose of time limits is to ensure that that the costs incurred and the resources devoted to the trial are proportionate, this is for the benefit of the parties. The judge will endeavour to secure agreement to any time limits imposed.)
- Directions in respect of the trial bundle: when it should be agreed and lodged; the contents and structure of the bundle; avoidance of duplication; whether witness statements and/or expert reports should be annotated with cross references to page numbers in the main bundle (see paragraph 12.3 above); and similar matters.
- Whether there should be a core bundle; if so how it should be prepared and what it should contain. (The court will order a core bundle in any case where (a) there is substantial documentation and (b) having regard to the issues it is appropriate and proportionate to put the parties to cost of preparing a core bundle).
- Rules governing any email communication during trial between the parties and the court.
- Any directions relating to the use of simultaneous transcription at trial (this subject to agreement between the parties).

TCC

14.5.2 The topics identified in paragraph 14.5.1 are discussed in greater detail in section 15 below.

Section 15.

The Trial

15.1 Arrangements prior to the trial—witnesses

2C–120 15.1.1 Prior to the trial the parties' legal representatives should seek to agree on the following matters, in so far as they have not been resolved at the PTR: the order in which witnesses are to be called to give evidence; which witnesses are not required for cross examination and whose evidence in consequence may be adduced entirely from their witness statements; the timetable for the trial and the length of time each advocate is to be allowed for a brief opening speech. When planning the timetable, it should be noted that trials normally take place on Mondays to Thursdays, since Fridays are reserved for applications.

15.1.2 The witnesses should be notified in advance of the trial as to: (a) when each is required to attend court and (b) the approximate period of time for which he or she will be required to attend.

15.1.3 It is the parties' responsibility to ensure that their respective witnesses are ready to attend court at the appropriate time. It is never satisfactory for witnesses to be interposed, out of their proper place. It would require exceptional circumstances for the trial to be adjourned for any period of time because of the unavailability of a witness.

15.2 Opening notes, trial bundle and oral openings

2C–121 15.2.1 <u>Opening notes.</u> Unless the court has ordered otherwise, each party's advocate should provide an opening note, which outlines that party's case in relation to each of the issues identified at the PTR. Each opening note should indicate which documents (giving their page numbers in the trial bundle) that party considers that the judge should pre-read. The claimant's opening note should include a neutral summary of the background facts, as well as a chronology and cast list. The other parties' opening notes should be shorter and should assume familiarity with the factual background. In general terms, all opening notes should be of modest length and proportionate to the size and complexity of the case. Subject to any specific directions at the PTR, the claimant's opening note should be served two working days before the start of the trial; the other parties opening notes should be served by 12 noon on the last working day before the trial.

15.2.2 <u>Trial bundles.</u> Subject to any specific directions at the PTR, the trial bundles should be delivered to court at least three working days before the hearing. It is helpful for the party delivering the trial bundles to liaise in advance with the judge's clerk, in order to discuss practical arrangements, particularly when a large number of bundles are to be delivered. The parties should provide for the court an agreed index of all trial bundles. There should also be an index at the front of each bundle. This should be a helpful guide to the contents of that bundle. (An interminable list, itemising every letter or sheet of paper is not a helpful guide. Nor are bland descriptions, such as "exhibit "JT3", of much help to the bundle user.) The spines of bundles should be clearly labelled.

15.2.3 As a general rule the trial bundles should be clearly divided between statements of case, orders, contracts, witness statements, expert reports and correspondence/ minutes of meetings. The correspondence/ minutes of meetings should be in a separate bundle or bundles and in chronological order. Documents should only be included, if they are relevant to the issues in the case or helpful as background material. Documents should not be duplicated. Exhibits to witness statements should generally be omitted, since the documents to which the witnesses are referring will be found elsewhere in the bundles. The bundles of contract documents and correspondence/ minutes of meetings should be paginated, so that every page has a discrete number. The other bundles could be dealt with in one of two ways:

- The statements of case, witness statements and expert reports could be placed in bundles and continuously paginated.
- Alternatively, the statements of case, witness statements and expert reports could be placed behind tabbed divider cards, and then the internal numbering of each such document can be used at trial. If the latter course is adopted, it is vital that the internal page numbering of each expert report continues sequentially through the appendices to that report.

The ultimate objective is to create trial bundles, which are user friendly and in which any page can be identified with clarity and brevity (e.g. "bundle G page 273" or "defence page 3" or "Dr Smith page 12"). The core bundle, if there is one (as to which see paragraph 14.5.1 above), will be a separate bundle with its own pagination

15.2.4 Opening speeches. Subject to any directions made at the PTR, each party will be permitted to make an opening speech. These speeches should be prepared and presented on the basis that the judge will have pre-read the opening notes and the documents identified by the parties for pre-reading. The claimant's advocate may wish to highlight the main features of the claimant's case and/or to deal with matters raised in the other parties' opening notes. The other parties' advocates will then make shorter opening speeches, emphasising the main features of their own cases and/or responding to matters raised in the claimant's opening speech.

15.2.5 It is not usually necessary or desirable to embark upon legal argument during opening speeches. It is, however, helpful to foreshadow those legal arguments which (a) explain the relevance of particular parts of the evidence or (b) will assist the judge in following a party's case that is to be presented during the trial.

15.2.6 Narrowing of issues. Experience shows that often that the issues between the parties progressively narrow as the trial advances. Sometimes this process begins during the course of opening speeches. Weaker contentions may be abandoned and responses to those contentions may become irrelevant. The advocates will co-operate in focussing their submissions and the evidence on the true issues between the parties, as those issues are thrown into sharper relief by the adversarial process.

15.3 Simultaneous transcription

15.3.1 Many trials in the TCC, including the great majority of the longer trials, are **2C–122** conducted with simultaneous transcripts of the evidence being provided. There are a number of transcribing systems available. It is now common for a system to be used involving simultaneous transcription onto screens situated in court. However, systems involving the production of the transcript in hard or electronic form at the end of the day or even after a longer period of time are also used. The parties must make the necessary arrangements with one of the companies who provide this service. The court can provide a list, on request, of all companies who offer such a service.

15.3.2 In long trials or those which involve any significant amount of detailed or technical evidence, simultaneous transcripts are helpful. Furthermore, they enable all but the shortest trials to be conducted so as to reduce the overall length of the trial appreciably, since the judge does not have to note the evidence or submissions in longhand as the trial proceeds. Finally, a simultaneous transcript makes the task of summarising a case in closing submissions and preparing the judgment somewhat easier. It reduces both the risk of error or omission and the amount of time needed to prepare a reserved judgment.

15.3.3 If possible, the parties should have agreed at or before the PTR whether a simultaneous transcript is to be employed. It is usual for parties to agree to share the cost of a simultaneous transcript as an interim measure pending the assessment or agreement of costs, when this cost is assessable and payable as part of the costs in the case. Sometimes, a party cannot or will not agree to an interim cost sharing arrangement. If so, it is permissible for one party to bear the cost, but the court cannot be provided with a transcript unless all parties have equal access to the

TCC

transcript. Unlike transcripts for use during an appeal, there is no available means of obtaining from public funds the cost of a transcript for use at the trial.

15.4 Time limits

2C–123 15.4.1 Generally trials in the TCC are conducted under some form of time limit arrangement. Several variants of time limit arrangements are available, but the TCC has developed the practice of imposing flexible guidelines in the form of directions as to the sharing of the time allotted for the trial. These are not mandatory but an advocate should ordinarily be expected to comply with them.

15.4.2 The practice is, in the usual case, for the court to fix, or for the parties to agree, at the PTR or before trial an overall length of time for the trial and overall lengths of time within that period for the evidence and submissions. The part of those overall lengths of time that will be allocated to each party must then be agreed or directed.

15.4.3 The amount of time to be allotted to each party will not usually be the same. The guide is that each party should have as much time as is reasonably needed for it to present its case and to test and cross examine any opposing case, but no longer.

15.4.4 Before the trial, the parties should agree a running order of the witnesses and the approximate length of time required for each witness. A trial timetable should be provided to the court when the trial starts and, in long trials, regularly updated.

15.4.5 The practice of imposing a strict guillotine on the examination or cross examination of witnesses, is not normally appropriate. Flexibility is encouraged, but the agreed or directed time limits should not ordinarily be exceeded without good reason. It is unfair on a party, if that party's advocate has confined cross-examination to the agreed time limits, but an opposing party then greatly exceeds the corresponding time limits that it has been allocated.

15.4.6 An alternative form of time limit, which is sometimes agreed between the parties and approved by the court, is the "chess clock arrangement". The available time is divided equally between the parties, to be used by the parties as they see fit. Thus each side has X hours. One representative on each side operates the chess clock. The judge has discretion "to stop the clock" in exceptional circumstances. A chess clock arrangement is only practicable in a two-party case.

15.5 Oral evidence

2C–124 15.5.1 Evidence in chief is ordinarily adduced by the witness confirming on oath the truth and accuracy of the previously served witness statement or statements. A limited number of supplementary oral questions will usually be allowed (a) to give the witness an opportunity to become familiar with the procedure and (b) to cover points omitted by mistake from the witness statement or which have arisen subsequent to its preparation.

15.5.2 In some cases, particularly those involving allegations of dishonest, disreputable or culpable conduct or where significant disputes of fact are not documented or evidenced in writing, it is desirable that the core elements of a witness's evidence-in-chief are given orally. The giving of such evidence orally will often assist the court in assessing the credibility or reliability of a witness.

15.5.3 If any party wishes such evidence to be given orally, a direction should be sought either at the PTR or during the openings to that effect. Where evidence in chief is given orally, the rules relating to the use of witness statements in cross-examination and to the adducing of the statement in evidence at any subsequent stage of the trial remain in force and may be relied on by any party.

15.5.4 It is usual for all evidence of fact from all parties to be adduced before expert evidence and for the experts to give evidence in groups with all experts in a particular discipline giving their evidence in sequence. Usually, but not invariably, the order of witnesses will be such that the claimant's witnesses give their evidence first, followed by all the witnesses for each of the other parties in turn. If a party wishes a different order of witnesses to that normally followed, the agreement of the parties or a direction from the judge must be obtained in advance.

15.5.5 In a multi-party case, attention should be given (when the timetable is being discussed) to the order of cross-examination and to the extent to which particular topics will be covered by particular cross-examiners. Where these matters cannot be agreed, the order of cross-examination will (subject to any direction of the judge) follow the order in which the parties are set out in the pleadings. The judge will seek to limit cross examination on a topic which has been covered in detail by a preceding cross examination.

15.5.6 The coaching of witnesses or the suggestion of answers that may be given, before that witness starts to give evidence, is not permitted. Any prior discussion between the lawyers and the witness about the giving of evidence should be confined to factual information about the evidence-giving process. In short, witness familiarisation is permissible, but witness coaching is not. The boundary between witness familiarisation and witness coaching is discussed by the Court of Appeal in *R v Momodou* [2005] EWCA Crim 177 at [61]–[62]. Once a witness has started giving evidence, he cannot discuss the case or his evidence either with the lawyers or with anyone else until he has finally left the witness box. Occasionally a dispensation is needed (for example, an expert may need to participate in an experts' meeting about some new development). In those circumstances the necessary dispensation will either be agreed between the advocates or ordered by the judge.

15.6 Submissions during the trial

15.6.1 Submissions and legal argument should be kept to a minimum during the course of the trial. Where these are necessary, (a) they should, where possible, take place when a witness is not giving evidence and (b) the judge should be given forewarning of the need for submissions or legal argument. Where possible, the judge will fix a time for these submissions outside the agreed timetable for the evidence. **2C–125**

15.7 Closing submissions

15.7.1 The appropriate form of closing submissions can be determined during the course of the trial. Those submissions may take the form of (a) oral closing speeches or (b) written submission alone or (c) written submissions supplemented by oral closing speeches. In shorter or lower value cases, oral closing speeches immediately after the evidence may be the most cost effective way to proceed. Alternatively, if the evidence finishes in the late afternoon, a direction for written closing submissions to be delivered by specified (early) dates may avoid the cost of a further day's court hearing. In longer and heavier cases the judge may (in consultation with the advocates) set a timetable for the delivery of sequential written submissions (alternatively, an exchange of written submissions) followed by an oral hearing. In giving directions for oral and/or written closing submissions, the judge will have regard to the circumstances of the case and the overriding objective. **2C–126**

15.7.2 It is helpful if, in advance of preparing closing submissions, the parties can agree on the principal topics or issues that are to be covered. It is also helpful for the written and oral submissions of each party to be structured so as to cover those topics in the same order.

15.7.3 It is both customary and helpful for the judge to be provided with a photocopy of each authority and statutory provision that is to be cited in closing submissions.

15.8 Views

15.8.1 It is sometimes necessary or desirable for the judge to be taken to view the subjectmatter of the case. In normal circumstances, such a view is best arranged to take place immediately after the openings and before the evidence is called. However, if the subject matter of the case is going to be covered up or altered prior **2C–127** to the trial, the view must be arranged earlier. In that event, it becomes particularly important to avoid a change of judge. Accordingly, the court staff will note on the trial diary the fact that the assigned judge has attended a view. In all subsequent communications between the parties and court concerning trial date, the need to avoid a change of judge must be borne firmly in mind.

15.8.2 The matters viewed by the judge form part of the evidence that is received and may be relied on in deciding the case. However, nothing said during the view to (or in the earshot of) the judge, has any evidential status, unless there has been an agreement or order to that effect.

15.8.3 The parties should agree the arrangements for the view and then make those arrangements themselves. The judge will ordinarily travel to the view unaccompanied and, save in exceptional circumstances when the cost will be shared by all parties, will not require any travelling costs to be met by the parties.

15.9 Judgments

2C–128 15.9.1 Depending on the length and complexity of the trial, the judge may (a) give judgment orally immediately after closing speeches; (b) give judgment orally on the following day or soon afterwards; or (c) deliver a reserved judgment in writing at a later date.

15.9.2 Where judgment is reserved. The judge will normally indicate at the conclusion of the trial what arrangements will be followed in relation to (a) the making available of any draft reserved judgment and (b) the handing down of the reserved judgment in open court. If a judgment is reserved, it will be handed down as soon as possible. Save in exceptional circumstances, any reserved judgment will be handed down within 3 months of the conclusion of the trial. Any enquiries as to the progress of a reserved judgment should be addressed in the first instance to the judge's clerk, with notice of that enquiry being given to other parties. If concerns remain following the judge's response to the parties, further enquiries or communication should be addressed to the judge in charge of the TCC.

15.9.3 If the judge decides to release a draft judgment in advance of the formal hand down, this draft judgment will be confidential to the parties and their legal advisers. Solicitors and counsel on each side should send to the judge a note (if possible, agreed) of any clerical errors or slips which they note in the judgment. However, this is not to be taken as an opportunity to re-argue the issues in the case.

15.10 Disposal of judge's bundle after conclusion of the case

2C–129 15.10.1 The judge will have made notes and annotations on the bundle during the course of the trial. Accordingly, the normal practice is that the entire contents of the judge's bundle are disposed of as confidential waste. The empty ring files can be recovered by arrangement with the judge's clerk.

15.10.2 If any party wishes to retrieve from the judge's bundle any particular items of value which it has supplied (e.g. plans or photographs), a request for these items should be made to the judge's clerk promptly at the conclusion of the case. If the judge has not made annotations on those particular items, they will be released to the requesting party.

SECTION 16.
COSTS

16.1 General

2C–130 16.1.1 All disputes as to costs will be resolved in accordance with CPR Part 44, and in particular CPR rule 44.3.

16.1.2 The judge's usual approach will be to determine which party can be properly described as 'the successful party', and then to investigate whether there are any good reasons why that party should be deprived of some or all of their costs.

16.1.3 It should be noted that, in view of the complex nature of TCC cases, a consideration of the outcome on particular issues or areas of dispute can sometimes be an appropriate starting point for any decision on costs.

16.2 Summary Assessment of Costs

16.2.1 Interlocutory hearings that last one day or less will usually be the subject of a summary assessment of costs in accordance with CPR 44.7 and section 13 of the Costs Practice Direction. The parties must ensure that their statements of costs, on which the summary assessment will be based, are provided to each other party, and the Court, no later than **24 hours** before the hearing in question: see paragraph 6.9.3 above. **2C–131**

16.2.2 The *Supreme Court Costs Office Guide to the Summary Assessment of Costs* sets out clear advice and guidance as to the principles to be followed in any summary assessment. Generally summary assessment proceeds on the standard basis. In making an assessment on the standard basis, the court will only allow a reasonable amount in respect of costs reasonably incurred and any doubts must be resolved in favour of the paying party.

16.2.3 In arguments about the hourly rates claimed, the judge will have regard to the principles set out by the Court of Appeal in *Wraith v Sheffield Forgemasters Ltd* [1998] 1 WLR 132: i.e. the judge will consider whether the successful party acted reasonably in employing the solicitors who had been instructed and whether the costs they charged were reasonable compared with the broad average of charges made by similar firms practising in the same area.

16.2.4 In addition, when considering hourly rates, the judge in the TCC may have regard to the guideline rates published from time to time by TecSA.

16.2.5 The court will also consider whether unnecessary work was done or an unnecessary amount of time was spent on the work.

16.2.6 It may be that, because of pressures of time, and/or the nature and extent of the disputes about the level of costs incurred, the court is unable to carry out a satisfactory summary assessment of the costs. In those circumstances, the court will direct that costs be assessed on the standard (or indemnity) basis and will order an amount to be paid on account of costs under CPR Rule 44.3(8).

16.3 Costs Cap Orders

16.3.1 In exercising case management powers, the judge may make costs cap orders which, in normal circumstances, will be prospective only. He should only do so, however, where there is a real and substantial risk that, without such an order: **2C–132**
  (a) costs will be disproportionately or unreasonably incurred and
  (b) such costs cannot be controlled by conventional case management and a detailed assessment of costs after a trial, and
  (c) it is just to make such an order.

See CPR rule 3.1 and the notes to that rule in the White Book headed "Prospective costs cap orders".

16.3.2 The possibility of a costs cap order should be considered at the first CMC. The later such an order is sought, the more difficult it may be to impose an effective costs cap.

16.4 Costs: Miscellaneous

16.4.1 The court may at any stage order any party to file and serve on the other parties an estimate of costs: see CPR rule 3.1(2)(ii) and section 6 of the Costs Practice Direction. The case management information sheet for the first CMC requires such **2C–133**

TCC

costs information. This information allows the court properly to exercise its case management functions. In appropriate cases (and where it is proportionate to do so) the judge will exercise his power under paragraph 3 of the Costs Practice Direction to direct the parties to file estimates of costs prepared in such a way as to demonstrate the likely effects of giving or not giving or not giving a particular case management direction.

16.4.2 Pursuant to CPR Rule 44.2 and Section 7 of the Costs Practice Direction, solicitors have a duty to tell their clients within 7 days if an order for costs was made against the clients and they were not present at the hearing, explaining how the order came to be made. They must also give the same information to anyone else who has instructed them to act on the case or who is liable to pay their fees.

Section 17.

Enforcement

17.1 General

2C–134 17.1.1 The TCC is concerned with the enforcement of judgments and orders given by the TCC and with the enforcement of adjudicators' decisions and arbitrators' awards. Adjudication and arbitration enforcement have been dealt with in, respectively, sections 9 and 10 above.

17.2 High Court

2C–135 17.2.1 <u>London.</u> A party wishing to make use of any provision of the CPR concerned with the enforcement of judgments and orders made in the TCC in London can use the TCC Registry in London or any other convenient TCC District Registry listed in **Appendix A**.

17.2.2 <u>Outside London.</u> Where the judgment or order in respect of which enforcement is sought was made by a judge of the TCC out of London, the party seeking enforcement should use the Registry of the court in which the judgment or order was made.

17.2.3 Where orders are required or sought to support enforcement of a TCC judgment or order, a judge of the TCC is the appropriate judge for that purpose. If available, the judge who gave the relevant judgment or made the relevant order is the appropriate judge to whom all applications should be addressed.

17.3 County Court

2C–136 17.3.1 A TCC county court judgment (like any other county court judgment):
    (a) if for less than £600, must be enforced in the county court;
    (b) if for between £600 and £4999, can be enforced in either the county court or the High Court, at the option of the judgment creditor;
    (c) if for £5,000 or more, must be enforced in the High Court.

17.3.2 If a judgment creditor in a TCC county court wishes to transfer any enforcement proceedings to any other county court (whether a TCC county court or not), he must make a written request to do so pursuant to section 2 of the Practice Direction supplementing Part 70. Alternatively, at the end of the trial the successful party may make an oral application to the trial judge to transfer the proceedings to some other specified county court for the purposes of enforcement.

17.4 Enforcement on paper

2C–137 17.4.1 Where the application or order is unopposed or does not involve any substantial dispute, the necessary order should be sought by way of a paper application.

SECTION 18.

THE TCC JUDGE AS ARBITRATOR

18.1 General

18.1.1 Section 93(1) of the Arbitration Act 1996 provides that a judge of the TCC **2C–138** (previously an Official Referee) may "if in all the circumstances he thinks fit, accept appointment as a sole arbitrator or as an umpire by or by virtue of an arbitration agreement." Judges of the TCC may accept appointments as arbitrators or umpires pursuant to these statutory provisions. A judge of the TCC may also accept an appointment as a member of a three-member panel of arbitrators pursuant to these provisions.

18.1.2 A TCC judge cannot accept such an appointment unless the Lord Chief Justice "has informed him that, having regard to the state of (TCC) business, he can be made available": see section 93(3) of the 1996 Act.

18.1.3 Application should be made in the first instance to the judge whose acceptance of the appointment is sought. If the judge is willing to accept the appointment, he will make application on behalf of the appointing party or parties, through the judge in charge of the TCC, to the Lord Chief Justice for his necessary approval. He will inform the party or parties applying for his appointment once the consent or refusal of consent has been obtained.

18.1.4 Subject to the workload of the court, such requests for judge arbitrators will generally be accepted. Particular advantages have been noted by both TECBAR and TeCSA in the appointment of a TCC judge to act as arbitrator where the dispute centres on the proper interpretation of a clause or clauses within one of the standard forms of building and engineering contracts.

18.2 Arbitration Management and Fees

18.2.1 Following the appointment of the judge arbitrator, the rules governing the **2C–139** arbitration will be decided upon, or directed, at the First Preliminary Meeting, when other appropriate directions will be given. The judge arbitrator will manage the reference to arbitration in a similar way to a TCC case.

18.2.2 The judge sitting as an arbitrator will sit in a TCC court room (suitably rearranged) unless the parties and the judge arbitrator agree to some other arrangement.

18.2.3 Fees are payable to the Court Service for the judge arbitrator's services and for any accommodation provided. The appropriate fee for the judge arbitrator, being a daily rate, is published in the Fees Order and should be paid through the TCC Registry.

18.3 Appeals

18.3.1 Section 2 of Schedule 2 to the Arbitration Act 1996 provides that any appeal **2C–140** from a judge arbitrator is to be heard, in the first instance, by the Court of Appeal.

Appendix A

Case Management Information Sheet

Appendix A to Part 60 Practice Direction—reproduced at para. 2C–27. **2C–141**

Appendix B

Case Management Directions Form

Appendix B to the Part 60 Practice Direction—reproduced at para. 2C–28. **2C–142**

TCC

Appendix C

Pre-Trial Review Questionnaire

2C–143 Appendix C to the Part 60 Practice Direction—reproduced at para. 2C–29.

Appendix D

Contact Details for Technology and Construction Court

2C–144 The High Court of Justice, Queen's Bench Division
Technology and Construction Court
St Dunstan's House
133-137 Fetter Lane
London EC4A 1HD

(a) Management

2C–145 Court Manager: Kevin Johnson
Case Administration Unit Manager/Registry Manager

Registry: Tel: 020 7947 6022/7427
Fax: 020 7947 7428

Case Administration Unit: Tel: 020 7947 7156
Fax: 020 7947 6465

(b) TCC Judges

2C–146 Mr Justice Rupert Jackson
Clerk: Mrs Pembe Overson (pembe.overson@hmcourts-service.gsi.gov.uk)
Tel: 020 7947 6484
Fax: 020 7947 6803

His Honour Judge Richard Havery QC
Clerk: Ms Sarah Landau (sarah.landau@hmcourts-service.gsi.gov.uk)
Tel: 020 7947 7445

His Honour Judge Anthony Thornton QC
Clerk: Ms Anne Farrelly (anne.farrelly@hmcourts-service.gsi.gov.uk)
Tel: 020 7947 6457

His Honour Judge David Wilcox
Clerk: Ms Pam Gilham (pamela.gilham@hmcourts-service.gsi.gov.uk)
Tel: 020 7947 6450

His Honour Judge John Toulmin CMG QC
Clerk: Ms Kim Andrews (kim.andrews@hmcourts-service.gsi.gov.uk)

Tel: 020 7947 6456

His Honour Judge Peter Coulson QC
Clerk: Mr Steve Jones (stephen.jones3@hmcourts-service.gsi.gov.uk)
Tel: 020 7947 6547

- The following five High Court Judges will be available, when necessary and by arrangement with the Vice-President of the Queen's Bench Division, to sit in the TCC:
    Mr Justice Elias
    Mr Justice Field
    Mr Justice Ouseley
    Mr Justice Simon
    Mr Justice Christopher Clarke
- The Case Administration Unit administers cases classified as "HCJ" (see section 3.7 of guide).

Birmingham District Registry: Birmingham County Court
33 Bull Street
Birmingham B4 6DS
TCC listing and clerk to HH Judge Kirkham: Peter Duke
Tel: 0121 681 3181
Fax: 0121 681 3121
e-mail: peter.duke@hmcourts-service.gsi.gov.uk

TCC Judges
Her Honour Judge Frances Kirkham (full time TCC Judge)
Her Honour Judge Caroline Alton (Mercantile Judge)
His Honour Judge Alastair Norris Q.C (Chancery Judge)

Each judge has his or her own diary with a first fixture. If the first fixture settles, the Judge in question will take a case from a shared list (which includes TCC, Mercantile and Chancery work).

Other judges in Birmingham who have been nominated to deal with TCC business are: His Honour Judge MacDuff Q.C and His Honour Judge Patrick McCahill Q.C

Bristol District Registry: Bristol County Court
TCC Listing Office
The Law Courts
Small Street
Bristol BS1 1DA
TCC Listing officers: Liz Bodman and Louise Piotrowski
Tel: 0117 976 3098
Fax: 0117 976 3074
e-mail: louise.piotrowski@hmcourts-service.gsi.gov.uk

TCC Judges
His Honour Judge Mark Havelock-Allan QC (principal TCC judge)
His Honour Judge Rupert Bursell QC

Cardiff District Registry: Cardiff County Court
Cardiff Civil Justice Centre
2 Park Street
Cardiff CF10 1 ET
Main switchboard: 02920 376 400
Fax: 02920 376 475
Listing office: 02920 376 412

TCC Judges
His Honour Judge Gary Hickinbottom (principal TCC judge)
His Honour Judge Nicholas Chambers QC
His Honour Judge Wyn Williams QC

Central London Civil Justice Centre
13-14 Park Crescent,
London WIN 4HT
Listing office for TCC, Chancery and Mercantile Courts
Tel: 0207 917 7889/ 7821
Fax: 0207 917 7935

TCC Judges
His Honour Judge Brian Knight QC (principal TCC judge)
His Honour Judge Michael Dean QC
His Honour Judge Michael Rich QC
His Honour Judge David Mackie QC

Chester District Registry: Chester County Court
The Chester Civil Justice Centre
Trident House
Little St John Street
Chester CH1 1SN
Tel: 01244 404200
Fax: 01244 404300

TCC Judge
His Honour Judge Derek Halbert

Leeds Combined Court Centre
The Courthouse
1 Oxford Row
Leeds LS1 3BG

High Court Civil Listing Officers: Chris Waring and Ms Sam Cox
Tel: 0113 254 2607
Fax: 0113 242 6380
e-mail: chris.waring@hmcourts-service.gsi.gov.uk

TCC Judges
His Honour Judge John Cockroft (principal TCC judge)
His Honour Judge John Behrens
His Honour Judge Peter Langan QC
His Honour Judge Simon Grenfell
His Honour Judge Simon Hawkesworth QC

Leicester District Registry: Leicester County Court
PO Box 3
90 Wellington Street
Leicester LE1 6ZZ
Tel : 0116 222 5700

TCC Judges
His Honour Judge David Brunning
His Honour Judge Hugh Mayor QC

Liverpool Combined Court Centre
QE 11 Law Court
Derby Square
Liverpool L2 1XA
TCC listing officer: Joseph Kelly
Tel: 0151 471 1069/ 1091
Fax: 0151 471 1095

The Chancery and Mercantile listing officer, Helen Davidson, on
the same telephone and fax numbers also assists with TCC matters
when necessary.

TCC Judges
His Honour Judge David Mackay (full time TCC judge)
His Honour Judge David Harris QC
His Honour Judge Stephen Stewart QC
His Honour Judge Nigel Gilmour QC

Newcastle upon Tyne Combined Court Centre
The Law Courts
Quayside
Newcastle upon Tyne NE1 3LA
Tel: 0191 201 2000

TCC Judge
His Honour Judge Christopher Walton

Nottingham District Registry: Nottingham County Court
60 Canal Street
Nottingham NG1 7EJ
Tel 0115 910 3500
Fax: 0115 910 3510

TCC Judge
His Honour Judge Richard Inglis

Plymouth Combined Court Centre
The Law Courts
10 Armada Way
Plymouth
Devon PL1 2ER
Tel: 01752 677 400

TCC Judge
His Honour Judge Sean Overend

Salford District Registry: SalfordCounty Court
Prince William House
Peel Cross Road
Salford M5 4RR
TCC clerks: Isobel Rich and Colette Worthington
Tel: 0161 745 7511
Fax: 0161 745 7202
e-mail: hearings@salford.countycourt.gsi.gov.uk

TCC Judges
His Honour Judge David Gilliland QC (full time TCC judge)
His Honour Judge Phillip Raynor QC

The following judges at Manchester are nominated to deal with
TCC business: His Honour Judge Brian Hegarty QC and His Honour Judge Michael Kershaw QC

Sheffield Combined Court Centre
The Law Courts
50 West Bar
Sheffield S3 8PH
Tel: 0114 281 2419
Fax: 0114 281 2585

TCC Judge
His Honour Judge John Bullimore

Southampton Combined Court Centre
Courts of Justice
London Road
Southampton SO15 2XQ
Diary Manager: Mr Wayne Hacking
Tel: 023 8021 3254
Fax: 023 8021 3232

TCC Judge
His Honour Judge Hughes QC

Appendix E

Draft ADR Order

1. By [   ] the parties shall exchange lists of three neutral individuals who **2C–147**
have indicated their availability to conduct a mediation/ENE in this case prior to
[   ].

2. By [   ] the parties shall agree an individual from the exchanged lists to
conduct the mediation/ENE by [   ]. If the parties are unable to agree on the
neutral individual, they will apply to the Court in writing by [   ] and the
Court will choose one of the listed individuals to conduct the mediation/ENE.

3. There will be a stay of the proceedings until [   ] to allow the
mediation/ENE to take place. On or before that date, the Court shall be informed as
to whether or not the case has been finally settled. If it has not been finally settled,
the parties will:
   a) comply with all outstanding directions made by the Court;
   b) attend for a review CMC on [   ].

Appendix F

Draft Directions in Adjudication Enforcement Proceedings

Upon reading the Claim Form, Particulars of Claim, the Claimant's without notice ap- **2C–148**
plication dated the   day of   200   and the evidence in
support thereof

IT IS ORDERED THAT:

1. The Claimant's solicitor shall [as soon as practicable after receipt of this Order/ by
4pm on   day of   ] serve upon the Defendant
   a. The Claim Form and Response Pack
   b. This Order
   c. The Claimant's Application Pursuant to Part 24 and the Claimant's evidence in
support.

2. The time for the Defendant to file its acknowledgement of service is abridged to
[   ] days.

3. The Claimant hereby has permission to issue an application pursuant to CPR Part
24 without an acknowledgement of service or Defence having been filed.

4. The Part 24 application will be heard on the   day of   at
       am/pm at   . Estimated Length of Hearing   hours]

5. Any further evidence in relation to the Part 24 Application shall be served and filed

   a. By the Defendant, [14 days after the service of the documents in Paragraph 1 above/ at least 5 working days before the date fixed for the hearing of the Application] [on the   day of   ]

   b. By the Claimant, in response to that of the Defendant, [at least 3 working days before the date fixed for the hearing of the Application] [on the   day of   200   ]

and in either case no later than 4.00pm upon that day.

6. The Claimant's solicitor shall file a paginated bundle comprising

   a. The witness statements provided in support of the application, together with any exhibits;

   b. The witness statements provided in opposition to the application together with exhibits;

   c. Any witness statements in reply, together with exhibits;

   d. Photocopies of relevant authorities.

This bundle is to be provided no later than [2 working days before the hearing of the Application] [on day   of   ].

7. The parties shall file and serve skeleton arguments by no later than [4.00pm one clear working day before the hearing/ 1pm the last working day before the hearing]* [on the day   of   ]

8. The costs of and incidental to these directions are reserved to the Part 24 hearing. Permission to apply in respect of such costs in the absence of such hearing.

9. The parties have permission to apply to the court on 48 hours written notice to the other to seek to set aside or vary these directions.

* Depending whether the hearing is estimated to last in excess of 1/2 day or not

2D ADMIRALTY JURISDICTION AND PROCEEDINGS

PART 61—ADMIRALTY CLAIMS AND THE PRACTICE
DIRECTION—ADMIRALTY CLAIMS

Contents

Editorial Introduction

This Part and its supplementing Practice Direction do not provide a complete code **2D–1** for these proceedings but have to be read in conjunction with the other Civil Procedure Rules. The application of the Civil Procedure Rules and the Practice Directions which supplement them is in Admiralty proceedings subject to the provisions of this Practice Direction. Part 61 also assigns certain claims to the QBD and provides that they are to be taken by the Admiralty court.

The following points are of importance:

— There is now no jurisdiction in the County Court in Admiralty matters (see Civil Courts (Amendment) (No. 2) Order 1999 (S.I. 1999 No. 1011).

— All Admiralty claims *in rem* or *in personam* should be commenced in the Admiralty and Commercial Registry at the RCJ. In cases of urgency out of London reference should be made to the Admiralty and Commercial Registry at the RCJ. See further under para. .

— All arrests will be dealt with by the Admiralty Marshal at the Admiralty and Commercial Registry in London.

— As a general rule in cases where there is an arrest, the file and matter will be retained in the Admiralty and Commercial Registry for all purposes save as may be otherwise specifically ordered.

— All arrests are to be supported by a Solicitor's undertaking to pay the Marshal's arrest expenses or disbursements or by a payment in in respect thereof.

— The caveat system is preserved, but caveats are now termed cautions.

— An acknowledgment of service must be filed in every Admiralty claim *in rem* and in every other Admiralty claim formerly called claims *in personam* unless liability is admitted on **ADM16** in a limitation claim. Such acknowledgment must be filed within 14 days of service of the claim form irrespective of whether or not particulars of claim are served with it.

— An Admiralty other claim (see the Practice Direction – Admiralty Claims, para. 12.1) is subject to the same rules as an ordinary claim where service is to be affected out of the jurisdiction save for the special rules set out in CPR rule 6.20(17A) and as regards a limitation claim form only in rule 61.11(5) and a collision claim form in rule 61.4.

— There are special rules as to times for service of a claim *in rem*.

ADMIRALTY

(a) The validity for service of an *in rem* claim form is 12 months, see rule 61.3(5)(b).

(b) The time for service of particulars of claim in an *in rem* claim if not served with the *in rem* claim form is 75 days after service of the *in rem* claim form, see rule 61.3(3)(b).

Collision and limitation claims have their own special procedures see rules 61.4 and 6.11 respectively. The Preliminary Act procedure still applies in collision claims but Preliminary Acts are now termed Collision Statements of Case.

Related Sources

2D–2
- Supreme Court Act 1981, ss.20–24, s.27 and s.150 (see paras 2D–139 *et seq.*)
- Hovercraft Act 1968, ss.2–4 (see paras 2D–193 *et seq.*)
- Merchant Shipping Act 1995, ss.92–93, ss.185–189, ss.190, 192, 224 and 229–230 (see paras 2D–200 *et seq.*)
- The Admiralty and Commercial Courts Guide.

Forms

2D–3
- **ADM1** Claim form (Admiralty claim form *in rem*)
- **ADM1A** Claim form (Admiralty claim form for other claims)
- **ADM1C** Notes for defendant on replying to an *in rem* claim form
- **ADM2** Acknowledgment of service/response pack (Admiralty claim *in rem*)
- **ADM3** Collision Statement of Case
- **ADM4** Application and undertaking for arrest and custody
- **ADM5** Outline form of declaration in support of application for warrant of arrest
- **ADM6** Notice to consular officer of intention to apply for warrant of arrest
- **ADM7** Request for caution against arrest
- **ADM9** Warrant of arrest
- **ADM10** Standard directions to the admiralty marshal
- **ADM11** Request for caution against release
- **ADM12** Application and undertaking for release
- **ADM12A** Request for withdrawal of caution against release
- **ADM13** Application for judgment in default of filing an acknowledgment of service and/or defence or collision statement of case
- **ADM14** Order for sale of a ship
- **ADM15** Claim form (Admiralty limitation claim)
- **ADM15B** Notes for defendant (Admiralty limitation claim)
- **ADM16** Notice of admission of right of claimant to limit liability
- **ADM16A** Defence to admiralty limitation claim
- **ADM16B** Acknowledgment of service/response pack (Admiralty limitation claim)
- **ADM17** Application for restricted decree of limitation
- **ADM17A** Application for general limitation decree
- **ADM18** Restricted decree of limitation
- **ADM19** Decree of limitation
- **ADM20** Defendant's claim in a limitation claim
- **ADM21** Outline form of declaration as to inability of a defendant to file and serve statement of case under a decree of limitation

2D–3.1   *Note* —**ADM1A**—An Admiralty Claim *in personam* shall be commenced on a Part 7 claim form as adapted for a Commercial Court claim, save for taking into consideration any logical or textual modifications made to the "Notes for Claimant on completing a claim form" in the Commercial Court, in order to accord with the practice of the Admiralty Court.

The formats for Part 7 and Part 8 claim forms for Commercial Court claims, the notes and response packs thereto together with certain other forms as adapted shall apply to an Admiralty action *in personam* (or *in rem*, if applicable) with the appropriate alterations.

Scope and interpretation[1]

61.1—(1) This Part applies to admiralty claims. **2D–4**

(2) In this Part—

(a) "admiralty claim" means a claim within the Admiralty jurisdiction of the High Court as set out in section 20 of the Supreme Court Act 1981[2];

(b) "the Admiralty Court" means the Admiralty Court of the Queen's Bench Division of the High Court of Justice;

(c) "claim in rem" means a claim in an admiralty action in rem;

(d) "collision claim" means a claim within section 20(3)(b) of the Supreme Court Act 1981;

(e) "limitation claim" means a claim under the Merchant Shipping Act 1995[3] for the limitation of liability in connection with a ship or other property;

(f) "salvage claim" means a claim—

(i) for or in the nature of salvage;

(ii) for special compensation under; Article 14 of Schedule 11 to the Merchant Shipping Act 1995

(iii) for the apportionment of salvage; and

(iv) arising out of or connected with any contract for salvage services;

(g) "caution against arrest" means a caution entered in the Register under rule 61.7;

(h) "caution against release" means a caution entered in the Register under rule 61.8;

(i) "the Register" means the Register of cautions against arrest and release which is open to inspection as provided by the practice direction;

(j) "the Marshal" means the Admiralty Marshal;

(k) "ship" includes any vessel used in navigation; and

(l) "the Registrar" means the Queen's Bench Master with responsibility for Admiralty claims.

(3) Part 58 (Commercial Court) applies to claims in the Admiralty Court except where this Part provides otherwise.

(4) The Registrar has all the powers of the Admiralty judge except where a rule or practice direction provides otherwise.

Admiralty jurisdiction

As to the Admiralty jurisdiction of the High Court see SCA 1981, ss.20 to 24 (paras **2D–5** 2D–139 *et seq.* below), the Hovercraft Act 1968 as amended by SCA 1981 (paras 2D–193 *et seq.* below), the Merchant Shipping Act 1995, s.166.

---

[1] Amended by Civil Procedure (Amendment No. 5) Rules 2001 (S.I. 2001 No. 4015).

[2] 1981 c.54; section 20 was amended by the Merchant Shipping (Salvage and Pollution) Act 1994 (c.28), section 1(6) and Schedule 2, paragraph 6; the Merchant Shipping Act 1995 (c.21), section 314(2) and Schedule 13, paragraph 59 and by the Merchant Shipping and Maritime Security Act 1997 (c.28), section 29(1) and Schedule 6, paragraph 2.

[3] 1995 c.21

361

The Court is seised of a claim *in rem* from the moment of service of the claim form or of arrest of a ship (whichever is the earlier). Where, however, proceedings are brought against a ship already under arrest in High Court proceedings, the Court will be seised of jurisdiction from the moment the claim form is issued. The Court cannot have jurisdiction over a ship which does not come within the jurisdiction (*The Freccia del Nord* [1989] 1 Lloyd's Rep. 388). The Court is seised of a claim *in personam* (see Practice Direction—Admiralty Claims, para. 12, Other Claims) when the defendant is served with the claim form (*Neste Chemicals SA v. D.K. Line SA The Sargasso* [1993] 1 Lloyd's Rep. 424, affirmed [1994] 3 All E.R. 180; [1994] 2 Lloyd's Rep. 6, CA). This is so whether service is to be effected within or without the jurisdiction and in the latter case may have first involved an application for permission to serve out of the jurisdiction. This is a matter of importance when considering Arts 21 and 22 of the Convention on Jurisdiction and the Enforcement of Judgments in Civil and Commercial Matters 1968.

Further, for cases subject to EC law, Council Regulation (EC) No. 44/2001 on jurisdiction and the recognition and enforcement of judgments in civil and commercial matters, effective from March 1, 2002, Section 9, *Lis pendens–* related actions, Article 30 provides:

For the purposes of this Section, a court shall be deemed to be seised:

1. at the time when the document instituting the proceedings or an equivalent document is lodged with the court, provided that the plaintiff has not subsequently failed to take the steps he was required to take to have service effected on the defendant, or

2. if the document has to be served before being lodged with the court, at the time when it is received by the authority responsible for service, provided that the plaintiff has not subsequently failed to take the steps he was required to take to have the document lodged with the court.

Article 2 of the 1968 Brussels Convention on Jurisdiction and the Enforcement of Judgments in Civil and Commercial Matters covers all forms of proceedings in civil and commercial matters whether *in rem* or *in personam* and the word "sued" in Arts 2 and 3 of the Convention should be construed accordingly (*The Deichland* [1989] 2 Lloyd's Rep. 113, CA). Where an arrest within Art.1(2) of the 1952 Arrest Convention is effected, the claimant is entitled to rely upon Art.57 of the 1968 Convention as excluding the exclusive jurisdiction of another convention country which would otherwise apply under Art.2 of the 1968 Convention in the absence of some exempting factor under Art.5 of the 1968 Convention, see *The Anna H* [1994] 1 Lloyd's Rep. 287. Affirmed CA [1995] 1 Lloyd's Rep. 11. The Court of Appeal further held that the Arrest Convention required only that the legal consequences of judicial detention of the ship should be that it became security for a maritime claim not that the claimant's commercial motive must be to obtain security.

In *Canada Trust Co. and Others v. Stolzenberg and Others* [2000] 4 All E.R. 481, the House of Lords held that on the true construction of Articles 2 and 6 of the Lugano Convention on Jurisdiction and the Enforcement of Judgments in Civil and Commercial Matters, 1988 (identical for present purposes to the terms of the 1968 Brussels Convention referred to above), the word "sued" referred to the initiation of proceedings, and accordingly the English court took jurisdiction over a defendant, for the purposes of those provisions, on the date that the writ [claim form] was issued. Such a conclusion was supported by the language of the convention which used the concepts "sued", "bring proceedings" and "instituted proceedings" interchangeably.

Admiralty Court

2D–6 This is part of the QBD. It has jurisdiction in all causes and matters assigned by SCA 1981 to that division which involve the exercise of the High Court's Admiralty jurisdiction or its jurisdiction as a prize court. See SCA 1981, ss.5, 6, 61 and 62 and Sched.1.

Claim in rem

2D–7 Admiralty claims may be either *in rem* or *in personam*. (now known as other Admiralty Claims).

An Admiralty claim *in rem* is in effect a claim against a *res*. (*The Longford* (1888) 14 P.D. 34, *per* Lord Esher M.R. at 37; *The City of Mecca* (1879) 5 P.D. 28 at 33; 6 P.D. 106; *The Burns* [1907] P. 137; SCA 1981, s.21 (para. 2D–169 below). A *res* is usually a ship but may in some cases be cargo or freight, an aircraft or hovercraft. In such a claim the claimant may cause the *res* to be arrested if it is within the jurisdiction (see rules 61.5 *et seq.*). If the *res* is arrested and the claimant's claim is successful then unless the *res* has been released (as to which see rules 61.8 *et seq.*) judgment may be given against the *res* and an order made for its appraisement and sale. The proceeds of sale will be paid into Court and will, after deduction of the fees and expenses of the Admiralty Marshal in connection with the arrest, custody, appraisement and the sale of the *res*, be available in or towards satisfaction of the claimant's judgment. If, as is frequently the case, there is more than one claim against the *res*, payment out of the proceeds of sale will be ordered in accordance with the Admiralty rules as to the priorities of claims, claims of the same priority ranking *pari passu*. As to proceedings for the determination of priority of claims (see rule 61.10).

A claim *in rem* may also be instituted against the proceeds of sale by the Court of a *res*.

If in a claim *in rem* issue or service of the claim form has been acknowledged and the claim form is not set aside, the personal liability of the defendant who has appeared is added and judgment may be given against him as well as against the *res*. See *The Gemma* [1899] P.285, CA and *The August 8* [1983] 2 A.C. 450; [1983] 1 Lloyd's Rep. 351, PC.

In *Republic of India v. India Steamship Co. Ltd* [1997] 3 W.L.R. 818; [1998] 1 Lloyd's Rep. 1 HL(E) it was held that for the purposes of section 34 of the Civil Jurisdiction and Judgments Act 1982, "a [claim] *in rem* is an action against the owners from the moment that the Admiralty Court is seised with jurisdiction. The jurisdiction of the Admiralty Court is invoked by the service of a [claim form], or, where a [claim form] is deemed to be served, as a result of the acknowledgment of the issue of the [claim form] by the defendant before service (*The Banco* [1971] P.137). From that moment the owners are parties *in rem*". Dicta of Lord Brandon in *The August 8* [1983] 2 A.C. 450; [1983] 2 W.L.R. 419 at 456, PC, and *The Deichland* [1990] 1 Q.B. 361, CA, applied and *The Nordglimt* [1988] Q.B. 183 overruled. The case reviews claims *in rem* generally and states that the idea that a ship can be a defendant in legal proceedings was always a legal fiction which can now be discarded holding that in reality a claim *in rem* is an action against the owners. *Quaere* the extent and effect of the reasoning in this case in claims *in rem* generally. The position in respect of cases involving a maritime lien was expressly reserved as requiring separate consideration. See too *The Irina Zharkikh* [2001] 2 Lloyd's Rep. 319 (N.Z. Ct.).

A defendant who has acknowledged issue or service of the claim form may provide security in order to avoid the arrest of the *res* or to obtain its release if it has been arrested.

Sale by the Court in a claim *in rem* is a sale of the whole property and it is sold free of all claims, encumbrances, liens, etc., with a clean title (see, *e.g. The Acrux* [1962] 1 Lloyd's Rep. 405) all existing claims, etc., being transferred to the proceeds of sale, against which claims begun after the sale must be brought. See also *The Blitz* [1992] 2 Lloyd's Rep. 441—sale of vessel by a local authority pursuant to its powers under section 44 of the Harbours, Docks and Piers Clauses Act 1847 is a sale free from mortgages. The position regarding maritime liens is unclear.

In *The Cerro Colorado* [1993] 1 Lloyd's Rep. 58, the Court declared that any conduct which impedes or is likely to impede the ability of the Admiralty Marshal to achieve a fair market value upon the sale of the vessel (including but not limited to published statements that the vessel will, after sale by the Admiralty Marshal, remain encumbered with existing claims) is an interference with the administration of justice. Such conduct may expose anyone responsible to proceedings for contempt of court.

The following are the main matters of procedure peculiar to a claim *in rem*:

(a) a special form of claim form is used. See PD61, para. 3.1;

(b) service of the claim form must be in a manner prescribed by PD61, para. 3.6;

(c) judgment in default of acknowledgment of service, defence, defence to counterclaim or the filing of a collision statement of case must be applied for by application under rule 61.9;

(d) a claim form *in rem* cannot be served outside the jursidiction;

Claims against two or more "sister" ships

When the AJA 1956 came into force it became possible in many cases for a claimant **2D–8** to proceed *in rem* against any one of a number of ships in the same beneficial ownership, see s.3(4). The practice soon became established in such cases of issuing one claim form against some or all of the ships against which the claimant was entitled to proceed and later amending the claim form by striking out the names of all ships save the one in respect of which the claim form had been served or against which a warrant of arrest had been issued. The claim form should be amended immediately after service by deleting all but one of the ship's names upon it (*The Freccia del Nord* [1989] 1 Lloyd's Rep. 388 at 391).

In *The Banco* [1971] P. 137; [1971] 1 Lloyd's Rep. 49, CA, in which it was held that only one ship could be served with a claim form *in rem* or arrested in respect of one cause of action, the practice described above was, by a majority, approved. See now SCA 1981, s.21(8) (paras 2D–169 and 2D–181 below).

Claims in rem and other claims

2D–9 If it is desired to commence proceedings both *in rem* and *in personam* separate claim forms must be issued. See para. 2D–135.

Cautions

2D–10 See rules 61.7 and 61.8.

Limitation Claim

2D–11 See para. 1.4, *British Shipping Laws*, Vols 1 and 11 (but note the change of onus of proof introduced since last publication of volumes 1 and 11). Limitation actions must be assigned to the Queen's Bench Division and taken by the Admiralty Court (rule 61.2(i)(c)). For special rules relating to limitation actions see rule 61.11 below.

Ship

2D–12 Compare the definition of ship in SCA 1981, s.24 and see note "Ship" at para. 2D–144 below.

A ship is equipment within the meaning of s.1 of the Employers' Liability (Defective Equipment) Act 1969 (*The Derbyshire* [1988] A.C. 276; [1988] 1 Lloyd's Rep. 109, HL).

Limitation of claims

2D–13 There are special periods, subject to Court's discretion, in collision and salvage: Merchant Shipping Act 1995, ss.190 and 195.

Admiralty claims[1]

2D–14 **61.2—(1) The following claims must be started in the Admiralty Court—**

> (a) **a claim—**
>> (i) **in rem;**
>> (ii) **for damage done by a ship;**
>> (iii) **concerning the ownership of a ship;**
>> (iv) **under the Merchant Shipping Act 1995;**
>> (v) **for loss of life or personal injury specified in section 20(2)(f) of the Supreme Court Act 1981;**
>> (vi) **by a master or member of a crew for wages;**
>> (vii) **in the nature of towage; or**
>> (viii) **in the nature of pilotage;**
> (b) **a collision claim;**
> (c) **a limitation claim; or**
> (d) **a salvage claim.**

(2) Any other admiralty claim may be started in the Admiralty Court.

---

[1] Amended by Civil Procedure (Amendment No. 5) Rules 2001 (S.I. 2001 No. 4015) and Civil Procedure (Amendment No. 4) Rules 2005 (S.I. 2005 No. 3515).

(3) **Rule 30.5 applies to claims in the Admiralty Court except that the Admiralty Court may order the transfer of a claim to—**
  (a) **the Commercial list;**
  (b) **a Mercantile Court;**
  (c) **the Mercantile list at the Central London County Court; or**
  (d) **any other appropriate court.**

Restrictions on Admiralty jurisdiction

(1) Collision and similar actions if in personam —See SCA 1981, s.22 (para. 2D–182). **2D–15**

(2) Wages actions — Section 4 of the Consular Relations Act 1968, provides that **2D–16** Orders in Council may be made to exclude or limit the jurisdiction to entertain proceedings relating to the pay or conditions of service of the master or crew of any ship or aircraft belonging to a state specified in the Order unless the Consul has first been notifed of the intention to invoke the jurisdiction of the Court and has not objected. Orders have been made in respect of Austria, Belgium, Bulgaria, Denmark, Federal Republic of Germany, Greece, Hungary, Italy, Japan, Mexico, Norway, Poland, Romania, Spain, Sweden, Yugoslavia, Czechoslovakia and Egypt. (See Statutory Instruments 1970 Nos. 1903–1905, 1907–1914, 1917, 1918 and 1920, 1971 No. 1846, 1978 No. 275 1976/768 and 1986/217.) Each of these orders provides for a period of two weeks for objection. Following the dissolution of Yugoslavia the position in respect of the individual former constituent member states is uncertain. It is suggested that the Consul of the individual state concerned is notified.

The above-mentioned Orders in Council additionally require a statement to the effect that the consular officer of the state concerned has been notified of the intention to invoke the jurisdiction of the court and has not objected within a period of two weeks from the date of such notification to be included among the details on which the claim is based at the time when the proceedings are commenced.

Further Orders in Council may be issued from time to time.

In *The Andrea Ursula* [1971] Fo. 61 and 81, it was held that proceedings were a nullity for non-compliance with the above mentioned statutory requirements.

(3) Crown —No claim *in rem* lies against the Crown, but in certain circumstances **2D–17** such a claim may be allowed to continue as if *in personam*: Crown Proceedings Act 1947, s.29 (Vol. 2, Section 21L, para.).

(4) Foreign sovereign states, etc. —As to claims against foreign sovereigns, foreign **2D–18** sovereign states, ambassadors and diplomatic agents, members of their suites and certain international organisations generally, see CPR, r.12.10. As to claims *in rem* against state owned ships and cargoes see also the State Immunity Act 1978, ss.10, 12 and 13.

A ship, belonging to private owners, requisitioned by the Crown, cannot be arrested while in Government service though if a maritime lien attaches it may be enforced after derequisitioning (*The Broadmayne* [1916] P. 64) and though a claim lies against the owners of the ship if the crew remain their servants (*The Messicano* (1916) 32 T.L.R. 519; *The Crindon* (1918) 35 T.L.R. 81; *The Eolo* [1918] 2 Ir.R. 78).

(5) Rhine Navigation Convention 1868 —No Court in England or Wales has jurisdic- **2D–19** tion in cases falling to be determined in accordance with the provisions of this convention. See SCA 1981, s.23 (para. 2D–185).

(6) Nuclear Installations Act 1965 —This Act consolidates and repeals the Nuclear **2D–20** Installations (Licensing and Insurance) Act 1959, and (with one exception relating to the Electricity (Amendment) Act 1961) the Nuclear Installations (Amendment) Act 1965. In the event of an occurrence involving nuclear matter, reference should be made to the Act; in particular, s.14 (protection for ships and aircraft) makes claims *in rem* against ships or aircraft and limitation of liability under the Merchant Shipping Act 1995 unavailable: the Act substitutes a new approach. This Act was amended by the Nuclear Installations Act 1969.

ADMIRALTY

2D–21   *(7) Liquidation and bankruptcy* —As to liquidation see the Insolvency Act 1986, s.130. See also *The Constellation* [1966] 1 W.L.R. 272; [1965] 2 Lloyd's Rep. 538; *Re Aro Co Ltd* [1980] Ch. 196; [1980] 1 All E.R. 1067, CA.

Claims in rem[1]

2D–22   **61.3**—(1) **This rule applies to claims in rem.**

(2) **A claim in rem is started by the issue of an in rem claim form as set out in the practice direction.**

(3) **Subject to rule 61.4, the particulars of claim must—**

    (a) **be contained in or served with the claim form; or**

    (b) **be served on the defendant by the claimant within 75 days after service of the claim form.**

(4) **An acknowledgment of service must be filed within 14 days after service of the claim form.**

(5) **The claim form must be served—**

    (a) **in accordance with the practice direction; and**

    (b) **within 12 months after the date of issue and rules 7.5 and 7.6 are modified accordingly.**

(6) **If a claim form has been issued (whether served or not), any person who wishes to defend the claim may file an acknowledgment of service.**

Claim in rem

2D–23   A claim *in rem* may properly be issued only when the jurisdiction can be invoked by proceedings *in rem* under section 21(2), (3), (4) or (5) of SCA, 1981 (paras 2D-169 and 2D-170 to 180). See too note "Claim in rem" under r.61.1.3 above.

Renewal of claim form

2D–24   As to renewal of a claim form *in rem* on grounds of impossibility of service on the ship see *The Berny* [1979] Q.B. 80; [1978] 1 All E.R. 1065; [1977] 2 Lloyd's Rep. 533. As to renewal of claim form generally see CPR, r.7.6 and notes thereto.

Acknowledgment of service before actual service

2D–25   In a claim *in rem* or limitation claim *issue* of the claim form may be acknowledged, see r.61.3(6) above.

Methods of service

2D–26   For methods of service of a claim form *in rem* see PD61 para. 3.6 which includes service by an alternative method under CPR, r.6.8 so long as *res* is within the jurisdiction.

Special provisions relating to collision claims[2]

2D–27   **61.4**—(1) **This rule applies to collision claims.**

(2) **A claim form need not contain or be followed by particulars of claim and rule 7.4 does not apply.**

(3) **An acknowledgment of service must be filed.**

(4) **A party who wishes to dispute the court's jurisdiction must make an application under Part 11 within 2 months after filing his acknowledgment of service.**

---

[1] Amended by Civil Procedure (Amendment No. 5) Rules 2001 (S.I. 2001 No. 4015).

[2] Amended by Civil Procedure (Amendment No. 5) Rules 2001 (S.I. 2001 No. 4015).

(5) **Every party must—**
- (a) **within 2 months after the defendant files the acknowledgment of service; or**
- (b) **where the defendant applies under Part 11 within 2 months after the defendant files the further acknowledgment of service,**

file at the court a completed collision statement of case in the form specified in the practice direction.

(6) **A collision statement of case must be—**
- (a) **in the form set out in the practice direction; and**
- (b) **verified by a statement of truth.**

(7) **A claim form in a collision claim may not be served out of the jurisdiction unless—**
- (a) **the case falls within section 22(2)(a), (b) or (c) of the Supreme Court Act 1981[1]; or**
- (b) **the defendant has submitted to or agreed to submit to the jurisdiction; and**

the court gives permission in accordance with Section III of Part 6.

(8) **Where permission to serve a claim form out of the jurisdiction is given, the court will specify the period within which the defendant may file an acknowledgment of service and, where appropriate, a collision statement of case.**

(9) **Where, in a collision claim in rem ("the original claim")—**
- (a)
  - (i) **a Part 20 claim; or**
  - (ii) **a cross-claim in rem**

arising out of the same collision or occurrence is made; and
- (b)
  - (i) **the party bringing the original claim has caused the arrest of a ship or has obtained security in order to prevent such arrest; and**
  - (ii) **the party bringing the Part 20 claim or cross-claim is unable to arrest a ship or otherwise obtain security,**

the party bringing the Part 20 claim or cross claim may apply to the court to stay the original claim until sufficient security is given to satisfy any judgment that may be given in favour of that party.

(10) **The consequences set out in paragraph (11) apply where a party to a claim to establish liability for a collision claim (other than a claim for loss of life or personal injury)—**
- (a) **makes an offer to settle in the form set out in paragraph (12) not less than 21 days before the start of the trial;**
- (b) **that offer is not accepted; and**
- (c) **the maker of the offer obtains at trial an apportionment equal to or more favourable than his offer.**

---

[1] 1981 c.54

(11) **Where paragraph (10) applies the parties will, unless the court considers it unjust, be entitled to the following costs—**

    (a) **the maker of the offer will be entitled to—**

        (i) **all his costs from 21 days after the offer was made; and**

        (ii) **his costs before then in the percentage to which he would have been entitled had the offer been accepted; and**

    (b) **all other parties to whom the offer was made—**

        (i) **will be entitled to their costs up to 21 days after the offer was made in the percentage to which they would have been entitled had the offer been accepted; but**

        (ii) **will not be entitled to their costs thereafter.**

(12) **An offer under paragraph (10) must be in writing and must contain—**

    (a) **an offer to settle liability at stated percentages;**

    (b) **an offer to pay costs in accordance with the same percentages;**

    (c) **a term that the offer remain open for 21 days after the date it is made; and**

    (d) **a term that, unless the court orders otherwise, on expiry of that period the offer remains open on the same terms except that the offeree should pay all the costs from that date until acceptance.**

Collision statement of case, formerly called preliminary act

2D–28   "The object of the collision statement of case is to obtain from the parties statements of the facts at a time when they are fresh in their recollection" (*per* Sir Robert Phillimore, in *The Frankland* (1872) L.R. 3 A. & E. 511). The other main purpose is to force the parties to "plead blind" (*The Vortigern* (1859) Sw. 518). A statement of fact in a collision statement of case is a formal admission, binding the party making it, and can only be departed from by special permission (*per* Fletcher Moulton L.J. in *The Seacombe, The Devonshire* [1912] P.21, 59, *The Devonshire* [1912] P. 21, 59; see *The Ladybell* (1933) 49 T.L.R. 595; 46 Ll.L.Rep. 342). As a rule, therefore, the Court will not allow either party subsequently to alter anything in his collision statement of case, not even to correct a clerical error (*The Miranda* (1882) 7 P.D. 185). But in *The Esso Brussels* (1968) Fo. 373 (unrep.) on this point, permission was given during the trial to amend Articles xii and xiv. Permission, however, is sometimes asked for and given to lead evidence not in accordance with the party's collision statement of case; if witnesses give evidence not in accordance with the collision statement of case and no leave is asked for, the Court may hold the party to what is in the collision statement of case (see *The Semiramis* [1952] 2 Lloyd's Rep. 86 at 93). The Court is not bound by the admissions in any collision statement of case (see, *e.g. The Vanessa* [1960] 1 Lloyd's Rep. 82; *The Geo. W. McKnight* (1947) 80 Ll.L.R. 419, HL). A party who has filed a defective collision statement of case, which does not give the information required by the rule, may be ordered on application by the other party to amend it (*The Godiva* (1886) 11 P.D. 20) or to give particulars.

    Note that the present and previous rules are wider than the rule which they replaced. The old rule referred to "actions for damage by collision between vessels..."; *The El Oso* (1925) 21 Ll.L.Rep. 340; *Armstrong v. Gaselee* (1889) 22 QBD 250; *Secretary of State for India v. Hewitt & Co* (1888) 6 Asp. 384; *The John Boyne* (1877) 36 L.T. 29; 3 Asp. M.L.C. 346, are cases decided under that rule. Each party is required in his collision statement of case to state the material facts upon which he founds his case and the Court may order the costs of a collision statement of case which differs widely from the facts proved at the trial to be disallowed on taxation (*The Pelican I* (1926) 25

Ll.L.Rep. 150). The information must be given fully; any concealment will be viewed by the Court with suspicion and, as stated, on the application of the other party, the Court may order amendment (*The Godiva*, above) or particulars so that all the questions are answered properly. When a ship in a river is on a fixed course as opposed to a course which is constantly changed, either the magnetic or the true course should be stated (*The Rievaulx Abbey* (1910) 11 Asp. 437). In a collision case in which one ship is, or both ships are, at anchor, the collision statement of case or collision statements of case filed on behalf of the owners of the anchored ship or both anchored ships should state in Art. vii the heading of the ship at anchor (*The Macroom* (1927) 17 Asp. 288 (one ship at anchor, the other under way): *The Erna* (1927) 27 Ll.L.Rep. 170 (a dragging case; both ships at anchor)). In *The Judith M.* (1968) 112 S.J. 859, a statement in the claimant's collision statement of case (Art.(ix)(b)) and elsewhere that the defendants' ship was heading "across the bows" of the claimant's ship "from port to starboard" was criticised by Brandon J.; it was desirable to state such heading with greater particularity. A defendant is not entitled to demand of another defendant whom he blames in his defence that he shall file a collision statement of case, unless he issues a claim form against him (*The Carlston and the Balcombe* [1926] P. 82).

Section 20(3)(b)(i) SCA 1981 ". . . collision between ships . . ."

A floating landing stage is not a ship, therefore no collision statements of case are **2D–29** required in an action arising from a collision between a steamship and it (*The Craighall* [1910] P. 207). On the other hand, where claimants whose ship, A, was in collision with another, B, blamed the owners of B and also the dock authority which had some measure of control over B it was held that all three parties must file collision statements of case; the dock authority were obliged to do the best they could to answer the questions in the collision statement of case (*The Beaverford* [1961] 1 W.L.R. 793; [1960] 3 All E.R. 612; [1960] 2 Lloyd's Rep. 216). This case was followed in *British Oil & Cake Mills Ltd v. John H. Whitaker (Tankers) Ltd (The Grainger's No. 4)* [1964] 1 W.L.R. 1474; [1964] 3 All E.R. 705; [1964] 2 Lloyd's Rep. 415. A collision statement of case is required of a widow whose husband has been killed in a collision (see *Webster v. M. S. & L. Ry.* [1884] W.N. 1). This is so even where the ship has been sunk in the collision with the loss of all hands. See as to further information concerning information contained in collision statements of case: (*The Isle of Cyprus* (1890) 15 P.D. 134; *The Bernard* [1905] W.N. 73; *The Biola* (1876) 34 L.T. 185; *The Radnorshire* (1880) 5 P.D. 172).

Dispensing with or limiting collision statement of case

It is considered that the Court retains power to order dispensing with or limiting **2D–30** the requirement under this paragraph of collision statements of case under its general CPR powers or inherent jurisdiction in appropriate though rare cases. An order to dispense with or limit the filing of collision statements of case will not be made on a consent application; the Court will always require the parties to attend and explain the reasons for the application. Application is made by application notice before the Registrar.

Expert Witnesses etc

For guidance in use of expert witnesses, illustrative plotting and computer stimula- **2D–31** tion, see *Owners of the Pelopidas v. Owners of the TRSL Concord* [1999] 2 All E.R. (Comm) 737.

Arrest[1]

61.5—(1) In a claim in rem—   **2D–32**

(a) **a claimant; and**

(b) **a judgment creditor**

may apply to have the property proceeded against arrested.

(2) **The practice direction sets out the procedure for applying for arrest.**

---

[1] Amended by Civil Procedure (Amendment No. 5) Rules 2001 (S.I. 2001 No. 4015).

ADMIRALTY

(3) A party making an application for arrest must—

    (a) request a search to be made in the Register before the warrant is issued to determine whether there is a caution against arrest in force with respect to that property; and

    (b) file a declaration in the form set out in the practice direction.

(4) A warrant of arrest may not be issued as of right in the case of property in respect of which the beneficial ownership, as a result of a sale or disposal by any court in any jurisdiction exercising admiralty jurisdiction in rem, has changed since the claim form was issued.

(5) A warrant of arrest may not be issued against a ship owned by a State where by any convention or treaty, the United Kingdom has undertaken to minimise the possibility of arrest of ships of that State until—

    (a) notice in the form set out in the practice direction has been served on a consular officer at the consular office of that State in London or the port at which it is intended to arrest the ship; and

    (b) a copy of that notice is attached to any declaration under paragraph (3)(b).

(6) Except—

    (a) with the permission of the court; or

    (b) where notice has been given under paragraph (5),

a warrant of arrest may not be issued in a claim in rem against a foreign ship belonging to a port of a State in respect of which an order in council has been made under section 4 of the Consular Relations Act 1968,[1] until the expiration of 2 weeks from appropriate notice to the consul.

(7) A warrant of arrest is valid for 12 months but may only be executed if the claim form—

    (a) has been served; or

    (b) remains valid for service at the date of execution.

(8) Property may only be arrested by the Marshal or his substitute.

(9) Property under arrest—

    (a) may not be moved unless the court orders otherwise; and

    (b) may be immobilised or prevented from sailing in such manner as the Marshal may consider appropriate.

(10) Where an in rem claim form has been issued and security sought, any person who has filed an acknowledgment of service may apply for an order specifying the amount and form of security to be provided.

General note

2D–33   Where the Admiralty jurisdiction of the High Court may be and is invoked by a

---

[1] 1968 c.18

claim *in rem* the *res* proceeded against may be arrested if it is within the territorial jurisdiction of the Court. For the circumstances in which the jurisdiction *in rem* may be invoked see SCA 1981, s.21 (para. 2D–169). It will be observed that in some cases only the property concerned may be proceeded against *in rem* (s.21(2) *ibid.*) and that if a maritime lien has attached, a claim *in rem* may be brought against the ship or property in question regardless of any change of ownership since the cause of action arose other than by a judicial sale. In all other cases it is necessary to look at the person, if any, who was liable *in personam* at the time the cause of action arose; a claim *in rem* may be brought against ships of which he is the beneficial owner or demise charterer at the time of the issue of the claim provided he was the owner or charterer or in possession or control of the ship in connection with which the claim arose at the time when the claim arose. The expression "claim is brought" means "when the claim form is issued" (*The Carmania II* [1963] 2 Lloyd's Rep. 152). Once a claim is brought against a ship by issue of a claim form a sale of the ship by her owner will not deprive the claimant of any rights he may have (*The Monica S* [1968] P. 741; [1967] 3 All E.R. 740; [1967] 2 Lloyd's Rep. 113). But *quaere* the effect of *The Blitz* [1992] 2 Lloyd's Rep. 441. As to the requirements regarding personal liability in actions *in rem* generally and where there is a maritime lien in particular, see *The Father Thames* [1979] 2 Lloyd's Rep. 364.

Until the Civil Jurisdiction and Judgments Act 1982 the sole purpose of an action *in rem* was to obtain security in respect of a judgment of the Court (or a sum due under a settlement) in that claim, the Court had no jurisdiction to arrest ships or to keep ships under arrest for other purposes, see *The Cap Bon* [1967] 1 Lloyd's Rep. 543. Now section 26 of the 1982 Act enables the Admiralty Court to retain the security of the *res* or the security for the purpose of arbitration or other proceedings in a United Kingdom or overseas Court. See also *The Jalamatsyr* [1987] 2 Lloyd's Rep. 164.

The issue of a warrant of arrest is not a discretionary remedy. If the statutory requirements set out in PD 61, para. 61.5.3 are complied with the claimant is entitled to issue the warrant of arrest and if there is such compliance there is no further scope for the application of any duty of full and frank disclosure, *The Varna* [1993] 2 Lloyd's Rep. 253.

A vessel cannot remain in the custody of the Admiralty Marshal and yet be allowed to trade outside the jurisdiction (*The Bazias 3, The Bazias 4* [1993] Q.B. 673; [1993] 2 W.L.R. 854; [1993] 2 All E.R. 964; [1993] 1 Lloyd's Rep. 101, CA).

The Admiralty Marshal may pursuant to the undertaking in **ADM4** call for money on account of the expenses of an arrest as occasion demands.

Merchant Shipping Act 1995

2D–34 Where a state has enacted legislation giving effect to the provisions of the International Convention Relating to the Limitation of the Liability of Owners of Sea-Going Ships 1957, but not the International Convention on Limitation of Liability for Maritime Claims 1976, the setting up of a limitation fund in such a state will not prevent the arrest of a ship in another state which has enacted legislation giving effect to the 1976 Convention.

Crown: foreign sovereign states, etc.

2D–35 See notes under paras 2D–17 and 18 above. Since the termination of the 1968 Treaty and Protocols between the UK and the USSR there is no longer any treaty or convention within 61.5(5) in force.

Delay in prosecution of claim

2D–36 The Marshal is not a shipkeeper and parties should not delay in prosecuting an action in which a vessel is under arrest (*The Italy II* [1987] 2 Lloyd's Rep. 162).

Wrongful arrest

2D–37 Whether a caution has been entered or not, if property is arrested by reason of *mala fides* or *crassa negligentia*, damages may be recovered in Admiralty or, indeed, at common law (*The Walter D. Wallett* [1893] P. 202; *The Evangelismos* (1858) 12 Moo. P.C. 352; Swa. 378; *The Strathnaver* (1875) 1 App. Cas. 58; *The Cathcart* (1867) L.R. 1 A. & E. 314; *The Eudora* (1879) 4 P.D. 208). Damages may also be recovered where an arrest has been unduly continued (*The Cheshire Witch* (1858) Br. & Lush. 362; *The Margaret and Jane* (1869) L.R. 2 A. & E. 345). As to claims for damages where release has been delayed owing to a caution against release and payment having been entered without good and sufficient reason, see r.61.8(5). See also r.61.7(5)(b).

ADMIRALTY

Rule 61.5(8)

2D-38   The warrant may only be executed by being served by the Marshal or his substitute upon the ship or property concerned in accordance with PD 61, para. 61.5.5. The Marshal's officer acts as his substitute in London; elsewhere Customs officers and County Court bailiffs do so. See too *The Berny* [1977] 2 Lloyd's Rep. 533 at 548.

> "The Court has to bear in mind that the duty of arresting a ship, and often at the time of serving a [claim form] on her, falls on the Admiralty Marshal or his deputies, and it should not adopt an approach to the matter which would or might expose these persons to unreasonable difficulties or dangers."

The claim form and warrant are frequently served at approximately the same time, but either may be served first. As to effect of failure to comply with the requirements as to service, see *The Prins Bernhard* [1964] P. 117; [1963] 3 All E.R. 735; [1963] 2 Lloyd's Rep. 236. As to the non-fatal character of a minor failure, see *The Sullivar* [1965] 2 Lloyd's Rep. 350.

Freight, being incorporeal, cannot be arrested nor can a claim form be served upon it, but where a claim is brought against freight, or cargo and freight, or ship, cargo and freight, the claim form can as against freight, be served on the cargo concerned or the ship in which it was carried, see PD61, para. 61.3.6(1) and a warrant can be executed against the cargo or ship or both (PD61, para. 61.5.5) in the manner prescribed.

Contempt of court

2D-39   To move a ship from where she is lying with knowledge of the fact that a warrant has been issued, is contempt of Court (*The Seraglio* (1885) 10 P.D. 120) and *a fortiori* after the warrant has been served. As to various acts amounting to contempt see *The Petrel* (1836) 3 Hagg. 299; *The Bure* (1850) 14 Jur. Pt 1, 1123; *The Armenian* (Sh.Gaz. March 1874); *The Rhenania* (Sh.Gaz. November 1909); *The Selina Stanford Times*, November 17, 1908. For modern examples see *The Jarlinn* [1965] 1 W.L.R. 1098; [1965] 2 All E.R. 886; [1965] 2 Lloyd's Rep. 191; *The Jarvis Brake* [1976] 2 All E.R. 886; [1976] 2 Lloyd's Rep. 320; *The Merdeka* [1982] 1 Lloyd's Rep. 401.

It is contempt to attempt to sell a ship in respect of which an order for sale by the Court is in force (*The Jarvis Brake* [1976] 2 All E.R. 886. See also *Cerro Colorado* [1993] 1 Lloyd's Rep. 58).

Security in claim in rem[1]

2D-40   **61.6—(1) This rule applies if, in a claim in rem, security has been given to—**

> **(a) obtain the release of property under arrest; or**
>
> **(b) prevent the arrest of property.**

> **(2) The court may order that the—**
>
> > **(a) amount of security be reduced and may stay the claim until the order is complied with; or**
> >
> > **(b) claimant may arrest or re-arrest the property proceeded against to obtain further security.**

(3) The court may not make an order under paragraph (2)(b) if the total security to be provided would exceed the value of the property at the time—

> **(a) of the original arrest; or**
>
> **(b) security was first given (if the property was not arrested).**

Rule 61.6.2(b)

2D-41   In *The Prinsengracht* [1993] 1 Lloyd's Rep. 41, applying *The Arctic Star*, *The Times*, February 5, 1985; it was held that arrest or re-arrest after security is given and before

---

[1] Amended by Civil Procedure (Amendment No. 5) Rules 2001 (S.I. 2001 No. 4015).

judgment is to be viewed in the light of whether the arrest or re-arrest is oppressive and vexatious in the circumstances of the particular case.

Cautions against arrest[1]

61.7—**(1) Any person may file a request for a caution against** 2D–42 **arrest.**

(2) **When a request under paragraph (1) is filed the court will enter the caution in the Register if the request is in the form set out in the practice direction and—**

(a) **the person filing the request undertakes—**

(i) **to file an acknowledgment of service; and**

(ii) **to give sufficient security to satisfy the claim with interest and costs; or**

(b) **where the person filing the request has constituted a limitation fund in accordance with Article 11 of the Convention on Limitation of Liability for Maritime Claims 1976[2] he—**

(i) **states that such a fund has been constituted; and**

(ii) **undertakes that the claimant will acknowledge service of the claim form by which any claim may be begun against the property described in the request.**

(3) **A caution against arrest—**

(a) **is valid for 12 months after the date it is entered in the Register; but**

(b) **may be renewed for a further 12 months by filing a further request.**

(4) **Paragraphs (1) and (2) apply to a further request under paragraph (3)(b).**

(5) **Property may be arrested if a caution against arrest has been entered in the Register but the court may order that—**

(a) **the arrest be discharged; and**

(b) **the party procuring the arrest pays compensation to the owner of or other persons interested in the arrested property.**

Rule 61.7(2)(b)

The 1976 Convention is now to be found in Sched.7 to the Merchant Shipping Act   2D–43
1995.

Entry of caution against arrest

The entry of a caution does not in fact prevent the issue or execution of a warrant   2D–44 of arrest but a person who causes property to be arrested despite the existence of a caution and without good and sufficient reason may be ordered to pay damages. See r.61.7(5).

Withdrawal of caution against arrest

If a cautioner wishes to withdraw a current caution against arrest, application for   2D–44A

---

[1] Amended by Civil Procedure (Amendment No. 5) Rules 2001 (S.I. 2001 No. 4015).

[2] The text of the Convention is set out in Schedule 7 to the Merchant Shipping Act 1995 (c.21).

such withdrawal must be made to the Court, "The Iberian Ocean" (October 25, 2002, Admiralty Court).

Release and cautions against release[1]

2D–45   61.8—(1) Where property is under arrest—

    (a) an in rem claim form may be served upon it; and

    (b) it may be arrested by any other person claiming to have an in rem claim against it.

(2) Any person who—

    (a) claims to have an in rem right against any property under arrest; and

    (b) wishes to be given notice of any application in respect of that property or its proceeds of sale,

may file a request for a caution against release in the form set out in the practice direction.

(3) When a request under paragraph (2) is filed, a caution against release will be entered in the Register.

(4) Property will be released from arrest if—

    (a) it is sold by the court;

    (b) the court orders release on an application made by any party;

    (c)

        (i) the arresting party; and

        (ii) all persons who have entered cautions against release

file a request for release in the form set out in the practice direction; or

    (d) any party files—

        (i) a request for release in the form set out in the practice direction (containing an undertaking); and

        (ii) consents to the release of the arresting party and all persons who have entered cautions against release.

(5) Where the release of any property is delayed by the entry of a caution against release under this rule any person who has an interest in the property may apply for an order that the person who entered the caution pay damages for losses suffered by the applicant because of the delay.

(6) the court may not make an order under paragraph (5) if satisfied that there was good reason to—

    (a) request the entry of; and

    (b) maintain

the caution.

(7) Any person—

[1] Amended by Civil Procedure (Amendment No. 5) Rules 2001 (S.I. 2001 No. 4015).

(a) **interested in property under arrest or in the proceeds of sale of such property; or**

(b) **whose interests are affected by any order sought or made,**

may be made a party to any claim in rem against the property or proceeds of sale.

(8) **Where—**

  (a)

   (i) **a ship is not under arrest but cargo on board her is; or**

   (ii) **a ship is under arrest but cargo on board her is not; and**

  (b) **persons interested in the ship or cargo wish to discharge the cargo,**

they may, without being made parties, request the Marshal to authorise steps to discharge the cargo.

(9) **If—**

  (a) **the Marshal considers a request under paragraph (8) reasonable; and**

  (b) **the applicant gives an undertaking in writing acceptable to the Marshal to pay—**

   (i) **his fees; and**

   (ii) **all expenses to be incurred by him or on his behalf**
   on demand,

the Marshall will apply to the court for an order to permit the discharge of the cargo.

(10) **Where persons interested in the ship or cargo are unable or unwilling to give an undertaking as referred to in paragraph (9)(b), they may—**

  (a) **be made parties to the claim; and**

  (b) **apply to the court for an order for—**

   (i) **discharge of the cargo; and**

   (ii) **directions as to the fees and expenses of the Marshal with regard to the discharge and storage of the cargo.**

Caution against release—General note

A caution under this paragraph may be entered by any person, whether he has **2D–46** begun a claim against the property under arrest (or the proceeds of sale) or not. A person entering a caution whose claim carries no maritime lien should consider the desirability of issuing a claim *in rem* in addition, to entering a caution because, if the *res* is sold by the owner while under arrest, the claimant's remedy against that *res* will be lost, though he may in some circumstances be able to proceed in a claim against a "sister ship". See SCA 1981, s.21(4). The effect of entering a caution is to prevent the release of the property or payment out of the proceeds of sale without the consent of the person entering a caution or order of the Court. See rr.61.8(2) and 61.8(4). A party applying for an order for release or payment out notwithstanding the existence of a caution, should serve the application notice on any persons entering a caution. The principle is "no caution, no notice". All arrestors should consider advisability of entering caution.

Use of the caution procedure normally makes it unnecessary for a claimant in a claim *in rem* against property which is under arrest in another claim to issue a warrant

ADMIRALTY

for the arrest of that property. A claimant who has issued a claim *in rem* against a ship which is under arrest and has entered a caution under this paragraph will be considered as a secured creditor for the purpose of deciding whether or not the discretion of the court should be exercised in his favour under s.231 of the Companies Act 1948 (now Insolvency Act 1986, s.130) (*Re Aro Co Ltd* [1980] Ch. 196; [1980] 1 All E.R. 1067, CA).

Release of property in usual case

2D–47   The owner may obtain the consent of the arresting party to the release by giving security to his satisfaction. There are many forms of security accepted but in almost all cases the arresting party is satisfied with a guarantee or undertaking given out of court, *e.g.* by the Defendant's P & I Club or by a bank or insurance company. Payment into court is sometimes used. Bail by bond is now a rarity.

The arresting party is "entitled to sufficient security to cover the amount of his claim with interest and costs on the basis of his reasonably arguable best case". (*The Moscanthy* [1971] 1 Lloyd's Rep. 37 at 44). Where the right to limit liability under the Merchant Shipping Acts is not disputed it seems that the proper amount is the limitation figure with interest and costs. It seems also that in no case can the amount exceed the value of the *res*. See *The Charlotte* [1920] P. 78. Where there is a dispute as to the amount of security to be provided, an application can be made to the court to determine the amount. See, for example, *The Moscanthy* [1971] 1 Lloyd's Rep. 37. The application should normally be made to the Admiralty Registrar by application notice in the claim asking for the release of the property upon provision of security for a stated amount. Where security has been provided in an excessive amount *e.g.*, in order to obtain the prompt release of the property, an application may be made to the court for reduction of the amount of security.

It is, of course, always open to a party not to provide security and to allow his property to remain under arrest.

A party demanding excessive security may have to pay (1) the costs of a successful application to reduce the amount of that security and (2) the expense of providing the excess. Further as to security and release see British Shipping Laws, Vol. 1. The power to exact security must not be used oppressively; where there is a genuine dispute or discussion about the appropriate amount, the party seeking security ought to put his cards on the table and explain to the other party or his solicitors the grounds on which he claims to exercise this strong power: (*The Moscanthy* [1971] 1 Lloyd's Rep. 37 at 46–47).

Letters of undertaking

2D–48   See *C Itoh & Co. Ltd v. Campanhia De Navegaçao Lloyd Brasileiro and Steamship Mutual Underwriting Association (Bermuda) Ltd* [1999] 1 Lloyd's Rep. 115; *Same v. Republic Federativa Do Brasil (The Rio Assu) (No. 2)* [1999] 1 Lloyd's Rep. 115, CA held *inter alia* that on the true construction of the letter of undertaking the liability of the demise charterers' P & I Club under the letter of undertaking survived the demise of the demise charterer of the vessel.

See too *Galaxy Energy International Ltd & Another v. Assuranceforeningen Skuld (The Oakwell)* [1999] 1 Lloyd's Rep. 249 held *inter alia* that on a true construction of the letter of undertaking the obligation to instruct solicitors to accept service of the claim was unaffected by the fact that the vessel had been sold post provision of the letter and before proceedings issued.

Release when claim stayed

2D–49   In *The Bazias 3, The Bazias 4* [1993] Q.B. 673; [1993] 2 W.L.R. 854; [1993] 1 Lloyd's Rep. 101, the Court of Appeal held that the effect of section 26 of the Civil Jurisdiction and Judgments Act 1982 was to assimilate *in rem* proceedings in the Admiralty Court with arbitration claims so that the discretion to release an arrested vessel was the same in both cases. Accordingly on an application to release a vessel held as security for a claim in arbitration the court would in accordance with the usual practice only exercise its discretion to release on provision of sufficient security to cover the claim, plus interest and costs on the basis of the claimant's reasonably arguable best case. Inconvenience and difficulty in finding sufficient liquid financial resources were not sufficient grounds for departing from the usual practice. There would be no cross-undertaking as to damages under s.26(2). The court granted a stay of action under s.1 of the Arbitration Act 1975 and ordered both vessels to remain under arrest pending further order.

Release by setting aside warrant of arrest

E.g. where the declaration leading to warrant of arrest contains material inaccuracies relating to the statutory requirements set out in PD 61, para. 61.5.3 and arrest cannot be validly maintained: in *The Varna* [1993] 2 Lloyd's Rep. 253, CA, the Court held that beyond the establishment of the facts then required by O.75, r.5(9) and now by PD 61, para. 61.5.3 there was no further scope for an attack upon the issue not being a discretionary remedy. The Court of Appeal, however, stated that a warrant might be set aside as a result of the claim *in rem* being struck out or the proceedings stayed and that there might be a general discretionary power on a with notice application to set aside the warrant on the basis that its continuance was in all the circumstances unjust.

2D–50

Release pursuant to Merchant Shipping Act 1995

Section 185 and Sched.7 provide that the Court may, and in certain circumstances must, order the release of a ship or other property which has been arrested, or the security given to prevent, or obtain release from, arrest. See also *The Putbus* [1969] P. 136; [1969] 2 All E.R. 676; [1969] 1 Lloyd's Rep. 253, CA).

2D–51

Rule 61.8(5)

For cases see *The Cormer* (1863) Br. & L. 161; *The Don Ricardo* (1880) 5 P.D. 121; 4 Asp. M.L.C. 225.

2D–52

Rule 61.8(7)

The object of this provision is to enable a person who has a substantial interest in the *res* to intervene, if this interest may be injuriously affected by the claim against the *res* and to protect his interests (*The Dowthorpe* (1843) 2 W.Rob. 73, 77). The rights of an intervener are limited to the protection of his interest in the *res*, and he has no *locus standi* to raise issues which are not material to his purpose (*The Lord Strathcona* [1925] P. 143; see also *The Byzantion* (1922) 127 L.T. 756; 16 Asp. M.L.C. 19, as to defences which an intervener may and those which he may not set up). Application is to the Admiralty Registrar.

2D–53

Inherent jurisdiction

The Court has inherent jurisdiction to allow a person who has no interest in the property under arrest to intervene, if the effect of the arrest is to cause him serious hardship, difficulty or danger (*The Mardina Merchant* [1975] 1 W.L.R. 147; [1974] 3 All E.R. 749; [1974] 2 Lloyd's Rep. 424, in which the interests of a harbour authority were adversely affected by the presence of the arrested ship at one of their quays).

As to intervention for the purpose of applying to be added as a defendant or for other purposes see CPR, r.19.

2D–54

Judgment in default[1]

61.9—(1) In a claim in rem (other than a collision claim) the claimant may obtain judgment in default of—

    (a) an acknowledgment of service only if—

        (i) the defendant has not filed an acknowledgment of service; and

        (ii) the time for doing so set out in rule 61.3(4) has expired; and

    (b) defence only if—

        (i) a defence has not been filed; and

        (ii) the relevant time limit for doing so has expired.

(2) In a collision claim, a party who has filed a collision statement of case within the time specified by rule 61.4(5) may obtain judgment in default of a collision statement of case only if—

2D–55

---

[1] Amended by Civil Procedure (Amendment No. 5) Rules 2001 (S.I. 2001 No. 4015).

    (a) **the party against whom judgment is sought has not filed a collision statement of case; and**

    (b) **the time for doing so set out in rule 61.4(5) has expired.**

(3) **An application for judgment in default—**

    (a) **under paragraph (1) or paragraph (2) in an in rem claim must be made by filing—**

        (i) **an application notice as set out in the practice direction;**

        (ii) **a certificate proving service of the claim form; and**

        (iii) **evidence proving the claim to the satisfaction of the court; and**

    (b) **under paragraph (2) in any other claim must be made in accordance with Part 12 with any necessary modifications.**

(4) **An application notice seeking judgment in default and, unless the court orders otherwise, all evidence in support, must be served on all persons who have entered cautions against release on the Register.**

(5) **The court may set aside or vary any judgment in default entered under this rule.**

(6) **The claimant may apply to the court for judgment against a party at whose instance a notice against arrest was entered where—**

    (a) **the claim form has been served on that party;**

    (b) **the sum claimed in the claim form does not exceed the amount specified in the undertaking given by that party in accordance with rule 61.7(2)(a)(ii); and**

    (c) **that party has not fulfilled that undertaking within 14 days after service on him of the claim form.**

Arrest of the res

2D–56   The rule does not require the arrest of the *res* as a condition precedent to judgment in default (*The Nautik* [1895] P. 121).

Practice

2D–57   It should be noted that before judgment in default can be obtained under this provision there must be adduced "evidence proving the claim to the satisfaction of the Admiralty Court". See rule 61.9(3). It is therefore necessary for the claimant's case to be properly proved.

    The usual practice is for evidence to be given by affidavit or certified statements and the Court usually refuses to allow oral evidence to be adduced. See *The Nettuno*, Lloyd's List and Shipping Gazette, January 30, 1969.

    The application notice and any evidence should be filed in the registry in good time in order that figures, etc. may be checked there before the hearing. If this is done it may be possible to obtain judgment for a specified sum and so avoid the expense of a reference. Any document in a foreign language must be accompanied by a translation which must itself be proved. If an order for appraisement and sale (rule 61.10 below) is desired this should be stated in the application notice.

Priorities

2D–58   If cautions have been entered under rule 61.8(2) any decree made on the hearing of the application for judgment will usually reserve all questions of priorities. As to the determination of priorities and orders that may be made in connection therewith on an application for a judgment under this rule, see r.61.10.

Payment out of proceeds of sale

See r.61.10(5) below.   **2D–59**

Setting aside judgment

It is not necessary for the defendant to have acknowledged service of the claim   **2D–60**
form when applying to set aside a judgment given in default (*The Ruben Martinez Vil-
lena* [1987] 1 Lloyd's Rep. 621).

Rule 61.10—Sale by the court, priorities and payment out

**61.10—(1)An application for an order for the survey, appraise-   2D–61
ment or sale of a ship may be made in a claim in rem at any stage
by any party.**

(2) **If the court makes an order for sale, it may—**

    (a) **set a time within which notice of claims against the
proceeds of sale must be filed; and**

    (b) **the time and manner in which such notice must be
advertised.**

(3) **Any party with a judgment against the property or proceeds
of sale may at any time after the time referred to in paragraph (2)
apply to the court for the determination of priorities.**

(4) **An application notice under paragraph (3) must be served
on all persons who have filed a claim against the property.**

(5) **Payment out of the proceeds of sale will be made only to
judgment creditors and—**

    (a) **in accordance with the determination of priorities; or**

    (b) **as the court orders.**

Res must be under arrest

The *res* must be in the hands of the Court before an order for sale will be made   **2D–62**
(*The Wexford* (1888) 13 P.D. 10) but in special circumstances an order for arrest, appraisement and sale may be made where it is not (*The Berriz* 1905 Fo. 497). In *The Ri-
cuna* 1974 Fo. 380 (unrep.) the practice of requiring that the *res* be under arrest in the
claim in which an order for appraisement and sale is sought was approved. The power
of the court in an Admiralty claim to order a court sale cannot be invoked in a claim *in
personam* (*The Lady Tahilla* [1967] 1 Lloyd's Rep. 591 at 601). Appraisement and sale
may be ordered *pendente lite*. As to the circumstances in which such an order will be
made see *The Myrto* [1977] 2 Lloyd's Rep. 243 at 259. Such a sale was ordered on the
defendant's application in *The Westport (No. 1)* [1965] 1 W.L.R. 796.

The Court may order a sale by the Admiralty Marshal without Appraisement to a
specific buyer for a specific price.

An order for appraisement and sale however can only be made in claim in which
the property is under arrest. Therefore, if the arresting claimant is dilatory or does
not proceed with his claim it will become necessary for the claimant in a second or
subsequent claim to issue a warrant and procure its execution so as to be in a position
when he moves for judgment to apply for an order for appraisement and sale. The
costs of a second or subsequent arrest are not normally allowed except in such
circumstances.

Property not under arrest

If a ship under arrest is being adversely affected by property on board (*e.g.*   **2D–63**
perishables) which is not under arrest, an order, if granted, may include an order for
sale of that property.

Sale in foreign currency

The Admiralty Marshal may if he thinks fit in order to obtain the best price in any   **2D–64**
particular case, invite offers and sell the property for a price in a foreign currency (*The
Halcyon the Great* [1975] 1 W.L.R. 515; [1975] 1 All E.R. 882; [1975] 1 Lloyd's Rep.
518).

Rule 61.10(3)

2D–65   An application under this paragraph should be made in the claim brought by the applicant. Notice of application must be served on all persons who have obtained judgment against the ship and on all cautioners. The names and addresses for service of these persons can be obtained from the Admiralty and Commercial Registry.

Note

2D–66   As to priorities, see *British Shipping Laws, McGuffie: Admiralty Practice* and Halsbury's *Laws of England*; and Meeson, *Admiralty Jurisdiction and Practice*. See also as to variation of order determining priorities, *The Fairport (No. 4)* [1967] 1 W.L.R. 964; [1967] 2 All E.R. 914n; [1967] 1 Lloyd's Rep. 602. For examples of subrogation of mortgagees to the rights and priorities of master and crew upon payment, *with permission of the court*, by the mortgagees of the master's and crew's wages, see *The Berostar* [1970] 2 Lloyd's Rep. 403 and *The Vasilia* [1972] 1 Lloyd's Rep. 51.

In *The Ruta* [2000] 1 W.L.R. 2068; [2001] 1 All E.R. 450, it was held that questions of priority were not capable of being compartmentalised in the form of strict rules of ranking, since the courts had adopted a broad discretionary approach, rival claims being ranked by reference to considerations of equity, public policy and commercial expediency, with the ultimate aim of doing that which was just in the circumstances of each case; and that, since the wage claimants had no alternative form of redress against the vessel owners and the only remedy open to them was to recover their unpaid wages from the proceeds of sale of the vessel, considerations of public policy justified according them a very high level of priority, giving them precedence over the damage claims and the contractual claim of the caveator.

Payment out from proceeds of sale under rule 61.10(3) and (4)

2D–67   The Court has no jurisdiction to order payment out from the proceeds of a sale by order of the Court, to persons other than judgment holders or, in the case of the residue after all claims have been satisfied, the defendant (*The Saxon King* 1975 Fo. 253 (unrep.)). Exceptionally, payment out may be ordered to any person where the defendants and all other parties interested in the proceeds of sale (judgment holders, interveners and caveators) consent (*The Valiant* 1977 Fo. 446 (unrep.)). A payment out on account may be ordered where all parties consent, or where the priorities are such that it is clear the claimant will ultimately be entitled to at least the amount ordered. See *The Reina (No. 2)* [1963] 2 Lloyd's Rep. 513.

Charging and stop orders

2D–68   Payment out from proceeds of sale may be affected by a charging order or stop order pursuant to CPR Pt 74 or an application or order under CPR Pt 72, r.72.10.

Note

2D–69   As to apportionment of a payment in a salvage action, see *The Talamba and the Troll* [1965] P. 433; [1965] 2 All E.R. 775; [1965] 2 Lloyd's Rep. 128.

In particular, note the observations of Sheen J. in *The Vasili Shelgunov* [1988] 2 Lloyd's Rep. 34, at 38 in relation to Admiralty claims *in personam*. Approved by Court of Appeal [1989] 1 Lloyd's Rep. 542, CA.

Limitation claims[1]

2D–70   **61.11—(1) This rule applies to limitation claims.**

(2) A claim is started by the issue of a limitation claim form as set out in the practice direction.

          (3) The—
                    (a) claimant; and
                    (b) at least one defendant
must be named in the claim form, but all other defendants may be described.

---

[1] Amended by Civil Procedure (Amendment No. 5) Rules 2001 (S.I. 2001 No. 4015).

(4) The claim form—

    (a) must be served on all named defendants and any other defendant who requests service upon him; and

    (b) may be served on any other defendant.

(5) The claim form may not be served out of the jurisdiction unless—

    (a) the claim falls within section 22(2)(a), (b) or (c) of the Supreme Court Act 1981[1];

    (b) the defendant has submitted to or agreed to submit to the jurisdiction of the court; or

    (c) the Admiralty Court has jurisdiction over the claim under any applicable Convention; and

the court grants permission in accordance with Section III of Part 6.

(6) An acknowledgment of service is not required.

(7) Every defendant upon whom a claim form is served must—

    (a) within 28 days of service file—

        (i) a defence; or

        (ii) a notice that he admits the right of the claimant to limit liability; or

    (b) if he wishes to—

        (i) dispute the jurisdiction of the court; or

        (ii) argue that the court should not exercise its jurisdiction,

file within 14 days of service (or where the claim form is served out of the jurisdiction, within the time specified in rule 6.22) an acknowledgment of service as set out in the practice direction.

(8) If a defendant files an acknowledgment of service under paragraph (7)(b) he will be treated as having accepted that the court has jurisdiction to hear the claim unless he applies under Part 11 within 14 days after filing the acknowledgment of service.

(9) Where one or more named defendants admits the right to limit—

    (a) the claimant may apply for a restricted limitation decree in the form set out in the practice direction; and

    (b) the court will issue a decree in the form set out in the practice direction limiting liability only against those named defendants who have admitted the claimant's right to limit liability.

(10) A restricted limitation decree—

    (a) may be obtained against any named defendant who fails to file a defence within the time specified for doing so; and

    (b) need not be advertised, but a copy must be served on the defendants to whom it applies.

[1] 1981 c.54.

(11) Where all the defendants upon whom the claim form has been served admit the claimant's right to limit liability—

    (a) the claimant may apply to the Admiralty Registrar for a general limitation decree in the form set out in the practice direction; and

    (b) the court will issue a limitation decree.

(12) Where one or more of the defendants upon whom the claim form has been served do not admit the claimant's right to limit, the claimant may apply for a general limitation decree in the form set out in the practice direction.

(13) When a limitation decree is granted the court—

    (a) may—

        (i) order that any proceedings relating to any claim arising out of the occurrence be stayed;

        (ii) order the claimant to establish a limitation fund if one has not been established or make such other arrangements for payment of claims against which liability is limited; or

        (iii) if the decree is a restricted limitation decree, distribute the limitation fund; and

    (b) will, if the decree is a general limitation decree, give directions as to advertisement of the decree and set a time within which notice of claims against the fund must be filed or an application made to set aside the decree.

(14) When the court grants a general limitation decree the claimant must—

    (a) advertise it in such manner and within such time as the court directs; and

    (b) file—

        (i) a declaration that the decree has been advertised in accordance with paragraph (a); and

        (ii) copies of the advertisements.

(15) No later than the time set in the decree for filing claims, each of the defendants who wishes to assert a claim must file and serve his statement of case on—

    (a) the limiting party; and

    (b) all other defendants except where the court orders otherwise.

(16) Any person other than a defendant upon whom the claim form has been served may apply to the court within the time fixed in the decree to have a general limitation decree set aside.

(17) An application under paragraph (16) must be supported by a declaration—

    (a) stating that the applicant has a claim against the claimant arising out of the occurrence; and

    (b) setting out grounds for contending that the claimant is not entitled to the decree, either in the amount of limitation or at all.

(18) **The claimant may constitute a limitation fund by making a payment into court.**

(19) **A limitation fund may be established before or after a limitation claim has been started.**

(20) **If a limitation claim is not commenced within 75 days after the date the fund was established—**

    (a) **the fund will lapse; and**

    (b) **all money in court (including interest) will be repaid to the person who made the payment into court.**

(21) **Money paid into court under paragraph (18) will not be paid out except under an order of the court.**

(22) **A limitation claim for—**

    (a) **a restricted decree may be brought by counterclaim; and**

    (b) **a general decree may only be brought by counterclaim with the permission of the court.**

Limitation Claim

For definition see rule 61.1(2)(e). These claims are assigned to the Queen's Bench Division and taken by the Admiralty Court, see rule 61.2(1)(c). See also SCA 1981, s.20(1)(b) and (3)(c). Limitation of liability may be relied on by way of defence to a claim or counterclaim. **2D–71**

A limitation decree or declaration can be granted before liability is established. The establishment of liability either by trial or agreement is not a precondition to the seeking and granting of a limitation decree or declaration, see *Bouygues Offshore S.A. v. Caspian Shipping Co and Others* [1998] 2 Lloyd's Rep. 461. See further *The "Western Regent"* [2005] EWHC 240 (Admlty); [2005] 2 Lloyd's Rep 54 at para. 20:

"...an ability to constitute a limitation fund under Article 11.1 of the 1976 Convention is neither a pre-condition of the jurisdiction to hear and determine a limitation claim nor of the power given to the Court in an appropriate case to grant a limitation decree." (Affirmed [2005] EWCA Civ 985; [2005] 2 Lloyd's Rep 359, CA)

In *Herceg Novi (Owners) v. Ming Galaxy (Owners)* [1998] 4 All E.R. 238; [1998] 2 Lloyd's Rep. 454, CA, the Court held that the 1976 Convention was not an internationally sanctioned and objective view of where substantial justice was viewed as lying, but was simply the view of some 30 states. Moreover, the preference for the 1976 Convention had no greater justification than for the 1957 regime and, in terms of abstract justice, neither convention was objectively more just than the other. Accordingly, since substantial justice would be done in Singapore, the appeal would be allowed and an unconditional stay of the English action would be granted.

In *MSC Mediterranean Shipping Co SA v. Delmur BVBA and others (The Rosa M)* [2000] 2 All E.R. (Comm) 458, the court held that for it to be established that the claimant's liability was not limited under Art.4 of the Convention, it was necessary for the defendant to prove that the casualty was caused by the personal act or omission of the charterers, that those personal acts or omissions were committed recklessly and at the time of those acts or omissions the *alter ego* of the charterers actually knew that the casualty would probably result. In the absence of any allegation of intent, the authorities made it clear that a person challenging the right to limit had to establish both reckless conduct and knowledge that the relevant loss would probably result, and "shut-eye" knowledge did not constitute "knowledge" for the purposes of Art.4, which required actual knowledge. This approach has been affirmed by the Court of Appeal in *The Leerort* [2001] 2 Lloyd's Rep. 291, the court holding that it is only the personal act or omission of a shipowner which defeats the right to limit. A shipowner is defined in art 1 as the owner, charterer, manager or operator of a seagoing ship. Thus, to defeat the right to limit, it is necessary to identify the causative act or omission on the part of such a person that caused the loss. Furthermore, it is only conduct committed with intent to cause such loss, or recklessly with knowledge that such loss would probably result, that defeats the right to limit. It seems that person challenging the right to limit

ADMIRALTY

must establish both reckless conduct *and* knowledge that the relevant loss would probably result. In considering the relevant loss the court continued that it seems that
where the loss in respect of which a claim is made resulted from a collision between
ship A and ship B, the owners of ship A, or cargo in ship A, will only defeat the right
to limit liability on the owner of ship B if they can prove that the owner of ship B
intended that it should collide with ship A, or acted recklessly with the knowledge that
it was likely to do so (para. 13).

The alternative, which is perhaps arguable, is that the claimant merely has to prove
that the owner of ship B intended that his ship should collide with another ship, or
acted recklessly with the knowledge that it was likely to do so (*ibid*, para. 17).

On the facts of this case it is not necessary to decide which alternative is correct. In
either event the reality is that when damage results from a collision the shipowner will
only lose his right to limit if it can be proved that he deliberately or recklessly acted in
way which he knew was likely to result in the loss of or damage to the property of another in circumstances where, inevitably, the same consequences would be likely to
flow to his own vessel (*ibid*, para. 18).

Article 2.1(a) of the 1976 Convention does not extend the right to limit to a claim
for damage to the vessel by reference to the tonnage of which limitation is to be
calculated, see *CMA CGM SA v. Classica Shipping Co Ltd (The CMA Djakarta)* [2004]
EWCA Civ 114; [2004] 1 Lloyd's Rep. 460, CA. Nor does the Convention provide for
a limitation on liablity for the costs of litigation, see *Thompson v. Masterton* [2004] 1
Lloyd's Rep 304 [Roy. Ct. Guernsey]. See too *Newcastle Port Corp v. Pevitt (The Robert
Whitmore)* [2004] 2 Lloyd's Rep. 47 (NSWSC), fund is exclusive of costs

Claim Form
2D-72 Special Admiralty Forms, Admiralty Limitation claim form, see the Civil Procedure
Forms Volume.

Service
2D-73 The claim form must be served on all named defendants in the claim form and not
merely described. As to service out of the jurisdiction see r.61.11(5).

In the *ICL Shipping Ltd v. Chin Tai Steel Enterprise Co Ltd (The ICL Vikraman)* [2003]
EWHC 2320; [2004] 1 W.L.R. 2254; [2004] 1 Lloyd's Rep. 21 the Court held that in
CPR, r.61.11(5)(c) the "claim" referred to is the claim to limit rather than any underlying claim and the words "any applicable convention" should be construed as covering
the 1976 Convention. This case also concerns the construction and scope of Arts 11
and 13 of the 1976 Convention.

Restricted decree
2D-74 When a claimant in a limitation claim is satisfied that there will be no claims upon
the fund other than the claims of the defendants who have acknowledged issue or service of the claim form the claimant may not want a decree which is good against the
world. The claimant may apply to the Admiralty Registrar to amend the claim form by
deleting reference to any defendants other than those named. The application should
be accompanied by a letter signed by all consenting parties stating that in their view it
is not anticipated that any further claims will emerge. The Registrar may then order
payment out of the limitation fund in Court.

If further claimants do emerge after payment out the claimant will be obliged to
constitute a new fund should they wish to limit their liability against the new claimants.
This practice arises from a decision of Sheen J. in an unreported case (*The Rena* [1979]
Fo. 138).

Owner-master
2D-75 As to the right of an owner-master to limit his liability, see *The Annie Hay* [1968] P.
341; [1968] 1 All E.R. 657; [1968] 1 Lloyd's Rep. 141.

Charterers
2D-76 Charterers cannot limit their liability under the 1976 Convention in respect of
claims brought by owners against them: see *Aegean Sea Traders Corporation v. Repsol Pe-
troleo SA and Another* [1998] 2 Lloyd's Rep. 39. See further *CMA CGM SA v. Classica
Shipping Co Ltd (The CMA Djakarta)* [2004] EWCA Civ 114; [2004] 1 Lloyd's Rep. 460,
CA. The term charterers is to be given its ordinary meaning. Accordingly, the

charterer's ability to limit will depend on the type of claim brought against him and not the capacity (*e.g.* qua owner) in which he was acting when his liability was incurred.

Costs of application

The costs of an application for a decree of limitation under the former s.17 of the   **2D–77**
Merchant Shipping Act 1979, now s.185 of the Merchant Shipping Act 1995, should normally follow the event, see *The Capitan San Luis* [1994] Q.B. 465; [1994] 2 W.L.R. 465; [1994] 2 W.L.R. 299; [1994] 1 All E.R. 1016; [1993] 2 Lloyd's Rep. 573. In this case it was held that the shipowners should pay the costs of proving the matters which he had to establish in order to obtain the decree and that the claimant should pay the costs of investigating and determining the facts which the Convention provided he must prove, if at the end of the day he failed to establish those facts.

Rule 61.11.13(a)(iii)

It seems that in a distribution pursuant to this paragraph, the court would order   **2D–78**
interest accrued on the limitation fund in court to be apportioned *pro rata* to the distribution.

Stay of proceedings[1]

61.12 Where the court orders a stay of any claim in rem—   **2D–79**

(a) any property under arrest in the claim remains under arrest; and

(b) any security representing the property remains in force,

unless the court orders otherwise.

Assessors[2]

61.13 The court may sit with assessors when hearing—   **2D–80**

(a) collision claims; or

(b) other claims involving issues of navigation or seamanship, and

the parties will not be permitted to call expert witnesses unless the court orders otherwise.

Assessors

In the specified cases, nautical assessors usually advise the Court of Appeal and the   **2D–81**
Judge of the Admiralty Court upon questions of navigation and seamanship if such questions arise. In some cases only one nautical assessor is called in and occasionally their attendance is dispensed with altogether. In the Admiralty Court, the assessors are usually two of the Elder Brethren of Trinity House neither of whom should have been in the service of any party to the claim (*The Bremen* (1931) 47 T.L.R. 505) save where an Elder Brother is a retired officer of the Royal Navy and one of H.M. ships is involved. If Trinity House is a party, one or two of such Court of Appeal assessors as are not Elder Brethren may be called on. Where nautical assessors are present, evidence in the nature of expert opinion on matters of nautical skill and practice, and as to the deductions to be drawn from nautical facts, is usually inadmissible (*The Gazelle* (1842) 1 W.Rob. 471). In *The St Chad* [1965] 2 Lloyd's Rep. 1, affirming; [1965] 1 Lloyd's Rep. 107, however, an order made provided for a fishery assessor to assist the court and also for each side to be at liberty to call an experienced trawler skipper to give general evidence on the system of work in trawlers of the relevant type, as the system was said to have changed so recently that the new developments might be outside the practical experience of a fishery assessor. A comparable order was made in

---

[1] Amended by Civil Procedure (Amendment No. 5) Rules 2001 (S.I. 2001 No. 4015).

[2] Amended by Civil Procedure (Amendment No. 5) Rules 2001 (S.I. 2001 No. 4015).

ADMIRALTY

The Bedford Earl 1954 Fo. 218 (unrep.), but this case never came to trial. As to the Court of Appeal, see para. 9A–275.

See generally CPR, r.35.15 and Practice Direction—Experts and Assessors para. 6.1 at 35–006 and the Admiralty and Commercial Courts Guide, section N.14 and para. 2D–134 below.

Assessors may be called in to assist the Registrar at a reference, see PD61 para. 13.3. The function of nautical assessors is to advise the court upon nautical matters (*The City of Berlin* [1908] P. 110; see *The New Pelton* [1891] P. 258; *The River Derwent* (1891) 7 Asp. 467). There is no right of cross-examination. The decision of the case rests entirely with the judge (*The Gannet* [1900] A.C. 234; *Owners of SS. Australia v. Owners of SS. Nautilus* [1927] A.C. 145; *Owners of S.S. Melanie v. Owners of SS. San Ono-fre (No. 1)* [1927] A.C. 162n; *Owners of SS. Artemisia v. Owners of S.S. Douglas* [1927] A.C. 164n); this equally applies in the Court of Appeal (*The Llanelly* (1926) 25 Ll.L.Rep. 37, p.39, HL) and House of Lords (*The Marinegra* [1960] 2 Lloyd's Rep. 1). Even in purely nautical matters the judge is not bound to follow the advice of his assessors, if it does not agree with his own opinion (see *The Magna Charta* (1872) 1 Asp. 153; *The Aid* (1881) 6 P.D. 84; *The Beryl* (1884) 9 P.D. 137, 141; *The Swanland* (1855) 2 Sp. 107; *The Fred* (1895) 7 Asp. 550; *Owners of SS. Melanie v. Owners of SS. San Onofre (No. 1)*; *Owners of SS. Australia v. Owners of Cargo of SS. Nautilus*, above; *The Spero* (1948) 81 Ll.L.Rep. 350 at 354 see *The British Resource* (1941) 70 Ll.L.Rep. 93 at 102, *per* du Parcq L.J., and *The Carrick Coast* (1948) 81 Ll.L.Rep. 447 at 451, *per* Willmer J.) as to judging ordinary navigating officers by the exceptionally high standard of knowledge and experience of the Elder Brethren. The assessors should not be asked any question that is tantamount to asking them whether they would find for the claimant or the defendant (see *The Ausomia* (1920) 2 L.L.Rep. 123 at 124, HL). The assessors in an appeal court are not substituted for those previously consulted. They are additional but not to be preferred to them unless the advice given is such as in itself is more acceptable to the appellate court (*The Sobieski* (1949) 82 Ll.L.Rep. 370 at 379). There is no question of appeal from one set of assessors to another set (*Owners of SS. Australia v. Owners of Cargo of SS. Nautilus*. See also *The Fina Canada* [1962] 2 Lloyd's Rep. 445). In *The St Chad* [1965] 2 Lloyd's Rep. 1, CA, Willmer L.J. pointed out that nautical assessors in the Court of Appeal and the court below were of equal standing. He also said that it was their function to advise on nautical questions put to them by the court whether or not such question had been canvassed by counsel. If there is a difference of opinion between assessors and a judge cannot decide which advice is sound he must regard the point as not proven (see *The Dageld* (1947) 80 Ll.L.Rep. 517, reversing (1947) 80 Ll.L.Rep. 225 at 230; *Owners of S.S. Australiav. Owners of Cargo of SS. Nautilus*) but he may reach a decision by rejecting the advice of one assessor and accepting that of the other (see *The Taiwan* (1947) 80 Ll.L.Rep. 580 at 586).

In order to comply with Art.6(1) of the European Convention for the Protection of Human Rights and Fundamental Freedoms when a Court has received evidence from an assessor it is appropriate, except in cases where such discussion is unnecessary in the light of submissions made earlier, that the preferable modern practice of putting questions to the assessors after discussion with counsel should be complemented by a practice of disclosing their answers to counsel, either orally or in writing—in order that any inappropriate submission can be made as to whether the judge should accept this advice, *Owners of the Bow Spring v. Owners of the Manzanillo* [2004] EWCA Civ 1007; [2005] 1 W.L.R. 144; [2004] 4 All E.R. 899; [2005] 1 Lloyd's Rep 1, CA.

The Court of Appeal has been known to adopt the advice of Elder Brethren in the lower court, rejecting that of their own assessors (*The Sobieski*, above; see also *The Mira-flores and The Abadesa* [1966] P. 18; [1966] 1 All E.R. 553; [1966] 1 Lloyd's Rep. 97 at 108, *per* Willmer L.J. A judge will not infrequently state in his judgment that he has sought advice on certain points, giving the results of having done so without detail, and saying whether he accepts or rejects the advice tendered (contrast *The Aurelian* [1957] 2 Lloyd's Rep. 417 at 422, where Willmer J. set out verbatim in his judgment the questions put to the Elder Brother). Questions and answers are in writing in the Court of Appeal.

As to assessors' fees, see para. 2D–134 below; *mutatis mutandis* the fees in the High Court and CA are the same.

PRACTICE DIRECTION—ADMIRALTY CLAIMS
This Practice Direction supplements CPR Part 61

Scope

1.1 The Practice Direction supplementing Part 58 (Commercial **2D–82** Claims) also applies to Admiralty claims except where it is inconsistent with Part 61 or this practice direction.

Admiralty and Commercial Registry

RCJ Room EB13 (Tel. 020 7947 6112). Hours: 10.00–16.30. See PD to CPR Part 2, **2D–83** at 2PD.2.

Inquiries as to practice may be made in person or by telephone. The Admiralty and Commercial Registry was initially established by *Practice Direction* [1987] 3 All E.R 616 issued by the Lord Chief Justice with the concurrence of the Admiralty judge and the judge in charge of the Commercial List. In relation to Admiralty and Commercial matters it replaces and carries out all the functions of the Central Office including the issuing of processes. Fees are paid to the Supreme Court Accounts Office, but the Registry may accept payment of a fee for a single item by way of a Solicitor's cheque.

Issue of claim form by fax

See Practice Direction—Commercial Court, para. 2.2 and Appendix A thereto.   **2D–84**

Use of postal facilities in the Registry

Section N12 of the Admiralty and Commercial Courts Guide provides as follows: **2D–84A**
N12.1 Applications together with the requisite documents may be posted to:
> The Admiralty and Commercial Registry,
> Room EB13,
> Royal Courts of Justice,
> Strand,
> London WC2 2LL.

N12.2 In addition to the classes of business for which the use of postal facilities is permitted by the CPR or the Commercial Court Guide, the filing of the following classes of documents is also permitted in Admiralty matters:
> (i) Requests for cautions;
> (ii) Collision Statements of Case

N12.3
> (a) Documents sent by post for filing must be accompanied by two copies of a list of the documents sent and an envelope properly addressed to the sender.
> (b) On receipt of the documents in the Registry, the court officer will, if the circumstances are such that had the documents been presented personally they would have been filed, cause them to be filed and will, by post, notify the sender that this has been done. If the documents would not have been accepted if presented personally the court officer will not file them but will retain them in the Registry for collection by the sender and will, by post, so inform the sender.
> (c) When documents received through the post are filed by the court officer they will be sealed and entered as filed on the date on which they were received in the Registry.

Issuance of Admiralty Claim Forms and Warrants of Arrest out of High Court District Registries post March 25, 2002

It is not intended that the facility to issue Admiralty Claim Forms and Warrants of **2D–84B** Arrest from District Registries of the High Court be removed under the new Part 61 and its associated Practice Direction. This facility should be continued. There must however be prior consultation with the Admiralty Marshal before any Warrant of Arrest is issued as has happened hitherto and the Court file must be sent immediately upon the issue of the Claim Form and any Warrant of Arrest to the Admiralty and Commercial Registry at the Royal Courts of Justice as before in order that the

ADMIRALTY

Admiralty Registrar may issue case management directions as required by the new Admiralty Practice Direction.

In so far as the new rule and Practice Direction read in conjunction with Part 58 and its Practice Direction provide that such facilities are to be provided out of the Admiralty and Commercial Registry the issuing District Registry will be deemed as providing the same on behalf of the Admiralty and Commercial Registry so long as the procedure outlined above is followed. District Registry numbering will continue to be used in the first place on issue. (Admiralty Registrar, March 18, 2002).

Case management

2D–85   **2.1** After a claim form is issued the Registrar will issue a direction in writing stating—

   (1) whether the claim will remain in the Admiralty Court or be transferred to another court; and

   (2) if the claim remains in the Admiralty Court–

      (a) whether it will be dealt with by–

         (i) the Admiralty judge; or

         (ii) the Registrar; and

      (b) whether the trial will be in London or elsewhere.

2.2 In making these directions the Registrar will have regard to–

   (1) the nature of the issues and the sums in dispute; and

   (2) the criteria set in rule 26.8 so far as they are applicable.

2.3 Where the Registrar directs that the claim will be dealt with by the Admiralty judge, case management directions will be given and any case management conference or pre-trial review will be heard by the Admiralty judge.

Application to Judge and to Admiralty Registrar

2D–86   Any party wishing to make an application to an Admiralty Judge should apply to the Admiralty and Commercial Registry (Listing Office) where all necessary arrangements will be made. Applications to the Admiralty Registrar should be applied for in the Admiralty and Commercial Registry (General Office).

Claims in rem

2D–87   **3.1** A claim form in rem must be in Form **ADM1**.

3.2 The claimant in a claim in rem may be named or may be described, but if not named in the claim form must identify himself by name if requested to do so by any other party.

3.3 The defendant must be described in the claim form.

3.4 The acknowledgment of service must be in Form **ADM2**. The person who acknowledges service must identify himself by name.

3.5 The period for acknowledging service under rule 61.3(4) applies irrespective of whether the claim form contains particulars of claim.

3.6 A claim form in rem may be served in the following ways:

   (1) on the property against which the claim is brought by fixing a copy of the claim form–

      (a) on the outside of the property in a position which may reasonably be expected to be seen; or

      (b) where the property is freight, either–

         (i) on the cargo in respect of which the freight was earned; or

(ii) on the ship on which the cargo was carried;

(2) if the property to be served is in the custody of a person who will not permit access to it, by leaving a copy of the claim form with that person;

(3) where the property has been sold by the Marshal, by filing the claim form at the court;

(4) where there is a notice against arrest, on the person named in the notice as being authorised to accept service;

(5) on any solicitor authorised to accept service;

(6) in accordance with any agreement providing for service of proceedings; or

(7) in any other manner as the court may direct under rule 6.8 provided that the property against which the claim is brought or part of it is within the jurisdiction of the court.

3.7 In claims where the property—

(1) is to be arrested; or

(2) is already under arrest in current proceedings,

the Marshal will serve the in rem claim form if the claimant requests the court to do so.

3.8 In all other cases in rem claim forms must be served by the claimant.

3.9 Where the defendants are described and not named on the claim form (for example as "the Owners of the Ship X"), any acknowledgment of service in addition to stating that description must also state the full names of the persons acknowledging service and the nature of their ownership.

3.10 After the acknowledgment of service has been filed, the claim will follow the procedure applicable to a claim proceeding in the Commercial list except that the claimant is allowed 75 days to serve the particulars of claim.

3.11 A defendant who files an acknowledgment of service to an in rem claim does not lose any right he may have to dispute the jurisdiction of the court (see rule 10.1(3)(b) and Part 11).

3.12 Any person who pays the prescribed fee may, during office hours, search for, inspect and take a copy of any claim form in rem whether or not it has been served.

Amendment of claim form

Where after the issue of a claim in an action *in rem* the defendants' vessel is sold, the title of the defendants should be amended to read "The Owners of the ship X, now named Y". (*The Mawan* [1988] 2 Lloyd's Rep. 459 at 460.)   **2D–88**

Paragraph 61.3.6(3)

The property must have been sold by the court and part of the proceeds of sale must still be in court. Where property has been sold by an agent who retains the proceeds, a claim form cannot be served on those proceeds (*The Optima* (1905) 74 L.T.P. 94; *The Fornjot* (1907) 24 T.L.R. 26). In *The Eva* (1950) 84 Ll.L.R. 20 wartime compensation money was held not to be a *res* or represent a *res*.   **2D–89**

Collision claims

4.1 A collision statement of case must be in Form **ADM3**.   **2D–90**

4.2 A collision statement of case must contain—

(a) in Part 1 of the form, answers to the questions set out in that Part; and

(b) in Part 2 of the form, a statement—

    (i) of any other facts and matters on which the party filing the collision statement of case relies;

    (ii) of all allegations of negligence or other fault which the party filing the collision statement of case makes; and

    (iii) of the remedy which the party filing the collision statement of case claims.

4.3 When he files his collision statement of case each party must give notice to every other party that he has done so.

4.4 Within 14 days after the last collision statement of case is filed each party must serve a copy of his collision statement of case on every other party.

4.5 Before the coming into force of Part 61, a collision statement of case was known as a Preliminary Act and the law relating to Preliminary Acts will continue to apply to collision statements of case.

Arrest

2D–91   **5.1** An application for arrest must be—

    (1) in Form **ADM4** (which must also contain an undertaking); and

    (2) accompanied by a declaration in Form **ADM5**.

5.2 When it receives an application for arrest that complies with the rules and the practice direction the court will issue an arrest warrant.

5.3 The declaration required by rule 61.5(3)(b) must be verified by a statement of truth and must state—

    (1) in every claim–

        (a) the nature of the claim or counterclaim and that it has not been satisfied and if it arises in connection with a ship, the name of that ship;

        (b) the nature of the property to be arrested and, if the property is a ship, the name of the ship and her port of registry; and

        (c) the amount of the security sought, if any.

    (2) in a claim against a ship by virtue of section 21(4) of the Supreme Court Act 1981—

        (a) the name of the person who would be liable on the claim if it were not commenced in rem;

        (b) that the person referred to in sub-paragraph (a) was, when the right to bring the claim arose

            (i) the owner or charterer of; or

            (ii) in possession or in control of,

        the ship in connection with which the claim arose; and

        (c) that at the time the claim form was issued the person referred to in sub-paragraph (a) was either—

            (i) the beneficial owner of all the shares in the ship in respect of which the warrant is required; or

            (ii) the charterer of it under a charter by demise;

    (3) in the cases set out in rules 61.5(5) and (6) that the relevant notice has been sent or served, as appropriate; and

(4) in the case of a claim in respect of liability incurred under section 153 of the Merchant Shipping Act 1995, the facts relied on as establishing that the court is not prevented from considering the claim by reason of section 166(2) of that Act.

5.4 The notice required by rule 61.5(5)(a) must be in Form **ADM6**.

5.5 Property is arrested—

(1) by service on it of an arrest warrant in Form **ADM9** in the manner set out at paragraph 3.6(1); or

(2) where it is not reasonably practicable to serve the warrant, by service of a notice of the issue of the warrant—

(a) in the manner set out in paragraph 3.6(1) on the property; or

(b) by giving notice to those in charge of the property.

5.6 When property is arrested the Registrar will issue standard directions in Form **ADM10**.

5.7 The Marshal does not insure property under arrest.

Specific Applications

An application to move a vessel under arrest (see r.61.5(9)) or to sell the same below the appraised value are made to the Admiralty Registrar or as he may direct.   **2D–92**

As to the practice to be followed by the Marshal when a ship is under arrest and a harbour or dock authority claims or purports to exercise a statutory power of detention or sale in respect of unpaid dock dues, see *The Queen of the South* [1968] P. 449; [1968] 1 All E.R. 1163; [1968] 1 Lloyd's Rep. 182 and *The Freightline One* [1986] 1 Lloyd's Rep. 266. In *The Girl Irene* [1991] Fo. 774; (unrep.), the court directed that the Marshal was to follow the same practice in respect of a claim by Trinity House for unpaid light dues. Where some doubt arises as to the right of a harbour or dock authority to detain a ship, that authority should seek a declaration from the court (*The Baltico* (1982) H. No. 140. Hartlepool District Registry).

Mooring charges do not constitute "ship dues" within the meaning of s.26(3) of the Harbours Act 1964 and as defined by s.57(1) of the 1964 Act. Accordingly there is no power to distain for non-payment of mooring charges under s.44 of the Harbours, Docks and Piers Clauses Act 1847: see *R. v. Carrick District Council, Ex p. Prankerd (The Winnie Rigg)* [1998] 2 Lloyd's Rep. 675; [1999] Q.B. 1119.

As to applications to discharge cargo where ship or cargo is under arrest, see r.61.8(8) and (9).

Applications under r.61.5(4) and (6) are made without notice to the Admiralty Registrar.

Insurance premiums

Premiums paid by claimants to insure their interest in arrested property were held in *The Fairport* [1965] 2 Lloyd's Rep. 183 at 186, to be recoverable as costs but not to constitute a head of claim under A.J.A. 1956, s.1 (see now SCA 1981, s.20).   **2D–93**

Insurance of arrested property

Section N13 of the Admiralty and Commercial Courts Guide provides as follows: **2D–94**

N13.1 The Marshal will not insure any arrested property for the benefit of parties at any time during the period of arrest (whether before or after the lodging of an application for sale, if any).

N13.2 The Marshal will use his best endeavours (but without any legal liability for failure to do so) to advise all parties known to him as being on the record in actions in rem against the arrested property, including those who have filed cautions against release of that property, before any such property moves or is moved beyond the area covered by the usual port risks policy.

N13.3 In these circumstances, practitioners' attention is drawn to the necessity of considering the questions of insuring against port risks for the amount of their clients' interest in any property arrested in an Admiralty action and the inclusion in any policy of a "Held Covered "clause in case the ship moves or is moved outside the area

ADMIRALTY

covered by the usual port risks policy. The usual port risks policy provides, among other things, for a ship to be moved or towed from one berth to another up to a distance of five miles within the port where she is lying.

Declarations

2D–95   As to the contents of these declarations see PD61, para. 61.5.3 above.

Para. 61.5.3 "... her port of registry ..."

2D–96   The object of this requirement is to minimise the risk of the arrest of a different ship bearing the same name as the ship intended to be arrested. If the port of registry is not known this should be stated in the declaration.

Practice

2D–97   The declaration, warrant and a copy of it are taken to or transmitted to the Admiralty and Commercial Registry and a search of the Register requested. A clerk in the Registry will search the Register and inform the applicant whether a caution against arrest of the property is in force. If there is no caution against arrest in force or if it is desired to issue a warrant despite the existence of a caution, the declaration is filed and the warrant and copy lodged. The proper officer, if he is satisfied that the declaration complies with the requirements of this rule (or if permission to issue despite non-compliance has been given) will issue the warrant. The warrant and copy are retained in the Registry.

False or inaccurate statement in declaration to lead warrant of arrest

2D–98   If the statutory requirements set out in para. 61.5.3 are complied with then there is no further scope for the application of any duty of full and frank disclosure see *The Varna* [1993] 2 Lloyd's Rep. 253 but as to such statutory requirements it is the duty of a declarant to correct promptly and frankly any false or inaccurate statement that he finds he has made in his declaration (*The Nordglimt* [1988] Q.B. 183; [1987] 2 Lloyd's Rep. 470).

Cautions against arrest

2D–99   **6.1** The entry of a caution against arrest is not treated as a submission to the jurisdiction of the court.

6.2 The request for a caution against arrest must be in form ADM7.

6.3 On the filing of such a request, a caution against arrest will be entered in the Register.

6.4 The Register is open for inspection when the Admiralty and Commercial Registry is open.

Para. 61.6.2 and 3 "... the Register..."

2D–100   There is only one book in which all cautions in Admiralty are entered; it is kept in the Admiralty and Commercial Registry at the Royal Courts of Justice in London where all cautions must be entered. As to cautions against arrest see r.61.7 and against release see r.61.8. As to searches see r.61.5 and PD61, para. 6.4.

Release and cautions against release

2D–101   **7.1** The request for a caution against release must be in Form **ADM11**.

7.2 On the filing of such a request, a caution against release will be entered in the Register.

7.3 The Register is open for inspection when the Admiralty and Commercial Registry is open.

7.4 A request for release under rule 61.8(4)(c) and (d) must be in Form **ADM12**.

7.5 A withdrawal of a caution against release must be in form **ADM12A**.

Application to secure release

2D–102   In cases where an applicant wishes to secure release of his property whether held at the instance of the arrestor or any person who has entered a caution, the procedure in the Admiralty and Commercial Registry will be as set out below. The purpose of this procedure is to arrange that such an application is dealt with by the tribunal likely to be able to dispose of it most expeditiously and cheaply.

(1) The application notice should be issued normally before the Registrar with the date left blank.

(2) The applicant should attend at the Admiralty and Commercial Registry upon the issue of the application notice for the purpose of obtaining a direction by the Registrar as to whether the application will be heard before the Registrar or before the judge. Unless there is attendance at the Registry the application will be issued before the Registrar.

(3) The applicant attending upon the issue of the application notice should, if it is desired that the application be heard initially by the judge, be prepared to indicate orally why the application is more suitable for the judge than the Registrar (*e.g.* substantial savings in costs or time would normally be reasons militating in favour of initial hearing by the judge).

(4) A direction as to the hearing will normally be given forthwith and date and time set for the hearing.

Release of vessels out of hours

Section N11 of the Admiralty and Commercial Courts Guide provides as follows: **2D–102.1**

N11.1 This section makes provision for release from arrest when the Registry is closed.

N11.2 An application for release under rule 61.8(4)(c) or (d) may, when the Registry is closed, be made in, and only in, the following manner:

   (i) The solicitor for the arrestor or the other party applying must telephone the security staff at the Royal Courts of Justice (020 7947 6260) and ask to be contacted by the Admiralty Marshal, who will then respond as soon as practicably possible;

  (ii) Upon being contacted by the Admiralty Marshal the solicitor must give oral instructions for the release and an oral undertaking to pay the fees and expenses of the Admiralty Marshal as required in Form **ADM12**;

 (iii) The arrestor or other party applying must then send a written request and undertaking on Form **ADM12** by fax to a number given by the Admiralty Marshal;

 (iv) The solicitor must provide written consent to the release from all persons who have entered cautions against release (and from the arrestor if the arrestor is not the party applying) by sending such consents by fax to the number supplied by the Admiralty Marshal;

  (v) Upon the Admiralty Marshal being satisfied that no cautions against release are in force, or that all persons who have entered cautions against release, and if necessary the arrestor, have given their written consent to the release, the Admiralty Marshal shall effect the release as soon as practicable.

N11.3 Practitioners should note that the Admiralty Marshal is not formally on call and therefore at times may not be available to assist. Similarly the practicalities of releasing a ship in some localities may involve the services of others who may not be available outside court hours.

N11.4 This service is offered to practitioners for use during reasonable hours and on the basis that if the Admiralty Marshal is available and can be contacted he will use his best endeavours to effect instructions to release but without guarantee as to their success.

Withdrawal of cautions

A caution against release may be withdrawn by lodging a written request in Form   **2D–103**
ADM12A (see para. 7.5 above). Where a solicitor acts for more than one cautioner and wishes to withdraw some or all of their cautions, this may be done by a single request, adapted as necessary.

"... the Register..."

See under para. 2D–100 above.   **2D–104**

Judgment in default

8.1 An application notice for judgment in default must be in form   **2D–105**
ADM13.

ADMIRALTY

Sale by the court and priorities

2D–106 **9.1** Any application to the court concerning–

(1) the sale of the property under arrest; or

(2) the proceeds of sale of property sold by the court

will be heard in public and the application notice served on–

(a) all parties to the claim;

(b) all persons who have requested cautions against release with regard to the property or the proceeds of sale; and

(c) the Marshal.

9.2 Unless the court orders otherwise an order for sale will be in form **ADM14**.

9.3 An order for sale before judgment may only be made by the Admiralty judge.

9.4 Unless the Admiralty judge orders otherwise, a determination of priorities may only be made by the Admiralty judge.

9.5 When—

(1) proceeds of sale are paid into court by the Marshal; and

(2) such proceeds are in a foreign currency,

the funds will be placed on one day call interest bearing account unless the court orders otherwise.

9.6 Unless made at the same time as an application for sale, or other prior application, an application to place foreign currency on longer term deposit may be made to the Registrar.

9.7 Notice of the placement of foreign currency in an interest bearing account must be given to all parties interested in the fund by the party who made the application under paragraph 9.6.

9.8 Any interested party who wishes to object to the mode of investment of foreign currency paid into court may apply to the Registrar for directions.

Court Fees on Sale

2D–106A On the sale of a ship or goods —

Subject to a minimum fee of £200,

(a) for every £100 or fraction of £100 of the price up to £100,000.   £1

(b) for every £100 or fraction of £100 of the price exceeding £100,000 . . . .   50p

Where there is sufficient proceeds of sale in court, fee 5.2 shall be taken by transfer from the proceeds of sale in court.

(See item 5.2 of Supreme Court Fees Order 1999, as amended). For other related charges see paras 2D–132 and 2D–133 below.

Limitation Claims

2D–107 **10.1** The claim form in a limitation claim must be—

(1) in form **ADM15**; and

(2) accompanied by a declaration—

(a) setting out the facts upon which the claimant relies; and

(b) stating the names and addresses (if known) of all persons who, to the knowledge of the claimant, have claims against him in respect of the occurrence to which the claim relates (other than named defendants), verified by a statement of truth.

10.2 A defence to a limitation claim must be in form **ADM16A**.

10.3 A notice admitting the right of the claimant to limit liability in a limitation claim must be in form **ADM16**.

10.4 An acknowledgment of service in a limitation claim must be in form **ADM16B**.

10.5 An application for a restricted limitation decree must be in form **ADM17** and the decree issued by the court on such an application must be in form **ADM18**.

10.6 An application for a general limitation decree must be in form **ADM17A**.

10.7 Where—

(1) the right to limit is not admitted; and

(2) the claimant seeks a general limitation decree in form **ADM17A**,

the claimant must, within 7 days after the date of the filing of the defence of the defendant last served or the expiry of the time for doing so, apply for an appointment before the Registrar for a case management conference.

10.8 On an application under rule 61.11(12) the Registrar may—

(1) grant a general limitation decree; or

(2) if he does not grant a decree—

    (a) order service of a defence;

    (b) order disclosure by the claimant; or

    (c) make such other case management directions as my be appropriate.

10.9 The fact that a limitation fund has lapsed under rule 61.11(20)(a) does not prevent the establishment of a new fund.

10.10 Where a limitation fund is established, it must be—

(1) the sterling equivalent of the number of special drawing rights to which [the claimant] claims to be entitled to limit his liability under the Merchant Shipping Act 1995; together with

(2) interest from the date of the occurrence giving rise to his liability to the date of payment into court.

10.11 Where the claimant does not know the sterling equivalent referred to in paragraph 10.10(1) on the date of payment into court he may—

(1) calculate it on the basis of the latest available published sterling equivalent of a special drawing right as fixed by the International Monetary Fund; and

(2) in the event of the sterling equivalent of a special drawing right on the date of payment into court being different from that used for calculating the amount of that payment into court the claimant may—

    (a) make up any deficiency by making a further payment into court which, if made within 14 days after the payment into court, will be treated, except for the purpose of the rules relating to the accrual of interest on money paid into court, as if made on the date of that payment into court; or

    (b) apply to the court for payment out of any excess amount (together with any interest accrued) paid into court.

10.12 An application under paragraph 10.11(2)(b)—

(1) may be made without notice to any party; and

(2) must be supported by evidence proving, to the satisfaction of the court, the sterling equivalent of the appropriate number of special drawing rights on the date of payment into court.

10.13 The claimant must give notice in writing to every named defendant of—

(1) any payment into court specifying—

    (a) the date of the payment in;

    (b) the amount paid in;

    (c) the amount and rate of interest included; and

    (d) the period to which it relates; and

(2) any excess amount (and interest) paid out to him under paragraph 10.11(2)(b).

10.14 A claim against the fund must be in form **ADM20**.

10.15 A defendant's statement of case filed and served in accordance with rule 61.11(15) must contain particulars of the defendant's claim.

10.16 Any defendant who is unable to file and serve a statement of case in accordance with rule 61.11(15) and paragraph 10.15 must file a declaration, verified by a statement of truth, in form **ADM21** stating the reason for his inability.

10.17 No later than 7 days after the time for filing claims [or declarations], the Registrar will fix a date for a case management conference at which directions will be given for the further conduct of the proceedings.

10.18 Nothing in rule 61.11 prevents limitation being relied on by way of defence.

Limitation fund and interest

2D–108   Any person wishing to constitute a limitation fund must pay into Court a fund constituted in accordance with s.185 and Sched.7 of the Merchant Shipping Act 1995, together with interest thereon from the date of the occurrence giving rise to his liability until the date of the constitution of the limitation fund pursuant to para. 8(1) of Pt II of Sched.7 to the Act. The rate of interest is now fixed by the Merchant Shipping (Liability of Shipowners and Others) (Rate of Interest) Order 1999 (S.I. 1999 No. 1922), effective September 1, 1999; by the Merchant Shipping (Liability of Shipowners and Others) (Rate of Interest) (Amendment) Order 2003 (S.I. 2003 No. 3136) effective December 31, 2003 and the Merchant Shipping (Liability of Shipowners and Others) (New Rate of Interest) Order 2004 (S.I. 2004 No. 931) effective April 28, 2004.

    The rate of interest is;

    (a) where the occurrence takes place before September 1, 1999 but the fund is constituted on or after that date:

        (i) 12 per cent from the date of the occurrence until December 31, 1994;

        (ii) 6.75 per cent on and after January 1, 1995 until August 31, 1998;

        (iii) 8.5 per cent on and after September 1, 1998 until August 31, 1999, and

        (iv) the prescribed rate on and after September 1, 1999, until December 30, 2003; or

    (b) where the occurrence takes place on or after September 1, 1999, but before December 31, 2003 the prescribed rate.

    Further, article 2 of S.I. 2003 No. 3136 provides as follows:

"2. The rate of interest for the purposes of article 11(1) of the Convention on Limitation of Liability for Maritime Claims 1976 (b) shall be the prescribed rate—

(a) where the occurrence takes place before 31st December 2003, but the fund is constituted on or after that date; and

(b) where the occurrence takes place on or after 31st December 2003".

The prescribed rate is defined as one per cent more than the base rate quoted from time to time by the Bank of England or the rate of interest set by any body which may supercede it and, where there is for the time being more than one such rate, the lowest of them (Article 2 of the S.I. 2004 No. 931).

Tonnage

The limitation tonnage is usually proved in the case of a British registered ship by a certified copy of the Tonnage Certificate. As to the tonnage of ships of a foreign country which has adopted the British tonnage regulations, see Merchant Shipping Act 1995, s.12. For a list of these countries see *British Shipping Laws*, Vol. 11, under s.84 of the Merchant Shipping Act 1894, now s.12 of the 1995 Act. See too the Merchant Shipping (Liability of Shipowners and Others) (Calculation of Tonnage) Order 1986 (S.I. 1986 No. 1040); the Merchant Shipping (Tonnage) Regulations 1997 (S.I. 1997 No. 1510) and the Merchant Shipping (Tonnage) (Fishing Vessels) Amendment Regulations 1998 (S.I. 1998 No. 1916).   **2D–109**

Sterling equivalents

For ascertainment of sterling equivalents, see Sched.7, Pt II, para. 7 to the Merchant Shipping Act 1995.   **2D–110**

Paras 10.8 and 10.17 "… directions …"

An order will usually be made providing for statements of case, disclosure, and any other directions deemed necessary and the imposition of a set timetable for expeditious disposal of the matter.   **2D–111**

Proceeding against or concerning the International Oil Pollution Compensation Fund

11.1 For the purposes of section 177 of the Merchant Shipping Act 1995 ("the Act") and the corresponding provision of Schedule 4 to the Act, the Fund may be given notice of proceedings by any party to a claim against an owner or guarantor in respect of liability under—   **2D–112**

(1) section 153 or section 154 of the Act; or

(2) the corresponding provisions of Schedule 4 to the Act

by that person serving a notice in writing on the Fund together with copies of the claim form and any statements of case served in the claim.

11.2 The Fund may intervene in any claim to which paragraph 11.1 applies, (whether or not served with the notice) by serving notice of intervention on the—

(1) owner;

(2) guarantor; and

(3) court.

11.3 Where a judgment is given against the Fund in any claim under—

(1) section 175 of the Act; or

(2) the corresponding provisions of Schedule 4 to the Act,

the Registrar will arrange for a stamped copy of the judgment to be sent to the Fund by post.

11.4 Notice to the Registrar of the matters set out in-

(1) section 176(3)(b) of the Act; or

(2) the corresponding provisions of Schedule 4 to the Act,

must be given by the Fund in writing and sent to the court.

Pollution damage

2D–112A   A claim by fish processors for the loss of profitable sales of processed whelks held to be secondary, derivative, relational and/or indirect, lacking in proximity and thus too remote. The "Sea Empress", [2002] EWHC 1095 (Admiralty); [2002] 2 All E.R. (Comm) 416; [2003] 1 Lloyd's Rep. 123, applying *Landcatch Ltd v. The International Oil Pollution Compensation Fund* [1999] 2 Lloyd's Rep. 316; affirmed [2003] EWCA Civ 65 [2003] 2 All E.R. (Comm.) 1; [2003] 1 Lloyd's Rep 327, CA.

Other claims

2D–113   **12.1** This section applies to admiralty claims which, before the coming into force of Part 61, would have been called claims in personam. Subject to the provisions of Part 61 and this practice direction relating to limitation claims and to collision claims, the following provisions apply to such claims.

12.2 All such claims will proceed in accordance with Part 58 (Commercial Court).

12.3 The claim form must be in Form **ADM1A** and must be served by the claimant.

12.4 The claimant may be named or may be described, but if not named in the claim form must identify himself by name if requested to do so by any other party.

12.5 The defendant must be named in the claim form.

12.6 Any person who files a defence must identify himself by name in the defence.

Claims in personam (now called other claims)

2D–114   An Admiralty action *in personam* is like an action in tort or contract in the QBD. It differs from such an action however in that it is subject to the rules of this order which modify those applicable to an ordinary QB action, *e.g.* collision cases, r.61.4 and the application of Pt 58 thereto unless inconsistent with Pt 61 and this practice direction.

Duration of Admiralty Claim in personam (other claims) for service out of the jurisdiction

2D–115   The period of validity of a claim form *in personam* in admiralty proceedings for service out of the jurisdiction is six months.

References to the Registrar

2D–116   **13.1** The court may at any stage in the claim refer any question or issue for determination by the Registrar (a "reference").

13.2 Unless the court orders otherwise, where a reference has been ordered—

(1) if particulars of claim have not already been served, the claimant must file and serve particulars of claim on all other parties within 14 days after the date of the order; and

(2) any party opposing the claim must file a defence to the claim within 14 days after service of the particulars of claim on him.

13.3 Within 7 days after the defence is filed, the claimant must apply for an appointment before the Registrar for a case management conference.

General note

2D–117   It is the long-established practice of the Admiralty Court after liability has been determined, to refer to the Admiralty Registrar the matter of the assessment of the amount of the claimant's claim and of the counterclaim if there be one. There is, however, no rule that the assessment of damages must be referred (*The Fremantle* [1954] 2 Lloyd's Rep. 20) and in personal injury and Fatal Accidents Acts cases it is not unusual for the judge to assess damages. See, *e.g. Connell v. Hellyer Brothers Ltd* [1963] 2 Lloyd's Rep. 249; *The St Chad (No. 2)* [1965] 2 Lloyd's Rep. 347.

Questions of amount have occasionally been referred before trial. (See, *e.g. The Happy Return* (1828) 2 Hagg. 198 at 207) but this has not been done for many years. In *The Lathara* (1930) 37 Ll.L.Rep. 160, it seems that all issues in the claim were referred to the Registrar.

Where the assessment of damages involves a question of causation this is in some cases decided by the judge at the trial or thereafter. See, *e.g. The Maid of Kent* (1881) 6 P.D. 178, *The Guildford* [1956] 2 Lloyd's Rep. 74; *The Lucile Bloomfield* [1967] 2 Lloyd's Rep. 308. If it is desired to have such questions decided by the judge at the trial this matter should be raised on the case management conference. In exercising its discretion the Court will be guided by the consideration whether the matter is one which can better be dealt with by the Court at the trial, or later at the reference (*The Maid of Kent* (1881) 6 P.D. 178, *ibid.*).

Assessors

In modern practice the Registrar decides questions without the assistance of merchants. Nautical and other assessors, however, are sometimes appointed. If the parties agree in desiring the Registrar to sit with a merchant (the full title is "merchant assessor") or other assessor, they should apply by letter to the Admiralty and Commercial Registry. In the event of disagreement between the parties an application should be made on notice.

2D–118

How references may rise

A reference may arise out of the judgment or decree made on the trial or the hearing of an application; out of the decree in a limitation claim made on the hearing of an application under r.61.11, or an order on a consent application.

Where in an action *in personam* (other claim) judgment in default is entered "for an amount of money to be decided by the Court" there can be no reference and the assessment is governed by CPR, r.12.7.

2D–119

Claim in reference. See para. 13.2 above

The claim referred to in this provision should in the first place state in a few words how the claim arises; thus in a collision claim it would begin with a short statement giving the date of the collision, the voyage on which the vessel was engaged, and, if she was repaired, the place and date and duration of such repair. In every case the several heads of claim should then be set out and numbered consecutively. It is not correct and is confusing, to call the claim a statement of case. It is a claim in a reference. For content and format of forms of claim see *Atkin's Encyclopaedia of Court Forms in Civil Proceedings*, Vol. 3, Form 181 (2003 Issue).

2D–120

Limitation references

In references in limitation claim a claimant need not serve a copy of his claim on any other party. Any claimant may, however, on the payment of the proper fee, inspect and obtain a copy of the claim and any other documents filed by any other claimant against the fund. See CPR, 5.4(1). In practice copies of these documents are supplied on request by the solicitors concerned on payment of the usual copying charges.

If any claimant wishes to dispute the claim of another he should so inform the Admiralty and Commercial Registry by letter in order that he can be given notice of the appointment fixed for the hearing of that other's claim.

In a claim arising out of a collision between ships A and B if there are cross claims and both ships have been held to blame (or the matter has been settled on a both to blame basis) and the owners of A obtain a limitation decree it may be necessary to assess their claim in order to arrive at the amount which the owners of B are entitled to claim against the fund. It will be necessary to do this if there are other claimants against the fund. See *The Stoom vart Maatschappf Nederland v. The Peninsular and Oriental Steam Navigation Co* (1882) 7 App. Cas. 795. In this event the practice is for the owners of B to put forward in their claim a deduction in respect of the appropriate

2D–121

ADMIRALTY

proportion of the damages of the owners of A as agreed or, failing agreement, estimated. This figure may be disputed by any other claimant.

Filing amended claims

2D–122 A claimant should not amend his filed claim but should file another claim in amended form. No leave is required. If, however, the alterations are of such a character and are made at such a late stage as to embarrass the paying party at the reference, the Registrar may, in his discretion, adjourn the reference or take some other course as he thinks fit.

Evidence

2D–123 The ordinary rules of evidence apply on the hearing of a reference but are, by agreement between the parties, frequently relaxed in order to save time and expense.

Proved recoverable amount

2D–124 The convention of awarding one per cent of proved recoverable amount to compensate for disruption to business and expenditure of management available to shipowners does not extend to cargo owners (*Owners of the Ship Kumanova v. Owners of the Ship Massira* [1998] 2 Lloyd's Rep. 301. The convention itself was re-affirmed in "*The Charlotte C*" [2005] 2 Lloyd's Rep 626.

Hearing; general note

2D–125 A party to a reference may be represented by counsel, solicitor, legal executive or solicitor's clerk.

If a sum has been paid into court and the award is less than the amount paid in, the party who made the payment in is entitled to an order enabling him to take the balance out of court (*The Mona* [1894] P. 265).

Inquiry regarding a shorthand record at references may be made of the Registry.

Delay; interest

2D–126 See *The Nassau* [1965] 1 Lloyd's Rep. 236 and cases cited.

Interest: date for addition

2D–127 On compromising an Admiralty claim for collision damages interest should be added to each claim before striking the balance, such balance to be struck on the date of assessment or of agreement of claims; see *The Lu Shan* [1993] 2 Lloyd's Rep. 259.

Interest in personal injury and fatal accident cases

2D–128 See SCA 1981, s.35A (see para. 9A–103).

Costs of reference

2D–129 The costs of the reference are in the Registrar's discretion. Where two vessels are held to blame in a collision claim the costs in the reference of each claimant are dealt with on the basis of the reference being a separate proceeding from the claim (*The Consett* (1880) 5 P.D. 77). As to the effect of failure to give notice of survey, see *The Solace (No. 2)* (1936) 55 Ll.L.Rep. 201. Usually where the claimant recovers a substantial proportion of the sum claimed he is given the costs of the reference, and where an offer has been made and the amount awarded in the reference is less, the offeror will usually be entitled to the costs after the offer was made (see *The Norseman* [1957] 1 Lloyd's Rep. 503; *The Reading* [1908] P. 162). If one claimant in a reference in a limitation claim puts forward a claim which is contested successfully by another, the former may be condemned to pay the costs of the successful claimant in contesting the claim, *i.e.* the costs over and above those of proving his own claim (*The Clan Canning*, 1906, Fo. 206 (unrep.)).

Undertakings

2D–130 **14.1** Where, in [Part 61] or this practice direction, any undertaking to the Marshal is required it must be given—

(1) in writing and to his satisfaction; or

(2) in accordance with such other arrangements as he may require.

14.2 Where any party is dissatisfied with a direction given by the Marshal in this respect he may apply to the Registrar for a ruling.

Note

The personal undertaking of the party's solicitor is normally given. Where the expenses of effecting or maintaining the arrest are more than minimal, successive demands are likely to be made by the Marshal beginning soon after the arrest.

2D–131

As to recovery from the proceeds of sale of sums paid to the Marshal by an arresting party, see *The Falcon* [1981] 1 Lloyd's Rep. 13. The Marshal's expenses of maintaining the arrest from the time of the order for appraisement and sale and the expenses of the sale are payable in the first instance by the party applying therefor. *The Falcon* [1981] 1 Lloyd's Rep. 13, above at 17. As to liability for the expenses of a second and subsequent arrests see *ibid.* As to recovery from the proceeds of sale of sums paid to the Marshal, insurance premiums, solicitors' costs of arrest, etc., crew's wages, interveners' costs and interest, see *The World Star* [1987] 1 Lloyd's Rep. 452.

For priorities and the method of determining the same see *British Shipping Laws*, Vol. 1, para. 1574, *The Falcon* [1981] 1 Lloyd's Rep. 13, above. *The World Star* [1987] 1 Lloyd's Rep. 452, above, and *The Rubi Sea* [1992] 1 Lloyd's Rep. 634.

The fees and commission paid by the Marshal to Brokers in addition to their reasonable expenses for carrying out a Judicial sale of a vessel are as follows:

Scale of valuation fees as from May 25, 1998

Not exceeding £20,000: £200
Exceeding £20,000: £400

2D–132

Where the condition of the ship and/or the state of the market make it advisable that there should be a dual valuation for both trading and demolition purposes the full fee will apply in respect of the valuation for trading and in addition a fee at half the above rates will apply in respect of the valuation for demolition.

Scale of Commission as from May 25, 1998

6 per cent on the first £5,000
5 per cent on the next £10,000 up to £15,000
3 per cent on the next £15,000 up to £30,000
1 per cent on the balance over £30,000.

2D–133

ADMIRALTY

REMUNERATION OF NAUTICAL AND OTHER ASSESSORS
PRACTICE DIRECTION [1994] 1 W.L.R. 599

2D–134   1.   This Practice Direction is issued by direction of the Lord Chief Justice and the Master of the Rolls.

2.   In the absence of special directions given in a particular case the remuneration payable to Trinity Masters, and nautical and other assessors summoned to assist the Court of Appeal, the Admiralty Court on the trial of an action, or a Divisional Court of the Queen's Bench Division hearing an appeal under Order 74 of [Schedule 1 of the Civil Procedure Rules] shall be:—

   (i)   For each day of the hearing (except where (ii) or (iiii) applies) £300.00

   (ii)   For a day on which the hearing finishes before the midday adjournment................ £150.00

   (iii)   For a day on which the hearing commences after the midday adjournment, the assessor not having attended, or having been engaged in another case, before such an adjournment . £150.00

   (iv)   For attending the Court on a day on which £40.00 the case is not heard.............................. per hour

   (v)   For consultation with the Court on a day on which the case is not heard £150.00

   (vi)   For attending to hear reserved judgment (including any consultation with the Court on the same say) £75.00

   (vii)   If notice of attendance is countermanded less than two days before the hearing............... £150.00

3.   Assessors shall in addition to the above scale be entitled to receive reasonable sums in respect of travelling expenses and subsistence.

4.   Where there is a cross appeal, or where appeals are heard together, or where actions are consolidated or tried together, the proceedings shall be deemed to be one appeal or action as the case may be.

5.   In the absence of special directions given in a particular case, the remuneration and expenses shall be paid by the appellant or the party setting down the action as the case may be without prejudice to any right to recover from any other party the amount so paid on taxation.

6.   This Practice Direction is to apply to all actions and appeals the hearing of which begins on or after 1st April, 1994.

USE OF CLAIM FORMS IN REM AND IN PERSONAM/OTHER CLAIMS

If it is desired to commence proceedings both *in rem* and *in personam* **2D–135**
separate claim forms must be issued.

See Practice Direction (Admiralty: [Claim Form]) [1979] 1 W.L.R.
426; [1979] 2 All E.R. 155.

TAXATION OF COSTS

At the request of the Admiralty Registrar, all costs [other than **2D–136**
those summarily assessed] in Admiralty matters will be taxed in the
Supreme Court Taxing Office.

Practice Direction (Admiralty Taxation of Costs) [1986] 1 W.L.R. 1310.

Supreme Court Act 1981

(1981 c.54)   **2D–137**

ARRANGEMENT OF SECTIONS

PART II

JURISDICTION

ADMIRALTY JURISDICTION

Introductory note

Sections 20–24 of this Act replace with amendments A.J.A. 1956, ss.1 and 3–8 as **2D–138**
amended. These sections were repealed by s.152 of and Sched.7 to this Act. Section 2
had been repealed by the Courts Act 1971, Sched.11. Amendments to ss.20–24 have
been made from time to time and latterly by and consequent upon the Merchant
Shipping Act 1995 which came into force on January 1, 1996.

The 1956 Act had replaced s.22 of the Judicature Act 1925 and extended the
Admiralty jurisdiction to give effect to much of the International Convention Relating
to the Arrest of Seagoing Ships and the International Convention on Certain Rules
concerning Civil Jurisdiction in Matters of Collision both of which were signed at
Brussels on May 10, 1952. See British Shipping Laws (Singh, International Maritime
Law Conventions (1983)) for the texts of these conventions.

Admiralty jurisdiction of High Court

2D–139   **20.**—(1) The Admiralty jurisdiction of the High Court shall be as follows, that is to say—

   (a) jurisdiction to hear and determine any of the questions and claims mentioned in subsection (2);

   (b) jurisdiction in relation to any of the proceedings mentioned in subsection (3);

   (c) any other Admiralty jurisdiction which it had immediately before the commencement of this Act; and

   (d) any jurisdiction connected with ships or aircraft which is vested in the High Court apart from this section and is for the time being by rules of court made or coming into force after the commencement of this Act assigned to the Queen's Bench Division and directed by the rules to be exercised by the Admiralty Court.

   (2) The questions and claims referred to in subsection (1)(a) are—

   (a) any claim to the possession or ownership of a ship or to the ownership of any share therein;

   (b) any question arising between the co-owners of a ship as to possession, employment or earnings of that ship;

   (c) any claim in respect of a mortgage of or charge on a ship or any share therein;

   (d) any claim for damage received by a ship;

   (e) any claim for damage done by a ship;

   (f) any claim for loss of life or personal injury sustained in consequence of any defect in a ship or in her apparel or equipment, or in consequence of the wrongful act, neglect or default of—

   (i) the owners, charterers or persons in possession or control of a ship; or

   (ii) the master or crew of a ship, or any other person for whose wrongful acts, neglects or defaults the owners, charterers or persons in possession or control of a ship are responsible.

being an act, neglect or default in the navigation or management of a ship, in the loading, carriage or discharge of goods on, in or from the ship, or in the embarkation, carriage or disembarkation of persons on, in or from the ship;

   (g) any claim for loss of or damage to goods carried in a ship;

   (h) any claim arising out of any agreement relating to the carriage of goods in a ship or to the use or hire of a ship;

   (j) any claim—

        (i) under the Salvage Convention 1989;

      (ii) under any contract for or in relation to salvage services; or

    (iii) in the nature of salvage not falling within (i) or (ii) above;

or any corresponding claim in connection with an aircraft.

  (k) any claim in the nature of towage in respect of a ship or an aircraft;

  (l) any claim in the nature of pilotage in respect of a ship or an aircraft;

(m) any claim in respect of goods or materials supplied to a ship for her operation or maintenance;

  (n) any claim in respect of the construction, repair or equipment of a ship or dock charges or dues;

  (o) any claim by a master or member of the crew of a ship for wages (including any sum allotted out of wages or adjudged by a superintendent to be due by way of wages);

  (p) any claim by a master, shipper, charterer or agent in respect of disbursements made on account of a ship;

  (q) any claim arising out of an act which is or is claimed to be a general average act;

  (r) any claim arising out of bottomry;

  (s) any claim for the forfeiture or condemnation of a ship or of goods which are being or have been carried, or have been attempted to be carried, in a ship, or for the restoration of a ship or any such goods after seizure, or for droits of Admiralty.

(3) The proceedings referred to in subsection (1)(b) are—

  (a) any application to the High Court under the Merchant Shipping Act 1995.

  (b) any action to enforce a claim for damage, loss of life or personal injury arising out of—

        (i) a collision between ships; or

      (ii) the carrying out of or omission to carry out a manoeuvre in the case of one or more of two or more ships; or

    (iii) non-compliance, on the part of one or more of two or more ships, with the collision regulations;

  (c) any action by shipowners or other persons under the Merchant Shipping Act 1995 for the limitation of the amount of their liability in connection with a ship or other property.

(4) The jurisdiction of the High Court under subsection (2)(b) includes power to settle any account outstanding and unsettled between the parties in relation to the ship, and to direct that the ship, or any share thereof, shall be sold, and to make such other order as the court thinks fit.

(5) Subsection (2)(e) extends to—

ADMIRALTY

(a) any claim in respect of a liability incurred under Chapter III of Part VI of the Merchant Shipping Act 1995; and

(b) any claim in respect of a liability falling on the International Oil Pollution Compensation Fund, or on the International Oil Pollution Compensation Fund 1992, under Chapter IV of Part VI of the Merchant Shipping Act 1995.

(6) In subsection 2(j)—

(a) the "Salvage Convention 1989" means the International Convention on Salvage, 1989 as it has effect under section 224 of the Merchant Shipping Act 1995;

(b) the reference to salvage services includes services rendered in saving life from a ship and the reference to any claim under any contract for or in relation to salvage services includes any claim arising out of such a contract whether or not arising during the provision of the services;

(c) the reference to a corresponding claim in connection with an aircraft is a reference to any claim corresponding to any claim mentioned in sub-paragraph (i) or (ii) of paragraph (j) which is available under section 87 of the Civil Aviation Act 1982.

(7) The preceding provisions of this section apply—

(a) in relation to all ships or aircraft, whether British or not and whether registered or not and wherever the residence or domicile of their owners may be;

(b) in relation to all claims, wherever arising (including, in the case of cargo or wreck salvage, claims in respect of cargo or wreck found on land); and

(c) so far as they relate to mortgages and charges, to all mortgages or charges, whether registered or not and whether legal or equitable, including mortgages and charges created under foreign law;

Provided that nothing in this subsection shall be construed as extending the cases in which money or property is recoverable under any of the provisions of the Merchant Shipping Act 1995.

Admiralty jurisdiction generally

2D–140   The Admiralty Court can entertain a claim transferred to it, though it could not have been properly instituted in that court (*The Montrosa* [1917] P. 1).

The jurisdiction *in personam* is, in collision and similar cases, restricted (see s.22 and rule 61.4(7) and rule 61.11(5) and see rule 6.20(17A). For other restrictions on the jurisdiction see paras 2D–15 *et seq*.

As to the jurisdiction to restrain by injunction an act on the high seas, see *The Tubantia* [1924] P. 78.

Specific performance may be ordered in an Admiralty claim *in rem* (or *in personam*) (*The Conoco Britannia* [1972] 2 Q.B. 543; [1972] 2 All E.R. 283; [1972] 1 Lloyd's Rep. 342).

It is now possible for a judgment creditor in a claim *in rem* to arrest both in respect of a national judgment *in rem* as well as a foreign judgment *in rem*. See rule 61.5(1) above at para. 2D–32. Formerly it was only possible to arrest to enforce a foreign judgment *in rem*, see *The Despina G.K.* [1982] 3 W.L.R. 950; [1982] 2 Lloyd's Rep. 555.

The existence of an unsatisfied judgment *in personam* or arbitration award does not prevent the bringing of a claim *in rem* on the same cause of action. See *The Rena K*

[1978] 1 Lloyd's Rep. 545 at 560 and cases there cited. See also *The Saint Anna* [1983] 1 Lloyd's Rep. 637. But see *The Bumbesti* noted at para. 2D–155 below.

Admiralty claims *in personam* are now termed "other claims". See Practice Direction—Admiralty Claims, para. 61.12.

s.20(1)(c)

Paragraph (c) of this subsection replaces the "sweeping up" provisions at the end of s.1(1) of the A.J.A. 1956. In *The Queen of the South* [1968] P. 449; [1968] 1 All E.R. 1163; [1968] 1 Lloyd's Rep. 182, Brandon J., while expressing no concluded opinion, said that it appeared that the effect of this "sweeping up" provision in the A.J.A., s.1(1) was to preserve to the court the jurisdiction over, *inter alia*, claims for what were known, before the coming into force of that Act, as "necessaries," a term not reproduced in it. **2D–141**

Construction of paragraphs (a)-(s)

Where any provision of this Act which appears to be intended to give effect to the Arrest Convention of 1952 is capable of more than one meaning the court may look at the Convention in order to gain assistance in deciding which meaning is to be preferred. See *The Eschersheim* [1975] 1 W.L.R. 83 at 89; [1974] 3 All E.R. 307 at 314; [1974] 2 Lloyd's Rep. 188 at 192 and cases there cited. See also [1976] 1 W.L.R. 430 at 434; [1976] 1 All E.R. 920 at 924; [1976] 2 Lloyd's Rep. 1 at 6, HL(E). **2D–142**

As to resort to the *travaux préparatoires* of the Convention as an aid to interpretation, see *Gatoil International Inc v. Arkwright-Boston Manufacturers Mutual Insurance Co* [1985] A.C. 255; [1985] 1 All E.R. 129, HL(Sc).

Paragraph "(2)(a) any claim to the possession or ownership of a ship or to the ownership of any share therein ..." — Jurisdiction

Jurisdiction to hear a claim for a declaration that the plaintiff is entitled to be registered as the owner of a British ship is given by this paragraph (*The Bineta* [1966] 2 Lloyd's Rep. 419). **2D–143**

"Ship"

See s.24(1), para. 2D–188. See too s.313 of the Merchant Shipping Act 1995 which replaces s.742 of the Merchant Shipping Act 1894 and the cases cited in British Shipping Laws, (Temperley, *Merchant Shipping Acts* (7th ed., 1976)) under s.742 of the Merchant Shipping Act 1894. A sailing dinghy used on a reservoir for pleasure was held not to be a "vessel in navigation" within s.742 aforesaid, see *Curtis v. Wild* [1991] 4 All E.R. 172; and a jet-ski was held not to be "a ship", see *Steedman v. Scofield* [1992] 2 Lloyd's Rep. 163. See also the Hovercraft Act 1968, s.2(1), paras 2D–215 and 2D–216. **2D–144**

Foreigners

The court has jurisdiction to entertain a claim between foreigners as to possession of a ship within the jurisdiction, see subs.(7)(a). But it seems it may refuse to adjudicate (*The Jupiter (No. 2)* [1925] P. 69, CA). **2D–145**

Paragraph "(2)(b) any question arising between the co-owners of a ship as to possession, employment or earnings of that ship"

Note —This paragraph must be read with subs.(4) of this section. **2D–146**

Paragraph "(2)(c) any claim in respect of a mortgage of or charge on a ship or any share therein"

Note —See also subs.(7)(c), which provides that this paragraph shall apply to all mortgages and charges on ships. As to the meaning of "charge" see the note to s.21, paras 2D–169 to 2D–180. **2D–147**

As to the circumstances in which a mortgagee can recover payments made by him for insurance of the mortgaged ship, see *The Basildon* [1967] 2 Lloyd's Rep. 134.

Paragraph "(2)(d) any claim for damage received by a ship"

Note —This includes damage done by something other than a ship; see *Mersey Docks* **2D–148** *and Harbour Board v. Turner, The Zeta* [1893] A.C. 469 (collision with pierhead); *The Upcerne* [1912] P. 160 (collision with gas buoy).

Section 21, which provides for the mode of exercise of Admiralty jurisdiction, makes no provision for proceedings *in rem* in respect of claims falling within this paragraph. In practice, many such claims will fall within para. (2)(e) also.

Paragraph "(2)(e) any claim for damage done by a ship"

2D–149   *Note* —This paragraph must be read with subs.(5), which extends it to certain claims in connection with oil pollution.

Damage done by a ship carries a maritime lien in the usual case; this is subject, however, to exceptions, *e.g.* no lien attaches under present law to a government ship.

"Done by a ship"

2D–150   "The figurative phrase 'damage done by a ship' is a term of art in maritime law whose meaning is well settled by authority (*The Vera Cruz (No. 2)* (1884) 9 P. D. 96; *Currie v. M'Knight* [1897] A.C. 97). To fall within the phrase not only must the damage be the direct result or natural consequence of something done by those engaged in the navigation of the ship but the ship itself must be the actual instrument by which the damage was done. The commonest case is that of collision, which is specifically mentioned in the Convention: but physical contact between the ship and whatever object sustains the damage is not essential—a ship may negligently cause a wash by which some other vessel or some property on shore is damaged." *per* Lord Diplock, *The Eschersheim* [1976] 1 W.L.R. 430 at 438; [1976] 1 All E.R. 920 at 926; [1976] 2 Lloyd's Rep. 1 at 8. See also the judgments in the Court of Appeal [1976] 1 W.L.R. 339; [1976] 1 All E.R. 441; [1976] 1 Lloyd's Rep. 81. See also *The Minerva* [1933] P. 224; 46 Ll.L.Rep. 212 (part of a ship's derrick fell damaging a barge alongside); *The Chr. Knudsen* [1932] P. 153; 43 Ll.L.Rep. 423 (damage to dock by barge being sunk in it) and *The Dagmara and Ama Antxine* [1988] 1 Lloyd's Rep. 431(claimant's vessel forced to leave fishing grounds due to alleged dangerous navigation of defendant's vessel).

See too *The Rama* [1996] 2 Lloyd's Rep. 281; damages for deceit and/or for negligent misrepresentation in relation to a charterparty where the ship was not the active cause of the damage or the noxious instrument or the instrument in the physical sense of the loss was not damage done by a ship within s.20(2)(e) so as to give rise to a maritime lien.

Paragraph "(2)(f) any claim for loss of life or personal injury"

2D–151   *Note* —This paragraph should be read together with subs.(1)(b) and subs.(3)(b).

Paragraph "(2)(g) any claim for loss of or damage to goods carried in a ship" — "Loss"

2D–152   It is arguable that "loss" is wide enough to include a claim for conversion against a carrier (*The Wildgans*, 1976, Fo. 947).

"Goods"

2D–153   "Goods" includes baggage, see s.24(1), para. 2D–188. The term "baggage," however, covers the baggage of passengers or travellers only. The belongings of those on board a ship as employees of the shipowners in order to man and operate her are not baggage nor are they goods under this paragraph. (*The Eschersheim* [1975] 1 W.L.R. 83; [1974] 3 All E.R. 307; [1974] 2 Lloyd's Rep. 188).

The claims of crew members for lost or damaged belongings will in many cases come within para. (2)(e).

Paragraph "(2)(h) any claim arising out of any agreement relating to the carriage of goods in a ship or to the use or hire of a ship"

2D–154   *Note* —Although this paragraph is in different terms from s.22(1)(a) (xii) of the J.A. 1925, which it replaces, it is wide enough to cover claims, whether in contract or in tort, arising out of any agreement relating to the carriage of goods in a ship (*The St Elefterio* [1957] P. 179; [1957] 2 All E.R. 374; [1957] 1 Lloyd's Rep. 283). This case was followed in *The Moscanthy* [1971] 1 Lloyd's Rep. 37.

An agreement for the payment of premiums on an insurance policy over goods to be carried by sea is not connected with the carriage of goods in a ship in a sufficiently direct sense to be capable of coming within this paragraph. See *Gatoil International Inc v. Arkwright-Boston Manufacturers Mutual Insurance Co* [1985] A.C. 255; [1985] 1 All E.R. 129, HL(Sc.). See also *The Sea Friends* [1991] 2 Lloyd's Rep. 322.

An agreement for the hire by shipowners of containers to be carried in a ship is not within this paragraph (*ibid.*, at pp.263, 271 and 131, 137 of the respective reports). (See also the note to para. (m)). Nor is a claim on a salvage agreement for damages for breach of an undertaking to obtain security from cargo owners. (*The Tesaba* [1982] 1 Lloyd's Rep. 397, which is referred to in *Gatoil* above at pp.263, 268 and 131, 135 of the respective reports).

"Arising out of"

These words are to be given the wider meaning of "connected with" and not the narrower meaning of "arising under" (*The Antonis P. Lemos* [1985] A.C. 711; [1985] 1 All E.R. 695; [1985] 1 Lloyd's Rep. 283, HL). In *The Hamburg Star* [1994] 1 Lloyd's Rep. 399 claims for indemnity and contribution under the Civil Liability (Contribution) Act 1978 were held to be claims arising out of an agreement for carriage of containers and their contents.

2D–155

In *The Bumbesti* [2000] Q.B. 559; [1999] 2 Lloyd's Rep. 481, the Court held (*inter alia*) that the claim was an action on an arbitration award and arose out of an agreement to refer disputes which had arisen under a bare-boat charterparty and that such agreement to refer was not "an agreement in relation to the use and hire of a ship" but one distinct from the principal contract, *i.e.* the bare-boat charterparty. Accordingly the claim did not fall within subsection (h).

"Goods"

See note to para. (2)(g).

2D–156

"Use or hire"

In deciding whether a particular agreement is an agreement relating to the use of a ship or not the court will look at the substances of the matter. See *The Eschersheim*, para. 2D–142 in which it was held that a salvage agreement on Lloyd's form was, on the facts of that case, an agreement for the use of a ship.

2D–157

In *The Stella Nora*, 1981, Com.L.R. 200 it was held that a management agreement, which provided that the managers would be solely entitled to enter into charterparties for the owners of the ship they were to manage, was an agreement relating to the use or hire of that ship.

To come within this paragraph the claim need not have its origin in an agreement between the claimant and the defendant (*The Antonis P. Lemos* [1985] A.C. 711; [1985] 1 All E.R. 695; [1985] 1 Lloyd's Rep. 283, HL).

Paragraph "(2)(j) any claim ... Salvage Convention 1989 ..."

Note —Derivation— s.1(6) and Sched.2 of the Merchant Shipping (Salvage and Pollution) Act 1994. The 1994 Act was repealed by the Merchant Shipping Act 1995 with saving and amendment of this provision and providing by s.224 the enactment of the Salvage Convention 1989 with a commencement date of January 1, 1995.

2D–158

This paragraph must be read together with subss.(6) and (7)(b).

See, generally, British Shipping Laws (Kennedy, *Civil Salvage* (7th ed., 2002)); *Halsbury's Laws of England* (4th ed., 2001 Reissue).

This paragraph does not cover a claim by the owners of property salved against salvors for negligence in the salvage operations. *The Eschersheim* [1976] 1 W.L.R. 339 at 346, 353 and 359; [1976] 1 All E.R. 441 at 446, 452 and 458; [1976] 1 Lloyd's Rep. 81 at 89, 90 and 95.

The court has power to award interest on a salvage award (*The Aldora* [1975] Q.B. 748; [1975] 2 All E.R. 69; [1975] 1 Lloyd's Rep. 617).

Salvage services rendered in non-tidal waters do not give rise to a claim for salvage reward (*The Goring* [1988] 1 Lloyd's Rep. 397, HL).

In *The Sava Star* [1995] 2 Lloyd's Rep. 134; the court held that there was no reason in principle why cargo owners could not issue a salvage claim against an owner where services of a salvage nature were rendered voluntarily in the sense that they were not rendered pursuant to a duty owed to the ship owners and were not part of what

ADMIRALTY

might ordinarily be expected of a cargo owner such as providing advice about the characteristics of the cargo.

Paragraph "(2)(k) any claim in the nature of towage in respect of a ship or an aircraft"

2D–159   *Note* —A "claim in the nature of towage" may include escorting without actually making fast: *The Leoborg* [1962] 2 Lloyd's Rep. 146. "Towage" in relation to an aircraft means towage when it is waterborne. See s.24(1), para. 2D–186.

Paragraph "(2)(l) any claim in the nature of pilotage in repsect of a ship or an aircraft"

2D–160   *Note* — "Pilotage" in relation to an aircraft means pilotage when it is waterborne. See s.24(1), para. 2D–186.

Paragraph "(2)(m) any claim in respect of goods or materials supplied to a ship for her operation or maintenance"

2D–161   *Note* —In *The Fairport (No. 5)* [1967] 2 Lloyd's Rep. 162 it was held that claims under this paragraph are certainly no narrower than claims which were formerly described as claims for necessaries in the Supreme Court of Judicature (Consolidation) Act 1925, and since there is authority that the word "necessaries" covers payment by way of advances to enable necessaries to be purchased then a similar construction should be given to this paragraph.

The words "in respect of" are wide words which should not be unduly restricted. They cover a claim for repayment of sums paid to sub-agents who had supplied goods to ships. *Centro Latino Americano de Commercio Exterior SA v. Owners of the Ship Kommunar (No. 1)* [1997] 1 Lloyd's Rep. 1.

Containers (in the sense in which that word is used in a commercial context) supplied whether by sale or lease to a shipowner to contain cargo loaded on board his ship or any sister ship available to him, are not supplied to that ship for her operation or maintenance within the meaning of this paragraph (*The River Rima* [1987] 2 Lloyd's Rep. 106, CA. Approved by HL [1988] 2 Lloyd's Rep. 193).

In *The Edinburgh Castle* [1999] 2 Lloyd's Rep. 362 the following were held to fall within s.20(2)(m) namely food, drink and other consumables supplied for use of the officers and crew; food, drink and other consumables supplied for the use or consumption of the passengers on the vessel; the provision of services, in particular, the provision of officers and crew of suitable calibre for the operation and manning of the vessel and a wide range of equipment supplied to the vessel. See too "Nore Challenger" and "Nore Commander" [2001] 2 Lloyd's Rep. 103.

Paragraph "(2)(n) any claim in respect of the construction, repair or equipment of a ship or dock charges or dues"

2D–162   *Note* —In the *Stinne Peter* 1986 Fo. 171, Sheen J., on an *ex parte* motion, held that a classification certificate was part of the equipment of a ship and the classification society's claim for issuing it fell within this paragraph.

Paragraph "(2)(o) any claim by a master or member of the crew of a ship for wages"

2D–163   *Note* —The jurisdiction in respect of wages is in relation to the ships of some foreign countries restricted by Orders in Council made under s.4 of the Consular Relations Act 1968, see para. 2D–16. Furthermore, the court may refuse to entertain a claim for wages by the master or a member of the crew of a ship which is not a British ship, see s.24(2), para. 2D–186.

As to the recovery as wages of or other emoluments and sums payable but not paid by an employer in respect of, *e.g.* taxes, insurance and pension contributions, see *The Halcyon Skies* [1977] Q.B. 14; [1976] 1 All E.R. 856; [1976] 1 Lloyd's Rep. 461 and cases cited therein.

In *The Fairport* [1967] P. 167; [1966] 2 Lloyd's Rep. 7, it was held that *The Carolina* (1875) 3 Asp.M.C. 141 was wrongly decided and that accordingly the institution of a wages claim did not terminate a contract of service; wages thereafter accruing might be recovered as such in the action.

It is well settled that there is a maritime lien for wages. See *The Halcyon Skies* [1977] Q.B. 14; [1976] 1 All E.R. 856; [1976] 1 Lloyd's Rep. 461 at 26, 864 and 467 of the respective reports. See too *The Ever Success* [1999] 1 Lloyd's Rep. 824. This maritime lien applies only to the ship aboard which the wages were earned (*The El Hussein* 1982 Fo. 693). There is a right *in rem* in respect of wages earned aboard a sister ship. Thus, where a claim is brought against ship A for wages earned aboard her and aboard a sister ship B, on payment out of proceeds of sale, wages earned in A will rank before, and wages earned in B after, any mortgage. This should be considered together with s.21(8), at para. 2D–169, before joining a claim for wages earned aboard a sister ship to a claim for wages earned aboard the ship proceeded against.

A master's claim for wages ranks *pari passu* with the claims of seamen (*The Royal Wells* [1984] 2 Lloyd's Rep. 255, not following earlier cases).

Severence pay is not wages within this sub-section and as opposed to wages does not give rise to a maritime lien (*The Tacoma City* [1991] 1 Lloyd's Rep. 330).

In *The Turiddu* [1999] 2 Lloyd's Rep. 401, CA, it was held that foreign members of a ship's crew requesting an allotted part of their wages to be paid through an agency to an identified person in their home country retained the benefit of a maritime lien over the vessel for unpaid wages in relation to that alloted part.

Paragraph "(2)(p) any claim by a master, shipper, charterer or agent in respect of disbursements made on account of a ship"

Note —A master has a maritime lien for his wages and for all disbursements or li- **2D–164** abilities properly made or incurred by him on account of the ship. See the Merchant Shipping Act 1995, s.41 replacing the Merchant Shipping Act 1970, s.18 and the notes to that section in *British Shipping Laws* (Temperley, *Merchant Shipping Acts* (7th ed., 1976)). See also *The Fairport (No. 3)* [1966] 2 Lloyd's Rep. 253.

"Agent"
It is arguable that the term agent in this paragraph is not restricted to a person car- **2D–165** rying on a business as a ship's agent in the usually accepted sense but is wide enough to include a manager of a ship (*The Corona Energy*, 1977, Fo. 174). However, the term agent does not extend to an insurance broker seeking to recover premiums paid out on behalf of ship's owners (*The Sea Friends* [1991] 2 Lloyd's Rep. 322).

Fees charged by agents for their services may be "disbursements" (*The Westport (No. 3)* [1966] 1 Lloyd's Rep. 342).

Paragraph "(2)(q) ... general average act ..." Paragraph "(2)(r) ... bottomry ..." Paragraph "(2)(s) ... forfeiture or condemnation of a ship or of goods"

Note —In *The Skylark* [1965] P. 474; [1965] 2 Lloyd's Rep. 250, it was held that the **2D–166** Commissioners of Customs and Excise had a right to proceed *in rem* under the equivalent paragraph of the AJA 1956 for forfeiture of a ship under the Temporary Importation (Private Vehicles, Vessels and Aircraft) Regulations 1961.

"Arising out of"
See the first note at para. 2D–155 above. **2D–167**

Subs. (7)
This paragraph applies only to aircraft referred to in s.20(2)(j), (k) and (l). The **2D–168** Admiralty jurisdiction does not extend, therefore, to a claim in respect of a mortgage of an aircraft (*The Glider Standard Austria S.H.* [1965] P. 463; [1965] 2 All E.R. 1022; [1965] 2 Lloyd's Rep. 189).

Mode of exercise of Admiralty jurisdiction

21.—(1) Subject to section 22, an action in personam may be **2D–169** brought in the High Court in all cases within the Admiralty jurisdiction of that court.

(2) In the case of any such claim as is mentioned in section

411

20(2)(a), (c) or (s) or any such question as is mentioned in section 20(2)(b), an action in rem may be brought in the High Court against the ship or property in connection with which the claim or question arises.

(3) In any case in which there is a maritime lien or other charge on any ship, aircraft or other property for the amount claimed, an action in rem may be brought in the High Court against that ship, aircraft or property.

(4) In the case of any such claim as is mentioned in section 20(2)(e) to (r), where—

   (a) the claim arises in connection with a ship; and
   (b) the person who would be liable on the claim in an action in personam ("the relevant person") was, when the cause of action arose, the owner or charterer of, or in possession or in control of, the ship,

an action in rem may (whether or not the claim gives rise to a maritime lien on that ship) be brought in the High Court against—

   (i) that ship, if at the time when the action is brought the relevant person is either the beneficial owner of that ship as respects all the shares in it or the charterer of it under a charter by demise; or
   (ii) any other ship of which, at the time when the action is brought, the relevant person is the beneficial owner as respects all the shares in it.

(5) In the case of a claim in the nature of towage or pilotage in respect of an aircraft, an action in rem may be brought in the High Court against that aircraft if, at the time when the action is brought, it is beneficially owned by the person who would be liable on the claim in an action *in personam*.

(6) Where, in the exercise of its Admiralty jurisdiction, the High Court orders any ship, aircraft or other property to be sold, the court shall have jurisdiction to hear and determine any question arising as to the title to the proceeds of sale.

(7) In determining for the purposes of subsections (4) and (5)whether a person would be liable on a claim in an action in personam it shall be assumed that he has his habitual residence or a place of business within England or Wales.

(8) Where, as regards any such claim as is mentioned in section 20(2)(e) to (r), a ship has been served with a writ or arrested in an action in rem brought to enforce that claim, no other ship may be served with a writ or arrested in that or any other action in rem brought to enforce that claim: but this subsection does not prevent the issue, in respect of any one such claim, of a writ naming more than one ship or of two or more writs each naming a different ship.

2D–170   *Note* —Generally as to claims *in rem*, see CPR Part 61.3 and notes thereunder and *British Shipping Laws*, Vol. 1, *Admiralty Practice*.

subs.(3) "... maritime lien ..."

2D–171   It is well settled that there is a maritime lien in respect of the following claims: damage done by a ship, salvage, wages, master's disbursements and bottomry. It is doubtful whether there is a maritime lien for pilotage. This question was left open in *The Ambatielos*; *The Cephalonia* [1923] P. 68. As to maritime liens generally see *The Tolten* [1946] P. 135 at 144 and 145 and cases there cited by Scott L.J. See also *The Father Thames* [1979] 2 Lloyd's Rep. 364.

subs.(3) "... other charge ..."

See *The St. Merriel* [1963] P. 247; [1963] 1 Lloyd's Rep. 63; *The Acrux* [1965] P. 391 at 403; [1965] 1 Lloyd's Rep. 565 at 572.   **2D–172**

subs.(4) "... in connection with a ship ..."

As to the effect of these words in s.3(4) of the 1956 Act, see the passage in the speech of Lord Diplock in *The Eschersheim* [1976] 1 W.L.R. 430 at 436H; [1976] 1 All E.R. 920 at 925d; [1976] 2 Lloyd's Rep. 1, HL(E), in the respective reports. In *The Span Terza* [1982] 1 Lloyd's Rep. 225, the Court of Appeal held that this passage was *obiter* and by a majority allowed the arrest of the ship "X" where the claimant (owner of the ship "Y") was claiming for charter hire in a claim *in rem* against the ship "X" which was owned by the person to whom the "Y" had been chartered by the claimant.   **2D–173**

subs.(4) "... liable ... in personam ..."

The purpose of the words "the person who would be liable on the claim in an action *in personam*" is to identify the person or persons whose ship or ships may be arrested (*The St Elefterio* [1957] P. 179 at 186; [1957] 2 All E.R. 374 at 377; [1957] 1 Lloyd's Rep. 283 at 287). But only one ship may be arrested, see subs.(8).   **2D–174**

subs.(4) "... beneficial owner ..."

For the meaning of beneficial owner in this subsection see *The Andrea Ursula* [1973] Q.B. 265; [1971] 1 All E.R. 821; [1971] 1 Lloyd's Rep. 145 and *The I Congreso del Partido* [1981] 1 Lloyd's Rep. 536 at 560 *et seq.* in which *The Andrea Ursula* was not followed. See also *The Father Thames*, [1979] 2 Lloyd's Rep. 364 at 366 and 367.   **2D–175**

subs.(4)(b)(i) "... charterer ..."

The effect of these words in sub-para. (i) is to enable a claim *in rem* to be brought against a ship on demise charter if the demise charterer of it when the claim form is issued is the person who would be liable *in personam*, and was when the cause of action arose the owner, charterer or in possession or in control of the ship in connection with which the claim arose.   **2D–176**

The "relevant person" can be a demise charterer within this subsection even in the absence of a consensual agreement between the parties in the nature of a demise charter if the legal relationship between the parties invests the "relevant person" with the right of a demise character against the owner of the vessel. See *Bridge Oil Ltd v. Owners and/or Demise Charterers of the Ship Giuseppe di Vittorio* [1998] 1 Lloyd's Rep. 136, CA.

A slot charterer of spaces on a container ship for the carriage of goods is capable of coming within the definition of a charterer in s.21(4)(b) of the Supreme Court Act 1981 despite the fact that a slot charter gave control of only part of the vessel to the charterer, *MSC Mediterranean Shipping Company SA v. Polish Ocean Lines (The Tychy)* [1999] 2 Lloyd's Rep. 11, CA.

subs.(4) "... when the action is brought ..."

This means when the claim form is issued (*The Carmania 11* [1963] 2 Lloyd's Rep. 152).   **2D–177**

subs.(4) "... owner ..."

Section 21 does not confer a right to arrest a ship owned by a sister company of the owners of the ship giving rise to the cause of action (*The Evpo Agnic* [1988] 2 Lloyd's Rep. 411, CA). See too *The Nazym Khikmet and Other Ships* [1996] 2 Lloyd's Rep. 362, CA.   **2D–178**

subs.(4)(b)

It is not sufficient that the cause of action, being one falling within s.20(2)(e) to (r), should arise probably, but not necessarily, in connection with a ship owned by or demise chartered to or in the possession or control of the relevant person as defined by   **2D–179**

ADMIRALTY

s.21(4)(b) (*The River Rima* [1987] 2 Lloyd's Rep. 106, CA. Approved by *HL* [1988] 2 Lloyd's Rep. 193). See too *The Lloyd Pacifico* [1995] 1 Lloyd's Rep. 54.

Change of ownership after issue of claim form

2D–180   This does not affect the claimant's right of claim *in rem* against the ship or prevent her arrest in the claim (*The Monica S* [1968] P. 741; [1967] 3 All E.R. 740; [1967] 2 Lloyd's Rep. 113 and see *The Andria*, renamed *The Vasso* (1984) 81 L.S.Gaz. 592).

subs.(8)

2D–181   Subsection (8) gives statutory effect to the decision of the Court of Appeal in *The Banco* [1971] P. 137; [1971] 1 All E.R. 524; [1971] 1 Lloyd's Rep. 49.

Where the claim form includes claims in respect of more than one ship, *e.g.* claims in respect of repairs to two or more ships in the same ownership, service of the claim form on or the arrest of any of the ships named in it will normally prevent valid service of that claim form on or the arrest of, any other ship named in it. Furthermore, after such service or arrest no other claim form *in rem* may be served or ship arrested in respect of any of the claims specified in the first claim form.

It seems however that in a case such as this if the claim form clearly shows what claims are made against each ship and there is no overlapping, all the ships against which claims are made in the claim form may be arrested and/or served with the claim form.

This subsection does not prevent the arrest of a ship where another has previously been arrested in the mistaken belief that she was a sister ship. The affidavit in support of the application for the second arrest should refer to the previous mistaken arrest and the reasons for it (*The Stephan J.* [1985] 2 Lloyd's Rep. 344).

Restrictions on entertainment of actions in personam in collision and other similar cases

2D–182   **22.**—(1) This section applies to any claim for damage, loss of life or personal injury arising out of—

    (a) a collision between ships; or

    (b) the carrying out of, or omission to carry out, a manoeuvre in the case of one or more of two or more ships; or

    (c) non-compliance, on the part of one or more of two or more ships, with the collision regulations.

(2) The High Court shall not entertain any action in personam to enforce a claim to which this section applies unless—

    (a) the defendant has his habitual residence or a place of business within England or Wales; or

    (b) the cause of action arose within inland waters of England or Wales or within the limits of a port of England or Wales; or

    (c) an action arising out of the same incident or series of incidents is proceeding in the court or has been heard and determined in the court.

In this subsection—

"inland waters" includes any part of the sea adjacent to the coast of the United Kingdom certified by the Secretary of State to be waters falling by international law to be treated as within the territorial sovereignty of Her Majesty apart from the operation of that law in relation to territorial waters;

"port" means any port, harbour, river, estuary, haven, dock, canal or other place so long as a person or body of persons is empowered by or under an Act to make charges in respect of ships entering it or using the facilities therein, and "limits of a port" means the limits thereof as fixed by or under the Act in question or, as the case may be, by the relevant charter or custom;

"charges" means any charges with the exception of light dues, local light dues and any other charges in respect of lighthouses, buoys or beacons and of charges in respect of pilotage.

(3) The High Court shall not entertain any action in personam to enforce a claim to which this section applies until any proceedings previously brought by the plaintiff in any court outside England and Wales against the same defendant in respect of the same incident or series of incidents have been discontinued or otherwise come to an end.

(4) Subsections (2) and (3) shall apply to counterclaims (except counterclaims in proceedings arising out of the same incident or series of incidents) as they apply to actions, the references to the plaintiff and the defendant being for this purpose read as references to the plaintiff on the counterclaim and the defendant to the counterclaim respectively.

(5) Subsections (2) and (3) shall not apply to any action or counterclaim if the defendant thereto submits or has agreed to submit to the jurisdiction of the court.

(6) Subject to the provisions of subsection (3), the High Court shall have jurisdiction to entertain an action in personam to enforce a claim to which this section applies whenever any of the conditions specified in subsections (2)(a) to (c) is satisfied, and the rules of court relating to the service of process outside the jurisdiction shall make such provision as may appear to the rule-making authority to be appropriate having regard to the provisions of this subsection.

(7) Nothing in this section shall prevent an action which is brought in accordance with the provisions of this section in the High Court being transferred, in accordance with the enactments in that behalf, to some other court.

(8) For the avoidance of doubt it is hereby declared that this section applies in relation to the jurisdiction of the High Court not being Admiralty jurisdiction, as well as in relation to its Admiralty jurisdiction.

subs.(2)(c)

In *The World Harmony* [1967] P. 341; [1965] 2 All E.R. 139; [1965] 1 Lloyd's Rep. **2D–183** 244, it was held that the critical date under the equivalent provision in the A.J.A. 1956(s.4(1)(c)), was the date when the claim form was issued and that when two claims are begun in two places on the same day, neither is previous or subsequent to the other.

subs.(6) "... rules of court ..."

See CPR Pt 61.4(7) and Pt 6.20(17A). **2D–184**

High Court not to have jurisdiction in cases within Rhine Convention

23. The High Court shall not have jurisdiction to determine any **2D–185**

ADMIRALTY

claim or question certified by the Secretary of State to be a claim or question which, under the Rhine Navigation Convention, falls to be determined in accordance with the provisions of that Convention; and any proceedings to enforce such a claim which are commenced in the High Court shall be set aside.

Supplementary provisions as to Admiralty jurisdiction

2D–186   24.—(1) In sections 20 to 23 and this section, unless the context otherwise requires—

"collision regulations" means safety regulations under section 85 of the Merchant Shipping Act 1995;

"goods" includes baggage;

"master" has the same meaning as in the Merchant Shipping Act 1995, and accordingly includes every person (except a pilot) having command or charge of a ship;

"the Rhine Navigation Convention" means the Convention of the 7th October 1868 as revised by any subsequent Convention;

"ship" includes any description of vessel used in navigation and (except in the definition of "port" in section 22(2)and in subsection (2)(c) of this section) includes, subject to section 2(3)of the Hovercraft Act 1968, a hovercraft;

"towage" and "pilotage", in relation to an aircraft, mean towage and pilotage while the aircraft is waterborne.

(2) Nothing in sections 20 to 23 shall—

(a) be construed as limiting the jurisdiction of the High Court to refuse to entertain an action for wages by the master or a member of the crew of a ship, not being a British ship;

(b) affect the provisions of section 226 of the Merchant Shipping Act 1995 (power of a receiver of wreck to detain a ship in respect of a salvage claim); or

(c) authorise proceedings in rem in respect of any claim against the Crown, or the arrest, detention or sale of any of Her Majesty's ships or Her Majesty's aircraft, or, subject to section 2(3)of the Hovercraft Act 1968, Her Majesty's hovercraft, or of any cargo or other property belonging to the Crown.

(3) In this section—

"Her Majesty's ships" and "Her Majesty's aircraft" have the meanings given by section 38(2) of the Crown Proceedings Act 1947;

"Her Majesty's hovercraft" means hovercraft belonging to the Crown in right of Her Majesty's Government in the United Kingdom or Her Majesty's Government in Northern Ireland.

2D–187   *Note* —Amended by the Merchant Shipping Act 1995, Sched.13.

Ship

2D–188   See further as to the meaning of ship, para. 2D–144.

Other particular fields of jurisdiction

* * * *

Prize jurisdiction of High Court

27. The High Court shall, in accordance with section 19(2), have as a prize court— **2D–189**

(a) all such jurisdiction as is conferred on it by the Prize Acts 1864 to 1944 (in which references to the High Court of Admiralty are by virtue of paragraph 1 of Schedule 4 to this Act to be construed as references to the High Court); and

(b) all such other jurisdiction on the high seas and elsewhere as it has as a prize court immediately before the commencement of this Act.

Note —Derived from the J.A. 1925, s.23. **2D–190**

Part VI

Miscellaneous and Supplementary

Supplementary

* * * *

Admiralty jurisdiction: provisions as to Channel Islands, Isle of Man, colonies, etc.

150.—(1) Her Majesty may by Order in Council— **2D–191**

(a) direct that any of the provisions of sections 20 to 24 specified in the Order shall extend, with such exceptions, adaptations and modifications as may be so specified, to any of the Channel Islands or the Isle of Man; or

(b) make, for any of the Channel Islands or the Isle of Man, provision for any purposes corresponding to the purposes of any of the provisions of those sections.

(2) Her Majesty may by Order in Council direct, either generally or in relation to particular courts or territories, that the Colonial Courts of Admiralty Act 1890 shall have effect as if for the reference in section 2(2) of that Act to the Admiralty jurisdiction of the High Court in England there were substituted a reference to the Admiralty jurisdiction of that court as defined by section 20 of this Act, subject, however, to such adaptations and modifications of section 20 as may be specified in the Order.

(3) Her Majesty may by Order in Council direct that any of the provisions of sections 21 to 24 shall extend, with such exceptions, adaptations and modifications as may be specified in the Order, to any colony or to any country outside Her Majesty's dominions in which Her Majesty has jurisdiction in right of the government of the United Kingdom.

(4) Subsections (1) and (3) shall each have effect as if the provisions there mentioned included section 2(2) of the Hovercraft Act

1968 (application of the law relating to maritime liens in relation to hovercraft and property connected with them).

2D–192   *Note* —Derived from the A.J.A. 1956, s.56.

Hovercraft Act 1968

2D–193   (1968 c.59)

1. [Power to make Orders in Council with respect to hovercraft.]

Admiralty jurisdiction, etc.

2D–194   **2.**—(1) Subject to subsection (3) of this section, the following enactments, that is to say, Part V of the Administration of Justice Act 1956, Part I of Schedule 1 to that Act and sections 27 to 29, 30(1) and 31 of the County Courts Act 1984 (which among other things relate to Admiralty jurisdiction) shall have effect as if references to ships (except references to Her Majesty's ships and the reference in paragraph 4(1) of the said Part I and the second reference in paragraph 8(1)of that Part) included references to hovercraft and as if references to Her Majesty's ships included references to hovercraft belonging to the Crown in right of the Government of the United Kingdom or the Government of Northern Ireland; and section 4 of the Sheriff Courts (Scotland) Act 1907 (which relates to the jurisdiction of the sheriffs) shall apply in relation to hovercraft as it applies in relation to ships.

(2) Subject to subsection (3) of this section, the law relating to maritime liens shall apply in relation to hovercraft and property connected with hovercraft as it applies in relation to ships and property connected with ships, and shall so apply notwithstanding that the hovercraft is on land at any relevant time.

(3) Her Majesty may by Order in Council provide that the enactments mentioned in subsection (1) and the law mentioned in subsection (2) of this section as extended by those subsections shall not apply in relation to hovercraft in such circumstances as may be specified in the Order or shall have effect, in all circumstances involving hovercraft or such circumstances involving hovercraft as may be specified in the Order, subject to such modifications as may be so specified; and subsection (3) of section 1 of this Act shall apply to an Order under this subsection as it applies to an Order under that section but as if paragraphs (c) (e) and (f) were omitted.

(3A) Subsection (3) of this section shall have effect as if the reference to the enactments mentioned in subsection (1) as extended by that subsection included a reference to sections 20 to 24 of the Supreme Court Act 1981.

(4) No recommendation shall be made to Her Majesty in Council to make an Order under this section unless a draft of the Order has been approved by a resolution of each House of Parliament.

(5) [*Repealed by SCA 1981 , s.152(4) and Sched.7.*]

(6) Subsection (1) of this section shall apply for the purposes of any proceedings begun on or after the date of the coming into operation of this section, whenever the cause of action arose, but shall not affect any proceedings begun before that date.

Note —Amended by the SCA 1981, s.152(1) and Sched.5. **2D–195**

Application of certain enactments to hovercraft

3. The enactments mentioned in the Schedule to this Act shall **2D–196** have effect subject to the modifications there specified (which provide for the application of those enactments in relation to hovercraft).

Interpretation, etc.

4.—(1) In this Act— **2D–197**

"contravention" includes failure to comply;

"enactment" includes an enactment of the Parliament of Northern Ireland, an enactment contained in a local Act and an enactment contained in any Act passed after and in the same Session as this Act;

"hovercraft" means a vehicle which is designed to be supported when in motion wholly or partly by air expelled from the vehicle to form a cushion of which the boundaries include the ground, water or other surface beneath the vehicle;

"hoverport" means any area, whether on land or elsewhere, which is designed, equipped, set apart or commonly used for affording facilities for the arrival and departure of hovercraft;

"modifications" includes additions, omissions and amendments; and

"prescribed" means prescribed by an Order in Council under section 1of this Act or by an instrument made under such an Order.

(2) Subject to section 2(5) of this Act, any reference in this Act to any enactment or instrument is a reference to it as amended, and includes a reference to it as applied, by or under any other enactment.

(3) Except as otherwise provided by or under this Act or an enactment passed before the date of the passing of this Act, a hovercraft shall not be treated as being a ship, aircraft or motor vehicle for the purposes of any such enactment or any instrument having effect by virtue of any such enactment.

5. [*Northern Ireland.*] **2D–198**

6. [*Financial provisions.*]

7. [*Short title and commencement.*]

Merchant Shipping Act 1995

(1995 c.21)

An Act to consolidate the Merchant Shipping Acts 1894 to 1994 and other enactments relating to merchant shipping.

[*July 19, 1995.*]

[Modifications of enactments].

PART IV

SAFETY

* * * * *

ASSISTANCE AT SEA

Duty of ship to assist the other in case of collision

92.—(1) In every case of collision between two ships, it shall be the
duty of the master of each ship, if and so far as he can do so without
danger to his own ship, crew and passengers (if any)— **2D–200**

> (a) to render to the other ship, its master, crew and pas-
> sengers (if any) such assistance as may be practicable,
> and may be necessary to save them from any danger
> caused by the collision, and to stay by the other ship
> until he has ascertained that it has no need of further as-
> sistance; and

> (b) to give to the master of the other ship the name of his
> own ship and also the names of the ports from which it
> comes and to which it is bound.

(2) The duties imposed on the master of a ship by subsection (1)
above apply to the masters of United Kingdom ships and to the
masters of foreign ships when in United Kingdom waters.

(3) The failure of the master of a ship to comply with the provisions of this section shall not raise any presumption of law that the
collision was caused by his wrongful act, neglect, or default.

(4) [Penalties for non compliance].

2D–201   *Note* —Derivation— Merchant Shipping Act 1894, s.422(1); the Merchant Shipping (Registration) Act 1993, Sched.4, para. 6(2); and the Maritime Conventions Act 1911, s.4(2).

Duty to assist aircraft in distress

2D–202   **93.**—(1) The master of a ship, on receiving at sea a signal of distress from an aircraft or information from any source that an aircraft is in distress, shall proceed with all speed to the assistance of the persons in distress (informing them if possible that he is doing so) unless he is unable, or in the special circumstances of the case considers it unreasonable or unnecessary, to do so, or unless he is released from this duty under subsection (4) or (5) below.

(2) [Omitted by S.I. 1998 No. 1691].

(3) The duties imposed on the master of a ship by subsection (1) above apply to the masters of United Kingdom ships and to the masters of foreign ships when in United Kingdom waters.

(4) [Omitted by S.I. 1998 No. 1691].

(5) A master shall be released from the duty imposed by subsection (1) above, if he is informed by the persons in distress, or by the master of any ship that has reached the persons in distress, that assistance is no longer required.

(6) [Penalties for non compliance].

(7) Compliance by the master of a ship with the provisions of this section shall not affect his right, or the right of any other person, to salvage.

2D–203   *Note* —Derivation— Merchant Shipping (Safety Convention) Act 1949, s.22(1) and (2); the Merchant Shipping (Registration, etc.) Act 1993, Sched.4, para. 6(2); and the Merchant Shipping (Safety Convention) Act 1949, s.22(3), (4), (5) and (8) and s.37(3).

Section 93 has been amended by The Merchant Shipping (Distress Messages) Regulation 1998 (S.I. 1998 No. 1691), reg. 2.

subs. (1)

2D–204   A vessel which puts herself into unusual peril by reason of rendering assistance under this section is not to be regarded as negligent on that account. The principles of the common law as laid down in *Haynes v. Harwood* [1935] 1 K.B. 146, apply (*The Gusty and the Daniel M.* [1940] P. 159, a case on the former s.6 of the Maritime Conventions Act 1911, see para. 2D–212, below).

subs. (7)

2D–205   *The Tower Bridge* [1936] P. 30 is a case in which salvage is awarded in such circumstances.

PART VII

LIABILITY OF SHIPOWNERS AND OTHERS

* * * *

LIMITATION OF LIABILITY OF SHIPOWNERS, ETC., AND SALVORS FOR

MARITIME CLAIMS

Limitation of liability for maritime claims

2D–206   **185.**—(1) The provisions of the Convention on Limitation of Liability for Maritime Claims 1976 as set out in Part I of Schedule 7 (in this section and Part II of that Schedule referred to as "the Convention") shall have the force of law in the United Kingdom.

(2) The provisions of Part II of that Schedule shall have effect in connection with the Convention, and subsection (1) above shall have effect subject to the provisions of that Part.

(2A) Her Majesty may by Order in Council make such modifications of Parts I and II of Schedule 7 as She considers appropriate in consequence of the revision of the Convention by the Protocol of 1996 amending the Convention (in this section referred to as "the 1996 Protocol").

(2B) If it appears to Her Majesty in Council that the Government of the United Kingdom has agreed to any further revision of the Convention or to any revision of article 8 of the 1996 Protocol, She may by Order in Council make such modifications of Parts I and II of Schedule 7 and subsections (2C) and (2D) below as She considers appropriate in consequence of the revision.

(2C) The Secretary of State may by order make such amendments of Parts I and II of Schedule 7 as appear to him to be appropriate for the purpose of giving effect to any amendment of a relevant limit which is adopted in accordance with article 8 of the 1996 Protocol.

(2D) In subsection (2C) above "a relevant limit" means any of the limits for the time being specified in either of the following provisions of the Convention—

    (a) article 6, paragraph 1, and

    (b) article 7, paragraph 1.

(2E) No modification made by virtue of subsection (2A), (2B) or (2C) above shall affect any rights or liabilities arising out of an occurrence which took place before the day on which the modification comes into force.

(3) The provisions having the force of law under this section shall apply in relation to Her Majesty's ships as they apply in relation to other ships.

(4) The provisions having the force of law under this section shall not apply to any liability in respect of loss of life or personal injury caused to, or loss of or damage to any property of, a person who is on board the ship in question or employed in connection with that ship or with the salvage operations in question if—

    (a) he is so on board or employed under a contract of service governed by the law of any part of the United Kingdom; and

    (b) the liability arises from an occurrence which took place after the commencement of this Act.

In this subsection, "ship" and "salvage operations" have the same meaning as in the Convention.

(5) A draft of an Order in Council proposed to be made by virtue of subsection (2A) or (2B) above shall not be submitted to Her Majesty in Council unless it has been approved by a resolution of each House of Parliament.

ADMIRALTY

2D–207 *Note* —Derivation— Merchant Shipping Act 1979, s.17, s.35(2) and Sched.5, para. 3. Subsections (2A) to (2E) inserted by the Merchant Shipping and Maritime Security Act 1997, s.15. These subsections are now in force. As at December 2002 see only under s.185(2A), the Merchant Shipping (Convention on Limitation of Liability for Maritime Claims) (Amendment) Order 1998 (S.I. 1998 No. 1258)—not in force until the 1996 Protocol amending the 1976 Convention on Liability for Maritime Claims comes into force internationally.

Exclusion of liability

2D–208 **186.**—(1) Subject to subsection (3) below, the owner of a United Kingdom ship shall not be liable for any loss or damage in the following cases, namely—

    (a) where any property on board the ship is lost or damaged by reason of fire on board the ship; or

    (b) where any gold, silver, watches, jewels or precious stones on board the ship are lost or damaged by reason of theft, robbery or other dishonest conduct and their nature and value were not at the time of shipment declared by their owner or shipper to the owner or master of the ship in the bill of lading or otherwise in writing.

(2) Subject to subsection (3) below, where the loss or damage arises from anything done or omitted by any person in his capacity of master or member of the crew or (otherwise than in that capacity) in the course of his employment as a servant of the owner of the ship, subsection (1) above shall also exclude the liability of—

    (a) the master, member of the crew or servant; and

    (b) in a case where the master or member of the crew is the servant of a person whose liability would not be excluded by that subsection apart from this paragraph, the person whose servant he is.

(3) This section does not exclude the liability of any person for any loss or damage resulting from any such personal act or omission of his as is mentioned in Article 4 of the Convention set out in Part I of Schedule 7.

(4) This section shall apply in relation to Her Majesty's ships as it applies in relation to other ships.

(5) In this section "owner", in relation to a ship, includes any part owner and any charterer, manager or operator of the ship.

2D–209 *Note* —Derivation— Merchant Shipping Act 1979, s.18; and the Merchant Shipping (Registration, etc.) Act 1993, Sched.4, para. 6(1).

MULTIPLE FAULT, APPORTIONMENT, LIABILITY AND CONTRIBUTION

Damage or loss: apportionment of liability

2D–210 **187.**—(1) Where, by the fault of two or more ships, damage or loss is caused to one or more of those ships, to their cargoes or freight, or to any property on board, the liability to make good the damage or loss shall be in proportion to the degree in which each ship was in fault.

(2) If, in any such case, having regard to all the circumstances, it is not possible to establish different degrees of fault, the liability shall be apportioned equally.

(3) This section applies to persons other than the owners of a ship who are responsible for the fault of the ships, as well as to the owners of a ship and where, by virtue of any charter or demise, or for any other reason, the owners are not responsible for the navigation and management of the ship, this section applies to the charterers or other persons for the time being so responsible instead of the owners.

(4) Nothing in this section shall operate so as to render any ship liable for any loss or damage to which the fault of the ship has not contributed.

(5) Nothing in this section shall affect the liability of any person under a contract of carriage or any contract, or shall be construed as imposing any liability upon any person from which he is exempted by any contract or by any provision of law, or as affecting the right of any person to limit his liability in the manner provided by law.

(6) In this section "freight" includes passage money and hire.

(7) In this section references to damage or loss caused by the fault of a ship include references to any salvage or other expenses, consequent upon that fault, recoverable at law by way of damages.

Note —Derivation— Maritime Conventions Act 1911, s.1(1), s.1(1) proviso (a), (b) and (c), s.1(2) and s.9(4). **2D–211**

General note

The Merchant Shipping Act 1995 came into force on January 1, 1996, see s.315 of **2D–212** the 1995 Act. The 1995 Act is described as an act to consolidate the Merchant Shipping Acts 1894 to 1994 and other enactments relating to merchant shipping. Among those other enactments was the Maritime Conventions Act 1911 the text of which is to be found in the 1995 edition and earlier editions of this publication. In relation to s.1 of the 1911 Act (now s.187 of the 1995 Act set out above), s.3(1) of the Law Reform (Contributory Negligence) Act 1945 provided that the 1945 Act should not apply to any claim to which s.1 of the 1911 Act applied and that the 1911 Act should have effect as if the 1945 had not been passed. The intention of the 1911 Act and now of the provisions of the 1995 Act derived therefrom and of the 1945 Act is the same so that similar principles should be applied by the common law courts and the admiralty courts in the same way. See *Davies v. Swan Motor Co (Swansea Corp Ltd and James, Third Parties)* [1949] 2 K.B. 291 at 319, *per* Evershed L.J. See also *The Miraflores and the Abadesa* [1966] P. 18 at 33; [1966] 1 Lloyd's Rep. 97 at 110, *per* Willmer L.J. Section 185 now applies in the case of ships belonging to Her Majesty as it applies in the case of other ships, see s.192(1) and (2) of the Merchant Shipping Act 1995. On the basis that the 1995 Act is a consolidating act case law previously appearing in the notes to the provisions of the 1911 Act has been retained.

"Fault of two or more ships"

For definition of "ship", see the Merchant Shipping Act 1995, s.313. See too the **2D–213** definitions of "vessel" and "ship" in the Merchant Shipping Act 1894, s.742 and the cases cited in the notes to that section in *British Shipping Laws* (Temperley, *Merchant Shipping Acts* (7th ed., 1976)). A sailing dinghy used on a reservoir for pleasure has been held not to be a "vessel in navigation" within s.742 aforesaid, see *Curtis v. Wild* [1991] 4 All E.R. 172; and a jet-ski not to be a "ship", see *Steedman v. Scofield* [1992] 2 Lloyd's Rep. 163.

Of the Maritime Conventions Act 1911 (see under General Note above) it was said: "The ... Act personifies the vessel, treating it at one time as the actor, at another as suffering damage or loss, and at another as liable to make good such damage or loss. The truth is, of course, that for the purpose of ascertaining the legal effect, the word in one context connotes those responsible for the navigation of the vessel; in another, those who are interested in her, her cargo or freight; and in another, those who are in law answerable for the conduct of those in charge.", *per* Warrington J. in *The Cairnbahn* [1914] P. 25 at 34, CA.

ADMIRALTY

The words "by the fault of two or more ships", and the words of s.190 "by the fault of that ship", are entirely general, and are wide enough to include not only faults of navigation but other faults as well. See *The Norwhale* [1975] Q.B. 589; [1975] 2 All E.R. 501; [1975] 1 Lloyd's Rep. 610, a case decided under ss.1(1) and 8 of the Maritime Conventions Act 1911.

As to the proof of "fault," the rule is the same as in common law cases, namely, that the onus is on the party setting up a case of negligence to prove both the breach of duty and the consequent damage (*SS. Heranger (Owners) v. SS. Diamond (Owners)* [1939] A.C. 94). However, in *The Minosa* (1944) 77 L.R. 218 at 219, the judge said: "The fact that one ship does not allege any fault against the other seems to me to be quite immaterial if the court after inquiring into all the facts finds that such fault exists. I think, therefore, that this is a case in which liability should be apportioned." See also *The Shelbrit IV* (1945) 78 Ll.L.Rep. 50.

It should be noted, however, that the negligence of an officer on board a ship is not always to be treated as "the fault of the ship"; see *The Sobieski* [1949] P. 313, and *The Glaucus and the City of Florence* [1948] P. 95. In the former case a collision occurred between two ships, the S and the E, as the result of the negligence of each of them and as the result, also, of the negligence of a senior escort officer, L, on board a naval ship, the L A, which was escorting the S. L's negligence consisted of his failure to transmit information of the approach, detected by radar, of the E. It was held that L's negligence was not the negligence of his ship, the L A. Therefore, the court held, the Maritime Conventions Act (see under General Note above) had no application to the claim of the S against L, and that claim failed also at common law because of the contributory negligence of the S, the collision having occurred before the coming into force of the Law Reform (Contributory Negligence) Act 1945.

"Damage or loss"

2D–214 As to what may be recovered under the head of damages in a collision action, see *British Shipping Laws* (Marsden, Collisions at Sea).

"The word 'loss' is wide enough to include that form of pecuniary prejudice which consists in compensating third parties for wrong done to them by the fault of persons for whose conduct the party prejudiced must answer," *per* Lord Sumner in *The Cairnbahn* [1914] P. 25 at 33, CA. In *The Abadesa* [1966] 1 Lloyd's Rep. 118, a case under the Maritime Conventions Act 1911, however, it was decided that " Sect. 1 deals with material claims, claims for material damage; Sects. 2 and 3 with personal injuries and loss of life." The corresponding sections are now ss.187, 188 and 189.

"One or more of those ships"

2D–215 An innocent third ship, not being one of "those ships" who were "at fault," can, it seems, still recover the whole of her damages from either of the vessels by the fault of which damage to her has been caused, leaving the ship which has paid to recover a proportionate share from the other ship at fault; see *The Cairnbahn* [1914] P. 25, where a collision occurred between a steamship and a barge in tow of and controlled by a tug. The tug-owners had no interest in the barge. The steamship and tug were found equally to blame for the collision. The owners of the innocent barge recovered the full amount of their damage from the steamship. In a subsequent claim against the tug the steamship was held entitled to include in her claim for damages half the amount of damages which she had paid to the barge. To bring the case within the section it is not necessary that the two ships on whom lies the liability to make good the damage should themselves have been in collision.

With this should be contrasted the decision in *The Umona* [1914] P. 141, where a collision occurred between a steamship and a dumb-barge in tow of and controlled by a tug whose owners also owned the barge. The fault was apportioned as to three-fourths to the steamship and one-fourth to the tug. The owners of cargo laden on the barge were held only entitled to recover from the steamship three-quarters of their damage in accordance with the doctrine enunciated in *The Milan* (1860) Lush. 388; 31 L.J.Ad. 105; followed in *The Drumlanrig* [1911] A.C. 16.

Only damage or loss to ships is within the section; so that, in *Manchester Ship Canal Co (Alpha) v. Helgoy* (1924) 18 Ll.L.Rep. 191, a jetty belonging to the owners of ship A was damaged in collision between ships A and B, for which both A and B were equally to blame. Though a moiety of the damage to A and B was recoverable from the owners of B and A respectively, no part of the damage to the jetty was recoverable from the owners of B for the claim in respect of the damage to the jetty is a common law claim and, as the collision causing the damage occurred before the coming into force of the Law Reform (Contributory Negligence) Act 1945, was defeated by the defence based on the contributory negligence of the servants of the owners of A. *Quaere*, however, whether this decision is consistent with certain passages in the judgment in *The Cairnbahn* [1914] P. 25, which suggests that all forms of pecuniary loss suffered by owners of ships involved in a collision are within the section. See, too, as to collision with wreck, *The Manorbier Castle* (1922) 129 L.T. 31; 16 Asp.M.L.C. 151.

"Cargoes"

The innocent owner of cargo on board either of the colliding ships could, prior to **2D–216** the J.A. 1873, recover in a common law action in tort the whole of his damages from either of the wrong-doing ships unless defeated as regards the carrying ship by the terms of the contract of carriage. In Admiralty, he could only recover half his damages against the other ship if both were found to blame for the collision (*The Milan* (1860) Lush. 388; 31 L.J.Adm. 105). From 1873 until 1911 this Admiralty rule prevailed in all courts. Since the Maritime Conventions Act 1911 and now, under this Act, he can recover from the other ship a share of his damages proportionate to the degree in which such ship was in fault (*The Umona* [1914] P. 141). Nothing in this rule or the Act prevents the cargo owner from recovering his damages in full from the carrying ship should the terms of the contract of carriage permit (*The Bushire* (1886) 5 Asp.M.L.C. 416; 52 L.T. 740).

"Liability to make good the damage or loss"

These words are equivalent to "the burden of the damage or loss"; *per* Warrington **2D–217** J. in *The Cairnbahn* [1914] P. 25 at 37. Further as to liability, see para. 2D–218.

Of s.1 of the Maritime Conventions Act 1911 (see under General Note above) it was said: Section 1 "is mandatory. It does not say that the liability shall be apportioned equally unless different degrees of fault are shown. It is the other way round. It says that the court must apportion the liability in proportion to the degree in which each vessel was at fault unless it is impossible to do so" (*per* Davies L.J., *The Anneliese* [1970] 1 Lloyd's Rep. 355 at 362, CA; see cases cited therein).

Application of rule of division of loss when liability is limited

In *Stoomvaart Maatschappy Nederland v. Peninsular and Oriental S. N. Co. [The Voor-* **2D–218** *waarts; The Khedive]* (1882) 7 App. Cas. 795, the House of Lords, following the rule laid down in *The Woodrop-Sims* (1815) 2 Dods. Ad. 83; *The Lord Melville* (1815) 5 Shaws Sc. App. Cas. 395; *The Petersfield and the Judith Randolph* (1789) Marsd. Ad. Cas. 332, decided that upon a finding of both to blame only one liability arose, namely, a liability upon the part of the owners of the ship that had done the greater damage to pay to the owners of the other ship the difference between the moieties of the losses suffered by the two ships, and that where the former limited their liability under the Merchant Shipping Acts (now the Merchant Shipping Act) the latter were only entitled to prove against the fund in court for this difference.

It is submitted that there is nothing in the present section to affect this rule as to unity of liability; but its application where both ships are held to blame with unequal degrees of fault may give rise to anomalous results even more striking than those which occurred under the old rule. It may happen that the ship which has been found to be at fault in the greater degree will, nevertheless, if she has also received the greater damage be entitled to some payment. Thus, for example, where the damage done to A amounts to £10,000 and to B £30,000, and the degree of fault in A is found to be one-third and in B two-thirds, A, though only one-third to blame, will have to pay B £3,333, *i.e.* the difference between £10,000 (one-third of B's damage) and £6,666 (two-thirds of A's damage). If A limits her liability, B can prove against the fund for £3,333.

Three ships involved

Where A, being towed by B, collides with C, and the court finds A and B one-half **2D–219** to blame and C one-half to blame, there is no obligation on the court to apportion the blame as between A and B. There is a joint and several liability in A and B to reimburse C in respect of a moiety of C's damage and a single liability in C to reimburse A and B in respect of a moiety of the damage, if any, sustained by them respectively (*The Socrates and the Champion* [1923] P. 76).

Where A collides with B while B is towing C, and the court finds that B and C are

ADMIRALTY

separately and distinctly at fault, the court will apportion blame as between B and C; see *The M.S.C. Panther and the Ericbank* [1957] P. 143 (distinguishing *The Socrates and the Champion* [1923] P. 76).

Where A goes aground negligently in avoiding B and C which have negligently collided, "the liability of each ship involved shall be assessed by comparison of her fault with the fault of each of the other ships involved individually, separately and in no way conjunctively." See *The Miraflores and the Abadesa* [1966] P. 18 at 37; [1966] 1 Lloyd's Rep. 97 at 113, *per* Winn L.J., affirmed by the House of Lords [1967] 1 A.C. 826; [1967] 1 All E.R. 672; [1967] 1 Lloyd's Rep. 191.

No collision

2D–220   The section is not confined to cases where two ships have actually been in collision. For example, where A, by her wash due to her excessive speed caused B, which was improperly moored, to break adrift and suffer damage, the loss was found to be due to the fault of both A and B, and was accordingly apportioned. *The Batavier III* (1925) 134 L.T. 155; 42 T.L.R. 8. See too, *The Cairnbahn* [1914] P. 25.

"Fault"

2D–221   No definition of "fault" is given in the Act or the Convention (see Schedule 7, Parts I & II). The basis of liability in a claim of damage by collision under the old Admiralty rule, and also, it seems, under the present section, is negligence causing or contributing to the *loss*. See, for example, *The Margaret* (1881) 6 P.D. 76, where, in a collision between a schooner at anchor and a dumb barge, the schooner, whose only fault consisted in having an anchor improperly suspended in such a position that it holed and sank the barge was held liable to pay for half the loss suffered by the barge, whose sole negligence caused the collision. See, too, *The Monte Rosa* [1893] P. 23, and presumably the same principle would be applied to cases under the present section. It is true that in *The Peter Benoit* (1915) 84 L.J.P. 197; 31 T.L.R. 227, CA; 85 L.J.P. 12; 32 T.L.R. 124, H.L.R. the Court of Appeal and the House of Lords held that the fault for which the liability is to be apportioned under this section must be "fault causing or contributing to the collision." But this decision must be read *secundum subjectam materiam*. The court was considering the effect of a breach of a local by-law (which, in fact, contributed neither to the collision nor to the loss) and must not be taken to have questioned the proposition of law illustrated above by *The Margaret* (1881) 6 P.D. 76, namely, that liability attaches to acts of negligence causing or contributing to the loss; see *The Kaiser Wilhelm II* (1916) 85. L.J.P. 34; 31 T.L.R. 615.

It is now well established that in assessing degrees of fault and apportioning blame, regard must be had both to the blameworthiness or culpability of the conduct and also its causative potency as a factor contributing to the collision and damage. See *Stapley v. Gypsum Mines Ltd* [1953] A.C. 663 and *The British Aviator* [1965] 1 Lloyd's Rep. 271 at 277.

Costs

2D–222   Until the case of *The Modica* [1926] P. 72, the regular practice from the commencement of the Maritime Conventions Act in 1911 was that, where in a collision action it was found that each ship had been to blame, although in different degrees, the court would apply in cases under this Act the old rule of making each ship pay her own costs. This practice was based upon the rulings of Bargrave Deane J. in *The Rosalia* [1912] P. 109, and of Sir Samuel Evans P. in *The Bravo* (1912) 29 T.L.R. 122. In *The Modica*, however, Hill J., after reviewing the authorities, laid down the principle that the court, being guided by the particular circumstances in each case, was at liberty in a proper case to give to the party least in fault such proportion of that party's costs as on the particular facts appeared just, and in modern practice an order apportioning the costs is frequently made. It is, however, in each case, both in the court of first instance and in the appellate tribunals, a matter of pure discretion and not of legal right, and, unless the judge can be shown to have taken into consideration matters which are immaterial to the issue, his decision as to costs is unappealable: *The Young Sid* [1929] P. 190.

In *The Osprey* [1967] 1 Lloyd's Rep. 76 at 94, in which the plaintiffs' ship was held three-fifths and the defendants' ship two-fifths to blame, Brandon J. said, after hearing argument on costs and referring to *The Modica*, and to the then in force RSC O.62, rr.2(4) and 3(2): "It seems to me that if costs are to follow the event in a case where one party has done better than the other then the fact that party has done better than the other ought to be reflected in some way in the order for costs." The judge discussed three ways in which this might be done and finally ordered that the plaintiffs pay one-fifth of the defendants' costs. *The Osprey* has been followed in a number of cases.

Appeal as to apportionment

See *The Peter Benoit* (1915) 84 L.J.P. 197; 31 T.L.R. 227, CA; 85 L.J.P. 12; 32 T.L.R. 124, HL. "I do not think this court ought lightly to interfere with the decision of the court below on the question of apportionment, unless it sees quite clearly that there has been some mistake of fact or some mistake of law which has led the learned judge to the conclusion to which he came": *per* Bankes L.J. at 91. See, too, *The Karamea* [1921] P. 76, CA; [1992] 1 A.C. 68; *The Clara Camus* (1926) 134 L.T. 50, CA; 136 L.T. 291, HL. In *The Testbank* [1942] P. 75 the Court of Appeal indicated that they regarded the principles laid down in *The Karamea* as placing too strict a limitation on the discretion of the Court of Appeal. But in *The MacGregor* [1943] A.C. 197, the House of Lords expressly approved *The Karamea* and disapproved the statement of principle in *The Testbank*. **2D–223**

The Court of Appeal will set aside the apportionment of the trial judge if persuaded that he has taken a wrong view of the material facts; see *The British Aviator* [1965] 1 Lloyd's Rep. 271 at 278.

"(3) ... persons other than the owners of a ship who are responsible ..."

Similar words under the former s.9(4) of the 1911 Act were held to include the commanding officer of a ship of the Royal Navy. *H.M.S. Archer* [1919] P. 1. See also *The Norwhale* [1975] Q.B. 589; [1975] 2 All E.R. 501; [1975] 1 Lloyd's Rep. 610. **2D–224**

"Liability ... a contract"

See, for example, *Chartered Mercantile Bank of India v. Netherlands India Steam Navigation Co* (1883) 10 Q.B.D. 521, where the owner of cargo damaged in collision between two ships both belonging to the same shipowner and equally to blame, was held only to be entitled to recover from the shipowner half the amount of the damage, *i.e.* the half attaching to the non-carrying ship, the claim for the other half being defeated by the negligence clause in the bill of lading under which the goods were carried. **2D–225**

"Limit his liability"

For the provisions as to limitation of liability, see s.185 and Sched.7 replacing s.17 and Pts I and II of Sched.4 to the Merchant Shipping Act 1979, which itself came into force on December 1, 1986. **2D–226**

Loss of life or personal injuries: joint and several liability

188.—(1) Where loss of life or personal injuries are suffered by any person on board a ship owing to the fault of that ship and of any other ship or ships, the liability of the owners of the ships shall be joint and several. **2D–227**

(2) Subsection (3) of section 187 applies also to this section.

(3) Nothing in this section shall be construed as depriving any person of any right of defence on which, apart from this section, he might have relied in an action brought against him by the person injured, or any person or persons entitled to sue in respect of such loss of life, or shall affect the right of any person to limit his liability in the manner provided by law.

(4) Subsection (7) of section 187 applies also for the interpretation of this section.

Note —Derivation— Maritime Conventions Act 1911, s.2, s.9(4), s.2 proviso and s.1(2). **2D–228**

Crown ships

This section now applies to ships belonging to Her Majesty as it applies in the case of other ships; see s.192(1) and (2) of the Merchant Shipping Act 1995. **2D–229**

ADMIRALTY

Loss of life and personal injuries

2D–230   Proceedings in respect of such damages may now be brought *in rem* or *in personam* (see the SCA 1981, s.20(1)(f), para. 2D–139).

"Fault"

2D–231   As to the personification of the ship, see s.187, at paras 2D–210 and 2D–213.

"Owners"

2D–232   For meaning of this expression, see s.187(3) and para. 2D–224.

"Provided that ..."

2D–233   Examples of defences preserved by this proviso are contributory negligence and an exempting term in a contract for the carriage of a passenger.

"Limit his liability"

2D–234   For the provisions as to limitation of liability, see s.185 of and Sched.7 to the 1995 Act.

Loss of life or personal injuries: right of contribution

2D–235   **189.**—(1) Where loss of life or personal injuries are suffered by any person on board a ship owing to the fault of that ship and any other ship or ships, and a proportion of the damages is recovered against the owners of one of the ships which exceeds the proportion in which the ship was in fault, they may recover by way of contribution the amount of the excess from the owners of the other ship or ships to the extent to which those ships were respectively in fault.

(2)   Subsection (3) of section 187 applies also to this section.

(3)   Nothing in this section authorises the recovery of any amount which could not, by reason of any statutory or contractual limitation of, or exemption from, liability, or which could not for any other reason, have been recovered in the first instance as damages by the persons entitled to sue therefore.

(4)   In addition to any other remedy provided by law, the persons entitled to any contribution recoverable under this section shall, for the purposes of recovering it, have the same rights and powers as the persons entitled to sue for damages in the first instance.

2D–236   *Note* —Derivation— Maritime Conventions Act 1911, s.3(1), s.9(4), s.3(1) proviso and s.3(2).

Crown ships

2D–237   This section now applies in the case of ships belonging to Her Majesty as it applied in the case of other vessels; see the Merchant Shipping Act 1995, s.192(1) and (2).

General Note

2D–238   If an innocent passenger on board ship A receives personal injuries in a collision between A and B, for which both ships are equally to blame, and recovers damages against A, A can recover a moiety from B subject to B's right to limit his liability in appropriate cases, for the passenger could have recovered against B in the first place.

An illustration of the working of subs.(3) formerly the proviso to s.3 of the Maritime Conventions Act 1911 is afforded by *The Cedric* [1920] P. 193. The representatives of the crew of a French sailing ship lost in collision with a British ship, for which both were equally to blame, had recovered in full the amount of the claims from the British ship. The owners of the latter were unable to recover a moiety of their damages in respect of these life claims in contribution from the French owners, on proof that by French law the representatives of the crew would have had no valid claim against the French ship.

"Fault"

As to the personification of the ship, see s.187 at paras 2D–210, 2D–213. See too **2D–239** para. 2D–221.

Costs

Costs incurred in unreasonably disputing liability cannot be made the subject of **2D–240** contribution (*The Cairnbahn (No. 2)* (1914) 30 T.L.R. 309, CA).

"Recover by way of contribution"

It seems that this right of contribution can be enforced by the third party proce- **2D–241** dure provided for by CPR Pt20.

Proceedings to endorse contribution must be commenced within one year of the date of payment (see s.190, below).

"Statutory ... limitation"

As to limitation of liability see s.185 of and Sched.7 to the Merchant Shipping Act **2D–242** 1995 which came into force on January 1, 1996 replacing s.17 and Pts I and II of Sched.4 to the Merchant Shipping Act 1979.

"The same rights and powers"

i.e. a person claiming contribution can proceed *in rem* or *in personam*. See the SCA **2D–243** 1981, s.20(1)(f), para. 2D–139.

TIME LIMIT FOR PROCEEDINGS AGAINST OWNERS OR SHIP

Time limit for proceedings against owners or ship

190.—(1) This section applies to any proceedings to enforce any **2D–244** claim or lien against a ship or her owners—

> (a) in respect of damage or loss caused by the fault of that ship to another ship, its cargo or freight or any property on board it; or
>
> (b) for damages for loss of life or personal injury caused by the fault of that ship to any person on board another ship.

(2) The extent of the fault is immaterial for the purposes of this section.

(3) Subject to subsections (5) and (6) below, no proceedings to which this section applies shall be brought after the period of two years from the date when—

> (a) the damage or loss was caused; or
>
> (b) the loss of life or injury was suffered.

(4) Subject to subsections (5) and (6) below, no proceedings under any of sections 187 to 189 to enforce any contribution in respect of any overpaid proportion of any damages for loss of life or personal injury shall be brought after the period of one year from the date of payment.

(5) Any court having jurisdiction in such proceedings may, in ac- cordance with rules of court, extend the period allowed for bringing proceedings to such extent and on such conditions as it thinks fit.

(6) Any such court, if satisfied that there has not been during any period allowed for bringing proceedings any reasonable opportunity of arresting the defendant ship within—

> (a) the jurisdiction of the court, or

ADMIRALTY

> (b) the territorial sea of the country to which the plaintiff's ship belongs or in which the plaintiff resides or has his principal place of business,

shall extend the period allowed for bringing proceedings to an extent sufficient to give a reasonable opportunity of so arresting the ship.

2D-245 *Note* —Derivation— Maritime Conventions Act 1911, s.8 and s.8 proviso.

General note

2D-246 This section applies to claims against a ship or her owners for (1) damage sustained by a ship (2) damage sustained by cargo or goods aboard a ship (3) loss of life or personal injury of persons aboard a ship (4) contribution under s.189 of the Act. Further, in relation to the second and third types of claim it applies only to claims made against a ship (or the owners of a ship) other than the ship in which the cargo or goods or persons killed or injured were carried. See *The Niceto de Larrinaga* [1966] P. 80; [1965] 2 All E.R. 930; [1965] 2 Lloyd's Rep. 134.

H.M. Ships

2D-247 With the exception of subsection (6) this section applies to H.M. ships, see the Merchant Shipping Act 1995, s.192(1).

"...shall be brought"

2D-248 The effect of this section, like that of most of statutes of limitation, is not to extinguish the cause of action, but merely to bar the right to maintain the claim. See *The P.L.M. 8* [1920] P. 236; *The Dorie S.S. Co. v. Kamanetz Podolsk* (1923) 14 Ll.L.Rep. 512(Sc.).

The defence must be specifically pleaded; see CPR Pt 16 and Practice Direction— Statements of Case. As to the effect of omitting to plead, see *Re Robinson's Settlement* [1912] 1 Ch. 717 at 728, *per* Buckley L.J.

An entry of an acknowledgment of service to a claim form does not prevent the defendant from raising this defence (*The Llandovery Castle* [1920] P. 119).

If the defendant desires to raise any defence based on this section, he should raise it as a preliminary objection by way of application whether the claim is *in personam* or *in rem*. See *The Niceto de Larrinaga* [1965] 2 Lloyd's Rep. 134. On the hearing of such application the claimant may apply to the court for the exercise of its discretion in extending the time. If the objection is upheld the proper order is not that the claim form should be set aside, but that the claim is not maintainable; see *The P.L.M. 8* [1920] P. 236.

Section 190(3)(b) envisaged that there might be cases where time did not run from the date of collision and provided for cases where the date of loss of life or injury was not the same as the date of collision, see *Sweet v. Owners of Blyth Lifeboat, The Times*, February 22, 2002 where time began to run from the date on which the claimant first developed a recognised psychiatric injury rather than from the date of collision between the vessels.

"Owners"

2D-249 For the meaning of "owners," see s.187(3) and para. 2D-224.

"Damages for loss of life"

2D-250 In *The Alnwick sub nom. Robinson v. Owners of the Motor Tug Alnwick* [1965] P. 357, CA, it was held that s.8 the precursor of this section was not affected by s.3 of the Law Reform (Limitation of Actions, etc.) Act 1954 and that the relevant period of limitation for an action in respect of loss of life which fell within s.8 was therefore two years. See the Limitation Act 1980, ss.31 *et seq.*

"... caused by the fault of that ship ..."

2D-251 See para. 2D-221.

"... No proceedings ... shall be brought after the period of two years [or as appropriate, one year] ... "

2D-252 In *The Espanoleto* [1920] P. 223; 36 T.L.R. 554, it was held that inasmuch as the period of limitation provided by the precursor (s.8 of the Maritime Conventions Act) of this section was not absolute, the court should consider an application to renew on its merits and inquire whether the circumstances were such that the court would have given permission to *issue* the claim form notwithstanding that the time had expired, on the ground that the claimant had exercised due diligence in prosecuting his claim. If permission to issue the claim form would have been given, *a fortiori* a renewal of a claim form taken out within the prescribed time should be granted. See also *The World Harmony* [1965] 1 Lloyd's Rep. 244; [1967] P. 341; [1965] 2 All E.R. 139.

Where liability for damage has been proved or admitted, and the party liable has obtained a decree entitling him to limit his liability, claimants against the limitation fund may challenge the right of proof of other claimants who have not commenced proceedings within the periods prescribed by this section, for they are entitled to raise any defence which would have been open to the limiting person. But in such a case the Court will generally consider the fact that limitation proceedings have been instituted as a sufficient ground for extending the time for commencing proceedings: *The Dispenser* [1920] P. 228. *Secus*, if the non-issue of the claim form resulted from the deliberate election of the claimant not to sue in this country (*The Nedenes* (1925) 23 Lloyd's Rep. 57).

"May ... extend"

Substantial grounds must be shown before the court will exercise its discretion to deprive the defendant of the limitation which he prima facie enjoys; and the Court of Appeal will not interfere with the exercise of this discretion unless it is shown that a wrong principle has been applied (*The Kashmir* [1923] P. 85, CA; *The James Westoll* [1923] P. 94n., CA, or, *semble*, unless the Court of Appeal considers that there were special circumstances or substantial reasons calling for an extension of the limitation period: *Robinson v. Alnwick (Owners), The Alnwick* [1965] P. 357; [1965] 3 W.L.R. 118, CA; *sub nom. The Alnwick* [1965] 1 Lloyd's Rep. 69, revd. *ibid.*, 320, CA. See also *The Hesselmoor and the Sergeant* [1951] 1 Lloyd's Rep. 146 (where Willmer J. reviewed some of the earlier authorities) *The Sauria and the Trent* [1957] 1 Lloyd's Rep. 396, CA (where it was successfully contended that an informal admission of liability amounted to a contractual undertaking not to plead the defence of limitation of action) and three later decisions illustrating the application of the proviso to the Maritime Conventions Act 1911, s.8 from which this section is derived, *Bartlett v. Admiralty (The Vadne)* [1959] 2 Lloyd's Rep. 480 (discretion exercised) and *The Vadne* [1960] 1 Lloyd's Rep. 260; and *The Sunpak* [1960] 2 Lloyd's Rep. 213 (exercise of discretion refused)). For a case in which the court exercised its discretion in favour of a counterclaiming defendant, see *The Fairplay XIV* [1939] P. 57. See also *The World Harmony* (exercise of discretion refused). In *The Al Tahith* [1995] 2 Lloyd's Rep. 336 a case under the former s.8, M.C.A. 1911, it was said that the test to be applied is the same as under the former RSC O.6, r.8 but note that CPR, r.7.6 which replaces O.6, r.8 introduces a new approach.

There is no antithesis between subs. (5) and subs. (6). Thus, even in cases where there has been reasonable opportunity of arresting, the court may extend the period if satisfied that there were reasonable grounds for not issuing the claim form earlier, *The Arraiz* (1924) 19 Lloyd's Rep. 382; 132 L.T. 715, a case on the proviso to the former s.8 from which both present subss. (5)and (6)are derived.

"And shall ... extend"

Subsection (6) does not extend to Her Majesty's ships, see s.192(1) below.

"Reasonable opportunity"

The fact that the vessel has been within the jurisdiction for a few days within the period does not necessarily disprove lack of reasonable opportunity to arrest (*The Largo Law* (1920) 123 L.T. 560; 15 Asp.M.L.C. 104). See also *The Berny* [1977] 2 Lloyd's Rep. 533 at 547–549, where the question of reasonable opportunity to serve the claim form arose in connection with renewal of a claim form *in rem*.

APPLICATION TO CROWN AND ITS SHIPS

* * * *

Application to Crown and its ships

192.—(1) Sections 185, 186, 187, 188, 189 and 190 (except subsec-

2D–253

2D–254

2D–255

2D–256

ADMIRALTY

tion (6)) apply in the case of Her Majesty's ships as they apply in relation to other ships and section 191 applies to the Crown in its capacity as an authority or person specified in subsection (1).

(2) In this section "Her Majesty's ships" means—

    (a) ships of which the beneficial interest is vested in Her Majesty;

    (b) ships which are registered as Government ships;

    (c) ships which are for the time being demised or sub-demised to or in the exclusive possession of the Crown; except that it does not include any ship in which Her Majesty is interested otherwise than in right of Her Government in the United Kingdom unless that ship is for the time being demised or sub-demised to Her Majesty in right of Her Government in the United Kingdom or in the exclusive possession of Her Majesty in that right.

(3) In the application of subsection (2) above to Northern Ireland, any reference to Her Majesty's Government in the United Kingdom includes a reference to Her Government in Northern Ireland.

2D–257   *Note* —Derivation— Crown Proceedings Act 1947, ss.5, 6, 7, 30(1) and 38(2); the Merchant Shipping Act 1979, Sched.5, para. 3; and the Crown Proceedings Order 1981, (S.I. 1981 No. 233), Art.30(1).

Compulsory insurance or security

2D–258   192A.—(1) Subject to subsections (2) and (3) below, the Secretary of State may make regulations requiring that, in such cases as may be prescribed by the regulations, while a ship is in United Kingdom waters, there must be in force in respect of the ship—

    (a) a contract of insurance insuring such person or persons as may be specified by the regulations against such liabilities as may be so specified and satisfying such other requirements as may be so specified, or

    (b) such other security relating to those liabilities as satisfies requirements specified by or under the regulations.

(2) Regulations under this section shall not apply in relation to—

    (a) a qualifying foreign ship while it is exercising—

        (i) the right of innocent passage, or

        (ii) the right of transit passage through straits used for international navigation,

    (b) any warship, or

    (c) any ship for the time being used by the government of any State for other than commercial purposes.

(3) Regulations under this section may not require insurance or security to be maintained in respect of a ship in relation to any liability in any case where an obligation to maintain insurance or security in respect of that ship in relation to that liability is imposed by section 163 or by or under an Order in Council under section 182B.

(4) Regulations under this section may require that, where a person is obliged to have in force in respect of a ship a contract of in-

surance or other security, such documentary evidence as may be specified by or under the regulations of the existence of the contract of insurance or other security must be carried in the ship and produced on demand, by such persons as may be specified in the regulations, to such persons as may be so specified.

(5) Regulations under this section may provide—

(a) that in such cases as are prescribed a ship which contravenes the regulations shall be liable to be detained and that section 284 shall have effect, with such modifications (if any) as are prescribed by the regulations, in relation to the ship,

(b) that a contravention of the regulations shall be an offence punishable on summary conviction by a fine of an amount not exceeding £50,000, or such less amount as is prescribed by the regulations, and on conviction on indictment by a fine, and

(c) that any such contravention shall be an offence punishable only on summary conviction by a fine of an amount not exceeding £50,000, or such less amount as is prescribed by the regulations.

(6) Regulations under this section may—

(a) make different provision for different cases,

(b) make provision in terms of any document which the Secretary of State or any person considers relevant from time to time, and

(c) include such incidental, supplemental and transitional provision as appears to the Secretary of State to be expedient for the purposes of the regulations.

Note —Inserted by the Merchant Shipping and Maritime Security Act 1997, s.16. **2D–259** This provision is now in force. As at December 2002 see hereunder the Merchant Shipping (Ship Receiving Transhipped Fish) Regulations 1998 (S.I. 1998 No. 209), effective April 1998.

PART IX

SALVAGE AND WRECK

CHAPTER I

SALVAGE

Salvage Convention 1989 to have force of law

224.—(1) The provisions of the International Convention on **2D–260** Salvage, 1989 as set out in Part I of Schedule 11 (in this Chapter referred to as "the Salvage Convention") shall have the force of law in the United Kingdom.

(2) The provisions of Part II of that Schedule shall have effect in connection with the Salvage Convention, and subsection (1) above shall have effect subject to the provisions of that Part.

(3) If it appears to Her Majesty in Council that the Government of the United Kingdom has agreed to any revision of the Salvage

ADMIRALTY

Convention She may by Order in Council make such modifications of Parts I and II of Schedule 11 as She considers appropriate in consequence of the revision.

(4) Nothing in subsection (1) or (2) above shall affect any rights or liabilities arising out of any salvage operations started or other acts done before 1st January 1995.

(5) Nothing in any modification made by virtue of subsection (3) above shall affect any rights or liabilities arising out of any salvage operations started or other acts done before the day on which the modification comes into force.

(6) As respects any period before the entry into force of the Salvage Convention any reference in the Salvage Convention to a State Party to the Convention shall be read as a reference to the United Kingdom.

(7) A draft of an Order in Council proposed to be made by virtue of subsection (3) above shall not be submitted to Her Majesty in Council unless the draft has been approved by a resolution of each House of Parliament.

2D–261   *Note* —Derivation— Merchant Shipping (Salvage and Pollution) Act 1994. The derivation of Sched.7 (*q.v.*) is as to Pt I, Merchant Shipping Act 1979, Sched.4, Pt I and as to Pt II, Merchant Shipping Act 1979, s.49(5), Sched.4, Pt II: Merchant Shipping (Survey and Certification) Regulations 1995 (S.I. 1995 No. 1210), reg. 1(8).

Apportionment of salvage by the court

2D–262   229.—(1) Where—

    (a) the aggregate amount of salvage payable in respect of salvage services rendered in United Kingdom waters has been finally determined and exceeds £5,000; or

    (b) the aggregate amount of salvage payable in respect of salvage services rendered outside United Kingdom waters (of whatever amount) has been finally determined; but

    (c) in either case, any delay or dispute arises as to the apportionment of the amount,

the court may cause the amount of salvage to be apportioned among the persons entitled to it in such manner as it thinks just.

(2) Any decision of the court under this section shall be made on the basis of the criteria contained in Article 13 of the Salvage Convention.

(3) For the purpose of making that apportionment, the court may—

    (a) appoint any person to carry that apportionment into effect;

    (b) compel any person in whose hands or under whose control the amount may be to distribute it or to pay it into court to be dealt with as the court directs; and

    (c) issue such process as it thinks fit.

(4) In this section "the court" means the High Court or, in Scotland, the Court of Session or a sheriff.

Note —Derivation— Merchant Shipping Act 1894, s.556; the Merchant Shipping **2D–263** (Registration, etc.) Act 1993, Sched.4, para. 30; and the Merchant Shipping (Salvage and Pollution) Act 1994, Sched.2, para. 1(5).

Salvage claims against the Crown and Crown rights of salvage and regulation thereof

230.—(1) Subject to section 29 of the Crown Proceedings Act 1947 **2D–264** (exclusion of proceedings in rem against the Crown) (so far as consistent with the Salvage Convention) the law relating to civil salvage, whether of life or property, except sections 225, 226 and 227, shall apply in relation to salvage services in assisting any of Her Majesty's ships, or in saving life therefrom, or in saving any cargo or equipment belonging to Her Majesty in right of Her Government in the United Kingdom, in the same manner as if the ship, cargo or equipment belonged to a private person.

(2) Where salvage services are rendered by or on behalf of Her Majesty, whether in right of Her Government in the United Kingdom or otherwise, Her Majesty shall be entitled to claim salvage in respect of those services to the same extent as any other salvor, and shall have the same rights and remedies in respect of those services as any other salvor.

(3) No claim for salvage services by the commander or crew, or part of the crew, of any of Her Majesty's ships shall be finally adjudicated upon without the consent of the Secretary of State to the prosecution of the claim.

(4) Any document purporting to give the consent of the Secretary of State for the purposes of subsection (3)above and to be signed by an officer of the Ministry of Defence shall be evidence of that consent.

(5) If a claim is prosecuted without the consent required by subsection (3) above the claim shall be dismissed with costs.

(6) The reference in subsection (5) above to dismissal with costs shall in Scotland be construed as a reference to dismissal with the defender being found entitled to expenses.

(7) "Her Majesty's ships" has the same meaning in this section as in section 192.

(8) In the application of this section to Northern Ireland, any reference to Her Majesty's Government in the United Kingdom includes a reference to Her Government in Northern Ireland.

Note —Derivation— Crown Proceedings Act 1947, s.8, s.38(2); the Merchant Ship- **2D–265** ping Act 1894, s.557; the Merchant Shipping (Salvage and Pollution) Act 1994, Sched.2, para. 3; the Defence (Transfer of Functions) Act 1964, ss.1(2), 3(2); and the Crown Proceedings (Northern Ireland) Order 1981 (S.I. 1981 No. 233), Art. 30(1).

ADMIRALTY

2E ARBITRATION PROCEEDINGS

PART 62—ARBITRATION CLAIMS

Contents

Editorial Introduction

2E–1
Part I of Part 62 is concerned with applications to which the Arbitration Act 1996 applies, Pt II is concerned with matters to which the old law applies, and Pt III with common enforcement procedures.

"The old law" means the enactments specified in section 107 of the Arbitration Act 1996 as they stood before their amendment or repeal by the 1996 Act, namely the Arbitration Act 1950 (see SCP 1999, Vol. 2, Section 21A, paras 21A–1 *et seq.*); the Arbitration Act 1975 (see SCP 1999, Vol. 2, Section 21B, paras 21B–1 *et seq.*) and the Arbitration Act 1979 (see SCP 1999, Vol. 2, Section 21C, paras 21C–1 *et seq.*).

The old law is preserved as a result of the provisions of section 109(2) of the Arbitration Act 1996 which provided that any order bringing the Act into force might contain any transitional provisions as might appear necessary and the provisions of the Arbitration Act 1996 (Commencement No. 1) Order 1996, made on December 16, 1996, by way of transitional provision, provide that:

2. The old law shall continue to apply to:
   (a) arbitral proceedings commenced before the appointed day [January 31, 1997];
   (b) arbitration applications commenced or made before the appointed day;
   (c) arbitration applications commenced or made on or after the appointed day relating to arbitral proceedings commenced before the appointed day;
and the provisions of the Act which would otherwise be applicable shall not apply.

Note

With the passage of time since the coming into force of the 1996 Act (January 31, **2E–1.1**

1997) the transitional concept of the "old law" is now (July 2005 onwards) considered to be for all practical purposes in a state of desuetude if not without any effect. See further at 2E–18.1 .

Part II of the 1950 Act together with the First Schedule thereto were not repealed by the 1996 Act and survive in their own right independently of the transitional concept of "the old law" but are now rarely relied upon.

The Application

2E–2   Arbitration applications under the 1996 Act (see Section I of Part 62) save for application under s.9, are made by use of an arbitration claim form (see rule 62.3, the Practice Direction—Arbitration and the reference to the form set out at Appendix A to the practice direction). Applications under s.9 are made by ordinary application process in the existing proceedings. The courts where the arbitration claim form may be issued are set out in the Practice Direction—Arbitration, para. 62.2.3.

Applications under "the old law" see (Section II of Part 62) save for s.4 of the 1950 Act applications are made by the use of an arbitration claim form and must be stated in the Commercial Court and issued out of the Admiralty and Commercial Registry at the R.C.J. London and where required to be heard by a judge must be heard by a judge of that court unless he otherwise directs, see rule 62.12 and Practice Direction—Arbitration, para. 62.14.1. Claims for the attendance of witnesses within the area of a district registry may be started within the relevant district registry, see rule 62.14 and see the Practice Direction, para. 7.2.

Applications for enforcement should be made using an arbitration claim form and may be considered by a Judge, Master, Admiralty Registrar or District Judge.

Related Sources

2E–3
- Arbitration Act 1950, Pt II (see paras 2E–50 *et seq.*).
- Arbitration Act 1996 (see paras 2E–76 *et seq.*).
- The preserved "old law"
  — Arbitration Act 1950, Pt I (see SCP 1999, Vol. 2, Section 21A).
  — Arbitration Acts 1975 and 1979 (see SCP 1999, Vol. 2, Sections 21B and 21C).
- High Court and County Court (Allocation of Arbitration Proceedings) Order 1996 (S.I. 1996 No. 3215), as amended.
- CPR 6.
- CPR 8.
- CPR 11
- CPR 25.
- CPR 34.
- CPR 58 and 59.
- CPR 74.
- The Admiralty and Commercial Courts Guide, Section O.
- The Technology and Construction Court Guide, Section 10.

Forms

2E–4
- **N8** Claim form (arbitration)
- **N8A** Notes for claimant
- **N8B** Notes for defendant
- **N15** Acknowledgment of service (arbitration claims)

Scope of this Part and interpretation[1]

2E–5   **62.1—(1) This Part contains rules about arbitration claims.**

(2) **In this Part—**

(a) **"the 1950 Act" means the Arbitration Act 1950;**

(b) **"the 1975 Act" means the Arbitration Act 1975;**

---

[1] Amended by Civil Procedure (Amendment No. 5) Rules 2001 (S.I. 2001 No. 4015).

(c) "the 1979 Act" means the Arbitration Act 1979;

(d) "the 1996 Act" means the Arbitration Act 1996;

(e) references to—

(i) the 1996 Act; or

(ii) any particular section of that Act

include references to that Act or to the particular section of that Act as applied with modifications by the ACAS Arbitration Scheme (England and Wales) Order 2001; and

(f) "arbitration claim form" means a claim form in the form set out in the practice direction.

(3) Part 58 (Commercial Court) applies to arbitration claims in the Commercial Court, Part 59 (Mercantile Court) applies to arbitration claims in the Mercantile Court and Part 60 (Technology and Construction Court claims) applies to arbitration claims in the Technology and Construction Court, except where this Part provides otherwise.

I. Claims under the 1996 Act

Interpretation[1]

62.2—(1) In this Section of this Part "arbitration claim" means—

2E-6

(a) any application to the court under the 1996 Act;

(b) a claim to determine—

(i) whether there is a valid arbitration agreement;

(ii) whether an arbitration tribunal is properly constituted; or what matters have been submitted to arbitration in accordance with an arbitration agreement;

(c) a claim to declare that an award by an arbitral tribunal is not binding on a party; and

(d) any other application affecting—

(i) arbitration proceedings (whether started or not); or

(ii) an arbitration agreement.

(2) This Section of this Part does not apply to an arbitration claim to which Sections II or III of this Part apply.

Starting the claim[2]

62.3—(1) Except where paragraph (2) applies an arbitration claim must be started by the issue of an arbitration claim form in accordance with the Part 8 procedure.

2E-7

(2) An application under section 9 of the 1996 Act to stay legal proceedings must be made by application notice to the court dealing with those proceedings.

---

[1] Amended by Civil Procedure (Amendment No. 5) Rules 2001 (S.I. 2001 No. 4015).

[2] Amended by Civil Procedure (Amendment No. 5) Rules 2001 (S.I. 2001 No. 4015) and Civil Procedure (Amendment No. 4) Rules 2005 (S.I. 2005 No. 3515).

(3) **The courts in which an arbitration claim may be started are set out in the practice direction.**

(4) **Rule 30.5 applies with the modification that a judge of the Technology and Construction Court may transfer the claim to any other court or specialist list.**

Note

2E–8   For the practice direction see below. See too the High Court and County Courts (Allocation of Arbitration Proceedings) Order 1996 at paras 2E–348 *et seq.*

Arbitration claim form[1]

2E–9   **62.4—(1) An arbitration claim form must—**

(a) **include a concise statement of—**

(i) **the remedy claimed; and**

(ii) **any questions on which the claimant seeks the decision of the court;**

(b) **give details of any arbitration award challenged by the claimant, identifying which part or parts of the award are challenged and specifying the grounds for the challenge;**

(c) **show that any statutory requirements have been met;**

(d) **specify under which section of the 1996 Act the claim is made;**

(e) **identify against which (if any) defendants a costs order is sought; and**

(f) **specify either—**

(i) **the persons on whom the arbitration claim form is to be served, stating their role in the arbitration and whether they are defendants; or**

(ii) **that the claim is made without notice under section 44(3) of the 1996 Act and the grounds relied on.**

(2) **Unless the court orders otherwise an arbitration claim form must be served on the defendant within 1 month from the date of issue and rules 7.5 and 7.6 are modified accordingly.**

(3) **Where the claimant applies for an order under section 12 of the 1996 Act (extension of time for beginning arbitral proceedings or other dispute resolution procedures), he may include in his arbitration claim form an alternative application for a declaration that such an order is not needed.**

Service out of the jurisdiction[2]

2E–10   **62.5—(1) The court may give permission to serve an arbitration claim form out of the jurisdiction if—**

(a) **the claimant seeks to—**

---

[1] Amended by Civil Procedure (Amendment No. 5) Rules 2001 (S.I. 2001 No. 4015).
[2] Amended by Civil Procedure (Amendment No. 5) Rules 2001 (S.I. 2001 No. 4015).

(i) **challenge; or**

(ii) **appeal on a question of law arising out of,**

an arbitration award made within the jurisdiction;

(The place where an award is treated as made is determined by section 53 of the 1996 Act).

(b) **the claim is for an order under section 44 of the 1996 Act; or**

(c) **the claimant—**

(i) **seeks some other remedy or requires a question to be decided by the court affecting an arbitration (whether started or not), an arbitration agreement or an arbitration award; and**

(ii) **the seat of the arbitration is or will be within the jurisdiction or the conditions in section 2(4) of the 1996 Act are satisfied.**

(2) **An application for permission under paragraph (1) must be supported by written evidence—**

(a) **stating the grounds on which the application is made; and**

(b) **showing in what place or country the person to be served is, or probably may be found.**

(3) **Rules 6.24 to 6.29 apply to the service of an arbitration claim form under paragraph (1).**

(4) **An order giving permission to serve an arbitration claim form out of the jurisdiction must specify the period within which the defendant may file an acknowledgment of service.**

Note

Rule 62.5 applies only to applications by and against parties to an arbitration and does not allow service out of the jurisdiction on a non-party, *Vale Do Doce Navegacao S.A. v. Shanghai Bao Steel Ocean Shipping Co Ltd* [2000] 2 Lloyd's Rep. 1 (attempt to serve brokers) a case under the forerunner to this rule. **2E–11**

Notice[1]

62.6—(1) Where an arbitration claim is made under section 24, 28 or 56 of the 1996 Act, each arbitrator must be a defendant. **2E–12**

(2) **Where notice must be given to an arbitrator or any other person it may be given by sending him a copy of—**

(a) **the arbitration claim form; and**

(b) **any written evidence in support.**

(3) **Where the 1996 Act requires an application to the court to be made on notice to any other party to the arbitration, that notice must be given by making that party a defendant.**

Case management[2]

62.7—(1) Part 26 and any other rule that requires a party to file an allocation questionnaire does not apply. **2E–13**

---

[1] Amended by Civil Procedure (Amendment No. 5) Rules 2001 (S.I. 2001 No. 4015).

[2] Amended by Civil Procedure (Amendment No. 5) Rules 2001 (S.I. 2001 No. 4015).

(2) Arbitration claims are allocated to the multi-track.

(3) Part 29 does not apply.

(4) The automatic directions set out in the practice direction apply unless the court orders otherwise.

Stay of legal proceedings[1]

2E–14   **62.8**—(1) An application notice seeking a stay of legal proceedings under section 9 of the 1996 Act[2] must be served on all parties to those proceedings who have given an address for service.

(2) A copy of an application notice under paragraph (1) must be served on any other party to the legal proceedings (whether or not he is within the jurisdiction) who has not given an address for service, at—

    (a) his last known address; or

    (b) a place where it is likely to come to his attention.

(3) Where a question arises as to whether—

    (a) an arbitration agreement has been concluded; or

    (b) the dispute which is the subject-matter of the proceedings falls within the terms of such an agreement,

the court may decide that question or give directions to enable it to be decided and may order the proceedings to be stayed pending its decision.

Variation of time[3]

2E–15   **62.9**—(1) The court may vary the period of 28 days fixed by section 70(3) of the 1996 Act for—

    (a) challenging the award under section 67 or 68 of the Act; and

    (b) appealing against an award under section 69 of the Act.

(2) An application for an order under paragraph (1) may be made without notice being served on any other party before the period of 28 days expires.

(3) After the period of 28 days has expired—

    (a) an application for an order extending time under paragraph (1) must—

        (i) be made in the arbitration claim form; and

        (ii) state the grounds on which the application is made;

    (b) any defendant may file written evidence opposing the extension of time within 7 days after service of the arbitration claim form; and

    (c) if the court extends the period of 28 days, each defendant's time for acknowledging service and serving

---

[1] Amended by Civil Procedure (Amendment No. 5) Rules 2001 (S.I. 2001 No. 4015).

[2] 1996 c.23.

[3] Amended by Civil Procedure (Amendment No. 5) Rules 2001 (S.I. 2001 No. 4015).

evidence shall start to run as if the arbitration claim form had been served on the date when the court's order is served on that defendant.

Hearings[1]

62.10—(1) The court may order that an arbitration claim be heard either in public or in private.   **2E–16**

(2) Rule 39.2 does not apply.

(3) Subject to any order made under paragraph (1)—
    (a) the determination of—
        (i) a preliminary point of law under section 45 of the 1996 Act; or
        (ii) an appeal under section 69 of the 1996 Act on a question of law arising out of an award,
will be heard in public; and
    (b) all other arbitration claims will be heard in private.

(4) Paragraph (3)(a) does not apply to—
    (a) the preliminary question of whether the court is satisfied of the matters set out in section 45(2)(b); or
    (b) an application for permission to appeal under section 69(2)(b).

Note

In *Moscow City Council v. Bankers Trust Co* [2004] EWCA Civ 314; [2005] Q.B. 207;   **2E–16.1**
[2004] 3 W.L.R. 533; [2004] 4 All E.R. 746; [2004] 2 Lloyd's Rep. 179, the Court of Appeal reviewed the several considerations material to deciding whether the hearing of an arbitration claim should be in public or in private and whether publication of any judgment given or order made should be restricted or not. At paragraph 34, Mance L.J. said:

"The consideration that parties have elected to arbitrate confidentially and privately cannot dictate the position is respect of arbitration claims brought to court under CPR 62.10. CPR 62.10 therefore only represents a starting point. Such proceedings are no longer consensual. The possibility of pursuing them exists in the public interest. The courts, when called upon to exercise the supervisory role assigned to them under the Arbitration Act 1996, are acting as a branch of the state, not as a mere extension of the consensual arbitral process. Nevertheless, they are acting in the public interest to facilitate the fairness and well-being of a consensual method of dispute resolution, and both the Rule Committee and the courts can still take into account the parties' expectations regarding privacy and confidentiality when agreeing to arbitrate."

And at paragraphs 38 and 39:

"...In arbitration claims relating to such arbitrations, the starting point may easily give way to a public hearing. In every case, while it will be appropriate to start the hearing in private as contemplated by CPR 62.10, the court should be ready to hear representations from one or other party that the hearing should be continued in public, and should anyway if appropriate raise this possibility with the parties, as Lord Woolf stressed in *ex p. Kaim Todner*.

Further, even though the hearing may have been in private, the court should, when preparing and giving judgment, bear in mind that any judgment should be given in public, where this can be done without disclosing significant confidential information."

And at paragraph 42:

"...It is, I think, better to describe CPR 62.10 and indeed 39.2 as establishing start-

---

[1] Amended by Civil Procedure (Amendment No. 5) Rules 2001 (S.I. 2001 No. 4015).

ing points, rather than as presumptions. If neither the parties nor the judge of his or her own motion raises any question about the appropriateness of private hearing, where that is the starting position, then the hearing will remain private. But, once the question of publication is raised, the judge's task is to weigh all relevant circumstances; and even where it is not raised by the parties, he or she may if appropriate raise it of his own motion."

II. Other Arbitration Claims

Scope of this Section[1]

2E–17   **62.11—(1) This Section of this Part contains rules about arbitration claims to which the old law applies.**

> (2) **In this Section—**
>> (a) **"the old law" means the enactments specified in Schedules 3 and 4 of the 1996 Act as they were in force before their amendment or repeal by that Act; and**
>> (b) **"arbitration claim" means any application to the court under the old law and includes an appeal (or application for permission to appeal) to the High Court under section 1(2) of the 1979 Act[2].**
>
> (3) **This Section does not apply to—**
>> (a) **a claim to which Section III of this Part applies; or**
>> (b) **a claim on the award.**

Note

2E–18   "The old law", namely the Arbitration Act 1950; the Arbitration Act 1975; and the Arbitration Act 1979, the texts of which are set out in SCP 1999, Vol. 2, Section 21 at paras 21A-1 *et seq.*, 21B–1 *et seq.*, and 21C–1 *et seq.* respectively. See too under Note at 2E–1.1 above.

Other Arbitration Claims—Section II

2E–18.1   It is important to note that the provisions of Section II of Part 62 and Section II of its associated Practice Direction apply only to arbitration claims under "the old law". Such provisions should not be applied by analogy or otherwise to claims under the 1996 Act for which a more flexible regime consistent with the modern approach to arbitration is provided. In particular for 1996 Act claims a more flexible point of entry and jurisdiction is provided (see PD62.2.3) allowing an arbitration claim to be issued and considered as appropriate to its subject matter in the Chancery Division, the Technology and Construction Court, the Mercantile lists (where established) and TCC lists of the High Court District Registries and the Mercantile list of the Central London County Court as well as the Commercial Court as hitherto. Applications for a stay under s.4 of the 1950 Act or under s.9 of the 1996 Act were and are in any event made in whatever Court is dealing with the proceedings concerned.

Applications to Judge[3]

2E–19   **62.12 A claim—**
> (a) **seeking permission to appeal under section 1(2) of the 1979 Act;**

---

[1] Amended by Civil Procedure (Amendment No. 5) Rules 2001 (S.I. 2001 No. 4015).

[2] 1979 c.42; repealed by the Arbitration Act 1996 (c.23), section 107(2) and Schedule 4 but continues to apply to claims commenced before January 31, 1997 by virtue of the Arbitration Act 1996 (Commencement No. 1) Order 1996 (S.I. 1996 No. 3146), article 4 and Schedule 2.

[3] Amended by Civil Procedure (Amendment No. 5) Rules 2001 (S.I. 2001, No.4015).

(b) **under section 1(5) of that Act (including any claim seeking permission); or**

(c) **under section 5 of that Act,**

must be made in the High Court and will be heard by a judge of the Commercial Court unless any such judge directs otherwise.

Effect of rule

In connection with the following commentary it is suggested that reference be made first to the Note at 2E–1.1 and the Note at 2E–18.1 above.   2E–20

Applications under s.1(5) of the 1979 Act must be made to a judge. These are applications to order the arbitrator or umpire concerned to state the reasons for his award in sufficient detail to enable the court, should an appeal be brought under s.1 of the 1979 Act, to consider any questions of law arising out of the award. The reason for this requirement is because of the likely complexity and importance of the questions which will probably arise in considering whether the award does or does not sufficiently set out the reasons for the award. An application under s.1(5) of the 1979 Act, including any application for permission is made by an arbitration form in accordance with Pt 8, which must be served on the arbitrator or umpire, as the case may be, and on all the parties to the reference (see r.62.13(3)).

Applications under s.5 of the 1979 Act must be made to a judge. These are applications to empower the arbitrator or umpire to continue with the reference in default of acknowledgment of service by any party or of non-compliance by a party with an order made by the arbitrator or umpire in the same manner as a Judge of the High Court might continue with proceedings where a party fails to comply with an order of the court or a requirement of the rules of court.

Applications for permission to appeal to the court under s.1(2) of the 1979 Act must be made to a judge. Section 1(2) provides that an appeal shall lie to the court on any question of law arising out of an award made on an arbitration agreement and in s.1(3) it is stated that an appeal may be brought by any of the parties to the reference (a) with the consent of all the other parties or (b) with the permission of the court.

Applications under this rule must be made, where a claim is pending by application notice in the claim, and in any other case by a Pt 8 arbitration claim form (see r.62.13(1) and (2).

It should further be noted that applications under this rule which are required to be heard by a Judge must be heard by a Commercial judge, unless he directs otherwise (see the practice direction para. 62.14(1).

Apart from the matters specified in this rule, all other applications arising under the Arbitration Act 1950, may be made in chambers and heard by the judge, Master or Admiralty Registrar. They include applications to stay proceedings under s.4, to appoint an arbitrator or umpire under s.10, for the issue of a witness summons, and all other matters included in s.12(6) of the Arbitration Act 1950. The effect of this rule is to negative the decisions in *Raymond and Reid v. Granger* [1952] 2 All E.R. 1952, and *Kruger Townwear Ltd v. Northern Assurance Co* [1953] 1 W.L.R. 1049; [1953] 2 All E.R. 727n.

Without notice applications for injunctions

CPR, r.25.2, which permits applications for injunctive relief in cases in urgency, before the issue of a Part 7 claim form or a Part 8 claim form. Where injunctive relief is granted in such circumstances, however, the claim form should be issued promptly thereafter. It is unacceptable that a *Mareva* injunction, for example, granted in aid of an arbitration, should remain in force for two months after its grant without any originating process to sustain it; accordingly such an injunction will be discharged (*Siporex Trade SA v. Comdel Commodities Ltd* [1986] 2 Lloyd's Rep. 428; (1986) 136 N.L.J. 538).   2E–21

Starting the claim[1]

62.13—(1) Except where paragraph (2) applies an arbitration   2E–22

---

[1] Amended by Civil Procedure (Amendment No. 5) Rules 2001 (S.I. 2001 No. 4015).

claim must be started by the issue of an arbitration claim form in accordance with the Part 8 procedure.

(2) Where an arbitration claim is to be made in existing proceedings—

    (a) it must be made by way of application notice; and

    (b) any reference in this Section of this Part to an arbitration claim form includes a reference to an application notice.

(3) The arbitration claim form in an arbitration claim under section 1(5) of the 1979 Act (including any claim seeking permission) must be served on—

    (a) the arbitrator or umpire; and

    (b) any other party to the reference.

Claims in District Registries[1]

2E–23   62.14 If—

    (a) a claim is to be made under section 12(4) of the 1950 Act[2] for an order for the issue of a witness summons to compel the attendance of the witness before an arbitrator or umpire; and

    (b) the attendance of the witness is required within the district of a District Registry,

the claim may be started in that Registry.

Time limits and other special provisions about arbitration claims[3]

2E–24   62.15—(1) An arbitration claim to—

    (a) remit an award under section 22 of the 1950 Act[4];

    (b) set aside an award under section 23(2) of that Act[5] or otherwise; or

    (c) direct an arbitrator or umpire to state the reasons for an award under section 1(5) of the 1979 Act,

must be made, and the arbitration claim form served, within 21 days after the award has been made and published to the parties.

(2) An arbitration claim to determine any question of law arising in the course of a reference under section 2(1) of the Arbitration Act 1979 must be made, and the arbitration claim form served, within 14 days after—

---

[1] Amended by Civil Procedure (Amendment No. 5) Rules 2001 (S.I. 2001 No. 4015).

[2] 1950 c.27; section 12(4) was repealed by the Arbitration Act 1996 (c.23), section 107(2) and Schedule 4 but continues to apply to claims commenced before January 31, 1997 by virtue of the Arbitration Act 1996 (Commencement No. 1) Order 1996 (S.I. 1996 No. 3146), article 4 and Schedule 2.

[3] Amended by Civil Procedure (Amendment No. 5) Rules 2001 (S.I. 2001, No.4015).

[4] 1950 c.27; section 22 was repealed by the Arbitration Act 1996 (c.23), section 107(2) and Schedule 4 but continues to apply to claims commenced before January 31, 1997 by virtue of the Arbitration Act 1996 (Commencement No. 1) Order 1996 (S.I. 1996 No. 3146), article 4 and Schedule 2.

[5] 1950 c.27; section 23(2) was repealed by the Arbitration Act 1996 (c.23), section 107(2) and Schedule 4 but continues to apply to claims commenced before January 31, 1997 by virtue of the Arbitration Act 1996 (Commencement No. 1) Order 1996 (S.I. 1996 No. 3146), article 4 and Schedule 2.

ARBITRATION

    (a) **the arbitrator or umpire gave his consent in writing to the claim being made; or**

    (b) **the other parties so consented.**

(3) **An appeal under section 1(2) of the 1979 Act must be filed, and the arbitration claim form served, within 21 days after the award has been made and published to the parties.**

(4) **Where reasons material to an appeal under** section 1(2) **of the 1979 Act are given on a date subsequent to the publication of the award, the period of 21 days referred to in paragraph (3) will run from the date on which reasons are given.**

(5) **In every arbitration claim to which this rule applies—**

    (a) **the arbitration claim form must state the grounds of the claim or appeal;**

    (b) **where the claim or appeal is based on written evidence, a copy of that evidence must be served with the arbitration claim form; and**

    (c) **where the claim or appeal is made with the consent of the arbitrator, the umpire or the other parties, a copy of every written consent must be served with the arbitration claim form.**

(6) **In an appeal under section 1(2) of the 1979 Act—**

    (a) **a statement of the grounds for the appeal specifying the relevant parts of the award and reasons; and**

    (b) **where permission is required, any written evidence in support of the contention that the question of law concerns—**

        (i) **a term of a contract; or**

        (ii) **an event,**

which is not a "one-off" term or event,

must be filed and served with the arbitration claim form.

(7) **Any written evidence in reply to written evidence under paragraph (6)(b) must be filed and served on the claimant not less than 2 days before the hearing.**

(8) **A party to a claim seeking permission to appeal under section 1(2) of the 1979 Act who wishes to contend that the award should be upheld for reasons not expressed or fully expressed in the award and reasons must file and serve on the claimant, a notice specifying the grounds of his contention not less than 2 days before the hearing.**

General Note to 2E–25.1 and 2E–27 to 2E–31

2E–25
In connection with the above mentioned commentaries reference should be made first to the Note at 2E–1.1 and the Note at 2E–18.1 .

Time for applying

2E–25.1
The–21–day time limit imposed by r.62.15(1) applies both to an application to set aside an award under s.23(2) of the Arbitration Act 1950 and to an application at common law for a declaration that an award is void on the grounds of the arbitrator's conduct. The time–limit cannot be circumvented simply by avoiding the use of the term "misconduct" in the application (*Cook International Inc v. B.V. Handelsmaatschappij Jean Delvaux* [1985] 2 Lloyd's Rep. 225 at 233). The 21–day–time limit is not mandatory. The court has jurisdiction to extend time, see *Nagusina Naviera v. Allied*

Maritime Inc [2002] C.L.C. 385 (a case under s.1(2) of the Arbitration Act 1979 and concerning the relevance of CPR, r.7.6).

"Made and published"

2E–26 An award is made and published when the arbitrator gives notice to the parties that it is ready. Delay in taking up the award does not extend the time for appealing or applying (*The Archipelagos* [1979] Lloyd's Rep. 289; *Selous Street Properties Ltd v. Oronel Fabrics Ltd* (1984) 270 E.G. 643).

Appeal under section 1(2) of the Arbitration Act 1979—practice

2E–27 The practice is regulated by the provisions of r.62.15, and, in particular, by sub-rules (3) to (8) thereof inclusive. See too Section O of the Admiralty and Commercial Courts Guide and in particular paras O.16.1 *et seq.* which provide as follows:

O16 Challenging the award

Challenge by way of appeal

2E–27.1 O16.1 A party wishing to appeal against the award of an arbitrator or umpire must file and serve with the arbitration claim form a statement of the grounds for the appeal, specifying the relevant part(s) of the award and reasons: rule 62.15(6).

O16.2 A party seeking permission to appeal must also file and serve with the arbitration claim form any written evidence in support of the contention that the question of law concerns a term of the contract or an event which is not "one off": rule 62.15(6).

O16.3 Any written evidence in reply must be filed and served not less than 2 days before the hearing of the application for permission to appeal: rule 62.15(7).

O16.4 A party who wishes to contend that the award should be upheld for reasons other than those set out in the award and reasons must file and serve on the claimant a notice specifying the grounds of his contention not less than 2 days before the hearing of the application for permission to appeal: rule 62.15(8).

O16.5 Applications for permission to appeal will be heard orally, but will not normally be listed for longer than half an hour. Skeleton arguments should be lodged.

Claims to set aside or remit the award

2E–27.2 O16.6 A claim to set aside or remit an award on the grounds of misconduct should not be regarded as an alternative to, or a means of supporting, an application for permission to appeal.

O16.7 The directions set out in 62PD 6.2–6.7 should be followed unless the court orders otherwise.

Service out of the jurisdiction[1]

2E–28 **62.16—(1) Subject to paragraph (2)—**

(a) **any arbitration claim form in an arbitration claim under the 1950 Act or the 1979 Act; or**

(b) **any order made in such a claim,**

may be served out of the jurisdiction with the permission of the court if the arbitration to which the claim relates—

(i) **is governed by the law of England and Wales; or**

(ii) **has been, is being, or will be, held within the jurisdiction.**

(2) An arbitration claim form seeking permission to enforce an award may be served out of the jurisdiction with the permission of

---

[1] Amended by Civil Procedure (Amendment No. 5) Rules 2001 (S.I. 2001 No. 4015).

the court whether or not the arbitration is governed by the law of England and Wales.

(3) An application for permission to serve an arbitration claim form out of the jurisdiction must be supported by written evidence—

(a) stating the grounds on which the application is made; and

(b) showing in what place or country the person to be served is, or probably may be found.

(4) Rules 6.24 to 6.29 apply to the service of an arbitration claim form under paragraph (1).

(5) An order giving permission to serve an arbitration claim form out of the jursidiction must specify the period within which the defendant may file an acknowledgment of service.

Note

This rule is really an extension of CPR Part 6, r.6.20 *et seq.*, and an additional case **2E–29** in which service out of the jurisdiction is permissible with the permission of the court. For observations on the differences between service out of jurisdiction under the former RSC, O.11 the forerunner of this rule and under this rule, see *Mayer Newman Co Ltd v. Al Ferro Commodities Corporation SA* [1990] 2 Lloyd's Rep. 290 at 293, CA, *per* Bingham L.J. The basis of the jurisdiction under this rule is that the "arbitration is to be or has been held within the jurisdiction". The practice under this rule is the same in all respects as under CPR Part 6, r.6.20 *et seq.*, including the requirement under CPR Part 6, r.6.28 that translations be provided of documents for service on a foreign state in arbitration proceedings unless the official language or an official language of that State is English.

Civil Jurisdiction and Judgments Acts 1982

Art.1 of the Brussels Convention, which forms the first Schedule to the Act, provides **2E–30** that the convention shall not apply to arbitration. The word "arbitration" in Art.1 covers all matters connected with arbitration, including the question whether there is a valid arbitration agreement (*Marc Rich & Co AG v. Societa Italiana Impianti PA, The Atlantic Emperor, Independent*, November 21, 1988). Thus where a claimant issues a Pt 8 arbitration claim form seeking the appointment of an arbitrator under s.10(3) of the Arbitration Act 1950, the Italian defendant having denied the existence of the alleged arbitration agreement, the claimant may properly seek permission to serve the Pt 8 arbitration claim form out of the jurisdiction under this rule, and should not attempt to serve without leave in Italy under the convention (*ibid.*).

Application

This rule is concerned only with applications by and against parties to an arbitra- **2E–31** tion which relate to the arbitration to which they are parties. Thus the natural meaning of the para. is that the application must be against the other party to the reference and not a non-party (as case under the pre-1997 RSC O.73, r.7 being *The Cienvik* [1996] 2 Lloyd's Rep. 395). The reasoning of the court in *The Cienvik* was adopted by the Court of Appeal in *Tate and Lyle Industries Ltd v. CIA Usina Bulhoes and Cargill Inc* [1997] 1 Lloyd's Rep. 355, when holding that there is no jurisdiction to issue a without notice injunction against a proposed defendant not a party to the arbitration under s.12 of the 1950 Act.

III. Enforcement

Scope of this Section[1]

2E-32   62.17 **This Section of this Part applies to all arbitration enforcement proceedings other than by a claim on the award.**

Enforcement of awards[2]

2E-33   62.18—(1) **An application for permission under—**

(a) **section 66 of the 1996 Act**[3]**;**

(b) **section 101 of the 1996 Act;**

(c) **section 26 of the 1950 Act**[4]**; or**

(d) **section 3(1)(a) of the 1975 Act,**[5]

to enforce an award in the same manner as a judgment or order may be made without notice in an arbitration claim form.

(2) **The court may specify parties to the arbitration on whom the arbitration claim form must be served.**

(3) **The parties on whom the arbitration claim form is served must acknowledge service and the enforcement proceedings will continue as if they were an arbitration claim under Section I of this Part.**

(4) **With the permission of the court the arbitration claim form may be served out of the jurisdiction irrespective of where the award is, or is treated as, made.**

(5) **Where the applicant applies to enforce an agreed award within the meaning of section 51(2) of the 1996 Act—**

(a) **the arbitration claim form must state that the award is an agreed award; and**

(b) **any order made by the court must also contain such a statement.**

(6) **An application for permission must be supported by written evidence—**

(a) **exhibiting—**

(i) **where the application is made under section 66 of the 1996 Act or under section 26 of the 1950 Act, the arbitration agreement and the original award (or copies);**

(ii) **where the application is under section 101 of the**

---

[1] Amended by Civil Procedure (Amendment No. 5) Rules 2001 (S.I. 2001 No. 4015).

[2] Amended by Civil Procedure (Amendment No. 5) Rules 2001 (S.I. 2001 No. 4015).

[3] 1996 c.23.

[4] 1950 c.27; section 26 was repealed by the Arbitration Act 1996 (c. 23), section 107(2) and Schedule 4 but continues to apply to claims commenced before January 31, 1997 by virtue of the Arbitration Act 1996 (Commencement No. 1) Order 1996 (S.I. 1996 No. 3146), article 4 and Schedule 2.

[5] 1975 c.3; repealed by the Arbitration Act 1996 (c.23), section 107(2) and Schedule 4 but continues to apply to claims commenced before January 31, 1997 by virtue of the Arbitration Act 1996 (Commencement No. 1) Order 1996 (S.I. 1996 No. 3146), article 4 and Schedule 2.

1996 Act, the documents required to be produced by section 102 of that Act; or

    (iii) where the application is under section 3(1)(a) of the 1975 Act, the documents required to be produced by section 4 of that Act;

(b) stating the name and the usual or last known place of residence or business of the claimant and of the person against whom it is sought to enforce the award; and

(c) stating either—

    (i) that the award has not been complied with; or

    (ii) the extent to which it has not been complied with at the date of the application.

(7) An order giving permission must—

(a) be drawn up by the claimant; and

(b) be served on the defendant by—

    (i) delivering a copy to him personally; or

    (ii) sending a copy to him at his usual or last known place of residence or business.

(8) An order giving permission may be served out of the jurisdiction—

(a) without permission; and

(b) in accordance with rules 6.24 to 6.29 as if the order were an arbitration claim form.

(9) Within 14 days after service of the order or, if the order is to be served out of the jurisdiction, within such other period as the court may set—

(a) the defendant may apply to set aside the order; and

(b) the award must not be enforced until after—

    (i) the end of that period; or

    (ii) any application made by the defendant within that period has been finally disposed of.

(10) The order must contain a statement of—

(a) the right to make an application to set the order aside; and

(b) the restrictions on enforcement under rule 62.18(9)(b).

(11) Where a body corporate is a party any reference in this rule to place of residence or business shall have effect as if the reference were to the registered or principal address of the body corporate.

Written evidence in support of application

As to the importance of full and frank disclosure in any affidavit and by like token **2E–34** in any witness statement in support of application which in the first instance is made without notice, and the relevant considerations where non-disclosure is established (see *Curacao Trading Co B.V. v. Harkisandas & Co* [1992] 21 Lloyd's Rep. 186).

Copies of draft order/Contents of affidavit/Witness statement in support

In addition to any written evidence Section O, para. O18.4(a) requires two copies of **2E–35** a draft order to be provided and requires that care be taken to see that the affidavit or witness statement and the draft order meet the requirements of this provision.

Interest on awards[1]

2E–36   62.19—(1) Where an applicant seeks to enforce an award of interest the whole or any part of which relates to a period after the date of the award, he must file a statement giving the following particulars—

(a) whether simple or compound interest was awarded;

(b) the date from which interest was awarded;

(c) where rests were provided for, specifying them;

(d) the rate of interest awarded; and

(e) a calculation showing—

(i) the total amount claimed up to the date of the statement; and

(ii) any sum which will become due on a daily basis.

(2) A statement under paragraph (1) must be filed whenever the amount of interest has to be quantified for the purpose of—

(a) obtaining a judgment or order under section 66 of the 1996 Act (enforcement of the award); or

(b) enforcing such a judgment or order.

Registration in High Court of foreign awards[2]

2E–37   62.20—(1) Where—

(a) an award is made in proceedings on an arbitration in any part of a United Kingdom Overseas Territory (within the meaning of rule 6.18(f)) or other territory to which Part I of the Foreign Judgments (Reciprocal Enforcement) Act 1933[3] ("the 1933 Act") extends;

(b) Part II of the Administration of Justice Act 1920[4] extended to that part immediately before Part I of the 1933 Act was extended to that part; and

(c) an award has, under the law in force in the place where it was made, become enforceable in the same manner as a judgment given by a court in that place,

rules 74.1 to 74.7 and 74.9 apply in relation to the award as they apply in relation to a judgment given by the court subject to the modifications in paragraph (2).

(2) The modifications referred to in paragraph (1) are as follows—

(a) for references to the State of origin are substituted references to the place where the award was made; and

(b) the written evidence required by rule 74.4 must state (in addition to the matters required by that rule) that to the best of the information or belief of the maker of the

---

[1] Amended by Civil Procedure (Amendment No. 5) Rules 2001 (S.I. 2001 No. 4015).

[2] Amended by Civil Procedure (Amendment No. 5) Rules 2001 (S.I. 2001 No. 4015) and Civil Procedure (Amendment) Rules 2002 (S.I. 2002 No. 2058).

[3] 1933 c.13 (23 & 24 Geo. 5).

[4] 1920 c.81 (10 & 11 Geo. 5); section 10 of Part II was substituted by the Civil Jurisdiction and Judgments Act 1982 (c.27), section 35(2) and section 14 of Part II was amended by the Civil Jurisdiction and Judgments Act 1982 (c.27), section 35(3).

statement the award has, under the law in force in the place where it was made, become enforceable in the same manner as a judgment given by a court in that place.

Note

A foreign award expressed in a foreign currency must not be converted into sterling for the purposes of registration, see Rate of Exchange, para. 74.11.9 in Volume 1.

2E–38

Registration of awards under the Arbitration (International Investment Disputes) Act 1966[1]

62.21—(1) In this rule—

(a) "the 1966 Act" means the Arbitration (International Investment Disputes) Act 1966[2];

(b) "award" means an award under the Convention;

(c) "the Convention" means the Convention on the settlement of investment disputes between States and nationals of other States which was opened for signature in Washington on 18th March 1965[3];

(d) "judgment creditor" means the person seeking recognition or enforcement of an award; and

(e) "judgment debtor" means the other party to the award.

(2) Subject to the provisions of this rule, the following provisions of Part 74 apply with such modifications as may be necessary in relation to an award as they apply in relation to a judgment to which Part I of the Foreign Judgments (Reciprocal Enforcement) Act 1933 applies—

(a) rule 74.1;

(b) rule 74.3;

(c) rule 74.4(1) , (2)(a) to (d) , and (4);

(d) rule 74.6 (except paragraph (3)(c) to (e)); and

(e) rule 74.9(2).

(3) An application to have an award registered in the High Court under section 1 of the 1966 Act[4] must be made in accordance with the Part 8 procedure.

(4) The written evidence required by rule 74.4 in support of an application for registration must—

(a) exhibit the award certified under the Convention instead of the judgment (or a copy of it); and

(b) in addition to stating the matters referred to in rule 74.4(2)(a) to (d), state whether—

(i) at the date of the application the enforcement of

2E–39

---

[1] Amended by Civil Procedure (Amendment No. 5) Rules 2001 (S.I. 2001, No. 4015) and Civil Procedure (Amendment) Rules 2002 (S.I. 2002, No. 2058).

[2] 1966 c.41.

[3] The text of the Convention is set out in the Schedule to the Arbitration (International Investment Disputes) Act 1966 (c.41).

[4] 1966 c.41; section 1 was amended by the Administration of Justice Act 1977 (c.38), sections 4 and 32(4) and Schedule 5, Part I and by the Supreme Court Act 1981 (c.54), section 152(1) and Schedule 5.

> the award has been stayed (provisionally or otherwise) under the Convention; and
>
> > (ii) any, and if so what, application has been made under the Convention, which, if granted, might result in a stay of the enforcement of the award.

(5) Where, on granting permission to register an award or an application made by the judgment debtor after an award has been registered, the court considers—

> (a) that the enforcement of the award has been stayed (whether provisionally or otherwise) under the Convention; or
>
> (b) that an application has been made under the Convention which, if granted, might result in a stay of the enforcement of the award,

the court may stay the enforcement of the award for such time as it considers appropriate.

Scope of rule

2E–40   This rule provides the machinery for the registration of an award rendered pursuant to the Convention set out in the Schedule to the Arbitration (International Investment Disputes) Act 1966. The procedure follows, in large measure, but with the necessary modifications, the provisions of CPR r.74, since this Act is in many respects similar to the Foreign Judgments (Reciprocal Enforcement) Act 1933.

Rule 62.21(2) makes it unecessary to convert an award under this Act expressed in foreign currency into sterling for the purposes of its registration.

PRACTICE DIRECTION—ARBITRATION
This Practice Direction supplements CPR Part 62   2E–41

Section I

1.1 This Section of this Practice Direction applies to arbitration claims to which Section I of Part 62 applies.

1.2 In this Section "the 1996 Act" means the Arbitration Act 1996.

1.3 Where a rule provides for a document to be sent, it may be sent—

(1)   by first class post—

(2)   through a document exchange; or

(3)   fax, electronic mail or other means of electronic communication.

62.3 Starting the Claim

2.1 An arbitration claim under the 1996 Act (other than under section 9) must be started in accordance with the High Court and County Courts (Allocation of Arbitration Proceedings) Order 1996 by the issue of an arbitration claim form.

2.2 An arbitration claim form must be substantially in the form set out in Appendix A to this practice direction.

2.3 Subject to paragraph 2.1, an arbitration claim form—

(1)   may be issued at the courts set out in column 1 of the table below and will be entered in the list set out against that court in column 2;

(2)   relating to a landlord and tenant or partnership dispute must be issued in the Chancery Division of the High Court.

2.3A An arbitration claim form must, in the case of an appeal, or application for permission to appeal, from a judge-adjudicator, be issued in the Civil Division of the Court of Appeal. The judge hearing the application may adjourn the matter for oral argument before two judges of that court.

Court	List
Admiralty and Commercial Registry at the Royal Courts of Justice, London	Commercial list
Technology and Construction Court Registry, St. Dunstan's House, London	TCC list
District Registry of the High Court (where mercantile court established)	Mercantile list
District Registry of the High Court (where arbitration claim form marked 'Technology and Construction Court' in top right hand corner)	TCC list

Central London County Court	Mercantile list

Note

2E–42   "...the High Court and County Courts (Allocation of Arbitration Proceedings) Order 1996" is S.I. 1996 No. 3215 in force on January 31, 1997. It has been amended by S.I. 1999 No. 1010.

Appendix A

2E–42.1   The forms **N8,N8A**, **N8B** and **N15** can be found in the Forms Volume to this publication, Section: *Civil Procedure Forms*.

Fees

2E–43   See the Supreme Court Fees Order 1999 (S.I. 1999 No. 687) and, in particular, items 1.2: 2.4 and 2.5: 4.4 and 4.5.

62.4 Arbitration claim form Service

3.1 Service

2E–44   The court may exercise its powers under rule 6.8 to permit service of an arbitration claim form at the address of a party's solicitor or representative acting for him in the arbitration.

3.2 Where the arbitration claim form is served by the claimant he must file a certificate of service within 7 days of service of the arbitration claim form. (Rule 6.10 specifies what a certificate of service must show).

Acknowledgment of service or making representations by arbitrator or ACAS

4.1 Where—

(1)   an arbitrator; or

(2)   ACAS (in a claim under the 1996 Act as applied with modifications by the ACAS Arbitration Scheme (England and Wales) Order 2001)

is sent a copy of an arbitration claim form (including an arbitration claim form sent under rule 62.6(2)), that arbitrator or ACAS (as the case may be) may—

(a) apply to be made a defendant; or

(b) make representations to the court under paragraph 4.3.

4.2 An application under paragraph 4.1(2)(a) to be made a defendant-

(1)   must be served on the claimant; but

(2)   need not be served on any other party.

4.3 An arbitrator or ACAS may make representations by filing written evidence or in writing to the court.

Supply of documents from court records

5.1 An arbitration claim form may only be inspected with the permission of the court.

62.7 Case management

6.1 The following directions apply unless the court orders otherwise.

6.2 A defendant who wishes to rely on evidence before the court must file and serve his written evidence—

    (1)   within 21 days after the date by which he was required to acknowledge service; or,

    (2)   where a defendant is not required to file an acknowledgement of service, within 21 days after service of the arbitration claim form.

6.3 A claimant who wishes to rely on evidence in reply to written evidence filed under paragraph 6.2 must file and serve his written evidence within 7 days after service of the defendant's evidence.

6.4 Agreed indexed and paginated bundles of all the evidence and other documents to be used at the hearing must be prepared by the claimant.

6.5 Not later than 5 days before the hearing date estimates for the length of the hearing must be filed together with a complete set of the documents to be used.

6.6 Not later than 2 days before the hearing date the claimant must file and serve—

    (1)   a chronology of the relevant events cross-referenced to the bundle of documents;

    (2)   (where necessary) a list of the persons involved; and

    (3)   a skeleton argument which lists succinctly—

        (a) the issues which arise for decision;

        (b) the grounds of relief (or opposing relief) to be relied upon;

        (c) the submissions of fact to be made with the references to the evidence; and

        (d) the submissions of law with references to the relevant authorities.

6.7 Not later than the day before the hearing date the defendant must file and serve a skeleton argument which lists succinctly—

    (1)   the issues which arise for decision;

    (2)   the grounds of relief (or opposing relief) to be relied upon;

    (3)   the submissions of fact to be made with the references to the evidence; and

    (4)   the submissions of law with references to the relevant authorities.

Securing the attendance of witnesses

7.1 A party to arbitral proceedings being conducted in England or Wales who wishes to rely on section 43 of the 1996 Act to secure the attendance of a witness must apply for a witness summons in accordance with Part 34.

7.2 If the attendance of the witness is required within the district of a district registry, the application may be made at that registry.

7.3 A witness summons will not be issued until the applicant files written evidence showing that the application is made with—

    (1)   the permission of the tribunal; or

    (2)   the agreement of the other parties.

Interim remedies

8.1 An application for an interim remedy under section 44 of the 1996 Act must be made in an arbitration claim form.

Applications under sections 32 and 45 of the 1996 Act

9.1 This paragraph applies to arbitration claims for the determination of—

(1)   a question as to the substantive jurisdiction of the arbitral tribunal under section 32 of the 1996 Act; and

(2)   a preliminary point of law under section 45 of the 1996 Act.

9.2 Where an arbitration claim is made without the agreement in writing of all the other parties to the arbitral proceedings but with the permission of the arbitral tribunal, the written evidence or witness statements filed by the parties must set out any evidence relied on by the parties in support of their contention that the court should, or should not, consider the claim.

9.3 As soon as practicable after the written evidence is filed, the court will decide whether or not it should consider the claim and, unless the court otherwise directs, will so decide without a hearing.

Decisions without a hearing

10.1 Having regard to the overriding objective the court may decide particular issues without a hearing. For example, as set out in paragraph 9.3, the question whether the court is satisfied as to the matters set out in section 32(2)(b) or section 45(2)(b) of the 1996 Act.

10.2 The court will generally decide whether to extend the time limit under section 70(3) of the 1996 Act without a hearing. Where the court makes an order extending the time limit, the defendant must file his written evidence within 21 days from service of the order.

62.9 Variation of time

11.1 An application for an order under rule 62.9(1)—

(1)   before the period of 28 days has expired, must be made in a Part 23 application notice; and

(2)   after the period of 28 days has expired, must be set out in a separately identified part in the arbitration claim form.

Applications for permission to appeal

12.1 Where a party seeks permission to appeal to the court on a question of law arising out of an arbitration award, the arbitration claim form must—

(1)   identify the question of law; and

(2)   state the grounds
      on which the party alleges that permission should be given.

12.2 The written evidence in support of the application must set out any evidence relied on by the party for the purpose of satisfying the court—

(1)   of the matters referred to in section 69(3) of the 1996 Act; and

(2)   that permission should be given.

12.3 The written evidence filed by the respondent to the application must—

(1)   state the grounds on which the respondent opposes the grant of permission;

460

(2) set out any evidence relied on by him relating to the matters mentioned in section 69(3) of the 1996 Act; and

(3) specify whether the respondent wishes to contend that the award should be upheld for reasons not expressed (or not fully expressed) in the award and, if so, state those reasons.

12.4 The court will normally determine applications for permission to appeal without an oral hearing.

12.5 Where the court refuses an application for permission to appeal without an oral hearing, it must provide brief reasons.

12.6 Where the court considers that an oral hearing is required, it may give such further directions as are necessary.

Section II

13.1 This Section of this Practice Direction applies to arbitration claims to which Section II of Part 62 applies.

14.1 An arbitration claim must be started in the Commercial Court and, where required to be heard by a judge, be heard by a judge of that court unless he otherwise directs.

Effect of rule

The commentary which follows together with that at 2E–46 and 47 should be read **2E–45** subject to the Note at 2E–1.1 and the Note at 2E–18.1 to which reference should be made. It is important to note that the requirement to channel arbitration applications through the Commercial Court as in necessary for Section II claims has been replaced in the case of 1996 Act claims by a more flexible regime. See further at 2E–18.1 and PD62.2.3.

This rule has the effect of channelling all applications under Section II of Pt 62 in the first instance to the Commercial Court. The rule thus recognises that in practice the subject of arbitration is substantially a commercial matter and should be dealt with by a Commercial Judge both as a matter of convenience and the proper distribution of business in the High Court and also to enable uniformity of practice and procedure to be fostered and encouraged.

On the other hand, of course, there is a great volume of important arbitrations which may be described as "non-commercial" in the sense that the subject matter does not fall within the definition of a "commercial claim" and applications relating to such arbitrations which require to be heard by a judge under rule 62.12, will no doubt be directed by a Commercial Judge to be heard by another judge of the High Court.

The normal practice should be that all applications for permission to appeal to the High Court are to be heard by a Commercial Judge unless any such judge otherwise directs, and if permission is granted, consideration could then be given to whether there should be a direction that the appeal itself should be heard by a judge who is not a Commercial Judge (*per* Donaldson L.J. in *F. G. Whitley & Sons Co Ltd v. Clwyd County Council, The Times*, August 6, 1982).

In Ashbank Property Co Ltd v. Department of Transport, The Times, July 25, 1994; (1994) *Independent*, October 3, 1994; held that where a notice of application to set aside an arbitration award had been incorrectly issued in the Chancery Division it was inappropriate to transfer the same to the Commercial Court as that would be to grant an inappropriate extension of time for an appeal.

It is the practice in the Commercial Court for one Judge to hear the application for permission to appeal under s.1(2) of the 1979 Act and for another judge to hear the appeal itself but there are exceptional cases where it would be quite right that the same judge should hear the appeal; ultimately, it must be a matter for the judge's discretion (*Hiscox v. Outhwaite (No. 2)* [1991] 1 W.L.R. 545, CA).

Application

By arbitration claim form in accordance with Pt 8 procedure, unless claim made in **2E–46** existing proceedings by way of application notice. Matters referred to in r.62.12 and application in respect of maters referred to in r.62.15(1) and (2) are to be made by issuing an arbitration claim form and will be heard by a judge of the Commercial Court unless such judge otherwise directs.

Where permission to appeal is required, it should be applied for to a judge in private by an application in existing proceedings or by a Pt 8 claim if no existing proceedings issued in the Admiralty and Commercial Registry. Such permission is required under s.1(3) of the Act of 1979, unless all parties to the reference consent.

2E–47   For ss.22 and 23 of the Arbitration Act 1950 and ss.1 and 2 of the Arbitration Act 1979, see SCP 1999 Vol.2, section 21.

Section III

2E–48   **15.1** This Section of this Practice Direction applies to enforcement proceedings to which Section III of Part 62 applies.

62.21 Registration of awards under the Arbitration (International Investment Disputes) Act 1966

16.1 Awards ordered to be registered under the 1966 Act and particulars will be entered in the Register kept for that purpose at the Admiralty and Commercial Registry.

Editorial Note

2E–49   With the exception of ss.35 to 42 and the First and Second Schedule to the Arbitration Act 1950, the texts of the Arbitration Act 1950, of the Arbitration Act 1975 and of the Arbitration Act 1979 (the "old law") are not printed in this publication. Such texts and related annotations are to be found in SCP 1999, Vol. 2 at Section 21A, paras 21A–1 *et seq.*, (the 1950 Act), paras 21B–1 *et seq.* (the 1975 Act) and paras 21C–1 *et seq.* (the 1979 Act) to which reference should be made as necessary.

Appendix A

2E–49.1   The form contained in Appendix A is to be found in the Forms Volume—Civil Procedure Forms Section, Form N8.

Arbitration Act 1950

2E–50   (14 GEO. 6 C.27)

ARRANGEMENT OF SECTIONS

PART II

ENFORCEMENT OF CERTAIN FOREIGN AWARDS

PART II

ENFORCEMENT OF CERTAIN FOREIGN AWARDS

Application of Part II

2E–51   **35.**—(1) This Part of this Act applies to any award made after the twenty-eighth day of July, nineteen hundred and twenty-four—

(a) in pursuance of an agreement for arbitration to which the Protocol set out in the First Schedule to this Act applies; and

(b) between persons of whom one is subject to the jurisdiction of some one of such Powers as His Majesty, being satisfied that reciprocal provisions have been made, may by Order in Council declare to be parties to the convention set out in the Second Schedule to this Act, and of whom the other is subject to the jurisdiction of some other of the Powers aforesaid; and

(c) in one of such territories as His Majesty, being satisfied that reciprocal provisions have been made, may by Order in Council declare to be territories to which the said Convention applies,

and an award to which this Part of this Act applies is in the Part of this Act referred to as "a foreign award."

(2) His Majesty may by a subsequent Order in Council vary or revoke any Order previously made under this section.

(3) Any Order in Council under section one of the Arbitration (Foreign Awards) Act, 1930, which is in force at the commencement of this Act shall have effect as if it had been made under this section.

"Order in Council"

By virtue of the Arbitration (Foreign Awards) Order 1984 (S.I. 1984 No. 1168) the **2E–52** territories to which the Geneva Convention applies as follows:

List of Territories to which the Geneva Convention applies:

The United Kingdom of Great Britain and Northern Ireland

Anguilla	Republic of Ireland
British Virgin Islands	Israel
Cayman Islands	Italy
Falkland Islands	Japan
Falkland Islands Dependencies	Kenya
Gibraltar	Luxembourg
Montserrat Turks and Caicos Islands	Malta
Antigua and Barbuda	Mauritius
Austria	Netherlands (including Curacao)
Bahamas	New Zealand
Bangladesh	Pakistan
Belgium	Portugal
Belize	Romania
†Czechoslovakia	Saint Christopher and Nevis
Denmark	St. Lucia
Dominica	Spain
Finland	Sweden
Federal Republic of Germany	Switzerland
France	Tanzania
*German Democratic Republic	Thailand
Greece	Western Samoa
Grenada	†Yugoslavia
Guyana	Zambia
India	

*The German Democratic Republic is now part of the Federal Republic of Germany.

†The position of Yugoslavia, Czechoslovakia and their former constituent states in relation to international treaties is, at present, uncertain.

Effect of foreign awards

36.—(1) A foreign award shall, subject to the provisions of this Part **2E–53**

of this Act, be enforceable in England either by action or in the same manner as the award of an arbitrator is enforceable by virtue of section sixty-six of the Arbitration Act 1966.

(2) Any foreign award which would be enforceable under this Part of this Act shall be treated as binding for all purposes on the persons as between whom it was made, and may accordingly be relied on by any of those persons by way of defence, set off or otherwise in any legal proceedings in England, and any references in this Part of this Act to enforcing a foreign award shall be construed as including references to relying on an award.

Effect of foreign awards

2E-54   Pt 2 of this Act is intended to put a foreign award in the same position as an English award subject of course to fulfilling the conditions laid down in s.37 (*Union Nationale des Co-operatives, etc. v. Robert Catterall & Co. Ltd* [1959] 2 Q.B. 44, CA).

Conditions for enforcement of foreign awards

2E-55   37.—(1) In order that a foreign award may be enforceable under this Part of this Act it must have—

(a) been made in pursuance of an agreement for arbitration which was valid under the law by which it was governed;

(b) been made by the tribunal provided for in the agreement or constituted in manner agreed upon by the parties;

(c) been made in conformity with the law governing the arbitration procedure;

(d) become final in the country in which it was made;

(e) been in respect of a matter which may lawfully be referred to arbitration under the law of England;

and the enforcement thereof must not be contrary to the public policy or the law of England.

(2) Subject to the provisions of this subsection, a foreign award shall not be enforceable under this Part of this Act if the Court dealing with the case is satisfied that—

(a) the award has been annulled in the country in which it was made; or

(b) the party against whom it is sought to enforce the award was not given notice of the arbitration proceedings in sufficient time to enable him to present his case, or was under some legal incapacity and was not properly represented; or

(c) the award does not deal with all the questions referred or contains decisions on matters beyond the scope of the agreement for arbitration:

Provided that, if the award does not deal with all the questions referred, the Court may, if it thinks fit, either postpone the enforcement of the award or order its enforcement subject to the giving of such security by the person seeking to enforce it as the Court may think fit.

(3) If a party seeking to resist the enforcement of a foreign award proves that there is any ground other than the non-existence of the conditions specified in paragraphs (a) (b) and (c) of subsection (1) of

this section, or the existence of the conditions specified in paragraphs (b) and (c) of subsection (2) of this section, entitling him to contest the validity of the award, the Court may, if it thinks fit, either refuse to enforce the award or adjourn the hearing until after the expiration of such period as appears to the Court to be reasonably sufficient to enable that party to take the necessary steps to have the award annulled by the competent tribunal.

Final award

A foreign award is final for the purposes of this section, even though it may not be **2E–56** directly enforceable in the country in which it was obtained until a judgment has been obtained in that country based on the award (*Union Nationale des Co-operatives Agricoles de Céreals v. Robert Catterall & Co Ltd* [1959] 2 Q.B. 44).

Subs.(2)(b)

It will be observed that the mere fact that a party does not attend the proceedings **2E–57** will not of itself make the award unenforceable.

Evidence

38.—(1) The party seeking to enforce a foreign award must pro- **2E–58** duce—

> (a) the original award or a copy thereof duly authenticated in manner required by the law of the country in which it was made; and
>
> (b) evidence proving that the award has become final; and
>
> (c) such evidence as may be necessary to prove that the award is a foreign award and that the conditions mentioned in paragraphs (a) (b) and (c) of subsection (1) of the last foregoing section are satisfied.

(2) In any case where any document required to be produced under subsection (1) of this section is in a foreign language, it shall be the duty of the party seeking to enforce the award to produce a translation certified as correct by a diplomatic or consular agent of the country to which that party belongs, or certified as correct in such other manner as may be sufficient according to the law of England.

(3) Subject to the provisions of this section, rules of Court may be made under section 84 of the Supreme Court Act 1981, with respect to the evidence which must be furnished by a party seeking to enforce an award under this Part of this Act.

"Rules of Court"

No Rules were made under the earlier s.4(3) of the Arbitration (Foreign Awards) **2E–59** Act 1930. The current relevant rules are made by the Civil Procedure Rule Committee pursuant to ss.1 and 2 of the Civil Procedure Act 1997.

Meaning of "final award"

39. For the purposes of this Part of this Act, an award shall not be **2E–60** deemed final if any proceedings for the purpose of contesting the validity of the award are pending in the country in which it was made.

Saving for other rights, etc.

40. Nothing in this Part of this Act shall— **2E–61**

(a) prejudice any rights which any person would have had of enforcing in England any award or of availing himself in England of any award if neither this Part of this Act nor Part I of the Arbitration (Foreign Awards) Act 1930, had been enacted; or

(b) apply to any award made on an arbitration agreement governed by the law of England.

Application of Part II to Scotland

2E–62   **41.**—(1) The following provisions of this section shall have effect for the purpose of the application of this Part of this Act to Scotland.

(2) For the references to England there shall be substituted references to Scotland.

(3) For subsection (1) of section thirty-six there shall be substituted the following subsection:—

> "(1) A foreign award shall, subject to the provisions of this Part of this Act, be enforceable by action, or, if the agreement for arbitration contains consent to the registration of the award in the Books of Council and Session for execution and the award is so registered, it shall, subject as aforesaid, be enforceable by summary diligence."

(4) For subsection (3) of section thirty-eight there shall be substituted the following subsection:—

> "(3) The Court of Session shall, subject to the provisions of this section, have power, exercisable by statutory instrument, to make provision by Act of Sederunt with respect to the evidence which must be furnished by a party seeking to enforce in Scotland an award under this Part of this Act, and the Statutory Instruments Act 1946, shall apply to a statutory instrument containing an Act of Sederunt made under this subsection as if the Act of Sederunt had been made by a Minister of the Crown."

Application of Part II to Northern Ireland

2E–63   **42.**—(1) The following provisions of this section shall have effect for the purpose of the application of this Part of this Act to Northern Ireland.

(2) For the references to England there shall be substituted references to Northern Ireland.

(3) [...]

(4) For subsection (3) of section thirty-eight there shall be substituted the following subsection:

> "(3) Subject to the provisions of this section, rules may be made under section 7 of the Northern Ireland Act 1962, with respect to the evidence which must be furnished by a party seeking to enforce an award under this Part of this Act."

466

SECTION 35　　　　　　FIRST SCHEDULE

PROTOCOL ON ARBITRATION CLAUSES SIGNED ON BEHALF OF HIS MAJESTY AT
A MEETING OF THE ASSEMBLY OF THE LEAGUE OF NATIONS HELD ON THE
TWENTY-FOURTH DAY OF SEPTEMBER, NINETEEN HUNDRED AND TWENTY-THREE

The undersigned, being duly authorised, declare that they accept, on behalf of the **2E–64**
countries which they represent, the following provisions:—

1. Each of the Contracting States recognises the validity of an agreement whether
relating to existing or future differences between parties, subject respectively to the jurisdiction of different Contracting States by which the parties to a contract agree to
submit to arbitration all or any differences that may arise in connection with such
contract relating to commercial matters or to any other matter capable of settlement
by arbitration, whether or not the arbitration is to take place in a country to whose jurisdiction none of the parties is subject.Each Contracting State reserves the right to
limit the obligation mentioned above to contracts which are considered as commercial
under its national law. Any Contracting State which avails itself of this right will notify
the Secretary-General of the League of Nations, in order that the other Contracting
States may be so informed.

2. The arbitral procedure, including the constitution of the arbitral tribunal, shall be
governed by the will of the parties and by the law of the country in whose territory the
arbitration takes place.The Contracting States agree to facilitate all steps in the procedure which require to be taken in their own territories, in accordance with the provisions of their law governing arbitral procedure applicable to existing differences.

3. Each Contracting State undertakes to ensure the execution by its authorities and
in accordance with the provisions of its national laws of arbitral awards made in its
own territory under the preceding articles.

4. The tribunals of the Contracting Parties, on being seised of a dispute regarding a
contract made between persons to whom Article 1 applies and including an arbitration
agreement whether referring to present or future differences which is valid in virtue
of the said article and capable of being carried into effect, shall refer the parties on the
application of either of them to the decision of the arbitrators. Such reference shall
not prejudice the competence of the judicial tribunals in case the agreement or the
arbitration cannot proceed or become inoperative.

5. The present Protocol, which shall remain open for signature by all States, shall be
ratified. The ratifications shall be deposited as soon as possible with the Secretary-
General of the League of Nations, who shall notify such deposit to all the signatories
in case the agreement or the arbitration cannot proceed or becomes inoperative.

6. The present Protocol shall come into force as soon as two ratifications have been
deposited. Thereafter it will take effect, in the case of each Contracting State, one
month after the notification by the Secretary-General of the deposit of its ratification.

7. The present Protocol may be denounced by any Contracting State on giving one
year's notice. Denunciation shall be effected by a notification addressed to the
Secretary-General of the League, who will immediately transmit copies of such notification to all the other signatory States and inform them of the date on which it was
received. The denunciation shall take effect one year after the date on which it was
notified to the Secretary-General, and shall operate only in respect of the notifying
State.

8. The Contracting States may declare that their acceptance of the present Protocol
does not include any or all of the under-mentioned territories: that is to say, their colonies, overseas possessions or territories, protectorates or the territories over which
they exercise a mandate.The said States may subsequently adhere separately on behalf
of any territory thus excluded. The Secretary-General of the League of Nations shall
be informed as soon as possible of such adhesions. He shall notify such adhesions to all
signatory States. They will take effect one month after the notification by the Secretary-
General to all signatory States.The Contracting States may also denounce the Protocol
separately on behalf of any of the territories referred to above. Article 7 applies to
such denunciation.

SECTION 35 # SECOND SCHEDULE

CONVENTION ON THE EXECUTION OF FOREIGN ARBITRAL AWARDS SIGNED AT GENEVA ON BEHALF OF HIS MAJESTY ON THE TWENTY-SIXTH DAY OF SEPTEMBER, NINETEEN HUNDRED AND TWENTY-SEVEN

Article 1

2E-65   In the territories of any High Contracting Party to which the present Convention applies, an arbitral award made in pursuance of an agreement, whether relating to existing or future differences (hereinafter called "a submission to arbitration") covered by the Protocol on Arbitration Clauses, opened at Geneva on September 24, 1923, shall be recognised as binding and shall be enforced in accordance with the rules of the procedure of the territory where the award is relied upon, provided that the said award has been made in a territory of one of the High Contracting Parties to which the present Convention applies and between persons who are subject to the jurisdiction of one of the High Contracting Parties.

To obtain such recognition or enforcement, it shall, further, be necessary:—

(a) That the award has been made in pursuance of a submission to arbitration which is valid under the law applicable thereto;

(b) That the subject-matter of the award is capable of settlement by arbitration under the law of the country in which the award is sought to be relied upon;

(c) That the award has been made by the Arbitral Tribunal provided for in the submission to arbitration or constituted in the manner agreed upon by the parties and in conformity with the law governing the arbitration procedure;

(d) That the award has become final in the country in which it has been made, in the sense that it will not be considered as such if it is open to *opposition, appel* or *pourvoi en cassation* (in the countries where such forms of procedure exist) or if it is proved that any proceedings for the purpose of contesting the validity of the award are pending;

(e) That the recognition or enforcement of the award is not contrary to the public policy or to the principles of the law of the country in which it is sought to be relied upon.

Article 2

2E-66   Even if the conditions laid down in Article 1 hereof are fulfilled, recognition and enforcement of the award shall be refused if the Court is satisfied:—

(a) That the award has been annulled in the country in which it was made;

(b) That the party against whom it is sought to use the award was not given notice of the arbitration proceedings in sufficient time to enable him to present his case; or, that, being under a legal incapacity, he was not properly represented;

(c) That the award does not deal with the differences contemplated by or falling within the terms of the submission to arbitration or that it contains decisions on matters beyond the scope of the submission to arbitration.

If the award has not covered all the questions submitted to the arbitral tribunal, the competent authority of the country where recognition or enforcement of the award is sought can, if it think fit, postpone such recognition or enforcement or grant it subject to such guarantee as that authority may decide.

Article 3

2E-67   If the party against whom the award has been made proves that, under the law governing the arbitration procedure, there is a ground, other than the grounds referred to in Article 1(a) and (c) and Article 2(b) and (c) entitling him to contest the validity of the award in a Court of Law, the Court may, if it thinks fit, either refuse recognition or enforcement of the award or adjourn the consideration thereof, giving such party a reasonable time within which to have the award annulled by the competent tribunal.

Article 4

2E-68   The party relying upon an award or claiming its enforcement must supply, in particular:—

(1) The original award or a copy thereof duly authenticated, according to the requirements of the law of the country in which it was made;

(2) Documentary or other evidence to prove that the award has become final, in the sense defined in Article 1(d) in the country in which it was made;

(3) When necessary, documentary or other evidence to prove that the conditions laid down in Article 1, paragraph 1 and paragraph 2(a) and (c) have been fulfilled.

A translation of the award and of other documents mentioned in this Article into the official language of the country where the award is sought to be relied upon may be demanded. Such translation must be certified correct by a diplomatic or consular agent of the country to which the party who seeks to rely upon the award belongs or by a sworn translator of the country where the award is sought to be relied upon.

Article 5

The provisions of the above Articles shall not deprive any interested party of the right of availing himself of an arbitral award in the manner and to the extent allowed by the law or the treaties of the country where such award is sought to be relied upon. **2E–69**

Article 6

The present Convention applies only to arbitral awards made after the coming into force of the Protocol on Arbitration Clauses, opened at Geneva on September 24, 1923. **2E–70**

Article 7

The present Convention, which will remain open to the signature of all the signatories of the Protocol of 1923 on Arbitration Clauses, shall be ratified. **2E–71**

It may be ratified only on behalf of those Members of the League of Nations and non-Member States on whose behalf the Protocol of 1923 shall have been ratified.

Ratifications shall be deposited as soon as possible with the Secretary-General of the League of Nations, who will notify such deposit to all the signatories.

Article 8

The present Convention shall come into force three months after it shall have been ratified on behalf of two High Contracting Parties. Thereafter, it shall take effect in the case of each High Contracting Party, three months after the deposit of the ratification on its behalf with the Secretary-General of the League of Nations. **2E–72**

Article 9

The present Convention may be denounced on behalf of any Member of the League or non-Member State. Denunciation shall be notified in writing to the Secretary-General of the League of Nations, who will immediately send a copy thereof, certified to be in conformity with the notification, to all the other Contracting Parties, at the same time informing them of the date on which he received it. **2E–73**

The denunciation shall come into force only in respect of the High Contracting Party which shall have notified it and one year after such notification shall have reached the Secretary-General of the League of Nations.

The denunciation of the Protocol on Arbitration Clauses shall entail ipso facto the denunciation of the present Convention.

Article 10

The present Convention does not apply to the Colonies, Protectorates or territories under suzerainty or mandate of any High Contracting Party, unless they are specially mentioned. **2E–74**

The application of this Convention to one or more of such Colonies, Protectorates or territories to which the Protocol on Arbitration Clauses, opened at Geneva on September 24, 1923, applies, can be effected at any time by means of a declaration addressed to the Secretary-General of the League of Nations by one of the High Contracting Parties.

Such declarations shall take effect three months after the deposit thereof.

The High Contracting Parties can at any time denounce the Convention for all or any of the Colonies, Protectorates or territories referred to above. Article 9 hereof applies to such denunciation.

Article 11

2E-75　A certified copy of the present Convention shall be transmitted by the Secretary-General of the League of Nations to every Member of the League of Nations and to every non-Member State which signs the same.

Arbitration Act 1996

2E-76　(1996 c.23)

Introductory note

2E-77　The provisions of the Arbitration Act 1996 save for a few exceptions were brought into force on January 31, 1997 by the Arbitration Act 1996 (Commencement No. 1) Order 1996, made December 16, 1996. That Order also provides that "the old law" shall continue to apply to:

(a) arbitral proceedings commenced before the appointed day (*i.e.* January 31, 1997);

(b) arbitration applications commenced or made before the appointed day;

(c) arbitration applications commenced or made on or after the appointed day relating to arbitral proceedings commenced before the appointed day;

and that the provisions of the Act which would otherwise be applicable shall not apply.

The Order also provides that the provisions of the Act which it brings into force shall apply to any other legal proceedings even though arbitral proceedings have not been commenced.

Accordingly as from January 31, 1997 there are two alternative regimes though the enforcement provisions of Pt II of the Arbitration Act 1950 are common to both. It will be necessary therefore to determine according to the above application provisions which regime is appropriate. These application provisions are reflected in CPR Part 62—Arbitration Claims and the Practice Direction—Arbitration supplementing CPR Pt 62.

The "old law" is defined in the said Order as the enactments mentioned in s.107 of the Act (the Consequential amendments and repeals provision). Included and now preserved in respect of the arbitral and legal proceedings referred to under (a), (b) and (c) above are the Arbitration Act 1950, the Arbitration Act 1975, and the Arbitration Act 1979.

General note

2E-78　The preamble to the 1996 Act states that it is "An act to restate and improve the law relating to arbitration pursuant to an arbitration agreement; to make other provision relating to arbitration and arbitration awards; and for connected purposes".

The 1996 Act applies to all arbitrations commenced after January 31, 1997 and to all applications made to the court on or after January 31, 1997, in respect of arbitrations yet to be commenced at the time of the application.

The Act enlarges the extent to which the principles of arbitration law are expressed in statutory form. It uses language that is "user friendly". It increases the authority of the parties to arbitral proceedings to regulate the proceedings themselves and restricts the role of the court to supporting the arbitral process save where court intervention is required to achieve justice between the parties.

Thus, for example access to the Court to intervene is denied where the agreement provides a mechanism for resolving the question unless that mechanism has been tried and failed. The circumstances in which an award can be challenged are now more precisely defined as are the circumstances in which leave can be given for appealing against an award. There is statutory expression of an arbitral tribunal's powers to rule on matters affecting its own jurisdiction and of the guidelines developed by the court since 1979 on the circumstances in which leave to appeal against an award may be granted. The Act further specifies the grounds on which an award may be set aside or remitted or an arbitration removed thus removing the general discretion available under "the old law".

The Court

2E-79　This is defined by s.105 of the Arbitration Act 1996 as meaning the High Court or a county court subject to powers vested in the Lord Chancellor by order to allocate and to impose restrictions in terms of specified proceedings and court.

By the High Court and County Courts (Allocation of Arbitration Proceedings) Order 1996 (S.I. 1996 No. 3215) set out in full at paras 2E–348 *et seq.*, which came into force on January 31, 1997, it was *inter alia* provided:

2. Subject to articles 3 to 5, proceedings under the Act shall be commenced and taken in the High Court.

3. Proceedings under section 9 of the Act (stay of legal proceedings) shall be commenced in the court in which the legal proceedings are pending.

4. Proceedings under sections 66 and 101(2) (enforcement of awards) of the Act may be commenced in any county court.

5. Proceedings under the Act may be commenced and taken in the Central London County Court Mercantile List.

[THE NEXT PARAGRAPH IS 2E–84.]

The Application

2E–84 Arbitration applications under the 1996 Act (see Section I of Part 62) save for application under s.9, are made by use of an arbitration claim form (see rule 62.3, the Practice Direction—Arbitration and the reference to the form set out at Appendix A to the practice direction). Applications under s.9 are made by ordinary application process in the existing proceedings. The courts where the arbitration claim form may be issued are set ou in the Practice Direction—Arbitration.

Applications under "the old law" see (Section II of Part 62) save for s.4 of the 1950 Act applications are made by the use of an arbitration claim form and must be stated in the Commercial Court and issued out of the Admiralty and Commercial Registry at the R.C.J. London and where required to be heard by a judge must be heard by a judge of that court unless he otherwise directs, see rule 62.12 and Practice Direction—Arbitration, para. 14.1. Claims for the attendance of witnesses within the aread of a district registry may be started within the relevant district registry, see rule 62.14.

Applications for enforcement should be made using an arbitration claim form and may be considered by a Judge, Master, Admiralty Regular or District Judge.

Definitions

2E–85 The following expressions are defined or otherwise explained by the provisions indicated:

"agree"	section 5(1)
"agreement in writing"	section 5(2)–(6)
"arbitration agreement"	section 5(1) and 6
"arbitrator"	section 82(1)
"available arbitral process"	section 82(1)
"claimant"	section 82(1)
"commencement of arbitral proceedings"	section 14
"costs of arbitration"	section 82(1)
"court (the)"	section 105
"dispute"	section 82(1)
"enactment"	section 82(1)
"legal proceedings"	section 82(1)
"limitation Acts"	section 13(4)
"notice"	section 76(6)
"notice (upon)"	section 80
"party"	sections 82(2) and 106(4)
"peremptory order"	section 82(1)
"question of law"	section 82(1)
"recoverable costs"	sections 63 and 64
"seat of arbitration"	section 3

"serve and service"	section 76(6)
"statutory arbitration"	section 94(1)
"substantive jurisdiction"	sections 82(1) and 30(1)(a) to (c)
"time and periods"	section 78

PART I

ARBITRATION PURSUANT TO AN ARBITRATION AGREEMENT

INTRODUCTORY

General principles

2E–86   **1.** The provisions of this Part are founded on the following principles, and shall be construed accordingly—

(a) the object of arbitration is to obtain the fair resolution of disputes by an impartial tribunal without unnecessary delay or expense;

(b) the parties should be free to agree how their disputes are resolved, subject only to such safeguards as are necessary in the public interest;

(c) in matters governed by this Part the court should not intervene except as provided by this Part.

Scope of application of provisions

2E–87   **2.**—(1) The provisions of this Part apply where the seat of the arbitration is in England and Wales or Northern Ireland.

(2) The following sections apply even if the seat of the arbitration is outside England and Wales or Northern Ireland or no seat has been designated or determined—

(a) sections 9 to 11 (stay of legal proceedings, etc.), and

(b) section 66 (enforcement of arbitral awards).

(3) The powers conferred by the following sections apply even if the seat of the arbitration is outside England and Wales or Northern Ireland or no seat has been designated or determined—

(a) section 43 (securing the attendance of witnesses), and

(b) section 44 (court powers exercisable in support of arbitral proceedings);

but the court may refuse to exercise any such power if, in the opinion of the court, the fact that the seat of the arbitration is outside England and Wales or Northern Ireland, or that when designated or determined the seat is likely to be outside England and Wales or Northern Ireland, makes it inappropriate to do so.

(4) The court may exercise a power conferred by any provision of this Part not mentioned in subsection (2) or (3) for the purpose of supporting the arbitral process where—

(a) no seat of the arbitration has been designated or determined, and

(b) by reason of a connection with England and Wales or

472

Northern Ireland the court is satisfied that it is appropriate to do so.

(5) Section 7 (separability of arbitration agreement) and section 8 (death of a party) apply where the law applicable to the arbitration agreement is the law of England and Wales or Northern Ireland even if the seat of the arbitration is outside England and Wales or Northern Ireland or has not been designated or determined.

"...makes it inappropriate to do so"

In *Commerce & Industry Co of Canada v. Certain Underwriters at Lloyd's of London* **2E–87.1** [2002] 1 W.L.R. 1323; [2002] 2 All E.R. (Comm) 204; [2002] 1 Lloyd's Rep 219, Court held it inappropriate to order pursuant to provisons of s.44 of the 1996 Act the examination of two witnesses in connection with New York arbitration proceedings on basis that the procedure adopted under the curial law of New York differed from that of England and Wales and of Northern Ireland in particular with regard to discovery of information by witness testimony.

The seat of the arbitration

3. In this Part "the seat of the arbitration" means the juridical seat **2E–88** of the arbitration designated—

(a) by the parties to the arbitration agreement, or

(b) by any arbitral or other institution or person vested by the parties with powers in that regard, or

(c) by the arbitral tribunal if so authorised by the parties,

or determined, in the absence of any such designation, having regard to the parties' agreement and all the relevant circumstances.

"the juridical seat of the arbitration"

For factors relevant to the determination of the juridical seat of the arbitration, see **2E–89** *Dubai Islamic Bank PJSC v. Paymentech Merchant Services Inc* [2001] 1 Lloyd's Rep. 65.

Mandatory and non-mandatory provisions

4.—(1) The mandatory provisions of this Part are listed in Sched- **2E–90** ule 1 and have effect notwithstanding any agreement to the contrary.

(2) The other provisions of this Part (the "non-mandatory provisions") allow the parties to make their own arrangements by agreement but provide rules which apply in the absence of such agreement.

(3) The parties may make such arrangements by agreeing to the application of institutional rules or providing any other means by which a matter may be decided.

(4) It is immaterial whether or not the law applicable to the parties' agreement is the law of England and Wales or, as the case may be, Northern Ireland.

(5) The choice of a law other than the law of England and Wales or Northern Ireland as the applicable law in respect of a matter provided for by a non-mandatory provision of this Part is equivalent to an agreement making provision about that matter.

For this purpose an applicable law determined in accordance with the parties' agreement, or which is objectively determined in the absence of any express or implied choice, shall be treated as chosen by the parties.

Agreements to be in writing

5.—(1) The provisions of this Part apply only where the arbitration **2E–91**

agreement is in writing, and any other agreement between the parties as to any matter is effective for the purposes of this Part only if in writing. The expressions "agreement", "agree" and "agreed" shall be construed accordingly.

(2) There is an agreement in writing—

 (a) if the agreement is made in writing (whether or not it is signed by the parties),

 (b) if the agreement is made by exchange of communications in writing, or

 (c) if the agreement is evidenced in writing.

(3) Where parties agree otherwise than in writing by reference to terms which are in writing, they make an agreement in writing.

(4) An agreement is evidenced in writing if an agreement made otherwise than in writing is recorded by one of the parties, or by a third party, with the authority of the parties to the agreement.

(5) An exchange of written submissions in arbitral or legal proceedings in which the existence of an agreement otherwise than in writing is alleged by one party against another party and not denied by the other party in his response constitutes as between those parties an agreement in writing to the effect alleged.

(6) References in this Part to anything being written or in writing include its being recorded by any means.

2E–92   *Note*—Compare s.32 of the 1950 Act and s.7(1) of the 1975 Act.

THE ARBITRATION AGREEMENT

Definition of arbitration agreement

2E–93   **6.**—(1) In this Part an "arbitration agreement" means an agreement to submit to arbitration present or future disputes (whether they are contractual or not).

(2) The reference in an agreement to a written form of arbitration clause or to a document containing an arbitration clause constitutes an arbitration agreement if the reference is such as to make that clause part of the agreement.

2E–94   *Note*—Compare s.32 of the 1950 Act and s.7(1) of the 1975 Act.

Agreement to submit to arbitration

2E–95   An agreement which gives one party alone the right to refer a dispute to arbitration was held to be a valid agreement to refer future disputes to arbitration within s.32 of the 1950 Act (*Pittalis v. Sherefettin* [1986] 2 W.L.R. 1003; [1986] 2 All E.R. 227, CA). See too NB *Three Shipping Ltd v. Harebell Shipping Ltd* [2004] EWHC 2001 (Comm); [2005] 1 Lloyd's Rep. 509 (a 1996 Act case).

The fact that a contractual agreement to refer disputes to arbitration depended upon the exercise of an option, even by the party claiming arbitration, does not prevent it from being "an agreement to refer future disputes" within s.27 of the 1950 Act (*Navigazione Alta Italia S.p.A. v. Concordia Maritime Chartering A.B.* [1990] 2 Lloyd's Rep. 234).

Where a bill of lading directs the reader to the charterparty which contains a clause providing for arbitration of disputes "arising … out of his contract" the bill of lading incorporates the arbitration clause and the parties are bound by its terms (*Astro Valiente Compania Naviera SA v. Pakistan Ministry of Food and Agriculture (No. 2), The Emanuel Colocotronis* [1982] 1 W.L.R. 1096; [1982] 1 All E.R. 823).

A clause in a charterparty providing that "either party may elect to have the dispute referred to arbitration" is merely an agreement to agree to arbitrate, but once a valid election is made no further agreement is needed or contemplated for the arbitration to take place, and therefore once the election is duly made and the option to arbitrate exercised, and both the agreement and the option are expressed in writing, a binding written arbitration agreement comes into existence and there is no want of mutuality since either party could make election (*Westfal-Larsen & Co A/S v. Ikerigi Compania Naviera SA, The Messiaki Bergen* [1983] 1 All E.R. 382; [1983] 1 Lloyd's Rep. 424).

The words in sub-clause (2) "if the reference is such as to make that clause part of the agreement" were held in *Trygg Hansa Insurance Co v. Equitas Ltd* [1998] 2 Lloyd's Rep. 439, to preserve the pre-existing law that general words of incorporation in an agreement were not appropriate to incorporate an arbitration clause. See too *Cigna Life Insurance v. Intercaser S.A.* [2001] Lloyd's Rep. I.R. 821.

Separability of arbitration agreement

7. Unless otherwise agreed by the parties, an arbitration agreement which forms or was intended to form part of another agreement (whether or not in writing) shall not be regarded as invalid, non-existent or ineffective because that other agreement is invalid, or did not come into existence or has become ineffective, and it shall for that purpose be treated as a distinct agreement. **2E–96**

Whether agreement discharged by death of a party

8.—(1) Unless otherwise agreed by the parties, an arbitration agreement is not discharged by the death of a party and may be enforced by or against the personal representatives of that party. **2E–97**

(2) Subsection (1) does not affect the operation of any enactment or rule of law by virtue of which a substantive right or obligation is extinguished by death.

Note —Compare s.52(1) and (3) of the 1950 Act. For Bankruptcy position, see s.349A of the 1986 Act, inserted by para. 46 of Sched.3 to this Act. This section does not apply to statutory arbitrations. On the dissolution of a company an arbitration lapses and cannot be revived (*Morris v. Harris* [1927] A.C. 252; *Baytur v. Finagro* [1992] Q.B. 610). **2E–98**

STAY OF LEGAL PROCEEDINGS

Stay of legal proceedings

9.—(1) A party to an arbitration agreement against whom legal proceedings are brought (whether by way of claim or counterclaim) in respect of a matter which under the agreement is to be referred to arbitration may (upon notice to the other parties to the proceedings) apply to the court in which the proceedings have been brought to stay the proceedings so far as they concern that matter **2E–99**

(2) An application may be made notwithstanding that the matter is to be referred to arbitration only after the exhaustion of other dispute resolution procedures.

(3) An application may not be made by a person before taking the appropriate procedural step (if any) to acknowledge the legal proceedings against him or after he has taken any step in those proceedings to answer the substantive claim.

(4) On an application under this section the court shall grant a stay unless satisfied that the arbitration agreement is null and void, inoperative, or incapable of being performed.

(5) If the court refuses to stay the legal proceedings, any provision that an award is a condition precedent to the bringing of legal proceedings in respect of any matter is of no effect in relation to those proceedings.

2E–100   *Note*—Compare s.4(1) of the 1950 Act and s.1 of the 1975 Act. This is a mandatory provision (see s.4) and applies even though the seat of arbitration is outside England and Wales or where no seat of arbitration has been designated (see s.2). Section 9(5) does not apply to statutory arbitrations.

Appeal

2E–101   There is a right of appeal to the Court of Appeal, see *INCO Europe Ltd v. First Choice Distribution* [1999] 1 W.L.R. 270; [1999] 1 All E.R. 820; [1999] C.L.C. 165, CA. The court held that the general terms of s.107 and Schedule 3 of the 1996 Act (*q.v.*) were not to be construed as removing the right of appeal which had existed under earlier legislation (affirmed by HL(E) [2000] 1 W.L.R. 586; [2000] 2 All E.R. 109; [2000] 1 Lloyd's Rep 467.

A Party to an arbitration agreement

2E–102   By s.82(2) a party to an arbitration agreement includes any person claiming under or through a party to the agreement.

Who may apply

2E–103   It is not necessary that all parties to the submission, other than the claimant in the claim, should join in application to stay (see *Willesford v. Watson* (1873) 8 Ch.App. 473).

The Application

2E–104   This is in by ordinary application notice and is made to the court in which the legal proceedings are pending.

Form of Order

2E–105   See Queen's Bench Masters' Practice Forms, Form **PF 167**, see Civil Procedure Forms Volume.

"... or after he has taken any step in those proceedings to answer the substantive claim"

2E–106   Though the application cannot precede the taking of the appropriate step if any to acknowledge the legal proceedings, the application must be made before taking any step to answer the substantive claim. So an application for security for costs was held to bar the defendant from obtaining a stay hereunder (*Adams v. Cattley* (1892) 66 L.T. 687); so also the issue of an application for disclosure, see *Chappell v. North* [1891] 2 Q.B. 252, cited above; so also attending an application for directions issued by the claimant and agreeing to or obtaining an order thereon (*County Theatres, etc. Ltd v. Knowles* [1902] 1 K.B. 480; *Richardson v. Le Maitre* [1903] 2 Ch. 222; *Stein v. Buncle* [1902] W.N. 44; *Cohen v. Arthur* (1912) 56 S.J. 344); or without an order being made, but an undertaking given to furnish an account (*Ochs v. Ochs Bros.* [1909] 2 Ch. 121). After defence it is too late (*West London, etc. Co v. Abbott* (1881) 29 W.R. 584). Also after defendant has obtained time to plead and agreed to take short notice of trial (*Smith v. British Marine* [1883] W.N. 176). Opposition to an application for final judgment may constitute a step in the action; but no "step" is taken by a defendant opposing an application who not merely raises the matter of the arbitration clause in his affidavit, but also at the same time takes out an application to stay the claim (*Pitchers Ltd v. Plaza (Queensbury) Ltd* [1940] 1 All E.R. 151, CA). *Cf.* also *Parker, Gaines & Co Ltd v. Turpin* [1918] 1 K.B. 358.

The defendant must, however, act timeously. Thus if a defendant resists summary judgment proceedings by serving an affidavit or certified witness statement in opposition, but omits to issue an application to stay the claim until after a first hearing of the claimant's application which is merely adjourned for a further and fuller hearing, he will be deemed to have taken a step in the claim (*Turner & Goudy v. McConnell* [1985] 1 W.L.R. 898; [1985] 2 All E.R. 34, CA; *Rumput (Panama) SA v. Islamic Republic of Iran Shipping Lines, The League* [1984] 2 Lloyd's Rep. 259). A party who initiates an application for a stay pending an arbitration does not take a "step" in the proceedings within the meaning of s.9(3) of the 1996 Act if he, either simultaneously or subsquently, invokes or accepts the court's jurisdiction provided he does so only conditionally on his stay application failing, *Capital Trust Investments Ltd v. Radio Design TJ AB* [2001] 3 All E.R. 756. Affirmed [2002] 2 All E.R. 159, CA.

Similarly, if a defendant issues an application for an extension of time for defence, but omits to issue an application to stay until after the application for has been dealt with, he will be held to have taken a step in the proceedings (*Ford's Hotel Co Ltd v. Bartlett* [1896] A.C. 1, HL). If, on the other hand, a defendant issues an application to stay, and, at the same time, issues an application for an extension of time for defence until after the hearing of the application to stay, he is unlikely to be held to have taken a step in the proceedings by the issue of the further time application (*London Sack & Bag Co Ltd v. Dixon & Lugton Ltd* [1943] 2 All E.R. 763, CA).

Where defendant gave notice demanding particulars of case, that was held to be no step in the claim (*Ives v. Willans* [1894] 1 Ch. 68; affirmed 2 Ch. 478; and *cf. Patteson v. Northern Accident Ins. Soc.* [1901] 2 Ir.R. 262) and the same where the defendant before defence wrote to claimant under the former O.3, r.5 for further time to plead and obtained it (*Brighton Marine, etc. Co v. Woodhouse* [1893] 2 Ch. 486); and where the defendant filed affidavits in the claim in answer to the claimant's affidavits in support of an application for a receiver, that was held to be no step in the claim (*Zalinoff v. Hammond* [1898] 2 Ch. 92). The distinction seems to be that negotiation or correspondence between parties or their solicitors does not constitute a step in the claim, but an application, or the service of a pleading does. An application to strike out may be a step in the proceedings (*Leigh v. English Property* [1976] 2 Lloyd's Rep. 298; *Eagle Star Insurance Co Ltd v. Yuval Insurance Ltd* [1978] 1 Lloyd's Rep. 357).

A defendant did not take any step to answer the substantive claim so as to lose his right to apply for a stay by applying for relief which was otiose to the relief he needed in addition to the relief he did need, see *Patel v. Patel* [2000] Q.B. 551, CA. In this case the defendant asked for the default judgment to be set aside (the relief he needed) but in addition and unnecessarily for leave to defend and counterclaim which he was entitled to do once default judgment was set aside.

The institution of an action within the time limit in a competent court in the United States between the same parties which was subsequently stayed because it was brought in breach of a London arbitration clause would not be regarded as steps having been taken under s.9 of the Arbitration Act 1996 when considering an application subsequently made out of time to appoint an arbitrator. *Thyssen Inc v. Calypso Shipping Corporation S.A.* [2000] 2 Lloyd's Rep. 243.

Whether additional matters sought to be raised by way of amendment to existing proceedings attract the stay provisions of s.9 of the 1996 Act depends on whether such additional matters "were part and parcel of the dispute of which the court was already seised or whether they were discrete matters in respect of which s.9 entitled the defendant to insist that they be arbitrated", *M Ahad v S Uddin* [2005] EWCA Civ 883.

Onus of showing that claim should proceed

It rests on the claimant to show that the dispute ought not to be referred to arbitration (*Hodgson v. Ry. Passengers Assn. Co* (1882) 9 QBD 188; and see *Vawdrey v. Simpson* [1896] 1 Ch. 166). The rule is now mandatory if the matters within subs.(4) are established. It is to be noted that the words "or that there was not in fact any dispute between the parties with regard to the matter agreed to be referred" (see s.1(1) of the 1975 Act) have not been re-enacted in s.9. Accordingly, where an amount due under an agreement was either disputed or simply not paid there was a dispute as to the amount due even though no answer to the claim existed in law or in fact. Such dispute was within the arbitration clause and proceedings at law brought to recover it had to be stayed (see *Halki Shipping Corporation v. Sopex Oils Ltd* [1997] 1 W.L.R. 1268; [1997] 3 All E.R. 833; [1998] 1 Lloyd's Rep. 49; affirmed by CA by a majority of 2:1, [1998] 1 W.L.R. 726; [1998] 2 All E.R. 23; [1998] 1 Lloyd's Rep. 465.

In *Wealands v. C.L.C. Contractors Ltd* [1998] C.L.C. 808, the Court held on an application by a sub-contractor for third party proceedings against it by the contractor to be stayed under s.9 of the Arbitration Act 1996 that despite the disadvantages of the claim against the third party going to arbitration (if the plaintiff did not join the third party as a defendant) the 1996 Act gave priority to party autonomy and entitled the third party as of right to the stay which is sought (affirmed [1999] 2 Lloyd's Rep. 739, CA).

Where a party objected under s.9 of the 1996 Act to a matter being considered

2E–107

other than by arbitrators then a dispute as to whether or not an arbitration agreement was time barred by limitation should be considered by the arbitrators even though the claimant might if he failed on such issue need to seek the exercise of the Court's discretion under s.12 of the 1996 Act; *Grimaldi Compagnia di Navigazione SpA v. Sekihyo Line Ltd* [1999] 1 W.L.R. 708; [1998] 3 All E.R. 943.

In *Ahmad Al-Naimi (T/A Buildmaster Construction Services) v. Islamic Press Agency Inc* [2000] 1 Lloyd's Rep. 522 CA the Court held that—

(1) If the Court decided that it was the Court which should determine whether the matters the subject of the action were the subject of an arbitration clause, unless the parties were agreed that the matter should be resolved on affidavit, then, if there was a triable issue directions should be given for trying that issue: under the CPR the Court had a wider discretion to rule what evidence it needed to decide any particular point; and

(2) On a proper construction of s.9 it could be said with force that a Court should be satisfied (a) that that there was an arbitration clause and (b) that the subject of the action was within that clause before the Court could grant a stay under that section; but a stay under the inherent jurisdiction might in fact be sensible in a situation where the Court could not be sure of these matters but could see that good sense and litigation management made it desirable for an arbitrator to consider the whole matter first.

In *Sonatrach Petroleum Corporation (BVI) v. Ferrell International Ltd* [2002] 1 All E.R. (Comm) 627 (head-charter provided for arbitration in Japan but sub-charter gave jurisdiction to English courts) held that the unenforceability of method of proper law selection in sub-charter did not mean the choice of forum was also void as the latter was free-standing and a stay was granted in respect of a claim brought under the sub-charter.

Section 9 does not apply to petitions under s.459 of the Companies Act 1985 as the shareholders statutory right to petition is inalienable and cannot be diminished by a contact for arbitration, *Exeter City AFC Ltd v. Football Conference Ltd* [2004] EWHC 831(Ch); [2004] 1 W.L.R. 2910; [2004] 4 All E.R. 1179.

Inoperative

2E–108   An arbitration agreement is inoperative where a defendant had shown an intention not to be bound by the agreement to refer and the other party (the claimant) had accepted such repudiation, *Downing v. Al Tameer Establishment* [2002] EWCA Civ 721; [2002] 2 All E.R. (Comm) 545, CA.

"Incapable of being performed"

2E–108A   The words in s.1(1) of the 1979 Act "incapable of being performed" were held to refer only to the question whether an arbitration agreement is capable of being performed up to the point when it results in an award and should not be construed as extending to the question whether, once an award has been made, the party against whom it is made will be incapable of satisfying it, for the impecuniosity of the loser rendering him unable to pay the amount of the award does not make the arbitration incapable of being performed (*The Rena K* [1979] Q.B. 377; [1979] 1 All E.R. 397; [1978] 1 Lloyd's Rep. 545). Nor was an arbitration agreement incapable of being performed within the meaning of s.1(1) of the Act merely because one party cannot afford the arbitration (*Paczy v. Haendler & Natermann GmbH* [1981] F.S.R. 250).

Reference of interpleader issue to arbitration

2E–109   **10.**—(1) Where in legal proceedings relief by way of interpleader is granted and any issue between the claimants is one in respect of which there is an arbitration agreement between them, the court granting the relief shall direct that the issue be determined in accordance with the agreement unless the circumstances are such that proceedings brought by a claimant in respect of the matter would not be stayed.

(2) Where subsection (1) applies but the court does not direct that the issue be determined in accordance with the arbitration agreement, any provision that an award is a condition precedent to the

bringing of legal proceedings in respect of any matter shall not affect the determination of that issue by the court.

Note—Compare s.5 of the 1950 Act. This is a mandatory provision (see s.4) and ap- **2E–110** plies even though the seat of arbitration is outside England and Wales or where no seat of arbitration has been designated. Subsection (2) does not apply to statutory arbitrations.

Retention of security where Admiralty proceedings stayed

11.—(1) Where Admiralty proceedings are stayed on the ground **2E–111** that the dispute in question should be submitted to arbitration, the court granting the stay may, if in those proceedings property has been arrested or bail or other security has been given to prevent or obtain release from arrest—

> (a) order that the property arrested be retained as security for the satisfaction of any award given in the arbitration in respect of that dispute, or
>
> (b) order that the stay of those proceedings be conditional on the provision of equivalent security for the satisfaction of any such award.

(2) Subject to any provision made by rules of court and to any necessary modifications, the same law and practice shall apply in relation to property retained in pursuance of an order as would apply if it were held for the purposes of proceedings in the court making the order.

Note—See s.26 of the Civil Jurisdiction and Judgments Act 1982. This is a manda- **2E–112** tory provision (see s.4).

COMMENCEMENT OF ARBITRAL PROCEEDINGS

Power of court to extend time for beginning arbitral proceedings, etc.

12.—(1) Where an arbitration agreement to refer future disputes **2E–113** to arbitration provides that a claim shall be barred, or the claimant's right extinguished, unless the claimant takes within a time fixed by the agreement some step—

> (a) to begin arbitral proceedings, or
>
> (b) to begin other dispute resolution procedures which must be exhausted before arbitral proceedings can be begun,

the court may by order extend the time for taking that step.

(2) Any party to the arbitration agreement may apply for such an order (upon notice to the other parties), but only after a claim has arisen and after exhausting any available arbitral process for obtaining an extension of time.

(3) The court shall make an order only if satisfied—

> (a) that the circumstances are such as were outside the reasonable contemplation of the parties when they agreed the provision in question, and that it would be just to extend the time, or
>
> (b) that the conduct of one party makes it unjust to hold the

other party to the strict terms of the provision in question.

(4) The court may extend the time for such period and on such terms as it thinks fit, and may do so whether or not the time previously fixed (by agreement or by a previous order) has expired.

(5) An order under this section does not affect the operation of the Limitation Acts (see section 13).

(6) The leave of the court is required for any appeal from a decision of the court under this section.

2E–114   *Note* —Compare s.27 of the 1950 Act. This is a mandatory provision (see s.4). This section does not apply to statutory arbitrations.

"Claim

2E–115   Under s.27 of the 1950 Act, it was held that the word claims therein was not to be construed as meaning "causes of action", but should be given a wide and liberal interpretation and it will thus extend to any claim to have determined by arbitration a matter in issue between the parties, *e.g.* a claim for arbitration so as to assess the proper amount of a salvage award (*Sioux Inc. v. China Salvage Co Kwangchow Branch* [1980] 1 W.L.R. 996; [1980] 3 All E.R. 154, CA).

"... the Court may by order extend the time for taking that step"

2E–116   The court's powers hereunder are only in respect of provisions laying down time limits for commencing proceedings. Thus in *Crown Estate Commissioners v. John Mowlem & Co Ltd* 70 B.L.R. 1 the Court of Appeal, disapproving *McLaughlin & Harvey Plc v. P&O Developments Ltd* 55 B.L.R. 101, held that the court does not have power under this section to extend the time for commencing arbitration proceedings under clause 30.9.3. of the JCT Standard Form of Building Contract (1980 PwQ) since on its true construction that clause does not lay down any time limit for commencing proceedings but is concerned solely with the evidential effect of a final certificate in any proceedings which may be *commenced* and accordingly there was nothing for the court to extend (a case under s.27 of the 1950 Act).

Section 12 of the 1996 Act is markedly more restricted than its predecessor, s.27 of the 1950 Act. See in particular sub-section 3. It is now not possible to extend time because the court concludes in general terms that it would be just to do so (*Cathiship SA v. Allanasons Ltd, The Catherine Helen* [1998] 3 All E.R. 714).

A party's failure properly to read a contractual provision relating to the time limit for commencing an arbitration was not a circumstance which triggered the court's power under section 12(3)(a) of the Arbitration Act 1996, to permit an extension of time for bringing arbitral proceedings. The aim of s.12(3) was to allow the court to consider an extension in relation to circumstances where the parties would not reasonably have contemplated them as being ones where the time-bar would apply (*Harbour and General Works Ltd v. Environment Agency* [2000] 1 W.L.R. 950; [1999] 2 All E.R. (Comm) 686; [2000] 1 All E.R. 50; [2001] 1 Lloyd's Rep. 65, CA).

Application of Limitation Acts

2E–117   13.—(1) The Limitation Acts apply to arbitral proceedings as they apply to legal proceedings.

(2) The court may order that in computing the time prescribed by the Limitation Acts for the commencement of proceedings (including arbitral proceedings) in respect of a dispute which was the subject matter—

    (a) of an award which the court orders to be set aside or declares to be of no effect, or

    (b) of the affected part of an award which the court orders to be set aside in part, or declares to be in part of no effect, the period between the commencement of the arbitration and the date of the order referred to in paragraph (a) or (b) shall be excluded.

(3) In determining for the purposes of the Limitation Acts when a cause of action accrued, any provision that an award is a condition precedent to the bringing of legal proceedings in respect of a matter to which an arbitration agreement applies shall be disregarded.

(4) In this Part "the Limitation Acts" means—

   (a) in England and Wales, the Limitation Act 1980, the Foreign Limitation Periods Act 1984 and any other enactment (whenever passed) relating to the limitation of actions;

   (b) in Northern Ireland, the Limitation (Northern Ireland) Order 1989, the Foreign Limitation Periods (Northern Ireland) Order 1985 and any other enactment (whenever passed) relating to the limitation of actions.

Note —This is a mandatory provision (see s.4).   **2E–118**

Commencement of arbitral proceedings

14.—(1) The parties are free to agree when arbitral proceedings   **2E–119** are to be regarded as commenced for the purposes of this Part and for the purposes of the Limitation Acts.

(2) If there is no such agreement the following provisions apply.

(3) Where the arbitrator is named or designated in the arbitration agreement, arbitral proceedings are commenced in respect of a matter when one party serves on the other party or parties a notice in writing requiring him or them to submit that matter to the person so named or designated.

(4) Where the arbitrator or arbitrators are to be appointed by the parties, arbitral proceedings are commenced in respect of a matter when one party serves on the other party or parties notice in writing requiring him or them to appoint an arbitrator or to agree to the appointment of an arbitrator in respect of that matter.

(5) Where the arbitrator or arbitrators are to be appointed by a person other than a party to the proceedings, arbitral proceedings are commenced in respect of a matter when one party gives notice in writing to that person requesting him to make the appointment in respect of that matter.

"... when one party serves ... a notice in writing requiring him ... to appoint an arbitrator ..."

A notice which does no more than state a dispute is referred to arbitration in accor-   **2E–120** dance with an agreement has been held to be insufficient to commence the arbitration as it did not imply a request to appoint an arbitrator (see *Vosnoc Ltd v. Transglobal Projects Ltd* [1998] 1 W.L.R. 101; [1998] 2 All E.R. 990; [1998] 1 Lloyd's Rep. 711, a case under s.34(3)(a) of the Limitation Act 1980, now superseded by s.14 of the Arbitration Act 1996). But this case was not followed in *Allianz Versicherungs-Aktiengesellschaft v. Fortuna Inc (The Baltic Universal)* [1999] 1 W.L.R. 2117; [1999] 2 All E.R. 625; [1999] 1 Lloyd's Rep. 497, nor in *Charles M. Willie & Co (Shipping) Ltd v. Ocean Laser Shipping Ltd* [1999] 1 Lloyd's Rep. 225 which held that it was sufficient that an intention to commence arbitration/invoke the arbitration agreement was clear in the notice even though it did not as such request the appointment of an arbitrator. See too *Seabridge*

Shipping AB v. AC Orssleff's Eftf's A/S [1999] 2 Lloyd's Rep. 685, letter from charters to a member of the LMAA asking him to accept appointment as arbitrator, copied to owners and by its terms asking owners to indicate whether they would accept addressee as sole arbitrator held objectively to be a notice in writing within s.14 which was to be interpreted broadly and flexibly.

2E–120.1   Note — A referral to adjudication under the Housing Grants Construction and Regeneration Act 1996 did not preclude a subsequent referral to arbitration of the same dispute arising under a construction contract subject to ICE Conditions of Contract, see *Trustees of the Harbours of Peterhead v. Lilley Construction Ltd, (Court of Senion, Outer House), The Times*, April 24, 2003.

THE ARBITRAL TRIBUNAL

The arbitral tribunal
2E–121   15.—(1) The parties are free to agree on the number of arbitrators to form the tribunal and whether there is to be a chairman or umpire.

(2) Unless otherwise agreed by the parties, an agreement that the number of arbitrators shall be two or any other even number shall be understood as requiring the appointment of an additional arbitrator as chairman of the tribunal.

(3) If there is no agreement as to the number of arbitrators, the tribunal shall consist of a sole arbitrator.

2E–122   Note —Compare ss.6, 8 and 9 of the 1950 Act.

Procedure for appointment of arbitrators
2E–123   16.—(1) The parties are free to agree on the procedure for appointing the arbitrator or arbitrators, including the procedure for appointing any chairman or umpire.

(2) If or to the extent that there is no such agreement, the following provisions apply.

(3) If the tribunal is to consist of a sole arbitrator, the parties shall jointly appoint the arbitrator not later than 28 days after service of a request in writing by either party to do so.

(4) If a tribunal is to consist of two arbitrators, each party shall appoint one arbitrator not later than 14 days after service of a request in writing by either party to do so.

(5) If the tribunal is to consist of three arbitrators—

    (a) each party shall appoint one arbitrator not later than 14 days after service of a request in writing by either party to do so, and

    (b) the two so appointed shall forthwith appoint a third arbitrator as the chairman of the tribunal.

(6) If the tribunal is to consist of two arbitrators and an umpire—

    (a) each party shall appoint one arbitrator not later than 14 days after service of a request in writing by either party to do so, and

    (b) the two so appointed may appoint an umpire at any time after they themselves are appointed and shall do so before any substantive hearing or forthwith if they cannot agree on a matter relating to the arbitration.

(7) In any other case (in particular, if there are more than two parties) section 18 applies as in the case of a failure of the agreed appointment procedure.

Power in case of default to appoint sole arbitrator

17.—(1) Unless the parties otherwise agree, where each of two parties to an arbitration agreement is to appoint an arbitrator and one party ("the party in default") refuses to do so, or fails to do so within the time specified, the other party, having duly appointed his arbitrator, may give notice in writing to the party in default that he proposes to appoint his arbitrator to act as sole arbitrator.

(2) If the party in default does not within 7 clear days of that notice being given—

(a) make the required appointment, and

(b) notify the other party that he has done so,

the other party may appoint his arbitrator as sole arbitrator whose award shall be binding on both parties as if he had been so appointed by agreement.

(3) Where a sole arbitrator has been appointed under subsection (2), the party in default may (upon notice to the appointing party) apply to the court which may set aside the appointment.

(4) The leave of the court is required for any appeal from a decision of the court under this section.

Note—Compare ss.7(b) and 10(3B) of the 1950 Act.   **2E–125**

2E–124

Extent of section

The former s.7 was held not apply to a reference to three arbitrators, one to be appointed by each of the parties, and the third by the two so appointed, though it would apply to a reference to two arbitrators and an umpire (see *Re Smith and Nelson Arbn.* (1890) 25 QBD 545).   **2E–126**

The procedure prescribed by the former s.7 was required to be strictly complied with; thus, where one party fails to appoint an arbitrator after service of a default notice under s.7(b), the arbitrator appointed by the other party has no jurisdiction to make an award until he has been appointed sole arbitrator in accordance with the section (*Ministry of Food, Government of Bangladesh v. Bengal Liner, The Bengal Pride* [1986] 1 Lloyd's Rep. 167).

"Notice to appoint"

Semble, these words mean notice to appoint or to concur in the appointment within seven days of an acceptable arbitrator. Where the notice was not worded strictly in accordance with the section, though its meaning was clear, and the party receiving it refused to concur in the appointment of any arbitrator, the Court appointed one (*Re Eyre and Corporation of Leicester* [1892] 1 Q.B. 136).   **2E–127**

Failure of appointment procedure

18.—(1) The parties are free to agree what is to happen in the event of a failure of the procedure for the appointment of the arbitral tribunal. There is no failure if an appointment is duly made under section 17 (power in case of default to appoint sole arbitrator), unless that appointment is set aside.   **2E–128**

(2) If or to the extent that there is no such agreement any party to the arbitration agreement may (upon notice to the other parties) apply to the court to exercise its powers under this section.

(3) Those powers are—

(a) to give directions as to the making of any necessary appointments;

(b) to direct that the tribunal shall be constituted by such appointments (or any one or more of them) as have been made;

(c) to revoke any appointments already made;

(d) to make any necessary appointments itself.

(4) An appointment made by the court under this section has effect as if made with the agreement of the parties.

(5) The leave of the court is required for any appeal from a decision of the court under this section.

2E–129   *Note* —Compare s.10 of the 1950 Act.

Consolidation by court

2E–130   In a case under s.10 of the 1950 Act it was held that the Court had power to appoint a single arbitrator in respect of two arbitrations, and it is highly desirable to do so to avoid the danger of inconsistent findings, where disputes between employers, main contractors and sub-contractors involve interrelated and also separate issues of fact and law in both arbitrations, but the Court in such case, will add an order for liberty to apply, to enable that arbitrator to arrange a pre-trial conference at which the issues in the two arbitrations may be segregated and if the single arbitrator should find that some issues are inseparable or other difficulties arise, he might think it right to be relieved of the further stages in the arbitration and apply to be replaced by a new arbitrator in respect of the inseparable issues or if the parties should think there is a risk of prejudice arising from the joint arbitration, they could apply to the Court presumably for separate arbitrations (see *Abu Dhabi Gas Liquefaction Co Ltd v. Eastern Bechtel Corp* [1982] Com.L.R. 215; [1982] 2 Lloyd's Rep. 425, CA).

Court to have regard to agreed qualifications

2E–131   **19.** In deciding whether to exercise, and in considering how to exercise, any of its powers under section 16 (procedure for appointment of arbitrators) or section 18 (failure of appointment procedure), the court shall have due regard to any agreement of the parties as to the qualifications required of the arbitrators.

Chairman

2E–132   **20.**—(1) Where the parties have agreed that there is to be a chairman, they are free to agree what the functions of the chairman are to be in relation to the making of decisions, orders and awards.

(2) If or to the extent that there is no such agreement, the following provisions apply.

(3) Decisions, orders and awards shall be made by all or a majority of the arbitrators (including the chairman).

(4) The view of the chairman shall prevail in relation to a decision, order or award in respect of which there is neither unanimity nor a majority under subsection (3).

2E–133   *Note* —Compare s.9 of the 1950 Act.

Umpire

2E–134   **21.**—(1) Where the parties have agreed that there is to be an umpire, they are free to agree what the functions of the umpire are to be, and in particular—

    (a) whether he is to attend the proceedings, and

    (b) when he is to replace the other arbitrators as the tribunal with power to make decisions, orders and awards.

(2) If or to the extent that there is no such agreement, the following provisions apply.

(3) The umpire shall attend the proceedings and be supplied with the same documents and other materials as are supplied to the other arbitrators.

(4) Decisions, orders and awards shall be made by the other arbitrators unless and until they cannot agree on a matter relating to the arbitration.

In that event they shall forthwith give notice in writing to the parties and the umpire, whereupon the umpire shall replace them as the tribunal with power to make decisions, orders and awards as if he were sole arbitrator.

(5) If the arbitrators cannot agree but fail to give notice of that fact, or if any of them fails to join in the giving of notice, any party to the arbitral proceedings may (upon notice to the other parties and to the tribunal) apply to the court which may order that the umpire shall replace the other arbitrators as the tribunal with power to make decisions, orders and awards as if he were sole arbitrator.

(6) The leave of the court is required for any appeal from a decision of the court under this section.

Note—Compare s.8(2) and (3) of the 1950 Act.   **2E–135**

Decision-making where no chairman or umpire

22.—(1) Where the parties agree that there shall be two or more **2E–136** arbitrators with no chairman or umpire, the parties are free to agree how the tribunal is to make decisions, orders and awards.

(2) If there is no such agreement, decisions, orders and awards shall be made by all or a majority of the arbitrators.

Revocation of arbitrator's authority

23.—(1) The parties are free to agree in what circumstances the **2E–137** authority of an arbitrator may be revoked.

(2) If or to the extent that there is no such agreement the following provisions apply.

(3) The authority of an arbitrator may not be revoked except—

    (a) by the parties acting jointly, or

    (b) by an arbitral or other institution or person vested by the parties with powers in that regard.

(4) Revocation of the authority of an arbitrator by the parties acting jointly must be agreed in writing unless the parties also agree (whether or not in writing) to terminate the arbitration agreement.

(5) Nothing in this section affects the power of the court—

    (a) to revoke an appointment under section 18 (powers

exercisable in case of failure of appointment procedure), or

(b) to remove an arbitrator on the grounds specified in section 24.

2E–138   *Note* —Compare s.1 of the 1950 Act.

Power of court to remove arbitrator

2E–139   **24.**—(1) A party to arbitral proceedings may (upon notice to the other parties, to the arbitrator concerned and to any other arbitrator) apply to the court to remove an arbitrator on any of the following grounds—

(a) that circumstances exist that give rise to justifiable doubts as to his impartiality;

(b) that he does not possess the qualifications required by the arbitration agreement;

(c) that he is physically or mentally incapable of conducting the proceedings or there are justifiable doubts as to his capacity to do so;

(d) that he has refused or failed—

(i) properly to conduct the proceedings, or

(ii) to use all reasonable despatch in conducting the proceedings or making an award,

and that substantial injustice has been or will be caused to the applicant.

(2) If there is an arbitral or other institution or person vested by the parties with power to remove an arbitrator, the court shall not exercise its power of removal unless satisfied that the applicant has first exhausted any available recourse to that institution or person.

(3) The arbitral tribunal may continue the arbitral proceedings and make an award while an application to the court under this section is pending.

(4) Where the court removes an arbitrator, it may make such order as it thinks fit with respect to his entitlement (if any) to fees or expenses, or the repayment of any fees or expenses already paid.

(5) The arbitrator concerned is entitled to appear and be heard by the court before it makes any order under this section.

(6) The leave of the court is required for any appeal from a decision of the court under this section.

2E–140   *Note* —Compare ss.13(3), 23 and 24(1) of the 1950 Act. This is a mandatory provision (see s.4).

"(a) circumstances exist that give rise to justifiable doubts as to his impartiality" etc.

2E–141   In *Petroships Pte Ltd v. Petec Trading and Investment Corporation* (The "Petro Ranger"), [2001] 2 Lloyd's Rep. 348 the Court stated that careful regard should be had to paras 105 and 106 of the report on the Arbitration Bill by the Departmental Advisory Committee on Arbitration Law, which provide as follows:

"105. We have included, as grounds for removal, the refusal or failure of an arbitrator properly to conduct the proceedings, as well as failing to use all reasonable despatch in conducting the proceedings or making an award, where the result has caused or will cause substantial injustices to the applicant. We trust that the courts will not allow the first of these matters to be abused by those intent on disrupting the arbitral process. To this end we have included a provision allowing the tribunal to continue while an application is made. There is also Clause 73 which effectively requires a party to "put up or shut up" if a challenge is to be made.

106. We have every confidence that the courts will carry through the intent of this part of the Bill, which is that it should only be available where the conduct of the arbitrator is such as to go so beyond anything that could reasonably be defended that substantial injustice has resulted or will result. The provision is not intended to allow the Court to substitute its own view as to how the arbitral proceedings should be conducted. Thus the choice by an arbitrator of a particular proceedure, unless it breaches the duty laid on arbitrators by Clause 33, should on no view justify the removal of an arbitrator, even if the court would not itself have adopted that procedure. In short, this ground only exists to cover what we hope will be the very rare case where an arbitrator so conducts the proceedings that it can fairly be said that instead of carrying through the object of arbitration as stated in the Bill, he is in effect frustrating that object. Only if the Court confines itself in this way can this power of removal be justified as a measure supporting rather than subverting the arbitral process."

Where circumstances have made the arbitrator an interested party (*e.g.* litigation between the arbitrator and one of the parties) leave to revoke will be given (*Re Baring Bros. & Co and Doulton & Co* (1892) 61 L.J.Q. 704). But the mere fact that one of the parties has issued a claim form against the arbitrator is not sufficient to disqualify the latter from acting where he has taken no positive step in retaliation (*Belcher v. Roedean School Site, etc. Ltd* (1901) 85 L.T. 468). The test is the same as that which applied to all who made judicial decisions, namely whether there was any real danger that the arbitrator was biased. "…when deciding whether bias has been established, the Court personifies the reasonable man. The Court considers on all the material which is placed before it whether there is any real danger of unconscious bias on the part of the decision maker. This is the case irrespective of whether it is a Judge or an arbitrator who is the subject of the allegation of bias". See *AT&T Construction v. Saudi Cable Co* [2000] CLC 220; [2000] 2 Lloyd's Rep 127, CA at 136.

In *Laker Airways Inc v. FLS Aerospace Ltd* [1999] 2 Lloyd's Rep. 45 (Barristers from the same Chambers appointed applicants' and respondents' arbitrators) the Court stated at p.48, "The test is an objective one – whether circumstances exist that give rise to justifiable doubts as to an arbitrator's impartiality. The test is thus objective in at least two respects: the Court must find that circumstances exist, and are not merely believed to exist (although I suppose that a belief may itself be a circumstance); and secondly, those cicumstances must justifiable or perhaps unreasonable doubt is not sufficient: it is not enough honestly to say that one has lost confidence in the arbitrator's impartiality. On the other hand, doubts, if justifiable, are sufficient: it is not necessary to prove actual bias".

The test for bias under s.24(1) is the same as that irregularity under s.68 where the application is made on the grounds of bias, see *Rustal Trading Ltd v. Gill & Duffus SA* [2000] 1 Lloyd's Rep. 14.

Abortive arbitration

"When an arbitration for any reason becomes abortive it is the duty of a court of law, in working out a contract of which such arbitration is part of the practical machinery, to supply the defect which has occurred. It is the duty of a court in such circumstances to come to the assistance of parties by removal of the impasse and the extrication of their rights" (*Cameron v. Caddy* [1914] A.C. 651 at 656). So in *Neal v. Richardson* [1938] 1 All E.R. 753, CA, where an architect being appointed to act as arbitrator, refused to grant certificates or to arbitrate, the Court refused to stay a claim in which the builder sought relief *aliunde*. On the other hand apart from the specific agreement the architect does not act as an arbitrator between the parties in issuing interim certificates (*Sutcliffe v. Thackrah* [1974] A.C. 727; [1974] 1 All E.R. 859, overruling *Chambers v. Goldthorpe* [1901] 1 K.B. 624, CA).

2E–142

Resignation of arbitrator

25.—(1) The parties are free to agree with an arbitrator as to the consequences of his resignation as regards—

2E–143

(a) his entitlement (if any) to fees or expenses, and

(b) any liability thereby incurred by him.

(2) If or to the extent that there is no such agreement the following provisions apply.

(3) An arbitrator who resigns his appointment may (upon notice to the parties) apply to the court—

(a) to grant him relief from any liability thereby incurred by him, and

(b) to make such order as it thinks fit with respect to his entitlement (if any) to fees or expenses or the repayment of any fees or expenses already paid.

(4) If the court is satisfied that in all the circumstances it was reasonable for the arbitrator to resign, it may grant such relief as is mentioned in subsection (3)(a) on such terms as it thinks fit.

(5) The leave of the court is required for any appeal from a decision of the court under this section.

Death of arbitrator or person appointing him

2E–144   26.—(1) The authority of an arbitrator is personal and ceases on his death.

(2) Unless otherwise agreed by the parties, the death of the person by whom an arbitrator was appointed does not revoke the arbitrator's authority.

2E–145   *Note* — Section 26(1) is a mandatory provision (see s.4). For s.26(2) compare s.2(2) of the 1950 Act.

Filling of vacancy, etc.

2E–146   27.—(1) Where an arbitrator ceases to hold office, the parties are free to agree—

(a) whether and if so how the vacancy is to be filled,

(b) whether and if so to what extent the previous proceedings should stand, and

(c) what effect (if any) his ceasing to hold office has on any appointment made by him (alone or jointly).

(2) If or to the extent that there is no such agreement, the following provisions apply.

(3) The provisions of sections 16 (procedure for appointment of arbitrators) and 18 (failure of appointment procedure) apply in relation to the filling of the vacancy as in relation to an original appointment.

(4) The tribunal (when reconstituted) shall determine whether and if so to what extent the previous proceedings should stand.

This does not affect any right of a party to challenge those proceedings on any ground which had arisen before the arbitrator ceased to hold office.

(5) His ceasing to hold office does not affect appointment by him (alone or jointly) of another arbitrator, in particular any appointment of a chairman or umpire.

Note —Compare s.25 of the 1950 Act. **2E–147**

Section 27(3)

The time limit of 14 days under s.16 referred to in s.27(3) applied only where there **2E–147.1** was no agreement on the time limit to be applied. The statutory provision does not prevail over party autonomy. It was a default provision to which resort was necessary only to the extent there was no agreement on the matter, see *Federal Insurance Co v. Transamerica Occidental Life Insurance Co* [1999] 2 Lloyd's Rep. 286 (30 day agreed time limit applied).

Joint and several liability of parties to arbitrators for fees and expenses

28.—(1) The parties are jointly and severally liable to pay to the **2E–148** arbitrators such reasonable fees and expenses (if any) as are appropriate in the circumstances.

(2) Any party may apply to the court (upon notice to the other parties and to the arbitrators) which may order that the amount of the arbitrators' fees and expenses shall be considered and adjusted by such means and upon such terms as it may direct.

(3) If the application is made after any amount has been paid to the arbitrators by way of fees or expenses, the court may order the repayment of such amount (if any) as is shown to be excessive, but shall not do so unless it is shown that it is reasonable in the circumstances to order repayment.

(4) The above provisions have effect subject to any order of the court under section 24(4) or 25(3)(b) (order as to entitlement to fees or expenses in case of removal or resignation of arbitrator).

(5) Nothing in this section affects any liability of a party to any other party to pay all or any of the costs of the arbitration (see sections 59 to 65) or any contractual right of an arbitrator to payment of his fees and expenses.

(6) In this section references to arbitrators include an arbitrator who has ceased to act and an umpire who has not replaced the other arbitrators.

Note —This is a mandatory provision (see s.4). **2E–149**

Immunity of arbitrator

29.—(1) An arbitrator is not liable for anything done or omitted in **2E–150** the discharge or purported discharge of his functions as arbitrator unless the act or omission is shown to have been in bad faith.

(2) Subsection (1) applies to an employee or agent of an arbitrator as it applies to the arbitrator himself.

(3) This section does not affect any liability incurred by an arbitrator by reason of his resigning (but see section 25).

Note —This is a mandatory provision (see s.4). **2E–151**

JURISDICTION OF THE ARBITRAL TRIBUNAL

Competence of tribunal to rule on its own jurisdiction

30.—(1) Unless otherwise agreed by the parties, the arbitral **2E–152** tribunal may rule on its own substantive jurisdiction, that is, as to—

(a) whether there is a valid arbitration agreement,

(b) whether the tribunal is properly constituted, and

(c) what matters have been submitted to arbitration in accordance with the arbitration agreement.

(2) Any such ruling may be challenged by any available arbitral process of appeal or review or in accordance with the provisions of this Part.

2E–153 *Note* —This is a mandatory provision (see s.4). For adaptation of s.30(1)(a) in case of statutory arbitration see s.96 below.

Counterclaims

2E–153.1 Factors determining whether arbitrators may entertain a counterclaim are the true construction of the agreement to refer and whether the counterclaim is a transaction set-off or other true defence as opposed to a completely independent set-off, see *Metal Distributors (UK) Ltd v. ZCCM Investment Holdings PLC* [2005] EWHC 156 (Comm); [2005] 2 Lloyd's Rep.37 .

Objection to substantive jurisdiction of tribunal

2E–154 **31.**—(1) An objection that the arbitral tribunal lacks substantive jurisdiction at the outset of the proceedings must be raised by a party not later than the time he takes the first step in the proceedings to contest the merits of any matter in relation to which he challenges the tribunal's jurisdiction. A party is not precluded from raising such an objection by the fact that he has appointed or participated in the appointment of an arbitrator.

(2) Any objection during the course of the arbitral proceedings that the arbitral tribunal is exceeding its substantive jurisdiction must be made as soon as possible after the matter alleged to be beyond its jurisdiction is raised.

(3) The arbitral tribunal may admit an objection later than the time specified in subsection (1) or (2) if it considers the delay justified.

(4) Where an objection is duly taken to the tribunal's substantive jurisdiction and the tribunal has power to rule on its own jurisdiction, it may—

(a) rule on the matter in an award as to jurisdiction, or

(b) deal with the objection in its award on the merits.

If the parties agree which of these courses the tribunal should take, the tribunal shall proceed accordingly.

(5) The tribunal may in any case, and shall if the parties so agree, stay proceedings whilst an application is made to the court under section 32 (determination of preliminary point of jurisdiction).

2E–155 *Note* —This is a mandatory provision (see s.4). The prescribed circumstances without which the application will not be considered are to be noted.

Determination of preliminary point of jurisdiction

2E–156 **32.**—(1) The court may, on the application of a party to arbitral proceedings (upon notice to the other parties), determine any question as to the substantive jurisdiction of the tribunal. A party may lose the right to object (see section 73).

(2) An application under this section shall not be considered unless—

    (a) it is made with the agreement in writing of all the other parties to the proceedings, or

    (b) it is made with the permission of the tribunal and the court is satisfied—

        (i) that the determination of the question is likely to produce substantial savings in costs,

        (ii) that the application was made without delay, and

        (iii) that there is good reason why the matter should be decided by the court.

(3) An application under this section, unless made with the agreement of all the other parties to the proceedings, shall state the grounds on which it is said that the matter should be decided by the court.

(4) Unless otherwise agreed by the parties, the arbitral tribunal may continue the arbitral proceedings and make an award while an application to the court under this section is pending.

(5) Unless the court gives leave, no appeal lies from a decision of the court whether the conditions specified in subsection (2) are met.

(6) The decision of the court on the question of jurisdiction shall be treated as a judgment of the court for the purposes of an appeal.

But no appeal lies without the leave of the court which shall not be given unless the court considers that the question involves a point of law which is one of general importance or is one which for some other special reason should be considered by the Court of Appeal.

Note —This is a mandatory provision (see s.4).   **2E–157**

Application of section

Guidance on the circumstances in which the Court can entertain an application **2E–157.1** under s.32 by a party to arbitral proceedings is contained in *Vale do Rio doce Navegacao SA v. Shanghai Bao Steel Ocean Shipping Co Ltd* [2000] 2 Lloyd's Rep. 1. The Court should not intervene except in the limited circumstances specified. Where the other alleged party to an arbitration agreement denies he is a party thereto the Court stated at para. 54:

> "The Act sets out in very clear terms the steps that a party who contends that there is another party to an arbitration agreement should take. First he should appoint an arbitrator. If the other party appoints an arbitrator, then s.31(1) makes it clear that his appointment of an arbitrator does not prevent him challenging the substantive jurisdiction of the tribunal. If the other party does not appoint an arbitrator, then the default provisions (s.17) or failure to appoint procedures (s.18) apply. Once the arbitral tribunal is constituted, then in accordance with the policy of the Act it is for that tribunal to rule on its own jurisdiction, save in the circumstances specified in s.32. Any award made can then be changed under s.67. The rights of the party who challenges the existence of the arbitration agreement and takes no part are protected by s.72; he is given the right to recourse to the Courts in the circumstances set out."

There is no jurisdiction under s.32 as regards non-parties to the arbitration (*e.g.* brokers). See further para. 23-11 above.

THE ARBITRAL PROCEEDINGS

General duty of the tribunal

    33.—(1) The tribunal shall—   **2E–158**

        (a) act fairly and impartially as between the parties, giving each party a reasonable opportunity of putting his case and dealing with that of his opponent, and

    (b) adopt procedures suitable to the circumstances of the particular case, avoiding unnecessary delay or expense, so as to provide a fair means for the resolution of the matters falling to be determined.

(2) The tribunal shall comply with that general duty in conducting the arbitral proceedings, in its decisions on matters of procedure and evidence and in the exercise of all other powers conferred on it.

2E-159   *Note* —This is a mandatory provision (see s.4).

Procedural and evidential matters

2E-160   **34.**—(1) It shall be for the tribunal to decide all procedural and evidential matters, subject to the right of the parties to agree any matter.

(2) Procedural and evidential matters include—

    (a) when and where any part of the proceedings is to be held

    (b) the language or languages to be used in the proceedings and whether translations of any relevant documents are to be supplied;

    (c) whether any and if so what form of written statements of claim and defence are to be used, when these should be supplied and the extent to which such statements can be later amended;

    (d) whether any and if so which documents or classes of documents should be disclosed between and produced by the parties and at what stage;

    (e) whether any and if so what questions should be put to and answered by the respective parties and when and in what form this should be done;

    (f) whether to apply strict rules of evidence (or any other rules) as to the admissibility, relevance or weight of any material (oral, written or other) sought to be tendered on any matters of fact or opinion, and the time, manner and form in which such material should be exchanged and presented;

    (g) whether and to what extent the tribunal should itself take the initiative in ascertaining the facts and the law;

    (h) whether and to what extent there should be oral or written evidence or submissions.

(3) The tribunal may fix the time within which any directions given by it are to be complied with, and may if it thinks fit extend the time so fixed (whether or not it has expired).

Consolidation of proceedings and concurrent hearings

2E-161   **35.**—(1) The parties are free to agree—

    (a) that the arbitral proceedings shall be consolidated with other arbitral proceedings, or

    (b) that concurrent hearings shall be held,

on such terms as may be agreed.

(2) Unless the parties agree to confer such power on the tribunal, the tribunal has no power to order consolidation of proceedings or concurrent hearings.

Note —For adaptation where a statutory arbitration is involved, see s.96(3) below. **2E–162**

Legal or other representation

36. Unless otherwise agreed by the parties, a party to arbitral **2E–163** proceedings may be represented in the proceedings by a lawyer or other person chosen by him.

Power to appoint experts, legal advisers or assessors

37.—(1) Unless otherwise agreed by the parties— **2E–164**

  (a) the tribunal may—

  (i) appoint experts or legal advisers to report to it and the parties, or

  (ii) appoint assessors to assist it on technical matters,

and may allow any such expert, legal adviser or assessor to attend the proceedings; and

  (b) the parties shall be given a reasonable opportunity to comment on any information, opinion or advice offered by any such person.

(2) The fees and expenses of an expert, legal adviser or assessor appointed by the tribunal for which the arbitrators are liable are expenses of the arbitrators for the purposes of this Part.

Note — Section 37(2) is a mandatory provision (see s.4). **2E–165**

General powers exercisable by the tribunal

38.—(1) The parties are free to agree on the powers exercisable by **2E–166** the arbitral tribunal for the purposes of and in relation to the proceedings.

(2) Unless otherwise agreed by the parties the tribunal has the following powers.

(3) The tribunal may order a claimant to provide security for the costs of the arbitration.

This power shall not be exercised on the ground that the claimant is—

  (a) an individual ordinarily resident outside the United Kingdom, or

  (b) a corporation or association incorporated or formed under the law of a country outside the United Kingdom, or whose central management and control is exercised outside the United Kingdom.

(4) The tribunal may give directions in relation to any property which is the subject of the proceedings or as to which any question arises in the proceedings, and which is owned by or is in the possession of a party to the proceedings—

  (a) for the inspection, photographing, preservation, custody or detention of the property by the tribunal, an expert or a party, or

(b) ordering that samples be taken from, or any observation be made of or experiment conducted upon, the property.

(5) The tribunal may direct that a party or witness shall be examined on oath or affirmation, and may for that purpose administer any necessary oath or take any necessary affirmation.

(6) The tribunal may give directions to a party for the preservation for the purposes of the proceedings of any evidence in his custody or control.

2E–167   *Note* —Compare s.12(1)–(3) and s.6(a) of the 1950 Act. The power to order security was new.

Power to make provisional awards

2E–168   **39.**—(1) The parties are free to agree that the tribunal shall have power to order on a provisional basis any relief which it would have power to grant in a final award.

(2) This includes, for instance, making—

(a) a provisional order for the payment of money or the disposition of property as between the parties, or

(b) an order to make an interim payment on account of the costs of the arbitration.

(3) Any such order shall be subject to the tribunal's final adjudication; and the tribunal's final award, on the merits or as to costs, shall take account of any such order.

(4) Unless the parties agree to confer such power on the tribunal, the tribunal has no such power.

This does not affect its powers under section 47 (awards on different issues, etc.).

2E–168.1   *Note* —Under this provision an arbitrator has power to make a freezing order on a provisional basis if the parties have so agreed, see *Kastner v. Jason* [2004] EWHC 592 (Ch); [2004] 2 Lloyd's Rep. 233(Ch). Further reviewed and analysed on appeal [2004] EWCA Civ 1599; [2005] 1 Lloyd's Rep. 397.

General duty of parties

2E–169   **40.**—(1) The parties shall do all things necessary for the proper and expeditious conduct of the arbitral proceedings.

(2) This includes—

(a) complying without delay with any determination of the tribunal as to procedural or evidential matters, or with any order or directions of the tribunal, and

(b) where appropriate, taking without delay any necessary steps to obtain a decision of the court on a preliminary question of jurisdiction or law (see sections 32 and 45).

2E–170   *Note* —This is a mandatory provision (see s.4).

Powers of tribunal in case of party's default

2E–171   **41.**—(1) The parties are free to agree on the powers of the tribunal in case of a party's failure to do something necessary for the proper and expeditious conduct of the arbitration.

(2) Unless otherwise agreed by the parties, the following provisions apply.

(3) If the tribunal is satisfied that there has been inordinate and inexcusable delay on the part of the claimant in pursuing his claim and that the delay—

> (a) gives rise, or is likely to give rise, to a substantial risk that it is not possible to have a fair resolution of the issues in that claim, or
>
> (b) has caused, or is likely to cause, serious prejudice to the respondent,

the tribunal may make an award dismissing the claim.

(4) If without showing sufficient cause a party—

> (a) fails to attend or be represented at an oral hearing of which due notice was given, or
>
> (b) where matters are to be dealt with in writing, fails after due notice to submit written evidence or make written submissions,

the tribunal may continue the proceedings in the absence of that party or, as the case may be, without any written evidence or submissions on his behalf, and may make an award on the basis of the evidence before it.

(5) If without showing sufficient cause a party fails to comply with any order or directions of the tribunal, the tribunal may make a peremptory order to the same effect, prescribing such time for compliance with it as the tribunal considers appropriate.

(6) If a claimant fails to comply with a peremptory order of the tribunal to provide security for costs, the tribunal may make an award dismissing his claim.

(7) If a party fails to comply with any other kind of peremptory order, then, without prejudice to section 42 (enforcement by court of tribunal's peremptory orders), the tribunal may do any of the following—

> (a) direct that the party in default shall not be entitled to rely upon any allegation or material which was the subject matter of the order;
>
> (b) draw such adverse inferences from the act of non-compliance as the circumstances justify;
>
> (c) proceed to an award on the basis of such materials as have been properly provided to it;
>
> (d) make such order as it thinks fit as to the payment of costs of the arbitration incurred in consequence of the non-compliance.

Note—Compare s.13A of the 1950 Act. **2E–172**

Unless otherwise agreed ... the following provisions apply

The provisions reflect the principles laid down in *Birkett v. James* [1978] A.C. 297, **2E–173** HL, and *Department of Transport v. Smaller (Chris) Transport Ltd* [1989] A.C. 1197, HL. Thus in *James Lazenby & Co v. McNicholas Construction Co Ltd* [1995] 1 W.L.R. 615;

[1995] 2 Lloyd's Rep. 30, it was held that it was an error of law for an arbitrator to dismiss a claim within its limitation period in the absence of exceptional circumstances.

Application

2E-174   Under the old law (s.13A) an arbitrator had power to dismiss a claim on the basis of inordinate and inexcusable delay occurring before (as well as after) the section came into force on January 1, 1992 and to such extent the provision has retrospective effect (*L'Office Cherifien des Phosphates and Unitramp SA v. Yamashita-Shinnihom Steamship Co Ltd* [1994] 1 A.C. 486; [1994] 2 W.L.R. 39; [1994] 1 All E.R. 20; [1994] 1 Lloyd's Rep. 251, HL).

POWERS OF COURT IN RELATION TO ARBITRAL PROCEEDINGS

Enforcement of peremptory orders of tribunal

2E-175   **42.**—(1) Unless otherwise agreed by the parties, the court may make an order requiring a party to comply with a peremptory order made by the tribunal.

(2) An application for an order under this section may be made—

(a) by the tribunal (upon notice to the parties),

(b) by a party to the arbitral proceedings with the permission of the tribunal (and upon notice to the other parties), or

(c) where the parties have agreed that the powers of the court under this section shall be available.

(3) The court shall not act unless it is satisfied that the applicant has exhausted any available arbitral process in respect of failure to comply with the tribunal's order.

(4) No order shall be made under this section unless the court is satisfied that the person to whom the tribunal's order was directed has failed to comply with it within the time prescribed in the order or, if no time was prescribed, within a reasonable time.

(5) The leave of the court is required for any appeal from a decision of the court under this section.

2E-176   *Note* —Compare s.5 of the 1979 Act. This section was amended by Scheme for Construction Contracts (England and Wales) Regulations 1998 (S.I. 1998 No. 649) so far as construction contracts are concerned in that art.24 thereof provides as follows:

" **24.** Section 42 of the Arbitration Act 1996 shall apply to this Scheme subject to the following modifications—

(a) in subsection (2) for the word "tribunal" wherever it appears there shall be substituted the word "adjudicator",

(b) in subparagraph (b) of subsection (2) for the words "arbitral proceedings" there shall be substituted the word "adjudication",

(c) subparagraph (c) of subsection (2) shall be deleted, and

(d) subsection (3) shall be deleted."

Securing the attendance of witnesses

2E-177   **43.**—(1) A party to arbitral proceedings may use the same court procedures as are available in relation to legal proceedings to secure the attendance before the tribunal of a witness in order to give oral testimony or to produce documents or other material evidence.

(2) This may only be done with the permission of the tribunal or the agreement of the other parties.

(3) The court procedures may only be used if—

    (a) the witness is in the United Kingdom, and

    (b) the arbitral proceedings are being conducted in England and Wales or, as the case may be, Northern Ireland.

(4) A person shall not be compelled by virtue of this section to produce any document or other material evidence which he could not be compelled to produce in legal proceedings.

Note —Compare s.12(4) and (5) of the 1950 Act. This is a mandatory provision (see s.4). **2E–178**

"A witness summons"

Normally issues at the Admiralty and Commercial Registry at the Royal Courts of Justice, Strand, London WC2A 2LL, or a district registry where attendance of witness required within the district of the district registry (see Practice Direction—Arbitration, paras 7.1 to 7.3). **2E–179**

Perjury

It was held that perjury committed in an arbitration under the Workmen's Compensation Act was perjury at Common Law and punishable as such (*R. v. Crossley* (1909) 100 L.T. 463, CA). See the Perjury Act 1911. **2E–180**

Note —There is no power under s.43 for a Court to order disclosure against a third party as opposed to issuing a witness summons for the production in evidence of specific documents. Nor are the Courts powers under CPR, r.31.17 to be translated into the context of arbitration, see *BNP Paribas v. Deloitte and Touch LLP* [2003] EWHC 2874 (Comm); [2004] 1 Lloyd's Rep. 233. **2E–180.1**

Court powers exercisable in support of arbitral proceedings

44.—(1) Unless otherwise agreed by the parties, the court has for the purposes of and in relation to arbitral proceedings the same power of making orders about the matters listed below as it has for the purposes of and in relation to legal proceedings. **2E–181**

(2) Those matters are—

    (a) the taking of the evidence of witnesses;

    (b) the preservation of evidence;

    (c) making orders relating to property which is the subject of the proceedings or as to which any question arises in the proceedings—

        (i) for the inspection, photographing, preservation, custody or detention of the property, or

        (ii) ordering that samples be taken from, or any observation be made of or experiment conducted upon, the property;

and for that purpose authorising any person to enter any premises in the possession or control of a party to the arbitration;

    (d) the sale of any goods the subject of the proceedings;

    (e) the granting of an interim injunction or the appointment of a receiver.

(3) If the case is one of urgency, the court may, on the application of a party or proposed party to the arbitral proceedings, make such orders as it thinks necessary for the purpose of preserving evidence or assets.

(4) If the case is not one of urgency, the court shall act only on the application of a party to the arbitral proceedings (upon notice to the other parties and to the tribunal) made with the permission of the tribunal or the agreement in writing of the other parties.

(5) In any case the court shall act only if or to the extent that the arbitral tribunal, and any arbitral or other institution or person vested by the parties with power in that regard, has no power or is unable for the time being to act effectively.

(6) If the court so orders, an order made by it under this section shall cease to have effect in whole or in part on the order of the tribunal or of any such arbitral or other institution or person having power to act in relation to the subject-matter of the order.

(7) The leave of the court is required for any appeal from a decision of the court under this section.

2E–182   *Note* —Compare s.12(6) of the 1950 Act.

Examination of Witness Order
2E–183   In *Commerce & Industry Co. of Canada v. Certain Underwriters at Lloyd's of London* [2002] 1 W.L.R. 1323; [2002] 2 All E.R. (Comm) 204; [2002] 1 Lloyd's Rep. 219, the Court (a) declined a letter of request from New York arbitrators on the basis the reference in s.1 of the Evidence (Proceedings in Other Jurisdictions) Act 1975 to a "tribunal" did not include a private arbitral tribunal and (b) declined to exercise its power under s.44 in respect of ordering the taking of the evidence of witnesses which may be exercised even where the seat arbitration is outside England and Wales or Northern Ireland on the basis that it was inappropriate to do (see s.2(3) of the 1996 Act above) because of differences in procedure, namely the discovery of information by witness testimony under the curial law of New York which had never been part of English procedure.

Preservation of Evidence etc.
2E–183.1   Whilst s.44(2) did not provide for an order for disclosure by a non-party it permitted an order for the inspection, photocopying and preservation of documents in the hands of third parties for the purpose of resolving an issue in the arbitration, (a feasibility study for deepening harbour in a breach of safe berth warranty claim) *Assimina Maritime Ltd v. Pakistan National Shipping; The Tasmin Spirit* [2004] EWHC 3005 (Comm); [2005] 1 All E.R. (Comm) 460; [2005] 1 Lloyd's Rep. 525 .

Interim Injunctions
2E–183.2   In *Channel Tunnel Group Ltd v. Balfour Beatty Construction Ltd* [1993] A.C. 334; [1993] 2 W.L.R. 262; [1993] 1 All E.R. 664; [1993] 1 Lloyd's Rep. 291, the House of Lords held that on the true construction of s.12(6)(h) of the Arbitration Act 1950 there was no power to grant an interim injunction in respect of a foreign arbitration but that an interim injunction pursuant to s.37(1) of the Supreme Court Act 1981 could be granted to assist or reinforce a foreign arbitration if circumstances so required even though a stay of English proceedings was ordered. In the cited case an interim injunction was refused as to grant the same would have pre-empted the very decision the support of which formed the raison d'être of the injunction. The House of Lords also held the Court had an inherent power to stay proceedings brought before it in breach of agreement to decide disputes by an alternative method whether or not the procedure agreed amounted to an arbitration agreement within s.1 of the Arbitration Act 1975.

In *Cetelem SA v Roust Holdings Ltd* [2005] EWCA Civ 618; [2005] 1 W.L.R. 3555; [2005] 4 All E.R. 52; [2005] 2 Lloyd's Rep. 494 (an interim injunction case) the Court of Appeal held that "on the true construction of s.44(3) of the 1996 Act if the case is one of urgency the court only has jurisdiction to make such orders as it thinks necessary for the purpose of preserving evidence or assets" not following the wider approach of *Hiscox Underwriting Ltd v. Dickson* [2004] EWHC 479; [2004] 1 All E.R. (Comm) 753; [2004] 2 Lloyd's Rep. 438 that s.44(3) was permissive and not restrictive of the powers conferred by s.44(1) and (2) and further holding that a contractual right could be an asset for the purposes of s.44(3).

Time when powers exercisable

It is doubtful that there is jurisdiction under this provision to order pre-delivery **2E–184** tests and inspection of a vessel before a cause of action had arisen for defective condition upon delivery or circumstances giving rise to an injunction under (formerly) RSC, O.29, r.1; see *Tsakos Shipping & Trading SA v. Orizon Tanker Co Ltd (The Centaurus Mar)* [1998] C.L.C. 1003.

Sub-section (7)

For the purposes of s.44(7) "the court" means the court of first instance but "...a **2E–184.1** decision of a judge which the court had no jurisdiction to make is not a decision 'under the section' within the meaning of s.44(7) of the 1996 Act", see *Cetelem SA* at para. 2E–183.2, above.

Determination of preliminary point of law

45.—(1) Unless otherwise agreed by the parties, the court may on **2E–185** the application of a party to arbitral proceedings (upon notice to the other parties) determine any question of law arising in the course of the proceedings which the court is satisfied substantially affects the rights of one or more of the parties. An agreement to dispense with reasons for the tribunal's award shall be considered an agreement to exclude the court's jurisdiction under this section.

(2) An application under this section shall not be considered unless—

    (a) it is made with the agreement of all the other parties to the proceedings, or

    (b) it is made with the permission of the tribunal and the court is satisfied—

        (i) that the determination of the question is likely to produce substantial savings in costs, and

        (ii) that the application was made without delay.

(3) The application shall identify the question of law to be determined and, unless made with the agreement of all the other parties to the proceedings, shall state the grounds on which it is said that the question should be decided by the court.

(4) Unless otherwise agreed by the parties, the arbitral tribunal may continue the arbitral proceedings and make an award while an application to the court under this section is pending.

(5) Unless the court gives leave, no appeal lies from a decision of the court whether the conditions specified in subsection (2) are met.

(6) The decision of the court on the question of law shall be treated as a judgment of the court for the purposes of an appeal.

But no appeal lies without the leave of the court which shall not be given unless the court considers that the question is one of general importance, or is one which for some other special reason should be considered by the Court of Appeal.

Note —Compare s.2 of the 1979 Act. **2E–186**

Determination of preliminary point of law

The Act has a procedure under which an application may be made to the Court to **2E–187** determine any question of law arising in the course of the reference, but restrictions are imposed on the making of such applications and the right to make an application may in specified circumstances also be excluded by agreement between the parties.

It should, however, be emphasised that s.45 provides for an essentially speedy procedure designed to interrupt the arbitration to the minimum possible extent and it is an exception to the general rule that the Courts do not intervene in the course of an arbitration, and therefore, save in wholly exceptional cases, *e.g.* where the preliminary question of law would determine the whole dispute between the parties it is not to be used to obtain definitive decisions from the Court of Appeal or the House of Lords (*per*Donaldson L.J. in *Babanaft International Co SA v. Avant Petroleum Inc* [1982] 1 W.L.R. 871 at 882; [1982] 3 All E.R. 244 at 252) a case on s.2 of the 1979 Act.

THE AWARD

Rules applicable to substance of dispute

2E–188   46.—(1) The arbitral tribunal shall decide the dispute—
(a) in accordance with the law chosen by the parties as applicable to the substance of the dispute, or
(b) if the parties so agree, in accordance with such other considerations as are agreed by them or determined by the tribunal.

(2) For this purpose the choice of the laws of a country shall be understood to refer to the substantive laws of that country and not its conflict of laws rules.

(3) If or to the extent that there is no such choice or agreement, the tribunal shall apply the law determined by the conflict of laws rules which it considers applicable.

2E–189   *Note* —For adaptation in case of a statutory arbitration, see s.96(4) below.

Awards on different issues, etc.

2E–190   47.—(1) Unless otherwise agreed by the parties, the tribunal may make more than one award at different times on different aspects of the matters to be determined.

(2) The tribunal may, in particular, make an award relating—
(a) to an issue affecting the whole claim, or
(b) to a part only of the claims or cross-claims submitted to it for decision

(3) If the tribunal does so, it shall specify in its award the issue, or the claim or part of a claim, which is the subject matter of the award.

2E–191   *Note* —Compare s.14 of the 1950 Act.

Remedies

2E–192   48.—(1) The parties are free to agree on the powers exercisable by the arbitral tribunal as regards remedies.

(2) Unless otherwise agreed by the parties, the tribunal has the following powers.

(3) The tribunal may make a declaration as to any matter to be determined in the proceedings.

(4) The tribunal may order the payment of a sum of money, in any currency.

(5) The tribunal has the same powers as the court—
(a) to order a party to do or refrain from doing anything;

    (b) to order specific performance of a contract (other than a contract relating to land);

    (c) to order the rectification, setting aside or cancellation of a deed or other document.

Note —Compare s.15 of the 1950 Act.   **2E–193**

"(4)...in any currency"

    Unless otherwise agreed the tribunal may order the payment of a sum of money in   **2E–193A**
any currency and any agreement to the contrary is effective only if it is in writing (Sections 5(1) and 48 of the 1996 Act) *Lesotho Highlands Development Authority v. Impregilo SpA* [2005] UKHL 43; [2005] 3 W.L.R. 129; [2005] 3 All E.R. 789 , a case in which it was held that the power under s.48(4) was unrestrained and available to the Tribunal: See further at 2E-197 and 2E-242.

"Specific performance ... contract"

    For example, for the delivery of specific goods under the Sale of Goods Act 1979,   **2E–194**
s.52.

Interest

    49.—(1) The parties are free to agree on the powers of the tribunal   **2E–195**
as regards the award of interest.

    (2) Unless otherwise agreed by the parties the following provisions apply.

    (3) The tribunal may award simple or compound interest from such dates, at such rates and with such rests as it considers meets the justice of the case—

    (a) on the whole or part of any amount awarded by the tribunal, in respect of any period up to the date of the award;

    (b) on the whole or part of any amount claimed in the arbitration and outstanding at the commencement of the arbitral proceedings but paid before the award was made, in respect of any period up to the date of payment.

    (4) The tribunal may award simple or compound interest from the date of the award (or any later date) until payment, at such rates and with such rests as it considers meets the justice of the case, on the outstanding amount of any award (including any award of interest under subsection (3) and any award as to costs).

    (5) References in this section to an amount awarded by the tribunal include an amount payable in consequence of a declaratory award by the tribunal.

    (6) The above provisions do not affect any other power of the tribunal to award interest.

Note —Compare ss.19A and 20 of the 1950 Act.   **2E–196**

Interest

    In *Walker & Others v. Rowe* [2001] 1 Lloyd's Rep. 116 it was held that under the   **2E–197**
1996 Act, if an award was entered as a judgment it had to be entered "in terms of the award"; so that if an award was made for a certain sum of money (with or without "pre-award interest") and there was no award of "post-award" interest, then the judgment had to be entered in these terms; to add s.35A interest to an award which had not been granted "post-award" interest would amount to an alteration by the court of

the arbitrator's award; and s.1(c) of the 1996 Act made it a principle that the Court should not intervene in matters that were covered by Part 1 which included ss.49(4) and 66; Parliament must have intended that once the arbitrators had decided on whether "post-award" interest should be granted that was the end of the matter. Thus the combined effect of ss.1(c), 49(4) and 66 of the 1996 Act was that the Court had no power to grant interest under s.35A on a sum which was awarded by arbitrators but remained unpaid after the award.

In *Lesotho Highlands Development Authority v. Impregilo SpA* [2005] UKHL 43; [2005] 3 W.L.R. 129; [2005] 3 All E.R. 789, the House of Lords held that the Tribunal's finding that it has power under s.49(3) to award interest was correct, that the governing law of the main contract (the law of Losotho) was not an agreement to the contrary in writing and that Section 49(6) does not state that any other power to award interest excludes the operation of s.49(3) but s.49(6) provides that the powers conferred by ss.49(1)–(5) do not necessarily oust any other power to award interest. It is no more than a saving provision. It does not confer priority on any such "other power".

Extension of time for making award

2E-198 **50.**—(1) Where the time for making an award is limited by or in pursuance of the arbitration agreement, then, unless otherwise agreed by the parties, the court may in accordance with the following provisions by order extend that time.

(2) An application for an order under this section may be made—
  (a) by the tribunal (upon notice to the parties), or
  (b) by any party to the proceedings (upon notice to the tribunal and the other parties),
but only after exhausting any available arbitral process for obtaining an extension of time.

(3) The court shall only make an order if satisfied that a substantial injustice would otherwise be done.

(4) The court may extend the time for such period and on such terms as it thinks fit, and may do so whether or not the time previously fixed (by or under the agreement or by a previous order) has expired.

(5) The leave of the court is required for any appeal from a decision of the court under this section.

2E-199 *Note*—Compare s.13(2) of the 1950 Act. It is to be noted that arbitral processes for obtaining an extension are to be exhausted first.

Settlement

2E-200 **51.**—(1) If during arbitral proceedings the parties settle the dispute, the following provisions apply unless otherwise agreed by the parties.

(2) The tribunal shall terminate the substantive proceedings and, if so requested by the parties and not objected to by the tribunal, shall record the settlement in the form of an agreed award.

(3) An agreed award shall state that it is an award of the tribunal and shall have the same status and effect as any other award on the merits of the case.

(4) The following provisions of this Part relating to awards (sections 52 to 58) apply to an agreed award.

(5) Unless the parties have also settled the matter of the payment of the costs of the arbitration, the provisions of this Part relating to costs (sections 59 to 65) continue to apply.

Form of award

52.—(1) The parties are free to agree on the form of an award.

(2) If or to the extent that there is no such agreement, the following provisions apply.

(3) The award shall be in writing signed by all the arbitrators or all those assenting to the award.

(4) The award shall contain the reasons for the award unless it is an agreed award or the parties have agreed to dispense with reasons.

(5) The award shall state the seat of the arbitration and the date when the award is made.

2E–201

Place where award treated as made

53.—(1) Unless otherwise agreed by the parties, where the seat of the arbitration is in England and Wales or Northern Ireland, any award in the proceedings shall be treated as made there, regardless of where it was signed, despatched or delivered to any of the parties.

2E–202

Date of award

54.—(1) Unless otherwise agreed by the parties, the tribunal may decide what is to be taken to be the date on which the award was made.

(2) In the absence of any such decision, the date of the award shall be taken to be the date on which it is signed by the arbitrator or, where more than one arbitrator signs the award, by the last of them.

2E–203

Notification of award

55.—(1) The parties are free to agree on the requirements as to notification of the award to the parties.

(2) If there is no such agreement, the award shall be notified to the parties by service on them of copies of the award, which shall be done without delay after the award is made.

(3) Nothing in this section affects section 56 (power to withhold award in case of non-payment).

2E–204

Power to withhold award in case of non-payment

56.—(1) The tribunal may refuse to deliver an award to the parties except upon full payment of the fees and expenses of the arbitrators.

(2) If the tribunal refuses on that ground to deliver an award, a party to the arbitral proceedings may (upon notice to the other parties and the tribunal) apply to the court, which may order that—

    (a) the tribunal shall deliver the award on the payment into court by the applicant of the fees and expenses demanded, or such lesser amount as the court may specify,

    (b) the amount of the fees and expenses properly payable shall be determined by such means and upon such terms as the court may direct, and

    (c) out of the money paid into court there shall be paid out such fees and expenses as may be found to be properly

2E–205

payable and the balance of the money (if any) shall be paid out to the applicant.

(3) For this purpose the amount of fees and expenses properly payable is the amount the applicant is liable to pay under section 28 or any agreement relating to the payment of the arbitrators.

(4) No application to the court may be made where there is any available arbitral process for appeal or review of the amount of the fees or expenses demanded.

(5) References in this section to arbitrators include an arbitrator who has ceased to act and an umpire who has not replaced the other arbitrators.

(6) The above provisions of this section also apply in relation to any arbitral or other institution or person vested by the parties with powers in relation to the delivery of the tribunal's award.

As they so apply, the references to the fees and expenses of the arbitrators shall be construed as including the fees and expenses of that institution or person.

(7) The leave of the court is required for any appeal from a decision of the court under this section.

(8) Nothing in this section shall be construed as excluding an application under section 28 where payment has been made to the arbitrators in order to obtain the award.

2E–206   *Note* —Compare s.19 of the 1950 Act. This is a mandatory provision (see s.4).

Correction of award or additional award

2E–207   57.—(1) The parties are free to agree on the powers of the tribunal to correct an award or make an additional award.

(2) If or to the extent there is no such agreement, the following provisions apply.

(3) The tribunal may on its own initiative or on the application of a party—

> (a) correct an award so as to remove any clerical mistake or error arising from an accidental slip or omission or clarify or remove any ambiguity in the award, or
>
> (b) make an additional award in respect of any claim (including a claim for interest or costs) which was presented to the tribunal but was not dealt with in the award.

These powers shall not be exercised without first affording the other parties a reasonable opportunity to make representations to the tribunal.

(4) Any application for the exercise of those powers must be made within 28 days of the date of the award or such longer period as the parties may agree.

(5) Any correction of an award shall be made within 28 days of the date the application was received by the tribunal or, where the correction is made by the tribunal on its own initiative, within 28 days of the date of the award or, in either case, such longer period as the parties may agree.

(6) Any additional award shall be made within 56 days of the date of the original award or such longer period as the parties may agree.

(7) Any correction of an award shall form part of the award.

Note —Compare ss.17 and 18(4) of the 1950 Act. **2E–208**

Construction of section

"Clerical" applies to "mistake" only, and not to "error arising from ...". "Accidental" **2E–209** applies to both "slip" and "omission" (*Sutherland and Co v. Hannevig Bros. Ltd* [1921] 1 K.B. 336; a case under the former s.17 of the Arbitration Act 1950).

The power under the former s.17 to correct errors or mistakes in an award applies to errors attributable to the parties as well as to errors attributable to the arbitrator or other tribunal; it does not, however, extend to oversights or errors in production of evidence or argument (*Craske v. Norfolk County Council* [1991] J.P.L. 760).

Section 57(3)(b) applies to a claim which has been presented to the tribunal but which had not been dealt with. It is inapplicable to an issue which remains undetermined as part of a claim which in circumstances of ambiguity or need of clarification could properly fall within s.57(3)(a), see *Torch Offshore LLC v. Cable Shipping Inc* [2004] EWHC 787 (Comm); [2004] 2 All E.R. (Comm) 365.

Effect of award

58.—(1) Unless otherwise agreed by the parties, an award made by **2E–210** the tribunal pursuant to an arbitration agreement is final and binding both on the parties and on any persons claiming through or under them.

(2) This does not affect the right of a person to challenge the award by any available arbitral process of appeal or review or in accordance with the provisions of this Part.

Note —Compare s.16 of the 1950 Act. **2E–211**

Form of Order

See Queen's Bench Masters' Practice Forms, Form **PF 166**, Civil Procedure Forms **2E–212** Volume.

COSTS OF THE ARBITRATION

Costs of the arbitration

59.—(1) References in this Part to the costs of the arbitration are **2E–213** to—

    (a) the arbitrators' fees and expenses,

    (b) the fees and expenses of any arbitral institution concerned, and

    (c) the legal or other costs of the parties.

(2) Any such reference includes the costs of or incidental to any proceedings to determine the amount of the recoverable costs of the arbitration (see section 63).

Agreement to pay costs in any event

60. An agreement which has the effect that a party is to pay the **2E–214** whole or part of the costs of the arbitration in any event is only valid if made after the dispute in question has arisen.

Note —Compare s.18(3) of the 1950 Act. This is a mandatory provision (see s.4). **2E–215**

Award of costs

2E–216   **61.**—(1) The tribunal may make an award allocating the costs of the arbitration as between the parties, subject to any agreement of the parties.

(2) Unless the parties otherwise agree, the tribunal shall award costs on the general principle that costs should follow the event except where it appears to the tribunal that in the circumstances this is not appropriate in relation to the whole or part of the costs.

2E–217   *Note* —Compare s.18(1) of the 1950 Act.

Effect of agreement or award about costs

2E–218   **62.** Unless the parties otherwise agree, any obligation under an agreement between them as to how the costs of the arbitration are to be borne, or under an award allocating the costs of the arbitration, extends only to such costs as are recoverable.

The recoverable costs of the arbitration

2E–219   **63.**—(1) The parties are free to agree what costs of the arbitration are recoverable.

(2) If or to the extent there is no such agreement, the following provisions apply.

(3) The tribunal may determine by award the recoverable costs of the arbitration on such basis as it thinks fit.

If it does so, it shall specify—
    (a) the basis on which it has acted, and
    (b) the items of recoverable costs and the amount referable to each.

(4) If the tribunal does not determine the recoverable costs of the arbitration, any party to the arbitral proceedings may apply to the court (upon notice to the other parties) which may—
    (a) determine the recoverable costs of the arbitration on such basis as it thinks fit, or
    (b) order that they shall be determined by such means and upon such terms as it may specify.

(5) Unless the tribunal or the court determines otherwise—
    (a) the recoverable costs of the arbitration shall be determined on the basis that there shall be allowed a reasonable amount in respect of all costs reasonably incurred, and
    (b) any doubt as to whether costs were reasonably incurred or were reasonable in amount shall be resolved in favour of the paying party.

(6) The above provisions have effect subject to section 64 (recoverable fees and expenses of arbitrators).

(7) Nothing in this section affects any right of the arbitrators, any expert, legal adviser or assessor appointed by the tribunal, or any arbitral institution, to payment of their fees and expenses.

2E–220   *Note* —Compare s.18(1) and (2) of the 1950 Act.

Recoverable fees and expenses of arbitrators

64.—(1) Unless otherwise agreed by the parties, the recoverable **2E–221** costs of the arbitration shall include in respect of the fees and expenses of the arbitrators only such reasonable fees and expenses as are appropriate in the circumstances.

(2) If there is any question as to what reasonable fees and expenses are appropriate in the circumstances, and the matter is not already before the court on an application under section 63(4), the court may on the application of any party (upon notice to the other parties)—

(a) determine the matter, or
(b) order that it be determined by such means and upon such terms as the court may specify.

(3) Subsection (1) has effect subject to any order of the court under section 24(4) or 25(3)(b) (order as to entitlement to fees or expenses in case of removal or resignation of arbitrator).

(4) Nothing in this section affects any right of the arbitrator to payment of his fees and expenses.

Note —Compare s.19 of the 1950 Act. **2E–222**

Power to limit recoverable costs

65.—(1) Unless otherwise agreed by the parties, the tribunal may **2E–223** direct that the recoverable costs of the arbitration, or of any part of the arbitral proceedings, shall be limited to a specified amount.

(2) Any direction may be made or varied at any stage, but this must be done sufficiently in advance of the incurring of costs to which it relates, or the taking of any steps in the proceedings which may be affected by it, for the limit to be taken into account.

Enforcement of the award

66.—(1) An award made by the tribunal pursuant to an arbitration **2E–224** agreement may, by leave of the court, be enforced in the same manner as a judgment or order of the court to the same effect.

(2) Where leave is so given, judgment may be entered in terms of the award.

(3) Leave to enforce an award shall not be given where, or to the extent that, the person against whom it is sought to be enforced shows that the tribunal lacked substantive jurisdiction to make the award.

The right to raise such an objection may have been lost (see section 73).

(4) Nothing in this section affects the recognition or enforcement of an award under any other enactment or rule of law, in particular under Part II of the Arbitration Act 1950 (enforcement of awards under Geneva Convention) or the provisions of Part III of this Act relating to the recognition and enforcement of awards under the New York Convention or by an action on the award.

Note —Compare s.26(1) of the 1950 Act. This is a mandatory provision (see s.4). **2E–225**

"By leave of the Court"

2E-226   Where the Court is of opinion that the award is legally invalid, it may refuse permission to enforce it. *Cf. Re Stone and Hastie Arb.* [1903] 2 K.B. 463, CA. Permission should be given in nearly all cases to enforce an award as a judgment unless there is real ground for doubting the validity of the award, and the ambit of this section should not be circumscribed (*Middlemiss & Gould v. Hartlepool Corp* [1972] 1 W.L.R. 1643; [1973] 1 All E.R. 172, CA, and see *Curacac Trading Co B.V. v. Harkisandas & Co* [1992] 2 Lloyd's Rep. 186 at 192 approving statement in Mustill and Boyd on Commercial Arbitration (2nd ed.), p.419 to the effect that the court would probably now only refuse the application where the objection cannot properly be disposed of without trial.

"Be enforced"

2E-227   This may be done by permission at any time, though the time for setting the award aside has not expired.

A person who obtains permission under this section to enforce an award is not thereby prevented from bringing a claim on the award (*China Steam Navigation Co v. Van Laun* (1905) 22 T.L.R. 26). It is an implied term of an arbitration agreement that an award for the payment of money should be in a form which is capable of being enforced in the same manner as a judgment, and the Court has power to remit such an award so that it may be amended to put it in such a form (*Margulies Ltd v. Dafnis Thomaides Ltd* [1958] 1 W.L.R. 398; [1958] 1 All E.R. 777).

A confidentiality or non-disclosure agreement in respect of an arbitration should not be construed so as to prevent in terms of enforcement a party relying on an award in respect of rights declared in his favour by the award, *Associated Electric and Gas Insurance Services Ltd v. European Reinsurance Co of Zurich* [2003] UKPC 11; [2003] 1 W.L.R. 1041.

In *Michael Carter v. Harold Simpson Associates (Architects) Ltd*; [2004] UKPC 29; [2005] 1 W.L.R. 919; [2004] 2 Lloyd's Rep. 512, PC, (a case concerning Jamaican law) the Privy Council held that the unremitted parts of an award remain valid and can properly form the subject matter of enforcement. Effect of *Johnson v. Latham* (1851) 20 L.J. Q.B. 236 considered.

Claim on the award

2E-228   "It is well settled that procedure by [claim] upon an award is one that ought to be pursued where the objections raised are such as to render the validity of the award a matter of doubt. Where there are matters which may gravely affect the validity of the award, no order should be made giving [permission] to proceed summarily under the award." *Per* Swinfen Eady, M.R., *Re Boks & Co and Peters, Rushton & Co Arbn.* [1919] 1 K.B. 491. In this case Lush J. in Chambers refused permission to enforce the award as the contract between the parties was an illegal one. In *May v. Mills* (1914) 30 T.L.R. 287, there was a doubt on the face of the proceedings whether there had been a valid arbitration. The Master refused leave to enforce the award. The Judge in Chambers reversed this decision, which was restored by the CA, who left the claimant to bring a claim on the award. The defendant had refused throughout to take any part in the arbitration. In the claim judgment was given for the defendant with costs of all the proceedings.

An application under s.66 is not a suitable procedure in a case where an objection is taken to the award which cannot properly be disposed of without a trial (*Allied Vision Ltd v. VPS Film Entertainment GmbH* [1991] 1 Lloyd's Rep. 392), a case under s.26 of the 1950 Act.

When confronted with a clause which purports to provide that the rights of the parties shall be governed by a system of law which is neither English law nor the law of any other state, or which is a serious modification of such law, the court has to decide (a) whether the parties intend to create legally enforceable rights and obligations (b) whether the resulting agreement is sufficiently certain to constitute a legally enforceable contract, and (c) whether it will be contrary to public policy to enforce the award because there is some illegality present, or because enforcement will clearly be injurious to the public good (*Deutsche Schachtbau- und Tiefbohr GmbH v. Ras Al Khaimah National Oil Co* [1987] 3 W.L.R. 1023; [1987] 2 All E.R. 796, CA reversed on another point *sub nom. Deutsche Schachtbau- und Tiefbohr GmbH v. Shell International Petroleum Co Ltd* [1988] 3 W.L.R. 230; [1988] 2 All E.R. 833, HL). An award made by I.C.C. arbitrators in Geneva, applying a system of law which represented a common denominator of the principles underlying the laws of contract of various nations was held to be enforceable on application of these tests (*ibid.*).

Counterclaim

In a claim on an award the defendant is not estopped from counterclaiming for rectification of the agreement to refer (*Crane v. Hegeman-Harris Co Inc* [1939] 1 All E.R. 662). **2E–229**

Appeal from order to enforce award

The principles applicable to obtaining permission to appeal out of time (see *C.M. Van Stillevoldt BV v. E.L. Carviers Inc* [1983] 1 W.L.R. 207; and *Norwich and Peterborough Building Society v. Steed* [1991] 1 W.L.R. 449) provided an appropriate guide to the court in exercising its discretion whether to extend time for permission to appeal where permission had been granted to enforce an award as a judgment and judgment had been entered (*Soinco Savi v. Novokuznetsk Aluminium Plant* [1998] 2 Lloyd's Rep. 337, CA). **2E–230**

Limitation

On a claim to enforce or an application for permission to enforce an arbitration award in the same way as a judgment, the cause of action accrues when the party against whom the award has been made fails to honour the award, not when the breach of contract to which the award relates occurs (*Agromet Motoimport v. Maulden Engineering Co (Beds) Ltd* [1985] 1 W.L.R. 762; [1985] 2 All E.R. 436). **2E–231**

Practice — Methods of enforcement

There are two methods of enforcement of an award which are open to the applicant namely: **2E–232**

1. By application directly to enforce the award (see next n., "Application") and if permission is granted.
2. By entering judgment in terms of the award and so to enforce the judgment by one or more of the usual forms of execution award.

These methods are not alternative, but successive. The applicant may apply for permission to enforce the award in the same manner as a judgment or order to the same effect, and if such permission is given, he may then proceed to enter judgment in the terms of the award. There is no need for a further application for permission to enter such a judgment, but it should be noted that there may be advantages in proceeding to the second stage of entering judgment instead of being content with an order granting leave to enforce the award as a judgment, *e.g.* by suing upon the judgment or otherwise proceeding by execution or registration or other method of enforcement in a foreign court or by obtaining the recognition of the judgment in a foreign court or by relying on the judgment as *res judicata*.

Application

(See generally CPR Part 62—Arbitration Claims, r.62.18) In the light of the wider point of entry for enforcement matters application for permission to enforce an award under this section should be made in the first instance without notice to a Master, Admiralty Registrar or district judge of the district registry. The application should be made upon an arbitration claim form supported by written evidence such as an affidavit or witness statement which, in the QBD in London, should be left with the Admiralty and Commercial Registry in Room E200A. The affidavit or witness statement should exhibit the arbitration agreement and the original award or copies thereof, and should state the name and the usual or last known place of abode or business of the applicant and the person against whom it is sought to enforce the award, and either that the award has not been complied with or the extent to which it has not been complied with at the date of the application (see Pt 62, r.62.18(6)). Where the application is under s.101 of the 1996 Act or s.3(1)(a) of the 1975 Act, different documents must be exhibited as specified in subss. 6(a)(ii) and (iii). The Master may either grant the application on a without notice basis or direct the application to be issued. It should ask for "permission to enforce the award dated—in the above arbitration in the same manner as a judgment or order to the same effect"; and "that the respondent do pay the costs of this application to be taxed". The applicant must produce before the Master the original award (or a duplicate) and a copy thereof, together with an affidavit or witness statement intituled as above, verifying both the original, the copy award, **2E–233** and the arbitration agreement. On issuing execution without entering judgment, the copy award must be filed (no fee) at the Admiralty and Commercial Registry, together with the order for permission to enforce it. But if a judgment is to be signed, the award should first be filed and an office copy produced on signing judgment. In the QBD a reference number will be given on signing judgment or issuing execution as on the commencement of a claim. The award will be marked with a seal to indicate that execution has issued on it. All subsequent proceedings should bear the reference number. In the Chancery Division the papers are lodged in Chancery Chambers and a similar practice followed.

Costs

2E-234   The costs of the application for permission to enforce the award should be included in the order, no matter how small the amount awarded and the certificate for such costs produced on issuing execution.

Taxation of costs under the award may be obtained on production of the award either before or after permission to enforce it has been obtained. And this applies to taxation of the charges of the arbitrator, provided he has not himself taxed and fixed the amount of the costs of the reference and award by, and as part of, his award.

Costs where judgment may be entered

2E-235   If it is desired to enter judgment for the amount awarded, the application should be so framed as to provide for "the costs of any judgment which may be entered hereunder". If this precaution is not taken, it may be impossible to secure an order for the costs incurred in signing judgment.

Service out of the jurisdiction

2E-236   The application may, with permission, be served out of the jurisdiction, see r.62.18(4). Service out of the jurisdiction of an order giving permission to enforce does not require permission, see r.62.18(8).

"Judgment ... in terms of the award"

2E-237   A judgment so entered may be enforced in the usual way. But it is important to notice that no provision is made for the costs which may be incurred in making the necessary application under this section. The incidence of such costs will no doubt be settled, in the ordinary course, by the Master who hears that application, and his order can be enforced as if it were a judgment; but if it is proposed to enforce the award as a judgment—*e.g.* by suing upon it in a foreign Court—no terms other than those to be found in the award can be included in the judgment. See for instance *Walker v. Rowe* [2000] 1 Lloyd's Rep. 116—there is no power to add s.35 Supreme Court Act 1981 interest to an award which made no provision for post award interest because to do so would be to alter the terms of the award rather than entering judgment in terms of the award.

Challenging the award: substantive jurisdiction

2E-238   **67.**—(1) A party to arbitral proceedings may (upon notice to the other parties and to the tribunal) apply to the court—

(a) challenging any award of the arbitral tribunal as to its substantive jurisdiction; or

(b) for an order declaring an award made by the tribunal on the merits to be of no effect, in whole or in part, because the tribunal did not have substantive jurisdiction.

A party may lose the right to object (see section 73) and the right to apply is subject to the restrictions in section 70(2) and (3).

(2) The arbitral tribunal may continue the arbitral proceedings and make a further award while an application to the court under this section is pending in relation to an award as to jurisdiction.

(3) On an application under this section challenging an award of the arbitral tribunal as to its substantive jurisdiction, the court may by order—

(a) confirm the award,

(b) vary the award, or

(c) set aside the award in whole or in part.

(4) The leave of the court is required for any appeal from a decision of the court under this section.

Note—Compare ss.22 and 23 of the 1950 Act. This is a mandatory provision (see **2E–239** s.4). A challenge under this section involves a re-hearing rather than a review, see *Azov Shipping Co v. Baltic Shipping Co (No.1)* [1999] 1 All E.R. 476; [1999] 1 Lloyd's Rep. 68; *Peterson Farms Inc. v. C&M Farming Ltd* [2004] EWHC 121 (Comm); [2004] 1 Lloyd's Rep. 603.

The identification of parties to an aribitration agreement is a matter of substantive not procedural law, see *Peterson Farms Inc v. C&M Farming Ltd* above in which award in favour of non-parties which were within the same group of companies as the company named in the arbitration agreement held to have been made without jurisdiction.

Section 67(1)(b)

See *Mohsin v. The Commonwealth Secretariat* [2002] EWHC 377 (Comm); March 1, **2E–239A** 2002 for interplay of this section and s.73 of the 1996 Act (loss of right to object).

The leave of the court is required

Only the trial judge can grant permission to appeal against a decision under section **2E–239B** 67. There is no jurisdiction in the Court of Appeal to do so, *Athletic Union of Constantinople v. National Basketball Association* [2002] 1 W.L.R. 2863; [2002] 3 All E.R. 897, CA. (See similarly *Henry Boot Construction v. Malmaison Hotel* under para. 2E–247 below.

Effect of an order pursuant to s.67(3)(c)

Upon an order setting aside the award or a declaration that the award was of no ef- **2E–239C** fect, the arbitration reverted to the position it was in before the arbitrator published his award so that the arbitrator was not *functus officio, Hussman (Europe) Ltd v. Pharaon* [2003] EWCA Civ 266; [2003] 1 All E.R. (Comm) 879, CA.

Challenging the award: serious irregularity

68.—(1) A party to arbitral proceedings may (upon notice to the **2E–240** other parties and to the tribunal) apply to the court challenging an award in the proceedings on the ground of serious irregularity affecting the tribunal, the proceedings or the award. A party may lose the right to object (see section 73) and the right to apply is subject to the restrictions in section 70(2) and (3).

(2) Serious irregularity means an irregularity of one or more of the following kinds which the court considers has caused or will cause substantial injustice to the applicant—

(a) failure by the tribunal to comply with section 33 (general duty of tribunal);

(b) the tribunal exceeding its powers (otherwise than by exceeding its substantive jurisdiction: see section 67);

(c) failure by the tribunal to conduct the proceedings in accordance with the procedure agreed by the parties;

(d) failure by the tribunal to deal with all the issues that were put to it;

(e) any arbitral or other institution or person vested by the parties with powers in relation to the proceedings or the award exceeding its powers;

(f) uncertainty or ambiguity as to the effect of the award;

(g) the award being obtained by fraud or the award or the way in which it was procured being contrary to public policy;

(h) failure to comply with the requirements as to the form of the award; or

(i) any irregularity in the conduct of the proceedings or in the award which is admitted by the tribunal or by any arbitral or other institution or person vested by the parties with powers in relation to the proceedings or the award.

(3) If there is shown to be serious irregularity affecting the tribunal, the proceedings or the award, the court may—

(a) remit the award to the tribunal, in whole or in part, for reconsideration,

(b) set the award aside in whole or in part, or

(c) declare the award to be of no effect, in whole or in part.

The court shall not exercise its power to set aside or to declare an award to be of no effect, in whole or in part, unless it is satisfied that it would be inappropriate to remit the matters in question to the tribunal for reconsideration.

(4) The leave of the court is required for any appeal from a decision of the court under this section.

2E–241   *Note* —Compare ss.22 and 23 of the 1950 Act. This is a mandatory provision (see s.4).

"On the ground of serious irregularity"

2E–242   This means irregularity of one or more of the kinds set out in sub-para. (2) which the court considers has or will cause substantial injustice to the applicant. In *Petroships Pte Ltd v. Petec Trading and Investment Corp (The "Petro Ranger")* [2001] 2 Lloyd's Rep. 348, the following commentary on this section appears at p.351:

1. Section 68 sets out a closed list of irregularities (which it is not open to the Court to extent).

2. Section 68 reflects the internationally accepted view that the Court should be able to correct serious failure to comply with the "due process" of arbitral proceedings: *cf.* art.34 of the Model Law.

3. A serious irregularity has to pass the test of causing "substantial injustice" before the Court can act (s.68(2)).

4. The test of "substantial injustice" is intended to be applied by way of support for the arbitral process, not by way of interference with that process. Thus it is only in those cases where it can be said that what has happened is so far removed from what could reasonably be expected of the arbitral process, that the Court will take action.

5. The test is not what would have happened had the matter been litigated. To apply such a test wouls be to ignore the fact that the parties have agreed to arbitrate not litigate.

6. Having chosen arbitration, the parties cannot complain of substantial injustice, unless what has happened cannot on any view be defended as an acceptable consequence of that choice.

7. Section 68 is designed as a longstop, only available in extreme cases, where the tribunal has gone so wrong in its conduct of the arbitration in one of the respects listed in s.68, that justice calls out for it to be corrected.

8. Section 68 must not be used as a means of circumventing the restrictions upon the Court's power to intervene in arbitral proceedings. Further, the distinction between s.68 and s.69 must be maintained. In addition, the Court's powers under s.70(4) should be borne in mind (see below).

9. Section 68(2)(d) ("failure by the tribunal to deal with all issues which were put to it") does not require a tribunal to set out each step by which they reached their conclusion or to deal with each point made by a party. There is a distinction between criticism of the reasoning and a failure to deal with an issue (Mr Justice Thomas in *Hussmann (Europe) Ltd v. Al Ameen Development & Trade Co* [2002] 2 Lloyd's Rep. 83, at p.97, col. 1).

In *Losotho Highlands Development Authority v. Impregilo SpA* [2005] UKHL 43; [2005] 3 W.L.R. 129; [2005] 3 All E.R. 789 a case where "the issue was whether the tribunal had exceeded its powers within the meaning of s.68(2)(b)" and concerned ss.48(4) and 49(3) of the 1996 Act, Lord Steyn said:

"**28**... This is a mandatory provision. The policy in favour of party autonomy does not permit derogation from the provisions of section 68. A number of preliminary observations about section 68 are pertinent. First, unlike the position under the old law, intervention under section 68 is only permissible *after* an award has been made. Secondly, the requirement is a serious irregularity. It is a new concept in English arbitration law. Plainly a high threshold must be satisfied. Thirdly, it must be established that the irregularity caused or will cause substantial injustice to the applicant. This is designed to eliminate technical and unmeritorious challenges. It is also a new requirement in English arbitration law. Fourthly, the irregularity must fall within the closed list of categories set out in paragraphs (a) to (i).

29 It will be observed that the list of irregularities under section 68 may be divided into those which affect the arbitral procedure, and those which affect the award. But nowhere in section 68 is there any hint that a failure by the tribunal to arrive at the "correct decision" could afford a ground for challenge under section 68. On the other hand, section 68 has a meaningful role to play...

31 By its very terms section 68(2)(b) assumes that the tribunal acted within its substantive jurisdiction. It is aimed at the tribunal *exceeding its powers* under the arbitration agreement, terms of reference or the 1996 Act. Section 68(2)(b) does not permit a challenge on the ground that the tribunal arrived at a wrong conclusion as a matter of law or fact. It is not apt to cover a mere error of law. The view is reinforced if one takes into account that a mistake in interpreting the contract is the paradigm of a "question of law" which may in the circumstances specified in section 69 be appealed unless the parties have excluded that right by agreement. In cases where the right of appeal has by agreement, sanctioned by the Act, has been excluded, it would be curious to allow a challenge under section 68(2)(b) to be based on a mistaken interpretation of the underlying contract. Moreover, it would be strange where there is no exclusion agreement, to allow parallel challenges under section 68(2)(b) and section 69.

32 In order to decide whether section 68(2)(b) is engaged it will be necessary to focus intensely on the particular power under an arbitration agreement, the terms of reference, or the 1996 Act which is involved, judged in all the circumstances of the case. In making this general observation it must always be borne in mind that the erroneous exercise of an available power cannot by itself amount to an excess of power. A mere error of law will not amount to an excess of power under section 68(2)(b)."

See too *Profilati Italia SRL v. Painewebber Inc* [2001] 1 Lloyd's Rep. 715 (a case of innocent failure to disclosure) the Court held that even where a successful party was said to have procured the award in a way which was contrary to public policy it would normally be necessary to satisfy the Court that some form of reprehensible or unconscionable conduct on his part had contributed in a substantial way to obtaining an award in his favour; and the Court should not be quick to interfere under s.68. Applied in *The Mariana* [2005] EWHC 219 (Comm); [2005] 1 Lloyd's Rep. 640 .

See too *Cuflet Chartering v. Carousel Shipping Co Ltd (The "Marie H")* [2001] 1 Lloyd's Rep. 707 (conduct alleged to have induced other party into believing that steps to obtaining an award would not be taken while negotiations were current), held that nothing short of unconscionable conduct (of which there had to be cogent evidence) would justify setting aside the award. Inadvertent conduct, however, careless would would not suffice.

In *Hussmann (Europe) Ltd v. Al Ameen Development & Trade Co* (see above) it was also held that a meeting between the tribunal and an expert witness in the absence of the parties and without their knowledge which was subsequently brought to the attention of the parties during oral examination of the expert with opportunity to cross-examine him, did not constitute a serious irregularity within the section.

A failure to address central issue by GAFA constituted a serious irregularity within s.68(2)(d), see *Ascot Commodities NV v. Olam International Ltd* [2002] C.L.C 277.

For the interplay of s.73 (loss of right to object) of the 1996 Act upon s.68 see *Moshin v. The Commonwealth Secretariat* [2002] EWHC 377 (Comm), March 1, 2002.

The Court has a discretion to allow an arbitrator's confidential reasons to be adduced in evidence despite any agreement to treat the same as confidential. Indeed in the light of the issues raised by s.68 the Court would allow confidential reasons to be adduced unless it was unnecessary to do so, or the allegations made were clearly groundless or there was some other exceptional reason not to do so, *Tame Shipping Ltd v. Easy Navigation Ltd*, [2004] EWHC 1862 (Comm); [2004] 2 All E.R. (Comm) 521; [2004] 2 Lloyd's Rep. 626, para. 27.

For the extent to which and the circumstances in which an arbitrator may rely upon his own experience/knowledge without breaching his obligation under s.33 or so as to commit a serious irregularity under s.68 of the 1996 Act, see *Checkpoint Ltd v. Strathclyde Pension Fund* [2003] EWCA Civ 84; *The Times*, February 12, 2003, CA, citing *Fox v. P.G. Wellfair Ltd* [1981] 2 Lloyd's Rep 514, CA.

The following pre-1996 Act cases may still provide examples of irregularity:

(1) If the arbitrator, without proper notice to both parties, gave audience to one of the parties in the absence of the other, that is a good reason for setting aside the award (*Re Gregson and Armstrong Arbn.* (1894) 70 L.T. 106; and see *The Warwick* (1890) 15 PD 189). Where the arbitrator heard the evidence of each party in the absence of the other, the award was set aside, although the party moving to set the award aside had made no objection at the time (*Ramsden & Co. Ltd v. Jacobs* [1922] 1 K.B. 640) but where a charterparty contained a clause that in the event of a dispute arising it should be referred to arbitration, each party to nominate an arbitrator, who was to be a commercial man, and that if the arbitrators differed they should appoint an umpire, and the umpire so appointed made his award after hearing the arbitrators, but without giving notice to or hearing the parties, it was held that, in view of the practice in commercial arbitrations, the award must stand (*French Government v. Owners of S.S. Tsurushima Maru* (1921) 37 T.L.R. 961, CA).

(2) If the arbitrator wrongly rejects relevant evidence, his award will be set aside (*Trayfoot v. Lock* [1957] 1 All E.R. 423). It is a settled principle that arbitrators must not take evidence in secret and therefore where an arbitrator who is an expert having special knowledge of the particular subject-matter is minded to use his special knowledge to form a different view of the facts from that given in evidence by expert witnesses called by the parties he should not do so without giving them an opportunity of dealing with it, and especially so where one party only appears before him (*Fisher v. P.G. Wellfair Ltd* [1981] Com.L.R. 140; [1981] 2 Lloyd's Rep. 514, CA).

An arbitrator should use his special expertise to evaluate evidence, not to supply it. Furthermore he should not receive evidence in the absence of one of the parties or use any particular factual knowledge acquired by him in other proceedings (*Top Shop Estates Ltd v. Danino* (1985) 273 E.G. 197).

Jurisdiction of arbitrator on remission

2E–243 Where an award was remitted under s.22 of the Arbitration Act 1950 the arbitrator's jurisdiction was held to be limited to consideration of matters previously raised, together with any additional matters specified by the court in its order; he was not empowered to consider other issues (*Interbulk Ltd v. Aiden Shipping Co Ltd*; *The Vimiera (No. 3)* [1986] 2 Lloyd's Rep. 75).

Appeal on point of law

2E–244 **69.**—(1) Unless otherwise agreed by the parties, a party to arbitral proceedings may (upon notice to the other parties and to the tribunal) appeal to the court on a question of law arising out of an award made in the proceedings. An agreement to dispense with reasons for the tribunal's award shall be considered an agreement to exclude the court's jurisdiction under this section.

(2) An appeal shall not be brought under this section except—

    (a) with the agreement of all the other parties to the proceedings, or

    (b) with the leave of the court.

The right to appeal is also subject to the restrictions in section 70(2) and (3).

(3) Leave to appeal shall be given only if the court is satisfied—

    (a) that the determination of the question will substantially affect the rights of one or more of the parties,

    (b) that the question is one which the tribunal was asked to determine,

    (c) that, on the basis of the findings of fact in the award—

        (i) the decision of the tribunal on the question is obviously wrong, or

        (ii) the question is one of general public importance and the decision of the tribunal is at least open to serious doubt, and

    (d) that, despite the agreement of the parties to resolve the matter by arbitration, it is just and proper in all the circumstances for the court to determine the question.

(4) An application for leave to appeal under this section shall identify the question of law to be determined and state the grounds on which it is alleged that leave to appeal should be granted.

(5) The court shall determine an application for leave to appeal under this section without a hearing unless it appears to the court that a hearing is required.

(6) The leave of the court is required for any appeal from a decision of the court under this section to grant or refuse leave to appeal.

(7) On an appeal under this section the court may by order—

    (a) confirm the award,

    (b) vary the award,

    (c) remit the award to the tribunal, in whole or in part, for reconsideration in the light of the court's determination, or

    (d) set aside the award in whole or in part.

The court shall not exercise its power to set aside an award, in whole or in part, unless it is satisfied that it would be inappropriate to remit the matters in question to the tribunal for reconsideration.

(8) The decision of the court on an appeal under this section shall be treated as a judgment of the court for the purposes of a further appeal.

But no such appeal lies without the leave of the court which shall not be given unless the court considers that the question is one of general importance or is one which for some other special reason should be considered by the Court of Appeal.

Note —Compare ss.1 and 3 of the 1979 Act.

2E–245

Appeal to the High Court

If no question of English law arises, there is no power in the English Court to grant leave to appeal under s.69(1) interpolating the wording of s.82 of the Act, see *Reliance Industries Ltd v. Enron Oil & Gas India Ltd* [2002] 1 Lloyd's Rep. 645 (arbitrators applying Indian law in construing contract). Case also emphasised importance under s.69 to establish that, despite the agreement of the parties to resolve the matter by arbitration, it is just and proper in all the circumstances for the court to determine the question.

2E–246

A judge should give sufficient reason for his decision so as to enable a party to understand why he had won or lost. What is sufficient will depend upon the issues involved in a particular case. The Antaios [1985] A.C. 1 guidance no longer holds good, see *North Range Shipping Ltd v. Seatrans Shipping Corporation (The Western Triumph)* [2002] EWCA Civ 405; [2002] 1 W.L.R. 2397; [2002] 4 All E.R. 390; [2002] 2 Lloyd's Rep. 1. The Court said:

> "Section 69(3) contains a variety of threshold tests. At the very least we think an unsuccessful applicant for leave should be told which of those tests he has failed...But does the judge need to go further and explain in every case why the relevant threshold test has been failed? We think the answer to this question is "No". If the question is not one of law, does not substantially affect the rights of one or more of the parties or is not one which the tribunal was asked to determine, an adequate reason for the judge's decision will in almost all cases have been given simply by identifying the test or tests which the applicant has failed without the need to say more. The same applies we think to the question of general public importance. However, when one gets to whether the tribunal's decision was obviously wrong or not open to serious doubt, we do not think that it is possible to give an unqualified answer to the question we have posed. It may be enough simply to refer to the statutory test, but we do not think it is possible to say that this will always be so. It would be enough to say "For the reasons given by the arbitrators" if that was the judge's reason. Otherwise it may be necessary to go further. But any further reasons need only be brief so as to show the losing party why he has lost. Such reasons will of course be given against a background of a full hearing, a reasoned award and detailed submissions as to why leave to appeal should be granted. In other words, the judge's brief reasons are directed to a fully informed applicant."

See too the last paragraph of 2E–247 below.

In *The Agios Dimitrios* [2004] EWHC 2232 (Comm); [2005] 1 Lloyd's Rep. 23 the Court at paras 5, 6 and 7 stated:

> "5. The philosophy and purpose underlying the s.69 procedure requires the achievement of finality of awards consistently with the on-going judicial development of English commercial law. The s.69(3) tests are designed to reflect this philosophy and purpose. Section 69(3)(c) therefore distinguishes between cases where the material question of law is one of general public interest and cases where it is not. A different threshold test is to be applied in the former case (the serious doubt test) from the latter (the obviously wrong test), but in both cases the test is to be applied to the question of law strictly 'on the basis of the findings of facts in the award'. In other words the Court takes the findings of fact as an immutable basis for testing the correctness of the arbitrators' decision on the question of law unless the Court takes the view that the award does not contain reasons or 'does not set out the tribunal's reasons in sufficient detail to enable the Court properly to consider the application or appeal', in which case it can order the arbitrators to give reasons in sufficient detail under s.70(3).
>
> 6. The Court's function under s.69 is thus to look exclusively at the award for the purpose of ascertaining whether the threshold tests under s.69(3) have been satisfied. Above all, it does not go behind what appears on the face of the award and it is not concerned with the circumstances in which the award came to be made and in particular with whether those circumstances were such as to amount to serious irregularity which has caused or will cause substantial injustice to either of the parties. The Act provides, by s.68, an entirely self-contained procedural regime for dealing with such circumstances.
>
> 7. Consequently, the combination in one hearing of applications under both sections involves two quite distinct processes of judicial analysis. In many cases determination of the s.69 application for leave to appeal before that of the s.68 application may be logically preferable. This is because the determination by the Court of the question whether there has obviously been an error of law on such facts as have been found or whether there is serious doubt as to that, will often have a direct bearing on the question whether if there has been the serious irregularity complained of for the purposes of the s.68 application such irregularity has given rise to substantial injustice. In each case, however, it is a matter for the Court whether the application for leave to appeal should be tried first. There may be cases where the procedural irregularity complained of is of such a kind that it would be logically preferable for the s.68 application to be determined first so that, if it succeeds, the award can be set aside or remitted to the arbitrators before leave to appeal is considered. After all, following remission, the issue of law in question might not eventually arise."

s.69(3)(c)(ii)

The requirement that the decision of the arbitrators is at least open to serious **2E–246A** doubt is broader than that propounded by Lord Diplock in *"The Nema"* [1982] A.C. 724 (at p.743D) that there was a strong *prima facie* case that the arbitrator's decision was wrong, see *CMA CGM SA v. Beteiligungs-Kommanditgesellscaft MS "Northern Pioneer" Schiffahrtgesellschaft MBH* [2002] EWCA Civ 1878; [2003] 1 W.L.R. 1015; [2003] 1 Lloyd's Rep 212; [2003] 3 All E.R. 330; [2003] 1 All E.R. (Comm) 204, CA.

Appeals to the Court of Appeal

In furtherance of the policy of injecting speed and finality in relation to arbitration **2E–247** awards, the Act re-enacts the far-reaching limitations on the right of appeal from decisions or orders of the High Court to the Court of Appeal.

Thus, it is provided that no appeal shall be to the Court of Appeal from a decision of the High Court on an appeal against an arbitration award under s.69 of the Act or from a decision determining a preliminary question of law (s.45) unless two conditions are satisfied, namely,

(a) the High Court or the Court of Appeal gives permission, and

(b) it is considered by the High Court that the question of law to which its decision relates, is either one of general public importance or is one which for some other special reason should be considered by the Court of Appeal under ss.69(8) and 45(6) of the Act,

Restrictions on the right of appeal to the Court of Appeal are contained in the Supreme Court Act 1981, s.18.

The mere fact that a High Court judge reaches a different conclusion from that of arbitrators he considers very experienced does not constitute a "special reason" justifying the granting of permission to appeal to the Court of Appeal (*Pera Shipping Corp. v. Petroship SA*, [1985] 2 Lloyd's Rep. 103, CA).

In *Henry Boot Construction (UK) Ltd v. Malmaison Hotel (Manchester) Ltd* [2000] 2 Lloyd's Rep. 625 [2001] Q.B. 388; [2001] 1 All E.R. 257 CA, the Court held (1) that on the true construction of s.69(8) of the Arbitration Act 1996 a party who wished to appeal from a decision of the High Court or a county court on appeal from an arbitration award required the permission of the High Court or the county court, as the case might be; and that the Court of Appeal had no jurisdiction either to grant permission itself or to review a refusal of the High Court or a county court to grant permission and (2) that s.55 of the Access to Justice Act 1999, which limited the right of appeal where there had already been one appeal, did not impliedly repeal s.69(8) of the Arbitration Act 1996; and that, accordingly (by a 2:1 majority), since s.55 of the Act of 1999 had no effect on s.69(8) of the Act of 1996, where the court which heard an appeal from an arbitrator gave permission to the Court of Appeal, there was no additional requirement to obtain the permission of the Court of Appeal.

Challenge or appeal: supplementary provisions

70.—(1) The following provisions apply to an application or appeal **2E–248** under section 67, 68 or 69.

(2) An application or appeal may not be brought if the applicant or appellant has not first exhausted—

(a) any available arbitral process of appeal or review, and

(b) any available recourse under section 57 (correction of award or additional award).

(3) Any application or appeal must be brought within 28 days of the date of the award or, if there has been any arbitral process of appeal or review, of the date when the applicant or appellant was notified of the result of that process.

(4) If on an application or appeal it appears to the court that the award—

(a) does not contain the tribunal's reasons, or

(b) does not set out the tribunal's reasons in sufficient detail

517

to enable the court properly to consider the application or appeal,

the court may order the tribunal to state the reasons for its award in sufficient detail for that purpose.

(5) Where the court makes an order under subsection (4), it may make such further order as it thinks fit with respect to any additional costs of the arbitration resulting from its order.

(6) The court may order the applicant or appellant to provide security for the costs of the application or appeal, and may direct that the application or appeal be dismissed if the order is not complied with.

The power to order security for costs shall not be exercised on the ground that the applicant or appellant is—

(a) an individual ordinarily resident outside the United Kingdom, or

(b) a corporation or association incorporated or formed under the law of a country outside the United Kingdom, or whose central management and control is exercised outside the United Kingdom.

(7) The court may order that any money payable under the award shall be brought into court or otherwise secured pending the determination of the application or appeal, and may direct that the application or appeal be dismissed if the order is not complied with.

(8) The court may grant leave to appeal subject to conditions to the same or similar effect as an order under subsection (6) or (7).

This does not affect the general discretion of the court to grant leave subject to conditions.

2E–249   *Note*—Compare s.23(3) of the 1950 Act, and s.1(5) and (6) of the 1979 Act. This is a mandatory provision (see s.4).

Time for appeal/Exhaustion of Specified Remedies s.70(2)

2E–250   There is a 28 day time limit and the appellant must first have exhausted any available arbitral process of appeal or review or any available recourse under s.57.

This time limit may be extended, see s.80(5) below. For factors relevant to an application to extend time, see *Aoot Kalmneft v. Glencore International AG* [2001] 2 All E.R. (Comm) 577.

For a case on exhaustion of any available recourse under s.57 see *Torch Offshore LLC v. Cable Shipping Inc* [2004] EWHC 787 (Comm); [2004] 2 All E.R. (Comm) 365.

Reasons for awards

2E–251   By s.52(4) of the 1996 Act an award must contain reasons for the award unless it is an agreed award or the parties have agreed to dispense with reasons. S.70(4) extends the power of the Court to order reasons to applications under ss.67 and 68 as well as to applications under s.69. For an example of the existence of this power see *Petroships Pte Ltd v. Petec Trading & Investment Corporation* [2001] 2 Lloyd's Rep. 348.

Terms

2E–252   In granting permission to appeal, the High Court may impose such conditions as it considers reasonable (*ibid.*) as for example, that the minimum sum due to the successful party should be paid over to him or that the sum in dispute should be in some way secured, *e.g.* by payment into court or otherwise.

Section 70(7)

2E–252.1   In *Peterson Farms Inc v. C&M Farming Ltd* [2003] EWHC 2298; [2004] 1 Lloyd's

Rep. 614 the Court considered factors material to the exercise of its discretion under s.70(7) holding inter alia that in most cases, it is likely that demonstration by the party against whom the jurisdictional challenge is made that the challenge is flimsy or otherwise lacks substance is likely to be regarded as a threshold requirement for the court's consideration whether in all the circumstances it is appropriate to require, as a condition of proceeding under s.67,that money payable under the award shall be brought into Court or otherwise secured pending the determination of the application.

Challenge or appeal: effect of order of court

71.—(1) The following provisions have effect where the court makes an order under section 67, 68 or 69 with respect to an award.   **2E–253**

(2) Where the award is varied, the variation has effect as part of the tribunal's award.

(3) Where the award is remitted to the tribunal, in whole or in part, for reconsideration, the tribunal shall make a fresh award in respect of the matters remitted within three months of the date of the order for remission or such longer or shorter period as the court may direct.

(4) Where the award is set aside or declared to be of no effect, in whole or in part, the court may also order that any provision that an award is a condition precedent to the bringing of legal proceedings in respect of a matter to which the arbitration agreement applies, is of no effect as regards the subject matter of the award or, as the case may be, the relevant part of the award.

Note—Compare s.22(2) of the 1950 Act, and s.1(8) of the 1979 Act. This is a mandatory provision (see s.4). Section 71(4) does not apply to statutory arbitrations.   **2E–254**

MISCELLANEOUS

Saving for rights of person who takes no part in proceedings

72.—(1) A person alleged to be a party to arbitral proceedings but who takes no part in the proceedings may question—   **2E–255**

    (a) whether there is a valid arbitration agreement,

    (b) whether the tribunal is properly constituted, or

    (c) what matters have been submitted to arbitration in accordance with the arbitration agreement,

by proceedings in the court for a declaration or injunction or other appropriate relief.

(2) He also has the same right as a party to the arbitral proceedings to challenge an award—

    (a) by an application under section 67 on the ground of lack of substantive jurisdiction in relation to him, or

    (b) by an application under section 68 on the ground of serious irregularity (within the meaning of that section) affecting him;

and section 70(2) (duty to exhaust arbitral procedures) does not apply in his case.

Note—This is a mandatory provision (see s.4). See *Arab National Bank v. El-Abdali* [2004] EWHC 2381 (Comm); [2005] 1 Lloyd's Rep. 541 injunction granted restraining publication of award.   **2E–256**

Loss of right to object

2E-257   73.—(1) If a party to arbitral proceedings takes part, or continues to take part, in the proceedings without making, either forthwith or within such time as is allowed by the arbitration agreement or the tribunal or by any provision of this Part, any objection—

    (a) that the tribunal lacks substantive jurisdiction,

    (b) that the proceedings have been improperly conducted,

    (c) that there has been a failure to comply with the arbitration agreement or with any provision of this Part, or

    (d) that there has been any other irregularity affecting the tribunal or the proceedings,

he may not raise that objection later, before the tribunal or the court, unless he shows that, at the time he took part or continued to take part in the proceedings, he did not know and could not with reasonable diligence have discovered the grounds for the objection.

(2) Where the arbitral tribunal rules that it has substantive jurisdiction and a party to arbitral proceedings who could have questioned that ruling—

    (a) by any available arbitral process of appeal or review, or

    (b) by challenging the award,

does not do so, or does not do so within the time allowed by the arbitration agreement or any provision of this Part, he may not object later to the tribunal's substantive jurisdiction on any ground which was the subject of that ruling.

2E-258   *Note* —This is a mandatory provison (see s.4). See too *Rustal Trading Ltd v. Gill & Duffus SA* [2002] 1 Lloyd's Rep. 14.

Examples:

2E-258.1   See *Rustal Trading Ltd v. Gill & Duffus SA* [2000] 1 Lloyd's Rep. 14 and *Moshin v. The Commonwealth Secretariat* [2002] EWHC 377 (Comm), March 1, 2002 (both cases of continuing to participate in the arbitral proceedings without objection with full knowledge and/a means of knowledge). See too *VEE Networks Ltd v. Econet Wireless International Ltd* [2004] EWHC 2909; [2005] 1 All E.R. (Comm) 303; [2005] 1 Lloyd's Rep. 192 .

Immunity of arbitral institutions, etc

2E-259   74.—(1) An arbitral or other institution or person designated or requested by the parties to appoint or nominate an arbitrator is not liable for anything done or omitted in the discharge or purported discharge of that function unless the act or omission is shown to have been in bad faith.

(2) An arbitral or other institution or person by whom an arbitrator is appointed or nominated is not liable, by reason of having appointed or nominated him, for anything done or omitted by the arbitrator (or his employees or agents) in the discharge or purported discharge of his functions as arbitrator.

(3) The above provisions apply to an employee or agent of an arbitral or other institution or person as they apply to the institution or person himself.

2E-260   *Note* —This is a mandatory provision (see s.4).

Charge to secure payment of solicitors' costs

75. The powers of the court to make declarations and orders under **2E–261** section 73 of the Solicitors Act 1974 or Article 71H of the Solicitors (Northern Ireland) Order 1976 (power to charge property recovered in the proceedings with the payment of solicitors' costs) may be exercised in relation to arbitral proceedings as if those proceedings were proceedings in the court.

Note —Compare s.18(5) of the 1950 Act. This is a mandatory provision. **2E–262**

Service of notices, etc

76.—(1) The parties are free to agree on the manner of service of **2E–263** any notice or other document required or authorised to be given or served in pursuance of the arbitration agreement or for the purposes of the arbitral proceedings.

(2) If or to the extent that there is no such agreement the following provisions apply.

(3) A notice or other document may be served on a person by any effective means.

(4) If a notice or other document is addressed, pre-paid and delivered by post—

    (a) to the addressee's last known principal residence or, if he is or has been carrying on a trade, profession or business, his last known principal business address, or

    (b) where the addressee is a body corporate, to the body's registered or principal office,

it shall be treated as effectively served.

(5) This section does not apply to the service of documents for the purposes of legal proceedings, for which provision is made by rules of court.

(6) References in this Part to a notice or other document include any form of communication in writing and references to giving or service a notice or other document shall be construed accordingly.

Powers of court in relation to service of documents

77.—(1) This section applies where service of a document on a **2E–264** person in the manner agreed by the parties, or in accordance with provisions of section 76 having effect in default of agreement, is not reasonably practicable.

(2) Unless otherwise agreed by the parties, the court may make such order as it thinks fit—

    (a) for service in such manner as the court may direct, or

    (b) dispensing with service of the document.

(3) Any party to the arbitration agreement may apply for an order, but only after exhausting any available arbitral process for resolving the matter.

(4) The leave of the court is required for any appeal from a decision of the court under this section.

Reckoning periods of time

78.—(1) The parties are free to agree on the method of reckoning **2E–265**

521

periods of time for the purposes of any provision agreed by them or any provision of this Part having effect in default of such agreement.

(2) If or to the extent there is no such agreement, periods of time shall be reckoned in accordance with the following provisions.

(3) Where the act is required to be done within a specified period after or from a specified date, the period begins immediately after that date.

(4) Where the act is required to be done a specified number of clear days after a specified date, at least that number of days must intervene between the day on which the act is done and that date.

(5) Where the period is a period of seven days or less which would include a Saturday, Sunday or a public holiday in the place where anything which has to be done within the period falls to be done, that day shall be excluded.

In relation to England and Wales or Northern Ireland, a "public holiday" means Christmas Day, Good Friday or a day which under the Banking and Financial Dealings Act 1971 is a bank holiday.

Power of court to extend time limits relating to arbitral proceedings

2E-266 **79.**—(1) Unless the parties otherwise agree, the court may by order extend any time limit agreed by them in relation to any matter relating to the arbitral proceedings or specified in any provision of this Part having effect in default of such agreement. This section does not apply to a time limit to which section 12 applies (power of court to extend time for beginning arbitral proceedings, etc.).

(2) An application for an order may be made—

    (a) by any party to the arbitral proceedings (upon notice to the other parties and to the tribunal), or

    (b) by the arbitral tribunal (upon notice to the parties).

(3) The court shall not exercise its power to extend a time limit unless it is satisfied—

    (a) that any available recourse to the tribunal, or to any arbitral or other institution or person vested by the parties with power in that regard, has first been exhausted, and

    (b) that a substantial injustice would otherwise be done.

(4) The court's power under this section may be exercised whether or not the time has already expired.

(5) An order under this section may be made on such terms as the court thinks fit.

(6) The leave of the court is required for any appeal from a decision of the court under this section.

Notice and other requirements in connection with legal proceedings

2E-267 **80.**—(1) References in this Part to an application, appeal or other step in relation to legal proceedings being taken "upon notice" to the other parties to the arbitral proceedings, or to the tribunal, are to such notice of the originating process as is required by rules of court and do not impose any separate requirement.

(2) Rules of court shall be made—

    (a) requiring such notice to be given as indicated by any provision of this Part, and

    (b) as to the manner, form and content of any such notice.

(3) Subject to any provision made by rules of court, a requirement to give notice to the tribunal of legal proceedings shall be construed—

    (a) if there is more than one arbitrator, as a requirement to give notice to each of them; and

    (b) if the tribunal is not fully constituted, as a requirement to give notice to any arbitrator who has been appointed.

(4) References in this Part to making an application or appeal to the court within a specified period are to the issue within that period of the appropriate originating process in accordance with rules of court.

(5) Where any provision of this Part requires an application or appeal to be made to the court within a specified time, the rules of court relating to the reckoning of periods, the extending or abridging of periods, and the consequences of not taking a step within the period prescribed by the rules, apply in relation to that requirement.

(6) Provision may be made by rules of court amending the provisions of this Part—

    (a) with respect to the time within which any application or appeal to the court must be made,

    (b) so as to keep any provision made by this Part in relation to arbitral proceedings in step with the corresponding provision of rules of court applying in relation to proceedings in the court, or

    (c) so as to keep any provision made by this Part in relation to legal proceedings in step with the corresponding provision of rules of court applying generally in relation to proceedings in the court.

(7) Nothing in this section affects the generality of the power to make rules of court.

Section 80(5)

The effect of s.80(5) is to introduce the broad discretionary approach under CPR r.3.12(a) into applications for the extension of the 28 day time limit under ss.67 to 69 of the 1996 Act, see *Kalmneft JSC v. Glencore International AG* [2002] 1 All E.R. 76, [2002] 1 Lloyd's Rep. 128. The case also identifies a number of specific considerations which are likely to be material. **2E–267A**

Saving for certain matters governed by common law

81.—(1) Nothing in this Part shall be construed as excluding the operation of any rule of law consistent with the provisions of this Part, in particular, any rule of law as to— **2E–268**

    (a) matters which are not capable of settlement by arbitration;

    (b) the effect of an oral arbitration agreement; or

(c) the refusal of recognition or enforcement of an arbitral
award on grounds of public policy.

(2) Nothing in this Act shall be construed as reviving any jurisdiction of the court to set aside or remit an award on the ground of errors of fact or law on the face of the award.

Minor definitions

2E–269   82.—(1) In this Part—

"arbitrator", unless the context otherwise requires, includes an
umpire;

"available arbitral process", in relation to any matter, includes
any process of appeal to or review by an arbitral or other
institution or person vested by the parties with powers in
relation to that matter;

"claimant", unless the context otherwise requires, includes a
counterclaimant, and related expressions shall be construed accordingly;

"dispute" includes any difference;

"enactment" includes an enactment contained in Northern
Ireland legislation;

"legal proceedings" means civil proceedings in the High Court
or a county court;

"peremptory order" means an order made under section 41(5)
or made in exercise of any corresponding power conferred
by the parties;

"premises" includes land, buildings, moveable structures,
vehicles, vessels, aircraft and hovercraft;

"question of law" means—

(a) for a court in England and Wales, a question of
the law of England and Wales, and

(b) for a court in Northern Ireland, a question of the
law of Northern Ireland;

"substantive jurisdiction", in relation to an arbitral tribunal,
refers to the matters specified in section 30(1)(a) to (c),
and references to the tribunal exceeding its substantive jurisdiction shall be construed accordingly.

(2) References in this Part to a party to an arbitration agreement
include any person claiming under or through a party to the
agreement.

Index of defined expressions: Part I

2E–270   83. In this Part the expressions listed below are defined or
otherwise explained by the provisions indicated—

agreement, agree and agreed   section 5(1)
agreement in writing   section 5(2) to (5)
arbitration agreement   sections 6 and 5(1)
arbitrator   section 82(1)
available arbitral process   section 82(1)

claimant	section 82(1)
commencement (in relation to arbitral proceedings)	section 14
costs of the arbitration	section 59
the court	section 105
dispute	section 82(1)
enactment	section 82(1)
legal proceedings	section 82(1)
Limitation Acts	section 13(4)
notice (or other document)	section 76(6)
party—	
—in relation to an arbitration agreement	section 82(2)
—where section 106(2) or (3) applies	section 106(4)
peremptory order	section 82(1) (and see section 41(5))
premises	section 82(1)
question of law	section 82(1)
recoverable costs	sections 63 and 64
seat of the arbitration	section 3
serve and service (of notice or other document)	section 76(6)
substantive jurisdiction (in relation to an arbitral tribunal)	section 82(1) (and see section 30(1)(a) to (c))
upon notice (to the parties or the tribunal)	section 80
written and in writing	section 5(6)

Transitional provisions

84.—(1) The provisions of this Part do not apply to arbitral **2E–271** proceedings commenced before the date on which this Part comes into force.

(2) They apply to arbitral proceedings commenced on or after that date under an arbitration agreement whenever made.

(3) The above provisions have effect subject to any transitional provision made by an order under section 109(2) (power to include transitional provisions in commencement order).

Note—Compare s.33 of the 1950 Act. **2E–272**

PART II

OTHER PROVISIONS RELATING TO ARBITRATION

DOMESTIC ARBITRATION AGREEMENTS

Modification of Part I in relation to domestic arbitration agreement

2E–273   **85.**—(1) In the case of a domestic arbitration agreement the provisions of Part I are modified in accordance with the following sections.

(2) For this purpose a "domestic arbitration agreement" means an arbitration agreement to which none of the parties is—

(a) an individual who is a national of, or habitually resident in, a state other than the United Kingdom, or

(b) a body corporate which is incorporated in, or whose central control and management is exercised in, a state other than the United Kingdom,

and under which the seat of the arbitration (if the seat has been designated or determined) is in the United Kingdom.

(3) In subsection (2) "arbitration agreement" and "seat of the arbitration" have the same meaning as in Part I (see sections 3, 5(1) and 6).

2E–274   *Note* —Compare s.1(4) of the 1975 Act. Not brought into force by (S.I. 1996 No. 3146).

Staying of legal proceedings

2E–275   **86.**—(1) In section 9 (stay of legal proceedings), subsection (4) (stay unless the arbitration agreement is null and void, inoperative, or incapable of being performed) does not apply to a domestic arbitration agreement.

(2) On an application under that section in relation to a domestic arbitration agreement the court shall grant a stay unless satisfied—

(a) that the arbitration agreement is null and void, inoperative, or incapable of being performed, or

(b) that there are other sufficient grounds for not requiring the parties to abide by the arbitration agreement.

(3) The court may treat as a sufficient ground under subsection (2)(b) the fact that the applicant is or was at any material time not ready and willing to do all things necessary for the proper conduct of the arbitration or of any other dispute resolution procedures required to be exhausted before resorting to arbitration.

(4) For the purposes of this section the question whether an arbitration agreement is a domestic arbitration agreement shall be determined by reference to the facts at the time the legal proceedings are commenced.

2E–276   *Note* —Compare s.4(1) of the 1950 Act, and s.1(1) of the 1975 Act. Not brought into force by (S.I. 1996 No. 3146).

"... the Court shall grant a stay unless ..."

The discretion under s.4 of the Arbitration Act 1950 has been replaced by specified **2E–277** circumstances and the Court is now required to grant a stay unless one or more of the specified circumstances is established.

Note —For s.9 generally, "a party to an arbitration agreement"; "who may apply"; **2E–278** "the application"; "... or after he has taken any step in those proceedings to answer the substantive claim"; "onus of showing that the action should proceed"; and "incapable of being performed".

"... other sufficient grounds ..."

It is considered that the matters referred to under the following sub-headings may, **2E–279** if this section is brought into force, be held to be sufficient grounds within subs.(2)(b) or not to be sufficient grounds depending upon whether under the old law a stay was refused or granted.

Claim going beyond arbitration agreement

Where a clause in an insurance policy provided for arbitration "where a difference **2E–280** has arisen as to adjustment of a loss," and the defendant company applied for a stay on the ground that by storing petroleum on the premises the claimant had violated the contract and thus created a difference as to the adjustment of the loss, the Irish Court refused a stay holding that the defendant had set up a defence against the right to recover at all under the contract, which went beyond the arbitration clause (*O'Connor v. Norwich Union, etc. Co* [1894] 2 I.R. 723). And where an arbitration clause in a private Act provided for arbitration as to reasonableness of charges, and on being sued for the amount charged the defendant denied the right of the plaintiff company to make any charge at all, it was held that there was no dispute within the arbitration clause and stay was refused (*L. & N.W. and G.W. Rys v. Billington* [1899] A.C. 79).

Absence of real dispute between parties

Where there is no sustainable dispute between the parties with regard to the matter **2E–281** agreed to be referred, *e.g.* where the case raised by the defendant does not afford a defence and is not available as a ground for a set-off or counterclaim, the Court has held that there is no jurisdiction to stay the action (*Nova (Jersey) Knit Ltd v. Kammgarn Spinnerei GmbH* [1977] 1 W.L.R. 713; [1977] 2 All E.R. 463, HL). Compare and contrast position under s.9, see *Halki Shipping Corp v. Sopex Oils Ltd*, noted at para. 2E–107, above.

Agreement to refer disputes to foreign Court

This is a good ground for granting a stay (*Kirchner and Co v. Gruban* [1909] 1 Ch. **2E–282** 413; and see *Racecourse Betting Control Board v. Secretary for Air* [1944] Ch. 114, *per* MacKinnon L.J.).

Building contracts

A claim to recover the amount of interim certificates issued by an architect under a **2E–283** standard form of building contract may be stayed by reason of a bona fide set-off or counterclaim for unliquidated damages alleged to have been suffered by the building owner (*Modern Engineering (Bristol) Ltd v. Gilbert-Ash (Northern) Ltd* [1974] A.C. 689; [1973] 3 All E.R. 195, HL, overruling *Dawnays Ltd v. F.G. Minter Ltd* [1971] 1 W.L.R. 1205; [1971] 2 All E.R. 1389, CA).

A claim to recover the amount due under an interim certificate may also be stayed where there is a dispute about the correctness of the certificate; such a stay may be made conditional, in appropriate circumstances, upon the defendant providing security (*C.M. Pillings & Co Ltd v. Kent Investments Ltd* (1985) 1 Const.L.J. 393; *The Times*, May 14, 1985, CA).

Company—articles of association

Articles of association of a company provided that any difference arising between **2E–284** the company and any of the members as to the construction of the articles should be settled by arbitration. Where differences arose between two rival sets of directors, it was held that the arbitration clause did not apply, as the difference was not between the company and one of its members in his capacity of member, but between different groups of directors (*Isaacs v. Chapman* (1916) 32 T.L.R. 183, affirmed [1916] W.N. 28).

Delay

2E–285   Where the object of the defendant was merely to delay the plaintiff a stay was refused (*Lury v. Pearson* (1856) 1 C.B.(N.S.) 639).

Difficult questions of law

2E–286   The mere fact that the subject-matter of a submission involves questions of law or is of a nature eminently suitable for trial in a Court of law is not sufficient ground for refusing to stay the claim (*Re Phoenix Timber Co's Application* [1958] 2 Q.B. 1). But if difficult questions of law are likely to arise which would be better to have argued in a Court of first instance, the Court has jurisdiction to refuse to stay the claim (*Clough v. County Livestock Assn. Ltd* (1916) 85 L.J. K.B. 1185).

Charge of fraud

2E–287   When fraud is charged, and the person charged with fraud wishes the matter to be heard in court, a stay will be refused. Where, however, it is the party alleging fraud who seeks to resist a stay, it is a matter for the court's discretion whether to grant or refuse a stay depending on all the circumstances of the case. If the only circumstance relied upon by the party alleging fraud is the charge of fraud, the normal approach of the court will be to grant a stay (*Russell v. Russell* (1880) 14 Ch D 471; *Camilla Cotton Oil Co v. Granadex SA* [1976] 2 Lloyd's Rep. 10, HL; *Cunningham-Reid v. Buchanan-Jardine* [1988] 1 W.L.R. 678; [1988] 2 All E.R. 438, CA). But where the parties had agreed by arbitration that the ascertainment of the amount in dispute was to be a condition precedent to liability, the Court upheld the submission, though fraud was charged. In that case it followed that the party charged with fraud had no right to proceed by claim. Until after arbitration there was no liability; until the liability was created there was no right of action; and until the right of action existed the issue as to fraud could not be said to exist either (*Trainor v. Phoenix Fire Assoc. Co* (1891) 65 L.T. 825).

Charge against professional reputation or of dishonesty

2E–288   Where the claimant is required to meet allegations of actual dishonesty involving his professional reputation, he is entitled to have his case tried by a Judge in open court, and the Court will refuse to stay his claim (*Radford v. Hair* (1971) Ch. 758; [1971] 2 All E.R. 1089). Where allegations of incompetence, negligence and impropriety are made so that a man's professional reputation is at stake, he ought to have the benefit of a trial in the High Court, even though no allegations of actual fraud or dishonesty are involved, since such allegations can shade into one another (*Turner v. Fenton* [1982] 1 W.L.R. 52; [1982] 1 All E.R. 8).

Matters unsuitable for arbitration

2E–289   The onus of showing this rests on the claimant (*Hodgson v. Ry. Passengers Assoc. Co* (1882) 9 QBD 188). Where the question was one as to dissolution of partnership and construction of the deed, a stay was refused on this among other grounds (*Bonnin v. Neame* [1910] 1 Ch. 732). In that case the claim sought to be stayed was brought by the mortgagees of the share of one of the partners, and it was held that they were not bound by the arbitration clause in the deed of partnership.

Multiplicity of proceedings

2E–290   A stay will be refused where the result of the stay would be the duplication of proceedings with all the consequences with regard to delay, additional costs and the risk of conflicting decisions which such duplication would involve (*The Eschersheim* [1975] 1 W.L.R. 83; [1974] 3 All E.R. 307, applying *Taunton-Collins v. Cromie* [1964] 1 W.L.R. 633; [1964] 2 All E.R. 322, CA and *Halifax Overseas Freighters Ltd v. Rasno Export*; *The Pine Hill* [1958] 2 Lloyd's Rep. 146). The case of *W. Bruce Ltd v. J. Strong* [1951] 2 K.B. 447, where the contrary was held, was a very special case.

Poverty and legally aided claimant

2E–291   Poverty which produces an inability to arbitrate is not in itself a ground for refusing to grant a stay to which the defendant is entitled. If poverty is caused by the breach on the part of the other party, such can be a ground for refusing a stay, see *Fakes v. Taylor Woodrow Construction Ltd* [1973] Q.B. 436; [1973] 1 All E.R. 670, CA (on this point), also see *Chrisphine Othieno v. Cooper & Cooper* 57 B.L.R. 128. See too *Trustee of the property of Andrews & Brock Builders (Kessingland)* [1997] Q.B. 674; [1997] 3 W.L.R. 124.

On its true construction, s.31(1) of the Legal Aid Act 1988 precludes the court from taking into account the fact that the claimant would be unable to receive legal aid for arbitration (*Edwin Jones v. Thyssen (G.B.) Ltd* 57 B.L.R. 116, CA, not following *Fakes v. Taylor Woodrow Construction Ltd* on the construction of s.1(7) of the Legal Aid and Advice Act 1949 which is in the same terms on this point). The question which the court must ask itself is, if the claimant was not legally aided, would it be proper to grant a stay of the arbitration, *per* Parker L.J. in *Edwin Jones v. Thyssen (G.B.) Ltd*

See too *Connelly v. R.T.Z. Corporation plc* [1997] 3 W.L.R. 373; [1997] 4 All E.R. 335, HL.

Exceptional case

In an exceptional case (a number of other interested persons: Court better placed **2E–292** to protect other interested parties: clause of wide interest and not considered in any reported case: desirable for issues to be decided by application of rules of evidence applied in Commercial Court) it was appropriate to refuse a stay, see *John Rew v. Malcolm John Cox* [1996] C.L.C. 472.

Effectiveness of agreement to exclude court's jurisdiction

87.—(1) In the case of a domestic arbitration agreement any agree- **2E–293** ment to exclude the jurisdiction of the court under—

    (a) section 45 (determination of preliminary point of law), or

    (b) section 69 (challenging the award: appeal on point of law),

is not effective unless entered into after the commencement of the arbitral proceedings in which the question arises or the award is made.

(2) For this purpose the commencement of the arbitral proceedings has the same meaning as in Part I (see section 14).

(3) For the purposes of this section the question whether an arbitration agreement is a domestic arbitration agreement shall be determined by reference to the facts at the time the agreement is entered into.

Note —Compare s.3(6) of the 1979 Act. Not brought into force by (S.I. 1996 No. **2E–294** 3146).

Exclusion agreements

The Act recognises the basic fundamental feature of a submission to arbitration for **2E–295** the resolution of civil disputes, namely, that it is consensual and voluntary that therefore, at any rate within specified limits, the parties should be entitled to exercise their freedom of contract in regulating the procedure of achieving speed and finality in resolving their disputes. Accordingly, the Act empowers the parties to enter into a written agreement, under which they can exclude the right of appeal against an arbitration award under s.69 of the Act or the right to apply to the Court for the determination of a preliminary point of law under s.45 of the Act. But an exclusion agreement will have no effect in relation to a domestic arbitration agreement unless it is entered into *after* the commencement of the arbitration (see s.87(1)).

Power to repeal or amend sections 85 to 87

88.—(1) The Secretary of State may by order repeal or amend the **2E–296** provisions of sections 85 to 87.

(2) An order under this section may contain such supplementary, incidental and transitional provisions as appear to the Secretary of State to be appropriate.

(3) An order under this section shall be made by statutory instru-

ment and no such order shall be made unless a draft of it has been laid before and approved by a resolution of each House of Parliament.

CONSUMER ARBITRATION AGREEMENTS

Application of unfair terms regulations to consumer arbitration agreements

2E–297 **89.**—(1) The following sections extend the application of the Unfair Terms in Consumer Contracts Regulations 1994 in relation to a term which constitutes an arbitration agreement. For this purpose "arbitration agreement" means an agreement to submit to arbitration present or future disputes or differences (whether or not contractual).

(2) In those sections "the Regulations" means those regulations and includes any regulations amending or replacing those regulations.

(3) Those sections apply whatever the law applicable to the arbitration agreement.

Regulations apply where consumer is a legal person

2E–298 **90.** The Regulations apply where the consumer is a legal person as they apply where the consumer is a natural person.

Arbitration agreement unfair where modest amount sought

2E–299 **91.**—(1) A term which constitutes an arbitration agreement is unfair for the purposes of the Regulations so far as it relates to a claim for a pecuniary remedy which does not exceed the amount specified by order for the purposes of this section.

(2) Orders under this section may make different provision for different cases and for different purposes.

(3) The power to make orders under this section is exercisable—

(a) for England and Wales, by the Secretary of State with the concurrence of the Lord Chancellor,

(b) for Scotland, by the Secretary of State [...]

(c) for Northern Ireland, by the Department of Economic Development for Northern Ireland with the concurrence of the Lord Chancellor.

(4) Any such order for England and Wales or Scotland shall be made by statutory instrument which shall be subject to annulment in pursuance of a resolution of either House of Parliament.

(5) Any such order for Northern Ireland shall be a statutory rule for the purposes of the Statutory Rules (Northern Ireland) Order 1979 and shall be subject to negative resolution, within the meaning of section 41(6) of the Interpretation Act (Northern Ireland) 1954.

2E–300 Note —The sum of £5,000 is specified for the purposes of s.91(1) by the Unfair Arbitrations Agreements (Specified Amounts) Order 1999 (S.I. 1999 No. 2167), effective January 1, 2000.

Amended by the Transfer of Functions (Lord Advocate and Secretary of State) Order 1999 (S.I. 1999 No. 678), art.6.

Exclusion of Part I in relation to small claims arbitration in the county court

92. Nothing in Part I of this Act applies to arbitration under section 64 of the County Courts Act 1984.   2E–301

Note —Compare s.7(3) of the 1979 Act.   2E–302

APPOINTMENT OF JUDGES AS ARBITRATORS

Appointment of judges as arbitrators

93.—(1) A judge of the Commercial Court or an official referee   2E–303 may, if in all the circumstances he thinks fit, accept appointment as a sole arbitrator or as umpire by or by virtue of an arbitration agreement.

(2) A judge of the Commercial Court shall not do so unless the Lord Chief Justice has informed him that, having regard to the state of business in the High Court and the Crown Court, he can be made available.

(3) An official referee shall not do so unless the Lord Chief Justice has informed him that, having regard to the state of official referees' business, he can be made available.

(4) The fees payable for the services of a judge of the Commercial Court or official referee as arbitrator or umpire shall be taken in the High Court.

(5) In this section—

"arbitration agreement" has the same meaning as in Part I; and

"official referee" means a person nominated under section 68(1)(a) of the Supreme Court Act 1981 to deal with official referees' business.

(6) The provisions of Part I of this Act apply to arbitration before a person appointed under this section with the modifications specified in Schedule 2.

Note —Compare s.11 of the 1950 Act.   2E–304

STATUTORY ARBITRATIONS

Application of Part I to statutory arbitrations

94.—(1) The provisions of Part I apply to every arbitration under   2E–305 an enactment (a "statutory arbitration"), whether the enactment was passed or made before or after the commencement of this Act, subject to the adaptations and exclusions specified in sections 95 to 98.

(2) The provisions of Part I do not apply to a statutory arbitration if or to the extent that their application—

(a) is inconsistent with the provisions of the enactment concerned, with any rules or procedure authorised or recognised by it, or

(b) is excluded by any other enactment.

(3) In this section and the following provisions of this Part "enactment"—

    (a) in England and Wales, includes an enactment contained in subordinate legislation within the meaning of the Interpretation Act 1978;

    (b) in Northern Ireland, means a statutory provision within the meaning of section 1(f) of the Interpretation Act (Northern Ireland) 1954.

2E–306   *Note* —Compare s.31 of the 1950 Act.

"Under an enactment ... etc."

2E–307   See the Lands Clauses Consolidation Act 1845, s.130; the Companies Clauses Consolidation Act 1845, ss.128–134; the Local Govt. Act 1888, s.63 (repealed with savings by SL(R) Act 1975), *Re Kent County Council and Sandgate, etc. Arb.* [1895] 2 Q.B. 43; and the Electricity Act 1989, s.23(1)(a) and (b). As to Friendly Societies Act see *Re Gollings and Tradesmen's Friendly Society Arb.* (1891) 64 T.L.R. 775 decided under the 1875 Act (see now 1974 Act).

By virtue of s.92 of the Arbitration Act 1996 the reference in subs.(1) to arbitrations under any other Act does not extend to arbitration under s.64 of the County Courts Act 1984 (cases in which proceedings are to be, or may be referred to arbitration) and accordingly nothing in Pt I of the Arbitration Act 1996 applies to arbitration under s.64 of the County Courts Act 1984.

"is inconsistent" or "is excluded"

2E–308   See *Re Knight and the Tabernacle Permanent Building Society Arbn.* [1891] 2 Q.B. 63, and *Tabernacle, etc. Building Society v. Knight* [1892] A.C. 298.

By virtue of the Trade Union and Labour Relations (Consolidation) Act 1992, ss.212(5), 263(6), Pt 1 of the Arbitration Act 1996 does not apply to an arbitration under s.212 of the 1992 Act, or to proceedings before the Central Arbitration Committee. The sections of the 1992 Act are amended pursuant to the consequential amendments in Sched.3 of the 1996 Arbitration Act. Pt I of the 1996 Act does not for like reasons apply to arbitrations under the Agricultural Holdings Act 1986 (see s.84, as amended by the 1996 Act).

General adaptation of provisions in relation to statutory arbitrations

2E–309   **95.**—(1) The provisions of Part I apply to a statutory arbitration—

    (a) as if the arbitration were pursuant to an arbitration agreement and as if the enactment were that agreement, and

    (b) as if the persons by and against whom a claim subject to arbitration in pursuance of the enactment may be or has been made were parties to that agreement.

(2) Every statutory arbitration shall be taken to have its seat in England and Wales or, as the case may be, in Northern Ireland.

2E–310   *Note* —Compare s.31 of the 1950 Act.

"As if the arbitration were pursuant to an arbitration agreement"

2E–311   The effect of this section is not in any way to introduce into arbitrations conducted under this Act provisions for arbitration contained in other Acts, but merely to apply the provisions of this Act to arbitrations under other Acts so far as such arbitrations are not conducted under statutory provisions inconsistent with the provisions of this Act (*Zelma Gold Mining Co v. Hoskins* [1895] A.C. 100).

Specific adaptations of provisions in relation to statutory arbitrations

2E–312   **96.**—(1) The following provisions of Part I apply to a statutory arbitration with the following adaptations.

(2) In section 30(1) (competence of tribunal to rule on its own jurisdiction), the reference in paragraph (a) to whether there is a valid arbitration agreement shall be construed as a reference to whether the enactment applies to the dispute or difference in question.

(3) Section 35 (consolidation of proceedings and concurrent hearings) applies only so as to authorise the consolidation of proceedings, or concurrent hearings in proceedings, under the same enactment.

(4) Section 46 (rules applicable to substance of dispute) applies with the omission of subsection (1)(b) (determination in accordance with considerations agreed by parties).

Note —Compare s.31 of the 1950 Act.   **2E–313**

Provisions excluded from applying to statutory arbitrations

97. The following provisions of Part I do not apply in relation to a **2E–314** statutory arbitration—

(a) section 8 (whether agreement discharged by death of a party);

(b) section 12 (power of court to extend agreed time limits);

(c) sections 9(5), 10(2) and 71(4) (restrictions on effect of provision that award condition precedent to right to bring legal proceedings).

Note —Compare s.31 of the 1950 Act.   **2E–315**

Power to make further provision by regulations

98.—(1) The Secretary of State may make provision by regulations **2E–316** for adapting or excluding any provision of Part I in relation to statutory arbitrations in general or statutory arbitrations of any particular description.

(2) The power is exercisable whether the enactment concerned is passed or made before or after the commencement of this Act.

(3) Regulations under this section shall be made by statutory instrument which shall be subject to annulment in pursuance of a resolution of either House of Parliament.

Note —Compare s.31 of the 1950 Act.   **2E–317**

PART III

RECOGNITION AND ENFORCEMENT OF CERTAIN FOREIGN AWARDS

ENFORCEMENT OF GENEVA CONVENTION AWARDS

Continuation of Part II of the Arbitration Act 1950

99. Part II of the Arbitration Act 1950 (enforcement of certain **2E–318** foreign awards) continues to apply in relation to foreign awards within the meaning of that Part which are not also New York Convention awards.

Note —Compare ss.35 to 42 of the 1950 Act, and s.2 of the 1975 Act.   **2E–319**

Geneva Convention Countries

2E–320   Section 99 does not apply to countries which are also New York Convention States and the list below should be checked against the list at para. 2E–323, below.

List of Territories to which the Geneva Convention applies:

The United Kingdom of Great Britain and Northern Ireland

Anguilla	India
British Virgin Islands	Republic of Ireland
Cayman Islands	Israel
Falkland Islands	Italy
Falkland Islands Dependencies	Japan
Gibraltar	Kenya
Montserrat	Luxembourg
Turks and Caicos Islands	Malta
Antigua and Barbuda	Mauritius
Austria	Netherlands (including Curacao)
Bahamas	New Zealand
Bangladesh	Pakistan
Belgium	Portugal
Belize	Romania
†Czechoslovakia	Saint Christopher and Nevis
Denmark	St. Lucia
Dominica	Spain
Finland	Sweden
Federal Republic of Germany	Switzerland
France	Tanzania
*German Democratic Republic	Thailand
Greece	Western Samoa
Grenada	†Yugoslavia
Guyana	Zambia

*The German Democratic Republic is now part of the Federal Republic of Germany.

†The position of Yugoslavia, Czechoslovakia and their former constituent states in relation to international treaties is, at present, uncertain.

RECOGNITION AND ENFORCEMENT OF NEW YORK CONVENTION AWARDS

New York Convention awards

2E–321   **100.**—(1) In this Part a "New York Convention award" means an award made, in pursuance of an arbitration agreement, in the territory of a state (other than the United Kingdom) which is a party to the New York Convention.

(2) For the purposes of subsection (1) and of the provisions of this Part relating to such awards—

> (a) "arbitration agreement" means an arbitration agreement in writing, and

> (b) an award shall be treated as made at the seat of the arbitration, regardless of where it was signed, despatched or delivered to any of the parties.

In this subsection "agreement in writing" and "seat of the arbitration" have the same meaning as in Part I.

(3) If Her Majesty by Order in Council declares that a state specified in the Order is a party to the New York Convention, or is a party in respect of any territory so specified, the Order shall, while in force, be conclusive evidence of that fact.

(4) In this section "the New York Convention" means the Convention on the Recognition and Enforcement of Foreign Arbitral Awards

adopted by the United Nations Conference on International Commercial Arbitration on 10th June 1958.

Note —Compare s.7 of the 1975 Act.   **2E–322**

New York Convention States

The following states have been specified by Order in Council (as amended from   **2E–323**
time to time by the Arbitration (Foreign Awards) (Orders) as being parties to the New
York Convention, namely:

Algeria	Republic of Ireland
Antigua and Barbuda	Israel
Argentina	Italy
Australia (including all the external	Japan
territories for the international rela-	Jordan
tions of which Australia is responsible)	Kenya
Austria	Korea
Bahrain	Kuwait
Belgium	Luxembourg
Belize	Madagascar
Benin	Malaysia
Botswana	Mexico
Bulgaria	Monaco
Burkina Faso	Morocco
Byelorussian Soviet Socialist Republic	Netherlands (including the
Cambodia	Netherlands Antilles)
Cameroon	New Zealand
Canada	Niger
Central African Republic	Nigeria
Chile	Norway
China	Panama
Colombia	Peru
Costa Rica	Philippines
Cuba	Poland
Cyprus	Romania
Czechoslovakia‡	San Marino
Denmark (including Greenland and	Singapore
the Faroe Islands)	South Africa
Djibouti	Spain
Dominica	Sri Lanka
Ecuador	Sweden
Egypt	Switzerland
Finland	Syria
France (including all the territories of	Tanzania
the French Republic)	Thailand
Federal Republic of Germany	Trinidad and Tobago
German Democratic Republic*	Tunisia
Ghana	Ukrainian Soviet Socialist Republic**
Greece	Union of Soviet Socialist Republics†
Guatemala	United States of America (including all
Haiti	the territories for the international re-
Holy See	lations of which the United States of
Hungary	America is responsible)
India	Uruguay
Indonesia	Yugoslavia‡

*The German Democratic Republic is now part of the Federal Republic of
Germany.
** The Ukrainian Soviet Socialist Republic is now the Ukraine.
†The Union of Soviet Socialist Republics is now dissolved. In many respects the
Russian Federation has succeeded to its international obligations but the precise
position is uncertain. The position of the countries which previously formed part
of the Union of Soviet Socialist Republics is also uncertain.
‡The position of Yugoslavia, Czechoslovakia and their former constituent states in
relation to international treaties is, at present, uncertain.

Note

2E–323.1   The list at para. 2E–323,above, identifies those signatories to the New York Convention in respect of whom an Order in Council envisaged under subsection (3) has been made. Not all signatories to the Convention are the subject of such an Order in Council. For a complete list of signatories recourse should be had to the website of the International Chamber of Commerce—Arbitration, or the website of the United Nations Commission on International Trade Law.

Recognition and enforcement of awards

2E–324   **101.**—(1) A New York Convention award shall be recognised as binding on the persons as between whom it was made, and may accordingly be relied on by those persons by way of defence, set-off or otherwise in any legal proceedings in England and Wales or Northern Ireland.

(2) A New York Convention award may, by leave of the court, be enforced in the same manner as a judgment or order of the court to the same effect.

As to the meaning of "the court" see section 105.

(3) Where leave is so given, judgment may be entered in terms of the award.

2E–325   *Note* —Compare s.3 of the 1975 Act.

Evidence to be produced by party seeking recognition or enforcement

2E–326   **102.**—(1) A party seeking the recognition or enforcement of a New York Convention award must produce—

(a) the duly authenticated original award or a duly certified copy of it, and

(b) the original arbitration agreement or a duly certified copy of it.

(2) If the award or agreement is in a foreign language, the party must also produce a translation of it certified by an official or sworn translator or by a diplomatic or consular agent.

2E–327   *Note* —Compare s.4 of the 1975 Act.

Refusal of recognition or enforcement

2E–328   **103.**—(1) Recognition or enforcement of a New York Convention award shall not be refused except in the following cases.

(2) Recognition or enforcement of the award may be refused if the person against whom it is invoked proves—

(a) that a party to the arbitration agreement was (under the law applicable to him) under some incapacity;

(b) that the arbitration agreement was not valid under the law to which the parties subjected it or, failing any indication thereon, under the law of the country where the award was made;

(c) that he was not given proper notice of the appointment of the arbitrator or of the arbitration proceedings or was otherwise unable to present his case;

(d) that the award deals with a difference not contemplated

by or not falling within the terms of the submission to arbitration or contains decisions on matters beyond the scope of the submission to arbitration (but see subsection (4));

(e) that the composition of the arbitral tribunal or the arbitral procedure was not in accordance with the agreement of the parties or, failing such agreement, with the law of the country in which the arbitration took place;

(f) that the award has not yet become binding on the parties, or has been set aside or suspended by a competent authority of the country in which, or under the law of which, it was made.

(3) Recognition or enforcement of the award may also be refused if the award is in respect of a matter which is not capable of settlement by arbitration, or if it would be contrary to public policy to recognise or enforce the award.

(4) An award which contains decisions on matters not submitted to arbitration may be recognised or enforced to the extent that it contains decisions on matters submitted to arbitration which can be separated from those on matters not so submitted.

(5) Where an application for the setting aside or suspension of the award has been made to such a competent authority as is mentioned in subsection (2)(f), the court before which the award is sought to be relied upon may, if it considers it proper, adjourn the decision on the recognition or enforcement of the award.

It may also on the application of the party claiming recognition or enforcement of the award order the other party to give suitable security.

Note—Compare s.5 of the 1975 Act.   **2E–329**

Enforcing court and curial court the same

Where the enforcing court and the court of the country whose law governs the **2E–330** award (the curial court) are the same, and application is made to that court to set aside or suspend a Convention award, that court may exercise both the curial court's power to set aside or suspend the award and, at the same time, the enforcing court's discretion to permit the pending supervisory process to continue and to refuse enforcement of the award if that process will result in the award being set aside or suspended by itself as the curial court, since, where the application is made to itself, as the curial court, to set aside or suspend the award it has as the enforcing court power under s.5(2) (now s.103(2)) to refuse enforcement of or reliance on the award and power under s.5(5) (now s.103(5)) to adjourn the proceedings, notwithstanding that the only proceedings consist of the application to itself as the curial court to set aside the award in which necessarily the award upon by the party seeking to have it set aside (*Hiscox v. Outhwaite (No. 1)* [1991] 3 All E.R. 641, HL).

In *Minmetals Germany GmbH v. Ferco Steel Ltd*, *The Times*, March 1, 1999 it was held that by agreeing the place of a foreign arbitration, a party not only agreed to submit all contractual disputes to arbitration but also agreed that the conduct of the arbitration should be subject to the supervisory jurisdiction of the courts of that place. Further the Court stated that in a case where a party against whom enforcement was sought alleged that a New York Convention award should not be enforced on the ground that such enforcement would lead to substantial injustice and therefore be contrary to English public policy the following must normally be included among the relevant considerations:

1. The nature of the procedural injustice.
2. Whether that party had invoked the supervisory jurisdiction of the seat of the arbitration.

3. Whether a remedy was available under that jurisdiction.
4. Whether the courts of that jurisdiction had conclusively determined the enforcee's complaint in favour of upholding the award.
5. If that party had failed to invoke that remedial jurisdiction, what reason had he and, in particular, whether he was acting, unreasonably in failing to do so.

Grounds of refusal

2E-331   In *Roseel N.V. v. Oriental Commercial & Shipping Co (UK) Ltd* [1991] 2 Lloyd's Rep. 625, held that an agreement in parallel New York legal proceedings prior to award that any proceedings to confirm or vacate arbitration will be brought in New York did not constitute a ground within s.5(2)(f) of the Arbitration Act 1975 (now s.103(2)(f)) to refuse enforcement nor was it a precondition to enforcement that there should be assets within the jurisdiction.

In *Omnium de Traitement et de Valorisation SA v. Hilmarton Ltd* [1999] 2 Lloyd's Rep. 222 (ICC arbitration where proper law of contract was Swiss law and curial seat of arbitration was the Canton of Geneva in a matter involving a business practice unlawful under Algerian law but involving no bribery or corruption and lawful under Swiss law) the Court said that it was not adjudicating upon the underlying contract but deciding whether or not an arbitration award should be enforced in England and that in such context it seemed "that (absent a finding of fact of corrupt practices which would give rise to obvious public policy considerations) the fact that English law would or might have arrived at a different result is nothing to the point. Indeed the reason for the different result is that Swiss law is different from English law, and the parties chose Swiss law and Swiss arbitration. If anything, this consideration dictates (as a matter of policy of the upholding of international arbitral awards) that the award should be enforced."

Subs.(5)

2E-332   On an application to adjourn an application for leave to enforce a foreign arbitration award because of a legal challenge to the validity of the award in a foreign jurisdiction, the Court should consider the strength or otherwise of the argument for setting aside the award and the ease or difficulty of enforcing the award if an order for security was not made, together with any other relevant considerations (*Soleh Boneh International Ltd v. Government of the Republic of Uganda* [1993] 2 Lloyd's Rep. 208).

Saving for other bases of recognition or enforcement

2E-333   **104.** Nothing in the preceding provisions of this Part affects any right to rely upon or enforce a New York Convention award at common law or under section 66.

2E-334   *Note*—Compare s.6 of the 1975 Act.

PART IV

GENERAL PROVISIONS

Meaning of "the court": jurisdiction of High Court and county court

2E-335   **105.**—(1) In this Act "the court" means the High Court or a county court, subject to the following provisions.

(2) The Lord Chancellor may by order make provision—

(a) allocating proceedings under this Act to the High Court or to county courts; or

(b) specifying proceedings under this Act which may be commenced or taken only in the High Court or in a county court.

(3) The Lord Chancellor may by order make provision requiring

proceedings of any specified description under this Act in relation to which a county court has jurisdiction to be commenced or taken in one or more specified county courts.

Any jurisdiction so exercisable by a specified county court is exercisable throughout England and Wales or, as the case may be, Northern Ireland.

(4) An order under this section—

    (a) may differentiate between categories of proceedings by reference to such criteria as the Lord Chancellor sees fit to specify, and

    (b) may make such incidental or transitional provision as the Lord Chancellor considers necessary or expedient.

(5) An order under this section for England and Wales shall be made by statutory instrument which shall be subject to annulment in pursuance of a resolution of either House of Parliament.

(6) An order under this section for Northern Ireland shall be a statutory rule for the purposes of the Statutory Rules (Northern Ireland) Order 1979 which shall be subject to annulment in pursuance of a resolution of either House of Parliament in like manner as a statutory instrument and section 5 of the Statutory Instruments Act 1946 shall apply accordingly.

Note—The proceedings under the Act have been allocated by the High Court and County Courts (Allocation of Arbitration Proceedings) Order 1996 (S.I. 1996 No. 3215) at para. 2E–248. **2E–336**

Crown application

106.—(1) Part I of this Act applies to any arbitration agreement to which Her Majesty, either in right of the Crown or of the Duchy of Lancaster or otherwise, or the Duke of Cornwall, is a party. **2E–337**

(2) Where Her Majesty is party to an arbitration agreement otherwise than in right of the Crown. Her Majesty shall be represented for the purposes of any arbitral proceedings—

    (a) where the agreement was entered into by Her Majesty in right of the Duchy of Lancaster, by the Chancellor of the Duchy or such person as he may appoint, and

    (b) in any other case, by such person as Her Majesty may appoint in writing under the Royal Sign Manual.

(3) Where the Duke of Cornwall is party to an arbitration agreement, he shall be represented for the purposes of any arbitral proceedings by such person as he may appoint.

(4) References in Part I to a party or the parties to the arbitration agreement or to arbitral proceedings shall be construed, where subsection (2) or (3) applies, as references to the person representing Her Majesty or the Duke of Cornwall.

Note—Compare s.30 of the 1950 Act. **2E–338**

Consequential amendments and repeals

107.—(1) The enactments specified in Schedule 3 are amended in accordance with that Schedule, the amendments being consequential on the provisions of this Act. **2E–339**

(2) The enactments specified in Schedule 4 are repealed to the extent specified.

Extent

2E–340 **108.**—(1) The provisions of this Act extend to England and Wales and, except as mentioned below, to Northern Ireland.

(2) The following provisions of Part II do not extend to Northern Ireland—

section 92 (exclusion of Part I in relation to small claims arbitration in the county court), and

section 93 and Schedule 2 (appointment of judges as arbitrators).

(3) Sections 89, 90 and 91 (consumer arbitration agreements) extend to Scotland and the provisions of Schedules 3 and 4 (consequential amendments and repeals) extend to Scotland so far as they relate to enactments which so extend, subject as follows.

(4) The repeal of the Arbitration Act 1975 extends only to England and Wales and Northern Ireland.

2E–341 *Note* —Compare s.34 of the 1950 Act, s.8(4) of the 1975 Act, and s.8(4) of the 1979 Act.

Commencement

2E–342 **109.**—(1) The provisions of this Act come into force on such day as the Secretary of State may appoint by order made by statutory instrument, and different days may be appointed for different purposes.

(2) An order under subsection (1) may contain such transitional provisions as appear to the Secretary of State to be appropriate.

Short title

2E–343 **110.** This Act may be cited as the Arbitration Act 1996.

SCHEDULES

SECTION 4(1)   SCHEDULE 1

MANDATORY PROVISIONS OF PART I

2E–344
    sections 9 to 11 (stay of legal proceedings);

    section 12 (power of court to extend agreed time limits);

    section 13 (application of Limitation Acts);

    section 24 (power of court to remove arbitrator);

    section 26(1) (effect of death of arbitrator);

    section 28 (liability of parties for fees and expenses of arbitrators);

    section 29 (immunity of arbitrator);

    section 31 (objection to substantive jurisdiction of tribunal);

    section 32 (determination of preliminary point of jurisdiction);

    section 33 (general duty of tribunal);

    section 37(2) (items to be treated as expenses of arbitrators);

    section 40 (general duty of parties);

    section 43 (securing the attendance of witnesses);

    section 56 (power to withhold award in case of non-payment);

    section 60 (effectiveness of agreement for payment of costs in any event);

    section 66 (enforcement of award);

    sections 67 and 68 (challenging the award: substantive jurisdiction and serious irregularity), and sections 70 and 71 (supplementary provisions; effect of order of court) so far as relating to those sections;

section 72 (saving for rights of person who takes no part in proceedings);

section 73 (loss of right to object);

section 74 (immunity of arbitral institutions, etc.);

section 75 (charge to secure payment of solicitors' costs).

SECTION 93(6)   # SCHEDULE 2

MODIFICATIONS OF PART I IN RELATION TO JUDGE-ARBITRATORS

Introductory

1. In this Schedule "judge-arbitrator" means a judge of the Commercial Court **2E–345** or official referee appointed as arbitrator or umpire under section 93.

General

2.—(1) Subject to the following provisions of this Schedule, references in Part I to the court shall be construed in relation to a judge-arbitrator, or in relation to the appointment of a judge-arbitrator, as references to the Court of Appeal.

(2) The references in sections 32(6), 45(6) and 69(8) to the Court of Appeal shall in such a case be construed as references to the *Supreme Court*.

Arbitrator's fees

3.—(1) The power of the court in section 28(2) to order consideration and adjustment of the liability of a party for the fees of an arbitrator may be exercised by a judge-arbitrator.

(2) Any such exercise of the power is subject to the powers of the Court of Appeal under sections 24(4) and 25(3)(b) (directions as to entitlement to fees or expenses in case of removal or resignation).

Exercise of court powers in support of arbitration

4.—(1) Where the arbitral tribunal consists of or includes a judge-arbitrator the powers of the court under sections 42 to 44 (enforcement of peremptory orders, summoning witnesses, and other court powers) are exercisable by the High Court and also by the judge-arbitrator himself.

(2) Anything done by a judge-arbitrator in the exercise of those powers shall be regarded as done by him in his capacity as judge of the High Court and have effect as if done by that court.Nothing in this sub-paragraph prejudices any power vested in him as arbitrator or umpire.

Extension of time for making award

5.—(1) The power conferred by section 50 (extension of time for making award) is exercisable by the judge-arbitrator himself.

(2) Any appeal from a decision of a judge-arbitrator under that section lies to the Court of Appeal with the leave of that court.

Withholding award in case of non-payment

6.—(1) The provisions of paragraph 7 apply in place of the provisions of section 56 (power to withhold award in the case of non-payment) in relation to the withholding of an award for non-payment of the fees and expenses of a judge-arbitrator.

(2) This does not affect the application of section 56 in relation to the delivery of such an award by an arbitral or other institution or person vested by the parties with powers in relation to the delivery of the award.

7.—(1) A judge-arbitrator may refuse to deliver an award except upon payment of the fees and expenses mentioned in section 56(1).

(2) The judge-arbitrator may, on an application by a party to the arbitral proceedings, order that if he pays into the High Court the fees and expenses demanded, or such lesser amount as the judge-arbitrator may specify—

    (a) the award shall be delivered,

    (b) the amount of the fees and expenses properly payable shall be determined by such means and upon such terms as he may direct, and

    (c) out of the money paid into court there shall be paid out such fees and expenses as may be found to be properly payable and the balance of the money (if any) shall be paid out to the applicant.

(3) For this purpose the amount of fees and expenses properly payable is the amount the applicant is liable to pay under section 28 or any agreement relating to the payment of the arbitrator.

(4) No application to the judge-arbitrator under this paragraph may be made where there is any available arbitral process for appeal or review of the amount of the fees or expenses demanded.

(5) Any appeal from a decision of a judge-arbitrator under this paragraph lies to the Court of Appeal with the leave of that court.

(6) Where a party to arbitral proceedings appeals under sub-paragraph (5), an arbitrator is entitled to appear and be heard.

Correction of award or additional award

8. Subsections (4) to (6) of section 57 (correction of award or additional award: time limit for application or exercise of power) do not apply to a judge-arbitrator.

Costs

9. Where the arbitral tribunal consists of or includes a judge-arbitrator the powers of the court under section 63(4) (determination of recoverable costs) shall be exercised by the High Court.

10.—(1) The power of the court under section 64 to determine an arbitrator's reasonable fees and expenses may be exercised by a judge-arbitrator.

(2) Any such exercise of the power is subject to the powers of the Court of Appeal under sections 24(2) and 25(3)(b) (directions as to entitlement to fees or expenses in case of removal or resignation).

Enforcement of award

11. The leave of the court required by section 66 (enforcement of award) may in the case of an award of a judge-arbitrator be given by the judge-arbitrator himself.

Solicitors' costs

12. The powers of the court to make declarations and orders under the provisions applied by section 75 (power to charge property recovered in arbitral proceedings with the payment of solicitors' costs) may be exercised by the judge-arbitrator.

Powers of court in relation to service of documents

13.—(1) The power of the court under section 77(2) (powers of court in relation to service of documents) is exercisable by the judge-arbitrator.

(2) Any appeal from a decision of a judge-arbitrator under that section lies to the Court of Appeal with the leave of that court.

Powers of court to extend time limits relating to arbitral proceedings

14.—(1) The power conferred by section 79 (power of court to extend time limits relating to arbitral proceedings) is exercisable by the judge-arbitrator himself.

(2) Any appeal from a decision of a judge-arbitrator under that section lies to the Court of Appeal with the leave of that court.

2E–345.1   *Note* —Words underlined prospectively repealed and words in square brackets and italics substituted by the Constitutional Reform Act 2005, s.40, Sch.9, para.60, with effect from a date to be appointed.

SECTION 107(1)   # SCHEDULE 3

CONSEQUENTIAL AMENDMENTS

Merchant Shipping Act 1894 (c. 60)

2E–346   1. In section 496 of the Merchant Shipping Act 1894 (provisions as to deposits by owners of goods), after subsection (4) insert—

"(5) In subsection (3) the expression "legal proceedings" includes arbitral proceedings and as respects England and Wales and Northern Ireland the provisions of section 14 of the Arbitration Act 1996 apply to determine when such proceedings are commenced."

Stannaries Court (Abolition) Act 1896 (c. 45)

2. In section 4(1) of the Stannaries Court (Abolition) Act 1896 (references of certain disputes to arbitration), for the words from "tried before" to "any such reference" substitute "referred to arbitration before himself or before an arbitrator agreed on by the parties or an officer of the court".

Tithe Act 1936 (c. 43)

3. [...].

Education Act 1944 (c. 31)

4. [...].

Commonwealth Telegraphs Act 1949 (c. 39)

5. In section 8(2) of the Commonwealth Telegraphs Act 1949 (proceedings of referees under the Act) for "the Arbitration Acts 1889 to 1934, or the Arbitration Act (Northern Ireland) 1937," substitute "Part I of the Arbitration Act 1996".

Lands Tribunal Act 1949 (c. 42)

6. In section 3 of the Lands Tribunal Act 1949 (proceedings before the Lands Tribunal)—

(a) in subsection (6)(c) (procedural rules: power to apply Arbitration Acts), and

(b) in subsection (8) (exclusion of Arbitration Acts except as applied by rules),for "the Arbitration Acts 1889 to 1934" substitute "Part I of the Arbitration Act 1996".

Wireless Telegraphy Act 1949 (c. 54)

7. [...].

Patents Act 1949 (c. 87)

8. In section 67 of the Patents Act 1949 (proceedings as to infringement of pre-1978 patents referred to comptroller), for "The Arbitration Acts 1889 to 1934" substitute " Part I of the Arbitration Act 1996".

National Health Service (Amendment) Act 1949 (c. 93)

9. In section 7(8) of the National Health Service (Amendment) Act 1949 (arbitration in relation to hardship arising from the National Health Service Act 1946 or the Act), for "the Arbitration Acts 1889 to 1934" substitute "Part I of the Arbitration Act 1996" and for "the said Acts" substitute "Part I of that Act".

Arbitration Act 1950 (c. 27)

10. In section 36(1) of the Arbitration Act 1950 (effect of foreign awards enforceable under Part II of that Act) for "section 26 of this Act" substitute "section 66 of the Arbitration Act 1996".

Interpretation Act (Northern Ireland) 1954 (c. 33 (N.I.))

11. In section 46(2) of the Interpretation Act (Northern Ireland) 1954 (miscellaneous definitions), for the definition of "arbitrator" substitute—

""arbitrator" has the same meaning as in Part I of the Arbitration Act 1996;".

Agricultural Marketing Act 1958 (c. 47)

12. In section 12(1) of the Agricultural Marketing Act 1958 (application of provisions of Arbitration Act 1950)—

(a) for the words from the beginning to "shall apply" substitute "Sections 45 and 69 of the Arbitration Act 1996 (which relate to the determination by the court of questions of law) and section 66 of that Act (enforcement of awards) apply"; and

(b) for "an arbitration" substitute "arbitral proceedings".

Carriage by Air Act 1961 (c. 27)

13.—(1) The Carriage by Air Act 1961 is amended as follows.

(2) In section 5(3) (time for bringing proceedings)—

(a) for "an arbitration" in the first place where it occurs substitute "arbitral proceedings"; and

(b) for the words from "and subsections (3) and (4)" to the end substitute "and the provisions of section 14 of the Arbitration Act 1996 apply to determine when such proceedings are commenced.".

(3) In section 11(c) (application of section 5 to Scotland)—

(a) for "subsections (3) and (4)" substitute "the provisions of section 14 of the Arbitration Act 1996"; and

(b) for "an arbitration" substitute "arbitral proceedings".

Factories Act 1961 (c. 34)

14. In the Factories Act 1961, for section 171 (application of Arbitration Act 1950), substitute—

Application of the Arbitration Act 1996

"171. Part I of the Arbitration Act 1996 does not apply to proceedings under this Act except in so far as it may be applied by regulations made under this Act.".

Clergy Pensions Measure 1961 (No. 3)

15. In the Clergy Pensions Measure 1961, section 38(4) (determination of questions), for the words "The Arbitration Act 1950" substitute "Part I of the Arbitration Act 1996".

Transport Act 1962 (c. 46)

16.—(1) The Transport Act 1962 is amended as follows.

(2) In section 74(6)(f) (proceedings before referees in pension disputes), for the words "the Arbitration Act 1950" substitute "Part I of the Arbitration Act 1996".

(3) In section 81(7) (proceedings before referees in compensation disputes), for the words "the Arbitration Act 1950" substitute "Part I of the Arbitration Act 1996".

(4) In Schedule 7, Part IV (pensions), in paragraph 17(5) for the words "the Arbitration Act 1950" substitute "Part I of the Arbitration Act 1996".

Corn Rents Act 1963 (c. 14)

17. In the Corn Rents Act 1963, section 1(5) (schemes for apportioning corn rents, etc.), for the words "the Arbitration Act 1950" substitute "Part I of the Arbitration Act 1996".

Plant Varieties and Seeds Act 1964 (c. 14)

18. [...].

Lands Tribunal and Compensation Act (Northern Ireland) 1964 (c. 29 (N.I.))

19. In section 9 of the Lands Tribunal and Compensation Act (Northern Ireland) 1964 (proceedings of Lands Tribunal), in subsection (3) (where Tribunal acts as arbitrator) for "the Arbitration Act (Northern Ireland) 1937" substitute "Part I of the Arbitration Act 1996".

Industrial and Provident Societies Act 1965 (c. 12)

20.—(1) Section 60 of the Industrial and Provident Societies Act 1965 is amended as follows.

(2) In subsection (8) (procedure for hearing disputes between society and member, etc.)—

(a) in paragraph (a) for "the Arbitration Act 1950" substitute "Part I of the Arbitration Act 1996"; and

(b) in paragraph (b) omit "by virtue of section 12 of the said Act of 1950".

(3) For subsection (9) substitute—

"(9) The court or registrar to whom any dispute is referred under subsections (2) to (7) may at the request of either party state a case on any question of law arising in the dispute for the opinion of the High Court or, as the case may be, the Court of Session.".

Carriage of Goods by Road Act 1965 (c. 37)

21. In section 7(2) of the Carriage of Goods by Road Act 1965 (arbitrations: time at which deemed to commence), for paragraphs (a) and (b) substitute—

> "(a) as respects England and Wales and Northern Ireland, the provisions of section 14(3) to (5) of the Arbitration Act 1996 (which determine the time at which an arbitration is commenced) apply;".

Factories Act (Northern Ireland) 1965 (c. 20 (N.I.))

22. In section 171 of the Factories Act (Northern Ireland) 1965 (application of Arbitration Act), for "The Arbitration Act (Northern Ireland) 1937" substitute "Part I of the Arbitration Act 1996".

Commonwealth Secretariat Act 1966 (c. 10)

23. In section 1(3) of the Commonwealth Secretariat Act 1966 (contracts with Commonwealth Secretariat to be deemed to contain provision for arbitration), for "the Arbitration Act 1950 and the Arbitration Act (Northern Ireland) 1937" substitute "Part I of the Arbitration Act 1996".

Arbitration (International Investment Disputes) Act 1966 (c. 41)

24. In the Arbitration (International Investment Disputes) Act 1966, for section 3 (application of Arbitration Act 1950 and other enactments) substitute—

"Application of provisions of Arbitration Act 1996

3.—(1) The Lord Chancellor may by order direct that any of the provisions contained in sections 36 and 38 to 44 of the Arbitration Act 1996 (provisions concerning the conduct of arbitral proceedings, etc.) shall apply to such proceedings pursuant to the Convention as are specified in the order with or without any modifications or exceptions specified in the order.

(2) Subject to subsection (1), the Arbitration Act 1996 shall not apply to proceedings pursuant to the Convention, but this subsection shall not be taken as affecting section 9 of that Act (stay of legal proceedings in respect of matter subject to arbitration).

(3) An order made under this section—
> (a) may be varied or revoked by a subsequent order so made, and
> (b) shall be contained in a statutory instrument.".

Poultry Improvement Act (Northern Ireland) 1968 (c. 12 (N.I.))

25. In paragraph 10(4) of the Schedule to the Poultry Improvement Act (Northern Ireland) 1968 (reference of disputes), for "The Arbitration Act (Northern Ireland) 1937" substitute "Part I of the Arbitration Act 1996".

Industrial and Provident Societies Act (Northern Ireland) 1969 (c. 24 (N.I.))

26.—(1) Section 69 of the Industrial and Provident Societies Act (Northern Ireland) 1969 (decision of disputes) is amended as follows.

(2) In subsection (7) (decision of disputes)—
> (a) in the opening words, omit the words from "and without prejudice" to "1937";
> (b) at the beginning of paragraph (a) insert "without prejudice to any powers exercisable by virtue of Part I of the Arbitration Act 1996,"; and
> (c) in paragraph (b) omit "the registrar or" and "registrar or" and for the words from "as might have been granted by the High Court" to the end substitute "as might be granted by the registrar".

(3) For subsection (8) substitute—

> "(8) The court or registrar to whom any dispute is referred under subsections (2) to (6) may at the request of either party state a case on any question of law arising in the dispute for the opinion of the High Court.".

Health and Personal Social Services (Northern Ireland) Order 1972 (N.I.14)

27. In Article 105(6) of the Health and Personal Social Services (Northern Ireland) Order 1972 (arbitrations under the Order), for "the Arbitration Act (Northern Ireland) 1937" substitute "Part I of the Arbitration Act 1996".

Consumer Credit Act 1974 (c. 39)

28.—(1) Section 146 of the Consumer Credit Act 1974 is amended as follows.

(2) In subsection (2) (solicitor engaged in contentious business), for " section 86(1) of the Solicitors Act 1957" substitute " section 87(1) of the Solicitors Act 1974".

(3) In subsection (4) (solicitor in Northern Ireland engaged in contentious business), for the words from "business done" to "Administration of Estates (Northern Ireland) Order 1979" substitute "contentious business (as defined in Article 3(2) of the Solicitors (Northern Ireland) Order 1976".

Friendly Societies Act 1974 (c. 46)

29.—(1) The Friendly Societies Act 1974 is amended as follows.

(2) For section 78(1) (statement of case) substitute—

"(1) Any arbitrator, arbiter or umpire to whom a dispute falling within section 76 above is referred under the rules of a registered society or branch may at the request of either party state a case on any question of law arising in the dispute for the opinion of the High Court or, as the case may be, the Court of Session.".

(3) In section 83(3) (procedure on objections to amalgamations etc. of friendly societies), for "the Arbitration Act 1950 or, in Northern Ireland, the Arbitration Act (Northern Ireland) 1937" substitute "Part I of the Arbitration Act 1996".

Industry Act 1975 (c. 68)

30. In Schedule 3 to the Industry Act (arbitration of disputes relating to vesting and compensation orders), in paragraph 14 (application of certain provisions of Arbitration Acts)—

    (a) for "the Arbitration Act 1950 or, in Northern Ireland, the Arbitration Act (Northern Ireland) 1937" substitute "Part I of the Arbitration Act 1996", and

    (b) for "that Act" substitute "that Part".

Industrial Relations (Northern Ireland) Order 1976 (N.I.16)

31. In Article 59(9) of the Industrial Relations (Northern Ireland) Order 1976 (proceedings of industrial tribunal), for "The Arbitration Act (Northern Ireland) 1937" substitute "Part I of the Arbitration Act 1996".

Aircraft and Shipbuilding Industries Act 1977 (c. 3)

32. In Schedule 7 to the Aircraft and Shipbuilding Industries Act 1977 (procedure of Arbitration Tribunal), in paragraph 2—

    (a) for "the Arbitration Act 1950 or, in Northern Ireland, the Arbitration Act (Northern Ireland) 1937" substitute " Part I of the Arbitration Act 1996", and

    (b) for "that Act" substitute "that Part".

Patents Act 1977 (c. 37)

33. In section 130 of the Patents Act 1977 (interpretation), in subsection (8) (exclusion of Arbitration Act) for "The Arbitration Act 1950" substitute "Part I of the Arbitration Act 1996".

Judicature (Northern Ireland) Act 1978 (c. 23)

34.—(1) The Judicature (Northern Ireland) Act 1978 is amended as follows.

(2) In section 35(2) (restrictions on appeals to the Court of Appeal), after paragraph (f) insert—

    (fa) except as provided by Part I of the Arbitration Act 1996, from any decision of the High Court under that Part;".

(3) In section 55(2) (rules of court) after paragraph (c) insert—

    "(cc) providing for any prescribed part of the jurisdiction of the High Court in relation to the trial of any action involving matters of account to be exercised in the prescribed manner by a person agreed by the parties and for the remuneration of any such person;".

Health and Safety at Work (Northern Ireland) Order 1978 (N.I.9)

35. In Schedule 4 to the Health and Safety at Work (Northern Ireland) Order 1978 (licensing provisions), in paragraph 3, for "The Arbitration Act (Northern Ireland) 1937" substitute "Part I of the Arbitration Act 1996".

County Courts (Northern Ireland) Order 1980 (N.I.3)

36.—(1) The County Courts (Northern Ireland) Order 1980 is amended as follows.

(2) In Article 30 (civil jurisdiction exercisable by district judge)—

    (a) for paragraph (2) substitute—

"(2) Any order, decision or determination made by a district judge under this Article (other than one made in dealing with a claim by way of arbitration under paragraph (3)) shall be embodied in a decree which for all purposes (including the right of appeal under Part VI) shall have the like effect as a decree pronounced by a county court judge.";

    (b) for paragraphs (4) and (5) substitute—

"(4) Where in any action to which paragraph (1) applies the claim is dealt with by way of arbitration under paragraph (3)—

    (a) any award made by the district judge in dealing with the claim shall be embodied in a decree which for all purposes (except the right of appeal under Part VI) shall have the like effect as a decree pronounced by a county court judge;

    (b) the district judge may, and shall if so required by the High Court, state for the determination of the High Court any question of law arising out of an award so made;

    (c) except as provided by sub-paragraph (b), any award so made shall be final; and

    (d) except as otherwise provided by county court rules, no costs shall be awarded in connection with the action.

(5) Subject to paragraph (4), county court rules may—

    (a) apply any of the provisions of Part I of the Arbitration Act 1996 to arbitrations under paragraph (3) with such modifications as may be prescribed;

    (b) prescribe the rules of evidence to be followed on any arbitration under paragraph (3) and, in particular, make provision with respect to the manner of taking and questioning evidence.

(5A) Except as provided by virtue of paragraph (5)(a), Part I of the Arbitration Act 1996 shall not apply to an arbitration under paragraph (3)".

(3) After Article 61 insert—

"Appeals from decisions under Part I of Arbitration Act 1996

61A.—(1) Article 61 does not apply to a decision of a county court judge made in the exercise of the jurisdiction conferred by Part I of the Arbitration Act 1996.

(2) Any party dissatisfied with a decision of the county court made in the exercise of the jurisdiction conferred by any of the following provisions of Part I of the Arbitration Act 1996, namely—

    (a) section 32 (question as to substantive jurisdiction of arbitral tribunal);

    (b) section 45 (question of law arising in course of arbitral proceedings);

    (c) section 67 (challenging award of arbitral tribunal: substantive jurisdiction);

    (d) section 68 (challenging award of arbitral tribunal: serious irregularity);

    (e) section 69 (appeal on point of law),

may, subject to the provisions of that Part, appeal from that decision to the Court of Appeal.

(3) Any party dissatisfied with any decision of a county court made in the exercise of the jurisdiction conferred by any other provision of Part I of the Arbitration Act 1996 may, subject to the provisions of that Part, appeal from that decision to the High Court.

(4) The decision of the Court of Appeal on an appeal under paragraph (2) shall be final".

Supreme Court Act 1981 (c. 54)

37.—(1) The Supreme Court Act 1981 is amended as follows.

(2) In section 18(1) (restrictions on appeals to the Court of Appeal), for paragraph (g) substitute—

"(g) except as provided by Part I of the Arbitration Act 1996, from any decision of the High Court under that Part;".

(3) In section 151 (interpretation, etc.), in the definition of "arbitration agreement", for "the Arbitration Act 1950 by virtue of section 32 of that Act;" substitute "Part I of the Arbitration Act 1996;".

Merchant Shipping (Liner Conferences) Act 1982 (c. 37)

38. In section 7(5) of the Merchant Shipping (Liner Conferences) Act 1982 (stay of legal proceedings), for the words from "section 4(1)" to the end substitute "section 9 of the Arbitration Act 1996 (which also provides for the staying of legal proceedings)".

Agricultural Marketing (Northern Ireland) Order 1982 (N.I.12)

39. In Article 14 of the Agricultural Marketing (Northern Ireland) Order 1982 (application of provisions of Arbitration Act (Northern Ireland) 1937)—
    (a) for the words from the beginning to "shall apply" substitute " Section 45 and 69 of the Arbitration Act 1996 (which relate to the determination by the court of questions of law) and section 66 of that Act (enforcement of awards)" apply; and
    (b) for "an arbitration" substitute "arbitral proceedings".

Mental Health Act 1983 (c. 20)

40. In section 78 of the Mental Health Act 1983 (procedure of Mental Health Review Tribunals), in subsection (9) for "The Arbitration Act 1950" substitute "Part I of the Arbitration Act 1996".

Registered Homes Act 1984 (c. 23)

41. [...].

Housing Act 1985 (c. 68)

42. In section 47(3) of the Housing Act 1985 (agreement as to determination of matters relating to service charges) for "section 32 of the Arbitration Act 1950" substitute "Part I of the Arbitration Act 1996".

Landlord and Tenant Act 1985 (c. 70)

43. [...].

Credit Unions (Northern Ireland) Order 1985 (N.I.12)

44.—(1) Article 72 of the Credit Unions (Northern Ireland) Order 1985 (decision of disputes) is amended as follows.

(2) In paragraph (7)—
    (a) in the opening words, omit the words from "and without prejudice" to "1937";
    (b) at the beginning of sub-paragraph (a) insert "without prejudice to any powers exercisable by virtue of Part I of the Arbitration Act 1996,"; and
    (c) in sub-paragraph (b) omit "the registrar or" and "registrar or" and for the words from "as might have been granted by the High Court" to the end substitute "as might be granted by the registrar".

(3) For paragraph (8) substitute—

"(8) The court or registrar to whom any dispute is referred under paragraphs (2) to (6) may at the request of either party state a case on any question of law arising in the dispute for the opinion of the High Court".

Agricultural Holdings Act 1986 (c. 5)

45. In section 84(1) of the Agricultural Holdings Act 1986 (provisions relating to arbitration), for "the Arbitration Act 1950" substitute "Part I of the Arbitration Act 1996".

Insolvency Act 1986 (c. 45)

46. In the Insolvency Act 1986, after section 349 insert—

"Arbitration agreements to which bankrupt is party

349A.—(1) This section applies where a bankrupt had become party to a contract containing an arbitration agreement before the commencement of his bankruptcy.

(2) If the trustee in bankruptcy adopts the contact, the arbitration agreement is enforceable by or against the trustee in relation to matters arising from or connected with the contract.

(3) If the trustee in bankruptcy does not adopt the contract and a matter to which the arbitration agreement applies requires to be determined in connection with or for the purposes of the bankruptcy proceedings—

(a) the trustee with the consent of the creditors' committee, or

(b) any other party to the agreement,

may apply to the court which may, if it thinks fit in all the circumstances of the case, order that the matter be referred to arbitration in accordance with the arbitration agreement.

(4) In this section—

"arbitration agreement" has the same meaning as in Part I of the Arbitration Act 1996; and

"the court" means the court which has jurisdiction in the bankruptcy proceedings".

Building Societies Act 1986 (c. 53)

47. In Part II of Schedule 14 to the Building Societies Act 1986 (settlement of disputes: arbitration), in paragraph 5(6) for "the Arbitration Act 1950 and the Arbitration Act 1979 or, in Northern Ireland, the Arbitration Act (Northern Ireland) 1937" substitute "Part I of the Arbitration Act 1996".

Mental Health (Northern Ireland) Order 1986 (N.I.4)

48. In Article 83 of the Mental Health (Northern Ireland) Order 1986 (procedure of Mental Health Review Tribunal), in paragraph (8) for "The Arbitration Act (Northern Ireland) 1937" substitute "Part I of the Arbitration Act 1996".

Multilateral Investment Guarantee Agency Act 1988 (c. 8)

49. For section 6 of the Multilateral Investment Guarantee Agency Act 1988 (application of Arbitration Act) substitute—

"Application of Arbitration Act

6.—(1) The Lord Chancellor may by order made by statutory instrument direct that any of the provisions of sections 36 and 38 to 44 of the Arbitration Act 1996 (provisions in relation to the conduct of the arbitral proceedings, etc.) apply, with such modifications or exceptions as are specified in the order, to such arbitration proceedings pursuant to Annex II to the Convention as are specified in the order.

(2) Except as provided by an order under subsection (1) above, no provision of Part I of the Arbitration Act 1996 other than section 9 (stay of legal proceedings) applies to any such proceedings".

Copyright, Designs and Patents Act 1988 (c. 48)

50. In section 150 of the Copyright, Designs and Patents Act 1988 (Lord Chancellor's power to make rules for Copyright Tribunal), for subsection (2) substitute—

"(2) The rules may apply in relation to the Tribunal, as respects proceedings in England and Wales or Northern Ireland, any of the provisions of Part I of the Arbitration Act 1996".

Fair Employment (Northern Ireland) Act 1989 (c. 32)

51. [...].

Limitation (Northern Ireland) Order 1989 (N.I.11)

52. In Article 2(2) of the Limitation (Northern Ireland) Order 1989 (interpretation), in the definition of "arbitration agreement", for "the Arbitration Act (Northern Ireland) 1937" substitute "Part I of the Arbitration Act 1996".

Insolvency (Northern Ireland) Order 1989 (N.I.19)

53. In the Insolvency (Northern Ireland) Order 1989, after Article 320 insert—

"Arbitration agreements to which bankrupt is party

320A.—(1) This Article applies where a bankrupt had become party to a contract containing an arbitration agreement before the commencement of his bankruptcy.

(2) If the trustee in bankruptcy adopts the contract, the arbitration agreement is enforceable by or against the trustee in relation to matters arising from or connected with the contract.

(3) If the trustee in bankruptcy does not adopt the contract and a matter to which the arbitration agreement applies requires to be determined in connection with or for the purposes of the bankruptcy proceedings—

(a) the trustee with the consent of the creditors' committee, or

(b) any other party to the agreement,

may apply to the court which may, if it thinks fit in all the circumstances of the case, order that the matter be referred to arbitration in accordance with the arbitration agreement.

(4) In this Article—

"arbitration agreement" has the same meaning as in Part I of the Arbitration Act 1996; and

"the court" means the court which has jurisdiction in the bankruptcy proceedings".

Social Security Administration Act 1992 (c. 5)

54. [...].

Social Security Administration (Northern Ireland) Act 1992 (c. 8)

55. [...].

Trade Union and Labour Relations (Consolidation) Act 1992 (c. 52)

56. In sections 212(5) and 263(6) of the Trade Union and Labour Relations (Consolidation) Act 1992 (application of Arbitration Act) for "the Arbitration Act 1950" substitute "Part I of the Arbitration Act 1996".

Industrial Relations (Northern Ireland) Order 1992 (N.I.5)

57. In Articles 84(9) and 92(5) of the Industrial Relations (Northern Ireland) Order 1992 (application of Arbitration Act) for "The Arbitration Act (Northern Ireland) 1937" substitute "Part I of the Arbitration Act 1996".

Registered Homes (Northern Ireland) Order 1992 (N.I.20)

58. In Article 33(3) of the Registered Homes (Northern Ireland) Order 1992 (procedure of Registered Homes Tribunal) for "The Arbitration Act (Northern Ireland) 1937" substitute "Part I of the Arbitration Act 1996".

Education Act 1993 (c. 35)

59. [...].

Roads (Northern Ireland) Order 1993 (N.I.15)

60.—(1) The Roads (Northern Ireland) Order 1993 is amended as follows.

(2) In Article 131 (application of Arbitration Act) for "the Arbitration Act (Northern Ireland) 1937" substitute "Part I of the Arbitration Act 1996".

(3) In Schedule 4 (disputes), in paragraph 3(2) for "the Arbitration Act (Northern Ireland) 1937" substitute "Part I of the Arbitration Act 1996".

Merchant Shipping Act 1995 (c. 21)

61. In Part II of Schedule 6 to the Merchant Shipping Act 1995 (provisions having effect in connection with Convention Relating to the Carriage of Passengers and Their Luggage by Sea), for paragraph 7 substitute—

"7. Article 16 shall apply to arbitral proceedings as it applies to an action; and, as respects England and Wales and Northern Ireland, the provisions of section 14 of the Arbitration Act 1996 apply to determine for the purposes of that Article when an arbitration is commenced".

Industrial Tribunals Act 1996 (c. 17)

62. In section 6(2) of the Industrial Tribunals Act 1996 (procedure of industrial tribunals), for "The Arbitration Act 1950" substitute "Part I of the Arbitration Act 1996".

Note —Amended by the Education Act 1996, Sched.38, Pt I; the Housing Act 1996, Sched.19, Pt III; the Plant Varieties Act 1997, Sched.4; S.I. 1998 No. 3162 (N.I. 21), art. 105, Sched.5, the Social Security Act 1998 (c. 14), s.86, Sched.8, by S.I. 1998 No. 150 (N.I. 10), art. 78, Sched.7; Communications Act 2003, Sched.19, para.1, subject to transitional provisions specified in (2003, Sched.18, para.13 and S.I. 2003 No. 1900, art.3(1)), Care Standards Act 2000, Sched.6, para.1, and Statute Law (Repeals) Act, s.1(1), Sch.1, Pt I.

SECTION 107(2)

SCHEDULE 4

REPEALS

2E–347

Chapter	Short title	Extent of repeal
1892 c. 43.	Military Lands Act 1892.	In section 21(b), the words "under the Arbitration Act 1889".
1922 c. 51.	Allotments Act 1992.	In section 21(3), the words "under the Arbitration Act 1889".
1937 c. 8 (N.I.)	Arbitration Act (Northern Ireland) 1937.	The whole Act.
1949 c. 54.	Wireless Telegraphy Act 1949.	In Schedule 2, paragraph 3(3).
1949 c. 97.	National Parks and Access to the Countryside Act 1949.	In section 18(4), the words from "Without prejudice"' to "England or Wales".
1950 c. 27.	Arbitration Act 1950.	Part I. Section 42(3).
1958 c. 47.	Agricultural Marketing Act 1958.	Section 53(8).
1962 c. 46.	Transport Act 1962.	In Schedule 11, Part II, paragraph 7.
1964 c. 14.	Plant Varieties and Seeds Act 1964.	In section 10(4) the words from "or in section 9" to "three arbitrators)". Section 39(3)(b)(i).
1964 c. 29 (N.I.).	Lands Tribunal and Compensation Act (Northern Ireland) 1964.	In section 9(3) the words from "so, however, that" to the end.
1965 c. 12.	Industrial and Provident Societies Act 1965.	In section 60(8)(b), the words "by virtue of section 12 of the said Act of 1950".
1965 c. 37.	Carriage of Goods by Road Act 1965.	Section 7(2)(b).
1965 c. 13 (N.I.).	New Towns Act (Northern Ireland) 1965.	In section 27(2), the words from "under and in accordance with" to the end.

1969 c. 24 (N.I.)	Industrial and Provident Societies Act (Northern Ireland) 1969.	In section 69(7)— (a) in the opening words, the words from "and without prejudice" to "1937"; (b) in paragraph (b), the words "the registrar or" and "registrar or".
1970 c. 31.	Administration of Justice Act 1970.	Section 4. Schedule 3.
1973 c. 41.	Fair Trading Act 1973.	Section 33(2)(d).
1973 N.I. 1.	Drainage (Northern Ireland) Order 1973.	In Article 15(4), the words from "under and in accordance" to the end. Article 40(4). In Schedule 7, in paragraph 9(2), the words from "under and in accordance" to the end.
1974 c. 47.	Solicitors Act 1974.	In section 87(1), in the definition of "contentious business", the words "appointed under the Arbitration Act 1950".
1975 c. 3.	Arbitration Act 1975.	The whole Act.
1975 c. 74.	Petroleum and Submarine Pipe-Lines Act 1975.	In Part II of Schedule 2— (a) in model clause 40(2), the words "in accordance with the Arbitration Act 1950"; (b) in model clause 40(2B), the words "in accordance with the Arbitration Act (Northern Ireland) 1937". In Part II of Schedule 3, in model clause 38(2) the words "in accordance with the Arbitration Act 1950".
1976 N.I. 12.	Solicitors (Northern Ireland) Order 1976.	In Article 3(2), in the entry "contentious business", the words "appointed under the Arbitration Act (Northern Ireland) 1937". Article 71H(3).

552

1977 c. 37.	Patents Act 1977.	In section 52(4) the words " section 21 of the Arbitration Act 1950 or, as the case may be, section 22 of the Arbitration Act (Northern Ireland) 1937 (statement of cases by arbitrators); but". Section 131(e).
1977 c. 38.	Administration of Justice Act 1977.	Section 17(2).
1978 c. 23.	Judicature (Northern Ireland) Act 1978.	In section 35(2), paragraph (g)(v). In Schedule 5, the amendment to the Arbitration Act 1950.
1979 c. 42.	Arbitration Act 1979.	The whole Act.
1980 c. 58.	Limitation Act 1980.	Section 34.
1980 N.I. 3.	County Courts (Northern Ireland) Order 1980.	Article 31(3).
1981 c. 54.	Supreme Court Act 1981.	Section 148.
1982 c. 27.	Civil Jurisdiction and Judgments Act 1982.	Section 25(3)(c) and (5). In section 26— (a) in subsection (1), the words "to arbitration or"; (b) in subsection (1)(a)(i), the words "arbitration or"; (c) in subsection (2), the words "arbitration or".
1928 c. 53.	Administration of Justice Act 1982.	Section 15(6). In Schedule 1, Part IV.
1984 c. 5.	Merchant Shipping Act 1984.	Section 4(8).
1984 c. 12.	Telecommunications Act 1984.	Schedule 2, paragraph 13(8).
1984 c. 16.	Foreign Limitation Periods Act 1984.	Section 5.
1984 c. 28	County Courts Act 1984.	In Schedule 2, paragraph 70.
1985 c. 61.	Administration of Justice Act 1985.	Section 58. In Schedule 9, paragraph 15.
1985 c. 68.	Housing Act 1985.	In Schedule 18, in paragraph 6(2) the words from "and the Arbitration Act 1950" to the end.
1985 N.I. 12.	Credit Unions (Northern Ireland) Order 1985.	In Article 72(7)— (a) in the opening words, the words from "and without prejudice" to "1937"; (b) in sub-paragraph (b), the words "the registrar or" and "registrar or".

1986 c. 45.	Insolvency Act 1986.	In Schedule 14, the entry relating to the Arbitration Act 1950.
1988 c. 8.	Multilateral Investment Guarantee Agency Act 1988.	Section 8(3).
1988 c. 21.	Consumer Arbitration Agreements Act 1988.	The whole Act.
1989 N.I. 11.	Limitation (Northern Ireland) Order 1989.	Article 72. In Schedule 3, paragraph 1.
1989 N.I. 19.	Insolvency (Northern Ireland) Order 1989.	In Part II of Schedule 9, paragraph 66.
1990 c. 41.	Courts and Legal Services Act 1990.	Sections 99 and 101 to 103.
1991 N.I. 7.	Food Safety (Northern Ireland) Order 1991.	In Articles 8(8) and 11(10) the words from "and the provisions" to the end.
1992 c. 40.	Friendly Societies Act 1992.	In Schedule 16, paragraph 30(1).
1995 c. 8.	Agricultural Tenancies Act 1995.	Section 28(4).
1995 c. 21.	Merchant Shipping Act 1995.	Section 96(10). Section 264(9).
1995 c. 42.	Private International Law (Miscellaneous Provisions) Act 1995.	Section 3.

High Court and County Courts (Allocation of Arbitration Proceedings) Order 1996

(S.I. 1996 No. 3215)

The Lord Chancellor, in exercise of the powers conferred on him by section 105 of the Arbitration Act 1996, hereby makes the following Order:—

2E–348 **1.**—(1) This Order may be cited as the High Court and County Courts (Allocation of Arbitration Proceedings) Order 1996 and shall come into force on 31st January 1997.

(2) In this Order, "the Act" means the Arbitration Act 1996.

2E–349 **2.** Subject to articles 3 to 5, proceedings under the Act shall be commenced and taken in the High Court.

2E–350 **3.** Proceedings under section 9 of the Act (stay of legal proceedings) shall be commenced in the court in which the legal proceedings are pending.

2E–351 **4.** Proceedings under sections 66 and 101(2) (enforcement of awards) of the Act may be commenced in any county court.

2E–352 **5.**—(1) Proceedings under the Act may be commenced and taken in the Central London County Court Mercantile List.

(2) Where, in exercise of the powers conferred by sections 41 and 42 of the County Courts Act 1984(b) the High Court or the judge in charge of the Central London County Court Mercantile List orders the transfer of proceedings under the Act which were commenced in the Central London County Court Mercantile List to the High Court, those proceedings shall be taken in the High Court.

(3) Where, in exercise of its powers under section 40(2) of the County Courts Act 1984(c) the High Court orders the transfer of proceedings under the Act which were commenced in the High Court to the Central London County Court Mercantile List, those proceedings shall be taken in the Central London County Court Mercantile List.

(4) In exercising the powers referred to in paragraphs (2) and (3) regard shall be had to the following criteria—

(a) the financial substance of the dispute referred to arbitration, including the value of any claim or counterclaim;

(b) the nature of the dispute referred to arbitration (for example, whether it arises out of a commercial or business transaction or relates to engineering, building or other construction work);

(c) whether the proceedings are otherwise important and, in particular, whether they raise questions of importance to persons who are not parties and

(d) the balance of convenience points to having the proceedings taken in the Central London County Court Mercantile List,

and, where the financial substance of the dispute exceeds £200,000, the proceedings shall be taken in the High Court unless the proceedings do not raise questions of general importance to persons who are not parties.

(5) The value of any claim or counterclaim shall be calculated in accordance with rule 16.3(6) of the Civil Procedure Rules 1998.

(6) In this article "the Central London County Court Mercantile List" means the Mercantile Court established at the Central London County Court pursuant to Part 59 of the Civil Procedure Rules 1998.

6. Nothing in this Order shall prevent the judge in charge of the **2E–353** commercial list (within the meaning of section 62(3) of the Supreme Court Act 1981) from transferring proceedings under the Act to another list, court or Division of the High Court to which he has power to transfer proceedings and, where such an order is made, the proceedings may be taken in that list, court or Division as the case may be.

Note —As amended by The High Court and County Courts (Allocation of Arbitration Proceedings) (Amendment) Order 1999 (S.I. 1999 No. 1010) and the Civil Procedure (Modification of Enactments) Order 2002.

Note —Throughout the Arbitration Act 1996, references to "the court" mean the **2E–354** High Court or a county court, but the jurisdiction of the two levels of court is not concurrent. By this Order, by exercise of powers under s.105, "proceedings under the Act" are allocated to the High Court and the county courts and proceedings which may be commenced or taken only in the High Court or in a county court are specified. The general rule stated in art.5 is that proceedings under the Act shall be commenced and taken in the High Court, however, in certain circumstances, such proceedings may be commenced and taken in the Central London County Court Mercantile List. This general rule is qualified by arts 3 and 4. It should also be noted that the High Court and County Courts Jurisdiction Order 1991, art.2(1)(c) provides that the county courts (as well as the High Court) shall have jurisdiction under s.26 of the Arbitration Act 1950. Where proceedings are transferred from the High Court to the Central London County Court Mercantile List or *vice versa*, regard must be had to the criteria in art.5(4). Where the financial substance of the dispute exceeds £200,000, the proceedings shall be taken in the High Court unless the proceedings do not raise questions of general importance to persons who are not parties. See also Pt 62 Arbitration Claims, r.62.1(3) and the Practice Direction–Arbitration, para. 2, which is to be read in conjunction with this Order.

2F INTELLECTUAL PROPERTY PROCEEDINGS

PART 63—PATENTS AND OTHER INTELLECTUAL PROPERTY CLAIMS AND THE PRACTICE DIRECTION—PATENTS AND INTELLECTUAL PROPERTY CLAIMS

Contents

Editorial Introduction

These Rules insert into the Civil Procedure Rules 1998, as Part 63, new rules **2F–1** governing the procedure for intellectual property rights, in particular patents, registered designs and registered trade marks. They also apply to unregistered intellectual property rights, and in particular copyright, design right and passing off cases. They supersede the rules in Practice Direction 49E. This part and its supplementing Practice Direction do not provide a complete guide for intellectual property proceedings. They should be read in conjunction with other Civil Procedure Rules. The application of the other Civil Procedure Rules and their practice directions is subject to the provisions of this practice direction.

Related Sources

- The Patents Court Guide, available on the Court Service website: **2F–2** www.courtservice.gov.uk, along with the Patents Court Diary.

Scope of this Part and interpretation[1]

2F–3   63.1—(1) This Part applies to all intellectual property claims including—

    (a) registered intellectual property rights such as—

        (i) patents;

        (ii) registered designs; and

        (iii) registered trade marks; and

    (b) unregistered intellectual property rights such as—

        (i) copyright;

        (ii) design right;

        (iii) the right to prevent passing off; and

        (iv) the other rights set out in the practice direction.

    (2) In this Part—

    (a) "the 1977 Act" means the Patents Act 1977[2];

    (b) "the 1988 Act" means the Copyright, Designs and Patents Act 1988[3];

    (c) "the 1994 Act" means the Trade Marks Act 1994[4];

    (d) "the Comptroller" means the Comptroller General of Patents, Designs and Trade Marks;

    (e) "patent" means a patent under the 1977 Act and includes any application for a patent or supplementary protection certificate granted under—

        (i) the Patents (Supplementary Protection Certificates) Rules 1997[5] ;

        (ii) the Patents (Supplementary Protection Certificate for Medicinal Products) Regulations 1992[6] ; and

        (iii) the Patents (Supplementary Protection Certificate for Plant Protection Products) Regulations 1996[7] ;

    (f) "Patents Court" means the Patents Court of the High Court constituted as part of the Chancery Division by section 6(1) of the Supreme Court Act 1981[8];

    (g) "Patents County Court" means a county court designated as a Patents County Court under section 287(1) of the 1988 Act;

    (gg) "patents judge" means a person nominated under section 291(1) of the 1988 Act as the patents judge of a patents county court[9];

    (h) "the register" means whichever of the following registers is appropriate—

---

[1] Amended by Civil Procedure (Amendment No. 4) Rules 2005 (S.I. 2005 No. 3515).

[2] 1977 c.37.

[3] 1988 c.48.

[4] 1994 c.26.

[5] S.I. 1997 No. 64.

[6] S.I. 1992 No. 3091.

[7] S.I. 1996 No. 3120.

[8] 1981 c.54.

[9] S.I. 2005 No. 2292.

(i) **patents maintained by the Comptroller under section 32 of the 1977 Act**

(ii) **designs maintained by the registrar under section 17 of the Registered Designs Act 1949**[1] **;**

(iii) **trade marks maintained by the registrar under section 63 of the 1994 Act;**

(iv) **Community trade marks maintained by the Office for Harmonisation in the Internal Market under Article 83 of Council Regulation (EC) 40/94**[2] **; and**

(v) **Community designs maintained by the Office for Harmonisation in the Internal Market under Article 72 of Council Regulation (EC) 6/2002**[3] **; and**

(i) **"the registrar" means—**

(i) **the registrar of trade marks; or**

(ii) **the registrar of registered designs, whichever is appropriate.**

(3) **Claims to which this Part applies are allocated to the multi-track.**

Application of the Civil Procedure Rules

63.2 These Rules and their practice directions apply to intel- 2F–4 lectual property claims unless this Part or a practice direction provides otherwise.

See *SmithKline Beecham Plc v. Apotex Europe Ltd (Costs) (No.2)* [2004] EWCA Civ 1703 . In respect of all intellectual property matters the general rule is now that the Civil Procedure Rules apply unless a rule in Part 63 provides otherwise.

I. Patents and registered designs

Scope of Section I

63.3—(1) This Section of this Part applies to claims in—   2F–5

(a) **the Patents Court; and**

(b) **a Patents County Court.**

(2) **Claims in the court include any claim relating to matters arising out of—**

(a) **the 1977 Act;**

(b) **the Registered Designs Act 1949; and**

(c) **the Defence Contracts Act 1958**[4]**.**

Specialist list

63.4 Claims in the Patents Court and a Patents County Court 2F–6 form specialist lists for the purpose of rule 30.5.

Rule 63.4A—Patents Judge

Patents Judge

63.4A—(1) Subject to paragraph (2), proceedings in the patents 2F–6A county court shall be dealt with by the patents judge.

---

[1] 1949 c.88.
[2] OJ No. L11, 14.1.1994, p.1.
[3] OJ No. L3, 5.1.2002, p.1.
[4] 1958, c.38.

(2) **When a matter needs to be dealt with urgently and it is not practicable or appropriate for the patents judge to deal with such matter, the matter may be dealt with by another judge with appropriate specialist experience who shall be nominated by the Vice-Chancellor.**

Transfer between Divisions and to and from a specialist list

2F–7   Rule 30.5 provides that the High Court may order proceedings in any Division of the High Court to be transferred to another Division and order proceedings to be transferred to or from a specialist list. Applications for the transfer of proceedings must be made to a judge dealing with claims in that list.

In order to ensure access to justice for parties with limited financial resources, s.289 of the Copyright, Designs and Patents Act 1988 contains special provisions concerning transfer of proceedings between the High Court and a patents county court.

Actions within the special jurisdiction of a patents county court may be ordered to be transferred to such a court by the High Court either of its own motion or on the application of any party to the proceedings. In considering whether to make such an order, the High Court shall have regard to the financial position of the parties and may order transfer notwithstanding that the proceedings are likely to raise an important question of law or fact.

Such actions may also be ordered to be transferred from a patents county court to the High Court by the county court either of its own motion or on the application of any party to the proceedings. The county court is required to have regard to the financial position of the parties and may refrain from ordering transfer notwithstanding that the proceedings are likely to raise an important question of law or fact.

The High Court does not have the power to order proceedings within the special jurisdiction of a patents county court to be transferred from the Patents County Court.

When an action is transferred to the Patents County Court, the court will, after consultation with the parties, give any directions deemed appropriate for the purpose of bringing the pleadings and any other documents in the case and outstanding procedural steps into conformity with its own procedures.

Role of a Patent County Court

2F–8   It is the role of a Patent County Court to make litigation cheaper and more accessible in the more straightforward disputes. In *Warheit v. Olympia Tools Ltd (Costs)*, unreported, there was further argument on costs following an appeal from a two-day trial in Patents County Court in which the costs claimed were in excess of £250,000. It was held that the costs should be subject to detailed assessment, and it was made clear that these costs were far in excess of what Lord Chancellor envisaged when setting up Patents County Court. In future, efforts should be made to keep costs in proportion with the complexity of the proceedings. See *e.g. Unilin Beheer BV v. Berry Floor NV* [2004] F.S.R. 14 on the wisdom of conducting experiments in the Patents County Court.

Starting the claim

2F–9   **63.5 Claims to which this Section of this Part applies must be started—**

(a) **by issuing a Part 7 claim form; or**

(b) **in existing proceedings under Part 20.**

Without Notice Applications

2F–10   As the court is only being presented with one side of the story when a without notice application is made, there must be *complete disclosure of all material facts*. Failure to make disclosure of matters which are or may be adverse to the party making the application may result in any order being subsequently set aside on the ground of non-disclosure. It may also have serious consequences for any person who has made an affidavit in support of the application and any professional person representing the applicant. See *Elvee Ltd v. Taylor* [2001] EWCA Civ 1943—search and seizure orders; *The Gadget Shop Ltd v. The Bug.com Ltd* [2001] F.S.R. 383—search orders, Part 25, CPR proper execution; *Memory Corporation plc v. Sidhu* [2000] F.S.R. 921—freezing orders.

Where allegations of copying made, search and seizure orders should be made in the Chancery Division; see *Elvee Ltd v. Taylor* [2001] EWCA Civ 1943.

Except in the case of a "search and seizure" (old Anton Piller) order or a "freezing" (old Mareva) injunction, the court may require notice to be given to any person affected by the application.

Security for Costs

The general principle is that parties to proceedings are not required to give security for the costs of other parties. However, a claimant or a counterclaiming defendant (except a defendant in a patent or design action whose counterclaim raises only the invalidity of the patent or design) may be ordered to give such security if ordinarily resident out of England and Wales or if it is a limited company and there is credible evidence that there is reason to believe that it will be unable to pay the other side's costs.

2F–11

Affidavit evidence in support of an application for security of costs should deal *inter alia* with any alleged practical difficulties of enforcing an order for costs.

Successive applications for security can be made. However, applications should always be made at the earliest possible moment: delay is a ground for refusal. The assistance of the registrar may be sought in assessing the amount of costs likely to be awarded on taxation.

Pleadings

In a claim for infringement of a patent, the claim form must show which of the claims in the specification of the patent are alleged to be infringed and give at least one example of each type of infringement alleged, and a copy of each document referred to in the claim form (with translation if necessary) must be served with the claim form (See practice direction supplementing Pt 63, para. 11.1).

2F–12

The statement of case should be full but concise. It must set out all facts, matters and arguments relied on as establishing the allegations made and justifying the relief sought. It is the duty of the claimant to plead case on liability and relief (*e.g.* springboard relief) in advance (*Kirin-Amgen Inc v. Transkaryotic Therapies Inc. (No. 2)* [2002] R.P.C. 3). That case sets out the factors that should be taken into account in considering whether it is just to permit the claimant to subsequently broaden relief.

Guild v. Eskander Ltd [2003] F.S.R. 23—Allegations of conscious copying ought to be strictly pleaded and proved.

Amendment to particulars of claim

Patent actions are subject to the general provisions of CPR Pt 17 and the overriding objective that cases should be dealt with fairly. In general therefore amendments ought to be allowed so that the real dispute between the parties can be adjudicated upon. Although the requirements of the Civil Procedure Rules are mandatory there is an element of discretion as to when the mandatory conditions need to be satisfied – See *Dendron GmbH v. University of California (Amendment of Claim)* [2003] EWHC 2771.

2F–12.1

There is no special rule in patent cases that permits a patentee to amend its pleaded claim after judgment – see *Nikken Kosakusho Works v. Pioneer Trading Co* [2005] EWCA Civ 906 .

Particulars of infringements

The onus always rests on the claimant to prove infringement (*Whatmough v. Morris Motors* (1940) 57 R.P.C. 177).

2F–13

The patentee need not give his construction of his patent, the function of particulars of infringements being merely to point out to the defendant what specific act on his part is complained of so as to prevent surprise at the trial (*Wenham Co Ltd v. Champion Gas Lamp Co.* (1891) 8 R.P.C. 22; *Marsden v. Albrecht* (1910) 27 R.P.C. 785). See also *Lux Traffic Controls Ltd v. Staffordshire Public Works Company Ltd* [1991] R.P.C. 73.

If the particulars allege as an instance a sale to A., and the defendants admit the sale of an exactly similar article to B., this will be admissible (*Sykes v. Howarth* (1879) 12 Ch D 826 at 829).

Each type of infringement alleged constitutes a separate cause of action and must be separately particularised (*Sorata Ltd v. Gardex Ltd* [1984] R.P.C. 317, CA) however see also *Building Product Design Ltd v. Sandtoft Roof Tiles Ltd* [2004] F.S.R. 40 where products of a different material to those complained of in the particulars of infringement were also held to infringe, and *Building Product Design Ltd v. Sandtoft Roof Tiles*

Ltd (No.2) [2004] F.S.R. 41 —the requirements of the Civil Procedure Rules 1998 Pt 63 that each type of infringement had to be specifically pleaded in a patent infringement action recognised the importance of economy with regard to costs as well as in relation to the court's resources, the implementation of public policy regarding the finality of litigation and practical good sense.

As to particulars of acts alleged to have been performed by directors of a company personally joined as defendants in an action against the company, see *British Thomson-Houston Co Ltd v. Irradiant Lamp Works Ltd* (1924) 41 R.P.C. 338.

Amendment of particulars of infringements

2F-14   If the Claimant wants to recover relief for infringement of a claim of a patent, it must amend the pleadings to plead infringement of that claim. The request for further and other relief is not wide enough to encompass such an allegation. Moreover, a claimant seeking to so amend cannot require that the defendant shows it would have run its case differently in the light of such an amendment. A serious possibility that it would have done so was enough. See *Kirin Amgen Inc v. Transkaryotic Therapies Inc* [2003] EWCA Civ 1096; [2003] R.P.C. 3.

Sandvik Aktiebolag v. K. R. Pfiffner (UK) Limited [2000] F.S.R. 17—"holding pleadings"; there is no automatic right to amend even if the other side could be compensated by costs; although the jurisdiction to strike out pleadings should be sparingly used.

In *Godfrey L. Cabot Inc v. Philblack Ltd* [1961] R.P.C. 19, leave was given in a summons of the claimant to amend its own particulars of breaches to delete therefrom one instance of infringement and replace it by two others, even though the defendant objected that the two remaining instances of infringement were not sufficiently particularised. It was stated that the defendant's right to apply for fuller particulars of these two instances was not prejudiced by the amendment allowed.

Abandonment of specific particulars was held not to be a discontinuance, in relation to subject-matter thereof, in *Anxionnaz v. Rolls-Royce Ltd* [1963] R.P.C. 81. In *General Tire and Rubber Co v. International Synthetic Rubber Co* [1968] R.P.C. 161, re-amendment of the statement of claim to allege a joint infringement was allowed.

In *Dow Chemical AG v. Spence Bryson and Co Ltd* [1982] F.S.R. 397, where the original particulars clearly complained of an infringement by manufacture, and all parties knew that manufacture had only taken place in Northern Ireland by the first defendant who operated there, an amendment to extend the particulars so as to more securely found an application for disclosure relating to Northern Ireland was allowable as involving no new cause of action.

Whilst the practice in patent actions is that if one act of infringement is proved, a claimant will generally be granted an injunction in general terms to restrain infringement, and an inquiry as to damages suffered from infringing acts is not limited to the particular infringing act which has been pleaded and proved, it does not follow in the least that the particulars of infringement are no part of the cause of action, and that a claim in respect of a different manufactured product is necessarily part of the same cause of action as the original claim. The form of order for the inquiry as to damages, and the form of injunction, are matters of relief only, rather than indicating the cause of action for which relief is granted; *Sorata Ltd v. Gardex Ltd* [1984] R.P.C. 317. For the appropriate scope of patent injunctions, see *Coflexip S.A. v Stolt Comex Seaway MS Ltd* [2001] R.P.C. 9, CA.

A proposed amendment to make a conditional allegation of infringement, on the basis that the claimant would only allege infringement of a second patent if unsuccessful in relation to an earlier, different patent is not a proper alternative plea and should not be allowed (*Beloit Technologies Inc. v. Valmet Paper Machinery Inc* [1994] R.P.C. 664).

The court has a complete discretion to impose terms where a claimant seeks to withdraw an allegation of infringement, and it is the practice of the Patents Court to require some kind of undertaking from the claimant in relation to future claims (*Albright & Wilson Ltd v. SB Chemicals* [1994] R.P.C. 608).

Terms of amendment

2F-15   The imposition of terms is in the discretion of the court, and save in the strongest case the CA will not interfere (*Wilson v. Wilson* (1899) 16 R.P.C. 315).

Further and better particulars

2F-16   If the defendant is unable to ascertain from the particulars with sufficient precision what type of machine or process is complained of, the onus will lie on him to apply for further and better particulars, and to give some evidence to show that the information given is insufficient (*Haslam & Co v. Hall* (1887) 4 R.P.C. 203); he should not wait until the trial to complain, but in appropriate cases further particulars will not be ordered until after disclosure and inspection (*Mullard Radio Valve Co Ltd v. Tungsram Electric Lamp Works (Great Britain) Ltd* (1932) 49 R.P.C. 279).

The exchange of witness statements may make the ordering of burdensome particulars undesirable (*Lux Traffic Controls Ltd v. Staffordshire Public Works Company Ltd* [1991] R.P.C. 73).

Action by exclusive licensee under patent

By s.67 of the 1977 Act an exclusive licensee may take proceedings in respect of **2F–17** infringements committed after the date of his licence. The patentee must be either joined as claimant or added as defendant (subs.(2)). An interim injunction may be refused if the defendants did not know of the fact that the claimants were exclusive licensees (*Christian Salvesen (Oil Services) Ltd v. Odfjell Drilling and Consulting Co (UK) Ltd* [1985] R.P.C. 569).

Parties

For proper parties and amendments to add parties see *PLG Research Ltd v. Ardon* **2F–18** *International Ltd* [1992] F.S.R. 59. An equitable owner of a patent is entitled to commence proceedings without joining the assignor provided that at a later date the legal owner is made a party to proceedings; see *Baxter International Inc v. Nederlands Produktielaboratorium voor Bloedtransusiapparatuur BV* [1998] R.P.C. 250. Exclusive licensees may sue for damages, but their licence must be registered; whilst a mere record of an older licence will justify damages from the date of the older licence, registration of a modification will not (*M.M.M. v. Rennicks (UK) Ltd* [1992] F.S.R. 118). A director who merely facilitates infringement does not necessarily procure it: he will not be liable unless his involvement would be such as to render him liable as a joint tortfeasor if the company had not existed (*PLG Research Ltd v. Ardon International Ltd* [1993] F.S.R. 197).

Threats in patent proceedings

Section 70 of the 1977 Act provides a remedy for groundless threats of patent in- **2F–19** fringement proceedings. Section 70 permits threats to bring proceedings for an infringement alleged to consist of making or importing a product for disposal or of using a process. Section 70(4) allows threats to be made against primary infringers only in respect of acts of primary infringement, and does not allow threats against a primary infringer in relation to secondary acts of infringement, which remain actionable (*Cavity Trays Ltd v. RMC Panel Products Ltd* [1996] R.P.C. 361).

Mere notification of the existence of a patent does not constitute a threat.

The threats may be direct or indirect, and the action may be brought by any person aggrieved thereby. Threats in respect of acts done while a patent application is pending are actionable within s.70(1) of the Patents Act 1977, as are threats to sue once the patent is granted. An individual intimately connected with the management of a company against which threats are directed is a person aggrieved and able to sue for threats. See *Brain v. Ingledew Brown Bennison and Garret* [1995] F.S.R. 552 (partially reversed on appeal, but not as to the legal findings). The threats must have been made within the jurisdiction (*Egg Fillers and Containers (Aust.) Proprietary Ltd v. Holed-Tite Packing Corp and Packing Products Corp* (1934) 51 R.P.C. 9). The remedies are a declaration, injunction and damages unless the defendant proves that the act the subject of the threats would constitute an infringement of a patent or of rights arising from publication of a complete specification, in respect of a claim not shown by the claimant to be invalid. A defendant who pleads that any threat was justifiable must give particulars identifying the acts relied on as being infringing acts of the claimant in respect of which proceedings were threatened (*Reymes-Cole v. Elite Hosiery Co Ltd* [1961] R.P.C. 277). The claimant is not entitled to relief even though some of the patents to which the threats related are invalid or uninfringed, if other such patents are valid and infringed. The defendant may counterclaim in respect of infringement, under the ordinary rules relating to counterclaims. Where the threats are admitted, the onus of proof shifts to the defendant who alleges infringement, and the defendant should then open the case (*Lewis Faulk v. Jacobwitz* [1944] Ch. 64). A claim for threats may be made by way of counterclaim in an action for infringement (see, *e.g. Norton & Gregory*

Ltd v. Jacobs (1937) 54 R.P.C. 271). The fact that threats are malicious does not entitle the claimant to increased damages (*Berkeley & Young Ltd v. Stillwell* (1940) 57 R.P.C. 291). An interlocutory injunction to restrain threats may be granted, even where threats are made only in solicitors' letters before action (*H.V.E. (Electric) Ltd v. Cuffin Holdings Ltd* [1964] 1 W.L.R. 378; [1964] 1 All E.R. 674; [1964] R.P.C. 149, CA).

Threats in registered design right proceedings

2F–20   Section 26 of the 1949 Act provides a remedy for groundless threats of registered design right infringement proceedings. Section 26 permits threats to bring proceedings for an infringement alleged to consist of the making or importing of anything.

A mere notification that a design is registered does not constitute a threat.

Discontinuance

2F–21   The normal rule in the event of a claimant discontinuing a claim is that the claimant has to pay the defendant's costs. The CPR gives the court a discretion however—see *Coca-Cola Company, The v. Mabe* [2002] F.S.R. 731.

Defence and reply

2F–22   **63.6 Part 15 applies with the modification—**

(a) to rule 15.4 that in a claim for infringement under rule 63.9, the defence must be filed within 42 days of service of the claim form; and

(b) to rule 15.8 that the claimant must—

(i) file any reply to a defence; and

(ii) serve it on all other parties,

within 21 days of service of the defence.

Time for defence

2–23   The general rule is that a defence must be served 14 days after service of a particulars of claim or, if the defendant files an acknowledgment of service, 28 days after service of the particulars of claim. Where the claim is a claim for infringement under r.63.9 however, the defendant has 42 days from the service of the *claim form* to serve a defence. Rule 63.9(1) sets out that in a claim for infringement or an application in which validity is challenged, the statement of case must particularise that challenge. Rule 63.9(2) sets out that in a claim for infringement the extended time period of 42 days applies. In the past it was this extended time period applied only to those infringement cases in which the validity of a patent or registered design was challenged. It would now appear that in accordance with r.63.9(2) the extended time for serving a defence now applies to all claims for infringement, and not just those where the validity is challenged. This may simply reflect the fact that in the vast majority of infringement actions validity is in issue. This reading of the Rules does make the words "under rule 93.9" otiose however.

Separate representation

2F–24   *Bristol Myers Squibb Co v. Baker Norton Pharmaceuticals Inc* [2001] R.P.C. 1—separately defended. Defendants will only fail to recover costs if it was unreasonable to have sought separate representation.

Defence that the patentee has granted licences with prohibited conditions

2F–25   This defence, given by the Patents Act 1977, s.44 exists where the patentee has imposed on licensees or purchasers or hirers certain conditions in restraint of trade attaching to the sale or use of the invention.

If the prohibited contract has effect in the UK it is irrelevant that it is governed by a foreign law which does not have a provision similar to that in the UK (*Chiron Corp v. Organon Teknika Ltd (No. 2)* [1992] 3 C.M.L.R. 813; [1993] F.S.R. 324).

Where a defendant succeeds on a s.44 defence there is jurisdiction to allow the claimant to alter the offending agreement after judgment and amend his pleadings after which the successful defence disappears; but leave to amend was refused in *Chiron Corp v. Organon Teknika Ltd (No. 4)* [1994] F.S.R. 252.

A s.44 defence which is good against a claim by the patentee may fail against an exclusive licensee who was not a party to, and did not consent to, the offending agreement (*Chiron Corp v. Organon Tekuka Ltd (No. 12)* [1995] F.S.R. 153).

Defence that use is for service of the Crown

An action against the Crown for infringement of patent will be struck out; *Dory v. Sheffield Health Authority* [1991] F.S.R. 221.

2F–26

Striking out defences

For an example of striking out Euro defences judged incapable of success see *Chiron Corp v. Organon Teknika Ltd (No. 2)* [1992] 3 C.M.L.R. 813; [1993] F.S.R. 324, upheld on appeal: [1994] F.S.R. 187.

2F–27

Where the defendants had been guilty of a number of significant breaches of court orders such that a fair trial was no longer possible it was appropriate to make a finding of contumacious default and strike out the defence see *Nutrinova Nutrition Specialties & Food Ingredients* [2002] EWHC 1729; (2002) 25(9) I.P.D. 25065.

Challenge of validity

See paragraphs below.

2F–28

Time for reply

Rule 15.8 stipulates that a claimant must file any reply to the defence at the same time as serving his allocation questionnaire and serve his reply on the other parties at the same time as he files it. Since r.26.3(6) which sets out the period for filing the allocation questionnaire is deemed not to apply by r.63.7(2) below, the period for filing any reply is set at within 21 days of service of the defence.

2F–29

Case management[1]

63.7—(1) *[Omitted]*

2F–30

(2) **Part 26 and any other rule that requires a party to file an allocation questionnaire do not apply.**

(3) **The following provisions only of Part 29 apply—**

    (a) **rule 29.3(2) (legal representatives to attend case management conferences);**

    (b) **rule 29.4 (the court's approval of agreed proposals for the management of proceedings); and**

    (c) **rule 29.5 (variation of case management timetable) with the exception of paragraph (1)(b) and (c).**

(4) **As soon as practicable the court will hold a case management conference which must be fixed in accordance with the practice direction.**

Case Management

The usual provisions relating to case management at the preliminary stage, *i.e.* those set out in r.26, do not apply to patent and registered design proceedings. The court will hold a case management conference as soon as practicable. Paragraphs 4.1–4.12 of the Practice Direction supplementing Pt 63 (see para. 63PD.4 below) deal generally with the procedure to be adopted in relation to case management. Paragraph 5 (except sub-para. 5.9) and paragraph 7 of the Practice Direction supplementing Pt 29 still apply, but only insofar as the provisions in that Practice Direction are consistent with the provisions of the Practice Direction supplementing Pt 63.

2F–31

Legal representation at case management conferences

The first provision that still applies is 29.3(2), which stipulates that parties legal

2F–32

---

[1] Amended by Civil Procedure (Amendment No. 5) Rules 2003 (S.I. 2003 No. 3361) and Civil Procedure (Amendment No. 4) Rules 2005 (S.I. 2005 No. 3515).

representatives at a case management conference should be familiar with the case and should have sufficient authority to deal with any issues that are likely to arise. As with Pt 29.3(2), if non-compliance with this rule leads to an adjournment the court will expect to make a wasted costs order (for which seer.48.7).

Agreed directions/case management

2F-33   If the parties can agree proposals for the management of the case they should notify the court and inform the court what the agreed proposals are. If the court thinks the agreed proposals suitable, a hearing may be unnecessary. Even if not all the proposals are suitable, those which are will be taken into account by the court when setting down directions. This is obviously beneficial in terms of time and cost. The parties should therefore attempt to come to some agreement about directions wherever possible in order to help the court to further the overriding objective (r.1.3). Parties who do so will be rewarded in costs. Parties who are combative are liable to be penalised in costs whether or not their case succeeds at trial.

Variation of case management timetable

2F-34   Rule 29.5 still applies with the exception of r.29.5(1)(c), which relates to listing questionnaires (r.29.6 relating to listing questionnaires (previously called pre-trial check lists) does not apply to patent and registered design right cases). Paragraphs 6.1 to 6.5 of the Practice Direction supplementing Pt 29 deal generally with the procedure to be adopted in order to obtain a variation in the directions given, however in accordance with the Practice Direction to Pt 63 these provisions no longer apply to patents and registered design cases.

Experiments

2F-35   Where a party seeks to establish any fact by experimental proof conducted for the purpose of litigation he must, at least 21 days before service of the application notice for directions under paragraph 9.3 of the practice direction, or within such other time as the court may direct, serve on all parties a notice stating the facts which he seeks to establish and giving full particulars of the experiments proposed to establish them. A party served with notice under paragraph 9.1 of the practice direction must within 21 days after such service, serve on the other party a notice stating whether or not he admits each fact and may request the opportunity to inspect a repetition of all or a number of the experiments identified in the notice served under paragraph 9.1. Where any fact which a party seeks to establish by experimental proof is not admitted, he must apply to the court for permission and directions by application notice (see practice direction paragraphs 9.1 to 9.3). However, no automatic provisions for experiments should be made during the course of case management, and no permission at all should be granted for experiments that are directed at the issue of construction – see *Merck & Co Inc v. Generics (UK) Ltd* [2003] EWHC 2842 (Pat) .

Although experiments were not necessarily inappropriate in Patents County Court litigation, their appropriateness should be considered at the case management stage and adverse cost consequences may flow from any failure to take account of the realities of the case – see *Unilin Beheer BV v. Berry Floor NV* [2004] F.S.R. 14 (overturned on appeal though no adverse comment made in relation to the above).

Where a party fails to permit the other party to see a repetition of an experiment, it is possible for that other party to apply to have the notice of experiments struck out. Whether this will be done depends on the circumstances (*American Cyanamid Co v. Ethicon Ltd* [1978] R.P.C. 667, experiment not repeated because trial would be delayed and party wanting inspection partly to blame).

Late applications to introduce experiments or like matter which may result in further delay and expense are likely to be refused (*H. & R. Johnson Tiles Ltd v. Candy Tiles Ltd* [1985] F.S.R. 253 (late photographs relating to infringement refused)).

To prove that a skilled man carrying out a recipe would be able to do so using his ordinary skills, the recipe should ideally be given to a scientist of ordinary skills to try. There is a benefit if the experiment is carried out by a single court appointed expert, which the parties ought to consider when they apply for leave to adduce such evidence. See *SmithKline Beecham Plc v. Apotex Europe Ltd* [2004] EWCA Civ 1568.

Use of models

2F-36   Where a party intends to rely on any model or apparatus, he must apply to the court for directions at the first case management conference (see practice direction 10.1).

Expert evidence

A shipping case in the Commercial Court contains a discussion of the duties and responsibilities of expert witnesses which should be widely applicable (*The Ikarian Reefer* [1993] F.S.R. 563). See Cantor *Fitzgerald International v. Tradition (UK) Ltd* [2000] R.P.C. 95 for the dangers of an expert acting as advocate or holding back relevant information. Expert witnesses are relied upon by the court to express a disinterested view. Any pressure, and any act which may have the effect of placing pressure, on a witness may be a contempt of court and dealt with accordingly. See *Glaxo Group Ltd's Patent* [2004] EWHC 477 (Ch).

2F–37

In a patent case the role of an expert is principally to educate the court in the technology so that it can establish what the skilled man would have thought. However the court must be careful not to weigh an expert's ability to teach or give evidence over the reasons for his views. What ultimately matters is what the skilled man would have thought – see *SmithKline Beecham Plc v. Apotex Europe Ltd* [2004] EWCA Civ 1568. See also *Kirin Amgen Inc v. Hoechst Marion Roussel Ltd* [2004] UKHL 46 , in which the appointment of a court expert to give the court a series of seminars in the material technology was approved of. It was suggested that such a course might usefully be adopted in future if the technology was "complex and undisputed" and the parties consented.

A party should not have more than one independent expert witness on each topic (*Gerber Garment Technology Inc v. Lectra Systems Ltd* [1994] F.S.R. 471). Whilst sometimes it is of value for experts to tutor the Court as to the differences between works of the parties, evidence as to whether or not there has been copying in a copyright case is unlikely to be useful. See *IPC Media Ltd v. Highbury Leisure Publishing Ltd* [2004] EWHC 2985 (Ch) . Likewise the experts' views as to whether an article is commonplace are not helpful since this is a question for the court (even though such evidence is admissible under the Civil Evidence Act 1972). What matters are the reasons for any such opinion – See *Lambretta Clothing Co Ltd v. Teddy Smith (UK) Ltd* [2004] EWCA (Civ) 886 .

Expert evidence in design right cases

Thermos Ltd v. Alladdin Sales and Marketing Ltd [2000] F.S.R. 402—the calling of expert evidence served little purpose in registered design actions concerned with ordinary consumer articles. In accordance with the CPR the court would need to be informed precisely at what areas the expert evidence would be directed, and it would exercise caution before admitting expert evidence. See also *Oren (Isaac) v. Red Box Toy Factory Ltd* [1999] F.S.R. 785.

2F–38

Similar fact evidence

See *Mattel Inc v. Woolbro (Distributors) Ltd* [2003] EWHC 2412 (Ch) in which it was held that there was no automatic admission of "similar fact" evidence in cases involving copying – it would depend on the probative value of the evidence. The Court should be careful not to allow the introduction of evidence which was unfair or oppressive.

2F–38.1

Agreed statements

In cases involving technical complexities, it has become the practice for the parties to prepare, where possible, an agreed statement of background technical facts (see, *e.g.* the "Phenothiazine Primer" used in *Olin Mathieson Chemical Corp v. Biorex Laboratories Ltd* [1970] R.P.C. 157 at 197). In such cases the parties may also prepare written summaries of their submissions upon disputed matters. This was done, for example, in *Valensi v. British Radio Corp Ltd* [1972] R.P.C. 373. In this case in the Court of Appeal, the defendants prepared a greatly extended explanatory document called a "Primer", and, although not an agreed document, it was greatly relied on by the court: [1973] R.P.C. 337 at 351, in *American Cyanamid Co's Patent* [1970] R.P.C. 306, the whole case was decided on agreed facts. See also *Evans Medical Ltd's Patent* [1998] R.P.C. 517 and *Hoechst Celanese Corp v. BP Chemicals Ltd* [1998] F.S.R. 586 for duties of parties in relation to primers. This is reflected in the practice direction at para. 4.10(2), which states that at the case management conference the court may direct that a document setting out basic undisputed technology should be prepared.

2F–39

Scientific adviser

At the case management conference the court may direct that a scientific adviser

2F–40

under s.70(3) of the Supreme Court Act 1981 be appointed (it should be noted that r.35.15 applies to scientific advisers).

Disclosure and inspection

2F–41   **63.8 Part 31 is modified to the extent set out in the practice direction.**

Product descriptions

2F–42   Standard disclosure does not require the disclosure of documents relating to the infringement of a patent by a product or process if, before serving a list of documents, the defendant has served on the claimant and any other parties full particulars of the product or process alleged to infringe and any drawings or other illustrations explaining the product and process should they be necessary (See practice direction supplementing Pt 63, para. 5.1(1)). As for the duties incumbent on those serving product descriptions, see *Alfred Taylor v. Ishida (Europe) Ltd* [2000] F.S.R. 224; "...the function of a product description is in all respects equivalent to that of disclosure. The duties of all parties, both the professionals and of the parties themselves, in relation to a product description, are the same as they would be in relation to disclosure...". See also *Consafe Engineering (UK) Ltd v. Emtunga UK Ltd* [1999] R.P.C. 154—a description of the product in general terms or including tendentious assertions is not acceptable.

It was appropriate to grant an application by the claimants for disclosure, subject to appropriate safeguards, of the defendant's product description to technically qualified American attorneys in circumstances where, in the absence of such disclosure, it was impossible for the claimant's UK advisers to formulate any sensible request for further information—*Intel Corp v. VIA Technologies Inc. (Application; Disclosure)* [2002] EWHC 1434. *Rockwater Ltd v. Coflexip SA* [2004] EWCA Civ 381 – where an alleged infringer provides a description of a product or process under CPR Pt 63, Practice Direction para. 5.1, it should be formally proved by a witness at trial if required by the other party.

Disclosure in relation to validity

2F–43   Standard disclosure does not require the disclosure of documents relating to any ground on which the validity of a patent is put in issue, except documents which fall in the period starting two years before the earliest claimed priority date and two years following that date (See practice direction supplementing Pt 63, para. 5.1(2)). See *Nokia Corp v. Interdigital Technology Corp* [2004] EWHC 2920 .

Disclosure in relation to commercial success

2F–44   Standard disclosure does not require the disclosure of documents relating to commercial success except as set out in the practice direction (See practice direction supplementing Pt 63, paras 5.1(3) and 5.2). This reflects the fact that virtually every commercial document produced relating to a product or process may be relevant to the success of that product or process. In order to rationalise the disclosure relating to the commercial success of a product therefore, the patentee must serve a schedule: identifying the article or product (for example by product code number) made in accordance with the claims of the patent; a summary by convenient periods of sales of any such articles; a summary by convenient periods of any equivalent prior article or product marketed before the article in question (if any); and a summary by convenient periods of any advertising or promotional expenditure on the article. In relation to a process, the patentee must serve a schedule: identifying the process made in accordance with the claims of the patent; a summary by convenient periods of revenue received by the use of the process; a summary by convenient periods of any equivalent prior art process; and a summary by convenient periods of any expenditure supporting the use of the process.

Disclosure generally

2F–45   A defendant's obligation to give disclosure is confined to the issues raised in the particulars of infringements. He need not normally give disclosure of all his sales (*Belegging, etc. v. Witten* [1979] F.S.R. 59, CA). Late applications for disclosure are very undesirable, but should not necessarily be refused on this ground alone (*Poseidon Industri A/B v. Cerosa Ltd* [1975] F.S.R. 122). In *Kahn (David) Inc v. Conway Stewart* [1972]

R.P.C. 572 very late notice for inspection of the claimant's documents was permitted where no delay was likely to be caused.

Correspondence between the patentee and the patent office relating to the application which matured into a patent in suit is not discoverable because it is not relevant (*Poseidon Industri A/B v. Cerosa Ltd* [1975] F.S.R. 122). Documents relating to the patentee's research leading to and concerned with the invention are disclosable when obviousness, insufficiency or inutility are pleaded, *Halcon International Inc v. Shell Transport, etc. (Discovery No. 2)* [1979] R.P.C. 459. *Wellcome Foundation v. V.R. Laboratories (Australia) Pty Ltd* [1981] R.P.C. 35 and [1982] R.P.C. 343. Evidence may be called generally on the issue of common general knowledge, but if it is apparent that the defendant is going to rely on particular documents, they should be disclosed as and when they come to hand (*Aluma Systems Inc v. Hunnebeck GmbH* [1982] F.S.R. 239). Since the reasons for alleged invalidity have to be specified in the particulars of objections it is not possible to get disclosure of the pleadings in earlier actions against different parties which were settled, on the suspicion—howsoever justified—that they disclosed much more relevant prior art (*Intalite Internationals N.V. v. Cellular Ceilings Ltd (No. 1)* [1987] R.P.C. 185).

Disclosure of documents relating to why foreign patents have more restricted claims will not be ordered as the question of fair basis is entirely a matter of construction for the court (*Schering Agrochemicals Ltd v. A. B. M. Chemicals Ltd* [1987] R.P.C. 185). In *Vickers Plc v. Horsell Graphic Industries Ltd* [1988] R.P.C. 421, it emerged on disclosure that the patentee had expressed opinions in US proceedings that carrying out the process of a particular piece of prior art did not disclose his invention. Disclosure was ordered of documents relating to the like opinions expressed in yet other jurisdictions as disclosing the patentee's counter to attacks on validity and his approach to infringement. This case was not followed in *Glaverbel SA v. British Coal Corp (No. 2)* [1993] R.P.C. 90; [1992] F.S.R. 642, where documents relating to the patentees' opinion on obviousness were held not relevant; the effect on the need for disclosure of the modern practice of disclosing witness statements and the preferability of dealing with some matters by affidavit rather than disclosure were discussed; no disclosure of documents will be ordered unless it is certain they exist. Where an alleged infringer is a licensee who imports without knowledge of the manufacturing process, and his licence entitles him to have information made available to him for the purposes of the licence, these purposes do not include litigation, and he will not be ordered to procure documents relating to manufacture (*Unilever Plc v. Gillette UK Ltd* [1988] R.P.C. 416).

Documents relating to a defendant's reaction to the claimant's patent and the indemnities he gives to his customers will not normally be relevant to the issue of obviousness and will not be ordered to be discovered (*Fuji Photo Film Co Ltd v. Carr's Paper* [1989] R.P.C. 713).

In a case involving benefit to an employer from a patent from an invention made by an employee, disclosure of documents relating to profit on patented articles is only relevant if the patent plays a major part in securing sales. *Memco-Med Ltd's Patent* [1992] R.P.C. 403.

A patentee's equivalent foreign specifications cannot assist with construction of a U.K. patent and disclosure of the same will not be ordered (*Glaverbel S.A. v. British Coal Corp (No. 2)* [1993] R.P.C. 90; [1992] F.S.R. 642).

Disclosure in relation to common general knowledge or an allegation of commonplace design

It is not normal for disclosure to be made in relation to common general knowledge, and it is only in the most exceptional circumstances that disclosure will be ordered in relation to the issue of whether or not a design was commonplace at the material time. See *Ultraframe Ltd v. Eurocell Building Plastics Ltd* [2003] EWHC 3258 (Ch).

2F–45.1

Use of disclosed documents

In *Bourns Inc v. Raychem Corporation (No. 2)* [2000] F.S.R. 841, it was held that there was an implied undertaking to use the documents disclosed only for purposes of taxation. See also *Smithkline Beecham Plc v. Generics (UK) Ltd* [2003] EWCA Civ 1109 in which permission had been granted to the claimant to use disclosed documents in a co-pending revocation action brought by a third party, and the claimant had sought permission to use disclosed documents in a further action, and also *Dendron GmbH v. University of California (No. 2)* [2004] EWHC 589 (Pat).

2F–46

Disclosure as against non-parties

2F-47 See *American Home Products Corp v. Novartis Pharmaceuticals UK Ltd (No. 2)* [2001] F.S.R. 784, in which the Court of Appeal held that s.34 of the Supreme Court Act 1981 provided jurisdiction to order disclosure of documents relevant to an issue, and the discretion to order such disclosure should be exercised when it would aid the administration of justice. See also *Coca-Cola Company, The v. British Telecommunications plc* [1999] F.S.R. 518 for appropriate considerations and factors to be taken into account.

Where a claim is made against an innocent defendant for disclosure only (or also under the protective jurisdiction for any injunction) the claimant will normally bear the costs as against him, but will be able to recover these from the true infringer, either in the same or subsequent action (*Smith, Kline & French Laboratories Ltd v. R. D. Harbottle (Mercantile) Ltd* [1980] R.P.C. 363; *Morton-Norwich Inc. v. Intercen* [1981] F.S.R. 337). See *Totalise plc v The Motley Fool Ltd* [2002] F.S.R. 779 for the appropriate cost order to be made in *Norwich Pharmacal* Orders as against an innocent third party.

Disclosure of infringing parties

2F-48 An action solely for an order compelling a defendant to give disclosure of the names and addresses of persons who are infringing the claimant's patent will lie against a defendant against whom the claimant has another cause of action (*e.g.* for infringement or breach of an equitable duty not to part with goods knowing that they infringe) and will also lie against an innocent defendant who, through no fault of his own and whether voluntarily or not, facilitated the infringement (*Norwich Pharmacal Co v. Commrs. of Customs and Excise* [1974] A.C. 133; [1973] 2 All E.R. 943; [1974] R.P.C. 101, HL).

The question of whether, and in what circumstances, information relating to the infringement of other parties' rights discovered in the execution of an Anton Piller order can be passed to those other parties was considered in *Cobra Golf Inc v. Rata* [1996] F.S.R. 819.

Documents showing grounds of invalidity not specifically pleaded

2F-49 In *Intel Corp v. General Instrument Corp* [1989] F.S.R. 640, the authorities being conflicting, the court left open whether disclosure of this class of documents could be ordered. (One case that does not appear to have been cited in that case was *Avery Ltd v. Ashworth, Son & Co Ltd* (1915) 32 R.P.C. 561, in which it was said that disclosure can be obtained from the claimant only of such matters as are relevant to the plea of invalidity as made out in the particulars of objections, and he cannot be compelled to disclose any documents affecting the validity otherwise than as such documents were specifically pleaded).

Disclosure and inspection of secret process

2F-50 Where a defendant claims that the allegedly infringing process is a trade secret, he can claim limited disclosure. As to the principles upon which this is granted, see *Warner-Lambert & Co v. Glaxo Laboratories Ltd* [1975] R.P.C. 354, CA; *Roussel Uclaf v. Imperial Chemical Industries Plc* [1989] R.P.C. 59, CA (disclosure to expert in France refused because of danger of leak). For further developments see *Roussel Uclaf v. Imperial Chemical Industries Plc (No. 2)* [1990] R.P.C. 45; [1990] F.S.R. 25; *British Thomson-Houston Co v. Duram Ltd* (1915) 37 R.P.C. 121; *Coloured Asphalte Co Ltd v. British Asphalt and Bitumen Ltd* (1936) 53 R.P.C. 89; *British Celanese Ltd v. Courtaulds Ltd* (1932) 49 R.P.C. 345; *Helitune Ltd v. Stewart Hughes Ltd* [1994] F.S.R. 422.

Even non-confidential documents discovered in English proceedings may not be authorised to be proffered in foreign proceedings in which it is impossible to protect confidence, lest confidential documents have to be produced to explain them (*Halcon International v. Shell Transport and Trading Co* [1979] R.P.C. 97).

Documents containing commercial secrets

2F-51 Extensive guidance was given by Whitford J. as to the circumstances in which documents filed in the Patent Office and subsequently in the Patents Court should be treated as confidential. (1) The fact that a document is said to contain "sensitive commercial information" does not necessarily mean that this material, which would otherwise become public property is to be excluded from public inspection; apart from generalities there must be some real indication as to why disclosure would be harmful. (2) Those requesting confidentiality should put in evidence. (3) Material which is going to form no part of the decision can remain confidential. (4) Material supplied by a third party on the basis of confidence which involves minimal excisions from a decision should be maintained as confidential unless there is some overwhelming public interest which makes it desirable that the public should have sight of it. (5) The appropriate procedure is for the matter to be dealt with before hearing so that if ruled against the person proffering the document can make up his mind whether he will go forward publicly, or have the material withdrawn (*Diamond Shamrock Technologies SA's Patent* [1987] R.P.C. 91). (See also *Lilly Icos Ltd v. Pfizer Ltd* [2002] 809 in which it was said that the Court will only depart from normal rule of publicity of trials if very good reasons are given).

This position is somewhat different when a claimant wins a case and is then forced to disclose potentially confidential documents before the account of profits or assessment of damages can take place. Just such a situation arose in *Dyson Limited v. Hoover Limited (No. 3)* [2002] R.P.C. 42. In that case it was said that it is only in exceptional cases that a party can be prevented from having access to information which would play a substantial part in the case. The burden is on the party seeking to restrict disclosure to show that the case was sufficiently exceptional that significant restrictions on disclosure had to be maintained. It is for the party trying to restrict disclosure to justify it and to show why, in all the circumstances, notwithstanding onerous undertakings as to confidentiality and the like, documents should not be shown to the other party. See also *Smithkline Beecham Plc v. Generics (UK) Ltd* [2003] EWCA Civ 1109 for discussion of the protection available to a party who discloses commercially sensitive documents in an action.

Inspection

In an action in which the validity of a patent is challenged, the court may order the inspection of machinery or apparatus where a party alleges such machinery or apparatus was used before the priority date of the claim (See practice direction supplementing Pt 63, para.11.5(2)).   **2F–52**

Privilege

Apart from the usual legal professional privilege, privilege for communications with patent agents has been established by the Copyright Designs and Patents Act 1988, s.280. For a case involving both heads see *Soc. Francaise Hoechst v. Allied Colloids Ltd* [1992] F.S.R. 66. Privilege at common law may extend to foreign lawyers giving advice on English law (*IBM v. Phoenix International Computers Ltd* [1995] F.S.R. 184).   **2F–53**

See *David Instance v. Denny Bros. Printing Ltd* [2000] F.S.R. 869 for discussion of privilege in documents created for the purposes of negotiating settlements and mediation and their use in subsequent litigation.

A defendant cannot rely on privilege against self-incrimination when he has accidentally handed over evidence of his own dishonesty; see *Bell Cablemedia plc v. Simmons* [2002] F.S.R. 34.

Claim for infringement and challenge to validity[1]

63.9—(1) In a claim for infringement or an application in which the validity of a patent or registered design is challenged, the statement of case must contain particulars as set out in the practice direction.   **2F–54**

(2) In a claim for infringement, the period for service of the defence or Part 20 claim is 42 days after service of the claim form.

Claims for infringement in which validity is challenged

The language used in r.63.9(1) does not make it entirely clear whether this rule applies to all claims for infringement *and* applications in which the validity of patents or designs is challenged, or only claims for infringement (and any other applications) in which validity is challenged. The practice direction only sets out stipulations for the   **2F–55**

---

[1] Amended by Civil Procedure (Amendment No. 5) Rules 2003 (S.I. 2003 No. 3361).

statement of case in respect of claims in which validity is challenged, so it may be assumed that the latter interpretation is correct. There appears to be no such ambiguity in respect of r.63.9(2), which suggests that for all claims for infringement the period of service for the defence or Part 20 claim is 42 days after service of the claim form.

Counterclaims for invalidity

2F–56   *Stay against one of several defendants who does not challenge validity* —Where one of two defendants does not raise the issue of invalidity, the action may be stayed against that defendant until after the action against the other defendant has been determined (*McCreath v. Mayor, etc., of South Shields* (1932) 49 R.P.C. 349). As to addition of defendant, see *Anxionnaz v. Rolls-Royce Ltd* [1963] R.P.C. 81.

2F–57   *Grounds of invalidity: general* —The objections which may be taken against the validity of a patent, in an action for infringement or in revocation proceedings, are set out in s.72 of the Patents Act 1977 (including European Patents (UK)).

The statement of case must contain particulars of the relief sought and the issues except those relating to validity, which should be contained in a separate document annexed to it headed "Grounds of Invalidity". The "Grounds of Invalidity" must specifiy the grounds on which validity is challenged. Grounds of Invalidity were previously called "Particulars of Objections".

The separate grounds of invalidity must be stated, for, apart from granting leave to amend, the court will not consider objections not pleaded, even if they appear on the evidence. See Judgment of Lord Loreburn L.C. in *Alsop Flour Process Co v. Flour Oxidising Co.* (1908) 25 R.P.C. 490, and CA in *British United Shoe Machinery Co v. Fussell & Co* (1908) 25 R.P.C. 631. Also, upon objection, the court may refuse to allow the admission of evidence or cross-examination relating to an insufficiently particularised plea of invalidity (*British Thomson-Houston Co Ltd v. Tungstalite Ltd* (1940) 57 R.P.C. 271 at 275).

Particulars of objection to validity:

2F–58   *(1) Want of novelty and want of any inventive step* —the particulars must specify such details of the matter in the state of the art relied on, namely—
   (1) in the case of matter made available to the public by written description—
      (a) the date on which and the means by which it was so made available, unless this is clear from the face of the matter; and
      (b) the identifying information allowing the public to access the matter; and
   (2) in the case of matter made available to the public by use—
      (a) the date or dates of such use;
      (b) the name of all persons making such use;
      (c) any written material which identifies such use;
      (d) the existence and location of any apparatus employed in such use; and
      (e) all facts and matters relied on to establish that such matter was made available to the public.
See practice direction paragraphs 11.3 and 11.4.

If a defendant also decides to rely upon common general knowledge he should plead it distinctly (*Phillips v. Ivel Cycle Co Ltd* (1890) 7 R.P.C. 77). Ordinarily a defendant need not give particulars of common general knowledge. However, particulars were in one case ordered of those portions of the specification relied upon by the defendant alleged to be common general knowledge (*Solaflex Signs Amalgamated Ltd v. Allen Manufacturing Co Ltd* (1931) 48 R.P.C. 577). They were refused in *McCreath v. Mayor, etc., of South Shields* (1932) 49 R.P.C. 349, but see *British Thomson-Houston Ltd v. Tungstalite Ltd* (1940) 57 R.P.C. 271, where defendants failed to give particulars ordered.

2F–59   *(2) Insufficiency* —the particulars must state, if appropriate, which examples of the invention cannot be made to work and in which respects they do not work or do not work as described in the specification (See practice direction paragraph 11.3(2)).

In response to a plea of insufficiency a patentee cannot be made to plead a positive case as against the whole world that his specification does sufficiently and fairly describe his invention and the manner of performing it. But in appropriate cases he can be made to give, in relation to each pleaded particular of insufficiency, particulars of the passage or passages in his complete specification alleged to contain a sufficient and fair description of that part of the invention and of the method by which it is to be performed, specifying in each case what it is alleged that a man skilled in the art would do in respect of that invention (*Polaroid Corp's Patent-Insufficiency Appeal* [1977] F.S.R. 233). However in most cases it seems that it will not be appropriate to order such particulars before experiments have been carried out (*Halcon International Inc v. Shell Transport & Trading Co* [1977] F.S.R. 458).

Amendment of particulars of objections—

(a) Before trial

(1) The rule is that the patentee is to be placed in the same position as to **2F–60** discontinuing the action, or disclaiming a portion of his invention, as if the new particulars had formed a part of the old particulars. The form which has been consistently followed in the past is that in *Baird v Moule's Patent Earth Closet Co Ltd* (1881) L.R. 17 Ch. D. 139 (Note) set out in *Edison Telephone Co v. India Rubber Co* (1881) L.R. 17 Ch. D. 137. In *See v. Scott-Paine* (1933) 50 R.P.C. 56, where there was a counterclaim for revocation, the order provided that if the patentee elected to discontinue the action he should also consent to an order for revocation of his patent. However, see *Cil International Ltd v. Vitrashop Ltd* [2002] F.S.R. 4 as to whether a *See v. Scott-Paine* or *Earth Closet* order is necessarily appropriate. A *See v. Scott-Paine* order is discretionary and the court must consider the merits in each case; its aim is not to penalise a defendant but to encourage the pleading of all the objections known to him. See also *Robert Hewitt v. P. McCann Ltd* [1998] F.S.R. 688 where a *See v. Scott-Paine* order was refused where no serious criticism could be levelled at the defendant.

In *Instance v. Denny Bros. Printing Ltd* [1994] F.S.R. 396 the defendant sought a qualification on the usual *See v. Scott-Paine* order that it be entitled to withdraw the amendments proposed at its election if the Claimant chose to discontinue. The qualification was rejected on the basis that amendment is an indulgence. A defendant must decide whether to amend.

(b) Amendment at the trial—

will only be permitted if the new evidence could not by reasonable diligence have been found before: North P. in *Moss v. Malings* (1886) L.R. 33 Ch D 603. Where on the evidence it appeared that the invention was insufficiently described (see note to r.21) and this was not alleged in the particulars, leave was given to amend, the patentees to have a fortnight to elect whether they would discontinue, the terms to be argued after election (*Badische Anilin and Soda Fabrik v. La Societe Chimique* (1897) 14 R.P.C. 875).

The eminently sensible implication of *Helitune Ltd v. Stewart Hughes Ltd* [1991] R.P.C. 78 is that if knowledge of a ground of invalidity (typically prior use by the patentee) comes to light only during cross examination, an amendment of the particulars of objections ought not to be subject to an Earth Closet order. Further a distinction may be drawn between prior documents and prior uses. In the case of the latter, the defendant may only be able to discover them by chance, and in such circumstances it may not be appropriate to grant a *See v. Scott-Paine* order (*La Baigne Magiglo v. Multiglow Fires* [1994] R.P.C. 295). For a case in which an *Earth Closet* Order was not made even though amendment was sought late and the party seeking revocation had been aware of the new prior art for some time, see *GEC Alsthom's Patent* [1996] F.S.R. 415. The purpose of Earth Closet Orders is to put the patentee in the position he would have been in from the point of view of costs and discontinuance if the particulars of objections had been fully and properly pleaded from the start. They are not to put the patentee in a "preferential" position (*Aumac Ltd's Patent* [1996] F.S.R. 843).

Amendment of pleadings, sought however late, ought to be allowed so as to determine the dispute between the parties (provided no injustice is caused) because it is the public interest that the validity of a patent should be fully tested (*Helitune* case, above).

Where a point is foreshadowed in witness statements, amendments of pleadings will be allowed if necessary; *Glaverbel SA v. British Coal Corp. (No.3)* [1993] F.S.R. 478.

Where the claimant in a patent infringement action opted following the making of a *See v. Scott-Paine* order to discontinue, and then sought to designate the UK in relation to a similar European divisional patent, the Court would not re-open the *See v. Scott Paine* order so as to prevent the claimant from suing on the European patent (*Aumac's Patent* [1995] F.S.R. 501).

Whilst the requirements of para. 11 of the Practice Direction that particulars must be given in relation to an attack on novelty are mandatory, nonetheless the Court has a discretion whether to allow amendments before they have been properly particularised (*Dendron GmbH v. University of California (Amendment of Claim)* [2003] EWHC 2771 (Ch) Ch D, unrep.). The Court should exercise that discretion to prevent amendments being made with a view to obtaining documents to discover a cause of action or defence. The Court must judge whether the amendment is tantamount to a fishing expedition or not. (See *Visx Inc. v. Nidek Co Ltd (No. 2)* [1999] F.S.R. 91).

Estoppel

2F–61   In *Chiron Corp v. Organon Teknika Ltd (No. 6)* [1994] F.S.R. 448, a defendant sued for a second time on the same patent, having unsuccessfully counterclaimed for its revocation in the first action, may not put the validity of the patent in issue in the second action (except possibly in exceptional circumstances). The matter was *res judicata* between the parties. *Chiron Corp v. Organon Teknika Ltd (No. 6)* has been reported in the Court of Appeal, where leave to appeal was obtained and then set aside (*Chiron Corp v. Organon Teknika Ltd (No. 14)* [1996] F.S.R. 701.

Whether and to what extent estoppel may arise from the findings of foreign Courts in parallel patent proceedings was considered in *Kirin Amgen Inc v. Boehringer Mannheim GmbH* [1997] F.S.R. 289 and (regarding an unsuccessful opposition in the European Patent Office) *Buehler AG v. Chronos Richardson Ltd* [1998] R.P.C. 609.

Commercial success

2F–62   In some cases a patentee may seek to rely upon the commercial success of his invention to rebut an allegation of obviousness. However such a case inherently involves a number of substantial questions, *e.g.* is the success due to what is claimed, or to other matters such as advertising, or good manufacture, or the later development of the details (whether further inventions or not) which make for commercial success? Whether there was a long-felt want met by the alleged invention is likewise often a question of significance. In *Raychem Corp's Patents* [1998] R.P.C. 31, Laddie J. went so far as to say that a plea of commercial success normally only added time and expense to the proceedings and served no useful purpose.

Paragraph 11.5(1) of the practice direction suggests that a patentee relying on commercial success must state the grounds on which he so relies on his claim form. This is plainly wrong. A patentee will not know (though he may fear) that a counterclaim for invalidity will be made at the time that he serves his claim form. It may be that the words "claim form" one should read "statement of case".

For disclosure in relation to commercial success, see para. 2F–44 above.

Foreign commercial success may be relevant (*Unilever plc v. Gillette (UK) Ltd* [1989] R.P.C. 417).

Application to amend a patent specification in existing proceedings

2F–63   **63.10—(1) An application under section 75 of the 1977 Act for permission to amend the specification of a patent by the proprietor of the patent must be made by application notice.**

    (2) The application notice must—

        (a) give particulars of—

            (i) the proposed amendment sought; and

            (ii) the grounds upon which the amendment is sought;

    (b) **state whether the applicant will contend that the claims prior to amendment are valid; and**

    (c) **be served by the applicant on all parties and the Comptroller within 7 days of its issue.**

(3) **The application notice must, if it is reasonably possible, be served on the Comptroller electronically.**

(4) **Unless the court otherwise orders, the Comptroller will forthwith advertise the application to amend in the journal.**

(5) **The advertisement will state that any person may apply to the Comptroller for a copy of the application notice.**

(6) **Within 14 days of the first appearance of the advertisement any person who wishes to oppose the application must file and serve on all parties and the Comptroller a notice opposing the application which must include the grounds relied on.**

(7) **Within 28 days of the first appearance of the advertisement the applicant must apply to the court for directions.**

(8) **Unless the court otherwise orders, the applicant must within 7 days serve on the Comptroller any order of the court on the application.**

(9) **In this rule, "the journal" means the journal published pursuant to rules made under section 123(6) of the 1977 Act.**

Amendment

See *Oxford Gene Technology Ltd v. Affymetrix Inc. (No. 2)* [2001] R.P.C. 310—privilege and disclosure in relation to amendment of patents.   **2F–64**

Terms on which amendment allowed

The form of the order will depend on the circumstances, and there is no form which is invariably to be followed in all cases (*per* Lindley L.J., in *Bray v. Gardner* (1887) 4 R.P.C. 40 at 44). For terms on which liberty to apply to amend under the Act of 1883 was granted, see *Ludington Cigarette Machine Co v. Baron Cigarette Machine Co* [1900] 1 Ch. 513; *Deeley v. Perkes* [1896] A.C. 496; 13 R.P.C. 581; *Re Geipel's Patent* [1903] 2 Ch. 715; [1904] 1 Ch. 239; 20 R.P.C. 545; 21 R.P.C. 279. The form in the last-mentioned case was substantially followed in similar cirumstances in *Gillette Safety Razor Co v. Luna Safety Razor Co* (1910) 27 R.P.C. 527, followed in *Rheinische Gummi and Celluloid Fabrik v. British Xylonite Co Ltd* (1912) 29 R.P.C. 672, where the order is set out in full. This form of order was slightly varied in *N.V. Hollandsche Glas-en Metaalbank v. Rockware Glass Syndicate Ltd* (1931) 48 R.P.C. 181; see also *Lilley v. Artistic Novelties Ltd* (1913) 30 R.P.C. 18, *Rowland Edwards & C Ltd v. Three Star Accumulators Ltd* (1934) 51 R.P.C. 370, and *White's Application* [1958] R.P.C. 287. The motion may be ordered to come on for hearing with the trial of the action (*British Celanese Ltd v. Courtaulds Ltd* (1932) 49 R.P.C. 345; *Re Nier's Patent* (1938) 55 R.P.C. 1; *Astra A/B v. Pharmaceutical Mfg Co.* (1952) 69 R.P.C. 312) but this course may sometimes be inconvenient (*British Acoustic Films Ltd v. Nettleford Productions* (1935) 52 R.P.C. 296; 53 R.P.C. 221, at 241; *Drysdale v. Davey, Paxman & Co (Colchester) Ltd* (1938) 55 R.P.C. 95, at 108). The motion may be allowed on the terms that consequential amendments may be made in the pleadings, in which case the defendant (or petitioner) will usually be given the costs occasioned thereby. See *Haslam Foundry and Engineering Co v. Goodfellow* (1888) 5 R.P.C. 28; *Re Chatwood's Patent* (1899) 16 R.P.C. 370; *N.V. Hollandsche Glas-en Metaalbank v. Rockware Glass Syndicate Ltd* (1931) 48 R.P.C. 425; *Chrome-Alloying Co. Ltd v. Metal Diffusions Ltd* [1962] R.P.C. 33. Leave to amend was given in *Electrical & Musical Industries Ltd's Patent* [1963] R.P.C. 241, but the question of terms was deferred to the full hearing.   **2F–65**

Where a perpetual injunction had been granted several years before the application to amend, the Court as a term of the permission to amend dissolved the injunction (*Re Kenrick and Jefferson's Patent* (1912) 29 R.P.C. 25).

In general it requires a special case before the Court imposes conditions when permitting amendment (*Wilkinson Sword Ltd v. Gillette Industries Ltd* [1975] R.P.C. 101; *General Tire & Rubber Co (Frost's) Patent* [1974] F.S.R. 433).

After amendment, a patentee must start a fresh action rather than seek to enforce any relief he has obtained in a previous action. That practice is based upon the fact that there has been no judgment on infringement and validity in relation to the amended patent and upon the statutory provisions that an amendment dates back to the grant (*PLG Research Ltd v. Ardon International Ltd (No. 2)* [1993] F.S.R. 698).

Costs may be awarded to a successful patentee even though he later amends his specification and throws away all other relief obtained prior to amendment (*ibid.*).

Full disclosure of facts

2F–65.1 In amendment proceedings full disclosure is not always necessary since obligation primarily met by the statement of reasons; see *Intel Corporation's Patent* [2002] R.P.C. 957.

Discretion to refuse amendment

2F–66 Amendment will not be allowed where the object is delay (*Re Stahlwerk, etc. Patent* (1918) 36 R.P.C. 13). However, amendment to validate an invalid claim is very different from amendment to delete an invalid claim. The latter kind of amendment is much easier to make (*Chiron Corp v. Organon Teknika Ltd (No. 7)* [1994] F.S.R. 458, and *Johnson Electric Industrial Manufactory Ltd v. Mabuchi Motor KK (No.2)* [1996] F.S.R. 93). Even grave error is not the same as deliberately seeking an excessive monopoly (*Johnson v. Mabuchi*, above). Where an error in the patent specification was brought to the patentee's attention by the defendants in their Particulars of Objection (now called "Grounds of Invalidity"), but where the patentee had to wait for further particulars of other objections, a delay of over two years in bringing the motion to amend was excused (*Alliance Flooring Co Ltd v. Winsoflor Ltd* [1961] R.P.C. 95). It is not unreasonable to delay finalising amendments until the attack on the patent is pleaded (*Rediffusion Simulation Ltd v. Link-Miles Ltd* [1993] F.S.R. 369). The conduct of the patentee in allowing the unamended patent to be placed or remain on the register may be a bar to amendment. See, *e.g. V.D. Ltd v. Boston Deep Sea Fishing and Ice Co Ltd* (1936) 52 R.P.C. 303; *Chrome-Alloying Co Ltd v. Metal Diffusions Ltd* [1962] R.P.C. 33; *Van der Lely (C.) N.V. v. Bamfords Ltd* [1964] R.P.C. 54. But in general mere delay in applying to amend is not a ground for exercising the court's discretion against the patentee. There must have been some detriment caused to the opponents or the general public (which will generally require proof) or the patentee must have persisted in maintaining his patent with a specification which he knows or has been warned is suspect (*Matbro Ltd v. Michigan (GB) Ltd* [1973] R.P.C. 823; *Bristol Myers Co v. Manon Frères Ltd* [1973] R.P.C. 836; *Wilkinson Sword Ltd v. Gillette Industries Ltd* [1975] R.P.C. 101). Discretion to permit amendment will be withheld where the patentee is highly negligent in failing to seek amendment earlier (*Western Electric Co Ltd v. Racal-Milgo Ltd* [1981] R.P.C. 253). A patentee will be held to have delayed unreasonably where he knows his claims may be suspect but takes no steps for a substantial time to investigate the matter further, even where the public will not be put at a disadvantage in the meantime (*Smith Kline & French Laboratories Ltd v. Evans Medical Ltd* [1989] F.S.R. 561). Where litigation had been on foot for five and a half years, the Court of Appeal refused leave to apply for an amendment because of the delay and the unfairness to the defendant which would be caused by amendment proceedings (*Procter & Gamble Co v. Peaudouce (UK) Ltd* [1989] F.S.R. 614). Where delay is in issue, the fact that "without prejudice" negotiations took place is permissible to explain delay; and it may be that some evidence of what then took place is admissible, but this should not be decided as a preliminary matter (*Rediffusion Simulation Ltd v. Link Miles Ltd* [1992] F.S.R. 195). Covetousness is a ground for refusing amendment and the test for covetousness is discussed in *Donaldson Co Inc's Patent* [1986] R.P.C. 1. Where a patentee has knowingly permitted some claims to go forward on too broad a basis and fails to provide an adequate explanation, although he may not be permitted to narrow the claims, he may be permitted to delete the claims concerned altogether and retain any existing claims which are not open to the objection concerned (*Bentley Engineering Co's Patent* [1981] R.P.C. 361). The burden of proof that a claim as originally drafted was covetous, or that a claim was so wide that assertions of the useful results to be obtained by materials within the claim were so reckless as to amount to a fraudulent representation, lies on an opponent (*American Cyanamid Co (Wilkinson and Shepherd's Patent)* [1977] R.P.C. 349).

Where a patentee applied to amend after judgment to delete claims found invalid, the defendants in the action were not entitled to plead in opposition to the amendments sought that the valid claims were not supported by the description in the specification. There was no nexus between the support for those claims and the amendments sought and the reasons for seeking them (*Chiron Corp v. Organon Teknika (No. 11)* [1995] F.S.R. 589, CA).

However where the specification had been amended once (in opposition) and the application to amend further was made only shortly before the trial, amendment was refused on the ground, *inter alia*, of discretion (*Farmhand Inc. v. Spadework Ltd* [1974] F.S.R. 425).

The terms of the order are in the discretion of the Judge, and the Court of Appeal will not interfere save in the strongest cases. See *Allen v. Doulton* (1887) 4 R.P.C. 377 at 383; *Re Geipel's Patent* [1904] 1 Ch. 239; *Re Patent of British Thomson-Houston Co Ltd* (1922) 39 R.P.C. 251; *British Celanese Ltd v. Courtaulds Ltd* (1932) 49 R.P.C. 345. The position in the Court of Appeal is different, however, where the exercise of discretion by the judge below was obiter, the amendment having been refused below on other grounds (*Farmhand Inc v. Spadework Ltd* [1975] R.P.C. 617).

In an appropriate case, where a patentee applies to the court for leave to amend his specification following an initial finding of invalidity, it may be proper to have the matter adjourned, the amendments advertised and the question argued, see *e.g.* *Hallen v. Brabantia* [1989] R.P.C. 307. But this is not an appropriate case where there is no reasonable scope for a valid amendment or where such a course would be oppressive (*Windsurfing International Inc v. Tabor Marine (G.B.) Ltd* [1985] R.P.C. 59, CA). Because of the effect of amendment on the recovery of damages (see para. 104/2/37) an advertised amendment may be sought to be withdrawn or to be enlarged to a deletion. For discretion to allow and discussion on re-advertisement see *Quantel Ltd v. Spaceward Microsystems Ltd* [1990] R.P.C. 83.

Only in exceptional circumstances will the Patents Court on appeal from the Patent Office consider amendments to the specification which make the specification substantially different to that considered in the decision of the patent office; here the exceptional circumstances were that there was a relevant decision of the CA intervening (*Schering Biotech Corp's Application* [1993] R.P.C. 249).

Court's determination of question or application

63.11 Where the Comptroller—   **2F–67**

(a) **declines to deal with a question under section 8(7), 12(2), 37(8) or 61(5) of the 1977 Act;**

(b) **declines to deal with an application under section 40(5) of the 1977 Act; or**

(c) **certifies under section 72(7)(b) of the 1977 Act that the court should determine the question whether a patent should be revoked,**

any person seeking the court's determination of that question or application must issue a claim form within 14 days of the Comptroller's decision.

Application by employee for compensation

63.12—(1) An application by an employee for compensation **2F–68** **under section 40(1) or (2) of the 1977 Act must be made—**

(a) **in a claim form; and**

(b) **within the period prescribed by paragraphs (2) and (3).**

(2) **The prescribed period begins on the date of the grant of the patent and ends one year after the patent has ceased to have effect.**

(3) **Where a patent has ceased to have effect as a result of failure to pay the renewal fees within the period prescribed under rule 39**

of the Patents Rules 1995([1]), and an application for restoration is made to the Comptroller under section 28 of the 1977 Act, the period prescribed under paragraph (2)—

    (a) if restoration is ordered, continues as if the patent had remained continuously in effect; or

    (b) if restoration is refused, is treated as expiring one year after the patent ceased to have effect, or six months after the refusal, whichever is the later.

II. Registered trade marks and other intellectual property rights

Allocation

2F–69   63.13—(1) This Section of this Part applies to—

    (a) claims relating to matters arising out of the 1994 Act; and

    (b) other intellectual property rights as set out in the practice direction.

    (2) [...]

    (3) Claims to which this Section of this Part applies must be brought in—

    (a) the Chancery Division;

    (b) a Patents County Court; or

    (c) a county court where there is also a Chancery district registry.

Clarity of Pleadings

2F–70   Where a party seeks to revoke a trade mark from a date earlier than the date of the application for revocation, it should set out in the statement of grounds the date it contended for and explicitly allege that the grounds for revocation existed at an appropriate earlier date. See *Omega SA v. Omega Engineering Inc* [2003] EWCA 1334; [2003] F.S.R. 49.

Discontinuance

2F–71   The normal rule in the event of a Claimant discontinuing a claim is that the claimant has to pay the defendant's costs. The CPR gives the Court a discretion however— see *Coca-Cola Company, The v. Mabe* [2002] F.S.R. 731.

Claims under the 1994 Act

2F–72   63.14 In a claim under the 1994 Act, the claim form or application notice must be served on the registrar where the relief sought would, if granted, affect an entry in the United Kingdom register.

Claim for infringement of registered trade mark

2F–73   63.15—(1) In a claim for infringement of a registered trade mark the defendant may—

    (a) in his defence, challenge the validity of the registration of the trade mark; and

    (b) apply by Part 20 claim for—

        (i) revocation of the registration;

---

[1] S.I. 1995 No. 2093

(ii) **a declaration that the registration is invalid; or**

(iii) **rectification of the register.**

(2) **Where a defendant applies under paragraph (1)(b) and the relief sought would, if granted, affect an entry in the United Kingdom register, he must serve on the registrar a copy of his claim form.**

Pleadings

Julian Higgins' Trade Mark Application [2000] R.P.C. 321 and *Club Europe Trade Mark* [2000] R.P.C. 329—Trade mark notice of oppositions and statements of grounds are in effect pleadings—it is the function of pleadings to define the issues between the parties.

    The provision of material facts upon which an allegation was based is particularly important where an applicant for a declaration of invalidity relies upon s.5(4) of the 1994 Act. *Geobank Trade Mark* [1999] R.P.C. 682.

2F–74

Injunctive relief

Aktiebolaget Volvo v. Heritage (Leicester) Ltd [2000] F.S.R. 253—trade marks; breadth of injunction; wide injunction appropriate when evidence of behaviour not in accordance with honest business practices.

2F–75

III. Service

Service[1]

63.16—(1) **Subject to paragraph (2), Part 6 applies to service of a claim form and any document under this Part.**

(2) **A claim form relating to a registered right may be served—**

    (a) **on a party who has registered the right at the address for service given for that right in the United Kingdom Patent Office register, provided the address is within the jurisdiction; or**

    (b) **in accordance with rule 6.19(1) or (1A) on a party who has registered the right at the address for service given for that right in the appropriate register at—**

        (i) **the United Kingdom Patent Office; or**

        (ii) **the Office for Harmonisation in the Internal Market.**

2F–76

Service out of the jurisdiction

A foreign parent company and its UK subsidiary may have as good a common design to infringe a UK patent as any other joint tortfeasors, and if so, service outside the jurisdiction is proper (*Intel Corp v. General Instrument Corp* [1991] R.P.C. 235). See also *Lubrizol v. Esso (No.1)* [1992] R.P.C. 467, CA, where the parent company had not by taking procedural steps submitted to the jurisdiction, but was held to have admitted common design and the claimants had shown a good arguable case on infringement; but the joinder of the parent involved a new claim and relief against it would only run from six years previous to service upon it.

    Molins plc v. G.D SpA [2000] F.S.R. 893—service of proceedings.

2F–77

IV. Appeals

Appeals from the Comptroller

63.17—(1) **Part 52 applies to appeals from the Comptroller.**

2F–78

---

[1] Amended by Civil Procedure (Amendment No. 5) Rules 2003 (S.I. 2003 No. 3361).

(2) **Patent appeals are to be made to the Patents Court, and other appeals to the Chancery Division.**

(3) **Where Part 52 requires a document to be served, it must also be served on the Comptroller or registrar, as appropriate.**

Nature of Appeal from the Comptroller
2F–79 See *Ladney and Hendry's International Application* [1998] R.P.C. 319.

Costs on appeal
2F–80 The normal rule in relation to appeals concerning matters arising under the 1977 Act is that the successful party is awarded his costs (*Extrude Hone Corp's Patent* [1982] R.P.C. 361, Whitford J.; *Omron's Patent* [1981] R.P.C. 125). This rule also applies to appeals to which the Comptroller is a party. If there is any further appeal the CA apply the usual rule of assessed costs (*Associated British Combustion Ltd's Patent* [1978] R.P.C. 58). Costs may be awarded on an application to the Court of Appeal for leave to appeal (*International Paint Co's Appn* [1982] R.P.C. 247).

Cross-examination on appeal
2F–81 This will not normally be allowed. The proper time to ask for cross-examination is before the superintending examiner (*J. Sainsbury Ltd's Appn* [1981] F.S.R. 406).

Trade mark appeals
2F–82 For the principles on which new evidence should be allowed in an appeal from the Trade Marks Registry, see *Label Rouge Trade Mark* [2003] F.S.R. 13 and also *WUNDERKIND Trade Mark* [2002] R.P.C. 923, *Du Pont Trade Mark* [2003] EWCA Civ 1368,and *Omega Engineering Inc v. Omega SA* [2004] EWHC 2315 (Ch) .

The specific provisions for patent and trade mark appeals in ss. 16 and 23 respectively of Practice Direction 49E no longer apply. By virtue of new r.63.17, all appeals to the court from the comptroller are governed by Pt 52 of the Civil Procedure Rules and (see rr 52.1(4) and 52.2) its supplementary Practice Direction 52. This affects the period to file the notice of appeal at the court; extension of that period; and the nature of the appeal. (N.B. The new Rules apply only to the courts in England and Wales.) See *Patent Office Practice Notice 1/2003 (Revised)* [2003] R.P.C. 46. For the role of the appellate court in trade mark appeals, see also Harrison's Trade Mark Application ("Chinawhite") [2002] EWHC 3009, *REEF Trade Mark* [2003] R.P.C. 5, CA, *POLICE Trade Mark* [2004] R.P.C. 35 and *Du Pont Trade Mark* [2003] EWCA Civ 1368

Period for appeal: Practice Direction 52 para. 17.3
2F–82A Notice of appeal must be filed at the court within 28 days after the date of the comptroller's decision. There is no discretion for the comptroller to direct a different period.

For trade mark appeals a period of 28 days already applied. However, the period prescribed by s.16.3 for patent appeals (14 days for matters of procedure and six weeks in other cases) is abolished, with the consequence that it is no longer necessary in patent proceedings for the hearing officer to determine whether the decision relates to a matter of procedure. In accordance with rr.52.4(3) and 63.17(3) and para. 17.5 of Practice Direction 52, the appeal notice must be served on each respondent and on the comptroller as soon as practicable and in any event not later than seven days after it is filed. The period of 21 days prescribed by ss.16.8 and 23.4 of Practice Direction 49E is abolished.

Extension of the appeal period: CPR, r.52.6
2F–82B Any application to extend the period for appeal must be made to the court. The parties cannot extend the period by agreement (r.52.6(2)). Further, it is no longer possible for the comptroller to extend the period at the request of a party.

An appellant who applies for an extension from the court must state the reasons for the delay and the steps taken prior to the application being made. The respondent has a right to be heard on the application.

The nature of the appeal: CPR, r.52.11
2F–82C In general, in accordance with r.52.11 the appeal will be limited to a review of the

comptroller's decision. Section 16.15 of Practice Direction 49E, whereby patents appeals were by way of a rehearing rather than a review (although further evidence was prohibited on appeal except with the leave of the court) will no longer apply.

Appeals to the Appointed Person and the Registered Designs Appeal Tribunal

Appointed Person —The period for appeal to the Appointed Person is 28 days **2F–82D** under the Trade Marks Rules and the comptroller has sole jurisdiction to extend this period. In relation to the nature of the appeal, the Appointed Person is not bound by the Civil Procedure Rules but is generally guided by the court's approach to the distinction between review and rehearing.

Registered Designs Appeal Tribunal —The Registered Designs Appeal Tribunal Rules 1950 (as amended 1970) govern appeals to the Tribunal under s.28 of the Registered Designs Act 1949 (as amended by the Copyright, Designs and Patents Act 1988) and s.249 of the 1988 Act. Under these Rules the period for appeal is 14 days for a decision on a matter of procedure and six weeks for other decisions, and the comptroller may extend the period upon request made prior to its expiry.

PATENTS

PRACTICE DIRECTION—PATENTS AND OTHER INTELLECTUAL PROPERTY CLAIMS

This Practice Direction supplements CPR Part 63

Contents of this Practice Direction

2F–83 **1.1** This practice direction is divided into three sections—

- Section I—Provisions about patents and registered designs;
- Section II—Provisions about registered trade marks and other intellectual property rights;
- Section III—Provisions about appeals.
- Section IV—Provisions about final orders

I. PROVISIONS ABOUT PATENTS AND REGISTERED DESIGNS

2F–84 **2.1** This Section of this practice direction applies to claims in the Patents Court and a Patents County Court.

2.2 The following claims must be dealt with in the court—

   (1) any matter arising out of the 1977 Act, including—

      (a) infringement actions;

      (b) revocation actions;

      (c) threats under section 70 of the 1977 Act; and

      (d) disputes as to ownership;

   (2) registered designs;

   (3) Community registered designs; and

   (4) semiconductor topography rights.

Starting the claim (rule 63.5)

2F–85 **3.1** A claim form to which this Section of this Part applies must be marked in the top right hand corner "Patents Court" below the title of the court in which it is issued.

Case management (rule 63.7)

2F–86 **4.1** The following parts only of the practice direction supplementing Part 29 apply—

   (1) paragraph 5 (case management conferences)—

      (a) excluding paragraph 5.9; and

      (b) modified so far as is made necessary by other specific provisions of this practice direction; and

   (2) paragraph 7 (failure to comply with case management directions).

4.2 Case management shall be dealt with by—

   (1) a judge of the court; or

   (2) a Master or district judge where a judge of the court so directs.

4.3 The claimant must apply for a case management conference within 14 days of the date when all defendants who intend to file and serve a defence have done so.

4.4 Where the claim has been transferred, the claimant must apply for a case management conference within 14 days of the date of the order transferring the claim, unless the court—

   (1) held; or

   (2) gave directions for

a case management conference, when it made the order transferring the claim.

4.5 Any party may, at a time earlier than that provided in paragraphs 4.3 and 4.4, apply in writing to the court to fix a case management conference.

4.6 If the claimant does not make an application in accordance with paragraphs 4.3 and 4.4, any other party may apply for a case management conference.

4.7 The court may fix a case management conference at any time on its own initiative.

4.8 Not less than 4 days before a case management conference, each party must file and serve an application notice for any order which that party intends to seek at the case management conference.

4.9 Unless the court orders otherwise, the claimant, or the party who makes an application under paragraph 4.6, in consultation with the other parties, must prepare a case management bundle containing—

    (1)   the claim form;

    (2)   all statements of case (excluding schedules), except that, if a summary of a statement of case has been filed, the bundle should contain the summary, and not the full statement of case;

    (3)   a pre-trial timetable, if one has been agreed or ordered;

    (4)   the principal orders of the court; and

    (5)   any agreement in writing made by the parties as to disclosure,

and provide copies of the case management bundle for the court and the other parties at least 4 days before the first case management conference or any earlier hearing at which the court may give case management directions.

4.10 At the case management conference the court may direct that—

    (1)   a scientific adviser under section 70(3) of the Supreme Court Act 1981 be appointed; and

    (2)   a document setting out basic undisputed technology should be prepared.

        (Rule 35.15 applies to scientific advisers).

4.11 Where a trial date has not been fixed by the court, a party may apply for a trial date by filing a certificate which must—

    (1)   state the estimated length of the trial, agreed if possible by all parties;

    (2)   detail the time required for the judge to consider the documents;

    (3)   identify the area of technology; and

    (4)   assess the complexity of the technical issues involved by indicating the complexity on a scale of 1 to 5 (with 1 being the least and 5 the most complex).

4.12 The claimant, in consultation with the other parties, must revise and update the documents referred to in paragraph 4.9 appropriately as the case proceeds. This must include making all necessary revisions and additions at least 7 days before any subsequent hearing at which the court may give case management directions.

Disclosure and inspection (rule 63.8)

2F–87 **5.1** Standard disclosure does not require the disclosure of documents where the documents relate to—

(1) the infringement of a patent by a product or process if, before or at the same time as serving a list of documents, the defendant has served on the claimant and any other party—

(a) full particulars of the product or process alleged to infringe; and

(b) drawings or other illustrations, if necessary;

(2) any ground on which the validity of a patent is put in issue, except documents which came into existence within the period—

(a) beginning two years before the earliest claimed priority date; and

(b) ending two years after that date; and

(3) the issue of commercial success.

5.2 Where the issue of commercial success arises, the patentee must, within such time limit as the court may direct, serve a schedule containing—

(1) where the commercial success relates to an article or product—

(a) an identification of the article or product (for example by product code number) which the patentee asserts has been made in accordance with the claims of the patent;

(b) a summary by convenient periods of sales of any such article or product;

(c) a summary for the equivalent periods of sales, if any, of any equivalent prior article or product marketed before the article or product in sub-paragraph (a); and

(d) a summary by convenient periods of any expenditure on advertising and promotion which supported the marketing of the articles or products in sub-paragraphs (a) and (c); or

(2) where the commercial success relates to the use of a process—

(a) an identification of the process which the patentee asserts has been used in accordance with the claims of the patent;

(b) a summary by convenient periods of the revenue received from the use of such process;

(c) a summary for the equivalent periods of the revenues, if any, received from the use of any equivalent prior art process; and

(d) a summary by convenient periods of any expenditure which supported the use of the process in sub-paragraphs (a) and (c).

Short applications

6.1 Where any application is listed for a short hearing, the parties **2F–88** must file all necessary documents, skeleton arguments and drafts of any orders sought, by no later than 3.00 p.m. on the preceding working day.

6.2 A short hearing is any hearing which is listed for no more than 1 hour.

Timetable for trial

7.1 Not less than one week before the beginning of the trial, each **2F–89** party must inform the court in writing of the estimated length of its—

(1) oral submissions;

(2) examination in chief, if any, of its own witnesses; and

(3) cross-examination of witnesses of any other party.

7.2 At least four days before the date fixed for the trial, the claimant must file—

(1) the trial bundle; and

(2) a Reading Guide for the judge.

7.3 The Reading Guide filed under paragraph 7.2 must—

(1) be short and if possible, agreed;

(2) set out the issues, the parts of the documents that need to be read on each issue and the most convenient order that they should be read;

(3) identify the relevant passages in text books and cases, if appropriate; and

(4) not contain argument.

Jurisdiction of Masters

8.1 A Master may only deal with— **2F–90**

(1) orders by way of settlement, except settlement of procedural disputes;

(2) orders on applications for extension of time;

(3) applications for leave to serve out of the jurisdiction;

(4) applications for security for costs;

(5) other matters as directed by a judge of the court; and

(6) enforcement of money judgments.

Experiments

9.1 Where a party seeks to establish any fact by experimental proof **2F–91** conducted for the purpose of litigation he must, at least 21 days before service of the application notice for directions under paragraph 9.3, or within such other time as the court may direct, serve on all parties a notice—

(1) stating the facts which he seeks to establish; and

(2) giving full particulars of the experiments proposed to establish them.

9.2 A party served with notice under paragraph 9.1—

(1) must within 21 days after such service, serve on the other

PATENTS

party a notice stating whether or not he admits each fact; and

(2) may request the opportunity to inspect a repetition of all or a number of the experiments identified in the notice served under paragraph 9.1.

9.3 Where any fact which a party seeks to establish by experimental proof is not admitted, he must apply to the court for permission and directions by application notice.

Use of models or apparatus

2F–92 **10.1** Where a party intends to rely on any model or apparatus, he must apply to the court for directions at the first case management conference.

Claim for infringement and challenge to validity (rule 63.9)

2F–93 **11.1** In a claim for infringement of a patent—

(1) the statement of case must—
  (a) show which of the claims in the specification of the patent are alleged to be infringed; and
  (b) give at least one example of each type of infringement alleged; and

(2) a copy of each document referred to in the statement of case, and where necessary a translation of the document, must be served with the statement of case.

11.2 Where the validity of a patent or registered design is challenged—

(1) the statement of case must contain particulars of—
  (a) the relief sought; and
  (b) the issues except those relating to validity of the patent or registered design;

(2) the statement of case must have a separate document annexed to it headed "Grounds of Invalidity" specifying the grounds on which validity of the patent is challenged;

(3) a copy of each document referred to in the Grounds of Invalidity, and where necessary a translation of the document, must be served with the Grounds of Invalidity; and

(4) the Comptroller must be sent a copy of the Grounds of Invalidity and where any such Grounds of Invalidity are amended, a copy of the amended document, at the same time as the Grounds of Invalidity are served or amended.

11.3 Where, in an application in which validity of a patent or a registered design is challenged, the Grounds of Invalidity include an allegation—

(1) that the invention is not a patentable invention because it is not new or does not involve an inventive step, the particulars must specify such details of the matter in the state of art relied on, as set out in paragraph 11.4;

(2) that the specification of the patent does not disclose the invention clearly enough and completely enough for it to be performed by a person skilled in the art, the particulars must state, if appropriate, which examples of the invention

cannot be made to work and in which respects they do not work or do not work as described in the specification; or

(3) that the registered design is not new, the particulars must specify such details of the matter in the state of art relied on, as set out in paragraph 11.4.

11.4 The details required under paragraphs 11.3(1) and 11.3(3) are—

(1) in the case of matter or a design made available to the public by written description the date on which and the means by which it was so made available, unless this is clear from the face of the matter; and

(2) in the case of matter or a design made available to the public by use—

    (a) the date or dates of such use;

    (b) the name of all persons making such use;

    (c) any written material which identifies such use;

    (d) the existence and location of any apparatus employed in such use; and

    (e) all facts and matters relied on to establish that such matter was made available to the public.

11.5 In any proceedings in which the validity of a patent is challenged—

(1) on the ground that the invention did not involve an inventive step, a party who wishes to rely on the commercial success of the patent must state the grounds on which he so relies in his statement of case; and

(2) the court may order inspection of machinery or apparatus where a party alleges such machinery or apparatus was used before the priority date of the claim.

Application to amend a patent specification in existing proceedings (rule 63.10)

12.1 Not later than two days before the first hearing date the applicant, the Comptroller if he wishes to be heard, the parties to the proceedings and any other opponent, must file and serve a document stating the directions sought. **2F–94**

12.2 Where the application notice is served on the Comptroller electronically under rule 63.10(3), it must comply with any requirements for the sending of electronic communications to the Comptroller.

Application by employee for compensation (rule 63.12)

13.1 Where an employee applies for compensation under section 40(1) or (2) of the 1977 Act, the court must at the case management conference give directions as to— **2F–95**

(1) the manner in which the evidence, including any accounts of expenditure and receipts relating to the claim, is to be given at the hearing of the claim and if written evidence is to be given, specify the period within which witness statements or affidavits must be filed; and

(2) the provision to the claimant by the defendant or a person

deputed by him, of reasonable facilities for inspecting and taking extracts from the accounts by which the defendant proposes to verify the accounts in sub-paragraph (1) or from which those accounts have been derived.

Communication of information to the European Patent Office

2F–96   **14.1** The court may authorise the communication of any such information in the court files as the court thinks fit to—

(1)   the European Patent Office; or

(2)   the competent authority of any country which is a party to the European Patent convention.

14.2 Before authorising the disclosure of information under paragraph 14.1, the court shall permit any party who may be affected by the disclosure to make representations, in writing or otherwise, on the question of whether the information should be disclosed.

Order affecting entry in the register of patents or designs

2F–97   **15.1** Where any order of the court affects the validity of an entry in the register, the court and the party in whose favour the order is made, must serve a copy of such order on the Comptroller within 14 days.

15.2 Where the order is in favour of more than one party, a copy of the order must be served by such party as the court directs.

Claim for rectification of the register of patents or designs

2F–98   **16.1** Where a claim is made for the rectification of the register of patents or designs, the claimant must at the same time as serving the other parties, serve a copy of—

(1)   the claim form; and

(2)   accompanying documents

on the Comptroller or registrar, as appropriate.

16.2 Where documents under paragraph 16.1 are served on the Comptroller or registrar, he shall be entitled to take part in the proceedings.

European Community designs

2F–99   **17.1** The Patents Court and the Central London County Court are the designated Community design courts under Article 80(5) of Council Regulation (EC) 6/2002.

17.2 Where a counterclaim is filed at the Community design court, for a declaration of invalidity of a registered Community design, the Community design court shall inform the Office for Harmonisation in the Internal Market of the date on which the counterclaim was filed, in accordance with Article 86(2) of Council Regulation (EC) 6/2002.

17.3 On filing a counterclaim under paragraph 17.2, the party filing it must inform the court in writing that it is a counterclaim to which paragraph 17.2 applies and that the Office for Harmonisation in the Internal Market needs to be informed of the date on which the counterclaim was filed.

17.4 Where a Community design court has given a judgment which has become final on a counterclaim for a declaration of invalidity of a registered Community design, the Community design court shall send a copy of the judgment to the Office for Harmonisation in the Internal Market, in accordance with Article 86(4) of Council Regulation (EC) 6/2002.

17.5 The party in whose favour judgment is given under paragraph 17.4 must inform the Community design court at the time of judgment that paragraph 17.4 applies and that the Office for Harmonisation in the Internal Market needs to be sent a copy of the judgment.

II. PROVISIONS ABOUT REGISTERED TRADE MARKS AND OTHER INTELLECTUAL PROPERTY RIGHTS

Allocation (rule 63.13)

18.1 Any of the following claims must be brought in the Chancery Division, a Patents County Court or a county court where there is also a Chancery district registry—   **2F–100**

(1)   copyright;

(2)   rights in performances;

(3)   rights conferred under Part VII of the 1988 Act;

(4)   design right;

(5)   Community design right;

(6)   Olympic symbols;

(7)   plant varieties;

(8)   moral rights;

(9)   database rights;

(10)   unauthorised decryption rights;

(11)   hallmarks;

(12)   technical trade secrets litigation;

(13)   passing off;

(14)   geographical indications;

(15)   registered marks; and

(16)   Community registered trade marks.

18.2 There are Chancery district registries at Birmingham, Bristol, Cardiff, Leeds, Liverpool, Manchester and Newcastle upon Tyne.

Starting the claim

19.1 A claim form to which this Section of this Part applies must be marked in the top right hand corner "Chancery Division, Intellectual Property" below the title of the court in which it is issued.   **2F–101**

Claims under the 1994 Act (rule 63.14)

20.1 Where the registrar refers to the court an application made to him under the 1994 Act, then unless within one month of receiving notification of the decision to refer, the applicant makes the application to the court, he shall be deemed to have abandoned it.   **2F–102**

20.2 The period prescribed under paragraph 20.1 may be extended by—

(1)   the registrar; or

589

(2) the court

where a party so applies, even if such application is not made until after the expiration of the period prescribed.

20.3 Where an application is made under section 19 of the 1994 Act, the applicant must serve his claim form or application notice on all identifiable persons having an interest in the goods, materials or articles within the meaning of section 19 of the 1994 Act.

Claim for infringement of registered trade mark (rule 63.15)

2F–103   **21.1** Where a document under rule 63.15(2) is served on the registrar, he—

(1) may take part in the proceedings; and

(2) need not serve a defence or other statement of case, unless the court otherwise orders.

Order affecting entry in the register of trade marks

2F–104   **22.1** Where any order of the court affects the validity of an entry in the register, the provisions of paragraphs 15.1 and 15.2 shall apply.

Claim for rectification of the register of trade marks

2F–105   **23.1** Where a claim is made for the rectification of the register of trade marks, the provisions of paragraphs 16.1 and 16.2 shall apply.

European Community trade marks

2F–106   **24.1** The Chancery Division of the High Court, a PatentsCounty Court or a county court where there is also a Chancery district registry are designated Community trade mark courts under Article 91(1) of Council Regulation (EC) 40/94.

24.2 Where a counterclaim is filed at the Community trade mark court, for revocation or for a declaration of invalidity of a Community trade mark, the Community trade mark court shall inform the Office for Harmonisation in the Internal Market of the date on which the counterclaim was filed, in accordance with Article 96(4) of Council Regulation (EC) 40/94.

24.3 On filing a counterclaim under paragraph 24.2, the party filing it must inform the court in writing that it is a counterclaim to which paragraph 24.2 applies and that the Office for Harmonisation in the Internal Market needs to be informed of the date on which the counterclaim was filed.

24.4 Where the Community trade mark court has given a judgment which has become final on a counterclaim for revocation or for a declaration of invalidity of a Community trade mark, the Community trade mark court shall send a copy of the judgment to the Office for Harmonisation in the Internal Market, in accordance with Article 96(6) of Council Regulation (EC) 40/94.

24.5 The party in whose favour judgment is given under paragraph 24.4 must inform the Community trade mark court at the time of judgment that paragraph 24.4 applies and that the Office for Harmonisation in the Internal Market needs to be sent a copy of the judgment.

Claim for additional damages under section 97(2) or section 229(3) of the 1988 Act

25.1 Where a claimant seeks to recover additional damages under section 97(2) or section 229(3) of the 1988 Act, the particulars of claim must include— **2F–107**

(1) a statement to that effect; and

(2) the grounds for claiming them.

Application for delivery up or forfeiture under the 1988 Act

26.1 Where a claimant applies under sections 99, 114, 195, 204, 230 or 231 of the 1988 Act for delivery up or forfeiture he must serve— **2F–108**

(1) the claim form; or

(2) application notice, where appropriate,

on all identifiable persons who have an interest in the goods, material or articles within the meaning of sections 114 or 204 of the 1988 Act.

Olympic symbols

27.1 In this practice direction "the Olympic Symbol Regulations" means the Olympic Association Right (Infringement Proceedings) Regulations 1995. **2F–109**

27.2 Where an application is made under regulation 5 of the Olympic Symbol Regulations, the applicant must serve his claim form or application notice on all identifiable persons having an interest in the goods, materials or articles within the meaning of regulation 5 of the Olympic Symbol Regulations.

III. PROVISIONS ABOUT APPEALS

Appeals and references from the Comptroller (rule 63.17)

28.1 Where— **2F–110**

(1) a person appointed by the Lord Chancellor to hear and decide appeals under section 77 of the 1994 Act, refers an appeal to the Chancery Division of the High Court under section 76(3) of the 1994 Act; or

(2) the Comptroller refers the whole proceedings or a question or issue to the Chancery Division of the High Court under section 251(1) of the 1988 Act,

the appeal or reference must be brought within 14 days of the reference.

IV. PROVISIONS ABOUT FINAL ORDERS

29.1 Where the court makes an order for delivery up or destruction of infringing goods, or articles designed or adapted to make such goods, the defendant will pay the costs of complying with that order unless the court orders otherwise. **2F–110A**

29.2 Where the court finds that an intellectual property right has been infringed, the court may, at the request of the applicant, order appropriate measures for the dissemination and publication of the judgment to be taken at the defendant's expense.

Patents Court Guide

1. Introduction

2F-111   The general guidance applicable to matters in the Chancery Division, as set out in the Chancery Guide, also applies to patent actions unless specifically mentioned below. "PD63" refers to the Practice Direction—Patents and Other Intellectual Property Claims which supplements CPR Part 63. This Guide applies as appropriate to both the Patents Court and the Patents County Court.

2. General

2F-112   Actions proceeding in the Patents Court are allocated to the multi-track (CPR 63.7(1)). Attention is drawn to CPR 63(7) and its associated PD (case management).

3. The Patent Judges

2F-113   The two principal Patent Judges are in future Laddie and Pumfrey JJ. Their clerks are:

> Peter Smith (Clerk to Laddie J.) telephone: 020 7947 6518, fax: 020 7947 6439 e-mail: peter.smith@courtservice.gsi.gov.uk
> Bob Glen (Clerk to Pumfrey J.) telephone: 020 7947 7482, fax: 020 7947 6593 e-mail: robert.glen@courtservice.gsi.gov.uk

The other assigned Patents Judges are:

> Neuberger J. (Clerk: Don Bennett, telephone: 020 7947 7280, fax: 020 7947 6894) e-mail: donald.bennett@courtservice.gsi.gov.uk
> Patten J. (Clerk: Richard Trout, telephone: 020 7947 7617, fax: 020 7947 6693) e-mail: richard.trout@courtservice.gsi.gov.uk
> Lewison J. (Clerk: Denise Dolan, telephon: 020 7947 6039, fax: 020 7947 6739) e-mail: denise.dolan@courtservice.gsi.gov.uk

4. Patents County Court

2F-114   The Patents County Court judge is HHJ Fysh QC. All written communications to his Court must be clearly marked "Patents". The Court details are as follows:

The Patents County Court
Field House
15-25 Breams Buildings
London
EC4A 1DX
Clerk: Sarah Cox
Telephone: 020 7073 4251
Fax: 020 7073 4253

5. Arrangements for Listing

2F-115   With effect from August 1, 2003 the Chancery Listing Office will take over the responsibility for the listing of all patents work.

The offices are located in Room WG04 in the Royal Courts of Justice. The offices are open to the public from 10.00am to 4.30pm each day. The telephone numbers are: 020 7947 6778/6690 and the fax number is: 020 7947 7345.

Appointments to fix trials and intercolutory applications are dealt with on Mondays and Thursdays between 11.00am and 12.00 noon. The applicant should first obtain an appointment from the Listing Office and notify all interested parties of the date and time fixed.

Short applications (before the normal court day starts at 10.30am) can be issued and the hearing date arranged at any time by attendance at the Listing Office.

These are listed for hearing before the normal court day starts at 10.30am, for instance at 9.30 or 10.00am. Attention is drawn to PD63.6. Accurate time estimates are essential and a guillotine may be imposed on oral submissions if estimates show signs of being exceeded.

6. September Sittings

2F-116   Although the previous experiment of the court sitting in September for routine business is not being continued, the Patents Court will endeavour, if the parties so desire and the case is urgent, to sit in September.

7. Appeals from the Comptroller General of Patents, Trade Marks and Designs

Patents

By virtue of statute these lie only to the High Court and not the Patents County **2F–117**
Court. They are now governed by CPR Part 52 (see CPR 63.17). Permission to appeal
is not required. Note that the Comptroller must be served with a Notice of Appeal
(CPR 63.17(3)). The appellant has the conduct of the appeal and he or his representative should within two weeks of lodging the appeal, contact the clerk in charge of the
Patents List with a view to arranging a hearing date. The appellant shall ensure that
the appeal is set down as soon as is reasonably practicable after service of the notice of
appeal. Parties are reminded that the provisions about the service of skeleton arguments apply to appeals from the Comptroller.

Trade Marks

These are assigned to the Chancery Division as a whole, not the Patents Court (CPR
63.17(2)). Permission to appeal is not required.

Appeals on Paper only

The Court will hear appeals on the papers only if that is what the parties desire. If the
appellant is willing for the appeal to be heard on paper only, he should contact the respondent and the Patent Office at the earliest opportunity to discover whether such a
way of proceeding is agreed. If it is, the clerk to the Patents Judge should be informed
as soon as possible. The parties (and the Office if it so desires) should liase amongst
themselves for early preparation of written submissions and bundles and provide the
court with all necessary materials.

Appeals concerning Registered Designs

These go to the Registered Designs Appeal Tribunal. This consists of one of the patent
judges sitting as a tribunal. The CPR and PD do not apply to such appeals. Where
such an appeal is desired, contact should be made direct to the clerk in charge of the
Patents List.

8. Applications without Notice

A party wishing to apply without notice to the respondent(s) should contact the **2F–118**
Chancery Listing Office. In cases of emergency in vacation or out of normal court
hours the application should be made to the duty Chancery Judge. In the Patents
County Court, contact should be made with the Court Office.

9. Documents

(a) Bundling is of considerable importance and should be approached intelligently. **2F–119**
    The general guidance given in Appendix 2 of the Chancery Guide should be
    followed. Solicitors or patent agents who fail to do so may be required to
    explain why and may be penalised personally in costs.

(b) Copies of documents referred to in a statement of case (*e.g.* an advertisement
    referred to in a claim of infringement form or documents cited in Grounds of
    Invalidity) should be served with the statement of case. Where any such docu-
    ment requires translation, a translation should be served at the same time.

(c) If it is known which judge will be taking the case, papers for the case should
    be lodged directly with that judge's clerk. Faxed documents of significance
    (and particularly skeleton arguments) should be followed up by clean direct
    prints. By agreement documents may also be sent by e-mail with to the clerk
    of the Judge concerned.

(d) It is the responsibility of both parties to ensure that all relevant documents are
    lodged with the clerk of the judge who will be taking the case by noon two
    days before the date fixed for hearing unless some longer or shorter period
    has been ordered by the judge or is prescribed by this Guide.

(e) The judges request that all important documents also be supplied to them on
    disk in a format convenient for the judge's use (normally Microsoft Word 7 for
    Windows). These will include skeleton arguments, the witness statements and
    expert reports.

10. Streamlined Procedure

(a) Nature of a streamlined procedure.

A streamlined procedure is one in which, save and to the extent that it is otherwise **2F–120**
ordered:

    i. all factual and expert evidence is in writing;

    ii. there is no requirement to give disclosure of documents;

    iii. there are no experiments,

    iv. cross-examination is only permitted on any topic or topics where it is necessary and is confined to those topics;

    v. the total duration of the trial fixed is and will normally be not more than one day;

    vi. the date for trial will be fixed when the Order for a streamlined trial is made and will normally be about six months thereafter.

A streamlined procedure also includes minor variants of the above (*e.g.* disclosure confined to a limited issue).

(b) Criteria for a streamlined procedure

The court will order a streamlined procedure by agreement or, in the absence of agreement, where application of the overriding objective indicates that it is appropriate. Particular emphasis will be placed on proportionality, the financial position of each of the parties, degree of complexity and the importance of the case.

(c) When to apply for streamlined procedure

Any party may apply at any time after commencement of the action for a streamlined procedure. Any such application should be made at the earliest time reasonably possible, which will generally be at the case management conference required by PD63 within 14 days after service of the defence.

(d) How to apply for a streamline procedure

A party wishing for a streamlined procedure should, in the first instance, invite the other party(ies) to agree, setting out the proposed procedural steps in a draft Order. If there is agreement, the court will normally make the Order on a written application signed on behalf of each party. The parties should liase with each other and the clerk to the Patents Court or the Patents County court concerning a date for trial so that this can be fixed.

If there is no agreement, the party wishing for a streamlined procedure must make an application for it, setting forth the proposed procedural directions in his application notice and requesting that the application be determined on paper. He should support the application by a witness statement addressing the criteria in CPR Rule 1(2). The opposing party must, unless he obtains an extension of time (by consent or from the court) make and serve on the opposite party a witness statement in response within 10 days of service upon him of the application notice.

The court will determine the matter provisionally on paper alone and make a provisional judgment and order accordingly. Unless either side seeks an oral hearing the provisional order will come into effect 7 days after its service on the parties.

If a party is desirous of an oral hearing, it must, within 7 days of service upon it of the provisional order, seek an oral hearing in the immediate future by contacting the clerk to the Judge in charge of the patent list. Such an oral hearing will fixed as soon as is practicable, either by way of a telephone hearing or a short application.

(e) Duty to inform clients

The parties' legal advisers must draw their clients' attention to the availability of a streamlined procedure in the Patents Court and the Patents County Court.

    The court will take the streamlined procedure seriously, and in particular is proposing to take seriously and monitor compliance with the requirement that parties' legal advisors had drawn their attention to the streamlined procedure – see *Merck & Co Inc v.Generics (UK) Ltd* [2003] EWHC 2842 (Pat) .

11. Timetable for trial, Reading Guide, Time Estimates, common general knowledge

2F–121   Attention is drawn to PD63.7. Further the parties should endeavour to produce a composite document setting forth the matters alleged to form part of the common general knowledge and, where they disagree, what that disagreement is.

12. Narrowing of Issues

2F–122   As early as possible the patentee should identify which of the claims of its patent are contended to have independent validity and which of those claims are said to be infringed and should communicate a list of those claims to the other party.

This position should be kept under constant review. If there is any alteration in the number of claims said to have independent validity the patentee must forthwith notify the other parties.

13. Admissions

With a view to early elimination of non-issues, practitioners are reminded of the necessity of making admissions in accordance with CPR Rule 32.18 at an early stage. It should be done as early as possible, for instance, in a defence or reply. Thus in a defence a party may admit the acts complained of or that his article/process has certain of the features of a claim. In a reply a patentee may be able to admit prior publication of cited documents.

2F–123

Parties should also consider making a request to identify points not in dispute. Technically a request seeking admissions in respect of particular integers of a claim may involve a mixed question of fact and law and so not be within the rules about admissions. By asking whether or not the defendant disputes that his article/process has certain features of the claim the real dispute can be narrowed. Thus the ambit of disclosure and of witness and expert statements will be narrowed.

14. Skeleton Arguments, Pre-Trial and after the Evidence

In addition to the Reading Guide parties should lodge skeleton arguments in time for the Judge to read them before trial. That should normally be at least two days before commencement of the trial, but in substantial cases a longer period (to be discussed with the clerk to the Judge concerned) may be needed. It is desirable that each party should summarise what it contends to be the common general knowledge of the man skilled in the art.

2F–124

Following the evidence in a substantial trial a short adjournment may be granted to enable the parties to summarise their arguments in writing before oral argument.

In trials where a transcript of evidence is being made and supplied to the Judge, the transcript should be accompanied by a version on disk.

15. Jurisdiction of Masters

Masters have only a limited jurisdiction in patent matters (see PD63.8). Generally it is more convenient for consent orders (on paper or in court) to be made by a judge even where a Master has jurisdiction to do so.

2F–125

Where a Master makes a consent order disposing of an action which has been fixed, it is the duty of all the parties' representatives to inform both the clerk in charge of the Patents list and the Listing Office that the case has settled.

16. Agreed Orders

The court is normally willing to make consent orders without the need for the attendance of any parties. A draft of the agreed order and the written consent of all the parties' respective solicitors or counsel should be supplied to the clerk in charge of the Patents list. Where a draft has been substantially amended by hand, it is helpful for a disk of the unamended version to be supplied in accordance with paragraph 9.6 of the Chancery Guide. Unless the judge considers a hearing is needed he will make the order in the agreed terms by initialling it. It will be drawn up accordingly and sent to the parties.

2F–126

17. Telephone Applications

For short (20 minutes or less) matters, the Patents Judges are willing, unless a matter of general public importance is involved, to hear applications by telephone conference in accordance with the Practice Direction under CPR Part 23.

2F–127

It is possible for the application to be recorded, and if recording by the Patents Court rather than by British Telecom (or other service provider) is requested arrangements should be made with the clerk in charge of the Patents list. The recording will not be transcribed. The tape will be kept for a period of six months. Arrangements for transcription, if needed, must be made by the parties.

This procedure should be used where it will save costs.

18. Patents Judges able and willing to sit out of London

If the parties so desire, for the purpose of saving time or costs, the Patents Court will sit out of London. Before any approach is made to the clerk in charge of the Patents list, the parties should discuss between themselves the desirability of such

2F–128

course. If there is a dispute as to venue the court will resolve the matter on an application. Where there is no dispute, the clerk should be contacted as soon as possible so that arrangements can be put in place well before the date of the proposed hearing. The Patents County Court may also be able to sit out of London.

19. Intellectual Property Court Users' Committee

2F–129   This considers the problems and concerns of intellectual property litigation generally. Membership of the committee includes the principal Patents Judges, the Patents County Court Judge, a representative of each of the Patent Bar Association, the Intellectual Property Lawyers Association, the Chartered Institute of Patent Agents, the Institute of Trade Mark Agents and the Trade Marks Designs and Patents Federation. It will also include one or more other Chancery Judges. Anyone having views concerning the improvement of intellectual property litigation is invited to make his or her views known to the committee, preferably through the relevant professional representative on the committee. The Patents County Court also has a Users' Committee.

20. Orders following judgment

2F–130   Where a judgment is made available in draft before being given in open court the parties should, in advance of that occasion, exchange drafts of the desired consequential order. It is highly undesirable that one party should spring a proposal on the other for the first time when judgment is given. Where the parties are agreed as to the consequential order and have supplied a copy of the same signed by all parties or their representatives, attendance at the handing down of the judgment is not necessary.

21. Applications for interim remedies: trial dates

2F–131   When an application for an interim remedy is made the claimant should, where practicable, make prior investigations as to the estimated length of trial and possible trial dates.

22. Specimen minute of order for directions

2F–132   The general form minute of order for directions annexed to this practice direction has the approval of the Patents Judges. It is intended only as a guide and may need adaptation for particular circumstances.

ANNEX

2F–133   *STANDARD FORM OF ORDER FOR DIRECTIONS*
(* indicates a provision which may be necessary when a rule has not been compiled with, for example, standard disclosure in accordance with the Practice Direction supplementing CPR Part 63.)
[RECITALS AS NECESSARY]

Transfer

1. [This Action and Counterclaim be transferred to the Patents County Court.] (If this order is made, no other Order will generally be necessary, though it will generally be desirable for procedural orders to be made at this time to save the costs of a further conference in the County Court).

Proof of Documents

2. Legible copies of the specification of the Patent in suit [and any patent specifications or other documents cited in the Particulars of Objections] may be used at the trial without further proof thereof or of their contents.

Amendments to Pleadings

3. The Claimants have leave to amend their Claim Form shown in red on the copy [annexed to the Application Notice/as signed by the solicitors for the parties/annexed hereto] and [to re-serve the same on or before [date]/and that re-service be dispensed with] and that the Defendants have leave to serve a consequentially amended Defence within [number] days [thereafter/hereafter] and that the Claimants have leave to serve a consequentially amended Reply (if so advised) within [number] days thereafter.

4. (a) The Defendants have leave to amend their Defence [and Part 20 Claim and Grounds of Invalidity] as shown in red on the copy [annexed to the Application notice/as signed by the solicitors for the parties/annexed hereto] and [to reserve the same within [number] days/on or before[date]] [and that re-service be dispensed with] and that the Claimants have leave to serve a consequentially amended Reply (if so advised) within [number] days thereafter.

(b) The Claimants do on or before [date] elect whether they will discontinue this Claim and withdraw their Defence to Part 20 Claim and consent to an Order for the revocation of Patent No. ...("the patent in suit") AND IF the Claimants shall so elect and give notice thereof in the time aforesaid IT IS ORDERED THAT the patent in suit be revoked [and that it be referred to the Costs Judge to assess the costs of the Defendants and this Action and Grounds of Invalidity up to and including [date] being the date of service of the [amended] Grounds of Invalidity and Part 20 Claim to the date of this Order [except so far as the same have been increased by the failure of the Defendants originally to deliver the Defence and Grounds of Invalidity in its amended form], and to assess the costs of the Claimants in this Action and Part 20 Claim from [date] [insofar as they have been increased by the failure of the Defendants aforesaid] AND IT IS ORDERED that the said Costs Judge is to set off the costs of the Defendants and of the Claimants when so assessed as aforesaid and to certify to which of them the balance after such set-off is due.]/[Order for payment of sums determined by the Court on a summary assessment].

Further Information and Clarification

5. (a) The [Claimants/Defendants] do on or before [date] serve on the [Defendants/Claimants] the Further Information or Clarification of the [specify Statement of case] as requested by the [Claimants/Defendants] by their Request served on the [Defendants/Claimants] on [date] [and/or]

(b) The [Claimants/Defendants] do on or before [date] serve on the [Defendants/Claimants] a response to their Request for Further Information or Clarification of the [identify statement of case] served on the [Defendants/Claimants] on [date].

Admissions*

6. The [Claimants/Defendants] do on or before [date] state in writing whether or not they admit the facts specified in the [Defendants'/Claimants'] Notice to Admit facts dated [date].

Security

7. The Claimants do provide security for the Defendants' costs in the sum of £[state sum] by [specify manner in which security to be given] and that in the meantime all further proceedings be stayed.

Lists of Documents*

8. (a) The Claimants and the Defendants respectively do on or before [state date] make and serve on the other of them a list in accordance with form **N265** of the documents in their control which they are required to disclose in accordance with the obligation of standard disclosure in accordance with CPR Part 31 as modified by paragraph 5 of the Practice Direction - Patents etc. supplementing CPR Part 63.

(b) In respect of those issues identified in Schedule [number] hereto disclosure shall be limited to those [documents/categories of documents] listed in Schedule [number].

Inspection*

9. If any party wishes to inspect or have copies of such documents as are in another party's control it shall give notice in writing that it wishes to do so and such inspection shall be allowed at all reasonable times upon reasonable notice and any copies shall be provided within [number] working days of the request upon the undertaking of the party requesting the copies to pay the reasonable copying charges.

Experiments*

10. (a) Where a party desires to establish any fact by experimental proof, including an experiment conducted for the purposes of litigation or otherwise not being an experiment conducted in the normal course of research, that party shall on or before [date] serve on all the other parties a notice stating the facts which it desires to establish and giving full particulars of the experiments proposed to establish them.

(b) A party upon whom a notice is served under the preceding sub-paragraph shall within [number] days, serve on the party serving the notice a notice stating in respect of each fact whether or not that party admits it.

(c) Where any fact which a party wishes to establish by experimental proof is not admitted that party shall apply to the Court for further directions in respect of such experiments. [Or where paragraph 9 of the Practice Direction – Patents etc. supplementing CPR Part 63 has been complied with.]

11. (a) The Claimants/Defendants are to afford to the other parties an opportunity, if so requested, of inspecting a repetition of the experiments identified in paragraphs [specify them] of the Notice[s] of Experiments served on [date]. Any such inspection must be requested within [number] days of the date of this Order and shall take place within [number] days of the date of the request.

(b) If any party shall wish to establish any fact in reply to experimental proof that party shall on or before [date] serve on all the other parties a notice stating the facts which it desires to establish and giving full particulars of the experiments proposed to establish them.

(c) A party upon whom a notice is served under the preceding sub-paragraph shall within [number] days serve on the party serving the notice a notice stating in respect of each fact whether or not that party admits it.

(d) Where any fact which a party wishes to establish by experimental proof in reply is not admitted the party may apply to the Court for further directions in respect of such experiments.

Notice of Models, etc.

12. (a) If any party wishes to rely at the trial of this action upon any model, apparatus, drawing, photograph, cinematograph or video film whether or not the same is contained in a witness statement, affidavit or expert's report that party shall on or before [date] give notice thereof to all the other parties; shall afford the other parties an opportunity within [number] days of the service of such notice of inspecting the same and shall, if so requested, furnish the other party with copies of any such drawing or photograph and a sufficient drawing photograph or other illustration of any model or apparatus.

(b) If any party wishes to rely upon any such materials in reply to any matter of which notice was given under sub-paragraph (a) of this paragraph, that party shall within [number] days after the last inspection to be made in pursuance of the said sub-paragraph (a) give to the other parties a like notice, and if so requested within [number] days of delivery of such notice shall afford like opportunities of inspection which shall take place within [number] days of such request; and shall in like manner furnish copies of any drawing or photograph and illustration of any such model or apparatus.

(c) No further or other model apparatus drawing photograph cinematograph or video film shall be relied upon in evidence by either party save with consent or by leave of the Court.

Written Evidence

13. (a) Each party may call up to [number] expert witnesses in this Action and Part 20 Claim provided that the said party:

    i. supplies the name of such expert to the other parties and to the Court on or before [date]; and

    ii. no later than [date/[number days] before the date set for the hearing of this Action and Part 20 Claim] serve upon the other parties a report of each such expert comprising the evidence which that expert intends to give at trial.

(b) Each party shall on or before [date] serve on the other parties [signed] written statements of the oral evidence which the party intends to lead on any issues of fact to be decided at the trial, such statements to stand as the evidence in chief of the witness unless the Court otherwise directs;

(c) The parties shall [here insert the particular directions sought, *e.g.* within 21 days after service of the other party's expert reports and written statements state in writing the facts and matters in those reports and statements which are admitted].

Admissibility of Evidence

14. A party who objects to any statements of any witness being read by the Judge prior to the hearing of the trial, shall serve upon each other party a notice in writing to that effect setting out the grounds of the objection.

Non-Compliance

15. Where either party fails to comply with the directions relating to experiments and written evidence it shall not be entitled to adduce evidence to which such directions relate without the leave of the Court.

Trial Bundles

16. Each party shall no later than [number] days before the date fixed for the trial of this Action and Counterclaim serve upon the parties a list of all the documents to be included in the trial bundles. The Claimants shall no later than [number] days before the date fixed for trial serve upon the Defendants...sets of the bundles for use at trial.

Trial

17. The trial of these proceedings shall be before an Assigned Judge alone in [London], estimated length [number] days and a pre-reading estimate for the Judge of [number] days.

Liberty to Apply

18. The parties are to be at liberty on two days' notice to apply for further directions and generally.

Costs

19. The costs of this Application are to be costs in the Action and Part 20 Claim.

PATENTS

2G   APPLICATIONS UNDER THE COMPANIES ACT 1985

PRACTICE DIRECTION—APPLICATIONS UNDER THE COMPANIES ACT 1985 AND OTHER LEGISLATION RELATING TO COMPANIES

This Practice Direction supplements CPR Part 49 and replaces, with modifications, RSC Order 102 and CCR Order 49, Rule 3   **2G–1**

General

1.(1) In this practice direction—

"the Act" means the Companies Act 1985 and includes the Act as applied to limited liability partnerships by the Limited Liability Partnerships Regulations 2001.

"the CJPA" means the Criminal Justice and Police Act 2001;

"the companies court registrar" means any officer of the High Court who is a registrar within the meaning of any rules for the time being in force relating to the winding-up of companies;

"the court" includes the companies court registrar;

"the EC Regulation" means Council Regulation (EC) No 2157/2001 of 8 October 2001 on the Statute for a European company (SE);

"the ICA" means the Insurance Companies Act 1982;

"Part VII FISMA means Part VII of the Financial Services and Markets Act 2000;

"the Rules" means the Civil Procedure Rules 1998;

"SE" means a European public limited-liability company (Societas Europaea) within the meaning of Article 1 of the EC Regulation.

(2) Applications under the Act may be made in the county court if the county court would have jurisdiction to wind up the company in question (see the definition of "the court" in section 744 of the Act). A company can be wound up in the county court if its paid-up capital is not more than £120,000 (s.117(2) Insolvency Act 1986).

(3) Every claim form or petition by which an application under the Act, Part VII FISMA or the ICA is begun and all affidavits, witness statements, notices and other documents in those proceedings must be entitled in the matter of the company in question and in the matter of the Act, Part VII FISMA or the ICA as the case may be.

Commencement of proceedings

2.(1) Except in the case of the applications mentioned in sub-paragraph (4) below–   **2G–2**

(a) every application under the Act, whether made in the High Court or in the county court;

(b) every application under Part VII FISMA;

(c) every application under Articles 25 and 26 of the EC Regulation; and

(d) every application under section 59 of the CJPA,

must be made by the issue of a claim form and the use of the procedure set out in CPR Part 8, subject to any modification of that procedure under this practice direction or any other practice direction relating to applications under the Act.

(2) Notice of an application under section 721 of the Act need not be given to the respondent and the claim form need not be served on him.

(3) A claim form issued under this paragraph must, in the High Court, be issued out of the office of the companies court registrar or a chancery district registry, or in the county court, out of a county court office.

(4) This paragraph does not apply to applications under sections 459 or 460 of the Act or to any of the applications specified in paragraph 4(1) of this practice direction.

3. All High Court applications to which this practice direction applies shall be assigned to the Chancery Division.

Applications under Part VII FISMA

2G–3   **3A.**(1) From 1st December 2001 applications to sanction insurance business transfer schemes or banking business transfer schemes must be made under Part VII FISMA, Schedule 2C of the ICA, subject to minor modifications, will continue to apply to applications to sanction or approve transfers of insurance business which are made up to and including 30th November 2001 (see the Financial Services and Markets Act 2000 (Transitional Provisions and Savings) (Business Transfers) Order 2001).

(2) Any application under Part VII FISMA must comply with the requirements of the Control of Business Transfers (Requirements on Applicants) Regulations 2001.

(3) In relation to insurance transfer schemes, the Supervision Manual of the Financial Services Authority ("FSA"), available on the FSA's website (www.fsa.gov.uk), contains rules and guidance with regard to the operation of Part VII FISMA and the FSA's role thereunder which should be referred to before any application under Part VII FISMA is made.

(4) Paragraphs 10 to 13 of this practice direction apply to applications under Part VII FISMA.

Applications under the EC Regulation

2G–4   **3B.**(1) An application for a certificate under Article 25(2) of the EC Regulation must—

(a) be issued in the Chancery Division of the High Court;

(b) identify the pre-merger acts and formalities applicable to the applicant company, and be accompanied by evidence that those acts and formalities have been completed;

(c) be accompanied by copies of:

(i) the draft terms of merger as provided for in Article 20 of the EC Regulation;

> (ii) the entry in the Gazette containing the particulars specified in Article 21 of the EC Regulation;
>
> (iii) a report drawn up and adopted by the directors of the applicant company containing the same information as would be required by paragraph 4 of Schedule 15B to the Act if there were to be a scheme of arrangement under sections 425 and 427A of the Act;
>
> (iv) the expert's report to the members of the applicant company drawn up in accordance with paragraph 5 of Schedule 15B to the Act or Article 22 of the EC Regulation; and
>
> (v) the resolution of the applicant company approving the draft terms of merger in accordance with Article 23 of the EC Regulation.

(2) Attention is drawn to Article 26(2) of the EC Regulation. Where it is proposed that the registered office of an SE should be in England or Wales, each of the merging companies is required, within 6 months after a certificate is issued in respect of that company under Article 25(2), to submit the certificate to the High Court in order that it may scrutinise the legality of the merger.

(3) Where a merging company is required to submit a certificate to the High Court under Article 26(2) of the EC Regulation, if no other merging company has commenced proceedings under Article 26, that company shall commence such proceedings by issuing a claim form in the Chancery Division.

(4) The claim form must—

(a) identify the SE and all of the merging companies;

(b) be accompanied by the documents referred to in paragraph 3B(6); and

(c) be served on each of the other merging companies.

(5) Where a merging company is required to submit a certificate to the High Court under Article 26(2) of the EC Regulation and proceedings under Article 26 have already been commenced, that company shall—

(a) file an acknowledgment of service not more than 14 days after service of the claim form, and serve the acknowledgment of service on each of the other merging companies; and

(b) file the documents referred to in paragraph 3B(6) within the time limit specified in Article 26(2), and serve copies of those documents on each of the other merging companies.

(6) Each merging company must file and serve the following documents in proceedings under Article 26 of the EC Regulation—

(a) the certificate issued under Article 25(2) in respect of that company;

> (b) a copy of the draft terms of merger approved by that company;
>
> (c) evidence that arrangements for employee involvement have been determined by that company pursuant to Council Directive 2001/86/EC of 8 October 2001 supplementing the Statute for a European company with regard to the involvement of employees; and
>
> (d) evidence that the SE has been formed in accordance with the requirements of Article 26(4) of the EC Regulation.

(7) Proceedings under Article 25 and Article 26 of the EC Regulation will be heard by a High Court judge.

(8) Paragraphs 10 to 13 of this practice direction apply to proceedings under Article 25 and 26 of the EC Regulation.

Applications made by petition

2G–5   4.(1) The following applications under the Act in addition to applications under sections 459 and 460 of the Act and applications under the ICA must be made by petition, namely, applications:

> (a) under section 5 to cancel the alteration of a company's objects,
>
> (b) under section 17 to cancel the alteration of a condition contained in a company's memorandum,
>
> (c) under section 130 to confirm a reduction of the share premium account of a company,
>
> (d) under section 136 to confirm a reduction of the share capital of a company,
>
> (e) under section 127 to cancel any variation or abrogation of the rights attached to any class of shares in a company,
>
> (f) under section 425 to sanction a compromise or arrangement between a company and its creditors or any class of them or between a company and its members or any class of them,
>
> (g) under section 653 for an order restoring the name of a company to the register, where the application is made in conjunction with an application for the winding up of the company,
>
> (h) under section 690 to cancel the alteration of the form of a company's constitution,
>
> (i) under section 727 for relief from liability of an officer of a company or a person employed by a company as auditor,
>
> (j) under section 54(1) to cancel resolution to which that section applies,
>
> (k) under sections 157(2) or 176(1) to cancel a special resolution to which either of those sections applies, and
>
> (l) under section 170 in relation to the reduction of capital redemption reserve.

(2)   Paragraphs 5 to 14 of this practice direction apply to the applications specified in sub-paragraph (1).

5.(1)   After the presentation of a petition by which any application **2G–6** mentioned in paragraph 4 is made, the petitioner, except where his application is one of those mentioned in sub-paragraph (2), must apply for directions by filing an application notice.

(2)   The exceptions referred to in sub-paragraph (1) are:

    (a) an application under section 425 of the Act to sanction a compromise or arrangement unless there is included in the petition for such sanction an application for an order under section 427 of the Act,

    (b) an application under section 653 of the Act for an order restoring the name of a company to the register,

    (c) an application under section 54(1) of the Act for an order cancelling a special resolution to which that section applies, and

    (d) an application under section 157(2) or 176(1) of the Act for an order cancelling a special resolution to which those sections apply.

(3)   At the directions hearing the court may by order give such directions for the hearing of the application as it thinks fit including, in particular, directions for the publication of notices and the making of any inquiry.

(4)   Where the application made by the petition is to confirm a reduction of the share capital, the share premium account, or the capital redemption reserve, of a company the Court may give directions:

    (a) for an inquiry to be made as to the debts of, and claims against, the company or as to any class or classes of such debts or claims,

    (b) as to the proceedings to be taken for settling the list of creditors entitled to object to the reduction and fixing the date by reference to which the list is to be made,

and the power of the court under section 136(6) of the Act to direct that section 136(3) to (5) thereof shall not apply as regards any class of creditors may be exercised at any directions hearing.

Reduction of capital and schemes of arrangement

6.(1)   The consent of a creditor to such reduction as is mentioned **2G–7** in paragraph 5(4) may be proved in such manner as the Court thinks sufficient.

(2)   The evidence in support of a petition to confirm a reduction of capital need not show as regards any issue of shares made since 1900 for a consideration other than cash that the statutory requirements as to registration were complied with. It is sufficient to state in the petition the extent to which any issued shares (other than shares issued otherwise than for cash before 1901) are or are deemed to be paid up.

(3)   The existing practice will remain unaltered in respect of is-

sues of shares otherwise than for cash made before 1901 whilst s.25 of the Companies Act 1867 remained in operation.

2G–8   7.(1) This paragraph applies to:

    (a) schemes of arrangement under sections 425 to 427A of the Companies Act 1985, whether made with creditors or members,

    (b) schemes for the transfer of the whole or part of the long-term business of an insurance company to which schedule 2C to the ICA applies, and

    (c) reductions of capital, share premium account or capital redemption reserve.

References in this and subsequent paragraphs to "schemes" are to schemes falling within (a) or (b) above, and references to "reductions" are to reductions falling within (c) above.

(2) Petitions to sanction schemes will be heard by the Companies Court Judge.

(3) Petitions to confirm reductions will be heard by the Companies Court Registrar unless otherwise ordered. The Registrar will hear petitions to confirm reductions in open court on a Wednesday each week after completion of the list of winding up petitions.

Schemes and reductions in the long vacation

2G–9   8.(1) The following requirements must be satisfied for a hearing to be fixed to sanction a scheme and/or confirm a reduction in the Long Vacation:

    (a) The application is one in which for financial, commercial or economic reasons a hearing before the end of the Long Vacation is desirable. This category will include cases of mergers and takeovers which arise in the summer and are likely to be affected by market fluctuations.

    (b) The application is one which could not with reasonable diligence have been made and prosecuted in time to be heard before the Long Vacation begins.

(2) An informal application in chambers, to the Court Manager, accompanied by an advocate's certificate that requiremens (a) and (b) are satisfied, must be made as soon as possible so that a suitable timetable may be settled, including a date for hearing.

(3) In the case of reductions to be heard by the Registrar, certain applications which do not fall within the above categories will be heard provided (i) that there is an urgent need for a hearing or (ii) that there is sufficient time available after the Registrar has disposed of the urgent applications.

(4) Applications to the Registrar in chambers for orders convening meetings to consider schemes and for directions on reduction applications will continue to be heard during the Long Vacation. Provided notice is given to the court before

the Long Vacation begins, a timetable will be fixed which will enable any necessary documents to be settled in chambers and enable the Registrar to hear the application.

(5) The Vacation Judge will be available to hear petitions to sanction schemes and any petitions to confirm reductions which require to be heard by a judge on one Wednesday in August and two Wednesdays in September on dates to be arranged and subsequently notified in the Long Vacation Notice which is printed in the Daily Cause List.

(6) The Vacation Judge may also hear petitions to sanction schemes or confirm reductions on other days if he thinks fit.

9.(1) Attention is drawn to the undesirability of asking as a matter **2G–10** of course for a winding up order as an alternative to an order under s.459 Companies Act 1985. The petition should not ask for a winding up order unless that is the relief which the petitioner prefers or it is thought that it may be the only relief to which the petitioner is entitled.

(2) Whenever a winding up order is asked for in a contributory's petition, the petition must state whether the petitioner consents or objects to an order under s.127 of the Act in the standard form. If he objects, the written evidence in support must contain a short statement of his reasons.

(3) If the petitioner objects to a s.127 order in the standard form but consents to such an order in a modified form, the petition must set out the form of order to which he consents, and the written evidence in support must contain a short statement of his reasons for seeking the modification.

(4) If the petition contains a statement that the petitioner consents to a s.127 order, whether in the standard or a modified form, but the petitioner changes his mind before the first hearing of the petition, he must notify the respondents and may apply on notice to a Judge for an order directing that no. s.127 order or a modified order only (as the case may be) shall be made by the Registrar, but validating dispositions made without notice of the order made by the Judge.

(5) If the petition contains a statement that the petitioner consents to a s.127 order, whether in the standard or a modified form, the Registrar shall without further enquiry make an order in such form at the first hearing unless an order to the contrary has been made by the Judge in the meantime.

(6) If the petition contains a statement that the petitioner objects to a s.127 order in the standard form, the company may apply (in the case of urgency, without notice) to the Judge for an order.

(7) Section 127 Order—Standard Form:
(Title, etc.)
ORDER that notwithstanding the presentation of the said Petition
(1) payments made into or out of the bank accounts of the

Company in the ordinary course of the business of the Company and

(2) dispositions of the property of the Company made in the ordinary course of its business for proper value between the date of presentation of the Petition and the date of judgment on the Petition or further order in the meantime

shall not be void by virtue of the provisions of section 127 of the Insolvency Act 1986 in the event of an Order for the winding up of the Company being made on the said Petition Provided that (the relevant bank) shall be under no obligation to verify for itself whether any transaction through the company's bank accounts is in the ordinary course of business, or that it represents full market value for the relevant transaction.

This form of Order may be departed from where the circumstances of the case require.

Case management

2G–11   **10.** Every application to which this practice direction applies shall be allocated to the multi-track and the CPR relating to allocation questionnaires and track allocation will not apply.

Service

2G–12   **11.** Service of documents in proceedings in the High Court to which this practice direction applies will be the responsibility of the parties and will not be undertaken by the court. Subject to that CPR Part 6 applies.

Filing of documents

2G–13   **12.**(1) Where an application to which this practice direction relates is proceeding in any Chancery district registry, all affidavits and witness statements made in connection with the application must be filed in that registry.

(2)   Where an application to which this practice direction relates in proceeding in any county court, all affidavits and witness statements made in connection with the application must be filed in the office of that county court.

Drawing up of orders

2G–14   **13.** The court will draw up all orders with the following exceptions:

(a)   orders by the Registrar on the application of the Official Receiver or for which the Treasury Solicitor is responsible under the existing practice,

(b)   orders by the court in relation to reductions or schemes.

Applications under section 59 of the CJPA

2G–15   **14.**(1) This paragraph applies to applications under section 59 of the CJPA in respect of property seized in the exercise of the power conferred by section 448(3) of the Act (including any additional powers of seizure conferred by section 50 of the CJPA which are exercisable by reference to that power).

(2) An application to which this paragraph applies should be made to a judge of the Chancery Division.

(3) The defendant to an application under section 59(2) or 59(5)(c) of the CJPA shall be the person for the time being having possession of the property to which the application relates.

(4) On an application under section 59(2) or 59(5)(c) of the CJPA, the claim form and the claimant's evidence must be served on—

    (a) the person for the time being having possession of the property to which the application relates;

    (b) in the case of an application under section 59(2) for the return of seized property, the person specified as the person to whom notice of such an application should be given by any notice served under section 52 of the CJPA when the property was seized;

    (c) in the case of an application under section 59(5)(c), the person from whom the property was seized (if not the claimant); and

    (d) in all cases, any other person appearing to have a relevant interest in the property within the meaning of section 59(11) of the CJPA.

(5) An application under section 59(2) or 59(5)(c) of the CJPA must be supported by evidence—

    (a) that the claimant has a relevant interest in the property to which the application relates within the meaning of section 59(11) of the CJPA; and

    (b) in the case of an application under section 59(2), that one or more of the grounds set out in section 59(3) of the CJPA is satisfied in relation to the property.

(6) The defendants to an application under section 59(5)(b) of the CJPA by a person for the time being in possession of seized property shall be—

    (a) the person from whom the property was seized; and

    (b) any other person appearing to have a relevant interest in the property to which the application relates within the meaning of section 59(11) of the CJPA.

(7) If an application to which this paragraph applies would not otherwise be served on the person who seized the property, and the identity of that person is known to the applicant, notice of the application shall be given to the person who seized the property.

(8) In all applications to which this paragraph applies, when the court issues the claim form it will fix a date for the hearing.

2G–16 *Note*—Amended by Civil Procedure (Amendment No. 3) Rules 2004 (S.I. 2004 No. 3129). The commencement date of these amendments is dependant on s.100 of the Courts Act 2003. At the time of the *White Book* going to press, it has not been indicated when it will be in force.

Companies Court Practice Direction — Commentary

Companies Court

2G–17 Companies Court is not a separate and distinct part of the High Court but a descriptive term for the part of the Chancery Division of the High Court which deals with cases which are generally commenced before the bankruptcy registrar sitting in Companies Court from time to time (*Re Shilena Hosiery Co Ltd* [1980] Ch 219). Cases so commenced are generally those involving the Companies Acts and the Financial Services and Markets Act 2000 (Part VII). The Insurance Companies Act 1982 has largely been repealed (by S.I. 2001 No. 3649, art.3(1)(b); see S.I. 2001 No. 3639, S.I. 2001 No. 3646 and S.I. 2001 No. 3650 for saving provisions): insurance or banking business transfer schemes with the sanction of the court are now governed by the provisions of Part VII Financial Services and Markets Act 2000. The Companies Court also deals with cases under the Insolvency Act 1986, the Company Directors Disqualification Act 1986 and related legislation.

Jurisdiction

2G–18   The Companies Act gives jurisdiction to the court to make a wide range of orders granting relief in relation to companies. "The court" is defined in relation to a company as the court having jurisdiction to wind up the company (s.744 of the Companies Act 1985). Section 117(1) of the Insolvency Act 1986 provides that the High Court has jurisdiction to wind up any company registered in England and Wales, and s.117(2) gives concurrent jurisdiction to the county court of the district in which the company's registered office is situated where the amount of the company's share capital paid up or credited as paid up does not exceed £120,000. Every court in England and Wales having winding up jurisdiction has for the purposes of that jurisdiction all the powers of the High Court (s.117(5) of the Insolvency Act 1986). A company's registered office for the purpose of s.117 of the Insolvency Act 1986 is the place which has longest been its registered office during the six months immediately preceding the presentation of a petition for winding up (s.117(6)). The relevant date for the purpose of determining jurisdiction is the date when proceedings are commenced, which need not be the date on which the company went into liquidation (*Re Lichfield Freight Terminal Ltd* [1997] BCC 11).

Company

2G–19   "Company" means a company formed and registered under the Companies Act 1985 or under the former Companies Acts (*i.e.* the Joint Stock Companies Acts, the Companies Act 1862, the Companies (Consolidation) Act 1908, the Companies Act 1929 and the Companies Acts 1948 to 1983) but excluding those in what is now Ireland (s.735(1) of the Companies Act 1985).

Issuing proceedings

2G–20   All applications and petitions under the Companies Act are listed for directions before the registrar save for applications for injunctions. The majority of petitions and applications are heard and finally determined by the registrar. The following are always heard and tried by the judge: final hearings of petitions to sanction a scheme of arrangement under ss.425 *et seq.* of the Companies Act 1985 or applications to do so under the Financial Services and Markets Act 2000; petitions under ss.459 *et seq.* of the Companies Act 1985; applications for injunctions; and cases involving new or complex points of law or which are likely to last more than half a day.

All applications to be heard by the registrar should be issued and listed in the issue section of Companies Court on the second floor of Thomas More Building in the Royal Courts of Justice.

Urgent applications to be heard by the registrar may be listed by arrangement with the Companies Court clerks to be heard at 10.15 a.m. Urgent applications to be heard by the judge should be fixed through the Chancery Listing Office, Room WG4, West Green Building, Royal Courts of Justice.

Other practice directions and practice notes

2G–21   The present Practice Direction is not framed so as to supersede other earlier practice directions and practice notes affecting the business of the Companies Court. Thus, it would seem, for example, that the following may still have application in the Companies Court: *Practice Direction* [1947] W.N. 116 (on valuation of assets in capital reductions, but as to which see para. 2G–32), *Practice Direction* [1965] 1 All E.R. 43; [1965] 1 W.L.R. 120 (on change of name of a company (see para. 2G–21)), *Practice Direction (Companies: Reduction of Capital)* [1966] 2 All E.R. 146; [1966] 1 W.L.R. 836 and *Practice Direction (Companies Court: Contributory's Petition)* (No. 1 of 1990)

[1990] 1 W.L.R. 490 (on contributories' petitions and s.127 of the Insolvency Act 1986). See also *Practice Statement (Companies: Schemes of Arrangement)* [2002] 1 W.L.R. 1345 (on schemes of arrangement, replacing *Practice Note* [1934] W.N. 142).

The Chancery Guide (October 2002) also provides general guidance on procedure in the Chancery Division (see in particular Chapter 20).

Change in company name

Where a company which is a party to proceedings changes its name in the course of **2G–22** proceedings, the new name should be substituted and the old name mentioned in brackets thereafter (*Practice Direction* [1965] 1 All E.R. 43; [1965] 1 W.L.R. 120).

Applications made by petition

Applications which must be made by petition rather than by claim form are those **2G–23** set out in paragraph 4.(1) of the Practice Direction (see paragraph 2G-5). In the High Court the petition should be headed In the High Court of Justice, Chancery Division, Companies Court and entitled "In the matter of [ ] Limited And in the matter of the Companies Act 1985" (or as the case may be). It should be addressed to Her Majesty's High Court of Justice and begin, "The petition of [ ] shows as follows:", followed by basic statutory information about the relevant company (its name, date of incorporation, registered office, principal objects ("...and other objects set out in the company's memorandum of association") and details of its share capital. Thereafter the petitioner should set out brief details of the matters complained of and end, "Your petitioner(s) therefore pray(s) as follows:), setting out the relief to be sought.

Petitions are issued on the second floor, Thomas More Building of the Royal Courts of Justice or in the equivalent office of any district registry or county court having jurisdiction. Sufficient copies of the petition should be submitted for sealing, allowing for an original for the court file, sufficient copies for the petitioner and for service on any respondents, and copies to exhibit to any evidence of service or evidence verifying the petition which may later have to be filed.

The petition will be endorsed with a hearing date. Where an application is required for directions, sufficient time should be allowed between the directions hearing and the final hearing of the petition. Petitions or other applications in connection with schemes of arrangement or capital or other reductions should be listed by arrangement with the Companies Court schemes and reductions case manager, Room TM 410, Thomas More Building, Royal Courts of Justice, to whom inquiries may also be made by telephone (020 7947 6727).

Para. (a) Applications to cancel the alteration of a company's objects (s.5(1)).

A company may generally change its objects without reference to the court by **2G–24** means of a special resolution. However, application may be made to the court for any amendment to the company's memorandum to be cancelled. The application may be made by the holders of not less in the aggregate than 15 per cent in nominal value of the company's issued share capital or any class thereof, or, if the company is not limited by shares, not less than 15 per cent of the company's members; or by the holders of not less than 15 per cent of the company's debentures entitling the holders to object to an alteration of the company's objects (subs.(2)). A person who has consented to or voted in favour of the alteration may not apply (subs.(2)). Consent or acquiescence may in certain circumstances be as good as a special resolution (*Re Home Treat Ltd* [1991] BCLC 705). (Debentures entitling the holders to object are limited to those secured by a floating charge which were issued or first issued before December 1, 1947 or form part of the same series as any debentures so issued (subs.(8)). The application must be made within 21 days after the date on which the resolution altering the objects was passed (subs.(3)). The date on which the resolution was passed is excluded for the purpose of calculating the 21 day period (*Dodds v. Walker* [1981] 2 All E.R. 609, HL). The period within which the application may be made expires at the end of the last day of the period (*Manorlike Ltd v. Le Vitas Travel Agency and Consultancy Services Ltd* [1986] 1 All E.R. 573, CA).

Petition

The petition should contain statutory information about the company (see para. **2G–25** 2G-23), details of the meeting of the company at which the resolution to alter the company's objects was passed, the wording of the resolution complained of, the statutory basis entitling the petitioner(s) to apply, that the petitioner did not vote for the alteration, and the nature of the prejudice caused by the alteration. It should also show the authority of the petitioners to make the application and, where appropriate, that they have been authorised in writing where they act for others (cf. *Re Suburban and Provincial Stores Ltd* [1943] Ch 156; [1943] 1 All E.R. 342; *Re Sound City (Films) Ltd* [1947] Ch 169; [1946] 2 All E.R. 521). The company, once served, is required to give notice of the petition to the registrar of companies (s.6(1)(b)).

Evidence

2G–26   The statements in the petition need to be verified by affidavit or witness statement.

Directions

2G–27   An application notice will generally be required so that the court may give directions for the hearing of the petition. This may include a direction that the petition be advertised.

Order

2G–28   The court may make an order confirming the alteration to the objects in whole or in part and on such terms and conditions as it thinks fit, may adjourn the proceedings to enable arrangements to be made to purchase the shares of dissenting members, may provide for the purchase of members' shares and for the reduction of capital and may make any alterations to the memorandum necessary to give effect thereto (subss.(4)–(5)). The court may direct that the order be advertised (*Re Lancaster Banking Co* [1897] W.N. 3).

Within 15 days from the date of any order cancelling or confirming the alteration, the company must deliver to the registrar of companies an office copy of the order and, in the case of an order confirming the alteration, a printed copy of the memorandum as altered (s.6(1)(b)(ii)). Time may be extended by the court (s.6(2)).

Para. (b) Applications to cancel the alteration of a condition in a company's memorandum (s.17(3))

2G–29   Any condition contained in a company's memorandum which could lawfully have been contained in the articles of association instead of the memorandum of the company may be altered by special resolution, but save as mentioned below the section gives the same right of objection to members as in cases under s.5 (s.17(3)). The section does not apply where the memorandum provides for or prohibits the alteration of all or any of such conditions and does not authorise any variation of abrogation of the special rights of any class of members (subs.(2)(b)). The section is also subject to the provisions of s.16 (under which alterations increasing liability to contribute to share capital do not bind existing members without their consent) and Part XVII (which enables a member to apply to the court in case of conduct which is unfairly prejudicial). Debenture holders have no right to apply. As to the relief available, see *Re Hampstead Garden Suburb Trust Ltd* [1962] Ch 806; [1962] 2 All E.R. 879.

Paras (c) and (d) Applications to sanction reductions of the share premium account or of share capital (ss.130 and 136)

2G–30   Part V, Chapter III of the Companies Act 1985 deals with share premiums. A company which issues shares at a premium must transfer a sum equal to the aggregate value of the premium to an account called the share premium account (s.130(1)). There are restrictions in the manner in which funds in the share premium account may be applied (s.130(2)). However, the provisions of the Companies Act relating to the reduction of a company's share capital apply as if the share premium account were part of the company's paid up share capital (s.130(3)). Section 131 (merger relief) and 132 (relief in respect of group reconstructions) give relief from the requirements of s.130.

Sections 135–141 (Part V, Chapter IV) deal generally with the reduction of a company's share capital and the requirement for an application to be made to the court confirming the reduction. See also the *Practice Direction (Companies: Reduction of Capital)* [1966] 2 All E.R. 146; [1966] 1 W.L.R. 836 which appears to have been supplemented but not replaced by the current Companies Act practice direction.

The company begins the process of capital reduction by passing a special resolution in accordance with powers contained in its articles (s.135). If the proposed reduction involves a diminution of liability in respect of unpaid share capital or the payment to a shareholder of any paid up share capital the company may apply to the court for confirmation of the reduction (s.136(1) and (2)). Every creditor of the company who would be admissible to proof is entitled to object, and the court is required to settle a list of such creditors and to ensure that notice is given so that they may object (s.136 (3) and (4)). In practice the company will generally seek the consent of creditors or give an undertaking to protect their interests and seek an order at the directions stage dispensing with the settlement of a list of creditors.

The petition

2G–31 The petition, which is a petition of the company, should contain statutory information about the company (see para. 2G–23 above) including full details of its capital broken down by types of share. It should state that the company has the power under the terms of its articles to pass a resolution for the reduction of capital and give details of the resolution passed and the meeting at which it was passed. The purpose of the reduction should be stated (usually, but not always, to eliminate a deficit on the profit and loss account or because the capital is in excess of the company's want). The form of minute proposed to be registered should be recited. The petition will generally end by seeking "that the reduction of the capital of the company proposed to be effected by the written resolution referred to in paragraph [] of the petition may be confirmed and the foregoing minute may be approved by the court" together with any further order, enquiry or direction as may be necessary. There is no requirement to serve the petition.

Evidence

2G–32 The evidence must be filed for checking at least two clear working days prior to the fist hearing.

The evidence in support of the petition must be provided by a director of the company and should exhibit a copy of the petition (confirming the truth of its contents), the certificate of incorporation (and any certificate recording any change of name), the memorandum and articles in force at the date of the passing of the special resolution, a copy of the notice convening the meeting to pass the special resolution, a certified copy of the minutes of the meeting at which the special resolution was passed, signed by the chairman (or a certified copy signed by all the members), if the meeting was held on less than 21 days' notice, a copy of the special resolution endorsed with the written consent to short notice of all shareholders entitled to attend and vote and holding not less than 95 per cent in nominal value, the latest set of accounts, and, if there has been a previous reduction, a copy of the court order confirming the reduction together with a certificate issued by the registrar of companies. The practice of requiring the original minute book to be put in evidence (as required by Practice Direction (Companies Reduction of Capital) [1966] 2 All E.R. 146; [1966] 1 W.L.R. 836) has been abandoned for practical reasons.

Evidence of service of notice of the meeting must also be produced where it cannot be shown that all shareholders have consented to the proposed reduction. This will generally be in the form of evidence from those who maintain the register of members. The evidence should demonstrate that the register has been kept under the personal supervision of the witness and contained the names and addresses of all the shareholders as at a specific date (the record date) chosen by the company in accordance with the Uncertificated Securities Regulations 1995 (S.I. 1995 No. 3272) (see para. 2G–45). It should give detail as to how notices of the meeting were addressed and despatched, and if any other person was involved in the operation (*e.g.* a printer or mailing company), that person should give personal evidence as to the tasks he undertook. Copies of the relevant notices, forms of proxy and other documents posted should be exhibited. In cases where share capital is written off as lost or not represented by available assets and the company relies on valuation, the practice was to insist that evidence from the valuer be filed (*Practice Direction* [1947] W.N. 116). This is now frequently waived where there is no hidden value accruing to the benefit of the company and in the light of the developed law on valuers' duties.

Application for directions

2G–33 It is generally necessary to issue an application for directions as to advertisement of the petition (which is generally directed to take place no later than the Tuesday eight days before the hearing of the petition) and for an order dispensing with the settling of a list of creditors pursuant to s.136(2). This will normally be ordered on the company's providing evidence of the consent of any creditors to the reduction or an undertaking to secure or safeguard the rights of creditors who have not consented by a means satisfactory to them or to the court. Where the company has long term liabilities under a lease, it is not normal to insist that the company should provide security for the whole of the unexpired term, as this would be unduly onerous. A draft order should be produced to the registrar at the directions hearing. After the directions hearing the order initialled (and amended, if necessary) by the registrar should be taken to room 410 in the Thomas More Building together with two clean copies and two copies of the proposed advertisement.

Hearings

2G-34   The hearing of the application for directions normally takes place before the registrar. The petition is heard in court on Wednesdays designated for the purpose of hearing reduction petitions or otherwise following the hearing of winding-up petitions.

Arrangements for hearings should be made with the Companies Court schemes and reductions case manager, Room 410 of the Thomas More Building, Royal Courts of Justice, to whom enquiries may also be made by telephone (020 7947 6727).

Order

2G-35   A draft order should be produced to the court at the hearing of the petition. If the court is satisfied that the reduction should be confirmed and that no objections have been made to it, the order will be made. If there are objections, the court will give directions for the objection to be heard. The order and the minute or reduction must be sent to the registrar of companies (s.138(1)). The reduction is of no effect until the order and the minute have been registered (s.138(2)). The order will provide for advertisement of the reduction, usually in the same newspaper in which the petition was advertised (as to the form of which see *Re Oceana Development Co* [1912] W.N. 121 at 138).

Para.(e) Applications to cancel any variation or abrogation of the rights attached to shares (s.127)

2G-36   Application to cancel a variation or abrogation of the rights attached to shares of a particular class may be made where variation or abrogation has been effected pursuant to a provision in the memorandum or articles authorising the rights of any class of shareholder to be altered with the consent of a specified proportion of the shares in such class or with the sanction of a resolution passed at a class meeting. The application may be made by holders of not less than 15 per cent of the issued shares of the class in question, provided the applicants are persons who did not consent to or vote in favour of the resolution (subs.(2)). The court may cancel the variation if it is satisfied, having regard to all the circumstances, that the variation would unfairly prejudice the shareholders of the relevant class, or, if satisfied, it may confirm the variation (subs.(4)). The application must be made within 21 days after the date on which consent was given to the resolution (subs.(3)).

Petition

2G-37   The petition must contain the usual statutory information concerning the company (see para. 2G–23 above) and give details of the special rights attached to the various classes of shares, the provisions in the memorandum and articles authorising the variation, details of the resolution and the manner in which it was passed, details of the requisite percentage of shareholders applying, and the reasons for opposing the variation. It should also show that the holders of the class are unfairly prejudiced.

Evidence

2G-38   The statements in the petition need to be verified by affidavit or witness statement.

Application notice

2G-39   An application notice should be issued at the same time as the petition so that directions may be given for the conduct of the petition. This will generally include a direction that the petition be advertised.

Order

The court may disallow the variation or confirm it (subs.(4)). **2G–40**

A copy of the order must be sent to the registrar of companies within 15 days of the making of the order (subs.(5)).

No appeal lies from the order, the decision of the court on such an application being final (subs.(4)).

Para. (f) Applications to sanction a compromise or arrangement (s.425 et seq.)

Whilst the sanctioning of a scheme of arrangement under s.425 of the Companies **2G–41** Act 1985 is one of the statutory purposes for which a petition may be presented for an administration order under Part II of the Insolvency Act 1986 (see s.8(3)(c) of the Insolvency Act 1986), a petition may be presented to sanction such a scheme without recourse to administration. Whilst a scheme of arrangement with the creditors of a company may (but need not necessarily) require the statutory protections offered by administration, a scheme designed to vary the rights of classes of shareholders or to effect a reconstruction, amalgamation or a transfer of assets to a new company frequently does not. Schemes may also be used to tidy up the capital structure of a company where, for example, shares have been wrongly issued, and may involve a capital reduction, in which case regard must also be had to the provisions of ss.135 *et seq.* of the Companies Act 1985. The only limitation on the form of the scheme is that it must be a compromise or arrangement (*Re NFU Development Trust Ltd* [1972] 1 W.L.R. 1548).

As to the court's jurisdiction in respect of foreign companies, see *Re Drax Holdings Ltd*; *Re In Power Ltd* [2004] 1 All E.R. 903.

The claim form

Although a petition will also have to be presented, the proceedings to sanction a **2G–42** scheme of arrangement are commenced by a Part 8 claim form presented by the company or any member or creditor (or in the case of a winding up or administration by the liquidator or administrator). The claim form will be issued returnable before the registrar who will give directions as to the convening of court meetings of creditors or members or both and as to the classes to be established for voting purposes. Guidance as to the approach to proceedings to sanction a scheme is to be found in the Practice Statement (Companies: Schemes of Arrangement) [2002] 1 W.L.R. 1345; [2002] 3 All E.R. 96 (superseding the Practice Statement of Eve J. reported at [1934] W.N. 142).

Evidence

The claim form should be supported by evidence (which will generally be from a **2G–43** director of the company) in the form of an affidavit or witness statement to which the latest proof of the scheme documentation (including any explanatory statements), the proposed form(s) of notice of the meeting(s) and form(s) of proxy for use thereat should be exhibited. If the company has power to maintain a branch register or to issue share warrants to bearer, the evidence should contain a statement that the company has not issued such shares and does not keep a branch register (or state what the position is if such is not the case). The evidence should be filed in Room 404, Thomas More Building at least two working days before the hearing for directions.

Directions

At the directions hearing, the court will (if appropriate) give directions for the **2G–44** convening of the court meetings and will approve the scheme documentation, the latest draft of which should be produced to be initialled by the registrar, the notices and forms of proxy, which should also be initialled by the register. Where the documentation has been substantially finalised but may be subject to minor amendments, the court may approve the documentation "subject to the completion of blanks and such minor amendments as counsel may advise". A draft order should also be produced for the court to approve.

CREST system shares

The shares in many listed companies are held in the CREST system which is **2G–45** regulated by the Uncertificated Securities Regulations 1995 (S.I. 1995 No. 3272). The court will generally exercise its discretion to permit the use of a record date as close as possible to the date of sending out the notice of the relevant meeting when determining the company members entitled to receive notice.

The petition

2G–46   The petition to sanction the scheme is issued after the court meetings have been held and is heard by the judge.

The petition should contain statutory information about the company (see para. 2G–23 above) and in particular full details of the classes of shareholders, since the court, at the directions stage as well as at the hearing of the petition, will have regard to the manner in which different classes of creditors and/or shareholders are dealt with for the purpose of voting on the scheme. The petition should therefore contain full details of the proceedings at the court meetings, including the voting figures for the class meetings.

Evidence

2G–47   The evidence must be filed for checking at least two clear working days prior to the first hearing.

An affidavit or witness statement verifying the petition must be filed and should exhibit the report of the chairman of the meetings and a full report of the proceedings thereat, setting out the voting figures for and against the scheme proposals. The report should be signed and dated by the chairman and a print of the scheme should be attached to the report.

Evidence of service

2G–48   Evidence of service will be required as in capital reductions (see para. 2G–31 above).

Function of the court

2G–49   The functions of the court in exercising its power of sanction is to see that the provisions of the statute have been complied with, that the class was fairly represented by those attending the meeting and that any minority has not been coerced to promote adverse interests and to ensure that the arrangement is one that intelligent and honest members of the class might reasonably approve (see *Re National Bank Ltd* [1966] 1 All E.R. 1006, in particular the approval of the relevant passage from *Buckley* at p.1012). The test as to whether more than one meeting of creditors should be held is whether the rights of the creditors are so dissimilar as to make it impossible for them to consult with a view to their common interest (*Re Osiris Insurance Ltd* [1999] 1 BCLC 182, *Re Hawk Insurance Co Ltd* [2001] 2 BCLC 480 and *Re UDL Argos Engineering & Heavy Industries Co Ltd* (unreported decision of the Court of Final Appeal of the Hong Kong Special Administrative Region No. 11 of 2001 (Civil), December 3, 2001). See also *Re PT Garuda Indonesia* [2001] EWCA Civ 1696 and *Re Telewest Communications plc* [2004] EWHC 924; [2004] BCC 342 as to the determination of groups of creditors of the company. The court should not act as a rubber stamp to approve a scheme (*Re Osiris Insurance Ltd* [1999] 1 BCLC 182).

Hearings

2G–50   The hearing for directions normally takes place before the registrar. The petition is heard in court by the judge. Arrangements for hearings should be made with the Companies Court schemes and reductions case manager, Room 410 of the Thomas More Building, Royal Courts of Justice, to whom enquiries may also be made by telephone (020 7947 6727).

Order

2G–51   If appropriate, the court, on the hearing of the petition, will sanction the scheme as proposed or as modified at the meetings. It will order the company to deliver a copy of the order to the registrar of companies, since the scheme will have no effect unless it has been so delivered (subs.(3)). A copy of the scheme is annexed to the order.

The court may require undertakings to cover possible lacunae in the scheme (*Re Osiris Insurance Ltd* [1999] 1 BCLC 182).

As to the human rights implications of a scheme of arrangements, see *Re Waste Recycling Group Plc* [2004] 1 BCLC 352.

As to schemes governed by the Financial Services and Markets Act 2000 see paras 2G–131 *et seq.*

Para. (g) Applications to restore the name of a company to the register in conjunction with a winding up (s.653)

Applications for the restoration of the name of a company to the register of **2G–52** companies is most commonly made by claim form (see paras 2G–134 *et seq.*). The court may restore the name of the company on an application by the company, a member or a creditor made before the expiration of 20 years from publication in the Gazette of notice to strike off pursuant to s.652 of the Companies Act 1985 provided it is satisfied that the company was at the time of the striking off carrying on business or in operation or it is otherwise just to restore the name (subs.(2)). A petitioner for the winding up of the company may seek such relief in his winding up petition as well as an order that the company be wound up by the court (see para. 3E–67). Provided the petition is in order, the court will make an order restoring the name of the company and winding it up (commonly called a "double barrelled order"). The court will need to be satisfied that the registrar of companies does not oppose the restoration and that the treasury solicitor consents to forego the crown's right to *bona vacantia* (although this requirement is waived where the petition is the crown's).

As to applications to restore the name of a company generally, see para. 2G–124 *et seq.*

Para.(h) Applications to cancel the alteration of the form of a company's constitution (s.690)

A company not formed under the companies legislation but authorised to register **2G–53** (see Part XXII, Chapter II of the Companies Act 1985) may by special resolution alter the form of its constitution by substituting a memorandum and articles for a deed of settlement (subs.(1)). "Deed of settlement" includes any contract of copartnery or other instrument constituting or regulating the company, not being an Act of parliament, a royal charter or letters patent (subs.(4)). Many companies were registered under Part VII of the Companies Act 1862 after the execution of a deed embodying provisions of a memorandum and articles. Not less than seven nor more than 20 members were permitted. Such a company could be treated as registered (*Re Geo. Newman & Co* [1895] 1 Ch. 674). Section 690 applies to such companies and to any other company registered but not formed under any of the former Companies Acts, though not registered under Part XXII of the Act (*Re Sherborne Gas Co Ltd* [1936] W.N. 20).

The practice on such an application is analogous to that described under para. 2G–29(a) above. An office copy of the order with a print of the substituted memorandum and articles must be delivered to the registrar of companies within 15 days (s.5(1)). The registrar will then issue a certificate.

Para.(i) Applications for relief from liability of an officer of a company or an auditor (s.727)

An officer of a company (defined by s.744 of the Companies Act 1985 as including a **2G–54** director, manager or secretary) or persons employed as auditors, whether or not they are officers, may petition the court for relief if they have reason to apprehend that a claim may be made against them in respect of negligence, default, breach of duty or breach of trust. The petitioner must show that he has acted honestly and reasonably, and that having regard to all the circumstances he ought fairly to be excused (subs.(1)). Subsection (1) gives the court power to grant relief in the context of existing proceedings. Subsection (2) would appear to indicate that the relief available by petition is prospective and that a petition cannot therefore be represented after such proceedings have been commenced. The relief available may extend to transactions which were *ultra vires* the company (*Re Claridge's Patent Asphalte Co* [1921] 1 Ch 543), but cannot be invoked against a claim for debt due to a third party (*Customs & Excise Commissioners v. Hedon Alpha Ltd* [1981] 2 All E.R. 697). Relief is not available against proceedings brought under s.214 of the Insolvency Act 1986 for misfeasance (*Re Produce Marketing Consortium Ltd* [1989] 3 All E.R. 1), nor generally in favour of a liquidator or other office holder (see *Buckley on the Companies Act*, para. 727.7 for a discussion of this topic).

COMPANIES ACT

The petition should contain statutory information relating to the company (see para. 2G–23) and details of the nature of and reasons for the relief sought and should be supported by evidence verifying the petition and detailing the circumstances giving rise to the default and full reasons why the court should grant relief. The petition should be served on the company. Directions should initially be sought as to whether any parties other than the company should be joined as respondents to the petition. It may be appropriate to join shareholders where their rights are likely to be affected. The court will not generally grant relief against a liability to repay money without ascertaining the views of the shareholders or, in the case of an insolvent company, the creditors (*Re Barry and Staines Linoleum Ltd* [1934] Ch 227).

Para.(j) Applications to cancel a resolution for re-registration as a private company (s.54)

2G–55   A public company may be re-registered as a private company (s.53 of the Companies Act 1985) provided that a special resolution is passed in accordance with subs.(2).

Where a special resolution has been passed by a public company to be re-registered under s.53 as a private company, an application may be made to the court for cancellation of that resolution (s.54(1)). The application may be made by the holders of not less in the aggregate than 5 per cent in nominal value of the issued share capital of the company (or any class thereof), or, if the company is not limited by shares, by not less than 5 per cent of members, or by not less than 50 of the company's members, but not by any person who has consented to or voted in favour of the resolution (subs.(2)). The application must be made within 28 days after the passing of the resolution (subs.(3)).

If such an application is made, the company must give notice to the registrar of companies (subs.(4)).

The petition, evidence and procedure are broadly as described in para. 2G–29(a) above.

On the hearing of the application the court may cancel or confirm the resolution on such terms as it thinks fit or may adjourn to enable an arrangement to be made for the purchase of the interests of dissenting members. The order may also provide for the purchase by the company of the shares of any of its members and for the reduction of capital, and it may order any consequential alterations in the memorandum and articles (subs.(5) and (6)).

The company must deliver a copy of the order to the registrar of companies within 15 days from the date it is made or such longer period as the court may direct (subs.(7)).

Para.(k) Applications to cancel a special resolution (ss.157(2) and 176(1))

2G–56   Chapter VI of the Companies Act 1985 provides for the circumstances in which a company can give financial assistance for the purchase of its own shares. Where a resolution is passed under s.155 approving the giving of financial assistance an application may be made to the court for the cancellation of the resolution by the holders of not less in the aggregate than 10 per cent in nominal value of the company's issued share capital or any class thereof, or if the company is not limited by shares, by not less than 10 per cent of its members. The application may not be made by any person who has consented to or voted in favour of the resolution (s.157(2)).

Chapter VII of the Companies Act 1985 deals with redeemable shares and the purchase by a company of its own shares. Where a private company passes a special resolution approving for the purposes of Chapter VII any payment out of capital for the redemption or purchase of any of its shares any member of the company other than one who has consented to or voted in favour of the resolution and any creditor of the company may apply to court for the cancellation of the resolution. The application must be made within 5 weeks of the date on which the resolution was passed (s.176(1)).

The procedure is analogous to that described in para. 2G–53 above.

Petitions for the protection of members against unfair prejudice (ss.459 and 460)

2G–57   A member of a company may apply to the court by petition for an order on the ground that the company's affairs are being or have been conducted in a manner which is unfairly prejudicial to the interests of its members or some part of its members or that some proposed act or omission would be prejudicial (subs.(1)). A person who is not a member but to whom shares in the company have been transferred or transmitted by operation of law may also apply (subs.(2)), as may the Secretary of State for Trade and Industry (s.460).

The petition

The petition should set out details of the company (see para. 2G-23) and of the acts **2G–58** or omissions complained of. It should also set out the relief sought. It should do so as economically as possible (*Re Oriental Gas Co Ltd* [1999] BCC 237). The aggrieved member will be the petitioner. The company is invariably joined as a respondent, but should not take an active role in the proceedings.

The conduct of the petition is regulated by the Companies (Unfair Prejudice Applications) Proceedings Rules 1986 (S.I. 1986 No. 2000). See also the Practice Direction (Companies Court: Contributory's Petition) [1990] 1 All E.R. 1056; [1990] 1 W.L.R. 490; [1990] B.C.L.C. 452.

Directions

The petition will be listed initially before the registrar for directions. These may **2G–59** provide for the petition to proceed by way of points of claim (or for the petition to stand as such), points of defence and points of reply, or may provide for the petition to be dealt with on the basis of an exchange of written evidence. If appropriate, directions will be given for disclosure, the exchange of witness statements and expert evidence. The registrar will also generally give directions for the parties to meet in order to narrow and identify the issues for trial.

Generally an order will be sought that the petition be not advertised: the court has power to regulate whether or not the petition should be advertised. To advertise without a direction from the court to do so or to disclose the existence of the petition to a third party may constitute an abuse and result in the petition being struck out (*Re A Company* (No. 002015 of 1996) [1997] 2 BCLC 1). Where, in addition to the usual relief, winding up is sought, consideration must be given to whether interim relief is required to avoid the potential consequences of s.127 of the Insolvency Act 1986 (see para. 2G–58 below). Note, however, that the courts have discouraged applications to wind up on the just and equitable ground in conjunction with applications for relief under s.459 (see Practice Direction (Companies Court: Contributory's Petition) [1990] 1 All E.R. 1056; [1990] 1 W.L.R. 490; [1990] BCLC 452; *Re A Company* (No. 00415 of 1986 [1997] 1 B.C.L.C. 479). Such relief should only be claimed if it is what the petitioner prefers or is the only relief to which he considers he may be entitled (Practice Direction, para.1). If the company is in reality a partnership and there is deadlock it may be appropriate to claim winding up on the just and equitable ground (*Re Yenidje Tobacco Company Limited* [1916] 2 Ch 426).

Section 127 relief

Where a prayer for winding up is included in a contributory's petition, the petition **2G–60** must include a statement as to whether the petitioner consents or objects to an order under s.127 of the Insolvency Act 1986 (*Practice Direction (Companies Court: Contributory's Petition)* [1990] 1 W.L.R. 490, para. 2). If an order is made it will be in the following terms: "that notwithstanding the presentation of the said petition (1) payments made into or out of the bank accounts of the company in the ordinary course of the business of the company and (2) dispositions of the property of the company made in the ordinary course of its business for proper value between the date of presentation of the petition and the date of judgment on the petition or further order in the meantime shall not be void by virtue of the provisions of s.127 of the Insolvency Act 1986 in the event of an order for the winding up of the company being made on the said petition provided that [the relevant bank] should be under no obligation to verify for itself whether any transaction through the company's bank accounts is in the ordinary course of business or that it represents full market value for the relevant transaction" (*Practice Direction (Companies Court: Contributory's Petition); as to the proviso see Re a Company* (No. 00687 of 1991) [1991] BCC 210 at p.212).

Order

The petition is tried before the judge. If the court is satisfied that the petition is **2G–61** well founded it may grant wide ranging relief which may include (but is not limited to) regulating the future conduct of the company's affairs, requiring the company to do any act or refrain from doing any act, authorising proceedings to be brought and providing for the purchase of the shares of any members by other members, or by the company itself, and (in the case of a purchase by the company itself) providing for a capital reduction (s.461). If an order is made altering the memorandum or articles of the company the order will provide for delivery of the same to the registrar of companies (s.461(5)). See, generally, *O'Neill v. Phillips* [1999] 1 W.L.R. 1092 for guidance as to the court's approach.

Other petitions

2G–62 As to petitions to wind up a company on the grounds of insolvency, on the just and equitable ground or in the public interest, see paras 2G–53 *et seq.*

Applications made by claim form

2G–63 Save for applications made by petition (see para. 2G–5), all applications made under the Companies Acts, the Insurance Companies Act and Part VII of the Financial Services and Markets Act 2000 are made by claim form, and the procedure applicable is as set out in CPR Part 8. The claim form should be headed "In the High Court of Justice, Chancery Division, Companies Court", if the claim is issued in the High Court in London, and identify the District Registry if issued out of one of the district registries. If the claim is issued in a county court it is headed "In the [ ] County Court". The claim form and any evidence or other documents subsequently filed should be entitled "In the matter of [name of company] And in the matter of [the Companies Act 1985 [or as the case may be]]" and should identify the claimant(s) and defendant(s).

Applications to extend time for registering documents (s.6(2))

2G–64 Where a company passes a resolution altering its objects (see ss.4–5 of the Companies Act 1985) it must deliver a copy of its altered memorandum to the registrar of companies within 15 days (s.6(1)). An application to extend the time in which to do so may be made (s.6(2)).

Claim form

2G–65 The claim form should set out details of the memorandum or other document in respect of which the extension is sought. If the application is made in existing proceedings so that an extension of time is sought to comply with the delivery of a court order to the registrar of companies, the application may be made by application notice in the existing proceedings. It may be made without notice, although it may be necessary to join the registrar of companies. This, and whether or not evidence in support will be required, will depend on the nature of the default and the length of time that has elapsed since registration was required.

Such applications are generally made where there has been a failure to comply with the requirement to deliver a copy order to the registrar of companies following the making of an order under ss.4–5.

Evidence

2G–66 The claim form should be supported by evidence giving details of the reason for the delay and explaining any other relevant circumstances.

Applications for relief in cases of default in delivering documents (s.88(6))

2G–67 When a company makes an allotment of shares, within one month it must deliver to the registrar of companies a return of the allotment in the prescribed form and certain other particulars (s.88(2)). Default may result in a fine (s.88(5)).

Application for relief may be made to the court, and, if the court is satisfied that the omission to deliver the document in question was accidental or inadvertent, or that it is just and equitable, it may extend time for delivery for such period as it thinks proper (s.88(6)).

The claim form should set out details of the relief claimed and be supported by evidence giving details of the reason for the default and the documents to which the application relates. The company will generally be the claimant and the registrar of companies should be the defendant.

Ignorance or misunderstanding of the statutory requirements may be a ground for granting relief (*Re Jackson & Co Ltd* [1899] 1 Ch 348; *Re Whitefriars Financial Co Ltd* [1899] 1 Ch 184).

The order will provide for a copy of it to be delivered to the registrar of companies within a given period of time.

Applications relating to the delivery of share certificates or debentures (s.185(6))

2G–68 The claim form should set out details of the claim and the relief sought. The company should be a defendant, but generally any other party should be included against whom relief is sought (usually the directors). Details should be given as to whether there are provisions in the articles of the company restricting the disposition of any shares in question.

Applications to inspect any register of debenture holders or for a copy of the register or of any trust deed securing the issue of debentures (s.191(5))

2G–69 The claim form should set out details of the claim and of the relief sought. The company should be a defendant, although other parties may be included. The claim form should be supported by a witness statement giving details of any request for inspection and any refusal to provide it.

Applications to summon a meeting of debenture holders (s.192(4))

2G–70 Section 192(1) provides that any provision contained in a trust deed for securing an issue of debentures or in a contract with the holders of debentures secured by a trust deed shall be void in so far as it would have the effect of exempting a trustee thereof from or indemnifying him against liability for breach of trust where he fails to show that he has exercised the degree of care and diligence required of him as a trustee, having regard to the provisions of the trust deed. This does not invalidate any provision in force on July 1, 1948 so long as any person then entitled to the benefit of the provision or afterwards given the benefit thereof under subs.(4) remains a trustee of the deed in question (subs.(3)). While any trustee of a trust deed remains entitled to the benefit of a provision saved by subs.(3) the benefit of such provision may be given to either all trustees of the deed, present or future, or any named trustees or proposed trustees thereof by a resolution passed by a three-fourths in value of the debenture holders at a meeting summoned for the purpose in accordance with the provisions of the deed or, if the deed makes no provision for a meeting to be summoned, in any manner approved by the court.

Claim form

2G–71 The Act does not provide for who can make the application, but as a general rule the application will be made by the company or the trustees or a debenture holder.

Evidence

2G–72 The evidence in support must prove a trust deed or contract in force on July 1, 1948 containing the provisions exempting the trustee from liability or indemnifying him, that there is at least one trustee of the trust deed entitled to the benefit of the provision, that it is desired to summon a meeting for the purpose of considering a resolution to give the benefit of the provision to other trustees, and that the deed makes no provision for summoning a meeting. The evidence should propose a time, date and place for the proposed meeting and give details of the manner in which notice of it is to be given.

Applications for an order directing that any shares should not be subject to restrictions imposed by Part XV Companies Act

2G–73 Section 212 of the Companies Act provides that any public company may require any person who the company knows or has reasonable cause to believe to be, or within the preceding three years to have been, interested in its voting shares to confirm that fact and to provide certain other information. If the information is not provided the company may apply to the court for an order directing that the shares in question be subject to the restrictions imposed by Part XV of the Companies Act, *i.e.* that any transfer of the shares be void, that no voting rights shall be exercisable in respect of them, that no further shares be issued and that, except in the liquidation of the company, no payment shall be made of any sums due from the company on the shares, whether in respect of capital or otherwise (s.454).

The purpose of s.212 is to enable a public company to obtain information as to the beneficial ownership of shares (*Re Geers Gross plc* [1987] 1 W.L.R. 837). Incomplete information is not sufficient to comply with the statutory obligation (*Re TR Technology Investment Trust Ltd* [1988] BCLC 256). Although a public company has a prima facie right to know who owns its shares, the court has a discretion, and the right to information may be outweighed by other factors, such as interference with a takeover bid (*Re Ricardo Group plc (No. 3)* [1989] 2 B.C.L.C. 771).

Claim form

2G-74   The claim form may seek both interim and final relief. The company is the claimant. Any person to whom notice has been given under s.212 should be named as defendant.

The evidence

2G-75   The evidence in support should set out as fully as possible the grounds for the company's belief that the person served with notice under s.212 has an interest in the shares in question and must prove service of the notice, give details of the information required and demonstrate failure to provide it on time in accordance with the notice.

Order

2G-76   The court may order the information to be given or may decline to grant relief. As to the question of costs see *Re Lonrho plc (No. 2)* [1989] B.C.L.C. 309 and *Re Bestwood plc* [1989] B.C.L.C. 606.

Applications to remove or amend an entry in the register of interests in shares (s.217)

2G-77   Section 211 of the Companies Act 1985 requires every public company to keep a register of known interests in its voting shares. Section 217(3) enables a person whose name has been included in the register to apply to the company for removal of the entry where the information is incorrect, and s.217(4) enables persons identified in the register as having been party to an agreement which includes provision for the acquisition of interests in shares to apply to the company for inclusion in the register of the information that he has ceased to be a party to the agreement. If the company refuses the application the applicant may apply to court for an order directing the company to remove the entry or include the information.

Claim form

2G-78   The claim form should set out the relief claimed under s.217. The applicant will be the claimant and the company the defendant.

Evidence

2G-79   The claim must be supported by written evidence setting out all the facts and matters relied on.

Applications to inspect the register of interests in shares (s.219(4))

2G-80   The claim form should set out details of the claim and of the relief sought. The company should be a defendant, although other parties may also be included. The claim form should be supported by a witness statement giving details of any request for inspection and of any refusal to allow it.

Applications relating to default in delivering accounts (s.242(1))

2G-81   Any member or creditor of a company which has failed to comply with its obligation to lay its accounts before a general meeting or to file accounts may apply to the court for an order requiring the default to be remedied.

The Secretary of State for Trade and Industry may give notice to a company that its accounts do not comply with the provisions of the Companies Acts and specify a period of not less than one month for the directors to provide an explanation of the accounts and to prepare revised accounts (s.242(5)A(1)). In the absence of compliance the Secretary of State may apply to the court for an order requiring the directors to prepare revised accounts.

Claim form

The member, creditor or Secretary of State will be the claimant and the company **2G–82** and any director in respect of whose conduct complaint is made will be the defendant. Notice of the application should be given to the registrar of companies.

Evidence

The evidence should indicate the status of the claimant to apply and contain details **2G–83** of the default complained of.

The court may order the director responsible for the default to pay the costs of the application.

Applications for an order declaring that company accounts do not comply with the requirements of the Companies Act (s.245B(1))

Section 238 of the Companies Act requires a copy of the company's annual ac- **2G–84** counts, together with a copy of the directors' report for the financial year and of the auditors' report on the accounts, to be sent to every member of the company and to every debenture holder and every person entitled to receive notice of general meetings not less than 21 days before the date of the meetings at which copies of those documents are to be laid in accordance with s.241. Section 245A provides that where it appears to the Secretary of State that there is, or may be, a question whether the accounts comply with the requirements of the Companies Act he may give notice to the directors indicating the respects in which it appears that such a question arose or may arise and specifying a period of not less than one month for the directors to give him an explanation of the accounts or prepare revised accounts. If at the end of that period, or such further period as may be allowed, no satisfactory explanation has been given and the accounts have not been revised, the Secretary of State may apply to the court for a declaration that the annual accounts do not comply with the requirements of the Act and for an order requiring the directors to prepare revised accounts.

Claim form

The Secretary of State will be the claimant and the company and any defaulting **2G–85** directors will be the defendants. Notice of the application should be given to the registrar of companies.

Evidence

Full evidence of the defaults complained of should be given on behalf of the Secre- **2G–86** tary of State.

Order

A copy of the order must be served on the registrar of companies for registration, **2G–87** and the order itself should provide for that. If the application succeeds costs may be awarded against the company, its directors or all of them.

Applications to inspect the register of directors and secretaries of a company (s.288(5))

The claim form should set out details of the claim. The company should be a defen- **2G–88** dant, although other parties may also be added. The claim form should be supported by a witness statement setting out details of any request for inspection or the relevant information and any refusal to provide it.

Applications relating to directors' or auditors' representations, etc. regarding removal or resignation (ss.304(4); 391A and 392A; 394)

Section 304(2) contains provisions entitling a director in respect of whom notice has **2G–89** been given of a proposed resolution to remove him from office to request notification to members of the company of representations made by him in relation to the resolution, and if a copy of them is not sent, to require that they be read out at the meeting. Sections 391A, 392A and 394 contain similar provisions in respect of auditors of a company. The court has power to make an order dispensing with such representations.

Claim form

2G–90   The claimant must be a person who claims to be aggrieved unless the application is made under s.394, in which case it must be the company. If the company is not the claimant it should be made a defendant along with the director or auditor against whom the relief is sought.

Evidence

2G–91   The claim form should be supported by evidence proving the notice of the meeting and of the intended resolution and details of any facts relied on to indicate that the statutory provisions are likely to be abused.

Applications to inspect directors' service contracts (s.318(9))

2G–92   Section 318(1) imposes a duty on a company to keep copies of directors' service contracts or (if there is no contract in writing) a written memorandum setting out the terms of any such service contracts. Details must be available for inspection by members of the company free of charge. If inspection is refused the court may make an order to allow inspection (subs. (9)).

Claim form

2G–93   The claimant will be the member to whom inspection has been refused. The company should be a defendant. Any director whose conduct in refusing inspection is a matter of complaint may also be joined as a defendant.

Evidence

2G–94   The claim form should be supported by evidence giving details of the contracts which the member has asked to inspect and of any refusal complained of.

Applications to inspect the register of directors' interests in shares and debentures (s.326(6))

2G–95   The claim form and procedure follow that described in relation to s.219(4) above.

Applications to inspect the register of members or the index of names of members of a company or to obtain copies of the register (s.356(6))

2G–96   The claim form should set out details of the claim. The company should be a defendant, although other parties may also be added. It should generally be supported by a witness statement setting out details of any refusal to provide inspection and any reasons given.

The order will provide that the company give inspection, for example by making the register available to the claimant, and will provide (if appropriate) for payment of the fee prescribed by s.356(3).

Applications to rectify the register of members of a company (s.359(1))

2G–97   If the name of a person is without sufficient cause entered in or omitted from a company's register of members, or there is default or unnecessary delay in entering on the register the fact of a person ceasing to be a member, the person aggrieved, any member of the company or the company itself may apply to the court for rectification of the register.

Claim form

2G–98   The claim form should set out precisely the terms of the rectification sought. The claimant may be the person aggrieved, a member of the company or the company. If the company is not a claimant it should be joined as a defendant. It may be necessary to join others who are likely to be affected by the order. The registrar of companies should only be joined if an order is sought rectifying the register as held by the registrar. The registrar should not be joined or served where rectification affects only the internal records of the company. The directors of the company should be joined if costs are to be sought against them. The directors may be ordered to pay costs even if they have acted on legal advice (*Re Morgan Insurance Brokers Ltd* [1993] BCLC 676).

Evidence

Evidence must be filed in support of the application. The court will grant the relief **2G–99** or give directions if the application is disputed. This may include service of points of claim and points and defence as well as directions for disclosure of documents where there is a substantial factual dispute (*Re Swarren Ltd* unrep. Decision of Lawrence J. of January 27, 1922).

Order

The court may refuse the application or order rectification and payment of costs. It **2G–100** may also award damages (subs.(2)) and decide any question relating to the title of any party to have his name entered on or omitted from the register and decide any question necessary or expedient (subs.(3)). Where the company is required to send a list of its members to the registrar of companies the order will direct that notice of the making of the order be sent to him (subs.(4)).

Applications for an order to convene a meeting of a company (s.371(1))

Such an application may be made by any director or member of the company who **2G–101** would be entitled to vote at the meeting. The section applies to cases where it is impracticable to call or conduct a meeting in the manner prescribed by the articles or the Act, *i.e.* where there is no director or no quorum is available. Relief may also be sought under this provision where certain members refuse to attend meetings making it impossible to obtain a quorum and conduct the business of the company (*Re El Sombrero Ltd* [1958] Ch 900; *Re H R Paul & Son Ltd* 118 S.J. 166; *Re Opera Photographic Ltd* [1989] 1 W.L.R. 634, [1989] B.C.L.C. 763; *Re Sticky Fingers Restaurant Ltd* [1991] B.C.C. 754; *Re Whitchurch Consultants Ltd* [1993] B.C.L.C. 1359). The section is procedural and is not designed to give substantive relief, *e.g.* by affecting voting rights so as to override a deadlock (*Harman v. BML Group* [1994] 1 W.L.R. 634; *Ross v. Telford* [1998] 1 B.C.L.C. 82).

The claim form should set out details of the claim and of the relief sought. The company should be a defendant, although it will often be necessary to join other directors or members. The claim form should be supported by a witness statement setting out all the facts relied on.

The order will generally give the claimant permission to convene a meeting of the company for any necessary purpose and provide for any notice period necessary. It may also direct that a specified number of members or directors should constitute a quorum for the purpose of the meeting.

Applications for an order that a company should not be bound to circulate a section 376 statement (s.377(3))

Section 376(1) imposes on a company a duty, if requisitioned by a sufficient number **2G–102** of members, to circulate to members entitled to receive notice of any general meeting a statement of not more than 1,000 words with respect to the matter referred to in any proposed resolution or business to be dealt with at a meeting. Section 377(3) provides that the company shall not be bound to circulate such a statement if, on the application of the company or of any other person aggrieved, the court is satisfied that the rights conferred by s.376 are being abused to secure needless publicity for defamatory matter (s.377(3)). The court may also order the company's costs to be paid in whole or in part by the requisitioners, even if they are not parties to the application.

Claim form

The claim form should set out details of the claim and of the relief sought. The **2G–103** company or person aggrieved should be the claimant. A person aggrieved is one who has suffered a legal grievance, one against whom a decision has been made which has wrongly deprived him of something, one who has been wrongfully refused something or one whose title to something has been wrongfully affected (*Re Sidebotham Ex p. Sidebotham* [1880] 14 Ch 458; *Re Read Bower & Co Ex p. Official Receiver* [1887] 19 QBD 174). The company should be joined as a defendant if it is not the claimant or one of the claimants. The court will usually require some or all of the requisitioners to be joined as defendants.

Evidence

2G–104   The evidence should prove the summoning of the meeting in relation to which relief is sought, the requisition by a sufficient number of members (as to which see s.376(2)) requiring the company to circulate a statement (the requisition and the statement should be exhibited), demonstrate that the statement contains defamatory matter and such facts as are necessary to demonstrate to the court that the provisions of s.376 are being abused to secure needless publicity. The names and addressees of any parties not named as defendants against whom a costs order is sought should also appear in the evidence.

Applications to inspect the minutes of proceedings at general meetings of a company or to obtain copies thereof (s.383(5))

2G–105   The company should be made a defendant to the application. If an order for inspection is made it will usually be on an undertaking from the claimant to pay the fee prescribed by s.383(2) and will direct the company to provide a copy of the minutes within a certain number of days.

Applications to extend time for registering a charge or to rectify an omission or mis-statement (o.404)

2G–106   Section 404 enables a party to apply for relief from the consequences of failing to register on time and omissions or misstatements in a memorandum of satisfaction to be rectified under s.403. The provisions as to registration are set out in ss.395–403 and 409.

The claim form should identify the charge in relation to which relief is sought and indicate the section of the Act under which the obligations to register arose (s.395 or s.400). The company is the claimant and the registrar of companies is the defendant.

The claim should be supported by evidence as to the circumstances under which the documents in question were not registered, setting out in detail the sequence of events surrounding the default. It must show that the omission to register (or misstatement of any particulars) was (a) accidental or (b) due to inadvertence (the nature of the inadvertence being set out) or (c) some other sufficient cause or (d) is not of a nature to prejudice the position of creditors or shareholders or (e) that there are other grounds on which it is just and equitable to grant relief. It should exhibit a copy of the document to be registered. Evidence of solvency should be filed confirming that no winding-up order has been made or resolution for winding-up passed, and that no winding up petition is pending, that no notice of a resolution to wind up has been given, that the company is continuing to carry on business, and that no judgment has been given against the company which remains unsatisfied (*Re Bootle Cold Storage Co* [1901] WN 54; *Re Telomatic Ltd* [1993] BCC 404). Such evidence of solvency must be given by an officer of the company. Evidence of solvency is not, however, required where the application is to extend time for registration following the acquisition by the company of property subject to a charge registrable under s.400, or is of a kind which could not prejudice creditors (*e.g.* to reduce the amount of the secured debt).

The original document to be registered should be produced at the hearing.

In extending time the court will generally add to the order a provision that it is made without prejudice to the rights of any person acquired between the date of the creation of the charge and the date of its actual registration (*Re Joplin Brewery* [1902] 1 Ch 79; *Watson v. Duff Morgan & Vermont (Holdings) Ltd* [1974] 1 All E.R. 794; *Re I. C. Johnson & Co* [1902] 2 Ch 101). For an exceptional case where the rights of intervening mortgagees were not preserved, see *Re Fablehill Ltd* [1991] B.C.L.C. 830.

The words in the order referred to above have been held not to put an unsecured creditor on the same footing as a debenture holder applying for an extension unless he has taken steps to enforce his debt or unless a winding up has intervened (*Re Ehrmann Bros.* [1906] 2 Ch 697) before actual registration (*Re Anglo Oriental Co* [1903] 1 Ch 914); but the court will not insert further words to protect unsecured creditors (*Re M. I. G. Trust Ltd* [1933] Ch 542, CA, affirmed in *Peat v. Gresham Trust* [1934] AC 252).

As to the limits of the court's jurisdiction (*e.g.* to order the removal of unnecessary information) see *igroup Ltd v. Ocwen* [2003] EWHC 2431 (Ch), [2003] 4 All E.R. 1063 and in *Re A Company (No. 007466) of 2003* [2004] 1 W.L.R. 1357. The court may, however, grant declaratory relief.

Re Charles orders

Where at the date of the making of the order a winding up is likely the order may **2G–107** reserve the right of the liquidator to apply to discharge the order within 21 days of commencement of the winding up if it occurred within a month of the making of the order (*Re L. H. Charles & Co* [1935] WN 15; *Exeter Trust Ltd v. Screenways Ltd* [1991] BCLC 888). The order, if made, will extend time for registration (or rectification) but subject to a proviso "that the company, acting by any liquidator or administrator, or any unsecured creditor of the company shall be at liberty to apply to discharge or vary this order within [a period of time] after the commencement of any voluntary winding up of the company or any order for the winding up of the company" (or as the case may be). Such an order may be made where, exceptionally, there is no evidence of solvency (*Re Kris Cruisers Ltd* [1949] Ch 138). However, *Kris Cruisers Ltd* was not followed in *Re Ashpurton Estates Ltd* [1983] Ch 110; [1982] 3 All E.R. 665 in which it was held that imminent liquidation was a factor to be taken into account and that an order extending time should not be made after a company has gone into liquidation (see *Re Resinoid and Mica Products Ltd (Note)* [1983] Ch 132; [1982] 3 All ER 677, but *cf.* R. M. Arnold & Co Ltd [1984] BCLC 505 where the circumstances were exceptional; see also *Re Braemar Investments Ltd* [1988] 3 W.L.R. 596; [1988] BCLC 556, where the court ordered a motion by the liquidator to discharge the registrar's order extending time). In *Re Chantry House Developments plc* [1990] BCLC 813 the court made an order extending time, notwithstanding the company being in administrative receivership, but on an undertaking that the mortgagee would notify substantial unsecured creditors of the company within seven days of the making of the order and on terms that they could apply within 14 days to discharge the order and that the mortgagee would abide by any order made in such circumstances. Generally, however, where insolvent liquidation seems inevitable the court should decline to extend time (*Re Barrow Borough Transport Ltd* [1989] 3 W.L.R. 858 and *Re Telomatic Ltd* [1993] BCC 404).

The court will only extend time in an application under s.404; it will not decide whether or not documents require registration (*Re Cunard Steamship Co* [1908] WN 160).

In *Exeter Trust Ltd v. Screenways Ltd* [1991] BCLC 888 it was held that even if an order extending time was set aside the registrar of companies' certificate as to registration was conclusive evidence of the valid registration of the charge.

Applications to inspect copies of instruments creating a charge and to inspect the register of charges (s.408(4))

The claim form should set out details of the claim and the relief sought. The **2G–108** company should be a defendant, although other parties may be included. The claim form should generally be supported by a witness statement setting out details of any request for inspection and any refusal to provide it.

Applications to pay into court (s. 430(11))

Part XIIIA of the Companies Act 1985 deals with takeover offers and the manner **2G–109** in which an offeror who has acquired or contracted to acquire not less than nine-tenths in value of a companies shares may give notice to acquire the shares of minority shareholders (s.429). The offeror may give notice to the minority shareholders, whereupon he is entitled and bound to acquire the shares in respect of which notice has been given (s.430(2)), and in the absence of acceptance of the consideration must pay it to the company (s.430(5)) which holds it on trust (s.430(9)). Where after reasonable inquiry the person entitled to the consideration held on trust cannot be found and twelve years have elapsed since the consideration was received, or the company is wound up, the consideration must be paid into court (s.430(11)).

As to payments into court generally see Section 6A.

Claim form

Where the company is not in liquidation, the application to pay into court should **2G–110** be made by claim form. Where the company is in liquidation the application should be made by application in the winding up.

Evidence

The application should be supported by evidence from an officer of the company or **2G–111**

COMPANIES ACT

the liquidator setting out full details of the takeover, the notices given by the offeror, the consideration paid and the inquiries which have been undertaken. A schedule should be exhibited setting out the name of the shareholder on whose behalf the consideration is held, details of any dividend payments made in respect of shares that formed any part of the consideration, the period to which such payments relate and details of any interest that has accrued, and the total figure which it is intended should be paid in in relation to the shareholder concerned.

Order

2G–112   The order will provide for the relevant sum or sums to be paid into court or, where the consideration is shares, for the shares to be paid into court. It should have annexed to it the schedule exhibited to the evidence (modified or updated, if appropriate).

Payment out

2G–113   Payment out may be sought without the making of a formal application by filing written evidence setting out the basis on which the applicant claims to be entitled to the monies or shares paid into court. Where the payment out exceeds £500 details of a bank or building society account into which payment can be made should be given.

Applications for a declaration that the affairs of a company ought to be investigated (s.431-432)

2G–114   Section 431 of the Companies Act 1985 provides that the Secretary of State for trade and Industry may appoint inspectors to investigate and report on the affairs of a company.

The application is made to the judge and should be supported by full evidence of all facts and matters relied on. It should be served on the solicitor for the DTI (*Practice Direction* [1954] 1 W.L.R. 563; [1954] 1 All E.R. 604).

Applications to inquire into the case of officers or agents who have refused to produce documents (s.436)

2G–115   Section 431(1) provides that inspectors appointed to investigate the affairs of a company under ss.431–432 may certify the refusal of an officer or agent of a company under investigation to produce any book or document which it is his duty to produce, or the refusal of such a person to answer questions regarding the affairs of the company. The court may then enquire into the case and, after hearing evidence, punish the offending person as if he were guilty of contempt. The certificate should be lodged with the registrar of companies.

The application is made to the judge. The Secretary of State is the claimant. The evidence in support from the inspector should exhibit the certificate and set out all the facts and matters relied on.

The defendant may seek to impugn the validity of the inspector's appointment. However, the fact that inspectors appointed for the purpose of determining facts which would have a bearing on the guilt or innocence of the persons being investigated did not result in their appointment being invalid (*Re London United Investments plc* [1992] BCLC 91 and [1992] BCLC 285, CA). As to the human rights implications of evidence obtained under compulsion see *Saunders v. United Kingdom* [1998] 1 BCLC 362, ECHR and *Re Westminster Property Management Ltd, Official Receiver v. Stern* [2000] 1 W.L.R. 2230; [2001] BCC 121.

Applications for orders removing or relaxing restrictions imposed under Part XV and orders for sale of shares (ss.456-457)

2G–116   Where shares in a company are by order made the subject of restrictions under Part XV of the Companies Act 1985 the court may, on application, remove or relax the restriction and direct that certain acts should not constitute a breach of the restrictions under Part XV (subs.(1) and (1A)). Such an order may be made where the rights of third parties are affected. The court may also order the shares to be sold (subs.(4)).

Claim form

2G–117   Where the application is made by a person other than the Secretary of State for Trade and Industry, he should be joined as a defendant. Where the application includes a claim for sale of the shares under subs.(4) and directions as to the sale or transfer of the shares are sought under subs.(5), the application may be made by the Secretary of State (unless the restrictions were imposed by order under s.216), the company, a person appointed to effect the sale or any person interested in the shares (subs.(5)).

Evidence

The court must be satisfied that the relevant facts have been disclosed to the **2G–118** company and that no unfair advantage has accrued to any person as a result of an initial failure to make disclosure; alternatively that the shares are to be transferred for valuable consideration and that the Secretary of State approves the transfer. The court may refuse to lift the restriction on the sale of shares even though it is intended to sell, and in exercising its discretion was entitled to take into account the refusal to disclose relevant facts (*Re Geers Gross plc* [1988] BCLC 140).

Order

The order, if made with a view to permitting a transfer of the shares, may continue **2G–119** the restriction either in whole or in part. The proceeds of any sale (less costs) must be paid into court for the benefit of the beneficial owner who may apply for payment out (s.457(1)).

Applications for an order declaring the dissolution of a company void (s.651)

Where a company has been dissolved (as opposed to struck off) the court may, on **2G–120** an application by the liquidator or any other person interested, make an order declaring the dissolution to have been void. The application is most commonly made where the company has been dissolved following completion of a winding up by a liquidator seeking to recover an asset which was overlooked in the winding up (*Morris v. Harris* [1927] AC 252) or to enable a creditor to bring proceedings (*Stanhope Pension Trust Ltd v. Registrar of Companies* [1994] 1 BCLC 628). The application may be combined with one for relief under s.653, but there is no jurisdiction to order the restoration of a company to the register (as opposed to declaring the dissolution void) if a company has been dissolved following winding up. For a comparison between the two jurisdictions see *Re M Belmont & Co Ltd* [1952] Ch 10, [1951] 2 All E.R. 447; *Re Test Holdings (Clifton) Ltd* [1970] Ch 285, [1969] 3 All E.R. 517; *Re Townreach Ltd* [1995] Ch 28; [1994] 3 W.L.R. 983.

Claim form

The claim form should contain the same information as a claim made under s.653 **2G–121** but setting out that relief is claimed under s.651. It should be served on the Treasury Solicitor, and if the company is not in liquidation the registrar of companies should be named as a defendant (*Re Test Holdings (Clifton) Ltd* above).

The application may not generally be made after the end of two years from the dissolution of the company (subs.(4)). However, an application may be made at any time for the purpose of bringing proceedings for damages in respect of personal injuries (including funeral expenses) or for damages under the Fatal Accidents Act 1976, although the court will not make an order if it appears that such proceedings would fail by virtue of any enactment as to time (subs.(5)).

Evidence

The claim should be supported by full evidence of the circumstances leading up to **2G–122** the dissolution of the company, the nature of the claim to be brought (or other purpose for which the order is sought) and should deal, if appropriate, with the limitation question.

Evidence of service should also be produced exhibiting the *bona vacantia* letter (see para. 2G–126.

The hearing

Applications are generally listed for hearing on Friday at 2.00 p.m., but urgent ap- **2G–123** plications may be heard at other times.

The court may allow an interested third party to appear and to be joined as a defendant (*Re Workvale Ltd* [1991] B.C.L.C. 528; *Re Forte's (Manufacturing) Ltd* [1994] B.C.C. 84).

As to the circumstances in which the court may make a consent order without a hearing, see para. 2G–129 *et seq.*

Order

2G–124   The general order will declare the dissolution of the company void. It may provide for the appointment of a liquidator, and will order the claimant to deliver a copy of the order to the registrar of companies (s.651(3)). Where the order has been brought with a view to commencing proceedings it will often order that the costs be in the discretion of the court hearing the proposed claim.

As to the power of the court to make a "limitation override order" see the conflicting dicta in *Re Mixhurst Ltd* [1994] 2 B.C.L.C. 19, in *Re Townreach Ltd* [1995] Ch 28 and *Re Philip Powys Ltd* [1998] B.C.L.C. 440 (in which Morritt L.J. held that where the application was made after the two year period it could only be made for the purposes specified by the Act, but if made within the two year period it could be made for any legitimate purpose, which could include purposes beyond bringing personal injuries proceedings) and *Regent Leisuretime Ltd v. NatWest Finance Ltd (formerly County NatWest Ltd)* [2003] EWCA Civ 391. As to the need for the court to hear persons affected, including insurers, see *Smith v. White Knight Laundry Ltd* [2002] 1 W.L.R. 616.

The court has power to direct that a liquidation which purportedly took place while the company was dissolved would be deemed valid and effective (*Re A Company (No. 002081 of 1994)* [1994] BCC 933, not following *Re Mixhurst Ltd* above). However, the court has no power to validate proceedings commenced before the company was dissolved (*Re Philip Powis Ltd* [1997] 2 BCLC 481 (the appeal against which was allowed on other grounds), following *Morris v. Harris* [1927] AC 252; *Foster Yates & Thom Ltd v. H W Edgehill Equipment Ltd* (1978) 122 SJ 860; and distinguishing *Re Townreach Ltd* [1995] Ch 28).

The court has no power to direct that the name of a dissolved company be changed so as not to conflict with the name of a newly formed company (*Re Selectclass Ltd* unrep. Decision of Arden J., February 3, 1995).

Applications to restore the name of a company to the register (ss.653(2) and 653(2B))

2G–125   Where the registrar of companies has reasonable cause to believe that a company is not carrying on business or is not in operation, or where a company makes application to the registrar for the name of the company to be struck off, the registrar may, after giving the prescribed notices, strike the name of the company from the register and, upon publication of notice thereof in the *London Gazette*, the company is dissolved. The court, on an application by the company, a member or creditor, may, if satisfied that the company was at the time it was struck off, carrying on business or was in operation or that it is for some other reason just, make an order restoring the name of the company to the register. In the case of striking off under s.652A any "notifiable person" (as defined in s.653(2C)) may apply. In addition, the Secretary of State for Trade and Industry may apply if it is in the public interest to do so (s.653(2D)). The application may be made at any time before the expiration of 20 years from the date of publication in the *London Gazette* of notice under s.652 or 652A(4).

Claim form

2G–126   An application under s.653(2) may be made by the company even though it has ceased to exist. A member may apply, as may any personal representative of a deceased member (*Re Bayswater Trading Co Ltd* [1970] 1 W.L.R. 343; [1970] 1 All E.R. 608). A creditor may apply, as may a contingent or prospective creditor (*Re Harvest Lane Motor Bodies Ltd* [1969] 1 Ch 457; [1968] 2 All E.R. 1012) at the time of striking off (*Re Aga Estate Agencies Ltd* [1986] B.C.L.C. 346). If the company is not a claimant it should be joined as a defendant to an application made by any member, in particular if any undertaking is to be given by it. However, as a general rule where the application is made by a creditor, neither the creditor nor any member is entitled to be heard (*Re H. Clarkson (Overseas) Ltd* (1987) 3 B.C.C. 606). The court may also join as a defendant any interested party whose rights may be affected by the order (*Re Jayham Ltd* [1995] 2 B.C.L.C. 455).

Evidence

2G–127   The evidence in support of the application should contain particulars of the interest of the claimant, the date of incorporation of the company, the registered office, the company's objects, the share capital and an explanation as to the circumstances surrounding the striking off of the company (*e.g.* failure to file annual returns) and as to why notices served by the registrar of companies were not complied with, together with any other material facts (*Practice Note* [1974] 1 W.L.R. 1459; [1974] 3 All E.R. 933). It should also state the date on which the company was struck off and the date of publication of notice thereof in the London Gazette. If the application is made by a member the evidence should confirm that the company is solvent.

Evidence of service on the registrar of companies (at Registration Office, Crown Way, Maindy, Cardiff CF4 3UZ) and on the treasury solicitor as bona vacantia agent of the Crown (at *Bona Vacantia* Division, Queen Anne's Chambers, 28 Broadway, London SW1H 9JS) should also be filed exhibiting a copy of the Crown's *bona vacantia* letter indicating that the Crown has no objection to the making of the order (Practice Notes [1928] WN 218 and [1931] WN 199).

The hearing

Routine applications are listed for hearing at 2.00p.m. each Friday. Urgent applications (*e.g.* where a limitation period is about to expire) may be dealt with at other times. In appropriate cases the court will require undertakings to be given to remedy any default. The undertaking is generally required to be given in the terms proposed by the treasury solicitor who will hand to the registrar his letter setting out the undertakings which will be initialled by the registrar and retained on the court file.

2G–128

As to the circumstances in which the court may make a consent order without a hearing, see para. 2G–130 *et seq.*

Order

The court will draw up the order, which will generally provide for payment of the treasury solicitor's costs (unless the registrar of companies was at fault in striking off the company). A sealed copy should be sent to the registrar of companies at the address above.

2G–129

The effect of an order restoring the name of a company is to put all parties concerned in the same position as if the company has never been struck off (s.653(3)). Thus, s.653(3) provides that the court may give such directions and make such provisions as seem just for that purpose. In certain circumstances the court may direct that the period between the date on which the company was struck off and the date of restoration should not count for limitation purposes (*Re Donald Kenyon Ltd* [1956] 1 W.L.R. 1397, [1956] 3 All E.R. 596). No such direction will be given unless it is necessary (*Re Huntingdon Poultry Ltd* [1969] 1 W.L.R. 204), nor when the company is in liquidation (*Re Vickers and Bott Ltd* [1968] 2 All E.R. 264).

Where the effect of such an order amounts to the same as granting relief under s.33 of the Limitation Act 1980 it may be appropriate to hear any party likely to be affected (*Re Advance Insulation Ltd* [1989] 5 BCC 55 and *cf. Smith v. White Knight Laundry Ltd* [2002] 1 W.L.R. 616). Thus, where insurers were affected they could apply to set aside any such order (*Re Regent Insulation Ltd*, *The Times*, November 5, 1981). The general practice of the court is not to allow interveners to appear on restoration applications, but the court may do so if it is right to take their interests into account in deciding whether it is just to order restoration (*Re Blenheim Leisure Restaurants Ltd* [2000] BCC 554).

The court may order restoration on terms (*Re Shire Court Residents Ltd* [1995] BCC 821). As a general rule it will exercise its discretion in favour of restoration unless there are strong grounds for refusing it (*City of Westminster Assurance Co Ltd v. Registrar of Companies* [1997] B.C.C. 960, CA, unrep.); *Re Priceland* [1997] 1 BCLC 467).

For the procedure to restore the name of a company in conjunction with a petition seeking a winding up order see para. 2G-52.

Companies Court — Practice Note 1 of 2003

Claims for an order restoring the name of a company to the Register or declaring the dissolution of a company void (ss.651 and 653 Companies Act 1985)

With effect from 29th April 2003 claims for order of this type issued in the High Court in London will be given a return date three months in advance of the date of issue. This is designed to enable the applicant(s) to have sufficient opportunity to

2G–130

complete the requirements of the Registrar of Companies. In this way it is intended to prevent repeated adjournments pending completion of those requirements and to save the expense of unnecessary and repeated attendance at court by the parties.

When the requirements of the Registrar of Companies have been met and the Treasury Solicitor is able to approve the application, a consent order may be filed for approval by the court without attendance. If an undertaking is required to be given to the court it must be given by the solicitor (partner) for the claimant(s) in Form **U1** (attached) or by the claimant in person in Form **U2** (attached).

In such circumstances the papers which must be filed at court by the claimant(s) with the consent order are:

1. A copy of the claim
2. A copy of the witness statement in support
3. Original evidence of service of the application on the company (where appropriate)
4. Original evidence of service of the application on the Registrar of Companies
5. Original evidence of service of the application on the Treasury Solicitor dealing with bona vacantia assets on behalf of the Crown, or on the solicitor for the Duchy of Lancaster or the Duke of Cornwall dealing with bona vacantia assets in those areas, exhibiting in either case the bona vacantia waiver letter received in reply
6. The original signed copy of any undertaking required to be given to the court
7. Four copies of the agreed consent order, one of which should be signed by or on behalf of each party by way of consent to the form of order

In the normal course the above documents will be seen by the Registrar within three working days of delivery to the court. If the papers are in order, the Registrar will make the agreed order and the court will send two sealed copies of the order to the applicant and one to the Treasury Solicitor. If the papers are not in order (or the court for some reason requires), the matter will be listed for the parties to attend at the earliest convenient date and notice of this appointment will be given by the court to the parties.

Chief Bankruptcy Registrar
Royal Courts of Justice, Strand, London, WC2A 2LL
April 2003

Application for Order to restore name of company to the Register or declare dissolution of company void

Form U1 — Undertaking by solicitor on behalf of the claimant(s)   **2G–131**

IN THE HIGH COURT OF JUSTICE   **Claim No**
CHANCERY DIVISION
COMPANIES COURT

IN THE MATTER OF   LIMITED

AND IN THE MATTER OF SECTION [ ]OF THE COMPANIES ACT 1985

Between:

                                       Claimant(s)

AND

THE REGISTRAR OF COMPANIES

                                       Defendant

I *   , a partner in the firm Messrs   of

     the solicitors for the claimant(s), am duly authorised to give the following

undertakings and do hereby give those undertakings to the court:

1. [Insert undertakings]

I have explained to the claimants the meaning of these undertakings and the consequences of failing to keep promises given to the court.
Dated this   day of   200

Signed..

*Print name in full

Form U2 — Undertaking by member on behalf of himself and the company

IN THE HIGH COURT OF JUSTICE   **Claim No**
CHANCERY DIVISION
COMPANIES COURT

IN THE MATTER OF   **LIMITED**

AND IN THE MATTER OF SECTION [   ] OF THE COMPANIES ACT 1985

Between:

Claimant(s)

AND

THE REGISTRAR OF COMPANIES

Defendant

I *   of   , on behalf of

myself and my co-claimant   Limited, do hereby

give the following undertakings to the court:

1. [Insert undertakings]

I understand the undertakings which I have given to the court and that if I break any of my promises to the court I may be sent to prison for contempt.

Dated   this   day of   200

Signed...

*Print full name

Applications for a vesting order in relation to the property of a dissolved company

2G–132   On dissolution a company ceases to exist and its property is deemed bona vacantia (s.654(1)). Where property has been held by the company on trust, legal title vests in the crown but an application may be made for a vesting order (*Re Strathblaine Estate Ltd* [1948] Ch 228, [1948] 1 All E.R. 162). The Treasury Solicitor should be named as defendant to the application.

Applications to enforce the duty of a company to deliver documents to the registrar of companies (s.713(1) as amended by s.127(4) Companies Act 1989)

2G–133   The claim form should set out details of the claim and the relief sought. The application may be made by any member of the company. The company should be a defendant, but the usual practice is to join the director or officer responsible for the default. The claim should be supported by a witness statement setting out details of the default and confirming service by the claimant of notice pursuant to s.713(1) requiring the company to make good its default and exhibiting a copy. Fourteen days' notice is required.

Applications for the production and inspection of books or papers (s.721)

Application may be made to inspect or have produced the books or papers of a **2G–134** company if there is cause to believe that an offence has been committed in connection with the management of a company's affairs. The application may be made by the DPP, the Secretary of State for Trade and Industry or a chief officer of police and is made to a judge of the High Court (subs.(1)), from whose decision there is no appeal (subs.(4)).

Applications relating to the transfer of insurance or banking business (Part VII Financial Services and Markets Act 2000)

Part VII of the Financial Services and Markets Act 2000 (replacing the provisions of **2G–135** ss.49–52B and Sched.2C of the Insurance Companies Act 1982) controls schemes for the transfer of insurance and banking business. No insurance or banking business transfer scheme has effect unless an order sanctioning it has been made by the court under s.111(1) of the Act (s.104).

Claim form

The application may be made by claim form by an authorised person within the **2G–136** meaning of s.105 of the Act, the transferee within the meaning of ss.105-106 or both (s.107(2)). The application may be made only to the High Court (s.107(4)(a)). The claim form itself will generally be expressed simply as seeking the sanction of the court under s.111 of the Act of the scheme and the making of provision under s.112 of the Act. No defendant is named. Detailed requirements in relation to the application are imposed by the Financial Services and Markets Act 2000 (Control of Business Transfers) (Requirements on Applicants) Regulations 2001 (S.I. 2001 No. 3625) (s.108(1)). In particular, the Regulations provide for notice to be given to relevant parties including the Financial Services Authority.

No petition is issued.

Evidence

The evidence in support of the application should be given by a director of the **2G–137** claimant company and should give statutory information about the claimant similar to that which would otherwise appear in a petition (see para. 2G–23) details of the background to the scheme and the reasons for its proposal, a summary of its effects and details of the timing and method of the proposed transfer and the proposed means of notifying policyholders concerned. It should also deal with relevant authorisations by the Financial Services Authority. All relevant documents should be exhibited.

Evidence should also be filed by the proposed transferee.

Hearings

The application is dealt with in a similar manner to that which applies to schemes **2G–138** under ss.425 *et seq.* of the Companies Act 1985. Arrangements for hearings should be made with the companies court schemes and arrangements case manager, Room 410, Thomas More Building, Royal Courts of Justice, to whom enquiries may also be made by telephone (020 7947 6727).

The application comes initially before the registrar for directions as to the giving of notices and advertisement (see the Financial Services and Markets Act 2000 (Control of Business Transfers) (Requirements on Applicants) Regulations 2001 (S.I. 2001 No. 3625)). The court will also be concerned to establish that the requisite approvals have been obtained from the Financial Services Authority. The order will normally recite that the court is satisfied with the steps taken or to be taken to comply with the Financial Services and Markets Act (Control of Business Transfers) (Requirements on Applicants) Regulations 2001, provide for notice pursuant to reg. 3(2) to be given in approved form and advertised, for the posting of the proposed circular and notice to policyholders, any ancillary matters, and for the application to be listed and heard by a judge, who will (if appropriate) make the order sanctioning the scheme. The order may (in appropriate circumstances) dispense with the sending of notice to every individual policy holder pursuant to reg. 3(2)(b) (*e.g.* where policies may have been assigned or there are other circumstances where the beneficiaries of all policies cannot be identified and given notice directly). An application in respect of an insurance business transfer scheme must be accompanied by a scheme report made by a person approved by the Financial Services Authority (s.109). The Financial Services Authority and any person (including an employee) who alleges that he would be adversely affected by the scheme is entitled to be heard (s.110). The court must be satisfied before sanctioning the scheme that the appropriate certificates provided for by Pts I and II of Sched.12 of the Act have been obtained and that the transferee has the authorisation to enable the business to be carried on in the place to which it is to be transferred; it must also consider whether in all the circumstances it is appropriate to sanction the scheme (s.111).

Order

2G–139   If it is satisfied that it is appropriate to do so the court will make an order sanctioning the scheme. When doing so the court may make a wide range of other orders (s.112).

SECTION 3

OTHER PROCEEDINGS

3A HOUSING

Common Law Procedure Act 1852

(15 & 16 Vict. c.76)

3A–1

ARRANGEMENT OF SECTIONS

Proceedings in ejectment by landlord for non-payment of rent

210. In all cases between landlord and tenant, as often as it shall 3A–2 happen that one half year's rent shall be in arrear, and the landlord or lessor, to whom the same is due, hath right by law to re-enter for the non-payment thereof, such landlord or lessor shall and may, without any formal demand or re-entry, serve a writ in ejectment for the recovery of the demised premises, ... which service ... shall stand in the place and stead of a demand and re-entry; and in case of judgment against the defendant for nonappearance, if it shall be made appear to the court where the said action is depending, by affidavit, or be proved upon the trial in case the defendant appears, that half a year's rent was due before the said writ was served, and that no sufficient distress was to be found on the demised premises, countervailing the arrears then due, and that the lessor had power to re-enter, then and in every such case the lessor shall recover judgment and execution, in the same manner as if the rent in arrear had been legally demanded, and a re-entry made; and in case the lessee or his assignee, or other person claiming or deriving under the said lease, shall permit and suffer judgment to be had and recovered on such trial in ejectment, and execution to be executed thereon, without paying the rent and arrears, together with full costs, and without proceeding for relief in equity within six months after such execution executed, then and in such case the said lessee, his assignee, and all other persons claiming and deriving under the said lease, shall be barred and foreclosed from all relief or remedy in law or equity, other than by bringing error for reversal of such judgment, in case the same shall be erroneous, and the said landlord or lessor shall from thenceforth hold the said demised premises discharged from such lease; ... provided that nothing herein contained shall extend to bar the right of any mortgagee of such lease, or any part thereof, who shall not be in possession, so as such mortgagee shall and do, within six months after such judgment obtained and execution executed pay all rent in arrear, and all costs and damages sustained by such lessor or person entitled to the remainder or reversion as aforesaid, and perform all the covenants and agreements which, on the part and behalf of the first lessee, are and ought to be performed.

Note—Amended by the Statute Law Revision Act 1892. 3A–3

Proceedings in ejectment by landlord for non-payment of rent
  Claims for forfeiture of residential premises let under Rent Act 1977, Housing Act 3A–4

1985 or Housing Act 1988 are generally brought in the county court since no costs are recoverable if proceedings are commenced in the High Court (see the Rent Act 1977, s.141(4); the Housing Act 1985, s.110(3); and the Housing Act 1988, s.40(4)).

Section 210 provides that in claims for forfeiture based on at least half a year's arrears of rent, lessees are barred from all relief from forfeiture if they do not seek relief within six months of execution.

See too the Supreme Court Act 1981, s.38, below and, in the county court, County Courts Act 1984, ss.138–140, below. For forfeiture based on other breaches of covenant see the Law of Property Act 1925, s.146, below.

For the restriction on forfeiture or re-entry for arrears of service charges see the Housing Act 1996, s.81, below.

Lessee proceeding in equity not to have injunction or relief without payment of rent and costs

3A–5   **211.** In case the said lessee, his assignee, or other person claiming any right, title, or interest, in law or equity, of, in, or to the said lease, shall, within the time aforesaid, proceed for relief in any court of equity, such person shall not have or continue any injunction against the proceedings at law on such ejectment, unless he does or shall, within forty days next after a full and perfect answer shall be made by the claimant in such ejectment, bring into court, the lodge with the proper officer such sum and sums of money as the lessor or landlord shall in his answer swear to be due and in arrear over and above all just allowances, and also the costs taxed in the said suit, there to remain till the hearing of the cause, or to be paid out to the lessor or landlord on good security, subject to the decree of the court; and in case such proceedings for relief in equity shall be taken within the time aforesaid, and after execution is executed, the lessor or landlord shall be accountable only for so much and no more as he shall really and bona fide, without fraud, deceit, or wilful neglect, make of the demised premises from the time of his entering into the actual possession thereof; and if what shall be so made by the lessor or landlord happen to be less than the rent reserved on the said lease, then the said lessee or his assignee, before he shall be restored to his possession, shall pay such lessor or landlord, what the money so by him made fell short of the reserved rent for the time such lessor or landlord held the said lands.

Lessee proceeding in equity not to have injunction or relief without payment of rent and costs

3A–6   The effect of s.211 is that a tenant is not to have relief without payment of rent due and costs.

Tenant paying all rent, with costs, proceedings to cease

3A–7   **212.** If the tenant or his assignee do or shall, at any time before the trial in such ejectment, pay or tender to the lessor or landlord, his executors or administrators, or his or their attorney in that cause, or pay into the court where the same cause is depending, all the rent and arrears, together with the costs, then and in such case all further proceedings on the said ejectment shall cease and be discontinued; and if such lessee, his executors, administrators, or assigns, shall, upon such proceedings as aforesaid, be relieved in equity, he and they shall have, hold, and enjoy the demised lands, according to the lease thereof made, without any new lease.

"Tenant pay all rent ..."

Under s.212 where at least half a year's rent is in arrears, a tenant may stay any **3A–8** proceedings at any time before trial by paying all rent, arrears and costs.

Law of Property Act 1925

(15 & 16 GEO. 5 C.20)   **3A–9**

ARRANGEMENT OF SECTIONS

PART III

Sale of mortgaged property in action for redemption or foreclosure

91.—(1) Any person entitled to redeem mortgaged property may **3A–10** have a judgment or order for sale instead of for redemption in an action brought by him either for redemption alone, or for sale alone, or for sale or redemption in the alternative.

(2) In any action, whether for foreclosure, or for redemption, or for sale, or for the raising and payment in any manner of mortgage money, the court, on the request of the mortgagee, or of any person interested either in the mortgage money or in the right of redemption, and, notwithstanding that—

    (a) any other person dissents; or

    (b) the mortgagee or any person so interested does not appear in the action;

and without allowing any time for redemption or for payment of any mortgage money, may direct a sale of the mortgaged property, on such terms as it thinks fit, including the deposit in court of a reasonable sum fixed by the court to meet the expenses of sale and to secure performance of the terms.

(3) But, in an action brought by a person interested in the right of redemption and seeking a sale, the court may, in the application of any defendant, direct the plaintiff to give such security for costs as the court thinks fit, and may give the conduct of the sale to any defendant, and may give such directions as it thinks fit respecting the costs of the defendants or any of them.

(4) In any case within this section the court may, if it thinks fit,

direct a sale without previously determining the priorities of incumbrancers.

(5) This section applies to actions brought either before or after the commencement of this Act.

(6) In this section "mortgaged property" includes the estate or interest which a mortgagee would have had power to convey if the statutory power of sale were applicable.

(7) For the purposes of this section the court may, in favour of a purchaser, make a vesting order conveying the mortgaged property, or appoint a person to do so, subject or not to any incumbrance, as the court may think fit; or, in the case of an equitable mortgage, may create and vest a mortgage term in the mortgagee to enable him to carry out the sale as if the mortgage had been made by deed by way of legal mortgage.

[(8) The county court has jurisdiction under this section where the amount owing in respect of the mortgage or charge at the commencement of the proceedings does not exceed £30,000].

3A–11   *Note* —Amended by the County Courts Act 1984, s.148(1), Sched.2, Pt II, para. 3(1); and the High Court and County Courts Jurisdiction Order 1991 (S.I. 1991 No. 724), art.2(4) and (8).

"mortgage"
3A–12   See s.205(xvi).

"property"
3A–13   See s.205(xx).

"sale"
3A–14   See s.205(xxiv).

"Sale of mortgaged property ..."
3A–15   Under this section the court (which includes the county court if the amount owing in respect of the mortgage at the commencement of proceedings does not exceed £30,000) on the application of any person entitled to redeem the mortgaged property may direct the sale of the premises on such terms as it thinks fit. The court has a wide discretion and may order a sale of mortgaged property against the wishes of the lender where it would be unfair to the borrower to postpone sale, even if the mortgage would not be redeemed. In exercising that discretion, the court should have regard to the interests of all concerned and to what is just and equitable (see *Palk v. Mortgage Funding Services* [1993] Ch. 330; [1993] 2 W.L.R. 415; [1993] 2 All E.R. 481, CA; and *Polonski v. Lloyds Bank* (1999) 31 H.L.R. 721; *The Times,* May 6, 1997, Ch D).

In *Cheltenham and Gloucester Building Society v. Krausz* [1997] 1 W.L.R. 1558; [1997] 1 All E.R. 21, CA, Phillips L.J. stated that he did not consider:

> "that the County Court, as part of its inherent jurisdiction, can properly suspend an order or warrant for possession in order to enable a mortgagor to apply to the High Court for an order under s.91. It [is] incumbent on the mortgagor to seek from the High Court any relief which the court is empowered to give before the warrant takes effect."

He noted that Administration of Justice Act 1970, s.36 (see below) makes it clear that parliament did not intend that the court should have power to curtail mortgagees' rights to possession unless the proceeds of sale were likely to discharge the mortgage debt. Millett L.J. expressed serious doubts as to whether *Barrett v. Halifax Building Society* (1995) 28 H.L.R. 634, Ch D, where an order allowing the borrowers to sell even though the proceeds of sale would not discharge the mortgage debt, was correctly decided.

If the proceeds of sale are likely to be sufficient to redeem the mortgage, it is normal for the court to give conduct of the sale to the borrower since he or she has a greater incentive to achieve the best price. In *Cheltenham and Gloucester plc v. Booker* [1997] 19 E.G. 155; (1997) 73 P. & C.R. 412; (1997) 29 H.L.R. 634, CA, where the proceeds of sale were not likely to be sufficient to redeem the mortgage and where the court was unable to exercise its discretion under Administration of Justice Act 1970, s.36 (see below) it was held that the court may give conduct of the sale of premises to the lender while postponing execution of a warrant for possession until completion of the sale, thus allowing the borrower to remain in occupation. There is no reason in principle for the court to accede to a lender's insistence upon immediate possession if:

(a) possession will only be required on completion;

(b) the presence of the borrowers pending completion will enhance, or at least not depress, the sale price;

(c) the borrowers will co-operate in the sale; and

(d) they will give possession to the purchasers on completion.

However, Millett L.J. stated these conditions are seldom likely to be satisfied and the circumstances in which such a course would be appropriate are hard to imagine. Such an order would "certainly be a rarity".

* * * *

PART V

LEASES AND TENANCIES

Restrictions on and relief against forfeiture of leases and underleases

146.—(1) A right of re-entry or forfeiture under any proviso or stipulation in a lease for a breach of any covenant or condition in the lease shall not be enforceable, by action or otherwise, unless and until the lessor serves on the lessee a notice— **3A–16**

(a) specifying the particular breach complained of; and

(b) if the breach is capable of remedy, requiring the lessee to remedy the breach; and

(c) in any case, requiring the lessee to make compensation in money for the breach;

and the lessee fails, within a reasonable time thereafter, to remedy the breach, if it is capable of remedy, and to make reasonable compensation in money, to the satisfaction of the lessor, for the breach.

(2) Where a lessor is proceeding, by action by otherwise, to enforce such a right of re-entry or forfeiture, the lessee may, in the lessor's action, if any, or in any action brought by himself, apply to the court for relief; and the court may grant or refuse relief, as the court, having regard to the proceedings and conduct of the parties under the foregoing provisions of this section, and to all the other circumstances, thinks fit; and in case of relief may grant it on such terms, if any, as to costs, expenses, damages, compensation, penalty, or otherwise, including the granting of an injunction to restrain any like breach in the future, as the court, in the circumstances of each case, thinks fit.

(3) A lessor shall be entitled to recover as a debt due to him from a lessee, and in addition to damages (if any), all reasonable costs and expenses properly incurred by the lessor in the employment of a solicitor and surveyor or valuer, or otherwise, in reference to any

HOUSING

breach giving rise to a right of re-entry or forfeiture which, at the request of the lessee, is waived by the lessor, or from which the lessee is relieved, under the provisions of this Act.

(4) Where a lessor is proceeding by action or otherwise to enforce a right of re-entry or forfeiture under any covenant, proviso, or stipulation in a lease, or for non-payment of rent, the court may, on application by any person claiming as under-lessee any estate or interest in the property comprised in the lease or any part thereof, either in the lessor's action (if any) or in any action brought by such person for that purpose, make an order vesting, for the whole term of the lease or any less term, the property comprised in the lease or any part thereof in any person entitled as under-lessee to any estate or interest in such property upon such conditions as to execution of any deed or other document, payment of rent, costs, expenses, damages, compensation, giving security, or otherwise, as the court in the circumstances of each case may think fit, but in no case shall any such under-lessee be entitled to require a lease to be granted to him for any longer term than he had under this original sub-lease.

(5) For the purposes of this section—

(a) "Lease" includes an original or derivative under-lease; also an agreement for a lease where the lessee has become entitled to have his lease granted; also a grant at a fee farm rent, or securing a rent by condition;

(b) "Lessee" includes an original or derivative under-lessee, and the persons deriving title under a lessee; also a grantee under any such grant as aforesaid and the persons deriving title under him;

(c) "Lessor" includes an original or derivative under-lessor, and the persons deriving title under a lessor; also a person making such grant as aforesaid and the persons deriving title under him;

(d) "Under-lease" includes an agreement for an underlease where the underlessee has become entitled to have his underlease granted;

(e) "Underlessee" includes any person deriving title under an underlessee.

(6) This section applies although the proviso or stipulation under which the right of re-entry or forfeiture accrues is inserted in the lease in pursuance of the directions of any Act of Parliament.

(7) For the purposes of this section a lease limited to continue as long only as the lessee abstains from committing a breach of covenant shall be and take effect as a lease to continue for any longer term for which it could subsist, but determinable by a proviso for re-entry on such a breach.

(8) This section does not extend—

(i) To a covenant or condition against assigning, underletting, parting with the possession, or disposing of the land leased where the breach occurred before the commencement of this Act; or

(ii) In the case of a mining lease, to a covenant or condition for allowing the lessor to have access to or inspect books, accounts, records, weighing machines or other things, or to enter or inspect the mine or the working thereof.

(9) This section does not apply to a condition for forfeiture on the bankruptcy of the lessee or on taking in execution of the lessee's interest if contained in a lease of—

(a) Agricultural or pastoral land;

(b) Mines or minerals;

(c) A house used or intended to be used as a public-house or beershop;

(d) A house let as a dwelling-house, with the use of any furniture, books, works of art, or other chattels not being in the nature of fixtures;

(e) Any property with respect to which the personal qualifications of the tenant are of importance for the preservation of the value or character of the property, or on the ground of neighbourhood to the lessor, or to any person holding under him.

(10) Where a condition of forfeiture on the bankruptcy of the lessee or on taking in execution of the lessee's interest is contained in any lease, other than a lease of any of the classes mentioned in the last subsection, then—

(a) if the lessee's interest is sold within one year from the bankruptcy or taking in execution, this section applies to the forfeiture condition aforesaid;

(b) if the lessee's interest is not sold before the expiration of that year, this section only applies to the forfeiture condition aforesaid during the first year from the date of the bankruptcy or taking in execution.

(11) This section does not, save as otherwise mentioned, affect the law relating to re-entry or forfeiture or relief in case of non-payment of rent.

(12) This section has affect notwithstanding any stipulation to the contrary.

(13) The county court has jurisdiction under this section.

Note —Amended by the High Court and County Courts Jurisdiction Order (S.I. 1991 No. 724), art. 2(1)(a) and (8). Subsection (13) was added by the County Courts Act 1984, s.148(1), Sched. 2 and then amended by High Court and County Courts Jurisdiction Order 1991 (S.I. 1991 No. 724), art.2(1)(a) and (8). County courts now have unlimited jurisdiction. **3A–17**

No forfeiture notice before determination of breach.

Commonhold and Leasehold Reform Act 2002, s.168 provides that a landlord under a long lease of a dwelling may not serve a notice under Law of Property Act 1925, s.146(1) unless it has been finally determined on an application under subsection s.168(4) that the breach has occurred; or the tenant has admitted the breach; or a court in any proceedings, or an arbitral tribunal in proceedings pursuant to a post-dispute arbitration agreement, has finally determined that the breach has occurred. Section 168 is printed at para. 3A–1507 below. Comonhold and Leasehold Reform Act 2002, s.76 provides that a lease is a long lease if it (a) is granted for a term of years certain exceeding 21 years; (b) is for a term fixed by law under a grant with a covenant or obligation for perpetual renewal (c) takes effect under Law of Property Act 1925, s.149(6) (leases terminable after a death or marriage); (d) was granted under the **3A–18** right to buy provisions of Housing Act 1985, Part 5; (e) is a shared ownership lease; or (f) under Housing Act 1996, s.17 (the right to acquire). Section 77 contains certain exceptions.

"rent"

3A–19   See s.205(xxiii).

"lease", "lessee", "lessor", "under-lease" and "under-lessor"

3A–20   See s.146(5).

"Restrictions on and relief against forfeiture ..."

3A–21   Note that this section does not, save as is otherwise mentioned, affect the law relating to re-entry or forfeiture or relief in the case of non-payment of rent (s.146(11)). See the Common Law Procedure Act 1852, ss.210–212, above, the Supreme Court Act 1981, s.38, below, and the County Courts Act 1984, ss.138–140, below.

For the restriction on forfeiture or re-entry for arrears of service charges see the Housing Act 1996, s.81, below.

For a statement of the circumstances in which a tenant may apply for relief, see *Billson v. Residential Apartments Ltd* [1992] 1 A.C. 494; [1992] 2 W.L.R. 15; [1992] 1 All E.R. 141, HL, where Lord Templeman said:

"A tenant may apply for ... relief from forfeiture under section 146(2) after the issue of a section 146 notice but he is not prejudiced if he does not do so. A tenant cannot apply for relief after a landlord has forfeited a lease by issuing and serving a writ, has recovered judgment and has entered into possession pursuant to that judgment. If the judgment is set aside or succesfully appealed, the tenant will be able to apply for relief in the landlord's action but the court in deciding whether to grant relief will take into account any consequences of the original order and repossession and the delay of the tenant. A tenant may apply for relief after a landlord has forfeited by re-entry without first obtaining a court order for that purpose, but the court in deciding whether to grant relief will take into account all the circumstances including delay on the part of the tenant."

Lord Templeman also indicated that he considered the practice of awarding indemnity costs as a condition of granting relief was ripe for reconsideration (but *cf. Church Commissioners v. Ibrahim* [1997] 1 E.G.L.R. 13, CA and CPR, r.48.3). See too *Fairview Investments Ltd v. Sharma* March 2000 Legal Action, January 11, 2000, CA where the Court of Appeal stated that although costs are in the court's discretion, where there is a contractual right to costs, the discretion should ordinarily be exercised so as to reflect that contractual right (*Gomba Holdings (UK) Ltd v. Minories Finance Ltd (No. 2)* [1993] Ch. 171 at p.194B, CA). If a lessee is to be relieved from forfeiture, it should be on terms that reflect the lessee's breach of covenant and the lessor should not be left out of pocket by taking proper steps to protect his interests. Where a lessor has bargained for the protection afforded by a clause providing for payment of costs, a court should be slow to deprive him or her of that protection and should not do so without good reason.

Relief against notice to effect decorative repairs

3A–22   **147.**—(1) After a notice is served on a lessee relating to the internal decorative repairs to a house or other building, he may apply to the court for relief, and if, having regard to all the circumstances of the case (including in particular the length of the lessee's term or interest remaining unexpired), the court is satisfied that the notice is unreasonable, it may, by order, wholly or partially relieve the lessee from liability for such repairs.

(2) This section does not apply—

    (i) where the liability arises under an express covenant or agreement to put the property in a decorative state of repair and the covenant or agreement has never been performed;

    (ii) to any matter necessary or proper—

       (a) for putting or keeping the property in a sanitary condition, or

       (b) for the maintenance or preservation of the structure;

   (iii) to any statutory liability to keep a house in all respects reasonably fit for human habitation;

   (iv) to any covenant or stipulation to yield up the house or other building in a specified state of repair at the end of the term.

(3) In this section "lease" includes an underlease and an agreement for a lease, and "lessee" has a corresponding meaning and includes any person liable to effect the repairs.

(4) This section applies whether the notice is served before or after the commencement of this Act, and has effect notwithstanding any stipulation to the contrary.

(5) The county court has jurisdiction under this section.

Note —Subs. (5) added by the County Courts Act 1984, s.148(1), Sched.2; repealed **3A–23** in part by the High Court and County Courts Jurisdiction Order 1991 (S.I. 1991 No. 724), art.2(8), Sched. County courts now have unlimited jurisdiction.

NOTICES

Regulations respecting notices

   196.—(1) Any notice required or authorised to be served or given **3A–24** by this Act shall be in writing.

(2) Any notice required or authorised by this Act to be served on a lessee or mortgagor shall be sufficient, although only addressed to the lessee or mortgagor by that designation, without his name, or generally to the persons interested, without any name, and notwithstanding that any person to be affected by the notice is absent, under disability, unborn, or unascertained.

(3) Any notice required or authorised by this Act to be served shall be sufficiently served if it is left at the last-known place of abode or business in the United Kingdom of the lessee, lessor, mortgagee, mortgagor, or other person to be served, in case of a notice required or authorised to be served on a lessee or mortgagor, is affixed or left for him on the land or any house or building comprised in the lease or mortgage, or, in case of a mining lease, is left for the lessee at the office or counting-house of the mine.

(4) Any notice required or authorised by this Act to be served shall also be sufficiently served, if it is sent by post in a registered letter addressed to the lessee, lessor, mortgagee, mortgagor, or other person to be served, by name, at the aforesaid place of abode or business, office, or counting-house, and if that letter is not returned by the postal operator (within the meaning of the Postal Services Act 2000) concerned undelivered; and that service shall be deemed to be made at the time at which the registered letter would in the ordinary course be delivered.

(5) The provisions of this section shall extend to notices required

to be served by any instrument affecting property executed or coming into operation after the commencement of this Act unless a contrary intention appears.

(6) This section does not apply to notices served in proceedings in the court.

3A–25   *Note* —Amended by the Leasehold Property (Repairs) Act 1938, s.72; the Reserve and Auxiliary Forces (Protection of Civil Interests) Act 1951, s.29(b); the Recorded Delivery Service Act 1962, s.1, Sched.; and the Postal Services Act 2000 (Consequential Modifications No.1) Order (S.I. 2001 No. 1149), Sched.1, para.7.

notices

3A–26   It is good practice for landlords by an express provision to incorporate this section into tenancy agreements. If they do not do so, it cannot be implied. In the absence of express incorporation, landlords must prove that notices to quit or notices of intention to seek possession have come to the attention of the tenant (see *Wandsworth LBC v. Attwell* (1995) 27 H.L.R. 536; (1996) 01 E.G. 100; (1996) 94 L.G.R. 419, CA; and *Enfield LBC v. Devonish* (1997) 29 H.L.R. 691; *The Times*, December 12, 1996, CA.

* * * *

Part XII

Construction, Jurisdiction, and General Provisions

General definitions

3A–27   **205.**—(1) In this Act unless the context otherwise requires, the following expressions have the meanings hereby assigned to them respectively, that is to say:

(i)–(viii) [...]

(ix) "Land" includes land of any tenure, and mines and minerals whether or not held apart from the surface, buildings or parts of buildings (whether the division is horizontal, vertical or made in any other way) and other corporeal hereditaments; also a manor, an advowson, and rent and other incorporeal hereditaments, and an easement, right, privilege, or benefit in, over, or derived from land; and "mines and minerals" include any strata or seam of minerals or substances in or under any land, and powers of working and getting the same; and "manor" includes a lordship and reputed manor or lordship; and "hereditament" means any real property which on an intestacy occurring before the commencement of this Act might have devolved upon an heir;

(x)–(xv) [...]

(xvi) "Mortgage" includes any charge or lien on any property for securing money or money's worth; "legal mortgage" means a mortgage by demise or subdemise or a charge by way of legal mortgage and "legal mortgagee" has a corresponding meaning; "mortgage money" means money or money's worth secured by a mortgage; "mortgagor" includes any person from time to time deriving title under the original mortgagor or entitled to redeem a mortgage according to his estate interest or right in the mortgaged property; "mortgagee" includes a chargee by way of legal mortgage and any person from time to time deriving title under the original mortgagee; and "mortgagee in possession" is, for the purposes of this Act, a mortgagee who, in right of the mortgage, has entered into and is in possession of the mortgaged property; and "right of redemption" includes an option to repurchase only if the option in effect creates a right of redemption;

(xvii)–(xxi) [...]

(xxii) "Registered land" has the same meaning as in the Land Registration Act 2002;

(xxiii) "Rent" includes a rent service or a rentcharge, or other rent, toll duty, royalty, or annual or periodical payment in money or money's worth, reserved or issuing out of or charged upon land, but does not include mortgage interest; "rentcharge" includes a fee farm rent; "fine" includes a premium or foregift and any payment consideration, or benefit in the nature of a nature of a fine, premium or foregift; "lessor" includes an underlessor and a person deriving title under a lessor or underlessor; and "lessee" includes an underlessee and a person deriving title under a lessee or underlessee, and "lease" includes an underlease or other tenancy;

(xxiv)–
(xxxi) [...]
(1A) [...]
(2) [...]
(3) [...]

Note —Amended by the County Courts Act 1984, Sched.2; the Finance Act 1949, **3A–28**
Sched.11; the Trusts of Land and Appointment of Trustees Act 1996, Sched.4; the Mental Health Act 1983, Sched.4; the Mental Health Act 1959, Sched.7; the Transfer of Functions (Ministry of Food) Order 1955 (S.I. 1955 No. 554); the Administration of Justice Act 1965, Sched.1; the High Court and County Courts Jurisdiction Order 1991 (S.I. 1991 No. 724), art.2(8), Sched.; and the Land Registration Act 2002, Sched.11, para.2(13)(a).

National Assistance Act 1948

(11 & 12 GEO. 6C.29)

PART III

LOCAL AUTHORITY SERVICES

PROVISION OF ACCOMMODATION

Duty of local authorities to provide accommodation

21.—(1) Subject to and in accordance with the provisions of this **3A–29**

Part of this Act, a local authority may with the approval of the Secretary of State, and to such extent as he may direct shall, make arrangements for providing—

    (a) residential accommodation for persons aged eighteen or over who by reason of age, illness, disability or any other circumstances are in need of care and attention which is not otherwise available to them; and

    (aa) residential accommodation for expectant and nursing mothers who are in need of care and attention which is not otherwise available to them.

    (b) [...]

(1A) A person to whom section 115 of the Immigration and Asylum Act 1999 (exclusion from benefits) applies may not be provided with residential accommodation under subsection (1)(a) if his need for care and attention has arisen solely—

    (a) because he is destitute; or

    (b) because of the physical effects, or anticipated physical effects, of his being destitute.

(1B) Subsections (3) and (5) to (8) of section 95, of the Immigration and Asylum Act 1999 and paragraph 2 of Schedule 8 to that Act, apply for the purposes of subsection (1A) as they apply for the purposes of that section, but for the references in subsections (5) and (7) of that section and in that paragraph to the Secretary of State substitute references to a local authoity.

(2) In [making any such arrangements] a local authority shall have regard to the welfare of all persons for whom accommodation is provided, and in particular to the need for providing accommodation of different descriptions suited to different descriptions of such persons as are mentioned in the last foregoing subsection.

(2A) In determining for the purposes of paragraph (a) or (aa) of subsection (1) of this section whether care and attention are otherwise available to a person, a local authority shall disregard so much of the person's resources as may be specified in, or determined in accordance with, regulations made by the Secretary of State for the purposes of this subsection.

(2B) In subsection (2A) of this section the reference to a person's resources is a reference to his resources within the meaning of regulations made for the purposes of that subsection.

(3) [...]

(4) Subject to the provisions of section 26 of this Act. Accommodation provided by a local authority in the exercise of their functions under this section shall be provided in premises managed by the authority or, to such extent as may be determined in accordance with the arrangements under this section, in such premises managed by another local authority as may be agreed between the two authorities and on such terms, including terms as to the reimbursement of expenditure incurred by the said other authority, as may be so agreed.

(5) References in this Act to accommodation provided under this Part thereof shall be construed as references to accommodation

provided in accordance with this and the five next following sections, and as including references to board and other services, amenities and requisites provided in connection with the accommodation except where in the opinion of the authority managing the premises their provision is unnecessary.

(6) References in this Act to a local authority providing accommodation shall be construed, in any case where a local authority agree with another local authority for the provision of accommodation in premises managed by the said other authority, as references to the first-mentioned local authority.

(7) Without prejudice to the generality of the foregoing provisions of this section, a local authority may—

(a) provide, in such cases as they may consider appropriate, for the conveyance of persons to and from premises in which accommodation is provided for them under this Part of the Act;

(b) make arrangements for the provision on the premises in which accommodation is being provided for such other services as appear to the authority to be required.

(8) [...] nothing in this section shall authorise or require a local authority to make any provision authorised or required to be made (whether by that or by any other authority) by or under any enactment not contained in this Part of this Act [or for authorised or required to be provided under the National Health Service Act 1977.]

Note —Amended by the Local Government Act 1972, ss.195(6), 272(1), Sched.23, **3A–30** para. 2(1), Sched.30; the National Health Service Reorganisation Act 1973, s.57(1), (2), Sched.4, para. 44, Sched.5; the Housing (Homeless Persons) Act 1977, s.20(4), Sched.; the Children Act 1989, s.108(5), Sched.13, para. 11(1); the National Health Service and Community Care Act 1990, s.42(1), 66, Sched.9, para. 5(1)–(3), Sched.10; the Immigration and Asylum Act 1999, s.116; and by the Health and Social Care Act 2001, s.53.

Editorial Introduction

The National Assistance Act 1948, s.21(1)(a) gives social services authorities power **3A–31** to make arrangements for the accommodation of adults who are in need of care and attention not otherwise available to them as a result of age, illness, disability or any other circumstances. The Secretary of State has directed that authorities shall make arrangements under s.21(1)(a) to provide accommodation for adults who are ordinarily resident in their areas or are in urgent need thereof and who, by reason of age, illness, disability or any other circumstance, are in need of care and attention not otherwise available to them. Note that s.21 was amended by Immigration and Asylum Act 1999, s.116 to exclude the provision of accommodation under s.21 to destitute asylum seekers.

Section 21 is not a safety net on which any person short of money can rely. The proper test is whether a person is "in need of care and attention" (*R. v. Newham LBC, Ex p. Plastin* (1997) 30 H.L.R. 261, QBD). In *R. v. Southwark, Ex p. Hong Cui* (1999) 31 H.L.R. 639, QBD David Pannick QC sitting as a deputy judge held that: (1) an applicant must show that s/he is in desperate need of care and attention and that otherwise there is a risk that there would be damage to his/her health or for some other reason assistance is urgently required. It is not enough to be destitute; and (2) authorities must consider the circumstances of each individual case.

There is no express provision that obliges a local authority to meet the needs of an individual child after assessment. National Assistance Act 1948, s.21 involves the notion of a target duty that becomes crystallised and enforceable after a needs assessment (see *R. v. Kensington & Chelsea RLBC, Ex p. Kujtim* [1999] 4 All E.R. 161). However, the language and structure of Children Act 1989, s.17 are entirely different from s.21. A

HOUSING

child previously accommodated by s.21 is catered for by s.20 of the 1989 Act. Where a child requires accommodation of a particular kind and is in a family unit so that s.20 is not invoked, provision would generally be made through the housing legislation. Section 17 of the 1989 Act creates a general duty to safeguard and promote the welfare of children in need. However in *A and W v. Lambeth LBC*; *G v. Barnet LBC* (also reported as *R.(G) v. Barnet LBC*) [2003] UKHL 57; [2003] 3 W.L.R. 1194; [2004] 1 All E.R. 97, the House of Lords rejected claims that Children Act 1989, s.17 gives rise to an enforceable duty to accommodate the children with their families. Social services departments are not statutorily required to arrange or provide accommodation for families with children who are not entitled to be housed through the usual channels, although they can do so. Section 17(1) is an overriding duty, a statement of general principle. It provides the broad aims which local authorities are to bear in mind when performing other duties set out in the Children Act and the specific duties for facilitating the discharge of those general duties which were set out in Pt I of Sched. 2. A child in need within the meaning of s.17(10) is eligible for the provision of those services, but has no absolute right to them. Section 17(1) sets out duties of a general character which are intended to be for the benefit of children in need in the local social services authority's area in general. The other duties and the specific duties which follow have to be performed in each individual case by reference to the general duties which s.17(1) sets out. Section 17 refers to a range and level of services appropriate to the children's needs. It is broadly expressed, with a view to giving the greatest possible scope to the local social services authority as to what it chooses to do in the provision of those services. Although the services which the authority provide may include the provision of accommodation (see s.17(6)), the provision of residential accommodation to house a child in need so that he or she can live with the family is not the principal or primary purpose of the legislation. Housing is the function of the local housing authority. Detailed provisions for the acquisition and management of housing stock are contained in the Housing Acts. Provisions of that kind are entirely absent from the Children Act. The expenditure of limited resources on the provision of residential accommodation for housing children with their families would be bound to mean that there was less available for expenditure on other services designed for the performance of the general duty which s.17(1) identified. It would also sit uneasily with the legislation in the Housing Acts.

local authority

3A–32   See s.33 below.

destitute

3A–33   See the Immigration and Asylum Act 1999, s.95(3).

resources

3A–34   Where a local authority is satisfied that a person is in need of care and attention which is not otherwise available, lack of funds does not excuse it from performing its duty to make appropriate arrangements (*R. v. Sefton MBC, Ex p. Help the Aged* [1997] 1 CCLR 40, CA).

accommodation

3A–35   In *R. v. Newham LBC, Ex p. Medical Foundation of the Care of Victims of Torture* (1998) 30 H.L.R. 955, QBD, Moses J. held that the phrase "residential accommodation" means no more than where a person lives. It does not mean "accommodation with an institutional quality". See too *R. v. Newham LBC, Ex p. C* (1999) 31 H.L.R. 567, QBD.

Termination of duty

3A–36   See Immigration and Asylum Act 1999, Pt VI. The duty of central government to provide support to asylum seekers under Immigration and Asylum Act 1999, s.95 applies only where need arises solely from destitution rather than sickness, age or disability. Otherwise local authorities are obliged to provide accommodation under s.21. Regulation 6(4)of the Asylum Support Regulations 2000 (S.I. 2000 No. 704) requires the secretary of state to take into account any other support available to an asylum seeker when determining whether that asylum seeker is destitute for the purposes of s.95(1). That regulation includes accomodation that the local authority is obliged to provide by s.21. See *R. (Westminster CC) v. National Asylum Support Service* [2002] UKHL 38; [2002] 1 W.L.R. 2956.

Where a person's needs satisfy the criteria contained in the National Assistance Act 1948, s.21(1)(a), the authority has a continuing duty to provide accommodation while the person's needs remain the same. However an authority is entitled to treat its duty as discharged and to refuse to provide further accommodation if the person refuses accommodation offered or, following its provision manifests by his or her conduct a persistent and unequivocal refusal to observe the authority's reasonable requirements in relation to occupation of such accommodation. Before concluding that there has been such a refusal it is desirable that the authority write a final warning letter. Any decision by the authority to treat its duty as discharged by conduct requires a reassessment both of current need and careful consideration of the nature of that conduct, including any medical condition or infirmity known to the authority (*R. v. Kensington and Chelsea RBC, Ex p. Kutjim* [1999] 4 All E.R. 161, CA).

Asylum Seekers

Asylum seekers are to be supported under the Immigration and Asylum Act 1999, **3A–37** Pt VI until the conclusion of any appeal. Thereafter, if they have a need for care and attention that does not arise solely because of destitution, they qualify under s.21. See *R v. Wandsworth LBC Ex p. O; R v. Leicester CC Ex p. Bhika* [2000] 1 W.L.R. 2539; [2000] 4 All E.R. 590 where Simon Brown L.J. accepted submissions that:

"if an applicant's need for care and attention is to any material extent made more acute by some circumstances other than the mere lack of accommodation and funds, then, despite being subject to immigration control, he qualifies for assistance. Other relevant circumstances include, of course, age, illness and disability, all of which are expressly mentioned in section 21(1) itself. If, for example, an immigrant, as well as being destitute, is old, ill or disabled, he is likely to be yet more vulnerable and less well able to survive than if he were merely destitute."

All other categories or persons from abroad, whether or not they have any pending immigration appeal qualify for assistance under s.21 if their need does not arise solely because of destitution. Where a destitute 'asylum-seeker' within the terms of Immigration and Asylum Act 1999, s.94(1) with children requires accommodation, a local authority's duty does not extend to accommodating the children. Responsibility for them falls on NASS rather than on the local authority and they are to be treated as "destitute" even though actually sheltered with their parent. In such circumstances, the appropriate practical solution is for the council to accommodate the whole family with NASS meeting the cost of accommodating the children (*R.(O) v. Haringey LBC* [2004] EWCA Civ 535; [2004] H.L.R.44).

The fact that someone is unlawfully present in the United Kingdom does not preclude them from seeking accommodation under s.21 (*R. v. Wandsworth LBC Ex p. O; R v. Leicester CC Ex p. Bhika* [2000] 1 W.L.R. 2539; [2000] 4 All E.R. 590 where Simon Brown L.J. said:

"section 21(1) affords the very last possibility of relief, the final hope of keeping the needy off the streets. Not even illegality should to my mind bar an applicant who otherwise qualifies for support. For my part I would hold that the local authority has no business with the applicant's immigration status save only for the purpose of learning why the care and attention 'is not otherwise available to them' as section 21(1) requires — and indeed... for reporting such applications to the immigration authorities if they conclude that the Home Office is unaware of their presence here."

Under National Assistance Act 1948, s.21(1A) the responsibility for meeting the care and accommodation needs of disabled asylum-seekers falls upon the local authorities, not the NASS. For the purposes of National Assistance Act 1948, s.21(1A), local authorities have to decide whether applicants are in need of care and attention not otherwise available to them. They cannot take into account the provision of asylum support under the Immigration and Asylum Act 1999 because the Asylum Support Regulations 2000 required them to disregard the provision of asylum support when deciding whether a person was destitute (*Murua and Gichura v. Croydon LBC* (2002) 5 C.C.L.R. 51, QBD Admin Ct).

A local authority is not relieved of its duty to provide residential accomodation under s.21 even if the asylum seeker has applied to NASS and has been accepted for provision of support by them. (Asylum Support Regulations 2000 (S.I. 2000 No. 704), reg.23 and *R.(Mani) v. Lambeth LBC* [2003] EWCA Civ 836; [2004] H.L.R. 5.

discharge of duty

See *Anufrijeva v. Southwark LBC* [2003] EWCA Civ 1406; [2004] 2 W.L.R. 603; **3A–38**

HOUSING

[2004] 1 All E.R. 833 where the claimants unsuccessfully brought proceedings for damages under the Human Rights Act 1998 for breach of ECHR Art.8 claiming that the defendant council had failed to discharge its duty under s.21 because a property in which they had been housed was unsuitable. The Court of Appeal held that there is a stage at which the dictates of humanity require the state to intervene to prevent any person within its territory suffering dire consequences as a result of deprivation of sustenance. If support is necessary to prevent a person in this country reaching the point of Art.3 degradation, then that support should be provided. If such a basic standard exists, it must require intervention by the state, whether the claimant is an asylum seeker who has not sought asylum promptly on entry or is a citizen entitled to all the benefits of our system. Article 8 is capable of imposing on a state a positive obligation to provide support (*R. (Bernard) v. Enfield LBC* [2002] EWHC 2282 (Admin); [2003] U.K.H.R.R. 148). Those obligations are not however absolute. There must be some ground for criticising the failure to act—an element of culpability and knowledge that the claimant's private and family life are at risk. If there is delay, there is no infringement of Art.8 unless substantial prejudice has been caused to the applicant. Maladministration does not infringe Art.8 unless the consequences are serious. Isolated acts of even significant carelessness are unlikely to suffice. At first instance courts dealing with claims for maladministration should adopt a broad-brush approach, without a close examination of authorities or a prolonged examination of the facts. Remedies have to be just and appropriate and necessary to afford just satisfaction. Levels of damages awarded in tort, by the CICB and local government ombudsmen might all provide some rough guidance. Courts should look critically at any attempt to recover damages for maladministration under the Human Rights Act 1998 other than in the Administrative Court. Before giving permission to apply for judicial review, the Administrative Court should require the claimant to explain why it is not more appropriate to use any internal complaints procedure.

Local and Central Authorities

Local Authorities for purposes of Part III

3A–39　**33.**—(1) In this Part of this Act the expression "local authority" means a council which is a local authority for the purposes of the Local Authority Social Services Act 1970 in England or Wales, and a council constituted under section 2 of the Local Government, etc. (Scotland) Act 1994 in Scotland:

(2) [...]

Administration of Justice Act 1970

3A–40　(1970 c.31)

Arrangement of Sections

Part IV

Actions by Mortgagees for Possession

Part IV

Actions by Mortgagees for Possession

Additional powers of court in action by mortgagee for possession of dwelling-house

3A–41　**36.**—(1) Where the mortgagee under a mortgage of land which consists of or includes a dwelling-house brings an action in which he claims possession of the mortgaged property, not being an action for foreclosure in which a claim for possession of the mortgaged property is also made, the court may exercise any of the powers conferred on it by subsection (2)below if it appears to the court that in the event of its exercising the power the mortgagor is likely to be able within a reasonable period to pay any sums due under the mortgage or to remedy a default consisting of a breach of any other obligation arising under or by virtue of the mortgage.

(2) The court—

    (a) may adjourn the proceedings, or

    (b) on giving judgment, or making an order, for delivery of possession of the mortgaged property, or at any time before the execution of such judgment or order, may—

        (i) stay or suspend execution of the judgment or order, or

        (ii) postpone the date for delivery of possession,

for such period or periods as the court thinks reasonable.

(3) Any such adjournment, stay, suspension or postponement as is referred to in subsection (2) above may be made subject to such conditions with regard to payment by the mortgagor of any sum secured by the mortgage or the remedying of any default as the court thinks fit.

(4) The court may from time to time vary or revoke any condition imposed by virtue of this section.

(5) [. . .][1]

(6) In the application of this section to Northern Ireland, "the court" means a judge of the High Court in Northern Ireland, and in subsection (1) the words from "not being" to "made" shall be omitted.

"Additional powers of court ..."

For definitions of "dwelling-house", "mortgage", "mortgagee" and "mortgagor" see s.39 below.

See too the Administration of Justice Act 1973, s.8 (below).

At common law, where, under an instalment mortgage, by reason of default by the borrower, the whole money advanced has become payable, the lender is entitled to possession and the court has no jurisdiction to decline to make an order for possession or to adjourn the hearing, whether on terms of keeping up payments or paying arrears, if the mortgagee cannot be persuaded to agree to this course. To this the *sole exception* is that the application may be adjourned for a short time to afford the mortgagor a chance of paying off the mortgagee in full or otherwise satisfying him; but this should not be done if there is no reasonable prospect of this occurring (*Birmingham Citizens Permanent Building Society v. Caunt* [1962] Ch. 883 at 912, Ch D). However, the Administration of Justice Act 1970, s.36 and the Administration of Justice Act 1973, s.8 (see below) give courts in mortgage possession proceedings power to adjourn, stay, suspend or postpone the date for the giving up of possession if it is likely that the arrears of instalments and interest can be repaid during a reasonable period. A bankrupt may make an application to the court for relief under Administration of Justice Acts 1970 and 1973 (*Nationwide BS v. Purvis* [1998] B.P.I.R. 625, CA).

In *Royal Bank of Scotland v. Miller* [2001] EWCA Civ 344; [2002] Q.B. 255; [2001] 3 W.L.R. 523, CA, it was held that (1) the relevant time for determining whether land

3A–42

---

[1] Repealed by Statute Law (Repeals) Act 2004, s.1(1), Sch.1, Pt 1.

consists of or includes a dwelling-house within the meaning of s.36 is the time when the mortgagee claims possession, not the date when the legal charge is entered into; and (2) breach of a term of the mortgage (*e.g.* occupation by a third party without consent) does not prevent s.36 from applying.

Section 8 does not apply to "all moneys" charges, since:

(a) the principal does not become due and cannot be sued upon until a written demand is made; and

(b) the charge does not provide for deferment after a written demand is made (*Habib Bank v. Tailor* [1982] 1 W.L.R. 1218; [1982] 3 All E.R. 561, CA).

Accordingly a mortgagor with an all moneys charge against whom possession is sought can only rely upon s.36 if it is likely that all sums due (*i.e.* principal, interest and any other sums due under the mortgage) can be paid within a reasonable period.

An agreement to pay off outstanding sums drawn down from an overdraft facility secured by a charge by monthly instalments does not come within s.36 or s.8 either (*Rees Investments Ltd v. Groves* June 27, 2001, Ch D, unreported).

Administration of Justice Act 1970, s.36 has not abrogated the mortgagee's common law right to take possession of property (see *Western Bank Ltd v. Schindler* [1977] Ch. 1, CA, and *Ropaigealach v. Barclays Bank Plc* [2000] 1 Q.B. 263; [1999] 3 W.L.R. 17; [1999] 4 All E.R. 235, CA). Parliament did not intend s.36 to give mortgagors protection from mortgagees who took possession without the assistance of the Court (*cf.* Criminal Law Act 1977, s.6 and Consumer Credit Act 1974, s.126 where specific protection has been given to mortgagors from forcible re-entry).

Where the court exercises its power under s.36 to stay or suspend execution for such period as the court thinks reasonable, that period must be defined or rendered ascertainable. It is wrong to suspend in general terms without fixing any period for the length of the suspension (*Royal Trust Co of Canada v. Markham* [1975] 3 All E.R. 433, CA).

The court cannot suspend an order for possession under s.36, however hard the circumstances, if there is no prospect of the borrower reducing the arrears (*Abbey National Mortgages v. Bernard* (1995) 71 P. & C.R. 257, CA; see too *Abbey National Building Society v. Mewton* [1995] 9 C.L. 346, CA).

Note also *Hyde Park Funding Ltd v. Ioannou* [1999] 3 C.L.D. 428 (Barnet County Court) where mortgagees brought possession proceedings and a possession order was granted. Later they obtained a warrant. On the morning of the proposed eviction the borrower applied to a district judge to suspend the warrant. That application was dismissed and the borrower was evicted. The borrower appealed to a circuit judge. The lender contended that as the warrant had been executed, the court no longer had jurisdiction to suspend under Administration of Justice Act 1970, s.36. HHJ Connor allowed the appeal. On appeal from a district judge, a circuit judge can exercise all of the jurisdiction that the district judge had and can make any order that the district judge could have made. In view of new evidence adduced on the appeal, the correct order was to suspend on terms. The district judge's order was set aside and possession restored.

"a reasonable period"

3A–43   What is a reasonable period depends on the individual circumstances of each case, particularly the extent to which the mortgage and arrears are secured by the value of the property (*Bristol and West Building Society v. Ellis* (1996) 73 P. & C.R. 158; (1996) 29 H.L.R. 282, CA). "The court should take as its starting point the full term of the mortgage and pose at the outset the question: would it be possible for the mortgagor to maintain payment-off of the arrears by instalments over that period?" (*Cheltenham and Gloucester Building Society v. Norgan* [1996] 1 All E.R. 449 at 458; (1995) 28 H.L.R. 443; (1996) 72 P. & C.R. 46, CA, see too *First Middlesbrough Trading and Mortgage Co Ltd v. Cunningham* (1974) 28 P. & C.R. 69, CA; and *Western Bank v. Schindler* [1977] Ch. 1; [1976] 2 All E.R. 393, CA).

The court may exercise its discretion under s.36 without hearing formal sworn evidence on the basis of information given by defendants. "It must be possible for [judges] to act without evidence, especially where, as here, the mortgagor was present in court and available to be questioned and no objection to the reception of informal material is made by the mortgagee" (*Cheltenham and Gloucester Building Society v. Grant* (1994) 26 H.L.R. 703 at 707, CA).

The court's powers under s.36 cease after a warrant has been executed (*Cheltenham and Gloucester Building Society v. Obi* (1996) 28 H.L.R. 22, CA; and *National and Provincial Building Society v. Ahmed* [1995] 38 E.G. 138, CA) unless the original order itself can be set aside, the warrant is obtained by fraud or there has been abuse of the process or oppression in its execution (*Hammersmith and Fulham LBC v. Hill* [1994] 35 E.G. 124; (1995) 27 H.L.R. 368; [1994] 2 E.G.L.R. 51, CA).

See also *Mortgage Agency Services v. Bal* (1998) 95(28) L.S.G. 31, CA (s.36 ceases to apply after execution of warrant).

Forms of order

See County Court Forms **N29** (Order for possession (mortgaged property)) and **N31** (Order for possession of mortgaged land suspended under the Administration of Justice Act 1970, s.36 and the Administration of Justice Act 1973, s.8) as specified in the Practice Direction to CPR Pt 4, Table 3.   **3A–44**

European Convention of Human Rights

There is no inconsistency between Administration of Justice Act 1970, s.36 and Convention rights under Art.8 or Art.1 of the First Protocol. (*Barclays Bank v. Alcorn* [2002] EWCA Civ 817; June 17, 2002)   **3A–45**

38A. This Part of this Act shall not apply to a mortgage securing an agreement which is a regulated agreement within the meaning of the Consumer Credit Act 1974.   **3A–46**

Note —Inserted by the Consumer Credit Act 1974, s.192(3)(a), Sched.4, Pt 1, para. 30.   **3A–47**

Statutory protection

For the statutory protection given to borrowers under the Consumer Credit Act 1974, see below.   **3A–48**

Interpretation of Part IV

39.—(1) In this Part of this Act—   **3A–49**

"dwelling-house" includes any building or part thereof which is used as a dwelling;

"mortgage" includes a charge and "mortgagor" and "mortgagee" shall be construed accordingly;

"mortgagor" and "mortgagee" includes any person deriving title under the original mortgagor or mortgagee.

(2) The fact that part of the premises comprised in a dwelling-house is used as a shop or office or for business, trade or professional purposes shall not prevent the dwelling-house from being a dwelling-house for the purposes of this Part of this Act.

Defective Premises Act 1972

(1972 c.35)   **3A–50**

ARRANGEMENT OF SECTIONS

Duty to build dwellings properly

1.—(1) A person taking on work for or in connection with the pro-   **3A–51**

HOUSING

vision of a dwelling (whether the dwelling is provided by the erection or by the conversion or enlargement of a building) owes a duty—

    (a) if the dwelling is provided to the order of any person, to that person; and

    (b) without prejudice to paragraph (a) above, to every person who acquires an interest (whether legal or equitable) in the dwelling;

to see that the work which he takes on is done in a workman-like or, as the case may be, professional manner, with proper materials and so that as regards that work the dwelling will be fit for habitation when completed.

(2) A person who takes on any such work for another on terms that he is to do it in accordance with instructions given by or on behalf of that other shall, to the extent to which he does it properly in accordance with those instructions, be treated for the purposes of this section as discharging the duty imposed on him by subsection (1) above except where he owes a duty to that other to warn him of any defects in the instructions and fails to discharge that duty.

(3) A person shall not be treated for the purposes of subsection (2)above as having given instructions for the doing of work merely because he has agreed to the work being done in a specified manner, with specified materials or to a specified design.

(4) A person who—

    (a) in the course of a business which consists of or includes providing or arranging for the provision of dwellings or installations in dwellings; or

    (b) in the exercise of a power of making such provision or arrangements conferred by or by virtue of any enactment;

arranges for another to take on work for or in connection with the provision of a dwelling shall be treated for the purposes of this section as included among the persons who have taken on the work.

(5) Any cause of action in respect of a breach of the duty imposed by this section shall be deemed, for the purposes of the Limitation Act 1939, the Law Reform (Limitation of Actions, &c.) Act 1954 and the Limitation Act 1963, to have accrued at the time when the dwelling was completed, but if after that time a person who has done work for or in connection with the provision of the dwelling does further work to rectify the work he has already done, any such cause of action in respect of that further work shall be deemed for those purposes to have accrued at the time when the further work was finished.

Duty to build dwellings properly

3A–52   This section imposes a duty to carry out work (whether by new building or conversion) for or in connection with the provision of a dwelling in a professional or workmanlike manner so that the premises are fit for habitation. It applies both to damage caused by the actual work and damage caused by failure to undertake necessary works (*Andrews v. Schooling* [1991] 3 All E.R. 723; (1991) 23 H.L.R. 316, CA and *Mirza v. Bhandal* August 1999, Legal Action 24, QBD).

For cases excluded from s.1, see s.2, below.

The duty only applies to work carried out after January 1, 1974.

As to limitation, see s.1(5) and *Alderson v. Beetham Organisation Ltd* [2003] EWCA Civ 408; [2003] H.L.R. 60.

Cases excluded from the remedy under section 1

2.—(1) Where— 3A–53

    (a) in connection with the provision of a dwelling or its first sale or letting for habitation any rights in respect of defects in the state of the dwelling are conferred by an approved scheme to which this section applies on a person having or acquiring an interest in the dwelling; and

    (b) it is stated in a document of a type approved for the purposes of this section that the requirements as to design or construction imposed by or under the scheme have, or appear to have, been substantially complied with in relation to the dwelling;

no action shall be brought by any person having or acquiring an interest in the dwelling for breach of the duty imposed by section 1 above in relation to the dwelling.

(2) A scheme to which this section applies—

    (a) may consist of any number of documents and any number of agreements or other transactions between any number of persons; but

    (b) must confer, by virtue of agreements entered into with persons having or acquiring an interest in the dwellings to which the scheme applies, rights on such persons in respect of defects in the state of the dwellings.

(3) In this section "approved" means approved by the Secretary of State, and the power of the Secretary of State to approve a scheme or document for the purposes of this section shall be exercisable by order, except that any requirements as to construction or design imposed under a scheme to which this section applies may be approved by him without making any order or, if he thinks fit, by order.

(4) The Secretary of State—

    (a) may approve a scheme or document for the purposes of this section with or without limiting the duration of his approval; and

    (b) may by order revoke or vary a previous order under this section or, without such an order, revoke or vary a previous approval under this section given otherwise than by order.

(5) The production of a document purporting to be a copy of an approval given by the Secretary of State otherwise than by order and certified by an officer of the Secretary of State to be a true copy of the approval shall be conclusive evidence of the approval, and without proof of the handwriting or official position of the person purporting to sign the certificate.

(6) The power to make an order under this section shall be exercisable by statutory instrument which shall be subject to annulment in pursuance of a resolution by either House of Parliament.

HOUSING

(7) Where an interest in a dwelling is compulsorily acquired—

    (a) no action shall be brought by the acquiring authority for breach of the duty imposed by section 1 above in respect of the dwelling; and

    (b) if any work for or in connection with the provision of the dwelling was done otherwise than in the course of a business by the person in occupation of the dwelling at the time of the compulsory acquisition, the acquiring authority and not that person shall be treated as the person who took on the work and accordingly as owing that duty.

Duty of care with respect to work done on premises not abated by disposal of premises

3A–54   **3.**—(1) Where work of construction, repair, maintenance or demolition or any other work is done on or in relation to premises, any duty of care owed, because of the doing of the work, to persons who might reasonably be expected to be affected by the defects in the state of the premises created by the doing of the work shall not be abated by the subsequent disposal of the premises by the persons who owed the duty.

(2) This section does not apply—

    (a) in the case of premises which are let, where the relevant tenancy of the premises commenced, or the relevant tenancy agreement of the premises was entered into, before the commencement of this Act;

    (b) in the case of premises disposed of in any other way, when the disposal of the premises was completed, or a contract for their disposal was entered into, before the commencement of this Act; or

    (c) in either case, where the relevant transaction disposing of the premises is entered into in pursuance of an enforceable option by which the consideration for the disposal was fixed before the commencement of this Act.

"disposal"

3A–55   For the definition of "disposal", see s.6 below.

Landlord's duty of care in virtue of obligation or right to repair premises demised

3A–56   **4.**—(1) Where premises are let under a tenancy which puts on the landlord an obligation to the tenant for the maintenance or repair of the premises, the landlord owes to all persons who might reasonably be expected to be affected by defects in the state of the premises a duty to take such care as is reasonable in all the circumstances to see that they are reasonably safe from personal injury or from damage to their property caused by a relevant defect.

(2) The said duty is owed if the landlord knows (whether as the result of being notified by the tenant or otherwise) or if he ought in all the circumstances to have known of the relevant defect.

(3) In this section "relevant defect" means a defect in the state of

the premises existing at or after the material time and arising from, or continuing because of, an act or omission by the landlord which constitutes or would if he had had notice of the defect, have constituted a failure by him to carry out his obligation to the tenant for the maintenance or repair of the premises; and for the purposes of the foregoing provision "the material time"means—

    (a) where the tenancy commenced before this Act, the commencement of this Act; and

    (b) in all other cases, the earliest of the following times, that is to say—

        (i) the time when the tenancy commences;

        (ii) the time when the tenancy agreement is entered into;

        (iii) the time when possession is taken of the premises in contemplation of the letting.

(4) Where premises are let under a tenancy which expressly or impliedly gives the landlord the right to enter the premises to carry out any description of maintenance or repair of the premises, then, as from the time when he first is, or by notice or otherwise can put himself, in a position to exercise the right and so long as he is or can put himself in that position, he shall be treated for the purposes of subsections (1) to (3) above (but for no other purpose) as if he were under an obligation to the tenant for that description of maintenance or repair of the premises; but the landlord shall not owe the tenant any duty by virtue of this subsection in respect of any defect in the state of the premises arising from, or continuing because of, a failure to carry out an obligation expressly imposed on the tenant by the tenancy.

(5) For the purposes of this section obligations imposed or rights given by any enactment in virtue of a tenancy shall be treated as imposed or given by the tenancy.

(6) This section applies to a right of occupation given by contract or any enactment and not amounting to a tenancy as if the right were a tenancy, and "tenancy" and cognate expressions shall be construed accordingly.

"Landlord's duty of care ..."

    Section 4 imposes on landlords a duty of care to all persons who might reasonably **3A–57** be affected by defects in the premises. The duty is to take such care as is reasonable in all the circumstances to see that they are reasonably safe from pesonal injury or from damage to their property (see, *e.g. Clarke v. Taff Ely BC* (1983) 10 H.L.R. 44, QBD). The duty is owed if the landlord has the express or implied right under the agreement to enter the premises to carry out any description of maintenance or repair of the premises (*e.g. McAuley v. Bristol City Council* [1992] 1 All E.R. 749; (1991) 23 H.L.R. 586; [1991] 46 E.G. 155, CA). See too the Rent Act 1977, ss.3(2) and 148 (below); and the Housing Act 1988, s.16 (below).

    A tenant relying upon s.4 merely has to show a failure on the part of the landlord to take such care as is reasonable in the circumstances to see that the tenant is reasonably safe from personal injury. That duty is owed if the landlord "ought in all circumstances" to have known of the relevant defect. That is a general test of negligence. There is no express or implied exclusion of the tenant from the category of persons who might be affected. The burden of a tenant in establishing a breach of duty under s.4 should not be equated with the need under Landlord and Tenant Act 1987, s.11 to demonstrate notice (actual or constructive) of the actual defect giving rise to injury (*Sykes v. Harry* [2001] EWCA Civ 167; [2001] QB 1014).

The word "premises" may include a paved area built by a previous tenant outside a house (*Smith v. Bradford MDC* (1982) 4 H.L.R. 86; (1982) P. & C.R. 171, CA).

As to liability at common law, see *Targett v. Torfaen B.C.* [1992] 3 All E.R. 27; (1992) 24 H.L.R. 164, CA.

Works required to remedy a defect in design are not works of "repair", giving that word the meaning that it has to bear in this context. In such circumstances s.4 is not engaged. (*Lee v. Leeds City Council* [2002] All E.R. 124; [2002] 1 W.L.R. 1488, CA).

Application to Crown

3A–58   **5.** This Act shall bind the Crown, but as regards the Crown's liability in tort shall not bind the Crown further than the Crown is made liable in tort by the Crown Proceedings Act 1947.

Supplemental

3A–59   **6.**—(1) In this Act—

"disposal", in relation to premises, includes a letting, and an assignment or surrender of a tenancy, of the premises and the creation by contract of any other right to occupy the premises, and "dispose" shall be construed accordingly;

"personal injury" includes any disease and any impairment of a person's physical or mental condition;

"tenancy" means—

(a) a tenancy created either immediately or derivatively out of the freehold, whether by a lease or underlease, by an agreement for a lease or underlease or by a tenancy agreement, but not including a mortgage term or any interest arising in favour of a mortgagor by his attorning tenant to his mortgagee; or

(b) a tenancy at will or a tenancy on sufferance; or

(c) a tenancy, whether or not constituting a tenancy at common law, created by or in pursuance of any enactment;

and cognate expressions shall be construed accordingly.

(2) Any duty imposed by or enforceable by virtue of any provision of this Act is in addition to any duty a person may owe apart from that provision.

(3) Any term of an agreement which purports to exclude or restrict, or has the effect of excluding or restricting, the operation of any of the provisions of this Act, or any liability arising by virtue of any such provision, shall be void.

(4) Section 4 of the Occupiers' Liability Act 1957 (repairing landlord's duty to visitors to premises) is hereby repealed.

Administration of Justice Act 1973

(1973 c.15)

PART II

MISCELLANEOUS

Extension of powers of court in action by mortgagee of dwelling-house

8.—(1) Where by a mortgage of land which consists of or includes **3A–60** a dwelling-house, or by any agreement between the mortgagee under such a mortgage and the mortgagor, the mortgagor is entitled or is to be permitted to pay the principal sum secured by instalments or otherwise to defer payment of it in whole or in part, but provision is also made for earlier payment in the event of any default by the mortgagor or of a demand by the mortgagee or otherwise, then for purposes of section 36 of the Administration of Justice Act 1970 (under which a court has power to delay giving a mortgagee possession of the mortgaged property so as to allow the mortgagor a reasonable time to pay any sums due under the mortgage) a court may treat as due under the mortgage on account of the principal sum secured and of interest on it only such amounts as the mortgagor would have expected to be required to pay if there had been no such provision for earlier payment.

(2) A court shall not exercise by virtue of subsection (1) above the powers conferred by section 36 of the Administration of Justice Act 1970 unless it appears to the court not only that the mortgagor is likely to be able within a reasonable period to pay any amounts regarded (in accordance with subsection (1) above) as due on account of the principal sum secured, together with the interest on those amounts, but also that he is likely to be able by the end of that period to pay any further amounts that he would have expected to be required to pay by then on account of that sum and of interest on it if there had been no such provision as is referred to in subsection (1)above for earlier payment.

(3) Where subsection (1) above would apply to an action in which a mortgagee only claimed possession of the mortgaged property, and the mortgagee brings an action for foreclosure (with or without also claiming possession of the property), then section 36 of the Administration of Justice Act 1970 together with subsections (1) and (2) above shall apply as they would apply if it were an action in which the mortgagee only claimed possession of the mortgaged property, except that—

(a) section 36(2)(b) shall apply only in relation to any claim for possession; and

(b) section 36(5) shall not apply.

(4) For purposes of this section the expressions "dwelling-house", "mortgage", "mortgagee" and "mortgagor" shall be construed in the same way as for the purposes of Part IV of the Administration of Justice Act 1970.

(5) [. . .][1]

(6) In the application of this section to Northern Ireland, subsection (3) shall be omitted.

"Extension of powers of court ..."

3A–61   See the Administration of Justice Act 1970, s.36, above and the commentary thereto.

The purpose of s.8 is to allow courts to exercise their powers to adjourn, stay, suspend or postpone the date for the giving up of possession in mortgage possession proceedings if it is likely that the arrears of instalments and interest can be repaid during a reasonable period, *cf. Halifax Building Society v. Clark* [1973] Ch. 307; [1973] 2 All E.R. 33, where, prior to the passing of the 1973 Act, it was held that s.36 only applied where it was likely that all sums due (including the whole of the capital) could be paid during a reasonable period. Section 8 extends the possibility of relief under s.36 to mortgagors with endowment mortgages (*Bank of Scotland v. Grimes* [1985] 2 All E.R. 254 and *Royal Bank of Scotland v. Miller* [2001] EWCA Civ 344; [2002] QB 255; [2001] 3 W.L.R. 523; see too *Habib Bank v. Tailor* [1982] 1 W.L.R. 1218; [1982] 3 All E.R. 561).

Welsh Development Agency Act 1975

SCHEDULE 4

Displacement of legislation preventing possession

3A–62   16. If the Secretary of State certifies that possession of a house which—

(a) has been acquired by the Agency under s.21A above; and

(b) is for the time being held by the Agency for the purposes for which it was acquired, is immediately required for those purposes, nothing in the Rent (Agriculture) Act 1976 , the Rent Act 1977 or the Housing Act 1988 shall prevent the Agency from obtaining possession of the house.

3A–63   *Note* —Amended by Government of Wales Act 1998, Sched.13.

The Agency

3A–64   *i.e.* The Welsh Development Agency.

Section 21A

3A–65   This gives the Welsh Development Agency power to acquire land by agreement or compulsorily if authorised to do so by the Secretary of State.

Protection from Eviction Act 1977

3A–66   (1977 c.43)

ARRANGEMENT OF SECTIONS

PART I

UNLAWFUL EVICTION AND HARASSMENT

---

[1] Repealed by the Statute Law (Repeals) Act 2004, s.1(1), Sch.1, Pt 1.

* * * *

PART I

UNLAWFUL EVICTION AND HARASSMENT

Restriction on re-entry without due process of law

2. Where any premises are let as a dwelling on a lease which is **3A–67** subject to a right of re-entry or forfeiture it shall not be lawful to enforce that right otherwise than by proceedings in the court while any person is lawfully residing in the premises or part of them.

* * * *

"court"

See s.9.   **3A–68**

"let"

See s.8(2).   **3A–69**

The purpose of this section is to prevent peaceable re-entry of premises "let as a dwelling" while there is "any person lawfully residing" in them or any part of them. In such circumstances possession proceedings must be brought in court.

For the restriction on forfeiture or re-entry for arrears of service charges see the Housing Act 1996, s.81, and, generally, Commonhold and Leasehold Reform Act 2002, ss.167–171, below.

Prohibition of eviction without due process of law

3.—(1) Where any premises have been let as a dwelling under a **3A–70** tenancy which is neither a statutorily protected tenancy nor an excluded tenancy and—

> (a) the tenancy (in this section referred to as the former tenancy) has come to an end, but
>
> (b) the occupier continues to reside in the premises or part of them,

it shall not be lawful for the owner to enforce against the occupier, otherwise than by proceedings in the court, his right to recover possession of the premises.

(2) In this section "the occupier", in relation to any premises, means any person lawfully residing in the premises or part of them at the termination of the former tenancy.

(2A) Subsections (1) and (2) above apply in relation to any restricted contract (within the meaning of the Rent Act 1977) which—

> (a) creates a licence; and
>
> (b) is entered into after the commencement of section 69 of the Housing Act 1980;

HOUSING

as they apply in relation to a restricted contract which creates a tenancy.

(2B) Subsections (1) and (2) above apply in relation to any premises occupied as a dwelling under a licence, other than an excluded licence, as they apply in relation to premises let as a dwelling under a tenancy, and in those subsections the expressions "let" and "tenancy" shall be construed accordingly.

(2C) References in the preceding provisions of this section and section 4(2A) below to an excluded tenancy do not apply to—

(a) a tenancy entered into before the date on which the Housing Act 1988 came into force, or

(b) a tenancy entered into on or after that date but pursuant to a contract made before that date,

but, subject to that, "excluded tenancy" and "excluded licence" shall be construed in accordance with section 3A below.

(3) This section shall, with the necessary modifications, apply where the owner's right to recover possession arises on the death of the tenant under a statutory tenancy within the meaning of the Rent Act 1977 or the Rent (Agriculture) Act 1976.

3A–71 *Note*—Amended by the Housing Act 1980, s.69(1); and the Housing Act 1988, ss.30 and 40.

"tenancy" and "statutorily protected tenancy"

3A–72 See s.8(1).

"excluded tenancy"

3A–73 See s.3A.

"owner"

3A–74 See s.8(3).

"court"

3A–75 See s.9.

"let"

3A–76 See s.8(2).

Prohibition of eviction without due process of law

3A–77 This section prevents eviction without a court order. It applies to occupiers who are not statutorily protected (*i.e.* those who lack full security of tenure as defined in s.8(1), *i.e.* under Rent Act 1977, Rent (Agriculture) Act 1976, Landlord and Tenant Act 1954 Part II, Agricultural Holdings Act 1986, Housing Act 1988 and Agricultural Tenancies Act 1995). Eviction of such tenants without a court order is unlawful.

It does not however apply to excluded tenants (see s.3A below). Excluded occupiers can be evicted without court orders.

Breach of s.3 is an actionable tort.

It has been held that:

(a) the 1977 Act was not intended to apply to temporary housing provided by local authorities under the Housing Act 1985, s.63; and

(b) temporary accommodation in a hotel or hostel cannot be "premises occupied as a dwelling under a licence" for the purposes of s.3(2B) (*Mohamed v. Manek and Kensington and Chelsea RLBC* (1995) 94 L.G.R. 211; (1995) 27 H.L.R. 439, CA).

Excluded tenancies and licences

3A–78 3A.—(1) Any reference in this Act to an excluded tenancy or an

666

excluded licence is a reference to a tenancy or licence which is excluded by virtue of any of the following provisions of this section.

(2) A tenancy or licence is excluded if—

(a) under its terms the occupier shares any accommodation with the landlord or licensor; and

(b) immediately before the tenancy or licence was granted and also at the time it comes to an end, the landlord or licensor occupied as his only or principal home premises of which the whole or part of the shared accommodation formed part.

(3) A tenancy or licence is also excluded if—

(a) under its terms the occupier shares any accommodation with a member of the family of the landlord or licensor;

(b) immediately before the tenancy or licence was granted and also at the time it comes to an end, the member of the family of the landlord or licensor occupied as his only or principal home premises of which the whole or part of the shared accommodation formed part; and

(c) immediately before the tenancy or licence was granted and also at the time it comes to an end, the landlord or licensor occupied as his only or principal home premises in the same building as the shared accommodation and that building is not a purpose-built block of flats.

(4) For the purposes of subsections (2) and (3) above, an occupier shares accommodation with another person if he has the use of it in common with that person (whether or not also in common with others) and any reference in those subsections to shared accommodation shall be construed accordingly, and if, in relation to any tenancy or licence, there is at any time more than one person who is the landlord of licensor, any reference in those subsections to the landlord or licensor shall be construed as a reference to any one of those persons.

(5) In subsections (2) to (4) above—

(a) "accommodation" includes neither an area used for storage nor a staircase, passage, corridor or other means of access;

(b) "occupier" means, in relation to a tenancy, the tenant and, in relation to a licence, the licensee; and

(c) "purpose-built block of flats" has the same meaning as in Part III of Schedule 1 to the Housing Act 1988;

and section 113 of the Housing Act 1985 shall apply to determine whether a person is for the purposes of subsection (3) above a member of another's family as it applies for the purposes of Part IV of that Act.

(6) A tenancy or licence is excluded if it was granted as a temporary expedient to a person who entered the premises in question or any other premises as a trespasser (whether or not, before the beginning of that tenancy or licence, another tenancy or licence to occupy the premises or any other premises had been granted to him).

(7) A tenancy or licence is excluded if—

(a) it confers on the tenant or licensee the right to occupy the premises for a holiday only; or

(b) it is granted otherwise than for money or money's worth.

(7A) A tenancy or licence is excluded if it is granted in order to provide accommodation under Part VI of the Immigration and Asylum Act 1999.

(7B) Section 32 of the Nationality, Immigration and Asylum Act 2002 (accommodation centre: tenure) provides for a resident's licence to occupy an accommodation centre to be an excluded licence.

(7C) A tenancy or licence is excluded if it is granted in order to provide accommodation under the Displaced Persons (Temporary Protection) Regulations 2005.

(8) A licence is excluded if it confers rights of occupation in a hostel, within the meaning of the Housing Act 1985, which is provided by—

(a) the council of a county, county borough, district or London Borough, the Common Council of the City of London, the Council of the Isles of Scilly, the Inner London Education Authority, the London Fire and Emergency Planning Authority, a joint authority within the meaning of the Local Government Act 1985 or a re-siduary body within the meaning of that Act;

(b) a development corporation within the meaning of the New Towns Act 1981;

(c) the Commission for the New Towns;

(d) an urban development corporation established by an order under section 135 of the Local Government, Planning and Land Act 1980;

(e) a housing action trust established under Part III of the Housing Act 1988;

(f) [...]

(g) the Housing Corporation;

(ga) the Secretary of State under section 89 of the Housing Associations Act 1985;

(h) a housing trust (within the meaning of the Housing Associations Act 1985) which is a charity or a registered social landlord (within the meaning of the Housing Act 1985); or

(i) any other person who is, or who belongs to a class of person which is, specified in an order made by the Secretary of State.

(9) The power to make an order under subsection (8)(i) above shall be exercisable by statutory instrument which shall be subject to annulment in pursuance of a resolution of either House of Parliament.

3A–79 *Note* —Added by the Housing Act 1988, s.31. Amended by the Local Government (Wales) Act 1994, Sched.8, para. 4(1); the Housing Act 1996 (Consequential Provisions) Order 1996 (S.I. 1996 No. 2325), art.5, Sched.2, para. 7; the Government of Wales Act 1998, s.140 and Sched.16, para. 2 and Sched.18, Pt IV the Immigration and Asylum Act 1996, Sched.14, para. 73; Greater London Authority Act 1999, Sched.29,

para.27; and by the Nationality, Immigration and Asylum Act 2002, s.32(5); and by
S.I. 2005 No. 1379.

Excluded tenancies

For a case in which the Court of Appeal considered s.3A(2) see *Sumeghova v. McMa-* **3A–80**
hon [2002] EWCA Civ 1581; [2003] H.L.R. 26, and for a case where Elias J. considered
whether premises were "a hostel" (s.3A(8)), see *Rogerson v. Wigan MBC* [2004] EWHC
(QB) 1677; [2005] HLR 10 (residents allocated bedrooms with their own locks in flat
but shared the facilities with other residents, warden with master key and terms of occupation including a nightly curfew, a prohibition on alcohol and drugs. The premises
met the statutory definition of a "hostel" in Housing Act 1985, s.622 in that they
provided residential accommodation with facilities for preparation of food "otherwise
than in separate or self contained accommodation"). See too *Mohamed v. Manek and
Kensington and Chelsea RLBC* (1995) 27 H.L.R. 439,CA.

* * * *

PART II

NOTICE TO QUIT

* * * *

Validity of notices to quit

5.—(1) Subject to subsection (1B) below no notice by a landlord or **3A–81**
a tenant to quit any premises let (whether before or after the commencement of this Act) as a dwelling shall be valid unless—

> (a) it is in writing and contains such information as may be
> prescribed, and
>
> (b) it is given not less than 4 weeks before the date on which
> it is to take effect.

(1A) Subject to subsection (1B) below, no notice by a licensor or a
licensee to determine a periodic licence to occupy premises as a
dwelling (whether the licence was granted before or after the passing
of this Act) shall be valid unless—

> (a) it is in writing and contains such information as may be
> prescribed, and
>
> (b) it is given not less than 4 weeks before the date on which
> it is to take effect.

(1B) Nothing in subsection (1) or subsection (1A) above applies
to—

> (a) premises let on an excluded tenancy which is entered
> into on or after the date on which the Housing Act 1988
> came into force unless it is entered into pursuant to a
> contract made before that date; or
>
> (b) premises occupied under an excluded licence.

(2) In this section "prescribed" means prescribed by regulations
made by the Secretary of State by statutory instrument, and a statutory instrument containing any such regulations shall be subject to
annulment in pursuance of a resolution of either House of
Parliament.

(3) Regulations under this section may make different provision

in relation to different descriptions of lettings and different circumstances.

3A–82   *Note* —Amended by the Housing Act 1988, s.32.

Excluded tenancies

3A–83   Note that this section does not apply to excluded tenancies (see s.3A above and *Mohamed v. Manek and Kensingson and Chelsea RLBC* (1995) 94 L.G.R. 211; (1995) 27 H.L.R. 439, CA).

"let ... as a dwelling"

3A–84   Premises let as an agricultural holding, even if there is a dwelling upon the holding, do not constitute "premises let as a dwelling" for the purposes of this section (see *National Trust for Places of Historic Interest v. Knipe* [1997] 40 E.G. 151; *The Times*, June 21, 1997, CA).

"not less than 4 weeks"

3A–85   The statutory four-week period should be reckoned as a period which includes the first day of the notice but excludes the last day. The requirement for a minimum of four weeks' notice does not mean "28 clear days" (*Schnabel v. Allard* [1967] 1 Q.B. 627; [1966] 3 All E.R. 816, CA). Note that the test generally applicable when interpreting a notice to quit is "Is the notice quite clear to a reasonable tenant reading it? Is it plain that he cannot be misled by it?" (*Carradine Properties Ltd v. Aslam* [1976] 1 W.L.R. 442; [1976] 1 All E.R. 573, Ch D, where on September 6, 1974 landlords served a notice stating that they intended to terminate the lease on September 27, 1973. Their intention had been to determine it on September 27, 1975, but the reference to 1973 was a clerical error. The notice was held to be valid because the tenant reading the notice must have seen the mistake and realised that it was "obvious" that the landlord meant 1975. The decision in *Carradine Properties Ltd v. Aslam* was approved by the House of Lords in *Mannai Investment Co Ltd v. Eagle Star Life Assurance Co Ltd* [1997] A.C. 749; [1997] 2 W.L.R. 945; [1997] 3 All E.R. 352, HL.

It has been held that it is possible for a landlord and the tenant to waive the requirements of Protection from Eviction Act 1977, s.5 (*Hackney LBC v. Snowden* (2001) 33 H.L.R. 554, CA; *Lewisham LBC v. Lasisi-Agiri* [2003] EWHC 2392 (Ch); [2003] 45 E.G. 175 (CS)).

"such information as may be prescribed"

3A–86   See the Notices to Quit (Prescribed Information) Regulations 1988 (S.I. 1988 No. 2201) which apply to notices to quit served by landlords. It is as follows:

(1) If the tenant or licensee does not leave the dwelling, the landlord or licensor must get an order for possession from the court before the tenant or licensee can lawfully be evicted. The landlord or licensor cannot apply for such an order before the notice to quit or notice to determine has run out.

(2) A tenant or licensee who does not know if he has any right to remain in possession after a notice to quit or notice to determine runs out can obtain advice from a solicitor. Help with all or part of the cost of legal advice and assistance may be available under the Legal Aid Scheme. He should also be able to obtain information from a Citizens' Advice Bureau, a Housing Aid Centre or a Rent Officer.

There is no prescribed information for notices to quit served by tenants.

It is not necessary that the precise form of wording of the current regulations should be set out (see *Beckerman v. Durling* (1983) 6 H.L.R. 87, CA; and *Swansea CC v. Hearn* (1991) 23 H.L.R. 284, CA, and *Tadema Holdings v. Ferguson*, [2000] 32 H.L.R. 866, cases where landlords used forms of notice to quit which complied with earlier regulations which had been superseded and where in substance all the information required by the then current regulations was contained in the notice served.

As to service of notices to quit, see *Wandsworth LBC v. Attwell* (1995) 27 H.L.R. 536; [1996] 01 E.G. 100; (1996) 94 L.G.R. 419, CA; and *Enfield LBC v. Devonish* (1997) 29 H.L.R. 691, CA.

PART III

SUPPLEMENTAL PROVISIONS

* * * *

Interpretation

8.—(1) In this Act "statutorily protected tenancy" means—   **3A–87**

    (a) a protected tenancy within the meaning of the Rent Act 1977 or a tenancy to which Part I of the Landlord and Tenant Act 1954 applies;

    (b) a protected occupancy or statutory tenancy as defined in the Rent (Agriculture) Act 1976;

    (c) a tenancy to which Part II of the Landlord and Tenant Act 1954 applies;

    (d) a tenancy of an agricultural holding within the meaning of the Agricultural Holdings Act 1986 which is a tenancy in relation to which that Act applies.

    (e) an assured tenancy or assured agricultural occupancy under Part I of the Housing Act 1988;

    (f) a tenancy to which Schedule 10 to the Local Government and Housing Act 1989 applies;

    (g) a farm business tenancy within the meaning of the Agricultural Tenancies Act 1995.

(2) For the purposes of Part I of this Act a person who, under the terms of his employment, had exclusive possession of any premises other than as a tenant shall be deemed to have been a tenant and the expressions "let" and "tenancy" shall be construed accordingly.

(3) In Part I of this Act "the owner", in relation to any premises, means the person who, as against the occupier, is entitled to possession thereof.

(4) In this Act "excluded tenancy" and "excluded licence" have the meaning assigned by section 3A of this Act.

(5) If, on or after the date on which the Housing Act 1988 came into force, the terms of an excluded tenancy or excluded licence entered into before that date are varied, then—

    (a) if the variation affects the amount of the rent which is payable under the tenancy or licence, the tenancy or licence shall be treated for the purposes of sections 3(2C) and 5(1B) above as a new tenancy or licence entered into at the time of the variation; and

    (b) if the variation does not affect the amount of the rent which is so payable, nothing in this Act shall affect the determination of the question whether the variation is such as to give rise to a new tenancy or licence.

(6) Any reference in subsection (5) above to a variation affecting

the amount of the rent which is payable under a tenancy or licence does not include a reference to—

    (a) a reduction or increase effected under Part III or Part VI of the Rent Act 1977 (rents under regulated tenancies and housing association tenancies), section 78 of that Act (power of rent tribunal in relation to restricted contracts) or sections 11 to 14 of the Rent (Agriculture) Act 1976; or

    (b) a variation which is made by the parties and has the effect of making the rent expressed to be payable under the tenancy or licence the same as a rent for the dwelling which is entered in the register under Part IV or section 79 of the Rent Act 1977.

3A–88   *Note* —Amended by the Agricultural Holdings Act 1986, Sched.14, para. 61; the Housing Act 1988, s.33; the Local Government and Housing Act 1989, Sched.11, para. 54; and the Agricultural Tenancies Act 1995, Sched., para. 29.

The court for purposes of Part I

3A–89   **9.**—(1) The court for the purposes of Part I of this Act shall, subject to this section, be—

    (a) the county court, in relation to premises with respect to which the county court has for the time being jurisdiction in actions for the recovery of land; and

    (b) the High Court, in relation to other premises.

(2) Any powers of a county court in proceedings for the recovery of possession of any premises in the circumstances mentioned in section 3(1) of this Act may be exercised with the leave of the judge by any registrar of the court, except in so far as rules of court otherwise provide.

(3) Nothing in this Act shall affect the jurisdiction of the High Court in proceedings to enforce a lessor's right of re-entry or forfeiture or to enforce a mortgagee's right of possession in a case where the former tenancy was not binding on the mortgagee.

(4) Nothing in this Act shall affect the operation of—

    (a) section 59 of the Pluralities Act 1838;

    (b) section 19 of the Defence Act 1842;

    (c) section 6 of the Lecturers and Parish Clerks Act 1844;

    (d) paragraph 3 of Schedule 1 to the Sexual Offences Act 1956; or

    (e) section 13 of the Compulsory Purchase Act 1965.

Rent Act 1977

3A–90   **(1977 c.42)**

ARRANGEMENT OF SECTIONS

PART I

PRELIMINARY

PROTECTED AND STATUTORY TENANCIES

SECT.

HOUSING

* * * *

PART I

PRELIMINARY

PROTECTED AND STATUTORY TENANCIES

Protected tenants and tenancies

3A–91   **1.** Subject to this Part of this Act, a tenancy under which a dwelling-house (which may be a house or part of a house) is let as a separate dwelling is a protected tenancy for the purposes of this Act. Any reference in this Act to a protected tenant shall be construed accordingly.

"let", "protected tenancy", "protected tenant" and "tenancy"

3A–92   See s.152, below.

Protected tenants and tenancies

3A–93   The Rent Act 1977 provided security of tenure and rent regulation for many tenancies created before January 15, 1989. The Housing Act 1988, s.34 (see below) lists three circumstances in which tenancies created on or after January 15, 1989 may also be within Rent Act protection. Otherwise private sector tenancies created after the implementation of the Housing Act 1988 are either assured tenancies, assured shorthold tenancies or tenancies with no security of tenure.

There can be no Rent Act protection if the occupant has a licence, as opposed to a tenancy (but see, *e.g. Street v. Mountford* [1985] A.C. 809; [1985] 2 W.L.R. 877; [1985] 2 All E.R. 289, HL; *AG Securities v. Vaughan* and *Antoniades v. Villiers and Bridger* [1990] 1 A.C. 417; [1988] 3 W.L.R. 1205; [1988] 3 All E.R. 1058, HL; *Duke v. Wynne* [1989] 3 All E.R. 130, CA; *Hadjiloucas v. Crean* [1988] 1 W.L.R. 1006; [1987] 3 All E.R. 1008, CA; *Nicolau v. Pitt* (1989) 21 H.L.R. 487; [1989] 21 E.G. 71, CA; *Aslan v. Murphy* [1989] 3 All E.R. 130, CA; and *Crancour Ltd v. Da Silvaesa* (1986) 18 H.L.R. 265; (1986) 278 E.G. 618, CA) or if any of the exceptions listed in Pt I of the Rent Act apply. Rent Act security of tenure operates by preventing landlords from recovering possession after termination of contractual tenancies unless they can prove a ground for possession and, when relying on certain grounds for possession, prove that it is reasonable to make a possession order (see the Rent Act 1977, s.98 and Sched.15, below).

See too *Gray v. Taylor* [1998] 4 All E.R. 17, CA; and *Meynell Family Properties Ltd v. Meynell*, June 1998, Legal Action 12, CA.

"as a separate dwelling"

3A–94   See *Goodrich v. Paisner* [1957] A.C. 65; [1956] 2 All E.R. 176, HL; *Central London YMCA Housing Association Ltd v. Goodman* (1992) 24 H.L.R. 109, CA; *Central London*

YMCA Housing Association Ltd v. Saunders (1991) 23 H.L.R. 212, CA; *Horford Investments v. Lambert* [1976] Ch. 39; [1974] 1 All E.R. 131, CA; *Kavanagh v. Lyroudias* [1985] 1 All E.R. 560, CA; *Mortgage Corporation v. Ubah* (1997) 73 P. & C.R. 500; (1997) 29 H.L.R. 48, CA; and *St. Catherine's College v. Dorling* [1980] 1 W.L.R. 66; [1979] 3 All E.R. 250, CA.

The word "dwelling" is not a term of art with a specialised legal meaning. It is "the place where [an occupier] lives and to which he returns and which forms the centre of his existence ... No doubt he will sleep there and usually eat there; he will often prepare at least some of his meals there." However there is no legislative requirement that cooking facilities must be available for premises to qualify as a dwelling. In deciding whether an occupant has security of tenure:

"The first step is to identify the subject-matter of the tenancy agreement. If this is a house or part of a house of which the tenant has exclusive possession with no element of sharing, the only question is whether, at the date when proceedings were brought, it was the tenant's home. If so, it was his dwelling ... The presence or absence of cooking facilities in the part of the premises of which the tenant has exclusive occupation is not relevant."

(See *Uratemp Ventures Ltd v. Collins and Carrell* [2001] UKHL 43; [2001] 3 W.L.R. 806; [2002] 1 All E.R. 46.)

Statutory tenants and tenancies

2.—(1) Subject to this Part of this Act—   **3A–95**

    (a) after the termination of a protected tenancy of a dwelling-house the person who, immediately before that termination, was the protected tenant of the dwelling-house shall, if and so long as he occupies the dwelling-house as his residence, be the statutory tenant of it; and

    (b) Part I of Schedule 1 to this Act shall have effect for determining what person (if any) is the statutory tenant of a dwelling-house or, as the case may be, is entitled to an assured tenancy of a dwelling-house by succession at any time after the death of a person who, immediately before his death, was either a protected tenant of the dwelling-house or the statutory tenant of it by virtue of paragraph (a) above.

(2) In this Act a dwelling-house is referred to as subject to a statutory tenancy when there is a statutory tenant of it.

(3) In subsection (1)(a) above and in Part I of Schedule 1, the phrase "if and so long as he occupies the dwelling-house as his residence" shall be construed as it was immediately before the commencement of this Act (that is to say, in accordance with section 3(2) of the Rent Act 1968).

(4) A person who becomes a statutory tenant of a dwelling-house as mentioned in subsection (1)(a) above is, in this Act, referred to as a statutory tenant by virtue of his previous protected tenancy.

(5) A person who becomes a statutory tenant as mentioned in subsection (1)(b) above is, in this Act, referred to as a statutory tenant by succession.

Note —Amended by the Housing Act 1988, s.39(1).   **3A–96**

"dwelling-house"
See ss.1 and 26.   **3A–97**

"let", "protected tenancy", "protected tenant" and "tenancy"
See s.152 below.   **3A–98**

Statutory tenants and tenancies

3A–99   Section 2 provides that after termination of a contractual tenancy a statutory tenancy comes into existence if the tenant is still occupying the premises as a residence.

If two people are joint tenants under a protected tenancy, but one ceases to occupy the premises as a residence, the remaining tenant will become the statutory tenant on termination of the tenancy if s/he is still occupying them as a residence (*Lloyd v. Sadler* [1978] Q.B. 774; [1978] 2 W.L.R. 721; [1978] 2 All E.R. 529, CA).

If tenants cease to occupy as a residence, there can be no statutory tenancy, and, if the contractual tenancy has been determined, tenants who cease to reside lose security of tenure (Rent Act 1977, s.2(1)(a)). Tenants who are temporarily absent may nevertheless still be occupying as a residence if they can show a *de facto* intention to return and some formal outward and visible sign of that intention—an *animus possidendi* and a *corpus possessionis*. A considerable body of case-law on this subject has built up over the years. See, *e.g. Hampstead Way Investments Ltd v. Lewis-Weare* [1985] 1 W.L.R. 164; [1985] 1 All E.R. 564, HL; *Bevington v. Crawford* (1974) 232 E.G. 191, CA; *Blanway Investments Ltd v. Lynch* (1993) 25 H.L.R. 378, CA; *Brickfield Properties Ltd v. Hughes* (1988) 20 H.L.R. 108; [1988] 24 E.G. 95, CA; *Brown v. Brash* [1948] 2 K.B. 247; [1948] 1 All E.R. 922, CA; *DF Crocker Securities (Portsmouth) Ltd v. Johal* (1989) 42 E.G. 103, CA; *Duke v. Porter* (1986) 280 E.G. 633; (1987) 19 H.L.R. 1, CA; *Gofor Investments v. Roberts* (1975) 29 P. & C.R. 366, CA; *Hall v. King* (1987) 19 H.L.R. 440, CA; *Regalian Securities Ltd v. Scheuer* (1982) 5 H.L.R. 48; (1982) 263 E.G. 973; (1982) 47 P. & C.R. 362, CA; *Richards v. Green* (1984) 11 H.L.R. 1; (1983) 268 E.G. 443, CA; *Robert Thackray's Estate Ltd v. Kaye* (1989) 21 H.L.R. 160, CA; *Tickner v. Hearn* [1961] 1 All E.R. 65, CA; *Wigley v. Leigh* [1950] 1 All E.R. 73, CA and *Prince v. Robinson* (1999) 31 H.L.R. 89.

Terms and conditions of statutory tenancies

3A–100   **3.**—(1) So long as he retains possession, a statutory tenant shall observe and be entitled to the benefit of all the terms and conditions of the original contract of tenancy, so far as they are consistent with the provisions of this Act.

(2) It shall be a condition of a statutory tenancy of a dwelling-house that the statutory tenant shall afford to the landlord access to the dwelling-house and all reasonable facilities for executing therein any repairs which the landlord is entitled to execute.

(3) Subject to section 5 of the Protection from Eviction Act 1977 (under which at least 4 weeks' notice to quit is required), a statutory tenant of a dwelling-house shall be entitled to give up possession of the dwelling-house if, and only if, he gives such notice as would have been required under the provisions of the original contract of tenancy, or, if no notice would have been so required, on giving not less than 3 months' notice.

(4) Notwithstanding anything in the contract of tenancy, a landlord who obtains an order for possession of a dwelling-house as against a statutory tenant shall not be required to give to the statutory tenant any notice to quit.

(5) Part II of Schedule 1 to this Act shall have effect in relation to the giving up of possession of statutory tenancies and the changing of statutory tenants by agreement.

"dwelling-house"

3A–101   See ss.1 and 26.

"statutory tenant"

3A–102   See ss.2 and 152.

"let", "protected tenancy", "protected tenant", and "tenancy"

3A–103   See ss.1 and 152.

EXCEPTIONS

Dwelling-houses above certain rateable values

4.—(1) A tenancy which is entered into before April 1, 1990 or **3A–104** (where the dwelling-house had a rateable value on March 31, 1990) is entered into on or after April 1, 1990 in pursuance of a contract made before that date is not a protected tenancy if the dwelling-house falls within one of the Classes set out in subsection (2) below.

(2) Where alternative rateable values are mentioned in this subsection, the higher applies if the dwelling-house is in Greater London and the lower applies if it is elsewhere.

Class A

The appropriate day in relation to the dwelling-house falls or fell on or after April 1, 1973 and the dwelling-house on the appropriate day has or had a rateable value exceeding £1,500 or £750.

Class B

The appropriate day in relation to the dwelling-house fell on or after March 22, 1973, but before April 1, 1973, and the dwelling-house—

(a) on the appropriate day had a rateable value exceeding £600 or £800, and

(b) on April 1, 1973 had a rateable value exceeding £1,500 or £750.

Class C

The appropriate day in relation to the dwelling-house fell before March 22, 1973 and the dwelling-house—

(a) on the appropriate day had a rateable value exceeding £400 or £200, and

(b) on March 22, 1973 had a rateable value exceeding £600 or £300, and

(c) on April 1, 1973 had a rateable value exceeding £1,500 or £750.

(3) If any question arises in any proceedings whether a dwelling-house falls within a Class in subsection (2) above, by virtue of its rateable value at any time, it shall be deemed not to fall within that Class unless the contrary is shown.

(4) A tenancy is not a protected tenancy if—

(a) it is entered into on or after April 1, 1990 (otherwise than, where the dwelling-house had a rateable value on March 31, 1990, in pursuance of a contract made before April 1, 1990), and

(b) under it the rent payable for the time being is payable at a rate exceeding £25,000 a year.

(5) In subsection (4) above "rent" does not include any sum payable by the tenant as is expressed (in whatever terms) to be payable in respect of rates, council tax, services, repairs, maintenance or insurance, unless it could not have been regarded by the parties as a sum so payable.

(6) If any question arises in any proceedings whether a tenancy is

precluded from being a protected tenancy by subsection (4) above, the tenancy shall be deemed to be a protected tenancy unless the contrary is shown.

(7) The Secretary of State may by order replace the amount referred to in subsection (4) above by an amount specified in the order; and such an order shall be made by statutory instrument which shall be subject to annulment in pursuance of a resolution of either House of Parliament.

3A–105   *Note* —Amended by the References to Rating (Housing) Regulations 1990 (S.I. 1990 No. 434), reg. 2, Sched., paras 15 and 16; and (S.I. 1993 No. 651), Sched.1, para. 3.

Dwelling-houses above certain rateable values

3A–106   The retrospective alteration of the rateable value does not bring a tenancy within protection (*Guest Heath plc v. Mirza* (1990) 22 H.L.R. 399, QBD).

Tenancies at low rents

3A–107   **5.**—(1) A tenancy which was entered into before April 1, 1990 or (where the dwelling-house under the tenancy had a rateable value on March 31, 1990) is entered into on or after April 1, 1990 in pursuance of a contract made before that date is not a protected tenancy if under the tenancy either no rent is payable or, the rent payable is less than two-thirds of the rateable value which is or was the rateable value of the dwelling-house on the appropriate day.

(2) Where—

    (a) the appropriate day in relation to a dwelling-house fell before March 22, 1973, and

    (b) the dwelling-house had on the appropriate day a rateable value exceeding, if it is in Greater London, £400 or, if it is elsewhere, £200.

subsection (1) above shall apply in relation to the dwelling-house as if the reference to the appropriate day were a reference to March 22, 1973.

(2A) A tenancy is not a protected tenancy if—

    (a) it is entered into on or after April 1, 1990 (otherwise than, where the dwelling-house had a rateable value on March 31, 1990, in pursuance of a contract made before April 1, 1990), and

    (b) under the tenancy for the time being either no rent is payable or the rent is payable at a rate of, if the dwelling-house is in Greater London, £1,000 or less a year, and, if the dwelling-house is elsewhere, £250 or less a year.

(2B) Subsection (7) of section 4 above shall apply to any amount referred to in subsection (2A) above as it applies to the amount referred to in subsection (4) of that section.

(3) In this Act a tenancy falling within subsection (1) above is referred to as a "tenancy at a low rent".

(4) In determining whether a long tenancy is a tenancy at a low rent, there shall be disregarded such part (if any) of the sums payable by the tenant as is expressed (in whatever terms) to be payable in respect of rates, council tax, services, repairs, maintenance, or in-

surance, unless it could not have been regarded by the parties as a part so payable.

(5) In subsection (4) above "long tenancy" means a tenancy granted for a term certain exceeding 21 years, other than a tenancy which is, or may become, terminable before the end of that term by notice given to the tenant.

Note —Amended by the Housing Act 1980, s.152 and Sched.26; the References to Rating (Housing) Regulations 1990 (S.I. 1990 No. 434), paras 17 and 18; and the Local Government Finance (Housing) (Consequential Amendments) Order 1993 (S.I. 1993 No. 651), Sched.1, para. 4. **3A–108**

Tenancies at low rents

The Court of Appeal in *Bostock v. Bryant* (1990) 22 H.L.R. 449; [1990] 39 E.G. 64, CA, stated that "if parties to an agreement describe a payment ... as rent, the court will normally accept that it is properly so described", but in that case "the more natural inference to be drawn from the payments by the tenants of the gas and electricity bills was that it was simply a payment of their part of the expenses incurred and a sharing of the expenses of the house" ((1990) 22 H.L.R. at 452). In those circumstances the inference should not be drawn that the payments were rent. **3A–109**

Certain shared ownership leases

5A.—(1) A tenancy is not a protected tenancy if it is a qualifying shared ownership lease, that is— **3A–110**

    (a) a lease granted in pursuance of the right to be granted a shared ownership lease under Part V of the Housing Act 1985, or

    (b) a lease granted by a housing association and which complies with the conditions set out in subsection (2) below.

(2) The conditions referred to in subsection (1)(b) above are that the lease—

    (a) was granted for a term of 99 years or more and is not (and cannot become) terminable except in pursuance of a provision for re-entry or forfeiture;

    (b) was granted at a premium, calculated by reference to the value of the dwelling-house or the cost of providing it, of not less than 25 per cent, or such other percentage as may be prescribed, of the figure by reference to which it was calculated;

    (c) provides for the tenant to acquire additional shares in the dwelling-house on terms specified in the lease and complying with such requirements as may be prescribed;

    (d) does not restrict the tenant's powers to assign, mortgage or charge his interest in the dwelling-house;

    (e) if it enables the landlord to require payment for outstanding shares in the dwelling-house, does so only in such circumstances as may be prescribed;

    (f) provides, in the case of a house, for the tenant to acquire the landlord's interest on terms specified in the lease and complying with such requirements as may be prescribed; and

    (g) states that the landlord's opinion that by virtue of this section the lease is excluded from the operation of this Act.

(3) The Secretary of State may by regulations prescribe anything requiring to be prescribed for the purposes of subsection (2) above.

(4) The regulations may—

(a) make different provision for different cases or descriptions of case, including different provision for different areas, and

(b) contain such incidental, supplementary or transitional provisions as the Secretary of State considers appropriate,

and shall be made by statutory instrument which shall be subject to annulment in pursuance of a resolution of either House of Parliament.

(5) In any proceedings the court may, if of opinion that it is just and equitable to do so, treat a lease as a qualifying shared ownership lease notwithstanding that the condition specified in subsection (2)(g) above is not satisfied.

(6) In this section—

"house" has the same meaning as in Part I of the Leasehold Reform Act 1967;

"housing association" has the same meaning as in the Housing Associations Act 1985; and

"lease" includes an agreement for a lease, and references to the grant of a lease shall be construed accordingly.

3A–111   *Note* —Inserted by the Housing and Planning Act 1986, s.18 and Sched.4.

Dwelling-houses let with other land

3A–112   **6.** Subject to section 26 of this Act, a tenancy is not a protected tenancy if the dwelling-house which is subject to the tenancy is let together with land other than the site of the dwelling-house.

"dwelling-house"
3A–113   See ss.1 and 26.

"let", "protected tenancy", "protected tenant" and "tenancy"
3A–114   See ss.1 and 152.

Payments for board or attendance

3A–115   **7.**—(1) A tenancy is not a protected tenancy if under the tenancy the dwelling-house is bona fide let at a rent which includes payments in respect of board or attendance.

(2) For the purposes of subsection (1) above, a dwelling-house shall not be taken to be bona fide let at a rent which includes payments in respect of attendance unless the amount of rent which is fairly attributable to attendance, having regard to the value of the attendance to the tenant, forms a substantial part of the whole rent.

"dwelling-house"
3A–116   See ss.1 and 26.

"let", "protected tenancy", "protected tenant" and "tenancy"
3A–117   See ss.1 and 152.

Payments for board of attendance

A tenancy cannot be a Rent Act protected tenancy if the rent includes "payment in **3A–118** respect of board or attendance ... [and] the value of the attendance to the tenant forms a substantial part of the whole rent".

In *Otter v. Norman* [1988] 3 W.L.R. 321; [1988] 2 All E.R. 897, HL, Lord Bridge approved *dicta* in *Wilkes v. Goodwin* [1923] 2 K.B. 86 that any amount of board suffices, provided it is not *de minimis*, but stressed the need for the tenant's rent to include "not only the cost of the food and drink provided but also all the housekeeping chores which must be undertaken in shopping for provisions, preparation and service of meals on the premises and cleaning and washing up after meals" ([1988] 2 All E.R. at 901). It is clear that the provision of a box of uncooked and unprepared groceries once a week is not sufficient to constitute board, although this might amount to an "attendance". Lord Bridge also pointed out that the "courts have consistently set their face against artificial and contrived devices whereby landlords have sought to deny to tenants the protection intended to be conferred by the Rent Acts" (at 901). "Attendance" means "services personal to the tenant" and the question of "proportionality" is a question of fact for the trial judge (*Nelson Developments Ltd v. Taboada* [1992] 34 E.G. 72; (1992) 24 H.L.R. 462, CA).

Lettings to students

8.—(1) A tenancy is not a protected tenancy if it is granted to a **3A–119** person who is pursuing, or intends to pursue, a course of study provided by a specified educational institution and is so granted either by that institution or by another specified institution or body of persons.

(2) In subsection (1) above "specified" means specified, or of a class specified, for the purposes of this section by regulations made by the Secretary of State by statutory instrument.

(3) A statutory instrument containing any such regulations shall be subject to annulment in pursuance of a resolution of either House of Parliament.

"protected tenancy", and "tenancy"

See ss.1 and 152. **3A–120**

"specified educational institution"

See the Assured and Protected Tenancies (Lettings to Students) Regulations 1998 **3A–121** (S.I. 1998 No. 1967) which define SEIs—basically any institution which provides higher or further education which is publicly funded and various other named institutions.

Holiday lettings

9. A tenancy is not a protected tenancy if the purpose of the **3A–122** tenancy is to confer on the tenant the right to occupy the dwelling-house for a holiday.

"dwelling-house"

See ss.1 and 26. **3A–123**

"let", "protected tenancy", "protected tenant" and "tenancy"

See ss.1 and 152. **3A–124**

Holiday lettings

In *Buchmann v. May* [1978] 2 All E.R. 993, CA, the Court of Appeal held that the **3A–125** labels put on a transaction are not conclusive, but that where a tenancy agreement expressly states the purpose for which it is made, that statement is evidence of that purpose unless the tenant can establish that it does not correspond with the true purpose, either because the express label is a sham or because it is a false label. Although a court will be "astute to detect a sham where it appears that a provision has been inserted for the purpose of depriving the tenant of statutory protection under the Rent Acts" ([1978] 2 All E.R. at 999), the burden of proof lies on the tenant. In that case there was no evidence which displaced the express purpose and accordingly there was no Rent Act protection. The court accepted the dictionary definition of a holiday as "a period of cessation of work, or period of recreation".

See too *R. v. Rent Officer for Camden LBC, Ex p. Plant* (1980) 257 E.G. 713; (1983) 7 H.L.R. 15, QBD, where there was "clear evidence that all the parties knew that [the applicants] were going to occupy it for the purpose of their work as students" and that that was "conclusive of the matter", and *McHale v. Daneham* (1979) 249 E.G. 969, where H.H.J. Edwards, sitting at Bloomsbury and Marylebone County Court, held that there was "no reason why a working holiday should not fall within the provisions of s.9 of the Rent Act".

Agricultural holdings

3A–126   **10.**—(1) A tenancy is not a protected tenancy if—

(a) the dwelling-house is comprised in an agricultural holding and is occupied by the person responsible for the control (whether as tenant or as servant or agent of the tenant) of the farming of the holding, or

(b) the dwelling-house is comprised in the holding held under a farm business tenancy and is occupied by the person responsible for the control (whether as tenant or as servant or agent of the tenant) of the management of the holding.

(2) In subsection (1) above—

"agricultural holding" means any agricultural holding within the meaning of the Agricultural Holdings Act 1986 held under a tenancy in relation to which that Act applies, and

"farm business tenancy" and "holding" in relation to such a tenancy, have the same meaning as in the Agricultural Tenancies Act 1995.

3A–127   *Note* —Substituted by the Agricultural Tenancies Act 1995, Sched., para. 27.

Licensed premises

3A–128   **11.** A tenancy of a dwelling-house which consists of or comprises premises licensed for the sale of intoxicating liquors for consumption on the premises shall not be a protected tenancy, nor shall such a dwelling-house be the subject of a statutory tenancy.

Resident landlords

3A–129   **12.**—(1) Subject to subsection (2) below, a tenancy of a dwelling-house granted on or after August 14, 1974 shall not be a protected tenancy at any time if—

(a) the dwelling-house forms part only of a building and, except in a case where the dwelling-house also forms part of a flat, the building is not a purpose-built block of flats; and

(b) the tenancy was granted by a person who, at the time when he granted it, occupied as his residence another dwelling-house which—

(i) in the case mentioned in paragraph (a) above, also forms part of the flat; or

682

> > (ii) in any other case, also forms part of the building; and
>
> (c) subject to paragraph 1 of Schedule 2 to this Act, at all times since the tenancy was granted the interest of the landlord under the tenancy has belonged to a person who, at the time he owned that interest, occupied as his residence another dwelling-house which—
>
> > (i) in the case mentioned in paragraph (a) above, also formed part of the flat; or
> >
> > (ii) in any other case, also formed part of the building.

(2) This section does not apply to a tenancy of a dwelling-house which forms part of a building if the tenancy is granted to a person who, immediately before it was granted, was a protected or statutory tenant of that dwelling-house or of any other dwelling-house in that building.

(3) [...]

(4) Schedule 2 to this Act shall have effect for the purpose of supplementing this section.

Note —Amended by the Housing Act 1980, ss.65(1) and 69(4).   **3A–130**

"dwelling-house"
See ss.1 and 26.   **3A–131**

"statutory tenant"
See ss.2 and 152.   **3A–132**

"let", "protected tenancy", "protected tenant" and "tenancy"
See ss.1 and 152.   **3A–133**

"purpose-built block of flats"
See Sched.2, para. 4.   **3A–134**

Resident landlords
In *Cooper v. Tait* (1984) 15 H.L.R. 98; (1984) 271 E.G. 105, CA, the Court of Appeal   **3A–135**
held that the residence requirements may be fulfilled by just one out of several joint landlords.

When courts are considering whether a landlord is a resident landlord within the meaning of s.12 they should use the same test as when deciding whether a statutory tenant continues to occupy premises as a residence for the purposes of the Rent Act 1977, s.2 (see above). Landlords who are temporarily absent must leave in the premises some personal and visible sign of their intention to return (*Jackson v. Pekic* [1989] 47 E.G. 141, CA).

Questions as to whether or not premises are part of the same building are essentially a question of fact for the county court judge. In *Griffiths v. English* (1981) 2 H.L.R. 134; (1982) 261 E.G. 257, CA; *Barnes v. Goresuch* (1982) 43 P. & C.R. 294; (1982) 263 E.G. 253; (1976) 2 H.L.R. 134, CA; *Bardrick v. Haycock* (1976) 1 P. & C.R. 420; (1981) 2 H.L.R. 118, CA; *Lewis-Graham v. Conacher* [1992] 02 E.G. 171, CA, and *Wolff v. Waddington* [1989] 47 E.G. 148, CA, the Court of Appeal declined to interfere with such findings.

Landlord's interest belonging to Crown

13.—(1) Except as provided by subsection (2) below—   **3A–136**

> (a) a tenancy shall not be a protected tenancy at any time when the interest of the landlord under the tenancy belongs to Her Majesty in right of the Crown or to a

government department or is held in trust for Her Majesty for the purposes of a government department; and

(b) a person shall not at any time be a statutory tenant of a dwelling-house if the interest of his immediate landlord would at that time belong or be held as mentioned in paragraph (a) above.

(2) An interest belonging to Her Majesty in right of the Crown shall not prevent a tenancy from being a protected tenancy or a person from being a statutory tenant if the interest is under the management of the Crown Estate Commissioners.

3A–137   *Note* —Substituted by the Housing Act 1980, s.73. See also the National Health Service and Community Care Act 1990, Sched.8, para. 19.

"dwelling-house"
3A–138   See ss.1 and 26.

"statutory tenant"
3A–139   See ss.2 and 152.

"protected tenancy" and "tenancy"
3A–140   See ss.1 and 152.

"landlord"
3A–141   See s.152(1).

Landlord's interest belonging to local authority, etc.

3A–142   **14.** A tenancy shall not be a protected tenancy at any time when the interest of the landlord under that tenancy belongs to—

(a) the council of a county or county borough;

(b) the council of a district or, in the application of this Act to the Isles of Scilly, the Council of the Isles of Scilly;

(bb) the Broads Authority;

(bc) a National Park Authority;

(c) the council of a London borough or the Common Council of the City of London;

(ca) [...]

(caa) a police authority established under section 3 of the Police Act 1996;

(caaa) [...];

(cb) a joint authority established by Part IV of the Local Government Act 1985;

(d) the Commission for the New Towns;

(e) a development corporation established by an order made, or having effect as if made, under the New Towns Act 1981; or

(f) [...]

(g) an urban development corporation within the meaning of Part XVI of the Local Government, Planning and Land Act 1980;

(h) a housing action trust established under Part III of the Housing Act 1988;

(i) the Residuary Body of Wales (Corff Gweddilliol Cymru);

nor shall a person at any time be a statutory tenant of a dwelling-house if the interest of his immediate landlord would belong at that time to any of those bodies.

Note —Amended by Local Government (Wales) Act 1994, Scheds 8 and 13; the Police and Magistrates' Courts Act 1994, Sched.4; the Environment Act 1995, Sched.10; S.I. 1985 No. 1884; the Local Government, Planning and Land Act 1980, s.155; the New Towns Act 1981, Sched.12; the Local Government Act 1985, Scheds 14 and 17; the Norfolk and Suffolk Broads Act 1988, ss.21, 23, 27, Sched.6; the Housing Act 1988, s.62; the Education Reform Act 1988, s.237, Sched.13; the Police Act 1997, Sched.9, para. 39; the Government of Wales Act 1998, Sched.18, Pt IV; and by the Criminal Justice and Police Act 2001, Sched.7, Pt 5. **3A–143**

"dwelling-house"

See ss.1 and 26. **3A–144**

"statutory tenant"

See ss.2 and 152. **3A–145**

"protected tenancy", "protected tenant" and "tenancy"

See ss.1 and 152. **3A–146**

"landlord"

See s.152(1). **3A–147**

Welsh Development Agency

Note that some tenants of the Welsh Development Agency do not enjoy security of tenure. See para. 3A-62 , The Welsh Development Agency Act 1975, Sched.4 as inserted by Government of Wales Act 1998, Sched.13. **3A–148**

Landlord's interest belonging to housing association, etc.

15.—(1) A tenancy shall not be a protected tenancy at any time **3A–149** when the interest of the landlord under that tenancy belongs to a housing association falling within subsection (3) below; nor shall a person at any time be a statutory tenant of a dwelling-house if the interest of his immediate landlord would belong at that time to such a housing asociation.

(2) A tenancy shall not be a protected tenancy at any time when the interest of the landlord under that tenancy belongs to—

    (a) the Housing Corporation; or

    (aa) [...]

    (b) a housing trust which is a charity within the meaning of the Charities Act 1993; nor shall a person at any time be a statutory tenant of a dwelling-house if the interest of his immediate landlord would belong at that time to any of those bodies.

(3) A housing association falls within this subsection if—

    (a) it is a registered social landlord within the meaning of the Housing Act 1985(see section 5(4) and (5) of that Act); or

    (b) it is a co-operative housing association within the meaning of the Housing Associations Act 1985; or

    (c) [...]

    (d) [...]

  (4) [...]

HOUSING

(5) In subsection (2) above "housing trust" means a corporation or body of persons which—

(a) is required by the terms of its constituent instrument to use the whole of its funds, including any surplus which may arise from its operations, for the purpose of providing housing accommodation; or

(b) is required by the terms of its constituent instrument to devote the whole, or substantially the whole, of its funds to charitable purposes and in fact uses the whole, or substantially the whole, of its funds for the purpose of providing housing accommodation.

(6) [...]

3A–150 *Note* —Amended by the Housing Act 1980, ss.74 and 152 and Sched.26; the Housing (Consequential Provisions) Act 1985, s.4, Sched.2; the Housing Act 1988, s.140, Sched.17, para. 99; the Charities Act 1993, s.98(1), Sched.6; and Order 1996, art.5, Sched.2, para. 66 and the Government of Wales Act 1998, Sched.18, Pt IV.

"dwelling-house"
3A–151 See ss.1 and 26.

"statutory tenant"
3A–152 See ss.2 and 152.

"protected tenancy", "protected tenant" and "tenancy"
3A–153 See ss.1 and 152.

"landlord"
3A–154 See ss.152(1).

"registered social landlord"
3A–155 See the Housing Act 1996, ss.1–7.

"co-operative housing association"
3A–156 See the Housing Associations Act 1985, s.1, which defines a housing association as a "society, body of trustees or company (a) which is established for the purpose of, or amongst whose objects or powers are included those of, providing, constructing, improving or managing, or facilitating or encouraging the construction or improvement of, housing accommodation, and (b) which does not trade for profit or whose constitution or rules prohibit the issue of capital with interest or dividend exceeding such rate as may be prescribed by the treasury, whether with or without differentiation between share and loan capital" and a co-operative housing association as "a fully mutual housing association which is a friendly society registered under the Industrial and Provident Societies Act 1965 ..."

Landlord's interest belonging to housing co-operative

3A–157 **16.** A tenancy shall not be a protected tenancy at any time when the interest of the landlord under that tenancy belongs to a housing co-operative, within the meaning of section 27B of the Housing Act 1985 (agreements with housing co-operatives under certain superseded provisions) and the dwelling-house is comprised in a housing co-operative agreement within the meaning of that section.

3A–158 *Note* —Amended by the Housing and Planning Act 1986, s.24(1), (2), Sched.5, para. 15.

"dwelling-house"
3A–159 See ss.1 and 26.

"protected tenancy" and "tenancy"
See ss.1 and 152.

3A–160

"housing co-operative"
See the Housing Act 1985, s.5.

3A–161

CONTROLLED AND REGULATED TENANCIES

* * * *

Regulated tenancies

18.—(1) Subject to sections 24(3) and 143 of this Act, a "regulated **3A–162**
tenancy" is, for the purposes of this Act, a protected or statutory
tenancy.

(2) Where a regulated tenancy is followed by a statutory tenancy
of the same dwelling-house, the two shall be treated for the purposes
of this Act as together constituting one regulated tenancy.

(3) [...]

(4) [...]

Note —Amended by the Housing Act 1980, Scheds 25, and 26. **3A–163**

"dwelling-house"
See ss.1 and 26.

3A–164

"statutory tenant"
See ss.2 and 152.

3A–165

"protected tenancy" and "tenancy"
See ss.1 and 152.

3A–166

Modification of Act for controlled tenancies converted into regulated tenancies

18A. Schedule 17 to this Act applies for the purpose of modifying **3A–167**
the provisions of this Act in relation to a tenancy which, by virtue of
any of the following enactments, was converted from a controlled
tenancy into a regulated tenancy, that is to say—

(a) section 18(3) of this Act;

(b) paragraph 5 of Schedule 2 to the Rent Act 1968 (which was
superseded by section 18(3));

(c) Part VIII of this Act;

(d) Part III of the Housing Finance Act 1972 (which was
superseded by Part VIII);

(e) Part IV of the Act of 1972 (conversion by reference to rateable
values);

(f) section 64 of the Housing Act 1980 (conversion of remaining
controlled tenancies into regulated tenancies).

Note —Added by the Housing Act 1980, Sched.25. **3A–168**

*   *   *   *

Tenant sharing accommodation with persons other than landlord

3A-169 **22.**—(1) Where a tenant has the exclusive occupation of any accommodation ("the separate accommodation") and—

(a) the terms as between the tenant and his landlord on which he holds the separate accommodation include the use of other accommodation ("the shared accommodation") in common with another person or other persons, not being or including the landlord, and

(b) by reason only of the circumstances mentioned in paragraph (a) above, the separate accommodation would not, apart from this section, be a dwelling-house let on or subject to a protected or statutory tenancy,

the separate accommodation shall be deemed to be a dwelling-house let on a protected tenancy or, as the case may be, subject to a statutory tenancy and the following provisions of this section shall have effect.

(2) For the avoidance of doubt it is hereby declared that where, for the purpose of determining the rateable value of the separate accommodation, it is necessary to make an apportionment under this Act, regard is to be had to the circumstances mentioned in subsection (1)(a) above.

(3) While the tenant is in possession of the separate accommodation (whether as a protected or statutory tenant), any term or condition of the contract of tenancy terminating or modifying, or providing for the termination or modification of, his right to use any of the shared accommodation which is living accommodation shall be of no effect.

(4) Where the terms and conditions of the contract of tenancy are such that at any time during the tenancy the persons in common with whom the tenant is entitled to the use of the shared accommodation could be varied, or their number could be increased, nothing in subsection (3) above shall prevent those terms and conditions from having effect so far as they relate to any such variation or increase.

(5) Without prejudice to the enforcement of any order made under subsection (6) below, while the tenant is in possession of the separate accommodation, no order shall be made for possession of any of the shared accommodation, whether on the application of the immediate landlord of the tenant or on the application of any person under whom that landlord derives title, unless a like order has been made, or is made at the same time, in respect of the separate accommodation; and the provisions of section 98(1) of this Act shall apply accordingly.

(6) On the application of the landlord, the county court may make such order either—

688

(a) terminating the right of the tenant to use the whole or any part of the shared accommodation other than living accommodation, or

(b) modifying his right to use the whole or any part of the shared accommodation, whether by varying the persons or increasing the number of persons entitled to the use of that accommodation, or otherwise,

as the court thinks just.

(7) No order shall be made under subsection (6) above so as to effect any termination or modification of the rights of the tenant which, apart from subsection (3) above, could not be effected by or under the terms of the contract of tenancy.

(8) In this section "living accommodation" means accommodation of such a nature that the fact that it constitutes or is included in the shared accommodation is (or, if the tenancy has ended, was) sufficient, apart from this section, to prevent the tenancy from constituting a protected tenancy of a dwelling-house.

"dwelling-house"

See ss.1 and 26.   3A–170

"statuory tenant"

See ss.2 and 152.   3A–171

"landlord", "protected tenancy" and "tenant"

See ss.1 and 152.   3A–172

SUBLETTINGS

Certain sublettings not to exclude any part of sub-lessor's premises from protection

23.—(1) Where the tenant of any premises, consisting of a house   3A–173
or part of a house, has sublet a part but not the whole of the premises, then, as against his landlord or any superior landlord, no part of the premises shall be treated as not being a dwelling-house let on or subject to a protected or statutory tenancy by reason only that—

(a) the terms on which any person claiming under the tenant holds any part of the premises include the use of accommodation in common with other persons; or

(b) part of the premises is let to any such person at a rent which includes payments in respect of board or attendance.

(2) Nothing in this section shall affect the rights against, and liabilities to, each other of the tenant and any person claiming under him, or of any two such persons.

"dwelling-house"

See ss.1 and 26.   3A–174

"statuory tenant"

See ss.2 and 152.   3A–175

"landlord" and "protected tenancy"

See ss.1 and 152.   3A–176

BUSINESS PREMISES

Premises with a business use

3A–177   **24.**—(1) [...]

(2) [...]

(3) A tenancy shall not be a regulated tenancy if it is a tenancy to which Part II of the Landlord and Tenant Act 1954 applies (but this provision is without prejudice to the application of any other provision of this Act to a sub-tenancy of any part of the premises comprised in such a tenancy).

3A–178   *Note* —Amended by the Housing Act 1980, s.152 and Sched.26.

Premises with business use

3A–179   Section 24 provides that a tenancy cannot be a regulated tenancy if it is a business tenancy to which the Landlord and Tenant Act 1954, Pt II applies. The Landlord and Tenant Act 1954, s.23(2) provides that "'business' includes trade, profession or employment".

Premises are only occupied "for the purposes of a business" where the business activity on the premises is a significant purpose of the occupation or part of the reason for the occupation. Where, however, the business use is merely incidental to residential occupation, there is Rent Act protection (*Cheryl Investments Ltd v. Saldanha* [1979] 1 All E.R. 5; [1978] 1 W.L.R. 1329, CA). This is essentially a question of fact for the trial judge—*Gurton v. Parrott* (1991) 23 H.L.R. 418; [1991] 18 E.G. 161, CA; *Pulleng v. Curran* (1982) 44 P. & C.R. 58, CA; and *Wright v. Mortimer* (1996) 28 H.L.R. 719; [1996] E.G.C.S. 51, CA, where the Court of Appeal held that whether or not business user is a significant element of occupation is a question of fact and degree which is particularly within the trial judge's ability to decide. It is permissible for the judge to take into account the tenant's attachment to the flat and the fact that an informed or reasonable person would conclude that the tenant is not carrying on a business at the premises.

See too *Florent v. Horez* (1983) 268 E.G. 807; (1984) 12 H.L.R. 1; (1984) 48 P. & C.R. 166, CA, where the Court of Appeal stated that the phrase "business user" has a broad meaning and approved a statement by Lindley L.J. in *Rolls v. Miller* (1884) 27 Ch D 71 at 88, that business "means almost anything which is an occupation, as distinguished from a pleasure—anything which is an occupation or duty which requires attention is a business".

MISCELLANEOUS

Rateable value and meaning of "appropriate day"

3A–180   **25.**—(1) Except where this Act otherwise provides, the rateable value on any day of a dwelling-house shall be ascertained for the purposes of this Act as follows—

(a) if the dwelling-house is a hereditament for which a rateable value is then shown in the valuation list, it shall be that rateable value;

(b) if the dwelling-house forms part only of such a hereditament or consists of or forms part of more than one such hereditament, its rateable value shall be taken to be such value as is found by a proper apportionment or aggregation of the rateable value or values so shown.

(2) Any question arising under this section as to the proper apportionment or aggregation of any value or values shall be determined by the county court, and the decision of the county court shall be final.

(3) In this Act "the appropriate day"—

(a) in relation to any dwelling-house which, on March 23, 1965, was or formed part of a hereditament for which a rateable value was shown in the valuation list then in force, or consisted or formed part of more than one such hereditament, means that date, and

(b) in relation to any other dwelling-house, means the date on which such a value is or was first shown in the valuation list.

(4) Where, after the date which is the appropriate day in relation to any dwelling-house, the valuation list is altered so as to vary the rateable value of the hereditament of which the dwelling-house consists or forms part and the alteration has effect from a date not later than the appropriate day, the rateable value of the dwelling-house on the appropriate day shall be ascertained as if the value shown in the valuation list on the appropriate day had been the value shown in the list as altered.

(5) This section applies in relation to any other land as it applies in relation to a dwelling-house.

Land and premises let with dwelling-house

26.—(1) For the purposes of this Act, any land or premises let **3A–181** together with a dwelling-house shall, unless it consists of agricultural land exceeding two acres in extent, be treated as part of the dwelling-house.

(2) For the purposes of subsection (1) above "agricultural land" has the meaning set out in section 26(3)(a) of the General Rate Act 1967(exclusion of agricultural land and premises from liability for rating).

* * * *

PART VII

SECURITY OF TENURE

LIMITATIONS ON RECOVERY OF POSSESSION OF DWELLING-HOUSES LET ON PROTECTED TENANCIES OR SUBJECT TO STATUTORY TENANCIES

Grounds for possession of certain dwelling-houses

98.—(1) Subject to this Part of this Act, a court shall not make an **3A–182** order for possession of a dwelling-house which is for the time being let on a protected tenancy or subject to a statutory tenancy unless the court considers it reasonable to make such order and either—

(a) the court is satisfied that suitable alternative accommodation is available for the tenant or will be available for him when the order in question takes effect, or

(b) the circumstances are as specified in any of the Cases in Part I of Schedule 15 to this Act.

HOUSING

(2) If, apart from subsection (1) above, the landlord would be entitled to recover possession of a dwelling-house which is for the time being let on or subject to a regulated tenancy, the court shall make an order for possession if the circumstances of the case are as specified in any of the Cases in Part II of Schedule 15.

(3) Part III of Schedule 15 shall have effect in relation to Case 9 in that Schedule and for determining the relevant date for the purposes of the Cases in Part II of that Schedule.

(4) Part IV of Schedule 15 shall have effect for determining whether, for the purposes of subsection (1)(a) above, suitable alternative accommodation is or will be available for a tenant.

(5) Part V of Schedule 15 shall have effect for the purpose of setting out conditions which are relevant to Cases 11 and 12 of that Schedule.

3A–183   *Note*—Amended by the Housing Act 1980, s.66.

Grounds for possession of certain dwelling-houses

3A–184   Section 98 contains the kernal of Rent Act security of tenure. In order to obtain possession a landlord must satisfy the court that a ground for possession (*i.e.* the availability of suitable alternative accommodation or one of the grounds in Sched.15) is made out, and, if the ground is a discretionary one, that it is reasonable to make an order for possession.

"[I] f there is before the court a claim that the defendant is entitled to the benefit of the Rent Acts, the court may not make an order for possession unless it is satisfied, either by evidence or by admission by or on behalf of the defendant, that he is not entitled to that protection". (*per* Glidewell J. in *R. v. Bloomsbury and Marylebone County Court, Ex p. Blackburne* (1984) 14 H.L.R. 56 at 67, QBD, approved by the Court of Appeal (1985) 275 E.G. 1273 at 1274). See also *Hounslow LBC v. McBride* (1999) 31 H.L.R. 143, CA and *R. v. Birmingham County Council, Ex p. Foley*, March 2001, Legal Action 29, Queen's Bench Division.

Although not stated in s.98, landlords also have to ensure that any contractual tenancy has been determined.

"dwelling-house"

3A–185   See ss.1 and 26.

"statuory tenant"

3A–186   See ss.2 and 152.

"landlord" and "protected tenancy"

3A–187   See ss.1 and 152.

"regulated tenancy"

3A–188   See ss.18 and 152.

Suitable alternative accommodation

3A–189   See too Sched.15, Pt IV, below. Paragraph 5 provides that alternative accommodation must be reasonably suitable to the needs of the tenant and his family. In that context "needs" means "the needs for housing" or "need for accommodation for the purpose of habitation"—see *Hill v. Rochard* [1983] 1 W.L.R. 478, CA and *Montross Associated Investments v. Stone* March 2000, Legal Action 29, CA.

The court can properly take into account environmental matters (*e.g.* where the alternative accommodation offered had no garden, was on a busy thoroughfare, was next door to a fried-fish shop, near to a hospital, cinema and public house and with an open space to the rear which the local authority proposed to use as a transport depot), both when considering suitability to the tenant's needs and reasonableness (*Redspring v. Francis* [1973] 1 W.L.R. 134; [1973] 1 All E.R. 640, CA), but only in so far as they relate to the property itself (not, *e.g.* matters such as the location of the tenant's friends, his mosque or cultural interests (*Siddiqui v. Rashid* [1980] 1 W.L.R. 1018; [1980] 3 All E.R. 184, CA).

Part of a tenant's existing accommodation can amount to suitable alternative accommodation (see *Mykolyshyn v. Noah* [1970] 1 W.L.R. 1271; [1971] 1 All E.R. 48, CA; *Thompson v. Rolls* [1926] 2 K.B. 426; *Parmee v. Mitchell* [1950] 1 All E.R. 872, CA; *McIntyre v. Hardcastle* [1948] 1 All E.R. 696, CA; and *Scrace v. Windust* [1955] 2 All E.R. 104, CA).

Reasonable

See also commentary to the Housing Act 1985, s.84.

3A–190

The question of reasonableness is an "overriding requirement" (*Smith v. McGoldrick* (1976) 242 E.G. 1047) and gives the court a very wide discretion (*Bell London and Provincial Properties Ltd v. Reuben* [1946] 2 All E.R. 547; and *Plaschkes v. Jones* (1982) 9 H.L.R. 110). In *Cumming v. Danson* [1942] 2 All E.R. 653 at 655, Lord Greene M.R. said:

> "in considering reasonableness ... it is, in my opinion, perfectly clear that the duty of the Judge is to take into account all relevant circumstances as they exist at the date of the hearing. That he must do in what I venture to call a broad common-sense way as a man of the world, and come to his conclusion giving such weight as he thinks right to the various factors in the situation. Some factors may have little or no weight, others may be decisive, but it is quite wrong for him to exclude from his consideration matters which he ought to take into account."

In *Shrimpton v. Rabbits*, 131 L.T. 478, KBD, Swift J. said that in considering the question of reasonableness the court "must consider all the circumstances affecting the holding of the premises by the person who holds them and as they relate to the landlord who wants to hold them". Acton J. said, "Because a [landlord's] wish is reasonable, it does not follow that it is reasonable in a court to gratify it."

In relation to rent arrears cases Denning L.J. (as he then was) has stated:

> "It would be very unusual indeed for the tenant to be ordered out on the ground of non-payment of rent when the full amount was already paid into court. If the tenant is in arrear, in these cases under the Rent Restriction Acts the everyday practice is to make an order for possession, but to suspend it so long as the current weekly rent and a payment on account of the rent in arrear are paid." (*Hayman v. Rowlands* [1957] 1 W.L.R. 317; [1957] 1 All E.R. 321, CA; but *cf. Dellenty v. Pellow* [1951] 2 All E.R. 716, CA; and *Lee-Steere v. Jennings* (1987) 20 H.L.R. 1, CA).

The first requirement for a judge who has found a ground for possession to be proved is to ask whether it is reasonable to make a possession order at all and then to ask whether the order should be stayed or suspended under s.100(2). The correct approach is to determine the extent of the rent arrears and how quickly those are likely to be paid. It is wrong to take into account matters which have not been pleaded

> "In considering whether it is reasonable to make an order ... the judge should consider all the relevant circumstances: but that is not a consideration at large. It is, or should be, a consideration in accordance with the pleadings. In my judgment, the matters proposed to be relied upon by the landlord in support of the contention that it would be reasonable to make an order for possession ... must be pleaded by the landlord." (*per* Sir Richard Scott V.-C. in *Laimond Properties Ltd v. Raeuchle* April 2000, Legal Action 31; (2001) 33 H.L.R. 113, CA); *cf. Taj v. Ali* 97/17 L.S. Gaz., April 28, 2000, p.36, [2000] 43 E.G. 183; (2001) 33 H.L.R. 37, CA where it was said that a suspended possession order should not extend "into the mists of time" or where there were "no sensible terms on which the order could be suspended" (suspended possession order providing for payment of arrears over 55 years replaced with 28 day possession order).

Courts must consider whether it is reasonable to make an order for possession at the date of the hearing and not at an earlier stage (*Smith v. McGoldrick* (1977) 242 E.G. 1047, CA). A judge's failure to consider reasonableness makes an order for possession a nullity (*Minchbourn Estates Ltd v. Fernandez (No. 2)* (1987) 19 H.L.R. 29; (1986) 280 E.G. 770, CA; and *Hounslow LBC v. McBride* (1999) 31 H.L.R. 143, CA and *R. v. Birmingham County Council, Ex p. Foley* March 2001, Legal Action 29, QBD), even where an order is made "by consent" and money is paid to the tenant in return for the giving of vacant possession (*R. v. Bloomsbury and Marylebone County Court, Ex p. Blackburne*

(1985) 275 E.G. 1273, CA). However, the Court of Appeal will "assume that the county court judge has taken all the relevant matters into account unless the contrary is clearly shown", and will only overrule a county court judge on the question of reasonableness "on very strong grounds" (*Dame Margaret Hungerford Charity Trustees v. Beazeley* [1993] 29 E.G. 100, CA). See too *Battlespring Ltd v. Gates* (1983) 268 E.G. 355, CA; *Dawncar Investments Ltd v. Plews* [1993] 13 E.G. 110; (1993) 25 H.L.R. 639, CA; *Empson v. Forde* [1990] 18 E.G. 99, CA and *Holloway v. Povey* (1984) 15 H.L.R. 104; (1984) 271 E.G. 195, CA.

Appeals on questions of reasonableness

3A–191   Although County Courts Act 1984, s.77(6) excludes appeals against judges' findings of fact, it does not exclude, in a proper case, the possibility of an appeal against a finding of reasonableness (*Castle Vale Housing Action Trust v. Gallagher* [2001] EWCA Civ 944; (2001) 33 H.L.R. 810).

ECHR Art 8 and reasonableness

3A–192   The Court of Appeal has doubted whether Article 8 makes any difference to the way in which courts have approached questions of the reasonableness of making possessions order. Article 8 does, however, reinforce the importance of only making an order depriving someone of his or her home in circumstances where a clear case is made out (*Castle Vale Housing Action Trust v. Gallagher* [2001] EWCA Civ 944; (2001) 33 H.L.R. 810, CA. See too *Newham LBC v. Neal* [2003] EWCA Civ 541 February 25, 2003.). There is a need to find a fair balance and to protect the rights of the neighbours and other members of the public (*Lambeth LBC v. Howard* [2001] EWCA Civ 468; (2001) 33 H.L.R. 636). See too *Harrow LBC v. Qazi* [2003] UKHL 43; [2003] 3 W.L.R. 792, where Lord Hope and Lord Scott said that contractual and property rights cannot be defeated by a defence based on Article 8. See too *Newham LBC v. Kibata* [2003] EWCA Civ 1785; [2004] HLR 28 and *Bradney v. Birmingham CC*; *Birmingham CC v. McCann* [2003] EWCA Civ 1783; [2004] HLR 27.

* * * *

Extended discretion of court in claims for possession of certain dwelling-houses

3A–193   **100.**—(1) Subject to subsection (5) below, a court may adjourn, for such period or periods as it thinks fit, proceedings for possession of a dwelling-house which is let on a protected tenancy or subject to a statutory tenancy.

(2) On the making of an order for possession of such a dwelling-house, or at any time before the execution of such an order (whether made before or after the commencement of this Act), the court, subject to subsection (5) below, may—

(a) stay or suspend execution of the order, or

(b) postpone the date of possession.

for such period or periods as the court thinks fit.

(3) On any such adjournment as is referred to in subsection (1) above or any such stay, suspension or postponement as is referred to in subsection (2) above, the court shall, unless it considers that to do so would cause exceptional hardship to the tenant or would otherwise be unreasonable, impose conditions with regard to payment by the tenant of arrears of rent (if any) and rent or payments in respect of occupation after termination of the tenancy (mesne profits) and may impose such other conditions as it thinks fit.

(4) If any such conditions as are referred to in subsection (3) above are complied with, the court may, if it thinks fit, discharge or rescind any such order as is referred to in subsection (2) above.

(4A) Subsection (4B) below applies in any case where—

    (a) proceedings are brought for possession of a dwelling-house which is let on a protected tenancy or subject to a statutory tenancy;

    (b) the tenant's spouse or former spouse, having rights of occupation under the Matrimonial Homes Act 1967, is then in occupation of the dwelling-house; and

    (c) the tenancy is terminated as a result of those proceedings.

(4B) In any case to which this subsection applies, the spouse or former spouse shall, so long as he or she remains in occupation, have the same rights in relation to, or in connection with, any such adjournment as is referred to in subsection (1) above or any such stay, suspension or postponement as is referred to in subsection (2) above, as he or she would have if those rights of occupation were not affected by the termination of the tenancy.

(5) This section shall not apply if the circumstances are as specified in any of the Cases in Part II of Schedule 15.

Note —Amended by the Housing Act 1980, s.75.   **3A–194**

"dwelling-house"
See ss.1 and 26.   **3A–195**

"statuory tenant"
See ss.2 and 152.   **3A–196**

"protected tenancy"
See ss.1 and 152.   **3A–197**

"tenant"
See s.152.   **3A–198**

Extended discretion of court in claims for possession of certain dwelling-houses
See commentary to the Housing Act 1985, s.85 and the Housing Act 1988, s.9.   **3A–199**

Overcrowded dwelling-houses

101. At any time when a dwelling-house is overcrowded, within the meaning of Part X of the Housing Act 1985, in such circumstances as to render the occupier guilty of an offence, nothing in this Part of this Act shall prevent the immediate landlord of the occupier from obtaining possession of the dwelling-house.   **3A–200**

Note —Substituted by the Housing (Consequential Provisions) Act 1985, Sched.2, para. 35.   **3A–201**

"overcrowding"
See the Housing Act 1985, ss.324–328.   **3A–202**

Overcrowded dwelling-houses
The Court of Appeal has held that where there is statutory overcrowding there is no jurisdiction to make a suspended possession order (*Henry Smith's Charity v. Bartosiak-Jentys* (1992) 24 H.L.R. 627, CA).   **3A–203**

Compensation for misrepresentation or concealment in Cases 8 and 9

102. Where, in such circumstances as are specified in Case 8 or Case 9 in Schedule 15 to this Act, a landlord obtains an order for   **3A–204**

possession of a dwelling-house let on a protected tenancy or subject to a statutory tenancy and it is subsequently made to appear to the court that the order was obtained by misrepresentation or concealment of material facts, the court may order the landlord to pay to the former tenant such sum as appears sufficient as compensation for damage or loss sustained by that tenant as a result of the order.

"dwelling-house"

3A–205   See ss.1 and 26.

"statuory tenant"

3A–206   See ss.2 and 152.

"protected tenancy"

3A–207   See ss.1 and 152.

"landlord" and "tenant"

3A–208   See s.152.

Compensation for misrepresentation or concealment in Cases 8 and 9

3A–209   See, *e.g. Thorne v. Smith* [1947] K.B. 307, CA and *Clements v. Simmonds* [2002] EWHC 1652 (QB); [2002] 41 E.G. 178. Note that the power of the court to award compensation under s.102 where possession has been obtained as a result of misrepresentation or concealment is limited to Case 8 (former employee) and Case 9 (dwelling reasonably required for occupation by landlord or landlord's family) (*cf.* Housing Act 1988, s.12). There is, however, no reason why a tenant should not bring proceedings based upon the common law tort of deceit (see, *e.g. Mafo v. Adams* [1970] 1 Q.B. 548, CA).

* * * *

MISCELLANEOUS

Interpretation of Part VII

3A–210   **107.**—(1) In this Part of this Act, except where the context otherwise requires—

"dwelling" means a house or part of a house;

"lessee" means the person to whom is granted, under a restricted contract, the right to occupy the dwelling in question as a residence and any person directly or indirectly deriving title from the grantee; and

"lessor" means the person who, under a restricted contract, grants to another the right to occupy the dwelling in question as a residence and any person directly or indirectly deriving title from the grantor.

(2) References in this Part of this Act to a party to a contract include references to any person directly or indirectly deriving title from such a party.

* * * *

PART XI

GENERAL

SUBLETTINGS

Effect on sub-tenancy of determination of superior tenancy

3A–211   **137.**—(1) If a court makes an order for possession of a dwelling-house from—

    (a) a protected or statutory tenant, or

    (b) a protected occupier or statutory tenant as defined in the Rent (Agriculture) Act 1976,

and the order is made by virtue of section 98(1) or 99(2) of this Act or, as the case may be, under Part I of Schedule 4 to that Act, nothing in the order shall affect the right of any sub-tenant to whom the dwelling-house or any part of it has been lawfully sublet before the commencement of the proceedings to retain possession by virtue of this Act, nor shall the order operate to give a right to possession against any such sub-tenant.

(2) Where a statutorily protected tenancy of a dwelling-house is determined, either as a result of an order for possession or for any other reason, any sub-tenant to whom the dwelling-house or any part of it has been lawfully sublet shall, subject to this Act, be deemed to become the tenant of the landlord on the same terms as if the tenant's statutorily protected tenancy had continued.

(3) Where a dwelling-house—

    (a) forms part of premises which have been let as a whole on a superior tenancy but do not constitute a dwelling-house let on a statutorily protected tenancy; and

    (b) is itself subject to a protected or statutory tenancy,

then, from the coming to an end of the superior tenancy, this Act shall apply in relation to the dwelling-house as if, in lieu of the superior tenancy, there had been separate tenancies of the dwelling-house and of the remainder of the premises, for the like purposes as under the superior tenancy, and at rents equal to the just proportion of the rent under the superior tenancy.

In this subsection "premises" includes, if the sub-tenancy in question is a protected or statutory tenancy to which section 99 of this Act applies, an agricultural holding within the meaning of the Agricultural Holdings Act 1986 held under a tenancy to which that Act applies, and land comprised in a farm business tenancy within the meaning of the Agricultural Tenancies Act 1995.

(4) In subsections (2) and (3) above "statutorily protected tenancy" means—

    (a) a protected or statutory tenancy;

    (b) a protected occupancy or statutory tenancy as defined in the Rent (Agricultural) Act 1976; or

    (c) if the sub-tenancy in question is a protected or statutory tenancy to which section 99 of this Act applies,

        (i) a tenancy of an agricultural holding within the meaning of the Agricultural Holdings Act 1986 which is a tenancy in relation to which that Act applies, or

        (ii) a farm business tenancy within the meaning of the Agricultural Tenancies Act 1995.

(5) Subject to subsection (6) below, a long tenancy of a dwelling-house which is also a tenancy at a low rent but which, had it not been a tenancy at a low rent, would have been a protected tenancy or an assured tenancy within the meaning of Part I of the Housing Act 1988, shall be treated for the purposes of subsection (2) above as a statutorily protected tenancy.

(6) Notwithstanding anything in subsection (5) above, subsection (2) above shall not have effect where the sub-tenancy in question was created (whether immediately or derivatively) out of a long tenancy falling within subsection (5) above and, at the time of the creation of the sub-tenancy—

    (a) a notice to terminate the long tenancy had been given under section 4(1) of the Landlord and Tenant Act 1954 or, as the case may be, served under paragraph 4(1) of Schedule 10 to the Local Government and Housing Act 1989; or

    (b) the long tenancy was being continued by section 3(1) of the said Act of 1954 or, as the case may be, paragraph 3 of the said Schedule 10;

unless the sub-tenancy was created with the consent in writing of the person who at the time when it was created was the landlord, within the meaning of Part I of the said Act of 1954 or, as the case may be, the said Schedule 10.

(7) This section shall apply equally where a protected occupier of a dwelling-house, or part of a dwelling-house, has a relevant licence as defined in the Rent (Agriculture) Act 1976, and in this section "tenancy" and all cognate expressions shall be construed accordingly.

3A–212   *Note*—Amended by the Agricultural Holdings Act 1986, Sched.14; the Housing Act 1988, s.140, Scheds 17 and 18; the Local Government and Housing Act 1989, s.195, Sched.11, para. 53; and the Agricultural Tenancies Act 1995, s.40, Sched.

Effect on sub-tenancy of determination of superior tenancy

3A–213   Section 137 provides that in some cases, on termination of a head tenancy, the subtenant of any dwelling house which has been lawfully sublet is deemed to become the tenant of the landlord and so gives some protection to subtenants when head tenancies come to an end.

In three appeals heard together, reported as *Wellcome Trust v. Hamad* [1998] Q.B. 638; [1998] 2 W.L.R. 156, CA, the Court of Appeal considered the construction of s.137(3) and the protection which it affords to sub-tenants. In each case buildings which comprised business premises (such as shops) on the ground floor and flats upstairs were let on long leases. These leases came within the provisions of the Landlord and Tenant Act 1954, Pt II. Subsequently Rent Act protected sub-tenancies of the residential parts of the buildings were granted. In all three cases county court judges relying on *Pittalis v. Grant* [1989] Q.B. 605, CA, found that, after the termination of the head leases, the subtenants fell outside Rent Act protection. The subtenants appealed, contending that *Pittalis v. Grant* had been decided *per incuriam*. After giving detailed consideration to the Rent Acts from a historical perspective the Court of Appeal granted the tenants' appeals and in two cases set aside possession orders made against them. Rent Act 1977, s.137(3) "appears to contemplate that where there is a flat over a shop, and the flat is lawfully sublet for residential use, so as to afford the sub-tenant protection under the Rent Act as against the tenant, the sub-tenant should continue to enjoy the same protection against the head landlord when the superior letting comes to an end". *Pittalis v. Grant* had been decided *per incuriam* because:

    (1) the argument relied upon that if a tenancy is not regulated, the premises cannot be treated as a dwelling house, was fallacious. Premises may amount to a dwelling house without being let on a regulated tenancy; and

    (2) the Court of Appeal had overlooked all of the authorities in which the accepted principles referred to by Lord Wilberforce in *Maunsell v. Olins* [1975] A.C. 373, HL, were contained. In each of the three cases the premises concerned constituted a dwelling-house and accordingly s.137(3) did afford protection to the sub-tenants.

A statutory tenant cannot grant an effective sub-tenancy, at least so far as the landlord is concerned. If a statutory tenant moves out and purports to sub-let, the premises cannot be lawfully sub-let under s.137 (*Moreland Properties (UK) Ltd v. Dhokia* [2003] EWCA Civ 1639; October 21, 2003).

Effect on furnished sub-tenancy of determination of superior unfurnished tenancy

138.—(1) If, in a case where section 137(2) of this Act applies, the **3A–214** conditions mentioned in subsection (2) below are fulfilled, the terms on which the sub-tenant is, by virtue of section 137(2), deemed to become the tenant of the landlord shall not include any terms as to the provision by the landlord of furniture or services.

(2) The conditions are—

    (a) that the statutorily protected tenancy which is determined as mentioned in section 137(2) was neither a protected furnished tenancy nor a statutory furnished tenancy; and

    (b) that, immediately before the determination of that statutorily protected tenancy, the sub-tenant referred to in section 137(2) was the tenant under a protected furnished tenancy or a statutory furnished tenancy; and

    (c) that the landlord, within the period of six weeks beginning with the day on which the statutorily protected tenancy referred to in section 137(2) is determined, serves notice on the sub-tenant that this section is to apply to his tenancy or statutory tenancy.

(3) In this section "statutorily protected tenancy" has the same meaning as it has for the purposes of section 137(2) of this Act.

Note —Amended by the Housing Act 1980, s.152, Sched.25, para. 51.　　**3A–215**

"statutory furnished tenancy"
See ss.2 and 152.　　**3A–216**

"protected tenancy"
See ss.1 and 152.　　**3A–217**

"statutorily protected tenancy"
See s.138(3).　　**3A–218**

"landlord" and "tenant"
See s.152.　　**3A–219**

* * * *

JURISDICTION AND PROCEDURE

County court jurisdiction

141.—(1) A county court shall have jurisdiction, either in the course **3A–220** of any proceedings relating to a dwelling or on an application made for the purpose by the landlord or the tenant, to determine any question—

    (a) as to whether a tenancy is a protected tenancy or whether any person is a statutory tenant of a dwelling-house; or

HOUSING

(b) as to the rent limit; or

(c) [...]

(d) as to the application of Part V and sections 103 to 106 of this Act to a contract; or

(e) as to whether a protected, statutory or regulated tenancy is a protected, statutory or regulated furnished tenancy;

or as to any matter which is or may become material for determining any such question.

(2) [...]

(3) A county court shall have jurisdiction to deal with any claim or other proceedings arising out of any of the provisions of this Act specified in subsection (5) below, notwithstanding that by reason of the amount of the claim or otherwise the case would not, apart from this subsection, be within the jurisdiction of a county court.

(4) If, under any of the provisions of this Act specified in subsection (5) below, a person takes proceedings in the High Court which he could have taken in the county court, he shall not be entitled to recover any costs.

(5) The provisions referred to in subsections (3) and (4) above are—

(a) [...]

(b) in Part III, section 57;

(c) Part VII, except sections 98(2) and 101;

(d) in Part IX, sections 125 and 126;

(e) in Part X, sections 133(1), 134 and 135; and

(f) in this Part of this Act, sections 145 and 147.

3A–221   *Note* —Amended by the Housing Act 1980, s.152, Sched.26.

"dwelling-house"

3A–222   See ss.1 and 26.

"statutory furnished tenancy"

3A–223   See ss.1 and 152.

"protected tenancy" and "protected furnished tenancy"

3A–224   See ss.1 and 152.

"statutorily protected tenancy"

3A–225   See s.138(3).

"landlord"and "tenant"

3A–226   See s.152.

"regulated tenancy"

3A–227   See ss.18 and 152.

Rules as to procedure

3A–228   **142.**—(1) The Lord Chancellor may make such rules and give such directions as he thinks fit for the purpose of giving effect to the provisions of this Act and may, by those rules or directions, provide for the conduct so far as desirable in private of any proceedings for the purposes of those provisions and for the remission of any fees.

(2) The power vested in the Lord Chancellor by subsection (1) above may, when the Great Seal is in commission, be exercised by any Lord Commissioner.

(3) The power conferred by subsection (1) above shall not be exercisable in relation to the following provisions of this Act—

(a) Part IV, except section 75(2);

(b) Part V;

(c) Part VI;

(d) sections 103 to 106, except subsection (4).

(4) Any rules made under this section shall be contained in a statutory instrument.

* * * *

MISCELLANEOUS

* * * *

Implied term in all protected tenancies

148. It shall be a condition of a protected tenancy of a dwelling-house that the tenant shall afford to the landlord access to the dwelling-house and all reasonable facilities for executing therein any repairs which the landlord is entitled to execute. **3A–229**

"protected tenancy"
See ss.1 and 152. **3A–230**

"landlord" and "tenant"
See s.152. **3A–231**

"dwelling-house"
See ss.1 and 26. **3A–232**

SUPPLEMENTAL

* * * *

Interpretation

152.—(1) In this Act, except where the context otherwise requires— **3A–233**
   "the appropriate day" has the meaning assigned to it by section 25(3) of this Act;
   "landlord" includes any person from time to time deriving title under the original landlord and also includes, in relation to any dwelling-house, any person other than the tenant who is, or but for Part VII of this Act would be, entitled to possession of the dwelling-house;
   "let" includes "sublet";
   "long tenancy" means a tenancy granted for a term of years certain exceeding 21 years, whether or not subsequently extended by act of the parties or by any enactment;
   "protected furnished tenancy", "regulated furnished tenancy"

701

HOUSING

and "statutory furnished tenancy" means a protected or, as the case may be, regulated or statutory tenancy—

(a) under which the dwelling-house concerned is bona fide let at a rent which includes payments in respect of furniture, and

(b) in respect of which the amount of rent which is fairly attributable to the use of furniture, having regard to the value of that use to the tenant, forms a substantial part of the whole rent;

"protected tenant" and "protected tenancy" shall be construed in accordance with section 1 of this Act;

"rates" includes water rates and charges but does not include an owner's drainage rate as defined in section 63(2)(a) of the Land Drainage Act 1976;

"rateable value" shall be construed in accordance with section 25 of this Act;

"regulated tenancy" shall be construed in accordance with section 18 of this Act;

"rent tribunal" has the meaning given by section 76(1) of this Act;

"rental period" means a period in respect of which a payment of rent falls to be made;

"restricted contract" shall be construed in accordance with section 19 of this Act;

"statutory tenant" and "statutory tenancy" shall be construed in accordance with section 2 of this Act;

"tenant" includes statutory tenant and also includes a sub-tenant and any person deriving title under the original tenant or sub-tenant;

"tenancy" includes "sub-tenancy";

"tenancy at a low rent" has the meaning assigned to it by section 5 of this Act.

(2) Except in so far as the context otherwise requires, any reference in this Act to any other enactment shall be taken as referring to that enactment as amended by or under any other enactment, including this Act.

3A–234 *Note*—Amended by the Housing Act 1980, s.152, Sched.26.

SCHEDULES

SECTIONS 2 AND 3 ## SCHEDULE 1

STATUTORY TENANCIES

PART I

STATUTORY TENANTS BY SUCCESSION

3A–235 1. Paragraph 2 below shall have effect, subject to section 2(3) of this Act, for the purpose of determining who is the statutory tenant of a dwelling-house by succession after the death of the person (in this Part of this Schedule referred to as "the original tenant") who, immediately before his death, was a protected tenant of the dwelling-house or the statutory tenant of it by virtue of his previous protected tenancy.

2.—(1) The surviving spouse (if any) of the original tenant, if residing in the dwelling-house immediately before the death of the original tenant, shall after the death be the statutory tenant if and so long as he or she occupies the dwelling-house as his or her residence.

(2) For the purposes of this paragraph, a person who was living with the original tenant as his or her wife or husband shall be treated as the spouse of the original tenant.

(3) If, immediately after the death of the original tenant, there is, by virtue of sub-paragraph (2) above, more than one person who fulfils the conditions in sub-paragraph (1) above, such one of them as may be decided by agreement or, in default of agreement, by the county court shall be treated as the surviving spouse for the purposes of this paragraph.

3.—(1) Where paragraph 2 above does not apply, but a person was a member of the original tenant's family was residing with him in the dwelling-house at the time of and for the period of 2 years immediately before his death then, after his death, that person or if there is more than one such person such one of them as may be decided by agreement, or in default of agreement by the county court, shall be entitled to an assured tenancy of the dwelling-house by succession.

(2) If the original tenant died within the period of 18 months beginning on the operative date, then, for the purposes of this paragraph, a person who was residing in the dwelling-house with the original tenant at the time of his death and for the period which began 6 months before the operative date and ended at the time of his death shall be taken to have been residing with the original tenant for the period of 2 years immediately before his death.

4. A person who becomes the statutory tenant of a dwelling-house by virtue of paragraph 2 above is in this Part of this Schedule referred to as "the first successor".

5. If, immediately before his death, the first successor was still a statutory tenant, paragraph 6 below shall have effect for the purpose of determining who is entitled to an assured tenancy of the dwelling-house by succession after the death of the first successor.

6.—(1) Where a person who—

    (a) was a member of the original tenant's family immediately before that tenant's death, and

    (b) was a member of the first successor's family immediately before the first successor's death,

was residing in the dwelling-house with the first successor at the time of, and for the period of two years immediately before, the first successor's death, that person or, if there is more than one such person, such one of them as may be decided by agreement or, in default of agreement, by the county court shall be entitled to an assured tenancy of the dwelling-house by succession.

(2) If the first successor died within the period of 18 months beginning on the operative date, then, for the purposes of this paragraph, a person who was residing in the dwelling-house with the first successor at the time of his death and for the period which began six months before the operative date and ended at the time of his death shall be taken to have been residing with the first successor for the period of two years immediately before his death.

7. [...]

8. [...]

9. Paragraphs 5 to 8 above do not apply where the statutory tenancy of the original tenant arose by virtue of section 4 of the Requisitioned Houses and Housing (Amendment) Act 1955 or section 20 of the Rent Act 1965.

10.—(1) Where after a succession the successor becomes the tenant of the dwelling-house by the grant to him of another tenancy, "the original tenant" and "the first successor" in this Part of this Schedule shall, in relation to that other tenancy, mean the persons who were respectively the original tenant and the first successor at the time of the succession, and accordingly—

    (a) if the successor was the first successor, and, immediately before his death he was still the tenant (whether protected or statutory), paragraphs 6 and 7 above shall apply on his death,

(b) if the successor was not the first successor; no person shall become a statutory tenant on his death by virtue of this Part of this Schedule.

(2) Sub-paragraph (1) above applies—

(a) even if a successor enters into more than one other tenancy of the dwelling-house, and

(b) even if both the first successor and the successor on his death enter into other tenancies of the dwelling-house.

(3) In this paragraph "succession" means the occasion on which a person becomes the statutory tenant of a dwelling-house by virtue of this Part of this Schedule and "successor" shall be construed accordingly.

(4) This paragraph shall apply as respects a succession which took place before August 27, 1972 if, and only if, the tenancy granted after the succession, or the first of those tenancies, was granted on or after that date, and where it does not apply as respects a succession, no account should be taken of that succession in applying this paragrpah as respects any later succession.

11.—(1) Paragraphs 5 to 8 above do not apply where—

(a) the tenancy of the original tenant was granted on or after the operative date within the meaning of the Rent (Agriculture) Act 1976, and

(b) both that tenancy and the statutory tenancy of the first successor were tenancies to which section 99 of this Act applies.

(2) If the tenants under both of the tenancies falling within sub-paragraph (1)(b) above were persons to whom paragraph 7 of Schedule 9 to the Rent (Agriculture) Act 1976 applies, the reference in sub-paragraph (1)(a) above to the operative date shall be taken as a reference to the date of operation for forestry workers within the meaning of that Act.

11A. In this Part of this Schedule "the operative date" means the date on which Part I of the Housing Act 1988 came into force.

PART II

RELINQUISHING TENANCIES AND CHANGING TENANTS

Payments demanded by statutory tenants as a condition of giving up possession

3A–236

12.—(1) A statutory tenant of a dwelling-house who, as a condition of giving up possession of the dwelling-house, asks for or receives the payment of any sum, or the giving of any other consideration, by any person other than the landlord, shall be guilty of an offence.

(2) Where a statutory tenant of a dwelling-house requires that furniture or other articles shall be purchased as a condition of his giving up possession of the dwelling-house, the price demanded shall, at the request of the person on whom the demand is made, by stated in writing, and if the price exceeds the reasonable price of the articles the excess shall be treated, for the purposes of sub-paragraph (1) above, as a sum asked to be paid as a condition of giving up possession.

(3) A person guilty of an offence under this paragraph shall be liable to a fine not exceeding level 3 on the standard scale.

(4) The court by which a person is convicted of an offence under this paragraph may order the payment—

(a) to the person who made any such payment, or gave any such consideration, as is referred to in sub-paragraph (1) above, of the amount of that payment or the value of that consideration, or

(b) to the person who paid any such price as is referred to in sub-paragraph (2) above, of the amount by which the price paid exceeds the reasonable price.

Change of statutory tenant by agreement

3A–237

13.—(1) Where it is so agreed in writing between a statutory tenant ("the outgoing tenant") and a person proposing to occupy the dwelling ("the incoming tenant"), the incoming tenant shall be deemed to be the statutory tenant of the dwelling as from such date as may be specified in the agreement ("the transfer date").

(2) Such an agreement shall not have effect unless the landlord is a party thereto, and, if the consent of any superior landlord would have been required to an assignment of the previous contractual tenancy, the agreement shall not have effect unless the superior landlord is a party thereto.

(3) If the outgoing tenant is the statutory tenant by virtue of his previous protected tenancy, then, subject to sub-paragraph (6) below, this Act shall have effect, on and after the transfer date, as if the incoming tenant had been a protected tenant and had become the statutory tenant by virtue of his previous protected tenancy.

(4) Subject to sub-paragraphs (5) and (6) below, if the outgoing tenant is a statutory tenant by succession, then, on and after the transfer date—

    (a) this Act shall have effect as if the incoming tenant were a statutory tenant by succession, and

    (b) the incoming tenant shall be deemed to have become a statutory tenant by virtue of that paragraph of Part I of this Schedule by virtue of which the outgoing tenant became (or is deemed to have become) a statutory tenant.

(5) If the outgoing tenant is a statutory tenant by succession, the agreement may provide that, notwithstanding anything in sub-paragraph (4) above, on and after the transfer date, this Act shall have effect, subject to sub-paragraph (6) below, as if the incoming tenant had been a protected tenant and had become the statutory tenant by virtue of his previous protected tenancy.

(6) Unless the incoming tenant is deemed, by virtue of sub-paragraph (4)(b) above, to have become a statutory tenant by virtue of paragraph 6 or 7 of Part I of this Schedule, paragraphs 5 to 7 of that Part shall not apply where a person has become a statutory tenant by virtue of this paragraph.

(7) In this paragraph "the dwelling" means the aggregate of the premises comprised in the statutory tenancy of the outgoing tenant.

No pecuniary consideration to be required on change of tenant under paragraph 13

3A–238

14.—(1) Any person who requires the payment of any pecuniary consideration for entering into such an agreement as is referred to in paragraph 13(1) above shall be liable to a fine not exceeding level 3 on the standard scale.

(2) The court by which a person is convicted of an offence under sub-paragraph (1) above may order the amount of the payment to be repaid by the person to whom it was paid.

(3) Without prejudice to sub-paragraph (2) above, the amount of any such payment as is referred to in sub-paragraph (1) above shall be recoverable by the person by whom it was made either by proceedings for its recovery or, if it was made to the landlord by a person liable to pay rent to the landlord, by deduction from any rent so payable.

(4) Notwithstanding anything in sub-paragraph (1) above, if apart from this paragraph he would be entitled to do so, the outgoing tenant may require the payment by the incoming tenant—

    (a) of so much of any outgoings discharged by the outgoing tenant as is referable to any period after the transfer date;

    (b) of a sum not exceeding the amount of any expenditure reasonably incurred by the outgoing tenant in carrying out any structural alteration of the dwelling or in providing or improving fixtures therein, being fixtures which, as against the landlord, the outgoing tenant is not entitled to remove;

    (c) where the outgoing tenant became a tenant of the dwelling by virtue of an assignment of the previous protected tenancy, of a sum not exceeding any reasonable amount paid by him to his assignor in respect of expenditure incurred by the assignor, or by any previous assignor of the tenancy, in carrying out any such alteration or in providing or improving any such fixtures as are mentioned in paragraph (b) above; or

    (d) where part of the dwelling is used as a shop or office, or for business, trade or professional purposes, of a reasonable amount in respect of any goodwill of the business, trade or profession, being goodwill transferred to the incoming tenant in connection with his becoming a statutory tenant of the dwelling or accruing to him in consequence thereof.

(5) In this paragraph "outgoing tenant", "incoming tenant", "the transfer date" and "the dwelling" have the same meanings as in paragraph 13 above.

3A–239   *Note* —Amended by the Housing Act 1980, s.152, Sched.26; the Criminal Justice Act 1982, ss.38 and 46; and the Housing Act 1988, Scheds.4 and 18.

Sched.1 should be read in conjunction with ss.2 and 3 (see paras 3A–106 to 3A–100).

Note: Para. 2 of this schedule has been amended by Civil Partnership Act 2004 s.81 and Sched. 8 . The amendment is not yet in force, but is printed at para. 3A–1525 .

Member of the original tenant's family
3A–240   A person of the same sex who has lived with the tenant for many years in a stable homosexual relationship may be a member of the tenant's family for the purposes of succession to a Rent Act tenancy (*Fitzpatrick v. Sterling HA* [2001] 1 A.C. 27; [1999] 3 W.L.R. 1113; [1999] 4 All E.R. 705, HL). Further, same sex couples may be treated in the same way as a husband and wife. The House of Lords has held that the words "as his or her wife or husband" in para. 2(2) must be read to mean "as if they were his or her wife or husband" in order to comply with the ECHR. Accordingly the survivor of a same sex couple who has been living in a loving and monogamous relationship with a tenant may acquire a statutory tenancy (*Ghaidan v. Mendoza* [2004] UKHL 30; [2004] 3 W.L.R. 113).

SECTION 12(3)   SCHEDULE 2

RESIDENT LANDLORDS

PART I

PROVISIONS FOR DETERMINING APPLICATION OF SECTION 12

3A–241   1. In determining whether the condition in section 12(1)(c) of this Act is at any time fulfilled with respect to a tenancy, there shall be disregarded—

(a) any period of not more than 28 days beginning with the date on which the interest of the landlord under the tenancy becomes vested at law and in equity in an individual who, during that period, does not occupy as his residence another dwelling-house which forms part of the building or, as the case may be, flat concerned;

(b) if, within a period falling within paragraph (a) above, the individual concerned notifies the tenant in writing of his intention to occupy as his residence another dwelling-house in the building or, as the case may be, flat concerned, the period beginning with the date on which the interest of the landlord under the tenancy becomes vested in that individual as mentioned in that paragraph and ending—

(i) at the expiry of the period of six months beginning on that date, or

(ii) on the date on which that interest ceases to be so vested, or

(iii) on the date on which the condition in section 12(1)(c) again applies,whichever is the earlier; and

(c) any period of not more than two years beginning with the date on which the interest of the landlord under the tenancy becomes, and during which it remains, vested—

(i) [...]

(ii) in trustees as such; or

(iii) by virtue of section 9 of the Administration of Estates Act 1925, in the Probate Judge or the Public Trustee.

2. During any period when—

(a) the interest of the landlord under the tenancy referred to in section 12(1) is vested in trustees as such, and

(b) that interest is held on trust for any person who occupies as his residence a dwelling-house which forms part of the building or, as the case may be, flat referred to in section 12(1)(a),the condition in section 12(1)(c) shall be deemed to be fulfilled and, accordingly, no part of that period shall be disregarded by virtue of paragraph 1 above.

2A.—(1) The tenancy referred to in section 12(1) falls within this paragraph if the interest of the landlord under the tenancy becomes vested in the personal representatives of a deceased person acting in that capacity.

(2) If the tenancy falls within this paragraph, the condition in section 12(1)(c) shall be deemed to be fulfilled for any period, beginning with the date on which the interest becomes vested in the personal representatives and not exceeding two years, during which the interest of the landlord remains so vested.

3. Throughout any period which, by virtue of paragraph 1 above, falls to be disregarded for the purpose of determining whether the condition in section 12(1)(c) is fulfilled with respect to a tenancy, no order shall be made for possession of the dwelling-house subject to that tenancy, other than an order which might be made if that tenancy were or, as the case may be, had been a regulated tenancy.

4. For the purposes of section 12, a building is a purpose-built block of flats if as constructed it contained, and it contains, two or more flats; and for this purpose "flat" means a dwelling-house which—

(a) forms part only of a building; and

(b) is separated horizontally from another dwelling-house which forms part of the same building.

5. For the purposes of section 12, a person shall be treated as occupying a dwelling-house as his residence if, so far as the nature of the case allows, he fulfils the same conditions as, by virtue of section 2(3) of this Act, are required to be fulfilled by a statutory tenant of a dwelling-house.

PART II

TENANCIES CEASING TO FALL WITHIN SECTION 12

6.—(1) In any case where—

(a) a tenancy which, by virtue only of section 12, was precluded from being a protected tenancy ceases to be so precluded and accordingly becomes a protected tenancy, and

(b) before it became a protected tenancy a rent was registered for the dwelling concerned under Part V of this Act,

the amount which is so registered shall be deemed to be registered under Part IV of this Act as the rent for the dwelling-house which is let on that tenancy, and that registration shall be deemed to take effect on the day the tenancy becomes a protected tenancy.

(2) Section 67(3) of this Act shall not apply to an application for the registration under Part IV of a rent different from that which is deemed to be registered as mentioned in sub-paragraph (1) above.

(3) [...]

(4) If, immediately before a tenancy became a protected tenancy as mentioned in sub-paragraph (1)(a) above, the rates in respect of the dwelling-house concerned were borne as mentioned in sub-section (3) of section 79 of this Act and the fact that they were so borne was noted as required by that sub-section then, in the application of Part IV in relation to the protected tenancy, section 71(2) of this Act shall be deemed to apply.

7. If, in a case where a tenancy becomes a protected tenancy as mentioned in sub-paragraph (1)(a) above—

(a) a notice to quit had been served in respect of the dwelling concerned before the date on which the tenancy became a protected tenancy, and

(b) the period at the end of which that notice to quit takes effect had, before that date, been extended under Part VII of this Act, and

(c) that period has not expired before that date,

the notice to quit shall take effect on the day following that date (whenever it would otherwise take effect) and, accordingly, on that day the protected tenancy shall become a statutory tenancy.

3A–242

HOUSING

3A–243   *Note* —Amended by the Housing Act 1980, s.65, Sched.26; the Housing Act 1988, Sched.18; the Trusts of Land and Appointment of Trustees Act 1996, Sched.4; and the Law of Property (Miscellaneous Provisions) Act 1994, s.21(1), Sched.1.

Sched.2 should be read in conjunction with s.12 (see para. 3A–140).

SCHEDULE 15 - GROUNDS FOR POSSESSION OF DWELLING-HOUSES LET ON OR SUBJECT TO PROTECTED OR STATUTORY TENANCIES

3A–244

* * * *

SECTION 98   SCHEDULE 15

PART I

CASES IN WHICH COURT MAY ORDER POSSESSION

Case 1

Where any rent lawfully due from the tenant has not been paid, or any obligation of the protected or statutory tenancy which arises under this Act, or—

(a) in the case of a protected tenancy, any other obligation of the tenancy, in so far as is consistent with the provisions of Part VII of this Act, or

(b) in the case of a statutory tenancy, any other obligation of the previous protected tenancy which is applicable to the statutory tenancy,

has been broken or not performed.

Case 2

3A–245   Where the tenant or any person residing or lodging with him or any sub-tenant of his has been guilty of conduct which is a nuisance or annoyance to adjoining occupiers, or has been convicted of using the dwelling-house or allowing the dwelling-house to be used for immoral or illegal purposes.

Case 3

3A–246   Where the condition of the dwelling-house has, in the opinion of the court, deteriorated owing to acts of waste by, or the neglect or default of, the tenant or any person residing or lodging with him or any sub-tenant of his and, in the case of any act of waste by, or the neglect or default of, a person lodging with the tenant or sub-tenant of his, where the court is satisfied that the tenant has not, before the making of the order in question, taken such steps as he ought reasonably to have taken for the removal of the lodger or sub-tenant, as the case may be.

Case 4

3A–247   Where the condition of any furniture provided for use under the tenancy has, in the opinion of the court, deteriorated owing to ill-treatment by the tenant or any person residing or lodging with him or any sub-tenant of his and, in the case of any ill-treatment by a person lodging with the tenant or a sub-tenant of his, where the court is satisfied that the tenant has not, before the making of the order in question, taken such steps as he ought reasonably to have taken for the removal of the lodger or sub-tenant, as the case may be.

Case 5

3A–248   Where the tenant has given notice to quit and, in consequence of that notice, the landlord has contracted to sell or let the dwelling-house or has taken any other steps as the result of which he would, in the opinion of the court, be seriously prejudiced if he could not obtain possession.

Case 6

3A–249   Where, without the consent of the landlord, the tenant has, at any time after—

(a) [...]

(b) 22nd March, 1973, in the case of a tenancy which became a regulated tenancy by virtue of section 14 of the Counter-Inflation Act 1973;

(bb) the commencement of section 73 of the Housing Act 1980, in the case of a tenancy which became a regulated tenancy by virtue of that section;

(c) 14th August, 1974, in the case of a regulated furnished tenancy; or

(d) 8th December, 1965, in the case of any other tenancy,

assigned or sublet the whole of the dwelling-house or sublet part of the dwelling-house, the remainder being already sublet.

Case 7

[...] **3A–250**

Case 8

Where the dwelling-house is reasonably required by the landlord for occupation as **3A–251** a residence for some person engaged in his whole-time employment, or in the whole-time employment of some tenant from him or with whom, conditional on housing being provided, a contract for such employment has been entered into, and the tenant was in the employment of the landlord or a former landlord, and the dwelling-house was let to him in consequence of that employment and he has ceased to be in that employment.

Case 9

Where the dwelling-house is reasonably required by the landlord for occupation as **3A–252** a residence for—

(a) himself, or

(b) any son or daughter of his over 18 years of age, or

(c) his father or mother, or

(d) if the dwelling-house is let on or subject to a regulated tenancy, the father or mother of his wife or husband,

and the landlord did not become landlord by purchasing the dwelling-house or any interest therein after—

(i) 7th November, 1956, in the case of a tenancy which was then a controlled tenancy;

(ii) 8th March, 1973, in the case of a tenancy which became a regulated tenancy by virtue of section 14 of the Counter-Inflation Act 1973;

(iii) 24th May, 1974, in the case of a regulated furnished tenancy; or

(iv) 23rd March, 1965, in the case of any other tenancy.

Case 10

Where the court is satisfied that the rent charged by the tenant— **3A–253**

(a) for any sublet part of the dwelling-house which is a dwelling-house let on a protected tenancy or subject to a statutory tenancy is or was in excess of the maximum rent for the time being recoverable for that part, having regard to Part III of this Act, or

(b) for any sublet part of the dwelling-house which is subject to a restricted contract is or was in excess of the maximum (if any) which it is lawful for the lessor, within the meaning of Part V of this Act to require or receive having regard to the provisions of that Part.

PART II

CASES IN WHICH COURT MUST ORDER POSSESSION WHERE DWELLIING-HOUSE SUBJECT TO REGULATED TENANCY

Case 11

Where a person (in this case referred to as the "owner-occupier") who let the dwelling- **3A–254** house on a regulated tenancy had, at any time before the letting, occupied it as his residence and—

(a) not later than the relevant date the landlord gave notice, in writing to the tenant that possession might be recovered under this Case, and

(b) the dwelling-house has not, since—

HOUSING

(i) March 22, 1973, in the case of a tenancy which became a regulated tenancy by virtue of section 14 of the Counter-Inflation Act 1973;

(ii) August 14, 1974, in the case of a regulated furnished tenancy; or

(iii) December 8, 1965, in the case of any other tenancy,

been let by the owner-occupier on a protected tenancy with respect to which the condition mentioned in paragraph (a) above was not satisfied, and

(c) the court is of the opinion that of the conditions set out in Part V of this Schedule one of those in paragraphs (a) and (c) to (f) is satisfied.

If the court is of the opinion that, notwithstanding that the condition in paragraph (a) or (b) above is not complied with, it is just and equitable to make an order for possession of the dwelling-house, the court may dispense with the requirements of either or both of these paragraphs, as the case may require.

The giving of a notice before August 14, 1974 under section 79 of the Rent Act 1968 shall be treated, in the case of a regulated furnished tenancy, as compliance with paragraph (a) of this Case.

Where the dwelling-house has been let by the owner-occupier on a protected tenancy (in this paragraph referred to as "the earlier tenancy") granted on or after November 16, 1984 but not later than the end of he period of two months beginning with the commencement of the Rent (Amendment) Act 1985 and either—

(i) the earlier tenancy was granted for a term certain (whether or not to be followed by a further term or to continue thereafter from year to year or some other period) and was during that term a protected shorthold tenancy as defined in section 52 of the Housing Act 1980, or

(ii) the conditions mentioned in paragraphs (a) to (c) of Case 20 were satisfied with respect to the dwelling-house and the earlier tenancy,

then for the purposes of paragraph (b) above the condition in paragraph (a) above is to be treated as having been satisfied with respect to the earlier tenancy.

Case 12

3A–255   Where the landlord (in this Case referred to as "the owner") intends to occupy the dwelling-house as his residence at such time as he might retire from regular employment and has let it on a regulated tenancy before he has so retired and—

(a) not later than the relevant date the landlord gave notice in writing to the tenant that possession might be recovered under this Case; and

(b) the dwelling-house has not, since August 14, 1974, been let by the owner paragraph (a) above was not satisfied; and

(c) the court is of the opinion that of the conditions set out in Part V of this Schedule one of those in paragraphs (b) to (e) is satisfied.

If the court is of the opinion that, notwithstanding that the condition in paragraph (a) or (b) above is not complied with, it is just and equitable to make an order for possession of the dwelling-house, the court may dispense with the requirements of either or both of those paragraphs, as the case may require.

Case 13

3A–256   Where the dwelling-house is let under a tenancy for a term of years certain not exceeding eight months and—

(a) not later than the relevant date the landlord gave notice in writing to the tenant that possession might be recovered under this Case; and

(b) that dwelling-house was, at some time within the period of 12 months ending on the relevant date, occupied under a right to occupy it for a holiday.

For the purposes of this Case a tenancy shall be treated as being for a term of years certain notwithstanding that it is liable to determination by re-entry or on the happening of any event other than the giving of notice by the landlord to determine the term.

Case 14

3A–257   Where the dwelling-house is let under a tenancy for a term of years certain not exceeding 12 months and—

(a) not later than the relevant date the landlord gave notice in writing to the tenant that possession might be recovered under this Case; and

(b) at some time within the period of 12 months ending on the relevant date, the dwelling-house was subject to such a tenancy as is referred to in section 8(1) of this Act.

For the purposes of this Case a tenancy shall be treated as being for a term of years certain notwithstanding that it is liable to determination by re-entry or on the happening of any event other than the giving of notice by the landlord to determine the term.

Case 15

3A-258

Where the dwelling-house is held for the purpose of being available for occupation by a minister of religion as a residence from which to perform the duties of his office and—

(a) not later than the relevant date the tenant was given notice in writing that possession might be recovered under this Case, and

(b) the court is satisfied that the dwelling-house is required for occupation by a minister of religion as such a residence.

Case 16

3A-259

Where the dwelling-house was at any time occupied by a person under the terms of his employment as a person employed in agriculture, and

(a) the tenant neither is nor at any time was so employed by the landlord and is not the widow of a person who was so employed, and

(b) not later than the relevant date, the tenant was given notice in writing that possession might be recovered under this Case, and

(c) the court is satisfied that the dwelling-house is required for occupation by a person employed, or to be employed, by the landlord in agriculture.

For the purposes of this Case "employed", "employment" and "agriculture" have the same meanings as in the Agricultural Wages Act 1948.

Case 17

3A-260

Where proposals for amalgamation, approved for the purposes of a scheme under section 26 of the Agriculture Act 1967, have been carried out and, at the time when the proposals were submitted, the dwelling-house was occupied by a person responsible (whether as owner, tenant, or servant or agent of another) for the control of the farming of any part of the land comprised in the amalgamation and

(a) after the carrying out of the proposals, the dwelling-house was let on a regulated tenancy otherwise than to, or to the widow of, either a person ceasing to be so responsible as part of the amalgamation or a person who is, or at any time was, employed by the landlord in agriculture, and

(b) not later than the relevant date the tenant was given notice in writing that possession might be recovered under this Case, and

(c) the court is satisfied that the dwelling-house is required for occupation by a person employed, or to be employed, by the landlord in agriculture, and

(d) the proceedings for possession are commenced by the landlord at any time during the period of five years beginning with the date on which the proposals for the amalgamation were approved or, if occupation of the dwelling-house after the amalgamation continued in, or was first taken by, a person ceasing to be responsible as mentioned in paragraph (a) above or his widow, during a period expiring three years after the date on which the dwelling-house next became unoccupied.

For the purposes of this Case "employed" and "agriculture" have the same meanings as in the Agricultural Wages Act 1948 and "amalgamation" has the same meaning as in Part II of the Agriculture Act 1967.

Case 18

3A-261

Where—

(a) the last occupier of the dwelling-house before the relevant date was a person, or the widow of a person, who was at some time during his occupation responsible (whether as owner, tenant, or servant or agent of another) for the control of the farming of land which formed, together with the dwelling-house, an agricultural unit within the meaning of the Agriculture Act 1947, and

HOUSING

 (b) the tenant is neither—

  (i) a person, or the widow of a person, who is or has at any time been responsible for the control of the farming of any part of the said land, nor

  (ii) a person, or the widow of a person, who is or at any time was employed by the landlord in agriculture, and

 (c) the creation of the tenancy was not preceded by the carrying out in connection with any of the said land of an amalgamation approved for the purposes of a scheme under section 26 of the Agriculture Act 1967, and

 (d) not later than the relevant date the tenant was given notice in writing that possession might be recovered under this Case, and

 (e) the court is satisfied that the dwelling-house is required for occupation either by a person responsible or to be responsible (whether as owner, tenant, or servant or agent of another) for the control of the farming of any part of the said land or by a person employed or to be employed by the landlord in agriculture, and

 (f) in a case where the relevant date was before August 9, 1972, the proceedings for possession are commenced by the landlord before the expiry of five years from the date on which the occupier referred to in paragraph (a) above went out of occupation.

For the purposes of this Case "employed" and "agriculture" have the same meanings as in the Agricultural Wages Act 1948 and "amalgamation" has the same meaning as in Part II of the Agriculture Act 1967.

Case 19

3A–262 Where the dwelling-house was let under a protected shorthold tenancy (or is treated under section 55 of the Housing Act 1980 as having been so let) and—

 (a) there either has been no grant of a further tenancy of the dwelling-house since the end of the protected shorthold tenancy or, if there was such a grant, it was to a person the dwelling-house as a protected or statutory tenant; and

 (b) the proceedings for possession were commenced after appropriate notice by the landlord to the tenant and not later than three months after the expiry of the notice.

A notice is appropriate for this Case if—

 (i) it is in writing and states that proceedings for possession under this Case may be brought after its expiry; and

 (ii) it expires not earlier than three months after it is served nor, if, when it is served, the tenancy is a periodic tenancy, before that periodic tenancy could be brought to an end by a notice to quit served by the landlord on the same day;

 (iii) it is served—

  (a) in the period of three months immediately preceding the date on which the protected shorthold tenancy comes to an end; or

  (b) if that date has passed, in the period of three months immediately preceding any anniversary of that date; and

 (iv) in a case where a previous notice has been served by the landlord on the tenant in respect of the dwelling-house, and that notice was an appropriate notice, it is served not earlier than three months after the expiry of the previous notice.

Case 20

3A–263 Where the dwelling-house was let by a person (in this Case referred to as "the owner") at any time after the commencement of section 67 of the Housing Act 1980 and—

 (a) at the time when the owner acquired the dwelling-house he was a member of the regular armed forces of the Crown;

 (b) at the relevant date the owner was a member of the regular armed forces of the Crown;

 (c) not later than the relevant date the owner gave notice in writing to the tenant that possession might be recovered under this Case;

 (d) the dwelling-house has not, since the commencement of section 67 of the Act of 1980 been let by the owner on a protected tenancy with respect to which the condition mentioned in paragraph (c) above was not satisfied; and

(e) the court is of the opinion that—

  (i) the dwelling-house is required as a residence for the owner; or

  (ii) of the conditions set out in Part V of this Schedule one of those in paragraphs (c) to (f) is satisfied.

If the court is of the opinion that, notwithstanding that the condition in paragraph (c) or (d) above is not complied with, it is just and equitable to make an order for possession of the dwelling-house, the court may dispense with the requirements of either or both of these paragraphs, as the case may require.

For the purposes of this Case "regular armed forces of the Crown" has the same meaning as in section 1 of the House of Commons Disqualification Act 1975.

PART III

PROVISIONS APPLICABLE TO CASE 9 AND PART II OF THIS SCHEDULE

Provision for Case 9

3A–264

1. A court shall not make an order for possession of a dwelling-house by reason only that the circumstances of the case fall within Case 9 in Part I of this Schedule if the court is satisfied that, having regard to all the circumstances of the case, including the question whether other accommodation is available for the landlord or the tenant, greater hardship would be caused by granting the order than by refusing to grant it.

Provision for Part II

3A–265

2. Any reference in Part II of this Schedule to the relevant date shall be construed as follows—

(a) except in a case falling within paragraph (b) or (c) below, if the protected tenancy, or, in the case of a statutory tenancy, the previous contractual tenancy, was created before December 8, 1965, the relevant date means June 7, 1966; and

(b) except in a case falling within paragraph (c) below, if the tenancy became a regulated tenancy by virtue of section 14 of the Counter-Inflation Act 1973 and the tenancy or, in the case of a statutory tenancy, the previous contractual tenancy, was created before March 22, 1973, the relevant date means September 22, 1973; and

(c) in the case of a regulated furnished tenancy, if the tenancy, or, in the case of a statutory furnished tenancy, the previous contractual tenancy was created before August 14, 1974, the relevant date means February 13, 1975; and

(d) in any other case, the relevant date means the date of the commencement of the regulated tenancy in question.

PART IV

SUITABLE ALTERNATIVE ACCOMMODATION

3A–266

3. For the purposes of section 98(1)(a) of this Act, a certificate of the local housing authority for the district in which the dwelling-house in question is situated, certifying that the authority will provide suitable alternative accommodation for the tenant by a date specified in the certificate, shall be conclusive evidence that suitable alternative accommodation will be available for him by that date.

4.—(1) Where no such certificate as is mentioned in paragraph 3 above is produced to the court, accommodation shall be deemed to be suitable for the purposes of section 98(1)(a) of this Act if it consists of either—

(a) premises which are to be let as a separate dwelling such that they will then be let on a protected tenancy (other than one under which the landlord might recover possession of the dwelling-house under one of the cases in Part II of this Schedule), or

(b) premises to be let as a separate dwelling on terms which will, in the opinion of the court, afford to the tenant security of tenure reasonably equivalent to the security afforded by Part VII of this Act in the case of a protected tenancy of a kind mentioned in paragraph (a) above,

713

and, in the opinion of the court, the accommodation fulfils the relevant conditions as defined in paragraph 5 below.

(2) [...]

5.—(1) For the purposes of paragraph 4 above, the relevant conditions are that the accommodation is reasonably suitable to the needs of the tenant and his family as regards proximity to place of work, and either—

(a) similar as regards rental and extent to the accommodation afforded by dwelling-houses provided in the neighbourhood by any local housing authority for persons whose needs as regards extent are, in the opinion of the court, similar to those of the tenant and of his family; or

(b) reasonably suitable to the means of the tenant and to the needs of the tenant and his family as regards extent and character; and

that if any furniture was provided for use under the protected or statutory tenancy in question, furniture is provided for use in the accommodation which is either similar to that so provided or is reasonably suitable to the needs of the tenant and his family.

(2) For the purposes of sub-paragraph (1)(a) above, a certificate of a housing authority stating—

(a) the extent of the accommodation afforded by dwelling-houses provided by the authority to meet the needs of tenants with families of such number as may be specified in the certificate, and

(b) the amount of the rent charged by the authority for dwelling-houses affording accommodation of that extent,

shall be conclusive evidence of the facts so stated.

6. Accommodation shall not be deemed to be suitable to the needs of the tenant and his family if the result of their occupation of the accommodation would be that it would be an overcrowded dwelling-house for the purposes of Part X of the Housing Act 1985.

7. Any document purporting to be a certificate of a local housing authority named therein issued for the purposes of this Schedule and to be signed by the proper officer of that authority shall be received in evidence and, unless the contrary is shown, shall be deemed to be such a certificate without further proof.

8. In this Part "local housing authority" and "district" in relation to such an authority have the same meaning as in the Housing Act 1985.

PART V

PROVISIONS APPLYING TO CASES 11, 12 AND 20

3A-267　　1. In this Part of this Schedule—

"mortgage" includes a charge and "mortgagee" shall be construed accordingly;

"owner" means, in relation to Case 11, the owner-occupied; and

"successor in title" means any person deriving title from the owner, other than a purchaser for value or a person deriving title from a purchaser for value.

2. The conditions referred to in paragraph (c) in each of Cases 11 and 12 and in paragraph (e)(ii) of Case 20 are that—

(a) the dwelling-house is required as a residence for the owner or any member of his family who resided with the owner when he last occupied the dwelling-house as a residence;

(b) the owner has retired from regular employment and requires the dwelling-house as a residence;

(c) the owner has died and the dwelling-house is required as a residence for a member of his family who was residing with him at the time of his death;

(d) the owner has died and the dwelling-house is required by a successor in title as his residence or for the purpose of disposing of it with vacant possession;

(e) the dwelling-house is subject to a mortgage, made by deed and granted before the tenancy, and the mortgagee—

(i) is entitled to exercise a power of sale conferred on him by the mortgage or by section 101 of the Law of Property Act 1925; and

(ii) requires the dwelling-house for the purpose of disposing of it with vacant possession in exercise of that power; and

(f) the dwelling-house is not reasonably suitable to the needs of the owner, having regard to his place of work, and he requires it for the purpose of disposing of it with vacant possession and of using the proceeds of that disposal in acquiring, as his residence, a dwelling-house which is more suitable to those needs.

Note —Amended by the Housing Act 1980, ss.55, 66 and 67, Scheds 7, 8 and 25; the **3A–268** Housing (Consequential Provisions) Act 1985, s.4, Sched.2, para. 35; the Rent (Amendment) Act 1985, ss.1, 66; the Housing and Planning Act 1986, s.13; and the Housing Act 1988, s.140, Sched.18.

Schedule 15 should be read in conjunction with s.98 (see para. 3A-182).

Note: Case 9 has been amended by the Civil Partnership Act 2004 s.81 and Sched.8. The amendment is not yet in force, but is printed at para. 3A–1525.

Cases 1 to 10 are discretionary grounds

The court may only make a possession order if it considers it reasonable to do so **3A–269** and the court has discretion to suspend any other in accordance with s.100 (see above). Cases 11 to 19 are mandatory grounds—if the ground is proved, the court must make a possession order to take effect in 14 days, or if there is exceptional hardship, a maximum of 42 days (see the Housing Act 1980, s.89, below).

Case 1

A landlord must prove either that there are rent arrears or that there has been a **3A–270** breach of a term or other obligation of the tenancy.

Rent arrears —A landlord must prove two things, first that rent was lawfully due **3A–271** from the tenant and second that some rent remained unpaid, at the date of issue of the claim. This applies only to rent which is due from the actual tenant against whom possession is claimed and not to that due from a predecessor of the present tenant (*Tickner v. Clifton* [1929] 1 K.B. 207). Rent becomes lawfully due at midnight on the day when it is payable (*Aspinall v. Aspinall* [1961] Ch. 526). If rent is tendered after the due date, but before the commencement of proceedings, that prevents rent from being "lawfully due" unless time has been made the essence of the contract. The words "lawfully due" mean that the obligation to pay rent must have arisen and not been discharged (*Bird v. Hildage* [1948] 1 K.B. 91; [1947] 2 All E.R. 7, CA). However, once a landlord shows that there were arrears of rent at the commencement of proceedings, the court has jurisdiction to make a possession order even if rent arrears are paid before the hearing (*Dellenty v. Pellow* [1951] 2 K.B. 858; [1951] 2 All E.R. 716, CA). *Prima facie* it would not ordinarily be reasonable to make a possession order in such circumstances (see *Hayman v. Rowlands* [1957] 1 W.L.R. 317; [1957] 1 All E.R. 321, CA) but where the tenant has frequently been in arrears and proceedings have been issued on a number of occasions, it may be reasonable to make a possession order (*Dellenty v. Pellow, supra*. See too *Lee-Steere v. Jennings* (1987) 20 H.L.R. 1, CA). See also *Laimond Properties Ltd v. Raeuchle*, also reported as *Raeuchle v. Laimond Properties Ltd* [2000] L & TR 319, December 1999 Legal Action 21, CA, April 2000 Legal Action 31, CA.

Failure to provide a rent book does not disentitle a landlord from recovering rent (*Shaw v. Groom* [1970] 2 Q.B. 504; [1970] 2 W.L.R. 299; [1970] 1 All E.R. 702, CA).

Breach of any other tenancy obligation —This limb of Case 1 is similar to the Hous- **3A–272** ing Act 1988, Sched.2, Ground 12 (see below).

It should be noted that the original terms of the contractual tenancy continue to bind a statutory tenant in so far as they are consistent with the provisions of the Rent Act 1977 (see s.3(1) above).

A proviso in a contractual tenancy giving the landlord a right of re-entry if the tenant becomes bankrupt is an obligation under the subsequent statutory tenancy within the meaning of Case 1 *Cadogan Estates Ltd v. McMahon* [2001] A.C. 378; [2000] 3 W.L.R. 1555; [2000] 4 All E.R. 897, HL.

Case 2

Nuisance or annoyance —"Nuisance" and "annoyance" are both used in the natural **3A–273** sense of the words. This ground may be satisfied by drunkenness, abusive behaviour, noise, obstructive behaviour towards other occupiers or violence (*per* Wood J. in *Cobstone Investments Ltd v. Maxim* [1984] 2 All E.R. 635). Unknown people coming to the

HOUSING

premises at all hours of the day and night may amount to an annoyance (*Florent v. Horez* (1984) 12 H.L.R. 1; (1983) 268 E.G. 807, CA).

It is not necessary for the premises of people complaining of nuisance or annoyance to be contiguous in the sense that they are physically joined to the dwelling-house rented by a defendant. The word "adjoining" is used in the wider sense of "neighbouring" (*Cobstone Investments Ltd v. Maxim* [1985] Q.B. 140; [1983] 3 W.L.R. 563; [1984] 2 All E.R. 635, CA). See too *Northampton B.C. v. Lovatt* (1998) 30 H.L.R. 875; (1998) 07 E.G. 142; *The Times*, January 3, 1998, CA.

3A-274   *Immoral of illegal purposes* —Where a landlord relies upon a conviction for using the dwelling-house or allowing the dwelling-house to be used for immoral or illegal purposes it is necessary to show that the crime has actually been committed on the premises and that the premises have been used for the purpose of committing the offence (*Abrahams v. Wilson* [1971] 2 Q.B. 88; [1971] 2 W.L.R. 923; [1971] 2 All E.R. 114, CA). For example, there is a difference between drugs being in a defendant's immediate possession, on the one hand, and on the other hand the tenant using the premises to store drugs.

In a claim for possession based on nuisance or annoyance to adjoining occupiers, a judge may infer that adjoining occupiers have been affected, even if none of them gives evidence of actual nuisance (*Frederick Platts Co Ltd v. Grigor* [1950] 1 All E.R. 941, CA).

Case 3

3A-275   This ground is similar to Ground 13 in the Housing Act 1988, Sched.2, see below.

There is no need for a landlord to give advance warning of an intention to issue proceedings relying on this ground (*Lowe v. Lendrum* (1950) 159 E.G. 423, CA) although failure to do so may be relevant when the court considers reasonableness and costs. See too *Holloway v. Povey* (1984) 15 H.L.R. 104; (1984) 271 E.G. 195, CA.

Case 5

3A-276   There must be a valid notice to quit before a landlord can rely on this ground for possession (*De Vries v. Sparks* (1927) 137 L.T. 441). The words "notice to quit" have their normal technical meaning and the disappearance of a tenant followed by the return by him of the keys does not amount to "notice to quit" (*Standingford v. Bruce* [1926] 1 K.B. 466).

Case 6

3A-277   The ground applies even if there is no prohibition against assigning or subletting in the tenancy agreement and covers a vesting assent made by executors of a deceased tenant which takes effect as an assignment (*Pazgate Ltd v. McGrath* (1984) 17 H.L.R. 127). It does not however apply unless all of the premises rented have been disposed of by assigning or subletting. In practice the ground is normally only of significance where there is subletting or assignment by a contractual tenant. If a statutory tenant sublets the whole of premises, Rent Act protection is lost because the tenant can no longer occupy the premises as his or her residence (see s.2 above, and *Poland v. Cadogan (Earl)* [1980] 3 All E.R. 544, CA, dealing with similar provisions in the Leasehold Reform Act 1967 where the comparable wording is slightly different).

Case 8

3A-278   This ground for possession is far more restrictive than Ground 16 in Sched.2 to the Housing Act 1988 (see below) which applies to assured tenants.

In order to succeed under this ground a landlord must prove that—

     (a) *the tenant was in the employment of the landlord or a former landlord at the time when the premises were let* (*Fuggle (RF) Ltd v. Gadsden* [1948] 2 K.B. 236). "Tenant" refers to the original contractual tenant (*Bolsover Colliery Co Ltd v. Abbott* [1946] K.B. 8);

     (b) *premises were let in consequence of that employment.* This is a question of fact in each case (*Long Eaton Co-op. v. Smith* [1949] 1 All E.R. 633). The questions to be asked are—

         (i) "What was the reason for the landlord letting the premises to the tenant?"

         (ii) "What was in the mind of the person who let the premises?"

(iii) "Was it let because of the tenant's employment or was there another reason?"

(Braithwaite & Co Ltd v. Elliot [1946] 2 All E.R. 537 at 539);

(c) *employment has ceased*; and

(d) *the premises are reasonably required by the landlord for occupation as a residence by someone engaged in the whole-time employment of the landlord or someone with whom a contract of employment has been entered into which is conditional on housing being provided.* When the court considers whether or not the proposed new occupant is employed or whether a contract of employment has been entered into, the relevant date is the date of the court hearing *(Benninga v. Bijstra* [1945] 2 All E.R. 433). Note that the premises must be reasonably required.

A tenant may be entitled to compensation if a landlord obtains an order for possession under Case 8 by misrepresentation or concealment. See s.102 above.

Case 9

"Reasonably required"—Case 9 applies where the premises are reasonably required as **3A–279** a residence by the landlord or certain specified members of the landlord's family. The words "reasonably required" mean more than a "desire" on the landlord's part, but less than "absolute necessity" *(Aitken v. Shaw* 1933 S.L.T. 21; *Kennealy v. Dunne* [1977] Q.B. 837). The court should consider whether this requirement is reasonable on the landlord's part, and in doing so the tenant's interests are not relevant *(Funnell v. Armstrong* [1962] E.G.D. 319). The relevant date for deciding whether the premises are required is the date of the hearing, not the date of commencement of proceedings *(Alexander v. Mohamadzadeh* (1985) 276 E.G. 1258, CA).

Where there are two or more joint beneficial owners, possession can be claimed under Case 9 only if possession is required for occupation as a residence for all or both of them *(McIntyre v. Hardcastle* [1948] 2 K.B. 82; [1948] 1 All E.R. 696, CA. The position is different under Case 11—see *Tilling v. Whiteman* [1979] 1 All E.R. 737, HL).

Landlord by purchase

Landlords are not entitled to rely on Case 9 if they became landlords by purchasing **3A–280** the premises after specified dates.

"Greater hardship"

Tenants have a complete defence to possession proceedings brought under Case 9 **3A–281** if they can prove that greater hardship would be caused to them by a possession order than would be caused to the landlord by refusing to grant the possession order. The burden of proving this lies on the tenant *(Smith v. Penny* [1947] K.B. 230; [1946] 2 All E.R. 672, CA; *Sims v. Wilson* [1946] 2 All E.R. 261). The court should consider how the balance of hardship will operate at the time when a possession order would take effect *(Wheeler v. Evans* [1948] 1 K.B. 459). The "greater hardship test" gives the court a very wide discretion to take into account all factors which may affect both landlord and tenant *(Robinson v. Donovan* [1946] 2 All E.R. 731).

Questions of greater hardship are essentially matters for county court judges, and their findings will normally only be overturned if no reasonable county court judge could have reached the same conclusion or if the decision was perverse. *(Hodges v. Blee* (1987) 283 E.G. 1215; (1988) 20 H.L.R. 32, CA; *cf.*, however, *Manaton v. Edwards* (1985) 276 E.G. 1256, CA, where, unusually, a county court judge's finding on greater hardship was overturned on appeal).

A tenant may be entitled to compensation if a landlord obtains an order for possession under Case 9 by misrepresentation or concealment. See s.102 above.

Case 11

This ground should be read in conjunction with Sched.15, Pt III, and Pt V. **3A–282**

The purpose of Case 11 was to allow owner-occupiers who intended to go away for a limited period but then to return home, to let the premises while they were away *(per* Griffiths L.J. in *Bradshaw v. Baldwin-Wiseman* (1985) 17 H.L.R. 260; (1985) 49 P.&C.R. 382 at 264).

To rely on Case 11 a landlord must prove that—

(a) *prior to the granting of the tenancy in question, the landlord had at some time in the past occupied the premises as his or her residence.* It is no longer necessary for landlords to prove that they occupied the premises immediately before the

Housing

granting of the tenancy. Residence at any time in the past is sufficient. It is sufficient for such previous residence to have been temporary and intermittent, although visits to a house by a landlord to stay with a girlfriend who lives there do not count as "occupation as a residence"(*Naish v. Curzon* (1984) 17 H.L.R. 220, CA; *Mistry v. Isidore* (1990) 22 H.L.R. 281; [1990] 2 E.G.L.R. 97, CA; and *Ibie v. Trubshaw* (1990) 22 H.L.R. 191, CA);

(b) *notice of his or her intention to rely on Case 11 was given before the commencement of the tenancy.* The schedule provides that such notice must be in writing, although no particular form is necessary. It has been said that it is "of the utmost importance to a tenant that he should appreciate when he takes rented property whether or not he is obtaining security of tenure" (*Bradshaw v. Baldwin-Wiseman, supra*). Alternatively, the landlord may satisfy the court that it is just and equitable to dispense with service of the notice. The criteria which apply are the same as under the Housing Act 1988, Sched.2, Pt I and the Housing Act 1985, s.83(1)(b) (as amended) (see below).

(c) *all tenants to whom the premises have previously been let since the dates specified in Case 11 have been given written notice.* Again there is a provision which entitles the court to dispense with this requirement if it is considered just and equitable; and

(d) *one of the requirements in* sub-paragraphs (a), (c), (d), (e) or (f) in Sched.15, Pt V *is satisfied.* The most important of these is that the premises are "required as a residence". All that is required is that the landlord "bona fide wants" or "genuinely has the immediate intention" of occupying the premises (*Kennealy v. Dunne* [1977] Q.B. 837, CA). The landlord need not require the premises as a permanent residence and fairly intermittent residence will be sufficient (*Naish v. Curzon* (1984) 17 H.L.R. 220, CA; and *Davies v. Peterson* (1989) 21 H.L.R. 63; (1989) 06 E.G. 130, CA). This is a question of fact in each case. It is sufficient if only one of two joint landlords requires the premises as a residence (*Tilling v. Whiteman* [1979] 1 All E.R. 737, HL).

Case 13

3A–283   *"right to occupy it for a holiday"* —See s.9 and commentary thereto, *supra*.

Case 14

3A–284   See s.8 and annotations thereto, *supra*.

Case 16

3A–285   The court cannot dispense with the requirement that notice must be served prior to the commencement of the tenancy. A term in a tenancy agreement that the tenant will vacate on 28 days' notice if the premises are required for another farm worker is not sufficient (*Fowler v. Minchin* (1987) 19 H.L.R. 224, CA), but a certificate of fair rent which was handed to the tenant before the commencement of the tenancy and which stated that the tenancy was to be subject to Case 16 has been held to be sufficient (*Springfield Investments v. Bell* (1990) 22 H.L.R. 440, CA).

Housing Act 1980

3A–286

(1980 c.51)

ARRANGEMENT OF SECTIONS

PART IV

JURISDICTION AND PROCEDURE

SECT.

* * * * *

PART IV

JURISDICTION AND PROCEDURE

Discretion of court in certain proceedings for possession

88.—(1) Where, under the terms of a rental purchase agreement, **3A–287** a person has been let into possession of a dwelling-house and, on the termination of the agreement or of his right to possession under it, proceedings are brought for the possession of the dwelling-house, the court may—

    (a) adjourn the proceedings; or

    (b) on making an order for the possession of the dwelling-house, stay or suspend execution of the order or postpone the date of possession;

for such period or periods as the court thinks fit.

(2) On any such adjournment, stay, suspension or postponement the court may impose such conditions with regard to payments by the person in possession in respect of his continued occupation of the dwelling-house and such other conditions as the court thinks fit.

(3) The court may revoke or from time to time vary any condition imposed by virtue of this section.

(4) In this section "rental purchase agreement" means an agreement for the purchase of a dwelling-house (whether freehold or leasehold property) under which the whole or part of the purchase price is to be paid in three or more instalments and the completion of the purchase is deferred until the whole or a specified part of the purchase price has been paid.

(5) This section extends to proceedings for the possession of a dwelling-house which were begun before the commencement of this section unless an order for the possession of the dwelling-house was made in the proceedings and executed before the commencement of this section.

"rental purchase agreement"
    See s.88(4).   **3A–288**

Restriction on discretion of court in making orders for possession of land

89.—(1) Where a court makes an order for the possession of any **3A–289** land in a case not falling within the exceptions mentioned in subsection (2) below, the giving up of possession shall not be postponed (whether by the order or any variation, suspension or stay of execution) to a date later than fourteen days after the making of the order, unless it appears to the court that exceptional hardship would be caused by requiring possession to be given up by that date; and shall not in any event be postponed to a date later than six weeks after the making of the order.

(2) The restrictions in subsection (1) above do not apply if—

    (a) the order is made in an action by a mortgagee for possession; or

(b) the order is made in an action for forfeiture of a lease; or

(c) the court had power to make the order only if it considered it reasonable to make it; or

(d) the order relates to a dwelling-house which is the subject of a restricted contract (within the meaning of section 19 of the 1977 Act); or

(e) the order is made in proceedings brought as mentioned in section 88(1) above.

Restriction on discretion of court in making orders for possession of land

3A–290   At common law judges had a discretion to allow occupiers a reasonable time before a possession order took effect even if they had no security of tenure (*Air Ministry v. Harris* [1951] 2 All E.R. 862 (six months too long for licensees); *Sheffield Corp. v. Luxford* [1929] 2 K.B. 180 (one year too long); *Jones v. Savery* [1951] 1 All E.R. 820 (one month reasonable)). However, this discretion was largely taken away by the Housing Act 1980. Apart from the exceptions contained in the section, county court orders for possession must now take effect not later than 14 days after the making of the order unless it would cause exceptional hardship, in which case the order can be postponed to a date which is not more than six weeks after the making of the order.

In *Hackney LBC v. Side by Side (Kids) Ltd* [2003] EWHC 1813 (QBD); [2004] 1 W.L.R. 363, Stanley Burnton J. held that Housing Act 1980, s.89 applies as much to orders made in the High Court as to those made in the county court. The decision of Harman J. in *Bain & Co. v. Church Commissioners for England* [1989] 1 W.L.R. 24, Ch D, that "a court" meant "a county court" was clearly wrong. Further, Stanley Burnton J. held that the general words of s.89 "did not permit him to find that it did not apply to consent orders".

There are no reported decisions on the meaning of "exceptional hardship".

Supreme Court Act 1981

(1981 c.54)

Relief against forfeiture for non-payment of rent

3A–291   **38.**—(1) In any action in the High Court for the forfeiture of a lease for non-payment rent, the court shall have power to grant relief against forfeiture in a summary manner, and may do so subject to the same terms and conditions as to the payment of rent, costs or otherwise as could have been imposed by it in such an action immediately before the commencement of this Act.

(2) Where the lessee or a person deriving title under him is granted relief under this section, he shall hold the demised premises in accordance with the terms of the lease without the necessity for a new lease.

Relief against forfeiture for non-payment of rent

3A–292   Relief from forfeiture for non-payment of rent may be obtained under the Common Law Procedure Act 1852, ss.210 to 212, or in a summary way under s.38 of the 1981 Act. "The Court, in exercising its jurisdiction to grant relief in cases of non-payment of rent is, of course, proceeding on the old principles of the Court of Equity which always regarded the condition of re-entry as being merely security for the payment of the rent and gave relief if the landlord could get his rent" (*Chandless-Chandless v. Nicholson* [1942] 2 K.B. 321, CA, at 323 *per* Lord Greene M.R.). Save in exceptional circumstances, therefore, the Court grants relief where all the rent and costs have been paid or tendered (*Gill v. Lewis* [1956] 2 Q.B. 1, CA).

Where an order is made giving relief in terms to be performed within a specified time, the Court has power to extend the time, even though the original order did not expressly reserve "liberty to apply" (see *Chandless-Chandless v. Nicholson*, above). Since the Court can grant relief under this section in the exercise of the same powers as it could "immediately before the commencement of this Act," if relief from forfeiture is granted, the lessee will hold the demised premises according to the terms of the lease and without the necessity of any new lease (see s.46 of the Supreme Court of Judicature (Consolidation) Act 1925).

A statutory tenant under the Rent Act cannot claim relief under this section or s.146 of the LPA 1925 (see *Brewer v. Jacobs* [1923] 1 K.B. 528).

As to relief against breaches of other covenants, see the LPA 1925, s.146.

Note also the County Courts Act 1984, s.138 (Provisions as to forfeiture for non-payment of rent), para. 3A–294, below, and notes thereto, and, in particular, the explanation there of the effect of, and the legislative response to, *Di Palma v. Victoria Square Property Co. Ltd* [1986] Ch. 150; [1985] 2 All E.R. 676, CA.

County Courts Act 1984

(1984 c.28)   3A–293

ARRANGEMENT OF SECTIONS

FORFEITURE FOR NON-PAYMENT OF RENT

FORFEITURE FOR NON-PAYMENT OF RENT

Provisions as to forfeiture for non-payment of rent

138.—(1) This section has effect where a lessor is proceeding by ac-   3A–294
tion in a county court (being an action in which the county court has jurisdiction) to enforce against a lessee a right of re-entry or forfeiture in respect of any land for non-payment of rent.

(2) If the lessee pays into court or to the lessor not less than 5 clear days before the return day all the rent in arrear and the costs of the action, the action shall cease, and the lessee shall hold the land according to the lease without any new lease.

(3) If—
    (a) the action does not cease under subsection (2); and
    (b) the court at the trial is satisfied that the lessor is entitled to enforce the right of re-entry or forfeiture,
the court shall order possession of the land to be given to the lessor at the expiration of such period, not being less than 4 weeks from the date of the order, as the court thinks fit, unless within that period the lessee pays into court or to the lessor all the rent in arrear and the costs of the action.

(4) The court may extend the period specified under subsection (3) at any time before possession of the land is recovered in pursuance of the order under that subsection.

(5) [...] if—
    (a) within the period specified in the order; or
    (b) within that period as extended under subsection (4),
the lessee pays into court or to the lessor—
      (i) all the rent in arrear; and

      (ii) the costs of the action,

he shall hold the land acording to the lease without any new lease.

(6) Subsection (2) shall not apply where the lessor is proceeding in the same action to enforce a right of re-entry or forfeiture on any other ground as well as for non-payment of rent, or to enforce any other claim as well as the right of re-entry or forfeiture and the claim for arrears of rent.

(7) If the lessee does not—

      (a) within the period specified in the order; or

      (b) with that period as extended under subsection (4), pay into court or to the lessor—

          (i) all the rent in arrear; and

          (ii) the costs of the action,

the order shall be enforceable in the prescribed manner and so long as the order remains unreversed the lessee shall, subject to subsections (8) and (9A), be barred from all relief.

(8) The extension under subsection (4) of a period fixed by a court shall not be treated as relief from which the lessee is barred by subsection (7) if he fails to pay into court or to the lessor all the rent in arrear and the costs of the action within that period.

(9) Where the court extends a period under subsection (4) at a time when—

      (a) that period has expired; and

      (b) a warrant has been issued for the possession of the land, the court shall suspend the warrant for the extended period; and, if before the expiration period, the lessee pays into court or to the lessor all the rent in arrear and all the costs of the action, the court shall cancel the warrant.

(9A) Where the lessor recovers possession of the land at any time after the making of the order under subsection (3) (whether as a result of the enforcement of the order or otherwise) the lessee may, at any time within six months from the date on which the lessor recovers possession, apply to the court for relief; and on any such application the court may, if it thinks fit, grant to the lessee such relief, subject to such terms and conditions, as it thinks fit.

(9B) Where the lessee is granted relief on an application under subsection (9A) he shall hold the land according to the lease without any new lease.

(9C) An application under subsection (9A) may be made by a person with an interest under a lease of the land derived (whether immediately or otherwise) from the lessee's interest therein in like manner as if he were the lessee; and on any such application the court may make an order which (subject to such terms and conditions as the court thinks fit) vests the land in such a person, as lessee of the lessor, for the remainder of the term of the lease under which he has any such interest as aforesaid, or for any lesser term.

In this subsection any reference to the land includes a reference to a part of the land.

(10) Nothing in this section or section 139 shall be taken to affect—

(a) the power of the court to make any order which it would otherwise have power to make as respects a right of re-entry or forfeiture on any ground other than non-payment of rent; or

(b) section 146(4) of the Law of Property Act 1925 (relief against forfeiture).

Note —Amended by the Administration of Justice Act 1985, ss.55 and 67(2), and **3A–295**
Sched.8; and the Courts and Legal Services Act 1990, s.125(2), Sched.17, para. 17.
See Form N27 (PD to CPR Pt 4, Table 3).

General note

Forfeiture is a remedy which may be available to a lessor against a lessee prior to **3A–296**
expiry of a fixed term lease; it has the effect of dispossessing the lessee. The remedy
may be available, not only where the lessee fails to pay rent, but also in other circumstances (*e.g.* breach of any other covenant). This section has effect where a lessor is
proceeding by action in a county court to enforce against a lessee a right of re-entry or
forfeiture in respect of any land for non-payment of rent. Where proceedings to
enforce a right of re-entry or forfeiture are brought for non-payment of rent and for
some other reason, or for some other reason alone, the Law of Property Act 1925,
s.146 is likely to apply. The 1925 Act may also apply where land has been forfeited,
not by action, but by the lessor's re-entry without action; see also s.139(2), below.

Peaceable re-entry of premises "let as a dwelling" is unlawful while there is "any
person lawfully residing" in them or any part of them (see the Protection from Eviction Act 1977, s.2, above). In such circumstances possession proceedings must be
brought in court.

For the restriction on forfeiture or re-entry for arrears of service charges see the
Housing Act 1996, s.81, below.

In relation to proceedings in the High Court, legislation dealing with forfeiture for
non-payment of rent is found in the Common Law Procedure Act 1852, ss.210 to 212
(re-enacting provisions in the Landlord and Tenant Act 1730). But this legislation is
not as elaborate as s.138; case law supplies the deficiencies. Note also the SCA 1981,
s.38 (summary relief against forfeiture for non-payment of rent) (see para. 3A–291
and commentary thereto).

In the CCA 1959, provisions as to the enforcement by action of a right of re-entry
or forfeiture for non-payment of rent were found in s.191 (as amended by the
Administration of Justice Act 1965, s.23). This section created certain difficulties, not
all of which were remedied by the re-enactment of s.191, with some modifications, as
s.138 of the 1984 Act. Consequently, the Administration of Justice Act 1985, s.55
added subss.(9A) to (9C) and made some minor amendments to subss.(5) and (7). The
principal difficulty which had arisen was that the extent of the powers of the High
Court, on the one hand, and of the county courts, on the other, differed and the relationship between the respective powers was a matter for doubt (see *Di Palma v. Victoria
Square Property Co. Ltd* [1986] Ch. 150; [1985] 2 All E.R. 676, CA).

As a result of the Courts and Legal Services Act 1990, s.1 and Orders made under
that section certain financial limits on the jurisdiction of county courts in relation to
actions of the type referred to in subs.(1) of this section were removed and the jurisdictions of the High Court and the county courts became, in effect, co-terminous. At the
same time, for the purpose of removing unnecessary distinctions between the two
levels of jurisdiction, the words "or to the lessor" were added to subss.(2), (3), (5), (7),
(8) and (9) by Sched.17, para. 17 of the 1990 Act.

In effect, s.138 codifies an old equitable jurisdiction. The policy of the law stated in
the section is to give lessees, against whom a right of re-entry or forfeiture may be
enforced by a lessor for non-payment of rent, protections he would not otherwise
enjoy, and which have the potential for enabling him to continue in occupation as lessee; where the protections apply, the lessee is relieved against forfeiture.

The section has no application to a case where there are arrears of service charges
not deemed by the terms of the lease to be additional rent (*Escalus Properties Ltd v.
Robinson* [1996] Q.B. 231; [1995] 3 W.L.R. 524, CA).

HOUSING

Service by the lessor on the lessee of a notice under the Law of Property Act 1925, s.146, forfeiting a lease on grounds other than non-payment of rent, does not prevent the lessor subsequently claiming from the lessee under s.138 forfeiture for non-payment of rent due before service of the notice (*Church Commissioners for England v. Nodjoumi* (1986) 51 P. & C.R. 155).

The broad scheme of s.138 is as follows. Subs.(2) states that, where a lessor brings an action to enforce a right of re-entry of forfeiture for non-payment of rent (but not for some other reason) and the action is not a mixed claim (see subs.(6)), then if the lessee pays arrears and costs within the time stipulated in that subsection he is relieved from forfeiture automatically; the action shall "cease" and the lease shall continue. Subss.(3) to (5) state that if the tenant does not so pay up and the court at trial is satisfied that the lessor is entitled to his remedy the court shall suspend the order for possession giving the lessee further time to pay. The time limit may be extended (and any warrant for possession suspended accordingly, see subs.(9)). If the tenant pays during the period of suspension, again he is relieved from forfeiture automatically (and any warrant is cancelled, see subs.(9)). If the tenant fails to pay, subs.(7) comes into play. This provision states that in these circumstances the order shall be enforceable in the prescribed manner and so long as the order remains unreversed the lessee shall "be barred from all relief", not only relief in any county court but also in the High Court. The lessor may proceed with a warrant for possession for the purpose of recovering possession. However, even in this event, from the tenant's point of view, all is not lost. At this late stage, if the lessor has not recovered possession (in pursuance of an order under subs.(3)), the tenant may still apply under subs.(4) for an extension (or a further extension) of the period for suspension of the order for possession fixed under subs.(3). It has been held in a county court that the divorced wife of a lessee, although not herself a lessee within the meaning of s.138, was a beneficial co-owner and so entitled to apply for an extension of time under s.138(4) and to pay the arrears on behalf of the lessee (*Bassett Road HA v. Gough* [1998] 5 C.L.Y. 3653, Central London County Court). Further, if the lessor has recovered possession (whether as a result of the enforcement of the order or otherwise) the lessee may at any time within six months from the date on which the lessor recovered possession, apply to the court for relief (subs.(9A)). On such application relief is not automatic but discretionary; the court may grant relief as it thinks fit. (An application under subs.(9A) may be made by a person with an interest under a lease of land derived from the lessee's interest, subs.(9C), see further below.) In these two respects the lessee is not, in the terms of subs.(7), "barred from all relief" for his failure to pay within the period specified in the order for possession or as extended (as the case may be).

"lessor","lessee","lease"

3A–297   For definitions, see s.140(1). "Lessee" includes mortgagee (*United Dominions Trust Ltd v. Shellpoint Trustees Ltd* [1993] 4 All E.R. 310, CA).

Service of claim

3A–298   If (a) one-half-year's rent is in arrear at the time of the commencement of the action, and (b) the lessor has a right to re-enter for non-payment of that rent, and (c) no sufficient distress is to be found on the premises countervailing the arrears then due, the service of the claim in the action shall stand in lieu of a demand and re-entry (s.139(1)). As to proof of insufficient distress, see *Rickett v. Green* [1910] 1 K.B. 253.

"not less than 5 clear days before the return day" (subs.(2))

3A–299   Section 147(1) states that "return day" means the day appointed in any summons or proceeding for the appearance of the defendant or any other day fixed for the hearing of any proceedings. In subs.(2) "return day" means the day so fixed, and not any later date upon which the action would fall actually to be tried in the absence of a payment under the subsection (*Swordheath Properties Ltd v. Bolt* [1992] 2 E.G.L.R. 68; [1992] 38 E.G. 152, CA, following *R. v. Registrar of the County Court at Leeds* (1886) 16 Q.B.D. 691, DC).

Lessee paying into court or to lessor (subss.(2), (3), (5), (7), (8) & (9))

3A–300   Where payment into court or (semble) to the lessor of arrears of rent and costs is made by a person other than the lessee and that person does not make the payment on behalf of the lessee (*e.g.* an underlessee or mortgagee), the action does not "cease" by operation of subs.(2) as "lessee" in that subsection means the lessee against whom the action is brought as referred to in subs.(1) (*Matthews v. Dobbins* [1963] 1 W.L.R. 227; [1963] 1 All E.R. 417, CA).

"the court shall order possession" (subs.(3))

Subs.(3) states that, if (a) the action does not cease under subs.(2), and (b) the court at the trial is satisfied that the lessor is entitled to enforce the right of re-entry or for-feiture, "the court shall order possession of the land". Where without doubt a lessor has established his claim he should be given judgment and the trial should not be adjourned against the wishes of the lessor except for good reason (*R. v. Circuit Judge (sitting at Norwich Court), ex p. Wathen* (1977) 33 P. & C.R. 423; (1976) 238 E.G. 45— in that case to give the lessee the opportunity to pay off the arrears).

3A–301

Possession to be given at expiration of specified period

An order for possession under subs.(3) must be suspended as provided by that subsection. Subs.(4) provides that the period may be extended at any time before pos-session of the land is recovered "in pursuance of the order" under subs.(3). There is some authority for the proposition that recovery of possession "in pursuance of the or-der" means recovery under a warrant for possession and not by other means (*Gadsby and Mitchell v. Price and Harrison* [1985] C.L.Y. 1877).

3A–302

"lessee pays...all the rent in arrear" (subss.(2), (3), (5), (7) & (9))

The lease comes to an end when the claim is served. Rent is payable to the date of service and mesne profits thereafter. To facilitate the calculation of rent payable to date of service where rent is paid in arrears, the particulars of claim should state the daily rate at which the rent in arrear is to be calculated (PD 55, para. 2.3(3)). Where the rent is payable in advance the lessor is entitled to be paid any rent due on a rent day which falls between issue and service (*Canas Property Co. v. KL Television Services* [1970] 2 Q.B. 433; [1970] 2 All E.R. 795, CA, see also *Capital and City Holdings Ltd v. Dean Warburg Ltd* (1989) 58 P. & C.R. 346, CA).

3A–303

In *Maryland Estates v. Joseph* [1999] 1 W.L.R. 83; [1998] 3 All E.R. 193, CA, the Court of Appeal, held that the words used in County Courts Act 1984, s.138(3) ("the lessee pays into court... all the rent in arrear") are not to be construed to mean that the court can order payment only of the rent in arrear at the date of the claim. It is to be assumed that leases continue after service of claims and that tenants remain under an obligation to pay sums reserved in leases as rent and that "all the rent in arrear" means the rent payable up to the date stated in the order.

Lessee's application for relief under subs.(9A)

Where the lessor recovers possession at any time after the making of the order for possession under subs.(3), whether as a result of the enforcement of the order or otherwise (*e.g.* where the lessee left voluntarily) the lessee may at any time within six months from the date on which the lessor recovers possession apply to the court for relief. Upon such application, the court "may, if it thinks fit, grant to the lessee such relief, subject to such terms and conditions, as it thinks fit". Guidance on the exercise of the power to grant relief was given in *Chandless-Chandless v. Nicholson* [1942] 2 K.B. 321; [1942] 2 All E.R. 315, CA, and *Gill v. Lewis* [1956] 2 Q.B. 1; [1956] 2 W.L.R. 962, CA. See also *Silverman v. AFCO (UK) Ltd* (1988) 56 P. & C.R. 185, CA (very late ap-plication made after a new lease to a third party had been executed properly refused); *Varndean Estates Ltd v. Buckland and Buckland* (1967) 111 S.J. 684, CA (period of 18 months for the payment of the arrears of rent reasonable in the special circumstances, and arrears should include amount owing under earlier judgment in respect of ar-rears); *Brompton Securities Ltd (No. 2), Re* [1988] 3 All E.R. 677 (save in exceptional cir-cumstances, relief may be granted notwithstanding lessor has been bad payer in past); *Three Stars Property Holdings v. Driscoll* [1986] CA Transcript 927; [1988] C.L.Y. 2795 (full payment of costs incurred by lessor may be imposed as a condition notwithstand-ing lessee legally aided with a nil contribution).

3A–304

Application "by a person with an interest... derived... from the lessee's interest" (subs.(9C))

PD 55, para 2.4 states that where the lessor knows of any person entitled to claim relief against forfeiture as underlessee (including a mortgagee) under subs.(9C) he shall give the name and address of that person in his particulars of claim and file a copy of the particulars for service on him. The holder of a charging order who has

3A–305

HOUSING

registered his interest is "a person with an interest under a lease" and may apply for relief from forfeiture under s.138(9C) (*Croydon (Unique) Ltd v. Wright* [2001] Ch. 318; [2000] 2 W.L.R. 683; [1999] 4 All E.R. 257, CA).

An underlessee or mortgagee who fails to avail himself of the procedure for automatic relief provided for by subss.(2) and (5) may, by virtue of subs.(7), be barred from all relief, subject only to his right to apply for discretionary relief under subss.(9A) and (9C) within the specified six month period (*United Dominions Trust Ltd v. Shellpoint Trustees Ltd* [1993] 4 All E.R. 310, CA; see also *Escalus Properties Ltd v. Robinson* [1996] Q.B. 231; [1995] 3 W.L.R. 524, CA).

Law of Property Act 1925, s.146(4)

3A–306   Section 138 has effect only where proceedings are brought for non-payment of rent. Subs.(10) states that nothing in this section (or in s.139) shall be taken to affect the power of the court to make any order which it would otherwise have power to make as respects a right of re-entry or forfeiture "on any ground other than non-payment of rent". Consequently, for example, the section does not affect the power of the court to grant relief from forfeiture to a lessee under s.146(2) of the 1925 Act, or to under-lessees claiming relief under s.146(4) of that Act. Relief from forfeiture may not be granted to a lessee under s.146(2) in proceedings based only on non-payment of rent (see s.146(11)). However, relief in proceedings based only on non-payment of rent, as well as proceedings based on other grounds (either additionally or alternatively), may be granted to an under-lessee under s.146(4). Because of this distinction between subss.(2) and (4) of s.146 of the 1925 Act, subs.(10) of this section further provides that nothing in s.138 (or in s.139) shall be taken to affect s.146(4).

Service of summons and re-entry

3A–307   **139.**—(1) In a case where section 138 has effect, if—

    (a) one-half-year's rent is in arrear at the time of the commencement of the action; and

    (b) the lessor has a right to re-enter for non-payment of that rent; and

    (c) no sufficient distress is to be found on the premises countervailing the arrears then due,

the service of the summons in the action in the prescribed manner shall stand in lieu of a demand and re-entry.

(2) Where a lessor has enforced against a lessee, by re-entry without action, a right of re-entry or forfeiture as respects any land for non-payment of rent, the lessee may ... at any time within six months from the date on which the lessor re-entered apply to the county court for relief, and on any such application the court may, if it thinks fit, grant to the lessee such relief as the High Court could have granted.

(3) Subsections (9B) and (C) of section 138 shall have effect in relation to an application under subsection (2) of this section as they have effect in relation to an application under subsection (9A) of that section.

3A–308   *Note* —Amended by the Administration of Justice Act 1985, s.55; and the High Court and County Courts Jurisdiction Order 1991 (S.I. 1991 No. 724), Schedule, Pt I.

The county court has unlimited jurisdiction.

"lease", "lessee", "lessor", "under-lease", "under-lessee"

3A–309   See s.140.

Interpretation of sections 138 and 139

3A–310   **140.** For the purposes of sections 138 and 139—

"lease" includes—

    (a) an original or derivative under-lease;

    (b) an agreement for a lease where the lessee has become entitled to have his lease granted; and

    (c) a grant at a fee farm rent, or under a grant securing a rent by condition;

"lessee" includes—

    (a) an original or derivative under-lessee;

    (b) the persons deriving title under a lessee;

    (c) a grantee under a grant at a fee farm rent, or under a grant securing a rent by condition; and

    (d) the persons deriving title under such a grantee;

"lessor" includes—

    (a) an original or derivative under-lessor;

    (b) the persons deriving title under a lessor;

    (c) a person making a grant at a fee farm rent, or a grant securing a rent by condition; and

    (d) the persons deriving title under such a grantor;

"under-lease" includes an agreement for an under-lease where the under-lessee has become entitled to have his under-lease granted; and

"under-lessee" includes any person deriving title under an under-lessee.

Housing Act 1985

(1985 c.68)

3A–311

PART I

INTRODUCTORY PROVISIONS

LOCAL HOUSING AUTHORITIES

Local housing authorities

3A–312 **1.** In this Act "local housing authority" means a district council, a London borough council, the Common Council of the City of London, a Welsh county council or county borough council, or the Council of the Isles of Scilly.

Note—Amended by the Local Government (Wales) Act 1994, Sched.8, para. 5(1). **3A–313**

* * * *

OTHER AUTHORITIES AND BODIES

Other descriptions of authority

4. In this Act—   **3A–314**

(a) "housing authority" means a local housing authority, or a new town corporation;

(b) "new town corporation" means a development corporation or the Commission for the New Towns;

(c) "development corporation" means a development corporation established by an order made, or having effect as if made, under the New Towns Act 1981;

(d) "urban development corporation" means an urban development corporation established under Part XVI of the Local Government, Planning and Land Act 1980;

(e) "local authority" means a county, county borough, district or London borough council, the Common Council of the City of London or the Council of the Isles of Scilly, in sections 43, 44 and 232 includes the Broads Authority, in sections 438, 441, 442, 443, and 458 includes the Broads Authority and a joint authority established by Part IV of the Local Government Act 1985 and the London Fire and Emergency Planning Authority, and in sections 45(2)(b), 50(2), 51(6), 80(1), 157(1), 171(2), 573(1), paragraph 2(1) of Schedule 1, grounds 7 and 12 in Schedule 2, ground 5 in Schedule 3, paragraph 7(1) of Schedule 4, paragraph 5(1)(b) of Schedule 5 and Schedule 16 includes the Broads Authority, a police authority established under section 3 of the Police Act 1996, [...] a joint authority established by Part IV of the Local Government Act 1985 and the London Fire and Emergency Planning Authority.

(f) "housing action trust" means a housing action established under Part III of the Housing Act 1988.

Note—Amended by S.I. 1986 No. 1; the Norfolk and Suffolk Broads Act 1988, s.21, **3A–315** Sched.6, para. 25; the Education Reform Act 1988, s.237(2), Sched.13; the Housing Act 1988, s.62(7); the Local Government (Wales) Act 1994, s.22(2), Sched.8, para. 5(3); the Police and Magistrates' Courts Act 1994, ss.43, 93, Scheds 4 and 9; the Police Act 1996, s.103(1) Sched.7; the Police Act 1997, Sched.9, para. 49; the Government of Wales Act 1998, Sched.15, para. 7; the Greater London Authority Act 1999, Sched.29, para.42; the Criminal Justice and Police Act 2001, Sched.7, Pt 5 and the Police Reform Act 2002, Sched.8, para.1.

Housing associations

5.—(1) In this Act "housing association" means a society, body of **3A–316** trustees or company—

(a) which is established for the purpose of, or amongst whose objects or powers are included those of, providing, constructing, improving or managing, or facilitating

HOUSING

729

or encouraging the construction or improvement of, housing accommodation, and

(b) which does not trade for profit or whose constitution or rules prohibit the issue of capital with interest or dividend exceeding such rate as may be prescribed by the Treasury, whether with or without differentiation as between share and loan capital.

(2) In this Act "fully mutual", in relation to a housing association, means that the rules of the association—

(a) restrict membership to persons who are tenants or prospective tenants of the association, and

(b) preclude the granting or assignment of tenancies to persons other than members;

and "co-operative housing association" means a fully mutual housing association which is a society registered under the Industrial and Provident Societies Act 1965.

(3) In this Act "self-build society" means a housing association whose object is to provide, for sale to, or occupation by, its members, dwellings built or improved principally with the use of its members' own labour.

(4) In this Act "registered social landlord" means—

(a) a housing association registered in the register maintained by the Housing Corporation under section 1 of the Housing Act 1996, or

(b) a housing association registered in the register maintained by the Secretary of State under section 1 of the Housing Act 1996,

subject as follows.

(5) References to registered social landlords include, where the context so permits, references to housing associations registered in the register maintained by Scottish Homes under section 3 of the Housing Associations Act 1985 (Scottish registered housing associations).

3A–317   *Note* —Amended by the Housing Act 1996 (Consequential Provisions) Order 1996 (S.I. 1996 No. 2325), Art. 5, Sched.2, para. 14(1), (2); and the Government of Wales Act 1998, s.140 and Sched.16, para. 6. See too *Qazi v. Harrow LBC* [2003] UKHL 43; [2003] 3 WLR 792; [2003] 4 All ER 461; The Times, August 1, 2003, where Lord Hope and Lord Scott said that contractual and property rights cannot be defeated by a defence based on Article 8.

Housing associations and the Human Rights Act 1998

3A–318   Whilst the activities of a housing association need not involve the performance of public functions, in taking over the responsibilities of a local housing authority as landlord of a tenant who had been granted a non-secure tenancy pending the determination of her application as a homeless person and in deciding to bring possession proceedings, the functions of a housing association were so closely assimilated to the council that it was properly to be regarded as a functional public authority within the meaning of the Human Rights Act 1998, s.6(1) (*Poplar HARCA v. Donoghue* [2002] Q.B. 48; [2001] 3 W.L.R. 183; [2001] 4 All E.R. 606, CA.

Housing trusts

3A–319   **6.** In this Act "housing trust" means a corporation or body of persons which—

(a) is required by the terms of its constituent instrument to use the whole of its funds, including any surplus which may arise from its operations, for the purpose of providing housing accommodation, or

(b) is required by the terms of its constituent instrument to devote the whole, or substantially the whole, of its funds for charitable purposes and in fact uses the whole, or substantially the whole, of its funds for the purpose of providing housing accommodation.

Relevant Authority

6A.—(1) In this Act "the Relevant Authority" means the Housing Corporation, the Secretary of State or Scottish Homes, subject as follows. **3A–320**

(2) In relation to a housing association which is—

(a) a registered charity which has its address for the purposes of registration by the Charity Commissioners in Wales,

(b) a society registered under the Industrial and Provident Societies Act 1965 which has its registered office for the purposes of that Act in Wales, or

(c) a company registered under the Companies Act 1985 which has its registered office for the purposes of that Act in Wales,

"the Relevant Authority" means the Secretary of State.

(3) In relation to a housing association which is a society registered under the Industrial and Provident Societies Act 1965 which has its registered office for the purposes of that Act in Scotland, "the Relevant Authority" means Scottish Homes.

(4) In relation to any other housing association which is a registered charity, a society registered under the Industrial and Provident Societies Act 1965 or a company registered under the Companies Act 1985, "the Relevant Authority" means the Housing Corporation.

(5) In this section "registered charity" means a charity which is registered under section 3 of the Charities Act 1993 and is not an exempt charity within the meaning of that Act.

Note—Inserted by the Housing Act 1988, Sched.17; substituted by the Housing Act 1996 (Consequential Provisions) Order 1996 (S.I. 1996 No. 2325), art.5, Sched.2, para. 14(1), (3). Amended by the Government of Wales Act 1998, s.140 and Sched.16, paras 5 and 7. **3A–321**

* * * *

PART IV

SECURE TENANCIES AND RIGHTS OF SECURE TENANTS

SECURITY OF TENURE

Secure tenancies

79.—(1) A tenancy under which a dwelling-house is let as a sepa- **3A–322**

rate dwelling is a secure tenancy at any time when the conditions described in sections 80 and 81 as the landlord condition and the tenant condition are satisfied.

(2) Subsection (1) has effect subject to—

(a) the exceptions in Schedule 1 (tenancies which are not secure tenancies),

(b) sections 89(3) and (4) and 90(3) and (4) (tenancies ceasing to be secure after death of tenant), and

(c) sections 91(2) and 93(2) (tenancies ceasing to be secure in consequence of assignment or subletting).

(3) The provisions of this Part apply in relation to a licence to occupy a dwelling-house (whether or not granted for a consideration) as they apply in relation to a tenancy.

(4) Subsection (3) does not apply to a licence granted as a temporary expedient to a person who entered the dwelling-house or any other land as a trespasser (whether or not, before the grant of that licence, another licence to occupy that or another dwelling-house had been granted to him).

"separate dwelling"

3A–323   See annotations to Rent Act 1977, s.1 above.

"dwelling-house"

3A–324   See s.112.

"landlord condition"

3A–325   See s.80.

"tenant condition"

3A–326   See s.81.

Secure tenancies

3A–327   This section provides the basic definition of a "secure tenancy" (or, in most circumstances, licence—see s.79(3) and (4)). The exceptions to security of tenure are set out in Sched.1, ss.89(3) and (4), 90(3) and (4), and 91(2) and (3). It is doubtful whether Parliament intended that a tenancy at will could be a secure tenancy, even where the conditions in ss.80 and s.81 are satisfied (*Banjo v. Brent LBC* [2005] EWCA Civ 292; [2005] 1 WLR 2520 .

Sub-tenancies

3A–328   A secure tenancy for the purpose of s.79 is one in which there is a direct landlord and tenant relationship between a landlord, satisfying the landlord condition in s.80, and a tenant, satisfying the tenant condition in s.81. If a local housing authority grants a lease to a charitable housing trust which in turn grants a sub-tenancy to an individual who lives in the property, the occupier's secure sub-tenancy persists while the intermediate lease continues, so long as the parties continue to meet the landlord and tenant conditions. As soon as either of them ceases to do so or the sub-lease in respect of which s.79 provided security ceases to exist, so also does the secure sub-tenancy (*Lambeth LBC v. Kay* [2004] EWCA Civ 926; [2004] H.L.R. 56 and *Bruton v. London and Quadrant Housing Trust* [2000] 1 A.C. 406; [1999] 3 W.L.R. 150, HL).

The landlord condition

3A–329   **80.**—(1) The landlord condition is that the interest of the landlord belongs to one of the following authorities or bodies—

a local authority,

a new town corporation,

a housing action trust,

an urban development corporation, or

housing co-operative to which this section applies.

(2) [...]

(3) If a co-operative housing association ceases to be a registered social landlord, it shall, within the period of 21 days beginning with the date on which it ceases to be a registered social landlord, notify each of its tenants who thereby becomes a secure tenant, in writing, that he has become a secure tenant.

(4) This section applies to a housing co-operative within the meaning of section 27B (agreements under certain superseded provisions) where the dwelling-house is comprised in a housing co-operative agreement within the meaning of that section.

Note —Amended by the Housing Act 1996 (Consequential Provisions) Order 1996 **3A–330** (S.I. 1996 No. 2325), art.5, Sched.2; the Housing Act 1988, Sched.18; the Housing and Planning Act 1986, Sched.5 and the Government of Wales Act 1998, Sched.18, Pt IV.

"local authority"

See s.4. **3A–331**

"housing action trust"

See s.4. **3A–332**

"an urban development corporation"

See s.4. **3A–333**

"housing co-operative"

See s.4. **3A–334**

"registered social landlord"

See the Housing Act 1996, ss.1–7. **3A–335**

The landlord condition

Note.that if a housing association granted a tenancy before January 15, 1989, and **3A–336** all the other requirements of a secure tenancy exist, that tenancy remains a secure tenancy (see s.80(1) prior to amendment by the Housing Act 1988 and the Housing Act 1988, s.35). Tenancies granted by housing associations on or after January 15, 1989 are likely to be assured tenancies within the meaning of the Housing Act 1988.

The Court of Appeal has held that the landlord condition is not satisfied if there are joint landlords and only one of the joint landlords comes within the list of bodies specified in s.80(1) (see *R. v. Council of City of Plymouth and Cornwall CC, Ex p. Freeman* (1987) 19 H.L.R. 328, CA). See too *Knowsley Housing Trust v. Revell; Helena Housing Ltd v. Curtis* [2003] EWCA Civ 496; [2003] H.L.R. 63; *The Times*, April 17, 2003.

The tenant condition

81. The tenant condition is that the tenant is an individual and oc- **3A–337** cupies the dwelling-house as his only or principal home; or, where the tenancy is a joint tenancy, that each of the joint tenants is an individual and at least one of them occupies the dwelling-house as his only or principal home.

"dwelling-house"

See s.112. **3A–338**

The tenant condition

In order to gain or retain public sector security of tenure tenants must occupy **3A–339** premises as their "only or principal home"(*cf.* the Housing Act 1988, s.1(1)(b) ("as his only or principal home") the Leasehold Reform Act 1967, s.1 ("as his residence"), and the Rent Act 1977, s.2 ("as his residence")). Security of tenure and associated rights, such as the right to buy, are lost if secure tenants cease to occupy premises as their only or principal home (*Sutton LBC v. Swann* (1986) 18 H.L.R. 140, CA) or if they sublet or part with possession of the whole (the Housing Act 1985, s.93). However, it is possible for tenants or licensees to have two or more homes in the public rented sector, but only the one which is the "principal" home can be secure.

In order to maintain a "home" a tenant need not be physically resident, so long as there is an intention to return after a temporary absence and some physical sign of continued occupation (*e.g.* furniture and possessions in the property). Two houses can be occupied as a home at the same time—*Crawley BC v. Sawyer* (1988) 20 H.L.R. 98, CA, where a council tenant went to live with his "girlfriend" for a period of approximately one-and-a-half years during which time the gas and electricity supplies to the premises which he rented from the council were cut off. Held that the rented premises remained his principal home throughout the period.

Temporary absence may be lengthy. In *Amoah v. Barking and Dagenham LBC* (2001) 81 P. & C.R. D12; March 2001 Legal Action 27, Ch D a secure tenant was sentenced to 12 years' imprisonment. He left items of furniture in the property and appointed a relative to act as "caretaker" in his absence and intended to return on his release. Etherton J. held that he had retained his secure status.

The court should consider whether the tenant has an intention to return at the date of expiry of the notice to quit. It should focus on "the enduring intention" of the tenant and not on "fleeting changes of mind". This is particularly true of an elderly tenant in poor health whose intentions "may well have fluctuated from time to time and even from day to day". *Hammersmith & Fulham LBC v. Clarke* (2001) 33 H.L.R. 881, CA.

It is possible for a tenant to lose security of tenure by reason of non-occupation but to regain it by re-occupying the property before service or a notice to quit—see *Hussey v. Camden LBC* (1995) 27 H.L.R. 5, CA, where, as the tenant was occupying the property as his only or principal home at the time of service of the notice to quit, the Court of Appeal held that the earlier loss of security was irrelevant.

Sub-letting of the whole of premises means that any tenancy ceases to be secure (see *Jennings v. Epping Forrest DC* (1993) 25 H.L.R. 241, CA; *Poland v. Cadogan* [1980] 3 All E.R. 544, CA (the Leasehold Reform Act, s.93(2)); *Muir Group Housing Association Ltd v. Thornley* (1993) 25 H.L.R. 89, CA; *Brent LBC v. Cronin* (1997) 30 H.L.R. 43, CA and *Ujima Housing Association v. Asnah* (1998) 30 H.L.R. 831, CA (assured tenancy) *cf. Merton LBC v. Salama* (1989) CAT No 89/169; June 1989 Legal Action 25, CA (parting with possession of part of premises)). Parting with possession is not to be inferred simply from the fact that another person has been allowed to use and occupy a tenant's home during his temporary absence (*Lam Kee Ying v. Lam Shes Tong* [1975] A.C. 247, PC).

The Court of Appeal has held that (1) there is nothing in the Housing Act 1985 which renders it impossible or unlawful to grant a tenancy to a person not lawfully in this country; and (2) there is no public policy requirement that the word "lawfully" should be inserted into s.81 to limit security of tenure to those lawfully in occupation of their homes, see *Akinbolu v. Hackney LBC* (1997) 29 H.L.R. 259, CA, where the council's claims that a tenancy was void because the tenant was an illegal overstayer and the council accordingly had no power to provide housing for him were rejected.

Security of tenure

3A–340   **82.**—(1) A secure tenancy which is either—
            (a) a weekly or other periodic tenancy, or
            (b) a tenancy for a term certain but subject to termination
                by the landlord,
        cannot be brought to an end by the landlord except by obtaining
an order mentioned in subsection (1A);
        (1A) These are the orders—
            (a) an order of the court for the possession of the dwelling-
                house;

    (b) an order under subsection (3);

    (c) a demotion order under section 82A.

(2) Where the landlord obtains an order for the possession of the dwelling-house, the tenancy ends on the date on which the tenant is to give up possession in pursuance of the order.

(3) Where a secure tenancy is a tenancy for a term certain but with a provision for re-entry or forfeiture, the court shall not order possession of the dwelling-house in pursuance of that provision, but in a case where the court would have made such an order it shall instead make an order terminating the tenancy on a date specified in the order and section 86 (periodic tenancy arising on termination of fixed term) shall apply.

(4) Section 146 of the Law of Property Act 1925 (restriction on and relief against forfeiture), except subsection (4) (vesting in under-lessee), and any other enactment or rule of law relating to forfeiture, shall apply in relation to proceedings for an order under subsection (3) of this section as if they were proceedings to enforce a right of re-entry or forfeiture.

Note—Section 82 has been amended by Anti-social Behaviour Act 2003, s.14(1). **3A–341** This amendment was brought into force in England on June 30, 2004 by the Anti-social Behaviour Act 2003 (Commencement No.3 and Savings) Order 2004 (S.I. 2004 No. 1502) (c.61). It does not have effect in relation to any proceedings for the posses-sion of a dwelling-house begun before June 30, 2004. It was brought into force in Wales on 30 April 2005 by the Anti-social Behaviour Act 2003 (Commencement No.4) (Wales) Order 2005 (S.I. 2005 No. 1225) (W.83) (C.55) . The amendment allows a secure tenancy to be brought to an end by a demotion order.

Demotion order
See s.82A.   **3A–342**

"dwelling-house"
See s.112.   **3A–343**

"secure tenancy"
See s.79.   **3A–344**

Security of tenure
This important section provides that a secure tenancy cannot be brought to an end **3A–345** by a *landlord* except by obtaining an order of the court. It does not apply where the tenancy has ceased to be secure (*e.g.* as a result of the tenant ceasing to occupy as his or her only or principal home—see s.81, but note the need for a court order under the Protection from Eviction Act 1977) or where the termination is brought about by the action of a tenant (see, *e.g. Hammersmith and Fulham LBC v. Monk* [1992] 1 A.C. 478; [1991] 3 W.L.R. 1144; [1992] 1 All E.R. 1, HL; *Harrow LBC v. Johnstone* [1997] 1 W.L.R. 459; [1997] 1 All E.R. 929, HL; and *Greenwich LBC v. McGrady* (1982) 81 L.G.R. 288; (1982) 46 P. & C.R. 223; (1983) 6 H.L.R. 361; (1982) 267 E.G. 515, CA and *Notting Hill Housing Trust v. Brackley* [2001] EWCA Civ 601; [2001] 35 E.G. 106; [2002] H.L.R. 212; [2001] L. & T.R. 467). The Court of Appeal has held that there was no breach of ECHR Article 8 where a local authority took possession proceedings against the wife of a sole tenant after the husband (the tenant) had served a valid no-tice to quit upon the council (*Kensington and Chelsea v. O'Sullivan* [2003] EWCA Civ 371; *The Times*, March 27, 2003. See too *Harrow LBC v. Qazi* [2003] UKHL 43; [2003] 3 W.L.R. 792).

For the prerequisites for a possession order, see s.83 (notice of intention to bring proceedings) s.84 and Sched.2 (grounds for possession).

The tenancy ends on the date specified by the court (see, *e.g. Thompson v. Elmbridge BC* [1987] 1 W.L.R. 1425; (1987) 19 H.L.R. 526, CA; *Leicester City Council v. Aldwinkle*

(1992) 24 H.L.R. 40, CA; and *Brent LBC v. Knightley* (1997) 29 H.L.R. 857; *The Times*, February 26, 1997).

Demotion because of anti-social behaviour

3A–346 **82A.**—(1) This section applies to a secure tenancy if the landlord is—

    (a) a local housing authority;

    (b) a housing action trust;

    (c) a registered social landlord.

(2) The landlord may apply to a county court for a demotion order.

(3) A demotion order has the following effect—

    (a) the secure tenancy is terminated with effect from the date specified in the order;

    (b) if the tenant remains in occupation of the dwelling-house after that date a demoted tenancy is created with effect from that date;

    (c) it is a term of the demoted tenancy that any arrears of rent payable at the termination of the secure tenancy become payable under the demoted tenancy;

    (d) it is also a term of the demoted tenancy that any rent paid in advance or overpaid at the termination of the secure tenancy is credited to the tenant's liability to pay rent under the demoted tenancy.

(4) The court must not make a demotion order unless it is satisfied—

    (a) that the tenant or a person residing in or visiting the dwelling-house has engaged or has threatened to engage in conduct to which section 153A or 153B of the Housing Act 1996 (anti-social behaviour or use of premises for unlawful purposes) applies, and

    (b) that it is reasonable to make the order.

(5) Each of the following has effect in respect of a demoted tenancy at the time it is created by virtue of an order under this section as it has effect in relation to the secure tenancy at the time it is terminated by virtue of the order—

    (a) the parties to the tenancy;

    (b) the period of the tenancy;

    (c) the amount of the rent;

    (d) the dates on which the rent is payable.

(6) Subsection (5)(b) does not apply if the secure tenancy was for a fixed term and in such a case the demoted tenancy is a weekly periodic tenancy.

(7) If the landlord of the demoted tenancy serves on the tenant a statement of any other express terms of the secure tenancy which are to apply to the demoted tenancy such terms are also terms of the demoted tenancy.

(8) For the purposes of this section a demoted tenancy is—

    (a) a tenancy to which section 143A of the Housing Act 1996

applies if the landlord of the secure tenancy is a local housing authority or a housing action trust;

(b) a tenancy to which section 20B of the Housing Act 1988 applies if the landlord of the secure tenancy is a registered social landlord.

Editorial note

This section was inserted by Anti-social Behaviour Act 2003, s.14(2). This amendment was brought into force in England on June 30, 2004 by the Anti-social Behaviour Act 2003 (Commencement No.3 and Savings) Order 2004 (S.I. 2004 No. 1502) (c.61). It was brought into force in Wales on 30 April 2005 by the Anti-social Behaviour Act 2003 (Commencement No.4) (Wales) Order 2005 (S.I. 2005 No. 1225) (W.83) (C.55).

3A–347

Section 82A provides that a local authority, a housing action trust or a registered social landlord can apply for a demotion order. A demotion order ends the secure tenancy on a specified date. If the tenant remains in occupation, a new demoted tenancy begins on the same date. The court may only make the order if the tenant, another resident of or visitor to the tenant's home has behaved in a way which is capable of causing nuisance or annoyance or if such a person has used the premises for illegal purposes. In addition the court must be satisfied that it is reasonable to make the order. Demoted tenancies lack security of tenure. If the landlord follows the procedure set out in Housing Act 1996, ss.143E and F, the court must make an order for possession (see Housing Act 1996, s.143D). Under a demoted tenancy, the parties, the period of the tenancy (unless it was for a fixed term) and rental terms remain the same, but a landlord may, apparently unilaterally, serve a statement of any other express terms of the secure tenancy which are to apply to the demoted tenancy.

Demoted tenancy

See s.82A(8), Housing Act 1996, s.143A and Housing Act 1988, s.20B. Section 82A(3)(c) and (d) confirm that any rent owed or overpaid on the tenant's rent account under the secure tenancy should be transferred across to the demoted tenancy. Section 82A(5) sets out certain basic terms of the demoted tenancy at the point at which it is created.

3A–348

Secure tenancy

See s.79.

3A–349

A local housing authority

See Housing Act 1996, s.230 and Housing Act 1985, ss.1 and 2(2).

3A–350

A housing action trust

See Housing Act 1996, s.230 and Housing Act 1988 Part III.

3A–351

A registered social landlord

See Housing Act 1996 Part I, ss.1 to 3.

3A–352

Anti-social behaviour or use of premises for unlawful purposes

See Housing Act 1996, ss.153A and 153B.

3A–353

Proceedings for possession or termination: notice requirements

83.—(1) The court shall not entertain proceedings for an order mentioned in section 82(1A) unless—

3A–354

(a) the landlord has served a notice on the tenant complying with the provisions of this section, or

(b) the court considers it just and equitable to dispense with the requirement of such a notice.

(2) A notice under this section shall—

    (a) be in a form prescribed by regulations made by the Secretary of State,

    (b) specify the ground on which the court will be asked to make the order, and

    (c) give particulars of that ground.

(3) Where the tenancy is a periodic tenancy and the ground or one of the grounds specified in the notice is Ground 2 in Schedule 2 (nuisance or other anti-social behaviour), the notice—

    (a) shall also—

        (i) state that proceedings for the possession of the dwelling-house may be begun immediately, and

        (ii) specify the date sought by the landlord as the date on which the tenant is to give up possession of the dwelling-house, and

    (b) ceases to be in force twelve months after the date so specified.

(4) Where the tenancy is a periodic tenancy and Ground 2 in Schedule 2 is not specified in the notice, the notice—

    (a) shall also specify the date after which proceedings for the possession of the dwelling-house may be begun, and

    (b) ceases to be in force twelve months after the date so specified.

(4A) If the proceedings are for a demotion order under section 82A the notice—

    (a) must specify the date after which the proceedings may be begun;

    (b) ceases to be in force twelve months after the date so specified.

(5) The date specified in accordance with subsection (3), (4) or (4A) must not be earlier than the date on which the tenancy could, apart from this Part, be brought to an end by notice to quit given by the landlord on the same date as the notice under this section.

(6) Where a notice under this section is served with respect to a secure tenancy for a term certain, it has effect also with respect to any periodic tenancy arising on the termination of that tenancy by virtue of section 86; and subsections (3) to (5) of this section do not apply to the notice.

(7) Regulations under this section shall be made by statutory instrument and may make different provision with respect to different cases or descriptions of case, including different provision for different areas.

3A–355   *Note*—Substituted by the Housing Act 1996, s.147.

    Section 83 has been amended by Anti-social Behaviour Act 2003, s.14(3) and Sched.1. The amendments were brought into force in England on June 30, 2004 by the Anti-social Behaviour Act 2003 (Commencement No.3 and Savings) Order 2004 (S.I. 2004 No. 1502) (c.61). It was brought into force in Wales on 30 April 2005 by the Anti-social Behaviour Act 2003 (Commencement No.4) (Wales) Order 2005 (S.I. 2005 No. 1225) (W.83) (C.55).

Proceedings for possession or termination: notice requirements

3A–356   The Housing Act 1996, s.147 introduced completely new ss.83 and 83A which apply to notices served on or after February 12, 1997 (Housing Act 1996 (Commencement No. 6) Order 1997 (S.I. 1997 No. 66)). They are in similar form to the old s.83, but with two significant modifications, *viz.* the court may dispense with the requirement for a notice if it considers it just and equitable to do, and the notice may state that proceedings under new Ground 2 (nuisance or anti-social behaviour—see below) may be begun immediately.

For the prescribed forms of notice, see the Secure Tenancies (Notices) Regulations 1987 (S.I. 1987 No.775) (as amended by the Secure Tenancies (Notices) (Amendment) Regulations 1997 (S.I. 1997 No. 71), the Secure Tenancies (Notices) (Amendment No.2) Regulations 1997 (S.I. 1997 No. 377) ; the Secure Tenancies (Notices) (Amendment) (England) Regulations 2004 (S.I. 2004 No. 1627) and the Secure Tenancies (Notices) (Amendment) (Wales) Regulations 2005 S.I. 2005 No. 1226 (W.84)). Paragraph 2(1) of the Regulations states that the notice should be "substantially to the same effect" as that contained in the Regulations. For cases where landlords used old versions of prescribed forms, see: *Beckerman v. Durling* (1983) 6 H.L.R. 87, CA; *Swansea CC v. Hearn* (1991) 23 H.L.R. 284, CA; and *Tadema Holdings v. Ferguson* (2000) 32 H.L.R. 866, CA.

If the court does not consider it just and equitable to dispense with the notice requirement, s.83 precludes the court from granting an order for possession of a secure tenancy unless satisfied that a notice of intention to seek possession complying with the requirements of that section has been served. Such a notice must state the ground for possession and give "particulars" of the ground (s.83(2)(c)).

As to service see *Wandsworth LBC v. Attwell* (1995) 27 H.L.R. 536; [1996] 01 E.G. 100; (1996) 94 L.G.R. 419, CA; *Enfield LBC v. Devonish* (1997) 29 H.L.R. 691, CA and *Tadema Holdings v. Ferguson* (2000) 32 H.L.R. 866, CA. If there are joint tenants, it should be addressed to all of them (*Newham LBC v. Okotoro*, March 1993, Legal Action 11, Bow County Court).

Notices must specify a date which must not be earlier than the date on which the tenancy could otherwise be brought to an end by a notice to quit served by the landlord. (See also the Protection from Eviction Act 1977, s.5). However, a notice may state that proceedings under Ground 2 (nuisance or anti-social behaviour) may be begun immediately. In that case, the notice should state this and specify the date sought by the landlord as the date on which the tenant is to give up possession (s.83(3)).

Notices cease to be in force 12 months after the date specified in the notice. If that date passes, a new notice must be served (s.83(3)(b) and s.83A).

"particulars of the ground"

In rent arrears cases the particulars given must at least show the amount claimed, **3A–357** and in all cases the notice must be sufficiently particularised to "tell the tenant what he had to do to put matters right before proceedings are commenced" (*Torridge DC v. Jones* (1986) 18 H.L.R. 107 at 114; (1985) 276 E.G. 1253, CA). ("The reasons for taking this action are non-payment of rent" not sufficient—notice invalid). See too *East Devon DC v. Williams and Mills*, December 1996, Legal Action 13, Exeter County Court (possession claimed under Sched.2, Ground 1 (breach of the terms of the tenancy). The notice set out the relevant terms but in the section marked "Particulars" merely repeated the terms in full, without indicating the conduct relied upon—possession claim struck out); *Slough BC v. Robbins* [1996] 12 C.L. 353, Slough County Court (notice seeking possession giving as particulars: "Numerous complaints have been received over a period of time that annoyance and nuisance is being caused to your neighbours by noise and disruptive behaviour. This nuisance and annoyance has been investigated by my staff and I believe the complaints to be substantiated" held to be defective, proceedings struck out); and *South Buckinghamshire CC v. Frances* [1985] 11 C.L. 152; [1985] C.L.Y. 1900, Slough County Court (where it was held that the Housing Act 1980, s.33(2) (now the Housing Act 1985, s.83(2)(c)) required detailed particulars which should be similar to those required under the Law of Property Act 1925, s.146. It must be obvious to tenants what they must do. Although there was discretion to allow amendment of the notice (now contained in the Housing Act 1985, s.84(3)), the council would not be permitted "at a late stage" in the proceedings to amend the notice to include a schedule of dilapidations and particulars of nuisance which ought to have been included in the original notice).

However, in *Dudley MBC v. Bailey* [1991] 10 E.G. 140; (1990) 22 H.L.R. 424, CA, Ralph Gibson L.J. stated that:

"The question is whether, at the date of the notice, the landlord has in good faith stated the ground and given the particulars of that ground. The requirement of particulars is satisfied, in my judgment, if the landlord has stated in summary form the facts which he then intends to prove in support of the stated ground for possession. Error in the particulars does not, in my judgment, invalidate the notice, although it may well affect the decision of the court on the merits". ((1990) 22 H.L.R. 424 at 431).

See too *Marath v. MacGillivray* (1996) 28 H.L.R. 484, CA, noted under the Housing Act 1988, s.8.

Section 83 expressly enables a court to give leave for a landlord to add to or alter the "grounds" on which possession is claimed (s.83(4)), but is silent about the addition or alteration of the "particulars" required by the notice. In *Camden LBC v. Oppong* (1996) 28 H.L.R. 701, CA, the Court of Appeal held the s.83(4) power *ipso facto* extended to a power to add to or alter the particulars. The court stated that such leave would be granted only in circumstances where it would be just to do so and that the nature and extent of the addition or alteration would always be a critical factor.

The form of notice is prescribed by the Secure Tenancies (Notices) Regulations 1987 (S.I. 1987 No. 775) (as amended by the Secure Tenancies (Notices) (Amendment) Regulations 1997 (S.I. 1997 No. 71) ; the Secure Tenancies (Notices)(Amendment No. 2) Regulations 1997 (S.I. 1997 No. 377) ; the Secure Tenancies (Notices) (Amendment) (England) Regulations 2004 (S.I. 2004 No. 1627) ; and the Secure Tenancies (Notices) (Amendment) (Wales) Regulations 2005 (S.I. 2005 No. 1226) (W.84)). Paragraph 2(1) of the Regulations states that the notice should be "substantially to the same effect" as that contained in the Regulations. Minor variations are unlikely to invalidate a notice—see *Dudley MBC v. Bailey* [1991] 10 E.G. 140; (1990) 22 H.L.R. 424, CA, where Ralph Gibson L.J. held that a notice, although not precisely in the prescribed form, was "substantially to the same effect". In *City of London v. Devlin* (1995) 29 H.L.R. 58, CA, the Court of Appeal held that a notice seeking possession which had not been signed by the Director of Housing above that description which appeared on the printed form was "substantially to the same effect" as that prescribed and accordingly valid. Simon Brown L.J. stated that:

"The reality here is that a series of aridly technical points raised by the applicant at trial were defeated by a series of creative, largely procedural rulings".

which were not even arguably impermissible.

"the court considers it just and equitable to do dispense with the requirement of such a notice" (s.83(1)(b))

3A–358
This provision brings secure tenancies into line with assured tenancies (*cf.* the Housing Act 1988, s.8(1)(b)). It is "obviously only in relatively exceptional cases where the court should be prepared to dispense with a section 83 notice". (*Braintree DC v. Vincent* [2004] EWCA Civ 415—a case where the Court of Appeal held that a judge was entitled to dispense with the notice on unusual facts. A s.83 notice would have been of no benefit to the tenant—indeed it would have been to her disadvantage because it would have postponed the date for possession and added to her liability for rent.) In *Kelsey H.A. v. King* (1995) 28 H.L.R. 270, CA, it was held that it was just and equitable to dispense with the notice requirement where a notice served was found to be invalid because it had not given adequate particulars of the complaints of nuisance. The court had regard, *inter alia*, to:

(a) developments since the commencement of proceedings; and

(b) the late stage in the proceedings at which any point about the deficiency in the notice was taken.

See too *North British HA v. Sheridan* [1999] 2 E.G.L.R. 138; [2000] L. & T.R. 115; (2000) 32 H.L.R. 346; (1999) 78 P. & C.R. D38.

Although the effect is different, the same wording is also used in the Rent Act 1977 Sched.15, Case 11, and the Housing Act 1988, Sched.2, Ground 1, where the court may dispense with the requirement that notice be served *before the grant* of certain tenancies. Those provisions have been considered by the Court of Appeal in *Fernandes v. Parvardin* (1982) 5 H.L.R. 33; *Bradshaw v. Baldwin-Wiseman* (1985) 17 H.L.R. 260; (1985) 49 P.&C.R. 382; and *Boyle v. Verrall* (1996) 29 H.L.R. 436. The decisions in those cases indicate that although the power to dispense with notices is not limited to exceptional cases and may be exercised where oral notice has been given, it is unlikely to be exercised where no intimation of an intention to require possession has been given.

Additional requirements in relation to certain proceedings for possession

83A.—(1) Where a notice under section 83 has been served on a tenant containing the information mentioned in subsection (3)(a) of that section, the court shall not entertain proceedings for the possession of the dwelling-house unless they are begun at a time when the notice is still in force.

(2) Where—

    (a) a notice under section 83 has been served on a tenant, and

    (b) a date after which proceedings may be begun has been specified in the notice in accordance with subsection (4)(a) of that section,

the court shall not entertain proceedings for the possession of the dwelling-house unless they are begun after the date so specified and at a time when the notice is still in force.

(3) Where—

    (a) the ground or one of the grounds specified in a notice under section 83 is Ground 2A in Schedule 2 (domestic violence), and

    (b) the partner who has left the dwelling-house as mentioned in that ground is not a tenant of the dwelling-house,

the court shall not entertain proceedings for the possession of the dwelling-house unless it is satisfied that the landlord has served a copy of the notice on the partner who has left or has taken all reasonable steps to serve a copy of the notice on that partner.

This subsection has effect subject to subsection (5).

(4) Where—

    (a) Ground 2A in Schedule 2 is added to a notice under section 83 with the leave of the court after proceedings for possession are begun, and

    (b) the partner who has left the dwelling-house as mentioned in that ground is not a party to the proceedings,

the court shall not continue to entertain the proceedings unless it is satisfied that the landlord has served a notice under subsection (6) on the partner who has left or has taken all reasonable steps to serve such a notice on that partner.

This subsection has effect subject to subsection (5).

(5) Where subsection (3) or (4) applies and Ground 2 in Schedule 2 (nuisance or other anti-social behaviour) is also specified in the notice under section 83, the court may dispense with the requirements as to service in relation to the partner who has left the dwelling-house if it considers it just and equitable to do so.

(6) A notice under this subsection shall—

    (a) state that proceedings for the possession of the dwelling-house have begun,

    (b) specify the ground or grounds on which possession is being sought, and

    (c) give particulars of the ground or grounds.

3A–360   *Note* —Added by the Housing Act 1996, s.147.

Additional requirements in relation to certain proceedings for possession

3A–361   This section contains special provisions concerning Ground 2A (domestic violence) (see Sched.2 below).

Grounds for orders for possession

3A–362   84.—(1) The court shall not make an order for the possession of a dwelling-house let under a secure tenancy except on one or more of the grounds set out in Schedule 2.

(2) The court shall not make an order for possession—

(a) on the grounds set out in Part I of that Schedule (grounds 1 to 8), unless it considers it reasonable to make the order,

(b) on the grounds set out in Part II of that Schedule (grounds 9 to 11), unless it is satisfied that suitable accommodation will be available for the tenant when the order takes effect,

(c) on the grounds set out in Part III of that Schedule (grounds 12 to 16), unless it both considers it reasonable to make the order and is satisfied that suitable accommodation will be available for the tenant when the order takes effect;

and Part IV of that Schedule has effect for determining whether suitable accommodation will be available for a tenant.

(3) Where a notice under section 83 has been served on the tenant, the court shall not make such an order on any of those grounds above unless the ground is specified in the notice; but the grounds so specified may be altered or added to with the leave of the court.

(4) Where a date is specified in a notice under section 83 in accordance with subsection (3) of that section, the court shall not make an order which requires the tenant to give up possession of the dwelling-house in question before the date so specified.

3A–363   *Note* —Amended by the Housing Act 1996, s.147.

"dwelling-house"

3A–364   See s.112.

"secure tenancy"

3A–365   See s.79.

"notice"

3A–366   See s.83. As to the alteration of grounds in notices, see the commentary to s.83.

"suitable accommodation will be available"

3A–367   see Sched.2, Pt IV.

Grounds for orders for possession

3A–368   The court may not make an order for possession against a secure tenant unless satisfied that one of the grounds for possession listed in Sched.2 is proved and in addition that, depending upon the ground, it is reasonable to make an order for possession, or that suitable alternative accommodation will be available, or that it is both reasonable to make an order for possession and suitable alternative accommodation will be available.

The service of a notice exercising the right to buy (Housing Act 1985, Pt V) does not prevent a public sector landlord from seeking possession of the property on any of the grounds permitted by the Housing Act 1985, Sched.2. However, if the ground requires the court to consider "reasonableness", the fact that the tenant has exercised the right to buy is a circumstance to be taken into account (*Enfield LBC v. McKeon* [1986] 1 W.L.R. 1007; [1986] 2 All E.R. 730, CA). See too *Bristol CC v. Lovell* [1998] 1 W.L.R. 446; [1998] 1 All E.R. 775, HL.

"reasonable"

See too the commentary to the Rent Act 1977, s.98. It is for the landlord to satisfy **3A–369** the court that it is reasonable to make a possession order.

The first requirement for a judge who has found a ground for possession to be proved is to ask whether it is reasonable to make a possession order at all and then to ask whether the order should be stayed or suspended under s.100(2). The correct approach is to determine the extent of the rent arrears and how quickly those were likely to be paid. It is wrong to take into account matters which have not been pleaded.

> "In considering whether it is reasonable to make an order...the judge should consider all the relevant circumstances: but that is not a consideration at large. It is, or should be, a consideration in accordance with the pleadings. In my judgment, the matters proposed to be relied upon by the landlord in support of the contention that it would be reasonable to make an order for possession...must be pleaded by the landlord." (*per* Sir Richard Scott V.-C. in *Laimond Properties Ltd v. Raeuchle*, April 2000 Legal Action 31; (2001) 33 H.L.R. 113, CA.

In view of the requirement that the appropriate grounds and conditions must be made out (*e.g.* as to reasonableness) "consent orders" have no place in public-sector proceedings. The court can have jurisdiction only if the necessary matters are proved by evidence or if there is express admission of the relevant facts (*Wandsworth LBC v. Fadayomi* [1987] 3 All E.R. 474; (1987) 19 H.L.R. 512, CA; and *Hounslow LBC v. McBride* (1999) 31 H.L.R. 143, CA, where after agreement between the parties in possession proceedings based upon Housing Act 1985 Grounds 1 and 2 a District Judge made a suspended possession order by consent without hearing evidence. Later the council alleged that Ms McBride had broken the conditions of the suspended order and applied for a warrant of possession. The Court of Appeal confirmed that both the possession order and the warrant should be set aside). See too *R. v. Birmingham CC, Ex p. Foley*, March 2001, Legal Action 29, Queen's Bench Division. A distinction has to be drawn between a form of order which contains an admission as to those matters on which the jurisdiction to make the order rests (*e.g.* reasonableness) and an order such as this one which did not.

"reasonable"—rent arrears

In rent arrears cases, the importance of ascertaining the position in respect of **3A–369.1** welfare benefits was stressed by the Court of Appeal in *Second WRVS Housing Society v. Blair* (1987) 19 H.L.R. 104, CA, where the tenant became affected by a psychiatric illness. His life "fell apart" and arrears mounted. He received supplementary benefit towards the housing costs but spent it on food. The county court judge, finding that there were arrears of £1,198 and that the tenant was still on supplementary benefit, ordered possession (suspended for two months in case the debt could be cleared in that time) and costs of £140. The Court of Appeal set aside the order, as the judge had failed to consider in detail the question of reasonableness and, in particular, the available welfare benefits. The case was sent back for reconsideration to ascertain "more fully the benefits which could be obtained from DHSS in relation to arrears and more generally in relation to [the tenant's] condition". Dillon L.J. stated "it is well known that arrangements can be made with the DHSS when housing benefit is payable to see that the rent is paid direct to the landlord and I feel that is a matter which should have been taken into account".

Also important are the tenant's past record and the reason for the arrears. See *Woodspring D.C. v. Taylor* (1982) 4 H.L.R. 95, CA, where the defendants, who were in their mid-fifties, had been tenants of the council for 24 years. They had a good rent record. However, Mr Taylor was made redundant and received a large tax demand. His wife became ill. As a result rent arrears accrued. They owed £557 at the launch of possession proceedings and £700 at the date of the hearing. By this time they were receiving benefit and the DHSS was paying current rent plus £1 per week off the arrears. In the county court a registrar made an absolute possession order. The Court of Appeal set aside the order, finding that no reasonable registrar could have found that it was reasonable to make the order. Waller L.J. stated that it was "hard to understand a conclusion that it was reasonable to make an order turning them out of their house" (at 99).

See also *Brent LBC v. Marks* (1999) 31 H.L.R. 343, CA: appeal by tenant against suspended possession on terms that the tenant pay current rent and £2.50 allowed. Following *Second WRVS Housing Society Ltd v. Blair*, the judge ought to have had more regard to the fact that current rent was being paid by deductions made by the DSS quarterly in arrears and that the benefit system was both causing and then dealing with the arrears. Looking at the overall position this was a responsible tenant whose position had stabilised. On a new exercise of the court's discretion, a possession order might not be made.

If a defendant counterclaims unsuccessfully for breach of repairing obligations, in ordinary circumstances, it is not reasonable to make a possession order, if the tenant has made arrangements, in the event of the failure of his counterclaim, for the early discharge of the arrears. However, in exceptional circumstances where there has been a bad history of persistent delay in paying rent, it may be reasonable to make an absolute order for possession (*Haringey LBC v. Stewart* (1991) 23 H.L.R. 557; [1991] 2 E.G.L.R. 252, CA).

In *Drew-Morgan v. Hamid-Zadeh* (2000) 32 H.L.R. 316; [1999] 25 E.G. 156, CA the Court of Appeal held that a judge was entitled to conclude that it was reasonable to make a possession order in the light of persistent non-payment which was inexcusable because the tenant had received housing benefit. The non-payment was plainly deliberate and avoidable. The fact that the tenant paid arrears during the hearing underlined the fact that she had been in a position to pay but had chosen not to do so until the last moment. The judge was also entitled to take into account false allegations made by the tenant.

"reasonable"—nuisance and annoyance

3A–369.2   The proper approach in a case of the commission of "a most serious breach" of the tenancy agreement is that it will be reasonable to order possession in the absence of some exceptional circumstance—*Bristol CC v. Mousah* (1997) 30 H.L.R. 32, CA (serious drug dealing). See too *Glasgow DC v. Heffron* [1997] October C.L.D. 618, Sheriff Court ("Any drug dealer would have to show genuine remorse and an intention not to return to old habits in order to avoid eviction"); and *Glasgow City Council v. Lockhart*, 1997 Hous.L.R. 99; [1997] C.L.D. 633, Sheriff Court.

Similarly, where there is an admitted breach of covenant and an intention to continue with the breach a landlord should only be refused possession in a "very special case" (*Sheffield CC v. Green* (1994) 26 H.L.R. 349, CA; *cf. Bell London & Provincial Properties Ltd v. Rueben* [1947] K.B. 157, CA). It is in the public interest that necessary and reasonable conditions in tenancy agreements are enforced fairly and effectively *Sheffield CC v. Jepson* (1993) 25 H.L.R. 299, CA (tenant keeping a dog in breach of an express term of the tenancy agreement. Although there was little evidence about the defendant's dog in particular, reasonable to make suspended possession order). In a case involving the parking of a caravan in a front garden in breach of the terms of a tenancy agreement, the Court of Appeal held that the propriety of the council's policy was not a factor relevant to the exercise of discretion. The judge should not have been concerned with the propriety or impropriety of the policy rule. His concern should have been with the reasonableness in the particular case of ordering possession; *Barking and Dagenham LBC v. Hyatt and Hyatt* (1992) 24 H.L.R. 406, CA, *cf. Wandsworth LBC v. Hargreaves* (1994) 27 H.L.R. 142, CA (in breach of a term of the tenancy a visitor brought petrol into the flat to make petrol bombs, which were thrown from the window. A fire started in the flat from spilt petrol, causing £14,000 worth of damage. The Court of Appeal dismissed the council's appeal against a refusal of the county court judge to order possession); and *Grogan v. Greenwich LBC* (2001) 33 H.L.R. 140, CA (17 year-old tenant pleaded guilty to handling stolen goods on the premises, sentenced to six months' youth custody. The Court of Appeal suspended the possession order for twelve months. In exercising its discretion, the court could take into account the wider public interest. The tenant was a young man trying to live a life free of crime and there was a serious possibility that that attempt would fail if he lost his flat. The council had a duty to consider its other tenants and people on its waiting list, but the balance was in favour of suspending the order). See too *Camden LBC v. Gilsenan* (1999) 31 H.L.R. 81, CA: decision by circuit judge that it was reasonable to make a possession order upheld. The trial judge had differentiated between acts done by the defendant and acts done by her visitors; and *Newcastle Upon Tyne CC v. Morrison* (2000) 32 H.L.R. 891, CA (single parent unable to control her "rampaging, destructive, intimidating and sometimes dangerous sons" with "quite appalling behaviour over a period of more than six years" involving "plain, repeated and grave breaches of the tenancy agreement, numerous offences affecting the neighbourhood and a dreadful catalogue of incidents". The Court of Appeal substituted a 28 day possession order for a suspended possession order). For a case in which a first instance judge dismissed a claim for possession but the Court of Appeal decided that it was reasonable to make a suspended possession order, see *Norwich City Council v. Famuyiwa* [2004] EWCA Civ 1770; *The Times*, January 24, 2005.

An outright possession order may not be appropriate where the anti-social behaviour was not caused by the tenant, but by a member of the tenant's family who has since left the premises, with the result that the chances of recurrence are reduced. (*Castle Vale Housing Action Trust v. Gallagher* [2001] EWCA Civ 944; (2001) 33 H.L.R. 810, CA). See too *Moat Housing Group South Ltd v. Harris and Hartless* [2005] EWCA Civ 287; [2005]HLR 33, where having regard to good school reports, the absence of any criminal records or any serious record of police involvement with the tenant's family, and favourable testimonies given about the tenant, the Court of Appeal concluded that it would be right to suspend a possession order on the terms that there were no further breaches of the tenancy agreement. *Cf.* Kensington and *Chelsea RLBC v. Simmonds* (1997) 29 H.L.R. 507, CA; *Northampton BC v. Lovatt* (1998) 30 H.L.R. 875, CA; and *Portsmouth City Council v. Bryant* (2000) 32 H.L.R. 906; [2000] E.G.L.R. 287, CA).

In nuisance cases, the authority's obligations towards other tenants should be borne in mind; *Woking BC v. Bystram* (1995) 27 H.L.R. 1; [1993] E.G.C.S. 208, CA (nuisance continuing—appropriate course was to make a suspended possession on terms that any further nuisance would lead to repossession in 28 days). See too *Solon South West Housing Association Ltd v. James*, [2004] EWCA Civ 1847; [2005] H.L.R. 24 (outright order confirmed by Court of appeal).

A local authority's housing obligations towards the defendant if made homeless, and in particular the question of whether rehousing is likely to be refused as a result of intentional homelessness may have greater or lesser weight when considering reasonableness, depending on the circumstances—*cf. Rushcliffe BC v. Watson* (1992) 24 H.L.R. 124, CA (the prospect that, if evicted, the tenant would probably be found to be intentionally homeless a very real consideration); *Bristol CC v. Mousah* (1997) 30 H.L.R. 32, CA (whether the tenant would be rehoused as homeless was a matter for the council and not for the court); *Darlington BC v. Sterling* (1996) 29 H.L.R. 309, CA (a decision by a Circuit Judge that as a District Judge had formed the view that the tenant ought not to be roofless he should not have ordered possession unless the council could show it would provide suitable alternative accommodation overturned by the Court of Appeal); and *Shrewsbury and Atcham BC v. Evans* (1997) 30 H.L.R. 123, CA (the judge had not needed to consider how a tenant who had "flagrantly and deliberately lied about her circumstances" in order to obtain council housing would be rehoused).

See too *Lewisham LBC v. Adeyemi* (2000) 32 H.L.R. 414, CA where the court dismissed a tenant's appeal against a possession order, where the tenant claimed that the judge, when considering reasonableness had failed to take into account whether the local authority would have a duty to rehouse under the Housing Act 1996, Pt VII. It is not for the court to make a pre-emptive decision on the possible outcome of an application that might or might not be made to the local authority. Entitlement to Pt VII accommodation is confined to the judgement of the local authority. It is not for the court to anticipate the outcome of that decision. The judge was well aware of the self-evident consequence of a possession order. The legal and practical consequences of homelessness however were not before the court, nor need they have been as they were for the local authority to determine.

appeals on questions of reasonableness

Although County Courts Act 1984, s.77(6) excludes appeals against judges' findings of fact, it does not exclude, in a proper case, the possibility of an appeal against a finding of reasonableness (*Castle Vale Housing Action Trust v. Gallagher* [2001] EWCA Civ 944; (2001) 33 H.L.R. 810).

3A–370

ECHR Art 8 and reasonableness

The Court of Appeal has doubted whether Art.8 makes any difference to the way in

3A–371

which courts have always approached questions of the reasonableness of making possessions order. Article 8 does, however, reinforce the importance of only making an order depriving someone of his or her home in circumstances where a clear case is made out (*Castle Vale Housing Action Trust v. Gallagher* [2001] EWCA Civ 944; (2001) 33 H.L.R. 810). See too *Newham LBC v. Neal* [2003] EWCA Civ 541; February 25, 2003. There is a need to find a fair balance and to protect the rights of the neighbours and other members of the public (*Lambeth LBC v. Howard* [2001] EWCA Civ 468; (2001) 33 H.L.R. 636). See too *Harrow LBC v. Qazi* [2003] UKHL 43; [2003] 3 W.L.R. 792, where Lord Hope and Lord Scott said that contractual and property rights cannot be defeated by a defence based on Art.8. See too *Newham LBC v. Kibata* [2003] EWCA Civ 1785; [2004] HLR 28 and *Bradney v. Birmingham CC*; *Birmingham CC v. McCann* [2003] EWCA Civ 1783; [2004] HLR 27.

Disability Discrimination Act 1995

3A-372
The effect of Disability Discrimination Act 1995, s.22(3)(c) is that it is unlawful to discriminate "by evicting [a] disabled person or subjecting him to any other detriment". Although unlawfulness under the Disability Discrimination Act is not a bar to a landlord seeking a possession order under the Housing Act, the fact that the eviction is unlawful and not justified is a highly relevant consideration for the s.7 discretion of whether or not to make a possession order. The Disability Discrimination Act contains its own code which requires a higher threshold than the Housing Act to justify an eviction (*North Devon Homes Ltd v. Brazier* [2003] EWHC 574 (QB)). In *Manchester CC v. Romano* [2004] EWCA (Civ) 834; [2005]1 WLR 2775, the Court of Appeal, in a very thorough review of the legislation, stated that when a court considers the Disability Discrimination Act 1995 in the context of possession proceedings, the first matter which has to be determined is whether the person who complains about disability discrimination is a "disabled person" within the meaning of the Disability Discrimination (Meaning of Disability) Regulations 1996 (S.I. 1996 No. 1455), Sched.1, ss.1–3, and the *Guidance on matters to be taking into account in determining questions relating to the definition of disability* issued by the Secretary of State. Secondly, the court should consider whether or not there has been discrimination—*i.e.* treating a disabled person less favourably for a reason which relates to the disabled person's disability. Thirdly, the court should consider whether the landlord's treatment of the tenant is justified. It is only justified if in the landlord's opinion the treatment (*viz* the decision to set in motion proceedings for possession) is necessary in order not to endanger the health or safety of any of the people living in neighbouring houses and it is reasonable, in all the circumstances, for the landlord to hold that opinion. The landlord must prove that if it does not take this action someone's health or safety would be endangered. It does not have to prove that that person's health or safety has actually been damaged. The 1995 Act does not explicitly provide a defence for disabled persons who wish to assert that the reason why their landlord brought possession proceedings related to disability. It is though open to such disabled persons to counterclaim for a declaration that they have been unlawfully discriminated against and/or to counterclaim for injunctive relief. Furthermore, if tenants can prove that the landlord's conduct amounts to unlawful discrimination, this is bound to be a relevant factor when the court is determining whether it is reasonable to make an order for possession. The Court of Appeal stated that it is preferable, in cases involving a secure tenancy or an assured tenancy, for tenants to assert that it is unreasonable for the court to make a possession order, rather than to complicate the proceedings by adding a formalistic counterclaim for a declaration or an injunction. Landlords whose tenants hold secure or assured tenancies must consider the position carefully before they decide to serve a notice seeking possession or to embark on possession proceedings against a tenant who is or might be mentally impaired. They should liase closely with local social services authorities at an early stage.

Forms of order

3A-373
Forms **N26** (Order for possession) and **N28** (Order for Possession (possession suspended) (rented property)) have been retained by the Practice Direction to CPR Pt 4, Table 3.

Extended discretion of court in certain proceedings for possession

3A-374
85.—(1) Where proceedings are brought for possession of a

dwelling-house let under a secure tenancy on any of the grounds set out in Part I or Part III of Schedule 2 (grounds 1 to 8 and 12 to 16: cases in which the court must be satisfied that it is reasonable to make a possession order), the court may adjourn the proceedings for such period or periods as it thinks fit.

(2) On the making of an order for possession of such a dwelling-house on any of those grounds, or at any time before the execution of the order, the court may—

    (a) stay or suspend the execution of the order, or

    (b) postpone the date of possession,

for such period or periods as the court thinks fit.

(3) On such an adjournment, stay, suspension or postponement the court—

    (a) shall impose conditions with respect to the payment by the tenant of arrears of rent (if any) and rent or payments in respect of occupation after the termination of the tenancy (mesne profits), unless it considers that to do so would cause exceptional hardship to the tenant or would otherwise be unreasonable, and

    (b) may impose such other conditions as it thinks fit.

(4) If the conditions are complied with, the court may, if it thinks fit, discharge or rescind the order for possession.

(5) Where proceedings are brought for possession of a dwelling-house which is let under a secure tenancy and—

    (a) the tenant's spouse or former spouse, having matrimonial home rights under Part IV of the Family Law Act 1996 is then in occupation of the dwelling-house, and

    (b) the tenancy is terminated as a result of those proceedings,

the spouse or former spouse shall, so long as he or she remains in occupation, have the same rights in relation to, or in connection with, any adjournment, stay, suspension or postponement in pursuance of this section as he or she would have if those matrimonial home rights were not affected by the termination of the tenancy.

(5A) If proceedings are brought for possession of a dwelling-house which let under a secure tenancy and—

    (a) an order is in force under section 35 of the Family Law Act 1996 conferring rights on the former spouse of the tenant or an order is in force under section 36 of that Act conferring rights on a cohabitant or former cohabitant (within the meaning of that Act) of the tenant,

    (b) the former spouse, cohabitant, or former cohabitant is then in occupation of the dwelling-house and

    (c) the tenancy is terminated as a result of those proceedings,

the former spouse, cohabitant or former cohabitant shall, so long as he or she remains in occupation, have the same rights in relation to, or in connection with any adjournment, stay, suspension or postponement in pursuance of this section as he or she would have if the rights conferred by the order referred to in paragraph (a) were not affected by the termination of the tenancy.

3A-375   *Note* —Amended by the Family Law Act 1996, Sched.8, para. 53.

"dwelling-house"

3A-376   See s.112.

"secure tenancy"

3A-377   See s.79. See too Housing Act 1988, s.9.

Extended discretion of court in certain proceedings for possession

3A-378   The court's power to stay or suspend execution or postpone the date of possession may be exercised when making an order for possession or "at any time before the execution of the order" (s.85(2)).

A tenant against whom an outright order has been made under a discretionary ground is entitled to make a fresh application to a district judge to stay or suspend execution. Such an application "is not in any way affected or fettered by the reasons given by [the district judge who heard the possession claim]...on such an application the district judge can take all relevant circumstances into account as they appear at the time of the application. Those will include any medical evidence which is before the court, any evidence as to the defendant's behaviour since the original order and the effect of an immediate order for possession which is not suspended upon the likelihood of the applicant being rehoused under the Housing Act 1996". There is a continuing remedy in the county court (*Plymouth CC v. Hoskin* [2002] EWCA Civ 684; May 1, 2002). See too *Ujima Housing Association v. Smith* April 2001 Legal Action 21; October 16,2000 ChD.

For the circumstances in which it is reasonable to suspend a possession order, see the commentary to s.84 above. Section 85(2) gives the court a wide discretion and expressly allows the court to suspend for such period as it thinks fit. The court practice is to be merciful to tenants and to give them a realistic opportunity to pay arrears. The question of whether it is appropriate for a tenant who owes substantial arrears to have the threat of losing her home hanging over her for years is a political question and does not go to the correctness of making an order (*Henry v. Lambeth LBC* (2000) 32 H.L.R. 874, CA).

Where there is a substantial dispute about the amount claimed and the tenant's compliance with the order, the up-to-date position has to be clearly and accurately established before considering an application to suspend under s.85 (*Haringey LBC v. Powell* (1996) 28 H.L.R. 798, CA).

When exercising its powers under s.85 the court shall impose conditions with respect to the repayment of arrears of rent and mesne profits unless it considers that to do so would cause exceptional hardship (s. 85(3)). There have been no reported Court of Appeal decisions as to what might constitute "exceptional hardship".

Note that the form of suspended possession order in former County Court Form N28 stated: "When you have paid the total amount mentioned, the plaintiff will not be able to take any steps to evict you as a result of this order"

If this Form of order was used, a suspended possession order becomes unenforceable at the moment that the balance of arrears is paid (see *Merton LBC v. Hashmi CAT 94/1147*; September 1995, Legal Action 13, CA (former Form N28, cheque for arrears handed to council on morning of execution. The council's contention that the judgment had not been satisfied because the cheque for £300 had not cleared before execution was rejected, since the tenants had been told that the further payment would satisfy all that was owed)).

The right to apply for a postponement of an order for possession under s.85 is not an interest in land which is capable of being inherited. It is only available to the tenant, the tenant's spouse or former spouse in occupation (s.85(5) and *Brent LBC v. Knightley* (1997) 29 H.L.R. 857, CA) and *Marshall v. Bradford MBC* [2001] EWCA Civ 594; [2002] H.L.R. 22.

Effect of breach of a suspended possession order

3A-379   A secure tenancy comes to an end on the first occasion that the terms of a suspended possession order are breached (*e.g.* by failing to pay the current rent or instalments towards the arrears) (*Thompson v. Elmbridge BC* [1987] 1 W.L.R. 1425; (1987) 19 H.L.R. 526, CA; and *Burrows v. Brent LBC* [1996] 1 W.L.R. 1448; [1996] 4 All E.R. 577, HL). In this "limbo" period there is neither a tenancy nor a licence. Accordingly, there can be no breach of any express or implied obligations or duties relevant to tenancies or licences (*e.g.* to repair). See *Thompson v. Elmbridge B.C.* [1987] 1 W.L.R. 1425; (1987) 19 H.L.R. 526, CA (no jurisdiction to transfer tenancy to spouse under the Matrimonial Homes Act 1983 after breach of suspended possession order); *Leicester City Council v. Aldwinkle* (1992) 24 H.L.R. 40, CA; *Tower Hamlets LBC v. Azad and Another* (1998) 30 H.L.R. 241, CA; *Brent LBC v. Knightley* (1997) 29 H.L.R. 857, CA (no right to succeed under s.87 after death of tenant if breach of suspended possession order); *Newham LBC v. Hawkins* [2005] EWCA Civ 451; April 22, 2005 (right to succeed lost); *R. v. Sheffield CC, Ex p. Creaser and Jarvis*, September 1991, Legal Action 15, QBD (no right to internal review of decision to evict as required by the council's standard tenancy agreement after breach of suspended possession order); and *Marshall v. Bradford MBC* [2001] EWCA Civ 594; [2002] H.L.R. 22 (claim for breach of repairing obligations struck out). However, a tolerated trespasser may bring proceedings in nuisance against the "landlord" (*Pemberton v. Southwark LBC* [2000] 1 W.L.R. 1672; [2000] 3 All E.R. 924, CA (cockroach infestation from common parts)).

An agreement to forbear from evicting a former tenant after breach of a suspended possession order does not restore the old tenancy but simply means the occupier is in a legal limbo as a "tolerated trespasser" until either the agreement to forbear is broken (in which case the landlord can seek a warrant) or the former tenant applies successfully to the court to discharge, rescind or modify the order so as to revive the earlier tenancy (*Burrows v. Brent LBC* [1996] 1 W.L.R. 1448; [1996] 4 All E.R. 577, HL; *Marshall v. Bradford MBC* above and *Greenwich LBC v. Regan* (1996) 28 H.L.R. 469; (1996) 72 P. & C.R. 507, CA, see too *Newham LBC v. Hawkins* [2005] EWCA Civ 451; 22 April 2005; *The Times* May 3, 2005; *Lambeth LBC v. O'Kane*; *Helena Housing v. Pinder* [2005] EWCA Civ 1010; 28 July 2005 (sending notice of variation of tenancy conditions and four notices of revision of rent and water charges to tolerated trespasser did not create new tenancy); *cf. Swindon BC (formerly Thamesdown BC) v. Aston* [2002] EWCA Civ 1850; [2003] HLR 42; [2003] L&TR 18; (conduct of both landlord and tenant after possession order, including the provision of a new tenancy agreement, was sensibly referable only to the existence of a new tenancy). Occupiers are not, however, homeless because they continue in occupation by "rule of law" (Housing Act 1996, s.175(1)(c)).

If either party wishes to revive the old tenancy for the purpose of enforcing its express or implied terms, they can apply to the court for an order varying the date on which possession is to be given so that the old tenancy can be resurrected (s.85(2)). It is possible for a court to exercise the discretion to postpone the date for possession (Housing Act 1985, s.85(2)(a)) after the terms of a suspended possession order have been breached, with the effect that the tenancy and its obligations revive retrospectively (unless the court otherwise directs (s.85(3)(b)). See *Routh v. Leeds CC* June 1998, Legal Action 11, CA and *Lambeth LBC v. Rogers* (2000) 32 H.L.R. 361; [2000] 03 E.G. 127, CA.

When considering an application to revive retrospectively a tenancy, the court should bear in mind: (i) the tenant's previous payment record; (ii) whether all parties were before the court; and (iii) whether the tenant was seeking merely the execution of works of repair or also damages for past disrepair (*Marshall v. Bradford MBC* above).

Relevance of other conduct

(a) *on a landlord's application*—After a suspended possession order has been made, liberty to apply to the court by the landlord is implicit, without the need to start new proceedings for possession. If a landlord wishes to put new allegations before the court, the court can make a new order, even if the old order has not expired. Such a new order may provide for possession to be given up forthwith. The court has, on such an application, to bear in mind the guidance given in cases such as *Sheffield City Council v. Hopkins* [2001] EWCA Civ 1023; [2002] H.L.R. 12; [2001] 26 E.G. 163, as to the exercise of its discretion in such a situation, and should be astute to ensure that tenants are not taken by surprise. However, that does not necessarily extend to insisting that the proceedings be delayed by the equivalent of the extra time that would have been taken had the landlord had to begin new proceedings (*Manchester City Council v. Finn* [2002] EWCA Civ 1998; [2003] H.L.R. 41).

(b) *on a tenant's application*—The court, exercising its discretion on an application to suspend a warrant under s.85, may take account of matters (*e.g.* breaches of the terms of the tenancy agreement or anti-social behaviour) other than those relied upon as grounds for making the original possession order—although it

3A-380

is not always right to do so (*Sheffield City Council v. Hopkins* [2001] EWCA Civ 1023; [2002] H.L.R. 12; [2001] 26 E.G. 163). Whilst not attempting to fetter the discretion of District Judges, the Court of Appeal stated that the following points are relevant: (1) The discretion should be used so as to further the policy of Housing Act 1985, Part IV, reinforced by ECHR Art.8. The policy is only to evict after a serious breach of an obligation, where it is reasonable to do so and where the tenant is proved to have breached any condition of suspension; (2) The overriding objective of the Civil Procedure Rules, especially the need for applications to be dealt with in a summary and proportionate way, means that wider issues may not be able to be dealt with on an application to suspend or vary. They may need to be dealt with in some other way; (3) The tenant should have clear evidence of what is alleged, especially where the allegations were not contained in the original claim; (4) The fact that the landlord had or had not included the allegations as part of the original proceedings is relevant; (5) The discretion to consider other allegations should generally be exercised more readily in respect of matters occurring after commencement of the proceedings; (6) The court should also consider the practicalities of dealing with matters on the execution of a warrant; (7) The fact that the tenant is at the mercy of the court and the responsibilities of a public landlord to its other tenants. The list is not exhaustive. District Judges have to exercise the discretion bearing in mind the importance of the issue to the tenant, at risk of losing his home, and the responsibilities of social landlords to their other tenants. However it would appear that the court cannot take into account allegations which have not been proved or admitted by the tenant.

After execution of a warrant

3A–381 The court's power to stay or suspend execution or postpone the date of possession only applies before the execution of the order (*Hammersmith and Fulham LBC v. Hill* (1995) 27 H.L.R. 368; [2001] L. & T.R. 423; [1994] 2 E.G.L.R. 51, CA and *Leicester CC v. Aldwinkle* (1992) 24 H.L.R. 40, CA). After execution an occupier can only be restored to possession if either the possession order is set aside (see, *e.g. Governors of Peabody Donation Fund v. Hay* (1987) 19 H.L.R. 145, CA; *Hackney LBC v. White* (1995) 28 H.L.R. 219, CA; and *Tower Hamlets LBC v. Abadie* (1990) 22 H.L.R. 264, CA) or the warrant has been obtained by fraud, abuse of process or oppression (*Hammersmith and Fulham LBC v. Hill* (1995) 27 H.L.R. 368; [2001] L. & T.R. 423; [1994] 2 E.G.L.R. 51, CA (arguable that the council had behaved "oppressively" where the tenant claimed that after issue of the warrant, but before execution, council officers had said that the defendant would have no chance of having the warrant suspended unless she was able to pay £1,000 within 24 hours); *Saint v. Barking and Dagenham LBC* (1999) 31 H.L.R. 620, CA (oppression where warrant executed without prior notification to tenant who was in prison and without inviting him to renew his application for housing benefit); and *William Sutton HT v. Breen*, February 2000, Legal Action. See too *Islington LBC v. Harridge*, *The Times*, June 30, 1993, CA.

In *Southwark LBC v. Sarfo* (2000) 32 H.L.R. 602, CA, Roch L.J. said:

"Oppression may be very difficult if not impossible to define, but it is not difficult to recognise. It is the insistence by a public authority on its strict rights in circumstances which make that insistence manifestly unfair. The categories of oppression are not closed because no-one can envisage all the sets of circumstances which could make the execution of a warrant oppressive".

"Oppression" is not limited to acts by the landlord. Misleading information from a court office, depriving a tenant of taking steps to have execution of a warrant for possession stayed prior to execution, may amount to oppression (*Hammersmith and Fulham LBC v. Lemeh* (2001) 33 H.L.R. 23; [2001] L & T R. 423, CA). See too *Lambeth LBC v. Hughes* (2001) 33 H.L.R. 350, CA where the Court of Appeal held that:

(1) a council's letter that only payment in full could prevent eviction was misleading and oppressive;

(2) the failure of the court office to advise the defendant of the procedure when he sought assistance in person was oppressive and

(3) the failure to despatch the bailiff's letter in sufficient time for it to be received and acted upon again made the execution oppressive.

However it has also been held that (1) a possession warrant obtained and executed against a secure tenant without fault on anyone's part cannot properly be set aside as oppressive or an abuse of process; (2) oppression cannot exist without the unfair use of court procedures; and (3) something more than the mere use of the eviction process "some action on someone's part which was open to criticism" is required before the court's procedures can be said to have been unfairly used (*Jephson Homes HA v. Moisejevs* [2001] 2 All E.R. 901, CA). See too *Circle 33 Housing Trust v.Ellis* [2005] EWCA Civ 1233; 23 September 2005.

There is no power under s.85(2) to stay or postpone the date for giving up possession under an existing possession order if tenants have already given up possession without the need for execution of the order. The words "at any time before the execution of the order" in s.85(2) have to be read subject to the qualification "and for so long as execution is required to give effect to that order" (*Dunn v. Bradford MDC* [2002] EWCA Civ 1137; [2003] H.L.R. 15, *Marston v. Leeds City Council* [2002] EWCA Civ 1137; [2003] H.L.R. 15).

Warrants and the ECHR

The Court of Appeal has held that the procedure which allows the issue of a warrant of possession and the arrangements for execution following breach of a suspended possession order do not infringe tenants' rights under ECHR Arts 6, 8 or 14. Tenants' rights to possession of premises are determined, when suspended possession orders are made. The issue of the warrant of possession is simply a step authorised to be taken to enforce that order. It does not alter the legal status of the tenant or make any kind of decision in relation to his or her rights, and so is not required to be the subject of a separate hearing. Secondly, although possession proceedings may interfere with tenants' right of respect for their homes, they are clearly in accordance with the law and are a legitimate and proportionate response to non-payment of rent. (*Southwark LBC v. St. Brice* [2001] EWCA Civ 1138; [2001] 1 W.L.R. 1537) and see too *Harrow LBC v. Qazi* [2003] UKHL 43; [2003] 3 W.L.R. 792; *Newham LBC v. Kibata* [2003] EWCA Civ 1785; [2004] HLR 28 and *Bradney v. Birmingham CC*; *Birmingham CC v. McCann* [2003] EWCA Civ 1783; [2004] HLR 27.

Nevertheless, the Lord Chancellor's Department (LCD) has improved the information available to occupiers when an eviction is due to take place. Bailiffs must deliver Form **N54** (Notice of Eviction) to all addresses where evictions are due to take place and hand it to the defendant personally or leave it at the property in an envelope addressed to the defendant(s) by name and "any other occupiers". The notice points out that in some circumstances the court can decide to suspend the warrant and explains the procedure to be followed. In *Southwark LBC v. St. Brice*, Kennedy L.J. said: "It is important that so far as possible tenants should receive such notice in time to enable time to take advice and, if so advised, bring the matter back to the court before the date fixed for eviction."

3A–382

Proceedings for possession: anti-social behaviour

85A—(1) This section applies if the court is considering under section 84(2)(a) whether it is reasonable to make an order for possession on ground 2 set out in Part 1 of Schedule 2 (conduct of tenant or other person).

(2) The court must consider, in particular—

    (a) the effect that the nuisance or annoyance has had on persons other than the person against whom the order is sought;

    (b) any continuing effect the nuisance or annoyance is likely to have on such persons;

    (c) the effect that the nuisance or annoyance would be likely to have on such persons if the conduct is repeated.

3A–383

Editorial note

This section was inserted by Anti-social Behaviour Act 2003, s.16. It was brought into force in England on June 30, 2004 by the Anti-social Behaviour Act 2003 (Commencement No.3 and Savings) Order 2004 (S.I. 2004 No. 1502) (c.61). It does not have effect in relation to any proceedings for the possession of a dwelling-house begun before June 30, 2004. It was brought into force in Wales on April 30, 2005 by the

3A–384

HOUSING

Anti-social Behaviour Act 2003 (Commencement No. 4) (Wales) Order 2005 (S.I. 2005 No. 1225) (W.83) (C.55).

Reasonable

3A–385   When considering whether or not to make a possession order and/or whether or not to make a suspended possession order under Schedule 2 Ground 2, the court must consider whether it is reasonable to make such an order—see the commentary to s.84 at para. 3A–379. Section 85A adds to that general consideration a requirement that the court must consider, in particular, the effect that the nuisance or annoyance has had and would be likely to have if continued on persons other than the defendant, *e.g.* neighbours.

Periodic tenancy arising on termination of fixed term

3A–386   **86.**—(1) Where a secure tenancy ("the first tenancy") is a tenancy for a term certain and comes to an end—

(a) by effluxion of time, or

(b) by an order of the court under section 82(3) (termination in pursuance of provision for re-entry or forfeiture),

a periodic tenancy of the same dwelling-house arises by virtue of this section, unless the tenant is granted another secure tenancy of the same dwelling-house (whether a tenancy for a term certain or a periodic tenancy) to begin on the coming to an end of the first tenancy.

(2) Where a periodic tenancy arises by virtue of this section—

(a) the periods of the tenancy are the same as those for which rent was last payable under the first tenancy, and

(b) the parties and the terms of the tenancy are the same as those of the first tenancy at the end of it;

except that the terms are confined to those which are compatible with a periodic tenancy and do not include any provision for re-entry or forfeiture.

"dwelling-house"

3A–387   See s.112.

"secure tenancy"

3A–388   See s.79. See *Banjo v. Brent LBC* [2005] EWCA Civ 292; (2005) *The Times* March 29, 2005 , where the Court of Appeal held that no periodic tenancy arose on the determination a long lease, either under s.86 (because the fixed term tenancy which the tenant had previously held was not itself a secure tenancy) or by implication from the demand, payment or acceptance of rent. Security of tenure is dependent on there being a tenancy that the landlord cannot bring to an end without obtaining an order for possession.

SUCCESSION ON DEATH OF TENANT

Persons qualified to succeed tenant

3A–389   **87.** A person is qualified to succeed the tenant under a secure tenancy if he occupies the dwelling-house as his only or principal home at the time of the tenant's death and either—

(a) he is the tenant's spouse, or

(b) he is another member of the tenant's family and has resided with the tenant throughout the period of twelve months ending with the tenant's death;

unless, in either case, the tenant was himself a successor, as defined in section 88.

Note —This section has been amended by Civil Partnership Act 2004 s.81 and **3A–389.1**
Sched. 8 . The amendment is not yet in force, but is printed at para. 3A–1525.

"dwelling-house"
See s.112.   **3A–390**

"secure tenancy"
See s.79.   **3A–391**

"member of the tenant's family"
See s.113.   **3A–392**

"successor"
See s.88.   **3A–393**

Persons qualified to succeed tenant
On the death of a secure tenant, another person living in the dwelling as his/her **3A–394**
only or principal home may succeed to the tenancy if s/he is either the spouse of the
tenant or a member of the tenant's family who has resided with the tenant throughout
the 12 months ending with the death. Co-habitees count as family members (s.113). In
"family member" succession cases, the burden of proof is on successors to show that
they are family members, that they have lived with the tenant for the 12 months and
that the dwelling is their only or principal home (*Peabody Donation Fund Governors v.
Grant* (1983) 6 H.L.R. 41; (1982) 264 E.G. 925, CA). Section 87 is also relevant to the
question of assignment of secure tenancies, since one of the exceptions to the general
prohibition against assignment of secure tenancies (s.91) applies where the assignee is
"a person who would be qualified to succeed the tenant if the tenant died immediately
before the assignment".

Security of tenure is commonly lost when a tenant dies and there is no person
qualified to succeed to the tenancy. In such circumstances the tenancy passes to the
late tenant's executors or administrators. In the case of intestacy, the tenancy now passes to the Public Trustee (Law of Property (Miscellaneous Provisions) Act 1994, s.14).
A Practice Direction (Probate: Notice to Quit [1995] 1 W.L.R. 1120) indicates how a
notice to quit may be served on the Public Trustee to bring the continuing tenancy to
an end. See too Sched.2, Ground 16 (ground for possession where dwelling more
extensive than reasonably required after succession).

It is not possible for there to be a joint succession to a secure tenancy (*Newham LBC
v. Phillips* (1998) 30 H.L.R. 859; (1998) 96 L.G.R. 788, CA).

The twelve month residence requirement may be satisfied by residence with the
deceased council tenant in any premises or combination of premises (not necessarily
subject to secure tenancies for the whole period) for the one year ending with the date
of death (*Waltham Forest LBC v. Thomas* [1992] 2 A.C. 198; [1992] 3 W.L.R. 131; [1992]
3 All E.R. 244, HL, overruling *South Northamptonshire DC v. Power* [1987] 1 W.L.R.
1433, CA).

The term "residence" is interpreted in much the same way as in the Rent Act 1977,
s.2, the Housing Act 1985, s.81, and the Housing Act 1988, s.1. Periods of temporary
absence (if there is an intention to return and a physical manifestation of that intention) or residence at other premises do not necessarily prevent "residence" continuing.
See, *e.g. Peabody Donation Fund Governors v. Grant* (1983) 6 H.L.R. 41; (1982) 264 E.G.
925, CA (daughter moved in to live with father who was ill for part of each week in
order to look after him. She stayed in her father's flat four nights a week, kept her
clothes and books there and regarded the flat as her home. She was entitled to succeed); *Camden LBC v. Goldenberg* (1996) 28 H.L.R. 727; (1997) 73. P & C.R. 376, CA
(grandson moved out after marriage, but he and his wife could not find alternative accommodation and as a result he moved back after ten weeks) and *Marsh v. Lewisham
LBC* December 1989, Legal Action 14, CA.

The Court of Appeal has held that the Housing Act 1985, s.87, when read together
with the words "living together as husband and wife" in s.113, means that in order to
be entitled to succeed a cohabitee must not only have lived with the deceased for a

year but have lived as "husband or wife" for the whole year. Succession cannot be established where the cohabitation "as husband and wife" has been for only part of the 12 months of co-residence (*Westminster CC v. Peart* (1992) 24 H.L.R. 389, CA).

Same sex couples may be treated in the same way as a husband and wife. The House of Lords has held that the words "as his or her wife or husband" in Rent Act 1977, Sched.1, para.2(2) must be read to mean "as if they were his or her wife or husband" in order to comply with the ECHR. Accordingly the survivor of a same sex couple who has been living in a loving and monogamous relationship with a tenant may be able to succeed to a secure tenancy (see *Ghaidan v. Mendoza* [2004] UKHL 30; [2004] 3 W.L.R. 113; *cf. Harrogate BC v. Simpson* (1985) 17 H.L.R. 205, CA and *Fitzpatrick v. Sterling Housing Association* [2001] 1 AC 27; [1999] 3 W.L.R. 1113; [1999] 4 All E.R. 705, HL).

The term "member of the family" can only be satisfied by the relationships listed in Housing Act 1985, s.113. First cousins, even if thought of as brothers in African culture, cannot be within the section (*Brent LBC v. Fofana*, September 1999, Legal Action 28, CA).

The right to succeed only applies where a secure tenancy is still in existence. It comes to an end if the terms of a suspended possession order have been breached (s.85(5), and *Brent LBC v. Knightley* (1997) 29 H.L.R. 857, CA). A minor who satisfies the succession conditions may succeed to a secure tenancy. In that case a secure tenancy in equity vests in the minor. The Trusts of Land and Appointment of Trustees Act 1996, Sched.1 operates in such a way that the legal tenancy to which the minor succeeded is held on trust until the age of majority is reached (*Kingston-Upon-Thames RLBC v. Prince* (1999) 31 H.L.R. 794, CA and *Newham LBC v. Ria* [2004] EWCA Civ 41; January 15, 2004).

Cases where the tenant is a successor

3A–395 **88.**—(1) The tenant is himself a successor if—

    (a) the tenancy vested in him by virtue of section 89 (succession to a periodic tenancy), or

    (b) he was a joint tenant and has become the sole tenant, or

    (c) the tenancy arose by virtue of section 86 (periodic tenancy arising on ending of term certain) and the first tenancy there mentioned was granted to another person or jointly to him and another person, or

    (d) he became the tenant on the tenancy being assigned to him (but subject to subsections (2) and (3)), or

    (e) he became the tenant on the tenancy being vested in him on the death of the previous tenant, or

    (f) the tenancy was previously an introductory tenancy and he was a successor to the introductory tenancy.

(2) A tenant to whom the tenancy was assigned in pursuance of an order under section 23A or 24 of the Matrimonial Causes Act 1973 (property adjustment orders in connection with matrimonial proceedings) or section 17(1) of the Matrimonial and Family Proceedings Act 1984 (property adjustment orders after overseas divorce) is a successor only if the other party to the marriage was a successor.

(3) A tenant to whom the tenancy was assigned by virtue of section 92 (assignments by way of exchange) is a successor only if he was a successor in relation to the tenancy which he himself assigned by virtue of that section.

(4) Where within six months of the coming to an end of a secure tenancy which is a periodic tenancy ("the former tenancy") the tenant becomes a tenant under another secure tenancy which is a periodic tenancy, and—

(a) the tenant was a successor in relation to the former tenancy, and

(b) under the other tenancy either the dwelling-house or the landlord, or both, are the same as under the former tenancy,

the tenant is also a successor in relation to the other tenancy unless the agreement creating that tenancy otherwise provides.

Note —Amended by the Housing Act 1996, Sched.14, para. 1, Sched.18, para. 9; **3A–396** and the Family Law Act 1996, Sched.8, para. 34. This section has been amended by the Civil Partnership Act 2004, s.81 and Sched. 8 . The amendment is not yet in force, but is printed at para. 3A–1525.

"dwelling-house"
See s.112.   **3A–397**

"secure tenancy"
See s.79.   **3A–398**

"introductory tenancy"
See s.115A and the Housing Act 1996, s.124.   **3A–399**

Succession to periodic tenancy

89.—(1) This section applies where a secure tenant dies and the **3A–400** tenancy is a periodic tenancy.

(2) Where there is a person qualified to succeed the tenant, the tenancy vests by virtue of this section in that person, or if there is more than one such person in the one to be preferred in accordance with the following rules—

(a) the tenant's spouse is to be preferred to another member of the tenant's family;

(b) of two or more other members of the tenant's family such of them is to be preferred as may be agreed between them or as may, where there is no such agreement, be selected by the landlord.

(3) Where there is no person qualified to succeed the tenant, the tenancy ceases to be a secure tenancy—

(a) where it is vested or otherwise disposed of in the course of the administration of the tenants' estate, unless the vesting or other disposal is in pursuance of an order made under—

(i) section 23A or 24 of the Matrimonial Causes Act 1973 (property adjustment orders made in connection with matrimonial proceedings),

(ii) section 17(1) of the Matrimonial and Family Proceedings Act 1984 (property adjustment orders after overseas divorce), or

(iii) paragraph 1 of Schedule 1 to the Children Act 1989 (orders for financial relief against parents); or

(b) When it is known that when the tenancy is so vested or disposed of it will not be in pursuance of such an order.

HOUSING

(4) A tenancy which ceases to be a secure tenancy by virtue of this section cannot subsequently become a secure tenancy.

3A–401 *Note* —Amended by the Housing Act 1996, Sched.18, para. 10; and the Family Law Act 1996, Sched.8, para. 34. This section has been amended by the Civil Partnership Act 2004, s.81 and Sched. 8. The amendment is not yet in force, but is printed at para. 3A–1525.

"secure tenancy"

3A–402 See s.79. The right to succeed is lost if the terms of a suspended possession order are breached and the tenant becomes a tolerated trespasser before death (*Newham LBC v. Hawkins* [2005] EWCA Civ 451; 22 April 2005 and *Brent LBC v. Knightley* (1997) 29 HLR 857., CA).

"member of the tenant's family"

3A–403 See s.113. Section 113 contains an exhaustive list of categories of family members eligible to succeed a secure tenant. Although that section is discriminatory in relation to a matter within the scope of ECHR Art.8 (the "home") and so Art.14 is engaged, there is an objective justification for establishing a "closed" list in s.113, namely "certainty" in determining which members of a secure tenant's family are eligible to succeed and accordingly Art.14 is not infringed. The fact that the Rent Acts contain no exhaustive definition of "member of the family" is not relevant to the construction of the section because the schemes of the Rent Act and the Housing Act tenancies are so different that a potential successor in one scheme has no "comparator" in the other scheme. On a claim for possession against a non-successor, the county court is not required to investigate the individual circumstances of the defendant in order to find the conditions of ECHR Art.8(2) made out. (*Michalak v. Wandsworth LBC* [2002] EWCA Civ 271; [2003] 1 W.L.R. 617). See too *R. (Gangera) v. Hounslow LBC* [2003] EWHC 794 Admin; [2003] H.L.R. 68 (where Moses J. held that the provisions prohibiting people in categories other than those listed in s.113 from succeeding to secure tenancies do not infringe ECHR Article 14 read with Article 8) and *Harrow LBC v. Qazi* [2003] UKHL 43; [2003] 3 W.L.R. 792; (where Lord Hope and Lord Scott approved these decisions and said that contractual and property rights cannot be defeated by a defence based on Article 8). See too *Newham LBC v. Kibata* [2003] EWCA Civ 1785; [2004] HLR 28 and *Bradney v. Birmingham CC*; *Birmingham CC v. McCann* [2003] EWCA Civ 1783; [2004] HLR 27.

"qualified to succeed"

3A–404 See s.87.
It has been held that if a minor would be entitled to succeed, by operation of the Trusts of Land and Appointment of Trustees Act 1996, Sched.1, the tenancy should be held on trust for him or her: *Kingston upon Thames RLBC v. Prince* (1999) 31 H.L.R. 794; [1999] L.G.R. 333, CA.

Devolution of term certain

3A–405 **90.**—(1) This section applies where a secure tenant dies and the tenancy is a tenancy for a term certain.

(2) The tenancy remains a secure tenancy until—

   (a) it vested or otherwise disposed of in the course of the administration of the tenant's estate, as mentioned in subsection (3), or

   (b) it is known that when it is so vested or disposed of it will not be a secure tenancy.

(3) The tenancy ceases to be a secure tenancy on being vested or otherwise disposed of in the course of administration of the tenant's estate, unless—

   (a) the vesting or other disposal is in pursuance of an order made under—

      (i) section 23A or 24 of the Matrimonial Causes Act 1973 (property adjustment orders in connection with matrimonial proceedings),

     (ii) section 17(1) of the Matrimonial and Family Proceedings Act 1984 (property adjustment orders after overseas divorce), or

    (iii) paragraph 1 of Schedule 1 to the Children Act 1989 (orders for financial relief against parents), or

  (b) the vesting or other disposal is to a person qualified to succeed the tenant.

(4) A tenancy which ceases to be a secure tenancy by virtue of this section cannot subsequently become a secure tenancy.

Note —Amended by the Housing Act 1996, Sched.18, para. 11; and the Family Law Act 1996. This section has been amended by the Civil Partnership Act 2004, s.81 and Sched. 8. The amendment is not yet in force, but is printed at para. 3A–1525.   **3A–406**

"secure tenancy"
See s.79.   **3A–407**

"qualified to succeed"
See s.87.   **3A–408**

ASSIGNMENT, LODGERS AND SUBLETTING

91.—(1) A secure tenancy which is—   **3A–409**
  (a) a periodic tenancy, or
  (b) a tenancy for a term certain granted on or after 5th November 1982, is not capable of being assigned except in the cases mentioned in subsection (3).

(2) If a secure tenancy for a term certain granted before 5th November 1982 is assigned, then, except in the cases mentioned in subsection (3), it ceases to be a secure tenancy and cannot subsequently become a secure tenancy.

(3) The exceptions are—
  (a) an assignment in accordance with section 92 (assignment by way of exchange);
  (b) an assignment in pursuance of an order made under—
     (i) section 23A or 24 of the Matrimonial Causes Act 1973 (property adjustment orders in connection with matrimonial proceedings),
    (ii) section 17(1) of the Matrimonial and Family Proceedings Act 1984 (property adjustment orders after overseas divorce), or
    (iii) paragraph 1 of Schedule 1 to the Children Act 1989 (orders for financial relief against parents),
  (c) an assignment to a person who would be qualified to succeed the tenant if the tenant died immediately before the assignment.

Note —Amended by the Housing Act 1996, Sched.18, para. 12; and the Family Law Act 1996, Sched.8, para. 34. This section has been amended by the Civil Partnership   **3A–410**

Act 2004, s.81 and Sched. 8. The amendment is not yet in force, but is printed at para. 3A–1525.

"secure tenancy"

3A–411　　See s.79.

"qualified to succeed"

3A–412　　See s.87.

Deed of Release

3A–413　　The prohibition on assignment in s.91(1) applies equally to deeds of assignment and deeds of release (*Burton v. Camden LBC* [2000] 2 A.C. 399; [2000] 2 W.L.R. 427, [2000] 1 All E.R. 943, HL).

Assignments by way of exchange

3A–414　　**92.**—(1) It is a term of every secure tenancy that the tenant may, with the written consent of the landlord, assign the tenancy to another secure tenant who satisfies the condition in subsection (2) or to an assured tenant who satisfies the conditions in subsection 2A.

(2) The condition is that the other secure tenant has the written consent of his landlord to an assignment of his tenancy either to the first-mentioned tenant or to another secure tenant who satisfies the condition in this subsection.

(2A) The conditions to be satisfied with respect to an assured tenant are—

(a) that the landlord under is assured tenancy is either the Housing Corporation, the Secretary of State, a registered housing association or a housing trust which is a charity; and

(b) that he intends to assign his assured tenancy to the secure tenant referred to in subsection (1) or to another secure tenant who satisfies the condition in subsection (2).

(3) The consent required by virtue of this section shall not be withheld except on one or more of the grounds set out in Schedule 3, and if withheld otherwise than on one of those grounds shall be treated as given.

(4) The landlord may not rely on any of the grounds set out in Schedule 3 unless he has, within 42 days of the tenant's application for the consent, served on the tenant a notice specifying the ground and giving particulars of it.

(5) Where rent lawfully due from the tenant has not been paid or an obligation of the tenancy has been broken or not performed, the consent required by virtue of this section may be given subject to a condition requiring the tenant to pay the outstanding rent, remedy the breach or perform the obligation.

(6) Except as provided by subsection (5), a consent required by virtue of this section cannot be given subject to a condition, and a condition imposed otherwise than as so provided shall be disregarded.

3A–415　　*Note*—Amended by the Local Government and Housing Act 1989, s.163; the Housing Act 1996 (Consequential Provisions) Order 1996 (S.I. 1996 No. 2325), art.5,

Sched.2, para. 14 and the Government of Wales Act 1998, s.140 and Sched.16, para. 10 and Sched.18, Pt VI.

"secure tenancy"

See s.79.   3A–416

"term"

See s.116.   3A–417

"assured tenancy"

See ss. 117 and 622, and the Housing Act 1988, s.1. See too Sched.2, Ground 6   3A–418
(ground for possession where premium charged on mutual exchange), and Sched.3
(grounds for withholding consent to assignment).

Assignments by way of exchange

The right to "mutual exchange" may be exercised between secure and assured ten-   3A–419
ants provided that they have the written consent of their landlords. Consent may only
be withheld on the grounds set out in Sched.3. If it is withheld other than on such
grounds, it is to be treated as having been given (s.91(3)).

To be effective an assignment must be by deed (Law of Property Act 1925, s.52, and
Crago v. Julian [1992] 1 W.L.R. 372; (1991) 24 H.L.R. 306, CA).

See also *Sanctuary Housing Association v. Baker* (1998) 30 H.L.R. 809, CA.

Lodgers and subletting

93.—(1) It is a term of every secure tenancy that the tenant—   3A–420
    (a) may allow any persons to reside as lodgers in the
        dwelling-house, but
    (b) will not, without the written consent of the landlord,
        sublet or part with possession of part of the dwelling-
        house.

(2) If the tenant under a secure tenancy parts with the possession
of the dwelling-house or sublets the whole of it (or sublets first part
of it and then the remainder), the tenancy ceases to be a secure
tenancy and cannot subsequently become a secure tenancy.

"secure tenancy"

See s.79.   3A–421

"dwelling-house"

See s.112.   3A–422

"lodgers"

Not defined in the Housing Act 1985, but see *Street v. Mountford* [1985] A.C. 809;   3A–423
[1985] 2 W.L.R. 877; [1985] 2 All E.R. 289; (1985) 17 H.L.R. 402, HL; *Aslan v. Murphy*
[1989] 3 All E.R. 130; [1989] 38 E.G. 109; (1989) 21 H.L.R. 532, CA; *Crancour Ltd v.
Da Silvaesa* (1986) 18 H.L.R. 265; (1986) 278 E.G. 618, CA; *Huwyer v. Ruddy* (1995) 28
H.L.R. 550, CA; and *Monmouth BC v. Marlog* (1994) 27 H.L.R. 30, CA.

"sub-letting or parting with possession"

See *Muir Group Housing Association Ltd v. Thornley* (1993) 25 H.L.R. 89, CA; and   3A–424
Brent LBC v. Cronin (1997) 30 H.L.R. 43, CA, *cf. Merton LBC v. Salama* (1989) CAT No.
89/169; June 1989, Legal Action 25, CA (parting with possession of part of premises);
and *Hussey v. Camden LBC* (1994) 27 H.L.R. 5, CA. Parting with possession is not to be
inferred simply from the fact that another person has been allowed to use and occupy
a tenant's home during his temporary absence (*Lam Kee Ying v. Lam Shes Tong* [1975]
A.C. 247, PC). See too the commentary to s.81. Section 93(2) is not incompatible with
ECHR Art.8 or Art.1 of the First Protocol (*Delson v. Lambeth LBC* [2002] EWCA Civ
1894; November 19, 2002).

"consent of the landlord"

See s.94.   3A–425

Consent to subletting

3A–426   94.—(1) This section applies to the consent required by virtue of section 93(1)(b)(landlord's consent to subletting of part of dwelling-house).

(2) Consent shall not be unreasonably withheld (and if unreasonably withheld shall be treated as given), and if a question arises whether the withholding of consent was unreasonable it is for the landlord to show that it was not.

(3) In determining that question the following matters, if shown by the landlord, are among those to be taken into account—

    (a) that the consent would lead to overcrowding of the dwelling-house within the meaning of Part X (overcrowding);

    (b) that the landlord proposes to carry out works on the dwelling-house, or on the building of which it forms part, and that the proposed works will affect the accommodation likely to be used by the sub-tenant who would reside in the dwelling-house as a result of the consent.

(4) Consent may be validly given notwithstanding that it follows, instead of preceding, the action requiring it.

(5) Consent cannot be given subject to a condition (and if purporting to be given subject to a condition shall be treated as given unconditionally).

(6) Where the tenant has applied in writing for consent, then—

    (a) if the landlord refuses to give consent, it shall give the tenant a written statement of the reasons why consent was refused, and

    (b) if the landlord neither gives nor refuses to give consent within a reasonable time, consent shall be taken to have been withheld.

"dwelling-house"
3A–427   See s.112.

"overcrowding"
3A–428   See s.324.

Assignment or subletting where tenant condition not satisfied

3A–429   95.—(1) This section applies to a tenancy which is not a secure tenancy but would be if the tenant condition referred to in section 81 (occupation by the tenant) were satisfied.

(2) Sections 91 and 93(2) (restrictions on assignment or subletting of whole dwelling-house) apply to such a tenancy as they apply to a secure tenancy, except that—

    (a) section 91(3)(b) and (c) (assignments expected from restrictions) do not apply to such a tenancy for a term certain granted before 5th November 1982, and

    (b) references to the tenancy ceasing to be secure shall be disregarded, without prejudice to the application of the

760

remainder of the provisions in which those references occur.

"secure tenancy"
See s.79.   **3A–430**

"tenant condition"
See s.81.   **3A–431**

Acquisition of dwelling-house subject to statutory tenancy

109A. Where an authority or body within section 80 (the landlord **3A–432** condition for secure tenancies) becomes the landlord of a dwelling-house subject to a statutory tenancy, the tenancy shall be treated for all purposes as if it were a contractual tenancy on the same terms, and the provisions of this Part apply accordingly.

Note —Inserted by Housing and Planning Act 1986 s.24(1)(b), Sched. 5, Part 1, **3A–433** para. 2.

* * * *

SUPPLEMENTARY PROVISIONS

Jurisdiction of county court

110.—(1) A county court has jurisdiction to determine questions **3A–434** arising under this Part and to entertain proceedings brought under this Part and claims, for whatever amount, in connection with a secure tenancy.

(2) That jurisdiction includes jurisdiction to entertain proceedings on the following questions—

   (a) whether a consent required by section 92 (assignment by way of exchange) was withheld otherwise than on one or more of the grounds set out in Schedule 3,

   (b) whether a consent required by section 93(1)(b) or 97(1) (landlord's consent to subletting of part of dwelling-house or to carrying out of improvements) was withheld or unreasonably withheld, or

   (c) whether a statement supplied in pursuance of section 104(2)(b)(written statement of certain terms of tenancy) is accurate,

notwithstanding that no other relief is sought than a declaration.

(3) If a person takes proceedings in the High Court which, by virtue of this section, he could have taken in the county court, he is not entitled to recover any costs.

County court rules and directions

111.—(1) The Lord Chancellor may make such rules and give such **3A–435** directions as he thinks fit for the purpose of giving effect to—

   (a) section 85 (extended discretion of court in certain proceedings for possession), and

   (b) section 110 (jurisdiction of county court to determine questions arising under this Part).

(2) The rules and directions may provide—

    (a) for the exercise by a registrar of a county court of any jurisdiction exercisable under the provisions mentioned in subsection (1), and

    (b) for the conduct of proceedings in private.

(3) The power to make rules is exercisable by statutory instrument which shall be subject to annulment in pursuance of a resolution of either House of Parliament.

Introductory tenancies

3A–436   **111A.** Sections 102(1), (2) and (3)(a), 103 and 108 apply in relation to introductory tenancies as they apply in relation to secure tenancies.

3A–437   *Note* —Inserted by the Housing Act 1996 (Consequential Amendments) Order 1997 (S.I. 1997 No. 74), art.2, Sched., para. 3(a), (i).

    See also s.115A and the Housing Act 1996, s.124.

Meaning of "dwelling-house"

3A–438   **112.**—(1) For the purposes of this Part a dwelling-house may be a house or a part of a house.

(2) Land let together with a dwelling-house shall be treated for the purposes of this Part as part of the dwelling-house unless the land is agricultural land (as defined in section 26(3)(a) of the General Rate Act 1967) exceeding two acres.

Members of a person's family

3A–439   **113.**—(1) A person is a member of another's family within the meaning of this Part if—

    (a) he is the spouse of that person, or he and that person live together as husband and wife, or

    (b) he is that person's parent, grandparent, child, grandchild, brother, sister, uncle, aunt, nephew or niece.

(2) For the purpose of subsection (1)(b)—

    (a) a relationship by marriage shall be treated as a relationship by blood,

    (b) a relationship of the half-blood shall be treated as a relationship of the whole blood,

    (c) the stepchild of a person shall be treated as his child, and

    (d) an illegitimate child shall be treated as the legitimate child of his mother and reputed father.

3A–439.1   *Note* —This section has been amended by the Civil Partnership Act 2004, s.81 and Sched.8. The amendment is not yet in force, but is printed at para. 3A–1525.

Members of a person's family

3A–440   See commentary to s.87.

Meaning of "landlord authority"

3A–441   **114.**—(1) In this Part "landlord authority" means—

    a local housing authority,

a registered social landlord other than a co-operative housing association,

a housing trust which is a charity,

a development corporation,

a housing action trust, or

an urban development corporation

other than an authority in respect of which an exemption certificate has been issued.

(2) The Secretary of State may, on an application duly made by the authority concerned, issue an exemption certificate to—

a development corporation,

a housing action trust, or

an urban development corporation,

if he is satisfied that it has transferred, or otherwise disposed of, at least three-quarters of the dwellings which have at any time before the making of the application been vested in it.

(3) The application shall be in such form and shall be accompanied by such information as the Secretary of State may, either generally or in relation to a particular case, direct.

Note —Amended by the Housing Act 1988, s.83; the Housing Act 1996 (Consequential Provisions) Order 1996 (S.I. 1996 No. 2325), Art. 5, Sched.2, para. 14 and the Government of Wales Act 1998, Sched.15, para. 10 and Sched.18, Pt IV.   **3A–442**

"local housing authority"
See ss.1 and 2.   **3A–443**

"housing action trust"
See s.4.   **3A–444**

"housing trust"
See s.6.   **3A–445**

"an urban development corporation"
See s.4.   **3A–446**

"development corporation"
See s.4.   **3A–447**

"registered social landlord"
See the Housing Act 1996, ss.1–7.   **3A–448**

Meaning of "long tenancy"

115.—(1) The following are long tenancies for the purposes of this **3A–449** Part, subject to subsection (2)—

> (a) a tenancy granted for a term certain exceeding 21 years, whether or not it is (or may become) terminable before the end of that term by notice given by the tenant or by re-entry or forfeiture;
>
> (b) a tenancy for a term fixed by law under a grant with a covenant or obligation for perpetual renewal, other than a tenancy by sub-demise from one which is not a long tenancy;

(c) any tenancy granted in pursuance of Part V (the right to buy), including any tenancy granted in pursuance of that Part as it has effect by virtue of section 17 of the Housing Act 1996 (the right to acquire).

(2) A tenancy granted so as to become terminable by notice after a death is not a long tenancy for the purposes of this Part, unless—

(a) it is granted by a housing association which at the time of the grant is a registered social landlord

(b) it is granted at a premium calculated by reference to a percentage of the value of the dwelling-house or of the cost of providing it, and

(c) at the time it is granted it complies with the requirements of the regulations then in force under section 140(4)(b) of the Housing Act 1980 or paragraph 4(2)(b) of Schedule 4A to the Leasehold Reform Act 1967 (conditions for exclusion of shared ownership leases from Part I of the Leasehold Reform Act 1967) or, in the case of a tenancy granted before any such regulations were brought into force, with the first such regulations to be in force.

3A–450   *Note* —Amended by the Housing Act 1988, s.140, Sched.17, para. 40; and the Housing Act 1996 (Consequential Provisions) Order 1996 (S.I. 1996 No. 2325), art.5, Sched.2, para. 14; and the Housing Act 1996 (Consequential Amendments No. 2) Order 1997 (S.I. 1997 No. 627), Sched.2, para. 3.

Meaning of "introductory tenancy"
3A–451   **115A.** In this Part "introductory tenancy" has the same meaning as in Chapter I of Part V of the Housing Act 1996.

3A–452   *Note* —Inserted by the Housing Act 1996, s.141(1), Sched.14, para. 3. See also the Housing Act 1996, s.124.

Minor definitions
3A–453   **116.** In this Part—

"common parts", in relation to a dwelling-house let under a tenancy, means any part of a building comprising the dwelling-house and any other premises which the tenant is entitled under the terms of the tenancy to use in common with the occupiers of other dwelling-houses let by the landlord;

"housing purposes" means the purposes for which dwelling-houses are held by local housing authorities under Part II (provision of housing) or purposes corresponding to those purposes;

"rental period" means a period in respect of which a payment of rent falls to be made;

"term", in relation to a secure tenancy, includes a condition of the tenancy.

Index of defined expressions: Part IV
3A–454   **117.** The following Table shows provisions defining or otherwise

explaining expressions used in this Part (other than provisions defining or explaining an expression in the same section or paragraph)—

assured tenancy	section 622
cemetery	section 622
charity	section 622
common parts (in relation to a dwelling-house let under a tenancy)	section 116
consent	Schedule 3A, para. 2(3)
co-operative housing association	section 5(2)
development corporation	section 4(c)
dwelling-house	section 112
family (member of)	section 113
housing association	section 5(1)
housing authority	section 4(a)
housing purposes	section 116
housing trust	section 6
improvement	section 97(2)
introductory tenancy	section 115A
landlord	Schedule 2 Part V, para. 7
landlord authority	section 114
local authority	section 4(e)
local housing authority	section 1, 2(2)
long tenancy	section 115
management agreement and manager	section 27(2) and 27B(4)
new town corporation	section 4(b)
qualified to succeed (on the death of a secure tenant)	section 87
registered social landlord	section 5(4) and (5)
relevant Authority	section 6A
rental period	section 116
secure tenancy	section 79
term (in relation to a secure tenancy)	section 116

Note—Amended by the Housing and Planning Act 1986, s.24(1), (2), Sched.5; the Housing Act 1988, s.140, Sched.17; the Housing Act 1996, s.141(1), Sched.14, para. 4; the Housing Act 1996 (Consequential Provisions) Order 1996 (S.I. 1996 No. 2325), art.5, Sched.2, para. 14 and the Government of Wales Act 1998, Sched.16, para. 11 and Sched.18, Pt VI. **3A–455**

* * * *

DEMOLITION ORDERS

Demolition orders: recovery of possession of building to be demolished

270.—(1) Where a demolition order has become operative with re- **3A–456**

spect to any premises, the local housing authority shall serve on any occupier of the premises or any part of the premises a notice—

    (a) stating the effect of the order,

    (b) specifying the date by which the order requires the premises to be vacated, and

    (c) requiring him to quit the premises before that date or before the expiration of 28 days from the service of the notice, whichever may be the later.

(2) If any person is in occupation of the premises, or any part of them, at any time after the date on which the notice requires the premises to be vacated, the local housing authority or an owner of the premises may apply to the county court which shall thereupon order vacant possession of the premises or part to be given to the applicant within such period, of not less than two or more than four weeks, as the court may determine.

(3) Nothing in the Rent Acts or Part I of the Housing Act 1988 affects the provisions of this section relating to the obtaining possession of any premises.

(4) Expenses incurred by the local housing authority under this section in obtaining possession of any premises, or part of any premises, may be recovered by them by action from the owner, or from any of the owners, of the premises.

(5) A person who, knowing that a demolition order has become operative and applies to any premises—

    (a) enters into occupation of the premises, or a part of them, after the date by which the order requires them to be vacated, or

    (b) permits another person to enter into such occupation after that date,

commits a summary offence and is liable on conviction to a fine not exceeding level 5 on the standard scale and to a further fine not exceeding £5 for every day or part of a day on which the occupation continues after conviction.

3A–457   *Note*—Amended by the Local Government and Housing Act 1989, Sched.9; and the Housing Act 1988, Sched.17.

"demolition order"

3A–458   Is defined by s.267 as "an order requiring that the premises—(a) be vacated within a specified period (of at least 28 days) from the date on which the order becomes operative, and (b) be demolished within six weeks after the end of that period, after the date on which it is vacated or, in either case, within such longer period as in the circumstances the local housing authority consider it reasonable to specify."

"local housing authority"

3A–459   See ss.1 and 2.

"owner"

3A–460   Is defined by s.322:

    "(a) ... a person (other than a mortgagee not in possession) who is for the time being entitled to dispose of the fee simple in premises, whether in possession or in the reversion, and

    (b) includes also a person holding or entitled to the rents and profits of the premises under a lease of which the unexpired term exceeds three years."

"premises"

Are defined by s.322 as "the dwelling-house, house in multiple occupation, building
or part of building in respect of which the closing order or, as the case may be, demolition order is made." "Dwelling house" includes "any yard, garden outhouses and appurtenances belonging to it or usually enjoyed with it ..."   **3A–461**

"Rent Acts"

Are defined by s.622 as the Rent Act 1977 and the Rent (Agriculture) Act 1976.   **3A–462**

Demolition orders

A tenant is not entitled to rely upon the protection of the Rent Act 1977 or the   **3A–463**
Housing Act 1988 when a demolition order is in force in relation to the premises (see
Marela v. Machorowski [1953] 1 Q.B. 565; and *Beaney v. Branchett* (1987) 19 H.L.R. 471,
CA). The effect of a demolition order is to remove security of tenure (*Johnson v. Felton*;
(1995) 27 H.L.R. 265, CA). However, any tenancy must still be terminated in the
normal way (*e.g.* by notice to quit) (see *Aslan v. Murphy (No. 2)* [1990] 1 W.L.R. 766;
[1989] 3 All E.R. 130, CA).

* * * *

CLOSING ORDERS

Closing orders: recovery of possession of house

276. Nothing in the Rent Acts or Part I of the Housing Act 1988   **3A–464**
prevents possession being obtained by the owner of premises in respect of which a closing order is in force.

Note — Section 276 was repealed by Housing Act 2004 Sched 16. However the   **3A–465**
repeal has not yet been implemented.
Amended by the Housing Act 1988, Sched.17, para. 47.

"owner"

See commentary to s.270.   **3A–466**

"premises"

See commentary to s.270.   **3A–467**

"closing order"

Is defined by s.267 as "an order prohibiting the use of the premises to which it re-   **3A–468**
lates for any purpose not approved by the local housing authority."

"Rent Acts"

Are defined by s.622 as the Rent Act 1977 and the Rent (Agriculture) Act 1976.   **3A–469**

Closing orders

A closing order brings security of tenure to an end in much the same was as a de-   **3A–470**
molition order (see the commentary to s.270 above).

SCHEDULES

SECTION 79   **SCHEDULE 1**

TENANCIES WHICH ARE NOT SECURE TENANCIES

Long leases

1. A tenancy is not a secure tenancy if it is a long tenancy.   **3A–471**

Introductory tenancies

1A. A tenancy is not a secure tenancy if it is an introductory tenancy or a   **3A–472**
tenancy which has ceased to be an introductory tenancy—

(a) by virtue of section 133(3) of the Housing Act 1996 (disposal on death to non-qualifying person), or

(b) by virtue of the tenant, or in the case of a joint tenancy every tenant, ceasing to occupy the dwelling-house as his only or principal home.

Demoted tenancies

3A–473   1B. A tenancy is not a secure tenancy if it is a demoted tenancy within the meaning of section 143A of the Housing Act 1996.

Premises occupied in connection with employment

3A–474   2.—(1) Subject to sub-paragraph 4B, a tenancy is not a secure tenancy if the tenant is an employee of the landlord or of—

a local authority,

a new town corporation,

a housing action trust,

an urban development corporation, or

the governors of an aided school,

and his contract of employment requires him to occupy the dwelling-house for the better performance of his duties.

(2) Subject to sub-paragraph 4B, a tenancy is not a secure tenancy if the tenant is a member of a police force and the dwelling-house is provided for him free of rent and rates in pursuance of regulations made under section 50 of the Police Act 1996(general regulations as to government, administration and conditions of service of police forces).

(3) Subject to sub-paragraph 4B, a tenancy is not a secure tenancy if the tenant is an employee of a fire and rescue authority and—

(a) his contract of employment requires him to live in close proximity to a particular fire station, and

(b) the dwelling-house was let to him by the authority in consequence of that requirement;

(4) Subject to sub-paragraph (4A) and (4B), a tenancy is not a secure tenancy if—

(a) within the period of three years immediately preceding the grant the conditions mentioned in sub-paragraph (1), (2) or (3) have been satisfied with respect to a tenancy of the dwelling-house, and

(b) before the grant the landlord notified the tenant in writing of the circumstances in which this exception applies and that in its opinion the proposed tenancy would fall within this exception;

(4A) Except where the landlord is a local housing authority, a tenancy under sub-paragraph (4) shall become a secure tenancy when the periods during which the conditions mentioned in sub-paragraph (1), (2) or (3) are not satisfied with respect to the tenancy amount in aggregate to more than three years.

(4B) Where the landlord is a local housing authority, a tenancy under sub-paragraph (1), (2), (3) or (4) shall become a secure tenancy if the authority notify the tenant that the tenancy is to be regarded as a secure tenancy.

(5) In this paragraph "contract of employment" means a contract of service or apprenticeship, whether express or implied and (if express) whether oral or in writing.

Land acquired for development

3A–475   3.—(1) A tenancy is not a secure tenancy if the dwelling-house is on land which has been acquired for development and the dwelling-house is used by the landlord, pending development of the land, as temporary housing accommodation.

(2) In this paragraph "development" has the meaning given by section 55 of the Town and Country Planning Act 1990 (general definition of development for purposes of that Act).

Accommodation for homeless persons

3A–476   4. A tenancy granted in pursuance of any function under Part VII of the Housing Act 1996 (homelessness) is not a secure tenancy unless the local housing authority concerned have notified the tenant that the tenancy is to be regarded as a secure tenancy.

Accommodation for Asylum Seekers

3A–477

4A.—(1) A tenancy is not a secure tenancy if it is granted in order to provide accommodation under Part VI of the Immigration and Asylum Act 1999.

(2) A tenancy mentioned in sub-paragraph (1) becomes a secure tenancy if the landlord notifies the tenant that it is to be regarded as a secure tenancy.

Temporary accommodation for persons taking up employment

3A–478

5.—(1) Subject to sub-paragraphs (1A and 1B), a tenancy is not a secure tenancy if—

    (a) the person to whom the tenancy was granted was not, immediately before the grant, resident in the district in which the dwelling-house is situated,

    (b) before the grant of the tenancy, he obtained employment, or an offer of employment, in the district or its surrounding area,

    (c) the tenancy was granted to him for the purpose of meeting his need for temporary accommodation in the district or its surrounding area in order to work there, and of enabling him to find permanent accommodation there, and

    (d) the landlord notified him in writing of the circumstances in which this exception applies and that in its opinion the proposed tenancy would fall within this exception;

(1A) Except where the landlord is a local housing authority, a tenancy under sub-paragraph (1) shall become a secure tenancy on the expiry of one year from the grant or on earlier notification by the landlord to the tenant that the tenancy is to be regarded as a secure tenancy.

(1B) Where the landlord is a local housing authority, a tenancy under sub-paragraph (1) shall become a secure tenancy is at any time the authority notify the tenant that the tenancy is to be regarded as a secure tenancy.

(2) In this paragraph—

    "district" means district of a local housing authority; and

    "surrounding area", in relation to a district, means the area consisting of each district that adjoins it.

Short-term arrangements

3A–479

6. A tenancy is not a secure tenancy if—

    (a) the dwelling-house has been leased to the landlord with vacant possession for use as temporary housing accommodation,

    (b) the terms on which it has been leased include provision for the lessor to obtain vacant possession from the landlord on the expiry of a specified period or when required by the lessor,

    (c) the lessor is not a body which is capable of granting secure tenancies, and

    (d) the landlord has no interest in the dwelling-house other than under the lease in question or as a mortgagee.

Temporary accommodation during works

3A–480

7. A tenancy is not a secure tenancy if—

    (a) the dwelling-house has been made available for occupation by the tenant (or a predecessor in title of his) while works are carried out on the dwelling-house which he previously occupied as his home, and

    (b) the tenant or predecessor was not a secure tenant of that other dwelling-house at the time when he ceased to occupy it as his home.

Agricultural holding etc.

3A–481

8.—(1) A tenancy is not secure if—

    (a) the dwelling-house is comprised in an agricultural holding and is occupied by the person responsible for the control (whether as tenant or as servant or agent of the tenant) of the farming of the holding, or

(b) the dwelling-house is comprised in the holding held under a farm business tenancy and is occupied by the person responsible for the control (whether a tenant or as servant or agent of the tenant) of the management of the holding.

(2) In sub-paragraph (1) above—

"agricultural holding" means any agricultural holding within the meaning of the Agricultural Holdings Act 1986 held under a tenancy in relation to which that Act applies, and

"farm business tenancy" and

"holding" in relation to such a tenancy, have the same meaning as in the Agricultural Tenancies Act 1995.

Licensed premises

3A–482   9. A tenancy is not a secure tenancy if the dwelling-house consists of or includes premises licensed for the sale of intoxicating liquor for consumption on the premises.

Student lettings

3A–483   10.—(1) Subject to sub-paragraphs (2A) and (2B), a tenancy of a dwelling-house is not a secure tenancy if—

(a) it is granted for the purpose of enabling the tenant to attend a designated course at an educational establishment, and

(b) before the grant of the tenancy the landlord notified him in writing of the circumstances in which this exception applies and that in its opinion the proposed tenancy would fall within this exception.

(2) A landlord's notice under sub-paragraph (1)(b) shall specify the educational establishment which the person concerned proposes to attend.

(2A) Except where the landlord is a local housing authority, a tenancy under sub-paragraph (1) shall become a secure tenancy on the expiry of the period specified in sub-paragraph (3) or on earlier notification by the landlord to the tenant that the tenancy is to be regarded as a secure tenancy.

(2B) Where the landlord is a local housing authority, a tenancy under sub-paragraph (1) shall become a secure tenancy if at any time the authority notify the tenant that the tenancy is to be regarded as a secure tenancy.

(3) The period referred to in sub-paragraph (2A) is—

(a) in a case where the tenant attends a designated course at the educational establishment specified in the landlord's notice, the period ending six months after the tenant ceases to attend that (or any other) designated course at that establishment;

(b) in any other case, the period ending six months after the grant of the tenancy.

(4) In this paragraph—

"designated course" means a course of any kind designated by regulations made by the Secretary of State for the purposes of this paragraph;

"educational establishment" means a university or institution which provides higher education or further education (or both); and for the purposes of this definition

"higher education" and "further education" have the same meaning as in the Education Act 1996.

(5) Regulations under sub-paragraph (4) shall be made by statutory instrument and may make different provision with respect to different cases or descriptions of case, including different provision for different areas.

1954 Act tenancies

3A–484   11. A tenancy is not a secure tenancy if it is one to which Part II of the Landlord and Tenant Act 1954 applies (tenancies of premises occupied for business purposes).

Almshouses

3A–485   12. A licence to occupy a dwelling-house is not a secure tenancy of—

(a) the dwelling-house is an almshouse, and

770

(b) the licence was granted by or on behalf of a charity which—

    (i) is authorised under its trusts to maintain the dwelling-house as an almshouse, and

    (ii) has no power under its trusts to grant a tenancy of the dwelling-house;

and in this paragraph "almshouse" means any premises maintained as an almshouse, whether they are called an almshouse or not and "trusts" in relation to a charity, means the provisions establishing it as a charity and regulating its purposes and administration, whether those provisions take effect by way of trust or not.

Note—Amended by the Housing Act 1988, s.83; the Planning (Consequential Provisions) Act 1990, the Charities Act 1992; the Agricultural Holdings Act 1986, Sched.14; the Education Reform Act 1988, Sched.12; the Housing Act 1996, Scheds 16 and 17; the Education Act 1996, Sched.7; the Agricultural Tenancies Act 1995, s.40, Sched.; the Police Act 1996, s.103, Sched.7, para. 40 the Government of Wales Act 1998, Sched.18, Pt IV; the Immigration and Asylum Act 1999, Sched.14, para. 81; the Anti-social Behaviour Act 2003, s.14(5) and Sched.1; and by the Fire and Rescue Services Act 2004, s.53(1), Sch.1, para.62(1), (3). **3A–486**

Sched.1 lists those types of tenancies and licences (see s.79) which cannot be secure.

Schedule 1 has been amended by Anti-social Behaviour Act 2003, s.14(5) and Sched.1. It was brought into force in England on June 30, 2004 by the Anti-social Behaviour Act 2003 (Commencement No.3 and Savings) Order 2004 (S.I. 2004 No. 1502) (c.61). It was brought into force in Wales on 30 April 2005 by the Anti-social Behaviour Act 2003 (Commencement No.4) (Wales) Order 2005 (S.I. 2005 No. 1225) (W.83) (C.55).

Sched.1, para. 1A—introductory tenancies
See para. 3A-996. **3A–487**

Sched.1 para. 1B—Demoted Tenancies
This paragraph was inserted by the Anti-social Behaviour Act 2003. See 3A–357. **3A–488**

Sched.1, para. 2—employees
Sched.1, para. 2 excepts from security of tenure tenants who are employees of public sector landlords where their contract of employment requires occupation of the accommodation for the better performance of employment duties. The requirement may arise expressly or by implication from the contract of employment (para. 2(5)). (Compare Sched.5, para. 5 (5.13)—exception to right to buy where dwelling house is let in connection with employment *and* is within the curtilage of a building held for mainly non-housing purposes.) **3A–489**

In *Hughes v. Greenwich LBC* [1994] 1 A.C. 170; [1993] 3 W.L.R. 821; [1993] 4 All E.R. 577, HL, the House of Lords rejected the council's assertion that a term which provided that a headmaster was required to occupy a house for the better performance of his duties should be implied into his contract in the absence of an express clause to that effect. This should be done only for a "compelling reason", *i.e.* if the council could prove that the employee could not perform his duties unless he occupied the particular accommodation.

The correct approach to be taken by a court in the light of *Hughes v. Greenwich LBC* is to find out what duties the employee was required to perform. Having regard to the nature of these duties, the court should then ask itself the question whether or not it was practicable for those duties to be carried out if the employee did not live on the premises in question. Where there was a requirement to attend at the premises where the occupant was employed both in and out of hours and where it would not be practicable to carry out those duties without living at the provided premises, such occupation was "for the better performance of his duties". (See *Surrey County Council v. Lamond* (1999) 31 H.L.R. 1051; [1999] 12 E.G. 170, CA where it was held that there was a clear distinction between the position of a caretaker and that of a headmaster as in *Hughes v. Greenwich LBC*).

The word "requires" means no more than that it is a term of the contract of employment with which the employee is required as a matter of fact to comply in order to perform his duty (*Brent LBC v. Charles* (1997) 29 H.L.R. 876, CA). Retirement does not revive security (*South Glamorgan CC v. Griffiths* (1992) 24 H.L.R. 334, CA). In determining whether an employee occupies for the "better performance of duties" the court is entitled to look beyond the written particulars of the contract of employment to the factual background leading to the tenant's occupation of the dwelling (*Campbell v. City of Edinburgh DC* 1987 S.L.T. 51, Court of Session).

As Sched.1, para. 2 uses the present tense "is" in setting out the conditions for exemption from security, the question is therefore whether the conditions are presently satisfied. In *Elvidge v. Coventry CC* [1994] Q.B. 241; [1993] 3 W.L.R. 976; [1993] 4 All E.R. 903, CA, an employee/tenant lost his security of tenure by taking a new employment contract which expressly required him to occupy the cottage where he was already living for the better performance of his duties, even though the contractual tenancy itself had continued throughout. In contrast in *Greenfield v. Berkshire CC* (1996) 28 H.L.R. 691; (1996) 73 P. & C.R. 280; (1996) 96 L.G.R. 327, CA a school caretaker who was granted a tenancy of a bungalow in school grounds for the better performance of his duties but was then made redundant acquired security of tenure when he found another job with the council at a different school and was allowed to stay in the bungalow until accommodation at the new school became available since by the date of the termination of the tenancy it was no longer a condition of his employment that he should occupy the particular property. As he had had new and different employment, his current occupation of the bungalow was not "referable" back to his last job (distinguishing *South Glamorgan CC v. Griffiths* (1992) 24 H.L.R. 334, CA).

The phrase "the better performance of his duties" means that the tenant/employee's duties would not be so well performed if he or she lived elsewhere (*De Fontenay v. Strathclyde Regional Council* 1990 S.L.T. (Ex. Div.) 605; *Fisher v. Fife Regional Council* 1989 S.L.T. (Lands Tr.) 26; and *Stevenson v. West Lothian DC* 1985 S.L.T. (Lands Tr.) 9).

Sched.1, para. 3—temporary use pending development

3A–490   Sched.1, para. 3 provides that a tenancy of premises acquired for development and temporarily used as housing accommodation pending that or other development is not secure.

There are two distinct requirements, firstly, that the premises are on land acquired for development, and secondly, that they are used as temporary accommodation pending development. The immediate landlord need not be the body which acquired the land for development (*Hyde Housing Association Ltd v. Harrison* (1991) 23 H.L.R. 57, CA.

In *Attley v. Cherwell DC* (1989) 21 H.L.R. 613, CA, the Court of Appeal found development was intended and so the tenancy was not secure, even though the development might not be the same type of development as had originally been envisaged (*cf. Lillieshall Road Housing Co-operative Ltd v. Brennan* (1992) 24 H.L.R. 193, CA).

Sched.1, para. 4—accommodation for homeless persons

3A–491   Article 8 does not entitle non-secure local authority tenants to have a county court judge (or the judicial review court) decide on the particular facts whether eviction was disproportionate to the council's aim of managing its housing stock properly. The effect of this would be to convert non-secure tenancies enjoyed by homeless persons into a form of secure tenancy. The balance of interests arising under Article 8(2) has in all its essentials been struck by the legislature when enacting the current scheme for the housing of homeless persons and their eviction (*Sheffield CC v. Smart* [2002] EWCA Civ 04; [2002] H.L.R. 34).

See too *Harrow LBC v. Qazi* [2003] UKHL 43; [2003] 3 W.L.R. 792, where Lord Hope and Lord Scott said that contractual and property rights cannot be defeated by a defence based on Article 8, although in exceptional cases where defendants believe that local authorities are acting unfairly or from improper notices, they can apply to the High Court for judicial review (*per* Lord Millett). Also *Newham LBC v. Kibata* [2003] EWCA Civ 1785; [2004] HLR 28 and *Bradney v. Birmingham CC*; *Birmingham CC v. McCann* [2003] EWCA Civ 1783; [2004] HLR 27.

Sched.1, para. 6—private sector leasing

3A–492   Sched.1, para. 6 excepts premises let under what are commonly called "private sector leasing" schemes. It applies when a private owner leases a property with vacant possession for use as temporary housing to a public landlord, which then sublets to an individual occupier. The subtenancy is excepted from secure status to ensure that vacant possession can be obtained at the expiry of the head lease.

See *Tower Hamlets LBC v. Abdi* (1992) 91 L.G.R. 300; (1993) 25 H.L.R. 80, CA; *Hackney LBC v. Lambourne* (1993) 25 H.L.R. 172, CA.

SECTION 84

SCHEDULE 2

GROUNDS FOR POSSESSION OF DWELLING-HOUSES LET UNDER SECURE TENANCIES

PART I

Ground 1

Rent lawfully due from the tenant has not been paid or an obligation of the tenancy has been broken or not performed. **3A–493**

Ground 2

The tenant or a person residing in or visiting the dwelling-house— **3A–494**

(a) has been guilty of conduct causing or likely to cause a nuisance or annoyance to a person residing, visiting or otherwise engaging in a lawful activity in the locality, or

(b) has been convicted of—

(i) using the dwelling-house of allowing it to be used for immoral or illegal purposes, or

(ii) an arrestable offence committed in, or in the locality of, the dwelling-house.

Ground 2A

The dwelling-house was occupied (whether alone or with others) by a married couple or a couple living together as husband and wife and— **3A–495**

(a) one or both of the partners is a tenant of the dwelling-house,

(b) one partner has left because of violence or threats of violence by the other towards—

(i) that partner, or

(ii) a member of the family of that partner who was residing with that partner immediately before the partner left, and

(c) the court is satisfied that the partner who has left is unlikely to return.

Ground 3

The condition of the dwelling-house or of any of the common parts has deteriorated owing to acts of waste by, or the neglect or default of, the tenant or a person residing in the dwelling-house and, in the case of an act of waste by, or the neglect or default of, a person lodging with the tenant or a sub-tenant of his, the tenant has not taken such steps as he ought reasonably to have taken for the removal of the lodger or sub-tenant. **3A–496**

Ground 4

The condition of furniture provided by the landlord for use under the tenancy, or for use in the common parts, has deteriorated owing to ill-treatment by the tenant or a person residing in the dwelling-house and, in the case of ill-treatment by a person lodging with the tenant or a sub-tenant of his, the tenant has not taken such steps as he ought reasonably to have taken for the removal of the lodger or sub-tenant. **3A–497**

Ground 5

The tenant is the person, or one of the persons, to whom the tenancy was granted and the landlord was induced to grant the tenancy by a false statement made knowingly or recklessly by **3A–498**

(a) the tenant, or

(b) a person acting at the tenants instigation.

Ground 6

The tenancy was assigned to the tenant, or to a predecessor in title of his who is a member of his family and is residing in the dwelling-house, by an assignment made by **3A–499** virtue of section 92 (assignments by way of exchange) and a premium was paid either in connection with that assignment or the assignment which the tenant or predecessor himself made by virtue of that section.

In this paragraph "premium" means any fine or other like sum and any other pecuniary consideration in addition to rent.

Ground 7

3A–500   The dwelling-house forms part of, or is within the curtilage of, a building which, or so much of it as is held by the landlord, is held mainly for purposes other than housing purposes and consists mainly of accommodation other than housing accommodation, and—

(a) the dwelling-house was let to the tenant or a predecessor in title of his in consequence of the tenant or predecessor being in the employment of the landlord, or of—

a local authority,

a new town corporation,

a housing action trust,

an urban development corporation, or

the governors of an aided school,

and

(b) the tenant or a person residing in the dwelling-house has been guilty of conduct such that, having regard to the purpose for which the building is used, it would not be right for him to continue in occupation of the dwelling-house.

Ground 8

3A–501   The dwelling-house was made available for occupation by the tenant (or a predecessor in title of his) while works were carried out on the dwelling-house which he previously occupied as his only or principal home and—

(a) the tenant (or predecessor) was a secure tenant of the other dwelling-house at the time when he ceased to occupy it as his home,

(b) the tenant (or predecessor) accepted the tenancy of the dwelling-house of which possession is sought on the understanding that he would give up occupation when, on completion of the works, the other dwelling-house was again available for occupation by him under a secure tenancy, and

(c) the works have been completed and the other dwelling-house is so available.

PART II

GROUNDS ON WHICH THE COURT MAY ORDER POSSESSION IF SUITABLE ALTERNATIVE ACCOMMODATION IS AVAILABLE

Ground 9

3A–502   The dwelling-house is overcrowded, within the meaning of Part X, in such circumstances as to render the occupier guilty of an offence.

Ground 10

3A–503   The landlord intends, within a reasonable time of obtaining possession of the dwelling-house—

(a) to demolish or reconstruct the building or part of the building comprising the dwelling-house, or

(b) to carry out work on that building or on land let together with, and thus treated as part of, the dwelling-house.

and cannot reasonably do so without obtaining possession of the dwelling-house.

Ground 10A

3A–504   The dwelling-house is in an area which is the subject of a redevelopment scheme approved by the Secretary of State or the Housing Corporation or Scottish Homes in accordance with Part V of this Schedule and the landlord intends a reasonable time of obtaining possession to dispose of the dwelling-house in accordance with the scheme.

or

Part of the dwelling-house is in such an area and the landlord intends within a reasonable time of obtaining possession to dispose of that part in accordance with the scheme and for that purpose reasonably requires possession of the dwelling-house.

Ground 11

The landlord is a charity and the tenant's continued occupation of the dwelling- **3A–505** house would conflict with the objects of the charity.

PART III

Ground 12

The dwelling-house forms part of, or is within the curtilage of, a building which, or **3A–506** so much of it as is held by the landlord, is held mainly for purposes other than housing purposes and consists mainly of accommodation other than housing accommodation, or is situated in a cemetery, and—

(a) the dwelling-house was let to the tenant or a predecessor in title of his in consequence of the tenant or predecessor being in the employment of the landlord or of—

a local authority,

a new town corporation,

a housing action trust,

an urban development corporation, or

the governors of an aided school,

and that employment has ceased, and

(b) the landlord reasonably requires the dwelling-house for occupation as a residence for some person either engaged in the employment of the landlord, or of such a body, or with whom a contract for such employment has been entered into conditional on housing being provided.

Ground 13

The dwelling-house has features which are substantially different from those of **3A–507** ordinary dwelling-houses and which are designed to make it suitable for occupation by a physically disabled person who requires accommodation of a kind provided by the dwelling-house and—

(a) there is no longer such a person residing in the dwelling-house, and

(b) the landlord requires it for occupation (whether alone or with members of his family) by such a person.

Ground 14

The landlord is a housing association or housing trust which lets dwelling-houses **3A–508** only for occupation (whether alone or with others) by persons whose circumstances (other than merely financial circumstances) make it especially difficult for them to satisfy their need for housing, and—

(a) either there is no longer such a person residing in the dwelling-house or the tenant has received from a local housing authority an offer of accommodation in premises which are to be let as a separate dwelling under a secure tenancy, and

(b) the landlord requires the dwelling-house for occupation (whether alone or with members of his family) by such a person.

Ground 15

The dwelling-house is one of a group of dwelling-houses which it is the practice of **3A–509** the landlord to let for occupation by persons with special needs and—

(a) a social service or special facility is provided in close proximity to the group of dwelling-houses in order to assist persons with those special needs,

(b) there is no longer a person with those special needs residing in the dwelling-house, and

(c) the landlord requires the dwelling-house for occupation (whether alone or with members of his family) by a person who had those special needs.

Ground 16

The accommodation afforded by the dwelling-house is more extensive than is rea- **3A–510** sonably required by the tenant and—

(a) the tenancy vested in the tenant by virtue of section 89 (succession to periodic tenancy), the tenant being qualified to succeed by virtue of section 87(b)(members of family other than spouse), and

(b) notice of the proceedings for possession was served under section 83 or, where no such notice was served, the proceedings for possession were begun more than six months but less than twelve months after the date of the previous tenant's death.

The matters to be taken into account by the court in determining whether it is reasonable to make an order on this ground include—

(a) the age of the tenant,

(b) the period during which the tenant has occupied the dwelling-house as his only or principal home, and

(c) any financial or other support given by the tenant to the previous tenant.

Part IV

Suitability of Accommodation

3A–511 1. For the purposes of section 84(2)(b) and (c) (case in which court is not to make an order for possession unless satisfied that suitable accommodation will be available) accommodation is suitable if it consists of premises—

(a) which are to be let as a separate dwelling under a secure tenancy, or

(b) which are to be let as a separate dwelling under a protected tenancy, not being a tenancy under which the landlord might recover possession under one of the Cases in Part II of Schedule 15 to the Rent Act 1977 (cases where court must order possession),

(c) which are to be let as a separate dwelling under an assured tenancy which is neither an assured shorthold tenancy, within the meaning of Part I of the Housing Act 1988, nor a tenancy under which the landlord might recover possession under any of Grounds 1 to 5 in Schedule 2 to that Act,

and, in the opinion of the court, the accommodation is reasonably suitable to the needs of the tenant and his family.

2. In determining whether the accommodation is reasonably suitable to the needs of the tenant and his family, regard shall be had to—

(a) the nature of the accommodation which it is the practice of the landlord to allocate to persons with similar needs;

(b) the distance of the accommodation available from the place of work or education of the tenant and of any members of his family;

(c) its distance from the home of any member of the tenant's family if proximity to it is essential to that member's or the tenant's well-being;

(d) the needs (as regards extent of accommodation) and means of the tenant and his family;

(e) the terms on which the accommodation is available and the terms of the secure tenancy;

(f) if furniture was provided by the landlord for use under the secure tenancy, whether furniture is to be provided for use in the other accommodation, and if so the nature of the furniture to be provided.

3. Where possession of a dwelling-house is sought on ground 9 (overcrowding such as to render occupier guilty of offence), other accommodation may be reasonably suitable to the needs of the tenant and his family notwithstanding that the permitted number of persons for that accommodation, as defined in section 326(3) (overcrowding: the space standard), is less than the number of persons living in the dwelling-house of which possession is sought.

4.—(1) A certificate of the appropriate local housing authority that they will provide suitable accommodation for the tenant by a date specified in the certificate is conclusive evidence that suitable accommodation will be available for him by that date.

(2) The appropriate local housing authority is the authority for the district in which the dwelling-house of which possession is sought is situated.

(3) This paragraph does not apply where the landlord is a local housing authority.

Part V

Approval of Redevelopment Schemes for Purposes of Ground 10A

3A–512 1.—(1) The Secretary of State may, on the application of the landlord, approve for the purposes of ground 10A in Part II of this Schedule a scheme for the disposal and redevelopment of an area of land consisting of or including the whole or part of one or more dwelling-houses.

(2) For this purpose—

(a) "disposal" means a disposal of any interest in the land (including the grant of an option), and

(b) "redevelopment" means the demolition or reconstruction of buildings or the carrying out of other works to buildings or land;

and it is immaterial whether the disposal is to precede or follow the redevelopment.

(3) The Secretary of State may on the application of the landlord approve a variation of a scheme previously approved by him and may, in particular, approve a variation adding land to the area subject to the scheme.

2.—(1) Where a landlord proposes to apply to the Secretary of State for the approval of a scheme or variation it shall serve a notice in writing on any secure tenant of a dwelling-house affected by the proposal stating—

(a) the main features of the proposed scheme or, as the case may be, the scheme as proposed to be varied,

(b) that the landlord proposes to apply to the Secretary of State for approval of the scheme or variation, and

(c) the effect of such approval, by virtue of section 84 and ground 10A in Part II of this Schedule, in relation to proceedings for possession of the dwelling-house,

and informing the tenant that he may, within such period as the landlord may allow (which shall be at least 28 days from service of the notice), make representations to the landlord about the proposal.

(2) The landlord shall not apply to the Secretary of State until it has considered any representations made to it within that period.

(3) In the case of a landlord to which section 105 applies (consultation on matters of housing management) the provisions of this paragraph apply in place of the provisions of that section in relation to the approval or variation of a redevelopment scheme.

3.—(1) In considering whether to give his approval to a scheme or variation the Secretary of State shall take into account, in particular—

(a) the effect of the scheme on the extent and character of housing accommodation in the neighbourhood,

(b) over what period of time it is proposed that the disposal and redevelopment will take place in accordance with the scheme, and

(c) to what extent the scheme includes provision for housing provided under the scheme to be sold or let to existing tenants or persons nominated by the landlord;

and he shall take into account any representations made to him and, so far as they are brought to his notice, any representations made to the landlord.

(2) The landlord shall give to the Secretary of State such information as to the representations made to it, and other relevant matters, as the Secretary of State may require.

4. The Secretary of State shall not approve a scheme or variation so as to include in the area subject to the scheme—

(a) part only of one or more dwelling-houses, or

(b) one or more dwelling-houses not themselves affected by the works involved in redevelopment but which are proposed to be disposed of along with other land which is so affected,

unless he is satisfied that the inclusion is justified in the circumstances.

5.—(1) Approval may be given subject to conditions and may be expressed to expire after a specified period.

(2) The Secretary of State, on the application of the landlord or otherwise, may vary an approval so as to—

(a) add, remove or vary conditions to which the approval is subject; or

(b) extend or restrict the period after which the approval is to expire.

(3) Where approval is given subject to conditions, the landlord may serve a notice under section 83 (notice of proceedings for possession) specifying ground 10A

notwithstanding that the conditions are not yet fulfilled but the court shall not make an order for possession on that ground unless satisfied that they are or will be fulfilled.

6. Where the landlord is a social landlord registered in the register maintained by the Housing Corporation under section 1 of the Housing Act 1996 or a housing association registered in the register maintained by Scottish Homes under section 3 of the Housing Associations Act 1985, the Housing Corporation, or Scottish Homes (and not the Secretary of State), has the functions conferred by this Part of this Schedule.

7. In this Part of this Schedule references to the landlord of a dwelling-house include any authority or body within section 80 (the landlord condition for secure tenancies) having an interest of any description in the dwelling-house.

3A–513 *Note* —Schedule 2 amended by the Housing and Planning Act 1986, s.9; the Housing Act 1988, s.83 and Sched.17, para. 65; the Housing Act 1996, ss.144–146; the Housing Act 1996 (Consequential Provisions) Order 1996 (S.I. 1996 No. 2325) and the Government of Wales Act 1998, s.140 and Sched.16, para. 21 and Sched.18, Pt IV. Ground 2A has been amended by the Civil Partnership Act 2004, s.81 and Sched. 8 . The amendment is not yet in force, but is printed at para. 3A–1525 .

Sched.2, Ground 1—arrears or breach of obligation
3A–514 See the commentary to the Rent Act 1977, Sched.15, Case 1.

As to reasonableness in claims for possession under "Ground 1", see commentary to s.84, above.

Sched.2, Ground 2—nuisance or annoyance
3A–515 As substituted by Housing Act 1996, s.144. In *Kensington & Chelsea RLBC v. Simmonds* (1997) 29 H.L.R. 507; *The Times*, July 15, 1996, CA, where conduct which was a nuisance or annoyance had persisted over a number of months, the Court of Appeal held that there was ample basis for the judge's findings that the tenant had allowed her son to abuse the neighbours. The Court also rejected the argument that it was necessary to show "fault" on the part of the tenant before a possession order could be made. The Court had to consider not only the interests of the tenant but also those of neighbours. It would be quite intolerable if neighbours were deprived of the possibility of relief because the tenant was incapable of controlling her son. See too *Portsmouth City Council v. Bryant* (2000) 32 H.L.R. 906; [2000] E.H.L.R. 287, CA (claimant does not have to establish fault or even knowledge on part of tenant, but the extent of personal fault is relevant when considering reasonableness.) In *Northampton BC v. Lovatt* (1998) 30 H.L.R. 875; [1998] 07 E.G. 142; *The Times*, January 3, 1998, CA, the Court of Appeal confirmed that a tenant can be held responsible for acts of a minor child.

As to reasonableness in claims for possession under Ground 2, see commentary to s.84, above.

Sched.2, Ground 2A—domestic violence
3A–516 As inserted by the Housing Act 1996, s.145.

The Housing Act 1996, s.145 introduced this ground for possession where there has been domestic violence. Ground 2A applies where one or both partners is a tenant and:

(a) one partner has left because of violence or threats of violence by the other towards that partner or a member of that partner's family; and

(b) the court is satisfied that the partner who has left is unlikely to return.

Landlords seeking to rely upon this ground must satisfy the court that notice of proceedings for possession has been served on the partner who has left the home or that they have taken reasonable steps to effect service (Housing Act 1996, s.147).

Where possession is sought under Ground 2A, it is not sufficient that the alleged violence or threats of violence were merely one of a range of causes of equal efficacy in the victim's departure from the property. For the ground to be made out it has to be established that the alleged violence or threat of violence was the dominant, principal and real cause of the departure (*Camden LBC v. Mallett* (2001) 33 H.L.R. 20, CA).

Sched.2, Ground 5—tenancy obtained by false statement
3A–517 The Housing Act 1996, s.146 amended Ground 5 by widening it to include a statement made by "a person acting at the tenant's instigation". The word "instigate"

means "to bring about or initiate". The Latin source of the word is *instigare*, to urge or incite. The Ground refers to "instigation" and not merely to someone "acting on behalf of the tenant". To come within Ground 5, the instigation must be of the false statement and not merely instigation of action in general on behalf of the tenant (*Merton LBC v. Richards* [2005] EWCA Civ 639; 11 May 2005).

In *Rushcliffe BC v. Watson* (1992) 24 H.L.R. 124, CA, Nourse L.J. approved comments made by the judge at first instance that the burden of proof in cases brought under Ground 5 was akin to the criminal standard because of the seriousness of the allegation. See too *Waltham Forest LBC v. Roberts* [2004] EWCA Civ 940; [2005] HLR 2.

In *Shrewsbury and Atcham BC v. Evans* (1997) 30 H.L.R. 123, CA, where the tenant had "flagrantly and deliberately lied about her circumstances" in order to obtain council housing, Beldam L.J. said that:

> "It would have been an affront to those who put forward their claims honestly, wait patiently and rely upon the local authority to deal fairly with their claims, if a judge had concluded that in the circumstances of this case it was not reasonable to make an order for possession."

As to reasonableness in claims for possession under Ground 5, see commentary to s.84, above and *Lewisham LBC v. Adeyenni* (2000) 32 H.L.R. 414, CA.

Sched.2, Ground 10—property required for demolition or redevelopment

This ground for possession may arise if a public landlord requires possession in order to carry out demolition or redevelopment work and cannot reasonably carry out the work without obtaining possession.

In *Wansbeck DC v. Marley* (1988) 20 H.L.R. 247, CA, the Court of Appeal held that it was for the landlord to prove:

(a) that it intended to carry out works; and

(b) that such work could not reasonably be done without obtaining possession.

In this case there was no evidence on which the judge could have reached such conclusions. The tenant's appeal against a possession order was allowed.

Sched.2, Ground 10A—redevelopment

As inserted by the Housing and Planning Act 1986, s.9.

Sched.2, Ground 16—dwelling more extensive than reasonably required after succession

As amended by the Housing Act 1996, s.147(3).

3A–518

3A–519

3A–520

Landlord and Tenant Act 1985

(1985 c.70)

3A–521

ARRANGEMENT OF SECTIONS

HOUSING

REPAIRING OBLIGATIONS

Repairing obligations in short leases

3A–522   **11.**—(1) In a lease to which this section applies (as to which, see sections 13 and 14) there is implied a covenant by the lessor—

(a) to keep in repair the structure and exterior of the dwelling-house (including drains, gutters and external pipes),

(b) to keep in repair and proper working order the installations in the dwelling-house for the supply of water, gas and electricity and for sanitation (including basins, sinks, baths and sanitary conveniences, but not other fixtures, fittings and appliances for making use of the supply of water, gas or electricity), and

(c) to keep in repair and proper working order the installations in the dwelling-house for space heating and heating water.

(1A) If a lease to which this section applies is a lease of a dwelling-house which forms part only of a building, then, subject to subsection (1B), the covenant implied by subsection (1) shall have effect as if—

(a) the reference in paragraph (a) of that subsection to the dwelling-house included a reference to any part of the building in which the lessor has an estate or interest; and

(b) any reference in paragraphs (b) and (c) of that subsection to an installation in the dwelling-house included a reference to an installation which, directly or indirectly, serves the dwelling-house and which either—

(i) forms part of any part of a building in which the lessor has an estate or interest; or

(ii) is owned by the lessor or under his control.

(1B) Nothing in subsection (1A) shall be construed as requiring the lessor to carry out any works or repairs unless the disrepair (or failure to maintain in working order) is such as to affect the lessee's enjoyment of the dwelling-house or of any common parts, as defined in section 60(1) of the Landlord and Tenant Act 1987, which the lessee, as such, is entitled to use.

(2) The covenant implied by subsection (1) ("the lessor's repairing covenant") shall not be construed as requiring the lessor—

    (a) to carry out works or repairs for which the lessee is liable by virtue of his duty to use the premises in a tenant-like manner, or would be so liable but for an express covenant on his part,

    (b) to rebuild or reinstate the premises in the case of destruction or damage by fire, or by tempest, flood or other inevitable accident, or

    (c) to keep in repair or maintain anything which the lessee is entitled to remove from the dwelling-house.

(3) In determining the standard of repair required by the lessor's repairing covenant, regard shall be had to the age, character and prospective life of the dwelling-house and the locality in which it is situated.

(3A) In any case where—

    (a) the lessor's repairing covenant has effect as mentioned in subsection (1A), and

    (b) in order to comply with the covenant the lessor needs to carry out works or repairs otherwise than in, or to an installation in, the dwelling-house, and

    (c) the lessor does not have a sufficient right in the part of the building or the installation concerned to enable him to carry out the required works or repairs,

then, in any proceedings relating to a failure to comply with the lessor's repairing covenant, so far as it requires the lessor to carry out the works or repairs in question, it shall be a defence for the lessor to prove that he used all reasonable endeavours to obtain, but was unable to obtain, such rights as would be adequate to enable him to carry out the works or repairs.

(4) A covenant by the lessee for the repair of the premises is of no effect so far as it relates to the matters mentioned in subsection (1)(a) to (c), except so far as it imposes on the lessee any of the requirements mentioned in subsection (2)(a) or (c).

(5) The reference in subsection (4) to a covenant by the lessee for the repair of the premises includes a covenant—

    (a) to put in repair or deliver up in repair,

    (b) to paint, point or render,

    (c) to pay money in lieu of repairs by the lessee, or

    (d) to pay money on account of repairs by the lessor.

(6) In a lease in which the lessor's repairing covenant is implied there is also implied a covenant by the lessee that the lessor, or any person authorised by him in writing, may at reasonable times of the day and on giving 24 hours' notice in writing to the occupier, enter

the premises comprised in the lease for the purpose of viewing their condition and state of repair.

3A–523   *Note* —Amended by the Housing Act 1988, s.116.

"dwelling-house"

3A–524   See s.16.

"lease"

3A–525   See s.16.

"lessor"

3A–526   See s.16.

Protocol

3A–527   There is a Pre-action Protocol for Housing Disrepair Cases. See Vol. 1, C10–001

Repairing obligations in short leases

3A–528   The Landlord and Tenant Act 1985, s.11 (which re-enacts with some modifications the Housing Act 1961, s.32) implies into leases granted on or after October 24, 1961 (see s.13) for a term of less than seven years a covenant requiring landlords to keep in repair the structure and exterior of dwellings let to tenants. This includes drains, gutters and external pipes. Landlords are also obliged to keep in repair and proper working order installations in dwelling-houses for the supply of water, gas and electricity, for sanitation, for space heating and for heating hot water. To be in breach of this implied contractual duty landlords must:

  (a) have knowledge of the defect; and
  (b) then fail to carry out the repair within a reasonable period.

The repairing obligation cannot be transferred to tenants by express terms in the tenancy agreement (s.11(4), but see s.12 below). It does not apply to tenancies for a term of seven years or more.

Two important changes were made by the Housing Act 1988, s.116 to the landlord's obligations to repair found in s.11. First, the covenant to repair the "structure and exterior" was extended beyond the tenant's dwelling to cover "any part of the same building in which the lessor has an estate or interest". Secondly, the obligation to repair and maintain installations was extended from those in the dwelling to any installation which "directly or indirectly" serves the dwelling and is either part of the same building or owned by the landlord. Only tenancies granted after the commencement of the Housing Act 1988 (January 15, 1989) are affected by these changes. As to common parts, see though *Liverpool City Council v. Irwin* [1977] A.C. 239; [1976] 2 All E.R. 39; (1984) 13 H.L.R. 38, HL.

Local authorities do not owe a higher repairing obligation under s.11 than other landlords (*Wainwright v. Leeds City Council* (1984) 13 H.L.R. 117; (1984) 270 E.G. 1289, CA).

Section 11 does not apply where the Crown is the landlord (*Department of Transport v. Egoroff* (1986) 278 E.G. 1361; (1986) 18 H.L.R. 326, CA) unless the lease is under the management of the Crown Estates Commissioners or a government department or a person holding in trust for Her Majesty for the purposes of a government department (s.14(5)).

Notice

3A–529   A landlord is not in breach of the implied covenant until a reasonable period has elapsed after the giving of notice of the defect (*O'Brien v. Robinson* [1973] A.C. 912; [1973] 2 W.L.R. 393; [1973] 1 All E.R. 583, HL—collapse of bedroom ceiling due to a latent defect. Neither the tenant nor the landlord was aware of the defect until the collapse occurred. The House of Lords held that no liability under the Housing Act 1961, s.32 (now the Landlord and Tenant Act 1985, s.11) arose until the landlord had information about the existence of a defect in the premises which would put a reasonable person on enquiry as to whether works of repair were needed). See too *McGreal v. Wake* (1984) 269 E.G. 1254; (1984) 13 H.L.R. 107, CA. The onus of proving that a reasonable period has passed is on the tenant (*Morris v. Liverpool City Council* (1988) 14 E.G. 59; (1988) 20 H.L.R. 498, CA).

Notice of disrepair need not specify the precise nature or degree of want of repair. A letter from the solicitors which did not give details or enclose estimates or a report will normally be sufficient to put the landlord under an obligation to attend and inspect and thereafter carry out the repair (*Al Hassani v. Merrigan* [1988] 03 E.G. 88; (1988) 20 H.L.R. 238, CA). The Court of Appeal has also held that a landlord local authority had notice of disrepair where an officer of the environmental health department had visited the property and seen the defects and the chief executive had received a report from the district valuer—prepared after a right to buy application—which drew attention to the defects, even though the tenancy agreement stated that notice of disrepair should be given direct to the architectural service of the council (*Dinefwr B.C. v. Jones* (1987) 19 H.L.R. 445, CA). See too *Hall v. Howard* (1988) 20 H.L.R. 566, CA (inspection report setting out items of disrepair taken into account in reaching a valuation of the property); and *Sheldon v. West Bromwich Corporation* (1984) 13 H.L.R. 23; (1984) 25 P. & C.R. 360, CA, where the Court of Appeal held that the state of discoloration of the water in a tank and the tank's age were sufficient to give the landlords actual knowledge of the need to repair. Information about the existence of such a defect which would put a reasonable person on inquiry as to whether works of repair are needed is sufficient for the landlord's repairing obligation to commence.

The requirement for notice to the landlord does not apply where reliance is placed upon the Defective Premises Act 1972, s.4 (see above) or where the disrepair is within part of a building retained by the landlord. See *British Telecommunications Plc v. Sun Life Plc* [1995] 3 W.L.R. 622; [1995] 4 All E.R. 44; [1996] Ch. 69, CA, where Nourse L.J. stated:

"The general rule is that a covenant to keep premises in repair obliges the covenantor to keep them in repair at all times, so that there is breach of the obligation immediately a defect occurs. There is an exception where the obligation is the landlord's and the defect occurs in the demised premises themselves, in which case he is in breach of his obligation only when he has information about the existence of a defect such as would put a reasonable landlord on enquiry as to whether works of repair are needed and he has failed to carry out the works with reasonable expedition thereafter" ([1995] 4 All E.R. at 52).

In *Loria v. Hammer* E.G.L.R. 249, Ch D, the cause of dampness was a failure to keep in repair the water tanks in the roof space and gutters around the roof. As these were in the common parts of a building, the landlord was held to be liable to repair irrespective of any notice.

"structure and exterior"

Outside walls of premises are part of the structure and so covered by the implied covenant, even if the lease expressly excludes them from the demise (*Campden Hill Towers Ltd v. Gardner* [1977] Q.B. 823; [1977] 1 All E.R. 739; (1984) 13 H.L.R. 64, CA). The roof above a flat is capable of being part of the structure and exterior' of the dwelling comprising the flat within the meaning of the Housing Act 1961, s.32 (now the Landlord and the Tenant Act 1985, s.11), whether or not the roof is part of the demised premises (*Douglas-Scott v. Scorgie* [1984] 1 W.L.R. 716; [1984] 1 All E.R. 1086, CA). See too *Ravenseft Properties Ltd v. Davstone (Holdings) Ltd* [1980] Q.B. 12; [1979] 2 W.L.R. 897; [1979] 1 All E.R. 929, QBD.

However, in *Brown v. Liverpool Corporation* [1969] 3 All E.R. 1345; (1984) 13 H.L.R. 1, CA, the Court of Appeal held that four shallow steps and a path made of flagstones between the house and the street were not part of the structure of the house and so not within the implied covenant. Similarly, in *Hopwood v. Cannock Chase DC (formerly Rugeley UDC)* [1975] 1 W.L.R. 373; [1975] 1 All E.R. 796, CA, where the widow of the tenant tripped and fell on the edge of a paving slab in the yard behind the house, the Court of Appeal held that the yard did not form part of the essential means of access to the property and so was not part of the structure or exterior of the dwelling house for the purposes of the Housing Act 1961, s.32 (now the Landlord and Tenant Act 1985, s.11). See too *King v. South Northamptonshire DC* [1992] 06 E.G. 152; (1992) 24 H.L.R. 284, CA.

In *Irvine v. Morgan* (1992) 24 H.L.R. 1; [1991] 1 E.G.L.R. 261, QBD, Recorder Thayne Forbes, Q.C. held that the words "structure and exterior" do not mean that landlords are liable to repair the whole of the house. On the other hand, "structure" is not limited to the load-bearing parts. It consists of those elements of the overall dwelling-house which give it its essential stability and shape. The expression does not extend to the many and various ways in which the dwelling-house will be fitted out,

3A–530

equipped, decorated and generally made habitable. Applying that test to the specific items, he held that:

- the separate garage and gates were not within the implied covenant;
- internal wall plaster and door furniture were decorative and therefore not part of the structure;
- external windows and doors and their constituent parts (including sashes) were either part of the structure or exterior;
- external painting was part of the obligation to repair the exterior;
- internal decorative painting of installations such as radiators was purely decorative and not part of the implied covenant.

See too *Quick v. Taff Ely Borough Council* [1986] 1 Q.B. 809; [1985] 3 W.L.R. 981; [1985] 3 All E.R. 321, CA (very severe condensation making house virtually unfit for human habitation not a breach of the s.11 covenant in the absence of evidence of disrepair to the structure or exterior) where Dillon L.J. stated:

"In the present case the liability of the council was to keep the structure and exterior of the house in repair—not the decorations. Though there is ample evidence of damage to the decorations and to bedding, clothing and other fabrics, evidence of damage to the subject-matter of the covenant, the structure and exterior of the house, is far too seek ... there is no evidence at all of physical damage to the walls—as opposed to the decorations—or the windows" ([1985] 3 All E.R. at 326).

Lawton L.J. stated:

"It follows that, on the evidence in this case, the trial judge should first have identified the parts of the exterior and structure of the house which were out of repair and then have gone on to decide whether, in order to remedy the defects, it was reasonably necessary to replace the concrete lintels over the windows, which caused 'cold bridging', and the single-glazed metal windows ..." (*ibid.*, at 328).

In *Lee v. Leeds City Council* [2002] 1 WLR 1488; [2002] All E.R. 124, CA the Court of Appeal held that: (1) *Quick* was not decided per incuriam because of a failure to consider the meaning given to "repair" in *Proudfoot v. Hart* (1890) 25 QBD 42. Even if *Quick* was decided in ignorance of *Proudfoot*, both cases were before the court in *Post Office v. Aquarius Properties Ltd* [1987] 1 All E.R. 1055 and the court did not regard them as inconsistent; and (2) In view of an express covenant to keep the structure in repair and the similar covenant which was otherwise implied under s.11, the court would not imply into local authority tenancies a term that the landlord was to keep the property "in good condition".

However, in *Staves v. Leeds City Council* (1991) 23 H.L.R. 107; [1992] 29 E.G. 119, CA, where the condensation was so bad that the wall plaster had become saturated in places, the council conceded that the internal plasterwork was part of the structure. It argued, however, that, although the plaster was saturated, the patches concerned were minimal and the plaster was not in "disrepair". The Court of Appeal upheld H.H.J. Coles Q.C.'s finding that plaster when saturated is in disrepair and dismissed the *de minimis* argument. The plaster was in such poor condition that it required complete renewal. An award of £5,000 general damages (December 1990, Legal Action 17) was not disturbed. See too *Hussein v. Mehman* [1992] 32 E.G. 59, Wood Green Trial Centre, where Assistant Recorder Sedley held that defective plaster on a bedroom ceiling was part of the "structure" for the purposes of s.11.

"age, character and prospective life of the dwelling-house"—(s.11(3))

3A–531

In *Dame Margaret Hungerford Charity Trustees v. Beazeley* [1993] 29 E.G. 100, CA, the main allegation was that the landlords had failed to keep in repair a stone tile and wooden peg roof, probably 150 to 180 years old. The trial judge was satisfied that by 1989 the roof was in need of complete repair but that since that date the landlords had simply undertaken "running repairs" by replacing individual rotten pegs and slipped tiles. Preferring the evidence of the landlords' expert, and having regard to the age, character and prospective life of the dwelling, he held that the landlords were not in breach of the repairing covenant. Although replacing the roof would be ideal, it was no breach simply to keep patching up the old roof. The Court of Appeal dismissed the tenant's appeal, declining to interfere with the judge's findings of fact. See too *Newham LBC v. Patel* (1984) 13 H.L.R. 77, CA; and *Murray v. Birmingham City Council* (1988) 20 H.L.R. 39, CA, where the roof of a rented property built in 1908 had repeatedly failed, causing six incidents of rainwater penetration in six years. Although each had "sooner or later" been repaired by retiling or other minor work, the tenant pressed for complete replacement. The Court of Appeal dismissed the tenant's appeal against a county court finding in favour of the landlord. Slade L.J. said:

"I accept that in any case where a landlord or a tenant for that matter is under an obligation to keep in repair an old roof, the stage may come where the only practicable way of performing that covenant is to replace the roof altogether." (p.43)

However, dismissing the appeal, the Court of Appeal found that by the end of the tenancy in 1982 that stage had not been reached. If a tenant wanted to make good the assertion that the whole roof should be replaced, it would require evidence as to its general condition, its construction, the condition of battens and joists, the fixing of slates and expert evidence as to why piecemeal repair was no longer practicable.

On the other hand, a landlord was not entitled to rely upon s.11(3) where the property which was not near the end of its life, had been in disrepair for three years and would cost only £1,200 to repair (*McLean v. Liverpool City Council* (1988) 20 H.L.R. 25; (1987) 283 E.G. 1395, CA).

"repair"

Section 11 obliges landlords to repair. The distinction between what is a repair and **3A–532** an improvement is therefore important. In *McDougall v. Easington DC* (1989) 21 H.L.R. 310, CA (where the works involved reducing each property to its original concrete framework and then fitting new roofs, new windows and new internal fittings and retiling the floors), Mustill L.J. stated that:

"... three different tests may be discerned, which may be applied separately or concurrently as the circumstances of the individual case may demand, but all are to be approached in the light of the nature and age of the premises, their condition when the tenant went into occupation, and the other express terms of the tenancy—

(i) whether the alterations went to the whole of the structure or only to a subsidiary part;

(ii) whether the effect of the alterations was to produce a building of a wholly different character than that which had been let;

(iii) what was the cost of the works in relation to the previous value of the building, and what was their effect on the value and lifespan of the building." (p.316)

See too *Wainwright v. Leeds City Council* (1984) 13 H.L.R. 117; (1984) 270 E.G. 1289, CA, a case involving rising damp, where the Court of Appeal rejected the tenant's contention that the defendants were in breach of the Housing Act 1961, s.32 (now the Landlord and Tenant Act 1985, s.11) because they had failed to install a damp-proof course in a house which had originally been built without one. Landlords have no obligation to go beyond repairing the subject-matter of the demise (in that case a house with no damp-proof course); *cf. Elmcroft Developments Ltd v. Tankersley-Sawyer* (1984) 15 H.L.R. 63; (1984) 270 E.G. 140, CA, where a landlord was obliged to repair a *defective* damp proof course.

In *Stent v. Monmouth DC* (1987) 19 H.L.R. 269; (1987) 282 E.G. 705, CA, where the accumulation of water beneath the front door caused parts of the door to rot and required repeated replacement, the Court of Appeal held that the landlord was obliged to replace the existing door with a weatherproof door.

Proper working order

An installation for the supply of water is in proper working order if it is able to **3A–533** function under those conditions of supply that it is reasonable to anticipate will prevail. An unanticipated change in the nature of the supply of a utility may occur in a varierty of circumstances. If a change is imposed deliberately because of some scientific or technical advance, the change is likely to be introduced in a manner and subject to conditions under which it is reasonable to expect customers to modify their installations to accomodate the change and business efficacy would suggest that the landlord's duty to keep installations in proper working order would require him to make necessary modifications. In other circumstances, if the change is likely to be short-lived, the cost of modification might be disproportionate. Where the changed circumstances are likely to persist for a lengthy period it might seem wholly unreason-

HOUSING

able for the landlord to leave his tenants deprived of a satisfactory supply of water for want of relatively modest expenditure on modifications. (*O'Connor v. Old Etonians Housing Association Ltd* [2002] EWCA Civ 150; [2002] Ch. 295)—water pipes reduced from 1.25 inch diameter to 1 inch—unable to supply water during period when water pressure reduced).

The Court of Appeal has held that landlords were not obliged by the Housing Act 1961, s.32 (now the Landlord and Tenant Act 1985, s.11) to lag pipes which function satisfactorily in all but the most extreme weather conditions. Accordingly there was no liability on the part of landlords for damage caused by the bursting of an unlagged pipe in very severe cold (*Wycombe Health Authority v. Barnett* (1982) 5 H.L.R. 84; (1982) 264 E.G. 619, CA).

The implied covenant to repair under s.11(1A)(b)(i) does not extend to installations located in parts of a building in which the lessor does not have an estate or interest, even if the lessor has an estate or interest in other parts of the same building (*Niazi Services Ltd v. Van der Loo* [2004] EWCA Civ 53; [2004] 1 W.L.R. 1254—inadequate water pressure in top floor flat caused by works in ground floor/basement restaurant in which the mesne lessor of the top floor had no interest).

Specific performance

3A–534   See s.17, below.

Damages

3A–535   "The object of awarding damages against a landlord for breach of his covenant to repair is not to punish the landlord but, so far as money can, to restore the tenant to the position he would have been in had there been no breach. This object will not be acheived by applying one set of rules to all cases regardless of particular circumstances of the case. The facts of each case must be looked at carefully to see what damage the tenant has suffered and how he may be fairly compensated by a monetary award."

per Griffiths L.J. in *Calabar Properties Ltd v. Stitcher* [1984] 1 W.L.R. 287; [1983] 3 All E.R. 759 at 768, CA).

In *Wallace v. Manchester City Council* (1998) 30 H.L.R. 1111; *The Times*, July 23, 1998; [1998] 41 E.G. 223, CA, Morritt L.J. said:

"First, the question in all cases of damages for breach of obligation to repair is what sum will, so far as money can, place the tenant in the position he would have been in if the obligation to repair had been duly performed by the landlord. Second, the answer to that question inevitably involves a comparison of the property as it was for the period when the landlord was in breach of his obligation with what it would have been if the obligation had been performed. Third, for the periods when the tenant remained in occupation of the property, notwithstanding the breach of the obligation to repair the loss to him requiring compensation is the loss of comfort and convenience which results from living in a property which was not in the state of repair it ought to have been if the landlord performed his obligation ... Fourth, if the tenant does not remain in occupation but, being entitled to do so, is forced by the landlord's failure to repair to sell or sublet the property he may diminution of the price or recoverable rent occasioned by the landlord's failure to perform his covenant to repair."

He continued:

"... the sum required to compensate the tenant for the distress and inconvenience ... may be ascertained in a number of different ways, including but not limited to a notional reduction in the rent. Some judges may prefer to use that method alone ... some may prefer a global award for discomfort and inconvenience ... and others may prefer a mixture of the two ... But, in my judgment, they are not bound to assess damages separately under heads of both diminution in value and discomfort because in cases within the third proposition those heads are alternative ways of expressing the same concept."

Morritt L.J. said that the source of the money with which to pay the rent (*e.g.* housing benefit) is irrelevant to the extent of the discomfort and inconvenience suffered by the tenant and what would be proper monetary compensation for it.

In *Shine v. English Churches Housing Group* [2004] EWCA Civ 434; [2004] H.L.R. 42, the Court of Appeal stated that although the guidelines in *Wallace* "are not to be applied in a mechanistic or dogmatic way", and that there are cases "where the level of distress or inconvenience experienced by a tenant may require an award in excess of the level of rent payable" if an award is made in excess of the rent payable, "clear reasons need to be given". The Court referred to "a basic rule of thumb that—all other things being equal—the maximum award of damages should be the rental value of the premises." Where a global award of damages is made, it should be cross-checked against the annual rent to ensure that damages are neither too high nor too low.

The fact that offers of alternative accommodation have been made but not taken up "cannot … affect the question of damages" (*per* Parker L.J. in *Lubren v. Lambeth LBC* (1988) 20 H.L.R. 165, CA).

Even if a landlord is not at fault in carrying out its repairing obligations, there is an obligation to reinstate the property after completion of works to a reasonable standard, and that includes putting right damage done to decorations (*Bradley v. Chorley Borough Council* (1985) 17 H.L.R. 305, CA). See too *McGreal v. Wake* (1984) 269 E.G. 1254; (1984) 13 H.L.R. 107, CA.

Damages may include loss of rent where it was foreseeable that the tenant might sub-let (*Mira v. Aylmer Square Investments Ltd* [1990] 22 E.G. 61; (1990) 22 H.L.R. 182, CA).

Registration of a fair rent does not preclude recovery of damages for breach of repairing covenants (*Sturolson and Co v. Mauroux* (1988) 20 H.L.R. 332, CA).

As to *quantum* generally, see *Brent LBC v. Murphy (Carmel)* (1996) 28 H.L.R. 203, CA; *Chiodi v. De Marney* [1988] 41 E.G. 80; (1989) 21 H.L.R. 6, CA; *Davies v. Peterson* (1989) 21 H.L.R. 63, CA; *Dean v. Ainley* [1987] 3 All E.R. 748, CA; *Elmcroft Developments Ltd v. Tankersley-Sawyer* (1984) 15 H.L.R. 63, CA; *Taylor v. Knowsley BC* (1985) 17 H.L.R. 376, CA; and *Televantos v. McCulloch* [1991] 19 E.G. 18; (1991) 23 H.L.R. 412, CA.

Repairing obligations and the ECHR

In *Lee v. Leeds City Council* [2002] EWCA Civ 6; [2002] 1 W.L.R. 1488; [2002] All **3A–536** E.R. 124, CA, the Court of Appeal held that Human Rights Act 1998, s.6 imposes an obligation on local authority landlords to take steps to ensure that the condition of dwelling houses which they let for social housing are such that the tenants' rights to respect for home and family life under Art.8 are not infringed. However rights under Art.8 are not unqualified (*Southwark LBC v. Tanner* [2001] 1 A.C. 1) and there is nothing in the Strasbourg jurisprudence to support the proposition that s.6 and Art.8 impose a general and unqualified obligation on local authorities in relation to the condition of their housing stock. There might though be cases where a local authority that had let a property that was unfit for human habitation or prejudicial to health would be in breach of the positive duty imposed by s.6 and Art.8. In this case there was no such breach of duty. The conditions complained of did not seem to be sufficiently serious (*Lopez Ostra v. Spain* (1994) 20 EHRR 277).

Restriction on contracting out of s.11

12.—(1) A covenant or agreement, whether contained in a lease to **3A–537** which section 11 applies or in an agreement collateral to such a lease, is void in so far as it purports—

(a) to exclude or limit the obligations of the lessor or the immunities of the lessee under that section, or

(b) to authorise any forfeiture or impose on the lessee any penalty, disability or obligation in the event of his enforcing or relying upon those obligations or immunities,

unless the inclusion of the provision was authorised by the county court.

(2) The county court may, by order made with the consent of the parties, authorise the inclusion in a lease, or in an agreement collateral to a lease, of provisions excluding or modifying in relation to the lease, the provisions of section 11 with respect to the repairing obligations of the parties if it appears to the court that it is reasonable to do

so, having regard to all the circumstances of the case, including the other terms and conditions of the lease.

"lease"

3A–538   See s.16.

"lessor"

3A–539   See s.16.

"lessee"

3A–540   See s.16.

Leases to which s.11 applies: general rule

3A–541   **13.**—(1) Section 11 (repairing obligations) applies to a lease of a dwelling-house granted on or after 24th October 1961 for a term of less than seven years.

(2) In determining whether a lease is one to which section 11 applies—

(a) any part of the term which falls before the grant shall be left out of account and the lease shall be treated as a lease for a term commencing with the grant,

(b) a lease which is determinable at the option of the lessor before the expiration of seven years from the commencement of the term shall be treated as a lease for a term of less than seven years, and

(c) a lease (other than a lease to which paragraph (b) applies) shall not be treated as a lease for a term of less than seven years if it confers on the lessee an option for renewal for a term which, together with the original term, amounts to seven years or more.

(3) This section has effect subject to—

section 14 (leases to which section 11 applies: exceptions), and

section 32(2) (provisions not applying to tenancies within Part II of the Landlord and Tenant Act 1954).

"dwelling-house"

3A–542   See s.16.

"lease"

3A–543   See s.16.

"lessor"

3A–544   See s.16.

"lessee"

3A–545   See s.16.

"for a term of less than seven years"

3A–546   In *Brikom Investments Ltd v. Seaford* [1981] 1 W.L.R. 863; [1981] 2 All E.R. 783, CA, a tenant was allowed into possession in accordance with an agreement for a lease for a term of seven years on November 1. The lease was executed some days later but provided for a term of seven years commencing on November 1. The landlord contended that the Housing Act 1961, s.32 (now the Landlord and the Tenant Act 1985, s.11) did not apply because of the reference in s.32(1) to any lease "for a term of less than seven years". The Court of Appeal held that, in view of s.33(5) (now s.13(2)(a)), for the purposes of s.32 the commencement of the term was November 1 (*cf. Roberts v. Church Commissioners* [1972] 1 Q.B. 278, CA). However, the landlord was estopped from denying that s.32 (now s.11) applied where the rent officer had registered a rent on the basis that the implied covenant applied, the rent registered had not been challenged or rectified and the landlord had been receiving the higher rent (*cf. Demetriou v. Poolaction Ltd* [1991] 25 E.G. 113, CA). See too *Tomkins v. Basildon DC* [2002] EWCA Civ 876; [2002] 43 E.G. 206.

Leases to which s.11 applies: exceptions

14.—(1) Section 11 (repairing obligations) does not apply to a new **3A–547** lease granted to an existing tenant, or to a former tenant still in possession, if the previous lease was not a lease to which section 11 applied (and, in the case of a lease granted before 24th October 1961, would not have been if it had been granted on or after that date).

(2) In subsection (1)—

"existing tenant" means a person who is when, or immediately before, the new lease is granted, the lessee under another lease of the dwelling-house;

"former tenant still in possession" means a person who—

(a) was the lessee under another lease of the dwelling-house which terminated at some time before the new lease was granted, and

(b) between the termination of that other lease and the grant of the new lease was continuously in possession of the dwelling-house or of the rents and profits of the dwelling-house; and

"the previous lease" means the other lease referred to in the above definitions.

(3) Section 11 does not apply to a lease of a dwelling-house which is a tenancy of an agricultural holding within the meaning of the Agricultural Holdings Act 1986 and in relation to which that Act applies or to a farm business tenancy within the meaning of the Agricultural Tenancies Act 1995.

(4) Section 11 does not apply to a lease granted on or after 3rd October 1980 to—

a local authority,

a National Park authority

a new town corporation,

an urban development corporation,

the Development Board for Rural Wales,

a registered social landlord,

a co-operative housing association, or

an educational institution or other body specified, or of a class specified, by regulations under section 8 of the Rent Act 1977or paragraph 8 of Schedule I to the Housing Act 1988 (bodies making student lettings).

a housing action trust established under Part III of the Housing Act 1988.

(5) Section 11 does not apply to a lease granted on or after 3rd October 1980 to—

(a) Her Majesty in right of the Crown (unless the lease is under the management of the Crown Estate Commissioners), or

(b) a government department or a person holding in trust for Her Majesty for the purposes of a government department.

3A–548   *Note* —Amended by the Agricultural Holdings Act 1986, Sched.14, para. 64; the Housing Act 1988, s.116; the Local Government and Housing Act 1989, Sched.11, para. 89; the Housing Act 1996 (Consequential Provisions) Order 1996 (S.I. 1996 No. 2325), Sched.2, para. 16; and the Agricultural Tenancies Act 1995, Sched.

"dwelling-house"
3A–549   See s.16.

"lease"
3A–550   See s.16.

"lessor"
3A–551   See s.16.

"lessee"
3A–552   See s.16.

"local authority"
3A–553   See s.38.

"new town corporation"
3A–554   See s.38.

"registered social landlord"
3A–555   See s.38, the Housing Act 1985, s.5, and the Housing Act 1996, ss.1–7.

"co-operative housing association"
3A–556   See s.38 and the Housing Associations Act 1985, s.1 which defines a housing association as a "society, body of trustees or company (a) which is established for the purpose of, or amongst whose objects or powers are included those of, providing, constructing, improving or managing, or facilitating or encouraging the construction or improvement of, housing accommodation, and (b) which does not trade for profit or whose constitution or rules prohibit the issue of capital with interest or dividend exceeding such rate as may be prescribed by the Treasury, whether with or without differentiation between share and loan capital" and a co-operative housing association as "a fully mutual housing association which is a friendly society registered under the Industrial and Provident Societies Act 1965..."

Jurisdiction of county court
3A–557   **15.** The county court has jurisdiction to make a declaration that section 11 (repairing obligations) applies, or does not apply, to a lease—

   (a) whatever the net annual value of the property in question, and

   (b) notwithstanding that no other relief is sought than a declaration.

Meaning of "lease" and related expressions
3A–558   **16.** In sections 11 to 15 (repairing obligations in short leases)—

   (a) "lease" does not include a mortgage term;

   (b) "lease of a dwelling-house" means a lease by which a building or part of a building is let wholly or mainly as a private residence, and "dwelling-house" means that building or part of a building;

(c) "lessee" and "lessor" mean, respectively, the person for the time being entitled to the term of a lease and to the reversion expectant on it.

Specific performance of landlord's repairing obligations

17.—(1) In proceedings in which a tenant of a dwelling alleges a **3A–559** breach on the part of his landlord of a repairing covenant relating to any part of the premises in which the dwelling is comprised, the court may order specific performance of the covenant whether or not the breach relates to a part of the premises let to the tenant and notwithstanding any equitable rule restricting the scope of the remedy, whether on the basis of a lack of mutuality or otherwise.

(2) In this section—

    (a) "tenant" includes a statutory tenant,

    (b) in relation to a statutory tenant the reference to the premises let to him is to the premises of which he is a statutory tenant,

    (c) "landlord", in relation to a tenant, includes any person against whom the tenant has a right to enforce a repairing covenant, and

    (d) "repairing covenant" means a covenant to repair, maintain, renew, construct or replace any property.

"dwelling"
See s.38.   **3A–560**

"landlord"
See s.36.   **3A–561**

"statutory tenant"
See s.37 and the Rent Act 1977, s.2, and the Rent (Agriculture) Act 1976.   **3A–562**

"tenant"
See s.36.   **3A–563**

See too *Jeune v. Queen's Cross Properties* [1974] Ch. 97; [1973] 3 W.L.R. 378; [1973] 3 All E.R. 97.

SERVICE CHARGES

Meaning of "service charge" and "relevant costs"

18.—(1) In the following provisions of this Act "service charge" **3A–564** means an amount payable by a tenant of a dwelling as part of or in addition to the rent—

    (a) which is payable, directly or indirectly, for services, repairs, maintenance, improvements or insurance or the landlord's costs of management, and

    (b) the whole or part of which varies or may vary according to the relevant costs.

(2) The relevant costs are the costs or estimated costs incurred or to be incurred by or on behalf of the landlord, or a superior landlord, in connection with the matters for which the service charge is payable.

(3) For this purpose—

    (a) "costs" includes overheads, and

(b) costs are relevant costs in relation to a service charge whether they are incurred, or to be incurred, in the period for which the service charge is payable or in an earlier or later period.

3A–565 *Note* —Amended by the Landlord and Tenant Act 1987, Sched.2, para. 1. Commonhold and Leasehold Reform Act 2002, Sched.9, para. 7 amends s.18(1)(a) by inserting the word "improvements" after "maintenance".

Commonhold and Leasehold Reform Act 2002, s.172 provides that Landlord and Tenant Act 1985, ss.18 to 30 apply in relation to Crown land as in relation to other land. The phrase "Crown land" is defined by Commonhold and Leasehold Reform Act 2002, s.172. As to implementation, see the Commonhold and Leasehold Reform Act 2002 (Commencement No.2 and Savings) (England) Order 2003 (S.I. 2003 No. 1986) (C.82) and the Commonhold and Leasehold Reform Act 2002 (Commencement No.2 and Savings) (Wales) Order 2004 (S.I. 2004 No. 669) (W.62) (C.25).

"dwelling"

3A–566 See s.38.

"landlord"

3A–567 See s.36.

"tenant"

3A–568 See s.36.

"service charge" and "relevant costs"

3A–569 It is normal for long leases of residential flats to include provisions enabling the lessor to recover from the lessee a proportion of the expenditure spent in maintaining, repairing and managing the building. The amount of service charges recoverable depends on two factors, firstly, the provisions of the lease in question and secondly, the statutory restrictions on the recovery of service charges, now contained in this Act. For example, s.19 provides that service charges are only recoverable to "the extent that they are reasonably incurred" and where "services or works are of a reasonable standard". Section 20 provides that where lessors wish to recover a proportion of the cost of major works from lessees they should first serve a notice giving details of estimates obtained, and then consult with the lessees. "Major works" are defined as either works costing more than £1,000 or more than £50 multiplied by the number of flats, whichever is the greater (see Service Charge (Estimates and Consultation) Order 1988 (S.I. 1988 No. 1285).

Limitation of service charges: reasonableness

3A–570 **19.**—(1) Relevant costs shall be taken into account in determining the amount of a service charge payable for a period—

(a) only to the extent that they are reasonably incurred, and

(b) where they are incurred on the provision of services or the carrying out of works, only if the services or works are of a reasonable standard;

and the amount payable shall be limited accordingly.

(2) Where a service charge is payable before the relevant costs are incurred, no greater amount than is reasonable is so payable, and after the relevant costs have been incurred any necessary adjustment shall be made by repayment, reduction or subsequent charges or otherwise.

(2A) [...]

(2B) [...]

(2C) [...]

(3) [...]

(4) [...]

(5) If a person takes any proceedings in the High Court in pursuance of any of the provisions of this Act relating to service charges and he could have taken those proceedings in the county court, he shall not be entitled to recover any costs.

Note —Amended by the Landlord and Tenant Act 1987, s.41, Sched.2; the Courts **3A–571** and Legal Services Act 1990, Sched.20; the Housing Act 1996, s.83, Sched.19, Pt III; the Arbitration Act 1996, Sched.3, para. 43; and the Commonhold and Leasehold Reform Act 2002 s.180 and Sched.14.

"dwelling"
See s.38.   **3A–572**

"tenant"
See s.36.   **3A–573**

"relevant costs"
See s.18.   **3A–574**

"service charges"
See s.18.   **3A–575**

Limitation of service charges: reasonableness

Service charges calculated by reference to expenditure by a management company, **3A–576** rather than by a landlord are subject to Landlord and Tenant Act 1985, s.19. Although s.18 defines relevant costs for service charges as "costs incurred or to be incurred by or on behalf of the landlord", the definition of "landlord" in s.30 includes "any person who has a right to enforce payment of a service charge." See *Cinnamon Ltd v. Morgan* [2001] EWCA 1616; [2002] 2 P. & C.R. 10.

The Court of Appeal has held that:

(a) where services provided do not reach a reasonable standard the judge is not bound to disallow the whole amount claimed by the freeholder, but may deduct a proportion and;

(b) only in exceptional circumstances should reductions be disallowed because they are *de minimis*.

Although such matters may be "small in quantum [they] may be of considerable moment to the parties" (*Yorkbrook Investments Ltd v. Batten* (1985) 52 P. & C.R. 51; [1985] 2 E.G.L.R. 100; (1986) 18 H.L.R. 25, CA).

For a case where lessees contended that the cost of insurance included in service charges was more than reasonable, see *Abbots Heath Management v. Sinclair Gardens Investments* [1995] N.P.C. 19; [1995] 11 C.L. 442, Mayor's and City of London County Court (held the costs were not unreasonably incurred).

Limitation of service charges: consultation requirements

20.—(1) Where this section applies to any qualifying works or **3A–577** qualifying long term agreement, the relevant contributions of tenants are limited in accordance with subsection (6) or (7) (or both) unless the consultation requirements have been either—

(a) complied with in relation to the works or agreement, or

(b) dispensed with in relation to the works or agreement by (or on appeal from) a leasehold valuation tribunal.

(2) In this section "relevant contribution", in relation to a tenant and any works or agreement, is the amount which he may be required under the terms of his lease to contribute (by the payment of service charges) to relevant costs incurred on carrying out the works or under the agreement.

(3) This section applies to qualifying works if relevant costs incurred on carrying out the works exceed an appropriate amount.

(4) The Secretary of State may by regulations provide that this section applies to a qualifying long term agreement—

(a) if relevant costs incurred under the agreement exceed an appropriate amount, or

(b) if relevant costs incurred under the agreement during a period prescribed by the regulations exceed an appropriate amount.

(5) An appropriate amount is an amount set by regulations made by the Secretary of State; and the regulations may make provision for either or both of the following to be an appropriate amount—

(a) an amount prescribed by, or determined in accordance with, the regulations, and

(b) an amount which results in the relevant contribution of any one or more tenants being an amount prescribed by, or determined in accordance with, the regulations.

(6) Where an appropriate amount is set by virtue of paragraph (a) of subsection (5), the amount of the relevant costs incurred on carrying out the works or under the agreement which may be taken into account in determining the relevant contributions of tenants is limited to the appropriate amount.

(7) Where an appropriate amount is set by virtue of paragraph (b) of that subsection, the amount of the relevant contribution of the tenant, or each of the tenants, whose relevant contribution would otherwise exceed the amount prescribed by, or determined in accordance with, the regulations is limited to the amount so prescribed or determined.

Implementation

3A–578 Commonhold and Leasehold reform Act 2002, s.151, introducing new Landlord and Tenant Act 1985, ss.20 and 20ZA was brought into force on October 31, 2003 in England and on March 30, 2004 in Wales by the Commonhold and Leasehold Reform Act 2002 (Commencement No.2 and Savings) (England) Order 2003 (S.I. 2003 No. 1986) (C.82) and the Commonhold and Leasehold Reform Act 2002 (Commencement No.2 and Savings) (Wales) Order 2004 (S.I. 2004 No. 669) (W.62) (C.25) but has no effect in relation to qualifying works begun before the commencement date. Note also the Service Charges (Consultation Requirements) (England) Regulations 2003 (S.I. 2003 No. 1987) and the Service Charges (Consultation Requirements) (Amendment) (Wales) Regulations 2005 (S.I. 2005 No. 1357) (W.105).

tenant
see s.36.

service charges
3A–579 See Landlord and Tenant Act 1985, s.18 as amended by Commonhold and Leasehold Reform Act 2002, Sched.9.

qualifying works
See s.20ZA.

qualifying long term agreement
See s.20ZA, the Service Charges (Consultation Requirements) (England) Regulations 2003 (S.I. 2003 No. 1987) and the Service Charges (Consultation Requirements) (Amendment No. 2) (England) Regulations 2004 (S.I. 2004 No. 2939) which apply to

certain agreements entered into, by or on behalf of a landlord or superior landlord, for a term of more than twelve months ("qualifying long term agreements"), where relevant costs (defined in section 18(2)) incurred under the agreement in any accounting period exceed an amount which results in the relevant contribution of any tenant being more than £100. For Wales, see the Service Charges (Consultation Requirements) (Wales) Regulations 2004 (S.I. 2004 No. 684) (W.72) and the Service Charges (Consultation Requirements) (Amendment) (Wales) Regulations 2005 (S.I. 2005 No. 1357) (W.105).

consultation requirements

See s.20ZA(4).

relevant contribution, relevant costs

See s.20(2).

appropriate amount

See s.20(5) and the Service Charge (Estimates and Consultation) Order 1988 (S.I. 1988 No. 1285)—*i.e.* £1,000 or £50 multiplied by the number of flats, whichever is the greater.

dispensed with

See the commentary to s.20ZA below.

Consultation requirements: supplementary

20ZA.—(1) Where an application is made to a leasehold valuation 3A–580 tribunal for a determination to dispense with all or any of the consultation requirements in relation to any qualifying works or qualifying long term agreement, the tribunal may make the determination if satisfied that it is reasonable to dispense with the requirements.

(2) In section 20 and this section—
> "qualifying works" means works on a building or any other premises, and
> "qualifying long term agreement" means (subject to subsection (3)) an agreement entered into, by or on behalf of the landlord or a superior landlord, for a term of more than twelve months.

(3) The Secretary of State may by regulations provide that an agreement is not a qualifying long term agreement—
> (a) if it is an agreement of a description prescribed by the regulations, or
> (b) in any circumstances so prescribed.

(4) In section 20 and this section "the consultation requirements" means requirements prescribed by regulations made by the Secretary of State.

(5) Regulations under subsection (4) may in particular include provision requiring the landlord—
> (a) to provide details of proposed works or agreements to tenants or the recognised tenants' association representing them,
> (b) to obtain estimates for proposed works or agreements,
> (c) to invite tenants or the recognised tenants' association to propose the names of persons from whom the landlord should try to obtain other estimates,

795

(d) to have regard to observations made by tenants or the recognised tenants' association in relation to proposed works or agreements and estimates, and

(e) to give reasons in prescribed circumstances for carrying out works or entering into agreements.

(6) Regulations under section 20 or this section—

(a) may make provision generally or only in relation to specific cases, and

(b) may make different provision for different purposes.

(7) Regulations under section 20 or this section shall be made by statutory instrument which shall be subject to annulment in pursuance of a resolution of either House of Parliament."

consultation requirements

3A–581   See s.20ZA(4).

regulations

see the Service Charges (Consultation Requirements) (England) Regulations 2003 (S.I. 2003 No. 1987) and the Service Charges (Consultation Requirements) (Amendment No. 2) (England) Regulations 2004 (S.I. 2004 No. 2939) which apply to certain agreements entered into, by or on behalf of a landlord or superior landlord, for a term of more than 12 months ("qualifying long term agreements"), where relevant costs (defined in s.18(2)) incurred under the agreement in any accounting period exceed an amount which results in the relevant contribution of any tenant being more than £100.

landlord, tenant, lease, tenancy

see Landlord and Tenant Act 1985, s.36.

recognised tenants' association

see Landlord and Tenant Act 1985, s.29.

Dispensing with Consultation Requirements

3A–582   In *Broadwater Court Management Co Ltd v. Jackson-Mann* [1997] E.G.C.S. 145, (transcript available) CA the defendant long lessee defended forfeiture proceedings, *inter alia*, on the grounds that the plaintiff had failed to comply with the requirements of s.20 with regard to estimates and consultation. At first instance the recorder hearing the case noted that a quotation for the works had been sent to the defendant's predecessor in title, the lowest tender was chosen, the costs were reasonable and that the plaintiffs were a management company, not a building company or commercial landlord. He dispensed with the requirement for a s.20 notice and gave judgment for the plaintiffs on their claim. The lessee appealed. The Court of Appeal held that the judge had exercised his discretion under s.20(9) to dispense with the notice on a proper appreciation of the facts and in accordance with the proper principles and accordingly there was no cause to interfere with that exercise of discretion.

For another example of circumstances where the court dispensed with the s.20 requirement see *Gardner v. Jones* February 1996, C.L.D. 460, Axminster and Chard County Court, where it was accepted that the landlord's expedition had much reduced the cost of works since it made it possible to utilise scaffolding which was already in place cf. though *Martin v. Maryland Estates Ltd* [1999] 26 E.G. 151; (2000) 32 H.L.R. 116, CA where at first instance a judge refused to grant landlords a dispensation under s.20(9), holding that they had not acted reasonably in failing to inform the tenants of the need for additional works. The landlords' appeal was dismissed. The cost of all the works, including the additional items, was almost double the amount estimated in the s.20 notice. Although it had not been practical for the landlords to comply with all the requirements, that did not justify a total dismissal of the requirements resulting in the tenants not being informed of the additional works. The judge had been entitled to conclude that the landlords had not acted reasonably. The Court of Appeal also held that the judge had been correct to dismiss the landlords' claim under s.20(1) for £1,000 towards the cost of the additional works. A common sense approach is required when deciding how one batch of "qualifying works" is to be divided from another for the purposes of s.20(1).

See *Taber v. MacDonald* (1999) 31 H.L.R. 73, QBD: held that a landlord had a reasonable excuse for not producing documentation regarding the composite charge for several properties because the lease provided that the lessee could refer the matter to arbitration. As he had not availed himself of that opportunity the landlords had a reasonable excuse for not producing the documents. **3A–583**

Limitation of service charges: grant-aided works

20A.—(1) Where relevant costs are incurred or to be incurred on **3A–584** the carrying out of works in respect of which a grant has been or is to be paid under section 523 of the Housing Act 1985 ... (assistance for provision of separate service pipe for water supply) or any provision of Part I of the Housing Grants, Construction and Regeneration Act 1996 (grants, etc. for renewal of private sector housing) or any corresponding earlier enactment, or article 3 of the Regulatory Reform (Housing Assistance) (England and Wales) Order 2002 (power of local housing authorities to provide assistance) the amount of the grant shall be deducted from the costs and the amount of the service charge payable shall be reduced accordingly.

(2) In any case where—

    (a) relevant costs are incurred or to be incurred on the carrying out of works which are included in the external works specified in a group repair scheme, within the meaning of Part I of the Housing Grants, Construction and Regeneration Act 1996, and

    (b) the landlord participated or is participating in that scheme as an assisted participant,

the amount which, in relation to the landlord, is the balance of the cost determined in accordance with section 69(3) of the Housing Grants, Construction and Regeneration Act 1996 shall be deducted from the costs, and the amount of the service charge payable shall be reduced accordingly.

Note —Inserted by the Housing and Planning Act 1986 and amended by the Local **3A–585** Government and Housing Act 1989, Sched.11; the Housing Grants, Construction and Regeneration Act 1996, Sched.2, para. 12; and the Regulatory Reform (Housing Assistance) (England and Wales) Order 2002 (S.I. 2002 No. 1860), Sched.1, para.2.

"relevant costs"
See s.18. **3A–586**

"service charges"
See s.18. **3A–587**

Limitation of service charges: time limits on making demands

20B.—(1) If any of the relevant costs taken into account in **3A–588** determining the amount of any service charge were incurred more than 18 months before a demand for payment of the service charge is served on the tenant, then (subject to subsection (2)), the tenant shall not be liable to pay so much of the service charge as reflects the costs so incurred.

(2) Subsection (1) shall not apply if, within the period of 18 months beginning with the date when the relevant costs in question were incurred, the tenant was notified in writing that those costs had been incurred and that he would subsequently be required under the terms of his lease to contribute to them by the payment of a service charge.

3A–589   *Note* —Inserted by the Landlord and Tenant Act 1987, Sched.2.

"relevant costs"

3A–590   See s.18.

"service charges"

3A–591   See s.18.

"tenant"

3A–592   See s.30.

Limitation of service charges: time limits on making demands

3A–593   It has been held in the county court that s.20B is mandatory and that landlords "are required to adhere strictly to the code" contained in ss.18 to 30. In *Westminster City Council v. Hammond*, December 1995, Legal Action 19, Central London County Court, H.H.J. Martin Reynolds, QC found that costs were "incurred" at the time when the landlord was obliged to pay them, *i.e.* when each interim certificate was issued in accordance with the JCT building works contract which governed the works.

Limitation of service charges: costs of proceedings

3A–594   **20C.**—(1) A tenant may make an application for an order that all or any of the costs incurred, or to be incurred, by the landlord in connection with proceedings before a court , residential property tribunal or leasehold valuation tribunal, or the Lands Tribunal, or in connection with arbitration proceedings, are not to be regarded as relevant costs to be taken into account in determining the amount of any service charge payable by the tenant or any other person or persons specified in the application.

(2) The application shall be made—

> (a) in the case of court proceedings; to the court before which the proceedings are taking place or, if the application is made after the proceedings are concluded, to a county court;
>
> (aa) in the case of proceedings before a residential property tribunal, to a leasehold valuation tribunal;
>
> (b) in the case of proceedings before a leasehold valuation tribunal, to the tribunal before which the proceedings are taking place or, if the application is made after the proceedings are concluded, to any leasehold valuation tribunal;
>
> (c) in the case of proceedings before the Lands Tribunal, to the tribunal;
>
> (d) in the case of arbitration proceedings, to the arbitral tribunal or, if the application is made after the proceedings are concluded, to a county court.

(3) The court or tribunal to which the application is made may make such order on the application as it considers just and equitable in the circumstances.

Note —Inserted by the Landlord and Tenant Act 1987, Sched.2; s.20C substituted by the Housing Act 1996, s.83 and amended by Housing Act 2004 Sched.15, para. 32 . The amendment is not yet in force. It is due to be brought into force by a commencement order..   **3A–595**

"service charges"

See s.18.   **3A–596**

Limitation of service charges: costs of proceedings

In *Iperion Investments Corporation v. Broadwalk House Residents Ltd* [1995] 46 E.G. 188; **3A–597** (1995) 27 H.L.R. 196; (1996) 71 P. & C.R. 34, CA, the Court of Appeal upheld an order made under s.20C by a deputy judge sitting on Official Referee's Business that the costs of the proceedings were not to be taken into account in determining the amount of any service charge payable by the tenant or any other person, even though on the construction of the lease those costs could in normal circumstances have been recovered as service charges. Peter Gibson L.J. said that in general the landlord should not "get through the back door what has been refused at the front". It was unattractive that a tenant who had been substantially successful in litigation against his landlord and who had been told by the court that not only need he pay no part of his landlord's costs but also had an award of costs in his favour should find himself having to pay the landlord's costs through service charges.

Request for summary of relevant costs

21.—(1) A tenant may require the landlord in writing to supply **3A–598** him with a written summary of the costs incurred—

>   (a) if the relevant accounts are made up for periods of twelve months, in the last such period ending not later than the date of the request, or
>
>   (b) if the accounts are not so made up, in the period of twelve months ending with the date of the request, and which are relevant costs in relation to the service charges payable or demanded as payable in that or any other period.

(2) If the tenant is represented by a recognised tenant's association and he consents, the request may be made by the secretary of the association instead of by the tenant and may then be for the supply of the summary to the secretary.

(3) A request is duly served on the landlord if it is served on—

>   (a) an agent of the landlord named as such in the rent book or similar document, or
>
>   (b) the person who receives the rent on behalf of the landlord;

and a person on whom a request is so served shall forward it as soon as may be to the landlord.

(4) The landlord shall comply with the request within one month of the request or within six months of the end of the period referred to in subsection (1)(a) or (b) whichever is the later.

(5) The summary shall state whether any of the costs relate to works in respect of which a grant has been or is to be paid under section 523 of the Housing Act 1985 (assistance for provision of separate service pipe for water supply) or any provision of Part I of the Housing Grants, Construction and Regeneration Act 1996 (grants, etc. for renewal of private sector housing) or any corresponding earlier enactment and set out the costs in a way showing how they

have been or will be reflected in demands for service charges and, in addition, shall summarise each of the following items, namely—

    (a) any of the costs in respect of which no demand for payment was received by the landlord within the period referred to in subsection (1)(a) or (b),

    (b) any of the costs in respect of which—

        (i) a demand for payment was so received, but

        (ii) no payment was made by the landlord within that period, and

    (c) any of the costs in respect of which—

        (i) a demand for payment was so received, and

        (ii) payment was made by the landlord within that period, and specify the aggregate of any amounts received by the landlord down to the end of that period on account of service charges in respect of relevant dwellings and still standing to the credit of the tenants of those dwellings at the end of that period.

(5A) In subsection (5) "relevant dwelling." means a dwelling whose tenant is either—

    (a) the person by or with the consent of whom the request was made, or

    (b) a person whose obligations under the terms of his lease as regards contributing to relevant costs relate to the same costs as the corresponding obligations of the person mentioned in paragraph (a) above relate to.

(5B) The summary shall state whether any of the costs relate to works which are included in the external works specified in a group repair scheme, within the meaning of Chapter II of Part I of the Housing Grants, Construction and Regeneration Act 1996 or any corresponding earlier enactment in which the landlord participated or is participating as an assisted participant.

(6) If the service charges in relation to which the costs are relevant costs as mentioned in subsection (1) are payable by the tenants of more than four dwellings, the summary shall be certified by a qualified accountant as.

    (a) in his opinion a fair summary complying with the requirements of subsection (5), and

    (b) being sufficiently supported by accounts, receipts and other documents which have been produced to him.

3A–599   *Note* —Amended by the Housing and Planning Act 1986, Sched.5, para. 9; the Landlord and Tenant Act 1987, Sched.2, para. 5; the Local Government and Housing Act 1989, Sched.11, para. 91; and the Housing Grants, Construction and Regeneration Act 1996, Sched.2, para. 12. Commonhold and Leasehold Reform Act 2002, s.152 provided for this section to be replaced by a new section 21. Although the new section was brought into force in so far as it confers power to make regulations (see the Commonhold and Leasehold Reform Act 2002 (Commencement No.1, Savings and Transitional Provisions) (England) Order 2002 (S.I. 2002 No. 1912) (C.58) and the Commonhold and Leasehold Reform Act 2002 (Commencement No.1, Savings and Transitional Provisions) (Wales) Order 2002 (S.I. 2002 No. 3012) (W.284) (C.96), the government announced in July 2005 that there would be a delay until the substantive provisions are brought into force (ODPM news release 2005/0156—see *www.odpm.gov.uk*). The new section is printed in Civil Procedure 2005, Vol. 2, para. 3A–598.

service charges

See Landlord and Tenant Act 1985, s.18 as amended by Commonhold and **3A–600**
Leasehold Reform Act 2002, Sched. 9.

relevant contribution, relevant costs

See s.20(2).

accounting period

See s.21(9).

qualified accountant

See Landlord and Tenant Act 1985, s.28 as amended.

regulations

at present, there are no regulations.

dwelling

see Landlord and Tenant Act 1985, s.38.

landlord, tenant, lease, tenancy

see Landlord and Tenant Act 1985, s.36.

Trivial offences

Failure to comply with s.21 is a criminal offence—see s.25. In *R. v. Marylebone Mag-* **3A–601**
istrates' Court, Ex p. Westminster City Council (2000) 32 H.L.R. 266, QBD, a landlady of
six flats, was summonsed for failing without reasonable cause to perform a duty
imposed by Landlord and Tenant Act 1985, s.21. A stipendiary magistrate stayed the
summons because he was satisfied that the offence allegedly committed was "so trivial
that it did not justify the bringing of proceedings". Westminster, who had prosecuted
the case, applied for judicial review. Although leave was refused because the case was
"extremely old" and "stale", Collins J. said "it would be wrong for a court to decide
that it was an abuse of the process of the court to prosecute if the summary did not
contain all that was required by Parliament. Of course, the court might take the view
that no penalty should follow. It might even take the view in an appropriate case that
that be coupled with some sort of costs sanction." Section 21 is not limited to cases
where there is a "wilful and inexcusable" failure to produce documents. Collins J. also
said that it is better for such challenges to be brought by way of case stated rather than
by judicial review since it would mean that the court was provided with the magistrates' reasons in every case.

Withholding of service charges

21A.—(1) A tenant may withhold payment of a service charge if— **3A–602**
    (a) the landlord has not supplied a document to him by the
        time by which he is required to supply it under section
        21, or
    (b) the form or content of a document which the landlord
        has supplied to him under that section (at any time)
        does not conform exactly or substantially with the
        requirements prescribed by regulations under subsec-
        tion (4) of that section.

    (2) The maximum amount which the tenant may withhold is an
amount equal to the aggregate of—
    (a) the service charges paid by him in the accounting period
        to which the document concerned would or does relate,
        and

HOUSING

(b) so much of the aggregate amount required to be dealt with in the statement of account for that accounting period by section 21(1)(c)(i) as stood to his credit.

(3) An amount may not be withheld under this section—

(a) in a case within paragraph (a) of subsection (1), after the document concerned has been supplied to the tenant by the landlord, or

(b) in a case within paragraph (b) of that subsection, after a document conforming exactly or substantially with the requirements prescribed by regulations under section 21(4) has been supplied to the tenant by the landlord by way of replacement of the one previously supplied.

(4) If, on an application made by the landlord to a leasehold valuation tribunal, the tribunal determines that the landlord has a reasonable excuse for a failure giving rise to the right of a tenant to withhold an amount under this section, the tenant may not withhold the amount after the determination is made.

(5) Where a tenant withholds a service charge under this section, any provisions of the tenancy relating to non-payment or late payment of service charges do not have effect in relation to the period for which he so withholds it.

Note —The government announced in July 2005 that there would be a delay until new section 21A is brought into force (ODPM news release 2005/0156—see *www.odpm.gov.uk*).

service charges

3A–603   See Landlord and Tenant Act 1985, s.18 as amended by Commonhold and Leasehold Reform Act 2002, Sched.9.

regulations

At present, there are no regulations.

landlord, tenant, lease, tenancy

See Landlord and Tenant Act 1985, s.36.

accounting period

See s.21(9).

statement of account

See 21.

Notice to accompany demands for service charges

3A–604   **21B.**—(1) A demand for the payment of a service charge must be accompanied by a summary of the rights and obligations of tenants of dwellings in relation to service charges.

(2) The Secretary of State may make regulations prescribing requirements as to the form and content of such summaries of rights and obligations.

(3) A tenant may withhold payment of a service charge which has been demanded from him if subsection (1) is not complied with in relation to the demand.

(4) Where a tenant withholds a service charge under this section, any provisions of the lease relating to non-payment or late payment

of service charges do not have effect in relation to the period for which he so withholds it.

(5) Regulations under subsection (2) may make different provision for different purposes.

(6) Regulations under subsection (2) shall be made by statutory instrument which shall be subject to annulment in pursuance of a resolution of either House of Parliament.

Implementation

Commonhold and Leasehold Reform Act 2002 section 153 (introducing new Landlord and Tenant Act 1985, s.21B) was brought into force in so far as it confers power to make regulations on July 26, 2002 in England and on January 1, 2003 in Wales by the Commonhold and Leasehold Reform Act 2002 (Commencement No.1, Savings and Transitional Provisions) (England) Order 2002 (S.I. 2002 No. 1912) (C.58) and the Commonhold and Leasehold Reform Act 2002 (Commencement No.1, Savings and Transitional Provisions) (Wales) Order 2002 (S.I. 2002 No. 3012) (W.284) (C.96).   **3A–605**

service charges

See Landlord and Tenant Act 1985, s.18 as amended by Commonhold and Leasehold Reform Act 2002, Sched. 9.   **3A–606**

dwelling

See Landlord and Tenant Act 1985, s.38.

regulations

At present, there are no regulations.

landlord, tenant, lease, tenancy

See Landlord and Tenant Act 1985, s.36.

withhold payment

See s.21A.

Inspection etc. of documents

22.—(1) A tenant may by notice in writing require the landlord—   **3A–607**

    (a) to afford him reasonable facilities for inspecting accounts, receipts or other documents relevant to the matters which must be dealt with in a statement of account required to be supplied to him under section 21 and for taking copies of or extracts from them, or

    (b) to take copies of or extracts from any such accounts, receipts or other documents and either send them to him or afford him reasonable facilities for collecting them (as he specifies).

(2) If the tenant is represented by a recognised tenants' association and he consents, the notice may be served by the secretary of the association instead of by the tenant (and in that case any requirement imposed by it is to afford reasonable facilities, or to send copies or extracts, to the secretary).

(3) A notice under this section may not be served after the end of the period of six months beginning with the date by which the tenant is required to be supplied with the statement of account under section 21.

(4) But if—

(a) the statement of account is not supplied to the tenant on or before that date, or

(b) the statement of account so supplied does not conform exactly or substantially with the requirements prescribed by regulations under section 21(4),

the six month period mentioned in subsection (3) does not begin until any later date on which the statement of account (conforming exactly or substantially with those requirements) is supplied to him.

(5) A notice under this section is duly served on the landlord if it is served on—

(a) an agent of the landlord named as such in the rent book or similar document, or

(b) the person who receives the rent on behalf of the landlord;

and a person on whom such a notice is so served must forward it as soon as may be to the landlord.

(6) The landlord must comply with a requirement imposed by a notice under this section within the period of twenty-one days beginning with the day on which he receives the notice.

(7) To the extent that a notice under this section requires the landlord to afford facilities for inspecting documents—

(a) he must do so free of charge, but

(b) he may treat as part of his costs of management any costs incurred by him in doing so.

(8) The landlord may make a reasonable charge for doing anything else in compliance with a requirement imposed by a notice under this section.

landlord, tenant, lease, tenancy
3A–608 See Landlord and Tenant Act 1985, s.36.

recognised tenants' association
See Landlord and Tenant Act 1985, s.29.

regulations
At present, there are no regulations.

qualified accountant
See Landlord and Tenant Act 1985, s.28 as amended.

statement of account
See s.21.

Information held by superior landlord
3A–609 **23.**—(1) If a statement of account which the landlord is required to supply under section 21 relates to matters concerning a superior landlord and the landlord is not in possession of the relevant information—

(a) he may by notice in writing require the person who is his landlord to give him the relevant information (and so on, if that person is not himself the superior landlord), and

    (b) the superior landlord must comply with the requirement within a reasonable time.

  (2) If a notice under section 22 imposes a requirement in relation to documents held by a superior landlord—

    (a) the landlord shall immediately inform the tenant or secretary of that fact and of the name and address of the superior landlord, and

    (b) section 22 then applies in relation to the superior landlord (as in relation to the landlord).

  The Commonhold and Leasehold Reform Act 2002, Sched.10 substituted a new **3A–610** s.23. It was brought into force on September 30, 2003 by the Commonhold and Leasehold Reform Act 2002 (Commencement No. 2 and Savings (England) Order 2003 (S.I. 2003 No. 1986) (c.82) and the Commonhold and Leasehold Reform Act 2002 (Commencement No.2 and Savings) (Wales) Order 2004 (S.I. 2004 No. 669) (W.62) (C.25).

statement of account
See s.21.   **3A–611**

landlord, tenant, lease, tenancy
see Landlord and Tenant Act 1985, s.36, para. 3A–608.

Effect of change of landlord

23A.—(1) This section applies where, at a time when a duty **3A–612** imposed on the landlord or a superior landlord by or by virtue of any of sections 21 to 23 remains to be discharged by him, he disposes of the whole or part of his interest as landlord or superior landlord to another person.

  (2) If the landlord or superior landlord is, despite the disposal, still in a position to discharge the duty to any extent, he remains responsible for discharging it to that extent.

  (3) If the other person is in a position to discharge the duty to any extent, he is responsible for discharging it to that extent.

  (4) Where the other person is responsible for discharging the duty to any extent (whether or not the landlord or superior landlord is also responsible for discharging it to that or any other extent)—

    (a) references to the landlord or superior landlord in sections 21 to 23 are to, or include, the other person so far as is appropriate to reflect his responsibility for discharging the duty to that extent, but

    (b) in connection with its discharge by the other person, section 22(6) applies as if the reference to the day on which the landlord receives the notice were to the date of the disposal referred to in subsection (1).

  landlord, tenant, lease, tenancy —See Landlord and Tenant Act 1985, s.36, para. 3A- **3A–613** 642 .

Effect of assignment

24. The assignment of a tenancy does not affect any duty imposed **3A–614** by or by virtue of any of sections 21 to 23A; but a person is not required to comply with more than a reasonable number of requirements imposed by any one person.

3A–615   *Note* —This section was substituted by Commonhold and Leasehold Reform Act 2002, Sched.10.

Failure to comply with ss.21, 22 or 23 an offence

3A–616   **25.**—(1) It is a summary offence for a person to fail, without reasonable excuse, to perform a duty imposed on him by or by virtue of any of sections 21 to 23A.

(2) A person committing such an offence is liable on conviction to a fine not exceeding level 4 on the standard scale.

3A–617   *Note* — The section was amended by Commonhold and Leasehold Reform Act 2002, Sched.10.

Exception: tenants of certain public authorities

3A–618   **26.**—(1) Sections 18 to 25 (limitation on service charges and statements of amount and inspection etc. of documents) do not apply to a service charge payable by a tenant of—

a local authority,

a National Park authority, or

a new town corporation,

unless the tenancy is a long tenancy, in which case sections 18 to 24 apply but section 25 (offence of failure to comply) does not.

(2) The following are long tenancies for the purposes of subsection (1), subject to subsection (3)—

(a) a tenancy granted for a term certain exceeding 21 years, whether or not it is (or may become) terminable before the end of that term by notice given by the tenant or by re-entry or forfeiture;

(b) a tenancy for a term fixed by law under a grant with a covenant or obligation for perpetual renewal, other than a tenancy by subdemise from one which is not a long tenancy;

(c) any tenancy granted in pursuance of Part V of the Housing Act 1985 (the right to buy), including any tenancy granted in pursuance of that Part as it has effect by virtue of section 17 of the Housing Act 1996 (the right to acquire).

(3) A tenancy granted so as to become terminable by notice after a death is not a long tenancy for the purposes of subsection (1), unless—

(a) it is granted by a housing association which at the time of the grant is a registered social landlord,

(b) it is granted at a premium calculated by reference to a percentage of the value of the dwelling-house or the cost of providing it, and

(c) at the time it is granted it complies with the requirements of the regulations then in force under section 140(4)(b) of the Housing Act 1980 or paragraph 4(2)(b) of Schedule 4A to the Leasehold Reform Act 1967 (conditions for exclusion of shared ownership leases from Part I of Leasehold Reform Act 1967) or, in the case of a tenancy granted before any such regulations were brought into force, with the first such regulations to be in force.

Note —Amended by the Housing Act 1988, Sched.17, para. 67; the Housing Act **3A–619** 1996 (Consequential Provisions) Order 1996 (S.I. 1996 No. 2325); and (S.I. 1997 No. 627); the Environment Act 1995, s.78, Sched.10, para. 25(1) and the Government of Wales Act, Sched.15, para. 12 and Sched.18, Pt IV. The section was also amended by Commonhold and Leasehold Reform Act 2002, Sched.10.

"local authority"
See s.38.　　　　　　　　　　　　　　　　　　　　　　　　　　**3A–620**

"new town corporation"
See s.38.　　　　　　　　　　　　　　　　　　　　　　　　　　**3A–621**

"service charges"
See s.18.　　　　　　　　　　　　　　　　　　　　　　　　　　**3A–622**

"tenant"
See s.30.　　　　　　　　　　　　　　　　　　　　　　　　　　**3A–623**

Exception: rent registered and not entered as variable

27. Sections 18 to 25 (limitation on service charges and statements **3A–624** of amount and inspection etc. of documents) do not apply to a service charge payable by the tenant of a dwelling the rent of which is registered under Part IV of the Rent Act 1977, unless the amount registered is, in pursuance of section 71(4) of that Act, entered as a variable amount.

Note —Amended by the Landlord and Tenant Act 1987, Sched.2, para. 8. The sec- **3A–625** tion was also amended by Commonhold and Leasehold Reform Act 2002, Sched.10.

"dwelling"
See s.38.　　　　　　　　　　　　　　　　　　　　　　　　　　**3A–626**

"service charges"
See s.18.　　　　　　　　　　　　　　　　　　　　　　　　　　**3A–627**

"tenant"
See s.30.　　　　　　　　　　　　　　　　　　　　　　　　　　**3A–628**

Liability to pay service charges: jurisdiction

27A.—(1) An application may be made to a leasehold valuation **3A–629** tribunal for a determination whether a service charge is payable and, if it is, as to—

　　(a) the person by whom it is payable,
　　(b) the person to whom it is payable,
　　(c) the amount which is payable,
　　(d) the date at or by which it is payable, and
　　(e) the manner in which it is payable.

　(2) Subsection (1) applies whether or not any payment has been made.

　(3) An application may also be made to a leasehold valuation

tribunal for a determination whether, if costs were incurred for services, repairs, maintenance, improvements, insurance or management of any specified description, a service charge would be payable for the costs and, if it would, as to—

    (a) the person by whom it would be payable,

    (b) the person to whom it would be payable,

    (c) the amount which would be payable,

    (d) the date at or by which it would be payable, and

    (e) the manner in which it would be payable.

(4) No application under subsection (1) or (3) may be made in respect of a matter which—

    (a) has been agreed or admitted by the tenant,

    (b) has been, or is to be, referred to arbitration pursuant to a post-dispute arbitration agreement to which the tenant is a party,

    (c) has been the subject of determination by a court, or

    (d) has been the subject of determination by an arbitral tribunal pursuant to a post-dispute arbitration agreement.

(5) But the tenant is not to be taken to have agreed or admitted any matter by reason only of having made any payment.

(6) An agreement by the tenant of a dwelling (other than a post-dispute arbitration agreement) is void in so far as it purports to provide for a determination—

    (a) in a particular manner, or

    (b) on particular evidence,

        of any question which may be the subject of an application under subsection (1) or (3).

(7) The jurisdiction conferred on a leasehold valuation tribunal in respect of any matter by virtue of this section is in addition to any jurisdiction of a court in respect of the matter.

Implementation

3A–630   This section was inserted by Commonhold and Leasehold Reform Act 2002 s.155 and was brought into force on September 30, 2003 in England and on March 30, 2004 in Wales by the Commonhold and Leasehold Reform Act 2002 (Commencement No.2 and Savings) (England) Order 2003 (S.I. 2003 No. 1986) (C.82) and the Commonhold and Leasehold Reform Act 2002 (Commencement No.2 and Savings) (Wales) Order 2004 (S.I. 2004 No. 669) (W.62) (C.25) but does not apply to any application made to the Leasehold Valuation Tribunal or case transferred to the Leasehold Valuation Tribunal before the commencement date.

service charges

see Landlord and Tenant Act 1985, s.18 as amended by Commonhold and Leasehold Reform Act 2002, Sched. 9.

dwelling

See Landlord and Tenant Act 1985, s.38.

landlord, tenant, lease, tenancy

See Landlord and Tenant Act 1985, s.36.

by reason only of having made any payment

Section 27A(2) and (5) reverse the effect of *R. (Daejan Properties Ltd) v. London*

Leasehold Valuation Tribunal [2001] EWCA Civ 1095; [2001] 43 EG 187; [2002] H.L.R. 25.

arbitration agreement, arbitral tribunal
   See s.169(5) and Arbitration Act 1996, Part 1.

post-dispute arbitration agreement
   See s.169(5). It means an arbitration agreement made after a breach has occurred (or is alleged to have occurred).

Meaning of "qualified accountant"

28.—(1) The reference to a "qualified accountant" in section 21(3)(a) (certification of statements of account) is to a person who, in accordance with the following provisions, has the necessary qualification and is not disqualified from acting.   **3A–631**

   (2) A person has the necessary qualification if he is eligible for appointment as a company auditor under section 25 of the Companies Act 1989.

   (3) [...]

   (4) The following are disqualified from acting—

   (a) [...];

   (b) an officer, employee or partner of the landlord or, where the landlord is a company, of an associated company;

   (c) a person who is a partner or employee of any such officer or employee.

   (d) an agent of the landlord who is a managing agent for any premises to which the statement of account in question relates;

   (e) an employee or partner of any such agent.

   (5) For the purposes of subsection (4)(b) a company is associated with a landlord company if it is (within the meaning of section 736 of the Companies Act 1985) the landlord's holding company, a subsidiary of the landlord or another subsidiary of the landlord's holding company.

   (5A) For the purposes of subsection (4)(d) a person is a managing agent for any premises to which a statement of account relates if he has been appointed to discharge any of the landlord's obligations relating to the management by him of the premises and owed to the tenants who may be required under the terms of their leases to contribute to costs covered by the statement of account by the payment of service charges.

   (6) Where the landlord is an emanation of the Crown, a local authority, a National Park authority, or a new town corporation—

   (a) the persons who have the necessary qualification include members of the Chartered Institute of Public Finance and Accountancy, and

   (b) subsection (4)(b) (disqualification of officers and employees of landlord) does not apply.

Note —Amended by the Landlord and Tenant Act 1987, Sched.2; and the Companies Act 1989 (Eligibility for Appointment as Company Auditor) (Consequential Amendments) Regulations 1991 (S.I. 1991 No. 1997); the Environment Act 1995, s.78,   **3A–632**

Sched.10, para. 25(2) and the Government of Wales Act, Sched.15, para. 13. The section was also amended by Commonhold and Leasehold Reform Act 2002, Sched.10.

Meaning of "recognised tenants' association"

3A–633   **29.**—(1) A recognised tenants' association is an association of qualifying tenants (whether with or without other tenants) which is recognised for the purposes of the provisions of this Act relating to service charges either—

> (a) by notice in writing given by the landlord to the secretary of the association, or
>
> (b) by a certificate of a member of the local rent assessment committee panel.

(2) A notice given under subsection (1)(a) may be withdrawn by the landlord by notice in writing given to the secretary of the association not less than six months before the date on which it is to be withdrawn.

(3) A certificate given under subsection (1)(b) may be cancelled by any member of the local rent assessment committee panel.

(4) In this section the "local rent assessment committee panel" means the persons appointed by the Lord Chancellor under the Rent Act 1977 to the panel of persons to act as members of a rent assessment committee for the registration area in which the dwellings let to the qualifying tenants are situated, and for the purposes of this section a number of tenants are qualifying tenants if each of them may be required under the terms of his lease to contribute to the same costs by the payment of a service charge.

(5) The Secretary of State may by regulations specify—

> (a) the procedure which is to be followed in connection with an application for, or for the cancellation of, a certificate under subsection (1)(b);
>
> (b) the matters to which regard is to be had in giving or cancelling such a certificate;
>
> (c) the duration of such a certificate; and
>
> (d) any circumstances in which a certificate is not to be given under subsection (1)(b).

(6) Regulations under subsection (5)—

> (a) may make different provisions with respect to different cases or descriptions of case, including different provision for different areas, and
>
> (b) shall be made by statutory instrument which shall be subject to annulment in pursuance of a resolution of either House of Parliament.

3A–634   *Note* —Amended by the Landlord and Tenant Act 1987, Sched.2.

Meaning of "flat", "landlord" and "tenant"

3A–635   **30.** In the provisions of this Act relating to service charges—

> "landlord" includes any person who has a right to enforce payment of a service charge;
>
> "tenant" includes
>
> > (a) a statutory tenant, and

810

(b) where the dwelling or part of it is sub-let, the sub-tenant.

Note—Amended by the Landlord and Tenant Act 1987, Scheds 2 and 5.   3A–636

"dwelling"
See s.38.   3A–637

"service charges"
See s.18.   3A–638

"statutory tenant"
See s.37 and the Rent Act 1977, s.3 and the Rent (Agriculture) Act 1976.   3A–639

MISCELLANEOUS

* * * *

Transfer of cases from county court
31C. [...]   3A–640

Note — Sections 31A to 31C were repealed by the Commonhold and Leasehold   3A–641
Reform Act 2002, s.180 and Sched.14.

SUPPLEMENTARY PROVISIONS

* * * *

Meaning of "lease" and "tenancy" and related expressions
36.—(1) In this Act "lease" and "tenancy" have the same meaning.   3A–642

(2) Both expressions include—

(a) a sub-lease or sub-tenancy, and

(b) an agreement for a lease or tenancy (or sub-lease or sub-tenancy).

(3) The expressions "lessor" and "lessee" and "landlord" and "tenant", and references to letting, to the grant of a lease or to covenants or terms, shall be construed accordingly.

Meaning of "statutory tenant" and related expressions
37. In this Act—   3A–643

(a) "statutory tenancy" and "statutory tenant" mean a statutory tenancy or statutory tenant within the meaning of the Rent Act 1977 or the Rent (Agriculture) Act 1976; and

(b) "landlord", in relation to a statutory tenant, means the person who, apart from the statutory tenancy, would be entitled to possession of the premises.

Minor definitions
38. In this Act—   3A–644

"address" means a person's place of abode or place of business or, in the case of a company, its registered office,

HOUSING

"arbitration agreement", "arbitration proceedings" and "arbitral tribunal" have the same meaning as in Part I of the Arbitration Act 1996; and "post-dispute arbitration agreement", in relation to any matter, means an arbitration agreement made after a dispute about the matter has arisen;

"co-operative housing association" has the same meaning as in the Housing Associations Act 1985;

"dwelling" means a building or part of a building occupied or intended to be occupied as a separate dwelling, together with any yard, garden, outhouses and appurtenances belonging to it or usually enjoyed with it;

"housing association" has the same meaning as in the Housing Associations Act 1985;

"local authority" means a district, county, county borough or London borough council, the Common Council of the City of London or the Council of the Isles of Scilly and in sections 14(4), 26(1) and 28(6) includes the Broads Authority, a Police authority established under section 3 of the Police Act 1996, the Services Authority for the National Criminal Intelligence Service, the Service Authority for the National Crime Squad and a joint authority established by Part IV of the Local Government Act 1985;

"local housing authority" has meaning given by section 1 of the Housing Act 1985;

"new town corporation" means—

(a) a development corporation established by an order made, or treated as made, under the New Towns Act 1981, or

(b) the Commission for the New Towns;

"protected tenancy" has the same meaning as in the Rent Act 1977;

"registered social landlord" has the same meaning as in the Housing Act 1985(see section 5(4) and (5) of that Act);

"restricted contract" has the same meaning as in the Rent Act 1977;

"urban development corporation" has the same meaning as in Part XVI of the Local Government, Planning and Land Act 1980.

3A–645 *Note* —Amended by the Norfolk and Suffolk Broads Act 1988, Sched.6, para. 26; the Education Reform Act 1988, Sched.13, Pt I; the Local Government (Wales) Act 1994, Sched.8, para. 7; the Police and Magistrates' Court Act 1994, Sched.4, para. 60; the Housing Act 1996, s.83; the Housing Act (Consequential Provisions) Order 1996 (S.I. 1996 No. 2325), art.5, Sched.2, para. 16 and the Police Act 1997, Sched.9, para. 57. Commonhold and Leasehold Reform Act 2002, s.155(2) has amended s.38. It was implemented on September 30, 2003—see the Commonhold and Leasehold Reform Act 2002 (Commencement No. 2 and Savings) (England) Order 2003 (S.I. 2003 No. 1986) (C.82) and the Commonhold and Leasehold Reform Act 2002 (Commencement No.2 and Savings) (Wales) Order 2004 (S.I. 2004 No. 669) (W.62) (C.25). In Wales, this amendment was brought into force on March 30, 2004 subject to savings specified in the Commonhold and Leasehold Reform Act 2002 (Commencement No. 2 and Savings) (Wales) Order 2004 (S.I. 2004 No. 669), Sched.2, para.6 by the Commonhold and Leasehold Reform Act 2002, s.155(2).

Index of defined expressions

39. The following Table shows provisions defining or otherwise **3A–646** explaining expressions used in this Act (other than provisions defining or explaining an expression in the same section):

address	section 38
arbitration agreement, arbitral tribunal and post-dispute arbitration agreement	section 38
co-operative housing association	section 38
dwelling	section 38
dwelling-house (in the provisions relating to repairing obligations)	section 16
fit for human habitation	section 10
flat (in provisions relating to service charges)	section 30
housing association	section 38
landlord	
(generally)	section 36(3)
(in sections 1 and 2)	section 1(3)
(in the provisions relating to rent books)	section 4(3)
(in the provisions relating to service charges)	section 30
(in relation to a statutory tenancy)	section 37(b)
lease, lessee and lessor—	
(generally)	section 36
(in the provisions relating to repairing obligations)	section 16
local authority	section 38
local housing authority	section 38
new town corporation	section 38
protected tenancy	section 38
qualified accountant (for the purposes of section 21(3)(a))	section 28
registered social landlord	section 38
recognised tenants' association	section 29
relevant costs (in relation to a service charge)	section 18(2)
restricted contract	section 38
service charge	section 18(1)
statutory tenant	section 37(a)
tenancy and tenant—	
(generally)	section 36
(in sections 1 and 2)	section 1(3)
(in the provisions relating to rent books)	section 4(3)

813

(in the provisions relating to service   section 30
charges)

urban development corporation   section 38

3A–647   *Note* —Amended by the Housing Act 1996, s.83; and the Housing Act (Consequential Provisions) Order 1996 (S.I. 1996 No. 2325), art.5, Sched.2, para. 16. Commonhold and Leasehold Reform Act 2002, s.155(3) and Sched.10 have amended s.39. It was implemented on September 30, 2003—see the Commonhold and Leasehold Reform Act 2002 (Commencement No. 2 and Savings) (England) Order 2003 (S.I. 2003 No. 1986) (C.82). The amendments are printed at para. 3A–1475 below. In Wales, this amendment was brought into force on March 30, 2004 subject to savings specified in the Commonhold and Leasehold Reform Act 2002 (Commencement No. 2 and Savings) (Wales) Order 2004 (S.I. 2004 No. 669), Sched.2, para.6 by the Commonhold and Leasehold Reform Act 2002, s.155(2).

Landlord and Tenant Act 1987

3A–648 (1987 c.31)

ARRANGEMENT OF SECTIONS

PART VI

INFORMATION TO BE FURNISHED TO TENANTS

* * * *

PART VI

INFORMATION TO BE FURNISHED TO TENANTS

Application of Part VI, etc.

3A–649   **46.**—(1) This Part applies to premises which consist of or include a dwelling and are not held under a tenancy to which Part II of the Landlord and Tenant Act 1954 applies.

(2) In this Part "service charge" has the meaning given by section 18(1) of the 1985 Act.

(3) In this Part "administration charge" has the meaning given by paragraph 1 of Schedule 11 to the Commonhold and Leasehold Reform Act 2002.

3A–650   *Note* —Amended by the Commonhold and Leasehold Reform Act 2002, Sched.11, para.9.

Application

3A–651   Commonhold and Leasehold Reform Act 2002, s.172 provides that Landlord and Tenant Act 1987, ss.46 to 49 apply in relation to Crown land as in relation to other land. The phrase "Crown land" is defined by Commonhold and Leasehold Reform Act 2002, s.172.

Landlord's name and address to be contained in demands for rent, etc.

3A–652   **47.**—(1) Where any written demand is given to a tenant of premises to which this Part applies, the demand must contain the following information, namely—

> (a) the name and address of the landlord, and
> (b) if that address is not in England and Wales, an address in England and Wales at which notices (including notices in proceedings) may be served on the landlord by the tenant.

(2) Where—

> (a) a tenant of any such premises is given such a demand, but
> (b) it does not contain any information required to be contained in it by virtue of subsection (1),

then (subject to subsection (3)) any part of the amount demanded which consists of a service charge ("the relevant amount") shall be treated for all purposes as not being due from the tenant to the landlord at any time before that information is furnished by the landlord by notice given to the tenant.

(3) The relevant amount shall not be so treated in relation to any time when, by virtue of an order of any court or tribunal, there is in force an appointment of a receiver or manager whose functions include the receiving of service charges from the tenant.

(4) In this section "demand" means a demand for rent or other sums payable to the landlord under the terms of the tenancy.

Note—Amended by the Commonhold and Leasehold Reform Act 2002, Sched.13, para.10.   **3A–653**

"premises"

See s.46.   **3A–654**

"tenant" and "landlord"

See s.59(2) which states that tenancy "includes "a sub-lease or sub-tenancy", and **3A–655** "an agreement for a lease or tenancy (or for a sub-lease or sub-tenancy)" and that the words "landlord" and "tenant" should be "construed accordingly". See also s.60 which states that "tenancy" includes "statutory tenancy".

"service charge"

See s.46 and the Landlord and Tenant Act 1985, s.18 and commentary thereto.   **3A–656**

"receiver or manager"

The power to appoint a receiver and manger is contained in the Landlord and **3A–657** Tenant Act 1987, Pt II, as amended by the Housing Act 1996.

"court"

See s.60—it includes the High Court and county court.   **3A–658**

Notification by landlord of address for service of notices

48.—(1) A landlord of premises to which this Part applies shall by **3A–659** notice furnish the tenant with an address in England and Wales at which notices (including notices in proceedings) may be served on him by the tenant.

(2) Where a landlord of any such premises fails to comply with subsection (1), any rent or service charge otherwise due from the tenant to the landlord shall (subject to subsection (3)) be treated for

all purposes as not being due from the tenant to the landlord at any time before the landlord does comply with that subsection.

(3) Any such rent or service charge shall not be so treated in relation to any time when, by virtue of an order of any court or tribunal, there is in force an appointment of a receiver or manager whose functions include the receiving of rent or (as the case may be) service charges from the tenant.

3A–660 *Note* —Amended by the Commonhold and Leasehold Reform Act 2002, Sched.13, para.11.

"premises", "tenant" and "landlord", "service charge", "receiver or manager and "court"

3A–661 See commentary to s.47, above.

Notification by landlord of address for service of notices

3A–662 In view of the contents of s.46, the requirements of s.48 apply to agricultural tenancies which include a dwelling house. The word "premises" means the subject matter of the letting and may include land which is the subject matter of the same letting (*Dallhold Estates (UK) Pty Ltd v. Lindsey Trading Properties Ltd* [1994] 17 E.G. 148, CA).

Section 48 applies to tenancies created and rent arrears in existence before the Act came into force on February 1, 1988 (*Hussain v. Singh* [1993] 31 E.G. 75, CA).

Notice under s.48 cannot be given orally (*Rogan v. Woodfield Building Services* (1994) 27 H.L.R. 78; [1995] 20 E.G. 132, CA). However, Ralph Gibson L.J. in *Rogan* said:

"... in the ordinary case, where the address of the landlord is stated without qualification in the written tenancy agreement, the requirement of section 48(1) is thereby satisfied provided that the address is an address in England and Wales."

Stuart-Smith L.J. agreed, saying that in such circumstances it is a necessary implication that the landlord "can be communicated at that address and hence it is an address to which notices can be sent." He distinguished *Dallhold Estates (UK) Pty Ltd v. Lindsey Trading Properties Ltd* [1994] 17 E.G. 148, CA, where Ralph Gibson L.J. had said that a s.48 notice must state at what address notices "including notices in proceedings"must be served on two grounds—firstly that in *Dallhold* the company was registered and incorporated in Panama, and secondly, that the only address in the jurisdiction was that of the landlord's solicitors. He said that the decision in *Dallhold* should be confined to its own facts. Russell L.J. said in *Rogan* that the test is "whether the circumstances of the individual case are such that a reasonable tenant must be taken to understand the purport and purpose of the notice."

A notice requiring possession against an assured shorthold tenant served under the Housing Act 1988, s.21, whether or not it is valid in its own right as a s.21 notice, may constitute notice within the meaning of s.48(1) if it informs the tenant of the name and address of the landlord's agent without limitation or qualification. The fact that it is not served for the purposes of s.48(1) and that it does not state that the address is one at which "notices (including notices in proceedings) may be served" on the landlord may be irrelevant. There may be cases where a suitably worded possession summons served with another document might constitute notice within s.48—see *Drew-Morgan v. Hamid-Zadeh* (2000) 32 H.L.R. 266; [1999] 26 E.G. 156, CA.

Housing Act 1988

3A–663 (1988 c.50)

HOUSING

PART I

RENTED ACCOMMODATION

CHAPTER I

ASSURED TENANCIES

MEANING OF ASSURED TENANCY ETC.

Assured tenancies

3A–664   **1.**—(1) A tenancy under which a dwelling-house is let as a separate dwelling is for the purposes of this Act an assured tenancy if and so long as—

    (a) the tenant or, as the case may be, each of the joint tenants is an individual; and

    (b) the tenant or, as the case may be, at least one of the joint tenants occupies the dwelling-house as his only or principal home; and

    (c) the tenancy is not one which, by virtue of subsection (2) or subsection (6) below, cannot be an assured tenancy.

    (2) Subject to subsection (3) below, if and so long as a tenancy falls within any paragraph in Part I of Schedule 1 to this Act, it cannot be an assured tenancy; and in that Schedule—

    (a) "tenancy" means a tenancy under which a dwelling-house is let as a separate dwelling;

    (b) Part II has effect for determining the rateable value of a dwelling-house for the purposes of Part I; and

    (c) Part III has effect for supplementing paragraph 10 in Part I.

    (2A) The Secretary of State may by order replace any amount referred to in paragraphs 2 and 3A of Schedule 1 to this Act by such amount as is specified in the order; and such an order shall be made by statutory instrument which shall be subject to annulment in pursuance of a resolution of either House of Parliament.

    (3) Except as provided in Chapter V below, at the commencement of this Act, a tenancy—

    (a) under which a dwelling-house was then let as a separate dwelling, and

(b) which immediately before that commencement was an assured tenancy for the purposes of sections 56 to 58 of the Housing Act 1980 (tenancies granted by approved bodies),

shall become an assured tenancy for the purposes of this Act.

(4) In relation to an assured tenancy falling within subsection (3) above—

(a) Part I of Schedule 1 to this Act shall have effect, subject to subsection (5) below, as if it consisted only of paragraphs 11 and 12; and

(b) sections 56 to 58 of the Housing Act 1980 (and Schedule 5 to that Act) shall not apply after the commencement of this Act.

(5) In any case where—

(a) immediately before the commencement of this Act the landlord under a tenancy is a fully mutual housing association, and

(b) at the commencement of this Act the tenancy becomes an assured tenancy by virtue of subsection (3) above,

then, so long as that association remains the landlord under that tenancy (and under any statutory periodic tenancy which arises on the coming to an end of that tenancy), paragraph 12 of Schedule 1 to this Act shall have effect in relation to that tenancy with the omission of sub-paragraph (1)(h).

(6) [...]

(7) [...]

Note —Subsection (2A) added by the References to Rating (Housing) Regulations 1990 (S.I. 1990 No. 434), para. 27. Subsections (6) and (7) repealed by the Housing Act 1996, Sched.19, Pt VIII. **3A–665**

"tenant"

See s.45. **3A–666**

"dwelling-house"

See s.45. **3A–667**

"let"

See s.45. **3A–668**

"fully mutual housing association"

See the Housing Associations Act 1985, s.1, which defines a housing association as a **3A–669** "society, body of trustees or company (a) which is established for the purpose of, or amongst whose objects or powers are included those of, providing, constructing, improving or managing, or facilitating or encouraging the construction or improvement of, housing accommodation, and (b) which does not trade for profit or whose constitution or rules prohibit the issue of capital with interest or dividend exceeding such rate as may be prescribed by the treasury, whether with or without differentiation between share and loan capital".

"A tenancy under which a dwelling-house is let"

Section 1 refers to: "A tenancy under which a dwelling-house is let ..." Therefore, **3A–670** there can only be an assured tenancy if there is a tenancy. There can be no such thing as an "assured licence". For the distinction between tenancies and licences see, *e.g. Street v. Mountford* [1985] A.C. 809; [1985] 2 W.L.R. 877; [1985] 2 All E.R. 289, HL; *AG Securities v. Vaughan* and *Antoniades v. Villiers and Bridger* [1990] 1 A.C. 417; [1988]

3 W.L.R. 1205; [1988] 3 All E.R. 1058, HL; *Duke v. Wynne* [1989] 3 All E.R. 130, CA; *Hadjiloucas v. Crean* [1988] 1 W.L.R. 1006; [1987] 3 All E.R. 1008, CA; *Nicolau v. Pitt* (1989) 21 H.L.R. 487; [1989] 21 E.G. 71, CA; *Aslan v. Murphy* [1989] 3 All E.R. 130, CA; and *Crancour Ltd v. Da Silvaesa* (1986) 18 H.L.R. 265; (1986) 78 E.G. 618, CA).

Section 1 contains four pre-requisites for the creation of an assured tenancy:

(a) The dwelling-house must be let as a separate dwelling. This is the well known phrase which appears in the Rent Act 1977, s.1. If a tenancy comprises two or more separate units of accommodation which are let together to a tenant, there can be no assured tenancy (*St Catherine's College v. Dorling* [1980] 1 W.L.R. 66; and *Kavanaghv. Lyroudias* [1985] 1 All E.R. 560). See also *Central YMCA Housing Association v. Goodman* (1992) 24 H.L.R. 109, CA, where Dillon L.J. referring to a furnished twin-bedded room in a hostel with a private bathroom and lavatory en suite, said that "...this room was no more a dwelling-house than a hotel room is a dwelling-house"); *Central YMCA Housing Association v. Saunders* (1990) 23 H.L.R. 212, CA; *Parkins v. Westminister CC* (1998) 30 H.L.R. 894, CA; and *R. v. Rent Officer for Nottingham, Ex p. Allen* (1985) 17 H.L.R. 481.

The word "dwelling" is not a term of art with a specialised legal meaning. It is "the place where [an occupier] lives and to which he returns and which forms the centre of his existence...No doubt he will sleep there and usually eat there; he will often prepare at least some of his meals there." However there is no legislative requirement that cooking facilities must be available for premises to qualify as a dwelling. In deciding whether an occupant has security of tenure "The first step is to identify the subject-matter of the tenancy agreement. If this is a house or part of a house of which the tenant has exclusive possession with no element of sharing, the only question is whether, at the date when proceedings were brought, it was the tenant's home. If so, it was his dwelling...The presence or absence of cooking facilities in the part of the premises of which the tenant has exclusive occupation is not relevant." (See *Uratemp Ventures Ltd v. Collins and Carrell* [2002] 1 A.C. 301; [2001] UKHL 43; [2001] 3 W.L.R. 806; [2002] 1 All E.R. 46, HL).

Section 3 provides that if a tenant enjoys exclusive occupation of some rented accommodation with a right to share other accommodation with other people, apart from the landlord, the mere fact that the other accommodation is shared, does not prevent the tenant from occupying the accommodation which is not shared as a separate dwelling (compare the Rent Act 1977, s.22 and the Housing Act 1985, s.79).

(b) The tenant, or if there are joint tenants, each of the joint tenants, must be individuals. A genuine letting to a company can never be an assured tenancy. See, *e.g. Hiller v. United Dairies* [1934] 1 K.B. 57, CA; *Hilton v. Plustitle Ltd* [1989] 1 W.L.R. 149; [1988] 3 All E.R. 1051, CA; *Kaye v. Massbetter Ltd and Kanter* (1992) 24 H.L.R. 28, CA; and *Estavest Investments Ltd v. Commercial Express Travel Ltd* (1989) 21 H.L.R. 106, CA and *Eaton Square Properties Ltd v. O'Higgins* (2001) 33 H.L.R. 771, CA. In such cases, the tenancy is unprotected and may come to an end by effluxion of time or may be terminated by service of a notice to quit. If this occurs, a landlord who brings possession proceedings is automatically entitled to possession without having to prove any ground for possession.

(c) The tenant, or if there are joint tenants, at least one of them, must occupy the premises as his or her only or principal home (*cf.* the Housing Act 1985, s.81 ("as his only or principal home"), the Leasehold Reform Act 1967, s.1 ("as his residence") and the Rent Act 1977, s.2 ("as his residence"). It is not possible for assured tenants to maintain assured tenancies in more than one home at the same time, although there is no reason why an assured tenant should not be temporarily absent from the premises in question provided that they remain his or her only or main home. Tenancies cease to be assured if tenants cease to occupy premises as their only or principal home (*cf. Sutton LBC v. Swann* (1986) 18 H.L.R. 140, CA).

In order to maintain a "home" a tenant need not be physically resident, so long as there is an intention to return after a temporary absence and some physical sign of continued occupation (*e.g.* furniture and possessions in the property). Two houses can be occupied as a home at the same time—*Crawley*

BC v. Sawyer (1988) 20 H.L.R. 98, CA, where a council tenant went to live with his "girlfriend" for a period of approximately one and a half years during which time the gas and electricity supplies to the premises which he rented from the council were cut off. Held that the rented premises remained his principal home throughout the period. However, if two houses are occupied, they cannot both be assured tenancies.

It is possible for a tenant to lose security of tenure by reason of non-occupation but to regain it by re-occupying the property before service of a notice to quit—see *Hussey v. Camden LBC* (1995) 27 H.L.R. 5, CA, where, as the tenant was occupying the property as his only or principal home at the time of service of the notice to quit, the Court of Appeal held that the earlier loss of security was irrelevant.

Sub-letting of the whole of premises means that any tenancy cases to be assured—see *Ujima Housing v. Ansah* (1998) 30 H.L.R. 831, CA; *Jennings v. Epping Forest DC* (1993) 25 H.L.R. 241, CA; *Poland v. Cadogan* [1980] 3 All E.R. 544, CA (Leasehold Reform Act 1993, s.93(2)); *Muir Group Housing Association Ltd v. Thornley* (1993) 25 H.L.R. 89, CA; and *Brent LBC v. Cronin* (1997) 30 H.L.R. 43, CA, *cf. Waltham Forest CBHA v. Fanning* July 2001 Legal Action 33, (2001) March 12, QBD and *Merton LBC v. Salama* (1989) CAT No. 89/169; June 1989, *Legal Action 25*, CA (parting with possession of part of premises). Parting with possession is not to be inferred simply from the fact that another person has been allowed to use and occupy a tenant's home during his temporary absence (*Lam Kee Ying v. Lam Shes Tong* [1975] A.C. 247, PC).

(d) A tenancy cannot be an assured tenancy if any of the exceptions listed in Schedule 1 applies (see below). Many of these exceptions are similar to those set out in the Rent Act 1977, Pt I.

Note also that a tenancy granted by a private landlord under arrangements made by a local housing authority in accordance with their functions under Housing Act 1996, ss.188, 190, 200 or 204 (interim duties towards the homeless) cannot be an assured tenancy within twelve months of the date of notification of the local authority's decision or the determination of any Housing Act 1996, s.202 review or s.204 appeal, unless the landlord notifies the tenant that the tenancy is to be an assured shorthold tenancy—see Housing Act 1996, s.209 as substituted by Homelessness Act 2002, Schedule 1, para 19.

Letting of a dwelling-house together with other land

2.—(1) If, under a tenancy, a dwelling-house is let together with **3A–671** other land then, for the purposes of this Part of this Act—

    (a) if and so long as the main purpose of the letting is the provision of a home for the tenant or, where there are joint tenants, at least one of them, the other land shall be treated as part of the dwelling-house; and

    (b) if and so long as the main purpose of the letting is not as mentioned in paragraph (a) above, the tenancy shall be treated as not being one under which a dwelling-house is let as a separate dwelling.

(2) Nothing in subsection (1) above affects any question whether a tenancy is precluded from being an assured tenancy by virtue of any provision of Schedule 1 to this Act.

"tenancy"
See s.45.   **3A–672**

"tenant"
See s.45.   **3A–673**

"dwelling-house"
See s.45.   **3A–674**

"let"

3A–675   See s.45.

Tenant sharing accommodation with persons other than landlord

3A–676   **3.**—(1) Where a tenant has the exclusive occupation of any accommodation (in this section referred to as "the separate accommodation") and—

> (a) the terms as between the tenant and his landlord on which he holds the separate accommodation include the use of other accommodation (in this section referred to as "the shared accommodation") in common with another person or other persons, not being or including the landlord, and
>
> (b) by reason only of the circumstances mentioned in paragraph (a) above, the separate accommodation would not, apart from this section, be a dwelling-house let on an assured tenancy,

the separate accommodation shall be deemed to be a dwelling-house let on an assured tenancy and the following provisions of this section shall have effect.

(2) For the avoidance of doubt it is hereby declared that where, for the purpose of determining the rateable value of the separate accommodation, it is necessary to make an apportionment under Part II of Schedule 1 to this Act, regard is to be had to the circumstances mentioned in subsection (1)(a) above.

(3) While the tenant is in possession of the separate accommodation, any term of the tenancy terminating or modifying, or providing for the termination or modification of, his right to the use of any of the shared accommodation which is living accommodation shall be of no effect.

(4) Where the terms of the tenancy are such that, at any time during the tenancy, the persons in common with whom the tenant is entitled to the use of the shared accommodation could be varied or their number could be increased, nothing in subsection (3) above shall prevent those terms from having effect so far as they relate to any such variation or increase.

(5) In this section "living accommodation" means accommodation of such a nature that the fact that it constitutes or is included in the shared accommodation is sufficient, apart from this section, to prevent the tenancy from constituting an assured tenancy of a dwelling-house.

"assured tenancy"

3A–677   See s.1.

"tenancy"

3A–678   See s.45.

"tenant"

3A–679   See s.45.

"dwelling-house"

3A–680   See s.45.

"let"
See s.45.　　　　　　　　　　　　　　　　　　　　　　　　　　**3A–681**

Sharing accommodation
Note *Miller v. Eyo* (1999) 31 H.L.R. 306, CA where the terms of the plaintiff's **3A–682**
tenancy were that she had exclusive use of her bedroom with shared use of a living
room, kitchen and bathroom/WC. Initially the only other bedroom in the flat was occupied by another tenant, but when she moved out the landlord and her family
moved into the other bedroom and started to share the other parts of the flat with the
plaintiff. Following *Gray v. Brown* (1993) 25 H.L.R. 144, CA the Court of Appeal held
that in the absence of an express term in the tenancy that the landlord had the right
to re-enter and occupy, the tenancy came with s.3 and was assured. For a landlord to
avoid this situation, a landlord's right to re-enter must be "clear and specific".

Certain sublettings not to exclude any part of sub-lessor's premises from assured tenancy

4.—(1) Where the tenant of a dwelling-house has sub-let a part but **3A–683**
not the whole of the dwelling-house, then, as against his landlord or
any superior landlord, no part of the dwelling-house shall be treated
as excluded from being a dwelling-house let on an assured tenancy
by reason only that the terms on which any person claiming under
the tenant holds any part of the dwelling-house include the use of
accommodation in common with other persons.

(2) Nothing in this section affects the rights against, and liabilities
to, each other of the tenant and any person claiming under him, or
of any two such persons.

"assured tenancy"
See s.1.　　　　　　　　　　　　　　　　　　　　　　　　　　**3A–684**

"tenancy"
See s.45.　　　　　　　　　　　　　　　　　　　　　　　　　　**3A–685**

"tenant"
See s.45.　　　　　　　　　　　　　　　　　　　　　　　　　　**3A–686**

"dwelling-house"
See s.45.　　　　　　　　　　　　　　　　　　　　　　　　　　**3A–687**

"let"
See s.45.　　　　　　　　　　　　　　　　　　　　　　　　　　**3A–688**

SECURITY OF TENURE

Security of tenure

5.—(1) An assured tenancy cannot be brought to an end by the **3A–689**
landlord except by obtaining an order of the court in accordance
with the following provisions of this Chapter or Chapter II below or,
in the case of a fixed term tenancy which contains power for the
landlord to determine the tenancy in certain circumstances, by the
exercise of that power and, accordingly, the service by the landlord
of a notice to quit shall be of no effect in relation to a periodic assured tenancy.

(2) If an assured tenancy which is a fixed term tenancy comes to
an end otherwise than by virtue of—

(a) an order of the court, or

(b) a surrender or other action on the part of the tenant,

then, subject to section 7 and Chapter II below, the tenant shall be entitled to remain in possession of the dwelling-house let under that tenancy and, subject to subsection (4) below, his right to possession shall depend upon a periodic tenancy arising by virtue of this section.

(3) The periodic tenancy referred to in subsection (2) above is one—

(a) taking effect in possession immediately on the coming to an end of the fixed term tenancy;

(b) deemed to have been granted by the person who was the landlord under the fixed term tenancy immediately before it came to an end to the person who was then the tenant under that tenancy;

(c) under which the premises which are let are the same dwelling-house as was let under the fixed term tenancy;

(d) under which the periods of the tenancy are the same as those for which rent was last payable under the fixed term tenancy; and

(e) under which, subject to the following provisions of this Part of this Act, the other terms are the same as those of the fixed term tenancy immediately before it came to an end, except that any term which makes provision for determination by the landlord or the tenant shall not have effect while the tenancy remains an assured tenancy;

(4) The periodic tenancy referred to in subsection (2) above shall not arise if, on the coming to an end of the fixed term tenancy, the tenant is entitled, by virtue of the grant of another tenancy, to possession of the same or substantially the same dwelling-house as was let to him under the fixed term tenancy.

(5) If, on or before the date on which a tenancy is entered into or is deemed to have been granted as mentioned in subsection (3)(b) above, the person who is to be the tenant under that tenancy—

(a) enters into an obligation to do any act which (apart from this subsection) will cause the tenancy to come to an end at a time when it is an assured tenancy, or

(b) executes, signs or gives any surrender, notice to quit or other document which (apart from this subsection) has the effect of bringing the tenancy to an end at a time when it is an assured tenancy,

the obligation referred to in paragraph (a) above shall not be enforceable or, as the case may be, the surrender, notice to quit or other document referred to in paragraph (b) above shall be of no effect.

(5A) Nothing in subsection (5) affects any right of pre-emption—

(a) which is exercisable by the landlord under a tenancy in circumstances where the tenant indicates his intention to dispose of the whole of his interest under the tenancy, and

824

(b) in pursuance of which the landlord would be required to pay, in respect of the acquisition of that interest, an amount representing its market value.

"Dispose" means dispose by assignment or surrender, and "acquisition" has a corresponding meaning.[1]

(6) If, by virtue of any provision of this Part of this Act, Part I of Schedule 1 to this Act has effect in relation to a fixed term tenancy as if it consisted only of paragraphs 11 and 12, that Part shall have the like effect in relation to any periodic tenancy which arises by virtue of this section on the coming to an end of the fixed term tenancy.

(7) Any reference in this Part of this Act to a statutory periodic tenancy is a reference to a periodic tenancy arising by virtue of this section.

"assured tenancy"
See s.1.   3A–690

"tenancy"
See s.45.   3A–691

"tenant"
See s.45.   3A–692

"dwelling-house"
See s.45.   3A–693

"let"
See s.45.   3A–694

"fixed term tenancy"
See s.45.   3A–695

Security of tenure

Section 5 provides that a periodic assured tenancy can only be brought to an end   3A–696
by a landlord by obtaining an order of the court or by surrender. Section 5(1) makes it
clear that notices to quit served by landlords have no effect upon periodic assured
tenancies. Service of a notice to quit by a tenant does terminate an assured tenancy
(see, *e.g. Hammersmith and Fulham LBC v. Monk* [1992] 1 A.C. 478; [1991] 3 W.L.R.
1144; [1992] All E.R. 1, HL; *Harrow LBC v. Johnstone* [1997] 1 W.L.R. 459; [1997] All
E.R. 929, HL; and *Greenwich LBC v. McGrady* (1982) 81 L.G.R. 288; (1982) 46 P. &
C.R. 223; (1983) 6 H.L.R. 361; (1982) 267 E.G. 515, CA and *Notting Hill Housing Trust
v. Brackley* [2001] EWCA Civ 601; [2002] H.L.R. 212; [2001] L. & T.R. 467; [2001] 35
E.G. 106, CA).

If a contractual fixed term assured tenancy is brought to an end, other than by an
order of a court or by surrender, a periodic assured tenancy (called a "statutory
periodic tenancy") normally comes into existence immediately after the fixed term
tenancy has come to an end. In some ways this is similar to a Rent Act statutory
tenancy, but there are differences. The most important of these is the provision for
fixing the terms of the statutory periodic tenancy. The basic rule is that the terms of
the new statutory periodic tenancy are the same as for the former contractual assured
tenancy (s.5(3)(e)).

Fixing of terms of statutory periodic tenancy

6.—(1) In this section, in relation to a statutory periodic tenancy—   3A–697
(a) "the former tenancy" means the fixed term tenancy on

---

[1] Amended by the Housing Act 2004, s.222(1), (2).

the coming to an end of which the statutory periodic tenancy arises, and

(b) "the implied terms" means the terms of the tenancy which have effect by virtue of section 5(3)(e) above, other than terms as to the amount of the rent;

but nothing in the following provisions of this section applies to a statutory periodic tenancy at a time when, by virtue of paragraph 11 or paragraph 12 in Part I of Schedule 1 to this Act, it cannot be an assured tenancy.

(2) Not later than the first anniversary of the day on which the former tenancy came to an end, the landlord may serve on the tenant, or the tenant may serve on the landlord, a notice in the prescribed form proposing terms of the statutory periodic tenancy different from the implied terms and, if the landlord or the tenant considers it appropriate, proposing an adjustment of the amount of the rent to take account of the proposed terms.

(3) Where a notice has been served under subsection (2) above—

(a) within the period of three months beginning on the date on which the notice was served on him, the landlord or the tenant, as the case may be, may, by an application in the prescribed form, refer the notice to a rent assessment committee under subsection (4) below; and

(b) if the notice is not so referred, then, with effect from such date, not falling within the period referred to in paragraph (a) above, as may be specified in the notice, the terms proposed in the notice shall become terms of the tenancy in substitution for any of the implied terms dealing with the same subject matter and the amount of the rent shall be varied in accordance with any adjustment so proposed.

(4) Where a notice under subsection (2) above is referred to a rent assessment committee, the committee shall consider the terms proposed in the notice and shall determine whether those terms, or some other terms (dealing with the same subject matter as the proposed terms), are such as, in the committee's opinion, might reasonably be expected to be found in an assured periodic tenancy of the dwelling-house concerned, being a tenancy—

(a) which begins on the coming to an end of the former tenancy; and

(b) which is granted by a willing landlord on terms which, except in so far as they relate to the subject matter of the proposed terms, are those of the statutory periodic tenancy at the time of the committee's consideration.

(5) Whether or not a notice under subsection (2) above proposes an adjustment of the amount of the rent under the statutory periodic tenancy, where a rent assessment committee determine any terms under subsection (4) above, they shall, if they consider it appropriate, specify such an adjustment to take account of the terms so determined.

(6) In making a determination under subsection (4) above, or

specifying an adjustment of an amount of rent under subsection (5) above, there shall be disregarded any effect on the terms or the amount of the rent attributable to the granting of a tenancy to a sitting tenant.

(7) Where a notice under subsection (2) above is referred to a rent assessment committee, then, unless the landlord and the tenant otherwise agree, with effect from such date as the committee may direct—

    (a) the terms determined by the committee shall become terms of the statutory periodic tenancy in substitution for any of the implied terms dealing with the same subject matter; and

    (b) the amount of the rent under the statutory periodic tenancy shall be altered to accord with any adjustment specified by the committee;

but for the purposes of paragraph (b) above the committee shall not direct a date earlier than the date specified, in accordance with subsection (3)(b) above, in the notice referred to them.

(8) Nothing in this section requires a rent assessment committee to continue with a determination under subsection (4) above if the landlord and tenant give notice in writing that they no longer require such a determination or if the tenancy has come to an end.

"tenancy"
  See s.45.   **3A–698**

"tenant"
  See s.45.   **3A–699**

"fixed term tenancy"
  See s.45.   **3A–700**

"landlord"
  See s.45.   **3A–701**

"statutory periodic tenancy"
  See s.5(7).   **3A–702**

"prescribed"
  See s.45 and the Assured Tenancies and Agricultural Occupancies (Forms) Regula- **3A–703** tions 1997 (S.I. 1997 No. 194). Note that a notice conforms with the regulations if it is "substantially to the same effect" as that prescribed (para. 2).

Fixing of terms of statutory periodic tenancy
  Section 6 provides a mechanism by which landlords and tenants may propose new **3A–704** terms for a statutory period tenancy which has come into existence by virtue of s.5. At any time up to one year after the former tenancy has come to an end, either party may serve a notice proposing new terms. The notice must be in "the prescribed form" (see Assured Tenancies and Agricultural Occupancies (Forms) Regulations 1997 (S.I. 1997 No. 194). If either party wishes to object to the proposed new terms, he or she may apply to the Rent Assessment Committee to determine whether they are terms which "might reasonably be expected to be found in an assured periodic tenancy of the dwelling-house concerned" granted by a willing landlord. The RAC may specify an adjustment of rent, even if none is sought, to take into account any new terms, if they consider it appropriate.

  An application to a RAC must be made within three months of service of the notice proposing new terms. If no application is made to the RAC within the three-month time limit, the proposed new terms automatically take effect.

Demotion because of anti-social behaviour

3A–705 6A—(1) This section applies to an assured tenancy if the landlord is a registered social landlord.

(2) The landlord may apply to a county court for a demotion order.

(3) A demotion order has the following effect—

(a) the assured tenancy is terminated with effect from the date specified in the order;

(b) if the tenant remains in occupation of the dwelling-house after that date a demoted tenancy is created with effect from that date;

(c) it is a term of the demoted tenancy that any arrears of rent payable at the termination of the assured tenancy become payable under the demoted tenancy;

(d) it is also a term of the demoted tenancy that any rent paid in advance or overpaid at the termination of the assured tenancy is credited to the tenant's liability to pay rent under the demoted tenancy.

(4) The court must not make a demotion order unless it is satisfied—

(a) that the tenant or a person residing in or visiting the dwelling-house has engaged or has threatened to engage in conduct to which section 153A or 153B of the Housing Act 1996 (anti-social behaviour or use of premises for unlawful purposes) applies, and

(b) that it is reasonable to make the order.

(5) The court must not entertain proceedings for a demotion order unless—

(a) the landlord has served on the tenant a notice under subsection (6), or

(b) the court thinks it is just and equitable to dispense with the requirement of the notice.

(6) The notice must—

(a) give particulars of the conduct in respect of which the order is sought;

(b) state that the proceedings will not begin before the date specified in the notice;

(c) state that the proceedings will not begin after the end of the period of twelve months beginning with the date of service of the notice.

(7) The date specified for the purposes of subsection (6)(b) must not be before the end of the period of two weeks beginning with the date of service of the notice.

(8) Each of the following has effect in respect of a demoted tenancy at the time it is created by virtue of an order under this section as it has effect in relation to the assured tenancy at the time it is terminated by virtue of the order—

(a) the parties to the tenancy;

(b) the period of the tenancy;

(c) the amount of the rent;

(d) the dates on which the rent is payable.

(9) Subsection (8)(b) does not apply if the assured tenancy was for a fixed term and in such a case the demoted tenancy is a weekly periodic tenancy.

(10) If the landlord of the demoted tenancy serves on the tenant a statement of any other express terms of the assured tenancy which are to apply to the demoted tenancy such terms are also terms of the demoted tenancy.

(11) For the purposes of this section a demoted tenancy is a tenancy to which section 20B of the Housing Act 1988 applies.

Editorial note

This section was inserted by Anti-social Behaviour Act 2003, s.14(4). It was brought **3A–706** into force in England on June 30, 2004 by the Anti-social Behaviour Act 2003 (Commencement No.3 and Savings) Order 2004 (S.I. 2004 No. 1502) (c.61). It was brought into force in Wales on 30 April 2005 by the Anti-social Behaviour Act 2003 (Commencement No.4) (Wales) Order 2005 (S.I. 2005 No. 1225) (W.83) (C.55). Section 6A provides that a demotion order ends an assured tenancy on a specified date. If the tenant remains in occupation, a new demoted assured shorthold tenancy begins on the same date. The court may only make the order if the tenant, another resident of or visitor to the tenant's home has behaved in a way which is capable of causing nuisance or annoyance or if such a person has used the premises for illegal purposes. In addition the court must be satisfied that it is reasonable to make the order. Sections 6A(3)(c) and (d) confirm that any rent owed or overpaid on the tenant's rent account under the secure tenancy should be transferred across to the new demoted tenancy. Section 6A(5) requires landlords to serve notice on assured tenants before issuing demotion proceedings, and specify the information which the notice should contain. However the court may dispense with the requirement for notice if it thinks it is just and equitable to do so. For consideration of the words "just and equitable" in other contexts, see the commentary at paras 3A–368 and 3A-733.

Registered social landlord

See Housing Act 1996, s.230, subss.1 to 3. **3A–707**

Housing Act 1988, s.20B

See para. 3A–814. **3A–708**

Orders for possession

7.—(1) The court shall not make an order for possession of a **3A–709** dwelling-house let on an assured tenancy except on one or more of the grounds set out in Schedule 2 to this Act; but nothing in this Part of this Act relates to proceedings for possession of such a dwelling-house which are brought by a mortgagee, within the meaning of the Law of Property Act 1925, who has lent money on the security of the assured tenancy.

(2) The following provisions of this section have effect, subject to section 8 below, in relation to proceedings for the recovery of possession of a dwelling-house let on an assured tenancy.

(3) If the court is satisfied that any of the grounds in Part I of Schedule 2 to this Act is established then, subject to subsections (5A) and (6) below, the court shall make an order for possession.

(4) If the court is satisfied that any of the grounds in Part II of Schedule 2 to this Act is established, then, subject to subsections (5A) and (6) below, the court may make an order for possession if it considers it reasonable to do so.

(5) Part III of Schedule 2 to this Act shall have effect for supplementing Ground 9 in that Schedule and Part IV of that Schedule shall have effect in relation to notices given as mentioned in Grounds 1 to 5 of that Schedule.

(5A) The court shall not make an order for possession of a dwelling-house let on an assured periodic tenancy arising under Schedule 10 to the Local Government and Housing Act 1989 on any of the following grounds, that is to say,—

    (a) Grounds 1, 2 and 5 in Part I of Schedule 2 to this Act;

    (b) Ground 16 in Part II of that Schedule; and

    (c) if the assured periodic tenancy arose on the termination of a former 1954 Act tenancy, within the meaning of the said Schedule 10, Ground 6 in Part I of Schedule 2 to this Act.

(6) The court shall not make an order for possession of a dwelling-house to take effect at a time when it is let on an assured fixed term tenancy unless—

    (a) the ground for possession is Ground 2 or Ground 8 in Part I of Schedule 2 to this Act or any of the grounds in Part II of that Schedule, other than Ground 9 or Ground 16; and

    (b) the terms of the tenancy make provision for it to be brought to an end on the ground in question (whether that provision takes the form of a provision for re-entry, for forfeiture, for determination by notice or otherwise).

(7) Subject to the preceding provisions of this section, the court may make an order for possession of a dwelling-house on grounds relating to a fixed term tenancy which has come to an end; and where an order is made in such circumstances, any statutory periodic tenancy which has arisen on the ending of the fixed term tenancy shall end (without any notice and regardless of the period) on the day on which the order takes effect.

3A–710   *Note*—Amended by the Local Government and Housing Act 1989, Sched.11.

"assured tenancy"

3A–711   See s.1.

"tenancy"

3A–712   See s.45.

"dwelling-house"

3A–713   See s.45.

"let"

3A–714   See s.45.

"fixed term"

3A–715   See s.45.

Orders for possession

3A–716   Like the Rent Act 1977, s.98 and the Housing Act 1985, s.84, this section provides that a court may only make an order for possession against an assured tenant if a ground for possession is made out. The grounds are specified in Sched.2 (see below). In addition, depending upon the ground relied upon, the landlord may have to satisfy the court that it is reasonable to make an order for possession. For reasonableness, see the commentary to the Housing Act 1985, s.84, above. As to reasonableness (s.7(4)) see *West Kent Housing Association v. Davis* (1991) 31 H.L.R. 415, CA; *New Charter Housing (North) Ltd v. Ashcroft* [2004] EWCA Civ 310; [2004] H.L.R. 36 and *Moat Housing Group South Ltd v. Harris and Hartless* [2005] EWCA Civ 287; [2005] HLR 33.

A fixed term assured or assured shorthold tenancy can be terminated during the fixed term if the landlord can prove that any of Grounds 2 (premises required by mortgagee), 8 (two months' rent arrears), 10 (rent arrears), 11 (persistent rent arrears), 12 (breach of obligation), 13 (deterioration), 14 (nuisance or annoyance) or 15 (deterioration of furniture) (see Sched.2) exist and provided that the tenancy contains a provision entitling the landlord to do so (see s.7(6)).

Where a landlord is seeking possession under one of the mandatory grounds for possession (*e.g.* Ground 8) during the fixed term of a tenancy, the court has no power to grant relief from forfeiture under the County Courts Act 1984, s.138. In *Artesian Residential Investments Ltd v. Beck* [2000] 2 W.L.R. 357; [1999] 3 All E.R. 113; [1999] 22 E.G. 145; [2001] QB 541, CA a fixed term assured tenancy agreement included a proviso for re-entry and determination if the rent was at any stage fourteen days in arrears. The defendant fell into rent arrears before the expiry of the term and, the landlord brought possession proceedings relying on the Housing Act 1988, Sched.2, Grounds 8 and 10. A possession order was made, but the defendant later paid all the arrears and applied for suspension of the possession order, relying upon the relief from forfeiture provisions of the County Courts Act 1984, s.138. H.H.J. Mitchell granted relief but the Court of Appeal held that the Housing Act 1988, s.5(1) sets out the only routes for bringing an assured tenancy to an end. There is no need for a parallel claim for forfeiture to prevent the contractual tenancy continuing after the granting of an order for possession under the Act. By its express words, s.5(1) makes it abundantly clear that an order for possession brings a tenancy to an end. This construction is also borne out by s.7(7) which provides that, when the court makes an order for possession on grounds relating to a fixed term tenancy which has come to an end, any ensuing statutory periodic tenancy which arises on the ending of the fixed term tenancy ends (without any notice or regardless of the period) on the day on which the order takes effect.

Furthermore, s.7(3) is explicit, obliging the court mandatorily to make an order for possession if satisfied that any of the grounds in Sched.2 is established subject, *inter alia*, to s.6. Section 7(6)(b) does no more than require provision for, *e.g.*, forfeiture to be included in the terms of the tenancy, and does not set up forfeiture as an independent ground for terminating the tenancy. As a matter of principle there is no room for applying s.138. As there is no exercise of a right of re-entry or forfeiture for non-payment of rent, its requirements are not met.

Difficulties may arise where arrears are due to housing benefit problems. In *North British Housing Association Limited v. Matthews* [2004] EWCA Civ 1736; [2005] 1 WLR 3133; [2005] 2 All E.R. 667 , when dismissing appeals by tenants who had been refused adjournments in order to attempt to resolve housing benefit problems, the Court of Appeal held that:

- The court cannot be satisfied that the landlord is entitled to possession before the date of the hearing. The date of the hearing is the date when the claim is heard. It is not the date fixed for the hearing if, on that date, an adjournment is granted without a hearing taking place at all.
- There is no doubt that it is a perfectly proper exercise of the court's discretion to adjourn, if a case has to be taken out of the list because there is no judge available, or because there has been over-listing, or because the defendant is prevented by ill-health from attending court.
- The court retains jurisdiction to grant an adjournment before it is satisfied that the landlord is entitled to possession. It may be a proper exercise of discretion to adjourn the hearing before the court is satisfied that the landlord is entitled to possession — *e.g.* where there is an arguable claim for damages which can be set-off against arrears; where the tenant shows that there is an arguable defence based on accord and satisfaction or estoppel arising from an agreement whereby the landlord accepts an offer by the tenant to pay off the current rent and arrears at a certain rate in return for not pursuing the claim for possession; or where the court is satisfied that there is a real chance that the tenant would be given permission to apply for judicial review of the landlord's decision to claim possession because of abuse of power.

- However it is not legitimate to adjourn to enable the tenant to pay off arrears and so defeat the claim for possession, unless there are exceptional circumstances — *e.g.* if a tenant is robbed on the way to court, or if a computer failure prevents the housing benefit authority from being able to pay benefit due until the day after the hearing date. The fact that arrears are attributable to maladministration on the part of the housing benefit authority is not an exceptional circumstance.
- Once the court has expressed the conclusion that it is satisfied that the landlord is entitled to possession, there is no power to grant an adjournment in any circumstances (seess.7(3) and 9(6)). The court cannot be "satisfied" within the meaning of s.9(6) until the judge has given a judgment and effect is given to that judgment in a perfected order of the court.
- The Housing Corporation may consider it wise to expand its advice in Regulatory Circular 07/04 (see November 2004 Legal Action 23) about the need for effective liaison between landlords and housing benefit departments right up to the time when a possession claim for rent arrears is heard.

In a case where an outright order for possession was made under Ground 8, but the landlord subsequently accepted the tenant's offer to pay rent and £100 per month off arrears, the Court of Appeal held that the landlord had done nothing to affect the legal relations between the parties. No new or different terms were come to. The landlord had no intention to create a new tenancy. The legal relations between the parties were governed by the terms of the order until the landlord took a position inconsistent with the order (*Stirling v. Leadenhall Residential 2 Ltd* [2001] EWCA Civ 1011; [2001] 3 All E.R. 645; [2002] 1 W.L.R. 499, CA).

Where an order for possession is made under one of the mandatory grounds in the Housing Act 1988, Sched.2, then that ground should be stated on the face of the order. It is not proper to return to the judge at a later date to find out the grounds on which he made the order to find out if it was made in exercise of his discretion. Accordingly, where an order for possession under those grounds failed to state the ground on the face of the order, it could be regarded as having been granted on uncertain grounds, and in those circumstances, a court could revisit the exercise of discretion by the previous judge (*Diab v. Countrywide Rentals 1 Plc* (2001) July 10, Ch D).

Disability Discrimination Act 1995

3A-717   The effect of Disability Discrimination Act 1995, s.22(3)(c) is that it is unlawful to discriminate "by evicting [a] disabled person or subjecting him to any other detriment". Although unlawfulness under the Disability Discrimination Act is not a bar to a landlord seeking a possession order under the Housing Act, the fact that the eviction is unlawful and not justified is a highly relevant consideration for the s.7 discretion of whether or not to make a possession order. The Disability Discrimination Act contains its own code which requires a higher threshold than the Housing Act to justify an eviction (*North Devon Homes Ltd v. Brazier* [2003] EWHC 574 (QB); [2003] 22 EG 141). In *Manchester CC v. Romano* [2004] EWCA Civ 834; [2005] 1 WLR 2775, the Court of Appeal, in a very thorough review of the legislation, stated that when a court considers the Disability Discrimination Act 1995 in the context of possession proceedings, the first matter which has to be determined is whether the person who complains about disability discrimination is a "disabled person" within the meaning of the Disability Discrimination (Meaning of Disability) Regulations 1996 S.I. 1996 No. 1455, Sched.1, ss.1-3 and the *Guidance on matters to be taking into account in determining questions relating to the definition of disability* issued by the Secretary of State. Secondly, the court should consider whether or not there has been discrimination— *i.e.* treating a disabled person less favourably for a reason which relates to the disabled person's disability. Thirdly, the court should consider whether the landlord's treatment of the tenant is justified. It is only justified if in the landlord's opinion the treatment (*viz* the decision to set in motion proceedings for possession) is necessary in order not to endanger the health or safety of any of the people living in neighbouring houses and it is reasonable, in all the circumstances, for the landlord to hold that opinion. The landlord must prove that if it does not take this action someone's health or safety would be endangered. It does not have to prove that that person's health or safety has actually been damaged. The 1995 Act does not explicitly provide a defence for disabled persons who wish to assert that the reason why their landlord brought possession proceedings related to disability. It is though open to such disabled persons to counterclaim for a declaration that they have been unlawfully discriminated against and/or to counterclaim for injunctive relief. Furthermore, if tenants can prove that the landlord's conduct amounts to unlawful discrimination, this is bound to be a relevant factor when the court is determining whether it is reasonable to make an order for possession. The Court of Appeal stated that it is preferable, in cases involving a secure tenancy or an assured tenancy, for tenants to assert that it is unreasonable for the court to make a possession order, rather than to complicate the proceedings by adding a formalistic counterclaim for a declaration or an injunction. Landlords whose tenants hold secure or assured tenancies must consider the position carefully before they decide to serve a notice seeking possession or to embark on possession proceedings against a tenant who is or might be mentally impaired. They should liase closely with local social services authorities at an early stage.

"consent orders"

The jurisdiction of the court to make an order for possession under s.7 is limited. If **3A–718** the court is not satisfied that a ground under Sched.2 has been established it does not have jurisdiction to make the order. A court is under a duty to determine whether the relevant ground has been established, whether or not it has been raised by the parties. Where a court lacks jurisdiction, it cannot be conferred merely by consent. To confer jurisdiction an admission that a ground is satisfied, either express or implied, has to be clearly shown. Any consent order should clearly spell out in express terms the admission made by the tenant, or the court should ask the tenant what admission was being made, so that there can be no room for confusion or doubt in the future (*Baygreen Properties Ltd v. Gil* [2002] EWCA Civ 1340; [2003] H.L.R. 12; [2002] 49 EG 126—"possession order by consent" approved by circuit judge set aside).

appeals on questions of reasonableness

Although County Courts Act 1984 s.77(6) excludes appeals against judges' findings **3A–719** of fact, it does not exclude, in a proper case, the possibility of an appeal against a finding of reasonableness *Castle Vale Housing Action Trust v. Gallagher* [2001] EWCA Civ 944; (2001) 33 H.L.R. 810, CA.

ECHR art 8 and reasonableness

The Court of Appeal has doubted whether Art.8 makes any difference to the way in **3A–720** which courts have always approached questions of the reasonableness of making possessions order. Article 8 does, however, reinforce the importance of only making an order depriving someone of his or her home in circumstances where a clear case is made out (*Castle Vale Housing Action Trust v. Gallagher* [2001] EWCA Civ 944; (2001) 33 H.L.R. 810. See too *Newham LBC v. Neal* [2003] EWCA Civ 541, February 25, 2003.) There is a need to find a fair balance and to protect the rights of the neighbours and other members of the public. (*Lambeth LBC v. Howard* [2001] EWCA Civ 468; (2001) 33 H.L.R. 636. See too *Harrow LBC v. Qazi* [2003] UKHL 43; [2003] 3 W.L.R. 792; *The Times,* July 31, 2003, where Lord Hope and Lord Scott said that contractual and property rights cannot be defeated by a defence based on Art.8. See too *Newham LBC v. Kibata* [2003] EWCA Civ 1785; [2004] HLR 28 and *Bradney v. Birmingham CC; Birmingham CC v. McCann* [2003] EWCA Civ 1783; [2004] HLR 27).

Forms of order

See Forms **N26A** (Order that Claimant have possession (Assured tenancies)) and **3A–721** **N28** (Order for Possession (possession suspended) (rented property)) as specified in the Practice Direction to CPR Pt 4, Table 3.

Notice of proceedings for possession

8.—(1) The court shall not entertain proceedings for possession of **3A–722** dwelling-house let on an assured tenancy unless—

> (a) the landlord or, in the case of joint landlords, at least one of them has served on the tenant a notice in accordance with this section and the proceedings are begun within the time limits stated in the notice in accordance with subsections (3) to (4B) below, or
>
> (b) the court considers it just and equitable to dispense with the requirement of such a notice.

(2) The court shall not make an order for possession on any of the grounds in Schedule 2 to this Act unless that ground and particulars of it are specified in the notice under this section; but the grounds specified in such a notice may be altered or added to with the leave of the court.

(3) A notice under this section is one in the prescribed form informing the tenant that—

    (a) the landlord intends to begin proceedings for possession of the dwelling-house on one or more of the grounds specified in the notice; and

    (b) those proceedings will not begin earlier than a date specified in the notice in accordance with subsections (4) to (4B) below; and

    (c) those proceedings will not begin later than twelve months from the date of service of the notice.

(4) If a notice under this section specifies in accordance with subsection (3)(a) above Ground 14 in Schedule 2 to this Act (whether with or without other grounds), the date specified in the notice as mentioned in subsection (3)(b) above shall not be earlier than the date of the service of the notice.

(4A) If a notice under this section specifies in accordance with subsection (3)(a) above, any of Grounds 1, 2, 5 to 7, 9 and 16 in Schedule 2 to this Act (whether without other grounds or with any ground other than Ground 14), the date specified in the notice as mentioned in subsection (3)(b) above shall not be earlier than—

    (a) two months from the date of service of the notice; and

    (b) if the tenancy is a periodic tenancy, the earliest date on which, apart from section 5(1) above, the tenancy could be brought to an end by a notice to quit given by the landlord on the same date as the date of service of the notice under this section.

(4B) In any other case, the date specified in the notice as mentioned in subsection (3)(b) above shall not be earlier than the expiry of the period of two weeks from the date of the service of the notice.

(5) The court may not exercise the power conferred by subsection (1)(b) above if the landlord seeks to recover possession on Ground 8 in Schedule 2 to this Act.

(6) Where a notice under this section—

    (a) is served at a time when the dwelling-house is let on a fixed term tenancy, or

    (b) is served after a fixed term tenancy has come to an end but relates (in whole or in part) to events occurring during that tenancy,

the notice shall have effect notwithstanding that the tenant becomes or has become tenant under a statutory periodic tenancy arising on the coming to an end of the fixed term tenancy.

3A-723   *Note* —Amended by the Housing Act 1996, s.151.

"assured tenancy"

3A-724   See s.1.

"landlord", "tenancy" and "tenant"

See s.45.   **3A–725**

"dwelling-house"

See s.45.   **3A–726**

"fixed term"

See s.45.   **3A–727**

"prescribed"

See s.45 and the Assured Tenancies and Agricultural Occupancies (Forms) Regula-   **3A–728**
tions 1997 (S.I. 1997 No. 194). For cases where landlords used old versions of
prescribed forms, see: *Beckerman v. Durling* (1983) 6 H.L.R. 87, CA; *Swansea CC v.
Hearn* (1991) 23 H.L.R. 284, CA; and *Tadema Holdings v. Ferguson*, (2000) 32 H.L.R.
866; *The Times*, November 25, 1999, CA.

Notice of proceedings for possession

Before bringing possession proceedings against assured tenants, landlords must ei-   **3A–729**
ther serve a "notice of proceedings for possession" in accordance with the Housing Act
1988, s.8, or (in cases other than Ground 8) persuade the court that it is just and equitable to dispense with that requirement. The relevant form is contained in the Assured
Tenancies and Agricultural Occupancies (Forms) Regulations 1997 (S.I. 1997 No.
194). Note that a notice conforms with the regulations if it is "substantially to the same
effect" as that prescribed (para.2). The relevant form (Form 3) states that the landlord
must, *inter alia*, "give the full text ... of each ground which is being relied upon". It is
similar to the form of notice used in connection with public sector secure tenancies
(Housing Act 1985, s.83). Particulars of the grounds relied upon have to be included,
as well as the ground itself.

Normally notices of intention to bring possession proceedings against assured tenants only have to give two weeks notice, but in the case of Grounds 1 (landlord's occupation), 2 (mortgagee seeking to exercise power of sale), 5 (ministers of religion), 6
(housing association wishing to demolish or reconstruct), 7 (death of tenant), 9 (suitable alternative accommodation) and 16 (letting in consequence of employment) (all
set out below) at least two months notice or notice equivalent to the contractual period
of the tenancy, whichever is longer, has to be given. If the landlord relies upon
Ground 14 (nuisance or annoyance) proceedings may be begun immediately after service (s.8(4)).

Proceedings must be begun within 12 months of service of the notice, otherwise a
new notice must be served. There is no need for a landlord of an assured tenant to
serve a notice to quit as well as a notice of intention to bring proceedings (s.5(1)).

As to assured tenancy agreements that provide that (1) before bringing possession
proceedings landlords will give four weeks notice and (2) that they will only rely upon
certain grounds for possession, see *North British H.A. v. Sheridan* (2000) 32 H.L.R. 346;
[2000] L & T.R. 115, CA.

Service of section 8 notices

The word "service" in ss.8 and 13 is an ordinary English word connoting delivery   **3A–730**
of a document to a particular person. It carries no implication that the document has
to be read, understood or indeed known by the recipient to have been delivered as
long as delivery is to the correct address. Such meaning does not change according to
the capacity of the intended recipient. See *Tadema Holdings v. Ferguson* (2000) 32
H.L.R. 866, CA.

"ground"

Although the full text of the ground as set out in the Housing Act 1988, Sched.2   **3A–731**
may not have to be repeated verbatim, "the words used [must] set out fully the
substance of the ground so that the notice is adequate to achieve the legislative purpose
of the provision. That purpose ... is to give ... information ... to enable the tenant to
consider what she should do and, with or without advice, to do that which is in her
power and which will best protect her against the loss of her home" (*Mountain v. Hastings* [1993] 29 E.G. 96; (1993) 25 H.L.R. 427 at 433, CA, where the notice was held to
be defective because it had omitted the words "both at the date of service of the

Notice...and at the date of the hearing" and the explanation that " 'rent' means rent lawfully due from the tenant"). In *Mountain v. Hastings* the Court of Appeal also held that the words in s.8(2) which allow a court to alter or add to the grounds specified in a notice assume that there is a valid notice and are solely directed to the possibility of adding to or deleting grounds.

particulars of the ground (s.8(2))

3A–732   See also the commentary to the Housing Act 1985, s.83.

The Court of Appeal has held that the particulars in a notice from a landlord to a tenant relying upon Ground 8 comply with the Housing Act 1988, s.8 provided that "it is made clear...that more than [two] months rent is at the date of that notice unpaid and due and provided also that in some way or other that notice makes it clear either how much, or how the tenant can ascertain how much, is alleged to be due". It is not necessary for the notice to contain a schedule of the arrears (*Marath v. MacGillivray* (1996) 28 H.L.R. 484, CA, where the notice stated, as particulars of the arrears: "At a meeting between the landlord and tenant on July 24, 1994 the arrears were agreed at £103.29...Since that date no payments of rent have been made..." without giving a figure for the arrears as at the date of the notice was given). In *Marath* the Court of Appeal also indicated that under s.8(2) a court may allow particulars to be added if they have not been given earlier.

"the court considers it just and equitable to dispense with the requirement of such a notice" (s.8(1)(b))

3A–733   See the commentary to the Housing Act 1985, s.83(1)(b). Note that there is no power to dispense with service of a notice if Ground 8 (*i.e.* 8 weeks' arrears) is relied upon.

It is "obviously only in relatively exceptional cases where the court should be prepared to dispense with a...notice". (*Braintree DC v. Vincent* [2004] EWCA Civ 415—a case where the Court of Appeal held that a judge was entitled to dispense with a statutory notice on unusual facts. A notice would have been of no benefit to the tenant—indeed it would have been to her disadvantage because it would have postponed the date for possession and added to her liability for rent). In *Kelsey HA v. King* (1995) 28 H.L.R. 270, CA, it was held that in deciding whether it is just and equitable to dispense with service a court should "weigh all the factors before it" and "take all the circumstances into account, both from the view of the landlord and the tenant". In many cases, the fact that tenants have not been given "an opportunity to put right what it is alleged had gone wrong" would be significant, but in this case where full particulars were annexed to the Particulars of Claim the Defendant had had ample time.

See too the Rent Act cases such as *Fernandes v. Parvardin* (1982) 264 E.G. 49; (1982) 5 H.L.R. 33, CA; and *Bradshaw v. Baldwin-Wiseman* (1985) 17 H.L.R. 260; (1985) 49 P.&C.R. 382, CA.

Applications to strike out possession proceedings where there has been a failure to comply with s.8 should be made promptly.

Where local authority landlords transfer their housing stock to registered social landlords, and as a result, the landlords are no longer within the landlord condition (Housing Act 1985, s.80(1)), tenancies cease to be secure and, by virtue of Housing Act 1988, s.1(1), become assured tenancies. In such circumstances courts have no jurisdiction to entertain possession claims unless s.8 notices are served, or the court exercises the power to dispense with notice under s.8(1)(b). This applies even where local authorities serve notices seeking possession under Housing Act 1985, s.83 before the stock transfer. The court's discretion is wide enough to allow substitution of the new landlord as claimant and dispensation of a s.8 notice where the reality is that the new landlord relies upon the same breach of the same term and the relief sought is no different. However, it is not legitimate for a court to dispense with s.8 notices without some consideration of any objection which might be taken by tenants by reference to the facts of their cases (*Knowsley Housing Trust v. Revell*; *Helena Housing Ltd v. Curtis* [2003] EWCA Civ 496; *The Times*, April 17, 2003). See too *North British HA v. Sheridan*, (2000) 32 H.L.R. 346; [1999] 2 E.G.L.R. 138, CA.

In *McShane v. William Sutton Trust* (1997) 1 L. & T. Rev. D67; December 1997, Legal Action 13, Warrington County Court, H.H.J. Daley held that although there is nothing in the rules preventing a landlord from applying *ex parte* to dispense with service of a s.8 notice, following *Kelsey HA v. King* (1995) 28 H.L.R. 270, CA, it is not possible for a judge deciding whether or not to dispense with service to weigh up all factors from both points of view without the tenant being in court and that a decision by a district judge *ex parte* to dispense with service was "plainly wrong".

See too *Hegab v. Shamash*, June 1998 Legal Action 13, CA: appeal by tenant against decision to dispense with requirement for notice allowed because the judge had failed to take into account two matters, namely the fact that the tenant had paid a deposit of £4,000 in relation to a proposed purchase of the premises which had not been refunded and that the landlord had not paid the costs of the earlier proceedings concerning an illegal eviction.

Additional notice requirements: ground of domestic violence

8A.—(1) Where the ground specified in a notice under section 8 (whether with or without other grounds) is Ground 14A in Schedule 2 to this Act and the partner who has left the dwelling-house as mentioned in that ground is not a tenant of the dwelling-house, the court shall not entertain proceedings for possession of the dwelling-house unless— **3A–734**

> (a) the landlord or, in the case of joint landlords, at least one of them has served on the partner who has left a copy of the notice or has taken all reasonable steps to serve a copy of the notice on that partner, or
>
> (b) the court considers it just and equitable to dispense with such requirements as to service.

(2) Where Ground 14A in Schedule 2 to this Act is added to a notice under section 8 with the leave of the court after proceedings for possession are begun and the partner who has left the dwelling-house as mentioned in that ground is not a party to the proceedings, the court shall not continue to entertain the proceedings unless—

> (a) the landlord or, in the case of joint landlords, at least one of them has served a notice under subsection (3) below on the partner who has left or has taken all reasonable steps to serve such a notice on that partner, or
>
> (b) the court considers it just and equitable to dispense with the requirement of such a notice.

(3) A notice under this subsection shall—

> (a) state that proceedings for the possession of the dwelling-house have begun,
>
> (b) specify the ground or grounds on which possession is being sought, and
>
> (c) give particulars of the ground or grounds.

Note—Added by the Housing Act 1996, s.150. **3A–735**

"landlord", "tenancy" and "tenant"

See s.45. **3A–736**

"dwelling-house"

See s.45. **3A–737**

"notice"

See s.8. **3A–738**

"the court considers it just and equitable to dispense with the requirement of such a notice"

See s.8(1)(b). See also commentary to Ground 14A, below. **3A–739**

Extended discretion of court in possession claims

3A–740   9.—(1) Subject to subsection (6) below, the court may adjourn for such period or periods as it thinks fit proceedings for possession of a dwelling-house let on an assured tenancy.

(2) On the making of an order for possession of a dwelling-house let on an assured tenancy or at any time before the execution of such an order, the court, subject to subsection (6) below, may—

(a) stay or suspend execution of the order, or

(b) postpone the date of possession,

for such period or periods as the court thinks just.

(3) On any such adjournment as is referred to in subsection (1) above or on any such stay, suspension or postponement as is referred to in subsection (2) above, the court, unless it considers that to do so would cause exceptional hardship to the tenant or would otherwise be unreasonable, shall impose conditions with regard to payment by the tenant of arrears of rent (if any) and rent or payments in respect of occupation after the termination of the tenancy (mesne profits) and may impose such other conditions as it thinks fit.

(4) If any such conditions as are referred to in subsection (3) above are complied with, the court may, if it thinks fit, discharge or rescind any such order as is referred to in subsection (2) above.

(5) In any case where—

(a) at a time when proceedings are brought for possession of a dwelling-house let on an assured tenancy, the tenant's spouse or former spouse, having matrimonial home rights under Part IV of the Family Law Act 1996 is in occupation of the dwelling-house, and

(b) the assured tenancy is terminated as a result of those proceedings,

the spouse or former spouse, so long as he or she remains in occupation, shall have the same rights in relation to, or in connection with, any such adjournment as is referred to in subsection (1) above or any such stay, suspension or postponement as is referred to in subsection (2) above, as he or she would have if those matrimonial home rights were not affected by the termination of the tenancy.

(5A) In any case where—

(a) at a time when proceedings are brought for possession of a dwelling-house let on an assured tenancy—

(i) an order is in force under section 35 of the Family Law Act 1996 conferring rights on the former spouse of the tenant, or

(ii) an order is in force under section 36 of that Act conferring rights on a cohabitant or former cohabitant (within the meaning of that Act) of the tenant,

(b) that cohabitant, former cohabitant or former spouse is then in occupation of the dwelling-house, and

(c) the assured tenancy is terminated as a result of those proceedings, the cohabitant, former cohabitant or former spouse shall have the same rights in relation to, or in connection with, any such adjournment as is referred to in subsection (1) above or any such stay, suspension or postponement as is referred to in subsection (2) above as he or she would have if the rights conferred by the order referred to in paragraph (a) above were not affected by the termination of the tenancy.

(6) This section does not apply if the court is satisfied that the landlord is entitled to possession of the dwelling-house—

    (a) on any of the grounds in Part I of Schedule 2 to this Act, or

    (b) by virtue of subsection (1) or subsection (4) of section 21 below.

Note—Amended by the Family Law Act 1996, Sched.8, para. 59.   **3A–741**

"assured tenancy"
See s.1.   **3A–742**

"landlord", "tenancy" and "tenant"
See s.45.   **3A–743**

"dwelling-house"
See s.45.   **3A–744**

Extended discretion of court in possession claims

See also commentary to the Housing Act 1985, s.85. This section gives the court a   **3A–745** wide discretion, firstly at trial when considering the form of possession order to make and secondly after the making of a possession order at " *any time before the execution of such an order*." See, *e.g. R. v. Ilkeston County Court; Ex p. Kruza* (1985) 17 H.L.R. 539, QBD, s.9 "gives a wide power to stay or suspend an order for possession which is applicable to all cases except those where it is expressly excluded by statute." The power may be exercised where circumstances have changed since the original hearing, even where an outright order was made by a different judge, (*Ujima HA v. Smith* Legal Action 22, October 16, 2000, Ch D, April 2001, where the defendant was by the time of the application to suspend accepting her legal responsibility for serious damage to a shared kitchen and offering to pay £150 in compensation). See too *Plymouth CC v. Hoskin* [2002] EWCA Civ 684; May 1, 2002 noted at para. 3A–378 where the Court of Appeal said "There is a continuing remedy in the county court." However, the power only applies where there is a discretionary ground for possession (as opposed to a mandatory ground where the court's discretion is limited by the Housing Act 1980, s.89 (see above).

When exercising its powers under s.9 the court should impose conditions with respect to the repayment of arrears of rent and mesne profits unless it considers that to do so would cause exceptional hardship (s.9(3)). There have been no reported Court of Appeal decisions as to what might constitute "exceptional hardship".

Where there is a substantial dispute about the amount claimed and the tenant's compliance with the order, the up-to-date position has to be clearly and accurately established before considering an application to suspend under s.9 (*Haringey LBC v. Powell* (1996) 28 H.L.R. 798, CA).

The court, exercising its discretion on an application to suspend a warrant under s.9, may take account of matters (*e.g.* breaches of the terms of the tenancy agreement or anti-social behaviour) other than those relied upon as grounds for making the original possession order—although it is not always be right to do so. (See *Sheffield City Council v.Hopkins* [2001] EWCA Civ 1023; [2002] H.L.R. 12, CA) and the more detailed commentary at para. 3A–387).

After execution an occupier can only be restored to possession if either the whole proceedings are set aside (see the commentary at 3A–381; *Leicester City Council v. Aldwinkle* (1992) 24 H.L.R. 40, CA; *cf. Governors of Peabody Donation Fund v. Hay* (1987) 19

H.L.R. 145, CA; and *Tower Hamlets LBC v. Abadie* (1990) 22 H.L.R. 264, CA) or the warrant had been obtained by fraud, abuse of process or oppression (see *Hammersmith and Fulham LBC v. Hill* (1995) 27 H.L.R. 368; [1994] 2 E.G.L.R. 51, CA; *Hackney LBC v. White* (1995) 28 H.L.R. 219, CA; and *Tower Hamlets LBC v. Azad* (1998) 30 H.L.R. 241, CA; but *cf. Islington LBC v. Harridge, The Times*, 30 June, 1993, CA).

See also *Saint v. Barking and Dagenham LBC* (1999) 31 H.L.R. 620, CA (oppression where warrant executed without prior notification to tenant who was in prison and without inviting him to renew his application for housing benefit).

On any of the grounds in Part I

3A–746   The extended discretion to stay or suspend does not apply where the landlord has satisfied one of the mandatory grounds for possession—s.9(6). See however *Capital Prime Plus Plc v. Wills* (1999) 31 H.L.R. 926, CA where the landlord had consented to the suspension of the original possession order even though there were over two months' arrears. The Court of Appeal held that the order had not been made under Ground 8 and so, on subsequent default, the court did have power to suspend a warrant and *Diab v. Countrywide Rentals 1 Plc*, October 2001 Legal Action 15, noted at para. 3A–708.

Proceedings for possession: anti-social behaviour

3A–747   **9A.**—(1) This section applies if the court is considering under section 7(4) whether it is reasonable to make an order for possession on ground 14 set out in Part 2 of Schedule 2 (conduct of tenant or other person).

(2) The court must consider, in particular—

(a) the effect that the nuisance or annoyance has had on persons other than the person against whom the order is sought;

(b) any continuing effect the nuisance or annoyance is likely to have on such persons;

(c) the effect that the nuisance or annoyance would be likely to have on such persons if the conduct is repeated.

Editorial note

3A–748   This section was inserted by Anti-social Behaviour Act 2003, s.14(6). It was brought into force in England on June 30, 2004 by the Anti-social Behaviour Act 2003 (Commencement No.3 and Savings) Order 2004 (S.I. 2004 No. 1502) (C.61). It was brought into force in Wales on April 30, 2005 by the Anti-social Behaviour Act 2003 (Commencement No. 4) (Wales) Order 2005SI No. 1225 (W.83)(C.55).

Reasonable

3A–749   When considering whether or not to make a possession order and/or whether or not to make a suspended possession order under Schedule 2 Ground 14, the court must consider whether it is reasonable to make such an order—see the commentary to s.7 at paras 3A–716 and 3A–369. Section 9A adds to that general consideration a requirement that the court must consider, in particular, the effect that the nuisance or annoyance has had and would be likely to have if continued on persons other than the defendant, *e.g.* neighbours.

Special provisions applicable to shared accommodation

3A–750   **10.**—(1) This section applies in a case falling within subsection (1) of section 3 above and expressions used in this section have the same meaning as in that section.

(2) Without prejudice to the enforcement of any order made under subsection (3) below, while the tenant is in possession of the separate accommodation, no order shall be made for possession of any of the shared accommodation, whether on the application of the

immediate landlord of the tenant or on the application of any person under whom that landlord derives title, unless a like order has been made, or is made at the same time, in respect of the separate accommodation; and the provisions of section 6 above shall have effect accordingly.

(3) On the application of the landlord, the court may make such order as it thinks just either—

(a) terminating the right of the tenant to use the whole or any part of the shared accommodation other than living accommodation; or

(b) modifying his right to use the whole or any part of the shared accommodation, whether by varying the persons or increasing the number of persons entitled to the use of that accommodation or otherwise.

(4) No order shall be made under subsection (3) above so as to effect any termination or modification of the rights of the tenant which, apart from section 3(3) above, could not be effected by or under the terms of the tenancy.

"landlord", "tenancy" and "tenant"
See s.45.   **3A–751**

"separate accommodation"
See s.3.   **3A–752**

"shared accommodation"
See s.3.   **3A–753**

Payment of removal expenses in certain cases

11.—(1) Where a court makes an order for possession of a **3A–754** dwelling-house let on an assured tenancy on Ground 6 or Ground 9 in Schedule 2 to this Act (but not on any other ground), the landlord shall pay to the tenant a sum equal to the reasonable expenses likely to be incurred by the tenant in removing from the dwelling-house.

(2) Any question as to the amount of the sum referred in subsection (1) above shall be determined by agreement between the landlord and the tenant or, in default of agreement, by the court.

(3) Any sum payable to a tenant by virtue of this section shall be recoverable as a civil debt due from the landlord.

"assured tenancy"
See s.1.   **3A–755**

"landlord", and "tenant"
See s.45.   **3A–756**

"dwelling-house"
See s.45.   **3A–757**

Payment of removal expenses in certain cases
The court may only order a landlord to pay removal expenses if possession is **3A–758** claimed under Ground 6 (housing association wishing to demolish or reconstruct), or Ground 9 (suitable alternative accommodation).

Compensation for misrepresentation or concealment

12. Where a landlord obtains an order for possession of a dwelling- **3A–759** house let on an assured tenancy on one or more of the grounds in

Schedule 2 to this Act and it is subsequently made to appear to the court that the order was obtained by misrepresentation or concealment of material facts, the court may order the landlord to pay to the former tenant such sum as appears sufficient as compensation for damage or loss sustained by that tenant as a result of the order.

"assured tenancy"

3A–760   See s.1.

"landlord" and "tenant"

3A–761   See s.45.

"dwelling-house"

3A–762   See s.45.

Compensation for misrepresentation or concealment

3A–763   *cf.* the Rent Act 1977, s.102. See also *Mafo v. Adams* [1970] 1 Q.B. 548, CA (proceedings based upon the common law tort of deceit).

RENT AND OTHER TERMS

Increase of rent under assured periodic tenancies

3A–764   **13.**—(1) This section applies to—

(a) a statutory periodic tenancy other than one which, by virtue of paragraph 11 or paragraph 12 in Part I of Schedule 1 to this Act, cannot for the time being be an assured tenancy; and

(b) any other periodic tenancy which is an assured tenancy, other than one in relation to which there is a provision, for the time being binding on the tenant, under which the rent for a particular period of the tenancy will or may be greater than the rent for an earlier period.

(2) For the purpose of securing an increase in the rent under a tenancy to which this section applies, the landlord may serve on the tenant a notice in the prescribed form proposing a new rent to take effect at the beginning of a new period of the tenancy specified in the notice, being a period beginning not earlier than—

(a) the minimum period after the date of the service of the notice; and

(b) except in the case of a statutory tenancy—

(i) in the case of an assured agricultural occupancy, the first anniversary of the date on which the first period of the tenancy began;

(ii) in any other case, on the date that falls 52 weeks after the date on which the first period of the tenancy began; and;

(c) if the rent under the tenancy has previously been increased by virtue of a notice under this subsection or a determination under section 14 below—

(i) in the case of an assured agricultural occupancy, the first anniversary of the date on which the increased rent took effect;

842

(ii) in any other case, the appropriate date.

(3) The minimum period referred to in subsection (2) above is—

(a) in the case of a yearly tenancy, six months;

(b) in the case of a tenancy where the period is less than a month, one month; and

(c) in any other case, a period equal to the period of the tenancy,

(3A) The appropriate date referred to in subsection (2)(c)(ii) above is—

(a) in a case to which subsection (3B) below applies, the date that falls 53 weeks after the date on which the increased rent took effect;

(b) in any other case, the date that falls 52 weeks after the date on which the increased rent took effect.

(3B) This subsection applies where—

(a) the rent under the tenancy has been increased by virtue of a notice under this section or a determination under section 14 below on at least one occasion after the coming into force of the Regulatory Reform (Assured Periodic Tenancies) (Rent Increases) Order 2003; and

(b) the fifty-third week after the date on which the last such increase took effect begins more than six days before the anniversary of the date on which the first such increase took effect.

(4) Where a notice is served under subsection (2) above, a new rent specified in the notice shall take effect as mentioned in the notice unless, before the beginning of the new period specified in the notice—

(a) the tenant by an application in the prescribed form refers the notice to a rent assessment committee; or

(b) the landlord and the tenant agree on a variation of the rent which is different from that proposed in the notice or agree that the rent should not be varied.

(5) Nothing in this section (or in section 14 below) affects the right of the landlord and the tenant under an assured tenancy to vary by agreement any term of the tenancy (including a term relating to rent).

Note —Amended by the Regulatory Reform (Assured Periodic Tenancies) (Rent **3A–765** Increases) Order 2003 (S.I. 2003 No. 259). The amendment was designed to overcome the argument that a strict interpretation of former s.13(2)(c) rendered many rent increases made by registered social landlords invalid because, although increases may have occurred annually, in some years they may have purported to take effect a few days earlier than "the first anniversary of the date" when the last increase took effect. The effect of the amendment is to enable landlords to set a fixed day (*e.g.* the first Monday in April) on which rent increases are to take effect. The first time that the rent is increased after the Order came into force on February 10, 2003, the increase may take effect not less than 52 weeks after the start of the tenancy or, if the rent has already been increased, not less than 52 weeks after the date of the last increase. On the second and subsequent occasions, the increase may take effect not less than 52 weeks after the last increase, unless that would result in the increase taking effect on a date falling a week or more before the anniversary of the first increase after the date on which the Order comes into force. In such a case the increase may not take effect until

53 weeks after the date of the last increase. As a result of this change the Assured Tenancies and Agricultural (Forms) (Amendment) (England) Regulations 2003 (S.I. 2003 No. 260) prescribe new forms to be used by landlords when proposing new rents under s.13(2) from April 11, 2003. The Assured Tenancies and Agricultural Occupancies (Forms) (Amendment) (Wales) Regulations 2003 (S.I. 2003 No. 307) (W.46) prescribe the new forms to be used in Wales.

"assured tenancy"

3A–766   See s.1.

"landlord", and "tenant"

3A–767   See s.45.

"dwelling-house"

3A–768   See s.45.

"statutory periodic tenancy"

3A–769   See s.5(7).

"refers"

3A–770   The word "refers" in s.13(4)(b) bears the ordinary and obvious meaning "deliver to". A rent assessment committee has no jurisdiction unless the application is received before the beginning of the new period. An application cannot be referred until it has been received (*R. (Lester) v. London Rent Assessment Committee* [2003] EWCA Civ 319; [2003] 1 W.L.R. 1449).

"prescribed"

3A–771   See s.45 and the Assured Tenancies and Agricultural Occupancies (Forms) Regulations 1997 (S.I. 1997 No. 194). Note that a notice conforms with the regulations if it is "substantially to the same effect" as that prescribed (para. 2).

In *Tadema Holdings v. Ferguson* (2000) 32 H.L.R. 866, CA landlords, seeking to rely upon s.13, used an older version of the prescribed form since replaced by the Assured Tenancies and Agricultural Occupancies (Forms) Regulations 1997, Form 4. It gave the landlord's address as being "c/o the agent" and an annualised figure rather than a monthly figure for rent. It also stipulated the wrong date for the date on which each new period of tenancy started. Arrears accrued. The landlord served a s.8 notice and brought possession proceedings. The tenant defended claiming that the s.13 notice was invalid. The tenant appealed unsuccessfully against a possession order. There was no basis for confusion.

Increase of rent under assured periodic tenancies

3A–772   Sections 13 and 14 give Rent Assessment Committees power to determine the rent payable by an assured tenant where there is a periodic tenancy which does not contain a contractual provision allowing for the variation of rent or a statutory periodic tenancy. The rent to be determined is the rent at which "the dwelling house concerned might reasonably be expected to be let in the open market by a willing landlord under an assured tenancy" (see s.14(1)).

Service

3A–773   The word "service" in ss.8 and 13 is an ordinary English word connoting delivery of a document to a particular person. It carries no implication that the document has to be read, understood or indeed known by the recipient to have been delivered as long as delivery is to the correct address. Such meaning does not change according to the capacity of the intended recipient. See *Tadema Holdings v. Ferguson* (2000) 32 H.L.R. 866, CA.

Determination of rent by rent assessment committee

3A–774   **14.**—(1) Where, under subsection (4)(a) of section 13 above, a tenant refers to a rent assessment committee a notice under subsection (2) of that section, the committee shall determine the rent at which, subject to subsections (2) and (4) below, the committee consider that the dwelling-house concerned might reasonably be expected to be let in the open market by a willing landlord under an assured tenancy—

    (a) which is a periodic tenancy having the same periods as those of the tenancy to which the notice relates;

    (b) which begins at the beginning of the new period specified in the notice;

    (c) the terms of which (other than relating to the amount of the rent) are the same as those of the tenancy to which the notice relates; and

    (d) in respect of which the same notices, if any, have been given under any of Grounds 1 to 5 of Schedule 2 to this Act, as have been given (or have effect as if given) in relation to the tenancy to which the notice relates.

(2) In making a determination under this section there shall be disregarded—

    (a) any effect on the rent attributable to the granting of a tenancy to a sitting tenant;

    (b) any increase in the value of the dwelling-house attributable to a relevant improvement carried out by a person who at the time it was carried out was the tenant, if the improvement—

        (i) was carried out otherwise than in pursuance of an obligation to his immediate landlord, or

        (ii) was carried out pursuant to an obligation to his immediate landlord being an obligation which did not relate to the specific improvement concerned but arose by reference to consent given to the carrying out of that improvement; and

    (c) any reduction in the value of the dwelling-house attributable to a failure by the tenant to comply with any terms of the tenancy.

(3) For the purposes of subsection (2)(b) above, in relation to a notice which is referred by a tenant as mentioned in subsection (1) above, an improvement is a relevant improvement if either it was carried out during the tenancy to which the notice relates or the following conditions are satisfied, namely—

    (a) that it was carried out not more than twenty-one years before the date of service of the notice; and

    (b) that, at all times during the period beginning when the improvement was carried out and ending on the date of service of the notice, the dwelling-house has been let under an assured tenancy; and

    (c) that, on the coming to an end of an assured tenancy at any time during that period, the tenant (or, in the case of joint tenants, at least one of them) did not quit.

(3A) In making a determination under this section in any case where under Part I of the Local Government Finance Act 1992 the landlord or a superior landlord is liable to pay council tax in respect of a hereditament ("the relevant hereditament") of which the dwelling-house forms part, the rent assessment committee shall have regard to the amount of council tax which, as at the date on which the notice under section 13(2) above was served, was set by the billing authority—

    (a) for the financial year in which that notice was served, and

    (b) for the category of dwellings within which the relevant hereditament fell on that date,

but any discount or other reduction affecting the amount of council tax payable shall be disregarded.

(3B) In subsection (3A) above—

    (a) "hereditament" means a dwelling within the meaning of Part I of the Local Government Finance Act 1992,

    (b) "billing authority" has the same meaning as in that Part of that Act, and

    (c) "category of dwellings" has the same meaning as in section 30(1) and (2) of that Act.

(4) In this section "rent" does not include any service charge, within the meaning of section 18 of the Landlord and Tenant Act 1985, but, subject to that, includes any sums payable by the tenant to the landlord on account of the use of furniture, in respect of council tax, or for any of the matters referred to in subsection (1)(a) of that section, whether or not those sums are separate from the sums payable for the occupation of the dwelling-house concerned or are payable under separate agreements.

(5) Where any rates in respect of the dwelling-house concerned are borne by the landlord or a superior landlord, the rent assessment committee shall make their determination under this section as if the rates were not so borne.

(6) In any case where—

    (a) a rent assessment committee have before them at the same time the reference of a notice under section 6(2) above relating to a tenancy (in this subsection referred to as "the section 6 reference") and the reference of a notice under section 13(2) above relating to the same tenancy (in this subsection referred to as "the section 13 reference"), and

    (b) the date specified in the notice under section 6(2) above is not later than the first day of the new period specified in the notice under section 13(2) above, and

    (c) the committee propose to hear the two references together,

the committee shall make a determination in relation to the section 6 reference before making their determination in relation to the section 13 reference and, accordingly, in such a case the reference in subsection (1)(c) above to the terms of the tenancy to which the notice relates shall be construed as a reference to those terms as varied by virtue of the determination made in relation to the section 6 reference.

(7) Where a notice under section 13(2) above has been referred to a rent assessment committee, then, unless the landlord and the

tenant otherwise agree, the rent determined by the committee (subject, in a case where subsection (5) above applies, to the addition of the appropriate amount in respect of rates) shall be the rent under the tenancy with effect from the beginning of the new period specified in the notice or, if it appears to the rent assessment committee that that would cause undue hardship to the tenant, with effect from such later date (not being later than the date the rent is determined) as the committee may direct.

(8) Nothing in this section requires a rent assessment committee to continue with their determination of a rent for a dwelling-house if the landlord and tenant give notice in writing that they no longer require such a determination or if the tenancy has come to an end.

(9) This section shall apply in relation to an assured shorthold tenancy as if in subsection (1)the reference to an assured tenancy were a reference to an assured shorthold tenancy.

Note —Amended by the Local Government Finance (Housing) (Consequential Amendments) Order 1993 (S.I. 1993 No. 651); and the Housing Act 1996, Sched.8, para. 2(2).　　**3A–775**

"assured tenancy"
See s.1.　　**3A–776**

"landlord", and "tenant"
See s.45.　　**3A–777**

"dwelling-house"
See s.45.　　**3A–778**

Determination of rent by rent assessment committee

Section 14(1) requires RACs to assess the rent at which "the dwelling-house **3A–779** concerned might reasonably be expected to be let in the open market by a willing landlord under an assured tenancy" even if the rent assessed by the RAC is in excess of £25,000 and this means the tenancy ceases to be an assured tenancy. Parliament did not intend the References to Rating (Housing) Regulations 1990 (S.I. 1990 No. 434) (para. 29) (tenancies at a high rent cannot be assured tenancies) to introduce a rent cap (*R. v. London RAP, Ex p. Cadogan Estates* [1997] 3 W.L.R. 833, QBD).

In *N & D (London) Ltd v. Gadson* (1992) 24 H.L.R. 64; [1992] 02 E.G. 176, QBD, Auld J. held that Housing Act 1988, s.14(2)(c), when stating that rent assessment committees should disregard "any reduction in the value of the dwelling-house attributable to a failure by the tenant to comply with any terms of the tenancy" only referred to default by the current tenant. They were obliged to take into account the current condition of the premises, even if that had been brought about by the default of the tenant's father before his death.

When applying the disregard for tenant's improvements (s.14(2)) the committee should not apply a de-capitalised discount based upon the cost of the works. They should simply take as the value of the property its current value less the improvements carried out (*Rowe v. South West Rent Assessment Panel* [2001] EWHC 865 (Admin), October 23, 2001).

Note that ss.14A and 14B (inserted by the Local Government Finance (Housing) (Consequential Amendments) Order 1993 (S.I. 1993 No. 651), provided for interim increases prior to April 1, 1994 where the landlord was liable for council tax.

Where a property is in disrepair, there is no requirement that the RAC should perform a two stage process of first calculating the open market rental of the property in good condition, and then indicating by a figure or percentage discount what allowance has been made for the actual condition of the property (*Ghani v. London Rent Assessment Committee* [2002] EWHC 1167 (Admin); May 28, 2002).

Interim increase before 1st April 1994 of rent under assured periodic tenancies in certain cases where landlord liable for council tax

14A.—(1) In any case where—　　**3A–780**

(a) under Part I of the Local Government Finance Act 1992 the landlord of a dwelling-house let under an assured tenancy to which section 13 above applies or a superior landlord is liable to pay council tax in respect of a dwelling (within the meaning of that Part of that Act) which includes that dwelling-house,

(b) under the terms of the tenancy (or an agreement collateral to the tenancy) the tenant is liable to make payments to the landlord in respect of council tax,

(c) the case falls within subsection (2) or subsection (3) below, and

(d) no previous notice under this subsection has been served in relation to the dwelling-house,

the landlord may serve on the tenant a notice in the prescribed form proposing an increased rent to take account of the tenant's liability to make payments to the landlord in respect of council tax, such increased rent to take effect at the beginning of a new period of the tenancy specified in the notice being a period beginning not earlier than one month after the date on which the notice was served.

(2) The case falls within this subsection if—

(a) the rent under the tenancy has previously been increased by virtue of a notice under section 13(2) above or under a determination under section 14 above, and

(b) the first anniversary of the date on which the increased rent took effect has not yet occurred.

(3) The case falls within this subsection if a notice has been served under section 13(2) above before 1st April 1993 but no increased rent has taken effect before that date.

(4) No notice may be served under subsection (1) above after 31st March 1994.

(5) Where a notice is served under subsection (1) above, the new rent specified in the notice shall take effect as mentioned in the notice unless, before the beginning of the new period specified in the notice—

(a) the tenant by an application in the prescribed form refers the notice to a rent assessment committee, or

(b) the landlord and the tenant agree on a variation of the rent which is different from that proposed in the notice or agree that the rent should not be varied.

(6) Nothing in this section (or in section 14B below) affects the right of the landlord and the tenant under an assured tenancy to vary by agreement any term of the tenancy (including a term relating to rent).

3A–781   *Note*—Note that ss.14A and 14B (inserted by the Local Government Finance (Housing) (Consequential Amendments) Order 1993 (S.I. 1993 No. 651), provided for interim increases prior to April 1, 1994 where the landlord was liable for council tax.

Interim determination of rent by rent assessment committee

3A–782   **14B.**—(1) Where, under subsection (5)(a) of section 14A above, a tenant refers to a rent assessment committee a notice under subsection (1) of that section, the committee shall determine the amount by which, having regard to the provisions of section 14(3A) above, the existing rent might reasonably be increased to take account of the tenant's liability to make payments to the landlord in respect of council tax.

(2) Where a notice under section 14A(1) above has been referred to a rent assessment committee, then, unless the landlord and the tenant otherwise agree, the existing rent shall be increased by the amount determined by the committee with effect from the beginning of the new period specified in the notice or, if it appears to the committee that that would cause undue hardship to the tenant, with effect from such later date (not being later than the date the increase is determined) as the committee may direct.

(3) In any case where—

(a) a rent assessment committee have before them at the same time the reference of a notice under section 13(2) above relating to a tenancy (in this subsection referred to as "the section 13 reference") and the reference of a notice under section 14A(1) above relating to the same tenancy (in this subsection referred to as "the section 14A reference"); and

(b) the committee propose to hear the two references together,

the committee shall make a determination in relation to the section 13 reference before making their determination in relation to the section 14A reference, and if in such a case the date specified in the notice under section 13(2) above is later than the date specified in the notice under section 14A(1) above, the rent determined under the section 14A reference shall not take effect until the date specified in the notice under section 13(2).

(4) In this section "rent" has the same meaning as in section 14 above; and section 14(4) above applies to a determination under this section as it applies to a determination under that section.

Note —Added by the Local Government Finance (Housing) (Consequential Amendments) Order 1993 (S.I. 1993 No. 651), Sched.2.   **3A–783**

Limited prohibition on assignment etc. without consent

15.—(1) Subject to subsection (3) below, it shall be an implied term **3A–784** of every assured tenancy which is a periodic tenancy that, except with the consent of the landlord, the tenant shall not—

(a) assign the tenancy (in whole or in part); or

(b) sub-let or part with possession of the whole or any part of the dwelling-house let on the tenancy.

(2) Section 19 of the Landlord and Tenant Act 1927 (consents to assign not to be unreasonably withheld etc.) shall not apply to a term which is implied into an assured tenancy by subsection (1) above.

(3) In the case of a periodic tenancy which is not a statutory periodic tenancy or an assured periodic tenancy arising under Schedule 10 to the Local Government and Housing Act 1989, subsection (1) above does not apply if—

(a) there is a provision (whether contained in the tenancy or not) under which the tenant is prohibited (whether absolutely or conditionally) from assigning or sub-letting or parting with possession or is permitted (whether absolutely or conditionally) to assign, sub-let or part with possession; or

(b) a premium is required to be paid on the grant or renewal of the tenancy.

(4) In subsection (3)(b) above "premium" includes—

(a) any fine or other like sum;

(b) any other pecuniary consideration in addition to rent; and

(c) any sum paid by way of deposit, other than one which does not exceed one-sixth of the annual rent payable under the tenancy immediately after the grant or renewal in question.

3A–785   *Note* —Amended by the Local Government and Housing Act 1989, Sched.11, para. 102.

"assured tenancy"

3A–786   See s.1.

"landlord", and "tenant"

3A–787   See s.45.

"dwelling-house"

3A–788   See s.45

"statutory periodic tenancy"

3A–789   See s.5(7).

Access for repairs

3A–790   **16.** It shall be an implied term of every assured tenancy that the tenant shall afford to the landlord access to the dwelling-house let on the tenancy and all reasonable facilities for executing therein any repairs which the landlord is entitled to execute.

"assured tenancy"

3A–791   See s.1.

"landlord", "tenancy" and "tenant"

3A–792   See s.45.

"dwelling-house"

3A–793   See s.45.

MISCELLANEOUS

Succession to assured periodic tenancy by spouse

3A–794   **17.**—(1) In any case where—

(a) the sole tenant under an assured periodic tenancy dies, and

(b) immediately before the death, the tenant's spouse was

occupying the dwelling-house as his or her only or principal home, and

   (c) the tenant was not himself a successor, as defined in subsection (2) or subsection (3) below,

then, on the death, the tenancy vests by virtue of this section in the spouse (and, accordingly, does not devolve under the tenant's will or intestacy).

(2) For the purposes of this section, a tenant is a successor in relation to a tenancy if—

   (a) the tenancy became vested in him either by virtue of this section or under the will or intestacy of a previous tenant; or

   (b) at some time before the tenant's death the tenancy was a joint tenancy held by himself and one or more other persons and, prior to his death, he became the sole tenant by survivorship; or

   (c) he became entitled to the tenancy as mentioned in section 39(5) below.

(3) For the purposes of this section, a tenant is also a successor in relation to a tenancy (in this subsection referred to as "the new tenancy") which was granted to him (alone or jointly with others) if—

   (a) at some time before the grant of the new tenancy, he was, by virtue of subsection (2) above, a successor in relation to an earlier tenancy of the same or substantially the same dwelling-house as is let under the new tenancy; and

   (b) at all times since he became such a successor he has been a tenant (alone or jointly with others) of the dwelling-house which is let under the new tenancy or of a dwelling-house which is substantially the same as that dwelling-house.

(4) For the purposes of this section, a person who was living with the tenant as his or her wife or husband shall be treated as the tenant's spouse.

(5) If, on the death of the tenant, there is, by virtue of subsection (4) above, more than one person who fulfils the condition in subsection (1)(b) above, such one of them as may be decided by agreement or, in default of agreement, by the county court shall be treated as the tenant's spouse for the purposes of this section.

Note —This section has been amended by the Civil Partnership Act 2004, s.81 and Sched. 8.The amendment is not yet in force, but is printed at para. 3A–1525.　**3A–794.1**

"assured tenancy"
See s.1.　**3A–795**

"landlord", "tenancy" and "tenant"
See s.45.　**3A–796**

"dwelling-house"
See s.45.　**3A–797**

Succession to assured periodic tenancy by spouse
   This section provides for succession to an assured tenancy by a spouse who was occupying the dwelling-house as his or her only or principal home. "Spouse" includes "a　**3A–798**

person who was living with the tenant as his or her wife or husband" even if they were not married. Same sex couples may be treated in the same way as a husband and wife. The House of Lords has held that the words "as his or her wife or husband" in Rent Act 1977, Sched.1, para.2(2) must be read to mean "as if they were his or her wife or husband" in order to comply with the ECHR. Accordingly the survivor of a same sex couple who has been living in a loving and monogamous relationship with a tenant may be able to succeed to an assured tenancy (see *Ghaidan v. Mendoza* [2004] UKHL 30; [2004] 3 W.L.R. 113; *cf. Harrogate BC v. Simpson* (1985) 17 H.L.R. 205, CA and *Fitzpatrick v. Sterling Housing Association* [2001] 1 A.C. 27; [1999] 3 W.L.R. 1113; [1999] 4 All E.R. 705, HL). In *Southern Housing Group Ltd v. Nutting* [2004] EWHC 2982 (Ch); [2005] HLR 25 Evans-Lombe J. held that without a lifetime commitment at least at some point in a same sex relationship, there is no sufficient similarity to marriage. Such a relationship must be "openly and unequivocally displayed to the outside world".

Note that Ground 7 does not apply to a successor under this section since the tenancy has not "devolved under the will or intestacy".

Provisions as to reversions on assured tenancies

3A–799   **18.**—(1) If at any time—

   (a) a dwelling-house is for the time being lawfully let on an assured tenancy, and

   (b) the landlord under the assured tenancy is himself a tenant under a superior tenancy, and

   (c) the superior tenancy comes to an end,

then, subject to subsection (2) below, the assured tenancy shall continue in existence as a tenancy held of the person whose interest would, apart from the continuance of the assured tenancy, entitle him to actual possession of the dwelling-house at that time.

   (2) Subsection (1) above does not apply to an assured tenancy if the interest which, by virtue of that subsection, would become that of the landlord, is such that, by virtue of Schedule 1 to this Act, the tenancy could not be an assured tenancy.

   (3) Where, by virtue of any provision of this Part of this Act, an assured tenancy which is a periodic tenancy (including a statutory periodic tenancy) continues beyond the beginning of a reversionary tenancy which was granted (whether before, on or after the commencement of this Act) so as to begin on or after—

   (a) the date on which the previous contractual assured tenancy came to an end, or

   (b) a date on which, apart from any provision of this Part, the periodic tenancy could have been brought to an end by the landlord by notice to quit,

the reversionary tenancy shall have effect as if it had been granted subject to the periodic tenancy.

   (4) The reference in subsection (3) above to the previous contractual assured tenancy applies only where the periodic tenancy referred to in that subsection is a statutory periodic tenancy and is a reference to the fixed-term tenancy which immediately preceded the statutory periodic tenancy.

"assured tenancy"

3A–800   See s.1.

"landlord", and "tenant"

3A–801   See s.45.

"dwelling-house"
See s.45.

3A–802

"statutory periodic tenancy"
See s.5(7).

3A–803

Restriction on levy of distress for rent

19.—(1) Subject to subsection (2) below, no distress for the rent of 3A–804 any dwelling-house let on an assured tenancy shall be levied except with the leave of the county court; and, with respect to any application for such leave, the court shall have the same powers with respect to adjournment, stay, suspension, postponement and otherwise as are conferred by section 9 above in relation to proceedings for possession of such a dwelling-house.

(2) Nothing in subsection (1) above applies to distress levied under section 102 of the County Courts Act 1984.

"assured tenancy"
See s.1.

3A–805

"dwelling-house"
See s.45.

3A–806

Chapter II

Assured Shorthold Tenancies

Assured shorthold tenancies: post-Housing Act 1996 tenancies

19A. An assured tenancy which—

3A–807

    (a) is entered into on or after the day on which section 96 of the Housing Act 1996 comes into force (otherwise than pursuant to a contract made before that day), or

    (b) comes into being by virtue of section 5 above on the coming to an end of an assured tenancy within paragraph (a) above,

is an assured shorthold tenancy unless it falls within any paragraph in Schedule 2A to this Act.

Note —Added by the Housing Act 1996, s.96(1).

3A–808

"assured tenancy"
See s.1.

3A–809

Assured shorthold tenancies: post-Housing Act 1996 tenancies

Housing Act 1996, s.96 and Sched.7 take effect as a new Housing Act 1988, s.19A 3A–810 and Sched.2A. They provide that all new tenancies entered into after this provision came into force on February 28, 1997 which would otherwise have been assured tenancies are automatically *assured shorthold* tenancies lacking long term security of tenure. This applies whether the tenancy is granted orally or by a written agreement. In other words, the requirement of a s.20 notice (see below) informing the tenant that the tenancy will be an assured shorthold tenancy has been abolished. There are though several exceptions. The new rule does not apply where:

    • the new tenancy is made pursuant to a contract made before the new provisions come into force (Housing Act 1996, s.96); or

    • the landlord serves a notice before entering into the tenancy stating that the tenancy is not to be an assured shorthold tenancy (Housing Act 1996, Sched.7, para. 1); or

- the landlord serves a notice after the grant of the tenancy stating that the tenancy is no longer an assured shorthold tenancy (Housing Act 1996, Sched.7, para. 2); or

- there is a provision in the tenancy agreement stating that the tenancy is not an assured shorthold tenancy (Housing Act 1996, Sched.7, para. 3); or

- the tenancy is an assured tenancy by succession—*i.e.* a spouse or member of the family of a statutory tenant under the Rent Act 1977 or the Rent (Agriculture) Act 1976 became an assured tenant after the death of the original tenant (Rent Act 1977, s.2(1)(b) and Sched.1; Housing Act 1988, s.39; and Housing Act 1996, Sched.7, para. 4); or

- the tenancy was formerly a secure tenancy and became an assured tenancy, *e.g.* on transfer of housing stock from a local housing authority to a housing association or other landlord (Housing Act 1985, Pt IV; Housing Act 1988, s.38; and Housing Act 1996, Sched.7, para. 5); or

- an assured tenancy came into existence on the ending of a long residential tenancy (Landlord and Tenant Act 1954, Pt I; Local Government and Housing Act 1989, s.186 and Sched.10; and Housing Act 1996, Sched.7, para. 6); or

- the tenancy is granted to someone who immediately before its grant was an assured tenant (as opposed to an assured *shorthold* tenant) and is granted by someone who was the landlord under the old tenancy (Housing Act 1996, Sched.7, para. 7); or

- in some cases the tenancy or licence is an assured agricultural occupancy (Rent (Agriculture) Act 1976; Housing Act 1988, s.24 and Sched.3; and Housing Act 1996, Sched.7, para. 9).

Assured shorthold tenancies: pre-Housing Act 1996 tenancies

3A–811   **20.**—(1) Subject to subsection (3) below, an assured tenancy which is not one to which section 19A above applies is an assured shorthold tenancy if—

(a) it is a fixed term tenancy granted for a term certain of not less than six months,

(b) there is no power for the landlord to determine the tenancy at any time earlier than six months from the beginning of the tenancy, and

(c) a notice in respect of it is served as mentioned in subsection (2) below.

(2) The notice referred to in subsection (1)(c) above is one which—

(a) is in such form as may be prescribed;

(b) is served before the assured tenancy is entered into;

(c) is served by the person who is to be the landlord under the assured tenancy on the person who is to be the tenant under that tenancy; and

(d) states that the assured tenancy to which it relates is to be a shorthold tenancy.

(3) Notwithstanding anything in subsection (1) above, where—

(a) immediately before a tenancy (in this subsection referred to as "the new tenancy") is granted, the person to whom it is granted or, as the case may be, at least one of the persons to whom it is granted was a tenant under an assured tenancy which was not a shorthold tenancy, and

854

(b) the new tenancy is granted by the person who, immediately before the beginning of the tenancy, was the landlord under the assured tenancy referred to in paragraph (a) above,

the new tenancy cannot be an assured shorthold tenancy.

(4) Subject to subsection (5) below, if, on the coming to an end of an assured shorthold tenancy (including a tenancy which was an assured shorthold but ceased to be assured before it came to an end), a new tenancy of the same or substantially the same premises comes into being under which the landlord and the tenant are the same as at the coming to an end of the earlier tenancy, then, if and so long as the new tenancy is an assured tenancy, it shall be an assured shorthold tenancy, whether or not it fulfils the conditions in paragraphs (a) to (c) of subsection (1) above.

(5) Subsection (4) above does not apply if, before the new tenancy is entered into (or, in the case of a statutory periodic tenancy, takes effect in possession), the landlord serves notice on the tenant that the new tenancy is not to be a shorthold tenancy.

(5A) Subsections (3) and (4) above do not apply where the new tenancy is one to which section 19A above applies.

(6) In the case of joint landlords—

(a) the reference in subsection (2)(c) above to the person who is to be the landlord is a reference to at least one of the persons who are to be joint landlords; and

(b) the reference in subsection (5) above to the landlord is a reference to at least one of the joint landlords.

Note —Amended by the Housing Act 1996, Scheds 8 and 19. **3A–812**

"assured tenancy"

See s.1. **3A–813**

"landlord", and "tenant"

See s.45. **3A–814**

"statutory periodic tenancy"

See s.5(7). **3A–815**

"prescribed"

See s.45 and the Assured Tenancies and Agricultural Occupancies (Forms) Regula- **3A–816**
tions 1988 (S.I. 1988 No. 2203). Note that a notice conforms with the regulations if it
is "substantially to the same effect" as that prescribed (para. 2).

Assured shorthold tenancies: pre-Housing Act 1996 tenancies

This section now only applies to tenancies granted prior to February 28, 1997 (but **3A–817**
note the exceptions listed in s.19A). For tenancies granted after that date, see s.19A,
above.

Section 20 provides that for a tenancy granted before February 28, 1997 to be an
assured shorthold tenancy:

(a) there had to be a tenancy granted for a fixed term of not less than six months
(A tenancy granted for "a term certain of one year... and... thereafter from
month to month" is a tenancy granted for a term certain within the meaning
of s.20(1)(a) which was capable of being an assured shorthold tenancy. (*Goodman v. Evely* [2001] EWCA Civ 104; [2002] H.L.R. 53; [2001] L.& T.R. 436,
CA)); and

(b) there could be no power enabling the landlord to determine the tenancy within the first six months;

Section 45(4) provides that a power of re-entry or forfeiture for breach of a condition does *not* count as a provision enabling the landlord to determine the tenancy for this purpose; and

(c) a notice in the prescribed form had to be served on the prospective tenant before the tenancy was entered into, stating that the tenancy was to be an assured shorthold tenancy.

This requirement was *mandatory*. There is no provision which allows the court to dispense with the service of a notice before the initial grant of a pre-February 28, 1997 assured shorthold tenancy.

Service earlier on the day when the tenancy commenced was sufficient (*Bedding v. Mc-Carthy* [1994] 41 E.G. 151, CA). This is a pure question of fact. It was good practice, although not a statutory requirement, for landlords to ensure that tenants endorsed a note confirming receipt on a copy of the notice. A s.20 notice may be served upon a prospective tenant's agent (*Yenula Properties Ltd v. Naidu* [2002] EWCA Civ 719; [2003] H.L.R. 18; [2002] 42 E.G.162).

Section 20 notices have been held to be invalid where the landlord inserted an incorrect date (*Panayi v. Roberts* (1993) 25 H.L.R. 421, CA), where the dates in the notice and the tenancy were "in complete conflict" (*Clickex Ltd v. McCann* (2000) 32 HLR 324; [1999] 30 EG 96, CA; where the four bullet points giving instructions and advice to the tenant were omitted (*Manel v. Memon* [2000] 33 E.G. 74, CA), where no date for termination was inserted (*Mistry v. Dave*, June 1995, Legal Action 20(cc)), where the landlord's name, address and telephone number were missing (*Stephens v. Lamb*, March 1996, Legal Action 12(cc)), and where the landlord's name was spelt incorrectly and the notice was not signed (*Symons v. Warren* [1995] C.L.W. 33/95(cc)).

However all these cases now have to be reconsidered in the light of cases such as *Ravenseft Proeprties Ltd v. Hall* and *B. Osborn & Co Ltd v. Dior* [2003] H.L.R. 45 where the Court of Appeal held that there is no statutory or common law doctrine of "obvious mistake" or any requirement to apply a two-stage test in which the court has first to consider whether the error in the notice is obvious or evident before proceeding to consider whether the notice read in context is sufficiently clear to leave a reasonable recipient in no reasonable doubt as to the terms of the notice. There is only one statutory question, which is whether, notwithstanding any errors or omissions, the notice is "substantially to the same effect" as a correct notice in accomplishing the purpose of telling the proposed tenant of the special nature of an assured shorthold tenancy (*Mannai Investment Co Ltd v. Eagle Star Life Assurance Co Ltd* [1997] A.C. 749, HL). This is a matter of fact and degree in each case. The resolution of that question is not a decision on a point of law that is binding on later courts (*White v. Chubb; Kasseer v. Freeman* [2001] EWCA Civ 2034; *Ravenseft Properties Ltd v. Hall* [2001] EWCA Civ 2034; [2002] H.L.R. 33; [2002] 11 E.G. 156.

See too *York and Ross v. Casey* (1999) 31 H.L.R. 209; [1998] 30 E.G. 110, CA where, following *Mannai Investment Co Ltd v. Eagle Star Life Assurance Co Ltd* [1997] A.C. 749; [1997] 2 W.L.R. 945; [1997] 3 All E.R. 352, HL, the Court of Appeal held that a notice is valid even if it contains a minor misdescription if, in its contextual setting, it informs a reasonably minded recipient how the notice is to operate. There is no material difference between contractual and statutory notices and accordingly the *Mannai* test is equally applicable to statutory notices. In this case where the section 20 notice gave a commencement date of September 28, 1996 but a date for termination of the tenancy of September 6, 1996, there was no doubt that the termination date was wrong. The real question was whether the correct termination date was sufficiently clear. In looking at a letter which accompanied the notice, there was no doubt that the termination date was understood to be March 27, 1997. See too *Garston v. Scottish Widows* [1998] 1 W.L.R. 1583, CA.

See too *B. Osborn & Co Ltd v. Dior* [2003] H.L.R. 45 where it was held that omission of landlords' particulars from a s.20 notice is not fatal. The question is whether the form is substantially to the same effect as the prescribed form.

Tenancy of same premises

3A–818   Note though that if a new tenancy of substantially the same premises was granted and at least one of the tenants was previously an assured shorthold tenant of the same landlord, the new tenancy automatically became an assured shorthold tenancy even if conditions (a) to (c) were not complied with (s.20(4)).

Post-Housing Act 1996 tenancies: duty of landlord to provide statement as to terms of tenancy

20A.—(1) Subject to subsection (3) below, a tenant under an as- **3A–819** sured shorthold tenancy to which section 19A above applies may, by notice in writing, require the landlord under that tenancy to provide him with a written statement of any term of the tenancy which—

    (a) falls within subsection (2) below, and

    (b) is not evidenced in writing.

(2) The following terms of a tenancy fall within this subsection, namely—

    (a) the date on which the tenancy began or, if it is a statutory periodic tenancy or a tenancy to which section 39(7) below applies, the date on which the tenancy came into being,

    (b) the rent payable under the tenancy and the dates on which that rent is payable,

    (c) any term providing for a review of the rent payable under the tenancy, and

    (d) in the case of a fixed term tenancy, the length of the fixed term.

(3) No notice may be given under subsection (1) above in relation to a term of the tenancy if—

    (a) the landlord under the tenancy has provided a statement of that term in response to an earlier notice under that subsection given by the tenant under the tenancy, and

    (b) the term has not been varied since the provision of the statement referred to in paragraph (a) above.

(4) A landlord who fails, without reasonable excuse, to comply with a notice under subsection (1) above within the period of 28 days beginning with the date on which he received the notice is liable on summary conviction to a fine not exceeding level 4 on the standard scale.

(5) A statement provided for the purposes of subsection (1) above shall not be regarded as conclusive evidence of what was agreed by the parties to the tenancy in question.

(6) Where—

    (a) a term of a statutory periodic tenancy is one which has effect by virtue of section 5(3)(e) above, or

    (b) a term of a tenancy to which subsection (7) of section 39 below applies is one which has effect by virtue of subsection (6)(e) of that section,

subsection (1) above shall have effect in relation to it as if paragraph (b) related to the term of the tenancy from which it derives.

(7) In subsections (1) and (3) above—

    (a) references to the tenant under the tenancy shall, in the case of joint tenants, be taken to be references to any of the tenants, and

(b) references to the landlord under the tenancy shall, in the case of joint landlords, be taken to be references to any of the landlords.

3A–820   *Note* —Added by the Housing Act 1996, s.97.

"assured shorthold tenancy"

3A–821   See ss.19A and 20.

"landlord", and "tenant"

3A–822   See s.45.

Demoted assured shorthold tenancies

3A–823   **20B.**—(1) An assured tenancy is an assured shorthold tenancy to which this section applies (a demoted assured shorthold tenancy) if—

(a) the tenancy is created by virtue of an order of the court under section 82A of the Housing Act 1985 or section 6A of this Act (a demotion order), and

(b) the landlord is a registered social landlord.

(2) At the end of the period of one year starting with the day when the demotion order takes effect a demoted assured shorthold tenancy ceases to be an assured shorthold tenancy unless subsection (3) applies.

(3) This subsection applies if before the end of the period mentioned in subsection (2) the landlord gives notice of proceedings for possession of the dwelling house.

(4) If subsection (3) applies the tenancy continues to be a demoted assured shorthold tenancy until the end of the period mentioned in subsection (2) or (if later) until one of the following occurs—

(a) the notice of proceedings for possession is withdrawn;

(b) the proceedings are determined in favour of the tenant;

(c) the period of six months beginning with the date on which the notice is given ends and no proceedings for possession have been brought.

(5) Registered social landlord has the same meaning as in Part 1 of the Housing Act 1996.

Editorial note

3A–824   This section was inserted by Anti-social Behaviour Act 2003, s.15(1). It was brought into force in England on June 30, 2004 by the Anti-social Behaviour Act 2003 (Commencement No.3 and Savings) Order 2004 (S.I. 2004 No. 1502) (C.61). It was brought into force in Wales on 30 April 2005 by the Anti-social Behaviour Act 2003 (Commencement No.4) (Wales) Order 2005 (S.I. 2005 No. 1225) (W.83) (C.55).

Section 20B sets out the legal basis for the form of demoted tenancy that can be used by registered social landlords. A demoted assured shorthold tenancy is an assured shorthold tenancy during the demoted period but there is provision for the demoted assured shorthold tenancy automatically to turn into an assured tenancy after one year unless the landlord has issued a notice of proceedings for possession during that year. If a notice is issued, the tenancy remains a demoted assured shorthold tenancy beyond the first year until the notice is withdrawn or six months have passed and no proceedings have been issued; or, if proceedings have been issued, until they are determined in favour of the tenant. A demoted assured shorthold tenancy can be ended at any time during the demotion period. Unlike non-demoted assured shorthold tenancies a possession order granted on the basis that the landlord has given the required notice under s.21(4) of the Housing Act 1988 can take effect within the first six months of the tenancy.

Assured tenancy

See s.1.

3A–825

Assured shorthold tenancy

See ss.19A and 20.

3A–826

Registered social landlord

See Housing Act 1996 Part I, ss.1 to 3.

3A–827

Recovery of possession on expiry or termination of assured shorthold tenancy

21.—(1) Without prejudice to any right of the landlord under an assured shorthold tenancy to recover possession of the dwelling-house let on the tenancy in accordance with Chapter I above, on or after the coming to an end of an assured shorthold tenancy which was a fixed term tenancy, a court shall make an order for possession of the dwelling-house if it is satisfied— 3A–828

> (a) that the assured shorthold tenancy has come to an end and no further assured tenancy (whether shorthold or not) is for the time being in existence, other than an assured shorthold periodic tenancy (whether statutory or not); and
>
> (b) the landlord or, in the case of joint landlords, at least one of them has given to the tenant not less than two months' notice in writing stating that he requires possession of the dwelling-house.

(2) A notice under paragraph (b) of subsection (1) above may be given before or on the day on which the tenancy comes to an end; and that subsection shall have effect notwithstanding that on the coming to an end of the fixed term tenancy a statutory periodic tenancy arises.

(3) Where a court makes an order for possession of a dwelling-house by virtue of subsection (1) above, any statutory periodic tenancy which has arisen on the coming to an end of the assured shorthold tenancy shall end (without further notice and regardless of the period) on the day on which the order takes effect.

(4) Without prejudice to any such right as is referred to in subsection (1) above, a court shall make an order for possession of a dwelling-house let on an assured shorthold tenancy which is a periodic tenancy if the court is satisfied—

> (a) that the landlord or, in the case of joint landlords, at least one of them has given to the tenant a notice in writing stating that, after a date specified in the notice, being the last day of a period of the tenancy and not earlier than two months after the date the notice was given, possession of the dwelling-house is required by virtue of this section; and
>
> (b) that the date specified in the notice under paragraph (a) above is not earlier than the earliest day on which, apart from section 5(1) above, the tenancy could be brought to an end by a notice to quit given by the landlord on the same date as the notice under paragraph (a) above.

(5) Where an order for possession under subsection (1) or (4) above is made in relation to a dwelling-house let on a tenancy to which section 19A above applies, the order may not be made so as to take effect earlier than—

    (a) in the case of a tenancy which is not a replacement tenancy, six months after the beginning of the tenancy, and

    (b) in the case of a replacement tenancy, six months after the beginning of the original tenancy.

(5A) Subsection (5) above does not apply to an assured shorthold tenancy to which section 20B (demoted assured shorthold tenancies) applies.

(6) In subsection (5)(b) above, the reference to the original tenancy is—

    (a) where the replacement tenancy came into being on the coming to an end of a tenancy which was not a replacement tenancy, to the immediately preceding tenancy, and

    (b) where there have been successive replacement tenancies, to the tenancy immediately preceding the first in the succession of replacement tenancies.

(7) For the purposes of this section, a replacement tenancy is a tenancy—

    (a) which comes into being on the coming to an end of an assured short-hold tenancy, and

    (b) under which, on its coming into being—

        (i) the landlord and tenant are the same as under the earlier tenancy as at its coming to an end, and

        (ii) the premises let are the same or substantially the same as those let under the earlier tenancy as at that time.

3A–829   *Note* —Amended by the Local Government and Housing Act 1989, Sched.11, and the Housing Act 1996, ss.98 and 99.

    Section 21 has been amended by Anti-social Behaviour Act 2003, s.15(2). The amendment was brought into force in England on June 30, 2004 by the Anti-social Behaviour Act 2003 (Commencement No. 3 and Savings) Order 2004 (S.I. 2004 No. 1502) (C.61). It was brought into force in Wales on 30 April 2005 by the Anti-social Behaviour Act 2003 (Commencement No.4) (Wales) Order 2005 (S.I. 2005 No. 1225) (W.83) (C.55).

"assured shorthold tenancy"
3A–830   See ss.19A and 20.

"landlord", and "tenant"
3A–831   See s.45.

"statutory periodic tenancy"
3A–832   See s.5(7).

Tenancy deposits and s.21 notices
3A–832.1   Housing Act 2004 s.215(1) provides that if a tenancy deposit (see Housing Act s.212(8)) has been paid in connection with an assured shorthold tenancy, no s.21 notice may be given in relation to the tenancy at any time when (a) the deposit is not being held in accordance with an authorised scheme (see Housing Act 2004 s.213(4)), or

(b) the initial requirements of such a scheme (see s.213(4)) have not been complied with in relation to the deposit. These provisions are not yet in force. They will be brought into force by commencement order.

Recovery of possession on expiry or termination of assured shorthold tenancy

Assured shorthold tenancies lack long-term security of tenure. If the initial tenancy **3A–833** was for a fixed term and the tenant continues to occupy premises as his or her only or principal home, a statutory periodic tenancy arises, but all that a landlord need do to recover possession is to:

(a) prove that any fixed term tenancy has come to an end and that no new fixed term tenancy has been granted; and

(b) give at least two months notice to the tenant that the landlord requires possession. Such notice may be given before the fixed term expires.

There are no requirements as to the form of the notice, although it should be in writing (s.21(1)(b) and s.21(4)(a), as amended by the Housing Act 1996, s.98).

Although s.21(4)(a) refers to "a date specified in the notice", the Court of Appeal has held that no date need be specified in a s.21 notice provided that "the tenant knows or can easily ascertain the date referred to...The word 'specified' ...means no more than 'made clear'". (*Lower Street Properties v. Jones* (1996) 28 H.L.R. 877; [1996] 2 E.G.L.R. 67). Accordingly a notice which does not contain a date, but which provides a formula for calculating a date which complies with s.21(4)(a) (*e.g.* "at the end of the period of your tenancy which will end next after the expiration of two months from the service upon you of this notice") is valid.

If landlords comply with these requirements, they are automatically entitled to possession. The court has no power to suspend possession orders, apart from the Housing Act 1980, s.89(1) (see above). It has been held in the county court that a s.21 notice served before the commencement of the tenancy is not valid because at that stage there was no relationship of landlord and tenant, as required by s.21(1)(b)—see *Turpitt v. Elizabeth*, August 1998, Legal Action 21, Edmonton County Court—although the better view is that such a notice is valid.

Uncertainty has been caused by the dichotomy between the Housing Act 1988, s.21(1)(b) and s.21(4)(a). Section 21(1)(b) merely provides that the landlord must give "the tenant not less than two months' notice stating that he requires possession of the dwelling-house". However, s.21(4)(a) provides that the date specified in a notice where there is "a periodic tenancy" shall be "the last day of a period of the tenancy". Although it has been argued that s.21(1) and s.21(4) are simply alternatives that may be used as landlords choose, the better view is that there is no need for the two months notice to expire on "the last day of a period of the tenancy" if the notice is served during a fixed term assured shorthold but this requirement has to be satisfied if the notice is served after the expiry of a fixed term (*i.e.* during a statutory periodic assured shorthold tenancy). The use of the words "without prejudice ... to ... subsection (1)" in s.21(4) clearly shows that the two subsections are alternatives and that s.21(4) is not an additional requirement for all s.21(1) notices. The words in s.21(2) ("A notice under paragraph (b) of subsection (1) above may be given before or on the day on which the tenancy comes to an end") indicate that a s.21(1) notice is one which can be served during a fixed term. In contrast, the use of the words "let on an assured shorthold tenancy which is a periodic tenancy" in s.21(4) indicate that the s.21(4)(b) requirement applies whenever a notice is served during a periodic tenancy—and that includes a statutory periodic tenancy (*cf.* s.13(1)(a) and (b) and s.15(3)). This approach is also supported by the Housing Act 1996, s.98 which refers to s.21(1) notices as being given "under a fixed term" and s.21(4) as the "corresponding provision for periodic tenancies".

In *Gracechurch SA v. Tribhovan and Abdul* (2001) 33 H.L.R. 263, CA, Simon Brown L.J., while hearing an appeal on another issue, described the dismissal of possession proceedings, because a notice requiring possession from a periodic tenant did not expire on the last day of a period of the tenancy, as "clearly correct". This was confirmed by the Court of Appeal in *McDonald v. Fernandez* [2003] EWCA Civ 1219; [2004] 1 W.L.R. 1027, when rejecting a landlord's contention that s.21 should be construed in the same way as the common law rules relating to notices to quit. It might be possible to give a notice to quit that expired on either the first day or the last day of a period of the tenancy, but that was not because there were two last days. It was because the last day ended at midnight and the first day of the new period would begin thereafter. A s.21 notice is not a notice to quit. The niceties of contractual no-

HOUSING

tices to quit should not be imported into the plain words of the statute. Section 21(4)(a) requires the notice to specify the last date of the period. It is not a situation where the legislation permits the form to be substantially to the same effect. The subsection is clear and precise. Accordingly, a notice served during a periodic assured shorthold tenancy which does not expire "on the last day of a period of the tenancy" is unlikely to be valid.

In order to be valid, a notice served upon a periodic assured shorthold tenant—

(1) must specify a date after which possession is required—either by inserting a particular date or by using a formula, as in *Lower Street Properties v. Jones* (above);

(2) give a date which is the last day of a period of the tenancy, and not any other day. The fact that the notice is too long does not save it from being defective. (*McDonald v. Fernandez* [2003] EWCA Civ 1219 (above));

(3) make it clear that possession is required after that date, not on it. This can be done either by stating "I require possession after [the date]" or by saying "This notice will expire on [the date]. Proceedings cannot be commenced until after that date". It cannot be done by stating "I require possession on [the date]" because "on [the date]" and "after [the date]" are not the same thing.

The Housing Act 1996, s.99, by inserting subsections (5) to (7), provides that possession orders made against tenants occupying under the Housing Act 1988, s.19A assured shorthold tenancies cannot take effect earlier than six months after the beginning of the tenancy. There is, however, no reason why a s.21(4) notice should not be served and proceedings commenced within six months of the grant of the tenancy.

A landlord relying upon s.21 may in most circumstances use the Accelerated Possession Procedure, using Form **N5A**, which if not defended, may result in a possession order without a hearing—(see CPR, rr.55.11 to 55.19). In *Manel v. Memon* [2000] 33 E.G. 74, CA, Holman J. said "[The accelerated possession procedure] is a robust machinery. It depends upon district judges rigorously considering the documents which have been filed. Some replies may be little more than a plea, however genuine, for mercy. But if, on the face of the reply, a matter has been raised which, if true, might arguably raise a defence; or if the documents filed by the claimant might arguably disclose a defect in his claim, then the district judge must necessarily be "not satisfied" within the meaning of CCR O.49, r.6A(16) and a hearing on notice must be fixed."

The same applies to cases brought under CPR, rr.55.11 to 55.19.

Section 21 and ECHR Article 8

3A–834   Notwithstanding its mandatory terms, the right to possession contained in s.21(4) does not conflict with the tenant's right to family life under ECHR Article 8. The section is clearly necessary in a democratic society insofar as there has to be a procedure for recovering possession of property at the end of a tenancy. The court would defer to Parliament as to whether the restricted power of the court under that section was legitimate and proportionate (*Donoghue v. Poplar HARCA* [2001] 3 W.L.R. 183, CA); also reported as *Poplar HARCA v. Donoghue* [2002] QB 48; [2001] 4 All E.R. 606. (Note that in *Harrow LBC v. Qazi* [2003] UKHL 43; [2003] 3 W.L.R. 792, Lord Scott stated that this case was correctly decided, but for the wrong reason).

Reference of excessive rents to rent assessment committee

3A–835   **22.**—(1) Subject to section 23 and subsection (2) below, the tenant under an assured shorthold tenancy may make an application in the prescribed form to a rent assessment committee for a determination of the rent which, in the committee's opinion, the landlord might reasonably be expected to obtain under the assured shorthold tenancy.

(2) No application may be made under this section if—

(a) the rent payable under the tenancy is a rent previously determined under this section;

(aa) the tenancy is one to which section 19A above applies and more than six months have elapsed since the beginning of the tenancy or, in the case of a replacement tenancy, since the beginning of the original tenancy; or

(b) the tenancy is an assured shorthold tenancy falling within subsection (4) of section 20 above (and, accordingly, is one in respect of which notice need not have been served as mentioned in subsection (2) of that section).

(3) Where an application is made to a rent assessment committee under subsection (1) above with respect to the rent under an assured shorthold tenancy, the committee shall not make such a determination as is referred to in that subsection unless they consider—

(a) that there is a sufficient number of similar dwelling-houses in the locality let on assured tenancies (whether shorthold or not); and

(b) that the rent payable under the assured shorthold tenancy in question is significantly higher than the rent which the landlord might reasonably be expected to be able to obtain under the tenancy, having regard to the level of rents payable under the tenancies referred to in paragraph (a) above.

(4) Where, on an application under this section, a rent assessment committee make a determination of a rent for an assured shorthold tenancy—

(a) the determination shall have effect from such date as the committee may direct, not being earlier than the date of the application;

(b) if, at any time on or after the determination takes effect, the rent which, apart from this paragraph, would be payable under the tenancy exceeds the rent so determined, the excess shall be irrecoverable from the tenant; and

(c) no notice may be served under section 13(2) above with respect to a tenancy of the dwelling-house in question until after the first anniversary of the date on which the determination takes effect.

(5) Subsections (4), (5) and (8) of section 14 above apply in relation to a determination of rent under this section as they apply in relation to a determination under that section and, accordingly, where subsection (5) of that section applies, any reference in subsection (4)(b) above to rent is a reference to rent exclusive of the amount attributable to rates.

(5A) Where—

(a) an assured tenancy ceases to be an assured shorthold tenancy by virtue of falling within paragraph 2 of Schedule 2A to this Act, and

(b) at the time when it so ceases to be an assured shorthold tenancy there is pending before a rent assessment committee an application in relation to it under this section, the fact that it so ceases to be an assured shorthold tenancy shall, in relation to that application, be disregarded for the purposes of this section.

(6) In subsection (2)(aa) above, the references to the original tenancy and to a replacement tenancy shall be construed in accordance with subsections (6) and (7) respectively of section 21 above.

3A–836 *Note* —Amended by the Housing Act 1996, s.10, Sched.8, para. 2, Sched.19, Pt IV.

"assured shorthold tenancy"
3A–837 See ss.19A and 20.

"landlord", and "tenant"
3A–838 See s.45.

"statutory periodic tenancy"
3A–839 See s.5(7).

"dwelling-house"
3A–840 See s.45.

Reference of excessive rents to rent assessment committee
3A–841 Assured shorthold tenants may apply to the rent assessment committee if they consider that the rent is excessive. This right cannot be exercised if more than six months have elapsed from the beginning of a s.19A tenancy.

Termination of rent assessment committee's functions

3A–842 **23.**—(1) If the Secretary of State by order made by statutory instrument so provides, section 22 above shall not apply in such cases or to tenancies of dwelling-houses in such areas or in such other circumstances as may be specified in the order.

(2) An order under this section may contain such transitional, incidental and supplementary provisions as appear to the Secretary of State to be desirable.

(3) No order shall be made under this section unless a draft of the order has been laid before, and approved by a resolution of, each House of Parliament.

"dwelling-house"
3A–843 See s.45.

"tenancy"
3A–844 See s.45.

* * * *

CHAPTER IV

PROTECTION FROM EVICTION

Damages for unlawful eviction

3A–845 **27.**—(1) This section applies if, at any time after 9th June 1988, a landlord (in this section referred to as "the landlord in default") or any person acting on behalf of the landlord in default unlawfully deprives the residential occupier of any premises of his occupation of the whole or part of the premises.

(2) This section also applies if, at any time after 9th June 1988, a landlord (in this section referred to as "the landlord in default") or any person acting on behalf of the landlord in default—

    (a) attempts unlawfully to deprive the residential occupier of any premises of his occupation of the whole or part of the premises, or

    (b) knowing or having reasonable cause to believe that the conduct is likely to cause the residential occupier of any premises—

        (i) to give up his occupation of the premises or any part thereof, or

        (ii) to refrain from exercising any right or pursuing any remedy in respect of the premises or any part thereof,

does acts likely to interfere with the peace or comfort of the residential occupier or members of his household, or persistently withdraws or withholds services reasonably required for the occupation of the premises as a residence,

and, as a result, the residential occupier gives up his occupation of the premises as a residence.

(3) Subject to the following provisions of this section, where this section applies, the landlord in default shall, by virtue of this section, be liable to pay to the former residential occupier, in respect of his loss of the right to occupy the premises in question as his residence, damages assessed on the basis set out in section 28 below.

(4) Any liability arising by virtue of subsection (3) above—

    (a) shall be in the nature of a liability in tort; and

    (b) subject to subsection (5) below, shall be in addition to any liability arising apart from this section (whether in tort, contract or otherwise).

(5) Nothing in this section affects the right of a residential occupier to enforce any liability which arises apart from this section in respect of his loss of the right to occupy premises as his residence; but damages shall not be awarded both in respect of such a liability and in respect of a liability arising by virtue of this section on account of the same loss.

(6) No liability shall arise by virtue of subsection (3) above if—

    (a) before the date on which proceedings to enforce the liability are finally disposed of, the former residential occupier is reinstated in the premises in question in such circumstances that he becomes again the residential occupier of them; or

    (b) at the request of the former residential occupier, a court makes an order (whether in the nature of an injunction or otherwise) as a result of which he is reinstated as mentioned in paragraph (a) above;

and, for the purposes of paragraph (a) above, proceedings to enforce a liability are finally disposed of on the earliest date by which the proceedings (including any proceedings on or in consequence of an appeal) have been determined and any time for appealing or further appealing has expired, except that if any appeal is abandoned, the proceedings shall be taken to be disposed of on the date of the abandonment.

(7) If, in proceedings to enforce a liability arising by virtue of subsection (3) above, it appears to the court—

    (a) that, prior to the event which gave rise to the liability, the conduct of the former residential occupier or any person living with him in the premises concerned was such that it is reasonable to mitigate the damages for which the landlord in default would otherwise be liable, or

    (b) that, before the proceedings were begun, the landlord in default offered to reinstate the former residential occupier in the premises in question and either it was unreasonable of the former residential occupier to refuse that offer or, if he had obtained alternative accommodation before the offer was made, it would have been unreasonable of him to refuse that offer if he had not obtained that accommodation,

the court may reduce the amount of damages which would otherwise be payable by such amount as it thinks appropriate.

(8) In proceedings to enforce a liability arising by virtue of subsection (3) above, it shall be a defence for the defendant to prove that he believed, and had reasonable cause to believe—

    (a) that the residential occupier had ceased to reside in the premises in question at the time when he was deprived of occupation as mentioned in subsection (1) above or, as the case may be, when the attempt was made or the acts were done as a result of which he gave up his occupation of those premises; or

    (b) that, where the liability would otherwise arise by virtue only of the doing of acts or the withdrawal or withholding of services, he had reasonable grounds for doing the acts or withdrawing or withholding the services in question.

(9) In this section—

    (a) "residential occupier", in relation to any premises, has the same meaning as in section 1 of the 1977 Act;

    (b) "the right to occupy", in relation to a residential occupier, includes any restriction on the right of another person to recover possession of the premises in question;

    (c) "landlord", in relation to a residential occupier, means the person who, but for the occupier's right to occupy, would be entitled to occupation of the premises and any superior landlord under whom that person derives title;

    (d) "former residential occupier", in relation to any premises, means the person who was the residential occupier until he was deprived of or gave up his occupation as mentioned in subsection (1) or subsection (2) above (and, in relation to a former residential occupier, "the right to occupy" and "landlord" shall be construed accordingly).

"landlord"

3A–846   See subs.(9).

"residential occupier"

See subs.(9) and the Protection from Eviction Act 1977, s.1 which defines "residen- **3A–847** tial occupier" as "a person occupying the premises as a residence, whether under a contract or by virtue of any enactment or rule of law giving him the right to remain in occupation or restricting the right of any other person to recover possession of the premises."

"the 1977 Act"

See s.33 which, for the purposes of this Chapter, states that this means the Protec- **3A–848** tion from Eviction Act 1977.

Damages for unlawful eviction

Section 27 provides a cause of action where a landlord or any person acting on **3A–849** behalf of the landlord:

   (i) Unlawfully deprives a residential occupier of the whole or part of any premises which are occupied; or

   (ii) Attempts unlawfully to deprive a residential occupier or the whole or part of any premises which are occupied; or

   (iii) Causes a residential occupier to give up premises by either—

      (a) Doing "acts likely to interfere with the peace or comfort of the residential occupier" or members of his or her household, or

      (b) Persistently withdrawing or withholding services reasonably required for the occupation of premises as a residence, and

      (c) the landlord or person acting on behalf of the landlord knows or has reasonable cause to believe that this conduct is likely to cause the residential occupier to give up occupation of the premises or to refrain from exercising any right or pursuing any remedy in respect of the premises.

Much of the wording of the section is derived from the Protection from Eviction Act 1977.

It has been held by the Court of Session in Scotland, that the expression "acting on his behalf" in Housing (Scotland) Act 1988, s.36 (the Scottish equivalent to Housing Act 1988, s.27) is clear and unambiguous and encompasses anyone who is acting either as direct agent of the landlord, or as someone employed to do a particular act, or to undertake the management of the property with no particular fetter. It should not be read as imposing liability only where a landlord instigated or at least connived at his agent's illegitimate activities (*Scott v. Thomson*, 2003 S.L.T. 99, Court of Session, Ex Div.)

The word "unlawfully" means that the section applies not only to acts or omissions which are a trespass or a breach of contract, but also to acts which amount to breaches of the Protection from Eviction Act 1977, s.2 (Re-entry without court order), and s.3 (Eviction of former unprotected tenant or licensee without taking court proceedings).

Purchasers who are let into occupation as licensees before completion of the sale of premises may come within the definition of "landlord" in s.27(9)(c) (*Jones v. Miah* (1992) 24 H.L.R. 578; [1992] 33 E.G. 59, CA). However, ss.27 and 28 impose liability on landlords alone to pay damages and accordingly no claim under these sections can lie against a landlord's agent as a joint tortfeasor (*Sampson v. Wilson* [1996] Ch. 39; [1995] 3 W.L.R. 455, CA).

Landlords have a defence to proceedings if they can show that they "believed, or had reasonable cause to believe" that the occupier had ceased to occupy the premises, or that there were "reasonable grounds" for withdrawing or withholding services. It should also be noted that no damages are recoverable under ss.27 and 28 if the residential occupier is reinstated in the premises by the time at which any civil proceedings are disposed of or if a landlord has offered to reinstate the tenant and it was unreasonable of the tenant to refuse the offer of reinstatement (s.27(6) and (7)). In *Tagro v. Cafane and Patel* [1991] 2 All E.R. 235, CA, the Court of Appeal held that, even though the tenant had obtained an injunction and even though the landlords had offered a key to a room which had been "wrecked", there had not been a reinstatement satisfying the Housing Act 1988, s.27(6)(b). See too *Wandsworth LBC v. Osei-Bonsu* [1999] 1 All E.R. 265, CA.

A landlord's contention that s.27 only applies where "the seriousness of the landlord's conduct is established to a high degree and where he makes the tenant's position so intolerable that he is driven out of the property" was rejected by the Court of Appeal in *Abbott v. Bayley* (2000) 32 H.L.R. 72, CA.

The real significance of s.27 is not the scope of the cause of action, which is narrower than the covenant for quiet enjoyment, but the way in which damages are to be assessed (see commentary to s.28 below).

The measure of damages

3A–850   **28.**—(1) The basis for the assessment of damages referred to in section 27(3) above is the difference in value, determined as at the time immediately before the residential occupier ceased to occupy the premises in question as his residence, between—

    (a) the value of the interest of the landlord in default determined on the assumption that the residential occupier continues to have the same right to occupy the premises as before that time; and

    (b) the value of that interest determined on the assumption that the residential occupier has ceased to have that right.

(2) In relation to any premises, any reference in this section to the interest of the landlord in default is a reference to his interest in the building in which the premises in question are comprised (whether or not that building contains any other premises) together with its curtilage.

(3) For the purposes of the valuations referred to in subsection (1) above, it shall be assumed—

    (a) that the landlord in default is selling his interest on the open market to a willing buyer;

    (b) that neither the residential occupier nor any member of his family wishes to buy; and

    (c) that it is unlawful to carry out any substantial development of any of the land in which the landlord's interest subsists or to demolish the whole or part of any building on that land.

(4) In this section "the landlord in default" has the same meaning as in section 27 above and subsection (9) of that section applies in relation to this section as it applies in relation to that.

(5) Section 113 of the Housing Act 1985 (meaning of "members of a person's family") applies for the purposes of subsection (3)(b) above.

(6) The reference in subsection (3)(c) above to substantial development of any of the land in which the landlord's interest subsists is a reference to any development other than—

    (a) development for which planning permission is granted by a general development order for the time being in force and which is carried out so as to comply with any condition or limitation subject to which planning permission is so granted; or

    (b) a change of use resulting in the building referred to in subsection (2) above or any part of it being used as, or as part of, one or more dwelling-houses;

and in this subsection "general development order" has the meaning given in section 56(6) of the Town and Country Planning Act 1990 and other expressions have the same meaning as in that Act.

Note —Amended by the Planning (Consequential Provisions) Act 1990, Sched.2, para. 79(1).   **3A–851**

"landlord"
See s.27(9).   **3A–852**

"residential occupier"
See s.27(9) and the Protection from Eviction Act 1977, s.1, which defines "residential occupier" as "a person occupying the premises as a residence, whether under a contract or by virtue of any enactment or rule of law giving him the right to remain in occupation or restricting the right of any other person to recover possession of the premises."   **3A–853**

"member of his family"
See the Housing Act 1985, s.113.   **3A–854**

The measure of damages
Section 28 provides that damages are to be determined by subtracting the value of the premises if the tenant had remained in occupation from the value of the premises with vacant possession. In making such valuations, it is assumed that: **3A–855**

(i) The landlord is selling on the open market to a willing buyer; and
(ii) Neither the tenant nor any member of the tenant's family wishes to buy; and
(iii) No substantial development on the premises can be carried out unless planning permission has been granted by general development order within the meaning of the Town & County Planning Act 1990, s.56(6)).

Where a tenant is wrongfully evicted, but the eviction makes no difference to the value of the landlord's interest in the property, no damages can be awarded under the Housing Act 1988, ss.27 and 28 (*Melville v. Bruton* (1997) 29 H.L.R. 319, CA).

In *Regalgrand Ltd v. Dickerson* (1997) 29 H.L.R. 620; (1997) 75 P. & C.R. 313, CA, the judge reduced the tenants' damages from £12,000 to £1,500 pursuant to s.27(7)(a) because their conduct "was such that it [was] reasonable to mitigate the damages". The relevant conduct which she took into acount were:

(a) the withholding of rent without giving prior notice and without justification;
(b) the tenants' failure to inform the landlord that his installation of a new boiler had failed to cure the heating problems; and
(c) their intention to vacate in any event.

The tenants appealed on the grounds that the landlord had failed to plead mitigation, that the judge had failed to specify how she had arrived at the figure of £1,500, that their omissions were not "conduct" and that the judge had been wrong to take into account the arrears of rent. The Court of Appeal dismissed the appeal. Failure to pay rent was conduct. Although a mere intention (*e.g.* to leave) cannot amount to conduct, here the intention to leave has been partly acted upon because the tenants had moved their belongings and only very occasionally resided in the flat.

In view of s.27(5), damages awarded at common law for the loss of the right to occupy premises should be set off against damages awarded under ss.27 and 28 (*Mason v. Nwokorie* (1994) 26 H.L.R. 60; [1994] 05 E.G. 155, CA). However, *Mason v. Nwokorie* was distinguished in *Kaur (Kashmir) v. Gill, The Times*, June 15, 1995, CA, where an award of general damages in addition to ss.27-28 damages was upheld because the damages had not been awarded for any loss of right to occupy, but rather for breaches of the covenant for quite enjoyment. Note that:

"... where damages have been awarded to the tenant against the landlord under sections 27 and 28, there is no place for a further award of exemplary damages against either the landlord or against the person who assisted her in the eviction", but that principle does not prevent the award of aggravated damages" (*per* Sir Iain Glidewell in *Francis v. Brown* (1997) 30 H.L.R. 143, CA).

In relation to damages, see also *Murray v. Aslam* (1995) 27 H.L.R. 284, CA; *Francis v. Brown* (1997) 30 H.L.R. 143, CA; *King v. Jackson* (1998) 30 H.L.R. 541; [1998] 03 E.G. 138, CA and *Wandsworth LBC v. Osei-Bonsu* [1999] 1 All E.R. 265, CA.

* * * *

CHAPTER V

PHASING OUT OF RENT ACTS AND OTHER TRANSITIONAL PROVISIONS

New protected tenancies and agricultural occupancies restricted to special cases

3A–856   **34.**—(1) A tenancy which is entered into on or after the commencement of this Act cannot be a protected tenancy, unless—

>   (a) it is entered into in pursuance of a contract made before the commencement of this Act; or
>
>   (b) it is granted to a person (alone or jointly with others) who, immediately before the tenancy was granted, was a protected or statutory tenant and is so granted by the person who at that time was the landlord (or one of the joint landlords) under the protected or statutory tenancy; or
>
>   (c) it is granted to a person (alone or jointly with others) in the following circumstances—
>
>   > (i) prior to the grant of the tenancy, an order for possession of a dwelling-house was made against him (alone or jointly with others) on the court being satisfied as mentioned in section 98(1)(a) of, or Case 1 in Schedule 16 to the Rent Act 1977 or Case 1 in Schedule 4 to the Rent (Agriculture) Act 1976 (suitable alternative accommodation available); and
>   >
>   > (ii) the tenancy is of the premises which constitute the suitable alternative accommodation as to which the court was so satisfied; and
>   >
>   > (iii) in the proceedings for possession the court considered that, in the circumstances, the grant of an assured tenancy would not afford the required security and, accordingly, directed that the tenancy would be a protected tenancy; or
>
>   (d) it is a tenancy under which the interest of the landlord was at the time the tenancy was granted held by a new town corporation, within the meaning of section 80 of the Housing Act 1985, and, before the date which has effect by virtue of paragraph (a) or paragraph (b) of subsection (4) of section 38 below, ceased to be so held by virtue of a disposal by the commission for the New Towns made pursuant to a direction under section 37 of the New Towns Act 1981.

(2) In subsection (1)(b) above "protected tenant" and "statutory tenant" do not include—

>   (a) a tenant under a protected shorthold tenancy;
>
>   (b) a protected or statutory tenant of a dwelling-house which was let under a protected shorthold tenancy which ended before the commencement of this Act and in re-

spect of which at that commencement either there has been no grant of a further tenancy or any grant of a further tenancy has been to the person who, immediately before the grant, was in possession of the dwelling-house as a protected or statutory tenant;

and in this subsection "protected shorthold tenancy" includes a tenancy which, in proceedings for possession under Case 19 in Schedule 15 to the Rent Act 1977, is treated as a protected shorthold tenancy.

(3) In any case where—

    (a) by virtue of subsections (1) and (2) above, a tenancy entered into on or after the commencement of this Act is an assured tenancy, but

    (b) apart from subsection (2) above, the effect of subsection (1)(b) above would be that the tenancy would be a protected tenancy, and

    (c) the landlord and the tenant under the tenancy are the same as at the coming to an end of the protected or statutory tenancy which, apart from subsection (2) above, would fall within subsection (1)(b) above,

the tenancy shall be an assured shorthold tenancy (whether or not in the case of a tenancy to which the provision applies it fulfils the conditions in section 20(1) above) unless, before the tenancy is entered into, the landlord serves notice on the tenant that it is not to be a shorthold tenancy.

(4) A licence or tenancy which is entered into on or after the commencement of this Act cannot be a relevant licence or relevant tenancy for the purposes of the Rent (Agriculture) Act 1976 (in this subsection referred to as "the 1976 Act") unless—

    (a) it is entered into in pursuance of a contract made before the commencement of this Act, or

    (b) it is granted to a person (alone or jointly with others) who, immediately before the licence or tenancy was granted, was a protected occupier or statutory tenant, within the meaning of the 1976 Act, and is so granted by the person who at that time was the landlord or licensor (or one of the joint landlords or licensors) under the protected occupancy or statutory tenancy in question.

(5) Except as provided in subsection (4) above, expressions used in this section have the same meaning as in the Rent Act 1977.

Note—Amended by the Local Government and Housing Act 1989, s.195, Sched.11; **3A–857**
and the Housing Act 1996, s.104, Sched.8, para. 2.

"commencement of this Act"
See s.141(2), which provides that Pt I shall come into force "at the expiry of the pe- **3A–858**
riod of two months beginning on the day it is passed"—*i.e.* January 15, 1989.

"assured shorthold tenancy"
See ss.19A and 20. **3A–859**

"protected shorthold tenancy"
See the Housing Act 1980, s.52. **3A–860**

871

"landlord", and "tenancy"

3A–861   See s.45.

New protected tenancies and agricultural occupancies restricted to special cases

3A–862   Section 34 provides that no new Rent Act protected tenancies can be created after the Act came into force unless one of three exceptions applies. All new tenancies created on or after January 15, 1989 are assured or assured shorthold tenancies or totally unprotected tenancies unless:

(1) The tenancy was entered into in pursuance of a contract made before January 15, 1989, or

(2) The tenancy was granted to an existing 1977 Rent Act protected or statutory tenant by the same landlord. If there are joint tenants or joints landlords, it is sufficient for only one of the joint tenants to have been a protected tenant and for only one of the joint landlords to have been the landlord of the existing tenant or tenants. In *Secretarial Nominee Co. Ltd v. Thomas* [2005] EWCA Civ 1008; (2005) *The Times* September 20, the Court of Appeal held that s.34 "begins with the concept of a person who, after the commencement of the 1988 Act, is both a Rent Act tenant and has entered into a new tenancy. Such a person, moreover, has to have been a Rent Act tenant already before the new tenancy". The words "and prior to the commencement of this Act" in s.34 "have to be understood (in addition to the express requirement of "immediately before the tenancy was granted") as inherently qualifying the words "was a protected or statutory tenant". It is for the sake of such a tenant, and no other that the transitional protection of a protected tenancy is extended." The statutory language shows that the protection is for a particular person. Section 34 accordingly gave no rights to a person who had never been a joint tenant with a Rent Act tenant.

> It is clear from *Hansard* (June 30, 1988, cols 75 and 87) that Parliament's intention was that this exception should apply even if the tenant was a protected tenant in other accommodation but has been granted a new post-January 15, 1989 tenancy in, say, a different building. This was confirmed by the Court of Appeal in *Laimond Properites Ltd v. Al-Shakarchi* (1998) 30 H.L.R. 1099, CA, where the Court of Appeal held that s.34(1)(a), (b) and (c) deal with three separate situations. Section 34(1)(b) has no application in a case where the landlords have obtained an order for possession since the court "will have considered whether the new tenancy affords 'the required security' and whether the court should direct that the new tenancy be a protected tenancy". Roch L.J. also: (1) accepted submissions that s.34(1)(b) was mandatory, not permissive; and (2) approving *Gorringe v. Twinsectra Ltd*, June 1994, Legal Action 11(cc), held that s.34(1)(b) protection applies both to new tenancies of the same premises and to tenancies of other premises granted by the same landlords. See too *Rajah v. Arogol Co Ltd* [2001] EWCA Civ 454; [2002] H.L.R. 21, CA. It is the identity of the landlord and tenant that matters, not the identity of the premises. Further, the fact that the landlord has changed between the grant of the two tenancies does not affect the position. Section 34(1)(b) clearly refers to a grant at a later date by the person who was the landlord at the time of the later grant. Note too in *McAllister v. Queens Cross Housing Association Ltd*, 2003 S.L.T. 971, a case involving a similar provision in Housing (Scotland) Act 1987, s.43(3)(c), where it was held that there is no requirement that the earlier tenancy should be of the same premises.

(3) Before the grant of the new tenancy an order for possession was made on the grounds of suitable alternative accommodation against a protected or statutory tenant (Rent Act 1977, s.98(1)(a) or Sched.16, Case 1) and in the possession proceedings relating to the earlier tenancy, the court directed that the tenancy of the suitable alternative accommodation shall be held on a protected tenancy. The court may make such a direction if an assured tenancy "would not afford the required security".

restricted contracts

3A–863   For the effect of Housing Act 1988 ss.34(1) and 36(2)(a) on restricted contracts, see *Rowe v. Matthews* (2001) 33 H.L.R. 921, QBD.

Removal of special regimes for tenancies of housing associations etc.

35.—(1) In this section "housing association tenancy" has the same **3A–864** meaning as in Part VI of the Rent Act 1977.

(2) A tenancy which is entered into on or after the commencement of this Act cannot be a housing association tenancy unless—

    (a) it is entered into in pursuance of a contract made before the commencement of this Act, or

    (b) it is granted to a person (alone or jointly with others) who, immediately before the tenancy was granted, was a tenant under a housing association tenancy and is so granted by the person who at that time was the landlord under that housing association tenancy; or

    (c) it is granted to a person (alone or jointly with others) in the following circumstances—

        (i) prior to the grant of the tenancy, an order for possession of a dwelling-house was made against him (alone or jointly with others) on the court being satisfied as mentioned in paragraph (b) or paragraph (c) of subsection (2) of section 84 of the Housing Act 1985; and

        (ii) the tenancy is of the premises which constitute the suitable accommodation as to which the court was so satisfied; and

        (iii) in the proceedings for possession the court directed that the tenancy would be a housing association tenancy; or

    (d) it is a tenancy under which the interest of the landlord was at the time the tenancy was granted held by a new town corporation, within the meaning of section 80 of the Housing Act 1985, and, before the date which has effect by virtue of paragraph (a) or paragraph (b) of subsection (4) of section 38 below, ceased to be so held by virtue of a disposal by the Commission for the New Towns made pursuant to a direction under section 37 of the New Towns Act 1981.

(3) Where, on or after the commencement of this Act, a registered social landlord, within the meaning of the Housing Act 1985 (see section 5(4) and (5) of that Act), grants a secure tenancy pursuant to an obligation under section 554(2A) of the Housing Act 1985 (as set out in Schedule 17 to this Act) then, in determining whether that tenancy is a housing association tenancy, it shall be assumed for the purposes only of section 86(2)(b) of the Rent Act 1977 (tenancy would be a protected tenancy but for section 15 or 16 of that Act) that the tenancy was granted before the commencement of this Act.

(4) Subject to section 38(4A) below a tenancy or licence which is entered into on or after the commencement of this Act cannot be a secure tenancy unless—

    (a) the interest of the landlord belongs to a local authority, a new town corporation or an urban development

873

corporation, all within the meaning of section 80 of the Housing Act 1985, or a housing action trust established under Part III of this Act; or

(b) the interest of the landlord belongs to a housing co-operative within the meaning of section 27B of the Housing Act 1985 (agreements between local housing authorities and housing co-operatives) and the tenancy or licence is of a dwelling-house comprised in a housing co-operative agreement falling within that section, or

(c) it is entered into in pursuance of a contract made before the commencement of this Act, or

(d) it is granted to a person (alone or jointly with others) who, immediately before it was entered into, was a secure tenant and is so granted by the body which at that time was the landlord or licensor under the secure tenancy, or

(e) it is granted to a person (alone or jointly with others) in the following circumstances—

   (i) prior to the grant of the tenancy or licence, an order for possession of a dwelling-house was made against him (alone or jointly with others) on the court being satisfied as mentioned in paragraph (b) or paragraph (c) of subsection (2) of section 84 of the Housing Act 1985; and

   (ii) the tenancy or licence is of the premises which constitute the suitable accommodation as to which the court was so satisfied; and

   (iii) in the proceedings for possession the court considered that, in the circumstances, the grant of an assured tenancy would not afford the required security and, accordingly, directed that the tenancy or licence would be a secure tenancy; or

(f) it is granted pursuant to an obligation under section 554(2A) of the Housing Act 1985 (as set out in Schedule 17 to this Act).

(5) If, on or after the commencement of this Act, the interest of the landlord under a protected or statutory tenancy becomes held by a housing association, a housing trust or the Housing Corporation or, where that interest becomes held by him as a result of the exercise by him of the functions under Part III of the Housing Associations Act 1985, the Secretary of State, nothing in the preceding provisions of this section shall prevent the tenancy from being a housing association tenancy or a secure tenancy and, accordingly, in such a case section 80 of the Housing Act 1985 (and any enactment which refers to that section) shall have effect without regard to the repeal of provisions of that section effected by this Act.

(6) In subsection (5) above "housing association" and "housing trust" have the same meaning as in the Housing Act 1985.

3A–865   Note —Amended by the Local Government and Housing Act 1989, s.195, Sched.11; the Housing Act 1996 (Consequential Provisions) Order 1996 (S.I. 1996 No. 2325),

Art. 5, Sched.2, para. 18, Government of Wales Act 1998, Sched.15, para. 15 and the Government of Wales Act 1998 (Housing) (Amendments) Order 1999 (S.I. 1999 No. 61).

"commencement of this Act"
See s.141(2) which provides that Pt I shall come into force "at the expiry of the pe- **3A–866** riod of two months beginning on the day it is passed"—*i.e.* January 15, 1989.

"housing association tenancy"
See the Rent Act 1977, s.86.   **3A–867**

"secure tenancy"
See s.45 and the Housing Act 1985, s.79 (above).   **3A–868**

"landlord" and "tenancy"
See s.45.   **3A–869**

New restricted contracts limited to transitional cases

36.—(1) A tenancy or other contract entered into after the com- **3A–870** mencement of this Act cannot be a restricted contract for the purposes of the Rent Act 1977 unless it is entered into in pursuance of a contract made before the commencement of this Act.

(2) If the terms of a restricted contract are varied after this Act comes into force then, subject to subsection (3) below,—

> (a) if the variation affects the amount of the rent which, under the contract, is payable for the dwelling in question, the contract shall be treated as a new contract entered into at the time of the variation (and subsection (1) above shall have effect accordingly); and

> (b) if the variation does not affect the amount of the rent which, under the contract, is so payable, nothing in this section shall affect the determination of the question whether the variation is such as to give rise to a new contract.

(3) Any reference in subsection (2) above to a variation affecting the amount of the rent which, under a contract, is payable for a dwelling does not include a reference to—

> (a) a reduction or increase effected under section 78 of the Rent Act 1977(power of rent tribunal); or

> (b) a variation which is made by the parties and has the effect of making the rent expressed to be payable under the contract the same as the rent for the dwelling which is entered in the register under section 79 of the Rent Act 1977.

(4) In subsection (1) of section 81A of the Rent Act 1977 (cancellation of registration of rent relating to a restricted contract) paragraph (a) (no cancellation until two years have elapsed since the date of the entry) shall cease to have effect.

(5) In this section "rent" has the same meaning as in Part V of the Rent Act 1977.

"restricted contract"
See the Rent Act 1977, ss.19 and 20. For the effect of Housing Act 1988, ss.34(1) **3A–871** and 36(2)(a) on restricted contracts, see *Rowe v. Matthews* (2001) 33 H.L.R. 921, QBD.

"commencement of this Act"

3A–872   See s.141(2), which provides that Pt I shall come into force "at the expiry of the period of two months beginning on the day it is passed"—*i.e.* January 15, 1989.

"landlord" and "tenancy"

3A–873   See s.45.

"rent"

3A–874   See the Rent Act 1977, s.85(3).

* * * *

Chapter VI

General Provisions

Jurisdiction of county courts

3A–875   **40.**—(1) A county court shall have jurisdiction to hear and determine any question arising under any provision of—

(a) Chapters I to III and V above, or

(b) sections 27 and 28 above,

other than a question falling within the jurisdiction of a rent assessment committee by virtue of any such provision.

(2) [...]

(3) Where any proceedings under any provision mentioned in subsection (1) above are being taken in a county court, the court shall have jurisdiction to hear and determine any other proceedings joined with those proceedings, notwithstanding that, apart from this subsection, those other proceedings would be outside the court's jurisdiction.

(4) If any person takes any proceedings under any provision mentioned in subsection (1) above in the High Court, he shall not be entitled to recover any more costs of those proceedings than those to which he would have been entitled if the proceedings had been taken in a county court: and in such a case the taxing master shall have the same power of directing on what county court scale costs are to be allowed, and of allowing any item of costs, as the judge would have had if the proceedings had been taken in a county court.

(5) Subsection (4) above shall not apply where the purpose of taking the proceedings in the High Court was to enable them to be joined with any proceedings already pending before that court (not being proceedings taken under any provision mentioned in subsection (1) above).

3A–876   *Note* —Amended by the High Court and County Courts Jurisdiction Order 1991 (S.I. 1991 No. 724).

3A–877   * * * *

Interpretation of Part I

45.—(1) In this part of this Act, except where the context otherwise requires,—

"dwelling-house" may be a house or part of a house;

"fixed term tenancy" means any tenancy other than a periodic tenancy;

"fully mutual housing association" has the same meaning as in Part I of the Housing Associations Act 1985;

"landlord" includes any person from time to time deriving title under the original landlord and also includes, in relation to a dwelling-house, any person other than a tenant who is, or but for the existence of an assured tenancy would be, entitled to possession of the dwelling-house;

"let" includes "sub-let";

"prescribed" means prescribed by regulations made by the Secretary of State by statutory instrument;

"rates" includes water rates and charges but does not include an owner's drainage rate, as defined in section 63(2)(a) of the Land Drainage Act 1976;

"secure tenancy" has the meaning assigned by section 79 of the Housing Act 1985;

"statutory periodic tenancy" has the meaning assigned by section 5(7) above;

"tenancy" includes a sub-tenancy and an agreement for a tenancy or sub-tenancy; and

"tenant" includes a sub-tenant and any person deriving title under the original tenant or sub-tenant.

(2) Subject to paragraph 11 of Schedule 2 to this Act, any reference in this Part of this Act to the beginning of a tenancy is a reference to the day on which the tenancy is entered into or, if it is later, the day on which, under the terms of any lease, agreement or other document, the tenant is entitled to possession under the tenancy.

(3) Where two or more persons jointly constitute either the landlord or the tenant in relation to a tenancy, then, except where this Part of this Act otherwise provides, any reference to the landlord or to the tenant is a reference to all the persons who jointly constitute the landlord or the tenant, as the case may require.

(4) For the avoidance of doubt, it hereby declared that any reference in this Part of this Act (however expressed) to a power for a landlord to determine a tenancy does not include a reference to a power of re-entry or forfeiture for breach of any term or condition of the tenancy.

(5) Regulations under subsection (1) above may make different provision with respect to different cases or descriptions of case, including different provisions for different areas.

prescribed

See the Assured Tenancies and Agricultural Occupancies (Forms) Regulations (S.I. 1988 No. 2203), amended by the Assured Tenancies and Agricultural Occupancies (Forms) (Amendment) Regulations (S.I. 1989 No.146); the Assured Tenancies and Agricultural Occupancies (Forms) (Amendment) Regulations 1990 (S.I. 1990 No. 1532); the Assured Tenancies and Agricultural Occupancies (Forms) (Amendment) Regulations 1993 (S.I. 1993 No. 654); the Assured Tenancies and Agricultural Occupancies (Forms) Regulations 1997 (S.I. 1997 No. 194) and the Assured Tenancies and Agricultural (Forms) (Amendment) (England) Regulations 2003 (S.I. 2003 No. 260).

3A–878

* * * *

3A–879

SECTION 1

SCHEDULE 1

TENANCIES WHICH CANNOT BE ASSURED TENANCIES

PART I

THE TENANCIES

Tenancies entered into before commencement

1. A tenancy which is entered into before, or pursuant to a contract made before, the commencement of this Act.

Tenancies of dwelling-houses with high rateable values

3A–880 2.—(1) A tenancy—

(a) which is entered into on or after 1st April 1990 (otherwise than, where the dwelling-house had a rateable value on 31st March 1990, in pursuance of a contract made before 1st April 1990), and

(b) under which the rent payable for the time being is payable at a rate exceeding £25,000 a year.

(2) In sub-paragraph (1) "rent" does not include any sum payable by the tenant as is expressed (in whatever terms) to be payable in respect of rates, council tax, services, management, repairs, maintenance or insurance, unless it could not have been regarded by the parties to the tenancy as a sum so payable.

(2A.) A tenancy—

(a) which was entered into before the 1st April 1990, or on or after that date in pursuance of a contract made before that date, and

(b) under which the dwelling-house had a rateable value on 31st March 1990 which, if it is in Greater London, exceeded £1,500 and, if it is elsewhere, exceeded £750.

Tenancies at a low rent

3A–881 3. A tenancy under which for the time being no rent is payable.

(3A.) A tenancy—

(a) which is entered into on or after 1st April 1990 (otherwise than, where the dwelling-house had a rateable value on 31st March 1990, in pursuance of a contract made before 1st April 1990), and

(b) under which the rent payable for the time being is payable at a rate of, if the dwelling-house is in Greater London, £1,000 or less a year and, if it is elsewhere, £250 or less a year.

(3B.) A tenancy—

(a) which was entered into before 1st April 1990 or, where the dwelling-house had a rateable value on the 31st March 1990, on or after 1st April 1990 in pursuance of a contract made before that date, and

(b) under which the rent for the time being payable is less than two-thirds of the rateable value of the dwelling-house on 31st March 1990.

(3C.) Paragraph 2(2) above applies for the purposes of paragraphs 3, 3A and 3B as it applies for the purposes of paragraph 2(1).

Business tenancies

3A–882 4. A tenancy to which Part II of the Landlord and Tenant Act 1954 applies (business tenancies).

Licensed premises

3A–883 5. A tenancy under which the dwelling-house consists of or comprises premises licensed for the sale of intoxicating liquors for consumption on the premises.

Tenancies of agricultural land

3A–884 6.—(1) A tenancy under which agricultural land, exceeding two acres, is let together with the dwelling-house.

(2) In this paragraph "agricultural land" has the meaning set out in section 26(3)(a) of the General Rate Act 1967(exclusion of agricultural land and premises from liability for rating).

Tenancies of agricultural holdings etc

3A–885

7.—(1) A tenancy under which the dwelling-house—

(a) is comprised in an agricultural holding, and

(b) is occupied by the person responsible for the control (whether as tenant or as servant or agent of the tenant) of the farming of the holding.

(2) A tenancy under which the dwelling-house—

(a) is comprised in the holding held under a farm business tenancy, and

(b) is occupied by the person responsible for the control (whether as tenant or as servant or agent of the tenant) of the management of the holding.

(3) In this paragraph—

"agricultural holding" means any agricultural holding within the meaning of the Agricultural Holdings Act 1986 held under a tenancy in relation to which that Act applies, and

"farm business tenancy" and "holding", in relation to such a tenancy, have the same meaning as in the Agricultural Tenancies Act 1995.

Lettings to students

3A–886

8.—(1) A tenancy which is granted to a person who is pursuing, or intends to pursue, a course of study provided by a specified educational institution and is so granted either by that institution or by another specified institution or body of persons.

(2) In sub-paragraph (1) above "specified" means specified, or of a class specified, for the purposes of this paragraph by regulations made by the Secretary of State by statutory instrument.

(3) A statutory instrument made in the exercise of the power conferred by sub-paragraph (2) above shall be subject to annulment in pursuance of a resolution of either House of Parliament.

Holiday lettings

3A–887

9. A tenancy the purpose of which is to confer on the tenant the right to occupy the dwelling-house for a holiday.

Resident landlords

3A–888

10.—(1) A tenancy in respect of which the following conditions are fulfilled—

(a) that the dwelling-house forms part only of a building and, except in a case where the dwelling-house also forms part of a flat, the building is not a purpose-built block of flats, and

(b) that, subject to Part III of this Schedule, the tenancy was granted by an individual who, at the time when the tenancy was granted, occupied as his only or principal home another dwelling-house which,—

(i) in the case mentioned in paragraph (a) above, also forms part of the flat; or

(ii) in any other case, also forms part of the building; and

(c) that, subject to Part III of this Schedule, at all times since the tenancy was granted the interest of the landlord under the tenancy has belonged to an individual who, at the time he owned that interest, occupied as his only or principal home another dwelling-house which,—

(i) in the case mentioned in paragraph (a) above, also formed part of the flat, or

(ii) in any other case, also formed part of the building; and

(d) that the tenancy is not one which is excluded from this sub-paragraph by sub-paragraph (3) below.

(2) If a tenancy was granted by two or more persons jointly, the reference in sub-paragraph (1)(b) above to an individual is a reference to any one of those persons and if the interest of the landlord is for the time being held by two or more persons jointly, the reference in sub-paragraph (1)(c) above to an individual is a reference to any one of those persons.

(3) A tenancy (in this sub-paragraph referred to as "the new tenancy") is excluded from sub-paragraph (1) above if—

    (a) it is granted to a person (alone, or jointly with others) who, immediately before it was granted, was a tenant under an assured tenancy (in this sub-paragraph referred to as "the former tenancy") of the same dwelling-house or of another dwelling-house which forms part of the building in question; and

    (b) the landlord under the new tenancy and under the former tenancy is the same person or, if either of those tenancies is or was granted by two or more persons jointly, the same person is the landlord or one of the landlords under each tenancy.

Crown tenancies

3A-889   11.—(1) A tenancy under which the interest of the landlord belongs to Her Majesty in right of the Crown or to a government department or is held in trust for Her Majesty for the purpose of a government department.

(2) The reference in sub-paragraph (1) above to the case where the interest of the landlord belongs to Her Majesty in right of the Crown does not include the case where that interest is under the management of the Crown Estate Commissioners or it is held by him as a result of the exercise by him of the functions under Part III 1985 of the Housing Associations Act 1985.

Local authority tenancies etc.

3A-890   12.—(1) A tenancy under which the interest of the landlord belongs to—

    (a) a local authority, as defined in sub-paragraph (2) below;

    (b) the Commission for the New Towns;

    (c) [...]

    (d) an urban development corporation established by an order under section 135 of the Local Government, Planning and Land Act 1980;

    (e) a development corporation, within the meaning of the New Towns Act 1981;

    (f) an authority established under section 10 of the Local Government Act 1985 (waste disposal authorities);

    (g) a residuary body, within the meaning of the Local Government Act 1985; or

    (gg) The Residuary Body for Wales (Corff Gweddilliol Cymru);

    (h) a fully mutual housing association; or

    (i) a housing action trust established under Part III of this Act.

(2) The following are local authorities for the purposes of sub-paragraph (1)(a) above—

    (a) the council of a county, county borough, district or London borough;

    (b) the Common Council of the City of London;

    (c) the Council of the Isles of Scilly;

    (d) the Broads Authority;

    (da) a National Park authority;

    (e) the Inner London Education Authority; and

    (f) a joint authority, within the meaning of the Local Government Act 1985.

    (g) a police authority established under section 3 of the Police Act 1964.

Accommodation for asylum-seekers

3A-891   12A.—(1) A tenancy granted by a private landlord under arrangements for the provision of support for asylum-seekers or dependants or asylum-seekers made under Part VI of the Immigration and Asylum Act 1999.

(2) Private landlord means a landlord who is not within section 80(1) of the Housing Act 1985.

12B.—(1) A tenancy granted by a private landlord under arrangements for the provision of accommodation for persons with temporary protection made under the Displaced Persons (Temporary Protection) Regulations 2005.

(2) "Private landlord" means a landlord who is not within section 80(1) of the Housing Act 1985.

Transitional cases

3A-892   13.—(1) A protected tenancy, within the meaning of the Rent Act 1977.

(2) A housing association tenancy, within the meaning of Part VI of that Act.

(3) A secure tenancy.

(4) Where a person is a protected occupier of a dwelling-house, within the meaning of the Rent (Agriculture) Act 1976, the relevant tenancy, within the meaning of that Act, by virtue of which he occupies the dwelling-house.

PART II

RATEABLE VALUES

14.—(1) The rateable value of a dwelling-house at any time shall be ascertained for **3A–893** the purposes of Part I of this Schedule as follows—

    (a) if the dwelling-house is a hereditament for which a rateable value is then shown in the valuation list, it shall be that rateable value;

    (b) if the dwelling-house forms part only of such a hereditament or consists of or forms part of more than one such hereditament, its rateable value shall be taken to be such value as is found by a proper apportionment or aggregation of the rateable value or values so shown.

(2) Any question arising under this Part of this Schedule as to the proper apportionment or aggregation of any value or values shall be determined by the county court and the decision of that court shall be final.

15. Where, after the time at which the rateable value of a dwelling-house is material for the purposes of any provision of Part I of this Schedule, the valuation list is altered so as to vary the rateable value of the hereditament of which the dwelling-house consists (in whole or in part) or forms part and the alteration has effect from that time or from an earlier time, the rateable value of the dwelling-house at the material time shall be ascertained as if the value shown in the valuation list at the material time had been the value shown in the list as altered.

16. Paragraphs 14 and 15 above apply in relation to any other land which, under section 2 of this Act, is treated as part of a dwelling-house as they apply in relation to the dwelling-house itself.

PART III

PROVISIONS FOR DETERMINING APPLICATION OF PARAGRAPH 10 (RESIDENT LANDLORDS)

17.—(1) In determining whether the condition in paragraph 10(1)(c) above is at any **3A–894** time fulfilled with respect to a tenancy, there shall be disregarded—

    (a) any period of not more than twenty-eight days, beginning with the date on which the interest of the landlord under the tenancy becomes vested at law and in equity in an individual who, during that period, does not occupy as his only or principal home another dwelling-house which forms part of the building or, as the case may be, flat concerned;

    (b) if, within a period falling within paragraph (a) above, the individual concerned notifies the tenant in writing of his intention to occupy as his only or principal home another dwelling-house in the building or, as the case may be, flat concerned, the period beginning with the date on which the interest of the landlord under the tenancy becomes vested in that individual as mentioned in that paragraph and ending—

        (i) at the expiry of the period of six months beginning on that date, or

        (ii) on the date on which that interest ceases to be so vested, or

        (iii) on the date on which that interest becomes again vested in such an individual as is mentioned in paragraph 10(1)(c) or the condition in that paragraph becomes deemed to be fulfilled by virtue of paragraph 18(1) or paragraph 20 below,

        whichever is the earlier; and

    (c) any period of not more than two years beginning with the date on which the interest of the landlord under the tenancy becomes, and during which it remains, vested—

        (i) in trustees as such; or

(ii) by virtue of section 9 of the Administration of Estates Act 1925, in the Probate Judge or the Public Trustee, within the meaning of that Act.

(2) Where the interest of the landlord under a tenancy becomes vested at law and in equity in two or more persons jointly, of whom at least one was an individual, sub-paragraph (1) above shall have effect subject to the following modifications—

(a) in paragraph (a) for the words from "an individual" to "occupy" there shall be substituted "the joint landlords if, during that period none of them occupies"; and

(b) in paragraph (b) for the words "the individual concerned" there shall be substituted "any of the joint landlords who is an individual"and for the words "that individual" there shall be substituted "the joint landlords".

18.—(1) During any period when—

(a) the interest of the landlord under the tenancy referred to in paragraph 10 above is vested in trustees as such, and

(b) that interest is held on trust for any person who or for two or more persons of whom at least one occupies as his only or principal home a dwelling-house which forms part of the building or, as the case may be, flat referred to in paragraph 10(1)(a),

the condition in paragraph 10(1)(c) shall be deemed to be fulfilled and accordingly, no part of that period shall be disregarded by virtue of paragraph 17 above.

(2) If a period during which the condition in paragraph 10(1)(c) is deemed to be fulfilled by virtue of sub-paragraph (1) above comes to an end on the death of a person who was in occupation of a dwelling-house as mentioned in paragraph (b) of that sub-paragraph, then, in determining whether that condition is at any time thereafter fulfilled, there shall be disregarded any period—

(a) which begins on the date of the death;

(b) during which the interest of the landlord remains vested as mentioned in sub-paragraph (1)(a) above; and

(c) which ends at the expiry of the period of two years beginning on the date of the death or on any earlier date on which the condition in paragraph 10(1)(c)becomes again deemed to be fulfilled by virtue of sub-paragraph (1) above.

19. In any case where—

(a) immediately before a tenancy comes to an end the condition in paragraph 10(1)(c) is deemed to be fulfilled by virtue of paragraph 18(1) above, and

(b) on the coming to an end of that tenancy the trustees in whom the interest of the landlord is vested grant a new tenancy of the same or substantially the same dwelling-house to a person (alone or jointly with others) who was the tenant or one of the tenants under the previous tenancy,

the condition in paragraph 10(1)(b) above shall be deemed to be fulfilled with respect to the new tenancy.

20.—(1) The tenancy referred to in paragraph 10 above falls within this paragraph if the interest of the landlord under the tenancy becomes vested in the personal representatives of a deceased person acting in that capacity.

(2) If the tenancy falls within this paragraph, the condition in paragraph 10(1)(c) shall be deemed to be fulfilled for any period, beginning with the date on which the interest becomes vested in the personal representatives and not exceeding two years, during which the interest of the landlord remains so vested.

21. Throughout any period which, by virtue of paragraph 17 or paragraph 18(2) above, falls to be disregarded for the purpose of determining whether the condition in paragraph 10(1)(c) is fulfilled with respect to a tenancy, no order shall be made for possession of the dwelling-house subject to that tenancy, other than an order which might be made if that tenancy were or, as the case may be, had been an assured tenancy.

22. For the purposes of paragraph 10 above, a building is a purpose-built block of flats if as constructed it contained, and it contains, two or more flats; and for this purpose "flat" means a dwelling-house which—

(a) forms part only of a building; and

(b) is separated horizontally from another dwelling-house which forms part of the same building.

Note —Amended by the Reference to Rating (Housing) Regulations 1990 (S.I. 1990 **3A–895**
No. 434); the Local Government (Wales) Act 1994, Sched.9, para. 9, and Sched.13, para. 31; the Law of Property (Miscellaneous Provisions) Act 1994, Sched.1, para. 11; the Local Government Finance (Housing) (Consequential Amendments) Order 1993 (S.I. 1993 No. 651); and the Police and Magistrates' Court Act 1994, Sched.4, para. 62; the Environmental Act 1995, s.78, Sched.10, para. 28; the Agricultural Tenancies 1995, Schedule, para. 34; the Trusts of Land and Appointment of Trustees Act 1996, s.25(2), Sched.4; the Government of Wales Act 1998, Sched.18, Pt IV; the Government of Wales Act 1998 (Housing) (Amendments) Order 1999 (S.I. 1999 No. 61); the-Immigration and Asylum Act 1999, Sched.14, para. 88; and by S.I. 2005 No. 1379.

Sched.1
This Schedule lists types of tenancies which cannot be assured tenancies: **3A–896**

Para. 1
A tenancy which is entered into before or pursuant to a contract made before Janu- **3A–897**
ary 15, 1989.

"commencement of this Act"
See s.141(2) which provides that Pt I shall come into force "at the expiry of the pe- **3A–898**
riod of two months beginning on the day it is passed"—*i.e.* January 15, 1989.

Para. 2
Tenancies of dwelling-houses with high rateable values—*i.e.* over £1,500 in Greater **3A–899**
London, over £750 elsewhere (compare the Rent Act 1977, s.4). Note that the References to Rating (Housing) Regulations 1990 (S.I. 1990 No. 434) provide that where tenancies are granted after April 1, 1990, they cannot be assured if the rent is more than £25,000 per annum. "Rent" does not include sums paid in respect of services, repairs, maintenance or insurance.

In *Bankway Properties v. Dunsford* [2001] EWCA Civ 528; [2001] 1 W.L.R. 1369, CA the Court of Appeal found that a clause permitting a landlord to increase the rent of a tenant in receipt of housing benefit to £25,000 per annum was a mere device, which enabled the landlord, effectively when it chose, to recover possession. In those circumstances it was unenforceable and the landlord's claim for possession based upon arrears was dismissed.

Para. 3
Tenancies at a low rent—either where no rent is payable or where the rent is less **3A–900**
than two thirds of the rateable value. The date for determining whether a tenancy is a tenancy at a low rent is the date when the relevant issue arises (*Woozley v. Woodall Smith* [1950] 1 K.B. 325). In effect a tenancy may drift in and out of being an assured tenancy, subject to fluctuating costs (compare the Rent Act 1977, s.5). Note that The References to Rating (Housing) Regulations provide that tenancies granted after April 1, 1990 cannot be assured if the *rent* is less than £1,000 per annum in London or less than £250 per annum outside London.

Para. 4
Business tenancies—see Pt II of the Landlord & Tenant Act 1954 (compare the **3A–901**
Rent Act 1977, ss.2 and 24 and see commentary thereto).

Para. 5
Tenancies under which dwelling-houses consists of or comprise premises licensed **3A–902**
for the sale of intoxicating liquors for consumption on the premises (compare the Rent Act 1977, s.11).

Paras 6 & 7
Tenancies under which agricultural land, exceeding two acres is let together with **3A–903**
the dwelling-house and agricultural holdings within the meaning of the Agricultural Holdings Act 1986 (compare the Rent Act 1977, s.10).

Para. 8
Lettings to students by a specified educational institution. See the Assured and **3A–904**

Protected Tenancies (Lettings to Students) Regulations 1998 (S.I. 1998 No. 1967) which define SEIs—basically any institution which provides higher or further education which is publicly funded and various other named institutions. Note also that lettings by registered housing associations to students cannot be assured tenancies (compare the Rent Act 1977, s.8).

Para. 9

3A-905   Holiday lettings—where the purpose of the tenancy is to confer on the tenant the right to occupy the dwelling-house for a holiday (see commentary to the Rent Act 1977, s.9). In *Buchmann v. May* [1978] 2 All E.R. 993; (1976) 240 E.G. 49, CA, the Court of Appeal held that the labels put on a transaction are not conclusive, but that where a tenancy agreement expressly states the purpose for which it is made, that statement is evidence of that purpose unless the tenant can establish that it does not correspond with the true purpose, either because the express label is a sham or because it is a false label. Although a court will be "astute to detect a sham where it appears that a provision has been inserted for the purpose of depriving the tenant of statutory protection under the Rent Acts" ([1978] 2 All E.R. at 999), the burden of proof lies on the tenant. In that case there was no evidence which displaced the express purpose and accordingly there was no Rent Act protection. The court accepted the dictionary definition of a holiday as "a period of cessation of work, or period of recreation". See also *R. v. Rent Officer for Camden LBC, Ex p. Plant* (1980) 257 E.G. 713; (1983) 7 H.L.R. 15, QBD, where there was "clear evidence that all the parociations, Housing Action Trusts (compare the Rent Act 1977, ss.14–16).

Para. 10

3A-906   Compare the Rent Act 1977, s.12 and the commentary to that section.

The provision of "Board" is *not* an exception (compare the Rent Act 1977, s.7).

Para. 12

3A-907   Welsh Development Agency—Note that some tenants of the Welsh Development Agency do not enjoy security of tenure. See para. 3A-62,the Welsh Development Agency Act 1975, Sched.4 as inserted by the Government of Wales Act 1998, Sched.13.

If one of the exceptions in Sched.1 applies, the tenant has no security of tenure. Once a notice to quit has been served and has expired the tenant has no statutory protection, except, in some cases, for the Protection from Eviction Act 1977, s.3 which provides that it is unlawful for a landlord to evict such a tenant without taking court proceedings. The landlord need only prove that the contractual tenancy has been terminated.

SECTION 7   **SCHEDULE 2**

GROUNDS FOR POSSESSION OF DWELLING-HOUSES LET ON ASSURED TENANCIES

PART I

GROUNDS ON WHICH COURT MUST ORDER POSSESSION

Ground 1

3A-908   Not later than the beginning of the tenancy the landlord gave notice in writing to the tenant that possession might be recovered on this ground or the court is of the opinion that it is just and equitable to dispense with the requirement of notice and (in either case)—

(a) at some time before the beginning of the tenancy, the landlord who is seeking possession or, in the case of joint landlords seeking possession, at least one of them occupied the dwelling-house as his only or principal home; or

(b) the landlord who is seeking possession or, in the case of joint landlords seeking possession, at least one of them requires the dwelling-house as his or his spouse's only or principal home and neither the landlord (or, in the case of joint landlords, any one of them) nor any other person who, as landlord, derived title under the landlord who gave the notice mentioned above acquired the reversion on the tenancy for money or money's worth.

Ground 2

3A-909 The dwelling-house is subject to a mortgage granted before the beginning of the tenancy and—

884

(a) the mortgagee is entitled to exercise a power of sale conferred on him by the mortgage or by section 101 of the Law of Property Act 1925; and

(b) the mortgagee requires possession of the dwelling-house for the purpose of disposing of it with vacant possession in exercise of that power; and

(c) either notice was given as mentioned in Ground 1 above or the court is satisfied that it is just and equitable to dispense with the requirement of notice;

and for the purposes of this ground "mortgage" includes a charge and "mortgagee" shall be construed accordingly.

Ground 3

The tenancy is a fixed term tenancy for a term not exceeding eight months and— **3A–910**

(a) not later than the beginning of the tenancy the landlord gave notice in writing to the tenant that possession might be recovered on this ground; and

(b) at some time within the period of twelve months ending with the beginning of the tenancy, the dwelling-house was occupied under a right to occupy it for a holiday.

Ground 4

The tenancy is a fixed term tenancy for a term not exceeding twelve months and— **3A–911**

(a) not later than the beginning of the tenancy the landlord gave notice in writing to the tenant that possession might be recovered on this ground, and

(b) at some time within the period of twelve months ending with the beginning of the tenancy, the dwelling-house was let on a tenancy falling within paragraph 8 of Schedule 1 to this Act.

Ground 5

The dwelling-house is held for the purpose of being available for occupation by a **3A–912** minister of religion as a residence from which to perform the duties of his office and—

(a) not later than the beginning of the tenancy the landlord gave notice in writing to the tenant that possession might be recovered on this ground; and

(b) the court is satisfied that the dwelling-house is required for occupation by a minister of religion as such a residence.

Ground 6

The landlord who is seeking possession or, if that landlord is a registered social **3A–913** landlord or charitable housing trust, a superior landlord intends to demolish or reconstruct the whole or a substantial part of the dwelling-house or to carry out substantial works on the dwelling-house or any part thereof or any building of which it forms part and the following conditions are fulfilled—

(a) the intended work cannot reasonably be carried out without the tenant giving up possession of the dwelling-house because—

  (i) the tenant is not willing to agree to such a variation of the terms of the tenancy as would give such access and other facilities as would permit the intended work to be carried out, or

  (ii) the nature of the intended work is such that no such variation is practicable, or

  (iii) the tenant is not willing to accept an assured tenancy of such part only of the dwelling-house (in this sub-paragraph referred to as "the reduced part") as would leave in the possession of his landlord so much of the dwelling-house as would be reasonable to enable the intended work to be carried out and, where appropriate, as would give such access and other facilities over the reduced part as would permit the intended work to be carried out, or

  (iv) the nature of the intended work is such that such a tenancy is not practicable; and

(b) either the landlord seeking possession acquired his interest in the dwelling-house before the grant of the tenancy or that interest was in existence at the time of that grant and neither that landlord (or, in the case of joint landlords, any of them) nor any other person who, alone or jointly with others, has acquired that interest since that time acquired it for money or money's worth; and

HOUSING

(c) the assured tenancy on which the dwelling-house is let did not come into being by virtue of any provision of Schedule 1 to the Rent Act 1977, as amended
by Part I of Schedule 4 to this Act or, as the case may be, section 4 of the Rent
(Agriculture) Act 1976, as amended by Part II of that Schedule.

For the purposes of this ground, if, immediately before the grant of the tenancy, the
tenant to whom it was granted or, if it was granted to joint tenants, any of them was
the tenant or one of the joint tenants of the dwelling-house concerned under an
earlier assured tenancy or, as the case may be, under a tenancy to which Schedule 10
to the Local Government and Housing Act 1989 applied, any reference in paragraph
(b) above to the grant of the tenancy is a reference to the grant of that or, as the case
may be, to the grant of the tenancy to which the said Schedule 10 applied.

For the purposes of this ground "registered social landlord" has the same meaning
as in the Housing Act 1985 (see section 5(4) and (5) of that Act) and "charitable housing trust" means a housing trust, within the meaning of the Housing Associations Act
1985, which is a charity, within the meaning of the Charities Act 1993.

For the purposes of this ground, every acquisition under Part IV of this Act shall be
taken to be an acquisition for money or money's worth; and in any case where—

(i) the tenancy (in this paragraph referred to as "the current tenancy") was
granted to a person (alone or jointly with others) who, immediately before it
was granted, was a tenant under a tenancy of a different dwelling-house (in
this paragraph referred to as "the earlier tenancy"), and

(ii) the landlord under the current tenancy is the person who, immediately before
that tenancy was granted, was the landlord under the earlier tenancy, and

(iii) the condition in paragraph (b) above could not have been fulfilled with respect
to the earlier tenancy by virtue of an acquisition under Part IV of this Act
(including one taken to be such an acquisition by virtue of the previous operation of this paragraph),

the acquisition of the landlord's interest under the current tenancy shall be taken to
have been under that Part and the landlord shall be taken to have acquired that interest after the grant of the current tenancy.

Ground 7

3A–914 The tenancy is a periodic tenancy (including a statutory periodic tenancy) which has
devolved under the will or intestacy of the former tenant and the proceedings for the
recovery of possession are begun not later than twelve months after the death of the
former tenant or, if the court so directs, after the date on which, in the opinion of the
court, the landlord or, in the case of joint landlords, any one of them became aware of
the former tenant's death.

For the purposes of this ground, the acceptance by the landlord of rent from a new
tenant after the death of the former tenant shall not be regarded as creating a new
periodic tenancy, unless the landlord agrees in writing to a change (as compared with
the tenancy before the death) in the amount of the rent, the period of the tenancy, the
premises which are let or any other term of the tenancy.

Ground 8

3A–915 Both at the date of the service of the notice under section 8 of this Act relating to
the proceedings for possession and at the date of the hearing—

(a) if rent is payable weekly or fortnightly, at least eight weeks rent is unpaid;

(b) if rent is payable monthly, at least two months rent is unpaid;

(c) if rent is payable quarterly, at least one quarter's rent is more than three
months in arrears; and

(d) if rent is payable yearly, at least three months' rent is more than three months
in arrears;

and for the purpose of this ground "rent" means rent lawfully due from the tenant.

PART II

GROUNDS ON WHICH COURT MAY ORDER POSSESSION

Ground 9

3A–916 Suitable alternative accommodation is available for the tenant or will be available for
him when the order for possession takes effect.

Ground 10

Some rent lawfully due from the tenant— **3A–917**

  (a) is unpaid on the date on which the proceedings for possession are begun; and

  (b) except where subsection (1)(b) of section 8 of this Act applies, was in arrears at the date of the service of the notice under that section relating to those proceedings.

Ground 11

Whether or not any rent is in arrears on the date on which proceedings for possession **3A–918** are begun, the tenant has persistently delayed paying rent which has become lawfully due.

Ground 12

Any obligation of the tenancy (other than one related to the payment of rent) has **3A–919** been broken or not performed.

Ground 13

The condition of the dwelling-house or any of the common parts has deteriorated **3A–920** owing to acts of waste by, or the neglect or default of, the tenant or any other person residing in the dwelling-house and, in the case of an act of waste by, or the neglect or default of, a person lodging with the tenant or a sub-tenant of his, the tenant has not taken such steps as he ought reasonably to have taken for the removal of the lodger or sub-tenant.

For the purposes of this ground, "common parts" means any part of a building comprising the dwelling-house and any other premises which the tenant is entitled under the terms of the tenancy to use in common with the occupiers of other dwelling-houses in which the landlord has an estate or interest.

Ground 14

The tenant or a person residing in or visiting the dwelling-house— **3A–921**

  (a) has been guilty of conduct causing or likely to cause a nuisance or annoyance to a person residing, visiting or otherwise engaging in a lawful activity in the locality, or

  (b) has been convicted of—

    (i) using the dwelling-house or allowing it to be used immoral or illegal purposes, or

    (ii) an arrestable offence committed in, or in the locality of, the dwelling-house.

Ground 14A

The dwelling-house was occupied (whether alone or with others) by a married couple **3A–922** or a couple living together as husband and wife and—

  (a) one or both of the partners is a tenant of the dwelling-house,

  (b) the landlord who is seeking possession is a registered social landlord or a charitable housing trust,

  (c) one partner has left the dwelling-house because of violence or threats of violence by the other towards—

    (i) that partner, or

    (ii) children of the partnership.

  (d) the court is satisfied that the partner who has left is unlikely to return.

For the purposes of this ground "registered social landlord" and "member of the family" have the same meaning as in Part I of the Housing Act 1996 and "charitable housing trust" means a housing trust, within the meaning of the Housing Associations Act 1985, which is a charity within the meaning of the Charities Act 1993.

Ground 15

The condition of any furniture provided for use under the tenancy has, in the **3A–923** opinion of the court, deteriorated owing to ill-treatment by the tenant or any other person residing in the dwelling-house and, in the case of ill-treatment by a person lodging with the tenant or by a sub-tenant of his, the tenant has not taken such steps as he ought reasonably to have taken for the removal of the lodger or sub-tenant.

HOUSING

Ground 16

3A–924 The dwelling-house was let to the tenant in consequence of his employment by the landlord seeking possession or a previous landlord under the tenancy and the tenant has ceased to be in that employment.

For the purposes of this ground, at a time when the landlord is or was the Secretary of State, employment by a health service body, as defined in section 60(7) of the National Health Service and Community Care Act 1990, shall be regarded as employment by the Secretary of State.

Ground 17

3A–925 The tenant is the person, or one of the persons, to whom the tenancy was granted and the landlord was induced to grant the tenancy by a false statement made knowingly or recklessly by—

(a) the tenant or,

(b) a person acting at the tenant's instigation.

Part III

Suitable Alternative Accommodation

3A–926 1. For the purposes of Ground 9 above, a certificate of the local housing authority for the district in which the dwelling-house in question is situated, certifying that the authority will provide suitable alternative accommodation for the tenant by a date specified in the certificate, shall be conclusive evidence that suitable alternative accommodation will be available for him by that date.

2. Where no such certificate as is mentioned in paragraph 1 above is produced to the court, accommodation shall be deemed to be suitable for the purposes of Ground 9 above if it consists of either—

(a) premises which are to be let as a separate dwelling such that they will then be let on an assured tenancy, other than—

  (i) a tenancy in respect of which notice is given not later than the beginning of the tenancy that possession might be recovered on any of Grounds 1 to 5 above, or

  (ii) an assured shorthold tenancy, within the meaning of Chapter II of Part I of this Act, or

(b) premises to be let as a separate dwelling on terms which will, in the opinion of the court, afford to the tenant security of tenure reasonably equivalent to the security afforded by Chapter I of Part I of this Act in the case of an assured tenancy of a kind mentioned in sub-paragraph (a) above,

and, in the opinion of the court, the accommodation fulfils the relevant conditions as defined in paragraph 3 below.

3.—(1) For the purposes of paragraph 2 above, the relevant conditions are that the accommodation is reasonably suitable to the needs of the tenant and his family as regards proximity to place of work, and either—

(a) similar as regards rental and extent to the accommodation afforded by dwelling-houses provided in the neighbourhood by any local housing authority for persons whose needs as regards extent are, in the opinion of the court, similar to those of the tenant and of his family; or

(b) reasonably suitable to the means of the tenant and to the needs of the tenant and his family as regards extent and character; and

that if any furniture was provided for use under the assured tenancy in question, furniture is provided for use in the accommodation which is either similar to that so provided or is reasonably suitable to the needs of the tenant and his family.

(2) For the purposes of sub-paragraph (1)(a) above, a certificate of a local housing authority stating—

(a) the extent of the accommodation afforded by dwelling-houses provided by the authority to meet the needs of tenants with families of such number as may be specified in the certificate, and

(b) the amount of the rent charged by the authority for dwelling-houses affording accommodation of that extent, shall be conclusive evidence of the facts so stated.

4. Accommodation shall not be deemed to be suitable to the needs of the tenant and his family if the result of their occupation of the accommodation would be that it would be an overcrowded dwelling-house for the purposes of Part X of the Housing Act 1985.

5. Any document purporting to be a certificate of a local housing authority named therein issued for the purposes of this Part of this Schedule and to be signed by the proper officer of that authority shall be received in evidence and, unless the contrary is shown, shall be deemed to be such a certificate without further proof.

6. In this Part of this Schedule "local housing authority" and "district", in relation to such an authority, have the same meaning as in the Housing Act 1985.

PART IV

NOTICES RELATING TO RECOVERY OF POSSESSION

7. Any reference in Grounds 1 to 5 in Part I of this Schedule or in the following **3A–927** provisions of this Part to the landlord giving a notice in writing to the tenant is, in the case of joint landlords, a reference to at least one of the joint landlords giving such a notice.

8.—(1) If, not later than the beginning of a tenancy (in this paragraph referred to as "the earlier tenancy"), the landlord gives such a notice in writing to the tenant as is mentioned in any of Grounds 1 to 5 in Part I of this Schedule, then, for the purposes of the ground in question and any further application of this paragraph, that notice shall also have effect as if it had been given immediately before the beginning of any later tenancy falling within sub-paragraph (2) below.

(2) Subject to sub-paragraph (3) below, sub-paragraph (1) above applies to a later tenancy—

(a) which takes effect immediately on the coming to an end of the earlier tenancy; and

(b) which is granted (or deemed to be granted) to the person who was the tenant under the earlier tenancy immediately before it came to an end; and

(c) which is of substantially the same dwelling-house as the earlier tenancy.

(3) Sub-paragraph (1) above does not apply in relation to a later tenancy if, not later than the beginning of the tenancy, the landlord gave notice in writing to the tenant that the tenancy is not one in respect of which possession can be recovered on the ground in question.

9. Where paragraph 8(1) above has effect in relation to a notice given as mentioned in Ground 1 in Part I of this Schedule, the reference in paragraph (b) of that ground to the reversion on the tenancy is a reference to the reversion on the earlier tenancy and on any later tenancy falling within paragraph 8(2) above.

10. Where paragraph 8(1) above has effect in relation to a notice given as mentioned in Ground 3 or Ground 4 in Part I of this Schedule, any second or subsequent tenancy in relation to which the notice has effect shall be treated for the purpose of that ground as beginning at the beginning of the tenancy in respect of which the notice was actually given.

11. Any reference in Grounds 1 to 5 in Part I of this Schedule to a notice being given not later than the beginning of the tenancy is a reference to its being given not later than the day on which the tenancy is entered into and, accordingly, section 45(2) of this Act shall not apply to any such reference.

Note—Amended by the Local Government and Housing Act 1989, s.195, Sched.11, **3A–928** paras 108 and 109; the NHS and Community Care Act 1990, Sched.8; the Charities Act 1993, s.98(1), Sched.6; the Housing Act 1996, ss.10, 101, 102, 148 and 149, Sched.19, Pt IX; and the Housing Act 1996 (Consequential Provisions) Order 1996 (S.I. 1996 No. 2325), art.5, Sched.2, para. 18. Grounds 1 and 14A have been amended by the Civil Partnership Act 2004, s.81 and Sched. 8 . The amendment is not yet in force, but is printed at para. 3A–1525 .

Mandatory Grounds

Ground 1

Returning Owner Occupier: This ground is similar to Case 11 in the Rent Act 1977, **3A–929** Sched.15, but more widely drafted. A landlord must prove that:

(a) At, or before, the grant of the tenancy the landlord gave notice in writing that possession might be recovered on this ground. The notice need not be in any particular form and may be included as a recital in any tenancy agreement provided that the agreement does not operate retrospectively. The court has power to dispense with such a notice if it considers it just and equitable.

AND EITHER

(b) At some time before the grant of the tenancy the landlord, or if there are joint landlords, at least one of them, occupied the dwelling-house as his or her only or principal residence. A landlord's previous occupation may be temporary and intermittent in order to suffice (see *Naish v. Curzon* (1984) 17 H.L.R. 220; and *Mistry v. Isidore* (1990) 22 H.L.R. 281, *cf. Ibie v. Trubshaw* (1990) 22 H.L.R. 191).

OR

(c) The landlord (or at least one of them) "requires the dwelling-house as his or his spouse's only or principal home". The landlord need not show that the premises are reasonably required, merely that the landlord "bona fide wants" or "genuinely has the immediate intention" of occupying the premises (*Kennealy v. Dunne* [1977] Q.B. 837). Premises need not be required as a permanent residence and fairly intermittent residence will be sufficient (*Naish v. Curzon* (1984) 17 H.L.R. 220).

This ground for possession is not available to a new landlord who has acquired the premises "for money or money's worth" from an original landlord who gave a notice that possession might be recovered under this ground (*Epps v. Rothnie* [1945] K.B. 562).

Ground 2

3A–930 *Mortgagees:* This ground applies if:

(a) a mortgagee is entitled to exercise a power of sale (*e.g.* if the mortgagor has defaulted on instalments of the mortgage), and

(b) the mortgagee requires vacant possession to exercise that power, and

(c) a Ground 1 notice was given before the commencement of the tenancy or the court considers it just and equitable to dispense with the notice.

Note the comments of Lord Denning M.R. in *Quennell v. Maltby* [1979] 1 W.L.R. 318) that:

"A mortgagee will be restrained from getting possesion except when it is sought bona fide and reasonably for the purpose of enforcing the security and then only subject to such conditions as the court thinks fit to impose" (approved in *Albany Homes Ltd v. Massey* [1997] 2 All E.R. 609, CA).

Ground 3

3A–931 *Tenancy preceded by "holiday let":* This ground is almost identical to the Rent Act 1977, Sched.15, Case 13. A landlord must prove that:

(a) not later than the grant of the tenancy, notice was given that possession might be recovered under this ground and;

(b) at some time during the twelve months prior to the grant of the tenancy, the dwelling-house was occupied for a holiday.

The court has no power to dispense with service of the notice required prior to the grant of the tenancy (*Fowler v. Minchin* (1987) 19 H.L.R. 224, but *cf. Springfied Investments v. Bell* (1990) 22 H.L.R. 440).

Ground 4

3A–932 *Educational Institutions:* This ground applies where, during the twelve months preceding the tenancy, premises were let by a specified educational institution. As with Ground 3, notice stating that this ground may be relied upon has to be served before the commencement of the tenancy. It is almost identical to the Rent Act 1977, Sched.15, Case 14.

"specified educational institution"

See the Assured and Protected Tenancies (Lettings to Students) Regulations 1998 **3A–933**
(S.I. 1998 No. 1967) which also provide that lettings by registered housing associations
to students cannot be assured tenancies.

Ground 5

Ministers of Religion: This ground applies to premises which are "held for the **3A–934**
purpose of being available for occupation by a minister of religion as a residence from
which to perform duties of his office". Note that possession might be required must be
served before the grant of the tenancy and the landlord must satisfy the court that the
property is required for occupation by a minister of religion as a residence.

Ground 6

Demolition or Reconstruction: This ground is available for a landlord who "intends to **3A–935**
demolish or reconstruct the whole or a substantial part of the dwelling-house or to
carry out substantial works". This ground is very similar to the Landlord and Tenant
Act 1954, s.30(1)(f):

(a) It has been held that "reconstruction" means "a substantial interference with
the structure of the premises and then a rebuilding, in probably a different
form, of such part of the premises as has been demolished by reason of the
interference with the structure (*Joel v. Swaddle* [1957] 3 All E.R. 325 at 329;
see too *Barth v. Pritchard* [1990] 20 E.G. 65).

(b) The landlord must show that the intention will be fulfilled shortly after the
date of the hearing (*Betty's Cafe v. Phillips* [1958] 1 All E.R. 607, HL). There
are two elements to the concept of intention—

(i) a genuine desire that the result will come about, and

(ii) a reasonable prospect of bringing about that result. See too *Edwards v.
Thompson* [1990] 29 E.G. 41, where the landlord failed to prevent the
grant of a new tenancy because she had not found a developer at the
time of the hearing and "there was a real possibility that [she] would
not be in a position to carry out the entire development on the
termination of the current tenancy. ... She had failed to show that she
had the means and ability; she had not established the necessary
intention." It is not essential that a landlord obtain planning permission in advance if it can be shown that there is a reasonable prospect
of getting consent (*Gregson v. Cyril Lord* [1962] 3 All E.R. 907).

(c) The landlord must show that, because of one of four specified reasons, the
intended work cannot reasonably be carried out without the tenant giving
up possession of the premises. "Possession" means "putting an end to legal
rights of possession" and not merely access (*Heath v. Drown* [1972] 2 All E.R.
561; and the Housing Act 1988, s.16).

(d) This ground is not available to a landlord who has acquired his or her interest in the property by purchasing it after the grant of the tenancy.

(e) When a possession order is made under this ground the landlord must pay a
sum equal to the tenant's reasonable removal expenses (s.11(1)).

Ground 7

Death of the Tenant: Although an assured tenancy may pass by will or on intestacy af- **3A–936**
ter the death of a tenant, the landlord may obtain possession if proceedings are
brought within twelve months of the death of the tenant or the date upon which the
landlord became aware of the death. "Proceedings for possession" means court
proceedings, not the service of a s.8 notice (*Shepping v. Osada* (2001) 33 H.L.R. 13;
[2000] L. & T.R. 489; [2000] 2 E.G.L.R. 38, CA).This ground does not apply if a
spouse succeeds to the tenancy under s.17. The Act specifies that acceptance of rent after the death of the former tenant should not be regarded as creating a new tenancy
unless the landlord has agreed in writing to a change in the terms of the tenancy, such
as an increase in rent.

Ground 8

Two months' rent arrears: This is the first of three distinct grounds for possession **3A–937**
based on rent arrears, although in practice landlords frequently plead all three in the

alternative. Under Ground 8, two months' rent arrears (or eight weeks' arrears in the case of a weekly tenancy) give a landlord an automatic right to a possession order. However the landlord must prove that there are two months' arrears, both at the time when the notice of the landlord's intention to bring proceedings is served and at the date of the hearing. It should be borne in mind that delays on the part of a local authority or the Benefits Agency in making housing benefit payments do not provide a defence to proceedings brought under Ground 8 (*Marath v. MacGillivray* (1996) 28 H.L.R. 484, CA). As to the restrictions on the court's power to adjourn in such circumstances, see ss.7(3) and 9(6) and the commentary at 3A-716.

In *Day v. Coltrane* [2003] EWCA Civ 342; [2003] 1 W.L.R. 1379 a tenant, facing a Ground 8 possession claim, handed the landlord a cheque for all the arrears on the day of the hearing. The landlord accepted the cheque and it was paid on first presentation. The Court of Appeal, allowing an appeal from a possession order, held that delivery of a cheque is a conditional payment. If the cheque is met, it is an actual payment from the date of delivery (*Homes v. Smith* [2000] Lloyd's Rep Banking 139). That principle applies to Ground 8. If the cheque cleared, the debt was paid when the cheque was delivered. An uncleared cheque delivered to the landlord at or before the hearing and which was accepted by him, or which he was bound by an earlier agreement to accept, is to be treated as payment on the date of delivery provided it was subsequently paid on first presentation. At the date of the hearing there was jurisdiction to adjourn the claim to see whether the cheque would be paid.

Note that the court cannot dispense with the requirement for a s.8 notice when Ground 8 is relied upon (see s.8(5)).

Discretionary Grounds

Ground 9

3A-938   *Suitable Alternative Accommodation:* As with the Rent Act 1977, s.98(1)(a), the availability of suitable alternative accommodation, either at the time of the hearing or when the order is to take effect, is a ground for possession. (See commentary to the Rent Act 1977, s.98). Pt III of Sched.2 gives further clarification as to the matters to be taken into account when determining whether or not accommodation is suitable. They are similar to those set out in the Rent Act 1977, Sched.15, Pt IV.

When a possession order is made under this ground, the landlord must pay a sum equal to the tenant's reasonable removal expenses (s.11(1)).

Ground 10

3A-939   *Rent Arrears:* A landlord must prove that there were rent arrears both at the date when proceedings were begun and, unless the court considers it "just and equitable" to dispense with the need for service of a notice prior to issue, that there were arrears when the notice was served. This is the ground for possession which is most similar to Case 1 in Sched.15 to the Rent Act (see commentary thereto). A possession order may be made even if the arrears are paid off before the hearing, although in most circumstances there would be strong grounds for arguing that it would not be reasonable to make an order. See *Dellenty v. Pellow* [1951] 2 All E.R. 716, CA; and *Lee-Steere v. Jennings* (1987) 20 H.L.R. 1, CA.

Ground 11

3A-940   *Persistent Delay in Paying Rent:* Even if there are no arrears on the date when possession proceedings are issued, persistent delay in paying rent which is due is a ground for possession. The phrase "persistent delay" is not defined, but is likely to have the same meaning as in the Landlord and Tenant Act 1954, s.30(1)(b)—*i.e.* one instalment of rent has been in arrears for a significant period of time or instalments have persistently been paid late, or both (see *Hopcutt v. Carver* (1969) 209 E.G. 1069, CA; and *Horowitz v. Ferand* [1956] C.L.Y. 4843). For an example of the court's exercise of its powers under Landlord and Tenant Act 1954, s.30(1)(b) (persistent delay in paying rent), see *Hazel v. Akhtar* [2001] EWCA Civ 1883; [2002] 07 E.G. 124.

Ground 12

3A-941   *Breach of any obligation:* This ground for possession is similar to the second limb of Case 1 in the Rent Act 1977, Sched.15 and applies if "any obligation of the tenancy (other than one related to the payment of rent) has been broken or not performed". See commentary to Case 1.

Ground 13

Waste or Neglect: This ground is similar to Case 3 in the Rent Act 1977, Sched.15, **3A–942**
but slightly wider in that it applies not only to the premises let, but also to common
parts.

There is no need for a landlord to give advance warning of an intention to issue
proceedings relying on this ground (*Lowe v. Lendrum* (1950) 159 E.G. 423, CA) although failure to do so may be relevant when the court considers reasonableness and
costs. See too *Holloway v. Povey* (1984) 15 H.L.R. 104; (1984) 271 E.G. 195, CA.

Ground 14

Nuisance or annoyance or conviction for illegal or immoral user: The Housing Act 1996, **3A–943**
s.148 introduced new Ground 14 which replaces the former "nuisance or annoyance"
ground.

There is no requirement that any person visiting the premises and causing a
nuisance should be there lawfully. The ground is wide enough, for example, to
encompass behaviour by a former partner of a tenant who has been excluded, but
returns contrary to the tenant's wishes. The widening of the ground from conduct
which *is* a nuisance or annoyance to neighbours to conduct which is *likely to cause
nuisance or annoyance* is designed to meet two problems. Firstly the new ground avoids
the apparent need for landlords to produce neighbours as witnesses to whom nuisance
or annoyance has been caused (but *cf. Frederick Platts Co v. Grigor* [1950] 1 All E.R.
941, CA, where it was held that the court can infer that nuisance or annoyance has
been caused without hearing evidence from anyone affected.) Secondly, the amended
ground covers nuisance or annoyance to people who are not neighbours—*e.g.* housing
officers (but *cf.* the wide definition of "neighbour" adopted by the Court of Appeal in
Northampton BC v. Lovatt (1998) 30 H.L.R. 875; 91 L.G.R. 548; [1998] 07 E.G. 142, CA.
As to the meaning of locality in the context of Housing Act 1996, s.152, see *Manchester
CC v. Lawler* (1999) 31 H.L.R. 119, CA where it was said that it is a matter of fact for
the judge in each case to determine whether the conduct complained of has occurred
in the locality (held that an incident in a shopping centre three streets away from the
property was "in the locality").

Arrestable offences are defined by the Police and Criminal Evidence Act 1984, s.24
and include all offences for which the sentence is fixed by law (*e.g.* life imprisonment),
offences for which adults may be sentenced with terms of imprisonment of five years
or more, taking motor vehicles without authority and offences under the Sexual Offences Act 1956, ss.22 and 23 (causing prostitution of women and procuring girls
under 21).

Ground 14A

Domestic Violence: **3A–944**

"registered social landlord" —See the Housing Act 1996, ss.1–7 and the Housing Act
1985, s.5.

The Housing Act 1996, s.149 introduced a new ground for possession against assured tenants of registered social landlords or charitable housing trusts where there
has been domestic violence. Ground 14A applies where one partner is or both partners
are tenants and:

(a) one partner has left because of violence or threats of violence by the other
towards that partner or a member of that partner's family; and

(b) the court is satisfied that the partner who has left is unlikely to return.

Landlords seeking to rely upon this ground must satisfy the court that notice of
proceedings for possession has been served on the partner who has left the home or
that they have taken reasonable steps to effect service (Housing Act 1996, s.150, inserting new Housing Act 1988, s.8A).

Where possession is sought under Ground 14A, it is not sufficient that the alleged
violence or threats of violence were merely one of a range of causes of equal efficacy in
the victim's departure from the property. For the ground to be made out it has to be
established that the alleged violence or threat of violence was the dominant, principal
and real cause of the departure (*Camden LBC v. Mallett* (2001) 33 H.L.R. 20, CA).

Ground 15

Deterioration of furniture: cf. the Rent Act 1977, Sched.15, Case 4. **3A–945**

Ground 16

3A–946   *Premises let to employees:* An employer who has let accommodation to an employee "in consequence" of employment may claim possession if the tenant has "ceased to be in that employment". This ground for possession is wider than Case 8, the comparable Rent Act ground. It applies whether or not the employer requires the premises for another employee.

Ground 17

3A–947   See commentary to the Housing Act 1985, Sched.2, Ground 5.

SCHEDULE 2A

ASSURED TENANCIES: NON-SHORTHOLDS

Tenancies excluded by notice

3A–948   1.—(1) An assured tenancy in respect of which a notice is served as mentioned in sub-paragraph (2) below.

(2) The notice referred to in sub-paragraph (1) above is one which—

   (a) is served before the assured tenancy is entered into,

   (b) is served by the person who is to be the landlord under the assured tenancy on the person who is to be the tenant under that tenancy, and

   (c) states that the assured tenancy to which it relates is not to be an assured shorthold tenancy.

2.—(1) An assured tenancy in respect of which a notice is served as mentioned in sub-paragraph (2) below.

(2) The notice referred to in sub-paragraph (1) above is one which—

   (a) is served after the assured tenancy has been entered into,

   (b) is served by the landlord under the assured tenancy on the tenant under that tenancy, and

   (c) states that the assured tenancy to which it relates is no longer an assured shorthold tenancy.

Tenancies containing exclusionary provision

3A–949   3. An assured tenancy which contains a provision to the effect that the tenancy is not an assured shorthold tenancy.

Tenancies under section 39

3A–950   4. An assured tenancy arising by virtue of section 39 above, other than one to which subsection (7) of that section applies.

Former secure tenancies

3A–951   5. An assured tenancy which became an assured tenancy on ceasing to be a secure tenancy.

Former demoted tenancies

3A–952   5A. An assured tenancy which ceases to be an assured shorthold tenancy by virtue of section 20B(2) or (4).

Tenancies under Schedule 10 to the Local Government and Housing Act 1989

3A–953   6. An assured tenancy arising by virtue of Schedule 10 to the Local Government and Housing Act 1989 (security of tenure on ending of long residential tenancies).

Tenancies replacing non-shortholds

3A–954   7.—(1) An assured tenancy which—

   (a) is granted to a person (alone or jointly with others) who, immediately before the tenancy was granted, was the tenant (or, in the case of joint tenants, one of the tenants) under an assured tenancy other than a shorthold tenancy ("the old tenancy"),

   (b) is granted (alone or jointly with others) by a person who was at that time the landlord (or one of the joint landlords) under the old tenancy, and

(c) is not one in respect of which a notice is served as mentioned in sub-paragraph (2) below.

(2) The notice referred to in sub-paragraph (1)(c) above is one which—

(a) is in such form as may be prescribed,

(b) is served before the assured tenancy is entered into,

(c) is served by the person who is to be the tenant under the assured tenancy on the person who is to be the landlord under that tenancy (or, in the case of joint landlords, on at least one of the persons who are to be joint landlords), and

(d) states that the assured tenancy to which it relates is to be a shorthold tenancy.

8. An assured tenancy which comes into being by virtue of section 5 above on the coming to an end of an assured tenancy which is not a shorthold tenancy.

Assured agricultural occupancies

9.—(1) An assured tenancy— **3A–955**

(a) in the case of which the agricultural worker condition is, by virtue of any provision of Schedule 3 to this Act, for the time being fulfilled with respect to the dwelling-house subject to the tenancy, and

(b) which does not fall within sub-paragraph (2) or (4) below.

(2) An assured tenancy falls within this sub-paragraph if—

(a) before it is entered into, a notice—

(i) in such form as may be prescribed, and

(ii) stating that the tenancy is to be a shorthold tenancy,

is served by the person who is to be the landlord under the tenancy on the person who is to be the tenant under it, and

(b) it is not an excepted tenancy.

(3) For the purposes of sub-paragraph (2)(b) above, an assured tenancy is an excepted tenancy if—

(a) the person to whom it is granted or, as the case may be, at least one of the persons to whom it is granted was, immediately before it is granted, a tenant or licensee under an assured agricultural occupancy, and

(b) the person by whom it is granted or, as the case may be, at least one of the persons by whom it is granted was, immediately before it is granted, a landlord or licensor under the assured agricultural occupancy referred to in paragraph (a) above.

(4) An assured tenancy falls within this sub-paragraph if it comes into being by virtue of section 5 above on the coming to an end of a tenancy falling within sub-paragraph (2) above.

Note —Added by the Housing Act 1996, s.96, Sched.7. **3A–956**

Section 21 has been amended by Anti-social Behaviour Act 2003, s.15(2) and Para.5A has been inserted by Anti-social Behaviour Act 2003, s.15(3). The amendment was brought into force in England on June 30, 2004 by the Anti-social Behaviour Act 2003 (Commencement No. 3 and Savings) Order 2004 (S.I. 2004 No. 1502) (C.61). It was brought into force in Wales on 30 April 2005 by the Anti-social Behaviour Act 2003 (Commencement No.4) (Wales) Order 2005 (S.I. 2005 No. 1225) (W.83) (C.55).

Criminal Justice and Public Order Act 1994

(1994 c.33) **3A–957**

* * * *

Interim possession orders: false or misleading statements

75.—(1) A person commits an offence if, for the purpose of obtain- **3A–958** ing an interim possession order, he—

     (a) makes a statement which he knows to be false or misleading in a material particular; or

     (b) recklessly makes a statement which is false or misleading in a material particular.

(2) A person commits an offence if, for the purpose of resisting the making of an interim possession order, he—

     (a) makes a statement which he knows to be false or misleading in a material particular; or

     (b) recklessly makes a statement which is false or misleading in a material particular.

(3) A person guilty of an offence under this section shall be liable—

     (a) on conviction on indictment, to imprisonment for a term not exceeding two years or a fine or both;

     (b) on summary conviction, to imprisonment for a term not exceeding six months or a fine not exceeding the statutory maximum or both.

(4) In this section—

"interim possession order" means an interim possession order (so entitled) made under rules of court for the bringing of summary proceedings for possession of premises which are occupied by trespassers;

"premises" has the same meaning as in Part II of the Criminal Law Act 1977 (offences relating to entering and remaining on property); and

"statement", in relation to an interim possession order, means any statement, in writing or oral and whether as to fact or belief, made in or for the purposes of the proceedings.

premises

3A–959   See Criminal Law Act 1977, s.12(1) which states "(a) 'premises' means any building, any part of a building under separate occupation, any land ancillary to a building, the site comprising any building or buildings together with any land ancillary thereto..."

3A–960   Section 12(2) provides that references to a building shall apply also to any structure other than a movable one, and to any movable structure, vehicle or vessel designed or adapted for use for residential purposes. Part of a building is under separate occupation if anyone is in occupation or entitled to occupation of that part as distinct from the whole. Land is ancillary to a building if it is adjacent to it and used (or intended for use) in connection with the occupation of that building or any part of it.

interim possession order

3A–961   See s.75(4) and CPR, rr.55.22 to 55.28.

Editorial note

3A–962   Criminal Justice and Public Order Act 1994, ss.75 and 76 created interim possession orders (IPOs). They can only be granted against trespassers. Failure to comply with an IPO is a criminal offence. The IPO procedure can only be used if:

    — the claimant is only seeking possession. A claimant cannot seek an IPO if there is a claim for another remedy (*e.g.* damages);

    — the claimant has an immediate right to possession and has had such a right throughout the period of unlawful occupation;

    — the defendants entered premises as trespassers. It cannot be used against former licensees, tenants or sub-tenants.

The procedure for obtaining an IPO is set out in CPR, rr.55.22 to 55.28.

If an IPO has been made and served, any person who is present on the premises as **3A–963** a trespasser at any time during the currency of the order commits an offence unless he or she leaves the premises within 24 hours of service of the order (and does not return) or a copy of the order is not fixed to the premises. It is also an offence if a person who was on the premises when the order was served and who has left then reenters or attempts to do so as a trespasser after the expiry of the order but within one year of the date of service of the order. Offences are triable summarily.

Interim possession orders: trespassing during currency of order

76.—(1) This section applies where an interim possession order **3A–964** has been made in respect of any premises and served in accordance with rules of court; and references to "the order" and "the premises" shall be construed accordingly.

(2) Subject to subsection (3), a person who is present on the premises as a trespasser at any time during the currency of the order commits an offence.

(3) No offence under subsection (2) is committed by a person if—
  (a) he leaves the premises within 24 hours of the time of service of the order and does not return; or
  (b) a copy of the order was not fixed to the premises in accordance with rules of court.

(4) A person who was in occupation of the premises at the time of service of the order but leaves them commits an offence if he reenters the premises as a trespasser or attempts to do so after the expiry of the order but within the period of one year beginning with the day on which it was served.

(5) A person guilty of an offence under this section shall be liable on summary conviction to imprisonment for a term not exceeding six months or a fine not exceeding level 5 on the standard scale or both.

(6) A person who is in occupation of the premises at the time of service of the order shall be treated for the purposes of this section as being present as a trespasser.

(7) A constable in uniform may arrest without a warrant anyone who is, or whom he reasonably suspects to be, guilty of an offence under this section.

(8) In this section—
  "interim possession order" has the same meaning as in section 75 above and "rules of court" is to be construed accordingly; and
  "premises" has the same meaning as in that section that is to say the same meaning as in Part II of the Criminal Law Act 1977 (offences relating to entering and remaining on property).

interim possession order
  See s.75(4). **3A–965**

rules of court
  See CPR, rr.55.22 to 55.28. **3A–966**

premises
  See commentary to s.75 and Criminal Law Act 1977, s.12. **3A–967**

Housing Act 1996

3A–968

(1996 c.52)

Housing Act 1996, Pt I—Editorial Introduction

3A–969   The Housing Act 1996, Pt I contains detailed provisions concerning registration by social landlords, disposal of land by them, financial grants and the role of the Housing Corporation. All housing associations on the register kept by the Housing Corporation under the Housing Associations Act 1985, Pt I are automatically registered as social landlords. So far as future registration is concerned, bodies are eligible for registration as social landlords if they are:

    (a) registered charities which are housing associations;

    (b) societies registered under the Industrial and Provident Societies Act 1965 which are non profit making and established for the purpose of providing rented housing or hostels; or

(c) companies which are non profit making and established for the purpose of providing rented housing or hostels.

The Social Landlords (Permissible Additional Purposes or Objects) Order 1996 (S.I. 1996 No. 2256) adds to the permissible objects of social landlords under the Housing Act 1996, s.2.

Right to buy

New tenants of registered social landlords have the right to buy their dwelling if **3A–970** they are:

(a) secure or assured tenants (but *not* assured shorthold tenants); and

(b) the dwelling was provided with public money and has remained in the social rented sector; and

(c) the tenant satisfies the qualifying conditions under the Housing Act 1985, Pt V which sets out qualifying periods and exceptions, etc.

The procedure set out in Housing Act 1985, Pt V applies to tenants of registered social landlords, subject to any variations which may be set out in regulations made by the Secretary of State. The modifications are contained in the Housing (Right to Acquire) Regulations 1997 (S.I. 1997 No. 619). Sched.2 to the Regulations sets out the Housing Act 1985, Pt V as it applies to tenants of registered social landlords in full. The most important variation is a new Housing Act 1985, s.124A which provides that a registered social landlord which accepts that a tenant is entitled to exercise the right to buy may offer to make a disposal of an alternative dwelling house. Paragraph 40 of the Regulations provides that tenants of registered social landlords cannot exercise the right to buy if the dwelling house is:

• situated in a designated rural area;

• one of a group let to persons with special needs or who require intensive housing assistance; or

• charged with a debt which is equal to or greater than the purchase price plus discount.

The Regulations also exclude the right to buy on rent to mortgage terms and the preserved right to buy.

PART I

CHAPTER I

REGISTERED SOCIAL LANDLORDS

REGISTRATION

The register of social landlords

1.—(1) The Relevant Authority shall maintain a register of social **3A–971** landlords which shall be open to inspection at all reasonable times—

(1A) In this Part "the Relevant Authority" means the Housing Corporation or the Secretary of State, as provided by section 56.

(1B) The register maintained by the Housing Corporation shall be maintained at its head office.

Note—As amended by the Government of Wales Act 1998, Sched.16, paras 82 and **3A–972** 83 and Sched.18, Pt VI.

"housing association"

See s.230 which refers to the Housing Associations Act 1985 where s.1 defines a **3A–973** housing association as a "society, body of trustees or company (a) which is established for the purpose of, or amongst whose objects or powers are included those of, providing, constructing, improving or managing, or facilitating or encouraging the construction or improvement of, housing accommodation, and (b) which does not trade for profit or whose constitution or rules prohibit the issue of capital with interest or dividend exceeding such rate as may be prescribed by the treasury, whether with or without differentiation between share and loan capital".

Eligibility for registration

3A–974   **2.**—(1) A body is eligible for registration as a social landlord if it is—

(a) a registered charity which is a housing association,

(b) a society registered under the Industrial and Provident Societies Act 1965 which satisfies the conditions in subsection (2), or

(c) a company registered under the Companies Act 1985 which satisfies those conditions.

(2) The conditions are that the body is non-profit-making and is established for the purpose of, or has among its objects or powers, the provision, construction, improvement or management of—

(a) houses to be kept available for letting,

(b) houses for occupation by members of the body, where the rules of the body restrict membership to persons entitled or prospectively entitled (as tenants or otherwise) to occupy a house provided or managed by the body, or

(c) hostels,

and that any additional purposes or objects are among those specified in subsection (4).

(3) For the purposes of this section a body is non-profit-making if—

(a) it does not trade for profit, or

(b) its constitution or rules prohibit the issue of capital with interest or dividend exceeding the rate prescribed by the Treasury for the purposes of section 1(1)(b) of the Housing Associations Act 1985.

(4) The permissible additional purposes or objects are—

(a) providing land, amenities or services, or providing, constructing, repairing or improving buildings, for its residents, either exclusively or together with other persons;

(b) acquiring, or repairing and improving, or creating by the conversion of houses or other property, houses to be disposed of on sale, on lease or on shared ownership terms;

(c) constructing houses to be disposed of on shared ownership terms;

(d) managing houses held on leases or other lettings (not being houses within subsection (2)(a) or (b)) or blocks of flats;

(e) providing services of any description for owners or occupiers of houses in arranging or carrying out works of maintenance, repair or improvement, or encouraging or facilitating the carrying out of such works;

902

(f) encouraging and giving advice on the forming of housing associations or providing services for, and giving advice on the running of, such associations and other voluntary organisations concerned with housing, or matters connected with housing.

(5) A body is not ineligible for registration as a social landlord by reason only that its powers include power—

(a) to acquire commercial premises or businesses as an incidental part of a project or series of projects undertaken for purposes or objects falling within subsection (2) or (4);

(b) to repair, improve or convert commercial premises acquired as mentioned in paragraph (a) or to carry on for a limited period any business so acquired;

(c) to repair or improve houses, or buildings in which houses are situated, after a disposal of the houses by the body by way of sale or lease or on shared ownership terms.

(6) In this section—

"block of flats" means a building containing two or more flats which are held on leases or other lettings and which are occupied or intended to be occupied wholly or mainly for residential purposes;

"disposed of on shared ownership terms" means disposed of on a lease—

(a) granted on a payment of a premium calculated by reference to a percentage of the value of the house or of the cost of providing it, or

(b) under which the tenant (or his personal representatives) will or may be entitled to a sum calculated by reference directly or indirectly to the value of the house;

"letting" includes the grant of a licence to occupy;

"residents", in relation to a body, means persons occupying a house or hostel provided or managed by the body; and

"voluntary organisation" means an organisation whose activities are not carried on for profit.

(7) The Secretary of State may by order specify permissible purposes, objects or powers additional to those specified in subsections (4) and (5).

The order may (without prejudice to the inclusion of other incidental or supplementary provisions) contain such provision as the Secretary of State thinks fit with respect to the priority of mortgages entered into in pursuance of any additional purposes, objects or powers.

(8) An order under subsection (7) shall be made by statutory instrument which shall be subject to annulment in pursuance of a resolution of either House of Parliament.

"housing association"

See commentary to s.1.

3A–975

"registered charity"

3A–976   See s.58 which states that "charity" has the same meaning as under the Charities Act 1993 and that "registered charity" means a charity which is registered under s.3 of that Act and is not an exempt charity within the meaning of that Act.

"permissible purposes"

3A–977   See too the Social Landlords (Permissible Additional Purposes or Objects) Order 1996 (S.I. 1996 No. 2256); the Social Landlords (Additional Purposes or Objects) Order 1999 (S.I. 1999 No. 985); and the Social Landlords (Additional Purposes or Objects) (No. 2) Order 1999 (S.I. 1999 No. 1206).

"house"

3A–978   See s.63 which states that "'house' includes—(a) any part of a building occupied or intended to be occupied as a separate dwelling, and (b) any yard, garden, outhouses, and appurtenances belonging to it or usually enjoyed with it."

"hostel"

3A–979   See s.63 which states that "'hostel' means a building in which is provided for persons generally or for a class or classes of persons—(a) residential accommodation otherwise than in separate and self-contained premises, and (b) either board or facilities for the preparation of food adequate to the needs of those persons, or both."

PART III

* * * *

LANDLORD AND TENANT

CHAPTER I

TENANTS' RIGHTS

FORFEITURE

Restriction on termination of tenancy for failure to pay service charge

3A–980   **81.**—(1) A landlord may not, in relation to premises let as a dwelling, exercise a right of re-entry or forfeiture for failure by a tenant to pay a service charge or administartion charge unless—

    (a) it is finally determined by (or on appeal from) a leasehold valuation tribunal or by a court, or by an arbitral tribunal in proceedings pursuant to a post-dispute arbitration agreement, that the amount of the service charge or administration charge is payable by him, or

    (b) the tenant has admitted that it is so payable.

(2) The landlord may not exercise a right of re-entry or forfeiture by virtue of subsection (1)(a) until after the end of the period of 14 days beginning with the day after that on which the final determination is made.

(3) For the purposes of this section it is finally determined that the amount of a service charge or administration charge is payable—

    (a) if a decision that it is payable is not appealed against or otherwise challenged, at the end of the time for bringing an appeal or other challenge, or

    (b) if such a decision is appealed against or otherwise challenged and not set aside in consequence of the appeal or other challenge, at the time specified in subsection (3A).

(3A) The time referred to in subsection (3)(b) is the time when the appeal or other challenge is disposed of—

(a) by the determination of the appeal or other challenge and the expiry of the time for bringing a subsequent appeal (if any), or

(b) by its being abandoned or otherwise ceasing to have effect.

(4) The reference in subsection (1) to premises let as a dwelling does not include premises let on—

(a) a tenancy to which Part II of the Landlord and Tenant Act 1954 applies (business tenancies),

(b) a tenancy of an agricultural holding within the meaning of the Agricultural Holdings Act 1986 in relation to which that Act applies, or

(c) a farm business tenancy within the meaning of the Agricultural Tenancies Act 1995.

(4A) References in this section to the exercise of a right of re-entry or forfeiture include the service of a notice under section 146(1) of the Law of Property Act 1925 (restriction on re-entry or forfeiture).

(5) In this section—

(a) "administration charge" has the meaning given by Part 1 of Schedule 11 to the Commonhold and Leasehold Reform Act 2002,

(b) "arbitration agreement" and "arbitral tribunal" have the same meaning as in Part 1 of the Arbitration Act 1996 (c.23) and "post-dispute arbitration agreement", in relation to any matter, means an arbitration agreement made after a dispute about the matter has arisen,

(c) "dwelling" has the same meaning as in the Landlord and Tenant Act 1985 (c.70), and (d).

(5A) Any order of a court to give effect to a determination of a leasehold valuation tribunal shall be treated as a determination by the court for the purposes of this section.

(6) Nothing in this section affects the exercise of a right of re-entry or forfeiture on other grounds.

Note —This section was amended by Commonhold and Leasehold Reform Act 2002, s.170. Commonhold and Leasehold Reform Act 2002, s.172 provides that Housing Act 1996, s.81 applies in relation to Crown land as in relation to other land. The phrase "Crown land" is defined by Commonhold and Leasehold Reform Act 2002, s.172. That section was brought into force on September 30, 2003 by the Commonhold and Leasehold Reform Act (Commencement No. 2 and Savings) (England) Order 2003 (S.I. 2003 No. 1986) (c.82). The amendment was brought into force in England on February 28, 2005 by the Commonhold and Leasehold Reform Act 2002 (Commencement No.5 and Saving and Transitional Provision) Order 2004 (S.I. 2004 No. 3056) (C.127).   **3A–981**

"service charge"
See the Landlord and Tenant Act 1985, s.18, above.   **3A–982**

"arbitral tribunal"
See the Arbitration Act 1996, Pt I.   **3A–983**

"dwelling"

3A-984   See Landlord and Tenant Act 1985, s.38.

landlord, tenant, lease, tenancy

3A-985   see Landlord and Tenant Act 1985, s.36, para. 3A-608.

administration charge

see Sched. 11, Pt 1.

post-dispute arbitration agreement

see s.169(5). It means an arbitration agreement made after a breach has occurred (or is alleged to have occurred).

Restriction on termination of tenancy for failure to pay service charge

3A-986   Section 81 prevents landlords from exercising a right of re-entry or forfeiture of premises let as a dwelling for failure to pay service charges unless the amount claimed is either agreed or admitted by the lessee or has been determined by a court or an arbitral tribunal in accordance with the Arbitration Act 1996, Pt I. If the service charge has been determined by a court or tribunal, the landlord cannot commence forfeiture proceedings until 14 days after the determination. Section 82 provides that the Law of Property Act 1925, s.146 notices relating to arrears of service charges must refer to s.81 and state that s.81 has been complied with. "Service charge" has the same meaning as in the Landlord and Tenant Act 1985, s.18(1)—*i.e.* sums payable "directly or indirectly, for services, repairs, maintenance, improvements or insurance or the landlord's costs of management" and which vary according to the relevant costs. The aim of this provision was to prevent freeholders from pressurising lessees who have genuine disputes about service charges (or their mortgagees) into paying up rather than face forfeiture proceedings. It came into force on September 24, 1996 (Housing Act 1996, s.232(2)).

Courts are probably obliged to take s.81 into account even if it is not pleaded (*Mohammadi v. Anston Investments Ltd* [2003] EWCA Civ 981; [2004] H.L.R. 8).

In *Southwark LBC v. Tornaritis* [1999] 7 C.L.D. 330, Lambeth County Court, H.H.J. Cox held that an earlier default judgment in respect of service charge arrears was a "determination" within the meaning of Housing Act 1996, s.81. The phrase "determination by a court" does not require a judicial determination.

Section 81 has to be read in conjunction with the Landlord and Tenant Act 1985, s.19, as amended by the Housing Act 1996, s.83 which provides that lessors and lessees may apply to RACs sitting as Leasehold Valuation Tribunals (LVTs) to determine whether costs incurred for services, repairs, maintenance, etc. were reasonably incurred, whether such services or works were of a reasonable standard and whether sums payable by lessees before costs have been incurred are reasonable. There is a right of appeal to the Lands Tribunal, but only with the leave of the LVT or the Lands Tribunal (Housing Act 1996, s.83).

Notice under s.146 of the Law of Property Act 1925

3A-987   **82.**—(1) Nothing in section 81 (restriction on termination of tenancy for failure to pay service charge) affects the power of a landlord to serve a notice under section 146(1) of the Law of Property Act 1925 (restrictions on and relief against forfeiture: notice of breach of covenant or condition).

(2) But such a notice in respect of premises let as a dwelling and failure to pay a service charge is ineffective unless it complies with the following requirements.

(3) It must state that section 81 applies and set out the effect of subsection (1) of that section.

The Secretary of State may by regulations prescribe a form of words to be used for that purpose.

(4) The information or words required must be in characters not less conspicuous than those used in the notice—

(a) to indicate that the tenancy may be forfeited, or

(b) to specify the breach complained of

whichever is the more conspicuous.

(5) In this section "premises let as a dwelling" and "service charge" have the same meaning as in section 81.

(6) Regulations under this section—

(a) shall be made by statutory instrument, and

(b) may make different provision for different cases or classes of case including different areas.

"premises let as a dwelling"

See s.81(4).   **3A–988**

"service charge"

See commentary to s.81, and the Landlord and Tenant Act 1985, s.18.   **3A–989**

SERVICE CHARGES

* * * *

Right to appoint surveyor to advise on matters relating to service charges

84.—(1) A recognised tenants' association may appoint a surveyor **3A–990** for the purposes of this section to advise on any matters relating to, or which may give rise to, service charges payable to a landlord by one or more members of the association. The provisions of Schedule 4 have effect for conferring on a surveyor so appointed rights of access to documents and premises.

(2) A person shall not be so appointed unless he is a qualified surveyor.

For this purpose "qualified surveyor" has the same meaning as in section 78(4)(a) of the Leasehold Reform, Housing and Urban Development Act 1993 (persons qualified for appointment to carry out management audit).

(3) The appointment shall take effect for the purposes of this section upon notice in writing being given to the landlord by the association stating the name and address of the surveyor, the duration of his appointment and the matters in respect of which he is appointed.

(4) An appointment shall cease to have effect for the purposes of this section if the association gives notice in writing to the landlord to that effect or if the association ceases to exist.

(5) A notice is duly given under this section to a landlord of any tenants if it is given to a person who receives on behalf of the landlord the rent payable by those tenants; and a person to whom such a notice is so given shall forward it as soon as may be to the landlord.

(6) In this section—

"recognised tenants' association" has the same meaning as in the provisions of the Landlord and Tenant Act 1985 relating to service charges (see section 29 of that Act); and "service charge" means a service charge within the meaning of section 18(1) of that Act, other than one excluded from that section by section 27 of that Act (rent of dwelling registered and not entered as variable).

Application

3A–991   Commonhold and Leasehold Reform Act 2002, s.172 provides that Housing Act 1996, s.84 applies in relation to Crown land as in relation to other land. The phrase "Crown land" is defined by Commonhold and Leasehold Reform Act 2002, s.172. That section was brought into force on September 30, 2003 by the Commonhold and Leasehold Reform Act (Commencement No. 2 and Savings) (England) Order 2003 (S.I. 2003 No. 1986) (C.82).

"recognised tenants' association"

3A–992   See the Landlord and Tenant Act 1985, s.29 which refers to an association of qualifying tenants being recognised "either—(a) by a notice in writing given by the landlord to the secretary of the association, or (b) by a certificate of a member of the local rent assessment committee panel."

"service charge"

3A–993   See commentary to s.81 and the Landlord and Tenant Act 1985, s.18.

"qualified surveyor"

3A–994   See the Leasehold Reform, Housing and Urban Development Act 1993, s.78(4)(a) which states that a person is a "qualified surveyor" if "(a) ... he is a qualified surveyor; (b) he is not disqualified from acting within the meaning of the Landlord and Tenant Act 1985, s.28(1); and (c) he is not the tenant of any premises contained in the relevant premises." See also the Leasehold Reform, Housing and Urban Development Act 1993, s.78(5).

Schedule 4 gives such a surveyor the right to inspect documents and premises.

* * * * *

SUPPLEMENTARY

Jurisdiction of county courts

3A–995   **95.**—(1) Any jurisdiction expressed by a provision to which this section applies to be conferred on the court shall be exercised by a county court.

(2) There shall also be brought in a county court any proceedings for determining any question arising under or by virtue of any provision to which this section applies.

(3) Where, however, other proceedings are properly brought in the High Court, that court has jurisdiction to hear and determine proceedings to which subsection (1) or (2) applies which are joined with those proceedings.

(4) Where proceedings are brought in a county court by virtue of subsection (1) or (2), that court has jurisdiction to hear and determine other proceedings joined with those proceedings despite the fact that they would otherwise be outside its jurisdiction.

(5) The provisions to which this section applies are—

  (a) section 81 (restriction on termination of tenancy for failure to pay service charge), and

  (b) section 84 (right to appoint surveyor to advise on matters relating to service charges) and Schedule 4 (rights exercisable by surveyor appointed by tenants' association).

* * * *

PART V

CONDUCT OF TENANTS

CHAPTER I

INTRODUCTORY TENANCIES

GENERAL PROVISIONS

Introductory tenancies

124.—(1) A local housing authority or a housing action trust may
elect to operate an introductory tenancy regime.

(2) When such an election is in force, every periodic tenancy of a
dwelling-house entered into or adopted by the authority or trust
shall, if it would otherwise be a secure tenancy, be an introductory
tenancy, unless immediately before the tenancy was entered into or
adopted the tenant or, in the case of joint tenants, one or more of
them was—

    (a) a secure tenant of the same or another dwelling-house,
       or

    (b) an assured tenant of a registered social landlord (other-
       wise than under an assured shorthold tenancy) in re-
       spect of the same or another dwelling-house.

(3) Subsection (2) does not apply to a tenancy entered into or
adopted in pursuance of a contract made before the election was
made.

(4) For the purposes of this Chapter a periodic tenancy is adopted
by a person if that person becomes the landlord under the tenancy,
whether on a disposal or surrender of the interest of the former
landlord.

(5) An election under this section may be revoked at any time,
without prejudice to the making of a further election.

"local housing authority"

    See s.230 which refers to Housing Act 1985 (see the Housing Act 1985, ss.1 and 2
above).

"housing action trust"

    See s.230 which refers to the Housing Act 1988. See the Housing Act 1985, s.4
above.

"dwelling house"

    See s.139.

"secure tenant"

    See s.230 which refers to the Housing Act 1985, Pt IV. See the Housing Act 1985,
s.79 above.

"assured tenant"

    See s.230 which refers to the Housing Act 1988, Pt I. See the Housing Act 1988, s.1
above.

3A–996

3A–997

3A–998

3A–999

3A–1000

3A–1001

HOUSING

"assured shorthold tenancy"

3A–1002   See s.230 which refers to the Housing Act 1988, Pt I. See the Housing Act 1988, ss.19A and 20 above.

Introductory tenancies

3A–1003   Introductory tenancies are a form of probationary tenancy granted by some local authorities lacking security of tenure within the first year of the tenancy. Housing Act 1985, Sched.1, para. 1A provides that introductory tenancies cannot be secure tenancies (Housing Act 1996, Sched.14, para. 5).

Section 124 provides that "a local housing authority or housing action trust (HAT) may elect to operate an introductory tenancy regime". The Department of the Environment's Circular on Introductory Tenancies (2/97) suggests that local authorities should consult with existing tenants in accordance with the Housing Act 1985, s.105 before setting up an introductory tenancy regime (para. 6). Where such an election is made, all new periodic tenancies and licences (Housing Act 1996, s.126) which would otherwise be secure tenancies will be introductory tenancies or licences unless immediately before the new tenancy, one or more of the tenants was either a secure tenant or an assured tenant of a registered social landlord. Tenancies remain introductory tenancies until the end of the "trial period" which lasts for one year after the date on which the tenancy was entered into, or the date on which the tenant was first entitled to possession, whichever is later. Earlier periods when the tenant had another introductory tenancy or had an assured shorthold tenancy granted by a registered social landlord count towards the trial period provided that there is no gap between them.

Tenancies cease to be introductory tenancies if:

- the circumstances are such that the tenancy could not be secure; or
- a person or body other than a local housing authority or HAT becomes the landlord; or
- the election is revoked; or
- the tenant dies and there is no-one qualified to succeed (Housing Act 1996, ss.125 and 133(3)).

The Department of the Environment's Circular on Introductory Tenancies (2/97) suggests that landlords should ensure "that introductory tenancies can never be used as a weapon against vulnerable individuals and ensure that there are safeguards to protect such tenants...[They] must be vigilant to ensure that neighbours are not able to make a case for eviction against a vulnerable tenant whose behaviour may be different through no fault of their own (paras 9 and 11)". Where there are vulnerable tenants, they should liaise with social services and should have arrangements "for automatic notification to social services at an early stage once any problems arise (para. 12)". The Circular also states that "eviction is not necessarily appropriate when problems arise between a vulnerable tenant and neighbours (para. 14)" and that "landlords should have fair and rigorous procedures in place to investigate complaints against tenants (para. 19)." The local authority associations have produced comprehensive good practice guidance on running an introductory regime which should be read in conjunction with the circular.

Landlords may only bring introductory tenancies to an end by obtaining a possession order in court (Housing Act 1996, s.127). Before bringing proceedings landlords must serve notices giving reasons for the decision to seek a possession order and specifying a date after which court proceedings may be begun. The notice given must be equivalent to that which would otherwise be needed to terminate the tenancy by notice to quit. It must also inform tenants of their right to "request a review of the landlord's decision" and that they may seek advice from a CAB, housing aid centre, law centre or solicitor (Housing Act 1996, s.128). The circular states:

"As good practice landlords should include a full statement of the reasons for seeking possession which could include a case history of the sequence of events (para. 16)."

Where a landlord serves a Housing Act 1996, s.128 notice based upon the arrears, but then also relies upon allegations of nuisance, the correct procedure is normally for the landlord to serve an additional notice. However in a case where the tenant had not suffered any prejudice, and the same decision would have been reached, even without the allegations of nuisance, a tenant's challenge to the review process was dismissed (*R.(Laporte) v. Newham LBC* [2004] EWHC 227 (Admin); [2004] 2 All ER 874).

"The precise way in which a landlord chooses to conduct...a review is for each landlord to determine" (DoE Circular: 2/97, para. 22)." However, the Introductory Tenants (Review) Regulations 1997 (S.I. 1997 No. 72) set out certain basic requirements to be followed on reviews. Reviews are not to be by way of a hearing unless tenants inform their landlords that they wish to have an oral hearing (para. 2). A request for an oral hearing must be made within 14 days after receipt of the notice seeking possession. Reviews must be carried out by a person who was not involved in the original decision to seek possession (para. 3). If the review is not to be conducted by an oral hearing, the tenant may make written representations (para. 4). If there is an oral hearing, the tenant has a right to:

(a) be heard and accompanied or represented by another person;

(b) call persons to give evidence;

(c) put questions to anyone who gives evidence; and

(d) make representations in writing (para. 5).

The tenant must be notified of the time, date and place of any hearing. It must take place not less than five days after the request for a hearing (para. 6). The Regulations do not, however, specify a minimum period between notification of the date of the hearing and the hearing itself.

The review must be carried out and the tenant notified of the result before the date specified as the date after which proceedings may be begun.

If a landlord serves a notice which expires and then brings proceedings against an introductory tenant, the court must make a possession order. It is not necessary for the landlord to give evidence about the reason for seeking possession. All that is necessary is to prove that notice was served and that any review has been determined or that the period specified in the notice has expired (s.127). "Suspended possession orders ... are not appropriate for introductory tenancies. Applications to court for possession must lead to eviction" (DoE, para 20).

See too *Manchester City Council v. Cochrane* [1999] 1 W.L.R. 809, CA where the Court of Appeal held that the word "shall" in s.127(2) means that once the requirements of s.128 have been complied with, the county court has no discretion but to make an order for possession.

In a case where a landlord served a s.128 notice, but then told the tenant that proceedings would not be issued if she cleared the arrears at a rate of £3 per week, the Court of Appeal held that there was no requirement to give a further or second notice when the arrears started to increase again. Housing Act 1996, s.127 imposes a mandatory duty on the court to grant possession if "a" notice has been served in compliance with s.128. A requirement to serve a further notice would introduce unnecessary formality and might deter an authority from taking a humane "wait and see" approach before issuing proceedings. *Cardiff City Council v. Stone* [2002] EWCA Civ 298; [2003] H.L.R. 47, CA. However, for a case where there was in reality a decision to reverse or quash the original decision, albeit with a warning about future conduct, see *Forbes v. Lambeth LBC* [2003] EWHC 222 (Admin); [2003] H.L.R. 49. Crane J. stated that where the reasons for a decision have changed, the tenant ought at least to be given an opportunity to seek a review, not only to question the alleged facts, but also, crucially, to argue that it was not reasonable to require possession. If that were not done, the scheme of the Act would not be ECHR compliant.

The Act is silent as to the methods by which tenants may challenge review decisions. This is not dealt with in the Introductory Tenancies (Review) Regulations either and so tenants' only redress if they are dissatisfied with a review decision is to apply for judicial review. In view of the decisions in *Manchester CC v. Cochrane* [1999] 1 W.L.R. 809, CA, and *Avon CC v. Buscott* [1988] Q.B. 656; [1988] 1 All E.R. 841, CA, county courts hearing subsequent possession proceedings cannot hear public law defences based upon tenants' complaints about the review procedure or decisions. The private law rights of tenants under introductory tenancies are no more than a right to remain in possession until an order for possession is made. In such cases, tenants have to apply for the possession proceedings to be adjourned pending determination of their applications for judicial review.

In determining whether proceedings are started before the end of the trial period, proceedings are started by the issue of the claim form by the court (CPR, r.7.2 and PD7, para 5.1), not when the claim form is received by the court (*Salford City Council v. Garner* [2004] EWCA Civ 364; [2004] H.L.R. 35). If the "trial period" ends before determination of the possession proceedings, the tenancy will remain an introductory tenancy until the determination of proceedings or the date on which possession is to be given up, whichever is later (s.130(2)).

Although introductory tenants lack security of tenure, the Act gives them some rights which are equivalent to those of secure tenants, *e.g.* succession (Housing Act 1996, ss.131–133 and 140) and information and consultation (ss.136–137). The right to repair scheme (Housing Act 1985, s.96) has been extended to introductory tenancies by the Secure Tenancies (Right to Repair) (Amendment) Regulations 1997 (S.I. 1997 No. 73). Assignment of introductory tenancies is in general prohibited although they may be transferred by orders made under the Matrimonial Causes Act 1973, s.24, the Matrimonial and Family Proceedings Act 1984, the Children Act 1989, Sched.1 and to a person who would be qualified to succeed the tenant if the tenant died immediately before the assignment (Housing Act 1996, s.134).

The provisions relating to introductory tenancies were brought into force on February 12, 1997 by the Housing Act 1996 (Commencement No. 6 and Savings) Order 1997 (S.I. 1997 No. 66).

Introductory tenants and the Human Rights Act 1998

3A–1004   In *R. (McLellan) v. Bracknell Forest DC* [2001] EWCA Civ 1510; [2002] Q.B. 1129; [2002] 2 W.L.R. 1448; [2002] 1 All E.R. 899, the Court of Appeal held that:

(1) Eviction of an introductory tenant falls within ECHR Art.8(1) (*Lambeth LBC v. Howard* (2001) 33 HR 58, CA). Accordingly it is necessary to consider under Art.8(2) whether an eviction is in accordance with the law and whether it is necessary for the protection of the rights of others. A tenant under an introductory tenancy has the right to raise the question whether it is reasonable in the particular case to insist on eviction, i.e. whether the eviction can be justified under Art.8(2) (*Donoghue v. Poplar HARCA* [2001] EWCA Civ 595 also reported as *Poplar HARCA v. Donoghue* [2002] Q.B. 48; [2001] 3 W.L.R. 183; [2001] 4 All E.R. 606, and Human Rights Act 1998 s.7(1)(b)). The review procedure taken together with the availability of judicial review provides adequate protection. Section 127 does not prevent tenants from relying on Convention rights if the procedure in *Manchester City Council v. Cochrane* [1999] 1 W.L.R. 809 is followed. The fact that the tenant has failed to seek judicial review of the decision to seek possession does not deprive the county court of the power to consider whether there is arguably a breach of the Convention and to adjourn if necessary. Therefore the introductory tenancy scheme is not as such incompatible with Art 8 and there is no reason to think that individuals' rights will be infringed without remedy from the courts. If the pace of eviction is too fast the court may grant a limited extension of time under Housing Act 1980, s.89(1). Section 89 is not itself incompatible with Art.8.

(2) The decision of the review panel involves the determination of an introductory tenant's civil rights and so ECHR Art 6 is engaged. However the combination of the review panel plus judicial review is enough to meet the requirements of Art. 6. There is no requirement that a council must be satisfied that there has been a breach of the terms of the tenancy before serving notice - the question is whether, in the light of allegation and counter-allegation, it was reasonable for the council to take a decision to proceed with termination of the tenancy. There is no reason to believe that the review procedure will not be operated fairly, nor any reason to believe that judicial review will not provide an adequate safeguard to tenants enabling them to challenge any unfairness or infringement of their Convention rights, bearing in mind that the courts will "examine the decision maker's actions more rigorously" where a discretionary power is liable to interfere with fundamental human rights. Where a review has taken place it should be the norm for the council to set out in an affidavit before the county court how the review procedure was operated in each case so that the court has the necessary information to decide whether to adjourn pending an application for judicial review.

In *Merton LBC v. Williams* [2002] EWCA Civ 980; [2003] H.L.R. 20, the Court of Appeal confirmed (following *McLellan*) that county courts hearing possession claims against introductory tenants have a general duty to consider the procedure that has been followed and to ensure that it complies both with the statutory procedure and the tenant's rights under the ECHR—although in the instant case a possession order should have been made because was no realistic prospect that any judicial review proceedings would succeed. See though *Harrow LBC v. Qazi* [2003] UKHL 43; [2003] 3 W.L.R. 79 where Lord Hope and Lord Scott said that contractual and property rights cannot be defeated by a defence based on Art.8. Note that in *Harrow LBC v.*

Qazi [2003] UKHL 43; [2003] 3 W.L.R. 79, Lord Scott also stated that *McLellan* was correctly decided, but for the wrong reason.

Duration of introductory tenancy

125.—(1) A tenancy remains an introductory tenancy until the end **3A–1005** of the trial period, unless one of the events mentioned in subsection (5) occurs before the end of that period.

(2) The "trial period" is the period of one year beginning with—

    (a) in the case of a tenancy which was entered into by a local housing authority or housing action trust—

        (i) the date on which the tenancy was entered into, or

        (ii) if later, the date on which a tenant was first entitled to possession under the tenancy; or

    (b) in the case of a tenancy which was adopted by a local housing authority or housing action trust, the date of adoption;

    but this is subject to subsections (3) and (4) and to section 125A (extension of trial period by 6 months).

(3) Where the tenant under an introductory tenancy was formerly a tenant under another introductory tenancy, or held an assured shorthold tenancy from a registered social landlord, any period or periods during which he was such a tenant shall count towards the trial period, provided—

    (a) if there was one such period, it ended immediately before the date specified in subsection (2), and

    (b) if there was more than one such period, the most recent period ended immediately before that date and each period succeeded the other without interruption.

(4) Where there are joint tenants under an introductory tenancy, the reference in subsection (3) to the tenant shall be construed as referring to the joint tenant in whose case the application of that subsection produces the earliest starting date for the trial period.

(5) A tenancy ceases to be an introductory tenancy if, before the end of the trial period—

    (a) the circumstances are such that the tenancy would not otherwise be a secure tenancy,

    (b) a person or body other than a local housing authority or housing action trust becomes the landlord under the tenancy,

    (c) the election in force when the tenancy was entered into or adopted is revoked, or

    (d) the tenancy ceases to be an introductory tenancy by virtue of section 133(3)(succession).

(6) A tenancy does not come to an end merely because it ceases to be an introductory tenancy, but a tenancy which has once ceased to be an introductory tenancy cannot subsequently become an introductory tenancy.

(7) This section has effect subject to section 130 (effect of beginning proceedings for possession).

3A-1005.1 Section 125(2) was amended by Housing Act 2004 s.179 which provides for the extension of the trial period. It was brought into force in England on 6 June 2005 by the Housing Act 2004 (Commencement No.3) (England) Order 2005 (S.I. 2005 No. 1451). There will be a separate commencement order for Wales. Note that amendment made by Housing Act 2004 s.179 does not apply in relation to any tenancy entered into before, or in pursuance of an agreement made before, the day on which this section comes into force (s.179(4)).

Duration of introductory tenancy

3A-1006 See commentary to s.124.

"introductory tenancy"

3A-1007 See s.124.

"local housing authority"

3A-1008 See s.230 which refers to the Housing Act 1985 (see the Housing Act 1985, ss.1 and 2 above).

"housing action trust"

3A-1009 See s.230 which refers to the Housing Act 1988. See the Housing Act 1985, s.4 above.

"dwelling house"

3A-1010 See s.139.

"secure tenant"

3A-1011 See s.230 which refers to the Housing Act 1985, Pt IV. See the Housing Act 1985, s.79 above.

"assured tenant"

3A-1012 See s.230 which refers to the Housing Act 1988, Pt I. See the Housing Act 1988, s.1 above.

"assured shorthold tenancy"

3A-1013 See s.230 which refers to the Housing Act 1988, Pt I. See the Housing Act 1988, ss.19A and 20 above.

"registered social landlord"

3A-1014 See s.1.

Extension of trial period by 6 months

3A-1014.1 **125A.**—(1) If both of the following conditions are met in relation to an introductory tenancy, the trial period is extended by 6 months.

(2) The first condition is that the landlord has served a notice of extension on the tenant at least 8 weeks before the original expiry date.

(3) The second condition is that either—

    (a) the tenant has not requested a review under section 125B in accordance with subsection (1) of that section, or

    (b) if he has, the decision on the review was to confirm the landlord's decision to extend the trial period.

(4) A notice of extension is a notice—

    (a) stating that the landlord has decided that the period for which the tenancy is to be an introductory tenancy should be extended by 6 months, and

    (b) complying with subsection (5).

(5) A notice of extension must—

(a) set out the reasons for the landlord's decision, and

(b) inform the tenant of his right to request a review of the landlord's decision and of the time within which such a request must be made.

(6) In this section and section 125B "the original expiry date" means the last day of the period of one year that would apply as the trial period apart from this section.

This section was inserted by Housing Act 2004 s.179 . It provides for the extension **3A–1014.2** of the trial period. It was brought into force in England on 6 June 2005 by the Housing Act 2004 (Commencement No.3) (England) Order 2005 (S.I. 2005 No. 1451). The section does not apply to any tenancy entered into before, or in pursuance of an agreement made before that date: Housing Act 2004, s.179(4). There will be a separate commencement order for Wales.

trial period

See s.125(2). **3A–1014.3**

review

See s.125B. **3A–1014.4**

Review of decision to extend trial period

125B.—(1) A request for review of the landlord's decision that the **3A–1014.5** trial period for an introductory tenancy should be extended under section 125A must be made before the end of the period of 14 days beginning with the day on which the notice of extension is served.

(2) On a request being duly made to it, the landlord shall review its decision.

(3) The Secretary of State may make provision by regulations as to the procedure to be followed in connection with a review under this section.

Nothing in the following provisions affects the generality of this power.

(4) Provision may be made by regulations—

(a) requiring the decision on review to be made by a person of appropriate seniority who was not involved in the original decision, and

(b) as to the circumstances in which the person concerned is entitled to an oral hearing, and whether and by whom he may be represented at such a hearing.

(5) The landlord shall notify the tenant of the decision on the review.

If the decision is to confirm the original decision, the landlord shall also notify him of the reasons for the decision.

(6) The review shall be carried out and the tenant notified before the original expiry date.

This section was inserted by Housing Act 2004 s.179. It was brought into force in **3A–1014.6** England on 6 June 2005 by the Housing Act 2004 (Commencement No.3) (England) Order 2005 (S.I. 2005 No. 1451).The section does not apply to any tenancy entered into before, or in pursuance of an agreement made before that date: Housing Act 2004, s.179(4). There will be a separate commencement order for Wales.

regulations

At present there are no regulations. **3A–1014.7**

HOUSING

the original expiry date

3A–1014.8   See s.125A(6).

Licences

3A–1015   **126.**—(1) The provisions of this Chapter apply in relation to a licence to occupy a dwelling-house (whether or not granted for a consideration) as they apply in relation to a tenancy.

(2) Subsection (1) does not apply to a licence granted as a temporary expedient to a person who entered the dwelling-house or any other land as a trespasser (whether or not, before the grant of that licence, another licence to occupy that or another dwelling-house had been granted to him).

Licences

3A–1016   See commentary to s.124.

"dwelling house"

3A–1017   See s.139.

"temporary expedient"

3A–1018   *cf.* Housing Act 1985, s.79(4).

PROCEEDINGS FOR POSSESSION

Proceedings for possession

3A–1019   **127.**—(1) The landlord may only bring an introductory tenancy to an end by obtaining an order of the court for the possession of the dwelling-house.

(2) The court shall make such an order unless the provisions of section 128 apply.

(3) Where the court makes such an order, the tenancy comes to an end on the date on which the tenant is to give up possession in pursuance of the order.

Proceedings for possession

3A–1020   See commentary to s.124 and *Manchester City Council v. Cochrane* [1999] 1 W.L.R. 809, CA.

"dwelling house"

3A–1021   See s.139.

Notice of proceedings for possession

3A–1022   **128.**—(1) The court shall not entertain proceedings for the possession of a dwelling-house let under an introductory tenancy unless the landlord has served on the tenant a notice of proceedings complying with this section.

(2) The notice shall state that the court will be asked to make an order for the possession of the dwelling-house.

(3) The notice shall set out the reasons for the landlord's decision to apply for such an order.

(4) The notice shall specify a date after which proceedings for the possession of the dwelling-house may be begun.

The date so specified must not be earlier than the date on which the tenancy could, apart from this Chapter, be brought to an end by notice to quit given by the landlord on the same date as the notice of proceedings.

(5) The court shall not entertain any proceedings for possession of the dwelling-house unless they are begun after the date specified in the notice of proceedings.

(6) The notice shall inform the tenant of his right to request a review of the landlord's decision to seek an order for possession and of the time within which such a request must be made.

(7) The notice shall also inform the tenant that if he needs help or advice about the notice, and what to do about it, he should take it immediately to a Citizens' Advice Bureau, a housing aid centre, a law centre or a solicitor.

Notice of proceedings of possession
See commentary to s.124.   3A–1023

"dwelling house"
See s.139.   3A–1024

"introductory tenancy"
See s.124.   3A–1025

Review of decision to seek possession

129.—(1) A request for review of the landlord's decision to seek an   3A–1026
order for possession of a dwelling-house let under an introductory tenancy must be made before the end of the period of 14 days beginning with the day on which the notice of proceedings is served.

(2) On a request being duly made to it, the landlord shall review its decision.

(3) The Secretary of State may make provision by regulations as to the procedure to be followed in connection with a review under this section.

Nothing in the following provisions affects the generality of this power.

(4) Provision may be made by regulations—
  (a) requiring the decision on review to be made by a person of appropriate seniority who was not involved in the original decision, and
  (b) as to the circumstances in which the person concerned is entitled to an oral hearing, and whether and by whom he may be represented at such a hearing.

(5) The landlord shall notify the person concerned of the decision on the review.

If the decision is to confirm the original decision, the landlord shall also notify him of the reasons for the decision.

(6) The review shall be carried out and the tenant notified before the date specified in the notice of proceedings as the date after which proceedings for the possession of the dwelling-house may be begun.

Review of decision to seek possession
See commentary to s.124.   3A–1027

"dwelling house"

3A–1028   See s.139.

"introductory tenancy"

3A–1029   See s.124.

"regulations"

3A–1030   See The Introductory Tenants (Review) Regulations 1997 (S.I. 1997 No. 72).

Effect of beginning proceedings for possession

3A–1031   **130.**—(1) This section applies where the landlord has begun proceedings for the possession of a dwelling-house let under an introductory tenancy and—

> (a) the trial period ends, or
>
> (b) any of the events specified in section 125(5) occurs (events on which a tenancy ceases to be an introductory tenancy).

(2) Subject to the following provisions, the tenancy remains an introductory tenancy until—

> (a) the tenancy comes to an end in pursuance of section 127(3) (that is, on the date on which the tenant is to give up possession in pursuance of an order of the court), or
>
> (b) the proceedings are otherwise finally determined.

(3) If any of the events specified in section 125(5)(b) to (d) occurs, the tenancy shall thereupon cease to be an introductory tenancy but—

> (a) the landlord (or, as the case may be, the new landlord) may continue the proceedings, and
>
> (b) if he does so, section 127(2) and (3) (termination by landlord) apply as if the tenancy had remained an introductory tenancy.

(4) Where in accordance with subsection (3) a tenancy ceases to be an introductory tenancy and becomes a secure tenancy, the tenant is not entitled to exercise the right to buy under Part V of the Housing Act 1985 unless and until the proceedings are finally determined on terms such that he is not required to give up possession of the dwelling-house.

(5) For the purposes of this section proceedings shall be treated as finally determined if they are withdrawn or any appeal is abandoned or the time for appealing expires without an appeal being brought.

Effect of beginning proceedings for possession

3A–1032   See commentary to s.124.

"dwelling house"

3A–1033   See s.139.

"introductory tenancy"

3A–1034   See s.124.

"trial period"

3A–1035   See s.125(2).

* * * *

Jurisdiction of county court

138.—(1) A county court has jurisdiction to determine questions **3A–1036**
arising under this Chapter and to entertain proceedings brought
under this Chapter and claims, for whatever amount, in connection
with an introductory tenancy.

(2) That jurisdiction includes jurisdiction to entertain proceedings as to whether a statement supplied in pursuance of section
136(2)(b) (written statement of certain terms of tenancy) is accurate
notwithstanding that no other relief is sought than a declaration.

(3) If a person takes proceedings in the High Court which, by
virtue of this section, he could have taken in the county court, he is
not entitled to recover any costs.

(4) The Lord Chancellor may make such rules and give such
directions as he thinks fit for the purpose of giving effect to this
section.

(5) The rules and directions may provide—
> (a) for the exercise by a district judge of a county court of
> any jurisdiction exercisable under this section, and
> (b) for the conduct of proceedings in private.

(6) The power to make rules is exercisable by statutory instrument which shall be subject to annulment in pursuance of a resolution of either House of Parliament.

Meaning of "dwelling-house"

139.—(1) For the purposes of this Chapter a dwelling-house may **3A–1037**
be a house or a part of a house.

(2) Land let together with a dwelling-house shall be treated for
the purposes of this Chapter as part of the dwelling-house unless the
land is agricultural land which would not be treated as part of a
dwelling-house for the purposes of Part IV of the Housing Act 1985
(see section 112(2) of that Act).

* * * *

Members of a person's family: Chapter I

140.—(1) A person is a member of another's family within the **3A–1038**
meaning of this Chapter if—
> (a) he is the spouse of that person, or he and that person
> live together as husband and wife, or
> (b) he is that person's parent, grandparent, child, grand-
> child, brother, sister, uncle, aunt, nephew or niece.

(2) For the purpose of subsection (1)(b)—
> (a) a relationship by marriage shall be treated as a relation-
> ship by blood,
> (b) a relationship of the half-blood shall be treated as a rela-
> tionship of the whole blood, and

(c) the stepchild of a person shall be treated as his child.

3A–1038.1 *Note* —This section has been amended by the Civil Partnership Act 2004, s.81 and Sched.8. The amendment is not yet in force, but is printed at para. 3A–1525.

CHAPTER 1A

DEMOTED TENANCIES

GENERAL PROVISIONS

Demoted tenancies

3A–1039 **143A.**—(1) This section applies to a periodic tenancy of a dwelling-house if each of the following conditions is satisfied.

(2) The first condition is that the landlord is either a local housing authority or a housing action trust.

(3) The second condition is that the tenant condition in section 81 of the Housing Act 1985 is satisfied.

(4) The third condition is that the tenancy is created by virtue of a demotion order under section 82A of that Act.

(5) In this Chapter—

> (a) a tenancy to which this section applies is referred to as a demoted tenancy;
>
> (b) references to demoted tenants must be construed accordingly.

Editorial note

3A–1040 This section was inserted by Anti-social Behaviour Act 2003, s.14(5) and Sched. 1. It was brought into force in England on June 30, 2004 by the Anti-social Behaviour Act 2003 (Commencement No.3 and Savings) Order 2004 (S.I. 2004 No. 1502) (C.61). It was brought into force in Wales on 30 April 2005 by the Anti-social Behaviour Act 2003 (Commencement No.4) (Wales) Order 2005 (S.I. 2005 No. 1225) (W.83) (C.55).

Demoted tenancies lack security of tenure. If the landlord follows the procedure set out in Housing Act 1996, s.143E and F, the court must make an order for possession (see Housing Act 1996, s.143D).

dwelling house

3A–1041 See s.143O which provides that a dwelling house may be a house or a part of a house and that land let together with a dwelling-house must be treated for as part of the dwelling-house unless the land is agricultural land which would not be treated as part of a dwelling-house for the purposes of Housing Act 1985 Part 4.

Local housing authority

3A–1042 See Housing Act 1996, s.230 and Housing Act 1985, ss.1 and 2(2).

Housing action trust

3A–1043 See Housing Act 1996, s.230 and Housing Act 1988, Part III.

Tenant condition

3A–1044 See Housing Act 1985, s.81.

Duration of demoted tenancy

3A–1045 **143B.**—(1) A demoted tenancy becomes a secure tenancy at the end of the period of one year (the demotion period) starting with the day the demotion order takes effect; but this is subject to subsections (2) to (5).

(2) A tenancy ceases to be a demoted tenancy if any of the following paragraphs applies—

> (a) either of the first or second conditions in section 143A ceases to be satisfied;
>
> (b) the demotion order is quashed;
>
> (c) the tenant dies and no one is entitled to succeed to the tenancy.

(3) If at any time before the end of the demotion period the landlord serves a notice of proceedings for possession of the dwelling-house subsection (4) applies.

(4) The tenancy continues as a demoted tenancy until the end of the demotion period or (if later) until any of the following occurs—

> (a) the notice of proceedings is withdrawn by the landlord;
>
> (b) the proceedings are determined in favour of the tenant;
>
> (c) the period of 6 months beginning with the date on which the notice is served ends and no proceedings for possession have been brought.

(5) A tenancy does not come to an end merely because it ceases to be a demoted tenancy.

Editorial note

This section was inserted by Anti-social Behaviour Act 2003, s.14(5) and Sched. 1. It **3A–1046** was brought into force in England on June 30, 2004 by the Anti-social Behaviour Act 2003 (Commencement No.3 and Savings) Order 2004 (S.I. 2004 No. 1502) (C.61). It was brought into force in Wales on 30 April 2005 by the Anti-social Behaviour Act 2003 (Commencement No.4) (Wales) Order 2005 (S.I. 2005 No. 1225) (W.83) (C.55).

Secure tenancy

See Housing Act 1985, s.79. **3A–1047**

Demoted tenancy

See Housing Act 1985, s.82A and s.143A, above. This section only applies to former **3A–1048** secure tenancies while the tenant condition (see Housing Act 1985, s.81) continues to apply. Demoted tenancies lack security of tenure. If the landlord follows the procedure set out in Housing Act 1996, ss.143E and F, the court must make an order for possession (see Housing Act 1996, s.143D).

Change of landlord

143C.—(1) A tenancy continues to be a demoted tenancy for the **3A–1049** duration of the demotion period if—

> (a) at the time the demoted tenancy is created the interest of the landlord belongs to a local housing authority or a housing action trust, and
>
> (b) during the demotion period the interest of the landlord transfers to another person who is a local housing authority or a housing action trust.

(2) Subsections (3) and (4) apply if—

> (a) at the time the demoted tenancy is created the interest of the landlord belongs to a local housing authority or a housing action trust, and
>
> (b) during the demotion period the interest of the landlord transfers to a person who is not such a body.

(3) If the new landlord is a registered social landlord or a person who does not satisfy the landlord condition the tenancy becomes an assured shorthold tenancy.

(4) If the new landlord is not a registered social landlord and does satisfy the landlord condition the tenancy becomes a secure tenancy.

(5) The landlord condition must be construed in accordance with section 80 of the Housing Act 1985.

Editorial note

3A–1050   This section was inserted by Anti-social Behaviour Act 2003, s.14(5) and Sched. 1. It was brought into force in England on June 30, 2004 by the Anti-social Behaviour Act 2003 (Commencement No.3 and Savings) Order 2004 (S.I. 2004 No. 1502) (C.61). It was brought into force in Wales on 30 April 2005 by the Anti-social Behaviour Act 2003 (Commencement No.4) (Wales) Order 2005 (S.I. 2005 No. 1225) (W.83) (C.55).

Registered social landlord

3A–1051   See Housing Act 1996, s.230 referring back to Part I (ss.1 to 3).

Local housing authority

3A–1052   See Housing Act 1996, s.230 and Housing Act 1985, ss.1 and 2(2).

Housing action trust

3A–1053   See Housing Act 1996, s.230 and Housing Act 1988, Part III.

Demoted tenancy

3A–1054   See Housing Act 1985, s.82A and s.143A, above. This section only applies to former secure tenancies while the tenant condition (see Housing Act 1985, s.81) continues to apply.

Secure tenancy

3A–1055   See Housing Act 1985, s.79.

Landlord condition

3A–1056   See Housing Act 1985, s.80 and the commentary at para. 3A–346.

Assured shorthold tenancy

3A–1057   See Housing Act 1988, ss.19A and 20.

PROCEEDINGS FOR POSSESSION

Proceedings for possession

3A–1058   **143D.**—(1) The landlord may only bring a demoted tenancy to an end by obtaining an order of the court for possession of the dwelling-house.

(2) The court must make an order for possession unless it thinks that the procedure under sections 143E and 143F has not been followed.

(3) If the court makes such an order the tenancy comes to an end on the date on which the tenant is to give up possession in pursuance of the order.

Editorial note

3A–1059   This section was inserted by Anti-social Behaviour Act 2003, s.14(5) and Sched. 1. It was brought into force in England on June 30, 2004 by the Anti-social Behaviour Act 2003 (Commencement No.3 and Savings) Order 2004 (S.I. 2004 No. 1502) (C.61). It was brought into force in Wales on 30 April 2005 by the Anti-social Behaviour Act 2003 (Commencement No.4) (Wales) Order 2005 (S.I. 2005 No. 1225) (W.83) (C.55).

Demoted tenancy

See Housing Act 1985, s.82A and s.143A, above. This section only applies to former **3A–1060** secure tenancies while the tenant condition (see Housing Act 1985, s.81) continues to apply.

Notice of proceedings for possession

143E.—(1) Proceedings for possession of a dwelling-house let **3A–1061** under a demoted tenancy must not be brought unless the landlord has served on the tenant a notice of proceedings under this section.

(2) The notice must—

(a) state that the court will be asked to make an order for the possession of the dwelling-house;

(b) set out the reasons for the landlord's decision to apply for the order;

(c) specify the date after which proceedings for the possession of the dwelling-house may be begun;

(d) inform the tenant of his right to request a review of the landlord's decision and of the time within which the request must be made.

(3) The date specified under subsection (2)(c) must not be earlier than the date on which the tenancy could (apart from this Chapter) be brought to an end by notice to quit given by the landlord on the same date as the notice of proceedings.

(4) The court must not entertain proceedings begun on or before the date specified under subsection (2)(c).

(5) The notice must also inform the tenant that if he needs help or advice—

(a) about the notice, or

(b) about what to do about the notice,

he must take the notice immediately to a Citizen's Advice Bureau, a housing aid centre, a law centre or a solicitor.

Editorial note

This section was inserted by Anti-social Behaviour Act 2003, s.14(5) and Sched. 1. It **3A–1062** was brought into force in England on June 30, 2004 by the Anti-social Behaviour Act 2003 (Commencement No.3 and Savings) Order 2004 (S.I. 2004 No. 1502) (C.61). It was brought into force in Wales on 30 April 2005 by the Anti-social Behaviour Act 2003 (Commencement No.4) (Wales) Order 2005 (S.I. 2005 No. 1225) (W.83) (C.55).

Demoted tenancies lack security of tenure. If a landlord follows the procedure set out in ss.143E and F, the court must make an order for possession (see Housing Act 1996, s.143D).

Demoted tenancy

See Housing Act 1985, s.82A and s.143A, above. This section only applies to former **3A–1063** secure tenancies while the tenant condition (see Housing Act 1985, s.81) continues to apply.

Notice

A landlord must serve notice of proceedings on a demoted tenant before bringing **3A–1064** possession proceedings. There is no prescribed form of notice. The notice must, among other things, set out the reasons for the landlord's decision to apply for a possession order and specify the date after which proceedings for possession may be begun. The date specified must not be earlier than the date on which the tenancy could be brought to an end by notice to quit—in most cases, in view of Protection from Eviction Act 1977, s.5, 28 days. Court proceedings should not be begun before that date. The notice must also inform the tenant of the right to request a review of the landlord's decision and of the time within which the request must be made—see s.143F.

Review of decision to seek possession

3A–1065 **143F.**—(1) Before the end of the period of 14 days beginning with the date of service of a notice for possession of a dwelling-house let under a demoted tenancy the tenant may request the landlord to review its decision to seek an order for possession.

(2) If a request is made in accordance with subsection (1) the landlord must review the decision.

(3) The Secretary of State may by regulations make provision as to the procedure to be followed in connection with a review under this section.

(4) The regulations may include provision—

    (a) requiring the decision on review to be made by a person of appropriate seniority who was not involved in the original decision;

    (b) as to the circumstances in which the tenant is entitled to an oral hearing, and whether and by whom he may be represented at the hearing.

(5) The landlord must notify the tenant—

    (a) of the decision on the review;

    (b) of the reasons for the decision.

(6) The review must be carried out and notice given under subsection (5) before the date specified in the notice of proceedings as the date after which proceedings for possession of the dwelling-house may be begun.

Editorial note

3A–1066 This section was inserted by Anti-social Behaviour Act 2003, s.14(5) and Sched. 1. It was brought into force in England on June 30, 2004 by the Anti-social Behaviour Act 2003 (Commencement No.3 and Savings) Order 2004 (S.I. 2004 No. 1502) (C.61). It was brought into force in Wales on 30 April 2005 by the Anti-social Behaviour Act 2003 (Commencement No.4) (Wales) Order 2005 (S.I. 2005 No. 1225) (W.83) (C.55).

Regulations

3A–1067 See the Demoted Tenancies (Review of Decisions) (England) Regulations 2004 (S.I. 2004 No. 1679) and the Demoted Tenancies (Review of Decisions) (Wales) Regulations 2005 S.I. 2005 No. 1228 (W.86). .

Demoted tenancy

3A–1068 See Housing Act 1985, s.82A and s.143A, above. This section only applies to former secure tenancies while the tenant condition (see Housing Act 1985, s.81) continues to apply.

Request for review

3A–1069 A tenant who seeks to challenge a decision to bring proceedings may request that the landlord review its decision. However a request for a review must be made before the end of the period of 14 days beginning with the date of service of the notice for possession. The court has no power to grant an extension of time. The statutory framework is similar to that for introductory tenancies—see Housing Act 1996, s.129 and the commentary at para. 3A–1003.

Effect of proceedings for possession

143G.—(1) This section applies if the landlord has begun proceed- **3A–1070**
ings for the possession of a dwelling-house let under a demoted
tenancy and—

    (a) the demotion period ends, or

    (b) any of paragraphs (a) to (c) of section 143B(2) applies
        (circumstances in which a tenancy ceases to be a demoted
        tenancy).

(2) If any of paragraphs (a) to (c) of section 143B(2) applies the
tenancy ceases to be a demoted tenancy but the landlord (or the new
landlord as the case may be) may continue the proceedings.

(3) Subsection (4) applies if in accordance with subsection (2) a
tenancy ceases to be a demoted tenancy and becomes a secure
tenancy.

(4) The tenant is not entitled to exercise the right to buy unless—

    (a) the proceedings are finally determined, and

    (b) he is not required to give up possession of the dwelling-
        house.

(5) The proceedings must be treated as finally determined if—

    (a) they are withdrawn;

    (b) any appeal is abandoned;

    (c) the time for appealing expires without an appeal being
        brought.

Editorial note

This section was inserted by Anti-social Behaviour Act 2003, s.14(5) and Sched. 1. It **3A–1071**
was brought into force in England on June 30, 2004 by the Anti-social Behaviour Act
2003 (Commencement No.3 and Savings) Order 2004 (S.I. 2004 No. 1502) (C.61). It
was brought into force in Wales on 30 April 2005 by the Anti-social Behaviour Act
2003 (Commencement No.4) (Wales) Order 2005 (S.I. 2005 No. 1225) (W.83) (C.55).

Demoted tenancy

See Housing Act 1985, s.82A and s.143A, above. This section only applies to former **3A–1072**
secure tenancies while the tenant condition (see Housing Act 1985, s.81) continues to
apply.

Secure tenancy

See Housing Act 1985, s.79. **3A–1073**

Right to buy

See Housing Act 1985 Part V. **3A–1074**

SUCCESSION TO DEMOTED TENANCY

Succession to demoted tenancy

143H.—(1) This section applies if the tenant under a demoted **3A–1075**
tenancy dies

(2) If the tenant was a successor, the tenancy—

    (a) ceases to be a demoted tenancy, but

    (b) does not become a secure tenancy.

(3) In any other case a person is qualified to succeed the tenant
if—

(a) he occupies the dwelling-house as his only or principal home at the time of the tenant's death,

(b) he is a member of the tenant's family, and

(c) he has resided with the tenant throughout the period of 12 months ending with the tenant's death.

(4) If only one person is qualified to succeed under subsection (3) the tenancy vests in him by virtue of this section.

(5) If there is more than one such person the tenancy vests by virtue of this section in the person preferred in accordance with the following rules—

(a) the tenant's spouse or (if the tenant has no spouse) the person mentioned in section 143P(1)(b) is to be preferred to another member of the tenant's family;

(b) if there are two or more other members of the tenant's family the person preferred may be agreed between them or (if there is no such agreement) selected by the landlord.

Editorial note

3A–1076   This section was inserted by Anti-social Behaviour Act 2003, s.14(5) and Sched. 1. It was brought into force in England on June 30, 2004 by the Anti-social Behaviour Act 2003 (Commencement No.3 and Savings) Order 2004 S.I. 2004 No. 1502 (C.61). It was brought into force in Wales on 30 April 2005 by the Anti-social Behaviour Act 2003 (Commencement No.4) (Wales) Order 2005 (S.I. 2005 No. 1225) (W.83) (C.55).

Section 143H provides for succession to demoted tenancies by members of a deceased tenant's family—*cf.* Housing Act 1985, s.88 and the commentary at para. 3A–394. There can only be one succession.

Demoted tenancy

3A–1077   See Housing Act 1985, s.82A and s.143A, above. This section only applies to former secure tenancies while the tenant condition (see Housing Act 1985, s.81) continues to apply.

Secure tenancy

3A–1078   See Housing Act 1985, s.79.

Only or principal home

3A–1079   This is the phrase which is used in the tenant condition for secure tenancies—see Housing Act 1985, s.81 and the commentary at para. 3A–349.

Member of the tenant's family

3A–1080   See s.143P.

No successor tenant: termination

3A–1081   **143I.**—(1) This section applies if the demoted tenant dies and no person is qualified to succeed to the tenancy as mentioned in section 143H(3).

(2) The tenancy ceases to be a demoted tenancy if either subsection (3) or (4) applies.

(3) This subsection applies if the tenancy is vested or otherwise disposed of in the course of the administration of the tenant's estate unless the vesting or other disposal is in pursuance of an order under—

(a) section 23A or 24 of the Matrimonial Causes Act 1973

(property adjustment orders in connection with matrimonial proceedings);

    (b) section 17(1) of the Matrimonial and Family Proceedings Act 1984 (property adjustment orders after overseas divorce, etc);

    (c) paragraph 1 of Schedule 1 to the Children Act 1989 (orders for financial relief against parents).

(4) This subsection applies if it is known that when the tenancy is vested or otherwise disposed of in the course of the administration of the tenant's estate it will not be in pursuance of an order mentioned in subsection (3).

(5) A tenancy which ceases to be a demoted tenancy by virtue of this section cannot subsequently become a secure tenancy.

Editorial note

    This section was inserted by Anti-social Behaviour Act 2003, s.14(5) and Sched. 1. It **3A-1082** was brought into force in England on June 30, 2004 by the Anti-social Behaviour Act 2003 (Commencement No.3 and Savings) Order 2004 (S.I. 2004 No. 1502) (C.61). It was brought into force in Wales on 30 April 2005 by the Anti-social Behaviour Act 2003 (Commencement No.4) (Wales) Order 2005 (S.I. 2005 No. 1225) (W.83) (C.55).

Demoted tenancy

    See Housing Act 1985, s.82A and s.143A, above. This section only applies to former **3A-1083** secure tenancies while the tenant condition (see Housing Act 1985, s.81) continues to apply.

Secure tenancy

    See Housing Act 1985, s.79.   **3A-1084**

Person is qualified to succeed

    See ss.143H and 143P.   **3A-1085**

Successor tenants

143J.—(1) This section applies for the purpose of sections 143H **3A-1086** and 143I.

(2) A person is a successor to a secure tenancy which is terminated by a demotion order if any of subsections (3) to (6) applies to him.

(3) The tenancy vested in him—

    (a) by virtue of section 89 of the Housing Act 1985 or section 133 of this Act;

    (b) under the will or intestacy of the preceding tenant.

(4) The tenancy arose by virtue of section 86 of the Housing Act 1985 and the original fixed term was granted—

    (a) to another person, or

    (b) to him jointly with another person.

(5) He became the tenant on the tenancy being assigned to him unless—

    (a) the tenancy was assigned in proceedings under section 23A or 24 of the Matrimonial Causes Act 1973 (property adjustment orders in connection with matrimonial proceedings) or section 17(1) of the Matrimonial and Family Proceedings Act 1984 (property adjustment orders after overseas divorce, etc), and

(b) neither he nor the other party to the marriage was a successor.

(6) He became the tenant on assignment under section 92 of the Housing Act 1985 if he himself was a successor to the tenancy which he assigned in exchange.

(7) A person is the successor to a demoted tenancy if the tenancy vested in him by virtue of section 143H(4) or (5).

(8) A person is the successor to a joint tenancy if he has become the sole tenant.

Editorial note

3A–1087   This section was inserted by Anti-social Behaviour Act 2003, s.14(5) and Sched. 1. It was brought into force in England on June 30, 2004 by the Anti-social Behaviour Act 2003 (Commencement No.3 and Savings) Order 2004 (S.I. 2004 No. 1502) (C.61). It was brought into force in Wales on 30 April 2005 by the Anti-social Behaviour Act 2003 (Commencement No.4) (Wales) Order 2005 (S.I. 2005 No. 1225) (W.83) (C.55).

Demoted tenancy

3A–1088   See Housing Act 1985, s.82A and s.143A, above. This section only applies to former secure tenancies while the tenant condition (see Housing Act 1985, s.81) continues to apply.

Secure tenancy

3A–1089   See Housing Act 1985, s.79.

Successor

3A–1090   See ss.143H and 143P.

ASSIGNMENT

Restriction on assignment

3A–1091   **143K.**—(1) A demoted tenancy is not capable of being assigned except as mentioned in subsection (2).

(2) The exceptions are assignment in pursuance of an order made under—

(a) section 24 of the Matrimonial Causes Act 1973 (property adjustment orders in connection with matrimonial proceedings);

(b) section 17(1) of the Matrimonial and Family Proceedings Act 1984 (property adjustment orders after overseas divorce, etc.);

(c) paragraph 1 of Schedule 1 to the Children Act 1989 (orders for financial relief against parents).

Editorial note

3A–1092   This section was inserted by Anti-social Behaviour Act 2003, s.14(5) and Sched. 1. It was brought into force in England on June 30, 2004 by the Anti-social Behaviour Act 2003 (Commencement No.3 and Savings) Order 2004 (S.I. 2004 No. 1502) (C.61). It was brought into force in Wales on 30 April 2005 by the Anti-social Behaviour Act 2003 (Commencement No.4) (Wales) Order 2005 (S.I. 2005 No. 1225) (W.83) (C.55). Section 143K provides that a demoted tenancy cannot be assigned except in matrimonial proceedings or under Children Act 1989—*cf.* Housing Act 1985, s.91. There is no provision for mutual exchange—*cf.* Housing Act 1985, s.92.

Demoted tenancy

3A–1093   See Housing Act 1985, s.82A and s.143A, above. This section only applies to former secure tenancies while the tenant condition (see Housing Act 1985, s.81) continues to apply.

REPAIRS

Right to carry out repairs

143L. The Secretary of State may by regulations under section 96 of the Housing Act 1985 (secure tenants: right to carry out repairs) apply to demoted tenants any provision made under that section in relation to secure tenants.

3A–1094

Editorial note

This section was inserted by Anti-social Behaviour Act 2003, s.14(5) and Sched. 1. It was brought into force in England on June 30, 2004 by the Anti-social Behaviour Act 2003 (Commencement No.3 and Savings) Order 2004 (S.I. 2004 No. 1502) (C.61). It was brought into force in Wales on 30 April 2005 by the Anti-social Behaviour Act 2003 (Commencement No.4) (Wales) Order 2005 (S.I. 2005 No. 1225) (W.83) (C.55).

3A–1095

Demoted tenancy

See Housing Act 1985, s.82A and s.143A, above. This section only applies to former secure tenancies while the tenant condition (see Housing Act 1985, s.81) continues to apply.

3A–1096

Secure tenants: right to carry out repairs

See Housing Act 1985, s.96.

3A–1097

Regulations

There are not yet any regulations.

3A–1098

PROVISION OF INFORMATION

Provision of information

143M.—(1) This section applies to a local housing authority or a housing action trust if it is the landlord of a demoted tenancy.

3A–1099

(2) The landlord must from time to time publish information about the demoted tenancy in such form as it thinks best suited to explain in simple terms and so far as it considers appropriate the effect of—

    (a) the express terms of the demoted tenancy;

    (b) the provisions of this Chapter;

    (c) the provisions of sections 11 to 16 of the Landlord and Tenant Act 1985 (landlord's repairing obligations).

(3) The landlord must ensure that information published under subsection (2) is, so far as is reasonably practicable, kept up to date.

(4) The landlord must supply the tenant with—

    (a) a copy of the information published under subsection (2);

    (b) a written statement of the terms of the tenancy, so far as they are neither expressed in the lease or written tenancy agreement (if any) nor implied by law.

(5) The statement required by subsection (4)(b) must be supplied on the grant of the tenancy or as soon as practicable afterwards.

Editorial note

This section was inserted by Anti-social Behaviour Act 2003, s.14(5) and Sched. 1. It was brought into force in England on June 30, 2004 by the Anti-social Behaviour Act

3A–1100

2003 (Commencement No.3 and Savings) Order 2004 (S.I. 2004 No. 1502) (C.61). It was brought into force in Wales on 30 April 2005 by the Anti-social Behaviour Act 2003 (Commencement No.4) (Wales) Order 2005 (S.I. 2005 No. 1225) (W.83) (C.55).

Demoted tenancy

3A-1101   See Housing Act 1985, s.82A and s.143A, above. This section only applies to former secure tenancies while the tenant condition (see Housing Act 1985, s.81) continues to apply.

Sections 11 to 16 of the Landlord and Tenant Act 1985

3A-1102   See para. 3A-525.

SUPPLEMENTARY

Jurisdiction of county court

3A-1103   **143N.**—(1) A county court has jurisdiction—
   (a) to determine questions arising under this Chapter;
   (b) to determine questions arising under this Chapter;
   (c) to determine claims (for whatever amount) in connection with a demoted tenancy.

(2) The jurisdiction includes jurisdiction to entertain proceedings as to whether a statement supplied in pursuance of section 143M(4)(b) (written statement of certain terms of tenancy) is accurate.

(3) For the purposes of subsection (2) it is immaterial that no relief other than a declaration is sought.

(4) If a person takes proceedings in the High Court which, by virtue of this section, he could have taken in the county court he is not entitled to recover any costs.

(5) The Lord Chancellor may make such rules and give such directions as he thinks fit for the purposes of giving effect to this section.

(6) The rules and directions may provide—
   (a) for the exercise by a district judge of a county court of any jurisdiction exercisable under this section;
   (b) for the conduct of proceedings in private.

(7) The power to make rules must be exercised by statutory instrument subject to annulment in pursuance of a resolution of either House of Parliament.

Editorial note

3A-1104   This section was inserted by Anti-social Behaviour Act 2003, s.14(5) and Sched. 1. It was brought into force in England on June 30, 2004 by the Anti-social Behaviour Act 2003 (Commencement No.3 and Savings) Order 2004 (S.I. 2004 No. 1502) (C.61). It was brought into force in Wales on 30 April 2005 by the Anti-social Behaviour Act 2003 (Commencement No.4) (Wales) Order 2005 (S.I. 2005 No. 1225) (W.83) (C.55).

Demoted tenancy

3A-1105   See Housing Act 1985, s.82A and s.143A, above. This section only applies to former secure tenancies while the tenant condition (see Housing Act 1985, s.81) continues to apply.

Rules and directions

3A-1106   See CPR Part 65 and PD65.

Meaning of dwelling house

3A-1107   **143O.**—(1) For the purposes of this Chapter a dwelling-house may be a house or a part of a house.

(2) Land let together with a dwelling-house must be treated for the purposes of this Chapter as part of the dwelling-house unless the land is agricultural land which would not be treated as part of a dwelling-house for the purposes of Part 4 of the Housing Act 1985.

Editorial note

This section was inserted by Anti-social Behaviour Act 2003, s.14(5) and Sched. 1. It was brought into force in England on June 30, 2004 by the Anti-social Behaviour Act 2003 (Commencement No.3 and Savings) Order 2004 (S.I. 2004 No. 1502) (C.61). It was brought into force in Wales on 30 April 2005 by the Anti-social Behaviour Act 2003 (Commencement No.4) (Wales) Order 2005 (S.I. 2005 No. 1225) (W.83) (C.55). **3A–1108**

Members of a person's family

143P.—(1) For the purposes of this Chapter a person is a member **3A–1109**
of another's family if—

    (a) he is the spouse of that person;

    (b) he and that person live together as a couple in an enduring family relationship, but he does not fall within paragraph (c);

    (c) he is that person's parent, grandparent, child, grandchild, brother, sister, uncle, aunt, nephew or niece.

(2) For the purposes of subsection (1)(b) it is immaterial that two persons living together in an enduring family relationship are of the same sex.

(3) For the purposes of subsection (1)(c)—

    (a) a relationship by marriage must be treated as a relationship by blood;

    (b) a relationship of the half-blood must be treated as a relationship of the whole blood;

    (c) a stepchild of a person must be treated as his child.

Note —This section has been amended by the Civil Partnership Act 2004, s.81 and **3A–1109.1**
Sched.8. The amendment is not yet in force, but is printed at para. 3A–1525.

Member of another's family

Cf. Housing Act 1985, s.113 and the commentary at para. 3A–400. Section 143P(2) **3A–1110**
gives effect to the decision in *Ghaidan v. Godin-Mendoza* [2004] UKHL 30; [2004] 3 W.L.R. 113.

Editorial note

This section was inserted by Anti-social Behaviour Act 2003, s.14(5) and Sched. 1. It **3A–1111**
was brought into force in England on June 30, 2004 by the Anti-social Behaviour Act 2003 (Commencement No.3 and Savings) Order 2004 (S.I. 2004 No. 1502) (C.61). It was brought into force in Wales on 30 April 2005 by the Anti-social Behaviour Act 2003 (Commencement No.4) (Wales) Order 2005 (S.I. 2005 No. 1225) (W.83) (C.55).

CHAPTER III

INJUNCTIONS AGAINST ANTI-SOCIAL BEHAVIOUR

Power to grant injunctions against anti-social behaviour

152. [revoked] **3A–1112**

Power of arrest for breach of other injunctions against anti-social behaviour

153. [revoked] **3A–1118**

3A–1119 *Note* — Sections 152 and 153 were repealed by the Anti-social Behaviour Act 2003 Sched.3 and replaced by new provisions in that Act. In England the repeal and new ss.153A-E were implemented on June 30, 2004 by the Anti-social Behaviour Act 2003 (Commencement No.3 and Savings) Order 2004 (S.I. 2004 No. 1502) (C.61). In Wales this was brought into force on September 30, 2004 by the Anti-social Behaviour Act 2003 (Commencement No.2 and Savings) (Wales) Order 2004 (S.I. 2004 No. 2557).

[THE NEXT PARAGRAPH IS 3A–1128.]

Anti-social behaviour injunction

3A–1128 **153A.**—(1) This section applies to conduct—

(a) which is capable of causing nuisance or annoyance to any person, and

(b) which directly or indirectly relates to or affects the housing management functions of a relevant landlord.

(2) The court on the application of a relevant landlord may grant an injunction (an anti-social behaviour injunction) if each of the following two conditions is satisfied.

(3) The first condition is that the person against whom the injunction is sought is engaging, has engaged or threatens to engage in conduct to which this section applies.

(4) The second condition is that the conduct is capable of causing nuisance or annoyance to any of the following—

(a) a person with a right (of whatever description) to reside in or occupy housing accommodation owned or managed by the relevant landlord;

(b) a person with a right (of whatever description) to reside in or occupy other housing accommodation in the neighbourhood of housing accommodation mentioned in paragraph (a);

(c) a person engaged in lawful activity in or in the neighbourhood of housing accommodation mentioned in paragraph (a);

(d) a person employed (whether or not by the relevant landlord) in connection with the exercise of the relevant landlord's housing management functions.

(5) It is immaterial where conduct to which this section applies occurs.

(6) An anti-social behaviour injunction prohibits the person in respect of whom it is granted from engaging in conduct to which this section applies.

Editorial note

3A–1129 This section was inserted by Anti-social Behaviour Act 2003, s.13. It was brought into force in England on June 30, 2004 by the Anti-social Behaviour Act 2003 (Commencement No.3 and Savings) Order 2004 (S.I. 2004 No. 1502) (C.61). In Wales this was brought into force on September 30, 2004 by the Anti-social Behaviour Act 2003 (Commencement No.2 and Savings) (Wales) Order 2004 (S.I. 2004 No. 2557).

Section 153A(1) provides that the conduct to which that provision applies is conduct which is capable of causing nuisance or annoyance (even if no complaint has been received) and which directly or indirectly relates to or affects the landlord's management of its housing stock. Section 153A(2) to (5) sets out the conditions that have to be met before an injunction against anti-social behaviour can be granted. An injunction may be granted against any person whose behaviour could cause nuisance or annoyance to anyone in any of classes of people listed in s.153A(4). The conduct need not cause any such nuisance or annoyance to any specific individual. It is sufficient that it is capable of having that effect. Section 153A(5) provides that the anti-social behaviour need not occur in the vicinity of the landlord's housing accommodation. However the behaviour still needs to be related, at least indirectly, to the landlord's management of its accommodation. For example a landlord should be able to apply for an injunction to protect a tenant who has been regularly harassed by other residents of an estate even if the incident itself which gave rise to the injunction application happened elsewhere. The anti-social behaviour in this example is clearly related to the tenant's occupation of a home owned or managed by the landlord.

Relevant landlord

An application for an anti-social behaviour injunction may only be made by a relevant landlord. Section 153E(7) specifies bodies which may be relevant landlords. Housing action trusts (see Housing Act 1996, s.230 and Housing Act 1988 Part III), local authorities (see Housing Act 1985, s.4(e)) and registered social landlords (see Housing Act 1996, s.230 referring back to Part I (ss.1 to 3)) are all relevant landlords for the purposes of s.153A. A charitable housing trust which is not a registered social landlord is not a relevant landlord for the purposes of s.153A.   **3A–1130**

Court

This means either the High Court or a county court (s.153E(6)). In practice applications for anti-social behaviour injunctions should always be made to a county court.   **3A–1131**

Housing accommodation

See s.153E(9). Housing accommodation includes flats, lodging-houses and hostels and any yard, garden, outhouses and appurtenances belonging to the accommodation or usually enjoyed with it. In relation to a neighbourhood, it includes the whole of the housing accommodation owned or managed by a relevant landlord in the neighbourhood and any common areas used in connection with the accommodation. Housing accommodation is owned (s.153A(4)) by a relevant landlord if either it is a person (other than a mortgagee not in possession) who is for the time being entitled to dispose of the fee simple in the premises, whether in possession or in reversion or holds or is entitled to the rents and profits of the premises under a lease which (when granted) was for a term of not less than three years.   **3A–1132**

Housing management functions

See s.153E(11). The housing management functions of a relevant landlord include functions conferred by or under any enactment and the powers and duties of the landlord as the holder of an estate or interest in housing accommodation.   **3A–1133**

Minors

In *Enfield LBC v. B (A Minor)* [2000] 1 W.L.R. 2259, CA, the Court of Appeal doubted but left open the proposition that former s.152 could not apply to minors—but see *H v. H (A Child) (Occupation Order: Power of Arrest)* [2001] 1 F.L.R. 641; [2001] 1 F.C.R. 370; [2001] Fam. Law 261, CA. (The court has the power to attach a power of arrest to an occupation order made under Family Law Act 1996, s.47(2) against a minor. By suggesting that such a power of arrest could not be made against a 17 year old, wording was implied upon the provisions of s.47(2) of the Act that just was not there) and *Wookey v. Wookey* [1991] Fam. 121; [1991] 3 W.L.R. 135, CA. But see *G v. Harrow LBC* [2004] EWHC 17 (QB). (Complaints against 14 year old. The council obtained an injunction against him under Housing Act 1996, s.152 with a power of arrest. Roderick Evans J. granted the appeal. G was too young to be sent to prison for contempt. In the absence of evidence to the contrary, common sense and experience dictated that G would have no source of income or goods that could be sequestered. The injunction could not be properly or effectively enforced and so should not have been granted. Roderick Evans J. stated that if a council did seek an injunction against a minor, it should be in a position to place evidence before the judge of the minor's circumstances which would make enforcement by a way of a fine or sequestration of assets an effective sanction for breach).   **3A–1134**

Procedure

The County Court (Amendment) Rules 1997 set out the procedure to be followed   **3A–1135**

HOUSING

on applications for injunctions to restrain anti-social behaviour under Housing Act 1996, ss.152 and 153 by creating a new CCR O.49, r.6B, as amended by the Civil Procedure (Amendment No.4) Rules 2001. They have been replaced by a new CPR, Part 65 (Anti-social Behaviour and Harassment) and PD 65. CPR, Pt 65 also contains provisions dealing with demoted tenancies, ASBOs and the Protection from Harassment Act 1997. The old procedure was also partly governed by a Practice Direction made by the Lord Chancellor on August 28, 1997. It has been revoked and not replaced.

(i) *Applications for anti-social behaviour injunctions.* Applications for injunctions under ss.153A, 153B or 153D must be made in Form N16A and follow the Part 8 procedure. They must be made in the court for the district in which the defendant resides or the conduct complained of occurred. (CPR, r.65.3; PD65, para.1; *cf.* CCR O.49, r.6B(1)).

(ii) All applications must state the terms of the injunction applied for and be supported by written evidence. They must be made on two days notice unless the court otherwise directs. The defendant must be served personally. If the application is made without notice the affidavit should explain why notice has not been given. (CPR, r.65.3; *cf.* CCR O.49, r.6B(2)–(4))

(iii) Unless otherwise directed applications made on notice should be heard in public. (CPR, r.39.2; *cf.* PD to CCR O.49, r.6B(5)). In *Moat Housing Group South Ltd v. Harris and Hartless* [2005] EWCA Civ 287; [2005] HLR 33, giving the judgement of the Court, stressed that the grant of an injunction without notice is an exceptional remedy. "It is hard to envisage a more intrusive 'without notice' order than one which requires a mother and her four young children to vacate their home immediately. .... As a matter of principle no order should be made in civil or family proceedings without notice to the other side unless there is a very good reason for departing from the general rule that notice must be given. Needless to say, the more intrusive the order, the stronger must be the reasons for the departure. It is one thing to restrain a defendant from what would in any event be anti-social behaviour for a short time until a hearing can be arranged at which both sides can be heard. It is quite another thing to make a 'without notice' order directing defendants to leave their home immediately and banning them from re-entering a large part of the area where they live." After reviewing family law authorities on ouster injunctions, Brooke LJ said that when deciding whether to exercise their discretion to make ASBIs without notice, judges should follow the guidance given in Family Law Act 1996 s.45(2)(a) . Further, it is "inconceivable that a court would grant an ASBI without notice unless there was both violence (or a threat of violence) in the past and a risk of significant harm to one of the relevant persons during the short period between the time of service of the order and the time of the court hearing on notice."

(iv) Applications for injunctions must be made in Form N16A (PD65, para.1). Injunctions should be in Form N16. Wherever possible the claimant should file a draft of the order sought with the application and a disc with the draft order should be available to the court (PD25, para.2.4). Injunctions must be "framed in terms appropriate and proportionate to the facts of the case". If there is a risk of significant harm to a particular person or persons it is usually appropriate for the injunction to identify that person or those persons. However, in order to justify granting a wider injunction, restraining someone from causing a nuisance or annoyance to, "a person of a similar description," it is normally necessary for the judge to make a finding that there has been use or threats of violence to persons of a similar description, and that there is a risk of significant harm to persons of a similar description if an injunction is not granted in respect of them. (*Manchester City Council v. Lee* [2003] EWCA Civ 1256; [2004] 1 W.L.R. 349).

(v) If a power of arrest is sought, each provision which is to be subject to the power of arrest, must be set out in a separate clause of the injunction (CPR, r.65.4). Powers of arrest may be sought in claim forms, acknowledgements of service or Part 23 applications. They must be supported by written evidence. If made on notice, not less than two days notice must be given (CPR, r.65.9) It is important to spell out in the injunction the specific activities which are forbidden and confine the power of arrest to those specific activities alone. Under ECHR law, citizens must be able, if necessary with appropriate advice, to foresee to a reasonable degree the consequences that a given action may produce (*Silver v. United Kingdom* (1983) 5 E.H.H.R. 347, at paras 87-8). Summary arrest and detention are clearly an extremely serious interference with a person's private life, which can only be justified by an order which is "particularly precise" (*Kopp v. Switzerland* (1991) 27 E.H.R.R. 91, at para.72). See too *Manchester City Council v. Lee* [2003] EWCA Civ 1256; [2004] 1 W.L.R. 349 and, in a domestic violence context, *Hale v. Tanner* [2000] 1 W.L.R. 2377, CA, which suggests a power of arrest be attached only to paragraphs prohibiting violence or physical proximity. This is confirmed by s.153C.

(vi) A without notice court order with a power of arrest attached deserves and demands early re-consideration, ideally within 14 days. There is nothing wrong in a without notice order being for a duration of six months, provided that it is of a non-intrusive type (such as a typical non-molestation or non-nuisance order) and the on notice hearing takes place timeously (*Moat HousingGroup South Ltd v. Harris and Hartless* [2005] EWCA Civ 287; [2005] HLR 33).

(vii) The claimant must deliver a copy of an injunction with a Power of Arrest to any police station for the area where the conduct occurred—but if it was granted without notice, only after service on the defendant (CPR, r.65.4 and Form N110A; *cf.* CCR O.49, r.6B(6)). The claimant must immediately inform the police station if an injunction containing a power of arrest is varied or discharged.

(viii) The question of jurisdiction has been dealt with by an amendment to PD2B. The former position was that the jurisdiction of the court under ss.152 and 153 could be exercised by district judges as well as circuit judges. The amendment to PD2B makes it clear that district and deputy district judges have jurisdiction to grant anti-social behaviour injunctions and to commit for contempt. There is no longer any requirement that district judges and deputy district judges have to have had appropriate training before exercising the jurisdiction (*cf.* the Practice Direction made by the Lord Chancellor on August 28, 1997 which has been revoked and not replaced). Notwithstanding the suggestion in some quarters that the former rule giving district judges jurisdiction was *ultra vires*, it is now accepted that this is not the case—see County Courts Act 1984, s.75(3)(d), repealed by Civil Procedure Act 1997 Sched.2, but Sched.1 of that Act provides that the Civil Procedure Rules may deal with the subjects contained in the former rules.

(ix) An application for a warrant of arrest under s.155(3) must be made in accordance with CPR Part 23 and may be made without notice. A claimant seeking a warrant must file an affidavit setting out grounds for the application or give oral evidence. A warrant shall not be issued unless the application is substantiated on oath and the judge has reasonable grounds for believing the defendant has failed to comply with the injunction (CPR, r.65.5).

(x) The judge before whom an arrested person is brought may deal with the matter or adjourn proceedings (CPR, r.65.6). In such circumstances the arrested person may be remanded or released. If the person is released, the matter shall be dealt with by the same or another judge within 28 days of the date the arrested person appears in court. At least two days notice of the adjourned hearing must be given. (CPR, r.65.6; *cf.* CCR O.49, r.6B(8B)).

(xi) Applications for bail. An application for bail made by a person arrested under a power of arrest attached to an injunction or a warrant of arrest issued under s.155(3) may be made either orally or in an application notice. An application notice seeking bail must contain (1) the full name of the person making the application; (2) the address of the place where the person making the application is detained; (3) the address where s/he would reside if bail were granted; (4) the amount of any proposed recognizance; and (5) the grounds for the application and, where a previous application has been refused, full details of any change in circumstances which has occurred since that refusal. A copy of the application notice must be served on the person who obtained the injunction. (PD65, para.2; *cf.* PD to CCR O.49, r.6B)

(xii) If a person is bailed, subject to a recognizance, the recognizance may subsequently be taken by a judge, a justice of the peace, a justice's clerk, a senior police officer or the governor of a prison (CPR, r.65.7; *cf.* CCR O.49, r.6B(11)).

Sentences for breach of s.153A injunctions

In *Tower Hamlets LBC v. Long* (2000) 32 H.L.R. 219, CA, the Court of Appeal held **3A–1136** that an immediate sentence of imprisonment was appropriate where a tenant had waged a personal vendetta against another tenant in breach of an injunction. However a prison sentence of three months was reduced to three weeks. In *Nottingham City Council v. Cutts* (2001) 33 H.L.R. 7, CA, the Court of Appeal dismissed an appeal against an immediate sentence of twelve months imprisonment where there had been previous breaches and where the actual breaches consisted of attempts to punch, racist and other foul language, threats to kill and kicking and banging of doors. The judge "was undoubtedly right in the case to impose a substantial term of imprisonment". Although the sentence was "a stiff one" it was not "manifestly excessive". See too *Leicester City Council v. Lewis* (2001) 33 H.L.R. 37, CA.

In *Barnet LBC v. Hurst* [2002] EWCA Civ 1009; [2003] 1 W.L.R. 722, the Court of Appeal held that a sentence of nine months imprisonment for a defendant who had breached an undertaking not to assault, threaten, harass or cause nuisance to anyone residing in or visiting a block of flats where his father lived by being loud and noisy and disturbing the neighbours' sleep was manifestly too long. The sentence was reduced to three months. The maximum sentence of two years imprisonment should be reserved for the worst cases (*Turnbull v. Middlesbrough BC* [2003] EWCA Civ 1327).

Time spent in custody on remand is not deducted from the sentence imposed on a committal for contempt of court (*Delaney v. Delaney* [1996] Q.B. 387, CA; *Sevketoglu v. Sevketoglu* [2003] EWCA Civ 1570).

Injunction against unlawful use of premises

3A–1137   **153B.**—(1) This section applies to conduct which consists of or involves using or threatening to use housing accommodation owned or managed by a relevant landlord for an unlawful purpose.

(2) The court on the application of the relevant landlord may grant an injunction prohibiting the person in respect of whom the injunction is granted from engaging in conduct to which this section applies.

Editorial note

3A–1138   This section was inserted by Anti-social Behaviour Act 2003, s.13. It was brought into force in England on June 30, 2004 by the Anti-social Behaviour Act 2003 (Commencement No.3 and Savings) Order 2004 (S.I. 2004 No. 1502) (C.61). In Wales this was brought into force on September 30, 2004 by the Anti-social Behaviour Act 2003 (Commencement No.2 and Savings) (Wales) Order 2004 (S.I. 2004 No. 2557).

Relevant landlord

3A–1139   An application for an anti-social behaviour injunction may only be made by a relevant landlord. Section 153E(7) specifies bodies which may be relevant landlords. Housing action trusts (see Housing Act 1996, s.230 and Housing Act 1988 Part III), local authorities (see Housing Act 1985, s.4(e)) and registered social landlords (see Housing Act 1996, s.230 referring back to Part I (ss.1 to 3)) are all relevant landlords for the purposes of s.153A. A charitable housing trust which is not a registered social landlord is not a relevant landlord for the purposes of s.153B.

Court

3A–1140   This means either the High Court or a county court (s.153E(6)). In practice applications for anti-social behaviour injunctions should always be made to a county court.

Housing accommodation

3A–1141   See s.153E(9). Housing accommodation includes flats, lodging-houses and hostels and any yard, garden, outhouses and appurtenances belonging to the accommodation or usually enjoyed with it. In relation to a neighbourhood, it includes the whole of the housing accommodation owned or managed by a relevant landlord in the neighbourhood and any common areas used in connection with the accommodation. Housing accommodation is owned (s.153A(4)) by a relevant landlord if either it is a person (other than a mortgagee not in possession) who is for the time being entitled to dispose of the fee simple in the premises, whether in possession or in reversion or holds or is entitled to the rents and profits of the premises under a lease which (when granted) was for a term of not less than three years.

Unlawful purpose

3A–1142   This phrase is not defined. Clearly the section includes any conduct which amounts to a criminal offence. The most obvious examples are drug dealing or use of the premises as a brothel. In view of s.153D, it is unlikely that it includes conduct which is merely a breach of the terms of a tenancy agreement and not a criminal offence.

Injunctions: exclusion order and power of arrest

153C.—(1) This section applies if the court grants an injunction 3A–1143 under subsection (2) of section 153A or 153B and it thinks that either of the following paragraphs applies—

(a) the conduct consists of or includes the use or threatened use of violence;

(b) there is a significant risk of harm to a person mentioned in section 153A(4).

(2) The court may include in the injunction a provision prohibiting the person in respect of whom it is granted from entering or being in—

(a) any premises specified in the injunction;

(b) any area specified in the injunction.

(3) The court may attach a power of arrest to any provision of the injunction.

Editorial note

This section was inserted by Anti-social Behaviour Act 2003, s.13. It was brought 3A–1144 into force in England on June 30, 2004 by the Anti-social Behaviour Act 2003 (Commencement No.3 and Savings) Order 2004 (S.I. 2004 No. 1502) (C.61). In Wales this was brought into force on September 30, 2004 by the Anti-social Behaviour Act 2003 (Commencement No.2 and Savings) (Wales) Order 2004 (S.I. 2004 No. 2557).

Section 153C allows the court granting an injunction under ss.153A or 153B to attach a power of arrest or to exclude a person from specified premises or a specified area where there is the use or threat of violence or a significant risk of harm to any person mentioned in s.153A(4). Consequently a power of arrest is available in cases where there is a significant risk of harm even if there has been no actual or threatened violence.

Power of arrest

See s.154 and the commentary to that section. 3A–1145

Exclusion orders

Although courts have power to make ouster orders and/or exclusion orders without 3A–1145.1 notice if the facts are sufficiently serious to warrant such a draconian order, very great care is needed. Further, judges making such orders should generally be scrupulous to prescribe that the order may only be served at a reasonable time of the day (for example, between 9 am and 4.30 p.m. on a weekday) (*Moat Housing Group South Ltd v. Harris and Hartless* [2005] EWCA Civ 287; [2005] HLR 33).

Court

This means either the High Court or a county court (s.153E(6)). In practice ap- 3A–1146 plications for anti-social behaviour injunctions, exclusion orders and/or powers of arrest should always be made to a county court.

Harm

See s.153E(12). Harm includes serious ill-treatment or abuse (whether physical or 3A–1147 not). The government's intention (see the explanatory notes to the Act) was that it should include emotional or psychological harm. This could apply, for example, in cases of racial or sexual harassment. The former repealed provisions only allowed a power of arrest when there was either violence or threatened violence together with a significant risk of harm.

Injunction against breach of tenancy agreement

153D.—(1) This section applies if a relevant landlord applies for 3A–1148 an injunction against a tenant in respect of the breach or anticipated breach of a tenancy agreement on the grounds that the tenant—

937

(a) is engaging or threatening to engage in conduct that is capable of causing nuisance or annoyance to any person, or

(b) is allowing, inciting or encouraging any other person to engage or threaten to engage in such conduct.

(2) The court may proceed under subsection (3) or (4) if it is satisfied—

(a) that the conduct includes the use or threatened use of violence, or

(b) that there is a significant risk of harm to any person.

(3) The court may include in the injunction a provision prohibiting the person in respect of whom it is granted from entering or being in—

(a) any premises specified in the injunction;

(b) any area specified in the injunction.

(4) The court may attach a power of arrest to any provision of the injunction.

(5) Tenancy agreement includes any agreement for the occupation of residential accommodation owned or managed by a relevant landlord.

Editorial note

3A–1149   This section was inserted by Anti-social Behaviour Act 2003, s.13. It was brought into force in England on June 30, 2004 by the Anti-social Behaviour Act 2003 (Commencement No.3 and Savings) Order 2004 (S.I. 2004 No. 1502) (C.61). In Wales this was brought into force on September 30, 2004 by the Anti-social Behaviour Act 2003 (Commencement No.2 and Savings) (Wales) Order 2004 (S.I. 2004 No. 2557).

Section 153D applies in relation to injunctions sought by a local authority, a housing action trust, a registered social landlord or a charitable housing trust on the grounds of a breach or anticipated breach of a tenancy agreement by a tenant. If the behaviour is prohibited by the terms of the tenancy agreement and satisfies the criteria ss.153D(1)(a) and (b), the court may exclude a person from specified premises or a specified area and attach a power of arrest to any provision of the injunction. The breach (or anticipated breach) of the tenancy agreement must relate to conduct which is capable of causing nuisance or annoyance to any person. The tenant may have engaged or threatened to engage in the conduct directly or have allowed, incited or encouraged another person to engage in such conduct. In addition the conduct must include violence or the threat of violence or a significant risk of harm to any person.

Relevant landlord

3A–1150   An application for an anti-social behaviour injunction may only be made by a relevant landlord. Section 153E(7) specifies bodies which may be relevant landlords. Housing action trusts (see Housing Act 1996, s.230 and Housing Act 1988 Part III), local authorities (see Housing Act 1985, s.4(e)) and registered social landlords (see Housing Act 1996, s.230 referring back to Part I (ss.1 to 3)) are all relevant landlords for the purposes of s.153A. A charitable housing trust which is not a registered social landlord is not a relevant landlord for the purposes of s.153D (see s.153E(8)).

Court

3A–1151   This means either the High Court or a county court (s.153E(6)). In practice applications for injunctions to prevent a breach of a tenancy agreement should always be made to a county court.

Power of arrest

3A–1152   See s.154 and the commentary to that section.

Injunctions: supplementary

3A–1153   153E.—(1) This section applies for the purposes of sections 153A to 153D.

(2) An injunction may—
  (a) be made for a specified period or until varied or discharged;
  (b) have the effect of excluding a person from his normal place of residence.

(3) An injunction may be varied or discharged by the court on an application by—
  (a) the person in respect of whom it is made;
  (b) the relevant landlord.

(4) If the court thinks it just and convenient it may grant or vary an injunction without the respondent having been given such notice as is otherwise required by rules of court.

(5) If the court acts under subsection (4) it must give the person against whom the injunction is made an opportunity to make representations in relation to the injunction as soon as it is practicable for him to do so.

(6) The court is the High Court or a county court.

(7) Each of the following is a relevant landlord—
  (a) a housing action trust;
  (b) a local authority (within the meaning of the Housing Act 1985);
  (c) a registered social landlord.

(8) A charitable housing trust which is not a registered social landlord is also a relevant landlord for the purposes of section 153D.

(9) Housing accommodation includes—
  (a) flats, lodging-houses and hostels;
  (b) any yard, garden, outhouses and appurtenances belonging to the accommodation or usually enjoyed with it;
  (c) in relation to a neighbourhood, the whole of the housing accommodation owned or managed by a relevant landlord in the neighbourhood and any common areas used in connection with the accommodation.

(10) A landlord owns housing accommodation if either of the following paragraphs applies to him—
  (a) he is a person (other than a mortgagee not in possession) who is for the time being entitled to dispose of the fee simple in the premises, whether in possession or in reversion;
  (b) he is a person who holds or is entitled to the rents and profits of the premises under a lease which (when granted) was for a term of not less than three years.

(11) The housing management functions of a relevant landlord include—
  (a) functions conferred by or under any enactment;
  (b) the powers and duties of the landlord as the holder of an estate or interest in housing accommodation.

(12) Harm includes serious ill-treatment or abuse (whether physical or not).

939

Editorial note

3A-1154   This section was inserted by Anti-social Behaviour Act 2003, s.13. It was brought into force in England on June 30, 2004 by the Anti-social Behaviour Act 2003 (Commencement No.3 and Savings) Order 2004 (S.I. 2004 No. 1502) (C.61). In Wales this was brought into force on September 30, 2004 by the Anti-social Behaviour Act 2003 (Commencement No.2 and Savings) (Wales) Order 2004 (S.I. 2004 No. 2557).

Registered social landlord

3A-1155   See Housing Act 1996, s.230 referring back to Part I, ss.1 to 3.

Powers of arrest: ex-parte applications for injunctions

3A-1156   **154.**—(1) In determining whether to exercise its power under section 153C(3) or 153D(4) to attach a power of arrest to an injunction which it intends to grant on an ex-parte application, the High Court or a county court shall have regard to all the circumstances including—

(a) whether it is likely that the applicant will be deterred or prevented from seeking the exercise of the power if the power is not exercised immediately, and

(b) whether there is reason to believe that the respondent is aware of the proceedings for the injunction but is deliberately evading service and that the applicant or any person of a description mentioned in section 153A(4) (as the case may be) will be seriously prejudiced if the decision as to whether to exercise the power were delayed until substituted service is effected.

(2) Where the court exercises its power as mentioned in subsection (1), it shall afford the respondent an opportunity to make representations relating to the exercise of the power as soon as just and convenient at a hearing of which notice has been given to all the parties in accordance with rules of court.

Powers of arrest: ex parte applications for injunctions

3A-1157   See commentary to ss.153A–E.

Section 154 has been amended by Anti-social Behaviour Act, 2003 s.13(4).

The amendments were brought into force in England on June 30, 2004 by the Anti-social Behaviour Act 2003 (Commencement No.3 and Savings) Order 2004 (S.I. 2004 No. 1502) (C.61). In Wales they were brought into force on September 30, 2004 by the Anti-social Behaviour Act 2003 (Commencement No.2 and Savings) (Wales) Order 2004 (S.I. 2004 No. 2557).

Arrest and remand

3A-1158   **155.**—(1) If a power of arrest is attached to certain provisions of an injunction by virtue of section 153C(3) or 153D(4), a constable may arrest without warrant a person whom he has reasonable cause for suspecting to be in breach of any such provision or otherwise in contempt of court in relation to a breach of any such provision. A constable shall after making any such arrest forthwith inform the person on whose application the injunction was granted.

(2) Where a person is arrested under subsection (1)—

(a) he shall be brought before the relevant judge within the period of 24 hours beginning at the time of his arrest, and

(b) if the matter is not then disposed of forthwith, the judge may remand him.

In reckoning for the purposes of this subsection any period of 24 hours no account shall be taken of Christmas Day, Good Friday or any Sunday.

(3) If the court has granted an injunction in circumstances such that a power of arrest could have been attached under section 153C(3) or 153D(4) but—

(a) has not attached a power of arrest under the section in question to any provisions of the injunction, or

(b) has attached that power only to certain provisions of the injunction,

then, if at any time the applicant considers that the respondent has failed to comply with the injunction, he may apply to the relevant judge for the issue of a warrant for the arrest of the respondent.

(4) The relevant judge shall not issue a warrant on an application under subsection (3)unless—

(a) the application is substantiated on oath, and

(b) he has reasonable grounds for believing that the respondent has failed to comply with the injunction.

(5) If a person is brought before a court by virtue of a warrant issued under subsection (4) and the court does not dispose of the matter forthwith, the court may remand him.

(6) Schedule 15 (which makes provision corresponding to that applying in magistrates' courts in civil cases under sections 128 and 129 of the Magistrates' Courts Act 1980) applies in relation to the powers of the High Court and a county court to remand a person under this section.

(7) If a person remanded under this section is granted bail by virtue of subsection (6), he may be required by the relevant judge to comply, before release on bail or later, with such requirements as appear to the judge to be necessary to secure that he does not interfere with witnesses or otherwise obstruct the course of justice.

Note — Section 155 has been amended by Anti-social Behaviour Act 2003, s.13(5). **3A–1159**
The amendments were brought into force in England on June 30, 2004 by the Anti-social Behaviour Act 2003 (Commencement No.3 and Savings) Order 2004 (S.I. 2004 No. 1502) (C.61). In Wales they were brought into force on September 30, 2004 by the Anti-social Behaviour Act 2003 (Commencement No.2 and Savings) (Wales) Order 2004 (S.I. 2004 No. 2557).

"relevant judge"
See s.158 and the commentary at 3A–1135, para. (vii) **3A–1160**

Arrest and remand
See commentary to ss.152 and 153 and Form **N148**. **3A–1161**
Note that s.155(2)(b) and s.155(3)–(7) were implemented on October 15, 2001 by the Housing Act 1996 (Commencement No. 13) Order 2001 (S.I. 2001 No. 3164) (C.100). See too *Braintree District Council v. Clark* [1998] C.L.Y. 3724, CA. The county court has power to review a decision to grant bail or to remand in custody, especially when there has been a change in circumstance. Accordingly, the Court of Appeal's task on any appeal against a refusal to grant bail is one of review rather than rehearing. (*Newham LBC v. Jones* [2002] EWCA Civ 1779; November 19, 2002 a case where an appeal was dismissed. Although the circuit judge did not specifically refer to the Bail Act 1976 when refusing bail, he did express concerns over the seriousness of the allegations and further breaches of the injunction).

Remand for medical examination and report

3A-1162   **156.**—(1) If the relevant judge has reason to consider that a medical report will be required, any power to remand a person under section 155 may be exercised for the purpose of enabling a medical examination and report to be made.

(2) If such a power is so exercised the adjournment shall not be for more than 4 weeks at a time unless the judge remands the accused in custody.

(3) If the judge so remands the accused, the adjournment shall not be for more than 3 weeks at a time.

(4) If there is reason to suspect that a person who has been arrested—

     (a) under section 155(1), or

     (b) under a warrant issued under section 155(4),

is suffering from mental illness or severe mental impairment, the relevant judge shall have the same power to make an order under section 35 of the Mental Health Act 1983 (remand for report on accused's mental condition) as the Crown Court has under section 35 of that Act in the case of an accused person within the meaning of that section.

"relevant judge"

3A-1163   See s.158 and the commentary at 3A-1135, para. (vii).

Remand for medical examination and report

3A-1164   See commentary to ss.152 and 153.

Note that ss.155(2)(b) (remands in custody) and 155(3)–(7) (warrants for arrest), 156 (remand for medical examination), and Sched.15 (provisions corresponding with civil procedure in magistrates' courts) were implemented on October 15, 2001 by the Housing Act 1996 (Commencement No. 13) Order 2001 (S.I. 2001 No. 3164) (C.100).

Powers of arrest: supplementary provisions

3A-1165   **157.**—(1) If in exercise of its power under section 153C(3) or 153D(4) the High Court or a county court attaches a power of arrest to any provisions of an injunction, it may provide that the power of arrest is to have effect for a shorter period than the other provisions of the injunction.

(2) Any period specified for the purposes of subsection (1) may be extended by the court (on one or more occasions) on an application to vary or discharge the injunction.

(3) If a power of arrest has been attached to certain provisions of an injunction by virtue of section 153C(3) or 153D(4), the court may vary or discharge the injunction in so far as it confers a power of arrest (whether or not any application has been made to vary or discharge any other provision of the injunction).

(4) An injunction may be varied or discharged under subsection (3) on an application by the respondent or the person on whose application the injunction was made.

3A-1166   *Note* — Section 157 has been amended by Anti-social Behaviour Act, 2003 s.13(6).

They were brought into force in England on June 30, 2004 by the Anti-social Behaviour Act 2003 (Commencement No.3 and Savings) Order 2004 (S.I. 2004 No. 1502) (C.61). In Wales they were brought into force on September 30, 2004 by the

Anti-social Behaviour Act 2003 (Commencement No.2 and Savings) (Wales) Order 2004 (S.I. 2004 No. 2557).

Powers of arrest: supplementary provisions
See commentary at 3A–1135.

3A–1167

Interpretation: Chapter III

158.—(1) For the purposes of this Chapter—

3A–1168

"charitable housing trust" means a housing trust, within the meaning of the Housing Associations Act 1985, which is a charity within the meaning of the Charities Act 1993;

"child" means a person under the age of 18 years;

"harm"—

(a) in relation to a person who has reached the age of 18 years, means ill-treatment or the impairment of health, and

(b) in relation to a child, means ill-treatment or the impairment of health or development;

"health" includes physical or mental health;

"ill-treatment", in relation to a child, includes sexual abuse and forms of ill-treatment which are not physical;

"relevant judge", in relation to an injunction, means—

(a) where the injunction was granted by the High Court, a judge of that court,

(b) where the injunction was granted by a county court, a judge or district judge of that or any other county court;

"tenancy" includes a licence, and "tenant" and "landlord" shall be construed accordingly.

(2) Where the question of whether harm suffered by a child is significant turns on the child's health or development, his health or development shall be compared with that which could reasonably be expected of a similar child.

Note —The references in s.158(1) to "child", "harm", "health" and "ill-treatment" were repealed by the Anti-social Behaviour Act 2003, s.13(7) and Sched.3, as was s.158(2).

3A–1169

It was brought into force in England on June 30, 2004 by the Anti-social Behaviour Act 2003 (Commencement No.3 and Savings) Order 2004 (S.I. 2004 No. 1502) (C.61). In Wales this was brought into force on September 30, 2004 by the Anti-social Behaviour Act 2003 (Commencement No.2 and Savings) (Wales) Order 2004 (S.I. 2004 No. 2557).

Interpretation: Chapter III
See commentary to ss.152 and 153.

3A–1170

"relevant judge"
See the commentary at 3A–1122.1, para. (vii).

3A–1171

* * * * *

PART VII

HOMELESSNESS

3A–1172   Pt VII completely replaces the homelessness provisions formerly found in the Housing Act 1985, Pt III (see the Housing Act 1996, Sched.19, Pt VIII) with a new statutory code contained in ss.175 to 218). Some of the old provisions are re-enacted without alteration (*e.g.* s.189 (priority need)) or with only minor amendments (*e.g.* ss.175–177 (definition of homelessness), s.188 (interim duty to accommodate), ss.198–199 (local connection), and ss.211–212 (protection of property)). However, there are several very significant changes. Significant amendments to the 1996 Act were also made by the Homelessness Act 2002.

The homelessness provisions in Pt VII were brought into force on January 20, 1997 by the Housing Act 1996 (Commencement No. 5 and Transitional Provisions) Order 1996 (S.I. 1996 No. 2959) (C.88). (The Housing Act 1996 (Commencement No. 3 and Transitional Provisions) Order 1996 (S.I. 1996 No. 2402) brought into force on October 1, 1996 those sections in Pt VII enabling the Secretary of State to make regulations and issue guidance and some definitions).

Pt VII does not apply to anyone who applied to a local authority as a homeless person prior to implementation (Housing Act 1996, s.216(2) and the Schedule to the Housing Act 1996 (Commencement No. 5 and Transitional Provisions) Order 1996 (S.I. 1996 No. 2959)).

When implementing the provisions of Pt VII authorities must have regard to the Guidance issued by the Department of the Environment (s.182). The current *Code of Guidance* was issued in July 2002 by the Office of the Deputy Prime Minister to reflect changes introduced by the Homelessness Act 2002. Copies are available from the Office of the Deputy Prime Minister, PO Box 236, Wetherby, West Yorkshire LS23 7NB. Failure to consider the current edition of the *Code* may provide grounds for quashing a decision (*R. v. Newham LBC, ex p. Bones* (1993) 25 H.L.R. 357, QBD). However the Code of Guidance is not a source of law. Although councils must take it into account and give reasons for departing from it, it is not binding on them (*Khatun v. Newham LBC* [2004] EWCA Civ 55; [2004] 3 W.L.R. 417). Where the Code of Guidance is in conflict with the Act, the words of the Act prevail (*Griffin v. Westminster City Council* [2004] EWCA Civ 108; [2004] H.L.R. 32).

See too Homelessness Act 2002, Part I.

Homelessness and threatened homelessness

3A–1173   **175.**—(1) A person is homeless if he has no accommodation available for his occupation, in the United Kingdom or elsewhere, which he—

    (a) is entitled to occupy by virtue of an interest in it or by virtue of an order of a court,

    (b) has an express or implied licence to occupy, or

    (c) occupies as a residence by virtue of any enactment or rule of law giving him the right to remain in occupation or restricting the right of another person to recover possession.

(2) A person is also homeless if he has accommodation but—

    (a) he cannot secure entry to it, or

    (b) it consists of a moveable structure, vehicle or vessel designed or adapted for human habitation and there is no place where he is entitled or permitted both to place it and to reside in it.

(3) A person shall not be treated as having accommodation unless it is accommodation which it would be reasonable for him to continue to occupy.

(4) A person is threatened with homelessness if it is likely that he will become homeless within 28 days.

"available for his occupation"

3A–1174   See s.176. Prison is not accommodation. It does not fall within s.175(a), (b) or (c).

For accommodation to exist there has to be a right to occupy which is enforceable or defensible in law. A prisoner cannot be said to have such a right of occupation. Detention is the antithesis of any such right. (*Stewart v. Lambeth LBC* [2002] EWCA Civ 753; [2002] H.L.R. 40 and *R. (B) v. Southwark LBC* [2003] EWHC 1678 (Admin); [2004] H.L.R. 3).

"any enactment or rule of law"

A person remaining in possession of premises after the date on which an order for **3A–1175** possession has become effective but before the warrant for possession has been executed is occupying a residence by virtue of an enactment restricting the right of the landlord to recover possession within s.175(1)(c). Enactment in that section includes rules of court under which the warrant was obtained. That is the position under the Protection from Eviction Act 1977 (*Haniff v. Robinson* [1992] 3 W.L.R. 875). Therefore a person only becomes homeless when the warrant for possession is executed (*R. (Sacupima) v. Newham LBC* [2001] 1 W.L.R. 563, QBD). See too *R. v. Newham LBC, ex p. Khan and Hussain* (2001) 33 H.L.R. 269, QBD.

"reasonable to continue to occupy"

See s.177. **3A–1176**

Homelessness and threatened homelessness

Sections 175, 176 and 177 re-enact the provisions defining homelessness ("A person **3A–1177** is homeless if he has no accommodation available for his occupation ...") and what is accommodation which it is reasonable to occupy, formerly found in the Housing Act 1985, ss.58 and 75 with minor amendments. Section 177(3)provides that the Secretary of State may specify other circumstances to be taken into account in determining whether or not it is reasonable to continue in occupation. This has been done by the Homelessness (Suitability of Accommodation) Order 1996 (S.I. 1996 No. 3204) which states that in considering whether it would have been reasonable for a person to continue to occupy accommodation, authorities should take into account the applicant's financial resources, including various specified forms of income, various specified costs relating to accommodation and other reasonable living expenses. See *Odunsi v. Brent LBC*, unreported, 1999, Willesden County Court, where it was held that Homelessness (Suitability of Accommodation) Order 1996, art.2 requires councils to consider whether property is affordable. This is a mandatory obligation. The procedure is inquisitorial, not adversarial.

Cannot secure entry

The condition in section 175(2)(a) requiring a person to be able to secure entry to **3A–1178** accommodation refers to some kind of physical bar to gaining entry at the premises themselves (*e.g.* displacement by unlawful eviction, squatting and the like) and not to some difficulty, for whatever reason, of travelling to them (*Begum v. Tower Hamlets LBC*; [2000] Q.B. 133; [2000] 1 W.L.R. 306, CA).

reasonable to occupy

In *R. v. Westminster City Council, ex p. Alouat* (1989) 21 H.L.R. 477, QBD, Schiemann **3A–1179** J. held that in the Housing Act 1985, s.58(2A)(now the Housing Act 1996, s.175(3)) "reasonableness" is not limited to statutory factors—non-statutory overcrowding, medical need and other matters should also be considered by local authorities.

Domestic violence

The provisions relating to homelessness as a result of domestic violence (Housing **3A–1180** Act 1985, s.83(3)) have been re-enacted and broadened (Housing Act 1996, s.177(1)).

Even before the introduction of the specific reference to domestic violence in s.177(1), threats of violence were likely to be a relevant factor when considering whether or not it was reasonable for an applicant to continue to occupy premises. In *R. v. Broxbourne BC, ex p. Willmoth* (1990) 22 H.L.R. 118, CA, the Court of Appeal (following and applying *R. v. Kensington and Chelsea RBC, ex p. Hammell* [1989] 1 Q.B. 518; [1989] 2 W.L.R. 90; [1989] 1 All E.R. 1202, CA) held that s.58(2A) (now the Housing Act 1996, s.175(3)) required consideration of all matters related to continued occupation. Sir John Megaw said the reasonableness test is:

"not necessarily or solely confined to looking at the actual quality of the accommodation within the four walls of the house or the room or flat which is the ac-

945

commodation available. It may be the duty of the housing authority to consider also circumstances, matters and factors which may fall outside the limited consideration of the actual quality of physical accommodation itself ... Just as the difficulties created by a staircase or other approach to accommodation, to an applicant with physical infirmities, is relevant to reasonableness, so also are threats of violence, even though those threats come from one who is not resident in the accommodation (p.127)".

The Court of Appeal has held that the probability test in s.177(1), (namely whether it is probable that continued occupation would lead to domestic violence) is clear and unequivocal. It is a question of fact devoid of value judgments about what an applicant might or might not have done. Available measures that would probably prove effective in preventing actual or threatened violence might reduce the level of risk below one of probability. However, councils are not entitled to assume that such measures would be taken or would be effective if taken (*Bond v. Leicester City Council* [2001] EWCA Civ 1544; [2002] H.L.R. 6).

Other Violence

3A–1181   Homelessness Act 2002, s.10 amended s.177 so as to provide that violence other than domestic violence may mean that it is not reasonable to continue to occupy existing accommodation. Violence includes threats of violence which are likely to be carried out. In England, this amendment was brought into force on July 31, 2002 by the Homelessness Act 2002 (Commencement No.1) (England) Order 2002 (S.I. No. 1799) (C.56). In Wales, this amendment was brought into force on September 30, 2002 by the Homelessness Act 2002 (Commencement) (Wales) Order 2002 (S.I. 2002 No. 1736) (W.166) (C.53).

Temporary accommodation

3A–1182   The amendment of the definition of homelessness in the Housing Act 1985, s.58 by the Housing and Planning Act 1986, s.14(2), which added a new s.58(2A)(now the Housing Act 1996, s.175(3)) which states that, "a person shall not be treated as having accommodation unless it is accommodation which it would be reasonable for him to continue to occupy", and a new s.58(2B)(now the Housing Act 1996, s.177(2)) which states that in determining whether it is reasonable to continue to occupy accommodation, regard may be had to the general circumstances prevailing in relation to housing in the district of the local housing authority to whom the applicant has applied for accommodation, have reversed the effect of the decision of the House of Lords in *R. v. Hillingdon LBC, ex p. Puhlhofer* [1986] A.C. 484; [1986] 2 W.L.R. 259; [1986] 1 All E.R. 467, HL.

The mere fact that accommodation is temporary does not mean that a person is homeless. In *R. v. Brent LBC, ex p. Awua* [1995] 3 W.L.R. 215; [1995] 3 All E.R. 493, HL, Lord Hoffmann, giving the leading speech, observed that nothing in the Housing Act 1985, s.58 (now the Housing Act 1996, s.175) caused a person to be homeless simply because their accommodation was temporary, short-term or precarious until they were within 28 days of losing it (s.58(4)—now s.175(4)). He found it hard to imagine a case in which it could be said that it was not reasonable to continue to occupy accommodation simply on the basis it was temporary but he observed that:

"On the other hand, the extent to which the accommodation is physically suitable, so that it would be reasonable for a person to continue to occupy it, must be related to the time for which he has been there and is expected to stay. A housing authority could take the view that a family like the Puhlhofers, put into a cramped and squalid bedroom, can be expected to make do for a temporary period. On the other hand, there will come a time at which it is no longer reasonable to expect them to continue to occupy such accommodation. At this point they come back within the definition of homelessness in section 58(1)" (now s.175(1)) ([1995] 3 All E.R. 498).

A council does not have to be satisfied that accommodation has some degree of permanence before it can conclude that a person is not homeless by reason of the availability of accommodation which it would be reasonable for him to occupy under s.175(3) (*Begum v. Tower Hamlets LBC* [2000] Q.B. 133, CA).

Meaning of accommodation available for occupation

3A–1183   **176.** Accommodation shall be regarded as available for a person's occupation only if it is available for occupation by him together with—

(a) any other person who normally resides with him as a member of his family, or

(b) any other person who might reasonably be expected to reside with him.

References in this Part to securing that accommodation is available for a person's occupation shall be construed accordingly.

Meaning of accommodation available for occupation

See commentary to s.175.

3A–1184

Whether it is reasonable to continue to occupy accommodation

177.—(1) It is not reasonable for a person to continue to occupy 3A–1185 accommodation if it is probable that this will lead to domestic violence or other violenceagainst him, or against—

(a) a person who normally resides with him as a member of his family, or

(b) any other person who might reasonably be expected to reside with him.

(1A) For this purpose "violence" means—

(a) violence from another person; or

(b) threats of violence from another person which are likely to be carried out; and violence is "domestic violence" if it is from a person who is associated with the victim.

(2) In determining whether it would be, or would have been, reasonable for a person to continue to occupy accommodation, regard may be had to the general circumstances prevailing in relation to housing in the district of the local housing authority to whom he has applied for accommodation or for assistance in obtaining accommodation.

(3) The Secretary of State may by order specify—

(a) other circumstances in which it is to be regarded as reasonable or not reasonable for a person to continue to occupy accommodation, and

(b) other matters to be taken into account or disregarded in determining whether it would be, or would have been, reasonable for a person to continue to occupy accommodation.

Amended by Homelessness Act 2002, s.10. In England, this amendment was brought into force on July 31, 2002 by the Homelessness Act 2002 (Commencement No. 1) (England) Order 2002 (S.I. 2002 No. 1799) (C.56). In Wales, this amendment was brought into force on September 30, 2002 by the Homelessness Act 2002 (Commencement) (Wales) Order 2002 (S.I. 2002 No. 1736) (W.166) (C.53).

Whether it is reasonable to continue to occupy accommodation

See commentary to s.175.

3A–1186

Meaning of associated person

178.—(1) For the purposes of this Part, a person is associated with 3A–1187 another person if—

(a) they are or have been married to each other;

(b) they are cohabitants or former cohabitants;

(c) they live or have lived in the same household;

(d) they are relatives;

(e) they have agreed to marry one another (whether or not that agreement has been terminated);

(f) in relation to a child, each of them is a parent of the child or has, or has had, parental responsibility for the child.

(2) If a child has been adopted or falls within subsection (2A) two persons are also associated with each other for the purposes of this Part if—

(a) one is a natural parent of the child or a parent of such a natural parent, and

(b) the other is the child or a person—

(i) who has become a parent of the child by virtue of an adoption order or who has applied for an adoption order, or

(ii) with whom the child has at any time been placed for adoption.

(2A) A child falls within this subsection if—

(a) an adoption agency, within the meaning of section 2 of the Adoption and Children Act 2002, is authorised to place him for adoption under section 19 of that Act (placing children with parental consent) or he has become the subject of an order under section 21 of that Act (placement orders), or

(b) he is freed for adoption by virtue of an order made—

(i) in England and Wales, under section 18 of the Adoption Act 1976,

(ii) in Scotland, under section 18 of the Adoption (Scotland) Act 1978, or

(iii) in Northern Ireland, under Article 17(1) or 18(1) of the Adoption (Northern Ireland) Order 1987.

(3) In this section—

"adoption order" means an adoption order within the meaning of section 72(1) of the Adoption Act 1976 or section 46(1) of the Adoption and Children Act 2002;

"child" means a person under the age of 18 years;

"cohabitants" means a man and a woman who, although not married to each other, are living together as husband and wife, and "former cohabitants" shall be construed accordingly;

"parental responsibility" has the same meaning as in the Children Act 1989; and

"relative", in relation to a person, means—

(a) the father, mother, stepfather, stepmother, son, daughter, stepson, stepdaughter, grandmother, grandfather, grandson or granddaughter of that person or of that person's spouse or former spouse, or

(b) the brother, sister, uncle, aunt, niece or nephew (whether of the full blood or of the half blood or by affinity) of that person or of that person's spouse or former spouse, and includes, in relation to a person who is living or has lived with another person as husband and wife, a person who would fall within paragraph (a) or (b) if the parties were married to each other.

Note —This section has been amended by the Civil Partnership Act 2004, s.81 and **3A–1187.1** Sched.8. The amendment is not yet in force, but is printed at para. 3A–1525.

Amended by the Adoption and Children Act 2002, s.139(1), Sch.3, paras 89, 90, 91, 92, as from December 30, 2005 (S.I. 2005 No.2213).

Meaning of associated person
See commentary to s.175.   **3A–1188**

GENERAL FUNCTIONS IN RELATION TO HOMELESSNESS OR THREATENED

HOMELESSNESS

Duty of local housing authority to provide advisory services

179.—(1) Every local housing authority shall secure that advice **3A–1189** and information about homelessness, and the prevention of homelessness, is available free of charge to any person in their district.

(2) The authority may give to any person by whom such advice and information is provided on behalf of the authority assistance by way of grant or loan.

(3) A local housing authority may also assist any such person—

(a) by permitting him to use premises belonging to the authority,

(b) by making available furniture or other goods, whether by way of gift, loan or otherwise, and

(c) by making available the services of staff employed by the authority.

"local housing authority"
See ss.217, 218, and 230 which refers to the Housing Act 1985—see the Housing **3A–1190** Act 1985, ss.1 and 2 above.

Assistance for voluntary organisations

180.—(1) The Secretary of State or a local housing authority may **3A–1191** give assistance by way of grant or loan to voluntary organisations concerned with homelessness or matters relating to homelessness.

(2) A local housing authority may also assist any such organisation—

(a) by permitting them to use premises belonging to the authority,

(b) by making available furniture or other goods, whether by way of gift, loan or otherwise, and

(c) by making available the services of staff employed by the authority.

(3) A "voluntary organisation" means a body (other than a public or local authority) whose activities are not carried on for profit.

3A–1192   See ss.217, 218, and 230 which refers to the Housing Act 1985—see the Housing Act 1985, ss.1 and 2 above.

Terms and conditions of assistance

3A–1193   **181.**—(1) This section has effect as to the terms and conditions on which assistance is given under section 179 or 180.

(2) Assistance shall be on such terms, and subject to such conditions, as the person giving the assistance may determine.

(3) No assistance shall be given unless the person to whom it is given undertakes—

    (a) to use the money, furniture or other goods or premises for a specified purpose, and

    (b) to provide such information as may reasonably be required as to the manner in which the assistance is being used.

The person giving the assistance may require such information by notice in writing, which shall be complied with within 21 days beginning with the date on which the notice is served.

(4) The conditions subject to which assistance is given shall in all cases include conditions requiring the person to whom the assistance is given—

    (a) to keep proper books of account and have them audited in such manner as may be specified,

    (b) to keep records indicating how he has used the money, furniture or other goods or premises, and

    (c) to submit the books of account and records for inspection by the person giving the assistance.

(5) If it appears to the person giving the assistance that the person to whom it was given has failed to carry out his undertaking as to the purpose for which the assistance was to be used, he shall take all reasonable steps to recover from that person an amount equal to the amount of the assistance.

(6) He must first serve on the person to whom the assistance was given a notice specifying the amount which in his opinion is recoverable and the basis on which that amount has been calculated.

Guidance by the Secretary of State

3A–1194   **182.**—(1) In the exercise of their functions relating to homelessness and the prevention of homelessness, a local housing authority or social services authority shall have regard to such guidance as may from time to time be given by the Secretary of State.

(2) The Secretary of State may give guidance either generally or to specified descriptions of authorities.

"local housing authority"

3A–1195   See ss.217, 218, and 230 which refers to the Housing Act 1985—see the Housing Act 1985, ss.1 and 2 above.

"social services authority"

3A–1196   See s.217.

Guidance by the Secretary of State

When implementing the provisions of Pt VII authorities must have regard to the is- **3A-1197** sued by the Department of the Environment (s.182). The current *Code of Guidance* was issued in July 2002 by the Office of the Deputy Prime Minister to reflect changes introduced by the Homelessness Act 2002. Copies are available from the Office of the Deputy Prime Minister, PO Box 236, Wetherby, West Yorkshire LS23 7NB. The Code of Guidance is not a source of law. Although councils must take it into account and give reasons for departing from it, it is not binding on them (*R.(on the application of Khatun) v. Newham LBC* [2004] EWCA Civ 55; [2004] 3 W.L.R. 417). Where the Code of Guidance is in conflict with the Act, the words of the Act prevail (*Griffin v. Westminster City Council* [2004] EWCA Civ 108; [2004] H.L.R. 12.

APPLICATION FOR ASSISTANCE IN CASE OF HOMELESSNESS OR THREATENED HOMELESSNESS

Application for assistance

183.—(1) The following provisions of this Part apply where a **3A-1198** person applies to a local housing authority for accommodation, or for assistance in obtaining accommodation, and the authority have reason to believe that he is or may be homeless or threatened with homelessness.

(2) In this Part—

"applicant" means a person making such an application,

"assistance under this Part" means the benefit of any function under the following provisions of this Part relating to accommodation or assistance in obtaining accommodation, and

"eligible for assistance" means not excluded from such assistance by section 185 (persons from abroad not eligible for housing assistance).

(3) Nothing in this section or the following provisions of this Part affects a person's entitlement to advice and information under section 179 (duty to provide advisory services).

Note —Amended by Immigration and Asylum Act 1999, Sched.14, para. 116. **3A-1199**

"homeless"
See s.175. **3A-1200**

"threatened with homelessness"
See s.175. **3A-1201**

"local housing authority"
See ss.217, 218, and 230 which refers to the Housing Act 1985—see the Housing **3A-1202** Act 1985, ss.1 and 2, above.

"application"
The House of Lords has held that a child dependent on an adult cannot make an **3A-1203** application for accommodation capable of triggering the duties under the Housing Act 1985, Pt III (now the Housing Act 1996, Pt VII). The Housing Act 1985, s.59(1)(b) (now s.189(1)(b)) plainly indicates that parliament intended dependent children to be the subject of applications by their carer (*R. v. Oldham MBC, ex p. G* [1993] A.C. 509; [1993] 2 W.L.R. 609; [1993] 2 All E.R. 65 (also reported as *Garlick v. Oldham MBC*, HL). Similarly, an adult lacking mental capacity was not owed duties under the Housing Act 1985, Pt III (now the Housing Act 1996, Pt VII). It is for local authorities to determine whether an applicant has sufficient mental capacity (*i.e.* the capacity to

understand and deal with the concept of being offered accommodation) and their decisions can only be challenged if they are manifestly perverse or otherwise wrong on *Wednesbury* grounds (*R. v. Tower Hamlets LBC, ex p. Begum (Ferdous)* [1993] AC 509; [1993] 2 W.L.R. 609; [1993] 2 All E.R. 65, HL).

Inquiry into cases of homelessness or threatened homelessness

3A–1204   **184.**—(1) If the local housing authority have reason to believe that an applicant may be homeless or threatened with homelessness, they shall make such inquiries as are necessary to satisfy themselves—

(a) whether he is eligible for assistance, and

(b) if so, whether any duty, and if so what duty, is owed to him under the following provisions of this Part.

(2) They may also make inquiries whether he has a local connection with the district of another local housing authority in England, Wales or Scotland.

(3) On completing their inquiries the authority shall notify the applicant of their decision and, so far as any issue is decided against his interests, inform him of the reasons for their decision.

(4) If the authority have notified or intend to notify another local housing authority under section 198 (referral of cases), they shall at the same time notify the applicant of that decision and inform him of the reasons for it.

(5) A notice under subsection (3) or (4) shall also inform the applicant of his right to request a review of the decision and of the time within which such a request must be made (see section 202).

(6) Notice required to be given to a person under this section shall be given in writing and, if not received by him, shall be treated as having been given to him if it is made available at the authority's office for a reasonable period for collection by him or on his behalf.

"homeless"

3A–1205   See s.175.

"threatened with homelessness"

3A–1206   See s.175.

"local housing authority"

3A–1207   See ss.217, 218, and 230 which refers to the Housing Act 1985—see the Housing Act 1985, ss.1 and 2 above.

"applicant"

3A–1208   See s.183 and the commentary thereto.

"eligible for assistance"

3A–1209   See s.185.

"local connection"

3A–1210   See s.199.

Inquiry into cases of homelessness or threatened homelessness

3A–1211   Section 184 sets out the matters into which a council must enquire on receiving an application from a potentially homeless applicant. These are such enquiries as are necessary to satisfy themselves as to:

(a) whether he or she is eligible for assistance; and

(b) if so, whether any duty, and if so, what duty is owed.

Inadequate inquiries will leave a council decision (irrespective of its merit) open to challenge for failure to have regard to all relevant considerations.

In *Cramp v. Hastings LBC*; *Phillips v Camden LBC* [2005] EWCA Civ 1005;29 July 2005, the Court of Appeal stated that Parliament imposed the duty to make the necessary inquiries upon housing officers, and, if there is a review, upon senior housing officers. It is for councils to judge what inquiries are necessary, and they are susceptible to successful challenges on a point of law if and only if a judge in the county court considers that no reasonable council could have failed to regard as necessary the further inquiries suggested by the appellant. As a matter of law a quashing order cannot be justified on the grounds "that it would have been helpful" if particular inquiries had been made, or that "there might well have been additional information" which further inquiries might have produced. Whether to make such inquiries is a matter for the reviewing officer. The Court of Appeal stated that

> "these two cases evidence a worrying tendency in judges at [county court] level to overlook the fact that it will never be easy for a judge to say that an experienced senior housing officer on a homelessness review, who has considered all the reports readily available, and all the representations made by the applicant's solicitors, has made an error of law when she considered that it was unnecessary to put in train further detailed inquiries, not suggested by the applicant's solicitors, before she could properly make a decision on the review. The need to correct that tendency raises an important point of practice".

For other Court of Appeal decisions on the adequacy of inquiries under the 1985 Act, see *R. v. Brent LBC, ex p. Grossett* (1996) 28 H.L.R. 9, CA; *R. v. Exeter City Council, ex p. Tranckle* (1993) 26 H.L.R. 244, CA; *R. v. Kensington and Chelsea RBC, ex p. Bayani* (1990) 22 H.L.R. 406, CA; *R. v. Kensington and Chelsea RBC, ex p. Cunha* (1989) 21 H.L.R. 16, CA; *R. v. Northavon DC, ex p. Palmer* (1995) 27 H.L.R. 576; (1995) 94 L.G.R. 568, CA; *R. v. Sevenoaks DC, ex p. Reynolds* (1990) 22 H.L.R. 250, CA; *R. v. Tower Hamlets LBC, ex p. Shafia Khatun* (1995) 27 H.L.R. 465, CA and *Kacar v. Enfield LBC* (2001) 33 H.L.R. 64, CA. Faced with an application based upon threatened homelessness, a council has to take immediate steps under s.184 to determine whether the applicant is eligible for assistance and what duty is owed. Where satisfied that the applicant is threatened with homelessness, eligible for assistance and in priority need, the duty to take steps to secure accommodation arises under section 195. The council cannot remain inactive (*R v. Newham LBC, ex p. Khan and Hussain* (2001) 33 H.L.R. 269, QBD).

ELIGIBILITY FOR ASSISTANCE

Persons from abroad not eligible for housing assistance

185.—(1) A person is not eligible for assistance under this Part if **3A–1212** he is a person from abroad who is ineligible for housing assistance.

(2) A person who is subject to immigration control within the meaning of the Asylum and Immigration Act 1996 is not eligible for housing assistance unless he is of a class prescribed by regulations made by the Secretary of State.

(2A) No person who is excluded from entitlement to housing benefit by section 115 of the Immigration and Asylum Act 1999 (exclusion from benefits) shall be included in any class prescribed under subsection (2).

(3) The Secretary of State may make provision by regulations as to other descriptions of persons who are to be treated for the purposes of this Part as persons from abroad who are ineligible for housing assistance.

(4) A person from abroad who is not eligible for housing assistance shall be disregarded in determining for the purposes of this Part whether another person—

(a) is homeless or threatened with homelessness, or

(b) has a priority need for accommodation.

3A–1213 *Note* —Amended by the Immigration and Asylum Act 1999, s.117 and by Homelessness Act 2002, Sched.1, para. 7. The latter amendment came into force on February 26, 2002.

"assistance"

3A–1214 See s.183.

"regulations"

3A–1215 See below.

"homeless"

3A–1216 See s.175.

"threatened with homelessness"

3A–1217 See s.175.

"priority need"

3A–1218 See s.189.

Persons from abroad not eligible for housing assistance

3A–1219 Section 185 provides that applicants *are not eligible* for assistance under Pt VII if—

(a) they are persons from abroad who are subject to immigration control under the Asylum and Immigration Act 1996. (Under the Immigration and Asylum Act 1999 Part VI, all people who applied for asylum after April 3, 2000 must rely upon the National Asylum Support Service, which, in some circumstances is obliged to provide accommodation); or

(b) they are persons who are not habitually resident in the Common Travel Area (s.185(2A) and Homelessness (England) Regulations 2000 No. 701, para. 4).

Both these provisions are subject to exceptions contained in The Homelessness (England) Regulations 2000 No. 701. (For Wales, see the Homelessness (Wales) Regulations (S.I. 2000 No. 1079).

First, the Homelessness (England) Regulations 2000 No. 701, para. 3 sets out nine classes of persons who, although subject to immigration control, are eligible for housing assistance. These regulations are not affected by s.185(2A) (introduced by Homelessness Act 2002, Sched.1, para. 7) but the regulations limit the definition of "asylumseeker" to persons not under 18 who made a claim for asylum before April 3, 2000 and which has not been determined (para. 2(1)). (As indicated above, the intention of the government is that post-April 3, 2000 asylum seekers should seek accommodation through the National Asylum Support Service.) The classes eligible for housing assistance are:

- **Class A**—a person recorded by the Secretary of State as a refugee within the definition in Article 1 of the Refugee Convention;

- **Class B**—a person—

  (i) who has been granted by the Secretary of State exceptional leave to enter or remain in the United Kingdom outside the provisions of the immigration rules; and

  (ii) whose leave is not subject to a condition requiring him to maintain and accommodate himself, and any person who is dependent on him, without recourse to public funds;

- **Class C**—a person who has current leave to enter or remain in the United Kingdom which is not subject to any limitation or condition and who is habitually resident in the Common Travel Area other than a person—

  (i) who has been given leave to enter or remain in the United Kingdom upon an undertaking given by another person (his "sponsor" in writing in pursuance of the immigration rules to be responsible for his maintenance and accommodation;

  (ii) who has been resident in the United Kingdom for less than five years beginning on the date of entry or the date on which the undertaking was given in respect of him, whichever date is the later; and

    (iii) whose sponsor or, where there is more than one sponsor, at least one of whose sponsors, is still alive;

- **Class D**—a person who left the territory of Montserrat after November 1, 1995 because of the effect on that territory of a volcanic eruption;
- **Class E**—a person who is habitually resident in the Common Travel Area and who—

    (i) is a national of a state which has ratified the European Convention on Social and Medical Assistance done at Paris on December 11, 1953 or a state which has ratified the European Social Charter done at Turin on October 18, 1961 and is lawfully present in the United Kingdom; or

    (ii) before April 3, 2000 was owed a duty by a housing authority under Part III of the Housing Act 1985 (housing the homeless) or Part VII of the 1996 Act (homelessness) which is extant, and who is a national of a state which is a signatory to the European Convention on Social and Medical Assistance done at Paris on December 11, 1953 or a state which is a signatory to the European Social Charter done at Turin on October 18, 1961 (see *Szoma v. Secretary of State for Work & Pensions* [2005] UKHL 64; 27 October 2005, where the House of Lords held that *Kaya v. Haringey LBC* [2001] EWCA Civ 677, [2002] HLR 1 was wrongly decided and that a person granted "temporary admission" is "lawfully present" in the UK. Accordingly any asylum seeker granted temporary admission and meeting the other requirements of Class E is now "eligible" for homelessness assistance).

- **Class F**—a person who is an asylum-seeker and who made a claim for asylum—

    (i) which is recorded by the Secretary of State as having been made on his arrival (other than on his re-entry) in the United Kingdom from a country outside the Common Travel Area; and

    (ii) which has not been recorded by the Secretary of State as having been either decided (other than on appeal) or abandoned;

- **Class G**—a person who is an asylum-seeker and—

    (i) who was in Great Britain when the Secretary of State made a declaration to the effect that the country of which that person is a national is subject to such a fundamental change in circumstances that he would not normally order the return of a person to that country;

    (ii) who made a claim for asylum which is recorded by the Secretary of State as having been made within a period of three months from the day on which that declaration was made; and

    (iii) whose claim for asylum has not been recorded by the Secretary of State as having been either decided (other than on appeal) or abandoned

- **Class H**—a person who is an asylum-seeker and—

    (i) who made a relevant claim for asylum on or before 4th February 1996; and

    (ii) who was, on February 4, 1996, entitled to benefit under regulation 7A of the Housing Benefit (General) Regulations 1987 (persons from abroad); and

- **Class I**—a person who is on an income-based jobseeker's allowance or in receipt of income support and is eligible for that benefit other than because—

    (i) he has limited leave to enter or remain in the United Kingdom which was given in accordance with the relevant immigration rules; and

    (ii) he is temporarily without funds because remittances to him from abroad have been disrupted.

(The purpose of s.185(2A), an amendment brought about by Homelessness Act 2002, (as of the subsection originally inserted by Immigration and Asylum Act 1999) is to limit the power of the Secretary of State to make regulations prescribing classes of persons subject to immigration control who may be eligible for assistance under Part VII. Section 185, as amended, excludes from Housing Act 1996, Part VII people from abroad who are not entitled to housing benefit.)

Secondly, Homelessness (England) Regulations 2000 No. 701, para. 4, as amended by the Allocation of Housing & Homelessness (Amendment) (England) Regulations 2004 (S.I. 2004 No. 1235), lists four classes of persons who, even though they are not

HOUSING

habitually resident in the Common Travel Area, are eligible for housing assistance. They are—

(a) a person who is a worker for the purposes of Council Regulation (EEC) No.1612/68 or (EEC) No.1251/70;

(b) a person who is an accession state worker requiring registration who is treated as a worker for the purpose of the definition of "qualified person" in regulation 5(1) of the Immigration (European Economic Area) Regulations 2000 pursuant to regulation 5 of the Accession (Immigration and Worker Registration) Regulations 2004;

(c) a person with a right to reside pursuant to the Immigration (European Economic Area) Regulations 2000, which is derived from Council Directive No.68/360/EEC, No.73/148/EEC or No.75/34/EEC;

(d) a person who left the territory of Montserrat after November 1, 1995 because of the effect on that territory of a volcanic eruption.

Local authorities may request information from the Secretary of State about a person's immigration status (Housing Act 1996, s.187). When considering an application for interim accommodation under s.188, local authorities have a duty to make enquiries, but where the Secretary of State has refused a non-EEA national's application for a resident's permit, a local authority is entitled to take such a refusal at face value. It is reasonable not to make further enquiries (*R. (on the application of Burns) v. Southwark LBC* [2004] EWHC 1901 (Admin.)).

Persons from abroad and priority need

3A–1220   Section 185(4) provides that persons from abroad who are not eligible for housing assistance are to be disregarded when determining whether or not an applicant has priority need. That sub-section is incompatible with ECHR Article 14 to the extent that it requires a dependent child of a British citizen to be disregarded when determining whether the British citizen has a priority need for accommodation, when that child is subject to immigration control (*R. (Morris) v. Westminster City Council* [2005] EWCA Civ 1184; 14 October 2005 .

Asylum-seekers and their dependents

3A–1221   **186.** [...]

Note

3A–1222   This section was repealed by Immigration and Asylum Act 1999, s.117(5) and Sched.16. Any accommodation which is to be made available for asylum seekers and their dependents should now be provided by via the National Asylum Support Service. See the Immigration and Asylum Act 1999, ss.94–100 and the Homelessness (England) Regulations 2000 (S.I. 2000 No. 701), the Allocation of Housing (England) Regulations 2000 (S.I. 2000 No. 702) and the Persons Subject to Immigration Control (Housing Authority Accommodation and Homelessness) Order 2000 (S.I. 2000 No. 706) came into force on April 3, 2000. They:

- close access to homelessness legislation for asylum seekers who claim asylum after April 2, 2000;
- change the rules on access to the housing register and eligibility for homelessness assistance for nationals of signatory countries to the European Convention on Social and Medical Assistance or the European Social Charter;
- enable authorities to grant non-secure tenancies of hard to let accommodation directly to overseas students; and
- consolidate existing orders under Immigration and Asylum Act 1996, s.9(1) and existing regulations under Housing Act 1996, Parts VI and VII.

Provision of information by Secretary of State

3A–1223   **187.**—(1) The Secretary of State shall, at the request of a local housing authority, provide the authority with such information as they may require—

(a) as to whether a person is a person to whom section 115 of the Immigration and Asylum Act 1999 (exclusion from benefits) applies, and

(b) to enable them to determine whether such a person is eligible for assistance under this Part under section 185 (persons from abroad not eligible for housing assistance).

(2) Where that information is given otherwise than in writing, the Secretary of State shall confirm it in writing if a written request is made to him by the authority.

(3) If it appears to the Secretary of State that any application, decision or other change of circumstances has affected the status of a person about whom information was previously provided by him to a local housing authority under this section, he shall inform the authority in writing of that fact, the reason for it and the date on which the previous information became inaccurate.

Note —Amended by the Immigration and Asylum Act 1999, s.117(8).　　**3A–1224**

"asylum seeker"
See s.186.　　**3A–1225**

"dependent of asylum seeker"
See s.186.　　**3A–1226**

"local housing authority"
See ss.217, 218, and 230 which refers to the Housing Act 1985—see the Housing **3A–1227**
Act 1985, ss.1 and 2, above.

Provision of information by Secretary of State
See commentary to s.185.　　**3A–1228**

Interim duty to accommodate in case of apparent priority need

188.—(1) If the local housing authority have reason to believe that **3A–1229**
an applicant may be homeless, eligible for assistance and have a priority need, they shall secure that accommodation is available for his occupation pending a decision as to the duty (if any) owed to him under the following provisions of this Part.

(2) The duty under this section arises irrespective of any possibility of the referral of the applicant's case to another local housing authority (see sections 198 to 200).

(3) The duty ceases when the authority's decision is notified to the applicant, even if the applicant requests a review of the decision (see section 202).

The authority may secure that accommodation is available for the applicant's occupation pending a decision on a review.

Amended by Homelessness Act 2002 Sched.1, para. 8. In England, this amendment **3A–1230**
was brought into force on July 31, 2002 by the Homelessness Act 2002 (Commencement No. 1) (England) Order 2002 (S.I. 2002 No. 1799) (C.56). In Wales, this amendment was brought into force on September 30, 2002 by the Homelessness Act 2002 (Commencement) (Wales) Order 2002 (S.I. 2002 No. 1736) (W.166)(C.53).

"eligible for assistance"
See s.185.　　**3A–1231**

"assistance"
See s.183.　　**3A–1232**

"local housing authority"

3A–1233   See ss.217, 218, and 230 which refer to the Housing Act 1985—see the Housing Act 1985, ss.1 and 2, above.

"homeless"

3A–1234   See s.175.

"threatened with homelessness"

3A–1235   See s.175.

"applicant"

3A–1236   See s.183 and the commentary thereto.

"priority need"

3A–1237   See s.189.

"available for his occupation"

3A–1238   See s.176.

Interim duty to accommodate

3A–1239   See *R. v. Camden LBC, ex p. Mohammed* (1998) 30 H.L.R. 315, QBD (summarised at para. 3A–1330); *R. v. Newham LBC, ex p. Idowu*, August 1998, Legal Action 21, QBD; and *R. v. Haringey LBC, ex p. Erdogan*, August 1998, Legal Action 23, QBD.

Suitability of interim accommodation

3A–1240   Accommodation provided under the interim duty to accommodate must be suitable. Lack of resources does not relieve councils from this mandatory duty. Section 188, when read with s.176, does not permit councils to split families in accommodation in separate dwellings (*Ealing LBC. v. Surdonja* (1999) 31 H.L.R. 686, QBD affirmed on appeal; [2001] Q.B. 97; [2000] 2 All E.R. 597, CA and [2001] UKHL 57; [2002] 1 A.C. 547; [2001] 3 W.L.R. 1339; [2001] 1 All E.R. 176, HL). When discharging their interim duties under s.188 local authorities should give individual consideration to the circumstances of particular applicants. The duty cannot be met by booking all applicants into bed and breakfast accommodation—*R. v. Newham LBC, ex p. Ojuri (No. 3)* (1999) 31 H.L.R. 452, CA, (Collins J.).

The question whether or not the accommodation is suitable requires an assessment of all the qualities of the accommodation in the light of the needs and requirements of the homeless person and his or her family. That means that the location of the accommodation may be relevant to an assessment of suitability. A council may act unlawfully in failing to have regard to the particular educational, employment and medical requirements of the family (*R.(Sacupima) v. Newham LBC* [2001] 1 W.L.R. 563, CA, where a decision to provide bed and breakfast accommodation outside its area was quashed).

Priority need for accommodation

3A–1241   189.—(1) The following have a priority need for accommodation—

(a) a pregnant woman or a person with whom she resides or might reasonably be expected to reside;

(b) a person with whom dependent children reside or might reasonably be expected to reside;

(c) a person who is vulnerable as a result of old age, mental illness or handicap or physical disability or other special reason, or with whom such a person resides or might reasonably be expected to reside;

(d) a person who is homeless or threatened with homelessness as a result of an emergency such as flood, fire or other disaster.

(2) The Secretary of State may by order—

(a) specify further descriptions of persons as having a priority need for accommodation, and

(b) amend or repeal any part of subsection (1).

(3) Before making such an order the Secretary of State shall consult such associations representing relevant authorities, and such other persons, as he considers appropriate.

(4) No such order shall be made unless a draft of it has been approved by resolution of each House of Parliament.

Priority need for accommodation

An applicant may have priority need as a result of falling within any one of the four sub-paragraphs in the Housing Act 1996, s.189(1), namely: **3A–1242**

(a) She is pregnant or the applicant is a person with whom a pregnant woman resides or might reasonably be expected to reside.

(b) S/he has dependent children. There are two routes to priority need through dependent children (s.189(1)(b)). One is if dependent children are residing with the applicant. The other is if, although the children do not at present reside with the applicant, it is reasonable to expect them to do so in the future. The second route may apply if a parent who does not have day-to-day care and control of children but intends to have prolonged staying contact. The Act contains no definition of "dependent child" but the Homelessness Code of Guidance suggests that it should include "all children under 16, and all children aged 16 to 18 who are in, or are about to begin, full-time education or training" (para. 14.2).

(c) S/he is vulnerable as a result of old age, mental illness or handicap or physical disability or other special reason, or is someone with whom such a person resides or might reasonably be expected to reside (s.189(1)(c)).

(d) S/he is homeless or threatened with homelessness as a result of an emergency such as a flood, fire or other disaster (s.189(1)(d)). If such a person is not intentionally homeless, the local authority must ensure that permanent alternative accommodation is made available.

The Homelessness (Priority Need for Accommodation) (England) Order 2002

In addition the Homelessness (Priority Need for Accommodation) (England) Order 2002 (S.I. 2002 No. 2051) provides that the following categories of people have a priority need for accommodation for the purposes of Part 7 of the Housing Act 1996: **3A–1243**

Children aged 16 or 17

3.—(1) A person (other than a person to whom paragraph (2) below applies) aged sixteen or seventeen who is not a relevant child for the purposes of section 23A of the Children Act 1989.

(2) This paragraph applies to a person to whom a local authority owe a duty to provide accommodation under section 20 of that Act (provision of accommodation for children in need).

Young people under 21

4.—(1) A person (other than a relevant student) who—

(a) is under twenty-one; and

(b) at any time after reaching the age of sixteen, but while still under eighteen, was, but is no longer, looked after, accommodated or fostered.

Vulnerability: institutional backgrounds

5.—(1) A person (other than a relevant student) who has reached the age of twenty-one and who is vulnerable as a result of having been looked after, accommodated or fostered.

(2) A person who is vulnerable as a result of having been a member of Her Majesty's regular naval, military or air forces.

(3) A person who is vulnerable as a result of—

(a) having served a custodial sentence (within the meaning of section 76 of the Powers of Criminal Courts (Sentencing) Act 2000);

(b) having been committed for contempt of court or any other kindred offence;

(c) having been remanded in custody (within the meaning of paragraph (b), (c) or (d) of section 88(1) of that Act).

Vulnerability: fleeing violence or threats of violence

6. A person who is vulnerable as a result of ceasing to occupy accommodation by reason of violence from another person or threats of violence from another person which are likely to be carried out.

Priority need in Wales

3A-1244   The Homeless Persons (Priority Need) (Wales) Order 2001 (S.I. 2001 No. 607 (W.3)) extended the priority need categories in s.189 to include anyone applying as a homeless person in Wales who is:

- aged 16 or 17;
- aged 18, 19 or 20 (who had been in local authority care and is at particular risk of sexual or financial exploitation);
- fleeing domestic violence or in fear of such violence if s/he returns home;
- homeless since leaving the regular armed forces; or
- homeless since leaving custody as a prisoner (and who has a local connection with the authority applied to).

It came into force on March 1, 2001.

Priority need and the ECHR

3A-1245   The provisions of s.189 do not breach ECHR Art.8(1) in enacting a scheme of priorities whereby applications for accommodation by homeless persons are to be determined by local housing authorities. In assessing priorities, Parliament was entitled to take into account considerations such as vulnerability, which might or might not have an impact on family life, as well as those that inevitably did. Specifically Art.8(1) does not require applicants with child spouses to be given priority over applicants with adult spouses or over other categories of applicant. (*Hackney LBC v. Ekinci* [2001] EWCA Civ 776; [2002] H.L.R. 2).

Dependent children

3A-1246   The function of the priority need provisions relating to dependent children in Part VII is to keep families together. That brings them within the ambit of ECHR Art 8 dealing with the right to respect for "family life" (*R (Morris) v. Westminster City Council* [2005] EWCA Civ 1184; 14 October 2005). The term "dependent child" in s.189(1) does not include a wife under the age of 18 who is in full-time education and dependent upon her husband (*Ekinci v. Hackney LBC* [2001] EWCA Civ 1776, CA; [2002] H.L.R. 2).

A child in full-time employment cannot be dependent. However, there may be circumstances where 16 or 17-year-olds who are not financially dependent on their parents may be dependent on them in other ways, bringing them within s.189(1)(b). (*R. v. Kensington and Chelsea RBC, ex p. Hammell* [1989] 1 Q.B. 518, CA—son aged 16, who was on a two-year YTS course at a training workshop, not dependent).

See also *R. v. Kingswood BC, ex p. Smith-Morse* [1995] 2 FLR 137, QBD; *R. v. Lambeth LBC, ex p. Bodunrin* (1992) 24 H.L.R. 647, QBD.

It has been held that the test to be applied under Housing Act 1985, s.59(1)(b) (now Housing Act 1996, s.189(1)(b)) was whether dependent children resided with the applicant, not whether there was any "greater residency" with another adult (*R. v. Leeds CC, ex p. Collier*, June 1998, Legal Action 14, QBD).

Vulnerable

Vulnerable means vulnerable in housing terms (*R. v. Bath City Council, ex p. Sanger-* **3A-1247**
mano (1985) 17 H.L.R. 94, QBD). See too *R. v. Lambeth LBC, ex p. Carroll* (1988) 20
H.L.R. 142, QBD, where Webster J. confirmed that "vulnerable" means less able to
fend for oneself when homeless or in finding and keeping accommodation. Note that
the Housing Act 1996, s.189(1)(c) draws a distinction between mental illness and
mental handicap which is not concerned with illness but with either subnormality or
severe subnormality (*R. v. Bath City Council, ex p. Sangermano* (1985) 17 H.L.R. 94,
QBD).

In *R. v. Waveney DC, ex p. Bowers* [1983] Q.B. 238; [1982] 3 All E.R. 727, CA, the
Court of Appeal held that although alcoholism does not normally give an applicant
priority need, in this case Mr Bowers's brain injury, whether described as a mental
handicap or other social reason, had increased his vulnerability to such an extent that
he had priority need (*cf. R. v. Westminster City Council, ex p. Ortiz* (1995) 27 H.L.R. 364,
CA).

In relation to epilepsy, *cf. R. v. Reigate and Banstead BC, ex p. Di Dominico* (1988) 20
H.L.R. 153, QBD; and *R. v. Wandsworth BC, ex p. Banbury* (1987) 19 H.L.R. 76, QBD.

Although it is proper for a local authority to consider medical opinion, the question
of whether or not someone is vulnerable for "some other special reason" is to be
answered by the authority itself, not by the medical adviser. Local authorities are
therefore obliged to consider any other available evidence and make whatever appropriate enquiries are necessary beyond obtaining their own officers' opinions (*R. v.
Lambeth LBC, ex p. Carroll* (1988) 20 H.L.R. 142, QBD).

In *R. v. Camden LBC, ex p. Pereira* (1999) 31 H.L.R. 317, CA, after reviewing recent
authorities, the Court of Appeal stated that vulnerability involves not just the issue of
whether applicants can find and keep accommodation, but also whether they are less
able to fend for themselves in coping with the state of homelessness. The assessment
required is a composite one and an individual is not homeless under the "coping with
homelessness" approach unless s/he would suffer injury of detriment which an ordinary
homeless person would not. See too *Thorne v. Winchester CC*, April 2000, Legal Action
32, CA. Although the Code of Guidance (July 2002) para 8.13 states that the critical
test in applying s.189(1)(c) is whether an applicant is less likely to be unable to fend
for himself so that he is likely to suffer injury or detriment, the Court of Appeal has
noted that the word 'likelihood' does not appear in the relevant provisions of the Act.
Although local authorities must have regard to the Code of Guidance when exercising
their functions under the Act, where the Code of Guidance is in conflict with the Act,
the words of the Act prevail. The correct test under s.189(1)(c) is whether homeless
persons are less able to fend for themselves so that they will suffer injury or detriment,
not whether they are likely to suffer injury or detriment. It is not necessary to put the
gloss of likeliness into the statutory test (*Griffin v. Westminster City Council* [2004] EWCA
Civ 108; [2004] H.L.R. 32). See too *Chowdhoury v. Islington LBC* [2004] EWCA Civ 08,
Osmani v. Camden LBC [2004] EWCA Civ 1706 ; [2005] HLR 22 ; *Bellouti v Wandsworth
LBC* [2005] EWCA Civ 602 ; 20 May 2005; and *Tetteh v. Kingston-upon-Thames RLBC*
[2004] EWCA Civ 1775 ; [2005] HLR 21. As to the obligation of local authorities to
make inquiries, see s.184 and (in relation to alleged vulnerability) *Cramp v. Hastings
LBC* ; *Phillips v Camden LBC* [2005] EWCA Civ 1005 ; 29 July 2005.

emergency

The phrase "emergency such as a flood, fire or other disaster" involves the sudden **3A-1248**
and wholly unexpected loss of a home in circumstances outside an applicant's control.
It is not necessary to show that a home has been lost through some physical disaster.
The disappearance of a caravan in unexplained circumstances may be an emergency
under s.189(1)(d). (*Higgs v. Brighton and Hove City Council* [2003] EWCA Civ 895;
[2003] 1 W.L.R. 2241; [2003] 3 All E.R. 753. However a demolition order is not "an
emergency such as a flood, fire or any other disaster" (*Noble v. South Hertfordshire DC*
(1985) 17 H.L.R. 80, CA). Similarly, the Court of Appeal has held that a person made
homeless by an unlawful eviction is not homeless "as a result of an emergency" within
the Housing Act 1985, s.59(1)(d)(now s.189(1)(d)) (*R. v. Bristol City Council, ex p. Bradic*
(1995) 94 L.G.R. 257; 27 H.L.R. 584, CA). The word "emergency" is qualified by the
phrase "such as flood, fire or other disaster". However, emergencies giving rise to
priority need are not limited to those with "natural" causes. Fires or floods caused by
humans can give rise to priority need, but there must be physical damage which
causes the accommodation to be uninhabitable.

*DUTIES TO PERSONS FOUND TO BE HOMELESS OR THREATENED WITH
HOMELESSNESS*

Duties to persons becoming homeless intentionally

3A-1249   **190.**—(1) This section applies where the local housing authority are satisfied that an applicant is homeless and is eligible for assistance but are also satisfied that he became homeless intentionally.

(2) If the authority are satisfied that the applicant has a priority need, they shall—

    (a) secure that accommodation is available for his occupation for such period as they consider will give him a reasonable opportunity of securing accommodation for his occupation, and

    (b) provide him with (or secure that he is provided with) advice and assistance in any attempts he may make to secure that accommodation becomes available for his occupation.

(3) If they are not satisfied that he has a priority need, they shall provide him with (or secure that he is provided with) advice and assistance in any attempts he may make to secure that accommodation becomes available for his occupation.

(4) The applicant's housing needs shall be assessed before advice and assistance is provided under subsection (2)(b) or (3).

(5) The advice and assistance provided under subsection (2)(b) or (3) must include information about the likely availability in the authority's district of types of accommodation appropriate to the applicant's housing needs (including, in particular, the location and sources of such types of accommodation).

3A-1250   Amended by Homelessness Act 2002, Sched.1, paras 9 and 10. In England, this amendment was brought into force on July 31, 2002 by the Homelessness Act 2002 (Commencement No. 1) (England) Order 2002 (S.I. 2002 No. 1799) (C.56). In Wales, this amendment was brought into force on September 30, 2002 by the Homelessness Act 2002 (Commencement) (Wales) Order 2002 (S.I. 2002 No. 1736) (W.166) (C.53).

"eligible for assistance"
3A-1251   See s.185.

"assistance"
3A-1252   See s.183.

"local housing authority"
3A-1253   See ss.217, 218, and 230 which refer to the Housing Act 1985—see the Housing Act 1985, ss.1 and 2 above.

"homeless"
3A-1254   See s.175.

"applicant"
3A-1255   See s.183 and the commentary thereto.

"priority need"
3A-1256   See s.189.

"available for his occupation"

See s.176.

3A–1257

"homeless intentionally"

See s.191.

3A–1258

Duties to persons becoming homeless intentionally

Local authorities only have minimal obligations to applicants who are intentionally   3A–1259
homeless. The definition of intentional homelessness in the Housing Act 1996, s.191(1)
has five component parts. The homeless person must have:

    (a) done a deliberate act,

    (b) which caused the loss of housing,

    (c) which s/he ceased to occupy,

    (d) which was available to him or her, and

    (e) which it would have been reasonable to continue to occupy.

In addition a person is to be treated as becoming homeless intentionally if he or she
enters "into an arrangement under which he is required to cease to occupy accommodation which it would be reasonable for him to continue to occupy, and … the
purpose of the arrangement is to enable him to become entitled to assistance" in accordance with Part VII of the Act "and there is no other good reason why he is homeless" (Housing Act 1996, s.191(3)).

A person is threatened with homelessness intentionally if homelessness is the "likely
result" of his or her deliberate act or omission.

It is for each local authority to make its own enquiries and to form its own view as
to whether homelessness is intentional or not (*R. v. Slough BC, ex p. Ealing LBC* [1981]
Q.B. 801; [1981] 1 All E.R. 601; [1981] 2 W.L.R. 399, CA; *Noh v. Hammersmith and Fulham LBC* [2001] EWCA Civ 905; [2002] H.L.R. 54, and *R. v. Basingstoke and Deane DC,
ex p. Webb*; December 1989; Legal Action 15, QBD).

The material date for determining whether a person became homeless intentionally
or unintentionally is the date on which s/he left the accommodation. What may have
happened afterwards is irrelevant (*Din v. Wandsworth LBC* [1983] 1 A.C. 657; [1981] 3
All E.R. 881, HL). See too *R. v. Islington LBC, ex p. Hassan* (1995) 27 H.L.R. 485, QBD,
where Deputy Judge Roger Toulson, QC quashed a finding of intentional homelessness because the council had erred in believing that it could take account of developments after the applicant became homeless but before his actual departure from the
premises.

The burden is on local authorities to satisfy themselves that an applicant has become
homeless intentionally. If there is doubt or uncertainty, the issue must be resolved in
the applicant's favour (*R. v. Gravesham BC, ex p. Winchester* (1986) 18 H.L.R. 207,
QBD—finding upheld).

Note that a homeless person cannot be intentionally homeless for refusing an offer
of permanent accommodation, as it has never been occupied (*R. v. Brent LBC, ex p.
Awua* [1995] 3 W.L.R. 215; [1995] 3 All E.R. 493; [1996] AC 55], HL, below). However,
such a refusal may mean that a local authority has discharged its duty and owes no
further obligations towards the homeless person.

There is no practical or policy reason why a woman who has been sent to prison for
theft should not be regarded as having made herself intentionally homeless, even
though she moved house between the commission of the offence and the start of her
sentence (*Minchin v. Sheffield City Council, The Times*, April 26, 2000, CA). See too *Stewart v. Lambeth LBC* [2002] EWCA Civ 753; [2002] H.L.R. 40, noted above.

"deliberately does or fails to do …"

In *Dyson v. Kerrier DC* [1980] 1 W.L.R. 1205; [1980] 3 All E.R. 313, CA, the ap-   3A–1260
plicant had surrendered her tenancy of a council flat in Cambridgeshire and gone to
Cornwall where she had relatives. She took an unprotected holiday let for about four-
and-a-half months. Not long before the holiday let was due to expire she approached
the council for accommodation. It decided that her impending homelessness had been
caused "intentionally" by her giving up the flat in Cambridgeshire. The Court of Appeal held that the council was entitled to take into account the fact that if she had not
surrendered the Cambridgeshire tenancy she would not have become homeless. See
too *R. v. Barking and Dagenham LBC, ex p. Okuneye* (1996) 28 H.L.R. 174, QBD and *R.
v. Tower Hamlets LBC, ex p. Abdul Jolil*, October 1998, Legal Action 22, QBD.

HOUSING

However, in *R. v. Tower Hamlets LBC, ex p. Rouf* (1991) 23 H.L.R. 460, CA, the applicant who had been in Britain since 1963 returned to Bangladesh in 1985 for three years. During his absence, he allowed a friend to occupy his council flat. The friend did not pay the rent and the flat was repossessed. In 1988, after obtaining entry clearance for his family, the applicant returned to England with them. He found the flat boarded up and applied to the council as a homeless person. Following an interview during which the applicant gave details of the accommodation he had used in Bangladesh (two small rooms), the authority declared him intentionally homeless for leaving the family home in Bangladesh. The interviewing officer failed to raise with the applicant two of the crucial issues contained in the definition of intentional homelessness (Housing Act 1985, s.60(1)—now the Housing Act 1996, s.191(1))—first, was the accommodation available for his continued occupation, and secondly, was it reasonable for him to have continued in occupation? The interviewer "deduced" positive answers from the discussion with the applicant. The Court of Appeal quashed the decision. The applicant had returned to England unaware that his flat had been repossessed. He had accordingly acted in ignorance and his action could not be "deliberate" for the purposes of s.60(1), if he had acted in good faith (s.60(3)—now Housing Act 1996, s.191(2)). The council had not addressed the good faith point in either its enquiries or its decision letter. See too *Kacar v. Enfield LBC* (2001) 33 H.L.R. 64, CA.

A family cannot become intentionally homeless simply because they choose to have additional children (*R. v. Eastleigh BC, ex p. Beattie (No. 1)* (1983) 10 H.L.R. 134, QBD).

Eviction following arrears

3A-1261 See, *e.g. Hobbs v. Sutton LBC* (1994) 26 H.L.R. 132, CA (eviction following rent arrears but claims by the applicants that there had been confusion about the whereabouts of their landlord and their entitlement to housing benefit. Finding of intentional homeless upheld). Similarly, in *R. v. Barnet LBC, ex p. Rughooputh* (1993) 25 H.L.R. 607, CA, the applicant was made homeless following mortgage possession proceedings. The deliberate act which caused the loss of the home was the applicant's taking out a mortgage in 1987 beyond her means—she was unemployed, but had claimed to have an earned income of £18,000. The council's finding of intentional homelessness was upheld. The taking out of the mortgage was the act that caused the homelessness. It had been induced by fraudulent misrepresentation and so the Housing Act 1985, s.60(3) (now the Housing Act 1996, s.190(2)) could not apply to prevent the act from being "deliberate".

Although eviction as a result of rent arrears is not intentional if it is the result of spending assets on the necessities of life, the "necessities of life" may vary from family to family. It is for an authority to consider whether a failure to pay rent is deliberate or whether it is due to a tenant having insufficient money to pay for the necessities of life, not for the court. It is not for the authority to investigate every detail in an applicant's figures of income and expenditure and it is not necessary for them to put to applicants their opinion that certain items are not a necessity (*R. v. Brent LBC, ex p. Baruwa* (1997) 29 H.L.R. 915, CA, where a finding of intentional homelessness was upheld). See too *R. v. Brent LBC, ex p. Grossett* (1996) 28 H.L.R. 9, CA; *R. v. Exeter City Council, ex p. Tranckle* (1994) 26 H.L.R. 244, CA; and *R. v. Wandsworth LBC, ex p. Onwudiwe* (1994) 26 H.L.R. 302, CA.

On the other hand, in *R. v. Wandsworth LBC, ex p. Hawthorne* [1995] 2 All E.R. 331; (1995) 27 H.L.R. 59, CA, a finding of intentional homelessness was quashed where the applicant had been evicted from her council home for rent arrears of over £3,000. She claimed that she had been unable to afford the rent, having had so low an income after her husband left her that she had been driven to choose between maintaining her children and paying the council. Nourse L.J. stated:

"The purpose of Part III of the 1985 Act [now the Housing Act 1996, Pt VII] is to house the homeless. Admittedly, it is no part of that purpose to house those whose homelessness has been brought upon them by their own fault. But equally it is no part of it to refuse housing to those whose homelessness has been brought upon them without fault on their part, for example by disability, sickness, poverty or even a simple inability to make ends meet."

The council had not considered the matters which had caused the applicant not to pay her rent. That was a fatal omission. It was no answer to assert that there had been a considered decision not to pay. The true question is: "What caused that decision?" See too *R. v. Hillingdon LBC, ex p. Tinn* (1988) 20 H.L.R. 305, QBD, below; *R. v. Shrewsbury and Atcham BC, ex p. Griffiths* (1993) 25 H.L.R. 613, QBD (decision of intentional homelessness after eviction for mortgage arrears quashed); *R. v. Southwark LBC, ex p. Davies* (1994) 26 H.L.R. 677, QBD; and *R. v. Camden LBC, ex p. Cosma*, (1998) 30 H.L.R. 817, QBD (return to England following the failure of the applicant's restaurant enterprise in Cyprus. Finding of intentional homelessness quashed because of failure to make sufficient enquiries into the question of the arrangements the applicant might (or might not have been) able to make with lenders to stave off her eviction and accordingly whether it would have been reasonable for the applicant to have continued to occupy her home in Cyprus).

Eviction after anti-social behaviour

It is not necessary for authorities to show that the applicants have deliberately done **3A–1262** something with the intention of being evicted. See *Devenport v. Salford City Council* (1983) 8 H.L.R. 54, CA, where a finding of intentional homelessness was upheld after failure by parents to take any steps to control their children and the children's conduct resulted in the making of a possession order. Findings of intentional homelessness were also upheld in *R. v. Rochester-upon-Medway City Council, ex p. Williams* (1994) 26 H.L.R. 588, QBD (failure to control children), and *R. v. Hammersmith and Fulham LBC, ex p. P* (1990) 22 H.L.R. 21, QBD (anti-social and criminal behaviour leading to the loss of homes).

Acquiescence in conduct of partner

A woman who lives with a man who becomes intentionally homeless is not necessar- **3A–1263** ily barred from relief by his conduct or by the fact that he may benefit undeservingly. However, depending on the facts, an authority may be entitled to assume that, in the absence of evidence to the contrary, she had acquiesced in his conduct and that accordingly she herself had become intentionally homeless (*R. v. North Devon DC, ex p. Lewis* [1981] 1 W.L.R. 328; [1981] 1 All E.R. 27, QBD). See too *R. v. Nottingham CC, ex p. Caine* (1995) 28 H.L.R. 374, CA (the applicant's partner had decided to withhold rent, for which housing benefit was being paid, because of the landlord's failure to carry out repairs. As a result of the arrears, the couple were evicted. Finding of intentional homelessness upheld because the applicant had acquiesced in the decision not to pay the rent and to use the housing benefit in the family budget); *R. v. Tower Hamlets LBC, ex p. Khatun* (1995) 27 H.L.R. 344, CA (wife content in the marriage to leave decisions to her husband. The Court of Appeal held that she might properly be treated as having "joined" in her husband's decision to move accommodation); *R. v. Barnet LBC, ex p. O'Connor* (1990) 22 H.L.R. 486, QBD; *R. v. Ealing LBC, ex p. Salmons* (1991) 23 H.L.R. 272, QBD; *R. v. East Herts DC, ex p. Bannon* (1986) 18 H.L.R. 515, QBD (acquiescence in nuisance); *R. v. Swansea City Council, ex p. John* (1983) 9 H.L.R. 56, QBD (council entitled to reach conclusion that wife has acquiesced in husband's drunkenness which had led to eviction).

Cf. however, *R. v. East Northamptonshire DC, ex p. Spruce* (1988) 20 H.L.R. 508, QBD (finding of intentional homelessness quashed because of insufficient inquiries into alleged acquiescence); *R. v. Eastleigh BC, ex p. Beattie (No. 2)* (1985) 17 H.L.R. 168, QBD (decision not to pay mortgage instalments based on legal advice; evidence that Mrs Beattie had protested about her husband not paying the mortgage. Finding of intentional homelessness quashed); *R. v. Penwith DC, ex p. Trevena* (1985) 17 H.L.R. 526, QBD (no material on which the authority could conclude that Mr Trevena had been a party to the surrender of a tenancy by his wife or that it was a joint surrender or abandonment); *R.v. Mole Valley DC, ex p. Burton* (1988) 20 H.L.R. 479, QBD; and *R. v. Thanet DC, ex p. Groves* (1990) 22 H.L.R. 223, QBD (failure by council to have regard to wife's assertions that she did not know of, or participate in, the accumulation of arrears).

"act or omission in good faith"

When considering this question "there is a distinction between honest blundering **3A–1264** and carelessness on the one hand, where a person can still act in good faith, and dishonesty on the other, where there can be no question of the person acting in good faith" (*per* Roch J. in *R. v. Hammersmith and Fulham LBC, ex p. Lusi* (1991) 23 H.L.R. 260, QBD). See too *R. v. Westminster CC, ex p. Obeid* (1996) 29 H.L.R. 389, QBD (ignorance about housing benefit); and *R. v. Wandsworth LBC, ex p. Rose* (1984) 11 H.L.R. 107, QBD (applicant came to stay with her father but asked to leave because his accommodation was not satisfactory. The council was not entitled to assume, without making proper enquiries, that simply because the applicant had failed to ask

965

her father about accommodation, she had acted other than in good faith about a relevant fact).

In *R. v. Westminster CC, ex p. N'Dormadingar, The Times*, November 20, 1997, QBD, Lightman J. enumerated the following principles which apply where someone gives up accommodation but claims not to be intentionally homeless because he or she is unaware of a material fact:

(1) An applicant must show that he or she is unaware of some relevant fact existing at the date that he or she gave up accommodation;

(2) Whether an applicant makes enquiries into the existence of the fact is relevant to his or her awareness of it;

(3) A fact is relevant where, had the applicant been aware of it, he or she would have taken it into account in deciding to give up accommodation;

(4) A fact must be sufficiently clear and definite for its existence to be objectively determined;

(5) Lack of, or deficiency in, foresight of the future does not constitute unawareness of an existing fact. To establish such unawareness it is necessary to show the existence at the relevant date of a factual state of affairs which falsifies the applicant's predictions.

In a case turning on whether ignorance was in good faith, the council should in interview tell an applicant if it believes that he or she is not acting in good faith (*R. v. Westminster City Council, ex p. Moozary-Oraky* (1994) 26 H.L.R. 213, QBD).

"reasonable for him to continue to occupy"

3A-1265   In considering whether or not it is reasonable to continue to occupy accommodation, local authorities are not limited to housing issues and can have regard to things like employment prospects and loss of benefits in that locality (*per* Woolf J. in *R. v. Hammersmith and Fulham LBC, ex p. Duro-Rama* (1983) 9 H.L.R. 71, QBD). See too *R. v. Hillingdon LBC, ex p. Tinn* (1988) 20 H.L.R. 305, QBD, where Kennedy J. said:

"it cannot be reasonable [within the meaning of section 60 of the 1985 Act—(now Housing Act 1996, s.191)] for a person to continue to occupy accommodation when they can no longer discharge the fiscal obligations ... in relation to that accommodation without so straining their resources as to deprive themselves of the ordinary necessities of life, such as food, clothing, heat, transport and so forth" (p.308).

See too *R. v. Camden LBC, ex p. Aranda* (1997) 30 H.L.R. 76, CA (surrender of London council flat under a scheme involving the receipt of a substantial sum to help them to buy privately followed by acquisition of a bungalow in Columbia. Applicant returned to London after failure to find work and being abandoned by her husband without financial support. Camden's finding of intentional homelessness was quashed. Any finding that the giving up of the Columbian home was intentional was impossible—no reasonable authority could have found, given the financial circumstances, that it would have been reasonable to continue in occupation); *R. v. Basingstoke and Deane BC, ex p. Bassett* (1983) 10 H.L.R. 125, QBD (applicant not homeless as a result of leaving that accommodation, but rather as a result of the breakdown in the marriage and in particular her husband's conduct, which made it unreasonable for her to live with him); *R. v. Islington LBC, ex p. Bibi* (1997) 29 H.L.R. 498, QBD (applicant left her home in Bangladesh because she had no access to sufficient monies to feed her family. Finding of intentional homelessness quashed); and *R. v. Tower Hamlets LBC, ex p. Ojo* (1991) 23 H.L.R. 488, QBD (council gave "no proper consideration" to the question of whether, as a result of overcrowding of the applicant's home in Nigeria, it could be said that it was not reasonable to continue to occupy the accommodation).

See also *R. v. Hillingdon LBC, ex p. Islam* [1983] 1 A.C. 688; [1981] 3 W.L.R. 109; [1981] 3 All E.R. 901, HL (husband, wife and several children evicted from shared room); *De Falco v. Crawley BC* [1980] Q.B. 460; [1980] 2 W.L.R. 664; [1980] 1 All E.R. 913, CA (reasonable to have continued to occupy the accommodation in Italy); *cf. R. v. Westminster City Council, ex p. Guilarte*, June 1994, Legal Action 13, QBD (applicant left accommodation in Venezuela because of the poor economy and high inflation in that country and because he thought he would find a better standard of living in Britain. Decision quashed because the council had failed to make enquiries as to (a) whether he could have remained in the specific accommodation he occupied in Venezuela, and, if so (b) why he chose to leave it).

In *R. v. Wandsworth LBC, ex p. Henderson* (1986) 18 H.L.R. 522, QBD, there was acute disrepair and, as a result, the council served statutory notices. The tenants withheld rent and arrears accrued. The landlord began possession proceedings based on rent arrears. Even though the tenants counterclaimed and were represented by counsel, a possession order was made. The council decided that they had consented to the possession order and had become homeless intentionally. McNeill J. dismissed an application for judicial review. Even though the necessary repairs were very extensive and being carried out slowly, the local authority was entitled to decide that the tenants had "deliberately" left available accommodation. See too *R. v. Waltham Forest LBC, ex p. Green* December 1997, Legal Action 15, QBD.

As to living conditions in shared accommodation, contrast *R. v. Brent LBC, ex p. Yusuf* (1996) 29 H.L.R. 48, QBD; and *R. v. Brent LBC, ex p. Bariise* (1999) 31 H.L.R. 50, CA.

Departure after violence

See *R. v. Croydon LBC, ex p. Toth* (1988) 20 H.L.R. 576, CA (departure after threats   **3A–1266** by associates of applicant's husband, who had disappeared and was being sought in relation to an armed robbery. Finding of intentional homelessness upheld); *R. v. Newham LBC, ex p. McIlroy* (1991) 23 H.L.R. 570, QBD (council was entitled to conclude that the family could have continued in their home or temporary accommodation in Belfast pending an urgent transfer application notwithstanding sectarian violence which had led to one of the applicants being shot at); *cf. R. v. Brent LBC, ex p. McManus* (1993) 25 H.L.R. 643, CA (sectarian violence); *R. v. Hillingdon LBC, ex p. H* (1988) 20 H.L.R. 554, QBD (intimidation and violence in Northern Ireland); *R. v. Westminster City Council, ex p. Bishop* (1993) 25 H.L.R. 459, CA (departure of applicant's daughter from flat after she had been harassed and molested by drug-dealers followed by the applicant leaving as a result of violence and harassment from a former partner. Finding of intentional homelessness quashed); *R. v. Westminster City Council, ex p. Ermakov* [1996] 2 All E.R. 302, CA; *R. v. Barnet LBC, ex p. Babalola* (1996) 28 H.L.R. 196, QBD; *R. v. Hillingdon LBC v. ex p. McDowell*, December 1992, Legal Action 22, QBD (harassment from neighbours, culminating in the systematic wrecking of her car and ransacking of her flat. Finding of intentional homelessness quashed); *R. v. Tynedale DC, ex p. McCabe* (1992) 24 H.L.R. 384, QBD (domestic violence); *R. v. Northampton BC, ex p. Clarkson* (1992) 24 H.L.R. 529, QBD (sexual abuse) and *R. (McAuley and Stewart) v. Highland Council*, Court of Session (Outer House), July 22, 2003 (harassment, threats and violence).

Affordability

The question of whether accommodation is affordable and accordingly whether it is   **3A–1267** reasonable to continue to occupy is not to be "judged on a Micawber test as to whether one's income exceeds, or fails to measure up to, the rent one is required to pay" (*per* Sir Thomas Bingham M.R. in *R. v. Croydon LBC, ex p. Graham* (1994) 26 H.L.R. 286, CA, where the applicant had not acted unreasonably in moving (without prospect of homelessness) to cheaper suitable accommodation. See too *R. v. Tower Hamlets LBC, ex p. Ullah* (1992) 24 H.L.R. 680, QBD (applicant sold house to repay loans. Finding of intentional homelessness quashed because council had failed to enquire into the loans, their terms and all the surrounding circumstances to determine where on the scale of necessity this situation fell). But *cf. R. v. Leeds City Council, ex p. Adamiec* (1992) 24 H.L.R. 138, QBD, where although a home-owner fell into financial difficulties and mortgage arrears developed, no action was taken by the lender to enforce the loan and there was no threat of repossession proceedings. The owner sold the home, repaid the debt and applied to the council as a homeless person. The council decided that he was intentionally homeless. Webster J. dismissed an application for judicial review, but said "if [the family] had been threatened with repossession, then it would have been unreasonable for the council not to rehouse them". See also *R. v. Westminster City Council, ex p. Ali* (1997) 29 H.L.R. 580, QBD.

Settled accommodation

Where someone applies to a local authority after leaving accommodation which is   **3A–1268** not settled, the council must first identify the last "settled" accommodation, the loss of which caused the present homelessness. For someone to remain intentionally homeless, there must be a causal link between past intentionality and present homelessness. Such a link may be broken if the applicant secures further "settled accommodation" after the original intentional homelessness. See, *e.g. R. v. Brent LBC, ex p. Awua* [1996]

AC 55; [1995] 3 W.L.R. 215; [1995] 3 All E.R. 493, HL, where the applicant when originally homeless applied to Tower Hamlets LBC for accommodation. She accepted temporary accommodation pending enquiries. Subsequently, in discharge of the full housing duty, she was offered a housing association tenancy (Housing Act 1985, ss.65(2) and 69(1)(b)) but rejected it. Tower Hamlets accordingly terminated her right to occupy the temporary accommodation. The applicant then applied to Brent LBC, with which she also had a local connection. Brent declared her intentionally homeless due to her eviction from the temporary accommodation granted by Tower Hamlets. The House of Lords upheld Brent's decision. What Ms Awua had lost was plainly "accommodation". It did not matter whether that accommodation was temporary or otherwise. What mattered was whether by her act or omission she had lost it. On the facts, her failure to take up an offer of suitable permanent accommodation made through Tower Hamlets had caused the loss of the temporary accommodation and she was intentionally homeless. See too *R. v. East Herts DC, ex p. Hunt* (1986) 18 H.L.R. 51, QBD (accommodation provided pending full discharge of council's duty was settled accommodation); but *cf. R. v. Rushcliffe DC, ex p. Summerson and Buckley* (1993) 25 H.L.R. 577, QBD (a single hostel room without facilities intended for only very short-term occupation could not be regarded as settled); *Mohammed v. Westminster CC* [2005] EWCA Civ 796;15 June 2005 (assured shorthold tenancy where housing benefit was capped at less than the rent due, resultant arrears of rent and an order for possession. Council decision that applicant had not had "settled" accommodation since her last application because the private sector accommodation had been unaffordable and overcrowded from the outset and the loss of it had been inevitable, upheld by Court of Appeal); and *Stewart v. Lambeth LBC* [2002] EWCA Civ 753; [2002] H.L.R. 40, (tenant sentenced to imprisonment and then evicted for rent arrears. Held (1) the applicant had had no "settled accommodation" since the loss of his flat as prison could not be treated as a settled home. He had been detained against his will and so it was "incarceration" rather than a "home"; and (2) the causal connection between the offending and the homelessness had not been broken by an arrangement with the applicant's sister that she would pay the rent and her failure to perform it).

In *Lambert v. Ealing LBC* [1982] 1 W.L.R. 550; [1982] 2 All E.R. 394, CA, a French widower left accommodation in Grenoble and came to England with three teenage daughters to occupy premises in Ealing on a holiday let. When the holiday let was terminated, he sought accommodation from the local authority. The Court of Appeal held that the accommodation which a person left "intentionally" did not have to be the same as the accommodation inhabited immediately before his/her ultimate homelessness. As Mr Lambert had not acquired any settled accommodation in the UK, he had become homeless intentionally when he left the home in Grenoble. See too *R. v. Croydon LBC, ex p. Easom* (1993) 25 H.L.R. 262, QBD (series of tenancies in Australia where applicants were illegal immigrants not settled accommodation); *cf. R. v. Camden LBC, ex p. Aranda* (1997) 30 H.L.R. 76, CA.

An assured shorthold tenancy may be settled accommodation. In *Knight v. Vale Royal BC* [2003] EWCA Civ 1258; [2004] H.L.R. 9,the Court of Appeal stated that occupation under an assured shorthold tenancy is "likely to be settled rather than temporary" and that it is not right to assume that occupation for a period of as little as six months "is likely to be temporary rather than settled". However, it does not follow that occupation under an assured shorthold tenancy always constitutes settled accommodation. That remains a question of fact and degree "although the existence of an assured shorthold tenancy will normally be a significant pointer to the accommodation being settled". The question of whether or not such a tenancy is settled accommodation is a question of degree and judgment for the local authority (*R. v. Christchurch B.C., ex p. Conway* (1987) 19 H.L.R. 238, QBD (finding of intentional homelessness upheld); and *R. v. Rochester-upon-Medway City Council, ex p. Williams* (1994) 26 H.L.R. 588, QBD (application for judicial review dismissed). See too *R. v. Harrow LBC, ex p. Fahia* [1998] 1 W.L.R. 1396; [1998] 4 All E.R. 137, HL; *R. v. Hackney LBC, ex p. Ajayi* [1997] August C.L.D. 306; June 1997, Legal Action 23, CA; and *R. v. Merton LBC, ex p. Ruffle* (1989) 21 H.L.R. 361, QBD.

Becoming homeless intentionally

3A-1269   **191.**—(1) A person becomes homeless intentionally if he deliberately does or fails to do anything in consequence of which he ceases to occupy accommodation which is available for his occupation and which it would have been reasonable for him to continue to occupy.

(2) For the purposes of subsection (1) an act or omission in good faith on the part of a person who was unaware of any relevant fact shall not be treated as deliberate.

(3) A person shall be treated as becoming homeless intentionally if—

(a) he enters into an arrangement under which he is required to cease to occupy accommodation which it would have been reasonable for him to continue to occupy, and

(b) the purpose of the arrangement is to enable him to become entitled to assistance under this Part,

and there is no other good reason why he is homeless.

(4) [...]

Note —Amended by Homelessness Act 2002, Sched.2, para.1. In England, this amendment was brought into force on July 31, 2002 by the Homelessness Act 2002 (Commencement No.1) (England) Order 2002 (S.I. 2002 No. 1799) (C.56). In Wales, this amendment was brought into force on September 30, 2002 by the Homelessness Act 2002 (Commencement) (Wales) Order 2002 (S.I. 2002 No. 1736) (W.166) (C.53). Section 191(4) was been repealed by Housing Act 1996, Sched. 2. **3A–1270**

"available for his occupation"
See s.176. **3A–1271**

Becoming homeless intentionally
See commentary to s.190. **3A–1272**

Duty to persons not in priority need who are not homeless intentionally

192.—(1) This section applies where the local housing authority— **3A–1273**

(a) are satisfied that an applicant is homeless and eligible for assistance, and

(b) are not satisfied that he became homeless intentionally,

but are not satisfied that he has a priority need.

(2) The authority shall provide the applicant with (or secure that he is provided with) advice and assistance in any attempts he may make to secure that accommodation becomes available for his occupation.

(3) The authority may secure that accommodation is available for occupation by the applicant.

(4) The applicant's housing needs shall be assessed before advice and assistance is provided under subsection (2).

(5) The advice and assistance provided under subsection (2) must include information about the likely availability in the authority's district of types of accommodation appropriate to the applicant's housing needs (including, in particular, the location and sources of such types of accommodation).

Amended by Homelessness Act 2002, s.5(1) and Schedule 1, paras 11 and 12. In England, this amendment was brought into force on July 31, 2002 by the Homelessness Act 2002 (Commencement No.1) (England) Order 2002 (S.I. 2002 No. 1799) (C.56). In Wales, this amendment was brought into force on September 30, 2002 by **3A–1274** the Homelessness Act 2002 (Commencement) (Wales) Order 2002 (S.I. 2002 No. 1736) (W.166)(C.53).

"eligible for assistance"

3A–1275   See s.185.

"assistance"

3A–1276   See s.183.

"local housing authority"

3A–1277   See ss.217, 218, and 230 which refer to the Housing Act 1985—see the Housing Act 1985, ss.1 and 2, above.

"homeless"

3A–1278   See s.175.

"applicant"

3A–1279   See s.183 and the commentary thereto.

"priority need"

3A–1280   See s.189.

"homeless intentionally"

3A–1281   See s.191.

Duty and Power

3A–1282   The only *duty* to persons not in priority need who are homeless unintentionally is to provide advice and assistance. However the amendment effected by Homelessness Act 2002 gives local housing authorities a *power* to secure that accommodation is made available.

Duty to persons with priority need who are not homeless intentionally

3A–1283   **193.**—(1) This section applies where the local housing authority are satisfied that an applicant is homeless, eligible for assistance and has a priority need, and are not satisfied that he became homeless intentionally.

(2) Unless the authority refer the application to another local housing authority (see section 198), they shall secure that accommodation is available for occupation by the applicant.

(3) The authority are subject to the duty under this section until it ceases by virtue of any of the following provisions of this section.

(3A) The authority shall, on becoming subject to the duty under this section, give the applicant a copy of the statement included in their allocation scheme by virtue of section 167(1A) (policy on offering choice to people allocated housing accommodation under Part 6).

(5) The local housing authority shall cease to be subject to the duty under this section if the applicant, having been informed by the authority of the possible consequence of refusal and of his right to request a review of the suitability of the accommodation, refuses an offer of accommodation which the authority are satisfied is suitable for him and the authority notify him that they regard themselves as having discharged their duty under this section.

(6) The local housing authority shall cease to be subject to the duty under this section if the applicant—

(a) ceases to be eligible for assistance,

(b) becomes homeless intentionally from the accommodation made available for his occupation,

(c) accepts an offer of accommodation under Part VI (allocation of housing), or

(cc) accepts an offer of an assured tenancy (other than an assured shorthold tenancy) from a private landlord,

(d) otherwise voluntarily ceases to occupy as his only or principal home the accommodation made available for his occupation.

(7) The local housing authority shall also cease to be subject to the duty under this section if the applicant, having been informed of the possible consequence of refusal and of his right to request a review of the suitability of the accommodation, refuses a final offer of accommodation under Part 6.

(7A) An offer of accommodation under Part 6 is a final offer for the purposes of subsection (7) if it is made in writing and states that it is a final offer for the purposes of subsection (7).

(7B) The authority shall also cease to be subject to the duty under this section if the applicant accepts a qualifying offer of an assured shorthold tenancy which is made by a private landlord in relation to any accommodation which is, or may become, available for the applicant's occupation.

(7C) The applicant is free to reject a qualifying offer without affecting the duty owed to him under this section by the authority.

(7D) For the purposes of subsection (7B) an offer of an assured shorthold tenancy is a qualifying offer if—

(a) it is made, with the approval of the authority, in pursuance of arrangements made by the authority with the landlord with a view to bringing the authority's duty under this section to an end;

(b) the tenancy being offered is a fixed term tenancy (within the meaning of Part 1 of the Housing Act 1988 (c. 50)); and

(c) it is accompanied by a statement in writing which states the term of the tenancy being offered and explains in ordinary language that—

(i) there is no obligation to accept the offer, but

(ii) if the offer is accepted the local housing authority will cease to be subject to the duty under this section in relation to the applicant.

(7E) An acceptance of a qualifying offer is only effective for the purposes of subsection (7B) if the applicant signs a statement acknowledging that he has understood the statement mentioned in subsection (7D).

(7F) The local housing authority shall not—

(a) make a final offer of accommodation under Part 6 for the purposes of subsection (7); or

(b) approve an offer of an assured shorthold tenancy for the purposes of subsection (7B), unless they are satisfied that the accommodation is suitable for the applicant and that it is reasonable for him to accept the offer.

(8) For the purposes of subsection (7F) an applicant may reasonably be expected to accept an offer even though he is under contractual or other obligations in respect of his existing accommodation, provided he is able to bring those obligations to an end before he is required to take up the offer.

(9) A person who ceases to be owed the duty under this section may make a fresh application to the authority for accommodation or assistance in obtaining accommodation.

3A-1284 Amended by Homelessness Act 2002 ss.6, 7 and 8(1) and Schedule 1, para. 13. In Wales, this amendment was brought into force on September 30, 2002 by the Homelessness Act 2002 (Commencement) (Wales) Order 2002 (S.I. 2002 No. 1736) (W.166) (C.53). Section 193(4) has been repealed.

"assured tenancy"

3A-1285 See Housing Act 1988, s.1.

"assured shorthold tenancy"

3A-1286 See Housing Act 1988, ss.19A and 20.

"fixed term tenancy"

3A-1287 See Housing Act 1988, s.45.

"eligible for assistance"

3A-1288 See s.185.

"assistance"

3A-1289 See s.183.

"local housing authority"

3A-1290 See ss.217, 218, and 230 which refer to the Housing Act 1985—see the Housing Act 1985, ss.1 and 2 above.

"homeless"

3A-1291 See s.175.

"applicant"

3A-1292 See s.183 and the commentary thereto.

"priority need"

3A-1293 See s.189.

"homeless intentionally"

3A-1294 See s.191.

They are satisfied that the accommodation is suitable (s.193(7F))

3A-1295 See s.210 below and commentary at para. 3A–1284, sub-paragraph (b).

"accommodation is available for occupation"

3A-1296 See too s.206; *R. v. Newham LBC, ex p. Dada* [1996] Q.B. 507; [1995] 3 W.L.R. 540; [1995] 2 All E.R. 522; *R. v. Southwark LBC, ex p. Ryder*, September 1995, Legal Action 15, CA (CAT95/556); *R. v. Kensington and Chelsea R.L.B., ex p. Assiter*, September 1996, Legal Action 13, QBD and *R. v. Newham LBC, ex p. Chowdhury* (1999) 31 H.L.R. 383, QBD.

See also section 176. In *R. v. Newham LBC, ex p. Khan and Hussain* (2001) 33 H.L.R. 269, QBD Collins J. held that the decision to "split" a family who had lived together prior to homelessness was unlawful. Housing Act 1996, s.176 requires that accommodation be secured not only for occupation by an applicant, but also for "any other person who normally resides with him as a member of his family".

"available for his occupation"

See s.176.

3A-1297

Duty to persons with priority need who are not homeless intentionally

If local housing authorities are satisfied that applicants are homeless, eligible for assistance, in priority need and not satisfied that they became homeless intentionally, they have two possible courses of action:

3A-1298

(a) to refer to another local authority. This is almost exactly the same as the previous "local connection" provisions (Housing Act 1996, s.198— *cf.* Housing Act 1985, s.67), but it has been extended to include referral back to another authority where that other authority originally dealt with the applicant's homeless application and as a result placed the applicant in accommodation outside its boundaries; or

(b) secure that accommodation is made available for occupation (Housing Act 1996, s.193(2)). Such accommodation should be suitable not only for the applicant, but also for his or her family. (*R. v. Westminster County Council ex p. Abo-Ragheed*, April 2001, Legal Action 22, November 27, 2001, QBD Admin Ct). The requirement that accommodation be suitable means suitable for the persons to whom the duty is owed. It encompasses considerations of the range, nature and location of accommodation as well as its standard of condition, and likely duration of the applicant's occupancy (*Codona v. Mid-Bedfordshire DC* [2004] EWCA Civ 925; [2005] HLR 1). In considering whether accommodation is suitable authorities shall have regard to the Housing Act 1985, Pts IX, X and XI (slum clearance, overcrowding and HMOs and the applicant's financial resources, including various specified forms of income, various specified costs relating to accommodation and other reasonable living expenses (Housing Act 1996, s.210 and The Homelessness (Suitability of Accommodation) Order 1996 (S.I. 1996 No. 3204). In addition the Homelessness (Suitability of Accommodation) (England) Order 2003 (S.I. 2003 No. 3326) prescribes the accommodation which is suitable for a person with family commitments—*i.e.* someone who is pregnant or with whom a pregnant woman or dependent children reside or might reasonably be expected to reside. Accommodation is not to be regarded as suitable if it is "B&B accommodation". B&B accommodation is accommodation which, whether or not breakfast is provided, is not self contained or which involves sharing certain amenities with another household. However there are exceptions. If there is no available accommodation, other than B&B accommodation, a local housing authority may house someone with family commitments in B&B accommodation, but only for a period or total of periods not exceeding six weeks.

Once the conditions in s.193(1) are met, the duty to accommodate is triggered and it is unlawful to impose "any further hurdle or proviso before accepting that the duty arises". (*e.g.* service of notice to quit in relation to joint tenancy. See *R. (Hammia) v. Wandsworth LBC* [2005] EWHC 1127 (Admin) ; 17 May 2005.

Authorities cease to be under if a duty if the applicant:

- after being informed about the possible consequences of refusal, refuses an offer of accommodation which the authority are satisfied is suitable (Housing Act 1996, s.193(5)); or
- ceases to be eligible for assistance (Housing Act 1996, s.193(6)(a)); or
- becomes homeless intentionally from the accommodation made available for occupation (Housing Act 1996, s.193(6)(b)); or
- accepts an offer of housing under the Housing Act 1996, Pt VI or otherwise ceases to occupy as his or her only or principal home the accommodation made available (Housing Act 1996, s.193(6)(c) and (d)); or
- after being informed of the possible consequences refuses an offer of Pt VI accommodation which the authority are satisfied was suitable (Housing Act 1996, s.193(7)(a)).
- the applicant accepts an offer of an assured tenancy from a private landlord (s.193(7B)).

The offer of an assured shorthold tenancy from a private landlord only ends the local housing authority's duty if it is a qualifying offer of a fixed term tenancy. The authority must be satisfied that it is suitable for the applicant and that it is reasonable for him or her to accept it. The landlord's offer must be accompanied by a written statement setting out the terms of the tenancy being offered and explaining that there is no obligation to accept the offer.

Under s.193, it is only in exceptional circumstances, if at all, that councils are allowed to 'earmark' properties in advance because when a property actually becomes available it has to be offered to the family highest placed in the council's allocation scheme at that date (*R. (Amirun Begum) v. Tower Hamlets LBC* [2002] EWHC 633 (Admin); [2003] H.L.R. 8).

Under Housing Act 1996, s.193(6), unless there is fraud, a local authority does not cease to be under a duty to accommodate simply because an applicant ceases to have priority need. (*R. v. Brent LBC, ex p. Sadiq* (2001) 33 H.L.R. 525, CA). After a determination has been made, if a council considers that it was wrong, it may conduct a further 'extra-statutory review'. Decisions under Housing Act 1996 as to whether applicants are in priority need or whether they are intentionally homeless are questions of public law. Accordingly once a decision has been taken the authority is permitted to revisit its conclusion (*Crawley BC v. B* (2000) 32 H.L.R. 636, CA). See too *Porteous v. West Dorset DC* [2004] EWCA Civ 244).

No claim lies for damages in tort for breach of the statutory duties owed to the homeless (*O'Rourke v. Camden LBC* [1998] AC 188). Although ECHR Art.8 does not impose on the state a duty to provide a home and the simple fact of "homelessness" does not therefore breach Article 8, there may though be cases where it assists if homelessness causes interference with the claimant's family life or private life (*R. (Morris) v. Newham LBC* [2002] EWHC 1262 (Admin); May 24, 2002—on the facts, claim dismissed).

Refuses a final offer of accommodation (s.193(5) and (7))

3A-1298.1   The Court of Appeal considered the situation where an offer is refused, but a homeless person then makes a further application in *Tower Hamlets LBC v. Rikha Begum* [2005] EWCA Civ 340; [2005] 1 WLR 2103 . It held that there was no test of "material change of circumstances" and that (applying *R. v. Harrow LBC ex p. Fahia* [1998] 1 WLR 1396)—

- an authority has to accept and consider a second application if it is not factually "identical" to the earlier one;
- this test of "exactly the same facts" was harder for an authority to use to refuse an application than the "material change of circumstances" approach;
- any new facts raised in the second approach to a council (provided not trivial or fanciful) require that it be treated as a fresh application;
- the question is whether the facts as presented are "new" and comparison has to be made by contrasting the material put forward on the new approach with the facts as they had stood when the earlier application was "disposed of" by an initial or review decision (as opposed to the date that the earlier application had been made);
- that question does not involve any "inquiries" by an authority, nor any investigation as to whether the asserted new facts are accurate (per Neuberger and Keene LJJ). The issue is simply whether, in the purported new application, the applicant has put forward facts which are different and the differences are neither fanciful nor trivial. A safeguard against applicants "inventing" new facts is the possibility of criminal prosecution. Pill LJ, however, considered that "some inquiry" might be necessary to establish (a) what matters are now relied upon and (b) whether they are the same matters or new matters.

Reviews

3A-1299   A decision as to suitability of s.193 accommodation is amenable to review under s.202(1)(f) and subsequent appeal to the county court under s.204. That is the appropriate route for any challenge. Would-be applicants should bear in mind that remedy and should not apply for judicial review (*R. v. Merton LBC, ex p. Sembi* (2000) 32 H.L.R. 439, QBD). After a determination has been made, if a council considers that it was wrong, it may conduct a further "extra-statutory review". Decisions under Housing Act 1996 as to whether applicants are in priority need or whether they are intentionally homeless are questions of public law. Accordingly once a decision has been taken the authority is permitted to revisit its conclusion (*Crawley BC v. B* (2000) 32 H.L.R. 636, CA. See too *Porteous v. West Dorset DC* [2004] EWCA Civ 244; [2004] HLR 30).

Note — Section 194 has been repealed by Homelessness Act 2002, s.6(4) which **3A–1300** provides that Housing Act 1996, s.194 (power to continue to secure accommodation after minimum period of two years, formerly contained in s.193) shall cease to have effect. The section is unnecessary in the light of the abolition of the former provisions of s.193 limiting the duty to two years. In England, this amendment was brought into force on July 31, 2002 by the Homelessness Act 2002 (Commencement No. 1) (England) Order 2002 (S.I. 2002 No. 1799) (C.56). In Wales, this amendment was brought into force on September 30, 2002 by the Homelessness Act 2002 (Commencement) (Wales) Order 2002 (S.I. 2002 No. 1736) (W.166) (C.53). Any person for whom a local housing authority was exercising their power under s.194 to continue to secure accommodation, immediately before implementation, is to be treated as a person to whom the authority owe the main duty under s.193 (Homelessness Act 2002, s.6(4)).

Duties in case of threatened homelessness

195.—(1) This section applies where the local housing authority **3A–1301** are satisfied that an applicant is threatened with homelessness and is eligible for assistance.

(2) If the authority—

    (a) are satisfied that he has a priority need, and

    (b) are not satisfied that he became threatened with homelessness intentionally,

they shall take reasonable steps to secure that accommodation does not cease to be available for his occupation.

(3) Subsection (2) does not affect any right of the authority, whether by virtue of a contract, enactment or rule of law, to secure vacant possession of any accommodation.

(3A) The authority shall, on becoming subject to the duty under this section, give the applicant a copy of the statement included in their allocation scheme by virtue of section 167(1A) (policy on offering choice to people allocated housing accommodation under Part 6).

(4) Where in pursuance of the duty under subsection (2) the authority secure that accommodation other than that occupied by the applicant when he made his application is available for occupation by him, the provisions of section 193(3) to (9) (period for which duty owed) apply, with any necessary modifications, in relation to the duty under this section as they apply in relation to the duty under section 193.

(5) If the authority—

    (a) are not satisfied that the applicant has a priority need, or

    (b) are satisfied that he has a priority need but are also satisfied that he became threatened with homelessness intentionally,

they shall provide him with (or secure that he is provided with) advice and assistance; in any attempts he may make to secure that accommodation does not cease to be available for his occupation.

(6) The applicant's housing needs shall be assessed before advice and assistance is provided under subsection (5).

(7) The advice and assistance provided under subsection (5) must include information about the likely availability in the authority's district of types of accommodation appropriate to the applicant's housing needs (including, in particular, the location and sources of such types of accommodation)."

(8) If the authority decide that they owe the applicant the duty under subsection (5) by virtue of paragraph (b) of that subsection, they may, pending a decision on a review of that decision—

    (a) secure that accommodation does not cease to be available for his occupation; and

    (b) if he becomes homeless, secure that accommodation is so available.

(9) If the authority—

    (a) are not satisfied that the applicant has a priority need; and

    (b) are not satisfied that he became threatened with homelessness intentionally,

the authority may take reasonable steps to secure that accommodation does not cease to be available for the applicant's occupation."

3A–1302   Amended by Homelessness Act 2002, s.5(2) and Schedule 1, para. 14. In England, this amendment (except the insertion of subsection (3A)) was brought into force on July 31, 2002 by the Homelessness Act 2002 (Commencement No. 1) (England) Order 2002 (S.I. 2002 No. 1799) (C.56). In Wales, this amendment was brought into force on September 30, 2002 by the Homelessness Act 2002 (Commencement) (Wales) Order 2002 (S.I. 2002 No. 1736) (W.166) (C.53).

Duties in case of threatened homelessness

3A–1303   See commentary to s.193.

"local housing authority"

3A–1304   See ss.217, 218, and 230 which refer to the Housing Act 1985—see the Housing Act 1985, ss.1 and 2 above.

"available for his occupation"

3A–1305   See s.176.

"priority need"

3A–1306   See s.189.

"eligible for assistance"

3A–1307   See s.185.

Becoming threatened with homelessness intentionally

3A–1308   **196.**—(1) A person becomes threatened with homelessness intentionally if he deliberately does or fails to do anything the likely result of which is that he will be forced to leave accommodation which is available for his occupation and which it would have been reasonable for him to continue to occupy.

(2) For the purposes of subsection (1) an act or omission in good faith on the part of a person who was unaware of any relevant fact shall not be treated as deliberate.

(3) A person shall be treated as becoming threatened with homelessness intentionally if—

       (a) he enters into an arrangement under which he is required to cease to occupy accommodation which it would have been reasonable for him to continue to occupy, and

       (b) the purpose of the arrangement is to enable him to become entitled to assistance under this Part,

and there is no other good reason why he is threatened with homelessness.

    (4) [...]

Note —Subsection (4) was repealed by the Homelessness Act 2002, Sched. 2.   **3A–1309**

Becoming threatened with homelessness intentionally
See commentary to ss.190 and 193.   **3A–1310**

"available for his occupation"
See s.176.   **3A–1311**

"threatened with homelessness intentionally"
See s.195.   **3A–1312**

Duty where other suitable accommodation available
   Homelessness Act, s.9 provides that Housing Act 1996, s.197 (duty where other **3A–1313** suitable accomodation available in their district) shall cease to have effect. In England, this amendment was brought into force on July 31, 2002 by the Homelessness Act 2002 (Commencement No. 1) (England) Order 2002 (S.I. 2002 No. 1799) (C.56). In Wales, this amendment was brought into force on September 30, 2002 by the Homelessness Act 2002 (Commencement) (Wales) Order 2002 (S.I. 2002 No.1736) (W.166) (C.56)). Any person for whom a local housing authority was exercising their power under s.197, immediately before implementation, is to be treated as a person to whom the authority owe the duty under s.193 (the main homelessness duty) (Homelessness Act 2002, s.6(4)).

"local housing authority"
   See ss.217, 218, and 230 which refer to the Housing Act 1985—see the Housing Act **3A–1314** 1985, ss.1 and 2, above.

"available for his occupation"
See s.176.   **3A–1315**

Note —Section 197 has been repealed.   **3A–1316**

REFERRAL TO ANOTHER LOCAL HOUSING AUTHORITY

Referral of case to another local housing authority

   198.—(1) If the local housing authority would be subject to the **3A–1317** duty under section 193 (accommodation for those with priority need who are not homeless intentionally) but consider that the conditions are met for referral of the case to another local housing authority, they may notify that other authority of their opinion.

   (2) The conditions for referral of the case to another authority are met if—

       (a) neither the applicant nor any person who might reasonably be expected to reside with him has a local connection with the district of the authority to whom his application was made,

    (b) the applicant or a person who might reasonably be expected to reside with him has a local connection with the district of that other authority, and

    (c) neither the applicant nor any person who might reasonably be expected to reside with him will run the risk of domestic violence in that other district.

(2A) But the conditions for referral mentioned in subsection (2) are not met if—

    (a) the applicant or any person who might reasonably be expected to reside with him has suffered violence (other than domestic violence) in the district of the other authority; and

    (b) it is probable that the return to that district of the victim will lead to further violence of a similar kind against him.

(3) For the purposes of subsections (2) and (2A) "violence" means—

    (a) violence from another person; or

    (b) threats of violence from another person which are likely to be carried out; and violence is "domestic violence" if it is from a person who is associated with the victim.

(4) The conditions for referral of the case to another authority are also met if—

    (a) the applicant was on a previous application made to that other authority placed (in pursuance of their functions under this Part) in accommodation in the district of the authority to whom his application is now made, and

    (b) the previous application was within such period as may be prescribed of the present application.

(5) The question whether the conditions for referral of a case are satisfied shall be decided by agreement between the notifying authority and the notified authority or, in default of agreement, in accordance with such arrangements as the Secretary of State may direct by order.

(6) An order may direct that the arrangements shall be—

    (a) those agreed by any relevant authorities or associations of relevant authorities, or

    (b) in default of such agreement, such arrangements as appear to the Secretary of State to be suitable, after consultation with such associations representing relevant authorities, and such other persons, as he thinks appropriate.

(7) No such order shall be made unless a draft of the order has been approved by a resolution of each House of Parliament.

3A–1318   Amended by Homelessness Act 2002 s.10. In England, this amendment was brought into force on July 31, 2002 by the Homelessness Act 2002 (Commencement No. 1) (England) Order 2002 (S.I. 2002 No. 1799) (C.56). In Wales, this amendment was brought into force on September 30, 2002 by the Homelessness Act 2002 (Commencement) (Wales) Order 2002 (S.I. 2002 No. 1736) (W.166)(C.53).

Note —The Allocation of Housing and Homelessness (Review Procedures) Regula- **3A–1319**
tions 1999 (S.I. 1999 No. 71) include a specific provision for reviews of decisions made
under s.198(5). See too the Homelessness (Decisions on Referrals) Order 1998 (S.I.
1998 No. 1578).

"local housing authority"
See ss.217, 218, and 230 which refer to the Housing Act 1985—see the Housing Act **3A–1320**
1985, ss.1 and 2 above.

"district"
See s.217(3). **3A–1321**

Referral of case to another local housing authority
A local housing authority which finds itself subject to a duty under the Housing Act **3A–1322**
1996, s.193 to an applicant who is unintentionally homeless and in priority need may,
if the conditions in s.198 are fulfilled, refer the duty to another housing authority with
which the applicant has a local connection. By s.199 an applicant can have a local connection with an area for one of four reasons:
  (a) residence;
  (b) employment;
  (c) family; or
  (d) special circumstances.
The onus of establishing a local connection rests on the applicant. Applicants must
show that they have built up a real connection based on a period of residence, employment, family associations or other special circumstances. Where the claim is based on
residence there is no reason why a local authority should not have guidelines that residence short of six months in the preceding year does not suffice (*R. v. Eastleigh B.C.,
ex p. Betts* [1983] 2 A.C. 613; [1983] 3 W.L.R. 397; [1983] 2 All E.R. 1111, HL).

The House of Lords has held that (1) on a statutory review of a decision to refer an
application for accommodation to another authority on the basis that there is no local
connection, any occupation by the applicant of interim accommodation within the first
authority's district prior to the date of the review may constitute normal residence and
so be taken into account as evidence of a local connection. So long as the place where
someone eats and sleeps is voluntarily accepted by him, the reason why he is there
rather than somewhere else does not prevent that place from being his normal residence; (2) the correct date to decide whether a person has a local connection is the
date of the decision or, if there is a review, the date of the review – whether in the
meantime the applicant has acquired or lost, by moving away, his local connection
(*Mohamed v. Hammersmith and Fulham LBC* [2001] UKHL 57; [2002] 1 A.C. 547; [2001]
3 W.L.R. 1339; [2002] 1 All E.R. 176.

For cases in the Court of Appeal on "local connection", see *R. v. Greenwich LBC, ex
p. Patterson* (1994) 26 H.L.R. 159, CA; *R. v. Hammersmith & Fulham LBC, ex p.Duro-
Rama* (1983) 9 H.L.R. 71, CA; *R. v. Newham LBC, ex p. Tower Hamlets LBC* (1990) 23
H.L.R. 62, CA; *R. v. Slough BC, ex p. Ealing LBC* [1981] Q.B. 801; [1981] 1 All E.R.
601; [1981] 2 W.L.R. 399, CA; *R. v. Tower Hamlets LBC, ex p. Ali and Bibi* (1993) 25
H.L.R. 158, CA; *R. v. Westminster CC, ex p. Benniche* (1996) 29 H.L.R. 230, *The Times*,
April 15, 1996, CA. *R. v. Ealing LBC, ex p. Fox*, (1998) 95(11) L.S.G. 35; *The Times*,
March 9, 1998, QBD: voluntary work may be employment for the purposes of
s.199(1)(b)).

The effect of the decision in *Al-Ameri v. Kensington and Chelsea RLBC* [2004] UKHL
4; [2004] 2 W.L.R. 354 (that residence in a district in accommodation provided to a
destitute asylum seeker under Immigration and Asylum Act 1999 was not capable of
being regarded as residence in that district of the asylum seeker's own choice) has
been reversed by Asylum and Immigration (Treatment of Claimants, etc) Act 2004,
s.11 which added new ss.(6) and (7) to s.199.

There is no statutory right to review of an authority's decision not to refer an application under s.198. Accordingly there is no right of appeal to a county court on that
issue under s.204. The county court has no jurisdiction to consider on appeal whether
local authorities have a duty to investigate the issue of local connection (*Sareen v.
Hackney LBC* [2003] EWCA Civ 351; [2003] H.L.R. 54).

Violence
Note that a referral to another authority may not be made if the applicant or a **3A–1323**

person who might reasonably be expected to live with the applicant runs the risk of violence in the other district. Since the amendment of s.198 by Homelessness Act 2002, s.10, "violence" is not limited to "domestic violence". "Violence" includes threats of violence which are likely to be carried out.

Disputes

3A-1324 Homelessness (Decisions on Referrals) Order 1998 (S.I. 1998 No. 1578) provides a mechanism for resolving disputes between housing authorities about whether or not the conditions of referral from one authority to another exist. Such questions are to be decided by a person to be appointed from a panel established by the Local Government Association.

Local connection

3A-1325 **199.**—(1) A person has a local connection with the district of a local housing authority if he has a connection with it—

> (a) because he is, or in the past was, normally resident there, and that residence is or was of his own choice,
>
> (b) because he is employed there,
>
> (c) because of family associations, or
>
> (d) because of special circumstances.

(2) A person is not employed in a district if he is serving in the regular armed forces of the Crown.

(3) Residence in a district is not of a person's own choice if—

> (a) he becomes resident there because he, or a person who might reasonably be expected to reside with him, is serving in the regular armed forces of the Crown, or
>
> (b) he, or a person who might reasonably be expected to reside with him, becomes resident there because he is detained under the authority of an Act of Parliament.

(4) In subsections (2) and (3) "regular armed forces of the Crown" means the Royal Navy, the regular forces as defined by section 225 of the Army Act 1955, the regular air force as defined by section 223 of the Air Force Act 1955 and Queen Alexandra's Royal Naval Nursing Service.

(5) The Secretary of State may by order specify other circumstances in which—

> (a) a person is not to be treated as employed in a district, or
>
> (b) residence in a district is not to be treated as of a person's own choice.

(6) A person has a local connection with the district of a local housing authority if he was (at any time) provided with accommodation in that district under section 95 of the Immigration and Asylum Act 1999 (support for asylum seekers).

(7) But subsection (6) does not apply—

> (a) to the provision of accommodation for a person in a district of a local housing authority if he was subsequently provided with accommodation in the district of another local housing authority under section 95 of that Act, or
>
> (b) to the provision of accommodation in an accommodation centre by virtue of section 22 of the Nationality, Immigration and Asylum Act 2002 (c.41) (use of accommodation centres for section 95 support).

3A-1326

Note —Subsections (6) and (7) were added by the Asylum and Immigration (Treatment of Claimants, etc) Act 2004, s.11. They were brought into force on January 4, 2005 by the Asylum and Immigration (Treatment of Claimants etc.) Act 2004 (Commencement No. 2) Order 2004 S.I. 2004 No. 2999. The effect of the amendment is to reverse the effect of *Al-Ameri v. Kensington and Chelsea RLBC* [2004] UKHL 4; [2004] 2 W.L.R. 354; [2004] 1 W.L.R. 1104.

Local connection

See commentary to s.198.

3A-1327

"local housing authority"

See ss.217, 218, and 230 which refer to the Housing Act 1985—see the Housing Act 1985, ss.1 and 2, above.

3A-1328

"district"

See s.217(3).

3A-1329

Duties to applicant whose case is considered for referral or referred

200.—(1) Where a local housing authority notify an applicant that they intend to notify or have notified another local housing authority of their opinion that the conditions are met for the referral of his case to that other authority—

3A-1330

    (a) they cease to be subject to any duty under section 188 (interim duty to accommodate in case of apparent priority need), and

    (b) they are not subject to any duty under section 193 (the main housing duty),

but they shall secure that accommodation is available for occupation by the applicant until he is notified of the decision whether the conditions for referral of his case are met.

(2) When it has been decided whether the conditions for referral are met, the notifying authority shall notify the applicant of the decision and inform him of the reasons for it.

The notice shall also inform the applicant of his right to request a review of the decision and of the time within which such a request must be made.

(3) If it is decided that the conditions for referral are not met, the notifying authority are subject to the duty under section 193 (the main housing duty).

(4) If it is decided that those conditions are met, the notified authority are subject to the duty under section 193 (the main housing duty).

(5) The duty under subsection (1) ceases as provided in that subsection even if the applicant requests a review of the authority's decision (see section 202).

The authority may secure that accommodation is available for the applicant's occupation pending the decision on a review.

(6) Notice required to be given to an applicant under this section shall be given in writing and, if not received by him, shall be treated as having been given to him if it is made available at the authority's office for a reasonable period for collection by him or on his behalf.

3A-1331   Amended by Homelessness Act 2002, Schedule 1, para. 15. In England, this amendment was brought into force on July 31, 2002 by the Homelessness Act 2002 (Commencement No. 1) (England) Order 2002 (S.I. 2002 No. 1799) (C.56). In Wales, this amendment was brought into force on September 30, 2002 by the Homelessness Act 2002 (Commencement) (Wales) Order 2002 (S.I. 2002 No. 1736) (W.166) (C.53).

Duties to applicant whose case is considered for referral or referred

3A-1332   See commentary to ss.193 and 198.

"local housing authority"

3A-1333   See ss.217, 218, and 230 which refers to the Housing Act 1985—see the Housing Act 1985, ss.1 and 2 above.

"district"

3A-1334   See s.217(3).

"other suitable accommodation"

3A-1335   See s.197.

Application of referral provisions to cases arising in Scotland

3A-1336   **201.** Sections 198 and 200 (referral of application to another local housing authority and duties to applicant whose case is considered for referral or referred) apply—

    (a) to applications referred by a local authority in Scotland in pursuance of sections 33 and 34 of the Housing (Scotland) Act 1987, and

    (b) to persons whose applications are so transferred,

as they apply to cases arising under this Part (the reference in section 198 to this Part being construed as a reference to Part II of that Act).

Right to request review of decision

3A-1337   **202.**—(1) An applicant has the right to request a review of—

    (a) any decision of a local housing authority as to his eligibility for assistance,

    (b) any decision of a local housing authority as to what duty (if any) is owed to him under sections 190 to 193 and 195 to 196 (duties to persons found to be homeless or threatened with homelessness),

    (c) any decision of a local housing authority to notify another authority under section 198(1) (referral of cases),

    (d) any decision under section 198(5) whether the conditions are met for the referral of his case,

    (e) any decision under section 200(3) or (4) (decision as to duty owed to applicant whose case is considered for referral or referred), or

    (f) any decision of a local housing authority as to the suitability of accommodation offered to him in discharge of their duty under any of the provisions mentioned in paragraph (b) or (e) or as to the suitability of accommodation offered to him as mentioned in section 193(7).

    (1A) An applicant who is offered accommodation as mentioned in section 193(5) or (7) may under subsection (1)(f) request a review of the suitability of the accommodation offered to him whether or not he has accepted the offer.

(2) There is no right to request a review of the decision reached on an earlier review.

(3) A request for review must be made before the end of the period of 21 days beginning with the day on which he is notified of the authority's decision or such longer period as the authority may in writing allow.

(4) On a request being duly made to them, the authority or authorities concerned shall review their decision.

Amended by Homelessness Act 2002, s.8(2) and Sched.1, para. 16. In England, the **3A–1338** amendment to s.202(1)(b) was brought into force on July 31, 2002 by the Homelessness Act 2002 (Commencement No. 1) (England) Order 2002 (S.I. 2002 No. 1799) (C.56). In Wales, the amendment to s.202(1)(b) was brought into force on September 30, 2002 by the Homelessness Act 2002 (Commencement) (Wales) Order 2002 (S.I. 2002 No.1736) (W.166) (Homelessness Act 2002, s.8(3)).

"available for his occupation"
See s.176.   **3A–1339**

"threatened with homelessness intentionally"
See s.195.   **3A–1340**

"assistance"
See s.183.   **3A–1341**

"local housing authority"
See ss.217, 218, and 230 which refer to the Housing Act 1985—see the Housing Act **3A–1342** 1985, ss.1 and 2 above.

"homeless"
See s.175.   **3A–1343**

"applicant"
See s.183 and the commentary thereto.   **3A–1344**

Reviews
On concluding their enquiries authorities, when they notify applicants of their deci- **3A–1345** sions and give their reasons, are also obliged to inform applicants of the right to request a review of the decision in accordance with the Housing Act 1996, s.202 (Housing Act 1996, s.184(5)).

The *Code of Guidance* states that it is good practice to notify applicants of decisions within three working days of the decision being made. Where possible decisions should not only be provided in writing but also explained in person to the applicant (para. 17.3).

The Housing Act 1996, s.202 provides that applicants have a right to request a review of any decision within 21 days of notification. The 21 day period may be extended by the authority. The Allocation of Housing and Homelessness (Review Procedures) Regulations 1999 (S.I. 1999 No. 71) provide that:

- if the decision is to be reviewed by an officer of the authority, the review shall be carried out by a person who was not involved in the original decision and who is senior to the officer who made the original decision (*cf. Saunders v. Hammersmith and Fulham LBC* [1999] 6 C.L.D. 347, West London County Court, where the officer who had made the original decision participated in the review with a more senior officer, Appeal allowed);
- the applicant should be notified that written representations may be made and shall be informed of the procedure to be followed;
- If the reviewer considers that there is deficiency or irregularity in the original

983

HOUSING

decision or in the manner in which it was made but is minded nevertheless to make a decision which is against the interests of the applicant on one or more issues the reviewer shall notify the applicant (a) that the reviewer is so minded, and the reasons why; and (b) that the applicant, or someone acting on his behalf, may make representations to the reviewer orally or in writing or both orally and in writing (reg 8(2). In *Hall v. Wandsworth LBC*; *Carter v. Wandsworth LBC* [2004] EWCA Civ 1740; [2005] 2 All E.R. 192, Carnwath L.J. said (para. 30): "To summarise, the reviewing officer should treat regulation 8(2) as applicable, not merely when he finds some significant legal or procedural error in the decision, but whenever (looking at the matter broadly and untechnically) he considers that an important aspect of the case was either not addressed, or not addressed adequately, by the original decision-maker. In such a case, if he intends to confirm the decision, he must give notice of the grounds on which he intends to do so, and provide an opportunity for written and (if requested) oral representations."

● decisions on reviews shall be notified to applicants within eight weeks of the day on which the request is made or such longer period as may be agreed by the applicant in writing.

With regards the adequacy of reasons given, courts would be slow to intervene and would only interfere where it was clear that the process of review was capable of being described as unfair.

An officer conducting a review must consider all the facts afresh, including information relevant to the period before the first decision, but only obtained thereafter, and to matters occurring after the initial decision, (*Mohamed v. Hammersmith and Fulham LBC* [2001] UKHL 57; [2002] 1 A.C. 547; [2001] 3 W.L.R. 1339; [2002] 1 All E.R. 176, HL and *Sarahid v. Camden LBC* [2004] EWCA Civ 1485; October 26, 2004). Where issues have been put to an applicant in interview, there is no reason why a review panel should offer an oral hearing (*Lomotey v. Enfield LBC* [2004] EWCA Civ 627; [2004] H.L.R. 45. See too *Connors v. Northampton BC* [2004] EWCA Civ 427).

There is no statutory right to a review of an authority's decision not to refer an application under s.198 (referral of case to another local housing authority). Accordingly there is no right of appeal to a county court on that issue under s.204 (*Sareen v. Hackney LBC* [2003] EWCA Civ 351; [2003] H.L.R. 54).

Accomodation pending reviews and appeals

3A-1346   In *R. v. Camden LBC, ex p. Mohammed* (1998) 30 H.L.R. 315; *The Times*, June 20, 1997, QBD, Latham J. considered the circumstances in which authorities should provide accommodation pursuant to s.188(3) pending a review. Camden's policy was that no interim accommodation was to be made available to an applicant pending a review of a refusal of an application for housing assistance under the Housing Act 1996, Pt.VII unless there were exceptional circumstances. Latham J. dismissed an application for a declaration that the policy was *ultra vires*. He considered the Housing Act 1996, ss.188(3), 202 and 204 and found that the council had a wide discretion. Use of the phrase "exceptional reasons" was a rational way of describing the approach to be adopted provided that the council carried out a balancing act and considered:

(1) the merits of the case itself and the extent to which it could properly be said that the decision was contrary to the merits of the case or was one which was finely balanced which could go either way;

(2) whether there was any new material which could have a real effect upon the decision under review; and

(3) the personal circumstances of the applicant and the consequence of an adverse decision.

Section 204A, as inserted by Homelessness Act 2002, s.11, allows an applicant to appeal to the county court against a refusal by a local housing authority to exercise its powers to provide accommodation pending the hearing of a county court appeal, or against their decision to exercise the power for a limited period, or to cease from exercising that power. The county court should determine any such appeal on judicial review principles. There is however no right to appeal to the county court against a refusal to provide accommodation pending a review—any such challenge must still be brought by judicial review, as in *R. v. Camden LBC, ex p. Mohammed* (above).

The effect of s.202(1A) is to reverse the effect of *Alghile v. Westminster City Council* [2001] EWCA Civ 363; (2001) 33 H.L.R. 57 where it was held that an applicant could not accept accommodation *and* seek a review as to its suitability.

Failure to apply for review within 21 days

Councils have a discretion under s.202(3) to extend time to request a review, but **3A–1347** that discretion has to be exercised in a principled way. This requires a consideration of the statutory scheme. Reasons for delay and the prospects of success are relevant but do not have to be balanced against each other. (*R. (C) v. Lewisham LBC* [2003] EWCA Civ 927; [2003] 3 All E.R. 1277). See too *R.(Minhas) v. Wandsworth LBC* [2004] EWHC 805).

Reconsideration of review

Councils are not precluded from reconsidering review decisions, but there is no **3A–1348** requirement that they should do so. If a council fails to reconsider a review, the remedy for the applicant is to appeal the original review decision in the county court in accordance with s.204. The High Court should not entertain an application for judicial review in such circumstances because another remedy (*i.e.* appeal in the county court) is available—*R. v. Westminster CC, ex p. Ellioua* (1999) 31 H.L.R. 440, CA. In *Demetri v. Westminster CC* [2000] 1 W.L.R. 772, CA, the Court of Appeal held that: (1) while an applicant has no right to seek a review of a review decision (see s.202(2)) a council can agree to re-open its earlier decision (*R. v. Westminster CC, ex p. Ellioua* (1999) 31 H.L.R. 440). If it does so, the council should make clear whether it is treating the earlier review decision as withdrawn and is conducting a new review or is simply "reconsidering" its earlier decision; (2) where an applicant is legally represented, the onus is on the advisers either to lodge an appeal within 21 days of the original review decision or to obtain clear agreement from the council that the review is being re-run and the earlier decision treated as non-existent. In the instant case no appeal had been lodged in time, no clear agreement to withdraw the earlier decision had been reached, and the council's agreement to "reconsider" the review decision did not have the effect of extending the time for appealing against it. Any judicial review challenge to a decision made on an extra-statutory reconsideration is unlikely to succeed (*R. (C) v. Lewisham LBC* [2003] EWCA Civ 927; [2003] 3 All E.R. 1277 applying the test in *R. v. Brighton and Hove Council, ex p. Nacion* (1999) 31 H.L.R. 1095, CA).

The Court of Appeal has held that, in the absence of any exceptional circumstances, there is nothing objectionable in the same officer conducting a review and then (if it is agreed or ordered that there should be a further review) conducting a re-review or second review. This is because the reviewing officer does not review his or her own earlier decision but starts afresh to review a decision made by a more junior officer. There is nothing unfair about that. Further, as the Allocation of Housing and Homelessness (Review Procedures) Regulations 1999 (S.I. 1999 No. 71) give no guidance as to who is to conduct a review the second time and there is nothing to suggest that it has to be someone who was not involved in the first decision, there is no breach of those regulations if the same officer conducts the further review (*Feld v. Barnet LBC* [2004] EWCA Civ 1307; [2005] HLR 9; *Pour v. Westminster CC* [2004] EWCA Civ 1307; *The Times* October 26, 2004).

Reasons

Section 203 requires local housing authorities to give reasons if the decision on **3A–1349** review is to confirm the original decision. In *R. v. Westminster CC, ex p. Ermakov* [1996] 2 All E.R. 302, a case involving Housing Act 1985, s.64 (now Housing Act 1996, s.184(3)), Hutchison L.J. said that the Act "requires a decision and at the same time reasons and if no reasons, which is the reality of the present case, or wholly deficient reasons are given, the applicant is *prima facie* entitled to have the decision quashed as unlawful". He stated that the reasons given must be proper, adequate and intelligible and deal with the substantial points that have been raised. In *Hijazi v. Kensington and Chelsea RLBC* [2003] EWCA Civ 692; [2003] H.L.R. 72, a case in which a circuit judge hearing a s.204 appeal had allowed further evidence from the reviewing officer that he had taken a doctor's report into account but had found that it did not take matters further, the Court of Appeal, dismissing a further appeal, held that while further evidence ought not to be considered where it added to, or supplemented, the reasons given in a review decision (see *R. v. Westminster CC, ex p. Ermakov* (1996) 28 H.L.R. 819), the statement in this case simply elucidated the reasons already given. For a case in which the Court of Appeal considered the adequacy of reasons given on review, see *Bernard v. Enfield LBC* [2001] EWCA Civ 1831; [2002] H.L.R. 46.

Appeals

If the review results in confirmation of the original decision, reasons must be given. **3A–1350**

The Act does not specify that they must be in writing. There is a right of appeal from a review decision to the county court on a point of law. Prior to amendment by Homelessness Act 2002, Sched.1, appeals to the court had to be brought within 21 days of "the date on which [the applicant] should have been notified" of the review decision (Housing Act 1996, s.204).

For the procedure for appeals, see CPR 52 and the commentary at 3A–1359.

In *Begum v. Tower Hamlets LBC* [2000] Q.B. 133; [2000] 1 W.L.R. 306, CA it was held that the judge at first instance was right in construing the words "point of law" which qualify the right of appeal to the county court in s.204 as being wide enough to embrace any ground of challenge that would have been available in proceedings for judicial review (including *Wednesbury* irrationality). See too *Chief Adjudication Officer v. Foster* [1993] A.C. 754, HL.

Where there is an appeal to a county court, the question for the court is whether the whole of the circumstances justify any relief in public law. A new ground for refusing accommodation should only be ignored if it can be faulted on public law grounds (*Crawley BC v. B* (2000) 32 H.L.R. 636, CA). Where a court identifies procedural flaws in a local authority's decision making process, the decision may only be upheld if a court is satisfied that a properly directed local authority would inevitably have reached the same decision. The test of inevitability is a strict test. (*Ali and Nessa v. Newham LBC* [2001] EWCA Civ 73; [2002] H.L.R. 20).

Note —*Warsame v. Hounslow LBC* (2000) 32 H.L.R. 335; [2000] 1 W.L.R. 696, CA where the council decided that a duty which it had owed to the applicants under Housing Act 1996, s.193 ended upon the refusal by the applicants of an offer of a secure council tenancy made under Housing Act, Part VI, s.193(7). Reversing a circuit judge's decision that he had no jurisdiction to consider an appeal, the Court of Appeal held that a decision that "no duty was owed" was a decision as to "what duty (if any)" was owed by the council and accordingly was brought by Housing Act 1996, s.202(1)(b) within the statutory mechanism for review and appeal. It followed that the applicants could challenge the findings by the council which had led to the "no duty" decision (*e.g.* on the "suitability" and "acceptability" issues in s.193(7) itself). It would seem from the court's approach that a decision that "no (further) duty is owed" must be given in writing with reasons and must notify the right to review: Housing Act 1996, s.184.

Section 202 reviews, section 204 appeals and the ECHR

3A–1351 The House of Lords considered whether this procedure is ECHR compliant in *Begum (Runa) v. Tower Hamlets LBC* [2003] UKHL 5; [2003] 2 A.C. 430; [2003] 2 W.L.R. 388; [2003] 1 All E.R. 731. (1) The House of Lords assumed, without deciding, that decisions made under Housing Act 1996 Part VII do give rise to "civil rights" for the purposes of ECHR Art.6, although Lord Bingham stated that "to hold that the right enjoyed by [a homeless person] is a 'civil right' for the purposes of article 6 would … be to go further than the Strasbourg court has yet gone…". (2) The s.202 review process does not comply with article 6 because the reviewing officer is not an "independent and impartial tribunal"—an employee cannot be independent of the authority. (3) However an appeal to the county court on a point of law (s.204) gives a right of access to a court of "full jurisdiction" for article 6 purposes. For reasons of good administration, the absence of a full fact finding jurisdiction in the court or tribunal to which an appeal lies from an administrative decision making body does not disqualify it for the purposes of article 6. "'Full jurisdiction' in this context does not necessarily mean full jurisdiction on fact or law, but … 'jurisdiction to deal with the case as the nature of the decision requires.'" (Lord Millett) An authority's factual findings are "only staging posts on the way to much the broader judgments which the authority has to make." Lord Bingham stated that he "would expect the county court judge to be alert to any indication that an applicant's case might not have been resolved by the authority in a fair, objective and even-handed way" but could "see no warrant for applying in this context notions of "anxious scrutiny" … or [an] enhanced approach to judicial review … [or] "a close and rigorous analysis" if by that is meant an analysis closer or more rigorous than would ordinarily be conducted by a careful and competent judge determining an application for judicial review." Lord Hoffmann considered that the conventional principles of judicial review are sufficient.

The House of Lords declined to follow and apply dicta in *Adan v. Newham LBC* [2001] EWCA Civ 1916; [2002] 1 All E.R. 931 that the limited right of appeal under s.204 means that the county court is not a court of full jurisdiction and that a local authority may use its contracting-out powers under the Local Authorities (Contracting Out of Allocation of Housing and Homelessness Functions) Order 1996 (S.I. 1996 No. 3205) to appoint an independent and impartial tribunal to conduct the review in cases where a material dispute of primary fact has to be resolved.

Procedure on a review

203.—(1) The Secretary of State may make provision by regula- **3A–1352** tions as to the procedure to be followed in connection with a review under section 202. Nothing in the following provisions affects the generality of this power.

(2) Provision may be made by regulations—

    (a) requiring the decision on review to be made by a person of appropriate seniority who was not involved in the original decision, and

    (b) as to the circumstances in which the applicant is entitled to an oral hearing, and whether and by whom he may be represented at such a hearing.

(3) The authority, or as the case may be either of the authorities, concerned shall notify the applicant of the decision on the review.

(4) If the decision is—

    (a) to confirm the original decision on any issue against the interests of the applicant, or

    (b) to confirm a previous decision—

        (i) to notify another authority under section 198 (referral of cases), or

        (ii) that the conditions are met for the referral of his case,

they shall also notify him of the reasons for the decision.

(5) In any case they shall inform the applicant of his right to appeal to a county court on a point of law, and of the period within which such an appeal must be made (see section 204).

(6) Notice of the decision shall not be treated as given unless and until subsection (5), and where applicable subsection (4), is complied with.

(7) Provision may be made by regulations as to the period within which the review must be carried out and notice given of the decision.

(8) Notice required to be given to a person under this section shall be given in writing and, if not received by him, shall be treated as having been given if it is made available at the authority's office for a reasonable period for collection by him or on his behalf.

Procedure on a review

See the commentary to s.202. **3A–1353**

"regulations"

See the Allocation of Housing and Homelessness (Review Procedures) Regulations **3A–1354** 1999 (S.I. 1999 No. 71).

Right of appeal to county court on point of law

204.—(1) If an applicant who has requested a review under section **3A–1355** 202—

(a) is dissatisfied with the decision on the review, or

(b) is not notified of the decision on the review within the time prescribed under section 203,

he may appeal to the county court on any point of law arising from the decision or, as the case may be, the original decision.

(2) An appeal must be brought within 21 days of his being notified of the decision or, as the case may be, of the date on which he should have been notified of a decision on review.

(2A) The court may give permission for an appeal to be brought after the end of the period allowed by subsection (2), but only if it is satisfied—

(a) where permission is sought before the end of that period, that there is a good reason for the applicant to be unable to bring the appeal in time; or

(b) where permission is sought after that time, that there was a good reason for the applicant's failure to bring the appeal in time and for any delay in applying for permission.

(3) On appeal the court may make such order confirming, quashing or varying the decision as it thinks fit.

(4) Where the authority were under a duty under section 188, 190 or 200 to secure that accommodation is available for the applicant's occupation, or had the power under section 195(8) to do so, they may secure that accommodation is so available—

(a) during the period for appealing under this section against the authority's decision, and

(b) if an appeal is brought, until the appeal (and any further appeal) is finally determined.

3A–1356   Amended by Homelessness Act 2002 Sched. 1, para. 17. In Wales, this amendment was brought into force on September 30, 2002 by the Homelessness Act 2002 (Commencement) (Wales) Order 2002 (S.I. 2002 No. 1736) (W.166) (C.53). Section 204(2A) was brought into force in England on September 30, 2002 by the Homelessness Act 2002 (Commencement No. 2 and Transitional Provisions) (England) Order 2002 (S.I. 2002 No. 2324) but only in relation to appeals brought after that date.

Right of appeal to county court on point of law

3A–1357   See the commentary to s.202.

"review"

3A–1358   See ss.202 and 203.

Procedure for appeal

3A–1359   CPR Part 52 (Appeals), which was introduced by the Civil Procedure (Amendment) Rules 2000, applies to s.204 appeals with effect from May 2, 2000 (see Pt 52, PD para. 17.2). Appellants' notices in Form **N161** must be filed and served in all cases (para. 5.1). Appellants must also file bundles of documents with appellants' notices. Such bundles should include all documents which the appellant reasonably considers necessary to enable the court to reach its decision on the hearing of the appeal (para. 5.6). If it is not possible to file all documents, the appellant must indicate which documents have not yet been filed and the reasons why they are not currently available (para. 5.7).

Appeals to the county court provided by s.204 are appeals for the purposes of the Access to Justice Act 1999 (Destination of Appeals) Order 2000 (S.I. 2000 No. 1071). Accordingly appeals from the county court lie to the Court of Appeal and the more restrictive test for permission to appeal, as prescribed by Access to Justice Act 1999 s.55, applies (*Azimi v. Newham LBC* (2001) 33 H.L.R. 569, CA).

District judges may not hear appeals pursuant to s. 204 (CPR Pt 2, PD2B, para. 9A and *Crawley LBC v. B* [2002] 32 H.L.R. 636, CA).

Under CPR Part 2.3 an appeal is brought by filing the notice of appeal. Filing means delivering by post or otherwise. Delivery of the appeal notice to the appropriate court is sufficient to constitute filing within the CPR, even if the court offices are closed. There is no need for a person to have received or authenticated it. (*Van Aken v. Camden LBC* [2002] EWCA Civ 1724; [2003] 1 W.L.R. 684; [2003] 1 All E.R. 552). See to *Aadan v. Brent LBC* (2000) 32 H.L.R. 848, CA.

extension of time for bringing appeal

Section 204(2A) was inserted by Homelessness Act 2002, Sched.1. An extension of **3A–1360** time may only be granted if permission is sought before the end of the period allowed by s.204(2) or there is a good reason for the applicant's failure to bring the appeal in time and for any delay in applying for permission. The word "only" in s.204(2A) provides a threshold which has to be passed before the merits can be considered. It is not open to a judge to have regard to the criteria in CPR r.3.9, or any other criteria, other than those specified in s.204(2A). If a judge is not satisfied that there are good reasons for a failure to bring an appeal in time, it is not possible to go on to consider the merits (*Short v. Birmingham CC* [2004] EWHC 2112 (QB); [2005] HLR 6).

Judicial review

An application for judicial review is an abuse of the process, and not available, **3A–1361** where a homeless person does not exhaust the right to a statutory review and appeal to the county court under ss.202 and 204 (*R. (Campbell) v. Enfield LBC* (2001) May 22, QBD Admin Ct), but *cf. R. (Van der Stolk) v. Camden LBC* [2002] EWHC 1261 (Admin); July 2002 Legal Action 26 (although judicial review would not normally lie where the claimant had not availed himself of a county court appeal, judicial review allowed in "an unusual case" where the claimant's health was poor and deteriorating and the medical report did add materially to what had been known about its effects on the claimant. His homelessness application should be reconsidered in the light of it).

New evidence on appeal

In *Cramp v Hastings LBC* ; *Phillips v Camden LBC* [2005] EWCA Civ 1005 ; 29 July **3A–1361.1** 2005, the Court of Appeal stated that:

". . .judges in the county court need to be astute to ensure that evidential material over and above the contents of the housing file and the reviewing officer's decision is limited to that which is necessary to illuminate the points of law that are to be relied on in the appeal, or the issue of what, if any, relief ought to be granted. An undisciplined approach to the admission of new evidence may lead to the danger that the reviewing officer is found guilty of an error of law for not taking into account evidence that was never before her, notwithstanding the applicant's opportunity to make representations about the original decision."

Section 204(4): appeals

204A.—(1) This section applies where an applicant has the right to **3A–1362** appeal to the county court against a local housing authority's decision on a review.

(2) If the applicant is dissatisfied with a decision by the authority—

(a) not to exercise their power under section 204(4) ("the section 204(4) power") in his case;

(b) to exercise that power for a limited period ending before the final determination by the county court of his appeal under section 204(1) ("the main appeal"); or

(c) to cease exercising that power before that time,

he may appeal to the county court against the decision.

(3) An appeal under this section may not be brought after the final determination by the county court of the main appeal.

(4) On an appeal under this section the court—

(a) may order the authority to secure that accommodation is available for the applicant's occupation until the determination of the appeal (or such earlier time as the court may specify); and

(b) shall confirm or quash the decision appealed against,

and in considering whether to confirm or quash the decision the court shall apply the principles applied by the High Court on an application for judicial review.

(5) If the court quashes the decision it may order the authority to exercise the section 204(4) power in the applicant's case for such period as may be specified in the order.

(6) An order under subsection (5)—

(a) may only be made if the court is satisfied that failure to exercise the section 204(4) power in accordance with the order would substantially prejudice the applicant's ability to pursue the main appeal;

(b) may not specify any period ending after the final determination by the county court of the main appeal.

3A–1363   Inserted by Homelessness Act 2002, s.11. In Wales, this amendment was brought into force on September 30, 2002 by the Homelessness Act 2002 (Commencement) (Wales) Order 2002 (S.I. 2002 No. 1736) (W.166)(C.53). Section 204A was brought into force in England on September 30, 2002 by the Homelessness Act 2002 (Commencement No. 2 and Transitional Provisions) (England) Order 2002 (S.I. 2002 No. 2324) but only in relation to appeals brought after that date. Note that PD52, para. 24.2 provides that

- an appeal under s.204A should be made in the same appellant's notice (Form N161) as a s.204 appeal or (if that is not possible) in separate appellant's notices;

- an application for an interim injunction in a s.204A appeal may be included in the appellant's notice; and

- where such an interim injunction is made without notice to the housing authority, that order will normally require that accommodation is secured only until a hearing date on which the authority can make representations.

PD2B, para. 9 provides that appeals under s.204A may be not be heard by district judges.

When hearing a s.204A appeal, the county court should apply the same approach as directed in *R. v. Brighton & Hove Council, ex p. Nacion* (1999) 31 H.L.R. 1095, CA unless the court decides that the local authority did not direct itself in accordance with *R. v. London Borough of Camden, ex p. Mohammed* (1998) 30 H.L.R. 315, QBD. In that case it should quash the decision and decide whether it should itself exercise the s.204A(5) power to order the authority to provide temporary accommodation. There is no question of the county court embarking on an assessment of the merits of the appeal. That would be to go beyond the scope of the appeal as set out in *Nacion*. A challenge to the exercise of powers under s.188 of the Act still has to be brought by way of judicial review. (See *Francis v. Kensington and Chelsea RLBC* [2003] EWCA Civ 443; [2003] 1 W.L.R. 2248; [2003] 2 All E.R. 1052.)

SUPPLEMENTARY PROVISIONS

Discharge of functions: introductory

3A–1364   **205.**—(1) The following sections have effect in relation to the discharge by a local housing authority of their functions under this Part to secure that accommodation is available for the occupation of a person—

section 206 (general provisions),

section 208 (out-of-area placements),

section 209 (arrangements with private landlord).

(2) In sections 206 and 208 those functions are referred to as the authority's "housing functions under this Part".

Amended by Homelessness Act 2002, Sched. 1, para. 18. In England, this amend- **3A–1365**
ment was brought into force on July 31, 2002 by the Homelessness Act 2002 (Commencement No. 1) (England) Order 2002 (S.I. 2002 No. 1799) (C.56). In Wales, this amendment was brought into force on September 30, 2002 by the Homelessness Act 2002 (Commencement) (Wales) Order 2002 (S.I. 2002 No.1736) (W.166) (C.53).

Discharge of functions by local housing authorities

206.—(1) A local housing authority may discharge their housing **3A–1366**
functions under this Part only in the following ways—

(a) by securing that suitable accommodation provided by them is available,

(b) by securing that he obtains suitable accommodation from some other person, or

(c) by giving him such advice and assistance as will secure that suitable accommodation is available from some other person.

(2) A local housing authority may require a person in relation to whom they are discharging such functions—

(a) to pay such reasonable charges as they may determine in respect of accommodation which they secure for his occupation (either by making it available themselves or otherwise), or

(b) to pay such reasonable amount as they may determine in respect of sums payable by them for accommodation made available by another person.

Discharge of functions by local housing authorities
See the commentary to s.193. **3A–1367**

"local housing authority"
See ss.217, 218, and 230 which refer to the Housing Act 1985—see the Housing Act **3A–1368**
1985, ss.1 and 2, above.

Discharge of functions: provision of accommodation by the authority

207. [...] **3A–1369**
This section was repealed by Homelessness Act 2002, Sched. 2. **3A–1370**

Discharge of functions: out-of-area placements

208.—(1) So far as reasonably practicable a local housing authority **3A–1371**
shall in discharging their housing functions under this Part secure that accommodation is available for the occupation of the applicant in their district.

(2) If they secure that accommodation is available for the occupation of the applicant outside their district, they shall give notice to the local housing authority in whose district the accommodation is situated.

(3) The notice shall state—
- (a) the name of the applicant,
- (b) the number and description of other persons who normally reside with him as a member of his family or might reasonably be expected to reside with him,
- (c) the address of the accommodation,
- (d) the date on which the accommodation was made available to him, and
- (e) which function under this Part the authority was discharging in securing that the accommodation is available for his occupation.

(4) The notice must be in writing, and must be given before the end of the period of 14 days beginning with the day on which the accommodation was made available to the applicant.

Discharge of functions: out-of-area placements

3A-1372   See the commentary to s.193.

"local housing authority"

3A-1373   See ss.217, 218, and 230 which refer to the Housing Act 1985—see the Housing Act 1985, ss.1 and 2 above.

"district"

3A-1374   See s.217(3).

"available for his occupation"

3A-1375   See s.176.

Discharge of interim duties: arrangements with private landlord

3A-1376   **209.**—(1) This section applies where in pursuance of any of their housing functions under section 188, 190, 200 or 204(4) (interim duties) a local housing authority make arrangements with a private landlord to provide accommodation.

(2) A tenancy granted to the applicant in pursuance of the arrangements cannot be an assured tenancy before the end of the period of twelve months beginning with—
- (a) the date on which the applicant was notified of the authority's decision under section 184(3) or 198(5); or
- (b) if there is a review of that decision under section 202 or an appeal to the court under section 204, the date on which he is notified of the decision on review or the appeal is finally determined,

unless, before or during that period, the tenant is notified by the landlord (or in the case of joint landlords, at least one of them) that the tenancy is to be regarded as an assured shorthold tenancy or an assured tenancy other than an assured shorthold tenancy.

3A-1377   Amended by Homelessness Act 2002, Sched.1, para. 19. In England, this amendment was brought into force on July 31, 2002 by the Homelessness Act 2002 (Commencement No. 1) (England) Order 2002 (S.I. 2002 No.1799) (C. 56). In Wales, this amendment was brought into force on September 30, 2002 by the Homelessness Act 2002 (Commencement) (Wales) Order 2002 (S.I. 2002 No.1736) (W.166)(C.53).

private landlord
See s.217(1), as amended by Homelessness Act 2002 Schedule 1, para. 20.

assured shorthold tenancy
See Housing Act 1988, ss.19A and 20.

Discharge of functions: arrangements with private landlord
See the commentary to s.193.　　　　　　　　　　　　　　　　　　　　**3A–1378**

"local housing authority"
See ss.217, 218, and 230 which refer to the Housing Act 1985—see the Housing Act **3A–1379**
1985, ss.1 and 2 above.

"available for his occupation"
See s.176.　　　　　　　　　　　　　　　　　　　　　　　　　　　　**3A–1380**

"assured tenancy"
See s.230 which refers to the Housing Act 1988, Pt I. See the Housing Act 1988, s.1 **3A–1381**
above.

"registered social landlord"
See s.1.　　　　　　　　　　　　　　　　　　　　　　　　　　　　　**3A–1382**

Suitability of accommodation

210.—(1) In determining for the purposes of this Part whether ac- **3A–1383**
commodation is suitable for a person, the local housing authority
shall have regard to Parts 9 and 10 of the Housing Act 1985 (slum
clearance and overcrowding) and Parts 1 to 4 of the Housing Act
2004).

(2) The Secretary of State may by order specify—
> (a) circumstances in which accommodation is or is not to be
> regarded as suitable for a person, and
> (b) matters to be taken into account or disregarded in
> determining whether accommodation is suitable for a
> person.

amendment
Amended by Housing Act 2004 Sched.15, para. 43.The amendment is not yet in **3A–1383.1**
force. It is due to be brought into force by commencement order.

Suitability of accommodation
See the commentary to s.193 and the Homelessness (Suitability of Accommodation **3A–1384**
(England) Order 2003 (S.I. 2003 No. 3326).

"local housing authority"
See ss.217, 218, and 230 which refer to the Housing Act 1985—see the Housing Act **3A–1385**
1985, ss.1 and 2 above.

Protection of property of homeless persons and persons threatened with homelessness

211.—(1) This section applies where a local housing authority have **3A–1386**
reason to believe that—
> (a) there is danger of loss of, or damage to, any personal
> property of an applicant by reason of his inability to
> protect it or deal with it, and
> (b) no other suitable arrangements have been or are being
> made.

(2) If the authority have become subject to a duty towards the applicant under—

> section 188 (interim duty to accommodate),
>
> section 190, 193 or 195 (duties to persons found to be homeless or threatened with homelessness), or
>
> section 200 (duties to applicant whose case is considered for referral or referred),
>
> then, whether or not they are still subject to such a duty, they shall take reasonable steps to prevent the loss of the property or prevent or mitigate damage to it.

(3) If they have not become subject to such a duty, they may take any steps they consider reasonable for that purpose.

(4) The authority may decline to take action under this section except upon such conditions as they consider appropriate in the particular case, which may include conditions as to—

> (a) the making and recovery by the authority of reasonable charges for the action taken, or
>
> (b) the disposal by the authority, in such circumstances as may be specified, of property in relation to which they have taken action.

(5) References in this section to personal property of the applicant include personal property of any person who might reasonably be expected to reside with him.

(6) Section 212 contains provisions supplementing this section.

"local housing authority"

3A-1387   See ss.217, 218, and 230 which refer to the Housing Act 1985—see the Housing Act 1985, ss.1 and 2 above.

3A-1388   For there to be a cause of action for a claim under s.211 the local authority must have reason to believe that: (a) there is a danger of loss or damage to property as a result of the owner being unable to protect it; and (b) no other suitable arrangements can be made (see ss.211(1)(a) and (b)). In view of the use of the word "danger", there has to be a likelihood of harm and not just the possibility of injury. (*Deadman v. Southwark LBC* (2001) 33 H.L.R. 865, CA).

Protection of property: supplementary provisions

3A-1389   **212.**—(1) The authority may for the purposes of section 211 (protection of property of homeless persons or persons threatened with homelessness)—

> (a) enter, at all reasonable times, any premises which are the usual place of residence of the applicant or which were his last usual place of residence, and
>
> (b) deal with any personal property of his in any way which is reasonably necessary, in particular by storing it or arranging for its storage.

(2) Where the applicant asks the authority to move his property to a particular location nominated by him, the authority—

> (a) may, if it appears to them that his request is reasonable, discharge their responsibilities under section 211 by doing as he asks, and
>
> (b) having done so, have no further duty or power to take action under that section in relation to that property.

If such a request is made, the authority shall before complying with it inform the applicant of the consequence of their doing so.

(3) If no such request is made (or, if made, is not acted upon) the authority cease to have any duty or power to take action under section 211 when, in their opinion, there is no longer any reason to believe that there is a danger of loss of or damage to a person's personal property by reason of his inability to protect it or deal with it.

But property stored by virtue of their having taken such action may be kept in store and any conditions upon which it was taken into store continue to have effect, with any necessary modifications.

(4) Where the authority—
  (a) cease to be subject to a duty to take action under section 211 in respect of an applicant's property, or
  (b) cease to have power to take such action, having previously taken such action,
they shall notify the applicant of that fact and of the reason for it.

(5) The notification shall be given to the applicant—
  (a) by delivering it to him, or
  (b) by leaving it, or sending it to him, at his last known address.

(6) References in this section to personal property of the applicant include personal property of any person who might reasonably be expected to reside with him.

Co-operation between relevant housing authorities and bodies

213.—(1) Where a local housing authority—

3A–1390

  (a) request another relevant housing authority or body, in England, Wales or Scotland, to assist them in the discharge of their functions under this Part, or
  (b) request a social services authority, in England, Wales or Scotland, to exercise any of their functions in relation to a case which the local housing authority are dealing with under this Part,

the authority or body to whom the request is made shall co-operate in rendering such assistance in the discharge of the functions to which the request relates as is reasonable in the circumstances.

(2) In subsection (1)(a) "relevant housing authority or body" means—

  (a) in relation to England and Wales, a local housing authority, a new town corporation, a registered social landlord or a housing action trust;
  (b) in relation to Scotland, a local authority, a development corporation, a registered housing association or Scottish Homes.

Expressions used in paragraph (a) have the same meaning as in the Housing Act 1985; and expressions used in paragraph (b) have the same meaning as in the Housing (Scotland) Act 1987.

995

(3) Subsection (1) above applies to a request by a local authority in Scotland under section 38 of the Housing (Scotland) Act 1987 as it applies to a request by a local housing authority in England and Wales (the references to this Part being construed, in relation to such a request, as references to Part II of that Act).

"local housing authority"

3A–1391   See ss.217, 218, and 230 which refer to the Housing Act 1985—see the Housing Act 1985, ss.1 and 2, above.

"social services authority"

3A–1392   See s.217.

Co-operation in certain cases involving children

3A–1393   213A—(1) This section applies where a local housing authority have reason to believe that an applicant with whom a person under the age of 18 normally resides, or might reasonably be expected to reside—

    (a) may be ineligible for assistance;

    (b) may be homeless and may have become so intentionally; or

    (c) may be threatened with homelessness intentionally.

(2) A local housing authority shall make arrangements for ensuring that, where this section applies—

    (a) the applicant is invited to consent to the referral of the essential facts of his case to the social services authority for the district of the housing authority (where that is a different authority); and

    (b) if the applicant has given that consent, the social services authority are made aware of those facts and of the subsequent decision of the housing authority in respect of his case.

(3) Where the local housing authority and the social services authority for a district are the same authority (a "unitary authority"), that authority shall make arrangements for ensuring that, where this section applies—

    (a) the applicant is invited to consent to the referral to the social services department of the essential facts of his case; and

    (b) if the applicant has given that consent, the social services department is made aware of those facts and of the subsequent decision of the authority in respect of his case.

(4) Nothing in subsection (2) or (3) affects any power apart from this section to disclose information relating to the applicant's case to the social services authority or to the social services department (as the case may be) without the consent of the applicant.

(5) Where a social services authority—

    (a) are aware of a decision of a local housing authority that the applicant is ineligible for assistance, became homeless intentionally or became threatened with homelessness intentionally, and

996

(b) request the local housing authority to provide them with advice and assistance in the exercise of their social services functions under Part 3 of the Children Act 1989, the local housing authority shall provide them with such advice and assistance as is reasonable in the circumstances.

(6) A unitary authority shall make arrangements for ensuring that, where they make a decision of a kind mentioned in subsection (5)(a), the housing department provide the social services department with such advice and assistance as the social services department may reasonably request.

(7) In this section, in relation to a unitary authority

"the housing department" means those persons responsible for the exercise of their housing functions; and

"the social services department" means those persons responsible for the exercise of their social services functions under Part 3 of the Children Act 1989.

3A–1394

Inserted by Homelessness Act 2002, s.12. In Wales, this amendment was brought into force on September 30, 2002 by the Homelessness Act 2002 (Commencement) (Wales) Order 2002 (S.I. 2002 No.1736) (W.166) (C.53). It was brought into force in England on October 1, 2002 by the Homelessness Act 2002 (Commencement No. 1) (England) Order (S.I. 2002 No. 1799).

local housing authority—see Housing Act 1985, s.1.

ineligible for assistance—see s.185.

homeless intentionally—see s.191.

threatened with homelessness intentionally—see s.191.

unitary authority—see s.213A(3).

social services authority—see s.213A(7) and Children Act 1989, Part III.

Co-operation with social services authority—If a local housing authority decide that an applicant, with whom a person under the age of 18 normally resides, may be ineligible for assistance, intentionally homeless, or threatened with homelessness intentionally, they must, subject to the consent of the applicant, make arrangements to ensure that the essential facts of the case are referred to the social services authority.

Children Act 1989—Local authorities have a power to provide assistance by way of accommodation under Children Act 1989, s.17. However s.17 does not impose an enforceable duty to provide assistance—see *A and W v. Lambeth LBC; G v. Barnet LBC* (also reported as *R.(on the application of G) v. Barnet LBC*) [2003] UKHL 57; [2003] 3 W.L.R. 1194 and the commentary at 3A–31 above.

GENERAL PROVISIONS

False statements, withholding information and failure to disclose change of circumstances

214.—(1) It is an offence for a person, with intent to induce a local housing authority to believe in connection with the exercise of their functions under this Part that he or another person is entitled to accommodation or assistance in accordance with the provisions of this Part, or is entitled to accommodation or assistance of a particular description—

3A–1395

(a) knowingly or recklessly to make a statement which is false in a material particular, or

(b) knowingly to withhold information which the authority

have reasonably required him to give in connection with the exercise of those functions.

(2) If before an applicant receives notification of the local housing authority's decision on his application there is any change of facts material to his case, he shall notify the authority as soon as possible.

The authority shall explain to every applicant, in ordinary language, the duty imposed on him by this subsection and the effect of subsection (3).

(3) A person who fails to comply with subsection (2) commits an offence unless he shows that he was not given the explanation required by that subsection or that he had some other reasonable excuse for non-compliance.

(4) A person guilty of an offence under this section is liable on summary conviction to a fine not exceeding level 5 on the standard scale.

"local housing authority"

3A–1396 See ss.217, 218 and 230 which refer to the Housing Act 1985—see the Housing Act 1985, ss.1 and 2 above.

See too the Housing Act 1985, Sched.2, Ground 5 above.

Regulations and orders

3A–1397 **215.**—(1) In this Part "prescribed" means prescribed by regulations of the Secretary of State.

(2) Regulations or an order under this Part may make different provision for different purposes, including different provision for different areas.

(3) Regulations or an order under this Part shall be made by statutory instrument.

(4) Unless required to be approved in draft, regulations or an order under this Part shall be subject to annulment in pursuance of a resolution of either House of Parliament.

Transitional and consequential matters

3A–1398 **216.**—(1) The provisions of this Part have effect in place of the provisions of Part III of the Housing Act 1985 (housing the homeless) and shall be construed as one with that Act.

(2) Subject to any transitional provision contained in an order under section 232(4) (power to include transitional provision in commencement order), the provisions of this Part do not apply in relation to an applicant whose application for accommodation or assistance in obtaining accommodation was made before the commencement of this Part.

(3) The enactments mentioned in Schedule 17 have effect with the amendments specified there which are consequential on the provisions of this Part.

Minor definitions: Part VII

3A–1399 **217.**—(1) In this Part, subject to subsection (2)—

"private landlord" means a landlord who is not within section

80(1) of the Housing Act 1985 (c.68) (the landlord condition for secure tenancies); and

"relevant authority" means a local housing authority or a social services authority; and

"social services authority" means a local authority for the purposes of the Local Authority Social Services Act 1970, as defined in section 1 of that Act.

(2) In this Part, in relation to Scotland—

(a) "local housing authority" means a local authority within the meaning of the Housing (Scotland) Act 1988, and

(b) "social services authority" means a local authority for the purposes of the Social Work (Scotland) Act 1968.

(3) References in this Part to the district of a local housing authority—

(a) have the same meaning in relation to an authority in England or Wales as in the Housing Act 1985, and

(b) in relation to an authority in Scotland, mean the area of the local authority concerned.

Amended by Homelessness Act 2002, Sched. 1, para. 20. In England, this amendment was brought into force on July 31, 2002 by the Homelessness Act 2002 (Commencement No. 1) (England) Order 2002 (S.I. 2002 No.1799) (C.56)). In Wales, this amendment was brought into force on September 30, 2002 by the Homelessness Act 2002 (Commencement) (Wales) Order 2002 (S.I. 2002 No.1736) (W.166) (C.53).   **3A–1400**

Index of defined expressions: Part VII

218. The following Table shows provisions defining or otherwise   **3A–1401**
explaining expressions used in this Part (other than provisions defining or explaining an expression used in the same section)—

accommodation available for occupation	section 176
applicant	section 183(2)
assistance under this Part	section 183(2)
associated (in relation to a person)	section 178
assured tenancy and assured shorthold tenancy	section 230
district (of local housing authority)	section 217(3)
eligible for assistance	section 183(2)
homeless	section 175(1)
housing functions under this Part (in sections 206 and 208)	section 205(2)
intentionally homeless	section 191
intentionally threatened with homelessness	section 196
local connection	section 199
local housing authority—	
—in England and Wales	section 230
—in Scotland	section 217(2)(a)
minimum period (for purposes of section 193)	section 193(3) and (4)

prescribed	section 215(1)
priority need	section 189
private landlord	section 217(1)
reasonable to continue to occupy accommodation	section 177
registered social landlord	section 230
relevant authority	section 217(1)
social services authority	section 217(1) and (2)(b)
threatened with homelessness	section 175(4)

3A–1402   Amended by Homelessness Act 2002, Sched.1, para. 21. In England, this amendment was brought into force on July 31,2002 by the Homelessness Act 2002 (Commencement No. 1) (England) Order 2002 (S.I. 2002 No.1799) (C.56). In Wales, this amendment was brought into force on September 30, 2002 by the Homelessness Act 2002 (Commencement) (Wales) Order 2002 (S.I. 2002 No.1736) (W.166) (C.53).

Anti-social behaviour: landlords' policies and procedures

3A–1403   218A—(1) This section applies to the following landlords—

    (a) a local housing authority;

    (b) a housing action trust;

    (c) a registered social landlord.

(2) The landlord must prepare—

    (a) a policy in relation to anti-social behaviour;

    (b) procedures for dealing with occurrences of anti-social behaviour.

(3) The landlord must not later than 6 months after the commencement of section 12 of the Anti-social Behaviour Act 2003 publish a statement of the policy and procedures prepared under subsection (2).

(4) The landlord must from time to time keep the policy and procedures under review and, when it thinks appropriate, publish a revised statement.

(5) A copy of a statement published under subsection (3) or (4)—

    (a) must be available for inspection at all reasonable hours at the landlord's principal office;

    (b) must be provided on payment of a reasonable fee to any person who requests it.

(6) The landlord must also—

    (a) prepare a summary of its current policy and procedures;

    (b) provide without charge a copy of the summary to any person who requests it.

(7) In preparing and reviewing the policy and procedures the landlord must have regard to guidance issued—

    (a) by the Secretary of State in the case of a local housing authority or a housing action trust;

    (b) by the Relevant Authority under section 36 in the case of a registered social landlord.

(8) Anti-social behaviour is any conduct to which section 153A or 153B applies.

(9) Relevant Authority has the same meaning as in Part 1.

Editorial note
This section was inserted by Anti-social Behaviour Act 2003, s.12. It was brought **3A–1404**
into force in England on June 30, 2004 by the Anti-social Behaviour Act 2003 (Commencement No.3 and Savings) Order 2004 (S.I. 2004 No. 1502) (C.61). It was brought into force in Wales on 30 April 2005 by the Anti-social Behaviour Act 2003 (Commencement No.4) (Wales) Order 2005 (S.I. 2005 No. 1225) (W.83) (C.55).

a local housing authority
See Housing Act 1996, s.230 and Housing Act 1985, ss.1 and 2(2). **3A–1405**

a housing action trust
See Housing Act 1996, s.230 and Housing Act 1988 Part III. **3A–1406**

a registered social landlord
See Housing Act 1996, s.230 referring back to Part I (ss.1 to 3). **3A–1407**

Anti-social behaviour
See ss.153A and 153B above. **3A–1408**

Relevant Authority
See Housing Act 1996, s.56—*i.e.* the Housing Corporation or Housing for Wales. **3A–1409**

Guidance
Guidance may be issued to local housing authorities or housing action trusts in **3A–1410**
England by the Secretary of State or, in Wales, by the National Assembly for Wales. Guidance to registered social landlords may be issued by the Housing Corporation in England or, in Wales, by the National Assembly for Wales. At present no guidance has been issued.

PART VIII

MISCELLANEOUS AND GENERAL PROVISIONS

GENERAL

Meaning of "lease" and "tenancy" and related expressions

229.—(1) In this Act "lease" and "tenancy" have the same meaning. **3A–1411**

(2) Both expressions include—

    (a) a sub-lease or a sub-tenancy, and

    (b) an agreement for a lease or tenancy (or sub-lease or sub-tenancy).

(3) The expressions "lessor" and "lessee" and "landlord" and "tenant", and references to letting, to the grant of a lease or to covenants or terms, shall be construed accordingly.

SECTION 155(6) SCHEDULE 15

ARREST FOR ANTI-SOCIAL BEHAVIOUR: POWERS OF HIGH COURT AND COUNTY
COURT TO REMAND

Introductory

1.—(1) The provisions of this Schedule apply where the court has power to remand **3A–1412**
a person under section 155(2) or (5) (arrest for breach of injunction, &c.).

(2) In this Schedule "the court" means the High Court or a county court and includes—

(a) in relation to the High Court, a judge of that court, and

(b) in relation to a county court, a judge or district judge of that court.

Remand in custody or on bail

3A–1413 2.—(1) The court may—

(a) remand him in custody, that is, commit him to custody to be brought before the court at the end of the period of remand or at such earlier time as the court may require, or

(b) remand him on bail, in accordance with the following provisions.

(2) The court may remand him on bail—

(a) by taking from him a recognizance, with or without sureties, conditioned as provided in paragraph 3, or

(b) by fixing the amount of the recognizances with a view to their being taken subsequently, and in the meantime committing him to custody as mentioned in sub-paragraph (1)(a).

(3) Where a person is brought before the court after remand, the court may further remand him.

3.—(1) Where a person is remanded on bail, the court may direct that his recognizance be conditioned for his appearance—

(a) before that court at the end of the period of remand, or

(b) at every time and place to which during the course of the proceedings the hearing may from time to time be adjourned.

(2) Where a recognizance is conditioned for a person's appearance as mentioned in sub-paragraph (1)(b), the fixing of any time for him next to appear shall be deemed to be a remand.

(3) Nothing in this paragraph affects the power of the court at any subsequent hearing to remand him afresh.

4.—(1) The court shall not remand a person for a period exceeding 8 clear days, except that—

(a) if the court remands him on bail, it may remand him for a longer period if he and the other party consent, and

(b) if the court adjourns a case under section 156(1) (remand for medical examination and report), the court may remand him for the period of the adjournment.

(2) Where the court has power to remand a person in custody it may, if the remand is for a period not exceeding 3 clear days, commit him to the custody of a constable.

Further remand

3A–1414 5.—(1) If the court is satisfied that a person who has been remanded is unable by reason of illness or accident to appear or be brought before the court at the expiration of the period for which he was remanded, the court may, in his absence, remand him for a further time. This power may, in the case of a person who was remanded on bail, be exercised by enlarging his recognizance and those of any sureties for him to a later time.

(2) Where a person remanded on bail is bound to appear before the court at any time and the court has no power to remand him under sub-paragraph (1) the court may in his absence enlarge his recognizance and those of any sureties for him to a later time. The enlargement of his recognizance shall be deemed to be a further remand.

(3) Paragraph 4(1) (limit of period of remand) does not apply to the exercise of the powers conferred by this paragraph.

Postponement of taking of recognizance

3A–1415 6. Where under paragraph 2(2)(b) the court fixes the amount in which the principal and his sureties, if any, are to be bound, the recognizance may afterwards be taken by such person as may be prescribed by rules of court, with the same consequences as if it had been entered into before the court.

Schedule 15

See the commentary to ss.153 to 155 above.. **3A–1416**

Note that ss.155(2)(b) (remands in custody), 155(3)–(7) (warrants for arrest), 156 (remand for medical examination), and Sched.15 (provisions corresponding with civil procedure in magistrate's courts) were implemented on October 15, 2001 by the Housing Act 1996 (Commencement No. 13) Order 2001 (S.I. 2001 No. 3164).

Crime and Disorder Act 1998

(1998c.37) **3A–1417**

ARRANGEMENT OF SECTIONS

PART I

PREVENTION OF CRIME AND DISORDER

CHAPTER I

ENGLAND AND WALES

CRIME AND DISORDER: GENERAL

PART I

PREVENTION OF CRIME AND DISORDER

CHAPTER I

ENGLAND AND WALES

CRIME AND DISORDER: GENERAL

Anti-social behaviour orders

1.—(1) An application for an order under this section may be **3A–1418** made by a relevant authority if it appears to the authority that the following conditions are fulfilled with respect to any person aged 10 or over, namely—

(a) that the person has acted, since the commencement date, in an anti-social manner, that is to say, in a manner that caused or was likely to cause harassment, alarm or distress to one or more persons not of the same household as himself; and

(b) that such an order is necessary to protect relevant persons from further anti-social acts by him.

(1A) In this section and sections 1B, 1CA and 1E 'relevant authority' means —

(a) the council for a local government area;

(aa) in relation to England, a county council;

(b) the chief officer of police of any police force maintained for a police area;

(c) the chief constable of the British Transport Police Force;

(d) any person registered under section 1 of the Housing Act 1996 (c. 52) as a social landlord who provides or manages any houses or hostel in a local government area; or

(e) a housing action trust established by order in pursuance of section 62 of the Housing Act 1988.

(1B) In this section 'relevant persons' means—

(a) in relation to a relevant authority falling within paragraph (a) of subsection (1A), persons within the local government area of that council;

(aa) in relation to a relevant authority falling within paragraph (aa) of subsection (1A), persons within the county of the county council;

(b) in relation to a relevant authority falling within paragraph (b) of that subsection, persons within the police area;

(c) in relation to a relevant authority falling within paragraph (c) of that subsection—

(i) persons who are on or likely to be on policed premises in a local government area; or

(ii) persons who are in the vicinity of or likely to be in the vicinity of such premises;

(d) in relation to a relevant authority falling within paragraph (d) or (e) of that subsection—

(i) persons who are residing in or who are otherwise on or likely to be on premises provided or managed by that authority; or

(ii) persons who are in the vicinity of or likely to be in the vicinity of such premises.

[...]

(3) Such an application shall be made by complaint to the magistrates' court whose commission area includes the local government area or police area concerned.

(4) If, on such an application, it is proved that the conditions mentioned in subsection (1) above are fulfilled, the magistrates' court may make an order under this section (an "anti-social behaviour order") which prohibits the defendant from doing anything described in the order.

(5) For the purpose of determining whether the condition mentioned in subsection (1)(a) above is fulfilled, the court shall disregard any act of the defendant which he shows was reasonable in the circumstances.

(6) The prohibitions that may be imposed by an anti-social behaviour order are those necessary for the purpose of protecting persons (whether relevant persons or persons elsewhere in England and Wales) from further anti-social acts by the defendant.

(7) An anti-social behaviour order shall have effect for a period (not less than two years) specified in the order or until further order.

(8) Subject to subsection (9) below, the applicant or the defendant may apply by complaint to the court which made an anti-social behaviour order for it to be varied or discharged by a further order.

(9) Except with the consent of both parties, no anti-social behaviour order shall be discharged before the end of the period of two years beginning with the date of service of the order.

(10) If without reasonable excuse a person does anything which he is prohibited from doing by an anti-social behaviour order, he is guilty of an offence and liable—

    (a) on summary conviction, to imprisonment for a term not exceeding six months or to a fine not exceeding the statutory maximum, or to both; or

    (b) on conviction on indictment, to imprisonment for a term not exceeding five years or to a fine, or to both.

(10A) The following may bring proceedings for an offence under subsection (10)—

    (a) a council which is a relevant authority;

    (b) the council for the local government area in which a person in respect of whom an anti-social behaviour order has been made resides or appears to reside.

(10B) If proceedings for an offence under subsection (10) are brought in a youth court section 47(2) of the Children and Young Persons Act 1933 (c. 12) has effect as if the persons entitled to be present at a sitting for the purposes of those proceedings include one person authorised to be present by a relevant authority.

(10C) In proceedings for an offence under subsection (10), a copy of the original anti-social behaviour order, certified as such by the proper officer of the court which made it, is admissible as evidence of its having been made and of its contents to the same extent that oral evidence of those things is admissible in those proceedings.

(10D) In relation to proceedings brought against a child or a young person for an offence under subsection (10)—

    (a) section 49 of the Children and Young Persons Act 1933 (restrictions on reports of proceedings in which children and young persons are concerned) does not apply in respect of the child or young person against whom the proceedings are brought;

    (b) section 45 of the Youth Justice and Criminal Evidence Act 1999 (power to restrict reporting of criminal proceedings involving persons under 18) does so apply.

(10E) If, in relation to any such proceedings, the court does exercise its power to give a direction under section 45 of the Youth Justice and Criminal Evidence Act 1999, it shall give its reasons for doing so.

(11) Where a person is convicted of an offence under subsection (10) above, it shall not be open to the court by or before which he is so convicted to make an order under subsection (1)(b) (conditional discharge) of section 1A of the Powers of Criminal Courts Act 1973 ("the 1973 Act") in respect of the offence.

(12) In this section—

"British Transport Police Force" means the force of constables appointed under section 53 of the British Transport Commission Act 1949 (c. xxix);

"child" and "young person" shall have the same meaning as in the Children and Young Persons Act 1933;

"the commencement date" means the date of the commencement of this section;

"local government area" means —

    (a) in relation to England, a district or London borough, the City of London, the Isle of Wight and the Isles of Scilly;

    (b) in relation to Wales, a county or county borough.

"policed premises" has the meaning given by section 53(3) of the British Transport Commission Act 1949.

3A–1419   *Note* —Section 1 has been amended by the Police Reform Act 2002, s.61; the Antisocial Behaviour Act 2003, s.85; and by the Serious Organised Crime and Police Act 2005, ss 139(2), 140(2), 141(2), (for transitional provisions relating to the reference in subs.(10D)(b) and (10E) above to s.45 of the Youth Justice and Criminal Evidence Act 1999, see s.141(4) of the 2005 Act).

Anti-social behaviour order

3A–1420   Such an order (an ASBO) may be granted if a person has acted in an anti-social manner, that is to say, in a manner that caused or was likely to cause harassment, alarm or distress to one or more persons not of the same household as himself and such an order is necessary to protect relevant persons from further anti-social acts (s.1(1)). When considering whether a person's conduct has caused or is likely to cause harassment, alarm or distress to others within the meaning of Crime and Disorder Act 1998, s.1(1)(a) "likely" means "more probable than not". The likelihood has to be proved to the criminal standard (see *Chief Constable of Lancashire v. Potter* [2003] EWHC 2272 (Admin) and *R.(on the application of McCann) v. Manchester Crown Court* [2002] UKHL 39; [2003] 1 A.C. 787; [2002] 3 W.L.R. 1313). An ASBO may prohibit the defendant from doing anything described in the order. The prohibitions that may be imposed by an ASBO are "those necessary for the purpose of protecting persons (whether relevant persons or persons elsewhere in England and Wales) from further anti-social acts by the defendant" (s.1(4) and (6)). ASBOs have effect for the period (not less than two years) specified in the order or until further order (s.1(7)). Although ASBOs should be substantially and not just formally prohibitory, a restraint upon leaving or travelling between specified premises between particular times meets that test. Further there is nothing legally objectionable to a curfew provision in an ASBO if it is necessary for the protection of relevant people. Courts should however consider carefully the need for and duration of curfew provisions when making ASBOs. Just because ASBOs have to run for a minimum of two years, it does not follow that each and every prohibition within a particular ASBO has to endure for the life of the order (*R. (Lonergan) v. Lewes Crown Court* [2005] EWHC 457 (Admin); [2005] 1 W.L.R. 2570).

Breach of an ASBO may be punished on summary conviction by imprisonment for a term not exceeding six months or a fine or both; or on conviction on indictment, by imprisonment for a term not exceeding five years or to a fine, or to both (s.1(10)).

In *Moat Housing Group South Ltd v. Harris and Hartless* [2005] EWCA Civ 287; [2005] HLR 33 , the Court of Appeal left open "the important question whether a failure to control one's children from being a nuisance, although it may constitute a breach of a tenancy agreement, is an "act" of the type referred to in" Crime and Disorder Act 1998 s.1(1)(a) .

A relevant authority

3A–1421   See s.1(1A), namely the council for a local government area, a county council, the chief officer of police of any police force maintained for a police area, the chief constable of the British Transport Police Force, a social landlord who provides or manages any houses or hostel which is registered under Housing Act 1996, s.1 or a housing action trust (see Housing Act 1988, s.62).

Relevant persons

See s.1(1B).

3A–1422

An application

Applications for ASBOs could originally only be made by complaint in the Magistrates Court, but see s.1B below (introduced by Police Reform Act 2002, s.63) which provides that ASBOs can be made in the county court if a relevant authority considers it is reasonable to make such an application. If the relevant authority or the person against whom the ASBO is sought is not already a party to the principal proceedings, an application can be made for him or her to be joined as a party. However a person may only be joined if his or her anti-social acts are material in relation to the principal proceedings (see s.1B(3C) below).

3A–1423

Power of Secretary of State to add to relevant authorities

1A.—(1) The Secretary of State may by order provide that the chief officer of a body of constables maintained otherwise than by a police authority is, in such cases and circumstances as may be prescribed by the order, to be a relevant authority for the purposes of section 1 above.

3A–1424

(2) The Secretary of State may by order—

    (a) provide that a person or body of any other description specified in the order is, in such cases and circumstances as may be prescribed by the order, to be a relevant authority for the purposes of such of sections 1 above and 1B, 1CA, 1E and 1F below as are specified in the order; and

    (b) prescribe the description of persons who are to be "relevant persons" in relation to that person or body.[1]

By order

No such order has been made.

3A–1425

Orders in county court proceedings

1B.—(1) This section applies to any proceedings in a county court ('the principal proceedings').

3A–1426

(2) If a relevant authority—

    (a) is a party to the principal proceedings, and

    (b) considers that a party to those proceedings is a person in relation to whom it would be reasonable for it to make an application under section 1,

it may make an application in those proceedings for an order under subsection (4).

(3) If a relevant authority—

    (a) is not a party to the principal proceedings, and

    (b) considers that a party to those proceedings is a person in relation to whom it would be reasonable for it to make an application under section 1,

it may make an application to be joined to those proceedings to enable it to apply for an order under subsection (4) and, if it is so joined, may apply for such an order.

---

[1] Amended by the Serious Organised Crime and Police Act 2005, ss. 139(3), 142(2).

HOUSING

(3A) Subsection (3B) applies if a relevant authority is a party to the principal proceedings and considers—

    (a) that a person who is not a party to the proceedings has acted in an anti-social manner, and

    (b) that the person's anti-social acts are material in relation to the principal proceedings.

(3B) The relevant authority may—

    (a) make an application for the person mentioned in subsection (3A)(a) to be joined to the principal proceedings to enable an order under subsection (4) to be made in relation to that person;

    (b) if that person is so joined, apply for an order under subsection (4).

(3C) But a person must not be joined to proceedings in pursuance of subsection (3B) unless his anti-social acts are material in relation to the principal proceedings.

(4) If, on an application for an order under this subsection, it is proved that the conditions mentioned in section 1(1) are fulfilled as respects that other party, the court may make an order which prohibits him from doing anything described in the order.

(5) Subject to subsection (6), the person against whom an order under this section has been made and the relevant authority on whose application that order was made may apply to the county court which made an order under this section for it to be varied or discharged by a further order.

(6) Except with the consent of the relevant authority and the person subject to the order, no order under this section shall be discharged before the end of the period of two years beginning with the date of service of the order.

(7) Subsections (5) to (7) and (10) to (12) of section 1 apply for the purposes of the making and effect of orders made under this section as they apply for the purposes of the making and effect of anti-social behaviour orders.

3A-1427   *Note* —Section 1B was inserted by the Police Reform Act 2002, s.63 and has been amended by the Anti-social Behaviour Act 2003, s.85(5), (6).

A relevant authority

3A-1428   See s.1(1A), namely the council for a local government area, a county council, the chief officer of police of any police force maintained for a police area, the chief constable of the British Transport Police Force, a social landlord who provides or manages any houses or hostel which is registered under Housing Act 1996, s.1 or a housing action trust (see Housing Act 1988, s.62).

Anti-social acts

3A-1429   See s.1(1)(a) which refers to behaviour that has caused or was likely to cause harassment, alarm or distress.

Principal proceedings

3A-1430   See s.1B(1).

Procedure

3A-1431   Applications for relevant authorities or persons against whom ASBOs are sought to be joined to the principal proceedings are made in accordance with CPR Part 65. See

CPR, r.65.23 and the commentary thereto. Note that a person may only be joined if his or her "anti-social acts are material in relation to the principal proceedings" (s.1B(3C)). On October 1, 2004 pilot arrangements began running for 18 months in selected English county courts enabling ASBOs to be made against children—see the Anti-social Behaviour Act 2003 (Commencement No. 4) Order 2004 (S.I. 2004 No. 2168). Cases should not be transferred from non-pilot courts to pilot courts for the sole purpose of joining minors (*Orbit HA v. Smith Central London Civil Justice Centre*; December 6, 2004; February 2005 Legal Action 37). As ASBOs are civil and not criminal orders (*R. (McCann) v. Manchester Crown Court* [2002] UKHL 39; [2003] 1 AC 787) it follows that hearsay evidence is admissible under the Civil Evidence Act 1995 . See too *R. (on the application of W) v. Acton Youth Court* [2005] EWHC 954 (Admin) ; 19 May 2005. However "the willingness of a civil court to admit hearsay evidence carries with it inherent dangers". Claimants should state, by convincing direct evidence, why it is not reasonable and practicable to produce the original makers of statements as witnesses. If statements involve multiple hearsay, the route by which the original statement came to the attention of the person attesting to it should be identified as far as practicable. When hearing such applications, it is better for judges to start their judgements with an analysis of the direct oral evidence received, and then to move onto the evidence of the absent named witnesses and anonymous witnesses. (See *Moat Housing Group South Ltd v. Harris and Hartless* [2005] EWCA Civ 287; (2005); [2005] HLR 33 .)

[THE NEXT PARAGRAPH IS 3A–1434.]

Interim orders

1D.—(1) This section applies where—

3A–1434

    (a) an application is made for an anti-social behaviour order;

    (b) an application is made for an order under section 1B;

    (c) a request is made by the prosecution for an order under section 1C; or

    (d) the court is minded to make an order under section 1C of its own motion.

(2) If, before determining the application or request, or before deciding whether to make an order under section 1C of its own motion, the court considers that it is just to make an order under this section pending the determination of that application or request or before making that decision, it may make such an order.

(3) An order under this section is an order which prohibits the defendant from doing anything described in the order.

(4) An order under this section—

    (a) shall be for a fixed period;

    (b) may be varied, renewed or discharged;

    (c) shall, if it has not previously ceased to have effect, cease to have effect on the determination of the application or request mentioned in subsection (1), or on the court's making a decision as to whether or not to make an order under section 1C of its own motion.

(5) In relation to cases to which this section applies by virtue of paragraph (a) or (b) of subsection (1), subsection (6), (8) and (10) to (12) of section 1 apply for the purposes of the making and effect of orders under this section as they apply for the purposes of the making and effect of anti-social behaviour orders.

(6) In relation to cases to which this section applies by virtue of paragraph (c) or (d) of subsection (1)—

HOUSING

> (a) subsections (6) and (10) to (12) of section 1 apply for the purposes of the making and effect of orders under this section as they apply for the purposes of the making and effect of anti-social behaviour orders; and
>
> (b) section 1CA applies for the purposes of the variation or discharge of an order under this section as it applies for the purposes of the variation or discharge of an order under section 1C.

3A-1435 *Note* —Section 1D was inserted by Police Reform Act 2002, s.65; amended by the Serious Organised Crime and Police Act 2005, s.139(6)–(9).

Interim ASBOs

3A-1436 The court may make an interim ASBO if it considers that it is just to make such an order pending the determination of the main application. Interim ASBOs should be made for a fixed period, but may be varied, renewed or discharged. An interim ASBO obtained without notice to the defendant does not breach the right to a fair trial under ECHR Art.6 (*R.(M) v. Secretary of State for Constitutional Affairs* [2004] EWCA Civ 312; [2004] 1 W.L.R. 2298).

Consultation requirements

3A-1437 1E.—(1) This section applies to—

> (a) applications for an anti-social behaviour order; and
> (b) applications for an order under section 1B.

(2) Before making an application to which this section applies, the council for a local government area shall consult the chief officer of police of the police force maintained for the police area within which that local government area lies.

(3) Before making an application to which this section applies, a chief officer of police shall consult the council for the local government area in which the person in relation to whom the application is to be made resides or appears to reside.

(4) Before making an application to which this section applies, a relevant authority other than a council for a local government area or a chief officer of police shall consult—

> (a) the council for the local government area in which the person in relation to whom the application is to be made resides or appears to reside; and
> (b) the chief officer of police of the police force maintained for the police area within which that local government area lies.

(5) Subsection (4)(a) does not apply if the relevant authority is a county council for a county in which there are no districts.

3A-1438 *Note* —Section 1E was inserted by Police Reform Act 2002, s.66 and amended by the Anti-social Behaviour Act 2003, s.85.

A relevant authority

3A-1439 See s.1(1A), namely the council for a local government area, a county council, the chief officer of police of any police force maintained for a police area, the chief constable of the British Transport Police Force, a social landlord who provides or manages any houses or hostel which is registered under Housing Act 1996, s.1 or a housing action trust (see Housing Act 1988, s.62).

Consultation

3A-1440 See *McC v. Wigan MBC*, October 30, 2003 where the lead role in seeking ASBOs was taken by a management company, which, although solely owned by the council, was a separate entity to the council. As such, in the absence of authorisation form the council, it was not authorised to consult. It was also apparent that there was a lack of knowledge on the part of the tenancy relations manager about the Home Office Guidance and an unstructured approach to the process. However these failings did not result in a substantial failure to comply with the consultation requirements. The requirement for consultation between the police and local authority in s.1E is fulfilled by substantial compliance, even though there may not have been full compliance. Information had been exchanged before making the application.

In *Wareham v. Purbeck District Council* [2005] EWHC 358 (Admin); March 14, 2005; (2005) *The Times* March 28 , the Divisional Court, dismissing an appeal by way of case stated, held that a failure to invite the proposed defendant to put his view at an anti-social behaviour case conference convened prior to the decision to apply for an ASBO does not amount to an infringement of any right under ECHR. The defendant had a full opportunity to put his case before the magistrates' court.

Note —Serious Organised Crime and Police Act 2005 ss.142 and s.143 introduce new s.1F (contracting out of local authority functions) and 11 (special measures for witnesses). These provisions are not yet in force. Drugs Act 2005 s.20 inserts new sections 1G and 1H (intervention orders). These provisions are not yet in force.

Homelessness Act 2002

(2002 c.7)   3A–1441

ARRANGEMENT OF SECTIONS

Editorial Introduction
                          3A–1442

The Act contains provisions relating to homelessness and the allocation of housing accommodation which were outlined in the Government's Housing Green Paper, "Quality and Choice: A decent home for all" (April 2000) and the Government's Housing Policy Statement "The way forward for housing" (December 2000).

The Act is intended to:

- require housing authorities to take a more strategic, multi-agency approach to the prevention of homelessness and the re-housing of homeless households;
- ensure that everyone accepted by housing authorities as unintentionally homeless and in priority need must be provided with suitable accommodation until they obtain a settled housing solution;
- allow housing authorities greater flexibility to assist non-priority homeless households, principally through a new power for housing authorities to secure accommodation for such households where they have scope to do so; and
- facilitate lettings policies which offer more choice to homeless people and others in housing need with the aim of helping to create sustainable communities, tackle social exclusion and make better use of the national housing stock.

Sections 1 to 4 contain a requirement for housing authorities, with the assistance of social services authorities, and in consultation with other bodies including registered social landlords and voluntary organisations, to:

- carry out reviews of homelessness within their area;
- formulate and publish strategies for tackling and preventing homelessness problems based on the results of those reviews;

HOUSING

- publish the first strategy within 12 months of the coming into operation of these provisions; and
- publish a new strategy thereafter within five years of the previous strategy having been published.

The other provisions relating to homelessness are amendments to Housing Act 1996, Part VII. These are incorporated into the text of that Act (see paras 3A–1172 to 3A–1402). In brief they provide for:

- the abolition of the former two year period during which a housing authority was subject to the main homelessness duty;
- abolition of the former duty on housing authorities to consider whether other suitable accommodation was available before they could secure accommodation themselves;
- additional circumstances in which the applicant can bring the main homelessness duty to an end by accepting an assured tenancy;
- a new power for authorities to secure accommodation for homeless applicants who are not in priority need.

The government's framework for local authorities is set out in 'Homelessness Strategies—a good practice handbook', available from www.housing.dtlr.goc.uk/information/homelessness.

A revised statutory Code of Guidance (Homelessness: Code of Guidance for Local Authorities) was issued in July 2002 by the Office of the Deputy Prime Minister to reflect changes introduced by the Homelessness Act 2002. Copies are available from the Office of the Deputy Prime Minister, PO Box 236, Wetherby, West Yorkshire LS23 7NB. The Government has issued a revised statutory Code of Guidance on Allocations.

Implementation

3A–1443 Section 8 (entitlement to seek review of decisions as to suitability of accommodation whether or not they have accepted accommodation) and Schedule 1, paras 3 and 7 (exclusion from access to Housing Act 1996 Parts VI and VII of people from abroad who are not entitled to housing benefit) came into force on receipt of the Royal Assent—February 26, 2002 (see s.20). The remaining homelessness provisions come into force on such day as the Secretary of State may by order made by statutory instrument appoint. See the Homelessness Act 2002 (Commencement No. 1) (England) Order 2002 (S.I. 2002 No. 1799) (C.56) and the Homelessness Act 2002 (Commencement) (Wales) Order 2002 (S.I. 2002 No.1736) (W.166) (C.53); Homelessness Act 2002 (Commencement No. 2 and Transitional Provisions) (England) Order 2002 (S.I. 2002 No. 2324).

Homelessness reviews and strategies

Duty of local housing authority to formulate a homelessness strategy

3A–1444 **1.**—(1) A local housing authority ("the authority") may from time to time—

    (a) carry out a homelessness review for their district; and

    (b) formulate and publish a homelessness strategy based on the results of that review.

(2) The social services authority for the district of the authority (where that is a different local authority) shall give such assistance in connection with the exercise of the power under subsection (1) as the authority may reasonably require.

(3) The authority shall exercise that power so as to ensure that the first homelessness strategy for their district is published within the period of twelve months beginning with the day on which this section comes into force.

(4) The authority shall exercise that power so as to ensure that a new homelessness strategy for their district is published within the

period of five years beginning with the day on which their last home-lessness strategy was published.

(5) A local housing authority shall take their homelessness strategy into account in the exercise of their functions.

(6) A social services authority shall take the homelessness strategy for the district of a local housing authority into account in the exercise of their functions in relation to that district.

(7) Nothing in subsection (5) or (6) affects any duty or requirement arising apart from this section.

Implementation

In England, this section was brought into force on July 31, 2002 by the Homeless-**3A–1445** ness Act 2002 (Commencement No. 1) (England) Order 2002 (S.I. 2002 No.1799) (C.56). In Wales, this section was brought into force on September 30, 2002 by the Homelessness Act 2002 (Commencement) (Wales) Order 2002 (S.I. 2002 No. 1736)(W.166)(C.53).

district—see s.5 below and Housing Act 1985, s.2.

local housing authority—see s.5 below and Housing Act 1985, s.1.

social services authority—see s.5 below which refers to the Local Authority Social Services Act 1970.

homelessness—see Housing Act 1996, s.175. See too s.2(2)(b) below.

homelessness review—see s.2 below.

homelessness strategy—see s.3 below.

Reviews and strategy

Section 1 contains a duty to on all local housing authorities to ensure that a home-**3A–1446** lessness strategy is published within twelve months of the coming into force of the section and that a new strategy must be published at least every five years.

Homelessness reviews

2.—(1) For the purposes of this Act "homelessness review" means a **3A–1447** review by a local housing authority of—

> (a) the levels, and likely future levels, of homelessness in their district;
>
> (b) the activities which are carried out for any purpose mentioned in subsection (2) (or which contribute to their achievement); and
>
> (c) the resources available to the authority, the social services authority for their district, other public authorities, voluntary organisations and other persons for such activities.

(2) Those purposes are—

> (a) preventing homelessness in the district of the authority;
>
> (b) securing that accommodation is or will be available for people in the district who are or may become homeless;
>
> (c) providing support for people in the district—
>
>> (i) who are or may become homeless; or
>>
>> (ii) who have been homeless and need support to prevent them becoming homeless again.

(3) A local housing authority shall, after completing a homelessness review—

> (a) arrange for the results of the review to be available at its

principal office for inspection at all reasonable hours, without charge, by members of the public; and

(b) provide (on payment if required by the authority of a reasonable charge) a copy of those results to any member of the public who asks for one.

Implementation

3A-1448   In England, this section was brought into force on July 31, 2002 by the Homelessness Act 2002 (Commencement No. 1) (England) Order 2002 (S.I. 2002 No. 1799) (C.56). In Wales, this section was brought into force on September 30, 2002 by the Homelessness Act 2002 (Commencement) (Wales) Order 2002 (S.I. 2002 No. 1736) (W.166) (C.53).

district—see s.4 below and Housing Act 1985, s.2.

local housing authority—see s.4 below and Housing Act 1985, s.1.

social services authority —see s.4 below which refers to the Local Authority Social Services Act 1970.

homelessness—see Housing Act 1996, s.175. See too s.2(2)(b) below.

homelessness strategy—see s.3 below.

support—see s.4 below.

voluntary organisation —see s.4 below and Housing Act 1996, s.180(3).

Homelessness strategies

3A-1449   **3.**—(1) For the purposes of this Act "homelessness strategy" means a strategy formulated by a local housing authority for—

(a) preventing homelessness in their district;

(b) securing that sufficient accommodation is and will be available for people in their district who are or may become homeless;

(c) securing the satisfactory provision of support for people in their district—

(i) who are or may become homeless; or

(ii) who have been homeless and need support to prevent them becoming homeless again.

(2) A homelessness strategy may include specific objectives to be pursued, and specific action planned to be taken, in the course of the exercise of—

(a) the functions of the authority as a local housing authority; or

(b) the functions of the social services authority for the district.

(3) A homelessness strategy may also include provision relating to specific action which the authority expects to be taken—

(a) by any public authority with functions (not being functions mentioned in subsection (2)) which are capable of contributing to the achievement of any of the objectives mentioned in subsection (1); or

(b) by any voluntary organisation or other person whose activities are capable of contributing to the achievement of any of those objectives.

(4) The inclusion in a homelessness strategy of any provision relating to action mentioned in subsection (3) requires the approval of the body or person concerned.

(5) In formulating a homelessness strategy the authority shall consider (among other things) the extent to which any of the objectives mentioned in subsection (1) can be achieved through action involving two or more of the bodies or other persons mentioned in subsections (2) and (3).

(6) The authority shall keep their homelessness strategy under review and may modify it from time to time.

(7) If the authority modify their homelessness strategy, they shall publish the modifications or the strategy as modified (as they consider most appropriate).

(8) Before adopting or modifying a homelessness strategy the authority shall consult such public or local authorities, voluntary organisations or other persons as they consider appropriate.

(9) The authority shall—

    (a) make a copy of each document published under this section available at its principal office for inspection at all reasonable hours, without charge, by members of the public; and

    (b) provide (on payment if required by the authority of a reasonable charge) a copy of anything so published to any member of the public who asks for one.

Implementation

In England, this section was brought into force on July 31, 2002 by the Homelessness Act 2002 (Commencement No. 1) (England) Order 2002 (S.I. 2002 No. 1799) (C.56). In Wales, this section was brought into force on September 30, 2002 by the Homelessness Act 2002 (Commencement) (Wales) Order 2002 (S.I. 2002 No. 1736) (W.166) (C.53). This section has also been amended by Local Government Act 2003, Sched.7, para.81(b). **3A–1450**

    district—see s.4 below and Housing Act 1985, s.2.

    local housing authority—see s.4 below and Housing Act 1985, s.1.

    social services authority—see s.4 below which refers to the Local Authority Social Services Act 1970.

    homelessness—see Housing Act 1996, s.175. See too s.2(2)(b) below.

    homelessness review—see s.2 above.

    support—see s.2 above.

    voluntary organisation—see s.4 below and Housing Act 1996, s.180(3).

    consultation—note the duty to consult in s.3(8).

Sections 1 to 3: interpretation

4. In sections 1 to 3— **3A–1451**

    "homeless" and "homelessness" have the same meaning as in Part 7 of the Housing Act 1996 (c.52) (in this Act referred to as " the 1996 Act");

    "local housing authority" and "district" have the same meaning as in the Housing Act 1985 (c.68);

    "social services authority" means a local authority for the purposes of the Local Authority Social Services Act 1970 (c.42);

    "support" means advice, information or assistance; and

    "voluntary organisation" has the same meaning as in section 180(3) of the 1996 Act.

Implementation

In England, this section was brought into force on July 31, 2002 by the Homeless- **3A–1452**

HOUSING

ness Act 2002 (Commencement No. 1) (England) Order 2002 (S.I. 2002 No. 1799) (C.56). In Wales, this section was brought into force on September 30, 2002 by the Homelessness Act 2002 (Commencement) (Wales) Order 2002 (S.I. 2002 No. 1736) (W.166) (C.53).

* * * *

Abolition of minimum period for which an authority is subject to main homelessness duty

3A–1453   **6.**—(1) For subsections (3) and (4) of section 193 of the 1996 Act (period for which main homelessness duty is owed to person with priority need) there is substituted—

> "(3) The authority are subject to the duty under this section until it ceases by virtue of any of the following provisions of this section."

(2) Subsection (1) applies to a person who, immediately before the commencement of this section, is owed the duty under section 193 as it applies to a person who comes to be owed that duty after that commencement.

(3) Section 194 of the 1996 Act (power to continue to secure accommodation after minimum period) shall cease to have effect.

(4) Any person who, immediately before the commencement of this section, is a person in relation to whom a local housing authority are exercising their power under section 194 of the 1996 Act shall be treated at that commencement as a person to whom the authority owe the duty under section 193 of that Act.

Implementation

3A–1454   In England, this section was brough into force on July 31, 2002 by the Homelessness Act 2002 (Commencement No. 1) (England) Order 2002 (S.I. 2002 No. 1799) (C.56). In Wales, this section was brought into force on September 30, 2002 by the Homelessness Act 2002 (Commencement) (Wales) Order 2002 (S.I. 2002 No. 1736) (W.166) (C.53).

Abolition of minimum period

3A–1455   See commentary to Housing Act 1996, s.193.

* * * * *

Abolition of duty under section 197

3A–1456   **9.**—(1) Section 197 of the 1996 Act (duty where other suitable accommodation available) shall cease to have effect.

(2) A person who, immediately before commencement, is a person to whom a local housing authority owe the duty under section 197(2) (instead of the duty under section 193 or 195) shall be treated at commencement as a person to whom the authority owe the duty under section 193 (the main homelessness duty) or, if at that time he is threatened with homelessness, section 195(2) (duty in case of threatened homelessness).

(3) In subsection (2) "commencement" means the commencement of this section.

Implementation

3A–1457   In England, this section was brought into force on July 31, 2002 by the Homelessness Act 2002 (Commencement No. 1) (England) Order 2002 (S.I. 2002 No. 1799)

(C.56). In Wales, this section was brought into force on September 30, 2002 by the Homelessness Act 2002 (Commencement) (Wales) Order 2002 (S.I. 2002 No. 1736) (W.166) (C.53).

Abolition of duty under Housing Act 1996, s.197

See commentary to Housing Act 1996, s.197.　　　**3A–1458**

Supplementary

Wales

17.—(1) The reference to the 1996 Act in Schedule 1 to the **3A–1459** National Assembly for Wales (Transfer of Functions) Order 1999 (S.I. 1999 No. 672) is to be treated as referring to that Act as amended by this Act.

(2) Subsection (1) does not affect the power to make further Orders varying or omitting that reference.

Implementation

This section was brought into force on September 30, 2002 by the Homelessness **3A–1460** Act 2002 (Commencement) (Wales) Order 2002 (S.I. 2002 No. 1736) (W.166)(C.53).

Minor and consequential amendments and repeals

18.—(1) Schedule 1 (which contains minor and consequential **3A–1461** amendments) has effect.

(2) Schedule 2 (which contains repeals) has effect.

Implementation

In Wales, this section was brought into force on September 30, 2002 by the Home- **3A–1462** lessness Act 2002 (Commencement) (Wales) Order 2002 (S.I. 2002 No. 1736) (W.166)(C.53).

Financial provision

19. There shall be paid out of money provided by Parliament any **3A–1463** increase attributable to this Act in the sums payable out of money so provided under any other Act.

Implementation

In Wales, this section was brought into force on September 30, 2002 by the Home- **3A–1464** lessness Act 2002 (Commencement) (Wales) Order 2002 (S.I. 2002 No. 1736) (W.166)(C.53).

Commencement, transitional provision and general saving

20.—(1) The preceding provisions of this Act (and the Schedules), **3A–1465** other than section 8 and paragraphs 3 and 7 of Schedule 1, come into force on such day as the Secretary of State may by order made by statutory instrument appoint; and different days may be appointed for different purposes.

(2) The Secretary of State may by order made by statutory instrument make such transitional provisions and savings as he considers appropriate in connection with the coming into force of any provision of this Act.

(3) The powers conferred by subsection (1) and (2) are exercisable as respects Wales by the National Assembly for Wales (and not the Secretary of State).

(4) Nothing in this Act affects the operation of section 216(2) of the 1996 Act in relation to persons who applied for accommodation or assistance in obtaining accommodation before the commencement of Part 7 of that Act.

Commencement Orders

3A-1466   See the Homelessness Act 2002 (Commencement No. 1) (England) Order 2002 (S.I. 2002 No. 1799) (C.56) and the Homelessness Act 2002 (Commencement) (Wales) Order 2002 (S.I. 2002 No. 1736) (W.166)(C.53) and the Homelessness Act 2002 (Commencement No. 2 and Transitional Provisions) (England) Order 2002 (S.I. 2002 No. 2324).

Short title, extent and application to Isles of Scilly

3A-1467   **21.**—(1) This Act may be cited as the Homelessness Act 2002.

(2) This Act extends to England and Wales only.

(3) This Act applies to the Isles of Scilly subject to such exceptions, adaptations.

(4) The power to make such an order is exercisable by statutory instrument subject to annulment in pursuance of a resolution of either House of Parliament.

Land Registration Act 2002

3A-1468

ARRANGEMENT OF SECTIONS

PART 9

ADVERSE POSSESSION

PART 9

3A-1469   # ADVERSE POSSESSION

Editorial Introduction

3A-1470   Part 9 of the Land Registration Act 2002, which follows recommendations in Law Commission Report 254, *Land Registration for the Twenty-First Century*, provides a new scheme for adverse possession of registered land.

Prior to its implementation, Limitation Act 1980, s.15(1) provided that no action should be brought to recover any land after the expiration of the limitation period of twelve years. "Limitation...extinguishes the right of the true owner to recover the land, so that the squatter's possession becomes impregnable, giving him a title superior to all others." (*Buckinghamshire County Council v. Moran* [1990] Ch 623, 635, CA). Time ran from the commencement of adverse possession. That required a degree of occupation or physical control, coupled with an intention to possess without the consent of the paper owner. (*JA Pye (Oxford) Ltd v. Graham* [2002] UKHL 30; [2003] 1 A.C. 419). Adverse possession might cease (Limitation Act 1980, Sched.1) if the occupier gave a written acknowledgement of the true owner's title (ss.29 and 30); if the true owner granted a tenancy or licence to the occupier; or if the true owner physically re-entered upon the land.

After twelve years adverse possession, the paper proprietor of the land held it on trust for the squatter who might apply to be registered as proprietor of a new estate,

1018

where the registered land was freehold, or as proprietor of the registered estate where that estate was leasehold (Land Registration Act 1925, s.75).

However under the Land Registration Act 2002 adverse possession of itself, for however long, does not bar the owner's title to a registered estate in land (s.96). A squatter is entitled to apply to the Land Registry to be registered as proprietor after ten years' adverse possession (s.97 and Sched.6). The Land Registration Rules 2003 (S.I. 2003 No. 1417) set out the procedure to be followed. Applications have to be in Form ADV1 and accompanied, among other things, by a statutory declaration. The registered proprietor, any registered chargee, and certain other persons interested in the land should be notified of the application. If the application is not opposed by any of those notified, the squatter should be registered as proprietor of the land. Otherwise, adverse possession for ten years does not by itself give a right to registration. If any of the people notified opposes the application it should be rejected, unless the adverse possessor can bring him or herself within one or more of three conditions contained in Schedule 6, para. 5—either (a) it would be unconscionable because of an equity of estoppel for the registered proprietor to seek to dispossess the applicant; or (b) the applicant is for some reason entitled to be registered as a proprietor; or (c) in some circumstances, the land is adjacent to land belonging to the applicant. To come within this third category, "for at least 10 years of the period of adverse possession ending on the date of the application, the applicant (or any predecessor in title) [must] reasonably [have] believed the land to which the application relates belonged to him" (para. 5(4)(c)). This third ground will not be brought into force until October 13, 2004.

If the squatter's application for registration is refused but the squatter remains in adverse possession for a further two years, he or she is entitled to apply once again to be registered and should this time be registered as proprietor whether or not the registered proprietor objects. The purpose of the two year period is to enable the paper owner to evict the squatter. Where the registered proprietor brings proceedings to recover possession from a squatter in that intervening period, the Act allows the squatter to establish certain limited defences which are consistent with the three conditions in Sched.6. Ten years adverse possession by itself is not a defence. If a landowner obtains judgment for possession against someone who has been in adverse possession for ten years, that judgment ceases to be enforceable two years after the date of the judgment (s.98). If, in proceedings, a court determines that a squatter has a defence under s.98 or that a judgment for possession ceases to be enforceable under s.98(4), the court must direct the Land Registrar to register that person as proprietor of the estate.

Implementation and Transitional Provisions

Most of Part 9 came into force on October 13, 2003, although 98(1) and para.5(4) **3A–1471** and (5) of Sched.6 and, to the extent that it relates thereto, s.97 were not brought into force until October 13, 2004.

The Land Registration Act 2002 does not immediately affect the position of those who have already acquired possessory title prior to its implementation. Schedule 12, para. 18 provides that where a registered estate in land is held in trust for a person by virtue of Land Registration Act 1925, s.75(1) immediately before the coming into force of s.97, he or she is be entitled to be registered as the proprietor of the estate. Similarly a person has a defence to any action for the possession of land if he or she is entitled under Sched.12, para. 18 to be registered as the proprietor of an estate in the land. For three years after October 13, 2003 the squatter's unregistered interest will be an overriding interest whether or not he or she is in actual occupation and so will be binding on purchasers (Sched.12, paragraph 7). However after three years have passed any squatter who has not been registered as owner will only continue to have an overriding interest if he or she remains in occupation and Sched.3, para. 2 applies.

Disapplication of periods of limitation

96.—(1) No period of limitation under section 15 of the Limitation **3A–1472** Act 1980 (c.58) (time limits in relation to recovery of land) shall run against any person, other than a chargee, in relation to an estate in land or rentcharge the title to which is registered.

(2) No period of limitation under section 16 of that Act (time

limits in relation to redemption of land) shall run against any person in relation to such an estate in land or rentcharge.

(3) Accordingly, section 17 of that Act (extinction of title on expiry of time limit) does not operate to extinguish the title of any person where, by virtue of this section, a period of limitation does not run against him.

Limitation Act 1980

3A–1473   See Editorial Introduction above.

estate in land—see s.132 which provides that "land" includes (a) buildings and other structures, (b) land covered with water, and (c) mines and minerals, whether or not held with the surface.

Registration of adverse possessor

3A–1474   **97.** Schedule 6 (which makes provision about the registration of an adverse possessor of an estate in land or rentcharge) has effect.

Schedule 6—See para. 3A–1477 below.

adverse possession—See Schedule 6, para. 11.

Defences

3A–1475   **98.**—(1) A person has a defence to an action for possession of land if—

> (a) on the day immediately preceding that on which the action was brought he was entitled to make an application under paragraph 1 of Schedule 6 to be registered as the proprietor of an estate in the land, and
>
> (b) had he made such an application on that day, the condition in paragraph 5(4) of that Schedule would have been satisfied.

(2) A judgment for possession of land ceases to be enforceable at the end of the period of two years beginning with the date of the judgment if the proceedings in which the judgment is given were commenced against a person who was at that time entitled to make an application under paragraph 1 of Schedule 6.

(3) A person has a defence to an action for possession of land if on the day immediately preceding that on which the action was brought he was entitled to make an application under paragraph 6 of Schedule 6 to be registered as the proprietor of an estate in the land.

(4) A judgment for possession of land ceases to be enforceable at the end of the period of two years beginning with the date of the judgment if, at the end of that period, the person against whom the judgment was given is entitled to make an application under paragraph 6 of Schedule 6 to be registered as the proprietor of an estate in the land.

(5) Where in any proceedings a court determines that—

> (a) a person is entitled to a defence under this section, or
>
> (b) a judgment for possession has ceased to be enforceable against a person by virtue of subsection (4), the court must order the registrar to register him as the proprietor of the estate in relation to which he is entitled to make an application under Schedule 6.

1020

(6) The defences under this section are additional to any other defences a person may have.

(7) Rules may make provision to prohibit the recovery of rent due under a rentcharge from a person who has been in adverse possession of the rentcharge.

Defences

See Editorial Introduction above.

3A–1476

estate in land—see s.132 which provides that "land" includes (a) buildings and other structures, (b) land covered with water, and (c) mines and minerals, whether or not held with the surface.

Schedule 6—see para. 3A-1477 below.

Court—see s.132(3)(a) which provides that references to the court are to the High Court or a county court.

Registered—see s.132 which provides that "registered" means entered in the register.

Registrar — see s.132 which provides that "registrar" means the Chief Land Registrar.

adverse possession—see Schedule 6, para. 11.

SECTION 97

SCHEDULE 6

REGISTRATION OF ADVERSE POSSESSOR

Right to apply for registration

1.—(1) A person may apply to the registrar to be registered as the proprietor of a **3A–1477** registered estate in land if he has been in adverse possession of the estate for the period of ten years ending on the date of the application.

(2) A person may also apply to the registrar to be registered as the proprietor of a registered estate in land if—

    (a) he has in the period of six months ending on the date of the application ceased to be in adverse possession of the estate because of eviction by the registered proprietor, or a person claiming under the registered proprietor,

    (b) on the day before his eviction he was entitled to make an application under sub-paragraph (1), and

    (c) the eviction was not pursuant to a judgment for possession.

(3) However, a person may not make an application under this paragraph if—

    (a) he is a defendant in proceedings which involve asserting a right to possession of the land, or

    (b) judgment for possession of the land has been given against him in the last two years.

(4) For the purposes of sub-paragraph (1), the estate need not have been registered throughout the period of adverse possession.

Notification of application

2.—(1) The registrar must give notice of an application under paragraph 1 to— **3A–1478**

    (a) the proprietor of the estate to which the application relates,

    (b) the proprietor of any registered charge on the estate,

    (c) where the estate is leasehold, the proprietor of any superior registered estate,

    (d) any person who is registered in accordance with rules as a person to be notified under this paragraph, and

    (e) such other persons as rules may provide.

(2) Notice under this paragraph shall include notice of the effect of paragraph 4.

Treatment of application

3.—(1) A person given notice under paragraph 2 may require that the application **3A–1479** to which the notice relates be dealt with under paragraph 5.

HOUSING

(2) The right under this paragraph is exercisable by notice to the registrar given before the end of such period as rules may provide.

3A–1480   4. If an application under paragraph 1 is not required to be dealt with under paragraph 5, the applicant is entitled to be entered in the register as the new proprietor of the estate.

3A–1481   5.—(1) If an application under paragraph 1 is required to be dealt with under this paragraph, the applicant is only entitled to be registered as the new proprietor of the estate if any of the following conditions is met.

(2) The first condition is that—

    (a) it would be unconscionable because of an equity by estoppel for the registered proprietor to seek to dispossess the applicant, and

    (b) the circumstances are such that the applicant ought to be registered as the proprietor.

(3) The second condition is that the applicant is for some other reason entitled to be registered as the proprietor of the estate.

(4) The third condition is that—

    (a) the land to which the application relates is adjacent to land belonging to the applicant,

    (b) the exact line of the boundary between the two has not been determined under rules under section 60,

    (c) for at least ten years of the period of adverse possession ending on the date of the application, the applicant (or any predecessor in title) reasonably believed that the land to which the application relates belonged to him, and

    (d) the estate to which the application relates was registered more than one year prior to the date of the application.

(5) In relation to an application under paragraph 1(2), this paragraph has effect as if the reference in sub-paragraph (4)(c) to the date of the application were to the day before the date of the applicant's eviction.

Right to make further application for registration

3A–1482   6.—(1) Where a person's application under paragraph 1 is rejected, he may make a further application to be registered as the proprietor of the estate if he is in adverse possession of the estate from the date of the application until the last day of the period of two years beginning with the date of its rejection.

(2) However, a person may not make an application under this paragraph if—

    (a) he is a defendant in proceedings which involve asserting a right to possession of the land,

    (b) judgment for possession of the land has been given against him in the last two years, or

    (c) he has been evicted from the land pursuant to a judgment for possession.

3A–1483   7. If a person makes an application under paragraph 6, he is entitled to be entered in the register as the new proprietor of the estate.

Restriction on applications

3A–1484   8.—(1) No one may apply under this Schedule to be registered as the proprietor of an estate in land during, or before the end of twelve months after the end of, any period in which the existing registered proprietor is for the purposes of the Limitation (Enemies and War Prisoners) Act 1945 (8 & 9 Geo 6 c.16)—

    (a) an enemy, or

    (b) detained in enemy territory.

(2) No-one may apply under this Schedule to be registered as the proprietor of an estate in land during any period in which the existing registered proprietor is—

    (a) unable because of mental disability to make decisions about issues of the kind to which such an application would give rise, or

    (b) unable to communicate such decisions because of mental disability or physical impairment.

(3) For the purposes of sub-paragraph (2), "mental disability" means a disability or disorder of the mind or brain, whether permanent or temporary, which results in an impairment or disturbance of mental functioning.

(4) Where it appears to the registrar that sub-paragraph (1) or (2) applies in relation to an estate in land, he may include a note to that effect in the register.

Effect of registration

9.—(1) Where a person is registered as the proprietor of an estate in land in pursuance of an application under this Schedule, the title by virtue of adverse possession which he had at the time of the application is extinguished. **3A–1485**

(2) Subject to sub-paragraph (3), the registration of a person under this Schedule as the proprietor of an estate in land does not affect the priority of any interest affecting the estate.

(3) Subject to sub-paragraph (4), where a person is registered under this Schedule as the proprietor of an estate, the estate is vested in him free of any registered charge affecting the estate immediately before his registration.

(4) Sub-paragraph (3) does not apply where registration as proprietor is in pursuance of an application determined by reference to whether any of the conditions in paragraph 5 applies.

Apportionment and discharge of charges

10.—(1) Where— **3A–1486**

(a) a registered estate continues to be subject to a charge notwithstanding the registration of a person under this Schedule as the proprietor, and

(b) the charge affects property other than the estate, the proprietor of the estate may require the chargee to apportion the amount secured by the charge at that time between the estate and the other property on the basis of their respective values.

(2) The person requiring the apportionment is entitled to a discharge of his estate from the charge on payment of—

(a) the amount apportioned to the estate, and

(b) the costs incurred by the chargee as a result of the apportionment.

(3) On a discharge under this paragraph, the liability of the chargor to the chargee is reduced by the amount apportioned to the estate.

(4) Rules may make provision about apportionment under this paragraph, in particular, provision about—

(a) procedure,

(b) valuation,

(c) calculation of costs payable under sub-paragraph (2)(b), and

(d) payment of the costs of the chargor.

Meaning of "adverse possession"

11.—(1) A person is in adverse possession of an estate in land for the purposes of this Schedule if, but for section 96, a period of limitation under section 15 of the Limitation Act 1980 (c.58) would run in his favour in relation to the estate. **3A–1487**

(2) A person is also to be regarded for those purposes as having been in adverse possession of an estate in land—

(a) where he is the successor in title to an estate in the land, during any period of adverse possession by a predecessor in title to that estate, or

(b) during any period of adverse possession by another person which comes between, and is continuous with, periods of adverse possession of his own.

(3) In determining whether for the purposes of this paragraph a period of limitation would run under section 15 of the Limitation Act 1980, there are to be disregarded—

(a) the commencement of any legal proceedings, and

(b) paragraph 6 of Schedule 1 to that Act.

Trusts

12. A person is not to be regarded as being in adverse possession of an estate for the purposes of this Schedule at any time when the estate is subject to a trust, unless the interest of each of the beneficiaries in the estate is an interest in possession. **3A–1488**

3A-1489

13.—(1) Where—

(a) a person is in adverse possession of an estate in land,

(b) the estate belongs to Her Majesty in right of the Crown or the Duchy of Lancaster or to the Duchy of Cornwall, and

(c) the land consists of foreshore,

paragraph 1(1) is to have effect as if the reference to ten years were to sixty years.

(2) For the purposes of sub-paragraph (1), land is to be treated as foreshore if it has been foreshore at any time in the previous ten years.

(3) In this paragraph, "foreshore" means the shore and bed of the sea and of any tidal water, below the line of the medium high tide between the spring and neap tides.

Rentcharges

3A-1490

14. Rules must make provision to apply the preceding provisions of this Schedule to registered rentcharges, subject to such modifications and exceptions as the rules may provide.

Procedure

3A-1491

15. Rules may make provision about the procedure to be followed pursuant to an application under this Schedule.

Registration

3A-1492

See generally the Editorial Introduction above.

Registrar—see s.132 which provides that "registrar" means the Chief Land Registrar.

estate in land—see s.132 which provides that "land" includes (a) buildings and other structures, (b) land covered with water, and (c) mines and minerals, whether or not held with the surface.

adverse possession—see para. 11.

Registered—see s.132 which provides that "registered" means entered in the register.

Register—see s.132 which provides that "register" means the register of title.

Rules—see the Land Registration Rules 2003 (S.I. 2003 No. 1417).

* * * *

SCHEDULE 12

TRANSITION

Former overriding interests

3A-1493

7. For the period of three years beginning with the day on which Schedule 1 comes into force, it has effect with the insertion after paragraph 14 of— "15. A right acquired under the Limitation Act 1980 before the coming into force of this Schedule."

Transitional provisions—see Editorial Introduction above.

The day on which Schedule 1 comes into force October 13, 2003—see The Land Registration Act 2002 (Commencement No. 4) Order 2003 (S.I. 2003 No. 1725) (C.73).

* * * *

Adverse possession

3A-1494

18.—(1) Where a registered estate in land is held in trust for a person by virtue of section 75(1) of the Land Registration Act 1925 immediately before the coming into force of section 97, he is entitled to be registered as the proprietor of the estate.

(2) A person has a defence to any action for the possession of land (in addition to any other defence he may have) if he is entitled under this paragraph to be registered as the proprietor of an estate in the land.

(3) Where in an action for possession of land a court determines that a person is entitled to a defence under this paragraph, the court must order the registrar to reg-

ister him as the proprietor of the estate in relation to which he is entitled under this paragraph to be registered.

(4) Entitlement under this paragraph shall be disregarded for the purposes of section 131(1).

(5) Rules may make transitional provision for cases where a rentcharge is held in trust under section 75(1) of the Land Registration Act 1925 immediately before the coming into force of section 97.

Adverse possession

See generally editorial introduction above and Sched.6, para. 11.

Registered—see s.132 which provides that "registered" means entered in the register.

estate in land—see s.132 which provides that "land" includes (a) buildings and other structures, (b) land covered with water, and (c) mines and minerals, whether or not held with the surface.

the coming into force of section 97 October 13, 2003—see the Land Registration Act 2002 (Commencement No. 4) Order 2003 (S.I. 2003 No. 1725) (C.73).

Court—see s.132(3)(a) which provides that references to the court are to the High Court or a county court.

Registrar—see s.132 which provides that "registrar" means the Chief Land Registrar.

Register—see s.132 which provides that "register" means the register of title.

Rules—see the Land Registration Rules 2003 (S.I. 2003 No. 1417).

3A–1495

Commonhold and Leasehold Reform Act 2002

(2002 c.15)

3A–1496

ARRANGEMENT OF SECTIONS

Chapter 5 - Other Provisions About Leases

Editorial introduction

Chapter 5 of the Commonhold and Leasehold Reform Act 2002 makes a number of **3A–1497** changes to the leasehold management provisions of the Landlord and Tenant Act 1985. It

- extends the definition of 'service charge' for the purposes of the 1985 Act to include any charge which is required to be paid under the terms of the lease to cover the costs of improvements;
- extends the jurisdiction of Leasehold Valuation Tribunals so that they can determine whether or not leaseholders are liable to pay service charges as well as the reasonableness of such charges;
- makes a number of changes to the existing requirements in the Landlord and Tenant Acts.1985 and 1987 covering the accounting and safeguarding of ser-

HOUSING

vice charge monies. Under the Act service charge funds have to be held in separate designated trust accounts for each property or group of service charge payers. Leaseholders have a new right to withhold payment of further service charges if key requirements are not met;

- introduces a new concept of 'administration charge' covering charges which are required to be paid under leases for approvals, for the provision of information, as a result of a failure to pay rent or other charges on time, or as a result of a breach of a covenant or condition of a lease. It sets out a requirement that administration charges must be reasonable. Lessees may challenge the liability to pay such charges, or their reasonableness, in Leasehold Valuation Tribunals;

- replaces Landlord and Tenant Act 1985, s.20 (which provides that landlords must consult leaseholders before carrying out works costing more than a prescribed sum which are recoverable through service charges) with a revised section. This extends the consultation requirements to include contracts for works or other services of more than 12 months duration, but with a power to exempt, by regulations, specified types of contract or in specified circumstances. It enables the consultation procedures to be prescribed by regulations and provides that LVTs (rather than county courts) may grant dispensation from the procedures in particular cases where they consider it reasonable to do so; and

- introduces a new requirement that ground rent is not payable unless it has been demanded by giving the tenant a prescribed notice, and prevents the application of any provisions of a lease relating to late or non-payment (*e.g.* additional charges) if the rent is paid within 30 days of the demand being issued. It also introduces additional restrictions on the commencement of forfeiture proceedings for breaches of covenants or conditions of a lease. It modifies Housing Act 1996, s.81 to prohibit the commencement of forfeiture proceedings, including the issue of a notice under Law of Property Act 1925, s.146, in respect of non-payment of service charges or administration charges unless the charge has been agreed or admitted by the tenant, or a court or a Leasehold Valuation Tribunal has determined that it is reasonable and due. It also prohibits the commencement of forfeiture proceedings for other breaches unless a court or Leasehold Valuation Tribunal has determined that a breach has occurred.

The amendments to Landlord and Tenant Act 1985 have now been incorporated into the main text.

Implementation and Transitional Provisions

3A-1498   See the Commonhold and Leasehold Reform Act 2002 (Commencement No.1, Savings and Transitional Provisions) (England) Order 2002 (S.I. 2002 No. 1912) (C.58),the Commonhold and Leasehold Reform Act 2002 (Commencement No.1, Savings and Transitional Provisions) (Wales) Order 2002 (S.I. 2002 No. 3012) (W.284) (C.96), the Commonhold and Leasehold Reform Act 2002 (Commencement No.2 and Savings) (England) Order 2003 (S.I. 2003 No. 1986) (C.82) and the Commonhold and Leasehold Reform Act 2002 (Commencement No.2 and Savings) (Wales) Order 2004 (S.I. 2004 No. 669) (W.62) (C.25).

Administration charges

3A-1499   **158.** Schedule 11 (which makes provision about administration charges payable by tenants of dwellings) has effect.

* * * *

Implementation

3A-1500   Section 158 and Sched.11 were brought into force, subject to savings, on September 30, 2003 in England and on March 30, 2004 in Wales by the Commonhold and Leasehold Reform Act 2002 (Commencement No.2 and Savings) (England) Order 2003 (S.I. 2003 No. 1986) (C.82) and the Commonhold and Leasehold Reform Act 2002 (Commencement No.2 and Savings) (Wales) Order 2004 (S.I. 2004 No. 669) (W.62) (C.25).

GROUND RENT

Requirement to notify long leaseholders that rent is due

166.—(1) A tenant under a long lease of a dwelling is not liable to   **3A–1501**
make a payment of rent under the lease unless the landlord has
given him a notice relating to the payment; and the date on which
he is liable to make the payment is that specified in the notice.

(2) The notice must specify—

(a) the amount of the payment,

(b) the date on which the tenant is liable to make it, and

(c) if different from that date, the date on which he would
have been liable to make it in accordance with the lease,

and shall contain any such further information as may be
prescribed.

(3) The date on which the tenant is liable to make the payment
must not be—

(a) either less than 30 days or more than 60 days after the
day on which the notice is given, or

(b) before that on which he would have been liable to make
it in accordance with the lease.

(4) If the date on which the tenant is liable to make the payment
is after that on which he would have been liable to make it in accordance with the lease, any provisions of the lease relating to non-
payment or late payment of rent have effect accordingly.

(5) The notice—

(a) must be in the prescribed form, and

(b) may be sent by post.

(6) If the notice is sent by post, it must be addressed to a tenant
at the dwelling unless he has notified the landlord in writing of a different address in England and Wales at which he wishes to be given
notices under this section (in which case it must be addressed to him
there).

(7) In this section "rent" does not include—

(a) a service charge (within the meaning of section 18(1) of
the 1985 Act), or

(b) an administration charge (within the meaning of Part 1
of Schedule 11 to this Act).

(8) In this section "long lease of a dwelling" does not include—

(a) a tenancy to which Part 2 of the Landlord and Tenant
Act 1954 (c.56) (business tenancies) applies,

(b) a tenancy of an agricultural holding within the meaning
of the Agricultural Holdings Act 1986 (c.5) in relation to
which that Act applies, or

(c) a farm business tenancy within the meaning of the Agricultural Tenancies Act 1995 (c.8).

(9) In this section—

"dwelling" has the same meaning as in the 1985 Act,

"landlord" and "tenant" have the same meanings as in Chapter
1 of this Part,

"long lease" has the meaning given by sections 76 and 77 of this Act, and

"prescribed" means prescribed by regulations made by the appropriate national authority.

Implementation

3A–1502   Section 166 was brought into force in so far as it confers power to make regulations on July 26, 2002 in England and on January 1, 2003 in Wales by the Commonhold and Leasehold Reform Act 2002 (Commencement No.1, Savings and Transitional Provisions) (England) Order 2002 (S.I. 2002 No. 1912) (C.58) and the Commonhold and Leasehold Reform Act 2002 (Commencement No.1, Savings and Transitional Provisions) (Wales) Order 2002 (S.I. 2002 No. 3012) (W.284) (C.96). It was brought fully into force in England on February 28, 2005 by the Commonhold and Leasehold Reform Act 2002 (Commencement No.5 and Saving and Transitional Provision) Order 2004 (S.I. 2004 No. 3056) (C.127) and in Wales on May 31, 2005 by the Commonhold and Leasehold Reform Act 2002 (Commencement No.3 and Saving and Transitional Provision) (Wales) Order 2005 (S.I. 2005 No. 1353) (W.101) (C.59).

Editorial introduction

3A–1502.1   Section 166(1) provides that a long lessee is not liable to make a payment of rent unless notice has been served. Section 166(2) provides that such a notice must specify the amount due, the date on which the lessee is liable to make the payment and, if different, the date on which the lessee would have been liable to make the payment in accordance with the lease. Section 166(2) is supplemented by the Landlord and Tenant (Notice of Rent) (England) Regulations 2004 (S.I. 2004 No. 3096) and the Landlord and Tenant (Notice of Rent) (Wales) Regulations 2005 (S.I. 2005 No. 1355) (W.103) which contain additional requirements, namely notes for both lessees and lessors. The content of the notes is set out in the Schedule to the Regulations, as part of the prescribed form of notice under s.166(1) .

Dwelling

3A–1503   See Landlord and Tenant Act 1985, s.38.

landlord, tenant, lease, tenancy—see Landlord and Tenant Act 1985, s.36, para. 3A–608.

regulations— see the Landlord and Tenant (Notice of Rent) (England) Regulations 2004 (S.I. 2004 No. 3096) and the Landlord and Tenant (Notice of Rent) (Wales) Regulations 2005 (S.I. 2005 No. 1355) (W.103).

long lease —see s.76 which provides that a lease is a long lease if it (a) is granted for a term of years certain exceeding 21 years; (b) is for a term fixed by law under a grant with a covenant or obligation for perpetual renewal (c) takes effect under Law of Property Act 1925, s.149(6) (leases terminable after a death or marriage); (d) was granted under the right to buy provisions of Housing Act 1985, Part 5; (e) is a shared ownership lease; or (f) under Housing Act 1996, s.17 (the right to acquire). Section 77 contains certain exceptions.

administration charge —see Schedule 11, Part 1.

FORFEITURE OF LEASES OF DWELLINGS

Failure to pay small amount for short period

3A–1504   **167.**—(1) A landlord under a long lease of a dwelling may not exercise a right of re-entry or forfeiture for failure by a tenant to pay an amount consisting of rent, service charges or administration charges (or a combination of them) ("the unpaid amount") unless the unpaid amount—

(a) exceeds the prescribed sum, or

(b) consists of or includes an amount which has been payable for more than a prescribed period.

(2) The sum prescribed under subsection (1)(a) must not exceed £500.

(3) If the unpaid amount includes a default charge, it is to be treated for the purposes of subsection (1)(a) as reduced by the amount of the charge; and for this purpose "default charge" means an administration charge payable in respect of the tenant's failure to pay any part of the unpaid amount.

(4) In this section "long lease of a dwelling" does not include—

    (a) a tenancy to which Part 2 of the Landlord and Tenant Act 1954 (c.56) (business tenancies) applies,

    (b) a tenancy of an agricultural holding within the meaning of the Agricultural Holdings Act 1986 (c.5) in relation to which that Act applies, or

    (c) a farm business tenancy within the meaning of the Agricultural Tenancies Act 1995 (c.8).

(5) In this section—

"administration charge" has the same meaning as in Part 1 of Schedule 11,

"dwelling" has the same meaning as in the 1985 Act,

"landlord" and "tenant" have the same meaning as in Chapter 1 of this Part,

"long lease" has the meaning given by sections 76 and 77 of this Act, except that a shared ownership lease is a long lease whatever the tenant's total share,

"prescribed" means prescribed by regulations made by the appropriate national authority, and

"service charge" has the meaning given by section 18(1) of the 1985 Act.

Implementation

Section 167 was brought into force in so far as it confers power to make regulations **3A–1505** on July 26, 2002 in England and on January 1, 2003 in Wales by the Commonhold and Leasehold Reform Act 2002 (Commencement No.1, Savings and Transitional Provisions) (England) Order 2002 (S.I. 2002 No. 1912) (C.58) and the Commonhold and Leasehold Reform Act 2002 (Commencement No.1, Savings and Transitional Provisions) (Wales) Order 2002 (S.I. 2002 No. 3012) (W.284) (C.96). It was brought fully into force in England on February 28, 2005 by the Commonhold and Leasehold Reform Act 2002 (Commencement No.5 and Saving and Transitional Provision) Order 2004 (S.I. 2004 No. 3056) (C.127) and in Wales on May 31, 2005 by the Commonhold and Leasehold Reform Act 2002 (Commencement No.3 and Saving and Transitional Provision) (Wales) Order 2005 (S.I. 2005 No. 1353) (W.101) (C.59).

Editorial introduction

Section 167(1) prevents a landlord under a long lease of a dwelling from exercising **3A–1505.1** a right of re-entry or forfeiture for failure by a tenant to pay an amount consisting of rent, service charges or administration charges (or a combination of them) unless the unpaid amount exceeds the prescribed sum or consists of, or includes, an amount which has been payable for more than a prescribed period. The Rights of Re-entry and Forfeiture (Prescribed Sum and Period) (England) Regulations 2004 (S.I. 2004 No. 3086), and the Rights of Re-entry and Forfeiture (Prescribed Sum and Period) (Wales) Regulations 2005 (S.I. 2005 No. 1352) (W.100), which prescribe the sum of £350 and a period of three years.

service charges

See Landlord and Tenant Act 1985, s.18 as amended by Commonhold and **3A–1506** Leasehold Reform Act 2002, Sched.9..

    administration charge—see Schedule 11, Part 1.

    dwelling—see Landlord and Tenant Act 1985, s.38.

HOUSING

landlord, tenant, lease, tenancy—see Landlord and Tenant Act 1985, s.36.

regulations—See the Rights of Re-entry and Forfeiture (Prescribed Sum and Period) (England) Regulations 2004 (S.I. 2004 No. 3086) and the Rights of Re-entry and Forfeiture (Prescribed Sum and Period) (Wales) Regulations 2005 (S.I. 2005 No. 1352) (W.100).

long lease—see s.76 which provides that a lease is a long lease if it (a) is granted for a term of years certain exceeding 21 years; (b) is for a term fixed by law under a grant with a covenant or obligation for perpetual renewal (c) takes effect under Law of Property Act 1925, s.149(6) (leases terminable after a death or marriage); (d) was granted under the right to buy provisions of Housing Act 1985, Part 5; (e) is a shared ownership lease; or (f) under Housing Act 1996, s.17 (the right to acquire). Section 77 contains certain exceptions.

No forfeiture notice before determination of breach

3A-1507   **168.**—(1) A landlord under a long lease of a dwelling may not serve a notice under section 146(1) of the Law of Property Act 1925 (c.20) (restriction on forfeiture) in respect of a breach by a tenant of a covenant or condition in the lease unless subsection (2) is satisfied.

(2) This subsection is satisfied if—

(a) it has been finally determined on an application under subsection (4) that the breach has occurred,

(b) the tenant has admitted the breach, or

(c) a court in any proceedings, or an arbitral tribunal in proceedings pursuant to a post-dispute arbitration agreement, has finally determined that the breach has occurred.

(3) But a notice may not be served by virtue of subsection (2)(a) or (c) until after the end of the period of 14 days beginning with the day after that on which the final determination is made.

(4) A landlord under a long lease of a dwelling may make an application to a leasehold valuation tribunal for a determination that a breach of a covenant or condition in the lease has occurred.

(5) But a landlord may not make an application under subsection (4) in respect of a matter which—

(a) has been, or is to be, referred to arbitration pursuant to a post-dispute arbitration agreement to which the tenant is a party,

(b) has been the subject of determination by a court, or

(c) has been the subject of determination by an arbitral tribunal pursuant to a post-dispute arbitration agreement.

3A-1508   **implementation**—This section was brought into force in England on February 28, 2005 by the Commonhold and Leasehold Reform Act 2002 (Commencement No.5 and Saving and Transitional Provision) Order 2004 (S.I. 2004 No. 3056) (C.127) and in Wales on May 31, 2005 by the Commonhold and Leasehold Reform Act 2002 (Commencement No.3 and Saving and Transitional Provision) (Wales) Order 2005 (S.I. 2005 No. 1353) (W.101) (C.59).

dwelling— See Landlord and Tenant Act 1985, s.38.

landlord, tenant, lease, tenancy—see Landlord and Tenant Act 1985, s.36, para. 3A–608.

long lease —see s.169 and s.76 which provides that a lease is a long lease if it (a) is granted for a term of years certain exceeding 21 years; (b) is for a term fixed by law under a grant with a covenant or obligation for perpetual renewal (c) takes effect under Law of Property Act 1925, s.149(6) (leases terminable after a death or marriage); (d) was granted under the right to buy provisions of Housing Act 1985, Part 5;

(e) is a shared ownership lease; or (f) under Housing Act 1996, s.17 (the right to acquire). Section 77 contains certain exceptions.

arbitration agreement, arbitral tribunal—see s.169(5) and Arbitration Act 1996, Part 1.

post-dispute arbitration agreement —see s.169(5). It means an arbitration agreement made after a breach has occurred (or is alleged to have occurred).

Section 168: supplementary

169.—(1) An agreement by a tenant under a long lease of a dwell-   **3A–1509**
ing (other than a post-dispute arbitration agreement) is void in so far
as it purports to provide for a determination—

    (a) in a particular manner, or

    (b) on particular evidence,

of any question which may be the subject of an application under section 168(4).

(2) For the purposes of section 168 it is finally determined that a breach of a covenant or condition in a lease has occurred—

    (a) if a decision that it has occurred is not appealed against or otherwise challenged, at the end of the period for bringing an appeal or other challenge, or

    (b) if such a decision is appealed against or otherwise challenged and not set aside in consequence of the appeal or other challenge, at the time specified in subsection (3).

(3) The time referred to in subsection (2)(b) is the time when the appeal or other challenge is disposed of—

    (a) by the determination of the appeal or other challenge and the expiry of the time for bringing a subsequent appeal (if any), or

    (b) by its being abandoned or otherwise ceasing to have effect.

(4) In section 168 and this section "long lease of a dwelling" does not include—

    (a) a tenancy to which Part 2 of the Landlord and Tenant Act 1954 (c.56) (business tenancies) applies,

    (b) a tenancy of an agricultural holding within the meaning of the Agricultural Holdings Act 1986 (c.5) in relation to which that Act applies, or

    (c) a farm business tenancy within the meaning of the Agricultural Tenancies Act 1995 (c.8).

(5) In section 168 and this section—

    "arbitration agreement" and "arbitral tribunal" have the same meaning as in Part 1 of the Arbitration Act 1996 (c.23) and "post-dispute arbitration agreement", in relation to any breach (or alleged breach), means an arbitration agreement made after the breach has occurred (or is alleged to have occurred),

    "dwelling" has the same meaning as in the 1985 Act,

    "landlord" and "tenant" have the same meaning as in Chapter 1 of this Part, and

    "long lease" has the meaning given by sections 76 and 77 of this

Act, except that a shared ownership lease is a long lease whatever the tenant's total share.

(6) Section 146(7) of the Law of Property Act 1925 (c.20) applies for the purposes of section 168 and this section.

(7) Nothing in section 168 affects the service of a notice under section 146(1) of the Law of Property Act 1925 in respect of a failure to pay—

(a) a service charge (within the meaning of section 18(1) of the 1985 Act), or

(b) an administration charge (within the meaning of Part 1 of Schedule 11 to this Act).

3A–1510 **implementation**—This section was brought into force in England on February 28, 2005 by the Commonhold and Leasehold Reform Act 2002 (Commencement No.5 and Saving and Transitional Provision) Order 2004 (S.I. 2004 No. 3056) (C.127) and in Wales on May 31, 2005 by the Commonhold and Leasehold Reform Act 2002 (Commencement No.3 and Saving and Transitional Provision) (Wales) Order 2005 (S.I. 2005 No. 1353) (W.101) (C.59).

dwelling— See Landlord and Tenant Act 1985, s.38.

service charges—see Landlord and Tenant Act 1985, s.18 as amended by Commonhold and Leasehold Reform Act 2002, Sched.9.

landlord, tenant, lease, tenancy—see Landlord and Tenant Act 1985, s.36, para. 3A–608.

administration charge—see Sched.11, Part 1.

Power to prescribe additional or different requirements

3A–1511 **171.**—(1) The appropriate national authority may by regulations prescribe requirements which must be met before a right of re-entry or forfeiture may be exercised in relation to a breach of a covenant or condition in a long lease of an unmortgaged dwelling.

(2) The regulations may specify that the requirements are to be in addition to, or instead of, requirements imposed otherwise than by the regulations.

(3) In this section "long lease of a dwelling" does not include—

(a) a tenancy to which Part 2 of the Landlord and Tenant Act 1954 (c.56) (business tenancies) applies,

(b) a tenancy of an agricultural holding within the meaning of the Agricultural Holdings Act 1986 (c.5) in relation to which that Act applies, or

(c) a farm business tenancy within the meaning of the Agricultural Tenancies Act 1995 (c.8).

(4) For the purposes of this section a dwelling is unmortgaged if it is not subject to a mortgage, charge or lien.

(5) In this section—

"dwelling" has the same meaning as in the 1985 Act, and

"long lease" has the meaning given by sections 76 and 77 of this Act, except that a shared ownership lease is a long lease whatever the tenant's total share.

Implementation

3A–1512 Section 171 was brought into force in so far as it confers power to make regulations on July 26, 2002 in England and on January 1, 2003 in Wales by the Commonhold and Leasehold Reform Act 2002 (Commencement No.1, Savings and Transitional Provisions) (England) Order 2002 (S.I. 2002 No. 1912) (C.58) and the Commonhold and

Leasehold Reform Act 2002 (Commencement No.1, Savings and Transitional Provisions) (Wales) Order 2002 (S.I. 2002 No. 3012) (W.284) (C.96). It was brought fully into force in England on February 28, 2005 by the Commonhold and Leasehold Reform Act 2002 (Commencement No.5 and Saving and Transitional Provision) Order 2004 (S.I. 2004 No. 3056) (C.127).

regulations

At present, there are no regulations.   **3A–1513**

dwelling —see Landlord and Tenant Act 1985, s.38.

long lease — see s.76 which provides that a lease is a long lease if it (a) is granted for a term of years certain exceeding 21 years; (b) is for a term fixed by law under a grant with a covenant or obligation for perpetual renewal (c) takes effect under Law of Property Act 1925, s.149(6) (leases terminable after a death or marriage); (d) was granted under the right to buy provisions of Housing Act 1985, Part 5; (e) is a shared ownership lease; or (f) under Housing Act 1996, s.17 (the right to acquire). Section 77 contains certain exceptions.

CROWN APPLICATION

Application to Crown

172.—(1) The following provisions apply in relation to Crown land **3A–1514** (as in relation to other land)—

(a) sections 18 to 30B of (and the Schedule to) the 1985 Act (service charges, insurance and managing agents),

* * * *

(d) sections 46 to 49 of the 1987 Act (information to be furnished to tenants),

* * * *

(f) section 81 of the Housing Act 1996 (c. 52) (restriction on termination of tenancy for failure to pay service charge etc.),

(g) section 84 of (and Schedule 4 to) that Act (right to appoint surveyor), and

(h) in this Chapter, the provisions relating to any of the provisions within paragraphs (a) to (g), Part 1 of Schedule 11 and sections 164 to 171.

(2) Land is Crown land if there is or has at any time been an interest or estate in the land—

(a) comprised in the Crown Estate,

(b) belonging to Her Majesty in right of the Duchy of Lancaster,

(c) belonging to the Duchy of Cornwall, or

(d) belonging to a government department or held on behalf of Her Majesty for the purposes of a government department.

(3) No failure by the Crown to perform a duty imposed by or by virtue of any of sections 21 to 23A of, or any of paragraphs 2 to 4A of the Schedule to, the 1985 Act makes the Crown criminally liable; but the High Court may declare any such failure without reasonable excuse to be unlawful.

Implementation

Section 172 was partially brought into force, on 30 September 2003 in England and **3A–1515** on March 30, 2004 in Wales by the Commonhold and Leasehold Reform Act 2002

(Commencement No.2 and Savings) (England) Order 2003 (S.I. 2003 No. 1986) (C.82) and the Commonhold and Leasehold Reform Act 2002 (Commencement No.2 and Savings) (Wales) Order 2004 (S.I. 2004 No. 669) (W.62) (C.25). See too the Commonhold and Leasehold Reform Act 2002 (Commencement No.5 and Saving and Transitional Provision) Order 2004 (S.I. 2004 No. 3056) (C.127).

SCHEDULE 11

ADMINISTRATION CHARGES PART 1 REASONABLENESS OF ADMINISTRATION CHARGES

Meaning of "administration charge"

3A–1516 1.—(1) In this Part of this Schedule "administration charge" means an amount payable by a tenant of a dwelling as part of or in addition to the rent which is payable, directly or indirectly—

(a) for or in connection with the grant of approvals under his lease, or applications for such approvals,

(b) for or in connection with the provision of information or documents by or on behalf of the landlord or a person who is party to his lease otherwise than as landlord or tenant,

(c) in respect of a failure by the tenant to make a payment by the due date to the landlord or a person who is party to his lease otherwise than as landlord or tenant, or

(d) in connection with a breach (or alleged breach) of a covenant or condition in his lease.

(2) But an amount payable by the tenant of a dwelling the rent of which is registered under Part 4 of the Rent Act 1977 (c.42) is not an administration charge, unless the amount registered is entered as a variable amount in pursuance of section 71(4) of that Act.

(3) In this Part of this Schedule "variable administration charge" means an administration charge payable by a tenant which is neither—

(a) specified in his lease, nor

(b) calculated in accordance with a formula specified in his lease.

(4) An order amending sub-paragraph (1) may be made by the appropriate national authority.

Reasonableness of administration charges

3A–1517 2. A variable administration charge is payable only to the extent that the amount of the charge is reasonable.

3A–1518 3.—(1) Any party to a lease of a dwelling may apply to a leasehold valuation tribunal for an order varying the lease in such manner as is specified in the application on the grounds that—

(a) any administration charge specified in the lease is unreasonable, or

(b) any formula specified in the lease in accordance with which any administration charge is calculated is unreasonable.

(2) If the grounds on which the application was made are established to the satisfaction of the tribunal, it may make an order varying the lease in such manner as is specified in the order.

(3) The variation specified in the order may be—

(a) the variation specified in the application, or

(b) such other variation as the tribunal thinks fit.

(4) The tribunal may, instead of making an order varying the lease in such manner as is specified in the order, make an order directing the parties to the lease to vary it in such manner as is so specified.

(5) The tribunal may by order direct that a memorandum of any variation of a lease effected by virtue of this paragraph be endorsed on such documents as are specified in the order.

(6) Any such variation of a lease shall be binding not only on the parties to the lease for the time being but also on other persons (including any predecessors in title), whether or not they were parties to the proceedings in which the order was made.

Notice in connection with demands for administration charges

3A-1519

4.—(1) A demand for the payment of an administration charge must be accompanied by a summary of the rights and obligations of tenants of dwellings in relation to administration charges.

(2) The appropriate national authority may make regulations prescribing requirements as to the form and content of such summaries of rights and obligations.

(3) A tenant may withhold payment of an administration charge which has been demanded from him if sub-paragraph (1) is not complied with in relation to the demand.

(4) Where a tenant withholds an administration charge under this paragraph, any provisions of the lease relating to non-payment or late payment of administration charges do not have effect in relation to the period for which he so withholds it.

Liability to pay administration charges

3A-1520

5.—(1) An application may be made to a leasehold valuation tribunal for a determination whether an administration charge is payable and, if it is, as to—

(a) the person by whom it is payable,

(b) the person to whom it is payable,

(c) the amount which is payable,

(d) the date at or by which it is payable, and

(e) the manner in which it is payable.

(2) Sub-paragraph (1) applies whether or not any payment has been made.

(3) The jurisdiction conferred on a leasehold valuation tribunal in respect of any matter by virtue of sub-paragraph (1) is in addition to any jurisdiction of a court in respect of the matter.

(4) No application under sub-paragraph (1) may be made in respect of a matter which—

(a) has been agreed or admitted by the tenant,

(b) has been, or is to be, referred to arbitration pursuant to a post-dispute arbitration agreement to which the tenant is a party,

(c) has been the subject of determination by a court, or

(d) has been the subject of determination by an arbitral tribunal pursuant to a post-dispute arbitration agreement.

(5) But the tenant is not to be taken to have agreed or admitted any matter by reason only of having made any payment.

(6) An agreement by the tenant of a dwelling (other than a post-dispute arbitration agreement) is void in so far as it purports to provide for a determination—

(a) in a particular manner, or

(b) on particular evidence,

of any question which may be the subject matter of an application under sub-paragraph (1).

Interpretation

3A-1521

6.—(1) This paragraph applies for the purposes of this Part of this Schedule.

(2) "Tenant" includes a statutory tenant.

(3) "Dwelling" and "statutory tenant" (and "landlord" in relation to a statutory tenant) have the same meanings as in the 1985 Act.

(4) "Post-dispute arbitration agreement", in relation to any matter, means an arbitration agreement made after a dispute about the matter has arisen.

(5) "Arbitration agreement" and "arbitral tribunal" have the same meanings as in Part 1 of the Arbitration Act 1996 (c.23).

Asylum and Immigration (Treatment of Claimants, etc.) Act 2004

(2004 c.19)

3A-1522

ARRANGEMENT OF SECTIONS

Accommodation for asylum seekers: local connection

11.—(2) Subsection (3) applies where—

(a) a local housing authority would (but for subsection (3)) be obliged to secure that accommodation is available for occupation by a person under section 193 of the Housing Act 1996 (homeless persons),

(b) the person was (at any time) provided with accommodation in a place in Scotland under section 95 of the Immigration and Asylum Act 1999 (support for asylum seekers),

(c) the accommodation was not provided in an accommodation centre by virtue of section 22 of the Nationality, Immigration and Asylum Act 2002 (use of accommodation centres for section 95 support), and

(d) the person has neither—

(i) a local connection with the district of a local housing authority (in England or Wales) within the meaning of section 199 of the Housing Act 1996 as amended by subsection (1) above, nor

(ii) a local connection with a district (in Scotland) within the meaning of section 27 of the Housing (Scotland) Act 1987 (c. 26).

(3) Where this subsection applies—

(a) the duty of the local housing authority under section 193 of the Housing Act 1996 in relation to the person shall not apply, but

(b) the local housing authority—

(i) may secure that accommodation is available for occupation by the person for a period giving him a reasonable opportunity of securing accommodation for his occupation, and

(ii) may provide the person (or secure that he is provided with) advice and assistance in any attempts he may make to secure that accommodation becomes available for his occupation.

Implementation

3A–1523 This section was brought into force on January 4, 2005 by the Asylum and Immigration (Treatment of Claimants etc) Act 2004 (Commencement No. 2) Order 2004 S.I. 2004 No. 2999.

Note

3A–1524 The purpose of his section is to reverse the effect of *Al-Ameri v. Kensington and Chelsea RLBC* [2004] UKHL 4; [2004] 2 W.L.R. 354. Subsection (1) is an amendment to Housing Act 1996, s.199: see 3A–1325.

Civil Partnership Act 2004

3A–1525

(2004c.33)

ARRANGEMENT OF SECTIONS

SECT.

Housing and tenancies

81. Schedule 8 amends certain enactments relating to housing and tenancies.

SECTION 81   SCHEDULE 8

HOUSING AND TENANCIES

....   **3A–1526**

Rent Act 1977 (c. 42)

13.—(1) In Part 1 of Schedule 1 (statutory tenants by succession), amend paragraph 2 (succession by surviving spouse) as follows.

(2) In sub-paragraph (1), after "surviving spouse" insert ", or surviving civil partner,".

(3) For sub-paragraph (2) substitute—

"(2) For the purposes of this paragraph—

(a) a person who was living with the original tenant as his or her wife or husband shall be treated as the spouse of the original tenant, and

(b) a person who was living with the original tenant as if they were civil partners shall be treated as the civil partner of the original tenant."

(4) In sub-paragraph (3), for the words after "the county court" substitute "shall for the purposes of this paragraph be treated (according to whether that one of them is of the opposite sex to, or of the same sex as, the original tenant) as the surviving spouse or the surviving civil partner."

14. In Schedule 15 (grounds for possession), in Case 9 in Part 1 (dwelling required **3A–1527** as residence for landlord or member of his family), for "wife or husband" substitute "spouse or civil partner".

....

Housing Act 1985 (c. 68)

20. In section 87(a) (entitlement of tenant's spouse to succeed to secure tenancy), af- **3A–1528** ter "spouse" insert "or civil partner".

21.—(1) Amend section 88 (cases where secure tenant is a successor) as follows. **3A–1529**

(2) In subsection (1)(d), for "(2) and (3)" substitute "(2) to (3)".

(3) After subsection (2) insert—

"(2A) A tenant to whom the tenancy was assigned in pursuance of an order under Part 2 of Schedule 5, or paragraph 9(2) or (3) of Schedule 7, to the Civil Partnership Act 2004 (property adjustment orders in connection with civil partnership proceedings or after overseas dissolution of civil partnership, etc.) is a successor only if the other civil partner was a successor."

22.—(1) Amend section 89 (succession to periodic secured tenancy) as follows. **3A–1530**

(2) In subsection (2)(a) (tenant's spouse is preferred successor), after "spouse" insert "or civil partner".

(3) In subsection (3)(a), after "parents" in sub-paragraph (iii) insert ", or

(iv) Part 2 of Schedule 5, or paragraph 9(2) or (3) of Schedule 7, to the Civil Partnership Act 2004 (property adjustment orders in connection with civil partnership proceedings or after overseas dissolution of civil partnership, etc.)".

23. In section 90(3)(a) (secure tenancy for term certain does not cease to be secure **3A–1531** tenancy if vested under certain orders), after sub-paragraph (iii) insert—

"(iv) Part 2 of Schedule 5, or paragraph 9(2) or (3) of Schedule 7, to the Civil Partnership Act 2004 (property adjustment orders in connection with civil partnership proceedings or after overseas dissolution of civil partnership, etc.), or".

HOUSING

3A–1532 24. In section 91(3)(b) (assignments not prohibited if in pursuance of certain orders), after "parents)" in sub-paragraph (iii) insert—

", or

(iv) Part 2 of Schedule 5, or paragraph 9(2) or (3) of Schedule 7, to the Civil Partnership Act 2004 (property adjustment orders in connection with civil partnership proceedings or after overseas dissolution of civil partnership, etc.)".

... ...

3A–1533 27.—(1) Amend sections 113 and 186 (meaning of "member of a person's family" in Parts 3 and 4) as follows.

(2) In subsection (1)(a) —

(a) after "spouse" insert "or civil partner", and

(b) after "live together as husband and wife" insert "or as if they were civil partners".

(3) In subsection (2)(a) , after "a relationship by marriage" insert "or civil partnership".

... ...

3A–1534 33. In Part 1 of Schedule 2 (secure tenancies: grounds for possession if court considers possession reasonable), in ground 2A (violence by member of a couple)—

(a) for "a married couple or" substitute "a married couple, a couple who are civil partners of each other," and

(b) after "as husband or wife" insert "or a couple living together as if they were civil partners".

... ...

Housing Act 1988 (c. 50)

3A–1535 41.—(1) Amend section 17 (succession to assured periodic tenancy by spouse) as follows.

(2) In subsection (1) , after "spouse" (in each place) insert "or civil partner".

(3) For subsection (4) substitute—

"(4) For the purposes of this section—

(a) a person who was living with the tenant as his or her wife or husband shall be treated as the tenant's spouse, and

(b) a person who was living with the tenant as if they were civil partners shall be treated as the tenant's civil partner."

(4) In subsection (5) , for the words after "the county court" substitute "shall for the purposes of this section be treated (according to whether that one of them is of the opposite sex to, or of the same sex as, the tenant) as the tenant's spouse or the tenant's civil partner."

... ...

3A–1536 43.—(1) Amend Schedule 2 (assured tenancies: grounds for possession) as follows.

(2) In Part 1 (cases where court must order possession), in paragraph (b) of Ground 1 (landlord previously resident or requiring premises as residence for himself or his spouse), for "his or his spouse's" substitute "his, his spouse's or his civil partner's".

(3) In Part 2 (cases where court may order possession), in Ground 14A (violence by member of a couple)—

(a) for "a married couple or" substitute "a married couple, a couple who are civil partners of each other," and

(b) after "as husband or wife" insert "or a couple living together as if they were civil partners".

... ...

Housing Act 1996 (c. 52)

3A–1537 51.—(1) Amend sections 62 and 140 (meaning of "member of a person's family" in Part 1 and in Chapter 1 of Part 5) as follows.

(2) In subsection (1)(a) —

(a) after "spouse" insert "or civil partner", and

(b) after "live together as husband and wife" insert "or as if they were civil partners".

(3) In subsection (2)(a) , after "a relationship by marriage" insert "or civil partnership".

... ...

55. In section 143H(5)(a) (two or more successors to demoted tenancy), for "spouse or (if the tenant has no spouse)" substitute "spouse or civil partner or (if the tenant has neither spouse nor civil partner)". **3A–1538**

56. In section 143I(3) (tenancy does not cease to be demoted tenancy if vested pursuant to certain orders), after paragraph (c) insert— **3A–1539**

> "(d) Part 2 of Schedule 5, or paragraph 9(2) or (3) of Schedule 7, to the Civil Partnership Act 2004 (property adjustment orders in connection with civil partnership proceedings or after overseas dissolution of civil partnership, etc.)."

57. For paragraphs (a) and (b) of section 143J(5) (successor by assignment to secure tenancy terminated by demotion order) substitute— **3A–1540**

> "(a) the tenancy was assigned—
>
>> (i) in proceedings under section 24 of the Matrimonial Causes Act 1973 (property adjustment orders in connection with matrimonial proceedings) or section 17(1) of the Matrimonial and Family Proceedings Act 1984 (property adjustment orders after overseas divorce, etc.), or
>>
>> (ii) in proceedings under Part 2 of Schedule 5, or paragraph 9(2) or (3) of Schedule 7, to the Civil Partnership Act 2004 (property adjustment orders in connection with civil partnership proceedings or after overseas dissolution of civil partnership, etc.),
>
> (b) where the tenancy was assigned as mentioned in paragraph (a)(i), neither he nor the other party to the marriage was a successor, and
>
> (c) where the tenancy was assigned as mentioned in paragraph (a)(ii), neither he nor the other civil partner was a successor."

58. In section 143K(2) (demoted tenancy may be assigned only in pursuance of certain orders), after paragraph (c) insert— **3A–1541**

> "(d) Part 2 of Schedule 5, or paragraph 9(2) or (3) of Schedule 7, to the Civil Partnership Act 2004 (property adjustment orders in connection with civil partnership proceedings or after overseas dissolution of civil partnership, etc.)."

59.—(1) Amend section 143P (meaning of "member of another's family") as follows. **3A–1542**

(2) In subsection (1)(a) , after "spouse" insert "or civil partner".

(3) In subsection (3)(a) , after "marriage" insert "or civil partnership".

... ...

61.—(1) Amend section 178 (meaning of "associated person" in Part 7) as follows. **3A–1543**

(2) In subsection (1), after paragraph (a) insert—

> "(aa) they are or have been civil partners of each other;".

(3) In subsection (1), after paragraph (e) insert—

> "(ea) they have entered into a civil partnership agreement between them (whether or not that agreement has been terminated);".

(4) In subsection (3) , after the definition of "child" insert—

> " "civil partnership agreement" has the meaning given by section 73 of the Civil Partnership Act 2004;".

(5) In subsection (3) , for the definition of "cohabitants" substitute—

> " "cohabitants" mean —
>
>> (a) a man and a woman who, although not married to each other, are living together as husband and wife, or
>>
>> (b) two people of the same sex who, although not civil partners of each other, are living together as if they were civil partners; and "former cohabitants" shall be construed accordingly;".

(6) In subsection (3), in each of paragraphs (a) and (b) of the definition of "relative", for "spouse or former spouse" substitute "spouse, civil partner, former spouse or former civil partner".

(7) In paragraph (b) of that definition, for "affinity" substitute "marriage or civil partnership".

Housing Act 2004

3A–1544

2004c.34

ARRANGEMENT OF SECTIONS

CHAPTER 4

TENANCY DEPOSIT SCHEMES

CHAPTER 4

TENANCY DEPOSIT SCHEMES

Tenancy deposit schemes

3A–1545

212—(1) The appropriate national authority must make arrangements for securing that one or more tenancy deposit schemes are available for the purpose of safeguarding tenancy deposits paid in connection with shorthold tenancies.

(2) For the purposes of this Chapter a "tenancy deposit scheme" is a scheme which–

(a) is made for the purpose of safeguarding tenancy deposits paid in connection with shorthold tenancies and facilitating the resolution of disputes arising in connection with such deposits, and

(b) complies with the requirements of Schedule 10.

(3) Arrangements under subsection (1) must be arrangements made with any body or person under which the body or person ("the scheme administrator") undertakes to establish and maintain a tenancy deposit scheme of a description specified in the arrangements.

(4) The appropriate national authority may–

(a) give financial assistance to the scheme administrator;

(b) make payments to the scheme administrator (otherwise than as financial assistance) in pursuance of arrangements under subsection (1).

(5) The appropriate national authority may, in such manner and on such terms as it thinks fit, guarantee the discharge of any financial obligation incurred by the scheme administrator in connection with arrangements under subsection (1).

(6) Arrangements under subsection (1) must require the scheme administrator to give the appropriate national authority, in such manner and at such times as it may specify, such information and facilities for obtaining information as it may specify.

(7) The appropriate national authority may make regulations conferring or imposing–

(a) on scheme administrators, or

(b) on scheme administrators of any description specified in the regulations,

such powers or duties in connection with arrangements under subsection (1) as are so specified.

(8) In this Chapter–

"authorised", in relation to a tenancy deposit scheme, means that the scheme is in force in accordance with arrangements under subsection (1);

"custodial scheme" and "insurance scheme" have the meaning given by paragraph 1(2) and (3) of Schedule 10);

"money" means money in the form of cash or otherwise;

"shorthold tenancy" means an assured shorthold tenancy within the meaning of Chapter 2 of Part 1 of the Housing Act 1988 (c. 50);

"tenancy deposit", in relation to a shorthold tenancy, means any money intended to be held (by the landlord or otherwise) as security for–

(a) the performance of any obligations of the tenant, or

(b) the discharge of any liability of his, arising under or in connection with the tenancy.

(9) In this Chapter–

(a) references to a landlord or landlords in relation to any shorthold tenancy or tenancies include references to a person or persons acting on his or their behalf in relation to the tenancy or tenancies, and

(b) references to a tenancy deposit being held in accordance with a scheme include, in the case of a custodial scheme, references to an amount representing the deposit being held in accordance with the scheme.

implementation

This section is not yet in force. It will be brought into force by commencement order.

3A–1546

tenancy deposit

See s.212(8).

3A–1547

shorthold tenancy

See s.212(8) and (9) and Housing Act 1988 s.19.

3A–1548

Requirements relating to tenancy deposits

213—(1) Any tenancy deposit paid to a person in connection with a shorthold tenancy must, as from the time when it is received, be dealt with in accordance with an authorised scheme.

3A–1549

(2) No person may require the payment of a tenancy deposit in connection with a shorthold tenancy which is not to be subject to the requirement in subsection (1).

(3) Where a landlord receives a tenancy deposit in connection

with a shorthold tenancy, the initial requirements of an authorised scheme must be complied with by the landlord in relation to the deposit within the period of 14 days beginning with the date on which it is received.

(4) For the purposes of this section "the initial requirements" of an authorised scheme are such requirements imposed by the scheme as fall to be complied with by a landlord on receiving such a tenancy deposit.

(5) A landlord who has received such a tenancy deposit must give the tenant and any relevant person such information relating to–

> (a) the authorised scheme applying to the deposit,
>
> (b) compliance by the landlord with the initial requirements of the scheme in relation to the deposit, and
>
> (c) the operation of provisions of this Chapter in relation to the deposit,

as may be prescribed.

(6) The information required by subsection (5) must be given to the tenant and any relevant person–

> (a) in the prescribed form or in a form substantially to the same effect, and
>
> (b) within the period of 14 days beginning with the date on which the deposit is received by the landlord.

(7) No person may, in connection with a shorthold tenancy, require a deposit which consists of property other than money.

(8) In subsection (7) "deposit" means a transfer of property intended to be held (by the landlord or otherwise) as security for–

> (a) the performance of any obligations of the tenant, or
>
> (b) the discharge of any liability of his, arising under or in connection with the tenancy.

(9) The provisions of this section apply despite any agreement to the contrary.

(10) In this section–

> "prescribed" means prescribed by an order made by the appropriate national authority;
>
> "property" means moveable property;
>
> "relevant person" means any person who, in accordance with arrangements made with the tenant, paid the deposit on behalf of the tenant.

implementation

3A–1550 This section is not yet in force. It will be brought into force by commencement order.

tenancy deposit

3A–1551 See s.212(8).

shorthold tenancy

3A–1552 See s.212(8) and (9) and Housing Act 1988 s.19.

Proceedings relating to tenancy deposits

3A–1553 214—(1) Where a tenancy deposit has been paid in connection with a shorthold tenancy, the tenant or any relevant person (as defined by section 213(10)) may make an application to a county court on the grounds–

(a) that the initial requirements of an authorised scheme (see section 213(4)) have not, or section 213(6)(a) has not, been complied with in relation to the deposit; or

(b) that he has been notified by the landlord that a particular authorised scheme applies to the deposit but has been unable to obtain confirmation from the scheme administrator that the deposit is being held in accordance with the scheme.

(2) Subsections (3) and (4) apply if on such an application the court–

(a) is satisfied that those requirements have not, or section 213(6)(a) has not, been complied with in relation to the deposit, or

(b) is not satisfied that the deposit is being held in accordance with an authorised scheme,

as the case may be.

(3) The court must, as it thinks fit, either–

(a) order the person who appears to the court to be holding the deposit to repay it to the applicant, or

(b) order that person to pay the deposit into the designated account held by the scheme administrator under an authorised custodial scheme,

within the period of 14 days beginning with the date of the making of the order.

(4) The court must also order the landlord to pay to the applicant a sum of money equal to three times the amount of the deposit within the period of 14 days beginning with the date of the making of the order.

(5) Where any deposit given in connection with a shorthold tenancy could not be lawfully required as a result of section 213(7), the property in question is recoverable from the person holding it by the person by whom it was given as a deposit.

(6) In subsection (5) "deposit" has the meaning given by section 213(8).

implementation

This section is not yet in force. It will be brought into force by commencement order.　　　　　　　　　　　　　　　　　　　　　　　　　　　　　　　**3A–1554**

tenancy deposit

See s.212(8).　　　　　　　　　　　　　　　　　　　　　　　　　　　　　　**3A–1555**

relevant person

See s.213(10).　　　　　　　　　　　　　　　　　　　　　　　　　　　　　**3A–1556**

shorthold tenancy

See s.212(8) and (9) and Housing Act 1988 s.19.　　　　　　　　　　　　　**3A–1557**

authorised scheme

See s.213(4).　　　　　　　　　　　　　　　　　　　　　　　　　　　　　　**3A–1558**

Sanctions for non-compliance

3A–1559   215—(1) If a tenancy deposit has been paid in connection with a shorthold tenancy, no section 21 notice may be given in relation to the tenancy at a time when–

> (a) the deposit is not being held in accordance with an authorised scheme, or
>
> (b) the initial requirements of such a scheme (see section 213(4)) have not been complied with in relation to the deposit.

(2) If section 213(6) is not complied with in relation to a deposit given in connection with a shorthold tenancy, no section 21 notice may be given in relation to the tenancy until such time as section 213(6)(a) is complied with.

(3) If any deposit given in connection with a shorthold tenancy could not be lawfully required as a result of section 213(7), no section 21 notice may be given in relation to the tenancy until such time as the property in question is returned to the person by whom it was given as a deposit.

(4) In subsection (3) "deposit" has the meaning given by section 213(8).

(5) In this section a "section 21 notice" means a notice under section 21(1)(b) or (4)(a) of the Housing Act 1988 (recovery of possession on termination of shorthold tenancy).

implementation

3A–1560   This section is not yet in force. It will be brought into force by commencement order.

tenancy deposit

3A–1561   See s.212(8).

shorthold tenancy

3A–1562   See s.212(8) and (9) and Housing Act 1988 s.19.

authorised scheme

3A–1563   See s.213(4).

SECTION 212   **SCHEDULE 10**

PROVISIONS RELATING TO TENANCY DEPOSIT SCHEMES

Schemes to be custodial schemes or insurance schemes

3A–1564   1—(1)A tenancy deposit scheme must be either–

> (a) a custodial scheme, or
>
> (b) an insurance scheme.

(2) A "custodial scheme" is a scheme under which–

> (a) tenancy deposits in connection with shorthold tenancies are paid to the landlords under the tenancies,
>
> (b) amounts representing the deposits are then paid by the landlords into a designated account held by the scheme administrator, and
>
> (c) those amounts are kept by the scheme administrator in that account until such time as, in accordance with the scheme, they fall to be paid (wholly or in part) to the landlords or tenants under the tenancies,

(3) An "insurance scheme" is a scheme under which–

> (a) tenancy deposits in connection with shorthold tenancies are paid to the landlords under the tenancies,

1044

(b) such deposits are retained by the landlords on the basis that, at the end of the tenancies–

    (i) such amounts in respect of the deposits as are agreed between the tenants and the landlords will be repaid to the tenants, and

    (ii) such amounts as the tenants request to be repaid to them and which are not so repaid will, in accordance with directions given by the scheme administrator, be paid into a designated account held by the scheme administrator,

(c) amounts paid into that account are kept by the scheme administrator in the account until such time as, in accordance with the scheme, they fall to be paid (wholly or in part) to the landlords or tenants under the tenancies,

(d) landlords undertake to reimburse the scheme administrator, in accordance with directions given by him, in respect of any amounts in respect of the deposits paid to the tenants by the scheme administrator (other than amounts paid to the tenants as mentioned in paragraph (c)), and

(e) insurance is maintained by the scheme administrator in respect of failures by landlords to comply with such directions.

Provisions applying to custodial and insurance schemes

2—(1)A custodial scheme must conform with the following provisions–
paragraphs 3 and 4, and
paragraphs 9 and 10.

(2) An insurance scheme must conform with the following provisions–
paragraphs 5 to 8, and
paragraphs 9 and 10.

3A–1565

Custodial schemes: general

3—(1)This paragraph applies to a custodial scheme.

(2) The scheme must provide for any landlord who receives a tenancy deposit in connection with a shorthold tenancy to pay an amount equal to the deposit into a designated account held by the scheme administrator.

(3) The designated account must not contain anything other than amounts paid into it as mentioned in sub-paragraph (2) and any interest accruing on such amounts.

(4) Subject to sub-paragraph (5), the scheme administrator may retain any interest accruing on such amounts.

(5) The relevant arrangements under section 212(1) may provide for any amount paid in accordance with paragraph 4 to be paid with interest–

    (a) in respect of the period during which the relevant amount has remained in the designated account, and

    (b) at such rate as the appropriate national authority may specify by order.

(6) With the exception of any interest retained in accordance with sub-paragraph (4), nothing contained in the designated account may be used to fund the administration of the scheme.

(7) In this paragraph "the relevant amount", in relation to a tenancy deposit, means the amount paid into the designated account in respect of the deposit.

3A–1566

Custodial schemes: termination of tenancies

4—(1)A custodial scheme must make provision–

    (a) for enabling the tenant and the landlord under a shorthold tenancy in connection with which a tenancy deposit is held in accordance with the scheme to apply, at any time after the tenancy has ended, for the whole or part of the relevant amount to be paid to him, and

    (b) for such an application to be dealt with by the scheme administrator in accordance with the following provisions of this paragraph.

(2) Sub-paragraph (3) applies where the tenant and the landlord notify the scheme administrator that they have agreed that the relevant amount should be paid–

    (a) wholly to one of them, or

    (b) partly to the one and partly to the other.

3A–1567

(3) If, having received such a notification, the scheme administrator is satisfied that the tenant and the landlord have so agreed, the scheme administrator must arrange for the relevant amount to be paid, in accordance with the agreement, within the period of 10 days beginning with the date on which the notification is received by the scheme administrator.

(4) Sub-paragraph (5) applies where the tenant or the landlord notifies the scheme administrator that–

(a) a court has decided that the relevant amount is payable either wholly to one of them or partly to the one and partly to the other, and

(b) that decision has become final.

(5) If, having received such a notification, the scheme administrator is satisfied as to the matters mentioned in sub-paragraph (4)(a) and (b), the scheme administrator must arrange for the relevant amount to be paid, in accordance with the decision, within the period of 10 days beginning with the date on which the notification is received by the scheme administrator.

(6) For the purposes of this Schedule a decision becomes final–

(a) if not appealed against, at the end of the period for bringing an appeal, or

(b) if appealed against, at the time when the appeal (or any further appeal) is disposed of.

(7) An appeal is disposed of–

(a) if it is determined and the period for bringing any further appeal has ended, or

(b) if it is abandoned or otherwise ceases to have effect.

(8) In this paragraph "the relevant amount" has the meaning given by paragraph 3(7).

Insurance schemes: general

3A–1568   5—(1) This paragraph applies to an insurance scheme.

(2) The scheme must provide that any landlord by whom a tenancy deposit is retained under the scheme must give the scheme administrator an undertaking that, if the scheme administrator directs the landlord to pay him any amount in respect of the deposit in accordance with paragraph 6(3) or (7), the landlord will comply with such a direction.

(3) The scheme must require the scheme administrator to effect, and maintain in force, adequate insurance in respect of failures by landlords by whom tenancy deposits are retained under the scheme to comply with such directions as are mentioned in sub-paragraph (2).

(4) If the scheme provides for landlords participating in the scheme to be members of the scheme, the scheme may provide for a landlord's membership to be terminated by the scheme administrator in the event of any such failure on the part of the landlord.

(5) The scheme may provide for landlords participating in the scheme to pay to the scheme administrator–

(a) fees in respect of the administration of the scheme, and

(b) contributions in respect of the cost of the insurance referred to in sub-paragraph (3).

Insurance schemes: termination of tenancies

3A–1569   6—(1) An insurance scheme must make provision in accordance with this paragraph and paragraphs 7 and 8 in relation to the respective obligations of the landlord and the scheme administrator where–

(a) a tenancy deposit has been retained by the landlord under the scheme, and

(b) the tenancy has ended.

(2) Sub-paragraphs (3) to (9) apply where the tenant notifies the scheme administrator that–

(a) the tenant has requested the landlord to repay to him the whole or any part of the deposit, and

(b) the amount in question ("the outstanding amount") has not been repaid to him within the period of 10 days beginning with the date on which the request was made.

(3) On receiving a notification in accordance with sub-paragraph (2), the scheme administrator must direct the landlord–

    (a) to pay an amount equal to the outstanding amount into a designated account held by the scheme administrator, and

    (b) to do so within the period of 10 days beginning with the date on which the direction is received by the landlord.

(4) The following sub-paragraphs apply where the tenant or the landlord notifies the scheme administrator–

    (a) that a court has decided that the outstanding amount is payable either wholly to one of them or partly to the one and partly to the other and the decision has become final (see paragraph 4(6) and (7)), or

    (b) that the tenant and landlord have agreed that such an amount is to be paid either wholly to one of them or partly to the one and partly to the other.

(5) If the scheme administrator is satisfied as to the matters mentioned in sub-paragraph (4)(a) or (b) (as the case may be), he must–

    (a) pay to the tenant any amount due to him in accordance with the decision or agreement (and, to the extent possible, pay that amount out of any amount held by him by virtue of sub-paragraph (3)), and

    (b) comply with sub-paragraph (6) or (7), as the case may be.

(6) Where any amount held by the scheme administrator by virtue of sub-paragraph (3) is more than any amount due to the tenant in accordance with the decision or agreement, the scheme administrator must pay the balance to the landlord.

(7) Where any amount so held by the scheme administrator is less than any amount so due to the tenant, the scheme administrator must direct the landlord to pay him the difference within the period of 10 days beginning with the date on which the direction is received by the landlord.

(8) The scheme administrator must pay any amounts required to be paid to the tenant or the landlord as mentioned in sub-paragraph (5)(a) or (6) within 10 days beginning with the date on which the notification is received by the scheme administrator.

(9) The landlord must comply with any direction given in accordance with sub-paragraph (3) or (7).

7—(1)The designated account held by the scheme administrator must not contain **3A–1570** anything other than amounts paid into it as mentioned in paragraph 6(3) and any interest accruing on such amounts.

(2) Subject to sub-paragraph (3), the scheme administrator may retain any interest accruing on such amounts.

(3) The relevant arrangements under section 212(1) may provide for any amount paid in accordance with paragraph 6(5)(a) or (6) to be paid with interest–

    (a) in respect of the period during which the relevant amount has remained in the designated account, and

    (b) at such rate as the appropriate national authority may specify for the purposes of paragraph 3(5)(b).

(4) With the exception of any interest retained in accordance with sub-paragraph (2), nothing contained in the designated account may be used to fund the administration of the scheme.

(5) In this paragraph "the relevant amount", in relation to a tenancy deposit, means the amount, in respect of the deposit, paid into the designated account by virtue of a direction given in accordance with paragraph 6(3).

8—(1)The scheme must make provision for preventing double recovery by a tenant **3A–1571** in respect of the whole or part of the deposit, and may in that connection make provision–

    (a) for excluding or modifying any requirement imposed by the scheme in accordance with paragraph 6 or 7, and

    (b) for requiring the repayment of amounts paid to the tenant by the scheme administrator.

(2) In this paragraph "double recovery", in relation to an amount of a tenancy deposit, means recovering that amount both from the scheme administrator and from the landlord.

Notifications to tenants

9—(1)Every custodial scheme or insurance scheme must provide for the scheme **3A–1572** administrator to respond as soon as is practicable to any request within sub-paragraph (2) made by the tenant under a shorthold tenancy.

(2) A request is within this sub-paragraph if it is a request by the tenant to receive confirmation that a deposit paid in connection with the tenancy is being held in accordance with the scheme.

Dispute resolution procedures

3A–1573 10—(1)Every custodial scheme or insurance scheme must provide for facilities to be available for enabling disputes relating to tenancy deposits subject to the scheme to be resolved without recourse to litigation.

(2) The scheme must not, however, make the use of such facilities compulsory in the event of such a dispute.

Power to amend

3A–1574 11 The appropriate national authority may by order make such amendments of this Schedule as it considers appropriate.

Interpretation

3A–1575 12 In this Schedule references to tenants under shorthold tenancies include references to persons who, in accordance with arrangements made with such tenants, have paid tenancy deposits on behalf of the tenants.

3B   BUSINESS TENANCIES

Landlord and Tenant Act 1927

(17 & 18 GEO. 5 c.36)

PART I

*COMPENSATION FOR IMPROVEMENTS AND GOODWILL ON THE TERMINATION
OF TENANCIES OF BUSINESS PREMISES*

Tenant's right to compensation for improvements

1.—(1) Subject to the provisions of this Part of this Act, a tenant of a holding to which this Part of this Act applies shall, if a claim for the purpose is made in the prescribed manner [and within the time limited by section forty-seven of the Landlord and Tenant Act, 1954] be entitled, at the termination of the tenancy, on quitting his holding, to be paid by his landlord compensation in respect of any improvement (including the erection of any building) on his holding made by him or his predecessors in title, not being a trade or other fixture which the tenant is by law entitled to remove, which at the termination of the tenancy adds to the letting value of the holding: Provided that the sum to be paid as compensation for any improvement shall not exceed—

  (a) the net addition to the value of the holding as a whole which may be determined to be the direct result of the improvement; or

  (b) the reasonable cost of carrying out the improvement at the termination of the tenancy, subject to a deduction of an amount equal to the cost (if any) of putting the works constituting the improvement into a reasonable state of repair, except so far as such cost is covered by the liability of the tenant under any covenant or agreement as to the repair of the premises.

(2) In determining the amount of such net addition as aforesaid, regard shall be had to the purposes for which it is intended that the premises shall be used after the termination of the tenancy, and if it is shown that it is intended to demolish or to make structural alterations in the premises or any part thereof or to use the premises for a different purpose, regard shall be had to the effect of such demolition, alteration or change of user on the additional value attributable to the improvement, and to the length of time likely to elapse between the termination of the tenancy and the demolition, alteration or change of user.

(3) In the absence of agreement between the parties, all questions as to the right to compensation under this section, or as to the amount thereof, shall be determined by the tribunal hereinafter mentioned, and if the tribunal determines that, on account of the intention to demolish or alter or to change the user of the premises, no compensation or a reduced amount of compensation shall be

paid, the tribunal may authorise a further application for compensation to be made by the tenant if effect is not given to the intention within such time as may be fixed by the tribunal.

3B-3   *Note* —Section 1 was amended by Landlord and Tenant Act 1954, s.1(1)(a)(b) and s.47(5).

Editorial note
3B-4   Landlord and Tenant Act 1927 allows certain business tenants who carry out improvements to their holdings to claim compensation on quitting. This does not apply to tenants of mining leases (see s.25(1)) or tenancies of agricultural holdings (s.17(1)) or tenants who hold any office, appointment or employment from the landlord (s.17(2)). Tenants have to follow the strict procedures laid down in Part I of this Act and comply with the time limit provided by Landlord and Tenant Act 1954, s.47—*i.e.* within the period of three months beginning on the date on which notice is given.

Sections 4 to 7 were repealed by Landlord and Tenant Act 1954, s.45 and Sched.7, Pt I.

holding
3B-5   *I.e.* premises held under a lease. See s.17.

improvement
3B-6   There is no definition of improvement in the Act, but s.1(1) provides that it must be something which at the termination of the tenancy adds to the letting value of the holding. Erection of a new building on unoccupied land may be an improvement within the Act (s.1(1) and *National Electric Theatres v. Hudgell* [1939] Ch 553; [1939] 1 All E.R. 567). Section 2 provides that a tenant is not entitled to claim compensation in respect of certain types of improvements.

tenant
3B-7   Any person entitled in possession to the holding under any contract of tenancy, whether the interest of such tenant was acquired by original contract, assignment, operation of law or otherwise (s.25). This includes sub-tenants. Note that the designation of landlord and tenant continues to apply to the parties until the conclusion of any proceedings taken under or in pursuance of this Act in respect of compensation (s.25(2)).

landlord
3B-8   Any person who under a lease is, as between himself and the tenant or other lessee, for the time being entitled to the rents and profits of the demised premises payable under the lease (s.25).

trade or business
3B-9   There is no definition of trade or business in the 1927 Act. It is generally accepted that the phrase is to be interpreted in a narrower sense than in the 1954 Act (see *e.g. Stuchbery v. General Accident Fire and Life Assurance Corporation* [1949] 2 K.B. 256; [1949] 1 All E.R. 1026, CA—solicitors carrying on profession, not trade or business, not entitled to compensation under the 1927 Act, but see s.17(3) and (4)).

procedural requirements
3B-10   A tenant must serve on the landlord notice of intention to make improvements before carrying them out. The notice must be accompanied by a plan (s.3(1)). There is no prescribed form. Notice may be given in the form of a letter. See *Deerfield Travel Services v. Wardens and Society of the Mistery or Art of the Leather Sellers* (1983) 46 P& C.R. 132, CA. The tenant may carry out the works if the landlord raises no objection within three months, even if a covenant in the lease provides otherwise. If the landlord objects, the tenant may apply to the court for a certificate that the improvement is a proper one (s.3(1)).

tribunal
3B-11   *I.e.* a county court or the High Court. See s.21 and Landlord and Tenant Act 1954, s.63. For the procedure see Vol. 1, PD56, para. 5.

the amount of compensation

See s.1(1). The landlord pays for the benefit received from the improvement. The **3B–12** sum to be paid shall not exceed the net addition to the value of the holding as a whole or the reasonable cost of carrying out the improvement at the termination of the tenancy.

Limitation on tenant's right to compensation in certain cases

2.—(1) A tenant shall not be entitled to compensation under this **3B–13** Part of this Act—

(a) in respect of any improvement made before the commencement of this Act; or

(b) in respect of any improvement made in pursuance of a statutory obligation, or of any improvement which the tenant or his predecessors in title were under an obligation to make in pursuance of a contract entered into, whether before or after the passing of this Act, for valuable consideration, including a building lease; or

(c) in respect of any improvement made less than three years before the termination of the tenancy; or

(d) if within two months after the making of the claim under section one, subsection (1), of this Act the landlord serves on the tenant notice that he is willing and able to grant to the tenant, or obtain the grant to him of, a renewal of the tenancy at such rent and for such term as, failing agreement, the tribunal may consider reasonable; and, where such a notice is so served and the tenant does not within one month from the service of the notice send to the landlord an acceptance in writing of the offer, the tenant shall be deemed to have declined the offer.

(2) Where an offer of the renewal of a tenancy by the landlord under this section is accepted by the tenant, the rent fixed by the tribunal shall be the rent which in the opinion of the tribunal a willing lessee other than the tenant would agree to give and a willing lessor would agree to accept for the premises, having regard to the terms of the lease, but irrespective of the value attributable to the improvement in respect of which compensation would have been payable.

(3) The tribunal in determining the compensation for an improvement shall in reduction of the tenant's claim take into consideration any benefits which the tenant or his predecessors in title may have received from the landlord or his predecessors in title in consideration expressly or impliedly of the improvement.

Note—The effect of s.2(1)(b) is restricted by Landlord and Tenant Act 1954, s.48(1). **3B–14**

tenant

Any person entitled in possession to the holding under any contract of tenancy, **3B–15** whether the interest of such tenant was acquired by original contract, assignment, operation of law or otherwise (s.25). This includes sub-tenants. Note that the designation of landlord and tenant continues to apply to the parties until the conclusion of any proceedings taken under or in pursuance of this Act in respect of compensation (s.25(2)).

landlord

Any person who under a lease is, as between himself and the tenant or other lessee, **3B–16** for the time being entitled to the rents and profits of the demised premises payable under the lease (s.25).

improvement

3B–17   See commentary to s.1.

tribunal

3B–18   *i.e.* a county court or the High Court. See s.21 and Landlord and Tenant Act 1954, s.63.

Landlord's right to object

3B–19   **3.**—(1) Where a tenant of a holding to which this Part of this Act applies proposes to make an improvement on his holding, he shall serve on his landlord notice of his intention to make such improvement, together with a specification and plan showing the proposed improvement and the part of the existing premises affected thereby, and if the landlord, within three months after the service of the notice, serves on the tenant notice of objection, the tenant may, in the prescribed manner, apply to the tribunal, and the tribunal may, after ascertaining that notice of such intention has been served upon any superior landlords interested and after giving such persons an opportunity of being heard, if satisfied that the improvement—

    (a) is of such a nature as to be calculated to add to the letting value of the holding at the termination of the tenancy; and

    (b) is reasonable and suitable to the character thereof; and

    (c) will not diminish the value of any other property belonging to the same landlord, or to any superior landlord from whom the immediate landlord of the tenant directly or indirectly holds;

and after making such modifications (if any) in the specification or plan as the tribunal thinks fit, or imposing such other conditions as the tribunal may think reasonable, certify in the prescribed manner that the improvement is a proper improvement.

Provided that, if the landlord proves that he has offered to execute the improvement himself in consideration of a reasonable increase of rent, or of such increase of rent as the tribunal may determine, the tribunal shall not give a certificate under this section unless it is subsequently shown to the satisfaction of the tribunal that the landlord has failed to carry out his undertaking.

(2) In considering whether the improvement is reasonable and suitable to the character of the holding, the tribunal shall have regard to any evidence brought before it by the landlord or any superior landlord (but not any other person) that the improvement is calculated to injure the amenity or convenience of the neighbourhood.

(3) The tenant shall, at the request of any superior landlord or at the request of the tribunal, supply such copies of the plans and specifications of the proposed improvement as may be required.

(4) Where no such notice of objection as aforesaid to a proposed improvement has been served within the time allowed by this section, or where the tribunal has certified an improvement to be a

proper improvement, it shall be lawful for the tenant as against the immediate and any superior landlord to execute the improvement according to the plan and specification served on the landlord, or according to such plan and specification as modified by the tribunal or by agreement between the tenant and the landlord or landlords affected, anything in any lease of the premises to the contrary notwithstanding:

Provided that nothing in this subsection shall authorise a tenant to execute an improvement in contravention of any restriction created or imposed—

    (a) for naval, military or air force purposes;

    (b) for civil aviation purposes under the powers of the Air Navigation Act, 1920;

    (c) for securing any rights of the public over the foreshore or bed of the sea.

(5) A tenant shall not be entitled to claim compensation under this Part of this Act in respect of any improvement unless he has, or his predecessors in title have, served notice of the proposal to make the improvement under this section, and (in case the landlord has served notice of objection thereto) the improvement has been certified by the tribunal to be a proper improvement and the tenant has complied with the conditions, if any, imposed by the tribunal, nor unless the improvement is completed within such time after the service on the landlord of the notice of the proposed improvement as may be agreed between the tenant and the landlord or may be fixed by the tribunal, and where proceedings have been taken before the tribunal, the tribunal may defer making any order as to costs until the expiration of the time so fixed for the completion of the improvement.

(6) Where a tenant has executed an improvement of which he has served notice in accordance with this section and with respect to which either no notice of objection has been served by the landlord or a certificate that it is a proper improvement has been obtained from the tribunal, the tenant may require the landlord to furnish to him a certificate that the improvement has been duly executed; and if the landlord refuses or fails within one month after the service of the requisition to do so, the tenant may apply to the tribunal who, if satisfied that the improvement has been duly executed, shall give a certificate to that effect.

Where the landlord furnishes such a certificate, the tenant shall be liable to pay any reasonable expenses incurred for the purpose by the landlord, and if any question arises as to the reasonableness of such expenses, it shall be determined by the tribunal.

Note —Section 3 is restricted by Landlord and Tenant Act 1954, s.48(1).   **3B–20**

holding

    i.e. premises held under a lease. See s.17.   **3B–21**

tenant

    Any person entitled in possession to the holding under any contract of tenancy, **3B–22** whether the interest of such tenant was acquired by original contract, assignment, operation of law or otherwise (s.25). This includes sub-tenants. Note that the designation of landlord and tenant continues to apply to the parties until the conclusion of any proceedings taken under or in pursuance of this Act in respect of compensation (s.25(2)).

landlord

3B–23   Any person who under a lease is, as between himself and the tenant or other lessee, for the time being entitled to the rents and profits of the demised premises payable under the lease (s.25).

change of mind

3B–24   See commentary to s.1, above. Where a tenant serves a notice under s.3 stating an intention to carry out improvements, but then withdraws the notice after the landlord has served a counter notice, the landlord is not entitled to carry out the improvements (*Norfolk Capital Group Ltd v. Cadogan Estates Ltd* [2004] EWHC 384 (ChD); [2004] 32 E.G. 64; *The Times*, March 12, 2004).

improvement

3B–25   There is no definition of improvement in the Act, but s.1(1) provides that it must be something which at the termination of the tenancy adds to the letting value of the holding. See commentary to s.1, above.

tribunal

3B–26   *i.e.* a county court or the High Court. See s.21 and Landlord and Tenant Act 1954, s.63.

* * * *

Rights of mesne landlords

3B–27   8.—(1) Where, in the case of any holding, there are several persons standing in the relation to each other of lessor and lessee, the following provisions shall apply:— Any mesne landlord who has paid or is liable to pay compensation under this Part of this Act, shall, at the end of his term, be entitled to compensation from his immediate landlord in like manner and on the same conditions as if he had himself made the improvement [...] in question, except that it shall be sufficient if the claim for compensation is made at least two months before the expiration of his term: A mesne landlord shall not be entitled to make a claim under this section unless he has, within the time and in the manner prescribed, served on his immediate superior landlord copies of all documents relating to proposed improvements and claims which have been sent to him in pursuance of this Part of this Act: Where such copies are so served, the said superior landlord shall have, in addition to the mesne landlord, the powers conferred by or in pursuance of this Part of this Act in like manner as if he were the immediate landlord of the occupying tenant, and shall, in the manner and to the extent prescribed, be at liberty to appear before the tribunal and shall be bound by the proceedings:

(2) In this section, references to a landlord shall include references to his predecessors in title.

3B–28   *Note*—Section 8 was amended by Landlord and Tenant Act 1954, s.45 and Sched.7, Pts I and II.

holding

3B–29   *i.e.* premises held under a lease. See s.17.

tenant

Any person entitled in possession to the holding under any contract of tenancy, **3B–30** whether the interest of such tenant was acquired by original contract, assignment, operation of law or otherwise (s.25). This includes sub-tenants. Note that the designation of landlord and tenant continues to apply to the parties until the conclusion of any proceedings taken under or in pursuance of this Act in respect of compensation (s.25(2)).

landlord

Any person who under a lease is, as between himself and the tenant or other lessee, **3B–31** for the time being entitled to the rents and profits of the demised premises payable under the lease (s.25).

tribunal

i.e. a county court or the High Court. See s.21 and Landlord and Tenant Act 1954, **3B–32** s.63.

Restriction on contracting out

9. This Part of this Act shall apply notwithstanding any contract to **3B–33** the contrary, being a contract made at any time after the eighth day of February, nineteen hundred and twenty-seven.

Note —The former proviso to s.9 was repealed by Landlord and Tenant Act 1954, **3B–34** s.49.

Right of entry

10. The landlord of a holding to which this Part of this Act applies, **3B–35** or any person authorised by him may at all reasonable times enter on the holding or any part of it, for the purpose of executing any improvement he has undertaken to execute and of making any inspection of the premises which may reasonably be required for the purposes of this Part of this Act.

landlord

Any person who under a lease is, as between himself and the tenant or other lessee, **3B–36** for the time being entitled to the rents and profits of the demised premises payable under the lease (s.25).

holding

i.e. premises held under a lease. See s.17. **3B–37**

Right to make deductions

11.—(1) Out of any money payable to a tenant by way of compensa- **3B–38** tion under this Part of this Act, the landlord shall be entitled to deduct any sum due to him from the tenant under or in respect of the tenancy.

(2) Out of any money due to the landlord from the tenant under or in respect of the tenancy, the tenant shall be entitled to deduct any sum payable to him by the landlord by way of compensation under this Part of this Act.

tenant

Any person entitled in possession to the holding under any contract of tenancy, **3B–39** whether the interest of such tenant was acquired by original contract, assignment, operation of law or otherwise (s.25). This includes sub-tenants. Note that the designation of landlord and tenant continues to apply to the parties until the conclusion of any proceedings taken under or in pursuance of this Act in respect of compensation (s.25(2)).

landlord

3B–40   Any person who under a lease is, as between himself and the tenant or other lessee, for the time being entitled to the rents and profits of the demised premises payable under the lease (s.25).

Application of 13 & 14 Geo. 5. c.9. s.20

3B–41   **12.** Section twenty of the Agricultural Holdings Act, 1923 (which relates to charges in respect of money paid for compensation), as set out and modified in the First Schedule to this Act, shall apply to the case of money paid for compensation under this Part of this Act, including any proper costs, charges, or expenses incurred by a landlord in opposing any proposal by a tenant to execute an improvement, or in contesting a claim for compensation, and to money expended by a landlord in executing an improvement the notice of a proposal to execute which has been served on him by a tenant under this Part of this Act.

tenant

3B–42   Any person entitled in possession to the holding under any contract of tenancy, whether the interest of such tenant was acquired by original contract, assignment, operation of law or otherwise (s.25). This includes sub-tenants. Note that the designation of landlord and tenant continues to apply to the parties until the conclusion of any proceedings taken under or in pursuance of this Act in respect of compensation (s.25(2)).

landlord

3B–43   Any person who under a lease is, as between himself and the tenant or other lessee, for the time being entitled to the rents and profits of the demised premises payable under the lease (s.25).

Power to apply and raise capital money

3B–44   **13.**—(1) Capital money arising under the Settled Land Act, 1925 [...] section twenty-eight of the Law of Property Act, 1925, or under the University and College Estates Act, 1925, may be applied—

> (a) in payment as for an improvement authorised by the Act of any money expended and costs incurred by a landlord under or in pursuance of this Part of this Act in or about the execution of any improvement;
>
> (b) in payment of any sum due to a tenant under this Part of this Act in respect of compensation for an improvement [...] and any costs, charges, and expenses incidental thereto;
>
> (c) in payment of the costs, charges, and expenses of opposing any proposal by a tenant to execute an improvement.

(2) The satisfaction of a claim for such compensation as aforesaid shall be included amongst the purposes for which a tenant for life, statutory owner, trustee for sale, or personal representative may raise money under section seventy-one of the Settled Land Act, 1925.

(3) Where the landlord liable to pay compensation for an improvement [...] is a tenant for life or in a fiduciary position, he may require the sum payable as compensation and any costs, charges, and expenses incidental thereto, to be paid out of any capital money held on the same trusts as the settled land.

In this subsection "capital money" includes any personal estate held on the same trusts as the land, and "settled land" includes land held on trust for sale or vested in a personal representative.

Note —Section 13 was amended by Trusts of Land and Appointment of Trustees **3B–45** Act 1925, Sched.4 and by Landlord and Tenant Act 1954, s.45, Sched.7, Pt I.

tenant

Any person entitled in possession to the holding under any contract of tenancy, **3B–46** whether the interest of such tenant was acquired by original contract, assignment, operation of law or otherwise (s.25). This includes sub-tenants. Note that the designation of landlord and tenant continues to apply to the parties until the conclusion of any proceedings taken under or in pursuance of this Act in respect of compensation (s.25(2)).

landlord

Any person who under a lease is, as between himself and the tenant or other lessee, **3B–47** for the time being entitled to the rents and profits of the demised premises payable under the lease (s.25).

Power to sell or grant leases notwithstanding restrictions

14. Where the powers of a landlord to sell or grant leases are **3B–48** subject to any statutory or other restrictions, he shall, notwithstanding any such restrictions or any rule of law to the contrary, be entitled to offer to sell or grant any such reversion or lease as would under this Part of this Act relieve him from liability to pay compensation thereunder, and to convey and grant the same, and to execute any lease which he may be ordered to grant under this Part of this Act.

landlord

Any person who under a lease is, as between himself and the tenant or other lessee, **3B–49** for the time being entitled to the rents and profits of the demised premises payable under the lease (s.25).

Provisions as to reversionary leases

15.—(1) Where the amount which a landlord is liable to pay as **3B–50** compensation for an improvement under this Part of this Act has been determined by agreement or by an award of the tribunal, and the landlord had before the passing of this Act granted or agreed to grant a reversionary lease commencing on or after the termination of the then existing tenancy, the rent payable under the reversionary lease shall, if the tribunal so directs, be increased by such amount as, failing agreement, may be determined by the tribunal having regard to the addition to the letting value of the holding attributable to the improvement: Provided that no such increase shall be permissible unless the landlord has served or caused to be served on the reversionary lessee copies of all documents relating to the improvement when proposed which were sent to the landlord in pursuance of this Part of this Act.

(2) The reversionary lessee shall have the same right of objection to the proposed improvement and of appearing and being heard at any proceedings before the tribunal relative to the proposed improvement as if he were a superior landlord, and if the amount of compensation for the improvement is determined by the tribunal, any question as to the increase of rent under the reversionary lease shall, where practicable, be settled in the course of the same proceedings.

3B–51   *Note* —Section 15 was amended by Landlord and Tenant Act 1954, Sched.7, Pt II.

holding

3B–52   *i.e.* premises held under a lease. See s.17.

landlord

3B–53   Any person who under a lease is, as between himself and the tenant or other lessee, for the time being entitled to the rents and profits of the demised premises payable under the lease (s.25).

tribunal

3B–54   *i.e.* a county court or the High Court. See s.21 and Landlord and Tenant Act 1954, s.63.

Landlord's right to reimbursement of increased taxes, rates or insurance premiums

3B–55   **16.** Where the landlord is liable to pay any [...] rates (including water rate) in respect of any premises comprised in a holding, or has undertaken to pay the premiums on any fire insurance policy on any such premises, and in consequence of any improvement executed by the tenant on the premises under this Act the assessment of the premises or the rate of premium on the policy is increased, the tenant shall be liable to pay to the landlord sums equal to the amount by which—

(a) the [...] rates payable by the landlord are increased by reason of the increase of such assessment;

(b) the fire premium payable by the landlord is increased by reason of the increase in the rate of premium;

and the sums so payable by the tenant shall be deemed to be in the nature of rent and shall be recoverable as such from the tenant, [...].

3B–56   *Note* —Section 16 was amended by Rent Act 1968, s.67(2); Finance Act 1963, Sched.13, Pt IV; and Housing Act 1980, s.152 and Sched.26.

tenant

3B–57   Any person entitled in possession to the holding under any contract of tenancy, whether the interest of such tenant was acquired by original contract, assignment, operation of law or otherwise (s.25). This includes sub-tenants. Note that the designation of landlord and tenant continues to apply to the parties until the conclusion of any proceedings taken under or in pursuance of this Act in respect of compensation (s.25(2)).

landlord

3B–58   Any person who under a lease is, as between himself and the tenant or other lessee, for the time being entitled to the rents and profits of the demised premises payable under the lease (s.25).

holding

3B–59   *i.e.* premises held under a lease. See s.17.

Holdings to which Part I. applies

3B–60   **17.**—(1) The holdings to which this Part of this Act applies are any premises held under a lease, other than a mining lease, made whether before or after the commencement of this Act, and used wholly or partly for carrying on thereat any trade or business, and [not being—

(a) agricultural holdings within the meaning of the Agricultural Holdings Act 1986 held under leases in relation to which that Act applies, or

(b) holdings held under farm business tenancies within the meaning of the Agricultural Tenancies Act 1995]

(2) This Part of this Act shall not apply to any holding let to a tenant as the holder of any office, appointment or employment, from the landlord, and continuing so long as the tenant holds such office, appointment or employment, but in the case of a tenancy created after the commencement of this Act, only if the contract is in writing and expresses the purpose for which the tenancy is created.

(3) For the purposes of this section, premises shall not be deemed to be premises used for carrying on thereat a trade or business—

(a) by reason of their being used for the purpose of carrying on thereat any profession;

(b) by reason that the tenant thereof carries on the business of subletting the premises as residential flats, whether or not the provision of meals or any other service for the occupants of the flats is undertaken by the tenant.

Provided that, so far as this Part of this Act relates to improvements, premises regularly used for carrying on a profession shall be deemed to be premises used for carrying on a trade or business.

(4) In the case of premises used partly for purposes of a trade or business and partly for other purposes, this Part of this Act shall apply to improvements only if and so far as they are improvements in relation to the trade or business.

Note —Section 17 was amended by the Agricultural Tenancies Act 1995, Sched.1. **3B–61**

tenant

Any person entitled in possession to the holding under any contract of tenancy, **3B–62** whether the interest of such tenant was acquired by original contract, assignment, operation of law or otherwise (s.25). This includes sub-tenants. Note that the designation of landlord and tenant continues to apply to the parties until the conclusion of any proceedings taken under or in pursuance of this Act in respect of compensation (s.25(2)).

landlord

Any person who under a lease is, as between himself and the tenant or other lessee, **3B–63** for the time being entitled to the rents and profits of the demised premises payable under the lease (s.25).

mining lease

A lease for any mining purpose or purposes connected therewith, and "mining **3B–64** purposes" include the sinking and searching for, winning, working, getting, making merchantable, smelting or otherwise converting or working for the purposes of any manufacture, carrying away, and disposing of mines and minerals, in or under land, and the erection of buildings, and the execution of engineering and other works suitable for those purposes (s.25)

trade or business

There is no definition of trade or business in the 1927 Act. It is generally accepted **3B–65** that the phrase is to be interpreted in a narrower sense than in the 1954 Act (see *e.g. Stuchbery v. General Accident Fire and Life Assurance Corporation* [1949] 2 K.B. 256; [1949] 1 All E.R. 1026, CA—solicitors carrying on profession, not trade or business, not entitled to compensation under the 1927 Act, but see s.17(3) and (4)).

PART II

GENERAL AMENDMENTS OF THE LAW OF LANDLORD AND TENANT

Provisions as to covenants to repair

3B–66 18.—(1) Damages for a breach of a covenant or agreement to keep or put premises in repair during the currency of a lease, or to leave or put premises in repair at the termination of a lease, whether such covenant or agreement is expressed or implied, and whether general or specific, shall in no case exceed the amount (if any) by which the value of the reversion (whether immediate or not) in the premises is diminished owing to the breach of such covenant or agreement as aforesaid; and in particular no damage shall be recovered for a breach of any such covenant or agreement to leave or put premises in repair at the termination of a lease, if it is shown that the premises, in whatever state of repair they might be, would at or shortly after the termination of the tenancy have been or be pulled down, or such structural alterations made therein as would render valueless the repairs covered by the covenant or agreement.

(2) A right of re-entry or forfeiture for a breach of any such covenant or agreement as aforesaid shall not be enforceable, by action or otherwise, unless the lessor proves that the fact that such a notice as is required by section one hundred and forty-six of the Law of Property Act, 1925, had been served on the lessee was known either—

    (a) to the lessee; or

    (b) to an under-lessee holding under an under-lease which reserved a nominal reversion only to the lessee; or

    (c) to the person who last paid the rent due under the lease either on his own behalf or as agent for the lessee or under-lessee;

and that a time reasonably sufficient to enable the repairs to be executed had elapsed since the time when the fact of the service of the notice came to the knowledge of any such person.

Where a notice has been sent by registered post addressed to a person at his last known place of abode in the United Kingdom, then, for the purposes of this subsection, that person shall be deemed, unless the contrary is proved, to have had knowledge of the fact that the notice had been served as from the time at which the letter would have been delivered in the ordinary course of post.

This subsection shall be construed as one with section one hundred and forty-six of the Law of Property Act, 1925.

(3) This section applies whether the lease was created before or after the commencement of this Act.

3B–67 *Note* —Section 18 was amended by the Recorded Delivery Service Act 1962, s.1, Sched.

re-entry or forfeiture

3B–68 See the commentary to Law of Property Act 1925, s.146 at para. 3A–16.

deemed knowledge

3B–69 See the commentary to s.23 below.

Provisions as to covenants not to assign, &c. without licence or consent

19.—(1) In all leases whether made before or after the commence- **3B–70** ment of this Act containing a covenant condition or agreement against assigning, underletting, charging or parting with the possession of demised premises or any part thereof without licence or consent, such covenant condition or agreement shall, notwithstanding any express provision to the contrary, be deemed to be subject—

    (a) to a proviso to the effect that such licence or consent is not to be unreasonably withheld, but this proviso does not preclude the right of the landlord to require payment of a reasonable sum in respect of any legal or other expenses incurred in connection with such licence or, consent; and

    (b) (if the lease is for more than forty years, and is made in consideration wholly or partially of the erection, or the substantial improvement, addition or alteration of buildings, and the lessor is not a Government department or local or public authority, or a statutory or public utility company) to a proviso to the effect that in the case of any assignment, under-letting, charging or parting with the possession (whether by the holders of the lease or any under-tenant whether immediate or not) effected more than seven years before the end of the term no consent or licence shall be required, if notice in writing of the transaction is given to the lessor within six months after the transaction is effected.

(1A) Where the landlord and the tenant under a qualifying lease have entered into an agreement specifying for the purposes of this subsection—

    (a) any circumstances in which the landlord may withhold his licence or consent to an assignment of the demised premises or any part of them, or

    (b) any conditions subject to which any such licence or consent may be granted,

then the landlord—

        (i) shall not be regarded as unreasonably withholding his licence or consent to any such assignment if he withholds it on the ground (and it is the case) that any such circumstances exist, and

        (ii) if he gives any such licence or consent subject to any such conditions, shall not be regarded as giving it subject to unreasonable conditions;

and section 1 of the Landlord and Tenant Act 1988 (qualified duty to consent to assignment etc.) shall have effect subject to the provisions of this subsection.

(1B) Subsection (1A) of this section applies to such an agreement as is mentioned in that subsection—

    (a) whether it is contained in the lease or not, and

    (b) whether it is made at the time when the lease is granted or at any other time falling before the application for the landlord's licence or consent is made.

(1C) Subsection (1A) shall not, however, apply to any such agreement to the extent that any circumstances or conditions specified in it are framed by reference to any matter falling to be determined by the landlord or by any other person for the purposes of the agreement, unless under the terms of the agreement—

(a) that person's power to determine that matter is required to be exercised reasonably, or

(b) the tenant is given an unrestricted right to have any such determination reviewed by a person independent of both landlord and tenant whose identity is ascertainable by reference to the agreement,

and in the latter case the agreement provides for the determination made by any such independent person on the review to be conclusive as to the matter in question.

(1D) In its application to a qualifying lease, subsection (1)(b) of this section shall not have effect in relation to any assignment of the lease.

(1E) In subsection (1A) and (1D) of this section—

(a) "qualifying lease" means any lease which is a new tenancy for the purposes of section 1 of the Landlord and Tenant (Covenants) Act 1995 other than a residential lease, namely a lease by which a building or part of a building is let wholly or mainly as a single private residence; and

(b) references to assignment include parting with possession on assignment.

(2) In all leases whether made before or after the commencement of this Act containing a covenant condition or agreement against the making of improvements without a licence or consent, such covenant condition or agreement shall be deemed, notwithstanding any express provision to the contrary, to be subject to a proviso that such licence or consent is not to be unreasonably withheld; but this proviso does not preclude the right to require as a condition of such licence or consent the payment of a reasonable sum in respect of any damage to or diminution in the value of the premises or any neighbouring premises belonging to the landlord, and of any legal or other expenses properly incurred in connection with such licence or consent nor, in the case of an improvement which does not add to the letting value of the holding, does it preclude the right to require as a condition of such licence or consent, where such a requirement would be reasonable, an undertaking on the part of the tenant to reinstate the premises in the condition in which they were before the improvement was executed.

(3) In all leases whether made before or after the commencement of this Act containing a covenant condition or agreement against the alteration of the user of the demised premises, without licence or consent, such covenant condition or agreement shall, if the alteration does not involve any structural alteration of the premises, be deemed, notwithstanding any express provision to the contrary, to be subject

to a proviso that no fine or sum of money in the nature of a fine, whether by way of increase of rent or otherwise, shall be payable for or in respect of such licence or consent; but this proviso does not preclude the right of the landlord to require payment of a reasonable sum in respect of any damage to or diminution in the value of the premises or any neighbouring premises belonging to him and of any legal or other expenses incurred in connection with such licence or consent.

Where a dispute as to the reasonableness of any such sum has been determined by a court of competent jurisdiction, the landlord shall be bound to grant the licence or consent on payment of the sum so determined to be reasonable.

(4) This section shall not apply to leases of agricultural holdings within the meaning of the [Agricultural Holdings Act 1986], and paragraph (b) of subsection (1), subsection (2) and subsection (3) of this section shall not apply to mining leases.

Note —Section 19 has been superseded in relation to secure tenancies by Housing **3B–71** Act 1985, s.97, s.109. It was amended by Agricultural Holdings Act 1986, ss.99 and 100, Sched.13, para. 3 and Sched.14, para. 15. See too Landlord and Tenant Act 1988.

tenant

Any person entitled in possession to the holding under any contract of tenancy, **3B–72** whether the interest of such tenant was acquired by original contract, assignment, operation of law or otherwise (s.25). This includes sub-tenants. Note that the designation of landlord and tenant continues to apply to the parties until the conclusion of any proceedings taken under or in pursuance of this Act in respect of compensation (s.25(2)).

landlord

Any person who under a lease is, as between himself and the tenant or other lessee, **3B–73** for the time being entitled to the rents and profits of the demised premises payable under the lease (s.25).

mining lease

A lease for any mining purpose or purposes connected therewith, and "mining **3B–74** purposes" include the sinking and searching for, winning, working, getting, making merchantable, smelting or otherwise converting or working for the purposes of any manufacture, carrying away, and disposing of mines and minerals, in or under land, and the erection of buildings, and the execution of engineering and other works suitable for those purposes (s.25).

Apportionment of rents

20.—(1) An order of apportionment of a rent reserved by a lease **3B–75** or any such other rent or payment as is mentioned in section ten of the Inclosure Act, 1854, may be made by the under sections ten to fourteen of that Act, on the application of any person interested in the rent or payment, or any part thereof, or in the land in respect of which such rent or payment is payable, without the concurrence of any other person: Provided that the Minister may in any such case, on the application of any person entitled to the rent or payment or any part thereof, require as a condition of making the order that any apportioned part of the rent or payment which does not exceed the yearly sum of [£5] shall be redeemed forthwith [in accordance with sections 8 to 10 of the Rentcharges Act 1977(which, for the purposes of this section, shall have effect with the necessary modifications)].

[(1A) An order of apportionment under sections 10 to 14 of the said Act of 1854 may provide for the amount apportioned to any part of the land in respect of which the rent or payment is payable to be nil.]

(2) Where the reason for the application was due to any action taken by a person other than the applicant, the Minister shall, notwithstanding anything in section fourteen of the Inclosure Act, 1854, have power to direct by whom and in what manner the expenses of the application or any part thereof are to be paid.

3B–76 *Note*—Section 20 was amended by Housing Act 1980, s.143(1), the Rentcharges Act 1977, s.17(1) and Sched. 1, para. 3 and by Housing Act 1980, s.143(3). The functions of the Minister of Agriculture and Fisheries under s.20 are now exercisable by the Secretary of State: see Transfer of Functions (Ministry of Food) Order 1955 (S.I. 1995 No. 554); Minister of Land and Natural Resources Order 1965 (S.I. 1965 No. 143); Ministry of Land and Natural Resources (Dissolution) Order 1967 (S.I. 1967 No. 156) and Secretary of State for the Environment Order 1970 (S.I. 1970 No. 1681).

The tribunal

3B–77 **21.** The tribunal for the purposes of Part I of this Act shall be the court exercising jurisdiction in accordance with the provisions of section sixty-three of the Landlord and Tenant Act, 1954.

3B–78 *Note*—The current s.21 was substituted by Landlord and Tenant Act 1954, s.63(10).

* * * * *

Service of notices

3B–79 **23.**—(1) Any notice, request, demand or other instrument under this Act shall be in writing and may be served on the person on whom it is to be served either personally, or by leaving it for him at his last known place of abode in England or Wales, or by sending it through the post in a registered letter addressed to him there, or, in the case of a local or public authority or a statutory or a public utility company, to the secretary or other proper officer at the principal office of such authority or company, and in the case of a notice to a landlord, the person on whom it is to be served shall include any agent of the landlord duly authorised in that behalf.

(1A) Occupation or the carrying on of a business—

(a) by a company in which the tenant has a controlling interest; or

(b) where the tenant is a company, by a person with a controlling interest in the company,

shall be treated for the purposes of this section as equivalent to occupation or, as the case may be, the carrying on of a business by the tenant.

(1B) Accordingly references (however expressed) in this Part of this Act to the business of, or to use, occupation or enjoyment by, the tenant shall be construed as including references to the business of, or to use, occupation or enjoyment by, a company falling within subsection (1A)(a) above or a person falling within subsection (1A)(b) above.

(2) Unless or until a tenant of a holding shall have received notice that the person theretofore entitled to the rents and profits of the holding (hereinafter referred to as "the original landlord") has ceased to be so entitled, and also notice of the name and address of the person who has become entitled to such rents and profits, any claim, notice, request, demand, or other instrument which the tenant shall serve upon or deliver to the original landlord shall be deemed to have been served upon or delivered to the landlord of such holding.

Note —Section 23 was amended by the Recorded Delivery Service Act 1962, s.1.　　**3B–80**

tenant

Any person entitled in possession to the holding under any contract of tenancy, **3B–81** whether the interest of such tenant was acquired by original contract, assignment, operation of law or otherwise (s.25). This includes sub-tenants. Note that the designation of landlord and tenant continues to apply to the parties until the conclusion of any proceedings taken under or in pursuance of this Act in respect of compensation (s.25(2)).

landlord

Any person who under a lease is, as between himself and the tenant or other lessee, **3B–82** for the time being entitled to the rents and profits of the demised premises payable under the lease (s.25).

service of notices

Section 23 provides that any notice, request, demand or other instrument can be **3B–83** served personally or left at the last known place of abode (which includes place of business—*Price v. West London Investment Building Society Ltd* [1964] 1 W.L.R. 616; [1964] 2 All E.R. 318, CA; *cf. Arundel Corp v. Khokher* [2003] EWCA Civ 1784; [2004 148 S.J.L.B. 25) of the person to be served or posted by registered or recorded delivery (s.1 of the Recorded Delivery Service Act 1962). (As to change of landlords, see s.23(2)). If one of these methods of service is adopted, service is deemed to be effected even if the document is not received by the intended recipient, if, for example, it is returned by the Post Office (*Blunden v. Frogmore Investments Ltd* [2002] EWCA Civ 573; [2003] 2 P. & C.R. 6; [2003] 29 E.G. 153). If a notice is sent by recorded delivery, it is irrefutably deemed to have been served on the date that the notice was put in the post and not on the date of actual receipt (*Beanby Estates Ltd v. Egg Stores (Stamford Hill) Ltd* [2003] EWHC 1252 (Ch); [2003] 1 W.L.R. 2064) and *CA Webber (Transport) Ltd v. Network Rail Infrastructure Ltd (formerly Railtrack Plc)* [2003] EWCA Civ 1167; [2004] 1 W.L.R. 320; *The Times*, August 5, 2003).

Application to Crown, Duchy, ecclesiastical and charity lands

24.—(1) This Act shall apply to land belonging to His Majesty in **3B–84** right of the Crown or the Duchy of Lancaster and to land belonging to the Duchy of Cornwall, and to land belonging to any Government department, and for that purpose the provisions of the Agricultural Holdings Act, 1923, relating to Crown and Duchy lands, as set out and adapted in Part I of the Second Schedule to this Act, shall have effect.

(2) The provisions of the Agricultural Holdings Act, 1923, with respect to the application of that Act to ecclesiastical and charity lands, as set out and adapted in Part II of the Second Schedule to this Act, shall apply for the purposes of this Act.

(3) [Repealed by Endowments and Glebe Measure 1976 (No. 4), s. 47(4), Sch. 8].

(4) Where any land is vested in the [official custodian for chari-

ties] in trust for any charity, the trustees of the charity and not the [custodian] shall be deemed to be the landlord for the purposes of this Act.

3B–85 *Note* —Section 24 was amended by Charities Act 1960, Sched.6. The functions of the Ecclesiastical Commissioners are now exercisable by the Church Commissioners— see Church Commissioners Measure 1947 (No. 2), s.2.

Interpretation

3B–86 **25.**—(1) For the purposes of this Act, unless the context otherwise requires—

The expression "tenant" means any person entitled in possession to the holding under any contract of tenancy, whether the interest of such tenant was acquired by original contract, assignment, operation of law or otherwise;

The expression "landlord" means any person who under a lease is, as between himself and the tenant or other lessee, for the time being entitled to the rents and profits of the demised premises payable under the lease;

The expression "predecessor in title" in relation to a tenant or landlord means any person through whom the tenant or landlord has derived title, whether by assignment, by will, by intestacy, or by operation of law;

The expression "lease" means a lease, under-lease or other tenancy, assignment operating as a lease or under-lease, or an agreement for such lease, under-lease tenancy, or assignment;

The expression "mining lease" means a lease for any mining purpose or purposes connected therewith, and

"mining purposes" include the sinking and searching for, winning, working, getting, making merchantable, smelting or otherwise converting or working for the purposes of any manufacture, carrying away, and disposing of mines and minerals, in or under land, and the erection of buildings, and the execution of engineering and other works suitable for those purposes;

The expression "term of years absolute" has the same meaning as in the Law of Property Act, 1925;

The expression "statutory company" means any company constituted by or under an Act of Parliament to construct, work or carry on any [...], tramway, hydraulic power, dock, canal or railway undertaking;

and the expression "public utility company" means any company within the meaning of the Companies (Consolidation) Act, 1908, or a society registered under the Industrial and Provident Societies Acts, 1893 to 1913, carrying on any such undertaking;

The expression "prescribed" means [prescribed by rules of court or by a practice direction].

(2) The designation of landlord and tenant shall continue to apply to the parties until the conclusion of any proceedings taken under or in pursuance of this Act in respect of compensation.

Note —Section 25 was amended by the Gas Act 1986, s.67(3)(4), Sched.8, para. 17, **3B–87**
Sched.9, Pt 1, the Water Act 1989, s.190(3), Sched.27, Pt 1, the Electricity Act 1989,
s.112(3)(4), Sched.17, para. 35(1), Sched.18 and by S.I. 2001 No. 2717, art.3.

Short title, commencement and extent

26.—(1) This Act may be cited as the Landlord and Tenant Act **3B–88**
1927.

(2) [Repealed by Statute Law Revision Act 1950 (c. 6)]

(3) This Act shall extend to England and Wales only.

Landlord and Tenant Act 1954

(2 & 3 ELIZ. 2 c.56)

PART II

SECURITY OF TENURE FOR BUSINESS, PROFESSIONAL AND OTHER TENANTS

3B–89

Editorial note

Part II of the Landlord and Tenant Act 1954 contains provisions regulating secu- **3B–90**
rity of tenure as between landlords and tenants of business premises. Significant
amendments were made by the Regulatory Reform (Business Tenancies) (England
and Wales) Order 2003 (S.I. 2003 No. 3096). These amendments apply to cases where
the landlord gave a statutory notice of termination, or the tenant made a statutory
request for a new tenancy on or after June 1, 2004—see the Regulatory Reform (Business Tenancies) (England and Wales) Order 2003 (S.I. 2003 No. 3096) para. 29(1).
The full text of para. 29 is as at 3B–92:

Part II of the Act is reproduced as amended by the 2003 Reform Order. It will be **3B–91**
necessary to refer to the Act in its unamended form where the transitional provisions
apply.

The Order implements most of the recommendations of the Law Commission
contained in their 1992 paper Business Tenancies: A Periodic Review of the Landlord
and Tenant Act Pt II (Law Com No.208).

In brief, the Order—

- changes the procedures to be followed to renew a tenancy or to terminate it
  without renewal. Both landlords and tenants are permitted to apply to the
  court for the terms of a new tenancy to be settled. Landlords are permitted to
  apply for an order that the tenancy be terminated without renewal if they can
  make out one of the statutory grounds for opposition. The requirement for a
  tenant to serve a counter-notice to a landlord's notice of termination is
  abolished.
- substitutes new time limits for applications to the court to renew tenancies and
  enables the parties to agree to extend these.
- widens the circumstances in which landlord and tenant can operate the statutory procedures of Pt II. An individual and any company s/he controls should
  be treated as one and the same for the purposes of those procedures.
  Companies controlled by one individual should be treated as members of a
  group of companies.
- introduces several changes relating to interim rent. Tenants as well as landlords
  are allowed to apply to the court for interim rent. The date from which any
  interim rent determined by the court is payable becomes the earliest date for
  renewal of the tenancy which could have been specified in the statutory notice
  served by the landlord or tenant. A new method for the calculation of the
  amount of interim rent is introduced where the landlord does not oppose
  renewal. The interim rent is set at the same level as the rent for the new
  tenancy (*i.e.* usually, the open market rent), but subject to adjustment where

market conditions or the occupational terms of the tenancy change significantly during the interim period. In other circumstances, the rules for calculation of interim rent formerly in s.24A(3), and now contained in s.24D(2), continue to apply although in a slightly modified form.

- amends the rules relating to the compensation that tenants may claim where their tenancies are not renewed. It changes the method of calculation of compensation where the tenant has occupied different parts of premises for different periods of time, and where different landlords control different parts. It also enables a tenant to claim compensation if induced not to apply to court, or to withdraw an application for renewal, because of a misrepresentation.
- replaces the requirement for both parties to apply to court for approval to an agreement to exclude security of tenure or to surrender a tenancy. The new procedure requires a landlord to serve a prescribed notice on the tenant at least 14 days before the parties enter into such an agreement. Tenants must sign a simple declaration that they have received and accepted the consequences of the notice. If the parties wish to waive the 14 day period, tenants have to sign a statutory declaration, rather than a simple declaration, that they have received and accepted the consequences of the notice. In the case of an agreement to exclude security of tenure, the declaration must be made before the tenant enters into the tenancy or becomes contractually bound to do so. In the case of an agreement to surrender, the declaration must be made before entering into the agreement. The forms of the notice, the simple declaration and the statutory declaration are set out in Scheds 1 to 4 to the Order.
- increases the categories of information which a landlord and tenant can require the other to provide towards the end of a tenancy term, in order to enable effective use of the statutory renewal or termination process. They also impose an obligation to keep such information up to date for six months, make provision for parties which transfer their interests and clarify the powers of the court where a party fails to comply with obligations to provide or update information.
- clarifies what a tenant must do to terminate a tenancy to which Pt II applies. If a tenant has ceased to occupy the business premises at the expiry of the contractual term, no continuation tenancy arises. Where a tenancy has continued beyond the end of the fixed contractual term, the tenant must give three months notice, ending on any day. Where necessary, rent is apportioned.
- increases the length of the term of a new tenancy that the court may order from 14 to 15 years.

Transitional provisions

3B–92

Paragraph 29 of the 2003 Reform Order contains transitional provisions. The most important of these for the purposes of proceedings is contained in para. 29(1). The effect of this paragraph is that Pt II of the 1954 Act as amended only applies where the s.25 notice or s.26 request was served on or after June 1, 2004 (when the 2003 Reform Order came into force). Where the notice or request was served before that date Pt II in its unamended form continues to apply. The full text of para. 29 of the 2003 Reform Order is as follows:

29.—(1) Where, before this Order came into force—
    (a) the landlord gave the tenant notice under section 25 of the Act; or
    (b) the tenant made a request for a new tenancy in accordance with section 26 of the Act,
    nothing in this Order has effect in relation to the notice or request or anything done in consequence of it.

(2) Nothing in this Order has effect in relation—
    (a) to an agreement—
        (i) for the surrender of a tenancy which was made before this Order came into force and which fell within section 24(2)(b) of the Act; or
        (ii) which was authorised by the court under section 38(4) of the Act before this Order came into force; or
    (b) to a notice under section 27(2) of the Act which was given by the tenant to the immediate landlord before this Order came into force.

(3) Any provision in a tenancy which requires an order under section 38(4) of the Act to be obtained in respect of any subtenancy shall, so far as is necessary after the coming into force of this Order, be construed as if it required the procedure mentioned in section 38A of the Act to be followed, and any related requirement shall be construed accordingly.

(4) If a person has, before the coming into force of this Order, entered into an agreement to take a tenancy, any provision in that agreement which requires an order under section 38(4) of the Act to be obtained in respect of the tenancy shall continue to be effective, notwithstanding the repeal of that provision by Article 21(2) of this Order, and the court shall retain jurisdiction to make such an order.

(5) Article 20 above does not have effect where the tenant quit the holding before this Order came into force.

(6) Nothing in Articles 23 and 24 above applies to a notice under section 40 of the Act served before this Order came into force.

PART II

Tenancies to which Part II applies

23.—(1) Subject to the provisions of this Act, this Part of this Act **3B–93** applies to any tenancy where the property comprised in the tenancy is or includes premises which are occupied by the tenant and are so occupied for the purposes of a business carried on by him or for those and other purposes.

(1A) Occupation or the carrying on of a business—

    (a) by a company in which the tenant has a controlling interest; or

    (b) where the tenant is a company, by a person with a controlling interest in the company, shall be treated for the purposes of this section as equivalent to occupation or, as the case may be, the carrying on of a business by the tenant.

(1B) Accordingly references (however expressed) in this Part of this Act to the business of, or to use, occupation or enjoyment by, the tenant shall be construed as including references to the business of, or to use, occupation or enjoyment by, a company falling within subsection (1A)(a) above or a person falling within subsection (1A)(b) above.

(2) In this Part of this Act the expression "business" includes a trade, profession or employment and includes any activity carried on by a body of persons, whether corporate or unincorporate.

(3) In the following provisions of this Part of this Act the expression "the holding", in relation to a tenancy to which this Part of this Act applies, means the property comprised in the tenancy, there being excluded any part thereof which is occupied neither by the tenant nor by a person employed by the tenant and so employed for the purposes of a business by reason of which the tenancy is one to which this Part of this Act applies.

(4) Where the tenant is carrying on a business, in all or any part of the property comprised in a tenancy, in breach of a prohibition (however expressed) of use for business purposes which subsists under the terms of the tenancy and extends to the whole of that property, this Part of this Act shall not apply to the tenancy unless the immediate landlord or his predecessor in title has consented to the breach or the immediate landlord has acquiesced therein.

In this subsection the reference to a prohibition of use for business purposes does not include a prohibition of use for the purposes of a specified business, or of use for purposes of any but a specified business, but save as aforesaid includes a prohibition of use for the purposes of some one or more only of the classes of business specified in the definition of that expression in subsection (2) of this section.

3B–94   *Note* —Paragraphs (1A) and (1B) were added by para. 13 of the Regulatory Reform (Business Tenancies)(England and Wales) Order 2003 (S.I. 2003 No. 3096).

tenancy

3B–95   See s.69(1). The definition includes an agreement for a lease or underlease, but does not include a mortgage. It also makes it clear that the Act applies to tenancies which have already been renewed under the provisions of the Act. Part II applies to sub tenancies. If a sub tenancy is granted in breach of a covenant, the superior landlord is not bound by the sub tenancy and may exercise rights of forfeiture, but the sub tenant, as against the mesne landlord may exercise the rights given by the Act (see s.69(1), *HL Bolton Engineering Co Ltd v. TJ Graham & Sons Ltd* [1957] 1 Q.B. 159; [1956] 3 W.L.R. 804; [1956] 3 All E.R. 624, CA, and *D'Silva v. Lister House Developments Ltd* [1971] Ch. 17; [1970] 2 W.L.R. 563; [1970] 1 All E.R. 858 (ChD)).

However, Landlord and Tenant Act 1954 Pt II does not apply to licences—see *e.g. Shell-Mex and BP v. Manchester Garages* [1971] 1 W.L.R. 612; [1971] 1 All E.R. 841, CA (licence of petrol filling station) and *Dresden Estates v. Collinson* (1988) 55 P. & C.R. 47, CA (licence of workshop and store) *National Car Parks Ltd v. Trinity Development Co (Banbury) Ltd* [2001] L. & T.R. 33 (car park) and *Clear Channel UK Ltd v. Manchester City Council* [2004] EWHC 2873 (advertising hoardings). Tenancies at will are also excluded from statutory protection, although courts will look carefully at any agreements which are alleged to be tenancies at will (*Hagee (London) Ltd v. AB Erikson and Larson* [1976] Q.B. 209; [1975] 3 W.L.R. 272; [1975] 3 All E.R. 234; (1975) 29 P. & C.R. 512, CA and *Manfield & Sons v. Botchin* [1970] 2 Q.B. 612; [1970] 3 W.L.R 120; [1970] 3 All E.R. 143, QBD).

tenant

3B–96   If there are joint tenants, for the purposes of the Act, "tenant" means all the joint tenants in whom the legal estate is vested (*Jacobs v. Chaudhuri* [1968] 2 Q.B. 470; [1968] 2 W.L.R. 1098; [1968] 2 All E.R. 124, CA) As to partnerships, see s.41A below and for groups of companies, see s.42 below.

Occupation by tenant for purposes of a business

3B–97   See ss.23(1) and (2). Landlord and Tenant Act 1954 Pt II only applies where the property comprised in the tenancy is occupied by the tenant for the purposes of a business carried on by him. As to "business", see s.46 and s.23(2) which provides that "business" includes a trade, profession or employment and includes any activity carried on by a body of persons, whether corporate or unincorporate. Residential premises may be occupied for the purpose of a business if the business activity is "a significant purpose" (see *e.g. Cheryl Investments v. Saldanha* [1978] 1 W.L.R. 1329; [1979] 1 All E.R. 5, CA; *Gurton v. Parrott* (1991) 23 H.L.R. 418; [1991] 18 E.G. 161, CA; *Florent v. Horez* (1983) 12 H.L.R. 1; (1984) 48 P. & C.R. 166, CA; *Lewis v. Weldcrest* [1978] 1 W.L.R. 1107; [1978] 3 All E.R. 1226, CA; and *Wright v. Mortimer* (1996) 28 H.L.R. 719, CA).

Premises are occupied if the tenant physically uses them and is able to control the day to day use of them by other persons (*Commissioner of Valuation for Northern Ireland v. Fermanagh Protestant Board of Education* [1969] 1 W.L.R. 1708; [1969] 3 All E.R. 352, HL (a rating case). See too Hancock & Willis v. *G.M.S. Syndicate* [1983] 1 E.G.L.R. 70, CA; *Graysim Holdings Ltd v. P&O Property Holdings Ltd* [1994] 1 W.L.R. 992; [1994] 3 All E.R. 897, CA; [1996] A.C. 329; [1995] 3 W.L.R. 854; [1995] 4 All E.R. 831, HL) There can be no continuation tenancy if the tenant has ceased to occupy the premises for business purposes before the expiry of the contractual tenancy (*Esselte AB v. Pearl Assurance Plc* [1997] 1 W.L.R. 891; [1997] 2 All E.R. 41, CA and see now s.27(1A) below). Occupation for the purposes of a business is a question of fact and degree.

The mere fact that premises are empty does not take them outside Pt II—e.g. if structural repairs are needed (*I&H Caplan Ltd v. Caplan (No. 2)* [1963] 1 W.L.R. 1247; [1963] 2 All E.R. 930, Ch D—where the tenant closed down a general clothing and footwear business, sold off stock, but remained in occupation prior to re-opening solely selling ladies' garments). Premises may be occupied through employees, agents or managers (*Linden v. Department of Health and Social Security* [1986] 1 W.L.R. 164; [1986] 1 All E.R. 691, ChD.) Protection is not lost if premises are shared but if the whole of premises are sub-let, it is the sub-tenant who is likely to be in occupation, not the mesne tenant (*Graysim Holdings Ltd v. P&O Property Holdings Ltd* [1994] 1 W.L.R. 992; [1994] 3 All E.R. 897, CA; [1996] A.C. 329; [1995] 3 W.L.R. 854; [1995] 4 All E.R. 831, HL; *Bagettes Ltd v. GP Estates Co. Ltd* [1956] Ch. 290; [1956] 2 W.L.R. 773; [1956] 1 All E.R. 729, CA).

The county court has considered the question of shared occupation and its effect on security under Part II of the Act. In *Smith v Titanate* [2005] 20 E.G. 262 (HH Judge Roger Cooke at Central London County Court) the property was divided into six flats. The tenant ran a business of letting out the flats. The longer term lettings were on standard assured shorthold tenancies. Other lettings were on terms that included the provision of services but the judge held that these were tenancies. The question for the court was whether the tenant was in occupation of the individual flats for the purpose of a business. Held: No. The 1954 Act did not therefore apply (*Graysim Holdings Ltd v. P&O Property Holdings Ltd* [1996] A.C. 329 applied). The judge analysed three different types of situation that might arise:

- Cases where flats are let on conventional terms, with the landlord doing no more than receiving the rents and performing the landlord's covenants. In those cases there is no business occupation of the flats.
- At the other end of the spectrum cases such as common lodging houses, or hostel/student halls of residence, where there is a high degree of control and the services are performed in circumstances in which the landlord has an unfettered access to the rooms for that purpose.
- Cases in the middle where there is some degree of control and/or less restricted access and/or a greater degree of intrusive service provision. Depending on the facts these may fall on either side of the line.

If a tenant voluntarily moves out after issuing a claim for a new tenancy, the claim may be struck out. On the other hand if events over which the tenant has no control (*e.g.* a fire) lead to absence from the premises, the tenant may continue to claim occupancy (*Morrison Holdings Ltd v. Manders Property (Wolverhampton) Ltd* [1976] 1 W.L.R. 533; [1976] 2 All E.R. 205, CA and *Flairline Properties v. Hassan* [1999] 1 EGLR 138 Anthony Hacking QC, Deputy High Court Judge.

Premises occupied for the purpose of a business in breach of a covenant against business or trade use in general are outside Pt II, unless the immediate landlord or his predecessor in title has consented to the breach or the immediate landlord has acquiesced therein. However a business carried out in breach of a covenant stipulated or prohibiting a particular type of business may come within Pt II (see s.23(4)). For government departments, see s.56(3).

excluded tenancies

Part II does *not* apply to—   **3B–98**

— agricultural holdings (see s.43(1)(a));
— farm business tenancies (see s.43(1)(aa));
— mining leases (see s.43(1)(b));
— most premises licensed for the sale of intoxicating liquor for consumption on the premises (see s.43(1)(d) below, but note the exceptions);
— most residential tenancies (see Rent Act 1977, s.24(3); Housing Act 1985, Sched.1, para. 11 and Housing Act 1988, Sched.1, para. 4)
— tenancies granted by reason of office, appointment or employment (see s.43(2));
— tenancies not exceeding six months (see s.43(3), but note the exceptions);
— where contracting out was authorised under the old s.38(4);

holding

See s.23(3) and s.32—*i.e.* prima facie the whole subject-matter of the tenancy (*Heath* **3B–99** *v. Drown* [1973] A.C. 498; [1972] 2 W.L.R. 1306; [1976] 2 All E.R. 561, HL) except for those parts not occupied by the tenant or employees for business purposes.

the landlord

3B–100   See s.44(1) which provides that "the landlord" means the person (whether or not he is the immediate landlord) who is the owner of that interest in the property comprised in the relevant tenancy which for the time being fulfils the conditions contained in ss.44(1)(a) and (b).

procedure

3B–101   See CPR Pt 56, PD56 and the commentary thereto.

Continuation of tenancies to which Part II applies and grant of new tenancies

3B–102   **24.**—(1) A tenancy to which this Part of this Act applies shall not come to an end unless terminated in accordance with the provisions of this Part of this Act; and, subject to the following provisions of this Act either the tenant or the landlord under such a tenancy may apply to the court for an order for the grant of a new tenancy—

> (a) if the landlord has given notice under section 25 of this Act to terminate the tenancy, or
>
> (b) if the tenant has made a request for a new tenancy in accordance with section 26 of this Act.

(2) The last foregoing subsection shall not prevent the coming to an end of a tenancy by notice to quit given by the tenant, by surrender or forfeiture, or by the forfeiture of a superior tenancy, unless—

> (a) in the case of a notice to quit, the notice was given before the tenant had been in occupation in right of the tenancy for one month; or
>
> (b) [...]

(2A) Neither the tenant nor the landlord may make an application under subsection (1) above if the other has made such an application and the application has been served.

(2B) Neither the tenant nor the landlord may make such an application if the landlord has made an application under section 29(2) of this Act and the application has been served.

(2C) The landlord may not withdraw an application under subsection (1) above unless the tenant consents to its withdrawal.

(3) Notwithstanding anything in subsection (1) of this section—

> (a) where a tenancy to which this Part of this Act applies ceases to be such a tenancy, it shall not come to an end by reason only of the cesser, but if it was granted for a term of years certain and has been continued by subsection (1) of this section then (without prejudice to the termination thereof in accordance with any terms of the tenancy) it may be terminated by not less than three nor more than six months' notice in writing given by the landlord to the tenant;
>
> (b) where, at a time when a tenancy is not one to which this Part of this Act applies, the landlord gives notice to quit, the operation of the notice shall not be affected by reason that the tenancy becomes one to which this Part of this Act applies after the giving of the notice.

Note —The current s.24 was substituted by Law of Property Act 1969, s.15, Sched.1. **3B–103** It was amended by the Regulatory Reform (Business Tenancies) (England and Wales) Order 2003 (S.I. 2003 No. 3096) art.3. Subsection (2)(b) was repealed by Sched.6. See too Landlord and Tenant (Licensed Premises) Act 1990, s.1(2); Leasehold Reform Act 1967, s.35(2); Rent Act 1977, s.108(3) and Opencast Coal Act 1958, s.37, Sched.7, para. 22.

tenancy

See s.69(1) and the commentary to s.23 above. The definition includes an agree- **3B–104** ment for a lease or underlease, but does not include a mortgage.

notice to quit

Means a notice to quit given by the immediate landlord (see s.44(2)). **3B–105**

the landlord

See s.44(1) which provides that "the landlord" means the person (whether or not **3B–106** he is the immediate landlord) who is the owner of that interest in the property comprised in the relevant tenancy which for the time being fulfils the conditions contained in ss.44(1)(a) and (b).

continuation

Business tenancies within the ambit of Pt II do not come to an end, notwithstand- **3B–107** ing effluxion of time, unless terminated in accordance with the provisions of the Act. On effluxion they are continued automatically by s.24(1) until terminated by notice in the prescribed form given either by the landlord (as defined in s.44) or tenant. All the terms and conditions of the contractual tenancy (apart from those relating to termina- tion) continue to apply (see *e.g. Poster v. Slough Estates Ltd* [1969] 1 Ch. 495; [1968] 1 W.L.R. 1515; [1968] 3 All E.R. 257, ChD). The contractual rent continues to be pay- able, unless the landlord or the tenant applies to the court in accordance with s.24A for an interim rent. However, unless there is a clear and express provision in the contractual tenancy agreement, where the tenancy has been assigned, it is only the as- signee who is liable for rent under the continuation tenancy (*City of London Corp v. Fell* [1993] Q.B. 589; [1993] 3 W.L.R. 1164; [1993] 2 All E.R. 449, CA (affirmed in House of Lords, [1994] 1 A.C. 458; [1993] 2 W.L.R. 710; [1993] 4 All E.R. 968); *cf. GMS Syndicate Ltd v. Gary Elliott Ltd* [1982] Ch. 1; [1981] 2 W.L.R. 478; [1981] 1 All E.R. 619, ChD). If the tenant vacates before the contractual expiry of the tenancy, he is not in occupation, and so no continuation tenancy can arise. In such circumstances there is no continuing liability for rent, even if an application has been made to the court for a new tenancy (*Surrey CC v. Single Horse Properties Ltd* [2002] EWCA Civ 367; [2002] 1 W.L.R. 2106; [2002] 4 All E.R. 143).

termination

Business tenancies may be terminated by— **3B–108**
— a section 25 notice given by the landlord as defined by s.44, although, if agree- ment for a new tenancy is not reached, the tenant or the landlord may apply to the court for a new tenancy;
— a section 26 request by the tenant for a new tenancy. Again, if agreement is not reached, the tenant or the landlord may apply to the court for a new tenancy;
— a notice to quit, or notice exercising a break clause, given by the tenant (s.24(2), but note the exceptions);
— surrender (s.24(2) but see s.38 below); or
— forfeiture (s.24(2)).

application to the court

See s.29, CPR Pt 56 and PD 56. **3B–109**

Applications for determination of interim rent while tenancy continues

24A. **3B–110**

(1) Subject to subsection (2) below, if—

(a) the landlord of a tenancy to which this Part of this Act applies has given notice under section 25 of this Act to terminate the tenancy; or

(b) the tenant of such a tenancy has made a request for a new tenancy in accordance with section 26 of this Act,

either of them may make an application to the court to determine a rent (an "interim rent") which the tenant is to pay while the tenancy ("the relevant tenancy") continues by virtue of section 24 of this Act and the court may order payment of an interim rent in accordance with section 24C or 24D of this Act.

(2) Neither the tenant nor the landlord may make an application under subsection (1) above if the other has made such an application and has not withdrawn it.

(3) No application shall be entertained under subsection (1) above if it is made more than six months after the termination of the relevant tenancy.

3B–111   *Note* —New s.24A was inserted by the Regulatory Reform (Business Tenancies) (England and Wales) Order 2003 (S.I. 2003 No. 3096).

tenancy

3B–112   See s.69(1) and the commentary to s.23 above. The definition includes an agreement for a lease or underlease, but does not include a mortgage.

the landlord

3B–113   See s.44(1) which provides that "the landlord" means the person (whether or not he is the immediate landlord) who is the owner of that interest in the property comprised in the relevant tenancy which for the time being fulfils the conditions contained in ss.44(1)(a) and (b).

3B–114 Date from which interim rent is payable

24B.—(1) The interim rent determined on an application under section 24A(1) of this Act shall be payable from the appropriate date.

(2) If an application under section 24A(1) of this Act is made in a case where the landlord has given a notice under section 25 of this Act, the appropriate date is the earliest date of termination that could have been specified in the landlord's notice.

(3) If an application under section 24A(1) of this Act is made in a case where the tenant has made a request for a new tenancy under section 26 of this Act, the appropriate date is the earliest date that could have been specified in the tenant's request as the date from which the new tenancy is to begin.

3B–115   *Note* —New s.24B was inserted by the Regulatory Reform (Business Tenancies) (England and Wales) Order 2003 (S.I. 2003 No. 3096), art.18.

Amount of interim rent where new tenancy of whole premises granted and landlord not opposed

3B–116   **24C.**—(1) This section applies where—

(a) the landlord gave a notice under section 25 of this Act at a time when the tenant was in occupation of the whole of the property comprised in the relevant tenancy for purposes such as are mentioned in section 23(1) of this

Act and stated in the notice that he was not opposed to the grant of a new tenancy; or

(b) the tenant made a request for a new tenancy under section 26 of this Act at a time when he was in occupation of the whole of that property for such purposes and the landlord did not give notice under subsection (6) of that section, and the landlord grants a new tenancy of the whole of the property comprised in the relevant tenancy to the tenant (whether as a result of order for the grant of a new tenancy or otherwise).

(2) Subject to the following provisions of this section, the rent payable under and at the commencement of the new tenancy shall also be the interim rent.

(3) Subsection (2) above does not apply where—

(a) the landlord or the tenant shows to the satisfaction of the court that the interim rent under that subsection differs substantially from the relevant rent; or

(b) the landlord or the tenant shows to the satisfaction of the court that the terms of the new tenancy differ from the terms of the relevant tenancy to such an extent that the interim rent under that subsection is substantially different from the rent which (in default of such agreement) the court would have determined under section 34 of this Act to be payable under a tenancy which commenced on the same day as the new tenancy and whose other terms were the same as the relevant tenancy.

(4) In this section "the relevant rent" means the rent which (in default of agreement between the landlord and the tenant) the court would have determined under section 34 of this Act to be payable under the new tenancy if the new tenancy had commenced on the appropriate date (within the meaning of section 24B of this Act).

(5) The interim rent in a case where subsection (2) above does not apply by virtue only of subsection (3)(a) above is the relevant rent.

(6) The interim rent in a case where subsection (2) above does not apply by virtue only of subsection (3)(b) above, or by virtue of subsection (3)(a) and (b) above, is the rent which it is reasonable for the tenant to pay while the relevant tenancy continues by virtue of section 24 of this Act.

(7) In determining the interim rent under subsection (6) above the court shall have regard—

(a) to the rent payable under the terms of the relevant tenancy; and

(b) to the rent payable under any sub-tenancy of part of the property comprised in the relevant tenancy,

but otherwise subsections (1) and (2) of section 34 of this Act shall apply to the determination as they would apply to the determination of a rent under that section if a new tenancy of the whole of the property comprised in the relevant tenancy were granted to the tenant by order of the court and the duration of that new tenancy were the same as the duration of the new tenancy which is actually granted to the tenant.

(8) In this section and section 24D of this Act "the relevant tenancy" has the same meaning as in section 24A of this Act.

3B–117   Note —New s.24C was inserted by the Regulatory Reform (Business Tenancies) (England and Wales) Order 2003 (S.I. 2003 No. 3096), art.18.

Amount of interim rent in any other case

3B–118   **24D.**—(1) The interim rent in a case where section 24C of this Act does not apply is the rent which it is reasonable for the tenant to pay while the relevant tenancy continues by virtue of section 24 of this Act.

(2) In determining the interim rent under subsection (1) above the court shall have regard—

    (a) to the rent payable under the terms of the relevant tenancy; and

    (b) to the rent payable under any sub-tenancy of part of the property comprised in the relevant tenancy,

but otherwise subsections (1) and (2) of section 34 of this Act shall apply to the determination as they would apply to the determination of a rent under that section if a new tenancy from year to year of the whole of the property comprised in the relevant tenancy were granted to the tenant by order of the court.

(3) If the court—

    (a) has made an order for the grant of a new tenancy and has ordered payment of interim rent in accordance with section 24C of this Act, but

    (b) either—

        (i) it subsequently revokes under section 36(2) of this Act the order for the grant of a new tenancy; or

        (ii) the landlord and tenant agree not to act on the order,

the court on the application of the landlord or the tenant shall determine a new interim rent in accordance with subsections (1) and (2) above without a further application under section 24A(1) of this Act.

3B–119   Note —New s.24D was inserted by the Regulatory Reform (Business Tenancies) (England and Wales) Order 2003 (S.I. 2003 No. 3096), art.18.

Termination of tenancy by the landlord

3B–120   **25.**—(1) The landlord may terminate a tenancy to which this Part of this Act applies by a notice given to the tenant in the prescribed form specifying the date at which the tenancy is to come to an end (hereinafter referred to as "the date of termination"): Provided that this subsection has effect subject to the provisions of section 29B(4) of this Act and the provisions of Part IV of this Act as to the interim continuation of tenancies pending the disposal of applications to the court.

(2) Subject to the provisions of the next following subsection, a

notice under this section shall not have effect unless it is given not more than twelve nor less than six months before the date of termination specified therein.

(3) In the case of a tenancy which apart from this Act could have been brought to an end by notice to quit given by the landlord—

    (a) the date of termination specified in a notice under this section shall not be earlier than the earliest date on which apart from this Part of this Act the tenancy could have been brought to an end by notice to quit given by the landlord on the date of the giving of the notice under this section; and

    (b) where apart from this Part of this Act more than six months' notice to quit would have been required to bring the tenancy to an end, the last foregoing subsection shall have effect with the substitution for twelve months of a period six months longer than the length of notice to quit which would have been required as aforesaid.

(4) In the case of any other tenancy, a notice under this section shall not specify a date of termination earlier than the date on which apart from this Part of this Act the tenancy would have come to an end by effluxion of time.

(5) [...]

(6) A notice under this section shall not have effect unless it states whether the landlord is opposed to the grant of a new tenancy to the tenant.

(7) A notice under this section which states that the landlord is opposed to the grant of a new tenancy to the tenant shall not have effect unless it also specifies one or more of the grounds specified in section 30(1) of this Act as the ground or grounds for his opposition.

(8) A notice under this section which states that the landlord is not opposed to the grant of a new tenancy to the tenant shall not have effect unless it sets out the landlord's proposals as to—

    (a) the property to be comprised in the new tenancy (being either the whole or part of the property comprised in the current tenancy);

    (b) the rent to be payable under the new tenancy; and

    (c) the other terms of the new tenancy.

Note—Subsection (5) was repealed by the Regulatory Reform (Business Tenancies) **3B–121** (England and Wales) Order 2003 (S.I. 2003 No. 3096) which also inserted new subss. (6) to (8). Those amendments came into force June 1, 2004. They only apply where a landlord has given a tenant notice under s.25 or a tenant has made a request for a new tenancy in accordance with s.26 on or after that date.

tenancy

See s.69(1) and the commentary to s.23 above. The definition includes an agree- **3B–122** ment for a lease or underlease, but does not include a mortgage.

date of termination

See s.46 and s.25(1)—the date specified in the landlord's s.25 notice at which the **3B–123** tenancy is to come to an end.

termination

A s.25 notice is used to exercise a break clause, to terminate a tenancy which would **3B–124**

BUSINESS TENANCIES

have expired by effluxion of time at common law, to terminate a tenancy continuing under s.24 and to terminate a periodic tenancy.

notice to quit

3B-125   Means a notice to quit given by the immediate landlord (see s.44(2)). A s.25 notice is not technically a notice to quit, although it has the effect of terminating the tenancy.

Requirements of a s.25 notice

3B-126   A s.25 notice must:

   (a) **be given by the landlord**—see s.44(1) which provides that "the landlord" means the person (whether or not he is the immediate landlord) who is the owner of that interest in the property comprised in the relevant tenancy which for the time being fulfils the conditions contained in s.44(1)(a) and (b). Notice may be served by an agent with the landlord's authority (*Tennant v. London County Council* (1957) 121 J.P. 428, CA; *London County Council v. Farren* [1956] 1 W.L.R. 129; [1956] 3 All E.R. 401, CA) but the correct landlord must be named (*Morrow v. Nadeem* [1986] 1 W.L.R. 1381; [1987] 1 All E.R. 237, CA). If there are joint landlords, all must join in giving the notice (*Dodson Bull Carpet Co Ltd v. City of London Corp* [1975] 1 W.L.R. 781; [1975] 2 All E.R. 497, CA).

   (b) **be given to the tenant.** If there are joint tenants, notice must be given to all of them (*Jacobs v. Chaudhuri* [1968] 2 Q.B. 470; [1968] 2 W.L.R. 1098; [1968] 2 All E.R. 124, CA), but in the case of partners, see s.41A(4).

   (c) **relate to the whole of the property comprised in the tenancy.** A notice which purports to apply to only part of the premises is ineffective (*Dodson Bull Carpet Co Ltd v. City of London Corp.* [1975] 1 W.L.R. 781; [1975] 2 All E.R. 497, CA; *Kaiser Engineers & Contractors v. Suibb (E.R.) & Sons* [1971] E.G.D. 553, CA).

   (d) **specify a date for termination which complies with tenancy and the Act**—see ss.25(1) and (3). The date of termination specified in the notice cannot be earlier than the earliest date on which, contractually, the tenancy could be brought to an end by a notice to quit or break clause, or the date on which a fixed term tenancy would have expired by effluxion of time (*Crowhurst Park, Re* [1974] 1 W.L.R. 583; [1974] 1 All E.R. 991, Ch D). The notice must also be given not more than twelve nor less than six-months before the date of termination unless more than six months notice would have been required at common law. In calculating that period, the date on which the notice is given must be disregarded, with the result that the relevant period is the specified number of months which end on the corresponding day of the appropriate subsequent month (*Dodds v. Walker* [1981] 1 W.L.R. 1027; [1981] 2 All E.R. 609, HL, a case on s.29). An obvious error as to the date may be corrected where it is clear that the tenant cannot be misled (*Carradine Properties Ltd v. Aslam* [1976] 1 W.L.R. 442; [1976] 1 All E.R. 573, CA).

   (e) **be in the prescribed form or substantially to the like effect.** There have been a number of new prescribed forms since June 1, 2004 (when the 2003 Reform Order amending Pt II of the 1954 Act came into effect) dealing with various different situations (the Landlord and Tenant Act 1954, Part 2 (Notices)(England and Wales) Regulations 2004 (S.I. 2004 No.1005). A full list is set out in Sched.1 to those regulations; and the forms themselves are in Sched.2. The two main forms that will be used in most cases are: (i) Form 1—to be used where the landlord is not opposed to the grant of a new tenancy; and (ii) Form 2—to be used where the landlord is opposed to the grant of a new tenancy. Where the landlord is not opposed to a new tenancy he must, in his s.25 notice, set out his proposals as to (i) the property to be comprised in the new tenancy, being either the whole or part of the property comprised in the tenancy; (ii) the rent to be payable under the new tenancy and (iii) the other terms of the new tenancy. The landlord must use the appropriate form listed in the schedule or "a form substantially to the same effect" (reg. 2(2)). The notes on the back of each form are part of the prescribed form and must be used. If they are omitted they will not be regarded as being in "a form substantially to same effect". These are important parts of the form and must be included. The fact that the tenant is not misled by their omission is irrelevant (*Sabella Ltd v. Montgomery* [1998] 1 EGLR 65, CA).

service of notice

3B-127   See Landlord and Tenant Act 1927, s.23 which provides that any notice, request, demand or other instrument can be served personally or left at the last known place of abode (which includes place of business—*Price v. West London Investment Building Society Ltd* [1964] 1 W.L.R. 616; [1964] 2 All E.R. 318, CA) of the person to be served or posted by registered or recorded delivery. (As to change of landlords, see Landlord and Tenant Act 1927, s.23(2)). If one of these methods of service is adopted, service is deemed to be effected even if the document is not received by the intended recipient, if, for example, it is returned by the Post Office (*Blunden v. Frogmore Investments Ltd* [2002] EWCA Civ 573; [2003] 29 E.G. 153). If a notice is sent by recorded delivery it is irrefutably deemed to have been served on the date that the notice was put in the post and not on the date of actual receipt (*Beanby Estates Ltd v. Egg Stores (Stamford Hill) Ltd* [2003] EWHC 1252 (Ch); [2003] 1 W.L.R. 2064 and *CA Webber (Transport) Ltd v. Network Rail Infrastructure Ltd (formerly Railtrack Plc)* [2003] EWCA Civ 1167; [2004] 1 W.L.R. 320).

withdrawal of notice

For the limited circumstances in which a valid s.25 notice may be withdrawn, see Landlord and Tenant Act 1954, Sched.6, para. 6. **3B–128**

more than one notice

For the position where a party serves more than one notice and the notices are contradictory, see *Barclays Bank Plc v. Bee* [2001] EWCA Civ 1126; [2001] 37 E.G. 153. **3B–129**

Tenant's request for a new tenancy

26.—(1) A tenant's request for a new tenancy may be made where **3B–130** the current tenancy is a tenancy granted for a term of years certain exceeding one year, whether or not continued by section twenty-four of this Act, or granted for a term of years certain and thereafter from year to year.

(2) A tenant's request for a new tenancy shall be for a tenancy beginning with such date, not more than twelve nor less than six months after the making of the request, as may be specified therein:

Provided that the said date shall not be earlier than the date on which apart from this Act the current tenancy would come to an end by effluxion of time or could be brought to an end by notice to quit given by the tenant.

(3) A tenant's request for a new tenancy shall not have effect unless it is made by notice in the prescribed form given to the landlord and sets out the tenant's proposals as to the property to be comprised in the new tenancy (being either the whole or part of the property comprised in the current tenancy), as to the rent to be payable under the new tenancy and as to the other terms of the new tenancy.

(4) A tenant's request for a new tenancy shall not be made if the landlord has already given notice under the last foregoing section to terminate the current tenancy, or if the tenant has already given notice to quit or notice under the next following section; and no such notice shall be given by the landlord or the tenant after the making by the tenant of a request for a new tenancy.

(5) Where the tenant makes a request for a new tenancy in accordance with the foregoing provisions of this section, the current tenancy shall, subject to the provisions of sections 29B(4) and 36(2) of this Act and the provisions of Part IV of this Act as to the interim continuation of tenancies, terminate immediately before the date specified in the request for the beginning of the new tenancy.

(6) Within two months of the making of a tenant's request for a

new tenancy the landlord may give notice to the tenant that he will oppose an application to the court for the grant of a new tenancy, and any such notice shall state on which of the grounds mentioned in section thirty of this Act the landlord will oppose the application.

3B–131   *Note* —Section 26 is excluded by Leasehold Reform Act 1967, ss.17, 18, Sched.2, para. 6(1). It was amended by the Regulatory Reform (Business Tenancies) (England and Wales) Order 2003 (S.I. 2003 No. 3096). The amendment came into force June 1, 2004. It only applies where a landlord has given a tenant notice under s.25 or a tenant has made a request for a new tenancy in accordance with s.26 on or after that date.

tenancy

3B–132   See s.69(1) and the commentary to s.23 above. The definition includes an agreement for a lease or underlease, but does not include a mortgage.

current tenancy

3B–133   See s.46 and s.26(1)—the tenancy under which the tenant holds for the time being.

notice to quit

3B–134   Means a notice to quit given by the immediate landlord (see s.44(2)).

the landlord

3B–135   See s.44(1) which provides that "the landlord" means the person (whether or not he is the immediate landlord) who is the owner of that interest in the property comprised in the relevant tenancy which for the time being fulfils the conditions contained in ss.44(1)(a) and (b).

prescribed form

3B–136   See the Landlord and Tenant Act 1954, Part 2 (Notices) Regulations 2004 (S.I. 2004 No. 1005). Regulation 2(2) allows a "form substantially to the like effect" of those contained in the regulations. See the commentary to s.25 above.

tenant's request

3B–137   Section 26 does not apply where (i) the landlord has already served a s.25 notice; (ii) the tenant has already given notice to quit; (iii) or the tenant has already given a s.27 notice to avoid continuance under the Act. If there are joint tenants, all must join in the request, unless they are partners (see s.41A). The request must be served upon the competent landlord or the landlord's authorised agent and set out the tenant's proposals as to the new tenancy. The request brings the existing tenancy to an end, but an interim continuation tenancy then comes into being (s.26(2)). Within two months of receipt the landlord may give a counter-notice stating that the grant of a new tenancy will be opposed on one of the s.30 grounds. Failure to give a counter-notice during the prescribed period prevents the landlord opposing the grant of a new tenancy. There is no prescribed form for a landlord's counter-notice. As to contents, see *Marks (Morris) v. British Waterways Board* [1963] 1 W.L.R. 1008; [1963] 3 All E.R. 28, CA.

A tenant's motive for requesting a new tenancy is irrelevant (*Sun Life Assurance Plc v. Thales Tracs Ltd (formerly Racal Tracs Ltd)* [2001] EWCA Civ 704; [2001] 1 W.L.R. 1562; [2002] 1 All E.R. 64 notice served only to preserve compensation rights).

service

3B–138   See commentary to s.25.

Termination by tenant of tenancy for fixed term

3B–139   **27.**—(1) Where the tenant under a tenancy to which this Part of this Act applies, being a tenancy granted for a term of years certain, gives to the immediate landlord, not later than three months before the date on which apart from this Act the tenancy would come to an end by effluxion of time, a notice in writing that the tenant does not desire the tenancy to be continued, section 24 of this Act shall not have effect in relation to the tenancy, unless the notice is given before the tenant has been in occupation in right of the tenancy for one month.

(1A) Section 24 of this Act shall not have effect in relation to a tenancy for a term of years certain where the tenant is not in occupation of the property comprised in the tenancy at the time when, apart from this Act, the tenancy would come to an end by effluxion of time.

(2) A tenancy granted for a term of years certain which is continuing by virtue of section 24 of this Act shall not come to an end by reason only of the tenant ceasing to occupy the property comprised in the tenancy but may be brought to an end on any day by not less than three months' notice in writing given by the tenant to the immediate landlord, whether the notice is given after the date on which apart from this Act the tenancy would have come to an end or before that date, but not before the tenant has been in occupation in right of the tenancy for one month.

(3) Where a tenancy is terminated under subsection (2) above, any rent payable in respect of a period which begins before, and ends after, the tenancy is terminated shall be apportioned, and any rent paid by the tenant in excess of the amount apportioned to the period before termination shall be recoverable by him.

Note —The current s.27 was substituted by Law of Property Act 1969, s.15, Sched.1 **3B–140** and amended by the Regulatory Reform (Business Tenancies) (England and Wales) Order 2003 (S.I. 2003 No. 3096). The amendment came into force June 1, 2004. It does not have effect in relation to a notice given under s.27(2) prior to that date.

tenancy
See s.69(1) and the commentary to s.23 above. The definition includes an agree- **3B–141** ment for a lease or underlease, but does not include a mortgage.

the landlord
See s.44(1) which provides that "the landlord" means the person (whether or not **3B–142** he is the immediate landlord) who is the owner of that interest in the property comprised in the relevant tenancy which for the time being fulfils the conditions contained in ss.44(1)(a) and (b).

Renewal of tenancies by agreement

28. Where the landlord and tenant agree for the grant to the ten- **3B–143** ant of a future tenancy of the holding, or of the holding with other land, on terms and from a date specified in the agreement, the current tenancy shall continue until that date but no longer, and shall not be a tenancy to which this Part of this Act applies.

tenancy
See s.69(1) and the commentary to s.23 above. The definition includes an agree- **3B–144** ment for a lease or underlease, but does not include a mortgage.

current tenancy
See s.46 and s.26(1)—the tenancy under which the tenant holds for the time being. **3B–145**

holding
See s.46, s.32 and s.23(3) which provides that the expression "the holding" means **3B–146**

the property comprised in the tenancy, there being excluded any part thereof which is occupied neither by the tenant nor by a person employed by the tenant ... for the purposes of a business by reason of which the tenancy is one to which this Part of this Act applies.

the landlord

3B–147   See s.44(1) which provides that "the landlord" means the person (whether or not he is the immediate landlord) who is the owner of that interest in the property comprised in the relevant tenancy which for the time being fulfils the conditions contained in ss.44(1)(a) and (b).

agree

3B–148   Any agreement must be in writing (s.69(2)). Note too Law of Property (Miscellaneous Provisions) Act 1989, s.2.

3B–149   ## Order by court for grant of new tenancy or termination of current tenancy

29.—(1) Subject to the provisions of this Act, on an application under section 24(1) of this Act, the court shall make an order for the grant of a new tenancy and accordingly for the termination of the current tenancy immediately before the commencement of the new tenancy.

(2) Subject to the following provisions of this Act, a landlord may apply to the court for an order for the termination of a tenancy to which this Part of this Act applies without the grant of a new tenancy—

>   (a) if he has given notice under section 25 of this Act that he is opposed to the grant of a new tenancy to the tenant; or

>   (b) if the tenant has made a request for a new tenancy in accordance with section 26 of this Act and the landlord has given notice under subsection (6) of that section.

(3) The landlord may not make an application under subsection (2) above if either the tenant or the landlord has made an application under section 24(1) of this Act.

(4) Subject to the provisions of this Act, where the landlord makes an application under subsection (2) above—

>   (a) if he establishes, to the satisfaction of the court, any of the grounds on which he is entitled to make the application in accordance with section 30 of this Act, the court shall make an order for the termination of the current tenancy in accordance with section 64 of this Act without the grant of a new tenancy; and

>   (b) if not, it shall make an order for the grant of a new tenancy and accordingly for the termination of the current tenancy immediately before the commencement of the new tenancy.

(5) The court shall dismiss an application by the landlord under section 24(1) of this Act if the tenant informs the court that he does not want a new tenancy.

(6) The landlord may not withdraw an application under subsection (2) above unless the tenant consents to its withdrawal.

3B–150   *Note* —A new s.29 was substituted by the Regulatory Reform (Business Tenancies)

(England and Wales) Order 2003 (S.I. 2003 No. 3096), art.5. The amendment came into force June 1, 2004 but only applies where the s.25 notice or s.26 request was served on or after that date.

such property

See s.32.   **3B–151**

such rent

See s.34.   **3B–152**

such other terms

See s.35.   **3B–153**

tenancy

See section 69(1) and the commentary to s.23 above. The definition includes an **3B–154** agreement for a lease or underlease, but does not include a mortgage.

date of termination

See s.46 and s.25(1)—the date specified in the landlord's s.25 notice at which the **3B–155** tenancy is to come to an end.

the landlord

See s.44(1) which provides that "the landlord" means the person (whether or not **3B–156** he is the immediate landlord) who is the owner of that interest in the property comprised in the relevant tenancy which for the time being fulfils the conditions contained in ss.44(1)(a) and (b).

procedure

See CPR Part 56, Vol. 1, para. 56.0.1. Section 29 applications may be made to the **3B–157** county court (the norm—CPR, r.56.2) in which the land is situated or the High Court. They are Part 8 claims and Form N208 should be used.

Time limits for applications to court   **3B–158**

29A.—(1) Subject to section 29B of this Act, the court shall not entertain an application—

   (a) by the tenant or the landlord under section 24(1) of this Act; or

   (b) by the landlord under section 29(2) of this Act,

if it is made after the end of the statutory period.

   (2) In this section and section 29B of this Act "the statutory period" means a period ending—

   (a) where the landlord gave a notice under section 25 of this Act, on the date specified in his notice; and

   (b) where the tenant made a request for a new tenancy under section 26 of this Act, immediately before the date specified in his request.

   (3) Where the tenant has made a request for a new tenancy under section 26 of this Act, the court shall not entertain an application under section 24(1) of this Act which is made before the end of the period of two months beginning with the date of the making of the request, unless the application is made after the landlord has given a notice under section 26(6) of this Act.

Note—New s.29A was substituted by the Regulatory Reform (Business Tenancies) **3B–159** (England and Wales) Order 2003 (S.I. 2003 No. 3096). The amendment came into force June 1, 2004.

time limits

Under the law prior to June 1, 2004 the tenant's application for a new tenancy had **3B–160** to be made "not less than two nor more than four months" after the giving of the landlord's s.25 or as the case may be the tenant's s.26 request. Many tenants missed this window of opportunity and lost their right to apply for a new tenancy. Since June 1, 2004 the deadline in respect of notices served on or after that date has been:

- the date specified in the s.25 notice; or
- the date immediately before the date specified in the s.26 request (s.29A(2)).

However, it should be noted (by tenants in particular) that where a s.26 request has been made by the tenant an application for a new tenancy cannot be made until the landlord has served a counter-notice or the time for so doing has passed (s.29A(3)). Thus, there still remains a potential trap that could invalidate applications.

no application shall be entertained

3B–161   The court has no power to extend time (*Hodgson v. Armstrong* [1967] 2 Q.B. 299; [1967] 2 W.L.R. 311; [1967] 1 All E.R. 307, CA). Strict compliance with the timetable may be waived by the parties (*Kammins Ballrooms Co. Ltd v. Zenith Investments (Torquay) Ltd (No. 1)* [1971] A.C. 850; [1970] 2 All E.R. 871, HL), but the landlord cannot agree to confer jurisdiction which the court does not have (*e.g.* because the application was made after the tenant ceased to be a tenant—*Meah v. Sector Properties Ltd* [1974] 1 W.L.R. 547; [1974] 1 All E.R. 1074, CA). However note that the parties can agree to extend time before issue — see s.29B below.

If the tenant ceases to occupy for purposes of a business, the protection of Pt II is lost and the landlord may apply to have the claim dismissed or struck out (*I&H Caplan Ltd v. Caplan (No. 2)* [1963] 1 W.L.R. 1247; [1963] 2 All E.R. 930, Ch D).

Agreements extending time limits

3B–162   **29B.**—(1) After the landlord has given a notice under section 25 of this Act, or the tenant has made a request under section 26 of this Act, but before the end of the statutory period, the landlord and tenant may agree that an application such as is mentioned in section 29A(1) of this Act, may be made before the end of a period specified in the agreement which will expire after the end of the statutory period.

(2) The landlord and tenant may from time to time by agreement further extend the period for making such an application, but any such agreement must be made before the end of the period specified in the current agreement.

(3) Where an agreement is made under this section, the court may entertain an application such as is mentioned in section 29A(1) of this Act if it is made before the end of the period specified in the agreement.

(4) Where an agreement is made under this section, or two or more agreements are made under this section, the landlord's notice under section 25 of this Act or tenant's request under section 26 of this Act shall be treated as terminating the tenancy at the end of the period specified in the agreement or, as the case may be, at the end of the period specified in the last of those agreements.

3B–163   *Note* —New s.29B was substituted by the Regulatory Reform (Business Tenancies) (England and Wales) Order 2003 (S.I. 2003 No. 3096). The amendment came into force June 1, 2004 but only applies where the s.25 or s.26 notice was served on or after that date.

agreement in writing

3B–164   The agreement to extend the time limit must be in writing (s.69(2)). Is an agreement by e-mail in writing? Almost certainly yes. Section 5 and Sched.1 of the Interpretation Act 1978 provides that "writing" includes "typing, printing, lithography, photography and other modes of representing or reproducing words in a visible form, and expressions referring to writing are construed accordingly". However, any practitioner who has any doubt about this should insist upon an agreement in old fashioned correspondence. If the agreement is not forthcoming the application should be made before the time limit expires.

time of expiry

When agreeing a new deadline the parties should use whole days not specific moments in time (*e.g.* 3.30pm on ...). Although the statute does not expressly forbid times it does seem to follow from the definition of "the statutory period" in s.29A(2) that only whole days are allowed. Indeed, generally speaking, the law does not recognise parts of days when dealing with notices.

3B–165

agreement before time expires

If no application to the court is made before the expiry of the deadline or any agreed extension, the right to apply to the court will be lost and the tenancy will come to an end (s.29B(3)(4)).

3B–166

Opposition by landlord to application for new tenancy

30.—(1) The grounds on which a landlord may oppose an application under section 24(1) of this Act, or make an application under section 29(2) of this Act, are such of the following grounds as may be stated in the landlord's notice under section 25 of this Act or, as the case may be, under subsection (6) of section 26 thereof, that is to say:—

3B–167

> (a) where under the current tenancy the tenant has any obligations as respects the repair and maintenance of the holding, that the tenant ought not to be granted a new tenancy in view of the state of repair of the holding, being a state resulting from the tenant's failure to comply with the said obligations;
>
> (b) that the tenant ought not to be granted a new tenancy in view of his persistent delay in paying rent which has become due;
>
> (c) that the tenant ought not to be granted a new tenancy in view of other substantial breaches by him of his obligations under the current tenancy, or for any other reason connected with the tenant's use or management of the holding;
>
> (d) that the landlord has offered and is willing to provide or secure the provision of alternative accommodation for the tenant, that the terms on which the alternative accommodation is available are reasonable having regard to the terms of the current tenancy and to all other relevant circumstances, and that the accommodation and the time at which it will be available are suitable for the tenant's requirements (including the requirement to preserve goodwill) having regard to the nature and class of his business and to the situation and extent of, and facilities afforded by, the holding;
>
> (e) where the current tenancy was created by the sub-letting of part only of the property comprised in a superior tenancy and the landlord is the owner of an interest in reversion expectant on the termination of that superior tenancy, that the aggregate of the rents reasonably obtainable on separate lettings of the holding and the

remainder of that property would be substantially less than the rent reasonably obtainable on a letting of that property as a whole, that on the termination of the current tenancy the landlord requires possession of the holding for the purpose of letting or otherwise disposing of the said property as a whole, and that in view thereof the tenant ought not to be granted a new tenancy;

(f) that on the termination of the current tenancy the landlord intends to demolish or reconstruct the premises comprised in the holding or a substantial part of those premises or to carry out substantial work of construction on the holding or part thereof and that he could not reasonably do so without obtaining possession of the holding;

(g) subject as hereinafter provided, that on the termination of the current tenancy the landlord intends to occupy the holding for the purposes, or partly for the purposes, of a business to be carried on by him therein, or as his residence.

(1A) Where the landlord has a controlling interest in a company, the reference in subsection (1)(g) above to the landlord shall be construed as a reference to the landlord or that company.

(1B) Subject to subsection (2A) below, where the landlord is a company and a person has a controlling interest in the company, the reference in subsection (1)(g) above to the landlord shall be construed as a reference to the landlord or that person.

(2) The landlord shall not be entitled to oppose an application under section 24(1) of this Act, or make an application under section 29(2) of this Act, on the ground specified in paragraph (g) of the last foregoing subsection if the interest of the landlord, or an interest which has merged in that interest and but for the merger would be the interest of the landlord, was purchased or created after the beginning of the period of five years which ends with the termination of the current tenancy, and at all times since the purchase or creation thereof the holding has been comprised in a tenancy or successive tenancies of the description specified in subsection (1) of section 23 of this Act.

(2A) Subsection (1B) above shall not apply if the controlling interest was acquired after the beginning of the period of five years which ends with the termination of the current tenancy, and at all times since the acquisition of the controlling interest the holding has been comprised in a tenancy or successive tenancies of the description specified in section 23(1) of this Act.

(3) [...]

3B–168   *Note* —The current s.30 was substituted by the Law of Property Act 1969, s.15, Sched.1 and amended by the Regulatory Reform (Business Tenancies) (England and Wales) Order 2003 (S.I. 2003 No. 3096) arts 6, 14 and subs.(3) was repealed by Sched.6, para. 1. The amendments came into force June 1, 2004 but only apply where the s.25 notice or s.26 request was served after that date.

Business

3B–169   See s.46 and s.23(2) which provides that "business" includes a trade, profession or employment and includes any activity carried on by a body of persons, whether corporate or unincorporate. See too the commentary to s.23 above.

current tenancy

See s.46 and s.26(1)—the tenancy under which the tenant holds for the time being. **3B–170**

holding

See s.46, s.32 and s.23(3) which provides that the expression "the holding" means **3B–171** the property comprised in the tenancy, there being excluded any part thereof which is occupied neither by the tenant nor by a person employed by the tenant ... for the purposes of a business by reason of which the tenancy is one to which this Part of this Act applies.

the landlord

See s.44(1) which provides that "the landlord" means the person (whether or not **3B–172** he is the immediate landlord) who is the owner of that interest in the property comprised in the relevant tenancy which for the time being fulfils the conditions contained in ss.44(1)(a) and (b).

grounds

Landlords may only rely upon grounds for opposing the grant of a new tenancy or **3B–173** termination under s.29(2) if they are specified in a s.25 notice or a counter-notice served in response to a tenant's s.26 notice.

s.30(1)(a) state of repair

The state of repair of the holding is only a ground for opposing the grant of a new **3B–174** tenancy if it results form the tenant's failure to comply with obligations. To be relied upon, the neglect to repair must be "substantial" (*Lyons v. Central Commercial Properties* [1958] 1 W.L.R. 869; [1958] 2 All E.R. 767, CA). Even then, the court has a discretion and should have regard to the overall conduct of the tenant in relation to his obligations and the reason for any breach. There is no entitlement to compensation if this ground is established.

s.30(1)(b) persistent delay in paying rent

There may be "persistent delay" if one instalment of rent has been in arrears for a **3B–175** significant period of time or instalments have persistently been paid late, or both (*Hopcutt v. Carver* (1969) 209 E.G. 1069, CA; *Horowitz v. Ferrand* [1956] C.L.Y. 4843. In exercising its discretion, the court may take into account both the conduct of the tenant and the landlord in relation to the late payments (*Hazel v. Akhtar* [2001] EWCA Civ 1883; [2002] 07 E.G. 124—landlord who accepted late payment without complaint prevented form relying upon s.30(1)(b)). There is no entitlement to compensation if this ground is established.

s.30(1)(c) other substantial breaches of obligations, or any other reason connected with the tenant's use or management of the holding

The court has a discretion and should have regard to the overall conduct of the **3B–176** tenant in relation to his obligations and the reason for any breach (*Eichner v. Midland Bank Executor and Trustee Co* [1970] 1 W.L.R. 1120; [1970] 2 All E.R. 597, CA). There is no entitlement to compensation if this ground is established.

s.30(1)(d) offer of alternative accommodation for the tenant

Alternative accommodation must be suitable for the tenant's requirements. For a **3B–177** case in which possession was refused because the alternative accommodation would have adversely affected the way in which the tenant's business was conducted, see *Singh v. Malayan Theatres* [1953] A.C. 632; [1953] 3 W.L.R. 491, PC. The terms on which it is offered must be reasonable having regard to the terms of the current tenancy and all other circumstances. Accommodation must have been offered and still be available at the time of the court hearing. If this ground is established, the court has no discretion and must dismiss the application for a new tenancy. There is no entitlement to compensation if this ground is established.

s30(1)(e) aggregate of the rents reasonably obtainable on separate lettings less than the rent reasonably obtainable on a letting of that property as a whole

This ground is rarely used in practice. It is designed to prevent a landlord from **3B–178** suffering prejudice as a result of sub-lettings created by a tenant. Even if the ground is established, the court has a discretion.

s.30(1)(f) intention of landlord to demolish or reconstruct

3B–179   See too s.31A. The landlord must show that the intention to demolish or reconstruct exists at the time of the hearing and will be fulfilled shortly after the date of the hearing. (*Betty's Cafes Ltd v. Phillips Furnishing Stores Ltd (No. 1)* [1959] A.C. 20; [1958] 2 W.L.R. 513; [1958] 1 All E.R. 607, HL). The intention must be genuine, firm, and settled, and unlikely to be changed (*Fleet Electrics v. Jacey Investments* [1956] 1 W.L.R. 1027; [1956] 3 All E.R. 99, CA. There are two elements to the concept of intention: first, a genuine desire that the result will come about and, secondly, a reasonable prospect of bringing about that result. For example, in *Edwards v. Thompson* [1990] 29 E.G. 41, CA, a landlord failed to prevent the grant of a new tenancy because she had not found a developer at the time of the hearing and "there was a real possibility that [she] would not be in a position to carry out the entire development on the termination of the current tenancy...She had failed to show that she had the means and ability; she had not established the necessary intention." (See too *Capocci v. Goble* (1987) 284 E.G. 230, CA). A landlordís case is stronger if planning permission has been obtained in advance of the institution of court proceedings, but this is not essential if it can be shown that there is a reasonable prospect of getting consent (*Gregson v. Cyril Lord Ltd* [1963] 1 W.L.R. 41; [1962] 3 All E.R. 907, CA).

It has been held that "reconstruction" means "a substantial interference with the structure of the premises and then a rebuilding, in probably a different form, of such part of the premises as has been demolished by reason of the interference with the structure" (*Joel v. Swaddle* [1957] 1 W.L.R. 1094; [1957] 3 All E.R. 325 at p.329, CA—removal of internal walls and replacement with reinforced steel joists amounted to reconstruction of a substantial part). See too *Barth v. Pritchard [1990] 20 E.G. 65, CA and Cook* v. Mott (1961) 178 E.G. 637, CA). There is no requirement of demolition or construction of structural or load bearing features as a condition of applicability (*Ivory-grove Ltd v. Global Grange Ltd* [2003] EWHC 1409 (Ch); [2003] 1 W.L.R. 2090).

The landlord must also show that the intended work cannot reasonably be carried out without the tenant giving up possession of the premises. "Possession" means "putting an end to legal rights of possession" and not merely access. For example, in *Heath v. Drown* [1973] A.C. 498; [1972] 2 W.L.R. 1306; [1972] 2 All E.R. 561, HL a business tenant successfully defeated the landlordís claim even though the front wall of the premises had to be entirely rebuilt and it would not be possible to occupy the premises while such work was carried out. The landlord must show that the work cannot be carried out while the tenancy still exists.

If this ground is established, the court has no discretion and must dismiss the application for a new tenancy.

In *Wessex Reserve Forces & Cadets Association v. White* [2005] 49 EG 89 (CS) (CA) the landlord relied upon s.30(1)(f) as a ground of opposition, stating that it intended to demolish some huts on the land. However, the huts were tenants' fixtures. These were the most substantial structures on the land and under the terms of the lease the tenant was required to remove them upon termination of its tenancy. The landlord could not therefore establish that it was going to demolish them.

s.30(1)(g) intention of landlord to occupy the holding for the purposes of a business or as his residence

3B–180   For "intention" see the commentary to s.30(1)(f) above. The landlord need not intend to occupy personally. It is sufficient to intend to carry on the business through an agent or manager (*Hills (Patents) Ltd v. University College Hospital Board of Governors* [1956] 1 Q.B. 90; [1955] 3 W.L.R. 523; [1955] 3 All E.R. 365, CA). An intention to sub-let the whole is inconsistent with an intention to occupy (*Crowhurst Park, Re* [1974] 1 WLR 583; [1974] 1 All E.R. 991, Ch D). As to trustees, see s.41(2) and groups of companies, s.42(3).

Note that this ground cannot be relied upon by a landlord who has purchased within the preceding five years if the premises have been let during the whole of that period (s.30(2)—see too *Northcote Laundry v. Donnelly (Frederick)* [1968] 1 W.L.R. 562; [1968] 2 All E.R. 50, CA). The period of five years is calculated backwards from the date of determination of the current tenancy (see *Frederick Lawrence Ltd v. Freeman Hardy & Willis Ltd (No. 1)* [1959] Ch. 731; [1959] 3 W.L.R. 275; [1959] 3 All E.R. 77, CA). If this ground is established, the court has no discretion and must dismiss the application for a new tenancy.

application dismissed

Any continuation tenancy terminates on the expiry of three months beginning with **3B–181** the date on which the application is finally disposed of (Sched.6, para. 4(3)).

misrepresentation or concealment

If the court refuses a new tenancy, and it later appears that the court was induced **3B–182** to refuse it by misrepresentation or concealment, the court may order compensation (s.37A).

Dismissal of application for new tenancy where landlord successfully opposes

31.—(1) If the landlord opposes an application under subsection **3B–183** (1) of section twenty-four of this Act on grounds on which he is entitled to oppose it in accordance with the last foregoing section and establishes any of those grounds to the satisfaction of the court, the court shall not make an order for the grant of a new tenancy.

(2) Where the landlord opposes an application under section 24(1) of this Act, or makes an application under section 29(2) of this Act, on one or more of the grounds specified in section 30(1)(d) to (f) of this Act but establishes none of those grounds, and none of the other grounds specified in section 30(1) of this Act, to the satisfaction of the court, then if the court would have been satisfied on any of the grounds specified in section 30(1)(d) to (f) of this Act, if the date of termination specified in the landlord's notice or, as the case may be, the date specified in the tenant's request for a new tenancy as the date from which the new tenancy is to begin, had been such later date as the court may determine, being a date not more than one year later than the date so specified—

    (a) the court shall make a declaration to that effect, stating of which of the said grounds the court would have been satisfied as aforesaid and specifying the date determined by the court as aforesaid, but shall not make an order for the grant of a new tenancy;

    (b) if, within fourteen days after the making of the declaration, the tenant so requires the court shall make an order substituting the said date for the date specified in the said landlord's notice or tenant's request, and thereupon that notice or request shall have effect accordingly.

Note —Note s.31 was amended by the Regulatory Reform (Business Tenancies) **3B–184** (England and Wales) Order 2003 (S.I. 2003 No. 3096), art.7. The amendments came into force June 1, 2004 but only applies where the s.25 notice or s.26 request was served on or after that date.

date of termination

See s.46 and s.25(1)—the date specified in the landlord's s.25 notice at which the **3B–185** tenancy is to come to an end.

the landlord

See s.44(1) which provides that "the landlord" means the person (whether or not **3B–186** he is the immediate landlord) who is the owner of that interest in the property comprised in the relevant tenancy which for the time being fulfils the conditions contained in ss.44(1)(a) and (b).

Grant of new tenancy in some cases where s. 30(1)(f) applies

31A.—(1) Where the landlord opposes an application under sec- **3B–187**

tion 24(1) of this Act on the ground specified in paragraph (f) of section 30(1) of this Act, or makes an application under section 29(2) of this Act on that ground,the court shall not hold that the landlord could not reasonably carry out the demolition, reconstruction or work of construction intended without obtaining possession of the holding if—

    (a) the tenant agrees to the inclusion in the terms of the new tenancy of terms giving the landlord access and other facilities for carrying out the work intended and, given that access and those facilities, the landlord could reasonably carry out the work without obtaining possession of the holding and without interfering to a substantial extent or for a substantial time with the use of the holding for the purposes of the business carried on by the tenant; or

    (b) the tenant is willing to accept a tenancy of an economically separable part of the holding and either paragraph (a) of this section is satisfied with respect to that part or possession of the remainder of the holding would be reasonably sufficient to enable the landlord to carry out the intended work.

(2) For the purposes of subsection (1)(b) of this section a part of a holding shall be deemed to be an economically separate part if, and only if, the aggregate of the rents which, after the completion of the intended work, would be reasonably obtainable on separate lettings of that part and the remainder of the premises affected by or resulting from the work would not be substantially less than the rent which would then be reasonably obtainable on a letting of those premises as a whole.

3B–188   *Note* —Section 31A was inserted by Law of Property Act 1969, s.7(1) and amended by the Regulatory Reform (Business Tenancies) (England and Wales) Order 2003 (S.I. 2003 No. 3096), art.8. The amendment came into force June 1, 2004.

business

3B–189   See s.46 and s.23(2) which provides that "business" includes a trade, profession or employment and includes any activity carried on by a body of persons, whether corporate or unincorporate. See too the commentary to s.23 above.

holding

3B–190   See s.46, s.32 and s.23(3) which provides that the expression "the holding" means the property comprised in the tenancy, there being excluded any part thereof which is occupied neither by the tenant nor by a person employed by the tenant ... for the purposes of a business by reason of which the tenancy is one to which this Part of this Act applies.

the landlord

3B–191   See s.44(1) which provides that "the landlord" means the person (whether or not he is the immediate landlord) who is the owner of that interest in the property comprised in the relevant tenancy which for the time being fulfils the conditions contained in ss.44(1)(a) and (b).

Property to be comprised in new tenancy

3B–192   **32.**—(1) Subject to the following provisions of this section, an order under section 29 of this Act for the grant of a new tenancy shall be an order for the grant of a new tenancy of the holding; and in the absence of agreement between the landlord and the tenant as to the property which constitutes the holding the court shall in the order designate that property by reference to the circumstances existing at the date of the order.

(1A) Where the court, by virtue of paragraph (b) of section 31A(1) of this Act, makes an order under section 29 of this Act for the grant of a new tenancy in a case where the tenant is willing to accept a tenancy of part of the holding, the order shall be an order for the grant of a new tenancy of that part only.

(2) The foregoing provisions of this section shall not apply in a case where the property comprised in the current tenancy includes other property besides the holding and the landlord requires any new tenancy ordered to be granted under section 29 of this Act to be a tenancy of the whole of the property comprised in the current tenancy; but in any such case—

> (a) any order under the said section 29 for the grant of a new tenancy shall be an order for the grant of a new tenancy of the whole of the property comprised in the current tenancy, and

> (b) references in the following provisions of this Part of this Act to the holding shall be construed as references to the whole of that property.

(3) Where the current tenancy includes rights enjoyed by the tenant in connection with the holding, those rights shall be included in a tenancy ordered to be granted under section 29 of this Act, except as otherwise agreed between the landlord and the tenant or, in default of such agreement, determined by the court.

Note —The current s.32 was substituted by the Law of Property Act 1969, s.15, Sched.1. **3B–193**

holding

The tenant is only entitled to require the grant of a new tenancy of his or her holding. For holdings, see s.46, s.32 and s.23(3) which provides that the expression "the holding" means the property comprised in the tenancy, there being excluded any part thereof which is occupied neither by the tenant nor by a person employed by the tenant ... for the purposes of a business by reason of which the tenancy is one to which this Part of this Act applies. **3B–194**

current tenancy

See s.46 and s.26(1)—the tenancy under which the tenant holds for the time being. **3B–195**

the landlord

See s.44(1) which provides that "the landlord" means the person (whether or not he is the immediate landlord) who is the owner of that interest in the property comprised in the relevant tenancy which for the time being fulfils the conditions contained in ss.44(1)(a) and (b). **3B–196**

Duration of new tenancy

33. Where on an application under this Part of this Act the court makes an order for the grant of a new tenancy, the new tenancy shall be such tenancy as may be agreed between the landlord and the tenant, or, in default of such an agreement, shall be such a tenancy as **3B–197**

may be determined by the court to be reasonable in all the circumstances, being, if it is a tenancy for a term of years certain, a tenancy for a term not exceeding fifteen years, and shall begin on the coming to an end of the current tenancy.

3B–198 *Note* —Section 33 was amended by the Regulatory Reform (Business Tenancies) (England and Wales) Order 2003 (S.I. 2003 No. 3096), art.26. The amendment came into force June 1, 2004 but only applies where the s.25 notice or s.26 request was served on or after that date.

duration
3B–199 The norm is for the term of any new tenancy to be agreed between the landlord and the tenant. In the absence of agreement, the court determines a term which is "reasonable in all the circumstances". The court cannot order a tenancy for a term of more than fifteen years, but the parties are free to agree a longer term. The starting point is the length of the current term, but the court must strike a reasonable balance between conflicting considerations (*Edwards (J.H.) & Sons v. Central London Commercial Estates* [1984] 2 E.G.L.R. 103, CA; *Upsons v. Robins (E)* [1956] 1 Q.B. 131; [1955] 3 W.L.R. 584; [1955] 3 All E.R. 348, CA). For a list of the considerations that the court might take into account when deciding what term is "reasonable in all the circumstances", see *Woodfall*, para. 23.146.

current tenancy
3B–200 See s.46 and s.26(1)—the tenancy under which the tenant holds for the time being.

the landlord
3B–201 See s.44(1) which provides that "the landlord" means the person (whether or not he is the immediate landlord) who is the owner of that interest in the property comprised in the relevant tenancy which for the time being fulfils the conditions contained in ss.44(1)(a) and (b).

Rent under new tenancy
3B–202 **34.**—(1) The rent payable under a tenancy granted by order of the court under this Part of this Act shall be such as may be agreed between the landlord and the tenant or as, in default of such agreement, may be determined by the court to be that at which, having regard to the terms of the tenancy (other than those relating to rent), the holding might reasonably be expected to be let in the open market by a willing lessor, there being disregarded—

(a) any effect on rent of the fact that the tenant has or his predecessors in title have been in occupation of the holding,

(b) any goodwill attached to the holding by reason of the carrying on thereat of the business of the tenant (whether by him or by a predecessor of his in that business),

(c) any effect on rent of an improvement to which this paragraph applies,

(d) in the case of a holding comprising licensed premises, any addition to its value attributable to the licence, if it appears to the court that having regard to the terms of the current tenancy and any other relevant circumstances the benefit of the licence belongs to the tenant.

(2) Paragraph (c) of the foregoing subsection applies to any improvement carried out by a person who at the time it was carried out was the tenant, but only if it was carried out otherwise than in

pursuance of an obligation to his immediate landlord and either it was carried out during the current tenancy or the following conditions are satisfied, that is to say,—

    (a) that it was completed not more than twenty-one years before the application to the court was made; and

    (b) that the holding or any part of it affected by the improvement has at all times since the completion of the improvement been comprised in tenancies of the description specified in section 23(1) of this Act; and

    (c) that at the termination of each of those tenancies the tenant did not quit.

(2A) If this Part of this Act applies by virtue of section 23(1A) of this Act, the reference in subsection (1)(d) above to the tenant shall be construed as including—

    (a) a company in which the tenant has a controlling interest, or

    (b) where the tenant is a company, a person with a controlling interest in the company.

(3) Where the rent is determined by the court the court may, if it thinks fit, further determine that the terms of the tenancy shall include such provision for varying the rent as may be specified in the determination.

(4) It is hereby declared that the matters which are to be taken into account by the court in determining the rent include any effect on rent of the operation of the provisions of the Landlord and Tenant (Covenants) Act 1995.

Note —The current s.34 was substituted by the Law of Property Act 1969, s.15, Sched.1; s.34(4) was added by the Landlord and Tenant (Covenants) Act 1995, Sched.1 para. 3. Section 34(2)(a) was amended and s.34(2A) inserted by the Regulatory Reform (Business Tenancies) (England and Wales) Order 2003 (S.I. 2003 No. 3096), art.15.
       3B–203

rent

In the absence of agreement between the parties, the court determines the rent at which, having regard to the terms of the tenancy, the holding might reasonably be expected to be let in the open market by a willing lessor, subject to a number of disregards. In view of the requirement to have regard to the terms of the tenancy, the court should determine any other disputed terms, before deciding the rent. (*O'May v. City of London Real Property Co Ltd* [1983] 2 A.C. 726; [1982] 2 W.L.R. 407; [1982] 1 All E.R. 660, HL; *Cardshops v. Davies* [1971] 1 W.L.R. 591; [1971] 2 All E.R. 721, CA) The best evidence of a reasonable open market rent is normally that of valuers relying upon comparables. The disregards in s.34(1) are principally matters related to the particular tenant—*e.g.* the effect of the tenant's occupation, any goodwill derived from the tenant's business and the effect of any improvements to which the section applies. It is possible for the court to fix a rent which increases by instalments (s.34(3), *Fawke v. Viscount Chelsea* [1980] Q.B. 441; [1979] 3 W.L.R. 508; [1979] 3 All E.R. 568, CA and *88 High Road, Kilburn, Re* [1959] 1 W.L.R. 279; [1959] 1 All E.R. 527, Ch D—upwards only rent review).
       3B–204

business

See s.46 and s.23(2) which provides that "business" includes a trade, profession or employment and includes any activity carried on by a body of persons, whether corporate or unincorporate. See too the commentary to s.23 above.
       3B–205

current tenancy

See s.46 and s.26(1)—the tenancy under which the tenant holds for the time being.
       3B–206

holding

3B–207   See s.46, s.32 and s.23(3) which provides that the expression "the holding" means the property comprised in the tenancy, there being excluded any part thereof which is occupied neither by the tenant nor by a person employed by the tenant ... for the purposes of a business by reason of which the tenancy is one to which this Part of this Act applies.

the landlord

3B–208   See s.44(1) which provides that "the landlord" means the person (whether or not he is the immediate landlord) who is the owner of that interest in the property comprised in the relevant tenancy which for the time being fulfils the conditions contained in ss.44(1)(a) and (b).

Other terms of new tenancy

3B–209   **35.**—(1) The terms of a tenancy granted by order of the court under this Part of this Act (other than terms as to the duration thereof and as to the rent payable thereunder), including, where different persons own interests which fulfil the conditions specified in section 44(1) of this Act in different parts of it, terms as to the apportionment of the rent,shall be such as may be agreed between the landlord and the tenant or as, in default of such agreement, may be determined by the court; and in determining those terms the court shall have regard to the terms of the current tenancy and to all relevant circumstances.

(2) In subsection (1) of this section the reference to all relevant circumstances includes (without prejudice to the generality of that reference) a reference to the operation of the provisions of the Landlord and Tenant (Covenants) Act 1995.

3B–210   *Note* —Subsections (1) and (2) were inserted by the Landlord and Tenant (Covenants) Act 1995, Sched.1, paras 4(1) and (2) and amended by the Regulatory Reform (Business Tenancies) (England and Wales) Order 2003 (S.I. 2003 No. 3096), art.27(3). The amendment came into force June 1, 2004 but only applies where the s.25 notice or s.26 request was served on or after that date.

Other terms

3B–211   In the absence of agreement between the parties, the court determines any other terms, having regard to the terms of the current tenancy, and all relevant circumstances. The court will normally follow the terms of the current tenancy—any party wishing to depart from them must give a reason (*O'May v. City of London Real Property Co Ltd* [1983] 2 A.C. 726; [1982] 2 W.L.R. 407; [1982] 1 All E.R. 660, HL). Any change must be fair and reasonable and take into account the comparatively weak negotiating position of a sitting tenant seeking renewal (*Cardshops v. Davies* [1971] 1 W.L.R. 591; [1971] 2 All E.R. 721, CA. See too *No. 1 Albermarle Street, Re* [1959] Ch. 532; [1959] 1 All E.R. 250; Ch D).

current tenancy

3B–212   See s.46 and s.26(1)—the tenancy under which the tenant holds for the time being.

the landlord

3B–213   See s.44(1) which provides that "the landlord" means the person (whether or not he is the immediate landlord) who is the owner of that interest in the property comprised in the relevant tenancy which for the time being fulfils the conditions contained in ss.44(1)(a) and (b).

Carrying out of order for new tenancy

3B–214   **36.**—(1) Where under this Part of this Act the court makes an order for the grant of a new tenancy, then, unless the order is revoked under the next following subsection or the landlord and the tenant agree not to act upon the order, the landlord shall be bound to execute or make in favour of the tenant, and the tenant shall be bound to accept, a lease or agreement for a tenancy of the holding embodying the terms agreed between the landlord and the tenant or determined by the court in accordance with the foregoing provisions of this Part of this Act; and where the landlord executes or makes such a lease or agreement the tenant shall be bound, if so required by the landlord, to execute a counterpart or duplicate thereof.

(2) If the tenant, within fourteen days after the making of an order under this Part of this Act for the grant of a new tenancy, applies to the court for the revocation of the order the court shall revoke the order; and where the order is so revoked, then, if it is so agreed between the landlord and the tenant or determined by the court, the current tenancy shall continue, beyond the date at which it would have come to an end apart from this subsection, for such period as may be so agreed or determined to be necessary to afford to the landlord a reasonable opportunity for reletting or otherwise disposing of the premises which would have been comprised in the new tenancy; and while the current tenancy continues by virtue of this subsection it shall not be a tenancy to which this Part of this Act applies.

(3) Where an order is revoked under the last foregoing subsection any provision thereof as to payment of costs shall not cease to have effect by reason only of the revocation; but the court may, if it thinks fit, revoke or vary any such provision or, where no costs have been awarded in the proceedings for the revoked order, award such costs.

(4) A lease executed or agreement made under this section, in a case where the interest of the lessor is subject to a mortgage, shall be deemed to be one authorised by section ninety-nine of the Law of Property Act 1925 (which confers certain powers of leasing on mortgagors in possession), and subsection (13) of that section (which allows those powers to be restricted or excluded by agreement) shall not have effect in relation to such a lease or agreement.

Carrying out of order for new tenancy

If the court orders the grant of a new tenancy, the landlord is bound to make and the tenant is bound to accept a new lease embodying the terms agreed or determined by the court, unless— **3B–215**

(a) the landlord and the tenant agree not to act on the order; or

(b) the tenant elects not to take the tenancy on the terms ordered. In such circumstances the tenant may apply to the court within 14 days of the making of the order for the revocation of the order. On such an application the court must revoke the order (s.36(2)).

See *e.g. 88 High Road, Kilburn, Re* [1959]1 W.L.R. 279; [1959] 1 All E.R. 527 where the order was revoked, but the tenant was ordered to pay the costs of the action and of the application to revoke.

current tenancy

See s.46 and s.26(1)—the tenancy under which the tenant holds for the time being. **3B–216**

holding

See s.46, s.32 and s.23(3) which provides that the expression "the holding" means **3B–217**

BUSINESS TENANCIES

the property comprised in the tenancy, there being excluded any part thereof which is occupied neither by the tenant nor by a person employed by the tenant ... for the purposes of a business by reason of which the tenancy is one to which this Part of this Act applies.

the landlord

3B–218 See s.44(1) which provides that "the landlord" means the person (whether or not he is the immediate landlord) who is the owner of that interest in the property comprised in the relevant tenancy which for the time being fulfils the conditions contained in ss.44(1)(a) and (b).

Compensation where order for new tenancy precluded on certain grounds

3B–219 **37.**—(1) Subject to the provisions of this Act, in a case specified in subsection (1A), (1B) or (1C) below (a "compensation case") the tenant shall be entitled on quitting the holding to recover from the landlord by way of compensation an amount determined in accordance with this section.

(1A) The first compensation case is where on the making of an application by the tenant under section 24(1) of this Act the court is precluded (whether by subsection (1) or subsection (2) of section 31 of this Act) from making an order for the grant of a new tenancy by reason of any of the grounds specified in paragraphs (e), (f) and (g) of section 30(1) of this Act (the "compensation grounds") and not of any grounds specified in any other paragraph of section 30(1).

(1B) The second compensation case is where on the making of an application under section 29(2) of this Act the court is precluded (whether by section 29(4)(a) or section 31(2) of this Act) from making an order for the grant of a new tenancy by reason of any of the compensation grounds and not of any other grounds specified in section 30(1) of this Act.

(1C) The third compensation case is where—

    (a) the landlord's notice under section 25 of this Act or, as the case may be, under section 26(6) of this Act, states his opposition to the grant of a new tenancy on any of the compensation grounds and not on any other grounds specified in section 30(1) of this Act; and

    (b) either—

        (i) no application is made by the tenant under section 24(1) of this Act or by the landlord under section 29(2) of this Act; or

        (ii) such an application is made but is subsequently withdrawn.

(2) Subject to the following provisions of this section, compensation under this section shall be as follows, that is to say—

    (a) where the conditions specified in the next following subsection are satisfied in relation to the whole of the holding it shall be the product of the appropriate multiplier and twice the rateable value of the holding,

    (b) in any other case it shall be [the product of the appropriate multiplier and] the rateable value of the holding.

(3) The said conditions are—

    (a) that, during the whole of the fourteen years immediately preceding the termination of the current tenancy, premises being or comprised in the holding have been occupied for the purposes of a business carried on by the occupier or for those and other purposes;

    (b) that, if during those fourteen years there was a change in the occupier of the premises, the person who was the occupier immediately after the change was the successor to the business carried on by the person who was the occupier immediately before the change.

(3A) If the conditions specified in subsection (3) above are satisfied in relation to part of the holding but not in relation to the other part, the amount of compensation shall be the aggregate of sums calculated separately as compensation in respect of each part, and accordingly, for the purpose of calculating compensation in respect of a part any reference in this section to the holding shall be construed as a reference to that part.

(3B) Where section 44(1A) of this Act applies, the compensation shall be determined separately for each part and compensation determined for any part shall be recoverable only from the person who is the owner of an interest in that part which fulfils the conditions specified in section 44(1) of this Act.

(4) Where the court is precluded from making an order for the grant of a new tenancy under this Part of this Act in a compensation case, the court shall on the application of the tenant certify that fact.

(5) For the purposes of subsection (2) of this section the rateable value of the holding shall be determined as follows:—

    (a) where in the valuation list in force at the date on which the landlord's notice under section 25 or, as the case may be, subsection (6) of section 26 of this Act is given a value is then shown as the annual value (as hereinafter defined) of the holding, the rateable value of the holding shall be taken to be that value;

    (b) where no such value is so shown with respect to the holding but such a value or such values is or are so shown with respect to premises comprised in or comprising the holding or part of it, the rateable value of the holding shall be taken to be such value as is found by a proper apportionment or aggregation of the value or values so shown;

    (c) where the rateable value of the holding cannot be ascertained in accordance with the foregoing paragraphs of this subsection, it shall be taken to be the value which, apart from any exemption from assessment to rates, would on a proper assessment be the value to be entered in the said valuation list as the annual value of the holding;

and any dispute arising, whether in proceedings before the court or otherwise, as to the determination for those purposes of the rateable value of the holding shall be referred to the Commissioners of Inland Revenue for decision by a valuation officer.

An appeal shall lie to the Lands Tribunal from any decision of a valuation officer under this subsection, but subject thereto any such decision shall be final.

[(5A) If part of the holding is domestic property, as defined in section 66 of the Local Government Finance Act 1988—

(a) the domestic property shall be disregarded in determining the rateable value of the holding under subsection (5) of this section; and

(b) if, on the date specified in subsection (5)(a) of this section, the tenant occupied the whole or any part of the domestic property, the amount of compensation to which he is entitled under subsection (1) of this section shall be increased by the addition of a sum equal to his reasonable expenses in removing from the domestic property.

(5B) Any question as to the amount of the sum referred to in paragraph (b) of subsection (5A) of this section shall be determined by agreement between the landlord and the tenant or, in default of agreement, by the court.

(5C) If the whole of the holding is domestic property, as defined in section 66 of the Local Government Finance Act 1988, for the purposes of subsection (2) of this section the rateable value of the holding shall be taken to be an amount equal to the rent at which it is estimated the holding might reasonably be expected to let from year to year if the tenant undertook to pay all usual tenant's rates and taxes and to bear the cost of the repairs and insurance and the other expenses (if any) necessary to maintain the holding in a state to command that rent.

(5D) The following provisions shall have effect as regards a determination of an amount mentioned in subsection (5C) of this section—

(a) the date by reference to which such a determination is to be made is the date on which the landlord's notice under section 25 or, as the case may be, subsection (6) of section 26 of this Act is given;

(b) any dispute arising, whether in proceedings before the court or otherwise, as to such a determination shall be referred to the Commissioners of Inland Revenue for decision by a valuation officer;

(c) an appeal shall lie to the Lands Tribunal from such a decision but, subject to that, such a decision shall be final.]

[(5E) Any deduction made under paragraph 2A of Schedule 6 to the Local Government Finance Act 1988 (deduction from valuation of hereditaments used for breeding horses etc.) shall be disregarded, to the extent that it relates to the holding, in determining the rateable value of the holding under subsection (5) of this section.]

(6) The Commissioners of Inland Revenue may by statutory instrument make rules prescribing the procedure in connection with references under this section.

(7) In this section—

the reference to the termination of the current tenancy is a reference to the date of termination specified in the landlord's notice under section 25 of this Act or, as the case may be, the date specified in the tenant's request for a new tenancy as the date from which the new tenancy is to begin;

the expression "annual value" means rateable value except that where the rateable value differs from the net annual value the said expression means net annual value;

the expression "valuation officer" means any officer of the Commissioners of Inland Revenue for the time being authorised by a certificate of the Commissioners to act in relation to a valuation list.

(8) In subsection (2) of this section "the appropriate multiplier" means such multiplier as the Secretary of State may by order made by statutory instrument prescribe and different multipliers may be so prescribed in relation to different cases.

(9) A statutory instrument containing an order under subsection (8) of this section shall be subject to annulment in pursuance of a resolution of either House of Parliament.

Note—Section 37 was amended by the Local Government, Planning and Land Act 1980, Sched.33, paras 4(1) and 4(2); the Local Government and Housing Act 1989, s.149 and Sched.7, paras 2(2), 2(3), 2(4) and 4 and by the Local Government Finance (Miscellaneous Amendments and Repeal) Order 1990 (S.I. 1990 No. 1285) art.2, Sched. Pt I, para. 4(a) and by the Regulatory Reform (Business Tenancies) (England and Wales) Order 2003 (S.I. 2003 No. 3096), art.19. The latter amendment came into force June 1, 2004 but only applies where the s.25 notice or s.26 request was served on or after that date. **3B–220**

business

See s.46 and s.23(2) which provides that "business" includes a trade, profession or employment and includes any activity carried on by a body of persons, whether corporate or unincorporate. See too the commentary to s.23 above. **3B–221**

current tenancy

See s.46 and s.26(1)—the tenancy under which the tenant holds for the time being. **3B–222**

date of termination

See s.46 and s.25(1)—the date specified in the landlord's s.25 notice at which the tenancy is to come to an end. **3B–223**

holding

See s.46, s.32 and s.23(3) which provides that the expression "the holding" means the property comprised in the tenancy, there being excluded any part thereof which is occupied neither by the tenant nor by a person employed by the tenant ... for the purposes of a business by reason of which the tenancy is one to which this Part of this Act applies. **3B–224**

the landlord

See s.44(1) which provides that "the landlord" means the person (whether or not he is the immediate landlord) who is the owner of that interest in the property comprised in the relevant tenancy which for the time being fulfils the conditions contained in ss.44(1)(a) and (b). **3B–225**

compensation

Put simply, a tenant is entitled to compensation if a landlord successfully relies **3B–226**

BUSINESS TENANCIES

upon s.30(1)(e) (aggregate of the rents reasonably obtainable on separate lettings less than the rent reasonably obtainable on a letting of that property as a whole), s.30(1)(f) (intention of landlord to demolish or reconstruct) or s.30(1)(g) (intention of landlord to occupy the holding for the purposes of a business or as his residence). If a court refuses the grant of a new tenancy on any these three grounds it must certify that fact (s.37(4)). The amount of compensation is either the product of the appropriate multiplier and the rateable value or the product of the appropriate multiplier and twice the rateable value. (See s.37 and the Landlord and Tenant Act 1954 (Appropriate Multiplier) Order 1990 (S.I. 1990 No. 363)).

restriction on contracting out

3B–227 See s.38(2).

Compensation for possession obtained by misrepresentation

3B–228 37A.—(1) Where the court—

    (a) makes an order for the termination of the current tenancy but does not make an order for the grant of a new tenancy, or

    (b) refuses an order for the grant of a new tenancy,

and it subsequently made to appear to the court that the order was obtained, or the court was induced to refuse the grant, by misrepresentation or the concealment of material facts, the court may order the landlord to pay to the tenant such sum as appears sufficient as compensation for damage or loss sustained by the tenant as the result of the order or refusal.

    (2) Where—

    (a) the tenant has quit the holding—

        (i) after making but withdrawing an application under section 24(1) of this Act; or

        (ii) without making such an application; and

    (b) it is made to appear to the court that he did so by reason of misrepresentation or the concealment of material facts,

the court may order the landlord to pay to the tenant such sum as appears sufficient as compensation for damage or loss sustained by the tenant as the result of quitting the holding.

3B–229 *Note* —New s.37A was inserted by the Regulatory Reform (Business Tenancies) (England and Wales) Order 2003 (S.I. 2003 No. 3096), art.20. The amendment came into force June 1, 2004 but only where the tenant quit the holding before that date (reg.29(5) of 2003 Order) but only where the tenant quit the holding before that date (reg.29(5) of 2003 Order; para. 3B–92).

Restriction on agreements excluding provisions of Part II

3B–230 38.—(1) Any agreement relating to a tenancy to which this Part of this Act applies (whether contained in the instrument creating the tenancy or not) shall be void (except as provided by section 38A of this Act) in so far as it purports to preclude the tenant from making an application or request under this Part of this Act or provides for the termination or the surrender of the tenancy in the event of his making such an application or request or for the imposition of any penalty or disability on the tenant in that event.

    (2) Where—

(a) during the whole of the five years immediately preceding the date on which the tenant under a tenancy to which this Part of this Act applies is to quit the holding, premises being or comprised in the holding have been occupied for the purposes of a business carried on by the occupier or for those and other purposes, and

(b) if during those five years there was a change in the occupier of the premises, the person who was the occupier immediately after the change was the successor to the business carried on by the person who was the occupier immediately before the change,

any agreement (whether contained in the instrument creating the tenancy or not and whether made before or after the termination of that tenancy) which purports to exclude or reduce compensation under section 37 of this Act shall to that extent be void, so however that this subsection shall not affect any agreement as to the amount of any such compensation which is made after the right to compensation has accrued.

(3) In a case not falling within the last foregoing subsection the right to compensation conferred by section 37 of this Act may be excluded or modified by agreement.

(4) [...]

Note—The current s.38 was substituted by Law of Property Act 1969, s.15, Sched.1 **3B–231** and was amended by the Regulatory Reform (Business Tenancies) (England and Wales) Order 2003 (S.I. 2003 No. 3096), art.21 and Sched.5, para. 4. Subsection (4) was repealed by Sched.6, para. 1. The amendment came into force June 1, 2004. It does not apply to an agreement to contract out nor does it apply to an agreement for the surrender for a tenancy which was authorised by the court under s.38(4) before that date. (Regulation 29(2)(a)(ii) of the 2003 Order—for further transitional provisions see reg. 29(3) and (4); para. 3B–92).

Agreements to exclude provisions of Part 2

38A.—(1) The persons who will be the landlord and the tenant in **3B–232** relation to a tenancy to be granted for a term of years certain which will be a tenancy to which this Part of this Act applies may agree that the provisions of sections 24 to 28 of this Act shall be excluded in relation to that tenancy.

(2) The persons who are the landlord and the tenant in relation to a tenancy to which this Part of this Act applies may agree that the tenancy shall be surrendered on such date or in such circumstances as may be specified in the agreement and on such terms (if any) as may be so specified.

(3) An agreement under subsection (1) above shall be void unless—

(a) the landlord has served on the tenant a notice in the form, or substantially in the form, set out in Schedule 1 to the Regulatory Reform (Business Tenancies) (England and Wales) Order 2003 ("the 2003 Order"); and

(b) the requirements specified in Schedule 2 to that Order are met.

(4) An agreement under subsection (2) above shall be void unless—

(a) the landlord has served on the tenant a notice in the form, or substantially in the form, set out in Schedule 3 to the 2003 Order; and

(b) the requirements specified in Schedule 4 to that Order are met.

3B–233   *Note* —New s.38A was inserted by the Regulatory Reform (Business Tenancies) (England and Wales) Order 2003 (S.I. 2003 No. 3096). The amendment came into force June 1, 2004. Section 38A sets out a completely new procedure for contracting out of the security provisions of Part II of the 1954 Act and for agreements to surrender where Part II of the Act applies. The procedure in each case is based upon three elements (i) notice in a prescribed form served upon the tenant by the landlord, (ii) a declaration from the tenant acknowledging receipt of the notice and (iii) a reference to the notice in the lease/agreement to surrender. The details are contained in Scheds 1 to 4 of 2003 Reform Order—not set out in the *White Book*.

Saving for compulsory acquisitions.

3B–234   **39.**—(1) [...]

(2) If the amount of the compensation which would have been payable under section thirty-seven of this Act if the tenancy had come to an end in circumstances giving rise to compensation under that section and the date at which the acquiring authority obtained possession had been the termination of the current tenancy exceeds the amount of [the compensation payable under section 121 of the Lands Clauses Consolidation Act 1845 or section 20 of the Compulsory Purchase Act 1965in the case of a tenancy to which this Part of this Act applies], that compensation shall be increased by the amount of the excess.

(3) Nothing in section twenty-four of this Act shall affect the operation of the said section one hundred and twenty-one.

3B–235   *Note* —Amended by Land Compensation Act 1973, s.47(3). Subsection (1) was repealed by Land Compensation Act 1973, Sched. 3.

current tenancy

3B–236   See s.46 and s.26(1)—the tenancy under which the tenant holds for the time being.

3B–237 Duty of tenants and landlords of business premises to give information to each other

40.—(1) Where a person who is an owner of an interest in reversion expectant (whether immediately or not) on a tenancy of any business premises has served on the tenant a notice in the prescribed form requiring him to do so, it shall be the duty of the tenant to give the appropriate person in writing the information specified in subsection (2) below.

(2) That information is—

(a) whether the tenant occupies the premises or any part of them wholly or partly for the purposes of a business carried on by him;

(b) whether his tenancy has effect subject to any sub-tenancy on which his tenancy is immediately expectant and, if so—

(i) what premises are comprised in the sub-tenancy;

    (ii) for what term it has effect (or, if it is terminable by notice, by what notice it can be terminated);

    (iii) what is the rent payable under it;

    (iv) who is the sub-tenant;

    (v) (to the best of his knowledge and belief) whether the sub-tenant is in occupation of the premises or of part of the premises comprised in the sub-tenancy and, if not, what is the sub-tenant's address;

    (vi) whether an agreement is in force excluding in relation to the sub-tenancy the provisions of sections 24 to 28 of this Act; and

    (vii) whether a notice has been given under section 25 or 26(6) of this Act, or a request has been made under section 26 of this Act, in relation to the sub-tenancy and, if so, details of the notice or request; and

  (c) (to the best of his knowledge and belief) the name and address of any other person who owns an interest in reversion in any part of the premises.

(3) Where the tenant of any business premises who is a tenant under such a tenancy as is mentioned in section 26(1) of this Act has served on a reversioner or a reversioner's mortgagee in possession a notice in the prescribed form requiring him to do so, it shall be the duty of the person on whom the notice is served to give the appropriate person in writing the information specified in subsection (4) below.

(4) That information is—

  (a) whether he is the owner of the fee simple in respect of the premises or any part of them or the mortgagee in possession of such an owner,

  (b) if he is not, then (to the best of his knowledge and belief)—

    (i) the name and address of the person who is his or, as the case may be, his mortgagor's immediate landlord in respect of those premises or of the part in respect of which he or his mortgagor is not the owner in fee simple;

    (ii) for what term his or his mortgagor's tenancy has effect and what is the earliest date (if any) at which that tenancy is terminable by notice to quit given by the landlord; and

    (iii) whether a notice has been given under section 25 or 26(6) of this Act, or a request has been made under section 26 of this Act, in relation to the tenancy and, if so, details of the notice or request;

  (c) (to the best of his knowledge and belief) the name and address of any other person who owns an interest in reversion in any part of the premises; and

  (d) if he is a reversioner, whether there is a mortgagee in

1103

possession of his interest in the premises and, if so, (to the best of his knowledge and belief) what is the name and address of the mortgagee.

(5) A duty imposed on a person by this section is a duty—

(a) to give the information concerned within the period of one month beginning with the date of service of the notice; and

(b) if within the period of six months beginning with the date of service of the notice that person becomes aware that any information which has been given in pursuance of the notice is not, or is no longer, correct, to give the appropriate person correct information within the period of one month beginning with the date on which he becomes aware.

(6) This section shall not apply to a notice served by or on the tenant more than two years before the date on which apart from this Act his tenancy would come to an end by effluxion of time or could be brought to an end by notice to quit given by the landlord.

(7) Except as provided by section 40A of this Act, the appropriate person for the purposes of this section and section 40A(1) of this Act is the person who served the notice under subsection (1) or (3) above.

(8) In this section—

"business premises" means premises used wholly or partly for the purposes of a business;

"mortgagee in possession" includes a receiver appointed by the mortgagee or by the court who is in receipt of the rents and profits, and "his mortgagor" shall be construed accordingly;

"reversioner" means any person having an interest in the premises, being an interest in reversion expectant (whether immediately or not) on the tenancy;

"reversioner's mortgagee in possession" means any person being a mortgagee in possession in respect of such an interest; and

"sub-tenant" includes a person retaining possession of any premises by virtue of the Rent (Agriculture) Act 1976 or the Rent Act 1977 after the coming to an end of a sub-tenancy, and "sub-tenancy" includes a right so to retain possession.

3B–238 *Note* —New s.40 was inserted by the Regulatory Reform (Business Tenancies) (England and Wales) Order 2003 (S.I. 2003 No. 3096). The amendment came into force June 1, 2004. It does not apply to a notice under s.40 served before that date (reg. 29(6) of the 2003 Reform Order—see para. 3B–92).

tenancy

3B–239 See s.69(1) and the commentary to s.23 above. The definition includes an agreement for a lease or underlease, but does not include a mortgage.

business

3B–240 See s.46 and s.23(2) which provides that "business" includes a trade, profession or employment and includes any activity carried on by a body of persons, whether corporate or unincorporate. See too the commentary to s.23 above.

prescribed form

See the Landlord and Tenant Act 1954, Pt 2 (Notices) Regulations 2004 (S.I. 2004 **3B–241** No. 1005). Regulation 2(2) allows a "form substantially to the like effect" of those contained in the regulations.

notice to quit

Means a notice to quit given by the immediate landlord (see s.44(2)). **3B–242**

the landlord

See s.44(1) which provides that "the landlord" means the person (whether or not **3B–243** he is the immediate landlord) who is the owner of that interest in the property comprised in the relevant tenancy which for the time being fulfils the conditions contained in ss.44(1)(a) and (b).

Duties in transfer cases

40A.—(1) If a person on whom a notice under section 40(1) or (3) **3B–244** of this Act has been served has transferred his interest in the premises or any part of them to some other person and gives the appropriate person notice in writing—

    (a) of the transfer of his interest; and

    (b) of the name and address of the person to whom he transferred it,

on giving the notice he ceases in relation to the premises or (as the case may be) to that part to be under any duty imposed by section 40 of this Act.

    (2) If—

    (a) the person who served the notice under section 40(1) or (3) of this Act ("the transferor") has transferred his interest in the premises to some other person ("the transferee"); and

    (b) the transferor or the transferee has given the person required to give the information notice in writing—

        (i) of the transfer; and

        (ii) of the transferee's name and address,

the appropriate person for the purposes of section 40 of this Act and subsection (1) above is the transferee.

    (3) If—

    (a) a transfer such as is mentioned in paragraph (a) of subsection (2) above has taken place; but

    (b) neither the transferor nor the transferee has given a notice such as is mentioned in paragraph (b) of that subsection,

any duty imposed by section 40 of this Act may be performed by giving the information either to the transferor or to the transferee.

Note —New s.40A was inserted by the Regulatory Reform (Business Tenancies) **3B–245** (England and Wales) Order 2003 (S.I. 2003 No. 3096). The amendment came into force June 1, 2004. It does not apply to a notice under s.40 served before that date.

Proceedings for breach of duties to give information

40B. A claim that a person has broken any duty imposed by sec- **3B–246** tion 40 of this Act may be made the subject of civil proceedings for breach of statutory duty; and in any such proceedings a court may order that person to comply with that duty and may make an award of damages.

3B–247   *Note* —New s.40B was inserted by the Regulatory Reform (Business Tenancies) (England and Wales) Order 2003 (S.I. 2003 No. 3096). The amendment came into force June 1, 2004. It does not apply to a notice under s.40 served before that date.

Trusts

3B–248   **41.**—(1) Where a tenancy is held on trust, occupation by all or any of the beneficiaries under the trust, and the carrying on of a business by all or any of the beneficiaries, shall be treated for the purposes of section twenty-three of this Act as equivalent to occupation or the carrying on of a business by the tenant; and in relation to a tenancy to which this Part of this Act applies by virtue of the foregoing provisions of this subsection—

(a) references (however expressed) in this Part of this Act and in the Ninth Schedule to this Act to the business of, or to carrying on of business, use, occupation or enjoyment by, the tenant shall be construed as including references to the business of, or to carrying on of business, use, occupation or enjoyment by, the beneficiaries or beneficiary;

(b) the reference in paragraph (d) of [subsection (1) of] section thirty-four of this Act to the tenant shall be construed as including the beneficiaries or beneficiary; and

(c) a change in the persons of the trustees shall not be treated as a change in the person of the tenant.

(2) Where the landlord's interest is held on trust the references in paragraph (g) of subsection (1) of section thirty of this Act to the landlord shall be construed as including references to the beneficiaries under the trust or any of them; but, except in the case of a trust arising under a will or on the intestacy of any person, the reference in subsection (2) of that section to the creation of the interest therein mentioned shall be construed as including the creation of the trust.

3B–249   *Note* —Amended by the Law of Property Act 1969, s.1(2).

tenancy

3B–250   See s.69(1) and the commentary to s.23 above. The definition includes an agreement for a lease or underlease, but does not include a mortgage.

business

3B–251   See s.46 and s.23(2) which provides that "business" includes a trade, profession or employment and includes any activity carried on by a body of persons, whether corporate or unincorporate. See too the commentary to s.23 above.

the landlord

3B–252   See s.44(1) which provides that "the landlord" means the person (whether or not he is the immediate landlord) who is the owner of that interest in the property comprised in the relevant tenancy which for the time being fulfils the conditions contained in ss.44(1)(a) and (b).

Partnerships

3B–253   **41A.**—(1) The following provisions of this section shall apply where—

    (a) a tenancy is held jointly by two or more persons (in this section referred to as the joint tenants); and

    (b) the property comprised in the tenancy is or includes premises occupied for the purposes of a business; and

    (c) the business (or some other business) was at some time during the existence of the tenancy carried on in partnership by all the persons who were then the joint tenants or by those and other persons and the joint tenants' interest in the premises was then partnership property; and

    (d) the business is carried on (whether alone or in partnership with other persons) by one or some only of the joint tenants and no part of the property comprised in the tenancy is occupied, in right of the tenancy, for the purposes of a business carried on (whether alone or in partnership with other persons) by the other or others.

(2) In the following provisions of this section those of the joint tenants who for the time being carry on the business are referred to as the business tenants and the others as the other joint tenants.

(3) Any notice given by the business tenants which, had it been given by all the joint tenants, would have been—

    (a) a tenant's request for a new tenancy made in accordance with section 26 of this Act; or

    (b) a notice under subsection (1) or subsection (2) of section 27 of this Act;

shall be treated as such if it states that it is given by virtue of this section and sets out the facts by virtue of which the persons giving it are the business tenants; and references in those sections and in section 24A of this Act to the tenant shall be construed accordingly.

(4) A notice given by the landlord to the business tenants which, had it been given to all the joint tenants, would have been a notice under section 25 of this Act shall be treated as such a notice, and references in that section to the tenant shall be construed accordingly.

(5) An application under section 24(1) of this Act for a new tenancy may, instead of being made by all the joint tenants, be made by the business tenants alone; and where it is so made—

    (a) this Part of this Act shall have effect, in relation to it, as if the references therein to the tenant included references to the business tenants alone; and

    (b) the business tenants shall be liable, to the exclusion of the other joint tenants, for the payment of rent and the discharge of any other obligation under the current tenancy for any rental period beginning after the date specified in the landlord's notice under section 25 of this Act or, as the case may be, beginning on or after the date specified in their request for a new tenancy.

(6) Where the court makes an order under section 29 of this Act for the grant of a new tenancy it may order the grant to be made to the business tenants or to them jointly with the persons carrying on the business in partnership with them, and may order the grant to

be made subject to the satisfaction, within a time specified by the order, of such conditions as to guarantors, sureties or otherwise as appear to the court equitable, having regard to the omission of the other joint tenants from the persons who will be the tenants under the new tenancy.

(7) The business tenants shall be entitled to recover any amount payable by way of compensation under section 37 or section 59 of this Act.

Note —Section 41A was inserted by Law of Property Act 1969, s.9 and amended by by the Regulatory Reform (Business Tenancies) (England and Wales) Order 2003 (S.I. 2003 No. 3096), Sched.5, para. 5.

business

3B–254   See s.46 and s.23(2) which provides that "business" includes a trade, profession or employment and includes any activity carried on by a body of persons, whether corporate or unincorporate. See too the commentary to s.23 above.

current tenancy

3B–255   See s.46 and s.26(1)—the tenancy under which the tenant holds for the time being.

the landlord

3B–256   See s.44(1) which provides that "the landlord" means the person (whether or not he is the immediate landlord) who is the owner of that interest in the property comprised in the relevant tenancy which for the time being fulfils the conditions contained in ss.44(1)(a) and (b).

Groups of companies

3B–257   **42.**—(1) For the purposes of this section two bodies corporate shall be taken to be members of a group if and only if one is a subsidiary of the other or both are subsidiaries of a third body corporate or the same person has a controlling interest in both.

(2) Where a tenancy is held by a member of a group, occupation by another member of the group, and the carrying on of a business by another member of the group, shall be treated for the purposes of section 23 of this Act as equivalent to occupation or the carrying on of a business by the member of the group holding the tenancy; and in relation to a tenancy to which this Part of this Act applies by virtue of the foregoing provisions of this subsection—

> (a) references (however expressed) in this Part of this Act and in the Ninth Schedule to this Act to the business of or to use occupation or enjoyment by the tenant shall be construed as including references to the business of or to use occupation or enjoyment by the said other member;
>
> (b) the reference in paragraph (d) of subsection (1) of section 34 of this Act to the tenant shall be construed as including the said other member; and
>
> (c) an assignment of the tenancy from one member of the group to another shall not be treated as a change in the person of the tenant.

(3) Where the landlord's interest is held by a member of a group—

> (a) the reference in paragraph (g) of subsection (1) of sec-

tion 30 of this Act to intended occupation by the landlord for the purposes of a business to be carried on by him shall be construed as including intended occupation by any member of the group for the purposes of a business to be carried on by that member; and

(b) the reference in subsection (2) of that section to the purchase or creation of any interest shall be construed as a reference to a purchase from or creation by a person other than a member of the group.

Note —The current s.42 was substituted by the Law of Property Act 1969, s.15, **3B–258** Sched.1 and amended by Companies Act 1989, s.144(4), s.213(2), s.215(2), Sched.18 para. 3 and by the Regulatory Reform (Business Tenancies) (England and Wales) Order 2003 (S.I. 2003 No. 3096) but only applies where the s.25 notice or s.26 request was served on or after that date.

business

See s.46 and s.23(2) which provides that "business" includes a trade, profession or **3B–259** employment and includes any activity carried on by a body of persons, whether corporate or unincorporate.

the landlord

See s.44(1) which provides that "the landlord" means the person (whether or not **3B–260** he is the immediate landlord) who is the owner of that interest in the property comprised in the relevant tenancy which for the time being fulfils the conditions contained in ss.44(1)(a) and (b).

Tenancies excluded from Part II

43.—(1) This Part of this Act does not apply— **3B–261**

(a) to a tenancy of an agricultural holding [[which is a tenancy in relation to which the Agricultural Holdings Act 1986 applies or a tenancy which would be a tenancy of an agricultural holding in relation to which that Act applied if subsection (3) of section 2 of that Act] did not have effect or, in a case where approval was given under subsection (1) of that section], if that approval had not been given;]]

(aa) [to a farm business tenancy;]

(b) to a tenancy created by a mining lease;

(c) [...]

(d) [...]

(2) This Part of this Act does not apply to a tenancy granted by reason that the tenant was the holder of an office, appointment or employment from the grantor thereof and continuing only so long as the tenant holds the office, appointment or employment, or terminable by the grantor on the tenant's ceasing to hold it, or coming to an end at a time fixed by reference to the time at which the tenant ceases to hold it:

Provided that this subsection shall not have effect in relation to a tenancy granted after the commencement of this Act unless the tenancy was granted by an instrument in writing which expressed the purpose for which the tenancy was granted.

[(3) This Part of this Act does not apply to a tenancy granted for a term certain not exceeding six months unless—

(a) the tenancy contains provision for renewing the term or for extending it beyond six months from its beginning; or

(b) the tenant has been in occupation for a period which, together with any period during which any predecessor in the carrying on of the business carried on by the tenant was in occupation, exceeds twelve months.]

3B–262 *Note* —Amended by Agricultural Tenancies Act 1995, Sched. para.10; Agricultural Holdings Act 1986, s.99, s.100, Sched.13 para. 3, Sched.14, para. 21; Agriculture Act 1958, Sched.1, Pt I, para. 29; Housing Act 1980, Sched.26; Finance Act 1959, Sched.2, para. 5; Landlord and Tenant (Licensed Premises) Act 1990, s.1(1)(2), s.2(2)(a); and Law of Property Act 1969, s.15, Sched.1.

tenancy

3B–263 See s.69(1) and the commentary to s.23 above. The definition includes an agreement for a lease or underlease, but does not include a mortgage.

mining lease

3B–264 See s.46 and Landlord and Tenant Act 1927, s.25 which defines "mining lease" as a lease for any mining purpose or purposes connected therewith, and "mining purposes" include the sinking and searching for, winning, working, getting, making merchantable, smelting or otherwise converting or working for the purposes of any manufacture, carrying away, and disposing of mines and minerals, in or under land, and the erection of buildings, and the execution of engineering and other works suitable for those purposes.

Jurisdiction of county court to make declaration

3B–265 **43A.** Where the rateable value of the holding is such that the jurisdiction conferred on the court by any other provision of this Part of this Act is, by virtue of section 63 of this Act, exercisable by the county court, the county court shall have jurisdiction (but without prejudice to the jurisdiction of the High Court) to make any declaration as to any matter arising under this Part of this Act, whether or not any other relief is sought in the proceedings.

3B–266 *Note* —Section 43A was inserted by the Law of Property Act 1969, s.13. Claims under Pt II should normally be brought in the county court. Only exceptional circumstances justify starting such a claim in the High Court (CPR, r.56.2 and PD56.2).

holding

3B–267 See s.46, s.32 and s.23(3) which provides that the expression "the holding" means the property comprised in the tenancy, there being excluded any part thereof which is occupied neither by the tenant nor by a person employed by the tenant ... for the purposes of a business by reason of which the tenancy is one to which this Part of this Act applies.

Meaning of "the landlord" in Part II, and provisions as to mesne landlords, etc.

3B–268 **44.**—(1) Subject to subsections (1A) and (2) below, in this Part of this Act the expression "the landlord", in relation to a tenancy (in this section referred to as "the relevant tenancy"), means the person (whether or not he is the immediate landlord) who is the owner of that interest in the property comprised in the relevant tenancy which for the time being fulfils the following conditions, that is to say—

(a) that it is an interest in reversion expectant (whether immediately or not) on the termination of the relevant tenancy, and

(b) that it is either the fee simple or a tenancy which will not come to an end within fourteen months by effluxion of time and, if it is such a tenancy, that no notice has been given by virtue of which it will come to an end within fourteen months or any further time by which it may be continued under section 36(2) or section 64 of this Act, and is not itself in reversion expectant (whether immediately or not) on an interest which fulfils those conditions.

(1A) The reference in subsection (1) above to a person who is the owner of an interest such as is mentioned in that subsection is to be construed, where different persons own such interests in different parts of the property, as a reference to all those persons collectively.

(2) References in this Part of this Act to a notice to quit given by the landlord are references to a notice to quit given by the immediate landlord.

(3) The provisions of the Sixth Schedule to this Act shall have effect for the application of this Part of this Act to cases where the immediate landlord of the tenant is not the owner of the fee simple in respect of the holding.

Note —The current s.44 was substituted by the Law of Property Act 1969, s.15, **3B–269** Sched.1 and amended by the Regulatory Reform (Business Tenancies) (England and Wales) Order 2003 (S.I. 2003 No. 3096), art.27(2). The latter amendment came into force June 1, 2004 but only applies where the s.25 notice or s.26 request was served on or after that date.

landlord

Only the competent landlord may give a s.25 notice or receive a s.26 request for a **3B–270** new tenancy. There can only be one competent landlord at any given time. Effectively it is the first person in the chain of landlords who has more than a nominal reversion. A mesne landlord, whose own tenancy is continuing under s.24 may be the landlord in relation to a sub-tenant of part of the premises, despite the uncertain duration of his own tenancy (*Bowes Lyon v. Green* [1963] A.C. 420; [1961] 3 W.L.R. 1044; [1961] 3 All E.R. 843, HL). The landlord means the person with legal title to the land and so it is trustees rather than beneficiaries who are the competent landlord (*Biles v. Caesar* [1957] 1 W.L.R. 156; [1957] 1 All E.R. 151, CA; *Morar v. Chauhan* [1985] 1 W.L.R. 1263; [1985] 3 All E.R. 493, CA). Note s.40 which provides a mechanism allowing tenants to serve notices to obtain information as to the identity of the competent landlord.

holding

See s.46, s.32 and s.23(3) which provides that the expression "the holding" means **3B–271** the property comprised in the tenancy, there being excluded any part thereof which is occupied neither by the tenant nor by a person employed by the tenant ... for the purposes of a business by reason of which the tenancy is one to which this Part of this Act applies.

45. [Repealed by Statute Law (Repeals) Act 1974 (C.22), Pt XI] **3B–272**

Interpretation of Part II

46.—(1) In this Part of this Act:— **3B–273**

"business" has the meaning assigned to it by subsection (2) of section twenty-three of this Act;

"current tenancy" means the tenancy under which the tenant holds for the time being;

"date of termination" has the meaning assigned to it by subsection (1) of section twenty-five of this Act;

subject to the provisions of section thirty-two of this Act,

"the holding" has the meaning assigned to it by subsection (3) of section twenty-three of this Act;

"interim rent" has the meaning given by section 24A(1) of this Act;

"mining lease" has the same meaning as in the Landlord and Tenant Act 1927.

(2) For the purposes of this Part of this Act, a person has a controlling interest in a company, if, had he been a company, the other company would have been its subsidiary; and in this Part—

"company" has the meaning given by section 735 of the Companies Act 1985; and

"subsidiary" has the meaning given by section 736 of that Act.

3B–274 *Note* — Section 46 was amended by the Regulatory Reform (Business Tenancies) (England and Wales) Order 2003 (S.I. 2003 No. 3096). The amendment came into force June 1, 2004 but only applies where the s.25 notice or s.26 request was served on or after that date.

* * * * *

PART IV

MISCELLANEOUS AND SUPPLEMENTARY

Jurisdiction of court for purposes of Parts I and II and of Part I of Landlord and Tenant Act 1927

3B–275 63.—(1) Any jurisdiction conferred on the court by any provision of Part I of this Act shall be exercised by the county court.

(2) Any jurisdiction conferred on the court by any provision of Part II of this Act or conferred on the tribunal by Part I of the Landlord and Tenant Act 1927, shall, subject to the provisions of this section, be exercised [by the High Court or a county court]

(3) [...]

(4) The following provisions shall have effect as respects transfer of proceedings from or to the High Court or the county court, that is to say—

(a) where an application is made to the one but by virtue of [an Order under section 1 of the Courts and Legal Services Act 1990] cannot be entertained except by the other, the application shall not be treated as improperly made but any proceedings thereon shall be transferred to the other court;

(b) any proceedings under the provisions of Part II of this Act or of Part I of the Landlord and Tenant Act 1927, which are pending before one of those courts may by order of that court made on the application of any person interested be transferred to the other court, if it appears to the court making the order that it is desirable that the proceedings and any proceedings before the other court should both be entertained by the other court.

(5) In any proceedings where in accordance with the foregoing provisions of this section the county court exercises jurisdiction the powers of the judge of summoning one or more assessors under subsection (1) of section 91 of the County Courts Act 1959, may be exercised notwithstanding that no application is made in that behalf by any party to the proceedings.

(6) Where in any such proceedings an assessor is summoned by a judge under the said subsection (1),—

    (a) he may, if so directed by the judge, inspect the land to which the proceedings relate without the judge and report to the judge in writing thereon;

    (b) the judge may on consideration of the report and any observations of the parties thereon give such judgment or make such order in the proceedings as may be just;

    (c) the remuneration of the assessor shall be at such rate as may be determined by the Lord Chancellor with the approval of the Treasury and shall be defrayed out of moneys provided by Parliament.

(7) In this section the expression "the holding"—

    (a) in relation to proceedings under Part II of this Act, has the meaning assigned to it by subsection (3) of section twenty-three of this Act,

    (b) in relation to proceedings under Part I of the Landlord and Tenant Act 1927, has the same meaning as in the said Part I.

(8) [...]

(9) Nothing in this section shall prejudice the operation of section 41 of the County Courts Act 1984 (which relates to the removal into the High Court of proceedings commenced in a county court).

(10) In accordance with the foregoing provisions of this section, for section 21 of the Landlord and Tenant Act 1927, there shall be substituted the following section—

The Tribunal

21. The tribunal for the purposes of Part I of this Act shall be the court exercising jurisdiction in accordance with the provisions of section sixty-three of the Landlord and Tenant Act 1954.

Note —See the reference to s.63(2) in the High Court and County Courts Jurisdiction Order 1991 (S.I. 1991 No. 724).   **3B–276**

Interim continuation of tenancies pending determination by court

64.—(1) In any case where—   **3B–277**

    (a) a notice to terminate a tenancy has been given under Part I or Part II of this Act or a request for a new tenancy has been made under Part II thereof, and

    (b) an application to the court has been made under the

said Part I or under section 24(1) or 29(2) of this Act, as the case may be, and

  (c) apart from this section the effect of the notice or request would be to terminate the tenancy before the expiration of the period of three months beginning with the date on which the application is finally disposed of,

the effect of the notice or request shall be to terminate the tenancy at the expiration of the said period of three months and not at any other time.

(2) The reference in paragraph (c) of subsection (1) of this section to the date on which an application is finally disposed of shall be construed as a reference to the earliest date by which the proceedings on the application (including any proceedings on or in consequence of an appeal) have been determined and any time for appealing or further appealing has expired, except that if the application is withdrawn or any appeal is abandoned the reference shall be construed as a reference to the date of the withdrawal or abandonment.

Provisions as to reversions

3B–278   **65.**—(1) Where by virtue of any provision of this Act a tenancy (in this subsection referred to as "the inferior tenancy") is continued for a period such as to extend to or beyond the end of the term of a superior tenancy, the superior tenancy shall, for the purposes of this Act and of any other enactment and of any rule of law, be deemed so long as it subsists to be an interest in reversion expectant upon the termination of the inferior tenancy and, if there is no intermediate tenancy, to be the interest in reversion immediately expectant upon the termination thereof.

(2) In the case of a tenancy continuing by virtue of any provision of this Act after the coming to an end of the interest in reversion immediately expectant upon the termination thereof, subsection (1) of section one hundred and thirty-nine of the Law of Property Act 1925 (which relates to the effect of the extinguishment of a reversion) shall apply as if references in the said subsection (1) to the surrender or merger of the reversion included references to the coming to an end of the reversion for any reason other than surrender or merger.

(3) Where by virtue of any provision of this Act a tenancy (in this subsection referred to as "the continuing tenancy") is continued beyond the beginning of a reversionary tenancy which was granted (whether before or after the commencement of this Act) so as to begin on or after the date on which apart from this Act the continuing tenancy would have come to an end, the reversionary tenancy shall have effect as if it had been granted subject to the continuing tenancy.

(4) Where by virtue of any provision of this Act a tenancy (in this subsection referred to as "the new tenancy") is granted for a period beginning on the same date as a reversionary tenancy or for a period such as to extend beyond the beginning of the term of a reversionary tenancy, whether the reversionary tenancy in question was granted before or after the commencement of this Act, the reversionary

tenancy shall have effect as if it had been granted subject to the new tenancy.

Provisions as to notices

66.—(1) Any form of notice required by this Act to be prescribed **3B–279** shall be prescribed by regulations made by the Lord Chancellor by statutory instrument.

(2) Where the form of a notice to be served on persons of any description is to be prescribed for any of the purposes of this Act, the form to be prescribed shall include such an explanation of the relevant provisions of this Act as appears to the Lord Chancellor requisite for informing persons of that description of their rights and obligations under those provisions.

(3) Different forms of notice may be prescribed for the purposes of the operation of any provision of this Act in relation to different cases.

(4) Section twenty-three of the Landlord and Tenant Act 1927 (which relates to the service of notices) shall apply for the purposes of this Act.

(5) Any statutory instrument under this section shall be subject to annulment in pursuance of a resolution of either House of Parliament.

Wales

The functions of the Secretary of State, exercisable in relation to Wales, were **3B–280** transferred to the National Assembly for Wales, by the National Assembly for Wales (Transfer of Functions) Order 1999 (S.I. 1999 No. 672).

prescribed ... by statutory instrument

See the Landlord and Tenant Act 1954, Part 2 (Notices) Regulations 2004 (S.I. **3B–281** 2004 No. 1005). Regulation 2(2) of the 2004 Regulations allows a "form substantially to the like effect" of those contained in the regulations.

Provisions as to mortgagees in possession

67. Anything authorised or required by the provisions of this Act, **3B–282** other than subsection (3) of section forty, to be done at any time by, to or with the landlord, or a landlord of a specified description, shall, if at that time the interest of the landlord in question is subject to a mortgage and the mortgagee is in possession or a receiver appointed by the mortgagee or by the court is in receipt of the rents and profits, be deemed to be authorised or required to be done by, to or with the mortgagee instead of that landlord.

Note — Section 67 was amended by the Regulatory Reform (Business Tenancies) **3B–283** (England and Wales) Order 2003 (S.I. 2003 No. 3096). The amendment came into force June 1, 2004.

* * * *

Interpretation

69.—(1) In this Act the following expressions have the meanings **3B–284** hereby assigned to them respectively, that is to say:—

"agricultural holding" has the same meaning as in the [Agricultural Holdings Act 1986];

"development corporation" has the same meaning as in the New Towns Act 1946;

'farm business tenancy' has the same meaning as in the Agricultural Tenancies Act 1995;

"local authority" [[means any local authority within the meaning of the Town and Country Planning Act 1990, any National Park authority, the Broads Authority[, the London Fire and Emergency Planning Authority] or]... a joint authority established by Part IV of the Local Government Act 1985];

"mortgage" includes a charge or lien and "mortgagor" and "mortgagee" shall be construed accordingly;

"notice to quit" means a notice to terminate a tenancy (whether a periodical tenancy or a tenancy for a term of years certain) given in accordance with the provisions (whether express or implied) of that tenancy;

"repairs" includes any work of maintenance, decoration or restoration, and references to repairing, to keeping or yielding up in repair and to state of repair shall be construed accordingly;

"statutory undertakers" has the same meaning as in the Town and Country Planning Act 1971...;

"tenancy" means a tenancy created either immediately or derivatively out of the freehold, whether by a lease or underlease, by an agreement for a lease or underlease or by a tenancy agreement or in pursuance of any enactment (including this Act), but does not include a mortgage term or any interest arising in favour of a mortgagor by his attorning tenant to his mortgagee, and references to the granting of a tenancy and to demised property shall be construed accordingly;

"terms" , in relation to a tenancy, includes conditions.

(2) References in this Act to an agreement between the landlord and the tenant (except in section seventeen and subsections (1) and (2) of section thirty-eight thereof) shall be construed as references to an agreement in writing between them.

(3) References in this Act to an action for any relief shall be construed as including references to a claim for that relief by way of counterclaim in any proceedings.

3B–285 *Note* —Section 69 was amended by the Agricultural Holdings Act 1986, s.100, Sched.14, para. 22; the Agricultural Tenancies Act 1995, s.40, para. 12; the Local Government Act 1985, s.84, Sched.14, para. 36; the Environment Act 1995, s.78, Sched.10, para. 3; the Greater London Authority Act 1999, s.328, Sched.29, Pt I, para. 1; the Education Reform Act 1988, s.237, Sched.13, Pt I and by the Coal Industry Act 1994, s.67, Sched.9, para. 5, Sched.11, Pt II.

SECTION 44 SIXTH SCHEDULE

PROVISIONS FOR PURPOSES OF PART II WHERE IMMEDIATE LANDLORD IS NOT
3B–286 THE FREEHOLDER

Definitions
3B–287 1. In this Schedule the following expressions have the meanings hereby assigned to

them in relation to a tenancy (in this Schedule referred to as "the relevant tenancy"), that is to say:—

"the competent landlord" means the person who in relation to the tenancy is for the time being the landlord (as defined by section 44) of this Act) for the purposes of Part II of this Act;

"mesne landlord" means a tenant whose interest is intermediate between the relevant tenancy and the interest of the competent landlord; and

"superior landlord" means a person (whether the owner of the fee simple or a tenant) whose interest is superior to the interest of the competent landlord.

Power of court to order reversionary tenancies

2. Where the period for which in accordance with the provisions of Part II of this **3B–288** Act it is agreed or determined by the court that a new tenancy should be granted thereunder will extend beyond the date on which the interest of the immediate landlord will come to an end, the power of the court under Part II of this Act to order such a grant shall include power to order the grant of a new tenancy until the expiration of that interest and also to order the grant of such a reversionary tenancy or reversionary tenancies as may be required to secure that the combined effects of those grants will be equivalent to the grant of a tenancy for that period; and the provisions of Part II of this Act shall, subject to the necessary modifications, apply in relation to the grant of a tenancy together with one or more reversionary tenancies as they apply in relation to the grant of one new tenancy.

Acts of competent landlord binding on other landlords

3.—(1) Any notice given by the competent landlord under Part II of this Act to **3B–289** terminate the relevant tenancy, and any agreement made between that landlord and the tenant as to the granting, duration, or terms of a future tenancy, being an agreement made for the purposes of the said Part II, shall bind the interest of any mesne landlord notwithstanding that he has not consented to the giving of the notice or was not a party to the agreement.

(2) The competent landlord shall have power for the purposes of Part II of this Act to give effect to any agreement with the tenant for the grant of a new tenancy beginning with the coming to an end of the relevant tenancy, notwithstanding that the competent landlord will not be the immediate landlord at the commencement of the new tenancy, and any instrument made in the exercise of the power conferred by this sub-paragraph shall have effect as if the mesne landlord had been a party thereto.

(3) Nothing in the foregoing provisions of this paragraph shall prejudice the provisions of the next following paragraph.

4.—(1) If the competent landlord, not being the immediate landlord, gives any such **3B–290** notice or makes any such agreements as is mentioned in sub-paragraph (1) of the last foregoing paragraph without the consent of every mesne landlord, any mesne landlord whose consent has not been given thereto shall be entitled to compensation from the competent landlord for any loss arising in consequence of the giving of the notice or the making of the agreement.

(2) If the competent landlord applies to any mesne landlord for his consent to such a notice or agreement, that consent shall not be unreasonably withheld, but may be given subject to any conditions which may be reasonable (including conditions as to the modification of the proposed notice or agreement or as to the payment of compensation by the competent landlord).

(3) Any question arising under this paragraph whether consent has been unreasonably withheld or whether any conditions imposed on the giving of consent are unreasonable shall be determined by the court.

5. An agreement between the competent landlord and the tenant made for the **3B–291** purposes of Part II of this Act in a case where—

(a) the competent landlord is himself a tenant, and

(b) the agreement would apart from this paragraph operate as respects any period after the coming to an end of the interest of the competent landlord,

shall not have effect unless every superior landlord who will be the immediate landlord of the tenant during any part of that period is a party to the agreement.

6. Where the competent landlord has given a notice under section 25 of this Act to **3B–292**

terminate the relevant tenancy and, within two months after the giving of the notice, a superior landlord—

    (a) becomes the competent landlord; and

    (b) gives to the tenant notice in the prescribed form that he withdraws the notice previously given;

        the notice under section 25 of this Act shall cease to have effect, but without prejudice to the giving of a further notice under that section by the competent landlord.

3B–293   7. If the competent landlord's interest in the property comprised in the relevant tenancy is a tenancy which will come or can be brought to an end within sixteen months (or any further time by which it may be continued under section 36(2) or section 64 of this Act) and he gives to the tenant under the relevant tenancy a notice under section 25 of this Act to terminate the tenancy or is given by him a notice under section 26(3) of this Act:—

    (a) the competent landlord shall forthwith send a copy of the notice to his immediate landlord; and

    (b) any superior landlord whose interest in the property is a tenancy shall forthwith send to his immediate landlord any copy which has been sent to him in pursuance of the preceding sub-paragraph or this sub-paragraph.

Landlord and Tenant Act 1988

3B–294

(1988 c.26)

* * * *

Qualified duty to consent to assigning, underletting etc. of premises

3B–295   **1.**—(1) This section applies in any case where—

    (a) a tenancy includes a covenant on the part of the tenant not to enter into one or more of the following transactions, that is—

        (i) assigning,

        (ii) underletting,

        (iii) charging, or

        (iv) parting with the possession of,

the premises comprised in the tenancy or any part of the premises without the consent of the landlord or some other person, but

    (b) the covenant is subject to the qualification that the consent is not to be unreasonably withheld (whether or not it is also subject to any other qualification).

    (2) In this section and section 2 of this Act—

    (a) references to a proposed transaction are to any assignment, underletting, charging or parting with possession to which the covenant relates, and

    (b) references to the person who may consent to such a transaction are to the person who under the covenant may consent to the tenant entering into the proposed transaction.

(3) Where there is served on the person who may consent to a proposed transaction a written application by the tenant for consent to the transaction, he owes a duty to the tenant within a reasonable time—

(a) to give consent, except in a case where it is reasonable not to give consent,

(b) to serve on the tenant written notice of his decision whether or not to give consent specifying in addition—

(i) if the consent is given subject to conditions, the conditions,

(ii) if the consent is withheld, the reasons for withholding it.

(4) Giving consent subject to any condition that is not a reasonable condition does not satisfy the duty under subsection (3)(a) above.

(5) For the purposes of this Act it is reasonable for a person not to give consent to a proposed transaction only in a case where, if he withheld consent and the tenant completed the transaction, the tenant would be in breach of a covenant.

(6) It is for the person who owed any duty under subsection (3) above—

(a) if he gave consent and the question arises whether he gave it within a reasonable time, to show that he did,

(b) if he gave consent subject to any condition and the question arises whether the condition was a reasonable condition, to show that it was,

(c) if he did not give consent and the question arises whether it was reasonable, for him not to do so, to show that it was reasonable,

and, if the question arises whether he served notice under that subsection within a reasonable time, to show that he did.

reasonable time

See *e.g. Blockbuster Entertainment Ltd v. Barnsdale Properties Ltd* [2003] EWHC 2912, **3B–296** (Ch D); November 11, 2003 (landlord breached its statutory duty under s.1(3) by failing to consent to a proposed sublease within a reasonable time. There was a delay of two months and as a result the proposed sub-lessee withdrew its offer, leaving the premises empty for over a year. Lloyd J. held that there was no basis for withholding consent and the landlord should have consented within a week. Damages of over £70,000 were awarded to compensate the tenant for rent, contributions to insurance costs and rates).

In *NCR Ltd v. Riverland Portfolio No. 1 Ltd (No. 2)* [2005] EWCA Civ 312; [2005] 22 EG 134 there was a covenant not to sublet without consent not to be unreasonably withheld. The landlord refused to consent to the tenant's proposed subletting. The tenant made two complaints: (i) that there had been an unreasonable delay and (ii) that the refusal was unreasonable. The judge found in favour of T but his decision was overturned in the CA. The case essentially turns upon its own facts and the evidence, including expert evidence, before the court but it does contain a useful summary of the law (paragraph 11 of the judgment). On the question of the reasonableness of the time taken to give a decision the judge considered that a period of two weeks was sufficient time for a decision once all the relevant information was available. This was criticised by Carnwath LJ in the Court of Appeal, at para 21:

"In my view, whatever earlier discussions there had been, Riverland was entitled to adequate time following receipt of the completed application to consider the serious financial and legal implications of a refusal with its advisers, and if necessary to report to the relevant Board. In the absence of special exceptional circumstances, a period of less than three weeks (particularly in the holiday period) cannot in my view be categorised as inherently unreasonable for that process.".

Conditions

3B-296.1   A landlord imposing a condition can only rely upon written reasons given within a reasonable time of receiving the tenant's application and within a reasonable time of imposing the condition. The question of reasonableness is determined by the information available to the landlord at the time he imposed the condition (*London & Argyll Developments Ltd v. Mount Cook Land Ltd* [2002] 50 EG 111 (ChD).)

"covenant", "consent", "tenancy" and "tenant"

3B-297   See s.5 and *Go West Ltd v. Spigarolo* [2003] EWCA Civ 17; [2003] Q.B. 1140; [2003] 2 W.L.R. 986; [2003] 2 All E.R. 141; *The Times*, February 10, 2003, *Norwich Union Life Insurance Society v. Shopmoor Ltd* [1999] 1 W.L.R. 531; *Footwear Corporation Ltd v. Amplight Properties Ltd* [1999] 1 W.L.R. 551 and *Mount Eden Land Ltd v. Folia Ltd* [2003] EWHC 1815 (Ch); July 23, 2003 (minor breaches not a valid basis for refusing licence to under-let).

Once the landlord has given written notice with reasons refusing consent the period of reasonable time for giving consent has passed. The landlord cannot subsequently change his mind and say that the change has occurred within a reasonable time of the request. The fact that there were subsequent attempts to negotiate permission to assign did not deprive the tenant on the facts to its rights under the 1988 Act (*Go West Ltd v.Spigarolo*, above).

Duty to pass on applications

3B-298   **2.**—(1) If, in a case where section 1 of this Act applies, any person receives a written application by the tenant for consent to a proposed transaction and that person—

   (a) is a person who may consent to the transaction or (though not such a person) is the landlord, and

   (b) believes that another person, other than a person who he believes has received that application or a copy of it, is a person who may consent to the transaction,

he owes a duty to the tenant (whether or not he owes him any duty under section 1 of this Act) to take such steps as are reasonable to secure the receipt within a reasonable time by the other person of a copy of the application.

(2) The reference in section 1(3) of this Act to the service of an application on a person who may consent to a proposed transaction includes a reference to the receipt by him of an application or a copy of an application (whether it is for his consent or that of another).

"consent" and "tenancy"

3B-299   See s.5.

"person who may consent"

3B-300   See s.1(2).

"proposed transaction"

3B-301   See s.1(2).

Qualified duty to approve consent by another

3B-302   **3.**—(1) This section applies in any case where—

   (a) a tenancy includes a covenant on the part of the tenant

not without the approval of the landlord to consent to the sub-tenant—

    (i) assigning,

    (ii) underletting,

    (iii) charging, or

    (iv) parting with the possession of, the premises comprised in the sub-tenancy or any part of the premises, but

  (b) the covenant is subject to the qualification that the approval is not to be unreasonably withheld (whether or not it is also subject to any other qualification).

(2) Where there is served on the landlord a written application by the tenant for approval or a copy of a written application to the tenant by the sub-tenant for consent to a transaction to which the covenant relates the landlord owes a duty to the sub-tenant within a reasonable time—

  (a) to give approval, except in a case where it is reasonable not to give approval,

  (b) to serve on the tenant and the sub-tenant written notice of his decision whether or not to give approval specifying in addition—

    (i) if approval is given subject to conditions, the conditions,

    (ii) if approval is withheld, the reasons for withholding it.

(3) Giving approval subject to any condition that is not a reasonable condition does not satisfy the duty under subsection (2)(a) above.

(4) For the purposes of this section it is reasonable for the landlord not to give approval only in a case where, if he withheld approval and the tenant gave his consent, the tenant would be in breach of covenant.

(5) It is for a landlord who owed any duty under subsection (2) above—

  (a) if he gave approval and the question arises whether he gave it within a reasonable time, to show that he did,

  (b) if he gave approval subject to any condition and the question arises whether the condition was a reasonable condition, to show that it was,

  (c) if he did not give approval and the question arises whether it was reasonable for him not to do so, to show that it was reasonable,

and if the question arises whether he served notice under that subsection within a reasonable time, to show that he did.

"covenant", "consent", "landlord", "tenancy" and "tenant"

See s.5.

3B–303

not to be unreasonably withheld

Unless it can be shown that a trial judge has misdirected himself by erring in principle or by reaching a conclusion that no reasonable judge could have reached,

3B–304

the Court of Appeal will be slow to differ from his measurements of reasonableness (*Arundel Corp v. Khokher* [2003] EWCA Civ 1784; December 9, 2003).

"served"

3B–305   See s.5(2).

Breach of duty

3B–306   **4.** A claim that a person has broken any duty under this Act may be made the subject of civil proceedings in like manner as any other claim in tort for breach of statutory duty.

damages

3B–307   Where a landlord has all relevant information to enable it to make a decision under s.1(3) as to whether or not to give licence to assign, but fails to respond and operates in a cynical way designed to frustrate the assignment of premises, the court may mark its disapproval by awarding a sum of exemplary damages that would cause the landlord to consider seriously its future conduct (*Design Progression Ltd v. Thurloe Properties Ltd* [2004] EWHC 324, (Ch); *The Times*, March 2, 2004—award of £25,000 exemplary damages plus £75,000 for loss of a premium and some other sums).

Interpretation

3B–308   **5.**—(1) In this Act—

"covenant" includes condition and agreement,

"consent" includes licence,

"landlord" includes any superior landlord from whom the tenant's immediate landlord directly or indirectly holds,

"tenancy", subject to subsection (3) below, means any lease or other tenancy (whether made before or after the coming into force of this Act) and includes—

(a) a sub-tenancy, and

(b) an agreement for a tenancy and references in this Act to the landlord and to the tenant are to be interpreted accordingly, and

"tenant", where the tenancy is affected by a mortgage (within the meaning of the Law of Property Act 1925) and the mortgagee proposes to exercise his statutory or express power of sale, includes the mortgagee.

(2) An application or notice is to be treated as served for the purposes of this Act if—

(a) served in any manner provided in the tenancy, and

(b) in respect of any matter for which the tenancy makes no provision, served in any manner provided by section 23 of the Landlord and Tenant Act 1927.

(3) This Act does not apply to a secure tenancy (defined in section 79 of the Housing Act 1985) or to an introductory tenancy (within the meaning of Chapter I of Part V of the Housing Act 1996).

(4) This Act applies only to applications for consent or approval served after its coming into force.

3C CONTEMPT OF COURT ACT 1981

Contempt of Court Act 1981

(1981 c.49)

ARRANGEMENT OF SECTIONS

STRICT LIABILITY

STRICT LIABILITY

The strict liability rule

1. In this Act "the strict liability rule" means the rule of law whereby **3C-2** conduct may be treated as a contempt of court as tending to interfere with the course of justice in particular legal proceedings regardless of intent to do so.

Limitation of scope of strict liability

2.—(1) The strict liability rule applies only in relation to publica- **3C-3** tions, and for this purpose "publication" includes any speech, writing, programme included in a cable programme service or other communication in whatever form, which is addressed to the public at large or any section of the public.

(2) The strict liability rule applies only to a publication which creates a substantial risk that the course of justice in the proceedings in question will be seriously impeded or prejudiced.

(3) The strict liability rule applies to a publication only if the proceedings in question are active within the meaning of this section at the time of publication.

CONTEMPT

(4) Schedule 1 applies for determining the times at which proceedings are to be treated as active within the meaning of this section.

(5) In this section "programme service" has the same meaning as in the Broadcasting Act 1990.

3C–4   *Note* —Amended by the Cable and Broadcasting Act 1984, Sched.5, para. 39; and the Broadcasting Act 1990, s.203, Sched.20, para. 31.

Meaning of "substantial risk" and "seriously impeded or prejudiced"

3C–5   "Substantial" describes the degree of risk; "seriously" describes the degree of impediment or prejudice to the course of justice; in combination the two words are intended to exclude a risk that is only remote (*per* Lord Diplock in *Att.-Gen. v. English* [1983] 1 A.C. 116; [1982] 3 All E.R. 903 at 919, HL). See also *Att.-Gen. v. Times Newspapers Ltd; The Times*, February 12, 1983, CA; and *Attorney General v. BBC, Independent*, January 3, 1992.

"Substantial," as a qualification of "risk," does not have the meaning of "weighty," but rather "not insubstantial" or "not minimal"; the risk part of the test will usually be of importance in the context of the width of the publication, the court needing to consider whether there is an element of public interest in the publication which ought to be permitted and whether the proceedings sought to be protected are sufficiently proximate to the apprehended publication to require protection; proximity in time between the publication and the proceedings will probably have a greater bearing on the risk limb than on the seriousness limb, but may go to both (*Attorney General v. News Group Newspapers Ltd* [1987] Q.B. 1, CA). Where the trial will not take place for at least ten months, the impact of the publication may be blunted (*ibid.*). Thus where nine months had elapsed between a single broadcast of an ephemeral nature and publication in a newspaper of limited circulation and the eventual trial, no contempt was held to have been committed (*Attorney General v. Independent Television News Ltd* [1995] 2 All E.R. 370).

The publication of a statement that a defendant in criminal proceedings is awaiting trial on other charges does not, for the purposes of s.2(2) of the 1981 Act, necessarily create a substantial risk that the course of justice would be seriously impeded. The test is whether the statement created a substantial risk not whether it was the type of publication inherently liable to create such a risk. The risk has to be practical risk rather than a theoretical one (*Attorney General v. Guardian Newspapers Ltd (No.3)* [1992] 1 W.L.R. 874.

Assessment of the risk will involve a consideration of the possible impact of the publication upon readers. Where an article appeared in an obscure weekly publication the possibility of any prospective juror having read the publication would be small and that small risk would be overwhelmed by a lengthy and complex trial. *Att.-Gen. v. Sunday Newspapers Ltd* [1999] C.O.D. 11.

On an application under s.2(2) it is not necessary to demonstrate the degree of prejudice which would justify an order by the trial judge for a stay of the criminal proceedings. It is a sufficient basis for a finding of contempt that the publication created a seriously arguable ground of appeal against conviction. *Attorney General v. Birmingham Post and Mail Ltd* [1999] 1 W.L.R. 361 (Simon Brown L.J. and Thomas J.).

A distinction should be drawn between private pressure on a litigant, by an opposing litigant or a third party, and publication to a wide section of the public. As regards the latter, publication will not generally constitute contempt if it contains nothing more than fair and temperate criticism of a litigant; an article that goes beyond such criticism may create a substantial risk of prejudice (*Attorney General v. Hislop* [1991] 2 W.L.R. 219; [1991] 1 Q.B. 514, CA).

Expressions of regret cannot excuse a breach of the strict liability rule although they might mitigate penalty. This is so even where the publishers did not intend such a consequence to ensue from the publication or foresee that it would or might have such an effect (*Attorney General v. BBC, Independent*, January 3, 1992).

A publication referring to particular legal proceedings is less likely to be held to create a substantial risk that the course of justice in those proceedings will be seriously impeded or prejudiced if the proceedings are to be heard by a judge rather than tried by a jury. The possibility that an appellate court will be influenced is even more remote. Hence a publication which prejudges appeal proceedings pending before the House of Lords, and which is unlikely to deter the parties from contesting the appeal, does not constitute a contempt of court (*Re Lonrho plc* [1989] 2 All E.R. 1100, HL). A litigant who seeks a judicial remedy to compel a particular course of action is not guilty of contempt of court under s.2(2) of the Act if he resorts to self-help to obtain the remedy without the assistance of the courts, since the fact that the litigant thereby pre-empts the decision of the courts does not amount to impeding or prejudicing the course of justice (*ibid.*).

Documents in a court file do not become available for inspection unless access to a particular document is granted by operation of the rules or by leave of the court in a particular case. Where a person inspects documents in the court file by deception or subterfuge and then publishes that which he discovers he interferes with the administration of justice and commits a contempt of court *Dobson v. Hastings* (1991) 141 New L.J. 1625.

A stay of proceedings, which stops the continuance of proceedings before a court or tribunal, is not an order enforceable by proceedings for contempt because it is not capable of being breached by a party to the proceedings (*Minister of Foreign Affairs, Trade and Industry v. Vehicle and Supplies Ltd* [1991] 1 W.L.R. 550, PC; [1990] 4 All E.R. 65).

The fact that words were spoken in a humorous, irreverent and often rude television programme ("Have I Got News for You") some six months before the trial did not diminish the risk of serious prejudice to the course of justice (*Attorney General v. BBC*, [1997] E.M.L.R. 76).

In determining the degree of risk the court will look at each publication separately, but the mere fact that by reason of earlier publications there is already some risk of prejudice does not prevent a finding that the latest publication has created a further risk. The crucial matter will be the residual impact of the publication on a notional juror at the time of the trial. It may be proper for a trial judge to stay proceedings on the ground of prejudice albeit that no individual is subsequently found to be guilty of contempt (*Attorney General v. MGN Ltd* [1997] 1 All E.R. 456).

A third party will not be held liable for contempt in acting inconsistently with a court order unless that order is clear and precise both in its effect and scope. Moreover where it is sought to impose indirect liability on a third party it is not necessary to show that the relevant proceedings had been wholly frustrated or rendered utterly futile but rather some significant and adverse effect upon the administration of justice. Conduct by a third party which is inconsistent with a court order only in a trivial or technical way should not expose him to conviction for contempt (*Attorney General v. Newspaper Publishing Plc* [1997] 1 W.L.R. 926).

"... If the proceedings in question are active"

The rules for determining the times at which proceedings are to be treated as active **3C–6** are set out in Sched.1 (see para. 3C–54 *et seq.*, below). Proceedings in a Coroner's Court become active as soon as the inquest is opened, even where there has been an adjournment of all contentious matters after non-contentious matters have been dealt with (*Peacock v. London Weekend Television Ltd, The Times*, November 27, 1985, CA).

Whether or not an action is in the High Court warned list, or is less than three months from the date fixed for trial, are not matters which can be substituted for the test of "activity" prescribed by paras 12 and 13 of Sched.1 (see para. 3C–56, below) (*Att.-Gen. v. News Group Newspapers Ltd* [1987] Q.B. 1; [1986] 2 All E.R. 833, CA).

In cases where no active steps have been taken in any prosecution against a plaintiff (so that the strict liability rule under ss.1 and 2 of the Contempt of Court Act 1981 did not apply), but it is sought to restrain publication of material on the ground of contempt of court at common law, it is necessary for the court to be sure (a) that publication would create a risk of real prejudice if and when the prosecution proceeded, and (b) the material would be published with the specific intention of causing that risk (*Coe v. Central Television, Cook and Thorne, Independent*, August 11, 1993).

Defence of innocent publication or distribution

3.—(1) A person is not guilty of contempt of court under the strict **3C–7** liability rule as the publisher of any matter to which that rule applies if at the time of publication (having taken all reasonable care) he does not know and has no reason to suspect that relevant proceedings are active.

(2) A person is not guilty of contempt of court under the strict liability rule as the distributor of a publication containing any such matter if at the time of distribution (having taken all reasonable care) he does not know that it contains such matter and has no reason to suspect that it is likely to do so.

(3) The burden of proof of any fact tending to establish a defence afforded by this section to any person lies upon that person.

(4) [. . .]

Note —Subs.(4) repealed by the Statute Law (Repeals) Act 2004, s.1(1), Sch.1, Pt 1.

Contemporary reports of proceedings

3C–8 **4.**—(1) Subject to this section a person is not guilty of contempt of court under the strict liability rule in respect of a fair and accurate report of legal proceedings held in public, published contemporaneously and in good faith.

(2) In any such proceedings the court may, where it appears to be necessary for avoiding a substantial risk of prejudice to the administration of justice in those proceedings, or in any other proceedings pending or imminent, order that the publication of any report of the proceedings, or any part of the proceedings, be postponed for such period as the court thinks necessary for that purpose.

(2A) Where in proceedings for any offence which is an administration of justice offence for the purposes of section 54 of the Criminal Procedure and Investigations Act 1996 (acquittal tainted by an administration of justice offence) it appears to the court that there is a possibility that (by virtue of that section) proceedings may be taken against a person for an offence of which he has been acquitted, subsection (2) of this section shall apply as if those proceedings were pending or imminent.

(3) For the purposes of subsection (1) of this section a report of proceedings shall be treated as published contemporaneously—

(a) in the case of a report of which publication is postponed pursuant to an order under subsection (2) of this section, if published as soon as practicable after that order expires;

(b) in the case of a report of committal proceedings of which publication is permitted by virtue only of subsection (3) of section 8 of the Magistrates' Courts Act, if published as soon as practicable after publication is so permitted.

(4) [. . .]

3C–9 *Note* —Amended by the Criminal Justice and Public Order Act 1994, s.44, Sched.4, para. 50; the Criminal Procedure and Investigations Act 1996, s.57; and the Defamation Act 1996, s.16, Sched.2; subs.(4) repealed by the Statute Law (Repeals) Act 2004, s.1(1), Sch.1, Pt 1.

Legal proceedings held in public
3C–10 The expression "legal proceedings held in public" refers to court proceedings, and

not to events preceding them. Thus an arrest of a defendant is not a legal proceeding held in public and a film of the arrest cannot be the subject of an order under s.4(2); if the showing of the film is likely to prejudice the trial, the proper remedy is for the person affected to apply for an injunction in the High Court (*R. v. Rhuddlan Justices, ex p. HTV Ltd* [1986] Crim.L.R. 329, DC).

Postponement of reports of proceedings

A magistrates' court in considering whether to make or continue a reporting re- **3C–11** striction order under s.4(2) of the Contempt of Court Act 1981 has, like the Crown Court, a discretionary power to hear representations from the press and it was to be expected that the power would ordinarily be exercised when the media asked to be heard (*R. v. Clerkenwell Stipendiary Magistrates, ex p. The Telegraph plc* (1992) 142 New L.J. 1541; *Independent*, October 16, 1992).

In relation to committal proceedings s.8 of the Magistrates' Courts Act 1980 already imposes restrictions on the reporting of such proceedings and, as a matter of general policy, justices should therefore be slow to make additional orders under s.4(2) of the 1981 Act (*R. v. Beaconsfield Justices, ex p. Westminster Press Ltd, The Times*, June 28, 1994).

In considering whether to make an order under s.4(2) the court should seek to answer three questions: (i) was there a substantial risk of prejudice to the administration of justice? (ii) did it appear necessary for the avoidance of that prejudice that there should be some order made postponing publication of a report? (iii) if so, should the court, in its discretion, make an order and, if so, in what terms? *MGN Pensions Trustees Ltd v. Bank of America National Trust and Savings Association* [1995] 2 All E.R. 355 (Lindsay J.). In determining whether publication of matter would cause a substantial risk of prejudice to a future trial, a court should credit the jury with the will and ability to abide by the judge's direction to decide the case only on the evidence before them. The court should also bear in mind that the staying power and detail of publicity, even in cases of notoriety, are limited and that the nature of a trial is to focus the jury's minds on the evidence put before them, rather than on matters outside the courtroom. The Court of Appeal's function on an appeal under s.159 of the Criminal Justice Act 1988 was to form its own view on the material before it. *ex p. The Telegraph plc* [1993] 1 W.L.R. 980.

In considering whether it is "necessary" to make an order, both in the sense contemplated by s.4(2) and in the different sense contemplated by Art.10 of the European Convention on Human Rights, "restrictions ... as are prescribed by law and are necessary in a democratic society ..." the court should apply a three part test:

(1) Whether reporting would give rise to a "not unsubstantial" risk of prejudice to the administration of justice in the relevant proceedings. if not, that will be the end of the matter.

(2) If such a risk is perceived to exist, would a s.4(2) order eliminate it? If not there could be no necessity to impose such a ban and, again, that will be the end of the matter. If, however, an order would achieve the objective the judge must still consider whether the risk could be satisfactorily overcome by less restrictive means.

(3) If the judge concludes that there is indeed no other way of eliminating the risk of prejudice he must still ask whether the degree of risk contemplated should be regarded as tolerable in the sense of being "the lesser of two evils". At that stage value judgments may have to be made as to the priority between "competing public interests". *ex p. The Telegraph Group PLC and others* [2001] 1 W.L.R. 1983 (Longmore L.J., Douglas Brown and Eady JJ.).

Since it is necessary to keep a permanent record of all orders made under s.4(2), all such orders must be formulated in precise terms, having regard to the decision in *R. v. Horsham Justices, ex p. Farquharson* [1982] Q.B. 762; [1982] 2 All E.R. 269, and all orders under this section as well as under s.11 must be committed to writing either by the judge personally or by the clerk of the Court under the judges' direction. Such an order must state (a) its precise scope (b) the time at which it will cease to have effect if appropriate and (c) the specific purpose of making the order.

Courts will normally give notice to the press in some form that an order has been made under either section of the Act and court staff should be prepared to answer any inquiry about a specific case, but it is, and will remain, the responsibility of those reporting cases, and their editors, to ensure that no breach of any order occurs and the onus rests with them to make inquiry in any case of doubt (Practice Direction (Contempt: Reporting Restrictions) [1982] 1 W.L.R. 1475; [1983] 1 All E.R. 64).

CONTEMPT

When making an order the courts should be diligent in accommodating and understanding the legitimate interests of the press and such an order should be drafted and made public in a way which makes it clear what may or may not be published, both as regards the proceedings themselves and the terms of the order. It is desirable that it be made in advance of the trial and the judge is at liberty to adjourn consideration of reporting restrictions until the press have been heard (*Att.-Gen. v. Guardian Newspapers Ltd (No. 3)* [1992] 1 W.L.R. 874; [1992] 3 All E.R. 38).

Care should be taken over the wording of any notice pinned to the door of the court or given in some other form which may be read by jurors. Where the complete text of an order made under s.4(2), making it clear that the defendant faces further trials, is pinned to the door of the court and is seen to be read by a juror trying the case, there is a real possibility of prejudice to the defendant and the jury should be discharged (*R. v. Hutton* [1990] Crim.L.R. 875, CA (Crim. Div)).

Where a jury has retired to spend a night at an hotel it is not necessary to postpone reports of the proceedings on television or radio for fear that members of the jury may watch television or listen to the radio while at the hotel; if it is considered necessary to insulate the members of the jury from the media, they can be deprived of access to television or radio, just as they can be denied access to newspapers, while at the hotel (*Re Central Independent Television plc* [1991] 1 All E.R. 347, CA (Crim. Div)).

A Judge's decision whether or not to order reporting restrictions under s.4(2) involves an exercise of discretion based on fact, and does not involve any question of law such as to entitle the Court of Appeal to interfere with the decision, unless it can be demonstrated that such discretion has been exercised on a fundamentally flawed basis (*Re Saunders, The Times*, February 8, 1990; *Independent*, February 8, 1990, CA).

It is important that there should be freedom of information unless some necessity is shown to prevent it. Thus where the managers of a company are alleged to have removed assets in breach of their duties, and where a receiver is appointed to ensure that certain funds should be secured until the Court can decide who is the true owner, there is no reason to restrict reporting of the judgment whereby the receiver is appointed. Nothing in such a judgment is likely to prejudice a fair trial of the managers involved, and any report that does not make it clear that, as yet, there are only unsubstantiated allegations, will not be fair and accurate, and itself will be a contempt of court by virtue of s.4 (*Barlow Clowes Gilt Managers Ltd v. Clowes, The Times*, February 2, 1990).

Discussion of public affairs

3C–12   **5. A publication made as or as part of a discussion in good faith of public affairs or other matters of general public interest is not to be treated as a contempt of court under the strict liability rule if the risk of impediment or prejudice to particular legal proceedings is merely incidental to the discussion.**

Incidental to the discussion

3C–13   The protection afforded by s.5 is intended to prevent the suppression of bona fide discussion in the media of controversial matters of public interest, merely by reason that contemporaneous legal proceedings exist in which some particular instance of such matters may be in issue, and the burden is on the Attorney-General to prove that the publication does not fall within s.5 and that the risk of prejudice to a fair trial is not "merely incidental" to the discussion. Where a newspaper article forms part of a wider campaign and controversy as to the justiciability of mercy killing, it does not prejudice the fair trial of the doctor accused of the murder of a severely disabled baby, since it is no more than an incidental consequence of a discussion of a matter of general public interest, and is not a contempt of court (*Att.-Gen. v. English* [1983] A.C. 116; [1982] 2 All E.R. 903, HL. See also *Att.-Gen. v. Times Newspapers Ltd, The Times*, February 12, 1983, CA).

In considering whether a publication is a contempt of court by reason of prejudice to particular legal proceedings, or is merely incidental to discussion of matters of general public interest, it is appropriate to look at the subject matter of the discussion in the publication and to see how closely it relates to the particular legal proceedings; where the theme of the discussion is narrowly directed to the activities of a small group of identifiable persons, and where such activities are the subject matter of indictments charging one or more of those persons, it is impossible to categorise the discussion as no more than incidental to discussion of matters of general public interest (*Attorney General v. TVS Television Ltd, The Times*, July 7, 1989; *Independent*, July 7, 1989).

Savings

6. Nothing in the foregoing provisions of this Act— **3C–14**

(a) prejudices any defence available at common law to a charge of contempt of court under the strict liability rule;

(b) implies that any publication is punishable as contempt of court under that rule which would not be so punishable apart from those provisions;

(c) restricts liability for contempt of court in respect of conduct intended to impede or prejudice the administration of justice.

"Conduct intended to impede or prejudice the administration of justice"

A person not named in an interlocutory injunction may be in contempt of court by **3C–15** acting in a way contrary to the terms of that injunction. Such action may constitute "conduct intended to impede or prejudice the administration of justice", even though such intention is not the sole or principal intention of the contemnor (*Att.-Gen. v. Newspaper Publishing plc* [1987] 3 W.L.R. 942, CA. See also *Att.-Gen. v. Guardian Newspaper Publishing Ltd (No. 2), Independent*, October 17, 1987; *The Times*, October 20, 1987).

A person who is not a party to an action in which an injunction has been granted, commits a contempt of court if he knowingly does an act which is in breach of the injunction and which has the effect of destroying in whole or in part the subject matter of the action, so that the purpose of the trial of the action is wholly or partly nullified. (*Att.-Gen. v. Times Newspapers Ltd, The Times*, February 12, 1983, HL).

The purpose the Court seeks to achieve in granting a interlocutory injunction is to prevent the restrained acts from being done, pending a decision by the Court on the claims in the proceedings. Third parties will be in contempt if they wilfully interfere with the administration of justice by thwarting the achievement of *this* purpose in *those* proceedings. This is so, even if the injunction is drawn in seemingly over-wide terms. The remedy of the third party whose conduct is affected by the order is to apply to the court for the order to be varied. See *Attorney General v. Punch Ltd* [2002] UKHL 50; [2003] 1 A.C. 1046; [2003] 2 W.L.R. 49, an appeal from [2001] EWCA Civ 403.

The Act makes extensive provision for what may be called statutory contempts, but the saving contained in s.6(c) indicates that something which falls short of contempt under the statute may still be contempt at common law. Hence a newspaper which publishes articles with specific intention of interfering with the course of justice in criminal proceedings which, though not pending, are virtually certain to be commenced in the near future may be guilty of contempt at a common law even if the articles do not come within the strict liability provisions of sections 1 and 2 (*Att.-Gen. v. News Group Newspapers Ltd* [1988] 3 W.L.R. 163; [1988] 2 All E.R. 907).

In *Att.-Gen. v. Sport Newspapers Ltd* [1991] 1 W.L.R. 1194; [1992] 1 All E.R. 503, Bingham L.J. followed *Att.-Gen. v. News Group Newspapers plc* [1989] Q.B. 110, holding that, if publication creates a real risk of prejudice to the due administration of justice, and if the alleged contemnor publishes with the specific intent of causing such risk, contempt may be committed even though proceedings are neither in existence nor imminent. In the same case, however, Hogson J., disapproving *Att.-Gen. v. News Group Newspapers plc* (above), took the view that the time when the summary jurisdiction of judges over intentional publications contempts begins is when the relevant proceedings become pending, and that the ambit of such summary procedure should not be widened.

Consent required for institution of proceedings

7. Proceedings for a contempt of court under the strict liability **3C–16** rule (other than Scottish proceedings) shall not be instituted except by or with the consent of the Attorney-General or on the motion of a court having jurisdiction to deal with it.

Consent of the Attorney-General

3C-17   An application to commit a person for an alleged contempt which falls within the strict liability rule will be dismissed where the consent of the Attorney-General has not been obtained (*Roger Bullivant Ltd v. Ellis, Financial Times*, April 16, 1986).

Although a circuit judge has jurisdiction to deal with a contempt in the face of the court, he has no jurisdiction to deal with a contempt alleged to have been committed by the publication of a book, shortly before the commencement of criminal proceedings against a defendant, in which reference is made to the defendant being involved in serious organised crime, and which thereby tends, contrary to "the strict liability rule" prescribed by s.1, to interfere with the course of justice in those proceedings; except in the narrow range of cases where proceedings for contempt can be instituted under s.7 on the motion of the Court having jurisdiction to deal with the matter, proceedings for contempt under "the strict liability rule" can be commenced only by or with the consent of the Attorney-General (*Taylor v. Topping, The Times*, February 15, 1990; *Independent*, February 20, 1990). The decision of the law officers not to institute proceedings under s.7 cannot be challenged by way of an application for judicial review. *R. v. Solicitor General, ex p. Taylor and Taylor* [1996] C.O.D. 61).

OTHER ASPECTS OF LAW AND PROCEDURE

Confidentiality of jury's deliberations

3C-18   **8.**—(1) Subject to subsection (2) below, it is a contempt of court to obtain, disclose or solicit any particulars of statements made, opinions expressed, arguments advanced or votes cast by members of a jury in the course of their deliberations in any legal proceedings.

(2) This section does not apply to any disclosure of any particulars—

(a) in the proceedings in question for the purpose of enabling the jury to arrive at their verdict, or in connection with the delivery of that verdict, or

(b) in evidence in any subsequent proceedings for an offence alleged to have been committed in relation to the jury in the first mentioned proceedings,

or to the publication of any particulars so disclosed.

(3) Proceedings for a contempt of court under this section (other than Scottish proceedings) shall not be instituted except by or with the consent of the Attorney-General or on the motion of a court having jurisdiction to deal with it.

Confidentiality of jury's deliberations

3C-19   Any approach or attempt to take statements from jurors which might have the effect of breaching s.8 is to run the risk of committing a contempt of court or even of an attempt to pervert the course of justice. In relation to enquiries concerning the jury the trial judge is *functus officio* after verdict and sentence and in such cases the proper course is to seek the consent of the Court of Appeal (*R. v. Mickleburgh, The Times*, July 26, 1994).

The prohibitions contained in s.8 apply equally to the Court of Appeal as they do to others. It would therefore be a breach of s.8 for the court to enquire into the jury's deliberations in the retiring room. However, the section does not prevent the court from enquiring into what may have taken place at an hotel where the jury had stayed overnight before returning to court to resume its deliberations (*R. v. Young (Stephen)*, [1995] Q.B. 324). In s.8(1) the word "disclose" is apt to include not only disclosure by a juror but also disclosure by some other, but not the republication of information already in the public domain (*Att.-Gen. v. Associated Newspapers* [1994] 2 W.L.R. 277; [1994] 1 All E.R. 556, HL).

A request by a judge for the names of jurors to which a note related was a breach of section 8(1), which applies to the court as it does to others, and of the long established principle that there is no right in anyone to enquire as to what occurred in the jury room, a principle reaffirmed in *Andrew Brown* (1907) 7 N.S.W. St.Rep. 291 and *R. v. Thompson* [1962] 1 All E.R. 65 CA *R. v. Schot and Barclay, The Times*, May 14, 1997).

Use of tape recorders

9.—(1) Subject to subsection (4) below, it is a contempt of court— **3C–20**

    (a) to use in court, or bring into court for use, any tape recorder or other instrument for recording sound, except with the leave of the court;

    (b) to publish a recording of legal proceedings made by means of any such instrument, or any recording derived directly or indirectly from it, by playing it in the hearing of the public or any section of the public, or to dispose of it or any recording so derived, with a view to such publication;

    (c) to use any such recording in contravention of any conditions of leave granted under paragraph (a).

(2) Leave under paragraph (a) of subsection (1) may be granted or refused at the discretion of the court, and if granted may be granted subject to such conditions as the court thinks proper with respect to the use of any recording made pursuant to the leave; and where leave has been granted the court may at the like discretion withdraw or amend it either generally or in relation to any particular part of the proceedings.

(3) Without prejudice to any other power to deal with an act of contempt under paragraph (a) of subsection (1), the court may order the instrument, or any recording made with it, or both, to be forfeited; and any object so forfeited shall (unless the court otherwise determines on application by a person appearing to be the owner) be sold or otherwise disposed of in such manner as the court may direct.

(4) This section does not apply to the making or use of sound recordings for purposes of official transcripts of proceedings.

Use of tape recorders in court

The following Practice Direction was issued on November 19, 1981. See *Practice* **3C–21** *Direction (Tape Recorders)* [1981] 1 W.L.R. 1526; [1981] 3 All E.R. 848:

1. Section 9 of the Contempt of Court Act 1981 contains provisions governing the unofficial use of tape recorders in court. Among other things it provides that it is a contempt of court to use in court, or bring into court for use, any tape recorder or other instrument for recording sound, except with the leave of the court; and it is also a contempt of court to publish a recording of legal proceedings or to use any such recording in contravention of any conditions which the court may have attached to the grant of permission to use the machine in court. These provisions do not apply to the making or use of sound recordings for purposes of official transcripts of proceedings, on which the Act imposes no restriction whatever.

2. The discretion given to the court to grant, withhold or withdraw leave to use tape recorders or to impose conditions as to the use of the recording is unlimited, but the following factors may be relevant to its exercise:

    (a) the existence of any reasonable need on the part of the applicant for leave, whether a litigant or a person connected with the press or broadcasting, for the recording to be made;

    (b) in a criminal case, or a civil case in which a direction has been given excluding one or more witnesses from the court, the risk that the recording could be used for the purpose of briefing witnesses out of court;

    (c) any possibility that the use of a recorder would disturb the proceedings or distract or worry any witnesses or other participants.

3. Consideration should always be given whether conditions as to the use of a recording made pursuant to leave should be imposed. The identity and role of the applicant for leave and the nature of the subject matter of the proceedings may be relevant to this.

4. The particular restriction imposed by s.9(1)(b) of the 1981 Act applies in every case, but may not be present to the mind of every applicant to whom leave is given. It may, therefore, be desirable on occasion for this provision to be drawn to the attention of those to whom leave is given.

5. The transcript of a permitted recording is intended for the use of the person given leave to make it and is not intended to be used as, or to compete with, the official transcript mentioned in s.9(4) of the 1981 Act.

Sources of information

3C–22   **10.** No court may require a person to disclose, nor is any person guilty of contempt of court for refusing to disclose, the source of information contained in a publication for which he is responsible, unless it be established to the satisfaction of the court that disclosure is necessary in the interests of justice or national security or for the prevention of disorder or crime.

Application of section

3C–23   Section 10 is not directly applicable to a requirement made of a journalist by inspectors investigating possible offences under the Companies Acts, because such inspectors are not a court. The section, however, is indicative of the general policy prescribed by Parliament which should be applied by way of analogy on a reference arising out of such a requirement. If, therefore, the journalist is in a position to show that, if the inspectors were a court, he could rely on s.10 to support refusal to disclose his source of information, he has "reasonable excuse" for his refusal, within the meaning of s.178(2) of the Financial Services Act 1986, and will not be punishable as for a contempt of court under that section (*Re an Inquiry under the Company Securities (Insider Dealing) Act 1985* [1988] A.C. 660; [1988] 1 All E.R. 203, HL).

Interests of national security

3C–24   The prohibition in s.10 against the court making an order to disclose a source of information is of wide and general application, subject only to the four exceptions specified in the section, namely that disclosure is necessary in the interests of justice or national security or for the prevention of disorder or crime. Accordingly it is sufficient to attract the protection of s.10 if the order for disclosure might, but not necessarily would have the effect of disclosing a source of information. Moreover a publisher is not precluded from relying on s.10 in the face of a proprietary claim by an owner for the delivery up of his property. The onus of proving that the case falls within one of the four exceptions specified in the section lies on the party seeking the order, and the standard of proof required to satisfy the court that disclosure is necessary is the balance of probabilities. The interests of national security require that the identity of a person who discloses to a newspaper a memorandum of the Secretary of State for Defence classified as "secret" should be disclosed, where the risk to national security lies not in the publication of the particular document but in the possibility that the person who discloses it may in future disclose other classified documents, the disclosure of which would have more serious consequences for national security (*Secretary of State for Defence v. Guardian Newspapers Ltd* [1985] A.C. 339; [1984] 3 All E.R. 601, HL).

Interests of justice

3C–25   "The interests of justice" refer to the administration of justice in the course of legal proceedings in a court of law, a tribunal or a body exercising judicial power of the state, and not to the concept of justice in the abstract (*Secretary of State for Defence v. Guardian Newspapers Ltd* (above)). The words "in the interests of justice" are to be construed in the technical sense of the administration of legal proceedings in a court of law; s.10 requires it to be established that disclosure is necessary for the administration of justice in that sense, and not merely that disclosure is expedient (*Maxwell v. Pressdram Ltd* [1987] 1 W.L.R. 298; [1987] 1 All E.R. 656, CA). The public interest in the non-disclosure of journalists' sources may in a particular case outweigh the requirement that the sources be named in the interest of justice (*ibid.*).

To construe "justice" as the antonym of "injustice" is too wide but to confine it to the technical sense of the administration of justice in court of legal proceedings in a court of law is too narrow. It is in the interests of justice, within the meaning of the section, that persons should be enabled to exercise important legal rights and to protect themselves from serious legal wrongs, whether or not resort to legal proceedings in a court of law will be necessary to attain such objectives. It will not be sufficient, by itself, to establish the necessity of disclosure, for a party seeking disclosure of a source to show merely that he will be unable, without disclosure, to exercise the legal right or avert the threatened legal wrong on which he bases his claim. If the party seeking disclosure shows that his livelihood depends on it, that will put the case near one end of the spectrum. The greater the legitimate public interest in the information, the greater will be the importance of protecting the source. If the information is obtained illegally, that will diminish the importance of protecting the source unless, for example, the source has acted for the purpose of exposing iniquity (*X Ltd v. Morgan Grampian (Publishers) Ltd* [1990] 2 All E.R. 1, HL). Hence disclosure of a journalist's source of confidential information about a company is necessary in the interests of justice, where the importance of protecting the source, whose complicity in obtaining the information is not counterbalanced by any legitimate public interest in publication of the information, is outweighed by the threat of severe damage to the company's business which can be avoided only if the information is recovered (*ibid.*). But now see the decision of the European Court of Human Rights that the order requiring the journalist to reveal his source of information, and the fine imposed on him for having refused to do so, constituted a violation of Art.10 of the European Convention of Human Rights (*Goodwin v. UK, The Times*, March 28, 1996).

The question whether a publisher is to be required to disclose the source of information or return documents which would necessarily identify that source is to be determined in accordance with English law, as set out in s.10 and interpreted by the English courts in *X Ltd v. Morgan-Grampian (Publishers) Ltd* [1991] 1 A.C. 1 (it being clear and unambiguous) and not therefore by the application of the decision of the European Court of Human Rights in *Goodwin v. United Kingdom* (1996) 22 E.C.H.R. 123 (based on the same facts) and the interpretation of Art.10 of the ECHR (*Camelot Group plc v. Centaur Communications Ltd, The Times*, July 15, 1997, *per* Kay J.).

Before the court will require journalists to break the important professional obligation to protect a source, the minimum requirement is that other avenues of enquiry should be explored in an attempt to identify the source. A single leak of counsel's draft advice was not sufficient to warrant an order for disclosure under s.10 of the Act. *John and Others v. Express Newspapers and Others* [2000] 1 W.L.R.1931 (Lord Woolf M.R., Pill and May L.JJ.).

An order for disclosure may be made, even if the information is not required for the purpose of bringing an action. The important protection which both s.10 and Art.10 provide for freedom of expression required however that the Court should scrutinise diligently any request for relief which would result in the Court interfering with freedom of expression including ordering the disclosure of journalists services. Both s.10 and Art.10 of the European Convention on Human Rights are one in making clear that the Court has to be sure that a sufficiently strong positive case has been made out in favour of disclosure before it will be ordered, *Ashworth Hospital Authority v. MGN Ltd* [2002] 4 All E.R. 193 (House of Lords).

"Necessary for the prevention of crime"

"Necessary" has a meaning that lies somewhere between "indispensable" on the one **3C–26** hand and "useful" or "convenient" on the other. It is a word which takes colour from its context. Whether a particular measure is necessary in a particular case involves an exercise of judgment on the established facts. "The prevention of crime" refers to the prevention of crime generally rather than to the prevention of a particular identifiable future crime. The court must be presented with sufficient material to enable it to exercise an independent judgment on the extent of the need for disclosure. It will pay proper regard to the views of those seeking disclosure, but must not act as a rubber stamp for those views (*Re an Inquiry under the Company Securities (Insider Dealing) Act 1985* [1988] A.C. 660; [1988] 1 All E.R. 203, HL). Disclosure by a defendant cannot be said to be necessary for the prevention of crime in circumstances where the prevention of crime is not the plaintiff's task, and where a criminal investigation would not be a likely consequence if the defendant's source were disclosed (*X (Health Authority) v. Y.* [1988] 2 All E.R. 648). In considering whether it is "necessary" to require a journalist to reveal the source of a leaked document, the court will consider whether the applicant for the disclosure order has itself attempted to discover the source of the leak, otherwise than by applying to the Court (*Broadmoor Hospital v. Hyde, The Times*, March 18, 1994; *Independent*, March 4, 1994).

Publication of matters exempted from disclosure in court

3C–27   **11.** In any case where a court (having power to do so) allows a name or other matter to be withheld from the public in proceedings before the court, the court may give such directions prohibiting the publication of that name or matter in connection with the proceedings as appear to the court to be necessary for the purpose for which it was so withheld.

Directions prohibiting publication

3C–28   The jurisdiction to order disclosure of the identity of a wrongdoer is one of general application, exisiting in equity. The "interests of justice" in s.10 means interests which were justifiable, and was not confined to the technical sense of the administration of justice in the course of legal proceedings in a court of law, *Ashworth Hospital Authority v. MGN Ltd* [2001] 1 W.L.R. 515, (Lord Phillips of Worth Matravers M.R., May and Laws L.JJ.).

The Q.B. Divisional Court has no jurisdiction to entertain an application for judicial review of an order made under s.11 by a Crown Court in relation to a trial on indictment. The Divisional Court has noted, however, an increasing tendency to make orders under s.11, even where the name of a witness which it was forbidden to publish outside court had been referred to in the proceedings. It is doubtful whether s.11 has any application in such circumstances. It is of vital constitutional importance that criminal trials are held in public and freely reported. This consideration must outweigh the individual interests of particular persons who may feel embarrassment as a result of allegations made in the course of a trial (*R. v. Central Criminal Court, ex p. Crook* (1985) 82 L.S.Gaz. 1408, DC; *The Times*, November 8, 1984).

A court has no power under s.11 to prohibit the press from publishing the name of a defendant if, earlier in the proceedings, that name has not been withheld from the public (*R. v. Arundel JJ. ex p. Westminster Press Ltd* [1985] 1 W.L.R. 708; [1985] 2 All E.R. 390).

The general principle of law is that all evidence communicated to a court should be communicated publicly (*Att.-Gen. v. Leveller Magazine Ltd* [1979] A.C. 440, [1979] 2 All E.R. 745, HL). The general rule should not be departed from save where the nature of circumstances of the proceedings are such that its application would frustrate or render impracticable the administration of justice. Such circumstances are rare. It is a misuse of s.11 for magistrates to prohibit the publication of a defendant's address in order to protect him from possible harassment by his former wife (*R. v. Evesham Justices, ex p. McDonagh* [1988] Q.B. 553; [1988] 1 All E.R. 371). A magistrate making an order under s.37 of the Public Health (Control of Disease) Act 1984 directing the removal to hospital of a person with a "notifiable disease" is a court for the purposes of s.11 of the Contempt of Court Act 1981 and has power to allow a patient's name to be withheld from the public. It is however a constrained power and exercisable only in so far as reasonably necessary to serve the ends of justice. While it would be unfair to allow publication of a patient's identity when subject to an *ex parte* order, once all reasonable opportunity to challenge that order had passed, no interest of justice was any longer involved. Any wish to protect privacy or avoid embarrassment is not a ground for the continuance of such a prohibition. *Birmingham Post & Mail Ltd v. Birmingham City Council, Independent*, November 25, 1993). The power to make an order under s.11 must be exercised carefully and cannot be used simply to protect privacy or avoid embarrassment. In proceedings for judicial review any application for anonymity should usually be made at the same time as the application for leave to move. However, where the applicant's name alone might itself give rise to publicity, enquiry should first be made of the Crown Office, so that the application for an order under s.11 can be made as soon as the papers are lodged (*R. v. Westminster City Council, ex p. Castelli and Garcia, The Times*, August 14, 1995).

The fact that publication of the summonses giving rise to the proceedings may have dire economic consequences leading to the closure of the defendant's business does not constitute an exceptional circumstances justifying magistrates making an order restricting publication under s.11 (*R. v. Dover Justices, ex p. Dover District Council, The Times*, October 21, 1991; *Independent*, October 21, 1991). It would be very rare indeed to find circumstances justifying departure from the general rule to prevent publication of material relating to a defendant's acquittal (*ibid.*).

Where, however, application is made to a court to hear proceedings *in camera* and for a direction under s.11 prohibiting publication of the proceedings, the court should accede to a request to hear the reasons for the application *in camera*, so that a decision may be made whether there is substance in the application without prejudicing the applicant (*R. v. Tower Bridge Justices, ex p. Osborne* [1988] Crim.L.R. 382).

In relation to an application for judicial review it may sometimes be appropriate to make an interim order under s.11 of the Act at the *ex parte* leave stage so as to enable the applicant to provide more substantial evidence at the substantive hearing as to the damage which might be caused by disclosure. This case also contains an examination of the more recent authorities on s.11 (*R. v. Somerset Health Authority, ex p. S* [1996] C.O.D. 244, *per* Brooke J.).

Offences of contempt of magistrates' courts

12.—(1) A magistrates' court has jurisdiction under this section to **3C–29** deal with any person who—

    (a) wilfully insults the justice or justices, any witness before or officer of the court or any solicitor or counsel having business in the court, during his or their sitting or attendance in court or in going to or returning from the court; or

    (b) wilfully interrupts the proceedings of the court or otherwise misbehaves in court.

(2) In any such case the court may order any officer of the court, or any constable, to take the offender into custody and detain him until the rising of the court; and the court may, if it thinks fit, commit the offender to custody for a specified period not exceeding one month or impose on him a fine not exceeding £2,500, or both.

(2A) A fine imposed under subsection (2) above shall be deemed, for the purposes of any enactment, to be a sum adjudged to be paid by a conviction.

(3) [...]

(4) A magistrates' court may at any time revoke an order of committal made under subsection (2) and, if the offender is in custody, order his discharge.

(5) Section 135 of the Powers of Criminal Courts (Sentencing) Act 2000, Sched. 9, para. 83(a) and the following provisions of the Magistrates' Courts Act 1980 apply in relation to an order under this section as they apply in relation to a sentence on conviction or finding of guilty of an offence, namely: section 36 (restriction on fines in respect of young persons); sections 75 to 91 (enforcement); section 108 (appeal to Crown Court); section 136 (overnight detention in default of payment); and section 142(1) (power to rectify mistakes).

Note —Amended by the Criminal Justice Act 1991, s.17(3), Sched.4; and the Criminal Justice Act 1993, s.65(3) (4) and Sched.3. **3C–30**

Jurisdiction of magistrates' courts

A committal of a person to custody under s.12(2) for wilfully interrupting the **3C–31** proceedings of the Court does not amount to a summary conviction giving the person a right to legal representation before a sentence of imprisonment can be imposed. Nor does natural justice require the contemnor to be so represented (see *R. v. Newbury Justices, ex p. du Pont* (1984) 148 J.P. 248; (1984) 78 Cr.App.R. 255).

By virtue of s.1(1) of the Criminal Justice Act 1982 a magistrates' court has no power to commit a person under the age of 17 for contempt; by virtue of s.9(1) of that Act and s.12 of this Act such a court does have power to commit for contempt a person between the ages of 17 and 21, but such power should be exercised only if the court is of opinion that no other method of dealing with the person is appropriate (*R. v. Selby Justices, ex p. Frame* [1991] 2 All E.R. 344).

Where a defendant persisted in seeking to occupy that part of the court reserved for professional advocates, she was rightly held to be in contempt. The court should, however, never act in haste and should always give the alleged contemnor an opportunity to obtain legal advice and to apologise to the court (*R. v. Pateley Bridge Justices, ex p. Percy* [1994] C.O.D. 453).

"Wilfully insults"

3C–32   "Insult" is to be given its ordinary meaning in the English language. Hence an alleged contemnor who threatens a witness does not thereby "wilfully insult" him as to confer jurisdiction on justices with the matter under s.12(1)(a) (*R. v. Havant JJ., ex p. Palmer* (1985) 149 J.P. 609; [1985] Crim.L.R. 658).

The provisions of s.12 of the Contempt of Court Act 1981 give a good indication of the type of behaviour which may amount to contempt in the face of the court at common law. Thus a wolf whistle directed at a juror returning into court was potentially insulting, offensive and a serious interference with the administration of justice and the courts. Jurors did not come to courts in order to have comments made about their personal appearance. The appropriate penalty was a moderate fine or detention until the end of the day or over the luncheon adjournment (*R. v. Powell, The Times*, June 3, 1993).

Justices who peremptorily committed a solicitor to custody under s.12 of the Act for criticising the court's listing system had acted unreasonably. This was a classic case of a storm in a tea cup and like most storms so located no one had acted with entire good sense (*R. v. Tamworth Justices, ex p. Walsh, The Times*, March 3, 1994; [1994] C.O.D. 277).

"Wilfully interrupts"

3C–33   Magistrates have jurisdiction under s.12(1)(b) to deal with a person who "wilfully interrupts the proceedings of the court," whether the interruptions result from acts done inside or outside the court. In addition to the deliberate commission of the acts causing the interruptions, the mental element of intention that they should interrupt the proceedings must be established. Recklessness, in the sense that the interrupter knows that there is a risk that his acts will interrupt the proceedings but nevertheless goes on to do such acts, will be sufficient (*Bodden v. Commissioner of Police for the Metropolis* [1990] 2 W.L.R. 76; [1989] 3 All E.R. 833, CA).

Appeal to Crown Court

3C–34   The jurisdiction of the Crown Court under s.12(5) is limited to hearing an appeal against a penalty imposed on a finding of contempt by justices, and does not extend to hearing an appeal against the finding of contempt itself (*ibid.*).

Legal aid

3C–35   **13.** [*Repealed by the*, Legal Aid Act 1988, s.45, Sched.6, *and effectively replaced by* s.29 of that Act.]

PENALTIES FOR CONTEMPT AND KINDRED OFFENCES

Proceedings in England and Wales

3C–36   **14.**—(1) In any case where a court has power to commit a person to prison for contempt of court and (apart from this provision) no limitation applies to the period of committal, the committal shall (without prejudice to the power of the court to order his earlier discharge) be for a fixed term, and that term shall not on any occasion exceed two years in the case of committal by a superior court, or one month in the case of committal by an inferior court.

(2) In any case where an inferior court has power to fine a person for contempt of court and (apart from this provision) no limit applies to the amount of the fine, the fine shall not on any occasion exceed £2,500.

(2A) In the exercise of jurisdiction to commit for contempt of court or any kindred offence the court shall not deal with the offender by making an order under section 60 of the Powers of Criminal Courts (Sentencing) Act 2000 (an attendance centre order) if it appears to the court, after considering any available evidence, that he is under 17 years of age.

(3) [*Repealed by, Criminal Justice Act 1982 , Sched.16.*]

(4) Each of the superior courts shall have the like power to make a hospital order or guardianship order under section 37 of the Mental Health Act 1983 or an interim hospital order under section 38 of that Act in the case of a person suffering from mental illness or severe mental impairment who could otherwise be committed to prison for contempt of court as the Crown Court has under that section in the case of a person convicted of an offence.

(4A) Each of the superior courts shall have the like power to make an order under section 35 of the said Act of 1983 (remand for report on accused's mental condition) where there is reason to suspect that a person who could be committed to prison for contempt of court is suffering from mental illness or severe mental impairment as the Crown Court has under that section in the case of an accused person within the meaning of that section.

(4A) For the purposes of the preceding provisions of this section a county court shall be treated as a superior court and not as an inferior court.

(5) The enactments specified in Part II of Schedule 2 shall have effect subject to the amendments set out in that Part, being amendments relating to the penalties and procedure in respect of certain offences of contempt in coroners' courts, county courts and magistrates' courts.

Note—Amended by the Mental Health (Amendment) Act 1982, s.65(1), Sched.3; the **3C–37** Mental Health Act 1983, s.148, Sched.4; the County Courts (Penalties for Contempt) Act 1983, s.1; the Criminal Justice Act 1991, s.17(3), Sched.4; and the Criminal Justice Act 1993, s.65(3) (4), Sched.3. There are two subss.(2A) and (4A). The first subs.(2A) was inserted by the Criminal Justice Act 1982, s.77, Sched.14, para. 60 and is amended by the Powers of Criminal Courts (Sentencing) Act 2000, Sched.9, para. 84.

"In any case where a court has power to commit a person to prison for contempt of court

Section 14 applies to civil contempts (*Linnett v. Coles* [1987] Q.B. 555; [1986] 3 All **3C–38** E.R. 652, CA). For guidance on sentencing where the contempt is constituted by a witness's refusal to give evidence see *R. v. Montgomery (James)* [1995] 2 All E.R. 28. For general guidance on sentencing see *Hale v. Tanner* [2000] 1 W.L.R. 2377. However this guidance was modified by *Lomas v. Parle* [2002] EWCA Civ 1804 which pointed out that, if there are parallel criminal proceedings arising out of the same incident it is not for the first court to sentence to anticipate or allow for a likely further sentence. Rather it is for the second court to reflect the prior sentence to ensure that the defendant is not punished twice for the same act.

Mitigation

3C–39   Where an alleged contemnor is liable to imprisonment the court must afford him, whether or not he is legally represented, proper opportunity to mitigate, especially where the court has indicated that it was reluctant to consider any sentence other than one of immediate imprisonment (*Taylor v. Persico*, *The Times*, February 12, 1992, CA).

A judge exercising the jurisdiction to punish for contempt will be well advised to invite, although he cannot require, the alleged contemnor to be legally represented. In this way he will obtain the assistance of counsel or solicitors in considering his powers and the circumstances of the case (*R. v. Tyne Tees Television Ltd*, *The Times*, October 20, 1997, *per* Beldam L.J., Ognall and Buckley L.JJ.).

See further Practice Direction—Committal Applications at scpd52.1. This PD is distilled from a series of Court of Appeal decisions and should be treated as authoritative.

"A fixed term"

3C–40   The term, once imposed, may not be varied so as to increase its duration (*Westcott v. Westcott* (1985) Fam.Law. 278, CA). An order committing a person to prison for contempt for an indefinite period, even if suspended for a fixed number of days, is not a committal for a fixed term and is *ultra vires* (*Re C. (A Minor)*, *The Times*, November 15, 1985, CA).

Where, however, there has been no unfairness or material irregularity in the committal proceedings, and where there has been nothing more than an irregularity in the drawing up of the committal order, the irregularity can be corrected on appeal by virtue of A.J.A. 1960, s.13(3), and the term varied so as to make the order lawful (*Linnett v. Coles* [1987] Q.B. 555; [1986] 3 All E.R. 652, CA).

A Court dealing with a person for criminal contempt, whether at first instance or on appeal, has no power to make a probation order (*R. v. Palmer* [1992] 1 W.L.R. 568).

S.14(1) does not enable the court on any one occasion to impose consecutive sentences which cumulatively exceed the two year maximum. Thus where a judge purported to give a contemnor credit for admitting breaches of an undertaking, but thereafter imposed consecutive sentences to a total of two years he could not be said to have made the reduction in sentence which he had promised (*Re R. (a Minor) (Contempt Sentence)* [1994] 1 W.L.R. 487; [1994] 2 All E.R. 144). The court cannot, moreover, on the same occasion both activate a suspended sentence and impose a new consecutive sentence which together exceed the two year maximum (*Villiers v. Villiers* [1994] 2 All E.R. 149).

Where the contempt consists of a refusal to give evidence in a criminal trial the Court of Appeal, Criminal Division, has set out the principles to which a court should have regard in determining the appropriate sentence (*R. v. Montgomery*, *The Times*, July 19, 1994).

A judge sitting in the county court who has found a party guilty of contempt, in breaching an order or undertaking, has no power to detain the contemnor in custody pending consideration of the sentence to be imposed (*Delaney v. Delaney*, *The Times*, November 2, 1995). A High Court judge has only a very limited power (see *Wilkinson v. S & anor* [2003] 1 WLR 1254).

In considering what order to make against a local authority for its contempt in breaching its undertaking to perform its repairing obligations under a lease a judge was entitled to take judicial notice of numerous instances of past contempt in other claims against that authority by its tenants (*Hackney LBC v. Mullen*, *Independent*, November 18, 1996).

Superior Court

3C–41   For the meaning of superior court see s.19 below. The County Courts (Penalties for Contempt) Act 1983, which came into force on May 13, 1983, provides for county courts to be treated as superior courts for the purposes of this section (see subs.(4A) inserted by that Act), thus reversing the effect of the House of Lords' decision in *Peart v. Stewart* [1983] 2 A.C. 109; [1983] 1 All E.R. 859.

Inferior court

A coroner's court is an inferior court of record which has power to punish a person **3C–42** for contempt of court committed in the face of the court, since it was necessary for the coroner to keep order in the proceedings which he has the duty of conducting (*R. v. West Yorkshire Coroner, Ex p. Smith* [1985] Q.B. 1096; [1985] 1 All E.R. 100). An industrial tribunal is also an inferior court and the Queen's Bench Divisional Court therefore has power to punish for contempt of that tribunal (*Peach Grey & Co (a firm) v. Sommers* [1995] 2 All E.R. 513).

Suspension of order

A county court now has like power as the High Court to suspend a committal order **3C–43** for contempt of court upon stated conditions, and to impose consecutive sentences for separate contempts (*Lee v. Walker* [1985] Q.B. 1191; [1985] 1 All E.R. 781, CA).

* * * *

Enforcement of fines imposed by certain superior courts

16.—(1) Payment of a fine for contempt of court imposed by a **3C–44** superior court, other than the Crown Court or one of the courts specified in subsection (4) below, may be enforced upon the order of the court—

    (a) in like manner as a judgment of the High Court for the payment of money; or

    (b) in like manner as a fine imposed by the Crown Court.

(2) Where payment of a fine imposed by any court falls to be enforced as mentioned in paragraph (a) of subsection (1)—

    (a) the court shall, if the fine is not paid in full forthwith or within such time as the court may allow, certify to Her Majesty's Remembrancer the sum payable;

    (b) Her Majesty's Remembrancer shall thereupon proceed to enforce payment of that sum as if it were due to him as a judgment debt;

    (c) [...].

(3) Where payment of a fine imposed by any court falls to be enforced as mentioned in paragraph (b) of subsection (1), the provisions of sections 139 and 140 of the Powers of Criminal Courts (Sentencing) Act 2000 shall apply as they apply to a fine imposed by the Crown Court.

(4) Subsection (1) of this section does not apply to fines imposed by the criminal division of the Court of Appeal or by the <u>House of Lords</u> [*Supreme Court*] on appeal from that division.

(5) The Fines Act 1833 shall not apply to a fine to which subsection (1) of this section applies.

(6) [...].

Note—Amended by the Supreme Court Act 1981, s.152(4), Sched.7; the Industrial **3C–45** Tribunals Act 1996, s.45, Sched.3 and by the Powers of Criminal Courts (Sentencing) Act 2000, Sched.9, para. 85; words underlined prospectively repealed and words in square brackets and italics prospectively substituted by the Constitutional Reform Act 2005, s.40, Sch.9, para.35(2), with effect from a date to be appointed.

Superior Court

See s.19, para. 3C–48 and note under s.14, para. 3C–36.   **3C–46**

Disobedience to certain orders of magistrates' courts

17.—(1) The powers of a magistrates' court under subsection (3) of **3C–47**

CONTEMPT

section 63 of the Magistrates' Court Act 1980 (punishment by fine or committal for disobeying an order to do anything other than the payment of money or to abstain from doing anything) may be exercised either of the court's own motion or by order on complaint.

(2) In relation to the exercise of those powers the provisions of the Magistrates'Court Act 1980 shall apply subject to the modifications set out in Schedule 3 to this Act.

* * * *

SUPPLEMENTAL

Interpretation

3C–48   **19.** In this Act—

"court" includes any tribunal or body exercising the judicial power of the State, and "legal proceedings" shall be construed accordingly;

"publication" has the meaning assigned by subsection (1) of section 2, and "publish" (except in section 9) shall be construed accordingly;

"Scottish proceedings" means proceedings before any court, including the Courts-Martial Appeal Court, the Restrictive Practices Court and Employment Appeal Tribunal, sitting in Scotland, and includes proceedings before the House of Lords [*Supreme Court*] in the exercise of any appellate jurisdiction over proceedings in such a court;

"the strict liability rule" has the meaning assigned by section 1;

"superior court" means [*Supreme Court*] the Court of Appeal, the High Court, the Crown Court, the Courts-Martial Appeal Court, the Restrictive Practices Court, the Employment Appeal Tribunal and any other court exercising in relation to its proceedings powers equivalent to those of the High Court, and includes the House of Lords in the exercise of its appellate jurisdiction.

3C–49   *Note* —Amended by the Cable and Broadcasting Act 1984, Sched.5, para. 39; and the Broadcasting Act 1990, Scheds 20 and 21; words underlined prospectively repealed and words in square brackets and italics prospectively substituted or inserted by the Constitutional Reform Act 2005, ss 40, 146, Sched.9, para.35(3), Sched.18, Pt II, with effect from a date to be appointed.

Court

3C–50   A mental health review tribunal is a court for *inter alia* the purposes of s.19 (*Pickering v. Liverpool Daily Post & Echo Newspapers plc* [1990] 2 W.L.R. 494; [1990] 1 All E.R. 335, CA; affd. on this ground (although reversed on others) [1991] 1 All E.R. 622, HL). The decision to the contrary in *Att.-Gen. v. Associated Newspapers Group plc* [1989] 1 W.L.R. 322; [1989] 1 All E.R. 604, is wrong (*ibid.*). See also generally the note at para. 13A–45.

Superior Court

3C–51   See n. "Superior court", para. 3C–46.

Tribunals of Inquiry

3C–52   **20.**—(1) In relation to any tribunal to which the Tribunals of Inquiry (Evidence) Act 1921 applies, and the proceedings of such a tribunal, the provisions of this Act (except subsection (3) of section 9) apply as they apply in relation to courts and legal proceedings; and references to the course of justice or the administration of justice in legal proceedings shall be construed accordingly.

(2) The proceedings of a tribunal established under the said Act shall be treated as active within the meaning of section 2 from the time when the tribunal is appointed until its report is presented to Parliament.

Short title, commencement and extent

21.—(1) This Act may be cited as the Contempt of Court Act 1981. **3C–53**

(2) The provisions of this Act relating to legal aid in England and Wales shall come into force on such day as the Lord Chancellor may appoint by order made by statutory instrument; and the provisions of this Act relating to legal aid in Scotland and Northern Ireland shall come into force on such day or days as the Secretary of State may so appoint.

Different days may be appointed under this subsection in relation to different courts.

(3) Subject to subsection (2), this Act shall come into force at the expiration of the period of one month beginning with the day on which it is passed.

(4) Sections 7, 8(3), 12, 13(1) to (3), 14, 16, 17 and 18, Parts I and III of Schedule 2 and Schedules 3 and 4 of this Act do not extend to Scotland.

(5) This Act, except sections 15 and 17 and Schedules 2 and 3, extends to Northern Ireland.

SCHEDULE 1

TIMES WHEN PROCEEDINGS ARE ACTIVE FOR PURPOSES OF SECTION 2

Preliminary

1. In this Schedule "criminal proceedings" means proceedings against a person in **3C–54** respect of an offence, not being appellate proceedings or proceedings commenced by motion for committal or attachment in England and Wales or Northern Ireland; and "appellate proceedings" means proceedings on appeal from or for the review of the decision of a court in any proceedings.

2. Criminal, appellate and other proceedings are active within the meaning of section 2 at the times respectively prescribed by the following paragraphs of this Schedule; and in relation to proceedings in which more than one of the steps described in any of those paragraphs is taken, the reference in that paragraph is a reference to the first of those steps.

Criminal proceedings

3. Subject to the following provisions of this Schedule, criminal proceedings are ac- **3C–55** tive from the relevant initial step specified in paragraph 4 or 4A until concluded as described in paragraph 5.

4. The initial steps of criminal proceedings are—
  (a) arrest without warrant;
  (b) the issue, or in Scotland the grant, of a warrant for arrest;
  (c) the issue of a summons to appear, or in Scotland the grant of a warrant to cite;
  (d) the service of an indictment or other document specifying the charge;

(e) except in Scotland, oral charge.

4A. Where as a result of an order under section 54 of the Criminal Procedure and Investigations Act 1996 (acquittal tainted by an administration of justice offence) proceedings are brought against a person for an offence of which he has previously been acquitted, the initial step of the proceedings is a certification under subsection (2) of that section; and paragraph 4 has effect subject to this.

5. Criminal proceedings are concluded—

(a) by acquittal or, as the case may be, by sentence;

(b) by any other verdict, finding, order or decision which puts an end to the proceedings;

(c) by discontinuance or by operation of law.

6. The reference in paragraph 5(a) to sentence includes any order or decision consequent on conviction or finding of guilt which disposes of the case, either absolutely or subject to future events, and a deferment of sentence under section 1 of the Powers of Criminal Courts (Sentencing) Act 2000, s.219 or 432 of the Criminal Procedure (Scotland) Act 1975 or Article 14 of the Treatment of Offenders (Northern Ireland) Order 1976.

7. Proceedings are discontinued within the meaning of paragraph 5(c)—

(a) in England and Wales or Northern Ireland, if the charge or summons is withdrawn or a *nolle prosequi* entered;

(aa) in England and Wales, if they are discontinued by virtue of section 23 of the Prosecution of Offences Act 1985;

(b) in Scotland, if the proceedings are expressly abandoned by the prosecutor or are deserted *simpliciter*;

(c) in the case of proceedings in England and Wales or Northern Ireland commenced by arrest without warrant, if the person arrested is released, otherwise than on bail, without having been charged.

8. Criminal proceedings before a court-martial or standing civilian court are not concluded until the completion of any review of finding or sentence.

9. Criminal proceedings in England and Wales or Northern Ireland cease to be active if an order is made for the charge to lie on the file, but become active again if leave is later given for the proceedings to continue.

9A. Where proceedings in England and Wales have been discontinued by virtue of section 23 of the Prosecution of Offences Act 1985, but notice is given by the accused under subsection (7) of that section to the effect that he wants the proceedings to continue, they become active again with the giving of that notice.

10. Without prejudice to paragraph 5(b) above, criminal proceedings against a person cease to be active—

(a) if the accused is found to be under a disability such as to render him unfit to be tried or unfit to plead or, in Scotland, is found to be insane in bar of trial; or

(b) if a hospital order is made in his case under section 51(5) of the Mental Health Act 1983 or sparagraph (b) of subsection (2) of section 62 of the Mental Health Act (Northern Ireland) 1961 or, in Scotland, where a transfer order ceases to have effect by virtue of section 73(1) of the Mental Health (Scotland) Act 1984. but become active again if they are later resumed.

11. Criminal proceedings against a person which become active on the issue or the grant of a warrant for his arrest cease to be active at the end of the period of twelve months beginning with the date of the warrant unless he has been arrested within that period, but become active again if he is subsequently arrested.

Other proceedings at first instance

3C–56
12. Proceedings other than criminal proceedings and appellate proceedings are active from the time when arrangements for the hearing are made or, if no such arrangements are previously made, from the time the hearing begins, until the proceedings are disposed of or discontinued or withdrawn; and for the purposes of this paragraph any motion or application made in or for the purposes of any proceedings, and any pre-trial review in the county court, is to be treated as a distinct proceeding.

13. In England and Wales or Northern Ireland arrangements for the hearing of

proceedings to which paragraph 12 applies are made within the meaning of that paragraph—

(a) in the case of proceedings in the High Court for which provision is made by rules of court for setting down for trial, when the case is set down;

(b) in the case of any proceedings, when a date for the trial or hearing is fixed.

14. [*Proceedings in Scotland.*]

Appellate proceedings

15. Appellate proceedings are active from the time when they are commenced— **3C–57**

(a) by application for leave to appeal or apply for review, or by notice of such an application;

(b) by notice of appeal or of application for review;

(c) by other originating process,

until disposed of or abandoned, discontinued or withdrawn.

16. Where, in appellate proceedings relating to criminal proceedings, the court—

(a) remits the case to the court below; or

(b) orders a new trial or a *venire de novo*, or in Scotland grants authority to bring a new prosecution,

any further or new proceedings which result shall be treated as active from the conclusion of the appellate proceedings.

Note —Amended by the Mental Health Act 1983, Sched.4, paras 57(c) and 59(c); the **3–58** Prosecution of Offences Act 1985, s.31, Sched.1, paras 4 and 5; the Mental Health (Scotland) Act 1984, s.17, s.127(1), Sched.3, para. 48; the Criminal Procedure and Investigations Act 1996, s.57 and by the Powers of Criminal Courts (Sentencing) Act 2000, Sched.9, para. 86.

CROSS REFERENCE TO COUNTY COURTS ACT 1984

Power to commit for contempt

For the power of a County Court to commit for contempt see s.118 of the County **3C–59** Courts Act 1984 (para. 9A–740).

3D   PROCEEDINGS UNDER THE HUMAN RIGHTS ACT 1998

Human Rights Act 1998

(1998 c.42)

An Act to give further effect to rights and freedoms guaranteed under the European Convention on Human Rights; to make provision with respect to holders of certain judicial offices who become judges of the European Court of Human Rights; and for connected purposes.

[November 9, 1998]

INTRODUCTION

The Convention rights

3D–2   1.—(1) In this Act(1), "the convention rights" means the rights and fundamental freedoms set out in—

(a) Articles 2 to 12 and 14 of the Convention,

(b) Articles 1 to 3 of the First Protocol, and

(c) Article 1 of the Thirteenth Protocol.

as read with Articles 16 to 18 of the Convention.

(2) Those Articles are to have effect for the purposes of this Act subject to any designated derogation or reservation (as to which see sections 14 and 15).

(3) The Articles are set out in Schedule 1.

(4) The Secretary of State may by order make such amendments to this Act as he considers appropriate to reflect the effect, in relation to the United Kingdom, of a protocol.

(5) In subsection (4) "protocol" means a protocol to the Convention—

(a) which the United Kingdom has ratified; or

(b) which the United Kingdom has signed with a view to ratification.

(6) No amendment may be made by an order under subsection (4) so as to come into force before the protocol concerned is in force in relation to the United Kingdom.

Section 1(1)

3D–3   "The Convention" here means "the Convention ... as it has effect for the time being in relation to the United Kingdom", as defined in section 21(1). Thus if the effect of a provision of the Convention is limited or extinguished by some other, overriding provision of international law, such as a UN Security Council Resolution, that limitation affects the interpretation of the convention rights in the United Kingdom: *R (on the application of Hilal Abdul-Razzaq Ali Al-Jedda v. Secretary of State for Defence* [2005] EWHC 1809 (Admin); [2005] HRLR 39, paras 59-63 and 112.

Section 1(1)(c)

3D–4   Substituted by the Human Rights Act 1998 (Amendment) Order 2004 (S.I. 2004 No. 1574), art 2(1) to reflect the coming into force of Protocol 13 of the ECHR, concerning abolition of the death penalty.

Section 1(2)

3D–5   The United Kingdom entered a derogation to Article 5 of the ECHR in order to enact Pt IV of the Anti-Terrorism Crime and Security Act 2001. This was contained in the Human Rights Act 1998 (Designated Derogation) Order 2001 (S.I. 2001 No 3644). However, that Order was quashed by the House of Lords in *A v.Secretary of State for the Home Department* [2005] UKHL 71, (2005) 3 W.L.R. 1249, *The Times*, December 9, 2005. Part IV of the Anti-Terrorism Crime and Security Act 2001 was repealed by the Prevention of Terrorism Act 2005, with effect from 14 March 2005, and the Human Rights Act 1998 (Amendment) Order 2005 (S.I. 2005 No 1071), of 8 April 2005, reflected the withdrawal of the derogation from Article 5 in response to this.

Section 1(4)

3D–6   For procedure for making of an order under this section, see section 20(4).

Interpretation of Convention rights

3D–7   2.—(1) A court or tribunal determining a question which has arisen under this Act in connection with a Convention right must take into account any—

> (a) judgment, decision, declaration or advisory opinion of the European Court of Human Rights,
> (b) opinion of the Commission given in a report adopted under Article 31 of the Convention,
> (c) decision of the Commission in connection with Article 26 or 27(2) of the Convention, or
> (d) decision of the Committee of Ministers taken under Article 46 of the Convention,

whenever made or given, so far as, in the opinion of the court or tribunal, it is relevant to the proceedings in which that question has arisen.

(2) Evidence of any judgment, decision, declaration or opinion of which account may have to be taken under this section is to be given in proceedings before any court or tribunal in such manner as may be provided by rules.

(3) In this section "rules" means rules of court or, in the case of proceedings before a tribunal, rules made for the purposes of this section—

> (a) by the Secretary of State, in relation to any proceedings outside Scotland;
> (b) by the Secretary of State, in relation to proceedings in Scotland; or
> (c) by a Northern Ireland department, in relation to proceedings before a tribunal in Northern Ireland—
>> (i) which deals with transferred matters; and
>> (ii) for which no rules made under paragraph (a) are in force.

Note —Amended by the Secretary of State for Constitutional Affairs Order 2003 **3D–8**
(S.I. 2003 No. 1887), Sched.2, para. 10.

Section 2(1)

This requires any court or tribunal determining a question which has arisen under **3D–9** any Act in connection with a Convention right to "take into account" the decisions of the Strasbourg organs, whenever made or given so far as, in the opinion of the court or tribunal, it is relevant to the proceedings in which that question has arisen. The courts will not without good reason depart from the principles laid down in a carefully considered judgment of the ECtHR sitting as a Grand Chamber: *R (Anderson) v Secretary of State for the Home Department* [2002] UKHL 46; (2003) 1 AC 834; [2002] 2 WLR 1143; [2002] UKHRR 261 per Lord Bingham para 18. In the absence of some special circumstance, a court should follow any clear and consistent jurisprudence of the ECtHR: *R (on the application of Holding and Barnes plc) v Secretary of State for the Environment* [2001] UKHL 23, [2003] 2 AC 295, [2001] 2 WLR 1389 HL per Lord Slynn. It may, however, be appropriate for a court to decline to follow the reasoning of the ECtHR if it is unpersuasive: see *R v. Spear* [2002] UKHL 31, [2003] 1 AC 734 HL paras 12-13 and 65-66 and *R v. Lyons* [2002] UKHL 44, [2003] 1 AC 976 para 46.

The purpose of section 2 is to ensure that the same Convention rights are enforced under the HRA by courts within the United Kingdom as would be enforced by the ECtHR in Strasbourg. It is not intended to provide Convention rights with a domestically autonomous meaning: *N v. Secretary of State for the Home Department* [2005] UKHL 31; [2005] 2 A.C. 296; [2005] 2 W.L.R. 1124; [2005] 4 All E.R. 1017 per Lord Hope para 25 and *R (on the application of Hilal Abdul-Razzaq Ali Al-Jedda) v. Secretary of State for Defence* [2005] EWHC 1809; [2005] H.L.R. 39 (Admin) paras 41, 43 and 59 per

Moses J. A national court should not, without strong reason, dilute or weaken the effect of Strasbourg case-law. Nor should the provision of more generous rights be the product of interpretation of the Convention by the national courts, since the meaning of the Convention should be uniform throughout the states party to it: *R v. Special Adjudicator ex p. Ullah*, sub nom. *Doh v Secretary of State for the Home Department* [2004] UKHL 26, [2004] 2 AC 323; [2004] 3 WLR 23 per Lord Bingham.

However (per Moses J in *Al-Jedda*) at para 41, the "less than imperative terms" of the drafting were necessary to allow a distinction to be drawn between the ECtHR approach and that of a domestic court, in that, for example, domestic courts may have a narrower area of discretion. Note section 11 of the Act: reliance on Convention rights does not restrict other wider rights available otherwise.

In *Price v. Leeds City Council* [2005] EWCA Civ 289, [2005] 1 WLR 1825, [2005] 3 All E.R. 573; [2005] U.K.H.R.R. 413(NB—Judgment of House of Lords awaited at time of writing), appeal heard by House of Lords, hearing commenced December 12, 2005, the Court of Appeal concluded that the principle of stare decisis compelled it to follow the decision of the House of Lords even if it conflicted with later Strasbourg authority (per Lord Phillips MR paras 31-34).

Section 2(1)(b)

3D–10   This refers to Art.31 of the Convention before it was amended by the 11th Protocol, which dealt with the duty of the European Commission of Human Rights to report in the event that it did not secure a friendly settlement of an application which it had declared admissible. Article 31(1) provided "If a solution is not reached, the Commission shall draw up a Report on the facts and state its opinion as to whether the facts found disclose a breach by the State concerned of its obligations under the Convention. The opinions of all the members of the Commission on this point may be stated in the Report."

Section 2(1)(c)

3D–11   This refers to Art.26 of the Convention before it was amended by the 11th Protocol, which provided "The Commission may only deal with the matter [*i.e.* non-state applications] after all domestic remedies have been exhausted, according to the generally recognised rules of international law, and within a period of six months from the date on which the final decision was taken." Article 27(2) of the unamended Convention provided "3. The Commission shall declare inadmissible any individual application submitted under Art.25 which it considers incompatible with the provisions of the present Convention, manifestly ill-founded, or an abuse of the right of petition". See now Art.35 of the Convention as amended.

Section 2(1)(d)

3D–12   "Article 46—Binding force and execution of judgments
1. The High Contracting Parties undertake to abide by the final judgment of the Court in any case to which they are parties.
2. The final judgment of the Court shall be transmitted to the Committee of Ministers, which shall supervise its execution."

The reference to Art.46 includes a reference to Arts 32 and 54 of the Convention before it was amended by the 11th Protocol: see s.21(3). Article 32(1) provided that if, after the Commission had adopted a Report under Art.31, the case was not referred to the European Court of Human Rights, "the Committee of Ministers [of the Council of Europe] shall decide by a majority of two-thirds of the members entitled to sit on the Committee whether there has been a violation of the Convention". Article 54 was virtually identical to the new Art.46.

Section 2(2)

3D–13   As to citation of Strasbourg authorities, see para 8 of the Practice Direction—Miscellaneous Provisions Relating to Hearings: 39PD.8. Excessive citation of authority is to be avoided. Decisions of the ECtHR tend to repeat the same principles in successive cases in order to apply them to different situations. Citation of a single case may therefore be all that is required: *A v.B Plc* [2002] EWCA Civ 337, [2002] EHRLR 25 paras 8-9, CA.

Section 2(3)

3D–14   The power to make rules under this subsection for England and Wales is exercisable by statutory instrument: see section 20(2). It can be annulled by resolution of either House of Parliament: see section 20(5) and 20(7).

For citation of authorities concerning human rights see CPR Practice Direction supplementing rule 39, para 8.1.

LEGISLATION

Interpretation of legislation

3.—(1) So far as it is possible to do so, primary legislation and sub- **3D-15** ordinate legislation must be read and given effect in a way which is compatible with the Convention rights.

(2) This section—

    (a) applies to primary legislation and subordinate legislation whenever enacted;

    (b) does not affect the validity, continuing operation or enforcement of any incompatible primary legislation; and

    (c) does not affect the validity, continuing operation or enforcement of any incompatible subordinate legislation if (disregarding any possibility of revocation) primary legislation prevents removal of the incompatibility.

Like the court's general free-standing jurisdiction to declare the meaning of legisla- **3D-16** tion, the interpretative obligation in section 3(1) is a general one. A claimant seeking a declaration as to the meaning of legislation under section 3(1) need not be a victim: it is sufficient that he or she has an interest and standing: see *R (on the application of Rusbridger) v. AG* [2003] UKHL 38; [2004] AC 357; [2003] 3 W.L.R. 232 para 21 per Lord Steyn. However, see para.3D-18 concerning declarations of incompatibility.

Section 3(1) introduced a new canon of construction, a "strong adjuration" to interpret legislation compatibly with the Convention, which may involve adopting a meaning other than the natural and ordinary meaning of the statutory words: see *R v. DPP ex p. Kebilene* [2000] 2 AC 326; [1999] 3 W.L.R. 972; [1999] 4 All E.R. 801 per Lord Cooke of Thorndon. For a review of section 3 case-law, see the speech of Lord Steyn in *Ghaidan v. Godin-Mendoza* [2004] UKHL 30; [2004] 2 A.C. 557; [2004] 3 W.L.R. 113.

The particular statutory provision which is said to contravene Convention rights must be identified with precision by the claimant: see *R. v. A (Complainant's Sexual History)* [2001] UKHL 25; [2001] 1 A.C. 45; [2001] 2 W.L.R. 1546, HL per Lord Hope at 1582, 153 para 110; *R v. Lambert* [2001] 3 W.L.R. 206 at 234 para 8; *Re S (Care Order: Implementation of Care Plan)* [2002] UKHL 10; [2002] 2 A.C. 291; [2002] 2 W.L.R 720; [2002] 2 All E.R. 192 per Lord Nicholls at para 41.

The court must first ask whether, on ordinary construction, the statutory provision is compatible with Convention rights. If not, it must consider whether it is possible to read the provision in a manner which is compatible: *Brown v. Stott* [2003] 1 A.C. 681; [2001] 2 All E.R. 97. These steps require the Court to identify the scope of the Convention right in question: *Brown*, per Lord Roger. As to what is "possible" see the case law on European Community law, *e.g. Marleasing SA v. La Comercial Internacional de Alimentacion SA (C-106/89)* [1990] E.C.R. I04125 and *Litster v. Forth Dry Dock & Engineering Company Limited* [1990] 1 A.C. 546. Techniques involved may be reading down of express language in a statute, or reading in. Section 3 may require a court to depart from the unambiguous meaning which the legislation would bear other than by reference to the purpose of compatibility with the Convention: see *Ghaidan v. Godin-Mendoza* [2004] UKHL 30; [2004] 2 A.C. 557; [2004] 3 W.L.R. 113 per Lord Nicholls at para 30. This may involve departure from the intention of the Parliament which enacted the legislation. Parliament's intention is normally to be deduced from the statutory language. It is seldom necessary to have regard to matters stated in Parliament by resort to Hansard: *Wilson v. First County Trust Ltd (No.2)* [2003] UKHL 40; [2004] 1 A.C. 816; [2003] 3 W.L.R. 568; [2003] 4 All E.R. 97.

A compatible interpretation must be sought unless it is plainly impossible: the search is for a "possible" meaning, not one which is "reasonably possible": *R v. A (No 2)* [2001] UKHL 25; [2002] 1 A.C. 45; [2001] 2 W.L.R. 1546 HL; cf *R. (on the application of H) v. Mental Health Review Tribunal for North and East London Region* [2001] EWCA Civ 415; [2002] Q.B. 1; [2001] 3 W.L.R. 512). Only if no possible reading of the statute is compatible with the Convention will the court consider whether to make a declaration of incompatibility under section 4, which is an order of last resort.

The exercise is, however, one of interpretation not legislation. A Convention-compatible interpretation cannot be given to legislation if it is contrary to express statutory words of the necessary implication of the statute: *Poplar Housing & Regeneration Community Association Ltd v.Donoghue* [2001] EWCA Civ 595; [2002] Q.B. 48; [2001] 3 W.L.R. 183, CA; *R (Anderson) v. Secretary of State for the Home Department* [2002] UKHL 46; [2003] EHRLR 7. There are two circumstances in which it would not be possible to use section 3 to achieve compatibility. First, a meaning which departs substantially from a fundamental feature of an Act of Parliament is likely to have crossed the boundary between interpretation and amendment: *Re S (Care Order: Implementation of Care Plan)* [2002] 2 AC 291; [2002] 2 WLR 720; [2002] 2 All ER 192; [2002] 1 FLR 815 per Lord Nicholls at para 40. Secondly, compatible interpretation would be impossible where the legislation in issue had wide ramifications, raising policy issues ill-suited for determination by the courts or court procedures, or would require the construction of a wide-ranging new extra-statutory scheme: *Re S (supra)*; *Bellinger v. Bellinger* [2003] UKHL 21; [2003] 2 A.C. 467; [2003] 2 W.L.R. 1174; [2003] 2 All E.R. 593.

Where a court does rely on section 3 it should limit the extent of the modified meaning to that necessary to achieve compatibility: see *Poplar Housing & Regeneration Community Association Ltd v. Donoghue* [2001] EWCA Civ 595; [2002] Q.B. 48; [2001] 3 W.L.R. 183 (CA); *R (on the application of Middleton) v. HM Coroner for Western Somerset* [2004] UKHL 10; [2004] 2 WLR 800 HL (para 34).

Declaration of incompatibility

3D–17   **4.**—(1) Subsection (2) applies in any proceedings in which a court determines whether a provision of primary legislation is compatible with a Convention right.

(2) If the court is satisfied that the provision is incompatible with a Convention right, it may make a declaration of that incompatibility.

(3) Subsection (4) applies in any proceedings in which a court determines whether a provision of subordinate legislation, made in the exercise of a power conferred by primary legislation, is compatible with a Convention right.

(4) If the court is satisfied—

(a) that the provision is incompatible with a Convention right, and

(b) that (disregarding any possibility of revocation) the primary legislation concerned prevents removal of the incompatibility,

it may make a declaration of that incompatibility.

(5) In this section "court" means—

(a) the House of Lords;

(b) the Judicial Committee of the Privy Council;

(c) the Courts-Martial Appeal Court;

(d) in Scotland, the High Court of Justiciary sitting otherwise than as a trial court or the Court of Session;

(e) in England and Wales or Northern Ireland, the High Court or the Court of Appeal.

(6) A declaration under this section ("a declaration of incompatibility")—

(a) does not affect the validity, continuing operation or enforcement of the provision in respect of which it is given; and

(b) is not binding on the parties to the proceedings in which it is made.

There is no strict requirement that a person who seeks a declaration of incompatibility is a "victim" within section 7, provided he or she has a sufficient interest and standing: *R (on the application of Rusbridger) v. Attorney General* [2003] UKHL 38; [2004] 1 AC 357; [2003] 3 WLR 232 para 21 per Lord Steyn. Ordinarily, however, the court will only grant a declaration of incompatibility to a person who is a victim of an actual or proposed breach of a Convention right: *Re S (Care Order: Implementation of Care Plan)* [2002] 2 A.C. 291; [2002] 2 W.L.R. 720; [2002] 2 All E.R. 192; [2002] 1 F.L.R. 815 per Lord Nicholls; *Bellinger v. Bellinger* [2003] UKHL 21; [2003] 2 A.C. 467; [2003] 2 W.L.R. 1174; [2003] 2 All E.R. 593. In any event, a person cannot apply for a declaration of incompatibility on the basis of a hypothetical argument, nor unless they are adversely affected by the impugned measure: *Joseph Taylor v. Lancashire County Council and Secretary of State for the Environment, Food & Rural Affairs* [2005] EWCA Civ 284; [2005] H.R.L.R. 17; [2005] U.K.H.R.R. 766, per Woolf, CJ.

3D–18

Unlike a claim under section 7, which can be considered by any court, only superior courts of record can make declarations of incompatibility (section 4(5)). When considering whether to make an order transferring proceedings from the County Court to the High Court, the court must have regard to the question of whether the making of a declaration of incompatibility has arisen or may arise: CPR r.30.3(2)(g). It is not, however, necessary to transfer the proceedings to the High Court merely because a breach of a Convention right is alleged, nor where an application for a declaration of incompatibility has been made by stands no chance of success: *V (A Child) (Care Proceedings: Human Rights Claims, Re* [2004] EWCA Civ 54; [2004] 1 W.L.R. 1433 (CA).

A statutory lacuna is not the same as an incompatibility: see *S (Children) (Care Order: Implementation of Care Plan), Re* [2002] UKHL 10; [2002] 2 A.C. 291; [2002] 2 W.L.R. 720 per Lord Nicholls. See also section 6(3)(b) and s6(6): failure to legislate does not amount to a breach of section 6(1).

A declaration of incompatibility is a remedy of last resort: it must be avoided unless it is plainly impossible to do so: *R v. A (No 2)* [2001] UKHL 25; [2002] 1 A.C. 45; [2001] 2 W.L.R. 1546 (see also commentary on section 3, above). Even where it is not possible to interpret a provision compatibly with the ECHR, the Court retains a discretion as to whether to grant a declaration, to be exercised according to the normal principles governing the grant of declarations. As to circumstances in which a declaration might be made, see *Wilson v. First County Trust Ltd (No.2)* [2001] EWCA 633; [2002] Q.B. 74; [2001] 3 WLR 42 (CA) (overruled on other grounds in *Wilson v. first County Trust Ltd (No.2)* [2003] UKHL 40; [2004] 1 A.C. 816; [2003] 3 W.L.R. 568; [2003] 4 All E.R. 97).

Extrinsic evidence of legislative policy is admissible only in relation to a declaration of incompatibility: see also *Wilson v. First County Trust Ltd (No.2)* [2003] UKHL 40; [2004] 1 A.C. 816; [2003] 3 W.L.R. 568; [2003] 4 All E.R. 97 at paras 61-67 per Lord Nicholls; *Evans v. Amicus Healthcare Ltd* [2004] EWCA Civ 727 CA and *R (on the Application of Morris) v. Westminster City Council (No 3)* [2005] EWCA Civ 1184, *The Times*, October 19, 2005 para 39 per Sedley LJ.

The fact that another power may achieve the same result as that which is prohibited by the operation of section 6(2), and which results in a declaration of incompatibility, does not mean that a statement of incompatibility is unnecessary if the impugned measure is incompatible with a Convention right. Other forms of statutory protection are immaterial. See *R (on the Application of Morris) v. Westminster City Council (No 3)* [2005] EWCA Civ 1184; [2005] H.R.L.R. 43; *The Times* October 19, 2005, paras 53-55, 82.

As to the procedure for making declarations of incompatibility, see section 5 post, and r.19.4A CPR 1998, inserted by regulation 3 of the Civil Procedure (Amendment No 4) Rules 2000 (SI 2000 No. 2092).

A request for a declaration of incompatibility should not be made on the basis of a hypothetical argument because a person cannot apply for a declaration under section 4(2) unless they are adversely affected by the legislation in question: *Joseph Taylor (Appellant) v Lancashire County Council (Respondent) & Secretary of State for Environment, Food*

3D–19

and Rural Affairs (Intervener) [2005] EWCA Civ 284; [2005] H.R.L.R. 17, [2005] U.K.H.R.R. 766, paragraph 43, per Woolf, CJ.

Right of Crown to intervene

3D–20   **5.**—(1) Where a court is considering whether to make a declaration of incompatibility, the Crown is entitled to notice in accordance with rules of court.

(2) In any case to which subsection (1) applies—

    (a) a Minister of the Crown (or a person nominated by him),

    (b) a member of the Scottish Executive,

    (c) a Northern Ireland Minister,

    (d) a Northern Ireland department,

is entitled, on giving notice in accordance with rules of court, to be joined as a party to the proceedings.

(3) Notice under subsection (2) may be given at any time during the proceedings.

(4) A person who has been made a party to criminal proceedings (other than in Scotland) as the result of a notice under subsection (2) may, with leave, appeal to the House of Lords against any declaration of incompatibility made in the proceedings.

(5) In subsection (4)—

    "criminal proceedings" includes all proceedings before the Courts-Martial Appeal Court; and

    "leave" means leave granted by the court making the declaration of incompatibility or by the House of Lords.

3D–21   As to the procedure for giving notice to the Crown, see CPR, r.19.4A.

The parties should also give as much informal notice as possible to the Crown of the proceedings and the issues involved, and should copy this notice to the court: *Poplar Housing & Regeneration Community Association Ltd v. Donoghue* [2001] EWCA Civ 595; [2002] Q.B. 48; [2001] 4 All E.R. 604; [2001] 3 W.L.R. 183, CA. "The Crown" means a person named in a list under the Crown Proceedings Act 1947, s.17, *ibid.*

PUBLIC AUTHORITIES

Acts of public authorities

3D–22   **6.**—(1) It is unlawful for a public authority to act in a way which is incompatible with a Convention right.

(2) Subsection (1) does not apply to an act if—

    (a) as the result of one or more provisions of primary legislation, the authority could not have acted differently; or

    (b) in the case of one or more provisions of, or made under, primary legislation which cannot be read or given effect in a way which is compatible with the Convention rights, the authority was acting so as to give effect to or enforce those provisions.

(3) In this section "public authority" includes—

    (a) a court or tribunal, and

    (b) any person certain of whose functions are functions of a public nature, but does not include either House of Parliament or a person exercising functions in connection with proceedings in Parliament.

(4) In subsection (3) "Parliament" does not include the House of Lords in its judicial capacity.

(5) In relation to a particular act, a person is not a public authority by virtue only of subsection (3)(b) if the nature of the act is private.

(6) "An act" includes a failure to act but does not include a failure to—

> (a) introduce in, or lay before, Parliament a proposal for legislation; or
>
> (b) make any primary legislation or remedial order.

Section 6(1)

Section 6(1) only applies to territory to which relevant provisions of the law have **3D–23** been extended by the United Kingdom: *R (on the application of Quark Fishing Limited) v. Secretary of State for Foreign & Commonwealth Affairs* [2005] UKHL 57.

Section 6(1) and 6(3)

As to the meaning of "public authority" see: *Poplar Housing & Regeneration Com-* **3D–24** *munity Association Limited v. Donoghue* [2001] EWCA Civ 395; [2002] Q.B. 48; [2001] 3 W.L.R. 183 CA; *R (on the application of Heather v. Leonard Cheshire Foundation* [2002] EWCA Civ 366; (2002) 2 All E.R. 936, *Aston Cantlow & Wilmcote with Billesley Parochial Church Council v. Wallbank* [2003] UKHL 37; [2004] 1 A.C. 546; *Hampshire CC v. Beer (t/a Hammer Trout Farm) sub nom. R (on the application nof Beer (t/a Hammer Trout Farm)) v. Hampshire Farmers Markets Ltd* [2003] EWCA Civ 1056; [2004] 1 W.L.R. 233; (2003) 31 EG 67 (CS); *R (on the application of West) v. Lloyds of London* [2004] EWCA Civ 506; [2004] 3 All E.R. 251. See *Public Law* [2005] 785-805.

Section 6(2)

As to the extent and effect of section 6(2), see *Ghaidan v. Ghodin-Mendoza* [2004] **3D–25** UKHL 30; [2004] 2 A.C. 557; [2004] 3 W.L.R. 113 at paragraph 18; *Hooper v. Department for Work & Pensions* [2005] UKHL 29; [2005] 1 W.L.R. 1681; *The Times* May 6, 2005 at paragraphs 49-51.

Section 6(2) disapplies section 6(1) only if the public authority is acting so as to give effect to one or more provisions of primary legislation which cannot be read or given effect in a way which is compatible with Convention rights, having read the legislation, under section 3(1), in a way which is, if possible, compatible with the Convention: see *Brown v. Stott* [2001] 2 W.L.R. 817, [2001] 2 All E.R. 97, per Lord Roger.

As to the effect of a finding that section 6(2) applies on the exercise of another power, see *R (on the Application of Morris) v.Westminster City Council (No 3)* [2005] EWCA Civ 118; [2005] H.R.L.R. 43; *The Times*, October 19, 2005 paras 53-55, 82.

The fact that a statute provides a specific scheme of enforcement by reference to specified public authorities does not confine any section 6(1) action to those bodies: *Marcic v. Thames Water Utilities* [2003] UKHL 66; [2004] 2 A.C. 42; [2004 1 All E.R. 135; [2003] 3 W.L.R. 1603, HL.

Section 6(3)

The fact that courts are public authorities under section 6(1) may affect the ap- **3D–26** proach they adopt in proceedings between two private bodies: for example, in the approach they take to determining whether to award an interim injunction to give effect to arts 8 and 10 of the Convention: *A v. B plc* [2002] EWCA Civ 337; [2003] Q.B. 195; [2002] 3 W.L.R. 542.

Proceedings

7.—(1) A person who claims that a public authority has acted (or **3D–27** proposes to act) in a way which is made unlawful by section 6(1) may—

  (a) bring proceedings against the authority under this Act in the appropriate court or tribunal, or

  (b) rely on the Convention right or rights concerned in any legal proceedings,

but only if he is (or would be) a victim of the unlawful act.

(2) In subsection (1)(a) "appropriate court or tribunal" means such court or tribunal as may be determined in accordance with rules; and proceedings against an authority include a counterclaim or similar proceeding.

(3) If the proceedings are brought on an application for judicial review, the applicant is to be taken to have a sufficient interest in relation to the unlawful act only if he is, or would be, a victim of that act.

(4) If the proceedings are made by way of a petition for judicial review in Scotland, the applicant shall be taken to have title and interest to sue in relation to the unlawful act only is he is, or would be, a victim of that act.

(5) Proceedings under subsection (1)(a) must be brought before the end of—

  (a) the period of one year beginning with the date on which the act complained of took place; or

  (b) such longer period as the court or tribunal considers equitable having regard to all the circumstances,

but that is subject to any rule imposing a stricter time limit in relation to the procedure in question.

(6) In subsection (1)(b) "legal proceedings" includes—

  (a) proceedings brought by or at the instigation of a public authority; and

  (b) an appeal against the decision of a court or tribunal.

(7) For the purposes of this section, a person is a victim of an unlawful act only if he would be a victim for the purposes of Article 34 of the Convention if proceedings were brought in the European Court of Human Rights in respect of that act.

(8) Nothing in this Act creates a criminal offence.

(9) In this section "rules" means—

  (a) in relation to proceedings before a court or tribunal outside Scotland, rules made by the Secretary of State for the purposes of this section or rules of court,

  (b) in relation to proceedings before a court or tribunal in Scotland, rules made by the Secretary of State for those purposes,

  (c) in relation to proceedings before a tribunal in Northern Ireland—

    (i) which deals with transferred matters; and

    (ii) for which no rules made under paragraph (a) are in force, rules made by a Northern Ireland department for those purposes,

  and includes provision made by order under section 1 of the Courts and Legal Services Act 1990.

(10) In making rules regard must be had to section 9.

(11) The Minister who has power to make rules in relation to a particular tribunal may, to the extent he considers it necessary to ensure that the tribunal can provide an appropriate remedy in relation to an act (or proposed act) of a public authority which is (or would be) unlawful as a result of section 6(1), by order add to—

(a) the relief or remedies which the tribunal may grant; or

(b) the grounds on which it may grant any of them.

(12) An order made under subsection (11) may contain such incidental, supplemental, consequential or transitional provision as the Minister making it considers appropriate.

(13) "The Minister" includes the Northern Ireland department concerned.

Note —Amended by the Secretary of State for Constitutional Affairs Order (S.I. 2003 No. 1887), Sched.2, para. 10.   **3D–28**

Sections 7(1) "public authority"

As to meaning of public authority, see 3D-24above.   **3D–29**

Section 7(1), 7(3) and 7(7) "victim"

As to the meaning of "victim" in Article 34 (formerly Article 25) of the Convention, see: Lester & Pannick, eds, *Human Rights Law & Practice* (2nd Edn., Lexis Nexis, Butterworths, 2004) para 2.7.2; Wadham, Mountfield & Edmundson, *Blackstone's Guide to the Human Rights Act 1998*, (3rd Edn., OUP, 2003) paras 5.3.1-5.3.3. See too *Director General of Fair Trading* v. Proprietary Association of Great Britain & Another [2001] EWCA Civ 1217; [2002] 1 WLR 269 (CA) (association could not be a "victim" where its rights wer not affected and where it had not been formally declared to be the representative of its members' interests). A person may continue to claim to be a victim where there is a continuing violation of a positive procedural obligation, even if he has received compensation for feelings of frustration, distress and anxiety from the ECtHR: *Re McKerr* [2004] UKHL 12; [2004] 1 WLR 807; [2004] 2 All ER 409 HL.   **3D–30**

Section 7(1)(a) and 7(2) "appropriate court or tribunal"

This is determined by the subject matter of the claim, and rules issued under the Act. See the Civil Procedure (Amendment No 4) Rules 2000 (S.I. 2000 No. 2092) concerning procedure for treatment of human rights issues in the Administrative Court; the Family Proceedings (Amendment) Rules 2000 (S.I. 2000 No. 2267) for family courts; Part 33 CPR and Practice Direction 30 concerning transfer between courts; Criminal Appeals (Amendment) Rules 2000 (S.I. 2000 No. 2036) concerning human rights issues in criminal courts; and the House of Lords: Practice Directions and Standing Orders Applicable to Civil Appeals and Practice Directions and Standing Orders Applicable to Criminal Appeals.   **3D–31**

Practice Directions and Standard Orders Applicable to Civil Appeals and Practice Directions and Standing Orders Applicable to Criminal Appeals

It is not necessary to transfer proceedings to the High Court merely because a breach of a Convention right is alleged, or where there is a claim for a declaration of incompatibility if it has no chance of success: *V (A Child) (Care Proceedings: Human Rights Act Claims), Re* [2004] EWCA Civ 54; [2004] 1 W.L.R. 1433, CA.   **3D–32**

For employment claims where a declaration of incompatibility may be sought see *Whittaker v. Watson (t/a P & M Watson Haulage)* [2002] ICR 1244.

The Proscribed Organisation Appeals Commission is the appropriate tribunal in relation to matters related to proscription of a terrorist organisation under the Terrorism Act 2000: *R (Kurdistan Workers' Party) v. Secretary of State for the Home Department* [2002] EWHC 644 (Admin).

Section 7(2)

In *Anufrijeva v. Southwark LBC* [2004] Q.B. 1124; [2004] 2 W.L.R. 613; [2004] 1 All   **3D–33**

E.R. 833; [2003] EWCA Civ 1406, the Court of Appeal has given guidance as to the approach in considering claims for damages for breaches of Convention rights involving maladministration. The Court also laid down the following procedural guidelines:

(i) Courts should look critically at any attempt to recover HRA damages for maladministration by any procedure other than judicial review.

(ii) A claim for damages alone cannot be brought by judicial review (r.54.3(2)) but it should still be brought in the Administrative Court by an ordinary claim. (see also para. 53). Note, however, that this refers only to an ordinary claim before the Administrative Court, that is to say a claim asserting breach of a public law duty (*i.e.* maladministration) which requires permission to enable it to proceed: *Andrews v. Reading BC* [2004] EWHC 970; [2005] Env. L.R. 2; [2004] U.K.H.R.R. 599, para. 9 (Collins J).

(iii) Before giving permission to apply for judicial review, the Administrative Court judge should require the claimant to explain why it would not be more appropriate to use any available internal complaint procedure or proceed by making a claim to the Parliamentary or Local Government Ombudsman at least in the first instance.

(iv) If there is a legitimate claim for other relief, permission should if appropriate be limited to that relief and consideration given to deferring permission for the damages claim, adjourning or staying that claim until use has been made of ADR, whether by a reference to a mediator or an ombudsman or otherwise, or remitting that claim to a district judge or master if it cannot be dismissed summarily on grounds that in any event an award of damages is not required to achieve just satisfaction.

(v) It is hoped that in future, claims that have to be determined by the courts can be determined by the appropriate level of judge in a summary manner by the judge reading the relevant evidence. The citing of more than three authorities should be justified and the hearing should be limited to half a day except in exceptional circumstances.

These guidelines may create certain practical difficulties and, it is suggested, may not be appropriate outside the area to which the cases related, namely allegations of breaches of positive obligations in the social welfare and immigration fields, arising out of delay caused by maladministration.

Section 7(6)(b)

3D–34   Proceedings brought by or at the instigation of a public authority include not only the trial but also a victim's appeal in such proceedings: *R. v. DPP, ex p. Kebilene* [2000] 2 A.C. 326; [1999] 3 W.L.R. 972; [1999] 4 All E.R. 801, *per* Lord Steyn.

As to the requirements of a statement of case relying on the Human Rights Act 1998 see Practice Direction to Pt 16, para. 15.1 As to the requirements of an appellant's notice see Practice Direction to Pt 52, para. 5.1A and 5.1B.

Applications for judicial review are not brought by or at the instigation of a public authority: *R v. Haringey LBC, ex p. Ben-Abdelaziz*, [2001] EWCA Civ 803; [2001] 1 W.L.R. 1485, CA.

Section 7(9)

3D–35   The power to make rules under this subsection for England and Wales is exercisable by statutory instrument: see section 20(2). It can be annulled by resolution of either House of Parliament: see section 20(5) and 20(7).

Section 7(11)

3D–36   For the procedure for making orders under this sub-section, see section 20(4).

Judicial remedies

3D–37   8.—(1) In relation to any act (or proposed act) of a public authority which the court finds is (or would be) unlawful, it may grant such relief or remedy, or make such order, within its powers as it considers just and appropriate.

(2) But damages may be awarded only by a court which has power to award damages, or to order the payment of compensation, in civil proceedings.

(3) No award of damages is to be made unless, taking account of all the circumstances of the case, including—

    (a) any other relief or remedy granted, or order made, in relation to the act in question (by that or any other court), and

    (b) the consequences of any decision (of that or any other court) in respect of that act,

the court is satisfied that the award is necessary to afford just satisfaction to the person in whose favour it is made.

(4) In determining—

    (a) whether to award damages, or

    (b) the amount of an award,

the court must take into account the principles applied by the European Court of Human Rights in relation to the award of compensation under Article 41 of the Convention.

(5) A public authority against which damages are awarded is to be treated—

    (a) in Scotland, for the purposes of section 3 of the Law Reform (Miscellaneous Provisions) (Scotland) Act 1940 as if the award were made in an action of damages in which the authority has been found liable in respect of loss or damage to the person to whom the award is made;

    (b) for the purposes of the Civil Liability (Contribution) Act 1978 as liable in respect of damage suffered by the person to whom the award is made.

(6) In this section—

"court" includes a tribunal;

"damages" means damages for an unlawful act of a public authority; and

"unlawful" means unlawful under section 6(1).

Remedies available under section 8 of the Act are all those within the court's powers, unconstrained by any new principles except in relation to damages, where sections 8(2)-8(4) apply. **3D–38**

Sections 8(3) and 8(4)

As to the meaning of "just satisfaction", the principles applied by the ECtHR must be taken into account (though they are not binding). **3D–39**

A domestic court should not award damages under section 8 unless it is satisfied it is necessary to do so. A causal connection is required between the violation and the loss for which compensation is claimed (see *R (on the application of Greenfield) v. Secretary of State for the Home Department* [2005] UKHL 14; [2005] 1 W.L.R. 637; [2005] 2 All E.R. 240; [2005] H.R.L.R. 13, per Lord Bingham, paragraph 11). The Court of Appeal gave guidelines as to the award of damages in *Anufrijeva v. Southwark LBC* [2004] Q.B. 1124; [2004] 2 W.L.R. 613; [2004] 1 All E.R. 833; [2003] EWCA Civ 1406. The Court made clear its view that damages are not available as of right like damages for tort, but only as a discretionary remedy of last resort. The guiding remedial principle is *restitutio in integrum*, so that the claimant should, so far as possible, be put in the position in which he would have found himself if his Convention rights had not been infringed. But account must first be taken of the effect of any other remedies which the court has already been able to provide. Any remaining significant pecuniary loss caused by the breach should usually be assessed and awarded; but caution is to be exercised when deciding whether to award damages for non-pecuniary loss, and if so **3D–40** how much. The consequences of the breach must be serious, the damage must be more than distress and frustration, and the scale and manner of the violation can be taken into account. In cases of maladministration, awards by the Parliamentary or Local Government Ombudsman may be the only guide. The Court of Appeal also approved the approach of Sullivan J. in *R. (on the application of Bernard) v. Enfield LBC* [2002] EWHC 2282; [2003] H.R.L.R. 4; [2003] U.K.H.R.R. 148, where damages were awarded a severely disabled woman and her husband-carer, who had been left in unsuitable accommodation for 20 months in breach of Art.8. For an example of case in which damages were found to be necessary, see *Ali v. The Headteacher & Governors of Lord Grey School* [2004] EWCA Civ 382; [2004] QB 1231; [2004] 2 WLR 1442.

As to whether the Court should declare that a Defendant has acted in breach of s.6, compare the approaches of Simon Brown and Carnwarth L.JJ. in *R. (on the application of Purja) v. Ministry of Defence* [2003] EWCA Civ 1345; [2004] 1 W.L.R. 289; [2004] U.K.H.R.R. 309; *The Times*, October 16, 2003.

In *R. (on the application of H) v. Secretary of State for the Home Department* [2003] U.K.H.L. 1; [2003] H.R.L.R. 570; [2003] 1 W.L.R. 411; [2003] 1 All E.R. 497, the House of Lords declined to award damages to a mental health patient since the violation had been publicly acknowledged and his right had been vindicated, the law had been amended in a way which should prevent similar violations in future, and he had not been the victim of unlawful detention, which art.5 is intended to avoid.

For authority on obligation of the courts to ensure effective protection of fundamental rights and to fashion new remedies where necessary see *Gairy v. Attorney-General of Grenada*, [2001] UKPC 30; [2001] 3 W.L.R. 779, PC. The limitation in s.21(1) read with s.38(2) of the Crown Proceedings Act 1947 must now be reading accordance with the provisions of the Human Rights Act.

Judicial acts

3D–41   **9.**—(1) Proceedings under section 7(1)(a) in respect of a judicial act may be brought only—

(a) by exercising a right of appeal;

(b) on any application (in Scotland a petition) for judicial review; or

(c) in such other forum as may be prescribed by rules.

(2) That does not affect any rule of law which prevents a court from being the subject of judicial review.

(3) In proceedings under this Act in respect of a judicial act done in good faith, damages may not be awarded otherwise than to compensate a person to the extent required by Article 5(5) of the Convention.

(4) An award of damages permitted by subsection (3) is to be made against the Crown, but no award may be made unless the appropriate person, if not a party to the proceedings, is joined.

(5) In this section—

"appropriate person" means the Minister responsible for the court concerned, or a person or government department nominated by him;

"court" includes a tribunal;

"judge" includes a member of a tribunal, a justice of the peace and a clerk or other officer entitled to exercise the jurisdiction of a court;

"judicial act" means a judicial act of a court and includes an act done on the instructions, or on behalf, of a judge; and

"rules" has the same meaning as in section 7(9).

As to evidence in a claim in respect of a judicial act, see CPR, r.33.9. **3D–42**

It is arguable that in *R v. Director General of Fair Trading v. Proprietary Association of Great Britain and another* [2001] EWCA Civ. 1217; [2002] 1 W.L.R. 269, CA, the court should have found that there was a breach of ECHR, Art.6(1) arising out of the lack of independence of the first instance court, but refused the application for costs on the basis of s.9(3).

Section 9(2)

See s.29(3) of the Supreme Court Act 1981. Considered in *R. v. DPP, ex p. Kebiline* **3D–43** [2000] 2 AC 326; [1999] 3 W.L.R. 972; [1999] 4 All E.R. 801. See also *R. v. Hertfordshire CC, ex p. Green Environmental Industries Ltd* [2000] 2 A.C. 412; [2000] 2 W.L.R. 373; [2000] 1 All E.R. 733, *per* Lord Cooke of Thorndon and Lord Hobhouse of Woodborough.

REMEDIAL ACTION

Power to take remedial action

10.—(1) This section applies if— **3D–44**

    (a) a provision of legislation has been declared under section 4 to be incompatible with a Convention right and, if an appeal lies—

        (i) all persons who may appeal have stated in writing that they do not intended to do so;

        (ii) the time for bringing an appeal has expired and no appeal has been brought within that time; or

        (iii) an appeal brought within that time has been determined or abandoned; or

    (b) it appears to a Minister of the Crown or Her Majesty in Council that, having regard to a finding of the European Court of Human Rights made after the coming into force of this section in proceedings against the United Kingdom, a provision of legislation is incompatible with an obligation of the United Kingdom arising from the Convention.

(2) If a Minister of the Crown considers that there are compelling reasons for proceeding under this section, he may by order make such amendments to the legislation as he considers necessary to remove the incompatibility.

(3) If, in the case of subordinate legislation, a Minister of the Crown considers—

    (a) that it is necessary to amend the primary legislation under which the subordinate legislation in question was made, in order to enable the incompatibility to be removed; and

    (b) that there are compelling reasons for proceeding under this section,

he may by order make such amendments to the primary legislation as he considers necessary.

(4) This section also applies where the provision in question is in subordinate legislation and has been quashed, or declared invalid, by reason of incompatibility with a Convention right and the Minister proposes to proceed under paragraph 2(b) of Schedule 2.

(5) If the legislation is an Order in Council, the power conferred by subsection (2) or (3) is exercisable by Her Majesty in Council.

(6) In this section "legislation" does not include a Measure of the Church Assembly or of the General Synod of the Church of England.

(7) Schedule 2 makes further provision about remedial orders.

OTHER RIGHTS AND PROCEEDINGS

Safeguard for existing human rights

3D–45   11. A person's reliance on a Convention right does not restrict—

    (a) any other right or freedom conferred on him by or under any law having effect in any part of the United Kingdom; or

    (b) his right to make any claim or bring any proceedings which he could make or bring apart from sections 7 to 9.

Freedom of expression

3D–46   12.—(1) This section applies if a court is considering whether to grant any relief which, if granted might affect the exercise of the Convention right to freedom of expression.

(2) If the person against whom the application for relief is made ("the respondent") is neither present nor represented, no such relief is to be granted unless the court is satisfied—

    (a) that the applicant has taken all practicable steps to notify the respondent; or

    (b) that there are compelling reasons why the respondent should not be notified.

(3) No such relief is to be granted so as to restrain publication before trial unless the court is satisfied that the applicant is likely to establish that publication should not be allowed.

(4) The court must have particular regard to the importance of the Convention right to freedom of expression and, where the proceedings relate to material which the respondent claims, or which appears to the court, to be journalistic, literary or artistic material (or to conduct connected with such material), to—

    (a) the extent to which—

        (i) the material has, or is about to, become available to the public; or

        (ii) it is, or would be, in the public interest for the material to be published;

    (b) any relevant privacy code.

(5) In this section—

"court" includes a tribunal; and

"relief" includes any remedy or order (other than in criminal proceedings).

3D–47   The Court of Appeal gave guidance as to the application of s.12 in *A v. B Plc* [2002] EWCA Civ 337; [2003] Q.B. 195; [2002] H.R.L.R. 25.

Section 12(3)

In *Cream Holdings Ltd v. Bannerjee* [2004] UKHL 44; [2005] 1 AC 253 it was held **3D–48** that, at this interlocutory stage, the test of likelihood was higher than the normal threshold for the grant of an interlocutory injunction in *American Cyanamid v. Ethicon Ltd* [1975] AC 796 (whether the claim had a "real prospect" of success) but not so high as being that the claim was "more likely than not" to succeed, which standard was unworkable in practice. The standard is a flexible one: the degree of likelihood of success at trial needed to satisfy s.12(3) must depend on the circumstances. There is no automatic priority, or presumption that art. 10 ECHR has greater weight than art. 8, and the court should evaluate whether it is necessary in any given case to qualify the one right in order to protect the other: *Campbell v. MGN Limited* [2004] UKHL 22; [2004] 2 AC 457; [2004] 2 WLR 1232 para 55 (Lord Hoffmann) and para 141 (Baroness Hale"). See also *Douglas v. Hello! Ltd* [2001] QB 967 para 150 per Keene LJ.

Section 12(4)

The court cannot have "particular regard" to Art.10 without having regard to the **3D–49** qualifications in Art.10(2), such as the rights and freedoms of others: *Douglas v. Hello! Ltd* [2001] Q.B. 967, *per* Sedley L.J., para. 133. Thus, the sub-section does not give either Art.8 or 12 pre-eminence over the other: *S (A Child) (Identification: Restrictions on Publication), Re* [2004] UKHL 47; [2005] 1 A.C. 593; [2004] 3 W.L.R. 1129, Hale L.J. When the values of two rights are in conflict, it is necessary to focus intensely on their comparative importance. This includes consideration of the justifications for interfering with or restricting each right and the application of the proportionality test: *A Local Authority v. PD* [2005] EWHC 1832 .

The fact that an injunction will interfere with freedom of the press is of particular importance: *A v. B Plc* [2002] EWCA Civ 337; [2003] Q.B. 195; [2002] 3 W.L.R. 542; [2002] All E.R. 545, para. 11(iv). The reference to the "public interest" does not mean that the court is justified in interfering where there is no identifiable special public interest in any particular material to be published. Any interference with publication must be justified: *ibid.*, para. 11(v). "Any relevant privacy code" includes the Press Complaints Commission Code of Practice, but this is only one factor. Courts should discourage advocates from seeking to rely on individual PCC decisions: *ibid.*, paras 11(xiv) and 11(xv). Where the balance does not clearly point in either direction, interim relief should be refused: *ibid.*, para. 12. Note that although the lack of media challenge to an application does not in itself justify the grant of an order interfering with the rights of the press, it nevertheless demonstrates that the press does not believe that a significant inhibition of the exercise of its rights under Article 10 exists: *Maxine Carr v. News Group Newspapers Ltd and Others* [2005] EWHC 971 (QB) . See also Anonymity Orders and Media Censorship in the "New Era of Human Rights" Paul Dougan, Ent. L.R. 2005, 16(6), 150-152

Freedom of thought, conscience and religion

13.—(1) If a court's determination of any question arising under **3D–50** this Act might affect the exercise by a religious organisation (itself or its members collectively) of the Convention right to freedom of thought, conscience and religion, it must have particular regard to the importance of that right.

(2) In this section, "court" includes a tribunal.

DEROGATIONS AND RESERVATIONS

Derogations

14.—(1) In this Act "designated derogation" means any derogation **3D–51** by the United Kingdom from an Article of the Convention, or of any protocol to the Convention, which is designated for the purposes of this Act in an order made by the Secretary of State.

(2) The derogation referred to in subsection (1)(a) is set out in Part I of Schedule 3.

(3) If a designated derogation is amended or replaced it ceases to be a designated derogation.

(4) But subsection (3) does not prevent the Secretary of State from exercising his power under subsection (1) to make a fresh designation order in respect of the Article concerned.

(5) The Secretary of State must by order make such amendments to Schedule 3 as he considers appropriate to reflect—

(a) any designation order; or

(b) the effect of subsection (3).

(6) A designation order may be made in anticipation of the making by the United Kingdom of a proposed derogation.

Note —The text of the UK's derogation is contained in Schedule 3.

The power to make such an order is exercisable by statutory instrument: section 20(1). For procedure for making of an order under this section, see section 20(3).

3D–52 Amended by the Secretary of State for Constitutional Affairs Order 2003 (S.I. 2003 No. 1884) Sched.2 para. 10.

The original derogation in Pt I of Sched.3 of the Act as enacted was deleted by the Human Rights Act (Amendment) Order 2001 (S.I. 2001 No. 1216). A new derogation from art.5 ECHR was designated in order to enact Pt IV of the Anti-Terrorism Crime and Security Act 2001. This was contained in the Human Rights Act 1998 (Designated Derogation) Order 2001 (S.I. 2001 No. 3644). However, that Order was quashed by the House of Lords in *A & ors v. Secretary of State for the Home Department* [2004] UKHL 71; [2005] 3 W.L.R. 1249 *The Times*, December 9, 2005. Part IV of the Anti-Terrorism Crime and Security Act 2001 was repealed by the Prevention of Terrorism Act 2005, with effect from March 14, 2005, and the Human Rights Act 1998 (Amendment) Order 2005 (S.I. 2005 No. 1071), of April 8, 2005, reflected the withdrawal of the derogation from Art. 5 in response to this.

Reservations

3D–53 15.—(1) In this Act, "designated reservation" means—

(a) the United Kingdom's reservation to Article 2 of the First Protocol to the Convention; and

(b) any other reservation by the United Kingdom to an Article of the Convention, or of any protocol to the Convention, which is designated for the purposes of this Act in an order made by the Secretary of State.

(2) The text of the reservation referred to in subsection (1)(a) is set out in Part II of Schedule 3.

(3) If a designated reservation is withdrawn wholly or in part it ceases to be a designated reservation.

(4) But subsection (3) does not prevent the Secretary of State from exercising his power under subsection (1)(b) to make a fresh designation order in respect of the Article concerned.

(5) The Secretary of State must by order make such amendments to this Act as he considers appropriate to reflect—

(a) any designation order; or

(b) the effect of subsection (3).

Note —The text of the UK's reservation is contained in Schedule 3.

The power to make such an order is exercisable by statutory instrument: section 20(1). For procedure for making of an order under this section, see section 20(3).

Period for which designated derogations have effect

16.—(1) If it has not already been withdrawn by the United **3D–54** Kingdom, a designated derogation ceases to have effect for the purposes of this Act, at the end of the period of five years beginning with the date on which the order designating it was made.

(2) At any time before the period—

    (a) fixed by subsection (1), or

    (b) extended by an order under this subsection,

comes to an end, the Secretary of State may by order extend it by a further period of five years.

(3) An order under section 14(1) ceases to have effect at the end of the period for consideration, unless a resolution has been passed by each House approving the order.

(4) Subsection (3) does not affect—

    (a) anything done in reliance on the order; or

    (b) the power to make a fresh order under section 14(1).

(5) In subsection (3) "period for consideration" means the period of forty days beginning with the day on which the order was made.

(6) In calculating the period for consideration, no account is to be taken of any time during which—

    (a) Parliament is dissolved or prorogued; or

    (b) both Houses are adjourned for more than four days.

(7) If a designated derogation is withdrawn by the United Kingdom, the Secretary of State must by order make such amendments to this Act as he considers are required to reflect that withdrawal.

Note —Amended by the Secretary of State for Constitutional Affairs Order (S.I. **3D–55** 2003 No. 1887), Sched.2, para. 10.

Section 16(2)

The power to make such an order is exercisable by statutory instrument: section **3D–56** 20(1). For procedure for making an order under this sub-section, see section 20(4).

Section 16(7)

The power to make such an order is exercisable by statutory instrument: section **3D–57** 20(1). For procedure for making an order under this sub-section, see section 20(3).

Periodic review of designated reservations

17.—(1) The appropriate Minister must review the designated **3D–58** reservation referred to in section 15(1)(a)—

    (a) before the end of the period of five years beginning with the date on which section 1(2) came into force; and

    (b) if that designation is still in force, before the end of the period of five years beginning with the date on which the last report relating to it was laid under subsection (3).

(2) The appropriate Minister must review each of the other designated reservations (if any)—

    (a) before the end of the period of five years beginning with the date on which the order designating the reservation first came into force; and

(b) if the designation is still in force, before the end of the period of five years beginning with the date on which the last report relating to it was laid under subsection (3).

(3) The Minister conducting a review under this section must prepare a report on the result of the review and lay a copy of it before each House of Parliament.

JUDGES OF THE EUROPEAN COURT OF HUMAN RIGHTS

Appointment to European Court of Human Rights

3D–59   **18.**—(1) In this section "judicial office" means the office of—

(a) Lord Justice of Appeal, Justice of the High Court or Circuit judge, in England and Wales;

(b) judge of the Court of Session or sheriff, in Scotland;

(c) Lord Justice of Appeal, judge of the High Court or county court judge, in Northern Ireland.

(2) The holder of a judicial office may become a judge of the European Court of Human Rights ("the Court") without being required to relinquish his office.

(3) But he is not required to perform the duties of his judicial office while he is a judge of the Court.

(4) In respect of any period during which he is a judge of the Court—

(a) a Lord Justice of Appeal or Justice of the High Court is not to count as a judge of the relevant court for the purposes of section 2(1) or 4(1) of the Supreme Court Act 1981 (maximum number of judges) nor as a judge of the Supreme Court for the purposes of section 12(1) to (6) of that Act (salaries etc.);

(b) a judge of the Court of Session is not to count as a judge of that court for the purposes of section 1(1) of the Court of Session Act 1988 (maximum number of judges) or of section 9(1)(c) of the Administration of Justice Act 1973 ("the 1973 Act") (salaries etc.);

(c) a Lord Justice of Appeal or judge of the High Court in Northern Ireland is not to count as a judge of the relevant court for the purposes of section 2(1) or 3(1) of the Judicature (Northern Ireland) Act 1978 (maximum number of judges) nor as a judge of the Supreme Court of Northern Ireland for the purposes of section 9(1)(d) of the 1973 Act (salaries etc.);

(d) a Circuit judge is not to count as such for the purposes of section 18 of the Courts Act 1971 (salaries etc.);

(e) a sheriff is not to count as such for the purposes of section 14 of the Sheriff Courts (Scotland) Act 1907 (salaries etc.);

(f) a county court judge of Northern Ireland is not to count as such for the purposes of section 106 of the County Courts Act (Northern Ireland) 1959 (salaries etc.).

(5) If a sheriff principal is appointed a judge of the Court, section 11(1) of the Sheriff Courts (Scotland) Act 1971 (temporary appointment of sheriff principal) applies, while he holds that appointment, as if his office is vacant.

(6) Schedule 4 makes provision about judicial pensions in relation to the holder of a judicial office who serves as a judge of the Court.

(7) The Lord Chancellor or the Secretary of State may by order make such transitional provision (including, in particular, provision for a temporary increase in the maximum number of judges) as he considers appropriate in relation to any holder of a judicial office who has completed his service as a judge of the Court.

Note —The power to make such an order is exercisable by statutory instrument: section 20(1). A statutory instrument made under this section can be annulled by resolution of either House of Parliament: see section 20(5). **3D–60**

PARLIAMENTARY PROCEDURE

Statements of compatibility

19.—(1) A Minister of the Crown in charge of a Bill in either House **3D–61** of Parliament must, before Second Reading of the Bill—

(a) make a statement to the effect that in his view the provisions of the Bill are compatible with the Convention rights ("a statement of compatibility"); or

(b) make a statement to the effect that although he is unable to make a statement of compatibility the government nevertheless wishes the House to proceed with the Bill.

(2) The statement must be in writing and be published in such manner as the Minister making it considers appropriate.

Note —This section came into force on November 24, 1998: The Human Rights Act **3D–62** 1998 (Commencement) Order 1998 (S.I. 1998 No. 2882).

"The Convention" has been held to mean "The Convention as given effect by the **3D–63** Act for the time being in relation to the United Kingdom": that is, the Convention and rights of the same scope as would be perceived in Strasbourg: see *R (on the application of Hilal Abdul-Razzaq Ali Al-Jedda v. Secretary of State for Defence* [2005] EWHC 1809 (Admin); [2005] H.R.L.R. 39, paras 59-63 and 112.

SUPPLEMENTAL

Orders, etc., under this Act

20.—(1) Any power of a Minister of the Crown to make an order **3D–64** under this Act is exercisable by statutory instrument.

(2) The power of the Secretary of State to make rules (other than rules of court) under section 2(3) or 7(9) is exercisable by statutory instrument.

(3) Any statutory instrument made under section 14, 15 or 16(7) must be laid before Parliament.

(4) No order may be made by the Secretary of State under section 1(4), 7(11) or 16(2) unless a draft of the order has been laid before, and approved by, each House of Parliament.

(5) Any statutory instrument made under section 18(7) or Schedule 4, or to which subsection (2) applies, shall be subject to annulment in pursuance of a resolution of either House of Parliament.

(6) The power of a Northern Ireland department to make—

(a) rules under section 2(3)(c) or 7(9)(c), or

(b) an order under section 7(11),

is exercisable by statutory rule for the purposes of the Statutory Rules (Northern Ireland) Order 1979.

(7) Any rules made under section 2(3)(c) or 7(9)(c) shall be subject to negative resolution; and section 41(6) of the Interpretation Act (Northern Ireland) 1954 (meaning of "subject to negative resolution") shall apply as if the power to make the rules were conferred by an Act of the Northern Ireland Assembly.

(8) No order may be made by a Northern Ireland department under section 7(11) unless a draft of the order has been laid before, and approved by, the Northern Ireland Assembly.

3D–65   *Note* —Amended by the Secretary of State for Constitutional Affairs Order (S.I. 2003 No. 1887), Sched.2, para.10.

Interpretation, etc.

3D–66   **21.**—(1) In this Act—

"amend" includes repeal and apply (with or without modification);

"the appropriate Minister" means the Minister of the Crown having charge of the appropriate authorised government department (within the meaning of the Crown Proceedings Act 1947);

"the Commission" means the European Commission of Human Rights;

"the Convention" means the Convention for the Protection of Human Rights and Fundamental Freedoms, agreed by the Council of Europe at Rome on November 4, 1950 as it has effect for the time being in relation to the United Kingdom;

"declaration of incompatibility" means a declaration under section 4;

"Minister of the Crown" has the same meaning as in the Ministers of the Crown Act 1975;

"Northern Ireland Minister" includes the First Minister and the deputy First Minister in Northern Ireland;

"primary legislation" means any—

(a) public general Act;

(b) local and personal Act;

(c) private Act;

(d) Measure of the Church Assembly;

(e) Measure of the General Synod of the Church of England;

(f) Order in Council—

(i) made in exercise of Her Majesty's Royal Prerogative;

(ii) made under section 38(1)(a) of the Northern Ireland Constitution Act 1973 of the corresponding provision of the Northern Ireland Act 1998; or

(iii) amending an Act of a kind mentioned in paragraph (a), (b) or (c); and includes an order or other instrument made under primary legislation (otherwise than by the National Assembly for Wales, a member of the Scottish Executive, a Northern Ireland Minister or a Northern Ireland department) to the extent to which it operates to bring one or more provisions of that legislation into force or amends any primary legislation;

"the First Protocol" means the protocol to the Convention agreed at Paris on March 20, 1952;

"the Eleventh Protocol" means the protocol to the Convention (restructuring the control machinery established by the Convention) agreed at Strasbourg on May 11, 1994;

"the Thirteenth Protocol" means the protocol to the Convention (concerning the abolition of the death penalty in all circumstances) agreed at Vilnius on 3rd May 2002;

"remedial order" means an order under section 10;

"subordinate legislation" means any—

(a) Order in Council other than one—

(i) made in exercise of Her Majesty's Royal Prerogative;

(ii) made under section 38(1)(a) of the Northern Ireland Constitution Act 1973 or the corresponding provision of the Northern Ireland Act 1998; or;

(iii) amending an Act of a kind mentioned in the definition of primary legislation;

(b) Act of the Scottish Parliament;

(c) Act of the Parliament of Northern Ireland;

(d) Measure of the Assembly established under section 1 of the Northern Ireland Assembly Act 1973;

(e) Act of the Northern Ireland Assembly;

(f) order, rules, regulations, scheme, warrant, byelaw or other instrument made under primary legislation (except to the extent to which it operates to bring one or more provisions of that legislation into force or amends any primary legislation);

(g) order, rules, regulations, scheme, warrant, byelaw or other instrument made under legislation mentioned in paragraph (b), (c), (d) or (e) or made under an Order in Council applying only to Northern Ireland;

(h) order, rules, regulations, scheme, warrant, byelaw or other instrument made by a member of the Scottish Executive, a Northern Ireland Minister or Northern

Ireland department in exercise of prerogative or other executive functions of Her Majesty which are exercisable by such a person on behalf of Her Majesty;

"transferred matters" has the same meaning as in the Northern Ireland Act 1998; and

"tribunal" means any tribunal in which legal proceedings may be brought.

(2) The references in paragraphs (b) and (c) of section 2(1) to Articles are to Articles of the Convention as they had effect immediately before the coming into force of the 11th Protocol.

(3) The reference in paragraph (d) of section 2(1) to Article 46 includes a reference to Articles 32 and 54 of the Convention as they had effect immediately before the coming into force of the Eleventh Protocol.

(4) The references in section 2(1) to a report or decision of the Commission or a decision of the Committee of Ministers include references to a report or decision made as provided by paragraphs 3, 4 and 6 of Article 5 of the 11th Protocol (transitional provisions).

(5) Any liability under the Army Act 1955, the Air Force Act 1955 or the Naval Discipline Act 1957 to suffer death for an offence is replaced by a liability to imprisonment for life or any less punishment authorised by those Acts; and those Acts shall accordingly have effect with the necessary modifications.

3D–67 *Note* —Amended by the Human Rights Act 1998 (Amendment) Order (S.I. 2004 No. 1574), art.2(2).

Short title, commencement, application and extent

3D–68 **22.**—(1) This Act may be cited as the Human Rights Act 1998.

(2) Sections 18, 20 and 21(5) and this section come into force on the passing of this Act.

(3) The other provisions of this Act come into force on such day as the Secretary of State may by order appoint; and different days may be appointed for different purposes.

(4) Paragraph (b) of subsection (1) of section 7 applies to proceedings brought by or at the instigation of a public authority whenever the act in question took place; but otherwise that subsection does not apply to an act taking place before the coming into force of that section.

(5) This Act binds the Crown.

(6) This Act extends to Northern Ireland.

(7) Section 21(5), so far as it relates to any provision contained in the Army Act 1955, the Air Force Act 1955 or the Naval Discipline Act 1957, extends to any place to which that provision extends.

Section 22(2) & 22(3)

3D–69 The date on which the Act received Royal Assent was 9th November 1998. Section 19 came into force on 24th November 1998: The Human Rights Act 1998 (Commencement) Order 1998, SI 1998/2882. The remainder of the Act came into force on 2nd October 2000: The Human Rights Act 1998 (Commencement No 2) Order 2000 S.I. 2000 No. 1851.

Section 22(4)

As to what constitutes an act "brought by or at the instigation of a public authority", **3D–70**
see commentary to section 7, and *R. (on the application of Ben-Abdelaziz) v Haringey LBC*
[2001] EWCA Civ 803; [2001] 1 W.L.R. 1485, *AG for Scotland v. MacDonald; Pearce v.
Governing Body of Mayfield School* [2003] UKHL 34; [2004] 1 All E.R. 339; *Malcolm v.
Mackenzie* [2004] EWHC 339 (Ch).

The object of section 22(4) is to protect defendants to proceedings brought by or at
the instigation of a public authority: see *Wilson v First County Trust Ltd (No.2)* [2001]
EWCA Civ 633; [2002] Q.B. 74; [2001] 3 W.L.R. 42; [2001] 3 All E.R. 229, (CA), para
90. Whether rights and obligations of parties may be different now from what they
were when an agreement was entered into depend on whether sectin 3 has retrospective effect. This depends on the strength of on the application of the general presumption against retrospective effect, in the context of the particular case, in particular,
whether a party to the dispute has an accrued or vested right.

Limited retrospective effect of section 3 may be permitted if no unfairness would be
caused to any individual: *Commissioner of Police for the Metropolis v. Hurst* [2005] EWCA
Civ 890; [2005] HRLR 31; *The Times*, August 11, 2005.

Acts of courts or tribunals which took place before October 2, 2000, which were
required by primary legislation and which were done according to the meaning of the
legislation which applied at the time are not affected by the provisions of the Act: *R v.
Kansal* [2001] UKHL 62, [2002] 2 AC 69; [2001] 3 WLR 1562 and *R v. Lyons* [2002]
UKHL 44; [2003] HRLR 6. (Though cf *R v. Kebilene* [2002] 2 AC 326; [1999] 3 WLR
972; [1999] 4 All ER 801 HL and *R v. Lambert* [2001] 3 All ER 577 HL).

The Act cannot be relied upon to make conduct which was lawful at the time when
it took place retrospectively unlawful: see *Wainwright v. Home Office* [2001] EWCA Civ
2081, [2002] QB 1334, CA. However, a continuing failure to act dating from before
the entry into force of the Act may become unlawful from the entry into force of the
Act (*R. (on the application of Daly) v Secretary of State for the Home Department* [1999]
C.O.D. 388, though damages may only be claimed from the date of the coming into
force of the Act: *Marcic v. Thames Water Utilities* [2002] EWCA Civ 64 (overruled on the
grounds by *Marcic v Thames Water Utilities Ltd* [2003] UKHL 66; [2004] 2 A.C. 42;
[2003] 3 W.L.R. 1603; [2004] 1 All E.R. 135) and *R. (on the application of Wright) v. Secretary of State for the Home Department* [2001] EWHC Admin 520; [2002] H.R.L.R. 1;
[2001] U.K.H.R.R. 1399 .

For continuing violation of positive obligations to investigate under art 2 or art 3
see *Re McKerr* [2004] UKHL 12; [2004] 1 WLR 807, HL.

SCHEDULE 1

THE ARTICLES

PART I

THE CONVENTION

RIGHTS AND FREEDOMS

Article 2—Right to life

1. Everyone's right to life shall be protected by law. No one shall be deprived of his **3D–71**
life intentionally save in the execution of a sentence of a court following his conviction
of a crime for which this penalty is provided by law.

2. Deprivation of life shall not be regarded as inflicted in contravention of this
Article when it results from the use of force which is no more than absolutely necessary:

    (a) in defence of any person from unlawful violence;

    (b) in order to effect a lawful arrest or to prevent the escape of a person lawfully
        detained;

    (c) in action lawfully taken for the purpose of quelling a riot or insurrection.

Article 3—Prohibition of torture

No one shall be subjected to torture or to inhuman or degrading treatment or **3D–72**
punishment.

Article 4—Prohibition of slavery and forced labour

3D-73   1. No one shall be held in slavery or servitude.

2. No one shall be required to perform forced or compulsory labour.

3. For the purpose of this Article the term "forced or compulsory labour" shall not include:

(a) any work required to be done in the ordinary course of detention imposed according to the provisions of Article 5 of this Convention or during conditional release from such detention;

(b) any service of a military character or, in case of conscientious objectors in countries where they are recognised, service exacted instead of compulsory military service;

(c) any service exacted in case of an emergency or calamity threatening the life or well-being of the community;

(d) any work or service which forms part of normal civic obligations.

Article 5—Right to liberty and security

3D-74   1. Everyone has the right to liberty and security of person. No one shall be deprived of his liberty save in the following cases and in accordance with a procedure prescribed by law:

(a) the lawful detention of a person after conviction by a competent court;

(b) the lawful arrest or detention of a person for non-compliance with the lawful order of a court or in order to secure the fulfilment of any obligation prescribed by law;

(c) the lawful arrest or detention of a person effected for the purpose of bringing him before the competent legal authority on reasonable suspicion of having committed an offence or when it is reasonably considered necessary to prevent his committing an offence or fleeing after having done so;

(d) the detention of a minor by lawful order for the purpose of educational supervision or his lawful detention for the purpose of bringing him before the competent legal authority;

(e) the lawful detention of persons for the prevention of the spreading of infectious diseases, of persons of unsound mind, alcoholics or drug addicts or vagrants;

(f) the lawful arrest or detention of a person to prevent his effecting an unauthorised entry into the country or of a person against whom action is being taken with a view to deportation or extradition.

2. Everyone who is arrested shall be informed promptly, in a language which he understands, of the reasons for his arrest and of any charge against him.

3. Everyone arrested or detained in accordance with the provisions of paragraph 1(c) of this Article shall be brought promptly before a judge or other officer authorised by law to exercise judicial power and shall be entitled to trial within a reasonable time or to release pending trial. Release may be conditioned by guarantees to appear for trial.

4. Everyone who is deprived of his liberty by arrest or detention shall be entitled to take proceedings by which the lawfulness of his detention shall be decided speedily by a court and his release ordered if the detention is not lawful.

5. Everyone who has been the victim of arrest or detention in contravention of the provisions of this Article shall have an enforceable right to compensation.

Article 6—Right to a fair trial

3D-75   1. In the determination of his civil rights and obligations or of any criminal charge against him, everyone is entitled to a fair and public hearing within a reasonable time by an independent and impartial tribunal established by law. Judgment shall be pronounced publicly but the press and public may be excluded from all or part of the trial in the interest of morals, public order or national security in a democratic society, where the interests of juveniles or the protection of the private life of the parties so require, or to the extent strictly necessary in the opinion of the court in special circumstances where publicity would prejudice the interests of justice.

2. Everyone charged with a criminal offence shall be presumed innocent until proved guilty according to law.

3. Everyone charged with a criminal offence has the following minimum rights:

(a) to be informed promptly, in a language which he understands and in detail, of the nature and cause of the accusation against him;

(b) to have adequate time and facilities for the preparation of his defence;

(c) to defend himself in person or through legal assistance of his own choosing or, if he has not sufficient means to pay for legal assistance, to be given it free when the interest of justice so require;

(d) to examine or have examined witnesses against him and to obtain the attendance and examination of witnesses on his behalf under the same conditions as witnesses against him;

(e) to have the free assistance of an interpreter if he cannot understand or speak the language used in court.

Article 7—No punishment without law

1. No one shall be held guilty of any criminal offence on account of any act or omission which did not constitute a criminal offence under national or international law at the time when it was committed. Nor shall a heavier penalty be imposed than the one that was applicable at the time the criminal offence was committed. **3D–76**

2. The Article shall not prejudice the trial and punishment of any person for any act or omission which, at the time when it was committed, was criminal according to the general principles of law recognised by civilised nations.

Article 8—Right to respect for private and family life

1. Everyone has the right to respect for his private and family life, his home and his correspondence. **3D–77**

2. There shall be no interference by a public authority with the exercise of this right except such as is in accordance with the law and is necessary in a democratic society in the interests of national security, public safety or the economic well-being of the country, for the prevention of disorder or crime, for the protection of health or morals, or for the protection of the rights and freedoms of others.

Article 9—Freedom of thought, conscience and religion

1. Everyone has the right to freedom of thought, conscience and religion; this right includes freedom to change his religion or belief and freedom, either alone or in community with others and in public or private, to manifest his religion or belief, in worship, teaching, practice and observance. **3D–78**

2. Freedom to manifest one's religion or beliefs shall be subject only to such limitations as are prescribed by law and are necessary in a democratic society in the interests of public safety, for the protection of public order, health or morals, or for the protection of the rights and freedoms of others.

Article 10—Freedom of expression

1. Everyone has the right to freedom of expression. This right shall include freedom to hold opinions and to receive and impart information and ideas without interference by public authority and regardless of frontiers. This Article shall not prevent States from requiring the licensing of broadcasting, television or cinema enterprises. **3D–79**

2. The exercise of these freedoms, since it carries with it duties and responsibilities, may be subject to such formalities, conditions, restrictions or penalties as are prescribed by law and are necessary in a democratic society, in the interests of national security, territorial integrity or public safety, for the prevention of disorder or crime, for the protection of health or morals, for the protection of the reputation or rights of others, for preventing the disclosure of information received in confidence, or for maintaining the authority and impartiality of the judiciary.

Article 11—Freedom of assembly and association

1. Everyone has the right to freedom of peaceful assembly and to freedom of association with others, including the right to form and to join trade unions for the protection of his interests. **3D–80**

2. No restrictions shall be placed on the exercise of these rights other than such as are prescribed by law and are necessary in a democratic society in the interests of national security or public safety, for the prevention of disorder or crime, for the

protection of health or morals or for the protection of the rights and freedoms of others. This Article shall not prevent the imposition of lawful restrictions on the exercise of these rights by members of the armed forces, of the police or of the administration of the State.

Article 12—Right to marry

3D–81   Men and women of marriageable age have the right to marry and to found a family, according to the national laws governing the exercise of this right.

Article 14—Prohibition of discrimination

3D–82   The enjoyment of the rights and freedoms set forth in this Convention shall be secured without discrimination on any ground such as sex, race, colour, language, religion, political or other opinion, national or social origin, association with a national minority, property, birth or other status.

Article 16—Restrictions on political activity of aliens

3D–83   Nothing in Articles 10, 11 and 14 shall be regarded as preventing the High Contracting Parties from imposing restrictions on the political activity of aliens.

Article 17—Prohibition of abuse of rights

3D–84   Nothing in this Convention may be interpreted as implying for any State, group or person any right to engage in any activity or perform any act aimed at the destruction of any of the rights and freedoms set forth herein or at their limitation to a greater extent than is provided for in the Convention.

Article 18—Limitation on use of restrictions on rights

3D–85   The restrictions permitted under this Convention to the said rights and freedoms shall not be applied for any purpose other than those for which they have been prescribed.

Part II

The First Protocol

Article 1—Protection of property

3D–86   Every natural or legal person is entitled to the peaceful enjoyment of his possessions. No one shall be deprived of his possessions except in the public interest and subject to the conditions provided for by law and by the general principles of international law.

The preceding provisions shall not, however, in any way impair the right of a State to enforce such laws as it deems necessary to control the use of property in accordance with the general interest or to secure the payment of taxes or other contributions or penalties.

Article 2—Right to education

3D–87   No person shall be denied the right to education. In the exercise of any functions which it assumes in relation to education and to teaching, the State shall respect the right of parents to ensure such education and teaching in conformity with their own religious and philosophical convictions.

Article 3—Right to free elections

3D–88   The High Contracting Parties undertake to hold free elections at reasonable intervals by secret ballot, under conditions which will ensure the free expression of the opinion of the people in the choice of the legislature.

Part III

The Thirteenth Protocol

Article 1—Abolition of the death penalty

3D–89   The death penalty shall be abolished. No one shall be condemned to such penalty or executed.

3D–90   *Note* —Substituted by the Human Rights Act 1998 (Amendment) Order 2004 (S.I. 2004 No. 1574), art.2(3).

Article 2—Death penalty in time of war

A State may make provision in its law for the death penalty in respect of acts committed in time of war or of imminent threat of war; such penalty shall be applied only in the instances laid down in the law and in accordance with its provisions. The State shall communicate to the Secretary General of the Council of Europe the relevant provisions of that law.

3D–91

European Convention on Human Rights

Article 1

Obligation to respect human rights

The High Contracting Parties shall secure to everyone within their jurisdiction the rights and freedoms defined in Section I of this Convention.

3D–92

* * * *

Article 13

Right to an effective remedy

Everyone whose rights and freedoms as set forth in this Convention are violated shall have an effective remedy before a national authority notwithstanding that the violation has been committed by persons acting in an official capacity.

3D–93

Editorial Note —Although not among the Convention rights to which s.1(2) of the Human Rights Act 1998 gives effect, Arts 1 and 13 of the Convention are also of significance. Their text is set out above.

3D–94

3E   INSOLVENCY PROCEEDINGS

PRACTICE DIRECTION: INSOLVENCY PROCEEDINGS

Part One

1. General

1.1 In this Practice Direction: 3E–1

(1)   "The Act" means the Insolvency Act 1986 and includes the Act as applied to limited ability partnerships by the Limited Liability Partnerships Regulations 2001; and includes the Act as applied to limited ability partnerships by the Limited Liability Partnerships Regulations 2001;

(2)   "The Insolvency Rules" means the rules for the time being in force and made under s.411 and s.412 of the Act in relation to insolvency proceedings;

(3)   "CPR" means the Civil Procedure Rules and "CPR" followed by a Part or rule by number means the Part or rule with that number in those Rules;

(4)   "RSC" followed by an Order by number means the Order with that number set out in Schedule 1 to the CPR;

(5)   "Insolvency proceedings" means any proceedings under the Act, the Insolvency Rules, the Administration of Insolvent Estates of Deceased Persons Order 1986 (S.I. 1986 No. 1999), the Insolvent Partnership Order 1986 (S.I. 1986 No. 2142) or the Insolvent Partnerships Order 1994 (S.I. 1994 No. 2421).

(6)   References to a 'company' shall include a limited liability partnership and references to a 'contributory' shall include a member of a limited liability partnership.

1.2 This Practice Direction shall come into effect on 26th April 1999 and shall replace all previous Practice Notes and Practice Directions relating to insolvency proceedings.

1.3 Except where the Insolvency Rules otherwise provide, service of documents in insolvency proceedings in the High Court will be the responsibility of the parties and will not be undertaken by the court.

1.4 Where CPR Part 2.4 provides for the court to perform any act, that act may be performed by a Registrar in Bankruptcy for the purpose of insolvency proceedings in the High Court.

1.5 A writ of execution to enforce any order made in insolvency proceedings in the High Court may be issued on the authority of a Registrar.

1.6(1) This paragraph applies where an insolvency practitioner ("the outgoing office holder") holds office as a liquidator, administrator, trustee or supervisor in more than one case and dies, retires from practice as an insolvency practitioner or is otherwise unable or unwilling to continue in office.

(2)   A single application may be made to a Judge of the Chancery Division of the High Court by way of ordinary applica-

tion in Form 7.2 for the appointment of a substitute office holder or office holders in all cases in which the outgoing office holder holds office, and for the transfer of each such case to the High Court for the purpose only of making such an order.

(3) The application may be made by any of the following:
(i) the outgoing office holder (if he is able and willing to do so);
(ii) any person who holds office jointly with the outgoing office holder;
(iii) any person who is proposed to be appointed as a substitute for the outgoing office holder; or
(iv) any creditor in the cases where the substitution is proposed to be made.

(4) The outgoing office holder (if he is not the applicant) and every person who holds office jointly with the office holder must be made a respondent to the application, but it is not necessary to join any other person as a respondent or to serve the application upon any other person unless the Judge or Registrar in the High Court so directs.

(5) The application should contain schedules setting out the nature of the office held, the identity of the Court currently having jurisdiction over each case and its name and number.

(6) The application must be supported by evidence setting out the circumstances which have given rise to the need to make a substitution and exhibiting the written consent to act of each person who is proposed to be appointed in place of the outgoing office holder.

(7) The Judge will in the first instance consider the application on paper and make such order as he thinks fit. In particular he may do any of the following:
(i) make an order directing the transfer to the High Court of those cases not already within its jurisdiction for the purpose only of the substantive application;
(ii) if he considers that the papers are in order and that the matter is straightforward, make an order on the substantive application;
(iii) give any directions which he considers to be necessary including (if appropriate) directions for the joinder of any additional respondents or requiring the service of the application on any person or requiring additional evidence to be provided;
(iv) if he does not himself make an order on the substantive application when the matter is first before him, give directions for the further consideration of the substantive application by himself or another Judge of the Chancery Division or adjourn the substantive application to the Registrar for him to make such order upon it as is appropriate.

(8) An order of the kind referred to in sub-paragraph (6)(i) shall follow the draft order in Form PDIP 3 set out in the

Schedule hereto and an order granting the substantive application shall follow the draft order in Form PDIP 4 set out in the schedule hereto (subject in each case to such modifications as may be necessary or appropriate).

(9) It is the duty of the applicant to ensure that a sealed copy of every order transferring any case to the High Court and of every order which is made on a substantive application is lodged with the court having jurisdiction over each case affected by such order for filing on the court file relating to that case.

(10) It will not be necessary for the file relating to any case which is transferred to the High Court in accordance with this paragraph to be sent to the High Court unless a Judge or Registrar so directs.

Part Two

Companies

2. Advertisement of winding up petition

2.1 Insolvency Rule 4.11(2)(b) is mandatory, and designed to **3E–2** ensure that the class remedy of winding up by the court is made available to all creditors, and is not used as a means of putting pressure on the company to pay the petitioner's debt. Failure to comply with the rule, without good reason accepted by the court, may lead to the summary dismissal of the petition on the return date (Insolvency Rule 4.11(5)). If the court, in its discretion, grants an adjournment, this will be on condition that the petition is advertised in due time for the adjourned hearing. No further adjournment for the purpose of advertisement will normally be granted.

2.2 Copies of every advertisement published in connection with a winding up petition must be lodged with the Court as soon as possible after publication and in any event not later than the day specified in Insolvency Rule 4.14 of the Insolvency Rules 1986. This direction applies even if the advertisement is defective in any way (*e.g.* is published at a date not in accordance with the Insolvency Rules, or omits or misprints some important words) or if the petitioner decides not to pursue the petition (*e.g.* on receiving payment).

3. Certificate of compliance—time for filing

3.1 In the High Court in order to assist practitioners and the **3E–3** Court the time laid down by Insolvency Rule 4.14 of the Insolvency Rules 1986, for filing a certificate of compliance and a copy of the advertisement, is hereby extended to not later than 4.30 p.m. on the Friday preceding the day on which the petition is to be heard. Applications to file the certificate and the copy advertisement after 4.30 p.m. on the Friday will only be allowed if some good reason is shown for the delay.

4. Errors in petitions

4.1 Applications for leave to amend errors in petitions which are **3E–4** discovered subsequent to a winding up order being made should be made to the Court Manager in the High Court and to the District Judge in the county court.

4.2 Where the error is an error in the name of the company, the Court Manager in the High Court and the District Judge in the county court may make any necessary amendments to ensure that the winding up order is drawn with the correct name of the company inserted. If there is any doubt, *e.g.* where there might be another company in existence which could be confused with the company to be wound up, the Court Manager will refer the application to the Registrar and the District Judge may refer it to the Judge.

4.3 Where an error is an error in the registered office of the company and any director or member of the company claims that the company was unaware of the petition by reason of it having been served at the wrong registered office, it will be open to them to apply to rescind the winding up order in the usual way.

4.4 Where it is discovered that the company had been struck off the Register of Companies prior to the winding up order being made, the matter must be restored to the list before the order is entered to enable an order for the restoration of the name to be made as well as the order to wind up.

5. Distribution of business

3E-5   **5.1** The following applications shall be made direct to the Judge and, unless otherwise ordered, shall be heard in public—

(1)   Applications to commit any person to prison for contempt;

(2)   Applications for urgent interim relief (*e.g.* applications pursuant to s.127 of the Act prior to any winding up order being made);

(3)   Applications to restrain the presentation or advertisement of a petition to wind up; or

(4)   Applications for the appointment of a provisional liquidator;

(5)   Petitions for administration orders or an interim order upon such a Petition;

(6)   Applications after an administration order has been made pursuant to s.14(3) of the Act (for directions) or s.18(3) of the Act (to vary or discharge the order);

(7)   Petitions to discharge administration orders and to wind up;

(8)   Applications pursuant to s.5(3) of the Act (to stay a winding up or discharge an administration order or for directions) where a voluntary arrangement has been approved;

(9)   Appeals from a decision made by a County Court or by a Registrar of the High Court.

5.2 Subject to paragraph 5.4 below all other applications shall be made to the Registrar or the District Judge in the first instance who may give any necessary directions and may, in the exercise of his discretion, either hear and determine it himself or refer it to the Judge.

5.3 The following matters will also be heard in public—

(1)   Petitions to wind up;

(2)   Public examinations;

(3)   All matters and applications heard by the Judge, except those referred by the Registrar or the District Judge to be heard in private or so directed by the Judge to be heard.

5.4 In accordance with directions given by the Lord Chancellor the Registrar has authorised certain applications in the High Court to be dealt with by the Court Manager of the Companies Court, pursuant to Insolvency Rule 13.2(2). The applications are:

(1)   To extend or abridge time prescribed by the Insolvency Rules in connection with winding up (Insolvency Rule 4.3 and 12.9);

(2)   For substituted service of winding up petitions (Insolvency Rule 4.8(6));

(3)   To withdraw petitions (Insolvency Rule 4.15);

(4)   For the substitution of a petitioner (Insolvency Rule 4.19);

(5)   By the Official Receiver for limited disclosure of a statement of affairs (Insolvency Rule 4.35);

(6)   By the Official Receiver for relief from duties imposed upon him by the rules (Insolvency Rule 4.47);

(7)   By the Official Receiver for permission to give notice of a meeting by advertisement only (Insolvency Rule 4.59);

(8)   To transfer proceedings from the High Court to a County Court (Insolvency Rule 7.11);

(9)   For permission to amend any originating application.

[N.B. In District Registries all such applications must be made to the District Judge].

6. Drawing up of orders

6.1 The Court will draw up all orders except orders on the application of the Official Receiver or for which the Treasury Solicitor is responsible under the existing practice.   **3E–6**

7. Rescission of a winding up order

7.1 Any application for the rescission of a winding up order shall be made within seven days after the date on which the order was made (Insolvency Rule 7.47(4)). Notice of any such application must be given to the Official Receiver.   **3E–7**

7.2 Applications will only be entertained if made (a) by a creditor, or (b) by a contributory, or (c) by the company jointly with a creditor or with a contributory. The application must be supported by written evidence of assets and liabilities.

7.3 In the case of an unsuccessful application the costs of the petitioning creditor, the supporting creditors and of the Official Receiver will normally be ordered to be paid by the creditor or the contributory making or joining in the application. The reason for this is that if the costs of an unsuccessful application are made payable by the company, they fall unfairly on the general body of creditors.

7.4 Cases in which the making of the winding up order has not been opposed may, if the application is made promptly, be dealt with on a statement by the applicants legal representative of the circumstances; but apart from such cases, the court will normally require any application to be supported by written evidence.

7.5 There is no need to issue a form of application (Form 7.2) as the petition is restored before the Court.

8. Restraint of presentation of a winding-up petition

3E–8 **8.1** An application to restrain presentation of a Winding-up petition must be made to the Judge by the issue of an Originating Application (Form 7.1).

Part Three

Personal Insolvency—Bankruptcy

9. Distribution of business

3E–9 **9.1** The following applications shall be made direct to the Judge and unless otherwise ordered shall be heard in public:

(1) Applications for the committal of any person to prison for contempt;

(2) Application for injunctions or for the modification or discharge of injunctions;

(3) Applications for interlocutory relief or directions after the matter has been referred to the Judge.

9.2 All other applications shall be made to the Registrar or the District Judge in the first instance. He shall give any necessary directions and may, if the application is within his jurisdiction to determine, in his discretion either hear and determine it himself or refer it to the Judge.

9.3 The following matters shall be heard in public:

(1) The public examination of debtors;

(2) Opposed applications for discharge or for the suspension or lifting of the suspension of discharge;

(3) Opposed applications for permission to be a director;

(4) In any case where the petition was presented or the receiving order or order for adjudication was made before the appointed day, those matters and applications specified in Rule 8 of the Bankruptcy Rules 1952;

(5) All matters and applications heard by the Judge, except matters and applications referred by the Registrar or the District Judge to be heard by the Judge in private or directed by the Judge to be so heard.

9.4 All petitions presented will be listed under the name of the debtor.

9.5 In accordance with Directions given by the Lord Chancellor the Registrar has authorised certain applications in the High Court to be dealt with by the Court Manager of the Bankruptcy Court pursuant to Insolvency Rule 13.2(2). The applications are:

(1) by petitioning creditors: to extend time for hearing petitions (s.376 of the Act).

(2) by the Official Receiver:

(a) To transfer proceedings from the High Court to a County Court (Insolvency Rule 7.13);

(b) to amend the full title of the proceedings (Insolvency Rule 6.35 and 6.47).

[N.B. In District Registries all such applications must be made to the District Judge].

10. Service abroad of statutory demand

10.1 A statutory demand is not a document issued by the Court. **3E–10** Leave to serve out of the jurisdiction is not, therefore, required.

10.2 Insolvency Rule 6.3(2) ("Requirements as to service") applies to service of the statutory demand whether outside or within the jurisdiction.

10.3 A creditor wishing to serve a statutory demand outside the jurisdiction in a foreign country with which a civil procedure convention has been made (including the Hague Convention) may and, if the assistance of a British Consul is desired, must adopt the procedure prescribed by rule 6.25. In the case of any doubt whether the country is a "convention country", enquiries should be made of the Queen's Bench Masters' Secretary Department, Room E216, Royal Courts of Justice.

10.4 In all other cases, service of the demand must be effected by private arrangement in accordance with Insolvency Rule 6.3(2) and local foreign law.

10.5 When a statutory demand is to be served out of the jurisdiction, the time limits of 21 days and 18 days respectively referred to in the demand must be amended. For this purpose reference should be made to the table set out in the practice direction supplementing Section III of Part 6.

10.6 A creditor should amend the statutory demand as follows:

(1) For any reference to 18 days there must be substituted the appropriate number of days set out in the table plus 4 days, and

(2) for any reference to 21 days there must be substituted the appropriate number of days in the table plus 7 days.

Attention is drawn to the fact that in all forms of the statutory demand the figure 18 and the figure 21 occurs in more than one place.

11. Substituted service

Statutory demands

11.1 The creditor is under an obligation to do all that is reasonable **3E–11** to bring the statutory demand to the debtor's attention and, if practicable, to cause personal service to be effected. Where it is not possible to effect prompt personal service, service may be effected by other means such as first class post or by insertion through a letter box.

11.2 Advertisement can only be used as a means of substituted service where:

(1) The demand is based on a judgment or order of any Court;

(2) The debtor has absconded or is keeping out of the way with a view to avoiding service and,

INSOLVENCY

(3) There is no real prospect of the sum due being recovered by execution or other process.

As there is no statutory form of advertisement, the Court will accept an advertisement in the following form:

STATUTORY DEMAND

(Debt for liquidated sum payable immediately following a judgment or order of the Court)

_____

To (Block letters)

of

TAKE NOTICE that a statutory demand has been issued by:

Name of Creditor:

Address:

The creditor demands payment of £   the amount now due on a judgment or order of the (High Court of Justice   Division) (.........County Court) dated the   day of 199 .

The statutory demand is an important document and it is deemed to have been served on you on the date of the first appearance of this advertisement. You must deal with this demand within 21 days of the service upon you or you could be made bankrupt and your property and goods taken away from you. If you are in any doubt as to your position, you should seek advice immediately from a solicitor or your nearest Citizens' Advice Bureau. The statutory demand can be obtained or is available for inspection and collection from:

Name:

Address:

(Solicitor for) the Creditor

Tel. No.   Reference:

You have only 21 days from the date of the first appearance of this advertisement before the creditor may present a Bankruptcy Petition. You have only 18 days within which to apply to the Court to set aside the demand.

11.3 In all cases where substituted service is effected, the creditor must have taken all those steps which would justify the Court making an order for substituted service of a petition. The steps to be taken to obtain an order for substituted service of a petition are set out below. Failure to comply with these requirements may result in the Court declining to file the petition: Insolvency Rule 6.11(g).

Petitions

11.4 In most cases, evidence of the following steps will suffice to justify an order for substituted service:

(1) One personal call at the residence and place of business of the debtor where both are known or at either of such places as is known. Where it is known that the debtor has more than one residential or business address, personal calls should be made at all the addresses.

(2) Should the creditor fail to effect service, a first class prepaid letter should be written to the debtor referring to the call(s), the purpose of the same and the failure to meet with the debtor, adding that a further call will be made for the same purpose on the   day of   19   at   hours at (place). At least two business days notice should be given of the appointment and copies of the letter sent to all known addresses of the debtor. The appointment letter should also state that

   (a) in the event of the time and place not being convenient, the debtor is to name some other time and place reasonably convenient for the purpose;

   (b) (Statutory Demands) if the debtor fails to keep the appointment the creditor proposes to serve the debtor by [advertisement] [post] [insertion through a letter box] or as the case may be, and that, in the event of a bankruptcy petition being presented, the Court will be asked to treat such service as service of the demand on the debtor;

   (c) (Petitions) if the debtor fails to keep the appointment, application will be made to the Court for an order for substituted service either by advertisement, or in such other manner as the Court may think fit.

(3) In attending any appointment made by letter, inquiry should be made as to whether the debtor has received all letters left for him. If the debtor is away, inquiry should also be made as to whether or not letters are being forwarded to an address within the jurisdiction (England and Wales) or elsewhere.

(4) If the debtor is represented by a Solicitor, an attempt should be made to arrange an appointment for personal service through such Solicitor. The Insolvency Rules enable a Solicitor to accept service of a statutory demand on behalf of his client but there is no similar provision in respect of service of a bankruptcy petition.

(5) The written evidence filed pursuant to Insolvency Rule 6.11

should deal with all the above matters including all relevant facts as to the debtor's whereabouts and whether the appointment letter(s) have been returned.

11.5 Where the Court makes an order for service by first class ordinary post, the order will normally provide that service be deemed to be effected on the seventh day after posting. The same method of calculating service may be applied to calculating the date of service of a statutory demand.

12. Setting aside a statutory demand

3E–12　**12.1** The application (Form 6.4) and written evidence in support (Form 6.5) exhibiting a copy of the statutory demand must be filed in Court within 18 days of service of the statutory demand on the debtor. Where service is effected by advertisement in a newspaper the period of 18 days is calculated from the date of the first appearance of the advertisement. Three copies of each document must be lodged with the application to enable the Court to serve notice of the hearing date on the applicant, the creditor and the person named in Part B of the statutory demand.

12.2 Where, to avoid expense, copies of the documents are not lodged with the application in the High Court, any order of the Registrar fixing a venue is conditional upon copies of the documents being lodged on the next business day after the Registrar's order otherwise the application will be deemed to have been dismissed.

12.3 Where the statutory demand is based on a judgment or order, the Court will not at this stage go behind the judgment or order and inquire into the validity of the debt nor, as a general rule, will it adjourn the application to await the result of an application to set aside the judgment or order.

12.4 Where the debtor (a) claims to have a counterclaim, set off or cross demand (whether or not he could have raised it in the action in which the judgment or order was obtained) which equals or exceeds the amount of the debt or debts specified in the statutory demand or (b) disputes the debt (not being a debt subject to a judgment or order) the Court will normally set aside the statutory demand if, in its opinion, on the evidence there is a genuine triable issue.

12.5 A debtor who wishes to apply to set aside a statutory demand after the expiration of 18 days from the date of service of the statutory demand must apply for an extension of time within which to apply. If the applicant wishes to apply for an injunction to restrain presentation of a petition the application must be made to the Judge. Paragraphs 1 and 2 of Form 6.5 (Affidavit in Support of Application to set Aside Statutory Demand) should be used in support of the application for an extension of time with the following additional paragraphs:

"3. That to the best of my knowledge and belief the creditor(s) named in the demand has/have not presented a petition against me.

4. That the reasons for my failure to apply to set aside the demand within 18 days after service are as follows: ... "

If application is made to restrain presentation of a bankruptcy petition the following additional paragraph should be added:

"5. Unless restrained by injunction the creditor(s) may present a bankruptcy petition against me."

13. Proof of service of a statutory demand

13.1 Insolvency Rule 6.11(3) provides that, if the Statutory **3E–13** Demand has been served personally, the written evidence must be provided by the person who effected that service. Insolvency Rule 6.11(4) provides that, if service of the demand (however effected) has been acknowledged in writing, the evidence of service must be provided by the creditor or by a person acting on his behalf. Insolvency Rule 6.11(5) provides that, if neither paragraphs (3) or (4) apply, the written evidence must be provided by a person having direct knowledge of the means adopted for serving the demand.

13.2 Form 6.11 (Evidence of personal service of the statutory demand): this form should only be used where the demand has been served personally and acknowledged in writing (see Insolvency Rule 6.11(4)). If the demand has not been acknowledged in writing, the written evidence should be provided by the Process Server and Paragraphs 2 and 3 (part of Form 6.11) should be omitted (See Insolvency Rule 6.11(3)).

13.3 Form 6.12 (Evidence of Substituted Service of the Statutory Demand): this form can be used whether or not service of the demand has been acknowledged in writing. Paragraphs 4 and 5 (part) provide for the alternatives. Practitioners are reminded, however, that the appropriate person to provide the written evidence may not be the same in both cases. If the demand has been acknowledged in writing, the appropriate person is the creditor or a person acting on his behalf. If the demand has not been acknowledged, that person must be someone having direct knowledge of the means adopted for serving the demand.

Practitioners may find it more convenient to allow process servers to carry out the necessary investigation whilst reserving to themselves the service of the demand. In these circumstances Paragraph 1 should be deleted and the following paragraph substituted:

"1. Attempts have been made to serve the demand, full details of which are set out in the accompanying affidavit of ..."

13.4 "Written evidence" means an affidavit or a witness statement.

14. Extension of hearing date of petition

14.1 Late applications for extension of hearing dates under **3E–14** Insolvency Rule 6.28, and failure to attend on the Iisted hearing of a petition, will be dealt with as follows:

(1) If an application is submitted less than two clear working days before the hearing date (for example, later than Monday for Thursday, or Wednesday for Monday) the costs of the application will not be allowed under Insolvency Rule 6.28(3).

(2) If the petition has not been served and no extension has been granted the time fixed for the hearing of the petition, and if no one attends for the hearing, the petition will be re-listed for hearing about 21 days later. The Court will notify

the petitioning creditor's solicitors (or the petitioning creditor in person), and any known supporting or opposing creditors or their solicitors, of the new date and times. Written evidence should then be filed on behalf of the petitioning creditor explaining fully the reasons for the failure to apply for an extension or to appear at the hearing, and (if appropriate) giving reasons why the petition should not be dismissed.

(3) On the re-listed hearing the Court may dismiss the petition if not satisfied it should be adjourned or a further extension granted.

14.2 All applications for extension should include a statement of the date fixed for the hearing of the petition.

14.3 The petitioning creditor should attend (by solicitors or in person) on or before the hearing date to ascertain whether the application has reached the file and been dealt with. It should not be assumed that an extension will be granted.

15. Bankruptcy petition

3E–15 **15.** To help in the completion of the form of a creditor's bankruptcy petition, attention is drawn to the following points:

15.1 The petition does not require dating, signing or witnessing.

15.2 In the title it is only necessary to recite the debtor's name, *e.g.* Re John William Smith or Re J W Smith (Male). Any alias or trading name will appear in the body of the petition. This also applies to all other statutory forms other than those which require the "full title".

15.3 Where the petition is based on a statutory demand, only the debt claimed in the demand may be included in the petition.

15.4 In completing Paragraph 2 of the petition, attention is drawn to Insolvency Rule 6.8(1)(a) to (c), particularly where the "aggregate sum" is made up of a number of debts.

15.5 Date of service of the statutory demand (paragraph 4 of the petition):

(1) In the case of personal service, the date of service as set out in the affidavit of service should be recited and whether service is effected before/after 1700 hours on Monday to Friday or at any time on a Saturday or a Sunday: see CPR Part 6.7(2) and (3).

(2) In the case of substituted service (otherwise than by advertisement), the date alleged in the affidavit of service should be recited: see "11. Substituted Service" above.

(3) In the strictly limited case of service by advertisement under Insolvency Rule 6.3, the date to be alleged is the date of the advertisement's appearance or, as the case may be, its first appearance: see Insolvency Rules 6.3(3) and 6.11(8).

15.6 There is no need to include in the petition details of the person authorised to present it.

15.7 Certificates at the end of the petition:

(1) The period of search for prior petitions has been reduced to eighteen months.

(2) Where a statutory demand is based wholly or in part on a

County Court judgment, the following certificate is to be added:

"I/We certify that on the day of   19   I/We attended on the County Court and was/were informed by an officer of the Court that no money had been paid into Court in the action or matter   v   Claim No   pursuant to the statutory demand."

This certificate will not be required when the demand also requires payment of a separate debt, not based on a County Court judgment, the amount of which exceeds the bankruptcy level (at present £750).

15.8 Deposit on petition: the deposit will be taken by the Court and forwarded to the Official Receiver. In the High Court, the petition fee and deposit should be handed to the Supreme Court Accounts Office, Fee Stamping Room, who will record the receipt and will impress two entries on the original petition, one in respect of the Court fee and the other in respect of the deposit. In the County Court, the petition fee and deposit should be handed to the duly authorised officer of the Court's staff who will record its receipt.

In all cases cheque(s) for the whole amount should be made payable to "HM Paymaster General".

15.9 On the hearing of a petition for a bankruptcy order, in order to satisfy the Court that the debt on which the petition is founded has not been paid or secured or compounded the Court will normally accept as sufficient a certificate signed by the person representing the petitioning creditor in the following form:

"I certify that I have/my firm has made enquiries of the petitioning creditor(s) within the last business day prior to the hearing/adjourned hearing and to the best of my knowledge and belief the debt on which the petition is founded is still due and owing and has not been paid or secured or compounded save as to

Signed   Dated "

For convenience in the High Court this certificate will be incorporated in the attendance slip, which will be filed after the hearing. A fresh certificate will be required on each adjourned hearing.

15.10 On the occassion of the adjourned hearing of a petition for a bankruptcy order, in order to satisfy the Court that the petitioner will be required to file has complied with Insolvency Rule 6.29, the petitioner will be required to file written evidence of the manner in which notice of the making of the order of adjournment and of venue for the adjourned hearing has been sent to:

(i)   the debtor, and

(ii)   any creditor who has given notice under Insolvency Rule 6.23 but was not present at the hearing when the order for adjournment was made.

16. Orders without attendance

16.1 In suitable cases the Court will normally be prepared to make   **3E–16**

orders under Part VIII of the Act (Individual Voluntary Arrangements), without the attendance of either party, provided there is no bankruptcy order in existence and (so far as is known) no pending petition. The orders are:

(1) A fourteen day interim order with the application adjourned 14 days for consideration of the nominee's report, where the papers are in order, and the nominee's signed consent to act includes a waiver of notice of the application or a consent by the nominee to the making of an interim order without attendance.

(2) A standard order on consideration of the nominee's report, extending the interim order to a date 7 weeks after the date of the proposed meeting, directing the meeting to be summoned and adjourning to a date about 3 weeks after the meeting. Such an Order may be made without attendance if the nominee's report has been delivered to the Court and complies with Section 256(1) of the Act and Insolvency Rule 5.10(2) and (3) and proposes a date for the meeting not less than 14 days from that on which the nominee's report is filed in Court under Insolvency Rule 5.10 nor more than 28 days from that on which that report is considered by the Court under Insolvency Rule 5.12.

(3) A "concertina" Order, combining orders as under (1) and (2) above. Such an order may be made without attendance if the initial application for an interim order is accompanied by a report of the nominee and the conditions set out in (1) and (2) above are satisfied.

(4) A final order on consideration of the Chairman's report. Such an order may be made without attendance if the Chairman's report has been filed and complies with Insolvency Rule 5.22(1). The order will record the effect of the Chairman's report and may discharge the interim order.

16.2 Provided that the conditions as under 16.1(2) and (4) above are satisfied and that the appropriate report has been lodged with the Court in due time the parties need not attend or be represented on the adjourned hearing for consideration of the Nominee's report or of the Chairman's report (as the case may be) unless they are notified by the Court that attendance is required. Sealed copies of the order made (in all four cases as above) will be posted by the Court to the applicant or his Solicitor and to the Nominee.

16.3 In suitable cases the Court may also make consent orders without attendance by the parties. The written consent of the parties will be required. Examples of such orders are as follows:

(1) On applications to set aside a statutory demand, orders:

    (a) dismissing the application, with or without an order for costs as may be agreed (permission will be given to present a petition on or after the seventh day after the date of the order, unless a different date is agreed);

    (b) setting aside the demand, with or without an order for costs as may be agreed; or

    (c) giving permission to withdraw the application with or without an order for costs as may be agreed.

(2) On petitions: where there is a list of supporting or opposing creditors in Form 6.21, or a statement signed by or on behalf of the petitioning creditor that no notices have been received from supporting or opposing creditors, orders:

    (a) dismissing the petition, with or without an order for costs as may be agreed, or

    (b) if the petition has not been served, giving permission to withdraw the petition (with no order for costs).

(3) On other applications, orders:

    (a) for sale of property, possession of property, disposal of proceeds of sale

    (b) giving interim directions

    (c) dismissing the application, with or without an order for costs as may be agreed

    (d) giving permission to withdraw the application, with or without an order for costs as may be agreed.

If (as may often be the case with orders under subparagraphs (3)(a) or (b) above), an adjournment is required, whether generally with liberty to restore or to a fixed date, the order by consent may include an order for the adjournment. If adjournment to a date is requested, a time estimate should be given and the Court will fix the first available date and time on or after the date requested.

16.4 The above lists should not be regarded as exhaustive, nor should it be assumed that an order will be made without attendance as requested.

16.5 The procedure outlined above is designed to save time and costs but is not intended to discourage attendance.

16.6 Applications for consent orders without attendance should be lodged at least two clear working days (and preferably longer) before any fixed hearing date.

16.7 Whenever a document is lodged or a letter sent, the correct case number, code (if any) and year (for example 123/SD/99 or 234/99) should be quoted. A note should also be given of the date and time of the next hearing (if any).

16.8 Attention is drawn to Paragraph 4.4(4) of the Practice Direction relating to CPR Part 44.

16A. Bankruptcy Restriction Orders

Making the application

16A.1 An application for a bankruptcy restrictions order is made **3E–17** as an ordinary application in the bankruptcy.

16A.2 The application must be made within one year beginning with the date of the bankruptcy order unless the court gives permission for the application to be made after that period. The one year period does not run while the bankrupt's discharge has been suspended under section 279(3) of the Insolvency Act 1986.

16A.3 An application for a bankruptcy restrictions order may be made by the Secretary of State or the Official Receiver ('the

Applicant'). The application must be supported by a report which must include:

(a) a statement of the conduct by reference to which it is alleged that it is appropriate for a bankruptcy restrictions order to be made; and

(b) the evidence relied on in support of the application (r.6.241 Insolvency Rules 1986).

16A.4 The report is treated as if it were an affidavit (r.7.9(2) Insolvency Rules 1986) and is prima facie evidence of any matter contained in it (r.7.9(3)).

16A.5 The application may be supported by evidence from other witnesses which may be given by affidavit or (by reason of r.7.57(5) Insolvency Rules 1986) by witness statement verified by a statement of truth.

16A.6 The court will fix a first hearing which must be not less than 8 weeks from the date when the hearing is fixed (r.6.241(4) Insolvency Rules 1986).

16A.7 Notice of the application and the venue fixed by the court must be served by the Applicant on the bankrupt not more than 14 days after the application is made. Service of notice must be accompanied by a copy of the application together with the evidence in support and a form of acknowledgment of service.

16A.8 The bankrupt must file in court an acknowledgment of service not more than 14 days after service of the application on him, indicating whether or not he contests the application. If he fails to do so he may attend the hearing of the application but may not take part in the hearing unless the court gives permission.

Opposing the application

16A.9 If the bankrupt wishes to oppose the application, he must within 28 days of service on him of the application and the evidence in support (or such longer period as the court may allow) file in court and (within three days thereof) serve on the Applicant any evidence which he wishes the court to take into consideration. Such evidence should normally be in the form of an affidavit or a witness statement verified by a statement of truth.

16A.10 The Applicant must file any evidence in reply within 14 days of receiving the evidence of the bankrupt (or such longer period as the court may allow) and must serve it on the bankrupt as soon as reasonably practicable.

Hearings

16A.11 Any hearing of an application for a bankruptcy restrictions order must be in public (r.6.241(5) Insolvency Rules 1986). The hearing will generally be before the registrar or district judge in the first instance who may:

(1) adjourn the application and give directions;

(2) make a bankruptcy restrictions order; or

(3) adjourn the application to the judge.

Making a bankruptcy restrictions order

16A.12 When the court is considering whether to make a bankruptcy restrictions order, it must not take into account any conduct of the bankrupt prior to 1 April 2004 (art. 7 Enterprise Act (Commencement No. 4 and Transitional Provisions and Savings) Order 2003).

16A.13 The court may make a bankruptcy restrictions order in the absence of the bankrupt and whether or not he has filed evidence (r.6.244 Insolvency Rules 1986).

16A.14 When a bankruptcy restrictions order is made the court must send two sealed copies of the order to the Applicant (r.6.244(2) Insolvency Rules 1986), and as soon as reasonably practicable after receipt, the Applicant must send one sealed copy to the bankrupt (r.6.244(3)).

16A.15 A bankruptcy restrictions order comes into force when it is made and must specify the date on which it will cease to have effect, which must be between two and 15 years from the date on which it is made.

Interim bankruptcy restriction orders

16A.16 An application for an interim bankruptcy restrictions order may be made any time between the institution of an application for a bankruptcy restrictions order and the determination of that application (Sch 4A para. 5 Insolvency Act 1986). The application is made as an ordinary application in the bankruptcy.

16A.17 The application must be supported by a report as evidence in support of the application (r.6.246(1) Insolvency Rules 1986) which must include evidence of the bankrupt's conduct which is alleged to constitute the grounds for making an interim bankruptcy restrictions order and evidence of matters relating to the public interest in making the order.

16A.18 Notice of the application must be given to the bankrupt at least two business days before the date fixed for the hearing unless the court directs otherwise (r.6.245).

16A.19 Any hearing of the application must be in public (r.6.245).

16A.20 The court may make an interim bankruptcy restrictions order in the absence of the bankrupt and whether or not he has filed evidence (r.6.247).

16A.21 The bankrupt may apply to the court to set aside an interim bankruptcy restrictions order. The application is made by ordinary application in the bankruptcy and must be supported by an affidavit or witness statement verified by a statement of truth stating the grounds on which the application is made (r.6.248(2)).

16A.22 The bankrupt must send the Secretary of State, not less than 7 days before the hearing, notice of his application, notice of the venue, a copy of his application and a copy of the supporting affidavit. The Secretary of State may attend the hearing and call the attention of the court to any matters which seem to him to be relevant, and may himself give evidence or call witnesses.

16A.23 Where the court sets aside an interim bankruptcy restrictions order, two sealed copies of the order must be sent by the court, as soon as reasonably practicable, to the Secretary of State.

16A.24 As soon as reasonably practicable after receipt of sealed copies of the order, the Secretary of State must send a sealed copy to the bankrupt.

Bankruptcy restrictions undertakings

16A.25 Where a bankrupt has given a bankruptcy restrictions undertaking, the Secretary of State must file a copy in court and send a copy to the bankrupt as soon as reasonably practicable (r.6.250).

16A.26 The bankrupt may apply to annul a bankruptcy restrictions undertaking. The application is made as an ordinary application in the bankruptcy and must be supported by an affidavit or witness statement verified by a statement of truth stating the grounds on which it is made.

16A.27 The bankrupt must give notice of his application and the venue together with a copy of his affidavit in support to the Secretary of State at least 28 days before the date fixed for the hearing.

16A.28 The Secretary of State may attend the hearing and call the attention of the court to any matters which seem to him to be relevant and may himself give evidence or call witnesses.

16A.29 The court must send a sealed copy of any order annulling or varying the bankruptcy restrictions undertaking to the Secretary of State and the bankrupt.

Part Four

Appeals

17. Appeals

3E–18   **17.1** This Part shall come into effect on 2nd May 2000 and shall replace and revoke Paragraph 17 of, and be read in conjunction with the Practice Direction—Insolvency Proceedings which came into effect on 26th April 1999 as amended.

17.2(1) An appeal from a decision of a County Court (whether made by a District Judge or a Circuit Judge) or of a Registrar of the High Court in insolvency proceedings ("a first appeal") lies to a Judge of the High Court pursuant to s.375(2) of the Act and Insolvency Rules 7.47(2) and 7.48(2) (as amended by s.55 of the Access to Justice Act 1999).

(2)   The procedure and practice for a first appeal are governed by Insolvency Rule 7.49 which imports the procedure and practice of the Court of Appeal. The procedure and practice of the Court of Appeal is governed by CPR Part 52 and its Practice Direction, which are subject to the provisions of the Act, the Insolvency Rules and this Practice Direction: see CPR Part 52, rule 1(4).

(3)   A first appeal (as defined above) does not include an appeal from a decision of a Judge of the High Court.

17.3(1) Section 55 of the Access to Justice Act 1999 has amended s.375(2) of the Act and Insolvency Rules 7.47(2) and

1192

7.48(2) so that an appeal from a decision of a Judge of the High Court made on a first appeal lies, with the permission of the Court of Appeal, to the Court of Appeal.

(2) An appeal from a Judge of the High Court in insolvency proceedings which is not a decision on a first appeal lies, with the permission of the Judge or of the Court of Appeal, to the Court of Appeal (see CPR Part 52, rule 3);

(3) The procedure and practice for appeals from a decision of a Judge of the High Court in insolvency proceedings (whether made on a first appeal or not) are also governed by Insolvency Rule 7.49 which imports the procedure and practice of the Court of Appeal as stated at Paragraph 17.2(2) above.

17.4 CPR Part 52 and its Practice Direction and Forms apply to appeals from a decision of a Judge of the High Court in insolvency proceedings.

17.5 An appeal from a decision of a Judge of the High Court in insolvency proceedings requires permission as set out in Paragraph 17.3(1) and (2) above.

17.6 A first appeal does not require the permission of any court.

17.7 Except as provided in this Part, CPR Part 52 and its Practice Direction and Forms do not apply to first appeals, but Paragraphs 17.8 to 17.23 inclusive of this Part apply only to first appeals.

17.8 Interpretation:

(a) the expressions "appeal court", "lower court", "appellant", "respondent" and "appeal notice" have the meanings given in CPR Part 52.1(3);

(b) "Registrar of Appeals" means in relation to an appeal filed at the Royal Courts of Justice in London a Bankruptcy Registrar, and in relation to an appeal filed in a District Registry in accordance with Paragraph 17.10(2) and (3) below a District Judge of the relevant District Registry.

(c) "appeal date" means the date fixed by the appeal court for the hearing of the appeal or the date fixed by the appeal court upon which the period within which the appeal will be heard commences.

17.9 An appellant's notice and a respondent's notice shall be in Form **PDIP 1** and **PDIP 2** set out in the Schedule hereto.

17.10(1) An appeal from a decision of a Registrar in Bankruptcy shall, or from any decision made in any County Court may, be filed at the Royal Courts of Justice in London.

(2) An appeal from a decision made in the County Court exercising jurisdiction over an area within the Birmingham, Bristol, Cardiff, Leeds, Liverpool, Manchester, Newcastle upon Tyne or Preston Chancery District Registries may be filed in the Chancery District Registry of the High Court appropriate to the area in which the decision was made.

17.11(1) Where a party seeks an extension of time in which to file an appeal notice it must be requested in the appeal notice and the appeal notice should state the reason for the delay and the steps taken prior to the application being made; the court will fix a date for the hearing of the application and notify the parties of the date and place of hearing;

(2) The appellant must file the appellant's notice at the appeal court within—

    (a) such period as may be directed by the lower court; or

    (b) where the court makes no such direction, 14 days after the date of the decision of the lower court which the appellant wishes to appeal.

(3) Unless the appeal court orders otherwise, an appeal notice must be served by the appellant on each respondent—

    (a) as soon as practicable; and

    (b) in any event not later than 7 days, after it is filed.

17.12(1) A respondent may file and serve a respondent's notice.

(2) A respondent who wishes to ask the appeal court to uphold the order of the lower court for reasons different from or additional to those given by the lower court must file a respondent's notice.

(3) A respondent's notice must be filed within—

    (a) such period as may be directed by the lower court; or

    (b) where the court makes no such direction, 14 days after the date on which the respondent is served with the appellant's notice.

Unless the appeal court orders otherwise a respondent's notice must be served by the respondent on the appellant and any other respondent—

    (a) as soon as practicable; and

    (b) in any event not later than 7 days, after it is filed.

17.13(1) An application to vary the time limit for filing an appeal notice must be made to the appeal court.

(2) The parties may not agree to extend any date or time limit set by—

    (a) this Practice Direction; or

    (b) an order of the appeal court or the lower court.

17.14 Unless the appeal court or the lower court orders otherwise an appeal shall not operate as a stay of any order or decision of the lower court.

17.15 An appeal notice may not be amended without the permission of the appeal court.

17.16 A Judge of the appeal court may strike out the whole or part of an appeal notice where there is compelling reason for doing so.

17.17(1) In relation to an appeal the appeal court has all the powers of the lower court.

(2) The appeal court has power to—

    (a) affirm, set aside or vary any order or judgment made or given by the lower court;

    (b) refer any claim or issue for determination by the lower court;

(c) order a new trial or hearing;

(d) make a costs order.

(3)   The appeal court may exercise its powers in relation to the whole or part of an order of the lower court.

17.18(1) Every appeal shall be limited to a review of the decision of the lower court.

(2)   Unless it orders otherwise, the appeal court will not receive—

(a) oral evidence; or

(b) evidence which was not before the lower court.

(3)   The appeal court will allow an appeal where the decision of the lower court was—

(a) wrong; or

(b) unjust because of a serious procedural or other irregularity in the proceedings in the lower court.

(4)   The appeal court may draw any inference of fact which it considers justified on the evidence.

(5)   At the hearing of the appeal a party may not rely on a matter not contained in his appeal notice unless the appeal court gives permission.

17.19 The following applications shall be made to a Judge of the appeal court:

(1)   for injunctions pending a substantive hearing of the appeal;

(2)   for expedition or vacation of the hearing date of an appeal;

(3)   for an order striking out the whole or part of an appeal notice pursuant to Paragraph 17.16 above;

(4)   for a final order on paper pursuant to Paragraph 17.22(8) below.

17.20(1) All other interim applications shall be made to the Registrar of Appeals in the first instance who may in his discretion either hear and determine it himself or refer it to the Judge.

(2)   An appeal from a decision of a Registrar of Appeals lies to a Judge of the appeal court and does not require the permission of either the Registrar of Appeals or the Judge.

17.21 The procedure for interim applications is by way of ordinary application (see Insolvency Rule 12.7 and Schedule 4, Form 7.2).

17.22 The following practice applies to all first appeals to a Judge of the High Court whether filed at the Royal Courts of Justice in London, or filed at one of the other venues referred to in Paragraph 17.10 above:

(1)   on filing an appellant's notice in accordance with Paragraph 17.11(2) above, the appellant must file:

(a) two copies of the appeal notice for the use of the court, one of which must be stamped with the appropriate fee, and a number of additional copies equal to the number of persons who are to be served with it pursuant to Paragraph 17.22(4) below;

(b) a copy of the order under appeal; and

(c) an estimate of time for the hearing.

(2) the above documents may be lodged personally or by post and shall be lodged at the address of the appropriate venue listed below:

(a) if the appeal is to be heard at the Royal Courts of Justice in London the documents must be lodged at Room 110, Thomas More Building, The Royal Courts of Justice, Strand, London WC2A 2LL;

(b) if the appeal is to be heard in Birmingham, the documents must be lodged at the District Registry of the Chancery Division of the High Court, 33 Bull Street, Birmingham B4 6DS;

(c) if the appeal is to be heard in Bristol the documents must be lodged at the District Registry of the Chancery Division of the High Court, Third Floor, Greyfriars, Lewins Mead, Bristol, BS1 2NR;

(d) if the appeal is to be heard in Cardiff the documents must be lodged at the District Registry in the Chancery Division of the High Court, First Floor, 2 Park Street, Cardiff, CF10 1ET;

(e) if the appeal is to be heard in Leeds the documents must be lodged at the District Registry of the Chancery Division of the High Court, The Court House, 1 Oxford Row, Leeds LS1 3BG;

(f) if the appeal is to be heard in Liverpool the documents must be lodged at the District Registry of the Chancery Division of the High Court, Liverpool Combined Court Centre, Derby Square, Liverpool L2 1XA;

(g) if the appeal is to be heard in Manchester the documents must be lodged at the District Registry of the Chancery Division of the High Court, Courts of Justice, Crown Square, Manchester, M60 9DJ;

(h) if the appeal is to be heard at Newcastle upon Tyne the documents must be lodged at the District Registry of the Chancery Division of the High Court, The Law Courts, Quayside, Newcastle upon Tyne NE1 3LA;

(i) if the appeal is to be heard in Preston the documents must be lodged at the District Registry of the Chancery Division of the High Court, The Combined Court Centre, Ringway, Preston PR1 2LL

(3) if the documents are correct and in order the court at which the documents are filed will fix the appeal date and will also fix the place of hearing. That court will send letters to all the parties to the appeal informing them of the appeal date and of the place of hearing and indicating the time estimate given by the appellant. The parties will be invited to notify the court of any alternative or revised time estimates. In the absence of any such notification the estimate of the appellant will be taken as agreed. The court

will also send to the appellant a document setting out the court's requirement concerning the form and content of the bundle of documents for the use of the Judge. Not later than 7 days before the appeal date the bundle of documents must be filed by the appellant at the address of the relevant venue as set out in sub-paragraph 17.22(2) above and a copy of it must be served by the appellant on each respondent. The bundle should include an approved transcript of the judgment of the lower court or, where there is no officially recorded judgment, the document(s) referred to in paragraph 5.12 of the Practice Direction to CPR Part 52.

(4) the appeal notice must be served on all parties to the proceedings in the lower court who are directly affected by the appeal. This may include the Official Receiver, liquidator or trustee in bankruptcy.

(5) the appeal notice must be served by the appellant or by the legal representative of the appellant and may be effected by:

(a) any of the methods referred to in CPR Part 6 rule 2; or

(b) with permission of the court, an alternative method pursuant to CPR Part 6 rule 8.

(6) service of an appeal notice shall be proved by a Certificate of Service in accordance with CPR Part 6, rule 10 (CPR Form **N215**) which must be filed at the relevant venue referred to at Paragraph 17.22(2) above immediately after service.

(7) skeleton arguments, accompanied by a written chronology of events relevant to the appeal, should be filed at the address of the appropriate venue as set out in sub-paragraph 17.22(2) above, at least two clear days before the date fixed for the hearing. Failure to lodge may result in an adverse costs order being made by the Judge on the hearing of the appeal.

(8) appeal, the appeal may be disposed of on paper without a hearing. It may be dismissed by consent but the appeal court will not make an order allowing an appeal unless it is satisfied that the decision of the lower court was wrong. Any consent order signed by each party or letters of consent from each party must be lodged not later than 24 hours before the date fixed for the hearing of the appeal at the address of the appropriate venue as set out in sub-paragraph 17.22(2) above and will be dealt with by the Judge of the appeal court. Attention is drawn to paragraph 4.4(4) of the Practice Direction to CPR Part 44 regarding costs where an order is made by consent without attendance.

17.23 Only the following paragraphs of the Practice Direction to CPR Part 52, with any necessary modifications, shall apply to first appeals: 5.12 and 5.14 to 5.20 inclusive.

17.24(1) Where, under the procedure relating to appeals in insolvency proceedings prior to the coming into effect of this Part of this Practice Direction, an appeal has been set down in the High Court or permission to appeal to the Court of Appeal has been granted before 2nd May 2000, the procedure and practice set out in this Part of this Practice Direction shall apply to such an appeal after that date.

(2) Where, under the procedure relating to appeals in insolvency proceedings prior to the coming into effect of this Part of this Practice Direction, any person has failed before 2nd May 2000 either:

(a) in the case of a first appeal, to set down in the High Court an appeal which relates to an order made (County Court) or sealed (High Court) after March 27, 2000 and before May 2, 2000, or

(b) in the case of an appeal from a decision of a Judge of the High Court, to obtain any requisite permission to appeal to the Court of Appeal which relates to an order sealed in the same period, the time for filing an appeal notice is extended to May 16, 2000 and application for any such permission should be made in the appeal notice.

17.25 This paragraph applies where a judge of the High Court has made a Bankruptcy order or a winding-up order or dismissed an appeal against such an order and an application is made for a stay of proceedings pending appeal.

(1) The judge will not normally grant a stay of all proceedings but will confine himself to a stay of advertisement of the proceedings.

(2) where the judge has granted permission to appeal any stay of advertisement will normally be until the hearing of the appeal but on terms that the stay will determine without further order if an appellant's notice is not filed within the period prescribed by the rules.

(3) where the judge has refused permission to appeal any stay of advertisement will normally be for a period not exceeding 28 days. Application for any further stay of advertisement should be made to the Court of Appeal.

Insolvency proceedings

3E–19   The law relating to insolvency is found primarily in the Insolvency Act 1986 and the Insolvency Rules 1986. The Insolvency Act 2000 and Enterprise Act 2002 have brought about significant reforms. The law governing the insolvency of partnerships is to be found in the Insolvent Partnerships Order 1994 (S.I. 1994 No. 2421) as amended by the Insolvent Partnerships (Amendment) Order 2005 (S.I. 2005 No. 1516) and that governing the insolvency of limited liability partnerships in the Limited Liability Partnerships Act 2000 and related secondary legislation. The administration of the estates of deceased insolvent individuals is governed by the Administration of Insolvent Estates of Deceased Persons Order 1986 (S.I. 1986 No. 1999).

The Bankruptcy Act 1914 and the Bankruptcy Rules 1952 continue to govern bankruptcies commenced under that Act. The Companies Act 1948 and the Companies (Winding-Up) Rules 1949 (S.I. 1949 No. 330) continue to apply to corporate insolvencies commenced under the 1948 Act regime.

Insolvency proceedings are defined as proceedings under the Insolvency Act 1986 and the Insolvency Rules 1986 (S.I. 1986 No. 1925) (r.13.7, Insolvency Rules 1986).

Procedure

Insolvency proceedings are governed primarily by the Insolvency Act 1986 and the **3E–20** Insolvency Rules 1986 (as amended) and not by the CPR. However, where the Act and the Rules do not make provision for procedure, the CPR may be invoked (see para. 2.1.4 and r.7.51(1) of the Insolvency Rules 1986). All insolvency proceedings are multi-track (r.7.51(2) of the Insolvency Rules 1986).

Part 7 of the Insolvency Rules 1986 deals with particular matters applying to procedure in insolvency proceedings including rules as to the form and content of applications (r.7.3).

Rule 7.60 of the Insolvency Rules 1986 enables any party to insolvency proceedings to apply to the court for clarification, further information or disclosure in accordance with CPR Pts 18 and 31.

Applications in insolvency proceedings

Applications in insolvency proceedings (other than those made by petition) may **3E–21** only be made by originating application or ordinary application. An originating application is an application made to the court which is not an application in pending proceedings before the court. An ordinary application is any other application to the court (r.7.2(1)). Every application must be in the appropriate form (r.7.2(2)). Rule 7.3 provides general rules as to the form and content of applications. Particular rules deal with the form and content of other documents such as statutory demands and petitions as well as prescribing forms for particular uses.

Evidence in insolvency proceedings

Evidence may be given by witness statement or affidavit following the coming into **3E–22** force of the CPR, but the following evidence must be given by affidavit (r.7.57): (a) a bankrupt's statement of affairs to the official receiver, (b) further information by a bankrupt to the official receiver amplifying, modifying or explaining any matter in his statement of affairs or in accounts, (c) accounts submitted by a bankrupt to the official receiver, (d) a creditor's proof of debt or a claim of debt if required by the official receiver or trustee in bankruptcy, (e) the evidence of a respondent on private examination, (f) evidence in proceedings under the Insolvent Partnerships Order 1994 where evidence is described in the Order as an affidavit ((S.I. 1994 No. 2421), art.18).

The official receiver or a deputy official receiver may file a report; an administrator, liquidator, trustee in bankruptcy, provisional liquidator or interim receiver, a special manager or an insolvency practitioner appointed under s.273(2) may also file a report unless the application to which it relates involves other parties or the court otherwise directs (r.7.9).

Jurisdiction - Companies Court

Applications concerning companies and partnerships made under the Insolvency **3E–23** Act 1986, the Insolvency Act 2000 and the Insolvency Partnerships Order 1994 (S.I. 1994 No. 2421) are dealt with by the Companies Court. As to Companies Court generally and its jurisdiction and that of the county courts see paras 2G–17 *et seq.*

Although paragraph 5.1 of the Practice Direction has not been formally amended, on May 23, 2005 the Vice-Chancellor issued a Practice Note on the Hearing of Insolvency Proceedings which sets out a much simplified scheme for the distribution of work between the judges and registrars and district judges (see para. 3E-119).

Jurisdiction - Bankruptcy

Section 265(1) of the Insolvency Act 1986 provides that certain jurisdictional condi- **3E–24** tions have to be satisfied in respect of a debtor. The debtor must be domiciled in England and Wales, or personally present in England and Wales on the day on which the petition is presented, or at any time in the three year period ending with that day, have been ordinarily resident or had a place of residence in England and Wales or carried on business in England and Wales. Section 265 is now subject to Art.3 of the EC Regulation on Insolvency Proceedings (see s.265(3) and para. 3E–25).

Although 9 of the Practice Direction had not been formally amended, on May 23, 2005 the Vice-Chancellor issued a Practice Note on the Hearing of Insolvency Proceedings which sets out a much simplified scheme for the distribution of work between the judges and registrars and district judges (see para. 3E-119).

The EC Regulation on Insolvency Proceedings

3E-25   The Council of the European Union Regulation on Insolvency Proceedings No. 1346/2000 (OJ L 160, 30.6.2000) came into force on May 31, 2002 and has direct application as domestic law. It applies to all the EU member states, except Denmark. It applies to "collective insolvency proceedings which entail the partial or total divestment of a debtor and the appointment of a liquidator" (Art.1(1)). Such proceedings are: winding up by the court, creditors' voluntary winding up with confirmation of the court (as to which see para. 3E-83), administration, voluntary arrangements and bankruptcy (Art.2(a) and Annex A), and the term "liquidator" includes the relevant office holder in relation thereto (Art.2(b) and Annex C). The Regulation does not apply to insurance and certain other financial undertakings (Art.1(2)), nor does it apply to members' voluntary winding-up, schemes of arrangement, winding-up on the just and equitable ground or winding-up in the public interest (*Marann Brooks CSV Ltd, Re* [2003] B.P.I.R. 1159 (Dec)).

The Regulation provides for insolvency proceedings to be main proceedings or secondary (or territorial) proceedings (Art.3(1) and (2)). Jurisdiction is founded by reference to the debtor's centre of main interests, which in the case of a company is presumed (in the absence of proof to the contrary) to be its registered office (Art.3(1)) and in the case of an individual is likely to be the place of the debtor's business or his place of ordinary residence (in the absence of evidence to the contrary). Main proceedings are proceedings brought in the place of the debtor's centre of main interests and are universal in scope. Secondary or territorial proceedings may be brought in a country in which the debtor has an establishment, *i.e.* a "place of operations where the debtor carries out a non-transitory economic activity with human means and goods" (Arts.2(h) and 3(2)). Such proceedings are limited to assets within the territory. The court is thus obliged to consider whether it has jurisdiction before making an order, and when making an order, to state whether the Regulation applies and if so whether the proceedings are main, territorial or secondary. (For examples of the court's consideration of the jurisdictional issue see *a Company, Re (No.6394/2002)* [2002] All E.R. (D) 223 (Oct); *Marann Brooks CSV Ltd, Re* [2003] B.P.I.R. 1159; *BRAC Rent-A-Car Internaional Inc., Re* [2003] 2 All E.R. 201; [2003] 1 W.L.R. 1421; *Re Salvage Association* [2003] B.C.C. 504; *Skjevesland v. Geveran Trading Co Ltd* [2003] B.P.I.R. 73; [2003] B.P.I.R. 924, *a bankrupt, Re (No. 136 of 2003)* [2003] All E.R. (D) 36 (Dec); *Shierson v. Vlieland-Boddy* [2005] EWCA Civ 974).

The place where proceedings are opened (usually by the making of an order (Art.2(f)) determines the law applicable to the insolvency (Art.4(1)), but subject to various exceptions set out in detail in the Regulation.

The Regulation provides for automatic recognition of insolvency proceedings in member states (Arts.17 and 25). A creditors' voluntary liquidation requires "confirmation of the court" for such purposes (Annex A) (see para. 3E-85).

Amendments to give effect to the provisions of the Regulation (in particular by amending or introducing prescribed forms) have been made by the Insolvency Act 1986 (Amendment) Regulations 2002 (S.I. 2002 No. 1037), the Insolvency Act 1986 (Amendment) (No. 2) Regulations 2002 (S.I. 2002 No. 1240), the Insolvency (Amendment) Rules 2002 (S.I. 2002 No. 1307), the Insolvent Partnerships (Amendment) Order 2002 (S.I. 2002 No. 1308) and the Administration of Insolvent Estates of Deceased Persons Order 2002 (S.I. 2002 No. 1309).

Company

3E-26   "Company" means a company formed and registered under the Companies Act 1985 or under the former Companies Acts (*i.e.* the Joint Stock Companies Act, the Companies Act 1862, the Companies (Consolidation) Act 1908, the Companies Act 1929 and the Companies Act 1948 to 1983) but excluding those in what was Ireland (s.735(1) of the Companies Act 1985). As to jurisdiction in relation to a company incorporated by royal charter, see *Re Salvage Association* [2003] B.C.C. 504.

Partnerships

3E-27   The insolvency of partnerships is dealt with largely by reference to the legislation on company insolvency (with appropriate modifications) Thus a partnership may propose a partnership voluntary arrangement under provisions set out in Sched.1 of the Insolvent Partnerships Order 1994 (S.I. 1994 No. 2421) as amended by the Insolvent Partnerships (Amendments) (No. 2) Order 2002 (S.I. 2002 No. 2708) (see para. 3E–29 *et seq.*), seek an administration order under pre-Enterprise Act Pt II (see para. 3E–34) or be wound up under Pt V (see para. 3E–53 *et seq.*).

Limited liability partnerships

The Limited Liability Partnerships Act 2000 created a new legal entity, the limited **3E–28** liability partnership and provided for the recognition of oversea limited liability partnerships. Pursuant to s.14 of the Limited Liability Partnerships Act 2000 and the Limited Liability Partnership Regulations 2001 (S.I. 2001 No. 1090) Pts I, II, III, IV, VI and VII of the Insolvency Act 1986 apply with modifications to limited liability partnerships.

Company voluntary arrangements (Part I Insolvency Act 1986)

Company voluntary arrangements without moratorium

The directors of a company, its administrator (where an administration order is in **3E–29** force) or its liquidator (where the company is being wound up) may propose to the creditors of the company a composition in satisfaction of its debts or a scheme of arrangement (a company voluntary arrangement) (s.1). The proposal must be made to all the company's creditors, and it must be for a composition of debts or a scheme of arrangement (as to which see *March Estates plc v. Gunmark Ltd* [1996] 2 B.C.L.C. 1). Within 28 days (or any longer period the courts allows) the nominee must submit a report to the court stating whether a meeting of creditors and members of the company should be summoned to consider the proposal (s.2). The meetings must then be held at the time, date and place proposed (s.3(2)) The chairman of the meetings must report to the court the result of the meetings (s.4(6)). Members vote according to the rights attaching to their shares (r.1.18(1)) but are entitled to vote even where no voting rights attach to their shares (r.1.18(2)). A resolution to approve or modify the proposal must be passed by a majority in excess of three-quarters in value of creditors present in person or by proxy (r.1.19(1)).

Company voluntary arrangements with moratorium

Under the provisions of the Insolvency Act 2000, which came into force on January **3E–30** 1, 2003, an "eligible company" (as defined by ss.2–4 of Sched.A1 Insolvency Act 1986 as inserted by Insolvency Act 2000), which must be a small company (as defined by s.247(3) of the Companies Act 1985), may obtain a moratorium without making an application for an administration order (ss.1 and 2 and Scheds.1 and 2). The moratorium commences when the directors file in court the company's proposal, a statement of affairs, a statement that the company is eligible for a moratorium and a statement from the nominee that he has consented to act and that in his opinion (a) the arrangement has a reasonable prospect of being approved and implemented, (b) the company is likely to have sufficient funds available during the moratorium to enable it to carry on its business, and (c) meetings of the company and its creditors should be summoned to consider the proposal. The moratorium lasts for 28 days but may be extended by resolution for up to two months after the date when the meetings were first held.

Filing of company voluntary arrangements

In the High Court in London the proposal and accompanying documents should **3E–31** be filed in the issue room on the second floor, Thomas More Building, Royal Courts of Justice.

Partnership voluntary arrangements

A partnership voluntary arrangement is made in much in the same way as a **3E–32** company voluntary arrangement (Insolvent Partnerships Order 1994 (as amended by the Insolvent Partnerships (Amendment) Order 2005). The moratorium provisions also apply to a partnership voluntary arrangement (Insolvent Partnerships (Amendment)(No. 2) Order 2002 (S.I. 2002 No. 2708)). A limited liability partnership may also propose a voluntary arrangement.

Challenges

Within 28 days of the day on which the chairman's reports have been filed a person **3E–33** entitled to vote at a meeting or who would have been so entitled if he had notice of it, the nominee or his replacement, or (if applicable) the liquidator or administrator, may apply to challenge the approval of the arrangement on the ground of unfair prejudice or material irregularity at or in relation to the meetings (s.6). The application should be made initially to the registrar and be supported by written evidence detailing the matters complained of.

Administration orders (Part II Insolvency Act 1986)

3E-34 Section 248 of the Enterprise Act 2002 substituted a new Pt II Insolvency Act 1986 creating a new statutory regime for administrations the details of which are to be found in Insolvency Act 1986, Sched.B1 as inserted by Sched.16 of the new act which replaces old ss.8-27. The Insolvency (Amendment) Rules 2003 (S.I. 2003 No. 1730) substitute a new Pt 2 in the Insolvency Rules 1986 dealing with the rules governing the new forms of administration. The new regime (which came into operation on September 15, 2003) permits an administrator to be appointed by the court or out of court.

3E-35 It is no longer necessary to show that the administration is likely to achieve one of four specified objectives. Instead, para. 3(1) of Sched.B1 provides that the administrator must perform his functions with the objective of—

    (a) rescuing the company as a going concern, or

    (b) achieving a better result for the company's creditors as a whole than would be likely if the company were wound up (without first being in administration), or

    (c) realising property in order to make a distribution to one or more secured or preferential creditors. Paragraphs 3(3) and (4) make it clear that the objectives rank in order of priority.

3E-36 The administration reforms of the Enterprise Act 2002 go hand in hand with the virtual abolition of administrative receivership. Holders of "qualifying floating charges" (see para. 3E-42) will no longer be able to block the appointment of an administrator but will instead themselves be able to seek the appointment of an administrator of their choice.

As to the application of the company administration provisions to partnerships see the Insolvent Partnerships Order 1994 (S.I. 1994 No. 2421) as amended by the Insolvent Partnerships (Amendment Order) 2005 (S.I. 2005 No 1516).

Administration by court order

3E-37 An administrator may still be appointed by order of the court. The application may be made by the company, the directors of the company, one or more creditors of the company, the justices' chief executive for a magistrates' court (in relation to a fine) or any combination of the above (para. 12(1)). It is made by a new prescribed form of application (Form 2.1B) rather than by petition and must be supported by an affidavit containing details of the company's financial position (including assets and liabilities), details of any security held, details of any existing insolvency proceedings, (where more than one administrator is to be appointed) details of which functions are to be carried out by them jointly or separately (para. 100(2), Sched.B1), any other relevant matters, (where the application is made by the holder of a qualifying floating charge) details to satisfy the court of the charge holder's entitlement to appoint an administrator, a statement as to the application of the EC Regulation on Insolvency Proceedings and whether the proceedings are main or territorial (r.2.4 of the Insolvency (Amendment) Rules 2003 (S.I. 2003 No. 1730)).

3E-38 Notice of the making of the application must be given to any person who has appointed an administrative receiver, any person who may be entitled to appoint one, the holder of any qualifying floating charge (para. 12(2), Sched.B1); in addition the application must be served on any administrative receiver who has been appointed, any person who has presented a winding up petition, any liquidator appointed in main proceedings in a member state, the proposed administrator, the company (unless it is the applicant) and the supervisor of a voluntary arrangement under Pt I Insolvency Act 1986 (r.2.6, Insolvency (Amendment) Rules 2003).

3E-39 Before making an administration order the court must be satisfied that the company is or is likely to become unable to pay its debts and that the administration order is reasonably likely to achieve the purpose of the administration (para. 11, Sched. B1).

3E-40 On the hearing of the application the court may make the administration order, dismiss the application, adjourn the hearing conditionally or unconditionally, make an interim order, treat the application as a winding up petition and make any order it could make under s.125 of the Insolvency Act 1986 or make any other order it thinks appropriate (para. 13(1), Sched.B1).

Where a qualifying charge holder applies for an order (as opposed to appointing **3E–41** out of court) there is no obligation to satisfy the court that the company is or is likely to become unable to pay its debts, but the application must state that it is being made under para. 35 of Sched.B1.

Administration out of court

The holder of a qualifying floating charge may appoint an administrator out of **3E–42** court (paras 14 to 21 of Sched.B1, Insolvency Act 1986 and rr.2.15 to 2.19, Insolvency (Amendment) Rules 2003). A floating charge "qualifies" if it is created by an instrument which states that para. 14, Sched.B1 applies to it, purports to empower the holder to appoint an administrator, purports to empower the holder to make an appointment of what would otherwise be an administrative receiver (para. 14(2)).

The appointment becomes effective when a notice of appointment in the prescribed **3E–43** form accompanied by the administrator's consent to act and a statement by him that in his opinion the purpose of the administration is likely to be achieved have been filed in court. Rule 2.19 makes special provision for filing notice of appointment by fax out of business hours (Form 2.7B). The fax number for filing notice in the Royal Courts of Justice is 020 7947 6607.

Similar provisions (but excluding that relating to appointment out of hours) are **3E–44** made for the appointment of an administrator by the company or its directors (paras 22 to 34 and rr.2.20 to 2.26).

The effects of administration are set out in paras 40 to 45 of Sched.B1. On the mak- **3E–45** ing of an administration order any petition to wind up the company (except in the public interest or under the Financial Services and Markets Act 2000) must be dismissed or (in the case of an appointment by the holder of a qualifying charge) suspended and any administrative receiver must vacate office (paras 40 and 41).

Both court and out of court administrations create a statutory moratorium during **3E–46** which no resolution to wind up the company may be passed, no winding up order may be made (save in the public interest or under the Financial Services and Markets Act 2000), no steps may be taken to enforce any security or repossess goods subject to hire purchase except with the consent of the administrator or the permission of the court, no landlord may forfeit except with such consent or permission (paras 42 and 43) and no legal process (including legal proceedings, execution and distress) may be instituted or continued against the company or its property except with such consent or permission.

An application for an administration order creates an interim moratorium which **3E–47** has the same effect as paras 42 and 43, save that the proviso relating to the consent of the administrator does not apply (para. 44).

Application for directions

As to the ability of an administrator to apply to court for directions see *Re Transbus* **3E–48** *International Ltd* [2004] 2 All E.R. 911.

Receivership (Part III Insolvency Act 1986)

Applications to the court in relation to receiverships are relatively rare, since the **3E–49** conduct of the receivership is governed by the provisions of the Insolvency Act and the terms of the debenture under which the receiver has been appointed.

Applications for directions

Section 35 enables a receiver to apply to the court for directions. The application **3E–50** should be made initially to the registrar who will give directions for its determination either before himself or the judge.

Applications for extensions of time

The Act imposes on a receiver obligations to give various notices and to file returns, **3E–51** accounts and other documents in relation to the receivership. Application to extend the time limits for so doing are made to the registrar and should be supported by written evidence setting out the reasons why the extension is required. Application may also be made to extend time for the submission of a statement of affairs (s.47).

The Enterprise Act 2002

3E–52   The Enterprise Act 2002 permits the holders of floating charges to appoint an administrator as an alternative to an administrative receiver (see para. 3E–46 above). This is intended as an alternative to administrative receivership, since s.250 of the Enterprise Act 2002 (inserting new Chap. IV in the Insolvency Act 1986) will in future prevent the appointment of administrative receivers except in relation to charges created before the new act came into force and certain charges in relation to capital market, public-private partnership and utilities charges and similar (ss.72A-72H).

Winding-up petitions (Parts IV and V Insolvency Act 1986)

3E–53   Part IV of the Insolvency Act 1986 deals with the winding up of registered companies and Pt V with the winding up of unregistered companies.

Jurisdiction

3E–54   Section 117(1) of the Insolvency Act 1986 provides that the High Court has jurisdiction to wind up any company registered in England and Wales, and s.117(2) gives concurrent jurisdiction to the county court of the district in which the company's registered office is situated where the amount of the company's share capital paid up or credited as paid up does not exceed £120,000. A company which has no share capital (*e.g.* a company limited by guarantee) may be wound up only in the High Court (*Re North of England Iron Steamship Insurance Association* [1900] 1 Ch. 481). A company's registered office for the purpose of s.117 of the Insolvency Act 1986 is the place which has longest been its registered office during the six months immediately preceding the presentation of a petition for winding up (s.117(6)). The relevant date for the purpose of determining jurisdiction is the date when proceedings are commenced, which need not be the date on which the company went into liquidation (*Re Lichfield Freight Terminal Ltd* [1997] B.C.C. 11).

Proceedings taken in the wrong court are not invalidated (s.118(1)).

Grounds on which a company may be wound up

3E–55   A company may be wound up by the court if:

(a) it has resolved by special resolution that it be wound up by the court;

(b) it is a public limited company and fails within one year of registration as such to obtain a certificate from the registrar of companies under s.117 of the Companies Act 1985;

(c) it is an old public company within the meaning of the Companies Consolidation (Consequential Provisions) Act 1985 (*i.e.* it has failed to comply with the requirements of re-registration following the re-definition of a public company in the Companies Act 1980);

(d) it has not commenced its business within a year from its incorporation or suspends its business for a whole year;

(e) except in the case of a private company limited by shares or by guarantee, the number of members is reduced below two;

(f) the company is unable to pay its debts;

(g) the court is of the opinion that it is just and equitable that the company should be wound up (s.122(1)).

Inability to pay debts

3E–56   A company is deemed unable to pay its debts:

(a) if a creditor (by assignment or otherwise) to whom the company is indebted in a sum exceeding £750 then due has served on the company, by leaving at the company's registered office, a written demand in the prescribed form (a statutory demand) requiring the company to pay the sum so due, and the company has for three weeks thereafter neglected to pay the sum or to secure or compound for it to the reasonable satisfaction of the creditor; or

(b) if execution or other process issued on a judgment, decree or order of any court in favour of a creditor of the company is returned unsatisfied in whole or in part; or

(c) if it is proved to the satisfaction of the court that the company is unable to pay its debts as they fall due (other than by reason of its failure to satisfy a statutory demand);

(d) if it is proved to the satisfaction of the court that the value of the company's assets is less than the amount of its liabilities, taking into account its contingent and prospective liabilities (s.123(1) and (2)).

As to the form of a statutory demand for the purpose of s.123(1)(a) see rr.4.4-4.6 of the Insolvency Rules 1986.

Note that the minimum level of indebtedness (£750) applies only to proof of inability to pay by service of a statutory demand. It is open to a creditor to petition for a lesser sum, relying on ground (d) above. The court may refuse to make the order (as it did in *Re Fancy Dress Balls Co* [1899] W.N. 109), but it may make the order where the company flagrantly refuses to pay (*Re World Industrial Bank Ltd* [1909] W.N. 148).

Service of a statutory demand is not a necessary prerequisite to presentation of a petition. Inability to pay may be established without service of a statutory demand (*Re Taylor's Industrial Flooring Ltd* [1990] B.C.C. 44), since the creditor may demonstrate inability to pay by the company's failure to pay an undisputed debt (*Taylor's Industrial Flooring Ltd v. M & H Plant Hire (Manchester) Ltd* [1990] B.C.L.C. 217).

A creditor with a debt which is not disputed is entitled to a winding-up order as a matter of right (*Bowes v. Hope Life Insurance Co Ltd* [1895] All E.R. 1383). However, the court will not make a winding-up order where the petition has been issued improperly or simply as a debt collecting exercise, for some private purpose, or to put pressure on a solvent company to pay a debt (*Re Lympne Investments Ltd* [1972] 1 W.L.R. 523; *Re a Company* [1983] B.C.L.C. 492) nor will it make an order on the basis of a debt which is disputed on genuine grounds (see, for example, *Re London & Paris Banking Corporation* (1874) 19 Eq 44; *Re Richbell Strategic Holdings Ltd* [1997] 2 B.C.L.C. 429). The dispute must be genuine: a bare allegation that the debt is in dispute will not suffice to establish that the dispute is genuine (*Re a Company No. 006685 of 1996* [1997] B.C.C. 830). A winding-up order will not be made on a debt which is time barred (*Re Karnos Property Co Ltd* (1989) 5 B.C.C. 14).

The petition

A petition to wind up a company may be presented by the following: **3E–57**

(a) the company itself;

(b) its directors

(c) one or more of its creditors (including an actual, contingent or prospective creditor);

(d) one or more of its contributories;

(e) a clerk to a magistrates' court to enforce a fine;

(f) any combination of the above (s.124(1));

(g) the official receiver (where the company is in voluntary liquidation) (s.124(5));

(h) the supervisor of the company's voluntary arrangement (s.7(4)(b));

(i) an administrator (s.14(1)(b); Sched.1, para. 21);

(j) an administrative receiver (s.42(1); Sched.1, para. 1);

(k) a voluntary liquidator (s.165(3); Sched.4, Part II, para. 4).

It should contain statutory information about the company and state the basis on which it is contended the company is unable to pay its debts.It should deal with jurisdiction under the EC Regulation on Insolvency proceedings (see para. 3E-25). It should expressly state that "the company is insolvent and unable to pay its debts" and contend, "In the circumstances it is just and equitable that the company should be wound up". It should conclude with the prayers, "(1) that the company may be wound up by the court under the provisions of the Insolvency Act 1986; or (2) that such other order may be made as the court thinks fit".

Evidence

The petition must be verified by an affidavit or witness statement (r.4.7(1) and **3E–58** r.4.12).

Service and advertisement

The petition (unless it is the company's own petition) must be served (r.4.8; see also **3E–59** r.4.10), and service must be proved (r.4.9).

The petition must be advertised not less than seven business days after service on the company and not less than seven business days before the date appointed for the hearing of the petition (r.4.11). As to the contents of the advertisement see r.4.11(4).

Applications to restrain presentation or advertisement of a petition

3E–60   A company which has been served with a statutory demand or is otherwise made aware that it is intended to present a petition may apply with or without notice for an order restraining presentation of a petition or advertisement of any petition which has already been presented. The application should be supported by full written evidence in support setting out in detail why the petition should not be presented or advertised (usually because the petition debt is disputed). Since the application is for an injunction it is made direct to the judge. There is no provision to apply for a statutory demand to be set aside.

The court will not restrain a creditor from prosecuting a petition where the company can demonstrate solvency but has failed to pay a debt that is due (*Cornhill Insurance plc v. Improvement Services Ltd* [1986] 1 W.L.R. 114).

Failure to advertise

3E–61   Winding up is a class remedy. Accordingly the court attaches importance to the advertisement of a winding up petition. The petition should be advertised in the London Gazette (r.4.11(1)), but may be advertised elsewhere if the court so orders (r.4.11(3)). If a petition has not been advertised in accordance with r.4.11 the court may dismiss it (r.4.11(5) and para. 2 of the Practice Direction). The court will not, as a general rule, dismiss the petition by reason only of a failure to advertise, at the first hearing of the petition. It will, however, do so as a general rule if the petition has not been advertised by any adjourned hearing unless there are exceptional circumstances for not complying with the general rule. It will almost certainly dismiss any petition that has not been advertised with a view to holding the unadvertised petition over the company's head for the purpose of obtaining costs from the company without an order of the court. If the court does adjourn the petition as a result of a failure to advertise it may do so on terms that the petitioner should have no costs in respect of the ineffective hearing.

Premature advertisement of the petition may result in dismissal if the breach of the rule appears to have been culpable, but will generally be waived if the petition is unopposed and no prejudice has been suffered by the company. The court may waive up to two days lateness in advertisement but will generally adjourn if the advertisement is more than two days late. The court may also waive minor errors in the advertisement (*e.g.* misspelling of the company's address) so long as the name and identity of the company in the advertisement are clear.

Certificate of compliance

3E–62   The Petitioner must, at least five days before the hearing of the petition, file in court a certificate of compliance relating to service and advertisement of the petition (r.4.14(1)). It must show the date of presentation of the petition, the date fixed for the hearing, the dates of service and advertisement, and it must be accompanied by a copy of the advertisement of the petition. Failure to file a certificate of compliance may also result in dismissal of the petition (r.4.14(3)).

At present it is the practice in the High Court in London to accept certificates of compliance filed late provided they are filed no later than 4.30 p.m. on the Friday next before the Wednesday on which the petition was to be heard.

List of appearances

3E–63   Any person who intends to appear on the hearing of the petition must give notice to the petitioner of his intention to do so, state whether he intends to support or oppose the petition and give details of the amount and nature of his debt (r.4.16). The petitioner must prepare a list of the persons who have given notice under r.4.16 and hand a copy of the list to the court before the hearing (r.4.17).

Hearing of the petition

3E–64   In the High Court in London winding up petitions are heard on Wednesdays by the registrar.

At the hearing of the petition the petitioner may appear as may the company and any supporting or opposing creditor who has given notice under r.4.16 or has failed to give such notice but has been permitted by the court to appear (r.4.16(5)). The company may appear by a director or employee as well as by solicitors or counsel. However, the court will not generally allow accountants right of audience.

At the hearing, the court may dismiss the petition, adjourn it conditionally or unconditionally, or make an interim order or any other order it thinks fit (s.125(1)). It may also make an order that the company be wound up.

Petition contested —If the company opposes the making of a winding up order it should file in court and serve on the petitioner evidence in opposition not less than seven days before the date fixed for the hearing of the petition (r.4.18). In practice, if the company appears and indicates that it opposes the making of an order on grounds that appear to be substantial, the court will give directions for the filing and service of evidence in opposition and evidence in reply and order the petition to be heard at a later date, notwithstanding any failure to comply with the provisions of r.4.18. The directions may provide for the contested petition to be heard by the registrar or the judge. **3E–65**

Substitution of petitioner —Where the petitioner is unable to proceed with his petition (*e.g.* because the petition debt is disputed) or is unable to seek a winding up order (*e.g.* because restrained by injunction from advertising, because he has failed to advertise or otherwise comply with the rules) or does not seek a winding up order for some other reason (*e.g.* because his debt has been paid), a creditor or contributory who would himself be entitled to present a petition may seek substitution. The application may be made informally at the hearing and without notice. If more than one creditor seeks substitution the court will generally substitute the creditor with the largest debt or the debt least likely to be disputed. The court will direct that the petition be amended and re-verified; it may order re-service but will generally dispense with re-advertisement if the petition has already been advertised. It will adjourn the petition so as to allow sufficient time for those steps to be taken. **3E–66**

Dismissal of the petition —If the petitioner fails to appear, if the petitioner accepts that the petition debt is capable of dispute, or if the petition debt has been paid and no creditor or contributory seeks substitution, the court will generally dismiss the petition. It may also dismiss the petition for failure to advertise or for some other failure to comply with the Insolvency Rules 1986 (*e.g.* rr.4.11(5) and 4.14(3)). **3E–67**

The court must dismiss a petition for the winding up of a company in respect of which an administration order has been made (Sched.B1, para. 40(1)(a)). It must suspend the petition where an administration has been appointed by the holder of a floating charge (Sched.B1, para. 40(b).

Usual compulsory order —If the court is satisfied that the provisions of the Insolvency Act 1986 and the Insolvency Rules 1986 have been complied with and that the petition debt is not disputed on grounds which are substantial and that it is just and equitable to wind up the company it will make "the usual compulsory order", *i.e.* an order that the company be wound up by the court under the provisions of the Insolvency Act 1986. It will also make a declaration as to whether or not the EC Regulation on Insolvency Proceedings applies to the winding up and whether (if it does) the proceedings are main or secondary/territorial proceedings. **3E–68**

Double barrelled order —Where a company has been struck off the register by the registrar of companies the court may order the company to be restored and wound up (see para. 3E–52). **3E–69**

Appointment of liquidator —Where a winding-up order is made immediately on the discharge of an administration order, the court may appoint the former administrator as liquidator (s.140(1)). The court may also appoint as liquidator a person who was the supervisor of a voluntary arrangement under Pt I of the Act (s.140(2)). **3E–70**

Where a petition presented by an administrator or supervisor contains a request for his appointment as liquidator the person whose appointment is sought must, not less than two days before the return day of the petition, file in court a report including particulars of the date on which he notified creditors of his intention to seek appointment and details of any response received to such notification (r.4.7(10)).

A winding-up petition should not be used as a mechanism to oust a liquidator appointed in a creditors' voluntary liquidation to whose appointment the petitioning creditor objects (*Re Inside Sport Ltd (In Liquidation)* [2000] B.C.C. 40; [2000] 1 B.C.L.C. 302; *The Times*, November 27, 1998). **3E–71**

Costs —The court has a discretion as to the making of any order for costs. **3E–72**

Where an order is made for the company to be wound up, unless otherwise stated, the petitioner will be entitled to his costs as a claim in the winding up of the company. The supporting creditors may also be awarded one set of costs to be shared among them provided they have given notice of intention to appear or been given permission to appear (r.4.16). Such costs are payable out of the assets of the company in accordance with the order of priority prescribed by r.4.218 of the Insolvency Rules 1986 (see r.4.218(1)(h) as to the costs of the petitioner and any other person appearing).

Where the petition is dismissed because the petition debt has been paid, the court will generally award the petitioner his costs provided that the petitioner has complied with the provisions of the Act and the Rules or if the company consents to pay the costs.Where the petition is dismissed because it has been successfully opposed by the company, the court will generally order the petitioner to pay the company's costs.

Where the petition is dismissed because the company has obtained approval for a voluntary arrangement under Pt I of the Act or because an administration order has been made, the court will generally order the company to pay the petitioner's costs and may order such costs to be in the voluntary arrangement or the administration. The court will not without good reason order the costs of a petition to be in the voluntary winding up of the company where the company goes into creditors' voluntary liquidation, even if the liquidator agrees that they should be paid on that basis.

Where the petition is adjourned, unless the contrary is said, the costs will generally be in the petition.

If there is argument as to costs the registrar will normally adjourn the question of costs to be dealt with at a later date and give directions for evidence to be filed.

Withdrawal of petition

3E–73   The petitioner may apply to withdraw a winding up petition provided that the application is made at least five days before the date fixed for hearing the petition, the petition has not been advertised, no notices in support of or in opposition to the petition have been received and the company consents to an order being made (r.4.15). The order may also be made without the consent of the company if the company has not been served. The application may be made without notice by ordinary application and will generally be heard by the clerk to the companies court if made at least five days before the hearing. Otherwise the application should be made to the registrar. Permission to withdraw a petition will almost never be given after the petition has been heard in court or advertised.

Winding up unregistered companies

3E–74   The court has power to wind up an unregistered company (as defined by s.220) (s.221). The provision is generally applied in the case of a company incorporated outside England and Wales which has established a place of business within the jurisdiction or has some other sufficient connection with the jurisdiction (see para. 3E–75) or to wind up an insolvent partnership (which is treated as an unregistered company under the provisions of the Insolvent Partnerships Order 1994 (S.I. 1994 No. 2421)).

Winding up a foreign company

3E–75   The power of the court to wind up a foreign company as an unregistered company is now restricted by the terms of the EC Regulation on Insolvency Proceedings (see para. 3E–25). However, the power still has effect in relation to foreign companies not covered by the Regulation. Furthermore, the courts have construed the power in relation to foreign companies narrowly, so that the court will not assume jurisdiction over matters which properly lie in the competence of the courts of other countries (*Banque des Marchands de Moscou (Koupetschesky) v. Kindersley* [1951] Ch. 112; [1950] 2 All E.R. 549). The court will be reluctant to make an order where the foreign company is continuing to trade in its place of incorporation and elsewhere in the world save in exceptional circumstances (*Banco Nacional de Cuba v. Cosmos Trading Corp* [2000] B.C.C. 910; [2000] 1 B.C.L.C. 812).

The court will generally have to be satisfied, before assuming jurisdiction and making an order in relation to a foreign company, that (a) there is a sufficient connection with the jurisdiction, (b) that there is a reasonable possibility of a benefit to the petitioner if an order is made to wind-up the company, and (c) that one or more persons interested in the distribution of assets is a person over whom the court can exercise jurisdiction (*Stocznia Gdanska v. Latreefers Inc* [1999] 1 B.C.L.C. 271).

Winding up in the public interest

Where it appears to the Secretary of State for Trade and Industry that it is expedient in the public interest that a company should be wound up he may present a petition to the court for an order that the company be wound up (s.124A). A public interest petition is dealt with in the same way as any other petition under the Act, save that a contested public interest petition is always be heard by the judge. Uncontested public interest petitions as well as any interim applications in connection with such petitions (save for an application to appoint a provisional liquidator) are heard by the registrar.

The court will not generally accept an undertaking as an alternative to making an order (*Re Supporting Link Alliance Ltd* [2004] EWHC 523; [2004] 1 W.L.R. 1549). The Housing Corporation may petition for the winding up of a registered social landlord (Housing Act 1996, Sched. 1) and the Financial Services Authority may petition for the winding up of an authorised person or appointed representative (Financial Services and Markets Act 2000, s.367).

3E–76

Contributory's petition

A contributory's petition (unlike a creditor's petition) is not listed straight away for hearing but is given a first return date on which the petitioner and the company should attend before the registrar for directions to be given (r.4.22(2)). The petition must be served on the company at least 14 days before the hearing (r.4.22(4)). As to the range of directions which the court may give see r.4.23.

3E–77

Supervisor's petition

A winding up petition presented by the supervisor of a voluntary arrangement under Part I of the Act must be presented to the court in which the nominee's report was filed (r.4.7(8)) and is treated as a petition presented by a contributory (r.4.7(9)). As to the appointment of the supervisor as liquidator see para. 3E–70.

3E–78

Applications for relief from the effects of s.127

Section 127 of the Insolvency Act 1986 renders certain transactions made after commencement of the winding up void. Thus, advertisement of a winding up petition will generally have the effect of freezing any bank accounts of the company. The company may apply for relief from the effects of the provisions of s.127 to the judge (if the application is urgent) or otherwise to the registrar.Any order made is commonly referred to as a validation order. For the form of the order see para. 3E–60.

3E–79

Applications for the appointment of a provisional liquidator

The court may appoint a provisional liquidator of a company at any time after presentation of a winding up petition and before the making of a winding up order (s.135(1)). Such an appointment is generally made only where assets of the company are in jeopardy or in connection with a public interest petition. The application may be (and commonly is) made without notice to the company and is always made direct to the judge. It should be supported by full written evidence (as to the contents of which see r.4.25(2)).

3E–80

Applications in the liquidation of companies

The winding up of a company (whether voluntary or by the court) does not bring the life of the company to an end. The company, acting by its liquidator, may bring proceedings in its own name even after it has been wound up. Thus, the company may by its liquidator and in its own name issue proceedings to collect a debt or to enforce any other right. Such proceedings should generally be issued in the court having the appropriate jurisdiction: the county court, for example, in the case of a debt action, the Chancery Division in the case of an action regarding intellectual property rights, and so on. However, the breadth of proceedings which the companies court may entertain is wide (*Re Shilena Hosiery Co Ltd* [1980] Ch. 219).

3E–81

Applications to recover assets or relating to prior transactions

The Insolvency Act 1986 provides the administrator,administrative receiver or liquidator of a company with a wide range of remedies to enable him to recover assets of the company or undo the effects of prior transactions (see, for example in liquidations, s.127 (void transactions), ss.206–207 (fraud), s.212 (misfeasance etc.), ss.212–213

3E–82

(fraudulent and wrongful trading), s.238 (transactions at an undervalue), s.239 (preferences), s.244 (extortionate credit transactions), s.245 (avoidance of floating charges) and s.246 (liens etc.)). Any application to enforce a right of the liquidator or to review or appeal against the conduct of a liquidator should be made to the court having jurisdiction in the winding up. The application should be made by originating or ordinary application (see para. 3E–20) and be supported by written evidence. It will be listed for directions before the registrar and determined by him or the judge depending on the length and complexity of the case

Applications for directions in the winding up of a company

3E–83   Section 112 of the Insolvency Act 1986 allows a liquidator, contributory or creditor to apply to the court to determine any question arising in the winding up of a company. The application should be made by originating or ordinary application (see para. 3E–21) and supported by written evidence. It will be listed for directions before the registrar and determined by him or the judge depending on the length and complexity of the case.

Applications for private examinations

3E–84   Section 236 of the Insolvency Act 1986 enables an office holder to apply to the court for an order summoning to appear before it (a) any officer of the company, (b) any person known or suspected to have in his possession any property of the company or supposed to be indebted to the company, (c) any person whom the court thinks capable of giving information concerning the promotion, formation, business, dealings, affairs or property of the company (subs.2). Such person may be examined on oath (s.237(3) and (4)). Failure to attend may give rise to the issue of a warrant for the arrest of the person concerned (s.236(5)).

The case law relating to s.236 relief is voluminous and complex. The making of an order is a matter for the discretion of the court, but the discretion will generally be exercised in favour an office holder (*Joint Liquidators of Sasea Finance Ltd v. KPMG* [1998] B.C.C. 216) provided the application is made to enable him to carry out his proper functions (*British & Commonwealth Holdings plc v. Spicer & Oppenheim (Re British & Commonwealth Holdings plc (No. 2))* [1993] A.C. 426; [1992] B.C.C. 977. The formation of the liquidator of an intention to bring proceedings against the proposed examinee may be a factor weighing against the exercise of the discretion to make an order (*Re Castle New Homes Ltd* [1979] 1 W.L.R. 1075; [1979] 2 All E.R. 775 and *Re Cloverbay Ltd* [1991] Ch 90; [1990] B.C.C. 414; [1990] B.C.L.C. 449); an order will not be made to give the office holder a litigation advantage (*Re Atlantic Computers plc* [1998] B.C.C. 200); however an order may be made for the purpose of obtaining information other than for the administration of the liquidation (*e.g.* for the purposes of disqualification proceedings, *Re Pantmaenog Timber Co Ltd* [2001] EWCA Civ 1227, CA; *Official Receiver v. Meade-King* [2003] UKHL 49; [2003] 4 All E.R. 18, HL; [2003] 3 W.L.R. 767). As to the use of compelled evidence in subsequent criminal proceedings see *Saunders v. United Kingdom* [1997] E.H.R.R. 313; [1997] B.C.C. 872 and s.219(2A) Insolvency Act 1986.

Applications for confirmation by the court of a creditors' voluntary winding up

3E–85   The EC Regulation on Insolvency Proceedings (see para. 3E–25) applies to creditors' voluntary winding up with confirmation by the court (Annex A). Article 19 of the Regulation provides that the appointment of a liquidator must be evidenced by a copy of the decision appointing him or by some other certificate issued by the court with jurisdiction. The procedure for applying for an order confirming a creditors' voluntary winding up is provided for by Chap. 10 of the Insolvency (Amendment) Rules 2002 (S.I. 2002 No. 1307).

The application is made pursuant to r.7.62(1) and must be made by prescribed form 7.20 which incorporates the application, the evidence in support and the order to be made. The evidence must state the name of the applicant and of the company and its registered number, the date of the resolution to wind up the company, that the application is accompanied by the required documents and that the copies submitted are true copies, that the Regulation applies to the company, and whether the proceedings are main, territorial or secondary proceedings (r.7.62(2)). The application must be filed together with a copy and be accompanied by a copy of the resolution to wind up the company, evidence of the applicant's appointment as liquidator and the statement of affairs (r.7.62(3)). Whilst provision is made for the order to be made by a member of the court staff (r.7.62(7)), in the High Court the application should be made to the registrar who will make the order without a hearing provided that the papers are in order. The application need not be served on any other party (r.7.62(4)).

The order is made by the court completing and sealing the order section of the prescribed form and returning a completed and sealed copy to the applicant.

Applications to convert proceedings

The EC Regulation on Insolvency Proceedings provides that the liquidator in main proceedings may request that proceedings listed in Annex A (see para. 3E–24) previously opened in another member state be converted into winding up proceedings if this is in the interests of creditors in the main proceedings (Art.37). The court may, on such an application, order that any such proceedings be converted into one of the proceedings listed in Annex B (*i.e.* winding up by or subject to the supervision of the court, creditors' voluntary winding up with confirmation by the court (see para. 3E–85) or bankruptcy). The application may be made to the registrar or the judge.

3E–86

Individual Voluntary Arrangements (Part VIII Insolvency Act 1986)

Part VIII of the Insolvency Act 1986 allows a debtor to make a proposal to his creditors for what must be either a composition with his creditors or a scheme of arrangement of his affairs. A composition is effectively an agreement whereby creditors agree to accept a lesser sum in satisfaction of their debt; a scheme of arrangement may take any form which is acceptable to the parties but must provide for someone to act either as a trustee or otherwise for the purpose of supervising its implementation. As to compositions and schemes generally, see *Re Griffith* (1886) 3 Morr.111 and *Inland Revenue Commissioners v. Adam & Partners Ltd* [2001] 1 B.C.L.C. 222. In practice the procedure to be followed in each case is the same and can be summarised as follows. A proposal is formulated, reviewed by the nominee who will then present it to the creditors at a meeting summoned for that purpose; if approved by a majority of in excess of three quarters of creditors in value it then becomes binding on the creditors.

3E–87

The Insolvency Act 2000, ss.3 and 4 and Sched.3, and the Insolvency (Amendment) (No. 2) Rules 2002 (S.I. 2712 No. 2002) which came into force on January 1, 2003, enable the debtor to choose whether or not to apply for an interim order. If the debtor needs protection from his creditors, which now includes protection against peaceable re-entry by his landlord or distress (except with the permission of the court), then an interim order will be required and an application will need to be made to the court as before. The procedure has not changed and is set out in Pt 5 of the Insolvency Rules 1986. If protection is not required then the debtor may submit his proposal, which must comply with r.5.3 (as amended) and statement of affairs to the intended nominee who, if he is of the opinion that the debtor is an undischarged bankrupt or is able to petition for his own bankruptcy and is prepared to act, can call the meeting of creditors. The nominee must within 14 days (or such longer period as the court may allow) after receiving the proposal and statement of affairs submit a report to the court in which he must state whether in his opinion the voluntary arrangement has a reasonable prospect of being approved and implemented, whether a meeting of creditors should be summoned and if so the date, time and venue. This must be filed along with a copy of the proposal, the statement of affairs and form 5.5 (which contains the statement that it is not intended to apply for an interim order). The court will not read the report unless an application is made under the Act or Rules in relation to the proposal, for example to challenge the decision of the creditors' meeting under s.262 of the Insolvency Act 1986, (see r.5.14(1)).

3E–88

The appropriate court in which to file is the court in which the debtor should file his own bankruptcy petition (r.6.40), or if an undischarged bankrupt the court with the conduct of the bankruptcy. Where the debtor is an undischarged bankrupt the nominee must send copies of his report, the proposal and the statement of affairs to the official receiver or trustee and to any petitioning creditor if a petition has been filed (r.5.5A(3)).

The nominee or supervisor appointed must either be a licensed insolvency practitioner or a member of a body recognised by the secretary of state for that purpose. To date no other body has been given such recognition. In either case he must have in force security for the proper performance of his functions.

3E–89

In his report the nominee must state whether in his opinion the proposal has a reasonable prospect of being approved and implemented (ss.256 as amended by para. 3

and para. 5 of Sched.3 of the Insolvency Act 2000). An application may be made to the court for an order replacing a nominee where it is impractical or inappropriate for the nominee to continue to act. Section 260 of the Insolvency Act 1986 as amended by s.3 and para. 10 of Sched.3 of the Insolvency Act 2000 provides that approval of a voluntary arrangement binds every person who in accordance with the rules was entitled to vote at the meeting (whether or not he was present or represented at it), or would have been so entitled had he had notice of it. The classes of person who may challenge the outcome of the meeting under s.262 of the Insolvency Act 1986 includes any person who was entitled, in accordance with the rules, to vote at the creditors' meeting or would have been so entitled had he had notice of it (r.5.3(2)). The content of the debtor's proposal must now state how it is proposed to deal with the claims of any person who is bound by the arrangement by virtue of this provision.

Section 262A, Insolvency Act 1986, as enacted by s.3 and para. 12 of Sched.3 of the Insolvency Act 2000, makes it an offence for a debtor to make any false representation or fraudulently to do, or omit to do, anything for the purpose of obtaining the approval of his creditors to a proposal, whether approved or not.

The Proposal

3E–90   The debtor must ensure that his proposal complies with the requirements of r.5.3 of the Insolvency Rules 1986 as amended. In particular it must deal with the EC Regulation on Insolvency Proceedings (see para. 3E–24) and give details of the debtor's centre of main interests and/or his establishment (r.5.3(2)(q)). It is also necessary to set out not only the fees to be charged by the intended nominee but also to list the disbursements (r.5.3 (2)(g)).

Application for interim order

3E–91   If the debtor decides that he needs the protection of an interim order then the steps set out in Pt 5 of the Insolvency Rules must be followed. The debtor must give written notice of his proposal together with a copy of the proposal to the intended nominee (r.5.4(1)). If he is an undischarged bankrupt then he must also give notice to the or his trustee (r.5.4(5)). If the nominee is prepared to act he endorses his consent on the notice (r.5.4(3)) and returns it to the debtor. The debtor then has 7 days, or such longer period as the nominee may allow, to give the nominee his statement of affairs (r.5.8(2)).

The application may be made by the debtor where he is not bankrupt or by the debtor, the official receiver or his trustee where he is (s.253(3) of the Insolvency Act 1986). The application is by way of originating application accompanied by an affidavit or witness statement in support. The evidence must comply with r.5.1 of the Insolvency Rules 1986: it should give the reason for the application, details of any execution or other legal process, state whether the debtor is an undischarged bankrupt or able to file his own petition, confirm that there has been no other application within the last 12 months, name the nominee and confirm that he is qualified to act and is willing to act. A copy of the notice served upon the nominee endorsed with his consent to act must be exhibited to the written evidence (r.5.5(2)). If the nominee has completed his enquiries the application may be accompanied by his report.

Interim order

3E–92   Where it is not necessary to give any other party notice the court will often deal with the application in the absence of the parties and will only require a hearing if the papers are not in order. In the absence of a nominee's report the court will make an interim order for 14 days commencing the day following the making of the order and will fix a hearing date within the 14 day period to consider the nominee's report (r.5.6(3)). At the adjourned hearing if the nominee's report has not been filed the court may extend the 14 day period in certain circumstances, if appropriate. Where it has been filed and a date, time and venue have been given for the meeting of creditors (which is not less than 14 days from the date on which it was filed and not more than 28 days from the date on which it is considered by the court) the court will extend the interim order to a date 7 weeks after the proposed date of the meeting and adjourn the application to a date about 3 weeks after the date of the meeting for consideration of the chairman's report. The time scale allows for possible adjournment of the meeting. If the nominee's report accompanies the application the court may make a "concertina order" which combines the two orders set out above. The nominee must state in his report whether the debtor's proposal has a reasonable prospect of being approved (s.256 as amended). As to the obligations of a nominee in reporting to the court see *Greystoke v. Hamilton-Smith* [1996] 2 B.C.L.C. 429; [1997] B.P.I.R. 24).

Where it has been necessary to give notice to other parties a hearing date will be fixed for consideration of the application when the parties will have the opportunity to make representations to the court about the proposal.

The court has a discretion as to whether or not to make an interim order. It will not make an order if the proposal is not viable (*Cooper v. Fearnley* [1997] B.P.I.R. 20; *Hook v. Jewson Ltd* [1997] B.C.C. 752) or cannot achieve the requisite majority (*Re Cove* [1990] 1 All E.R. 949). As to the importance of adhering to the statutory regime applicable to interim orders and individual voluntary arrangements see, for example, *Greystoke v. Hamilton-Smith* [1996] 2 B.C.L.C. 429; [1997] B.P.I.R. 24; *Fletcher v. Vooght* [2000] B.P.I.R. 435 and *Re N (a debtor)* [2002] B.P.I.R. 1024.

Chairman's report

3E–93 The chairman's report must state whether the proposal was approved, with or without modifications, or rejected, set out the resolutions and the decision on each one, list the creditors who were present and how they voted, indicate whether it is governed by the E.C. Regulation on Insolvency Proceedings and if so whether the proceedings are main or territorial proceedings and include any other information he thinks should be made known to the court (r.5.22(2)). As to the chairman's obligations in conducting the meeting of creditors see *Re a Debtor (No. 222 of 1990) Ex p. Bank of Ireland* [1992] B.C.L.C. 137; [1993] B.C.L.C. 233; as to his obligations in reporting to the court see *Re N (a debtor)* [2002] B.P.I.R. 1024.

Challenges

3E–94 Within 28 days of the day on which the chairman's report was made to the court the debtor, a person entitled to vote at the creditors' meeting, the nominee, and, where the debtor is an undischarged bankrupt, the official receiver or trustee, may apply to challenge the approval of the arrangement on the ground of unfair prejudice or material irregularity at or in relation to the meeting (s.262 of the Insolvency Act 1986). The application is made initially to the registrar and must be supported by written evidence detailing the matters complained of. As to creditors bound who did not receive notice, see para. 3E–88, above.

Bankruptcy (Part IX Insolvency Act 1986)

3E–95 Part IX of the Act enables a petition for a bankruptcy order to be presented by a creditor or creditors, the debtor, a temporary administrator within the meaning of Art.38 of the EC Regulation, a liquidator within the meaning of Art.2(b) appointed in proceedings by virtue of article 3(1) of the EC Regulation and the supervisor of a voluntary arrangement (s.264(1) of the Insolvency Act 1986).

Presentation of petition

3E–96 A creditor's petition is normally presented to the court in whose insolvency district the debtor has carried on business; this may be different from the insolvency district in which the debtor resides.Petitions presented by government departments are always presented in the High Court. If the debtor is resident or carries on business in the London insolvency district or is not resident in England and Wales or his place of business or residence is not known the petition may also be presented in the High Court. See generally r.6.9 of the Insolvency Rules 1986.

Grounds of a creditor's petition

3E–97 The grounds for a creditor's petition are set out in s.267(2) of the Insolvency Act 1986. A creditor may present a petition where the amount of the debt or debts is equal to or greater than the bankruptcy level, currently £750, the debt or debts are for a liquidated sum payable either immediately or at some future time and are unsecured and the debtor appears either to be unable to pay or to have no reasonable prospect of paying the debt or debts. Also there must be no outstanding application to set aside a statutory demand. It is possible for creditors to join in the presentation of a creditor's petition: the debts do not need to be interrelated but can be entirely separate. The creditor has a duty to disclose whether he holds any security though he may undertake in the petition to give it up for the benefit of all the creditors (s.269(1)(a)).

3E–98   *Inability to pay debts* —The debtor is deemed to be unable to pay his debts if 3 weeks have elapsed since service of a statutory demand and the demand has not been complied with or set aside, or if execution of a judgment or court order in favour of the petitioner has been returned unsatisfied (s.268). As to the requirements in relation to unsatisfied execution see *Re a debtor (No. 340 of 1992)* [1996] 2 All E.R. 211.

Statutory demand

3E–99   The form of the statutory demand and the information it must contain is prescribed by rr.6.1 and 6.2. The form to be used will vary depending on the nature of the debt.

The creditor is under an obligation to do all that is reasonable to bring the demand to the debtor's attention and, if practicable, to cause personal service to be effected (r.6.3(2)). The Practice Direction sets out in detail the steps to be taken to effect service. Where substituted service is effected the court will need to satisfied that the creditor has taken all steps which would justify the court making an order for substituted service of a petition

Application to set aside statutory demand

3E–100   The debtor may apply to the court to set aside the statutory demand within 18 days of its service upon him. The court will consider the application and will dismiss it summarily if it considers that it has no real prospect of success (r.6.5(1)); for example where the demand is based on a judgment, the court will not go behind it at this stage. In all other cases a date will be fixed for a directions hearing. As to the grounds on which the court will set aside a demand see r.6.5(4) of the Insolvency Rules 1986.

A petition (other than an expedited petition) may not be presented until the application is dealt with.

Expedited petition

3E–101   Although the prescribed period for compliance with a statutory demand is 3 weeks, if a creditor can establish that there is a serious possibility that before the end of the 3 week period the value of the debtor's property will be significantly diminished then the court may allow a petition to be presented before the expiry of the 3 weeks but no bankruptcy order can be made until 3 weeks have elapsed (s.270).

Petition

3E–102   The content of the petition must be verified (r.6.12(1)) and if it relies upon an unsatisfied statutory demand written evidence must be filed establishing service of the demand. The requirements to satisfy the court that service has been properly affected are set out in para. 13 of the Practice Direction. If the petition relies upon a demand served more than 4 months before the filing of the petition the reason for the delay must be explained in the affidavit of verification, r.6.12(7).

The petition must be served personally. If this proves to be impossible then an application for substituted service may be made (see para. 11 of the Practice Direction). The court may order service by post or other appropriate means, advertisement in a national newspaper or (rarely) the London Gazette. Again the Practice Direction sets out the criteria for this. The petition must comply with the EC Regulation and state whether it will apply and if so whether the proceedings will be main, territorial or secondary proceedings and the debtor's centre of main interests. Once presented the court fixes a date, time and place for the hearing and seals sufficient copies for service.

Service of the petition

3E–103   The petition must be served at least 14 days before the hearing date, but if service proves to be difficult an application may be made to the court on paper for an extension of the hearing date of the petition (r.6.28 of the Insolvency Rules 1986 and para. 14 of the Practice Direction). The application should be made in advance of the hearing date; if made less than 2 days before the hearing costs will not be allowed.

A first extension will generally be granted without evidence, but where a further application is made by written evidence in support may be required.

Hearing of the petition

3E–104   The court will not make a bankruptcy order unless it is satisfied that the debt on which the petition is based is either (a) a debt which has not been paid, secured or compounded for or (b) a debt which the debtor has no reasonable prospect of being able to pay when it falls due (s.271(1)). Thus, at the hearing of the petition the court will need to satisfied that that the debt remains due and payable. The petitioner must complete a certificate of continuing debt so as to satisfy the court that the petition debt remains due (r.6.25). In the High Court in London this is incorporated in the attendance sheet. A fresh certificate is required for each adjourned hearing.

When a petition is adjourned the court will also need to be satisfied at the adjourned hearing that the petitioner has complied with r.6.29 and given written notice to the debtor of the adjourned hearing date and time, regardless of whether the debtor attended the previous hearing. The petitioner is also required to give notice to any creditor who has given notice under r.6.23 but was not present at the hearing when the adjournment was made.

At the hearing the petitioning creditor, the debtor, any supervisor under a voluntary arrangement and any other creditor who has given notice may be heard (r.6.18(3)). If the debtor intends to oppose the petition he must file with the court and serve the petitioning creditor with a notice setting out his grounds of opposition not less than 7 days before the hearing (r.6.21). The petitioning creditor must prepare a list of supporting/opposing creditors (r.6.24).

At the hearing the court, upon being satisfied that the papers are in order, may make a bankruptcy order noting in the record the time when the order was made. The court also has general power to dismiss stay or adjourn a petition for any reason and if stayed to impose conditions (s.266(3)). The court will not allow repeated adjournments to see if a debtor maintains payments by an instalment arrangement agreed with the petitioner.

Withdrawal, substitution and change of carriage of petition

Once issued a petition may not be withdrawn without the permission of the court **3E–105** (s.266(2)). Permission will only be given at a hearing.

At the hearing of the petition any creditor who has given notice and was in a position to issue his own petition at the date the petition was filed may apply to be substituted as petitioner (r.6.30). This will require amendment and possibly re-service of the petition.

Where a creditor who has given proper notice but was not in a position to file a petition at the time the petition was presented appears, and the petition debt remains unpaid, he may apply to the court for carriage of the petition (r.6.31). Amendment of the petition will not be necessary. As to change of carriage generally see *Re Purvis and another* [1997] 3 All E.R. 663.

Debtor's petition

The only ground upon which a debtor may present his own petition is that he is **3E–106** unable to pay his debts (s.272(1) and rr.6.37 to 6.50). The petition must contain sufficient information to establish that it is being brought in the right court and be accompanied by a statement of affairs detailing the debtor's assets and liabilities. The court will usually hear the petition immediately. Generally the High Court will make the order in the absence of the debtor. Where a bankruptcy order is made the court will notify the official receiver immediately. If it is apparent that the liabilities are less than £20,000 the court will make an order for summary administration (s.273(1)(a) of the Insolvency Act 1986 and Insolvency Proceedings (Monetary Limits) Order 1986 (S.I. 1986 No.1996)).

Review, rescind or vary

Section 375(1) of the Insolvency Act gives the court power to review, rescind or **3E–107** vary any order made by it in the exercise of its jurisdiction. This provision is of very broad application but should not be used in place of an appeal. The fact that an appeal is pending does not prevent to court from rehearing a matter and reviewing any order made. The exercise of the power should be confined to cases in which there has been a change of circumstance since the making of the original order. The court may apply this provision to a bankruptcy order in circumstances where annulment is not possible (*Fitch v. Official Receiver* [1996] 1 W.L.R. 242).

Annulment

The jurisdiction to annul a bankruptcy order is found in ss.261 and 282 of the **3E–108** Insolvency Act. Section 261(1)(a) allows a bankrupt to apply for the annulment of the bankruptcy order if his creditors have at a meeting called for the purpose approved a proposal for a voluntary arrangement. The court cannot make the order before the end of the period of 28 days beginning with the day on which the chairman's report was made to the court (s.261(2)). The official receiver and trustee (if appointed) are necessary parties and must be given notice of the application but they are not required to file any report. If the court feels that a relevant obligation under the arrangement has yet to be fulfilled, for example if a third party is to make a single lump sum payment, then the court may adjourn the annulment application until the payment has been received.

Section 282(1) gives the court power to annul a bankruptcy order on the basis that either (a) on grounds existing at the time the order was made it should not have been made or (b) the bankrupt has paid or secured his debts in full. Rules 6.206(1)(a), (2)–(4) as amended relate to ground (a) above. A report is required from the trustee or official receiver. The courts will generally be sympathetic if the debtor can provide a reasonable explanation for non-attendance in circumstances where his attendance would in all probability have led to the adjournment or dismissal of the petition. In such cases the annulment will be on terms that he pays the official receiver's fees, costs charges and expenses and the creditor's costs of the annulment application. Further, unless the creditor agrees to the petition being dismissed, it will be restored to the list for hearing. There is no point in annulling if the debtor is hopelessly insolvent or if the trustee's inquiries reveal that there is a strong case that the bankrupt has entered into antecedent transactions.

Annulment under s.282(1)(b) can only be granted where the official receiver or trustee confirms that he is satisfied it is appropriate and files with the court a detailed report to this effect (r.6.207). In the absence of such report the annulment cannot be granted. Note that before the court makes the order it must generally be satisfied that the debts and costs of the bankruptcy have been paid: the provisions relating to security for bankruptcy costs and debts relate only to those which are disputed or are claimed by creditors who cannot be traced (r.6.211).

The annulment of a bankruptcy order is a matter of discretion, and the court will not make an order where the bankrupt has not, for example, complied with his obligations to the official receiver or where there has been misconduct.

Where after the annulment has been granted a trustee wants an order for his release he must make a separate fee paid application.

Discharge

3E–109   Section 279 of the Insolvency Act 1986 (as inserted by s.256, Enterprise Act 2002) provides for automatic discharge for the majority of bankrupts after one year (s.279(1)) or earlier if the official receiver files notice (see r.6.214A) that the affairs of the bankrupt do not require investigation or that such investigation has been concluded (s.279(2)) in which case the bankrupt is discharged when the notice is filed. The trustee (where one has been appointed) or a creditor may, within 28 days of receiving notice from the official receiver of his intention to file a notice under s.279(2), inform the official receiver that he objects to the proposed course of action (r.6.214A(5)). Reasons for objection must be given. The official receiver may reject the objection, he must also give reasons and the trustee or creditor may appeal (r.6.214A(5)(b) and r.7.50, Insolvency Rules 1986). Any appeal must be made within 14 days of the notification by the official receiver of his decision (r.7.50(2)). The official receiver may still apply to suspend discharge if a bankrupt fails to comply with his obligations. Section 279(3) provides that the official receiver may apply to suspend discharge until the end of a specified period or until the fulfilment of a specified condition (see also r.6.215).

The bankrupt's home

3E–110   Section 283A of the Insolvency Act 1986 (inserted by s.261, Enterprise Act 2002) introduces restrictions on the right of a trustee to realise the home of the bankrupt. Under this provision, where the bankrupt had an interest in a dwelling-house which was the sole or principal residence of the bankrupt, the bankrupt's spouse or former spouse at the date of the bankruptcy order, that interest ceases to be comprised in the bankrupt's estate at the end of three years beginning with the date of the bankruptcy and revests automatically in the bankrupt unless the trustee makes an application within the three year period or takes any of the other steps set out in the section. The three year period may be extended (s.283A(6)).

Section 313A, Insolvency Act 1986 (inserted by s.261, Enterprise Act 2002) provides that the court must dismiss an application made in respect of a low value home. What will constitute a low value home is not yet clear.

Bankruptcy Restrictions Order

3E–111

Section 257 of the Enterprise Act 2002 (headed Post-discharge restrictions) inserts a new s.281A and Sched.4A into the Insolvency Act 1986 and thereby introduces the bankruptcy restrictions order and undertaking.

The Secretary of State for Trade and Industry or the official receiver may make the application for a bankruptcy restrictions order (para. 1, Sched.4A, Insolvency Act 1986). It is made as an ordinary application in the bankruptcy and must be supported by a report setting out the conduct relied on (r.6.241). The timing of the application is crucial and it must be made before the end of one year, beginning with the commencement of the bankruptcy (*i.e.* the making of the bankruptcy order) unless the discharge period has been suspended (para. 3, Sched.4A). The application and supporting evidence must be served not more than 14 days after making the application (r.6.242(1)) and the defendant must file an acknowledgment of service indicating whether or not he contests the application not more than 14 days after service upon him (r.6.242(3)). Evidence in opposition must be filed within 28 days of service of the application and served on the Secretary of State within 3 days of filing it at the court (r.6.243(1)). The Secretary of State must file any evidence in reply within 14 days of receipt of the evidence in opposition and serve this on the bankrupt as soon as is reasonably practicable (r.6.243(2)).

A number of grounds of conduct likely to lead to the making of an order are set out in para. 2(2) of Sched.4A but these are not exhaustive. The making of an order is obligatory if the court reaches the conclusion that it is appropriate to make one having regard to the bankrupt's conduct (para. 2(1), Sched.4A). The order comes into force when it is made and may be for a period of between two and fifteen years (para. 3, Sched.4A). The Act and the Rules also allow the court to make an interim bankruptcy restrictions order (see rr.6.245 to 6.248, Insolvency Rules 1986).

A bankrupt may enter into an undertaking, which has the same effect as an order (paras 7 to 9, Sched.4A; see also r.6.249, Insolvency Rules 1986).

Appeal

3E–112

Section 375(2) provides that an appeal from a decision of a County Court or a registrar of the High Court lies to a single judge of the High Court, and an appeal from the decision of that judge is to the Court of Appeal. Paragraph 17 of the Practice Direction sets out the procedure for first and second appeals. Permission is not required for a first appeal but the appeal must be lodged within 14 days from the date of the decision. The appeal is a true appeal limited to a review of the decision of the lower court (*Vadher v. Wesigard* [1997] B.C.C. 219) and will only be allowed if the decision was wrong or unjust because of a serious procedural irregularity or other irregularity in the proceedings. Permission is required for a second appeal and will only be given where either the appeal raises an important point of principle or practice or there is some other compelling reason. Where the first decision has been given by a judge of the High Court then either his permission is required or, if he refuses, the permission of the Court of Appeal is required before the appeal can proceed.

Applications to fix an office holder's remuneration

3E–113

The Insolvency Act 1986 and the Insolvency Rules 1986 allow an office holder to apply to the court for his remuneration to be fixed. An administrator may apply (rr.2.47(6) & 2.49(1)), as may a liquidator in relation to the remuneration of a receiver (s.36(1)) or in relation to his own remuneration (rr.4.130(1)) & 4.148A(6)). The court will not generally interfere in relation to the remuneration of a receiver unless it is excessive (*Re Potters Oils (No. 2)* [1986] 1 W.L.R. 201; [1985] 1 B.C.C. 99). The remuneration of a provisional liquidator must be fixed by the court (r.4.30(1)).

The application should be made by originating or ordinary application and supported by written evidence which should include a narrative of the case, details of the work done, the charging rates and charging units applied and any matters to which the court's attention should be drawn (*e.g.* the complexity of the case, urgency, the need to continue trading, exceptional demands on the office holder and his staff, the value of the property preserved or realised, the return or projected return to creditors and others affected by the insolvency). The application should normally be made to the registrar and should generally be listed (unless very straightforward) for half an hour to one hour.

The court has a broad discretion as to how it deals with applications to fix remuneration. Following the decision in *Mirror Group Newspapers v. Maxwell* [1998] B.C.C. 301 the practice of the court is to subject applications for remuneration to detailed scrutiny. The registrar will generally dispose of applications for remuneration up to £50,000, may deal himself with applications for remuneration up to £100,000, and may refer applications for remuneration in excess of £100,000 to a costs judge for a report. The costs judge will give directions to enable him to report to the registrar who will, on receipt of the report, fix a date for its consideration. A copy of the costs judge's report will be sent to the office holder's legal advisors to enable them to make submissions to the registrar at the final hearing: the report of the costs judge is a report to the court and is not binding on it. The court may also refer the application to the judge who may hear it alone or with assessors (*Re Independent Insurance Co Ltd* [2002] EWHC 1577 (Ch); [2002] 2 B.C.L.C 709 and *Re Independent Insurance Co Ltd (No.2)* [2003] EWHC 51 (Ch); [2003] 1 B.C.L.C. 640). Where remuneration is to be fixed periodically in relation to long-running insolvencies the court may order payments on account subject to claw-back provisions when the costs judge makes his final report. The court will not as a general rule make blanket orders for remuneration at the office holder's "usual rates".

Detailed guidance on office holders' remuneration is contained in the Report (July 1998), Statement of Insolvency Practice 9 (Recovery Professionals) and the Practice Statement—The Fixing and Approval of the Remuneration of Appointees (2004) the text of which is reproduced below.

PRACTICE STATEMENT—THE FIXING AND APPROVAL OF THE REMUNERATION OF APPOINTEES (2004)

Part One

General

3E-114   **1. Definitions and Interpretation**

1.1 In this Practice Statement:

   (1) "appointee" means:

   (i) a provisional liquidator appointed under Section 135 of the Insolvency Act;

   (ii) a special manager appointed under Section 177 or Section 370 of the Insolvency Act;

   (iii) a liquidator appointed by the members of a company or partnership or by the creditors of a company or partnership or by the Secretary of State pursuant to Section 137 of the Insolvency Act, or by the court pursuant to Section 140 of the Insolvency Act;

   (iv) an administrator of a company appointed to manage the property, business and affairs of that company under the Insolvency Act or other enactment and to which the provisions of the Insolvency Act are applicable;

   (v) a trustee in bankruptcy (other than the Official Receiver) appointed under the Insolvency Act;

   (vi) a nominee or supervisor of a voluntary arrangement under Part I or Part VIII of the Insolvency Act;

   (vii) a licensed insolvency practitioner appointed by the court pursuant to Section 273 of the Insolvency Act;

       (viii) an interim receiver appointed by the court pursu-
            ant to Section 286 of the Insolvency Act;

  (2) "appointment" means the appointment as an appointee;

  (3) "assessor" means a person appointed in accordance with
      Rule 35.15 of the CPR;

  (4) "CPR" means the Civil Procedure Rules 1998 (as amend-
      ed);

  (5) "the court" means the court exercising jurisdiction in re-
      spect of the appointment in accordance with the Insol-
      vency Act and the Insolvency Rules or other relevant
      enactment and/or applicable rules;

  (6) "the guiding principles" means the statements of
      principle contained in paragraph 3.4;

  (7) "Insolvency Act" means the Insolvency Act 1986 (as
      amended);

  (8) "Insolvency Rules" means the Insolvency Rules 1986 (as
      amended);

  (9) "the objective" means the objective stated in paragraph
      3.2.

1.2 References to paragraphs are references to paragraphs of this
Practice Statement.

2. Applicability

3E–115

2.1 This Practice Statement shall, save to the extent and as may
otherwise be ordered by the court, apply to all appointees in respect
of:

  (1) any application to the court by an appointee for the fix-
      ing and approval of his remuneration where his remu-
      neration has not otherwise already been fixed and ap-
      proved;

  (2) any application to the court by an appointee for the fix-
      ing and approval of his remuneration in circumstances
      where he considers that the amount of his remuneration
      as fixed and approved by resolution of the members of
      the partnership or company or the creditors' committee
      or the liquidation committee or by resolution of the gen-
      eral body of creditors (as appropriate) is insufficient;

  (3) any application by a person who may be permitted to
      apply under the Insolvency Act, the Insolvency Rules, or
      otherwise including by reference to the jurisdiction of
      the court to supervise the conduct of one of its officers
      and the inherent jurisdiction of the Supreme Court and
      is dissatisfied with the remuneration of an appointee that
      has otherwise been fixed and approved on the basis that
      such remuneration is excessive.

2.2 This Practice Statement shall come into effect on 1 October
2004 and shall apply to all applications for the fixing and approval of
the remuneration of an appointee issued after that date.

3. The Objective and the Guiding Principles

3E–116

3.1 This Practice Statement is supplemental to the Insolvency
Act, the Insolvency Rules and such other enactments or rules as have

been or may be introduced and which are relevant to the fixing and approval of the remuneration of an appointee.

3.2 The objective of this Practice Statement is to ensure that the remuneration of an appointee which is fixed and approved by the court is fair, reasonable and commensurate with the nature and extent of the work properly undertaken by the appointee in any given case and is fixed and approved by reference to a process which is consistent and predictable.

3.3 Set out below are the guiding principles by reference to which applications for the fixing and approval of the remuneration of appointees are to be considered both by applicants, in the preparation and presentation of their application, and by the court which is required to determine such applications.

3.4 The guiding principles are as follows:

(1) "Justification": It is for the appointee who seeks to be remunerated at a particular level and/or in a particular manner to justify his claim and in order to do so the appointee should be prepared to provide full particulars of the basis for and the nature of his claim for remuneration.

(2) "The benefit of the doubt": The corollary of guiding principle (1) is that on any application for the fixing and approval of the remuneration of an appointee, if after considering the evidence before it and after having regard to the guiding principles (in particular guiding principle (3)), the matters contained in paragraph 5.2 (in particular paragraph 5.2(10)) and the matters referred to in paragraph 5.3 (as appropriate) there remains any element of doubt as to the appropriateness, fairness or reasonableness of the amount sought to be fixed and approved (whether arising from a lack of particularity as to the basis for and the nature of the appointee's claim to remuneration or otherwise) such element of doubt should be resolved by the court against the appointee.

(3) "Professional integrity": The court should give weight to the fact that the appointee is a member of a regulated profession (where such is the case) and as such is subject to rules and guidance as to professional conduct and (where such is the case) the fact that the appointee is an officer of the court.

(4) "The value of the service rendered": the remuneration of an appointee should reflect and should be fixed and approved so as to reward the value of the service rendered by the appointee, not simply to reimburse the appointee in respect of time expended and cost incurred.

(5) "Fair and reasonable": the amount of the remuneration to be fixed and approved by the court should be fair and reasonable and represent fair and reasonable remuneration for the work properly undertaken or to be undertaken.

(6) "Proportionality":

  (i) "proportionality of information": in considering the nature and extent of the information which should be provided by an appointee in respect of an application for the fixing and approval of his remuneration the court, the appointee and any other parties to the application shall have regard to what is proportionate by reference to the amount of remuneration to be fixed and approved, the nature, complexity and extent of the work to be completed (where the application relates to future remuneration) or that has been completed by the appointee and the value and nature of the assets and liabilities with which the appointee will have to deal or has had to deal;

  (ii) "proportionality of remuneration": the amount of remuneration to be fixed and approved by the court should be proportional to the nature, complexity and extent of the work to be completed (where the application relates to future remuneration) or that has been completed by the appointee and the value and nature of the assets and/or potential assets and the liabilities and/or potential liabilities with which the appointee will have to deal or has had to deal, the nature and degree of the responsibility to which the appointee has been subject in any given case, the nature and extent of the risk (if any) assumed by the appointee and the efficiency (in respect of both time and cost) with which the appointee has completed the work undertaken;

(7) "Professional guidance": In respect of an application for the fixing and approval of the remuneration of an appointee, the appointee may have regard to the relevant and current statements of practice promulgated by any relevant regulatory and professional bodies in relation to the fixing and approval of the remuneration of an appointee. In considering an application for the fixing or approval of the remuneration of an appointee, the court may also have regard to such statements of practice and the extent of compliance with such statements of practice by the appointee.

(8) "Impracticability": where the appointee has not, either upon or shortly after the commencement of his appointment, sought to have the basis upon which his remuneration is to be fixed approved by the members of the partnership or the company, the creditors' committee, the liquidation committee or the general body of creditors (as appropriate) and in circumstances where the appointee considers that it will be impracticable to have his remuneration fixed and/or approved in such a manner,

1221

he may, as soon as reasonably practicable after his appointment, apply to the court to have the basis upon which he is to be remunerated fixed and for directions as to the manner in which his remuneration is to be approved (which may include provision for payments to be made on account). In circumstances where such an application may be made, to the extent that such an application is not made but the appointee subsequently makes an application to the court for the fixing and approval of the whole or any part of his remuneration, an explanation as to why no earlier application was made shall be provided to the court.

Part Two

The Fixing and Approval of Remuneration

3E–117 **4. Distribution of Business**

4.1 All applications for the fixing and approval of the remuneration of an appointee shall in the first instance (unless otherwise ordered by the court, having regard to the particular circumstances of an application) be made, where the court is the High Court to a Registrar or a District Judge in the appropriate District Registry of the High Court or, where the court is a County Court, a District Judge in the appropriate County Court.

4.2 On the hearing of the application the court shall consider the evidence then available to it and may either summarily determine the application or adjourn it giving such directions as it thinks appropriate. Such directions may include a direction that:

(1) an assessor or a Costs Judge prepare a report to the court in respect of the remuneration which is sought to be fixed and approved; and/or

(2) the application be heard by the Registrar or the District Judge sitting with or without an assessor or a Costs Judge or by a Judge sitting with or without an assessor or a Costs Judge.

4.3 In the usual course an application for the fixing and approval of the remuneration of an appointee should be determined by a Registrar or a District Judge sitting without an assessor or a Costs Judge and without the need for a report from an assessor or a Costs Judge.

4.4 The court may give the directions referred to in paragraphs 4.2(1) and (2) where it considers this to be appropriate having regard to the size and complexity of the case or in the event that the application gives rise to complicated issues of fact or of law. The court ought only to make an order for the involvement of a Costs Judge in circumstances where it considers the involvement of an assessor is (for whatever reason) not appropriate and that the application can only properly be determined by reference to the particular expertise and assistance that can be provided by a Costs Judge.

4.5 A list of suitably qualified persons appointed by the court to act as assessors in respect of applications for the fixing and approval of the remuneration of an appointee is available from the court.

4.6 The reasonable costs of an assessor appointed by the court shall be paid from the assets under the control of the appointee.

5. Relevant Criteria and Procedure 3E–118

5.1 When considering an application for the fixing and approval of the remuneration of an appointee the court shall have regard to the objective, the guiding principles and all relevant circumstances including the matters referred to in paragraph 5.2 and where appropriate paragraph 5.3, each of which should be addressed in the evidence placed before the court.

5.2 On any application for the fixing and approval of the remuneration of an appointee, the appointee should:

(1) Provide a narrative description and explanation of:

(i) the background to, the relevant circumstances of and the reasons for the appointment;

(ii) the work undertaken or to be undertaken in respect of the appointment and in respect of which work the remuneration of the appointee is sought to be fixed and approved, which description should be divided, insofar as possible, into individual tasks or categories of task. General descriptions of work, tasks, or categories of task should (insofar as possible) be avoided;

(iii) the reasons why it is or was considered reasonable and/or necessary and/or beneficial for such work to be conducted, giving details of why particular tasks or categories of task were undertaken and why such tasks or categories of task are to be undertaken or have been undertaken by particular individuals and in a particular manner;

(iv) the amount of time to be spent or that has been spent in respect of work to be completed or that has been completed and in respect of which the fixing and approval of remuneration is sought and which it is considered is fair, reasonable and proportionate;

(v) what is likely to be and has been achieved, the benefits that are likely to and have accrued as a consequence of the work that is to be or has been completed, the manner in which the work required in respect of the appointment is progressing and what, in the opinion of the appointee, remains to be achieved.

(2) Provide details sufficient for the court to determine the application by reference to the criteria which is required to be taken into account by reference to the Insolvency Rules and any other applicable enactments or rules relevant to the fixing and approval of the remuneration of an appointee.

(3) Provide a statement of the total number of hours of work undertaken or to be undertaken in respect of which the

INSOLVENCY

fixing and approval of remuneration is sought, together with a breakdown of such hours by individual member of staff and individual tasks or categories of tasks to be performed or that have been performed. Details should also be given of:

(i) the tasks or categories of tasks to be undertaken as a proportion of the total amount of work to be undertaken in respect of which the fixing and approval of remuneration is sought and the tasks or categories of tasks that have been undertaken as a proportion of the total amount of work that has been undertaken in respect of which the fixing and approval of remuneration is sought; and

(ii) the tasks or categories of task to be completed by individual members of staff or grade of personnel including the appointee as a proportion of the total amount of work to be completed by all members of staff including the appointee in respect of which the fixing and approval of remuneration is sought, or the tasks or categories of task that have been completed by individual members of staff or grade of personnel as a proportion of the total amount of work that has been completed by all members of staff including the appointee in respect of which the fixing and approval of remuneration is sought.

(4) Provide a statement of the total amount to be charged for the work to be undertaken or that has been undertaken in respect of which the fixing and approval of remuneration is sought which should include:

(i) a breakdown of such amounts by individual member of staff and individual task or categories of task performed;

(ii) details of the time expended and the remuneration charged in respect of each individual task or category of task as a proportion (respectively) of the total time expended and the total remuneration charged.

In respect of an application pursuant to which the amount of the appointee's remuneration is to be fixed and approved on the basis of a percentage of the value of the assets realised and/or distributed, the appointee shall provide (for the purposes of comparison) the same details as are required by this paragraph (4), but on the basis of what would have been charged had he been seeking remuneration on the basis of the time properly spent by him and his staff.

(5) Provide details of each individual to be engaged or who has been engaged in work in respect of the appointment and in respect of which the fixing and approval of remuneration is sought, including details of their relevant ex-

perience, training, qualifications and the level of their seniority.

(6) Provide an explanation of:

 (i) the steps, if any, to be taken or that have been taken by the appointee to avoid duplication of effort and cost in respect of the work to be completed or that has been completed in respect of which the fixing and approval of the remuneration is sought; and

 (ii) the steps to be taken or that have been taken to ensure that the work to be completed or that has been completed is to be or was undertaken by individuals of appropriate experience and seniority relative to the nature of the work to be or that has been undertaken.

(7) Provide details of the individual rates charged by the appointee and members of his staff in respect of the work to be completed or that has been completed and in respect of which the remuneration is sought to be fixed and approved. Such details should include:

 (i) a general explanation of the policy adopted in relation to the fixing or calculation of such rates;

 (ii) in relation to charges in respect of secretarial, administrative and cashiering services (and/or such other charges as might also otherwise be regarded as an overhead cost forming a component part of the rates charged by the appointee and members of his staff), an explanation as to why (where this is the case) such costs are to be or have been charged for separately together with confirmation that where such work is to be or has been charged for separately such work will not or has not also been charged for as part of the rates that are to be or have been charged by the appointee and/or members of his staff;

(8) Where the application for the fixing and approval of remuneration is in respect of a period of time during which the charge out rates of the appointee and/or members of his staff engaged in work in respect of the appointment have increased, provide an explanation of the nature, extent and reason for such increase and the date when such increase took effect. This paragraph (8) does not apply to applications to which paragraph 5.3 applies.

(9) Provide details of any remuneration previously fixed and approved in relation to the appointment (whether by the court or otherwise) including in particular the amounts that were previously sought to be fixed and approved and the amounts that were in fact fixed and approved and the basis upon which such amounts were fixed and approved.

INSOLVENCY

(10) In order that the court may be able to consider the views of those persons which the appointee considers have an interest in the assets that are under his control, provide details of:

(i) what (if any) consultation has taken place between the appointee and those persons and if no such consultation has taken place an explanation should be given as to the reason why; and

(ii) the number and value of the interests of the persons consulted including details of the proportion (by number and by value) of the interests of such persons by reference to the entirety of those persons having an interest in the assets under the control of the appointee.

(11) Provide such other relevant information as the appointee considers, in the circumstances, ought to be provided to the court.

5.3 This paragraph applies to applications where the remuneration of the appointee is to be fixed and approved on the basis of a percentage of the value of the assets realised and/or distributed. On such applications in addition to the matters referred to in paragraph 5.2 (as applicable) the appointee shall:

(1) Provide a full description of the basis of and reasons for his remuneration being sought to be fixed and approved by reference to a percentage of the value of the assets realised and/or distributed.

(2) Provide a full explanation of the basis upon which the percentage rates to be applied to the values of the assets realised and/or distributed have been chosen.

(3) Provide a statement that to the best of the appointee's belief the percentage rates which are sought to be applied are similar to the percentage rates that are applied or have been applied in respect of other appointments of a similar nature.

(4) By reference to the matters contained in paragraph 5.2 (as applicable), provide a comparison of the amount to be charged by reference to a percentage of the value of the assets realised and/or distributed and an estimate of the amount that would otherwise have been charged if the remuneration was to be fixed by reference to the time properly given by him and his staff.

(5) Provide a comparison between the amounts to be charged by reference to a percentage of the value of the assets realised and/or distributed using the percentage rates sought to be fixed and approved by the court and the percentage rates provided for by the scale of fees referred to in Schedule 6 to the Insolvency Rules.

5.4 If and insofar as any of the matters referred to in paragraph 5.2 or 5.3 (as appropriate) are not addressed in the evidence placed before the court on the hearing of an application for the fixing and approval of the remuneration of an appointee an explanation for why this is the case should be included in such evidence.

5.5 Notwithstanding that the expenses and disbursements of the appointee and his staff are not required to be approved by the court on any application by the appointee for the fixing and approval of his remuneration, a summary of the amount and nature of such expenses and disbursements incurred during the relevant period should be provided as should an explanation of the steps taken by the appointee to subject such expenses and disbursements to critical scrutiny.

5.6 There should be included in the evidence placed before the court by the appointee in respect of any application for the fixing and approval of the remuneration of an appointee the following documents:

(1) A copy of the most recent receipts and payments account;

(2) Copies of any reports by the appointee to the persons having an interest in the assets under his control relevant to the period for which the remuneration sought to be fixed and approved relates;

(3) Schedules or such other representations of the information referred to in paragraphs 5.2 and 5.3 such as are likely to be of assistance to the court in fixing and approving the remuneration of the appointee.

(4) Evidence of consultation with those persons having an interest in the assets under the control of appointee in relation to the fixing and approval of the remuneration of the appointee.

5.7 On any application for the fixing and approval of remuneration of an appointee the court may make an order permitting payments of remuneration to be made on account subject to final approval whether by the court or otherwise.

5.8 Unless otherwise ordered by the court (or as may otherwise be provided for in any enactment or rules of procedure) the costs of and occasioned by an application for the fixing and/or approval of the remuneration of an appointee shall be paid from the assets under the control of the appointee.

Chief Bankruptcy Registrar
Royal Courts of Justice, Strand, London, WC2A 2LL
15 July 2004

PRACTICE NOTE ON THE HEARING OF INSOLVENCY PROCEEDINGS

The following statement was issued by the Vice-Chancellor.

3E–119

This Practice Note supersedes all previous Practice Statements of the Bankruptcy Registrars dealing with jurisdiction and work distribution and the Guidelines issued by the Insolvency Court Users' Committee in November 1988.

As a general rule all petitions, claims and applications (except for those listed in paragraph 4 below) should be listed for initial hearing before a registrar or district judge in accordance with rule 7.6(2) Insolvency Rules 1986.

The following applications should always be listed before a judge:

Proceedings relating to insolvent companies
- applications for committal for contempt
- applications for an administration order
- applications for an injunction
- applications for the appointment of a provisional liquidator
- interim applications and applications for directions or case management after any proceedings have been referred or adjourned to the judge (except where liberty to apply to the registrar or district judge has been given);

Proceedings relating to insolvent individuals
- applications for committal for contempt
- applications for an injunction
- interim applications and applications for directions or case management after any proceedings have been referred or adjourned to the judge (except where liberty to apply to the registrar or district judge has been given).

When deciding whether to hear proceedings themselves or refer or adjourn them to the judge, the registrar or district judge should have regard to the following factors:

- the complexity of the proceedings
- whether the proceedings raise new or controversial points of law
- the likely date and length of the hearing
- public interest in the proceedings
- the availability in the court which is likely to hear the proceedings of relevant specialist expertise.

Litigants and their advisors are reminded that paragraph 17 of the Practice Direction on Insolvency Proceedings applies to appeals and that an appeal from a registrar, district judge or County Court judge lies, in the first instance and without permission, to a single judge of the High Court.

23rd May 2005

3F   PERSONAL INJURY

Contents

Introduction

Personal Injury Litigation forms a significant percentage of the work of the civil   **3F-1**
courts. This Section includes materials which will be of special use to practitioners in
this important area. Of course, the CPR apply to all types of litigation and this Section
therefore supplements the rules and commentary in Vol. 1. The CPR heralded a major change of direction for the adversarial system. Litigation is not the first option but
is to be resorted to because there is no alternative. Thus the Pre-Action Protocol for
Personal Injury Claims (C2–001) and the Pre-Action Protocol for Resolution of Clinical Disputes (C3–001) are the most widely used of the pre-action protocols.

A number of rules in the CPR make special provision for personal injury cases.
These include:

r.2.3(1)—definition of "claim for personal injuries"

r.16.3(3)—pleading requirement for "statement of value"

PD16, para. 4—pleading requirements for PI claims, including the requirement to
attach a medical report to the Particulars of Claim where the claimant is relying on the
evidence of a medical practitioner

PD16, para. 5—pleading requirements for Fatal Accident Act cases

r.26.6—different financial values in PI cases for purpose of allocation to track

Part 41—Provisional Damages

In addition the following rules, though not confined to PI cases, are often
encountered:

Part 25.1—Interim Remedies

PD25B—Interim Payments

PD26, para. 12.4—Disposal Hearings

Part 28—The Fast Track (most fast track cases are PI cases)

r.31.6—standard disclosure

r.31.16—pre-action disclosure

Part 35—Expert Evidence

Part 36—Offers to Settle and Payments into Court

Part 41 Section II—the courts powers to order periodical payments in PI cases

There are relatively few rules that have no application at all to PI cases. Thus Parts
not specifically mentioned here should be referred to as the need arises.

In addition to statutes thought to be of particular use to PI practitioners this Section includes the Rehabilitation Code of Practice. Rehabilitation is a welcome development and is something to be considered in all cases. It is of particular importance where the claimant has suffered serious injury. Rehabilitation concentrates on assessing the claimant's needs (including medical treatment) and for the defendant's insurers to meet the cost of providing them at an early stage. This marks a departure from thinking of claims solely in terms of money. Successful rehabilitation provides both a quicker and better outcome for the claimant and a lower cost for insurers. The Code provides a framework supported by all the main associations for insurers and PI lawyers in the UK. Note that the Rehabilitation Protocol now formally forms part of the Personal Injury Pre-Action protocol.

Material relevant to Personal Injury located elsewhere in this work

Access to Health Records Act 1990

3F–3   (1990 c.23)

ARRANGEMENT OF SECTIONS

General Note

3F–4   *The Access to Health Records Act 1990 came into force on 1st November 1991.*

The practical application of the parts of this Act included here, following the modifications introduced by the Data Protection Act 1998 is to enable the obtaining of the health records (as defined in s.1) of (in Scotland) persons who lack capacity, and more generally in relation to the medical records of deceased persons (where the application may be made by the Personal Representative of the Deceased or any person having a claim arising from the Deceased's death. The categories of persons entitled to apply under this Act were restricted in favour of the general personal data access regime contained in the Data Protection Act 1998, but use of the Access to Health Records Act 1990 may still be required for the two categories of application just referred to. Only the sections of direct relevance to personal injury claims are set out here.

Obtaining medical records: the 1990 Act and the Data Protection Act 1998

3F–5   In general patients (in the non-CPR sense of that term) have a right to have copies of their medical records, but in exceptional circumstances the law allows for records to be withheld. The Data Protection Act 1998 (most cases) and the Access to Health Records Act 1990 (in the two situations referred to in the preceding note) set out the legal code which applies, but in practice what is required in the first instance is to contact the medical professional concerned or to the Medical Records section or department in the case of larger institutions such as hospitals. The Clinical Disputes protocol at C3–001 in this work contains further information and pro-forma documents to assist. See also Health Service Circular HSC 2000/009 on the topic of patient information. A strictly limited fee may be charged for providing copies, under the provisions of the Data Protection Act 1998. (For a note on fees see the notes to section 4 below).

Disclosure of medical records under the 1990 Act may be refused on the basis set out in s.5.[1]

Medical Reports prepared for insurers/employers—Access to Medical Records Act 1988

For the law relating to access to medical reports prepared on behalf of insurers or employers, see s.1 of the Access to Medical Reports Act 1988 which states: **3F–6**

"It shall be the right of an individual to have access, in accordance with the provisions of this Act, to any medical report relating to the individual which is to be, or has been, supplied by a medical practitioner for employment purposes or insurance purposes".

That Act thus allows patients to obtain access to reports for insurers or employers and provides for the patient to ask for amendments. The patient can require that his/her own comments are appended if the report is not corrected. The Act also requires the patient's consent before any information is released to a third party in the context of reports requested by insurers or employers. The patient must be provided with the report before it is sent if the patient so wishes and the patient also has a right to refuse consent for the provision of a report.

Disclosure by doctor to own legal advisers

Note that there is some authority to the effect that a doctor who discloses a patient's **3F–7** medical records to his own solicitors, for the purpose of seeking legal advice as to whether the doctor is obliged to disclose the records in the course of litigation brought by the patient against him, does not thereby act in breach of the Data Protection legislation or the Access to Health Records Act 1990, or the general law of confidentiality (*Matthew Yeboah Mensah v. Robert H Jones* [2004] EWHC 2699 (Ch.D)). It was held that the disclosure was necessary to allow the doctor to obtain legal advice as to the extent of his obligation to make disclosure.

Relevant Pre-action Protocols

See the Protocol for the Resolution of Clinical Disputes in Vol. 1 of this work at C3– **3F–8** 001 and the Protocol for Obtaining Hospital Records at C3–019.

Definitions

"health record" "patient" "holder" see s.1 **3F–9**
"health professional" see s.2
"care" "general practitoner" "Health Authority" "Health Board" "health service
body" "information" "make" "Primary Care Trust" "Special Health
Authority" "Strategic Health Authority" see s.11

"Health record" and related expressions

1.—(1) In this Act "health record" means a record which— **3F–10**

(a) consists of information relating to the physical or mental
health of an individual who can be identified from that

---

[1] Similarly under the Data Protection Act 1998 a record holder may refuse to supply records if he/she believes that disclosure of the contents may have an adverse affect on the patient's health (Data Protection (Subject Access Modification) (Health) Order 2000 (S.I. 2000 No. 413)), or may identify a third party (Data Protection Act 1998 s.7(4)). Under the 1998 Act refusal is permitted if copying requires "disproportionate effort" for which see the provisions of the Data Protection (Conditions under Paragraph 3 of Part II of Schedule 1) Order 2000, (S.I. 2000 No. 185).

information, or from that and other information in the possession of the holder of the record; and

(b) has been made by or on behalf of a health professional in connection with the care of that individual;

[...]

(2) In this Act "holder", in relation to a health record, means—

(a) in the case of a record made by a health professional performing primary medical services under a general medical services contract made with a Primary Care Trust or Local Health Board, the person or body who entered into the contract with the Trust or Board (or, in a case where more than one person so entered into the contract, any such person);

(aa) in the case of a record made by a health professional performing such services in accordance with arrangements under section 28C of that Act with a Primary Care Trust, Strategic Health Authority or Local Health Board, the person or body which made the arrangements with the Trust, Authority or Board (or, in a case where more than one person so made the arrangements, any such person);

(b) in the case of a record made by a health professional for purposes connected with the provision of health services by a health service body (and not falling within paragraph (aa) above), the health service body by which or on whose behalf the record is held;

(c) in any other case, the health professional by whom or on whose behalf the record is held.

(3) In this Act "patient", in relation to a health record, means the individual in connection with whose care the record has been made.

Amendments

3F–11   Amended by the Data Protection Act 1998, s.74; and the Health and Social Care (Community Health and Standards) Act 2003, Sched.11, para. 57.

Note that subss.2(a) and 2(aa) were substituted for the previous words by the Health and Social Care (Community Health and Standards) Act 2003, Sched.11, para. 57.

Note

3F–12   Note that by subs.(3) the definition of "patient" is in wider terms than that under the Civil Procedure Rules and is closer to the conventional usage. For rights of access to medical reports prepared for insurers or employers as opposed to medical records, see the note Medical Reports prepared for insurers/employers—Access to Medical Records Act 1988 above.

Disclosure of another person's medical records to own legal advisers

3F–13   See *Matthew Yeboah Mensah v. Robert H Jones* [2004] EWHC 2699 where it was held that the 1990 Act could not impose on the respondent any obligation to obtain a court order before sending the applicant's health records to his solicitor for the purpose of obtaining legal advice on disclosure obligations.

Health professionals

3F–14   **2.** [In this Act "health professional" has the same meaning as in the Data Protection Act 1998].

Amendments

Text in square brackets substituted by Data Protection Act (1998 c.29), Sched.15 **3F–15**
para. 11.

"health professional"

The full definition of "health professional" given by s.69 of the Data Protection Act **3F–16**
1998 is as follows:

"**69.**—(1) In this Act "health professional" means any of the following— **3F–17**
    (a) a registered medical practitioner,
    (b) a registered dentist as defined by section 53(1) of the Dentists Act 1984,
    (bb) a Primary Care Trust established under section 16A of that Act,
    (bbb) a Local Health Board established under section 16BA of that Act,
    (c) a registered optician as defined by section 36(1) of the Opticians Act 1989,
    (d) a registered pharmaceutical chemist as defined by section 24(1) of the Pharmacy Act 1954 or a registered person as defined by Article 2(2) of the Pharmacy (Northern Ireland) Order 1976,
    (e) a registered nurse, midwife or health visitor,
    (f) a registered osteopath as defined by section 41 of the Osteopaths Act 1993,
    [(fa) an NHS foundation Trust,]
    (g) a registered chiropractor as defined by section 43 of the Chiropractors Act 1994,
    (h) any person who is registered as a member of a profession to which the Professions Supplementary to Medicine Act 1960 for the time being extends,
    (i) a clinical psychologist, child psychotherapist or speech therapist,
    (j) a music therapist employed by a health service body, and
    (k) a scientist employed by such a body as head of a department.

(2) In subsection (1)(a) "registered medical practitioner" includes any person who is provisionally registered under section 15 or 21 of the Medical Act 1983 and is engaged in such employment as is mentioned in subsection (3) of that section.

(3) In subsection (1) "health service body" means —
    (a) a Health Authority established under section 8 of the National Health Service Act 1977,
    (b) a Special Health Authority established under section 11 of that Act,
    (c) a Health Board within the meaning of the National Health Service (Scotland) Act 1978,
    (d) a Special Health Board within the meaning of that Act,
    (e) the managers of a State Hospital provided under section 102 of that Act,
    (f) a National Health Service trust first established under section 5 of the National Health Service and Community Care Act 1990 or section 12A of the National Health Service (Scotland) Act 1978,
    (g) a Health and Social Services Board established under Article 16 of the Health and Personal Social Services (Northern Ireland) Order 1972,
    (h) a special health and social services agency established under the Health and Personal Social Services (Special Agencies) (Northern Ireland) Order 1990, or
    (i) a Health and Social Services trust established under Article 10 of the Health and Personal Social Services (Northern Ireland) Order 1991".

Note: the text in square brackets was added by the Health and Social Care (Com- **3F–18**
munity Health and Standards) Act (2003 c.43) Sched.4 para. 107.

Right of access to health records

3.—(1) An application for access to a health record, or to any part **3F–19**
of a health record, may be made to the holder of the record by any
of the following, namely— [...]

[(ee) where the record is held in Scotland and the patient is incapable, within the meaning of the Adults with Incapacity (Scotland) Act 2000 (asp 4) in relation to making or authorising the application, any person entitled to act on behalf of the patient under that Act.]

(f) where the patient has died, the patient's personal representative and any person who may have a claim arising out of the patient's death.

(2) Subject to section 4 below, where an application is made under subsection (1) above the holder shall, within the requisite period, give access to the record, or the part of a record, to which the application relates—

(a) in the case of a record, by allowing the applicant to inspect the record or, where section 5 below applies, an extract setting out so much of the record as is not excluded by that section;

(b) in the case of a part of a record, by allowing the applicant to inspect an extract setting out that part or, where that section applies, so much of that part as is not so excluded; or

(c) in either case, if the applicant so requires, by supplying him with a copy of the record or extract.

(3) Where any information contained in a record or extract which is so allowed to be inspected, or a copy of which is so supplied, is expressed in terms which are not intelligible without explanation, an explanation of those terms shall be provided with the record or extract, or supplied with the copy.

(4) No fee shall be required for giving access under subsection (2) above other than the following, namely—

(a) where access is given to a record, or part of a record, none of which was made after the beginning of the period of 40 days immediately preceding the date of the application, a fee not exceeding such maximum as may be prescribed for the purposes of this section by regulations under section 7 of the Data Protection Act 1998; and

(b) where a copy of a record or extract is supplied to the applicant, a fee not exceeding the cost of making the copy and (where applicable) the cost of posting it to him.

(5) For the purposes of subsection (2) above the requisite period is—

(a) where the application relates to a record, or part of a record, none of which was made before the beginning of the period of 40 days immediately preceding the date of the application, the period of 21 days beginning with that date;

(b) in any other case, the period of 40 days beginning with that date.

(6) Where—

(a) an application under subsection (1) above does not

1234

contain sufficient information to enable the holder of the record to identify the patient or, to satisfy himself that the applicant is entitled to make the application; and

(b) within the period of 14 days beginning with the date of the application, the holder of the record requests the applicant to furnish him with such further information as he may reasonably require for that purpose,

subsection (5) above shall have effect as if for any reference to that date there were substituted a reference to the date on which that further information is so furnished.

Amendments

Text omitted in square brackets repealed by Data Protection Act 1998.   **3F–20**

The intention appears to have been to insert s.3(1)(ee) by Adults with Incapacity (Scotland) Act (2000 ASP.4), Sched.5 para. 21 (which in fact refers to s.3(3)(ee)).

Note

For a summary of the other principal rights of access to medical records and **3F–21** reports see the General Note above.

Fees

For the fees which may be charged by order under s.7 of the Data Protection Act **3F–22** 1998, applied to this section by subs.(4) see the Data Protection (Subject Access) (Fees and Miscellaneous Provisions) Regulations 2000 (S.I. 2000 No. 191) as amended by the Data Protection (Subject Access) (Fees and Miscellaneous Provisions) (Amendment) Regulations 2001 (S.I. 2001 No. 3223), and as substituted by the Secretary of State for Constitutional Affairs Order (S.I. 2003 No. 1887) Sched.2 para. 9 (1)(a).

Cases where right of access may be wholly excluded

4. [...]   **3F–23**

(3) Where an application is made under subsection (1)(f) of section 3 above, access shall not be given under subsection (2) of that section if the record includes a note, made at the patient's request, that he did not wish access to be given on such an application.

Amendments

Text omitted in square brackets repealed by Data Protection Act (1998 c.29), **3F–24** Sched.16(I) para. 1.

Cases where right of access may be partially excluded

5.—(1) Access shall not be given under section 3(2) above to any **3F–25** part of a health record—

(a) which, in the opinion of the holder of the record, would disclose—

    (i) information likely to cause serious harm to the physical or mental health of any individual; or

    (ii) information relating to or provided by an individual, other than the patient, who could be identified from that information; or

(b) which was made before the commencement of this Act.

(2) Subsection (1)(a)(ii) above shall not apply—

    (a) where the individual concerned has consented to the application; or

    (b) where that individual is a health professional who has been involved in the care of the patient;

and subsection (1)(b) above shall not apply where and to the extent that, in the opinion of the holder of the record, the giving of access is necessary in order to make intelligible any part of the record to which access is required to be given under section 3(2) above.

(3) [Access shall not be given under section 3(2) to any part of a health record] which, in the opinion of the holder of the record, would disclose—

    (a) information provided by the patient in the expectation that it would not be disclosed to the applicant; or

    (b) information obtained as a result of any examination or investigation to which the patient consented in the expectation that the information would not be so disclosed.

(4) Where an application is made under subsection (1)(f) of section 3 above, access shall not be given under subsection (2) of that section to any part of the record which, in the opinion of the holder of the record, would disclose information which is not relevant to any claim which may arise out of the patient's death.

(5) The Secretary of State may by regulations provide that, in such circumstances as may be prescribed by the regulations, access shall not be given under section 3(2) above to any part of a health record which satisfies such conditions as may be so prescribed.

Amendments

3F–26   Words in square brackets in subs.(3) substituted by the Data Protection Act (1998 c.29), Sched.15 para. 13.

Orders under this section

3F–27   See the Access to Health Records (Control of Access) Regulations 1993 (S.I. 1993 No. 746) in relation to non-disclosure of information showing that an identifiable individual was, or may have been, born in consequence of treatment services within the meaning of the Human Fertilisation and Embryology Act 1990.

Note

3F–28   For information concerning the (similar) limitations on disclosure under theData Protection Act 1998 see Obtaining Medical Records: the 1990 Act and the Data Protection Act 1998 under the General Note above.

Correction of inaccurate health records

3F–29   6.—(1) Where a person considers that any information contained in a health record, or any part of a health record, to which he has been given access under section 3(2) above is inaccurate, he may apply to the holder of the record for the necessary correction to be made.

(2) On an application under subsection (1) above, the holder of the record shall—

    (a) if he is satisfied that the information is inaccurate, make the necessary correction;

    (b) if he is not so satisfied, make in the part of the record in which the information is contained a note of the matters in respect of which the information is considered by the applicant to be inaccurate; and

    (c) in either case, without requiring any fee, supply the applicant with a copy of the correction or note.

(3) In this section "inaccurate" means incorrect, misleading or incomplete.

* * * *

Applications to the court

8.—(1) Subject to subsection (2) below, where the court is satisfied, **3F–30** on an application made by the person concerned within such period as may be prescribed by rules of court, that the holder of a health record has failed to comply with any requirement of this Act, the court may order the holder to comply with that requirement.

(2) The court shall not entertain an application under subsection (1) above unless it is satisfied that the applicant has taken all such steps to secure compliance with the requirement as may be prescribed by regulations made by the Secretary of State.

(3) For the purposes of subsection (2) above, the Secretary of State may by regulations require the holders of health records to make such arrangements for dealing with complaints that they have failed to comply with any requirements of this Act as may be prescribed by the regulations.

(4) For the purpose of determining any question whether an applicant is entitled to be given access under section 3(2) above to any health record, or any part of a health record, the court—

(a) may require the record or part to be made available for its own inspection; but

(b) shall not, pending determination of that question in the applicant's favour, require the record or part to be disclosed to him or his representatives whether by discovery (or, in Scotland, recovery) or otherwise.

* * * *

Interpretation

11. In this Act— **3F–31**

"application" means an application in writing and "apply" shall be construed accordingly;

"care" includes examination, investigation, diagnosis and treatment;

"general practitioner" means a medical practitioner who is—

(a) providing general medical services in accordance with arrangements made under section 29 of the National Health Service Act 1977 or section 19 of the National Health Service (Scotland) Act 1978; or

(b) performing personal medical services in accordance with arrangements made under section 28C of the 1977 Act or section 17C of the 1978 Act;

"Health Authority" means a Health Authority established under section 8 of the National Health Service Act 1977;

"Health Board" has the same meaning as in the National Health Service (Scotland) Act 1978;

"health service body" means —

(a) a Strategic Health Authority, Health Authority, Special Health Authority or Primary Care Trust;

(b) a Health Board;

(c) a State Hospital Management Committee constituted under section 91 of the Mental Health (Scotland) Act 1984;

(d) a National Health Service trust first established under section 5 of the National Health Service and Community Care Act 1990 or section 12A of the National Health Service (Scotland) Act 1978;

(e) an NHS foundation trust;

"information", in relation to a health record, includes any expression of opinion about the patient;

"make", in relation to such a record, includes compile;

"Primary Care Trust" means a Primary Care Trust established under section 16A of the National Health Service Act 1977;

"Special Health Authority" means a Special Health Authority established under section 11 of the National Health Service Act 1977.

["Strategic Health Authority" means a Strategic Health Authority established under section 8 of the National Health Service Act 1977].

Amendments

3F–32   The text in square brackets inserted by National Health Service Reform and Health Care Professions Act 2002 (Supplementary, Consequential etc. Provisions) Regulations (S.I. 2002 No. 2469), Sched.1(1) para. 17(b). Sub-paragraph (e) in the definition of "health service body" was inserted by the Health and Social Care (Community Health and Standards) Act 2003, Sched.4, paras 87 and 88.

* * * * *

Damages Act 1996

3F–33   (1996 c.48)

Note

3F–34   By s.8 (not reproduced in this work) this Act came into force two months after date of passage, *i.e.* in force from September 24, 1996.

The Courts Act 2003

3F–35   By s.100 and s.101 of the Courts Act 2003 , which received Royal Assent on November 20, 2003, and which came into force on April 1, 2005 (S.I. 2005 No. 910); ss.2, 2A, 2B and 4 were extensively substituted, and the text is shown here as amended by that Act.

Assumed rate of return on investment of damages

3F–36   **1.**—(1) In determining the return to be expected from the investment of a sum awarded as damages for future pecuniary loss in an action for personal injury the court shall, subject to and in accordance with rules of court made for the purposes of this section, take into account such rate of return (if any) as may from time to time be prescribed by an order made by the Lord Chancellor.

(2) Subsection (1) above shall not however prevent the court taking a different rate of return into account if any party to the proceedings shows that it is more appropriate in the case in question.

(3) An order under subsection (1) above may prescribe different rates of return for different classes of case.

(4) Before making an order under subsection (1) above the Lord Chancellor shall consult the Government Actuary and the Treasury; and any order under that subsection shall be made by statutory instrument subject to annulment in pursuance of a resolution of either House of Parliament.

[(5) In the application of this section to Scotland—
>   (a) for the reference to the Lord Chancellor in subsections (1) and (4) there is substituted a reference to the Scottish Ministers; and
>   (b) in subsection (4)–
>   (i) "and the Treasury" is omitted; and
>   (ii) for "either House of Parliament" there is substituted "the Scottish Parliament".]

Amendments

Subsection (5) substituted by (Scotland Act 1998 (Consequential Modifications) **3F–37**
(No.2) Order (S.I. 1999 No. 1820)), Sched.2(I) para. 126(2).

"personal injury"

By s.7 (not printed here), "personal injury" includes any disease and any impair- **3F–38**
ment of a person's physical or mental condition and references to a claim or action for personal injury include references to such a claim or action brought by virtue of the Law Reform (Miscellaneous Provisions) Act 1934 and to a claim or action brought by virtue of the Fatal Accidents Act 1976.

Orders and regulations under this section

The Damages (Personal Injury) Order 2001 (S.I. 2002 No. 2301). **3F–39**

Note

Section 10 of the Civil Evidence Act 1995 (see 9B–268) provides that the H.M. **3F–40**
Government Actuary's Department's tables known as the Ogden Tables are admissible in evidence when that section comes into force. In practice such tables are regularly used in court in any event: see *Wells v. Wells and Ors.* [1999] 1 AC 345 referred to more fully below, and *Longden v. British Coal Corp* (1998) AC 653 at 671; [1997] 3 W.L.R. 1336 and in Scotland it has been held that the court can take judicial notice of the Ogden Tables at least for some purposes: *O'Brien's Curator Bonis v. British Steel Plc* 1991 S.C. 315. In simple terms a claimant who receives a lump sum at trial representing future lost income is expected to be able to derive an investment income from that lump sum whilst also drawing down on the funds. An award of the full amount of the loss as a lump sum would overcompensate the claimant.

Section 1 of the Damages Act 1996 provides that the Lord Chancellor may by order specify a particular assumed rate of annual return for the calculation of lump sum awards for future pecuniary loss, representing what is in effect the presumed rate of investment return available on the money without undue risk to the capital, on the footing that the capital is gradually drawn down and should be precisely exhausted by the end of the period of anticipated loss. The courts are enjoined by subs.(1) to "take into account" such a specified rate of return in accordance with court rules.

The Lord Chancellor's discount rate

3F–41   By the Damages (Personal Injury) Order 2001 which came into force on June 28, 2001 the Lord Chancellor specified a rate of 2.5% for this purpose, frequently referred to as the "discount rate".

In practice the manner in which practitioners approach the calculation of future pecuniary loss in a straightforward case making use of the 2.5% rate is to consult the 2.5% discount rate column within the Ogden tables, at the row representing the period of time over which the loss will occur. That provides a multiplier for the loss which takes into account normal likelihood of death (other than where there is a particular raised chance of death over and above normal mortality levels) and takes into account the accelerated recovery due to an estimated 2.5% investment income on the lump sum whilst drawing down on the capital over the number of years specified as the loss period.

For general principles of calculation of lump sum damages see the judgment of Stephen J. in the High Court of Australia in *Todorovic v. Waller* [1981] 37 A.L.R. at 498 (approved in *Wells v. Wells; Thomas v. Brighton Health Authority; Page v. Sheerness Steel Co Plc* [1999] 1 AC 345; [1998] 3 All E.R. 481 HL.) See also *Kemp and Kemp Quantum of Damages* vol. 1, para. 7–010), Judgment of Lord Pearson in *Taylor v. O'Connor* [1971] AC 115, 140, and Lord Oliver of Aylmerton in *Hodgson v. Trapp* [1989] AC 807, 826.

Prior to the announcement of the 2.5% rate by the Lord Chancellor the prevailing rate was set by common law in the absence of any order under s.1. In *Wells v Wells; Thomas v. Brighton Health Authority; Page v. Sheerness Steel Co Plc* [1999] 1 AC 345; [1998] 3 All E.R. 481 HL the House of Lords set a guideline rate of 3% based on the average rate of return of Index Linked Government Securities, the House stressing that it was not in their view appropriate to assume a higher rate based on a premise that injured parties will invest in more hazardous forms of investment, *per* Lord Steyn:

> "The premise that plaintiffs, who have perhaps been very seriously injured, are in the same position as ordinary investors is not one that I can accept. Such plaintiffs have not chosen to invest: the tort and its consequences compel them to do so. For plaintiffs an investment in equities is inherently risky, notably in regard to the timing of the investment....
>
> Typically, by investing in equities an ordinary investor takes a calculated risk which he can bear in order to improve his financial position. On the other hand, the typical plaintiff requires the return from an award of damages to provide the necessities of life. For such a plaintiff it is not possible to cut back on medical and nursing care as well as other essential services. His objective must be to ensure that the damages awarded do not run out. It is money that he cannot afford to lose.... It is therefore unrealistic to treat such a plaintiff as an ordinary investor. It seems to me entirely reasonable for such a plaintiff to be cautious and conservative.... it seems to me difficult to say that an investment in index-linked securities by plaintiffs would be unreasonable."

The analysis of the underlying principles is informative notwithstanding the later decision of the Lord Chancellor to set a 2.5% rather than 3% rate and many of the reported cases between 1999 and 2001 refer to a 3% rate in accordance with the *Wells v. Wells* judgment.

Basis for the Lord Chancellor's decision to set the rate

3F–42   The Lord Chancellor has a wide discretion to decide upon the most appropriate rate. His reasons for setting the 2.5% were set out in his Reasons dated July 27, 2001 (http://www.dca.gov.uk/civil/discount.htm#part3) at length, *inter alia* basing his decision on then current average gross redemption yield figures for Index linked Government Stock:

> "it is highly desirable to exercise my powers under the Act so as to produce a situation in which claimants and defendants may have a reasonably clear idea about the impact of the discount rate upon their cases, so as to facilitate negotiation of settlements and the presentation of cases in court. In order to promote this objective, I have concluded that I should:
>
> a. set a single rate to cover all cases.
>
> b. set a rate which is easy for all parties and their lawyers to apply in practice and which reflects the fact that the rate is bound to be applied in a range of different circumstances over a period of time. For this reason, I consider it appropriate to set the discount rate to the nearest half per cent...."

c. set a rate which should obtain for the foreseeable future. I consider it would be very detrimental to the reasonable certainty which is necessary to promote the just and efficient resolution of disputes (by settlement as well as by hearing in court) to make frequent changes to the discount rate. Therefore, whilst I will remain ready to review the discount rate whenever I find there is a significant and established change in the relevant real rates of return to be expected, I do not propose to tinker with the rate frequently to take account of every transient shift in market conditions."

Court's discretion to depart from the 2.5% rate

Whilst the court must take the rate set under this section "into account" the court is **3F–43** not bound to apply it. By s.1(2) the court may take into account a different rate if any party shows that a different rate is more appropriate, though on the strict wording it appears that a court may not decide to take into account a different rate merely of its own motion in the absence of submissions by a party. The courts will be prepared to depart from the rate, it seems, only with great reluctance for example if the Lord Chancellor's reasons for setting a particular rate were demonstrably wrong or omitted to take into account a significant factor. For two failed attempts to vary the former 3% rate (decisions of the Court of Appeal in the period between judgment of the House of Lords in *Wells v. Wells* and the announcement of the Lord Chancellor's rate of 2.5%) see *Warriner v. Warriner* [2002] 1 W.L.R. 1703 and *Warren v. Northern General Hospital NHS Trust* [2000] 1 W.L.R. 1404.

Similarly, attempts to depart from the 2.5% rate by the "back door", based on evidence that future care costs for the claimant would increase at a significantly steeper rate than general inflation, failed in three conjoined appeals to the Court of Appeal handed down on October 16, 2003 (*Cooke v.United Bristol Healthcare NHS Trust* [2003] EWCA Civ 1370; *Sheppard v. Stibbe* and another; *Page v. Lee* [2003] EWCA Civ 1370) in which it was held that such would constitute an illegitimate attempt to subvert the "discount rate" set by the Lord Chancellor to be applied when assessing the multiplier for future loss.

In *Page v. Plymouth Hospitals NHS Trust* [2004] EWHC 1154 All E.R. 367 (QB), the courtrejected any argument that the Lord Chancellor when fixing the discount rate did so with the intention of abiding by the fudamental principle of full compensation, and had wished to achieve certainty and consistency. He was essentially prescribing the discount rate by reference to index-linked gilt-edged stock and not a mixed portfolio, and it was inherent in the Lord Chancellor's reasons for the 2001 Order that the costs of investment advice were taken into account in setting the discount rate. Accordingly predicted costs of investment advice and fund management charges incurred in the management of the claimant's award of damages could not be recovered as damages.

Periodical payments

2.—(1) A court awarding damages for future pecuniary loss in re- **3F–44** spect of personal injury—

> (a) may order that the damages are wholly or partly to take the form of periodicalpayments, and

> (b) shall consider whether to make that order.

(2) A court awarding other damages in respect of personal injury may, if the parties consent, order that the damages are wholly or partly to take the form of periodical payments.

(3) A court may not make an order for periodical payments unless satisfied that the continuity of payment under the order is reasonably secure.

(4) For the purpose of subsection (3) the continuity of payment under an order is reasonably secure if—

> (a) it is protected by a guarantee given under section 6 of or the Schedule to this Act,

    (b) it is protected by a scheme under section 213 of theFinancial Services and Markets Act 2000 (compensation) (whether or not as modified by section 4 of this Act), or

    (c) the source of payment is a government or health service body.

(5) An order for periodical payments may include provision—

    (a) requiring the party responsible for the payments to use a method (selected or to be selected by him) under which the continuity of payment is reasonably secure by virtue of subsection (4);

    (b) about how the payments are to be made, if not by a method under which the continuity of payment is reasonably secure by virtue of subsection (4);

    (c) requiring the party responsible for the payments to take specified action to secure continuity of payment, where continuity is not reasonably secure by virtue of subsection (4);

    (d) enabling a party to apply for a variation of provision included under paragraph (a), (b) or (c).

(6) Where a person has a right to receive payments under an order for periodical payments, or where an arrangement is entered into in satisfaction of an order which gives a person a right to receive periodical payments, that person's right under the order or arrangement may not be assigned or charged without the approval of the court which made the order; and—

    (a) a court shall not approve an assignment or charge unless satisfied that special circumstances make it necessary, and

    (b) a purported assignment or charge, or agreement to assign or charge, is void unless approved by the court.

(7) Where an order is made for periodical payments, an alteration of the method by which the payments are made shall be treated as a breach of the order (whether or not the method was specified under subsection (5)(b)) unless—

    (a) the court which made the order declares its satisfaction that the continuity of payment under the new method is reasonably secure,

    (b) the new method is protected by a guarantee given under section 6 of or the Schedule to this Act,

    (c) the new method is protected by a scheme under section 213 of the Financial Services and Markets Act 2000 (compensation) (whether or not as modified by section 4 of this Act), or

    (d) the source of payment under the new method is a government or health service body.

(8) An order for periodical payments shall be treated as providing for the amount of payments to vary by reference to the retail prices index (within the meaning of section 833(2) of the Income and Corporation Taxes Act 1988) at such times, and in such a manner, as may be determined by or in accordance with Civil Procedure Rules.

(9) But an order for periodical payments may include provision—

    (a) disapplying subsection (8), or

    (b) modifying the effect of subsection (8).

Amendments

The above new text of s.2, and the text of ss.2A and 2B (below) were substituted for **3F–45** the old text of s.2 with effect from April 1, 2005 by S.I. 2005 No. 901 by virtue of the Courts Act 2003, s.100. The Courts Act 2003 received Royal Assent on November 20, 2003. The 37th Update of the Civil Procedure Rules, published December 17, 2004, included provisions for periodical payments, and the amended rules appear in CPR 41 Part (II) . Those rules came into force on the date of entry into force of ss.100 and 101 of the Courts Act 2003 (namely April 1, 2005).

Note

For the court rules which relate to periodical payments, see CPR 41 Part II **3F–46** elsewhere in this work. The references to "government or health service body" in subs. (4)(c) and 7(d) are defined in section 2A below, and itemized in the Statutory Instrument which is referred to in the Note to that section below headed "Designated Government and Health Service Bodies".

Note

The original text of s.2 did not provide the court with the power to impose a **3F–47** periodical payments order in a personal injury case, rather the court could make such an order only with the consent of the parties. The new sections 2, 2A and 2B reproduced here and below brought in a regime from April 1, 2005 where consent is not required for such an order where the damages are for future pecuniary loss for personal injury (and the court is now—under the new section 2(b)— required to consider whether such an order should be made. (Consent remains necessary for other forms of loss). This was in accordance with the recommendation of the Law Commission Report No. 224 Cm. 2646 "Structured Settlements and Interim and Provisional Damages". The Law Commission recommended that in the absence of agreement there should be no judicial power to impose a structured settlement (paras 3.37–3.53 of the Report). Judicially however the power for the courts to order periodical payments was called for: See *per* Lord Steyn in *Wells v. Wells*; *Thomas v. Brighton Health Authority*; *Page v. Sheerness Steel Co Plc* [1999] 1 AC 345 at 384B where s.2(1) was described as a "dead letter".

See also the Lord Chancellor's consultative document "Damages For Future Loss: Giving the Courts the Power to Order Periodical Payments for Future Loss and Care Costs in Personal Injury Cases", March 2002, which resulted in the Courts Act 2003, ss.100 and 101 to address the absence of a power to order periodical payments. The result was the scheme now set iout in sections 2,2A and 2B reproduced below and which replaced this section from April 1, 2005 (S.I. 2005 No. 910)."

One of the potential problems with a periodical payment structured settlement, which can be over the course of the remainder of the claimant's life, is that the insurer or other source of funds for the payments may go into liquidation or otherwise cease to be able to pay at some date in the future, ss.4 to 6 provide a protective regime to deal with such eventualities.

Case law

For an example of s.2(1) in action, see *Peter Godbold v. Rashid Mahmood* [2005] **3F–48** EWHC 1002 (QB). A periodical payments order under s.2(1)(a) was made for care and related costs which would recur over time. It was held that a periodical payments order eliminated uncertainty and risks of unfairness, and met the Claimant's needs having regard to factors in CPR PD41B. The order was also preferred because it facilitated budgeting by the Claimant because his income was secure.

Periodical payments: supplementary

2A.—(1) Civil Procedure Rules may require a court to take speci- **3F–49** fied matters into account in considering—

    (a) whether to order periodical payments;

(b) the security of the continuity of payment;

(c) whether to approve an assignment or charge.

(2) For the purposes of section 2(4)(c) *and* (7)(d) "government or health service body" means a body designated as a government body or a health service body by order made by the Lord Chancellor.

(3) An order under subsection (2)—

(a) shall be made by statutory instrument, and

(b) shall be subject to annulment in pursuance of a resolution of either House of Parliament.

(4) Section 2(6) is without prejudice to a person's power to assign a right to the scheme manager established under section 212 of the Financial Services and Markets Act 2000.

(5) In section 2 "damages" includes an interim payment which a court orders a defendant to make to a claimant.

* * * *

(7) Section 2 is without prejudice to any power exercisable apart from that section.

Amendments

3F–50   The above new text of s.2A, and the text of s.2 (ante) B (below) were substituted for old the text of s.2 with effect from April 1, 2005 by S.I. 2005 No. 910 , by virtue of the Courts Act 2003, s.100. For relevant Court rules see CPR 41 Part II elsewhere in this work.

Designated Government and Health Service Bodies

3F–51   Note that the reference in s.2A(2) to section (7)(d) is presumably intended to be a reference to s.2(7)(d) of the amended Act. Under the section 2 regime a court may not make an order that damages for future pecuniary loss for personal injury are to be via periodical payments unless the continuity of payment is reasonably secure (s.2(4)) and by s.2(4)(c) one of the circumstances in which payment is reasonably secure is where the source of payment is a "designated government or health service body". Moreover later alterations in the method of payment are also permitted, under s.2(7), without the need for further approval by the court, where the source of payment is a designated government or health service body. By virtue of The Damages (Government and Health Service Bodies) Order 2005 (S.I. 2005 No. 474) coming into effect on April 1, 2005 the designated bodies are as follows:

> *Designated health service bodies*
> Department for Constitutional Affairs
> Department for Culture, Media and Sport
> Ministry of Defence
> Office of the Deputy Prime Minister
> Department for Education and Skills
> Department for Environment, Food and Rural Affairs
> Department of Health
> Home Office
> Foreign and Commonwealth Office
> Commissioners of Inland Revenue and Commissioners of Customs and Excise
> Department for International Development
> Northern Ireland Office
> Department of Trade and Industry
> Department for Transport
> HM Treasury
> Wales Office
> Department for Work and Pensions

National Assembly for Wales
Department of Health, Social Services and Public Safety (Northern Ireland)

Designated health service bodies
National Health Service Litigation Authority
In Wales, NHS Trusts
In Wales, Local Health Boards
In Northern Ireland, Health and Social Services Boards
In Northern Ireland, Health and Social Services Trusts
In Northern Ireland, Health and Personal Social Services Agencies and Special Agencies

Variation of orders and settlements

2B.—(1) The Lord Chancellor may by order enable a court which **3F–52** has made an order for periodical payments to vary the order in specified circumstances (otherwise than in accordance with section 2(5)(d)).

(2) The Lord Chancellor may by order enable a court in specified circumstances to vary the terms on which a claim or action for damages for personal injury is settled by agreement between the parties if the agreement—

    (a) provides for periodical payments, and

    (b) expressly permits a party to apply to a court for variation in those circumstances.

(3) An order under this section may make provision—

    (a) which operates wholly or partly by reference to a condition or other term of the court's order or of the agreement;

    (b) about the nature of an order which may be made by a court on a variation;

    (c) about the matters to be taken into account on considering variation;

    (d) of a kind that could be made by Civil Procedure Rules or, in relation to Northern Ireland, rules of court (and which may be expressed to be with or without prejudice to the power to make those rules).

(4) An order under this section may apply (with or without modification) or amend an enactment about provisional or further damages.

(5) An order under this section shall be subject to any order under section 1 of the Courts and Legal Services Act 1990 (allocation between High Court and county courts).

(6) An order under this section—

    (a) shall be made by statutory instrument,

    (b) may not be made unless the Lord Chancellor has consulted such persons as he thinks appropriate

    (c) may not be made unless a draft has been laid before and approved by resolution of each House of Parliament, and

    (d) may include transitional, consequential or incidental provision.

(7) In subsection (4)—

PERSONAL INJURY

"provisional damages" means damages awarded by virtue of subsection (2)(a) of section 32A of the Supreme Court Act 1981 *or* section 51 of the County Courts Act 1984 (or, in relation to Northern Ireland, paragraph 10(2)(a) *of* Schedule 6 to the Administration of Justice Act 1982), *and*

"further damages" means damages awarded by virtue of subsection (2)(b) of either of those sections (or, in relation to Northern Ireland, paragraph 10(2)(b) of Schedule 6 to the Administration of Justice Act 1982).

Commencement

3F–53   The above section came into force on April 1, 2005 by virtue of S.I. 2005 No. 910. For relevant court rules see CPR 41 Part II elsewhere in this work.

The Damages (Variation of Periodical Payments) Order 2005 S.I. 2005 No. 841

3F–54   Section 2B(6) allows the Lord Chancellor to specify the circumstances in which a court may vary a periodical payments order. The Damages (Variation of Periodical Payments) Order 2005 S.I. 2005 No. 841 provides for such circumstances and the text of the body of the Order appears below.

Citation, commencement, interpretation and extent

1.——(1) This Order may be cited as the Damages (Variation of Periodical Payments) Order 2005 and shall come into force on the fourteenth day after the day on which it is made.

(2) In this Order–

(a) "the Act" means the Damages Act 1996;

(b) "agreement" means an agreement by parties to a claim or action for damages which settles the claim or action and which provides for periodical payments;

(c) "damages" means damages for future pecuniary loss in respect of personal injury;

(d) "defence society" means the Medical Defence Union or the Medical Protection Society;

(e) "variable agreement" means an agreement which contains a provision referred to in Article 9(1);

(f) "variable order" means an order for periodical payments which contains a provision referred to in Article 2.

(3) In the application of this Order to Northern Ireland–

(a) "claimant" means plaintiff;

(b) "permission" means leave;

(c) "statements of case" means, in the High Court, the writ and pleadings and, in the county court, the civil bill and any notice of intention to defend, defence, notice for particulars, replies and counterclaim.

(4) This Order extends to England and Wales and Northern Ireland.

(5) This Order applies to proceedings begun on or after the date on which it comes into force.

Power to make variable orders

2. If there is proved or admitted to be a chance that at some definite or indefinite time in the future the claimant will–

(a) as a result of the act or omission which gave rise to the cause of action, develop some serious disease or suffer some serious deterioration, or

(b) enjoy some significant improvement, in his physical or mental condition, where that condition had been adversely affected as a result of that act or omission,

the court may, on the application of a party, with the agreement of all the parties, or of its own initiative, provide in an order for periodical payments that it may be varied.

Defendant's financial resources

3. Unless–

(a) the defendant is insured in respect of the claim,

(b) the source of payment under the order for periodical payments is a government or health service body within the meaning of section 2A(2) of the Act,

(c) the payment is guaranteed under section 6 of or the Schedule to the Act, or

(d) the order is made by consent and the claimant is neither a child, nor a patient within the meaning of Part VII of the Mental Health Act 1983 or of Part VIII of the Mental Health (Northern Ireland) Order 1986,

the court will take into account the defendant's likely future financial resources in considering whether to make a variable order.

Award of provisional damages

4. The court may make a variable order in addition to an order for an award of provisional damages made by virtue of section 32A of the Supreme Court Act 1981[1] or section 51 of the County Courts Act 1984 or, in relation to Northern Ireland, paragraph 10(2)(a) of Schedule 6 to the Administration of Justice Act 1982.

Contents of variable order

5. Where the court makes a variable order–

(a) the damages must be assessed or agreed on the assumption that the disease, deterioration or improvement will not occur;

(b) the order must specify the disease or type of deterioration or improvement;

(c) the order may specify a period within which an application for it to be varied may be made;

(d) the order may specify more than one disease or type of deterioration or improvement and may, in respect of each, specify a different period within which an application for it to be varied may be made;

(e) the order must provide that a party must obtain the

---

[1] Section 32A was inserted by the Administration of Justice Act 1982 (c. 53), section 6.

court's permission to apply for it to be varied, unless the court otherwise orders.

Applications to extend period for applying for permission to vary

6. Where a period is specified under Article 5(c) or (d)–

(a) a party may make more than one application to extend the period, and such an application is not to be treated as an application to vary a variable order for the purposes of Article 7;

(b) a party may not make an application for the variable order to be varied after the end of the period specified or such period as extended by the court.

Limit on number of applications to vary

7. A party may make only one application to vary a variable order in respect of each specified disease or type of deterioration or improvement.

Case file

8.——(1) Where the court makes a variable order, the case file documents must be preserved by the court until the end of the period or periods specified under Article 5(c) or (d) or of any extension of them or, if no such period was specified, until the death of the claimant.

(2) The case file documents are, unless the court otherwise orders–

(a) the judgment as entered;

(b) the statements of case;

(c) the schedule of expenses and losses;

(d) a transcript of the judge's oral judgment;

(e) all medical reports relied on;

(f) a transcript of any parts of the claimant's own evidence which the judge considers necessary;

(g) any subsequent orders.

(3) A court officer must ensure that the case file documents are provided by the parties where necessary and filed on the court file.

(4) Where a variable order has been made, the legal representatives of the parties and, if the parties are insured, their insurers, must also preserve their own case file until the end of the period or periods specified under Article 5(c) or (d) or of any extension of them or, if no such period was specified, until the death of the claimant.

Variable agreements

9.——(1) If there is agreed to be a chance that at some definite or indefinite time in the future the claimant will–

(a) as a result of the act or omission which gave rise to the cause of action, develop some serious disease or suffer some serious deterioration, or

(b) enjoy some significant improvement, in his physical or mental condition, where that condition had been adversely affected as a result of that act or omission,

the parties to an agreement may agree that a party to it may apply to the court subsequently for its terms to be varied.

(2) Where the parties agree to permit an application to vary the terms of an agreement, the agreement–

(a) must expressly state that a party to it may apply to the court for its terms to be varied;

(b) must specify the disease or type of deterioration or improvement;

(c) may specify a period within which an application for it to be varied may be made;

(d) may specify more than one disease or type of deterioration or improvement and may, in respect of each, specify a different period within which an application for it to be varied may be made.

(3) A party who is permitted by an agreement to apply for its terms to be varied must obtain the court's permission to apply for it to be varied.

Application for permission

10.——(1) An application for permission to apply for a variable order or a variable agreement to be varied must be accompanied by evidence–

(a) that the disease, deterioration or improvement specified in the order or agreement has occurred, and

(b) that it has caused or is likely to cause an increase or decrease in the pecuniary loss suffered by the claimant.

(2) Where the applicant is the claimant and he knows that the defendant is insured in respect of the claim and the identity of the defendant's insurers, he must serve the application notice on the insurers as well as on the defendant.

(3) Where the applicant is the claimant and he knows that the defendant is a member of a defence society and the identity of the defence society, he must serve the application notice on the defence society as well as on the defendant.

(4) The respondent to the application may, within 28 days after service of the application, serve written representations on the applicant and, if he does, must file them with the court.

(5) The court will deal with the application without a hearing.

Refusal of permission

11.——(1) Where permission is refused, the applicant may, within 14 days after service of the order, request the decision to be reconsidered at a hearing.

(2) No appeal lies from an order refusing permission after reconsideration.

Grant of permission

12.——(1) Where permission is granted, the court will also give directions as to the application for the variation of the variable order or the variable agreement.

(2) Directions must include directions as to–
- (a) the date by which the application for variation must be served and filed;
- (b) the service and filing of evidence.

(3) No appeal lies from an order granting permission.

Order for variation

13.——(1) On an application for the variation of a variable order or a variable agreement, if the court is satisfied–
- (a) that the disease, deterioration or improvement specified in the order or agreement has occurred, and
- (b) that it has caused or is likely to cause an increase or decrease in the pecuniary loss suffered by the claimant,

it may order–
  - (i) the amount of annual payments to be varied, either from the date of the application for permission or from the date of the application to vary if the order did not require the permission of the court for an application to vary, or from such later date as it may specify in the order;
  - (ii) how each payment is to be made during the year and at what intervals;
  - (iii) a lump sum to be paid in addition to the existing periodical payments.

(2) Section 2(3) to (9) of the Act applies to orders under this Order as it applies to orders for periodical payments.

Application of rules of court

14. In England and Wales, the Civil Procedure Rules 1998 and in Northern Ireland, rules of court apply to applications under this Order, except where this Order makes provision inconsistent with Civil Procedure Rules or rules of court.

Provisional damages and fatal accident claims

3F–55   **3.**—(1) This section applies where a person—
- (a) is awarded provisional damages; and
- (b) subsequently dies as a result of the act or omission which gave rise to the cause of action for which the damages were awarded.

(2) The award of the provisional damages shall not operate as a bar to an action in respect of that person's death under the Fatal Accidents Act 1976

(3) Such part (if any) of—
- (a) the provisional damages; and
- (b) any further damages awarded to the person in question before his death,

as was intended to compensate him for pecuniary loss in a period which in the event falls after his death shall be taken into account in assessing the amount of any loss of support suffered by the person or persons for whose benefit the action under the Fatal Accidents Act 1976 is brought.

(4) No award of further damages made in respect of that person after his death shall include any amount for loss of income in respect of any period after his death.

(5) In this section "provisional damages" means damages awarded by virtue of subsection (2)(a) of section 32A of the Supreme Court Act 1981 or section 51 of the County Courts Act 1984 and "further damages" means damages awarded by virtue of subsection (2)(b) of either of those sections.

(6) Subsection (2) above applies whether the award of provisional damages was before or after the coming into force of that subsection; and subsections (3) and (4) apply to any award of damages under the 1976 Act or, as the case may be, further damages after the coming into force of those subsections.

* * * *

Note

3F–56

This section clarifies the linkage between provisional damages, the rights of the dependants of the deceased under the Inheritance (Provision for Family and Dependants) Act 1976, and damages under the Fatal Accidents Act 1976. The section applies where a person was awarded provisional damages—(damages awarded on the basis that there is a recognised specific risk of future development of a medical condition, or of further deterioration, which has not yet resulted in harm) but which will entitle the claimant to pursue a "further" damages claim in the event that the risk crystallises. For "provisional damages" see s.32A(2)(a) of the SCA 1981 and s.51 of the CCA 1984.

If the claimant in due course dies as a result of the tort which gave rise to the cause of action for which provisional damages were awarded, the fact that that award was made will not amount to a bar on the commencement of a claim by the deceased's dependants under the Fatal Accidents Act 1976 (see subs.(2)).

To extent that the award of damages was intended to be compensation for loss covering a period which in the event fell after the deceased died, then by subs.(3) the amount of the damages for that period must be taken into account by the court when it comes to assess damages for loss of support under the Fatal Accidents Act 1976. Relatedly subs.(4) provides that courts may not award amounts of "further damages" in respect loss of income under a provisional damages order after that persons' death. This avoids a risk of double recovery by relatives under both the Fatal Accidents Act 1976 and under the terms of the provisional order made within the deceased's original personal injury claim. For the meaning of "further damages" see s.32A(2)(b) of the SCA 1981 and s.51(2)(b) of the CCA 1984.

Enhanced protection for periodical payments

3F–57

4.—(1) Subsection (2) applies where—

(a) a person has a right to receive periodical payments, and

(b) his right is protected by a scheme under section 213 of the Financial Services and Markets Act 2000 (compensation), but only as to part of the payments.

(2) The protection provided by the scheme shall extend by virtue of this section to the whole of the payments.

(3) Subsection (4) applies where—

(a) one person ("the claimant") has a right to receive periodical payments from another person ("the defendant"),

(b) a third person ("the insurer") is required by or in pursuance of an arrangement entered into with the defendant (whether or not together with other persons and whether before or after the creation of the claimant's right) to make payments in satisfaction of the claimant's right or for the purpose of enabling it to be satisfied, and

(c) the claimant's right to receive the payments would be wholly or partly protected by a scheme under section 213 of the Financial Services and Markets Act 2000 if it arose from an arrangement of the same kind as that mentioned in paragraph (b) but made between the claimant and the insurer.

(4) For the purposes of the scheme under section 213 of that Act—

(a) the claimant shall be treated as having a right to receive the payments from the insurer under an arrangement of the same kind as that mentioned in subsection (3)(b)

(b) the protection under the scheme in respect of those payments shall extend by virtue of this section to the whole of the payments, and

(c) no person other than the claimant shall be entitled to protection under the scheme in respect of the payments.

(5) In this section "periodical payments" means periodical payments made pursuant to—

(a) an order of a court in so far as it is made in reliance on section 2 above (including an order as varied), or

(b) an agreement in so far as it settles a claim or action for damages in respect of personal injury (including an agreement as varied).

(6) In subsection (5)(b) the reference to an agreement in so far as it settles a claim or action for damages in respect of personal injury includes a reference to an undertaking given by the Motor Insurers' Bureau (being the company of that name incorporated on 14th June 1946 under the Companies Act 1929), or an Article 75 insurer under the Bureau's Articles of Association, in relation to a claim or action in respect of personal injury.

Amendments

3F–58   The text above is now in force and replaced the old text of ss.4 and 5 from April 1, 2005 by S.I. 2005 No. 910 , by virtue of the Courts Act 2003, s.101(1) . The Courts Act 2003 received Royal Assent on November 20, 2003.

This section puts into place enhanced protection for persons who have a right to receive periodical payments under s.2 whether under an order or under a settlement agreement. By section 213 of the Financial Services and Markets Act 2000 the Financial Services Authority provides compensation arrangements to cover defaults by 'relevant persons', in this instance insurers, whenever they become unable, or are likely to be unable, to satisfy claims against them. This section provides that where an insurer is funding the periodical payments due to the Claimant, and those payments are covered by a compensation scheme under the 2000 Act then the compensation scheme extends to the whole of the periodical payments, thereby providing what amounts to extended protection for Claimants in receipt of periodical payments under s.2. The section contains provision in subs. (4)(a) that the Claimant is treated as being directly entitled to receive the payments from the insurer notwithstanding that the contractual relationship is between the Defendant and the insurer.

Guarantees for public sector settlements

6.—(1) This section applies where—   **3F–59**

    (a) a claim or action for damages for personal injury is settled [*on terms whereby the damages are to consist wholly or partly of periodical payments*]; or

    (b) a court awarding damages for personal injury makes an order incorporating such terms.

(2) If it appears to a Minister of the Crown that the payments are to be made by a body in relation to which he has, by virtue of this section power to do so, he may guarantee the payments to be made under the agreement or order.

(3) The bodies in relation to which a Minister may give such a guarantee shall, subject to subsection (4) below, be such bodies as are designated in relation to the relevant government department by guidelines agreed upon between that department and the Treasury.

(4) A guarantee purporting to be given by a Minister under this section shall not be invalidated by any failure on his part to act in accordance with such guidelines as are mentioned in subsection (3) above.

(5) A guarantee under this section shall be given on such terms as the Minister concerned may determine but those terms shall in every case require the body in question to reimburse the Minister, with interest, for any sums paid by him in fulfilment of the guarantee.

(6) Any sums required by a Minister for fulfilling a guarantee under this section shall be defrayed out of money provided by Parliament and any sums received by him by way of reimbursement or interest shall be paid into the Consolidated Fund.

(7) A Minister who has given one or more guarantees under this section shall, as soon as possible after the end of each financial year, lay before each House of Parliament a statement showing what liabilities are outstanding in respect of the guarantees in that year, what sums have been paid in that year in fulfilment of the guarantees and what sums (including interest) have been recovered in that year in respect of the guarantees or are still owing.

(8) In this section "government department" means any department of Her Majesty's government in the United Kingdom and for the purposes of this section a government department is a relevant department in relation to a Minister if he has responsibilities in respect of that department.

* * * *

Amendments

The text of subs.(1) in italics above was inserted by amendment with effect from   **3F–60**
April 1, 2005 by S.I. 2005 No. 901 by virtue of the Courts Act 2003, s.101(2) . See also
CPR 41 Pt II. The pre-amendment text formerly read " ...*on terms corresponding to those
of a structured settlement as defined in section 5 above except that the person to whom the payments are to be made is not to receive them as mentioned in subsection (1)(b) of that section; or* "

Note

Where a periodical payments settlement is entered into with a public body, the sit-   **3F–61** uation differs in practical terms from private sector settlements in that the public bodies such as the NHS have sufficient funds, and will probably continue to exist in the future, to be able to fund the settlement without the need for the purchase and assignment of annuities in the financial marketplace. Nevertheless because state bodies could in principle be dissolved or their responsibilities transferred elsewhere without being required to honour existing "self funded" settlements, this section creates a procedure whereby a minister responsible for a Government department may guarantee payments which will be made under settlements involving public bodies under that department's remit. The public bodies concerned are those to be agreed between the relevant department and the Treasury (subs.(2)). The guarantee, if provided, would in all cases have to require that the public body repays to the relevant Minister any sums paid out by him under the guarantee (subs.(5)). (Note that additionally in the case of the NHS liabilities are transferred to successor authorities under the National Health Service (Residual Liabilities) Act 1996 in any event).

The Damages (Personal Injury) Order 2001

(S.I. 2001 No. 2301)

3F–62   1. This Order may be cited as the Damages (Personal Injury) Order 2001 and shall come into force on 28th June 2001.

2. The rate of return referred to in section 1(1) of the Damages Act 1996 shall be 2.5 per cent.

Note

3F–63   This order sets the "discount rate" which the courts must take into account when awarding damages for future pecuniary loss in personal injury cases, under s.1 of the Damages Act 1996. Prior to the making of this Order the rate in use was fixed by Common Law at 3 per cent following the case of *Wells v. Wells*; *Thomas v. Brighton Health Authority*; *Page v. Sheerness Steel Co Plc* [1999] 1 AC 345; [1998] 3 All E.R. 481 HL.

For a detailed discussion of this Order in relation to section 1 of the Damages Act 1996 see the notes to that Act in this section, *supra*.

Fatal Accidents Act 1976

3F–64   ### (1976 c.30)

ARRANGEMENT OF SECTIONS

SECT.

* * * *

3F–65   *Note* —The Act still retains its regnal year though it was virtually re-enacted by s.3 of the AJA 1982, subs.(1) substituting the following ss.1 to 4, and subs.(2) amending section 5.

Right of action for wrongful act causing death

3F–66   **1.**—(1) If death is caused by any wrongful act, neglect or default which is such as would (if death had not ensued) have entitled the person injured to maintain an action and recover damages in respect thereof, the person who would have been liable if death had not ensued shall be liable to an action for damages, notwithstanding the death of the person injured.

(2) Subject to section 1A(2) below, every such action shall be for the benefit of the dependants of the person ("the deceased") whose death has been so caused.

(3) In this Act "dependant" means—

    (a) the wife or husband or former wife or husband of the deceased;

    (b) any person who—

        (i) was living with the deceased in the same household immediately before the date of the death; and

        (ii) had been living with the deceased in the same household for at least two years before that date; and

        (iii) was living during the whole of that period as the husband or wife of the deceased;

    (c) any parent or other ascendant of the deceased;

    (d) any person who was treated by the deceased as his parent;

    (e) any child or other descendant of the deceased;

    (f) any person (not being a child of the deceased) who, in the case of any marriage to which the deceased was at any time a party, was treated by the deceased as a child of the family in relation to that marriage;

    (g) any person who is, or is the issue of, a brother, sister, uncle or aunt of the deceased.

(4) The reference to the former wife or husband of the deceased in subsection (3)(a) above includes a reference to a person whose marriage to the deceased has been annulled or declared void as well as a person whose marriage to the deceased has been dissolved.

(5) In deducing any relationship for the purposes of subsection (3) above—

    (a) any relationship by affinity shall be treated as a relationship by consanguinity, any relationship of the half blood as a relationship of the whole blood, and the stepchild of any person as his child, and

    (b) an illegitimate person shall be treated as the legitimate child of his mother and reputed father.

(6) Any reference in this Act to injury includes any disease and any impairment of a person's physical or mental condition.

Bereavement

1A.—(1) An action under this Act may consist of or include a claim **3F–67** for damages for bereavement.

(2) A claim for damages for bereavement shall only be for the benefit—

    (a) of the wife or husband of the deceased; and

    (b) where the deceased was a minor who was never married—

        (i) of his parents, if he was legitimate; and

        (ii) of his mother, if he was illegitimate.

(3) Subject to subsection (5) below, the sum to be awarded as damages under this section shall be £10,000.

(4) Where there is a claim for damages under this section for the benefit of both the parents of the deceased, the sum awarded shall be divided equally between them (subject to any deduction falling to be made in respect of costs not recovered from the defendant).

(5) The Lord Chancellor may by order made by statutory instrument, subject to annulment in pursuance of a resolution of either House of Parliament, amend this section by varying the sum of the time being specified in subsection (3) above.

3F–68   *Note* — Amended by the Damages for Bereavement (Variation of Sum) (England and Wales) Order 2002 (S.I. 2002 No. 644), art.2.

Persons entitled to bring the action

3F–69   **2.**—(1) The action shall be brought by and in the name of the executor or administrator of the deceased.

(2) If—

    (a) there is no executor or administrator of the deceased, or

    (b) no action is brought within six months after the death by and in the name of an executor or administrator of the deceased,

the action may be brought by and in the name of all or any of the persons for whose benefit an executor or administrator could have brought it.

(3) Not more than one action shall lie for and in respect of the same subject matter of complaint.

(4) The plaintiff in the action shall be required to deliver to the defendant or his solicitor full particulars of the persons for whom and on whose behalf the action is brought and of the nature of the claim in respect of which damages are sought to be recovered.

"more than one action"

3F–70   Section 2(3) has to be construed compatibly with the ECHR (see Human Rights Act 1998, Sched.1), and "action" is to be interpreted as referring to "served process" (*Cachia v. Faluyl* [2001] EWCA Civ 998; [2001] 1 W.L.R. 1966, CA).

Assessment of damages

3F–71   **3.**—(1) In the action such damages, other than damages for bereavement, may be awarded as are proportioned to the injury resulting from the death to the dependants respectively.

(2) After deducting the costs not recovered from the defendant any amount recovered otherwise than as damages for bereavement shall be divided among the dependants in such shares as may be directed.

(3) In an action under this Act where there fall to be assessed damages payable to a widow in respect of the death of her husband there shall not be taken into account the re-marriage of the widow or her prospects of re-marriage.

(4) In an action under this Act where there fall to be assessed damages payable to a person who is a dependant by virtue of section

1(3)(b) above in respect of the death of the person with whom the dependant was living as husband or wife there shall be taken into account (together with any other matter that appears to the court to be relevant to the action) the fact that the dependant had no enforceable right to financial support by the deceased as a result of their living together.

(5) If the dependants have incurred funeral expenses in respect of the deceased, damages may be awarded in respect of those expenses.

(6) Money paid into court in satisfaction of a cause of action under this Act may be in one sum without specifying any person's share.

Assessment of damages

Where the husband was in receipt of a retirement pension from his former employers' pension fund which constituted the whole or part of his income, the widow on his death suffered a loss of dependency and thus an "injury" under s.3(1) of the Act for which she was entitled to damages, and the allowances paid to her after her husband's death could be disregarded, since these were benefits which accrued to her as a result of his death under s.4 (*Pidduck v. Eastern Scottish Omnibuses Ltd* [1990] 1 W.L.R. 993; [1990] 2 All E.R. 69, CA).   **3F–72**

Assessment of damages: disregard of benefits

4. In assessing damages in respect of a person's death in an action under this Act, benefits which have accrued or will or may accrue to any person from his estate or otherwise as a result of his death shall be disregarded.   **3F–73**

"Benefits"

A pension and a widow's allowance received from an employer's pension fund are benefits for the purposes of s.4 and are to be disregarded in assessing damages for the deceased's death (*Pidduck v. Eastern Scottish Omnibuses Ltd* [1989] 1 W.L.R. 317; [1989] 2 All E.R. 261).   **3F–74**

Contributory negligence

5. Where any person dies as the result partly of his own fault and partly by the fault of any other person or persons, and accordingly if an action were brought for the benefit of the estate under the Law Reform (Miscellaneous Provisions) Act 1934 the damages recoverable could be reduced under section 1(1) of the Law Reform (Contributory Negligence) Act 1945, any damages recoverable in an action under this Act shall be reduced by a proportionate extent.   **3F–75**

Note

Amended by the AJA 1982, s.3(2).   **3F–76**

Premature action by dependants

An action by the dependants of the deceased claiming damages as dependants under the Fatal Accidents Act commenced within six months of the death of deceased, although premature and perhaps irregular, is nevertheless valid and sustainable where it appears that no executor or administrator of the deceased started proceedings against the defendant within six months of the death of the deceased and that the defendant has not suffered any prejudice by the action by the dependants (*Austin v. Hart* [1983] 2 AC 640; [1983] 2 All E.R. 341, PC (decided on the provision in an Ordinance in Trinidad and Tobago substantially similar to the Fatal Accidents Act 1976, s.2)).   **3F–77**

Road Traffic Act 1988

3F–78

(1988 c.52)

Users of motor vehicles to be insured or secured against third-party risks

3F–79   **143.**—(1) Subject to the provisions of this Part of this Act—

(a) a person must not use a motor vehicle on a road or other public place unless there is in force in relation to the use of the vehicle by that person such a policy of insurance or such a security in respect of third party risks as complies with the requirements of this Part of this Act, and

(b) a person must not cause or permit any other person to use a motor vehicle on a road [or other public place] unless there is in force in relation to the use of the vehicle by that other person such a policy of insurance or such a security in respect of third party risks as complies with the requirements of this Part of this Act.

* * * *

Amendments

3F–80   The words in square brackets in subs.(1)(b) were inserted by (Motor Vehicles (Compulsory Insurance) Regulations (S.I. 2000 No. 726)), reg.2(2)(b).

Note

3F–81   This section puts in place the basic rule that persons using (etc) motor vehicles on roads or other public places must have in place a policy of insurance, or provide security, as is required by the Act, in respect of third party risks. The detailed minimum requirements for type of insurance cover appear in s.145, essentially being insurance in respect of damage to property up to a specified maximum of £250,000, and liability for third party injury and death. By the remainder of s.143 not reproduced here an offence is committed if s.143 is not complied with. Various public bodies (notably County Councils and London Boroughs, for example and NHS ambulances, the fire brigade etc.) are exempted from the requirements of this section under the provisions of s.144. For organisations which have sufficient funds, rather than take out a policy of insurance, they may, by s.144(1) deposit a sum with the Accountant General as follows:

"**144**—(1) Section 143 of this Act does not apply to a vehicle owned by a person who has deposited and keeps deposited with the Accountant General of the Supreme Court the sum of £500,000, at a time when the vehicle is being driven under the owner's control"

(1A) The Secretary of State may by order made by statutory instrument substitute a greater sum for the sum for the time being specified in subsection (1) above.

(1B) No order shall be made under subsection (1A) above unless a draft of it has been laid before and approved by resolution of each House of Parliament.

(2) Section 143 does not apply—

(a) to a vehicle owned—

(i) by the council of a county or county district in England and Wales, the Broads Authority, the Common Council of the City of London, the council of a London borough, a National Park authority, the Inner London Education Authority, the London Fire and Emergency Planning Authority, or a joint authority (other than a police authority) established by Part IV of the Local Government Act 1985,

   (ii) by a council constituted under section 2 of the Local Government etc. (Scotland) Act 1994 in Scotland, or

   (iii) by a joint board or committee in England or Wales, or joint committee in Scotland, which is so constituted as to include among its members representatives of any such council,

at a time when the vehicle is being driven under the owner's control,

(b) to a vehicle owned by a police authority at a time when it is being driven under the owner's control, or to a vehicle at a time when it is being driven for police purposes by or under the direction of a constable, or by a person employed by a police authority, or

(ba) to a vehicle owned by the Service Authority for the National Criminal Intelligence Service or the Service Authority for the National Crime Squad, at a time when it is being driven under the owner's control, or to a vehicle at a time when it is being driven for the purposes of the body maintained by such an Authority by or under the Direction of a constable, or by a person employed by such an Authority;

(c) to a vehicle at a time when it is being driven on a journey to or from any place undertaken for salvage purposes pursuant to Part IX Merchant Shipping Act 1995,

(d) to the use of a vehicle for the purpose of its being provided in pursuance of a direction under section 166(2)(b) of the Army Act 1955 or under the corresponding provision of the Air Force Act 1955,

(da) to a vehicle owned by a health service body, as de.ned in section 60(7) of the National Health Service and Community Care Act 1990 , by a Primary Care Trust established under section 16A of the National Health Service Act 1977 , by a Local Health Board established under section 16BA of that Act or by the Commission for Healthcare Audit and Inspection at a time when the vehicle is being driven under the owner's control,

(db) to an ambulance owned by a National Health Service trust established under Part I of the National Health Service and Community Care Act 1990 or the National Health Service (Scotland) Act 1978, at a time when a vehicle is being driven under the owner's control,

(dc) to an ambulance owned by an NHS foundation trust, at a time when the vehicle is being driven under the owner's control,

(e) to a vehicle which is made available by the Secretary of State to any person, body or local authority in pursuance of section 23 or 26 of the National Health Service Act 1977 at a time when it is being used in accordance with the terms on which it is so made available,

(f) to a vehicle which is made available by the Secretary of State to any local authority, education authority or voluntary organisation in Scotland in pursuance of section 15 or 16 of the National Health Service (Scotland) Act 1978 at a time when it is being used in accordance with the terms on which it is so made available".

(g) to a vehicle owned by the Commission for Social Care Inspection, at a time when the vehicle is being driven under the owner's control

Amended by the Health and Social Care (Community Health and Standards) Act 2003, Sched. 4, para. 74.

Subs. 2(da) amended, and subs. (g) inserted by the Health and Social Care (Community Health and Standards) Act 2003 (Commission for Healthcare Audit and Inspection and Commission for Social Care Inspection) (Consequential Provisions) Order 2004 (S.I. 2004 No. 2987).

Reference in subs.(1) to the Supreme Court will be amended from a date to be appointed by the Constitutional Reform Act 2005, Sch.11, para.4.

Validity of insurance

3F–82 By s.147(1) the delivery of an insurance certificate to the insured is essential (similar requirements apply to those providing security, by subs.(2)):

"**147**—(1) A policy of insurance shall be of no effect for the purposes of this Part of this Act unless and until there is delivered by the insurer to the person by whom the policy is effected a certificate (in this Part of this Act referred to as a "certificate of insurance") in the prescribed form and containing such particulars of any conditions subject to which the policy is issued and of any other matters as may be prescribed."

Agreement to exclude liability towards passengers is of no effect

3F–83 Any agreement to exclude liability towards to persons carried on or in the vehicle, where s.143 requires insurance, is of no effect. By s.149(2) and (3) in such circumstances:

"**149**—(2) If any other person is carried in or upon the vehicle while the user is so using it, any antecedent agreement or understanding between them (whether intended to be legally binding or not) shall be of no effect so far as it purports or might be held—

    (a) to negative or restrict any such liability of the user in respect of persons carried in or upon the vehicle as is required by section 145 of this Act to be covered by a policy of insurance, or

    (b) to impose any conditions with respect to the enforcement of any such liability of the user.

(3) The fact that a person so carried has willingly accepted as his the risk of negligence on the part of the user shall not be treated as negativing any such liability of the user."

Liability of insurer to repay NHS treatment costs

3F–84 By s.157 the insurer will be liable to repay NHS treatment costs to the NHS in the event of a finding of liability and judgment for damages against the insured. The insurer's liability for such costs is however capped at very modest levels by those sections (for non-emergency treatment, currently a maximum of £2,949 for each person treated as an in-patient or £295 for each person treated as an out-patient). Provisions for nominal payment of fees to an attending medical professional providing emergency treatment at the scene appear in s.158, payable only in limited circumstances.

* * * *

Duty of insurers or persons giving security to satisfy judgment against persons insured or secured against third-party risks

3F–85 **151.**—(1) This section applies where, after a certificate of insurance or certificate of security has been delivered under section 147 of this Act to the person by whom a policy has been effected or to whom a security has been given, a judgment to which this subsection applies is obtained.

(2) Subsection (1) above applies to judgments relating to a liability with respect to any matter where liability with respect to that matter is required to be covered by a policy of insurance under section 145 of this Act and either—

    (a) it is a liability covered by the terms of the policy or security to which the certificate relates, and the judgment is obtained against any person who is insured by the policy or whose liability is covered by the security, as the case may be, or

    (b) it is a liability, other than an excluded liability, which would be so covered if the policy insured all persons or, as the case may be, the security covered the liability of all persons, and the judgment is obtained against any person other than one who is insured by the policy or, as the case may be, whose liability is covered by the security.

(3) In deciding for the purposes of subsection (2) above whether a liability is or would be covered by the terms of a policy or security, so much of the policy or security as purports to restrict, as the case may be, the insurance of the persons insured by the policy or the operation of the security by reference to the holding by the driver of the vehicle of a licence authorising him to drive it shall be treated as of no effect.

(4) In subsection (2)(b) above "excluded liability" means a liability in respect of the death of, or bodily injury to, or damage to the property of any person who, at the time of the use which gave rise to the liability, was allowing himself to be carried in or upon the vehicle and knew or had reason to believe that the vehicle had been stolen or unlawfully taken, not being a person who—

(a) did not know and had no reason to believe that the vehicle had been stolen or unlawfully taken until after the commencement of his journey, and

(b) could not reasonably have been expected to have alighted from the vehicle. In this subsection the reference to a person being carried in or upon a vehicle includes a reference to a person entering or getting on to, or alighting from, the vehicle.

(5) Notwithstanding that the insurer may be entitled to avoid or cancel, or may have avoided or cancelled, the policy or security, he must, subject to the provisions of this section, pay to the persons entitled to the benefit of the judgment—

(a) as regards liability in respect of death or bodily injury, any sum payable under the judgment in respect of the liability, together with any sum which, by virtue of any enactment relating to interest on judgments, is payable in respect of interest on that sum,

(b) as regards liability in respect of damage to property, any sum required to be paid under subsection (6) below, and

(c) any amount payable in respect of costs.

(6) This subsection requires—

(a) where the total of any amounts paid, payable or likely to be payable under the policy or security in respect of damage to property caused by, or arising out of, the accident in question does not exceed £250,000, the payment of any sum payable under the judgment in respect of the liability, together with any sum which, by virtue of any enactment relating to interest on judgments, is payable in respect of interest on that sum,

(b) where that total exceeds £250,000, the payment of either—

1261

(i) such proportion of any sum payable under the judgment in respect of the liability as £250,000 bears to that total, together with the same proportion of any sum which, by virtue of any enactment relating to interest on judgments, is payable in respect of interest on that sum, or

(ii) the difference between the total of any amounts already paid under the policy or security in respect of such damage and £250,000, together with such proportion of any sum which, by virtue of any enactment relating to interest on judgments, is payable in respect of interest on any sum payable under the judgment in respect of the liability as the difference bears to that sum,

whichever is the less, unless not less than £250,000 has already been paid under the policy or security in respect of such damage (in which case nothing is payable).

(7) Where an insurer becomes liable under this section to pay an amount in respect of a liability of a person who is insured by a policy or whose liability is covered by a security, he is entitled to recover from that person—

(a) that amount, in a case where he became liable to pay it by virtue only of subsection (3) above, or

(b) in a case where that amount exceeds the amount for which he would, apart from the provisions of this section, be liable under the policy or security in respect of that liability, the excess.

(8) Where an insurer becomes liable under this section to pay an amount in respect of a liability of a person who is not insured by a policy or whose liability is not covered by a security, he is entitled to recover the amount from that person or from any person who—

(a) is insured by the policy, or whose liability is covered by the security, by the terms of which the liability would be covered if the policy insured all persons or, as the case may be, the security covered the liability of all persons, and

(b) caused or permitted the use of the vehicle which gave rise to the liability.

(9) In this section—

(a) "insurer" includes a person giving a security,

(b) [...]

(c) "liability covered by the terms of the policy or security" means a liability which is covered by the policy or security or which would be so covered but for the fact that the insurer is entitled to avoid or cancel, or has avoided or cancelled, the policy or security.

* * * *

Amendments

3F–86   The words in square brackets in subs.(9) repealed by the Road Traffic Act (1991 c.40), Sched. 8 para. 1.

Note

3F–87

By s.143(1) of this Act, every person who uses or causes, or who permits another person to use a motor vehicle on a road in a public place must be insured or must have given security, in respect of third party risks which are set out in Part VI of the Act (principally s.145). See the notes to s.143 *ante*.

The object of this section is to ensure that an insurer cannot normally escape or exclude liability to pay in respect of third party injury and loss if a judgment is made against the insured.

Subsection (2)(b) ensures that the driver of the vehicle does not have to be the insured person: the policy must in effect therefore cover any driver for the risks specified in the Act. By subs.(3) it is not permissible for an insurer to seek to exclude liability for unlicensed drivers of the vehicle, though the insurer may seek to recover sums paid out from the insured in such circumstances (subs.(7)).

An exception to the general rule is stated in subs.(4) in respect of persons knowingly riding in stolen or unlawfully taken vehicles save where they did not know and "had no reason to believe" that the vehicle had been stolen or unlawfully taken until after the commencement of the journey, and they could not reasonably have been expected to have alighted from the vehicle.

Subs.(4) "had no reason to believe"

3F–88

This expression is taken to mean "deliberately turned a blind eye" to the fact that the vehicle was stolen. (*White v. White* [2001] 1 W.L.R. 481, HL).

Exceptions to section 151

3F–89

152.—(1) No sum is payable by an insurer under section 151 of this Act—

    (a) in respect of any judgment unless, before or within seven days after the commencement of the proceedings in which the judgment was given, the insurer had notice of the bringing of the proceedings, or

    (b) in respect of any judgment so long as execution on the judgment is stayed pending an appeal, or

    (c) in connection with any liability if, before the happening of the event which was the cause of the death or bodily injury or damage to property giving rise to the liability, the policy or security was cancelled by mutual consent or by virtue of any provision contained in it, and also—

        (i) before the happening of that event the certificate was surrendered to the insurer, or the person to whom the certificate was delivered made a statutory declaration stating that the certificate had been lost or destroyed, or

        (ii) after the happening of that event, but before the expiration of a period of fourteen days from the taking effect of the cancellation of the policy or security, the certificate was surrendered to the insurer, or the person to whom it was delivered made a statutory declaration stating that the certificate had been lost or destroyed, or

        (iii) either before or after the happening of that event, but within that period of fourteen days, the insurer has commenced proceedings under this Act in respect of the failure to surrender the certificate.

    (2) Subject to subsection (3) below, no sum is payable by an

insurer under section 151 of this Act if, in an action commenced before, or within three months after, the commencement of the proceedings in which the judgment was given, he has obtained a declaration—

    (a) that, apart from any provision contained in the policy or security, he is entitled to avoid it on the ground that it was obtained—

        (i) by the non-disclosure of a material fact, or

        (ii) by a representation of fact which was false in some material particular, or

    (b) if he has avoided the policy or security on that ground, that he was entitled so to do apart from any provision contained in it.

[and, for the purposes of this section, "material" means of such a nature as to influence the judgment of a prudent insurer in determining whether he will take the risk and, if so, at what premium and on what conditions].

(3) An insurer who has obtained such a declaration as is mentioned in subsection (2) above in an action does not by reason of that become entitled to the benefit of that subsection as respects any judgment obtained in proceedings commenced before the commencement of that action unless before, or within seven days after, the commencement of that action he has given notice of it to the person who is the plaintiff (or in Scotland pursuer) in those proceedings specifying the non-disclosure or false representation on which he proposes to rely.

(4) A person to whom notice of such an action is so given is entitled, if he thinks fit, to be made a party to it.

Amendments

3F–90   The words in square brackets in subs.(2) inserted by the Road Traffic Act (1991 c.40), Sched.4 para. 66.

Note

3F–91   This section sets out the main additional exceptions to the broad cover provided by s.151. By subs.(1)(a) late notification of claim to the insurer (within seven days after commencement of proceedings) enables the insurer to decline to pay. Similarly no sum need be paid if there is a stay of execution pending appeal (subs.1(b)), or in the circumstances relating to voluntary cancellation of the policy detailed in subs.1(c) prior to the act leading to liability.

Misrepresentation and non-disclosure of material facts

3F–92   By subs.(2) in limited circumstances an insurer may avoid payment if a policy was obtained by misrepresentation or non-disclosure of a material fact and the insurer shows he is entitled to avoid the policy. To take advantage of the provision the insurer must first seek a declaration that it is entitled to avoid the policy. The insurer must however seek such a declaration from the court within three months of commencement of the proceedings against the insured.

By subs.(3) If the declaration is sought after the damages claim has been commenced against the insured the insurer will not be allowed to rely on the declaration unless within seven days after commencing the claim for a declaration it notifies the claimant in the main claim of the fact that it is applying for a declaration, and specifies the non-disclosure or misrepresentation relied on. The claimant in the main claim may if he chooses become a party to the declaration claim (subs.(4)).

"material" facts

3F–93   For the purposes of subs.(2), "material" means "of such a nature as to influence the judgment of a prudent insurer in determining whether he will take the risk and, if so, at what premium and on what conditions" (subs.(2)).

Bankruptcy, death and sequestration of assets do not affect cover

By s.153, if a person dies, becomes bankrupt or suffers sequestration of assets (or **3F–94** makes a composition or arrangement with his creditors, or grants a trust deed for his creditors) after the event which leads to liability, the insurer's obligation to pay does not cease merely for that reason. Similar provisions apply in the case of companies who are insured persons, also under s.153.

Law Reform (Personal Injuries) Act 1948

(11 & 12 GEO. 6 C.41)

An Act to abolish the defence of common employment, to amend the law relating to the measure of damages for personal injury or death, and for purposes connected therewith.

[30th June 1948] **3F–95**

ARRANGEMENT OF SECTIONS

PERSONAL INJURY

Common employment

1.—(1) It shall not be a defence to an employer who is sued in re- **3F–96** spect of personal injuries caused by the negligence of a person employed by him, that that person was at the time the injuries were caused in common employment with the person injured.

(2) Accordingly the Employers' Liability Act 1880, shall cease to have effect, and is hereby repealed.

(3) Any provision contained in a contract of service or apprenticeship, or in an agreement collateral thereto (including a contract or agreement entered into before the commencement of this Act) shall be void in so far as it would have the effect of excluding or limiting any liability of the employer in respect of personal injuries caused to the person employed or apprenticed by the negligence of persons in common employment with him.

Measure of damages

2.— [...] **3F–97**

(4) In an action for damages for personal injuries (including any such action arising out of a contract), there shall be disregarded, in determining the reasonableness of any expenses, the possibility of avoiding those expenses or part of them by taking advantage of facilities under the National Health Service Act 1977 or the National Health Service (Scotland) Act 1978, or of any corresponding facilities in Northern Ireland.

[...]

Note

Amended by the Fatal Accidents Act 1959; the Social Security (Consequential Provi- **3F–98** sions) Act 1975, s.1(3) and Sched.2. Social Security Pensions Act 1975, s.65(1) and

Sched.4; the National Health Service Act 1977, s.129 and Sched.15; the Health and Social Security Act 1984, Sched.4, para. 1; the Social Security Act 1989, Scheds 4 and 9; and the Social Security Act 1990, Sched.1; subs. (1), (1A), (3), and (6) omitted by the Social Security (Recovery of Benefits) Act 1997 (1997 c.27), Sched.3 para. 1.

"Rights"—"value of rights"

3F–99   For the procedure in relation to Recoupment of Benefits from damages awards in personal injury cases see the Social Security (Recovery of Benefits) Act 1997 (1997 c.27) and regulations thereunder.

Definition of "personal injury"

3F–100   **3. In this Act the expression "personal injury" includes any disease and any impairment of a person's physical or mental condition, and the expression "injured" shall be construed accordingly.**

Application to Crown

3F–101   **4. This Act shall bind the Crown.**

* * *

Short title and commencement

3F–102   **6.—(1) This Act may be cited as the Law Reform (Personal Injuries) Act 1948.**

(2) Section one and subsection (1) of section two of this Act shall apply only where the cause of action accrues on or after the day appointed for the National Insurance (Industrial Injuries) Act 1946, to take effect; but subsections (4) and (5) of the said section two shall apply whether the cause of action accrued or the action was commenced before or after the commencement of this Act.

CONDITIONAL FEE MATERIALS IN PERSONAL INJURY AND CLINICAL
NEGLIGENCE CASES

Contents

Introductory Note

3F–104   The materials here have been compiled in the light of substantial changes to conditional fee regulations which took place in November 2005. The notes and guidance in Volume 1 relating to the subject of costs generally should be referred to on more general costs points and in relation to detailed assessment of conditional fee costs. The materials here (more particularly the Solicitors' Practice (Client Care) Amendment Rule 2005, the Law Society model CFA agreement and the Law Society client information text) arise against a historical backdrop which it is beyond the proper scope of this work to set out in full but brief contextual information appears in the relevant footnotes to the materials.

Access to Justice Act 1999

1999 c.22

27—(1) For section 58 of the Courts and Legal Services Act 1990 **3F–105** substitute—

"Conditional fee agreements

58—(1) A conditional fee agreement which satisfies all of the conditions applicable to it by virtue of this section shall not be unenforceable by reason only of its being a conditional fee agreement; but (subject to subsection (5)) any other conditional fee agreement shall be unenforceable.

(2) For the purposes of this section and section 58A—

    (a) a conditional fee agreement is an agreement with a person providing advocacy or litigation services which provides for his fees and expenses, or any part of them, to be payable only in specified circumstances; and

    (b) a conditional fee agreement provides for a success fee if it provides for the amount of any fees to which it applies to be increased, in specified circumstances, above the amount which would be payable if it were not payable only in specified circumstances.

(3) The following conditions are applicable to every conditional fee agreement—

    (a) it must be in writing;

    (b) it must not relate to proceedings which cannot be the subject of an enforceable conditional fee agreement; and

    (c) it must comply with such requirements (if any) as may be prescribed by the Lord Chancellor.

(4) The following further conditions are applicable to a conditional fee agreement which provides for a success fee—

    (a) it must relate to proceedings of a description specified by order made by the Lord Chancellor[1];

    (b) must state the percentage by which the amount of the fees which would be payable if it were not a conditional fee agreement is to be increased; and

    (c)) that percentage must not exceed the percentage specified in relation to the description of proceedings to which the agreement relates by order made by the Lord Chancellor.[2]

(5) If a conditional fee agreement is an agreement to which section 57 of the Solicitors Act 1974 (non-contentious business agreements between solicitor and client) applies, subsection (1) shall not make it unenforceable.

---

[1] All proceedings which can be the subject of an enforceable conditional fee agreement under s. 58, other than proceedings under s. 82 of the Environmental Protection Act 1990, are specified for the purposes of s.58(4)(a) by r. 3 of The Conditional Fee Agreements Order 2000, SI 2000 No. 823.

[2] Presently r. 4 of The Conditional Fee Agreements Order 2000, SI 2000 No. 823 prescribes a maximum success fee of 100%.

Conditional fee agreements: supplementary

58A.—(1) The proceedings which cannot be the subject of an enforceable conditional fee agreement are—

> "(a) criminal proceedings, apart from proceedings under section 82 of the Environmental Protection Act 1990; and
>
> (b) family proceedings."

(2) In subsection (1) "family proceedings" means proceedings under any one or more of the following—

(a) the Matrimonial Causes Act 1973;

(b) the Adoption Act 1976;

(c) the Domestic Proceedings and Magistrates' Courts Act 1978;

(d) Part III of the Matrimonial and Family Proceedings Act 1984;

(e) Parts I, II and IV of the Children Act 1989;

(f) Part IV of the Family Law Act 1996; and

(g) the inherent jurisdiction of the High Court in relation to children.

(3) The requirements which the Lord Chancellor may prescribe under section 58(3)(c)—

(a) include requirements for the person providing advocacy or litigation services to have provided prescribed information before the agreement is made; and

(b) may be different for different descriptions of conditional fee agreements (and, in particular, may be different for those which provide for a success fee and those which do not).

(4) In section 58 and this section (and in the definitions of "advocacy services" and "litigation services" as they apply for their purposes) "proceedings" includes any sort of proceedings for resolving disputes (and not just proceedings in a court), whether commenced or contemplated.

(5) Before making an order under section 58(4), the Lord Chancellor shall consult—

(a) the designated judges;

(b) the General Council of the Bar;

(c) the Law Society; and

(d) such other bodies as he considers appropriate.

(6) A costs order made in any proceedings may, subject in the case of court proceedings to rules of court, include provision requiring the payment of any fees payable under a conditional fee agreement which provides for a success fee.

(7) Rules of court may make provision with respect to the assessment of any costs which include fees payable under a conditional fee agreement (including one which provides for a success fee)."

(8) In section 120(4) of the Courts and Legal Services Act 1990 (orders and regulations subject to affirmative procedure), for "58," substitute "58(4),".

Courts and Legal Services Act 1990 s.58 and The Access to Justice Act 1999 s.27

Prior to the enactment of the Courts and Legal Services Act 1990 the historical po- **3F–106**
sition had been that conditional fee agreements were not lawful. A solicitor acting for a
client in litigation was not entitled to agree with the client to accept a financial reward
which varied according to the success of the case. See the Court of Appeal's judgment
in *Thai Trading (A firm) v. Taylor* [1998] QB 781 for a summary of the early development of the law relating to Champerty and Maintenance. Following a policy review in
1988 and consultation, the original form of s.58 of the Courts and Legal Services Act
1990 was enacted, with Regulations following in 1995 to permit CFA's to be used in a
fairly circumscribed range of six types of case. New regulations in 1998 extended the
range of cases in which a CFA could be used but 'no win no fee' funding as it became
known had to await developments in case law and statute before becoming
commonplace. In early 1998 the Court of Appeal gave judgment in *Thai Trading (A
firm) v. Taylor* [1998] QB 781, holding that an agreement between solicitor and client
that the solicitor would charge no fee in the event of failure and only his normal fee in
the event of success was no longer contrary to public policy and was not an unlawful
agreement despite involving conduct by the solicitor which had been in breach of rule
8 of the then Solicitor's Practice Rules (which forbade conditional fee agreements).
Thai Trading was initially not followed at Divisional Court level (*Hughes v. Kingston
upon Hull City Council* [1999] QB 1193), on the basis that a dictum in the House of
Lords case of *Swain v. The Law Society* [1983] 1 AC 598, that the Solicitors' Practice
rules "had the force of a statute" was incompatible with the *Thai Trading* decision and
that *Swain* had not been considered in *Thai Trading*. Rule 8 of the Solicitor's Practice
rules was then swiftly amended to permit CFA agreements to be entered into provided
they were lawful either at common law or under statute.

In 1999 reform to the whole subject of litigation funding was considered by Parlia- **3F–107**
ment and the subject was placed on a new statutory footing in the guise of s.27 of the
Access to Justice Act 1999 above, which wholly replaced s.58 of the Courts and legal
Services Act 1990 and introduced s.58A. By these sections CFA agreements, provided
they complied with the Act and any relevant regulations, are no longer unenforceable
but any other forms of CFA are rendered unenforceable, a fact confirmed by the
Court of Appeal in *Awwad v. Geraghty & Co.* [2001] QB 570 to the effect that there was
no longer scope for development of the Common Law in the area of CFA agreements.

The Solicitors' Practice Rules

(Costs information and client care)
15 Solicitors shall: **3F–108**

(a) give information about costs and other matters, and

(b) operate a complaints handling procedure,

in accordance with a Solicitors' Costs Information and Client Care
Code made from time to time by the Council of the Law Society with
the concurrence of the Master of the Rolls, but subject to the notes.

Notes

(i) A serious breach of the code, or persistent breaches of a material nature, will be a breach of the rule, and may also be evidence of
inadequate professional services under section 37A of the Solicitors'
Act 1974.

(ii) Material breaches of the code which are not serious or persistent will not be a breach of the rule, but may be evidence of inadequate professional services under section 37A.

(iii) The powers of the Law Society on a finding of inadequate
professional services include:

(a) disallowing all or part of the solicitor's costs; and

PERSONAL INJURY

(b) directing the solicitor to pay compensation to the client up to a limit of £5,000.

(iv) Non-material breaches of the code will not be a breach of the rule, and will not be evidence of inadequate professional services under section 37A.

(v) Registered foreign lawyers practising in partnership with solicitors of the Supreme Court or registered European lawyers, or as members of recognised bodies which are limited liability partnerships, or as directors of recognised bodies which are companies, although subject to Rule 15 as a matter of professional conduct, are not subject to section 37A. However, such solicitors, registered European lawyers and recognised bodies are subject to section 37A for professional services provided by the firm.

The Solicitors' Practice (Client Care) Amendment Rule [2005]

3F–109 (1)At the end of paragraph 5 of the Solicitors' Costs Information and Client Care Code 1999 add:[1]

"Clients represented under a conditional fee agreement (including a collective conditional fee agreement)

(d) Where a client is represented under a conditional fee agreement, the solicitor should explain:

(i) the circumstances in which the client may be liable for their own costs and for the other party's costs;

(ii) the client's right to assessment of costs, wherever the solicitor intends to seek payment of any or all of their costs from the client; and

(iii) any interest the solicitor may have in recommending a particular policy or other funding."

(2)This rule will come into force on[2] [the date of notification of the Lord Chancellor's approval or the date of repeal of the Conditional Fee Agreements Regulations (2000), whichever is the later].

The Solicitors' Costs Information and Client Care Code 1999

3F–110 The Law Society published the Solicitors' Costs Information and Client Care Code in 1999 with the effect that solicitors were professionally obliged to provide to clients a wide range of information about charging and about funding options available to them, orally and in writing. This amendment to the Code was introduced in the light of the revocation in November 2005 of the Conditional Fees regulations of 2000 and 2003 (see notes to the Conditional Fee Agreements (Revocation) Regulations 2005 below).

The developing role of professional rules and guidance as to conditional fee agreements

3F–111 The history of the courts' approach to the consequences of breach of Law Society's practice rules in relation to CFA's might give encouragement to litigators seeking to

---

[1] Rule made by the Council of the Law Society under Pt II of the Solicitors Act 1974 and s.9 of the Administration of Justice Act 1985, with the concurrence of the Master of the Rolls under that section and the approval of the Lord Chancellor under Sch. 4 to the Courts and Legal services Act 1990, regulating the conduct of solicitors, registered European lawyers, registered foreign lawyers and recognised bodies.
[2] *i.e.* November 1, 2005 by virtue of The Conditional Fee Agreements (Revocation) Regulations 2005, S.I. 2005 No. 2305

raise challenges to the new-form CFA agreements if there are departures from the Code. If the strict letter of the Code supplied by the Law Society is not followed it may be that a challenge could be founded upon that breach on the basis that the guidance is made pursuant to Law Society rules. It will be recalled that in *Thai Trading (A Firm) v. Taylor* [1998] QB 781, the Court of Appeal had regarded a breach of rule 8 of the Solicitor's practice rules as not affecting the enforceability or lawfulness of a fee agreement, but that the Divisional Court in *Hughes v. Kingston upon Hull City Council* [1999] QB 1193, in refusing to follow *Thai Trading*, relied upon a dictum in *Swain v. The Law Society* [1983] 1 AC 598 that the Law Society's rules 'had the force of a statute. . . just as much as if the rules, . . . were set out in a Schedule to the Act ' (per Lord Brightman in *Swain* at page 621G, cited in *Hughes*).

It appears however that more recent re-interpretation of Swain given by the Court of Appeal in *Garbutt v. Edwards* [2005] EWCA Civ 1206 treats the Solicitors' Practice rules (in that instance rule 15) as a species of subordinate legislation the breach of which does not of itself necessarily render a funding contract unlawful and similarly decides that a breach of the Solicitors' Costs Information and Client Care Code does not necessarily have that consequence either. It is suggested that that is the correct approach, not least on the basis that to adopt too literal a reading of Lord Brightman's dictum in *Swain* quoted above might imply that the Law Society is empowered to create primary legislation. In a sense the *Thai Trading* public policy approach towards breaches of the Solicitors Practice rules has been revived, Per Arden LJ at para. 31 in *Garbutt v. Edward*:

> Estimates are required only by the Code (as defined above). The Code is made pursuant to Rule 15 of the Solicitors' Practice Rules. These Rules are made by the Council of the Law Society pursuant to section 31 of the 1974 Act (set out above). In making these Rules, the Council of the Law Society is acting in the public interest, and the Rules have the force of subordinate legislation: *Swain v. Law Society* [1983] A.C. 598. The inference I would draw is that the Code is there to protect the legitimate interests of the client, and the administration of justice, rather than to relieve paying parties of their obligations to pay costs which have been reasonably incurred.

The Conditional Fee Agreements (Revocation) Regulations 2005

S.I. 2005 No. 2305

Citation and commencement

1. These Regulations may be cited as the Conditional Fee Agreements (Revocation) Regulations 2005 and shall come into force on 1st November 2005.[1]

3F–112

Revocation

2. Subject to regulation 3, the Conditional Fee Agreements Regulations 2000 (the "CFA Regulations"), the Collective Conditional Fee Agreements Regulations 2000 (the "CCFA Regulations"), the Conditional Fee Agreements (Miscellaneous Amendments) Regulations 2003, and the Conditional Fee Agreements (Miscellaneous Amendments) (No. 2) Regulations 2003 are revoked.

Savings and transitional provisions

3.—(1) The CFA Regulations shall continue to have effect for the

---

[1] The official explanatory note to these regulations stated that parties may enter into Conditional Fee Agreements and Collective Conditional Fee Agreements on or after November 1, 2005 date based on the 'primary legislation', namely s.27 of the Access to Justice Act 1999. The Regulations were made on August 9, 2005, laid before Parliament on August 19, 2005 and came into force on November 1, 2005. The regulations were made by the Secretary of State in exercise of powers conferred upon the Lord Chancellor by ss. 58(3)(c), 58A(3), 119 and 120(3) of the Courts and Legal Services Act 1990.

purposes of a conditional fee agreement entered into before 1st November 2005.

(2) Paragraph (1) shall apply in relation to a collective conditional fee agreement as if there were substituted for a reference to the CFA Regulations a reference to the CCFA Regulations.

The 2000 & 2003 Regulations

3F–113   The protections provided in the Solicitors' Costs Information and Client Care Code 1999 were joined by a series of arguably precipitate regulations in circumstances which were described at paragraphs 25-30 of the Court of Appeal's judgment in the subsequent case of *Hollins v. Russell* [2003] EWCA 718. The Conditional Fee Agreements Regulations 2000 (S.I. 2000 No. 692), the Collective Conditional Fee Agreements Regulations 2000 (S.I. 2000 No. 2988), Conditional Fee Agreements (Miscellaneous Amendments) Regulations 2003 (S.I. 2003 No.1240), and the Conditional Fee Agreements (Miscellaneous Amendments) (No. 2) Regulations 2003 (S.I. 2003 No. 3344), were highly prescriptive and served to provide a technical battleground for challenges to CFA agreements by paying parties in the course of detailed assessment. The case history of technical challenges is lengthy: for a cross-section of challenges concerning the adherence to regulations see *Hollins v. Russell* [2003] EWCA 718, *Sarwar v. Alam* [2002] 1 WLR 125, *Bowen v. Bridgend Borough Council 25/3/2004 SCCO case no. 0309853*, *Richards v. Davis 25/11/2005 SCCO case no. PTH0504722*, *Hughes v. LB Newham 28/7/2005 SCCO case no. 0502314*, *Samonini v. London General Transport Services Limited 19/1/2005 SCCO case no. DOFL 0405618*, *Woods v. Chaleff, 30/4/2002 SCCO case no. PR0108754, 0108755*, and the numerous test and first instance cases which can be accessed through the Supreme Court Costs Office website at www.hmcourts-service.gov.uk/infoabout/scco/transcripts/index.htm

Revocation of the 2000 and 2003 Regulations

3F–114   In 2003 and 2004 the Government conducted consultation on the subject of the simplification of the regulatory legislation governing CFA's in the light of the state of affairs described above. The conclusion was that that the CFA regulations were not necessary or effective and to a large extent duplicated existing professional regulation and should be revoked so that the primary legislation in the form of s.27 of the Access to Justice Act 1999 would provide the basic legislative framework for the use of CFAs. The primary responsibility for client care, contractual and guidance aspects would be via the Law Society's Professional Rules and supporting guidance. The Conditional Fee Agreements (Revocation) Regulations 2005 (S.I. 2005 No. 2305), reproduced in this section were the result, together with the Solicitors' Practice (Client Care) Amendment Rule [2005] and the Law Society's model CFA and guidance text for clients which also appear here. The entire new regime—effectively revoking the whole of the body of regulations governing the form and content of CFA agreements—came into force on November 1, 2005 and has been observed judicially as being intended by Parliament to prevent further technical challenges. (See the judgment of the Senior Costs Judge in *Richards v. Davis 25/11/2005 SCCO case no. PTH0504722* at para. 91: '...in revoking the CFA regulations Parliament's desire is clearly to prevent further technical challenges. Such challenges take up a disproportionate amount of court time and prevent the proper development of the CFA and ATE market. The client's protection has not simply been abandoned, but the regulation of the funding regime has been taken on by the professional bodies, in particular, by the Law Society which has passed the Solicitors' Practice (Amendment) Rule 2005.')

Note that by reg. 3 the 2000 and 2003 regulations continue to have effect in respect of agreements entered into before November 1, 2005, though there is presumably no reason in law why a client and solicitor cannot elect to enter into a new fee agreement under the new regime after that date by mutual agreement notwithstanding that they had earlier contracted under the old regime.

Law Society Model Conditional Fee Agreement (2005) (Personal Injury and Clinical Negligence cases)

CFA[1]

3F–115

For use in personal injury and clinical negligence cases only.

This agreement is a binding legal contract between you and your solicitor/s. Before you sign, please read everything carefully. This agreement must be read in conjunction with the Law Society document "What you need to know about a CFA".

Agreement date
[..]
I/We, the solicitors/s [. . . .
]
You, the client[. . . .
]

What is covered by this agreement
- Your claim against [ ] for damages for personal injury suffered on [ ] *(if either the name of the opponent or the date of the incident are unclear then set out here in as much detail as possible to give sufficient information for the client and solicitor to understand the basis of the claim being pursued)*
- Any appeal by your opponent.
- Any appeal you make against an interim order.
- Any proceedings you take to enforce a judgment, order or agreement.
- Negotiations about and/or a court assessment of the costs of this claim.

What is not covered by this agreement
- Any counterclaim against you.
- Any appeal you make against the final judgment order.

Paying us
If you win your claim, you pay our basic charges, our disbursements and a success fee. You are entitled to seek recovery from your opponent of part or all of our basic charges, our disbursements, a success fee and insurance premium as set out in the document "What you need to know about a CFA."

It may be that your opponent makes a Part 36 offer or payment which you reject on our advice, and your claim for damages goes ahead to trial where you recover damages that are less than that offer or payment. If this happens, we will *[not add our success fee to the basic charges] [not claim any costs]* for the work done after we received notice of the offer or payment.

If you receive interim damages, we may require you to pay our disbursements at that point and a reasonable amount for our future disbursements.

If you receive provisional damages, we are entitled to payment of our basic charges our disbursements and success fee at that point.

If you lose you remain liable for the other side's costs.

The Success Fee
The success fee is set at [....................]% of basic charges, where the claim concludes at trial; or [....................]% where the claim concludes before a trial has commenced. In addition [....................]% relates to the postponement of payment of our fees and expenses and can not be recovered from your opponent. The Success fee inclusive of any additional percentage relating to postponement cannot be more than 100% of the basic charges in total.

---

[1] This model Conditional Fee Agreement for use in Personal Injury and Clinical Negligence cases is reproduced with the kind permission of the Law Society.

PERSONAL INJURY

Other points

The parties acknowledge and agree that this agreement is not a Contentious Business Agreement within the terms of the Solicitors Act 1974.

Signatures

Signed by the solicitor(s):...

Signed by the client: ....

Law Society Model CFA Agreement—Information for Clients (2005)

3F–116

Conditional Fee Agreements: what you need to know

Definitions of words used in this document and the accompanying CFA are explained at the end of this document.[1]

What do I pay if I win?

If you win your claim, you pay our basic charges, our disbursements and a success fee. The amount of these is not based on or limited by the damages. You can claim from your opponent part or all of our basic charges, our disbursements, a success fee and insurance premium.

It may be that your opponent makes a Part 36 offer or payment which you reject on our advice, and your claim for damages goes ahead to trial where you recover damages that are less than that offer or payment. Refer to the "Paying Us" section in the CFA document to establish costs we will be seeking for the work done after we received notice of the offer or payment.

If you receive interim damages, we may require you to pay our disbursements at that point as well as a reasonable amount for our future disbursements.

If you receive provisional damages, we are entitled to payment of our basic charges, our disbursements and success fee at that point.

If you win overall but on the way lose an interim hearing, you may be required to pay your opponent's charges of that hearing.

If on the way to winning or losing you are awarded any costs, by agreement or court order, then we are entitled to payment of those costs, together with a success fee on those charges if you win overall.

What do I pay if I lose?

If you lose, you pay your opponent's charges and disbursements. You may be able to take out an insurance policy against this risk. If you lose, you do not pay our charges but we may require you to pay our disbursements.

Ending this agreement

If you end this agreement before you win or lose, you pay our basic charges and disbursements. If you go on to win, you also pay a success fee.

We may end this agreement before you win or lose.

Basic charges

These are for work done from now until this agreement ends. These are subject to review.

How we calculate our basic charges

These are calculated for each hour engaged on your matter. Routine letters and telephone calls will be charged as units of one tenth of an hour. Other letters and telephone calls will be charged on a time basis. The hourly rates are:

---

[1] This document is the Information for Clients document published by the Law Society and is copyright (c) 2005 The Law Society. It is reproduced with their kind permission.

Grade of Fee Earner	Hourly Rate
1 Solicitors with over eight years post qualification experience including at least eight years litigation experience.	
2 Solicitors and legal executives with over four years post qualification experience including at least four years litigation experience.	
3 Other solicitors and legal executives and fee earners of equivalent experience	
4 Trainee solicitors, para legals and other fee earners.	

We review the hourly rate on [review date] and we will notify you of any change in the rate in writing.

Road Traffic Accidents

[If your claim is settled before proceedings are issued, for less than £10,000, our basic costs will be £800; plus 20% of the damages agreed up to £5,000; and 15% of the damages agreed between £5,000 and £10,000.] [If you live in London, these costs will be increased by 12.5%]. These costs are fixed by the Civil Procedure Rules.

Success fee

The success fee percentage set out in the agreement reflects the following:

(a) the fact that if you lose, we will not earn anything;

(b) our assessment of the risks of your case;

(c) any other appropriate matters;

(d) the fact that if you win we will not be paid our basic charges until the end of the claim;

(e) our arrangements with you about paying disbursements.

Value added tax (VAT)

We add VAT, at the rate (now [...............]%) that applies when the work is done, to the total of the basic charges and success fee.

The Insurance Policy

In all the circumstances and on the information currently available to us, we believe, that a contract of insurance with [............................] is appropriate to cover your opponent's charges and disbursements in case you lose.

This is because

> You do not have an existing or satisfactory insurance that would cover the costs of making this claim. The policy we recommend will pay:
>
> (a) the costs of the other party in the event that the claim fails, to a maximum of £X;
>
> (b) all your disbursements if your claim fails.
>
> (c) [add other key features where necessary such as, our costs and the other side's costs (without deduction from your damages) if you fail to beat an (Part 36) Offer to Settle your claim, which you rejected following our advice].

or:

> [We cannot identify a policy which meets your needs but our recommended policy is the closest that we can discover within the products that we have searched. It does not meet your needs in the following respects:
>
> (a) it has an excess of £Z
>
> (b) the maximum cover is £ZZ]

or:

> [We cannot obtain an insurance policy at this stage but we shall continue to look

PERSONAL INJURY

for one and if we are successful in our search then we shall advise you at that stage of the benefits of the policy and purchasing it]

[NB. The italicised reasons in set out are examples only. Your solicitor must consider your individual circumstances and set out the reasons that apply].

Law Society Conditions

The Law Society Conditions below are part of this agreement. Any amendments or additions to them will apply to you. You should read the conditions carefully and ask us about anything you find unclear.

Our responsibilities

We must:

- always act in your best interests, subject to our duty to the court;
- explain to you the risks and benefits of taking legal action;
- give you our best advice about whether to accept any offer of settlement;
- give you the best information possible about the likely costs of your claim for damages.

Your responsibilities

You must:

- give us instructions that allow us to do our work properly;
- not ask us to work in an improper or unreasonable way;
- not deliberately mislead us;
- co-operate with us;
- go to any medical or expert examination or court hearing.

Dealing with costs if you win

- You are liable to pay all our basic charges, our disbursements and success fee.
- Normally, you can claim part or all of our basic charges, our disbursements success fee and insurance premium from your opponent.
- If we and your opponent cannot agree the amount, the court will decide how much you can recover. If the amount agreed or allowed by the court does not cover all our basic charges and our disbursements, then you pay the difference.
- You will not be entitled to recover from your opponent the part of the success fee that relates to the cost to us of postponing receipt of our charges and our disbursements. This remains payable by you.
- You agree that after winning, the reasons for setting the success fee at the amount stated may be disclosed:
  - (i) to the court and any other person required by the court;
  - (ii) to your opponent in order to gain his or her agreement to pay the success fee.
- If the court carries out an assessment and reduces the success fee because the percentage agreed was unreasonable in view of what we knew or should have known when it was agreed, then the amount reduced ceases to be payable unless the court is satisfied that it should continue to be payable.
- If we agree with your opponent that the success fee is to be paid at a lower percentage than is set out in this agreement, then the success fee percentage will be reduced accordingly unless the court is satisfied that the full amount is payable.
- It may happen that your opponent makes an offer of one amount that includes payment of our basic charges and a success fee. If so, unless we consent, you agree not to tell us to accept the offer if it includes payment of the success fee at a lower rate than is set out in this agreement.
- If your opponent is receiving Community Legal Service funding, we are unlikely to get any money from him or her. So if this happens, you have to pay us our basic charges, disbursements and success fee.

As with the costs in general, you remain ultimately responsible for paying our success fee.

You agree to pay into a designated account any cheque received by you or by us from your opponent and made payable to you. Out of the money, you agree to let us take the balance of the basic charges; success fee; insurance premium; our remaining disbursements; and VAT.

You take the rest.

We are allowed to keep any interest your opponent pays on the charges.

If your opponent fails to pay

If your opponent does not pay any damages or charges owed to you, we have the right to take recovery action in your name to enforce a judgment, order or agreement. The charges of this action become part of the basic charges.

Payment for advocacy

The cost of advocacy and any other work by us, or by any solicitor agent on our behalf, forms part of our basic charges. We shall discuss with you the identity of any barrister instructed, and the arrangements made for payment.

Barristers who have a conditional fee agreement with us

If you win, you are normally entitled to recover their fee and success fee from your opponent. The barrister's success fee is shown in the separate conditional fee agreement we make with the barrister. We will discuss the barrister's success fee with you before we instruct him or her. If you lose, you pay the barrister nothing.

Barristers who do not have a conditional fee agreement with us

If you win, then you will normally be entitled to recover all or part of their fee from your opponent. If you lose, then you must pay their fee.

What happens when this agreement ends before your claim for damages ends?

(a) Paying us if you end this agreement

You can end the agreement at any time. We then have the right to decide whether you must:

- pay our basic charges and our disbursements including barristers' fees but not the success fee when we ask for them; or
- pay our basic charges, and our disbursements including barristers' fees and success fees if you go on to win your claim for damages.

(b) Paying us if we end this agreement

(i) We can end this agreement if you do not keep to your responsibilities. We then have the right to decide whether you must:

- pay our basic charges and our disbursements including barristers' fees but not the success fee when we ask for them; or
- pay our basic charges and our disbursements including barristers' fees and success fees if you go on to win your claim for damages.

(ii) We can end this agreement if we believe you are unlikely to win. If this happens, you will only have to pay our disbursements. These will include barristers' fees if the barrister does not have a conditional fee agreement with us.

(iii) We can end this agreement if you reject our opinion about making a settlement with your opponent. You must then:

- pay the basic charges and our disbursements, including barristers' fees;
- pay the success fee if you go on to win your claim for damages.

If you ask us to get a second opinion from a specialist solicitor outside our firm, we will do so. You pay the cost of a second opinion.

(iv) We can end this agreement if you do not pay your insurance premium when asked to do so.

(c) Death

This agreement automatically ends if you die before your claim for damages is concluded. We will be entitled to recover our basic charges up to the date of your death from your estate.

If your personal representatives wish to continue your claim for damages, we may offer them a new conditional fee agreement, as long as they agree to pay the success fee on our basic charges from the beginning of the agreement with you.

What happens after this agreement ends

After this agreement ends, we may apply to have our name removed from the record of any court proceedings in which we are acting unless you have another form of funding and ask us to work for you.

We have the right to preserve our lien unless another solicitor working for you undertakes to pay us what we are owed including a success fee if you win.

Explanation of words used

(a) Advocacy
Appearing for you at court hearings.

(b) Basic charges
Our charges for the legal work we do on your claim for damages.

(c) Claim
Your demand for damages for personal injury whether or not court proceedings are issued.

(d) Counterclaim
A claim that your opponent makes against you in response to your claim.

(e) Damages
Money that you win whether by a court decision or settlement.

(f) Our disbursements
Payment we make on your behalf such as:

- court fees;
- experts' fees;
- accident report fees;
- travelling expenses.

(g) Interim damages
Money that a court says your opponent must pay or your opponent agrees to pay while waiting for a settlement or the court's final decision.

(h) Interim hearing
A court hearing that is not final.

(i) Lien
Our right to keep all papers, documents, money or other property held on your behalf until all money due to us is paid. A lien may be applied after this agreement ends.

(j) Lose
The court has dismissed your claim or you have stopped it on our advice.

(k) Part 36 offers or payments
An offer to settle your claim made in accordance with Part 36 of the Civil Procedure Rules.

(l) Provisional damages
Money that a court says your opponent must pay or your opponent agrees to pay, on the basis that you will be able to go back to court at a future date for further damages if:

- you develop a serious disease; or
- your condition deteriorates;

in a way that has been proved or admitted to be linked to your personal injury claim.

(m) Success fee
The percentage of basic charges that we add to your bill if you win your claim for damages and that we will seek to recover from your opponent.

(n) Trial
The final contested hearing or the contested hearing of any issue to be tried separately

and a reference to a claim concluding at trial includes a claim settled after the trial has commenced or a judgment.

(o) Win

Your claim for damages is finally decided in your favour, whether by a court decision or an agreement to pay you damages or in any way that you derive benefit from pursuing the claim.

'Finally' means that your opponent:

- is not allowed to appeal against the court decision; or
- has not appealed in time; or
- has lost any appeal.

The Untraced Drivers' Agreement Department of Transport Motor Insurers' Bureau (Compensation of Victims of Untraced Drivers)

3F–117

14th February 2003

THIS AGREEMENT is made the seventh day of February 2003 between the **SECRETARY OF STATE FOR TRANSPORT** (hereinafter referred to as "the Secretary of State") and the **MOTOR INSURERS' BUREAU**, whose registered office is at Linford Wood House 6–12 Capital Drive Linford Wood Milton Keynes MK14 6XT (hereinafter referred to as "MIB").

IT IS HEREBY AGREED AS FOLLOWS:—

3F–118

Interpretation

General interpretation

1. (1) In this Agreement, unless the context otherwise requires, the following expressions have the following meanings—

"1988 Act" means the Road Traffic Act 1988;

"1996 Agreement" means the Agreement made on 14 June 1996 between the Secretary of State for Transport and MIB providing for the compensation of victims of untraced drivers;

"1999 Agreement" means the Agreement dated 13th August 1999 made between the Secretary of State for the Environment, Transport and the Regions and MIB providing for the compensation of victims of uninsured drivers;

"applicant" means the person who has applied for compensation in respect of a death, bodily injury or damage to property (or the person on whose behalf such an application has been made) and "application" means an application made by or on behalf of an applicant;

"arbitrator", where the arbitration takes place under Scottish law, includes an arbiter;

"award" means the aggregate of the sums which MIB is obliged to pay under this Agreement;

"bank holiday" means a day which is, or is to be observed as, a bank holiday under the Banking and Financial Dealings Act 1971;

"judgement" means, in relation to a court in Scotland, a court decree;

"property" means any property whether (in England and Wales) real or personal, or (in Scotland) heritable or moveable;

"relevant proceedings" means civil proceedings brought by the applicant (whether or not pursuant to a requirement made under this Agreement) against a person other than the unidentified person in respect of an event described in clause 4(1);

"specified excess" means £300 or such other sum as may from time to time be agreed in writing between the Secretary of State and MIB;

"unidentified person" means a person who is, or appears to be, wholly or partly liable in respect of the death, injury or damage to property to which an application relates and who cannot be identified.

(2) Save as otherwise herein provided, the Interpretation Act 1978 shall apply for the interpretation of this Agreement as it applies for the interpretation of an Act of Parliament.

(3) Where, under this Agreement, something is required to be done within a specified period after a date or the happening of a particular event, the period begins on the day after the happening of that event.

(4) Where, apart from this paragraph, the period in question, being a period of 7 days or less, would include a Saturday, Sunday, bank holiday, Christmas Day or Good Friday, that day shall be excluded.

(5) Save where expressly otherwise provided, a reference in this Agreement to a numbered clause is a reference to the clause bearing that number in this Agreement and a reference to a numbered paragraph is a reference to a paragraph bearing that number in the clause or schedule in which the reference occurs.

(6) In this Agreement—

(a) a reference (however framed) to the doing of any act or thing by or the happening of any event in relation to the applicant includes a reference to the doing of that act or thing by or the happening of that event in relation to a Solicitor or other person acting on his behalf, and

(b) a requirement to give notice or send documents to MIB shall, where MIB has appointed a Solicitor to act on its behalf in relation to the application, be satisfied by the giving of the notice or the sending of the documents, in the manner herein provided for, to that Solicitor.

Applicants' representatives

3F–119 2. Where, under and in accordance with this Agreement—

(a) any notice or other document is given to or by a Solicitor or other person acting on behalf of an applicant,

(b) any act or thing is done by or in respect of such Solicitor or other person,

(c) any decision is made by or in respect of such Solicitor or other person, or

(d) any payment is made to such Solicitor or other person,

then, whatever may be the age or other circumstances affecting the capacity of the applicant, that act, thing, decision or payment shall be treated as if it had been done to or by, or made to or in respect of an applicant of full age and capacity.

3F–120

Application of Agreement

Duration of Agreement

3. (1) This Agreement shall come into force on 14 February 2003.

(2) This Agreement may be determined by the Secretary of State or by MIB giving to the other not less than twelve months notice in writing to that effect.

(3) Notwithstanding the giving of notice of determination under paragraph (2) this Agreement shall continue to operate in respect of any application made in respect of death, bodily injury or damage to property arising from an event occurring on or before the date of termination specified in the notice.

Scope of Agreement

3F–121 4. (1) Save as provided in clause 5, this Agreement applies where—

(a) the death of, or bodily injury to, a person or damage to any property of a person has been caused by, or arisen out of, the use of a motor vehicle on a road or other public place in Great Britain, and

(b) the event giving rise to the death, bodily injury or damage to property occurred on or after fourteenth day February 2003, and

(c) the death, bodily injury or damage to property occurred in circumstances giving rise to liability of a kind which is required to be covered by a policy of insurance or a security under Part VI of the 1988 Act, and

(d) it is not possible for the applicant—
  (i)
  to identify the person who is, or appears to be, liable in respect of the death, injury or damage, or
  (ii)
  (where more than one person is or appears to be liable) to identify any one or more of those persons,

and

(e) the applicant has made an application in writing to MIB for the payment of an award in respect of such death, bodily injury or damage to property (and in a case where they are applicable the requirements of paragraph (2) are satisfied), and

(f) the conditions specified in paragraph (3), or such of those conditions as are relevant to the application, are satisfied.

(2) Where an application is signed by a person who is neither the applicant nor a Solicitor acting on behalf of the applicant MIB may refuse to accept the application (and shall incur no liability under this Agreement) until it is reasonably satisfied that, having regard to the status of the signatory and his relationship with the applicant, the applicant is fully aware of the content and effect of the application but subject thereto MIB shall not refuse to accept an application by reason only of the fact that it is signed by a person other than the applicant or his Solicitor.

(3) The conditions referred to in paragraph (1)(f) are that—

(a) except in a case to which sub-paragraph (b) applies, the application must have been made not later than —
  (i)
  three years after the date of the event which is the subject of the application in the case of a claim for compensation for death or bodily injury (whether or not damage to property has also arisen from the same event), or
  (ii)
  nine months after the date of that event in the case of a claim for compensation for damage to property (whether or not death or bodily injury has also arisen from the same event);

(b) in a case where the applicant could not reasonably have been expected to have become aware of the existence of bodily injury or damage to property, the application must have been made as soon as practicable after he did become (or ought reasonably to have become) aware of it and in any case not later than—
  (i)
  fifteen years after the date of the event which is the subject of the application in the case of a claim for compensation for death or bodily injury (whether or not damage to property has also arisen from the same event), or
  (ii)
  two years after the date of that event in the case of a claim for compensation for damage to property (whether or not death or bodily injury has also arisen from the same event);

(c) the applicant, or a person acting on the applicant's behalf, must have reported that event to the police—
  (i)
  in the case of an event from which there has arisen a death or bodily injury alone, not later than 14 days after its occurrence, and
  (ii)
  in the case of an event from which there has arisen property damage (whether or not a death or bodily injury has also arisen from it), not later than 5 days after its occurrence,

but where that is not reasonably possible the event must have been reported as soon as reasonably possible;

(d) the applicant must produce satisfactory evidence of having made the report required under sub-paragraph (c) in the form of an acknowledgement from the relevant force showing the crime or incident number under which that force has recorded the matter;

(e) after making, or authorising the making of, a report to the police the applicant must have co-operated with the police in any investigation they have made into the event.

(4) Where both death or bodily injury and damage to property have arisen from a single event nothing contained in this clause shall require an applicant to make an application in respect of the death or bodily injury on the same occasion as an application in respect of the damage to property and where two applications are made in respect of one event the provisions of this Agreement shall apply separately to each of them.

Exclusions from Agreement

3F–122   5. (1) This Agreement does not apply where an application is made in any of the following circumstances (so that where an application is made partly in such circumstances and partly in other circumstances, it applies only to the part made in those other circumstances)—

(a) where the applicant makes no claim for compensation in respect of death or bodily injury and the damage to property in respect of which compensation is claimed has been caused by, or has arisen out of, the use of an unidentified vehicle;

(b) where the death, bodily injury or damage to property in respect of which the application is made has been caused by or has arisen out of the use of a motor vehicle which at the time of the event giving rise to such death, injury or damage was owned by or in the possession of the Crown, unless at that time some other person had undertaken responsibility for bringing into existence a policy of insurance or security satisfying the requirements of the 1988 Act;

(c) where, at the time of the event in respect of which the application is made the person suffering death, injury or damage to property was voluntarily allowing himself to be carried in the responsible vehicle and before the commencement of his journey in the vehicle (or after such commencement if he could reasonably be expected to have alighted from the vehicle) he knew or ought to have known that the vehicle—

(i)

had been stolen or unlawfully taken, or

(ii)

was being used without there being in force in relation to its use a contract of insurance or security which complied with the 1988 Act; or

(iii)

was being used in the course or furtherance of crime; or

(iv)

was being used as a means of escape from or avoidance of lawful apprehension;

(d) where the death, bodily injury or damage to property was caused by, or in the course of, an act of terrorism;

(e) where property damaged as a result of the event giving rise to the application is insured against such damage and the applicant has recovered the full amount of his loss from the insurer on or before the date of the application (but without prejudice to the application of the Agreement in the case of any other claim for compensation made in respect of the same event);

(f) where a claim is made for compensation in respect of damage to a motor vehicle (or losses arising therefrom) and, at the time when the damage to it was sustained—

(i)

there was not in force in relation to the use of that vehicle such a contract of insurance as is required by Part VI of the 1988 Act, and

ii)

the person suffering damage to property either knew or ought to have known that was the case

(but without prejudice to the application of the Agreement in the case of any other claim for compensation made in respect of the same event);

(g) where the application is made neither by a person suffering injury or property damage nor by the personal representative of such a person nor by a dependant claiming in respect of the death of another person but is made in any of the following circumstances, namely—

(i)

where a cause of action or a judgment has been assigned to the applicant, or

(ii)

where the applicant is acting pursuant to a right of subrogation or a similar contractual or other right belonging to him.

(2) The burden of proving that the person suffering death, injury or damage to property knew or ought to have known of any matter set out in paragraph (1)(c) shall be on MIB but, in the absence of evidence to the contrary, proof by MIB of any of the following matters shall be taken as proof of his knowledge of the matter set out in paragraph (1)(c)(ii)—

(a) that he was the owner or registered keeper of the vehicle or had caused or permitted its use;

(b) that he knew the vehicle was being used by a person who was below the minimum age at which he could be granted a licence authorising the driving of a vehicle of that class;

(c) that he knew that the person driving the vehicle was disqualified for holding or obtaining a driving licence;

(d) that he knew that the user of the vehicle was neither its owner nor registered keeper nor an employee of the owner or registered keeper nor the owner or registered keeper of any other vehicle.

(3) Where—

(a) the application includes a claim for compensation both in respect of death or bodily injury and also in respect of damage to property, and

(b) the death or injury and the property damage has been caused by, or has arisen out of, the use of an unidentified vehicle,

the Agreement does not apply to the claim for compensation in respect of the damage to property.

(4) For the purposes of paragraphs (1) and (2)—

(a) references to a person being carried in a vehicle include references to his being carried in or upon, or entering or getting on to or alighting from the vehicle;

(b) knowledge which a person has or ought to have for the purposes of sub-paragraph (c) includes knowledge of matters which he could reasonably be expected to have been aware of had he not been under the self-induced influence of drink or drugs;

(c) "crime" does not include the commission of an offence under the Traffic Acts, except an offence under section 143 (use of a motor vehicle on a road without there being in force a policy of insurance), and "Traffic Acts" means the Road Traffic Regulation Act 1984, the Road Traffic Act 1988 and the Road Traffic Offenders Act 1988;

(d) "responsible vehicle" means the vehicle the use of which caused (or through the use of which there arose) the death, bodily injury or damage to property which is the subject of the application;

(e) "terrorism" has the meaning given in section 1 of the Terrorism Act 2000;

(f) "dependant" has the same meaning as in section 1(3) of the Fatal Accidents Act 1976.

Limitation on application of Agreement

6. (1) This clause applies where an applicant receives compensation or other payment **3F–123**

PERSONAL INJURY

in respect of the death, bodily injury or damage to property otherwise than in the circumstances described in clause 5(1)(e) from any of the following persons—

    (a) an insurer or under an insurance policy (other than a life assurance policy) or arrangement between the applicant or his employer and the insurer, or

    (b) a person who has given a security pursuant to the requirements of 1988 Act under an agreement between the applicant and the security giver, or

    (c) any other source other than a person who is an identified person for the purposes of clauses 13 to 15 or an insurer of, or a person who has given a security on behalf of, such a person.

(2) Where the compensation or other payment received is equal to or greater than the amount which MIB would otherwise be liable to pay under the provisions of clauses 8 and 9 MIB shall have no liability under those provisions (to the intent that this Agreement shall immediately cease to apply except to the extent that the applicant is entitled to a contribution to his legal costs under clause 10).

(3) Where the compensation or other payment received is less than the amount which MIB would otherwise be liable to pay under the provisions of clauses 8 and 9 MIB's liability under those provisions shall be reduced by an amount equal to that compensation or payment.

3F–124

Principal Terms and Conditions

MIB's obligation to investigate claims and determine amount of award

7. (1) MIB shall, at its own cost, take all reasonable steps to investigate the claim made in the application and—

    (a) if it is satisfied after conducting a preliminary investigation that the case is not one to which this Agreement applies and the application should be rejected, it shall inform the applicant accordingly and (subject to the following provisions of this Agreement) need take no further action, or

    (b) in any other case, it shall conduct a full investigation and shall as soon as reasonably practicable having regard to the availability of evidence make a report on the applicant's claim.

(2) Subject to the following paragraphs of this clause, MIB shall, on the basis of the report and, where applicable, any relevant proceedings—

    (a) reach a decision as to whether it must make an award to the applicant in respect of the death, bodily injury or damage to property, and

    (b) where it decides to make an award, determine the amount of that award.

(3) Where MIB reaches a decision that the Agreement applies and that it is able to calculate the whole amount of the award the report shall be treated as a full report and the award shall (subject to the following provisions of this Agreement) be treated as a full and final award.

(4) Where MIB reaches a decision that the Agreement applies and that it should make an award but further decides that it is not at that time able to calculate the final amount of the award (or a part thereof), it may designate the report as an interim report and where it does so—

    (a) it may, as soon as reasonably practicable, make one or more further interim reports, but

    (b) it must, as soon as reasonably practicable having regard to the availability of evidence, make a final report.

(5) Where it makes an interim or final report MIB shall, on the basis of that report and, where applicable, any relevant proceedings—

    (a) in the case of an interim report, determine the amount of any interim award it wishes to make, and

1284

(b) in the case of its final report, determine the whole amount of its award which shall (subject to the following provisions of this Agreement) be treated as a full and final award.

(6) MIB shall be under an obligation to make an award only if it is satisfied, on the balance of probabilities, that the death, bodily injury or damage to property was caused in such circumstances that the unidentified person would (had he been identified) have been held liable to pay damages to the applicant in respect of it.

(7) MIB shall determine the amount of its award in accordance with the provisions of clauses 8 to 10 and (in an appropriate case) clauses 12 to 14 but shall not thereby be under a duty to calculate the exact proportion of the award which represents compensation, interest or legal costs.

Compensation

8. (1) MIB shall include in its award to the applicant, by way of compensation for the death, bodily injury or damage to property, a sum equivalent to the amount which a court— **3F–125**

(a) applying the law of England and Wales, in a case where the event giving rise to the death, injury or damage occurred in England or Wales, or

(b) applying the law of Scotland, in a case where that event occurred in Scotland,

would have awarded to the applicant (where applying English law) as general and special damages or (where applying the law of Scotland) as solatium and patrimonial loss if the applicant had brought successful proceedings to enforce a claim for damages against the unidentified person.

(2) In calculating the sum payable under paragraph (1), MIB shall adopt the same method of calculation as the court would adopt in calculating damages but it shall be under no obligation to include in that calculation an amount in respect of loss of earnings suffered by the applicant to the extent that he has been paid wages or salary (or any sum in lieu of them) whether or not such payments were made subject to an agreement or undertaking on his part to repay the same in the event of his recovering damages for the loss of those earnings.

(3) Where an application includes a claim in respect of damage to property, MIB's liability in respect of that claim shall be limited in accordance with the following rules—

(a) if the loss incurred by an applicant in respect of any one event giving rise to a claim does not exceed the specified excess, MIB shall incur no liability to that applicant in respect of that event;

(b) if the aggregate of all losses incurred by both the applicant and other persons in respect of any one event giving rise to a claim ("the total loss") exceeds the specified excess but does not exceed £250,000—
(i)
MIB's liability to an individual applicant shall be the amount of the claim less the specified excess, and
(ii)
MIB's total liability to applicants in respect of claims arising from that event shall be the total loss less a sum equal to the specified excess multiplied by the number of applicants who have incurred loss through damage to property;

(c) if the total loss exceeds £250,000—
(i)
MIB's liability to an individual applicant shall not exceed the amount of the claim less the specified excess, and
(ii)
MIB's total liability to applicants in respect of claims arising from that event shall be £250,000 less a sum equal to the specified excess multiplied by the number of applicants who have incurred loss due to property damage.

(4) MIB shall not be liable to pay compensation to an appropriate authority in

respect of any loss incurred by that authority as a result of its failure to recover a charge for the recovery, storage or disposal of an abandoned vehicle under a power contained in the Refuse Disposal (Amenity) Act 1978 or Part VIII of the Road Traffic Regulation Act 1984 (and in this paragraph "appropriate authority" has the meaning given in the Act under which the power to recover the charge was exercisable).

Interest

3F-126 9. (1) MIB shall in an appropriate case also include in the award a sum representing interest on the compensation payable under clause 8 at a rate equal to that which a court—

(a) applying the law of England and Wales, in a case where the event giving rise to the death, bodily injury or damage to property occurred in England or Wales, or

(b) applying the law of Scotland, in a case where that event occurred in Scotland,

would have awarded to a successful applicant.

(2) MIB is not required by virtue of paragraph (1) to pay a sum representing interest in respect of the period before the date which is one month after the date on which MIB receives the police report (but, where MIB has failed to seek and obtain that report promptly after the date of the application, interest shall run from the date which falls one month after the date on which it would have received it had it acted promptly).

Contribution towards legal costs

3F-127 10. (1) MIB shall, in a case where it has decided to make a compensation payment under clause 8, also include in the award a sum by way of contribution towards the cost of obtaining legal advice from a Solicitor, Barrister or Advocate in respect of—

(a) the making of an application under this Agreement;

(b) the correctness of a decision made by MIB under this Agreement; or

(c) the adequacy of an award (or a part thereof) offered by MIB under this Agreement

that sum to be determined in accordance with the Schedule to this Agreement.

(2) MIB shall not be under a duty to make a payment under paragraph (1) unless it is satisfied that the applicant did obtain legal advice in respect of any one or more of the matters specified in that paragraph.

Conditions precedent to MIB's obligations

3F-128 11. (1) The applicant must—

(a) make his application in such form,

(b) provide in support of the application such statements and other information (whether in writing or orally at interview), and

(c) give such further assistance,

as may reasonably be required by MIB or by any person acting on MIB's behalf to enable an investigation to be carried out under clause 7 of this Agreement.

(2) The applicant must provide MIB with written authority to take all such steps as may be reasonably necessary in order to carry out a proper investigation of the claim.

(3) The applicant must, if MIB reasonably requires him to do so before reaching a decision under clause 7, provide MIB with a statutory declaration, made by him, setting out to the best of his knowledge and belief all the facts and circumstances upon which his application is based or such facts and circumstances in relation to the application as MIB may reasonably specify.

(4) The applicant must, if MIB reasonably requires him to do so before it reaches a decision or determination under clause 7 and subject to the following provisions of this clause—

(a) at MIB's option (and subject to paragraph (5)) either—

(i)

bring proceedings against any person or persons who may, in addition or alternatively to the unidentified person, be liable to the applicant in respect of the death, bodily injury or damage to property (by virtue of having caused or contributed to that death, injury or damage, by being vicariously liable in respect of it or having failed to effect third party liability insurance in respect of the vehicle in question) and co-operate with MIB in taking such steps as are reasonably necessary to obtain judgement in those proceedings, or

(ii) authorise MIB to bring such proceedings and take such steps in the applicant's name;

(b) at MIB's expense, provide MIB with a transcript of any official shorthand or recorded note taken in those proceedings of any evidence given or judgement delivered therein;

(c) assign to MIB or to its nominee the benefit of any judgement obtained by him (whether or not obtained in proceedings brought under subparagraph (a) above) in respect of the death, bodily injury or damage to property upon such terms as will secure that MIB or its nominee will be accountable to the applicant for any amount by which the aggregate of all sums recovered by MIB or its nominee under the judgement (after deducting all reasonable expenses incurred in effecting recovery) exceeds the award made by MIB under this Agreement in respect of that death, injury or damage;

(d) undertake to assign to MIB the right to any sum which is or may be due from an insurer, security giver or other person by way of compensation for, or benefit in respect of, the death, bodily injury or damage to property and which would (if payment had been made before the date of the award) have excluded or limited MIB's liability under the provisions of clause 6.

(5) If, pursuant to paragraph (4)(a), MIB requires the applicant to bring proceedings or take steps against any person or persons (or to authorise MIB to bring such proceedings or take such steps in his name) MIB shall indemnify the applicant against all costs and expenses reasonably incurred by him in complying with that requirement.

(6) Where the applicant, without having been required to do so by MIB, has commenced proceedings against any person described in paragraph (4)(a)—

(a) the applicant shall as soon as reasonably possible notify MIB of such proceedings and provide MIB with such further information about them as MIB may reasonably require, and

(b) the applicant's obligations in paragraph (4)(a) to (c) shall apply in respect of such proceedings as if they had been brought at MIB's request.

3F–129

Joint and Several Liability

Joint and several liability: interpretation

12. In clauses 13 to 15—

"identified person" includes an identified employer or principal of a person who is himself unidentified;

"original judgement" means a judgement obtained against an identified person at first instance in relevant proceedings;

"three month period" means the period of three months specified in clause 13(3); and

"unidentified person's liability" means—

(a) the amount of the contribution which (if not otherwise apparent) would, on the balance of probabilities, have been be recoverable from the unidentified person in an action brought —

(i) in England and Wales, under the Civil Liability (Contribution) Act 1978, or

1287

(ii) in Scotland, under the Law Reform (Miscellaneous Provisions) (Scotland) Act 1940, by an identified person who had been held liable in full in an earlier action brought by the applicant, and

(b) where a court has awarded the applicant interest or costs in addition to damages, an appropriate proportion of that interest or those costs.

MIB's liability where wrongdoer is identified

3F–130 13. (1) This clause applies where the death, bodily injury or damage to property in respect of which the application is made is caused, or appears on the balance of probabilities to have been caused—

(a) partly by an unidentified person and partly by an identified person, or

(b) partly by an unidentified person and partly by another unidentified person whose employer or principal is identified,

in circumstances making (or appearing to make) the identified person liable, or vicariously liable, to the applicant in respect of the death, injury or damage.

(2) Where this clause applies, MIB's liability under this Agreement shall not exceed the unidentified person's liability and the following provisions shall apply to determine MIB's liability in specific cases.

(3) Where the applicant has obtained a judgement in relevant proceedings in respect of the death, injury or damage which has not been satisfied in full by or on behalf of the identified person within the period of three months after the date on which the applicant became entitled to enforce it—

(a) if that judgement is wholly unsatisfied within the three month period MIB shall make an award equal to the unidentified person's liability;

(b) if the judgement is satisfied in part only within the three month period, MIB shall make an award equal to—
(i)
the unsatisfied part, if it does not exceed the unidentified person's liability; and
(ii)
the unidentified person's liability, if the unsatisfied part exceeds the unidentified person's liability.

(4) A judgment given in any relevant proceedings against an identified person shall be conclusive as to any issue determined in those proceedings which is relevant to the determination of MIB's liability under this Agreement.

(5) Where the applicant has not obtained (or been required by MIB to obtain) a judgement in respect of the death, injury or damage against the identified person but has received an agreed payment from the identified person in respect of the death, bodily injury or damage to property, that payment shall be treated for the purposes of this Agreement as a full settlement of the applicant's claim and MIB shall be under no liability under this Agreement in respect thereof.

(6) Where the applicant has not obtained (or been required by MIB to obtain) a judgement in respect of the death, injury or damage against the identified person nor received any payment by way of compensation in respect thereof from the identified person MIB shall make an award equal to the unidentified person's liability.

Appeals by identified persons

3F–131 14. (1) This clause applies where an appeal against, or other proceeding to set aside, the original judgement is commenced within the three month period.

(2) If, as a result of the appeal or other proceeding—

(a) the applicant ceases to be entitled to receive any payment in respect of the death, bodily injury or damage to property from any identified person, clause 13 shall apply as if he had neither obtained nor been required by MIB to obtain a judgement against that person;

    (b) the applicant becomes entitled to recover an amount different from that which he was entitled to recover under the original judgement the provisions of clause 13(3) shall apply, but as if for each of the references therein to the original judgement there were substituted a reference to the judgement in that appeal or other proceeding;

    (c) the applicant remains entitled to enforce the original judgement the provisions of clause 13(3) shall apply, but as if for each of the references therein to the three month period there were substituted a reference to the period of three months after the date on which the appeal or other proceeding was disposed of.

(3) Where the judgement in the appeal or other proceeding is itself the subject of a further appeal or similar proceeding the provisions of this clause shall apply in relation to that further appeal or proceeding in the same manner as they apply in relation to the first appeal or proceeding.

(4) Nothing in this clause shall oblige MIB to make a payment to the applicant until the appeal or other proceeding has been determined.

Compensation recovered under Uninsured Drivers Agreements

15. (1) Where, in a case to which clause 13 applies, judgement in the relevant **3F–132** proceedings is given against an identified person in circumstances which render MIB liable to satisfy that judgement under any of the Uninsured Drivers Agreements, MIB shall not be under any liability under this Agreement in respect of the event to which the relevant proceedings relate.

(2) In this clause "Uninsured Drivers Agreements" means—

    (a) the Agreement dated 21st December 1988 made between the Secretary of State for Transport and MIB providing for the compensation of victims of uninsured drivers,

    (b) the 1999 Agreement, and

    (c) any agreement made between the Secretary of State and MIB (or their respective successors) which supersedes (whether immediately or otherwise) the 1999 Agreement.

3F–133

Notification of Decision and Payment of Award

Notification of decision

16. MIB shall give the applicant notice of a decision or determination under clause 7 in writing and when so doing shall provide him—

    (a) if the application is rejected because a preliminary investigation has disclosed that it is not one made in a case to which this Agreement applies, with a statement to that effect;

    (b) if the application has been fully investigated, with a statement setting out—

        (i) all the evidence obtained during the investigation, and

        (ii) MIB's findings of fact from that evidence which are relevant to the decision;

    (c) if it has decided to make an interim award on the basis of an interim report under clause 7(4), with a copy of the report and a statement of the amount of the interim award;

    (d) if it has decided to make a full report under clause 7(3) or a final report under clause 7(4)(b), with a copy of the report and a statement of the amount of the full and final award;

    (e) in a case to which clause 13 applies, with a statement setting out the way in which the amount of the award has been computed under the provisions of that clause; and

    (f) in every case, with a statement of its reasons for making the decision or determination.

Acceptance of decision and payment of award

17. (1) Subject to the following paragraphs of this clause, if MIB gives notice to the **3F–134** applicant that it has decided to make an award to him, it shall pay him that award—

(a) in the case of an interim award made pursuant to clause 7(5)(a), as soon as reasonably practicable after the making of the interim report to which the award relates;

(b) in the case of a full and final award made pursuant to clause 7(3) or (5)(b)—

(i)

where the applicant notifies MIB in writing that he accepts the offer of the award unconditionally, not later than 14 days after the date on which MIB receives that acceptance, or

(ii)

where the applicant does not notify MIB of his acceptance in accordance with sub-paragraph (a) but the period during which he may give notice of an appeal under clause 19 has expired without such notice being given, not later than 14 days after the date of expiry of that period,

and that payment shall discharge MIB from all liability under this Agreement in respect of the death, bodily injury or damage to property for which the award is made.

(2) MIB may, upon notifying an applicant of its decision to make an award, offer to pay the award in instalments in accordance with a structure described in the decision letter (the "structured settlement") and if the applicant notifies MIB in writing of his acceptance of the offer—

(a) the first instalment of the payment under the structured settlement shall be made not later than 14 days after the date on which MIB receives that acceptance, and

(b) subsequent payments shall be made in accordance with the agreed structure.

(3) Where an applicant has suffered bodily injury and believes either that there is a risk that he will develop a disease or condition other than that in respect of which he has made a claim or that a disease or condition in respect of which he has made a claim will deteriorate, he may—

(a) by notice given in his application, or

(b) by notice in writing received by MIB before the date on which MIB issues notification of its full or (as the case may be) final report under clause 16,

state that he wishes MIB to make a provisional award and if he does so paragraphs (4) and (5) shall apply.

(4) The applicant must specify in the notice given under paragraph (3)—

(a) each disease and each type of deterioration which he believes may occur, and

(b) the period during or within which he believes it may occur.

(5) Where MIB receives a notice under paragraph (3) it shall, not later than 14 days after the date of such receipt (or within such longer period as the applicant may agree)—

(a) accept the notice and confirm that any award it makes (other than an interim award made pursuant to clause 7(5)(a)) is to be treated as a provisional award, or

(b) reject the notice and inform the applicant that it is not willing to make a provisional award.

6) Where MIB has notified the applicant that it accepts the notice, an award which would otherwise be treated a full or final award under this Agreement shall be treated as a provisional award only and the applicant may make a supplementary application under this Agreement but—

(a) only in respect of a disease or a type of deterioration of his condition specified in his notice, and

(b) not later than the expiration of the period specified in his notice.

(7) Where MIB has notified the applicant that it rejects the notice, subject to any decision to the contrary made by an arbitrator, no award which MIB makes shall be treated as a provisional award.

Appeals Against MIB's Decision

Right of appeal

18. Where an applicant is not willing to accept—

(a) a decision or determination made by MIB under clause 7 or a part thereof, or

(b) a proposal for a structured settlement or a rejection of the applicant's request for a provisional award under clause 17,

he may give notice (a "notice of appeal") that he wishes to submit the matter to arbitration in accordance with the provisions of clauses 19 to 25.

Notice of appeal

19. (1) A notice of appeal shall be given in writing to MIB at any time before the **3F–136** expiration of a period of 6 weeks from—

(a) the date on which the applicant receives notice of MIB's decision under clause 16;

(b) where he disputes a notification given under clause 17(5)(b), the date when such notification is given;

(c) in any other case, the date on which he is given notification of the decision, determination or requirement.

(2) The notice of appeal—

(a) shall state the grounds on which the appeal is made,

(b) shall contain the applicant's observations on MIB's decision,

(c) may be accompanied by such further evidence in support of the appeal as the applicant thinks fit, and

(d) shall contain an undertaking that (subject, in the case of an arbitration to be conducted England and Wales, to his rights under sections 67 and 68 of the Arbitration Act 1996) the applicant will abide by the decision of the arbitrator made under this Agreement.

Procedure following notice of appeal

20. (1) Not later than 7 days after receiving the notice of appeal MIB shall— **3F–137**

(a) apply to the Secretary of State for the appointment of a single arbitrator, or

(b) having notified the applicant of its intention to do so, cause an investigation to be made into any further evidence supplied by the applicant and report to the applicant upon that investigation and of any change in its decision which may result from it.

(2) Where the only ground stated in the notice of appeal is that the award is insufficient (including a ground contesting the degree of contributory negligence attributed to the applicant or, as the case may be, the person in respect of whose death the application is made), MIB may give notice to the applicant of its intention, if the appeal proceeds to arbitration, to ask the arbitrator to decide whether its award exceeds what a court would have awarded or whether the case is one in which it would make an award at all and shall in that notice set out such observations on that matter as MIB considers relevant to the arbitrator's decision.

(3) Where MIB has made a report under paragraph (1)(b) or given to the applicant notice under paragraph (2), the applicant may, not later than 6 weeks after the date on which the report or (as the case may be) the notice was given to him—

(a) notify MIB that he wishes to withdraw the appeal, or

(b) notify MIB that he wishes to continue with the appeal and send with that notification—

(i)

1291

any observations on the report made under paragraph (1)(b) which he wishes to have drawn to the attention of the arbitrator,

(ii) any observations on the contents of the notice given under paragraph (2), including any further evidence not previously made available to MIB and relevant to the matter, which he wishes to have drawn to the attention of the arbitrator.

(4) Where the applicant notifies MIB under paragraph (3)(b) of his wish to continue the appeal, or if the applicant fails within the specified period of 6 weeks to give notification of his wish either to withdraw or to continue with the appeal, MIB shall, not later than 7 days after receiving the notification or 7 days after the expiry of the said period (as the case may be)—

(a) apply to the Secretary of State for the appointment of an arbitrator, or

(b) having notified the applicant of its intention to do so, cause a further investigation to be made into the further evidence sent under paragraph (3)(b)(ii).

(5) Where MIB has caused an investigation to be made into any further evidence supplied by the applicant under paragraph (3)(b)(ii), it shall report to the applicant upon that investigation and of any change in a decision or determination made under clause 7 which may result from it and the applicant may, not later than 6 weeks after the date on which he receives the report—

(a) notify MIB that he wishes to withdraw the appeal, or

(b) notify MIB that he wishes to continue with the appeal.

(6) Where the applicant notifies MIB under paragraph (5)(b) of his wish to continue the appeal, or if the applicant fails within the specified period of 6 weeks to give notification of his wish either to withdraw or to continue with the appeal, MIB shall not later than 7 days after receiving the notification or 7 days after the expiry of the said period (as the case may be) apply to the Secretary of State for the appointment of an arbitrator.

(7) When applying to the Secretary of State for the appointment of an arbitrator MIB may send with the application such written observations as it wishes to make upon the applicant's notice of appeal but must at the same time send a copy of those observations to the applicant.

Appointment of arbitrator

3F–138 21. (1) In the event of MIB neither applying to the Secretary of State for the appointment of an arbitrator in accordance with the provisions of clause 20 nor taking such further steps as it may at its discretion take in accordance with that clause, the applicant may apply to the Secretary of State for the appointment of an arbitrator.

(2) For the purposes of the Arbitration Act 1996 (where the arbitration is to be conducted in England and Wales) the arbitral proceedings are to be regarded as commencing on the date of the making of the application by the Secretary of State or the applicant (as the case may be).

(3) The Secretary of State shall, upon the making of an application for the appointment of an arbitrator to hear the appeal, appoint the first available member, by rotation, of a panel of Queen's Counsel appointed for the purpose of determining appeals under this Agreement (where the event giving rise to the death, bodily injury or damage to property occurred in England and Wales) by the Lord Chancellor or (where the event giving rise to the death, bodily injury or damage to property occurred in Scotland) by the Lord Advocate and shall forthwith notify the applicant and MIB of the appointment.

Arbitration procedure

3F–139 22. (1) Upon receiving notification from the Secretary of State of the appointment of an arbitrator, MIB shall send to the arbitrator—

(a) the notice of appeal,

(b) (if appropriate) its request for a decision as to whether its award exceeds what a court would have awarded or whether the case is one in which it would make an award at all,

> (c) copies of—
>> (i)
>> the applicant's application,
>> (ii)
>> its decision; and
>> (iii)
>> all statements, declarations, notices, reports, observations and transcripts of evidence made or given under this Agreement by the applicant or MIB.

(2) The arbitrator may, if it appears to him to be necessary or expedient for the purpose of resolving any issue, ask MIB to make a further investigation and to submit a written report of its findings to him for his consideration and in such a case—

> (a) MIB shall undertake the investigation and send copies of the report to the arbitrator and the applicant,

> (b) the applicant may, not later than 4 weeks after the date on which a copy of the report is received by him, submit written observations on it to the arbitrator and if he does so he shall send a copy of those observations to MIB.

(3) The arbitrator shall, after considering the written submissions referred to in paragraphs (1) and (2), send to the applicant and MIB a preliminary decision letter setting out the decision he proposes to make under clause 23 and his reasons for doing so.

(4) Not later than 28 days after the date of sending of the preliminary decision letter (or such later date as the applicant and MIB may agree) the applicant and MIB may, by written notification given to the arbitrator and copied to the other, either—

> (a) accept the preliminary decision, or

> (b) submit written observations upon the preliminary decision or the reasons or both, or

> (c) request an oral hearing,

and if either of them should within that period fail to do any of those things (including a failure to provide the other person with a copy of his notification) he or it shall be treated as having accepted the decision.

(5) If the applicant submits new evidence with any written observations under paragraph (4)(b) MIB may at its discretion, but within 28 days or such longer period as the arbitrator may allow, do any of the following—

> (a) make an investigation into that evidence,

> (b) submit its own written observations on that evidence, and

> (c) if it has not already done so, request an oral hearing,

and, except where an oral hearing has been requested, the arbitrator shall (in exercise of his powers under section 34 of the Arbitration Act 1996 if the arbitration is being conducted in England and Wales) determine whether, and if so how, such evidence shall be admitted and tested.

(6) If both the applicant and MIB accept the reasoned preliminary decision that decision shall be treated as his final decision for the purposes of clause 23 (so that clause 23(2) shall not then apply) but if either of them submits observations on that decision the arbitrator must take those observations into account before making a final decision.

(7) If the applicant or MIB requests an oral hearing, the arbitrator shall determine the appeal in that manner and in such a case—

> (a) the hearing shall be held in public unless the applicant requests that it (or any part of it) be heard in private;

> (b) the hearing shall take place at a location—
>> (i)
>> in England or Wales, where the event giving rise to the death, bodily injury or damage to property occurred in England or Wales and the applicant is resident in England or Wales,
>> (ii)

in Scotland, where the event giving rise to the death, bodily injury or damage to property occurred in Scotland and the applicant is resident in Scotland, or

(iii)

in England, Wales or Scotland in any other case,

which in the opinion of the arbitrator (after consultation with each of them) is convenient for both MIB and the applicant as well as for himself;

(c) a party to the hearing may be represented by a lawyer or other person of that party's choosing;

(d) a party to the hearing shall be entitled to address the arbitrator, to call witnesses and to put questions to those witnesses and any other person called as a witness.

Arbitrator's decision

3F–140   23. (1) The arbitrator, having regard to the subject matter of the proceedings, may in an appropriate case—

(a) determine whether or not the case is one to which this Agreement applies;

(b) remit the application to MIB for a full investigation and a decision in accordance with the provisions of this Agreement;

(c) determine whether MIB should make an award under this Agreement and if so what that award should be;

(d) determine such other questions as have been referred to him as he thinks fit;

(e) (subject to the provisions of paragraph (4) of this clause and clause 24) order that the costs of the proceedings shall be paid by one party or allocated between the parties in such proportions as he thinks fit;

and where the arbitrator makes a determination under sub-paragraph (a) that the case is one to which this Agreement applies, all the provisions of this Agreement shall apply as if the case were one to which clause 7(1)(b) applies.

(2) The arbitrator shall notify MIB and the applicant of his decision in writing.

(3) MIB shall pay to the applicant any amount which the arbitrator has decided shall be awarded to him, and that payment shall discharge MIB from all liability under this Agreement in respect of the death, bodily injury or damage to property in respect of which that decision is given.

(4) Where an oral hearing has taken place at the request of the applicant and the arbitrator is satisfied that it was unnecessary and that the matter could have been decided on the basis of the written submissions referred to in clause 22(1) and (2) he shall take that into account when making an order under paragraph (1)(e).

Payment of arbitrator's fee and costs of legal representation

3F–141   24. (1) Subject to paragraph (2), MIB shall upon being notified of the decision of the arbitrator pay the arbitrator a fee approved by the Lord Chancellor or the Lord Advocate, as the case may be, after consultation with MIB.

(2) In a case where it appears to the arbitrator that, having regard to all the surrounding circumstances of the case, there were no reasonable grounds for making the appeal or bringing the question before him, the arbitrator may, in his discretion, order—

(a) the applicant or,

(b) where he considers it appropriate to do so, any Solicitor or other person acting on behalf of the applicant, to reimburse MIB the fee it has paid to the arbitrator or any part thereof.

(3) Where, pursuant to paragraph (2), the arbitrator orders—

(a) the applicant to reimburse MIB, MIB may deduct an amount equal to the fee from any amount which it pays to the applicant to discharge its liability under this Agreement;

(b) a Solicitor or other person to reimburse MIB, MIB may deduct an amount equal to the fee from any amount which it pays to that Solicitor or other person to discharge its liability to the applicant under this Agreement.

(4) Where there is an oral hearing and the applicant secures an award of compensation greater than that previously offered, then (unless the arbitrator orders otherwise) MIB shall make a contribution of £500 per half day towards the cost incurred by the applicant in respect of representation by a Solicitor, Barrister or Advocate.

Applicants under a disability

25. (1) If in any case it appears to MIB that, by reason of the applicant being a minor **3F–142** or of any other circumstance affecting his capacity to manage his affairs, it would be in the applicant's interest that all or some part of the award should be administered for him by an appropriate representative, MIB may establish for that purpose a trust of the whole or part of the award (such trust to take effect for such period and under such provisions as appears to MIB to be appropriate in the circumstances of the case) or, as the case may be, initiate or cause any other person in initiate the proceedings necessary to have the award administered by an appropriate representative and otherwise cause any amount payable under the award to be paid to and administered by the appropriate representative.

(2) In this clause "appropriate representative" means—

(a) in England and Wales—

    (i) the Family Welfare Association, or a similar body or person, as trustee of the trust, or

    (ii) the Court of Protection; and

(b) in Scotland—

    (i) a Judicial Factor, or

    (ii) a guardian under the Adults with Incapacity (Scotland) Act 2000, or

    (iii) (where the applicant is a child) the tutor or curator of the child or a person having parental responsibilities under the Children (Scotland) Act 1995.

3F–143

Accelerated Procedure

Instigation of accelerated procedure

26. (1) In any case where, after making a preliminary investigation under clause 7, MIB has decided that—

(a) the case is one to which this Agreement applies, and

(b) it is not one to which clause 13, applies,

MIB may notify the applicant of that decision and, instead of causing a full investigation and report to be made under clause 7, may make to the applicant an offer to settle his claim by payment of an award specified in the offer representing compensation assessed in accordance with clause 8 together, in an appropriate case, with interest thereon assessed in accordance with clause 9 and a contribution towards the cost of obtaining legal advice in respect of the making of the application.

(2) Where an offer is made under paragraph (1), MIB shall send to the applicant a statement setting out—

(a) the relevant evidence it has collected disclosing the circumstances in which the death, bodily injury or damage to property occurred, and

(b) its reasons for the assessment of the award.

Settlement by accelerated procedure

27. (1) The applicant shall not later than 6 weeks after he receives an offer under **3F–144** clause 26 notify MIB of his acceptance or rejection thereof.

(2) Where the applicant notifies MIB of his acceptance of the offer—

    (a) MIB shall not later than 14 days after receipt of the acceptance pay to the applicant the amount of the award, and

    (b) MIB shall be discharged from all liability under this Agreement in respect of the death, bodily injury or damage to property for which that payment is made.

(3) In the event of the applicant failing to accept the offer within the specified period, the application shall be treated as one to which clause 7(1)(b) applies.

3F–145

Miscellaneous

Referral of disputes to arbitrator

28. (1) Any dispute between the applicant and MIB concerning a decision, determination or requirement made by MIB under the terms of this Agreement, other than a dispute relating to MIB's decision for which provision is made by clause 18, shall be referred to and determined by an arbitrator.

(2) Where an applicant wishes to refer such a dispute to arbitration, he shall not later than 4 weeks after the decision, determination or requirement is communicated to him, give notice to MIB that he wishes the matter to be so resolved.

(3) For the purposes of the Arbitration Act 1996 (where the arbitration is to be conducted in England and Wales) the arbitral proceedings are to be regarded as commencing on the date of such application.

(4) Upon receipt of the applicant's notice MIB shall apply immediately to the Secretary of State for the appointment of an arbitrator and in the event of MIB failing to do so the applicant may make the application.

(5) The Secretary of State shall, upon receiving the application for the appointment of an arbitrator to hear the appeal, appoint the first available member, by rotation, of a panel of Queen's Counsel appointed for the purpose of determining appeals under this Agreement (where the event giving rise to the death, bodily injury or damage to property occurred in England and Wales) by the Lord Chancellor or (where the event giving rise to the death, bodily injury or damage to property occurred in Scotland) by the Lord Advocate and shall forthwith notify the applicant and MIB of the appointment.

(6) The applicant and MIB shall, not later than 4 weeks after receiving notification of the appointment of the arbitrator, submit to him a written statement of their respective cases with supporting documentary evidence where available.

(7) Subject to paragraphs (8) to (10), the arbitrator shall decide the appeal on the documents submitted to him under paragraph (6) and no further evidence shall be produced to him.

(8) The applicant may, by notice in writing given to the arbitrator and MIB not later than the date on which he submits the statement of his case, ask the arbitrator to determine the appeal by means of an oral hearing and shall submit to the arbitrator and MIB a written statement, with supporting documentary evidence where appropriate, in support of that request.

(9) The arbitrator shall in such a case seek the view of MIB on the need for an oral hearing and MIB may submit to the arbitrator and the applicant a written statement, with supporting documentary evidence where appropriate, in support of its view.

(10) If, after considering those written submissions, the arbitrator decides that an oral hearing is necessary to determine the dispute—

    (a) the hearing shall be held in public unless the applicant requests that it (or any part of it) be heard in private;

    (b) the hearing shall take place at a location—

      (i)

    in England or Wales, where the event giving rise to the death, bodily injury or damage to property occurred in England or Wales and the applicant is resident in England or Wales,

(ii)

in Scotland, where the event giving rise to the death, bodily injury or damage to property occurred in Scotland and the applicant is resident in Scotland, or

(iii)

in England, Wales or Scotland in any other case,

which in the opinion of the arbitrator (after consultation with each of them) is convenient for both MIB and the applicant as well as for himself;

(c) a party to the hearing may be represented by a lawyer or other person of that party's choosing;

(d) a party to the hearing shall be entitled to address the arbitrator, to call witnesses and to put questions to those witnesses and any other person called as a witness.

(11) The arbitrator may, having regard to the subject matter of the proceedings and in an appropriate case, order that his fee or the costs of the proceedings (as determined according to clause 10(1)(b) of, and the Schedule to, this Agreement) or both his fee and those costs shall be paid by one party or allocated between the parties in such proportions as he thinks fit.

(12) Unless otherwise agreed, the decision, determination or requirement in respect of which notice is given under paragraph (2) shall stand unless reversed by the arbitrator.

Services of notices, etc, on MIB

29. Any notice required to be served on or any other notification or document **3F–146** required to be given or sent to MIB under the terms of this Agreement shall be sufficiently served or given sent by fax or by Registered or Recorded Delivery post to MIB's registered office and delivery shall be proved by the production of a fax report produced by the sender's fax machine or an appropriate postal receipt.

Agents

30. MIB may perform any of its obligations under this Agreement by agents. **3F–147**

Contracts (Rights of Third Parties) Act 1999

31. (1) For the purposes of the Contracts (Rights of Third Parties) Act 1999 the **3F–148** following provisions shall apply.

(2) This Agreement may be—

(a) varied or rescinded without the consent of any person other than the parties hereto, and

(b) determined under clause 3(2) without the consent of any such person.

(3) Save for the matters specified in paragraph (4), MIB shall not have available to it against an applicant any matter by way of counterclaim or set-off which would have been available to it if the applicant rather than the Secretary of State had been a party to this Agreement.

(4) The matters referred to in paragraph (3) are any counterclaim or set-off arising by virtue of the provisions of—

(a) this Agreement;

(b) the 1996 Agreement;

(c) the 1999 Agreement;

(d) either of the agreements which were respectively superseded by the 1996 Agreement and the 1999 Agreement.

(5) This agreement, being made for the purposes of Article 1(4) of Council Directive 84/5/EEC of 30th December 1983—

(a) is intended to confer a benefit on an applicant but on no other person, and

(b) to confer such benefit subject to the terms and conditions set out herein.

Enforcement against MIB

3F–149 32. If MIB fail to pay compensation in accordance with the provisions of this agreement the applicant is entitled to enforce payment through the courts.

Transitional provisions

3F–150 33. The 1996 Agreement shall cease to have effect after the 13 February 2003 but shall continue in force in relation to any claim arising out of an event occurring on or before that date.

IN WITNESS whereof the Secretary of State has caused his Corporate Seal to be hereunto affixed and the Motor Insurer's Bureau has caused its Common Seal to be hereunto affixed the day and year first above written.

3F–151

SCHEDULE

MIB's Contribution Towards Applicant's Legal Costs

1. Subject to paragraph 4, MIB shall pay a contribution towards the applicant's costs of obtaining legal advice determined in accordance with paragraph 2,

3F–152 2. That amount shall be the aggregate of—

    (a) the fee specified in column (2) of the table below in relation to the amount of the award specified in column (1) of that table,

    (b) the amount of value added tax charged on that fee,

    (c) where the applicant has opted for an oral hearing under clause and

    (d) reasonable disbursements.

TABLE

Amount of the award (1)	Specified fee (2)
Not exceeding £150,000	15% of the amount of the award, subject to a minimum of £500 and a maximum of £3000
Exceeding £150,000	2% of the amount of the award

3F–153 3. For the purposes of paragraph 2—

    "amount of the award" means the aggregate of the sum awarded by way of compensation and interest under clauses 8 and 9, before deduction of any reimbursement due to be paid to the Secretary of State for Work and Pensions through the Compensation Recovery Unit (CRU) of his Department (or to any successor of that unit), but excluding the amount of any payment due in respect of benefits and hospital charges.

    "reasonable disbursements" means reasonable expenditure incurred on the applicant's behalf and agreed between the applicant and MIB before it is incurred (MIB's agreement not having been unreasonably withheld) but includes Counsel's fees only where the applicant is a minor or under a legal disability.

3F–154 4. The foregoing provisions of this Schedule are without prejudice to MIB's liability under the provisions of this Agreement to pay the costs of arbitration proceedings or an arbitrator's fee.

THE CORPORATE SEAL of the Secretary of State)

FOR TRANSPORT hereunto affixed is authenticated by:—)

Authorised by the Secretary of State

Richard Jones

THE COMMON SEAL of the Motor Insurers')

BUREAU was hereunto affixed in the presence of:—   )

J A Read R D Snook

Directors of the Board of Management

B Louisy

Secretary

Motor Insurers' Bureau (Compensation of Victims of Uninsured Drivers) Text of an Agreement dated the 13th August 1999 between the Secretary of State for the Environment, Transport and the Regions and Motor Insurers' Bureau together with some notes on its scope and purpose

3F–155

13th August 1999

THIS AGREEMENT is made the thirteenth day of August 1999 between the SEC-RETARY OF STATE FOR THE SECRETARY OF STATE FOR THE ENVIRON-MENT, TRANSPORT AND THE REGIONS (hereinafter referred to as "the Secretary of State") and the MOTOR INSURERS' BUREAU, whose registered office is at 152 Silbury Boulevard, Milton Keynes MK9 1NB (hereinafter referred to as "MIB") and is SUPPLEMENTAL to an Agreement (hereinafter called "the Principal Agreement") made the 31st Day of December 1945 between the Minister of War Transport and the insurers transacting compulsory motor insurance business in Great Britain by or on behalf of whom the said Agreement was signed and in pursuance of paragraph 1 of which MIB was incorporated.

IT IS HEREBY AGREED AS FOLLOWS:

3F–156

Interpretation

General definitions

1. In this Agreement, unless the context otherwise requires, the following expressions have the following meanings—
"1988 Act" means the Road Traffic Act 1988;
"1988 Agreement" means the Agreement made on 21 December 1988 between the Secretary of State for Transport and MIB;
"bank holiday" means a day which is, or is to be observed as, a bank holiday under the Banking and Financial Dealings Act 1971;
"claimant" means a person who has commenced or who proposes to commence relevant proceedings and has made an application under this Agreement in respect thereof;
"contract of insurance" means a policy of insurance or a security covering a relevant liability;
"insurer" includes the giver of a security;
"MIB's obligation" means the obligation contained in clause 5;
"property" means any property whether real, heritable or personal;
"relevant liability" means a liability in respect of which a contract of insurance must be in force to comply with Part VI of the 1988 Act;

"relevant proceedings" means proceedings in respect of a relevant liability (and "commencement", in relation to such proceedings means, in England and Wales, the date on which a Claim Form or other originating process is issued by a Court or, in Scotland, the date on which the originating process is served on the Defender);

"relevant sum" means a sum payable or remaining payable under an unsatisfied judgment, including—

(a) an amount payable or remaining payable in respect of interest on that sum, and

(b) either the whole of the costs (whether taxed or not) awarded by the Court as part of that judgment or, where the judgment includes an award in respect of a liability which is not a relevant liability, such proportion of those costs as the relevant liability bears to the total sum awarded under the judgment;

"specified excess" means £300 or such other sum as may from time to time be agreed in writing between the Secretary of State and MIB;

"unsatisfied judgment" means a judgment or order (by whatever name called) in respect of a relevant liability which has not been satisfied in full within seven days from the date upon which the claimant became entitled to enforce it.

Meaning of references

3F–157 2.1 Save as otherwise herein provided, the Interpretation Act 1978 shall apply for the interpretation of this Agreement as it applies for the interpretation of an Act of Parliament.

2.2 Where, under this Agreement, something is required to be done—

(a) within a specified period after or from the happening of a particular event, the period begins on the day after the happening of that event;

(b) within or not less than a specified period before a particular event, the period ends on the day immediately before the happening of that event.

2.3 Where, apart from this paragraph, the period in question, being a period of seven days or less, would include a Saturday, Sunday or bank holiday or Christmas Day or Good Friday, that day shall be excluded.

2.4 Save where expressly otherwise provided, a reference in this Agreement to a numbered clause is a reference to the clause bearing that number in this Agreement and a reference to a numbered paragraph is a reference to a paragraph bearing that number in the clause in which the reference occurs.

2.5 In this Agreement

(a) a reference (however framed) to the doing of any act or thing by or the happening of any event in relation to the claimant includes a reference to the doing of that act or thing by or the happening of that event In relation to a Solicitor or other person acting on his behalf, and

(b) a requirement to give notice to, or to serve documents upon, MIB or an insurer mentioned in clause 9(1)(a) shall be satisfied by the giving of the notice to, or the service of the documents upon, a Solicitor acting on its behalf in the manner provided for.

Claimants not of full age or capacity

3F–158 3.1 Where, under and in accordance with this Agreement—

(a) any act or thing is done to or by a Solicitor or other person acting on behalf of a claimant,

(b) any decision is made by or in respect of a Solicitor or other person acting on behalf of a claimant, or

(c) any sum is paid to a Solicitor or other person acting on behalf of a claimant, then, whatever may be the age or other circumstances affecting the capacity of the claimant, that act, thing, decision or sum shall be treated as if it had been done to or by, or made in respect of or paid to a claimant of full age and capacity.

Principal Terms

Duration of Agreement

4.1 This Agreement shall come into force on 1st October 1999 in relation to accidents occurring on or after that date and, save as provided by clause 23, the 1988 Agreement shall cease and determine immediately before that date.

4.2 This Agreement may be determined by the Secretary of State or by MIB giving to the other not less than twelve months' notice in writing but without prejudice to its continued operation in respect of accidents occurring before the date of termination.

MIB's obligation to satisfy compensation claims

5.1 Subject to clauses 6 to 17, if a claimant has obtained against any person in a Court in Great Britain a judgment which is an unsatisfied judgment then MIB will pay the relevant sum to, or to the satisfaction of, the claimant or will cause the same to be so paid.

5.2 Paragraph (1) applies whether or not the person liable to satisfy the judgment is in fact covered by a contract of insurance and whatever may be the cause of his failure to satisfy the judgment.

Exceptions to Agreement

6.1 Clause 5 does not apply in the case of an application made in respect of a claim of any of the following descriptions (and, where part only of a claim satisfies such a description, clause S does not apply to that part)

- (a) a claim arising out of a relevant liability incurred by the user of a vehicle owned by or in the possession of the Crown, unless—
  - (i) responsibility for the existence of a contract of insurance under Part VI of the 1988 Act in relation to that vehicle had been undertaken by some other person (whether or not the person liable was in fact covered by a contract of insurance), or
  - (ii) the relevant liability was in fact covered by a contract of insurance;
- (b) a claim arising out of the use of a vehicle which is not required to be covered by a contract of insurance by virtue of section 144 of the 1988 Act, unless the use is in fact covered by such a contract;
- (c) a claim by, or for the benefit of, a person ("the beneficiary") other than the person suffering death, injury or other damage which is made either—
  - (i) in respect of a cause of action or a judgment which has been assigned to the beneficiary,

  or
  - (ii) pursuant to a right of subrogation or contractual or other right belonging to the beneficiary;
- (d) a claim in respect of damage to a motor vehicle or losses arising there from where, at the time when the damage to it was sustained—
  - (i) there was not in force in relation to the use of that vehicle such a contract of insurance as is required by Part VI of the 1988 Act, and
  - (ii) the claimant either knew or ought to have known that that was the case;
- (e) a claim which is made in respect of a relevant liability described in paragraph (2) by a claimant who, at the time of the use giving rise to the relevant liability was voluntarily allowing himself to be carried in the vehicle and, either before the commencement of his journey in the vehicle or after such

commencement if he could reasonably be expected to have alighted from it, knew or ought to have known that—

    (i) the vehicle had been stolen or unlawfully taken,

    (ii) the vehicle was being used without there being in force in relation to its use such a contract of insurance as would comply with Part VI of the 1988 Act,

    (iii) the vehicle was being used in the course or furtherance of a crime, or

    (iv) the vehicle was being used as a means of escape from, or avoidance of, lawful apprehension.

6.2 The relevant liability referred to in paragraph (1)(e) is a liability incurred by the owner or registered keeper or a person using the vehicle in which the claimant was being carried.

6.3 The burden of proving that the claimant knew or ought to have known of any matter set out in paragraph (1)(e) shall be on MIB but, in the absence of evidence to the contrary, proof by MIB of any of the following matters shall be taken as proof of the claimant's knowledge of the matter set out in paragraph (1)(e)(ii)—

    (a) that the claimant was the owner or registered keeper of the vehicle or had caused or permitted its use;

    (b) that the claimant knew the vehicle was being used by a person who was below the minimum age at which he could be granted a licence authorising the driving of a vehicle of that class;

    (c) that the claimant knew that the person driving the vehicle was disqualified for holding or obtaining a driving licence;

    (d) that the claimant knew that the user of the vehicle was neither its owner nor registered keeper nor an employee of the owner or registered keeper nor the owner or registered keeper of any other vehicle.

6.4 Knowledge which the claimant has or ought to have for the purposes of paragraph (1)(e) includes knowledge of matters which he could reasonably be expected to have been aware of had he not been under the self-induced influence of drink or drugs.

6.5 For the purposes of this clause—

    (a) a vehicle which has been unlawfully removed from the possession of the Crown shall be taken to continue in that possession whilst it is kept so removed,

    (b) references to a person being carried in a vehicle include references to his being carried upon, entering, getting on to and alighting from the vehicle, and

    (c) "owner", in relation to a vehicle which is the subject of a hiring agreement or a hire-purchase agreement, means the person in possession of the vehicle under that agreement.

3F–162

Conditions Precedent to MIB's Obligation

Form of application

7.1 MIB shall incur no liability under MIB's obligation unless an application is made to the person specified in clause 9(1)—

    (a) in such form,

    (b) giving such information about the relevant proceedings and other matters relevant to this Agreement, and

    (c) accompanied by such documents as MIB may reasonably require.

7.2 Where an application is signed by a person who is neither the claimant nor a Solicitor acting on his behalf MIB may refuse to accept the application (and shall incur no liability under MIB's obligation) until it is reasonably satisfied that, having regard to the status of the signatory and his relationship to the claimant, the claimant is fully aware of the contents and effect of the application but subject thereto MIB shall not refuse to accept such an application by reason only that it is signed by a person other than the claimant or his Solicitor.

Service of notices etc.

8.1 Any notice required to be given or documents to be supplied to MIB pursuant to clauses 9 to 12 of this Agreement shall be sufficiently given or supplied only if sent by facsimile transmission or by Registered or Recorded Delivery post to MIB's registered office for the time being and delivery shall be proved by the production of a facsimile transmission report produced by the sender's facsimile machine or an appropriate postal receipt. **3F–163**

Notice of relevant proceedings

9.1 MIB shall incur no liability under MIB's obligation unless proper notice of the bringing of the relevant proceedings has been given by the claimant not later than fourteen days after the commencement of those proceedings— **3F–164**

    (a) in the case of proceedings in respect of a relevant liability which is covered by a contract of insurance with an insurer whose identity can be ascertained, to that insurer;

    (b) in any other case, to MIB.

9.2 In this clause "proper notice" means, except in so far as any part of such information or any copy document or other thing has already been supplied under clause 7—

    (a) notice in writing that proceedings have been commenced by Claim Form, Writ, or other means,

    (b) a copy of the sealed Claim Form, Writ or other official document providing evidence of the commencement of the proceedings and, in Scotland, a statement of the means of service,

    (c) a copy or details of any insurance policy providing benefits in the case of the death, bodily injury or damage to property to which the proceedings relate where the claimant is the insured party and the benefits are available to him,

    (d) copies of all correspondence in the possession of the claimant or (as the case may be) his Solicitor or agent to or from the Defendant or the Defender or (as the case may be) his Solicitor, insurers or agent which is relevant to—

        (i) the death, bodily in jury or damage for which the Defendant or Defender is alleged to be responsible, or

        (ii) any contract of insurance which covers, or which may or has been alleged to cover, liability for such death, injury or damage the benefit of which is, or is claimed to be, available to Defendant or Defender,

    (e) subject to paragraph (3), a copy of the Particulars of Claim whether or not indorsed on the Claim Form, Writ or other originating process, and whether or not served (in England and Wales) on any Defendant or (in Scotland) on any Defender, and

    (f) a copy of all other documents which are required under the appropriate rules of procedure to be served on a Defendant or Defender with the Claim Form, Writ or other originating process or with the Particulars of Claim,

    (g) such other information about the relevant proceedings as MIB may reasonably specify.

9.3 If, in the case of proceedings commenced in England or Wales, the Particulars of Claim (including any document required to be served therewith) has not yet been served with the Claim Form or other originating process paragraph (2)(e) shall be sufficiently complied with if a copy thereof is served on MIB not later than seven days after it is served on the Defendant.

Notice of service of proceedings

10.1 This clause applies where the relevant proceedings are commenced in England or Wales. **3F–165**

10.2 MIB shall incur no liability under MIB's obligation unless the claimant has, not later than the appropriate date, given notice in writing to the person specified in clause 9(1) of the date of service of the Claim Form or other originating process in the relevant proceedings.

10.3 In this clause, "the appropriate date" means the day falling—

(a) seven days after—

   (i) the date when the claimant receives notification from the Court that service of the Claim Form or other originating process has occurred,

   (ii) the date when the claimant receives notification from the Defendant that service of the Claim Form or other originating process has occurred, or

   (iii) the date of personal service, or

(b) fourteen days after the date when service is deemed to have occurred in accordance with the Civil Procedure Rules, whichever of those days occurs first.

Further information

3F–166 11.1 MIB shall incur no liability under MIB's obligation unless the claimant has, not later than seven days after the occurrence of any of the following events, namely—

(a) the filing of a defence in the relevant proceedings,

(b) any amendment to the Particulars of Claim or any amendment of or addition to any schedule or other document required to be served therewith, and

(c) either—

   (i) the setting down of the case for trial, or

   (ii) where the court gives notice to the claimant of the trial date, the date when that notice is received, given notice in writing of the date of that event to the person specified in clause 9.1 and has, in the case of the filing of a defence or an amendment of the Particulars of Claim or any amendment of or addition to any schedule or other document required to be served therewith, supplied a copy thereof to that person.

11.2 MIB shall incur no liability under MIB's obligation unless the claimant furnishes to the person specified in clause 9.1 within a reasonable time after being required to do so such further information and documents in support of his claim as MIB may reasonably require notwithstanding that the claimant may have complied with clause 7.1.

Notice of intention to apply for judgment

3F–167 12.1 MIB shall incur no liability under MIB's obligation unless the claimant has, after commencement of the relevant proceedings and not less than thirty-five days before the appropriate date, given notice in writing to the person specified in clause 9.1 of his intention to apply for or to sign judgment in the relevant proceedings.

12.2 In this clause, "the appropriate date" means the date when the application for judgment is made or, as the case may be, the signing of judgment occurs.

Section 154 of the 1988 Act

3F–168 13.1 MIB shall incur no liability under MIB's obligation unless the claimant has as soon as reasonably practicable—

(a) demanded the information and, where appropriate, the particulars specified in section 154(1) of the 1988 Act, and

(b) if the person of whom the demand is made fails to comply with the provisions of that subsection—

   (i) made a formal complaint to a police officer in respect of such failure, and

   (ii) used all reasonable endeavours to obtain the name and address of the registered keeper of the vehicle or, if so required by MIB, has authorised MIB to take such steps on his behalf.

Prosecution of proceedings

14.1 MIB shall incur no liability under MIB's obligation—

(a) unless the claimant has, if so required by MIB and having been granted a full indemnity by MIB as to costs, taken all reasonable steps to obtain judgment against every person who may be liable (including any person who may be vicariously liable) in respect of the injury or death or damage to property, or

(b) if the claimant, upon being requested to do so by MIB, refuses to consent to MIB being joined as a party to the relevant proceedings.

3F–169

Assignment of judgment and undertakings

15.1 MIB shall incur no liability under MIB's obligation unless the claimant has—

(a) assigned to MIB or its nominee the unsatisfied judgment, whether or not that judgment includes an amount in respect of a liability other than a relevant liability, and any order for costs made in the relevant proceedings, and

(b) undertaken to repay to MIB any sum paid to him—

  (i) by MIB in discharge of MIB's obligation if the judgment is subsequently set aside either as a whole or in respect of the part of the relevant liability to which that sum relates;

  (ii) by any other person by way of compensation or benefit for the death, bodily injury or other damage to which the relevant proceedings relate, including a sum which would have been deductible under the provisions of clause 17 if it had been received before MIB was obliged to satisfy MIB's obligation.

3F–170

3F–171

Limitations on MIB's Liability

Compensation for damage to property

16.1 Where a claim under this Agreement includes a claim in respect of damage to property, MIB's obligation in respect of that part of the relevant sum which is awarded for such damage and any losses arising therefrom (referred to in this clause as "the property damage compensation") is limited in accordance with the following paragraphs.

16.2 Where the property damage compensation does not exceed the specified excess, MIB shall incur no liability.

16.3 Where the property damage compensation in respect of any one accident exceeds the specified excess but does not exceed £250,000, MIB shall incur liability less the specified excess.

16.4 Where the property damage compensation in respect of any one accident exceeds £250,000, MIB shall incur liability only in respect of the sum of £250,000 less the specified excess.

Compensation received from other sources

17.1 Where a claimant has received compensation from—

(a) the Policyholders Protection Board under the Policyholders Protection Act 1975, or

(b) an insurer under an insurance agreement or arrangement, or

(c) any other source, in respect of the death, bodily injury or other damage to which the relevant proceedings relate and such compensation has not been taken into account in the calculation of the relevant sum MIB may deduct from the relevant sum, in addition to any sum deductible under clause 16, an amount equal to that compensation.

3F–172

3F–173

Miscellaneous

Notifications of decisions by MIB

18.1 Where a claimant—

    (a) has made an application in accordance with clause 7, and

    (b) has given to the person specified in clause 9.1 proper notice of the relevant proceedings in accordance with clause 9.2,

MIB shall—

    (i) give a reasoned reply to any request made by the claimant relating to the payment of compensation in pursuance of MIB's obligation, and

    (ii) as soon as reasonably practicable notify the claimant in writing of its decision regarding the payment of the relevant sum, together with the reasons for that decision.

Reference of disputes to the Secretary of State

3F–174 19.1 In the event of any dispute as to the reasonableness of a requirement made by MIB for the supply of information or documentation or for the taking of any step by the claimant, it may be referred by the claimant or MIB to the Secretary of State whose decision shall be final.

19.2 Where a dispute is referred to the Secretary of State—

    (a) MIB shall supply the Secretary of State and, if it has not already done so, the claimant with notice in writing of the requirement from which the dispute arises, together with the reasons for that requirement and such further information as MIB considers relevant, and

    (b) where the dispute is referred by the claimant, the claimant shall supply the Secretary of State and, if he has not already done so, MIB with notice in writing of the grounds on which he disputes the reasonableness of the requirement.

Recoveries

3F–175 20.1 Nothing in this Agreement shall prevent an insurer from providing by conditions in a contract of insurance that all sums paid by the insurer or by MIB by virtue of the Principal Agreement or this Agreement in or towards the discharge of the liability of the insured shall be recoverable by them or by MIB from the insured or from any other person.

Apportionment of damages, etc.

3F–176 21.1 Where an unsatisfied judgment which includes an amount in respect of a liability other than a relevant liability has been assigned to MIB or its nominee in pursuance of clause 15 MIB shall—

    (a) apportion any sum it receives in satisfaction or partial satisfaction of the judgment according to the proportion which the damages awarded in respect of the relevant liability bear to the damages awarded in respect of the other liability, and

    (b) account to the claimant in respect of the moneys received properly apportionable to the other liability.

21.2 Where the sum received includes an amount in respect of interest or an amount awarded under an order for costs, the interest or the amount received in pursuance of the order shall be dealt with in the manner provided in paragraph (1).

Agents

3F–177 22.1 MIB may perform any of its obligations under this agreement by agents.

Transitional provisions

3F–178 23.1 The 1988 Agreement shall continue in force in relation to claims arising out of accidents occurring before 1st October 1999 with the modifications contained in paragraph (2).

23.2 In relation to any claim made under the 1988 Agreement after this Agreement has come into force, the 1988 Agreement shall apply as if there were inserted after clause 6 thereof

> Where any person in whose favour a judgment In respect of a relevant liability has been made has—
>
>> (a) made a claim under this Agreement, and
>>
>> (b) satisfied the requirements specified in clause 5 hereof,
>
> MIB shall, if requested to do so, give him a reasoned reply regarding the satisfaction of that claim".

IN WITNESS whereof the Secretary of State has caused his Corporate Seal to be hereunto affixed and the Motor Insurers' Bureau has caused its Common Seal to be hereunto affixed the day and year first above written.

THE CORPORATE SEAL of the SECRETARY OF STATE FOR THE ENVIRONMENT ~ TRANSPORT AND THE REGIONS hereunto affixed is authenticated by:—

Authorised by the Secretary of State

THE COMMON SEAL of the MOTOR INSURERS'

Bureau was hereunto affixed in the presence of:

Directors of the Board of Management

Secretary

3F–179

Notes for the Guidance of Victims of Road Traffic Accidents

The following notes are for the guidance of anyone who may have a claim on the Motor Insurers' Bureau under this Agreement and their legal advisers. They are not part of the Agreement, their purpose being to deal in ordinary language with the situations which most readily occur. They are not in any way a substitute for reading and applying the terms of this or any other relevant Agreement.

At the request of the Secretary of State, these notes have been revised with effect from 15th April 2002 and in their revised form have been agreed and approved by MIB, the Law Society of England and Wales, the Law Society of Scotland, the Motor Accident Solicitors' Society and the Association of Personal Injury Lawyers. Any application made under the Agreement after this date (unless proceedings have already been issued) will be handled by MIB in accordance with these notes.

Where proceedings have been issued in Scotland, for the words "Claimant" and "Defendant" there shall be substituted in these Notes where appropriate the words "Pursuer" and "Defender" respectively.

Enquiries, requests for application forms and general correspondence In connection with the Agreement should be addressed to:—

Motor Insurers Bureau
Linford Wood House
6-12 Capital Drive
MILTON KEYNES
MK14 6XT
Tel: 01908 830001
Fax: 01908 671681
DX: 142620 Milton Keynes

1. Introduction—MIB's role and application of the Agreement

1.1 The role of MIB under this Agreement is to provide a safety net for innocent victims of drivers who have been identified but are uninsured. MIB's funds for this **3F–180** purpose are obtained from levies charged upon insurers and so come from the premiums which are charged by those insurers to members of the public.

1.2 MIB has entered into a series of Agreements with the Secretary of State and his predecessors in office. Under each Agreement MIB undertakes obligations to pay defined compensation in specific circumstances. There are two sets of Agreements, one relating to victims of uninsured drivers (the "Uninsured Drivers" Agreements) and the other concerned with victims of hit and run or otherwise untraceable drivers (the "Untraced Drivers" Agreements). These Notes are addressed specifically to the procedures required to take advantage of the rights granted by the Uninsured Drivers Agreements. However, it is not always certain which of the Agreements applies. For guidance in such cases please see the note on Untraced Drivers at paragraph 11 below.

1.3 In order to determine which of the Uninsured Drivers Agreements is applicable to a particular victim's claim, regard must be had to the date of the relevant accident. This Agreement only applies in respect of claims arising on or after 1st October 1999. Claims arising earlier than that are covered by the following Agreements:—

1.3.1 Claims arising in respect of an incident occurring between 1st July 1946 and 28th February 1971 are governed by the Agreement between the Minister of Transport and the Bureau dated 17th June 1946.

1.3.2 Claims arising in respect of an incident occurring between 1st March 1971 and 30th November 1972 are governed by the Agreement between the Secretary of State for the Environment and the Bureau dated 1st February 1971.

1.3.3 Claims arising in respect of an incident occurring between 1st December 1972 and 30th December 1988 are governed by the Agreement between the Secretary of State and the Bureau dated 22nd November 1972.

1.3.4 Claims arising in respect of an incident occurring between 31st December 1988 and 30th September 1999 are governed by the Agreement between the Secretary of State and the Bureau dated 21st December 1988.

2. MIB's obligation

3F–181 2.1 MIB's basic obligation (see clause 5) is to satisfy judgments which fall within the terms of this Agreement and which, because the Defendant to the proceedings is not insured, are not satisfied.

2.2 This obligation is, however, not absolute. It is subject to certain exceptions where MIB has no liability (see clause 6), there are a number of pre-conditions which the claimant must comply with (see clauses 7 to 15) and there are some limitations on MIB's liability (see clauses 16 and 17).

2.3 Nothing in the Agreement is intended to vary the limitation rules applying to claimants not of full age or capacity. Limitation for personal injury remains 3 years from the date of full age or capacity.

2.4 MIB does not have to wait for a judgment to be given; it can become party to the proceedings or negotiate and settle the claim if it wishes to do so.

3. Claims which MIB is not obliged to satisfy

3F–182 MIB is not liable under the Agreement in the case of the following types of claim.

3.1 A claim made in respect of an unsatisfied judgment which does not concern a liability against which Part VI of the Road Traffic Act 1988 requires a vehicle user to insure (see section 145 of the Act). An example would be a case where the accident did not occur in a place specified in the Act. See the definitions of "unsatisfied judgment" and "relevant liability" in clause 1.

3.2 A claim in respect of loss or damage caused by the use of a vehicle owned by or in the possession of the Crown (that is the Civil Service, the armed forces and so on) to which Part VI does not apply. If the responsibility for motor insurance has been undertaken by someone else or the vehicle is in fact insured, this exception does not apply. See clause 6(1)(a).

3.3 A claim made against any person who is not required to insure by virtue of section 144 of the Road Traffic Act 1988. See clause 6(1)(b).

3.4 A claim (commonly called subrogated) made in the name of a person suffering damage or injury but which is in fact wholly or partly for the benefit of another who has indemnified, or is liable to indemnify that person. See clause 6(1)(c).

It is not the intention of this Clause to exclude claims for the gratuitous provision of care, travel expenses by family members or friends, or miscellaneous expenses incurred on behalf of the Claimant, where the claimant is entitled to include such claims in his claim for damages.

3.5 A claim in respect of damage to a motor vehicle or losses arising from such **3F–183** damage where the use of the damaged vehicle was itself not covered by a contract of insurance as required by law. See clause 6(1)(d).

3.6 A claim made by a passenger in a vehicle where the loss or damage has been caused by the user of that vehicle if:—

    3.6.1 the use of the vehicle was not covered by a contract of insurance; and

    3.6.2 the claimant knew or could be taken to have known that the vehicle was being used without insurance, had been stolen or unlawfully taken or was being used in connection with crime.

See clause 6(1)(e), (2), (3) and (4).

For an interpretation of "knew or ought to have known" refer to the House of Lords judgment in *White v White of 1st March 2001*.

3.7 A claim in respect of property damage amounting to £300 or less, £300 being the "specified excess". See clause 16(2).

3.8 Where the claim is for property damage, the first £300 of the loss and so much of it as exceeds £250,000. See clause 16(3) and (4).

4. Procedure after the accident and before proceedings

4.1 The claimant must take reasonable steps to establish whether there is in fact any **3F–184** insurance covering the use of the vehicle which caused the injury or damage. First, a claimant has statutory rights under section 154 of the Road Traffic Act 1988 to obtain relevant particulars which he must take steps to exercise even if that involves incurring expense and MIB will insist that he does so. See clause 13(a).

MIB accept that if the MIB application form is sufficiently completed and signed by the Claimant, the Claimant will have complied with this Clause of the Agreement.

4.2 Other steps will include the following:

    4.2.1 The exchange of names, addresses and insurance particulars between those involved either at the scene of the accident or afterwards.

    4.2.2 Corresponding with the owner or driver of the vehicle or his representatives. He will be obliged under the terms of his motor policy to inform his insurers and a letter of claim addressed to him will commonly be passed to the insurers who may reply on his behalf. See clause 9(2)(d).

    4.2.3 Where only the vehicle's number is known, enquiry of the Driver and Vehicle Licensing Agency at Swansea SA99 1BP as to the registered keeper of the vehicle is desirable so that through him the identity of the owner or driver can be established or confirmed.

    4.2.4 Enquiries of the police (see clause 13(b) and Note 4.1 above).

4.3 If enquiries show that there is an insurer who is obliged to accept and does accept the obligation to handle the claim against the user of the vehicle concerned, even though the relevant liability may not be covered by the policy in question, then the claim should be pursued with such insurer.

PERSONAL INJURY

4.4 If, however, enquiries disclose that there is no insurance covering the use of the vehicle concerned or if the insurer cannot be identified or the insurer asserts that it is under no obligation to handle the claim or if for any other reason it is clear that the insurer will not satisfy any judgment, the claim should be directed to MIB itself.

5. When proceedings are commenced or contemplated

3F–185 5.1 As explained above, MIB does not have to wait for a judgment to be obtained before intervening. Claimants may apply to MIB before the commencement of proceedings. MIB will respond to any claim which complies with clause 7 and must give a reasoned reply to any request for compensation in respect of the claim (see clause 18) although normally a request for compensation will not be met until MIB is satisfied that it is properly based. Interim compensation payments are dealt with at paragraph 8 below.

Application Forms are available from MIB's office or their website: www.mib.org.uk.

Where a claim is made by the Claimant in person, who has not received legal advice, then if the claim is first made within 14 days prior to expiry of the limitation period, MIB will require the completed application form within the 21 days after the issue of proceedings.

5.2 It is important that wherever possible claims should be made using MIB's application form, fully completed and accompanied by documents supporting the claim, as soon as possible to avoid unnecessary delays. See clause 7(1). Copies of the form can be obtained on request made by post, telephone, fax or on the DX or on personal application to MIB's offices.

5.3 The claimant must give MIB notice in writing that he has commenced legal proceedings. The notice, the completed application form (if appropriate) and all necessary documents must be received by MIB no later than 14 days after the date of commencement of proceedings. See clause 9(1) and (2)(a). The date of commencement is determined in accordance with the definitions of "relevant proceedings" and "commencement" given in clause 1.

When it is decided to commence legal proceedings, MIB should be joined as a defendent (unless there is good reason not to do so). Once MIB is a defendant, the Court will advise the relevant events direct and clauses 9(3),11 and 12 will no longer apply.

The form of words set out below should be used for the joinder of MIB as second defendant:

1. The Second Defendant is a Company limited by guarantee under the Companies Act. Pursuant to an Agreement with the Secretary of State for the Environment Transport and the Regions dated 13th August 1999, the Second Defendant provides compensation in certain circumstances to persons suffering injury or damage as a result of the negligence of uninsured motorists.

2. The Claimant has used all reasonable endeavours to ascertain the liability of an insurer for the First Defendant and at the time of the commencement of these proceedings verily believes that the First Defendant is not insured.

3. The Claimant accepts that only if a final judgment is obtained against the First Defendant (which judgment is not satisfied in full within seven days from the date uponwhich the Claimant became entitled to enforce it) can the Second Defendant be required to satisfy the judgement and then only if the terms and conditions set out in the Agreement are satisfied. Until that time, any liability of the Second Defendant is only contingent .

4. To avoid the Second Defendant having later to apply to join itself to this action (which the Claimant must consent to in any event, pursuant to Clause 14(b) of the Agreement) the Claimant seeks to include the Second Defendant from the outset recognising fully the Second Defendant's position as reflected in 3 above and the

rights of the Second Defendant fully to participate in the action to protect its position as a separate party to the action.

5. With the above in mind, the Claimant seeks a declaration of the Second Defendant's contingent liability to satisfy the claimant's judgment against the First Defendant.

5.4 This notice must have with it the following:

5.4.1 a copy of the document originating the proceedings, usually in England and Wales a Claim Form and in Scotland a Sheriff Court Writ or Court of Session Summons (see clause 9(2)(b));

5.4.2 normally the Particulars of Claim endorsed on or served with the Claim Form or Writ (see clause 9(2)(e), although this document may be served later in accordance with clause 9(3) if that applies);

5.4.3 in any case the documents required by the relevant rules of procedure (see clause 9(2)(f).

Provided that the documents referred to above are forwarded to MIB, it is not necessary to enclose the Response Pack or the Notice of Issue.

5.5 In addition, other items as mentioned in clause 9(2), e.g. correspondence with the Defendant (or Defender) or his representatives, need to be supplied where appropriate.

5.6 It is for the claimant to satisfy himself that the notice has in fact been received by MIB. However, where the Claimant proves that service by DX, First Class Post, Personal Service or any other form of service allowed by the Civil Procedure Rules, was effected, MIB will accept that such notice has been served in the same circumstances in which a party to litigation would be obliged to accept that he had been validly served by such means.

5.7 It should be noted that when MIB has been given notice of a claim, it may elect to require the claimant to bring proceedings and attempt to secure a judgment against the party whom MIB alleges to be wholly or partly responsible for the loss or damage or who may be contracted to indemnify the claimant. In such a case MIB must indemnify the claimant against the costs of such proceedings. Subject to that, however, MIB's obligation to satisfy the judgment in the action will only arise if the claimant commences the proceedings and takes all reasonable steps to obtain a judgment. See clause 14(a).

6. Service of proceedings

6.1 If proceedings are commenced in England or Wales the claimant must inform **3F–186** MIB of the date of service (see clause 10(1) and (2)).

6.2 If service of the Claim Form is effected by the Court, notice should be given within 7 days from the earliest of the dates listed in clause 10(3)(a)(i) or (ii) or within 14 days from the date mentioned in clause 10(3)(b) (the date of deemed service under the court's rules of procedure). Claimants are advised to take steps to ensure that the court or the defendant's legal representatives inform them of the date of service as soon as possible. Although a longer period is allowed than in other cases, service may be deemed to have occurred without a Claimant knowing of it until some time afterwards.

6.3 Where proceedings are served personally, notice should be given 7 days from the date of personal service (clause 10(3)(a)(iii)).

6.4 However, by concession MIB will accept the notice referred to in note 6.1 above if it is received by MIB within 14 days from the dates referred to in notes 6.2 and 6.3.

6.5 In Scotland, proceedings are commenced at the date of service (see clause 1) so notice should already have been given under clause 9 and clause 10 does not apply there.

7. After service and before judgment

3F–187 See Note 5.3 above.

3F–188 7.1 Notice of the filing of a defence, of an amendment to the Statement or Particulars of Claim, and the setting down of the case for trial should be given not later than 7 days after the occurrence of such events and a copy of the document must be supplied (clause 11(1)).

7.2 However, by concession MIB will accept the notice referred to in note 7.1 above if it is received by MIB within 14 days after the proven date on which it was received by the claimant

7.3 MIB may request further information and documents to support the claim where it is not satisfied that the documents supplied with the application form are sufficient to enable it to assess its liability under the Agreement (see clause 11(2)).

7.4 If the claimant intends to sign or apply for judgment he must give MIB notice of the fact before doing so. This notice must be given at least 35 days before the application is to be made or the date when judgment is to be signed (see clause 12).

The 35 days notice does not apply where the court enters judgment of its own motion.

7.5 At no time must the claimant oppose MIB if it wishes to be joined as a party to proceedings and he must if requested consent to any application by MIB to be joined. Conflicts may arise between a Defendant and MIB which require MIB to become a Defendant or, in Scotland, a party Minuter if a defence is to be filed on its behalf (see clause 14(b)).

8. Interim payments

3F–189 In substantial cases, the claimant may wish to apply for an interim payment. MIB will consider such applications on a voluntary basis but otherwise the claimant has the right to apply to the court for an interim payment order which, if granted, will be met by MIB.

9. After judgment

3F–190 9.1 MIB's basic obligation normally arises if a judgment is not satisfied within 7 days after the claimant has become entitled to enforce it (see clause 1). However, that judgment may in certain circumstances be set aside and with it MIB's obligation to satisfy it. Sometimes MIB wishes to apply to set aside a judgment either wholly or partially. If MIB decides not to satisfy a judgment it will notify the claimant as soon as possible. Where a judgment is subsequently set aside, MIB will require the claimant to repay any sum previously paid by MIB to discharge its obligation under the Agreement (see clause 15(b)).

9.2 MIB is not obliged to satisfy a judgment unless the claimant has in return assigned the benefit to MIB or its nominee (see clause 15(a)). If such assignment is effected and if the subject matter of the judgment includes claims in respect of which MIB is not obliged to meet any judgment and if MIB effects any recovery on the judgment, the sum recovered will be divided between MIB and the claimant in proportion to the liabilities which were and which were not covered by MIB's obligation (see clause 21).

10. Permissible deductions from payments by MIB

3F–191 10.1 Claims for loss and damage for which the claimant has been compensated or indemnified, e.g. under a contract of insurance or under the Policyholders Protection Act 1975, and which has not been taken into account in the judgment, may be deducted from the sum paid in settlement of MIB's obligation (see clause 17).

10.2 If there is a likelihood that the claimant will receive payment from such a source after the judgment has been satisfied by MIB, MIB will require him to undertake to repay any sum which duplicates the compensation assessed by the court (see clause 15(b)).

11. Untraced drivers

11.1 Where the owner or driver of a vehicle cannot be identified application may be **3F–192** made to MIB under the relevant Untraced Drivers Agreement. This provides, subject to specified conditions, for the payment of compensation for personal injury. It does not provide for compensation in respect of damage to property.

11.2 In those cases where it is unclear whether the owner or driver of a vehicle has been correctly identified it is sensible for the claimant to register a claim under both this Agreement and the Untraced Drivers Agreement following which MIB will advise which Agreement will, in its view, apply in the circumstances of the particular case.

PERSONAL INJURY

3G   DATA PROTECTION ACT 1998

DATA PROTECTION ACT 1998

Introduction

The Data Protection Act ("the Act" or "DPA") was passed to implement Directive **3G–1**
95/46 of October 24, 1995 on the protection of individuals with regard to the processing of personal data and the free movement of such data ("Directive 95/46"). It repealed the Data Protection Act 1984 which had been passed to enable the UK to ratify
the Convention for the Protection of Individuals with regard to automatic processing
of Personal Data ("Treaty 108"). The courts have referred to the Directive, Treaty 108
and the Convention Rights, particularly Art.8, in interpreting cases on the Act. In case
law since the Act came into force the courts have tended to consider the law of
confidence and the emerging privacy rights under Art. 8 in conjunction with the Act.
Further specific rights in relation to telecommunications services and electronic
marketing are contained in the Privacy and Electronic Communications (EC Directive)
Regulations 2003 (see 3G–23).

Data Protection Act 1998

(1998 c.29)

PART I   **3G–2**

PRELIMINARY

Basic interpretative provisions

1.—(1) In this Act, unless the context otherwise requires—   **3G–3**
"data" means information which—

> (a) is being processed by means of equipment operat-
> ing automatically in response to instructions given for
> that purpose,
> (b) is recorded with the intention that it should be
> processed by means of such equipment,
> (c) is recorded as part of a relevant filing system or
> with the intention that it should form part of a rele-
> vant filing system,
> (d) does not fall within paragraph (a), (b) or (c) but
> forms part of an accessible record as defined by section
> 68;
> (e) is recorded information held by a public author-
> ity and does not fall within paragraphs (a) to (d).

Notes

"Data"—although the definition limits the scope of the Act by reference to the form   **3G–4**
in which information is held, material which would fall outside this definition may also
be covered because it is the product of the processing of data. In *Campbell v. Mirror
Group Newspapers* [2003] 2 W.L.R. 80 it was held that the Act covered text and
photographs printed in newspapers which were the immediate result of data
processing. See para. 3G–12 in relation to "processing". Confirmed (para. 230) in *Michael Douglas, Catherine Zeta-Jones and Northern Shell Plc v. Hello* [2003] EWHC 786.
Conversely information held in machine readable form which can no longer be accessed because the technology is no longer available should fall outside the definition.
However in *Smith v. Lloyds Bank Plc* [2005] EWHC 246 (Ch) the court rejected a

DATA PROTECTION

contention that hard copy should be regarded as "data" because it could be scanned and become data or because it was produced from data within 1(1)(a).

Some types of manual filing systems are caught by this provision. See the definition of "relevant filing system" and para. 3G–14.

"Accessible records" are manual records to which access was available under the Access to Health Records Act 1990 (health records) and the Access to Personal Files Act 1987 (personal information held for social work purposes by specified authorities and in relation to public sector tenancies). Accessible records are defined in s.68 and Scheds 11 and 12 of the Act. The rights of access are slightly modified in respect of such records. Such records are covered only by the rights of access and correction under the Act until October 2007, after which the Act applies in full.

Where information falls within the definition because it is intended to process it as data or include it in a relevant filing system s.1(3) provides that it is immaterial that the processing or inclusion should occur outside the EEA.

Subsection (e) was added by s.68 of the Freedom of Information Act 2000. "Public authority" has the same meaning as in that Act. The effect of this, and further amendments made by ss.69–72 is to extend the right of subject access (see 3G–16), rectification etc. (see 3G–28) and compensation for inaccuracy (see 3G–26) to all types of information after January 1, 2005. The amendments impact only on public sector bodies (see also note 3G–15).

3G–5 "data controller" means subject to subsection (4), a person who (either alone or jointly or in common with other persons) determines the purposes for which and the manner in which any personal data are, or are to be, processed.

Notes

3G–6 "Data controller"—this is a two part definition, the second part being in s.1(4). The terms "jointly" and "in common" are not defined.

The controller must determine both the manner and purpose of the processing. There may be two or more controllers sharing control in different ways. The Information Commissioner has suggested that:

"the determination of the purposes for which personal data are to be processed is paramount in deciding whether or not a person is a data controller"

Legal Guidance October 2001. The approach has not been tested by the courts and possibly should be treated with caution.

3G–7 "data processor", in relation to personal data, means any person (other than an employee of the data controller) who processes the data on behalf of the data controller.

Notes

3G–8 "Data processor"—a data controller who uses a data processor must ensure that the relationship is governed by a contract made or evidenced in writing covering security and control of the data. See Principle 7 Sched.1.

3G–9 "data subject" means an individual who is the subject of personal data.

3G–10 "personal data" means data which relate to a living individual who can be identified—

    (a) from those data, or

    (b) from those data and other information which is in the possession of, or is likely to come into the possession of, the data controller, and includes any expression of opinion about the individual and any indication of the intentions of the data controller or any other person in respect of the individual.

Notes

3G–11 "Personal data" was considered in *Durant v. Financial Services Authority* [2003] EWCA Civ 1746; [2004] F.S.R. 28; [2004] IP & T 814. Mr Durant had applied for access to information under s.7 of the Act. The court considered the meaning of the words "relate to" and the extent to which, if any, information must have the data subject as its focus, or main focus, before it is considered to relate to him. It held that the term has a narrow meaning:

"...not all information retrieved from a computer search against an individual's name is personal data within the Act. Mere mention of the data subject in a document held by a data controller does not necessarily amount to his personal data. Whether it does so in any particular instance depends on where it falls in a continuum of relevance or proximity to the data subject as distinct, say, from transactions or matters in which he may have been involved in a greater or lesser degree. It seems to me that there are two notions which may be of assistance. The first is whether the information is biographical in a significant sense, that is going beyond the recording of the putative data subject's involvement in a matter or an event that has no personal connotations, a life event in respect of which his privacy could not be said to be compromised. The second is one of focus. The information should have the putative data subject as its focus rather than some other person with whom he may have been involved or some other transaction or event in which he may have figured or had an interest, for example as in this case an investigation into some other person's or body's conduct that he may have instigated. In short it is information that affects his privacy, whether in his personal or family life, business or professional capacity."

per Auld L.J. at para. 28. It should be noted that he went on to refer to the judgment of the European Court in the case of criminal proceedings against *Lindqvist* Case C-101/01 in which the court held that the term "personal data" covered name and identifying data such as a telephone number. Thus the name, and information immediately associated with the name, such as a statement in a report of a meeting that Mr X was present, will fall within the definition but the remainder of the report will not be personal data about Mr X merely by virtue of that one reference.

It is arguable that the definition has been narrowed in transposition from the definition in Art. 2 of the Directive in which it covers identifiable natural persons that is:

"one who can be identified, directly or indirectly, in particular by reference to an identification number or to one or more factors specific to his physical, physiological, mental, economic, cultural or social identity".

In *Lindqvist* the court held that the name of a person or identification of him by some other means, for instance by giving his telephone number, or information about his working conditions or hobbies, constituted personal data about the individual. *Durant* was applied in *Johnson v. The Medical Defence Union Ltd* [2004] EWHC 2509.

The EU Commission has reviewed the question of UK compliance with Directive 95/46 but no infrigement proceedings have yet been issued.

"Sensitive personal data" is defined in s.2 as information about racial or ethnic origin, political opinions, religious beliefs and a number of other specific categories set out in the section. Particular care should be taken when processing such types of data. Before processing such data the controller must ensure that he can rely on one or more of the grounds set out in Sched.3 as well as the normal grounds set out in Sched.2 or S.I. 2000 No. 417. Considered in *Lindqvist* where the court held that information that an individual had injured her foot and was working half-time on medical grounds was sensitive personal data.

3G-12 "processing", in relation to information or data, means obtaining, recording or holding the information or data or carrying out any operation or set of operations on the information or data, including—

(a) organisation, adaptation or alteration of the information or data,

(b) retrieval, consultation or use of the information or data,

(c) disclosure of the information or data by transmission, dissemination or otherwise making available, or

(d) alignment, combination, blocking, erasure or destruction of the information or data.

Notes

3G-13 "Processing"—was considered by the Court of Appeal in *Campbell v. MGN* [2003] 2 W.L.R. 80 *per* Lord Phillips MR at para. 122 who held that the publication in hard copy, where data had previously been automatically processed, formed part of the processing and falls within the Act. The point was not specifically considered in the House of Lords but appears to have been accepted, *per* Lord Nicholls of Birkenhead at para. 32: "It is not necessary for me to pursue the claim based on the Data Protection Act 1998. The parties were agreed that this claim stands or falls with the outcome of the main claim." If the House did not accept that publication in these circumstances fell under the Data Protection Act, the claim under that Act would have failed irrespective of the failure or success of the main claim.

Information, as well as data, may be processed, thus the collection of information orally before it is captured as data may fall within the scope of the Act. This is made explicit in s.1(2).

3G–14   **"relevant filing system"** means any set of information relating to individuals to the extent that, although the information is not processed by means of equipment operating automatically in response to instructions given for that purpose, the set is structured, either by reference to individuals or by reference to criteria relating to individuals, in such a way that specific information relating to a particular individual is readily accessible.

Notes

3G–15   "Relevant filing system"—in *Durant* (see para. 3G–11 above) the Court of Appeal considered three files and a sheaf of papers and agreed with the ruling in the High Court that in each case the material did not satisfy all the elements necessary to fall within the definition:

— one file was not structured by reference to individuals at all;
— one was referenced to the claimant but documents were filed in date order only; the other was referenced by issues and although it did contain a section on the claimant, there was no further internal structure of the material so that specific information could not be said to be readily accessible.

"I conclude….that a "relevant filing system" for the purpose of the Act is limited to a system:

(1) in which the files forming part of it are structured or referenced in such a way as clearly to indicate at the outset of the search whether specific information capable of amounting to personal data of an individual requesting it under section 7 is held within the system, and, if so, in which file or files it is held; and

(2) which has, as part of its own structure or referencing mechanism, a sufficiently sophisticated and detailed means of readily indicating whether and where in an individual files or files specific criteria or information about the applicant can be located"

per Auld L.J. at para. 50.

The definition is the starting point for the new exclusory definitions of "recorded" and "unstructured" manual information in s.68 and s.69 of the Freedom of Information Act 2000. Section 69 inserts a new s.9A in the DPA which applies to public authorities in England, Wales and Northern Ireland. Equivalent amendments have been made to impact in Scotland by the Freedom of Information (Scotland) Act 2002 (consequential modifications) Order 2004 (S.I. 2004 No. 3089) made under the Scotland Act 2000 as the Freedom of Information (Scotland) Act 2002, being devolved legislation, could not be used to amend the Data Protection Act 1998. Thus the definition of a relevant filing system excludes material which would fall within these categories of information.

The term derives from "personal data filing system" in the Directive which provides that a data set may exist irrespective of whether the data set is: "centralised, decentralised or dispersed on a functional or geographic basis".

The Directive appears to allow Member States some margin of appreciation in how far they apply the Directive to manual files see Art. 4 and Recitals 15 and 27. The Government aimed at the narrowest possible coverage. Relevant material can be found in Hansard at Vol 587 No. 95 col 467 Lords Rep March 16, 1998.

"Grounds for processing"—a data controller may only process personal data if he can rely on one or more of the six grounds set out in Sched.2. Where sensitive personal data (defined s.2) are to be processed the controller must rely on one or more of the further grounds set out in Sched.3 or S.I. 2000 No. 417.

"Personal or domestic"—data processed only for the personal, domestic or recreational purposes by an individual are exempt from most of the Act including the Principles and the individual rights. It follows that no remedies will be available whatever the use where the controller processes for such purposes s.36.

In *Lindqvist* the European Court had regard to the relevant preamble to the Directive in interpreting the equivalent exemption in the Swedish law. The court held a narrow interpretation applied so material posted on the internet would not fall within the exemption.

Right of access to personal data

7.—(1) Subject to the following provisions of this section and to **3G–16** sections 8 and 9, an individual is entitled—

(a) to be informed by any data controller whether personal data of which that individual is the data subject are being processed by or on behalf of that data controller,

(b) if that is the case, to be given by the data controller a description of—

    (i) the personal data of which that individual is the data subject,

    (ii) the purposes for which they are being or are to be processed, and

    (iii) the recipients or classes of recipients to whom they are or may be disclosed,

(c) to have communicated to him in an intelligible form—

    (i) the information constituting any personal data of which that individual is the data subject, and

    (ii) any information available to the data controller as to the source of those data, and

(d) where the processing by automatic means of personal data of which that individual is the data subject for the purpose of evaluating matters relating to him such as, for example, his performance at work, his credit worthiness, his reliability or his conduct, has constituted or is likely to constitute the sole basis for any decision significantly affecting him, to be informed by the data controller of the logic involved in that decision-taking.

(2) A data controller is not obliged to supply any information under subsection (1) unless he has received—

(a) a request in writing, and

(b) except in prescribed cases, such fee (not exceeding the prescribed maximum) as he may require.

(3) Where a data controller—

(a) reasonably requires further information in order to satisfy himself as to the identity of the person making a request under this section and to locate the information which that person seeks, and

(b) has informed him of that requirement,

the data controller is not obliged to comply with the request unless he is supplied with that further information.

(4) Where a data controller cannot comply with the request without disclosing information relating to another individual who can be identified from that information, he is not obliged to comply with the request unless—

(a) the other individual has consented to the disclosure of the information to the person making the request, or

(b) it is reasonable in all the circumstances to comply with the request without the consent of the other individual.

(5) In subsection (4) the reference to information relating to an-

other individual includes a reference to information identifying that individual as the source of the information sought by the request; and that subsection is not to be construed as excusing a data controller from communicating so much of the information sought by the request as can be communicated without disclosing the identity of the other individual concerned, whether by the omission of names or other identifying particulars or otherwise.

(6) In determining for the purposes of subsection (4)(b) whether it is reasonable in all the circumstances to comply with the request without the consent of the other individual concerned, regard shall be had, in particular, to—

(a) any duty of confidentiality owed to the other individual,

(b) any steps taken by the data controller with a view to seeking the consent of the other individual,

(c) whether the other individual is capable of giving consent, and

(d) any express refusal of consent by the other individual.

(7) An individual making a request under this section may, in such cases as may be prescribed, specify that his request is limited to personal data of any prescribed description.

(8) Subject to subsection (4), a data controller shall comply with a request under this section promptly and in any event before the end of the prescribed period beginning with the relevant day.

(9) If a court is satisfied on the application of any person who has made a request under the foregoing provisions of this section that the data controller in question has failed to comply with the request in contravention of those provisions, the court may order him to comply with the request.

(10) In this section—

"prescribed" means prescribed by the Secretary of State by regulations:

"the prescribed maximum" means such amount as may be prescribed:

"the prescribed period" means forty days or such other period as may be prescribed:

"the relevant day", in relation to a request under this section, means the day on which the data controller receives the request or, if later, the first day on which the data controller has both the required fee and the information referred to in subsection (3).

(11) Different amounts or periods may be prescribed under this section in relation to different cases.

Notes

3G–17   Subject access is one of the "rights of data subjects" under Principle 6 of Sched.1 (interpretation of the provision at para. 8a of Pt II of Sched.1). Accordingly failure to comply with it may not only be the basis for an application to court by the data subject but also the subject of a request for assessment of processing by a data subject to the Information Commissioner under s.42. Failure to comply with a subject access request may give rise to the exercise of the Commissioner's supervisory jurisdiction. A data subject who has referred a failure to comply to the Commissioner is not bound to await the Commissioner's response before commencing action but may take independent action under s.7(9), *R (Lord) v. Secretary of State for the Home Department* [2003] EWHC 2073 (Admin).

Since the Human Rights Act 1998 came into force a court must have regard to any relevant jurisprudence of the Court of Human Rights when interpreting legislation. Section 7(5) derives from the judgment of the ECtHR in *Gaskin v. UK* [1990] 1 FLR 167; (1990) 12 E.H.R.R. 36 although the case was not referred to in *Lord* which considered (*inter alia*) this provision.

This section is one of the "subject information provisions" s.27(2). By virtue of s.27(5) the subject information provisions "shall have effect notwithstanding any enactment or rule of law prohibiting or restricting the disclosure or authorising the withholding of information" except as provided by Pt IV. Part IV sets out the exemptions. It follows that, if personal data (see para. 3G–10 above) are properly requested by a data subject from a data controller (see para. 3G–6 above) in accordance with this section the data controller must supply them unless one of the exemptions listed in Pt IV applies. Part IV incorporates the exemptions in Sched.7.

In a second case brought by Mr Johnson (see 3G–12 *supra*) *Johnson v. The Medical Defence Union Ltd* [2004] EWHC 2509 the court held that the fact that documents did not contain personal data, and were therefore not available to him under a subject access request, did not preclude a claimant from seeking disclosure under CPR, Pt 31.

Exemptions

Class exemptions apply to personal data processed only for domestic and recreational purposes (s.36) (see para. 3G–15 above), information available to the public by or under any enactment (s.34), references provided in confidence when in the hands of the giver only (para. 1 Sched.7), judicial appointments and honours (para. 3 Sched.7), certain Crown Offices exempt under Data Protection (Crown Appointments) Order 2000 (S.I. 2000 No. 416), examination scripts (para. 9 Sched.7) and where legal professional privilege or the equivalent privilege in Scotland, would apply (para. 10 Sched.7).

Other exemptions are limited in extent: national security if "required for the purpose of safeguarding national security", s.28. A claim for exemption under s.28 must be supported by a Ministerial certificate. The breadth of a certificate issued by the Home Secretary was successfully challenged under s.28(6) before the National Security Panel of the Information Tribunal in the case of *Norman Baker MP v. Secretary of State for the Home Department* [2001] U.K.H.R.R. 1275. The Panel concluded that the Minister was not justified in issuing a certificate which permitted the Security Service to issue a "neither confirm nor deny" response to a request made under s.7(1)(a) regardless of whether national security would be harmed in the particular case.

Access to a number of classes of personal data is affected by modification orders which apply specific exemptions. These cover health information in accordance with the Data Protection (Subject Access Modification) (Health) Order 2000 (S.I. 2000 No. 413), social work data in accordance with the Data Protection (Subject Access Modification)(Social Work) Order 2000 (S.I. 2000 No. 415) and the Data Protection (Subject Access Modification) (Social Work) (Amendment) Order 2005 , education information in accordance with the Data Protection (Subject Access Modification) (Education) Order 2000 (S.I. 2000 No. 414) and a variety of additional special cases, such as material about embryos and adoption, covered by the Data Protection (Miscellaneous Subject Access Exemption) Order 2000 (S.I. 2000 No. 419).

The remaining exemptions cover material held for the purposes of journalistic, literary or artistic work (s.32), information held for research purposes (s.33) (both exemptions only applicable where particular conditions apply), information which would be prejudicial to:

— the purposes of the detection of crime and related purposes (s.29);

— a range of regulatory activities (s.31);

— management forecasting or management planning (Sched.7 para. 5);

— and negotiation (Sched.7 para. 7).

In *R. (on the application of Alan Lord) v. Secretary of State for the Home Department* [2003] EWHC 2073 the Court held that s.29(1) requires the issue of whether disclosure is likely to prejudice the prevention or detection of crime to be determined in relation to each individual case (paras 122-127).

There are special provisions for access to examination marks to ensure that access rights cannot be used to obtain premature disclosure.

The remaining exemptions cover corporate finance under the Data Protection (Corporate Finance Exemption) Order 2000 (S.I. 2000 No. 184) and preserve the privilege against self incrimination (Sched.7 para. 11).

Information which is disclosed under a subject access obligation is not admissible against the disclosing data controller in proceedings for an offence under the Act, (Sched.7 para. 11). Note however that the Act itself does not restrict the use of material disclosed as evidence in a prosecution for any other offence. Material disclosed can be used in civil proceedings and a subject access request is often a precursor of proceedings.

Two new exemptions are inserted by the Freedom of Information Act 2000 covering material which would infringe the privileges of the Houses of Parliament (Sched.6 paras 2–5) and information relating to personnel matters (s.33A inserted by s.70). The latter will only apply to manual data held in structured and unstructured files (see para. 3G–15).

Note: the number and extent of exemptions has been criticised, as has the proliferation of class exemptions, as being open to challenge for being wider than those permissible under the Directive.

"Previous access rights"—access rights previously exercised by individuals under the Consumer Credit Act 1974, Access to Health Records Act 1990 and Access to Personal Files Act 1987 have been consolidated under the DPA although some of the detailed rules remain different.

For "data controller", "personal data" and "processed" see definitions above.

"Extent of obligations"—the controller must provide a description of the nature of the data and the purposes for which they are held as well as a copy of the information constituting the data. Note that the data subject has to be informed of the purposes for which the data are held and not the grounds for the processing relied on by the controller. Nevertheless the information provided may assist the data subject to determine whether he is entitled to exercise his right to object to processing under s.10 (see below). Where the information falls into the definition of unstructured personal data the data subject must describe the data requested and his request may be refused if it is estimated that the cost of compliance would exceed the appropriate limit (s.9A)

"Prescribed fee"—the fee is £10 for a subject access request, although different limits apply to applications for consumer credit files, medical data and unstructured personal data. Fees and time limits for response, which also differ with the type of application, are set out in the Data Protection (Subject Access) (Fees and Miscellaneous Provisions) Regulations 2000 (S.I. 2000 No. 191). A request for information under one part of s.7 is taken to be a request for information under the first three sub-sections but is only to be taken as applying to s.7(1)(d) if the application shows an express intention to that effect.

In *R. v. Chief Constable of B County Constabulary and the Director of the National Identification Service, ex p. R* (unreported November 1997) a case under the equivalent provisions of the 1984 Act, it was held that the section establishes a simple duty to supply the data subject with all the information held upon him when he makes a request, with the implication that the data subject may not, as the claimant wished in that case, cherry pick particular material or omit some from the record. As a matter of practice it is common for data controllers to ask the data subject which material he wishes to receive and for data subjects to limit their request to particular files or types of data. It is submitted that this is not incompatible with the judgment in *Ex p. R* and the two issues can be distinguished. The mischief addressed by the decision in *R* was the desire of the data subject for the data controller to "doctor" the response to omit specific material for presentation to a third party.

"Personal data"—only "personal data" of which the applicant is the subject is available to him in response to an access request; the mere fact that a document may be retrievable by reference to an individual's name does not entitle him to a copy of it. The court considered the purpose of the right in *Durant* as being:

"to enable him to check whether the data controller's processing of it unlawfully infringes his privacy and, if so, to take such steps as the Act provides, for example in section 10 to 14, to protect it"

per Auld L.J. at para. 27 (see para. 3G–11).

"Third party data"—material may be omitted or "redacted" where the disclosure of such material would encroach upon the legitimate privacy or confidentiality of a third party but the controller must apply an appropriate balancing test to ensure that the interests of both the data subject and the third party are protected. This follows the ruling of the ECtHR in *Gaskin v. UK* [1990]1 F.L.R. 167. The issue only arises where the personal data about the individual includes such third party material in such a manner that it is impossible to separate the two. If the "personal data" about the applicant can be provided by omitting material about others that course should be followed *i.e.* there should be no unnecessary or gratuitous disclosure of information about third parties.

In *R (on the application of Alan Lord) v. Secretary of State for the Home Department* [2003] EWHC 2073 held information about individuals in an employment capacity is personal data in which privacy interests subsist (para. 46). A blanket policy of non-disclosure does not meet the balancing test required by 7(4); a selective and targeted approach to redaction of third party information is required (para. 148).

The "data controller" must determine whether it is "reasonable in all the circumstances" to make the disclosure. The court when considering this will not review the entire sets of material but will proceed by examining the approach of the data controller to the decisions to omit material. It will ask what, if any, legitimate interest the data subject has in the disclosure of the identity of another individual named in or identifiable from personal data to which he is otherwise entitled (*Durant* para. 61) The court will generally not substitute its own view for the view of the data controller as long as the data controller is shown to have approached the decision in a balanced and fair way, taking account of the relevant considerations.

"Jurisdiction"—exercisable by the High Court or a county court or, in Scotland Court of Session or the sheriff s.15(1).

"Powers of the court"—applications for remedial orders may be made to the High Court or a county court. Section 7(9) provides that, where a court is satisfied on the application of a data subject that the data controller has failed to comply with a valid request, the court may order the controller to comply with the request. The judgments in the cases of *P v. Wozencroft* [2002] EWHC 1724, *Durant* and *Lord* appear to regard this as affording the court a wide discretion. In *Durant* the judge in the High Court commented on the applicant's motives for making the access request as relevant to the nature of the judgment which he would have been prepared to make. On appeal it was argued that such an approach diverges from the requirements of the Directive or even the Act itself. The Directive provides in Art.22 for Member States to provide for:

"the right of every person to a judicial remedy for any breach of the rights guaranteed him by the national law applicable to the processing in question,"

subject only to limited grounds of exemption. On appeal the court confirmed the breadth of judicial discretion. In the Act the considerations which are incorporated in s.8 are limited to whether the individual has made unreasonably frequent requests, whether the information would disclose a trade secret or whether the data relate to third parties, in addition the court may accept that the data should not be provided by means of a copy where to do so would involve disproportionate effort but the right may be satisfied by the adoption of another mechanism, for example inspection of the material. In *Lindqvist* the European Court addressed the issue of how prescriptive the terms of the Directive are where a private right may conflict with other rights or interests. It accepts that in some areas the State will have room to manoeuvre and must strike a balance between competing rights and interests (para. 85). In *Lord*, the court commented that where the court has held that there are no grounds to withhold data, whether under an exemption, s.7(4) or8(2)(a) the Act:

"points powerfully in favour of the Court exercising its discretion in favour of the data subject ... at least where as here it is the data subjects' liberty interests that are at stake" (para. 163).

A lower court does not appear to be able to order that an access request be complied with in part. In a case in which the court might be minded to seek to curtail the scope of an order it could deal with the problem by giving leave to amend the application for an order under its case management powers.

"Special purposes"—the special purposes are journalistic, literary and artistic purposes s.3. These are not further defined. Extensive exemptions are available to those who process personal data for the special purposes if publication would be in the public interest and compliance with the Act would be incompatible with the special purposes. In *Campbell v. MGN (No. 2)* the Court of Appeal overruled the High Court and held that the data controller has the benefit of s.32 **after** publication as well as before where the grounds are made out (para. 130). It was suggested by the court that news media would usually be entitled to rely on the exemption.

Where personal data are processed for the special purposes with a view to the publication of material not previously published a court must stay proceedings brought under this section until a determination has been made by the Commissioner under s.45 or the claim is withdrawn s.32(4) and (5). The Information Commissioner may provide legal assistance to a claimant where a case involves the special purposes s.53 and Sched.10.

Where a controller has refused to respond to a repeated request he may be able to apply to strike out an action against him for failure to provide access under CPR r.3.4 on the ground that the statement of claim discloses no reasonable ground for bringing a claim.

"Access to material to inspect"—a court considering an application under s.7(9) is entitled to inspect any relevant data or information as to the logic involved in any decision making in order to determine the case s.15(2). The court cannot permit disclosure to the claimant prior to the determination of the case. In the event that the court rules against the data controller the court must order access by the controller. It is not the role of the court itself to provide access.

"Position pending appeal"—under CPR r.52.7 unless the Appeal Court or the lower Court orders otherwise an appeal does not operate as a stay of an order or decision. A "data controller" who intends to appeal against an order that he provide access to personal data should apply to the Information Tribunal for an appropriate order on the grounds of r.52.7.1.

"Compensation for breach"—if a failure to provide subject access has caused the data subject to suffer damage he may seek compensation under s.13. Where damage has been suffered the subject may also claim for any associated distress. There is a defence of due diligence against a compensation claim s.13(3).

Provisions supplementary to section 7

3G–18   8.—(1) The Secretary of State may by regulations provide that, in such cases as may be prescribed, a request for information under any provision of subsection (1) of section 7 is to be treated as extending also to information under other provisions of that subsection.

(2) The obligation imposed by section 7(1)(c)(i) must be complied with by supplying the data subject with a copy of the information in permanent form unless—

> (a) the supply of such a copy is not possible or would involve disproportionate effort, or
>
> (b) the data subject agrees otherwise;

and where any of the information referred to in section 7(1)(c)(i) is expressed in terms which are not intelligible without explanation the copy must be accompanied by an explanation of those terms.

(3) Where a data controller has previously complied with a request made under section 7 by an individual, the data controller is not obliged to comply with a subsequent identical or similar request under that section by that individual unless a reasonable interval has elapsed between compliance with the previous request and the making of the current request.

(4) In determining for the purposes of subsection (3) whether requests under section 7 are made at reasonable intervals, regard shall be had to the nature of the data, the purposes for which the data are processed and the frequency with which the data are altered.

(5) Section 7(1)(d) is not to be regarded as requiring the provision of information as to the logic involved in any decision-taking if, and to the extent that, the information constitutes a trade secret.

(6) The information to be supplied pursuant to a request under section 7 must be supplied by reference to the data in question at the time when the request is received, except that it may take account of any amendment or deletion made between that time and the time when the information is supplied, being an amendment or deletion that would have been made regardless of the receipt of the request.

(7) For the purposes of section 7(4) and (5) another individual can be identified from the information being disclosed if he can be identified from that information, or from that and any other information which, in the reasonable belief of the data controller, is likely to be in, or to come into, the possession of the data subject making the request.

Notes

"Disproportionate effort"—in *R(Lord) v. SSHD* held 8(2)(a) cannot justify withholding information in the form in which the data subject would otherwise be entitled to receive it para. 155. **3G–19**

Right to prevent processing likely to cause damage or distress

10.—(1) Subject to subsection (2), an individual is entitled at any **3G–20** time by notice in writing to a data controller to require the data controller at the end of such period as is reasonable in the circumstances to cease, or not to begin, processing, or processing for a specified purpose or in a specified manner, any personal data in respect of which he is the data subject, on the ground that, for specified reasons—

    (a) the processing of those data or their processing for that purpose or in that manner is causing or is likely to cause substantial damage or substantial distress to him or to another, and

    (b) that damage or distress is or would be unwarranted.

(2) Subsection (1) does not apply—

    (a) in a case where any of the conditions in paragraphs 1 to 4 of Schedule 2 is met, or

    (b) in such other cases as may be prescribed by the Secretary of State by order.

(3) The data controller must within twenty-one days of receiving a notice under subsection (1) ("the data subject notice") give the individual who gave it a written notice—

    (a) stating that he has complied or intends to comply with the data subject notice, or

    (b) stating his reasons for regarding the data subject notice as to any extent unjustified and the extent (if any) to which he has complied or intends to comply with it.

(4) If a court is satisfied, on the application of any person who has given a notice under subsection (1) which appears to the court to be justified (or to be justified to any extent), that the data controller in question has failed to comply with the notice, the court may order him to take such steps for complying with the notice (or for complying with it to that extent) as the court thinks fit.

(5) The failure by a data subject to exercise the right conferred by subsection (1) or section 11(1) does not affect any other right conferred on him by this Part.

Notes

3G–21   This is one of the two rights to prevent processing; the other being an absolute right relating to use of personal data for direct marketing only in s.11.

The right to object to processing is limited to those cases in which the controller relies for his justification for processing on the general discretionary powers as set out in grounds 5 and 6 of Sched.2.

It appears that the burden of showing that the data controller was **not** relying on one of the other grounds falls on the claimant as the right to serve the notice does not apply where the relevant conditions in the Schedule are met.

Where sensitive personal data, as defined in s.2 (see para. 3G–11 above), are processed it is more likely that damage or distress may be caused to the individual however s.10 includes no specific reference to the categories of sensitive personal data.

In *Michael Douglas, Catherine Zeta Jones and Northern Shell Plc v. Hello!* [2003] EWHC 786 it was initially argued that the film stars had exercised their right of objection under the DPA when they had first heard of the proposal by *Hello!* magazine to publish unauthorised pictures of their wedding day but the point was not pursued at trial.

Note: the provision has been restrictively transposed from the Directive, Art.14 of which provides that the data subject must be granted the right to:

> "object at any time on compelling legitimate grounds relating to his particular situation to the processing of personal data relating to him....Where there is a justified objection, the processing instigated by the controller may no longer involve those data".

"Powers of the court"—s.10(4) a court may order the controller to desist from processing to the same extent that the individual could where it is satisfied that the controller has failed to comply with a valid notice.

"Special purposes"—where personal data are processed for the special purposes with a view to the publication of material not previously published a court must stay proceedings brought under this section until a determination has been made by the Commissioner under s.45 or the claim is withdrawn s.32(4) and (5). The information Commissioner may fund legal advice or representation for a claimant where a case concerns the special purposes s.53 and Sched.10.

"Jurisdiction"—exercisable by the High Court or a county court or, in Scotland Court of Session or the sheriff s.15(1).

The court has a wide discretion as to the appropriate remedy when dealing with an application under this section (contrast s.7 see above) and may require partial compliance with the notice.

"Form of order"—as the order will be binding on the controller and failure to comply may involve penalties orders should be drawn with the care exercised in relation to mandatory injunctions. The order should specify the processing in question, the purpose of the processing the duration and any other relevant matters.

"Non-disclosure exemptions"—the obligations to respond to notices of objection under ss.10 and 11 are included in the non-disclosure provisions by s.27(4)(c) and are disapplied in a number of cases where the disclosure would be inconsistent with the protection of the interest protected by the exemption. Non-disclosure exemptions apply where disclosures are required for the purposes of the prevention or detection of crimes.29, national security s.28, the special purposes s.32, information available under an enactment s.34 or disclosures required by law or for legal purposes s.35. Thus a data subject could not use a notice of objection to processing under s.10 to restrict a disclosure made for one of those purposes in accordance with the terms of the individual exemption.

"Compensation for breach"—if a failure to deal with a proper objection has caused the data subject to suffer damage he may seek compensation under s.13. Where damage has been suffered the subject may also claim for any associated distress. There is a defence of due diligence against a compensation claim s.13(3).

Right to prevent processing for purposes of direct marketing

3G–22   **11.**—(1) An individual is entitled at any time by notice in writing to a data controller to require the data controller at the end of such period as is reasonable in the circumstances to cease, or not to begin, processing for the purposes of direct marketing personal data in respect of which he is the data subject.

(2) If the court is satisfied, on the application of any person who has given a notice under subsection (1), that the data controller has failed to comply with the notice, the court may order him to take such steps for complying with the notice as the court thinks fit.

(3) In this section "direct marketing" means the communication (by whatever means) of any advertising or marketing material which is directed to particular individuals.

Notes

This is an absolute right.

3G–23

The terms advertising or marketing materials are not defined. The court took a very broad view of what amounts to processing for the purposes of direct marketing in *R. (on the application of Robertson) v. Wakefield MDC* [2001] EWHC Admin 915; [2002] Q.B. 1052; [2002] 2 W.L.R. 889 to include uses made of the data by third parties to whom the data are passed, as long as the controller is aware of those uses. Mr Robertson objected to the fact that the electoral roll was sold, pursuant to a statutory requirement in regulations, to any person who wished to purchase it. This resulted in the data derived from the roll being used in a wide range of commercial applications, including direct marketing. In a judicial review of the relevant provisions of the regulations the judge held that the Electoral Registration Officer (ERO) was acting in breach of s.11 and Art.14 of the Directive, as well as the right to a free and fair election under Art.3 of the First Protocol of the Convention Rights. The breach was the processing by the ERO to disclose the electoral roll without providing individuals with a right of objection in the knowledge that at least some of the purchasers would use the data for direct marketing. The judge found that the register was sold for marketing:

> "and for many years the data contained in the Register have been purchased by commercial interests and it has been obvious to EROs and to others that the data so purchased have been used, for among other things, direct marketing".

Additional provisions apply to marketing by telephone, facsimile and e-mail or short messaging services (SMS). From December 11, 2003 these are contained in the Privacy and Electronic Communication (EU Directive) Regulations 2003 (S.I. 2003 No. 2426) which replace the Telecommunications (Data Protection and Privacy) Regulations 1999. These are based on Directive 2002/58/EC. They apply in addition to the provisions of the DPA. In brief the use by any person of automated dialling machines for marketing requires prior consent of any subscriber; fax marketing to individual subscribers requires prior consent, other subscribers may opt-out of fax marketing; individual subscribers have a right to opt-out of telephone marketing both by registering on the Stop list and by notice to the person using the telephone line to carry out direct marketing, other subscribers can only opt-out by giving notice to the person using the telephone line to carry out direct marketing; any electronic marketing such as e-mail or SMS requires the consent of an individual subscriber except where the marketer is marketing similar goods and services to existing customers or prospects and the customer or prospect has been made aware, and continues to be made aware, of the opportunity to opt out of the use. The use of electronic mail for marketing to subscribers who are not individuals is subject to no restriction.

The provisions were extended by the Privacy and Electronic Communications (EC Directive) (Amendment) Regulations 2004 (S.I. 2004 No. 1039) . These regulations, which came into force on June 25, 2004, implement the corporate telephone preference service.

Note: the Regulations do not provide for a specific right to apply to the court for breach of the special rules relating to electronic marketing. The general right under this section applies irrespective of how the marketing complained of is carried out. The Commissioner's powers of enforcement and individual rights for compensation for breach apply to electronic marketing under the Regulations (see para. 3G–31 re appeals against enforcement notices and para. 3G–26 re compensation).

"Powers of the court"—a court which is satisfied that a data subject has made an objection in accordance with the Act under s.11 which has not been complied with by the data controller may order the controller to take appropriate steps to comply.

"Compensation for breach"—if a failure to respond to a proper objection has caused the data subject to suffer damage he may seek compensation under s.13. Where damage has been suffered the subject may also claim for any associated distress. There is a defence of due diligence against a compensation claim s.13(3).

"Jurisdiction"—exercisable by the High Court or a county court or, in Scotland Court of Session or the sheriff s.15(1).

Rights in relation to automated decision-taking

3G–24   12.—(1) An individual is entitled at any time, by notice in writing to any data controller, to require the data controller to ensure that no decision taken by or on behalf of the data controller which significantly affects that individual is based solely on the processing by automatic means of personal data in respect of which that individual is the data subject for the purpose of evaluating matters relating to him such as, for example, his performance at work, his credit worthiness, his reliability or his conduct.

(2) Where, in a case where no notice under subsection (1) has effect, a decision which significantly affects an individual is based solely on such processing as is mentioned in subsection (1)—

    (a) the data controller must as soon as reasonably practicable notify the individual that the decision was taken on that basis, and

    (b) the individual is entitled, within twenty-one days of receiving that notification from the data controller, by notice in writing to require the data controller to reconsider the decision or to take a new decision otherwise than on that basis.

(3) The data controller must, within twenty-one days of receiving a notice under subsection (2)(b) ("the data subject notice") give the individual a written notice specifying the steps that he intends to take to comply with the data subject notice.

(4) A notice under subsection (1) does not have effect in relation to an exempt decision; and nothing in subsection (2) applies to an exempt decision.

(5) In subsection (4) "exempt decision" means any decision—

    (a) in respect of which the condition in subsection (6) and the condition in subsection (7) are met, or

    (b) which is made in such other circumstances as may be prescribed by the Secretary of State by order.

(6) The condition in this subsection is that the decision—

    (a) is taken in the course of steps taken—

        (i) for the purpose of considering whether to enter into a contract with the data subject,

        (ii) with a view to entering into such a contract, or

        (iii) in the course of performing such a contract, or

    (b) is authorised or required by or under any enactment.

(7) The condition in this subsection is that either—

    (a) the effect of the decision is to grant a request of the data subject, or

(b) steps have been taken to safeguard the legitimate interests of the data subject (for example, by allowing him to make representations).

(8) If a court is satisfied on the application of a data subject that a person taking a decision in respect of him ("the responsible person") has failed to comply with subsection (1) or (2)(b), the court may order the responsible person to reconsider the decision, or to take a new decision which is not based solely on such processing as is mentioned in subsection (1).

(9) An order under subsection (8) shall not affect the rights of any person other than the data subject and the responsible person.

Notes

There is no case law on this section. It is a complex provision. There are two **3G–25** aspects to the right:
  (1) the right to stop a data controller from taking a relevant (non-exempt) decision by automated means; and
  (2) the right to object to such a decision after the event and require it to be reviewed.

In order to ensure that individuals are aware of automated decisions data controllers must notify data subjects where such decisions are made, although there is no sanction if the controller fails to do so. **Note**: that the court may make an order against the "responsible person". It appears therefore that a person other than the relevant data controller for the personal data processed may be held responsible for the making of an automated decision.

"Exempt decisions"—may either be in relation to contractual situations or where the controller is processing on the basis of a statutory power. Either the effect of the decision must have been to grant the request of the individual or his interests must be protected in some other way *e.g.* by being entitled to make representations about the decision.

"Powers of the court"—a court which is satisfied that a data subject has served a notice in accordance with the Act under s.12 which has not been complied with by the data controller may order the controller to take appropriate steps to comply.

"Special purposes"—where personal data are processed for the special purposes with a view to the publication of material not previously published a court must stay proceedings brought under this section until a determination has been made by the Commissioner under s.45 or the claim is withdrawn s.32(4) and (5). The Information Commissioner may fund legal advice or assistance for a claimant where a case concerns the special purposes s.53 and Sched.10.

"Compensation for breach"—if a failure to respond to a proper objection has caused the data subject to suffer damage he may seek compensation under s.13. Where damage has been suffered the subject may also claim for any associated distress. There is a defence of due diligence against a compensation claim s.13(3).

"Jurisdiction"—exercisable by the High Court or a county court or, in Scotland Court of Session or the sheriff s.15(1).

Compensation for failure to comply with certain requirements

13.—(1) An individual who suffers damage by reason of any **3G–26** contravention by a data controller of any of the requirements of this Act is entitled to compensation from the data controller for that damage.

(2) An individual who suffers distress by reason of any contravention by a data controller of any of the requirements of this Act is entitled to compensation from the data controller for that distress if—

> (a) the individual also suffers damage by reason of the contravention, or
>
> (b) the contravention relates to the processing of personal data for the special purposes.

(3) In proceedings brought against a person by virtue of this section it is a defence to prove that he had taken such care as in all the circumstances was reasonably required to comply with the requirement concerned.

Notes

3G–27   "Extent of right to compensation"—compensation is not only available for damage caused by failure to comply with the individual rights as noted above but for damage (and associated distress) caused by any contravention of the Act. The claimant need not be a data subject in order to bring proceedings, although it may be unlikely that damage will be caused to anyone who is not a data subject. The other provisions of the Act which might give rise to claims for damages are breach of the Principles, particularly Principle 7 which covers the requirements of adequate security for information. Under s.13(3) there is a defence of due diligence against a compensation claim.

In *Lord Ashcroft v. Attorney General* [2002] EWHC 1122; [2002] All E.R. (D) 521, QBD Lord Ashcroft, having been unsuccessful in his claim for damages for breach of Principle under the 1984 Act, claimed damages under s.13 for the continued holding of irrelevant and inaccurate data post March 2000, when the 1998 Act came into force. The judge agreed that it was an arguable claim however it did not proceed to hearing.

In *Abayomi Sofola v. Lloyds TSB Bank* [2005] EWHC 1335 Tugendhat J., in a hearing in which he gave permission for a claimant to re-open an appeal so that claims under the Act could be considered, considered it arguable that the retention of material alleging a fraud on file for nine years without evidence could breach Principles 4 and 5.

"Compensation"—November 2003 it was reported that the Chief Constable of Greater Manchester had paid compensation of £2000 for psychiatric harm to a lady whose details had been accessed by a police officer neighbour; in *A v. London Borough of Newham* it was reported that the Borough paid £5,000 to the parents of a child who was wrongly stigmatised as being HIV positive, the picture of the child having used on the front of a Council publication on HIV and Children. The Borough had continued to use the picture in that way even after the parents had complained. In *Michael Douglas and others v. Hello!* Michael Douglas and his wife, Catherine Zeta Jones, received modest damages of £3750 each plus expenses of £50 each by way of nominal damages for breach of the Act in the High Court. However they received damages for a breach of confidence, described by the court as "abuse of private information", and the court stated that the DPA should not be seen as adding a separate route to recovery for damage or distress beyond the nominal amount, (para. 239). The failure of the lower courts to grant the Douglases a permanent injunction and then to compensate for abuse of their private information was regretted by the Court of Appeal on appeal, *Douglas v. Hello! Ltd (No.6)* [2005] EWCA Civ 595,which confirmed the award of damages was an appropriate level.The Court of Appeal took same view in *Ogle v. Chief Constable of Thames Valley* [2001] EWCA Civ 598; [2001] All E.R. (D) 231, a claim for compensation arising from inaccurate data. The Claimant could not recover additional damages to those recovered on same facts for wrongful arrest.

"Special purposes"—where the processing is for those purposes but outside the scope of the exemptions the claimant can seek compensation for distress only, and need not show damage. In *Campbell v. MGN* [2002] EWCA Civ 1373 the model who had been surreptitiously photographed by the Mirror newspaper attending a clinic was awarded £2,500 for damage and hurt feelings plus £1,000 for aggravated damages for a subsequent offensive article, although the judgment was overturned by Court of Appeal it was reinstated by the House of Lords which considered the case under the application of the law of confidence rather than as a Data Protection Act claim, see para. 3G–13.

Where personal data are processed for the special purposes with a view to the publication of material not previously published a court must stay proceedings brought under this section until a determination has been made by the Commissioner under s.45 or the claim is withdrawn s.32(4) and (5). The Information Commissioner may fund legal advice or assistance for a claimant where a case concerns the special purposes s.53 and Sched.10.

"Injunction"—where the purpose of the claimant is to protect his privacy a claim may also lie in Art. 8 of the HRA 1998. There are difficulties for a claimant seeking to use the DPA in order to restrain the publication of material because of the provisions in ss.32 (4) which restrict the bringing of proceedings in relation to the special purposes until a determination has been made by the Commissioner under s.45.

"Jurisdiction"—exercisable by the High Court or a county court or, in Scotland Court of Session or the sheriff s.15(1).

"Data Protection Principles"—s.4 and Sched.1. It is the duty of a data controller to comply with the data protection principles in relation to all personal data in respect of which he is the data controller. The eight principles require that personal data:

(1) are processed fairly and lawfully and in accordance with the fair processing rules set out in the Schedule;

(2) are processed for limited purposes and not in a manner incompatible with the notified purposes;

(3) are adequate relevant and not excessive in relation to those purposes;

(4) are accurate;

(5) are not kept for longer than is necessary;

(6) are processed in accordance with the rights of data subjects;

(7) are kept secure and

(8) are not transferred outside the EEA without adequate protection.

Information may be disclosed without breach of the principles in reliance on one or more of the non-disclosure exemptions s.27. In *Matthew Yeboah Mensah v. Robert H Jones* [2004] EWHC 2699 (Ch) the data subject could not resist the disclosure of his medical records by his doctor for the purpose of seeking legal advice where the doctor had relied on the non-disclosure exemption in s.35(2).

In *Lindqvist* the European Court ruled that the posting of personal details on the internet where the site is hosted in the EEA does not amount to a transfer of the personal data.

The Privacy and Electronic Communications (EC Directive) Regulations 2003 include a mirror provision in reg.30 which entitles any person who has suffered damage (but not distress) by reason of a contravention of the Regulations by any other person to claim compensation for the damage, subject to a defence of due diligence. The damage would have to be specific to the electronic marketing and additional to damage suffered by reason of breach of the Act itself.

Rectification, blocking, erasure and destruction

14.—(1) If a court is satisfied on the application of a data subject **3G–28** that personal data of which the applicant is the subject are inaccurate, the court may order the data controller to rectify, block, erase or destroy those data and any other personal data in respect of which he is the data controller and which contain an expression of opinion which appears to the court to be based on the inaccurate data.

(2) Subsection (1) applies whether or not the data accurately record information received or obtained by the data controller from the data subject or a third party but where the data accurately record such information, then—

(a) if the requirements mentioned in paragraph 7 of Part II of Schedule 1 have been complied with, the court may, instead of making an order under subsection (1), make an order requiring the data to be supplemented by such statement of the true facts relating to the matters dealt with by the data as the court may approve, and

(b) if all or any of those requirements have not been complied with, the court may, instead of making an order under that subsection, make such order as it thinks fit for securing compliance with those requirements with or without a further order requiring the data to be supplemented by such a statement as is mentioned in paragraph (a).

(3) Where the court—

    (a) makes an order under subsection (1), or

    (b) is satisfied on the application of a data subject that personal data of which he was the data subject and which have been rectified, blocked, erased or destroyed were inaccurate,

it may, where it considers it reasonably practicable, order the data controller to notify third parties to whom the data have been disclosed of the rectification, blocking, erasure or destruction.

(4) If a court is satisfied on the application of a data subject—

    (a) that he has suffered damage by reason of any contravention by a data controller of any of the requirements of this Act in respect of any personal data, in circumstances entitling him to compensation under section 13, and

    (b) that there is a substantial risk of further contravention in respect of those data in such circumstances,

the court may order the rectification, blocking, erasure or destruction of any of those data.

(5) Where the court makes an order under subsection (4) it may, where it considers it reasonably practicable, order the data controller to notify third parties to whom the data have been disclosed of the rectification, blocking, erasure or destruction.

(6) In determining whether it is reasonably practicable to require such notification as is mentioned in subsection (3) or (5) the court shall have regard, in particular, to the number of persons who would have to be notified.

Notes

3G–29   "Accuracy"—personal data are inaccurate if they are "incorrect or misleading as to any matter of fact" s.70(2).

"Information received from a third party"—where data accurately reflect information received from the data subject or a third party and the controller has taken reasonable care to ensure accuracy, taking account of the purposes and, if the data subject notifies the controller that he regards the data as inaccurate, the controller marks the data to indicate that fact then there is no breach of the relevant Principle Sched.1 Pt II, para. 7, nevertheless the data subject may ask the court to order deletion, blocking etc.

"Rectification, blocking, erasure and destruction"—are not defined terms. If rectification involves the alteration or removal of data it may conflict with requirements to maintain an audit trail for security purposes. Blocking appears to cover the case where the data remain on the record but access is forbidden either generally or to specific persons or for specific purposes. Erasure and destruction appear to import different meanings. It is suggested that erasure takes place where the media on which the data are held is not destroyed and destruction where the media are also destroyed.

In *P v. Wozencroft* [2002] EWHC 1724, Fam the court considered an application under the DPA to amend an expert report which had been relied upon in family proceedings on the basis that the report was inaccurate. The judge ruled that it would be an abuse of process to seek to challenge an expert's report in satellite proceedings under the DPA and dismissed the case.

"Powers of the court"—a court which is satisfied that personal data are inaccurate may make any of the orders noted above as well as ordering enquiries to be made and data to be traced where it has been shown that inaccurate data have been disclosed to third parties.

"Special purposes"—where personal data are processed for the special purposes with a view to the publication of material not previously published a court must stay proceedings brought under this section until a determination has been made by the Commissioner under s.45 or the claim is withdrawn s.32(4) and (5). The Information Commissioner may fund legal advice or assistance for a claimant where a case concerns the special purposes s.53 and Sched.10.

"Compensation for breach"—if a failure to maintain accurate data or the dissemination of inaccurate data has caused the data subject to suffer damage he may seek compensation under s.13. Where damage has been suffered the subject may also claim for any associated distress. There is a defence of due diligence under s.13(3).

"Jurisdiction"—exercisable by the High Court or a county court or, in Scotland Court of Session or the sheriff s.15(1).

Part V

Appeals from that Tribunal may be made to the High Court. **3G–30**

Rights of appeal

48.—(1) A person on whom an enforcement notice, an information **3G–31** notice or a special information notice has been served may appeal to the Tribunal against the notice.

(2) A person on whom an enforcement notice has been served may appeal to the Tribunal against the refusal of an application under section 41(2) for cancellation or variation of the notice.

(3) Where an enforcement notice, an information notice or a special information notice contains a statement by the Commissioner in accordance with section 40(8), 43(5) or 44(6) then, whether or not the person appeals against the notice, he may appeal against—

> (a) the Commissioner's decision to include the statement in the notice, or
>
> (b) the effect of the inclusion of the statement as respects any part of the notice.

(4) A data controller in respect of whom a determination has been made under section 45 may appeal to the Tribunal against the determination.

(5) Schedule 6 has effect in relation to appeals under this section and the proceedings of the Tribunal in respect of any such appeal.

Notes

"Information Tribunal Rules"—the Act continued the Data Protection Tribunal **3G–32** which became the Information Tribunal following the implementation of s.18(2) of the Freedom of Information Act 2000. The Tribunal operates under the Data Protection Tribunal (Enforcement Appeals) Rules 2000 (S.I. 2000 No. 189), as amended by the Information Tribunal (Enforcement Appeal) (Amendment) Rules 2002 (S.I. 2002 No. 2722). The amending Regulations were necessary to provide for cases under the Freedom of Information Act 2000 before January 2005. Further amendments have been made in the Information Tribunal (Enforcement appeals) Rules 2005 (S.I. 2005 No. 14), The Information Tribunal (Enforcement Appeals) (Amendment) Rules 2005 (S.I. 2005 No.450) and the Information Tribunal (National Security Appeals) Rules 2005 (S.I. 2005 No. 13). Separate rules of procedure, the Data Protection Tribunal (National Security Appeals) Rules 2000 (S.I. 2000 No. 206), apply to hearings in relation to national security certificates under s.28(4).

"Appeals"—the Tribunal hears appeals against a range of orders which can be made by the Information Commissioner. Under the Data Protection Act 1998 it hears appeals against enforcement notices, information notices and special information notices, against the inclusion of urgency provisions in any of the notices, a determination that personal data are not held for the special purposes or the refusal to vary or cancel an enforcement notice. Sitting in special panel the Tribunal also hears appeals against the extent of national security certificates. Under the Freedom of Information Act 2000 it hears appeals against enforcement information notices, and decision notices under the Freedom of Information Act 2000 and the extent of national security certificates issued under that Act. Under the Privacy and Electronic Communications (EC Directive) Regulations 2003 it hears appeals against enforcement notices, information notices, against the inclusion of urgency provisions in a notice or the refusal to vary or cancel an enforcement notice.

In *R. v. Ewing (Terence Patrick)* [1983] Q.B. 1039 held that the Information Tribunal was, for the purpose of hearing appeals against the issue of certificates on the grounds of national security, a court within the meaning of s.42 Supreme Court Act 1981 and a vexatious litigant requires leave to bring such proceedings.

Determination of appeals

3G–33 **49.**—(1) If on an appeal under section 48(1) the Tribunal considers—

> (a) that the notice against which the appeal is brought is not in accordance with the law, or
> (b) to the extent that the notice involved an exercise of discretion by the Commissioner, that he ought to have exercised his discretion differently,

the Tribunal shall allow the appeal or substitute such other notice or decision as could have been served or made by the Commissioner; and in any other case the Tribunal shall dismiss the appeal.

(2) On such an appeal, the Tribunal may review any determination of fact on which the notice in question was based.

(3) If on an appeal under section 48(2) the Tribunal considers that the enforcement notice ought to be cancelled or varied by reason of a change in circumstances, the Tribunal shall cancel or vary the notice.

(4) On an appeal under subsection (3) of section 48 the Tribunal may direct—

> (a) that the notice in question shall have effect as if it did not contain any such statement as is mentioned in that subsection, or
> (b) that the inclusion of the statement shall not have effect in relation to any part of the notice,

and may make such modifications in the notice as may be required for giving effect to the direction.

(5) On an appeal under section 48(4), the Tribunal may cancel the determination of the Commissioner.

(6) Any party to an appeal to the Tribunal under section 48 may appeal from the decision of the Tribunal on a point of law to the appropriate court; and that court shall be—

> (a) the High Court of Justice in England if the address of the person who was the appellant before the Tribunal is in England or Wales,
> (b) the Court of Session if that address is in Scotland, and
> (c) the High Court of Justice in Northern Ireland if that address is in Northern Ireland.

(7) For the purposes of subsection (6)—

(a) the address of a registered company is that of its registered office, and

(b) the address of a person (other than a registered company) carrying on a business is that of his principal place of business in the United Kingdom.

Notes

The powers of the Tribunal in dealing with appeals apply also to appeals under the Privacy and Electronic Communications (EU Directive) Regulations 2003 and the Freedom of Information Act 2000.

3G–34

Powers of entry and inspection

50. Schedule 9 (powers of entry and inspection) has effect.

3G–35

SECTION 50   SCHEDULE 9

POWERS OF ENTRY AND INSPECTION

Issue of warrants

1.—(1) If a circuit judge is satisfied by information on oath supplied by the Commissioner that there are reasonable grounds for suspecting—

3G–36

(a) that a data controller has contravened or is contravening any of the data protection principles, or

(b) that an offence under this Act has been or is being committed,

and that evidence of the contravention or of the commission of the offence is to be found on any premises specified in the information, he may, subject to sub-paragraph (2) and paragraph 2, grant a warrant to the Commissioner.

(2) A judge shall not issue a warrant under this Schedule in respect of any personal data processed for the special purposes unless a determination by the Commissioner under section 45 with respect to those data has taken effect.

(3) A warrant issued under sub-paragraph (1) shall authorise the Commissioner or any of his officers or staff at any time within seven days of the date of the warrant to enter the premises, to search them, to inspect, examine, operate and test any equipment found there which is used or intended to be used for the processing of personal data and to inspect and seize any documents or other material found there which may be such evidence as is mentioned in that sub-paragraph.

2.—(1) A judge shall not issue a warrant under this Schedule unless he is satisfied—

3G–37

(a) that the Commissioner has given seven days' notice in writing to the occupier of the premises in question demanding access to the premises, and

(b) that either—

(i) access was demanded at a reasonable hour and was unreasonably refused, or

(ii) although entry to the premises was granted, the occupier unreasonably refused to comply with a request by the Commissioner or any of the Commissioner's officers or staff to permit the Commissioner or the officer or member of staff to do any of the things referred to in paragraph 1(3), and

(c) that the occupier, has, after the refusal, been notified by the Commissioner of the application for the warrant and has had an opportunity of being heard by the judge on the question whether or not it should be issued.

(2) Sub-paragraph (1) shall not apply if the judge is satisfied that the case is one of urgency or that compliance with those provisions would defeat the object of the entry.

3. A judge who issues a warrant under this Schedule shall also issue two copies of it and certify them clearly as copies.

3G–38

Execution of warrants

4. A person executing a warrant issued under this Schedule may use such reasonable force as may be necessary.

3G–39

3G–40   5. A warrant issued under this Schedule shall be executed at a reasonable hour unless it appears to the person executing it that there are grounds for suspecting that the evidence in question would not be found if it were so executed.

3G–41   6. If the person who occupies the premises in respect of which a warrant is issued under this Schedule is present when the warrant is executed, he shall be shown the warrant and supplied with a copy of it; and if that person is not present a copy of the warrant shall be left in a prominent place on the premises.

3G–42   7.—(1) A person seizing anything in pursuance of a warrant under this Schedule shall give a receipt for it if asked to do so.

(2) Anything so seized may be retained for so long as is necessary in all the circumstances but the person in occupation of the premises in question shall be given a copy of anything that is seized if he so requests and the person executing the warrant considers that it can be done without undue delay.

Matters exempt from inspection and seizure

3G–43   8. The powers of inspection and seizure conferred by a warrant issued under this Schedule shall not be exercisable in respect of personal data which by virtue of section 28 are exempt from any of the provisions of this Act.

3G–44   9.—(1) Subject to the provisions of this paragraph, the powers of inspection and seizure conferred by a warrant issued under this Schedule shall not be exercisable in respect of—

(a) any communication between a professional legal adviser and his client in connection with the giving of legal advice to the client with respect to his obligations, liabilities or rights under this Act, or

(b) any communication between a professional legal adviser and his client, or between such an adviser or his client and any other person, made in connection with or in contemplation of proceedings under or arising out of this Act (including proceedings before the Tribunal) and for the purposes of such proceedings.

(2) Sub-paragraph (1) applies also to—

(a) any copy or other record of any such communication as is there mentioned, and

(b) any document or article enclosed with or referred to in any such communication if made in connection with the giving of any advice or, as the case may be, in connection with or in contemplation of and for the purposes of such proceedings as are there mentioned.

(3) This paragraph does not apply to anything in the possession of any person other than the professional legal adviser or his client or to anything held with the intention of furthering a criminal purpose.

(4) In this paragraph references to the client of a professional legal adviser include references to any person representing such a client.

3G–45   10. If the person in occupation of any premises in respect of which a warrant is issued under this Schedule objects to the inspection or seizure under the warrant of any material on the grounds that it consists partly of matters in respect of which those powers are not exercisable, he shall, if the person executing the warrant so requests, furnish that person with a copy of so much of the material as is not exempt from those powers.

Return of warrants

3G–46   11. A warrant issued under this Schedule shall be returned to the court from which it was issued—

(a) after being executed, or

(b) if not executed within the time authorised for its execution;

and the person by whom any such warrant is executed shall make an endorsement on it stating what powers have been exercised by him under the warrant.

Offences

3G–47   12. Any person who—

(a) intentionally obstructs a person in the execution of a warrant issued under this Schedule, or

(b) fails without reasonable excuse to give any person executing such a warrant such assistance as he may reasonably require for the execution of the warrant, is guilty of an offence.

Vessels, vehicles etc.

13. In this Schedule "premises" includes any vessel, vehicle, aircraft or hovercraft, **3G–48** and references to the occupier of any premises include references to the person in charge of any vessel, vehicle, aircraft or hovercraft.

Scotland and Northern Ireland

14. In the application of this Schedule to Scotland—   **3G–49**
   (a) for any reference to a circuit judge there is substituted a reference to the sheriff,
   (b) for any reference to information on oath there is substituted a reference to evidence on oath, and
   (c) for the reference to the court from which the warrant was issued there is substituted a reference to the sheriff clerk.

15. In the application of this Schedule to Northern Ireland—   **3G–50**
   (a) for any reference to a circuit judge there is substituted a reference to a county court judge, and
   (b) for any reference to information on oath there is substituted a reference to a complaint on oath.

Notes

Privacy and Electronic Communications (EC Directive) Regulations 2003 the power **3G–51** to apply for warrant of entry is extended to circumstances where a person has contravened or is contravening the requirements of those Regulations (para. 10(a) Sched.1 PECR).

"Without notice"—warrant may be granted without notice having been given to the occupier in limited circumstances where the matter is one of urgency or compliance would defeat the object of the entry. The burden of establishing that notice would defeat the object of the entry falls upon the applicant for the warrant. The provisions are silent as to the standard of proof required. The issue and execution of a warrant will amount to a breach of the Art.8 rights of the occupier and therefore the requirement of proportionality will apply.

The Codes of Practices made pursuant to the Police and Criminal Evidence Act 1984 do not apply to warrants issued under this provision but it is thought that those executing warrants should ensure that equivalent standards are met.

"Seizure of property"—difficult questions may arise where the material which the investigator wishes to inspect appears to be held on computer. The officer executing the warrant is entitled to inspect, examine and test material on the premises and only to seize material which is evidence of breach of the Act. Therefore if the officer wishes to take a computer in order to carry out tests off site the consent of the occupier will be required to remove the computer or to take a forensic copy of the disk unless the inspection shows that the computer contains evidence of a breach.

"Copies"—the occupier must be provided with copies of material seized if he so requests. The Commissioner's office has in the past refused to provide copies if they were not requested at the execution of the warrant so anyone subject to a warrant is advised to require copies during the execution of the warrant.

"Legal privilege"—the investigator is not entitled to seize material which is subject to legal professional privilege. Note that this is an absolute provision and does not depend on the reasonable belief of the investigator that the material is not privileged.

Assistance by Commissioner in cases involving processing for the special purposes

53.—(1) An individual who is an actual or prospective party to any **3G–52** proceedings under section 7(9), 10(4), 12(8), 12A(3) or 14 or by virtue of section 13 which relate to personal data processed for the special purposes may apply to the Commissioner for assistance in relation to those proceedings.

DATA PROTECTION

(2) The Commissioner shall, as soon as reasonably practicable after receiving an application under subsection (1), consider it and decide whether and to what extent to grant it, but he shall not grant the application unless, in his opinion, the case involves a matter of substantial public importance.

(3) If the Commissioner decides to provide assistance, he shall, as soon as reasonably practicable after making the decision, notify the applicant, stating the extent of the assistance to be provided.

(4) If the Commissioner decides not to provide assistance, he shall, as soon as reasonably practicable after making the decision, notify the applicant of his decision and, if he thinks fit, the reasons for it.

(5) In this section—

    (a) references to "proceedings" include references to prospective proceedings, and

    (b) "applicant", in relation to assistance under this section, means an individual who applies for assistance.

(6) Schedule 10 has effect for supplementing this section.

SECTION 53(6)   SCHEDULE 10

FURTHER PROVISIONS RELATING TO ASSISTANCE UNDER SECTION 53

3G–53   1. In this Schedule "applicant" and "proceedings" have the same meaning as in section 53.

3G–54   2. The assistance provided under section 53 may include the making of arrangements for, or for the Commissioner to bear the costs of—

    (a) the giving of advice or assistance by a solicitor or counsel, and

    (b) the representation of the applicant, or the provision to him of such assistance as is usually given by a solicitor or counsel—

        (i) in steps preliminary or incidental to the proceedings, or

        (ii) in arriving at or giving effect to a compromise to avoid or bring an end to the proceedings.

3G–55   3. Where assistance is provided with respect to the conduct of proceedings—

    (a) it shall include an agreement by the Commissioner to indemnify the applicant (subject only to any exceptions specified in the notification) in respect of any liability to pay costs or expenses arising by virtue of any judgment or order of the court in the proceedings,

    (b) it may include an agreement by the Commissioner to indemnify the applicant in respect of any liability to pay costs or expenses arising by virtue of any compromise or settlement arrived at in order to avoid the proceedings or bring the proceedings to an end, and

    (c) it may include an agreement by the Commissioner to indemnify the applicant in respect of any liability to pay damages pursuant to an undertaking given on the grant of interlocutory relief (in Scotland, an interim order) to the applicant.

3G–56   4. Where the Commissioner provides assistance in relation to any proceedings, he shall do so on such terms, or make such other arrangements, as will secure that a person against whom the proceedings have been or are commenced is informed that assistance has been or is being provided by the Commissioner in relation to them.

3G–57   5. In England and Wales or Northern Ireland, the recovery of expenses incurred by the Commissioner in providing an applicant with assistance (as taxed or assessed in such manner as may be prescribed by rules of court) shall constitute a first charge for the benefit of the Commissioner—

    (a) on any costs which, by virtue of any judgment or order of the court, are payable to the applicant by any other person in respect of the matter in connection with which the assistance is provided, and

    (b) on any sum payable to the applicant under a compromise or settlement arrived at in connection with that matter to avoid or bring to an end any proceedings.

    6. In Scotland, the recovery of such expenses (as taxed or assessed in such manner as may be prescribed by rules of court) shall be paid to the Commissioner, in priority to other debts— **3G–58**

    (a) out of any expenses which, by virtue of any judgment or order of the court, are payable to the applicant by any other person in respect of the matter in connection with which the assistance is provided, and

    (b) out of any sum payable to the applicant under a compromise or settlement arrived at in connection with that matter to avoid or bring to an end any proceedings.

Notes

    See para. 3G–17 in relation to the actions in respect of which the data subject may wish to seek support from the Commissioner. **3G–59**

Notes

    "Provision"—gives the Tribunal power to deal with behaviour that might result in punishment for contempt of court were it to be perpetrated before a court. **3G–60**

3H CONSUMER CREDIT AND CONSUMER LAW

Consumer Credit Act 1974

(1974 c.39)

An Act to establish for the protection of consumers a new system, administered by the Director General of Fair Trading, of licensing and other control of traders concerned with the provision of credit, or the supply of goods on hire or hire-purchase, and their transactions, in place of the present enactments regulating moneylenders, pawnbrokers and hire-purchase traders and their transactions; and for related matters.

[31st July 1974] **3H–1**

CONSUMER

Consumer Credit Bill 2005

3H–1.1   The Consumer Credit Bill 2005 is expected to receive the Royal Assent sometime early in 2006. Once the Bill has become an Act, its provisions will be brought into force by statutory instruments. The Bill will have no substantive freestanding provisions but will make significant amendments to the Consumer Credit Act 1974. These will include amendments which:

- Remove the financial limit in the definition of regulated agreement (in ss.8 and 15 of the 1974 Act);
- Repeal subsections (3) to (5) of s.127 of the 1974 Act, which in certain circumstances make improperly executed agreements irredeemably unenforceable against the debtor or hirer;
- Widen the scope of the court's ability to re-open a credit bargain (under s.139 *et seq.* of the 1974 Act) as being "unfair" (the word "extortionate" no longer being used).
- Expand the definition of ancillary credit business (in s.145 of the 1974 Act) to include "debt administration" and "credit information services".
- Allow only simply interest to be charged on default sums owed by debtors and hirers under regulated agreements.
- Set up an ombudsman scheme for considering complaints from individuals.

Introductory note about procedure

Jurisdiction and parties

3H–2   The county court has exclusive jurisdiction to hear a claim to enforce a regulated agreement against a debtor or hirer, s.141. For requirements as to joinder of parties, see s.141(5). For procedural requirements where claim is brought by debtor or hirer or where the claim is to enforce an exempt agreement, see commentaries to ss.129, 139 and 141.

Land

3H–3   Claims for the possession of land, including mortgage possession actions, must be brought under the procedure set out in CPR Pt 55, as supplemented by the Practice Direction to that Part (see 55PD.1).

Goods

Claims to enforce regulated consumer hire agreements and regulated consumer **3H–4** credit agreements relating to goods shall be made in accordance with the "Consumer Credit Act procedure" (at para. 7BPD.1) in the Consumer Credit Practice Direction (which supplements CPR r.7.9). This procedure applies in addition to the rest of the CPR (which are modified only to the extent that they are inconsistent with it). This Consumer Credit Act procedure (para. 7BPD.1) includes requirements for what must be included in the particulars of claim, including specific requirements when the claim is for delivery of goods let, other than to a corporate body, under a regulated hire-purchase or conditional sale agreement. [For the requirements where the hire-purchase or conditional sale agreement is *not* regulated by the Consumer Credit Act, see (at para. 16PD.6) para. 6.1 of the Statements of Case Practice Direction (which supplements CPR Pt 16)].

Money claims

For money claims by the creditor or owner which do not relate to the recovery of **3H–5** land, the relevant procedure is as follows:

(a) Where the agreement relates to goods, the Consumer Credit Act procedure (para. 7BPD.1) applies.

(b) Where the agreement does not relate to goods but the creditor or owner, in order to be able to enforce the agreement (or security) against the defendant, requires a court order under any of ss.65(1), 86(2), 90, 92(1), 105(7)(a) or (b), 111(2), 124(1) or (2), the Consumer Credit Act procedure (para. 7BPD.1) applies.

(c) In other cases where the agreement relates only to money, the Consumer Credit Act procedure does not apply. Instead such a claim must be started by the issue of a Pt 7 claim form (see para. 7BPD.1, para. 3.3).

No doubt in many cases, the claimant will not know or believe, or will be unwilling to acknowledge, that he requires an order under one of the sections listed at (b), *e.g.* that the documentation requirements were not complied with when the agreement was made and that he consequently requires an order under s.65(1) in order to enforce the agreement. In that case if the agreement does not relate to goods or land, the claimant is likely to start proceedings by the issue of a Pt 7 claim form ignoring the Consumer Credit Act procedure. In that case, it is for the defendant to raise the issue by way of defence.

The Consumer Credit Act Procedure

Stated (at para. 7BPD.1) in the Consumer Credit Act Practice Direction which **3H–6** supplements CPR Rule 7.9, this procedure

- is a fixed-date procedure
- in which the claimant must serve the particulars of claim with the claim form,
- where the defendant is not required to, but may, serve an acknowledgement of service or file a defence
- where default judgment is not available.

See "Goods" and "Money claims" above for when this procedure is to be used.

Applications by debtor or hirer

Except where the claim relates to the recovery of land, the Consumer Credit Act **3H–7** procedure is to be used for originating applications by the debtor or hirer for a time order (under s.129) or to re-open an agreement as being an extortionate credit bargain (under s.139(1)). Where a regulated agreement is secured by a land mortgage, the position is not clear. Arguably, in such a case, an *originating* application for a time order or to re-open the agreement as being an extortionate credit bargain does not "relate to the recovery of land", in which case the Consumer Credit Act procedure is to be used. If it does "relate to the recovery of land", then the CPR appear to have no special provision for such an application, other than, in the case of an application for a time order, pointing to the use of form **N440** (CPR Pt 4, Table 3). Of course applications under ss.129 and 139 can be made by a defendant whatever procedure has been used by the claimant/creditor.

Default judgment

A judgment in default of acknowledgement of service or in default of defence is not **3H–8**

CONSUMER

obtainable on a claim for delivery of goods which are subject to a regulated agreement, CPR, r.12.2(a). It is not available in any case where the claimant is using the Consumer Credit Act procedure (para. 7BPD.5 at para. 5.5).

Hearings
3H–9   Proceedings brought under the Consumer Credit Act shall in the first instance be listed by the court as a hearing in private under CPR, r.39.2(3)(c)—see para. 39PD.1, para. 1.5.

Costs
3H–10   For claims for "fixed commencement costs" and for recovery of "fixed costs on entry of judgment" for delivery up of goods, see CPR Pt 45.

Bills of Sale
3H–11   For registration of bills of sale, renewals of registration, entry of satisfaction, search of the register and related matters, see paras sc95.0.1 to sc95.4.1 and the Practice Direction supplementing RSC O.95 (at scpd95.1).

* * * *

PART II

CREDIT AGREEMENTS, HIRE AGREEMENTS AND LINKED TRANSACTIONS

Consumer credit agreements
3H–12   **8.**—(1) A personal credit agreement is an agreement between an individual ("the debtor") and any other person ("the creditor") by which the creditor provides the debtor with credit of any amount.

(2) A consumer credit agreement is a personal credit agreement by which the creditor provides the debtor with credit not exceeding £25,000.

(3) A consumer credit agreement is a regulated agreement within the meaning of this Act if it is not an agreement (an "exempt agreement") specified in or under section 16.

3H–13   *Note* —Amended by the Consumer Credit (Increase of Monetary Limits) Order 1983 (S.I. 1983 No. 1878); and the Consumer Credit (Increase of Monetary Limits) (Amendment) Order 1998 (S.I. 1998 No. 996).

Consumer credit agreements
3H–14   As a general rule the Act and the regulations made under it apply only to "regulated" agreements. There are two kinds of regulated agreement:

    (i) those defined in this section, *i.e.* regulated consumer credit agreements; and

    (ii) those defined in s.15, *i.e.* regulated consumer hire agreements.

Referring just to this section, a "personal credit agreement", defined in s.8(1), is not a regulated agreement unless it is both:

    (a) a consumer credit agreement, *i.e.* within the financial limit in s.8(2), and also

    (b) not an exempt agreement.

Nevertheless, and by way of exception to the general rule stated above, there is one set of provisions in the Act (the extortionate credit bargain provisions in ss.137–140) which apply to personal credit agreements irrespective of whether they are consumer credit agreements or are exempt agreements.

No agreement will be a personal credit agreement or a regulated agreement unless the debtor is an "individual". A partnership is, but a corporate body is not, an individual. For the definition of this and other expressions used in the section, see s.189(1). For the meaning of "credit", see s.9.

When the Act came into force, the figure in s.8(2) was £5,000. From May 20, 1985 it became £15,000. In respect of any agreement made on or after May 1, 1998 the figure is £25,000. In relation to the figure in s.8(2), there is an important distinction between fixed-sum credit and running-account credit, which terms are defined in s.10. When dealing with fixed-sum credit, the important question is whether the amount of the *credit* exceeds the figure in s.8(2). A loan of £25,000 is within the limit in s.8(2) even though the repayments (*i.e.* including interest) will exceed £25,000. Similarly a hire-purchase or conditional sale agreement involving an initial down-payment of £2,000 and instalment payments totalling £27,000 will be within the £25,000 figure provided that the instalment payments included a figure of at least £2,000 for interest (or credit charge). Neither the down payment nor the credit charges form part of the "credit". (For the rule that credit charges do not form part of the credit, see s.9(4).) As a rule of thumb, when dealing with a hire-purchase, conditional sale or credit sale agreement, one can ascertain the amount of the credit by deducting the down payment and any trade-in allowance from the cash price of the item being purchased; the resulting figure is the amount which, in common parlance, is being "borrowed", *i.e.* is the amount of "credit" (see also Sched.II, Pt II, Example 10). When dealing with running-account credit, *e.g.* a credit card agreement or an overdraft, the important question is whether the "credit-limit" (defined in s.10(2)) exceeds the figure in s.8(2), though there are anti-avoidance provisions in s.10(3).

"Credit" can be provided under an agreement—and that agreement can thus be a personal credit agreement, a consumer credit agreement and a regulated agreement—even though the credit is never actually used. Thus a bank may agree to a customer having authority to go overdrawn to, say, a maximum of £5,000. Credit is provided even though the customer may subsequently choose not to use the overdraft facility. "Credit" is provided when the customer is granted the facility. Similarly credit is provided when a credit card agreement is made and a credit card issued to the customer. A credit card agreement will normally be a regulated consumer credit agreement, *i.e.* unless the debtor is a company or other corporate body. A charge card agreement, however, will normally be an exempt agreement under s.16.

Meaning of credit

9.—(1) In this Act "credit" includes a cash loan, and any other **3H–15** form of financial accommodation.

(2) Where credit is provided otherwise than in sterling it shall be treated for the purposes of this Act as provided in sterling of an equivalent amount.

(3) Without prejudice to the generality of subsection (1), the person by whom goods are bailed or (in Scotland) hired to an individual under a hire-purchase agreement shall be taken to provide him with fixed-sum credit to finance the transaction of an amount equal to the total price of the goods less the aggregate of the deposit (if any) and the total charge for credit.

(4) For the purposes of this Act, an item entering into the total charge for credit shall not be treated as credit even though time is allowed for its payment.

Meaning of credit

Subs. (1) —"Credit" appears intended to embrace the classic form of credit summed **3H–16** up in the phrase "Have now, pay later", or expressed as the deferment of an obligation to pay. An agreement for the provision of advertising services provided for payment to be made in full on the primary date (*i.e.* the signing of the agreement) or by instalments; this was held to be the provision of credit in that customers were permitted to defer payment beyond the primary date (*Stolink UK v. Thomas* [1996] 1 C.L.Y. 1225). The term "credit hire agreement" is sometimes used to describe a hire agreement under which payment for the hire of goods is deferred for a period after the hire has come to an end. It involves the provision of credit because the duty to pay is contractually deferred for a significant period after payment has been earned: *Hatfield v. Hiscock* [1998] C.C.L.R. 68 and *Dimond v. Lovell* [2000] 1 A.C. 384, HL. (See further the notes to s.11.)

CONSUMER

Whether a contract provides credit is to be determined as at the time the contract is made. Where at that time it is uncertain whether the arrangements between the parties will give rise to a debt at all, there is no "credit" merely because the contract postpones any obligation to pay until the possible indebtedness has crystallised: *Nejad v. City Index Ltd* [2000] C.C.L.R. 7; *McMillan Williams (A Firm) v. Range* [2004] C.C.L.R. 3; [2004] 1 W.L.R. 1858. A publishing contract, which provided for the author to be paid an advance on royalties coupled with a requirement for the author to repay after three years such amount of the advance as the sales in those three years had failed to earn, would not provide the author with credit. That conclusion might be different, however, if the amount of the advance was so great as to show that it was in reality a loan dressed up as an advance on royalties.

Professionally drafted contracts for the sale by J of a farm, for its lease-back to J and for J to have an option to re-purchase it later, were held not to amount to the provision of credit even though they were transactions made in order to enable J to cope with substantial financial problems: *Lavin v. Johnson* [2002] EWCA Civ 1138.

After the event (ATE) insurance: a claimant in a personal injury claim action may well fund the proceedings by a conditional fee arrangement (CFA). If the claimant loses, the claimant will not have to pay legal fees but may well have costs awarded against her requiring her to pay the defendant's legal costs. The claimant therefore may, at the time of entering her CFA, take out an insurance policy to cover herself against that risk. Such a policy, known as "after the event" (ATE) insurance, may provide that the premium is not payable until the conclusion of the case. If so, does that amount to the provision of "credit", *i.e.* insurance cover now, pay later? In *Tilby v. Perfect Pizza Ltd* [2003] C.C.L.R. 9 (also available on Court Service website), Senior Costs Judge Hurst held that there was no provision of "credit" unless payment of the premium was deferred for a significant period beyond the conclusion of the case. For the recoverability of an ATE insurance premium as part of a successful claimant's costs: see paras 44.3A.3 and 7A–33.1.

3H–17 *Subs. (2)* —This is relevant to the various financial limits in the Act. Most of these are relevant at the time the agreement is made. For example an agreement involving credit of more than £25,000 is not a regulated agreement (see s.8). Thus the relevant exchange rate to apply is that operative on the date of the making of the agreement. An agreement is either a regulated agreement or it is not; it cannot become one, or cease to be one, at some later date simply because the exchange rate has moved.

3H–18 *Subs. (3)* —This makes it clear that hire-purchase agreements are treated by the Act as consumer credit agreements and not as consumer hire agreements. Where the Act uses the terms "creditor or owner" and "debtor or hirer", in each case it is the former which is relevant to hire-purchase agreements. A hire-purchase agreement may itself use the terms "owner" and "hirer"; nevertheless, in the terminology employed in the Act, the parties are "creditor"and "debtor". The terms "owner" and "hirer", when used in the Act, refer only to the parties to consumer hire agreements.

3H–19 *Subs. (4)* —The "total charge for credit" is defined in the Consumer Credit (Total Charge for Credit) Regulations 1980, made under s.20. In determining whether a fixed-sum credit agreement is within the financial limit to bring it within the definition of a regulated consumer credit agreement (see s.8(2)), any item which is part of the total charge for credit is to be ignored. In *Humberclyde Finance Ltd v. Thompson* [1997] C.C.L.R. 23, CA, the debtor contracted to buy a car on conditional sale terms. The balance of the cash price (*i.e.* after deduction of the initial down payment which was paid by a part-exchange) was £14,497. However, the agreement contained also a payment waiver option which the debtor adopted and which provided that if the debtor (Mr Thompson) died within five years, Mrs Thompson would be relieved from having to pay any instalments which had not fallen due before his death. The fee for this option was £796. Despite the fact that, under the agreement, payment of this fee was a deferred obligation, it was held that the fee did not form part of the "credit", because it fell within the definition of the "total charge for credit". Thus the agreement involved "credit" of less than £15,000 (the then figure specified in s.8(2)) and was a regulated agreement. [*Query* whether the fee was *correctly* held to be within the definition of the total charge for credit—see Consumer Credit (Total Charge for Credit) Regulations 1980 below]. For further examples of the application of s.9(4), see *Huntpast Ltd v. Leadbeater* [1993] C.C.L.R. 15, CA and *Watchtower Investments Ltd v. Payne* [2001] EWCA

Civ. 1159; [2003] C.C.L.R. 10 and *McGinn v. Grangewood Securities Ltd* [2002] EWCA Civ 522; [2003] C.C.L.R. 11 and *London North Securities Ltd v. Meadows and Meadows* [2005] C.C.L.R. 7; [2005] EWCA Civ 956 —all explained at para. 3H–350 below. See also *Wilson v. First County Trust (No. 1)* [2001] Q.B. 407; [2003] C.C.L.R. 1—discussed in the commentary to s.127(3) below.

Running-account credit and fixed-sum credit

10.—(1) For the purposes of this Act—   **3H–20**

(a) running-account credit is a facility under a personal credit agreement whereby the debtor is enabled to receive from time to time (whether in his own person, or by another person) from the creditor or a third party cash, goods and services (or any of them) to an amount or value such that, taking into account payments made by or to the credit of the debtor, the credit limit (if any) is not at any time exceeded; and

(b) fixed-sum credit is any other facility under a personal credit agreement whereby the debtor is enabled to receive credit (whether in one amount or by instalments).

(2) In relation to running-account credit, "credit limit" means, as respects any period, the maximum debit balance which, under the credit agreement, is allowed to stand on the account during that period, disregarding any term of the agreement allowing that maximum to be exceeded merely temporarily.

(3) For the purposes of section 8(2), running-account credit shall be taken not to exceed the amount specified in that subsection ("the specified amount") if—

(a) the credit limit does not exceed the specified amount; or

(b) whether or not there is a credit limit, and if there is, notwithstanding that it exceeds the specified amount,—

(i) the debtor is not enabled to draw at any one time an amount which, so far as (having regard to section 9(4)) it represents credit, exceeds the specified amount, or

(ii) the agreement provides that, if the debit balance rises above a given amount (not exceeding the specified amount), the rate of the total charge for credit increases or any other condition favouring the creditor or his associate comes into operation, or

(iii) at the time the agreement is made it is probable, having regard to the terms of the agreement and any other relevant considerations, that the debit balance will not at any time rise above the specified amount.

Running-account credit and fixed-sum credit

Typical examples of fixed-sum credits are: hire-purchase, conditional sale and **3H–21** credit sale agreements, bank loans (whether advanced as a lump sum or in instalments), pawnbrokers' loans, check trading credit (see also Sched.II, Pt II, Examples 9, 10, 17 and 23). A "credit hire" agreement has been held to be an example of fixed-sum credit (see notes to s.11). Typical examples of running-account credit are: credit card agreements, bank overdraft agreements, shop budget accounts (see also Sched.II, Pt

II, Examples 15, 16, 18 and 23). The distinction is important for the purposes of calculation of the "specified amount" in s.8(2). As regards running-account agreements, the primary rule is that the credit limit is the determining factor. However, even if there is no credit limit or if the credit limit is higher than the specified amount (currently £25,000), the agreement may still be a regulated consumer credit agreement by virtue of s.10(3). S.10(3) is an anti-avoidance provision to cope with the situation where an unrealistically high credit limit is agreed. A term that the interest rate increases if the debit balance rises above £25,000 (or any lower figure), would cause the application of s.10(3)(b)(ii)—(see also Sched.II, Pt II, Example 6). If the agreement contains a term signifying that in the opinion of the parties s.10(3)(b)(iii) does not apply to the agreement, it (*i.e.* s.10(3)(b)(iii)) shall be taken not to apply unless the contrary is proved, see s.171(1)(see also Sched.II, Pt II, Example 6). By s.10(2) a term of the agreement allowing the debtor to exceed the credit limit merely temporarily is to be ignored (see also s.18(5) and Sched.II, Pt II, Examples 22 and 23).

Restricted-use credit and unrestricted-use credit

3H–22   **11.**—(1) A restricted-use credit agreement is a regulated consumer credit agreement—

> (a) to finance a transaction between the debtor and the creditor, whether forming part of that agreement or not, or
>
> (b) to finance a transaction between the debtor and a person (the "supplier") other than the creditor, or
>
> (c) to refinance any existing indebtedness of the debtor's, whether to the creditor or another person,

and "restricted-use credit"shall be construed accordingly.

(2) An unrestricted-use credit agreement is a regulated consumer credit agreement not falling within subsection (1), and "unrestricted-use credit" shall be construed accordingly.

(3) An agreement does not fall within subsection (1) if the credit is in fact provided in such a way as to leave the debtor free to use it as he chooses, even though certain uses would contravene that or any other agreement.

(4) An agreement may fall within subsection (1)(b) although the identity of the supplier is unknown at the time the agreement is made.

Restricted-use credit and unrestricted-use credit

3H–23   Credit is either restricted-use credit or unrestricted-use credit. These two definitions interrelate with those (in ss.12 and 13) of debtor-creditor agreement and debtor-creditor-supplier agreement. Also they are relevant to the definitions of some exempt agreements (see commentary to s.16). Where the credit is advanced in such a way that the debtor can spend it in any way he chooses (*e.g.* cash is put into the debtor's hands or into his current account), the credit is inevitably unrestricted-use credit (s.11(3)). That is so even if the debtor has agreed to use the credit only in a particular way. Where goods or services are supplied on credit, then the credit is tied to that particular purpose and the agreement will therefore fall within s.11(1)(a) or s.11(1)(b). It will be a s.11(1)(a) situation where the person providing the credit (the creditor) and the person contracting with the debtor to supply the goods or services (the supplier) are one and the same person, *e.g.* where a retailer supplies a fridge on terms that the debtor pays the retailer for it in instalments later. A s.11(1)(b) situation arises where the creditor and the supplier are two different persons, *e.g.* where the customer uses his regulated credit card to pay for goods or services. The credit card issuer (the creditor) provides credit to the customer to enable the customer to buy from the retailer. The customer's contract of purchase is with the retailer; his credit card agreement with the card issuer is a restricted-use credit agreement within s.11(1)(b). It is "restricted" use because, although the card can no doubt be used at many retail outlets, it is not available for use absolutely anywhere. If the card-holder (the debtor) is able to draw cash on his credit card account, he is, of course, free to use that cash as he chooses. In that case the credit card agreement is a "multiple agreement"(within s.18(1)(a)): when the debtor uses the card to pay for goods or services, the agreement is one for restricted-use credit within s.11(1)(b); when the debtor uses it to draw cash, it is an unrestricted-use credit agreement (see Sched.II, Pt II, Example 16).

Hatfield v. Hiscock [1998] C.C.L.R. 68, involved a "credit hire" agreement for the hire of a motor vehicle for a period not exceeding three months and under which the payment for the hire was deferred for a period after the hire had come to an end. This agreement was held to involve fixed-sum credit, albeit the amount of the credit was incapable of being quantified until some weeks or months after the agreement was made. In *Dimond v. Lovell* [2000] Q.B. 216; [1999] 3 W.L.R. 561, the Court of Appeal held a similar "credit hire" agreement to be: a personal credit agreement within s.8(1); a consumer credit agreement within s.8(2); an agreement for fixed-sum credit within s.10(1)(b), and; a debtor-credit-supplier agreement within s.12(a). This analysis was apparently approved when a further appeal in *Dimond v. Lovell* was dismissed by the House of Lords [2000] 1 A.C. 384; [2000] C.C.L.R. 57.

A hire-purchase agreement (or a conditional sale or credit sale agreement) entered into between the customer and a finance company to whom the customer has been introduced by a dealer for the purpose of enabling the customer to buy goods of the dealer on credit terms, may appear at first sight to be a s.11(1)(b)agreement. In fact it is not. In this scenario, the finance company buys the goods from the dealer and in turn contracts to supply them to the customer/debtor. The finance company is both creditor and supplier. It is the latter because under the hire-purchase contract the finance company contracts to supply the goods. It is to the finance company that the debtor can look if the goods are not delivered or if, say, there is a breach of the statutory implied terms (as to description, satisfactory quality, etc.). The credit in these cases is provided by the finance company to finance a transaction (*i.e.* for the supply of the goods) between the finance company and the debtor. Thus every regulated hire-purchase agreement, every regulated conditional sale agreement and every regulated credit sale agreement is a s.11(1)(a) agreement.

An agreement can be "to finance ..." or "to refinance ..." within s.11 only where it contains an express or implied term that the credit shall be used for that purpose. It is not enough that the parties had a common purpose or intention that the credit be used for that purpose, *National Westminster Bank v. Story and Pallister* [1999] C.C.L.R. 70, CA.

Debtor-creditor-supplier agreements

12. A debtor-creditor-supplier agreement is a regulated consumer **3H–24** credit agreement being—

    (a) a restricted-use credit agreement which falls within section 11(1)(a), or

    (b) a restricted-use credit agreement which falls within section 11(1)(b)and is made by the creditor under pre-existing arrangements, or in contemplation of future arrangements, between himself and the supplier, or

    (c) an unrestricted-use credit agreement which is made by the creditor under pre-existing arrangements between himself and a person (the "supplier") other than the debtor in the knowledge that the credit is to be used to finance a transaction between the debtor and the supplier.

Debtor-creditor-supplier agreements

Every regulated agreement is either a debtor-creditor-supplier agreement (within **3H–25** s.12) or a debtor-creditor agreement (within s.13). The former identifies regulated consumer credit agreements: first where the creditor and the supplier are one and the same person (s.12(a)); and, secondly, where, though the creditor and supplier are separate persons, there is a business link between them such that the credit contract and the supply contract are linked in a business sense (s.12(b) and (c)). Later sections provide for the dealer to be deemed to be agent of the creditor in antecedent negotiations (s.56) and for the creditor to be jointly and severally liable for misrepresentations and breaches of contract committed by the supplier when the supplier is a different person from the creditor (s.75). These sections do not apply to debtor-creditor agreements.

Every regulated hire-purchase agreement, every regulated conditional sale agreement and every regulated credit sale agreement is a debtor-creditor-supplier agreement within s.12(a) (see commentary to s.11 above). A regulated credit card agreement will be a debtor-creditor-supplier agreement within s.12(b) when the credit card is used to pay for goods or services and will be a debtor-creditor agreement within s.13(c) when used to withdraw cash (see commentary to s.11 above). A "credit hire" agreement is a debtor-creditor-supplier agreement within s.12(a)—see notes to s.11.

"Arrangements" is a key word intended to identify the link between the credit agreement and the supply agreement. The Crowther Report, which the Act was passed to implement, referred to the situation where the creditor and supplier were in effect in a "joint venture for mutual profit". For "arrangements", see s.187. An agreement for an individual to have an overdraft (with a credit limit of £25,000 or less) is a regulated consumer credit agreement; it is a debtor-creditor agreement. That is so irrespective of whether payment (for goods or services) out of that account is by means of either a cheque (whether or not backed by a cheque guarantee card) or an electronic debit card (*e.g.* Delta or Switch), see s.187(3) and (3A). It would be a debtor-creditor-supplier agreement (within s.12(b) or (c)) in the very unlikely event that the bank agreed to the overdraft pursuant to arrangements between the bank and a supplier whereby the bank agreed to grant credit to customers to enable them to make purchases from the supplier. Such a scenario would be more likely to occur, however, in the case of a bank loan (*i.e.* rather than an overdraft agreement). If that scenario did exist, the loan would be a debtor-creditor-supplier agreement even if the loan were advanced by means of unrestricted-use credit (*e.g.* if the bank advanced the credit, albeit under a separate loan agreement, by simply crediting it to the debtor's current account). In that case, if the loan was made under the arrangements between the bank and the supplier, and if the bank knew that it was to be used to finance a transaction between the debtor and the supplier, it would be a debtor-creditor-supplier agreement within s.12(c).

In relation to debtor-creditor-supplier and debtor-creditor agreements, see Sched.II, Pt II, Examples 8, 16, 17, 18 and 21.

Debtor-creditor agreements

3H–26   **13.** A debtor-creditor agreement is a regulated consumer credit agreement being—

> (a) a restricted-use credit agreement which falls within section 11(1)(b) but is not made by the creditor under pre-existing arrangements, or in contemplation of future arrangements, between himself and the supplier, or
>
> (b) a restricted-use credit agreement which falls within section 11(1)(c), or
>
> (c) an unrestricted-use credit agreement which is not made by the creditor under pre-existing arrangements between himself and a person (the "supplier") other than the debtor in the knowledge that the credit is to be used to finance a transaction between the debtor and the supplier.

Debtor-creditor agreements

3H–27   See commentary to s.12.

Credit-token agreements

3H–28   **14.**—(1) A credit-token is a card, check, voucher, coupon, stamp, form, booklet or other document or thing given to an individual by a person carrying on a consumer credit business, who undertakes—

(a) that on the production of it (whether or not some other action is also required) he will supply cash, goods and services (or any of them) on credit, or

(b) that where, on the production of it to a third party (whether or not any other action is also required), the third party supplies cash, goods and services (or any of them), he will pay the third party for them (whether or not deducting any discount or commission), in return for payment to him by the individual.

(2) A credit-token agreement is a regulated agreement for the provision of credit in connection with the use of a credit-token.

(3) Without prejudice to the generality of section 9(1), the person who gives to an individual an undertaking falling within subsection (1)(b) shall be taken to provide him with credit drawn on whenever a third party supplies him with cash, goods or services.

(4) For the purposes of subsection (1), use of an object to operate a machine provided by the person giving the object or a third party shall be treated as the production of the object to him.

Credit-token agreements

3H–29

The basic concept of a credit-token is of an object on production of which cash, goods or services may be supplied on credit. The credit card is the typical case, but the term also covers trading vouchers, trading checks, and in some circumstances electronic debit (Delta or Swift) cards.

This section contains two definitions: "credit-token"; and "credit-token agreement". Only a regulated agreement can be a credit-token agreement. A credit-token can exist, on the other hand in relation to an agreement which is not a regulated agreement—though it can only be a credit-token if it is given by someone carrying on a "consumer credit business". *Query* whether a token issued in relation to an exempt agreement (*e.g.* an exempt charge card) by someone who also carries on a "consumer credit business" (*e.g.* issues regulated credit cards) can be a "credit-token"? See the definition of "consumer credit business" in s.189(1). It seems that an electronic debit card which can be used only to withdraw cash from machines operated by the bank which issued the card will be a credit-token only if the bank has agreed to the card holder having a debit balance on his account, since if the card is to be used simply to withdraw money from an account with a credit balance, the card does not fall within s.14(1)(a), there being no "credit" involved. If, on the other hand, the card can be used to withdraw money from a machine operated by a third party (*e.g.* another bank) the card appears capable of falling within s.14(1)(b). In that case it appears to be irrelevant (if it is the case) that the card is able to be used only in relation to a credit balance, since by s.14(3) the issuing bank is "taken" to provide the card holder with credit. Or does the reference in s.14(1) to the object being given by a person carrying on a consumer credit business imply that it is confined to objects issued in relation to regulated consumer credit agreements?

It is an offence to give an unsolicited credit-token, s.51(1). In that context, it has been held that the word "undertakes" in s.14(1) does not imply a requirement of a contract or of a binding undertaking, *Elliott v. Director General of Fair Trading* [1980] 1 W.L.R. 977; [1980] C.C.L.R. 23. In that case a card having the appearance of a credit card was on its face stated to be a credit card available for immediate use. It was held that this was a credit-token even though a customer first presenting the card would have been required to enter a formal agreement and complete other formalities before getting credit.

Consumer hire agreements

3H–30

15.—(1) A consumer hire agreement is an agreement made by a person with an individual (the "hirer") for the bailment or (in Scotland) the hiring of goods to the hirer, being an agreement which—

(a) is not a hire-purchase agreement, and

(b) is capable of subsisting for more than three months, and

(c) does not require the hirer to make payments exceeding £25,000.

(2) A consumer hire agreement is a regulated agreement if it is not an exempt agreement.

3H–31   *Note* —Amended by the Consumer Credit (Increase of Monetary Limits) Order 1983 (S.I. 1983 No. 1878); and the Consumer Credit (Increase of Monetary Limits) (Amendment) Order 1988 (S.I. 1998 No. 996).

Consumer hire agreements

3H–32   For "individual", see commentary to s.8. A hire-purchase agreement cannot be a consumer hire agreement. Hire-purchase agreements are credit agreements (see s.9(2)). The parties to a consumer hire agreement are referred to in the Act as "owner" and "hirer". A hire agreement which is stated to have a duration of two months and which contains an option to renew the agreement for a further two months (whether exercisable by the hirer or the owner) is capable of subsisting for more than three months. When the Act came into force, the figure in s.15(1)(c) was £5,000. On May 20, 1985, it was raised to £15,000. For agreements made on or after May 1, 1998 the figure is £25,000. An agreement which is stated to last for seven years, which contains no clause entitling either party to terminate it before the expiry of the seven years, and which provides for quarterly rentals each of £1,000, is not a consumer hire agreement. This is because it requires the debtor to make payments amounting to £28,000, *i.e.* exceeding £25,000. If, on the other hand, the agreement contained a clause entitling the hirer to terminate the agreement at the end of three and a half years, it would be a consumer hire agreement because it would then require the hirer to make payments of only £14,000, *i.e.* not exceeding £25,000. See also Sched.II, Pt II, Examples 20 and 24. For "exempt" agreements, see s.16.

Credit-hire agreements

3H–33   If the *bailment* is not capable of subsisting for more than three months, then the agreement is not a consumer hire agreement. That is so, even if the agreement is a "credit-hire" agreement and thus the period allowed for payment of the hire charges is much longer than three months: *Lagden v. O'Connor* [2003] Q.B. 36; [2002] EWCA Civ 510. For whether a "credit-hire" agreement is a consumer credit agreement, see the commentaries to ss.8 and 11. For whether it is exempt, see commentary to s.16 (at the sixth bullet point).

Exempt agreements

3H–34   **16.**—(1) This Act does not regulate a consumer credit agreement where the creditor is a local authority, or a body specified, or of a description specified, in an order made by the Secretary of State, being—

(a) an insurer,

(b) a friendly society,

(c) an organisation of employers or organisation of workers,

(d) a charity,

(e) a land improvement company,

(f) a body corporate named or specifically referred to in any public general Act.

(ff) a body corporate named or specifically referred to in an order made under—

Section 156(4), 444(1), or 447(2)(a) of the Housing Act 1985,

Section 156(4) of that Act as it has effect by virtue of section 17 of the Housing Act 1996 (the right to acquire),

Section 2 of the Home Purchase Assistance and Housing Corporation Guarantee Act 1978 or section 31 of the Tenants' Rights, etc. (Scotland) Act 1980,

Section 223 or 229 of the Housing (Scotland) Act 1987, or

Article 154(1)(a) or 156AA of the Housing (Northern Ireland) Order 1981 or Article 10(6A) of the Housing (Northern Ireland) Order 1983; or

(g) a building society, or

(h) a deposit-taker.

(2) Subsection (1) applies only where the agreement is—

(a) a debtor-creditor-supplier agreement financing—

(i) the purchase of land, or

(ii) the provision of dwellings on any land, and secured by a land mortgage on that land; or

(b) a debtor-creditor agreement secured by any land mortgage; or

(c) a debtor-creditor-supplier agreement financing a transaction which is a linked transaction in relation to—

(i) an agreement falling within paragraph (a), or

(ii) an agreement falling within paragraph (b) financing—

(aa) the purchase of any land, or

(bb) the provision of dwellings on any land, and secured by a land mortgage on the land referred to in paragraph (a) or, as the case may be, the land referred to in sub-paragraph (ii).

(3) Before he makes, varies or revokes an order under subsection (1), the Secretary of State must undertake the necessary consultation.

(3A) The necessary consultation means consultation with the bodies mentioned in the following table in relation to the provision under which the order is to be made, varied or revoked:

TABLE

Provision of subsection (1)	Consultee
Paragraph (a) or (b)	The Financial Services Authority
Paragraph (d)	The Charity Commissioners
Paragraph (e), (f) or (ff)	Any Minister of the Crown with responsibilities in relation to the body in question
Paragraph (g) or (h)	The Treasury and the Financial Services Authority.

(4) An order under subsection (1) relating to a body may be limited so as to apply only to agreements by that body of a description specified in the order.

(5) The Secretary of State may by order provide that this Act shall not regulate other consumer credit agreements where—

(a) the number of payments to be made by the debtor does not exceed the number specified for that purpose in the order, or

(b) the rate of the total charge for credit does not exceed the rate so specified, or

(c) an agreement has a connection with a country outside the United Kingdom.

(6) The Secretary of State may by order provide that this Act shall not regulate consumer hire agreements of a description specified in the order where—

(a) the owner is a body corporate authorised by or under any enactment to supply electricity, gas or water, and

(b) the subject of the agreement is a meter or metering equipment,

or where the owner is a provider of a public electronic communications service who is specified in the order.

(6A) This Act does not regulate a consumer credit agreement where the creditor is a housing authority and the agreement is secured by a land mortgage of a dwelling.

(6B) In subsection (6A) "housing authority" means—

(a) as regards England and Wales, the Housing Corporation and an authority or body within section 80(1) of the Housing Act 1985 (the landlord condition for secure tenancies), other than a housing association or a housing trust which is a charity;

(b) as regards Scotland, a development corporation established under an order made, or having effect as if made under the New Towns (Scotland) Act 1968, the Scottish Special Housing Association or the Housing Corporation;

(c) as regards Northern Ireland, the Northern Ireland Housing Executive.

(6C) This Act does not regulate a consumer credit agreement if—

(a) it is secured by a land mortgage; and

(b) entering into that agreement as lender is a regulated activity for the purposes of the Financial Services and Markets Act 2000.

(6D) But section 126, and any other provision so far as it relates to section 126, applies to an agreement which would (but for subsection (6C)) be a regulated agreement.

(6E) Subsection (6C) must be read with—

(a) section 22 of the Financial Services and Markets Act 2000 (regulated activities: power to specify classes of activity and categories of investment);

(b) any order for the time being in force under that section; and

(c) Schedule 2 to that Act.

(7) Nothing in this section affects the application of sections 137 to 140 (extortionate credit bargains).

(8) In the application of this section to Scotland, subsection (3A) shall have effect as if the reference to the Charity Commissioners were a reference to the Lord Advocate.

(9) In the application of this section to Northern Ireland subsection (3A) shall have effect as if any reference to a Minister of the Crown were a reference to a Northern Ireland department, and any reference to the Charity Commissioners were a reference to the Department of Finance for Northern Ireland.

(10) In this section—

> (a) "deposit-taker" means—
>
> > (i) a person who has permission under Part 4 of the Financial Services and Markets Act 2000 to accept deposits,
> >
> > (ii) an EEA firm of the kind mentioned in paragraph 5(b) of Schedule 3 to that Act which has permission under paragraph 15 of that Schedule (as a result of qualifying for authorisation under paragraph 12 of that Schedule) to accept deposits,
> >
> > (iii) any wholly owned subsidiary (within the meaning of the Companies Act 1985) of a person mentioned in sub-paragraph (i), or
> >
> > (iv) any undertaking which, in relation to a person mentioned in sub-paragraph (ii), is a subsidiary undertaking within the meaning of any rule of law in force in the EEA State in question for purposes connected with the implementation of the European Council Seventh Company Law Directive of 13 June 1983 on consolidated accounts (No. 83/349/EEC), and which has no members other than that person;
>
> (b) "insurer" means—
>
> > (i) a person who has permission under Part 4 of the Financial Services and Markets Act 2000 to effect or carry out contracts of insurance, or
> >
> > (ii) an EEA firm of the kind mentioned in paragraph 5(d) of Schedule 3 to that Act, which has permission under paragraph 15 of that Schedule (as a result of qualifying for authorisation under paragraph 12 of that Schedule)) to effect or carry out contracts of insurance,
> >
> > but does not include a friendly society or an organisation of workers or of employers.

(11) Subsection (10) must be read with—

> (a) section 22 of the Financial Services and Markets Act 2000;
>
> (b) any relevant order under that section; and
>
> (c) Schedule 2 to that Act.

Note —Amended by the Employment Protection Act 1975, Sched.18; the Telecommunications Act 1984, Sched.4; the Building Societies Act 1986, Scheds 18 and 19; the Housing and Planning Act 1986, s.22; the Banking Act 1987, s.88; the Housing (Scotland) Act 1987, Sched.23; the Housing Act 1988, Sched.17; the Housing Act 1996, Sched.19, Pt XIV the Housing Act 1996 (Consequential Amendments) (No. 2) Order 1997 (S.I. 1997 No. 627); the Bank of England Act 1998, Sched.5, para. 36; the

3H–35

Government of Wales Act 1998, s.152, Sched.18, Pt VI; the Financial Services and Markets Act 2000 (Regulated Activities) Order 2001 (S.I. 2001 No. 544); the Financial Services and Markets Act 2000 (Consequential Amendments and Repeals) Order 2001 (S.I. 2001 No. 3649) and by the Communications Act 2003, Sched.17, para. 47. Subsections (6C) to (6E) were added, as from October 31, 2004, by the Financial Services and Markets Act (Regulated Activities) Order 2001 (S.I. 2001 No. 544) as amended by the Financial Services and Markets Act 2000 (Commencement of Mortgage Regulation) (Amendment) Order 2002 (S.I. 2002 No. 1777).

Exempt agreements

3H-36   This section enables agreements to be exempt but operates mainly through the Order which it authorises the Secretary of State to make. The current Order is the Consumer Credit (Exempt Agreements) Order 1989, as amended. The Order is detailed. That detail must be consulted in order to determine if any particular agreement falls within one of the exemptions. *Broadly*, the combined effect of s.16 and the Order is that there are the following categories of exempt agreements:

- Consumer credit agreements secured on land and made by a local authority.
- House purchase and improvement loans (for dwellings or sometimes for business premises) secured by mortgage and granted by a bank, building society or other body mentioned in s.16(1).
- Land mortgages which are regulated under the Financial Services and Markets Act 2000. [These are, broadly, any agreement (made on or after October 31, 2004) which satisfies three requirements: (i) it provides credit to an individual or trustee; (ii) it is secured by a first legal mortgage on land in the UK; and (iii) at least 40% of the land is, or is intended to be, used as a dwelling by the borrower or his family – see the Financial Services and Markets Act 2000 (Regulated Activities) Order 2001 (S.I. 2001 No. 544).
- A debtor-creditor-supplier agreement financing the purchase of land where the number of payments to be made by the debtor does not exceed four.
- A "running-account" "debtor-creditor-supplier" agreement where the debtor is required to pay the whole of each periodical account in a single payment. This exemption exempts the milk, newspaper and grocery accounts of many households. It also exempts those charge cards which (a) do not entitle the card holder to draw cash, and (b) require each periodic account to be settled in a single payment. This covers the traditional American Express card. American Express have more recently launched a card which allows the card holder extended credit, *i.e.* which does not require each account to be paid in full. This latter card therefore is not exempt and will be a regulated running-account consumer credit agreement—unless either the credit limit (a realistic one) exceeds £25,000 or else the debtor is a corporate body. The use by the issuer of the description "charge card" is not a sure guide to this exemption, since some card issuers use that description in relation to a credit card agreement which allows extended credit and is a regulated credit card agreement. A chargecard which requires the debtor to settle each account in a single payment but which allows the cardholder not only to use the card to pay for goods or services but also to draw cash, will not be entirely exempt. It is a multiple agreement within s.18 (see Sched.II, Pt II, Example 16). In so far as the card allows the cardholder to draw cash it is a debtor-creditor agreement and is not exempt. In so far as it allows the cardholder to use the card to pay for goods and services, it is exempt.
- A "fixed-sum" "debtor-creditor-supplier" agreement under which the debtor is to repay the credit in no more than four instalments within a period of 12 months. The twelve month period begins with, and includes, the date the agreement is made. An agreement requiring payments to be completed within 12 months after the date of the agreement will thus not qualify for this exemption, *Zoan v. Rouamba* [2000] 1 W.L.R. 1509; [2000] 2 All E.R. 620, CA. Nor will an agreement which requires payment "on expiry" of the twelve month period, *Ketley v. Gilbert* [2001] 1 W.L.R. 986; [2003] C.C.L.R. 3, CA. However, a contract term making the debtor "liable" to pay on expiry of 51 weeks from the date of the agreement did require payment within the twelve month period, *Clark v. Tull t/a Ardington Electrical Services* [2002] EWCA Civ 510; [2003] Q.B. 36; [2002] 3 W.L.R. 762. Similarly, agreements allowing the debtor to defer payment for a period of up to 12 months "from the start of the agree-

ment" and "from the date of this agreement (including the date of this agreement)" were held to require payment within the 12 month period and were within the exemption, *Thew v. Cole, King v. Daltry* [2003] EWCA Civ 1828; [2004] C.C.L.R. 2. For this exemption to apply, it is not necessary for there to be an express term spelling out that the number of payments (within the 12 month period) must not exceed four. It is sufficient that the agreement envisages, without expressly requiring, that the credit will be repaid in a single instalment (or in no more than four): *Clark v. Tull t/a Ardington Electrical Services*, above. In any case, hire-purchase agreements, conditional sale agreements, agreements financing the purchase of land and agreements secured by pledge cannot be within this exemption.

- A debtor-creditor agreement (made on or before July 31, 1999) where the cost of the credit is low, *i.e.* where the annual rate of the total charge for credit (the APR) does not exceed the higher of:

    (a) 13 per cent; or

    (b) a rate 1 per cent higher than the highest of the base rates operated by the main English and Scottish banks at the close of business 28 days before the making of the credit agreement.

- A debtor-creditor agreement which is of a type offered only to a certain class or classes of individuals and not offered to the public generally and where the cost of the credit is low, *i.e.* where there is no charge other than interest for the credit and where the annual rate of that interest (the APR) cannot exceed a rate 1 per cent higher than the highest of the base rates operated by the main English and Scottish banks 28 days earlier.

- A debtor-creditor agreement which is of a type offered only to a certain class or classes of individuals and not offered to the public generally, where there can be no increase in the charge for credit and where the cost of the credit is low, *i.e.* where the annual rate of the charge for credit (the APR) does not exceed a rate 1 per cent higher than the highest of the base rates operated by the main English and Scottish banks at the close of business 28 days before the date on which the agreement is made.

- A debtor-creditor agreement (made on or after August 1, 1999) where the creditor is a credit union and rate of the total charge for credit (the APR) does not exceed 12.7 per cent.

- Consumer credit agreements providing credit to be used by the debtor in connection with overseas trade.

- Consumer hire agreements for the hire of gas, water or electricity metering equipment from a corporate body authorised to supply that commodity.

An exempt agreement is not a "regulated agreement". Thus, with a couple of exceptions, exempt agreements are not regulated by the provisions of the Act. The first exception is that a personal credit agreement (defined in s.8(1)) is liable to be reopened under ss.137-140 if it is an extortionate credit bargain. That is so even if the personal credit agreement is an exempt agreement – unless it is exempt under s.16(6C). A further exception is stated in s.16(6D). Thus a land mortgage which (a) is exempt within s.16(6C) and (b) would otherwise be a regulated agreement, is subject to s.126 and thus cannot be enforced without a court order.

Small agreements

17.—(1) A small agreement is— **3H–37**

    (a) a regulated consumer credit agreement for credit not exceeding £50, other than a hire-purchase or conditional sale agreement; or

    (b) a regulated consumer hire agreement which does not require the hirer to make payments exceeding £50,

being an agreement which is either unsecured or secured by a guarantee or indemnity only (whether or not the guarantee or indemnity is itself secured).

(2) Section 10(3)(a) applies for the purposes of subsection (1) as it applies for the purposes of section 8(2).

(3) Where—

    (a) two or more small agreements are made at or about the same time between the same parties, and

    (b) it appears probable that they would instead have been made as a single agreement but for the desire to avoid the operation of provisions of this Act which would have applied to that single agreement but, apart from this subsection, are not applicable to the small agreements,

this Act applies to the small agreements as if they were regulated agreements other than small agreements.

(4) If, apart from this subsection, subsection (3) does not apply to any agreements but would apply if, for any party or parties to any of the agreements, there were substituted an associate of that party, or associates of each of those parties, as the case may be, then subsection (3) shall apply to the agreements.

3H–38   *Note* —Amended by the Consumer Credit (Increase of Monetary Limits) Order 1983 (S.I. 1983 No. 1878).

Small agreements

3H–39   This definition identifies agreements of low value and enables later sections to except some of them from some of the requirements of the Act, *e.g.* from the documentation requirements (see s.74). From the coming into force of the Act until January 1, 1984 the figure in s.17(1)(a) was £30. Since that date the figure has been £50. See Sched.II, Pt II, Examples 16, 17 and 22.

Multiple agreements

3H–40   18.—(1) This section applies to an agreement (a "multiple agreement") if its terms are such as—

    (a) to place a part of it within one category of agreement mentioned in this Act, and another part of it within a different category of agreement so mentioned, or within a category of agreement not so mentioned, or

    (b) to place it, or a part of it, within two or more categories of agreement so mentioned.

(2) Where a part of an agreement falls within subsection (1), that part shall be treated for the purposes of this Act as a separate agreement.

(3) Where an agreement falls within subsection (1)(b), it shall be treated as an agreement in each of the categories in question, and this Act shall apply to it accordingly.

(4) Where under subsection (2) a part of a multiple agreement is to be treated as a separate agreement, the multiple agreement shall (with any necessary modifications) be construed accordingly; and any sum payable under the multiple agreement, if not apportioned by the parties, shall for the purposes of proceedings in any court relating to the multiple agreement be apportioned by the court as may be requisite.

(5) In the case of an agreement for running-account credit, a term of the agreement allowing the credit limit to be exceeded merely temporarily shall not be treated as a separate agreement or as providing fixed-sum credit in respect of the excess.

(6) This Act does not apply to a multiple agreement so far as the agreement relates to goods if under the agreement payments are to be made in respect of the goods in the form of rent (other than a rentcharge) issuing out of land.

Multiple agreements

There is a controversy as to the proper interpretation of this section. Professor **3H–41** Goode in his *Consumer Credit Legislation* takes the view that an agreement can fall either within s.18(1)(a), or within s.18(1)(b), but not both. He takes the view that an agreement can fall within s.18(1)(a) only if it is a "multipart" agreement and not if it is a "unitary" agreement. (These terms are not to be found in the Act). This approach is inconsistent, however, with Examples 16 and 18 in Sched.II, Pt II. It is also inconsistent with s.18 operating, as it was surely meant to, as an anti-avoidance measure. Yet in *National Home Loans Corp. v. Hannah* [1997] C.C.L.R. 7, Professor Goode's thesis was followed apparently without any hesitation (or, indeed, acknowledgement). The case involved a loan agreement to lend over £52,000 which (a) was a refinancing of an existing loan of over £41,000, and also (b) provided extra spending of £10,915. It was held that even if the (a) part was for restricted-use credit and the (b) part was for unrestricted-use credit, it still did not fall within s.18(1)(a) and was not a multiple agreement. This was because it was a unitary agreement incapable of being split up without altering its essential character. The result was that something (*i.e.* part (b)) which, if looked at alone would have been a regulated agreement, escaped being designated as such by virtue of being included within an agreement outside the scope of the Act.

The opposing view to Professor Goode's is put by the draftsman of the Act, Francis Bennion, in *Multiple Agreements under the Consumer Credit Act 1974* [1999] C.I.C.C. 1. It is that an agreement, whether "unitary" or not, which falls into more than one category of agreement under the Act, is a multiple agreement and that those aspects of the agreement falling into any one such category are to be treated as a separate agreement—*i.e.* that part is to be treated as being, even though it is not in fact, a separate agreement. The difference between the two views can be vital because the effect of treating a part of an agreement as a separate agreement can be to cause that part to fall within the financial limits of the Act when otherwise it would not be a regulated agreement. When the matter surfaced in *National Westminster Bank v. Story and Pallister* [1999] C.C.L.R. 70, Bennion's article was not referred to and the Court of Appeal avoided the issue by deciding that the two different parts, or aspects, of the agreement in that case were both within the same catetory of agreement within the Act, both involving unrestricted-use credit. The matter surfaced again in the House of Lords in *Dimond v. Lovell* [2000] 1 A.C. 384; [2000] C.C.L.R. 57. It was argued that by virtue of section 18 a "credit-hire" agreement was a multiple agreement, one part being for the hire of a car (non-regulated) and other part being for the allowing of credit to pay the hire charges (regulated). Lord Hoffman, giving the leading speech, simply said "Whatever a multiple agreement may be, one cannot divide up a contract in that way." The matter was fully argued for the first time in *Ocwen v. Coxall and Coxall* [2004] C.C.L.R. 7, where H.H. Judge Holt held that Bennion's views were to be preferred to those of Professor Goode. In *London North Securities Ltd v. Williams and Williams* (unreported, Reading Cty Ct May 16, 2005) Recorder Gary Flather OBE QC entirely agreed with, and followed, that decision. In *London North Securities Ltd v Meadows and Meadows* [2005] C.C.L.R. 7; [2005] EWCA Civ 956 , the Court of Appeal set out the controversy but on the facts found it unnecessary to rule upon it. Francis Bennion's article and his addendum to it (written after the decision in *National Westminster Bank v. Story* [1999] Lloyd's Rep. Bank. 261; [1999] C.C.L.R. 70) can both be seen (as separate items) on Francis Bennion's website at www.francisbennion.com

Linked transactions

19.—(1) A transaction entered into by the debtor or hirer, or a rel- **3H–42** ative of his, with any other person ("the other party"), except one for the provision of security, is a linked transaction in relation to an actual or prospective regulated agreement (the "principal agreement") of which it does not form part if—

    (a) the transaction is entered into in compliance with a term of the principal agreement; or

(b) the principal agreement is a debtor-creditor-supplier agreement and the transaction is financed, or to be financed, by the principal agreement, or

(c) the other party is a person mentioned in subsection (2), and a person so mentioned initiated the transaction by suggesting it to the debtor or hirer, or his relative, who enters into it—

    (i) to induce the creditor or owner to enter into the principal agreement, or

    (ii) for another purpose related to the principal agreement, or

    (iii) where the principal agreement is a restricted-use credit agreement, for a purpose related to a transaction financed, or to be financed, by the principal agreement.

(2) The persons referred to in subsection (1)(c) are—

(a) the creditor or owner, or his associate;

(b) a person who, in the negotiation of the transaction, is represented by a credit-broker who is also a negotiator in antecedent negotiations for the principal agreement;

(c) a person who, at the time the transaction is initiated, knows that the principal agreement has been made or contemplates that it might be made.

(3) A linked transaction entered into before the making of the principal agreement has no effect until such time (if any) as that agreement is made.

(4) Regulations may exclude linked transactions of the prescribed description from the operation of subsection (3).

Linked transactions

3H–43   For the meaning of the many technical terms in this section, see s.189(1). Three provisions in particular have an impact upon linked transactions: ss.19(3), 69(1) and 96(1). If the debtor or hirer withdraws an offer to enter a regulated agreement or exercises his right to cancel a cancellable agreement, any linked transaction is automatically withdrawn from or cancelled (ss.19(3) and 69(1)). If for any reason the debtor's indebtedness is discharged early, the debtor is discharged from any further liability under any linked transaction (s.96(1)). However, by virtue of the Consumer Credit (Linked Transactions) (Exemptions) Regulations 1983 (S.I. 1983 No. 1560), three types of linked transaction are exempted from the three provisions just mentioned which would otherwise have applied to them. Those three types of linked transaction are:

    (i) contracts of insurance;

    (ii) written guarantees of goods; and

    (iii) any transaction which is (or is made under) an agreement for the operation of a savings, deposit or current account.

Total charge for credit

3H–44   **20.**—(1) The Secretary of State shall make regulations containing such provisions as appear to him appropriate for determining the true cost to the debtor of the credit provided or to be provided under an actual or prospective consumer credit agreement (the "total charge for credit"), and regulations so made shall prescribe—

(a) what items are to be treated as entering into the total

charge for credit, and how their amount is to be ascertained;

(b) the method of calculating the rate of the total charge for credit.

(2) Regulations under subsection (1) may provide for the whole or part of the amount payable by the debtor or his relative under any linked transaction to be included in the total charge for credit, whether or not the creditor is a party to the transaction or derives benefit from it.

Total charge for credit

The purpose of the section is to enable (a) a definition (*i.e.* of the "total charge for **3H–45** credit") to be produced which will show the true cost of the credit which is being advertised or provided, and (b) a common method of calculating the rate of charge (the APR) to be devised. APR = Annual Percentage Rate of the total charge for credit. The relevant regulations are the Consumer Credit (Total Charge for Credit) Regulations 1980 (see para. 3H–333, below).

PART III

LICENSING OF CREDIT AND HIRE BUSINESS

* * * *

MISCELLANEOUS

Enforcement of agreements made by unlicensed trader

40.—(1) A regulated agreement, other than a non-commercial **3H–46** agreement, if made when the creditor or owner was unlicensed, is enforceable against the debtor or hirer only where the OFT has made an order under this section which applies to the agreement.

(2) Where during any period an unlicensed person (the "trader") was carrying on a consumer credit business or consumer hire business, he or his successor in title may apply to the OFT for an order that regulated agreements made by the trader during that period are to be treated as if he had been licensed.

(3) Unless the OFT determines to make an order under subsection (2) in accordance with the application, it shall, before determining the application, by notice—

(a) inform the applicant, giving its reasons, that, as the case may be, it is minded to refuse the application, or to grant it in terms different from those applied for, describing them, and

(b) invite the applicant to submit to the OFT representations in support of his application in accordance with section 34.

(4) In determining whether or not to make an order under subsection (2) in respect of any period the OFT shall consider, in addition to any other relevant factors—

(a) how far, if at all, debtors or hirers under regulated agreements made by the trader during that period were prejudiced by the trader's conduct,

    (b) whether or not the OFT would have been likely to grant a licence covering that period on an application by the trader, and

    (c) the degree of culpability for the failure to obtain a licence.

(5) If the OFT thinks fit, it may in an order under subsection (2)—

    (a) limit the order to specified agreements, or agreements of a specified description or made at a specified time;

    (b) make the order conditional on the doing of specified acts by the applicant.

Section 40 shall have effect as if the reference in subsection (1) to a regulated agreement, other than a non-commercial agreement, made when the creditor or owner was unlicensed did not include a reference to such an agreement made when the creditor or owner was a relevant firm.

(6) This section does not apply to a regulated agreement, other than a non-commercial agreement, made by a consumer credit EEA firm unless at the time it was made that firm was precluded from entering into it as a result of—

    (a) a consumer credit prohibition imposed under section 203 of the Financial Services and Markets Act 2000; or

    (b) a restriction imposed on the firm under section 204 of that Act.

3H–47   *Note* —Amended by the Financial Services and Markets Act 2000 (Consequential Amendments and Repeals) Order 2001 (S.I. 2001 No. 3649) and by the Enterprise Act 2002, s.278 and Sched.25.

Enforcement of agreements made by unlicensed trader

3H–48   A licence is required to carry on: a "consumer credit business", a "consumer hire business" or an "ancillary credit business" (credit brokerage, debt adjusting, debt-counselling, debt-collecting, or operation of a credit reference agency; see ss.21 and 147). For definitions, including "consumer credit business" and "consumer hire business", see s.189(1). The latter definitions mean that no licence is required to carry on a business which grants credit (or supplies goods on hire) *only* to corporate bodies and/or in excess of the financial limit in ss.8(2) and 15(1)(c) and/or under exempt agreements. On the other hand a trader, whose principal business (*e.g.* a car dealer) is something not requiring a licence under this Act but who as part of it does also provide credit or goods under regulated agreements, must be licensed. A person is not, however, to be regarded as carrying on a particular kind of business merely because *occasionally* he enters into transactions belonging to a business of that type (s.189(2)). For this purpose there is no distinction between transactions initiated by the trader and those initiated by the customers (*R. v. Marshall* (1990) 90 Cr. App. R. 73; [1989] C.C.L.R. 47, CA). A car dealer who never normally provided credit but who on one occasion agreed to supply a car to a friend on hire-purchase, was not carrying on a consumer credit business (*Hare v. Shurek* [1993] C.C.L.R. 47, CA).

3H–49   *Standard and group licences* —A group licence can be issued covering the activities of particular groups of people. (A number of group licences have been issued covering such people as practising solicitors; liquidators; executors; administrators; trustees in bankruptcy; other trustees; Citizen's Advice Bureaus; chartered accountants; certified accountants; and higher education intitutions.) A standard licence is issued to a corporate body, a partnership, an unincorporated association or an individual. Any one of these whose activities should be licensed and who is not covered by the terms of a group licence, must be covered by a standard licence.

3H–50   *Canvassing off trade premises* —This is defined in s.48. Except to the extent that it contains express limitations, a licence to carry on a business covers all lawful activities done in the course of that business (s.23(1) & (2)). It does not, however, cover the canvassing off trade premises of debtor-creditor-supplier agreements or regulated consumer hire agreements except to the extent that it specifically so provides (s.23(3)).

The "Single Market Passport" and subs.(6) —This concept is that banks and invest- **3H–51**
ment firms in other EEA states should be subject to control just by their home State. The concept is now to be found in the Banking Consolidation Directive (No. 2000/12/EEC) and the Investment Services Directive (No. 92/22/EEC). These Directives are now implemented in the UK by the Financial Services and Markets Act 2000. The result is that EEA firms are regulated by their home state and, subject to some bureaucratic requirements, do not need to be licensed under the Consumer Credit Act: Financial Services and Markets Act 2000, Sched.3, para. 15. This disapplication of the licensing provisions does not apply if the EEA firm is the subject of a prohibition by the Office of Fair Trading. For the definition of "consumer credit EEA firm", see the Consumer Credit Act, s.189A (below).

Unlicensed trading —This is a criminal offence (s.39). Usually a much more severe **3H–52**
consequence is that it can also lead to the creditor or owner being unable to enforce agreements made when the creditor or owner was unlicensed (s.40). Furthermore, s.149 contains a provision similar to that in s.40, whereby a regulated agreement made by a debtor or hirer who, for the purpose of making that agreement, was introduced to the creditor or owner by an unlicensed credit-broker, is unenforceable against the debtor or hirer. As under s.40(2), so also under ss.148 and 149, a validating order can be applied for from the Director General of Fair Trading allowing agreements to be enforced.

* * * * *

PART V

ENTRY INTO CREDIT OR HIRE AGREEMENTS

PRELIMINARY MATTERS

Disclosure of information

55.—(1) Regulations may require specified information to be **3H–53**
disclosed in the prescribed manner to the debtor or hirer before a regulated agreement is made.

(2) A regulated agreement is not properly executed unless regulations under subsection (1) were complied with before the making of the agreement.

Pre-contract information

The Consumer Credit (Disclosure of Information) Regulations 2004 (S.I. 2004 No. **3H–54**
1481), which came into force on May 31, 2005, were the first regulations to be made under this section. They require certain stated information to be given to the debtor or hirer before a regulated agreement is made. The information must be provided in a document which is: (i) on paper or another durable medium; (ii) separate from the agreement itself; (iii) headed "Pre-contract Information", and; (iv) of such a nature that it can be removed by the debtor or hirer from the place where it is disclosed to him. The information must be legible, not generally interspersed with any other information and must all (apart from headings) be of equal prominence. Failure to comply with the regulations will result in the agreement being improperly executed (see ss.66(1) and 65). These sections—and the regulations—do not apply to agreements listed in ss.74(1) and 82(4). Also the regulations do not apply either to any agreement to which s.58 applies or to any regulated agreement which is a "distance contract" (as defined by the regulations). In the case of distance contracts, however, the Financial

Services (Distance Marketing) Regulations 2004 set out, with effect from May 31, 2005, pre-contract disclosure requirements where the debtor is an individual acting outside any business he may carry on.

Antecedent negotiations

3H–55   **56.**—(1) In this Act "antecedent negotiations" means any negotiations with the debtor or hirer—

> (a) conducted by the creditor or owner in relation to the making of any regulated agreement, or
>
> (b) conducted by a credit-broker in relation to goods sold or proposed to be sold by the credit-broker to the creditor before forming the subject-matter of a debtor-creditor-supplier agreement within section 12(a), or
>
> (c) conducted by the supplier in relation to a transaction financed or proposed to be financed by a debtor-creditor-supplier agreement within section 12(b) or (c), and "negotiator" means the person by whom negotiations are so conducted with the debtor or hirer.

(2) Negotiations with the debtor in a case falling within subsection (1)(b) or (c) shall be deemed to be conducted by the negotiator in the capacity of agent of the creditor as well as in his actual capacity.

(3) An agreement is void if, and to the extent that, it purports in relation to an actual or prospective regulated agreement—

> (a) to provided that a person acting as, or on behalf of, a negotiator is to be treated as the agent of the debtor or hirer, or
>
> (b) to relieve a person from liability for acts or omissions of any person acting as, or on behalf of, a negotiator.

(4) For the purposes of this Act, antecedent negotiations shall be taken to begin when the negotiator and the debtor or hirer first enter into communication (including communication by advertisement), and to include any representations made by the negotiator to the debtor or hirer and any other dealings between them.

Antecedent negotiations

Subs. (1)

3H–56   The definition of antecedent negotiations is significant for two reasons:

> (i) the agency provision in s.56(2);
>
> (ii) no agreement will be cancellable under s.67 unless oral representations were made during "antecedent negotiations".

Section 56(1)(b) covers the triangular situation where the dealer sells the goods to a finance company which in turn contracts with the debtor to supply the goods to the debtor on hire-purchase, conditional sale or credit sale agreement terms. In that situation the dealer who introduces the debtor to the finance company is a "credit-broker" (s.189(1)). Section 56(1)(b) does not, however, cover the situation where the contract made by the finance company with the customer is a regulated consumer hire agreement (*Moorgate Mercantile Leasing Ltd v. Gell and Ugolini* [1988] C.C.L.R. 1). Section 56(1)(c) covers the situation where, pursuant to arrangements between the creditor and the supplier, the creditor provides credit for the debtor to pay for goods or services supplied by the supplier, *e.g.* the debtor pays for the goods using his (regulated) credit card.

Deemed agency

3H–57   Subsection (2) reverses the common law rule whereby the dealer (*e.g.* in the hire-purchase triangular situation) is not normally the agent of the finance company (*Branwhite v. Worcester Works Finance* [1969] 1 A.C. 552). It means, *inter alia*, that statements, promises, etc., made to the debtor by the dealer are regarded as also made by the creditor who can accordingly be liable for misrepresentation or breach of a contractual promise. The deemed agency, in a s.56(1)(b) situation, relates only to statements and promises "in relation to" the goods being supplied to the debtor. This *does*, however, include, where the debtor has traded in a vehicle in part exchange for the new one (the "goods"), a promise by the dealer to use the part exchange allowance (or part of it) to discharge the debtor's indebtedness under the credit agreement by which the debtor acquired the traded in vehicle (*Forthright Finance Ltd v. Ingate* [1997] 4 All E.R. 99; [1997] C.C.L.R. 95). Negotiations relating to the part-exchange and to the new vehicle were all part of the same transaction.

For a situation where at common law the dealer was held (contrary to the usual position) to have been expressly authorised by the finance company to accept the debtor's offer to enter a conditional sale agreement, thereby making the agreement by releasing the vehicle to the debtor upon the latter signing the finance company's proposal form, see *Carlyle Finance Ltd v. Pallas Industrial Finance Ltd* [1999] C.C.L.R. 85, CA.

Withdrawal from prospective agreement

57.—(1) The withdrawal of a party from a prospective regulated **3H–58** agreement shall operate to apply this Part to the agreement, any linked transaction and any other thing done in anticipation of the making of the agreement as it would apply if the agreement were made and then cancelled under section 69.

(2) The giving to a party of a written or oral notice which, however expressed, indicates the intention of the other party to withdraw from a prospective regulated agreement operates as a withdrawal from it.

(3) Each of the following shall be deemed to be the agent of the creditor or owner for the purpose of receiving a notice under subsection (2)—

(a) a credit-broker or supplier who is the negotiator in antecedent negotiations, and

(b) any person who, in the course of a business carried on by him, acts on behalf of the debtor or hirer in any negotiations for the agreement.

(4) Where the agreement, if made, would not be a cancellable agreement, subsection (1) shall nevertheless apply as if the contrary were the case.

Withdrawal from prospective agreement

Deemed cancellation

By s.57(1) a prospective agreement which is withdrawn from, is deemed to have **3H–59** been made, to have been a cancellable one and to have been cancelled, with the result that ss.67–73 below apply. For those linked transactions to which this provision does not apply, see commentary to s.19.

Deemed agency

A wider range of persons than negotiator in antecedent negotiations is deemed **3H–60** agent of the creditor or owner for the purpose of receiving notice of the withdrawal. It could, for example, include the debtor's solicitor if he helped the debtor arrange the prospective agreement. A person deemed to receive a notice as agent of the creditor or owner is under a duty to transmit the notice to the creditor or owner forthwith (s.175).

Section 57 does not apply to agreements listed in ss.74 and 82(4).

Opportunity for withdrawal from prospective land mortgage

3H–61   **58.**—(1) Before sending to the debtor or hirer, for his signature, an unexecuted agreement in a case where the prospective regulated agreement is to be secured on land (the "mortgaged land"), the creditor or owner shall give the debtor or hirer a copy of the unexecuted agreement which contains a notice in the prescribed form indicating the right of the debtor or hirer to withdraw from the prospective agreement, and how and when the right is exercisable, together with a copy of any other document referred to in the unexecuted agreement.

(2) Subsection (1) does not apply to—

(a) a restricted-use credit agreement to finance the purchase of the mortgaged land, or

(b) an agreement for a bridging loan in connection with the purchase of the mortgaged land or other land.

Opportunity for withdrawal from prospective land mortgage

3H–62   In the case of cancellable agreements, the debtor or hirer is given a cooling off period after the agreement is made during which time he is free to cancel the agreement (ss.67–69). Those provisions do not apply, however, to any agreement secured on land. Section 58, read together with s.61(2) and (3), gives the debtor or hirer a right to a pre-contract "consideration period" of at least seven days free from sales pressure, before he becomes committed to the agreement. The form for the s.58(1) notice is prescribed in the Consumer Credit (Cancellation Notices and Copies of Documents) Regulations 1983 (S.I. 1983 No. 1557). Failure to comply with the requirements of the sections renders the agreement "improperly executed" (s.61(2)). For the consequences of improper execution, see s.65.

Sections 58 and 61 do not apply to agreements listed in ss.74 and 82(4).

Agreement to enter future agreement void

3H–63   **59.**—(1) An agreement is void if, and to the extent that, it purports to bind a person to enter as debtor or hirer into a prospective regulated agreement.

(2) Regulations may exclude from the operation of subsection (1) agreements such as are described in the regulations.

Agreement to enter future agreement void

3H–64   The section does not prevent the *creditor or owner* being bound to enter into a regulated agreement. It does not apply to agreements listed in ss.74(1) and 82(4). Nor does it apply to written agreements to enter into either of the two kinds of prospective agreement excluded from its application by the Consumer Credit (Agreements to enter Prospective Agreements) (Exemption) Regulations 1983 (S.I. 1983 No. 1552):

(i) consumer hire agreements where the hirer requires, or holds himself out as requiring, the goods for business purposes, and

(ii) restricted-use credit agreements for fixed-sum credit to finance the purchase of goods which the debtor requries, or holds himself as requiring, for business purposes.

The Regulations contain further detailed requirements for these two exclusions.

MAKING THE AGREEMENT

Form and content of agreements

3H–65   **60.**—(1) The Secretary of State shall make regulations as to the form and content of documents embodying regulated agreements, and the regulations shall contain such provisions as appear to him appropriate with a view to ensuring that the debtor or hirer is made aware of—

    (a) the rights and duties conferred or imposed on him by the agreement,

    (b) the amount and rate of the total charge for credit (in the case of a consumer credit agreement),

    (c) the protection and remedies available to him under this Act, and

    (d) any other matters which, in the opinion of the Secretary of State, it is desirable for him to know about in connection with the agreement.

(2) Regulations under subsection (1) may in particular—

    (a) require specified information to be included in the prescribed manner in documents, and other specified material to be excluded;

    (b) contain requirements to ensure that specified information is clearly brought to the attention of the debtor or hirer, and that one part of a document is not given insufficient or excessive prominence compared with another.

(3) If, on an application made to the OFT by a person carrying on a consumer credit business or a consumer hire business, it appears to the OFT impracticable for the applicant to comply with any requirement of regulations under subsection (1) in a particular case, it may, by notice to the applicant direct that the requirement be waived or varied in relation to such agreements, and subject to such conditions (if any), as it may specify, and this Act and the regulations shall have effect accordingly.

(4) The OFT shall give a notice under subsection (3) only if it is satisfied that to do so would not prejudice the interests of debtors or hirers.

Note —Amended by the Enterprise Act 2002, s.278 and Sched.25.   **3H–66**

Form and content of agreements

The Consumer Credit (Agreements) Regulations 1983 (S.I. 1983 No. 1553), as **3H–67** amended with effect from May 31, 2005 by the Consumer Credit (Agreements)(Amendment) Regulations 2004 (S.I. 2004 No. 1482), lay down detailed requirements as to form and content. Failure to comply with the regulations will result in the agreement being improperly executed (see ss.61(1) and 65). These sections—and the regulations—do not apply to agreements listed in ss.74 and 82(4).

Dispensations —Granted under subss. (3) and (4) by the Office of Fair Trading are **3H–68** entered in the Consumer Credit Public Register.

Signing of agreement

61.—(1) A regulated agreement is not properly executed unless—   **3H–69**

    (a) a document in the prescribed form itself containing all the prescribed terms and conforming to regulations under section 60(1) is signed in the prescribed manner both by the debtor or hirer and by or on behalf of the creditor or owner, and

    (b) the document embodies all the terms of the agreement, other than implied terms, and

CONSUMER

    (c) the document is, when presented or sent to the debtor or hirer for signature, in such a state that all its terms are readily legible.

(2) In addition, where the agreement is one to which section 58(1) applies, it is not properly executed unless—

    (a) the requirements of section 58(1) were complied with, and

    (b) the unexecuted agreement was sent, for his signature, to the debtor or hirer by an appropriate method not less than seven days after a copy of it was given to him under section 58(1), and

    (c) during the consideration period, the creditor or owner refrained from approaching the debtor or hirer (whether in person, by telephone or letter, or in any other way) except in response to a specific request made by the debtor or hirer after the beginning of the consideration period, and

    (d) no notice of withdrawal by the debtor or hirer was received by the creditor or the owner before the sending of the unexecuted agreement.

(3) In subsection (2)(c), "the consideration period" means the period beginning with the giving of the copy under section 58(1) and ending—

    (a) at the expiry of seven days after the day on which the unexecuted agreement is sent, for his signature, to the debtor or hirer, or

    (b) on its return by the debtor or hirer after signature by him,

whichever first occurs.

(4) Where the debtor or hirer is a partnership or an unincorporated body of persons, subsection (1)(a) shall apply with the substitution for "by the debtor or hirer" of "by or on behalf of the debtor or hirer".

3H–69.1   *Note* —Amended by the Consumer Credit Act 1974 (Electronic Communications) Order 2004 (S.I. 2004 No. 3236).

Signing of agreement

3H–70   Where there is more than one debtor or hirer (other than a partnership or unincorporated body), the requirements of s.61(1)(a) apply in relation to each of them (ss.185(1)(a) and 185(3)). Thus each must sign. For "embodies" in s.61(1)(b), see s.189(4). Failure to comply with the requirements of s.61 (including those of the Consumer Credit (Agreements) Regulations 1983) will result in the agreement being improperly executed. For consequences of improper execution, see s.65. An agreement signed by the debtor or hirer in blank before the financial details are completed will be improperly executed as not complying with s.61(1)(a) and will be unenforceable by the creditor or owner (*P.B. Leasing Ltd v. Patel and Patel* [1995] C.C.L.R. 82, see commentary to s.127). Section 61 does not apply to agreements listed in ss.74 and 82(4).

3H–71   *Subss. (2) and (3)* —See s.58 and commentary thereon.

Duty to supply copy of unexecuted agreement

3H–72   **62.**—(1) If the unexecuted agreement is presented personally to the debtor or hirer for his signature, but on the occasion when he signs it the document does not become an executed agreement, a copy of it, and of any other document referred to in it, must be there and then delivered to him.

(2) If the unexecuted agreement is sent to the debtor or hirer for his signature, a copy of it, and of any other document referred to in it, must be sent to him at the same time.

(3) A regulated agreement is not properly executed if the requirements of this section are not observed.

Duty to supply copy of unexecuted agreement

Sections 62 and 63 lay down requirements as to the service of copies on the debtor or hirer. Their effect is, broadly, as follows: **3H–73**

  (i) An agreement becomes "executed" only when it is signed by, or on behalf of, both parties.

  (ii) If the agreement becomes executed (*i.e.* signed by both parties) on the occasion when it is presented personally to the debtor or hirer, then the latter must be given a copy of the executed agreement on that occasion.

  (iii) If the agreement does not become executed on the occasion when it is presented personally to the debtor or hirer, then the latter must be given a copy of the unexecuted agreement on that occasion.

  (iv) If the agreement (by definition unexecuted) is sent to the debtor or hirer for his signature, a copy of that unexecuted agreement must be sent at the same time.

  (v) If the agreement does not become executed on the occasion when the debtor signs it, then a copy of the executed agreement must be served on the debtor within seven days of the making of the agreement; if the agreement is a cancellable one (within s.67), this copy must be sent by post.

Where there is more than one debtor or hirer (other than a partnership or unincorporated body) each must be served with the copy or copies required by ss.62 and s.63 (s.185(1)(a)). Section 180(1)(b) allows for regulations to authorise:

  (i) the omission from a copy, of material contained in the original; or

  (ii) its inclusion in condensed form.

Section 180(3) also allows for regulations to remove the duty to supply a copy of a document (*e.g.* an Act of Parliament) referred to in the agreement in the case of documents of specified kinds. These powers have been exercised in the Consumer Credit (Cancellation Notices and Copies of Documents) Regulations 1983 (S.I. 1983 No. 1557).

For consequences of improper execution, see s.65. Sections 62 and 63 do not apply to agreements listed in ss.74 and 82(4).

Duty to supply copy of executed agreement

63.—(1) If the unexecuted agreement is presented personally to **3H–74** the debtor or hirer for his signature, and on the occasion when he signs it the document becomes an executed agreement, a copy of the executed agreement, and of any other document referred to in it, must be there and then delivered to him.

(2) A copy of the executed agreement, and of any other document referred to in it, must be given to the debtor or hirer within the seven days following the making of the agreement unless—

    (a) subsection (1) applies, or

    (b) the unexecuted agreement was sent to the debtor or hirer for his signature and, on the occasion of his signing it, the document became an executed agreement.

(3) In the case of a cancellable agreement, a copy under subsection (2) must be sent by an appropriate method.

(4) In the case of a credit-token agreement, a copy under subsection (2) need not be given within the seven days following the making of the agreement if it is given before or at the time when the credit-token is given to the debtor.

(5) A regulated agreement is not properly executed if the requirements of this section are not observed.

3H–74.1   *Note* —Amended by the Consumer Credit Act 1974 (Electronic Communications) Order 2004 (S.I. 2004 No. 3236).

Duty to supply copy of executed agreement
3H–75   See commentary to s.62.

Duty to give notice of cancellation rights
3H–76   **64.**—(1) In the case of a cancellable agreement, a notice in the prescribed form indicating the right of the debtor or hirer to cancel the agreement, how and when that right is exercisable, and the name and address of a person to whom notice of cancellation may be given,—

    (a) must be included in every copy given to the debtor or hirer under section 62 or 63, and

    (b) except where section 63(2) applied, must also be sent by the appropriate method to the debtor or hirer within the seven days following the making of the agreement.

(2) In the case of a credit-token agreement, a notice under subsection (1)(b) need not be sent by the appropriate method within seven days following the making of the agreement if either—

    (a) it is sent by the appropriate method to the debtor or hirer before the credit-token is given to him, or

    (b) it is sent by the appropriate method to him together with the credit-token.

(3) Regulations may provide that except where section 63(2) applied a notice sent under subsection (1)(b) shall be accompanied by a further copy of the executed agreement, and of any other document referred to in it.

(4) Regulations may provide that subsection (1)(b) is not to apply in the case of agreements such as are described in the regulations, being agreements made by a particular person, if—

    (a) on application by that person to the OFT, the OFT has determined that, having regard to—

        (i) the manner in which antecedent negotiations for agreements with the applicant of that description are conducted, and

        (ii) the information provided to debtors or hirers before such agreements are made,

the requirement imposed by subsection (1)(b) can be dispensed with without prejudicing the interests of debtors or hirers; and

    (b) any conditions imposed by the OFT in making the determination are complied with.

(5) A cancellable agreement is not properly executed if the requirements of this section are not observed.

Note —Amended by the Enterprise Act 2002, s.278 and Sched.25 and by the **3H–77**
Consumer Credit Act 1974 (Electronic Communications) Order 2004 (S.I. 2004 No.
3236).

Duty to give notice of cancellation rights

For "cancellable agreement", see s.67. For the required form for the notice of **3H–78**
cancellation rights, see the Consumer Credit (Cancellation Notices and Copies of
Documents) Regulations 1983 (S.I. 1983 No. 1557). A notice in that form must be
included in each copy of the executed or unexecuted agreement required by ss.62 and
63. Where only one copy is required, then the notice must also be sent within seven
days of the making of the agreement either by post or, if the debtor or hirer has
agreed to electronic communication, by electronic transmission in accordance with
s.176A. Failure to comply with s.64(1) renders the agreement improperly executed; it
will be unenforceable against the debtor or hirer (ss.65 and 127(4)(b)). No regulations
have been made pursuant to s.64(3).

Dispensations —By virtue of s.64(4) and the Consumer Credit (Notice of Cancella- **3H–79**
tion Rights) (Exemptions) Regulations 1983 (S.I. 1983 No. 1558), the Office of Fair
Trading may grant dispensations in respect of certain types of mail order agreement.
Determinations granting such dispensations are recorded in the Consumer Credit
Public Register.

Section 64 does not apply to agreements listed in ss.74 and 82(4).

Consequences of improper execution

65.—(1) An improperly-executed regulated agreement is enforce- **3H–80**
able against the debtor or hirer on an order of the court only.

(2) A retaking of goods or land to which a regulated agreement
relates is an enforcement of the agreement.

Consequences of improper execution

An agreement is "improperly-executed" if the documentation requirements in **3H–81**
ss.57–63 are not complied with. The consequence is that the creditor will be unable to
enforce the agreement against the debtor or hirer without a court order. The court's
power to grant an order is restricted by s.127 (*q.v.*). Sometimes, as in the case of non-
compliance with s.64(1), the court must refuse such an order. Otherwise, the court has
a discretion. For the effect of this on "security", see s.113. Section 65(2) does not
preclude the re-taking of goods or land where it is done with the consent of the
debtor or hirer given at the time of the re-possession (see s.173(3)). If the debtor or
hirer has disposed of the goods wrongfully to a third party, then arguably recovery of
them from that third party would not be prohibited since it would not be an enforcement of the agreement "against the debtor or hirer". See the case law on the rather
different wording of s.90. Similarly, if say a hire purchase or consumer hire agreement
has terminated leaving the creditor with ownership, the creditor has a right to recover
the goods independently of the agreement, *i.e.* on the basis of his ownership, and,
arguably, in recovering the goods would not be enforcing the agreement but relying
on his ownership as the basis of the claim (see *Bowmaker v. Barnet Instruments Ltd* [1945]
K.B. 65). Section 65(2) appears to deny such an argument.

There is no sanction provided for breach of s.65 but such a breach may be taken
into account by the Office of Fair Trading in determining if the creditor or owner is fit
to have a licence (see s.170(1) and (2)).

Section 65 does not apply to agreements listed in ss.74 and 82(4).

Procedure

For the relevant procedural rules see the notes to s.127 and the Introductory Note **3H–82**
About Procedure at the start of this Act (above).

Acceptance of credit-tokens

66.—(1) The debtor shall not be liable under a credit-token agree- **3H–83**
ment for use made of the credit-token by any person unless the
debtor had previously accepted the credit-token, or the use constituted an acceptance of it by him.

(2) The debtor accepts a credit-token when—

    (a) it is signed, or

    (b) a receipt for it is signed, or

    (c) it is first used,

either by the debtor himself or by a person who, pursuant to the agreement, is authorised by him to use it.

Acceptance of credit-tokens

3H–84   This section provides for the earliest point at which the debtor may become liable in respect of use/misuse of a credit-token. See s.171(4)(a) for the burden of proof, and ss.83 and 84 for debtor's liability for subsequent misuse of credit facilities including credit-tokens. The Banking Code of Practice and the Finance and Leasing Association's Code of Practice contain similar provisions causing card issuers to bear the full losses of misuse before the card is received by the customer.

CANCELLATION OF CERTAIN AGREEMENTS WITHIN COOLING–OFF PERIOD

Cancellable agreements

3H–85   67. A regulated agreement may be cancelled by the debtor or hirer in accordance with this Part if the antecedent negotiations included oral representations made when in the presence of the debtor or hirer by an individual acting as, or on behalf of, the negotiator, unless—

    (a) the agreement is secured on land, or is a restricted-use credit agreement to finance the purchase of land or is an agreement for a bridging loan in connection with the purchase of land, or

    (b) the unexecuted agreement is signed by the debtor or hirer at premises at which any of the following is carrying on any business (whether on a permanent or temporary basis)—

        (i) the creditor or owner;

        (ii) any party to a linked transaction (other than the debtor or hirer or a relative of his);

        (iii) the negotiator in any antecedent negotiations.

Cancellable agreements

3H–86   A statement is not a "representation" unless it:

    (a) is a statement of fact or opinion or an undertaking as to the future; and

    (b) is capable of inducing the proposed debtor or hirer to enter the regulated agreement (*Moorgate Services Ltd v. Kabir* [1995] C.C.L.R. 74, CA).

A regulated agreement is cancellable if four conditions are satisfied:

    (i) antecedent negotiations included oral representations made in the presence of the debtor or hirer by or on behalf of the creditor or owner;

    (ii) the unexecuted agreement was signed by the debtor or hirer away from business premises identified in s.67(b);

    (iii) the agreement does not fall within s.67(a), s.74(1) or (2), or s.82(4) or (6);

    (iv) the agreement is not cancellable under the provisions of the Timeshare Act 1992.

Where negotiations are conducted by a dealer leading up to the common tripartite arrangement whereby the dealer sells the goods to a finance company which in turn contracts with the debtor to supply them to the debtor on hire-purchase terms, the first of these conditions will be satisfied. Where, however, the resultant agreement between the finance company is a consumer hire agreement, the negotiations between the dealer and the customer are not antecedent negotiations (*Lloyds Bowmaker Leasing*

Ltd v. MacDonald [1993] C.C.L.R. 65). For antecedent negotiations, see s.56. Note that an agreement may be cancellable if signed at the debtor's or hirer's own business premises. In relation to agreements within s.67(a), see ss.58 and 61(2) and (3). An agreement which is not cancellable (*i.e.* within the meaning of the Consumer Credit Act) may nevertheless be cancellable by virtue of other legislation, *e.g.* the Consumer Protection (Cancellation of Contracts Concluded away from Business Premises) Regulations 1987; or the Timeshare Act 1992. When an agreement appears to be cancellable under both the Consumer Credit Act 1974 and the 1987 Regulations just mentioned, the latter do not apply and it is cancellable only under the Consumer Credit Act. On the other hand where an agreement prima facie appears to be cancellable under both the Consumer Credit Act 1974 and the Timeshare Act 1992, it is in fact cancellable only under the Timeshare Act 1992. When the Timeshare Act 1992 was first enacted, the opposite solution was adopted (*i.e.* an agreement *prima facie* falling within the cancellation provisions of both enactments would in fact be cancellable only under the Consumer Credit Act). That position was reversed by s.1(6A) of the Timeshare Act 1992 which was inserted by the Timeshare Regulations 1997 (S.I. 1997 No. 1081).

An agreement which is not cancellable under the Consumer Credit Act may be cancellable under the Consumer Protection (Distance Selling) Regulations 2000. An agreement is unlikely to be cancellable under both, since for an agreement to be cancellable under the former there have to be representations made in the presence of the debtor or hirer, whereas the latter apply only to "distance contracts", namely where the contract is concluded entirely by distance communication. Broadly, an agreement is cancellable under the regulations if it is a "distance contract" and not an "excepted contract". For the meaning of these expressions see the commentary to s.83 at para. 3H–130 below. Besides "excepted contracts", certain other distance contracts are not cancellable under the regulations. These are: timeshare agreements (within the meaning of the Timeshare Act 1992); contracts for food, beverages or other goods used for everyday consumption and supplied to the consumer at his residence or workplace by regular roundsmen; contracts for accommodation, catering, transport or leisure services where the supplier undertakes to supply the services on a specific date or within a specific period. Where a distance contract is cancellable under the regulations and is cancelled, that cancellation operates (reg. 15) also to cancel any "related credit agreement". A "related credit agreement" is any agreement under which fixed-sum credit (fully or partly covering the price of the goods or services under the cancelled distance contract) is supplied either by the supplier or by another person under an arrangement between that person and the supplier. Regulations 15 and 16 provide for the consequences of such cancellation of a related credit agreement. They are modelled on s.71 of the Consumer Credit Act. Thus any credit which has already been advanced, the consumer remains liable to repay in accordance with conditions the same as those in s.71 (*q.v*).

Related to the concept of cancellation is that of canvassing off trade premises (defined in s.48). A regulated agreement made following canvassing off trade premises by someone whose licence did not specifically cover that activity may be unenforceable by virtue of s.40 (*q.v.*).

Distance credit contracts

A credit agreement made entirely by distance communication, though not cancel- **3H–86.1** lable under the Consumer Credit Act , may be cancellable under the Financial Services (Distance Marketing) Regulations 2004 (S.I. 2004 No. 2095) which implemented the European Directive on the distance marketing of financial services (2002/65/EC). Under these regulations a credit agreement concluded at a distance with a consumer (an individual acting outside any business of his) is cancellable by the consumer for a period of 14 days after the day on which the contract is made. This right of cancellation does not apply to: a "related credit agreement" cancelled under reg. 15(1) of the Consumer Protection (Distance Selling) Regulations 2000; a credit agreement cancelled under reg. 6A of the Timeshare Act 1992; a credit agreement where the consumer's obligation to repay is secured by a legal mortgage on land; a restricted-use credit agreement to finance the purchase of land or an existing building, or an agreement for a bridging loan in connection with the purchase of land or an existing building.

Cooling-off period

68. The debtor or hirer may serve notice of cancellation of a cancel- **3H–87**

lable agreement between his signing of the unexecuted agreement and—

(a) the end of the fifth day following the day on which he received a copy under section 63(2) or a notice under section 64(1)(b), or

(b) if (by virtue of regulations made under section 64(4)) section 64(1)(b) does not apply, the end of the fourteenth day following the day on which he signed the unexecuted agreement.

Cooling-off period

3H–88   The notice must be in writing (see ss.189(1) and 69(1) and must be sent by post or, if the person on whom it is served has agreed to electronic communication, by electronic communication in accordance with s.176A. It takes effect upon posting or, in the case of electronic communication, at the time of transmission. See generally, s.69; see also commentary to s.64 for agreements to which s.64(1)(b) does not apply).

Notice of cancellation

3H–89   **69.**—(1) If within the period specified in section 68 the debtor or hirer under a cancellable agreement serves on—

(a) the creditor or owner, or

(b) the person specified in the notice under section 64(1), or

(c) a person who (whether by virtue of subsection (6) or otherwise) is the agent of the creditor or owner,

a notice (a "notice of cancellation") which, however expressed and whether or not conforming to the notice given under section 64(1), indicates the intention of the debtor or hirer to withdraw from the agreement, the notice shall operate—

(i) to cancel the agreement, and any linked transaction, and

(ii) to withdraw any offer by the debtor or hirer, or his relative, to enter into a linked transaction.

(2) In the case of a debtor-creditor-supplier agreement for restricted-use credit financing—

(a) the doing of work or supply of goods to meet an emergency, or

(b) the supply of goods which, before service of the notice of cancellation, had by the act of the debtor or his relative become incorporated in any land or thing not comprised in the agreement or any linked transaction,

subsection (1) shall apply with the substitution of the following for paragraph (i)—

"(i) to cancel only such provisions of the agreement and any linked transaction as—

(aa) relate to the provisions of credit, or

(bb) require the debtor to pay an item in the total charge for credit, or

(cc) subject the debtor to any obligation other than to pay for the doing of the said work, or the supply of the said goods".

(3) Except so far as is otherwise provided, references in this Act to the cancellation of an agreement or transaction do not include a case within subsection (2).

(4) Except as otherwise provided by or under this Act, an agreement or transaction cancelled under subsection (1) shall be treated as if it had never been entered into.

(5) Regulations may exclude linked transactions of the prescribed description from subsection (1)(i) or (ii).

(6) Each of the following shall be deemed to be the agent of the creditor or owner for the purpose of receiving a notice of cancellation—

(a) a credit-broker or supplier who is the negotiator in antecedent negotiations, and

(b) any person who, in the course of a business carried on by him, acts on behalf of the debtor or hirer in any negotiations for the agreement.

(7) Whether or not it is actually received by him, a notice of cancellation sent to a person shall be deemed to be served on him—

(a) in the case of a notice sent by post, at the time of posting, and

(b) in the case of a notice transmitted in the form of an electronic communication in accordance with section 176A(1), at the time of the transmission.

Note —Subsection (7) substituted by the Consumer Credit Act 1974 (Electronic Communications) Order 2004 (S.I. 2004 No. 3236). **3H–89.1**

Notice of cancellation

Broadly, in order to cancel a cancellable agreement, the debtor or hirer must serve **3H–90** a written notice, however expressed, indicating his intention to withdraw from the agreement and must serve it on the creditor or owner or on one of the persons in s.69(6) and must do so before expiry of the deadline in s.68. It takes effect upon posting or, in the case of electronic communication, upon transmission (s.69(7)). A person deemed to receive a notice as agent of the creditor or owner is under a duty to transmit the notice to the creditor or owner forthwith (s.175). For linked transactions which will not be cancelled or withdrawn from by virtue of s.69(1), see commentary to s.19 above.

Effect of cancellation —This is stated in ss.69–73. The Act distinguishes between on **3H–91** the one hand consumer hire agreements and debtor-creditor-supplier agreements, and on the other hand other regulated agreements. For the effect of cancellation of the latter, see s.71. The rest of this commentary relates to the former category. Broadly, the debtor or hirer will not have to make any payments under the agreement and will be entitled to the recovery of any already paid (s.70) but will be required to return any goods already received by him (s.72)—though having a lien over them to enforce repayment of money he has already paid (s.70(1)). If he has given goods in part-exchange, he is entitled to their return (in substantially the same condition) within ten days of cancellation or, failing that, to their part-exchange allowance (s.73). There are exceptions or qualifications to this outline in the case of:

(i) goods or work supplied to meet an emergency; and

(ii) goods (*e.g.* spare parts or garden plants) which the debtor or hirer has incorporated into something else before cancellation (for goods or work in these two categories the debtor or hirer remains liable to pay (s.69(2)).

In any case, the debtor or hirer is not required to return:

(a) perishable goods;

(b) consumable goods which were consumed before cancellation;

(c) goods supplied to meet an emergency; and

(d) goods which before cancellation were incorporated (whether or not by the debtor or hirer) in anything else (s.72(9)).

For the effect of cancellation upon any security, see s.113(3) and (5).

Cancellation: recovery of money paid by debtor or hirer

3H–92 **70.**—(1) On the cancellation of a regulated agreement, and of any linked transaction—

    (a) any sum paid by the debtor or hirer, or his relative, under or in contemplation of the agreement or transaction, including any item in the total charge for credit, shall become repayable, and

    (b) any sum, including any item in the total charge for credit, which but for the cancellation is, or would or might become, payable by the debtor or hirer, or his relative, under the agreement or transaction shall cease to be, or shall not become, so payable, and

    (c) in the case of a debtor-creditor-supplier agreement falling within section 12(b), any sum paid on the debtor's behalf by the creditor to the supplier shall become repayable to the creditor.

(2) If, under the terms of a cancelled agreement or transaction, the debtor or hirer, or his relative, is in possession of any goods, he shall have a lien on them for any sum repayable to him under subsection (1) in respect of that agreement or transaction, or any other linked transaction.

(3) A sum repayable under subsection (1) is repayable by the person to whom it was originally paid, but in the case of a debtor-creditor-supplier agreement falling within section 12(b) the creditor and the supplier shall be under a joint and several liability to repay sums paid by the debtor, or his relative, under the agreement or under a linked transaction falling within section 19(1)(b) and accordingly, in such a case, the creditor shall be entitled, in accordance with rules of court, to have the supplier made a party to any proceedings brought against the creditor to recover any such sums.

(4) Subject to any agreement between them, the creditor shall be entitled to be indemnified by the supplier for loss suffered by the creditor in satisfying his liability under subsection (3), including costs reasonably incurred by him in defending proceedings instituted by the debtor.

(5) Subsection (1) does not apply to any sum which, if not paid by a debtor, would be payable by virtue of section 71, and applies to a sum paid or payable by a debtor for the issue of a credit-token only where the credit-token has been returned to the creditor or surrendered to a supplier.

(6) If the total charge for credit includes an item in respect of a fee or commission charged by a credit-broker, the amount repayable under subsection (1) in respect of that item shall be the excess over £5 of the fee or commission.

(7) If the total charge for credit includes any sum payable or paid by the debtor to a credit-broker otherwise than in respect of a fee or commission charged by him, that sum shall for the purpose of subsection (6) be treated as if it were such a fee or commission.

(8) So far only as is necessary to give effect to section 69(2), this section applies to an agreement or transaction within that subsection as it applies to a cancelled agreement or transaction.

Cancellation: recovery of money paid by debtor or hirer
See generally the commentary to s.69.   **3H–94**

Cancellation: repayment of credit

71.—(1) Notwithstanding the cancellation of a regulated consumer **3H–95**
credit agreement, other than a debtor-creditor-supplier agreement
for restricted-use credit, the agreement shall continue in force so far
as it relates to repayment of credit and payment of interest.

(2) If, following the cancellation of a regulated consumer credit
agreement, the debtor repays the whole or a portion of the credit—

   (a) before the expiry of one month following service of the
       notice of cancellation, or

   (b) in the case of a credit repayable by instalments, before
       the date on which the first instalment is due,

no interest shall be payable on the amount repaid.

(3) If the whole of a credit repayable by instalments is not repaid
on or before the date specified in subsection (2)(b), the debtor shall
not be liable to repay any of the credit except on receipt of a request
in writing in the prescribed form, signed by or on behalf of the creditor, stating the amounts of the remaining instalments (recalculated
by the creditor as nearly as may be in accordance with the agreement
and without extending the repayment period), but excluding any
sum other than principal and interest.

(4) Repayment of a credit, or payment of interest, under a
cancelled agreement shall be treated as duly made if it is made to
any person on whom, under section 69, a notice of cancellation could
have been served, other than a person referred to in section 69(6)(b).

Cancellation: repayment of credit
For the effect of cancellation on security, see s.113(3) and (5).   **3H–96**

Cancellation: return of goods

72.—(1) This section applies where any agreement or transaction **3H–97**
relating to goods, being—

   (a) a restricted-use debtor-creditor-supplier agreement, a
       consumer hire agreement, or a linked transaction to
       which the debtor or hirer under any regulated agree-
       ment is a party, or

   (b) a linked transaction to which a relative of the debtor or
       hirer under any regulated agreement is a party,

is cancelled after the debtor or hirer (in a case within paragraph
(a)) or the relative (in a case within paragraph (b)) has acquired possession of the goods by virtue of the agreement or transaction.

(2) In this section—

   (a) "the possessor" means the person who has acquired pos-
       session of the goods as mentioned in subsection (1),

   (b) "the other party" means the person from whom the pos-
       sessor acquired possession and

(c) "the pre-cancellation period" means the period beginning when the possessor acquired possession and ending with the cancellation.

(3) The possessor shall be treated as having been under a duty throughout the pre-cancellation period—

(a) to retain possession of the goods, and

(b) to take reasonable care of them.

(4) On the cancellation, the possessor shall be under a duty, subject to any lien, to restore the goods to the other party in accordance with this section, and meanwhile to retain possession of the goods and take reasonable care of them.

(5) The possessor shall not be under any duty to deliver the goods except at his own premises and in pursuance of a request in writing signed by or on behalf of the other party and served on the possessor either before, or at the time when, the goods are collected from those premises.

(6) If the possessor—

(a) delivers the goods (whether at his own premises or elsewhere) to any person on whom, under section 69, a notice of cancellation could have been served (other than a person referred to in section 69(6)(b)), or

(b) send the goods at his own expense to such a person.

he shall be discharged from any duty to retain the goods or deliver them to any person.

(7) Where the possessor delivers the goods as mentioned in subsection (6)(a), his obligation to take care of the goods shall cease; and if he sends the goods as mentioned in subsection (6)(b), he shall be under a duty to take reasonable care to see that they are received by the other party and not damaged in transit, but in other respects his duty to take care of the goods shall cease.

(8) Where, at any time during the period of 21 days following the cancellation, the possessor receives such a request as is mentioned in subsection (5), and unreasonably refuses or unreasonably fails to comply with it, his duty to take reasonable care of the goods shall continue until he delivers or sends the goods as mentioned in subsection (6), but if within that period he does not receive such a request his duty to take reasonable care of the goods shall cease at the end of that period.

(9) The preceding provisions of this section do not apply to—

(a) perishable goods, or

(b) goods which by their nature are consumed by use and which, before the cancellation, were so consumed, or

(c) goods supplied to meet an emergency, or

(d) goods which, before the cancellation, had become incorporated in any land or thing not comprised in the cancelled agreement or a linked transaction.

(10) Where the address of the possessor is specified in the executed agreement, references in this section to his own premises are to that address and no other.

(11) Breach of a duty imposed by this section is actionable as a breach of statutory duty.

Cancellation: return of goods

See generally the commentary to s.69.

3H–98

Cancellation: goods given in part-exchange

73.—(1) This section applies on the cancellation of a regulated agreement where, in antecedent negotiations, the negotiator agreed to take goods in part-exchange (the "part-exchange goods") and those goods have been delivered to him.

3H–99

(2) Unless, before the end of the period of ten days beginning with the date of cancellation, the part-exchange goods are returned to the debtor or hirer in a condition substantially as good as when they were delivered to the negotiator, the debtor or hirer shall be entitled to recover from the negotiator a sum equal to the part-exchange allowance, as defined in subsection (7)(b)).

(3) In the case of a debtor-creditor-supplier agreement within section 12(b), the negotiator and the creditor shall be under a joint and several liability to pay to the debtor a sum recoverable under subsection (2).

(4) Subject to any agreement between them, the creditor shall be entitled to be indemnified by the negotiator for loss suffered by the creditor in satisfying his liability under subsection (3), including costs reasonably incurred by him in defending proceedings instituted by the debtor.

(5) During the period of ten days beginning with the date of cancellation, the debtor or hirer, if he is in possession of goods to which the cancelled agreement relates, shall have a lien on them for—

    (a) delivery of the part-exchange goods in a condition substantially as good as when they were delivered to the negotiator, or

    (b) a sum equal to the part-exchange allowance;

and if the lien continues to the end of that period it shall thereafter subsist only as a lien for a sum equal to the part-exchange allowance.

(6) Where the debtor or hirer recovers from the negotiator or creditor, or both of them jointly, a sum equal to the part-exchange allowance, then, if the title of the debtor or hirer to the part-exchange goods has not vested in the negotiator, it shall so vest on the recovery of that sum.

(7) For the purposes of this section—

    (a) the negotiator shall be treated as having agreed to take goods in part-exchange if, in pursuance of the antecedent negotiations, he either purchased or agreed to purchase those goods or accepted or agreed to accept them as part of the consideration for the cancelled agreement, and

    (b) the part-exchange allowance shall be the sum agreed as such in the antecedent negotiations or, if no such agreement was arrived at, such sum as it would have been reasonable to allow in respect of the part-exchange goods if no notice of cancellation had been served.

(8) In an action brought against the creditor for a sum recoverable under subsection (2), he shall be entitled, in accordance with rules of court, to have the negotiator made a party to the proceedings.

Cancellation: goods given in part-exchange

3H–100   See commentary to s.69.

EXCLUSION OF CERTAIN AGREEMENTS FROM PART V

Exclusion of certain agreements from Part V

3H–101   74.—(1) This part (except section 56) does not apply to—

    (a) a non-commercial agreement, or

    (b) a debtor-creditor agreement enabling the debtor to overdraw on a current account, or

    (c) a debtor-creditor agreement to finance the making of such payments arising on, or connected with, the death of a person as may be prescribed.

(2) This Part (except sections 55 and 56) does not apply to a small debtor-creditor-supplier agreement for restricted-use credit.

(2A) In the case of an agreement to which the Consumer Protection (Cancellation of Contracts Concluded away from Business Premises) Regulations 1987 apply the reference in subsection (2) to a small agreement shall be construed as if in section 17(1)(a) and (b) "£35" were substituted for "£50".

(3) Subsection (1)(b) or (c) applies only where the OFT so determines, and such a determination—

    (a) may be made subject to such conditions as the OFT thinks fit, and

    (b) shall be made only if the OFT is of opinion that it is not against the interests of debtors.

(3A) Notwithstanding anything in subsection (3)(b) above, in relation to a debtor-creditor agreement under which the creditor is the Bank of England or a bank within the meaning of the Bankers' Books Evidence Act 1879, the OFT shall make a determination that subsection (1)(b) above applies unless it considers that it would be against the public interest to do so.

(4) If any term of an agreement falling within subsection (1)(c) or (2) is expressed in writing, regulations under section 60(1) shall apply to that term (subject to section 60(3)) as if the agreement were a regulated agreement not falling within subsection (1)(c) or (2).

3H–102   *Note* —Amended by the Banking Act 1979, s.38 and S.I. 1987 No. 2117, reg. 9 and by the Enterprise Act 2002, s.278 and Sched.25.

Exclusion of certain agreements from Part V

3H–103   For "non-commercial agreement" see s.189(1).

3H–104   *Subs.(1)(b)* —"current account" is not defined. The determination (dated December

21, 1989) of the Director General of Fair Trading (now the OFT) covers both formal and informal overdraft agreements where the creditor is a bank.

The determination contains conditions requiring the debtor to be given specified information as to the rate of interest and other credit charges incurred in relation to the overdraft. For interpretation of those conditions, see *Coutts & Co. v. Sebestyen* [2005] EWCA Civ 473, [2005] C.C.L.R. 4 .

Subs.(1)(c) —Covers only agreements financing payments prescribed by the **3H–105** Consumer Credit (Payments Arising on Death) Regulations 1983 (S.I. 1983 No. 1554), namely: capital transfer tax; court fees for grant of probate or of letters of administration (or the resealing in the UK of a Commonwealth or colonial grant); payments to a surety in connection with a guarantee required as a condition of the grant of probate or of letters of administration. The determination (dated December 21, 1989) of the Director General of Fair Trading (now the OFT) limits the effect of subs.(1)(c) to credit granted by a bank to a debtor who is acting in the course of his trade or profession.

PART VI

MATTERS ARISING DURING CURRENCY OF CREDIT OR HIRE AGREEMENTS

Liability of creditor for breaches by supplier

75.—(1) If the debtor under a debtor-creditor-supplier agreement **3H–106** falling within section 12(b) or (c) has, in relation to a transaction financed by the agreement, any claim against the supplier in respect of a misrepresentation or breach of contract, he shall have a like claim against the creditor, who, with the supplier, shall accordingly be jointly and severally liable to the debtor.

(2) Subject to any agreement between them, the creditor shall be entitled to be indemnified by the supplier for loss suffered by the creditor in satisfying his liability under subsection (1), including costs reasonably incurred by him in defending proceedings instituted by the debtor.

(3) Subsection (1) does not apply to a claim—

    (a) under a non-commercial agreement, or

    (b) so far as the claim relates to any single item to which the supplier has attached a cash price not exceeding £100 or more than £30,000.

(4) This section applies notwithstanding that the debtor, in entering into the transaction, exceeded the credit limit or otherwise contravened any term of the agreement.

(5) In an action brought against the creditor under subsection (1) he shall be entitled, in accordance with rules of court, to have the supplier made a party to the proceedings.

Note —Amended by the Consumer Credit (Increase of Monetary Limits) Order **3H–107** 1983 (S.I. 1983 No. 1878).

Liability of creditor for breaches by supplier

This section implements the recommendation of the Crowther Committee that **3H–108** there should be "connected lender liability" where the creditor and the supplier are two different persons and the creditor is, by arrangement with the supplier, providing credit to finance the debtor's purchase (of goods or services) from the supplier. The creditor is jointly and severally liable for the supplier's default but is entitled to an indemnity from the supplier. In the event of the supplier's insolvency the creditor will end up carrying the loss, unless the creditor can claim indemnity against anyone else, *e.g.* under the Civil Liability (Contribution) Act 1978. There is no doubt that s.75 applies where a (regulated) credit card is used by the debtor to pay for goods or services (within the limits in subs.(3)(b)). Credit card companies have variously maintained that s.75 does not apply:

(i) to cards (including replacement cards) issued under agreements made before July 1, 1997 (the commencement date of s.75);

(ii) where it is a second authorised card-holder on the debtor's account who used the card;

(iii) to "four party" credit card transactions *i.e.* where it was not the creditor (the card issuer) who was the "merchant acquirer" who signed up the particular retailer to the credit-card payment system (*e.g.* VISA);

(iv) where a British credit card is used to make a payment abroad.

The first two of these have not been determined in any reported decision. (i) is probably correct, but not in the case of an agreement which has been modified by agreement since July 1, 1977 (see s.82(2)); in any case the credit card companies have agreed "voluntarily" to accept s.75 liability (up to the amount of the credit used on the transaction in question) in relation to pre-July 1977 agreements. (ii) is arguable, but perhaps the second card holder *is* within the definition of "debtor" in s.189(1), see "credit" in s.9(1). (iii) and (iv) were considered in *Office of Fair Trading v. Lloyds TSB Bank Plc, Tesco Personal Finance Limited and American Express Services Europe Limited* [2005] 1 All E.R. 843; [2004] C.C.L.R. 9 (QBD Commercial Court, Nov 12, 2004), where Mrs Justice Gloster held that s.75(1) does apply to "four party" credit card agreements. Her Ladyship held that s.75(1) does not apply, however, where the contract between the debtor and the supplier of the goods or services (the supply contract) has the following characteristics: (a) it was made wholly outside the UK; (b) it was governed by a foreign law, and (c) the goods were delivered, or the services were supplied, outside the UK. Her Ladyship held that that rule is not affected (and s.75(1) still does not apply) where the acts of offer and acceptance (in relation to the supply contract) occurred partly within and partly outside the UK or the goods were despatched outside the UK for delivery within the UK. In *Bank of Scotland v. Alfred Truman* [2005] EWHC 583, [2005] C.C.L.R.3, customers of a car dealer used their credit cards to pay deposits on cars to be supplied by the dealer. The dealer did not have credit card payment processing facilities. The defendant firm of solicitors had such facilities, having signed a merchant services agreement with the firm's bank. The defendant firm used its card processing facilities to process, on behalf of the dealer, the payments of deposits by the car dealer's customers. It was held that section 75 applied to these *five* party credit card transactions.

In *Jarrett v. Barclays Bank and Royal Bank of Scotland* [1999] Q.B. 1; [1997] C.C.L.R. 32, CA, credit was advanced under a credit card agreement and under other regulated agreements to finance the purchase of timeshares in Portugal and Spain. Though in each case a claim by the debtor against the timeshare supplier was, by virtue of the Brussels Convention, subject to the exclusive jurisdiction of the Portuguese or Spanish court, it was held that that did not apply to actions under s.75 against the creditors, *i.e.* the British banks.

Where, relying on a breach of contract or misrepresentation, the debtor rescinds the supply agreement which was financed by a loan agreement within s.12(b) or (c), then a "like claim" under s.75 means a claim to rescind the loan agreement (*United Dominions Trust v. Taylor* [1980] S.L.T. (Sh. Ct.) 28; [1980] C.C.L.R. 29, followed, despite academic criticism, in *Forward Trust Ltd v. Hornsby* [1996] C.C.L.R. 18).

3H–109   *Subs. (3)* —The original figures were increased to the current ones of £100 and £30,000 as from January 1, 1984 (S.I. 1983 No. 1878). The limit refers to the cash price attached to the "item". This is arguably inconsistent with the Consumer Credit Directive (87/102/EEC) which allows a lower limit only where "the *transaction* in question is for an amount less than 200 ECU".

Duty to give notice before taking certain action

3H–110   **76.**—(1) The creditor or owner is not entitled to enforce a term of a regulated agreement by—

(a) demanding earlier payment of any sum, or
(b) recovering possession of any goods or land, or
(c) treating any right conferred on the debtor or hirer by the agreement as terminated, restricted or deferred,

except by or after giving the debtor or hirer not less than seven days' notice of his intention to do so.

(2) Subsection (1) applies only where—

(a) a period for the duration of the agreement is specified in the agreement, and
(b) that period has not ended when the creditor or owner does an act mentioned in subsection (1),

but so applies notwithstanding that, under the agreement, any party is entitled to terminate it before the end of the period so specified.

(3) A notice under subsection (1) is ineffective if not in the prescribed form.

(4) Subsection (1) does not prevent a creditor from treating the right to draw on any credit as restricted or deferred and taking such steps as may be necessary to make the restriction or deferment effective.

(5) Regulations may provide that subsection (1) is not to apply to agreements described by the regulations.

(6) Subsection (1) does not apply to a right of enforcement arising by reason of any breach by the debtor or hirer of the regulated agreement.

Duty to give notice before taking certain action
See commentary to s.98.   **3H–111**

Duty to give information to debtor under fixed sum credit agreement

77.—(1) The creditor under a regulated agreement for fixed-sum **3H–112** credit, within the prescribed period after receiving a request in writing to that effect from the debtor and payment of a fee of £1, shall give the debtor a copy of the executed agreement (if any) and of any other document referred to in it, together with a statement signed by or on behalf of the creditor showing, according to the information to which it is practicable for him to refer—

(a) the total sum paid under the agreement by the debtor;
(b) the total sum which has become payable under the agreement by the debtor but remains unpaid, and the various amounts comprised in that total sum, with the date when each became due; and
(c) the total sum which is to become payable under the agreement by the debtor, and the various amounts comprised in that total sum, with the date, or mode of determining the date, when each becomes due.

(2) If the creditor possesses insufficient information to enable him to ascertain the amounts and dates mentioned in subsection (1)(c), he shall be taken to comply with that paragraph if his statement under

subsection (1) gives the basis on which, under the regulated agreement, they would fall to be ascertained.

(3) Subsection (1) does not apply to—

    (a) an agreement under which no sum is, or will or may become, payable by the debtor, or

    (b) a request made less than one month after a previous request under that subsection relating to the same agreement was complied with.

(4) If the creditor under an agreement fails to comply with subsection (1)—

    (a) he is not entitled, while the default continues, to enforce the agreement; and

    (b) if the default continues for one month he commits an offence.

(5) This section does not apply to a non-commercial agreement.

3H–113   *Note* —Amended by the Consumer Credit (Further Increase of Monetary Amounts) Order 1998 (S.I. 1998 No. 997).

Duty to give information to debtor under fixed sum credit agreement

3H–114   The prescribed period is 12 working days (the Consumer Credit (Prescribed Period for Giving Information) Regulations 1983 (S.I. 1983 No. 1569)). For the binding nature of statements, see s.172.

Duty to give information to debtor under running-account credit agreement

3H–115   **78.**—(1) The creditor under a regulated agreement for running-account credit, within the prescribed period after receiving a request in writing to that effect from the debtor and payment of a fee of £1, shall give the debtor a copy of the executed agreement (if any) and of any other document referred to in it, together with a statement signed by or on behalf of the creditor showing, according to the information to which it is practicable for him to refer—

    (a) the state of the account, and

    (b) the amount, if any, currently payable under the agreement by the debtor to the creditor, and

    (c) the amounts and due dates of any payments which, if the debtor does not draw further on the account, will later become payable under the agreement by the debtor to the creditor.

(2) If the creditor possesses insufficient information to enable him to ascertain the amounts and dates mentioned in subsection (1)(c), he shall be taken to comply with that paragraph if his statement under subsection (1) gives the basis on which, under the regulated agreement, they would fall to be ascertained.

(3) Subsection (1) does not apply to—

    (a) an agreement under which no sum is, or will or may become, payable by the debtor, or

    (b) a request made less than one month after a previous request under that subsection relating to the same agreement was complied with.

(4) Where running-account credit is provided under a regulated agreement, the creditor shall give the debtor statements in the prescribed form, and with the prescribed contents—

    (a) showing according to the information to which it is practicable for him to refer, the state of the account at regular intervals of not more than twelve months, and

    (b) where the agreement provides, in relation to specified periods, for the making of payments by the debtor, or the charging against him of interest or any other sum, showing according to the information to which it is practicable for him to refer the state of the account at the end of each of those periods during which there is any movement in the account.

(5) A statement under subsection (4) shall be given within the prescribed period after the end of the period to which the statement relates.

(6) If the creditor under an agreement fails to comply with subsection (1)—

    (a) he is not entitled, while the default continues, to enforce the agreement; and

    (b) if the default continues for one month he commits an offence.

(7) This section does not apply to a non-commercial agreement, and subsections (4) and (5) do not apply to a small agreement.

Note —Amended by the Consumer Credit (Further Increase of Monetary Amounts) **3H–116** Order 1998 (S.I. 1998 No. 997).

Duty to give information to debtor under running-account credit agreement

  The prescribed period in s.78(1) is 12 working days (the Consumer Credit **3H–117** (Prescribed Period for Giving Information) Regulations 1983 (S.I. 1983 No. 1569)). For the binding nature of statements, see s.172. Section 78(4) requires the provision of regular periodic statements of account in relation to regulated running-account credit agreements. In relation to this duty the prescribed period varies according to the frequency of the use of the account, see the Consumer Credit (Running-account Credit Information) Regulations 1983 (S.I. 1983 No. 1570). The prescribed period is: where the statement includes a demand for payment, one calendar month; where it does not include a demand for payment and there has been no credit or debit balance on the account throughout the period to which it relates, twelve months after there is next a credit or debit balance on the account; where it does not include a demand for payment and, though there has been movement on the account in that period, there is no credit or debit balance on the account at the end of the period to which it relates, twelve months from the end of that period; in all other cases, six months.

Duty to give hirer information

79.—(1) The owner under a regulated consumer hire agreement, **3H–118** within the prescribed period after receiving a request in writing to that effect from the hirer and payment of a fee of £1, shall give to the hirer a copy of the executed agreement and of any other document referred to in it, together with a statement signed by or on behalf of the owner showing, according to the information to which it is practicable for him to refer, the total sum which has become payable under the agreement by the hirer but remains unpaid and the various amounts comprised in that total sum, with the date when each became due.

(2) Subsection (1) does not apply to—

    (a) an agreement under which no sum is, or will or may become, payable by the hirer, or

    (b) a request made less than one month after a previous request under that subsection relating to the same agreement was complied with.

(3) If the owner under an agreement fails to comply with subsection (1)—

    (a) he is not entitled, while the default continues, to enforce the agreement; and

    (b) if the default continues for one month he commits an offence.

(4) This section does not apply to a non-commercial agreement.

3H–119   *Note* —Amended by the Consumer Credit (Further Increase of Monetary Amounts) Order 1998 (S.I. 1998 No. 997).

Duty to give hirer information

3H–120   The prescribed period is 12 working days, (the Consumer Credit (Prescribed Period for Giving Information) Regulations 1983 (S.I. 1983 No. 1569)). For the binding nature of statements, see s.172.

Debtor or hirer to give information about goods

3H–121   **80.**—(1) Where a regulated agreement, other than a non-commercial agreement, requires the debtor or hirer to keep goods to which the agreement relates in his possession or control, he shall, within seven working days after he has received a request in writing to that effect from the creditor or owner, tell the creditor or owner where the goods are.

(2) If the debtor or hirer fails to comply with subsection (1), and the default continues for 14 days, he commits an offence.

Appropriation of payments

3H–122   **81.**—(1) Where a debtor or hirer is liable to make to the same person payments in respect of two or more regulated agreements, he shall be entitled, on making any payment in respect of the agreements which is not sufficient to discharge the total amount then due under all the agreements, to appropriate the sum so paid by him—

    (a) in or towards the satisfaction of the sum due under any one of the agreements, or

    (b) in or towards the satisfaction of the sums due under any two or more of the agreements in such proportions as he thinks fit.

(2) If the debtor or hirer fails to make any such appropriation where one or more of the agreements is—

    (a) a hire-purchase agreement or conditional sale agreement, or

    (b) a consumer hire agreement, or

    (c) an agreement in relation to which any security is provided,

the payment shall be appropriated towards the satisfaction of the sums due under the several agreements respectively in the proportions which those sums bear to one another.

Appropriation of payments

At common law, where the debtor owes two or more debts that have fallen due and they are payable by him to the same person (*e.g.* the debts are both owed to the same creditor, but under different contracts), then the debtor when he makes a payment can appropriate that payment as he chooses between the different debts. If when he pays he communicates no such appropriation to the payee (*i.e.* usually the creditor), the latter may appropriate the payments as the creditor chooses. No appropriation by the creditor is effective until it is communicated to the debtor. An unequivocal appropriation becomes both effective and irrevocable when communicated to the debtor (*Julian Hodge Bank Ltd v. Hall* [1998] C.C.L.R. 14, CA). Where it applies, s.81(2) removes the creditor's common law right of appropriation and provides its own automatic appropriation. It appropriates the payment according to the sums that have fallen "due" under the different agreements. This then takes no account of instalments that have not fallen due at the time of the repayment. Where s.81(2) does not apply, *e.g.* when allocating a payment as between (a) instalments that have already fallen due, and (b) default interest that has accrued under the same agreement for failing to pay the instalments on time, the common law rules apply. In the case of a regulated hire purchase agreement this can have crucial significance in determining whether goods are "protected goods" within s.90 (*Julian Hodge Bank Ltd v. Hall*, above).

3H–123

Variation of agreements

82.—(1) Where, under a power contained in a regulated agreement the creditor or owner varies the agreement, the variation shall not take effect before notice of it is given to the debtor or hirer in the prescribed manner.

3H–124

(2) Where an agreement (a "modifying agreement") varies or supplements an earlier agreement, the modifying agreement shall for the purposes of this Act be treated as—

(a) revoking the earlier agreement, and

(b) containing provisions reproducing the combined effect of the two agreements,

and obligations outstanding in relation to the earlier agreement shall accordingly be treated as outstanding instead in relation to the modifying agreement.

(2A) Subsection (2) does not apply if the modifying agreement is an exempt agreement as a result of section 16(6C).

(3) If the earlier agreement is a regulated agreement but (apart from this subsection) the modifying agreement is not then, unless the modifying agreement is—

(a) for running account credit; or

(b) an exempt agreement as a result of section 16(6C),

it shall be treated as a regulated agreement.

(4) If the earlier agreement is a regulated agreement for running-account credit, and by the modifying agreement the creditor allows the credit limit to be exceeded but intends the excess to be merely temporary, Part V (except section 56) shall not apply to the modifying agreement.

(5) If—

(a) the earlier agreement is a cancellable agreement, and

(b) the modifying agreement is made within the period applicable under section 68 to the earlier agreement, then, whether or not the modifying agreement would, apart from this subsection, be a cancellable agreement, it shall be treated as a cancellable agreement in respect of which a notice may be served under section 68 not later than the end of the period applicable under that section to the earlier agreement.

(5A) Subsection (5) does not apply where the modifying agreement is an exempt agreement as a result of section 16(6C).

(6) Except under subsection (5), a modifying agreement shall not be treated as a cancellable agreement.

(7) This section does not apply to a non-commercial agreement.

Note —Amended by the Financial Services and Markets Act 2000 (Consequential Amendments) Order 2005 (S.I. 2005 No. 2967).

Variation of agreements

3H–125   Subsection (1) deals with a variation which can be made unilaterally by the creditor or owner; *i.e.* because he has that power under the agreement. Subsections (2)–(5) deal with a variation which comes about by a subsequent agreement between the parties.

3H–126   *Unilateral variation* —The Consumer Credit (Notice of Variation of Agreements) Regulations 1977 (S.I. 1977 No. 328), as amended, prescribe a general rule that the debtor or hirer must be given at least seven days' written notice of the change, but that changes in interest rate may normally be given by public notices placed in newspapers and in the creditor's business premises.

3H–127   *Modifying agreements* —An agreement varying an earlier agreement is a modifying agreement. Section 82(2)(b)means that an agreed variation could turn an unregulated agreement into a regulated one. A fixed-sum credit agreement made in 1996 (*i.e.* when the specified figure in s.8(2) was £15,000) and providing the debtor, an individual, with £20,000 worth of credit would be unregulated. If in September 1998, at a time when some of the credit had been repaid and only £10,000 was outstanding, the parties agreed to vary the agreement by adding a further advance of £5,000, this is regarded as a termination of the old agreement and the making of a new agreement providing £15,000 of credit (see also Sched.II, Pt II, Example 24). A regulated modifying agreement will normally be subject to the documentation requirements in s.55 and ss.57–65, though not normally (see s.82(6)) to the cancellation provisions. The Consumer Credit (Agreements) Regulations 1983 (S.I. 1983 No. 1553) make provision for the form and contents of modifying agreements.

Liability for misuse of credit facilities

3H–128   **83.**—(1) The debtor under a regulated consumer credit agreement shall not be liable to the creditor for any loss arising from use of the credit facility by another person not acting, or to be treated as acting, as the debtor's agent.

(2) This section does not apply to a non-commercial agreement, or to any loss in so far as it arises from misuse of an instrument to which section 4 of the Cheques Act 1957 applies.

Liability for misuse of credit facilities

3H–129   Section 83(1) states a general rule which is subject to exceptions stated in s.84. The protection afforded does not, however, extend to the fraudulent use of payment cards (*e.g.* many charge cards) which are issued under exempt agreements (for "exempt agreements" see s.16 above). Similarly it does not apply to the unauthorised use of a cash withdrawal token to withdraw cash from an account, *e.g.* a current account, which has a credit balance—since the protection afforded by s.83 extends only to the unauthorised use of a "credit" facility. In the latter case the Banking Code of Practice (subscribed to by banks and building societies) offers a similar degree of protection to that afforded by ss.83 and 84 (taken together) in the case of misuse of a credit facility.

Fraudulent use of payment card in connection with distance contract

In the case of a distance contract, the Consumer Protection (Distance Selling) **3H–130**
Regulations 2000 (S.I. 2000 No. 2334) give protection to a consumer against the
fraudulent use of any "payment card". A "payment card" includes credit cards, charge
cards, debit cards and store cards. By reg. 21, a consumer is entitled to cancel a payment where fraudulent (unauthorised) use has been made of his payment card in connection with a distance contract. Upon cancelling a payment, the consumer is entitled
to be re-credited, or to have all sums returned by the card issuer. Regulation 21 does
not apply to any contract to which s.83(1) applies. Subject to that qualification, reg. 21
applies where fraudulent (unauthorised) use is made of the consumer's payment card
in connection with a "distance contract" other than an "excepted contract". A typical
distance contract is one which is made by mail order, over the internet, by fax or by
telephone. A contract is a distance contract, if four conditions are satisfied: (i) it
concerns goods or services; (ii) it is between a supplier acting for business purposes
and a consumer (an individual acting for purposes outside his business); (iii) it is
concluded under an organised distance sales or service provision scheme run by the
supplier; and, (iv) the supplier used exclusively distance communication up to, and at
the moment, the contract was made. "Excepted contracts" are: contracts made with a
telecommunications operator via a public pay phone operator; contracts made at an
auction; contracts made via automated vending machines or automated premises (*e.g.*
car parks); contracts for financial services; contracts (other than rental agreements) for
the sale or disposition of an interest in land or for the construction of a building
coupled with the sale or disposition of the land on which the construction is to take
place. For this purpose a rental agreement is one which does not have to be in writing
because of s.2(5)(a) of the Law of Property (Miscellaneous Provisions) Act 1989.

Misuse of credit-tokens

84.—(1) Section 83 does not prevent the debtor under a credit- **3H–131**
token agreement from being made liable to the extent of £50 (or the
credit limit if lower) for loss to the creditor arising from use of the
credit-token by other persons during a period beginning when the
credit-token ceases to be in the possession of any authorised person
and ending when the credit-token is once more in the possession of
an authorised person.

(2) Section 83 does not prevent the debtor under a credit-token
agreement from being made liable to any extent for loss to the creditor from use of the credit-token by a person who acquired possession of it with the debtor's consent.

(3) Subsections (1) and (2) shall not apply to any use of the credit-
token after the creditor has been given oral or written notice that it
is lost or stolen, or is for any other reason liable to misuse.

(3A) Subsections (1) and (2) shall not apply to any use, in connection with a distance contract (other than an excepted contract), of a
card which is a credit-token.

(3B) In subsection (3A), "distance contract" and "excepted
contract" have the meanings given in the Consumer Protection
(Distance Selling) Regulations 2000.

(4) Subsections (1) and (2) shall not apply unless there are
contained in the credit-token agreement in the prescribed manner
particulars of the name, address and telephone number of a person
stated to be the person to whom notice is to be given under subsection (3).

(5) Notice under subsection (3) takes effect when received, but
where it is given orally, and the agreement so requires, it shall be
treated as not taking effect if not confirmed in writing within seven
days.

(6) Any sum paid by the debtor for the issue of the credit-token, to the extent (if any) that it has not been previously offset by use made of the credit-token, shall be treated as paid towards satisfaction of any liability under subsection (1) or (2).

(7) The debtor, the creditor, and any person authorised by the debtor to use the credit-token, shall be authorised persons for the purposes of subsection (1).

(8) Where two or more credit-tokens are given under one credit-token agreement, the preceding provisions of this section apply to each credit-token separately.

3H–132 *Note* —Amended by the Consumer Credit (Further Increase of Monetary Amounts) Order 1998 (S.I. 1998 No. 997). Subss. (3A) and (3B) were added by the Consumer Protection (Distance Selling) Regulations 2000 (S.I. 2000 No. 2334).

Misuse of credit-tokens

3H–133 See commentary to s.83. The original figure of £30 in s.84(1) was raised to the current one of £50 as from May 20, 1985. The commonplace example is that of unauthorised use of a stolen credit card. For the burden of proof as to whether use was authorised or whether any unauthorised use occurred before or after notice had been given under s.84(3), see s.171(4)(b). The debtor has no liability in respect of use of a credit-token before he has "accepted" it (s.66). For "distance contract" and "excepted contract" in subss. (3A) and (3B) see commentary to s.83.

Duty on issue of new credit-tokens

3H–134 **85.**—(1) Whenever, in connection with a credit-token agreement, a credit-token (other than the first) is given by the creditor to the debtor, the creditor shall give the debtor a copy of the executed agreement (if any) and of any other document referred to in it.

(2) If the creditor fails to comply with this section—

    (a) he is not entitled, while the default continues, to enforce the agreement; and

    (b) if the default continues for one month he commits an offence.

(3) This section does not apply to a small agreement.

Death of debtor or hirer

3H–135 **86.**—(1) The creditor or owner under a regulated agreement is not entitled, by reason of the death of the debtor or hirer, to do an act specified in paragraphs (a) to (e) section 87(1) if at the death the agreement is fully secured.

(2) If at the death of the debtor or hirer a regulated agreement is only partly secured or is unsecured, the creditor or owner is entitled, by reason of the death of the debtor or hirer, to do an act specified in paragraphs (a) to (e) section 87(1) on an order of the court only.

(3) This section applies in relation to the termination of an agreement only where—

    (a) a period for its duration is specified in the agreement, and

    (b) that period has not ended when the creditor or owner purports to terminate the agreement,

but so applies notwithstanding that, under the agreement, any party is entitled to terminate it before the end of the period so specified.

(4) This section does not prevent the creditor from treating the right to draw on any credit as restricted or deferred, and taking such steps as may be necessary to make the restriction or deferment effective.

(5) This section does not affect the operation of any agreement providing for payment of sums—

    (a) due under the regulated agreement, or

    (b) becoming due under it on the death of the debtor or hirer,

out of the proceeds of a policy of assurance on his life.

(6) For the purposes of this section an act is done by reason of the death of the debtor or hirer if it is done under a power conferred by the agreement which is—

    (a) exercisable on his death, or

    (b) exercisable at will and exercised at any time after his death.

Death of debtor or hirer

The object is to prevent the creditor or owner being entitled to terminate an agree- **3H–136** ment (other than in the sense of refusing to allow further drawings of credit, *e.g.* under a credit card agreement) simply because of the death of the debtor or hirer (or of any one of the debtors or hirers—s.185(4)). If the agreement is not "fully secured" then the creditor may be able to terminate the agreement by an order of the court, but only if he can satisfy the requirements in s.128. The same restrictions apply to prevent the creditor doing any of the other acts listed in s.87(1). Even though the debtor may have died, s.86 does not, however, prevent the creditor being entitled to do one of those things for some reason other than the death, *e.g.* by reason of a breach of the agreement (providing in that case that s.87 is complied with). "Fully secured" is not defined, but presumably means an agreement in relation to which there is security which if realised at the time of the debtor's or hirer's death would cover the whole of the outstanding debt under the agreement.

Procedure

Where a court order is required under s.86(2) then the claim is governed by the **3H–137** Consumer Credit Act procedure in the Consumer Credit Practice Direction at para. 7BPD.1, unless the claim relates to the recovery of land. If it is a mortgage repossesion action, the procedure set out in CPR Pt 55 should be used. See further, the Introductory Note About Procedure at the start of this Act.

PART VII

DEFAULT AND TERMINATION

DEFAULT NOTICES

Need for default notice

87.—(1) Service of a notice on the debtor or hirer in accordance **3H–138** with section 88 (a "default notice") is necessary before the creditor or owner can become entitled, by reason of any breach by the debtor or hirer of a regulated agreement—

    (a) to terminate the agreement, or

    (b) to demand earlier payment of any sum, or

(c) to recover possession of any goods or land, or

(d) to treat any right conferred on the debtor or hirer by the agreement as terminated, restricted or deferred, or

(e) to enforce any security.

(2) Subsection (1) does not prevent the creditor from treating the right to draw upon any credit as restricted or deferred, and taking such steps as may be necessary to make the restriction or deferment effective.

(3) The doing of an act by which a floating charge becomes fixed is not enforcement of a security.

(4) Regulations may provide that subsection (1) is not to apply to agreements described by the regulations.

Need for default notice

3H–139   Section 87 does not give the creditor or owner the right to take any of the actions listed in s.87(1). Its effect is that if he has that right, *e.g.* by virtue of a provision in the agreement or because of a repudiation by the debtor, he will not be entitled to exercise it until a default notice has been served (and has expired without the default having been rectified). This restriction applies only where the right to do one of those acts arises by reason of a breach of the agreement by the debtor or hirer. Where, however, it arises by some other reason (*e.g.* the agreement gives the creditor the right to terminate the agreement on the debtor becoming unemployed), then ss.76 and 98 may require prior service of a notice. The inclusion of s.87(1)(b) in the list means that an accelerated payments clause cannot be activated without service of a default notice (or a notice under s.76). Copies of any default notice must be served on each debtor or hirer (*i.e.* where there is more than one), s.185(1)(a) and on any surety (s.111). Notices served on the debtor or hirer under ss.76(1), 87(1) and 98(1) must be given in paper form: the Consumer Credit (Enforcement, Default and Termination Notices) Regulations 1983 (S.I. 1983 No. 1561), as amended. The same regulations state that ss.76(1), 87(1) and 98(1) do not apply to non-commercial agreements in relation to which no security has been provided. For content and effect of default notice, see s.88. For default notice sent by post and never arriving, see s.176.

Contents and effect of default notice

3H–140   **88.**—(1) The default notice must be in the prescribed form and specify—

(a) the nature of the alleged breach;

(b) if the breach is capable of remedy, what action is required to remedy it and the date before which that action is to be taken;

(c) if the breach is not capable of remedy, the sum (if any) required to be paid as compensation for the breach, and the date before which it is to be paid.

(2) A date specified under subsection (1) must not be less than seven days after the date of service of the default notice, and the creditor or owner shall not take action such as is mentioned in section 87(1) before the date so specified or (if no requirement is made under subsection (1)) before those seven days have elapsed.

(3) The default notice must not treat as a breach failure to comply with a provision of the agreement which becomes operative only on breach of some other provision, but if the breach of that other provision is not duly remedied or compensation demanded under subsection (1) is not duly paid, or (where no requirement is made under subsection (1)) if the seven days mentioned in subsection (2) have

elapsed, the creditor or owner may treat the failure as a breach and section 87(1) shall not apply to it.

(4) The default notice must contain information in the prescribed terms about the consequences of failure to comply with it.

(5) A default notice making a requirement under subsection (1) may include a provision for the taking of action such as is mentioned in section 87(1) at any time after the restriction imposed by subsection (2) will cease, together with a statement that the provision will be ineffective if the breach is duly remedied or the compensation duly paid.

Contents and effects of default notice

For the prescribed form, see the Consumer Credit (Enforcement, Default and Termination Notices) Regulations 1983 (S.I. 1983 No. 1561). The usual default is a failure to pay instalments. In that case, the action required to remedy the default, and which s.88(1)(b) requires the default notice to specify, is payment of the arrears together with any default interest owing on those arrears. If the default notice specifies a figure more than the giver of the notice is entitled to demand, then the default notice is invalid, *Woodchester Lease Management Services Ltd v. Swain* [1999] 1 W.L.R. 263; [1999] C.C.L.R. 8, CA, although the court might overlook an error which was no more than *de minimis*. Besides complying with s.88 and with the regulations, the default notice must not put upon the debtor a repudiation when he has not committed one and must make clear when it expires (*Eshun v. Moorgate Mercantile Co.* [1971] 1 W.L.R. 722 (decided under the earlier provisions of the Hire Purchase Act 1965). If the debtor or hirer rectifies the breach (*i.e.* by taking the action specified in s.88(1)(b) or (c)) the breach is taken not to have occurred (s.89). As soon as a default notice is served, the debtor or hirer is eligible to apply for a time order under s.129, under which the court could grant extra time for paying off arrears or remedying the breach. Even if the debtor does not apply for a time order and the breach is not rectified before the default notice expires, the creditor or owner may still face a restriction on enforcing the agreement. Thus he may not be entitled to recover goods or enter land without a court order (ss.90 and 92) and, if he brings proceedings to enforce the agreement, the debtor or hirer may in those proceedings apply for a time order.

3H–141

Compliance with default notice

89. If before the date specified for that purpose in the default notice the debtor or hirer takes the action specified under section 88(1)(b) or (c) the breach shall be treated as not having occurred.

3H–142

FURTHER RESTRICTION OF REMEDIES FOR DEFAULT

Retaking of protected hire-purchase, etc., goods

90.—(1) At any time when—

    (a) the debtor is in breach of a regulated hire-purchase or a regulated conditional sale agreement relating to goods, and

    (b) the debtor has paid to the creditor one-third or more of the total price of the goods, and

    (c) the property in the goods remains in the creditor,

the creditor is not entitled to recover possession of the goods from the debtor except on an order of the court.

(2) Where under a hire-purchase or conditional sale agreement the creditor is required to carry out any installation and the agreement specifies, as part of the total price, the amount to be paid in respect of the installation (the "installation charge") the reference in

3H–143

CONSUMER

subsection (1)(b) to one-third of the total price shall be construed as a reference to the aggregate of the installation charge and one-third of the remainder of the total price.

(3) In a case where—

(a) subsection (1)(a) is satisfied, but not subsection (1)(b), and

(b) subsection (1)(b) was satisfied on a previous occasion in relation to an earlier agreement, being a regulated hire-purchase or regulated conditional sale agreement, between the same parties, and relating to any of the goods comprised in the later agreement (whether or not other goods were also included),

subsection (1) shall apply to the later agreement with the omission of paragraph (b).

(4) If the later agreement is a modifying agreement, subsection (3) shall apply with the substitution, for the second reference to the later agreement, of a reference to the modifying agreement.

(5) Subsection (1) shall not apply, or shall cease to apply, to an agreement if the debtor has terminated, or terminates, the agreement.

(6) Where subsection (1) applies to an agreement at the death of the debtor, it shall continue to apply (in relation to the possessor of the goods) until the grant of probate or administration, or (in Scotland) confirmation (on which the personal representative would fall to be treated as the debtor).

(7) Goods falling within this section are in this Act referred to as "protected goods".

Retaking of protected hire-purchase, etc., goods

3H–144   Forcing the creditor to have to apply for a court order to recover possession of protected goods, makes it more likely that the debtor may apply for a time order (s.129), hoping thereby to prevent what would usually otherwise be for the debtor the rather disastrous financial consequences of termination of a hire-purchase or conditional sale agreement. Section 90 prevents the creditor being entitled, without a court order, to recover possession of protected goods "from the debtor". This does not prevent recovery of them from someone to whom the debtor has sold them or if the debtor has abandoned them but does prevent recovery from someone to whom the debtor has temporarily bailed them (*e.g.* lent them to a friend or left them at a garage for repair) (*Bentinck v. Cromwell Engineering Ltd* [1971] 1 Q.B. 324). Nor does it prohibit recovery of the goods with the debtor's consent given at the time of the repossession (s.173(3)). For the consequences of recovering possession in contravention of s.90, see s.91.

3H–145   *Subs. (1)(b)* — "payment" includes tender (s.189(1)). The "total price" (s.189(1)) does not include default interest that may accrue following lateness in paying off instalments. If after having fallen into arrears and after default interest has accrued, the debtor makes a further payment he can appropriate that payment as between applying it to paying off (a) instalments overdue, or (b) the accrued default interest. If he does not, the creditor has the right to make such appropriation. Applying it to (a) will, but applying it to (b) will not, increase the amount of the total price that has been paid and may make the crucial difference as to whether one third or more of the total price has been paid (*Julian Hodge Bank Ltd v. Hall* [1998] C.C.L.R. 14, CA; and see s.81 as to appropriation of payments).

Procedure

3H–146   For a claim for a court order under s.90(1), the relevant procedure is the Consumer

Credit procedure, set out in the Consumer Credit Practice Direction at para. 7BPD.1. See, further, the Introductory Note About Procedure at the start of this Act.

Consequences of breach of s.90

91. If goods are recovered by the creditor in contravention of section 90— **3H–147**

    (a) the regulated agreement, if not previously terminated shall terminate, and

    (b) the debtor shall be released from all liability under the agreement, and shall be entitled to recover from the creditor all sums paid by the debtor under the agreement.

Recovery of possession of goods or land

92.—(1) Except under an order of the court, the creditor or owner **3H–148** shall not be entitled to enter any premises to take possession of goods subject to a regulated hire-purchase agreement, regulated conditional sale agreement or regulated consumer hire agreement.

(2) At any time when the debtor is in breach of a regulated conditional sale agreement relating to land, the creditor is entitled to recover possession of the land from the debtor, or any person claiming under him, on an order of the court only.

(3) An entry in contravention of subsection (1) or (2) is actionable as a breach of statutory duty.

Recovery of possesion of goods or land

Section 90 does not prevent recovery of the goods or land with consent of the rele- **3H–149** vant person(s) given at the time of the repossession (s.173(3)).

Procedure

The relevant procedural rules are: (i) for a claim under subs. (1), the Consumer **3H–150** Credit Act procedure in the Consumer Credit Practice Direction at para. 7BPD.1, and, (ii) for a claim under subs. (2), the procedure set out in CPR Pt 55. See further, the Introductory Note About Procedure at the start of this Act.

Interest not to be increased on default

93. The debtor under a regulated consumer credit agreement **3H–151** shall not be obliged to pay interest on sums which, in breach of the agreement, are unpaid by him at a rate—

    (a) where the total charge for credit includes an item in respect of interest, exceeding the rate of that interest, or

    (b) in any other case, exceeding what would be the rate of the total charge for credit if any items included in the total charge for credit by virtue of section 20(2) were disregarded.

Interest not to be increased on default

Section 93 prevents the debtor being charged default interest at a rate in excess of **3H–152** the rate of the APR payable under the agreement. For the effect of a contract clause providing for interest (at the same APR as that payable under the agreement as whole) to be payable on arrears, including after judgment has been given for those arrears, see commentary to s.136 below and at 3H–537.

Summary diligence not competent in Scotland

93A. Summary diligence shall not be competent in Scotland to **3H–153**

enforce payment of a debt due under a regulated agreement or under any security related thereto.

3H–154   *Note* —Added by the Debtors (Scotland) Act 1987, Sched.6. This section applies to Scotland only.

EARLY PAYMENT BY DEBTOR

Right to complete payments ahead of time

3H–155   **94.**—(1) The debtor under a regulated consumer credit agreement is entitled at any time, by notice to the creditor and the payment to the creditor of all amounts payable by the debtor to him under the agreement (less any rebate allowable under section 95), to discharge the debtor's indebtedness under the agreement.

(2) A notice under subsection (1) may embody the exercise by the debtor of any option to purchase goods conferred on him by the agreement, and deal with any other matter arising on, or in relation to, the termination of the agreement.

Right to complete payments ahead of time

3H–156   "notice" means notice in writing (s.189(1)).

Rebate on early settlement

3H–157   **95.**—(1) Regulations may provide for the allowance of a rebate of charges for credit to the debtor under a regulated consumer credit agreement where, under section 94, on refinancing, on breach of the agreement, or for any other reason, his indebtedness is discharged or becomes payable before the time fixed by the agreement, or any sum becomes payable by him before the time so fixed.

(2) Regulations under subsection (1) may provide for calculation of the rebate by reference to any sums paid or payable by the debtor or his relative under or in connection with the agreement (whether to the creditor or some other person), including sums under linked transactions and other items in the total charge for credit.

Rebate on early settlement

3H–158   The first regulations under this section were the Consumer Credit (Rebate on Early Settlement) Regulations 1983 (S.I. 1983 No. 1562). Those regulations were replaced by the Consumer Credit (Early Settlement) Regulations 2004 (S.I. 2004 No. 1483) in respect of any agreement made on or after May 31, 2005. In respect of an agreement made before that date, the 1983 regulations continue to apply until either May 31, 2007 (if the agreement was for a term of 10 years or less) or May 31, 2010 (if the agreement was for a term exceeding 10 years). The calculation of the rebate is different under the two sets of regulations. Both the 1983 and the 2004 regulations, however, provide for the statutory rebate where, on refinancing, breach of the agreement or for any other reason, the debtor's indebtedness becomes payable or discharged before the time fixed by the agreement, or any sum becomes payable by the debtor before the time fixed. The rebate therefore applies to accelerated payments clauses, so that the accelerated payment must be reduced by the amount of the rebate calculated according to the regulations. In relation to an accelerated payments clause, in *Forward Trust Plc v. Whymark* [1990] 2 Q.B. 670; [1990] C.C.L.R. 1, the Court of Appeal held that judgment could be entered for the full outstanding amount, even though that judgment debt could be discharged by payment of that amount less the amount of the statutory rebate.

Effect on linked transactions

3H–159   **96.**—(1) Where for any reason the indebtedness of the debtor under a regulated consumer credit agreement is discharged before the time fixed by the agreement, he, and any relative of his, shall at the same time be discharged from any liability under a linked transaction, other than a debt which has already become payable.

(2) Subsection (1) does not apply to a linked transaction which is itself an agreement providing the debtor or his relative with credit.

(3) Regulations may exclude linked transactions of the prescribed description from the operation of subsection (1).

Effect on linked transactions
For "linked transactions" and for those that are excepted from the operation of **3H–160**
s.96, see s.19 and commentary thereon.

Duty to give information

97.—(1) The creditor under a regulated consumer credit agree- **3H–161** ment, within the prescribed period after he has received a request in writing to that effect from the debtor, shall give the debtor a statement in the prescribed form indicating, according to the information to which it is practicable for him, to refer, the amount of the payment required to discharge the debtor's indebtedness under the agreement, together with the prescribed particulars showing how the amount is arrived at.

(2) Subsection (1) does not apply to a request made less than one month after a previous request under that subsection relating to the same agreement was complied with.

(3) If the creditor fails to comply with subsection (1)—

> (a) he is not entitled, while the default continues, to enforce the agreement; and
>
> (b) if the default continues for one month he commits an offence.

Duty to give information
Until May 31, 2005, the prescribed period was 12 working days (the Consumer **3H–162** Credit (Settlement Information) Regulations 1983 (S.I. 1983 No. 1564)). The prescribed period is reduced to seven working days in the case of an agreement made on or after May 31, 2005 (the same regulations as amended by S.I. 2004 No. 1483). In respect of an agreement made before that date, the prescribed period will continue to be 12 working days until either May 31, 2007 (if the agreement was for a term of 10 years or less) or May 31, 2010 (if the agreement was for a term exceeding 10 years). The 1983 regulations also prescribe the "form" and "particulars". Where the agreement provides for a rebate in excess of the statutory rebate (under s.95), the settlement figure shown in the statement issued in response to a request for a settlement, must be calculated on the basis of the more favourable rebate provided in the contract (*Home Insulation Ltd v. Wadsley* [1988] C.C.L.R. 25, DC). A contractual provision giving a rebate less than the statutory rebate, is void (s.173(1)).

TERMINATION OF AGREEMENTS

Duty to give notice of termination (non-default case)

98.—(1) The creditor or owner is not entitled to terminate a **3H–163** regulated agreement except by or after giving the debtor or hirer not less than seven days' notice of the termination.

(2) Subsection (1) applies only where—

(a) a period for the duration of the agreement is specified in
the agreement, and

(b) that period has not ended when the creditor or owner
does an act mentioned in subsection (1),

but so applies notwithstanding that, under the agreement, any
party is entitled to terminate it before the end of the period so
specified.

(3) A notice under subsection (1) is ineffective if not in the
prescribed form.

(4) Subsection (1) does not prevent a creditor from treating the
right to draw on any credit as restricted or deferred and taking such
steps as may be necessary to make the restriction or deferment
effective.

(5) Regulations may provide that subsection (1) is not to apply to
agreements described by the regulations.

(6) Subsection (1) does not apply to the termination of a regulated
agreement by reason of any breach by the debtor or hirer of the
agreement.

Duty to give notice of termination (non-default case)

3H–164   Sections 98 and 76 together provide for the position where, under an agreement of
specified duration, the creditor or owner might claim to be entitled to do one of the
things listed in s.87(1)(a)–(d) for a reason other than a breach of the agreement by the
debtor or hirer. For example, a clause in the agreement might give the creditor the
right to terminate the agreement or to activate an accelerated payments clause on an
event which is not a breach of the agreement, *e.g.* upon the debtor become
unemployed or insolvent. For the situation where the stated event is the debtor's or
hirer's death, see also s.86. Copies of a notice served under ss.76 or 98 must be served
on each debtor or hirer (s.185(1)(a)) and on any surety (s.111). As soon as a notice is
served under s.76 or s.98, the debtor becomes eligible to apply for a time order under
s.129. The Consumer Credit (Enforcement, Default and Termination Notices) Regulations 1983 (S.I. 1983 No. 1561) provide for the form of the notice (which must be
given in paper form) and for the exemption (under subs. (5)) of certain agreements
where no security is provided.

Right to terminate hire-purchase, etc., agreements

3H–165   **99.**—(1) At any time before the final payment by the debtor under
a regulated hire-purchase or regulated conditional sale agreement
falls due, the debtor shall be entitled to terminate the agreement by
giving notice to any person entitled or authorised to receive the sums
payable under the agreement.

(2) Termination of an agreement under subsection (1) does not
affect any liability under the agreement which has accrued before the
termination.

(3) Subsection (1) does not apply to a conditional sale agreement
relating to land after the title to the land has passed to the debtor.

(4) In the case of a conditional sale agreement relating to goods,
where the property in the goods, having become vested in the debtor,
is transferred to a person who does not become the debtor under the
agreement, the debtor shall not thereafter be entitled to terminate
the agreement under subsection (1).

(5) Subject to subsection (4), where a debtor under a conditional
sale agreement relating to goods terminates the agreement under

this section after the property in the goods has become vested in him, the property in the goods shall thereupon vest in the person (the "previous owner") in whom it was vested immediately before it became vested in the debtor:

Provided that if the previous owner has died, or any other event has occurred whereby that property, if vested in him immediately before that event, would thereupon have vested in some other person, the property shall be treated as having devolved as if it had been vested in the previous owner immediately before his death or immediately before that event, as the case may be.

Right to terminate hire-purchase, etc., agreements

The activation of an accelerated payments clause causes the whole outstanding debt **3H–166** (less any rebate due under s.95 or, if greater, under the terms of the contract) to fall due immediately. The activation of such a clause upon a breach of the agreement by the debtor, will require first the service of a default notice. If the default notice expires without the debtor rectifying his default, the accelerated payments clause will have been activated and the whole outstanding sum (*i.e.* the final payment) "falls due". After that, the debtor will have lost the right to terminate the agreement under s.99 (*Wadham Stringer Ltd v. Meaney* [1981] 1 W.L.R. 39). Upon termination under s.99, the debtor remains liable to pay all payments which fell due before termination. For other consequences of termination under s.99(1), see s.100.

Liability of debtor on termination of hire-purchase, etc., agreement

100.—(1) Where a regulated hire-purchase or regulated conditional **3H–167** sale agreement is terminated under section 99 the debtor shall be liable, unless the agreement provides for a smaller payment, or does not provide for any payment, to pay to the creditor the amount (if any) by which one-half of the total price exceeds the aggregate of the sums paid and the sums due in respect of the total price immediately before the termination.

(2) Where under a hire-purchase or conditional sale agreement the creditor is required to carry out any installation and the agreement specifies, as part of the total price, the amount to be paid in respect of the installation (the "installation charge") the reference in subsection (1) to one-half of the total price shall be construed as a reference to the aggregate of the installation charge and one-half of the remainder of the total price.

(3) If in any action the court is satisfied that a sum less than the amount specified in subsection (1) would be equal to the loss sustained by the creditor in consequence of the termination of the agreement by the debtor, the court may make an order for the payment of that sum in lieu of the amount specified in subsection (1).

(4) If the debtor has contravened an obligation to take reasonable care of the goods or land, the amount arrived at under subsection (1) shall be increased by the sum required to recompense the creditor for that contravention, and subsection (2) shall have effect accordingly.

(5) Where the debtor, on the termination of the agreement, wrongfully retains possession of goods to which the agreement relates, then, in any action brought by the creditor to recover possession of the goods from the debtor, the court, unless it is satisfied that

having regard to the circumstances it would not be just to do so, shall order the goods to be delivered to the creditor without giving the debtor an option to pay the value of the goods.

Liability of debtor on termination of hire-purchase, etc., agreement

3H–168   Taking ss.99(2) and 100 together, the effect of the debtor terminating the agreement under s.99(1) is as follows:

(i) he is to return the goods to the creditor;

(ii) he is liable for all arrears which fell due before termination;

(iii) he is liable to pay such extra sum, if any, as is necessary to bring the payments already made and the arrears still owing up to one half of the total price;

(iv) if the agreement required him to take reasonable care of the goods, damages in respect of any failure by him to do so.

Number (iii) in this list will be slightly greater if the total price included any installation charge. Number (iii) also assumes that the agreement provides for a payment of at least that amount and in any case the court can reduce that element (s.100(3)).

Right to terminate hire agreement

3H–169   **101.**—(1) The hirer under a regulated consumer hire agreement is entitled to terminate the agreement by giving notice to any person entitled or authorised to receive the sums payable under the agreement.

(2) Termination of an agreement under subsection (1) does not effect any liability under the agreement which has accrued before the termination.

(3) A notice under subsection (1) shall not expire earlier than 18 months after the making of the agreement, but apart from that the minimum period of notice to be given under subsection (1), unless the agreement provides for a shorter period, is as follows.

(4) If the agreement provides for the making of payments by the hirer to the owner at equal intervals, the minimum period of notice is the length of one interval or three months, whichever is less.

(5) If the agreement provides for the making of such payments at differing intervals, the minimum period of notice is the length of the shortest interval or three months, whichever is less.

(6) In any other case, the minimum period of notice is three months.

(7) This section does not apply to—

(a) any agreement which provides for the making by the hirer of payments which in total (and without breach of the agreement) exceed £1,500 in any year, or

(b) any agreement where—

(i) goods are bailed or (in Scotland) hired to the hirer for the purposes of a business carried on by him, or the hirer holds himself out as requiring the goods for those purposes, and

(ii) the goods are selected by the hirer, and acquired by the owner for the purposes of the agreement at the request of the hirer from any person other than the owner's associate, or

(c) any agreement where the hirer requires, or holds himself out as requiring, the goods for the purpose of bailing or hiring them to other persons in the course of a business carried on by him.

(8) If, on an application made to the OFT by a person carrying on a consumer hire business, it appears to the OFT that it would be in the interest of hirers to do so, it may by notice to the applicant direct that this section shall not apply to consumer hire agreements made by the applicant, and subject to such conditions (if any) as the OFT may specify, this Act shall have effect accordingly.

(9) In the case of a modifying agreement, subsection (3) shall apply with the substitution, for "the making of the agreement" of "the making of the original agreement".

Note —Amended by the Consumer Credit (Further Increase of Monetary Amounts) Order 1998 (S.I. 1998 No. 997) and by the Enterprise Act 2002, s.278 and Sched.25. **3H–170**

Right to terminate hire agreement

This section prevents the hirer being tied in indefinitely to a consumer hire agreement by giving him the right to terminate it after 18 months by giving notice. The minimum period of notice is the lesser of: **3H–171**

    (i) three months; and

    (ii) the interval between the due dates of the hirer's payments under the agreement.

The figure specified in s.101(7) was £300 when the Act came into force, was raised to £900 as from May 20, 1985 and to £1,500 as from May 1, 1998. The section does not apply to the agreements specified in subs. (7) nor to any in relation to which the OFT (formerly the Director General of Fair Trading) has made a direction under subs. (8). Directions given under subs. (8) are recorded in the Consumer Credit Public Register.

Agency for receiving notice of rescission

102.—(1) Where the debtor or hirer under a regulated agreement claims to have a right to rescind the agreement, each of the following shall be deemed to be the agent of the creditor or owner for the purpose of receiving any notice rescinding the agreement which is served by the debtor or hirer— **3H–172**

    (a) a credit-broker or supplier who was the negotiator in antecedent negotiations, and

    (b) any person who, in the course of a business carried on by him, acted on behalf of the debtor or hirer in any negotiations for the agreement.

(2) In subsection (1) "rescind" does not include—

    (a) service of a notice of cancellation, or

    (b) termination of an agreement under section 99 or 101 or by the exercise of a right or power in that behalf expressly conferred by the agreement.

Agency for receiving notice of rescission

"notice" means notice in writing (s.189(1)). Where someone receives a notice as a deemed agent he is under a duty to transmit it to the creditor or owner forthwith (s.175). **3H–173**

Termination statements

103.—(1) If an individual (the "customer") serves on any person (the "trader") a notice— **3H–174**

(a) stating that—

    (i) the customer was the debtor or hirer under a regulated agreement described in the notice, and the trader was the creditor or owner under the agreement, and

    (ii) the customer has discharged his indebtedness to the trader under the agreement, and

    (iii) the agreement has ceased to have any operation; and

(b) requiring the trader to give the customer a notice, signed by or on behalf of the trader, confirming that those statements are correct,

the trader shall, within the prescribed period after receiving the notice, either comply with it or serve on the customer a counter-notice stating that, as the case may be, he disputes the correctness of the notice or asserts that the customer is not indebted to him under the agreement.

(2) Where the trader disputes the correctness of the notice he shall give particulars of the way in which he alleges it to be wrong.

(3) Subsection (1) does not apply in relation to any agreement if the trader has previously complied with that subsection on the service of a notice under it with respect to that agreement.

(4) Subsection (1) does not apply to a non-commercial agreement.

(5) If the trader fails to comply with subsection (1), and the default continues for one month, he commits an offence.

Termination statements

3H–175   "notice" means notice in writing (s.189(1)). The prescribed period is 12 working days (Consumer Credit (Prescribed Period for Giving Notice) Regulations 1983 (S.I. 1983 No. 1569). For the binding nature of a termination statement, see s.172(2).

Goods not to be treated as subject to landlord's hypothec in Scotland

3H–176   **104.** Goods comprised in a hire-purchase agreement or goods comprised in a conditional sale agreement which have not become vested in the debtor shall not be treated in Scotland as subject to the landlord's hypothec—

(a) during the period between the service of a default notice in respect of the goods and the date on which the notice expires or is earlier complied with; or

(b) if the agreement is enforceable on an order of the court only, during the period between the commencement and termination of an action by the creditor to enforce the agreement.

3H–177   *Note*—This section applies to Scotland only.

Part VIII

Security

General

Form and content of securities

105.—(1) Any security provided in relation to a regulated agreement shall be expressed in writing. **3H–178**

(2) Regulations may prescribe the form and content of documents ("security instruments") to be made in compliance with subsection (1).

(3) Regulations under subsection (2) may in particular—

    (a) require specified information to be included in the prescribed manner in documents, and other specified material to be excluded;

    (b) contain requirements to ensure that specified information is clearly brought to the attention of the surety, and that one part of a document is not given insufficient or excessive prominence compared with another.

(4) A security instrument is not properly executed unless—

    (a) a document in the prescribed form, itself containing all the prescribed terms and conforming to regulations under subsection (2), is signed in the prescribed manner by or on behalf of the surety, and

    (b) the document embodies all the terms of the security, other than implied terms, and

    (c) the document, when presented or sent for the purpose of being signed by or on behalf of the surety, is in such state that its terms are readily legible, and

    (d) when the document is presented or sent for the purpose of being signed by or on behalf of the surety there is also presented or sent a copy of the document.

(5) A security instrument is not properly executed unless—

    (a) where the security is provided after, or at the time when, the regulated agreement is made, a copy of the executed agreement, together with a copy of any other document referred to in it, is given to the surety at the time the security is provided, or

    (b) where the security is provided before the regulated agreement is made, a copy of the executed agreement, together with a copy of any other document referred to in it, is given to the surety within seven days after the regulated agreement is made.

(6) Subsection (1) does not apply to a security provided by the debtor or hirer.

(7) If—

    (a) in contravention of subsection (1) a security is not expressed in writing, or

1405

(b) a security instrument is improperly executed,

the security, so far as provided in relation to a regulated agreement, is enforceable against the surety on an order of the court only.

(8) If an application for an order under subsection (7) is dismissed (except on technical grounds only) section 106 (ineffective securities) shall apply to the security.

(9) Regulations under section 60(1) shall include provision requiring documents embodying regulated agreements also to embody any security provided in relation to a regulated agreement by the debtor or hirer.

Form and content of securities

3H–179   Pt VIII (ss.105–126) deals with "security" (for definition see commentary to s.113).

3H–180   *Documentation* —Security provided by a third party must be in writing and the document must comply with subss. (4) and (5) and with the Consumer Credit (Guarantees and Indemnities) Regulations 1983 (S.I. 1983 No. 1556), made under subss. (1)–(6). The regulations do not apply to guarantees by way of mortgage, charge or pledge. The consequence of improper execution is that the security is unenforceable without an enforcement order granted by the court (see s.127). For the position where such an enforcement order is refused, see ss.105(8) and 106. For "embodies" (*e.g.* in s.105(4)(b)), see s.189(4). A regulated agreement is required to "embody" any security provided by the debtor or hirer himself (the Consumer Credit (Agreements) Regulations 1983 (made under ss.60(1) and 105(9))). If it does not, the regulated agreement is itself improperly executed (s.61).

Procedure

3H–181   For the relevant procedural rules see the notes to s.127 and the Introductory Note About Procedure at the start of this Act.

Ineffective securities

3H–182   **106.** Where, under any provision of this Act, this section is applied to any security provided in relation to a regulated agreement, then, subject to section 177 (saving for registered charges)—

(a) the security, so far as it is so provided, shall be treated as never having effect;

(b) any property lodged with the creditor or owner solely for the purposes of the security as so provided shall be returned by him forthwith;

(c) the creditor or owner shall take any necessary action to remove or cancel an entry in any register, so far as the entry relates to the security as so provided; and

(d) any amount received by the creditor or owner on realisation of the security shall, so far as it is referable to the agreement, be repaid to the surety.

Ineffective securities

3H–183   For where s.106 may be applied, see ss.105(8), 113 and 124(3). In *Wilson v. Howard Pawnbrokers* [2005] EWCA Civ 147, [2005] C.C.L.R. 2 it was held that moneys paid by the debtor to the creditor, a pawnbroker, in repayment of capital and interest, were received by the creditor on "realisation" of the pledge within the meaning of s.106(d). Thus when the creditor was refused an enforcement order, the debtor was entitled not just to the return of the pledged goods but also to repayment of those moneys which she had paid.

Duty to give information to surety under fixed-sum credit agreement

3H–184   **107.**—(1) The creditor under a regulated agreement for fixed-sum credit in relation to which security is provided, within the prescribed period after receiving a request in writing to that effect from the surety and payment of a fee of £1, shall give to the surety (if a different person from the debtor)—

    (a) a copy of the executed agreement (if any) and of any other document referred to in it;

    (b) a copy of the security instrument (if any); and

    (c) a statement signed by or on behalf of the creditor showing, according to the information to which it is practicable for him to refer—

        (i) the total sum paid under the agreement by the debtor,

        (ii) the total sum which has become payable under the agreement by the debtor but remains unpaid, and the various amounts comprised in that total sum, with the date when each became due, and

        (iii) the total sum which is to become payable under the agreement by the debtor, and the various amounts comprised in that total sum, with the date, or mode of determining the date, when each becomes due.

(2) If the creditor possesses insufficient information to enable him to ascertain the amounts and dates mentioned in subsection (1)(c)(iii), he shall be taken to comply with that sub-paragraph if his statement under subsection (1)(c) gives the basis on which, under the regulated agreement, they would fall to be ascertained.

(3) Subsection (1) does not apply to—

    (a) an agreement under which no sum is, or will or may become, payable by the debtor, or

    (b) a request made less than one month after a previous request under that subsection relating to the same agreement was complied with.

(4) If the creditor under an agreement fails to comply with subsection (1)—

    (a) he is not entitled, while the default continues, to enforce the security, so far as provided in relation to the agreement; and

    (b) if the default continues for one month he commits an offence.

(5) This section does not apply to a non-commercial agreement.

Note—Amended by the Consumer Credit (Further Increase of Monetary Amounts) Order 1998 (S.I. 1998 No. 997).   **3H–185**

Duty to give information

The fee payable under subs. (1) was raised to £1 with effect from May 1, 1998. The prescribed period is 12 working days (the Consumer Credit (Prescribed Period of Giving Information) Regulations 1983 (S.I. 1983 No. 1569)). For the binding nature of statements, see s.172. For the definition of "security" see the commentary to s.113.   **3H–186**

Duty to give information to surety under running-account credit agreement

108.—(1) The creditor under a regulated agreement for running-   **3H–187**

account credit in relation to which security is provided, within the prescribed period after receiving a request in writing to that effect from the surety and payment of a fee of £1, shall give to the surety (if a different person from the debtor)—

    (a) a copy of the executed agreement (if any) and of any other document referred to in it;

    (b) a copy of the security instrument (if any); and

    (c) a statement signed by or on behalf of the creditor showing, according to the information to which it is practicable for him to refer,—

        (i) the state of the account, and

        (ii) the amount, if any, currently payable under the agreement by the debtor to the creditor, and

        (iii) the amounts and due dates of any payments which, if the debtor does not draw further on the account, will later become payable under the agreement by the debtor to the creditor.

(2) If the creditor possesses insufficient information to enable him to ascertain the amounts and dates mentioned in subsection (1)(c)(iii), he shall be taken to comply with that sub-paragraph if his statement under subsection (1)(c) gives the basis on which, under the regulated agreement, they would fall to be ascertained.

(3) Subsection (1) does not apply to—

    (a) an agreement under which no sum is, or will or may become, payable by the debtor, or

    (b) a request made less than one month after a previous request under that subsection relating to the same agreement was complied with.

(4) If the creditor under an agreement fails to comply with subsection (1)—

    (a) he is not entitled, while the default continues, to enforce the security, so far as provided in relation to the agreement; and

    (b) if the default continues for one month he commits an offence.

(5) This section does not apply to a non-commercial agreement.

3H–188   *Note* —Amended by the Consumer Credit (Further Increase of Monetary Amounts) Order 1998 (S.I. 1998 No. 997).

Duty to give information to surety under running-account credit agreement

3H–189   See commentary to s.107 above.

Duty to give information to surety under consumer hire agreement

3H–190   **109.**—(1) The owner under a regulated consumer hire agreement in relation to which security is provided, within the prescribed period after receiving a request in writing to that effect from the surety and payment of a fee of £1, shall give to the surety (if a different person from the hirer)—

(a) a copy of the executed agreement and of any other document referred to in it;

(b) a copy of the security instrument (if any); and

(c) a statement signed by or on behalf of the owner showing, according to the information to which it is practicable for him to refer, the total sum which has become payable under the agreement by the hirer but remains unpaid and the various amounts comprised in that total sum, with the date when each became due.

(2) Subsection (1) does not apply to—

(a) an agreement under which no sum is, or will or may become, payable by the hirer, or

(b) a request made less than one month after a previous request under that subsection relating to the same agreement was complied with.

(3) If the owner under an agreement fails to comply with subsection (1)—

(a) he is not entitled, while the default continues, to enforce the security, so far as provided in relation to the agreement; and

(b) if the default continues for one month he commits an offence.

(4) This section does not apply to a non-commercial agreement.

Note —Amended by the Consumer Credit (Further Increase of Monetary Amounts) Order 1998 (S.I. 1998 No. 997). **3H–191**

Duty to give information to surety under consumer hire agreement
See the commentary to s.107 above. **3H–192**

Duty to give information to debtor or hirer

110.—(1) The creditor or owner under a regulated agreement, **3H–193** within the prescribed period after receiving a request in writing to that effect from the debtor or hirer and payment of a fee of £1, shall give the debtor or hirer a copy of any security instrument executed in relation to the agreement after the making of the agreement.

(2) Subsection (1) does not apply to—

(a) a non-commercial agreement, or

(b) an agreement under which no sum is, or will or may become, payable by the debtor or hirer, or

(c) a request made less than one month after a previous request under subsection (1) relating to the same agreement was complied with.

(3) If the creditor or owner under an agreement fails to comply with subsection (1)—

(a) he is not entitled, while the default continues, to enforce the security (so far as provided in relation to the agreement); and

(b) if the default continues for one month he commits an offence.

3H–194   *Note* —Amended by the Consumer Credit (Further Increase of Monetary Amounts) Order 1998 (S.I. 1998 No. 997).

Duty to give information to debtor or hirer

3H–195   See the commentary to s.107 above.

Duty to give surety copy of default, etc., notice

3H–196   **111.**—(1) When a default notice or a notice under section 76(1) or 98(1) is served on a debtor or hirer, a copy of the notice shall be served by the creditor or owner on any surety (if a different person from the debtor or hirer).

   (2) If the creditor or owner fails to comply with subsection (1) in the case of any surety, the security is enforceable against the surety (in respect of the breach or other matter to which the notice relates) on an order of the court only.

Duty to give surety copy of default, etc., notice

3H–197   For application for a court order under s.111, see s.127. For the relevant procedural rules see the notes to s.127 and the Introductory Note About Procedure at the start of this Act. For the definition of "security" see commentary to s.113.

Realisation of securities

3H–198   **112.** Subject to section 121, regulations may provide for any matters relating to the sale or other realisation, by the creditor or owner, of property over which any right has been provided by way of security in relation to an actual or prospective regulated agreement, other than a non-commercial agreement.

Realisation of securities

3H–199   No regulations have been made under s.112.

Act not to be evaded by use of security

3H–200   **113.**—(1) Where a security is provided in relation to an actual or prospective regulated agreement, the security shall not be enforced so as to benefit the creditor or owner, directly or indirectly, to an extent greater (whether as respects the amount of any payment or the time or manner of its being made) than would be the case if the security were not provided and any obligations of the debtor or hirer, or his relative, under or in relation to the agreement were carried out to the extent (if any) to which they would be enforced under this Act.

   (2) In accordance with subsection (1), where a regulated agreement is enforceable on an order of the court or the OFT only, any security provided in relation to the agreement is enforceable (so far as provided in relation to the agreement) where such an order has been made in relation to the agreement, but not otherwise.

   (3) Where—
   (a) a regulated agreement is cancelled under section 69(1) or becomes subject to section 69(2), or
   (b) a regulated agreement is terminated under section 91, or
   (c) in relation to any agreement an application for an order under section 40(2), 65(1), 124(1) or 149(2) is dismissed (except on technical grounds only), or

(d) a declaration is made by the court under section 142(1) (refusal of enforcement order) as respects any regulated agreement,

section 106 shall apply to any security provided in relation to the agreement.

(4) Where subsection (3)(d) applies and the declaration relates to a part only of the regulated agreement, section 106shall apply to the security only so far as it concerns that part.

(5) In the case of a cancelled agreement, the duty imposed on the debtor or hirer by section 71 or 72 shall not be enforceable before the creditor or owner has discharged any duty imposed on him by section 106 (as applied by subsection (3)(a)).

(6) If the security is provided in relation to a prospective agreement or transaction, the security shall be enforceable in relation to the agreement or transaction only after the time (if any) when the agreement is made; and until that time the person providing the security shall be entitled, by notice to the creditor or owner, to require that section 106 shall thereupon apply to the security.

(7) Where an indemnity or guarantee is given in a case where the debtor or hirer is a minor, or an indemnity is given in a case where he is otherwise not of full capacity, the reference in subsection (1) to the extent to which his obligations would be enforced shall be read in relation to the indemnity or guarantee as a reference to the extent to which those obligations would be enforced if he were of full capacity.

(8) Subsections (1) to (3) also apply where a security is provided in relation to an actual or prospective linked transaction, and in that case—

(a) references to the agreement shall be read as references to the linked transaction, and

(b) references to the creditor or owner shall be read as references to any person (other than the debtor or hirer, or his relative) who is a party, or prospective party, to the linked transaction.

Note —Amended by the Minor's Contracts Act 1987, s.4 and by the Enterprise Act 2002, s.278 and Sched.25. **3H–201**

Act not to be evaded by use of security

Section 113 prevents the provisions of the Act being circumvented by the use of security. Broadly, no security can be enforced to any greater extent than can the regulated agreement to which it relates. Thus an indemnity provided in relation to a regulated agreement at the request (express or implied) of the debtor or hirer, will be reduced in effect to a guarantee. **3H–202**

"Security" —The provisions of the Act apply only to "security". "Security" includes only security which is given by the debtor or hirer or at his express or implied request (s.189(1)). Thus an agreement whereby a dealer agrees to indemnify a finance house for defaults of any customer whom the dealer should introduce to the finance house will not be within the definition. Similarly outside the definition will be a recourse agreement, *e.g.* whereby a car dealer agrees to re-purchase from the creditor, any vehicle which is repossessed from any hire-purchase customer introduced to the creditor by the dealer. Some of the provisions in this Part apply only to security, *e.g.* a guarantee or indemnity, given by a third party. Others, including s.113, apply to security whether given by the third party or by the debtor or hirer himself. **3H–203**

CONSUMER

3H–204   *Subs.(2)* —For the position where a regulated agreement is enforceable on an order of the court only, see the sections referred to in s.127. Other provisions rendering a regulated agreement enforceable on an order of the court or of the OFT only are ss.40(1), 86(2), 90(1), 92, 149(1). Note, however, s.173(3) which allows something to be done in relation to a person provided that that person consents at the time it is done.

3H–205   *Subs.(7)* —Is in line with the general law relating to guarantees of the liabilities of minors after the Minor's Contracts Act 1987 and is an exception to the rule preventing enforcement of the security to any extent greater than the regulated agreement is enforceable. Where the only reason that a regulated agreement is unenforceable against the debtor or hirer is that the latter is (or at the time of the agreement was) a minor, then a guarantee or indemnity is not rendered unenforceable.

PLEDGES

Pawn-receipts

3H–206   **114.**—(1) At the time he receives the article, a person who takes any article in pawn under a regulated agreement shall give to the person from whom he receives it a receipt in the prescribed form (a "pawn-receipt").

(2) A person who takes any article in pawn from an individual whom he knows to be, or who appears to be and is, a minor commits an offence.

(3) This section and sections 115 to 122 do not apply to—
   (a) a pledge of documents of title or of bearer bonds, or
   (b) a non-commercial agreement.

3H–207   *Note* —Amended by the Banking Act 1979, s.38.

3H–208   *Pawn-receipts* — Sections 114–122 relate to pledges taken under regulated agreements. For "pawn" and "pledge", see s.189(1). The regulations prescribing the form of a pawn receipt are: where the pawn receipt is not separate from any document embodying the regulated agreement, the Consumer Credit (Agreements) Regulations 1983 (S.I. 1983 No. 1553); where they are in separate documents, the Consumer Credit (Pawn-Receipts) Regulations 1983 (S.I. 1983 No. 1566).

Penalty for failure to supply copies of pledge agreement, etc.

3H–209   **115.** If the creditor under a regulated agreement to take any article in pawn fails to observe the requirements of sections 62 to 64 or 114(1) in relation to the agreement he commits an offence.

Penalty for failure to supply copies of pledge agreement, etc.

3H–210   Normally, failure to observe the documentation requirements merely renders the agreement unenforceable without a court order (s.65). Where the creditor takes an article in pawn, it also is an offence.

Redemption period

3H–211   **116.**—(1) A pawn is redeemable at any time within six months after it was taken.

(2) Subject to subsection (1), the period within which a pawn is redeemable shall be the same as the period fixed by the parties for the duration of the credit secured by the pledge, or such longer period as they may agree.

(3) If the pawn is not redeemed by the end of the period laid down by subsections (1) and (2) (the "redemption period"), it never-

theless remains redeemable until it is realised by the pawnee under section 121 except where under section 120(1)(a) the property in it passes to the pawnee.

(4) No special charge shall be made for redemption of a pawn after the end of the redemption period, and charges in respect of the safe keeping of the pawn shall not be at a higher rate after the end of the redemption period than before.

Redemption period

In *Wilson v Robertsons (London) Ltd* [2005] EWHC 1425 Ch; [2005] 3 All E.R. 873; **3H–212** [2005] C.C.L.R.6 , Laddie J. held that s. 116(1) requires a pawnbroking agreement to contain a term allowing the debtor a minimum period of six months within which to redeem the pawn. The six months must extend from the date the pawn is "taken". That cannot be earlier than the date on which the agreement is entered into. If the agreement is backdated thereby reducing to less than six months the period allowed by the agreement for the debtor to redeem the pawn, section 116(1) is not complied with. That is so even if the backdating of the agreement was freely agreed to by the debtor, since section 173(1) prevents contracting out of these provisions.

Redemption procedure

117.—(1) On surrender of the pawn-receipt, and payment of the **3H–213** amount owing, at any time when the pawn is redeemable, the pawnee shall deliver the pawn to the bearer of the pawn-receipt.

(2) Subsection (1) does not apply if the pawnee knows or has reasonable cause to suspect that the bearer of the pawn-receipt is neither the owner of the pawn nor authorised by the owner to redeem it.

(3) The pawnee is not liable to any person in tort or delict for delivering the pawn where subsection (1) applies, or refusing to deliver it where the person demanding delivery does not comply with subsection (1) or, by reason of subsection (2), subsection (1) does not apply.

Loss, etc., of pawn-receipt

118.—(1) A person (the "claimant") who is not in possession of the **3H–214** pawn-receipt but claims to be the owner of the pawn or to be otherwise entitled or authorised to redeem it, may do so at any time when it is redeemable by tendering to the pawnee in place of the pawn-receipt—

(a) a statutory declaration made by the claimant in the prescribed form, and with the prescribed contents, or

(b) where the pawn is security for fixed-sum credit not exceeding £75 or running-account credit on which the credit limit does not exceed £75, and the pawnee agrees, a statement in writing in the prescribed form, and with the prescribed contents, signed by the claimant.

(2) On compliance by the claimant with subsection (1), section 117 shall apply as if the declaration or statement were the pawn-receipt, and the pawn-receipt itself shall become inoperative for the purposes of section 117.

Note—Amended by the Consumer Credit (Further Increase of Monetary Amounts) **3H–215** Order 1998 (S.I. 1998 No. 997).

CONSUMER

Loss, etc., of pawn-receipt

3H–216 The form and contents of the declaration or statement are prescribed by the Consumer Credit (Loss of Pawn-Receipt) Regulations 1983 (S.I. 1983 No. 1567). The declaration or statement takes the place of the pawn-receipt. Section 117(2), however, still applies.

Unreasonable refusal to deliver pawn

3H–217 **119.**—(1) If a person who has taken a pawn under a regulated agreement refuses without reasonable cause to allow the pawn to be redeemed, he commits an offence.

(2) On the conviction in England or Wales of a pawnee under subsection (1) where the offence does not amount to theft, section 148 of the Powers of Criminal Courts (Sentencing) Act 2000 (restitution orders), shall apply as if the pawnee had been convicted of stealing the pawn.

(3) On the conviction in Northern Ireland of a pawnee under subsection (1) where the offence does not amount to theft, section 27 (orders for restitution) of the Theft Act (Northern Ireland) 1969, and any provision of the Theft Act (Northern Ireland) 1969 relating to that section, shall apply as if the pawnee had been convicted of stealing the pawn.

Unreasonable refusal to deliver pawn

3H–218 Amended by the Powers of Criminal Courts (Sentencing) Act 2000, Sched.9, para. 45. For burden of proof as to reasonable cause to refuse to allow redemption, see s.171(6) of the Consumer Credit Act 1974.

Consequence of failure to redeem

3H–219 **120.**—(1) If at the end of the redemption period the pawn has not been redeemed—

    (a) notwithstanding anything in section 113, the property in the pawn passes to the pawnee where the redemption period is six months and the pawn is security for fixed-sum credit not exceeding £75 or running-account credit on which the credit limit does not exceed £75; or

    (b) in any other case the pawn becomes realisable by the pawnee.

(2) Where the debtor or hirer is entitled to apply to the court for a time order under section 129, subsection (1) shall apply with the substitution, for "at the end of the redemption period" of "after the expiry of five days following the end of the redemption period".

3H–220 *Note*—Amended by the Consumer Credit (Further Increase of Monetary Amounts) Order 1998 (S.I. 1998 No. 997).

Consequence of failure to redeem

3H–221 It seems that where a pawnee wishes to realise a pawn pursuant to s.120(1)(b), a default notice under s.87, as well as a notice of intention under s.121, should first be served. Regulations under s.87(4) have not dispensed with this requirement. The original figure in s.120(1)(a) was raised to the current figure of £75 as from May 1, 1998.

Realisation of pawn

3H–222 **121.**—(1) When a pawn has become realisable by him, the pawnee may sell it, after giving to the pawnor (except in such cases as may be prescribed) not less than the prescribed period of notice of the intention to sell, indicating in the notice the asking price and such other particulars as may be prescribed.

(2) Within the prescribed period after the sale takes place, the pawnee shall give the pawnor the prescribed information in writing as to the sale, its proceeds and expenses.

(3) Where the net proceeds of sale are not less than the sum which, if the pawn had been redeemed on the date of the sale, would have been payable for its redemption, the debt secured by the pawn is discharged and any surplus shall be paid by the pawnee to the pawnor.

(4) Where subsection (3) does not apply, the debt shall be treated as from the date of sale as equal to the amount by which the net proceeds of sale fall short of the sum which would have been payable for the redemption of the pawn on that date.

(5) In this section the "net proceeds of sale" is the amount realised (the "gross amount") less the expenses (if any) of the sale.

(6) If the pawnor alleges that the gross amount is less than the true market value of the pawn on the date of sale, it is for the pawnee to prove that he and any agents employed by him in the sale used reasonable care to ensure that the true market value was obtained, and if he fails to do so subsections (3) and (4) shall have effect as if the reference in subsection (5) to the gross amount were a reference to the true market value.

(7) If the pawnor alleges that the expenses of the sale were unreasonably high, it is for the pawnee to prove that they were reasonable, and if he fails to do so subsections (3) and (4) shall have effect as if the reference in subsection (5) to expenses were a reference to reasonable expenses.

Realisation of pawn

The Consumer Credit (Realisation of Pawn) Regulations 1983, as amended by the Consumer Credit (Realisation of Pawn) (Amendment) Regulations 1998 (S.I. 1998 No. 998), prescribe the minimum periods: for giving notice under s.121(1), 14 days; for giving information under s.121(2), 20 days. They also prescribe the particulars and information under those subsections. They also provide exemption from s.121(1) where the credit (or credit limit) does not exceed £100. Surplus money from the sale is held by the pawnee on trust for the pawnor and the pawnee thus is liable to pay interest on the surplus money if it is not immediately returned (*Mathew v. T M Sutton Ltd* [1994] 1 W.L.R. 1455; [1994] 4 All E.R. 793; [1994] C.C.L.R. 140).   **3H–223**

Order in Scotland to deliver pawn

3H–224

122.—(1) As respects Scotland where—
    (a) a pawn is either—
        (i) an article which has been stolen, or
        (ii) an article which has been obtained by fraud, and
           a person is convicted of any offence in relation to
           the theft or, as the case may be, the fraud; or
    (b) a person is convicted of an offence under section 119(1),
the court by which that person is so convicted may order delivery of the pawn to the owner or the person otherwise entitled thereto.

(2) A court making an order under subsection (1)(a) for delivery

of a pawn may make the order subject to such conditions as to payment of the debt secured by the pawn as it thinks fit.

3H–225   *Note* —This section applies to Scotland only.

NEGOTIABLE INSTRUMENTS

Restrictions on taking and negotiating instruments

3H–226   **123.**—(1) A creditor or owner shall not take a negotiable instrument, other than a bank note or cheque, in discharge of any sum payable—

> (a) by the debtor or hirer under a regulated agreement, or
> (b) by any person as surety in relation to the agreement.

(2) The creditor or owner shall not negotiate a cheque taken by him in discharge of a sum payable as mentioned in subsection (1) except to a banker (within the meaning of the Bills of Exchange Act 1882).

(3) The creditor or owner shall not take a negotiable instrument as security for the discharge of any sum payable as mentioned in subsection (1).

(4) A person takes a negotiable instrument as security for the discharge of a sum if the sum is intended to be paid in some other way, and the negotiable instrument is to be presented for payment only if the sum is not paid in that way.

(5) This section does not apply where the regulated agreement is a non-commercial agreement.

(6) The Secretary of State may by order provide that this section shall not apply where the regulated agreement has a connection with a country outside the United Kingdom.

Restrictions on taking and negotiating instruments

3H–227   "Cheque" is undefined in this statute but probably includes post-dated cheques. This section does not apply to payments relating to agreements which are exempt agreements (see s.16). Also the Consumer Credit (Negotiable Instruments) (Exemption) Order 1984 (S.I. 1984 No. 435), made under s.123(6), exempts consumer hire agreements having a connection with a country outside the U.K. provided the goods are hired in the course of the hirer's business. For consequences of contravening the section, see s.124.

Consequences of breach of s.123

3H–228   **124.**—(1) After any contravention of section 123 has occurred in relation to a sum payable as mentioned in section 123(1)(a), the agreement under which the sum is payable is enforceable against the debtor or hirer on an order of the court only.

(2) After any contravention of section 123 has occurred in relation to a sum payable by any surety, the security is enforceable on an order of the court only.

(3) Where an application for an order under subsection (2) is dismissed (except on technical grounds only) section 106 shall apply to the security.

Consequences of breach of s.123

3H–229   In relation to security enforceable on an order of the court only, see s.127. For the relevant procedural rules see the notes to s.127 and the Introductory Note About Procedure at the start of this Act.

Holders in due course

125.—(1) A person who takes a negotiable instrument in contravention of section 123(1) or (3) is not a holder in due course, and is not entitled to enforce the instrument.

3H–230

(2) Where a person negotiates a cheque in contravention of section 123(2), his doing so constitutes a defect in his title within the meaning of the Bills of Exchange Act 1882.

(3) If a person mentioned in section 123(1)(a) or (b) ("the protected person") becomes liable to a holder in due course of an instrument taken from the protected person in contravention of section 123(1) or (3), or taken from the protected person and negotiated in contravention of section 123(2), the creditor or owner shall indemnify the protected person in respect of that liability.

(4) Nothing in this Act affects the rights of the holder in due course of any negotiable instrument.

Holders in due course

The object is:

3H–231

(a) to prevent someone who takes a negotiable instrument in contravention of s.123 from gaining any rights to it;
(b) to preserve the rights of any other person who becomes a holder in due course;
(c) to provide an indemnity to the debtor or hirer (or surety) if he becomes liable to such a holder in due course.

LAND MORTGAGES

Enforcement of land mortgages

126. A land mortgage securing a regulated agreement is enforceable (so far as provided in relation to the agreement) on an order of the court only.

3H–232

Enforcement of land mortgages

This section also applies to a land mortgage which secures an agreement which is exempt by virtue of s.16(6C) and which would, but for s.16(6C), be a regulated agreement: see s.16(6D). Section 126 presumably prevents the creditor from retaking possession and from selling the property without a court order. It does not prevent anything, *e.g.* repossession, being done with the consent of the relevant person (the mortgagor?) given at the time of the repossession (s.173(3)). The relevant procedure for an application for an order under this section (being a claim for recovery of land) is the procedure set out in CPR Pt 55.

3H–233

PART IX

JUDICIAL CONTROL

ENFORCEMENT OF CERTAIN REGULATED AGREEMENTS AND SECURITIES

Enforcement orders in cases of infringement

127.—(1) In the case of an application for an enforcement order under—

3H–234

    (a) section 65(1) (improperly executed agreements), or

    (b) section 105(7)(a) or (b) (improperly executed security instruments), or

    (c) section 111(2) (failure to serve copy of notice on surety), or

    (d) section 124(1) or (2) (taking of negotiable instruments in contravention of section 123),

the court shall dismiss the application if, but (subject to subsection (3) and (4)) only if, it considers it just to do so having regard to—

    (i) prejudice caused to any person by the contravention in question, and the degree of culpability for it; and

    (ii) the powers conferred on the court by subsection (2) and sections 135 and 136.

(2) If it appears to the court just to do so, it may in an enforcement order reduce or discharge any sum payable by the debtor or hirer, or any surety, so as to compensate him for prejudice suffered as a result of the contravention in question.

(3) The court shall not make an enforcement order under section 65(1) if section 61(1)(a) (signing of agreements) was not complied with unless a document (whether or not in the prescribed form and complying with regulations under section 60(1)) itself containing all the prescribed terms of the agreement was signed by the debtor or hirer (whether or not in the prescribed manner).

(4) The court shall not make an enforcement order under section 65(1) in the case of a cancellable agreement if—

    (a) a provision of section 62 or 63 was not complied with, and the creditor or owner did not give a copy of the executed agreement, and of any other document referred to in it, to the debtor or hirer before the commencement of the proceedings in which the order is sought, or

    (b) section 64(1) was not complied with.

(5) Where an enforcement order is made in a case to which subsection (3) applies, the order may direct that the regulated agreement is to have effect as if it did not include a term omitted from the document signed by the debtor or hirer.

Enforcement orders in cases of infringement

No enforcement order possible

3H–235   In certain cases of improperly executed regulated agreements, the court must refuse to grant an enforcement order (s.127(3) and (4)). Subsection (3), however, applies only if the agreement has been improperly executed including no signing by the debtor or hirer of a document containing certain basic minimum terms (prescribed for this purpose by the Consumer Credit (Agreements) Regulations 1983 (S.I. 1983 No. 1553), reg. 6(1)). These basic minimum terms are, broadly: the amount of credit (possibly expressed simply as the cash price of the goods being purchased) or (in the case of running-account credit) the credit limit (or how it is determined); the rate of interest; how the debtor is to discharge his obligations (*e.g.* the number, frequency and amount of repayments instalments). For agreements unenforceable for failure to include basic minimum terms when the agreement was signed, see *Wilson v. First County Trust (No. 1)* [2001] Q.B. 407; [2003] C.C.L.R. 1 and *O'Hagan v. Wright* [2001] NICA 26; [2003] C.C.L.R. 6. For a "credit hire" agreement which was held to be unenforceable for failure to include basic minimum terms when the agreement was signed, see *Dimond v. Lovell* [2000] Q.B 216, confirmed in the House of Lords [2002] 1 A.C. 384; [2000] C.C.L.R. 57 and, further, the notes to ss.9 and 11.

The effect of no enforcement order being granted is severe: the creditor or owner cannot enforce the agreement or any security (s.113) : *Wilson v. First County Trust (No. 1)* [2001] Q.B. 407; [2003] C.C.L.R. 1. Nor is the creditor able to recover his security or losses via any restitutionary remedy: *Dimond v. Lovell* [2002] 1 A.C. 384; [2000] C.C.L.R. 57 and *Wilson v. First County Trust Ltd (No.2)* [2004] 1 A.C 816; [2003] UKHL 40; [2003] 3 W.L.R. 568; [2003] C.C.L.R. 14. In the case of a pledge agreement where the court refuses an enforcement order, the debtor will be entitled to the return of the goods given in pawn and also, apparently, to recover any payments of interest and capital which he has already made under the agreement: *Wilson v. Howard Pawnbrokers* [2005] EWCA Civ 147, [2005] C.C.L.R.2 (see notes to s.106 above). According to Lord Nicholls, obiter, in *Wilson v. First County Trust Ltd (No.2)* [2003] UKHL 40; [2004] 1 A.C. 816; [2003] C.C.L.R. 14, at paras 31 and 75, s.173(3) expressly permits consensual enforcement against the debtor and thus s.127(3) will not assist a debtor who consents to the enforcement of the agreement in ignorance of the fact that, without that consent, s.127(3) renders the agreement unenforceable against him. His Lordship's view is, however, inconsistent with *O'Hagan v. Wright* [2003] C.C.L.R. 6; [2001] NICA 26, where the Court of Appeal of Northern Ireland held, in relation to s.173(3), that where an agreement is unenforceable against the debtor by virtue of s.127(3), the debtor cannot render it enforceable by consenting to its enforcement. In *Wilson v. First County Trust Ltd (No.2)* the House of Lords reversed a decision where the Court of Appeal had held that s.127(3) is incompatible with the European Convention on Human Rights but indicated that the result might be different if the Act were amended so as to apply to credit agreements regardless of the amount of credit, *per* Lord Nicholls at para. 80.

Court's discretion

In other cases the court has a discretion to refuse to grant an enforcement order **3H–236** taking into account the factors spelt out in s.127(1)(i) and (ii). It might grant an enforcement order without any qualification if, despite the infringement, the debtor or hirer has suffered no prejudice (*Nissan Finance v. Lockhart* [1993] C.C.L.R. 39, CA). It might refuse to grant an enforcement order, *e.g.* where the debtor or hirer would not have entered the agreement if it had been properly executed (*P.B. Leasing Ltd v. Patel and Patel* [1995] C.C.L.R. 82). It might grant an enforcement order but (under ss.127(2) and 136) reduce the rate of interest where a failure to give the debtor an advance copy of the agreement and leave the debtor a pre-contract consideration period (under ss.58 and 61) has deprived the debtor of the opportunity of securing a loan elsewhere at a lower rate of interest (*National Guardian Mortgage Corp. v. Wilkes* [1993] C.C.L.R. 1). It might considerably reduce (under ss.127(2) and 136) the amount of an accelerated payment due after termination of a consumer hire agreement, where the documentation failed to include that information (*Rank Xerox v. Hepple* [1994] C.C.L.R. 1). The Court of Appeal will not normally interfere with the exercise of the judge's discretion under s.127 unless it has not been exercised on the right principles (*Nissan Finance UK v. Lockhart, supra*).

Procedure

In the case of an application under any of the sections referred to in s.127(1) the **3H–237** relevant procedural rules are as follows: (i) for a claim relating to the recovery of land, the procedure set out in CPR Pt 55; (ii) for any other claim, the Consumer Credit Act procedure in the Consumer Credit Practice Direction at para. 7BPD.1. See further the Introductory Note About Procedure at the start of this Act (above).

Enforcement orders on death of debtor or hirer

128. The court shall make an order under section 86(2) if, but **3H–238** only if, the creditor or owner proves that he has been unable to satisfy himself that the present and future obligations of the debtor or hirer under the agreement are likely to be discharged.

EXTENSION OF TIME

Time orders

129.—(1) Subject to subsection (3) below, if it appears to the court **3H–239** just to do so—

      (a) on an application for an enforcement order; or

      (b) on an application made by a debtor or hirer under this paragraph after service on him of—

          (i) a default notice, or

          (ii) a notice under section 76(1) or 98(1); or

      (c) in an action brought by a creditor or owner to enforce a regulated agreement or any security, or recover possession of any goods or land to which a regulated agreement relates,

the court may make an order under this section (a "time order").

(2) A time order shall provide for one or both of the following, as the court considers just—

      (a) the payment by the debtor or hirer or any surety of any sum owed under a regulated agreement or a security by such instalments, payable at such times, as the court, having regard to the means of the debtor or hirer and any surety, considers reasonable;

      (b) the remedying by the debtor or hirer of any breach of a regulated agreement (other than non-payment of money) within such period as the court may specify.

(3) Where in Scotland a time to pay direction or a time to pay order has been made in relation to a debt, it shall not thereafter be competent to make a time order in relation to the same debt.

3H–240   *Note* —Amended by the Debtors (Scotland) Act 1987, Sched.6.

Time orders

3H–241   The court's power under s.129(2)(a) to allow time for the payment is limited to "any sum owed". This must mean, and is confined to, sums that have actually fallen due, since otherwise there would be no need, in s.130(2), to extend the power, "in the case of a hire-purchase and conditional sale agreement only", to allow the court to grant the order in respect also of payments that have not yet fallen due. Where an accelerated payments clause has been activated (*i.e.* after expiry of a default notice under s.87), then the whole outstanding balance will have fallen due by virtue of the clause; in that case the court's power under s.129(2)(a) extends to the whole balance, irrespective of whether the agreement is a hire-purchase or conditional sale agreement. Where a land mortgage has been granted as security for a loan and, after the debtor's default, the creditor (no doubt after expiry of a default notice under s.87) commences repossession proceedings, that amounts to a "calling-in" of the loan entitling the creditor to the whole of the outstanding balance; in that case, the court's power under s.127(2)(a) extends to the whole debt including future instalments that would not otherwise have fallen due yet (*Southern District Finance plc v. Barnes* [1995] C.C.L.R. 62, CA). According to this case, when a time order is made, it should normally be for a stipulated period on account of temporary financial difficulty; the correct judicial approach is first to consider whether it is just to make a time order, bearing in mind the positions of both parties. See also *First National Bank plc v. Syed* [1991] 2 All E.R. 250; [1991] C.C.L.R. 37; there is no point making a time order involving payments that would be insufficient even to keep down the interest accruing on the account. If a time order is made, the court should suspend (see s.135) any possession order it also makes, for so long as the terms of the time order are complied with.

    For supplementary matters see s.130 and for the court's power to vary the rate of interest or otherwise amend the agreement in consequence of a term of a time order, see s.136.

    A time order is a final order (*Jenkins v. Cedar Holdings Ltd* [1988] C.C.L.R. 34).

Procedure

3H–242   An application under s.129(1) will no doubt often be made by way of defence to an action begun by the creditor. Unless it "relates to the recovery of land", an *originating* application for a time order (*i.e.* under s.129(1)(b)) should be made using the Consumer Credit Act procedure, set out in the Consumer Credit Practice Direction at para. 7BPD.1 and it should be made in the county court where the claimant resides or carries on business (para. 4.3 of the Consumer Credit Act procedure). See further the Introductory Note about Procedure at the start of this Act.

Supplemental provisions about time orders

130.—(1) Where in accordance with rules of court an offer to pay **3H–243** any sum by instalments is made by the debtor or hirer and accepted by the creditor or owner, the court may in accordance with rules of court make a time order under section 129(2)(a) giving effect to the offer without hearing evidence of means.

(2) In the case of a hire-purchase or conditional sale agreement only, a time order under section 129(2)(a) may deal with sums which, although not payable by the debtor at the time the order is made, would if the agreement continued in force become payable under it subsequently.

(3) A time order under section 129(2)(a) shall not be made where the regulated agreement is secured by a pledge if, by virtue of regulations made under section 76(5), 87(4) or 98(5), service of a notice is not necessary for enforcement of the pledge.

(4) Where, following the making of a time order in relation to a regulated hire-purchase or conditional sale agreement or a regulated consumer hire agreement, the debtor or hirer is in possession of the goods, he shall be treated (except in the case of a debtor to whom the creditor's title has passed) as a bailee or (in Scotland) a custodier of the goods under the terms of the agreement, notwithstanding that the agreement has been terminated.

(5) Without prejudice to anything done by the creditor or owner before the commencement of the period specified in a time order made under section 129(2)(b)("the relevant period"),—

    (a) he shall not while the relevant period subsists take in relation to the agreement any action such as is mentioned in section 87(1);

    (b) where—

        (i) a provision of the agreement ("the secondary provision") becomes operative only on breach of another provision of the agreement ("the primary provision"), and

        (ii) the time order provides for the remedying of such a breach of the primary provision within the relevant period,

he shall not treat the secondary provision as operative before the end of that period;

    (c) if while the relevant period subsists the breach to which the order relates is remedied it shall be treated as not having occurred.

(6) On the application of any person affected by a time order, the court may vary or revoke the order.

Supplemental provisions about time orders
See commentary to s.129. **3H–244**

PROTECTION OF PROPERTY PENDING PROCEEDINGS

Protection orders

3H-245   131. The court, on the application of the creditor or owner under a regulated agreement, may make such orders as it thinks just for protecting any property of the creditor or owner, or property subject to any security, from damage or depreciation pending the determination of any proceedings under this Act, including orders restricting or prohibiting use of the property or giving directions as to its custody.

Protection orders

3H-246   For powers to impose conditions or suspend the operation of the order or to vary agreements in consequence of the order, see ss.135 and 136. The Consumer Credit Act Practice Direction (para. 7BPD.1) makes no reference to claims under this section, which appear from the wording of the section to be necessarily interim applications. Presumably an application under s.131 must comply with the rules about Applications for Court Orders (CPR 23) and Interim Remedies (CPR 25).

HIRE AND HIRE-PURCHASE, ETC., AGREEMENTS

Financial relief for hirer

3H-247   132.—(1) Where the owner under a regulated consumer hire agreement recovers possession of goods to which the agreement relates otherwise than by action, the hirer may apply to the court for an order that—

    (a) the whole or part of any sum paid by the hirer to the owner in respect of the goods shall be repaid, and

    (b) the obligation to pay the whole or part of any sum owed by the hirer to the owner in respect of the goods shall cease,

and if it appears to the court just to do so, having regard to the extent of the enjoyment of the goods by the hirer, the court shall grant the application in full or in part.

(2) Where in proceedings relating to a regulated consumer hire agreement the court makes an order for the delivery to the owner of goods to which the agreement relates the court may include in the order the like provision as may be made in an order under subsection (1).

Financial relief for hirer

3H-248   In *Automotive Financial Services v. Henderson* [1993] C.C.L.R. 55; [1992] S.L.T. Sh.Ct. 63, the defenders suggested two different formulae for determining whether relief should be granted—one based on the interest and the administrative costs of the owner, the other based on the value of the goods supplied and their subsequent depreciation. The Sheriff Principal held that it would be wrong to control the application of s.132 by any formula not in the Act. Presumably, as with s.127 (see the commentary thereto), the Court of Appeal will not normally interfere with the exercise of the judge's discretion unless it has not been exercised on the right principles—or is patently unreasonable.

Hire-purchase, etc., agreements: special powers of court

3H-249   133.—(1) If, in relation to a regulated hire-purchase or conditional sale agreement, it appears to the court just to do so—

(a) on an application for an enforcement order or time order; or

(b) in an action brought by the creditor to recover possession of goods to which the agreement relates,

the court may—

(i) make an order (a "return order") for the return to the creditor of goods to which the agreement relates;

(ii) make an order (a "transfer order") for the transfer to the debtor of the creditor's title to certain goods to which the agreement relates ("the transferred goods"), and the return to the creditor of the remainder of the goods.

(2) In determining for the purposes of this section how much of the total price has been paid ("the paid-up sum"), the court may—

(a) treat any sum paid by the debtor, or owed by the creditor, in relation to the goods as part of the paid-up sum;

(b) deduct any sum owed by the debtor in relation to the goods (otherwise than as part of the total price) from the paid-up sum,

and make corresponding reductions in amounts so owed.

(3) Where a transfer order is made, the transferred goods shall be such of the goods to which the agreement relates as the court thinks just; but a transfer order shall be made only where the paid-up sum exceeds the part of the total price referable to the transferred goods by an amount equal to at least one-third of the unpaid balance of the total price.

(4) Notwithstanding the making of a return order or transfer order, the debtor may at any time before the goods enter the possession of the creditor, on payment of the balance of the total price and the fulfilment of any other necessary conditions, claim the goods ordered to be returned to the creditor.

(5) When, in pursuance of a time order or under this section, the total price of goods under a regulated hire-purchase agreement or regulated conditional sale agreement is paid and any other necessary conditions are fulfilled, the creditor's title to the goods vests in the debtor.

(6) If, in contravention of a return order or transfer order, any goods to which the order relates are not returned to the creditor, the court, on the application of the creditor, may—

(a) revoke so much of the order as relates to those goods, and

(b) order the debtor to pay the creditor the unpaid portion of so much of the total price as is referable to those goods.

(7) For the purposes of this section, the part of the total price referable to any goods is the part assigned to those goods by the agreement or (if no such assignment is made) the part determined by the court to be reasonable.

Hire-purchase, etc., agreements: special powers of court

Section 133 provides for two possible orders in the case of a regulated hire-purchase **3H–250** or conditional sale agreement. A transfer order will be possible only where the goods subject to the agreement are divisible. Another way of expressing the formula, is that a transfer order is not possible unless the debtor has paid both (a) that part of the total price referable to the "transferred goods" and also (b) one quarter of the rest of the total price. This formula may need adjusting, however, by virtue of subs. (2). In the usual case, the choice before the court will be whether to make a return order or whether to make, if one is applied for, a time order (under s.129). If it decides to make a time order, it could make a return order, suspended, *e.g.* for so long as the debtor observes the terms of the time order, see s.135.

Evidence of adverse detention in hire purchase, etc., cases

3H–251 **134.**—(1) Where goods are comprised in a regulated hire-purchase agreement, regulated conditional sale agreement or regulated consumer hire agreement, and the creditor or owner—

(a) brings an action or makes an application to enforce a right to recover possession of the goods from the debtor or hirer, and

(b) proves that a demand for the delivery of the goods was included in the default notice under section 88(5), or that, after the right to recover possession of the goods accrued but before the action was begun or the application was made, he made a request in writing to the debtor or hirer to surrender the goods,

then, for the purposes of the claim of the creditor or owner to recover possession of the goods, the possession of them by the debtor or hirer shall be deemed to be adverse to the creditor or owner.

(2) In subsection (1) "the debtor or hirer" includes a person in possession of the goods at any time between the debtor's or hirer's death and the grant of probate or administration, or (in Scotland) confirmation.

(3) Nothing in this section affects a claim for damages for conversion or (in Scotland) for delict.

SUPPLEMENTAL PROVISIONS AS TO ORDERS

Power to impose conditions, or suspend operation of order

3H–252 **135.**—(1) If it considers it just to do so, the court may in an order made by it in relation to a regulated agreement include provisions—

(a) making the operation of any term of the order conditional on the doing of specified acts by any party to the proceedings;

(b) suspending the operation of any term of the order either—

(i) until such time as the court subsequently directs, or

(ii) until the occurrence of a specified act or omission.

(2) The court shall not suspend the operation of a term requiring the delivery up of goods by any person unless satisfied that the goods are in his possession or control.

(3) In the case of a consumer hire agreement, the court shall not so use its powers under subsection (1)(b) as to extend the period for

which, under the terms of the agreement, the hirer is entitled to possession of the goods to which the agreement relates.

(4) On the application of any person affected by a provision included under subsection (1), the court may vary the provision.

Power to impose conditions, or suspend operation of order

These powers are relevant to ss.127(1)(ii), 129, 131, 132 and 133 (see commentaries to ss.127, 129 and 133). **3H–253**

Power to vary agreements and securities

136. The court may in an order made by it under this Act include such provision as it considers just for amending any agreement or security in consequence of a term of the order. **3H–254**

Power to vary agreements and securities

When a time order is made, then unless the contemplated amendment under s.136 is truly a consequence of the time order, and the making of it is also just, there is no power to make it (*Southern & District Finance plc v. Barnes* [1995] C.C.L.R. 62). When a time order is made in relation to future instalments that have not yet fallen due (*i.e.* in one of those limited types of case where that is possible), there will inevitably be consequences for the term of the loan or the rate of interest or both; in such a case the court has power to reduce the rate of interest in re-scheduling the debt (*ibid.*). The decision in *Southern & District Finance plc v. Barnes* was, however, rather ambiguous since in that case the Court of Appeal having confirmed the above mentioned limitations on the court's power conferred by section 136, nevertheless then went on to confirm its use in an apparently very wide set of circumstances. In *Director General of Fair Trading v. First National Bank* [2000] 1 W.L.R. 98; [2000] 1 All E.R. 240 Evans Lombe J. considered (*obiter*) that the court's powers under section 136 (as explained and applied in *Southern & District Finance v. Barnes*) were ample to prevent the imposition on a borrower of post-judgment interest where it would not be just to impose such interest. [The case was brought under the Unfair Terms in Consumer Contracts Regulations 1994 and ultimately reached the House of Lords – see para. 3H–537.] The court has wider powers to amend the agreement in the case of an extortionate credit bargain (ss.137-140). **3H–255**

EXTORTIONATE CREDIT BARGAINS

Extortionate credit bargains

137.—(1) If the court finds a credit bargain extortionate it may reopen the credit agreement so as to do justice between the parties. **3H–256**

(2) In this section and sections 138 to 140,—

    (a) "credit agreement" means any agreement (other than an agreement which is an exempt agreement as a result of section 16(6C)) between an individual (the "debtor") and any other person (the "creditor") by which the creditor provides the debtor with credit of any amount, and

    (b) "credit bargain"—

        (i) where no transaction other than the credit agreement is to be taken into account in computing the total charge for credit, means the credit agreement, or

        (ii) where one or more other transactions are to be so taken into account, means the credit agreement and those other transactions, taken together.

Note —The words "(other than an agreement which is an exempt agreement as a result of section 16(6C))" will be added by the Financial Services and Markets Act 2000 **3H–257**

(Regulated Activities) Order 2001 (S.I. 2001 No. 544) from a date to be specified (see S.I. 2002 No. 1777 and notes to s.16).

Extortionate credit bargains

3H–258   Sections 137–140 deal with extortionate credit bargains. They apply not just to regulated consumer credit agreements, but to any "personal credit agreement", *e.g.* an exempt agreement or an agreement to provide an individual with credit of £30,000. Section 137 enables the court to re-open a "credit agreement" where a "credit bargain" is found to be extortionate. The definition of "credit agreement" (identical to that of "personal credit agreement" in s.8(1)), is not as wide as that of "credit bargain". For the definition of extortionate, see s.138. For court's powers on re-opening a credit agreement, see s.139. For applications to re-open the credit agreement and for possible rules as to limitation, see s.139 and commentary thereon.

When bargains are extortionate

3H–259   **138.**—(1) A credit bargain is extortionate if it—

    (a) requires the debtor or a relative of his to make payments (whether unconditionally, or on certain contingencies) which are grossly exorbitant, or

    (b) otherwise grossly contravenes ordinary principles of fair dealing.

(2) In determining whether a credit bargain is extortionate, regard shall be had to such evidence as is adduced concerning—

    (a) interest rates prevailing at the time it was made,

    (b) the factors mentioned in subsections (3) to (5), and

    (c) any other relevant considerations.

(3) Factors applicable under subsection (2) in relation to the debtor include—

    (a) his age, experience, business capacity and state of health; and

    (b) the degree to which, at the time of making the credit bargain, he was under financial pressure, and the nature of that pressure.

(4) Factors applicable under subsection (2) in relation to the creditor include—

    (a) the degree of risk accepted by him, having regard to the value of any security provided;

    (b) his relationship to the debtor; and

    (c) whether or not a colourable cash price was quoted for any goods or services included in the credit bargain.

(5) Factors applicable under subsection (2) in relation to a linked transaction include the question how far the transaction was reasonably required for the protection of debtor or creditor, or was in the interest of the debtor.

When bargains are extortionate

Burden of proof

3H–260   Rests upon the creditor (s.171(7)).

"Evidence ... adduced"

3H–261   The court will normally have regard to the "evidence adduced" about the factors listed. However, the court can take judicial notice, relying on its own general knowledge, *e.g.* of interest rates (*Castle Phillips Finance v. Williams* [1986] C.C.L.R. 13).

Interest rates

The court should consider rates for similar types of transaction prevailing at the **3H–262** time the agreement was made. It is essential to compare like with like. For example, a short term loan will not be exorbitant simply because the interest rate is higher than that obtainable for long term loans. A different approach might be possible if, say, an unworldly debtor has been talked into making an agreement in an expensive sector of the market when she could have equally well have obtained the credit via a less expensive type of agreement. In making comparison between the interest rate under the agreement and prevailing rates the APR should be used (*Davies v. Direct Loans Ltd* [1986] 1 W.L.R. 823). Sometimes a credit agreement confers on the creditor a power to vary the rate of interest. In *Paragon Finance Plc v. Nash* [2002] 1 W.L.R. 685; [2002] C.C.L.R. 2 the Court of Appeal declined to follow *Lombard Tricity Finance v. Paton* [1989] 1 All E.R. 918, CA, and held: (i) post-contract variations to the rate of interest are irrelevant to whether the credit bargain is extortionate; (ii) the contractual power to vary the rate of interest is subject to an implied contractual term that the creditor will not exercise that power dishonestly, for an improper purpose, arbitrarily, capriciously or unreasonably. A creditor which raised its interest rate in an attempt to alleviate serious financial difficulties by passing on its increased costs to its borrowers, was held not to be in breach of that implied term – even though the variation increased the gap between the rate charged by the creditor and that charged by other lenders. A commercial lender is free to conduct its business in what it genuinely believes to be its best commercial interests: *Paragon Finance Ltd v. Pender and Pender* [2005] C.C.L.R. 5; [2005] EWCA Civ 760 . The implied terms which in *Paragon* the Court of Appeal was prepared to imply are all negative and *Paragon* does not open the door to an implied term that a lender may have a positive obligation to reduce a rate of interest: *Sterling Credit v. Rahman (No. 2)* [2002] EWHC 3008 (Ch); [2003] C.C.L.R. 13.

If a creditor has a policy of not exercising a contractual power to vary the interest rate (or the APR) even when market rates fall substantially, then failure to inform the debtor, at the time the agreement is made, about that policy is a relevant factor. If, however, the debtor would have entered the agreement even with that information, that factor is unlikely on its own to be sufficient to render the agreement extortionate: *Broadwick Financial Services Ltd v. Spencer* [2002] C.C.L.R. 3; [2002] EWCA Civ 35. There were two further aspects of *Broadwick*. First, the debtor, a non-status borrower, was allowed to make payments based on a lower rate of interest than the contractual rate. This was by virtue of a "concession letter" given to the debtor at the time the agreement was made. The letter stated that it was "not intended to be legally binding" and that the lower rate was an "*ex gratia* concession". Secondly, the agreement provided for a rebate on early settlement calculated according to the "Rule of 78". Both these features of the case were irrelevant to the issue of whether the agreement was extortionate: the first because the concession was not intended to be legally binding and the concessionary rate was not substantially lower than the contractual interest rate; the second because calculating the rebate according to the "Rule of 78" was sanctioned by the Consumer Credit (Rebate on Early Settlement) Regulations 1983.

Alternative challenges

A debtor may be able to challenge terms of the agreement (other than "core" terms, **3H–263** such as those which set the rate of interest payable under a loan agreement) as being "unfair" within the meaning of the Unfair Terms in Consumer Contracts Regulations 1994 (if the agreement was made after June 30, 1995 and before October 1, 1999) or the Unfair Terms in Consumer Contracts Regulations 1999 (if the agreement was made on or after October 1, 1999). For the 1999 regulations see para. 3H–533 below. In *Falco Finance Ltd v. Gough* [1999] C.C.L.R. 16 (Macclesfield County Court), the court considerd three features of a long term mortgage loan, namely: (i) its "dual rate" clause by which a lower ("concessionary") rate of interest was charged unless and until the debtor fell into arrears at any point; (ii) a clause providing for a rebate on redemption calculated on the "rule of 78" coupled with six months' notional deferral; and (iii) the charging of interest on a "flat rate" basis. The first was held to be extortionate within the meaning of s.138 while all three features were held to be unfair within the 1994 regulations. For an analysis of the application of the 1994 Regulations to a clause in a loan agreement imposing default interest at the contractual rate on outstanding arrears, including after judgment, see *Director General of Fair Trading v. First National Bank plc* at para. 3H–537 below.

Reopening of extortionate agreements

139.—(1) A credit agreement may, if the court thinks just, be **3H–264** reopened on the ground that the credit bargain is extortionate—

    (a) on an application for the purpose made by the debtor or any surety to the High Court, county court or sheriff court; or

    (b) at the instance of the debtor or a surety in any proceedings to which the debtor and creditor are parties, being proceedings to enforce the credit agreement, any security relating to it, or any linked transaction; or

    (c) at the instance of the debtor or a surety in other proceedings in any court where the amount paid or payable under the credit agreement is relevant.

(2) In reopening the agreement, the court may, for the purpose of relieving the debtor or a surety from payment of any sum in excess of that fairly due and reasonable, by order—

    (a) direct accounts to be taken, or (in Scotland) an accounting to be made, between any persons,

    (b) set aside the whole or part of any obligation imposed on the debtor or a surety by the credit bargain or any related agreement,

    (c) require the creditor to repay the whole or part of any sum paid under the credit bargain or any related agreement by the debtor or a surety, whether paid to the creditor or any other person,

    (d) direct the return to the surety of any property provided for the purposes of the security, or

    (e) alter the terms of the credit agreement or any security instrument.

(3) An order may be under subsection (2) notwithstanding that its effect is to place a burden on the creditor in respect of an advantage unfairly enjoyed by another person who is a party to a linked transaction.

(4) An order under subsection (2) shall not alter the effect of any judgment.

(5) In England and Wales an application under subsection (1)(a) shall be brought only in the county court in the case of—

    (a) a regulated agreement, or

    (b) an agreement (not being a regulated agreement) under which the creditor provides the debtor with fixed-sum credit or running-account credit.

(5A) [...]

(6) In Scotland an application under subsection (1)(a) may be brought in the sheriff court for the district in which the debtor or surety resides or carries on business.

(7) In Northern Ireland an application under subsection (1)(a) may be brought in the county court in the case of—

    (a) a regulated agreement, or

    (b) an agreement (not being a regulated agreement) under which the creditor provides the debtor with fixed-sum credit not exceeding £5,000 or running-account credit on which the credit limit does not exceed £5,000.

Note —Amended by the Debtors (Scotland) Act 1987, Sched.6; the Administration of **3H–265** Justice (Northern Ireland) Order 1975 (S.I. 1975 No. 816), art. 9(1), Sched.1; the County Courts Jurisdiction Order 1977 (S.I. 1977 No. 600); the County Courts Jurisdiction Order 1981 (S.I. 1981 No. 1123); the Administration of Justice Act 1982, Sched.3; the County Courts (Amendment) Rules (Northern Ireland) 1982 (S.I. 1982 No. 120); the County Courts Act, Sched.2; and the High Court and County Courts Jurisdiction Order 1991 (S.I. 1991 No. 724).

Reopening of extortionate agreements

Restrictions on court's ability to re-open agreement

An application under s.139(1) must be made within any relevant limitation period **3H–266** under the Limitation Act 1980. The proper approach, it is submitted, is that the Limitation Act has no application at all where the debtor makes the application to re-open the credit agreement (*e.g.* to be relieved of the obligation to pay a sum) as part of his *defence*, but that it may apply to a claim or counterclaim— see also *Extortionate Credit Bargain Claims and the Limitation Rules* (1998) 412 S.J. 274 and *Extortionate Loans: the Limitation Act revisited* (1999) 143 S.J. 646. Where an application under s.139 is for a remedy or remedies, other than for repayment of any sum, the claim is an action upon a specialty within s.8 of the Limitation Act 1980 and the relevant period limitation period expires 12 years after the agreement was made, *Rahman v. Sterling Credit Limited* [2001] 1 W.L.R. 496; [2002] C.C.L.R. 1. The period is six years where the remedy claimed is repayment of any sum, Limitation Act 1980, s.9. The Court of Appeal in *Rahman* did not decide, but nevertheless appeared to imply, that the six year period under s.9 began when the agreement was made. This is surely wrong, because the period does not start until the cause of action accrues and the cause of action to recover a sum of money cannot accrue until that sum has first been paid—see the articles referred to above. *Rahman* did not deal with the situation where an extortionate credit bargain claim is made purely by way of defence. It involved a secure loan made in 1989 in respect of which a possession order had been made in 1990 but never executed. In 1998, the debtor wished to apply, by way of a counterclaim in the possession proceedings, to have the agreement re-opened as being extortionate. Holding that the 12 year limitation period had not expired, the Court of Appeal granted him permission under CPR 20.4 to file that counterclaim (which did not include a claim for repayment of any sum). The court declined to refuse permission on the grounds of issue stoppel, since the counterclaim was part of the same original action in which the possession order had been claimed. It was not a new action in which the defendant was seeking to raise an issue which should have been raised in an earlier action.

Procedure

An application under s.139(1) will no doubt often be made by the debtor (or surety) **3H–267** in an action begun by the creditor. Written notice of an intention to make such an application should be served on the court and all other parties within 14 days after the service of the claim form on the applicant: see 7BPD.10. If such a notice is served, the applicant will be treated as having filed a defence. An originating application should be made using the Consumer Credit Act procedure, set out in the Consumer Credit Practice Direction at para. 7BPD.1, unless it relates to the recovery of land. See further the Introductory Note About Procedure at the start of this Act.

Interpretation of sections 137 to 139

140. Where the credit agreement is not a regulated agreement, **3H–268** expressions used in sections 137 to 139 which, apart from this section, apply only to regulated agreements, shall be construed as nearly as may be as if the credit agreement were a regulated agreement.

MISCELLANEOUS

Jurisdiction and parties

141.—(1) In England and Wales the county court shall have juris- **3H–269** diction to hear and determine—

    (a) any action by the creditor or owner to enforce a
        regulated agreement or any security relating to it;
    (b) any action to enforce any linked transaction against the
        debtor or hirer or his relative,

and such an action shall not be brought in any other court.

(2) Where an action or application is brought in the High Court which, by virtue of this Act, ought to have been brought in the county court it shall not be treated as improperly brought, but shall be transferred to the county court.

(3) In Scotland the sheriff court shall have jurisdiction to hear and determine any action referred to in subsection (1) and such an action shall not be brought in any other court.

(3A) Subject to subsection (3B) an action which is brought in the sheriff court by virtue of subsection (3) shall be brought only in one of the following courts, namely—

    (a) the court for the place where the debtor of hirer is
        domiciled (within the meaning of section 41 or 42 of the
        Civil Jurisdiction and Judgments Act 1982);
    (b) the court for the place where the debtor of hirer carries
        on business; and
    (c) where the purpose of the action is to assert, declare or
        determine proprietary or possessory rights, or rights of
        security, in or over moveable property, or to obtain
        authority to dispose of moveable property, the court for
        the place the property is situated.

(3B) Subsection (3A) shall not apply—

    (a) where Rule 3 of Schedule 8 to the said Act of 1982 ap-
        plies; or
    (b) where the jurisdiction of another court has been
        prorogated by an agreement entered into after the
        dispute has arisen.

(4) In Northern Ireland the county court shall have jurisdiction to hear and determine any action or application falling within subsection (1).

(5) Except as may be provided by rules of court, all the parties to a regulated agreement, and any surety, shall be made parties to any proceedings relating to the agreement.

3H–270   *Note* —Amended by the Civil Jurisdiction and Judgments Act 1982, Sched.12.

Jurisdiction and parties

3H–271   The Consumer Credit Practice direction (which supplements CPR 7.9) indicates in which county court a claim to recover goods, or an originating application for a time order (under s.129(1)(b)), may be started—generally the court in the district where the debtor or hirer resides or carries on business (para. 7BPD.1, para. 4).

    Subs.(2) —Despite the words "which shall not be treated as improperly brought", the court now has, by virtue of the County Courts Act 1984, s.40(1)(b) (as substituted by the Courts and Legal Services Act 1990), discretion to strike out the proceedings if satisfied that the claimant knew or ought to have known that they should have been brought in the County Court (*Barclays Bank Plc v. Brooks* [1997] C.C.L.R. 60). In any claim issued in the High Court in relation to a consumer credit agreement (*e.g.* a claim by the debtor or in relation to an exempt agreement), the particulars of claim must contain a statement that the action is not one to which s.141 applies (see para. 7.6 of the Practice Direction supplementing CPR Part 16 at para. 16PD.7).

Subs.(5) —For additional requirements as to parties and for the court's power to dispense with the requirements of this subsection, see para. 9 of the Consumer Credit Practice Direction (para. 7BPD.1).

Procedure

A claim by a creditor or owner to enforce a regulated agreement will be subject to one of the following three sets of procedure:　　　　　　　　　　　　　　　　**3H–272**

- The procedure set out in CPR Pt 55, if it is a claim relating to recovery of land;
- The Consumer Credit Act procedure, set out in the Consumer Credit Practice Direction at para. 7BPD.1, if either
  - (i) the agreement relates to goods, or
  - (ii) the agreement relates only to money and the claim involves an application for an order under any of ss.65(1), 86(2), 90, 92(1), 105(7)(a) or (b), 111(2), 124(1) or (2);
- A Pt 7 claim form (but not using the Consumer Credit Act procedure), if the agreement relates only to money and the claim does not involve an application under one of the above mentioned sections.

See further, the Introductory Note About Procedure at the start of this Act.

Power to declare rights of parties

142.—(1) Where under any provision of this Act a thing can be done by a creditor or owner on an enforcement order only, and either—　　　　　　　**3H–273**

- (a) the court dismisses (except on technical grounds only) an application for an enforcement order, or
- (b) where no such application has been made or such an application has been dismissed on technical grounds only, an interested party applies to the court for a declaration under this subsection,

the court may if it thinks just make a declaration that the creditor or owner is not entitled to do that thing, and thereafter no application for an enforcement order in respect of it shall be entertained.

(2) Where—

- (a) a regulated agreement or linked transaction is cancelled under section 69(1), or becomes subject to section 69(2), or
- (b) a regulated agreement is terminated under section 91,

and an interested party applies to the court for a declaration under this subsection, the court may make a declaration to that effect.

Power to declare rights of parties

For the effect on security of a declaration under subs. (1), see s.113(3)(d) and (4).　　**3H–274**

NORTHERN IRELAND

Jurisdiction of county court in Northern Ireland

143. Without prejudice to any provision which may be made by rules of court made in relation to county courts in Northern Ireland such rules may provide—　　　　　　　　　　　　　　　　　　　　　　　　**3H–275**

(a) that any action or application such as is mentioned in section 141(4) which is brought against the debtor or hirer in the county court may be brought in the county court for the division in which the debtor or hirer resided or carried on business at the date on which he last made a payment under the regulated agreement;

(b) that an application by a debtor or hirer or any surety under section 129(1)(b), 132(1), 139(1)(a), or 142(1)(b) which is brought in the county court may be brought in the county court for the division in which the debtor, or, as the case may be, the hirer or surety resides or carries on business;

(c) for service of process on persons outside Northern Ireland.

Appeal from county court in Northern Ireland

3H–276   **144.** Any person dissatisfied—

(a) with an order, whether adverse to him or in his favour, made by a county court in Northern Ireland in the exercise of any jurisdiction conferred by this Act, or

(b) with the dismissal or refusal by such a county court of any action or application instituted by him under the provisions of this Act,

shall be entitled to appeal from the order or from the dismissal or refusal as if the order, dismissal or refusal had been made in exercise of the jurisdiction conferred by Part III of the County Courts (Northern Ireland) Order 1980 and the appeal brought under Part VI of that Order and Articles 61 and 62 of that Order apply accordingly.

3H–277   *Note* —Amended by the County Courts (Northern Ireland) Order 1980 (S.I. 1980 No. 397)

PART X

ANCILLARY CREDIT BUSINESS

* * * *

LICENSING

* * * *

Agreement for services of unlicensed trader

3H–278   **148.**—(1) An agreement for the services of a person carrying on an ancillary credit business (the "trader"), if made when the trader was unlicensed, is enforceable against the other party (the "customer") only where the OFT has made an order under subsection (2) which applies to the agreement.

(2) The trader or his successor in title may apply to the OFT for

an order that agreements within subsection (1) are to be treated as if made when the trader was licensed.

(3) Unless the OFT determines to make an order under subsection (2) in accordance with the application, it shall, before determining the application, by notice—

    (a) inform the trader, giving its reasons, that, as the case may be, it is minded to refuse the application, or to grant it in terms different from those applied for, describing them, and

    (b) invite the trader to submit to the OFT representations in support of his application in accordance with section 34.

(4) In determining whether or not to make an order under subsection (2) in respect of any period the OFT shall consider, in addition to any other relevant factors,—

    (a) how far, if at all, customers under agreements made by the trader during that period were prejudiced by the trader's conduct;

    (b) whether or not the OFT would have been likely to grant a licence covering that period on an application by the trader, and

    (c) the degree of culpability for the failure to obtain a licence.

(5) If the OFT thinks fit, it may in an order under subsection (2)—

    (a) limit the order to specified agreements, or agreements of a specified description or made at a specified time;

    (b) make the order conditional on the doing of specified acts by the trader.

(6) This section does not apply to an agreement made by a consumer credit EEA firm unless at the time it was made that firm was precluded from entering into it as a result of—

    (a) a consumer credit prohibition imposed under section 203 of the Financial Services and Markets Act 2000; or

    (b) a restriction imposed on the firm under section 204 of that Act.

Note —Amended by the Financial Services and Markets Act 2000 (Consequential Amendments and Repeals) Order 2001 (S.I. 2001 No. 3649) and by the Enterprise Act 2002, s.278 and Sched.25.   **3H–279**

Agreement for services of unlicensed trader
  See commentary to s.40.   **3H–280**

Regulated agreements made on introductions by unlicensed credit-broker

149.—(1) A regulated agreement made by a debtor or hirer who, **3H–281** for the purpose of making that agreement, was introduced to the creditor or owner by an unlicensed credit-broker is enforceable against the debtor or hirer only where—

    (a) on the application of the credit-broker, the OFT has made an order under section 148(2) in respect of a period including the time when the introduction was made, and the order does not (whether in general terms or specifically) exclude the application of this paragraph to the regulated agreement, or

(b) the OFT has made an order under subsection (2) which applies to the agreement.

(2) Where during any period individuals were introduced to a person carrying on a consumer credit business or consumer hire business by an unlicensed credit-broker for the purpose of making regulated agreements with the person carrying on that business, that person or his successor in title may apply to the OFT for an order that regulated agreements so made are to be treated as if the credit-broker had been licensed at the time of the introduction.

(3) Unless the OFT determines to make an order under subsection (2) in accordance with the application, he shall, before determining the application, by notice—

(a) inform the applicant, giving its reasons, that, as the case may be, it is minded to refuse the application, or to grant it in terms different from those applied for, describing them, and

(b) invite the applicant to submit to the Director representations in support of his application in accordance with section 34.

(4) In determining whether or not to make an order under subsection (2) the OFT shall consider, in addition to any other relevant factors—

(a) how far, if at all, debtors or hirers under regulated agreements to which the application relates were prejudiced by the credit-broker's conduct, and

(b) the degree of culpability of the applicant in facilitating the carrying on by the credit-broker of his business when unlicensed.

(5) If the OFT thinks fit, it may in an order under subsection (2)—

(a) limit the order to specified agreements, or agreements of a specified description or made at a specified time;

(b) make the order conditional on the doing of specified acts by the applicant.

(6) For the purposes of this section, "unlicensed credit-broker" does not include a consumer credit EEA firm unless at the time the introduction was made that firm was precluded from making it as a result of—

(a) a consumer credit prohibition imposed under section 203 of the Financial Services and Markets Act 2000; or

(b) a restriction imposed on the firm under section 204 of that Act.

3H–282 *Note* —Amended by the Financial Services and Markets Act 2000 (Consequential Amendments and Repeals) Order 2001 (S.I. 2001 No. 3649) and by the Enterprise Act 2002, s.278 and Sched.25.

Regulated agreements made on introductions by unlicensed credit-broker

3H–283 See commentary to s.40

PART XI

ENFORCEMENT OF ACT

* * * *

No further sanctions for breach of Act

170.—(1) A breach of any requirement made (otherwise than by 3H–284 any court) by or under this Act shall incur no civil or criminal sanction as being such a breach, except to the extent (if any) expressly provided by or under this Act.

(2) In exercising its functions under this Act the OFT may take account of any matter appearing to it to constitute a breach of a requirement made by or under this Act, whether or not any sanction for that breach is provided by or under this Act and, if it is so provided, whether or not proceedings have been brought in respect of the breach.

(3) Subsection (1) does not prevent the grant of an injunction, or the making of an order of certiorari, mandamus or prohibition or as respects Scotland the grant of an interdict or of an order under section 91 of the Court of Session Act 1868 (order for specific performance of statutory duty).

Note—Amended by the Enterprise Act 2002, s.278 and Sched.25.   3H–285

Onus of proof in various proceedings

171.—(1) If an agreement contains a term signifying that in the 3H–286 opinion of the parties section 10(3)(b)(iii) does not apply to the agreement, it shall be taken not to apply unless the contrary is proved.

(2) It shall be assumed in any proceedings, unless the contrary is proved that when a person initiated a transaction as mentioned in section 19(1)(c) he knew the principal agreement had been made, or contemplated that it might be made.

(3) Regulations under section 44 or 52 may make provision as to the onus of proof in any proceedings to enforce the regulations.

(4) In proceedings brought by the creditor under a credit-token agreement—

  (a) it is for the creditor to prove that the credit-token was lawfully supplied to the debtor, and was accepted by him, and

  (b) if the debtor alleges that any use made of the credit-token was not authorised by him, it is for the creditor to prove either—

   (i) that the use was so authorised, or

   (ii) that the use occurred before the creditor had been given notice under section 84(3).

(5) In proceedings under section 50(1) in respect of a document received by a minor at any school or other educational establishment for minors, it is for the person sending it to him at that establishment

to prove that he did not know or suspect it to be such an establishment.

(6) In proceedings under section 119(1) it is for the pawnee to prove that he had reasonable cause to refuse to allow the pawn to be redeemed.

(7) If, in proceedings referred to in section 139(1), the debtor or any surety alleges that the credit bargain is extortionate it is for the creditor to prove the contrary.

Statements by creditor or owner to be binding

3H–287 **172.**—(1) A statement by a creditor or owner is binding on him if given under—

section 77(1),
section 78(1),
section 79(1),
section 97(1),
section 107(1)(c),
section 108(1)(c),
section 109(1)(c).

(2) Where a trader—

(a) gives a customer a notice in compliance with section 103(1)(b), or

(b) gives a customer a notice under section 103(1) asserting that the customer is not indebted to him under an agreement,

the notice is binding on the trader.

(3) Where in proceedings before any court—

(a) it is sought to rely on a statement or notice given as mentioned in subsection (1) or (2), and

(b) the statement or notice is shown to be incorrect,

the court may direct such relief (if any) to be given to the creditor or owner from the operation of subsection (1) or (2) as appears to the court to be just.

Statements by creditor or owner to be binding

3H–288 It would seem likely in exercising its discretion under subs. (3), the court will follow a very similar approach to that in estoppel cases. Indeed, a debtor may well seek to rely on s.172 and on estoppel as alternatives. For cases on estoppel see *United Overseas Bank v. Jiwani* [1976] 1 W.L.R. 964 (bank, which had credited debtor's account erroneously, not estopped from reclaiming money from debtor as debtor had not altered his position on basis of the error), and *Lombard North Central v. Stobart* [1990] C.C.L.R. 53, CA (creditor issuing settlement statement in relation to unregulated conditional sale agreement for purchase of car—statement understating amount required to pay off outstanding debt—debtor selling the car in consequence of error—creditor estopped from making claim in contract or conversion).

Contracting-out forbidden

3H–289 **173.**—(1) A term contained in a regulated agreement or linked transaction, or in any other agreement relating to an actual or prospective regulated agreement or linked transaction, is void if, and to the extent that, it is inconsistent with a provision for the protection of the debtor or hirer or his relative or any surety contained in this Act or in any regulation made under this Act.

(2) Where a provision specified the duty or liability of the debtor or hirer or his relative or any surety in certain circumstances, a term is inconsistent with that provision if it purports to impose, directly or indirectly, an additional duty or liability on him in those circumstances.

(3) Notwithstanding subsection (1), a provision of this Act under which a thing may be done in relation to any person on an order of the court or the OFT only shall not be taken to prevent its being done at any time with that person's consent given at that time, but the refusal of such consent shall not give rise to any liability.

Note —Amended by the Enterprise Act 2002, s.278 and Sched.25. **3H–290**

Consensual enforcement —For apparently conflicting rulings on whether s.173(3) **3H–291** enables a debtor to give effective consent to enforcement of the agreement against himself where, without that consent, s.127(3) renders the agreement unenforceable against him, see commentary to s.127 (para. 3H–235).

PART XII

SUPPLEMENTAL

GENERAL

* * * *

Service of documents

176.—(1) A document to be served under this act by one person **3H–292** ("the server") on another person ("the subject") is to be treated as properly served on the subject if dealt with as mentioned in the following subsections.

(2) The document may be delivered or sent by an appropriate method to the subject, or addressed to him by name and left at his proper address.

(3) For the purposes of this Act, a document sent by post to, or left at, the address last known to the server as the address of a person shall be treated as sent by post to, or left at, his proper address.

(4) Where the document is to be served on the subject as being the person having any interest in land, and it is not practicable after reasonable inquiry to ascertain the subject's name or address, the document may be served by—

    (a) addressing it to the subject by the description of the person having that interest in the land (naming it), and

    (b) delivering the document to some responsible person on the land or affixing it, or a copy of it, in a conspicuous position on the land.

(5) Where a document to be served on the subject as being a debtor, hirer or surety, or as having any other capacity relevant for the purposes of this Act, is served at any time on another person who—

    (a) is the person last known to the server as having that capacity, but

(b) before that time had ceased to have it,
the document shall be treated as having been served at that time on the subject.

(6) Anything done to a document in relation to a person who (whether to the knowledge of the server or not) has died shall be treated for the purposes of subsection (5) as service of the document on that person if it would have been so treated had he not died.

(7) The following enactments shall not be construed as authorising service on the Public Trustee (in England and Wales) or the Probate Judge (in Northern Ireland) of any document which is to be served under this Act—

section 9 of the Administration of Estates Act 1925;

section 3 of the Administration of Estates Act (Northern Ireland) 1955.

(8) References in the preceding subsections to the serving of a document on a person include the giving of the document to that person.

3H-293 Note —Amended by the Law of Property (Miscellaneous Provisions) Act 1994, Sched.1 and by the Consumer Credit Act 1974 (Electronic Communications) Order 2004 (S.I. 2004 No. 3236).

Service of documents
3H-294 in *Lombard North Central v. Power-Hines* [1995] C.C.L.R. 24, the debtor claimed in vain, that a default notice (under s.87) had not been received by him either because the postman was unreliable or because the debtor's young son had intercepted it. It was held that the fact that it did not come to the debtor's attention did not mean that he did not receive it. Section 176(2) was designed to apply where through no fault of the creditor the document does not come to the attention of the debtor. The court was entitled to assume that where the letter was not returned, it had been delivered.

Electronic transmission of documents
3H-295 176A.—(1) A document is transmitted in accordance with this subsection if—

(a) the person to whom it is transmitted agrees that it may be delivered to him by being transmitted to a particular electronic address in a particular electronic form,

(b) it is transmitted to that address in that form, and

(c) the form in which the document is transmitted is such that any information in the document which is addressed to the person to whom the document is transmitted is capable of being stored for future reference for an appropriate period in a way which allows the information to be reproduced without change.

(2) A document transmitted in accordance with subsection (1) shall, unless the contrary is proved, be treated for the purposes of this Act, except section 69, as having been delivered on the working day immediately following the day on which it is transmitted.

(3) In this section, "electronic address" includes any number or address used for the purposes of receiving electronic communications.

3H-296 Note —Section 176A was added by the Consumer Credit Act 1974 (Electronic Communications) Order 2004 (S.I. 2004 No. 3236).

* * * *

Arrangements between creditor and supplier

187.—(1) A consumer credit agreement shall be treated as entered **3H–297** into under pre-existing arrangements between a creditor and a supplier if it is entered into in accordance with, or in furtherance of, arrangements previously made between persons mentioned in subsection (4)(a), (b) or (c).

(2) A consumer credit agreement shall be treated as entered into in contemplation of future arrangements between a creditor and a supplier if it is entered into in the expectation that arrangements will subsequently be made between persons mentioned in subsection (4)(a), (b) or (c) for the supply of cash, goods and services (or any of them) to be financed by the consumer credit agreement.

(3) Arrangements shall be disregarded for the purposes of subsection (1) or (2) if—

    (a) they are arrangements for the making, in specified circumstances, of payments to the supplier by the creditor, and

    (b) the creditor holds himself out as willing to make, in such circumstances, payments of the kind to suppliers generally.

(3A) Subsections (1) and (2) do not apply to any disclosure of information by the Director to the Bank of England for the purpose of enabling or assisting the Bank to discharge its functions under the Banking Act 1987 or the Director to discharge his functions under this Act.

(4) The persons referred to in subsections (1) and (2) are—

    (a) the creditor and the supplier;

    (b) one of them and an associate of the other's;

    (c) an associate of one and an associate of the other's.

(5) Where the creditor is an associate of the supplier's, the consumer credit agreement shall be treated, unless the contrary is proved, as entered into under pre-existing arrangements between the creditor and the supplier.

Note —Amended by the Banking Act 1987, s.89. **3H–298**

Arrangements between creditor and supplier

See commentary to s.12. **3H–299**

Examples of use of new terminology

188.—(1) Schedule 2 shall have effect for illustrating the use of **3H–300** terminology employed in this Act.

(2) The examples given in Schedule 2 are not exhaustive.

(3) In the case of conflict between Schedule 2 and any other provision of this Act, that other provision shall prevail.

(4) The Secretary of State may by order amend Schedule 2 by adding further examples or in any other way.

Definitions

3H–301   189.—(1) In this Act, unless the context otherwise requires—

"advertisement" includes every form of advertising, whether in a publication, by television or radio, by display of notices, signs, labels, showcards or goods, by distribution of samples, circulars, catalogues, price lists or other material, by exhibition of pictures, models or films, or in any other way, and references to the publishing of advertisements shall be construed accordingly;

"advertiser" in relation to an advertisement, means any person indicated by the advertisement as willing to enter into transactions to which the advertisement relates;

"ancillary credit business" has the meaning given by section 145(1);

"antecedent negotiations" has the meaning given by section 56;

"appeal period" means the period beginning on the first day on which an appeal to the Secretary of State may be brought and ending on the last day on which it may be brought or, if it is brought, ending on its final determination, or abandonment;

"appropriate method" means (a) post, or (b) transmission in the form of an electronic communication in accordance with section 176A(1);

"assignment", in relation to Scotland, means assignation;

"associate" shall be construed in accordance with section 184;

"bill of sale" has the meaning given by section 4 of the Bills of Sale Act 1878 or, for Northern Ireland, by section 4 of the Bills of Sale (Ireland) Act 1879;

"building society" means a building society within the meaning of the Building Societies Act 1986;

"business" includes profession or trade, and references to a business apply subject to subsection (2);

"cancellable agreement" means a regulated agreement which, by virtue of section 67, may be cancelled by the debtor or hirer;

"canvass" shall be construed in accordance with sections 48 and 153;

"cash" includes money in any form;

"charity" means as respects England and Wales a charity registered under the Charities Act [1993]or an exempt charity (within the meaning of that Act), and as respects Scotland and Northern Ireland an institution or other organisation established for charitable purposes only ("organisation" including any persons administering a trust and "charitable" being construed in the same way as if it were contained in the Income Tax Acts);

"conditional sale agreement" means an agreement for the sale of goods or land under which the purchase price or part of it is payable by instalments, and the property in the goods or land is to remain in the seller (notwithstanding that the buyer is to be in possession of the goods or land) until such conditions as to the payment of instalments or otherwise as may be specified in the agreement are fulfilled;

"consumer credit agreement" has the meaning given by section 8, and includes a consumer credit agreement which is cancelled under section 69(1), or becomes subject to section 69(2), so far as the agreement remains in force;

"consumer credit business" means any business so far as it comprises or relates to the provision of credit under regulated consumer credit agreements;

"consumer hire agreement" has the meaning given by section 15;

"consumer hire business" means any business so far as it comprises or relates to the bailment or (in Scotland) the hiring of goods under regulated consumer hire agreements;

"controller", in relation to a body corporate, means a person—

    (a) in accordance with whose directions or instructions the directors of the body corporate or of another body corporate which is its controller (or any of them) are accustomed to act, or

    (b) who, either alone or with any associate or associates, is entitled to exercise, or control the exercise of, one third or more of the voting power at any general meeting of the body corporate or of another body corporate which is its controller;

"copy" shall be construed in accordance with section 180;

"costs", in relation to Scotland, means expenses;

"court" means in relation to England and Wales the county court, in relation to Scotland the sheriff court and in relation to Northern Ireland the High Court or the county court;

"credit" shall be construed in accordance with section 9;

"credit-broker" means a person carrying on a business of credit brokerage;

"credit brokerage" has the meaning given by section 145(2);

"credit limit" has the meaning given by section 10(2);

"creditor" means the person providing credit under a consumer credit agreement or the person to whom his rights and duties under the agreement have passed by assignment or operation of law, and in relation to a prospective consumer credit agreement, includes the prospective creditor;

"credit reference agency" has the meaning given by section 145(8);

"credit-sale agreement" means an agreement for the sale of goods, under which the purchase price or part of it is payable by instalments, but which is not a conditional sale agreement;

"credit-token" has the meaning given by section 14(1);

"credit-token agreement" means a regulated agreement for the provision of credit in connection with the use of a credit-token;

"debt-adjusting" has the meaning given by section 145(5);

"debt-collecting" has the meaning given by section 145(7);

"debt-counselling" has the meaning given by section 145(6);

"debtor" means the individual receiving credit under a consumer credit agreement or the person to whom his rights and duties under the agreement have passed by assignment or operation of law, and in relation to a prospective consumer credit agreement includes the prospective debtor;

"debtor-creditor agreement" has the meaning given by section 13;

"debtor-creditor-supplier agreement" has the meaning given by section 12;

"default notice" has the meaning given by section 87(1);

"deposit" means (except in section 16(10) and 25(1B)) any sum payable by a debtor or hirer by way of deposit or down-payment, or credited or to be credited to him on account of any deposit or down-payment, whether the sum is to be or has been paid to the creditor or owner or any other person, or is to be or has been discharged by a payment of money or a transfer or delivery of goods or by any other means;

"electric line" has the meaning given by the Electricity Act 1989 or, for Northern Ireland, the Electricity Supply (Northern Ireland) Order 1992;

"electronic communication" means an electronic communication within the meaning of the Electronic Communications Act 2000 (c.7);

"embodies" and related words shall be construed in accordance with subsection (4);

"enforcement authority" has the meaning given by section 161(1);

"enforcement order" means an order under section 65(1), 105(7)(a) or (b), 111(2) or 124(1) or (2);

"executed agreement" means a document, signed by or on behalf of the parties, embodying the terms of a regulated agreement, or such of them as have been reduced to writing;

"exempt agreement" means an agreement specified in or under section 16;

"finance" means to finance wholly or partly, and "financed" and "refinanced" shall be construed accordingly;

"file" and "copy of the file" have the meanings given by section 158(5);

"fixed-sum credit" has the meaning given by section 10(1)(b);

"friendly society" means a society registered or treated as registered under the Friendly Societies Act 1974 or the Friendly Societies Act 1992;

"future arrangements" shall be construed in accordance with section 187;

"general notice" means a notice published by the OFT at a time and in a manner appearing to it suitable for securing that the notice is seen within a reasonable time by persons likely to be affected by it;

"give" means deliver or send by an appropriate method to;

"goods" has the meaning given by section 61(1) of the Sale of Goods Act 1979;

"group licence" has the meaning given by section 22(1)(b);

"High Court" means Her Majesty's High Court of Justice, or the Court of Session in Scotland or the High Court of Justice in Northern Ireland;

"hire-purchase agreement" means an agreement, other than a conditional sale agreement, under which—

(a) goods are bailed or (in Scotland) hired in return for periodical payments by the person to whom they are bailed or hired, and

(b) the property in the goods will pass to that person if the terms of the agreement are complied with and one or more of the following occurs—

(i) the exercise of an option to purchase by that person,

(ii) the doing of any other specified act by any party to the agreement,

(iii) the happening of any other specified event;

"hirer" means the individual to whom goods are bailed or (in Scotland) hired under a consumer hire agreement, or the person to whom his rights and duties under the agreement have passed by assignment or operation of law, and in relation to a prospective consumer hire agreement includes the prospective hirer;

"individual" includes a partnership or other unincorporated body of persons not consisting entirely of bodies corporate;

"installation" means—

(a) the installing of any electric line or any gas or water pipe,

(b) the fixing of goods to the premises where they are to be used, and the alteration of premises to enable goods to be used on them,

(c) where it is reasonably necessary that goods should be constructed or erected on the premises where they are to be used, any work carried out for the purpose of constructing or erecting them on those premises;

"judgment" includes an order or decree made by any court;

"land", includes an interest in land, and in relation to Scotland includes heritable subjects of whatever description;

"land improvement company" means an improvement company

as defined by section 7 of the Improvement of Land Act, 1899;

"land mortgage" includes any security charged on land;

"licence" means a licence under Part III (including that Part as applied to ancillary credit businesses by section 147);

"licensed", in relation to any act, means authorised by a licence to do the act or cause or permit another person to do it;

"licensee", in the case of a group licence, includes any person covered by the licence;

"linked transaction" has the meaning given by section 19(1);

"local authority", in relation to England means a county council, a London borough council, a district council, the Common Council of the City of London, or the Council of the Isles of Scilly, in relation to Wales means a county council or a county borough council, and in relation to Scotland, means a council constituted under section 2 of the Local Government, etc. (Scotland) Act 1994, and, in relation to Northern Ireland, means a district council;

"minor", in relation to Scotland, includes pupil;

"modifying agreement" has the meaning given by section 82(2);

"mortgage", in relation to Scotland, includes any heritable security;

"multiple agreement" has the meaning given by section 18(1);

"negotiator" has the meaning given by section 56(1);

"non-commercial agreement" means a consumer credit agreement or a consumer hire agreement not made by the creditor or owner in the course of a business carried on by him;

"notice" means notice in writing;

"notice of cancellation" has the meaning given by section 69(1);

"OFT" means the Office of Fair Trading;

"owner" means a person who bails or (in Scotland) hires out goods under a consumer hire agreement or the person to whom his rights and duties under the agreement have passed by assignment or operation of law, and in relation to a prospective consumer hire agreement, includes the prospective bailor or person from whom the goods are to be hired;

"pawn" means any article subject to a pledge;

"pawn-receipt" has the meaning given by section 114;

"pawnee" and "pawnor" include any person to whom the rights and duties of the original pawnee or the original pawnor, as the case may be, have passed by assignment or operation of law;

"payment" includes tender;

"personal credit agreement" has the meaning given by section 8(1);

"pledge" means the pawnee's rights over an article taken in pawn;

"prescribed" means prescribed by regulations made by the Secretary of State;

"pre-existing arrangements" shall be construed in accordance with section 187;

"principal agreement" has the meaning given by section 19(1);

"protected goods" has the meaning given by section 90(7);

"quotation" has the meaning given by section 52(1)(a);

"redemption period" has the meaning given by section 116(3);

"register" means the register kept by the OFT under section 35;

"regulated agreement" means a consumer credit agreement, or consumer hire agreement, other than an exempt agreement, and "regulated" and "unregulated" shall be construed accordingly;

"regulations" means regulations made by the Secretary of State;

"relative", except in section 184, means a person who is an associate by virtue of section 184(1);

"representation" includes any condition or warranty, and any other statement or undertaking, whether oral or in writing;

"restricted-use credit agreement" and "restricted-use credit" have the meanings given by section 11(1);

"rules of court", in relation to Northern Ireland means, in relation to the High Court, rules made under section 7 of the Northern Ireland Act 1962, and, in relation to any other court, rules made by the authority having for the time being power to make rules regulating the practice and procedure in that court;

"running-account credit" shall be construed in accordance with section 10;

"security", in relation to an actual or prospective consumer credit agreement or consumer hire agreement, or any linked transaction, means a mortgage, charge, pledge, bond, debenture, indemnity, guarantee, bill, note or other right provided by the debtor or hirer, or at his request (express or implied), to secure the carrying out of the obligations of the debtor or hirer under the agreement;

"security instrument" has the meaning given by section 105(2);

"serve on" means deliver or send by an appropriate method to;

"signed" shall be construed in accordance with subsection (3);

"small agreement" has the meaning given by section 17(1), and "small" in relation to an agreement within any category shall be construed accordingly;

"specified fee" shall be construed in accordance with section 2(4) and (5);

"standard licence" has the meaning given by section 22(1)(a);

"supplier" has the meaning given by section 11(1)(b) or 12(c) or 13(c) or, in relation to an agreement falling within section 11(1)(a), means the creditor, and includes a person to whom the rights and duties of a supplier (as so defined) have passed by assignment or operation of law, or (in relation to a prospective agreement) the prospective supplier;

"surety" means the person by whom any security is provided, or the person to whom his rights and duties in relation to the security have passed by assignment or operation of law;

"technical grounds" shall be construed in accordance with subsection (5);

"time order" has the meaning given by section 129(1);

"total charge for credit" means a sum calculated in accordance with regulations under section 20(1);

"total price" means the total sum payable by the debtor under a hire-purchase agreement or a conditional sale agreement, including any sum payable on the exercise of an option to purchase, but excluding any sum payable as a penalty or as compensation or damages for a breach of the agreement;

"unexecuted agreement" means a document embodying the terms of a prospective regulated agreement, or such of them as it is intended to reduce to writing;

"unlicensed" means with a licence, but applies only in relation to acts for which a licence is required;

"unrestricted-use credit agreement" and "unrestricted-use credit" have the meanings given by section 11(2);

"working day" means any day other than—

    (a) Saturday or Sunday,

    (b) Christmas Day or Good Friday,

    (c) a bank holiday within the meaning given by section 1 of the Banking and Financial Dealings Act 1971.

(2) A person is not to be treated as carrying on a particular type of business merely because occasionally he enters into transactions belonging to a business of that type.

(3) Any provision of this Act requiring a document to be signed is complied with by a body corporate if the document is sealed by that body.

This subsection does not apply to Scotland.

(4) A document embodies a provision if the provision is set out either in the document itself or in another document referred to in it.

(5) An application dismissed by the court or the OFT shall, if the court or the OFT (as the case may be) so certifies, be taken to be dismissed on technical grounds only.

(6) Except in so far as the context otherwise requires, any reference in this Act to an enactment shall be construed as a reference to that enactment as amended by or under any other enactment, including this Act.

(7) In this Act, except where otherwise indicated—

    (a) a reference to a numbered Part, section or Schedule is a reference to the Part or section of, or the Schedule to this Act so numbered, and

    (b) a reference in a section to a numbered subsection is a reference to the subsection of that section so numbered, and

(c) a reference in a section, subsection or Schedule to a numbered paragraph is a reference to the paragraph of that section, subsection or Schedule so numbered.

Note —Amended by the Sale of Goods Act 1979, Sched.2; the Insurance Companies **3H–302** Act 1982, Sched.5; the Building Societies Act 1986, Sched.18; the Banking Act 1987, s.88; the Inheritance Act 1985, Sched.17; the Electricity Act 1989, Sched.16; the Charities Act 1993, Sched.6; the Local Government (Wales) Act 1994, Scheds 16 and 18; the Age of Legal Capacity (Scotland) Act 1991, Sched.2; the Friendly Societies Act 1992, Sched.22; the Financial Services and Markets Act 2000 (Consequential Amendments and Repeals) Order 2001 (S.I. 2001 No. 3649); the Enterprise Act 2002, s.278 and Sched.25 and the Consumer Credit Act 1974 (Electronic Communications) Order 2004 (S.I. 2004 No. 3236).

Meaning of "consumer credit EEA firm"

189A. In this Act "consumer credit EEA firm" means an EEA firm **3H–303** falling within sub-paragraph (a), (b) or (c) of paragraph 5 of Schedule 3 to the Financial Services and Markets Act 2000 carrying on, or seeking to carry on, consumer credit business, consumer hire business or ancillary credit business for which a licence would be required under this Act but for paragraph 15(3) of Schedule 3 to the Financial Services and Markets Act 2000.

Note —Section 189A was added by the Financial Services and Markets Act 2000 **3H–304** (Consequential Amendments and Repeals) Order 2001 (S.I. 2001 No. 3649).

Meaning of "consumer credit EEA firm"
See s.40(6) and commentary thereto at para. 3H–51 above. **3H–305**

* * * *

Special provisions as to Northern Ireland

191.—(1) The OFT may make arrangements with the Department **3H–306** of Commerce for Northern Ireland for the Department, on its behalf,—

(a) to receive applications, notices and fees;

(b) to maintain, and make available for inspection and copying, copies of entries in the register; and

(c) to provide certified copies of entries in the register,

to the extent that seems to it desirable for the convenience of persons in Northern Ireland.

(2) The OFT shall give general notice of any arrangements made under subsection (1).

(3) Nothing in this Act shall authorise any Northern Ireland department to incur any expenses attributable to the provisions of this Act until provision has been made for those expenses to be defrayed out of money appropriated for the purpose.

(4) The power of the Department of Commerce for Northern Ireland to make an order under section 178 shall be exercisable by statutory rule for the purposes of the Statutory Rules (Northern Ireland) Order 1979, and any such order shall be subject to negative resolution within the meaning of the Interpretation Act (Northern Ireland) 1954 as if it were a statutory instrument within the meaning of that Act.

(5) In this Act "enactment" includes an enactment of the Parliament of Northern Ireland or the Northern Ireland Assembly, and "Act" shall be construed in a corresponding manner; and (without prejudice to section 189(6)) any reference in this Act to such an enactment shall include a reference to any enactment re-enacting it with or without modifications.

(6) Section 38 of the Interpretation Act 1889 (effect of repeals) shall have the same operation in relation to any repeal by this Act of an enactment of the Parliament of Northern Ireland as it has in relation to the repeal of an Act of the Parliament of the United Kingdom, references in that section of the Act of 1889 to Acts and enactments being construed accordingly.

3H-307 *Note* —Amended by the Statutory Rules (Northern Ireland) Order 1979, S.O. 1979 No. 1573 (N.I.12) and the Enterprise Act 2002, s.278 and Sched. 25.

* * * *

SECTION 188(1)

SCHEDULE 2

EXAMPLES OF USE OF NEW TERMINOLOGY

PART I

LIST OF TERMS

3H-308

Term	Defined in section	Illustrated by example(s)
Advertisement	189(1)	2
Advertiser	189(1)	2
Antecedent negotiations	56	1, 2, 3, 4
Cancellable agreement	67	4
Consumer credit agreement	8	5, 6, 7, 15, 19, 21
Consumer hire agreement	15	20, 24
Credit	9	16, 19, 21
Credit-broker	189(1)	2
Credit limit	10(2)	6, 7, 19, 22, 23
Creditor	189(1)	1, 2, 3, 4
Credit-sale agreement	189(1)	5
Credit-token	14	3, 14, 16
Credit-token agreement	14	3, 14, 16, 22
Debtor-creditor agreement	13	8, 16, 17, 18
Debtor-creditor-supplier agreement	12	8, 16
Fixed-sum credit	10	9, 10, 17, 23
Hire-purchase agreement	189(1)	10
Individual	189(1)	19, 24

Term	Defined in section	Illustrated by example(s)
Linked transaction	19	11
Modifying agreement		24
	82(2)	
Multiple agreement	18	16, 18
Negotiator		1, 2, 3, 4
	56(1)	
Personal credit agreement		19
	8(1)	
Pre-existing arrangements	187	8, 21
Restricted-use credit	11	10, 12, 13, 14, 16
Running-account credit	10	15, 16, 18, 23
Small agreement	17	16, 17, 22
Supplier		3, 14
	189(1)	
Total charge for credit	20	5, 10
Total price		10
	189(1)	
Unrestricted-use credit	11	8, 12, 16, 17, 18

PART II

EXAMPLES

Example 1

Facts. Correspondence passes between an employee of a moneylending company **3H–309** (writing on behalf of the company) and an individual about the terms on which the company would grant him a loan under a regulated agreement.

Analysis. The correspondence constitutes antecedent negotiations falling within section 56(1)(a), the moneylending company being both creditor and negotiator.

Example 2

Facts. Representations are made about goods in a poster displayed by a shopkeeper **3H–310** near the goods, the goods being selected by a customer who has read the poster and then sold by the shopkeeper to a finance company introduced by him (with whom he has a business relationship). The goods are disposed of by the finance company to the customer under a regulated hire-purchase agreement.

Analysis. The representations in the poster constitute antecedent negotiations falling within section 56(1)(b), the shopkeeper being the credit-broker and negotiator and the finance company being the creditor. The poster is an advertisement and the shopkeeper is the advertiser.

Example 3

Facts. Discussions take place between a shopkeeper and a customer about goods the **3H–311** customer wishes to buy using a credit-card issued by the D Bank under a regulated agreement.

Analysis. The discussions constitute antecedent negotiations falling within section 56(1)(c), the shopkeeper being the supplier and negotiator and the D Bank the creditor. The credit-card is a credit-token as defined in section 14(1), and the regulated agreement under which it was issued is a credit-token agreement as defined in section 14(2).

Example 4

Facts. Discussions take place and correspondence passes between a secondhand car **3H–312** dealer and a customer about a car, which is then sold by the dealer to the customer under a regulated conditional sale agreement. Subsequently, on a revocation of that agreement by consent, the car is resold by the dealer to a finance company introduced

CONSUMER

by him (with whom he has a business relationship), who in turn dispose of it to the same customer under a regulated hire-purchase agreement.

Analysis. The discussions and correspondence constitute antecedent negotiations in relation both to the conditional sale agreement and the hire-purchase agreement. They fall under section 56(1)(a) in relation to the conditional sale agreement, the dealer being the creditor and the negotiator. In relation to the hire-purchase agreement they fall within section 56(1)(b), the dealer continuing to be treated as the negotiator but the finance company now being the creditor. Both agreements are cancellable if the discussions took place when the individual conducting the negotiations (whether the "negotiator" or his employee or agent) was in the presence of the debtor, unless the unexecuted agreement was signed by the debtor at trade premises (as defined in section 67(b)). If the discussion all took place by telephone however, or the unexecuted agreement was signed by the debtor on trade premises (as so defined) the agreements are not cancellable.

Example 5

3H–313   *Facts.* E agrees to sell to F (an individual) an item of furniture in return for 24 monthly instalments of £10 payable in arrear. The property in the goods passes to F immediately.

Analysis. This is a credit-sale agreement (see definition of "credit-sale agreement" in section 189(1)). The credit provided amounts to £240 less the amount which, according to regulations made under section 20(1), constitutes the total charge for credit. (The amount is required to be deducted by section 9(4).) Accordingly the agreement falls within section 8(2) and is a consumer credit agreement.

Example 6

3H–314   *Facts.* The G Bank grants H (an individual) an unlimited overdraft, with an increased rate of interest on so much of any debit balance as exceeds £2,000.

Analysis. Although the overdraft purports to be unlimited, the stipulation for increased interest above £2,000 bring the agreement within section 10(3)(b)(ii) and it is a consumer credit agreement.

Example 7

3H–315   *Facts.* J is an individual who owns a small shop which usually carries a stock worth about £1,000. K makes a stocking agreement under which he undertakes to provide on short-term credit the stock needed from time to time by J without any specified limit.

Analysis. Although the agreement appears to provide unlimited credit, it is probable, having regard to the stock usually carried by J, that his indebtedness to K will not at any item rise above £5,000. Accordingly the agreement falls within section 10(3)(b)(iii) and is a consumer credit agreement.

Example 8

3H–316   *Facts.* U, a moneylender, lends £500 to V (an individual) knowing he intends to use it to buy office equipment from W. W introduced V to U, it being his practice to introduce customers needing finance to him. Sometimes U gives W a commission for this and sometimes not. U pays the £500 direct to V.

Analysis. Although this appears to fall under section 11(1)(b), it is excluded by section 11(3) and is therefore (by section 11(2)) an unrestricted-use credit agreement. Whether it is a debtor-creditor agreement (by section 13(c)) or a debtor-creditor-supplier agreement (by section 12(c)) depends on whether the previous dealings between U and W amount to "pre-existing arrangements", that is whether the agreement can be taken to have been entered into "in accordance with, or in furtherance of" arrangements previously made between U and W, as laid down in section 187(1).

Example 9

3H–317   *Facts.* A agrees to lend B (an individual) £4,500 in nine monthly instalments of £500.

Analysis. This is a cash loan and is a form of credit (see section 9 and definition of "cash" in section 189(1)). Accordingly it falls within section 10(1)(b) and is fixed-sum credit amounting to £4,500.

Example 10

3H–318   *Facts.* C (in England) agrees to bail goods to D (an individual) in return for periodical payments. The agreement provides for the property in the goods to pass to D on payment of a total of £7,500 and the exercise by D of an option to purchase. The sum of £7,500 includes a down-payment of £1,000. It also includes an amount which, according to regulations made under section 20(1), constitutes a total charge for credit of £1,500.

Analysis. This is a hire-purchase agreement with a deposit of £1,000 and a total price of £7,500 (see definitions of "hire-purchase agreement", "deposit" and "total price" in section 189(1)). By section 9(3), it is taken to provide credit amounting to £7,500−(£1,500+£1,000), which equals £5,000. Under section 8(2), the agreement is therefore a consumer credit agreement, and under sections 9(3) and 11(1) it is a restricted-use credit agreement for fixed-sum credit. A similar result would follow if the agreement by C had been a hiring agreement in Scotland.

Example 11

Facts. X (an individual) borrows £500 from Y (Finance). As a condition of the grant- **3H–319**
ing of the loan X is required—

    (a) to execute a second mortgage on his house in favour of Y (Finance), and

    (b) to take out a policy of insurance on his life with Y (Insurances).

In accordance with the loan agreement, the policy is charged to Y (Finance) as collateral security for the loan. The two companies are associates within the meaning of section 184(3).

Analysis. The second mortgage is a transaction for the provision of security and accordingly does not fall within section 19(1), but the taking out of the insurance policy is a linked transaction falling within section 19(1)(a). The charging of the policy is a separate transaction (made between different parties) for the provision of security and again is excluded from section 19(1). The only linked transaction is therefore the taking out of the insurance policy. If X had not been required by the loan agreement to take out the policy, but it had been done at the suggestion of Y (Finance) to induce them to enter into the loan agreement, it would have been a linked transaction under section 19(1)(c)(i) by virtue of section 19(2)(a).

Example 12

Facts. The N Bank agrees to lend O (an individual) £2,000 to buy a car from P. To **3H–320**
make sure the loan is used as intended, the N Bank stipulates that the money must be paid by it direct to P.

Analysis. The agreement is a consumer credit agreement by virtue of section 8(2). Since it falls within section 11(1)(b), it is a restricted-use credit agreement, P being the supplier. If the N Bank had not stipulated for direct payment to the supplier, section 11(3) would have operated and made the agreement into one for unrestricted-use credit.

Example 13

Facts. Q, a debt-adjuster, agrees to pay off debts owed by R (an individual) to vari- **3H–321**
ous moneylenders. For this purpose the agreement provides for the making of a loan by Q to R in return for R's agreeing to repay the loan by instalments with interest. The loan money is not paid over to R but retained by Q and used to pay off the moneylenders.

Analysis. This is an agreement to refinance existing indebtedness of the debtor's, and if the loan by Q does not exceed £5,000 is a restricted-use credit agreement falling within section 11(1)(c).

Example 14

Facts. On payment of £1, S issues to T (an individual) a trading check under which **3H–322**
T can spend up to £20 at any shop which has agreed, or in future agrees, to accept S's trading checks.

Analysis. The trading check is a credit-token falling within section 14(1)(b). The credit-token agreement is a restricted-use credit agreement within section 11(1)(b), any shop in which the credit-token is used being the "supplier". The fact that further shops may be added after the issue of the credit-token is irrelevant in view of section 11(4).

Example 15

Facts. A retailer, L, agrees with M (an individual) to open an account in M's name **3H–323**
and, in return for M's promise to pay a specified minimum sum into the account each

CONSUMER

month and to pay a monthly charge for credit, agrees to allow to be debited to the account, in respect of purchases made by M from L, such sums as will not increase the debit balance at any time beyond the credit limit, defined in the agreement as a given multiple of the specified minimum sum.

Analysis. This arrangement provides credit falling within the definition of running-account credit in section 10(1)(a). Provided the credit limit is not over £5,000, the agreement falls within section 8(2) and is a consumer credit agreement for running-account credit.

Example 16

3H–324   *Facts.* Under an unsecured agreement, A (Credit), an associate of the A Bank, issues to B (an individual) a credit-card for use in obtaining cash on credit from A (Credit), to be paid by branches of the A Bank (acting as agent of A (Credit)), or goods or cash from suppliers or banks who have agreed to honour credit-cards issued by A (Credit). The credit limit is £30.

Analysis. This is a credit-token agreement falling within section 14(1)(a) and (b). It is a regulated consumer credit agreement for running-account credit. Since the credit limit does not exceed £30, the agreement is a small agreement. So far as the agreement relates to goods it is a debtor-creditor-supplier agreement within section 12(b), since it provides restricted-use credit under section 11(1)(b). So far as it relates to cash it is a debtor-credit agreement within section 13(c) and the credit it provides is unrestricted-use credit. This is therefore a multiple agreement. In that the whole agreement falls within several of the categories of agreement mentioned in this Act, it is, by section 18(3), to be treated as an agreement in each of those categories. So far as it is a debtor-creditor-supplier agreement providing restricted-use credit it is, by section 18(2), to be treated as a separate agreement; and similarly so far as it is a debtor-creditor agreement providing unrestricted-used credit. (See also Example 22)).

Example 17

3H–325   *Facts.* The manager of the C Bank agrees orally with D (an individual) to open a current account in D's name. Nothing is said about overdraft facilities. After maintaining the account in credit for some weeks, D draws a cheque in favour of E for an amount exceeding D's credit balance by £20. E presents the cheque and the Bank pay it.

Analysis. In drawing the cheque D, by implication, requests the Bank to grant him an overdraft of £20 on its usual terms as to interest and other charges. In deciding to honour the cheque, the Bank by implication accepts the offer. This constitutes a regulated small consumer credit agreement for unrestricted-use, fixed-sum credit. It is a debtor-creditor agreement, and falls within section 74(1)(b) if covered by a determination under section 74(3). (Compare Example 18).

Example 18

3H–326   *Facts.* F (an individual) has had a current account with the G Bank for many years. Although usually in credit, the account has been allowed by the Bank to become overdrawn from time to time. The maximum such overdraft has been is about £1,000. No explicit agreement has ever been made about overdraft facilities. Now, with a credit balance of £500, F draws a cheque for £1,300.

Analysis. It might well be held that the agreement with F (express or implied) under which the Bank operate his account includes an implied term giving him the right to overdraft facilities up to say £1,000. If so, the agreement is a regulated consumer credit agreement for unrestricted-use, running-account credit. It is a debtor-creditor agreement, and falls within section 74(1)(b) if covered by a direction under section 74(3). It is also a multiple agreement, part of which (*i.e.* the part not dealing with the overdraft), as referred to in section 18(1)(a), falls within a category of agreement not mentioned in this Act. (Compare Example 17).

Example 19

3H–327   *Facts.* H (a finance house) agrees with J (a partnership of individuals) to open an unsecured loan account in J's name on which the debit balance is not to exceed £7,000 (having regard to payments into the account made from time to time by J). Interest is to be payable in advance on this sum, with provision for yearly adjustments. H is entitled to debit the account with interest, a "setting-up" charge, and other charges. Before J has an opportunity to draw on the account it is initially debited with £2,250 for advance interest and other charges.

Analysis. This is a personal running-account credit agreement (see section 8(1) and 10(1)(a), and definition of "individual" in section 189(1)). By section 10(2) the credit limit is £7,000. By section 9(4) however the initial debit of £2,250, and any other charges later debited to the account by H, are not to be treated as credit even though time is allowed for their payment. Effect is given to this by section 10(3). Although the credit limit of £7,000 exceeds the amount (£5,000) specified in section 8(2) as the maximum for a consumer credit agreement, so that the agreement is not within section 10(3)(a), it is caught by section 10(3)(b)(i). At the beginning J can effectively draw (as credit) no more than £4,750, so the agreement is a consumer credit agreement.

Example 20

Facts. K (in England) agrees with L (an individual) to bail goods to L for a period of three years certain at £2,000 a year, payable quarterly. The agreement contains no provision for the passing of the property in the goods to L.

3H–328

Analysis. This is not a hire-purchase agreement (see paragraph (b) of the definition of that term in section 189(1)) and is capable of subsisting for more than three months. Paragraphs (a) and (b) ofsection 15(1) are therefore satisfied, but paragraph (c) is not. The payments by L must exceed £5,000 if he conforms to the agreement. It is true that under section 101 L has a right to terminate the agreement on giving K three months' notice expiring not earlier than eighteen months after the making of the agreement, but that section applies only where the agreement is a regulated consumer hire agreement apart from the section (see subsection (1)). So the agreement is not a consumer hire agreement, though it would be if the hire charge were say £1,500 a year, or there were a "break" clause in it operable by either party before the hire charges exceeded £5,000. A similar result would follow if the agreement by K had been a hiring agreement in Scotland.

Example 21

Facts. The P Bank decides to issue cheque cards to its customers under a scheme whereby the Bank undertakes to honour cheques of up to £30 in every case where the payee has taken the cheque in reliance on the cheque card, whether the consumer has funds in his account or not. The P Bank writes to the major retailers advising them of this scheme and also publicises it by advertising. The Bank issues a cheque card to Q (an individual), who uses it to pay by cheque for goods costing £20 bought by Q from R, a major retailer. At the time, Q has £500 in his account at the P Bank.

3H–329

Analysis. The agreement under which the cheque card is issued to Q is a consumer credit agreement even though at all relevant times Q has more than £30 in his account. This is because Q is free to draw out his whole balance and then use the cheque card, in which case the Bank has bound itself to honour the cheque. In other words the cheque card agreement provides Q with credit, whether he avails himself of it or not. Since the amount of the credit is not subject to any express limit, the cheque card can be used any number of times. It may be presumed however that section 19(3)(b)(iii) will apply. The agreement is an unrestricted-use debtor-creditor agreement (by section 13(c)). Although the P Bank wrote to R informing R of the P Bank's willingness to honour any cheque taken by R in reliance on a cheque card, this does not constitute pre-existing arrangements as mentioned in section 13(c) because section 187(3) operates to prevent it. The agreement is not a credit-token agreement within section 4(1)(b) because payment by the P Bank to R, would be a payment of the cheque and not a payment for the goods.

Example 22

Facts. The facts are as in Example 6. On one occasion B uses the credit-card in a way which increases his debit balance with A (Credit) to £40. A (Credit) writes to B agreeing to allow the excess on that occasion only, but stating that it must be paid off within one month.

3H–330

Analysis. In exceeding his credit limit B, by implication, requests A (Credit) to allow him a temporary excess (compare Example 17). A (Credit) is thus faced by B's action with the choice of treating it as a breach of contract or granting his implied request. He does the latter. If he had done the former, B would be treated as taking credit to which he was not entitled (section 14(3)) and, subject to the terms of his contract with A (Credit), would be liable to damages for breach of contract. As it is, the agreement to allow the excess varies the original credit-token agreement by adding a new term. Under section 10(2), the new term is to be disregarded in arriving at the credit limit, so that the credit-token agreement at no time ceases to be a small agreement. By section 82(2) the later agreement is deemed to revoke the original agreement and contain provisions reproducing the combined effect of the two agreements. By section 82(4), this latter agreement is exempted from Part V (except section 56).

Example 23

3H–331   *Facts.* Under an oral agreement made on 10th January, X (an individual) has an overdraft on his current account at the Y Bank with a credit limit of £100. On 15th February, when his overdraft standards at £90, X draws a cheque for £25. It is the first time that X has exceeded his credit limit, and on 16th February the bank honours the cheque.

Analysis. The agreement of 10th January is a consumer credit agreement for running-account credit. The agreement of 15th–16th February varies the earlier agreement by adding a term allowing the credit limit to be exceeded merely temporarily. By section 82(2) the later agreement is deemed to revoke the earlier agreement and reproduce the combined effect of the two agreements. By section 82(4), Part V of this Act (except section 56) does not apply to the later agreement. By section 18(5), a term allowing a merely temporary excess over the credit limit is not to be treated as a separate agreement, or as providing fixed-sum credit. The whole of the £115 owed to the Bank by X on 16th February is therefore running-account credit.

Example 24

3H–332   *Facts.* On 1st March 1975 Z (in England) enters into an agreement with A (an unincorporated body of persons) to bail to A equipment consisting of two components (component P and component Q). The agreement is not a hire-purchase agreement and is for a fixed term of 3 years, so paragraphs (a) and (b) of section 15(1) are both satisfied. The rental is payable monthly at a rate of £2,400 a year, but the agreement provides that this is to be reduced to £1,200 a year for the remainder of the agreement if at any time during its currency A returns component Q to the owner Z. On 5th May 1976 A is incorporated as A Ltd, taking over A's assets and liabilities. On 1st March 1977, A Ltd returns component Q. On 1st January 1978, Z and A Ltd agree to extend the earlier agreement by one year, increasing the rental for the final year by £250 to £1,450.

Analysis. When entered into on 1st March 1975, the agreement is a consumer hire agreement. A falls within the definition of "individual" in section 189(1) and if A returns component Q before 1st May 1976 the total rental will not exceed £5,000 (see section 15(1)(c)). When this date is passed without component Q having been returned it is obvious that the total rental must now exceed £5,000. Does this mean that the agreement then ceases to be a consumer hire agreement? The answer is no, because there has been no charge in the terms of the agreement, and without such a change the agreement cannot move from one category to the other. Similarly, the fact that A's rights and duties under the agreement pass to a body corporate on 5th May 1976 does not cause the agreement to cease to be a consumer hire agreement (see the definition of "hirer" in section 189(1)).

The effect of the modifying agreement on 1st January 1978 is governed by section 82(2), which requires it to be treated as containing provisions reproducing the combined effect of the two actual agreements, that is to say as providing that—

(a) obligations outstanding on 1st January 1978 are to be treated as outstanding under the modifying agreement;

(b) the modifying agreement applies at the old rate of hire for the months of January and February 1978, and

(c) for the year beginning 1st March 1978 A Ltd will be the bailee of component P at a rental of £1,450.

The total rental under the modifying agreement is £1,850. Accordingly the modifying agreement is a regulated agreement. Even if the total rental under the modifying agreement exceeded £5,000 it would still be regulated because of the provisions of section 82(3).

* * * * *

Consumer Credit (Total Charge for Credit) Regulations 1980

3H–333   (S.I. 1980 No. 51)

ARRANGEMENT OF REGULATIONS

The Secretary of State, in exercise of his powers under sections 20 and 182(2) of **3H–334** the Consumer Credit Act 1974, and of all other powers enabling him in that behalf, hereby makes the following Regulations:—

PART I

GENERAL

Citation, commencement, interpretation and revocation

1.—(1) These Regulations may be cited as the Consumer Credit **3H–335** (Total Charge for Credit) Regulations 1980 and shall come into operation on 28th April 1980.

(2) In these Regulations—

"the Act" means the Consumer Credit Act 1974;

"agreement" means a consumer credit agreement;

"land-related agreement" means an agreement which is—

(a) intended primary to finance the acquisition or retention of land, or

(b) intended to finance the renovation or improvement of a building, or any other agreement secured by a mortgage on land or, in Scotland, by a standard security within the meaning of the Conveyancing and Feudal Reform (Scotland) Act 1970;

"period rate of charge" means a percentage rate of charge for a period, comprising all charges included in the total charge for credit determined in accordance with Part II of these Regulations;

"the relevant date" means, in a case where a date is specified in or determinable under an agreement at the date of its making as that on which the debtor is entitled to require provision of anything the subject of the agreement, the earliest such date and, in any other case, the date of the making of the agreement; and

"transaction", except in regulation 5(1)(c) below, means an agreement, any transaction which is a linked transaction by virtue of section 19(1)(a) of the Act, any contract for the provision of security relating to the agreement, any credit brokerage contract relating to the agreement and any other contract to which the debtor or a relative of his is a party and which the creditor requires to be made or maintained as a condition of the making of the agreement,

and, except where the contrary intention appears, other expressions used in these Regulations have the same respective meanings as in the Act.

(3) For the purposes of these Regulations, references to the period for which credit is provided,—

(a) in the case of an agreement under which the period for which credit is to be provided is ascertainable at the date of the making of the agreement, are references to the period beginning with the relevant date and ending with the end of the period for which credit is to be provided;

(b) in the case of an agreement under which the period for which credit is to be provided can be ascertained at the relevant date if the assumption set out in regulation 13 below is applied, are references to the period beginning with the relevant date and ending with the end of the period for which credit would be provided under the agreement if the amount given by that assumption were the amount of the credit so provided; and

(c) in any other case, are references to the period of one year referred to in regulation 14 below.

(4) References in these Regulations to repayment of the credit under an agreement and of the total charge for credit include references to any repayment or payment, as the case may require, of any part of the credit and of the total charge for credit.

(5) The Consumer Credit (Total Charge for Credit) Regulations 1977 are hereby revoked.

3H–336   *Note* —Amended by the Consumer Credit (Total Charge for Credit and Rebate on Early Settlement) (Amendment) Regulations 1989 (S.I. 1989 No. 596) and the Consumer Credit (Total Charge for Credit, Agreements and Advertisements) (Amendment) Regulations 1999 (S.I. 1999 No. 3177).

Regulation 1

3H–337   These regulations provide for the calculation of (a) the total charge for credit and (b) the annual percentage rate of the total charge for credit (known as the APR). Part II (regs 3, 4 and 5) deals with the former. Part III (regs 6–11) deals with the latter. Pt IV (regs 12–18) provides assumptions to be made in making the calculations. Other assumptions required to be made are stated in reg. 2.

The regulations are stated here as amended (with effect from April 14, 2000), by the Consumer Credit (Total Charge for Credit, Agreements and Advertisements) (Amendment) Regulations 1999. The amendments were made, principally, to implement Directive 98/7/E.C., which amended the Consumer Credit Directive (87/102/ EEC). The amendments to the Consumer Credit Directive required there to be just one way of calculating the APR, where previously the 1980 regulations had provided three alternative ways of doing it. Those three ways were set out in regs 7, 8 and 9 (supplemented by reg. 10). Thus the effect of the amendments (as from April 14, 2000) is that the original regs 7–10 have been revoked and replaced with a new reg. 7 which sets out the single way of calculating the APR. The opportunity was also taken, in the 1999 amending regulations, to clarify one of the assumptions to be made in the case of low start mortgages, see regs 2(1)(e) and 15A and commentaries.

The "Relevant Date" —Is important in determining the period for which credit is **3H–338** provided (see reg. 1(3)). It will be normally the date of the making of the agreement unless the agreement makes it clear that the credit will not be provided before some later specified or ascertainable date. In the case of a contract for the purchase of goods on credit with a stated delivery date for the goods, the latter date is the "relevant date".

"Transaction" —Now includes a credit brokerage agreement. This change, relating **3H–339** to agreements made on or after June 30, 1989, was to ensure that credit brokerage charges were brought within the definition of the total charge for credit.

General provisions about calculation

2.—(1) Any calculation under these Regulations shall be made on **3H–340** the following assumptions—

> (a) the assumption that the debtor will not be entitled to any income tax relief relating to the transaction other than relief under section 19 of the Income and Corporation Taxes Act 1970 and Schedule 4 to the Finance Act 1976 (which afford relief in respect of premiums under certain policies of insurance) without any deduction under section 21 of the said Act of 1970;

> (b) the assumption that no assistance is given under the Home Purchase Assistance and Housing Corporation Guarantee Act 1978;

> (c)

>> (i) in the case of a transaction which provides for repayment of the credit or of the total charge for credit at or not later than a specified time or times, the assumption that the creditor will not exercise any right under the transaction to require repayment at any other time or times; and

>> (ii) in any other case, the assumption that the creditor will not exercise any right under the transaction to require repayment;

the debtor, in any case, performing all his obligations under the transaction; and

> (d) subject to sub-paragraph (e) below, in the case of a transaction which provides for variation of the rate or amount of any item included in the total charge for credit in consequence of the occurrence after the relevant date of any event, the assumption that the event will not occur; and, in this sub-paragraph, "event" means an act or

omission of the debtor or of the creditor or any other event (including where the transaction makes provision for variation upon the continuation of any circumstance, the continuation of that circumstance) but does not include an event which is certain to occur and of which the date of occurrence, or the earliest date of occurrence, can be ascertained at the date of the making of the agreement; and

(e) in the case of a land-related agreement which provides for the possibility of any variation of the rate of interest in consequence of the occurrence after the relevant date of any event (being an event which is certain to occur and of which the date of occurrence, or the earliest date of occurrence, can be ascertained at the date of the making of the agreement), the assumption that such a variation will, when the event occurs, take place.

(2) For the purposes of these Regulations—

(a) subject to sub-paragraph (b) below and regulation 18 below, in the case of any agreement each provision of credit and each repayment of the credit and of the total charge for credit shall be taken to be made:—

(i) at the earliest time provided under the transaction, and

(ii) in a case where any such provision or repayment is to be made at or not later than a specified time, at that time

and, where any such repayment is to be made before the relevant date, it shall be taken to be made on the relevant date;

(b) where under an agreement for running-account credit or an agreement for fixed-sum credit where the credit is not repayable at specified intervals or in specified amounts a constant period rate of charge in respect of periods of equal or of nearly equal length is charged, it shall be assumed for the purposes of calculations under these Regulations, notwithstanding regulation 17 below, that—

(i) the amount of credit outstanding at the beginning of a period is to remain outstanding throughout the period;

(ii) the amount of any credit provided during a period is provided immediately after the end of the period; and

(iii) any repayment of credit or of the total charge for credit made during a period is made immediately after the end of the period; and

(c) the assumption that the amount of any repayment of credit or of the total charge for credit will, at the time when the repayment is made, be the smallest for which the agreement provides.

(3) In determining the amount of the total of the interest on the

credit which may be provided under the agreement, any subsidy receivable by any person under Part II of the Housing Subsidies Act 1967 shall be deducted.

Note —Amended by the Consumer Credit (Total Charge for Credit, Agreements and Advertisements) (Amendment) Regulations 1999 (S.I. 1999 No. 3177).   **3H–341**

Regulation 2

Reg. 2(1)(a) —Calculations are to be made on gross charges (*i.e.* ignoring any tax **3H–342** relief) except in the case of those insurance premiums which are payable net of tax (*i.e.* certain life insurance premiums).

Reg. 2(1)(c) —It is assumed that the agreement will run its course and that the cred- **3H–343** itor will not, *e.g.*, exercise any power to call in the credit early.

Reg. 2(1)(d) and (e) —*Appear* to require: **3H–344**
   (a) where a variation in the charge for credit *will or may* occur on the occurrence of some future event which *may* occur, the making of the assumption that the event will not occur; but
   (b) where a variation in the charge for credit *will or may* occur on the occurrence of some future event which is *certain* to occur, the making of no such assumption.
   This caused difficulty in relation to certain low-start mortgage schemes, *i.e.* where the interest rate is low for an initial period of, say, one or two years and thereafter is to be at the standard variable rate of the lender. *National Westminster Bank v. Devon County Council* [1993] C.C.L.R. 69; *Scarborough Building Society v. Humberside Trading Standards Department* [1997] C.C.L.R. 47. To deal with this, the regulations were therefore amended, with effect from April 14, 2000, by, firstly, the addition of para. (e) (to which para. (d) is made subject) and, secondly, the addition of reg. 15A. The effect is that, in the case of low-start mortgages, it is to be assumed that the rate will be varied and that the rate as varied will be the lender's "initial standard variable rate" (as defined in reg. 15A).

Reg. 2(2) —States assumptions to be made about the dates when credit is to be **3H–345** provided or repayments (of credit and of the charge for credit) are to be made. Broadly the effect is as follows. Credit is assumed to be provided or repaid on the date on or before which, according to the agreement, it is to be done; if there is no such time specified, then it is assumed to be provided or repaid at the earliest time provided by the agreement. In the running-account and fixed-sum agreements specified in para. (b) (where a constant period rate of charge is applied, *e.g.* in respect of weekly or monthly periods), the assumption is made that a fixed amount of credit is outstanding throughout the period (*i.e.* ignoring withdrawals and repayments during the period). Where the debtor may repay more or less, it is to be assumed that he will make the smallest payment allowed.

PART II

TOTAL CHARGE FOR CREDIT

Total charge for credit

3. For the purposes of the Act, the total charge for the credit which **3H–346** may be provided under an actual or prospective agreement shall be the total of the amounts determined as at the date of the making of the agreement of such of the charges specified in regulation 4 below as apply in relation to the agreement but excluding the amount of the charges specified in regulation 5 below.

Regulation 3
The calculation of the total charge for credit is to be made as at the time the credit **3H–347**

agreement is made. It is done by adding up all the items that fall within the definition. It is a two stage definition. An item is within the definition if it is within reg. 4 and not within the exceptions stated in reg. 5. Any item within the definition is not within the "credit" provided, s.9(4) of "the Act" (and see reg.4 below).

Items included in total charge for credit

3H–348   **4.** Except as provided in regulation 5 below, the amounts of the following charges are included in the total charge for credit in relation to an agreement:—

(a) the total of the interest on the credit which may be provided under the agreement;

(b) other charges at any time payable under the transaction by or on behalf of the debtor or a relative of his whether to the creditor or any other person; and

(c) a premium under a contract of insurance, payable under the transaction by the debtor or a relative of his, where the making or maintenance of the contract of insurance is required by the creditor—

  (i) as a condition of making the agreement, and

  (ii) for the sole purpose of ensuring complete or partial repayment of the credit, and complete or partial payment to the creditor of such of those charges included in the total charge for credit as are payable to him under the transaction, in the event of the death, invalidity, illness or unemployment of the debtor,

notwithstanding that the whole or part of the charge may be repayable at any time or that the consideration therefor may include matters not within the transaction or subsisting at a time not within the duration of the agreement.

3H–349   *Note* —Amended by the Consumer Credit (Total Charge for Credit, Agreements and Advertisements) (Amendment) Regulations 1999 (S.I. 1999 No. 3177).

Regulation 4

3H–350   Reg. 4 seeks to identify any charge payable by the debtor or a relative under the "transaction", which term encompasses more than just the credit agreement (see reg. 1). Credit broker's fees are charges within reg. 4 (see commentary to reg. 1). Where a discount is allowed to a cash purchaser but not to a credit purchaser, that discount would appear to be a "charge" and, subject to reg. 5, part of the total charge for credit (*Metsoja v. H. Normal Pitt & Co. Ltd* [1990] C.C.L.R. 12, DC and see also *Holman v. Co-operative Wholesale Society Ltd* [2003] C.C.L.R 12, QB DC). A payment waiver premium payable by the debtor under a conditional sale agreement is a charge within reg. 4(b) (*Humberclyde Finance Ltd v. Thompson* [1997] C.C.L.R. 23, CA; but see commentary to reg. 5 below).

A secured short term bridging loan was advanced to the debtor after part of it had been deducted and used to pay an initial fire insurance premium and the lender's legal costs in connection with the transaction; these deductions, though they were not charges payable as a matter of contractual obligation, were deducted in accordance with general mortgage practice and were held to be charges "payable under the transaction by or on behalf of the debtor" and (not being within reg. 5 below) were thus within the total charge for credit (*Huntpast Ltd v. Leadbeater* [1993] C.C.L.R. 15, CA). It should be noted, however, that the insurance premium will now (after April 14, 2000) fall within reg. 5 unless it falls within reg. 4(c).

Reg. 4 does not define what it means by "charges". However, two things are mutually exclusive, namely the "credit" and anything entering into the "total charge for credit": s.9(4)of the Consumer Credit Act 1974. It would be absurd for anything to fall within the concept of a "charge" under reg. 4 which is in reality a part of the "credit". Thus where a debtor buys goods or services on credit, clearly the cash price of the goods or services is not one of the charges, even though payment of that price may well be a condition or term of the credit agreement. Equally, where the purpose (or one of the purposes) of a loan is to enable the debtor to pay off an existing debt, the amount advanced in order to pay off that debt is part of the credit and is not a *charge* for the credit – and that is so even if paying off that debt is a condition of the loan: *Watchtower Investments Ltd v. Payne* [2001] EWCA Civ 1159; [2003] C.C.L.R. 10. On the other hand, where paying off the debt owed by the debtor under an earlier agreement was not an objective purpose of the loan agreement but was merely something done (out of the amount of the loan) as a condition of the loan agreement, it was not part of the credit and was part of the total charge for credit: *McGinn v. Grangewood Securities Ltd* [2002] EWCA Civ 522; [2003] C.C.L.R. 11. In *London North Securities Ltd v.Meadows and Meadows* [2005] C.C.L.R.7, [2005] EWCA Civ 956 , the creditor insisted that the proposed loan be increased from £2,000 to £5,000 so that the extra £3,000 could be used to pay off the arrears under the debtor's existing mortgage agreement. The Court of Appeal followed Watchtower and distinguished McGinn as being "a case on very special and unusual facts", presumably in that there had in the pre-contract negotiations in McGinn been no mention of any of the credit being used to pay off the debtor's arrears under an existing mortgage agreement and the amount in question was no more than one instalment due under the debtor's existing agreement.

Insurance premiums —para. (c) was added to reg. 4 with effect from April 14, 2000. **3H–351** Before that date, an insurance premium had to be treated like any other charge, *i.e.* it was within the total charge for credit if it fell within reg. 4(a) or (b) and was not excluded by reg. 5. From April 14, 2000, the combination of reg. 4(c) and 5(1)(i) means that an insurance premium is within the total charge for credit only if it falls within reg. 4(c).

Unquantifiable charges —If charges (*e.g.* the lender's legal costs) cannot be quantified **3H–352** at the time the agreement is made, then the calculation of the total charge for credit would appear impossible. However, in advertisements a "typical" APR should be used (Consumer Credit (Advertisements) Regulations 2004 (S.I. 2004 No. 1484)) and in the agreement itself estimated information based on (stated) reasonable assumptions should be given (Consumer Credit (Agreements) Regulations 1983 (S.I. 1983 No. 1553), reg. 2(2)). Resort to such techniques will not be necessary (or indeed permitted) where the uncertainty is removed by one or more assumptions required to be made under the Consumer Credit (Total Charge for Credit) Regulations 1980, *e.g.* in the case of a low-start mortgage by reg. 2(1)(e) above (and see regs 12–18).

Items excluded from total charge for credit

5.—(1) The amounts of the following items are not included in the **3H–353** total charge for credit in relation to an agreement:—

    (a) any charge payable under the transaction to the creditor upon failure by the debtor or a relative of his to do or to refrain from doing anything which he is required to do or to refrain from doing, as the case may be;

    (b) any charge—

        (i) which is payable by the creditor to any person upon failure by the debtor or a relative of his to do or to refrain from doing anything which he is required under the transaction to do or to refrain from doing, as the case may be, and

        (ii) which the creditor may under the transaction require the debtor or a relative of his to pay to him or to another person on his behalf;

    (c) any charge relating to an agreement which is an agreement to finance a transaction of a description referred to

CONSUMER

in paragraph (a) or (b) of section 11(1) of this Act, being a charge which would be payable if the transaction were for cash;

(d) any charge (other than a fee or commission charged by a credit-broker) not within sub-paragraph (c) above—

    (i) of a description which relates to services or benefits incidental to the agreement and also to other services or benefits which may be supplied to the debtor, and

    (ii) which is payable pursuant to an obligation incurred by the debtor under arrangements effected before he applies to enter into the agreement, not being arrangements under which the debtor is bound to enter into any personal credit agreement;

(e) subject to paragraph (2) below, any charge under arrangements for the care, maintenance or protection of any land or goods;

(f) charges for money transmission services relating to an arrangement for a current account whereby the debtor may, by cheques or similar orders payable to himself or to any other person, obtain or have the use of money held or made available by the creditor and which records alterations in the financial relationship between the creditor and debtor, being charges which vary with the use made by the debtor of the arrangement;

(g) any charge for a guarantee other than a guarantee—

    (i) which is required by the creditor as a condition of making the agreement, and

    (ii) the purpose of which is to ensure complete or partial repayment of the credit and complete or partial payment to the creditor of such of those charges included in the total charge for credit as are payable to him under the transaction, in the event of the death, invalidity, illness or unemployment of the debtor;

(h) charges for the transfer of funds (other than charges within sub-paragraph (f) above) and charges for keeping an account intended to receive payments towards the repayment of the credit and the payment of interest and other charges, except where the debtor does not have reasonable freedom of choice in the matter and where such charges are abnormally high; but this sub-paragraph does not exclude from the total charge for credit charges for collection of the payments to which it refers, whether such payments are made in cash or otherwise;

(i) a premium under a contract of insurance other than a contract of insurance referred to in regulation 4(c) above.

(2) Paragraph (1) above has effect only—

(a) in the case of a charge within subparagraph (e), where, in pursuance of the arrangements—

    (i) the services are to be performed if, after the date of the making of the agreement, the condition of the land or goods becomes or is in immediate danger of becoming such that the land or goods cannot reasonably be enjoyed or used, and

    (ii) the charge will not accrue unless the services are performed; and

(b) in the case of any other charge within subparagraph (e)—

    (i) where provision of substantially the same description as that to which the arrangements relate is available under comparable arrangements from a person who is not the creditor or a supplier or a credit-broker who introduced the debtor and the creditor, and

    (ii) where the arrangements are made with a person chosen by the debtor, and

    (iii) if, in accordance with the transaction, the consent of the creditor or of a supplier or of the credit-broker who introduced the debtor and the creditor is required to the making of the arrangements where the transaction provides that such consent may not be unreasonably withheld whether because no incidental benefit will or may accrue to the creditor or to the supplier or to the credit-broker or on any other ground;

and references in this paragraph to the creditor, a supplier and a credit-broker include references to his near relative, his partner and a member of a group of which he is a member, to any person nominated by him or any such person in relation to the arrangements, and to a near relative of his partner; and "near relative" means, in relation to any person, the husband, wife, father, mother, brother, sister, son or daughter of that person and "group" means the person (including a company) having control of a company together with all the companies directly or indirectly controlled by him.

Note —Amended by the Consumer Credit (Total Charge for Credit) (Amendment) Regulations 1985 (S.I. 1985 No. 1192); the Consumer Credit (Total Charge for Credit and Rebate on Early Settlement) (Amendment) Regulations 1989 (S.I. 1989 No. 596); and the Consumer Credit (Total Charge for Credit, Agreements and Advertisements) (Amendment) Regulations 1999 (S.I. 1999 No. 3177).

3H–354

Regulation 5

Those charges which are excluded from the total charge for credit are, broadly: default charges (paras (1)(a) and (b)); charges that would be payable by a customer buying the same goods or services for cash instead of on credit terms (para. (1)(c)); certain club membership and similar charges (para. (1)(d)); certain charges for the care, maintenance or protection of goods or land (para. (1)(e)); variable bank charges (but not interest) on current accounts (para. (1)(f)); charges for guarantees (with one exception); charges for the transfer of funds (with exceptions); insurance premiums other than those falling within reg. 4(c). Club membership charges (*e.g.* membership

3H–355

of a motoring organisation) would, broadly, be excluded if, although membership were a condition of securing a loan at a given (preferential rate), the debtor was a member before entering the credit agreement and membership also conferred other benefits unconnected with the credit agreement. Maintenance, etc., charges are excluded, broadly:

(i) if they are payable only if something goes wrong (*e.g.* the dishwasher breaks down); or

(ii) if the debtor is allowed by the terms of the credit agreement (and in practice has) a free choice as to with whom he makes the maintenance agreement.

In *Humberclyde Finance Ltd v. Thompson* [1997] C.C.L.R. 23, CA (see commentary to s.9 of the Act), it was conceded that an optional payment waiver premium payable under a conditional sale agreement was not an *insurance* premium and that it was therefore not excluded from the total charge for credit by reg. 5. It is arguable, however, that it was insurance since in return for the premium, the debtor was promised that if he died within five years, he (*i.e.* in effect, his heirs) would be relieved from having to make any further payments under the agreement. If it were insurance, the premium would, after April 14, 2000, be excluded from the total charge for credit since, being optional, it would not fall within reg. 4(c).

PART III

RATE OF TOTAL CHARGE FOR CREDIT

Rate of total charge for credit

3H–356   **6.** The rate of the total charge for credit in the case of an actual or prospective agreement shall be the annual percentage rate of charge determined in accordance with the following provisions of this Part of these Regulations and (where it has more than one decimal place) rounded to one decimal place in accordance wtih regulation 6A below.

3H–357   *Note* —Amended by the Consumer Credit (Total Charge for Credit, Agreements and Advertisements) (Amendment) Regulations 1999 (S.I. 1999 No. 3177).

Regulation 6

3H–358   *Methods of calculation* —From April 14, 2000, only one method of calculation is permitted—see commentary to reg. 1. That method is found by application of the formula in reg. 7, rounded to one decimal place according to reg. 6A.

3H–359   *Tolerances* —Although the rate should in principle be determined correct to one decimal place, tolerances are allowed for APR's stated in advertisements (Consumer Credit (Advertisements) Regulations 1989 (S.I. 1989 No. 1125)) and in the agreement itself. As regards the latter, according to Sched.7 of the Consumer Credit (Agreements) Regulations 1983 (S.I. 1983 No. 1553), the following statement of the APR is permitted: a rate of up to 1 per cent over, or 0.1 per cent less than, the APR calculated according to the Consumer Credit (Total Charge for Credit) Regulations. There are other further minor tolerances in that Schedule covering situations where:

(i) all instalment intervals are equal but there is a longer period before instalments begin;

(ii) the amount of one instalment, usually the final one, differs from the others.

Other tolerances must not be combined with use of the *plus 1 per cent or minus 0.1 per cent* tolerance.

3H–360   **6A.** The annual percentage rate of charge referred to in regulation 6 above shall be rounded to one decimal place as follows—

(a) where the figure at the second decimal place is greater than or equal to 5, the figure at the first decimal place shall be increased by one and the decimal place (or places) following the first decimal place shall be disregarded; and

(b) where the figure at the second decimal place is less than 5, that decimal place and any decimal places following it shall be disregarded.

Note —Added by the Consumer Credit (Total Charge for Credit, Agreements and Advertisements) (Amendment) Regulations 1999 (S.I. 1999 No. 3177).   **3H–361**

7.—(1) Subject to paragraph (4) below, the annual percentage rate   **3H–362** of charge is the rate for *i* which satisfies the equation set out in paragraph (2) below, expressed as a percentage.

(2) The equation referred to in paragraph (1) above is—

$$\sum_{K=1}^{K=m} \frac{A_k}{(1+i)^{tK}} = \sum_{K'=1}^{K'=m'} \frac{A'_{k'}}{(1+i)^{tK'}}$$

where

K is the number identifying a particular advance of credit;

K' is the number identifying a particular instalment;

A_k is the amount of advance K;

$A'_{k'}$ is the amount of instalment K';

Σ represents the sum of all the terms indicated;

m is the number of advances of credit;

m' is the total number of instalments;

tK is the interval, expressed in years, between the relevant date and the date of the second advance and those of any subsequent advances numbered three to m; and

tK' is the interval, expressed in years, between the relevant date and the dates of instalments numbered one to m'.

(3) In paragraph (2) above, references to instalments are references to any payment made by or on behalf of the debtor or a relative of his which comprises—

(a) a repayment of all or part of the credit under the agreement;

(b) a payment of all or part of the total charge for credit; or

(c) both a repayment of all or part of the credit and a payment of all or part of the total charge for credit.

(4) Where more than one rate is given under paragraph (1) above, the annual percentage rate of charge is the positive rate nearest to zero or, if no positive rate is so given, the negative rate nearest to zero.

Note —Regulation 7 was substituted, and regulations 8, 9 and 10 were deleted, by   **3H–363** the Consumer Credit (Total Charge for Credit, Agreements and Advertisements) (Amendment) Regulations 1999 (S.I. 1999 No. 3177).

Computation of time

11.—(1) This regulation has effect for determining the length of   **3H–364**

any period for the purposes of calculations under this Part of these Regulations.

(2) A period which is not a whole number of calendar months or a whole number of weeks shall be counted in years and days.

(3) Subject to paragraph (4) below, a period which is a whole number of calendar months or a whole number of weeks shall be counted in calendar months or in weeks, as the case may be.

(4) Where a period is both a whole number of calendar months and a whole number of weeks and—

(a) one repayment only is to be made, the period shall be counted in calendar months, or

(b) more than one repayment is to be made,—

(i) if all such repayments are to be made at intervals from the relevant date of one or more weeks, the period shall be counted in weeks, and

(ii) in any other case, the period shall be counted in calendar months.

(5) A period which is to be counted—

(a) in calendar months shall be taken to be of a length equal to the relevant number of twelfth parts of a year, and

(b) in weeks, shall be taken to be of a length equal to the relevant number of fifty-second parts of a year.

(6) A day may be taken to be either—

(a) one three hundred and sixty-fifth part of a year or, if it is a leap year, one three hundred and sixty-sixth part of a year; or

(b) $\dfrac{1}{365.25}$ of a year.

(7) Every day shall be taken to be a working day.

3H–365   *Note* —Amended by the Consumer Credit (Total Charge for Credit, Agreements and Advertisements) (Amendment) Regulations 1999 (S.I. 1999 No. 3177).

PART IV

ASSUMPTIONS FOR CALCULATIONS

Effect of part IV

3H–366   **12.**—(1) The provisions of this Part of these Regulations shall have effect as the case may require for the purpose of the calculation of the total charge for credit under Part II above and of the rate of such charge under Part III above in relation to any actual or prospective agreement in respect of matters necessary for the calculation which cannot be ascertained by the creditor at the date of the making of the agreement.

(2) In a case where apart from this paragraph regulation 13 below and one or more other provisions of this Part would fall to be applied the said regulation 13 shall be applied first.

Regulation 12

The APR must be calculated as at the date the agreement is made. At that time **3H–367** certain information essential to the calculation may not be known. Therefore this Part (regs 12–18) states assumptions to be made in a number of such cases. Each of these regulations, except reg. 15, refers to "credit" being "provided". Despite the statement in reg. 2(2) that expressions not otherwise defined in that regulation are to have the same meaning as in the Act, the reference to credit being provided must be, not to the provision of a facility (*e.g.* an overdraft facility) upon which the debtor may or may not draw, but to the actual drawing upon that facility. There are other assumptions in reg. 2 above. When the APR is stated in an agreement for running-account credit, the Consumer Credit (Agreements) Regulations 1983 (S.I. 1983 No.1553) (as amended by S.I. 2004 No. 1482), provide a different set of assumptions which are to be used instead of those in Part IV of the Consumer Credit (Total Charge for Credit) Regulations 1980.

Assumption about the amount of credit

13. Where the amount of the credit to be provided under the **3H–368** agreement cannot be ascertained at the date of the making of the agreement,—

> (a) in the case of an agreement for running-account credit under which there is a credit limit, that amount shall be taken to be such credit limit, and
>
> (b) in any other case, that amount shall be taken to be £100.

Regulation 13

This assumption must be applied before any of the assumptions in regs 14–18 (see **3H–369** reg. 12(2)).

Assumption about period for which credit is provided

14. Where the period for which credit is to be provided is not as- **3H–370** certainable at the date of the making of the agreement, it shall be assumed that credit is provided for one year beginning with the relevant date.

Assumption about index-linked rates and amounts

15. Subject to regulation 15A below, where the rate or amount of **3H–371** any item included in the total charge for credit or the amount of any repayment of credit under a transaction falls to be ascertained thereunder by reference to the level of any index or other factor in accordance with any formula specified therein, the rate or amount, as the case may be, shall be taken to be the rate or amount so ascertained, the formula being applied as if the level of such index or other factor subsisting at the date of the making of the agreement were that subsisting at the date by reference to which the formula is to be applied.

Note —Amended by the Consumer Credit (Total Charge for Credit, Agreements **3H–372** and Advertisements) (Amendment) Regulations 1999 (S.I. 1999 No. 3177).

Regulation 15

Where an interest rate is variable by reference, say, to a lender's "base rate", then it **3H–373** will be assumed (either under this reg. or under reg. 2(1)(d)) that the base rate will remain throughout at the level it is when the agreement is made. There is a qualification to that, however, where reg. 15A applies.

Assumptions about variations of interest rates in land-related agreements

15A.—(1) This regulation applies to any land-related agreement **3H–374**

which provides for the possibility of any variation of the rate of interest if it is to be assumed, by virtue of regulation 2(1)(e) above, that the variation will take place but the amount of the variation cannot be ascertained at the date of the making of the agreement.

(2) In this regulation—

"initial standard variable rate" means—

(a) the standard variable rate of interest which would be applied by the creditor to the agreement on the date of the making of the agreement if the agreement provided for interest to be paid at the creditor's standard variable rate with effect from that date, or

(b) if there is no such rate, the standard variable rate of interest applied by the creditor on the date of the making of the agreement in question to other land-related agreements or, where there is more than one such rate, the highest such rate, taking no account (for the avoidance of doubt) of any discount or other reduction to which the debtor would or might be entitled; and

"varied rate" means any rate of interest charged when a variation of the rate of interest is to be assumed to take place by virtue of regulation 2(1)(e) above.

(3) Where a land-related agreement proides a formula for calculating a varied rate by reference to a standard variable rate of interest applied by the creditor, or any other fluctuating rate of interest, but does not enable the varied rate to be ascertained at the date of the making of the agreement because it is not known on that date what the standard variable rate will be or (as the case may be) at what level the fluctuating rate will be fixed when the varied rate falls to be calculated, it shall be assumed that that rate or level will be the same as the initial standard variable rate.

(4) Where a land-related agreement provides for the possibility of any variation in the rate of interest (other than a variation referred to in paragraph (3) above) which it is to be assumed, by virtue of regulation 2(1)(e) above, will take place but does not enable the amount of that variation to be ascertained at the date of the making of the agreement, it shall be assumed that the varied rate will be the same as the initial standard variable rate.

3H–375 *Note*—Regulation 15A was added, with effect from April 14, 2000, by the Consumer Credit (Total Charge for Credit, Agreements and Advertisements) (Amendment) Regulations 1999 (S.I. 1999 No. 3177).

Regulation 15A

3H–376 This applies, typically, to "low-start" mortgages. It is a characteristic of these that after the initial low interest period of, say, 1 year or 2 years, the mortgage loan will attract interest at a rate, usually, which is tied to (*e.g.* 2 per cent above) the lender's base rate. In these cases, the combined effect of reg. 2(1)(e) and reg. 15A is that the APR is to be calculated on the assumption that the rate will vary (*i.e.* at the end of the initial "low-start" period) and that the varied rate will be the "initial standard variable rate" as defined in regulation 15A(2). For "land-related agreement", see reg. 1(2). See also the commentary to reg. 2(1)(d) and (e).

Assumption about changes in charges

3H–377 **16.** Where—

    (a) the period for which the credit or any part thereof is to be or may be provided cannot be ascertained at the date of the making of the agreement; and

    (b) the rate or amount of any item included in the total charge for credit will change at a time provided in the transaction within one year beginning with the relevant date,

the rate or amount shall be taken to be the highest rate or amount at any time obtaining under the transaction in that year.

Assumption about time of provision of credit

17. Where the earliest date on which credit is to be provided can- **3H–378** not be ascertained at the date of the making of the agreement, it shall be assumed that credit is provided on that date.

Assumptions about time of payment of charges

18. In the case of any transaction it shall be assumed— **3H–379**

    (a) that a charge payable at a time which cannot be ascertained at the date of the making of the agreement shall be payable on the relevant date or, where it may reasonably be expected that a debtor will not make payment on that date, on the earliest date at which it may reasonably be expected that he will make payment; or

    (b) where more than one payment of a charge of the same description falls to be made at times which cannot be ascertained at the date of the making of the agreement, that the first such payment will be payable on the relevant date (or, where it may reasonably be expected that a debtor will not make payment on that date, at the earliest date on which it may reasonably be expected that he will make payment), that the last such payment will be payable at the end of the period for which credit is provided and that all other such payments (if any) will be payable at equal intervals between such times,

as the case may require.

List of Relevant Statutory Instruments

CONSUMER

- Consumer Credit (Rebate on Early Settlement) Regulations 1983 (S.I. 1983 No. 1562)
- Consumer Credit (Prescribed Periods for Giving Information) Regulations 1983 (S.I. 1983 No. 1569)
- Consumer Credit (Running Account Credit Information) Regulations 1983 (S.I. 1983 No. 1570)
- Consumer Credit (Increase of Monetary Limits) Order 1983 (S.I. 1983 No. 1878)
- Consumer Credit (Negotiable Instruments) (Exemptions) Order 1984 (S.I. 1984 No. 435)
- Consumer Protection (Cancellation of Contracts Concluded Away from Business Premises) Regulations 1987 (S.I. 1987 No. 2117)
- Consumer Credit (Exempt Agreements) Order 1989 (S.I. 1989 No. 869) (as amended)
- Consumer Credit (Increase of Monetary Limits) (Amendment) Order 1998 (S.I. 1998 No. 996)
- Consumer Credit (Further Increase of Monetary Amounts) Order 1998 (S.I. 1998 No. 997)
- Consumer Credit (Disclosure of Information) Regulations 2004 (S.I. 2004 No. 1481)
- Consumer Credit (Early Settlement) Regulations 2004 (S.I. 2004 No. 1483) (as amended)
- Consumer Credit (Advertisements) Regulations 2004 (S.I. 2004 No. 1484) (as amended)
- Financial Services (Distance Marketing) Regulations 2004 (S.I. 2004 No. 2095)
- Consumer Credit Act 1974 (Electronic Communications) Order 2004 (S.I. 2004 No. 3236)

Supply of Goods (Implied Terms) Act 1973

(1973 c.53)

General Note

3H–381   The only sections of this Act remaining unrepealed are those relating to the terms as to title, description, satisfactory quality, fitness for purpose, and sample which are implied in hire-purchase contracts. The sections that imply these terms in hire-purchase agreements are s.8 (title), s.9 (description), s.10 (satisfactory quality and fitness for purpose) and s.11 (sample). These implied terms are word for word the same as the equivalent sections (12–15) of the Sale of Goods Act 1979 (*q.v.*) except for necessary changes of wording to adapt the provisions to apply to hire-purchase agreements. Thus, instead of "seller" and "buyer" the terms "creditor" and "debtor" are used to describe the parties. These are the same terms as used by the Consumer Credit Act 1974 to describe the parties to a hire-purchase agreement. The terms implied by the Supply of Goods (Implied Terms) Act 1973 are implied into all hire-purchase agreements, not just those which are regulated by the Consumer Credit Act 1974.

Exclusion of liability

3H–382   The statutory restrictions on excluding liability for breach of these terms are exactly the same as they are in relation to the implied terms in ss.12–15 of the Sale of Goods Act 1979 (see, in particular, the Unfair Contract Terms Act 1977, s.6).

Remedies

3H–383   The same terms are conditions as are the equivalent implied terms in ss.12–15 of the Sale of Goods Act 1979. As with a contract of sale of goods, a breach of one of these conditions entitles the debtor to reject the goods. In sale of goods a buyer who is not "dealing as a consumer" has no right to reject the goods for breach of the implied conditions if the breach is so slight that it would be unreasonable to reject the goods (Sale of Goods Act 1979, s.15A). The position is exactly the same under the Supply of Goods (Implied Terms) Act 1973 for a debtor who is not "dealing as a consumer" (s.11A). One small difference in the law, however, is that the sale of goods doctrine that the right of rejection is lost by "acceptance" (within the meaning of the Sale of Goods Act 1979, s.35) does not apply to hire-purchase agreements. The difference is small because the debtor under a hire-purchase agreement is subject to the doctrine of affirmation whereby he loses any right of rejection he may have when he affirms the contract (*U.C.B. Leasing Ltd. v. Holtom* [1987] C.C.L.R. 101; [1987] R.T.R. 82, CA). See also *Feldaroll Foundry Plc v. Hermes Leasing (London) Ltd* [2004] EWCA Civ 747; [2004] C.C.L.R. 8.

Implied terms as to title

8.—(1) In every hire-purchase agreement, other than one to which **3H–384** subsection (2) below applies, there is—

> (a) an implied term on the part of the creditor that he will have a right to sell the goods at the time when the property is to pass; and
>
> (b) an implied term that—
>
>> (i) the goods are free, and will remain free until the time when the property is to pass, from any charge or encumbrance not disclosed or known to the person to whom the goods are bailed or (in Scotland) hired before the agreement is made, and
>>
>> (ii) that person will enjoy quiet possession of the goods except so far as it may be disturbed by any person entitled to the benefit of any charge or encumbrance so disclosed or known.

(2) In a hire-purchase agreement, in the case of which there appears from the agreement or is to be inferred from the circumstances of the agreement an intention that the creditor should transfer only such title as he or a third person may have, there is—

> (a) an implied term that all charges or encumbrances known to the creditor and not known to the person to whom the goods are bailed or hired have been disclosed to that person before the agreement is made; and
>
> (b) an implied term that neither—
>
>> (i) the creditor; nor
>>
>> (ii) in a case where the parties to the agreement intend that any title which may be transferred shall be only such title as a third person may have, that person; nor
>>
>> (iii) anyone claiming through or under the creditor or that third person otherwise than under a charge or encumbrance disclosed or known to the person to whom the goods are bailed or hired, before the agreement is made; will disturb the quiet possession of the person to whom the goods are bailed or hired.

(3) As regards England and Wales and Northern Ireland, the term implied by subsection (1)(a) above is a condition and the terms implied by subsections (1)(b), (2)(a) and 8(2)(b) above are warranties.

Note—Substituted by the Consumer Credit Act 1974 and amended by the Sale and **3H–385** Supply of Goods Act 1994, Sched.2, para. 4.

Implied terms as to title

3H–386   As explained in the general note above, these terms are identical to the equivalent terms in the Sale of Goods Act 1979. See generally the commentary to s.12 of that Act (at 3H–440).

3H–387   *Subs. (1)(a)* —This implied condition does not bite very early on because it is the nature of hire-purchase (almost always) that the property will not pass to the debtor until he has completed payments under the agreement, which will usually not be for years after the agreement is made. There is authority, however, that there is a term implied in a hire purchase agreement at common law that the creditor will have good title to the goods at the time the debtor takes delivery of them (*Mercantile Union Guarantee Corpn v. Wheatley* [1938] 1 K.B. 490).

Bailing or hiring by description

3H–388   **9.**—(1) Where under a hire-purchase agreement goods are bailed or (in Scotland) hired by description, there is an implied term that the goods will correspond with the description, and if under the agreement the goods are bailed or hired by reference to a sample as well as a description, it is not sufficient that the bulk of the goods correspond with the sample if the goods do not also correspond with the description.

(1A) As regards England and Wales and Northern Ireland, the term implied by subsection (1) above is a condition.

(2) Goods shall not be prevented from being bailed or hired by description by reason only that, being exposed for sale, bailment or hire, they are selected by he person to whom they are bailed or hired.

3H–389   *Note* —Subs.(1A) added by the Sale and Supply of Goods Act 1994, Sched.2, para. 4(3)(b).

Implied undertakings as to quality or fitness

3H–390   **10.**—(1) Except as provided by this section and section 11 below and subject to the provisions of any other enactment, including any enactment of the Parliament of Northern Ireland or the Northern Ireland Assembly, there is no implied term as to the quality or fitness for any particular purpose of goods bailed or (in Scotland) hired under a hire-purchase agreement.

(2) Where the creditor bails or hires goods under a hire-purchase agreement in the course of a business, there is an implied term that the goods supplied under the agreement are of satisfactory quality.

(2A) For the purposes of this Act, goods are of satisfactory quality if they meet the standard that a reasonable person would regard as satisfactory, taking account of any description of the goods, the price (if relevant) and all the other relevant circumstances.

(2B) For the purposes of this Act, the quality of goods includes their state and condition and the following (among others) are in appropriate cases aspects of the quality of goods—

    (a) fitness for all the purposes for which goods of the kind in question are commonly supplied,

    (b) appearance and finish,

    (c) freedom from minor defects,

    (d) safety, and

(e) durability.

(2C) The term implied by subsection (2) above does not extend to any matter making the quality of goods unsatisfactory—

(a) which is specifically drawn to the attention of the person to whom the goods are bailed or hied before the agreement is made,

(b) where that person examines the goods before the agreement is made, which that examination ought to reveal, or

(c) where the goods are bailed or hired by reference to a sample, which would have been apparent on a reasonable examination of the sample;

(2D) If the person to whom the goods are bailed or hired deals as consumer or, in Scotland, if the goods are hired to a person under a consumer contract, the relevant circumstances mentioned in subsection (2A) above include any public statements on the specific characteristics of the goods made about them by the creditor, the producer or his representative, particularly in advertising or on labelling.

(2E) A public statement is not by virtue of subsection (2D) above a relevant circumstance for the purposes of subsection (2A) above in the case of a contract of hire-purchase, if the creditor shows that—

(a) at the time the contract was made, he was not, and could not reasonably have been, aware of the statement,

(b) before the contract was made, the statement had been withdrawn in public or, to the extent that it contained anything which was incorrect or misleading, it had been corrected in public, or

(c) the decision to acquire the goods could not have been influenced by the statement.

(2F) Subsections (2D) and (2E) above do not prevent any public statement from being a relevant circumstance for the purposes of subsection (2A) above (whether or not the person to whom the goods are bailed or hired deals as consumer or, in Scotland, whether or not the goods are hired to a person under a consumer contract) if the statement would have been such a circumstance apart from those subsections.

(3) Where the creditor bails or hires goods under a hire-purchase agreement in the course of a business and the person to whom the goods are bailed or hired, expressly or by implication, makes known—

(a) to the creditor in the course of negotiations conducted by the creditor in relation to the making of the hire-purchase agreement, or

(b) to a credit-broker in the course of negotiations conduced by that broker in relation to goods sold by him to the creditor before forming the subject matter of the hire-purchase agreement,

any particular purpose for which the goods are being bailed or hired, there is an implied term that the goods supplied under the agreement are reasonably fit for that purpose, whether or not that is a purpose for which such goods are commonly supplied, except where the circumstances show that the person to whom the goods are bailed or hired does not rely, or that it is unreasonable for him to rely, on the skill or judgment of the creditor or credit-broker.

(4) An implied term as to quality or fitness for a particular purpose may be annexed to a hire-purchase agreement by usage.

(5) The preceding provisions of this section apply to a hire-purchase agreement made by a person who in the course of a business is acting as agent for the creditor as they apply to an agreement made by the creditor in the course of a business, except where the creditor is not bailing or hiring in the couse of a business and either the person to whom the goods are bailed or hired knows that fact or reasonable steps are taken to bring it to the notice of that person before the agreement is made.

(6) In subsection (3) above and this subsection—
    (a) "creditor-broker" means a person acting in the course of a business of credit brokerage;
    (b) "credit brokerage" means the effecting of introductions of individuals desiring to obtain credit—
        (i) to persons carrying on any business so far as it relates to the provision of credit, or
        (ii) to other persons engaged in credit brokerage.

(7) As regards England and Wales and Northern Ireland, the terms implied by subsections (2) and (3) above are conditions.

(8) In Scotland, "consumer contract" in this section has the same meaning as in section 12A(3) below.

3H–391   *Note* —Amended by the Sale and Supply of Goods Act 1994, Sched.2, para. 4(4)(c). Subss. (2D) to (2F) and (8) were added by the Sale and Supply of Goods to Consumers Regulations 2002 (S.I. 2002 No. 3045).

Samples

3H–392   **11.**—(1) Where under a hire-purchase agreement goods are bailed or (in Scotland) hired by reference to a sample, there is an implied term—
    (a) that the bulk will correspond with the sample in quality; and
    (b) that the person to whom the goods are bailed or hired will have a reasonable opportunity of comparing the bulk with the sample; and
    (c) that the goods will be free from any defect, making their quality unsatisfactory, which would not be apparent on reasonable examination of the sample.

(2) As regards England and Wales and Northern Ireland, the term implied by subsection (1) above is a condition.

3H–393   *Note* —Amended by the Sale and Supply of Goods Act 1994, Sched.2, para. 4(5)(c).

Modification of remedies for breach of statutory condition in non-consumer cases

3H–394   **11A.**—(1) Where in the case of a hire-purchase agreement—

(a) the person to whom the goods are bailed would, apart from this subsection, have the right to reject them by reason of a breach on the part of the creditor of a term implied by section 9, 10 or 11(1)(a) or (c) above, but

(b) the breach is so slight that it would be unreasonable for him to reject them,

then, if the person to whom the goods are bailed does not deal as consumer, the breach is not to be treated as a breach of condition, but may be treated as a breach of warranty.

(2) This section applies unless a contrary intention appears in, or is to be implied from, the agreement.

(3) It is for the creditor to show—

(a) that a breach fell within subsection (1)(b) above, and

(b) that the person to whom the goods were bailed did not deal as consumer.

(4) The references in this section to dealing as consumer are to be construed in accordance with Part I of the Unfair Contract Terms Act 1977.

(5) This section does not apply to Scotland.

Note—Inserted by the Sale and Supply of Goods Act 1994, Sched.2, para. 4(6). **3H–395**

Special provisions as to conditional sale agreements

14.—(1) Section 11(4) of the Sale of Goods Act 1979 (whereby in certain circumstances a breach of a condition in a contract of sale is treated only as a breach of warranty) shall not apply to a conditional sale agreement where the buyer deals as consumer within Part I of the Unfair Contract Terms Act 1977 [...] **3H–396**

(2) In England and Wales and Northern Ireland a breach of a condition (whether express or implied) to be fulfilled by the seller under any such agreement shall be treated as a breach of warranty, and not as grounds for rejecting the goods and treating the agreement as repudiated, if (but only if) it would have fallen to be so treated had the condition been contained or implied in a corresponding hire-purchase agreement as a condition to be fulfilled by the creditor.

Note—Amended by the Consumer Credit Act 1974, s.192(4), Sched.4, para. 36 and the Unfair Contract Terms Act, Sched.3. **3H–397**

Supplementary

15.—(1) In sections 8 to 14 above and this section— **3H–398**

"business" includes a profession and the activities of any government department (including a Northern Ireland department), or local or public authority;

"buyer" and "seller" includes a person to whom rights and duties under a conditional sale agreement have passed by assignment or operation of law;

"conditional sale agreement" means an agreement for the sale of goods under which the purchase price or part of it is payable by instalments, and the property in the goods is to remain in the seller (notwithstanding that the buyer is to be in possession of the goods) until such conditions as to the payment of instalments or otherwise as may be specified in the agreement are fulfilled;

"consumer sale" has the same meaning as in section 55 of the Sale of Goods Act 1979 (as set out in paragraph 11 of Schedule 1 to that Act)

"creditor" means the person by whom the goods are bailed or (in Scotland) hired under a hire-purchase agreement or the person to whom his rights and duties under the agreement have passed by assignment or operation of law; and

"hire-purchase agreement" means an agreement, other than conditional sale agreement, under which—

(a) goods are bailed or (in Scotland) hired in return for periodical payments by the person to whom they are bailed or hired, and

(b) the property in the goods will pass to that person if the terms of the agreement are complied with and one or more of the following occurs—

(i) the exercise of an option to purchase by that person,

(ii) the doing of any other specified act by any party to the agreement,

(iii) the happening of any other specified event.

"producer" means the manufacturer of goods, the importer of goods into the European Economic Area or any person purporting to be a producer by placing his name, trade mark or other distinctive sign on the goods.

(3) In section 14(2) above "corresponding hire-purchase agreement" means, in relation to a conditional sale agreement, a hire-purchase agreement relating to the same goods as the conditional sale agreement and made between the same parties and at the same time and in the same circumstances and, as nearly as may be, in the same terms as the conditional sale agreement.

(4) Nothing in sections 8 to 13 above shall prejudice the operation of any other enactment including any enactment of the Parliament of Northern Ireland or the Northern Ireland Assembly or any rule of law whereby any [...] term, other than one relating to quality or fitness, is to be implied in any hire-purchase agreement.

3H–399   *Note* —Amended by the Sale and Supply of Goods Act 1994, Sched.2, para. 4(9)(c) and by the Sale and Supply of Goods to Consumers Regulations 2002 (S.I. 2002 No. 3045).

Unfair Contract Terms Act 1977

(1977 c.50)

An Act to impose further limits on the extent to which under the law of England and Wales and Northern Ireland civil liability for breach of contract, or for negligence or other breach of duty, can be avoided by means of contract terms and otherwise, and under the law of Scotland civil liability can be avoided by means of contract terms.

[26th October 1977] **3H–400**

ARRANGEMENT OF SECTIONS

Introductory Note

This Act implemented, with some modifications, the recommendations in the **3H–401** Second Report on Exemption Clauses of the Law Commissions (Law. Com. No. 69; Scot. Law Com. No.39). The Act does not apply to all contract terms, but only to those which purport to exempt or limit the liability of one of the parties to the contract. It restricts the ability of the parties to exclude or limit liability for: breach of contract, negligence or misrepresentation. It also restricts the exclusion of tortious liability by non-contractual notices. For legislation which applies to other contractual terms which are unfair: see the Unfair Terms in Consumer Contracts Regulations 1999 (below) and (in relation to extortionate credit bargains) the Consumer Credit Act 1974, ss.137– 140. Hitherto the privity of contract rule meant that generally speaking, a third party (X) could not rely upon a contractual exclusion clause in a contract between A and B, *Scruttons v. Midland Silicones* [1962] A.C. 446. In such a case the provisions of the Unfair Contract Terms Act 1977 were irrelevant. The Contracts (Rights of Third Parties) Act 1999 has (subject to some exceptions) removed the inability of a third party to rely upon an exclusion clause where the clause was intended by the parties to benefit the third party and the third party was identified by name, class or description. In that case, the Unfair Contract Terms Act 1977 may then operate to restrict the effectiveness of the clause. A clause which is not affected by this Act may be rendered ineffective by the Unfair Terms in Consumer Contracts Regulations 1999 (see para. 3H–533 below).

PART I

Scope of Part I

1.—(1) For the purposes of this Part of this Act, "negligence" means **3H–402** the breach—

> (a) of any obligation, arising from the express or implied terms of a contract, to take reasonable care or exercise reasonable skill in the performance of the contract;

(b) of any common law duty to take reasonable care or exercise reasonable skill (but not any stricter duty);

(c) of the common duty of care imposed by the Occupiers' Liability Act 1957 or the Occupiers' Liability Act (Northern Ireland) 1957.

(2) This Part of this Act is subject to Part III; and in relation to contracts, the operation of sections 2 to 4 and 7 is subject to the exceptions made by Schedule 1.

(3) In the case of both contract and tort, sections 2 to 7 apply (except where the contrary is stated in section 6(4)) only to business liability, that is liability for breach of obligations or duties arising—

(a) from things done or to be done by a person in the course of a business (whether his own business or another's); or

(b) from the occupation of premises used for business purposes of the occupier;

and references to liability are to be read accordingly, but liability of an occupier of premises for breach of an obligation or duty towards a person obtaining access to the premises for recreational or educational purposes, being liability for loss or damage suffered by reason of the dangerous state of the premises, is not a business liability of the occupier unless granting that person such access for the purposes concerned falls within the business purposes of the occupier.

(4) In relation to any breach of duty or obligation, it is immaterial for any purpose of this Part of this Act whether the breach was inadvertent or intentional, or whether liability for it arises directly or vicariously.

3H–403   *Note* —Amended by the Occupiers' Liability Act 1984, s.2.

Scope of Part I

3H–404   *Subs. (2)* —The effect of Pt III is that the Act does not apply to: international supply contracts where possession or ownership of goods is to pass (s.26); foreign contracts where the parties have chosen English Law as the applicable law (s.27); exemption clauses allowed by U.K. legislation implementing international conventions (ss.28 and 29); and, contracts within Sched.1, para. 1 of the Act. The latter include: insurance contracts; land transactions; formation and dissolution of companies; securities transactions. A contract of employment, which excluded the employer's liability for the employee's loss of share option rights in the event that the employee was wrongfully dismissed, related to the creation or transfer of securities (share option rights) and to that extent was outside the scope of the Act, *Micklefield v. S.A.C. Technology Ltd* [1990] 1 W.L.R. 1002. Except in favour of a person dealing as a consumer, the Act, apart from s.2(1), does not apply to charterparties, marine salvage, contracts of carriage by ship or hovercraft (Sched.1, para. 2).

Subs. (3) —the expression "in the course of a business" has been held to have a restricted meaning in s.12. Even if that is correct in relation to s.12, it seems more likely that the expression here includes any transaction made by a business, whether or not such a transaction was the regular trade of that business. See the commentary to s.12.

Avoidance of Liability for Negligence, Breach of Contracts, etc.

Negligence liability

3H–405   **2.**—(1) A person cannot by reference to any contract term or to a notice given to persons generally or to particular persons exclude or restrict his liability for death or personal injury resulting from negligence.

(2) In the case of other loss or damage, a person cannot so exclude or restrict his liability for negligence except in so far as the term or notice satisfies the requirement of reasonableness.

(3) Where a contract term or notice purports to exclude or restrict liability for negligence a person's agreement to or awareness of it is not of itself to be taken as indicating his voluntary acceptance of any risk.

Negligence liability

Subs. (1)—Two cases both concerned the same standard clause in a contract to hire a crane and driver. The clause provided that as between supplier and hirer, the driver would be regarded for all purposes as employee of the hirer. In *Phillips Products Ltd v. Hyland* [1987] 1 W.L.R. 659 where the negligent driver drove the crane into a building belonging to the hirer, thereby damaging it, the hirer was the victim and claimed damages from the supplier for the negligence of the supplier's employee. The hirer succeeded in having the clause declared ineffective under subs. (2) as not satisfying the test of reasonableness. This case was distinguished in *Thomson v. T. Lohan (Plant Hire) Ltd* [1987] 1 W.L.R. 649 where the driver brought a claim (successfully) against one employer (the hirer) for his injuries and the hirer sought to recover contribution from the supplier. The supplier was able to rely on the clause, since a clause which does not restrict the victim's ability to bring a claim but which merely apportions or allocates liability between potential defendants is not affected by s.2. **3H–406**

Subs. (2)—For the requirement of reasonableness, see s.11. Even if a term satisfied the requirement of reasonableness, it would still be ineffective to exclude liability for negligence if either (a) it was not incorporated into the contract or (b) as a matter of construction, it does not operate to exclude liability for negligence or the loss in question. The language may not be sufficiently plain to exclude liability for negligence, *Hollier v. Rambler Motors* [1972] 2 Q.B. 71. A disclaimer by a professional valuer giving a valuation of a house to a prospective lender and foreseeably relied upon by the borrower/buyer has been held invalid under this provision, *Smith v. Eric S. Bush* [1990] 1 A.C. 381.

Liability arising in contract

3.—(1) This section applies as between contracting parties where one of them deals as consumer or on the other's written standard terms of business. **3H–407**

(2) As against that party, the other cannot by reference to any contract term—

    (a) when himself in breach of contract, exclude or restrict any liability of his in respect of the breach; or

    (b) claim to be entitled—

        (i) to render a contractual performance substantially different from that which was reasonably expected of him, or

        (ii) in respect of the whole or any part of his contractual obligation, to render no performance at all,

except in so far as (in any of the cases mentioned above in this subsection) the contract term satisfies the requirement of reasonableness.

Liability arising in contract

For the requirement of reasonableness, see s.11. For "deals as a consumer" see s.12. **3H–408**

CONSUMER

There is no definition of "standard terms of business". It certainly includes both (i) clauses prepared by a trade association or similar body for use generally in the trade and (ii) those prepared just by an individual contractor with no particular contract in mind.

Unreasonable indemnity clauses

3H–409 **4.**—(1) A person dealing as consumer cannot by reference to any contract term be made to indemnify another person (whether a party to the contract or not) in respect of liability that may be incurred by the other for negligence or breach of contract, except in so far as the contract term satisfies the requirement of reasonableness.

(2) This section applies whether the liability in question—

(a) is directly that of the person to be indemnified or is incurred by him vicariously:

(b) is to the person dealing as consumer or to someone else.

LIABILITY ARISING FROM SALE OR SUPPLY OF GOODS

"Guarantee" of consumer goods

3H–410 **5.**—(1) In the case of goods of a type ordinarily supplied for private use or consumption, where loss or damage—

(a) arises from the goods proving defective while in consumer use; and

(b) results from the negligence of a person concerned the manufacture or distribution of the goods,

liability for the loss or damage cannot be excluded or restricted by reference to any contract term or notice contained in or operating by reference to a guarantee of the goods.

(2) For these purposes—

(a) goods are to be regarded as "in consumer use" when a person is using them, or has them in his possession for use, otherwise than exclusively for the purposes of a business; and

(b) anything in writing is a guarantee if it contains or purports to contain some promise or assurance (however worded or presented) that defects will be made good by complete or partial replacement, or by repair, monetary compensation or otherwise.

(3) This section does not apply as between the parties to a contract under or in pursuance of which possession or ownership of the goods passed.

Sale and hire-purchase

3H–411 **6.**—(1) Liability for breach of the obligations arising from—

(a) section 12 of the Sale of Goods Act 1979 (seller's implied undertakings as to title, etc.);

(b) section 8 of the Supply of Goods (Implied Terms) Act 1973 (the corresponding thing in relation to hire-purchase),

cannot be excluded or restricted by reference to any contract term.

(2) As against *a* person dealing as consumer, liability for breach of the obligations arising from—

 (a) section 13, 14 or 15 of the 1979 Act (seller's implied undertakings as to conformity of goods with description or sample, or as to their quality or fitness for a particular purpose);

 (b) section 9, 10 or 11 of the 1973 Act (the corresponding things in relation to hire-purchase),

cannot be excluded or restricted by reference to any contract term.

(3) As against a person dealing otherwise than as consumer, the liability specified in subsection (2) above can be excluded or restricted by reference to a contract term, but only in so far as the term satisfies the requirement of reasonableness.

(4) The liabilities referred to in this section are not only the business liabilities defined by section 1(3), but include those arising under any contract of sale of goods or hire-purchase agreement.

Note —Amended by the Sale of Goods Act 1979, s.63(2) and Sched.2. **3H–412**

Sale and hire-purchase

 This section restates provisions previously stated in the Sale of Goods Act 1893, s.55 **3H–413** as amended by the Supply of Goods (Implied Terms) Act 1973 and in the 1973 Act itself. For "dealing as a consumer", see s.12. For "requirement of reasonableness", see s.11 and Sched.2.

Miscellaneous contracts under which goods pass

 7.—(1) Where the possession or ownership of goods passes under **3H–414** or in pursuance of a contract not governed by the law of sale of goods or hire-purchase, subsections (2) to (4) below apply as regards the effect (if any) to be given to contract terms excluding or restricting liability for breach of obligation arising by implication of law from the nature of the contract.

 (2) As against a person dealing as consumer, liability in respect of the goods' correspondence with description or sample, or their quality or fitness for any particular purpose, cannot be excluded or restricted by reference to any such term.

 (3) As against a person dealing otherwise than as consumer, that liability can be excluded or restricted by reference to such a term, but only in so far as the term satisfies the requirement of reasonableness.

 (3A) Liability for breach of the obligations arising under section 2 of the Supply of Goods and Services Act 1982 (implied terms about title etc. in certain contracts for the transfer of the property in goods) cannot be excluded or restricted by references to any such term.

 (4) Liability in respect of—

 (a) the right to transfer ownership of the goods, or give possession; or

 (b) the assurance of quiet possession to a person taking goods in pursuance of the contract, cannot (in a case to which subsection (3A) above does not apply) be excluded or restricted by reference to any such term except in so

CONSUMER

far as the term satisfies the requirement of reasonableness.

3H–415   *Note*—Amended, and subs. (3A) added, by the Supply of Goods and Services Act 1982, s.17; subs.(5) repealed by The Regulatory Reform (Trading Stamps) Order 2005 (S.I. 2005 No. 871).

Miscellaneous contracts

3H–416   The principal examples of contracts capable of falling within subs. (1) are: contracts of barter or exchange, contracts for services which involve the supply of goods; contracts of hire. See further, the commentary to the Sale of Goods Act 1979, s.2 (below).

OTHER PROVISIONS ABOUT CONTRACTS

Misrepresentation

3H–417   **8.**—(1) In the Misrepresentation Act 1967, the following is substituted for section 3— "Avoidance of provision excluding liability for misrepresentation

3. If a contract contains a term which would exclude or restrict—

(a) any liability to which a party to a contract may be subject by reason of any misrepresentation made by him before the contract was made; or

(b) any remedy available to another party to the contract by reason of such a misrepresentation,

the term shall be of no effect except in so far as it satisfies the requirement of reasonableness as stated in section 11(1) of the Unfair Contract Terms Act 1977; and it is for those claiming that the term satisfies that requirement to show that it does"

(2) The same section is substituted for section 3 of the Misrepresentation Act (Northern Ireland) 1967.

Misrepresentation

3H–418   This section does not in any way qualify the right of a principal to limit the authority (actual or ostensible) of his agent, *Overbrooke Estates v. Glencombe Park Properties* [1974] 1 W.L.R. 1335.

Effect of breach

3H–419   **9.**—(1) Where for reliance upon it a contract term has to satisfy the requirement of reasonableness, it may be found to do so and be given effect accordingly notwithstanding that the contract has been terminated either by breach or by a party electing to treat it as repudiated.

(2) Where on a breach the contract is nevertheless affirmed by a party entitled to treat it as repudiated, this does not of itself exclude the requirement of reasonableness in relation to any contract term.

Effect of breach

3H–420   If an exemption clause (a) is properly incorporated into the contract, (b), as a matter of construction, covers the breach in question and, (c) satisfies the requirement of reasonableness, then it may be relied upon notwithstanding the termination of the contract.

Evasion by means of secondary contract

3H–421   **10.** A person is not bound by any contract term prejudicing or taking away rights of his which arise under, or in connection with the performance of, another contract, so far as those rights extend to the enforcement of another's liability which this Part of this Act prevents that other from excluding or restricting.

Evasion by secondary contract

This section applies only to clauses in a contract which seek to modify or exempt **3H–422** future liability and does not affect retrospective waivers of existing claims, *Tudor Grange Holdings Ltd v. Citibank NA* [1992] Ch 53.

The "reasonableness" test

11.—(1) In relation to a contract term, the requirement of **3H–423** reasonableness for the purposes of this Part of this Act, section 3 of the Misrepresentation Act 1967 and section 3 of the Misrepresentation Act (Northern Ireland) 1967 is that the term shall have been a fair and reasonable one to be included having regard to the circumstances which were, or ought reasonably to have been, known to or in the contemplation of the parties when the contract was made.

(2) In determining for the purposes of section 6 or 7 above whether a contract term satisfies the requirement of reasonableness, regard shall be had in particular to the matters specified in Schedule 2 to this Act; but this subsection does not prevent the court or arbitrator from holding, in accordance with any rule of law, that a term which purports to exclude or restrict any relevant liability is not a term of the contract.

(3) In relation to a notice (not being a notice having contractual effect), the requirement of reasonableness under this Act is that it should be fair and reasonable to allow reliance on it, having regard to all the circumstances obtaining when the liability arose or (but for the notice) would have arisen.

(4) Where by reference to a contract term or notice a person seeks to restrict liability to a specified sum of money, and the question arises (under this or any other Act) whether the term or notice satisfies the requirement of reasonableness, regard shall be had in particular (but without prejudice to subsection (2) above in the case of contract terms) to—

　　(a) the resources which he could expect to be available to him for the purpose of meeting the liability should it arise; and

　　(b) how far it was open to him to cover himself by insurance.

(5) It is for those claiming that a contract term or notice satisfies the requirement of reasonableness to show that it does.

The reasonableness test

In applying the test, the courts have to weigh relevant factors. When applying it for **3H–424** the purposes of ss.6 and 7 the court is given guidelines in Sched.2. These, however, are not exhaustive of the factors to be taken into account. The judge's task in weighing the various factors is akin to the exercise of a discretion and his decision on the issue of reasonableness will not be disturbed by an appellate court unless it proceeded on some erroneous principle or was plainly and obviously wrong, *Mitchell (George) v. Finney Lock Seeds* [1983] 2 A.C. 803. In that case, a contract by which a farmer bought some seeds contained a clause limiting the liability of the sellers to no more than the purchase price of the seeds. The wrong seeds were supplied and the farmer's crop consequently failed. It was held in the House of Lords that the clause did not satisfy the test of reasonableness bearing in mind, *inter alia*, the following: (i) it had not been negotiated by any representative body; (ii) the buyers could not have discovered the error until after the crop had been sown; (iii) the buyers could not reasonably have been expected to cover the risk (of crop failure) by insurance whereas the sellers could easily, and at modest cost, have obtained liability insurance. An international computer firm's standard term limiting the firm's liability to a maximum of £100,000 has been held unreasonable, *St Albans District Council v. I.C.L. Ltd* [1996] 4 All E.R. 481, relevant factors including: (i) the parties were of unequal bargaining power; (ii) the limit of £100,000 was small in relation to the potential risk; (iii) the defendants held an aggregate of £50M of insurance cover world wide; (iv) the defendants were in a better position to insure. In assessing the reasonableness of a clause the court must consider the whole scope of the clause and not just that part upon which the defendant seeks to rely, *Stewart Gill Ltd. v. Horatio Myer & Co. Ltd* [1992] Q.B. 600. In principle, a standard form clause which removes one party's right of set-off is subject to the requirement of reasonableness by virtue of s.3 as extended by s.13. Whether it will satisfy the requirement may depend upon whether the clause contains a further limitation of liability. In *Overland Shoes Ltd v. Schenkers Ltd* [1998] 1 Lloyd's Rep. 498, a clause of the British International Freight Association which provided that customers must make prompt payment "without reduction or deferment on account of any claim, counterclaim or set-off" was held to satisfy the requirement. It had been drafted following wide consultation in the industry, was in common use, having been accepted by the trade as fair and reasonable and it merely defined the method of resolving competing claims, rather than seeking to limit liability. For more cases on the reasonableness test, see commentary to the Guidelines in Sched.2 below.

"Dealing as consumer"

3H–425   12.—(1) A party to a contract "deals as consumer" in relation to another party if—

> (a) he neither makes the contract in the course of a business nor holds himself out as doing so; and
>
> (b) the other party does make the contract in the course of a business; and
>
> (c) in the case of a contract governed by the law of sale of goods or hire-purchase, or by section 7 of this Act, the goods passing under or in pursuance of the contract are of a type ordinarily supplied for private use or consumption.

(1A) But if the first party mentioned in subsection (1) is an individual paragraph (c) of that subsection must be ignored.

(2) But the buyer is not in any circumstances to be regarded as dealing as consumer—

> (a) if he is an individual and the goods are second hand goods sold at public auction at which individuals have the opportunity of attending the sale in person;
>
> (b) if he is not an individual and the goods are sold by auction or by competitive tender.

3H–426   *Note* —Amended, and subs. (1A) added, by the Sale and Supply of Goods to Consumers Regulations 2002 (S.I. 2002 No. 3045).

In the course of a business

3H–427   Where a business buys something in which it deals (*e.g.* a butcher buying meat) that is clearly a purchase in the course of a business. Where, however, a business buys something which is incidental to its business (*e.g.* the butcher buys a car for his business), then it has been held that the purchase is not "in the course of a business" unless the business makes such transactions regularly—two or three times in five years being insufficiently regular— *R & B Customs Brokers Co. Ltd v. United Dominions Trust* [1988] 1 W.L.R. 321. This decision seemed very doubtful in the light of the reasoning and the decision in *Stevenson v. Rogers* [1999] 1 All E.R. 613, see commentary to Sale of Goods Act 1979, s.14. It was nevertheless followed and applied by the Court of Appeal in *Feldaroll Foundry Plc v. Hermes Leasing (London) Ltd* [2004] EWCA Civ 747; [2004] C.C.L.R. 8. The amendments effected by the Sale and Supply of Goods to Consumers Regulations 2002 brought the definition of "dealing as a consumer" as it applies to non-corporate customers into line with the Directive on Certain Aspects of Sale of Goods and Consumer Guarantees (1999/34/EC). See the Sale of Goods Act 1979, ss.14(2D) and 48A and commentaries, below.

Varieties of exemption clause

13.—(1) To the extent that this Part of this Act prevents the exclu-   **3H–428**
sion or restriction of any liability it also prevents—

- (a) making the liability or its enforcement subject to restrictive or onerous conditions;
- (b) excluding or restricting any right or remedy in respect of the liability, or subjecting a person to any prejudice in consequence of his pursuing any such right or remedy;
- (c) excluding or restricting rules of evidence or procedure;

and (to that extent) sections 2 and 5 to 7 also prevent excluding or restricting liability by reference to terms and notices which exclude or restrict the relevant obligation or duty.

(2) But an agreement in writing to submit present or future differences to arbitration is not to be treated under this Part of this Act as excluding or restricting any liability.

Varieties of exemption clause

A clause which removes one party's right of set-off is a clause which excludes or   **3H–429**
restricts a right or remedy, see commentary to s.11 above.

Interpretation of Part I

14. In this Part of this Act—   **3H–430**

"business" includes a profession and the activities of any government department or local or public authority;

"goods" has the same meaning as in the Sale of Goods Act 1979;

"hire-purchase agreement" has the same meaning as in the Consumer Credit Act 1974;

"negligence" had the meaning given by section 1(1);

"notice" includes an announcement, whether or not in writing, and any other communication or pretended communication; and

"personal injury" includes any disease and any impairment of physical or mental condition.

Note —Amended by the Sale of Goods Act 1979, s.63(2) and Sched.2.   **3H–431**

SCHEDULES

* * * *   **3H–432**

SCHEDULE 2

"GUIDELINES" FOR APPLICATION OF REASONABLENESS TEST

The matters to which regard is to be had in particular for the purposes of sections 6(3), 7(3) and (4), 20 and 21 are any of the following which appear to be relevant—

(a) the strength of the bargaining positions of the parties relative to each other, taking into account (among other things) alternative means by which the customer's requirements could have been met;

(b) whether the customer received an inducement to agree to the term, or in accepting it had an opportunity of entering into a similar contract with other persons, but without having to accept a similar term;

(c) whether the customer knew or ought reasonably to have known of the existence and extent of the term (having regard, among other things, to any custom of the trade and any previous course of dealing between the parties);

(d) where the term excludes or restricts any relevant liability if some condition is not complied with, whether it was reasonable at the time of the contract to expect that compliance with that condition would be practicable;

(e) whether the goods were manufactured, processed or adapted to the special order of the customer.

Guidelines for Application of Reasonableness Test

3H–433   An exclusion clause may well be incorporated into the contract by virtue of being part of the small print on a standard form contract of one of the parties. The other party, typically a buyer, may not be aware of its existence or extent, *e.g.* may not have read the form or may not have understood it fully before signing it. Paragraph (c) of the Guidelines does not equate the position of a party who knows of the existence of an exclusion clause with a party who "ought to have known" of its existence: *Britvic Soft Drinks Ltd v. Messer UK Ltd* [2002] 2 Lloyd's Rep. 368; [2002] EWCA Civ 548. A clause of which the buyer was unaware and which purported to exclude liability for lack of satisfactory quality or fitness for purpose in a contract to sell an ingredient for use in making soft drinks failed the test in *Britvic*. Where, on the other hand, the buyer was aware of and had succeeded in getting amended (albeit not substantially) a clause excluding liability for consequential loss in a contract to supply software (which is notoriously liable to present problems), the clause was held to pass the test: *Watford Electronics Ltd v. Sanderson CFL Ltd* [2001] 1 All E.R. (Comm) 696 and see also *SAM Business Systems Ltd v. Hedley & Co.* [2002] EWHC 2733; [2003] 1 All E.R.(Comm) 465.

Sale of Goods Act 1979

(1979 c.54)

An Act to consolidate the law relating to the sale of goods.

3H–434   *[6th December 1979]*

ARRANGEMENT OF SECTIONS

Contract of sale

3H–435   **2.**—(1) A contract of sale of goods is a contract by which the seller transfers or agrees to transfer the property in goods to the buyer for a money consideration, called the price.

(2) There may be a contract of sale between one part owner and another.

(3) A contract of sale may be absolute or conditional.

(4) Where under a contract of sale the property in the goods is transferred from the seller to the buyer the contract is called a sale.

(5) Where under a contract of sale the transfer of the property in the goods is to take place at a future time or subject to some condition later to be fulfilled the contract is called an agreement to sell.

(6) An agreement to sell becomes a sale when the time elapses or the conditions are fulfilled subject to which the property in the goods is to be transferred.

Contracts of sale of goods

Into contracts which are not contracts of sale of goods but which are analogous, terms are implied relating to goods supplied under the contract which terms are very similar to those implied in sale of goods contracts by ss.12–15 of the Sale of Goods Act. Those analogous contracts and the related implied terms provisions are as follows: hire-purchase agreements (Supply of Goods (Implied Terms) Act 1973, ss.8–11); contracts of barter and contracts for services which involve the passing of property in goods (Supply of Goods and Services Act 1982, ss.2–5A); contracts of hire (Supply of Goods and Services Act 1982, ss.6 to 10A). Where under a contract no property in goods transfers and no goods are hired, it is possible that nevertheless goods are consumed in the course of providing a service to the customer— *e.g.* shampoo used in washing hair. In that case the common law may imply terms as to quality similar to those implied by statute in the above mentioned contracts, *Ingham v. Emes* [1955] 2 Q.B. 366. A contract to supply computer software on disk is a sale of goods contract, whereas a contract to supply computer software in purely intangible form is not; in the latter case the court will be prepared to imply a term at common law that the software will be reasonably fit for its intended purpose, *St Albans District Council v. ICL* [1996] 4 All E.R. 481, CA.

3H–436

When condition to be treated as warranty

3H–437

11.—(1) This section does not apply to Scotland.

(2) Where a contract of sale is subject to a condition to be fulfilled by the seller, the buyer may waive the condition, or may elect to treat the breach of the condition as a breach of warranty and not as a ground for treating the contract as repudiated.

(3) Whether a stipulation in a contract of sale is a condition, the breach of which may give rise to a right to treat the contract as repudiated, or a warranty, the breach of which may give rise to a claim for damages but not to a right to reject the goods and treat the contract as repudiated, depends in each case on the construction of the contract, and a stipulation may be a condition, though called a warranty in the contract.

(4) Subject to section 35A below where a contract of sale is not severable and the buyer has accepted the goods or part of them, the breach of a condition to be fulfilled by the seller can only be treated as a breach of warranty, and not as a ground for rejecting the goods and treating the contract as repudiated, unless there is an express or implied term of the contract to that effect.

(5) [...]

(6) Nothing in this section affects a condition or warranty whose fulfilment is excused by law by reason of impossibility or otherwise.

(7) Paragraph 2 of Schedule 1 below applies in relation to a contract made before 22 April 1967 or (in the application of this Act to Northern Ireland) 28 July 1967.

3H–438 *Note* —Amended, and subs. (5) repealed, with effect from January 3, 1995 by the Sale and Supply of Goods Act 1994.

For "acceptance" and the loss of right of rejection see ss.35 and 35A and commentaries, below.

Conditional sale agreements

3H–439 Subsection (4) does not—and thus the doctrine of "acceptance" does not—apply to a conditional sale agreement where the buyer deals as a consumer within s.12 of the Unfair Contract Terms Act 1977 (*i.e.* irrespective of whether the conditional sale agreement is regulated by the Consumer Credit Act 1974). In such a case the buyer's right to reject goods for breach of a condition is not lost by his "acceptance" but may be lost, as in the case of a hire-purchase agreement, by his affirmation of the contract. That is the effect of s.14 of the Supply of Goods (Implied Terms) Act 1973.

Implied terms about title, etc.

3H–440 **12.**—(1) In a contract of sale, other than one to which subsection (3) below applies, there is an implied term on the part of the seller that in the case of a sale he has a right to sell the goods, and in the case of an agreement to sell he will have such a right at the time when the property is to pass.

(2) In a contract of sale, other than one to which subsection (3) below applies, there is also an implied term that—

    (a) the goods are free, and will remain free until the time when the property is to pass, from any charge or encumbrance not disclosed or known to the buyer before the contract is made, and

    (b) the buyer will enjoy quiet possession of the goods except so far as it may be disturbed by the owner or other person entitled to the benefit of any charge or encumbrance so disclosed or known.

(3) This subsection applies to a contract of sale in the case of which there appears from the contract or is to be inferred from its circumstances an intention that the seller should transfer only such title as he or a third person may have.

(4) In a contract to which subsection (3) above applies there is an implied term that all charges or encumbrances known to the seller and not known to the buyer have been disclosed to the buyer before the contract is made.

(5) In a contract to which subsection (3) above applies there is also an implied term that none of the following will disturb the buyer's quiet possession of the goods, namely—

    (a) the seller;

    (b) in a case where the parties to the contract intend that the seller should transfer only such title as a third person may have, that person;

    (c) anyone claiming through or under the seller or that third person otherwise than under a charge or encumbrance disclosed or known to the buyer before the contract is made.

(5A) As regards England and Wales and Northern Ireland, the term implied by subsection (1) above is a condition and the terms implied by subsections 12(2), 12(4) and 12(5) above are warranties.

(6) Paragraph 3 of Schedule 1 below applies in relation to a contract made before 18 May 1973.

Note —Amended, and subs. (5A) added, with effect from January 3, 1995 by the **3H–441** Sale and Supply of Goods Act 1994.

Title to goods

The classic example of a breach of the condition in s.12(1) is where the seller is not **3H–442** the owner and does not have the owner's authority to sell the goods. It makes no difference whether the seller knows that he is not the owner. He may honestly believe himself to be the owner (*e.g.* having in all innocence "bought" the goods from someone who had stolen them from the true owner). He is still in breach of this condition. It may be that the buyer does not discover until some months later that the seller was not the owner of the goods. If he then rejects the goods for breach of this condition, he is entitled to recover the whole of the purchase price as being money had and received on a total failure of consideration, *Rowland v. Divall* [1923] 2 K.B. 500. This is so notwithstanding that the buyer has had the enjoyment of the goods for several months. The position is exactly the same where the contract is not a contract of sale of goods but one of hire-purchase, *Warman v. Southern Counties Finance* [1949] 2 K.B. 576 (approved in *Barber v. N.W.S. Bank* [1996] 1 W.L.R. 641, CA). For the corresponding condition as to title in contracts of hire-purchase, see Supply of Goods (Implied Terms) Act 1973, s.8.

The buyer's right to reject the goods for breach of the condition in s.12(1) is, apparently, not lost by his "acceptance" of the goods within the meaning of s.35. It will be lost, however, if the title is "fed" to him, *Butterworth v. Kingsway Motors* [1954] 1 W.L.R. 1286. This typically occurs where the buyer buys goods from someone who acquired them on hire-purchase or conditional sale terms and who at the time of the sale has not become the owner (*i.e.* because he has not completed his instalment payments under the hire-purchase or conditional sale agreement). Here the seller is in breach of the implied condition as to title. If, however, at some later stage he completes his instalment payments, then the seller will at that moment acquire title which automatically and immediately will be fed to his buyer. If at that moment the buyer has not already rejected the goods, then he loses that right. He does, however, have a claim for damages (see s.53(1)) and the *prima facie* measure of damages will be the difference between the value of the goods at the time when the buyer should have acquired good title and their (lower) value at the time he did acquire good title, *Butterworth v. Kingsway Motors* (above).

Normally, someone who sells goods which he does not own (and who does not have the owner's authority to sell) cannot transfer title to the buyer. *Nemo dat quod non habet*—a seller cannot give a good title which he does not himself have (Sale of Goods Act 1979, s.21(1)). There are, however, some exceptions to this principle, the main ones being: (i) where the true owner is estopped from asserting that the sale was unauthorised; (ii) where the seller is a mercantile agent in possession of the goods with the consent of the owner, is acting in the ordinary course of business of a mercantile agent and sells the goods to someone who takes in good faith and is unaware that the seller has no authority to make the sale (Factors Act 1889, s.2(1)); (iii) where the seller has a voidable title to the goods and that title has not been avoided at the time of the sale and the seller sells to someone buying in good faith without notice of the seller's defect of title (Sale of Goods Act 1979, s.23); (iv) where the seller is someone who has already sold the goods to someone else but who has retained the goods (or documents of title) and who then sells and delivers them to the buyer who receives them in good faith without notice of the earlier sale (Sale of Goods Act 1979, s.24); (v) where the seller is someone who had agreed to buy the goods and who has taken delivery of them but to whom property (title) has not yet passed and who sells and delivers them (or the documents of title) to a buyer who receives them in good faith and without notice of the rights of the original seller (Sale of Goods Act 1979, s.25). The latter excep-

CONSUMER

tion (in s.25) does not apply where the contract under which the seller had acquired the goods was a hire-purchase agreement, because in that case the seller is not a "buyer", *i.e.* someone who has "bought or agreed to buy", *Helby v. Matthews* [1895] A.C. 471, *Close Asset Finance v. Care Graphics Machinery Ltd* [2000] C.C.L.R. 43. Nor does this exception apply where the contract under which the seller had acquired the goods is a conditional sale agreement which is a consumer credit agreement within the meaning of the Consumer Credit Act 1974 (Sale of Goods Act 1979, s.25(2)).

There is a further exception (in the Hire Purchase Act 1964, s.27) which applies only to the sale of motor vehicles. This applies where the seller is someone who is hiring the vehicle under a hire-purchase agreement or buying it under a conditional sale agreement and who, before he acquires title, sells the vehicle to a "private purchaser" who is bona fide and unaware of any relevant hire-purchase or conditional sale agreement. In that case the innocent private purchaser obtains good title to the vehicle (or, more accurately, such title as belonged to the person from whom the seller had acquired the vehicle on hire-purchase or conditional sale terms). A buyer who is aware only of a hire purchase agreement under which all the payments have been made is still an innocent purchaser (*Barker v. Bell* 1 W.L.R. 983) as also is a buyer who originally had suspicions but whose suspicions had at the time he bought the car been laid to rest, *Dodds v. Yorkshire Bank Finance Ltd* [1992] C.C.L.R. 92, CA. Someone who is carrying on business in the motor trade (whether as dealer or as finance house) is not a private purchaser—and that is so even if he is buying for his private (and not his business) purposes, *Stevenson v. Beverley Bentinck* [1976] 1 W.L.R. 483. Where the purchaser is not a private purchaser and then himself sells the vehicle, then the first private purchaser who buys the vehicle thereafter will, providing he is bona fide and without notice, acquire title by virtue of the Hire Purchase Act 1964, s.27. Notwithstanding that an innocent private purchaser obtains good title to the vehicle by virtue of s.27, he still has the same right to reject the vehicle (and reclaim all money paid) as if s.27 did not apply (*Barber v. NWS Bank* [1996] 1 W.L.R. 641). This is because nothing in s.27 exonerates the seller from any liability he would have been under apart from the section (s.27(3)).

Subs. (2) —Where the seller supplies goods which involve an infringement of the trade mark rights of a third party, that will amount to a breach of the condition in s.12(1) and also of the warranty of quiet possession, *Niblett Ltd. v. Confectioners' Materials Co.* [1921] 3 K.B. 387. Where after the sale a third party obtained a patent and brought patent proceedings against the buyers to enforce the patent, the sellers were not in breach of the condition in s.12(1) which related to the time of the sale but were in breach of the warranty that "the buyer *will* enjoy quiet possession", *Microbeads v. Vinhurst Road Markings* [1975] 1 W.L.R. 218.

Subs. (3) —A seller might, for example, acknowledge that he has only a limited title where he has found the goods which he is selling—a finder having only a limited, possessory, title.

Exclusion

3H–443   It is not possible to contract out of liability for breach of the undertakings under s.12 where the liability is a business liability, see ss.1(3) and 6(1) of the Unfair Contract Terms Act 1977.

Sale by description

3H–444   **13.**—(1) Where there is a contract for the sale of goods by description, there is an implied term that the goods will correspond with the description.

(1A) As regards England and Wales and Northern Ireland, the term implied by subsection (1) above is a condition.

(2) If the sale is by sample as well as by description it is not sufficient that the bulk of the goods corresponds with the sample if the goods do not also correspond with the description.

(3) A sale of goods is not prevented from being a sale by description by reason only that, being exposed for sale or hire, they are selected by the buyer.

(4) Paragraph 4 of of Schedule 1 below applies in relation to a contract made before 18 May 1973.

Note —The word "term" was substituted in subsection (1), and subs. (1A) was added, **3H–445** with effect from January 3, 1995 by the Sale and Supply of Goods Act 1994.

By description

It is a sale by description if the item is sold as corresponding to a description and **3H–446** the buyer placed some (but not necessarily exclusive) reliance upon the description, *Grant v. Australian Knitting Mills* [1936] A.C. 85; *Beale v. Taylor* [1967] 1 W.L.R. 1193. If it is not within the reasonable contemplation of the parties that the buyer is relying on the description, then it is not a sale by description, *Harlingdon & Leinster Enterprises Ltd v. Christopher Hull Fine Art Ltd* [1991] 1 Q.B. 564 (painting attributed by seller to a painter of the German impressionist school when both seller and buyer knew that the buyer had, and the seller did not have, expertise and knowledge of the German expressionist school). If some of the goods supplied are outside the contract description, then that amounts to a breach of the condition, *Pinnock Bros. v. Lewis & Peat* [1923] 1 K.B. 690 (castor oil included in goods supplied under contract to sell "copra cake"). The fact that the goods are of poor quality does not of itself indicate a failure to correspond with description. The key to the concept of description is "identification", not "quality", *Ashington Piggeries v. Hill* [1972] A.C. 441. An expression in the contract which refers to quality (*e.g.* "fair average quality for the season"), though usually not part of the description and therefore not relevant to a claim under s.13, will nevertheless amount to an express term (albeit probably only a warranty and not a condition) of the contract.

Exclusion and remedies

For the buyer's rights of rejection and to claim damages, see ss.11, 15A, 35, 35A **3H–447** and 53. For restrictions on the ability to exclude or limit the seller's liability, see Unfair Contract Terms Act 1977, ss.1–6.

Implied terms about quality or fitness

14.—(1) Except as provided by this section and section 15 below **3H–448** and subject to any other enactment, there is no implied term about the quality or fitness for any particular purpose of goods supplied under a contract of sale.

(2) Where the seller sells goods in the course of a business, there is an implied term that the goods supplied under the contract are of satisfactory quality.

(2A) For the purposes of this Act, goods are of satisfactory quality if they meet the standard that a reasonable person would regard as satisfactory, taking account of any description of the goods, the price (if relevant) and all the other relevant circumstances.

(2B) For the purposes of this Act, the quality of goods includes their state and condition and the following (among others) are in appropriate cases aspects of the quality of goods—

    (a) fitness for all the purposes for which goods of the kind in question are commonly supplied,

    (b) appearance and finish,

    (c) freedom from minor defects,

    (d) safety, and

    (e) durability.

(2C) The term implied by subsection (2) above does not extend to any matter making the quality of goods unsatisfactory—

    (a) which is specifically drawn to the buyer's attention before the contract is made,

CONSUMER

    (b) where the buyer examines the goods before the contract is made, which that examination ought to reveal, or

    (c) in the case of a contract for sale by sample, which would have been apparent on a reasonable examination of the sample.

(2D) If the buyer deals as consumer or, in Scotland, if a contract of sale is a consumer contract, the relevant circumstances mentioned in subsection (2A) above include any public statements on the specific characteristics of the goods made about them by the seller, the producer or his representative, particularly in advertising or on labelling.

(2E) A public statement is not by virtue of subsection (2D) above a relevant circumstance for the purposes of subsection (2A) above in the case of a contract of sale, if the seller shows that—

    (a) at the time the contract was made, he was not, and could not reasonably have been, aware of the statement,

    (b) before the contract was made, the statement had been withdrawn in public or, to the extent that it contained anything which was incorrect or misleading, it had been corrected in public, or

    (c) the decision to buy the goods could not have been influenced by the statement.

(2F) Subsections (2D) and (2E) above do not prevent any public statement from being a relevant circumstance for the purposes of subsection (2A) above (whether or not the buyer deals as consumer or, in Scotland, whether or not the contract of sale is a consumer contract) if the statement would have been such a circumstance apart from those subsections.

(3) Where the seller sells goods in the course of a business and the buyer, expressly or by implication, makes known—

    (a) to the seller, or

    (b) where the purchase price or part of it is payable by instalments and the goods were previously sold by a credit-broker to the seller, to that credit-broker,

any particular purpose for which the goods are being bought, there is an implied term that the goods supplied under the contract are reasonably fit for that purpose, whether or not that is a purpose for which such goods are commonly supplied, except where the circumstances show that the buyer does not rely, or that it is unreasonable for him to rely, on the skill or judgment of the seller or credit-broker.

(4) An implied term about quality or fitness for a particular purpose may be annexed to a contract of sale by usage.

(5) The preceding provisions of this section apply to a sale by a person who in the course of a business is acting as agent for another as they apply to a sale by a principal in the course of a business, except where that other is not selling in the course of a business and either the buyer knows that fact or reasonable steps are taken to bring it to the notice of the buyer before the contract is made.

(6) As regards England and Wales and Northern Ireland, the term implied by subsection (1) above is a condition.

(7) Paragraph 5 of Schedule 1 below applies in relation to a contract made on or after 18 May 1973 and before the appointed day, and paragraph 6 in relation to one made before 18 May 1973.

(8) In subsection (7) above and paragraph 5 of Schedule 1 below references to the appointed day are to the day appointed for the purposes of those provisions by an order of the Secretary of State made by statutory instrument.

Note —Amended with effect from January 3, 1995 by the Sale and Supply of Goods **3H–449** Act 1994—see satisfactory quality below. Subsections (2D) to (2F) added by Sale and Supply of Goods Regulations 2002 (S.I. 2002 No. 3045).

Goods supplied in the course of a business

The implied terms apply to second hand as well as new goods. They apply also not **3H–450** only to the goods bought but also to other goods "supplied", *e.g.* a returnable bottle, even though the ownership in those goods is not to transfer to the buyer, *Geddling v. Marsh* [1920] 1 K.B. 668. Apparently, in the case of a book or computer disk they apply not only to the tangible item but also to the information or program within it, *obiter* in *St Albans District Council v. ICL* [1996] 4 All E.R. 481, CA. The expression "in the course of a business" includes all sales of goods made by businesses, whether or not the sale of such goods was the regular trade of that business, *Stevenson v. Rogers* [1999] Q.B. 1028; [1999] 2 W.L.R. 1064; [1999] 1 All E.R. 613 (distinguishing *R & B Customs Brokers Co. Ltd v. United Dominions Trust* [1988] 1 W.L.R. 321, a case decided under Unfair Contract Terms Act 1977, s.12).

Subs. (5) —where the (selling) agent is acting in the course of a business and the principal (seller) is not selling in the course of a business and the buyer is unaware of the latter fact and reasonable steps have not been taken to bring it to the buyer's attention, the buyer is entitled to rely on s.14 to bring proceedings against the principal (the seller), *Boyter v. Thomson* [1995] 2 A.C. 628.

Satisfactory quality

The Sale and Supply of Goods Act 1994 implemented recommendations in the Law **3H–451** Commission Final Report, *Sale and Supply of Goods* (1987), (Law Com. No. 160 Cm. 137). Subss. 14(2) to (2C) replaced the previous subs. (2) thereby substituting "satisfactory quality" for the old expression "merchantable quality" and introducing the revised definition in subss. 14(2A) and 14(2B). This refers to the goods' fitness for the purposes for which such goods are commonly supplied. In the case of a motor vehicle those purposes include not merely the purpose of driving it from place to place but of doing so with the appropriate degree of comfort, ease of handling and pride in the vehicle's outward and interior appearance, *Rogers v. Parish (Scarborough) Ltd* [1987] Q.B. 933 (decided under the old definition of "merchantable quality" but still authoritative). The relative weight to be attached to the different characteristics of the vehicle depends on the market at which it is aimed. On a vehicle sold as new, the performance and finish to be expected are those of a model of average standard with no mileage—and no less is expected of a vehicle sold with a manufacturer's warranty. The same general approach is to be taken in the case of a second hand vehicle, though defects unacceptable on a new car, might be acceptable on a second hand model. It is a matter of degree, bearing in mind various factors including especially the price. Examples are: *Lee v. York Coach and Marine* [1977] R.T.R. 35 (car unmerchantable when brakes were in such a state that they would have failed if driver had to perform an emergency stop); *Bartlett v. Sydney Marcus* [1965] 1 W.L.R. 1013 (car not unmerchantable when one month after purchase it required new clutch—buyer had turned down seller's offer at time of sale to supply the car with new clutch fitted if buyer agreed to pay £25 extra); *Shine v. General Guarantee Finance Co. Ltd* [1988] 1 All E.R. 911 (20 month old Fiat held unmerchantable because, unknown to the buyer, it had been treated as a "write off" after being submerged in water for over 24 hours); *Crowther v. Shannon* [1975] 1 W.L.R. 30 (8 year old Jaguar with 82,000 miles on clock, seized up after 3 weeks and 2,300 miles—held unfit for purpose under subs. 14(3)); *Bramhill v. Edwards* [2004] EWCA Civ 403, [2004] 2 Lloyd's Rep. 653 (American motor-home 102 inches wide sold for use on UK roads where it was illegal to use such a vehicle exceeding 100 inches in width, held to be of satisfactory quality in the light of evidence that the authorities turned a blind eye to such illegality and that such motor-homes were used by enthusiasts who knew of their non-compliance with the regulations). For an extended discussion of the requirement of satisfactory quality in relation to a contract to supply a computer system comprising hardware and software to a business, see *Anglo Group Plc v. Winther Browne & Co. Ltd* (2000) 144 S.J.L.B. 197; [2000] I.T.C.L.R. 559, available on the Court Service website.

Subs. (2C) —(a) where the defect is drawn to the buyer's attention but he is reasonably of the (erroneous) opinion that the defect can and will be rectified at no cost to himself, then the implied term may well not be excluded, *per* Neill LJ in *R & B Customs Brokers Co. Ltd v. United Dominions Trust* [1988] 1 W.L.R. 321. (b) The buyer cannot complain of defects he should have discovered during any examination he made of the goods. Apparently, if the buyer made no examination, then this provision does not apply.

Subss. (2D) to (2F) —added by the Sale and Supply of Goods to Consumers Regulations 2002, these subsections implement Article 2 of Directive on Certain Aspects of Sale of Goods and Consumer Guarantees (1999/44/EC), which provides for the seller to be made liable for public statements made by the seller, the producer or his representative. Similar amendments were at the same time made to the Supply of Goods and Services Act 1982, ss.4 and 9 and to the Supply of Goods (Implied Terms) Act 1973, s.10. For the latter, see para. 3H–390 above.

Fitness for purpose

3H–452   For the condition to be implied the buyer must make known to the seller the particular purpose for which the goods are required. The buyer may have made known a particular purpose (*e.g.* that he wants a garment to wear) but failed to indicate some particular idiosyncrasy of his intended use of them (*e.g.* that his skin is abnormally sensitive to contracting dermatitis). There is no breach of the term as to fitness for purpose where the failure of the goods to meet the intended purpose arises from an abnormal feature or idiosyncrasy, not made known to the seller, in the buyer or in the circumstances of the use of the goods by the buyer, *Slater v. Finning* [1997] A.C. 473. That is so even if the buyer was himself unaware of the abnormal feature or idiosyncrasy.

Subsection (3)(b) applies to the situation where the buyer acquires the goods on conditional sale or credit sale terms in the typical triangular transaction, *i.e.* where the dealer (the credit broker) sells the goods to a finance company (the seller) which then contracts to supply them to the buyer on the aforesaid instalment terms; it is sufficient that the buyer has informed the dealer of the particular purpose. This is so irrespective of whether the resulting contract is a consumer credit agreement regulated by the Consumer Credit Act 1974. If, however, the resulting contract is one of hire-purchase, then the Sale of Goods Act does not apply to it but it will instead contain virtually identical terms (similar to those in ss.12–15 of the Sale of Goods Act) implied by the Supply of Goods (Implied Terms) Act 1973, ss.8–11.

Where goods are to be made to a specification supplied by the buyer, the buyer will still be placing reliance on the seller's skill and judgment in some respects (*e.g.* in regard to matters not covered by the specification). If the goods' subsequent unfitness for their intended purpose relates to the sphere of reliance placed upon the seller, the buyer will have a claim, *Cammell Laird & Co. Ltd v. Manganese Bronze & Brass Co. Ltd* [1934] A.C. 402.

The implied term requires the goods to continue to be fit for the intended purpose for a reasonable period after delivery, so long as they remain in the same apparent state and condition as when they were delivered, apart from normal wear and tear, *Lambert v. Lewis* [1982] A.C. 225. Often in practice, where goods are being put to a conventional use, there is little, if any, distinction between liability under s.14(3) and s.14(2), see *e.g. Crowther v. Shannon*, above. Liability is strict and does not depend upon proof of negligence, *Frost v. Aylesbury Dairy Co.* [1905] 1 K.B. 608.

Exclusion and remedies

3H–453   For the buyer's rights of rejection and to claim damages, see ss.11, 15A, 35, 35A and 53. For restrictions on the ability to exclude or limit the seller's liability, see Unfair Contract Terms Act 1977, ss.1–6.

Sale by sample

15.—(1) A contract of sale is a contract for sale by sample where **3H–454** there is an express or implied term to that effect in the contract.

(2) In the case of a contract for sale by sample there is an implied term—

(a) that the bulk will correspond with the sample in quality;

(b) [...]

(c) that the goods will be free from any defect, making their quality unsatisfactory, which would not be apparent on reasonable examination of the sample.

(3) As regards England and Wales and Northern Ireland, the term implied by subsection (2) above is a condition.

(4) Paragraph 7 of Schedule 1 below applies in relation to a contract made before 18 May 1973.

Note —Amended (and subs. (2)(b) repealed) with effect from January 3, 1995 by the **3H–455** Sale and Supply of Goods Act 1994, Sched.2, para. 5.

Modification of remedies for breach of condition in non-consumer cases

15A.—(1) Where in the case of a contract of sale— **3H–456**

(a) the buyer would, apart from this subsection, have the right to reject goods by reason of a breach on the part of the seller of a term implied by section 13, 14 or 15 above, but

(b) the breach is so slight that it would be unreasonable for him to reject them,

then, if the buyer does not deal as consumer, the breach is not to be treated as a breach of condition but may be treated as a breach of warranty.

(2) This section applies unless a contrary intention appears in, or is to be implied from, the contract.

(3) It is for the seller to show that a breach fell within subsection (1)(b) above.

(4) This section does not apply to Scotland.

Note —Section 15A was added with effect from January 3, 1995 by the Sale and **3H–457** Supply of Goods Act 1994, which implemented the recommendations in the Law Commission Final Report, *Sale and Supply of Goods* (1987), (Law Com. No. 160 Cm. 137). "Dealing as a consumer" has the same meaning as in the Unfair Contract Terms Act 1977, s.12 (see s.61(5A) of the Sale of Goods Act 1979, as inserted by the Sale and Supply of Goods Act 1994). For s.12 of the 1977 Act see para. 3H–425 above.

Buyer's right of examining goods

34.—(1) Unless otherwise agreed when the seller tenders delivery **3H–458** of the goods to the buyer, he is bound on request to afford the buyer a reasonable opportunity of examining the goods for the purpose of ascertaining whether they are in conformity with the contract and, in the case of a contract for sale by sample, of comparing the bulk with the sample.

Note —Amended with effect from January 3, 1995 by the Sale and Supply of Goods **3H–459** Act 1994. See further the commentary to s.35.

CONSUMER

Acceptance

3H–460   **35.**—(1) The buyer is deemed to have accepted the goods subject to subsection (2) below—

    (a) when he intimates to the seller that he has accepted them, or

    (b) when the goods have been delivered to him and he does any act in relation to them which is inconsistent with the ownership of the seller.

(2) Where goods are delivered to the buyer, and he has not previously examined them, he is not deemed to have accepted them under subsection (1) above until he has had a reasonable opportunity of examining them for the purpose—

    (a) of ascertaining whether they are in conformity with the contract, and

    (b) in the case of a contract for sale by sample, of comparing the bulk with the sample.

(3) Where the buyer deals as consumer or (in Scotland) the contract of sale is a consumer contract, the buyer cannot lose his right to rely on subsection (2) above by agreement, waiver or otherwise.

(4) The buyer is also deemed to have accepted the goods when after the lapse of a reasonable time he retains the goods without intimating to the seller that he has rejected them.

(5) The questions that are material in determining for the purposes of subsection (4) above whether a reasonable time has elapsed include whether the buyer has had a reasonable opportunity of examining the goods for the purpose mentioned in subsection (2) above.

(6) The buyer is not by virtue of this section deemed to have accepted the goods merely because—(a) he asks for, or agrees to, their repair by or under an arrangement with the seller, or (b) the goods are delivered to another under a sub-sale or other disposition.

(7) Where the contract is for the sale of goods making one or more commercial units, a buyer accepting any goods included in a unit is deemed to have accepted all the goods making the unit; and in this subsection "commercial unit" means a unit division of which would materially impair the value of the goods or the character of the unit.

(8) Paragraph 10 of Schedule 1 below applies in relation to a contract made before 22 April 1967 or (in the application of this Act to Northern Ireland) 28 July 1967.

3H–461   *Note*—Amended, and subs. (7) added, with effect from January 3, 1995 by the Sale and Supply of Goods Act 1994.

Acceptance

3H–462   Acceptance of the goods (within the meaning of s.35) removes any right the buyer might have to reject the goods for breach of condition (see s.11(4) above). Loss of that right still leaves the buyer with a claim for damages, see s.53. In *Bernstein v. Pamson Motors (Golders Green) Ltd* [1987] 2 All E.R. 220, it was held, at first instance, that acceptance occurred after lapse of a length of time which was reasonable for the buyer to try out the goods generally, which in that case was held to be less than three weeks after the buyer took delivery of a new car. That decision, however, no longer represents the law: *Clegg v. Andersson* (below). One purpose of the amendments made by the 1994 Act was to allow the buyer an opportunity to check the goods to see if they conform to the contract, before the buyer is deemed to have lost his right to reject the goods for breach of condition. It is quite possible that long, perhaps months or years, after the buyer examined them for conformity and (let us assume) was unable to find any suggestion of non-conformity, the goods might prove not to have been of satisfactory quality. A reasonable period of time will not necessarily last years, however. An opportunity to examine the goods for conformity is not a guarantee that such an examination will necessarily be capable of discovering any non-conformity. Another purpose of the 1994 amendments was to encourage informal attempts at cure. Thus the buyer is now not taken to have accepted the goods simply because he asks for or agrees to their repair: s.35(6). Similarly he is entitled to a reasonable period to ascertain what would be required for modification or repair. In *Clegg v. Andersson* [2003] EWCA Civ 320; [2003] 2 Lloyd's Rep. 32, the buyers had contracted to buy a new yacht costing £236,000, which when they took delivery had a keel which was dangerously overweight. The buyers returned the vessel to the seller after a few days and were not prepared to agree to repairs/modifications proposed by the seller until (a) the seller had first supplied them with details (with drawings and calculations) as to what was proposed and (b) the buyers had been able to take professional advice in the light of that information. When after approximately a further six months the seller supplied the information, the buyers took less than three weeks to reject the yacht. The Court held that the buyers had not accepted the yacht and had validly rejected it. A buyer is entitled to a reasonable period to ascertain what is required for modification or repair and in this case time had not begun to run until the buyers were given the requested information which was necessary for them to make a decision. There is, however, no general rule that acceptance cannot take place whilst the buyer is seeking information about possible alleged breaches of contract and possible cures for them: see *Jones v. Callagher* [2004] EWCA Civ 10; [2004] 1 Lloyd's Rep.377, an ordinary case, where the defects in the goods (kitchen fitments) were obvious needing no expert to identify them and where a purported rejection five months after delivery was held to be too late. *Truk (UK) Ltd v. Tokmakidis GmbH* [2000] 1 Lloyd's Rep. 543 involved a contract between two businesses for the sale and fitting of some lifting equipment to be paid for six months after delivery. The equipment was to be fitted to, and form part of, a towing vehicle which the buyer was then going to resell. Approximately six months after delivery the buyer was informed by a potential purchaser of the towing vehicle that the equipment was defective. The buyer immediately informed the seller and refused to pay the price pending investigation (by an appropriate company). About three months later, promptly upon receipt of the result of the investigation which confirmed the allegation, the buyer unequivocally rejected the goods. The judge held as follows. Where goods are sold for resale, a reasonable time in which to give notice of rejection should normally be the time actually taken to resell the goods, together with an additional period in which they can be inspected and tried out (by the sub-purchaser). Where the price is payable at a date after delivery, that reasonable period of time should normally last at least until the date for payment. The reasonable time had not expired when about six months after delivery, the buyer first questioned compliance. The buyer was entitled to a further period in which to investigate that issue. Accordingly the buyer had not accepted the goods when he validly rejected them nine months after delivery.

Commercial Unit

Subsection (7) creates an exception to the rule in s.35A which rule allows the buyer to accept conforming goods without losing the right to reject non-conforming goods. For example, accepting volume A to M of a two volume dictionary would amount to acceptance of the other volume and thus prevent the buyer being able to reject either volume. Whether a three-piece suite amounts to a commercial unit would be a nice question of fact.

3H–463

Right of partial rejection

35A.—(1) If the buyer—

    (a) has the right to reject the goods by reason of a breach on the part of the seller that affects some or all of them, but

3H–464

CONSUMER

      (b) accepts some of the goods, including, where there are any goods unaffected by the breach, all such goods.

he does not by accepting them lose his right to reject the rest.

(2) In the case of a buyer having the right to reject an instalment of goods, subsection (1) above applies as if references to the goods were references to the goods comprised in the instalment.

(3) For the purposes of subsection (1) above, goods are affected by a breach if by reason of the breach they are not in conformity with the contract.

(4) This section applies unless a contrary intention appears in, or is to be implied from, the contract.

3H–465   *Note* —Section 35A was added with effect from January 3, 1995 by the Sale and Supply of Goods Act 1994, s.3.

Right of partial rejection

3H–466   The amendments made by the 1994 Act were designed, amongst other things, to enable the buyer to accept conforming goods without thereby losing the right to reject goods which did not conform to the contract. Where the contract is not severable and the buyer accepts some *but not all* of the *conforming* goods, then subs. (1) will not apply, with the result that, applying s.11(4), the buyer will have lost the right to reject any of the goods whether conforming or not. Acceptance of part of a "commercial unit" amounts to acceptance of all of it, see s.35(7).

Buyer not bound to return rejected goods

3H–467   **36.** Unless otherwise agreed, where goods are delivered to the buyer, and he refuses to accept them, having the right to do so, he is not bound to return them to the seller, but it is sufficient if he intimates to the seller that he refuses to accept them.

3H–468   *Note* —The buyer is entitled to claim reasonably incurred storage expenses, if the seller fails to collect goods which the buyer has rightly rejected, *Kolfor Plant Ltd v. Tilbury Plant Ltd* (1977) 121 S.J. 390. The buyer has no lien over rejected goods to enforce the return of the purchase price, *Lyons v. May & Baker* [1923] 1 K.B. 695.

Introductory

3H–469   **48A.**—(1) This section applies if—

      (a) the buyer deals as consumer or, in Scotland, there is a consumer contract in which the buyer is a consumer, and

      (b) the goods do not conform to the contract of sale at the time of delivery.

(2) If this section applies, the buyer has the right—

      (a) under and in accordance with section 48B below, to require the seller to repair or replace the goods, or

      (b) under and in accordance with section 48C below—

            (i) to require the seller to reduce the purchase price of the goods to the buyer by an appropriate amount, or

            (ii) to rescind the contract with regard to the goods in question.

(3) For the purposes of subsection (1)(b) above goods which do not conform to the contract of sale at any time within the period of

six months starting with the date on which the goods were delivered to the buyer must be taken not to have so conformed at that date.

(4) Subsection (3) above does not apply if—

    (a) it is established that the goods did so conform at that date;

    (b) its application is incompatible with the nature of the goods or the nature of the lack of conformity.

Note —Part 5A of the Act comprises ss.48A to 48F and was added with effect from **3H–470** March 31, 2003 by the Sale and Supply of Goods to Consumers Regulations 2002 (S.I. 2002 No. 3045).

Consumer's additional rights for non-conformity

The Sale and Supply of Goods to Consumers Regulations 2002 implemented the **3H–471** Directive on Aspects of Sale of Goods and Consumer Guarantees (1999/44/EC). They introduced additional remedies for a buyer dealing as a consumer where there has been any breach of an express term of the contract or of the statutory implied terms as to description, satisfactory quality, fitness for purpose and sample. Those additional remedies are set out in ss.48A to 48F. They include the right to require the goods to be repaired or replaced (if that is not a disproportionate remedy) and, failing that, to rescind the contract or obtain a reduction in the price. These rights are entirely additional and do not take away any right (*e.g.* to reject the goods for breach of condition and/or to claim damages for consequential loss) which the buyer has independently of ss.48A to 48F. If, however, the buyer chooses to require repair or replacement, he cannot reject the goods and terminate the contract without allowing the seller a reasonable time to comply with his request. Section 61(5A) of the Sale of Goods Act provides that "dealing as a consumer" has the same meaning as in s.12 of the Unfair Contract Terms Act 1977. For the latter, see para. 3H–425 above. Similar provisions to those in ss.48A to 48F were added to the Supply of Goods and Services Act 1982 (s.11M to s.11S). Under the latter, the goods will also be non-conforming (and the buyer will thus be entitled to require repair or replacement) if, in installing the goods, the supplier has been in breach of the implied term that he will use reasonable care and skill. For the term as to reasonable care and skill, see Supply of Goods and Services Act 1982, s.13 at para. 3H–489 below.

"The time of delivery" —is normally when the goods are physically handed over to the buyer. Where the buyer deals as a consumer and the seller is authorised or required to send the goods to the buyer, delivery of the goods to a carrier does not constitute delivery: s.32(4). In that case delivery will occur only when the carrier delivers to the buyer.

Repair or replacement of the goods.

48B.—(1) If section 48A above applies, the buyer may require the **3H–472** seller—

    (a) to repair the goods, or

    (b) to replace the goods.

(2) If the buyer requires the seller to repair or replace the goods, the seller must—

    (a) repair or, as the case may be, replace the goods within a reasonable time but without causing significant inconvenience to the buyer;

    (b) bear any necessary costs incurred in doing so (including in particular the cost of any labour, materials or postage).

(3) The buyer must not require the seller to repair or, as the case may be, replace the goods if that remedy is—

    (a) impossible, or

CONSUMER

(b) disproportionate in comparison to the other of those remedies, or

(c) disproportionate in comparison to an appropriate reduction in the purchase price under paragraph (a), or rescission under paragraph (b), of section 48C(1) below.

(4) One remedy is disproportionate in comparison to the other if the one imposes costs on the seller which, in comparison to those imposed on him by the other, are unreasonable, taking into account—

(a) the value which the goods would have if they conformed to the contract of sale,

(b) the significance of the lack of conformity, and

(c) whether the other remedy could be effected without significant inconvenience to the buyer.

(5) Any question as to what is a reasonable time or significant inconvenience is to be determined by reference to—

(a) the nature of the goods, and

(b) the purpose for which the goods were acquired.

Repair or replacement of the goods

3H–473   See note and commentary to s.48A above.

Reduction of purchase price or rescission of contract

3H–474   48C.—(1) If section 48A above applies, the buyer may—

(a) require the seller to reduce the purchase price of the goods in question to the buyer by an appropriate amount, or

(b) rescind the contract with regard to those goods,

if the condition in subsection (2) below is satisfied.

(2) The condition is that—

(a) by virtue of section 48B(3) above the buyer may require neither repair nor replacement of the goods; or

(b) the buyer has required the seller to repair or replace the goods, but the seller is in breach of the requirement of section 48B(2)(a) above to do so within a reasonable time and without significant inconvenience to the buyer.

(3) For the purposes of this Part, if the buyer rescinds the contract, any reimbursement to the buyer may be reduced to take account of the use he has had of the goods since they were delivered to him.

Reduction of purchase price or rescission of contract

3H–475   See note and commentary to s.48A above

Reduction of purchase price or rescission of contract

3H–476   48D.—(1) If the buyer requires the seller to repair or replace the goods the buyer must not act under subsection (2) until he has given the seller a reasonable time in which to repair or replace (as the case may be) the goods.

(2) The buyer acts under this subsection if—

(a) in England and Wales or Northern Ireland he rejects the goods and terminates the contract for breach of condition;

(b) in Scotland he rejects any goods delivered under the contract and treats it as repudiated;

(c) he requires the goods to be replaced or repaired (as the case may be).

Reasonable time for repair or replacement of goods

See note and commentary to s.48A above.

3H–477

Powers of the court

48E.—(1) In any proceedings in which a remedy is sought by virtue of this Part the court, in addition to any other power it has, may act under this section.

3H–478

(2) On the application of the buyer the court may make an order requiring specific performance or, in Scotland, specific implement by the seller of any obligation imposed on him by virtue of section 48B above.

(3) Subsection (4) applies if—

(a) the buyer requires the seller to give effect to a remedy under section 48B or 48C above or has claims to rescind under section 48C, but

(b) the court decides that another remedy under section 48B or 48C is appropriate.

(4) The court may proceed—

(a) as if the buyer had required the seller to give effect to the other remedy, or if the other remedy is rescission under section 48C

(b) as if the buyer had claimed to rescind the contract under that section.

(5) If the buyer has claimed to rescind the contract the court may order that any reimbursement to the buyer is reduced to take account of the use he has had of the goods since they were delivered to him.

(6) The court may make an order under this section unconditionally or on such terms and conditions as to damages, payment of the price and otherwise as it thinks just.

Powers of the court

See note and commentary to s.48A above.

3H–479

Conformity with the contract

48F. For the purposes of this Part, goods do not conform to a contract of sale if there is, in relation to the goods, a breach of an express term of the contract or a term implied by section 13, 14 or 15 above.

3H–480

Conformity with the contract

See note and commentary to s.48A above.

3H–481

Remedy for breach of warranty

53.—(1) Where there is a breach of warranty by the seller or where

3H–482

the buyer elects (or is compelled) to treat any breach of a condition on the part of the seller as a breach of warranty, the buyer is not by reason only of such breach of warranty entitled to reject the goods; but he may—

    (a) set up against the seller the breach of warranty in diminution or extinction of the price, or

    (b) maintain an action against the seller for damages for the breach of warranty.

(2) The measure of damages for breach of warranty is the estimated loss directly and naturally resulting, in the ordinary course of events, from the breach of warranty.

(3) In the case of breach of warranty of quality such loss is prima facie the difference between the value of the goods at the time of delivery to the buyer and the value they would have had if they had fulfilled the warranty.

(4) The fact that the buyer has set up the breach of warranty in diminution or extinction of the price does not prevent him from maintaining an action for the same breach of warranty if he has suffered further damage.

(5) This section does not apply to Scotland.

3H–483   *Note* —Subsection (5) was substituted with effect from January 3, 1995 by the Sale and Supply of Goods Act 1994, Sched.2, para. 5.

Supply of Goods and Services Act 1982

(S.I. 1982 c.29)

An Act to amend the law with respect to the terms to be implied in certain contracts for the transfer of property in goods, in certain contracts for the hire of goods and in certain contracts for the supply of a service; and for connected purposes.

3H–484   *[13th July 1982]*

Implied terms as to description, quality and sample

3H–485   Terms as to title, description, quality and sample are implied in contracts of sale of goods by the Sale of Goods Act 1979, ss.12–15. Similar terms are implied by the Supply of Goods and Service Act 1982 in: contracts of barter or exchange, contracts whereby goods are exchanged for trading stamps and contracts for services under which the property is to pass (ss.1–5A); contracts of hire (other than hire-purchase) (ss.6–11). These terms apply only to the goods supplied, not to the services. As with the terms implied by the Sale of Goods Act, any clause purporting to exclude or limit liability in respect of them is subject to the provisions of the Unfair Contract Terms Act 1977 (in this case, in particular, s.7 of that Act.) Sections 12–16 imply into contracts for the supply of services (whether or not the contract is one of sale of goods) terms which relate to the services provided—terms as to care and skill, time for performance and the remuneration.

Consumer's additional rights for non-conformity

3H–486   Amendments to the Sale of Goods Act 1979 by the Sale and Supply of Goods to

Consumer Regulations 2002 (S.I. 2002 No. 3045) are mirrored by similar amendments to the Supply of Goods and Services Act 1982. Sections 48A to 48F of the former Act give the buyer additional rights in relation to non-conforming goods (including the right to require repair or replacement of the goods), see para. 3H–471above. The Supply of Goods and Services Act 1982 contains, in ss.11M to 11S, provisions which are, with one exception, identical apart from necessary changes of wording. The exception is as follows. Whereas under both Acts the goods will be non-conforming if there is a breach of any of the statutory implied terms as to description, satisfactory quality, fitness for purpose or sample, under the Supply of Goods of Services Act the goods will also be non-conforming if, in installing the goods, the supplier has been in breach of the implied term in s.13 that he will use reasonable care and skill. For s.13 see below.

The contracts concerned

12.—(1) In this Act a "contract for the supply of a service" means, subject to subsection (2) below, a contract under which a person ("the supplier") agrees to carry out a service.   **3H–487**

(2) For the purposes of this Act, a contract of service or apprenticeship is not a contract for the supply of a service.

(3) Subject to subsection (2) above, a contract is a contract for the supply of a service for the purposes of this Act whether or not the goods are also—

(a) transferred or to be transferred, or
(b) bailed or to be bailed by way of hire,

under the contract, and whatever is the nature of the consideration for which the service is to be carried out.

(4) The Secretary of State may by order provide that one or more of sections 13 to 15 below shall not apply to services of a description specified in the order, and such an order may make different provision for different circumstances.

(5) The power to make an order under subsection (4) above shall be exercisable by statutory instrument subject to annulment in pursuance of a resolution of either House of Parliament.

"Contracts for the supply of a service"

This concept will include not only contracts of which the substance is the provision of a service, but also a contract of sale of goods under which a service is also to be provided (*e.g.* the sale and installation of a washing machine).   **3H–488**

Implied term about care and skill

13. In a contract for the supply of a service where the supplier is acting in the course of a business, there is an implied term that the supplier will carry out the service with reasonable care and skill.   **3H–489**

Implied term about care and skill

For exclusion of liability see s.16. For case law on "in the course of a business", see commentary to Sale of Goods Act 1979, s.14. For the other party's right to require repair or replacement of goods where the supplier is in breach of the implied term as to care and skill in installing goods, see para. 3H–486.   **3H–490**

Implied term about time for performance

14.—(1) Where, under a contract for the supply of a service by a supplier acting in the course of a business, the time for the service to be carried out is not fixed by the contract, left to be fixed in a manner agreed by the contract or determined by the course of dealing   **3H–491**

between the parties, there is an implied term that the supplier will carry out the service within a reasonable time.

(2) What is a reasonable time in a question of fact.

3H–492   **Time for performance**—a related requirement appears in the Consumer Protection (Distance Selling) Regulations 2000 (S.I. 2000 No. 2334), which implemented the Distance Selling Directive (97/7/EC). By reg. 19(1), in the case of a "distance contract" which is not an "excepted contract", the supplier must, unless the parties agree otherwise, perform the contract within a period of 30 days, which period begins when the consumer forwarded his order to the supplier. For "distance contract" and "excepted contract", see the commentary to s.83 of the Consumer Credit Act (para. 3H–130 above). Reg. 19(1) does not apply to any excepted contract, nor to timeshare agreements (within the meaning of the Timeshare Act 1992), nor to the following agreements: contracts for food, beverages or other goods used for everyday consumption supplied to the consumer at his residence or workplace by regular roundsmen; contracts for accommodation, catering, transport or leisure services where the supplier undertakes to supply the services on a specific date or within a specific period. Where reg. 19(1) does apply and the supplier is unable to supply the goods or services ordered, reg. 19(7) allows the supplier to supply substitute goods or services of equivalent price and quality, if the contract provided for that possibility. Apart from that possibility, if reg. 19(1) applies and the supplier is unable, because the goods or services are not available, to perform the contract within the 30 days or such other period as the parties agree, reg. 19(2) to (6) come into play. These contain consequential provisions: the supplier is required to reimburse any sum paid by or on behalf of the consumer, including any sum paid by a creditor under a personal credit agreement with the consumer; the contract shall be treated as if never made (except for any rights or remedies arising from the non-performance); any security provided in relation to the contract is to be treated as if never having had any effect.

Implied term about consideration

3H–493   **15.**—(1) Where, under a contract for the supply of a service, the consideration for the service is not determined by the contract, left to be determined in a manner agreed by the contract or determined by the course of dealing between the parties, there is an implied term that the party contracting with the supplier will pay a reasonable charge.

(2) What is a reasonable charge is a question of fact.

Exclusion of implied terms, etc.

3H–494   **16.**—(1) Where a right, duty or liability would arise under a contract for the supply of a service by virtue of this Part of this Act, it may (subject to subsection (2) below and the 1977 Act) be negatived or varied by express agreement, or by the course of dealing between the parties, or by such usage as binds both parties to the contract.

(2) An express term does not negative a term implied by this Part of this Act unless inconsistent with it.

(3) Nothing in this Part of this Act prejudices—

    (a) any rule of law which imposes on the supplier a duty stricter than that imposed by section 13 or 14 above; or

    (b) subject to paragraph (a) above, any rule of law whereby any term not inconsistent with this Part of this Act is to be implied in a contract for the supply of a service.

(4) This Part of this Act has effect subject to any other enactment which defines or restricts the rights, duties or liabilities arising in connection with a service of any description.

Exclusion of implied terms

The 1977 Act referred to in subs. (1) is the Unfair Contract Terms Act 1977. Liability for breach of the implied term as to care and skill in s.13 is negligence liability within the meaning of the 1977 Act and thus any attempt to exclude such liability is subject to s.2 of the 1977 Act. If the recipient of the services contracts as a consumer or the exclusion clause is a standard term of the service provider, s.3 of the 1977 Act will apply as well. **3H–495**

The Package Travel, Package Holidays and Package Tours Regulations 1992

(S.I. 1992 No. 3288)

General Note

These regulations implemented the EC Directive on Package Travel, Package **3H–496** Holidays and Package Tours 90/314/EEC. In various respects they enhance holiday makers' rights compared with what they would or might otherwise be. The ordinary law of contract and tort continues to apply to any holiday which is outside the regulations (*i.e.* if it is not a "package" within reg. 2). Similarly, even where the holiday is a package within the regulations, the common law continues to apply in relation to matters not covered by the regulations. Thus, the regulations being silent on the matter, the assessment of damages is to be determined by decisions based on *Jarvis v. Swans Tours Ltd* [1973] Q.B. 233. For a case finder guide on damages in holiday cases, see an article "Wish We Weren't Here" at (2003) Vol. 147 Sol. Jo. 1103.

As an alternative to court action, the ABTA (Association of British Travel Agents) arbitration scheme administered by the Chartered Institute of Arbitrators allows a claim for up to £5,000 (or £15,000 per booking) to be referred to arbitration if it is against an ABTA member.

For an authoritative account of this area of the law, see *Holiday Law* by Grant and Mason (3rd ed., Sweet and Maxwell, 2003).

Citation and commencement

1. These Regulations may be cited as the Package Travel, Package **3H–497** Holidays and Package Tours Regulations 1992 and shall come into force on the day after the day on which they are made.

Interpretation

2.—(1) In these Regulations– **3H–498**

"brochure" means any brochure in which packages are offered for sale;

"contract" means the agreement linking the consumer to the organiser or to the retailer, or to both, as the case may be;

"the Directive" means Council Directive 90/314/EEC on package travel, package holidays and package tours;

"member State" means a member State of the European Community or another State in the European Economic Area;

"offer" includes an invitation to treat whether by means of advertising or otherwise, and cognate expressions shall be construed accordingly;

"organiser" means the person who, otherwise than occasionally, organises packages and sells or offers them for sale, whether directly or through a retailer;

"the other party to the contract" means the party, other than the consumer, to the contract, that is, the organiser or the retailer, or both, as the case may be;

"package" means the pre-arranged combination of at least two of the following components when sold or offered for sale at an inclusive price and when the service covers a period of more than twenty-four hours or includes overnight accommodation:–

    (a) transport;

    (b) accommodation;

    (c) other tourist services not ancillary to transport or accommodation and accounting for a significant proportion of the package, and

        (i) the submission of separate accounts for different components shall not cause the arrangements to be other than a package;

        (ii) the fact that a combination is arranged at the request of the consumer and in accordance with his specific instructions (whether modified or not) shall not of itself cause it to be treated as other than pre-arranged; and

"retailer" means the person who sells or offers for sale the package put together by the organiser.

(2) In the definition of "contract" in paragraph (1) above, "consumer" means the person who takes or agrees to take the package ("the principal contractor") and elsewhere in these Regulations "consumer" means, as the context requires, the principal contractor, any person on whose behalf the principal contractor agrees to purchase the package ("the other beneficiaries") or any person to whom the principal contractor or any of the other beneficiaries transfers the package ("the transferee").

3H–499   *Note*—Definition of "member state" added by the Package Travel, Package Holidays and Package Tours (Amendment) Regulations 1995 (S.I. 1995 No. 1648).

"contract"

3H–500   This definition is taken from the Directive. It would appear that it is possible for an agreement to fall within this definition even though it is not what would at common law be recognised as a contract. Thus a travel agent might on a given occasion arrange for the consumer (a) flights with an airline and (b) accommodation with an hotel. That would constitute a "package" and the travel agent would be the "organiser", see para. 3H–501below. Yet the contracts for flights and accommodation may well have been between the consumer and, respectively, the airline and the hotel. In this situation, it can perhaps be said that there was an "agreement" between the travel agent and the consumer which was a "contract" within the meaning of the regulations, albeit it may not have been a contract at common law, the agreement being that the travel agent would make, or try to make, the arrangements which the consumer wanted.

"the other party to the contract"

3H–501   This expression is not derived from the Directive. In the usual situation the tour operator will be "the other party to the contract"", the travel agent having been merely an agent to bring about a contract between the consumer and tour operator. The definition clearly contemplates, however, that the travel agent (the retailer) can also, either alone or as well as the tour operator, be "the other party to the contract". The vagueness created by the words "as the case may be" leaves a great deal of scope for judicial interpretation. It allows the courts to determine who is (or are) the other party(ies) to the contract according to the facts of different cases. It also leaves open the possibility that the identity of "the other party to the contract" may vary according to which of the substantive regulations is in point. According to Goldring J. in *ABTA v.*

Civil Aviation Authority [2006] EWHC 13 (Admin), at para. 161, "[T]he [regulations] do not exclude the application of the English law of contract...[W]hether the agreement links the consumer to the organiser or retailer or both depends upon the application of the English law of contract, in particular the law of agency. So too do decisions as to whether the organiser or retailer or both are parties to the contract or whether under regulation 15, the organiser or retailer or both are liable under it."

"Package"

Only those holidays which are "packages" are affected by the regulations.　　　**3H–502**

"Pre-arranged combination" —In *Club-Tour Viagens e Turismo SA v. Lobo Goncalves Garrido (C400/00)* [2002] ECR I-4051, the ECJ, in interpreting the Directive, determined two things: (i) arrangements put together by a travel agent at the request of, and according to the specifications of, a consumer (or defined group of consumers) can fall within the definition of a package; (ii) "pre-arranged combination" must be interpreted so as to include combinations of tourist services put together at the time when the contract is concluded between the travel agency and the consumer. Thus, where a travel agent had arranged both (a) a holiday at the destination resort and (b) the flights to reach the destination, that was a package within the regulations and, apparently, the travel agent was an "organiser" within the meaning of the regulations.

"Inclusive price" —The arrangement is not a package unless it is sold or offered "at an inclusive price". Thus an optional excursion which the consumer buys from the tour operator only after arrival at his holiday resort would not be part of the package. It would, however, be part of the package it if it was arranged (and the cost included) at the time the holiday was booked. In *Rechberger v. Austria (C140/97)* [1999] ECR I-3499; [2000] 2 C.M.L.R. 1, trips including travel and accommodation were offered (as part of an advertising campaign) to subscribers to a newspaper. The lucky travellers were to pay only airport taxes and, if they travelled alone, a single supplement. The price was held to be "inclusive", even though it did not equal the value of either the travel or the accommodation. Thus the trips were held to be "packages". According to Goldring J. in *ABTA v. Civil Aviation Authority* [2006] EWHC 13 (Admin), at para 156, "[T]he words 'inclusive price' should be given their ordinary and natural meaning...If the substance of a transaction is the sale by the travel agent of separate and discrete components of...a holiday, with no one part being connected with or dependent upon any other part (other than that they are sold together), ...the resultant price ...is no more an 'inclusive price' than is the total of goods at the checkout of a supermarket. For the sale of a package at an inclusive price the relationship between the component parts of the package must be such as to mean that the consumer is buying and paying for them as a whole; that the sale or offer for sale of one component part is in some way connected with or dependent on the sale or offer for sale of the others."

"Accommodation" —*Administrative Proceedings Concerning AFS Intercultural Programs Finland RY (C237/97)* [1999] ECR I-825; [2000] 1 C.M.L.R. 845 involved a student exchange arrangement whereby students would be sent from Finland to study in another country for a period of six months or more, lodging with families which put them up free of charge. AFS Finland organised the exchange by: arranging transport, selecting the host family, arranging the school to be attended by students during their visit abroad, preparing documentation relating to the host country and organising a preparatory course for the students and their families. The ECJ held that the combination of all three of the following factors meant that the lodging with the families was not "accommodation" within the meaning of the Directive: (i) the lodging was free, (ii) it was not in a hotel or similar establishment, and (iii) it was for a long time.

"Other tourist services..." —In the *AFS Finland* case (see "Accommodation" above), it was held that AFS Finland did not organise "other tourist services" within the meaning of the Directive, because: (i) selecting the school for the exchange student to attend was not a tourist service, since its specific purpose was education of the student; (ii) selection of the host family, if it was a tourist service, was ancillary to accommodation; (iii) preparation of the documentation and the courses followed by the students and parents prior to departure, though within the definition of "tourist services", did not account for a significant proportion of the package.

CONSUMER

"Organiser" and "retailer"

3H–503   A tour operator, whether it markets its package holidays directly or via travel agents, is clearly an "organiser". A travel agent who sells such a package holiday will be a "retailer" but not normally an "organiser". However, in two situations a travel agent might be an "organiser". The first is where, in addition to selling the conventional package holiday and as part of that same transaction, the travel agent himself arranges transport to the hotel or the airport, *c.f.* the *Club-Tour* case at para. 3H–500 above. Whilst the package travel company remains an "organiser" and the travel agent remains a "retailer" of the conventional package, the travel agent would appear to be "organiser" of the whole package, *i.e.* including the additional transport. The second situation is where in selling the package, the travel agent has acted as an undisclosed agent, *i.e.* held himself out, whether or not intentionally, as principal: *Hone v. Going Places Leisure Travel Ltd* (QBD Nov 16, 2000, confirmed in the Court of Appeal—see para. 3H–524 below).

Para. (2) —the definition of "consumer", coupled with the provisions of substantive regulations (including in particular reg. 15), means that the common law rule of privity of contract is effectively abrogated. The consumer, whether that be the purchaser of the package or someone else in the party, can proceed against "the other party to the contract" in respect of any improper performance of the contract. Where the regulations apply, therefore, the consumer will not need to rely on the Contracts (Rights of Third Parties) Act 1999. Re "transferee", see reg. 10 below.

Application of Regulations

3H–504   **3.**—(1) These Regulations apply to packages sold or offered for sale in the territory of the United Kingdom.

(2) Regulations 4 to 15 apply to packages so sold or offered for sale on or after 31st December 1992.

(3) Regulations 16 to 22 apply to contracts which, in whole or part, remain to be performed on 31st December 1992.

Application of the regulations

3H–505   Subsection (3) is an example of very sloppy drafting. It is generally accepted that regs 16 to 22 apply to "contracts" sold after December 31, 1992 as well as to those which had been made previously and on that date still remained to be fully performed.

Descriptive matter relating to packages must not be misleading

3H–506   **4.**—(1) No organiser or retailer shall supply to a consumer any descriptive matter concerning a package, the price of a package or any other conditions applying to the contract which contains any misleading information.

(2) If an organiser or retailer is in breach of paragraph (1) he shall be liable to compensate the consumer for any loss which the consumer suffers in consequence.

Misleading information

3H–507   Where the only remedy claimed is damages, this regulation makes unnecessary any consideration of whether the misleading information amounted to either (a) an actionable misrepresentation or (b) a term of the contract. In *Mawdsley v. Cosmosair Plc* [2002] EWCA Civ 587, the claimant and her husband booked a holiday for themselves and their two children. The defendant tour operator had advertised in its brochure that the hotel had "Lifts (in main building)". The restaurant, however, could be reached only via stairs because it was located on a mezzanine floor not served by the lifts. Whilst the claimant and her husband were descending the stairs carrying their baby daughter in a pushchair, the claimant lost her footing, fell and suffered injuries. It was held that "Lifts (in main building)" was a representation that all levels in the main building, including the restaurant, could be accessed by lift. That was "misleading information" for the purposes of Regulation 4, "with the result that [the defendant] is liable under that Regulation for all consequent damage", *per* Jonathan Parker L.J. at para. 45. His Lordship continued: "Since Regulation 6 ... provides that particulars in the brochure are implied warranties in the contract, it follows that [the defendant] was also in breach of contract in that respect." There was a sufficient causal link between the misrepresentation that the restaurant could be accessed by lift and the accident which occurred on the stairs. There had been no novus actus interveniens since the claimant and her husband had behaved perfectly reasonably in taking their daughter in her pushchair in the way that they had (*Quinn v. Burch Bros (Builders) Ltd* [1966] 2 Q.B. 370 distinguished).

Requirements as to brochures

5.— [Regulation 5 creates criminal offences in relation to brochures **3H–508** which do not include the price and information on the matters specified in Sched. 1 to the regulations.]

Circumstances in which particulars in brochure are to be binding

6.—(1) Subject to paragraphs (2) and (3) of this regulation, the **3H–509** particulars in the brochure (whether or not they are required by regulation 5(1) above to be included in the brochure) shall constitute implied warranties (or, as regards Scotland, implied terms) for the purposes of any contract to which the particulars relate.

(2) Paragraph (1) of this regulation does not apply–

    (a) in relation to information required to be included by virtue of paragraph 9 of Schedule 1 to these Regulations; or

    (b) where the brochure contains an express statement that changes may be made in the particulars contained in it before a contract is concluded and changes in the particulars so contained are clearly communicated to the consumer before a contract is concluded.

(3) Paragraph (1) of this regulation does not apply when the consumer and the other party to the contract agree after the contract has been made that the particulars in the brochure, or some of those particulars, should not form part of the contract.

Brochure contents as terms of the contract

Mawdsley v. Cosmosair Plc [2002] EWCA Civ 587 provides an example of the applica- **3H–510** tion of Regulation 6(1)—see para. 3H–507 above.

The information "required to be included by virtue of paragraph 9 of Schedule 1" is information about "the arrangements for security for money paid over and for the repatriation of the consumer in the event of insolvency".

Information to be provided before contract is concluded

7.— [Regulation 7 creates criminal offences for a failure by "the **3H–511** other party to the contract" to provide certain information to the intending consumer before the contract is made, namely information regarding: passport and visa requirements; health formalities; arrangements for security of money paid over and repatriation of the consumer in the event of insolvency.]

Information to be provided in good time

8.— [Regulation 8 creates criminal offences for a failure by "the **3H–512** other party to the contract" to provide certain information to the consumer before the start of the journey, namely information regarding: transport arrangements, connections, accommodation en route, contact details of local representatives, holiday/travel insurance.]

Contents and form of contract

3H–513   **9.**—(1) The other party to the contract shall ensure that–

(a) depending on the nature of the package being purchased, the contract contains at least the elements specified in Schedule 2 to these Regulations;

(b) subject to paragraph (2) below, all the terms of the contract are set out in writing or such other form as is comprehensible and accessible to the consumer and are communicated to the consumer before the contract is made; and

(c) a written copy of these terms is supplied to the consumer.

(2) Paragraph (1)(b) above does not apply when the interval between the time when the consumer approaches the other party to the contract with a view to entering into a contract and the time of departure under the proposed contract is so short that it is impracticable to comply with the sub-paragraph.

(3) It is an implied condition (or, as regards Scotland, an implied term) of the contract that the other party to the contract complies with the provisions of paragraph (1).

(4) In Scotland, any breach of the condition implied by paragraph (3) above shall be deemed to be a material breach justifying rescission of the contract.

Transfer of bookings

3H–514   **10.**—(1) In every contract there is an implied term that where the consumer is prevented from proceeding with the package the consumer may transfer his booking to a person who satisfies all the conditions applicable to the package, provided that the consumer gives reasonable notice to the other party to the contract of his intention to transfer before the date when departure is due to take place.

(2) Where a transfer is made in accordance with the implied term set out in paragraph (1) above, the transferor and the transferee shall be jointly and severally liable to the other party to the contract for payment of the price of the package (or, if part of the price has been paid, for payment of the balance) and for any additional costs arising from such transfer.

Transfer of bookings

3H–515   This regulation will sometimes enable a consumer to avoid having to pay cancellation charges by transferring his booking to someone else. It applies, however, only where the consumer is "prevented" from proceeding. It is not enough that the consumer has simply changed his mind.

Price revision

3H–516   **11.**—(1) Any term in a contract to the effect that the prices laid down in the contract may be revised shall be void and of no effect unless the contract provides for the possibility of upward or downward revision and satisfies the conditions laid down in paragraph (2) below.

(2) The conditions mentioned in paragraph (1) are that–

    (a) the contract states precisely how the revised price is to be calculated;

    (b) the contract provides that price revisions are to be made solely to allow for variations in:–

        (i) transportation costs, including the cost of fuel,

        (ii) dues, taxes or fees chargeable for services such as landing taxes or embarkation or disembarkation fees at ports and airports, or

        (iii) the exchange rates applied to the particular package; and

(3) Notwithstanding any terms of a contract,

        (i) no price increase may be made in a specified period which may not be less than 30 days before the departure date stipulated; and

        (ii) as against an individual consumer liable under the contract, no price increase may be made in respect of variations which would produce an increase of less than 2%, or such greater percentage as the contract may specify, ("non-eligible variations") and that the non-eligible variations shall be left out of account in the calculation.

Significant alterations to essential terms

12. In every contract there are implied terms to the effect that–   **3H–517**

    (a) where the organiser is constrained before the departure to alter significantly an essential term of the contract, such as the price (so far as regulation 11 permits him to do so), he will notify the consumer as quickly as possible in order to enable him to take appropriate decisions and in particular to withdraw from the contract without penalty or to accept a rider to the contract specifying the alterations made and their impact on the price; and

    (b) the consumer will inform the organiser or the retailer of his decision as soon as possible.

Withdrawal by consumer pursuant to regulation 12 and cancellation by organiser

13.—(1) The terms set out in paragraphs (2) and (3) below are   **3H–518** implied in every contract and apply where the consumer withdraws from the contract pursuant to the term in it implied by virtue of regulation 12(a), or where the organiser, for any reason other than the fault of the consumer, cancels the package before the agreed date of departure.

(2) The consumer is entitled–

    (a) to take a substitute package of equivalent or superior quality if the other party to the contract is able to offer him such a substitute; or

    (b) to take a substitute package of lower quality if the other party to the contract is able to offer him one and to re-

CONSUMER

cover from the organiser the difference in price between the price of the package purchased and that of the substitute package; or

(c) to have repaid to him as soon as possible all the monies paid by him under the contract.

(3) The consumer is entitled, if appropriate, to be compensated by the organiser for non-performance of the contract except where–

(a) the package is cancelled because the number of persons who agree to take it is less than the minimum number required and the consumer is informed of the cancellation, in writing, within the period indicated in the description of the package; or

(b) the package is cancelled by reason of unusual and unforeseeable circumstances beyond the control of the party by whom this exception is pleaded, the consequences of which could not have been avoided even if all due care had been exercised.

(4) Overbooking shall not be regarded as a circumstance falling within the provisions of sub-paragraph (b) of paragraph (3) above.

Pre-departure cancellation

3H–519   The regulations are silent as to the position where the consumer cancels the contract other than in the situations covered in reg. 12 (a price increase or other alteration to an essential term of the contract). Thus the consumer who cancels in any other situation will fall liable to pay the cancellation charges stated in the contract, unless they are challengeable under the Unfair Terms in Consumer Contracts Regulations 1999 (see para. 3H–532) or are inconsistent with the terms of a code (*e.g.* ABTA) subscribed to by the tour organiser. For post-departure cancellation, see regulation 14.

Para. (3)(b) —The wording here follows exactly that of the Directive in its definition of "force majeure". Sometimes the "unusual and unforeseeable circumstances" will amount to what at common law would be a frustrating event (*e.g.* the destination resort is completed destroyed by fire). Nevertheless, it seems clear that the contract will not be frustrated but rather the consumer, though not entitled to compensation, will be entitled to the appropriate remedy under para. (2).

Significant proportion of services not provided

3H–520   **14.**—(1) The terms set out in paragraphs (2) and (3) below are implied in every contract and apply where, after departure, a significant proportion of the services contracted for is not provided or the organiser becomes aware that he will be unable to procure a significant proportion of the services to be provided.

(2) The organiser will make suitable alternative arrangements, at no extra cost to the consumer, for the continuation of the package and will, where appropriate, compensate the consumer for the difference between the services to be supplied under the contract and those supplied.

(3) If it is impossible to make arrangements as described in paragraph (2), or these are not accepted by the consumer for good reasons, the organiser will, where appropriate, provide the consumer with equivalent transport back to the place of departure or to another place to which the consumer has agreed and will, where appropriate, compensate the consumer.

Force majeure

3H–521   This regulation contains no exception for force majeure and thus it applies whatever may be the reason that a significant proportion of the services cannot be, or are not, provided. Thus it seems clear that a post-departure event which would otherwise have frustrated the contract at common law will not do so in the case of a package to which the regulations apply. For the position regarding a pre-departure event, see commentary to reg. 13.

Compensation

Paragraphs (2) and (3) state that compensation is to be paid "where appropriate". It **3H–522** is submitted that this regulation is to be read together with reg. 15 and that payment of compensation under reg. 14 will not be "appropriate" where the failure to provide the services falls within paras (a) to (c) of reg. 15(2) and is not due to the fault of the organiser (or of another supplier of services). Similarly compensation would not be appropriate to the extent that liability to pay it is limited by an exclusion clause which is reasonable within the meaning of para. (4) of reg. 15.

Liability of other party to the contract for proper performance of obligations under contract

15.—(1) The other party to the contract is liable to the consumer **3H–523** for the proper performance of the obligations under the contract, irrespective of whether such obligations are to be performed by that other party or by other suppliers of services but this shall not affect any remedy or right of action which that other party may have against those other suppliers of services.

(2) The other party to the contract is liable to the consumer for any damage caused to him by the failure to perform the contract or the improper performance of the contract unless the failure or the improper performance is due neither to any fault of that other party nor to that of another supplier of services, because—

(a) the failures which occur in the performance of the contract are attributable to the consumer;

(b) such failures are attributable to a third party unconnected with the provision of the services contracted for, and are unforeseeable or unavoidable; or

(c) such failures are due to—

    (i) unusual and unforeseeable circumstances beyond the control of the party by whom this exception is pleaded, the consequences of which could not have been avoided even if all due care had been exercised; or

    (ii) an event which the other party to the contract or the supplier of services, even with all due care, could not foresee or forestall.

(3) In the case of damage arising from the non-performance or improper performance of the services involved in the package, the contract may provide for compensation to be limited in accordance with the international conventions which govern such services.

(4) In the case of damage other than personal injury resulting from the non-performance or improper performance of the services involved in the package, the contract may include a term limiting the amount of compensation which will be paid to the consumer, provided that the limitation is not unreasonable.

(5) Without prejudice to paragraph (3) and paragraph (4) above, liability under paragraphs (1) and (2) above cannot be excluded by any contractual term.

CONSUMER

(6) The terms set out in paragraphs (7) and (8) below are implied in every contract.

(7) In the circumstances described in paragraph (2)(b) and (c) of this regulation, the other party to the contract will give prompt assistance to a consumer in difficulty.

(8) If the consumer complains about a defect in the performance of the contract, the other party to the contract, or his local representative, if there is one, will make prompt efforts to find appropriate solutions.

(9) The contract must clearly and explicitly oblige the consumer to communicate at the earliest opportunity, in writing or any other appropriate form, to the supplier of the services concerned and to the other party to the contract any failure which he perceives at the place where the services concerned are supplied.

"Proper performance of the contract"

3H–524   Regulation 15 does not impose strict liability in all cases. Whether there has been proper performance "can only be determined by reference to the terms of the contract. There may be absolute obligations, *e.g.* as to the existence of a swimming-pool or any other matter, but, in the absence of the assumption of an absolute obligation, the implication will be that reasonable skill and care will be used in the rendering of the relevant service. There will thus be no improper performance of the air carriage unless there is an absence of reasonable skill and care in the provision of that service": *per* Longmore L.J. in *Hone v. Going Places Leisure Travel Ltd* [2001] EWCA Civ 947 at para. 15.

The "other party to the contract"

3H–525   Regulation 15 ensures that the other party to the contract (usually the tour operator) is responsible for the proper performance of the contract by those supplying the relevant service, whether transport, accommodation or another service, irrespective of whoever it is that actually performs that service. In the conventional package holiday situation, the tour operator will be the other party to the contract. Query whether reg. 15 imposes liability on a travel agent who, in addition to selling a tour operator's conventional package holiday and as part of that same transaction, himself arranges transport to the hotel or the airport. In that situation there are two "organisers", the tour operator and the agent, but arguably only the tour operator is the other party to the contract—see the commentary to reg. 5 at para. 3H–501 above. Where the travel agent has held himself out as principal (*i.e.* as the tour operator), he will on ordinary principles of the law of agency be liable as if he were the other party to the contract: see the High Court decision in *Hone v. Going Places Leisure Travel Ltd* (QBD, November 16, 2000, Manchester District Registry, No. MA993390, confirmed on appeal at [2001] EWCA Civ 947). In *Hone*, the consumer had viewed the defendant travel agent's teletext advertisement, which had failed to make clear that the travel agent was merely an agent for the tour operator, and had then booked the package by phone to the defendant travel agent.

"Damage"

3H–526   It is thought that nothing hangs on the use of the different words "loss" and "damage" in regs 4 and 15 respectively. The latter certainly includes more than personal injuries (see reg. 14(4)) and would appear to include any type of loss for which damages can be awarded for breach of contract. On assessment, see the General Note at the start of these regulations.

Exclusion clauses

3H–527   An exclusion clause is not effective except to the extent allowed under paras (3) and (4). The international conventions referred to in para. (3) include, but are not limited to: the Warsaw Convention on Carriage by Air; the Berne Convention on Carriage by Rail; the Athens Convention on Carriage by Sea; the Paris Convention on Liability of Hotel Keepers. Paragraph (4) allows a limitation (except in relation to personal injuries) which "is not unreasonable". This appears to involve a test similar to the requirement of reasonableness in s.11 of the Unfair Contract Terms Act 1977, see para. 3H–423above.

Unfair Contract Terms

Regulation 15 (apart from para. (9)) deals with the contractual liability of the other **3H–528** party to the contract (usually the tour operator) and not with that of the consumer. The regulations are silent as regards contractual obligations which can be said to be unfair to the consumer, *e.g.* a clause imposing unreasonably high cancellation charges. Such obligations are, however, challengeable under the Unfair Terms in Consumer Contracts Regulations 1999, see below.

Regulations 16-26

[Regulations 16-22 require arrangements to be in place to cover the risk of the tour **3H–529** operator becoming insolvent, so that there is security for the refund of money paid over and for the repatriation of the consumer.

Regulations 23-26 (and also Scheds 1 and 3) contain provisions relating to the criminal offences created by the regulations.]

Saving for civil consequences

27. No contract shall be void or unenforceable, and no right of ac- **3H–530** tion in civil proceedings in respect of any loss shall arise, by reason only of the commission of an offence under regulations 5, 7, 8, 16 or 22 of these Regulations.

Terms implied in contract

28. Where it is provided in these Regulations that a term (whether **3H–531** so described or whether described as a condition or warranty) is implied in the contract it is so implied irrespective of the law which governs the contract.

* * * * *

REGULATION 9   SCHEDULE 2

Elements to be included in the contract if relevant to the particular
PACKAGE

1. The travel destination(s) and, where periods of stay are involved, the relevant **3H–532** periods, with dates.

2. [Repealed by the Enterprise Act 2002 (Part 8 Notice to OFT of Intended Prosecution Specified Enactments, Revocation and Transitional Provision) Order (S.I. 2003 No. 1376), art.3.]

3. Where the package includes accommodation, its location, its tourist category or degree of comfort, its main features and, where the accommodation is to be provided in a member State, its compliance with the rules of that member State.

4. The meals which are included in the package.

5. Whether a minimum number of persons is required for the package to take place and, if so, the deadline for informing the consumer in the event of cancellation.

6. The itinerary.

7. Visits, excursions or other services which are included in the total price agreed for the package.

8. The name and address of the organiser, the retailer and, where appropriate, the insurer.

9. The price of the package, if the price may be revised in accordance with the term which may be included in the contract under regulation 11, an indication of the possibility of such price revisions, and an indication of any dues, taxes or fees chargeable for certain services (landing, embarkation or disembarkation fees at ports and airports and tourist taxes) where such costs are not included in the package.

10. The payment schedule and method of payment.

11. Special requirements which the consumer has communicated to the organiser or retailer when making the booking and which both have accepted.

12. The periods within which the consumer must make any complaint about the failure to perform or the inadequate performance of the contract.

Unfair Terms in Consumer Contracts Regulations 1999

(S.I. 1999 No. 2083)

General Note

3H–533   The European Directive on Unfair Terms in Consumer Contracts (93/13/EEC) was first implemented in the UK by the Unfair Terms in Consumer Contracts Regulations 1994, which came into effect on July 1, 1995. Those regulations therefore apply to contracts entered on or after that date and before October 1, 1999 when the present regulations came into force. The present regulations replicate most of what was in the 1994 regulations with some relatively minor modifications to reflect more closely the wording of the Directive.

Contracts affected

3H–534   The regulations apply to contracts concluded between on the one hand a seller or supplier who is acting for purposes related to his trade, business or profession (whether publicly or private owned) and on the other a consumer who is a natural person (not a corporate body) acting for purposes which are outside his trade business or profession. The regulations overlap with other enactments, including particularly the Consumer Credit Act 1974 and the Unfair Contract Terms Act 1977. A term of a regulated credit agreement could, for example, both render the agreement extortionate within ss.137–140 of the 1974 Act and also be rendered ineffective by the regulations. The range of contracts subject to the regulations is, in one respect, wider and, in another respect, narrower than those regulated by the Consumer Credit Act. It is wider in that it includes contracts involving all sorts of subject matter, and not just credit and hire agreements. It is narrower in that it does not cover contracts where the customer is making the contract for the purposes of his trade or profession. The scope of the two is the same in one respect, namely neither applies where the customer is a corporate body.

The overlap with the Unfair Contract Terms Act is that an exclusion clause could be rendered ineffective by either, or both of the regulations and the 1977 Act. Unlike the Act, the regulations do not apply (*e.g.* to standard form exclusion clauses) where both parties are acting for business purposes. On the other hand, where the regulations do apply to a contract, they apply, not just to exclusion clauses but also to other terms that may be unfair.

Effect of the regulations

3H–535
- All written terms are required to be in plain and intelligible language; if there is a doubt, the interpretation most favourable to the consumer applies (reg. 7).
- Any terms which (a) are not core terms, (b) have not been individually negotiated and, (c) are unfair, are not binding on the consumer (reg. 8). The validity of the rest of the contract is not affected, provided it is capable of continuing in existence without the unfair term. The test of unfairness is stated in reg. 5 and a non-exhaustive indicative list of unfair terms is given in Sched.2.
- In so far as they are in plain and intelligible language, the core terms of the contract (*i.e.* those relating to the definition of the main subject matter of the contract or the adequacy of the price or remuneration) are not subject to the requirement to be fair (reg. 6).

3H–536   Regulations 10 to 15 and Sched.1 which are not reproduced here, deal with the powers and duties of the Director General of Fair Trading (now the Office of Fair Trading) and other bodies under the regulations. Under the 1994 Regulations the Director General was given a duty to consider any complaint that a contract term drawn up for general use was unfair and was given a power to ask the court for an injunction to prohibit its use. The 1999 Regulations re-enact those provisions and extend the power to seek an injunction to a range of other regulatory bodies and to trading standards departments. They also extend the power to seek an injunction to the Consumers' Association. Pursuant to the 1994 and the 1999 Regulations, the Office of Fair Trading periodically publishes bulletins giving information on complaints received and undertakings taken from traders to change or abandon the use of particular clauses.

Case law

The regulations have no express exclusion for land transactions and thus do apply **3H–537** to tenancy agreements between tenants and a local authority: *Khatun v. Newham LBC* [2005] Q.B. 37; [2004] 3 W.L.R. 417. The protection provided for consumers by the Directive (which the regulations implement) entails the court being able of its own motion to determine whether a term of a contract (which is before the court) is unfair, when making its preliminary assessment as to whether to allow a claim to proceed, *Oceano Grupo Editorial SA v. Rocio Murciano Qunitero*, June 27, 2000 C-240/98, ECJ. That case involved a number of contracts by a company which had its principal place of business in Barcelona, each such contract being a contract to sell, on instalment credit terms, an encyclopedia to a consumer domiciled in another part of Spain. Each contract contained a clause, not individually negotiated, giving exclusive jurisdiction to the Barcelona courts, which is where the seller commenced proceedings against consumers who had defaulted on their repayments. It was held that the Barcelona court should of its own motion (a) determine whether the jurisdiction clause was fair and (b) it being unfair, decline the jurisdiction it conferred.

For an example of a successful challenge under the 1994 Regulations to the terms of a mortgage loan agreement, see *Falco Finance Ltd v. Gough* [1999] C.C.L.R. 16, noted in the commentary to the Consumer Credit Act 1974, s.138 (at para. 3H–263, above). In *Director General of Fair Trading v. First National Bank plc* [2002] 1 A.C. 48; [2003] C.C.L.R. 8, HL, the Director General sought an injunction (under the 1994 Regulations) in respect of a clause in the standard form loan agreement used by the defendant Bank. The contractual rate of interest was stated and was variable in accordance with changes in the Bank's Base Lending rate. Clause 3 of the agreement provided that that rate of interest was to be charged on a day to day basis on the outstanding balance and debited to the account in arrears. Clause 8 provided that the same rate of interest would be charged on arrears until payment. It further provided that interest would continue to be charged at the same rate after judgment, until the debt was paid. Clause 3 and the other contract provisions which fixed the contractual rate of interest were core terms (concerned with the adequacy of the remuneration) which could not be challenged as unfair under the regulations (see now reg.6 of the 1999 Regulations). Clause 8, however was assessable for fairness. It was part of the Director General's case that not infrequently a borrower, against whom the Bank had brought proceedings to recover the outstanding balance, would agree to a consent order being made, such judgment being for the balance to be payable by instalments over an extended period. The effects of clause 8 were: (i) to reverse the common law rule that the right to interest merged with the judgment debt and thus evaporated after judgment; (ii) to oust the application of the County Court (Interest on Judgments) Order 1991 (under which no interest is payable on judgments for money due under regulated consumer credit agreements). The House of Lords held that clause 8 was not unfair within the 1994 Regulations. The problems for consumers (debtors) arose from the fact that debtors were unaware of the reliefs which the court could give them at the default stage. Those reliefs included: (i) re-opening an extortionate agreement (under s.139 of the Consumer Credit Act 1974); and (ii) reducing the rate of interest (under s.136 when granting a time order under s.128 of the 1974 Act). It was, however, not customary (nor was it a statutory requirement) that the debtor be given notice of those possible reliefs when the contract was made. Clause 8 was not rendered unfair by the absence of procedural safeguards for the debtor at the default stage. *Cf. Bairstow Eves London Central v. Smith and Another* [2004] EWHC 263; [2004] E.G. 118, (QB), where the contract provided for an estate agent to be paid commission of 1.5% of the purchase price. A clause entitling the estate agent to claim commission at 3% if the commission was not paid in full within 10 days of completion of the sale, was held, (a) not to fall within regulation 6(2) and thus to be assessable for fairness and, (b) to be unfair.

Citation and commencement

1. These Regulations may be cited as the Unfair Terms in **3H–538**

CONSUMER

Consumer Contracts Regulations 1999 and shall come into force on 1st October 1999.

Revocation

3H–539 2. The Unfair Terms in Consumer Contracts Regulations 1994 are hereby revoked.

Interpretation

3H–540 3.—(1) In these Regulations—

"the Community" means the European Community;

"consumer" means any natural person who, in contracts covered by these Regulations, is acting for purposes which are outside his trade, business or profession;

"court" in relation to England and Wales and Northern Ireland means a county court or the High Court, and in relation to Scotland, the Sheriff or the Court of Session;

"Director" means the Director General of Fair Trading;

"EEA Agreement" means the Agreement on the European Economic Area signed at Oporto on 2nd May 1992 as adjusted by the protocol signed at Brussels on 17th March 1993;

"Member State" means a State which is a contracting party to the EEA Agreement;

"notified" means notified in writing;

"qualifying body" means a person specified in Schedule 1;

"seller or supplier" means any natural or legal person who, in contracts covered by these Regulations, is acting for purposes relating to his trade, business or profession, whether publicly owned or privately owned;

"unfair terms" means the contractual terms referred to in regulation 5.

(1A) The references—

(a) in regulation 4(1) to a seller or a supplier, and

(b) in regulation 8(1) to a seller or supplier,

include references to a distance supplier and to an intermediary.

(1B) In paragraph (1A) and regulation 5(6) "distance supplier" means—

(a) a supplier under a distance contract within the meaning of the Financial Services (Distance Marketing) Regulations 2004, or

(b) a supplier of unsolicited financial services within regulation 15 of those Regulations; and

"intermediary" has the same meaning as in those Regulations.

(2) In the application of these Regulations to Scotland for references to an "injunction" or an "interim injunction" there shall be substituted references to an "interdict" or "interim interdict" respectively.

3H–540.1 *Note* —Paragraphs (1A) and (1B) were added by the Financial Services (Distance Marketing) Regulations 2004 (S.I. 2004 No. 2095).

Terms to which these Regulations apply

3H–541 4.—(1) These Regulations apply in relation to unfair terms in contracts concluded between a seller or a supplier and a consumer.

(2) These Regulations do not apply to contractual terms which reflect—

(a) mandatory statutory or regulatory provisions (including such provisions under the law of any Member State or in Community legislation having effect in the United Kingdom without further enactment);

(b) the provisions or principles of international conventions to which the Member States or the Community are party.

Unfair Terms

5.—(1) A contractual term which has not been individually negoti- **3H–542** ated shall be regarded as unfair if, contrary to the requirement of good faith, it causes a significant imbalance in the parties' rights and obligations arising under the contract, to the detriment of the consumer.

(2) A term shall always be regarded as not having been individually negotiated where it has been drafted in advance and the consumer has therefore not been able to influence the substance of the term.

(3) Notwithstanding that a specific term or certain aspects of its in a contract has been individually negotiated, these Regulations shall apply to the rest of a contract if an overall assessment of it indicates that it is a pre-formulated standard contract.

(4) It shall be for any seller or supplier who claims that a term was individually negotiated to show that it was.

(5) Schedule 2 to these Regulations contains an indicative and non-exhaustive list of the terms which may be regarded as unfair.

(6) Any contractual term providing that a consumer bears the burden of proof in respect of showing whether a distance supplier or an intermediary complied with any or all of the obligations placed upon him resulting from the Directive and any rule or enactment implementing it shall always be regarded as unfair.

(7) In paragraph (6)—

"the Directive" means Directive 2002/65/EC of the European Parliament and of the Council of 23 September 2002 concerning the distance marketing of consumer financial services and amending Council Directive 90/619/EEC and Directives 97/7/EC and 98/27/EC; and

"rule" means a rule made by the Financial Services Authority under the Financial Services and Markets Act 2000 or by a designated professional body within the meaning of section 326(2) of that Act.

Note —Paragraphs (6) and (7) were added by the Financial Services (Distance **3H–543** Marketing) Regulations 2004 (S.I. 2004 No. 2095). See, generally, case law mentioned in the general note at the start of these Regulations.

Assessment of unfair terms

6.—(1) Without prejudice to regulation 12, the unfairness of a **3H–544** contractual term shall be assessed, taking into account the nature of the goods or services for which the contract was concluded and by

CONSUMER

referring, at the time of conclusion of the contract, to all the circumstances attending the conclusion of the contract and to all the other terms of the contract or of another contract on which it is dependent.

(2) In so far as it is in plain intelligible language, the assessment of fairness of a term shall not relate—

(a) to the definition of the main subject matter of the contract, or

(b) to the adequacy of the price or remuneration, as against the goods or services supplied in exchange.

3H–545 *Note*—See case law mentioned in the general note at the start of these Regulations.

Written contracts
3H–546 7.—(1) A seller or supplier shall ensure that any written term of a contract is expressed in plain, intelligible language.

(2) If there is no doubt about the meaning of a written term, the interpretation which is most favourable to the consumer shall prevail but this rule shall not apply in proceedings brought under regulation 12.

Effect of unfair term
3H–547 8.—(1) An unfair term in a contract concluded with a consumer by a seller or supplier shall not be binding on the consumer.

(2) The contract shall continue to bind the parties if it is capable of continuing in existence without the unfair term.

Choice of law clauses
3H–548 9. These Regulations shall apply notwithstanding any contract term which applies or purports to apply the law of a non-Member State, if the contract has a close connection with the territory of the Member States.

* * * *

SCHEDULES

REGULATION 5(5)   **SCHEDULE 2**

INDICATIVE AND NON-EXHAUSTIVE LIST OF TERMS WHICH MAY BE REGARDED AS UNFAIR

3H–549 1. Terms which have the object or effect of—

(a) excluding or limiting the legal liability of a seller or supplier in the event of the death of a consumer or personal injury to the latter resulting from an act or omission of that seller or supplier;

(b) inappropriately excluding or limiting the legal rights of the consumer *vis-à-vis* the seller or supplier or another party in the event of total or partial non-performance or inadequate performance by the seller or supplier of any of the contractual obligations, including the option of offsetting a debt owed to the seller or supplier against any claim which the consumer may have against him;

(c) making an agreement binding on the consumer whereas provision of services by the seller or supplier is subject to a condition whose realisation depends on his own will alone;

(d) permitting the seller or supplier to retain sums paid by the consumer where the latter decides not to conclude or perform the contract, without providing

1520

for the consumer to receive compensation of an equivalent amount from the seller or supplier where the latter is the party cancelling the contract;

(e) requiring any consumer who fails to fulfil his obligation to pay a disproportionately high sum in compensation;

(f) authorising the seller or supplier to dissolve the contract on a discretionary basis where the same facility is not granted to the consumer, or permitting the seller or supplier to retain the sums paid for services not yet supplied by him where it is the seller or supplier himself who dissolves the contract;

(g) enabling the seller or supplier to terminate a contract of indeterminate duration without reasonable notice except where there are serious grounds for doing so;

(h) automatically extending a contract of fixed duration where the consumer does not indicate otherwise, when the deadline fixed for the consumer to express his desire not to extend the contract is unreasonably early;

(i) irrevocably binding the consumer to terms with which he had no real opportunity of becoming acquainted before the conclusion of the contract;

(j) enabling the seller or supplier to alter the terms of the contract unilaterally without a valid reason which is specified in the contract;

(k) enabling the seller or supplier to alter unilaterally without valid reason any characteristics of the product or service to be provided;

(l) providing for the price of goods to be determined at the time of delivery or allowing a seller of goods or supplier of services to increase their price without in both cases giving the consumer the corresponding right to cancel the contract if the final price is too high in relation to the price agreed when the contract was concluded;

(m) giving the seller or supplier the right to determine whether the goods or services supplied are in conformity with the contract, or giving him the exclusive right to interpret any term of the contract;

(n) limiting the seller's or supplier's obligation to respect commitments undertaken by his agents or making his commitments subject to compliance with a particular formality;

(o) obliging the consumer to fulfil all his obligations where the seller or supplier does not perform his;

(p) giving the seller or supplier the possibility of transferring his rights and obligations under the contract, where this may serve to reduce the guarantees for the consumer, without the latter's agreement;

(q) excluding or hindering the consumer's right to take legal action or excercise any other legal remedy, particularly by requiring the consumer to take disputes exclusively to arbitration not covered by legal provisions, unduly restricting the evidence available to him or imposing on him a burden of proof which, according to the acpplicable law, should lie with another party to the contract.

2. Scope of paragraphs 1(g), (j) and (l)

(a) Paragraph 1(g) is without hindrance to terms by which a supplier of financial services reserves the right to terminate unilaterally a contract of indeterminate duration without notice where there is a valid reason, provided that the supplier is required to inform the other contracting party or parties thereof immediately.

(b) Paragraph 1(j) is without hindrance to terms under which a supplier of financial services reserves the right to alter the rate of interest payable by the consumer or due to the latter, or the amount of other charges for financial services without notice where there is a valid reason, provided that the supplier is required to inform the other contracting party or parties thereof at the earliest opportunity and that the latter are free to dissolve the contract immediately.

Paragraph 1(j) is also without hindrance to terms under which a seller or supplier reserves the right to alter unilaterally the conditions of a contract of indeterminate duration, provided that he is required to inform the consumer with reasonable notice and that the consumer is free to dissolve the contract.

(c) Paragraphs 1(g), (j) and (l) do not apply to:

– transactions in transferable securities, financial instruments and other products or services where the price is linked to fluctuations in a stock exchange quotation or index or a financial market rate that the seller or supplier does not control;

– contracts for the purchase or sale of foreign currency, traveller's cheques or international money orders denominated in foreign currency.

(d) Paragraph 1(1) is without hindrance to price indexation clauses, where lawful, provided that the method by which prices vary is explicitly described.

Sale and Supply of Goods to Consumers Regulations 2002

3H–550   (S.I. 2002 No. 3045)

General Note

3H–551   These regulations implemented the Directive on Certain Aspects of Sale of Goods and Consumer Guarantees (1999/44/EC). They made the seller liable for public statements made by the seller, the producer or his representative; they extended the range of remedies available to a consumer in the case of goods which fail to comply with statutory implied terms; they provide, in regulation 15, that a consumer guarantee takes effect as a contractual obligation. Regs 2 and 15 are the only free-standing provisions in the regulations. The other provisions all operate by making amendments to existing Acts, namely: Supply of Goods (Implied Terms) Act 1973; Supply of Goods and Services Act 1982; Unfair Contract Terms Act 1977; Sale of Goods Act 1979. See commentaries to ss.14(2D) and 48A of the Sale of Goods Act 1979 above.

Interpretation

3H–552   2. In these Regulations—

"consumer" means any natural person who, in the contracts covered by these Regulations, is acting for purposes which are outside his trade, business or profession;

"consumer guarantee" means any undertaking to a consumer by a person acting in the course of his business, given without extra charge, to reimburse the price paid or to replace, repair or handle consumer goods in any way if they do not meet the specifications set out in the guarantee statement or in the relevant advertising;

"court" in relation to England and Wales and Northern Ireland means a county court or the High Court, and in relation to Scotland, the sheriff or the Court of Session;

"enforcement authority" means the Director General of Fair Trading, every local weights and measures authority in Great Britain and the Department of Enterprise, Trade and Investment for Northern Ireland; "goods" has the same meaning as in section 61 of the Sale of Goods Act 1979;

"guarantor" means a person who offers a consumer guarantee to a consumer; and

"supply" includes supply by way of sale, lease, hire or hire-purchase.

Consumer guarantees

3H–553   15.—(1) Where goods are sold or otherwise supplied to a consumer which are offered with a consumer guarantee, the consumer guarantee takes effect at the time the goods are delivered as a contractual obligation owed by the guarantor under the conditions set out in the guarantee statement and the associated advertising.

(2) The guarantor shall ensure that the guarantee sets out in plain intelligible language the contents of the guarantee and the essential particulars necessary for making claims under the guarantee, notably the duration and territorial scope of the guarantee as well as the name and address of the guarantor.

(3) On request by the consumer to a person to whom paragraph (4) applies, the guarantee shall within a reasonable time be made available in writing or in another durable medium available and accessible to him.

(4) This paragraph applies to the guarantor and any other person who offers to consumers the goods which are the subject of the guarantee for sale or supply.

(5) Where consumer goods are offered with a consumer guarantee, and where those goods are offered within the territory of the United Kingdom, then the guarantor shall ensure that the consumer guarantee is written in English.

(6) If the guarantor fails to comply with the provisions of paragraphs (2) or (5) above, or a person to whom paragraph (4) applies fails to comply with paragraph (3) then the enforcement authority may apply for an injunction or (in Scotland) an order of specific implement against that person requiring him to comply.

(7) The court on application under this Regulation may grant an injunction or (in Scotland) an order of specific implement on such terms as it thinks fit.

Extended Warranties on Electrical Goods

In addition to the protection given under Regulation 15 above, a consumer who **3H–554** buys an extended guarantee (usually one lasting more than a year) relating to an electrical product may have further protection by virtue of the Supply of Extended Warranties on Domestic Electrical Goods Order 2005 (S.I. 2005 No. 37). The 2005 Order does not apply to a warranty unless the consumer gives a monetary consideration for it and thus does not apply where a warranty or guarantee comes free with the goods. Nor does it apply to extended warranties that are distance contracts. It is designed to deal with the situation where a consumer buys an electrical item (usually making the purchase in-store) and also (for an additional amount) buys an extended warranty (usually one lasting more than one year after purchase of the goods). The Order requires, where an extended warranty is available for purchase at the same time as electrical goods are bought, that in-store (or in-catalogue) information be displayed, close to where the goods are displayed (or advertised) clearly indicating that purchase of the extended guarantee is optional and stating its duration and price. The Order makes it unlawful for the trader to supply the consumer with an extended warranty lasting more than a year unless the consumer is allowed certain cancellation and termination rights. As regards cancellation, the consumer must be allowed, for 45 days after purchasing the warranty (and provided no claim has been made under it), to give notice, either written or oral, to cancel it and to obtain a complete refund of the price of it. As regards termination, the consumer must be allowed, regardless of whether a claim has been made under the warranty, to give oral or written notice to terminate it after the 45 day period and to obtain a pro-rata refund. Where the price of the warranty exceeds £20, the supplier must give the consumer written notice of the consumer's rights of cancellation and termination.

3I   DISCRIMINATION

Editorial Note

Proceedings for unlawful discrimination may be brought under the Sex Discrimina-   **3I–1**
tion Act 1975 and the Race Relations Act 1976. Part VII of the former Act and Part
VIII of the latter contain provisions dealing with (amongst other things) the bringing
of civil proceedings for discrimination. Those provisions are set out below (see paras.
3I–2 *et seq* to 3I–7). Extended commentary on these Parts then follows (see para. 3I–12
et seq). Proceedings for discrimination may also be brought under the Disability
Discrimination Act 1995. Selected provisions relating to the bringing of proceedings
under that Act are set out in paras 3I–18 *et seq*, followed by commentary (para. 3I–19).
As is indicated in the commentary, rules of court relating to proceedings under the
legislation referred to above are found in CPR Sched.2 CCR O.49, r.17 (see vol.1,
para. cc49.17).

Sex Discrimination Act 1975

(1975c.65)

PART VII

ENFORCEMENT

GENERAL

Restriction of proceedings for breach of Act

62.—(1) Except as provided by this Act no proceedings, whether   **3I–2**
civil or criminal, shall lie against any person in respect of an act by
reason that the act is unlawful by virtue of a provision of this Act.

(2) Subsection (1) does not preclude the making of an order of
certiorari, mandamus or prohibition.

(3) * * * *

ENFORCEMENT OF PART III

Claims under Part III

66.—(1) A claim by any person ("the claimant") that another   **3I–3**
person ("the respondent")—

    (a) has committed an act of discrimination or harassment
       against the claimant which is unlawful by virtue of Part
       III other than section 35A or 35B, or

    (b) is by virtue of section 41 or 42 to be treated as having
       committed such an act of discrimination or harassment
       against the claimant,

may be made the subject of civil proceedings in like manner as
any other claim in tort or (in Scotland) in reparation for breach of
statutory duty.

(2) Proceedings under subsection (1)—

    (a) shall be brought in England and Wales only in a county
       court, and

    (b) shall be brought in Scotland only in a sheriff court,

but all such remedies shall be obtainable in such proceedings as, apart from this subsection and section 62(1), would be obtainable in the High Court or the Court of Session, as the case may be.

(3) As respects an unlawful act of discrimination falling within section 1(1)(b) ... no award of damages shall be made if the respondent proves that the requirement or condition in question was not applied with the intention of treating the claimant unfavourably on the ground of his sex.

(3A) Subsection (3) does not affect the award of damages in respect of an unlawful act of discrimination falling within section 1(2)(b).

(4) For the avoidance of doubt it is hereby declared that damages in respect of an unlawful act of discrimination or harassment may include compensation for injury to feelings whether or not they include compensation under any other head.

(5) Civil proceedings in respect of a claim by any person that he has been discriminated against, or subjected to harassment, in contravention of section 22 or 23 by a body to which section 25(1) applies shall not be instituted unless the claimant has given notice of the claim to the Secretary of State and either the Secretary of State has by notice informed the claimant that the Secretary of State does not require further time to consider the matter, or the period of two months has elapsed since the claimant gave notice to the Secretary of State; but nothing in this subsection applies to a counterclaim.

(6) For the purposes of proceedings under subsection (1)—
    (a) section 63(1) (assessors) of the County Courts Act 1984 shall apply with the omission of the words "on the application of any party", and
    (b) * * * *

(7) * * * *

(8) A county court or sheriff court shall have jurisdiction to entertain proceedings under subsection (1) with respect to an act done on a ship, aircraft or hovercraft outside its district, including such an act done outside Great Britain.

Note —Amended by S.I. 2005 No. 2467.

Burden of proof: county and sheriff courts

3I–4   **66A.**—(1) This section applies to any claim brought under section 66(1) in a county court in England and Wales or a sheriff court in Scotland.

(2) Where, on the hearing of the claim, the claimant proves facts from which the court could, apart from this section, conclude in the absence of an adequate explanation that the respondent—
    (a) has committed an act of discrimination or harassment against the claimant which is unlawful by virtue of—
        (i) section 35A or 35B, or
        (ii) any other provision of Part 3 so far as it applies to vocational training, or
    (b) is by virtue of section 41 or 42 to be treated as having

committed such an act of discrimination or harassment against the claimant,

the court shall uphold the claim unless the respondent proves that he did not commit, or, as the case may be, is not to be treated as having committed, that act.

Note —Amended by S.I. 2005 No. 2467.

HELP FOR PERSONS SUFFERING DISCRIMINATION

Help for aggrieved persons in obtaining information etc

74.—(1) With a view to helping a person ("the person aggrieved") **3I–5**
who considers he may have been discriminated against or subjected to harassment in contravention of this Act to decide whether to institute proceedings and, if he does so, to formulate and present his case in the most effective manner, the Secretary of State shall by order prescribe—

  (a) forms by which the person aggrieved may question the respondent on his reasons for doing any relevant act, or on any other matter which is or may be relevant;

  (b) forms by which the respondent may if he so wishes reply to any questions.

(2) Where the person aggrieved questions the respondent (whether in accordance with an order under subsection (1) or not)—

  (a) the question, and any reply by the respondent (whether in accordance with such an order or not) shall, subject to the following provisions of this section, be admissible as evidence in the proceedings;

  (b) if it appears to the court or tribunal that the respondent deliberately, and without reasonable excuse, omitted to reply within the period applicable under subsection (2A) or that his reply is evasive or equivocal, the court or tribunal may draw any inference from that fact that it considers it just and equitable to draw, including an inference that he committed an unlawful act.

(2A) The period applicable for the purposes of subsection (2)(b) is—

  (a) eight weeks beginning with the day when the question was served on the respondent, if the question relates to discrimination under—

    (i) any provision of Part 2,

    (ii) section 35A or 35B, or

    (iii) any other provision of Part 3, so far as it applies to vocational training;

  (b) a reasonable period, as regards any other question.

(3) The Secretary of State may by order—

  (a) prescribe the period within which questions must be duly served in order to be admissible under subsection (2)(a), and

  (b) prescribe the manner in which a question, and any reply by the respondent, may be duly served.

(4) * * * *

(5) This section is without prejudice to any other enactment or rule of law regulating interlocutory and preliminary matters in proceedings before a county court, sheriff court or employment tribunal, and has effect subject to any enactment or rule of law regulating the admissibility of evidence in such proceedings.

(6) * * * *

Note —Amended by S.I. 2005 No. 2467.

PERIOD WITHIN WHICH PROCEEDINGS TO BE BROUGHT

Period within which proceedings to be brought

3I–6   **76.**—(1) * * * * *

(2) A county court or a sheriff court shall not consider a claim under section 66 unless proceedings in respect of the claim are instituted before the end of

(a) the period of six months beginning when the act complained of was done; or

(b) in a case to which section 66(5) applies, the period of eight months so beginning.

(2A) Where in England and Wales–

(a) proceedings or prospective proceedings under section 66 relate to the act or omission of a qualifying institution, and

(b) the dispute concerned is referred as a complaint under the student complaints scheme before the end of the period of six months mentioned in subsection (2)(a),

the period allowed by subsection (2)(a) shall be extended by two months.

(2B) In subsection (2A)–

"qualifying institution" has the meaning given by section 11 of the Higher Education Act 2004;

"the student complaints scheme" means a scheme for the review of qualifying complaints, as defined by section 12 of that Act, that is provided by the designated operator, as defined by section 13(5)(b) of that Act.

(3) An employment tribunal, county court or sheriff court shall not consider an application under section 72(2)(a) unless it is made before the end of the period of six months beginning when the act to which it relates was done; and a county court or sheriff court shall not consider an application under section 72(4) unless it is made before the end of the period of five years so beginning.

(4) * * * *

(5) A court or tribunal may nevertheless consider any such complaint, claim or application which is out of time if, in all the circumstances of the case, it considers that it is just and equitable to do so.

(6) For the purposes of this section—

(a) where the inclusion of any term in a contract renders the making of the contract an unlawful act that act shall be treated as extending throughout the duration of the contract, and

(b) any act extending over a period shall be treated as done at the end of that period, and

(c) a deliberate omission shall be treated as done when the person in question decided upon it,

and in the absence of evidence establishing the contrary a person shall be taken for the purposes of this section to decide upon an omission when he does an act inconsistent with doing the omitted act or, if he has done no such inconsistent act, when the period expires within which he might reasonably have been expected to do the omitted act if it was to be done.

Note —Amended by the Higher Education Act 2004, s.19(1).

Race Relations Act 1976

(1976 c.74)

PART VIII

ENFORCEMENT

Restriction of proceedings for breach of Act

53.—(1) Except as provided by this Act or the Special Immigra-   **3I–7** tion Appeals Commission Act 1997 or Part 5 of the Nationality, Immigration and Asylum Act 2002 no proceedings, whether civil or criminal, shall lie against any person in respect of an act by reason that the act is unlawful by virtue of a provision of this Act.

(2) Subsection (1) does not preclude the making of an order of certiorari, mandamus or prohibition.

(3) * * * *

(4) Subsections (2) and (3) do not, except so far as provided by section 76, apply to any act which is unlawful by virtue of section 76(5) or (9) or by virtue of section 76(10)(b), (11) and (11B).

Claims under Part III etc

57.—(1) A claim by any person ("the claimant") that another   **3I–8** person ("the respondent")—

(a) has committed an act against the claimant which is unlawful by virtue of Part III other than, in relation to discrimination on grounds of race or ethnic or national origins, or harassment, section 26A or 26B; or

(b) is by virtue of section 32 or 33 to be treated as having committed such an act against the claimant,

may be made the subject of civil proceedings in like manner as any other claim in tort or (in Scotland) in reparation for breach of statutory duty.

(2) Proceedings under subsection (1)—

(a) shall, in England and Wales, be brought only in a designated county court; and

(b) * * * * *

but all such remedies shall be obtainable in such proceedings as, apart from this subsection and section 53(1), would be obtainable in the High Court or the Court of Session, as the case may be.

(3) As respects an unlawful act of discrimination falling within section 1(1)(b), no award of damages shall be made if the respondent proves that the requirement or condition in question was not applied with the intention of treating the claimant unfavourably on racial grounds.

(4) For the avoidance of doubt it is hereby declared that damages in respect of an unlawful act of discrimination may include compensation for injury to feelings whether or not they include compensation under any other head.

(4A) As respects an act which is done, or by virtue of section 32 or 33 is treated as done, by a person in carrying out public investigator functions or functions as a public prosecutor and which is unlawful by virtue of section 19B, no remedy other than—

(a) damages; or

(b) a declaration or, in Scotland, a declarator;

shall be obtainable unless the court is satisfied that the remedy concerned would not prejudice a criminal investigation, a decision to institute criminal proceedings or any criminal proceedings.

(4B) In this section—

"criminal investigation" means —

(a) any investigation which a person in carrying out functions to which section 19B applies has a duty to conduct with a view to it being ascertained whether a person should be charged with, or in Scotland prosecuted for, an offence, or whether a person charged with or prosecuted for an offence is guilty of it;

(b) any investigation which is conducted by a person in carrying out functions to which section 19B applies and which in the circumstances may lead to a decision by that person to institute criminal proceedings which the person has power to conduct; or

(c) any investigation which is conducted by a person in carrying out functions to which section 19B applies and which in the circumstances may lead to a decision by that person to make a report to the procurator fiscal for the purpose of enabling him to determine whether criminal proceedings should be instituted; and

"public investigator functions" means functions of conducting criminal investigations or charging offenders;

and in this subsection "offence" includes any offence under the Army Act 1955, the Air Force Act 1955 or the Naval Discipline Act 1957 (and "offender" shall be construed accordingly).

(4C) Subsection (4D) applies where a party to proceedings under subsection (1) which have arisen by virtue of section 19B has applied for a stay or sist of those proceedings on the grounds of prejudice to—

    (a) particular criminal proceedings;

    (b) a criminal investigation; or

    (c) a decision to institute criminal proceedings.

(4D) The court shall grant the stay or sist unless it is satisfied that the continuance of the proceedings under subsection (1) would not result in the prejudice alleged.

(5) Civil proceedings in respect of a claim by any person that he has been discriminated against in contravention of section 17 or 18 by a body to which subsection (5A) applies shall not be instituted unless the claimant has given notice of the claim to the Secretary of State.

(5A) This subsection applies to—

    (a) local education authorities in England and Wales;

    (b) * * * * *

    (c) any body which is a responsible body in relation to an establishment falling within paragraph 3, 3B or 7B of the table in section 17.

(6) * * * * *

(7) This section has effect subject to section 57A.

Burden of proof: County and Sheriff Courts

57ZA.—(1) This section applies where a claim is brought under   **3I–9** section 57 and the claim is that the respondent–

    (a) has committed an act of discrimination, on grounds of race or ethnic or national origins, which is unlawful by virtue of any provision referred to in section 1(1B)(b) to (d), or Part IV in its application to those provisions, or

    (b) has committed an act of harassment.

(2) Where, on the hearing of the claim, the claimant proves facts from which the court could, apart from this section, conclude in the absence of an adequate explanation that the respondent–

    (a) has committed such an act of discrimination or harassment against the claimant, or

    (b) is by virtue of section 32 or 33 to be treated as having committed such an act of discrimination or harassment against the claimant,

the court shall uphold the claim unless the respondent proves that he did not commit or, as the case may be, is not to be treated as having committed, that act.

HELP FOR PERSONS SUFFERING DISCRIMINATION

Help for aggrieved persons in obtaining information etc

65.—(1) With a view to helping a person ("the person aggrieved")   **3I–10** who considers he may have been discriminated against or subjected to harassment in contravention of this Act to decide whether to institute proceedings and, if he does so, to formulate and present his case in the most effective manner, the Secretary of State shall by order prescribe—

>   (a) forms by which the person aggrieved may question the respondent on his reasons for doing any relevant act, or on any other matter which is or may be relevant; and

>   (b) forms by which the respondent may if he so wishes reply to any questions.

(2) Where the person aggrieved questions the respondent (whether in accordance with an order under subsection (1) or not)—

>   (a) the question, and any reply by the respondent (whether in accordance with such an order or not) shall, subject to the following provisions of this section, be admissible as evidence in the proceedings;

>   (b) if it appears to the court or tribunal that the respondent deliberately, and without reasonable excuse, omitted to reply within a reasonable period or, where the question relates to discrimination on grounds of race or ethnic or national origins, or to harassment, the period of eight weeks beginning with the day on which the question was served on him or that his reply is evasive or equivocal, the court or tribunal may draw any inference from that fact that it considers it just and equitable to draw, including an inference that he committed an unlawful act.

(3) The Secretary of State may by order—

>   (a) prescribe the period within which questions must be duly served in order to be admissible under subsection (2)(a); and

>   (b) prescribe the manner in which a question, and any reply by the respondent, may be duly served.

(4) *   *   *   *

(4A) In section 19B proceedings, subsection (2)(b) does not apply in relation to a failure to reply, or a particular reply, if the conditions specified in subsection (4B) are satisfied.

(4B) Those conditions are that—

>   (a) at the time of doing any relevant act, the respondent was carrying out public investigator functions or was a public prosecutor; and

>   (b) he reasonably believes that a reply or (as the case may be) a different reply would be likely to prejudice any criminal investigation, any decision to institute criminal proceedings or any criminal proceedings or would reveal the reasons behind a decision not to institute, or a decision not to continue, criminal proceedings.

(4C) For the purposes of subsections (4A) and (4B)—

"public investigator functions" has the same meaning as in section 57;

"section 19B proceedings" means proceedings in respect of a claim under section 57 which has arisen by virtue of section 19B.

(5) This section is without prejudice to any other enactment or rule of law regulating interlocutory and preliminary matters in proceedings before a county court, sheriff court or employment tribunal, and has effect subject to any enactment or rule of law regulating the admissibility of evidence in such proceedings.

(6) * * * *

(7) This section does not apply in relation to any proceedings under—

(a) the Special Immigration Appeals Commission Act 1997; or

(b) Part 5 of the Nationality, Immigration and Asylum Act 2002.

Period within which proceedings to be brought

68.—(1) * * * * *   **3I–11**

(2) Subject to subsection (2A) a county court or a sheriff court shall not consider a claim under section 57 unless proceedings in respect of the claim are instituted before the end of—

(a) the period of six months beginning when the act complained of was done;

(b) * * * *

(2A) In relation to an immigration claim within the meaning of section 57A, the period of six months mentioned in subsection (2)(a) begins on the expiry of the period during which, by virtue of section 57A(1)(a), no proceedings may be brought under section 57(1) in respect of the claim.

(3) Where, in relation to proceedings or prospective proceedings by way of a claim under section 57, an application for assistance under section 66 is made to the Commission before the end of the period of six months mentioned in paragraph (a) of subsection (2), the period allowed by that paragraph for instituting proceedings in respect of the claim shall be extended by two months.

(3A) Where in England and Wales–

(a) proceedings or prospective proceedings by way of a claim under section 57 relate to the act or omission of a qualifying institution,

(b) the dispute concerned is referred as a complaint under the student complaints scheme before the end of the period of six months mentioned in subsection (2), and

(c) subsection (3) does not apply,

the period allowed by subsection (2) for instituting proceedings in respect of the claim shall be extended by two months.

(3B) In subsection (3A)–

"qualifying institution" has the meaning given by section 11 of the Higher Education Act 2004;

"the student complaints scheme" means a scheme for the review of qualifying complaints, as defined by section 12 of that Act, that is provided by the designated operator, as defined by section 13(5)(b) of that Act.

(4) An employment tribunal, county court or sheriff court shall not consider an application under section 63(2)(a) unless it is made before the end of the period of six months beginning when the act to which it relates was done; and a county court or sheriff court shall not consider an application under section 63(4) unless it is made before the end of the period of five years so beginning.

(5) An employment tribunal shall not consider a complaint under section 64(1) unless it is presented to the tribunal before the end of the period of six months beginning when the act complained of was done.

(6) A court or tribunal may nevertheless consider any such complaint, claim or application which is out of time if, in all the circumstances of the case, it considers that it is just and equitable to do so.

(7) For the purposes of this section—

    (a) when the inclusion of any term in a contract renders the making of the contract an unlawful act, that act shall be treated as extending throughout the duration of the contract; and

    (b) any act extending over a period shall be treated as done at the end of that period; and

    (c) a deliberate omission shall be treated as done when the person in question decided upon it;

and in the absence of evidence establishing the contrary a person shall be taken for the purposes of this section to decide upon an omission when he does an act inconsistent with doing the omitted act or, if he has done no such inconsistent act, when the period expires within which he might reasonably have been expected to do the omitted act if it was to be done.

Notes on Part VII of the Sex Discrimination Act 1975 and Part VIII the Race Relations Act 1976

3I-12   Part VII of the Sex Discrimination Act 1975 (SDA) and Part VIII of the Race Relations Act 1976 (RRA) address enforcement and the evidential and procedural issues peculiar to the SDA and RRA.

Rules of court (CPR Sched. 2, CCR Ord.49, r.17)

3I-13   When the 1975 Act and the 1976 Act came into effect the County Court Rules 1984 were amended by the addition of r.17 to O.49 for the purpose of providing necessary rules of court. When the CPR came into effect, those provisions were carried forward into Sched.2 (see Vol.1, para.cc49.17). That rule has been amended from time to time, principally for the purpose of taking account of changes in primary legislation.

Jurisdiction and Proceedings

3I-14   Proceedings in respect of the unlawful acts created by the SDA and RRA may be brought only in the way provided for by the Acts themselves (s.62 SDA; s.53 RRA). Nothing in the SDA or RRA prevents an application being made in judicial review (SDA s.62; RRA s.53). However (outside the employment and related fields), jurisdiction is in the main exclusively conferred on the county courts. Where appropriate, proceedings may be brought by way of a defence and/or counter claim (*e.g.* in defence of a possession action, see *Manchester City Council v. Romano* [2004] EWCA Civ 834, CA June 29, 2004 unrep., paras 63–64). In England and Wales proceedings under Part III of the RRA (alone) may only be brought in a "designated" County Court (RRA s.57(2), as to which see RRA s.67; see too, s.57A for claims arising in certain immigration cases). In addition, by s.67(4) of the RRA, the judge hearing such a claim "shall, unless with the consent of the parties he sits without assessors, be assisted by two assessors". Assessors have a wide role (*Ahmed v. Governing Body of the University of Oxford*

[2002] EWCA Civ 1907; [2003] 1 W.L.R. 995, CA). They assist the judge in the broadest sense of helping him or her "evaluate the evidence in the area of race relations". They may therefore be involved in fact finding though the judge remains responsible for actually deciding the facts and the "ultimate decision has to be for the judge" (*ibid* para 32). The fact that the assessors' primary role is in the decision making process, "militates against any general obligation of disclosure prior to judgment" but there may be circumstances where disclosure will be necessary, "for example where a point arises as a result of the assistance of the assessors which the parties clearly did not have in mind and which they should be entitled to address". Furthermore assessors, despite their primary role, may provide a piece of information akin to expert evidence, and here, once again, disclosure should be made (*ibid*, para 34). The judge must ensure that it is apparent from his or her judgment that s.67(4) has been complied with and the assistance of his assessors has been used in reaching conclusions on issues relating to possible racism (*ibid*, para 35). Where the judge accepts the evaluation of the assessors it will normally form part of the reasoning for the conclusion ultimately reached and this aspect should be recorded in the judgment (*ibid*, para 36). Disagreement between the judge and the assessors on issues relating to racism should be rare, at least if the assessors themselves are agreed (*ibid*, para 37). Where there is disagreement between the judge and the assessors as to an important matter, this should be recorded in the judgment with the judge explaining his reasons for taking a different view or, where the assessors are not agreed, preferring the advice of one assessor rather than the other (*ibid*, paras 38–39). In addition, the SDA makes specific provision allowing for the appointment of assessors under s.63 of the County Courts Act 1984 (SDA s.66(6)). Certain claims (but not counter claims) under the education provisions of the SDA and RRA may only be instituted after the Claimant has given notice of the claim to the Secretary of State (SDA s.66(5) and RRA s.57(5)–(5A)) and, in the case of claims under the SDA, two months has elapsed since notice has been given or the Secretary of State has indicated that no further time is required (the same requirement in the RRA was removed by the Race Relations (Amendment) Act 2000). Provision is made allowing for the staying of proceedings under RRA s.19B where a party has applied for the same on the ground of prejudice to particular criminal proceedings; a criminal investigation or a decision to institute criminal proceedings when such a stay must be granted unless the court is satisfied that the continuance of the proceedings would not result in the prejudice alleged (RRA) s.57(4C) and (4D)).

The SDA has been recently amended by the Employment Equality (Sex Discrimination) Regulations 2005 S.I. 2005 No. 2467 so as to, amongst other things, introduce a statutory tort of harassment into certain parts of the SDA (already found in the RRA and Disability Discrimination Act 1995) and to move the unlawful acts applicable to the treatment of barristers, pupils and advocates from the jurisdiction of the County Court and to the Employment Tribunals. These changes took effect from October 1, 2005 though the jurisdiction changes do not apply to proceedings where the act complained of took place before that date (see transitional provisions in regs 1(1), 2(1)).

Time limits

Proceedings under Parts III of the SDA and RRA must be instituted within six months of when the act complained was done (SDA s.76(2)(a); RRA s.68(2), and see s.68(2A) for a modification in relation to certain immigration claims under RRA s.19B). In cases falling under ss.22 and 23 of the SDA (education) proceedings must be instituted within eight months of when the act complained of was done (SDA s.76(2)(b)). In cases where the dispute involves a higher education institution and the complaint has been referred as a complaint under the "student complaints scheme" the time limit for instituting proceedings is extended by two months (SDA s.76(2A); RRA s.68(3A)). Where an application is made for assistance to the CRE (only), the time limit for issuing proceedings under Part III RRA is extended by two months and then by an additional month if the requisite notice is given (see RRA s.68(3) and s.66(4)). As to when time begins to run, see SDA s.76(6); s.68(7) RRA s.68(7)). The circumstances in which an act might be said to "extend over a period" (usually described as a "continuing act") for the purposes of the time limits have proved problematic and controversial. A policy, rule or practice, in accordance with which decisions are taken from time to time, might constitute a "continuing act" for these purposes, even where such policy is unwritten and informal (*Owusu v. London Fire and Civil Defence Authority*

3I–15

[1995] I.R.L.R. 574, EAT; *Cast v. Croydon College* [1998] I.C.R. 500, CA). Likewise a continuing state of affairs may constitute a continuing act for these purposes (*Hendricks v. MPC* [2003] I.R.L.R. 96, even where the individual acts relied upon are done by different persons and are done at different places). In addition, in each case, a claim may be considered notwithstanding that it has been instituted outside of the time limit where it would be "just and equitable" to do so (SDA s.76(5); RRA s.68(6)); as to the factors which are likely to be relevant, see *Anderson v. Rover Group* (1999) 1426/99, EAT; *British Coal Corporation v. Keeble and Others* [1997] I.R.L.R. 336, EAT, at 338, and *London Borough of Southwark v. Afolabi* [2003] I.R.L.R. 220, presented nearly nine years after the expiry of the statutory time limit). Each case is likely to turn very much on its own facts.

Enforcement and Remedies

3I–16   The unlawful acts created by the SDA and RRA are statutory torts and in general terms the Courts have addressed their enforcement and remedies in relation to them in much the same way as with any other statutory tort. Thus, where an award of compensation is made in respect of joint tortfeasors, the award will be distributed according to what is just and equitable having regard to the extent of that person's responsibility for the damage in question (Civil Liability (Contribution) Act 1978; see *Prison Service v. Johnson* [1997] I.C.R. 275). Further, where a person has a cause of action under the SDA and RRA that cause of action survives his or her death for the benefit of his estate (Law Reform (Miscellaneous Provisions) Act 1934; *Lewisham and Guys Mental Health NHS Trust v. Harris* [2000] I.C.R. 707, CA). As to remedies under the SDA and RRA the county courts may make any order as would be available in the High Court (in England and Wales) and the Court of Session (in Scotland) and in particular awards of compensation, including an award for injury to feelings, and declarations may be made (SDA s.66(1)–(2) and (4) and RRA s.57(1)–(2) and (4)). In determining whether any particular losses are recoverable the test to be applied is whether such losses are caused by (or arise naturally and directly from) the discrimination found proved. There is no requirement of foreseeabilty (*Essa v. Laing Ltd* [2004] EWCA Civ 2; [2004] I.C.R. 746, CA). In relation to claims of indirect sex discrimination outside the employment field and certain claims of indirect race discrimination outside the employment field, no award of damages may be made if the defendant proves that the requirement or condition in question was not applied with the intention of treating the claimant unfavourably (SDA s.66(3); RRA s.57(3)) but a court may infer that a defendant had the requisite intention where he knew when he applied the offending requirement or condition that the discriminatory consequences would follow (*London Underground Limited v. Edwards* [1995] IRLR 355, EAT; *JH Walker Ltd v. Hussain* [1996] ICR 291, EAT).

Proving discrimination and the burden of proof

3I–17   There is much guidance from the appellate courts on proving the different forms of discrimination provided for under the SDA and RRA (see, for example, *Anya v. University of Oxford* [2001] EWCA Civ 405; [2001] I.C.R. 847, CA, at pp 851–855, *per* Sedley L.J.; *Qureshi v. Victoria University of Manchester* [2001] I.C.R. 863, EAT, for the very helpful guidance of Mummery L.J.; *Shamoon v Chief Constable of the Royal Ulster Constabulary* [2003] UKHL 11; [2003] ICR 337, HL; *Chief Constable of the West Yorkshire Police v. Khan* [2001] UKHL 48; [2001] I.C.R. 1065, HL). In addition, the SDA and RRA now make specific provision shifting the burden of proof in certain circumstances. Where a claimant proves facts from which a court could conclude in the absence of an adequate explanation that the defendant has committed an unlawful act, a court must uphold the complaint unless the defendant proves that he did not so act (SDA s.63A and s.66A; RRA s.54A and s.57ZA). This shift applies only in relation to certain of the unlawful acts created by the SDA and RRA, as the provisions themselves make clear. The impact of these provisions is as yet unclear though some guidance has been provided by the courts (*Barton v. Investec Securities Ltd* [2003] I.C.R. 1205, EAT; *Chamberlin Solicitors v. Emokpae* [2004] I.C.R. 1476, EAT; *University of Huddersfield v. Wolff*, [2004] I.C.R. 828, EAT; *Nelson v. Carillion Services Ltd* [2003] EWCA Civ 544; [2003] I.C.R. 1256, CA). The SDA and RRA also make provision for the service of "questionnaires" (SDA s.74 and RRA s.65; see too, Sex Discrimination (Questions and Replies) Order 1975 (S.I. 1975 No. 2048); Race Relations (Questions and Replies) Order 1977 (S.I. 1977 No. 842)). Time limits are prescribed for the purposes of serving and replying to such questionnaires and provision is made allowing for adverse inferences to be drawn in cases where a questionnaire is not replied to or not replied to within the time limit prescribed for so doing (SDA s.74 and RRA s.65). Carefully crafted questions can assist a complainant in properly identifying his complaints and in proving them, as can be seen from the guidance in *Barton, supra* (and see *West Midlands Passenger Transport Executive v. Singh* [1988] I.R.L.R. 186, CA). The statutory Codes of Practice also provide valuable guidance as to the proving of discrimination.

Disability Discrimination Act 1995

(1995 c.50)

PART IV

EDUCATION

Enforcement, remedies and procedure

28V—(1) A claim by a person–   3I–18

    (a) that a responsible body has discriminated against him in a way which is unlawful under this Chapter,

    (b) that a responsible body is by virtue of section 57 or 58 to be treated as having discriminated against him in such a way, or

    (c) that a person is by virtue of section 57 to be treated as having discriminated against him in such a way,

may be made the subject of civil proceedings in the same way as any other claim in tort or (in Scotland) in reparation for breach of statutory duty.

(2) For the avoidance of doubt it is hereby declared that damages in respect of discrimination in a way which is unlawful under this Chapter may include compensation for injury to feelings whether or not they include compensation under any other head.

(3) Proceedings in England and Wales may be brought only in a county court.

(4) Proceedings in Scotland may be brought only in a sheriff court.

(5) The remedies available in such proceedings are those which are available in the High Court or (as the case may be) the Court of Session.

(6) The fact that a person who brings proceedings under this Part against a responsible body may also be entitled to bring proceedings against that body under Part 2 is not to affect the proceedings under this Part.

(7) Part 4 of Schedule 3 makes further provision about the enforcement of this Part and about procedure.

Notes on Part IV of the Disability Discrimination Act 1995

When the 1995 Act came into effect the CCR O.49, r.17 was amended for the   3I–19
purpose of providing necessary rules of court; see now Sched. 2 CCR O.49, r.17 (Vol. 1, para. cc49.17). In 2004, that rule was amended to take account of the coming into effect of the Disability Rights Commission Act 1999.

Part IV, Chapters 1 and 2, of the Disability Discrimination Act 1995 (DDA) was inserted by the Special Educational Needs and Disability Act 2001 and it creates a number of unlawful acts in relation to schools and local education authorities in relation to pupils (ss. 28A–C and 28F); in relation to Further and Higher Education (s.28R to s.28T) and in relation to certain providers of statutory youth and community services including adult education in relation to students (s.28U and Sched.4C DDA). Claims under Part IV, Chapter 1 (discrimination in relation to pupils) are heard in Special Educational Need and Disability Tribunals (s.28I). Claims under Part IV Chapter 2 (discrimination in relation to students) are heard in the county courts (s.28V).

There are many similarities between the DDA, on the one hand, and the SDA and RRA on the other, but significant differences also. However, the DDA addresses remedies and enforcement in a similar way in respect of those unlawful acts it creates and, in particular, in respect of those justiciable in the county courts under Part III and IV DDA (Sched.3, paras. 2(1)–(2), 5(1)–(2), 9(1)–(2) and 12(1)–(2); ss.25(1), (2), (5), 28V(1)–(2), (5)). In addition the DDA provides for a shift in the burden of proof in respect of certain of the unlawful acts (s.17A(1C) and s.25(7)–(9)); provides for a questionnaire procedure (s.56 DDA and Disability Discrimination (Questions and Replies) Order 2004 (S.I. 2004 No. 1168)); addresses vicarious and secondary liability (ss. 57–58 and s.64A DDA) and time limits (Sched. 3, paras. 6 and 13) and the guidance provided by the courts on these matters in relation to the SDA and the RRA should be taken as applying equally to proceedings under the DDA. The DDA makes express provision allowing the Disability Rights Commission to facilitate conciliation (s.28 and s.31B).

SECTION 4

HOUSE OF LORDS APPEALS

4A   CIVIL APPEALS

Practice Directions Applicable to Civil Appeals

(with effect from 7 April 2005)

Part I Directions on Petitions for Leave to Appeal

1.

PERMISSION TO APPEAL

Introduction

1.1 Subject to certain conditions, appeals in civil matters may be brought to the **4A–1** House of Lords from the Court of Appeal in England and Wales and in Northern Ireland, from the High Court in England and Wales and in Northern Ireland under the "leapfrog" procedure, and from the Court of Session in Scotland.[1] The judicial procedures of the House are regulated by statute, by standing orders of the House and by practice directions.[2] Copies of these and other documents may be obtained free of charge from the Judicial Office of the House of Lords or downloaded from the Internet.

Terminology

1.2 The Appellate Jurisdiction Act 1876 is the basic Act governing the judicial **4A–2** function of the House of Lords. This booklet uses the terminology of that Act. The term "leave to appeal" means permission to appeal. A "petition for leave to appeal" is an application for permission to appeal.

Right of appeal

1.3 The right of appeal to the House of Lords is regulated by statute and subject to **4A–3** statutory restrictions. The relevant statutes for civil appeals are: the Administration of Justice (Appeals) Act 1934; the Administration of Justice Act 1960; the Administration of Justice Act 1969; the Judicature (Northern Ireland) Act 1978; the Court of Session Act 1988; and the Access to Justice Act 1999. Every applicant for leave to appeal must comply with the statutory requirements before the application can be considered by the House. The Human Rights Act 1998 applies to the House in its judicial capacity. But that Act does not confer any general right of appeal to the House, or any right of appeal in addition to or superseding any right of appeal provided for in Acts passed before the coming into force of the Human Rights Act 1998.

Stay of execution

1.4 See direction 43.   **4A–4**

Appeals from (i) the Court of Appeal in England & Wales; and (ii) the Court of Appeal in Northern Ireland

1.5 An appeal to the House of Lords from any order or judgment of the Court of **4A–5** Appeal in England and Wales or in Northern Ireland may only be brought with the leave of the Court of Appeal or of the House of Lords.[3]

1.6 An application for leave to appeal must be made first to the Court of Appeal and

---

[1] For appeals "in a criminal cause or matter", see the Red Book of *Practice Directions applicable to criminal appeals* (January 2006 ed) available from the Judicial Office and on www.parliament.uk.
[2] The orders are made pursuant to the Appellate Jurisdiction Act 1876 s 11.
[3] Administration of Justice (Appeals) Act 1934, s.1(1); Judicature (Northern Ireland) Act 1978, s.42.

only after that Court refuses leave may application be made to the House of Lords itself. Application is made by presenting a petition for leave to appeal.[1]

Appeals from the Court of Session in Scotland

4A–6   1.7 The House of Lords does not grant leave to appeal from the Court of Session.

1.8 In all cases where leave to appeal from the Court of Session is required, it must be obtained from the Inner House of the Court of Session.[2] In all such cases a refusal of the Court of Session to grant leave to appeal is final and no petition for leave to appeal may then be presented to the House of Lords.

1.9 An appeal lies to the House of Lords from an interlocutor of the Inner House of the Court of Session. As a general rule, leave to appeal is not required.[3] Standing Order I applies and the petition of appeal must be lodged within 3 months of the date of the interlocutor(s) appealed from. Standing Order IV also applies and the petition of appeal must be signed by two counsel who must also certify that the appeal is reasonable.

1.10 An appeal lies to the House of Lords from an interlocutory judgment of the Court of Session where there is a difference of opinion among the judges or where the interlocutory judgment is one sustaining a dilatory defence and dismissing the action. As a general rule, leave to appeal is not required. Standing Order IV applies and the petition of appeal must be signed by two counsel who must also certify that the appeal is reasonable.

1.11 An appeal lies to the House of Lords against any interlocutory judgment of the Court of Session other than one falling within direction 1.10 provided the Inner House of the Court of Session has granted leave to appeal.

Appeals from (i) High Court of Justice in England & Wales; and (ii) High Court of Justice in Northern Ireland

4A–7   1.12 In certain cases, and subject to certain conditions, an appeal lies direct from the High Court in England and Wales or in Northern Ireland to the House of Lords. A certificate of the High Court must first be obtained and the leave of the House of Lords then sought and given before the appeal may proceed (see direction 6).[4] No application may be made to the House of Lords without the certificate of the High Court.

Civil contempt of court cases

4A–8   1.13 In cases involving civil contempt of court, an appeal may be brought under s 13 of the Administration of Justice Act 1960.[5] Leave to appeal is required and an application for such leave must first be made to the court below. If that application is refused, a petition for leave to appeal may then be presented to the House of Lords. Where the decision of the court below is a decision on appeal under the same section of the same Act, leave to appeal to the House of Lords is only granted if the court below certifies that a point of law of general public importance is involved in that decision and if it appears to that court or to the House, as the case may be, that the point is one that ought to be considered by the House. Where the court below refuses to grant the certificate required, a petition for leave to appeal is not accepted for presentation to the House.

Admissibility of petitions

4A–9   1.14 Leave to appeal to the House of Lords is subject to conditions imposed by

---

[1] For form of petition, see Appendix A, Form 1.
[2] Court of Session Act 1988, s.40(1)(b).
[3] Court of Session Act 1988, s.40(1). The right of appeal may however be restricted or excluded by statute e.g. Transport Act 1985, s.117, Sched. 4, para. 14(1).
[4] Administration of Justice Act 1969, ss.12–15.
[5] Or, in Northern Ireland, under Judicature (Northern Ireland) Act 1978, s.44. Appeals involving criminal contempt of court are subject to the *Practice directions applicable to Criminal Appeals* (January 2006 ed).

Parliament in statute. The relevant statutes exclude certain types of petition from the House's jurisdiction. Petitions for leave to appeal are not admissible if they fall into any of the following categories:

(a) petitions for leave to appeal to the House of Lords from a refusal by the Court of Appeal to grant leave to appeal to that court from a judgment or order of a lower court, or from any other preliminary decision of the Court of Appeal in respect of a case in which leave to appeal to the Court of Appeal was not granted[1];

(b) petitions for leave to appeal to the House of Lords brought by a petitioner in respect of whom the High Court has made an order under s 42 of the Supreme Court Act 1981 (restriction of vexatious legal proceedings), except a petition for leave to appeal against the s 42 order itself;

(c) petitions for leave to appeal from a decision of the Court of Appeal on any appeal from a county court in any probate proceedings[2];

(d) petitions for leave to appeal from a decision of the Court of Appeal on an appeal from a decision of the High Court on a question of law under Part III of the Representation of the People Act 1983 (legal proceedings).[3]

1.15 If in the opinion of the Judicial Office a petition for leave to appeal appears to be inadmissible because it falls into one of the above categories, the petitioner is advised accordingly by letter. No fee is charged if the petition is then withdrawn.

1.16 If a petitioner who has been advised that a petition appears to be inadmissible nevertheless wishes the petition to be placed before an Appeal Committee, the petition is accepted for presentation to the House, provided that:

(i) the petition is properly served on the respondents;

(ii) all the required documents are supplied to the Judicial Office[4]; and

(iii) the prescribed fee is paid.

The fee paid in respect of such a petition is not refunded if the Appeal Committee finds the petition to be inadmissible.

1.17 If the Appeal Committee finds a petition to be inadmissible, the Judicial Office writes to the petitioner, informing them of the Appeal Committee's decision. The European Court of Human Rights accepts this letter (accompanied by the Committee's report and the Minutes of Proceedings of the House in which the report is recorded) or the letter referred to in direction 1.15 as setting out the jurisdiction of the House of Lords in the litigation, for the purpose of determining whether the petitioner has satisfied the requirement, laid down by Article 35 of the European Convention on Human Rights, that all domestic remedies must be exhausted before an appeal can be made to the Strasbourg Court.

Cross-appeals

1.18 See direction 30.   **4A–10**

Public funding/legal aid

1.19 See direction 41.   **4A–11**

Counsel

1.20 Petitioners and respondents to a petition for leave to appeal may instruct **4A–12** leading or junior counsel, but on taxation (assessment of costs) the House allows only

---

[1] See the decisions of the House in *Lane v. Esdaile* [1891] A.C. 10; also *R. v. Secretary of State for Trade and Industry ex p Eastaway* [2000] 1 W.L.R. 2222; Access to Justice Act 1999, s.54, and Pt 52 Civil Procedure Rules (as amended). No appeal lies to the House from an incidental decision of the Court of Appeal: Supreme Court Act 1981, s.58 (as amended by Access to Justice Act 1999, s.60).

[2] County Courts Act 1934, s.82.

[3] Representation of the People Act 1983, s.157(1).

[4] For documents required see direction 4.2.

junior counsel's fees for any stage of a petition for leave to appeal, even if a public funding or legal aid certificate provides for leading counsel. The only exception to this practice is where leading counsel who conducted the case in the court below are instructed by the Legal Services Commission or legal aid authorities to advise on the merits of an appeal.

2.

TIME LIMITS

4A–13 2.1 Subject to direction 2.5, a petition for leave to appeal to the House of Lords should be lodged in the Judicial Office within one month from the date of the order appealed from.[1] However, petitions for leave to appeal out of time are admissible.[2]

Petitions out of time

4A–14 2.2 A petition for leave to appeal lodged outside the one month period is accepted by the Judicial Office for presentation to the House provided that:
  (a) it has been drafted in the style required for such petitions and seeks leave to appeal out of time[3]; and
  (b) it sets out in the first paragraph the reason(s) why it was not lodged within the time limit; and
  (c) it is in order in all other respects

The reason(s) should not normally exceed one paragraph in length.

2.3 In considering a petition for leave to appeal out of time, the Appeal Committee may reject it solely on the ground that it is out of time; but the Appeal Committee may grant an extension of time and decide the application for leave on the merits.

2.4 The Appeal Committee does not usually grant leave to appeal if a petition for leave is lodged more than three months after the date of the order appealed from (i.e. more than two months out of time).

Contempt of court

4A–15 2.5 A petition for leave to appeal in a case involving civil contempt of court must be lodged in the Judicial Office within 14 days (not one month), beginning with the date of the refusal of leave by the court below (not the following day).[4]

3.

LODGMENT OF PETITION

Form of petition

4A–16 3.1 A petition for leave to appeal should be produced on durable quality A4 paper, bound on the left like a book, using both sides of the paper. The petition should set out briefly the facts and points of law; and conclude with a summary of the reasons why leave should be granted.[5] Petitions which are not legible or which are not produced in the required form are not accepted. A petition should not contain annexes or appendices. Parties may consult the Judicial Office at any stage of preparation of the petition, and may submit petitions in draft for approval.

---

[1] The one month period runs from the date of the substantive order appealed from, not the date of any subsequent procedural order, e.g., an order refusing leave to appeal (Standing Order II). For admissibility of petitions for leave, see direction 1.14. If a petitioner has applied for public funding, the period is extended to one month after the decision whether funding should be granted, including any appeals. The Judicial Office must be informed in writing within the one month period that public funding has been applied for (direction 41).
[2] Directions 2.2–2.4.
[3] For style see Appendix A, Form 3.
[4] Administration of Justice Act 1960, s.13 as amended.
[5] For style see Appendix A, Forms 1, 2.

3.2 Supporting documents other than those set out in direction 4.2 are not normally accepted.

3.3 Amendments to petitions and the lodging of supplementary petitions are allowed only in exceptional circumstances. The Head of the Judicial Office may allow amendments to petitions and the lodging of supplementary petitions if he is satisfied that this will assist the Appeal Committee and will not unfairly prejudice the respondents or cause undue delay. Any such amendments and supplementary petitions must be served on the respondents (see direction 3.12).

3.4 If a petition for leave to appeal
    (a) asks the House to depart from one of its own decisions;
    (b) raises issues relating to the Human Rights Act 1998; or
    (c) seeks a reference to the Court of Justice of the European Communities,

this point should be stated clearly in the petition.

3.5 A petition for leave to appeal must be signed by the petitioners or their agents

3.6 On the back of the petition for leave, underneath the certificate of service, there should be inserted the neutral citation of the judgment petitioned against, the references of any law report in the courts below, and subject matter catchwords for indexing (whether or not the case has been reported).

Case title

3.7 Petitions for leave to appeal to the House of Lords carry the same title as in the **4A–17** court below, except that the parties are described as petitioner(s) and respondent(s). For reference purposes, the names of parties to the original action who are not parties to the appeal should nevertheless be included in the title: their names should be enclosed in square brackets. The names of all parties should be given in the same sequence as in the title used in the court below.

3.8 Petitions in which trustees, executors etc. are parties are titled in the short form, for example *Trustees of John Black's Charity (Respondents) v. White (Petitioner)*.

3.9 In any petition concerning minors or where in the court below the title used has been such as to conceal the identity of one or more parties to the action, this fact should be clearly drawn to the attention of the Judicial Office at the time the petition is lodged, so that the title adopted in the House of Lords can take account of the need for anonymity. Petitions involving minors are normally given a title in the form *In re B* (see also direction 9.9).

3.10 In case titles involving the Crown, the abbreviation "R" meaning "Regina" is used. "R" is always given first. So case titles using this abbreviation take the form *R v Jones (Petitioner)* or *R v Jones (Respondent)* (as the case may be) or *R (on the application of Jones) (Petitioner) v Secretary of State for the Home Department (Respondent)*.

3.11 Apart from the above, Latin is not used in case titles.

Service

3.12 A copy of the petition must be served on the respondents or their agents, either **4A–18** by delivery in person or by first class post, before it is lodged in the Judicial Office. A certificate of such service (noting the full name and address of the respondents or their agents) must be endorsed on the back of the original petition and signed.[1]

Lodgment

3.13 Two top copies of the original petition must be lodged in the Judicial Office, **4A–19** together with a copy of the order appealed from and, if separate, a copy of the order

---

[1] For style see Appendix A, Form 2.

of the court below refusing leave to appeal. If the substantive order appealed against is not immediately available, the petition should nevertheless be lodged within the required time limits, and the order lodged as soon as possible thereafter.

3.14 An agent who attends the Judicial Office to lodge a petition for leave to appeal and/or accompanying papers must be familiar with the subject matter of the petition.

3.15 A petition for leave to appeal is presented to the House and recorded in the Minutes of Proceedings on the day it is lodged or on the next sitting day of the House.

Waiver of fee

4A–20 3.16 Standing Order XIII provides that a fee is payable when a petition for leave to appeal is lodged.

3.17 In circumstances where a petitioner would suffer financial hardship by the payment of fees to the House, the requirement to pay fees may be waived. Application should be made to the Judicial Office. In order to provide an objective test for determining financial hardship, and to keep in step with the courts below, the Judicial Office applies the provisions of the Civil Proceedings Fees Order 2004[1] to determine financial hardship for the purposes of standing order XIII. No waiver of fees can be granted unless the petitioner (i) has applied for and been refused public funding/legal aid to bring their appeal to the House of Lords; and (ii) is in receipt of one or more of the qualifying benefits set out in the 2004 Order, or has been granted a remission of fees in the court below.

Appearance for respondents

4A–21 3.18 Respondents or their agents enter appearance to a petition for leave as soon as they have received service. The respondents or their agents enter appearance by attending at the Judicial Office to enter their name and address or that of their firm and paying the prescribed fee, or by letter to the Judicial Office together with the fee. The fee is refunded if the petition is dismissed as inadmissible.

3.19 Respondents who do not intend to take part in the proceedings do not need to enter appearance, but the Judicial Office sends communications concerning a petition for leave to appeal only to those who have entered appearance.

3.20 An order for costs will not be made in favour of a respondent who has not entered an appearance.

Interventions in petitions for leave to appeal

4A–22 3.21 Save in exceptional circumstances, no application may be made to intervene in support of a petition for leave to appeal[2].

Communications by fax/e-mail

4A–23 3.22 See direction 26.2.

4.

APPEAL COMMITTEE

4A–24 4.1 Petitions for leave to appeal to the House of Lords are considered by an Appeal Committee consisting of three Lords of Appeal. Petitions are generally decided on the papers alone, without a hearing.

Additional papers

4A–25 4.2 The following additional papers for use by the Appeal Committee must be lodged within one week of lodgment of the petition:

---

[1] S.I. 2004 No. 3121.
[2] For interventions in appeals, see direction 37.

(a) four copies of the petition;

(b) four copies of the order appealed from;

(c) if separate, four copies of the order of the court below refusing leave to appeal to the House of Lords;

(d) five copies of the official transcript of the judgment of the court below[1];

(e) five copies of the order of the court of first instance;

(f) five copies of the official transcript of the judgment of the court of first instance[2];

(g) five copies of any unreported judgment cited in the petition or judgment of a court below;

(h) the form sent out by the Judicial Office to the petitioner(s) asking for details of the history of the action.

No other papers are required, and documents other than those listed above are not normally received.

4.3 Papers lodged in accordance with direction 4.2 above should be lodged as individual documents, double-sided, not bound together or inserted into ring binders. Documents which are not clearly legible or which are not in the required style or form (see direction 3.1) are not accepted.

4.4 Where the required papers are not lodged within three months of presentation of the petition and no good reason is given, the petition may at the direction of the Head of the Judicial Office be referred to an Appeal Committee without the required accompanying papers.

Consideration on the papers

4.5 The Appeal Committee decides first whether a petition for leave to appeal is admissible. The rules on admissibility are set out in direction 1.14. If the Appeal Committee determines that a petition is inadmissible, it may refuse leave on that ground alone and not consider the content of the petition. The Appeal Committee gives a reason for its decision that the petition is inadmissible. **4A–26**

4.6 If the Appeal Committee decides that a petition is admissible, the Committee may then:

(a) refuse leave (see direction 4.8);

(b) give leave outright (see direction 4.9);

(c) invite the respondents to lodge objections to the petition (see directions 4.10–4.14);

(d) give leave on terms (see direction 4.15);

(e) refer the petition for an oral hearing (see direction 4.16–4.21).

4.7 Leave to appeal is granted to petitions that raise an arguable point of law of general public importance which ought to be considered by the House at this time, bearing in mind that the matter will already have been the subject of judicial decision and reviewed on appeal. A petition which in the opinion of the Appeal Committee does not raise such a point of law is refused on that ground. The Appeal Committee gives brief reasons for refusing leave to appeal[3] but does not otherwise explain its decisions.[4]

Leave refused

4.8 If the Appeal Committee is unanimous that a petition should be refused, the parties are notified that the petition is dismissed. **4A–27**

---

[1] If the judgment has been published in a report which is ordinarily received in court, copies of the report may be lodged in lieu of transcripts. Transcripts of judgments marked "in draft" are not accepted without certification by the relevant court that the copy is the final version of the judgment.

[2] Or, in the case of a County Court, of the Judge's Notes.

[3] See also directions 34.2 and 34.3 for practice where a point of European Community law is raised on a petition for leave to appeal.

[4] See Appeal Committee, 38th Report (2002–03): *Petitions for leave to appeal: reasons for the refusal of leave* (HL Paper 89).

Leave given outright

4A–28 4.9 If the Appeal Committee is unanimous that a petition should be allowed without further proceedings, the House grants leave outright (without inviting respondents' objections).

Respondents' objections

4A–29 4.10 There is no requirement for respondents to submit written objections giving their reasons why leave to appeal should be refused. But respondents may submit written objections if they wish to do so. This must be done (a) within 14 days of the date of service on them of the petition for leave to appeal; or (b) within 14 days of any invitation by the Appeal Committee to do so; or (c) within 14 days of a petition for leave to appeal being referred for an oral hearing.

4.11 Respondents' objections set out briefly the reasons why the petition should be refused or make submissions as to the terms upon which leave should be granted (for example, on costs). One master plus six copies of the respondents' written objections must be lodged at the Judicial Office. The objections must be produced on durable quality A4 paper, securely fastened, using both sides of the paper.

4.12 A copy of the respondents' objections should be sent to the agents for the other parties. In certain circumstances the Appeal Committee may invite further submissions from the petitioners in the light of the respondents' objections, but petitioners do not have a right to comment on respondents' objections. Where the Appeal Committee does not require further submissions, and provided the Committee is unanimous in its decision to grant or refuse leave, it reports its decision to the House and the parties are informed. Where the Appeal Committee proposes terms for granting leave, direction 4.15 applies.

4.13 Respondents' objections are subject to any order for costs made by the Appeal Committee or, if leave to appeal is granted, become costs in the appeal (see direction 5).

4.14 Parties unable to meet the deadlines set out in direction 4.10 must write to the Head of the Judicial Office requesting an extension of time for lodging their written objections.

Leave given on terms

4A–30 4.15 If the Appeal Committee decides that leave to appeal should be given on terms, the Committee proposes the terms. The parties have the right to make submissions on the proposed terms within 14 days.

Petition referred for oral hearing

4A–31 4.16 In all cases where the members of the Appeal Committee are not unanimous, or where further argument is required, a petition for leave to appeal is referred for an oral hearing.

4.17 If the respondents have not already been invited to lodge objections, they should do so as soon as possible after being informed that the petition has been referred for a hearing (direction 4.10(c)).

4.18 When a petition is referred for an oral hearing, the petitioners and all respondents who have entered appearance are notified of the date of the hearing before the Appeal Committee.

4.19 Parties may be heard before the Appeal Committee by counsel, by agent, or in person, but one only may be heard on each side.

4.20 If counsel is briefed, agents should ensure that the Judicial Office is notified of their name. Only a junior counsel's fee is allowed on taxation (direction 1.20).

4.21 Authorities are not normally cited before the Appeal Committee or provided for the Committee's use at the hearing.

Lodgment of petition of appeal

4A–32 4.22 If leave to appeal is given, the petition of appeal (direction 9) must be lodged with the prescribed fee within two weeks of the date of the Appeal Committee's decision. Failure to meet this deadline results in the petition of appeal being lodged out of time and referred to an Appeal Committee pursuant to direction 7.3.

Order of the House

4A–33 4.23 Copies of the Minutes of Proceedings of the House recording the report of the Appeal Committee and the order of the House are sent to all parties who have entered appearance.

4.24 A formal order of the Appeal Committee is not normally issued but will be issued on written request and on payment of a fee. A formal order is not required for taxation of costs arising from the application for leave to appeal.

Expedition

4A–34 4.25 Once the required papers are lodged in the Judicial Office (direction 4.2), the procedure described above is normally completed within eight sitting weeks (excluding any oral hearing). However, in cases involving liberty of the subject, urgent medical intervention or the well-being of children, application for expedition may be made in writing to the Judicial Office.

5.

COSTS

4A–35 5.1 Where a petition for leave to appeal is determined without an oral hearing, costs may be awarded as follows:

    (a) to a publicly funded or legally aided petitioner, reasonable costs incurred in preparing papers for the Appeal Committee[1];

    (b) to a publicly funded or legally aided respondent, only those costs necessarily incurred in attending the client, attending the petitioner's agents, perusing the petition, entering appearance and, where applicable, preparing respondent's objections to the petition[2];

    (c) to an unassisted respondent where the petitioner is publicly funded or legally aided, payment out of the Community Legal Service Fund (pursuant to s 11 of the Access to Justice Act 1999 [3]) of costs as specified at (b) above;

    (d) to a respondent where neither party is publicly funded or legally aided, costs as specified at (b) above.

Where costs are sought under (c) or (d) above, the application may be made by letter addressed to the Judicial Office or may be included in a bill of costs lodged in the Judicial Office conditional upon the application being granted.

5.2 Where a petition for leave to appeal is referred for an oral hearing and is dismissed, application for costs must be made by the respondent at the end of the hearing. No order for costs is made unless requested at that time.

5.3 Where a petition for leave to appeal is allowed, costs of the petition become costs in the appeal.

5.4 Bills of costs for taxation must be lodged within three months from the date of the decision of the Appeal Committee or the date on which a petition for leave is

---

[1] See *Practice directions applicable to judicial taxations in the House of Lords and forms of bills of costs*, available on request from the Judicial Office.
[2] *ibid.*
[3] Also pursuant to r.5(2) Community Legal Service (Cost Protection) Regulations 2000 and in accordance with the procedural requirements of rr.9, 10 Community Legal Service (Costs) Regulations 2000 as amended; or Legal Aid Act 1988, s.18; or in Scotland pursuant to Legal Aid (Scotland) Act 1986, s.19; or in Northern Ireland pursuant to Legal Aid Advice and Assistance (N.I.) Order 1981, Art.16.

withdrawn in accordance with direction 45.1. If an extension of the three month period is desired, application must be made in writing to the Taxing Officer and copies of all such correspondence sent to all interested parties In deciding whether to grant an application for an extension of time made after the expiry of the three month period the Taxing Officer takes into account the circumstances set out in the practice directions applicable to judicial taxations.

5.5 The practice directions relating to judicial taxations and forms of bills of costs are available from the Judicial Office and on the internet at www.parliament.uk. Fees are payable on taxation of a bill of costs.

Withdrawal of petitions for leave to appeal

4A–36 5.6 See direction 45.1.

6.

PETITIONS BROUGHT DIRECT FROM THE HIGH COURT

4A–37 6.1 In certain cases an appeal lies direct from the High Court in England and Wales or in Northern Ireland to the House of Lords. A certificate of the High Court must first be obtained and the leave of the House of Lords then given before the appeal may proceed.[1] Such appeals are known as "leapfrog" appeals.

Judge's certificate

4A–38 6.2 An application for a certificate may be made by any of the parties to any civil proceedings in the High Court before a single judge or before a Divisional Court. The application should be made immediately after the trial judge gives judgment in the proceedings or, if no such application is made, within 14 days from the date on which judgment was given.

6.3 The judge may grant a certificate under s 12 of the Administration of Justice Act 1969 if he is satisfied (a) that the relevant conditions are fulfilled; (b) that a sufficient case has been made to justify taking to the House of Lords an application for leave; and (c) that all the parties to the proceedings consent to the grant of a certificate.

6.4 The relevant conditions are that a point of law of general public importance is involved in the judge's decision, and that that point of law either (a) relates wholly or mainly to the construction of an enactment or of a statutory instrument and has been fully argued in the proceedings and fully considered in the judgment of the judge in the proceedings,[2] or (b) is one in respect of which the judge is bound by a decision of the Court of Appeal or House of Lords in previous proceedings and was fully considered in the judgments of the Court of Appeal or House of Lords in those previous proceedings.[3]

6.5 The judge may not grant a certificate in cases where no appeal would lie (with or without leave) from the judge's decision to the Court of Appeal, apart from the provisions of the Administration of Justice Act 1969 . Similarly, a certificate may not be granted where no appeal would lie (with or without leave) from the Court of Appeal on an appeal from the judge's decision. Where no appeal would lie from the judge's decision to the Court of Appeal except with the leave of the judge or the Court of Appeal, no certificate may be granted unless it appears to the judge that it would be a proper case for granting such leave.

6.6 No certificate may be given where the judge's decision concerns punishment for contempt of court.

6.7 No appeal lies against the grant or refusal of a certificate, but if a certificate is

---

[1] Administration of Justice Act 1969. ss.12–15.
[2] Administration of Justice Act 1969, s.12(3)(a).
[3] Administration of Justice Act 1969, s.12(3)(b).

refused the applicant may appeal to the Court of Appeal from the High Court's decision in the normal way, once the time for applying for a certificate has expired.

Petition for leave to appeal direct from High Court

6.8 At any time within one month from the date on which the judge grants the certificate, or such extended time as the House of Lords may allow,[1] any of the parties may apply to the House of Lords for leave to appeal.[2] Application is made by petition. If any party to the action in the High Court is not a party to the petition, the petition must be endorsed with a certificate of service on that party.

4A–39

6.9 One copy of the judge's certificate must be lodged with the petition. The petition should indicate whether the judge's certificate was granted under s 12(3)(a) or s 12(3)(b) of the Administration of Justice Act 1969.

6.10 The following additional papers for use by the Appeal Committee must be lodged within one week of the lodgment of the petition:
   (a) four additional copies of the petition;
   (b) five copies of order of High Court;
   (c) four additional copies of the High Court's certificate, if not contained in the order; and
   (d) five copies of the transcript of the judgment of the High Court.[3]

No other papers are required, and documents other than those listed above are not normally received.

6.11 Petitions for leave are determined by an Appeal Committee without a hearing.

6.12 In petitions where the certificate has been granted by the judge under s 12(3)(a) of the 1969 Act , the House only grants leave to appeal where:
   (a) there is an urgent need to obtain an authoritative interpretation by the House of Lords;
   (b) the case is one in which leave to appeal to the House of Lords would have been granted if it had not been brought direct to the House and the judgment had been that of the Court of Appeal; and
   (c) it does not appear likely that any additional assistance could be derived from a judgment of the Court of Appeal.

Similarly, where the certificate has been granted under s 12(3)(b) of the 1969 Act, the House only grants leave where:
   (i) the case is not distinguishable from the case that was the subject of the previous decision;
   (ii) the previous case was fully considered in previous judgment after argument that appears to have been adequate; and
   (iii) the case is one in which leave to appeal to the House of Lords would have been granted if it had not been brought direct to the House and the judgment had been that of the Court of Appeal.

6.13 The Judicial Office notifies the parties of the Appeal Committee's decision.

Extensions of time

6.14 If an applicant cannot lodge the petition within one month from the date on which the judge's certificate was granted, the applicant must within the one month period lodge in the Judicial Office:

4A–40

---

[1] For applications to extend time see direction 6.14.
[2] Administration of Justice Act 1969, s.13(1).
[3] If the judgment has been published in a report which is ordinarily received in court, copies of the report may be lodged in lieu of transcripts. Transcripts of judgments marked as in draft are not acceptable without certification by the relevant court that the copy is the final version of the judgment.

(i) a request for an extension of time, giving reasons why an extension is needed; and

(ii) three copies of the transcript of the High Court's judgment.

The request is referred to an Appeal Committee and determined without a hearing. The Judicial Office notifies the applicant of the Appeal Committee's decision.

Proceedings after leave to appeal is granted or refused

4A–41 6.15 If the House grants leave to appeal direct from the High Court, no appeal from the decision of the judge lies to the Court of Appeal but only to the House of Lords. The appeal is brought by petition and the usual requirements apply. However, an appeal does lie to the Court of Appeal from the judge's decision (i) after the expiry of the one month period within which an application may be made for leave to the House of Lords and (ii) where leave to appeal direct to the House has been refused by the House of Lords.

Habeas corpus

4A–42 6.16 Proceedings for a writ of habeas corpus are subject to the procedures governing criminal appeals to the House of Lords. These are set out in the red booklet of criminal practice directions[1]. In proceedings for a writ of habeas corpus, an appeal lies from the Queen's Bench Divisional Court to the House of Lords at the instance of the defendant or prosecutor with the leave either of the Divisional Court or the House of Lords. No certificate stating a point of law of general public importance is required.[2]

Such a petition is considered by an Appeal Committee without an oral hearing. Parties are notified of the Committee's decision.

6.17 Such a petition is considered by an Appeal Committee without an oral hearing. Parties are notified of the Committee's decision.

Part II Directions Applying in All Appeals

7.

TIME LIMITS

4A–43 7.1 A petition of appeal must be lodged in the Judicial Office within three months of the date on which the order appealed against was made.[3]

7.2 However, this time limit may be varied by an order of the House when granting leave or by an order of the court below. The order appealed against is the substantive order complained of.

Out of time appeals

4A–44 7.3 Where a petition of appeal is not lodged within the time allowed, a petition for leave to present the appeal out of time may be lodged[4]. This petition is referred to an Appeal Committee.

Fees

4A–45 7.4 A fee is payable on a petition of appeal and on a petition for leave to present a petition of appeal out of time (see Appendix C).

---

[1] See n 1 on p 7 above.

[2] Administration of Justice Act 1969, ss.1, 15(3); Judicature (Northern Ireland) Act 1978, s.45(3).

[3] Standing Order I. The court below may reduce but may not extend the three month period. For extensions of time in publicly funded/legal aid cases, see direction 41.3–41.4.

[4] Adapt Appendix A, Form 4 using Form 3 as a model.

8.

LONDON AGENTS

8.1 Solicitors outside London may appoint London agents. Those who decide not to **4A–46** do so should note that any additional costs incurred as a result of that decision may be disallowed on taxation (assessment of costs).

9.

LODGMENT OF APPEAL

Form of petition of appeal

9.1 Petitions of appeal must be produced on durable quality A4 paper, bound on the **4A–47** left, using both sides of the paper[1].

9.2 Where leave to appeal has been obtained, it is enough for the petition of appeal to be signed by the appellants or their agents. In appeals where leave to appeal is not required (for example, in most Scottish appeals) the petition of appeal must be certified as reasonable by two counsel and signed by them.[2] In Scottish appeals a certificate of difference of opinion must also be included where appropriate.[3]

9.3 On the back page of the petition, below the certificate of service, there should be inserted the neutral citation of the judgment appealed against, the references of any law report of the case in the courts below and subject matter catchwords for indexing (whether or not the case has been reported).

Case title

9.4 Petitions of appeal to the House of Lords carry the same title as in the court **4A–48** below, except that the parties are described as appellant(s) and respondent(s). For reference purposes, the names of parties to the original action who are not parties to the appeal should nevertheless be included in the title: their names should be enclosed in square brackets. The names of all parties should be given in the same sequence as in the title used in the court below.

9.5 Petitions in which trustees, executors, etc. are parties are titled in the short form, for example *Trustees of John Black's Charity (Respondents) v. White (Appellant)*.

9.6 In any petition concerning minors or where in the court below the title used has been such as to conceal the identity of one or more parties to the action, this fact should be clearly drawn to the attention of the Judicial Office at the time the petition is lodged, so that the title adopted in the House of Lords can take account of the need for anonymity. Petitions involving minors are normally given a title in the form *In re B* (see also direction 9.9).

9.7 In case titles involving the Crown, the abbreviation "R" meaning "Regina" is used. "R" is always given first. Case titles using this abbreviation take the form *R v Jones (Appellant)* or *R v Jones (Respondent)* (as the case may be) or *R (on the application of Jones) (Appellant) v Secretary of State for the Home Department (Respondent)*.

9.8 Apart from the above, Latin is not used in case titles.

Anonymity and reporting restrictions

9.9 In any appeal concerning children the parties should, in addition to considering **4A–49** the case title to be used, also consider whether it would be appropriate for the House

---

[1] see Appendix A, Form 4 for style of petition and direction 24 for preparation of documents.
[2] Standing Order IV. In such cases, counsel's signatures are required even if the appellants propose to conduct the appeal in person. For the purposes of the Standing Order, "counsel" includes any solicitor who has obtained a Higher Courts Qualification in respect of civil proceedings.
[3] See Standing Order XI.

to make an order under s 39 of the Children and Young Persons Act 1933. The parties should always inform the Judicial Office if such an order has been made by a court below. A request for such an order to be made by the House should be made in writing, preferably on behalf of all parties to the appeal, as soon as possible after the appeal has been presented and not later than 14 days before the start of the hearing.

9.10 Direction 9.9 also applies to a request for an order under s 4 of the Contempt of Court Act 1981.

Human Rights Act 1998

4A–50   9.11 Appellants must notify the Judicial Office in writing when:
>   (a) the House is to be asked to consider whether to make, uphold or reverse a declaration that a provision of primary or subordinate legislation is incompatible with a European Human Rights Convention right[1], or is to be asked to consider any issue which may lead the House to make such a declaration, or where such an issue is or may be raised in respect of a judicial act;
>   (b) a party seeks to challenge an act of a public authority under the Human Rights Act 1998; or
>   (c) a party relies in whole or in part on the provisions of the Human Rights Act 1998.

Appellants should indicate whether notification is made under (a), (b) or (c) above (see direction 33.1). They should set out briefly the arguments involved; and state whether the point was taken in the courts below. In appeals in which (a) above is an issue, the Crown has a right to be joined as a party to the appeal (see direction 33.2).

Service

4A–51   9.12 A copy of the petition of appeal must be served on the respondents or their agents, either by delivery in person or by first class post, before lodgment in the Judicial Office. A certificate of such service noting the full name and address of the respondents or their agents must be endorsed on the back of the original petition and signed by the appellants or their agents.[2]

Lodgment

4A–52   9.13 The petition of appeal together with seven copies must be lodged in the Judicial Office with the prescribed fee. If leave to appeal was granted by the court below, a copy of the order appealed from must also be lodged and, if separate, a copy of the order granting leave to appeal to the House of Lords. If the order is not immediately available, the petition should be lodged in time and the order lodged as soon as possible thereafter.

9.14 Once the petition of appeal has been lodged, it is presented to the House and recorded in the Minutes of Proceedings of the House. A copy of the Minutes is sent to all parties who have entered appearance (see direction 9.10).

Appearance for respondents

4A–53   9.15 Respondents or their agents should enter appearance to an appeal as soon as they have received service of the petition of appeal. They enter appearance by attending at the Judicial Office to enter their name and address or that of their firm, and paying the fee. Respondents may enter appearance by letter to the Judicial Office together with the fee.

9.16 Respondents who do not intend to take part in the proceedings do not need to

---

[1] Human Rights Act 1998, which gives further effect in domestic law to much of the *Convention for the Protection of Human Rights and Fundamental Freedoms agreed by the Council of Europe at Rome on 4 November 1950.*
[2] For style see Appendix A, Form 5.

enter appearance, but the Judicial Office sends communications concerning the appeal only to those who have entered appearance. An order for costs will not be made in favour of a respondent who has not entered appearance.

Children

9.17 In a case involving a child, where delay might affect the facts of the case or the interests of the child, parties should draw these facts to the attention of the Head of the Judicial Office not later than the day of presentation of the petition of appeal. **4A–54**

[THE NEXT PARAGRAPH IS 4A–56.]

10.

SECURITY FOR COSTS

10.1 Appellants must give security for costs in the sum fixed by the House by payment into the House of Lords Security Fund Account within seven days of the presentation of an appeal. Failure to do so results in the appeal being dismissed by default.[1] **4A–56**

10.2 Payment is normally made by banker's draft or cheque made payable to 'House of Lords Security Fund Account'. If an appellant wishes to pay in cash, the Judicial Office may only accept cash up to £10,000, in order to comply with money laundering regulations. No interest is payable on security money.

Waiver of security

10.3 Provided that all the respondents agree that security for costs should be waived, the appellants may lodge a consent form asking the House to release the appellants from the obligation to pay security for costs. The consent must be signed by all the respondents and lodged with the prescribed fee within one week of the presentation of the appeal. An order is then made absolving the appellants from giving security. A copy of the form of consent is available from the Judicial Office. **4A–57**

10.4 The following are not required to give security for costs and no waiver is necessary:

(a) an appellant who has been granted a certificate of public funding/legal aid;

(b) an appellant in an appeal under the Child Abduction and Custody Act 1985;

(c) a Minister or Government department.[2]

10.5 No security for costs or waiver is required in cross-appeals.

10.6 The House has the power to vary or dispense with the requirement to give security for costs when the respondents do not agree to a waiver, but uses this power rarely, and only after an Appeal Committee has recommended that the requirement for security should be waived.[3] The Appeal Committee normally takes this decision on the papers alone, without an oral hearing.

11.

STATEMENT OF FACTS AND ISSUES

11.1 The appellants must lodge a Statement of the facts and issues (with an Appendix (see direction 12)) within six weeks of the presentation of the appeal, or longer period approved by the House (see direction 13.3). The Statement should be a succinct account of the main facts of the case, including an account of judicial proceedings up to that point and an account of the issues raised by the appeal. The appellants are responsible for drawing up the Statement in draft and they must **4A–58**

---

[1] Standing Order V(1).
[2] Standing Order V(2).
[3] See speech of Lord Chancellor Irvine of Lairg, HL Deb 26 July 1999, col 1292.

submit it to the respondents for discussion and agreement. The Statement must be a single document agreed between the parties. In the event of disagreement, disputed material should be removed from the draft Statement and included instead in each party's case (see direction 15). The Statement must be signed on behalf of each party by at least one counsel who appeared in the court below or who will appear at the hearing before the House.

Form of Statement of facts and issues

4A–59 11.2 The Statement of facts and issues should be produced on durable quality A4 paper and incorporate:

> (a) pages printed on both sides of the paper;
> (b) capital letters down the inside margins;
> (c) references on the outside margins to relevant pages of the Appendix;
> (d) on the front cover, the reference of every law report of the case in the courts below, together with the catchword summary of one of the reports;
> (e) on the front cover, a headnote summary, whether or not the case has been reported;
> (f) on the front cover, a statement of the time occupied in the courts below; and
> (g) at the end, the signatures of counsel for both parties above their printed names.

12.

APPENDIX

4A–60 12.1 It is the appellants' responsibility in consultation with the respondents to prepare and lodge an Appendix of documents considered necessary for the appeal. These documents include all the documents used in evidence or recording proceedings in the courts below.

12.2 The appellants bear the cost of preparing the Appendix, although these costs are ultimately subject to the decision of the House as to the costs of the appeal.

Contents of Appendix

4A–61 12.3 The Appendix contains only documents or extracts from documents that are necessary to support and understand the argument when the appeal is heard by the Appellate Committee. No document which was not used in evidence or does not record proceedings relevant to the action in the courts below may be included. Transcripts of arguments in the courts below may not be included unless remarks by a judge are relied on by any party or the arguments refer to facts which are admitted by all parties and as to which no evidence was called.

12.4 The Appendix consists of one or more parts. Part 1 must contain:

> (a) formal originating documents;
> (b) case stated (if any);
> (c) judgments and orders relating to the decisions at first instance and on appeal;
> (d) relevant legislative provisions including delegated legislation; and
> (e) any relevant document on which the action is founded (such as a will, contract, map, plan etc.) or an extract from such document.

Published documents under (b), (c) and (d) above may so far as is practicable be placed in a pocket attached to the inside of the back cover of the Appendix.

12.5 For judgments that have been published, unbound parts of the relevant Law Reports or the Weekly Law Reports should be used if available; otherwise the All England Reports, Tax Cases, Simons' Tax Cases, Reports of Patent Cases and Lloyd's List Reports may be used. In Scottish appeals, Session Cases should be used where available; otherwise, Scots Law Times and Scottish Civil Case Reports may be used. Where, at the time of preparation of the Appendix, a judgment of a court below has not been published, a transcript must be included, which may later be replaced by the published version. In such circumstances, 15 copies of the published version should be submitted to the Judicial Office. Judgments in draft are not accepted. For legislation, if the printed Act or set of Regulations is conveniently small; it should be used; if the provisions are bulky or numerous, the relevant provisions should be copied. Halsbury's statutes may be used.

12.6 Other documents should be included in Part 2 of the Appendix and, if the bulk of the documents makes it necessary, in Parts 3, 4 etc. The Appendix volume should only be numbered Part 1 if there is more than one Part.

Form of Appendix

12.7 The Appendix takes the following form: **4A–62**
  (a) it must be A4 size bound with a plastic comb binding and blue card covers (blue indicating a civil appeal);
  (b) documents must be printed on both sides of the paper;
  (c) documents must be numbered;
  (d) original documents under the size of A4 may be enlarged to A4 size with a broad outside margin;
  (e) if the Appendix has more than one Part, each Part must contain a list of its contents;
  (f) documents of an unsuitable size or form for binding (for example, booklets or charts) should be included in a pocket attached to the inside back cover of the appropriate Appendix volume.

Examination of Appendix

12.8 The Appendix is for the use of all parties and the contents of the Appendix **4A–63** must be agreed by appellants and respondents. Disputed documents (see direction 12.9) should not be included in the Appendix. As soon as proofs of the Appendix are available they should be examined against the originals by all parties, if possible at one joint examination. As soon as practicable after the examination, a final proof of the Appendix should be provided to each party.

Documents in readiness at hearing

12.9 Disputed documents and any document not included in the Appendix which **4A–64** may be required at the hearing should be held in readiness and, subject to leave being given by the Appellate Committee, may be introduced at an appropriate moment. Fifteen copies are required. All such documents are subject to previous examination by the other parties. Where the appellants refuse to include in the Appendix any documents that the respondents consider necessary, the respondents must prepare and reproduce the documents at their own expense, subject to the final order on costs.

Scottish Record

12.10 In all Scottish appeals the appellants are required to include in Part 1 of the **4A–65** Appendix:
  (1) a copy of the Record as authenticated by the Deputy Principal Clerk of Session or a Clerk of Session delegated by him;
  (2) a supplement containing an account, without argument or statement of other facts, of the further steps which have been taken in the appeal since the Record was completed; and
  (3) copies of the interlocutors (or parts of interlocutors) complained of.[1]

13.

LODGMENT OF STATEMENT AND APPENDIX

Time limits

13.1 The Statement and Appendix must be lodged by the appellants within six weeks **4A–66**

---

[1] Standing Order VI(2).

of the presentation of the appeal, or within such longer period as may be allowed on petition (see direction 13.3)[1].

13.2 If this time limit expires during a parliamentary recess, it is automatically extended to the third next sitting day of the House of Lords[2]; and if any party has applied for public funding/legal aid, the time limit is automatically extended to one month after the notification of the result of the funding decision, provided that the Judicial Office has been informed of the application.[3]

Petitions for extension of time—first extension

4A–67 13.3 Appellants who are unable to complete preparation of the Statement and Appendix within the initial six weeks' period may apply by petition for an extension of that time.[4] The petition takes the form common to all formal documents of the House. It should explain briefly the reason(s) why an extension is needed. Application may be made for an extension of up to six weeks from the original expiry date, and the petition must specify the date to which the extension is requested. If that date seems likely to fall in a parliamentary recess, the petition may request extension until '[specify date] or the third sitting day of the next ensuing meeting of the House'.[5]

13.4 A petition for extension of time must be signed by the appellants. It must be submitted to those respondents who have entered appearance for the endorsement of their consent, and it must bear their signature. One master of the petition plus one copy and prescribed fee must be lodged before the expiry of the six weeks initially allowed for lodging the Statement and Appendix.

Petitions for extension of time—second and subsequent extensions

4A–68 13.5 Up to three extensions of time are normally granted, provided that they do not prejudice the preparation for the hearing or its proposed date. A petition for a fourth extension of time, and any subsequent petitions, may, at the discretion of the Head of the Judicial Office, be referred to an Appeal Committee.

Respondents' consent

4A–69 13.6 Respondents are expected not to withhold unreasonably their consent to a petition for extension of time. If consent is refused the petition must be endorsed with a certificate that it has been served on the respondents. The petition is then referred to an Appeal Committee and decided after an oral hearing. In that event, eight copies of the petition must be lodged, together with the prescribed fee.

Lodgment

4A–70 13.7 When the Statement and Appendix are ready, one master plus seven copies of the Statement, eight copies of Part 1 of the Appendix and 15 copies of Parts 2 etc. (if any) must be lodged in the Judicial Office with the prescribed fee. The appellants must at the same time apply to set down the appeal for hearing.

---

[1] Standing Order VI(1). For extensions of time in publicly funded/legally aided cases, see direction 41.
[2] Standing Order VIII.
[3] See direction 41.3–41.4.
[4] For style see Appendix A, Form 6.
[5] As the "third sitting day" depends on future sittings of the House, the date of expiry is not fixed. The appellants should contact the Judicial Office from time to time to discover how sittings of the House affect this date.

14.

SETTING DOWN FOR HEARING

14.1 An appeal is set down for hearing at the same time as the appellants lodge the Statement and Appendix.[1] **4A–71**

14.2 Once an appeal has been set down for hearing, it may be called on at any time. Certain directions, for example direction 15.13, may be dispensed with to enable an appeal to be called on at short notice.

Estimates of length of time needed for hearing of appeal

14.3 Within seven days of the setting down of an appeal, each party must notify the Judicial Office of the number of hours that their counsel estimate to be necessary for each of them to address the Appellate Committee. The Listings Officer arranges the programme of hearings on the basis of these estimates, and so they should be as accurate as is reasonably possible. Subject to any directions by the Appellate Committee before or at the hearing, counsel are expected to confine their submissions to the time indicated in their estimates. The Judicial Office should be informed at once of any alteration to the original estimate. **4A–72**

14.4 In all appeals where combined estimates amount to more than 17½ hours (four sitting days), such estimates must be justified by letter to the Head of the Judicial Office and may be referred to the Law Lords.

15.

APPELLANTS' AND RESPONDENTS' CASES

15.1 The case is the statement of a party's argument in the appeal. **4A–73**

15.2 The case should be confined to the heads of argument that counsel propose to submit at the hearing and omit material contained in the Statement of facts and issues[2]. The members of the Appeal Committee who gave leave to appeal may not be sitting on the Appellate Committee; and so it cannot be assumed that the members of the Appellate Committee will be familiar with the arguments set out in the petition for leave to appeal.

15.3 Page 1 of the case should set out the title of the party on whose behalf it is lodged.

15.4 If either party is abandoning any point taken in the courts below, this should be made plain in their case. If they intend to apply in the course of the hearing for leave to introduce a new point not taken below, this should also be indicated in their case and the Judicial Office informed. If such a point involves the introduction of fresh evidence, application for leave must be made either in the case or by lodging a petition for leave to adduce the fresh evidence.

15.5 If a party intends to invite the House to depart from one of its own decisions, this intention must be clearly stated in a separate paragraph of their case, to which special attention must be drawn. A respondent who wishes to contend that a decision of the court below should be affirmed on grounds other than those relied on by that court must set out the grounds for that contention in their case.

15.6 Transcripts of unreported judgments should only be cited when they contain an authoritative statement of a relevant principle of law not to be found in a reported case or when are necessary for the understanding of some other authority.

15.7 All cases must conclude with a numbered summary of the reasons upon which the argument is founded, and must bear the signature of at least one counsel for

---

[1] For form of application for setting down, see Appendix A, Form 13.
[2] See Lord Diplock's speech in *M.V. Yorke Motors v. Edwards*, [1982] 1 W.L.R. 444; [1982] 1 All E.R. 1024.

each party to the appeal who has appeared in the court below or who will be briefed for the hearing before the House.

15.8 The lodgment of a case carries the right to be heard by two counsel, one of whom may be leading counsel. The fees of two counsel only for any party are allowed on taxation unless the Appellate Committee orders otherwise on application at the hearing.

Separate cases

4A–74 15.9 All the appellants must join in one case. All the respondents must also join in one case, unless it can be shown that the interests of one or more of the respondents are distinct from those of the rest. If the respondents' interests are distinct, the agents who first lodge their case must certify in a letter to the Judicial Office as follows:

(a) 'We, as agents for the respondent(s) [*name particular parties*], certify that opportunity has been offered by us for joining in one case to the respondent(s) [*name particular parties*] whose interests are, in our opinion, similar to those set out in the case lodged by us.'; or

(b) 'We, as agents for the respondent(s) [*name particular parties*], certify that the interests represented in the case lodged by us are, in our opinion, distinct from those of the remaining respondent(s).'

15.10 When one of the foregoing certificates has been given, all remaining respondents wishing to lodge a case must respectively petition to do so in respect of each of their separate cases. Such petitions (which must be lodged with the prescribed fee) must be consented to by the appellants, and must set out the reasons for separate lodgment.

15.11 Parties whose interests in the appeal are passive (for example, stakeholders, trustees, executors, etc.) are not required to lodge a separate case but should ensure that their position is explained in one of the cases lodged.

Joint case

4A–75 15.12 The lodgment of a joint case on behalf of both appellants and respondents may be permitted in certain circumstances.

Lodgment and exchange of cases

4A–76 15.13 No later than five weeks before the proposed date of the hearing, the appellants must lodge in the Judicial Office one master plus seven copies of their case and serve it on the respondents.

15.14 No later than three weeks before the proposed date of the hearing, the respondents must serve on the appellants a copy of their case in response and lodge at the Judicial Office one master plus seven copies of their case in response, as must any other party lodging a case (for example, an intervener or advocate to the court).

15.15 Where there is a cross-appeal, the cases on the original appeal must be lodged in accordance with direction 15.13. The cross-appellants' case for the cross-appeal must be lodged in accordance with direction 15.14, i.e. three weeks before the hearing as part of their reply to the original appellants' case. The original appellants/cross-respondents may reply to the case for the cross-appeal in their case lodged in the bound volumes.

15.16 The number of copies of cases exchanged should be enough to meet the requirements of counsel and agents and should not usually exceed eight. To enable the appellants to lodge the bound volumes, the respondents and any other party who has lodged a case must also provide the appellants with 15 further copies of their case.

15.17 Following the exchange of cases, further arguments by either side may not without leave be submitted in advance of the hearing.

Form of cases

15.18 Cases must be produced on durable quality A4 paper securely bound on the **4A–77**
left, with:
    (a) capital letters down the inside margins;
    (b) numbered paragraphs;
    (c) the signatures of counsel at the end above their printed names.

Scottish cases

15.19 Each party must include in their case to the House a copy of the case **4A–78**
presented by them to the Court of Session, with a short summary of any additional
reasons on which they propose to insist. If no case was presented to the Court of
Session, each party must set forth in their case as shortly and succinctly as possible
the reasons upon which they found their argument[1].

16.

BOUND VOLUMES

16.1 As soon as all cases have been exchanged, and no later than 14 days before the **4A–79**
proposed date of the hearing, the appellants must lodge (in addition to the
documents already lodged on setting down) 15 bound volumes, each containing:
    (a) petition(s) of appeal;
    (b) petition(s) of cross-appeal (if any);
    (c) Statement of facts and issues;
    (d) appellants' and respondents' cases, with cross-references to the Appendix and
        authorities volume(s);
    (e) case of the advocate to the court or intervener, if any;
    (f) Part 1 of the Appendix; and
    (g) index to the authorities volume(s).

Form of bound volumes

16.2 The bound volumes: **4A–80**
    (a) should be bound in the same manner as the Appendix, with plastic comb bind-
        ing and blue card covers;
    (b) must include cut-out indices for each of the documents set out in direction
        16.1, tabbed with the name of the document on the front sheet of each;
    (c) must show on the front cover a list of the contents and the names and ad-
        dresses of the agents for all parties;
    (d) must indicate on a sticker attached to the plastic spine the volume number and
        the short title of the appeal; and
    (e) should include a few blank pages at either end.

Provision of documents

16.3 To enable the appellants to produce the bound volumes, the respondents must **4A–81**
provide the appellants' agents with a further 15 copies of the respondents' case in
addition to the cases already exchanged.

16.4 Respondents should arrange with the appellants' agents for the delivery to them
of such bound volumes as the respondents' counsel and agents require.

17.

AUTHORITIES

17.1 Ten copies of all authorities that may be needed during the hearing must be **4A–82**

---

[1] Standing Order VI(2).

lodged at the same time as the bound volumes. The authorities should be collected together into one or more volumes. The appellants are responsible for producing the authorities' volumes and lodging them in the Judicial Office. To enable the appellants to lodge the volumes, the respondents must provide the appellants with ten copies of any authorities which the respondents require but which the appellants do not, or arrange with the appellants for their photocopying. Respondents should arrange with the appellants for the delivery to them of such authorities' volumes as the respondents' counsel and agents require.

Form and content of authorities' volumes

4A–83 17.2 The authorities' volumes should:

    (a) be A4 size, comb bound with green card covers;

    (b) have flexible covers;

    (c) separate each authority in the volume by numbered dividers;

    (d) contain an index to that volume; the first volume must also contain an index to all the volumes;

    (e) be numbered consecutively on the cover and spine with numerals at least point 72 in size for swift identification of different volumes during the hearing;

    (f) have printed clearly on the front cover the title of the appeal and the names of the agents for all parties;

    (g) have affixed to the plastic spine a sticker indicating clearly the volume number and short title of the appeal;

    (h) include a few blank pages at either end;

    (i) be not more than $2^1/_2$cm (1 inch) thick.

17.3 The first volume(s) should contain citations from the C and L series of the Official Journal of the European Union; the Law Reports; the All England Reports; the Weekly Law Reports; Session Cases; the Scots Law Times; and the current edition of Halsbury's Laws Subsequent volumes should contain all other material. In an appeal where there is a large number of authorities' volumes, it is helpful to produce an index of indexes, separate from the index contained in the first authorities volume.

17.4 The authorities' volumes should be lodged in the Judicial Office in separate containers from the Bound Volumes.

17.5 Where a case is not reported in the Law Reports or Session Cases, references to other recognised reports may be given (see direction 15.6). In Revenue appeals, Tax Cases may be cited but, wherever possible, references to the case in the Law Reports or Session Cases should also be given.

17.6 In order to produce the authorities' volumes, parties may download text from electronic sources; but the authorities' volumes may only be lodged in paper form.

17.7 In certain circumstances (e.g. when during the hearing before the Appellate Committee it becomes apparent that a particular authority is needed but is not in the authorities volume), the House of Lords Library can arrange for copies of authorities to be made available at the hearing[1]. Parties must themselves provide ten copies of any other authority or of unreported cases. They must similarly provide copies of any authority of which notice has not been given.

17.8 The cost of preparing the authorities' volumes falls to the appellants, but is ultimately subject to the decision of the House as to the costs of the appeal.

18.

NOTICE OF HEARING

4A–84 18.1 Once an appeal has been set down, it may be called on at any time, possibly at

---

[1] See Appendix B for a list of authorities held by the House of Lords Library.

short notice. However, the Judicial Office lists appeals to meet the convenience of all the parties.

18.2 The Judicial Office agrees provisional dates with the parties well in advance of the hearing and makes every effort to keep to these dates Counsel, agents and parties are however advised to hold themselves in readiness during the week before and the week following the provisional date given. Agents receive formal notification shortly before the hearing.

18.3 Parties should inform the Judicial Office as early as possible of the names of counsel they have briefed.

18.4 Appellate Committees usually hear appeals on Mondays from 11am–1pm and from 2–4pm, and on Tuesdays to Thursdays from 10.30am–1pm and 2–4pm. Hearings take place in Committee Rooms 1 and 2 on the Committee Corridor of the Palace of Westminster.

19.

COSTS

19.1 If counsel seek an order other than that costs should be awarded to the **4A–85** successful party, they should make submissions on costs at the conclusion of the argument before the Appellate Committee. Oral submissions should be followed up by written submissions within 14 days. If there have been no oral submissions, written submissions on costs may be made within 14 days of the conclusion of the hearing. One master plus seven copies of the written submissions must be lodged at the Judicial Office

Conditional fee agreements

19.2 Conditional fee agreements may properly be made by parties to appeals before **4A–86** the House of Lords[1]. It is open to the Taxing Officer to reduce the percentage uplift recoverable under a conditional fee agreement if he considers it to be excessive. The Taxing Officer decides questions of percentage uplift in accordance with the principles set out in *Designers Guild Limited v. Russell Williams (Textiles) Limited (trading as Washington DC)* [2003] 2 Costs L.R. 204. If a party appearing before the House seeks a ruling that the percentage uplift provided for in a conditional fee agreement should be wholly disallowed on legal grounds, such a ruling should (unless otherwise ordered) be expressly sought from the House before the end of the hearing[2].

Public funding and legal aid

19.3 In appeals involving legal service funding, a successful unassisted party who **4A–87** wishes to apply for costs against the Community Legal Service under s 11 of the Access to Justice Act 1999[3] should make the application at the conclusion of the hearing and also in writing within 14 days. They should inform the Legal Services Commission (the procedure is set out in regulations 9 and 10 of the Community Legal Service (Costs) Regulations 2000 as amended). It is the responsibility of the parties to bring to the attention of the Judicial Office any factor which might affect the making of such an order by the House[4].

Submissions at judgment

19.4 Leave may exceptionally be given to a party to make submissions on costs at the **4A–88**

---

[1] Conditional fee agreements are sanctioned by the Courts and Legal Services Act 1990, as amended by the Access to Justice Act 1999.

[2] See Appeal Committee, 58th Report (2001–02): *Conditional Fee Agreements* (HL Paper 78).

[3] Also pursuant to r.5(2) Community Legal Service (Cost Protection) Regulations 2000.

[4] This direction also applies to unassisted parties who, if successful, would seek an order for costs under Legal Aid Act 1988, s.18; Legal Aid (Scotland) Act 1986, s.19; or Legal Aid, Advice and Assistance (Northern Ireland) Order 1981 Article 16; such parties should inform the Scottish Legal Aid Board or the Legal Aid Committee respectively.

time the House meets to give judgment. Notice must be given in writing to the Judicial Office at least two days before the date of judgment. One master plus seven copies of the submissions must be lodged at the Judicial Office. A copy of the submissions must be sent to the other party or parties to arrive at least two days before the date of judgment.

19.5 The House may postpone making an order for costs to allow the parties to make written submissions in the light of the result of the appeal, usually within 14 days of the date on which judgment is given. One master plus seven copies of the submissions must be lodged at the Judicial Office.

20.
JUDGMENT

Place and time of judgment

4A–89   20.1 Judgments are given in the Chamber of the House of Lords, usually on Thursdays at 9.45am. Agents are notified of the date. One week's notice is normally given.

Attendance of counsel

4A–90   20.2 One junior of counsel for each party or group of parties who have lodged a case is required to attend at the Bar of the House when judgment is delivered. Queen's Counsel may attend instead, but only a junior's fee is allowed on taxation. It is the convention that Queen's Counsel wear full-bottomed wigs when appearing at the Bar of the House. Counsel instructed to attend judgment must be familiar with the subject matter of the appeal and with the options for its disposal.

Conditions under which judgments are released in advance

4A–91   20.3 The opinions of the Law Lords who sat on the Appellate Committee and the questions to be put to the House to dispose of the appeal are available to each party 24 hours before judgment is given, i.e. on a Tuesday morning when judgment is to be given at 9.45am on the Wednesday. The documents may be collected from the Judicial Office. In releasing these documents, the House gives permission for their contents to be disclosed to counsel, agents (including solicitors outside London who have appointed London agents) and in-house legal advisers in a client Government department. The contents of the documents and the result of the appeal must not be disclosed to the client parties themselves until judgment is given in the House.

20.4 It is the duty of counsel to check that the questions to be put to the House dispose of the appeal in accordance with the opinions of the members of the Appellate Committee. In the case of apparent error or ambiguity in the opinions, counsel are requested to inform the Judicial Office immediately.

20.5 Accredited members of the media may also be supplied in advance of judgment with the Appellate Committee's opinions and the questions to be put to the House to dispose of the appeal. The contents of these documents are subject to a strict embargo, and are not for publication, broadcast or use on club tapes before judgment has been delivered. The documents are issued in advance on the strict understanding that no approach is made to any person or organisation about their contents before judgment is given.

21.
ORDER OF THE HOUSE

Draft order

4A–92   21.1 After the House has given judgment, drafts of the order of the House are sent to all parties who lodged a case. The drafts must be returned to the Judicial Office within seven days of the date of receipt (unless otherwise directed), either approved or with suggested amendments. If amendments are proposed, they must be submitted to the agents for the other parties, who should indicate their approval or disagreement both to the agents submitting the proposals and to the Judicial Office. Where the amendments proposed are contrary to the questions put to and agreed by the House, a petition must be lodged.

Final order

21.2 The final order is sent free of charge to the agents for the successful parties. **4A–93**

21.3 Prints of the final order are sent free of charge to the agents for all parties who have entered appearance.

22.

BILLS OF COSTS

22.1 Bills of costs for taxation (assessment of costs) must be lodged within three **4A–94** months from the date of judgment [1] or the date on which a petition of appeal is withdrawn (see direction 45). For an extension of the three month period, direction 5.4 applies.

22.2 The practice directions relating to judicial taxations and forms of bills of costs are available on request from the Judicial Office and on the internet at www.parliament.uk. Fees are payable on taxation of a bill of costs.

23.

DISPOSAL OF SECURITY MONEY

23.1 When the appellants are ordered to pay the costs of the appeal, the **4A–95** respondents' costs are met in whole or in part by direct payment to the respondents of the money deposited in the Security Fund (see direction 10), unless the parties have come to some other arrangement.

23.2 If the total amount of the respondents' costs can be met from the money paid into the Security Fund, any balance is repaid to the party who paid it in.

23.3 If the respondents' costs are only partly met by such payment, any certificate of taxation which is forwarded to the respondents takes account of the amount so paid.

23.4 In appeals where more than one bill of respondents' costs is to be paid by the appellants, and the money deposited as security is not enough to meet all the bills, the money is divided between the bills in proportion to their amounts as allowed on taxation or in proportion to the amounts agreed by the respondents.

23.5 If the appellants are not ordered to pay the costs of the appeal, money paid into the Security Fund is returned to them when the final judgment order has been issued.

23.6 If an appeal is withdrawn before setting down or is dismissed for want of prosecution, or if the respondent fails to lodge a bill of costs or an application for extension of time within three months of the date of judgment (see direction 22), the appellants may apply in writing to the Judicial Office for the return to them of the money deposited in the Security Fund. The application must be accompanied by the written consent of all the respondents who have entered appearance. If any respondent refuses consent, the appellants may send them a written demand to lodge a bill of costs within four weeks from the date of notice. If the Clerk of the Parliaments is satisfied that such a demand was duly sent and if the respondent fails to lodge a bill of costs within the time specified, the money in the Security Fund is returned to the appellants.

---

[1] This period is not affected by suspended orders made under Legal Aid (Scotland) Act 1986, s.19 or Legal Aid Advice and Assistance (N.I.) Order 1981 Article 16.

24.

PREPARATION OF DOCUMENTS

General

4A–96 24.1 All formal documents to the House of Lords must be produced on durable quality A4 paper, securely bound on the left, using both sides of the paper.

24.2 Documents which are not legible or which are not produced in the authorised form or which are unsatisfactory for some other similar reason are not accepted.

24.3 Parties may consult the Judicial Office at all stages of preparation of documents and may submit proofs for approval where appropriate.

Number of documents required

4A–97 24.4 The following table shows the numbers of documents usually required for the hearing of an appeal. The numbers shown are the minimum prescribed in the directions. Actual requirements must be subject to agreement and depend on the number of parties, counsel and agents concerned, and on the special circumstances of each appeal. Copies for the use of the party originating the documents are not included in the numbers indicated.

The appellants must provide:

Document	For Judicial Office	For other side
Petition of appeal	Original and seven copies on lodgment	Two on service
Statement of facts and issues	Original and seven copies on setting down	As arranged
Appendix Part 1	Eight on setting down	One in advance otherwise as arranged
Appendix Part 2 and any subsequent Parts	15 on setting down	One in advance otherwise as arranged
Case	Original and seven copies no later than five weeks before the hearing	As arranged on exchange
Bound volumes	15 no later than two weeks before the hearing	As arranged
Authorities volumes	Ten no later than two weeks before the hearing	As arranged
Documents held in readiness at hearing (if any)	15 held at the Bar	at least three

The respondents (and any interveners) must provide:

Document	For Judicial Office	For other side
Case	Original and seven copies no later than 3 weeks before the hearing	as arranged on exchange; 15 for bound volumes
Respondents' additional documents (if any)	15 held at the Bar	as arranged

Form of Statement of facts and issues

4A–98 24.5 Statement of facts and issues: See direction 11.2.

24.6 Appendix: see direction 12.7.

24.7 Cases: see direction 15.18.

24.8 Bound volumes: see direction 16.2.

24.9 Authorities volumes: see direction 17.2.

[THE NEXT PARAGRAPH IS 4A–103.]

25.

DISPOSAL OF DOCUMENTS

25.1 All petitions and supporting documents lodged become the property of the **4A–103** House. No documents submitted in connection with an application for leave to appeal can be returned. Certain documents submitted in connection with an appeal may be returned, on application to the Judicial Office within 14 days of judgment in the appeal. Master documents are retained in the parliamentary archives.

25.2 Documents lodged for the use of the Appellate Committee may with the permission of the Committee be inspected by persons who are not a party to the appeal. Such persons must comply with any anonymity orders and data protection requirements.

26.

LODGMENT

26.1 'Lodgment' and 'lodging' mean delivery to the Judicial Office or to a member of **4A–104** the Judicial Office staff by post or in person during opening hours . Where the time for lodging a document expires on a Saturday, Sunday, bank holiday, or any other day on which the Judicial Office is closed, the document will be received by the Judicial Office if it is lodged on the first day on which the Office is next open.

26.2 Communications with the Judicial Office may be transmitted by facsimile (fax) only in urgent circumstances. No document which is to be presented to the House or on which a fee is payable may be transmitted by fax or email.

26.3 Any agent attending the Judicial Office to lodge papers must be familiar with the subject matter to be dealt with.

27.

WAIVER OF FEES

27.1 In circumstances where a party to an appeal would suffer financial hardship by **4A–105** the payment of fees to the House, the requirement to pay the fee may be waived. Direction 3.17 applies.

27.2 In order to provide an objective test for determining financial hardship, and to keep in step with the courts below, the Judicial Office applies the provisions of the Civil Proceedings Fees Order 2004 (SI 2004 No 3121) to determine financial hardship for the purposes of Standing Order XIII. No waiver of fee can be granted unless the petitioner (i) has applied for and been refused public funding/legal aid and (ii) is in receipt of one or more of the qualifying benefits set out in SI 2004 No 3121.

Part III Directions Applying in Certain Appeals Only

28.

BANKRUPTCY

28.1 If a party to an appeal is adjudicated bankrupt, their agent must give immediate **4A–106** notice in writing to the other parties and to the Judicial Office, who must also be provided with a certified copy of the bankruptcy order (Standing Order X). The bankrupt party must lodge a petition to render the appeal effective and the appeal cannot proceed until the petition has been agreed to by the House.

28.2 A petition to render the appeal effective must be lodged within three months of the date of the notice.

28.3 The form of petition and the procedure for any supplemental case follows that for abatement by death[1].

29.

CONSOLIDATION AND CONJOINDER

4A–107 29.1 Where the issues in two or more appeals are similar, it may be appropriate for them to be consolidated or conjoined.

29.2 Consolidation results in the appeals being conducted as a single cause with one set of counsel and one case only on each side and with a single Appendix of documents

29.3 Conjoinder is a looser linking of two or more appeals, and a number of variations is possible. Commons forms of conjoinder are where: the appellants lodge separate cases with a separate junior for each appellant but a single leader; or the appellants lodge a single case with a single set of counsel but the respondents lodge separate cases and are separately represented.

29.4 The Judicial Office should be consulted on whether consolidation or some form of conjoinder is likely to be appropriate. A principal consideration should be to avoid wherever possible separate representation by counsel, or any duplication in the submissions made or in documents produced for the hearing.

29.5 Applications to consolidate or to conjoin appeals are made by petition[2]. The petition must be signed by the agents for all petitioners and must be submitted to the agents for all the other parties who have entered appearance for the endorsement of their consent. If consent is refused, the petition must be endorsed with a certificate that it has been served on the agents in question.

29.6 If all parties consent to or join in the petition, one master plus one copy of the petition should be lodged, together with the prescribed fee.

29.7 If any party refuses their consent, one master plus five copies of the petition should be lodged, together with the prescribed fee. The petition is then referred to an Appeal Committee and may be determined after a hearing.

30.

CROSS-APPEALS

4A–108 30.1 The presentation of an appeal does not entitle a respondent to an appeal to present a cross-appeal. Leave to appeal is required. The respondents must first apply to the Court of Appeal for leave to cross-appeal and, if leave is refused, then to apply to the House.

30.2 For security of costs and cross-appeals, see direction 10.5.

30.3 A petition for leave to cross-appeal may only be lodged after leave to appeal has been granted to the original petitioner for leave to appeal; and if leave to cross-appeal is granted, the petition of cross-appeal must be lodged with the

---

[1] Standing Order X; direction 31. For style of petition, adapt Appendix A, Form 8.
[2] For style, see Appendix A, Form 7.

prescribed fee within six weeks of the presentation of the original appeal.[1] One master plus seven copies of the petition of cross-appeal must be lodged. A cross-appeal may be presented out of time in accordance with direction 7.3. In a petition of cross-appeal, the original respondent in the House of Lords is designated the original-respondent/cross-appellant and the original appellant is designated the original-appellant/cross-respondent.

30.4 Argument in respect of a cross-appeal must be included by each party in their case in the original appeal. Such an inclusive case must clearly state that it is lodged in respect of both the original and cross-appeals.

30.5 There is only one Appendix for the original appeal and cross-appeal, and documents in respect of the appeal and cross-appeal must be included in the same Appendix. The original-appellants/cross-respondents are responsible for lodging the Statement and Appendix and setting the appeal and cross-appeal down for hearing (including payment of the fee).

31.

DEATH OF A PARTY

31.1 If a party to an appeal dies before the hearing, the appeal abates from the date **4A–109** of death (Standing Order X). Immediate notice of the death must be given in writing to the Judicial Office and to the other parties. The addition of a new party to represent the deceased person's interest cannot proceed until a petition for reviving the appeal has been agreed to by the House.

31.2 The petition for revivor must be lodged with the prescribed fee within three months of the date of notice of death[2]. It must be accompanied by an affidavit explaining the circumstances in which it is being lodged. It must be endorsed with a certificate of service on the respondents.

31.3 If abatement takes place after the case for the deceased person has been lodged but before the appeal has been heard, the appellants must lodge a supplemental case setting out the orders of the House on reviving the appeal and information about the newly-added parties.

32.

DISPUTE BETWEEN PARTIES SETTLED

32.1 It is the duty of counsel and solicitors in any pending appeal, if an event occurs **4A–110** which arguably disposes of the dispute between the parties, either to ensure that the appeal is withdrawn by consent or, if there is no agreement on that course, to bring the facts promptly to the attention of the House, and to seek directions.

33.

EUROPEAN CONVENTION ON HUMAN RIGHTS

Appeals notified under direction 9.11(a), (b) or (c)

33.1 Where an appeal involves a point notified under direction 9.11(a), 9.6(b) or **4A–111** 9.6(c), the petition of appeal must include the words 'in accordance with the Human Rights Act 1998 ' at the appropriate place in the prayer of the petition[3]. Details of the Convention right[4] which it is alleged has been infringed and of the infringement

---

[1] Standing Order VII. For style of petition, see Appendix A, Form 4.
[2] Standing Order X. For style of petition, adapt Appendix A, Form 8.
[3] See Appendix A, Form 4.
[4] See Human Rights Act 1998, which gives further effect in domestic law to much of the *Convention for the Protection of Human Rights and Fundamental Freedoms agreed by the Council of Europe at Rome on 4 November 1950.*

must be set out in the Statement of facts and issues and dealt with in a separate paragraph of the cases of all parties to the appeal.

Appeals notified under direction 9.11(a)

4A-112 33.2 The Crown has the right to be joined as a party in any appeal where the House is considering whether to declare that a provision of primary or subordinate legislation is incompatible with a Convention right[1]. In any appeal where the House is considering, or is being asked to consider, whether to make, uphold or reverse such a declaration, whether or not the Crown[2] is already a party to the appeal, the Head of the Judicial Office notifies the appropriate Law Officer(s)[3].

33.3 Where such an issue is raised in respect of a judicial act[4], the Head of the Judicial Office notifies the Crown through the Treasury Solicitor as agent for the Lord Chancellor[5].

33.4 The person notified under direction 33.2 or 33.3 must within 21 days of receiving such notice, or such extended period as the Head of the Judicial Office may allow, serve on the parties and lodge in the Judicial Office a notice stating whether or not the Crown intends to intervene in the appeal; and the identity of the Minister or other person who is to be joined as a party to the appeal[6].

33.5 If a Minister or other person has already been joined to proceedings in the court below in accordance with the provisions of s 5 of the Human Rights Act 1998 , the leave of the House is not required for the continued intervention of the Crown.

33.6 Once joined to the appeal, the case for the Minister or other person must be lodged in accordance with direction 15.

33.7 The House may order the postponement or adjournment of the hearing of the appeal for the purpose of giving effect to the provisions of this direction or the requirements of the Act.

Appeals notified under direction 9.11(b) or (c)

4A-113 33.8 Except as prescribed in direction 33.1, no special steps are required for appeals notified under direction 9.11(b) or 9.11(c).

34.

EUROPEAN COURT OF JUSTICE

4A-114 34.1 Article 234 of the Treaty establishing the European Community provides:
  1. The Court of Justice shall have jurisdiction to give preliminary rulings concerning:
     (a) the interpretation of this Treaty ;
     (b) the validity and interpretation of acts of the institutions of the Community and of the European Central Bank;
     (c) the interpretation of the statutes of bodies established by an act of the Council, where those statutes so provide.

---

[1] Human Rights Act 1998, ss.4, 5.
[2] Through a Minister, governmental body or other person defined in Human Rights Act 1998, s.5(2).
[3] The Head of the Judicial Office notifies: (i) in appeals from England, the Attorney-General; (ii) in appeals from Scotland, the Advocate General for Scotland and the Lord Advocate; (iii) in appeals from Wales, if appropriate, the Counsel General of the National Assembly for Wales; (iv) in appeals from Northern Ireland, the Attorney General for Northern Ireland.
[4] Human Rights Act 1998, ss.7, 9(3) and 9(4).
[5] In appeals from Scotland, the Head of the Judicial Office notifies the Solicitor to the Scottish Executive; in appeals from Northern Ireland, he notifies the Crown Solicitor and the Departmental Solicitor.
[6] Human Rights Act 1998, ss.5(2) and 9(5).

2. Where such a question is raised before any court or tribunal of a Member State, that court or tribunal may, if it considers that a decision on the question is necessary to enable it to give judgment, request the Court of Justice to give a ruling thereon.

3. Where any such question is raised in a case pending before a court or tribunal of a Member State against whose decisions there is no judicial remedy under national law, that court or tribunal shall bring the matter before the Court of Justice.

34.2 When the House refuses leave to appeal to a petition which includes a contention that a question of Community law is involved, the House gives additional reasons for its decision not to grant leave to appeal (see direction 4.7). These reasons reflect the decision of the Court of Justice in *CILFIT v. Ministry of Health* (Case C-283/81) which laid down the categories of case where the Court of Justice considered that no reference should be made to it, namely (a) where the question raised is irrelevant; (b) where the Community provision in question has already been interpreted by the Court of Justice; (c) where the question raised is materially identical with a question which has already been the subject of a preliminary ruling in a similar case; and (d) where the correct application of Community law is so obvious as to leave no scope for any reasonable doubt[1].

34.3 The House may order a reference to the Court of Justice before determining whether to grant leave to appeal. In such circumstances proceedings on the petition for leave to appeal are stayed until the answer is received. The directions below apply as appropriate [2].

34.4 When the House intends to make a reference, the hearing is adjourned and the parties are invited to submit an agreed draft of the question(s) to be referred. A further Statement of facts and issues, for the use of the Court of Justice, may also be appropriate. The House then makes the reference, with or without opinions. At this stage the appeal may also be disposed of in part.

34.5 Within one month of the judgment of the Court of Justice, the parties must make written submissions on whether a further hearing before the Appellate Committee is necessary or on how the appeal is to be disposed of.

34.6 If a further hearing is required, the parties may seek leave to lodge supplemental cases.

34.7 The Court of Justice does not make orders for costs. The costs of the reference are included in the order of the House disposing of the appeal; and, if necessary, are taxed by the House's Taxing Officer.

35.

EXHIBITS

35.1 Parties who require exhibits (such as machines in a patent action) to be available **4A–115** for inspection at the hearing must apply to the Judicial Office for permission for the exhibits to be brought to the House before the hearing.

36.

FEES AND SECURITY FOR COSTS

36.1 Payments of fees and deposits of security money may be made in cash or by **4A–116** banker's draft or cheque. If an appellant wishes to pay in cash, the Judicial Office may only accept cash up to £10,000, in order to comply with money laundering regulations. Drafts and cheques for fees must be made payable to 'House of Lords

---

[1] Appeal Committee, 38th Report (2002–03): *Petitions for leave to appeal: reasons for the refusal of leave* (HL Paper 89).
[2] Ibid.

Account'. Drafts and cheques for security money must be made payable to 'House of Lords Security Fund Account'.

37.

INTERVENERS

4A–117 37.1 Participation in an appeal as an intervener in a court below does not entitle a person to intervene in the House of Lords.

37.2 Application for leave to intervene in an appeal must be made by petition[1], together with the prescribed fee. The petition may only be lodged after the petition of appeal has been presented to the House. One master plus seven copies of the petition for leave to intervene must be lodged. The petition must indicate whether leave is sought for oral and written interventions or for written intervention only. The petition should be certified with the consent of the parties in the case. If their consent is refused, the petition must be endorsed with a certificate of service on them. All petitions for leave to intervene, whether or not opposed by the parties, are referred to an Appeal Committee.

37.3 Subject to the discretion of the House, interveners bear the costs of their intervention.

37.4 Subject to the discretion of the House, any additional costs to the appellants and respondents resulting from an intervention are costs in the appeal.

37.5 If the Crown has been joined to proceedings in the court below in accordance with the provisions of s 5 of the Human Rights Act 1998 , the leave of the House is not necessary for the continued intervention of the Crown (direction 33.5).

37.6 For intervention in petitions for leave to appeal, see direction 3.21.

38.

NEW SUBMISSIONS

4A–118 38.1 If, after the conclusion of the argument on an appeal, a party wishes to bring to the notice of the House new circumstances which have arisen and which might affect the decision or order of the House, application must be made without delay (by letter to the Head of the Judicial Office) for leave to make new submissions. The application should indicate the circumstances and the submissions it is desired to make, and a copy must be sent to the agents for the other parties to the appeal.

39.

OPPOSED INCIDENTAL PETITIONS

4A–119 39.1 Unless the Head of the Judicial Office directs otherwise, opposed incidental petitions (including any interlocutory petition which relates to any petition of appeal) are referred to an Appeal Committee and may be decided after an oral hearing.

39.2 One master plus seven copies of the petition must be lodged, with the prescribed fee. The original petition must bear a certificate of service on the other parties and must clearly indicate whether the other parties consent or refuse to consent to the prayer of the petition.

39.3 If the Appeal Committee orders an oral hearing, the parties may apply at that time to hand in affidavits and such other documents as they may wish. Eight copies are required. Copies of such documents must be served on the other parties before the oral hearing. Authorities are not normally cited before the Appeal Committee.

40.

PATENTS: APPEAL FROM ORDER FOR REVOCATION OF

4A–120 40.1 This direction applies to any appeal direct from the High Court under ss 12 and

---

[1] See Appendix A, Form 8.

13 of the Administration of Justice Act 1969 , from an order for the revocation of a patent made under s 32 or 61 of the Patents Act 1949 or under s 72 of the Patents Act 1977.

40.2 Notice of intention to present an appeal, with a copy of the petition of appeal, must be served on the Comptroller-General of Patents, Designs and Trade Marks, as well as on the respondents.

40.3 If at any time before the appeal comes on for hearing the respondents decide not to appear on the appeal or not to oppose it, they must without delay serve notice of their decision on the Comptroller and on the appellants. Any such notice served on the Comptroller must be accompanied by a copy of the petition under s 32 of the 1949 Act or of the pleadings in the action and the affidavits filed therein.

40.4 The Comptroller must, within 14 days of receiving notice of the respondents' decision, serve on the appellant and lodge in the Judicial Office a notice stating whether or not he intends to enter appearance.

40.5 The Comptroller may appear and be heard in opposition to the appeal:
   (a) in any case where he has given notice of his intention to appear, and
   (b) in any other case (including in particular a case where the respondents withdraw opposition to the appeal during the hearing) if the House so directs or allows.

40.6 The House makes such orders for the postponement or adjournment of the hearing of the appeal as may appear necessary for the purpose of giving effect to the provisions of this direction.

41.

PUBLIC FUNDING AND LEGAL AID

41.1 The House of Lords does not provide public funding or legal aid. Application **4A–121** for public funding must be made in England and Wales to the Legal Services Commission, in Scotland to the Scottish Legal Aid Board, and in Northern Ireland to the Legal Aid Committee.

41.2 A party to whom a public funding or legal aid certificate has been issued must lodge a copy in the Judicial Office as soon as possible thereafter. Any emergency certificate and subsequent amendments and the authority for leading counsel must also be lodged.

41.3 Deadlines for the deposit of documents are extended while public funding or legal aid is being sought, provided the Judicial Office and the other parties have been notified in writing. Notification must be made within the original time limits. The original time limits are then extended to a date one month after the final decision is taken on the funding application (including appeals, if any).

41.4 Where a respondent to an appeal has applied for public funding or legal aid, the Judicial Office should be informed within the original time limit for lodging the Statement and Appendix[1]. The period is then extended to six weeks from the final determination of the legal aid application.

41.5 Where a certificate is granted, the relevant date for the purpose of time limits is the date of issue of the certificate.

42.

SPECIALIST ADVISERS

42.1 Any party to an appeal may apply in writing to the Judicial Office for Specialist **4A–122**

---

[1] See direction 13.

Advisers to attend the hearing[1]. Such advisers provide assistance to the Appellate Committee and are strictly independent of the parties to the appeal.

43.

Stay of Execution

4A-123   43.1 Presentation of a petition of appeal or a petition for leave to appeal does not in itself place a stay of execution on any order appealed from. A party seeking such a stay must apply to the court appealed from, not to the House of Lords. The House cannot stay an interlocutor of the Court of Session[2].

44.

Transcription

4A-124   44.1 Transcriptions are not made of hearings before the Appellate Committee. Any party may seek permission to arrange for its own transcription of a hearing, by writing to the Head of the Judicial Office. Permission is usually given. The service arranged must be silent. A single copy of the transcript should be lodged in the Judicial Office.

45.

Withdrawal of Petitions

Petitions for leave to appeal

4A-125   45.1 A petition for leave to appeal may be withdrawn by writing to the Head of the Judicial Office, stating that the parties to the petition have agreed how the costs should be settled. The respondents should notify the Judicial Office of their agreement.

Petitions of appeal

4A-126   45.2 An appeal that has not been set down for hearing may be withdrawn by writing to the Head of the Judicial Office, stating that the parties to the appeal have agreed the costs of the appeal. The nature of the agreement should be indicated. Where appropriate, the letter should also indicate how the money paid into the security fund (if any) should be disposed of. Written notification must also be given to the respondents who must notify the Judicial Office of their agreement to the withdrawal of the appeal and who must confirm that the costs have been agreed.

45.3 An appeal that has been set down for hearing may only be withdrawn by order of the House on petition[3]. Such a petition should include submissions on costs and, where appropriate, indicate how the security money should be disposed of. The petition must be submitted for their consent to those respondents who have entered appearance. The petition should be lodged with the prescribed fee.

Statements to the House

JUDICIAL PRECEDENT

4A-127   **26 July 1966—BY THE LORD CHANCELLOR (LORD GARDINER)**

'Before judgments are delivered today, I wish to make the following statement on behalf of myself and the Lords of Appeal in Ordinary:

"Their Lordships regard the use of precedent as an indispensable foundation upon

---

[1] Standing Order XIV. For Nautical Assessors, see also Supreme Court of Judicature Act 1891 s 3.

[2] Court of Session Act 1988, s.41(2).

[3] For style of petition, adapt Appendix A, Form 16.

which to decide what is the law and its application to individual cases It provides at least some degree of certainty upon which individuals can rely in the conduct of their affairs, as well as a basis for orderly development of legal rules.

"Their Lordships nevertheless recognise that too rigid adherence to precedent may lead to injustice in a particular case and also unduly restrict the proper development of the law. They propose therefore to modify their present practice and, while treating former decisions of this House as normally binding, to depart from a previous decision when it appears right to do so.

"In this connection they will bear in mind the danger of disturbing retrospectively the basis on which contracts, settlements of property and fiscal arrangements have been entered into and also the especial need for certainty as to the criminal law.

"This announcement is not intended to affect the use of precedent elsewhere than in this House.'"

PRINCIPLES FOR PARTICIPATION

22 June 2000—BY THE SENIOR LORD OF APPEAL IN ORDINARY (LORD BINGHAM OF CORNHILL)
4A–128

'My Lords, with the leave of the House, before the reports from the Appellate Committees are considered, I should like to make a statement on Recommendation 59 of the Royal Commission on the Reform of the House of Lords That recommendation is that "The Lords of Appeal should set out in writing and publish a statement of the principles which they intend to observe when participating in debates and votes in the second chamber and when considering their eligibility to sit on related cases."

'I should tell the House that my noble and learned friends have considered this recommendation and have agreed on the terms of a statement to give effect to it. I will now read the statement which has been agreed by all the Lords of Appeal in Ordinary:

General Principles

"As full members of the House of Lords the Lords of Appeal in Ordinary have a right to participate in the business of the House. However, mindful of their judicial role they consider themselves bound by two general principles when deciding whether to participate in a particular matter, or to vote: first, the Lords of Appeal in Ordinary do not think it appropriate to engage in matters where there is a strong element of party political controversy; and secondly the Lords of Appeal in Ordinary bear in mind that they may render themselves ineligible to sit judicially if they were to express an opinion on a matter which might later be relevant to an appeal to the House.

"The Lords of Appeal in Ordinary will continue to be guided by these broad principles They stress that it is impossible to frame rules which cover every eventuality. In the end it must be for the judgment of each individual Lord of Appeal to decide how to conduct himself in any particular situation.

Eligibility

"In deciding who is eligible to sit on an appeal, the Lords of Appeal agree to be guided by the same principles as apply to all judges These principles were restated by the Court of Appeal in the case of *Locabail (UK) Ltd v. Bayfield Properties Ltd and others and four other actions* [2000] 1 All E.R. 65 (CA)]."

'My Lords, that concludes the statement.'

46. Standing Orders

STANDING ORDER NO. 17 OF THE HOUSE OF LORDS RELATING TO PUBLIC BUSINESS

Recall of the House. 20 May 1970.

(1) If, during any adjournment of the House, the Lord Chancellor is satisfied that 4A–129

the public interest requires that the House should meet at a time earlier than that appointed, he may signify that he is so satisfied and notice shall be given and thereupon the House shall meet at the time stated in the notice, as if it had been duly adjourned to that time.

(2) If the Lord Chancellor is unable to act for the purposes of this Standing Order, the Chairman of Committees, after consultation with Her Majesty's Government, may act in his stead.

(3) Notwithstanding any adjournment of the House, the House may meet for judicial business at a time earlier than that appointed if the Lord Chancellor or, in his absence, the senior Lord of Appeal in Ordinary, is satisfied that it should do so and has signified that he is so satisfied and has given notice to such Lords as he thinks fit.

STANDING ORDER NO. 87 OF THE HOUSE OF LORDS RELATING TO PUBLIC BUSINESS

Appellate and Appeal Committees. 20 May 1970. 28 January 1984.

4A–130　　(1) For the purposes of its appellate jurisdiction, the House shall have Appellate and Appeal Committees, of which all Lords qualified under the Appellate Jurisdiction Acts 1876 and 1887 shall be members.

(2) These Committees shall be:

(a) two Appellate Committees, which shall hear any cause or matter referred to them and shall report thereon to the House;

(b) two Appeal Committees, which shall consider any Petition or application for leave to appeal that may be referred to them and any matter relating thereto, or to causes depending, or formerly depending, in this House, and shall report thereon to the House.

(3) In any criminal matter, or in any matter concerning extradition, an Appeal Committee may take decisions and give directions on behalf of the House.

(4) In any Appellate or Appeal Committee the Chair shall be taken by the Lord Chancellor or, in his absence, by the senior Lord of Appeal in Ordinary present, such seniority being determined in accordance with the Commission for the time being appointing Speakers for the purpose of the hearing and determination of Appeals.

(5) For the purposes of section 8 of the Appellate Jurisdiction Act 1876 , any Appellate Committee may sit and act while Parliament is prorogued.

STANDING ORDERS OF THE HOUSE OF LORDS REGULATING JUDICIAL BUSINESS, MADE IN PURSUANCE OF THE APPELLATE JURISDICTION ACT 1876 AND SUBSEQUENT ENACTMENTS.

4A–131　　The dates (round bracketed) are those of the original standing orders prior to 1876. The dates [square bracketed] are those of the original standing orders made in pursuance of the Appellate Jurisdiction Act 1876 . The dates without brackets are those of subsequent amendments.

Time limit for presenting Appeals

4A–132　　I. ORDERED, that no Petition of Appeal be received by this House unless the same be lodged in the Parliament Office for presentation to the House within the period of three months from the date of the last Order or Interlocutor appealed from.

(13 December 1661)

[14 August 1876]

26 February 1959

25 March 1964

Leave to Appeal from the Courts of Appeal

4A–133　　II. ORDERED, that, in all Appeals from the Court of Appeal, the Court of Appeal in Northern Ireland or the Court of Session in Scotland in which the leave of the House is required under the provisions of any Act of Parliament, a Petition for Leave to Appeal be lodged in the Parliament Office within one month from the date of the last Order or Judgment appealed from, and that such Petition be referred to an Appeal Committee to consider whether such leave should be granted.

[24 October 1935]

3 March 1966

3 December 1969

Leave to Appeal from the High Court

4A–134 III. ORDERED, that, in all cases where application is made for leave for an Appeal to be brought direct to the House from the High Court of Justice in England and Wales or from the High Court of Justice in Northern Ireland—

(a) a Petition for such leave, together with the certificate granted by the High Court under section 12 of the Administration of Justice Act 1969 , be lodged in the Parliament Office within one month from the date of the grant of such certificate or within such extended time as in any particular case the House may allow;

(b) any such Petition, and any application for extension of time or other incidental matter, be referred to an Appeal Committee for their consideration and report.

15 December 1969

Appeals to be signed and certified by counsel

4A–135 IV. ORDERED, that, except in cases where leave to appeal has been granted under the provisions of any Act of Parliament, all Petitions of Appeal be signed, and the reasonableness thereof certified, by two counsel.

(3 March 1697)

[14 August 1876]

3 March 1966

Security for costs

4A–136 V. (1) ORDERED, that, unless otherwise ordered by the House, in all Appeals the Appellants do give security for costs by paying into the House of Lords Security Fund Account within one week of the presentation of the Appeal such sum as shall be authorised from time to time by the House, to be subject to the Order of the House with regard to the costs of the Appeal.

On default by the Appellants in complying with the above conditions, the Appeal to stand dismissed.

(20 November 1680)

[14 August 1876]

7 August 1877

2 June 1959

12 April 1962

27 April 1976

9 March 1977

21 July 1988

26 July 1999

Exemptions

4A–137 (2) ORDERED, that this Standing Order shall not apply (a) to Appellants who have been granted public funding or legal aid, (b) to appellants in Appeals under the Child Abduction and Custody Act 1985,or (c) to a Minister or Government department.

15 December 1960

17 December 1991

10 October 2000

Time for lodging Statement

4A–138 VI.(1) ORDERED, that the Statement and the Appendix thereto be lodged in the Parliament Office within six weeks from the date of the presentation of the Appeal to the House; and the Appeal be set down for hearing on the first sitting day thereafter; on default by the Appellant, the Appeal to stand dismissed.

(12 July 1811)

[14 August 1876]

26 February 1959

17 December 1991

Scottish appeals

4A–139 (2) ORDERED, that in all Appeals from Scotland the Appellant in the Appendix shall lay before this House a copy of the record as authenticated by the Deputy

Principal Clerk of Session or a Clerk of Session delegated by him; together with a supplement containing an account, without argument or statement of other facts, of the further steps which have been taken in the cause since the record was completed, and containing also copies of the Interlocutors or parts of Interlocutors complained of; and each party shall in his Case lay before the House a copy of the case presented by him to the Court of Session, if any such case was presented there, with a short summary of any additional reasons upon which he means to insist; and if there shall have been no case presented to the Court of Session then each party shall set forth in his Case the reasons upon which he founds his argument, as shortly and succinctly as possible.

25 March 1964
17 December 1991

Statement to be signed by counsel

4A–140 (3) ORDERED, that the Statement be signed by one or more counsel for each party, who shall have attended as counsel in the Court below, or shall purpose attending as counsel at the hearing in this House.

(19 April 1698)
17 December 1991

Cross-appeals

4A–141 VII. ORDERED, that all Cross-appeals be presented to the House within the period allowed by Standing Order No. VI for lodging the Statement in the original Appeal.

(8 March 1763)
[14 August 1876]
17 December 1991

Expiry of time during parliamentary recess

4A–142 VIII. ORDERED, with regard to Appeals in which the periods under Standing Orders Nos V, VI and VII expire during the parliamentary recess of the House, that such periods be extended to the third sitting day of the next ensuing meeting of the House.

Provided that if the House is recalled in pursuance of Public Business Standing Order No. 16 or Proclamation, any day on which the House sits pursuant to such recall is not a sitting day for the purposes of this Standing Order.

[14 August 1876]
17 December 1991

Public funding and legal aid

4A–143 IX. ORDERED, that where a party to an Appeal has applied for public funding or legal aid, and the Clerk of the Parliaments has been informed of that application in writing before the expiration of the periods of time limited by Standing Orders Nos I, II or III, such periods of time shall be extended until one month after the date of the final determination of the application.

[15 December 1960]
3 March 1966
21 July 1988
19 May 1994
10 October 2000

Abatement or defect Revivor etc.

4A–144 X. ORDERED, that in the event of abatement by death or defect through bankruptcy, an Appeal shall not stand dismissed for default under Standing Orders Nos V or VI, provided that notice of such abatement or defect be given by a letter from the Appellant's Agent addressed to the Clerk of the Parliaments and lodged in the Judicial Office prior to the expiration of the period limited by the Standing Order under which the Appeal would otherwise have stood dismissed.

ORDERED, that all Appeals marked on the Cause List of the House as abated or defective shall stand dismissed unless, within three months from the date of the notice to the Clerk of the Parliaments of abatement or defect, if the House be then sitting, or, if not, then not later than the third sitting day of the next ensuing sittings of the House, a Petition shall be presented to the House for reviving the Appeal or for rendering the same effective.

[14 August 1876]
12 August 1884
26 February 1959
17 December 1991

Supplemental case

ORDERED, that when an Appeal has abated or become defective after the Cases have been lodged, and it is subsequently revived or rendered effective, a Supplemental Case shall be lodged by the Appellant setting forth the Order or Orders made by the House reviving the Appeal or rendering the same effective. **4A–145**

The like rule shall be observed by the Appellant and Respondent respectively, where any person or persons shall, by leave of the House, upon Petition or otherwise, be added as a party or parties to the said Appeal after the Cases in such Appeal shall have been lodged.

(20 March 1823)

Certificate of leave or difference of opinion in Scottish appeals

XI. ORDERED, that when any Petition of Appeal shall be presented to this House **4A–146** from any interlocutory Judgment of either division of the Lords of Session in Scotland, the counsel who shall sign the said Petition, or two of the counsel for the party or parties in the Court below, shall sign a certificate or declaration, stating either that leave was given by that division of the judges pronouncing such interlocutory Judgment to the Appellant or Appellants to present such Petition of Appeal or that there was a difference of opinion amongst the judges of the said division pronouncing such interlocutory Judgment.

[14 August 1876]

Taxation of costs

XII. ORDERED, that the Clerk of Parliaments shall appoint such person as he may **4A–147** think fit as Taxing Officer, and in all cases in which this House shall make any order for payment of costs by any party or parties in any cause, the amount thereof to be certified by the Clerk of the Parliaments, the Taxing Officer shall tax the Bill of Costs so ordered to be paid, and ascertain the amount thereof, and report the same to the Clerk of the Parliaments or Clerk Assistant: And it is further Ordered, that the same fees shall be demanded from and paid by the party applying for such taxation for and in respect thereof as are now charged or shall be authorised from time to time by the House; and such fees shall be added at the foot of the said Bill of Costs as taxed. And the Clerk of the Parliaments or Clerk Assistant may give a certificate of such costs, expressing the amount so reported to him as aforesaid, and in his certificate, as well as in the Taxing Officer's report, regard shall be had to any sum that has been paid in to the Security Fund Account of the House, as directed by Standing Order No. V; and the amount in money certified by him in such certificate shall be the sum to be demanded and paid under or by virtue of such order as aforesaid for payment of costs.

(3 April 1835)
[14 August 1876]
7 August 1877
2 June 1959
9 March 1977
27 June 1984

Fees

XIII. ORDERED, that fees be taken in this House on the documents specified in **4A–148** the Schedule hereto, that the fees to be charged shall be such as shall be authorised from time to time by the House, and that none of the said documents be issued from or received at the Parliament Office unless it shall have been endorsed with the date of lodgment and the amount of fee paid.

If the Clerk of the Parliaments is satisfied that a litigant who has been refused public funding or legal aid would suffer financial hardship by the payment of fees to this

House, he shall report the circumstances to the Appeal Committee. The Appeal Committee shall have power to waive, modify or suspend such fees, either wholly or in part, and shall report thereon to the House.

[10 March 1902]
26 March 1970
27 April 1976
9 March 1977
21 July 1988
17 December 1991
19 May 1994
17 October 1995
10 October 2000

SCHEDULE

4A–149

Petition for Leave to Appeal.

Interlocutory Petitions referred to an Appeal Committee (including the Report thereon).

Petition of Appeal.

Notice of Appearance.

Waiver of Security for costs.

Petition not referred to Appeal Committee.

Application to set down for hearing.

Petition to withdraw Appeal after setting down.

Specialist advisers

4A–150

XIV. (1) ORDERED, that the Lord Chancellor or the Lord Speaker may direct that one or more Specialist Advisers shall attend the hearing of any Appeal in which they consider the House would benefit from such attendance.

(2) ORDERED, that the parties or either party to an Appeal may apply by letter to the Clerk of the Parliaments requesting, upon grounds stated in the letter, the attendance of Specialist Advisers Such an application shall be referred to and determined by the Lord Chancellor or Lord Speaker.

(3) ORDERED, that in any Appeal concerning nautical matters in which the attendance of Specialist Advisers is required, Nautical Assessors may be appointed of whom one shall be an Officer, active or retired, of Her Majesty's Navy, and the other an Elder Brother of the Corporation of Trinity House.

(4) ORDERED, that the fees and expenses paid to each Specialist Adviser shall be such as shall have been agreed between the parties and the Advisers and approved by the Lord Chancellor or Lord Speaker, or, failing such agreement, such sum as shall be authorised by the Lord Chancellor or Lord Speaker.

(5) ORDERED, that unless the House otherwise directs, the fees referred to in paragraph (4) shall be paid by the party against whom the House awards costs.

23 November 1995

Appendix A: standard forms of key documents

FORM 1

PETITION for leave to appeal

(HL direction 3)

IN THE HOUSE OF LORDS

ON APPEAL FROM HER MAJESTY'S COURT OF APPEAL (CIVIL DIVISION) (ENGLAND) (*or relevant court*)

Court of Appeal Ref: (eg, B3/2003/0038)
Neutral citation of judgment appealed against: (eg, [2003] EWCA Civ 1575)

BETWEEN

AB (Respondent)
and
CD (Petitioners)
[and]
[(2) EF]
[and]
[(3) GH]

PETITION FOR LEAVE TO APPEAL

TO THE RIGHT HONOURABLE THE HOUSE OF LORDS

THE HUMBLE PETITION OF [*set out full name(s) and address(es) of petitioners*]
PRAYING FOR LEAVE TO APPEAL SHOWS—

1.   That ....[*set out briefly in numbered paragraphs such facts and arguments as may be necessary to enable the Appeal Committee to decide whether leave to appeal should be given*].
2.   ....
3.   ....etc.

[*Note: it is usually appropriate for petitions for leave to appeal to deal with some or all of the following:*

1. Narrative of the facts;
2. Statutory framework (*if any*);
3. Chronology of proceedings;
4. Orders made in the courts below;
5. Issues before Court of Appeal (*or court appealed from*);
6. Treatment of the issues by Court of Appeal (*or court appealed from*);
7. Issues in the petition for leave to appeal.]

[At end of numbered paragraphs insert]

YOUR PETITIONER(S) HUMBLY SUBMIT(S) that leave to appeal to Your Lordships' House should be granted for the following among other

REASONS

[list here numbered reasons summarising the arguments]

(1) ....
(2) ....
(3) ....etc.

AND YOUR PETITIONER(S) WILL EVER PRAY

Signed

....

Signature of petitioner(s) or agent(s) for the petitioner(s)

[Note: for leapfrog petitions (direction 6) the prayer of the petition uses the words:

THE HUMBLE PETITION OF *[set out full name(s) and address(es) of petitioners]* PRAYING FOR LEAVE FOR AN APPEAL TO BE BROUGHT DIRECT FROM THE HIGH COURT OF JUSTICE IN ACCORDANCE WITH PART II OF THE ADMINISTRATION OF JUSTICE ACT 1969 SHOWS—]

CERTIFICATE OF SERVICE TO BE ENDORSED ON BACK OF PETITION FOR LEAVE TO APPEAL

[I *or* We], [(Messrs) *(name)*, of *(address)*,(agents for)] the petitioner(s) within-named, hereby certify that on *(date)* [I *or* we] served [(Messrs) *(name)* of *(address)* (agents for)] *(name(s) of respondent(s))*, the within-named respondent(s), with a correct copy of the petition for leave to appeal and with notice that the petition would be presented to the House of Lords on behalf of the petitioner(s) as soon as conveniently may be.

(signature of petitioner(s) or their agent(s))

FORM 2

BACK OF PETITION for leave to appeal showing certificate of service to be endorsed on original petition

[I *or* We], [(Messrs) (*name*), of (*address*),(agents for)] the petitioner(s) within-named, hereby certify that on (*date*) [I *or* we] served [(Messrs) (*name*) of (*address*) (agents for)] (*name(s) of respondent(s)*), the within-named respondent(s), with a correct copy of the petition for leave to appeal and with notice that the petition would be presented to the House of Lords on behalf of the petitioner(s) as soon as conveniently may be. (*signature of petitioner(s) or their agents*)	IN THE HOUSE OF LORDS ON APPEAL FROM (*name court*) BETWEEN: (*set out title of cause*) <hr>PETITION FOR LEAVE TO APPEAL
(*neutral citation of judgment petitioned against*) (*references to law reports*) (*indexing catchwords*) (*head-note summary*)	(*set out full name, address, telephone number, and reference (if any) of petitioner(s) or their agents*)

4A–153

FORM 3
PETITION for leave to appeal out of time
(HL directions 2 and 3)

IN THE HOUSE OF LORDS

ON APPEAL FROM HER MAJESTY'S COURT OF APPEAL CIVIL DIVISION (ENGLAND) *(or relevant court)*]

Court of Appeal Ref: (eg, B3/2004/0039)
Neutral citation of judgment appealed against: (eg, [2004] EWCA Civ 3847)

BETWEEN
AB (Respondent)
and
CD (Petitioners)
[and]
[(2) EF]
[and]
[(3) GH]

PETITION FOR LEAVE TO APPEAL

TO THE RIGHT HONOURABLE THE HOUSE OF LORDS

THE HUMBLE PETITION OF [*set out full name(s) and address(es) of petitioners*]
PRAYING FOR LEAVE TO APPEAL NOTWITHSTANDING THAT THE TIME LIMITED
BY STANDING ORDER NUMBER II HAS EXPIRED SHOWS –

1. That (*set out briefly the reason(s) why the petition was not lodged in time*).
2. That ......(*continue as in Form 1, setting out briefly in numbered paragraphs such facts and arguments as may be necessary to enable the Appeal Committee to decide whether to give leave to appeal out of time*].
3.   ....
4.   ....etc.

Note: it is usually appropriate for petitions for leave to appeal to deal with some or all of the following:

1. Narrative of the facts;
2. Statutory framework (*if any*);
3. Chronology of proceedings;
4. Orders made in the courts below;
5. Issues before Court of Appeal (*or court appealed from*);
6. Treatment of the issues by Court of Appeal (*or court appealed from*);
7. Issues in the petition for leave to appeal.

[*At end of numbered paragraphs insert*]

YOUR PETITIONER(S) HUMBLY SUBMIT(S) that leave to appeal out of time to Your Lordships' House should be granted for the following among other

REASONS

[*list here numbered reasons summarising the arguments*]

(4) ....

(5) ....

(6) ....etc.

AND YOUR PETITIONER(S) WILL EVER PRAY

Signed

....

Signature of petitioner or agent(s) for the petitioner

CERTIFICATE OF SERVICE TO BE ENDORSED ON BACK OF PETITION FOR LEAVE TO APPEAL

[I *or* We], [(Messrs) (*name*), of (*address*),(agents for)] the petitioner(s) within-named, hereby certify that on (*date*) [I *or* we] served [(Messrs) (*name*) of (*address*) (agents for)] (*name(s) of respondent(s)*), the within-named respondent(s), with a correct copy of the petition for leave to appeal and with notice that the petition would be presented to the House of Lords on behalf of the petitioner(s) as soon as conveniently may be.

(*signature of petitioner(s) or their agents*)

4A–154

FORM 4

PETITION of appeal [or cross-appeal]

(HL direction 9)

IN THE HOUSE OF LORDS

ON APPEAL FROM HER MAJESTY'S COURT OF APPEAL (ENGLAND) *(or relevant court)*

BETWEEN:

AB (Respondents)
and
CD (Appellants)
[and]
[(2) EF]
[and]
[(3) GH]

(in a petition of cross appeal the original respondent lodging the cross appeal is designated as cross-appellant/original respondent and the original appellant is designated as original appellant/cross-respondent)

PETITION OF APPEAL

TO THE RIGHT HONOURABLE THE HOUSE OF LORDS

THE HUMBLE PETITION AND [CROSS-] APPEAL OF *(set out the full name(s) and address(es) of the appellant(s)).*

YOUR PETITIONER(S) humbly pray(s) that the matter of the Order(s)/Interlocutor(s) set forth in the Schedule hereto *[if Order is partly appealed against, insert the words: so far as therein stated to be appealed against]* may be reviewed before Her Majesty the Queen, in Her Court of Parliament, and that the said Order(s)/Interlocutor(s) *[if Order is partly appealed against, insert the words: so far as aforesaid]* may be reversed, varied or altered *[if appropriate, insert the words: in accordance with the Human Rights Act 1998]*, *[if specific relief is asked for, it should be so stated, prefaced by the words: and that]* or that the petitioner(s) may have such other relief in the premises as to Her Majesty the Queen, in Her Court of Parliament, may seem meet.

[signature(s) of appellant(s) or their agents or counsel, as appropriate].

THE SCHEDULE REFERRED TO ABOVE
FROM HER MAJESTY'S COURT OF APPEAL (CIVIL DIVISION) (ENGLAND) (*or relevant court*)

In a certain cause [*or other matter*] wherein (*insert name(s)*) was/were claimant(s) [*or other designation*] and (*insert name(s)*) was/were defendant(s) [*or other designation*]. (*The names of all parties to the action, whether originally in the cause or added by subsequent order, must be given.*)

The Order(s)/Interlocutor(s) of (*state court*) of (*date*) appealed from is/are in the words following, [*add, if appropriate, the words*: the portion(s) complained of being underlined]: (*The whole of each Order/Interlocutor, including the recital, must be set out. All and only those parts of the Order/Interlocutor appealed from must be underlined. The recital should not be underlined. Where an Order/Interlocutor includes leave to appeal to the House of Lords, that part should not be underlined. Where leave to appeal has been granted by a subsequent Order of the court, that Order must also be set out but should not be underlined.*)

[*Where leave to appeal has been granted by order of the House, the following words are added:*

And your Lordships gave leave to appeal to your Lordships' House on (*date*)]

[*Where leave to appeal is not required under the provisions of any Act of Parliament (see direction 9.2), the following must be added and signed as indicated:*

We humbly conceive this to be a proper case to be heard before your Lordships by way of appeal.]

(*signatures and names of two counsel*)]

[*The special certificate required by HL Standing Order XI in certain Scottish appeals is added here if necessary*]

4A–155

FORM 5

BACK OF PETITION OF [CROSS-] APPEAL, showing certificate of service to be endorsed on original petition

[I *or* We], [(Messrs) *(name)*, of *(address)*,(agents for)] the [*cross-*] appellant(s) within-named, hereby certify that on *(date)* [I *or* we] served [(Messrs) *(name)* of *(address)* (agents for)] *(name(s) of [cross-] respondent(s))*, the within-named [cross-] respondent(s), with a correct copy of the petition of [cross-] appeal and with notice that the petition would be presented to the House of Lords on behalf of the petitioner(s) as soon as conveniently may be.	IN THE HOUSE OF LORDS ON APPEAL FROM *(name court)* BETWEEN: *(set out title of cause)*
(signature of petitioner(s) or their agents)	
	PETITION OF [CROSS-] APPEAL
(neutral citation of judgment petitioned against) *(references to law reports)* *(indexing catchwords)* *(head-note summary)*	*(set out full name, address, telephone number, and reference (if any) of [cross-] appellant(s) or their agents)*

FORM 6

PETITION for extension of time to lodge Statement and Appendix

(HL direction 13)

IN THE HOUSE OF LORDS

ON APPEAL FROM HER MAJESTY'S COURT OF APPEAL (ENGLAND) (*or relevant court)*)

BETWEEN:

(set out title of appeal)

TO THE RIGHT HONOURABLE THE HOUSE OF LORDS

THE HUMBLE PETITION OF (*set out full name(s) of appellant(s)*) shows -

That your petitioner(s) presented a petition of appeal on (*date*) complaining of an Order of the (*state court*) dated (*date*).

That the time allowed by Standing Order VI for the appellant(s) to lodge the statement and appendix and to set down the cause for hearing [will expire *or* originally expired] on (*date*).

[That the House, pursuant to a petition from the appellant(s), granted an extension of time in which to lodge the statement and the appendix and set down the cause for hearing to (*date*).]

[That the House, pursuant to a further petition from the appellant(s), granted a second extension of time until (*date*).]

That the petitioner(s) will be unable to lodge the statement and appendix by the said date for the following reasons:

(set out brief reasons)

THEREFORE YOUR PETITIONER(S) HUMBLY PRAY(S)

That Your Lordships will be pleased to grant an extension of time until (*date*) to lodge the statement and appendix and set down the cause for hearing.

And your petitioner(s) will ever pray.

(signature of appellant(s) or their agents)

[Agents for the] Appellant(s) *(set out here name and address of appellant(s) or their agents)*

[I *or* We] consent to the prayer of the above petition.

(signature of respondent(s) or their agents)
[Agents for the] respondent(s) *(set out here name and address of respondent(s) or their agents)*

FORM 7

PETITION for Consolidation or Conjoinder

(HL direction 29)

IN THE HOUSE OF LORDS

ON APPEAL FROM HER MAJESTY'S COURT OF APPEAL (ENGLAND)

(set out title of first appeal)

AND

(set out title of second, third etc appeals)

TO THE RIGHT HONOURABLE THE HOUSE OF LORDS

THE HUMBLE PETITION OF *(set out full name(s) of appellant(s)* SHOWS—

That your petitioner(s) presented [a] petition(s) of appeal on *(date)* complaining of (an) Order(s) of the *(name relevant court below)* dated *(date)*.

That your petitioner(s) *(name appellant(s) in other appeal(s), if different)* presented [a] petition(s) of appeal on *(date)* complaining of [an] Order(s) of the *(name relevant court below)* dated *(date)*.

That the same matters of law are raised in each of the appeals [and that the appeals of *(name relevant parties)* to *(name relevant court below)* were heard and argued together and one Judgment was delivered in respect of the [two] appeals].

That it is expedient that your petitioners' said appeals be [consolidated *or* conjoined].

YOUR PETITIONERS THEREFORE HUMBLY PRAY

[Consolidation:
　That the said appeals may be consolidated and that they be allowed to lodge one statement, one case and one appendix and be jointly represented in respect of the *(insert relevant number)* appeals and that the respondents have leave to lodge one case in respect of the appeals.]

[Conjoinder:
　That the said appeals may be conjoined and that they be allowed to lodge separate statements and cases and one appendix in respect of the *(insert relevant number)* appeals and that the respondents have leave to lodge separate cases in respect of the appeals and be separately represented or that such other Order may be made with a view to the convenient conduct of the said appeals as to your Lordships may seem meet *(or such variation as is required).*]

And your petitioner(s) will ever pray.

(signature of appellant(s) to first appeal or their agents)

[Agents for the] Appellant(s) *(set out here name and address of appellant(s) or their agents)*

(signature of appellant(s) to other appeal(s) or their agents)

[Agents for the] Appellant(s)/co-petitioners *(set out here name and address of appellant(s)/co-petitioners or their agents)*

[I *or* We] consent to the prayer of the above petition.

(signature of respondent(s)to first appeal or their agents)

[Agents for the] Respondent(s) *to first appeal (set out here name and address of respondent(s) or their agents)*

(signature of respondent(s) to other appeal(s) or their agents)

[Agents for the] Respondent(s) *to other appeal(s) (set out here name and address of respondent(s) or their agents) etc*

4A–158

FORM 8

PETITION for leave to intervene

(HL direction 37)

IN THE HOUSE OF LORDS

ON APPEAL FROM HER MAJESTY'S COURT OF APPEAL (ENGLAND) *(or relevant court))*

BETWEEN:

(set out title of appeal)

TO THE RIGHT HONOURABLE THE HOUSE OF LORDS

THE HUMBLE PETITION OF *(set out full name(s) of prospective intervener(s))* PRAYING FOR LEAVE TO INTERVENE SHOWS—

1. That on *(date) (set out full name(s) of appellant(s))* presented a petition of appeal to your Lordships' House, complaining of an Order of the *(state court)* dated *(date)*.

2. That your petitioner(s) seek(s) your Lordships' leave to present written [*add, if appropriate, the words:* and oral] submissions in intervention in the said appeal.

3. That *(set out briefly in numbered paragraphs such facts and arguments as may be necessary to enable the Appeal Committee to report to the House whether leave to intervene should be granted)*.

YOUR PETITIONER(S) HUMBLY SUBMIT(S) that leave to intervene in the said appeal should be granted for the following among other

REASONS
(give numbered reasons summarising the arguments)

And your petitioner(s) will ever pray.

(signature of petitioner(s) or their agents)

[Agents for the] Petitioner(s) (set out here name and address of petitioner(s) or their agents)

[I *or* We] consent to the prayer of the above petition.

(signature of appellant(s) or their agents)

[Agents for the] Appellant(s) (set out here name and address of appellant(s) or their agents)

[I *or* We] consent to the prayer of the above petition.

(signature of respondent(s) or their agents)

[Agents for the] Respondent(s) (set out here name and address of respondent(s) or their agents)

FORM 9

4A–159

BACK OF PETITION for leave to intervene, showing certificate of service to be endorsed on original petition

[I *or* We], [(Messrs) *(name)*, of *(address)*,(agents for)] the petitioner(s) within-named, hereby certify that on *(date)* [I *or* we] served [(Messrs) *(name)* of *(address)* (agents for)] *(name(s) of appellant(s))*, the within-named appellant(s),and [*if different date, insert the words:* on *(date)*] [(Messrs) *(name)* of *(address)* (agents for)] *(name(s) of respondent(s))*, the within-named respondent(s),with a correct copy of the petition for leave to intervene and with notice that the petition would be presented to the House of Lords on behalf of the petitioner(s) as soon as conveniently may be.	IN THE HOUSE OF LORDS ON APPEAL FROM *(name court)* BETWEEN: *(set out title of cause)* _____ PETITION FOR LEAVE TO INTERVENE _____
(signature of petitioner(s) or their agents)	*(set out full name, address, telephone number, and reference (if any) of petitioner(s) or their agents)*

4A–160

FORM 10

PETITION for restoration of appeal when time for lodging Statement has expired

(HL direction 13)

IN THE HOUSE OF LORDS

ON APPEAL FROM HER MAJESTY'S COURT OF APPEAL (ENGLAND)

BETWEEN: AB (Appellant(s))

and

CD (Respondent(s))

TO THE RIGHT HONOURABLE THE HOUSE OF LORDS

THE HUMBLE PETITION OF AB SHOWS –

That your petitioner(s) presented a Petition of Appeal on *(date)* complaining of an Order of the [Court of Appeal *or relevant court*] dated *(date)*.

That the time allowed by Standing Order VI for the appellant(s) to lodge the Statement of facts and issues and the Appendix and to set down the cause for hearing expired on the *(date)*.

That your petitioner(s) has/have been unable to lodge their Statement and the Appendix by the said date for the following reasons:

(set out reasons).

YOUR PETITIONER(S) THEREFORE HUMBLY PRAY(S) that your Lordships will be pleased to order that their appeal be restored and to grant them an extension of time until *(date)* to lodge the Statement and the Appendix and to set down the cause for hearing.

And your petitioner(s) will ever pray.

> *(signature of appellant(s) or their agents)*
>
> [Agents for the] Appellant(s) *(set out here name and address of appellant(s) or their agents)*

[I *or* We] consent to the prayer of the above petition.

> *(signature of respondent(s) or their agents)*
> [Agents for the] respondent(s) *(set out here name and address of respondent(s) or their agents)*

FORM 11

4A–161

RESPONDENTS' CONSENT to incidental petition

(HL direction 13.6)

(The consent is endorsed on the petition)

We consent to the prayer of the above petition.

(signature)

Respondent(s)/Agents for the respondent(s)

FORM 12

4A–162

CONSENT to waiver of security for costs

(HL direction 10.3)

(Letter to be sent by respondent(s) or their agent(s) to the Judicial Office)

(date)

Dear Sirs,

AB v CD

[I or We], [as agents for] the Respondent(s) in the above appeal, consent to the appellant(s) being allowed to prosecute the appeal without giving the security for costs required by Standing Order V(1) regulating judicial business.

(signature)

Respondent(s)/Agents for
the respondent(s)

FORM 13

APPLICATION to set down cause for hearing

(HL direction 14)

IN THE HOUSE OF LORDS

ON APPEAL FROM HER MAJESTY'S COURT OF APPEAL (ENGLAND) (*or relevant court*)

BETWEEN: AB   Appellant(s)

and

CD   Respondent(s)

The appellant(s) having lodged a Statement of facts and issues and the Appendix thereto pursuant to order of the House,

My Lords,

Please to move, That this cause be set down for hearing after those causes already appointed.

(signature of appellant(s) or their agents)

Appellant/Agents for the appellant

(set out name and address of appellant(s) or their agent)

FORM 14

4A–164

FORM OF COVER for Bound Volume *(on blue card)*

IN THE HOUSE OF LORDS

ON APPEAL FROM HER MAJESTY'S COURT OF APPEAL (ENGLAND) *(or relevant court)*

BETWEEN:

(set out title of appeal)

Sticker on spine:

[Set out short title of cause]

BV

1

BOUND VOLUME

1

(The bound volume is only numbered if there is more than one volume)

PETITION OF APPEAL

[PETITION OF CROSS-APPEAL]

STATEMENT OF FACTS AND ISSUES

CASE FOR THE APPELLANTS

CASE FOR THE RESPONDENTS

APPENDIX - PART 1

LIST OF AUTHORITIES

(The above list is amended as appropriate)

(Name and address of agents for appellant(s))

(Name and address of agents for respondent(s))

FORM 15

FORM OF COVER for authorities' volume *(on green card)*

IN THE HOUSE OF LORDS

ON APPEAL FROM HER MAJESTY'S COURT OF APPEAL (ENGLAND) *(or relevant court))*

BETWEEN:

(set out title of appeal)

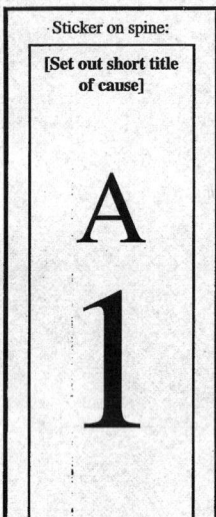

Sticker on spine:

[Set out short title of cause]

AUTHORITIES' VOLUME

(The authorities' volume is only numbered if there is more than one volume)

(Name and address of agents for appellant(s))   *(Name and address of agents for respondent(s))*

FORM 16

PETITION for withdrawal of appeal

(HL direction 45.2 - 45.3)

IN THE HOUSE OF LORDS

ON APPEAL FROM HER MAJESTY'S COURT OF APPEAL (ENGLAND)

BETWEEN: AB Appellant(s)

       and

      CD Respondent(s)

TO THE RIGHT HONOURABLE THE HOUSE OF LORDS

THE HUMBLE PETITION OF the Appellant(s) shows –

That your petitioner(s) presented a Petition of Appeal on *(date)* complaining of an Order of the Court of Appeal *(or relevant court)* dated *(date)*.

That as security for the costs of their appeal your petitioner(s) paid [£25,000] into the Security Fund Account.

That your petitioner'(s)(s') appeal was set down for hearing before your Lordships' House on *(date)*.

That your petitioner(s) and the respondent(s) have agreed to terms of settlement of all matters in dispute between them, as follows:

1. That your petitioner(s) and the respondent(s) should join in making an application to your Lordships' House for leave that your petitioner'(s)(s') appeal might be withdrawn; and

2. That *(set out terms of agreement)*.

YOUR PETITIONER(S) THEREFORE HUMBLY PRAY(S) that your Lordships will be pleased to order that:

(1) your petitioner'(s)(s') appeal be withdrawn;

(2) *(state costs order sought, to dispose of appeal)*

And your petitioner(s) will ever pray.

(signature)

Agents for the appellant(s)

Appendix B

List of Authorities Kept in House of Lords Library

(see direction 17.5)

The House of Lords Library keeps the following authorities:

All England Reports
Anglo American Law Review
British Yearbook of International Law
Cambrian Law Review
Cambridge Law Journal
Canadian Rights Reporter
Common Market Law Reports
Common Market Law Review
Cox's Criminal Law Cases (1843–49)
Criminal Appeal Reports
Criminal Appeal Reports (Sentencing)
Criminal Law Forum
Criminal Law Review
Crown Office Digest
English Reports
Estates Gazette Law Reports (1985—)
European Court Reports
European Human Rights Reports
European Law Digest
European Law Review
European Public Law
Family Law Reports
Financial Law Reports
Fleet Street Reports
Halsbury's Laws and Statutes
Housing Law Reports
Human Rights Law Journal
Immigration Appeal Reports
Industrial Cases Reports
Industrial Law Journal
Industrial Relations Law Reports
Industrial Tribunal Reports (1971–78)
International and Comparative Law Quarterly
International Litigation Procedure
Irish Jurist (1848–1866, 1935–1965)
Irish Jurist Reports
Irish Law Reports
Journal of Legal History
Journal of Legislative Studies
Journal of Planning and Environment Law
Journal of Social Welfare Law
Jurist—Reports of Cases in Law and Equity (1837–1866)
Justice of the Peace Reports
Law Journal Reports
Law Quarterly Review
Law Reports (1866—)
Law Times Reports
Legislative Studies Quarterly
Lloyd's Law Reports
Local Government Review Reports
Modern Law Review
New Law Journal
Northern Ireland Law Reports
Northern Ireland Legal Quarterly (Vol 34 (1983)—)
Northern Ireland Statutes
Oxford Journal of Legal Studies
Planning and Compensation Reports (1963–67)

Property and Compensation Reports (1968—)
Public Law (British Journal of Administrative Law)
Reports of Patent Cases
Road Traffic Reports
Rydes Rating Cases (1956–1979)
Scots Law Times
Scottish Civil Law Reports
Scottish Criminal Case Reports (1983—)
Scottish Jurist (1829–1873)
Scottish Law Reporter (1865–1924)
Scottish Planning Law and Practice
Session Cases
Simons Tax Cases (1981—)
Solicitors Journal
Statute Law Review
Statutes
Tax Cases
Times Law Reports
Weekly Law Reports
Weekly Notes (1866–1952)
Weekly Reporter (1852–1906)

Appendix C

Fees and Security Money

JUDICIAL FEES

4A–168

The following fees are payable at the time of lodgment or collection of documents:

Petitions for leave to appeal—mandatory fees

Presentation	£570
Entering appearance	£115

Petitions of appeal—mandatory fees

Presentation (following successful petition for leave to appeal)	£570
Presentation (not following petition for leave)	£1,140
Entering appearance	£230
Lodging Statement and Appendix and setting down	£3,420

Petitions of appeal—occasional fees

Waiver of security	£115
First petition for extension of time	£230
Second petition for extension	£340
Third petition for extension	£570
Fourth or subsequent petition for extension	£1,000
Petition for leave to intervene	£570
Other interlocutory petition, if agreed	£230
Any interlocutory petition, if opposed	£570
Appeal Committee Order or other certified document (except Judgment Order, for which there is no fee)	£12

In respect of a joint petition, only one fee is payable. Fees for presenting petitions in respect of a cross-appeal are the same as fees for petitions in respect of an appeal.

(27th July 2000 [1])

Drafts and cheques for judicial fees are payable to 'House of Lords Account'.

TAXING FEES

The fees payable upon the sums allowed by the Taxing Officer are as follows:

    (a) where the amount allowed does not exceed £500, a flat rate of £50;

    (b) where the amount allowed exceeds £500, for every £1 or fraction of £1, an amount of 5p.

The fees payable on the withdrawal of a bill of costs (subject to written confirmation of the withdrawal from both parties to the taxation) are as follows:

    (a) in respect of bills withdrawn within 21 days of the date appointed for taxation, 1 per cent. of the agreed sum or £50, whichever is the larger;

    (b) in respect of bills withdrawn within 7 days of the date appointed for taxation, 2 per cent. of the agreed sum or £50, whichever is the larger.

(27th July 2000 [2])

Drafts and cheques for taxing fees are payable to 'House of Lords Account'.

SECURITY MONEY

Security for costs, to be paid by the appellant(s)   £25,000

(27th July 2000 [3])

Drafts and cheques for security money are payable to
'House of Lords Security Fund Account'.

---

[1] House of Lords Offices Committee, 6th Report (1999–2000), HL Paper 97.
[2] Ibid.
[3] Ibid.

4B   CRIMINAL APPEALS

Practice Directions Applicable to Criminal Appeals

(with effect From 23 January 2006)

Part I: Directions on Petitions for Leave to Appeal

1.

LEAVE TO APPEAL

Introduction

1.1 The judicial procedures of the House of Lords are regulated by statute, by **4B–1** standing orders of the House and by practice directions[1]. Copies of these and other documents may be obtained free of charge from the Judicial Office of the House of Lords or downloaded from the Internet.

Terminology

1.2 The Appellate Jurisdiction Act 1876 is the basic Act governing the judicial **4B–2** function of the House of Lords. This booklet uses the terminology of that Act. The term "leave to appeal" means permission to appeal. A "petition for leave to appeal" is an application for permission to appeal.

Right of appeal

1.3 The right of appeal to the House of Lords is regulated by statute and subject to **4B–3** statutory restrictions. The relevant statutes for criminal appeals are: the Administration of Justice Act 1960; the Criminal Appeal Act 1968; the Courts-Martial (Appeals) Act 1968; the Administration of Justice Act 1969; the Judicature (Northern Ireland) Act 1978; the Criminal Appeal (Northern Ireland) Act 1980; the Extradition Act 2003; the Criminal Justice Act 2003; the Serious Organised Crime and Police Act 2005. Every applicant for leave to appeal must comply with the statutory requirements before the application can be considered by the House. The Human Rights Act 1998 applies to the House in its judicial capacity. But that Act does not confer any general right of appeal to the House, or any right of appeal in addition to or superseding any right of appeal provided for in Acts passed before the coming into force of the Human Rights Act 1998.

Stay of execution

1.4 See direction 39.   **4B–4**

England and Wales and Northern Ireland

1.5 An appeal to the House of Lords may only be brought with the leave of the court **4B–5** below or, if refused by that court, with the leave of the House of Lords. Subject to directions 2.2–2.4, in criminal matters such leave may not be granted unless the court below has issued the certificate referred to in direction 2.1.

1.6 Subject to directions 1.5 and 2, an application for leave to appeal to the House of Lords in a criminal matter may be made by either the defendant or the prosecutor, as follows:

---

[1] The orders are made pursuant to the Appellate Jurisdiction Act 1876, s.11.

(a) from any decision of the Court of Appeal Criminal Division in England and Wales on an appeal to that court[1];

(b) from any decision of the Courts-Martial Appeal Court on an appeal to that court[2];

(c) from any decision of the Court of Appeal in Northern Ireland on an appeal to that court by a person convicted on indictment[3];

(d) from any decision of the Court of Appeal in Northern Ireland in a criminal cause or matter on a case stated by a county court or magistrates' court[4];

(e) from any decision of the High Court of Justice in England and Wales in a criminal cause or matter[5];

(f) from any decision of the High Court of Justice in Northern Ireland in a criminal cause or matter[6].

Scotland

4B-6 1.7 No appeal lies to the House of Lords from the High Court of Justiciary in Scotland.

Criminal contempt of court

4B-7 1.8 In cases involving criminal contempt of court, an appeal lies to the House of Lords at the instance of the defendant only and, in respect of an application for committal or attachment, at the instance of the applicant from any decision of the Court of Appeal Criminal Division, the Courts-Martial Appeal Court or the High Court[7].

2.

CERTIFICATE OF POINT OF LAW

4B-8 2.1 Subject to directions 2.2–2.4, leave to appeal to the House of Lords in a criminal matter may only be granted if it is certified by the court below that a point of law of general public importance is involved in the decision of that court, and it appears to that court or to the House that the point is one that ought to be considered by the House [8]. A petition for leave to appeal without the required certificate may not be lodged (direction 4.8), except as provided by directions 2.2–2.4.

2.2 A certificate is not required for an appeal from a decision of the High Court in England and Wales or of the High Court in Northern Ireland on a criminal application for habeas corpus[9].

2.3 A certificate is not required for an appeal by a minister of the Crown or a person nominated by him, a member of the Scottish Executive, a Northern Ireland minister

---

[1] Criminal Appeal Act 1968, s.33(1) (as amended); Criminal Justice Act 2003, Part 9.

[2] Courts-Martial (Appeals) Act 1968, s.39(1).

[3] Judicature (Northern Ireland) Act 1978, s.40(1)(b); Criminal Appeal (Northern Ireland) Act 1980, s.31(1) (as amended). The practice directions are available on www.parliament.uk.

[4] Judicature (Northern Ireland) Act 1978, s.41(1)(b).

[5] Administration of Justice Act 1960 s 1(1)(a) (as amended); Extradition Act 2003, ss.32, 114.

[6] Judicature (Northern Ireland) Act 1978, s.41(1)(a); Extradition Act 2003, ss.32, 114.

[7] Administration of Justice Act 1960, s.13; Judicature (Northern Ireland) Act 1978, s.44. Appeals under either section in cases involving civil contempt of court are subject to the *Practice Directions applicable to Civil Appeals* (January 2006 ed).

[8] Criminal Appeal Act 1968, s.33(2); Administration of Justice Act 1960, s.1(2); Extradition Act 2003, ss.32(4), 114(4); Courts-Martial (Appeals) Act 1968, s.39(2); Judicature (Northern Ireland) Act 1978, s.41(2); Criminal Appeal (Northern Ireland) Act 1980, s.31(2); Extradition Act 2003, ss.32, 114; Proceeds of Crime Act (Appeals under Part 4) Order 2003, S.I. 2003 No. 458.

[9] Administration of Justice Act 1960, s.15(3) (as amended); Judicature (Northern Ireland) Act 1978, s.45(3).

or a Northern Ireland department when they have been joined as a party to any criminal proceedings other than in Scotland by a notice given under the Human Rights Act 1998 ss 5(1) and 5(2) and wish to appeal under s 5(4) of that Act against any declaration of incompatibility made in those proceedings.

2.4 A certificate is not required in contempt of court cases where the decision of the court below was not a decision on appeal[1].

3.

TIME LIMITS

Time within which to apply for leave to appeal

3.1 Application for leave to appeal to the House of Lords must first be made to the court below. If the court below refuses leave to appeal, application must then be made to the House of Lords.

4B–9

3.2 Application to the House of Lords for leave to appeal is made by petition (direction 4). An application for leave to appeal to the House of Lords (a) from a decision of the Court of Appeal under s 33(1) of the Criminal Appeal Act 1968 or (b) from a decision of a Divisional Court of the Queen's Bench Division in a criminal cause or matter under s 1(1)(a) of the Administration of Justice Act 1960 must be made within 28 days beginning with the date on which the application for such leave was refused by the court below (and not the following day). This date is not necessarily that on which the point of law was certified. Where the time prescribed expires on a Saturday, Sunday, bank holiday or other day on which the Judicial Office is closed, the application is accepted as being in time if it is received on the next day on which the Judicial Office is open.

3.3 An application for leave to appeal must be made within 14 days if made under one of the following provisions: ss 32(5), 114(5) of the Extradition Act 2003; ss 33, 44 and 66 of the Proceeds of Crime Act 2002[2]; and, ss 183, 193 and 214 of the Proceeds of Crime Act 2002.[3] A 14 day time limit also applies to an application to refer a case pursuant to the Attorney General's Reference procedure under s 36(5) of the Criminal Justice Act 1988.[4]

Application for extension of time to lodge petition for leave

3.4 Subject to direction 3.5, the House of Lords or the court below may, on application made at any time by the defendant and in certain limited circumstances the prosecutor[5], extend the time within which application for leave to appeal to the House may be made to the House or to that court[6]. Such an application to the House is incorporated in the petition for leave itself, and should set out briefly the reason(s) why the petition is being presented outside the statutory period. The reason(s) should not normally exceed a paragraph in length.[7]

4B–10

---

[1] Administration of Justice Act 1960, s.13(4); Judicature (Northern Ireland) Act 1978, s.44(4).

[2] Proceeds of Crime Act 2002 (appeals under Part 2) Order 2003 (S.I. 2003 No. 82), Part 3, Article 12.

[3] Proceeds of Crime Act 2002 (appeals under Part 4) Order 2003 (S.I. 2003 No. 483), Part 3, Article 11.

[4] Criminal Justice Act 1988, Sch 3, para 4.

[5] Criminal Appeal Act 1968, ss.33(1B), 34(2); see also Appeal Committee 13th Report (2000-01): Regina v. Weir (Respondent) (HL Paper 28).

[6] Criminal Appeal Act 1968, s.34(2); Administration of Justice Act 1960, s.2(3); Courts-Martial (Appeals) Act 1968, s.40(2); Criminal Appeal (Northern Ireland) Act 1980, s.32(2); Judicature (Northern Ireland) Act 1978, Sched. 1, para. 1(2). Section 1A of the Geneva Conventions Act 1957 makes, in relation to protected prisoners, certain extensions to the time limits in the Administration of Justice Act 1960, the Criminal Appeal Act 1968, the Courts-Martial (Appeals) Act 1968 and the Criminal Appeal (Northern Ireland) Act 1968.

[7] For form of petition, see Appendix A, Form 3.

3.5 No extension may be granted in respect of application made under ss 32 and 114 of the Extradition Act 2003.

Public funding and legal aid

4B–11   3.6 See direction 37.

4.

LODGMENT OF PETITION

Form of petition

4B–12   4.1 A petition for leave to appeal should be produced on durable quality A4 paper, securely bound on the left, using both sides of the paper. The petition should set out briefly the facts and points of law; and conclude with a summary of the reasons why leave should be granted[1]. Petitions which are not legible or which are not produced in the required form are not accepted. A petition should not contain annexes or appendices. Parties may consult the Judicial Office at any stage of preparation of the petition, and may submit petitions in draft for approval.

4.2 In petitions where a prosecuting authority is petitioner, the prosecuting authority should be described in the preamble to the petition as follows: "Director of Public Prosecutions (*or other prosecuting authority*) (on behalf of Her Majesty)".

4.3 Supporting documents other than those set out in direction 5.2 are not normally accepted.

4.4 Amendments to petitions and the lodging of supplementary petitions are allowed only in exceptional circumstances. The Head of the Judicial Office may allow amendments to petitions and the lodging of supplementary petitions if he is satisfied that this will assist the Appeal Committee and will not unfairly prejudice the respondents or cause undue delay. Any such amendments and supplementary petitions must be served on the respondents (direction 4.14).

4.5 If a petition for leave to appeal:
    (a) asks the House to depart from one of its own decisions;
    (b) raises issues relating to the Human Rights Act 1998 ; or
    (c) seeks a reference to the Court of Justice of the European Communities,

this point should be stated clearly in the petition.

4.6 A petition for leave to appeal must be signed by the petitioners or their agents

4.7 On the back of the petition for leave, underneath the certificate of service, there should be inserted the neutral citation of the judgment petitioned against, the references of any law report in the courts below, and subject matter catchwords for indexing (whether or not the case has been reported).

4.8 Subject to directions 2.2–2.4, the Judicial Office cannot accept for lodgment any petition for leave to appeal that is not accompanied by the certificate from the court below required by statute, certifying a point of law of general public importance (see direction 2)[2].

Case title

4B–13   4.9 Petitions for leave to appeal to the House of Lords carry the same title as in the court below, except that the parties are described as petitioner(s) and respondent(s). For reference purposes, the names of parties to the original action who are not parties to the appeal should nevertheless be included in the title: their names should

---

[1] For style see Appendix A, Forms 1, 2.
[2] See speech of Viscount Simonds in *Gelberg v. Miller* [1961] 1 All E.R. 618.

be enclosed in square brackets. The names of all parties should be given in the same sequence as in the title used in the court below.

4.10 Petitions in which trustees, executors etc. are parties are titled in the short form, for example *Trustees of John Black's Charity (Respondents) v. White (Petitioner)*.

4.11 In any petition concerning minors or where in the court below the title used has been such as to conceal the identity of one or more parties to the action, this fact should be clearly drawn to the attention of the Judicial Office at the time the petition is lodged, so that the title adopted in the House of Lords can take account of the need for anonymity. Petitions involving minors are normally given a title in the form *In re B* (see also direction 10.9).

4.12 In case titles involving the Crown, the abbreviation "R" meaning "Regina" is used. "R" is always given first. So case titles using this abbreviation take the form *R v Jones (Petitioner)* or *R v Jones (Respondent)* (as the case may be) or *R (on the application of Jones) (Petitioner) v Secretary of State for the Home Department (Respondent)*.

4.13 Apart from the above, Latin is not used in case titles.

Service

4.14 A copy of the petition must be served on the respondents or their agents, either by delivery in person or by first class post, before it is lodged in the Judicial Office. A certificate of such service (noting the full name and address of the respondents or their agents) must be endorsed on the back of the original petition and signed[1]. In habeas corpus appeals and/or in appeals concerning extradition, the petition must be served on the government that is seeking extradition or on the Director of Public Prosecutions if he is acting for that government.

4B–14

Lodgment

4.15 Two top copies of the original petition must be lodged in the Judicial Office, together with a copy of the order appealed from and, if separate, a copy of the order of the court below refusing leave to appeal. If the substantive order appealed against is not immediately available, the petition should nevertheless be lodged within the required time limits, and the order lodged as soon as possible thereafter.

4B–15

4.16 An agent who attends the Judicial Office to lodge a petition for leave to appeal and/or accompanying papers must be familiar with the subject matter of the petition.

Appearance for respondents

4.17 Respondents or their agents enter appearance to a petition for leave to appeal as soon as they have received service. The respondents or their agents enter appearance by attending at the Judicial Office to enter their name and address or that of their firm, or by letter to the Judicial Office.

4B–16

4.18 Respondents who do not intend to take part in the proceedings do not need to enter appearance, but the Judicial Office sends communications concerning a petition for leave to appeal only to those who have entered appearance.

4.19 An order for costs will not be made in favour of a respondent who has not entered appearance.

Communications by fax/e-mail

4.20 See direction 26.2.

4B–17

5.

APPEAL COMMITTEE

5.1 Petitions for leave to appeal to the House of Lords are considered by an Appeal

4B–18

---

[1] For style see Appendix A, Form 2.

Committee consisting of three Lords of Appeal. Petitions are generally decided on the papers alone, without a hearing.

Additional papers

4B–19 5.2 The following additional papers for use by the Appeal Committee must be lodged within one week of lodgment of the petition:

(a) four copies of the petition;

(b) four copies of the order appealed from;

(c) if separate, four copies of the order of the court below refusing leave to appeal to the House of Lords;

(d) five copies of the official transcript of the judgment of the court below[1];

(e) five copies of the order of the court of first instance;

(f) five copies of the official transcript of the judgment of the court of first instance[2];

(g) five copies of any unreported judgment cited in the petition or judgment of a court below;

(h) the form sent by the Judicial Office to the petitioner(s) asking for details of the history of the action.

No other papers are required, and documents other than those listed above are not normally received.

5.3 Papers lodged in accordance with direction 5.2 above should be lodged as individual documents, double-sided, not bound together or inserted into ring binders. Documents which are not clearly legible or which are not in the required style or form (see direction 4.1) are not accepted.

5.4 Where the required papers are not lodged within three months of presentation of the petition and no good reason is given, the petition may at the direction of the Head of the Judicial Office be referred to an Appeal Committee without the required accompanying papers.

Consideration on the papers

4B–20 5.5 The Appeal Committee decides first whether a petition for leave to appeal is admissible. The rules on admissibility are set out in directions 1 and 2. If the Appeal Committee determines that a petition is inadmissible, it may refuse leave on that ground alone and not consider the content of the petition. The Appeal Committee gives a reason for its decision that the petition is inadmissible.

5.6 If the Appeal Committee decides that a petition is admissible, the Committee may then:

(a) refuse leave (see direction 5.8);

(b) give leave outright (see direction 5.9);

(c) invite the respondents to lodge objections to the petition (see direction 5.10);

(d) give leave on terms (see direction 5.15);

(e) refer the petition for an oral hearing (see direction 5.16).

5.7 Leave to appeal is granted to petitions that raise an arguable point of law of general public importance which ought to be considered by the House at this time, bearing in mind that the matter will already have been the subject of judicial decision and reviewed on appeal. A petition which in the opinion of the Appeal Committee does not raise such a point of law is refused on that ground. The Appeal Committee

---

[1] If the judgment has been published in a report which is ordinarily received in court, copies of the report may be lodged in lieu of transcripts. Transcripts of judgments marked "in draft" are not accepted without certification by the relevant court that the copy is the final version of the judgment.

[2] Or, in the case of a County Court, of the Judge's Notes.

gives brief reasons for refusing leave to appeal[1] but does not otherwise explain its decisions[2].

Leave refused

5.8 If the Appeal Committee is unanimous that a petition should be refused, the parties are notified that the petition is dismissed. **4B–21**

Leave given outright

5.9 If the Appeal Committee is unanimous that a petition should be allowed without further proceedings, the House grants leave outright (without inviting respondents' objections). **4B–22**

Respondents' objections

5.10 There is no requirement for respondents to submit written objections giving their reasons why leave to appeal should be refused. But respondents may submit written objections if they wish to do so. This must be done (a) within 14 days of the date of service on them of the petition for leave to appeal; or (b) within 14 days of any invitation by the Appeal Committee to do so; or (c) within 14 days of a petition for leave to appeal being referred for an oral hearing. **4B–23**

5.11 Respondents' objections set out briefly the reasons why the petition should be refused or make submissions as to the terms upon which leave should be granted (for example, on costs). One master plus six copies of the respondents' written objections must be lodged at the Judicial Office. The objections must be produced on durable quality A4 paper, securely fastened, using both sides of the paper.

5.12 A copy of the respondents' objections should be sent to the agents for the other parties. In certain circumstances the Appeal Committee may invite further submissions from the petitioners in the light of the respondents' objections, but petitioners do not have a right to comment on respondents' objections. Where the Appeal Committee does not require further submissions, and provided the Committee is unanimous in its decision to grant or refuse leave, it reports its decision to the House and the parties are informed. Where the Appeal Committee proposes terms for granting leave, direction 5.15 applies.

5.13 Respondents' objections are subject to any order for costs made by the Appeal Committee or, if leave to appeal is granted, become costs in the appeal (see direction 6).

5.14 Parties unable to meet the deadlines set out in direction 5.10 must write to the Head of the Judicial Office requesting an extension of time for lodging their written objections.

Leave given on terms

5.15 If the Appeal Committee decides that leave to appeal should be given on terms, the Committee proposes the terms. The parties have the right to make submissions on the proposed terms within 14 days. **4B–24**

Petition referred for oral hearing

5.16 In all cases where the members of the Appeal Committee are not unanimous, or where further argument is required, a petition for leave to appeal is referred for an oral hearing. **4B–25**

5.17 If the respondents have not already been invited to lodge objections, they

---

[1] See also directions 33.2–33.3 for practice where a point of European Community law is raised on a petition for leave to appeal.

[2] See Appeal Committee 38th Report (2002–03): *Petitions for leave to appeal: reasons for the refusal of leave* (HL Paper 89).

should do so as soon as possible after being informed that the petition has been referred for a hearing (direction 5.10(c)).

5.18 When a petition is referred for an oral hearing, the petitioners and all respondents who have entered appearance are notified of the date of the hearing before the Appeal Committee.

5.19 Parties may be heard before the Appeal Committee by counsel, by agent, or in person, but one only may be heard on each side.

5.20 If counsel is briefed, agents should ensure that the Judicial Office is notified of their name. Only a junior counsel's fee is allowed on taxation (assessment of costs).

5.21 Authorities are not normally cited before the Appeal Committee or provided for the Committee's use at the hearing.

Lodgment of petition of appeal

4B–26 5.22 If leave to appeal is given, the petition of appeal (direction 10) must be lodged within two weeks of the date of the Appeal Committee's decision. Failure to meet this deadline results in the petition of appeal being lodged out of time and referred to an Appeal Committee pursuant to direction 8.4.

Order of the House

4B–27 5.23 Copies of the Minutes of Proceedings of the House recording the report of the Appeal Committee and the order of the House are sent to all parties who have entered appearance.

5.24 A formal order of the Appeal Committee is not normally issued but will be issued on written request and on payment of a fee. A formal order is not required for taxation of costs arising from the application for leave to appeal.

Expedition

4B–28 5.25 Once the required papers are lodged in the Judicial Office (direction 5.2), the procedure described above is normally completed within eight sitting weeks (excluding any oral hearing). However, in cases involving liberty of the subject, urgent medical intervention or the well-being of children, application for expedition may be made in writing to the Judicial Office.

6.

COSTS

4B–29 6.1 Where a petition for leave to appeal is determined without an oral hearing, costs may be awarded as follows:

  (a) to a publicly funded or legally aided petitioner, reasonable costs incurred in preparing papers for the Appeal Committee[1];
  (b) to a publicly funded or legally aided respondent, only those costs necessarily incurred in attending the client, attending the petitioner's agents, perusing the petition, entering appearance and, where applicable, preparing respondent's objections to the petition[2];
  (c) to an unassisted respondent where the petitioner is publicly funded or legally aided, payment out of the Community Legal Service Fund (pursuant to s 11 of the Access to Justice Act 1999[3])[4] of costs as specified at (b) above;
  (d) to a petitioner or respondent, payment out of central funds, pursuant to s 16

---

[1] See *Practice directions applicable to judicial taxations in the House of Lords and forms of bills of costs*, available on request from the Judicial Office and on the Internet at www.parliament.uk.
[2] *ibid*.
[3] Also pursuant to r. 5(2) Community Legal Service (Cost Protection) Regulations

or s 17 of the Prosecution of Offences Act 1985 , of costs incurred at (a) or (b) above, as the case may be;

(e) to a respondent where neither party is publicly funded or legally aided, costs as specified at (b) above to be paid by the petitioner[1].

Where costs are sought under (c), (d) or (e) above, the application may be made by letter addressed to the Judicial Office or may be included in a bill of costs lodged in the Judicial Office conditional upon the application being granted.

6.2 Where a petition for leave to appeal is referred for an oral hearing and is dismissed, application for costs must be made by the respondent at the end of the hearing. No order for costs will be made unless requested at that time.

6.3 Where a petition for leave to appeal is allowed, the costs of the petition will be costs in the ensuing appeal.

6.4 Bills of costs for taxation must be lodged within three months from the date of the decision of the Appeal Committee or the date on which a petition for leave is withdrawn in accordance with direction 42.1. If an extension of the three months period is desired, application must be made in writing to the Taxing Officer and copies of all such correspondence sent to all interested parties. In deciding whether to grant an application for an extension of time made after the expiry of the three month period the Taxing Officer takes into account the circumstances set out in the practice directions applicable to judicial taxations.

6.5 The practice directions relating to judicial taxations and forms of bills of costs are available on request from the Judicial Office and on the internet at www.parliament.uk. Fees are payable on taxation of a bill of costs.

7.

FEES

7.1 No fee is payable at any stage of a petition for leave to appeal in a criminal matter, except when a formal order of the House is requested[2]. Fees are payable on the taxation of a bill of costs.

4B–30

Part II Directions Applying in all Appeals

8.

TIME LIMITS

8.1 Save for appeals under the Extradition Act 2003 (direction 8.3), a petition of appeal must be lodged in the Judicial Office within three months of the date on which the order appealed from was made[3]. The order appealed from is the substantive order complained of.

4B–31

8.2 However, this time limit may be varied (but not increased) by an order of the House when granting leave or by an order of the court below. The order appealed against is the substantive order complained of.

2000 and in accordance with the procedural requirements of rr. 9, 10 Community Legal Service (Costs) Regulations 2000 as amended.

[4] Or s 18 Legal Aid Act 1988; or, in Scotland, pursuant to s 19 Legal Aid (Scotland) Act 1986 or, in Northern Ireland, pursuant to Article 16 Legal Aid Advice and Assistance (N.I.) Order 1981.

[1] See *Practice directions applicable to judicial taxations in the House of Lords and forms of bills of costs*, available on request from the Judicial Office and on the Internet at www.parliament.uk.

[2] See direction 5.24.

[3] Standing Order I. The court below may reduce but may not extend the three month period. For extensions of time in publicly funded/legal aid cases, see direction 37.

8.3 Appeals under the Extradition Act 2003 must be lodged within 28 days of the grant of leave, starting with the day on which leave is granted. The time for doing so may not be extended[1].

Out of time appeals

4B–32 8.4 Where a petition of appeal is not lodged within the time allowed, a petition for leave to present the appeal out of time may be lodged[2]. This petition is referred to an Appeal Committee.

Fees

4B–33 8.5 No fee is payable at any stage of a criminal appeal, except taxation (assessment of costs).

9.

LONDON AGENTS

4B–34 9.1 Solicitors outside London may appoint London agents. Those who decide not to do so should note that any additional costs incurred as a result of that decision may be disallowed on taxation (assessment of costs).

10.

LODGMENT OF APPEAL

Form of petition of appeal

4B–35 10.1 Petitions of appeal must be produced on durable quality A4 paper, bound on the left like a book, using both sides of the paper[3].

10.2 Where leave to appeal has been obtained from the court below or from the House, it is enough for the petition of appeal to be signed by the appellants or their agents.

10.3 On the back page of the petition, below the certificate of service, there should be inserted the neutral citation of the judgment appealed against, the references of any law report of the case in the courts below and subject matter catchwords for indexing (whether or not the case has been reported).

Case title

4B–36 10.4 Petitions of appeal to the House of Lords carry the same title as in the court below, except that the parties are described as appellant(s) and respondent(s). For reference purposes, the names of parties to the original action who are not parties to the appeal should nevertheless be included in the title: their names should be enclosed in square brackets. The names of all parties should be given in the same sequence as in the title used in the court below.

10.5 Petitions in which trustees, executors, etc. are parties are titled in the short form, for example *Trustees of John Black's Charity (Respondents) v. White (Appellant)*.

10.6 In any petition concerning minors or where in the court below the title used has been such as to conceal the identity of one or more parties to the action, this fact should be clearly drawn to the attention of the Judicial Office at the time the petition is lodged, so that the title adopted in the House of Lords can take account of the need for anonymity. Petitions involving minors are normally given a title in the form *In re B* .

---

[1] Extradition Act 2003 ss 32, 114.
[2] Adapt Appendix A, Form 4 using Form 3 as a model
[3] See Appendix A, Form 4 for style of petition and direction 24 for preparation of documents

10.7 In case titles involving the Crown, the abbreviation "R" meaning "Regina" is used. "R" is always given first. Case titles using this abbreviation take the form *R v Jones (Appellant)* or *R v Jones (Respondent)* (as the case may be) or *R (on the application of Jones) (Appellant) v Secretary of State for the Home Department (Respondent)*.

10.8 Apart from the above, Latin is not used in case titles.

Anonymity and reporting restrictions

10.9 In any appeal concerning children the parties should, in addition to considering the case title to be used, also consider whether it would be appropriate for the House to make an order under s 39 of the Children and Young Persons Act 1933. The parties should always inform the Judicial Office if such an order has been made by a court below. A request for such an order to be made by the House should be made in writing, preferably on behalf of all parties to the appeal, as soon as possible after the appeal has been presented and not later than 14 days before the start of the hearing.

4B–37

10.10 Direction 10.9 also applies to a request for an order under s 4 of the Contempt of Court Act 1981 .

Human Rights Act 1998

10.11 Appellants must notify the Judicial Office in writing when:

4B–38

   (a) the House is to be asked to consider whether to make, uphold or reverse a declaration that a provision of primary or subordinate legislation is incompatible with a European Human Rights Convention right[1], or is to be asked to consider any issue which may lead the House to make such a declaration, or where such an issue is or may be raised in respect of a judicial act;
   (b) a party seeks to challenge an act of a public authority under the Human Rights Act 1998; or
   (c) a party relies in whole or in part on the provisions of the Human Rights Act 1998.

Appellants should indicate whether notification is made under (a), (b) or (c) above (see direction 31.1). They should set out briefly the arguments involved; and state whether the point was taken in the courts below. In appeals in which (a) above is an issue, the Crown has a right to be joined as a party to the appeal (direction 31.2).

Service

10.12 A copy of the petition of appeal must be served on the respondents or their agents, either by delivery in person or by first class post, before lodgment in the Judicial Office. A certificate of such service noting the full name and address of the respondents or their agents must be endorsed on the back of the original petition and signed by the appellants or their agents[2].

4B–39

Lodgment

10.13 The original petition of appeal together with seven copies must be lodged at the Judicial Office. If leave to appeal was granted by the court below, a copy of the order appealed from must also be lodged and, if separate, a copy of the order granting leave to appeal to the House of Lords. If the order is not immediately available, the petition should be lodged in time and the order lodged as soon as possible thereafter.

4B–40

10.14 Once the petition of appeal has been lodged, it is presented to the House and recorded in the Minutes of Proceedings of the House. A copy of the Minutes is sent to all parties who have entered appearance (direction 10.15).

---

[1] Human Rights Act 1998, which gives further effect in domestic law to much of the Convention for the Protection of Human Rights and Fundamental Freedoms agreed by the Council of Europe at Rome on 4 November 1950.
[2] For style see Appendix A, Form 5.

HL CRIMINAL

Appearance for respondents

4B–41   10.15 Respondents or their agents should enter appearance to an appeal as soon as they have received service of the petition of appeal. They enter appearance by attending at the Judicial Office to enter their name and address or that of their firm. Respondents may enter appearance by letter to the Judicial Office. Respondents who do not intend to take part in the proceedings do not need to enter appearance, but the Judicial Office sends communications concerning the appeal only to those who have entered appearance. An order for costs will not be made in favour of a respondent who has not entered an appearance.

Children

4B–42   10.16 In a case involving a child, where delay might affect the facts of the case or the interests of the child, parties should draw these facts to the attention of the Head of the Judicial Office not later than the day of presentation of the petition of appeal.

[THE NEXT PARAGRAPH IS 4B–44.]

11.

SECURITY FOR COSTS AND FEES

4B–44   11.1 No security for costs is required to be lodged in criminal appeals to the House of Lords and no fee is payable, except on taxation.

12.

STATEMENT OF FACTS AND ISSUES

4B–45   12.1 The appellants must lodge a Statement of the facts and issues (with an Appendix (see direction 13) within six weeks of the presentation of the appeal, or longer period approved by the House (direction 14.3). The Statement should be a succinct account of the main facts of the case, including an account of judicial proceedings up to that point and an account of the issues raised by the appeal. The appellants are responsible for drawing up the Statement in draft and they must submit it to the respondents for discussion and agreement. The Statement must be a single document agreed between the parties. In the event of disagreement, disputed material should be removed from the draft Statement and included instead in each party's case (direction 16). The Statement must be signed on behalf of each party by at least one counsel who appeared in the court below or who will appear at the hearing before the House.

12.2 In any appeal under the Criminal Appeal Act 1968 , the Statement must state clearly whether any grounds of appeal have been left undetermined by the Court of Appeal[1] (see also direction 16.6).

Form of Statement of facts and issues

4B–46   12.3 The Statement of facts and issues should be produced on durable quality A4 paper and incorporate:
  (a) pages printed on both sides of the paper;
  (b) capital letters down the inside margins;
  (c) references on the outside margins to relevant pages of the Appendix;
  (d) on the front cover, the reference of every law report of the case in the courts below, together with the catchword summary of one of the reports;
  (e) on the front cover, a headnote summary, whether or not the case has been reported;
  (f) on the front cover, a statement of the time occupied in the courts below; and

---

[1] See penultimate paragraph of Lord Chancellor's speech in *R v Mandair* [1994] 2 All E.R. 715.

(g) at the end, the signatures of counsel for both parties above their printed names.

13.

APPENDIX

13.1 It is the appellants' responsibility in consultation with the respondents to prepare and lodge an Appendix of documents considered necessary for the appeal. These documents include all the documents used in evidence or recording proceedings in the courts below.

4B–47

13.2 The appellants bear the cost of preparing the Appendix, although these costs are ultimately subject to the decision of the House as to the costs of the appeal.

Contents of Appendix

13.3 The Appendix contains only documents or extracts from documents that are necessary to support and understand the argument when the appeal is heard by the Appellate Committee. No document which was not used in evidence or does not record proceedings relevant to the action in the courts below may be included. Transcripts of arguments in the courts below may not be included unless remarks by a judge are relied on by any party or the arguments refer to facts which are admitted by all parties and as to which no evidence was called.

4B–48

13.4 The Appendix consists of one or more parts. Part 1 must contain:
   (a) formal originating documents;
   (b) case stated (if any);
   (c) judgments and orders relating to the decisions at first instance and on appeal;
   (d) relevant legislative provisions including delegated legislation; and
   (e) any relevant document on which the action is founded (such as a will, contract, map, plan etc.) or an extract from such document.

Published documents under (b), (c) and (d) above may so far as is practicable be placed in a pocket attached to the inside of the back cover of the Appendix.

13.5 For judgments that have been published, unbound parts of the relevant Law Reports or the Weekly Law Reports should be used if available; otherwise the All England Reports, Tax Cases, Simons' Tax Cases, Reports of Patent Cases and Lloyd's List Reports may be used. In Scottish appeals, Session Cases should be used where available; otherwise, Scots Law Times and Scottish Civil Case Reports may be used. Where, at the time of preparation of the Appendix, a judgment of a court below has not been published, a transcript must be included, which may later be replaced by the published version. In such circumstances, 15 copies of the published version should be submitted to the Judicial Office. Judgments in draft are not accepted. For legislation, if the printed Act or set of Regulations is conveniently small; it should be used; if the provisions are bulky or numerous, the relevant provisions should be copied. Halsbury's Statutes may be used.

13.6 Other documents should be included in Part 2 of the Appendix and, if the bulk of the documents makes it necessary, in Parts 3, 4 etc. The Appendix volume should only be numbered Part 1 if there is more than one Part.

Form of Appendix

13.7 The Appendix takes the following form:
   (a) it must be A4 size bound with a plastic comb binding and red card covers (red indicating a criminal appeal);
   (b) documents must be printed on both sides of the paper;
   (c) documents must be numbered;
   (d) original documents under the size of A4 may be enlarged to A4 size with a broad outside margin;
   (e) if the Appendix has more than one Part, each Part must contain a list of its contents;

4B–49

(f) documents of an unsuitable size or form for binding (for example, booklets or charts) should be included in a pocket attached to the inside back cover of the appropriate Appendix volume.

Examination of Appendix

4B–50 13.8 The Appendix is for the use of all parties and the contents of the Appendix must be agreed by appellants and respondents. Disputed documents (see direction 13.9) should not be included in the Appendix. As soon as proofs of the Appendix are available they should be examined against the originals by all parties, if possible at one joint examination. As soon as practicable after the examination, a final proof of the Appendix should be provided to each party.

Documents in readiness at hearing

4B–51 13.9 Disputed documents and any document not included in the Appendix which may be required at the hearing should be held in readiness and, subject to leave being given by the Appellate Committee, may be introduced at an appropriate moment. Fifteen copies are required. All such documents are subject to previous examination by the other parties. Where the appellants refuse to include in the Appendix any documents that the respondents consider necessary, the respondents must prepare and reproduce the documents at their own expense, subject to the final order on costs.

14.

LODGMENT OF STATEMENT AND APPENDIX

Time limits

4B–52 14.1 The Statement and Appendix must be lodged by the appellants within six weeks of the presentation of the appeal, or within such longer period as may be allowed on petition (see direction 14.3)[1].

14.2 If this time limit expires during a parliamentary recess, it is automatically extended to the third next sitting day of the House of Lords[2]; and if any party has applied for public funding/legal aid, the time limit is automatically extended to one month after the notification of the result of the funding decision, provided that the Judicial Office has been informed of the application[3].

Applications for extension of time—first extension

4B–53 14.3 Appellants who are unable to complete preparation of the Statement and Appendix within the initial six weeks' period may apply for an extension of that time. The application should explain briefly the reason(s) why an extension is needed. Application may be made for an extension of up to six weeks from the original expiry date, and the application must specify the date to which the extension is requested. If that date seems likely to fall in a parliamentary recess, the application may request extension until '[specify date] or the third sitting day of the next ensuing meeting of the House'[4].

14.4 An application for extension of time is submitted to those respondents who have entered appearance, for information. It must be lodged before the expiry of the six weeks initially allowed for lodging the Statement and Appendix.

Petitions for extension of time—second and subsequent extensions

4B–54 14.5 Up to three extensions of time are normally granted, provided that they do not prejudice the preparation for the hearing or its proposed date. An application for a

---

[1] Standing Order VI(1). For extensions of time in publicly funded/legally aided cases, see direction 38.
[2] Standing Order VIII.
[3] See direction 38.1–38.3.
[4] As the "third sitting day" depends on future sittings of the House, the date of expiry is not fixed. The appellants should contact the Judicial Office from time to time to discover how sittings of the House affect this date.

fourth extension of time, and any subsequent applications, may, at the discretion of the Head of the Judicial Office, be referred to an Appeal Committee.

Respondents' consent

14.6 In criminal appeals it is not the practice to require the consent of the respondents to applications for extensions of time. **4B–55**

Lodgment

14.7 When the Statement and Appendix are ready, one master plus seven copies of **4B–56** the Statement, eight copies of Part 1 of the Appendix and 15 copies of Parts 2 etc (if any) must be lodged in the Judicial Office. The appellants must at the same time apply to set down the appeal for hearing.

15.
SETTING DOWN FOR HEARING

15.1 An appeal is set down for hearing at the same time as the appellants lodge the **4B–57** Statement and Appendix[1].

15.2 Once an appeal has been set down for hearing, it may be called on at any time. Certain directions, for example directions 16.14–16.15, may be dispensed with to enable an appeal to be called on at short notice.

Estimates of length of time needed for hearing of appeal

15.3 Within seven days of the setting down of an appeal, each party must notify the **4B–58** Judicial Office of the number of hours that their counsel estimate to be necessary for each of them to address the Appellate Committee. The Listings Officer arranges the programme of hearings on the basis of these estimates, and so they should be as accurate as is reasonably possible. Subject to any directions by the Appellate Committee before or at the hearing, counsel are expected to confine their submissions to the time indicated in their estimates. The Judicial Office should be informed at once of any alteration to the original estimate.

15.4 In all appeals where combined estimates amount to more than 17½ hours (four sitting days), such estimates must be justified by letter to the Head of the Judicial Office and may be referred to an Appeal Committee for a direction.

16.
APPELLANTS' AND RESPONDENTS' CASES

16.1 The case is the statement of a party's argument in the appeal. **4B–59**

16.2 The case should be confined to the heads of argument that counsel propose to submit at the hearing and omit material contained in the Statement of facts and issues[2]. The members of the Appeal Committee who gave leave to appeal may not be sitting on the Appellate Committee; and so it cannot be assumed that the members of the Appellate Committee will be familiar with the arguments set out in the petition for leave to appeal.

16.3 Page 1 of the case should set out the title of the party on whose behalf it is lodged.

16.4 If either party is abandoning any point taken in the courts below, this should be made plain in their case. If they intend to apply in the course of the hearing for leave to introduce a new point not taken below, this should also be indicated in their

---

[1] For form of application for setting down, see Appendix A, Form 12.
[2] See Lord Diplock's speech in *M.V.Yorke Motors v. Edwards* [1982] 1 W.L.R. 444, [1982] 1 All E.R. 1024.

case and the Judicial Office informed. If such a point involves the introduction of fresh evidence, application for leave must be made either in the case or by lodging a petition for leave to adduce the fresh evidence.

16.5 If a party intends to invite the House to depart from one of its own decisions, this intention must be clearly stated in a separate paragraph of their case, to which special attention must be drawn. A respondent who wishes to contend that a decision of the court below should be affirmed on grounds other than those relied on by that court must set out the grounds for that contention in their case.

16.6 In any appeal under the Criminal Appeal Act 1968 in which grounds of appeal have been left undetermined by the Court of Appeal (see direction 12.2), each party should include in their case submissions on the merits of those grounds and on how they would seek to have them disposed of by the House.

16.7 Transcripts of unreported judgments should only be cited when they contain an authoritative statement of a relevant principle of law not to be found in a reported case or when are necessary for the understanding of some other authority.

16.8 All cases must conclude with a numbered summary of the reasons upon which the argument is founded, and must bear the signature of at least one counsel for each party to the appeal who has appeared in the court below or who will be briefed for the hearing before the House[1].

16.9 The lodgment of a case carries the right to be heard by two counsel, one of whom may be leading counsel. The fees of two counsel only for any party are allowed on taxation unless the Appellate Committee orders otherwise on application at the hearing.

Separate cases

4B-60 16.10 All the appellants must join in one case. All the respondents must also join in one case, unless it can be shown that the interests of one or more of the respondents are distinct from those of the rest. If the respondents' interests are distinct, the agents who first lodge their case must certify in a letter to the Judicial Office as follows:

(a) 'We, as agents for the respondent(s) [name particular parties], certify that opportunity has been offered by us for joining in one case to the respondent(s) [name particular parties] whose interests are, in our opinion, similar to those set out in the case lodged by us.'; or

(b) 'We, as agents for the respondent(s) [name particular parties], certify that the interests represented in the case lodged by us are, in our opinion, distinct from those of the remaining respondent(s).'

16.11 When one of the foregoing certificates has been given, all remaining respondents wishing to lodge a case must respectively petition to do so in respect of each of their separate cases. Such petitions must be consented to by the appellants, and must set out the reasons for separate lodgment.

16.12 Parties whose interests in the appeal are passive (e.g. stakeholders, trustees, executors, etc.) are not required to lodge a separate case but should ensure that their position is explained in one of the cases lodged.

Joint case

4B-61 16.13 The lodgment of a joint case on behalf of both appellants and respondents may be permitted in certain circumstances.

Lodgment and exchange of cases

4B-62 16.14 No later than five weeks before the proposed date of the hearing, the

---

[1] Standing Order VI(3).

appellants must lodge in the Judicial Office one master plus seven copies of their case and serve it on the respondents.

16.15 No later than three weeks before the proposed date of the hearing, the respondents must lodge in the Judicial Office one master plus seven copies of their case in response, as must any other party lodging a case (for example, an intervener or advocate to the court).

16.16 The number of copies of cases exchanged should be enough to meet the requirements of counsel and agents and should not usually exceed eight. To enable the appellants to lodge the bound volumes, the respondents and any other party who has lodged a case must also provide the appellants with 15 further copies of their case.

16.17 Following the exchange of cases, further arguments by either side may not without leave be submitted in advance of the hearing.

Form of cases

16.18 Cases must be produced on durable quality A4 paper with: **4B–63**
    (a) capital letters down the inside margins;
    (b) numbered paragraphs;
    (c) the signatures of counsel at the end above their printed names

17.

Bound Volumes

17.1 As soon as all cases have been exchanged, and no later than 14 days before the **4B–64** proposed date of the hearing, the appellants must lodge (in addition to the documents already lodged on setting down) 15 bound volumes, each containing:
    (a) petition(s) of appeal;
    (b) petition(s) of cross-appeal (if any);
    (c) Statement of facts and issues;
    (d) appellants' and respondents' cases, with cross-references to the Appendix and authorities' volume(s);
    (e) case of the advocate to the court or intervener, if any;
    (f) Part 1 of the Appendix; and
    (g) index to the authorities' volume(s).

Form of bound volumes

17.2 The bound volumes: **4B–65**
    (a) should be bound in the same manner as the Appendix, with plastic comb binding and red card covers;
    (b) must include cut-out indices for each of the documents set out in direction 17.1, tabbed with the name of the document on the front sheet of each;
    (c) must show on the front cover a list of the contents and the names and addresses of the agents for all parties;
    (d) must indicate on a sticker attached to the plastic spine the volume number and the short title of the appeal; and
    (e) should include a few blank pages at either end.

Provision of documents

17.3 To enable the appellants to produce the bound volumes, the respondents must **4B–66** provide the appellants' agents with a further 15 copies of the respondents' case in addition to the cases already exchanged.

17.4 Respondents should arrange with the appellants' agents for the delivery to them of such bound volumes as the respondents' counsel and agents require.

HL Criminal

18.

AUTHORITIES

4B–67 18.1 Ten copies of all authorities that may be needed during the hearing must be lodged at the same time as the bound volumes[1]. The authorities should be collected together into one or more volumes. The appellants are responsible for producing the authorities' volumes and lodging them in the Judicial Office. To enable the appellants to lodge the volumes, the respondents must provide the appellants with ten copies of any authorities which the respondents require but which the appellants do not, or arrange with the appellants for their photocopying. Respondents should arrange with the appellants for the delivery to them of such authorities' volumes as the respondents' counsel and agents require.

Form and content of authorities' volumes

4B–68 18.2 The authorities' volumes should:

    (a) be A4 size, comb bound with green card covers;

    (b) have flexible covers;

    (c) separate each authority in the volume by numbered dividers;

    (d) contain an index to that volume; the first volume must also contain an index to all the volumes;

    (e) be numbered consecutively on the cover and spine with numerals at least point 72 in size for swift identification of different volumes during the hearing;

    (f) have printed clearly on the front cover the title of the appeal and the names of the agents for all parties;

    (g) have affixed to the plastic spine a sticker indicating clearly the volume number and short title of the appeal;

    (h) include a few blank pages at either end;

    (i) be not more than $2^{1}/_{2}$cm (1 inch) thick.

18.3 The first volume(s) should contain citations from the C and L series of the Official Journal of the European Union; the Law Reports; the All England Reports; the Weekly Law Reports; Session Cases; the Scots Law Times; and the current edition of Halsbury's Laws. Subsequent volumes should contain all other material. In appeals where there is a large number of authorities' volumes, it is helpful to produce an index of indexes, separate from the index contained in the first authorities' volume.

18.4 The authorities' volumes should be lodged in the Judicial Office in separate containers from the Bound Volumes.

18.5 Where a case is not reported in the Law Reports or Session Cases, references to other recognised reports may be given (see direction 16.7). In Revenue appeals, Tax Cases may be cited but, wherever possible, references to the case in the Law Reports or Session Cases should also be given.

18.6 In order to produce the authorities' volumes, parties may download text from electronic sources; but the authorities' volumes may only be lodged in paper form.

18.7 In certain circumstances (for example, when during the hearing before the Appellate Committee it becomes apparent that a particular authority is needed but is not in the authorities volume), the House of Lords Library can arrange for copies of authorities to be made available at the hearing[2]. Parties must themselves provide ten copies of any other authority or of unreported cases. They must similarly provide copies of any authority of which notice has not been given.

18.8 The cost of preparing the authorities volumes falls to the appellants, but is ultimately subject to the decision of the House as to the costs of the appeal.

---

[1] i.e, no later than two weeks before the proposed date of the hearing.
[2] See Appendix B for a list of authorities held by the House of Lords Library.

19.

NOTICE OF HEARING

19.1 Once an appeal has been set down, it may be called on at any time, possibly at **4B–69** short notice.

19.2 The Judicial Office lists appeals to meet the convenience of all the parties. The Judicial Office agrees provisional dates with the parties well in advance of the hearing and makes every effort to keep to these dates. Counsel, agents and parties are however advised to hold themselves in readiness during the week before and the week following the provisional date given. Agents receive formal notification shortly before the hearing.

19.3 Parties should inform the Judicial Office as early as possible of the names of counsel they have briefed.

19.4 Appellate Committees usually hear appeals on Mondays from 11am-1pm and from 2-4pm, and on Tuesdays to Thursdays from 10.30am-1pm and 2-4pm. Hearings take place in Committee Rooms 1 and 2 on the Committee Corridor of the Palace of Westminster.

20.

COSTS

20.1 If counsel seek an order other than that costs should be awarded to the **4B–70** successful party, they should make submissions on costs at the conclusion of the argument before the Appellate Committee. Oral submissions should be followed up by written submissions within 14 days. If there have been no oral submissions, written submissions on costs may be made with 14 days of the conclusion of the hearing. One master plus seven copies of the written submissions must be lodged at the Judicial Office.

Public funding and legal aid

20.2 In appeals involving legal service funding, a successful unassisted party who **4B–71** wishes to apply for costs against the Community Legal Service under s 11 of the Access to Justice Act 1999[1] should make the application at the conclusion of the hearing and also in writing within 14 days. They should inform the Legal Services Commission (the procedure is set out in regulations 9 and 10 of the Community Legal Service (Costs) Regulations 2000 (as amended)). It is the responsibility of the parties to bring to the attention of the Judicial Office any factor which might affect the making of such an order by the House[2].

Submissions at judgment

20.3 Leave may exceptionally be given to a party to make submissions on costs at the **4B–72** time the House meets to give judgment. Notice must be given in writing to the Judicial Office at least two days before the date of judgment. One master plus seven copies of the submissions must be lodged at the Judicial Office. A copy of the submissions must be sent to the other party or parties to arrive at least two days before the date of judgment.

20.4 The House may postpone making an order for costs to allow the parties to make written submissions in the light of the result of the appeal, usually within 14 days of

---

[1] Also pursuant to r.5(2) Community Legal Service (Cost Protection) Regulations 2000.

[2] This direction also applies to unassisted parties who, if successful, would seek an order for costs under Legal Aid Act 1988, s.18; Legal Aid (Scotland) Act 1986, s.19; or Legal Aid, Advice and Assistance (Northern Ireland) Order 1981, Art.16; such parties should inform the Scottish Legal Aid Board or the Legal Aid Committee respectively.

HL CRIMINAL

the date on which judgment is given. One master plus seven copies of the submissions must be lodged at the Judicial Office.

21.

JUDGMENT

Place and time of judgment

4B–73 21.1 Judgments are given in the Chamber of the House of Lords, usually on Wednesdays at 9.45am. Agents are notified of the date. One week's notice is usually given.

Attendance of counsel

4B–74 21.2 One junior of counsel for each party or group of parties who have lodged a case is required to attend at the Bar of the House when judgment is delivered. Queen's Counsel may attend instead, but only a junior's fee is allowed on taxation. It is the convention that Queen's Counsel wear full-bottomed wigs when appearing at the Bar of the House. Counsel instructed to attend judgment must be familiar with the subject matter of the appeal and with the options for its disposal.

Conditions under which judgments are released in advance

4B–75 21.3 The opinions of the Law Lords who sat on the Appellate Committee and the questions to be put to the House to dispose of the appeal are available to each party 24 hours before judgment is given, i.e. on a Tuesday morning when judgment is to be given at 9.45am on the Wednesday. The documents may be collected from the Judicial Office. In releasing these documents, the House gives permission for their contents to be disclosed to counsel, agents (including solicitors outside London who have appointed London agents) and in-house legal advisers in a client government department. The contents of the documents and the result of the appeal must not be disclosed to the client parties themselves until judgment is given in the House.

21.4 It is the duty of counsel to check that the questions to be put to the House dispose of the appeal in accordance with the opinions of the members of the Appellate Committee. In the case of apparent error or ambiguity in the opinions, counsel are requested to inform the Judicial Office immediately.

21.5 Accredited members of the media may also be supplied in advance of judgment with the Appellate Committee's opinions and the questions to be put to the House to dispose of the appeal.

The contents of these documents are subject to a strict embargo, and are not for publication, broadcast or use on club tapes before judgment has been delivered. The documents are issued in advance on the strict understanding that no approach is made to any person or organisation about their contents before judgment is given.

22.

ORDER OF THE HOUSE

Draft order

4B–76 22.1 After the House has given judgment, drafts of the order of the House are sent to all parties who lodged a case. The drafts must be returned to the Judicial Office within seven days of the date of receipt (unless otherwise directed), either approved or with suggested amendments. If amendments are proposed, they must be submitted to the agents for the other parties, who should indicate their approval or disagreement both to the agents submitting the proposals and to the Judicial Office. Where the amendments proposed are contrary to the questions put to and agreed by the House, a petition must be lodged.

Final order

4B–77 22.2 The final order is sent free of charge to the agents for the successful parties.

22.3 Prints of the final order are sent free of charge to the agents for all parties who have entered appearance.

23.

BILLS OF COSTS

23.1 Bills of costs for taxation (assessment of costs) must be lodged within three **4B–78** months from the date of judgment[1] or the date on which a petition of appeal is withdrawn (see direction 42). For an extension of the three month period, direction 6.4 applies.

23.2 The practice directions relating to judicial taxations and forms of bills of costs are available on request from the Judicial Office and on the internet at www.parliament.uk. Fees are payable on taxation of a bill of costs.

23.3 In conducting the taxation of bills of costs in criminal appeals the Taxing Officer follows the recommendations of the report of the Appeal Committee agreed to by the House on 14 October 1998[2].

24.

PREPARATION OF DOCUMENTS

General

24.1 All formal documents to the House of Lords must be produced on durable **4B–79** quality A4 paper, securely bound on the left, using both sides of the paper.

24.2 Documents which are not legible or which are not produced in the authorised form or which are unsatisfactory for some other similar reason are not accepted.

24.3 Parties may consult the Judicial Office at all stages of preparation of documents and may submit proofs for approval where appropriate.

Number of documents required

24.4 The following table shows the numbers of documents usually required for the **4B–80** hearing of an appeal. The numbers shown are the minimum prescribed in the directions. Actual requirements must be subject to agreement and depend on the number of parties, counsel and agents concerned, and on the special circumstances of each appeal. Copies for the use of the party originating the documents are not included in the numbers indicated.

The appellants must provide:

Document	For Judicial Office	For other side
Petition of appeal	Original and seven on lodgement	Two on service
Statement of facts and issues	Original and seven on setting down	As arranged
Appendix Part 1	Eight on setting down	One in advance otherwise as arranged
Appendix Part 2 and any subsequent Parts	15 on setting down	One in advance otherwise as arranged

[1] This period is not affected by suspended orders made under Legal Aid (Scotland) Act 1986, s.19 or Legal Aid Advice and Assistance (N.I.) Order 1981, Art.16.
[2] Report on the Clerk of the Parliaments' reference regarding criminal legal aid taxation, Session 1997-98, HL Paper 145.

Document	For Judicial Office	For other side
Case	Original and seven no later than five weeks before the hearing	As arranged on exchange
Bound volumes	15 no later than 2 two weeks before the hearing	As arranged
Authorities' volumes	Ten no later than two weeks before the hearing	As arranged
Documents held in readiness at hearing (if any)	15 held at the Bar	at least three

The respondents (and any interveners) must provide:

Document	For Judicial Office	For other side
Case	Original and seven no later than three weeks before the hearing	As arranged on exchange; 15 for bound volumes
Respondents' additional documents (if any)	15 held at the Bar	As arranged

Form of Statement of facts and issues

4B–81 24.5 See direction 12.3

24.6 Appendix: see direction 13.7.

24.7 Cases: see direction 16.18.

24.8 Bound volumes: see direction 17.2.

24.9 Authorities volume: see direction 18.2.

[THE NEXT PARAGRAPH IS 4B–86.]

25.

DISPOSAL OF DOCUMENTS

4B–86 25.1 All petitions and supporting documents lodged become the property of the House. No documents submitted in connection with an application for leave to appeal can be returned. Certain documents submitted in connection with an appeal may be returned, on application to the Judicial Office within 14 days of judgment in the appeal. Master documents are retained in the parliamentary archives.

25.2 Documents lodged for the use of the Appellate Committee may with the permission of the Committee be inspected by persons who are not a party to the appeal. Such persons must comply with any anonymity orders and data protection requirements.

26.

LODGMENT

4B–87 26.1 'Lodgment' and 'lodging' mean delivery to the Judicial Office or to a member of the Judicial Office staff by post or in person during opening hours . Where the time for lodging a document expires on a Saturday, Sunday, bank holiday, or any other day on which the Judicial Office is closed, the document will be received by the Judicial Office if it is lodged on the first day on which the Office is next open.

26.2 Communications with the Judicial Office may be transmitted by facsimile (fax) only in urgent circumstances. No document which is to be presented to the House or on which a fee is payable may be transmitted by fax or e-mail.

[THE NEXT PARAGRAPH IS 4B-89.]

Part III Directions Applying in Certain Appeals Only

27.

BAIL

27.1 The House of Lords does not grant bail. Applications for bail should be made to the court below. Where bail is granted to a party to an appeal to the House, the Judicial Office should be notified. **4B-89**

27.2 The attendance of a party to an appeal who is in custody is not normally required or permitted. Where the attendance of a party in custody is required, his agents will be informed by the Judicial Office in writing.

27.3 It should be noted that where a party was on bail pending the hearing of the appeal, surrender is usually required on the first day of the hearing.

28.

CONSOLIDATION AND CONJOINDER

28.1 Where the issues in two or more appeals are similar, it may be appropriate for them to be consolidated or conjoined. **4B-90**

28.2 Consolidation results in the appeals being conducted as a single cause with one set of counsel and one case only on each side and with a single Appendix of documents.

28.3 Conjoinder is a looser linking of two or more appeals, and a number of variations is possible. Commons forms of conjoinder are where: the appellants lodge separate cases with a separate junior for each appellant but a single leader; or the appellants lodge a single case with a single set of counsel but the respondents lodge separate cases and are separately represented.

28.4 The Judicial Office should be consulted on whether consolidation or some form of conjoinder is likely to be appropriate. A principal consideration should be to avoid wherever possible separate representation by counsel, or any duplication in the submissions made or in documents produced for the hearing.

28.5 Applications to consolidate or to conjoin appeals are made by petition[1]. The petition must be signed by the agents for all petitioners and must be submitted to the agents for all the other parties who have entered appearance for the endorsement of their consent. If consent is refused, the petition must be endorsed with a certificate that it has been served on the agents in question.

28.6 If all parties consent to or join in the petition, two copies of the petition should be lodged. The House then makes the appropriate order.

28.7 If any party refuses their consent, six copies of the petition should be lodged. The petition is then referred to an Appeal Committee and may be determined after a hearing[2].

29.

DEATH: ABATEMENT THROUGH

29.1 If a party to an appeal dies before the hearing, the appeal abates from the date of death (Standing Order X). Immediate notice of the death must be given in writing **4B-91**

---

[1] For style, see Appendix A, Form 7.
[2] See direction 37.

to the Judicial Office and to the other parties. The addition of a new party to represent the deceased person's interest cannot proceed until a petition for reviving the appeal has been agreed to by the House.

29.2 The petition for revivor must be lodged within three months of the date of notice of death[1]. It must be accompanied by an affidavit explaining the circumstances in which it is being lodged. It must be endorsed with a certificate of service on the respondents.

29.3 If abatement takes place after the case for the deceased person has been lodged but before the appeal has been heard, the appellants must lodge a supplemental case setting out the orders of the House on reviving the appeal and information about the newly-added parties.

30.

Dispute between Parties Settled

4B-92 30.1 It is the duty of counsel and solicitors in any pending appeal, if an event occurs which arguably disposes of the dispute between the parties, either to ensure that the appeal is withdrawn by consent or, if there is no agreement on that course, to bring the facts promptly to the attention of the House, and to seek directions.

31.

European Convention on Human Rights

Appeals notified under direction 10.6(a), (b) or (c)

4B-93 31.1 Where an appeal involves a point notified under direction 10.6(a), 10.6(b) or 10.6(c), the petition of appeal must include the words 'in accordance with the Human Rights Act 1998 ' at the appropriate place in the prayer of the petition[2]. Details of the Convention right which it is alleged has been infringed and of the infringement must be set out in the Statement of facts and issues and dealt with in a separate paragraph of the cases of all parties to the appeal[3].

Appeals notified under direction 10.6(a)

4B-94 31.2 The Crown has the right to be joined as a party in any appeal where the House is considering whether to declare that a provision of primary or subordinate legislation is incompatible with a Convention right[4] . In any appeal where the House is considering, or is being asked to consider, whether to make, uphold or reverse such a declaration, whether or not the Crown[5] is already a party to the appeal, the Head of the Judicial Office notifies the appropriate Law Officer(s)[6].

31.3 Where such an issue is raised in respect of a judicial act[7], the Head of the Judicial Office notifies the Crown through the Treasury Solicitor as agent for the Lord Chancellor[8].

---

[1] Standing Order X. For style of petition, adapt Appendix A, Form 8.

[2] See Appendix A, Form 4.

[3] See Human Rights Act 1998, which gives further effect in domestic law to much of the Convention for the Protection of Human Rights and Fundamental Freedoms agreed by the Council of Europe at Rome on 4 November 1950.

[4] Human Rights Act 1998, ss.4, 5.

[5] Through a Minister, governmental body or other person defined in Human Rights Act 1998, s.5(2).

[6] The Head of the Judicial Office notifies: (i) in appeals from England, the Attorney-General; (ii) in appeals from Scotland, the Advocate General for Scotland and the Lord Advocate; (iii) in appeals from Wales, if appropriate, the Counsel General of the National Assembly for Wales; (iv) in appeals from Northern Ireland, the Attorney General for Northern Ireland.

[7] Human Rights Act 1998. ss.7, 9(3) and 9(4).

[8] In appeals from Scotland, the Head of the Judicial Office notifies the Solicitor to

31.4 The person notified under direction 32.2 or 32.3 must within 21 days of receiving such notice, or such extended period as the Head of the Judicial Office may allow, serve on the parties and lodge in the Judicial Office a notice stating whether or not the Crown intends to intervene in the appeal; and the identity of the Minister or other person who is to be joined as a party to the appeal[1].

31.5 If a Minister or other person has already been joined to proceedings in the court below in accordance with the provisions of s 5 of the Human Rights Act 1998, the leave of the House is not required for the continued intervention of the Crown.

31.6 Once joined to the appeal, the case for the Minister or other person must be lodged in accordance with direction 16.

31.7 The House may order the postponement or adjournment of the hearing of the appeal for the purpose of giving effect to the provisions of this direction or the requirements of the Act.

Appeals notified under direction 10.6(b) or (c)

31.8 Except as prescribed in direction 32.1, no special steps are required for appeals notified under direction 10.6(b) or 10.6(c).　　**4B–95**

32.

EUROPEAN COURT OF JUSTICE

32.1 Article 234 of the Treaty establishing the European Community provides:　　**4B–96**

1. The Court of Justice shall have jurisdiction to give preliminary rulings concerning:

   (a) the interpretation of this Treaty;

   (b) the validity and interpretation of acts of the institutions of the Community and of the European Central Bank;

   (c) the interpretation of the statutes of bodies established by an act of the Council, where those statutes so provide.

2. Where such a question is raised before any court or tribunal of a Member State, that court or tribunal may, if it considers that a decision on the question is necessary to enable it to give judgment, request the Court of Justice to give a ruling thereon.

3. Where any such question is raised in a case pending before a court or tribunal of a Member State against whose decisions there is no judicial remedy under national law, that court or tribunal shall bring the matter before the Court of Justice.

32.2 When the House refuses leave to appeal to a petition which includes a contention that a question of Community law is involved, the House gives additional reasons for its decision not to grant leave to appeal (see direction 5.7). These reasons reflect the decision of the Court of Justice in *CILFIT v. Ministry of Health* (Case C-283/81) which laid down the categories of case where the Court of Justice considered that no reference should be made to it, namely (a) where the question raised is irrelevant; (b) where the Community provision in question has already been interpreted by the Court of Justice; (c) where the question raised is materially identical with a question which has already been the subject of a preliminary ruling in a similar case; and (d) where the correct application of Community law is so obvious as to leave no scope for any reasonable doubt[2].

32.3 The House may order a reference to the Court of Justice before determining

---

the Scottish Executive; in appeals from Northern Ireland, he notifies the Crown Solicitor and the Departmental Solicitor.

[1] Human Rights Act 1998, ss.5(2) and 9(5).

[2] Appeal Committee, 38th Report (2002–03): *Petitions for leave to appeal: reasons for the refusal of leave* (HL Paper 89).

whether to grant leave to appeal. In such circumstances proceedings on the petition for leave to appeal are stayed until the answer is received. The directions below apply as appropriate [1].

32.4 When the House intends to make a reference, the hearing is adjourned and the parties are invited to submit an agreed draft of the question(s) to be referred. A further Statement of facts and issues, for the use of the Court of Justice, may also be appropriate. The House then makes the reference, with or without opinions. At this stage the appeal may also be disposed of in part.

32.5 Within one month of the judgment of the Court of Justice, the parties must make written submissions on whether a further hearing before the Appellate Committee is necessary or on how the appeal is to be disposed of.

32.6 If a further hearing is required, the parties may seek leave to lodge supplemental cases.

32.7 The Court of Justice does not make orders for costs. The costs of the reference are included in the order of the House disposing of the appeal; and, if necessary, are taxed by the House's Taxing Officer.

33.

EXHIBITS

4B–97 33.1 Parties who require exhibits (such as machines in a patent action) to be available for inspection at the hearing must apply to the Judicial Office for permission for the exhibits to be brought to the House before the hearing.

34.

INTERVENERS

4B–98 34.1 Participation in an appeal as an intervener in a court below does not entitle a person to intervene in the House of Lords.

34.2 Application for leave to intervene in an appeal must be made by petition [2]. The petition may only be lodged after the petition of appeal has been presented to the House. One master plus seven copies of the petition for leave to intervene must be lodged. The petition must indicate whether leave is sought for oral and written interventions or for written intervention only. The petition should be certified with the consent of the parties in the case. If their consent is refused, the petition must be endorsed with a certificate of service on them. All petitions for leave to intervene, whether or not opposed by the parties, are referred to an Appeal Committee.

34.3 Subject to the discretion of the House, interveners bear the costs of their intervention.

34.4 Subject to the discretion of the House, any additional costs to the appellants and respondents resulting from an intervention are costs in the appeal.

34.5 If the Crown has been joined to proceedings in the court below in accordance with the provisions of s 5 of the Human Rights Act 1998, the leave of the House is not necessary for the continued intervention of the Crown.

36.

NEW SUBMISSIONS

4B–99 35.1 If, after the conclusion of the argument on an appeal, a party wishes to bring to the notice of the House new circumstances which have arisen and which might affect

---

[1] *ibid.*
[2] See Appendix A, Form 8.

the decision or order of the House, application must be made without delay (by letter to the Head of the Judicial Office) for leave to make new submissions. The application should indicate the circumstances and the submissions it is desired to make, and a copy must be sent to the agents for the other parties to the appeal.

36.

OPPOSED INCIDENTAL PETITIONS

36.1 Unless the Head of the Judicial Office directs otherwise, opposed incidental **4B–100** petitions (including any interlocutory petition which relates to any petition of appeal) are referred to an Appeal Committee and decided on the papers or, if the Committee so directs, after an oral hearing.

36.2 Eight copies of the petition must be lodged. The original petition must bear a certificate of service on the other parties and must clearly indicate whether the other parties consent or refuse to consent to the prayer.

36.3 If the Appeal Committee orders an oral hearing, the parties may apply at that time to hand in affidavits and such other documents as they may wish. Eight copies are required. Copies of such documents must be served on the other parties before the oral hearing. Authorities are not normally cited before the Appeal Committee.

37.

PUBLIC FUNDING AND LEGAL AID

37.1 The House of Lords does not grant public funding or legal aid. In criminal **4B–101** proceedings, depending on the route of appeal, application should be made to the court appealed from or, in Northern Ireland, to the Legal Aid Committee. Where an application for public funding/legal aid has been made but not determined within the statutory 28 days set out in direction 3.1 (for petitions for leave to appeal) or the three months stipulated by Standing Order I (for petitions of appeal), then provided the Judicial Office and the respondents to the proposed petition have been informed of the application for funding, the period within which the petition for leave to appeal or petition of appeal (as the case may be) must be lodged is extended to 28 days from the date of the final determination of the funding application. Such an extension may not be granted to a petitioner under the Extradition Act 2003[1]. Where public funding/legal aid has been applied for after the lodgement of a petition of appeal but not determined, the 6 weeks' period in which the statement of facts and issues must be lodged is automatically extended to one month after the legal aid application has been determined, provided the Judicial Office has been informed of the application.

37.2 A party to whom a funding certificate is issued must immediately lodge the certificate or a copy in the Judicial Office. Any emergency certificate and subsequent amendments, and the authority for leading counsel, must also be lodged.

37.3 Where a funding certificate is granted, the date of issue of the certificate is the date of final determination for the purpose of time limits.

38.

SPECIALIST ADVISERS

38.1 Any party to an appeal may apply in writing to the Head of the Judicial Office **4B–102** for Specialist Advisers to attend the hearing[2].

39.

STAY OF EXECUTION

39.1 Presentation of a petition of appeal or a petition for leave to appeal does not in **4B–103**

---

[1] Extradition Act 2003, ss.32, 114.
[2] See Standing Order XIV. For Nautical Assessors, see also Supreme Court of Judicature Act 1891, s.3.

itself place a stay of execution on any order appealed from. A party seeking such a stay must apply to the court appealed from, not to the House of Lords.

40.

TRANSCRIPTION

4B–104 40.1 Transcriptions are not made of hearings before the Appellate Committee. Any party may seek permission to arrange for its own transcription of a hearing, by writing to the Head of the Judicial Office. Permission is usually given. The service arranged must be silent. A single copy of the transcript should be lodged in the Judicial Office.

41.

VICTIMS' CODE OF PRACTICE

4B–104.1 41.1 The Victims' Code of Practice governs the services to be provided in England and Wales to victims of criminal conduct that has occurred in England and Wales. The Code is issued by the Home Secretary under s 32 of theDomestic Violence, Crime and Victims Act 2004. The House of Lords applies the Code to its judicial function.

41.2 Accordingly, all applications for permission to appeal and all appeals are examined to establish whether a victim can be identified and, if so, to determine what services are required to be provided to the victim by the Judicial Office.

41.3 In giving effect to direction 41.2 the Judicial Office may consult the Treasury Solicitor, the Court of Appeal Criminal Division and other relevant persons to obtain any necessary information.

41.4 The Judicial Office may either directly or through the joint police/CPS Witness Care Units contact victims to inform them that an application for permission to appeal or an appeal has been filed, to explain the appeals procedure, and to report progress on the application and/or appeal, including the date set for the hearing.

41.5 Victims may attend the hearing of an appeal or application for leave to appeal or the handing down of judgment. The Judicial Office arranges such attendance and provides the case papers.

41.6 If leave to appeal is granted by an Appeal Committee, the Judicial Office notifies the joint police/CPS Witness Care Units no later than one working day after the day on which leave to appeal has been granted.

41.7 The Judicial Office notifies the joint police/CPS Witness Care Units of the result of the appeal no later than one working day after the day of the result.

42.

WITHDRAWAL OF PETITIONS

Petitions for leave to appeal

4B–105 42.1 A petition for leave to appeal may be withdrawn by writing to the Head of the Judicial Office, stating that the parties to the petition have agreed how the costs should be settled. The respondents should notify the Judicial Office of their agreement.

Petitions of appeal

4B–106 42.2 An appeal that has not been set down for hearing may be withdrawn by writing to the Head of the Judicial Office, stating that the parties to the appeal have agreed the costs of the appeal. The nature of the agreement should be indicated. Where appropriate, the letter should also indicate how the money paid into the security fund (if any) should be disposed of. Written notification must also be given to the respondents who must notify the Judicial Office of their agreement to the withdrawal of the appeal and who must confirm that the costs have been agreed.

42.3 An appeal that has been set down for hearing may only be withdrawn by order of the House on petition. Such a petition should include submissions on costs. The petition must be submitted for their consent to those respondents who have entered appearance[1].

Statements to the House

JUDICIAL PRECEDENT

26 July 1966—BY THE LORD CHANCELLOR (LORD GARDINER)

4B–107

'Before judgments are delivered today, I wish to make the following statement on behalf of myself and the Lords of Appeal in Ordinary:

"Their Lordships regard the use of precedent as an indispensable foundation upon which to decide what is the law and its application to individual cases. It provides at least some degree of certainty upon which individuals can rely in the conduct of their affairs, as well as a basis for orderly development of legal rules.

"Their Lordships nevertheless recognise that too rigid adherence to precedent may lead to injustice in a particular case and also unduly restrict the proper development of the law. They propose therefore to modify their present practice and, while treating former decisions of this House as normally binding, to depart from a previous decision when it appears right to do so.

"In this connection they will bear in mind the danger of disturbing retrospectively the basis on which contracts, settlements of property and fiscal arrangements have been entered into and also the especial need for certainty as to the criminal law.

"This announcement is not intended to affect the use of precedent elsewhere than in this House."'

PRINCIPLES FOR PARTICIPATION

22 June 2000—BY THE SENIOR LORD OF APPEAL IN ORDINARY (LORD BINGHAM OF CORNHILL)

4B–108

'My Lords, with the leave of the House, before the reports from the Appellate Committees are considered, I should like to make a statement on Recommendation 59 of the Royal Commission on the Reform of the House of Lords. That recommendation is that "The Lords of Appeal should set out in writing and publish a statement of the principles which they intend to observe when participating in debates and votes in the second chamber and when considering their eligibility to sit on related cases.".

'I should tell the House that my noble and learned friends have considered this recommendation and have agreed on the terms of a statement to give effect to it. I will now read the statement which has been agreed by all the Lords of Appeal in Ordinary:

General Principles

"As full members of the House of Lords the Lords of Appeal in Ordinary have a right to participate in the business of the House. However, mindful of their judicial role they consider themselves bound by two general principles when deciding whether to participate in a particular matter, or to vote: first, the Lords of Appeal in Ordinary do not think it appropriate to engage in matters where there is a strong element of party political controversy; and secondly the Lords of Appeal in Ordinary bear in mind that they may render themselves ineligible to sit judicially if they were

---

[1] See Appendix A, Form 15.

to express an opinion on a matter which might later be relevant to an appeal to the House.

"The Lords of Appeal in Ordinary will continue to be guided by these broad principles. They stress that it is impossible to frame rules which cover every eventuality. In the end it must be for the judgment of each individual Lord of Appeal to decide how to conduct himself in any particular situation.

Eligibility

"In deciding who is eligible to sit on an appeal, the Lords of Appeal agree to be guided by the same principles as apply to all judges. These principles were restated by the Court of Appeal in the case of *Locabail (UK) Ltd v. Bayfield Properties Ltd* and others and four other actions [2000 1 All E.R. 65 (CA)]."

'My Lords, that concludes the statement.'

Standing Orders

STANDING ORDER NO. 17 OF THE HOUSE OF LORDS RELATING TO PUBLIC BUSINESS

Recall of the House. 20 May 1970.

4B–109   (1) If, during any adjournment of the House, the Lord Chancellor is satisfied that the public interest requires that the House should meet at a time earlier than that appointed, he may signify that he is so satisfied and notice shall be given and thereupon the House shall meet at the time stated in the notice, as if it had been duly adjourned to that time.

(2) If the Lord Chancellor is unable to act for the purposes of this Standing Order, the Chairman of Committees, after consultation with Her Majesty's Government, may act in his stead.

(3) Notwithstanding any adjournment of the House, the House may meet for judicial business at a time earlier than that appointed if the Lord Chancellor or, in his absence, the senior Lord of Appeal in Ordinary, is satisfied that it should do so and has signified that he is so satisfied and has given notice to such Lords as he thinks fit.

STANDING ORDER NO. 87 OF THE HOUSE OF LORDS RELATING TO PUBLIC BUSINESS

Appellate and Appeal Committees. 20 May 1970. 28 January 1984.

4B–110   (1) For the purposes of its appellate jurisdiction, the House shall have Appellate and Appeal Committees, of which all Lords qualified under the Appellate Jurisdiction Acts 1876 and 1887 shall be members.

(2) These Committees shall be:

(a) two Appellate Committees, which shall hear any cause or matter referred to them and shall report thereon to the House;

(b) two Appeal Committees, which shall consider any petition or application for leave to appeal that may be referred to them and any matter relating thereto, or to causes depending, or formerly depending, in this House, and shall report thereon to the House.

(3) In any criminal matter, or in any matter concerning extradition, an Appeal Committee may take decisions and give directions on behalf of the House.

(4) In any Appellate or Appeal Committee the Chair shall be taken by the Lord Chancellor or, in his absence, by the senior Lord of Appeal in Ordinary present, such seniority being determined in accordance with the Commission for the time being appointing Speakers for the purpose of the hearing and determination of Appeals.

(5) For the purposes of section 8 of the Appellate Jurisdiction Act 1876, any Appellate Committee may sit and act while Parliament is prorogued.

STANDING ORDERS OF THE HOUSE OF LORDS REGULATING JUDICIAL BUSINESS, MADE IN PURSUANCE OF THE APPELLATE JURISDICTION ACT 1876 AND SUBSEQUENT ENACTMENTS.

4B–111   The following Standing Orders regulating judicial business are not fully applied to criminal appeals because the right to bring such appeals is established and regulated by statute [1] . Parties are instead bound by the provisions of the statute by whose authority they petition the House. However it is recommended that parties should follow the Standing Orders wherever possible.

The dates (round bracketed) are those of the original Standing Orders prior to 1876. The dates [square bracketed] are those of the original Standing Orders made in pursuance of the Appellate Jurisdiction Act 1876 . The dates unbracketed are those of subsequent amendments.

Time limit for presenting appeals

I. ORDERED, that no petition of Appeal be received by this House unless the same **4B–112** be lodged in the Parliament Office for presentation to the House within the period of three months from the date of the last Order or Interlocutor appealed from.

(13 December 1661)

[14 August 1876]

26 February 1959

25 March 1964

Leave to appeal from the Courts of Appeal

II. ORDERED, that, in all Appeals from the Court of Appeal, the Court of Appeal **4B–113** in Northern Ireland or the Court of Session in Scotland in which the leave of the House is required under the provisions of any Act of Parliament, a Petition for leave to appeal be lodged in the Parliament Office within one month from the date of the last Order or Judgment appealed from, and that such Petition be referred to an Appeal Committee to consider whether such leave should be granted.

[24 October 1935]

3 March 1966

3 December 1969

Leave to appeal from the High Court

III. ORDERED, that, in all cases where application is made for leave for an appeal **4B–114** to be brought direct to the House from the High Court of Justice in England and Wales or from the High Court of Justice in Northern Ireland—

(a) a Petition for such leave, together with the certificate granted by the High Court under section 12 of the Administration of Justice Act 1969 , be lodged in the Parliament Office within one month from the date of the grant of such certificate or within such extended time as in any particular case the House may allow;

(b) any such Petition, and any application for extension of time or other incidental matter, be referred to an Appeal Committee for their consideration and report.

15 December 1969

Appeals to be signed and certified by counsel

IV. ORDERED, that, except in cases where leave to appeal has been granted under **4B–115** the provisions of any Act of Parliament, all Petitions of Appeal be signed, and the reasonableness thereof certified, by two counsel.

(3 March 1697)

[14 August 1876]

3 March 1966

Security for costs

V. (1) ORDERED, that in all Appeals the Appellants do give security for costs by **4B–116** paying into the House of Lords Security Fund Account within one week of the presentation of the Appeal such sum as shall be authorised from time to time by the House, to be subject to the Order of the House with regard to the costs of the Appeal.

On default by the Appellants in complying with the above conditions, the Appeal to stand dismissed.

(20 November 1680)

---

[1] The right was first established by the Criminal Appeal Act 1907. The first criminal appeal to the House was heard and determined in 1910: *Director of Public Prosecutions v. Ball*.

[14 August 1876]
7 August 1877
2 June 1959
12 April 1962
27 April 1976
9 March 1977
21 July 1988

Exemptions

4B–117 (2) ORDERED, that this Standing Order shall not apply (a) to Appellants who have been granted public funding or legal aid, (b) to appellants in appeals under the Child Abduction and Custody Act 1985,or (c) to a Minister or Government department.

15 December 1960
17 December 1991
10 October 2000

Time for lodging statement

4B–118 VI.(1) ORDERED, that the Statement and the Appendix thereto be lodged in the Parliament Office within six weeks from the date of the presentation of the appeal to the House; and the appeal be set down for hearing on the first sitting day thereafter; on default by the Appellant, the appeal to stand dismissed.

(12 July 1811)
[14 August 1876]
26 February 1959
17 December 1991

Scottish appeals

4B–119 (2) ORDERED, that in all appeals from Scotland the Appellant in the Appendix shall lay before this House a copy of the record as authenticated by the Deputy Principal Clerk of Session or a Clerk of Session delegated by him; together with a supplement containing an account, without argument or statement of other facts, of the further steps which have been taken in the cause since the record was completed, and containing also copies of the interlocutors or parts of interlocutors complained of; and each party shall in his Case lay before the House a copy of the case presented by him to the Court of Session, if any such case was presented there, with a short summary of any additional reasons upon which he means to insist; and if there shall have been no case presented to the Court of Session then each party shall set forth in his Case the reasons upon which he founds his argument, as shortly and succinctly as possible.

25 March 1964
17 December 1991

Statement to be signed by counsel

4B–120 (3) ORDERED, that the statement be signed by one or more counsel for each party, who shall have attended as counsel in the Court below, or shall purpose attending as counsel at the hearing in this House.

(19 April 1698)
17 December 1991

Cross-appeals

4B–121 VII. ORDERED, that all cross-appeals be presented to the House within the period allowed by Standing Order No. VI. for lodging the Statement in the original appeal.

(8 March 1763)
[14 August 1876]
17 December 1991

Expiry of time during recess

4B–122 VIII. ORDERED, with regard to appeals in which the periods under Standing Orders Nos. V., VI. and VII. expire during the recess of the House, that such periods be extended to the third sitting day of the next ensuing meeting of the House.

Provided that if the House is recalled in pursuance of Public Business Standing Order No. 14 or Proclamation, any day on which the House sits pursuant to such recall is not a sitting day for the purposes of this Standing Order.

[14 August 1876]
17 December 1991

Public funding and legal aid

4B–123

IX. ORDERED, that where a party to an appeal has applied for public funding or legal aid, and the Clerk of the Parliaments has been informed of that application in writing before the expiration of the periods of time limited by Standing Orders Nos. I, II. or III., such periods of time shall be extended until one month after the date of the final determination of the application.

[15 December 1960]
3 March 1966
21 July 1988
19 May 1994
10 October 2000

Abatement or defect Revivor etc.

4B–124

X. ORDERED, that in the event of abatement by death or defect through bankruptcy, an appeal shall not stand dismissed for default under Standing Orders Nos. V. or VI., provided that notice of such abatement or defect be given by a letter from the Appellant's Agent addressed to the Clerk of the Parliaments and lodged in the Judicial Office prior to the expiration of the period limited by the Standing Order under which the appeal would otherwise have stood dismissed.

ORDERED, that all appeals marked on the Cause List of the House as abated or defective shall stand dismissed unless, within three months from the date of the notice to the Clerk of the Parliaments of abatement or defect, if the House be then sitting, or, if not, then not later than the third sitting day of the next ensuing sittings of the House, a petition shall be presented to the House for reviving the appeal or for rendering the same effective.

[14 August 1876]
12 August 1884
26 February 1959
17 December 1991

Supplemental case

4B–125

ORDERED, that when an appeal has abated or become defective after the Cases have been lodged, and it is subsequently revived or rendered effective, a Supplemental Case shall be lodged by the Appellant setting forth the Order or Orders made by the House reviving the appeal or rendering the same effective.

The like rule shall be observed by the Appellant and Respondent respectively, where any person or persons shall, by leave of the House, upon petition or otherwise, be added as a party or parties to the said appeal after the Cases in such appeal shall have been lodged.

(20 March 1823)

Certificate of leave or difference of opinion in Scottish appeals

4B–126

XI. ORDERED, that when any petition of appeal shall be presented to this House from any interlocutory judgment of either division of the Lords of Session in Scotland, the counsel who shall sign the said petition, or two of the counsel for the party or parties in the Court below, shall sign a certificate or declaration, stating either that leave was given by that division of the judges pronouncing such interlocutory judgment to the Appellant or Appellants to present such petition of appeal or that there was a difference of opinion amongst the judges of the said division pronouncing such interlocutory judgment.

[14 August 1876]

Taxation of costs

4B–127

XII. ORDERED, that the Clerk of Parliaments shall appoint such person as he may think fit as Taxing Officer, and in all cases in which this House shall make any order for payment of costs by any party or parties in any cause, the amount thereof to be certified by the Clerk of the Parliaments, the Taxing Officer shall tax the Bill of Costs so ordered to be paid, and ascertain the amount thereof, and report the same to the Clerk of the Parliaments or Clerk Assistant: And it is further Ordered, that the same fees shall be demanded from and paid by the party applying for such taxation for and in respect thereof as are now charged or shall be authorised from time to time by the House; and such fees shall be added at the foot of the said Bill of Costs as taxed. And the Clerk of the Parliaments or Clerk Assistant may give a certificate of such costs, expressing the amount so reported to him as aforesaid, and in his certificate, as well as in the Taxing Officer's report, regard shall be had to any sum that has been paid in to the Security Fund Account of the House, as directed by Standing Order No. V.; and the amount in money certified by him in such certificate shall be the sum to be demanded and paid under or by virtue of such order as aforesaid for payment of costs.

> (3 April 1835)
> [14 August 1876]
> 7 August 1877
> 2 June 1959
> 9 March 1977
> 27 June 1984

Fees

4B–128   XIII. ORDERED, that fees be taken in this House on the documents specified in the Schedule hereto, that the fees to be charged shall be such as shall be authorised from time to time by the House, and that none of the said documents be issued from or received at the Parliament Office unless it shall have been endorsed with the date of lodgment and the amount of fee paid.

If the Clerk of the Parliaments is satisfied that a litigant who has been refused public funding or legal aid would suffer financial hardship by the payment of fees to this House, he shall report the circumstances to the Appeal Committee. The Appeal Committee shall have power to waive, modify or suspend such fees, either wholly or in part, and shall report thereon to the House.

> [10 March 1902]
> 26 March 1970
> 27 April 1976
> 9 March 1977
> 21 July 1988
> 17 December 1991
> 19 May 1994
> 17 October 1995
> 10 October 2000

SCHEDULE

Schedule

4B–129   Petition for leave to appeal.

Interlocutory Petitions referred to an Appeal Committee (including the Report thereon).

Petition of Appeal.

Notice of Appearance.

Waiver of Security for costs.

Petition not referred to Appeal Committee.

Application to set down for hearing.

Petition to withdraw Appeal after setting down.

Specialist advisers

4B–130   XIV. (1) ORDERED, that the Lord Chancellor or the Lord Speaker may direct that one or more Specialist Advisers shall attend the hearing of any appeal in which they consider the House would benefit from such attendance.

(2) ORDERED, that the parties or either party to an appeal may apply by letter to the Clerk of the Parliaments requesting, upon grounds stated in the letter, the attendance of Specialist Advisers. Such an application shall be referred to and determined by the Lord Chancellor or Lord Speaker.

(3) ORDERED, that in any appeal concerning nautical matters in which the attendance of Specialist Advisers is required, Nautical Assessors may be appointed of whom one shall be an Officer, active or retired, of Her Majesty's Navy, and the other an Elder Brother of the Corporation of Trinity House.

(4) ORDERED, that the fees and expenses paid to each Specialist Adviser shall be such as shall have been agreed between the parties and the Advisers and approved by the Lord Chancellor or Lord Speaker, or, failing such agreement, such sum as shall be authorised by the Lord Chancellor or Lord Speaker.

(5) ORDERED, that unless the House otherwise directs, the fees referred to in paragraph (4) shall be paid by the party against whom the House awards costs.

23 November 1995

Appendix A: standard forms of key documents

4B–131

FORM 1

PETITION for leave to appeal

(*HL direction 4*)

IN THE HOUSE OF LORDS

ON APPEAL FROM HER MAJESTY'S COURT OF APPEAL CRIMINAL DIVISION (ENGLAND) [*or* A DIVISIONAL COURT OF THE QUEEN'S BENCH DIVISION OF HER MAJESTY'S HIGH COURT OF JUSTICE *or* HER MAJESTY'S COURT OF APPEAL IN NORTHERN IRELAND (*or relevant court*)]

Court of Appeal Ref: (*for example,* 200406398 D5)
Neutral citation of judgment appealed against: (eg, [2004] EWCA Crim 3847)

BETWEEN

AB (Respondent)
and
CD (Petitioners)
[and]
[(2) EF]
[and]
[(3) GH]

PETITION FOR LEAVE TO APPEAL
TO THE RIGHT HONOURABLE THE HOUSE OF LORDS

THE HUMBLE PETITION OF [*set out full name(s) and address(es) of petitioners*]
PRAYING FOR LEAVE TO APPEAL IN ACCORDANCE WITH THE CRIMINAL APPEAL
ACT 1968 *or* ADMINISTRATION OF JUSTICE ACT 1960 (*or relevant statute*) SHOWS -

1. That ....[*set out briefly in numbered paragraphs such facts and arguments as may be necessary to enable the Appeal Committee to decide whether leave to appeal should be given*].
2. ....
3. ....etc.

[*Note: it is usually appropriate for petitions for leave to appeal to deal with some or all of the following:*
1. Narrative of the facts;
2. Statutory framework (*if any*);
3. Chronology of proceedings;
4. Orders made in the courts below;
5. Issues before Court of Appeal Criminal Division (*or court appealed from*);
6. Treatment of the issues by Court of Appeal Criminal Division (*or court appealed from*);
7. Issues in the petition for leave to appeal.]

[*At end of numbered paragraphs insert*]

YOUR PETITIONER(S) HUMBLY SUBMIT(S) that leave to appeal to Your Lordships' House should be granted for the following among other

REASONS

[*list here numbered reasons summarising the arguments*]

(1) ....

(2) ....

(3) ....etc.

AND YOUR PETITIONER(S) WILL EVER PRAY

Signed

....

Signature of petitioner or agent(s) for the petitioner

CERTIFICATE OF SERVICE TO BE ENDORSED ON BACK OF
PETITION FOR LEAVE TO APPEAL

[I *or* We], [(Messrs) (*name*), of (*address*),(agents for)] the petitioner(s) within-named, hereby certify that on (*date*) [I *or* we] served [(Messrs) (*name*) of (*address*) (agents for)] (*name(s) of respondent(s)*), the within-named respondent(s), with a correct copy of the petition for leave to appeal and with notice that the petition would be presented to the House of Lords on behalf of the petitioner(s) as soon as conveniently may be.

(*signature of petitioner(s) or their agents*)

4B–132

FORM 2

BACK OF PETITION for leave to appeal showing certificate of service to be endorsed on original petition

[I *or* We], [(Messrs) (*name*), of (*address*),(agents for)] the petitioner(s) within-named, hereby certify that on (*date*) [I *or* we] served [(Messrs) (*name*) of (*address*) (agents for)] (*name(s) of respondent(s)*), the within-named respondent(s), with a correct copy of the petition for leave to appeal and with notice that the petition would be presented to the House of Lords on behalf of the petitioner(s) as soon as conveniently may be. (*signature of petitioner(s) or their agents*)	IN THE HOUSE OF LORDS ON APPEAL FROM (*name court*) BETWEEN: (*set out title of cause*)
	_____ PETITION FOR LEAVE TO APPEAL
(*neutral citation of judgment petitioned against*) (*references to law reports*) (*indexing catchwords*) (*head-note summary*)	(*set out full name, address, telephone number, and reference (if any) of petitioner(s) or their agents*)

4B–133

FORM 3
PETITION for leave to appeal out of time

IN THE HOUSE OF LORDS

ON APPEAL FROM HER MAJESTY'S COURT OF APPEAL CRIMINAL DIVISION (ENGLAND) [*or* A DIVISIONAL COURT OF THE QUEEN'S BENCH DIVISION OF HER MAJESTY'S HIGH COURT OF JUSTICE *or* HER MAJESTY'S COURT OF APPEAL IN NORTHERN IRELAND (*or relevant court)*]

Court of Appeal Ref: (*for example,* 200406398 D5)
Neutral citation of judgment appealed against: (eg, [2004] EWCA Crim 3847)

BETWEEN
AB (Respondent)
and
CD (Petitioners)
[and]
[(2) EF]
[and]
[(3) GH]

PETITION FOR LEAVE TO APPEAL

TO THE RIGHT HONOURABLE THE HOUSE OF LORDS

THE HUMBLE PETITION OF [*set out full name(s) and address(es) of petitioners*] PRAYING FOR AN EXTENSION OF TIME WITHIN WHICH THE PETITION MAY BE LODGED AND PRAYING FOR LEAVE TO APPEAL IN ACCORDANCE WITH THE CRIMINAL APPEAL ACT 1968 *or* ADMINISTRATION OF JUSTICE ACT 1960 (*or relevant statute*) SHOWS –

1. That (*set out briefly the reason(s) why the petition was not lodged in time*).
2. That ......(*continue as in Form 1, setting out briefly in numbered paragraphs such facts and arguments as may be necessary to enable the Appeal Committee to decide whether to give leave to appeal out of time*].
3. ....
4. ....etc.

Note: it is usually appropriate for petitions for leave to appeal to deal with some or all of the following:

1. Narrative of the facts;
2. Statutory framework (*if any*);
3. Chronology of proceedings;
4. Orders made in the courts below;
5. Issues before Court of Appeal (*or court appealed from*);
6. Treatment of the issues by Court of Appeal (*or court appealed from*);
7. Issues in the petition for leave to appeal.

[At end of numbered paragraphs insert]

YOUR PETITIONER(S) HUMBLY SUBMIT(S) that leave to appeal to Your Lordships' House should be granted for the following among other

REASONS

[list here numbered reasons summarising the arguments]

(4) ....
(5) ....
(6) ....etc.

AND YOUR PETITIONER(S) WILL EVER PRAY

Signed

....

Signature of petitioner or agent(s) for the petitioner

CERTIFICATE OF SERVICE TO BE ENDORSED ON BACK OF PETITION FOR LEAVE TO APPEAL

[I *or* We], [(Messrs) (*name*), of (*address*),(agents for)] the petitioner(s) within-named, hereby certify that on (*date*) [I *or* we] served [(Messrs) (*name*) of (*address*) (agents for)] (*name(s) of respondent(s)*), the within-named respondent(s), with a correct copy of the petition for leave to appeal and with notice that the petition would be presented to the House of Lords on behalf of the petitioner(s) as soon as conveniently may be.

(signature of petitioner(s) or their agents)

FORM 4

4B–134

PETITION OF APPEAL

(HL direction 10)

IN THE HOUSE OF LORDS

ON APPEAL FROM HER MAJESTY'S COURT OF APPEAL CRIMINAL DIVISION (ENGLAND) [*or* A DIVISIONAL COURT OF THE QUEEN'S BENCH DIVISION OF HER MAJESTY'S HIGH COURT OF JUSTICE *or* HER MAJESTY'S COURT OF APPEAL IN NORTHERN IRELAND (*or relevant court*)]

BETWEEN

AB (Respondents)
and
CD (Appellants)
[and]
[(2) EF]
[and]
[(3) GH]

PETITION OF APPEAL

TO THE RIGHT HONOURABLE THE HOUSE OF LORDS

THE HUMBLE PETITION AND APPEAL OF [*set out full name(s) and address(es) of appellants*]

YOUR PETITIONER(S) has/have pursuant to [section 1 of the Administration of Justice Act 1960 *or* section 33 of the Criminal Appeal Act 1968 (*or other relevant statute*)] obtained the certificate of [*name court below*] set forth in the Schedule hereto that the decision of that court involves a point of law of general public importance.

YOUR PETITIONER(S) humbly pray(s) that the matter of the Order(s) set forth in the Schedule(s) hereto [*if Order is partly appealed against, insert the words:* so far as therein stated to be appealed against] may be reviewed before Her Majesty the Queen, in Her Court of Parliament, and that the said Order(s) [*if Order is partly appealed against, insert the words*: so far as aforesaid] may be reversed, varied or altered [*if appropriate, insert the words:* in accordance with the Human Rights Act 1998], [*if specific relief is asked for, it should be so stated, prefaced by the words*: and that] or that the petitioner(s) may have such other relief in the premises as to Her Majesty the Queen, in Her Court of Parliament, may seem meet.

[*signature(s) of appellant(s) or their agents, as appropriate*].

THE SCHEDULE REFERRED TO ABOVE

FROM HER MAJESTY'S COURT OF APPEAL CRIMINAL DIVISION (ENGLAND) (*or relevant court*)

FIRST SCHEDULE

In a certain criminal cause or matter wherein (*insert name(s)*) was/were the Prosecutor [*or other designation*] and (*insert name(s)*) was/were the defendant(s) [*or other designation*].

The Order(s) of [*state court*] of [*date*] appealed from is/are in the words following, the portion(s) complained of being underlined:

[*Set out here the whole of the order(s), with those parts complained of (and only those parts) underlined. The recital, the certified point of law and any decision on an application for leave to appeal to the House of Lords should be included but not underlined.*]

[*Where a point of law was not certified originally but later by a subsequent order of the court, the words 'FIRST SCHEDULE' should appear where indicated above and the following added:*]

SECOND SCHEDULE

The Order of [*state court*] of [*date*], by which that court certified that a point of law of general public importance was involved in its decision and granted/refused leave to appeal, is in the words following:

[*Set out here the whole of the order, including the recital*]

[*Then, at end add:*

Either

By an order of (*date*) the (*name of court below*) gave your petitioner(s) leave to appeal to Your Lordships' House from the said decision.

or

The Appeal Committee of Your Lordships' House on (*date*) gave your petitioner(s) leave to appeal against the said decision.]

FORM 5

BACK OF PETITION OF APPEAL, showing certificate of service to be endorsed on original petition

[I *or* We], [(Messrs) (*name*), of (*address*),(agents for)] the appellant(s) within-named, hereby certify that on (*date*) [I *or* we] served [(Messrs) (*name*) of (*address*) (agents for)] (*name(s) of respondent(s)*), the within-named respondent(s), with a correct copy of the petition of appeal and with notice that the petition would be presented to the House of Lords on behalf of the petitioner(s) as soon as conveniently may be.	IN THE HOUSE OF LORDS ON APPEAL FROM (*name court*) BETWEEN: (*set out title of cause*)
(*signature of petitioner(s) or their agents*)	
	PETITION OF APPEAL
(*neutral citation of judgment petitioned against*) (*references to law reports*) (*indexing catchwords*) (*head-note summary*)	(*set out full name, address, telephone number, and reference (if any) of appellant(s) or their agents*)

4B–136

FORM 6

PETITION FOR EXTENSION OF TIME to lodge Statement and Appendix

(HL direction 14)

IN THE HOUSE OF LORDS

ON APPEAL FROM HER MAJESTY'S COURT OF APPEAL CRIMINAL DIVISION (ENGLAND) (*or relevant court*)

BETWEEN:

(set out title of appeal)

TO THE RIGHT HONOURABLE THE HOUSE OF LORDS

THE HUMBLE PETITION OF (*set out full name(s) of appellant(s)*) SHOWS –

That your petitioner(s) presented a petition of appeal on (*date*) complaining of an Order of the (*state court*) dated (*date*).

That the time allowed by standing order VI for the appellant(s) to lodge the statement and appendix and to set down the cause for hearing [will expire *or* originally expired] on (*date*).

[That the House, pursuant to a petition from the appellant(s), granted an extension of time in which to lodge the statement and the appendix and set down the cause for hearing to (*date*).]

[That the House, pursuant to a further petition from the appellant(s), granted a second extension of time until (*date*).]

That the petitioner(s) will be unable to lodge the statement and appendix by the said date for the following reasons:

(set out brief reasons)

THEREFORE YOUR PETITIONER(S) HUMBLY PRAY(S)

That Your Lordships will be pleased to grant an extension of time until (*date*) to lodge the statement and appendix and set down the cause for hearing.

And your petitioner(s) will ever pray.

(signature of appellant(s) or their agents)

[Agents for the] Appellant(s) (set out here name and address of appellant(s) or their agents)

[I *or* We] consent to the prayer of the above petition.

(signature of respondent(s) or their agents)

[Agents for the] respondent(s) (set out here name and address of respondent(s) or their agents)

FORM 7

PETITION FOR CONSOLIDATION OR CONJOINDER

(HL direction 29)

IN THE HOUSE OF LORDS

ON APPEAL FROM HER MAJESTY'S COURT OF APPEAL CRIMINAL DIVISION
(ENGLAND) (*or relevant court*)

(set out title of first appeal)

AND

(set out title of second appeal)

TO THE RIGHT HONOURABLE THE HOUSE OF LORDS

THE HUMBLE PETITION OF (*set out full name(s) of appellant(s)* SHOWS—

That your petitioner(s) presented [a] petition(s) of appeal on (*date*) complaining of (an) Order(s) of the (*name relevant court below*) dated (*date*).

That your petitioner(s) (*name appellant(s) in other appeal(s), if different*) presented [a] petition(s) of appeal on (*date*) complaining of [an] Order(s) of the (*name relevant court below*) dated (*date*).

That the same matters of law are raised in each of the appeals [and that the appeals of (*name relevant parties*) to (*name relevant court below*) were heard and argued together and one Judgment was delivered in respect of the [two] appeals].

That it is expedient that your petitioners' said appeals be [consolidated *or* conjoined].

YOUR PETITIONERS THEREFORE HUMBLY PRAY

[Consolidation:
    That the said appeals may be consolidated and that they be allowed to lodge one statement, one case and one appendix and be jointly represented in respect of the (*insert relevant number*) appeals and that the respondents have leave to lodge one case in respect of the appeals.]

[Conjoinder:
    That the said appeals may be conjoined and that they be allowed to lodge separate statements and cases and one appendix in respect of the (*insert relevant number*) appeals and that the respondents have leave to lodge separate cases in respect of the appeals and be separately represented or that such other Order may be made with a view to the convenient conduct of the said appeals as to your Lordships may seem meet (*or such variation as is required)*.]

And your petitioner(s) will ever pray.

> (*signature of appellant(s) to first appeal or their agents*)
>
> [*Agents for the*] *Appellant(s)* (*set out here name and address of appellant(s) or their agents*)
>
> (*signature of appellant(s) to other appeal(s) or their agents*)
>
> [*Agents for the*] *Appellant(s)/co-petitioners* (*set out here name and address of appellant(s)/co-petitioners or their agents*)

[I *or* We] consent to the prayer of the above petition.

> (*signature of respondent(s)to first appeal or their agents*)
>
> [*Agents for the*] *Respondent(s) to first appeal* (*set out here name and address of respondent(s) or their agents*)
>
> (*signature of respondent(s) to other appeal(s) or their agents*)
>
> [*Agents for the*] *Respondent(s) to other appeal(s)* (*set out here name and address of respondent(s) or their agents*) etc

FORM 8

PETITION FOR LEAVE TO INTERVENE

(HL direction 35)

IN THE HOUSE OF LORDS

ON APPEAL FROM HER MAJESTY'S COURT OF APPEAL CRIMINAL DIVISION (ENGLAND) (*or relevant court*))

BETWEEN:

(set out title of appeal)

TO THE RIGHT HONOURABLE THE HOUSE OF LORDS
THE HUMBLE PETITION OF *(set out full name(s) of prospective intervener(s))* PRAYING FOR LEAVE TO INTERVENE SHOWS—

1. That on *(date)* *(set out full name(s) of appellant(s))* presented a petition of appeal to your Lordships' House, complaining of an Order of the *(state court)* dated *(date)*.

2. That your petitioner(s) seek(s) your Lordships' leave to present written [*add, if appropriate, the words:* and oral] submissions in intervention in the said appeal.

3. That *(set out briefly in numbered paragraphs such facts and arguments as may be necessary to enable the Appeal Committee to report to the House whether leave to intervene should be granted)*.

YOUR PETITIONER(S) HUMBLY SUBMIT(S) that leave to intervene in the said appeal should be granted for the following among other

REASONS
(give numbered reasons summarising the arguments)

And your petitioner(s) will ever pray.

(signature of petitioner(s) or their agents)

[Agents for the] Petitioner(s) (set out here name and address of petitioner(s) or their agents)

[I *or* We] consent to the prayer of the above petition.

(signature of appellant(s) or their agents)

[Agents for the] Appellant(s) (set out here name and address of appellant(s) or their agents)

[I *or* We] consent to the prayer of the above petition.

(signature of respondent(s) or their agents)

[Agents for the] Respondent(s) (set out here name and address of respondent(s) or their agents)

4B–139

FORM 9

BACK OF PETITION for leave to intervene, showing certificate of service to be endorsed on original petition

[I *or* We], [(Messrs) *(name)*, of *(address)*,(agents for)] the petitioner(s) within-named, hereby certify that on *(date)* [I *or* we] served [(Messrs) *(name)* of *(address)* (agents for)] *(name(s) of appellant(s))*, the within-named appellant(s),and [*if different date, insert the words:* on *(date)*] [(Messrs) *(name)* of *(address)* (agents for)] *(name(s) of respondent(s))*, the within-named respondent(s),with a correct copy of the petition for leave to intervene and with notice that the petition would be presented to the House of Lords on behalf of the petitioner(s) as soon as conveniently may be.	IN THE HOUSE OF LORDS ON APPEAL FROM *(name court)* BETWEEN: *(set out title of cause)* _____ PETITION FOR LEAVE TO INTERVENE
(signature of petitioner(s) or their agents)	*(set out full name, address, telephone number, and reference (if any) of petitioner(s) or their agents)*

FORM 10

PETITION for restoration of appeal when time for lodging Statement has expired

(HL direction 14)

IN THE HOUSE OF LORDS

ON APPEAL FROM HER MAJESTY'S COURT OF APPEAL CRIMINAL DIVISION (ENGLAND) *(or relevant court)*

BETWEEN: AB (Appellant(s))

                                       and

                                       CD (Respondent(s))

TO THE RIGHT HONOURABLE THE HOUSE OF LORDS

THE HUMBLE PETITION OF AB SHOWS –

That your petitioner(s) presented a Petition of Appeal on *(date)* complaining of an Order of the [Court of Appeal Criminal Division *or relevant court*] dated *(date)*.

That the time allowed by Standing Order VI for the appellant(s) to lodge the Statement of facts and issues and the Appendix and to set down the cause for hearing expired on the *(date)*.

That your petitioner(s) has/have been unable to lodge their Statement and the Appendix by the said date for the following reasons:

(set out reasons).

YOUR PETITIONER(S) THEREFORE HUMBLY PRAY(S) that your Lordships will be pleased to order that their appeal be restored and to grant them an extension of time until *(date)* to lodge the Statement and the Appendix and to set down the cause for hearing.

And your petitioner(s) will ever pray.

                    (signature of appellant(s) or their agents)

                    [Agents for the] Appellant(s) *(set out here name and address of appellant(s) or their agents)*

[I *or* We] consent to the prayer of the above petition.

                    (signature of respondent(s) or their agents)
                    [Agents for the] respondent(s) *(set out here name and address of respondent(s) or their agents)*

4B–141

FORM 11

RESPONDENTS' CONSENT to incidental petition

(HL direction 14.6)

(The consent is endorsed on the petition)

We consent to the prayer of the above petition.

(signature)

Respondent(s)/Agents for the respondent(s)

FORM 12

APPLICATION to set down cause for hearing

(HL direction 15)

IN THE HOUSE OF LORDS

ON APPEAL FROM HER MAJESTY'S COURT OF APPEAL CRIMINAL DIVISION (ENGLAND) (*or relevant court*)

BETWEEN: AB Appellant(s)

and

CD Respondent(s)

The appellant(s) having lodged a Statement of facts and issues and the Appendix thereto pursuant to order of the House,

My Lords,

Please to move, That this cause be set down for hearing after those causes already appointed.

(signature of appellant(s) or their agents)

Appellant/Agents for the appellant

(set out name and address of appellant(s) or their agent)

FORM 13

FORM OF COVER for Bound Volume *(on red card)*

IN THE HOUSE OF LORDS

ON APPEAL FROM HER MAJESTY'S COURT OF APPEAL CRIMINAL DIVISION (ENGLAND) *(or relevant court)*

BETWEEN:

(set out title of appeal)

Sticker on spine:

[Set out short title of cause]

BV 1

BOUND VOLUME

1

(The bound volume is only numbered if there is more than one volume)

PETITION OF APPEAL

[PETITION OF CROSS-APPEAL]

STATEMENT OF FACTS AND ISSUES

CASE FOR THE APPELLANTS

CASE FOR THE RESPONDENTS

APPENDIX - PART 1

LIST OF AUTHORITIES

(The above list is amended as appropriate)

(Name and address of agents for appellant(s))　　　　*(Name and address of agents for respondent(s))*

FORM 14

FORM OF COVER for authorities' volume *(on green card)*

IN THE HOUSE OF LORDS

ON APPEAL FROM HER MAJESTY'S COURT OF APPEAL CRIMINAL DIVISION (ENGLAND) *(or relevant court)*

BETWEEN:

(set out title of appeal)

Sticker on spine:

[Set out short title of cause]

AUTHORITIES' VOLUME

1

(The authorities' volume is only numbered if there is more than one volume)

(Name and address of agents for appellant(s))

(Name and address of agents for respondent(s))

HL CRIMINAL

4B–145

FORM 15

PETITION for withdrawal of appeal

(HL direction 42)

IN THE HOUSE OF LORDS

ON APPEAL FROM HER MAJESTY'S COURT OF APPEAL CRIMINAL DIVISION (ENGLAND) *(or relevant court)*

BETWEEN:
      AB   Appellant(s)

and

      CD   Respondent(s)

TO THE RIGHT HONOURABLE THE HOUSE OF LORDS

THE HUMBLE PETITION OF the Appellant(s) shows –

That your petitioner(s) presented a Petition of Appeal on *(date)* complaining of an Order of the Court of Appeal Criminal Division *(or relevant court)* dated *(date)*.

That your petitioner'(s)(s') appeal was set down for hearing before your Lordships' House on *(date)*.

That your petitioner(s) and the respondent(s) have agreed to terms of settlement of all matters in dispute between them, as follows:

1. That your petitioner(s) and the respondent(s) should join in making an application to your Lordships' House for leave that your petitioner'(s)(s') appeal might be withdrawn; and

2. That *(set out terms of agreement)*.

YOUR PETITIONER(S) THEREFORE HUMBLY PRAY(S) that your Lordships will be pleased to order that:

(1) your petitioner'(s)(s') appeal be withdrawn;

(2) *(state costs order sought, to dispose of appeal)*

And your petitioner(s) will ever pray.

(signature)

Agents for the appellant(s)

Appendix B

List of Authorities Kept in House of Lords Library

4B–146
(see direction 18.5)

The House of Lords Library keeps the following authorities:
    All England Reports
    Anglo American Law Review
    British Yearbook of International Law

Cambrian Law Review
Cambridge Law Journal
Canadian Rights Reporter
Common Market Law Reports
Common Market Law Review
Cox's Criminal Law Cases (1843–49)
Criminal Appeal Reports
Criminal Appeal Reports (Sentencing)
Criminal Law Forum
Criminal Law Review
Crown Office Digest
English Reports
Estates Gazette Law Reports (1985—)
European Court Reports
European Human Rights Reports
European Law Digest
European Law Review
European Public Law
Family Law Reports
Financial Law Reports
Fleet Street Reports
Halsbury's Laws and Statutes
Housing Law Reports
Human Rights Law Journal
Immigration Appeal Reports
Industrial Cases Reports
Industrial Law Journal
Industrial Relations Law Reports
Industrial Tribunal Reports (1971–78)
International and Comparative Law Quarterly
International Litigation Procedure
Irish Jurist (1848–866, 1935–1965)
Irish Jurist Reports
Irish Law Reports
Journal of Legal History
Journal of Legislative Studies
Journal of Planning and Environment Law
Journal of Social Welfare Law
Jurist—Reports of Cases in Law and Equity (1837–1866)
Justice of the Peace Reports
Law Journal Reports
Law Quarterly Review
Law Reports (1866—)
Law Times Reports
Legislative Studies Quarterly
Lloyd's Law Reports
Local Government Review Reports
Modern Law Review
New Law Journal
Northern Ireland Law Reports
Northern Ireland Legal Quarterly (Vol 34 (1983)—)
Northern Ireland Statutes
Oxford Journal of Legal Studies
Planning and Compensation Reports (1963–67)
Property and Compensation Reports (1968—)
Public Law (British Journal of Administrative Law)
Reports of Patent Cases

Road Traffic Reports
Rydes Rating Cases (1956–1979)
Scots Law Times
Scottish Civil Law Reports
Scottish Criminal Case Reports (1983—)
Scottish Jurist (1829–1873)
Scottish Law Reporter (1865–1924)
Scottish Planning Law and Practice
Session Cases
Simons Tax Cases (1981—)
Solicitors Journal
Statute Law Review
Statutes
Tax Cases
Times Law Reports
Weekly Law Reports
Weekly Notes (1866–1952)
Weekly Reporter (1852–1906)

Appendix C

Fees and Security Money

4B–147

JUDICIAL FEES

(1) JUDICIAL FEES

No fee is payable in a criminal cause or matter.

(2) TAXING FEE

The fees payable upon the sums allowed by the Taxing Officer are as follows:

(a) where the amount allowed does not exceed £500, a flat rate of £50;

(b) where the amount allowed exceeds £500, for every £1 or fraction of £1, an amount of 5p.

(27 July 2000)[1]

The fees payable on the withdrawal of a bill of costs (subject to written confirmation of the withdrawal from both parties to the taxation) are as follows:

(a) in respect of bills withdrawn within 21 days of the date appointed for taxation, 1 per cent of the agreed sum or £50, whichever is the larger;

(b) in respect of bills withdrawn within 7 days of the date appointed for taxation, 2 per cent of the agreed sum or £50, whichever is the larger.

(27 July 2000)[2]

Drafts and cheques for taxing fees are payable to 'House of Lords Account'.

(3) SECURITY MONEY

No security for costs is taken in criminal causes.

---

[1] Offices Committee, 6th Report (1999–2000), HL Paper 97.
[2] Offices Committee, 6th Report (1999–2000), HL Paper 97.

SECTION 5

EUROPEAN JURISDICTION

EUROPEAN JURISDICTION

GENERAL

The Brussels Convention

When the EEC Treaty (now called the EC Treaty (as a result of the Treaty of Maastricht on European Union) and also referred to as the Treaty of Rome) was signed in 1957, the six original Member States agreed by Art. 220 that they would enter into negotiations with each other "with a view to securing for the benefit of their nationals ... the simplification of formalities governing the reciprocal recognition and enforcement of judgments of courts or tribunals and of arbitration awards". Subsequently, the Convention on Jurisdiction and Enforcement of Judgments in Civil and Commercial Matters was signed at Brussels on September 23, 1968 on behalf of these States (the Brussels Convention). **5–1**

This Convention went beyond Art. 220 in that it was not confined to the recognition and enforcement of judgments, but also contained rules of jurisdiction applicable in all States. No provision was, however, made for the recognition of arbitration awards. In 1971 the Member States concluded a Protocol on the Interpretation of the 1968 Convention by the European Court of Justice (the 1971 Protocol). This provides for references for preliminary rulings on questions of interpretation of the Convention to be made to the Court by appellate courts of the Contracting States (see text of 1971 Protocol at para. 5–139 below).

The object of the Conventions is not to unify the rules of substantive law and of procedure of the different contracting states, but to determine which courts have jurisdiction in disputes relating to civil and commercial matters in relations between the contracting states and to facilitate enforcements of judgments (Case C–68/93 *Shevill v. Presse Alliance* [1995] I.L.Pr. 267). However, the Conventions establish an enforcement procedure which constitutes an autonomous and complete system independent of the legal systems of the contracting states (*Société d'Informatique Realisation Organisation v. Ampersand Software B.V.* [1995] All E.R. (EC) 783).

Accession of United Kingdom

When the United Kingdom, together with Denmark and Ireland, joined the European Community, it undertook to accede to any Conventions provided for by Art. 220 of the Treaty of Rome and "to enter into negotiations with the original Member States in order to make the necessary adjustments thereto". The result was a Convention signed on October 9, 1978 amending the Brussels Convention and the 1971 Protocol and providing for the accession to them of the United Kingdom, Denmark and Ireland. In this instance, the amendments went well beyond mere "necessary adjustments". **5–2**

Civil Jurisdiction and Judgments Act 1982

This Act has as its main purpose the implementation of the Brussels Convention as amended by the 1978 Accession Convention and the 1971 Protocol. The Act gives the Conventions the force of law in the United Kingdom and requires judicial notice to be taken of them. They are set out, as s.2 states, for "convenience of reference" in the Act. Thus, the English text of the Brussels Convention (as it was at that time) is found in Sched.1, the 1971 Protocol in Sched.2 and the relevant provisions of the Accession Convention are in Sched.3. It is open to the UK islands and territories to ask that the Brussels Convention should be extended to them (see in this respect the Civil Jurisdiction and Judgments Act 1982 (Gibraltar) Order 1997) at para. 5–161 below). **5–3**

The Civil Jurisdiction and Judgments Act 1982 also contains rules of jurisdiction and rules for the enforcement of judgments as between the constituent parts of the United Kingdom, England and Wales, Scotland, and Northern Ireland. To this end, the Act sets out in Sched.4 a modified version of the jurisdictional rules found in the Brussels Convention and in addition contains a number of special provisions dealing with recognition and enforcement of judgments. It should be noted that the provisions of the 1982 Act, including the Brussels Convention and the 1971 Protocol (amended as explained below), contained in this Section of *Civil Procedure*, are confined to those dealing with the allocation of jurisdiction among the courts of the EC Member States. Schedule 4 of the 1982 Act contains provisions modelled on the Convention for the allocation business between the three separate jurisdictions within the UK. Its interpretation is a matter solely within the jurisdiction of the United Kingdom national courts (Case C–346/93 *Kleinwort Benson Lid v. City of Glasgow District Council, The Times*, April 17, 1995).

The Civil Procedure Rules and the relevant Practice Directions give procedural effect to the provisions of the Act and the Conventions. The principal rules are CPR Pt 6 r.6.19 (service of Claim Form where the permission of the Court is not required), and Practice Direction 6B, paras 1.1 to 1.3 (form of certificates on claim form when service abroad is to be effected without permission). See also Sched.1 and RSC O.71 (reciprocal enforcement of judgments under the Conventions) and the Practice Direction supplementing O.71. For applications under RSC O.71 the appropriate Practice Forms should be used: see **PF 157QB** to **PF 165QB**.

Accession of Other States

5–4   Section 14(1) of the 1982 Act provides that the Act (including the texts of the Conventions in the Schedules) may be amended by Order in Council. The Civil Jurisdiction and Judgments Act 1982 (Amendment) Order 1989 (S.I. 1989 No. 1346) modified the Act in consequence of a revision of the Brussels Convention and the 1971 Protocol occasioned by the accession to them of Greece by a Convention signed in Luxemburg on October 25, 1982. The Civil Jurisdiction and Judgments Act 1982 (Amendment) Order 1990 (S.I. 1990 No. 2591) brought into effect in the UK revisions occasioned by the accession of Spain and Portugal as a result of the San Sebastian Convention signed on May 28, 1989 (as to ratification elsewhere, see para. 5–6 below). The revisions made to the Brussels Convention on these occasions have not always been confined to what could be called "necessary adjustments" to cope with the accessions of new jurisdictions but in addition have included some changes thought necessary in the light of problems encountered in operating the provisions of the Convention over the years within the Member States.

EC and EFTA—The Lugano Convention

5–5   The Lugano Convention on Jurisdiction and the Enforcement of Judgments in Civil Matters was made between the Member States of the EC and those of the European Free Trade Association (EFTA). This Convention is very closely modelled on the Brussels Convention although there is no provision for references on interpretation to be made to the European Court. The Civil Jurisdiction and Judgments Act 1991 (brought into effect on May 1, 1992) gives the Lugano Convention the force of law in the UK and amends the 1982 Act so as to incorporate references in it to this Convention (as to ratification elsewhere, see para. 5–6 below). By this statute the English text of the Convention is inserted in the 1982 Act as Sched.3C. Differences between the two Conventions are noted, except in relation to Titles VI and VII where the differences are more substantial.

Ratification

5–6   The San Sebastian Convention has been ratified by all Member States. (The UK ratified the San Sebastian Convention on September 13, 1991, with entry into force on December 1, 1991.) The Lugano Convention has been ratified by all EC and EFTA Member States. (The UK ratified the Lugano Convention on February 5, 1992, with entry into force on May 1, 1992).

Up-to-date information as to the progress of ratification by EFTA Member States acceding to the Brussels Convention may be obtained from the Lord Chancellor's Department, International Division, 28 Old Queen Street, London SW1H 9HP, or from the International Litigation Procedure Reports. The information contained therein is updated monthly.

Civil Jurisdiction and Judgments Act 1982

5–7   (1982 c.27)

ARRANGEMENT OF SECTIONS

PART I

IMPLEMENTATION OF THE CONVENTIONS

MAIN IMPLEMENTING PROVISIONS

SECT.

Introductory note

This Act incorporates into United Kingdom law the EC Convention on Jurisdiction **5–8** and Enforcement of Judgments in Civil and Commercial Matters of 1968, known as the "Brussels Convention". As stated in s.2(2), "for convenience of reference" the English text of this Convention is set out in Sched.1 to the Act. For the Articles of the Convention relating to jurisdiction, see paras 5–24 *et seq*.

PART I

IMPLEMENTATION OF THE CONVENTIONS

MAIN IMPLEMENTING PROVISIONS

Interpretation of references to the Conventions and Contracting States

1.—(1) In this Act—   **5–9**

EUROPE

"the 1968 Convention" means the Convention on jurisdiction and the enforcement of judgments in civil and commercial matters (including the Protocol annexed to that Convention), signed at Brussels on 27th September 1968;

"the 1971 Protocol" means the Protocol on the interpretation of the 1968 Convention by the European Court, signed at Luxembourg on 3rd June 1971;

"the Accession Convention" means the Convention on the accession to the 1968 Convention and the 1971 Protocol of Denmark, the Republic of Ireland and the United Kingdom, signed at Luxembourg on 9th October 1978;

"the 1982 Accession Convention" means the Convention on the accession of the Hellenic Republic to the 1968 Convention and the 1971 Protocol, with the adjustments made to them by the Accession Convention, signed at Luxembourg on 25th October 1982;

"the 1989 Accession Convention" means the Convention on the accession of the Kingdom of Spain and the Portuguese Republic to the 1968 Convention and the 1971 Protocol, with the adjustments made to them by the Accession Convention and the 1982 Accession Convention, signed at Donostia—San Sebastián on 26th May 1989;

"the Brussels Conventions" means the 1968 Convention, the 1971 Protocol, the Accession Convention, the 1982 Accession Convention and the 1989 Accession Convention;

"the Lugano Convention" means the Convention on jurisdiction and the enforcement of judgments in civil and commercial matters (including the Protocols annexed to that Convention) opened for signature at Lugano on 16th September 1988 and signed by the United Kingdom on 18th September 1989.

"the Regulation" means Council Regulation (EC) No. 44/2001 of 22nd December 2000 on jurisdiction and the recognition and enforcement of judgments in civil and commercial matters.

(2) In this Act, unless the context otherwise requires—

(a) references to, or to any provision of, the 1968 Convention or the 1971 Protocol are references to the Convention, Protocol or provision as amended by the Accession Convention, the 1982 Accession Convention and the 1989 Accession Convention; and

(b) any reference to a numbered Article without more is a reference—

(i) to the Article so numbered of the 1968 Convention, in so far as the provision applies in relation to that Convention, and

(ii) to the Article so numbered of the Lugano Convention, in so far as the provision applies in relation to that Convention,

and any reference to a sub-division of a numbered Article shall be construed accordingly.

(3) In this Act—

"Contracting State", without more, in any provision means—

(a) in the application of the provision in relation to the Brussels Conventions, a Brussels Contracting State; and

(b) in the application of the provision in relation to the Lugano Convention, a Lugano Contracting State;

"Brussels Contracting State" means Denmark (which is not bound by the Regulation, but was one of the parties acceding to the 1968 Convention under the Accession Convention);

"Lugano Contracting State" means one of the original parties to the Lugano Convention, that is to say—

Austria, Belgium, Denmark, Finland, France, the Federal Republic of Germany, the Hellenic Republic, Iceland, the Republic of Ireland, Italy, Luxembourg, the Netherlands, Norway, Portugal, Spain, Sweden, Switzerland and the United Kingdom,

being a State in relation to which that Convention has taken effect in accordance with paragraph 3 or 4 of Article 61.

"Regulation State" in any provision, in the application of that provision in relation to the Regulation, has the same meaning as "Member State" in the Regulation, that is all Member States except Denmark.

(4) Any question arising as to whether it is the Regulation, any of the Brussels Conventions, or the Lugano Convention which applies in the circumstances of a particular case shall be determined as follows—

(a) in accordance with Article 54B of the Lugano Convention (which determines the relationship between the Brussels Convention and the Lugano Convention); and

(b) in accordance with Article 68 of the Regulation (which determines the relationship between the Brussels Convention and the Regulation).

Note —Amended by the Civil Jurisdiction and Judgments Act 1982 (Amendment) **5–10** Order 1989 (S.I. 1989 No. 1346); the Civil Jurisdiction and Judgments Act 1982 (Amendment) Order 1990 (S.I. 1990 No. 2591); the Civil Jurisdiction and Judgments Act 1991, s.2; and by the Civil Jurisdiction and Judgments Order 2001 (S.I. 2001 No. 3929), Sched.2, para. 1(c).

The Conventions to have the force of law

2.—(1) The Brussels Conventions shall have the force of law in the **5–11** United Kingdom, and judicial notice shall be taken of them.

(2) For convenience of reference there are set out in Schedules 1, 2, 3, 3A and 3B respectively the English texts of—

(a) the 1968 Convention as amended by Titles II and III of the Accession Convention, by Titles II and IIIof the 1982 Accession Convention and by Titles II and III of, and Annex I(d) to, the 1989 Accession Convention;

(b) the 1971 Protocol as amended by Title IV of the Accession Convention, by Title IV of the 1982 Accession Convention and by Title IV of the 1989 Accession Convention;

   (c) Titles V and VI of the Accession Convention (transitional and final provisions) as amended by Title V of the 1989 Accession Convention;

   (d) Titles V and VI of the 1982 Accession Convention (transitional and final provisions); and

   (e) Titles VI and VII of the 1989 Accession Convention (transitional and final provisions),

   (f) Titles V and VI of the 1996 Accession Convention (transitional and final provisions),

being texts prepared from the authentic English texts referred to in Articles 37 and 41 of the Accession Convention, in Article 17 of the 1982 Accession Convention and in Article 34 of the 1989 Accession Convention.

5–12   *Note* —Amended by the Civil Jurisdiction and Judgments Act 1982 (Amendment) Order 1989 (S.I. 1989 No.1346); the Civil Jurisdiction and Judgments Act 1982 (Amendment) Order 1990 (S.I. 1990 No. 2591); the Civil Jurisdiction and Judgments Act 1991, s.3, Sched.2, para. 1; and by the Civil Jurisdiction and Judgments Act 1982 (Amendment) Order 2000 (S.I. 2000 No. 1824), art.6(e).

"1968 Convention ... 1971 Protocol"

5–13   This Convention, *i.e.* the Brussels Convention, and the attached 1971 Protocol are set out in, respectively, Sched.1 and 2 of the Act both of which are included in this Section of *The Supreme Court Practice* beginning at para. 5–48, below.

Interpretation of the Conventions

5–14   **3.**—(1) Any question as to the meaning or effect of any provision of the Brussels Convention shall, if not referred to the European Court in accordance with the 1971 Protocol, be determined in accordance with the principles laid down by and any relevant decision of the European Court.

(2) Judicial notice shall be taken of any decision of, or expression of opinion by, the European Court on any such question.

(3) Without prejudice to the generality of subsection (1), the following reports (which are reproduced in the Official Journal of the Communities), namely—

   (a) the reports by Mr P. Jenard on the 1968 Convention and the 1971 Protocol; and

   (b) the report by Professor Peter Schlosser on the Accession Convention; and

   (c) the report by Professor Demetrios I. Evrigenis and Professor K. D. Kerameus on the 1982 Accession Convention; and

   (d) the report by Mr. Martino de Almeida Cruz, Mr. Manuel Desantes Real and Mr P. Jenard on the 1989 Accession Convention,

may be considered in ascertaining the meaning or effect of any provision of the Conventions and shall be given such weight as is appropriate in the circumstances.

Note —Amended by the Civil Jurisdiction and Judgments Act 1982 (Amendment) **5–15**
Order 1989 (S.I. 1989 No. 1346); the Civil Jurisdiction and Judgments Act 1982
(Amendment) Order 1990 (S.I. 1990 No. 2591); and the Civil Jurisdiction and Judg-
ments Act 1991, s.3, Sched.2, para. 1.

The Lugano Convention to have the force of law

3A.—(1) The Lugano Convention shall have the force of law in the **5–16**
United Kingdom and judicial notice shall be taken of it.

(2) For convenience of reference there is set out in Schedule 3C
the English text of the Lugano Convention as amended on the accession of Poland to that Convention.

Note —Added by the Civil Jurisdiction and Judgments Act 1991, s.1(1). Amended by **5–17**
the Civil Jurisdiction and Judgments Act 1982 (Amendment) Order (S.I. 2000 No.
1824), art.11.

"Lugano Convention"
The text of this Convention is set out in Sched.3C of the Act as amended; it is not **5–18**
included in this Section of *The Supreme Court Practice*. The Lugano Convention is made
between the Member States of the EC and those of the European Free Trade Association (EFTA). It is very closely modelled on the Brussels Convention. The amendments
to the 1982 Act required to accommodate the Lugano Convention were introduced by
the Civil Jurisdiction and Judgments Act 1991. See further, para. 5–162 below.

Interpretation of the Lugano Convention

3B.—(1) In determining any question as to the meaning or effect **5–19**
of a provision of the Lugano Convention, a court in the United
Kingdom shall, in accordance with Protocol No.2 to that Convention,
take account of any principles laid down in any relevant decision
delivered by a court of any other Lugano Contracting State concerning provisions of the Convention.

(2) Without prejudice to any practice of the courts as to the matters which may be considered apart from this section, the report of
the Lugano Convention by Mr P. Jenard and Mr G. Möller (which is
reproduced in the Official Journal of the Communities of 28th July
1990) may be considered in ascertaining the meaning or effect of any
provision of the Convention and shall be given such weight as is appropriate in the circumstances.

Note —Added by the Civil Jurisdiction and Judgments Act 1991, s.1(1). For Jenard **5–20**
and Möller report, see O.J. 1990 No. C189/07.

* * * *

OTHER SUPPLEMENTARY PROVISIONS

Allocation within UK of jurisdiction with respect to trusts and consumer contracts

10.—(1) The provisions of this section have effect for the purpose **5–21**
of allocating within the United Kingdom jurisdiction in certain
proceedings in respect of which the 1968 Convention or the Lugano
Convention confers jurisdiction on the courts of the United Kingdom
generally and to which section 16 does not apply.

(2) Any proceedings which by virtue of Article 5(6) (trusts) are

brought in the United Kingdom shall be brought in the courts of the part of the United Kingdom in which the trust is domiciled.

(3) Any proceedings which by virtue of the first paragraph of Article 14 (consumer contracts) are brought in the United Kingdom by a consumer on the ground that he is himself domiciled there shall be brought in the courts of the part of the United Kingdom in which he is domiciled.

5–22   *Note* —Amended by the Civil Jurisdiction and Judgments Act 1991, s.3, Sched.2.

"To which section 16 does not apply"

5–23   Section 16 deals with the allocation within the UK of jurisdiction in certain civil proceedings. The provisions set out in Sched.4 to the Act (which contains a modified version of Title II of the Brussels Convention) have effect for determining, for each part of the UK, whether the courts of law of that part have jurisdiction.

* * * *

PART IV

MISCELLANEOUS PROVISIONS

PROVISIONS RELATING TO JURISDICTION

Interim relief and protective measures in cases of doubtful jurisdiction

5–24   24.—(1) Any power of a court in England and Wales or Northern Ireland to grant interim relief pending trial or pending the determination of an appeal shall extend to a case where—

(a) the issue to be tried, or which is the subject of the appeal, relates to the jurisdiction of the court to entertain the proceedings;

(b) the proceedings involve the reference of any matter to the European Court under the 1971 Protocol or

(c) the proceedings involve a reference of any matter relating to the Regulation to the European Court under Article 68 of the Treaty establishing the European Community.

(2) *[Applies to Scotland]*

(3) Subsections (1) and (2) shall not be construed as restricting any power to grant interim relief or protective measures which a court may have apart from this section.

5–24.1   *Note* —Subsection (1)(c) was added by the Civil Jurisdiction and Judgments Order 2001 (S.I. 2001 No. 3929), Sched.2, para. 9(b).

"The issue to be tried ... relates to the jurisdiction of the court"

5–25   For example, where the issue is whether the court, or a court in a Contracting State, has jurisdiction under the Brussels Convention. See also Art. 24 of the Brussels Convention.

Interim relief in England and Wales and Northern Ireland in the absence of substantive proceedings

5–26   25.—(1) The High Court in England and Wales or Northern Ireland shall have power to grant interim relief where—

(a) proceedings have been or are to be commenced in a Brussels or Lugano Contracting State or a Regulation State other than the United Kingdom or in a part of the United Kingdom other than that in which the High Court in question exercises jurisdiction; and

(b) they are or will be proceedings whose subject-matter is within the scope of the Regulation as determined by Article 1 of the Regulation (whether or not the Regulation has effect in relation to the proceedings).

(2) On an application for any interim relief under subsection (1) the court may refuse to grant that relief if, in the opinion of the court, the fact that the court has no jurisdiction apart from this section in relation to the subject- matter of the proceedings in question makes it inexpedient for the court to grant it.

(3) Her Majesty may by Order in Council extend the power to grant interim relief conferred by subsection (1) so as to make it exercisable in relation to proceedings of any of the following descriptions, namely—

(a) proceedings commenced or to be commenced otherwise than in a Brussels or Lugano Contracting State or Regulation State;

(b) proceedings whose subject-matter is not within the scope of the Regulation as determined by Article 1 of the Regulation;

(c) [...]

(4) An Order in Council under subsection (3)—

(a) may confer power to grant only specified descriptions of interim relief;

(b) may make different provision for different classes of proceedings, for proceedings pending in different countries or courts outside the United Kingdom or in different parts of the United Kingdom, and for other different circumstances; and

(c) may impose conditions or restrictions on the exercise of any power conferred by the order.

(5) [...]

(6) Any Order in Council under subsection (3) shall be subject to annulment in pursuance of a resolution of either House of Parliament.

(7) In this section "interim relief", in relation to the High Court in England and Wales or Northern Ireland, means interim relief of any kind which that court has power to grant in proceedings relating to matters within its jurisdiction, other than—

(a) a warrant for the arrest of property; or

(b) provision for obtaining evidence.

Note — Subsections (1)(a) and (3)(a) amended by the Civil Jurisdiction and Judgments Act 1991, s.3, Sched.2, para. 12(a); subs.(1)(b) amended by para. 12. Subss.(3)(c) and (5) repealed by the Arbitration Act 1996. The power to grant interim relief under subs.(1) has been extended by the Civil Jurisdiction and Judgments Act 1982 (Interim Relief) Order 1997 (see para. 5–160 below). Subsections (1)(a), (b) and (3)(b) were fur-

5–27

ther amended and by the Civil Jurisdiction and Judgments Order (S.I. 2001 No. 3929), Sched.2, para. 10(b)(ii).

Security in Admiralty proceedings in England and Wales or Northern Ireland in case of stay, etc.

5–28 **26.**—(1) Where in England and Wales or Northern Ireland a court stays or dismisses Admiralty proceedings on the ground that the dispute in question should be submitted to the determination of the courts of another part of the United Kingdom or of an overseas country, the court may, if in those proceedings property has been arrested or bail or other security has been given to prevent or obtain release from arrest—

> (a) order that the property arrested be retained as security for the satisfaction of any award or judgment which—
>
> > (i) is given in respect of the dispute in the legal proceedings in favour of which those proceedings are stayed or dismissed; and
> >
> > (ii) is enforceable in England and Wales or, as the case may be, in Northern Ireland, or
>
> (b) order that the stay or dismissal of those proceedings be conditional on the provision of equivalent security for the satisfaction of any such award or judgment.

(2) Where the court makes an order under subsection (1), it may attach such conditions to the order as it thinks fit, in particular conditions with respect to the institution or prosecution of the relevant legal proceedings.

(3) Subject to any provision made by rules of court and to any necessary modifications, the same law and practice shall apply in relation to property retained in pursuance of an order made by a court under subsection (1) as would apply if it were held for the purposes of proceedings in that court.

5–29 *Note* —Amended by the Arbitration Act 1996.

* * * * *

DOMICILE

Proceedings in England and Wales or Northern Ireland for torts to immovable property

5–30 **30.**—(1) The jurisdiction of any court in England and Wales or Northern Ireland to entertain proceedings for trespass to, or any other tort affecting, immovable property shall extend to cases in which the property in question is situated outside that part of the United Kingdom unless the proceedings are principally concerned with a question of the title, or the right to possession of, that property.

(2) Subsection (1) has effect subject to the 1968 Convention and the Lugano Convention and the Regulation and to the provisions set out in Schedule 4.

Note —Amended by the Civil Jurisdiction and Judgments Act 1991, s.3, Sched.2, **5–31** para. 13; and by the Civil Jurisdiction and Judgments Order (S.I. 2001 No. 3929), Sched.2, para. 13.

* * * * *

PART V

SUPPLEMENTARY AND GENERAL PROVISIONS

Note —Under the Brussels Convention, domicile rather than presence (or national- **5–32** ity), is the key to the allocation of jurisdiction among the courts of the Contracting States, see Arts 2 and 52, paras 5–50 and 5–122, below. Consequently, this Part of the Act, *inter alia*, enacts particular rules governing domicile.

Domicile of individuals

41.—(1) Subject to Article 52 (which contains provisions for **5–33** determining whether a party is domiciled in a Contracting State), the following provisions of this section determine, for the purposes of the 1968 Convention the Lugano Convention and this Act, whether an individual is domiciled in the United Kingdom or in a particular part of, or place in, the United Kingdom or in a state other than a Contracting State.

(2) An individual is domiciled in the United Kingdom if and only if—

    (a) he is resident in the United Kingdom; and

    (b) the nature and circumstances of his residence indicate that he has a substantial connection with the United Kingdom.

(3) Subject to subsection (5), an individual is domiciled in a particular part of the United Kingdom if and only if—

    (a) he is resident in that part; and

    (b) the nature and circumstances of his residence indicate that he has a substantial connection with that part.

(4) An individual is domiciled in a particular place in the United Kingdom if and only if he—

    (a) is domiciled in the part of the United Kingdom in which that place is situated; and

    (b) is resident in that place.

(5) An individual who is domiciled in the United Kingdom but in whose case the requirements of subsection (3)(b) are not satisfied in relation to any particular part of the United Kingdom shall be treated as domiciled in the part of the United Kingdom in which he is resident.

(6) In the case of an individual who—

    (a) is resident in the United Kingdom, or in a particular part of the United Kingdom; and

    (b) has been so resident for the last three months or more, the requirements of subsection (2)(b) or, as the case may be, subsection (3)(b) shall be presumed to be fulfilled unless the contrary is proved.

(7) An individual is domiciled in a state other than a Contracting State if and only if—

    (a) he is resident in that state; and

    (b) the nature and circumstances of his residence indicate that he has a substantial connection with that state.

5–34   *Note* — Subs.(1) amended by the Civil Jurisdiction and Judgments Act 1991, s.3, Sched.2, para. 16.

Domicile and seat of corporation or association

5–35   **42.**—(1) For the purposes of this Act the seat of a corporation or association (as determined by this section) shall be treated as its domicile.

(2) The following provisions of this section determine where a corporation or association has its seat—

    (a) for the purpose of Article 53 (which for the purposes of the 1968 Convention or, as the case may be, the Lugano Convention equates the domicile of such a body with its seat); and

    (b) for the purposes of this Act other than the provisions mentioned in section 43(1)(b) and (c).

(3) A corporation or association has its seat in the United Kingdom if and only if—

    (a) it was incorporated or formed under the law of a part of the United Kingdom and has its registered office or some other official address in the United Kingdom; or

    (b) its central management and control is exercised in the United Kingdom.

(4) A corporation or association has its seat in a particular part of the United Kingdom if and only if it has its seat in the United Kingdom and—

    (a) it has its registered office or some other official address in that part; or

    (b) its central management and control is exercised in that part; or

    (c) it has a place of business in that part.

(5) A corporation or association has its seat in a particular place in the United Kingdom if and only if it has its seat in the part of the United Kingdom in which that place is situated and—

    (a) it has its registered office or some other official address in that place; or

    (b) its central management and control is exercised in that place; or

    (c) it has a place of business in that place.

(6) Subject to subsection (7), a corporation or association has its seat in a state other than the United Kingdom if and only if—

    (a) it was incorporated or formed under the law of that state and has its registered office or some other official address there; or

    (b) its central management and control is exercised in that state.

(7) A corporation or association shall not be regarded as having its seat in a Contracting State other than the United Kingdom if it is shown that the courts of that state would not regard it as having its seat there.

(8) In this section—

"business" includes any activity carried on by a corporation or association, and "place of business" shall be construed accordingly; "official address", in relation to a corporation or association, means an address which it is required by law to register, notify or maintain for the purpose of receiving notices or other communications.

Note — Subs.(2)(a) amended by the Civil Jurisdiction and Judgments Act 1991, s.3, **5–36**
Sched.2, para. 17.

Seat of corporation or association for purposes of Article 16(2) and related provisions

43.—(1) The following provisions of this section determine where **5–37** a corporation or association has its seat for the purposes of—

(a) Article 16(2) of the 1968 Convention or of the Lugano Convention (which confers exclusive jurisdiction over proceedings relating to the formation or dissolution of such bodies, or to the decisions of their organs);

(b) Articles 5A and 16(2); in Schedule 4 and

(c) and Rules 2(12), 4(1)(b) in Schedule 8.

(2) A corporation or association has its seat in the United Kingdom if and only if—

(a) it was incorporated or formed under the law of a part of the United Kingdom; or

(b) its central management and control is exercised in the United Kingdom.

(3) A corporation or association has its seat in a particular part of the United Kingdom if and only if it has its seat in the United Kingdom and—

(a) subject to subsection (5), it was incorporated or formed under the law of that part; or

(b) being incorporated or formed under the law of a state other than the United Kingdom, its central management and control is exercised in that part.

(4) A corporation or association has its seat in a particular place in Scotland if and only if it has its seat in Scotland and—

(a) it has its registered office or some other official address in that place; or

(b) it has no registered office or other official address in Scotland, but its central management and control is exercised in that place.

(5) A corporation or association incorporated or formed under—

(a) an enactment forming part of the law of more than one part of the United Kingdom; or

(b) an instrument having effect in the domestic law of more than one part of the United Kingdom,

1673

shall, if it has a registered office, be taken to have its seat in the part of the United Kingdom in which that office is situated, and not in any other part of the United Kingdom.

(6) Subject to subsection (7), a corporation or association has its seat in a Contracting State other than the United Kingdom if and only if—

    (a) it was incorporated or formed under the law of that state; or

    (b) its central management and control is exercised in that state.

(7) A corporation or association shall not be regarded as having its seat in a Contracting State other than the United Kingdom if—

    (a) it has its seat in the United Kingdom by virtue of subsection 2(a); or

    (b) it is shown that the courts of that other state would not regard it for the purposes of Article 16(2) as having its seat there.

(8) In this section "official address" has the same meaning as in section 42.

5–38   *Note* — Subs.(1)(a) amended by the Civil Jurisdiction and Judgments Act 1991, s.3, Sched.2, para. 18.

Persons deemed to be domiciled in the United Kingdom for certain purposes

5–39   **44.**—(1) This section applies to—

    (a) proceedings within Section 3 of Title II of the 1968 Convention or Section 3 of Title II of the Lugano Convention (insurance contracts), and

    (b) proceedings within Section 4 of Title II of either of those Conventions (consumer contracts).

(2) A person who, for the purposes of proceedings to which this section applies arising out of the operations of a branch, agency or other establishment in the United Kingdom, is deemed for the purposes of the 1968 Convention or, as the case may be, of the Lugano Convention to be domiciled in the United Kingdom by virtue of—

    (a) Article 8, second paragraph (insurers); or

    (b) Article 13, second paragraph (suppliers of goods, services or credit to consumers),

shall, for the purposes of those proceedings, be treated for the purposes of this Act as so domiciled and as domiciled in the part of the United Kingdom in which the branch, agency or establishment in question is situated.

5–40   *Note* — Subs.(1) amended by the Civil Jurisdiction and Judgments Act 1991, s.3, Sched.2, para. 19.

Domicile of trusts

5–41   **45.**—(1) The following provisions of this section determine, for the purposes of the 1968 Convention the Lugano Convention and this Act, where a trust is domiciled.

(2) A trust is domiciled in the United Kingdom if and only if it is by virtue of subsection (3) domiciled in a part of the United Kingdom.

(3) A trust is domiciled in a part of the United Kingdom if and only if the system of law of that part is the system of law with which the trust has its closest and most real connection.

Note — Subsection (1) amended by the Civil Jurisdiction and Judgments Act 1991, **5–42** s.3, Sched.2, para. 20.

Domicile and seat of the Crown

46.—(1) For the purposes of this Act the seat of the Crown (as **5–43** determined by this section) shall be treated as its domicile.

(2) The following provisions of this section determine where the Crown has its seat—

    (a) for the purposes of the 1968 Convention and the Lugano Convention (in each of which Article 53 equates the domicile of a legal person with its seat); and

    (b) for the purposes of this Act.

(3) Subject to the provisions of any Order in Council for the time being in force under subsection (4)—

    (a) the Crown in right of Her Majesty's government in the United Kingdom has its seat in every part of, and every place in, the United Kingdom; and

    (aa) the Crown in right of the Scottish Administration has its seat in, and in every place in, Scotland; and

    (b) the Crown in right of Her Majesty's government in Northern Ireland has its seat in, and in every place in, Northern Ireland.

(4) Her Majesty may by Order in Council provide that, in the case of proceedings of any specified description against the Crown in right of Her Majesty's government in the United Kingdom, the Crown shall be treated for the purposes of the 1968 Convention the Lugano Convention and this Act as having its seat in, and in every place in, a specified part of the United Kingdom and not in any other part of the United Kingdom.

(5) An Order in Council under subsection (4) may frame a description proceedings in any way, and in particular may do so by reference to the government department or officer of the Crown against which or against whom they fall to be instituted.

(6) Any Order in Council made under this section shall be subject to annulment in pursuance of a resolution of either House of Parliament.

(7) Nothing in this section applies to the Crown otherwise than in right of Her Majesty's government in the United Kingdom, the Scottish Administration or Her Majesty's government in Northern Ireland.

Note — Subss.(2)(a) & (4) amended by the Civil Jurisdiction and Judgments Act **5–44** 1991, s.3, Sched.2, para. 21. Subss.(3) and (7) are amended by the Scotland Act 1998 (c.46), s.125, Sched.8, para. 18.

EUROPE

* * * * *

Saving for powers to stay, sist, strike out or dismiss proceedings

5–45   **49.** Nothing in this Act shall prevent any court in the United Kingdom from staying, sisting, striking out or dismissing any proceedings before it, on the ground of forum non conveniens or otherwise, where to do so is not inconsistent with the 1968 Convention or, as the case may be, the Lugano Convention.

5–46   *Note* —Amended by the Civil Jurisdiction and Judgments Act 1991, s.3, Sched.2, para. 24.

"Staying ... any proceedings"

5–47   This section should be read in conjunction with the Supreme Court Act 1981, s.49(3), see paras 9A–153, 9A–161, 9A–162.

* * * *

SCHEDULES

SECTION 2(2)(A)   **SCHEDULE 1**

TEXT OF 1968 CONVENTION, AS AMENDED

5–48   *Note* —The text set out below is the version of the 1968 Convention as inserted in Sched.1 to the 1982 Act by the Civil Jurisdiction and Judgments Act 1982 (Amendment) Order 1990 (S.I. 1990 No. 2591), art. 12(1), Sched.1, following upon the accession to the European Community of Spain and Portugal. For the earlier version of the Convention inserted following the accession of Greece, see the Civil Jurisdiction and Judgments Act 1982 (Amendment) Order 1989 (S.I. 1989 No. 1346), art. 9(1), Sched.1. Section 3(3) of the 1982 Act, as amended, states that:

> "the reports by Mr. P. Jenard on the 1968 Convention and the 1971 Protocol; and the reports by Professor Peter Schlosser, Professor Demetrios I. Evrigenis, Professor K.D. Kerameus, Mr. Martinho de Almedia Cruz, Mr. Manuel Desantes Real and Mr. P. Jenard on the various Accession Conventions between 1978 and 1989,"

may be considered in ascertaining the meaning or effect of any provision in the Convention and "shall be given such weight as is appropriate in the circumstances". These reports were published in the Official Journal of the European Communities. For a basic commentary on the text of Titles I and II see notes to RSC O.11 in SCP 1999, Vol. 1 and particularly notes at Vol. 1, paras 11/1/48 to 11/1/74. For a basic commentary on the text of Title III see notes to RSC O.71, rr.25–39 in SCP 1999, Vol. 1. For more detailed analysis of the Convention see the leading textbooks, *e.g.* Dicey & Morris, *Conflict of Laws* (12th ed.), and Briggs & Rees, *Civil Jurisdiction and Judgments* (2nd ed.).

For commentary on the text of Title II see notes to O.11 in SCP 1999, Vol. 1 and particularly notes at Vol. 1, paras 11/4/48 to 11/1/74. For commentary on the text of Title III see notes to O.71 rr.25–39 in SCP 1999, Vol. 1.

* * * *

TITLE I

SCOPE

Article 1

5–49   This Convention shall apply in civil and commercial matters whatever the nature of the court or tribunal. It shall not extend, in particular, to revenue, customs or administrative matters.

The Convention shall not apply to—

1. The status or legal capacity of natural persons, rights in property arising out of a matrimonial relationship, wills and succession.

2. Bankruptcy, proceedings relating to the winding-up of insolvent companies or other legal persons, judicial arrangements, compositions and analogous proceedings.

3. Social security.

4. Arbitration.

TITLE II

JURISDICTION

SECTION 1

GENERAL PROVISIONS

Article 2

Subject to the provisions of this Convention, persons domiciled in a Contracting State shall, whatever their nationality, be sued in the courts of that State.   **5–50**

Persons who are not nationals of the State in which they are domiciled shall be governed by the rules of jurisdiction applicable to nationals of that State.

"Persons domiciled in a Contracting State"

See ss.41–46 of the 1982 Act, paras 5–33 to 5–43, above.   **5–51**

Article 3

Persons domiciled in a Contracting State may be sued in the courts of another   **5–52**
Contracting State only by virtue of the rules set out in Sections 2 to 6 of this Title.

In particular the following provisions shall not be applicable as against them—

...

—in the United Kingdom: the rules which enable jurisdiction to be founded on:

(a) the document instituting the proceedings having been served on the defendant during his temporary presence in the United Kingdom; or

(b) the presence within the United Kingdom of property belonging to the defendant; or

(c) the seizure by the plaintiff of property situated in the United Kingdom.

Article 4

If the defendant is not domiciled in a Contracting State, the jurisdiction of the   **5–53**
courts of each Contracting State shall, subject to the provisions of Article 16, be determined by the law of that State.

As against such a defendant, any person domiciled in a Contracting State may, whatever his nationality, avail himself in that State of the rules of jurisdiction there in force, and in particular those specified in the second paragraph of Article 3, in the same way as the nationals of that State.

SECTION 2

SPECIAL JURISDICTION

Article 5

A person domiciled in a Contracting State may, in another Contracting State, be   **5–54**
sued—

1. In matters relating to a contract, in the courts for the place of performance of the obligation in question; in matters relating to individual contracts of employment, this place is that where the employee habitually carries out his work, or if the employee does not habitually carry out his work in any one country, the employer may also be sued in the courts for the place where the business which engaged the employee was or is now situated.

2. In matters relating to maintainance, in the courts for the place where the mainte-nance creditor is domiciled or habitually resident or, if the matter is ancillary to proceedings concerning the status of a person, in the court which, according to its own law, has jurisdiction to entertain those proceedings, unless that jurisdiction is based solely on the nationality of one of the parties.

3. In matters relating to tort, delict or quasi-delict, in the courts for the place where the harmful event occurred.

4. As regards a civil claim for damages or restitution which is based on an act giving rise to criminal proceedings, in the court seised of those proceedings, to the extent that that court has jurisdiction under its own law to entertain civil proceedings.

5. As regards a dispute arising out of the operations of a branch, agency or other establishment, in the courts for the place in which the branch, agency or other establishment is situated.

6. As settlor, trustee or beneficiary of a trust created by the operation of a statute, or by a written instrument, or created orally and evidenced in writing, in the courts of the Contracting State in which the trust is domiciled.

7. As regards a dispute concerning the payment of remuneration claimed in respect of the salvage of a cargo or freight, in the court under the authority of which the cargo or freight in question—

    (a) has been arrested to secure such payment, or

    (b) could have been so arrested, but bail or other security has been given;
           provided that this provision shall apply only if it is claimed that the defen-dant has an interest in the cargo or freight or had such an interest at the time of salvage.

"In matters relating to individual contracts of employment"

5–55   In Point 1 these words and the text following were added by Civil Jurisdiction and Judgments Act 1982 (Amendment) Order 1990 at the time of the revision of the 1968 Convention upon the accession of Spain and Portugal. The opportunity was taken to make this modification in the light of experience.

    The corresponding Point in Art. 5.1 of the Lugano Convention reads:

    "A person domiciled in a Contracting State may, in another Contracting State, be sued:

        1. In matters relating to a contract, in the courts for the place of perfor-mance of the obligation in question; in matters relating to individual contracts of employments, this place is that where the employee habitu-ally carries out his work, or if the employee does not habitually carry out his work in any one country, this place shall be the place of business through which he was engaged;".

Article 6

5–56 A person domiciled in a Contracting State may also be sued—

1. Where he is one of a number of defendants, in the courts for the place where any one of them is domiciled.

2. As a third party in an action on a warranty or guarantee or in any other third party proceedings, in the court seised of the original proceedings, unless these were instituted solely with the object of removing him from the jurisdiction of the court which would be competent in his case.

3. On a counter-claim arising from the same contract or facts on which the original claim was based, in the court in which the original claim is pending.

4. In matters relating to a contract, if the action may be combined with an action against the same defendant in matters relating to rights in rem in immovable prop-erty, in the court of the Contracting State in which the property is situated.

"In matters relating to a contract"

5–57   Point 4 of this Article was added by Civil Jurisdiction and Judgments Act 1982 (Amendment) Order 1990 at the time of the revision of the 1968 Convention upon the accession of Spain and Portugal. The opportunity was taken to make this modifica-tion in the light of experience.

Article 6a

5–58 Where by virtue of this Convention a court of a Contracting State has jurisdiction in actions relating to liability from the use or operation of a ship, that court, or any other court substituted for this purpose by the internal law of that State, shall also have jurisdiction over claims for limitation of such liability.

"Relating to liability from"

The corresponding Article in the Lugano Convention reads "relating to liability **5–59** arising from".

SECTION 3

JURISDICTION IN MATTERS RELATING TO INSURANCE

Article 7

In matters relating to insurance, jurisdiction shall be determined by this Section, **5–60** without prejudice to the provisions of Articles 4 and 5 point 5.

Article 8

An insurer domiciled in a Contracting State may be sued— **5–61**

1. in the courts of the State where he is domiciled, or

2. in another Contracting State, in the courts for the place where the policy-holder is domiciled, or

3. if he is a co-insurer, in the courts of a Contracting State in which proceedings are brought against the leading insurer.

An insurer who is not domiciled in a Contracting State but has a branch, agency or other establishment in one of the Contracting States shall, in disputes arising out of the operations of the branch, agency or establishment, be deemed to be domiciled in that State.

Article 9

In respect of liability insurance or insurance of immovable property, the insurer **5–62** may in addition be sued in the courts for the place where the harmful event occurred. The same applies if movable and immovable property are covered by the same insurance policy and both are adversely affected by the same contingency.

Article 10

In respect of liability insurance, the insurer may also, if the law of the court permits **5–63** it, be joined in proceedings which the injured party had brought against the insured.

The provisions of Articles 7, 8 and 9 shall apply to actions brought by the injured party directly against the insurer, where such direct actions are permitted.

If the law governing such direct actions provides that the policy-holder or the insured may be joined as a party to the action, the same court shall have jurisdiction over them.

"Injured party had brought"

The corresponding Article in the Lugano Convention reads "injured party has **5–64** brought".

Article 11

Without prejudice to the provisions of the third paragraph of Article 10, an insurer **5–65** may bring proceedings only in the courts of the Contracting State in which the defendant is domiciled, irrespective of whether he is the policy-holder, the insured or a beneficiary.

The provisions of this Section shall not affect the right to bring a counterclaim in the court in which, in accordance with this Section, the original claim is pending.

Article 12

The provisions of this Section may be departed from only by an agreement on juris- **5–66** diction—

1. which is entered into after the dispute has arisen, or

2. which allows the policy-holder, the insured or a beneficiary to bring proceedings in courts other than those indicated in this Section, or

EUROPE

1679

3. which is concluded between a policy-holder and an insurer, both of whom are domiciled in the same Contracting State, and which has the effect of conferring jurisdiction on the courts of that State even if the harmful event were to occur abroad, provided that such an agreement is not contrary to the law of that State, or

4. which is concluded with a policy-holder who is not domiciled in a Contracting State, except in so far as the insurance is compulsory or relates to immovable property in a Contracting State, or

5. which relates to a contract of insurance in so far as it covers one or more of the risks set out in Article 12a.

"Whom are domiciled in the same Contracting State"

5–67   *Cf.*, Art. 15(3). The corresponding Article in the Lugano Convention (and in some earlier versions of the Brussels Convention) reads "whom are at the time of conclusion of the contract domiciled or habitually resident in the same Contracting State".

Article 12a

5–68   The following are the risks referred to in point 5 of Article 12—

1. Any loss of or damage to—
   (a) sea-going ships, installations situated offshore or on the high seas, or aircraft, arising from perils which relate to their use for commercial purposes;
   (b) goods in transit other than passengers' baggage where the transit consists of or includes carriage by such ships or aircraft.

2. Any liability, other than for bodily injury to passengers or loss of or damage to their baggage—
   (a) arising out of the use or operation of ships, installations or aircraft as referred to in point 1(a) above in so far as the law of the Contracting State in which such aircraft are registered does not prohibit agreements on jurisdiction regarding insurance of such risks;
   (b) for loss or damage caused by goods in transit as described in point 1(b) above.

3. Any financial loss connected with the use or operation of ships, installations or aircraft as referred to in point 1(a) above, in particular loss of freight or charter-hire.

4. Any risk or interest connected with any of those referred to in points 1 to 3 above.

SECTION 4

JURISDICTION OVER CONSUMER CONTRACTS

Article 13

5–69   In proceedings concerning a contract concluded by a person for a purpose which can be regarded as being outside his trade or profession, hereinafter called "the consumer", jurisdiction shall be determined by this Section, without prejudice to the provisions of Article 4 and point 5 of Article 5, if it is—

1. a contract for the sale of goods on instalment credit terms, or

2. a contract for a loan repayable by instalments, or for any other form of credit, made to finance the sale of goods, or

3. any other contract for the supply of goods or a contract for the supply of services, and
   (a) in the State of the consumer's domicile the conclusion of the contract was preceded by a specific invitation addressed to him or by advertising; and
   (b) the consumer took in that State the steps necessary for the conclusion of the contract.

Where a consumer enters into a contract with a party who is not domiciled in a Contracting State but has a branch, agency or other establishment in one of the Contracting States, that party shall, in disputes arising out of the operations of the branch, agency or establishment, be deemed to be domiciled in that State.

This Section shall not apply to contracts of transport.

Article 14

5–70   A consumer may bring proceedings against the other party to a contract either in the courts of the Contracting State in which that party is domiciled or in the courts of the Contracting State in which he is himself domiciled.

Proceedings may be brought against a consumer by the other party to the contract only in the courts of the Contracting State in which the consumer is domiciled.

These provisions shall not affect the right to bring a counter-claim in the court in which, in accordance with this Section, the original claim is pending.

Article 15

The provisions of this Section may be departed from only by an agreement— **5–71**

1. which is entered into after the dispute has arisen, or

2. which allows the consumer to bring proceedings in courts other than those indicated in this Section, or

3. which is entered into by the consumer and the other party to the contract, both of whom are at the time of conclusion of the contract domiciled or habitually resident in the same Contracting State, and which confers jurisdiction on the courts of that State, provided that such an agreement is not contrary to the law of that State.

SECTION 5

EXCLUSIVE JURISDICTION

Article 16

The following courts shall have exclusive jurisdiction, regardless of domicile: **5–72**

   (a) in proceedings which have as their object rights *in rem* in immovable property or tenancies of immovable property, the courts of the Contracting State in which the property is situated;

   (b) however, in proceedings which have as their object tenancies of immovable property concluded for temporary private use for a maximum period of six consecutive months, the courts of the Contracting State in which the defendant is domiciled shall also have jurisdiction, provided that the landlord and the defendant are natural persons and are domiciled in the same Contracting State.

2. In proceedings which have as their object the validity of the constitution, the nullity or the dissolution of companies or other legal persons or associations of natural or legal persons, or the decisions of their organs, the courts of the Contracting State in which the company, legal person or association has its seat.

3. In proceedings which have as their object the validity of entries in public registers, the courts of the Contracting State in which the register is kept.

4. In proceedings concerned with the registration or validity of patents, trade marks, designs, or other similar rights required to be deposited or registered, the courts of the Contracting State in which the deposit or registration has been applied for, has taken place or is under the terms of an international convention deemed to have taken place.

5. In proceedings concerned with the enforcement of judgments, the courts of the Contracting State in which the judgment has been or is to be enforced.

"Tenancies of immovable property"

Alterations to the circumstances in which concurrent jurisdiction would be enjoyed **5–73**
by the courts of Contracting States were made by Civil Jurisdiction and Judgments Act 1982 (Amendment) Order 1990 at the time of the revision of the 1968 Convention upon the accession of Spain and Portugal. The opportunity was taken to make this modification in the light of experience.

Article 6.1(b) in the Lugano Convention reads:

"however, in proceedings which have as their object tenancies of immovable property concluded for temporary private use for a maximum period of six consecutive months, the courts of the Contracting State in which the defendant is domiciled shall also have jurisdiction, provided that the tenant is a natural person and neither party is domiciled in the Contracting State in which the property is situated;".

SECTION 6

PROROGATION OF JURISDICTION

Article 17

If the parties, one or more of whom is domiciled in a Contracting State, have **5–74**
agreed that a court or the courts of a Contracting State are to have jurisdiction to

EUROPE

settle any disputes which have arisen or which may arise in connection with a particular legal relationship, that court or those courts shall have exclusive jurisdiction. Such an agreement conferring jurisdiction shall be either—

(a) in writing or evidenced in writing, or

(b) in a form which accords with practices which the parties have established between themselves, or

(c) in international trade or commerce, in a form which accords with a usage of which the parties are or ought to have been aware and which in such trade or commerce is widely known to, and regularly observed by, parties to contracts of the type involved in the particular trade or commerce concerned.

Where such an agreement is concluded by parties, none of whom is domiciled in a Contracting State, the courts of other Contracting States shall have no jurisdiction over their disputes unless the court or courts chosen have declined jurisdiction.

The court or courts of a Contracting State on which a trust instrument has conferred jurisdiction shall have exclusive jurisdiction in any proceedings brought against a settlor, trustee or beneficiary, if relations between these persons or their rights or obligations under the trust are involved.

Agreements or provisions of a trust instrument conferring jurisdiction shall have no legal force if they are contrary to the provisions of Articles 12 or 15, or if the courts whose jurisdiction they purport to exclude have exclusive jurisdiction by virtue of Article 16.

If an agreement conferring jurisdiction was concluded for the benefit of only one of the parties, that party shall retain the right to bring proceedings in any other court which has jurisdiction by virtue of this Convention.

In matters relating to individual contracts of employment an agreement conferring jurisdiction shall have legal force only if it is entered into after the dispute has arisen or if the employee invokes it to seise courts other than those for the defendant's domicile or those specified in article 5(1).

5-75   *Note* —The first paragraph of this Article was substantially amended by the Civil Jurisdiction and Judgments Act 1982 (Amendment) Order 1990 at the time of the revision of the 1968 Convention upon the accession of Spain and Portugal. The opportunity was taken to make this modification in the light of experience. O.10, r.3 (service of writ in pursuance of contract) provides that where a contract contains an agreement conferring jurisdiction to which the 1982 Act applies and the writ is served under O.11, r.1(2) the writ shall be deemed to have been duly served on the defendant.

"Individual contracts of employment"

5-76   In the Lugano Convention the points within Art. 17 are numbered and the final point, numbered 5, reads as follows: "In matters relating to individual contracts of employment an agreement conferring jurisdiction shall have legal force only if it is entered into after the dispute has arisen."

Article 18

5-77   Apart from jurisdiction derived from other provisions of this Convention, a court of a Contracting State before whom a defendant enters an appearance shall have jurisdiction. This rule shall not apply where appearance was entered solely to contest the jurisdiction, or where another court has exclusive jurisdiction by virtue of Article 16.

"Enters an appearance"

5-78   For relationship between "appearance" and "acknowledgement of service" as provided for in O.12, see Vol. 1, para. 12.0.1.

SECTION 7

EXAMINATION AS TO JURISDICTION AND ADMISSIBILITY

Article 19

5-79   Where a court of a Contracting State is seised of a claim which is principally concerned with a matter over which the courts of another Contracting State have exclusive jurisdiction by virtue of Article 16, it shall declare of its own motion that it has no jurisdiction.

Article 20

Where a defendant domiciled in one Contracting State is sued in a court of another **5–80** Contracting State and does not enter an appearance, the court shall declare of its own motion that it has no jurisdiction unless its jurisdiction is derived from the provisions of the Convention.

The court shall stay the proceedings so long as it is not shown that the defendant has been able to receive the document instituting the proceedings or an equivalent document in sufficient time to enable him to arrange for his defence, or that all necessary steps have been taken to this end.

The provisions of the foregoing paragraph shall be replaced by those of Article 15 of the Hague Convention of 15th November 1965 on the service abroad of judicial and extrajudicial documents in civil or commercial matters, if the document instituting the proceedings or notice thereof had to be transmitted abroad in accordance with that Convention.

"Provisions of the Convention"

Would seem to mean "this" Convention, *i.e.* the Brussels Convention. **5–81**

SECTION 8

LIS PENDENS—RELATED ACTIONS

Article 21

Where proceedings involving the same cause of action and between the same parties **5–82** are brought in the courts of different Contracting States, any court other than the court first seised shall of its own motion stay its proceedings until such time as the jurisdiction of the court first seised is established.

Where the jurisdiction of the court first seised is established, any court other than the court first seised shall decline jurisdiction in favour of that court.

"Stay its proceedings"

This phrase and the words following it in the first paragraph of this Article were **5–83** substituted for the words "decline jurisdiction in favour of that court". The substitution was made by the Civil Jurisdiction and Judgments Act 1982 (Amendment) Order 1990 at the time of the revision of the 1968 Convention upon the accession of Spain and Portugal. The opportunity was taken to make this modification in the light of experience.

Article 22

Where related actions are brought in the courts of different Contracting States, any **5–84** court other than the court first seised may, while the actions are pending at first instance, stay its proceedings.

A court other than the court first seised may also, on the application of one of the parties, decline jurisdiction if the law of that court permits the consolidation of related actions and the court first seised has jurisdiction over both actions.

For the purposes of this Article, actions are deemed to be related where they are so closely connected that it is expedient to hear and determine them together to avoid the risk of irreconcilable judgments resulting from separate proceedings.

Article 23

Where actions come within the exclusive jurisdiction of several courts, any court **5–85** other than the court first seised shall decline jurisdiction in favour of that court.

SECTION 9

PROVISIONAL, INCLUDING PROTECTIVE, MEASURES

Article 24

Application may be made to the courts of a Contracting State for such provisional, **5–86** including protective, measures as may be available under the law of that State, even if,

EUROPE

under this Convention, the courts of another Contracting State have jurisdiction as to the substance of the matter.

* * * *

Title III

Recognition and Enforcement

Article 25

5–87 For the purposes of this Convention "judgment" means any judgment given by a court or tribunal of a Contracting State, whatever the judgment may be called, including a decree, order, decision or writ of execution, as well as the determination of costs or expenses by an officer of the court.

Section 1

Recognition

Article 26

5–88 A judgment given in a Contracting State shall be recognised in the other Contracting States without any special procedure being required.

Any interested party who raises the recognition of a judgment as the principal issue in a dispute may, in accordance with the procedures provided for in Sections 2 and 3 of this Title apply for a decision that the judgment be recognised.

If the outcome of proceedings in a court of a Contracting State depends on the determination of an incidental question of recognition that court shall have jurisdiction over that question.

Article 27

5–89 A judgment shall not be recognised:

1. if such recognition is contrary to public policy in the State in which recognition is sought;

2. where it was given in default of appearance, if the defendant was not duly served with the document which instituted the proceedings or with an equivalent document in sufficient time to enable him to arrange for his defence;

3. if the judgment is irreconcilable with a judgment given in a dispute between the same parties in the State in which recognition is sought;

4. if the court of the State of origin, in order to arrive at its judgment, has decided a preliminary question concerning the status or legal capacity of natural persons, rights in property arising out of a matrimonial relationship, wills or succession in a way that conflicts with a rule of the private international law of the State in which the recognition is sought, unless the same result would have been reached by the application of the rules of private international law of that State;

5. if the judgment is irreconcilable with an earlier judgment given in a non-contracting State involving the same cause of action and between the same parties, provided that this latter judgment fulfils the conditions necessary for its recognition in the state addressed.

Article 28

5–90 Moreover, a judgment shall not be recognised if it conflicts with the provisions of Sections 3, 4 or 5 of Title II, or in a case provided for in Article 59.

In its examination of the grounds if jurisdiction referred to in the foregoing paragraph, the court or authority applied to shall be bound by the findings of fact on which the court of the State of origin based its jurisdiction.

Subject to the provisions of the first paragraph, the jurisdiction of the court of the State of origin may not be reviewed; the test of public policy referred to in point 1 of Article 27 may not be applied to the rules relating to jurisdiction.

Lugano Convention

5–91 An additional paragraph has been inserted between paras 2 and 3 of this Article:

A judgment may furthermore be refused recognition in any case provided for in Article 54B(3) or 57(4).

Application

The mischief at which this Article is directed is the recognition and enforcement of a judgment of a court which did not have jurisdiction under Section 3, 4 or 5 of Title II to the Convention. It is not concerned with whether the foreign court had jurisdiction on an issue which would subsequently have fallen to be decided by the court of another Contracting State (*Berkeley Administration Inc. v. McClelland (No. 2)* [1995] I.L.Pr. 201).

5–92

Article 29

Under no circumstances may a foreign judgment be reviewed as to its substance.

5–93

Article 30

A court of a Contracting State in which recognition is sought of a judgment given in another Contracting State may stay the proceedings if an ordinary appeal against the judgment has been lodged.

5–94

A court of a Contracting State in which recognition is sought of a judgment given in Ireland or the United Kingdom may stay the proceedings if enforcement is suspended in the State of origin, by reason of an appeal.

SECTION 2

ENFORCEMENT

Article 31

A judgment given in a Contracting State and enforceable in that State shall be enforced in another Contracting State when, on the application of any interested party, it has been declared enforceable there.

5–95

However, in the United Kingdom, such a judgment shall be enforced in England and Wales, in Scotland, or in Northern Ireland when, on the application of any interested party, it has been registered for enforcement in that part of the United Kingdom.

Article 32

1. The application shall be submitted:

5–96

   — in Belgium, to the tribunal de première instance or rechtbank van eerste aanleg,
   — in Denmark, to the byret,
   — in the Federal Republic of Germany, to the presiding judge of a chamber of the Landgericht,
   — in Greece, to the Μονομελεζ Ποωτοδιχειο,
   — in Spain, to the Juzgado de Primera Instancia,
   — in France, to the presiding judge of the tribunal de grande instance,
   — in Ireland, to the High Court,
   — in Italy, to the corte d'appello,
   — in Luxembourg, to the presiding judge of the tribunal d'arrondissement,
   — in the Netherlands, to the presiding judge of the arrondissementsrechtbank,
   — in Portugal, to the Tribunal Judicial de Circulo,
   — in the United Kingdom:
      1. in England and Wales, to the High Court of Justice, or in the case of maintenance judgment to the Magistrates' Court on transmission by the Secretary of State;
      2. in Scotland, to the Court of Session, or in the case of a maintenance judgment to the Sheriff Court on transmission by the Secretary of State;
      3. in Northern Ireland, to the High Court of Justice, or in the case of a maintenance judgment to the Magistrates' Court on transmission by the Secretary of State.

2. The jurisdiction of local courts shall be determined by reference to the place of do-

micile of the party against whom enforcement is sought. If he is not domiciled in the State in which enforcement is sought, it shall be determined by reference to the place of enforcement.

Lugano Convention

5–97   the list of courts to which the application is made is supplemented in the Lugano Convention with courts of the additional Contracting States.

Article 33

5–98   The procedure for making the application shall be governed by the law of the State in which enforcement is sought.

The applicant must give an address for service of process within the area of jurisdiction of the court applied to. However, if the law of the State in which enforcement is sought does not provide for the furnishing of such an address, the applicant shall appoint a representative *ad litem*.

The documents referred to in Articles 46 and 47 shall be attached to the application.

Article 34

5–99   The court applied to shall give its decision without delay; the party against whom enforcement is sought shall not at this stage of the proceedings be entitled to make any submissions on the application.

The application may be refused only for one of the reasons specified in Articles 27 and 28.

Under no circumstances may the foreign judgment be reviewed as to its substance.

Article 35

5–100   The appropriate officer of the court shall without delay bring the decision given on the application to the notice of the applicant in accordance with the procedure laid down by the law of the State in which enforcement is sought.

Article 36

5–101   If enforcement is authorised, the party against whom enforcement is sought may appeal against the decision within one month of service thereof.

If that party is domiciled in a Contracting State other than that in which the decision authorising enforcement was given, the time for appealing shall be two months and shall run from the date of service, either on him in person or at his residence. No extension of time may be granted on account of distance.

Article 37

5–102   1. An appeal against the decision authorising enforcement shall be lodged in accordance with the rules governing procedure in contentious matters:
— in Belgium, with the tribunal de première instance or rechtbank van eerste aanleg,
— in Denmark, with the landsret,
— in the Federal Republic of Germany, with the Oberlandesgericht,
— in Greece, with the Eφετειο,
— in Spain, with the Audiencia Provincial,
— in France, with the cour d'appel,
— in Ireland, with the High Court,
— in Italy, with the corte d'appello,
— in Luxembourg, with the Court supérieure de justice sitting as a court of civil appeal,
— in the Netherlands, with the arrondissementsrechtbank,
— in Portugal, with the Tribunal de Relação,
— in the United Kingdom:
  (a) in England and Wales, with the High Court of Justice, or in the case of a maintenance judgment with the Magistrates' Court;
  (b) in Scotland, with the Court of Session, or in the case of a maintenance judgment with the Sheriff Court;
  (c) in Northern Ireland, with the High Court of Justice, or in the case of a maintenance judgment with the Magistrates' Court.

2. The judgment given on the appeal may be contested only:
— in Belgium, Greece, Spain, France, Italy, Luxembourg and in the Netherlands, by an appeal in cassation,
— in Denmark, by an appeal to the højesteret, with the leave of the Minister of Justice,
— in the Federal Republic of Germany, by a Rechtschwerde,
— in Ireland, by an appeal on a point of law to the Supreme Court,
— in Portugal, by an appeal on a point of law,
— in the United Kingdom, by a single further appeal on a point of law.

Lugano Convention

the list of courts to which the application shall be submitted is supplemented in the **5–103** Lugano Convention with courts of the additional Contracting States.

Article 38

The court with which the appeal under Article 37(1) is lodged may, on the applica- **5–104** tion of the appellant, stay the proceedings if an ordinary appeal has been lodged against the judgment in the State of origin or if the time for such an appeal has not yet expired; in the latter case, the court may specify the time within such an appeal is to be lodged.

Where the judgment was given in Ireland or the United Kingdom, any form of appeal available in the State of origin shall be treated as an ordinary appeal for the purposes of the first paragraph.

The court may also make enforcement conditional on the provision of such security as it shall determine.

Lugano Convention

The text of the first paragraph of Art. 38 differs and is set out below: **5–105**

The court with which the appeal under the first paragraph of Article 37 is lodged may, on the application of the appellant, stay the proceedings if an ordinary appeal has been lodged against the judgment in the State of origin or if the time for such an appeal has not yet expired; in the latter case, the court may specify the time within which such an appeal is to be lodged.

Article 39

During the time specified for an appeal pursuant to Article 36 and until any such **5–106** appeal has been determined, no measures of enforcement may be taken other than protective measures taken against the property of the party against whom enforcement is sought.

The decision authorising enforcement shall carry with it the power to proceed to any such protective measures.

Article 40

1. If the application for enforcement is refused, the applicant may appeal: **5–107**
— in Belgium, to the cour d'appel or hof van beroep,
— in Denmark, to the landsret,
— in the Federal Republic of Germany, to the Oberlandesgericht,
— in Greece, to the Εφετειο,
— in Spain, to the Audiencia Provincial,
— in France, to the court d'appel,
— in Ireland, to the High Court,
— in Italy, to the corte d'appello,
— in Luxembourg, to the Cour supérieure de justice sitting as a court of civil appeal,
— in the Netherlands, to the gerechtshof,
— in Portugal, to the Tribunal da Relação,
— in the United Kingdom,
  (a) in England and Wales, to the High Court of Justice, or in the case of a maintenance judgment to the Magistrates' Court;
  (b) in Scotland, to the Court of Session, or in the case of a maintenance judgment to the Sheriff Court,

(c) in Northern Ireland, to the High Court of Justice, or in the case of a maintenance judgment to the Magistrates' Court.

2. The party against whom enforcement is sought shall be summoned to appear before the appellate court. If he fails to appear, the provisions of the second and third paragraphs of Article 20 shall apply even where he is not domiciled in any of the Contracting States.

Lugano Convention

5–108   the list of courts to which the applicant may appeal is supplemented in the Lugano Convention with courts of the additional Contracting States.

Article 41

5–109   A judgment given on an appeal provided for in Article 40 may be contested only:
— in Belgium, Greece, Spain, France, Italy, Luxembourg and in the Netherlands, by an appeal in cassation,
— in Denmark, by an appeal to the højesteret, with the leave of the Minister of Justice,
— in the Federal Republic of Germany, by a Rechtsbeschwerde,
— in Ireland, by an appeal on a point of law to the Supreme Court,
— in Portugal, by an appeal on a point of law,
— in the United Kingdom, by a single further appeal on a point of law.

Lugano Convention

5–110   the list of courts to which a judgment on appeal may be contested is supplemented in the Lugano Convention with courts of the additional Contracting States.

Article 42

5–111   Where a foreign judgment has been given in respect of several matters and enforcement cannot be authorised for all of them, the court shall authorise the enforcement for one or more of them.

An applicant may request partial enforcement of a judgment.

Article 43

5–112   A foreign judgment which orders a periodic payment by way of a penalty shall be enforceable in the State in which enforcement is sought only if the amount of the payment has been finally determined by the courts of the State of origin.

Article 44

5–113   An applicant who, in the State of origin has benefited from complete or partial legal aid or exemption from costs or expenses, shall be entitled, in the procedures provided for in Articles 32 to 35, to benefit from the most favourable legal aid or the most extensive exemption from costs or expenses provided for by the law of the State addressed.

However, an applicant who requests the enforcement of a decision given by an administrative authority in Denmark in respect of a maintenance order may, in the State addressed, claim the benefits referred to in the first paragraph if he presents a statement from the Danish Ministry of Justice to the effect that he fulfils the economic requirements to qualify for the grant of complete or partial legal aid or exemption from costs or expenses.

Lugano Convention

5–114   The text of the second paragraph of Art. 44 differs and is set out below:

However, an applicant who requests the enforcement of a decision given by an administrative authority in Denmark or in Iceland in respect of a maintenance order may, in the State addressed, claim the benefits referred to in the first paragraph if he presents a statement from, respectively, the Danish Ministry of Justice or the Icelandic Ministry of Justice to the effect that he fulfils the economic requirements to qualify for the grant of complete or partial legal aid or exemption from costs or expenses.

Article 45

5–115   No security, bond or deposit, however described, shall be required of a party who in one Contracting State applies for enforcement of a judgment given in another

Contracting State on the ground that he is a foreign national or that he is not domiciled or resident in the State in which enforcement is sought.

SECTION 3

COMMON PROVISION

Article 46

A party seeking recognition or applying for enforcement of a judgment shall produce:

1. a copy of the judgment which satisfies the conditions necessary to establish its authenticity;

2. in the case of a judgment given in default, the original or a certified true copy of the document which establishes that the party in default was served with the document instituting the proceedings or with an equivalent document.

5–116

Article 47

A party applying for enforcement shall also produce:

1. documents which establish that, according to the law of the State of origin the judgment is enforceable and has been served;

2. where appropriate, a document showing that the applicant is in receipt of legal aid in the State of origin.

5–117

Article 48

If the documents specified in point 2 of Articles 46 and 47 are not produced, the court may specify a time for their production, accept equivalent documents or, if it considers that it has sufficient information before it, dispense with their production.

If the court so requires, a translation of the documents shall be produced; the translation shall be certified by a person qualified to do so in one of the Contracting States.

5–118

Article 49

No legalisation or other similar formality shall be required in respect of the documents referred to in Articles 46 or 47 or the second paragraph of Article 48, or in respect of a document appointing a representative *ad litem*.

5–119

TITLE IV

AUTHENTIC INSTRUMENTS AND COURT SETTLEMENTS

Article 50

A document which has been formally drawn up or registered as an authentic instrument and is enforceable in one Contracting State shall, in another Contracting State, be declared enforceable there, on application made in accordance with the procedures provided for in Article 31 *et seq*. The application may be refused only if enforcement of the instrument is contrary to public policy in the State addressed.

The instrument produced must satisfy the conditions necessary to establish its authenticity in the State of origin.

The provisions of Section 3 of Title III shall apply as appropriate.

5–120

Article 51

A settlement which has been approved by a court in the course of proceedings and is enforceable in the State in which it was concluded shall be enforceable in the State addressed under the same conditions as authentic instruments.

5–121

TITLE V

GENERAL PROVISIONS

Article 52

In order to determine whether a party is domiciled in the Contracting State whose courts are seised of a matter, the court shall apply its internal law.

5–122

EUROPE

If a party is not domiciled in the State whose courts are seised of the matter, then, in order to determine whether the party is domiciled in another Contracting State, the court shall apply the law of that State.

5-123 *Note* —A third paragraph in this Article was omitted by the Civil Jurisdiction and Judgments Act 1982 (Amendment) Order 1990 at the time of the revision of the 1968 Convention upon the accession of Spain and Portugal. The opportunity was taken to make this modification in the light of experience.

Article 53

5-124 For the purposes of this Convention, the seat of a company or other legal person or association of natural or legal persons shall be treated as its domicile. However, in order to determine that seat, the court shall apply its rules of private international law.

In order to determine whether a trust is domiciled in the Contracting State whose courts are seised of the matter, the court shall apply its rules of private international law.

TITLE VI

TRANSITIONAL PROVISIONS

Article 54

5-125 The provisions of the Convention shall apply only to legal proceedings instituted and to documents formally drawn up or registered as authentic instruments after its entry into force in the State of origin and, where recognition or enforcement of a judgment or authentic instruments is sought, in the State addressed.

However, judgments given after the date of entry into force of this Convention between the State of origin and the State addressed in proceedings instituted before that date shall be recognised and enforced in accordance with the provisions of Title III if jurisdiction was founded upon rules which accorded with those provided for either in Title II of this Convention or in a convention concluded between the State of origin and the State addressed which was in force when the proceedings were instituted.

If the parties to a dispute concerning a contract had agreed in writing before 1 June 1988 for Ireland or before 1 January 1987 for the United Kingdom that the contract was to be governed by the law of Ireland or of a part of the United Kingdom, the courts of Ireland or of that part of the United Kingdom shall retain the right to exercise jurisdiction in the dispute.

Article 54a

5-126 For a period of three years from 1 November 1986 for Denmark and from 1 June 1988 for Ireland, jurisdiction in maritime matters shall be determined in these States not only in accordance with the provisions of Title II, but also in accordance with the provisions of paragraphs 1 to 6 following. However, upon the entry into force of the International Convention relating to the arrest of sea-going ships, signed at Brussels on 10 May 1952, for one of these States, these provisions shall cease to have effect for that State.

1. A person who is domiciled in a Contracting State may be sued in the courts for one of the States mentioned above in respect of a maritime claim if the ship to which the claim relates or any other ship owned by him has been arrested by judicial process within the territory of the latter State to secure the claim, or could have been so arrested there but bail or other security has been given, and either:

(a) the claimant is domiciled in the latter State; or

(b) the claim arose in the latter State; or

(c) the claim concerns the voyage during which the arrest was made or could have been made; or

(d) the claim arises out of a collision or out of damage caused by a ship to another ship or to goods or persons on board either ship, either by the execution or non-execution of a manoeuvre or by the non-observance of regulations; or

(e) the claim is for salvage; or

(f) the claim is in respect of a mortgage or hypothecation of the ship arrested.

2. A claimant may arrest either the particular ship to which the maritime claim re-

lates, or any other ship which is owned by the person who was, at the time when the maritime claim arose, the owner of the particular ship. However, only the particular ship to which the maritime claim relates may be arrested in respect of the maritime claims set out in (5)(o), (p) or (q) of this Article.

3. Ships shall be deemed to be in the same ownership when all the shares therein are owned by the same person or persons.

4. When in the case of a charter by demise of a ship the charterer alone is liable in respect of a maritime claim relating to that ship, the claimant may arrest that ship or any other ship owned by the charterer, but no other ship owned by the owner may be arrested in respect of such claim. The same shall apply to any case in which a person other than the owner of a ship is liable in respect of a maritime claim relating to that ship.

5. The expression "maritime claim" means a claim arising out of one or more of the following:

(a) damage caused by any ship either in collision or otherwise;

(b) loss of life or personal injury caused by any ship or occurring in connection with the operation on any ship;

(c) salvage;

(d) agreement relating to the use or hire of any ship whether by charterparty or otherwise;

(e) agreement relating to the carriage of goods in any ship whether by charterparty or otherwise;

(f) loss of or damage to goods including baggage carried in any ship;

(g) general average;

(h) bottomry;

(i) towage;

(j) pilotage;

(k) goods or materials wherever supplied to a ship for her operation or maintenance;

(l) construction, repair or equipment of any ship or dock charges and dues;

(m) wages of masters, officers or crew;

(n) master's disbursements, including disbursements made by shippers, charterers or agents on behalf of a ship or her owner;

(o) dispute as to the title to or ownership of any ship;

(p) disputes between co-owners of any ship as to the ownership, possession, employment or earnings of that ship;

(q) the mortgage of hypothecation of any ship.

6. In Denmark, the expression "arrest" shall be deemed as regards the maritime claims referred to in 5(o) and (p) of this Article, to include a "forbud", where that is the only procedure allowed in respect of such a claim under Articles 646 to 653 of the law on civil procedure (lov om rettens pleje).

TITLE VII

RELATIONSHIP TO OTHER CONVENTIONS

Article 55

Subject to the provisions of the second paragraph of Article 54, the Article 56, this **5–127** Convention shall, for the States which are parties to it, supersede the following conventions concluded between two or more of them.

— the Convention between Belgium and France on jurisdiction and the validity and enforcement of judgments, arbitration awards and authentic instruments, signed at Paris on 8th July, 1899,

— the Convention between Belgium and the Netherlands on jurisdiction, bankruptcy, and the validity and enforcement of judgments, arbitration awards and authentic instruments, signed at Brussels on 28th March, 1925,

— the Convention between France and Italy on the enforcement of judgments in civil and commercial matters, signed at Rome on 3rd June, 1930,

- the Convention between the United Kingdom and the French Republic providing for the reciprocal enforcement of judgments in civil and commercial matters, with Protocol, signed at Paris on 18th January, 1934,
- the Convention between the United Kingdom and the Kingdom of Belgium, providing for the reciprocal enforcement of judgments in civil and commercial matters, with Protocol, signed at Brussels on 2nd May, 1934,
- the Convention between Germany and Italy on the recognition and enforcement of judgments in civil and commercial matters, signed at Rome on 9th March, 1936,
- the Convention between the Federal Republic of Germany and the Kingdom of Belgium on the mutual recognition and enforcement of judgments, arbitration awards and authentic instruments in civil and commercial matters, signed at Bonn on 30th June, 1958,
- the Convention between the Kingdom of the Netherlands and the Italian Republic on the recognition and enforcement of judgments in civil and commercial matters, signed at Rome on 17th April, 1959,
- the Convention between the United Kingdom and the Federal Republic of Germany for the reciprocal recognition and enforcement of judgments in civil and commercial matters, signed at Bonn on 15th July, 1960,
- the Convention between the Kingdom of Greece and the Federal Republic of Germany for the reciprocal recognition and enforcement of judgments, settlements and authentic instruments in civil and commercial matters, signed in Athens on 4th November, 1961,
- the Convention between the Kingdom of Belgium and the Italian Republic on the recognition and enforcement of judgments and other enforceable instruments in civil and commercial matters, signed at Rome on 6th April, 1962,
- the Convention between the Kingdom of the Netherlands and the Federal Republic of Germany on the mutual recognition and enforcement of judgments and other enforceable instruments in civil and commercial matters, signed at The Hague on 30th August, 1962,
- the Convention between the United Kingdom and the Republic of Italy for the reciprocal recognition and enforcement of judgments in civil and commercial matters, signed at Rome on 7th February, 1964, with amending Protocol signed at Rome on 14th July, 1970,
- the Convention between the United Kingdom and the Kingdom of the Netherlands providing for the reciprocal recognition and enforcement of judgments in civil matters, signed at The Hague on 17th November, 1967,
- the Convention between Spain and France on the recognition and enforcement of judgment and arbitration awards in civil and commercial matters, signed at Paris on 28th May, 1969,
- the Convention between Spain and Italy regarding legal aid and the recognition and enforcement of judgments in civil and commercial matters, signed at Madrid on 22nd May, 1973,
- the Convention between Spain and the Federal Republic of Germany on the recognition and enforcement of judgments, settlements and enforceable authentic instruments in civil and commercial matters, signed at Bonn on 14th November, 1983.

and, in so far as it is in force:

- the Treaty between Belgium, the Netherlands and Luxembourg on jurisdiction, bankruptcy, and the validity and enforcement of judgments, arbitration awards and authentic instruments, signed at Brussels on 24th November, 1961.

Article 56

5–128 The Treaty and the conventions referred to in Article 55 shall continue to have effect in relation to matters to which this Convention does not apply.

They shall continue to have effect in respect of judgments given and documents formally drawn up or registered as authentic instruments before the entry into force of this Convention.

Article 57

5–129 1. This Convention shall not affect any conventions to which the Contracting States are or will be parties and which in relation to particular matters, govern jurisdiction or the recognition or enforcement of judgments.

2. With a view to its uniform interpretation, paragraph 1 shall be applied in the following manner:

    (a) this Convention shall not prevent a court of a Contracting State which is a party to a convention on a particular matter from assuming jurisdiction in accordance with that Convention, even where the defendant is domiciled in another Contracting State which is not a party to that Convention. The court hearing the action shall, in any event, apply Article 20 of this Convention;

    (b) judgments given in a Contracting State by a court in the exercise of jurisdiction provided for in a convention on a particular matter shall be recognised and enforced in the other Contracting State in accordance with this Convention.

    Where a convention on a particular matter to which both the State of origin and the State addressed are parties lays down conditions for the recognition or enforcement of judgments, those conditions shall apply. In any event, the provisions of this Convention which concern the procedure for recognition and enforcement of judgments may be applied.

3. This Convention shall not affect the application of provisions which, in relation to particular matters, govern jurisdiction or the recognition or enforcement of judgments and which are or will be contained in acts of the institutions of the European Communities or in national laws harmonised in implementation of such acts.

Lis Pendens

When a specialised convention contains certain rules of jurisdiction but no provision as to *lis pendens*, Arts 21 and 22 of the Judgments Convention applies. The specialised convention will preclude the application of the Judgments Convention only in relation to questions governed by the specialised convention (*The Tatry* [1995] I.L.Pr. 81, E.C. Case No. 406/92). **5–130**

Article 58

Until such time as the Convention on jurisdiction and the enforcement of judgments in civil and commercial matters, signed at Lugano on 16th September, 1988, takes effect with regard to France and the Swiss Confederation, this Convention shall not affect the rights granted to Swiss nationals by the Convention between France and the Swiss Confederation on jurisdiction and enforcement of judgments in civil matters, signed at Paris on 15th June, 1869. **5–131**

Article 59

This Convention shall not prevent a Contracting State from assuming, in a convention on the recognition and enforcement of judgments, an obligation towards a third State not to recognise judgments given in other Contracting States against defendants domiciled or habitually resident in the third State where, in cases provided for in Article 4, the judgment could only be founded on a ground of jurisdiction specified in the second paragraph of Article 3. **5–132**

However, a Contracting State may not assume an obligation towards a third State not to recognise a judgment given in another Contracting State by a court basing its jurisdiction on the presence within that State of property belonging to the defendant, or the seizure by the plaintiff of property situated there:

    1. if the action is brought to assert or declare proprietary or possessory rights in that property, seeks to obtain authority to dispose of it, or arises from another issue relating to such property, or,

    2. if the property constitutes the security for a debt which is the subject-matter of the action.

[THE NEXT PARAGRAPH IS 5–134.]

Articles 61–63

Article 64

The Secretary-General of the Council of the European Communities shall notify the signatory State of: **5–134**

    (a) the deposit of each instrument of ratification;

(b) the date of entry into force of this Convention;

(c) ...

(d) any declaration received pursuant to Article IV of the Protocol;

(e) any communication made pursuant to Article VI of the Protocol.

Article 65

5–135   The Protocol annexed to this Convention by common accord of the Contracting States shall form an integral part thereof.

Article 66

5–136   This Convention is concluded for an unlimited period.

Article 67

5–137   Any Contracting State may request the revision of this Convention. In this event, a revision conference shall be convened by the President of the Council of the European Communities.

Article 68

5–138   *Note* —The annexed Protocol is not printed in this Section of *Civil Procedure*.

SECTION 2(2)(B)   SCHEDULE 2

TEXT OF 1971 PROTOCOL, AS AMENDED

5–139   *Note* —The text set out below is the version of the 1971 Protocol inserted in Sched.2 of the 1982 Act by the Civil Jurisdiction and Judgments Act 1982 (Amendment) Order 1990 (S.I. 1990 No. 2591), Art. 12(2), Sched.2, following upon the accession to the European Community of Spain and Portugal. It has the force of law in the United Kingdom, see s.3(1) of the 1982 Act. Section 3(3) of the 1982 Act, as amended, states that the report by Mr. P. Jenard on the 1971 Protocol may be considered in ascertaining the meaning or effect of any provision in the 1971 Protocol and "shall be given such weight as is appropriate in the circumstances". This report was published in the *Official Journal of the European Communities* (O.J.) 1979, C.59) and is re-printed in various European law texts.

Article 1

5–140   The Court of Justice of the European Communities shall have jurisdiction to give rulings on the interpretation of the Convention on jurisdiction and the enforcement of judgments in civil and commercial matters and of the Protocol annexed to that Convention, signed at Brussels on 27th September 1968, and also on the interpretation of the present Protocol.

"Court of Justice"

5–141   For procedure for references to European Court of Justice by High Court and Court of Appeal, see O.114.

Article 2

5–142   The following courts may request the Court of Justice to give preliminary rulings on questions of interpretation—

1. —... ...

— in the United Kingdom: the House of Lords and courts to which application has been made under the second paragraph of Article 37 or under Article 41 of the Convention.

2. The courts of the Contracting States when they are sitting in an appellate capacity.

3. In the case provided for in Article 37 of the Convention, the courts referred to in that Article.

Article 3

5–143   1. Where a question of interpretation of the Convention or of one of the other instruments referred to in Article 1 is raised in a case pending before one of the courts listed in point 1 of Article 2, that court shall, if it considers that a decision on the question is necessary to enable it to give judgment, request the Court of Justice to give a ruling thereon.

2. Where such a question is raised before any court referred to in point 2 or 3 of Article 2, that court may, under the conditions laid down in paragraph 1, request the Court of Justice to give a ruling thereon.

SCHEDULE 4

CHAPTER II OF THE REGULATION AS MODIFIED: RULES FOR ALLOCATION OF JURISDICTION WITHIN UK

General

1. Subject to the rules of this Schedule, persons domiciled in a part of the United Kingdom shall be sued in the courts of that part.

5–144

2. Persons domiciled in a part of the United Kingdom may be sued in the courts of another part of the United Kingdom only by virtue of rules 3 to 13 of this Schedule.

5–145

SECTION 2

Special jurisdiction

3. A person domiciled in a part of the United Kingdom may, in another part of the United Kingdom, be sued—

5–146

    (a) in matters relating to a contract, in the courts for the place of performance of the obligation in question;

    (b) in matters relating to maintenance, in the courts for the place where the maintenance creditor is domiciled or habitually resident or, if the matter is ancillary to proceedings concerning the status of a person, in the court which, according to its own law, has jurisdiction to entertain those proceedings, unless that jurisdiction is based solely on the nationality of one of the parties;

    (c) in matters relating to tort, delict or quasi-delict, in the courts for the place where the harmful event occurred or may occur;

    (d) as regards a civil claim for damages or restitution which is based on an act giving rise to criminal proceedings, in the court seised of those proceedings, to the extent that that court has jurisdiction under its own law to entertain civil proceedings;

    (e) as regards a dispute arising out of the operations of a branch, agency or other establishment, in the courts for the place in which the branch, agency or other establishment is situated;

    (f) as settlor, trustee or beneficiary of a trust created by the operation of a statute, or by a written instrument, or created orally and evidenced in writing, in the courts of the part of the United Kingdom in which the trust is domiciled;

    (g) as regards a dispute concerning the payment of remuneration claimed in respect of the salvage of a cargo or freight, in the court under the authority of which the cargo or freight in question—

        (i) has been arrested to secure such payment; or

        (ii) could have been so arrested, but bail or other security has been given;

  provided that this provision shall apply only if it is claimed that the defendant has an interest in the cargo or freight or had such an interest at the time of salvage;

    (h) in proceedings—

        (i) concerning a debt secured on immovable property; or

        (ii) which are brought to assert, declare or determine proprietary or possessory rights, or rights of security, in or over movable property, or to obtain authority to dispose of movable property;

  in the courts of the part of the United Kingdom in which the property is situated.

4. Proceedings which have as their object a decision of an organ of a company or other legal person or of an association of natural or legal persons may, without preju-

5–147

dice to the other provisions of this Schedule, be brought in the courts of the part of the United Kingdom in which that company, legal person or association has its seat.

5–148 5. A person domiciled in a part of the United Kingdom may, in another part of the United Kingdom, also be sued—

(a) where he is one of a number of defendants, in the courts for the place where any one of them is domiciled, provided the claims are so closely connected that it is expedient to hear and determine them together to avoid the risk of irreconcilable judgments resulting from separate proceedings;

(b) as a third party in an action on a warranty or guarantee or in any other third party proceedings, in the court seised of the original proceedings, unless these were instituted solely with the object of removing him from the jurisdiction of the court which would be competent in his case;

(c) on a counter-claim arising from the same contract or facts on which the original claim was based, in the court in which the original claim is pending;

(d) in matters relating to a contract, if the action may be combined with an action against the same defendant in matters relating to rights *in rem* in immovable property, in the court of the part of the United Kingdom in which the property is situated.

5–149 6. Where by virtue of this Schedule a court of a part of the United Kingdom has jurisdiction in actions relating to liability arising from the use or operation of a ship, that court, or any other court substituted for this purpose by the internal law of that part, shall also have jurisdiction over claims for limitation of such liability.

SECTION 4

Jurisdiction over consumer contracts

5–150 7.—(1) In matters relating to a contract concluded by a person, the consumer, for a purpose which can be regarded as being outside his trade or profession, jurisdiction shall be determined by this rule and rules 8 and 9, without prejudice to rule 3(e) and (h)(ii), if—

(a) it is a contract for the sale of goods on instalment credit terms; or

(b) it is a contract for a loan repayable by instalments, or for any other form of credit, made to finance the sale of goods; or

(c) in all other cases, the contract has been concluded with a person who pursues commercial or professional activities in the part of the United Kingdom in which the consumer is domiciled or, by any means, directs such activities to that part or to other parts of the United Kingdom including that part, and the contract falls within the scope of such activities.

(2) This rule shall not apply to a contract of transport other than a contract which, for an inclusive price, provides for a combination of travel and accommodation, or to a contract of insurance.

5–151 8.—(1) A consumer may bring proceedings against the other party to a contract either in the courts of the part of the United Kingdom in which that party is domiciled or in the courts of the part of the United Kingdom in which the consumer is domiciled.

(2) Proceedings may be brought against a consumer by the other party to the contract only in the courts of the part of the United Kingdom in which the consumer is domiciled.

(3) The provisions of this rule shall not affect the right to bring a counter-claim in the court in which, in accordance with this rule and rules 7 and 9, the original claim is pending.

5–152 9. The provisions of rules 7 and 8 may be departed from only by an agreement—

(a) which is entered into after the dispute has arisen; or

(b) which allows the consumer to bring proceedings in courts other than those indicated in those rules; or

(c) which is entered into by the consumer and the other party to the contract, both of whom are at the time of conclusion of the contract domiciled or habitually resident in the same part of the United Kingdom, and which confers jurisdiction on the courts of that part, provided that such an agreement is not contrary to the law of that part.

Jurisdiction over individual contracts of employment

10.—(1)In matters relating to individual contracts of employment, jurisdiction shall be determined by this rule, without prejudice to rule 3(e). **5–153**

(2) An employer may be sued—

    (a) in the courts of the part of the United Kingdom in which he is domiciled; or

    (b) in the courts of the part of the United Kingdom where the employee habitually carries out his work or in the courts of that part where he last did so; or

    (c) if the employee does not or did not habitually carry out his work in any one place, in the courts of the part of the United Kingdom where the business which engaged the employee is or was situated.

(3) An employer may bring proceedings only in the courts of the part of the United Kingdom in which the employee is domiciled.

(4) The provisions of this rule shall not affect the right to bring a counter-claim in the court in which, in accordance with this rule, the original claim is pending.

(5) The provisions of this rule may be departed from only by an agreement on jurisdiction—

    (a) which is entered into after the dispute has arisen; or

    (b) which allows the employee to bring proceedings in courts other than those indicated in this rule.

(5) in proceedings concerned with the enforcement of judgments, the courts of the **part of the United Kingdom** in which the judgment has been or is to be enforced.

Exclusive jurisdiction

11. The following courts shall have exclusive jurisdiction, regardless of domicile:— **5–154**

    (a)

        (i) in proceedings which have as their object rights *in rem* in immovable property or tenancies of immovable property, the courts of the part of the United Kingdom in which the property is situated;

        (ii) however, in proceedings which have as their object tenancies of immovable property concluded for temporary private use for a maximum period of six consecutive months, the courts of the part of the United Kingdom in which the defendant is domiciled shall also have jurisdiction, provided that the tenant is a natural person and that the landlord and the tenant are domiciled in the same part of the United Kingdom;

    (b) in proceedings which have as their object the validity of the constitution, the nullity or the dissolution of companies or other legal persons or associations of natural or legal persons, the courts of the part of the United Kingdom in which the company, legal person or association has its seat;

    (c) in proceedings which have as their object the validity of entries in public registers, the courts of the part of the United Kingdom in which the register is kept;

    (d) in proceedings concerned with the enforcement of judgments, the courts of the part of the United Kingdom in which the judgment has been or is to be enforced.

Prorogation of jurisdiction

12.—(1)If the parties have agreed that a court or the courts of a part of the United Kingdom are to have jurisdiction to settle any disputes which have arisen or which may arise in connection with a particular legal relationship, and, apart from this Schedule, the agreement would be effective to confer jurisdiction under the law of that part, that court or those courts shall have jurisdiction. **5–155**

(2) The court or courts of a part of the United Kingdom on which a trust instrument has conferred jurisdiction shall have jurisdiction in any proceedings brought

EUROPE

against a settlor, trustee or beneficiary, if relations between these persons or their rights or obligations under the trust are involved.

(3) Agreements or provisions of a trust instrument conferring jurisdiction shall have no legal force if they are contrary to the provisions of rule 9, or if the courts whose jurisdiction they purport to exclude have exclusive jurisdiction by virtue of rule 11.

5-156 13.—(1)Apart from jurisdiction derived from other provisions of this Schedule, a court of a part of the United Kingdom before which a defendant enters an appearance shall have jurisdiction.

(2) This rule shall not apply where appearance was entered to contest the jurisdiction, or where another court has exclusive jurisdiction by virtue of rule 11.

Examination as to jurisdiction and admissibility

5-157 14. Where a court of a part of the United Kingdom is seised of a claim which is principally concerned with a matter over which the courts of another part of the United Kingdom have exclusive jurisdiction by virtue of rule 11, it shall declare of its own motion that it has no jurisdiction.

5-158 15.—(1)Where a defendant domiciled in one part of the United Kingdom is sued in a court of another part of the United Kingdom and does not enter an appearance, the court shall declare of its own motion that it has no jurisdiction unless its jurisdiction is derived from the provisions of this Schedule.

(2) The court shall stay the proceedings so long as it is not shown that the defendant has been able to receive the document instituting the proceedings or an equivalent document in sufficient time to enable him to arrange for his defence, or that all necessary steps have been taken to this end.

Provisional, including protective, measures

5-159 16. Application may be made to the courts of a part of the United Kingdom for such provisional, including protective, measures as may be available under the law of that part, even if, under this Schedule, the courts of another part of the United Kingdom have jurisdiction as to the substance of the matter."

Civil Jurisdiction and Judgments Act 1982 (Interim Relief) Order 1997

(S.I. 1997 No. 302)

5-160 **1.** This Order may be cited as the Civil Jurisdiction and Judgments Act 1982 (Interim Relief) Order 1997 and shall come into force on 1st April 1997.

2. The High Court in England and Wales or Northern Ireland shall have power to grant interim relief under section 25(1) of the Civil Jurisdiction and Judgments Act 1982 in relation to proceedings of the following descriptions, namely—

(a) proceedings commenced or to be commenced otherwise than in a Brussels or Lugano Contracting State or Regulation State;

(b) proceedings whose subject-matter is not within the scope of the Regulation as determined by Article 1 of the Regulation.

Civil Jurisdiction and Judgments Act 1982 (Gibraltar) Order 1997

(S.I. 1997 No. 2602)

5-161 **1.** This Order may be cited as the Civil Jurisdiction and Judgments Act 1982 (Gibraltar) Order 1997 and shall come into force on 1st February 1998.

2.

(a) Provision corresponding to that made by the provisions of the 1968 Convention specified in paragraph (b) shall apply, so far as relevant, for the purpose of regulating, as between the United Kingdom and Gibraltar, the jurisdiction of courts and the recognition and enforcement of judgments.

(b) Those provisions are—

(i) Titles I–V;

(ii) Articles 54 and 57; and

(iii) Article 65 and the Protocol referred to therein.

3. For the purpose stated in Article 2 above the United Kingdom and Gibraltar shall be treated as if each were a separate Contracting State and the relevant provisions of the 1968 Convention and the 1982 Act shall be construed accordingly.

4. In determining any question as to the meaning or effect of the provision (or any part of the provision) made by Article 2 above—

(a) regard shall be had to any relevant principles laid down by the European Court in connection with Title II of the 1968 Convention and to any relevant decision of that court as to the meaning or effect of any provision of that Title; and

(b) without prejudice to the generality of paragraph (a), the reports mentioned in section 3(3) of the 1982 Act may be considered and shall, so far as relevant, be given such weight as is appropriate in the circumstances.

5. A judgment shall not be recognised under this Order if, had it been given in another Contracting State, recognition would be refused by virtue of an agreement to which Article 59 of the 1968 Convention applies.

6. This Order extends to Northern Ireland.

Civil Jurisdiction and Judgments Act 1991

(1991 c.12)

An Act to give effect to the Convention on jurisdiction and the enforcement of judgments in civil and commercial matters, including the Protocols annexed thereto, opened for signature at Lugano on 16th September 1988; and for purposes connected therewith.

[9th May 1991]

BE IT ENACTED by the Queen's most Excellent Majesty, by and with the advice and consent of the Lords Spiritual and Temporal, and Commons, in this present Parliament assembled, and by the authority of the same, as follows:—

5–162

Implementation and interpretation of the Lugano Convention

1.—(1) The Civil Jurisdiction and Judgments Act 1982 (in this Act referred to as "the 1982 Act") shall have effect with the insertion of the following after section 3—

5–162.1

The Lugano Convention to have the force of law

"**3A.**—(1) The Lugano Convention shall have the force of law in the United Kingdom, and judicial notice shall be taken of it.

(2) For convenience of reference there is set out in Schedule 3C the English text of the Lugano Convention.

Interpretation of the Lugano Convention

3B.—(1) In determining any question as to the meaning or effect of a provision of the Lugano Convention, a court in the United Kingdom shall, in accordance with Protocol No. 2 to that Convention, take account of any principles laid down in any relevant decision delivered by a court of any other Lugano Contracting State concerning provisions of the Convention.

(2) Without prejudice to any practice of the courts as to the matters which may be considered apart from this section, the report on the Lugano Convention by Mr P. Jenard and Mr G. Möller (which is reproduced in the Official Journal of the Communities of 28th July 1990) may be considered in ascertaining the meaning or effect of any provision of the Convention and shall be given such weight as is appropriate in the circumstasnces."

(2) In section 9 of that Act, after subsection (1) (which, as amended, will govern the relationship between other conventions and the 1968 and Lugano Conventions) there shall be inserted—

"(1A) Any question arising as to whether it is the Lugano Convention or any of the Brussels Conventions which applies in the circumstances of a particular case falls to be determined in accordance with the provisions of Article 54B of the Lugano Convention."

(3) After Schedule 3B to that Act there shall be inserted the Schedule 3C set out in Schedule 1 to this Act.

Interpretation of the 1982 Act

5–163   **2.**—(1) Section 1 of the 1982 Act (interpretation of references to the Conventions and Contracting States) shall be amended in accordance with the following provisions of this section.

(2) In subsection (1), in the definition of "the Conventions", for the words "the Conventions" there shall be substituted the words "the Brussels Conventions".

(3) At the end of that subsection there shall be added—

"the Lugano Convention" means the Convention on jurisdiction and the enforcement of judgments in civil and commercial matters (including the Protocols annexed to that Convention) opened for signature at Lugano on 16th September 1988 and signed by the United Kingdom on 18th September 1989."

(4) In subsection (2), for paragraph (b) (citation of Articles) there shall be substituted—

"(b) any reference in any provision to a numbered Article without more is a reference—

(i) to the Article so numbered of the 1968 Convention, in so far as the provision applies in relation to that Convention, and

(ii) to the Article so numbered of the Lugano

1700

Convention, in so far as the provision applies in relation to that Convention,

and any reference to a sub-division of a numbered Article shall be construed accordingly."

(5) In subsection (3) (definition of "Contracting State") for the words "In this Act "Contracting State" means—" there shall be substituted the words—

"In this Act—

"Contracting State", without more, in any provision means—

(a) in the application of the provision in relation to the Brussels Conventions, a Brussels Contracting State; and

(b) in the application of the provision in relation to the Lugano Convention, a Lugano Contracting State; "Brussels Contracting State" means—".

(6) At the end of that subsection there shall be added—

""Lugano Contracting State" means one of the original parties to the Lugano Convention, that is to say—Austria, Belgium, Denmark, Finland, France, the Republic of Germany, the Hellenic Republic, Iceland, the Republic of Ireland, Italy, Luxembourg, the Netherlands, Norway, Portugal, Spain, Sweden, Switzerland and the United Kingdom, being a State in relation to which the Convention has taken effect in accordance with paragraph 3 or 4 of Article 61."

Other amendments of the 1982 Act

3. The 1982 Act shall have effect with the amendments specified in **5–164** Schedule 2 to this Act, which are either consequential on the amendments made by sections 1 and 2 above or otherwise for the purpose of implementing the Lugano Convention.

Application to the Crown

4. The amendments of the 1982 Act made by this Act bind the **5–165** Crown in accordance with the provisions of section 51 of that Act.

Short title, interpretation, commencement and extent

5.—(1) This Act may be cited as the Civil Jurisdiction and Judg- **5–166** ments Act 1991.

(2) In this Act—

"the 1982 Act" means the Civil Juridiction and Judgments Act 1982;

"the Lugano Convention" has the same meaning as it has in the 1982 Act by virtue of section 2(3) above.

(3) This Act shall come into force on such day as the Lord Chancellor and the Lord Advocate may apopint in an order made by statutory instrument.

(4) This Act extends to Northern Ireland.

SCHEDULES

SECTION 1(3) SCHEDULE 1

SCHEDULE TO BE INSERTED AS SCHEDULE 3C TO THE 1982 ACT

SECTION 3A(2) "SCHEDULE 3C

TEXT OF THE LUGANO CONVENTION: CONVENTION ON JURISDICTION AND THE
ENFORCEMENT OF JUDGMENTS IN CIVIL AND COMMERCIAL MATTERS

5–167

PREAMBLE

The High Contracting Parties to this Convention, Anxious to strengthen in their
territories the legal protection of persons therein established, Considering that it
is necessary for this purpose to determine the international jurisdiction of their
courts, to facilitate recognition and to introduce an expeditious procedure for
securing the enforcement of judgments, authentic instruments and court settlements, Aware of the links between them, which have been sanctioned in the economic field by the free trade agreements concluded between the European Economic Community and the States members of the European Free Trade
Association, Taking into account the Brussels Convention of 27 September 1968
on jurisdiction and the enforcement of judgments in civil and commercial matters, as amended by the Accession Conventions under the successive enlargements
of the European Communities, Persuaded that the extension of the principles of
that Convention to the States parties to this instrument will strengthen legal and
economic co-operation in Europe, Desiring to ensure as uniform an interpretation as possible of this instrument, Have in this spirit decided to conclude this
Convention and Have agreed as follows:

TITLE I

SCOPE

Article 1

This Convention shall apply in civil and commercial matters whatever the nature **5–168** of the court or tribunal. It shall not extend, in particular, to revenue, customs or administrative matters.

The Convention shall not apply to:

1. the status or legal capacity of natural persons, rights in property arising out of a matrimonial relationship, wills and succession;
2. bankruptcy, proceedings relating to th winding-up of insolvent companies or other legal persons, judicial arrangements, compositions and analogous proceedings;
3. social security;
4. arbitration.

TITLE II

JURISDICTION

SECTION 1

GENERAL PROVISIONS

Article 2

Subject to the provisions of this Convention, persons domiciled in a Contracting **5–169** State shall, whatever their nationality, be sued in the courts of that State.

Persons who are not nationals of the State in which they are domiciled shall be governed by the rules of jurisdiction applicable to nationals of that State.

Article 3

Persons domiciled in a Contracting State may be sued in the courts of another Contracting State only by virute of the rules set out in Sections 2 to 6 of this Title.

In particular the following provisions shall not be applicable as against them:

— in Belgium: Article 15 of the civil code (Code civil—Burgerlijk Wetboek) and Article 638 of the judicial code (Code judiciaire—Gerechtelijk Wetboek),

— in Denmark: Article 246(2) and (3) of the law on civil procedure (Lov om rettens pleje),

— in the Federal Republic of Germany: Article 23 of the code of civil procedure (Zivilprozeßordnung),

— in Greece: Article 40 of the code of civil procedure (lgΚωδικας πολιτικῆς δικονομίας),

— in France: Articles 14 and 15 of the civil code (Code civil),

— in Ireland: the rules which enable jurisdiction to be founded on the document instituting the proceedings having been served on the defendant during his temporary presence in Ireland,

— in Iceland: Article 77 of the Civil Proceedings Act (lög um meðferð einkamála í héraði),

— in Italy: Articles 2 and 4, Nos 1 and 2 of the code of civil procedure (Codice di procedura civile),

— in Luxembourg: Articles 14 and 15 of the civil code (Code civil),

— in the Netherlands: Articles 126(3) and 127 of the code of civil procedure (Wetboek van Burgerlijke Rechtsvordering),

— in Norway: Section 32 of the Civil Proceedings Act (tvistemålsloven),

— in Austria: Article 99 of the Law on Court Jurisdiction (Jurisdiktionsnorm),

— in Portugal: Articles 65(1)(c), 65(2) and 65A(c) of the code of civil procedure (Código de Processo Civil) and Article 11 of the code of labour procedure (Código de Processo de Trabalho),

— in Switzerland: le for du lieu du séquestre/Gerichtsstand des Arrestortes/ foro del luogo del sequestro within the meaning of Article 4 of the loi fédérale sur le droit international privé/Bundesgesetz über das international Privatrecht/legge federale sul diritto internazionale privato,

— in Finland: the second, third and fourth sentences of Section 1 of Chapter 10 of the Code of Judicial Procedure (oikeudenkäymiskaari/ rättegångsbalken),

— in Sweden: the first sentence of Section 3 Procedure of Chapter 10 of the Code of Judicial (Rättegångsbalken),

— in the United Kingdom: the rules which enable jurisdiction to be founded on:

(a) the document instituting the proceedings having been served on the defendant during his temporary presence in the United Kingdom; or

(b) the presence within the United Kingdom of property belonging to the defendant; or

(c) the seizure by the plaintiff of property situated in the United Kingdom.

Article 4

If the defendant is not domiciled in a Contracting State, the jurisdiction of the courts of each Contracting State shall, subject to the provisions of Article 16, be determined by the law of that State.

As against such a defendant, any person domiciled in a Contracting State may, whatever his nationality, avail himself in that State of the rules of jurisdiction there in force, and in particular those specified in the second paragraph of Article 3, in the same way as the nationals of that State.

SECTION 2

SPECIAL JURISDICTION

Article 5

5–170   A person domiciled in a Contracting State may, in another Contracting State, be sued:

1. in matters relating to a contract, in the courts for the place of performance of the obligation in question; in matters relating to individual contracts of employment, this place is that where the employee habitually carries out his work, or if the employee does not habitually carry out his work in any one country, this place shall be the place of business through which he was engaged;

2. in matters relating to maintenance, in the courts for the place where the maintenance creditor is domiciled or habitually resident or, if the matter is ancillary to proceedings concerning the status of a person, in the court which, according to its own law, has jurisdiction to entertain those proceedings, unless that jurisdiction is based solely on the nationality of one of the parties;

3. in matters relating to tort, delict or quasi-delict, in the courts for the place where the harmful event occurred;

4. as regards a civil claim for damages or restitution which is based on an act giving rise to criminal proceedings, in the court seised of those proceedings, to the extent that that court has jurisdiction under its own law to entertain civil proceedings;

5. as regards a dispute arising out of the operations of a branch, agency or other establishment, in the courts for the place in which the branch, agency or other establishment is situated;

6. in his capacity as settlor, trustee or beneficiary of a trust created by the operation of a statute, or by a written instrument, or created orally and evidenced in writing, in the courts of the Contracting State in which the trust is domiciled;

7. as regards a dispute concerning the payment of remuneration claimed in respect of the salvage of a cargo or freight, in the court under the authority of which the cargo or freight in question:

    (a) has been arrested to secure such payment,

or

    (b) could have been so arrested, but bail or other security has been given;

provided that this provision shall apply only if it is claimed that the defendant has an interest in the cargo or freight or had such an interest at the time of salvage.

Article 6

A person domiciled in a Contracting State may also be sued:

1. where he is one of a number of defendants, in the courts for the place where any one of them is domiciled;

2. as a third party in an action on a warranty or guarantee or in any other third party proceedings, in the court seized of the original proceedings, unless these were instituted solely with the object of removing him from the jurisdiction of the court which would be competent in his case;

3. on a counterclaim arising from the same contract or facts on which the original claim was based, in the court in which the original claim is pending;

4. in matters relating to a contract, if the action may be combined with an action against the same defendant in matters relating to rights *in rem* in immovable property, in the court of the Contracting State in which the property is situated.

Article 6A

Where by virtue of this Convention a court of a Contracting State has jurisdiction in actions relating to liability arising from the use or operation of a ship, that court, or any other court substituted for this purpose by the internal law of that State, shall also have jurisdiction over claims for limitation of such liability.

SECTION 3

JURISDICTION IN MATTERS RELATING TO INSURANCE

Article 7

In matters relating to insurance, jurisdiction shall be determined by this Section, **5–171** without prejudice to the provisions of Article 4 and 5(5).

Article 8

An insurer domiciled in a Contracting State may be sued:

1. in the courts of the State where he is domiciled; or

2. in another Contracting State, in the courts for the place where the policy-holder is domiciled; or

3. if he is a co-insurer, in the courts of a Contracting State in which proceedings are brought against the leading insurer.

An insurer who is not domiciled in a Contracting State but has a branch, agency or other establishment in one of the Contracting States shall, in disputes arising out of the operations of the branch, agency or establishment, be deemed to be domiciled in that State.

Article 9

In respect of liability insurance or insurance of immovable property, the insurer may in addition be sued in the courts for the place where the harmful event occurred. The same applies if movable and immovable property are covered by the same insurance policy and both are adversely affected by the same contingency.

Article 10

In respect of liability insurance, the insurer may also, if the law of the court permits it, be joined in proceedings which the injured party has brought against the insured.

The provisions of Articles 7, 8 and 9 shall apply to actions brought by the injured party directly against the insurer, where such direct actions are permitted.

If the law governing such direct actions provides that the policy-holder or the insured may be joined as a party to the action, the same court shall have jurisdiction over them.

Article 11

Without prejudice to the provisions of the third paragraph of Article 10, an insurer may bring proceedings only in the courts of the Contracting State in which the defendant is domiciled, irrespective of whether he is the policy-holder, the insured or a beneficiary.

The provisions of this Section shall not affect the right to bring a counterclaim in the court in which, in accordance with this Section, the original claim is pending.

Article 12

The provisions of this Section may be departed from only by an agreement on jurisdiction:

1. which is entered into after the dispute has arisen; or
2. which allows the policy-holder, the insured or a beneficiary to bring proceedings in courts other than those indicated in this Section; or
3. which is concluded between a policy-holder and an insurer, both of whom are at the time of conclusion of the contract domiciled or habitually resident in the same Contracting State, and which has the effect of conferring jurisdiction on the courts of that State even if the hamful even were to occur abroad, provided that such an agreement is not contrary to the law of the State; or
4. which is concluded with a policy-holder who is not domiciled in a Contracting State, except in so far as the insurance is compulsory or relates to immovable property in a Contracting State; or
5. which relates to a contract of insurance in so far as it covers one or more of the risks set out in Article 12A.

Article 12A

The following are the risks referred to in Article 12(5):

1. any loss of or damage to:
   (a) sea-going ships, installations situated offshore or on the high seas, or aircraft arising from periods which relate to their use for commercial purposes;
   (b) goods in transit other than passengers' baggage where the transit consists of or includes carriage by such ships or aircraft;
2. any liability, other than for bodily injury to passengers or loss of or damage to their baggage;
   (a) arising out of the use or operation of ships, installations or aircraft as referred to in (1)(a) above in so far as the law of the Contracting State in which such aircraft are registered does not prohibit agreements on jurisdiction regarding insurance of such risks;
   (b) for loss or damage caused by goods in transit as described in (1)(b) above;
3. any financial loss connected with the use or operation of ships, installations or aircraft as referred to in (1)(a) above, in particular loss of freight or charter-hire;
4. any risk or interest connected with any of those referred to in (1) to (3) above.

SECTION 4

JURISDICTION OVER CONSUMER CONTRACTS

Article 13

5–172 In proceedings concerning a contract concluded by a person for a purpose which can be regarded as being outside his trade or profession, hereinafter called "the consumer", jurisdiction shall be determined by this Section, without prejudice to the provisions of Articles 4 and 5(5), if it is:

1. a contract for the sale of goods on instalment credit terms; or
2. a contract for a loan repayable by instalments, or for any other form of credit, made to finance the sale of goods; or
3. any other contract for the supply of goods or a contract for the supply of services, and
   (a) in the State of the consumer's domicile the conclusion of the contract was preceded by a specific invitation addressed to him or by advertising, and
   (b) the consumer took in that State the steps necessary for the conclusion of the contract.

Where a consumer enters into a contract with a party who is not domiciled in a Contracting State but has a branch, agency or other establishment in one of the Contracting States, that party shall, in disputes arising out of the operations of the branch, agency or establishment, be deemed to be domiciled in that State.

This section shall not apply to contracts of transport.

Article 14

A consumer may bring proceedings against the other party to a contract either in the courts of the Contracting State in which that party is domiciled or in the courts of the Contracting State in which he is himself domiciled.

Proceedings may be brought against a consumer by the other party to the contract only in the courts of the Contracting State in which the consumer is domiciled.

These provisions shall not affect the right to bring a counterclaim in the court in which, in accordance with this Section, the original claim is pending.

Article 15

The provisions of this Section may be departed from only by an agreement:

1. which is entered into after the dispute has arisen; or
2. which allows the consumer to bring proceedings in courts other than those indicated in this Section; or
3. which is entered into by the consumer and the other party to the contract, both of whom are at the time of conclusion of the contract domiciled or habitually resident in the same Contracting State, and which confers jurisdiction on the courts of that State, provided that such an agreement is not contrary to the law of that State.

SECTION 5

EXCLUSIVE JURISDICTION

Article 16

The following courts shall have exclusive jurisdiction, regardless of domiciled:　　　**5–173**

(a) in proceedings which have as their object rights *in rem* in immovable property or tenancies of immovable property, the courts of the Contracting State in which the property is situated;

(b) however, in proceedings which have as their object tenancies of immovable property concluded for temporary private use for a maximum period of six consecutive months, the courts of the Contracting State in which the defendant is domiciled shall also have jurisdiction, provided that the tenant is a natural person and neither party is domiciled in the Contracting State in which the property is situated;

2. in proceedings which have as their object the validity of the constitution, the nullity or the dissolution of companies or other legal persons or associations or natural or legal persons, or the decisions of their organs, the courts of the Contracting State in which the company, legal person or association has its seat;

3. in proceedings which have as their object the validity of entries in public registers, the courts of the Contracting State in which the register is kept;

4. in proceedings concerned with the registration or validity of patents, trade marks, designs, or other similar rights required to be deposited or registered, the courts of the Contracting State in which the deposit or registration has been applied for, has taken place or is under the terms of an international convention deemed to have taken place;

5. in proceedings concerned with the enforcement of judgments, the courts of the Contracting State in which the judgment has been or is to be enforced.

SECTION 6

PROROGATION OF JURISDICTION

Article 17

5–174   1. If the parties, one or more of whom is domiciled in a Contracting State, have agreed that a court or the courts of a Contracting State are to have jurisdiction to settle any disputes which have arisen or which may arise in connection with a particular legal relationship, that court or those courts shall have exclusive jurisdiction. Such an agreement conferring jurisdiction shall be either:

(a) in writing or evidenced in writing, or

(b) in a form which accords with practices which the parties have established between themselves, or

(c) in international trade or commerce, in a form which accords with a usage of which the parties are or ought to have been aware and which in such trade or commerce is widely known to, and regularly observed by, parties to contracts of the type involved in the particular trade or commerce concerned.

Where such an agreement is concluded by parties, none of whom is domiciled in a Contracting State, the courts of other Contracting States shall have no jurisdiction over their disputes unless the court or courts chosen have declined jurisdiction.

2. The court or courts of a Contracting State on which a trust instrument has conferred jurisdiction shall have exclusive jurisdiction in any proceedings brought against a settlor, trustee or beneficiary, if relations between these persons or their rights or obligations under the trust are involved.

3. Agreements or provisions of a trust instrument conferring jurisdiction shall have no legal force if they are contrary to the provisions of Article 12 or 15, or if the courts whose jurisdiction they purport to exclude have exclusive jurisdiction by virtue of Article 16.

4. If an agreement conferring jurisdiction was concluded for the benefit of only one of the parties, that party shall retain the right to bring proceedings in any other court which has jurisdiction by virtue of this Convention.

5. In matters relating to individual contracts of employment an agreement conferring jurisdiction shall have legal force only if it is entered into after the dispute has arisen.

Article 18

Apart from jurisdiction derived from other provisions of this Convention, a court of a Contracting State before whom a defendant enters an appearance shall have jurisdiction. This rule shall not apply where appearance was entered solely to contest the jurisdiction, or where another court has exclusive jurisdiction by virtue of Article 16.

SECTION 7

EXAMINATION AS TO JURISDICTION AND ADMISSIBILITY

Article 19

5–175   Where a court of a Contracting State is seised of a claim which is principally concerned with a matter over which the courts of another Contracting State have exclusive jurisdiction by virtue of Article 16, it shall declare of its own motion that it has no jurisdiction.

Article 20

Where a defendant domiciled in one Contracting State is sued in a court of another Contracting State and does not enter an appearance, the court shall declare of its own motion that it has no jurisdiction unless its jurisdiction is derived from the provisions of this Convention.

The court shall stay the proceedings so long as it is not shown that the defendant has been able to receive the document instituting the proceedings or an equivalent document in sufficient time to enable him to arrange for his defence, or that all necessary steps have been taken to this end.

The provisions of the foregoing paragraph shall be replaced by those of Article 15 of the Hague Convention of 15 November 1965 on the service abroad of judicial and extra judicial documents in civil or commercial matters, if the document insituting the proceedings or notice thereof had to be transmitted abroad in accordance with that Convention.

SECTION 8

LIS PENDENS—RELATED ACTIONS

Article 21

Where proceedings involving the same cause of action and between the same parties are brought in the courts of different Contracting States, any court other than the court first seized shall of its own motion stay its proceedings until such time as the jurisdiction of the court first seised is established. **5–176**

Where the jurisdiction of the court first seised is established, any court other than the court first seised shall decline jurisdiction in favour of that court.

Article 22

Where related actions are brought in the courts of different Contracting States, any court other than the court first seised may, while the actions are pending at first instance, stay its proceedings.

A court other than the court first seised may also, on the application of one of the parties, decline jurisdiction if the law of that court permits the consolidation of related actions and the court first seised has jurisdiction over both actions.

For the purposes of this Article, actions are deemed to be related where they are so closely connected that it is expedient to hear and determine them together to avoid the risk of irreconcilable judgments resulting from separate proceedings.

Article 23

Where actions come within the exclusive jurisdiction of several courts, any court other than the court first seised shall decline jurisdiction in favour of that court.

SECTION 9

PROVISIONAL, INCLUDING PROTECTIVE, MEASURES

Article 24

Application may be made to the courts of a Contracting State for such provisional, including protective, measures as may be available under the law of that State, even if, under this Convention, the courts of another Contracting State have jurisdiction as to the substance of the matter. **5–177**

TITLE III

RECOGNITION AND ENFORCEMENT

Article 25

For the purposes of this Convention, "judgment" means any judgment given by a court of tribunal of a Contracting State, whatever the judgment may be called, **5–178**

EUROPE

including a decree, order, decision of writ of execution, as well as the determination of costs or expenses by an officer of the court.

SECTION 1

RECOGNITION

Article 26

A judgment given in a Contracting State shall be recognised in the other Contracting States without any special procedure being required.

Any interested party who raises the recognition of a judgment as the principal issue in a dispute may, in accordance with the procedures provided for in Sections 2 and 3 of this Title, apply for a decision that the judgment be recognised.

If the outcome of proceedings in a court of a Contracting State depends on the determination of an incidental question of recognition that court shall have jurisdiction over that question.

Article 27

A judgment shall not be recognised:

1. if such recognition is contrary to public policy in the State in which recognition is sought;
2. Where it was given in default of appearance, if the defendant was not duly served with the document which instituted the proceedings or with an equivalent document in sufficient time to enable him to arrange for his defence;
3. if the judgment is irreconcilable with a judgment given in a dispute between the same parties in the State in which recognition is sought;
4. if the court of the State of origin, in order to arrive at its judgment, has decided a preliminary question concerning the status or legal capacity of natural persons, rights in property arising out of a matrimonial relationship, wills or succession in a way that conflicts with a rule of the private international law of the State in which the recognition is sought, unless the same result would have been reached by the application of the rules of private international law of that State;
5. if the judgment is irreconcilable with an earlier judgment given in a non-contracting State involving the same cause of action and between the same parties, provided that this latter judgment fulfils the conditions necessary for its recognition in the State addressed.

Article 28

Moreover, a judgment shall not be recognised if it conflicts with the provisions of Sections 3, 4 or 5 of Title II or in a case provided for in Article 59.

A judgment may furthermore be refused recognition in any case provided for in Article 54B(3) or 57(4).

In its examination of the grounds of jurisdiction referred to in the foregoing paragraphs, the court or authority applied to shall be bound by the findings of fact on which the court of the State of origin based its jurisdiction.

Subject to the provisions of the first and second paragraphs, the jurisdiction of the court of the State of origin may not be reviewed; the test of public policy referred to in Article 27(1) may not be applied to the rules relating to jurisdiction.

Article 29

Under no circumstances may a foreign judgment be reviewed as to its subtance.

Article 30

A court of a Contracting State in which recognition is sought of a judgment given in another Contracting State may stay the proceedings if an ordinary appeal against the judgment has been lodged.

A court of a Contracting State in which recognition is sought of a judgment given in Ireland or the United Kingdom may stay the proceedings if enforcement is suspended in the State of origin by reason of an appeal.

SECTION 2

ENFORCEMENT

Article 31

A judgment given in a Contracting State and enforceable in that State shall be **5–179** enforced in another Contracting State when, on the application of any interested party, it has been declared enforceable there.

However, in the United Kingdom, such a judgment shall be enforced in England and Wales, in Scotland, or in Northern Ireland when, on the application of any interested party, it has been registered for enforcement in that part of the United Kingdom.

Article 32

1. The application shall be submitted:
   — in Belgium, to the tribunal de premiére instance or rechtbank van eerste aanleg,
   — in Denmark, to the byret,
   — in the Federal Republic of Germany, to the presiding judge of a chamber of the Landgericht,
   — in Greece, to the μονομελές πρωτοδικείο,
   — in Spain, to the Juzgado de Primera Instancia,
   — in France, to the presiding judge of the tribunal de grande instance,
   — in Ireland, to the High Court,
   — in Iceland, to the héraðsdómari,
   — in Italy, to the corte d'appello,
   — in Luxembourg, to the presiding judge of the tribunal d'arrondissement,
   — in the Netherlands, to the presiding judge of the arrondissementsrecht-bank,
   — in Norway, to the herredsrett or byrett as namsrett,
   — in Austria, to the Landesgericht or the Kreisgericht,
   — in Portugal, to the Tribunal Judicial de Círculo,
   — in Switzerland:
   (a) in respect of judgments ordering the payment of a sum of money, to the juge de la mainlevée/Rechtsöffnungsrichter/giudice competente a pronunciare sul rigetto dell'opposizione, within the framework of the procedure governed by Articles 80 and 81 of the loi fédérale sur la poursuite pour dettes et la faillite/Bundesgesetz über Schuldbe-treibung und Konkurs/legge federale sulla esecuzione e sul fallimento;
   (b) in respect of judgments ordering a performance other than the payment of a sum of money, to the juge cantonal d'exequatur compétent/zuständiger kantonaler Vollstreckungsrichter/giudice cantonale competente a pronunciare l'exequatur,
   — in Finland, to the ulosotonhaltija/överexekutor,
   — in Sweden, to the Svea hovrätt,
   — in the United Kingdom:
   (a) in England and Wales, to the High Court of Justice, or in the case of a maintenance judgment to the Magistrates' Court on transmission by the Secretary of State;
   (b) in Scotland, to the Court of Session, or in the case of a maintenance judgment to the Sheriff Court on transmission by the Secretary of State;
   (c) in Northern Ireland, to the High Court of Justice, or in the case of a maintenance judgment to the Magistrates' Court on transmission by the Secretary of State.

2. The jurisdiction of local courts shall be determined by reference to the place of domicile of the party against whom enforcement is sought. If he is not domiciled in the State in which enforcement is sought, it shall be determined by reference to the place of enforcement.

Article 33

The procedure for making the application shall be governed by the law of the State in which enforcement is sought.

The applicant must give an address for service of process within the area of jurisdiction of the court applied to. However, if the law of the State in which enforcement is sought does not provide for the furnishing of such an address, the applicant shall appoint a representative *ad litem*.

The documents referred to in Articles 46 and 47 shall be attached to the application.

Article 34

The court applied to shall give its decision without delay; the party against whom enforcement is sought shall not at this stage of the proceedings be entitled to make any submissions on the application.

The application may be refused only for one of the reasons specified in Articles 27 and 28.

Under no circumstances may the foreign judgment be reviewed as to its substance.

Article 35

The appropriate officer of the court shall without delay bring the decision given on the application to the notice of the applicant in accordance with the procedure laid down by the law of the State in which enforcement is sought.

Article 36

If enforcement is authorised, the party against whom enforcement is sought may appeal against the decision within one month of service thereof.

If that party is domiciled in a Contracting State other than that in which the decision authorising enforcement was given, the time for appealing shall be two months and shall run from the date of service, either on him in person or at his residence. No extension of time may be granted on account of distance.

Article 37

1. An appeal against the decision authorising enforcement shall be lodged in accordance with the rules governing procedure in contentious matters:
   — in Belgium, with the tribunal de première instance or rechtbank van eerste aanleg,
   — in Denmark, with the landsret,
   — in the Federal Republic of Germany, with the Oberlandesgericht,
   — in Greece, with the εφετείο,
   — in Spain, with the Audiencia Provincial,
   — in France, with the cour d'appel,
   — in Ireland, wit hthe High Court,
   — in Iceland, with the héraðsdómari,
   — in Italy, with the corte d'appello,
   — in Luxembourg, with the Cour supérieure de justice sitting as a court of civil appeal,
   — in the Netherlands, with the arrondissementsrechtbank,
   — in Norway, with the lagmannsrett,
   — in Austria, with the Landesgericht or the Kreisgericht,
   — in Portugal, with the Tribunal da Relação,
   — in Finland, with the hovioikeus/hovrätt,
   — in Switzerland, with the tribunal cantonal/Kantonsgericht/tribunale cantonale,
   — in Sweden, with the Svea hovrätt,
   — in the United Kingdom:
      (a) in England and Wales, with the High Court of Justice, or in the case of a maintenance judgment with the Magistrates' Court;
      (b) in Scotland, with the Court of Session, or in the case of a maintenance judgment with the Sheriff Court;

1712

(c) in Nothern Ireland, with the High Court of Justice, or in the case of a maintenance judgment with the Magistrates' Court.

2. The judgment given on the appeal may be contested only:

— in Belgium, Greece, Spain, France, Italy, Luxembourg and in the Netherlands, by an appeal in cassation,

— in Denmark, by an appeal to the højesteret, with the leave of the Minister of Justice,

— in the Federal Repubic of Germany, by a Rechtsbeschwerde,

— in Ireland, by an appeal on a point of law to the Supreme Court,

— in Iceland, by an appeal to the Hæstiréttur,

— in Norway, by an appeal (kjæremål or anke) to the Hoyesteretts Kjæremålsutvalg or Hoyesterett,

— in Austria, in the case of an appeal, by a Revisionsrekurs and, in the case of opposition proceedings, by a Berufung with the possibility of a Revision,

— in Portugal, by an appeal on a point of law,

— in Switzerland, by a recours de droit public devant le tribunal fédéral/ staatsrechtliche Beschwerde beim Bundesgericht/ricorso di diritto pubblico davanti al tribunale federale,

— in Finland, by an appeal to the korkein oikeus/högsta domstolen,

— in Sweden, by an appeal to the högsta domstolen,

— in the United Kingdom, by a single further appeal on a point of law.

Article 38

The court with which the appeal under the first paragraph of Article 37 is lodged may, on the application of the appellant, stay the proceedings if an ordinary appeal has been lodged against the judgment in the State of origin or if the time for such an appeal has not yet expired; in the latter case, the court may specify the time within which such an appeal is to be lodged.

Where the judgment was given in Ireland or the United Kingdom, any form of appeal available in the State of origin shall be treated as an ordinary appeal for the purpose of the first paragraph.

The court may also make enforcement conditional on the provision of such security as it shall determine.

Article 39

During the time specified for an appeal pursuant to Article 36 and until any such appeal has been determined, no measures of enforcement may be taken other than protective measures taken against the property of the party against whom enforcement is sought.

The decision authorising enforcement shall carry with it the power to proceed to any such protective measures.

Article 40

1. If the application for enforcement is refused, the applicant may appeal:

— in Belgium, to the cour d'appel or hof van beroep,

— in Denmark, to the landsret,

— in the Federal Republic of Germany, to the Oberlandesgericht,

— in Greece, to the εφετείο,

— in Spain, to the Audiencia Provincial,

— in France, to the cour d'appel,

— In Ireland, to the High Court,

— in Iceland, to the héraðsdómari,

— in Italy, to the corte d'appello,

— in Luxembourg, to the Cour supérieure de justice sitting as a court of civil appeal,

— in the Netherlands, to the gerechtshof,

— in Norway, to the lagmannsrett,

— in Austria, to the Landesgericht or the Kreisgericht,

— in Portugal, to the Tribunal da Relação,

EUROPE

- in Switzerland, to the tribunal cantonal/Kantonsgericht/tribunale cantonale,
- in Finland, to the hovioikeus/hovrätt,
- in Sweden, the Svea hovrätt,
- in the United Kingdom:
  (a) in England and Wales, to the High Court of Justice, or in the case of a maintenance judgment to the Magistrates' Court;
  (b) in Scotland, to the Court of Session, or in the case of a maintenance judgment to the Sheriff Court;
  (c) in Nothern Ireland, to the High Court of Justice, or in the case of a maintenance judgment to the Magistrates' Court.

2. The party against whom enforcement is sought shall be summoned to appear before the appellate court. If he fails to appear, the provisons of the second and third paragraphs of Article 20 shall apply even where he is not domiciled in any of the Contracting States.

Article 41

A judgment given on an appeal provided for in Article 40 may be contested only:

- in Belgium, Greece, Spain, France, Italy, Luxembourg and in the Netherlands, by an appeal in cassation,
- in Denmark, by an appeal to the højesteret, with the leave of the Minister of Justice,
- in the Federal Republic of Germany, by a Rechtsbeschwerde,
- in Ireland, by an appeal on a point of law to the Supreme Court,
- in Iceland, by an appeal to the Hæstiréttur,
- in Norway, by an appeal (kjæremål or anke) to the Hoyesteretts kjæremålsutvalg or Hoyesterett,
- in Austria, by a Revisionsrekurs,
- in Portugal, by an appeal on a point of law,
- in Switzerland, by a recours de droit public devant le tribunal fédéral/staatsrechtliche Beschwerde beim Bundesgericht/ricorso di diritto pubblico davanti al tribunale federale,
- in Finland, by an appeal to the korkein oikeus/högsta domstolen,
- in Sweden, by an appeal to the högsta domstolen,
- in the United Kingdom, by a single further appeal on a point of law.

Article 42

Where a foreign judgment has been given in respect of several matters and enforcement cannot be authorised for all of them, the court shall authorise enforcement for one or more of them.

An applicant may request partial enforcement of a judgment.

Article 43

A foreign judgment which orders a periodic payment by way of a penalty shall be enforceable in the State in which enforcement is sought only if the amount of the payment has been finally determined by the courts of the State of origin.

Article 44

An applicant who, in the State of origin, has benefited from complete or partial legal aid or exemption from costs or expenses, shall be entitled, in the procedures provided for in Articles 32 to 35, to benefit from the most favourable legal aid or the most extensive exemption from costs or expenses provided for by the law of the State addressed.

However, an applicant who requests the enforcement of a decision given by an administrative authority in Denmark or in Iceland in respect of a maintenance order may, in the State addressed, claim the benefits referred to in the first paragraph if he presents a statement from, respectively, the Danish Ministry of Justice or the Icelandic Ministry of Justice to the effect that he fulfils the economic requirements to qualify for the grant of complete or partial legal aid or exemption from costs or expenses.

Article 45

No security, bond or deposit, however described, shall be required of a party who in one Contracting State applies for enforcement of a judgment given in another Contracting State on the ground that he is a foreign national or that he is not domiciled or resident in the State in which enforcement is sought.

SECTION 3

COMMON PROVIONS

Article 46

A party seeking recognition or applying for enforcement of a judgment shall produce:

1. a copy of the judgment which satisfies the conditions necessary to establish its authenticity;
2. in the case of a judgment given in default, the original or a certified true copy of the document which establishes that the party in default was served with the document instituting the proceedings or with an equivalent document.

5–180

Article 47

A party applying for enforcement shall also produce:

1. documents which establish that, according to the law of the State of origin, the judgment is enforceable and has been served;
2. where appropriate, a document showing that the applicant is in receipt of legal aid in the State of origin.

Article 48

If the documents specified in Article 46(2) and Article 47(2) are not produced, the court may specify a time for their production, accept equivalent documents or, if it considers that it has sufficient information before it, dispense with their production.

If the court so requires, a translation of the documents shall be produced; the translation shall be certified by a person qualified to do so in one of the Contracting States.

Article 49

No legislation or other similar formality shall be required in respect of the documents referred to in Article 46 or 47 or the second paragraph of Article 48, or in respect of a document appointing a representative *ad litem*.

TITLE IV

AUTHENTIC INSTRUMENTS AND COURT SETTLEMENTS

Article 50

A document which has been formally drawn up or registered as an authentic instrument and is enforceable in one Contracting State shall, in another Contracting State, be declared enforceable there, on application made in accordance with the procedures provided for in Articles 31 *et seq*. The application may be refused only if enforcement of the instrument is contrary to public policy in the State addressed.

5–181

The instrument produced must satisfy the conditions necessary to establish its authenticity in the State of origin.

The provisions of Section 3 of Title III shall apply as appropriate.

Article 51

A settlement which has been approved by a court in the course of proceeedings and is enforceable in the State in which it was concluded shall be enforceable in the State addressed under the same conditions as authentic instruments.

EUROPE

TITLE V

GENERAL PROVISIONS

Article 52

5–182   In order to determine whether a party is domiciled in the Contracting State whose courts are seised of a matter, the court shall apply its internal law.

If a party is not domiciled in the State whose courts are seised of the matter, then in order to determine whether the party is domiciled in another Contracting State, the court shall apply the law of that State.

Article 53

For the purposes of this Convention, the seat of a company or other legal person or association of natural or legal persons shall be treated as its domicile. However, in order to determine that seat, the court shall apply its rules of private international law.

In order to determine whether a trust is domiciled in the Contracting State whose courts are seised of the matter, the court shall apply its rules of private international law.

TITLE VI

TRANSITIONAL PROVISIONS

Article 54

5–183   The provisions of this Convention shall apply to legal proceedings instituted and to documents formally drawn up or registered as authentic instruments after its entry into force in the State of origin and, where recognition or enforcement of a judgment or authentic instrument is sought, in the State addressed.

However, judgments given after the date of entry into force of this Convention between the State of origin and the State addressed in proceedings instituted before that date shall be recognised and enforced in accordance with the provisions of Title III if jurisdiction was founded upon rules which accorded with those provided for either in Title II of this Convention or in a convention concluded between the State of origin and the State addressed which was in force when the proceedings were instituted.

If the parties to a dispute concerning a contract had agreed in writing before the entry into force of this Convention that the contract was to be governed by the law of Ireland or of a part of the United Kingdom, the courts of Ireland or of that part of the United Kingdom shall retain the right to exercise jurisdiction in the dispute.

Article 54A

For a period of three years from the entry into force of this Convention for Denmark, Greece, Ireland, Iceland, Norway, Finland and Sweden, respectively, jurisdiction in maritime matters shall be determined in these States not only in accordance with the provisions of Title II, but also in accordance with the provisions of paragraphs 1 to 7 following. However, upon the entry into force of the International Convention relating to the arrest of sea-going ships, signed at Brussels on 10 May 1952, for one of these States, these provisions shall cease to have effect for that State.

1. A person who is domiciled in a Contracting State may be sued in the courts of one of the States mentioned above in respect of a maritime claim if the ship to which the claim relates or any other ship owned by him has been arrested by judicial process within the territory of the latter State to secure the claim, or could have been so arrested there but bail or other security has been given, and either:

    (a) the claimant is domiciled in the latter State; or

    (b) the claim arose in the latter State; or

    (c) the claim concerns the voyage during which the arrest was made or could have been made; or

    (d) the claim arises out of a collision or out of damage caused by a ship to another ship or to goods or persons on board either ship, either by the execution or non-execution of a manoeuvre or by the non-observance of regulations; or

    (e) the claim is for salvage; or

    (f) the claim is in respect of a mortgage or hypothecation of the ship arrested.

2. A claimant may arrest either the particular ship to which the maritime claim relates, or any other ship which is owned by the person who was, at the time when the maritime claim arose, the owner of the particular ship. However, only the particular ship to which the maritime claim relates may be arrested in respect of the maritime claims set out in 5(o), (p) or (q) of this Article.

3. Ships shall be deemed to be in the same ownership when all the shares therein are owned by the same person or persons.

4. When in the case of a charter by demise of a ship the charterer alone is liable in respect of a maritime claim relating to that ship, the claimant may arrest that ship or any other ship owned by the charterer, but no other ship owned by the owner may be arrested in respect of such claim. The same shall apply to any case in which a person other than the owner of a ship is liable in respect of a maritime claim relating to that ship.

5. The expression 'maritime claim' means a claim arising out of one or more of the following:

    (a) damage caused by any ship either in collision or otherwise;

    (b) loss of life or personal injury caused by any ship or occurring in connection with the operation of any ship;

    (c) salvage;

    (d) agreement relating to the use or hire of any ship whether by charterparty or otherwise;

    (e) agreement relating to the carriage of goods in any ship whether by charterparty or otherwise;

    (f) loss of or damage to goods including baggage carried in any ship;

    (g) general average;

    (h) bottomry;

    (i) towage;

    (j) pilotage;

    (k) goods or materials wherever supplied to a ship for her operation or maintenance;

    (l) construction, repair or equipment or any ship or dock charges and dues;

    (m) wages of masters, officers or crew;

    (n) master's disbursements, including disbursements made by shippers, charterers or agents on behalf of a ship or her owner;

    (o) dispute as to the title to or ownership of any ship;

    (p) disputes between co-owners of any ship as to the ownership, possession, employment or earnings of that ship;

    (q) the mortgage or hypothecation of any ship.

6. In Demark, the expression 'arrest' shall be deemed, as regards the maritime claims referred to in 5.(o) and (p) of this Article, to include a 'forbud', where that is the only procedure allowed in respect of such a claim under Articles 646 to 653 of the law on civil procedure (lov om rettens pleje).

7. In Iceland, the expression 'arrest' shall be deemed, as regards the maritime claims referred to in 5.(o) and (p) of this Article, to include a 'lögbann', where that is the only procedure allowed in respect of such a claim under Chapter III of the law on arrest and injunction (lög um kyrrsetningu og lögbann).

TITLE VII

RELATIONSHIP TO THE BRUSSELS CONVENTION AND TO OTHER CONVENTIONS

Article 54B

5-184   1. This Convention shall not prejudice the application by the Member States of the European Communities of the Convention on Jurisdiction and the Enforcement of Judgments in Civil and Commercial Matters, signed at Brussels on 27 September 1968 and of the Protocol on interpretation of that Convention by the Court of Justice, signed at Luxembourg on 3 June 1971, as amended by the Conventions of Accession to the said Convention and the said Protocol by the States acceding to the European Communities, all of these Conventions and the Protocol being hereinafter referred to as the 'Brussels Convention'.

2. However, this Convention shall in any event be applied:

  (a) in matters of jurisdiction, where the defendant is domiciled in the territory of a Contracting State which is not a member of the European Communities, or where Article 16 or 17 of this Convention confers a jurisdiction on the courts of such a Contracting State;

  (b) in relation to a *lis pendens* or to related actions as provided for in Article 21 and 22, when proceedings are instituted in a Contracting State which is not a member of the European Communities and in a Contracting State which is a member of the European Communities;

  (c) in matters of recognition and enforcement, where either the State of origin or the State addressed is not a member of the Euroepan Communities.

3. In addition to the grounds provided for in Title III recognition or enforcement may be refused if the ground of jurisdiction on which the judgment has been based differs from that resulting from this Convention and recognition or enforcement is sought against a party who is domiciled in a Contracting State which is not a member of the European Communities, unless the judgment may otherwise be recognised or enforced under any rule of law in the State addressed.

Article 55

Subject to the provisions of the second paragraph of Article 54 and of Article 56, this Convention shall, for the States which are parties to it, supersede the following conventions concluded between two or more of them:

  — the Convention between the Swiss Confederation and France on jurisdiction and enforcement of judgments in civil matters, signed at Paris on 15 June 1869,

  — the Treaty between the Swiss Confederation and Spain on the mutual enforcement of judgments in civil or commercial matters, signed at Madrid on 19 November 1896,

  — the Convention between the Swiss Confederation and the German Reich on the recognition and enforcement of judgments and arbitration awards, signed at Berne on 2 November 1929,

  — the Convention between Denmark, Finland, Iceland, Norway and Sweden on the recognition and enforcement of judgments, signed at Copenhagen on 16 March 1932,

  — the Convention between the Swiss Confederation and Italy on the recognition and enforcement of judgments, signed at Rome on 3 January 1933,

  — the Convention between Sweden and the Swiss Confederation on the recognition and enforcement of judgments and arbitral awards, signed at Stockholm on 15 January 1936,

  — the Convention between the Kingdom of Belgium and Austria on the reciprocal recognition and enforcement of judgments and authentic instruments relating to maintenance obligations, signed at Vienna on 25 October 1957,

  — the Convention between the Swiss Confederation and Belgium on the recognition and enforcement of judgments and arbitration awards, signed at Berne on 29 April 1959,

1718

— the Convention between the Federal Republic of Germany and Austria on the reciprocal recognition and enforcement of judgments, settlements and authentic instruments in civil and commercial matters, signed at Vienna on 6 June 1959,

— the Convention between the Kingdom of Belgium and Austria on the reciprocal recognition and enforcement of judgments, arbitral awards and authentic instruments in civil and commercial matters, signed at Vienna on 16 June 1959,

— the Convention between Austria and the Swiss Confederation on the recognition and enforcement of judgments, signed at Berne on 16 December 1960,

— the Convention between Norway and the United Kingdom providing for the reciprocal recognition and enforcement of judgments in civil matters, signed at London on 12 June 1961,

— the Convention between the United Kingdom and Austria providing for the reciprocal rcognition and enforcement of judgments in civil and commercial matters, signed at Vienna on 14 July 1961, with amending Protocol signed at London on 6 March 1970,

— the Convention between the Kingdom of the Netherlands and Austria on the reciprocal recognition and enforcement of judgments and authentic instruments in civil and commercial matters, signed at The Hague on 6 February 1963,

— the Convention between France and Austria on the recognition and enforcement of judgments and authentic instruments in civil and commercial matters, signed at Vienna on 15 July 1966,

— the Convention between Luxembourg and Austria on the recognition and enforcement of judgments and authentic instruments in civil and commercial matters, signed at Luxembourg on 29 July 1971,

— the Convention between Italy and Austria on the recognition and enforcement of judgments in civil and commercial matters, of judicial settlements and of authentic instruments, signed at Rome on 16 November 1971,

— the Convention between Norway and the Federal Republic of Germany on the recognition and enforcement of judgments and enforceable documents, in civil and commercial matters, signed at Oslo on 17 June 1977,

— the Convention between Denmark, Finland, Iceland, Norway and Sweden on the recognition and enforcement of judgments in civil matters, signed at Copenhagen on 11 October 1977,

— the Convention between Austria and Sweden on the recognition and enforcement of judgments in civil matters, signed at Stockholm on 16 September 1982,

— the Convention between Austria and Spain on the recognition and enforcement of judgments, settlements and enforceable authentic instruments in civil and commercial matters, signed at Vienna on 17 February 1984,

— the Convention between Norway and Austria on the recognition and enforcement of judgments in civil matters, signed at Vienna on 21 May 1984, and

— the Convention between Finland and Austria on the recognition and enforcement of judgments in civil matters, signed at Vienna on 17 November 1986.

Article 56

The Treaty and the conventions referred to in Article 55 shall continue to have effect in relation to matters to which this Convention does not apply.

They shall continue to have effect in respect of judgments given and documents formally drawn up or registered as authentic instruments before the entry into force of this Convention.

Article 57

1. This Convention shall not affect any conventions to which the Contracting States

are or will be parties and which, in relation to particular matters, govern jurisdiction or the recognition or enforcement of judgments.

2. This Convention shall not prevent a court of a Contracting State which is party to a convention referred to in the first paragraph from assuming jurisdiction in accordance with that convention, even where the defendant is domiciled in a Contracting State which is not a party to that convention. The court hearing the action shall, in any event, apply Article 20 of this Convention.

3. Judgments given in a Contracting State by a court in the exercise of jurisdiction provided for in a convention referred to in the first paragraph shall be recognised and enforced in the other Contracting States in accordance with Title III of this Convention.

4. In addition to the grounds provided for in Title III, recognition or enforcement may be refused if the State addressed it not a contracting party to a convention referred to in the first paragraph and the person against whom recognition or enforcement is sought is domiciled in that State, unless the judgment may otherwise be recognised or enforced under any rule of law in the State addressed.

5. Where a convention referred to in the first paragraph to which both the State of origin and the State addressed are parties lays down conditions for the recognition or enforcement of judgments, those conditions shall apply. In any event, the provisions of this Convention which concern the procedures for recognition and enforcement of judgments may be applied.

Article 58(None)

Article 59

5–185   This Convention shall not prevent a Contracting State from assuming, in a convention on the recognition and enforcement of judgments, an obligation towards a third State not to recognise judgments given in other Contracting States against defendants domiciled or habitually resident in the third State where, in cases provided for in Article 4, the judgment could only be founded on a ground of jurisdiction specified in the second paragraph of Article 3.

However, a Contracting State may not assume an obligation towards a third State not to recognise a judgment given in another Contracting State by a court basing its jurisdiction on the presence within that State of property belonging to the defendant, or the seizure by the plaintiff of property situated there:

1. if the action is brought to assert or declare proprietary or possessory rights in that property, seeks to obtain authority to dispose of it, or arises from another issue relating to such property, or

2. if the property constitutes the security for a debt which is the subject-matter of the action.

TITLE VIII

FINAL PROVISIONS

Article 60

5–186   The following may be parties to this Convention:

(a) States which, at the time of the opening of this Convention for signature, are members of the European Communities or of the European Free Trade Association;

(b) States which, after the opening of this Convention for signature, become members of the European Communities or of the European Free Trade Association;

(c) States invited to accede in accordance with Article 62(1)(b).

Article 61

1. This Convention shall be opened for signature by the States members of the European Communities or of the European Free Trade Association.

2. The Convention shall be submitted for ratification by the signatory States. The instruments of ratification shall be deposited with the Swiss Federal Council.

3. The Convention shall enter into force on the first day of the third month following the date on which two States, of which one is a member of the European Com-

munities and the other a member of the European Free Trade Association, deposit their instruments of ratification.

4. The Convention shall take effect in relation to any other signatory State on the first day of the third month following the deposit of its instrument of ratification.

Article 62

1. After entering into force this Convention shall be open to accession by:
    (a) the States referred to in Article 60(b);
    (b) other States which have been invited to accede upon a request made by one of the Contracting States to the depositary State. The depositary State shall invite the State concerned to accede only if, after having communicated the contents of the communications that this State intends to make in accordance with Article 63, it has obtained the unanimous agreement of the signatory States and the Contracting States referred to in Article 60(a) and (b).

2. If an acceding State wishes to furnish details for the purposes of Protocol No. 1, negotiations shall be entered into to that end. A negotiating conference shall be convened by the Swiss Federal Council.

3. In respect of an acceding State, the Convention shall take effect on the first day of the third month following the deposit of its instrument of accession.

4. However, in respect of an acceding State referred to in paragraph 1(a) or (b), the Convention shall take effect only in relations between the acceding State and the Contracting States which have not made any objections to the accession before the first day of the third month following the deposit of the instrument of accession.

Article 63

Each acceding State shall, when depositing its instrument of accession, communicate the information required for the application of Articles 3, 32, 37, 40, 41 and 55 of this Convention and furnish, if need be, the details prescribed during the negotiations for the purposes of Protocol No. 1.

Article 64

1. This Convention is concluded for an initial period of five years from the date of its entry into force in accordance with Article 61(3), even in the case of States which ratify it or accede to it after that date.

2. At the end of the initial five-year period, the Convention shall be automatically renewed from year to year.

3. Upon the expiry of the initial five-year period, any Contracting State may, at any time, denounce the Convention by sending a notification to the Swiss Federal Council.

4. The denunciation shall take effect at the end of the calendar year following the expiry of a period of six months from the date of receipt by the Swiss Federal Council of the notification of denunciation.

Article 65

The following are annexed to this Convention:
    — a Protocol No. 1, on certain questions of jurisdiction, procedure and enforcement,
    — a Protocol No. 2, on the uniform interpretation of the Convention,
    — a Protocol No. 3, on the application of Article 57.
These Protocols shall forman integral part of the Convention.

Article 66

Any Contracting State may request the revision of this Convention. To that end, the Swiss Federal Council shall issue invitations to a revision conference within a period of six months from the date of the request for revision.

Article 67

The Swiss Federal Council shall notify the States represented at the Diplomatic Conference of Lugano and the States who have later acceded to the Convention of:

    (a) the deposit of each instrument of ratification or accession;

1721

(b) the dates of entry into force of this Convention in respect of the Contracting States;

(c) any denunciation received pursuant to Article 64;

(d) any declaration received pursuant to Article Ia of Protocol No. 1;

(e) any declaration received pursuant to Article Ib of Protocol No. 1;

(f) any declaration received pursuant to Article IV of Protocol No. 1;

(g) any communication made pursuant to Article VI of Protocol No. 1.

Article 68

This Convention, drawn up in a single original in the Danish, Dutch, English, Finnish, French, German, Greek, Icelandic, Irish, Italian, Norwegian, Portuguese, Spanish and Swedish languages, all fourteen texts being equally authentic, shall be deposited in the archives of the Swiss Federal Council. The Swiss Federal Council shall transmit a certified copy to the Government of each State represented at the Diplomatic Conference of Lugano and to the Government of each acceding State.

PROTOCOL No. 1

ON CERTAIN QUESTIONS OF JURISDICTION, PROCEDURE AND ENFORCEMENT

The High Contracting Parties have agreed upon the following provisions, which shall be annexed to the Convention:

Article I

Any person domiciled in Luxembourg who is sued in a court of another Contracting State pursuant to Article 5(1) may refuse to submit to the jurisdiction of that court. If the defendant does not enter an appearance the court shall declare of its own motion that it has no jurisdiction.

An agreement conferring jurisdiction, within the meaning of Article 17, shall be valid with respect to a person domiciled in Luxembourg only if that person has expressly and specifically so agreed.

Article Ia

1. Switzerland reserves the right to declare, at the time of depositing its instrument of ratification, that a judgment given in another Contracting State shall be neither recognised nor enforced in Switzerland if the following conditions are met:

(a) the jurisdiction of the court which has given the judgment is based only on Article 5(1) of this Convention; and

(b) the defendant was domiciled in Switzerland at the time of the introduction of the proceedings; for the purposes of this Article, a company or other legal person is considered to be domiciled in Switzerland if it has its registered seat and the effective centre of activities in Switzerland; and

(c) the defendant raises an objection to the recognition or enforcement of the judgment in Switzerland, provided that he has not waived the benefit of the declaration foreseen under this paragraph.

2. This reservation shall not apply to the extent that at the time recognition or enforcement is sought a derogation has been granted from Article 59 of the Swiss Federal Constitution. The Swiss Government shall communicate such derogations to the signatory States and the acceding States.

3. This reservation shall cease to have effect on 31 December 1999. It may be withdrawn at any time.

Article Ib

Any Contracting State may, by declaration made at the time of signing or of deposit of its instrument of ratification or of accession, reserve the right, notwithstanding the provisions of Article 28, not to recognise and enforce judgments given in the other Contracting States if the jurisdiction of the court of the State of origin is based, pursuant to Article 16(1)(b), exclusively on the domicile of the defendant in the State of origin, and the property is situated in the territory of the State which entered the reservation.

Article II

Without prejudice to any more favourable provisions of national laws, persons domiciled in a Contracting State who are being prosecuted in the criminal courts of another Contracting State of which they are not nationals for an offence which was not intentionally committed may be defended by persons qualified to do so, even if they do not appear in person.

However, the court seised of the matter may order appearance in person; in the case of failure to appear, a judgment given in the civil action without the person concerned having had the opportunity to arrange for his defence need not be recognised or enforced in the other Contracting States.

Article III

In proceedings for the issue of an order for enforcement, no charge, duty or fee calculated by reference to the value of the matter in issue may be levied in the State in which enforcement is sought.

Article IV

Judicial and extrajudicial documents drawn up in one Contracting State which have to be served on persons in another Contracting State shall be transmitted in accordance with the procedures laid down in the conventions and agreements concluded between the Contracting States.

Unless the State in which service is to take place objects by declaration to the Swiss Federal Council, such documents may also be sent by the appropriate public officers of the State in which the document has been drawn up directly to the appropriate public officers of the State in which the addressee is to be found. In this case the officer of the State of origin shall send a copy of the document to the officer of the State applied to who is competent to forward it to the addressee. The document shall be forwarded in the manner specified by the law of the State applied to. The forwarding shall be recorded by a certificate sent directly to the officer of the State of origin.

Article V

The jurisdiction specified in Articles 6(2) and 10 in actions on a warranty or guarantee or in any other third party proceedings may not be resorted to in the Federal Republic of Germany, in Spain, in Austria and in Switzerland. Any person domiciled in another Contracting State may be sued in the courts:

— of the Federal Republic of Germany, pursuant to Articles 68, 72, 73 and 74 of the code of civil procedure (Zivilprozeßordnung) concerning third-party notices,

— of Spain, pursuant to Article 1482 of the civil code,

— of Austria, pursuant to Article 21 of the code of civil procedure (Zivilprozeßordnung) concerning third-party notices,

— of Switzerland, pursuant to the appropriate provisions concerning third-party notices of the cantonal codes of civil procedure.

Judgments given in the other Contracting States by virtue of Article 6(2) or Article 10 shall be recognised and enforced in the Federal Republic of Germany, in Spain, in Austria and in Switzerland in accordance with Title III. Any effects which judgments given in these States may have on third parties by application of the provisions in the preceding paragraph shall also be recognised in the other Contracting States.

Article Va

In matters relating to maintenance, the expression 'court' includes the Danish, Icelandic and Norwegian administrative authorities.

In civil and commercial matters, the expression 'court' includes the Finnish ulosotonhaltija/överexekutor.

Article Vb

In proceedings involving a dispute between the master and a member of the crew of a sea-going ship registered in Denmark, in Greece, in Ireland, in Iceland, in Norway, in Portugal or in Sweden concerning remuneration or other conditions of service, a court in a Contracting State shall establish whether the

1723

diplomatic or consular officer responsible for the ship has been notified of the dispute. It shall stay the proceedings so long as he has not been notified. It shall of its own motion decline jurisdiction if the officer, having been duly notified, has exercised the powers accorded to him in the matter by a consular convention, or in the absence of such a convention has, within the time allowed, raised any objection to the exercise of such jurisdiction.

Article Vc (None)

Article Vd

Without prejudice to the jurisdiction of the European Patent Office under the Convention on the grant of European patents, signed at Munich on 5 October 1973, the courts of each Contracting State shall have exclusive jurisdiction, regardless of domicile, in proceedings concerned with the registration or validity of any European patent granted for that State which is not a Community patent by virtue of the provision of Article 86 of the Convention for the European patent for the common market, signed at Luxembourg on 15 December 1975.

Article VI

The Contracting States shall communicate to the Swiss Federal Council the text of any provisions of their laws which amend either those provisions of their laws mentioned in the Convention or the lists of courts specified in Section 2 of Title III.

PROTOCOL No. 2

ON THE UNIFORM INTERPRETATION OF THE CONVENTION

Preamble

5–187   The High Contracting Parties,

Having regard to Article 65 of this Convention,

Considering the substantial link between this Convention and the Brussels Convention,

Considering that the Court of Justice of the European Communities by virtue of the Protocol of 3 June 1971 has jurisdiction to give rulings on the interpretation of the provisions of the Brussels Convention,

Being aware of the rulings delivered by the Court of Justice of the European Communities on the interpretation of the Brussels Convention up to the time of signature of this Convention.

Considering that the negotiations which led to the conclusion of the Convention were based on the Brussels Convention in the light of these rulings.

Desiring to prevent, in full deference to the independence of the courts, divergent interpretations and to arrive at as uniform an interpretation as possible of the provisions of the Convention, and of these provisions and those of the Brussels Convention which are substantially reproduced in this Convention,

Have agreed as follows:

Article 1

The courts of each Contracting State shall, when applying and interpreting the provisions of the Convention, pay due account to the principles laid down by any relevant decision delivered by courts of the other Contracting States concerning provisions of this Convention.

Article 2

1. The Contracting Parties agree to set up a system of exchange of information concerning judgments delivered pursuant to this Convention as well as relevant judgments under the Brussels Convention. This system shall comprise:

   — transmission to a central body by the competent authorities of judgments delivered by courts of last instance and the Court of Justice of the European Communities as well as judgments of particular importance which have become final and have been delivered pursuant to this Convention or the Brussels Convention,

   — classification of these judgments by the central body including, as far as necessary, the drawing-up and publication of translations and abstracts,

   — communication by the central body of the relevant documents to the competent national authorities of all signatories and acceding States to the Convention and to the Commission of the European Communities.

2. The central body is the Registrar of the Court of Justice of the European Communities.

Article 3

1. A Standing Committee shall be set up for the purposes of this Protocol.

2. The Committee shall be composed of representatives appointed by each signatory and acceding State.

3. The European Communities (Commission, Court of Justice and General Secretariat of the Council) and the European Free Trade Association may attend the meetings as observers.

Article 4

1. At the request of a Contracting Party, the depositary of the Convention shall convene meetings of the Committee for the purpose of exchanging views on the functioning of the Convention and in particular on:

   — the development of the case-law as communicated under the first paragraph first indent of Article 2,

   — the application of Article 57 of the Convention.

2. The Committee, in the light of these exchanges, may also examine the appropriateness of starting on particular topics a revision of the Convention and make recommendations.

PROTOCOL No. 3

ON THE APPLICATION OF ARTICLE 57

The High Contracting Parties have agreed as follows:

5–188

1. For the purposes of the Convention, provisions which, in relation in particular matters, govern jurisdiction or the recognition or enforcement of judgments and which are, or will be, contained in acts of the institutions of the European Communities shall be treated in the same way as the conventions referred to in paragraph 1 of Article 57.

2. If one Contracting State is of the opinion that a provision contained in an act of the institutions of the European Communities is incompatible with the Convention, the Contracting States shall promptly consider amending the Convention pursuant to Article 66, without prejudice to the procedure established by Protocol No. 2.

SCHEDULE 2

OTHER AMENDMENTS OF THE 1982 ACT

Section 3

1. The words "Brussels Conventions" shall be substituted for the word "Conventions" wherever occurring in section 2 (the Conventions to have the force of law) and section 3 (interpretation of the Conventions). **5–189**

2. In section 4(1) (enforcement of judgments other than maintenance orders) and section 5(1) (recognition and enforcement of maintenance orders) after the words "an application under Article 31" there shall be inserted the words "of the 1968 Convention or of the Lugano Convention".

3. In section 6 (appeals under Article 37, second paragraph and Article 41)—

   (a) in subsection (1), after the words "referred to" there shall be inserted the words "in the 1968 Convention and the Lugano Convention"; and

   (b) in subsection (3), after the words "referred to" there shall be inserted the words "in each of those Conventions".

4. In section 9 (provisions supplementary to Title VII of the 1968 Convention) —in subsection 1(1)

(a) after the words "Title VII of the 1968 Convention" there shall be inserted the words "and, apart from Article 54B, of Title VII of the Lugano Convention"; and

(b) for the words "that convention" there shall be substituted the words "the Convention in question".

5. In section 10 (allocation within UK of jurisdiction in proceedings with respect to trusts and consumer contracts in respect of which the 1968 Convention confers jurisdiction on UK courts generally), in subsection (1) after the words "the 1968 Convention" there shall be inserted the words "or the Lugano Convention".

6. In section 11 (proof and admissibility of certain judgments and related documents for the purposes of the 1968 Convention), in subsection (1) after the words "For the purposes of the 1968 Convention" there shall be inserted the words "and the Lugano Convention".

7. In section 12 (provisions for issue of copies of, and certificates in connection with, UK judgments for purposes of the 1968 Convention) after the words "the 1968 Convention" there shall be inserted the words "or the Lugano Convention".

8. In section 13 (modifications to cover authentic instruments and court settlements) in subsection (1)—

(a) after the words "the 1968 Convention" in paragraph (a) there shall be inserted the words "or the Lugano Convention";

(b) after the words "Title IV of the 1968 Convention" there shall be inserted the words "or, as the case may be, Title IV of the Lugano Convention"; and

(c) for the words "that Convention" there shall be substituted the words "the Convention in question".

9. In section 14 (modifications consequential on revision of the Conventions)—

(a) for the words "any of the Conventions", wherever occuring in subsections (1) and (3), there shall be substituted the words "the Lugano Convention or any of the Brussels Conventions"; and

(b) in subsection (1), after the words "any revision connected with the accession to" there shall be inserted the words "the Lugano Convention or".

10. In section 15 (interpretation of Part I)—

(a) in subsection (1), in the definition of "maintenance order", after the words "maintenance judgment within the meaning of the 1968 Convention" there shall be inserted the words "or, as the case may be, the Lugano Convention"; and

(b) in subsection (3), after the words "authorised or required by the 1968 Convention" there shall be inserted the words "the Lugano Convention".

11. In section 16 (allocation within UK of jurisdiction in certain civil proceedings)—

(a) in paragraph (a) of subsection (1), for the words "the Convention" there shall be substituted the words "that or any other Convention";

(b) in paragraph (b) of that subsection, after the words "Article 16" there shall be inserted the words "of the 1968 Convention"; and

(c) in subsection (4), after the words "subject to the 1968 Convention" there shall be inserted the words "and the Lugano Convention".

12. The words "Brussels or Lugano Contracting State" shall be substituted for the words "Contracting State" wherever occurring in each of the following provisions, that is to say—

(a) in subsections (1)(a) and (3)(a) of section 25 (interim relief in England and Wales or Northern Ireland in the absence of substantive proceedings);

(b) in subsections (2)(a) and (3)(a) and (d) of section 27 (which makes for Scotland similar provision to that made by section 25 for England and Wales); and

(c) in section 28 (application of section 1 of the Administration of Justice (Scotland) Act 1972);and, in section 25(1)(b), for the words "the Convention" there shall be substituted the words "that or any other Convention".

13. In section 30 (proceedings in England and Wales or Northern Ireland for torts to immovable property) in subsection (2), after the words "subject to the 1968 Convention" there shall be inserted the words "and the Lugano Convention".

14. In section 32 (overseas judgments given in proceedings brought in breach of agreement for settlement of disputes) in subsection (4) (saving for judgments required to be recognised or enforced in UK under the 1968 Convention etc) in paragraph (a),

after the words "under the 1968 Convention" there shall be inserted the words "or the Lugano Convention".

15. In section 33 (certain steps not to amount to submission to the jurisdiction of an overseas court) in subsection (2) (saving for judgments required to be recognised or enforced in England and Wales or Northern Ireland under the 1968 Convention) after the words "under the 1968 Convention" there shall be inserted the words "or the Lugano Convention".

16. In section 41 (determination of domicile of individuals for the purposes of the 1968 Convention etc),in subsection (1) after the words "for the purposes of the 1968 Convention" there shall be inserted the words "the Lugano Convention".

17. In section 42 (domicile and seat of corporation or association) in subsection (2)(a), after the words "for the purposes of the 1968 Convention" there shall be inserted the words "or, as the case may be, the Lugano Convention".

18. In section 43 (seat of corporation or association for purposes of Article 16(2) and related provisions) in subsection (1)(a), after the words " Article 16(2)" there shall be inserted the words "of the 1968 Convention or of the Lugano Convention".

19.—(1) In section 44 (persons deemed to be domiciled in UK for certain purposes) in subsection (1)—

    (a) in paragraph (a) (which provides that the section applies to Proceedings within Section 3 of Title II of the 1968 Convention) after the words "the 1968 Convention" there shall be inserted the words "or Section 3 of Title II of the Lugano Convention"; and

    (b) in paragraph (b) (proceedings within Section 2 of that Title) for the words "that Title" there shall be substituted the words "Title II of either of those Conventions".

(2) In subsection (2) of that section, after the words "is deemed for the purposes of the 1968 Convention" there shall be inserted the words "or, as the case may be, of the Lugano Convention".

20. In section 45 (domicile of trusts) in subsection (1), after the words "for the purposes of the 1968 Convention" there shall be inserted the words "the Lugano Convention".

21.—(1) In section 46 (domicile and seat of the Crown) in subsection (2)(a), after the words "for the purposes of the 1968 Convention" there shall be inserted the words "and the Lugano Convention" and for the words "(in which" there shall be substituted the words "(in each of which".

(2) In subsection (4) of that section (Order in Council with respect to seat of the Crown) after the words "for the purposes of the 1968 Convention" there shall be inserted the words "the Lugano Convention".

22. In section 47 (modifications occasioned by decisions of the European Court as to meaning or effect of the Conventions) for the word "Conventions", wherever occuring, there shall be substituted the words "Brussels Conventions".

23. In section 48 (matters for which rules of court may provide)—

    (a) in subsection (1), for the words "or the Conventions" there shall be substituted the words "the Lugano Convention or the Brussels Conventions"; and

    (b) in subsection (3), for the words "the Conventions" there shall be substituted the words "the Lugano Convention, the Brussels Conventions".

24. In section 49 (saving for powers to stay, sist, strike out or dismiss proceedings where to do so is not inconsistent with the 1968 Convention) after the words "the 1968 Convention" there shall be inserted the words "or, as the case may be, the Lugano Convention".

25. In section 50 (general interpretation) the following definitions shall be inserted at the appropriate places—

                "Brussels Contracting State" has the meaning given by section 1(3)";

                "the Brussels Conventions" has the meaning given by section 1(1)";

                "Lugano Contracting State" has the meaning given by section 1(3)";

                "the Lugano Convention" has the meaning given by section 1(1)";

and the entry relating to "the Conventions" is hereby repealed.

The Civil Jurisdiction and Judgments (Authentic Instruments and Court Settlements) Order 2001

(S.I. 2001 No. 3928)

At the Court at Buckingham Palace, the 11th day of December 2001

Present,

The Queen's Most Excellent Majesty in Council

Whereas a Regulation on jurisdiction and the recognition and enforcement of judgments in civil and commercial matters[1] was done on 22nd December 2000:

Now, therefore, Her Majesty, in exercise of the powers conferred upon Her by section 2(2) of the European Communities Act 1972, is pleased, by and with the advice of Her Privy Council, to order, and it is hereby ordered, as follows:

5–190

5–191   **1.**—(1) This Order may be cited as the Civil Jurisdiction and Judgments (Authentic Instruments and Court Settlements) Order 2001 and shall come into force on 1st March 2002.

(2) In this Order—

"the Act" means the Civil Jurisdiction and Judgments Act 1982[2];

"the Regulation" means Council Regulation (EC) No. 44/2001 of 22nd December 2000 on jurisdiction and the recognition and enforcement of judgments in civil and commercial matters;

"Regulation State" in any provision, in the application of that provision in relation to the Regulation, has the same meaning as "Member State" in the Regulation, that is all Member States except Denmark;

"the 2001 Order" means the Civil Jurisdiction and Judgments Order 2001.

(3) In this Order—

(a) references to authentic instruments and court settlements are references to those instruments and settlements referred to in Chapter IV of the Regulation; and

(b) references to judgments and maintenance orders are references to judgments and maintenance orders to which the Regulation applies.

5–192   **2.**—(1) Subject to the modifications specified in paragraphs (2) and (3), paragraphs 1 to 6 of Schedule 1 to the 2001 Order shall apply, as appropriate, to authentic instruments and court settlements which—

(a) do not concern maintenance as if they were judgments,

(b) concern maintenance as if they were maintenance orders.

(2) In the application of paragraph 2(2) of Schedule 1 to the 2001 Order to authentic instruments and court settlements, for the words

---

[1] Council Regulation (EC) No. 44/2001.

[2] As amended by the Civil Jurisdiction and Judgments Act 1991 (c.12) and by S.I. 1989 No. 1346, S.I. 1990 No. 2591, S.I. 1993 No. 603 and S.I. 2000 No. 1824.

"as if the judgment had been originally given" there shall be substituted "as if it was a judgment which had been originally given".

(3) In the application of paragraph 3(3) of Schedule 1 to the 2001 Order to authentic instruments and court settlements, for the words "as if the order had been originally made" there shall be substituted the words "as if it was an order which had been originally made".

(4) Paragraph 8 of Schedule 1 to the 2001 Order shall apply to authentic instruments as if they were judgments and in its application—

    (a) for sub-paragraph (1)(b) there shall be substituted the following—

    "(b) a certificate obtained in accordance with Article 57 and Annex VI shall be evidence, and in Scotland sufficient evidence, that the authentic instrument is enforceable in the Regulation State of origin."

; and

    (b) for sub-paragraph (2) there shall be substituted the following—

"(2) A document purporting to be a copy of an authentic instrument drawn up or registered, and enforceable, in a Regulation State other than the United Kingdom is duly authenticated for the purposes of this paragraph if it purports to be certified to be a true copy of such an instrument by a person duly authorised in that Regulation State to do so.".

(5) Paragraph 8 of Schedule 1 to the 2001 Order shall apply to court settlements as if they were judgments and in its application for "Article 54" there shall be substituted "Article 58".

3. The disapplication of section 18 of the Act (enforcement of United Kingdom judgments in other parts of the United Kingdom) by section 18(7) will extend to authentic instruments and court settlements enforceable in a Regulation State outside the United Kingdom which will fall to be treated for the purposes of their enforcement as judgments of a court of law in the United Kingdom by virtue of registration under the Regulation.   **5–193**

4. Section 48[1] of the Act (matters for which rules of court may provide) will apply to authentic instruments and court settlements as if they were judgments or maintenance orders, as appropriate, to which the Regulation applies.   **5–194**

A.K. Galloway
Clerk of the Privy Council

The Civil Jurisdiction and Judgments Order 2001

(S.I. 2001 No. 3929)

At the Court at Buckingham Palace, the 11th day of December 2001   **5–195**

Present,

---

[1] Section 48 was amended by paragraph 23 of Schedule 2 to the Civil Jurisdiction and Judgments Act 1991 (c.12) and paragraph 17 of Schedule 2 of the Civil Jurisdiction and Judgments Order 2001 (S.I. 2001 No. 3929).

The Queen's Most Excellent Majesty in Council

Whereas a Convention on jurisdiction and the enforcement of judgments in civil and commercial matters was signed on 27th September 1968:

And whereas a Protocol on the interpretation of the Convention by the Court of Justice of the European Communities was signed on 3rd June 1971:

And whereas a Convention on the accession of the Kingdom of Denmark, Ireland and the United Kingdom of Great Britain and Northern Ireland to the Convention signed by Her Majesty's Government on 9th October 1978, was ratified on 7th October 1986 by Her Majesty's Government and entered into force for the United Kingdom on 1st January 1987:

And whereas the Civil Jurisdiction and Judgments Act 1982[1] gave the force of law to these Conventions and to the Protocol in the United Kingdom:

And whereas a Convention on jurisdiction and the enforcement of judgments in civil and commercial matters was opened for signature at Lugano on 16th September 1988 and signed by Her Majesty's Government on 18th September 1989:

And whereas the Civil Jurisdiction and Judgments Act 1982, as amended by the Civil Jurisdiction and Judgments Act 1991, gave the force of law to that Convention in the United Kingdom:

And whereas a Regulation on jurisdiction and the recognition and enforcement of judgments in civil and commercial matters[2] was done on 22nd December 2000:

Now, therefore, Her Majesty, in exercise of the powers conferred on Her by section 2(2) of the European Communities Act 1972, is pleased, by and with the advice of Her Privy Council, to order, and it is hereby ordered, as follows:

Citation and commencement

5–196 **1.** This Order may be cited as the Civil Jurisdiction and Judgments Order 2001 and shall come into force—

   (a) as to articles 1 and 2, paragraphs 1(a), 1(b)(ii) and 17 of Schedule 2 and, so far as it relates to those paragraphs, article 4, on 25th January 2002; and

   (b) as to the remainder of this Order, on 1st March 2002.

Interpretation

5–197 **2.**—(1) In this Order—

  "the Act" means the Civil Jurisdiction and Judgments Act 1982;

  "the Regulation" means Council Regulation (EC) No. 44/2001 of 22nd December 2000 on jurisdiction and the recognition and enforcement of judgments in civil and commercial matters;

  "Regulation State" in any provision, in the application of that provision in relation to the Regulation, has the same meaning as "Member State" in the Regulation, that is all Member States except Denmark.

---

[1] As amended by the Civil Jurisdiction and Judgments Act 1991 (c.12) and by S.I. 1989 No. 1346, S.I. 1990 No. 2591, S.I. 1993 No. 603 and S.I. 2000 No. 1824.
[2] Council Regulation (EC) No. 44/2001.

(2) In Schedule 2 to this Order, a section, Part, Schedule or paragraph referred to by number alone is a reference to the section, Part, Schedule or paragraph so numbered in the Act.

The Regulation

3. Schedule 1 to this Order (which applies certain provisions of the Act with modifications for the purposes of the Regulation) shall have effect.

5–198

Amendments to the Civil Jurisdiction and Judgments Act 1982

4. Schedule 2 to this Order (which makes amendments to the Act) shall have effect.

5–199

Consequential amendments

5. Schedule 3 to this Order (which makes consequential amendments) shall have effect.

5–200

Transitional provisions

6.—(1) Where proceedings are begun before 1st March 2002 in any part of the United Kingdom on the basis of jurisdiction determined in accordance with section 16 of, and Schedule 4 to, the Act, the proceedings may be continued as if the amendments made by paragraphs 3 and 4 of Schedule 2 to this Order had not been made and those amendments shall not apply in respect of any proceedings begun before that date.

5–201

(2) Where proceedings are begun before 1st March 2002 in any court in Scotland on the basis of jurisdiction determined in accordance with section 20 of, and Schedule 8 to, the Act, the proceedings may be continued as if the amendments made by paragraphs 6 and 7 of Schedule 2 to this Order had not been made and those amendments shall not apply in respect of any proceedings begun before that date.

A.K. Galloway
Clerk of the Privy Council

ARTICLE 3   SCHEDULE 1

THE REGULATION

Interpretation

1.—(1)In this Schedule—

5–202

"court", without more, includes a tribunal;

"judgment" has the meaning given by Article 32 of the Regulation;

"magistrates' court", in relation to Northern Ireland, means a court of summary jurisdiction;

"maintenance order" means a maintenance judgment within the meaning of the Regulation;

"part of the United Kingdom" means England and Wales, Scotland or Northern Ireland;

"payer", in relation to a maintenance order, means the person liable to make the payments for which the order provides;

"prescribed" means prescribed by rules of court.

(2) In this Schedule, any reference to a numbered Article or Annex is a reference to the Article or Annex so numbered in the Regulation, and any reference to a subdivision of a numbered Article shall be construed accordingly.

(3) References in paragraphs 2 to 8 to a judgment registered under the Regulation include, to the extent of its registration, references to a judgment so registered to a limited extent only.

(4) Anything authorised or required by the Regulation or paragraphs 2 to 8 to be done by, to or before a particular magistrates' court may be done by, to or before any magistrates' court acting in the same local justice area (or, in Northern Ireland, acting for the same petty sessions district) as that court.

Enforcement of judgments other than maintenance orders (section 4)

5–203 2.—(1)Where a judgment is registered under the Regulation, the reasonable costs or expenses of and incidental to its registration shall be recoverable as if they were sums recoverable under the judgment.

(2) A judgment registered under the Regulation shall, for the purposes of its enforcement, be of the same force and effect, the registering court shall have in relation to its enforcement the same powers, and proceedings for or with respect to its enforcement may be taken, as if the judgment had been originally given by the registering court and had (where relevant) been entered.

(3) Sub-paragraph (2) is subject to Article 47 (restriction on enforcement where appeal pending or time for appeal unexpired), to paragraph 5 and to any provision made by rules of court as to the manner in which and conditions subject to which a judgment registered under the Regulation may be enforced.

Recognition and enforcement of maintenance orders (section 5)

5–204 3.—(1)The Secretary of State's function (under Article 39 and Annex II) of transmitting an application for the recognition or enforcement in the United Kingdom of a maintenance order (made under Article 38) to a magistrates' court shall be discharged—

> (a) as respects England and Wales and Northern Ireland, by the Lord Chancellor;
>
> (b) as respects Scotland, by the Scottish Ministers.

(2) Such an application shall be determined in the first instance by the prescribed officer of the court having jurisdiction in the matter.

(3) A maintenance order registered under the Regulation shall, for the purposes of its enforcement, be of the same force and effect, the registering court shall have in relation to its enforcement the same powers, and proceedings for or with respect to its enforcement may be taken, as if the order had been originally made by the registering court.

(4) Sub-paragraph (3) is subject to Article 47 (restriction on enforcement where appeal pending or time for appeal unexpired), to paragraph 5 and to any provision made by rules of court as to the manner in which and conditions subject to which an order registered under the Regulation may be enforced.

(5) A maintenance order which by virtue of the Regulation is enforceable by a magistrates' court in England and Wales shall, subject to the modifications of sections 76 and 93 of the Magistrates' Courts Act 1980[1] specified in sections 5(5B) and 5(5C) of the Act[2], be enforceable in the same manner as a magistrates' court maintenance order made by that court.

In this sub-paragraph "magistrates' court maintenance order" has the same meaning as in section 150(1) of the Magistrates' Courts Act 1980[3].

(6) A maintenance order which by virtue of the Regulation is enforceable by a magistrates' court in Northern Ireland shall, subject to the modifications of Article 98

---

[1] Section 76 was amended by the Criminal Justice Act 1982 (c. 48), section 78, Schedule 16 and the Maintenance Enforcement Act 1991 (c.17), section 7; section 93 was amended by the Family Law Reform Act 1987 (c.42), section 33(1), Schedule 2, paragraph 84 and the Maintenance Enforcement Act 1991 (c.17), section 11(1), Schedule 2, paragraph 7.

[2] Sections 5(5B) and 5(5C) of that Act were inserted by the Maintenance Enforcement Act 1991 (c.17), section 10, Schedule 1, paragraph 21. Section 5(5B) was also amended by the Access to Justice Act 1999 (c.22), section 90(1), Schedule 13, paragraph 122.

[3] This definition was inserted by the Family Law Reform Act 1987 (c.42), section 33(1), Schedule 2, paragraph 88.

of the Magistrates' Courts (Northern Ireland) Order 1981 specified in section 5(6A) of the Act[1], be enforceable as an order made by that court to which that Article applies.

(7) The payer under a maintenance order registered under the Regulation in a magistrates' court in England and Wales or Northern Ireland shall give notice of any changes of address to the proper officer of that court.

A person who without reasonable excuse fails to comply with this sub-paragraph shall be guilty of an offence and liable on summary conviction to a fine not exceeding level 2 on the standard scale.

(8) In sub-paragraph (7) "proper officer" means—

    (a) in relation to a magistrates' court in England and Wales, the designated officer; and

    (b) in relation to a magistrates' court in Northern Ireland, the clerk of the court.

Appeals under Article 44 and Annex IV (section 6)

4.—(1)The single further appeal on a point of law referred to under Article 44 and Annex IV in relation to the recognition or enforcement of a judgment other than a maintenance order lies— **5–205**

    (a) in England and Wales or Northern Ireland, to the Court of Appeal or to the House of Lords in accordance with Part II of the Administration of Justice Act 1969 (appeals direct from the High Court to the House of Lords);

    (b) in Scotland, to the Inner House of the Court of Session.

(2) Paragraph (a) of sub-paragraph (1) has effect notwithstanding section 15(2) of the Administration of Justice Act 1969[2] (exclusion of direct appeal to the House of Lords in cases where no appeal to that House lies from a decision of the Court of Appeal).

(3) The single further appeal on a point of law referred to in Article 44 and Annex IV in relation to the recognition or enforcement of a maintenance order lies—

    (a) in England and Wales, to the High Court by way of case stated in accordance with section 111 of the Magistrates' Courts Act 1980;

    (b) in Scotland, to the Inner House of the Court of Session;

    (c) in Northern Ireland, to the Court of Appeal.

Interest on registered judgments (section 7)

5.—(1)Subject to sub-paragraph (3), where in connection with an application for **5–206** registration of a judgment under the Regulation the applicant shows—

    (a) that the judgment provides for the payment of a sum of money; and

    (b) that in accordance with the law of the Regulation State in which the judgment was given interest on that sum is recoverable under the judgment from a particular date or time,

the rate of interest and the date or time from which it is so recoverable shall be registered with the judgment and, subject to rules of court, the debt resulting, apart from paragraph 2(1), from the registration of the judgment shall carry interest in accordance with the registered particulars.

(2) Costs or expenses recoverable by virtue of paragraph 2(1) shall carry interest as if they were the subject of an order for the payment of costs or expenses made by the registering court on the date of registration.

(3) Interest on arrears of sums payable under a maintenance order registered under the Regulation in a magistrates' court in England and Wales or Northern Ireland shall not be recoverable in that court, but without prejudice to the operation in relation to any such order of section 2A of the Maintenance Orders Act 1958[3] or section 11A of the Maintenance and Affiliation Orders Act (Northern Ireland) 1966[4]

---

[1] Section 5(6A) was inserted by the Family Law (Northern Ireland) Order 1993 (S.I. 1993 No. 1576 (N.I.6)), article 11, Schedule 1, paragraph 16(b).

[2] This section was amended by the Administration of Justice Act 1977, section 32, Schedule 5, Part IV.

[3] Section 2A was inserted by the Civil Jurisdiction and Judgments Act 1982 (c.27), section 37, Schedule 1, Part II.

[4] 1966 c.53, section 11A was inserted by the Civil Jurisdiction and Judgments Act 1982 (c.27), paragraph 7 of Schedule 11.

(which enable interest to be recovered if the order is re-registered for enforcement in the High Court).

(4) Except as mentioned in sub-paragraph (3), debts under judgments registered under the Regulation shall carry interest only as provided by this paragraph.

Currency of payment under registered maintenance orders (section 8)

5–207   6.—(1)Sums payable in the United Kingdom under a maintenance order by virtue of its registration under the Regulation, including any arrears so payable, shall be paid in the currency of the United Kingdom.

(2) Where the order is expressed in any other currency, the amounts shall be converted on the basis of the exchange rate prevailing on the date of registration of the order.

(3) For the purposes of this paragraph, a written certificate purporting to be signed by an officer of any bank in the United Kingdom and stating the exchange rate prevailing on a specified date shall be evidence, and in Scotland sufficient evidence, of the facts stated.

Allocation within United Kingdom of jurisdiction with respect to trusts and consumer contracts (section 10)

5–208   7.—(1)The provisions of this paragraph have effect for the purpose of allocating within the United Kingdom jurisdiction in certain proceedings in respect of which the Regulation confers jurisdiction on the courts of the United Kingdom generally and to which section 16 of the Act does not apply.

(2) Any proceedings which by virtue of Article 5(6) (trusts) are brought in the United Kingdom shall be brought in the courts of the part of the United Kingdom in which the trust is domiciled.

(3) Any proceedings which by virtue of the Article 16(1) (consumer contracts) are brought in the United Kingdom by a consumer on the ground that he is himself domiciled there shall be brought in the courts of the part of the United Kingdom in which he is domiciled.

Proof and admissibility of certain judgments and related documents (section 11)

5–209   8.—(1)For the purposes of the Regulation—

    (a) a document, duly authenticated, which purports to be a copy of a judgment given by a court of a Regulation State other than the United Kingdom shall without further proof be deemed to be a true copy, unless the contrary is shown; and

    (b) a certificate obtained in accordance with Article 54 and Annex V shall be evidence, and in Scotland sufficient evidence, that the judgment is enforceable in the Regulation State of origin.

(2) A document purporting to be a copy of a judgment given by any such court as is mentioned in sub-paragraph (1)(a) is duly authenticated for the purposes of this paragraph if it purports—

    (a) to bear the seal of that court; or

    (b) to be certified by any person in his capacity as a judge or officer of that court to be a true copy of a judgment given by that court.

(3) Nothing in this paragraph shall prejudice the admission in evidence of any document which is admissible apart from this paragraph.

Domicile of individuals (section 41)

5–210   9.—(1)Subject to Article 59 (which contains provisions for determining whether a party is domiciled in a Regulation State), the following provisions of this paragraph determine, for the purposes of the Regulation, whether an individual is domiciled in the United Kingdom or in a particular part of, or place in, the United Kingdom or in a state other than a Regulation State.

(2) An individual is domiciled in the United Kingdom if and only if—

    (a) he is resident in the United Kingdom; and

    (b) the nature and circumstances of his residence indicate that he has a substantial connection with the United Kingdom.

(3) Subject to sub-paragraph (5), an individual is domiciled in a particular part of the United Kingdom if and only if—

    (a) he is resident in that part; and

    (b) the nature and circumstances of his residence indicate that he has a substantial connection with that part.

(4) An individual is domiciled in a particular place in the United Kingdom if and only if he—

    (a) is domiciled in the part of the United Kingdom in which that place is situated; and

    (b) is resident in that place.

(5) An individual who is domiciled in the United Kingdom but in whose case the requirements of sub-paragraph (3)(b) are not satisfied in relation to any particular part of the United Kingdom shall be treated as domiciled in the part of the United Kingdom in which he is resident.

(6) In the case of an individual who—

    (a) is resident in the United Kingdom, or in a particular part of the United Kingdom; and

    (b) has been so resident for the last three months or more,

the requirements of sub-paragraph (2)(b) or, as the case may be, sub-paragraph (3)(b) shall be presumed to be fulfilled unless the contrary is proved.

(7) An individual is domiciled in a state other than a Regulation State if and only if—

    (a) he is resident in that state; and

    (b) the nature and circumstances of his residence indicate that he has a substantial connection with that state.

Seat of company, or other legal person or association for purposes of Article 22(2) (section 43)

10.—(1)The following provisions of this paragraph determine where a company, legal person or association has its seat for the purposes of Article 22(2) (which confers exclusive jurisdiction over proceedings relating to the formation or dissolution of such bodies, or to the decisions of their organs).

5–211

(2) A company, legal person or association has its seat in the United Kingdom if and only if—

    (a) it was incorporated or formed under the law of a part of the United Kingdom; or

    (b) its central management and control is exercised in the United Kingdom.

(3) Subject to sub-paragraph (4), a company, legal person or association has its seat in a Regulation State other than the United Kingdom if and only if—

    (a) it was incorporated or formed under the law of that state; or

    (b) its central management and control is exercised in that state.

(4) A company, legal person or association shall not be regarded as having its seat in a Regulation State other than the United Kingdom if–

    (a) it has its seat in the United Kingdom by virtue of sub-paragraph (2)(a); or

    (b) it is shown that the courts of that other state would not regard it for the purposes of Article 22(2) as having its seat there.

Persons deemed to be domiciled in the United Kingdom for certain purposes (section 44)

11.—(1)This paragraph applies to

5–212

    (a) proceedings within Section 3 of Chapter II of the Regulation (insurance contracts),

    (b) proceedings within Section 4 of Chapter II of the Regulation (consumer contracts), and

    (c) proceedings within Section 5 of Chapter II of the Regulation (employment contracts).

(2) A person who, for the purposes of proceedings to which this paragraph applies arising out of the operations of a branch, agency or other establishment in the United Kingdom, is deemed for the purposes of the Regulation to be domiciled in the United Kingdom by virtue of—

    (a) Article 9(2) (insurers); or

    (b) Article 15(2) (suppliers of goods, services or credit to consumers), or

    (c) Article 18(2) (employers),

shall, for the purposes of those proceedings, be treated as so domiciled and as domiciled in the part of the United Kingdom in which the branch, agency or establishment in question is situated.

Domicile of trusts (section 45)

5–213   12.—(1)The following provisions of this paragraph determine for the purposes of the Regulation where a trust is domiciled.

(2) A trust is domiciled in the United Kingdom if and only if it is by virtue of sub-paragraph (3) domiciled in a part of the United Kingdom.

(3) A trust is domiciled in a part of the United Kingdom if and only if the system of law of that part is the system of law with which the trust has its closest and most real connection.

COUNCIL REGULATION (EC) NO 44/2001

5–214   THE COUNCIL OF THE EUROPEAN UNION,

Having regard to the Treaty establishing the European Community, and in particular Article 61(c) and Article 67(1) thereof,

Having regard to the proposal from the Commission (1),

Having regard to the opinion of the European Parliament (2),

Having regard to the opinion of the Economic and Social Committee (3),

(1) The Community has set itself the objective of maintaining and developing an area of freedom, security and justice, in which the free movement of persons is ensured. In order to establish progressively such an area, the Community should adopt, amongst other things, the measures relating to judicial cooperation in civil matters which are necessary for the sound operation of the internal market.

(2) Certain differences between national rules governing jurisdiction and recognition of judgments hamper the sound operation of the internal market. Provisions to unify the rules of conflict of jurisdiction in civil and commercial matters and to simplify the formalities with a view to rapid and simple recognition and enforcement of judgments from Member States bound by this Regulation are essential.

(3) This area is within the field of judicial cooperation in civil matters within the meaning of Article 65 of the Treaty.

(4) In accordance with the principles of subsidiarity and proportionality as set out in Article 5 of the Treaty, the objectives of this Regulation cannot be sufficiently achieved by the Member States and can therefore be better achieved by the Community. This Regulation confines itself to the minimum required in order to achieve those objectives and does not go beyond what is necessary for that purpose.

(5) On 27 September 1968 the Member States, acting under Article 293, fourth indent, of the Treaty, concluded the Brussels Convention on Jurisdiction and the Enforcement of Judgments in Civil and Commercial Matters, as amended by Conventions on the Accession of the New Member States to that Convention (hereinafter referred to as the "Brussels Convention"). On 16 September 1988 Member States and EFTA States concluded the Lugano Convention on Jurisdiction and the Enforcement of Judgments in Civil and Commercial Matters, which is a parallel Convention to the 1968 Brussels Convention. Work has been undertaken for the revision of those Conventions, and the Council has approved the content of the revised texts. Continuity in the results achieved in that revision should be ensured.

(6) In order to attain the objective of free movement of judgments in civil and commercial matters, it is necessary and appropriate that

the rules governing jurisdiction and the recognition and enforcement of judgments be governed by a Community legal instrument which is binding and directly applicable.

(7) The scope of this Regulation must cover all the main civil and commercial matters apart from certain well-defined matters.

(8) There must be a link between proceedings to which this Regulation applies and the territory of the Member States bound by this Regulation. Accordingly common rules on jurisdiction should, in principle, apply when the defendant is domiciled in one of those Member States.

(9) A defendant not domiciled in a Member State is in general subject to national rules of jurisdiction applicable in the territory of the Member State of the court seised, and a defendant domiciled in a Member State not bound by this Regulation must remain subject to the Brussels Convention.

(10) For the purposes of the free movement of judgments, judgments given in a Member State bound by this Regulation should be recognised and enforced in another Member State bound by this Regulation, even if the judgment debtor is domiciled in a third State.

(11) The rules of jurisdiction must be highly predictable and founded on the principle that jurisdiction is generally based on the defendant's domicile and jurisdiction must always be available on this ground save in a few well-defined situations in which the subject-matter of the litigation or the autonomy of the parties warrants a different linking factor. The domicile of a legal person must be defined autonomously so as to make the common rules more transparent and avoid conflicts of jurisdiction.

(12) In addition to the defendant's domicile, there should be alternative grounds of jurisdiction based on a close link between the court and the action or in order to facilitate the sound administration of justice.

(13) In relation to insurance, consumer contracts and employment, the weaker party should be protected by rules of jurisdiction more favourable to his interests than the general rules provide for.

(14) The autonomy of the parties to a contract, other than an insurance, consumer or employment contract, where only limited autonomy to determine the courts having jurisdiction is allowed, must be respected subject to the exclusive grounds of jurisdiction laid down in this Regulation.

(15) In the interests of the harmonious administration of justice it is necessary to minimise the possibility of concurrent proceedings and to ensure that irreconcilable judgments will not be given in two Member States. There must be a clear and effective mechanism for resolving cases of lis pendens and related actions and for obviating problems flowing from national differences as to the determination of the time when a case is regarded as pending. For the purposes of this Regulation that time should be defined autonomously.

(16) Mutual trust in the administration of justice in the Community justifies judgments given in a Member State being recognised automatically without the need for any procedure except in cases of dispute.

(17) By virtue of the same principle of mutual trust, the procedure for making enforceable in one Member State a judgment given in another must be efficient and rapid. To that end, the declaration that a judgment is enforceable should be issued virtually automatically after purely formal checks of the documents supplied, without there being any possibility for the court to raise of its own motion any of the grounds for non-enforcement provided for by this Regulation.

(18) However, respect for the rights of the defence means that the defendant should be able to appeal in an adversarial procedure, against the declaration of enforceability, if he considers one of the grounds for non-enforcement to be present. Redress procedures should also be available to the claimant where his application for a declaration of enforceability has been rejected.

(19) Continuity between the Brussels Convention and this Regulation should be ensured, and transitional provisions should be laid down to that end. The same need for continuity applies as regards the interpretation of the Brussels Convention by the Court of Justice of the European Communities and the 1971 Protocol(5) should remain applicable also to cases already pending when this Regulation enters into force.

(20) The United Kingdom and Ireland, in accordance with Article 3 of the Protocol on the position of the United Kingdom and Ireland annexed to the Treaty on European Union and to the Treaty establishing the European Community, have given notice of their wish to take part in the adoption and application of this Regulation.

(21) Denmark, in accordance with Articles 1 and 2 of the Protocol on the position of Denmark annexed to the Treaty on European Union and to the Treaty establishing the European Community, is not participating in the adoption of this Regulation, and is therefore not bound by it nor subject to its application.

(22) Since the Brussels Convention remains in force in relations between Denmark and the Member States that are bound by this Regulation, both the Convention and the 1971 Protocol continue to apply between Denmark and the Member States bound by this Regulation.

(23) The Brussels Convention also continues to apply to the territories of the Member States which fall within the territorial scope of that Convention and which are excluded from this Regulation pursuant to Article 299 of the Treaty.

(24) Likewise for the sake of consistency, this Regulation should not affect rules governing jurisdiction and the recognition of judgments contained in specific Community instruments.

(25) Respect for international commitments entered into by the Member States means that this Regulation should not affect conventions relating to specific matters to which the Member States are parties.

(26) The necessary flexibility should be provided for in the basic rules of this Regulation in order to take account of the specific procedural rules of certain Member States. Certain provisions of the Protocol annexed to the Brussels Convention should accordingly be incorporated in this Regulation.

(27) In order to allow a harmonious transition in certain areas which were the subject of special provisions in the Protocol annexed to the Brussels Convention, this Regulation lays down, for a transitional period, provisions taking into consideration the specific situation in certain Member States.

(28) No later than five years after entry into force of this Regulation the Commission will present a report on its application and, if need be, submit proposals for adaptations.

(29) The Commission will have to adjust Annexes I to IV on the rules of national jurisdiction, the courts or competent authorities and redress procedures available on the basis of the amendments forwarded by the Member State concerned; amendments made to Annexes V and VI should be adopted in accordance with Council Decision 1999/468/EC of 28 June 1999 laying down the procedures for the exercise of implementing powers conferred on the Commission (6),

HAS ADOPTED THIS REGULATION:

CHAPTER I — SCOPE

Article 1

1. This Regulation shall apply in civil and commercial matters whatever the nature **5–215** of the court or tribunal. It shall not extend, in particular, to revenue, customs or administrative matters.

2. The Regulation shall not apply to:
   (a) the status or legal capacity of natural persons, rights in property arising out of a matrimonial relationship, wills and succession;
   (b) bankruptcy, proceedings relating to the winding-up of insolvent companies or other legal persons, judicial arrangements, compositions and analogous proceedings;
   (c) social security;
   (d) arbitration.

3. In this Regulation, the term "Member State" shall mean Member States with the exception of Denmark.

CHAPTER II — JURISDICTION

SECTION 1 — GENERAL PROVISIONS

Article 2

1. Subject to this Regulation, persons domiciled in a Member State shall, whatever **5–216** their nationality, be sued in the courts of that Member State.

2. Persons who are not nationals of the Member State in which they are domiciled shall be governed by the rules of jurisdiction applicable to nationals of that State.

Article 3

1. Persons domiciled in a Member State may be sued in the courts of another **5–217** Member State only by virtue of the rules set out in Sections 2 to 7 of this Chapter.

2. In particular the rules of national jurisdiction set out in Annex I shall not be applicable as against them.

Article 4

5–218   1. If the defendant is not domiciled in a Member State, the jurisdiction of the courts of each Member State shall, subject to Articles 22 and 23, be determined by the law of that Member State.

2. As against such a defendant, any person domiciled in a Member State may, whatever his nationality, avail himself in that State of the rules of jurisdiction there in force, and in particular those specified in Annex I, in the same way as the nationals of that State.

SECTION 2 — SPECIAL JURISDICTION

Article 5

5–219   A person domiciled in a Member State may, in another Member State, be sued:

    (a) in matters relating to a contract, in the courts for the place of performance of the obligation in question;

    (b) for the purpose of this provision and unless otherwise agreed, the place of performance of the obligation in question shall be:

        – in the case of the sale of goods, the place in a Member State where, under the contract, the goods were delivered or should have been delivered,

        – in the case of the provision of services, the place in a Member State where, under the contract, the services were provided or should have been provided,

    (c) if subparagraph (b) does not apply then subparagraph (a) applies;

2. in matters relating to maintenance, in the courts for the place where the maintenance creditor is domiciled or habitually resident or, if the matter is ancillary to proceedings concerning the status of a person, in the court which, according to its own law, has jurisdiction to entertain those proceedings, unless that jurisdiction is based solely on the nationality of one of the parties;

3. in matters relating to tort, delict or quasi-delict, in the courts for the place where the harmful event occurred or may occur;

4. as regards a civil claim for damages or restitution which is based on an act giving rise to criminal proceedings, in the court seised of those proceedings, to the extent that that court has jurisdiction under its own law to entertain civil proceedings;

5. as regards a dispute arising out of the operations of a branch, agency or other establishment, in the courts for the place in which the branch, agency or other establishment is situated;

6. as settlor, trustee or beneficiary of a trust created by the operation of a statute, or by a written instrument, or created orally and evidenced in writing, in the courts of the Member State in which the trust is domiciled;

7. as regards a dispute concerning the payment of remuneration claimed in respect of the salvage of a cargo or freight, in the court under the authority of which the cargo or freight in question:

    (a) has been arrested to secure such payment, or

    (b) could have been so arrested, but bail or other security has been given; provided that this provision shall apply only if it is claimed that the defendant has an interest in the cargo or freight or had such an interest at the time of salvage.

Article 6

5–220   A person domiciled in a Member State may also be sued:

1. where he is one of a number of defendants, in the courts for the place where any one of them is domiciled, provided the claims are so closely connected that it is expedient to hear and determine them together to avoid the risk of irreconcilable judgments resulting from separate proceedings;

2. as a third party in an action on a warranty or guarantee or in any other third party proceedings, in the court seised of the original proceedings, unless these were instituted solely with the object of removing him from the jurisdiction of the court which would be competent in his case;

3. on a counter-claim arising from the same contract or facts on which the original claim was based, in the court in which the original claim is pending;

4. in matters relating to a contract, if the action may be combined with an action against the same defendant in matters relating to rights in rem in immovable property, in the court of the Member State in which the property is situated.

Article 7

Where by virtue of this Regulation a court of a Member State has jurisdiction in actions relating to liability from the use or operation of a ship, that court, or any other court substituted for this purpose by the internal law of that Member State, shall also have jurisdiction over claims for limitation of such liability.   **5–221**

SECTION 3 — JURISDICTION IN MATTERS RELATING TO INSURANCE

Article 8

In matters relating to insurance, jurisdiction shall be determined by this Section,   **5–222**
without prejudice to Article 4 and point 5 of Article 5.

Article 9

1. An insurer domiciled in a Member State may be sued: **5–223**
   (a) in the courts of the Member State where he is domiciled, or
   (b) in another Member State, in the case of actions brought by the policyholder, the insured or a beneficiary, in the courts for the place where the plaintiff is domiciled,
   (c) if he is a co-insurer, in the courts of a Member State in which proceedings are brought against the leading insurer.

Article 10

In respect of liability insurance or insurance of immovable property, the insurer   **5–224**
may in addition be sued in the courts for the place where the harmful event occurred. The same applies if movable and immovable property are covered by the same insurance policy and both are adversely affected by the same contingency.

Article 11

1. In respect of liability insurance, the insurer may also, if the law of the court   **5–225**
permits it, be joined in proceedings which the injured party has brought against the insured.

2. Articles 8, 9 and 10 shall apply to actions brought by the injured party directly against the insurer, where such direct actions are permitted.

3. If the law governing such direct actions provides that the policyholder or the insured may be joined as a party to the action, the same court shall have jurisdiction over them.

Article 12

5–226   1. Without prejudice to Article 11(3), an insurer may bring proceedings only in the courts of the Member State in which the defendant is domiciled, irrespective of whether he is the policyholder, the insured or a beneficiary.

2. The provisions of this Section shall not affect the right to bring a counter-claim in the court in which, in accordance with this Section, the original claim is pending.

Article 13

5–227   The provisions of this Section may be departed from only by an agreement:

1. which is entered into after the dispute has arisen, or

2. which allows the policyholder, the insured or a beneficiary to bring proceedings in courts other than those indicated in this Section, or

3. which is concluded between a policyholder and an insurer, both of whom are at the time of conclusion of the contract domiciled or habitually resident in the same Member State, and which has the effect of conferring jurisdiction on the courts of that State even if the harmful event were to occur abroad, provided that such an agreement is not contrary to the law of that State, or

4. which is concluded with a policyholder who is not domiciled in a Member State, except in so far as the insurance is compulsory or relates to immovable property in a Member State, or

5. which relates to a contract of insurance in so far as it covers one or more of the risks set out in Article 14.

SECTION 4 — JURISDICTION OVER CONSUMER CONTRACTS

Article 14

5–228   The following are the risks referred to in Article 13(5):

1. any loss of or damage to:

    (a) seagoing ships, installations situated offshore or on the high seas, or aircraft, arising from perils which relate to their use for commercial purposes;

    (b) goods in transit other than passengers' baggage where the transit consists of or includes carriage by such ships or aircraft;

2. any liability, other than for bodily injury to passengers or loss of or damage to their baggage:

    (a) arising out of the use or operation of ships, installations or aircraft as referred to in point 1(a) in so far as, in respect of the latter, the law of the Member State in which such aircraft are registered does not prohibit agreements on jurisdiction regarding insurance of such risks;

    (b) for loss or damage caused by goods in transit as described in point 1(b);

3. any financial loss connected with the use or operation of ships, installations or aircraft as referred to in point 1(a), in particular loss of freight or charter-hire;

4. which is concluded with a policyholder who is not domiciled in a Member State, except in so far as the insurance is compulsory or relates to immovable property in a Member State, or

5. notwithstanding points 1 to 4, all "large risks" as defined in Council Directive 73/239/EEC(7), as amended by Council Directives 88/357/EEC(8) and 90/618/EEC(9), as they may be amended.

Article 15

5–229   1. In matters relating to a contract concluded by a person, the consumer, for a purpose which can be regarded as being outside his trade or profession, jurisdiction shall be determined by this Section, without prejudice to Article 4 and point 5 of Article 5, if:

    (a) it is a contract for the sale of goods on instalment credit terms; or

    (b) it is a contract for a loan repayable by instalments, or for any other form of credit, made to finance the sale of goods; or

    (c) in all other cases, the contract has been concluded with a person who pursues commercial or professional activities in the Member State of the consumer's domicile or, by any means, directs such activities to that Member State or to several States including that Member State, and the contract falls within the scope of such activities.

2. Where a consumer enters into a contract with a party who is not domiciled in the Member State but has a branch, agency or other establishment in one of the Member States, that party shall, in disputes arising out of the operations of the branch, agency or establishment, be deemed to be domiciled in that State.

3. This Section shall not apply to a contract of transport other than a contract which, for an inclusive price, provides for a combination of travel and accommodation.

Article 16

1. A consumer may bring proceedings against the other party to a contract either in **5–230** the courts of the Member State in which that party is domiciled or in the courts for the place where the consumer is domiciled.

2. Proceedings may be brought against a consumer by the other party to the contract only in the courts of the Member State in which the consumer is domiciled.

3. This Article shall not affect the right to bring a counter-claim in the court in which, in accordance with this Section, the original claim is pending.

Article 17

The provisions of this Section may be departed from only by an agreement: **5–231**

1. which is entered into after the dispute has arisen; or

2. which allows the consumer to bring proceedings in courts other than those indicated in this Section; or

3. which is entered into by the consumer and the other party to the contract, both of whom are at the time of conclusion of the contract domiciled or habitually resident in the same Member State, and which confers jurisdiction on the courts of that Member State, provided that such an agreement is not contrary to the law of that Member State.

Section 5 — Jurisdiction over individual contracts of employment

Article 18

1. In matters relating to individual contracts of employment, jurisdiction shall be **5–232** determined by this Section, without prejudice to Article 4 and point 5 of Article 5.

2. Where an employee enters into an individual contract of employment with an employer who is not domiciled in a Member State but has a branch, agency or other establishment in one of the Member States, the employer shall, in disputes arising out of the operations of the branch, agency or establishment, be deemed to be domiciled in that Member State.

Article 19

An employer domiciled in a Member State may be sued: **5–233**

1. in the courts of the Member State where he is domiciled; or

2. in another Member State:

    (a) in the courts for the place where the employee habitually carries out his work or in the courts for the last place where he did so, or

    (b) if the employee does not or did not habitually carry out his work in any one country, in the courts for the place where the business which engaged the employee is or was situated.

Article 20

5–234   1. An employer may bring proceedings only in the courts of the Member State in which the employee is domiciled.

2. The provisions of this Section shall not affect the right to bring a counter-claim in the court in which, in accordance with this Section, the original claim is pending.

Article 21

5–235   The provisions of this Section may be departed from only be an agreement on jurisdiction:

1. which is entered into after the dispute has arisen; or

2. which allows the employee to bring proceedings in courts other than those indicated in this Section.

SECTION 6 — EXCLUSIVE JURISDICTION

Article 22

5–236   The following courts shall have exclusive jurisdiction, regardless of domicile:

1. in proceedings which have as their object rights in rem in immovable property or tenancies of immovable property, the courts of the Member State in which the property is situated. However, in proceedings which have as their object tenancies of immovable property concluded for temporary private use for a maximum period of six consecutive months, the courts of the Member State in which the defendant is domiciled shall also have jurisdiction, provided that the tenant is a natural person and that the landlord and the tenant are domiciled in the same Member State;

2. in proceedings which have as their object the validity of the constitution, the nullity or the dissolution of companies or other legal persons or associations of natural or legal persons, or of the validity of the decisions of their organs, the courts of the Member State in which the company, legal person or association has its seat. In order to determine that seat, the court shall apply its rules of private international law;

3. in proceedings which have as their object the validity of entries in public registers, the courts of the Member State in which the register is kept;

4. in proceedings concerned with the registration or validity of patents, trade marks, designs, or other similar rights required to be deposited or registered, the courts of the Member State in which the deposit or registration has been applied for, has taken place or is under the terms of a Community instrument or an international convention deemed to have taken place. Without prejudice to the jurisdiction of the European Patent Office under the Convention on the Grant of European Patents, signed at Munich on 5 October 1973, the courts of each Member State shall have exclusive jurisdiction, regardless of domicile, in proceedings concerned with the registration or validity of any European patent granted for that State;

5. in proceedings concerned with the enforcement of judgments, the courts of the Member State in which the judgment has been or is to be enforced.

SECTION 7 — PROROGATION OF JURISDICTION

Article 23

5–237   1. If the parties, one or more of whom is domiciled in a Member State, have agreed that a court or the courts of a Member State are to have jurisdiction to settle any disputes which have arisen or which may arise in connection with a particular legal relationship, that court or those courts shall have jurisdiction. Such jurisdiction shall be exclusive unless the parties have agreed otherwise. Such an agreement conferring jurisdiction shall be either:

   (a) in writing or evidenced in writing; or

   (b) in a form which accords with practices which the parties have established between themselves; or

   (c) in international trade or commerce, in a form which accords with a usage of which the parties are or ought to have been aware and which in such trade or commerce is widely known to, and regularly observed by, parties to contracts of the type involved in the particular trade or commerce concerned.

2. Any communication by electronic means which provides a durable record of the agreement shall be equivalent to "writing".

3. Where such an agreement is concluded by parties, none of whom is domiciled in a Member State, the courts of other Member States shall have no jurisdiction over their disputes unless the court or courts chosen have declined jurisdiction.

4. The court or courts of a Member State on which a trust instrument has conferred jurisdiction shall have exclusive jurisdiction in any proceedings brought against a settlor, trustee or beneficiary, if relations between these persons or their rights or obligations under the trust are involved.

5. Agreements or provisions of a trust instrument conferring jurisdiction shall have no legal force if they are contrary to Articles 13, 17 or 21, or if the courts whose jurisdiction they purport to exclude have exclusive jurisdiction by virtue of Article 22.

Article 24

Apart from jurisdiction derived from other provisions of this Regulation, a court of **5–238** a Member State before which a defendant enters an appearance shall have jurisdiction. This rule shall not apply where appearance was entered to contest the jurisdiction, or where another court has exclusive jurisdiction by virtue of Article 22.

SECTION 8 — EXAMINATION AS TO JURISDICTION AND ADMISSIBILITY

Article 25

Where a court of a Member State is seised of a claim which is principally concerned **5–239** with a matter over which the courts of another Member State have exclusive jurisdiction by virtue of Article 22, it shall declare of its own motion that it has no jurisdiction.

Article 26

1. Where a defendant domiciled in one Member State is sued in a court of another **5–240** Member State and does not enter an appearance, the court shall declare of its own motion that it has no jurisdiction unless its jurisdiction is derived from the provisions of this Regulation.

2. The court shall stay the proceedings so long as it is not shown that the defendant has been able to receive the document instituting the proceedings or an equivalent document in sufficient time to enable him to arrange for his defence, or that all necessary steps have been taken to this end.

3. Article 19 of Council Regulation (EC) No 1348/2000 of 29 May 2000 on the service in the Member States of judicial and extrajudicial documents in civil or commercial matters(10) shall apply instead of the provisions of paragraph 2 if the document instituting the proceedings or an equivalent document had to be transmitted from one Member State to another pursuant to this Regulation.

4. Where the provisions of Regulation (EC) No 1348/2000 are not applicable,

Article 15 of the Hague Convention of 15 November 1965 on the Service Abroad of Judicial and Extrajudicial Documents in Civil or Commercial Matters shall apply if the document instituting the proceedings or an equivalent document had to be transmitted pursuant to that Convention. Without prejudice to the jurisdiction of the European Patent Office under the Convention on the Grant of European Patents, signed at Munich on 5 October 1973, the courts of each Member State shall have exclusive jurisdiction, regardless of domicile, in proceedings concerned with the registration or validity of any European patent granted for that State;

SECTION 9 — LIS PENDENS - RELATED ACTIONS

Article 27

5–241   1. Where proceedings involving the same cause of action and between the same parties are brought in the courts of different Member States, any court other than the court first seised shall of its own motion stay its proceedings until such time as the jurisdiction of the court first seised is established.

2. Where the jurisdiction of the court first seised is established, any court other than the court first seised shall decline jurisdiction in favour of that court.

Article 28

5–242   1. Where related actions are pending in the courts of different Member States, any court other than the court first seised may stay its proceedings.

2. Where these actions are pending at first instance, any court other than the court first seised may also, on the application of one of the parties, decline jurisdiction if the court first seised has jurisdiction over the actions in question and its law permits the consolidation thereof.

3. For the purposes of this Article, actions are deemed to be related where they are so closely connected that it is expedient to hear and determine them together to avoid the risk of irreconcilable judgments resulting from separate proceedings.

Article 29

5–243   Where actions come within the exclusive jurisdiction of several courts, any court other than the court first seised shall decline jurisdiction in favour of that court.

Article 30

5–243   For the purposes of this Section, a court shall be deemed to be seised:

1. at the time when the document instituting the proceedings or an equivalent document is lodged with the court, provided that the plaintiff has not subsequently failed to take the steps he was required to take to have service effected on the defendant, or.

2. if the document has to be served before being lodged with the court, at the time when it is received by the authority responsible for service, provided that the plaintiff has not subsequently failed to take the steps he was required to take to have the document lodged with the court.

SECTION 10 — PROVISIONAL, INCLUDING PROTECTIVE, MEASURES

Article 31

5–244   Application may be made to the courts of a Member State for such provisional, including protective, measures as may be available under the law of that State, even if, under this Regulation, the courts of another Member State have jurisdiction as to the substance of the matter.

CHAPTER III — RECOGNITION AND ENFORCEMENT

Article 32

For the purposes of this Regulation, "judgment" means any judgment given by a court or tribunal of a Member State, whatever the judgment may be called, including a decree, order, decision or writ of execution, as well as the determination of costs or expenses by an officer of the court.

5–245

SECTION 1 — RECOGNITION

Article 33

1. A judgment given in a Member State shall be recognised in the other Member States without any special procedure being required.

5–246

2. Any interested party who raises the recognition of a judgment as the principal issue in a dispute may, in accordance with the procedures provided for in Sections 2 and 3 of this Chapter, apply for a decision that the judgment be recognised.

3. If the outcome of proceedings in a court of a Member State depends on the determination of an incidental question of recognition that court shall have jurisdiction over that question.

Article 34

A judgment shall not be recognised:

5–247

1. if such recognition is manifestly contrary to public policy in the Member State in which recognition is sought;

2. where it was given in default of appearance, if the defendant was not served with the document which instituted the proceedings or with an equivalent document in sufficient time and in such a way as to enable him to arrange for his defence, unless the defendant failed to commence proceedings to challenge the judgment when it was possible for him to do so;

3. if it is irreconcilable with a judgment given in a dispute between the same parties in the Member State in which recognition is sought;

4. if it is irreconcilable with an earlier judgment given in another Member State or in a third State involving the same cause of action and between the same parties, provided that the earlier judgment fulfils the conditions necessary for its recognition in the Member State addressed.

Article 35

1. Moreover, a judgment shall not be recognised if it conflicts with Sections 3, 4 or 6 of Chapter II, or in a case provided for in Article 72.

5–248

2. In its examination of the grounds of jurisdiction referred to in the foregoing paragraph, the court or authority applied to shall be bound by the findings of fact on which the court of the Member State of origin based its jurisdiction.

3. Subject to the paragraph 1, the jurisdiction of the court of the Member State of origin may not be reviewed. The test of public policy referred to in point 1 of Article 34 may not be applied to the rules relating to jurisdiction.

EUROPE

Article 36

5–249   Under no circumstances may a foreign judgment be reviewed as to its substance.

Article 37

5–250   1. A court of a Member State in which recognition is sought of a judgment given in another Member State may stay the proceedings if an ordinary appeal against the judgment has been lodged.

2. A court of a Member State in which recognition is sought of a judgment given in Ireland or the United Kingdom may stay the proceedings if enforcement is suspended in the State of origin, by reason of an appeal.

SECTION 2 — ENFORCEMENT

Article 38

5–251   1. A judgment given in a Member State and enforceable in that State shall be enforced in another Member State when, on the application of any interested party, it has been declared enforceable there.

2. However, in the United Kingdom, such a judgment shall be enforced in England and Wales, in Scotland, or in Northern Ireland when, on the application of any interested party, it has been registered for enforcement in that part of the United Kingdom.

Article 39

5–252   1. The application shall be submitted to the court or competent authority indicated in the list in Annex II.

2. The local jurisdiction shall be determined by reference to the place of domicile of the party against whom enforcement is sought, or to the place of enforcement.

Article 40

5–253   1. The procedure for making the application shall be governed by the law of the Member State in which enforcement is sought.

2. The applicant must give an address for service of process within the area of jurisdiction of the court applied to. However, if the law of the Member State in which enforcement is sought does not provide for the furnishing of such an address, the applicant shall appoint a representative ad litem.

3. The documents referred to in Article 53 shall be attached to the application.

Article 41

5–254   The judgment shall be declared enforceable immediately on completion of the formalities in Article 53 without any review under Articles 34 and 35. The party against whom enforcement is sought shall not at this stage of the proceedings be entitled to make any submissions on the application.

Article 42

5–255   1. The decision on the application for a declaration of enforceability shall forthwith be brought to the notice of the applicant in accordance with the procedure laid down by the law of the Member State in which enforcement is sought.

2. The declaration of enforceability shall be served on the party against whom enforcement is sought, accompanied by the judgment, if not already served on that party.

Article 43

5–256

1. The decision on the application for a declaration of enforceability may be appealed against by either party.

2. The appeal is to be lodged with the court indicated in the list in Annex III.

3. The appeal shall be dealt with in accordance with the rules governing procedure in contradictory matters.

4. If the party against whom enforcement is sought fails to appear before the appellate court in proceedings concerning an appeal brought by the applicant, Article 26(2) to (4) shall apply even where the party against whom enforcement is sought is not domiciled in any of the Member States.

5. An appeal against the declaration of enforceability is to be lodged within one month of service thereof. If the party against whom enforcement is sought is domiciled in a Member State other than that in which the declaration of enforceability was given, the time for appealing shall be two months and shall run from the date of service, either on him in person or at his residence. No extension of time may be granted on account of distance.

Article 44

5–257

The judgment given on the appeal may be contested only by the appeal referred to in Annex IV.

Article 45

5–258

1. The court with which an appeal is lodged under Article 43 or Article 44 shall refuse or revoke a declaration of enforceability only on one of the grounds specified in Articles 34 and 35. It shall give its decision without delay.

2. Under no circumstances may the foreign judgment be reviewed as to its substance.

Article 46

5–259

1. The court with which an appeal is lodged under Article 43 or Article 44 may, on the application of the party against whom enforcement is sought, stay the proceedings if an ordinary appeal has been lodged against the judgment in the Member State of origin or if the time for such an appeal has not yet expired; in the latter case, the court may specify the time within which such an appeal is to be lodged.

2. Where the judgment was given in Ireland or the United Kingdom, any form of appeal available in the Member State of origin shall be treated as an ordinary appeal for the purposes of paragraph 1.

3. The court may also make enforcement conditional on the provision of such security as it shall determine.

Article 47

5–260

1. When a judgment must be recognised in accordance with this Regulation, nothing shall prevent the applicant from availing himself of provisional, including protective, measures in accordance with the law of the Member State requested without a declaration of enforceability under Article 41 being required.

2. The declaration of enforceability shall carry with it the power to proceed to any protective measures.

3. During the time specified for an appeal pursuant to Article 43(5) against the declaration of enforceability and until any such appeal has been determined, no measures of enforcement may be taken other than protective measures against the property of the party against whom enforcement is sought.

Article 48

5–261 1. Where a foreign judgment has been given in respect of several matters and the declaration of enforceability cannot be given for all of them, the court or competent authority shall give it for one or more of them.

2. An applicant may request a declaration of enforceability limited to parts of a judgment.

Article 49

5–262 A foreign judgment which orders a periodic payment by way of a penalty shall be enforceable in the Member State in which enforcement is sought only if the amount of the payment has been finally determined by the courts of the Member State of origin.

Article 50

5–263 An applicant who, in the Member State of origin has benefited from complete or partial legal aid or exemption from costs or expenses, shall be entitled, in the procedure provided for in this Section, to benefit from the most favourable legal aid or the most extensive exemption from costs or expenses provided for by the law of the Member State addressed.

Article 51

5–264 No security, bond or deposit, however described, shall be required of a party who in one Member State applies for enforcement of a judgment given in another Member State on the ground that he is a foreign national or that he is not domiciled or resident in the State in which enforcement is sought.

Article 52

5–265 In proceedings for the issue of a declaration of enforceability, no charge, duty or fee calculated by reference to the value of the matter at issue may be levied in the Member State in which enforcement is sought.

SECTION 3 — COMMON PROVISIONS

Article 53

5–266 1. A party seeking recognition or applying for a declaration of enforceability shall produce a copy of the judgment which satisfies the conditions necessary to establish its authenticity.

2. A party applying for a declaration of enforceability shall also produce the certificate referred to in Article 54, without prejudice to Article 55.

Article 54

The court or competent authority of a Member State where a judgment was given **5–267** shall issue, at the request of any interested party, a certificate using the standard form in Annex V to this Regulation.

Article 55

1. If the certificate referred to in Article 54 is not produced, the court or competent **5–268** authority may specify a time for its production or accept an equivalent document or, if it considers that it has sufficient information before it, dispense with its production.

2. If the court or competent authority so requires, a translation of the documents shall be produced. The translation shall be certified by a person qualified to do so in one of the Member States.

Article 56

No legalisation or other similar formality shall be required in respect of the docu- **5–269** ments referred to in Article 53 or Article 55(2), or in respect of a document appointing a representative ad litem.

CHAPTER IV — AUTHENTIC INSTRUMENTS AND COURT SETTLEMENTS

Article 57

1. A document which has been formally drawn up or registered as an authentic **5–270** instrument and is enforceable in one Member State shall, in another Member State, be declared enforceable there, on application made in accordance with the procedures provided for in Articles 38, et seq. The court with which an appeal is lodged under Article 43 or Article 44 shall refuse or revoke a declaration of enforceability only if enforcement of the instrument is manifestly contrary to public policy in the Member State addressed.

2. A document which has been formally drawn up or registered as an authentic instrument and is enforceable in one Member State shall, in another Member State, be declared enforceable there, on application made in accordance with the procedures provided for in Articles 38, *et seq*. The court with which an appeal is lodged under Article 43 or Article 44 shall refuse or revoke a declaration of enforceability only if enforcement of the instrument is manifestly contrary to public policy in the Member State addressed.

3. The instrument produced must satisfy the conditions necessary to establish its authenticity in the Member State of origin.

4. Section 3 of Chapter III shall apply as appropriate. The competent authority of a Member State where an authentic instrument was drawn up or registered shall issue, at the request of any interested party, a certificate using the standard form in Annex VI to this Regulation.

Article 58

A settlement which has been approved by a court in the course of proceedings and **5–271** is enforceable in the Member State in which it was concluded shall be enforceable in

EUROPE

the State addressed under the same conditions as authentic instruments. The court or competent authority of a Member State where a court settlement was approved shall issue, at the request of any interested party, a certificate using the standard form in Annex V to this Regulation.

CHAPTER V — GENERAL PROVISIONS

Article 59

5–272   1. In order to determine whether a party is domiciled in the Member State whose courts are seised of a matter, the court shall apply its internal law.

2. If a party is not domiciled in the Member State whose courts are seised of the matter, then, in order to determine whether the party is domiciled in another Member State, the court shall apply the law of that Member State.

Article 60

5–273   1. For the purposes of this Regulation, a company or other legal person or association of natural or legal persons is domiciled at the place where it has its:

(a) statutory seat, or

(b) central administration, or

(c) principal place of business.

2. For the purposes of the United Kingdom and Ireland "statutory seat" means the registered office or, where there is no such office anywhere, the place of incorporation or, where there is no such place anywhere, the place under the law of which the formation took place.

3. In order to determine whether a trust is domiciled in the Member State whose courts are seised of the matter, the court shall apply its rules of private international law.

Article 61

5–274   Without prejudice to any more favourable provisions of national laws, persons domiciled in a Member State who are being prosecuted in the criminal courts of another Member State of which they are not nationals for an offence which was not intentionally committed may be defended by persons qualified to do so, even if they do not appear in person. However, the court seised of the matter may order appearance in person; in the case of failure to appear, a judgment given in the civil action without the person concerned having had the opportunity to arrange for his defence need not be recognised or enforced in the other Member States.

Article 62

5–275   In Sweden, in summary proceedings concerning orders to pay (betalningsföreläggande) and assistance (handräckning), the expression "court" includes the "Swedish enforcement service" (kronofogdemyndighet).

Article 63

5–276   1. A person domiciled in the territory of the Grand Duchy of Luxembourg and sued in the court of another Member State pursuant to Article 5(1) may refuse to submit to the jurisdiction of that court if the final place of delivery of the goods or provision of the services is in Luxembourg.

2. Where, under paragraph 1, the final place of delivery of the goods or provision of the services is in Luxembourg, any agreement conferring jurisdiction must, in order to be valid, be accepted in writing or evidenced in writing within the meaning of Article 23(1)(a).

3. The provisions of this Article shall not apply to contracts for the provision of financial services.

4. The provisions of this Article shall apply for a period of six years from entry into force of this Regulation.

Article 64

1. In proceedings involving a dispute between the master and a member of the crew of a seagoing ship registered in Greece or in Portugal, concerning remuneration or other conditions of service, a court in a Member State shall establish whether the diplomatic or consular officer responsible for the ship has been notified of the dispute. It may act as soon as that officer has been notified.

5–277

2. The provisions of this Article shall apply for a period of six years from entry into force of this Regulation.

Article 65

1. The jurisdiction specified in Article 6(2), and Article 11 in actions on a warranty of guarantee or in any other third party proceedings may not be resorted to in Germany and Austria. Any person domiciled in another Member State may be sued in the courts:

5–278

  (a) of Germany, pursuant to Articles 68 and 72 to 74 of the Code of Civil Procedure (Zivilprozessordnung) concerning third-party notices,

  (b) of Austria, pursuant to Article 21 of the Code of Civil Procedure (Zivilprozessordnung) concerning third-party notices.

2. Judgments given in other Member States by virtue of Article 6(2), or Article 11 shall be recognised and enforced in Germany and Austria in accordance with Chapter III. Any effects which judgments given in these States may have on third parties by application of the provisions in paragraph 1 shall also be recognised in the other Member States.

CHAPTER VI — TRANSITIONAL PROVISIONS

Article 66

1. This Regulation shall apply only to legal proceedings instituted and to documents formally drawn up or registered as authentic instruments after the entry into force thereof.

5–279

2. However, if the proceedings in the Member State of origin were instituted before the entry into force of this Regulation, judgments given after that date shall be recognised and enforced in accordance with Chapter III,

  (a) if the proceedings in the Member State of origin were instituted after the entry into force of the Brussels or the Lugano Convention both in the Member State or origin and in the Member State addressed;

  (b) in all other cases, if jurisdiction was founded upon rules which accorded with those provided for either in Chapter II or in a convention concluded between the Member State of origin and the Member State addressed which was in force when the proceedings were instituted.

CHAPTER VII — RELATIONS WITH OTHER INSTRUMENTS

Article 67

5–280   This Regulation shall not prejudice the application of provisions governing jurisdiction and the recognition and enforcement of judgments in specific matters which are contained in Community instruments or in national legislation harmonised pursuant to such instruments.

Article 68

5–281   1. This Regulation shall, as between the Member States, supersede the Brussels Convention, except as regards the territories of the Member States which fall within the territorial scope of that Convention and which are excluded from this Regulation pursuant to Article 299 of the Treaty.

2. In so far as this Regulation replaces the provisions of the Brussels Convention between Member States, any reference to the Convention shall be understood as a reference to this Regulation.

Article 69

5–282   Subject to Article 66(2) and Article 70, this Regulation shall, as between Member States, supersede the following conventions and treaty concluded between two or more of them:

- the Convention between Belgium and France on Jurisdiction and the Validity and Enforcement of Judgments, Arbitration Awards and Authentic Instruments, signed at Paris on 8 July 1899,
- the Convention between Belgium and the Netherlands on Jurisdiction, Bankruptcy, and the Validity and Enforcement of Judgments, Arbitration Awards and Authentic Instruments, signed at Brussels on 28 March 1925,
- the Convention between France and Italy on the Enforcement of Judgments in Civil and Commercial Matters, signed at Rome on 3 June 1930,
- the Convention between Germany and Italy on the Recognition and Enforcement of Judgments in Civil and Commercial Matters, signed at Rome on 9 March 1936,
- the Convention between Belgium and Austria on the Reciprocal Recognition and Enforcement of Judgments and Authentic Instruments relating to Maintenance Obligations, signed at Vienna on 25 October 1957,
- the Convention between Germany and Belgium on the Mutual Recognition and Enforcement of Judgments, Arbitration Awards and Authentic Instruments in Civil and Commercial Matters, signed at Bonn on 30 June 1958,
- the Convention between the Netherlands and Italy on the Recognition and Enforcement of Judgments in Civil and Commercial Matters, signed at Rome on 17 April 1959,
- the Convention between Germany and Austria on the Reciprocal Recognition and Enforcement of Judgments, Settlements and Authentic Instruments in Civil and Commercial Matters, signed at Vienna on 6 June 1959,
- the Convention between Belgium and Austria on the Reciprocal Recognition and Enforcement of Judgments, Arbitral Awards and Authentic Instruments in Civil and Commercial Matters, signed at Vienna on 16 June 1959,
- the Convention between Greece and Germany for the Reciprocal Recognition and Enforcement of Judgments, Settlements and Authentic Instruments in Civil and Commercial Matters, signed in Athens on 4 November 1961,

- the Convention between Belgium and Italy on the Recognition and Enforcement of Judgments and other Enforceable Instruments in Civil and Commercial Matters, signed at Rome on 6 April 1962,
- the Convention between the Netherlands and Germany on the Mutual Recognition and Enforcement of Judgments and Other Enforceable Instruments in Civil and Commercial Matters, signed at The Hague on 30 August 1962,
- the Convention between the Netherlands and Austria on the Reciprocal Recognition and Enforcement of Judgments and Authentic Instruments in Civil and Commercial Matters, signed at The Hague on 6 February 1963,
- the Convention between France and Austria on the Recognition and Enforcement of Judgments and Authentic Instruments in Civil and Commercial Matters, signed at Vienna on 15 July 1966,
- the Convention between Spain and France on the Recognition and Enforcement of Judgment Arbitration Awards in Civil and Commercial Matters, signed at Paris on 28 May 1969,
- the Convention between Luxembourg and Austria on the Recognition and Enforcement of Judgments and Authentic Instruments in Civil and Commercial Matters, signed at Luxembourg on 29 July 1971,
- the Convention between Italy and Austria on the Recognition and Enforcement of Judgments in Civil and Commercial Matters, of Judicial Settlements and of Authentic Instruments, signed at Rome on 16 November 1971,
- the Convention between Spain and Italy regarding Legal Aid and the Recognition and Enforcement of Judgments in Civil and Commercial Matters, signed at Madrid on 22 May 1973,
- the Convention between Finland, Iceland, Norway, Sweden and Denmark on the Recognition and Enforcement of Judgments in Civil Matters, signed at Copenhagen on 11 October 1977,
- the Convention between Austria and Sweden on the Recognition and Enforcement of Judgments in Civil Matters, signed at Stockholm on 16 September 1982,
- the Convention between Spain and the Federal Republic of Germany on the Recognition and Enforcement of Judgments, Settlements and Enforceable Authentic Instruments in Civil and Commercial Matters, signed at Bonn on 14 November 1983,
- the Convention between Austria and Spain on the Recognition and Enforcement of Judgments, Settlements and Enforceable Authentic Instruments in Civil and Commercial Matters, signed at Vienna on 17 February 1984,
- the Convention between Finland and Austria on the Recognition and Enforcement of Judgments in Civil Matters, signed at Vienna on 17 November 1986, and
- the Treaty between Belgium, the Netherlands and Luxembourg in Jurisdiction, Bankruptcy, and the Validity and Enforcement of Judgments, Arbitration Awards and Authentic Instruments, signed at Brussels on 24 November 1961, in so far as it is in force.

Article 70

1. The Treaty and the Conventions referred to in Article 69 shall continue to have effect in relation to matters to which this Regulation does not apply.

2. They shall continue to have effect in respect of judgments given and documents formally drawn up or registered as authentic instruments before the entry into force of this Regulation.

5–283

Article 71

1. This Regulation shall not affect any conventions to which the Member States are parties and which in relation to particular matters, govern jurisdiction or the recognition or enforcement of judgments.

5–284

2. With a view to its uniform interpretation, paragraph 1 shall be applied in the following manner:

    (a) this Regulation shall not prevent a court of a Member State, which is a party to a convention on a particular matter, from assuming jurisdiction in accordance with that convention, even where the defendant is domiciled in another Member State which is not a party to that convention. The court hearing the action shall, in any event, apply Article 26 of this Regulation;

    (b) judgments given in a Member State by a court in the exercise of jurisdiction provided for in a convention on a particular matter shall be recognised and enforced in the other Member States in accordance with this Regulation. Where a convention on a particular matter to which both the Member State of origin and the Member State addressed are parties lays down conditions for the recognition or enforcement of judgments, those conditions shall apply. In any event, the provisions of this Regulation which concern the procedure for recognition and enforcement of judgments may be applied.

Article 72

5–285   This Regulation shall not affect agreements by which Member States undertook, prior to the entry into force of this Regulation pursuant to Article 59 of the Brussels Convention, not to recognise judgments given, in particular in other Contracting States to that Convention, against defendants domiciled or habitually resident in a third country where, in cases provided for in Article 4 of that Convention, the judgment could only be founded on a ground of jurisdiction specified in the second paragraph of Article 3 of that Convention.

CHAPTER VIII — FINAL PROVISIONS

Article 73

5–286   No later than five years after the entry into force of this Regulation, the Commission shall present to the European Parliament, the Council and the Economic and Social Committee a report on the application of this Regulation. The report shall be accompanied, if need be, by proposals for adaptations to this Regulation.

Article 74

5–287   1. The Member States shall notify the Commission of the texts amending the lists set out in Annexes I to IV. The Commission shall adapt the Annexes concerned accordingly.

2. The updating or technical adjustment of the forms, specimens of which appear in Annexes V and VI, shall be adopted in accordance with the advisory procedure referred to in Article 75(2).

Article 75

5–288   1. The Commission shall be assisted by a committee.

2. Where reference is made to this paragraph, Articles 3 and 7 of Decision 1999/468/EC shall apply.

3. The Committee shall adopt its rules of procedure.

Article 76

5–289   This Regulation shall enter into force on 1 March 2002.

This Regulation is binding in its entirety and directly applicable in the Member States in accordance with the Treaty establishing the European Community. Done at Brussels, 22 December 2000.

For the Council

The President

C. Pierret

SECTION 6

ADMINISTRATION OF FUNDS, PROPERTY AND AFFAIRS

6A   COURT FUNDS

Supreme Court Act 1981

(1981 c.54)

Accountant General of the Supreme Court

97.—(1) There shall continue to be an Accountant General of, and **6A–1**
an accounting department for, the Supreme Court.

(2) The Lord Chancellor shall appoint such person as he thinks
fit to the office in the Supreme Court of Accountant General of the
Supreme Court, and the person so appointed shall hold and vacate
office in accordance with the terms of his appointment.

(3) The Accountant General shall be paid such salary or fees as
the Lord Chancellor determines with the consent of the Treasury.

(4) If one person holds office both as the Accountant General and
as the Public Trustee then, if he ceases to be the Public Trustee, he
shall also cease to be the Accountant General unless the Lord
Chancellor otherwise directs.

(5) If a vacancy occurs in the office of Accountant General or the
person appointed to hold the office is for any reason unable to act
for any period such person as the Lord Chancellor appoints as deputy in that office shall, during the vacancy or that period, perform
the functions of that office (and any property vested in the Accountant General may accordingly be dealt with by the deputy in all
respects as if it were vested in him instead).

Note —Amended by the Public Trustee and Administration of Funds Act 1986, **6A–2**
Sched.3, para. 5.

Court Funds Office

The name of this office has replaced the former name of the Supreme Court Pay **6A–3**
Office (see the Supreme Court Funds Rules 1975, r.3, paras 6A–18 *et seq.*). This office
is the office of the Accountant General of the Supreme Court (S.C.A. 1981, s.97). The
machinery of this office is governed by the Court Funds Rules 1987 made by the Lord
Chancellor, with the concurrence of the Treasury, under the powers conferred by
A.J.A. 1982, s.38(2) and (7). Pt VI of the A.J.A. 1982 was brought into force by the
Public Trustee and Administration of Funds Act 1986.

Administration of Justice Act 1982

(1982 c.53)   **6A–4**

ARRANGEMENT OF SECTIONS

PART VI

FUNDS IN COURT

* * * *

PART VI

FUNDS IN COURT

Management and investment of funds in court

6A–5 **38.**—(1) Subject to rules made under subsection (7) below, all sums of money, securities and effects paid and deposited in, or under the custody of—

(a) the High Court;

(b) a county court; or

(c) such other courts and tribunals as the Lord Chancellor may by rules made under that subsection prescribe,

shall be vested in the Accountant General.

(2) One or more accounts shall be opened and kept in the name of the Accountant General at such bank or banks as may be designed by the Lord Chancellor with the concurrence of the Treasury.

(3) Money and securities held by the Accountant General shall vest in his successor in office without any assignment or transfer.

(4) A sum of money paid and deposited in court may [...] be invested and reinvested by the Accountant General in any manner authorised by rules made under subsection (7) below.

(5) [...]

(6) The Accountant General may, in such cases as the Lord Chancellor may by rules made under subsection (7) below prescribe, apply to the court for an order for directions as to the manner in which a particular fund in court is to be dealt with.

(7) The Lord Chancellor, with the concurrence of the Treasury, may make provision as to the payment of interest on funds in court and may make rules as to the administration and management of funds in court including the deposit, payment, delivery and transfer in, into and out of any court of funds in court and regulating the evidence of such deposit, payment, delivery or transfer.

(8) Rules made under subsection (7) above may—

(a) provide for the discharge of the functions of the Accountant General under the rules by a person or persons appointed by him;

(b) provide for the transfer of money in court to and from the Commissioners;

(c) provide for money paid and deposited in a county court to be vested in, and accounted for by, a person other than the Accountant General;

(d) prescribe cases in which interest is to be paid on funds in court;

(e) prescribe cases in which funds in court are to be invested;

(f) make provision for the transfer of funds in court from one court to another; and

(g) prescribe cases in which moneys payable under a judgment or order shall be paid into court.

(9) Any such rules may make different provision for different cases.

Note —Amended by Public Trustee and Administration of Funds Act 1986, s.4.   **6A–6**

Investment of money transferred to National Debt Commissioners

39.—(1) The Commissioners may invest, in such manner as may be **6A–7** prescribed by regulations made by the Treasury, money transferred to them in pursuance of rules made under section 38(7) above or section 82(1) of the Judicature (Northern Ireland) Act 1978 and the interest or dividends accruing on investments made under this subsection.

(2) If in any accounting year the aggregate of the sums of money received by the Commissioners by way of interest and dividends on investments made by them under subsection (1)above, after deduction of—

(a) any sum required by the Treasury to be set aside to provide for depreciation in the value of investments so made;

(b) such sum as the Lord Chancellor may with the concurrence of the Treasury direct to be paid to him in respect of the cost to him in that year of administering funds in court, and

(c) an amount equal to the expenses incurred by the Commissioners in that year in making investments under subsection (1) above and disposing of investments so made

exceeds the aggregate of the sums due to be paid or credited in respect of that year by way of interest on funds in court, the excess shall be paid into the Consolidated Fund.

(3) If in any accounting year the aggregate of the sums of money received as mentioned in subsection (2) above, after deduction of the sum or sums falling to be deducted under paragraphs (a) to (c) of that subsection, is less than the aggregate of the sums due as mentioned in that subsection, the deficiency shall be made good out of the Consolidated Fund.

(4) The Commissioners shall pay to the Lord Chancellor any sum deducted by them under subsection (2)(b) above; and any sum received by the Lord Chancellor under this subsection shall be paid into the Consolidated Fund.

(4A) Any sum deducted by the Commissioners under subsection (2)(c)above shall be applied as an appropriation in aid of moneys provided by Parliament for the expenses of the National Debt Commissioners; and, so far as not so applied, shall be paid into the Consolidated Fund.

(5) If at any time the Commissioners are unable to pay—

(a) to the Accountant General a sum due from them to him under rules made under section 38(7) above; or

(b) to the Accountant General of the Supreme Court of Judicature of Northern Ireland a sum due from them to him under rules made under section 82(1) of the Judicature (Northern Ireland) Act 1978,

the Treasury shall provide them with it out of the Consolidated Fund.

6A–8 *Note* —Amended by the Public Trustee and Administration of Funds Act 1986, s.5.

Statutory deposits

6A–9 **40.**—(1) Where money or securities are deposited with the Accountant General under any enactment or subordinate legislation, whether passed or made before or after the commencement of this Part of this Act, they shall for the purposes of this Part of this Act be treated as if they were funds in court except in so far as—

(a) the enactment; or

(b) the subordinate legislation; or

(c) rules made under section 38(7) above,

provide to the contrary.

(2) In subsection (1) above "subordinate legislation" means Orders in Council, orders, rules, regulations and other instruments made or to be made under any Act.

Transfer of funds in court to Official Custodian for Charities and Church Commissioners

6A–10 **41.**—(1) Any funds for the time being vested in the Accountant General and held by him in trust for any charity or in trust for any ecclesiastical corporation in the Church of England may, if the Accountant General on an application made in that behalf to him by the Charity Commissioners or the Church Commissioners thinks fit so to direct, be transferred to the Official Custodian for Charities or the Church Commissioners, as the case may be.

(2) Any funds transferred by virtue of a direction given under subsection (1) above shall be vested in and held by the Official Custodian for Charities or the Church Commissioners respectively in trust for the charity or ecclesiastical corporation upon the trusts upon which the funds were held before the transfer.

(3) In this section "ecclesiastical corporation" means a capitular body within the meaning of the Cathedrals Measure 1963 or the incumbent of a benefice.

Common investment schemes

6A–11 **42.**—(1) The Lord Chancellor may continue to make schemes ("common investment schemes") establishing common investment funds for the purpose of investing funds in court and money held by any person who in accordance with subsection (5)(b) below may hold shares in common investment funds.

(2) A common investment scheme shall provide for the fund thereby established to be under the management and control of an investment manager appointed by the Lord Chancellor.

(3) A common investment scheme shall make provision for the investment by its investment manager in accordance with the provisions of this section of funds in court transferred to the fund under rules made by virtue of section 38(7) above and of any sums of money transferred to the fund by persons who in accordance with subsection (5)(b) below may hold shares in the fund.

(4) A common investment scheme shall make provision—

    (a) for treating the fund established by it as being divided into shares; and

    (b) for treating a sum invested in the fund as being represented by a number of shares determined by reference to that sum and the value of the fund at the time the investment was made.

(5) Shares in a common investment fund—

    (a) shall be allotted to and held by the Accountant General and

    (b) may be allotted to and held by the Accountant General of the Supreme Court of Judicature of Northern Ireland and any other person authorised by the Lord Chancellor.

(6) Where a person is authorised under subsection (5) above to hold shares in a common investment fund—

    (a) he may invest trust money in shares in the fund without obtaining and considering advice on whether to make such an investment; and

    (b) he may invest trust money in a common investment fund of which he is the investment manager.

(7) Moneys comprised in the fund established by a common investment scheme may, subject to the provisions of the scheme, be invested by the investment manager of the fund in any way in which he thinks fit, whether or not authorised by the general law in relation to trust funds.

(8) [...]

(9) The investment manager of a fund established by a common investment scheme shall not be required or entitled to take account of any trusts or equities affecting any share in the fund whether or not he is also a trustee of any such trust.

(10) The investment manager of a fund established by a common investment scheme shall be remunerated at such rates and in such manner as the Lord Chancellor shall with the concurrence of the Treasury determine.

(11) The salary or remuneration of an investment manager and his officers and such other expenses of executing his office or otherwise carrying this Part of this Act into effect as may be sanctioned by the Treasury shall be paid out of moneys provided by Parliament.

COURT FUNDS

(12) There shall be charged in respect of the running of a common investment scheme such fees, whether by way of percentage or otherwise, as the Lord Chancellor shall with the concurrence of the Treasury fix and such fees shall be collected and accounted for by such persons, and in such manner, and shall be paid to such account, as the Treasury direct.

(13) There shall be retained or paid out of a fund established by a common investment scheme any expenses which could be so retained or paid out of trust property if the investment manager of the fund were a trustee and such expenses shall be retained or paid in the same way as and in addition to fees charged in respect of the running of the scheme.

(14) Fees and expenses recovered under this section shall be paid into the Consolidated Fund.

(15) Money and securities held by an investment manager of a fund established by a common investment scheme shall vest in his successor in office without any assignment or transfer.

(16) The power conferred by subsection (1) above to make a common investment scheme shall include the power to vary or revoke such a scheme.

6A–12   *Note* — Subsection 8 repealed by Financial Services Act 1986, s.212(3), Sched.17, Pt 1.

Subsection 6 amended by Trustee Act 2000, see S.I. 2001 No. 49, art. 2.

Provision for making good defaults

6A–13   **43.** If the Lord Chancellor, whether on a recommendation made to him by any person interested or not, certifies—

    (a) that the Accountant General; or

    (b) that the manager of a common investment fund,

has been guilty of any default with respect to any money, securities and effects for which he is responsible under this Part of this Act, such sum as may be certified by the Lord Chancellor to be necessary for making good the default shall be paid out of moneys provided by Parliament or, if and so far as it is not so paid, shall be charged on and issued out of the Consolidated Fund.

Power to repeal and modify ss.42 and 43

6A–14   **44.**—(1) Her Majesty may by Order in Council—

    (a) repeal subsections (8), (10), (12), (14) and (15) of section 42 above and section 43 above; or

    (b) make such modifications to those enactments as Her Majesty considers appropriate.

(2) Any Order in Council made under subsection (1) above shall be subject to annulment in pursuance of a resolution of either House of Parliament.

Accounts

6A–15   **45.**—(1) Accounts shall be prepared and shall at such times as the Treasury shall direct be sent to the Comptroller and Auditor General—

(a) in respect of his transactions under section 38 above, by the Accountant General;

(b) in respect of their transactions under section 39 above, by the Commissioners; and

(c) in respect of transactions in a fund established by a common investment scheme, by the investment manager.

(2) The accounts shall be in such form and shall be prepared in respect of such periods as the Treasury may direct.

(3) The Comptroller and Auditor General shall examine, certify and report on accounts sent to him under subsection (1) above and lay copies of them and his report on them before each House of Parliament.

Supplemental

46.—(1) Any power conferred by this Part of this Act to make a **6A–16** scheme or rules or regulations shall be exercisable by statutory instrument which shall be subject to annulment in pursuance of a resolution of either House of Parliament.

(2) The following amendments shall have effect—

(a) the words "invested under section 38 of the Administration of Justice Act 1982" shall be substituted for the words "dealt with under section 6 of the Administration of Justice Act 1965" in each case where they occur in the following enactments—

(i) section 46 of the Chelsea and Kilmainham Hospitals Act 1826;

(ii) section 12 of the Ecclesiastical Houses of Residence Act 1842;

(iii) sections 70, 78 and 86 of the Lands Clauses Consolidation Act 1845; and

(iv) section 9 of the Tithe Act 1846;

(b) the words "section 42 of the Administration of Justice Act 1982" shall be substituted for the words " section 1 of the Administration of Justice Act 1965"—

(i) [*Repealed by*, Transport and Works Act 1992, s.68(1), and Sched.4.]

(ii) in section 20(1) of the Insurance Companies Act 1958;

(c) in section 7(1) of the Industrial Assurance Act 1923, for the words from the beginning of paragraph (a) to "1958" there shall be substituted—

"(a) the provision substituted by the Administration of Justice Act 1965 for section 19(1) of the Insurance Companies Act 1958 and the provision so substituted for section 20(1) of that Act, as amended by section 46(2)(c) of the Administration of Justice Act 1982,";

(d) [*Repealed by*, Transport and Works Act 1992, s.68(1) and Sched.4.]

(e) [*Repealed by*, Income and Corporation Taxes Act 1988, s.844 and Sched.31.]

(f) [*Repealed by* Taxation of Chargeable Gains Act 1992, s.290(3) and Sched.12.]

(g) in section 9(7) of the Insurance Companies Act 1981 for the words " section 7 of the Administration of Justice Act 1965" there shall be substituted the words "section 38(7) of the Administration of Justice Act 1982".

Interpretation

6A–17 47. In this Part—

"Accountant General" means the Accountant General of the Supreme Court;

"the Commissioners" means the National Debt Commissioners;

"a common investment scheme" means a scheme made under section 42 above;

"funds" or "funds in court" means—

(a) any money, securities or other investments (including foreign currency and assets) standing or to be placed to the account—

(i) of the Accountant General by virtue of section 38(1) above; or

(ii) of any other person by virtue of rules made under subsection (7) of that section;

(b) any effects deposited with the Accountant General by virtue of section 38(1) above; but does not include any statutory deposit referred to in section 40 above.

* * * *

Court Funds Rules 1987

(S.I. 1987 No. 821)

6A–18 [As amended by S.I. 1988 No. 817, S.I. 1990 No. 518, S.I. 1991 No. 1227, S.I. 1997 No. 177, S.I. 1999 No. 1021, S.I. 2000 No. 2918, S.I. 2001 No. 703, S.I. 2003 No. 375and S.I. 2003 No. 720.]

ARRANGEMENT OF RULES

PRELIMINARY

Court Funds

6A-19 *Note* —These Rules have been amended by the Court Funds (Amendment) Rules 1999 (S.I. 1999 No. 1021). For "plaintiff" wherever it appears, substitute "claimant"; and for "proper officer" substitute "court officer".

Preliminary

Citation, commencement and revocation

6A-20 1.—(1) **These Rules may be cited as the Court Funds Rules 1987 and shall come into force on 1st June 1987.**

(2) The Rules specified in the schedule to these Rules shall be hereby revoked, except that those Rules shall continue to apply to such extent as may be necessary for giving effect to any order or request made before 1st June 1987.

6A-21 *Note* —Amended by S.I. 1997 No. 177, and S.I. 1999 No. 1021.

Interpretation

6A-22 2.—(1) Unless the context otherwise requires, expressions used in these Rules shall have the same meaning as in the Civil Procedure Rules 1998, and those Rules are referred to in these Rules as the "CPR".

(2) The following expressions shall have the following meanings:
"Accountant General" means the Accountant General of the Supreme Court or an officer appointed by him under Rule 4;

"Appointed Officer" means an officer appointed by the Accountant General under Rule 4(1);

"Authenticated" means authenticated with the impression of a stamp issued by the Accountant General;

"Authorised Officer" means an officer authorised by the Accountant General under Rules 4(2);

"The Bank" means the Bank of England or such bank or banks as may be designated by the Lord Chancellor with the concurrence of the Treasury;

"Bankers' Automated Clearing System" means the method of payment whereby funds are transferred from one bank to another by means of an automated system;

"Basic Account" means a deposit account bearing interest as established under Rule 26;

"Carry over" means to transfer a fund in Court or any part thereof from one account to another in the books of the Court Funds Office;

"Common Investment Fund" means a fund established by a scheme made under section 42(1) of the Administration of Justice Act 1982;

"Court" includes, unless otherwise specified, the following:—

> The Supreme Court.
> Any county court.
> The Employment Appeal Tribunal.
> The Lands Tribunal;

"Any county court" means a judge or district judge exercising the powers of a county court in chambers as well as in open court;

"Court Funds Office" means the Court Funds Division of the Court Service;

"Court Funds Office account" means the cash account of the Accountant General at the Bank;

"Duty" means inheritance tax, or capital transfer tax, or estate, succession or legacy duty;

"Employment Appeal Tribunal" means the tribunal established under section 87 of the Employment Protection Act 1975;

"Foreign currency" means currency other than sterling;

"Fund" or "Fund in Court" has the meaning assigned by section 47 of the Administration of Justice Act 1982;

"Holding" means the units in any one common investment fund purchased on any one valuation day and held in respect of a particular long-term investment account;

"Interest" means interest accruing on funds and includes dividends;

"Interest bearing account" means an account of funds established under Rule 26;

"Lodge in court" means pay or transfer into court or deposit in court;

"Lodgment Schedule" means a schedule to an order directing funds to be lodged to the account of the Accountant General;

"Master" means a Master of the Supreme Court or Master of the Court of Protection and includes the Admiralty Registrar, a District Judge, a Registrar in Bankruptcy and the Registrar of the Employment Appeal Tribunal;

"Master of the Court of Protection" means the Master of the Court of Protection, the Public Trustee or any other officer nominated by the Lord Chancellor to act for the purposes of Part VII of the Mental Health Act 1983;

"National Savings Stock" means stock registered on the National Savings Stock Register;

"Order" means an order or judgment of the High Court or Court of Appeal or a county court, an order, certificate or direction under the seal of the Court of Protection, an order under the seal of the Employment Appeal Tribunal or an order under the seal of the Lands Tribunal;

"Patient" means a person who, by reason of mental disorder within the meaning of Part VII of the Mental Health Act 1983 is incapable of managing and administering his property and affairs;

"Payment Schedule" means a schedule to an order directing the payment of funds from the account of the Accountant General;

"Person under disability" means a person who is a child or a patient;

"Royal Courts of Justice" means the Supreme Court at the Royal Courts of Justice and does not include any District Registry

"Securities" includes units purchased and investments affected by placing money to special accounts;

"Special Account" means an investment account bearing interest as established under Rule 26;

"Unit" means one of the shares into which a common investment fund is treated as being divided.

(3) Unless the context otherwise requires, a Rule, or Part referred to by number means the Rule or Part so numbered in these Rules.

6A–23   *Note* —There must be no liability upon any security to be lodged in court (*per* Selborne L.C., *Re Stephens* (1873) L.R. 86 Ch.App. 465).

Amended by S.I. 1988 No. 817; S.I. 1991 No. 1227; S.I. 1997 No. 177; S.I. 1999 No. 1008; S.I. 1999 No. 1021; S.I. 2000 No. 2918; S.I. 2001 No. 703 and S.I. 2003 No. 375.

[THE NEXT PARAGRAPH IS 6A–26.]

Court Funds Office
6A–26   3. The office of the Accountant General shall continue to be known as the Court Funds Office.

Discharge of Accountant General's functions
6A–27   4.—(1) The functions of the Accountant General under these Rules may be discharged, to such extent as he may direct, by any officer appointed by him.

(2) The Accountant General, with the approval of the Treasury, may from time to time authorise in writing any officer to authenticate on his behalf any direction issued by him for the purpose of giving effect to these Rules and such authorisation may be either general or in respect of any particular class or classes of transaction.

Power to authorise use of forms

5. [Repealed by *S.I. 1988 No. 817 , r.5(1)*.]   6A–28

PART I

AUTHORITIES FOR LODGMENT, PAYMENT OUT, TRANSFER, ETC.

Lodgment Schedule

6.—(1) Where lodgment of funds in court is directed by an order 6A–29
or authorised by a Master, the Accountant General shall not make such lodgment until he has received:—

> (i) in proceedings in the Chancery Division, or in the Court of Protection, a lodgment schedule; or
> (ii) in proceedings in the Queen's Bench Division, Family Division, or any other court or tribunal, a copy of the order.

but in the case of proceedings mentioned in sub-paragraph (ii) he may refuse to make such lodgment until he has received a lodgment schedule.

(2) Where proceedings in which money has been lodged in court are ordered to be transferred to another court, the court officer of the transferring courts shall so advise the Accountant General in writing.

*Note —*Amended by S.I. 1999 No. 1021, r.2(b). With reference to 6(1)(i) above, in 6A–30
the Chancery Division in respect of a person liable to account and in the Court of Protection Division, it is not necessary for the sum to be lodged to be specified; if this sum is not ascertainable at the time that the lodgment schedule is drawn up, any sum tendered in respect of the lodgment will be accepted by the Accountant General.

Payment Schedule

7.—(1) Where an order directs the manner in which any fund in 6A–31
court is to be dealt with by the Accountant General, a payment schedule shall be lodged with him.

(2) Subject to paragraph (3) a payment schedule signed and authenticated by a court officer shall be sufficient authority to the Accountant General to deal with a fund in accordance with the schedule.

(3) Where money is lodged in court in proceedings under section 84 of the Law of Property Act 1925 and directions are given by the Lands Tribunal instructing the Accountant General to deal with that fund, such directions shall be sufficient authority to the Accountant General to deal with the fund accordingly.

6A–32   *Note* —Amended by S.I. 1999 No. 1021, r.2(b). When the payment schedule directs payment to a person who, subsequently to the date thereof, has changed his name, proof of the change may be furnished by an office copy of an affidavit by the payee exhibiting the instrument or authority under which the change has been made. (Form 301).

When the payment schedule directs payment to a company and its name has been changed since the date of the Order, proof of the change may be furnished by an office copy of an affidavit by the secretary exhibiting a certificate of the Registrar of Companies.

Where a dividend is to be paid to creditors, shareholders or debenture holders, the Schedule should direct the total amount of such dividend to be carried over to a separate account entitled: First [or as may be] dividend [*with any further necessary particulars*]. The names of the payees if they are fairly numerous should be inserted in the Schedule alphabetically and each item numbered.

When payment is dependent upon production of a solicitor's certificate that a debenture has been endorsed, and the debenture cannot be found, provision may be made by stating in the Order, "or if the debenture cannot be found, upon a certificate from the Master (or Registrar of the Companies Court) that such production may be dispensed with".

Where duty and costs are directed to be paid the first direction should be "Pay Duty".

The effect of opening a separate account in an action is to release it from the general questions in the suit, and to indicate in each heading the person interested in the fund placed to such separate account (*Edgar v. Plomley* [1900] A.C. 431) but so long as the fund remains in Court it is under the control of the Court (*Cloutte v. Storey* [1911] 1 Ch. 18, CA).

As to the payment and transfer of funds out of Court see Pt VII, rr.40–51.

Preparation and amendment of Schedules

6A–33   8.—(1) In any proceedings, other than proceedings in the Court of Protection, the Lands Tribunal or the Employment Appeal Tribunal, where an order is made for the lodgment of or dealing with funds in court, the party having carriage of the order shall prepare and submit the lodgment or payment schedule to the appropriate court office for authentication.

(2) Without prejudice to paragraph (1), the court officer of a court in which an order has been made for the lodgment of or dealing with funds in court, may prepare the lodgment or payment schedule where he considers it appropriate to do so.

(3) The court officer of the court in question shall sign and authenticate the lodgment or payment schedule and forward it to the Accountant General.

(4) Any amendment to a schedule needed to correct a clerical or accidental error or omission shall be signed by the court officer.

6A–33.1   *Note* —Amended by S.I. 1999 No. 1021, r.2(b).

[THE NEXT PARAGRAPH IS 6A–34.]

Regulations concerning the transmission of Schedules to the Accountant General

6A–34   All schedules will be transmitted to the Accountant General immediately after they have been authenticated by the court using the stamp provided by the Accountant General.

It will be observed that in no case will a schedule ever be in the hands of the solicitor, and as a fact, the Accountant General will refuse to accept schedules by any other means than through official channels. In this way a complete record will be preserved of all schedules in the hands of the Accountant General.

All charging or stop orders affecting funds in Court or to be lodged must be produced to the Court Funds Office by the solicitors obtaining them. The Accountant General otherwise receives no notification of these orders. A copy of the Order should be supplied for retention in the Court Funds Office.

In the Queen's Bench and Family Divisions, although payment schedules are prepared by the solicitors having carriage of the Orders, they reach the Accountant General only through official channels (by post as appropriate). The practice is, however, different in the Admiralty Registry: payment schedules are always prepared by the Registry and transmitted direct to the Accountant General.

In the Court of Protection all schedules are prepared by the Court and transmitted direct to the Accountant General.

Certificate of a Master or Taxing Master

9.—(1) Where a payment schedule directs a Master to ascertain **6A–35** and certify a sum to be dealt with by the Accountant General or directs that costs shall be assessed and paid out of funds in court, the Master or Costs Officer shall certify:—

    (i) the amount ascertained or the amount of the assessed costs (including the fees of detailed assessment); and

    (ii) the name and address of the person to whom payment is to be made;

and shall send the certificate to the Accountant General in the approved form.

(2) A certificate issued by a Master or Costs Officer following a detailed assessment shall, unless described as an interim certificate, be deemed to include all the costs directed to be assessed and paid out of funds in court.

Note —Amended by the Court Funds (Amendment) Rules 1999 (S.I. 1999 No. **6A–36** 1021).

If an interim certificate of detailed assessment is sent to the Court Funds Office it is acted upon, but no further payments which might be affected by the payment of costs will be made until after the final certificate of detailed assessment is received by the Accountant General.

When the costs officer states in his certificate that any party has made objections thereto, and that he has overruled the same, payment will not be made until the expiration of 14 days from the date of the certificate, being the time allowed for an appeal under CPR r.47.22.

Where it is desired to provide for the investment of a fund and payment of costs, the order should, unless there is any special reason to the contrary, direct investment of the whole fund and deal with interest thereon and then the sale of sufficient stock to raise the amount of the assessed costs and the payments thereof. The fund would then not be lying idle pending detailed assessment.

Particulars of interest ordered to be paid as directed in judgment or order

10.—(1) Where interest is directed by an order to be paid on any **6A–37** sum in court, the payment schedule shall state:—

    (i) the rate per cent. at which interest is payable

    (ii) the date from which and, if known, the date to which interest is to be calculated;

    (iii) whether the interest should be paid with or without deduction of income tax; and

    (iv) the amount of such interest, if ascertainable when the payment schedule is drawn up.

(2) If the amount of interest cannot be stated in the payment schedule, then either:—

    (i) the schedule shall direct that the amount be ascertained and certified by a Master or

    (ii) the party having carriage of the order shall agree in writing with the Accountant General the amount of interest.

(3) Whenever interest is required to be calculated for a period of less than a year, the interest shall be calculated on a daily basis in respect of that period.

6A–38   *Note*—Amended by S.I. 1988 No. 817.

Regular payments
6A–39   11. Where a payment schedule directs that regular payments (not being interest payable as it accrues due) are to be made by the Accountant General, the schedule shall state the dates on which payments are to be made and whether the payments are to be made with or without deduction of income tax at the basic rate.

Funds on which duty is payable
6A–40   12. Where a fund in court is subject to payment of duty but the order relating to it does not provide for such payment, the payment schedule shall state that the fund is subject to duty; and if the payment schedule directs the carry over of any part of a fund subject to duty, the words "subject to duty" shall be written boldly at the top of the first page of the schedule relating to the account to which the fund is to be carried over.

6A–41   *Note*—"Duty" does not include income tax which must be specially mentioned in the order.

Only duties presently payable will be provided for on payment out of Court (*Re Bowes* [1907] W.N. 198).

"Notice ... that duty is payable"
6A–42   The Inland Revenue "notice" operates as a restraint on the transfer or payment out of a fund and is recorded on any certificate of the fund under r.63. A "notice" given by the Inland Revenue solicitor must be withdrawn by him.

When duty separately chargeable against the shares of several beneficiaries is not stated in the order, a personal certificate apportioning the duty may be required from the solicitor having conduct of the proceedings. If possible, it is preferable for the Capital Taxes Office to apportion.

If the London solicitor having carriage of the order is unable to certify, the certificate of a country solicitor having knowledge of the facts will be accepted.

If death duties are to be satisfied by the transfer of securities the transfer is made to "The Commissioners of Inland Revenue on account of death duties." A requisition issued by the Capital Taxes Office of the Inland Revenue should accompany the request for transfer.

The certificate of the Capital Taxes Office regarding the clearance of liability to duty on a fund in Court should normally be on Inland Revenue Form No 33.

PART II

LODGMENT OF FUNDS IN COURT

Accountant General's directions for payment to the Bank
6A–43   13. Money shall not be paid directly to the Bank save on the direction of the Accountant General.

Lodgment on receipt of a Lodgment Schedule

14.—(1) Approval for the lodgment of funds in court shall be **6A–44** given by the Accountant General on receipt of a lodgment schedule in proceedings:—

    (i) in the Court of Protection and in the Employment Appeal Tribunal;

    (ii) in the Chancery Division of the High Court, where the lodgment is:

        (a) directed by a lodgment schedule;

        (b) made under the Life Assurance (Payment into Court) Act 1896 or the Trustee Act 1925, and the lodgment schedule is accompanied by a copy of a witness statement or affidavit filed in accordance with CPR rule 37.5;

    (iii) in a county court where money is paid into court under the Trustee Act 1925 in accordance with CPR rule 37.5, and the lodgment schedule has been authenticated by the court officer.

(2) Where the Accountant General receives from a company a notice of claim after the making of the witness statement or affidavit required under CPR rule 37.5, he shall note the account accordingly.

Note — Amended by the Court Funds (Amendment) Rules 2003 (S.I. 2003 No. **6A–45** 375).

Where the amount of funds to be lodged is not ascertained at the date of the order, the lodgment schedule should describe them so far as possible and state how they are to be verified, *e.g.* by a certificate of the Master, by affidavit or certificate of the solicitor or of the person directed to make the lodgment.

The affidavit or certificate should quote the account title, date of order, description and amount of funds to be lodged, name of person lodging and the details concerning such lodgment mentioned in the schedule.

The authority for lodgment of proceeds of sale of any property directed by an order to be sold and of balances due from persons liable to account may be a lodgment schedule signed by a Master, and it may contain a direction for investment and accumulation, and that the funds, whether capital or interest, or both, are not to be dealt with without notice.

Interest on securities directed to be lodged in Court, in cases other than in proceedings in the Court of Protection, which accrued due between the date of the order and the actual date of lodgment of the securities, will be payable into Court unless the order otherwise provides.

Stocks, shares, or bonds which cannot be accepted by the Accountant General, may be placed in a sealed packet or box, and a direction should then be inserted in the Schedule for the lodgment of such sealed packet or box, care being taken in the case of bonds with coupons to provide for the periodical delivery out and re-deposit of the box for the purpose of cutting off such coupons. See rule 17(3) as to providing the Accountant General with an inventory of the contents of a sealed packet or box deposited in court.

Security for costs of appeal

When money is ordered to be lodged in Court as security for costs of an appeal **6A–46** from the Ch.D., the time limited for such lodgment should be stated in the lodgment schedule. When the time limited is short payment in should be by cash or banker's draft.

[THE NEXT PARAGRAPH IS 6A–48.]

Note —The company shall not deduct any costs or expenses of or incidental to the **6A–48**

COURT FUNDS

payment into Court (Practice Direction (Miscellaneous Provisions About Payments Into Court) para. 7.1, see voVol. 1 para. 37PD.7).

The draft lodgment schedule should be submitted to the Court Funds Office before the affidavit is sworn. The lodgment schedule must be signed by the Commissioner for Oaths. before whom the affidavit is sworn.

Boxes and other effects are not accepted under this rule.

If a trustee is in doubt as to who is entitled to a fund in his hands, CPR Pt 64, s.I, is generally available for the purpose of getting the point decided, and this course should be followed instead of the fund being lodged in court under the Trustee Act (*Dix v. Great Western Railway* (1886) 34 W.R. 712).

"Witness statement or affidavit"

6A–49   See Practice Direction (Miscellaneous Provisions About Payments Into Court) para. 9.1, see Vol. 1 para. 37PD.9.

The witness statement or affidavit may be made by one of several trustees (*Anon.* (1885) 1 Jur.N.S. 974; Trustee Act 1925, s.63); though, where reasonably possible, all should join.

If an affidavit is supplied the Schedule must be signed by the Commissioner for Oaths before whom the affidavit is sworn.

The witness statement or affidavit may be written or printed; only an office copy of the lodgment schedule to the affidavit has to be left at the Court Funds Office.

The shares of several persons separately entitled may be lodged under a witness statement or an affidavit (*Re Wright* (1857) 3 K. & J. 419) but in the title of the account to be raised such shares must not be described as the "separate accounts of A.B. and C.D." A separate schedule should be used for each person's share where possible.

See notes to C.F.O. Form 103 as to the account title, statement as to duty and directions as to investment.

The beneficiary's name should appear first in the title, following the analogy of cases without affidavit where this form is compulsory.

Should the lodgment schedule require amendment or correction, a supplemental witness statement or affidavit may be filed with a corrected schedule. It is advisable before swearing trustee affidavits, to submit the draft schedule to the Court Funds Office for examination.

Notice

6A–50   As to notice of payment into court, "filed in accordance with CPR rule 37.5" see Practice Direction (Miscellaneous Provisions About Payments Into Court) paras 7.5 and 9.3 (Vol. 1 paras 37PD.7 and 37PD.9).

"Required under CPR rule 37.5"

6A–51   Provisions as to the written evidence "required under CPR rule 37.5" are found, not in r.37.5, but in Practice Direction (Miscellaneous Provisions About Payments Into Court) (Vol. 1 para. 37PD.1 *et seq*).

Lodgment on receipt of a written request

6A–52   15.—(1) Approval for the lodgment of funds in court shall be given by the Accountant General on receipt of a written request in proceedings:—

> (i) in the Queen's Bench or Family Divisions of the High Court or in a county court where the request is accompanied by a sealed copy order directing the lodgment, or where in Admiralty proceedings the request is made by the Admiralty Marshal;
>
> (ii) in the Chancery Division of the High Court where the lodgment is made in proceedings:—
>
>> (a) under section 84 of the Law of Property Act 1925; or
>>
>> (b) under the Trustee Act 1925 where the written

request is signed by or on behalf of the personal representative; or

(c) under any enactment other than those mentioned in Rule 14(1)(ii) or in this paragraph where it is accompanied by the appropriate document authorising lodgment where specific authority to lodge is required by the relevant enactment;

(iii) in any division of the High Court or in a county court where the lodgment is made under—

(a) CPR Part 36 in satisfaction of a claim and the request is accompanied by a copy of the claim form and the notice of payment into court; or

(b) CPR, rule 37.3 (where the defendant wishes to rely on a defence of tender before claim) and the request is accompanied by a copy of the claim form and a copy of the defence;

(iv) in the Admiralty Registry if the request is sealed by the Registry.

(2) The Accountant General may give approval for lodgment of funds in court notwithstanding that a request is not accompanied by a sealed copy order directing lodgment in accordance with paragraph (1)(i), provided that he is satisfied that such an order has been made and the reason why a copy of the order does not accompany the request is stated in the request.

Note —Instructions as to lodgment will be given on application to the Court Funds Office. As to form of request for lodgment see C.F.O. Form 100 for High Court and County Court lodgments, or C.F.O. Form 101 for Chancery lodgments except for lodgment under the Compulsory Purchase Act 1965 when C.F.O. Form 102 must be used. **6A–53**

[THE NEXT PARAGRAPH IS 6A–55.]

Note —Amended by the Court Funds (Amendment) Rules 1999 (S.I. 1999 No. 1021). **6A–55**

A claimant against whom a counterclaim is made may make a payment into court (see CPR Pt 36). Under former rules expressly providing for this (see RSC O.22, r.6) it was held that a claimant defending a counterclaim may pay money into court on C.F.O. Form No. 100 (*Hutchinson v. Barker* (1895) 71 L.T. 625).

As to payment of fund lodged in satisfaction on C.F.O. Form No. 100, see r.44; and see *Re Earl Stamford* (1885) 33 W.R. 909.

A lodgment of cash as security in QBD may be made on the authority of an order of certiorari under CPR Pt 54, C.F.O. Form No. 100.

Security for costs of election petition

A lodgment of cash in QBD for costs of an election petition is made on the *fiat* of a Master on C.F.O. Form No. 100. As there is a time limit of three days for payment in this should be by cash or banker's draft. **6A–56**

Admiralty actions

See *British Shipping Laws*, Vol. 1 (1964) paras 340 *et seq.* **6A–57**

The proceeds of the sale of a ship in U.S. dollars may be paid into court by the Admiralty Marshal without first converting them into sterling and placed in a dollar deposit account but an order of the court is necessary both for the payment into court of dollars and for placing them in a dollar deposit account (*The Halcyon the Great* [1975] 1 W.L.R. 515; [1975] 1 All E.R. 882).

[THE NEXT PARAGRAPH IS 6A–59.]

Lodgment of money in court

6A–59   16.—(1) Money to be lodged in accordance with Rules 14 or 15, except money representing the proceeds of sale or redemption of National Savings stock or money to be paid into court under rule 19, shall be paid directly into the Court Funds Office.

(2) [*Repealed by S.I. 1999 No. 1921.*]

(3) Where money is paid under paragraph (1), cheques or other instruments shall be made payable to the Accountant General of the Supreme Court.

(4) Money received in the Court Funds Office shall be paid into the Bank for the credit of the Accountant General's account as soon as practicable.

6A–60   *Note* — Amended by the Court Funds (Amendment) Rules 2003 (S.I. 2003 No. 375).

The Accountant General can take no responsibility for any delays, losses, etc., where, for whatever reason, a cheque or payable instrument on presentation is returned by the Bank as unacceptable, *i.e.* insufficient funds, unauthorised signatory, etc. It is the responsibility of the payer to notify the other parties of any delays, non-compliance, etc.

6A–61   (5) Lodgments of money which are not required to be paid into the Court Funds Office under this rule to which rule 19 applies shall be made directly to the bank to the credit of the Accountant General's account.

(6) The effective date of lodgment of money lodged under paragraph (1) shall be:—

(i) in the case of cash or a banker's draft, the date of its receipt in the Court Funds Office;

(ii) in the case of a cheque or instrument other than a banker's draft the date of its receipt in the Court Funds Office or such later date as the Accountant General may determine;

(iii) in the case of a lodgment to which paragraph (5) applies, the date certified by the Bank as that on which the money was placed to an account of the Accountant General.

(7) Any person who desires or is directed to pay money into a District Registry or county court under any enactment, other than a payment to which rule 15 applies, and who has complied with the requirements of the relevant Civil Procedure Rules shall pay the money into the appropriate court office, by a cheque or other instrument made payable to the Accountant General of the Supreme Court which shall be forwarded to the Accountant General within one working day of the date of receipt.

(8) The effective date of lodgment of money paid in under paragraph (7) shall be the date of its receipt in the court office.

6A–62   *Note* —Amended by S.I. 1988 No. 817 and S.I. 1999 No. 1021.

[THE NEXT PARAGRAPH IS 6A–64.]

Securities transferable by delivery and deposit of effects

6A–64   17.—(1) The lodgment in the Supreme Court of securities transferable by delivery and the deposit of effects shall be made either by delivery to the Court Funds Office or, if the Accountant General so directs, by delivery to the Bank.

(2) Where lodgment under paragraph (1) is made by delivery to the Bank:—

> (i) effects so delivered shall be secured in locked boxes or otherwise to the satisfaction of the Bank, and any person delivering effects shall, if the Bank so requires, permit them to be inspected in his presence by an officer of the Bank; and

> (ii) the Bank shall give a written receipt for the delivery of any securities or effects.

(3) Any person who deposits effects in court in accordance with these Rules shall provide the Accountant General with an inventory of those effects signed and certified by him as a true and accurate record.

(4) Any person who desires or is directed to deposit securities in a county court under any statute, and has complied with the requirements of the relevant Civil Procedure Rules, shall deposit the securities with the proper officer who shall give the depositor a receipt of the deposit and shall forward the security certificate or certificates to the Accountant General.

Note —Amended by the Court Funds (Amendment) Rules 1999 (S.I. 1999 No. 1021).

Return of lodgment directions

18.—(1) Where—   **6A–65**

> (i) money lodged directly with the Bank has been received and credited to the Accountant General's account, or

> (ii) securities transferable by delivery and effects have been delivered to the Bank, or

> (iii) securities (other than those transferable by delivery) have been transferred into the Accountant General's name in the books of the Bank or in the books of a company,

the Bank or Company, as the case may be, shall certify on the lodgment direction issued under rule 14 that the funds have been lodged and shall send it to the Court Funds Office.

Payment of money into a District Registry or county court

19.—(1) A litigant in person without a current account may pay **6A–66** money into a District Registry or a county court in accordance with paragraph (2).

(2) Where paragraph (1) applies payment shall be made—

> (i) in cash;

> (ii) at the appropriate court office during office hours on any day on which the office is open; and

> (iii) the court officer shall give a receipt for it.

(3) Payments shall be forwarded to the Accountant General within one working day of the date of receipt.

19A. The effective date of lodgment paid in under rule 19 shall be the date of its receipt in the court office.

20.[Revoked by S.I. 1990 No. 518.]

21.[Revoked by S.I. 2003 No. 375.]

22. An officer of a District Registry or county court who receives money under the process of the court shall give a written receipt for every sum so received in the form prescribed.

23.[Revoked by S.I. 2003 No. 375.]

24. Where—

    (a) money has been paid into court in a claim proceeding in the Royal Courts of Justice; and

    (b) the claim is transferred to a District Registry or county court, the court officer of the court to which the claim is transferred shall notify the Accountant General.

Note — Amended by the Court Funds (Amendment) Rules 2003 (S.I. 2003 No. 375).

PART III

APPROPRIATION

Appropriation

6A–67   **25.**—(1) Where a defendant has paid money into court in accordance with a court order and wishes to treat the whole or any part of the money paid into court as a CPR Part 36 payment (in these Rules referred to as "appropriation") he shall file a notice of appropriation with the Accountant General.

(2) The effective date of appropriation shall be the date of the receipt of the notice of appropriation by the Accountant General.

(3) [Omitted]

(4) On receipt of a notice of appropriation the Accountant General shall note the relevant account accordingly and shall withdraw the sum mentioned in the notice from the basic account.

(5) The Accountant General shall place money in the basic account 21 days after he has received the notice of appropriation, unless before that date he receives a request for payment from the claimant.

(6) Where, before appropriation, interest has accrued on the money in question the interest may be included in the appropriation, and this rule shall apply to the interest in the same way as it applies to the money lodged.

6A–68   *Note* — Amended by the Court Funds (Amendment) Rules 2003 (S.I. 2003 No. 375).

Where money lodged in court on or before March 31, 1983, and by that date had been directed by the court to be placed to short-term investment account, now special account, the money will remain so invested until the Accountant General receives a notice of appropriation under this rule or until alternative directions to deal with the money are received from the court. (See r.8(1) of S.I. 1983 No. 290).

The defendant is entitled to any part which has accrued on the sum which he has appropriated in satisfaction of the claim under this rule (see *Schroeder v. Accountant General* [1980] 1 W.L.R. 1314; [1980] 2 All E.R. 648).

PART IV

PLACING OF MONEY ON DEPOSIT AND INVESTMENT OF FUNDS

Establishment of interest bearing accounts

26. There shall be established the following two interest bearing **6A–69** accounts, namely a basic account (that is to say, a deposit account) and a special account (that is to say, an investment account) to which shall accrue, in accordance with these Rules, interest derived from the transfer to, and investment by, the National Debt Commissioners of the money placed to all the accounts of those kinds.

Note —This rule re-establishes the two interest bearing accounts under different **6A–70** names. Basic account and special account replace money on deposit and short term investment account respectively.

Interest on money placed to an interest bearing account

27.—(1) The rate at which interest on money placed to a basic ac- **6A–71** count or a special account is to accrue shall be as prescribed from time to time by a direction made by the Lord Chancellor with the concurrence of the Treasury.

(2) Interest on money placed to a basic account or a special account shall accrue from day to day from the day on which the money is placed to the account until the day preceding its withdrawal from the account.

(3) Unless the Accountant General directs otherwise, accrued interest shall be credited:—

(i) on the capital sum when it is withdrawn from the account; or

(ii) on transfer of the capital sum from a basic account to a special account; and

(iii) on the last Friday in March and the last Friday in September each year in respect of money placed to a basic account and on the last Friday in May and the last Friday in November each year in respect of money placed to a special account.

(4) Accrued interest shall be credited without deduction of income tax.

Note —Amended by S.I. 1988 No. 817; and S.I. 1999 No. 1021. **6A–72**

Time for placing money to an interest bearing account

28.—(1) Subject to the provisions of this part of the Rules and to **6A–73** any direction of the court, all money (including interest) shall be placed to a basic account or, in the case of a person under disability, to a special account, on the day on which the schedule or other authority is received in the Court Funds Office or on the effective date of lodgment of the money, whichever is the later.

(2) Where judgment is given in favour of a person under disability, or settlement of his claim is approved by the court the money to which he is entitled shall, subject to any directions of the court, be placed to a special account in his name as at the date of the judgment or on the effective date of lodgment of the money, whichever is the later, without further authority.

(3) Interest shall not accrue from a date earlier than that on which the money is placed to an interest bearing account in accordance with this Rule.

(4) This rules does not apply to money—

    (a) paid into court; or

    (b) appropriated

to which Rule 31 applies.

6A–74 *Note* —Amended by the Court Funds (Amendment) Rules 1999 (S.I. 1999 No. 1021).

Money not to be placed to a basic account

6A–75 29. Money, including interest, shall not be placed to a basic account where the money:—

    (i) has been directed by an order or another authority to be dealt with other than by being placed to a basic account; or

    (ii) has been carried over to an account of unclaimed balances under Rule 57; or

    (iii) stood to the credit of a fund in court before 1st October 1965, without a request that it be placed on deposit; or

    (iv) was paid into court in satisfaction of a claim before 1st April 1983, without a direction that it be placed on deposit; or

    (v) amounts to a sum which is less than £10.

Money to be placed to a special account

6A–76 30. Money, including interest, shall only be placed to a special account where the person entitled to it is under a disability, and it amounts to a sum which is not less than £10.

Money paid in satisfaction, etc.

6A–77 31.—(1) **Where money has been—**

    (a) paid into court in accordance with CPR Part 36; or

    (b) appropriated in accordance with CPR rule 37.2

in satisfaction of a claim, it shall only be placed to a basic account 21 days after the effective date of lodgment or appropriation and not before.

(2) [Omitted]

(2A) Paragraph (1) shall not apply where a request for payment from the claimant is received within the 21 days specified in that paragraph.

(3) [Omitted]

(4) Where money is remitted under rules 16(7) or 19(3) the remittance shall be accompanied by a notice stating the date and the reason why the money was paid into court.

(5) Where the claimant is under a disability money lodged or paid into court under paragraphs (1) or (2) shall be placed to a basic account in any event, whether or not he has accepted it, until the claim is determined or settlement is reached, unless the court otherwise directs.

Note — Amended by the Court Funds (Amendment) Rules 2003 (S.I. 2003 No. **6A–78** 375).

When money has been lodged in court but interest has not started to accrue on it before April 1, 1983, any party may apply for such money to be placed to a basic account and where the court makes such an order the money will be treated thereafter in accordance with the provisions of these rules.

Interest on money paid in satisfaction

32.—(1) Subject to paragraph (4), interest on money remitted to **6A–79** the Court Funds Office in satisfaction of a claim under rule 19(3) shall start to accrue 21 days after the effective date of payment into the District Registry or county court.

(2) Subject to paragraph (4), where money is paid into a District Registry or county court in such circumstances that it is to await the outcome of an order of court, whether it is paid into court as a condition of obtaining relief or otherwise, interest shall start to accrue from the effective date of payment into the District Registry or county court

(3) Where a court determines a claim, or, as the case may be, approves a settlement on behalf of a person under a disability, any interest which has accrued on the money in court shall be dealt with as the court orders.

(4) Where money has been—

(a) placed to a basic account under rule 31(1); and

(b) accepted by the claimant within the time limit specified in CPR rule 36.11

no interest shall be payable after the effective date of lodgment or appropriation, or where there has been more than one lodgment or appropriation, after the latest effective date of lodgment or appropriation.

Note — Amended by the Court Funds (Amendment) Rules 2003 (S.I. 2003 No. 375).

Withdrawal of money from an interest bearing account

33. Money shall only be withdrawn from an interest bearing account where the money, including any interest which has accrued at the time of withdrawal, is required to be withdrawn for the purpose of giving effect to a direction of the court or these Rules; provided that such interest shall not be used if directed by the court to be otherwise dealt with.

PART V

RANGE OF INVESTMENTS

Range of Investments

6A–81   34.—(1) Subject to paragraph (3), money under the control of, or subject to an order of the court, may be invested or reinvested by the Accountant General in accordance with these Rules, in the following ways:—

    (i) it may be placed to a basic account or; in the case of a person under a disability, to a special account;

6A–82   *Note* —Where money has been lodged in court on or before March 31, 1983, and by that date had been directed by the court to be placed to short term investment account, now special account, the money will remain so invested until the Accountant General receives from the court alternative directions to deal with the money.

6A–83   —

    (ii) it may be transferred to such of the funds established by common investment schemes as may be specified;

    (iii) it may be invested in any manner specified in Part I, paragraphs 1 to 10 and 12 of Part II and paragraphs 2, 2A and 3 of Part III of Schedule 1 to the Trustee Investments Act 1961, as supplemented by the provisions of Part IV of that Schedule;

    (iv) it may be invested in investment trust ordinary shares.

(2) Money subject to an order of the court may be invested or reinvested in accordance with instructions received by him from the Public Trustee.

(3) Money under the control of or subject to an order of the Court of Protection may be invested or reinvested by the Accountant General in such investments as that court may direct.

6A–84   *Note* —Amended by S.I. 1991 No. 1227; S.I. 1997 No. 177 and S.I. 2003 No. 720.

Time for investment

6A–85   35. Subject to the provisions of Part IV and this Part of the Rules and to any directions of the court, money, including interest, shall be invested as soon as it is available.

6A–86   *Note* —A commission for a purchase of a security is passed to the Private Client Fund Managers on the day following that on which the directions of the court have been received in the Court Funds Office or on which the money is available (whichever is the later). The security purchased will be credited to the suitor's account as soon as it is delivered by the brokers.

Amount for investment

6A–87   36.—(1) Notwithstanding Rule 34, no sum of money or interest shall be invested in any case where in the view of the Accountant General the cost of investment, by way of commission or otherwise, would be disproportionate to the amount of money involved.

(2) Any money which is not invested shall be placed, in the case of a person under a disability, to a special account and in all other

cases to a basic account and shall be drawn from the account and invested when it, together with the interest credited to it, and further sums of money or interest credited to the account which are required to be invested in the same manner, amount to a sum in respect of which the cost of investment is not disproportionate.

Investment in Common Investment Fund

37.—(1) Where funds are required to be invested in Common **6A–88** Investment Fund units or such units are required to be realised, the purchases and sales shall be effected on the first available valuation day.

(2) Funds shall not be directed to be invested in Common Investment Fund Units unless the authority giving the direction is satisfied that the funds are likely to remain so invested for at least five years: provided that this paragraph shall not apply in any case where there is an express request for investment in Common Investment Fund Units by or on behalf of one or more of the persons interested in the fund, or, if no such person is ascertained or traceable, by the person who pays the funds into court.

[THE NEXT PARAGRAPH IS 6A–90.]

PART VI

DEALING WITH FOREIGN CURRENCIES

Dealing with Foreign Currencies

38.—(1) Foreign currency may only be lodged in court when:— **6A–90**
    (i) it is lodged in the Supreme Court in accordance with CPR Part 36 in satisfaction of a claim for a debt or liquidated demand, and is in the currency in which the claim is made; or
    (ii) the court so directs or permits.

(2) Foreign currency lodged in accordance with paragraph (1) shall be paid into court in the manner approved by the Accountant General.

39.—(1) Where foreign currency is lodged in court, the court may **6A–91** direct that it shall be placed in an interest bearing account in that currency or any other currency, and any interest shall accrue from the date of the order or the date of placing it in the account, whichever is the later; and the Accountant General shall deal with the interest as the court may direct.

(2) Any charges incurred by placing foreign currency to an account shall be deducted from the currency so placed or from the accrued interest, as may be appropriate.

(3) Where income from a security in court is received in a foreign currency, the court may give such direction as it thinks fit, and in the absence of such direction the foreign currency shall be converted into sterling and invested in accordance with the provisions of Part IV.

COURT FUNDS

6A–92 *Note* —Amended by the Court Funds (Amendment) Rules 1999 (S.I. 1999 No. 1021).

As to the manner of dealing with foreign currency lodged into court, see Practice Direction (Offers to Settle and Payments Into Court) para. 9.1 (Vol. 1,para. 36PD.9).

Prior consultation is advisable with the Court Funds Office on all dealings with foreign currencies.

PART VII

PAYMENT, TRANSFER AND DELIVERY OF FUNDS OUT OF COURT

Payments out of money by post and identification of payees

6A–93   40.—(1) In this rule, the person entitled to the payment out of money lodged in court is referred to as the payee.

(2) Subject to paragraphs (4) and (10) below, the payment out of money lodged in court may be made by the Accountant General, to a bank in the United Kingdom by means of the Bankers' Automated Clearing System for the credit of the account of the payee at the bank.

(3) The Payment Schedule shall provide the necessary details of the payee's bank and account to enable a payment to be made under paragraph (2) above.

(4) In cases where:

    (i) the Payment Schedule or supplementary authority is dated not more than one year prior to the date on which the Accountant General is able to make payment, he shall make payment as soon as is practicable;

    (ii) the Payment Schedule or supplementary authority is dated more than one year prior to the date on which the Accountant General is able to make payment, he shall make payment on receipt of a written request from the payee.

(5) On receipt of a written request from a donee under a power of attorney given by the payee, the Accountant General may make payment by means of the Bankers' Automated Clearing System to a bank in the United Kingdom for the credit of the account of the payee at the bank.

(6) Where the Accountant General does not make a payment by means of the Bankers' Automated Clearing System under paragraph (2) above, he shall make the payment by a cheque crossed "account payee" by post in accordance with paragraph (8).

(7) In cases where:

    (i) the payee does not have an account which is suitable for the receipt of funds by means of the Bankers' Automated Clearing System; or

    (ii) there is a written request from the payee for the payment to be made by cheque;

the Accountant General shall make the payment by a cheque crossed "account payee".

(8) Where the Accountant General makes a payment under paragraph (6) or (7) above, it shall be sent by post as follows:

    (i) where the address of the payee is stated in the Payment Schedule or supplementary authority and that schedule or authority is dated not more than one year prior to the date on which the Accountant General is able to make payment, he shall make payment to the payee at the address so stated;

    (ii) where the Payment Schedule or supplementary authority is dated more than one year prior to the date on which the Accountant General is able to make payment, he shall make payment on receipt of a written request from the payee and, in a case where there has been a written request under paragraph (7)(ii) above, that request shall be sufficient for the purposes of this sub-paragraph.

(9) The Accountant General may, if he thinks fit:

    (i) refuse to make a payment until he is satisfied as to the identity and entitlement of any person claiming to be the payee and may require the personal attendance of the payee at the Court Funds Office or a court office as a condition of payment;

    (ii) refuse to make a payment by means of the Bankers' Automated Clearing System in any individual case if the Payment Schedule is not completed with sufficient information or for another good reason.

Note —Amended by S.I. 1997 No. 177.   **6A–94**

The Treasury has empowered the Accountant General at his discretion to dispense with evidence in the case of (1) holders of ecclesiastical benefices provided that remittance is made direct to *them*; (2) payment to treasurers and other officials of public bodies provided that the cheques are crossed to the accounts of the public bodies and remitted direct to their bankers; and (3) payments of dividends in Court of Protection matters.

There are, however, cases in the Court of Protection where evidence is required, *e.g.* where periodical payments are made to individuals who are not receivers.

As to the Form of Declaration by a person entitled to payment (Evidence of Life, etc.) see C.F.O. Form No. 206.

In the Chancery Division, as to Notice of Creditors see C.F.O. Form No. 207 and as to Notice to Security Holders see C.F.O. Form No. 208.

As to form of Request for Remittance to Payee's Bank see C.F.O. Form No. 205.

If payment is directed to be made to two or more payees the cheque will be remitted to the first named payee in the Schedule at his address stated therein.

When a request for payment is provided in accordance with para. (2)(i):

If the payment is to one of the two persons, or to two or more of a large number, a postal request will be acted upon if signed by the required minimum number of the payees.

If the payees are executors or administrators, the request need only be signed by one of them. The cheque will be crossed to the account of the payees as executors or administrators as the case may be.

In the case of unincorporated trustees all must sign the request, and the cheque will be crossed to the trust account.

Special arrangements apply to payments in foreign currencies and prior consultation with the Court Funds Office is advisable.

Payments to foreign companies under powers of attorney

Powers of attorney executed by foreign companies should have attached thereto an **6A–95** affidavit made preferably by a notary public before a British consular official, proving:—

 (1) that the company is duly constituted and registered in accordance with the local law of the foreign country;

 (2) that A., B., and C. (the signatories) are respectively directors and secretary (as the case may be) of the said company, and that it has no common seal (if such is the case); and

 (3) that the company is bound and engaged by the signature of A., B., and C., in accordance with the statutes (or articles of association) of the said company, and the local law.

 The reference in 40(2) to paragraph (10) is incorrect as there is no paragraph (10). It should refer to paragraph (9).

Payments to residents outside the United Kingdom

6A–96 In cases where payment is directed to a person who is resident outside the United Kingdom a request should be provided stating the bank in the United Kingdom to which payment may be made either for the credit of the payee's accounts there or for transfer to his account at a bank in the country in which he resides (this bank must also be stated).

Payment etc. after a change of name or style

6A–97 41. Where a person entitled to payment of a fund in court changes his name or style before the fund is paid, transferred or delivered to him, the Accountant General shall, except where payment is to be made to the person as Receiver under Part VII of the Mental Health Act 1983, require evidence of the change before dealing with the fund.

6A–98 *Note*—This rule enables the Accountant General to take proof of the marriage of a payee entitled to payment as legal personal representative or trustee as well as in her own right; there is now no limit to the amount that can be paid on proof of marriage. The rule further provides for the payment to a woman entitled as a receiver, who marries, upon the written request of the Master of the Court of Protection. On the marriage of a female child, payment to her guardian is continued unless the Court otherwise orders.

Payment pursuant to direction of the Court of Protection

6A–99 42. Where a patient is entitled to a fund in court (other than pursuant to an order made under Part VII of the Mental Health Act 1983) the Accountant General shall, on receipt of a direction from the Master of the Court of Protection, either pay the money to the patient's Receiver or carry it over to such account as the Master may direct.

Payment, etc. to representatives of deceased persons

6A–100 43.—(1) Where a person entitled to a fund in court either in his own right or as sole, or sole surviving, executor dies, the Accountant General may, where the fund exceeds £5,000, pay it to the personal representative of the deceased on production of a grant of probate or office copy thereof, or, where the deceased was entitled to the fund in his own right, letters of administration in respect of the deceased's estate.

 (2) Where a person entitled to a fund in court in his own right dies intestate and no grant of administration has been issued, the Accountant General may, where the assets of the deceased (including

the fund in court and after deduction of debts and funeral expenses) do not exceed £5,000, pay the fund to the person who appears to him to have the prior right to a grant of administration of the estate, on lodgment in the Court Funds Office of a written declaration of kinship.

(3) Where two or more persons were entitled to payment of a fund in court as personal representatives and any of them dies before the fund is dealt with, the Accountant General may pay the fund to the surviving personal representatives on proof of the death of the deceased personal representative; and where the fund does not exceed £5,000 the Accountant General may, unless a court otherwise directs, pay the fund to any one of them.

Payment out without order of money lodged in satisfaction

44.—(1) In this Rule and in Rule 45 a person in respect of whose **6A–101** cause of action a sum has been paid into court in satisfaction, whether by way of claim or counterclaim, is referred to as a claimant and a person against whom such a cause of action lies is referred to as a defendant.

(2) Subject to paragraph (2B), the Accountant General shall, on receipt of a written request, pay:

     (i) by cheque crossed "account payee" to the claimant, or

     (ii) to a bank in the United Kingdom by means of the Bankers' Automated Clearing System for the credit of the account of the claimant at the bank,

money lodged in court in satisfaction of a claim, or appropriated in accordance with Rule 25, and accepted by him in accordance with Rule of Court: provided that where a solicitor is acting for the claimant in the proceedings in which the money was lodged or appropriated by virtue of a certificate issued under the code approved under section 9 of the Access to Justice Act 1999 certifying a decision to fund services for the claimant as part of the Community Legal Service under sections 4 to 10 of that Act, the Accountant General shall pay the money to that solicitor, or to the Legal Services Commission if the claimant is no longer represented by the solicitor, but further provided that the Accountant General's obligation under this paragraph to pay the money to the solicitor or to the Legal Services Commission shall apply only to the extent that regulation 18(1) of the Community Legal Service (Costs) Regulations 2000 applies to that money.

(2A) The written request under paragraph (2) above shall, where payment is to be made under sub-paragraph (ii) of that paragraph, provide the necessary details of the claimant's bank and account.

(2B) In cases where:

     (i) the claimant does not have an account which is suitable for the receipt of funds by means of the Bankers' Automated Clearing System; or

     (ii) there is a written request from the claimant for the payment to be made by cheque;

the Accountant General shall make the payment by a cheque crossed "account payee", to the claimant by post.

(2C) The Accountant General may, if he thinks fit, refuse to make a payment by means of the Bankers' Automated Clearing System in any individual case if the claimant fails to provide him with sufficient information under paragraph (2A) above or for another good reason.

[THE NEXT PARAGRAPH IS 6A–103.]

6A–103

(3) [*Repealed by S.I. 1999 No. 1021.*]

(4) The Accountant General shall not make any payment under paragraph (2) where:—

    (i) money has been lodged by one, or some, only of several defendants sued jointly or in the alternative, unless the plaintiff discontinues the action against all the other defendants and those defendants consent in writing to the payment, and a copy of the notice of discontinuance and the written consent of each consenting defendant required by CPR rule 36.17(2) is lodged with the Accountant General; or

    (ii) a defence of tender before action has been pleaded; or

    (iii) the claim is made by, or on behalf of, a child or a patient; or

    (iv) money has been lodged in proceedings under the Fatal Accidents Act 1976 and the Law Reform (Miscellaneous Provisions) Act 1934, or under the first mentioned Act alone where more than one person is entitled to the money; or

        (a) payment into court has been made less than 21 days before the start of the trial; or

        (b) the claimant has not accepted a payment into court within the time limit in CPR rule 36.11(1);

    (v) except in the circumstances provided by CPR rule 36.11(2)(i).

6A–104   *Note*—Amended by S.I. 1997 No. 177 and S.I. 1999 No. 1021.

Payment out of interest

6A–105   45. Where money lodged or appropriated by the defendant in satisfaction of the whole of the claim has been accepted and paid to the claimant, the Accountant General shall pay any accrued interest remaining in court in respect of that claim to the defendant but no interest shall be payable after the date on which the claimant serves notice of acceptance.

   Note—Amended by the Court Funds (Amendment) Rules 1999 (S.I. 1999 No. 1021).

Payment out of interest on securities

6A–106   46. Where securities are lodged in court under Rule 15 or money lodged under that Rule is invested, any interest which accrues shall (subject to any contrary provision contained in the relevant enactment) be paid by the Accountant General to the person in whose name the lodgment was made.

Transfer or delivery of securities

47.—(1) Subject to paragraph (2) where pursuant to directions of **6A–107** the court or under these Rules the Accountant General is required to transfer or deliver any securities or effects held in his name he shall issue directions accordingly which shall be sufficient authority for the transfer or delivery and, in the case of a transfer of securities on sale, for the Bank to receive the proceeds of sale.

(2) The directions of the Accountant General shall not be required for the transfer of National Savings Stock, on sale or otherwise.

Note —Instructions as to transfer or delivery will be issued by the Court Funds Of- **6A–108** fice on receipt of the appropriate payments schedule.

A transfer may be liable to Inland Revenue Stamp Duty and, now very occasionally, a company registration fee.

The transfers will be effected by the Court Funds Office who will, in due course, forward the new stock certificates to the solicitors on the record without any request or production of the order of court.

Delivery of bearer securities etc. requires the personal attendance of an identified solicitor or bank official at the Court Funds Office and the Bank of England.

Charges on purchase or sale of securities

48. Except where Rule 34 applies and subject to any directions of **6A–109** the court:—

(i) where money in court is invested in the purchase of se- curities, the payment for the purchase shall include all applicable charges; and

(ii) where securities in court are sold, all applicable charges shall be deducted from the proceeds of sale:

provided that, if the schedule directing a purchase or sale also directs that charges are not to be deducted from the fund in court, the transaction shall not be completed until such charges have been paid either to the stockbroker or to the Accountant General, as the case may be.

Note —When a schedule directs a purchase or sale "without deducting any ap- **6A–110** plicable charges" (*i.e.* that these deductions are not to be charged to the account, but otherwise provided for) the Court Funds Office will notify the solicitor having carriage of the order of the amount of these charges and inform him that the purchase or sale as the case maybe, cannot be completed until the total amount of the charges has been paid.

Sales are effected by the Accountant General when, and to the extent that, the proceeds thereof can be applied as directed.

A commission for a sale of a security is passed to a broker on the day following receipt of the payment schedule or other subsidiary document. The proceeds of the sale will usually be credited to the suitor's account approximately five working days afterwards.

Application of funds dealt with before receipt of Payment Schedule

49. Unless otherwise directed by the court, where an order has **6A–111** been made dealing with a fund and, after the date of the order but before the Payment Schedule relating to it is received in the Court Funds Office, interest has accrued or money and interest have been dealt with in accordance with a previous direction of the court or under these Rules, the part of the fund attributable to accrued inter- est or to money or interest shall be treated as follows:—

    (i) interest on securities directed to be transferred, delivered or carried over shall be dealt with as the securities are directed to be dealt with under the Payment Schedule;

    (ii) interest which has accured on securities directed to be sold shall be dealt with as the proceeds of sale are directed to be dealt with under the Payment Schedule, except where the sale is to raise a specified sum of money, when the interest is included with the capital;

    (iii) where interest which has accrued on securities directed to be transferred, delivered or carried over has been invested in the purchase of further securities, the securities so purchased and any interest on them shall be dealt with as the original securities are directed to be dealt with;

    (iv) where interest which has accrued on securities directed to be sold has been invested in the purchase of further securities, the securities so purchased shall be sold and the proceeds of sale added to the proceeds of the original securities;

    (v) money or accrued interest which has been placed to a basic or special account shall be withdrawn and, together with any interest credited on withdrawal, applied as directed by the Payment Schedule: provided that where such money is directed to be invested, any interest credited on withdrawal shall be applied as interest accruing on the investment is directed to be applied.

Payment of suitors' money out of a District Registry or county court

6A–112   **50.** [Revoked by S.I. 2003 No. 375.]

Specially created account

6A–113   **51.**—(1) In apportioning to any account the interest received in respect of securities the Accountant General shall exclude all fraction of one penny and shall carry over the aggregate of such fractions to a specially created account.

    (2) The Accountant General shall from time to time transfer to the cash account of Her Majesty's Paymaster General, for the credit of the Administration of Justice: England and Wales (Lord Chancellor's Department) Vote all sums standing to the specially created account.

PART VIII

CONVERSION, ALLOTMENT AND WRITE-OFF OF SECURITIES

Application to the court concerning conversion and allotment

6A–114   **52.** Where a question has arisen as to an allotment or conversion of securities which have been paid into court under section 63 of the

Trustee Act 1925, or in any other case in which he considers it appropriate because no application will otherwise be made, the Accountant General may apply to the court for directions as to how the securities should be dealt with.

Conversion and allotment of securities

53.—(1) Where a security in court has been converted into another security the Accountant General shall write-off the original security from the account to which it is standing and shall place to that account the whole, or where appropriate a proportionate part, of the substituted security and shall, so far as practicable and unless otherwise directed by the court, deal with the substituted security and any interest on it in the same manner as the original security and interest. **6A–115**

(2) Where a security in court is paid off and the money received is invested or placed to an interest bearing account, the security purchased or money in the account and any interest on it shall, unless the court otherwise directs, be dealt with by the Accountant General in the same manner as the original security and interest.

(3) Where an allotment is made in respect of a security in court the Accountant General may:—

    (i) credit the whole, or where appropriate a proportionate part, of the allotment to the account of the original security if the allotment is fully paid; or

    (ii) sell the allotment and credit the whole, or a proportionate part, of the proceeds of sale to that account or otherwise as the Court may direct if the allotment is not fully paid; or

    (iii) sell any non-apportionable shares and apportion such proceeds as nearly as practicable to the appropriate account.

Note —The usual brokerage and VAT are charged by the broker for a sale under this rule. **6A–116**

When a bearer security is allotted in lieu of interest it may be delivered to the person entitled to the interest.

Arrangements with the Bank over paid off securities, etc.

54.—(1) Where bearer or similar bonds or securities deposited at the Bank to the credit of the Accountant General are being paid off, the Bank shall take the necessary steps to receive the principal money and interest due and shall inform the Accountant General in writing of the amounts of the securities paid off and of the principal money and interest received. **6A–117**

(2) Where the interest on securities in court is payable on the presentation of coupons in a series and the last coupon of any such series has been presented and paid, the Bank shall take the necessary steps to obtain a new series of coupons.

Note —Money received in respect of securities paid off will be placed to basic account (see r.28) except as provided by r.29, and interest received on such account may **6A–118** be dealt with in the same manner as the interest on the security paid off was dealt with, the basic account being regarded as a substituted security (see r.53(2)).

Securities of dissolved companies

6A–119 55. Where a company has been wound up and the Accountant General has received:—

> (i) written notice from the liquidator or from the Department of Trade that no assets are or will be distributable in respect of the securities of the company; and
>
> (ii) written notice from the Registrar of the Companies Registration Office that the company has been dissolved;

he shall withdraw from the Bank the certificate representing any security in that company and shall write-off any such security from the account to which it stands.

PART IX

NATIONAL DEBT COMMISSIONERS

National Debt Commissioners

6A–120 56.—(1) Where, in the opinion of the Accountant General, the cash balance in his account at the Bank exceeds the amount that he requires to satisfy current demands, he shall remit the excess to the National Debt Commissioners; and where, in his opinion the balance is insufficient to meet such demands, the Commissioners shall remit to that account such amount as the Accountant General may in writing request.

(2) As soon as practicable after half-yearly interest accruing on money placed to an interest bearing account has been credited to the appropriate account in accordance with these Rules, the Accountant General shall certify to the National Debt Commissioners the amount of the interest and the Commissioners shall credit that amount to the account kept by them of money received from the Accountant General.

PART X

UNCLAIMED FUNDS IN COURT

Unclaimed funds

6A–121 57.—(1) Subject to the provisions of this Rule, the Accountant General may carry over an unclaimed fund in court to an account of unclaimed balances when ten years have elapsed since an account was opened for the fund.

(2) Subject to paragraph (3), a fund shall be treated as unclaimed if:—

> (i) it stands to the credit of an account which has not been dealt with for a period of ten years otherwise than by the continuous investment or placing on deposit of ac-

crued interest, the compulsory conversion, redemption or acquisition of securities or the placing on deposit of any money arising therefrom; and

(ii) the Accountant General is satisfied that all reasonable steps have been taken to trace the person entitled to it and to pay it to him.

(3) Where a fund was lodged in court for the benefit of a minor, the period of ten years mentioned in paragraph 2(i) shall not begin to run until the minor's 18th birthday, or, if his date of birth is not known, until 18 years have elapsed since the account was opened.

(4) Where the person entitled to a fund was a patient, the Accountant General may at any time, if so requested by the court officer of the Court of Protection, and provided he is satisfied that all reasonable steps have been taken to trace the person entitled to the fund and to pay it to him, carry the fund over to an account of unclaimed balances.

(5) In the case of a fund paid into court by the Public Trustee under the Trustee Act 1925, the Accountant General may at any time, provided he is satisfied that all reasonable steps have been taken to trace the person entitled to the fund and to pay it to him, carry the fund over to an account of unclaimed balances.

(6) On receipt of a Payment Schedule directing a dealing with a fund carried over in accordance with this Rule, the Accountant General shall carry back the unclaimed balance to the appropriate account.

(7) Where a fund is carried back under paragraph (6) simple interest shall be credited to the fund in respect of the whole period during which the fund stood to an account of unclaimed balances at the rate of interest prescribed at the date when the fund is carried back, for money placed in a basic account.

Note —Amended by the Court Funds (Amendment) Rules 1999 (S.I. 1999 No. **6A–121.1** 1021), r.2(b), and S.I. 2000 No. 2918.

Lists of unclaimed funds

58.—(1) The Accountant General shall maintain a list of the ac- **6A–122** counts in respect of which funds have been carried over to an account of unclaimed balances under rule 57, which may be inspected at the Court Funds Office during normal office hours.

(2) The court officer of each county court shall maintain a list of unclaimed funds in the custody of that court, which may be inspected at the Court office; and he shall send to the Accountant General a copy of the list from time to time.

Note —Amended by the Court Funds (Amendment) Rules 1999 (S.I. 1999 No. **6A–123** 1021), r.2(b).

The Accountant General may in his discretion supply information regarding an unclaimed fund in court on receipt of a written request from a person claiming to have a beneficial interest in the fund or from a solicitor acting on his behalf. Such information will not be given verbally in the Court Funds Office.

As to the nature of the information which the Accountant General can provide see notice in paras 6A–163 to 6A–170.

Disposal of unclaimed effects in court

6A–124 59.—(1) Where effects have been deposited in court on or after 3rd July 1978 and have been carried over to an account of unclaimed balances under Rule 57, the Accountant General may send to the court a copy of an inventory provided to him in accordance with Rule 17(3) in respect of such effects when 25 years have elapsed since he received the authority for such lodgment.

(2) On receipt of an inventory sent in accordance with paragraph (1) the court may:—

  (i) cause enquiries to be made whether any party to the proceedings in which the effects were deposited wishes to make any application in respect of them, or whether any other person who may have an interest in the effects can be found; and

  (ii) of its own motion and without reference to any party or person (other than a party or person who may have an interest and whose whereabouts or the whereabouts of whose personal representatives are known), order the final disposal of the effects by sale, realisation or otherwise; provided that the court shall not order the destruction of any effects unless it is satisfied that they have no realisable value.

(3) For the purpose of any reference to a party or other person who may have an interest in the effects in question it shall not be necessary to revive any proceedings which may have abated or to issue any summons unless the court so directs and an order for such final disposal may be made after oral or written communication with such party or person.

(4) The amount of the net proceeds of any sale or realisation under paragraph (2) should be certified by the court officer and placed to the credit of the unclaimed balance account in which the effects were held prior to the sale or realisation.

6A–124.1 *Note* —Amended by the Court Funds (Amendment) Rules 1999 (S.I. 1999 No. 1021), r.2(b).

Disposal of unclaimed securities in court

6A–125 60.—(1) Where any securities (including Common Investment Fund units) are carried over under Rule 57, or are standing to an account of unclaimed balances on 1st June 1987 the Accountant General shall sell the securities and pay the proceeds into the account of unclaimed balances.

(2) The Accountant General shall write-off any securities carried over under Rule 57 or standing to an account of unclaimed balances on 1st June 1987 which have no value.

(3) Where any sum carried over under Rule 57 stands to an interest bearing account the Accountant General shall withdraw the sum and place it to the account of unclaimed balances.

Repayment of closed county court funds

6A–126 61.—(1) Where a fund in a county court has been closed a person may apply to the court at which the fund account was kept for repayment of all or part of the fund to him.

(2) Where the court is satisfied that the claimant is entitled to the whole or part of the fund, it may order the payment to him of money standing to the credit of the account as at the date of its closure or of a sum of money representing the value of the fund at the date of its closure.

(3) Where the Court makes an order under paragraph (2) the court officer shall send a sealed copy of the court's order to the Accountant General.

(4) On receipt of the order the Accountant General shall take such steps as may be necessary to give effect to it, and shall forward a remittance for the amount of the fund to the claimant.

Note —Amended by the Court Funds (Amendment) Rules 1999 (S.I. 1999 No. **6A–127** 1021), r.2(b).

Unclaimed money in county court

62. This part of these Rules shall apply, with such modifications as **6A–128** may be necessary, to unclaimed moneys in a county court which have not been dealt with for a period of one year immediately before the preceding 1st March.

Note —Amended by S.I. 1988 No. 817.   **6A–129**

The Court Manager of a court may in his discretion supply information regarding unclaimed money in that court on receipt of a written request from a person claiming to have a beneficial interest or from a solicitor acting on his behalf. Such information will not be given verbally.

PART XI

CERTIFICATES IN RESPECT OF FUNDS IN COURT

Certificates of funds in court, copies of accounts, etc.

63.—(1) The Accountant General may, on receipt of a written **6A–130** request from a person appearing to him to be interested in a fund in court, issue to him a certificate as to lodgment in court, non-payment into court under an order, carry over of the fund to an account of unclaimed balances or any other dealing with the fund; and the certificate shall, where appropriate, state the account to which the fund has been placed, the amount standing to its credit, and particulars of any charges or restraints on the fund of which the Accountant General is aware.

Note —The date of lodgment is the date defined in r.16(6) and is not necessarily the **6A–131** date on which a cheque is received in the Court Funds Office.

(2) On receipt of a written request the Accountant General may **6A–132** issue to a person appearing to him to be interested in a fund in court a copy of the account relating to the fund, which shall be authenticated by the National Audit Office if that person so requires.

(3) The Accountant General shall supply an annual statement of

any fund in court for the benefit of a child to that person or to his representative.

6A–133 *Note* —Copies of accounts will normally consist of computer produced copies and/or photo-copies of the suitor's account and will be available within one week of the day on which they are applied for.

If the account was opened prior to the introduction of a mechanised accounting system, a transcript book must be provided to cover that earlier period. In these circumstances it may be necessary to extend the period for preparation beyond one week.

Copies of accounts for the use of Masters and other officers of the courts will have precedence.

If so requested, the Accountant General will supply the prices at which securities have been purchased or realised with the copy of the account.

Should the copy of account require authentication, it may be sent by post to the National Audit Office, Buckingham Palace Road, Victoria, London SW1W 9SP. No fee is charged for the authentication.

As to the form of Request for Copy of Account see C.F.O. Form No. 300.

SCHEDULE

RULES REVOKED

6A–134

Title		Reference
Supreme Court Funds	Rules 1975	S.I. 1975/1803
Supreme Court Funds (Amendment)	Rules 1976	S.I. 1976/2235
Supreme Court Funds (Amendment)	Rules 1979	S.I. 1979/106
Supreme Court Funds (Amendment No. 2)	Rules 1979	S.I. 1979/1620
Supreme Court Funds (Amendment)	Rules 1980	S.I. 1980/1858
Supreme Court Funds (Amendment)	Rules 1981	S.I. 1981/1589
Supreme Court Funds (Amendment)	Rules 1982	S.I. 1982/123
Supreme Court Funds (Amendment No. 2)	Rules 1982	S.I. 1982/787
Supreme Court Funds (Amendment)	Rules 1983	S.I. 1983/290
Supreme Court Funds (Amendment)	Rules 1984	S.I. 1984/285
Supreme Court Funds (Amendment)	Rules 1986	S.I. 1986/1142
County Court Funds (Amendment)	Rules 1982	S.I. 1982/436
County Court Funds (Amendment No. 2)	Rules 1982	S.I. 1982/1140
County Court Funds (Amendment No. 3)	Rules 1982	S.I. 1982/1794
County Court Funds (Amendment)	Rules 1983	S.I. 1983/275
County Court Funds (Amendment No. 2)	Rules 1983	S.I. 1983/1716
County Court Funds (Amendment)	Rules 1984	S.I. 1984/576
County Court Funds (Amendment No. 2)	Rules 1984	S.I. 1984/878
County Court Funds (Amendment)	Rules 1985	S.I. 1985/566
County Court Funds (Amendment No. 2)	Rules 1985	S.I. 1985/1269
County Court Funds (Amendment)	Rules 1986	S.I. 1986/636
County Court Funds (Amendment No. 2)	Rules 1986	S.I. 1986/1189

6A–135 The forms relating to Court Funds are reproduced in the Civil Procedure Forms Volume.

[THE NEXT PARAGRAPH IS 6A–160.]

THE INVESTMENT OF FUNDS IN COURT

6A–160 *Note* —In addition to the investments authorised by CPR Pt 21; A.J.A. 1982, Pt VI provides for the continuing methods of investment in the Supreme Court and the Court of Protection, namely

    (a) investments in the common investment funds under the management and control of an investment manager appointed by the Lord Chancellor (as detailed below)—see the Court Funds Rules 1987, r.37;

    (b) investments in a special investment account for persons under a disability (also detailed below)—see the Court Funds Rules 1987, rr.28 and 30.

Common Investment Funds

The Lord Chancellor has made a scheme (the Common Investment Funds Scheme **6A–161** 2004 (S.I. 2004 No. 266)) under the powers conferred on him by the A.J.A. 1982, Pt VI for the establishment of common investment funds. These funds are administered by a fund manager in a manner similar to a unit trust and are intended for money which is likely to remain invested for a period of five years or more.

Special Investment Account (formerly short term investment account)

Money is placed in a basic account but in the case of a person under disability, **6A–162** money is placed in a special investment account (see the Court Fund Rules 1987, r.28). The special account is particularly suitable for money which is unlikely to remain invested for a long time and which may have to be withdrawn, in whole or in part, at comparatively short notice.

The money is transferred by the court to the National Debt Commissioner and invested by them; the return of the capital is guaranteed £ for £ and this guarantee is backed by the Consolidated Fund.

The manner of crediting interest is set out in the Court Funds Rules 1987, r.27(1). Interest accruing to a special investment account is credited without the deduction of income tax.

The rate of interest on this investment is fixed by the Lord Chancellor and the Treasury.

The current rate of interest is 6 per cent per annum and came into force on February 1, 2002. See list of rates set out at para. 6A–171.

Dormant funds in court

Dormant funds are generally cash accounts under the control of the court which **6A–163** have had no action on them for ten years. The majority are small accounts of under £150.

Until 1938, lists of funds with £50 or over were published every five years as supplements to the London Gazette. This was abolished in favour of annually prepared lists of accounts which can be inspected, free of charge, in the Court Funds Office, 22 Kingsway, London WC2B 6LE.

Applications for information

A search will be made on application in writing. The application should provide **6A–164** some evidence of beneficial interest. Whenever possible, the title of the court action or of an account title should be quoted and must relate solely to funds which have been, or are believed to have been, lodged in England and Wales.

It is unwise to send *original* documents such as certificates of birth, marriage or death with an application for search.

Applicants are notified of the results of searches and, when an account is traced, are given a statement of the funds credited to it and any other helpful information available.

The Court Funds Office is an accounting office which does not hold records of origin. It cannot answer queries regarding descent or relationship, or advise on the selection of legal advisers. It can only release a dormant fund, in an appropriate case, by an order of court and an order can only be sought from the court of origin.

Sources of information

The High Court of Justice

Enquiries regarding orders and documents of the High Court in London should be **6A–165** made as follows:—

(a) **Companies Winding Up Proceedings**
To inspect Orders, apply to:
Companies Court
Thomas More Building
Royal Courts of Justice
London WC2A 2LL

(b) **Chancery Chambers**
Apply in the first instance to:
Chancery Chambers
Royal Courts of Justice
London WC2A 2LL

(c) **Court of Protection**
Apply to:
Public Guardianship Office
Archway Tower
2 Junction Road
London N19 5SZ

(d) **Family Division**
Apply to:
Principal Registry of the Family
Division
First Avenue House
42–49 High Holborn
London WC1V 6NP

(e) **Other sources**
Wills, Probate and Letters of
Administration
Principal Probate Registry
First Avenue House
42–49 High Holborn
London WC1V 6NP

(f) **Public Trustee Matters**
Apply in the first instance to:
The Official Solicitor and Public
Trustee Office
81 Chancery Lane
London WC2A 1DD

(g) **Births, Marriages and Deaths**
Applications in person:
The Family Records Centre
1 Myddleton Street
London EC1R 1UW

Postal applications:
General Register Office
P.O. Box 2
Southport
Merseyside PR8 2JD

(h) **Public Records**
Public Records Office
Kew
Richmond
Surrey TW9 4DU

Scotland

6A–166   Enquiries concerning Scottish estates which have fallen to the Crown in default of heirs should be made to: Queen's and Lord Treasurer's Remembrancer, Crown Office, 25 Chambers Street, Edinburgh, EH1 1LA.

Enquiries concerning funds lodged in the Court of Session and other unclaimed sums resulting from company liquidations, bankruptcies, judicial factories etc. are held by Accountant of Court, Parliament House, Edinburgh EH1 1RQ for a period of seven years from the date of consignation. After this date, they are transferred to the Queen's and Lord Treasurer's Remembrancer at the address above.

Other enquiries may be made to the Keeper of the Records of Scotland, New Register House, 3 West Register Street, Edinburgh, EH1 3YT or Ladywell House, Ladywell Road, Edinburgh, EH12 7TF.

Republic of Ireland

6A–167   For funds under the control of the Supreme Court and High Court of Justice in Ireland write to the Accountant of the Courts of Justice, 3rd Floor, 15/24 Pheonix Street North, Smithfield, Dublin 7.

Northern Ireland

6A–168   For funds lodged in Court in Northern Ireland, write to the Accountant General, Court Funds Office, 3rd Floor, Bedford House, Bedford Street, Belfast, BT2 7DS.

[For records prior to the institution of the Supreme Court in Northern Ireland in 1921 contact The Accountant of the Courts of Justice in Dublin].

A caution

6A–169   You are cautioned against relying upon the statements of persons claiming to be "unclaimed money agents" at home or abroad, and to be able to recover money in Chancery on payment of fees or percentage, or to act on behalf of the "Court of Chancery". The Supreme Court of Judicature has no such agents.

It is recommended that independent advice should be taken before making a payment to any agency in respect of money alleged to be in Court.

Inspection of Orders of Court, etc.

Orders, reports and certificates and affidavits prior to 1954 are kept, in the case of **6A–170**
general Chancery proceedings, and in companies winding-up proceedings, if prior to 1949, at the Legal Room, Public Record Office, Kew, Richmond, Surrey TW9 4DU. If the date and description of the documents and the title of the cause be given, copies may be obtained on application to the Secretary, but it must be understood that no search can be undertaken by the officials of the Public Record Office.

Access to old Chancery orders, certificates and affidavits is available in Room TM3.07, Thomas More Building. Old Queen's Bench orders, certificates and affidavits are retained at the Royal Courts of Justice (Room E07).

Applications to inspect orders in companies' winding-up proceedings from 1949 to the present time, may be made at the Companies Winding-up Department, Thomas More Building, Royal Courts of Justice, London WC2A 2LL.

Applications for permission to inspect orders in Court of Protection matters may be made at the Public Guardianship Office, Archway Tower, 2 Junction Road, London N19 SZ.

Inquiries respecting wills, probates and letters of administration may be made at the Principal Probate Registry, First Avenue House, 42–49 High Holborn, London WC1V 6NP. Such inquiries should state the full names and the date of death of the testator or intestate.

Records of births, marriages and deaths, since July 1, 1837, are kept at the Family Records Centre, 1 Myddleton Street, London EC1R 1UW.

The above records can be inspected during official hours or copies obtained on payment of the prescribed fees.

Special and Basic rates from October 1, 1965

Set out below are the interest rates which accrue on: **6A–171**
   (a) the High Court and County Court Special Accounts, *i.e.* investment accounts, formerly the Short Term Investment accounts; and
   (b) the High Court and County Court Basic accounts, *i.e.* deposit accounts, formerly the Money on Deposit accounts.

| High Court Special (formerly S.T.I.) | | | High Court Basic (formerly M.O.D.) | | |
Date	Rate	S.I.	Date	Rate	S.I.
1.10.65	5	65/1466	1.10.65	2^1/$_2$	65/1466
1.09.66	5^1/$_2$	66/876	1.04.71	3^1/$_2$	71/259
1.03.68	6	68/106	1.04.73	4	73/231
1.03.69	6^1/$_2$	69/206	1.02.77	5	76/2235
1.03.70	7	70/121	1.04.83	9^1/$_2$	83/290
1.03.71	7^1/$_2$	71/259	1.04.84	8	84/285
1.03.73	8	73/231	1.08.86	7^1/$_2$	86/1142
1.03.74	9	74/207	1.01.87	8^1/$_2$	86/2115
1.02.77	10	76/2235	1.12.87	8	Lord Chancellor's direction d/d 23.11.87
1.03.79	12^1/$_2$	79/106			
1.01.80	15	79/1620			
1.01.81	12^1/$_2$	80/1858	1.05.88	7^1/$_2$	Lord Chancellor's direction d/d 22.4.88

High Court Special (formerly S.T.I.)			High Court Basic (formerly M.O.D.)		
Date	Rate	S.I.	Date	Rate	S.I.
1.12.81	15	81/1589			
1.03.82	14	82/123			
1.07.82	13	82/787	1.08.88	9	Lord Chancellor's direction d/d 19.7.88
1.04.83	12½	83/290			
1.04.84	12	84/285			
1.08.86	11½	86/1142	1.11.88	10¼	Lord Chancellor's direction d/d 22.10.88
1.01.87	12¼	86/2115			
1.04.87	11¾	Lord Chancellor's direction d/d 30.3.87	1.01.89	10¾	Lord Chancellor's direction d/d 21.12.88
1.11.87	11¼	Lord Chancellor's direction d/d 19.10.87	1.11.89	11¼	Lord Chancellor's direction d/d 27.10.89
1.12.87	11	Lord Chancellor's direction d/d 23.11.87	1.04.91	9½	Lord Chancellor's direction d/d 25.3.91
1.05.88	9½	Lord Chancellor's direction d/d 22.4.88	1.10.91	8	Lord Chancellor's direction d/d 20.9.91
1.08.88	11	Lord Chancellor's direction d/d 19.7.88	1.02.93	6	Lord Chancellor's direction d/d 27.1.93
1.11.88	12¼	Lord Chancellor's direction d/d 22.10.88	1.08.99	5¼	Lord Chancellor's direction d/d 14.7.99
			1.02.02	4	Lord Chancellor's direction d/d 7.1.02
1.01.89	13	Lord Chancellor's direction d/d 21.12.88			

High Court Special (formerly S.T.I.)			*High Court Basic (formerly M.O.D.)*		
Date	Rate	S.I.	Date	Rate	S.I.
1.11.89	14¼	Lord Chancellor's direction d/d 27.10.89			
1.04.91	12	Lord Chancellor's direction d/d 25.3.91			
1.10.91	10¼	Lord Chancellor's direction d/d 20.9.91			
1.02.93	8	Lord Chancellor's direction d/d 27.1.93			
1.08.99	7	Lord Chancellor's direction d/d 14.7.99			
1.02.02	6	Lord Chancellor's direction d/d 7.1.02			

County Court Special (formerly S.T.I.)			*County Court Basic (formerly M.O.D.)*		
Date	Rate	S.I.	Date	Rate	S.I.
1.10.65	5	65/1500	1.10.65	2½	65/1500
1.09.66	5½	66/875	1.03.71	3½	71/260
1.03.68	6	68/107	1.03.73	4	73/230
1.03.69	6½	69/204	1.03.77	5	76/2234
1.03.70	7	70/228	1.04.83	9½	83/291
1.03.71	7½	71/260	1.04.84	8	84/285
1.03.73	8	73/230	1.08.86	7½	86/1142
1.03.74	9	74/206	1.01.87	8½	86/2115
1.03.77	10	76/2234	1.12.87	8	Lord Chancellor's direction d/d 23.11.87
1.03.79	12½	79/105			
1.01.80	15	79/1619			

COURT FUNDS

County Court Special (formerly S.T.I.)			County Court Basic (formerly M.O.D.)		
Date	Rate	S.I.	Date	Rate	S.I.
1.01.81	12¹/₂	80/1857	1.05.88	7¹/₂	Lord Chancellor's direction d/d 22.4.88
1.12.81	15	81/1588			
1.03.82	14	82/124			
1.07.82	13	82/786	1.08.88	9	Lord Chancellor's direction d/d 19.7.88
1.04.83	12¹/₂	83/291			
1.04.84	12	84/285			
1.08.86	11¹/₂	86/1142	1.11.88	10¹/₄	Lord Chancellor's direction d/d 22.10.88
1.01.87	12¹/₄	86/2115			
1.04.87	11³/₄	Lord Chancellor's direction d/d 30.3.87			
			1.01.89	10³/₄	Lord Chancellor's direction d/d 20.12.88
1.11.87	11¹/₄	Lord Chancellor's direction d/d 19.10.87	1.11.89	11¹/₄	Lord Chancellor's direction d/d 27.10.89
1.12.87	11	Lord Chancellor's direction d/d 23.11.87	1.04.91	9¹/₂	Lord Chancellor's direction d/d 25.3.91
1.05.88	9¹/₂	Lord Chancellor's direction d/d 22.4.88	1.10.91	8	Lord Chancellor's direction d/d 20.9.91
1.08.88	11	Lord Chancellor's direction d/d 19.7.88	1.02.93	6	Lord Chancellor's direction d/d 27.1.93

County Court Special (formerly S.T.I.)			County Court Basic (formerly M.O.D.)		
Date	Rate	S.I.	Date	Rate	S.I.
1.11.88	12¼	Lord Chancellor's direction d/d 22.10.88	1.08.99	5¼	Lord Chancellor's direction d/d 14.7.99
1.01.89	13	Lord Chancellor's direction d/d 21.12.88			
1.11.89	14¼	Lord Chancellor's direction d/d 27.10.89	1.02.02	4	Lord Chancellors' direction d/d 7.1.02
1.04.91	12	Lord Chancellor's direction d/d 25.3.91			
1.10.91	10¼	Lord Chancellor's direction d/d 20.9.91			
1.02.93	8	Lord Chancellor's direction d/d 27.1.93			
1.08.99	7	Lord Chancellor's direction d/d 14.7.99			
1.02.02	6	Lord Chancellors' direction d/d 7.1.02			

COURT FUNDS

6B COURT OF PROTECTION

GENERAL

The Mental Health Act 1983

The Mental Health Act 1983, came into operation on September 30, 1983, and has **6B–1** effect with respect to the reception care and treatment of mentally disordered patients, the management of their property and other related matters. "Mental disorder" is a generic term, statutorily defined in s.1(2), embracing all forms of unsoundness of mind to which previous Acts applied. See para. 6B–185.

The terms "lunatic", "persons of unsound mind" and "defectives" are obsolete; they all fall into one class of "persons suffering from mental disorder".

So far as rendering a person liable to compulsory detention or guardianship is concerned, the Act recognises four forms of mental disorder, namely, mental illness, severe mental impairment, psychopathic disorder and mental impairment (see Mental Health Act 1983, ss.3(2) and 7(2)) but the particular form of mental disorder has no special significance when the question of ability to manage one's affairs is concerned.

The Act contains no definition of "mental illness". The words have to be construed in the way that ordinary sensible people would construe them (see *W. v. L. (Mental Health Patient)* [1974] Q.B. 711; [1973] 3 All E.R. 884).

Wherever possible patients are now admitted voluntarily for treatment with absence of formality (s.131). A magistrate's order is no longer necessary to secure the admission and detention of a patient against his will, this normally being secured by an application, duly supported by medical evidence, to the managers of the hospital or mental nursing home concerned (ss.3–6). Provision is also made for guardianship in suitable cases (ss.7–8).

Part VII of the Act (set out at paras 6B–186 *et seq.*) deals with the management of the property and affairs of mental patients and the jurisdiction of the Court of Protection. The rules are the Court of Protection Rules 2001 made pursuant to ss.106, 107 and 108 of the Mental Health Act 1983 and s.54(2) of the Trustee Act 1925.

The Court of Protection

The Court of Protection and the Protection Division of the Public Guardianship Of- **6B–2** fice (PGO) are situated at Archway Tower, 2 Junction Road, London, N19 5SZ. Tel: 0845 330 2900, DX: 141150 Archway 2, Fax: 0870 739 5780. The purpose of the jurisdiction of the court is to protect and administer the property and affairs of persons who are incapable by reason of mental disorder of managing and administering their own property and affairs (Mental Health Act 1983, ss.93(2) and 94(2)). The court also has jurisdiction in relation to the Enduring Powers of Attorney Act 1985 (see paras 6B–358 *et seq.*) It has no jurisdiction over the management or care of the patient's person (*Re W.* [1971] 1 Ch. 123) or whether the patient should undergo a surgical operation, including an operation for sterilisation (*F. v. West Berkshire Health Authority, sub nom. Re F.* [1989] 2 W.L.R. 1025).

The offices are open to the public between the hours of 10 a.m. and 4.30 p.m. on working days, which are as prescribed for the Supreme Court offices (O.64, r.7).

All correspondence should be sent to the above address and the case number and any court reference on correspondence should be quoted.

The Judge

Pursuant to s.93(1) of the Act, the Lord Chancellor has nominated all the judges for **6B–3** the time being of the Chancery Division to act for the purposes of Pt VII of the Mental Health Act 1983 (Court of Protection matters).

Any matters dealt with by the judge are taken at the Royal Courts of Justice. Sometimes this will be in the judge's private room, though more frequently in court as chambers; if the matter is to be heard in court, the usual practice is for it to be *in camera* but subject to the safeguard of anonymity, matters of principle, and particularly the judgments, should be dealt with in public (see *Re W. (E.E.M.)* [1971] Ch. 123).

The Court of Protection Registrar, subject to the provisions of r.55(3) arranges for parties to be notified of the time fixed for the hearing and draws and settles the order at the Court of Protection.

The Master

Generally speaking the jurisdiction of the judge under Pt VII of the Act and other **6B–4** enactments is exercised by the master, (and other nominated officers—see r.3 of the Court of Protection Rules and s.94), though certain matters are reserved to the Lord Chancellor or a nominated judge (see s.104(3)). Unless the contrary is stated or the context otherwise requires, the term "master" in these notes includes the Assistant masters or other nominated officer. In practice the master deals with applications for statutory wills, large gifts and complex disputes and the Assistant masters deal mainly with contentious receivership work.

All applications are returnable before the master who will usually deal with the matter although there is power to refer any matter to the nominated judge.

Consideration of applications

6B–5   It is primarily a matter for country solicitors whether or not London agents are instructed in matters relating to the Court of Protection. All first applications for the appointment of a receiver and formal applications, save those mentioned below, are stamped on issue "Attendance not required unless notified." Attendance will therefore be required only when the master so directs or the persons concerned wish to attend.

If the master requires the attendance of solicitors in connection with applications, country solicitors are at liberty either to instruct London agents or to attend themselves.

Patient or property outside England and Wales

6B–6   A receiver will be appointed in respect of a patient resident abroad but only where there is property within the jurisdiction, *i.e.* England and Wales (*Ex p. Southgate* (1751) 2 Ves. Sen. 401; *Re Scott* (1874) 22 W.R. 748; *Re Soltykoff* [1898] W.N. 77). As to reciprocal jurisdiction between Scotland and Northern Ireland and this country, see s.110 of the Mental Health Act 1983. Briefly, the effect is that, as between Scotland and Northern Ireland on the one hand and England and Wales on the other hand, so long as jurisdiction has been invoked in one country only (treating England and Wales as one country) that jurisdiction is effective to deal with property, other than land or interests in land, in the other country. As to the power of a foreign curator in respect of movable property in this country, see *Didisheim v. London and Westminster Bank* [1900] 2 Ch.15.

Section 100 of the Mental Health Act 1983 (see para. 6B–197) provides a convenient procedure where:

(a) stock, or the proceeds thereof is or are to be remitted to a foreign curator; or

(b) dividends only are to be remitted and the stock consists of gilt-edged or other securities suitable to be retained indefinitely; or

(c) although dividends only are to be remitted and although the stock consists of equities unsuitable for permanent retention, it is proposed that the stock be sold and re-invested in securities suitable to be retained indefinitely.

The procedure is *not* suitable where the stock is to be retained in this country and consists of or comprises equities or short-term gilts. In such cases a receiver will usually be required.

Where stock is to be retained and an order is made under s.100, it is usually convenient to lodge the securities in court. This has the advantages of safeguarding the stock certificates and providing for the court's fees.

It should be noted that s.100 of the Mental Health Act 1983, relates exclusively to stock, as defined by the section, *standing in the name of a patient* beneficially, so that stock vested in a foreign curator on behalf of a patient, the subject of foreign jurisdiction, would not fall to be dealt with thereunder. Further, the section should not be invoked if a receiver has already been appointed by the Court of Protection or where the stock in question stands in the name of the patient as trustee.

Where a receiver is to be appointed, it is usually convenient to appoint as receiver a nominee of the foreign curator residing in this country. A receiver can only be appointed if there is medical evidence before the court to satisfy the requirements of s.94(2) of the Mental Health Act 1983. There is no reason why an office copy of a medical affidavit sworn in the foreign proceedings should not, in suitable cases, be accepted as establishing the jurisdiction of the court (see r.27 of the Court of Protection Rules).

Generally as regards practice, see Heywood and Massey, *Court of Protection Practice*, 2002 Edition, 1–035 to 1–042.

As to court fees payable on any application and order made, see paras 6B–316 and 6B–337.

Jurisdiction of Chancery Division

The question of the jurisdiction of the Chancery Division to deal with property of **6B–7** persons of unsound mind has for long been the subject of many decisions, often conflicting. The whole subject and the authorities were exhaustively reviewed by Megarry J. in *Re K.'s Settlement Trusts* [1969] 2 Ch. 1, and he decided that the Chancery Division would exercise jurisdiction, assuming it existed at all, only if the property in question were small, the income therefrom would plainly all be used up in the patient's maintenance (so that there would be no likelihood of surplus income to be dealt with) and the Chancery Division already had some control of the property by reason of some pending proceedings, thus having "seisin". Further, such jurisdiction is at most discretionary and it is better that the Chancery Division "should leave to the Court of Protection that specialist jurisdiction which it exercises with such experience and understanding and not to attempt, with less adequate tools, to exercise an overlapping jurisdiction in a limited and ill-defined category of cases" (*Re K.'s Settlement Trusts*, above, p.7).

In the course of the judgment the further condition of its not being possible for an application to be made to the Court of Protection was also mentioned but, assuming evidence to satisfy s.94(2) of the Act were available, it is not readily seen how this situation could arise. In any event, where the patient's affairs are being dealt with by the Court of Protection, it would seem the Chancery Division would not exercise jurisdiction as this would be an interference with the control of the patient's affairs by the Court of Protection (see *Re Winkle* [1894] 2 Ch. 519; *CL v.C FW* [1928] P. 223; *Swettenham v. Swettenham (By her Guardian)* [1938] P. 218 and *Re A Debtor (No. 1 of 1941)* [1941] Ch. 487).

Minor (Infant) under mental disability

The jurisdiction of the Family Division over a minor ward is not ousted by his being **6B–8** in such a state as would, if he were adult, attract the jurisdiction of the Court of Protection (*Re Edwards* (1879) 10 Ch.D. 605). The Court of Protection has jurisdiction to deal with the affairs of a minor patient, and will do so in a proper case. See Heywood and Massey, *Court of Protection Practice* 2002 edition, para. 1–006. Where damages are recovered on behalf of a minor patient, the Court of Protection will now usually accept jurisdiction to administer such damages if the minor patient is likely to survive until attaining his majority and is not likely to recover before then.

Where judicial relief is only required to enable a minor's property to be applied for his maintenance and there are no family disputes as to what should be done, the jurisdiction of the Court of Protection is usually to be preferred to that of the Family Division, particularly when the minor is approaching his majority; where, however, questions of maintenance are mixed up with family disputes as to where he shall live, and under whose custody, the matter is one for the Family Division.

As to administration of damages by the court of Protection, see para. 6B–115.

As, with few exceptions, transfers in favour of a minor of stocks and shares cannot be registered, any investments on behalf of minors (including the purchase of equities) are usually made in the name of the Accountant General in court. Exceptionally, investment might be made in the name of the receiver or in the names of trustees.

Appeals

See s.105 and rr.54 and 55. On an appeal from the master to the judge, the notice **6B–9** of appeal is lodged in the Protection Division and is then forwarded to the appropriate nominated judge. The Court of Protection Registrar sits as Registrar not only on appeals to the judge but on appeals to the Court of Appeal (see "The Judge", para. 6B–3).

An appeal from the judge in a Court of Protection matter under s.105(2) of the Mental Health Act 1983 lies to the Court of Appeal without leave (*Re Cathcart* [1893] 1 Ch. 466; *Re Cathcart* [1902] W.N. 80; see also *Moore v. Commissioner of Metropolitan Police* [1968] 1 Q.B. 26; [1967] 2 All E.R. 827). Generally as to Court of Protection appeals, see Heywood and Massey, *Court of Protection Practice* 2002 Editon, paras 3–033 to 3–037.

See *Re D. (J.)* [1982] Ch. 237; [1982] 2 All E.R. 37 as to the discretion of the nominated judge in an appeal from the master against the contents of a statutory will.

Forms

See r. 2(2)(c) and the Schedule to the Rules. The following forms may be obtained **6B–10** (free) from the Protection Division:

Fees

6B–11   See rr.76–86 and the Appendix to the Rules. Payment of fees may be made as follows:

(i) in cash at the Protection Division, Archway Tower, 2 Junction Road, London N19 5SZ;

(ii) by cheque or postal order made payable to the Public Guardianship Office and crossed and sent by post to the Protection Division.

APPOINTMENT AND DISCHARGE OF RECEIVER

(a) First Application

General note

6B–12   The jurisdiction to appoint a receiver stems from ss.94(2) and 99 of the Mental Health Act 1983. In particular it must be noted that the jurisdiction is, normally, only exercisable where, after considering medical evidence, the court is satisfied that the person in question is incapable, by reason of mental disorder (see s.1) of managing and administering his property and affairs, though under s.98 there is jurisdiction to deal with cases of emergency without conclusive evidence of incapacity.

The question of the degree of incapability of managing and administering a patient's property and affairs must be related to the circumstances, including the state in which he lives and the complexity and importance of the property and affairs which he has to administer, and the court has a discretion of deciding whether in these circumstances and upon the facts it is right for a receiver to be appointed (*Re C. A. F.*, March 23, 1962; unrep., CA transcript 62/2367, *per* Wilberforce J.).

If the property of the patient does not exceed £16,000 in value, the application, using the same prescribed forms as for an application for the appointment of a receiver may ask for a Short Order enabling, *inter alia*, for a suitable person to apply the assets and income of the patient for his or her benefit. A Commencement fee of £240 is payable (see para. 6B–303).

Mode of application

6B–13   Proceedings are by way of application (r.7) usually in the form of a letter unless the court directs that it should be formed in which case it shall be made as in Form A in the Schedule to the Rules.

The application is issued in the Protection Division. A commencement fee of £240 payable (see para. 6B–303).

Withdrawal of application

6B–14   An application can only be withdrawn with the consent of the court. It is a matter for the master's discretion whether the master allows an application to be disposed of by withdrawal, dismissal or staying further proceedings, or whether the master appoints as receiver a person, willing to be so appointed, notwithstanding that the applicant or any other person objects.

Applicants and receivers

6B–15   The spouse or other nearest relative is normally the applicant and where the application is not so made the reason should be stated in the evidence. Relatives of a degree nearer than, or equal to, that of the applicant to the patient, should be notified and the court should be informed that this has been done (r.25). The Rules, however, do not lay down who is to apply and, accordingly, when the circumstances so require the application could be made by any person interested, *e.g.* the patient's solicitor, a trustee, a creditor or a friend.

It is usual to appoint a near relative as receiver. Until recent times it was not the normal practice to appoint the solicitor in the matter (see *Ex p. Pincke* (1817) 2 Mer. 453; *Re Lloyd* (1879) 12 Ch.D. 447), but in the absence of any other suitable person the court now often considers favourably such an appointment. In suitable cases the court will authorise the solicitor so appointed to charge profit costs for work not usually requiring professional assistance (see r.87). Where the appointment of some other professional person with remuneration is sought, *e.g.* an accountant or estate agent, directions as to remuneration should be asked for in the evidence of family and property and the suggested amount specified. The general practice is to direct remuneration (when granted) to be fixed subsequently, normally on the passing of the receiver's accounts. Generally as to remuneration see r.43.

An accounting party will not be appointed unless and until his accounts are clear. Joint receivers are not usually favoured.

Normally the court requires that the proposed receiver should be resident in England or Wales.

The court has power to direct that the application be made by an officer of the court or (if he consents) by the Official Solicitor (see r.11). In the absence of any suitable relative or other person the court may appoint a Panel Receiver or in exceptional circumstances an officer of the court to act as receiver.

Death of applicant

If the applicant dies before the application is considered or the entry of the order, **6B–16** the application cannot proceed until a new applicant is substituted, for which purpose the master's direction is required. The solicitor should file a statement giving the following information:

(i) The date of death of the applicant;

(ii) The name, address, occupation and relationship to the patient of the proposed new applicant;

(iii) The name, address, occupation and relationship to the patient of the proposed receiver (if other than originally proposed) together with the name, address and occupation of a referee;

(iv) Details of any change of the patient's circumstances caused by applicant's death;

(v) Whether service of notification has been effected on the patient and when.

The statement should be accompanied by a certificate of death of the applicant, and what is said above as to an original applicant and notification of relatives applies. The master's direction for substitution will be endorsed on the court's copy of the application (if any) and on the original and the application is then amended and sealed in the usual way. If service had been effected before the applicant's death no further service is required but, if not, the notification should be served on the patient showing, if necessary, the substituted receiver.

If the proposed receiver (not being the applicant) dies before the hearing or the entry of the order, some other person can be appointed without amendment of the proceedings.

Documents and evidence

The printed forms required for the application are obtainable free of charge (in **6B–17** sets) from the Protection Division. The following are necessary:

(i) Medical Certificate (Form C.P. 3)

(ii) Statement of assets and income (Form C.P. 5). The statement includes provision for details of the applicant and the proposed receiver.

(iii) Receiver's Declaration

Service of notice

The application itself is not served on the patient but notification of the application **6B–18** (Form C.P.6) is served on him personally (see r.24). The necessary forms are provided without request on the issue of the application.

Service of the notice (which is left with the patient) should be effected as soon as possible after the issue of the application, and at least 10 clear days before the return date (r.19). Otherwise service is bad and the case will have to be adjourned to another date to enable service to be effected in due time In any event the order may not be entered until the expiration of 10 clear days from service (r.46(1)). The patient is, of course, at liberty, if he is able, to instruct solicitors on his behalf or if he so wishes may communicate with the court by post, addressing his letter to "The Court of Protection, Archway Tower, 2 Junction Road, London, N19 5SZ"

Interim order and direction

In any case where the circumstances necessitate that immediate steps be taken a **6B–19** receiver *ad interim* may be appointed forthwith (r.42(1)(b)) before comliance with the requirements as to notification (r.46(2)). The solicitor should file the normal appropriate medical evidence unless, in an exceptional case, under the provision of s.98 of the Mental Health Act 1983, it is intended to endeavour to persuade the court to make the order on lay evidence only. The master may require the solicitors to attend before her/him at the time of the issue of the application or as soon thereafter as can be arranged.

The order is drafted immediately, and settled and engrossed without delay. It is usual for the receiver *ad interim* to be authorised to act at once before giving security and for him to be directed in the order to give security in the sum fixed as soon as he reasonably can. The order also states that a copy of the order is to be served upon the patient within a certain specified time (usually 14 days) and that he may apply within (usually) 14 days for reconsideration of the order (r.44(2)).

The usual practice as to the issue of orders applies (see "Entry and sealing of order," para. 6B–25). Evidence of service (which may be in certificate form unless the court otherwise directs) of the copy order *ad interim* should be filed before the date the formal application is due to be considered. Generally, see Heywood and Massey, *Court of Protection Practice* 2002 edition, paras 4–028 to 4–034.

If money is required for maintenance or other necessary requirements before the order appointing a receiver can be drawn up, or any other urgent matter arises but the circumstances of the case do not warrant the appointment of a receiver *ad interim*, it may well be possible to deal with the matter by an interim certificate or direction under r.42(1)(a). An *interim* sale of land will be authorised by order not by certificate.

A commencement fee of £240 is payable—see para. 6B–303.

Where the court makes an interim order for sale, the order will, if thought fit, contain directions for service on the patient as if it were an order appointing a receiver *ad interim* in accordance with the provisions of r.42(2).

The order

6B–20   As indicated in para. 6B–5 attendance on the consideration of the application will seldom be necessary. Where an attendance is required the persons concerned should first ask to see the appropriate Branch Officer who will then take them to the master concerned.

In making the appropriate order the master has to consider the case as a whole. The following are some of the more important points upon which it is usual to give directions on a first application:

   (i) The person to be appointed receiver.
   (ii) Amount of receiver's security (if any) (see para. 6B–24, "Security").
   (iii) Directions as to maintenance of the patient and, if necessary, any dependant; upkeep of establishment, etc. if the patient is living at home.
   (iv) Payment of debts.
   (v) Retention or sale of property, including, in the case of house property or land, letting powers for periods not exceeding three years.
   (vi) Carrying on or closing down of a patient's business.
   (vii) Deposit of securities and deeds and perhaps jewellery at a bank for safe custody. Patient's wills are usually allowed to remain deposited with the solicitor who prepared them—but otherwise they are deposited at a bank.
   (viii) Lodgment in court of securities or cash.
   (ix) Costs (see paras 6B–155 *et seq.*).

Objection by alleged patient

6B–21   It is the right of a person to require that the free use of his property, and personal freedom, shall not be taken away from him on the ground of alleged incapability without his being allowed the opportunity of establishing his capacity or denying his mental disorder (previously before a jury) not merely as a subject of inquiry (*Re Cumming* (1852) 1 De G.M. & G. 537 at 545). See also Heywood and Massey, *Court of Protection Practice* 2002 edition, para. 4–024 and para. 6B–159.

Draft order and settlement

6B–22   Only in exceptional circumstances are draft orders now sent out for approval. The order is drafted and any additional information called for. It is then engrossed and dispatched to the solicitors having carriage of the order.

Normally five copies of the engrossment are prepared by the court for use as follows:

(i) The original retained by the court.

(ii) The file copy also retained by the court.

(iii) The receiver's plain copy specially noted on the indorsement "This copy to be retained in the personal custody of the receiver."

(iv) Two office copies. It is, however, open to solicitors to request further copies, if required.

Where there is a lodgment and payment schedule to the order an additional copy of such schedule alone is prepared for the use of the Court Funds Office and is transmitted direct.

Note —If the order entails the execution of a deed, *e.g.* on a sale of land, an ad- **6B–23** ditional copy for placing with the title deeds should be requested.

Appointment Fee

An appointment fee of £315 is payable upon the appointment of a receiver for a **6B–23A** patient – r.77A as amended by the Court of Protection (Amendment) Rules 2002, 2004 and 2005.

A request for the fee is despatched when the Order is made. If the patient dies or the proceedings are otherwise terminated less than four weeks from the appointment of a receiver, the appointment fee will be refunded if it has been paid or, if it has not been paid, it will cease to be payable.

Security

Where the court directs that security be given (r.56) it is usually in such a sum as **6B–24** will with a reasonable margin cover the annual amount passing through the receiver's hands; and where at any time the receiver is directed to receive capital money temporary increase of such security may, in some cases, be directed. Security can be effected by one of the four following methods (r.57):

(a) *By a Bond with a Guarantee Society* in which case the proposal form must be fully completed by the receiver and forwarded to the company selected. The annual premium will be payable out of the Patient's estate. A list of the companies approved by the court is made available.

(b) *By use of a simplified arrangement with HSBC Insurance Brokers Limited* in which case an endorsement supplied by the Public Guardianship Office should be signed, witnessed and sent to HSBC Insurance Brokers Limited together with the premium.

(c) *By a Bond given by Personal Sureties*. This method is not advocated for many reasons, *e.g.* the expense incurred in the execution of a new bond on the death or bankruptcy of one of the sureties.

The bond is prepared as in (a) above, but the court's sanction is required; the solicitor prepares the affidavits of sufficiency and due execution.

The bond and the affidavits, when complete, are filed with the Public Guardianship Office. See as to maintenance of security by bond.

When it is directed that the security be increased, in a case where security has been given by bond with a guarantee society, a memorandum will be prepared by the PGO and sent to the solicitor. This document when duly executed is filed in the PGO and attached to the original bond. In the case of a bond with private sureties, a new bond will be required.

Where security is to be reduced the bond will be indorsed accordingly and the guarantee society will be notified by the PGO. Reduction of penalty in the case of private sureties is not likely to be sanctioned.

For vacation of security, see paras 6B–33, 6B–39, 6B–47 and 6B–57. Should default be made in a case where security has been effected by bond, a certificate of default will issue which, under the term of the bond, is conclusive evidence against the receiver and the sureties. Generally as to liability of sureties, etc. see Heywood and Massey, *Court of Protection Practice* 2002 edition, paras 4–038 to 4–042.

Entry and sealing of order

All orders are sealed and entered in the Sealing Room. Office copies are sent to the **6B–25** solicitors as soon as the engrossments are ready, but where security has been directed the order cannot normally be issued until security has been completed. See also r.46.

Carrying first order into effect

6B–26 An office copy of the order should be registered with all sources of income including those companies in which the patient has securities (or with banks at which any of the securities are domiciled) other than in respect of those securities which are to be lodged in court. Not to do so would amount to an irregularity and conversion; see *Re N. (decd.)* [1977] 1 W.L.R. 676; [1977] 2 All E.R. 687, CA.

Any necessary undertaking and inventory as to furniture and household effects or bankers' receipt and undertaking (Form C.P.12) should be filed as soon as possible.

In the case of the court directing any investigation, inquiry or report every effort should be made to ensure that the direction is complied with within the period limited by the order, or, if no time limited, as soon as possible.

Special consideration should be given to the detailed directions which are usually incorporated in an order directing the carrying on of a business. See "Business," para. 6B–101.

If a patient holds a driving licence, the licensing authority (Driver's Medical Branch, Driver and Vehicle Licensing Agency, Swansea SA99 1AB) should be notified by the Receiver by reference to the name, address, date of birth and sex of the patient.

Lodgments in Court

6B–27 Where stock or shares to be lodged stand in the name of a patient the lodgment is made by the proper officer of the company (r.73) and where they stand in the joint names of a patient and another the lodgment is made by the proper officer of the company and that other; the lodgment will, usually, only be directed where the patient is solely entitled thereto. In cases where the patient holds securities either solely or jointly as trustee the question of appointing a new trustee in place of the patient and obtaining any necessary vesting order would have to be considered. See paras 6B–59 *et seq.*

Funds to be lodged are transferred into the name of the Accountant General, usually to the general credit of the patient, but where any income is not required for maintenance or other necessary expenditure an "accumulating fund" is sometimes created, the Accountant General of the Supreme Court being directed to invest and accumulate the income. Accumulations are placed on Special Account pending investment.

On the sale of or realisation of specifically bequeathed or nominated property the proceeds may be directed to be lodged to a special credit or otherwise earmarked in accordance with s.101(4) of the Mental Health Act 1983. See also para. 6B–111.

(b) Appointment of New Receiver

When and by whom made

6B–28 Somewhat the same considerations arise as upon the first application, but where a receiver is retiring he should usually be the applicant. The appointment of a new receiver may become necessary for one of many reasons, *e.g.* the death or illness of the existing receiver, the default or other misdemeanour of the receiver, his permanent residence abroad, his desire to retire or perhaps his bankruptcy.

Whenever it becomes necessary to appoint a new receiver the application should be made without undue delay, as it is obviously imperative to have someone through whom the court can give directions and who will take an active and personal interest in the patient, his condition, welfare and estate.

If money is required for maintenance or other necessary requirements before the order appointing a new receiver can be drawn up, or any other urgent matter arises, it may well be possible to deal with the matter by interim order or direction, see para. 6B–19.

Proceedings are by way of formal application.

Documents and evidence

6B–29 The application should ask that "A. B." (name, address and occupation of proposed new receiver and relationship to patient—if any) "be appointed receiver in place of C.D., the receiver appointed by order dated—and that such other necessary directions be given." The address of the patient should be indorsed on the back of the application (court's copy) as should also the name, address and occupation of a referee with whom the court can communicate as to the proposed receiver's fitness to act.

The following are necessary:
  (i) Two copies of the formal application (Form C.P.9).
  (ii) On the death of the receiver—a certificate of death or production of the grant of representation (or office copy) to the deceased receiver's estate.
  (iii) A statement of facts showing the grounds of the application giving particulars of any change in the circumstances or property of the patient, *e.g.* any benefit to which the patient may be entitled under the will or intestacy of the late receiver.
  (iv) Certificate of the fund in court (if any). (*Note*—If there is none, a statement to this effect should be indorsed on the court's copy of the application.)
  (v) Receiver's Declaration

The formal application is not served on the patient but he is notified in the same way as on the issue of a first application for the appointment of a receiver (see para. 6B–18). A Transaction fee of £200 is payable — see paras 6B–316 and 6B–337. However, no additional appointment fee is payable.

The order

The following are some of the more important points in regard to which directions are usually given: **6B–30**
  (i) The person appointed new receiver.
  (ii) Receiver's security (if any).
  (iii) The discharge of the old receiver (if alive) and, in any case, directions as to the passing of, or dispensing with, his final account and discharge of his security (if any).
  (iv) Directions as to maintenance of the patient and, if necessary, any dependants; upkeep of establishment, etc.
  (v) The repetition of any previous authority or direction which is either of such a nature as to require continuance or has not yet been complied with.

Order, settlement, entry and sealing

As on first application (see paras 6B–22, 6B–23 and 6B–25).   **6B–31**

Security

As on first application (see para. 6B–24).   **6B–32**

Vacation of receiver's security

Where the court dispenses with a final account of the former receiver and discharges **6B–33** his security the security may be vacated forthwith and the bond will be returned duly vacated direct to the guarantee society (or to the solicitor when there are private sureties) and the solicitor informed accordingly.

If, as is more usually the case, the court directs that a final account of the former receiver be passed, either by that receiver or his personal representatives, the security cannot be vacated until such account is passed and the balance found due thereon paid over to the new receiver and (unless the new receiver is the personal representative of the late receiver) his receipt obtained and produced to the court.

Passing final account of former receiver

(See "Accounts", paras 6B–149 *et seq.*).   **6B–34**

(c) Application on Recovery of Patient

Recovery of patient

Under s.99(3) of the Mental Health Act 1983, a receiver must be discharged by or- **6B–35** der on the court being satisfied that the patient has become capable of managing and administering his property and affairs. The question must be divorced from such considerations as to whether or not he remains in an institution, or whether or not he continues to be liable to be detained under any compulsory powers (see *Re B. A. S.* [1898] 2 Ch. 392, where, under the Lunacy Act 1890, it was held that discharge of a reception order did not of itself determine the receivership). The test is, "Is the patient now capable of managing and administering his property and affairs?"

Proceedings are by way of formal application.

If the court is not satisfied that the patient is capable of managing and administering the whole of his affairs so as to satisfy the first part of the section, it may consider discharging the receiver on the grounds that it is "expedient to do so", *e.g.* if a settlement of the patient's property were first executed under an order of the court, see para. 6B–135. It must be noted, however, that "expedient" means "expedient for the patient" and not for any other purpose, see *Re N. (decd.)* [1977] 1 W.L.R. 676; [1977] 2 All E.R. 687, CA.

Documents and evidence

6B–36   A precedent for a medical certificate in support is given in para. 6B–187. If the certificate is to be made by the doctor who gave the medical evidence in support of the first application, the deponent should traverse his former evidence; if not, the deponent should state that he has read a copy of such former evidence. In either case the deponent must give the reasons upon which he bases his conclusions as to recovery, and must state that in his opinion the patient is capable of managing and administering his property and affairs. If not satisfied with such evidence the master may request one of the Lord Chancellor's Medical Visitors to visit the patient and report. See paras 6B–199 and 6B–206.

Where the same solicitors are acting on the application for the order determining proceedings as acted on the first application, no doubt (except in cases where the evidence was obtained direct by the court) they will have their completed draft of the original medical evidence from which to prepare a copy for the deponent as above, but if necessary an office copy should be bespoken. Where different solicitors are acting they should first apply to the solicitors who filed the original medical evidence who should, if necessary, bespeak an office copy (r.75). Such copies of medical evidence are for the use of the patient's medical and legal advisers and should not in any circumstances be disclosed to the patient or anyone else without the leave of the court.

The patient makes the application, and, if acting by the same solicitors, the receiver should be joined as an applicant, but if not the receiver should be notified and a copy of the application served on him at least two clear days before the hearing date (r.19). If the receiver is dead, a certificate of death or the grant of representation to his estate should be produced; but his personal representatives need not be notified unless the court so directs.

The application should ask that:

(1) The patient be restored to the management of his property and that the powers of the receiver be determined.

(2) The final account of the receiver be dispensed with, or passed and that his security (if any) may be discharged.

(3) The will, deeds, securities and other documents (if any) deposited with Bank   (or elsewhere) subject to the directions of the court may be delivered to the patient. The application should also ask for the release from restriction of any other assets, *e.g.* furniture and effects, building society or bank accounts (N.B. not receivership bank account) held subject to the directions of the court.

(4) The funds in court (if any) be transferred to the patient.

(5) The costs of the application (and the costs directed to be taxed or assessed by any previous order which may not yet have been taxed and paid) and any outstanding costs of general management may be assessed (unless agreed) and paid out of the fund in court (or paid by the patient). See also "Costs," paras 6B–155 to 6B–162. The following are necessary:

(i) Two copies of the formal application (Form C.P. 9).

(ii) Medical certificate in support (para. 6B–187).

(iii) Certificate of the fund in court (if any).

Order, settlement, entry and sealing

6B–37   As on first application, except that no "receiver's copy" of the order is issued (see paras 6B–22, 6B–23 and 6B–25).

Transfer out of fund in Court

6B–38   Subject to compliance with the procedure of the Court Funds Office the balance of the fund in court can be transferred to the patient immediately under the terms of the order unless:

(i) A final account is to be passed and any administration fees certified due upon the passing thereof paid out of the fund in court, or

(ii) The costs are to be assessed (unless agreed) and paid out of the fund in court.

Pending the disposal of such questions (if any) the whole fund cannot be transferred, but it is not unusual for the order to provide for the transfer of the greater part at once and the reservation of such a part only of the fund as is considered will be adequate to meet the above-mentioned payments. Any ultimate surplus is finally transferred as directed by the order after the two above-mentioned payments have been made.

Where the direction is for the costs to be assessed (unless agreed) and paid out of the fund in court, the Accountant General of the Supreme Court will accept a letter from the solicitors that such costs have been or will be agreed. As to realisation of Equity Index Tracker Fund units, see para. 6B–86.

Vacation of security

Where the court dispenses with a final account of the receiver and discharges his **6B–39** security the security may normally be vacated forthwith and the bond will be returned duly vacated to the guarantee society (or to the solicitor when private sureties) and the solicitor informed accordingly.

If a final account is to be passed the security will not be vacated until such account has been passed and any balance found due thereon paid to the recovered patient and his receipt therefor obtained and produced to the court when bespeaking the bond as above.

Passing final account of former receiver

See "Accounts," paras 6B–149 *et seq.* **6B–40**

(d) Final Order or Direction on Death of Patient

Death of patient

The court should be notified immediately of the death of the patient. A winding up **6B–41** fee £290 is payable on the death of a patient where a receiver has been appointed.

The jurisdiction of the Court of Protection ceases on the death of the patient (*Re Walker* [1907] 2 Ch. 120; *Re Wheater* [1928] 1 Ch. 223; and the powers of the receiver are automatically determined (*Re Walker*) and he is discharged from the office (without an order) by the death (Mental Health Act 1983, s.99(3)). Certain jurisdiction, incidental to the winding up of the proceedings, however, survives; as to costs, see r.84(3); as to remuneration, see r.43(2); as to administration fees, see r.78(4); as to final accounts, see r.65; as to transfer and delivery of funds, see r.74.

The Court of Protection will not administer the estate nor decide who is entitled to any fund in court or other property (*Ex p. Gilbert* (1810) 1 Ball & B. 297) nor order payment of debts (*Re Marman's Trusts* (1878) 26 W.R. 621) nor make the receiver or any one else account for any thing received after the death (*Re Walker*; but the Chancery Division may (*Scammell v. Light* (1863) 32 L.J.Ch. 53). In *Strangwayes v. Read* [1898] 2 Ch. 419, the committee of the person was made to account for money paid to him in advance for maintenance of the patient, who died within a short time after the receipt of the money.

Where since the death an order had been made in the Chancery Division for the administration of the patient's estate, the fund in court to the credit of the patient was by consent ordered to be carried over to the credit of the administrator's action, and an order of the Court of Protection for payment to creditors gives them no equitable charge on the fund (*Re Wheater*).

When order necessary

Should a patient die between the date of the first application and the entering of **6B–42** the order, the court requires proof of death, usually by production of a death certificate.

A receiver is automatically discharged on the death of a patient (Mental Health Act 1983, s.99(3); see para. 6B–195) but a final order or directions will be necessary to wind up the proceedings in the court. No order is usually required: a direction of the court is sufficient as to the passing or dispensing with the receiver's final account and discharging his security, the release of the funds in court (if any) and the release by formal authority under the seal of the court of any documents or assets held subject to the directions of the court where the restriction is not limited to "the lifetime of the patient". The majority of cases can be dealt with by a letter, accompanied by a state-ment of facts, asking for the required directions. Formal proceedings for a final order are only now required where it is anticipated that an order of the court will be neces-sary to enforce payment of costs in the proceedings.

Where there is a charge on the fund in court, it may be convenient to let the charg-ees make their own application to enforce their charge. If any surplus remains of the fund after payment of the charge, the order or directions would then provide for pay-ment of the residue to the personal representatives of the patient.

Representation to patient's estate

6B–43   Before application can be made for a final order, or final directions given, the ap-propriate grant of representation must, normally, be obtained. Where, however, the net estate is under £5,000 in value there is usually no need to obtain a grant and the matter can be dealt with under the provisions of r.74(3). If there is a fund in court directions can be given either for it to be transferred to the personal representatives of the patient (when constituted) under the Court Funds Rules 1987, r.43, or to a named payee, under the Court Funds Rules 1987, r.7, as may be appropriate.

To enable payment, transfer, delivery or release to be directed under r.74(3) a cer-tificate of death and the will (if any) should be lodged together with a statement show-ing (a) the total assets of the deceased and their value (b) the debts and whether paid or not and in the case of funeral expenses forward the undertaker's account and if paid say who paid them and (c) the names, addresses and relationship of the persons entitled and where the person applying is neither the executor nor the only person entitled a statement should be filed signed by the persons entitled nominating one of their number to collect the assets. If there is any minority interest a grant may be necessary.

A Scottish confirmation or Northern Irish grant of representation in respect of a patient who dies domiciled in Scotland or Northern Ireland, as the case may be, will be recognised without resealing in the Principal Probate Registry provided it contains a statement as to such domicile (see the Administration of Estates Act 1971, s.1). A Co-lonial grant which is to be acted upon in respect of estate of a patient in England and Wales will, however, require to be resealed before production to the Court of Protec-tion (see *ibid.*, s.11).

How application is made

6B–44   Where (as is rarely the case) an order is necessary, application is made by way of formal application.

Documents and evidence

6B–45   The application is made by the personal representatives of the deceased patient, and where the receiver is also a personal representative, such an applicant should be described in both capacities, but in the capacity of executor or administrator first.

The receiver, if he is not also a personal representative, should, where he is acting by the same solicitors, be joined as an applicant, but if not he should be notified and a copy of the application should be served on him at least two clear days before the return day (r.19). If the receiver is also dead, a certificate of death or the grant of rep-resentation (or a sealed office copy) to his estate should be produced; but his personal representatives need not be notified unless the court so directs.

The formal application should ask that:

(1) The receiver's final account be dispensed with or passed. and that the security (if any) be discharged.

(2) The deeds, securities or other documents (if any) deposited with the Bank (or elsewhere) be delivered to the executor or administrator. The application should also ask for the release from restriction of any other assets, *e.g.* furniture and effects, building society or bank accounts (*N.B.* not receivership bank ac-count) held subject to the directions of the court. Present-day orders provide for documents and items to be held subject to the directions of the court only *during the lifetime of the patient* and in those cases the documents, etc., can be released without further authority on the death of the patient.

(3) The fund in court be transferred to the executor or administrator or that the fund in court be sold and that after discharge of the charge thereon (if any) the balance of the proceeds be paid, etc. (as the case may require).

(4) The costs of the application (and the costs directed to be taxed or assessed by any previous order which may not yet have been assessed and paid) and any outstanding costs of general management be assessed (unless agreed) and paid out of the patient's estate or fund in court (as the case may require).

The grant of representation (or a sealed office copy), which will normally be accepted as sufficient evidence of death and identity, should support the application.

The following are necessary:

(i) Two copies of the formal application (Form C.P.9).

(ii) Certificate of the fund in court (if any).

Where (as is usually the case) only directions are required the following are necessary:

(i) A statement as explained above (see paras 6B–42 and 6B–43).

(ii) The grant of representation.

Where the receiver is the sole personal representative but is not the sole beneficiary, the consents in writing of the principal beneficiaries to dispensing with the final account of the receiver, if so desired, must be filed and, preferably, on the issue of the formal application or the filing of the statement as the case may be.

Where it is desired that funds should be transferred not to the personal representatives but to their solicitors or nominees, an authority and request to that effect signed by the personal representatives should be filed with the application (see *Woodhead v. Bates* [1963] 1 W.L.R. 926; [1963] 2 All E.R. 877).

Costs

Normally the final order will pick up any outstanding costs, but where at the death **6B–46** of a patient there is pending an application for a settlement or a gift or a statutory will under s.96(1)(d) or (e) of the principal Act, or under s.1(3) of the Variation of Trusts Act 1958, the final order to wind up the court of Protection proceedings would not normally deal with the costs of such a pending application; but if directions are required, the application in question should be restored to the list to enable the question of the costs thereof to be dealt with separately. The personal representatives (if constituted) should be the persons to be notified, but if they have not been constituted, the court would consider whether or not those entitled to the estate were sufficiently represented to enable the matter to be dealt with in the absence of the personal representatives, neither would the costs of a pending application relating to the appointment of new trustees be dealt with by the final order, and the application should similarly be restored to the list if an order as to costs is required.

Order, settlement, entry and sealing

Usually directions are given by way of a letter, but where an order is made it **6B–47** proceeds in much the same way as on a first application. See paras 6B–22 to 6B–25.

Transfer out of fund in Court

As on an order determining proceedings on recovery, see para. 6B–38. As to real- **6B–48** isation of Equity Index Tracker Fund units, see para. 6B–86.

Vacation of security

As on an order determining proceedings on recovery (see para. 6B–39) except that **6B–49** the receipt for the balance found due on the passing of the final account will be that of the personal representatives, unless the receiver is the sole personal representative.

Passing final account

See "Accounts", paras 6B–149 *et seq.*   **6B–50**

(e) Application to Raise Money out of the Fund in Court for Duty on Death of Patient

Note — "Duty" means Capital Transfer Tax, Inheritance tax or, where relevant, **6B–51** Estate, Succession or Legacy Duty.

Sometimes prior to grant of representation it is desired that part of the fund should be transferred to the Capital Taxes Office to meet duty. Should it be desired to tender any National Savings or Stocks on the National Savings Register not in court, the practice here indicated should be followed so far as applicable.

The application is made by way of formal application, unless the court otherwise directs.

Documents and evidence

6B–52   The application is made by the executors named in the will of the patient or (where the patient dies intestate) the persons entitled to apply for a grant of administration to his estate. The receiver, if acting by the same solicitors, should be joined as an applicant, but if not he should be notified and a copy of the application served on him at least two clear days before the return day (r.19). If the receiver is also dead, a certificate of death or the grant of administration (or sealed office copy) to his estate should be produced; but his personal representatives should not be notified unless so directed. The application should ask that:

(1) Sufficient of the stock in court be sold to meet the tax (and interest) now payable, and that the balance of such fund in court be transferred to the personal representatives of the patient when constituted.

(2) The deeds, securities, or other documents (if any) deposited with the Bank (or elsewhere) be delivered to such personal representatives when constituted. The application should also ask for the release from restriction of any other assets, *e.g.* furniture and effects, building society or bank accounts (*N.B.* not receivership bank account) held subject to the directions of the court. If the aforementioned items are held *only during the lifetime of the patient* subject to the directions of the court, no directions in the order will be required.

(3) Direction as to costs as in application for final order, paras 6B–44 and 6B–45.

The affidavit in support should state:

(1) The date of the death of the patient and whether the patient left a will and if so the date thereof and the executors (if any) appointed thereby and, if they are dead or if the patient dies intestate, that the applicants are the persons entitled to apply for administration.

(2) That representation has not yet been obtained but the necessary papers to lead to a grant have been completed and are ready to be lodged in the Probate Registry.

(3) The approximate amount of the tax.

(4) The stock which it is suggested should be sold to meet the tax.

(5) That the facts therein deposed to are within the deponent's own knowledge and are true and that, where necessary, the deponent is authorised by his co-executor or co-applicant to make the affidavit.

The following are necessary:

(i) Two copies of the formal application (Form C.P. 9).

(ii) Affidavit in support.

(iii) Certificate of Death.

(iv) Certificate of the fund in court.

Order, settlement, entry and sealing

6B–53   As on a first application except that no "receiver's copy" of the order is issued, see paras 6B–22 to 6B–25.

Certificate of duty

6B–54   When the order has been completed, an office copy should be produced to the Capital Taxes Office who will send a requisition for the amount of tax payable to the Court Funds Office.

Final directions as to account and security

6B–55   When the personal representatives have been constituted, directions as to passing or dispensing with a final account and vacation of security (if any) should be applied for by lodging a statement (formal application not necessary); the grant should be produced.

Transfer out of balance of fund

6B–56   The balance will be transferred out to the personal representatives when constituted upon the production of the grant to the Court Funds Office and, if the fund exceeds £5,000 in value, an affidavit of representation will also be required. See also paras 6B–38 and 6B–85.

Vacation of security

As on final order (para. 6B–47).

6B–57

Passing final account

See "Accounts", paras 6B–149 *et seq.*

6B–58

APPOINTMENT OF NEW TRUSTEES AND VESTING ORDERS

(a) Generally as to Jurisdiction

Statutory jurisdiction

The removal from his office of a trustee under mental disability and the appoint- **6B–59** ment, where necessary, of a new trustee in his place and the vesting of trust property are matters which may be effected out of court or may require relief either in the Court of Protection or the Chancery Division or county court, according to the circumstances.

The following enactments have special application:

(1) s.96(1)(k) of the Mental Health Act 1983—exercise of a patient's power of appointing new trustee or retiring from a trust with (if necessary) a vesting order under subs.(2).

(2) s.54(2) of the Trustee Act 1925—appointment by the Court of Protection of a new trustee in place of a patient with (if necessary) a vesting order.

(3) s.36(9) of the Trustee Act 1925—giving of leave to a continuing (or refusing or retiring) trustee to exercise his *statutory* power of appointment.

Which method to adopt

With a view to assisting the practitioner to decide what is the appropriate course **6B–60** and procedure to be followed in any particular case, the following working rules are given:

(a) Where the Patient is not a Trustee

(1) Where the patient has no beneficial interest, and the assistance of the court is **6B–61** required, relief should be asked for in the Chancery Division (or county court, where appropriate; see Trustee Act 1925, s.67) but see note (4) below.

(2) s.54(2) of the Trustee Act 1925, does not apply.

(3) The only jurisdiction in the Court of Protection is under s.96(1)(k) of the Mental Health Act 1983, exercising a power of appointment (if any) vested in the patient, with, if necessary, a consequential vesting order under subs. (2).

(4) Where the patient is the person nominated by the trust instrument to exercise the power of appointing new trustees, such power should be exercised in the Court of Protection if the patient is beneficially interested and a receiver has been appointed (see *Re Blake* [1887] W.N. 173); otherwise new trustees may be appointed out of court by any of the persons so empowered by s.36 of the Trustee Act 1925. Where, however, the patient was the settlor it is appropriate for the power to be exercised in the Court of Protection under note (3) above, whether or not the patient has a beneficial interest.

(5) If the power vested in the patient is purely statutory, and there is no other person with a power capable of exercising the same, application may be made to the Court of Protection to exercise the power.

(b) Where the Patient is a Trustee

(1) Where the patient has no beneficial interest and the assistance of the court is **6B–62** required, relief should be asked for in the Chancery Division (or other court, where appropriate; see Trustee Act 1925, s.67) but see note (5) below.

(2) If a vesting order is required and the matter is one coming within the scope of s.54(2) of the Trustee Act 1925, proceed under that section for an order appointing and vesting. This course is advocated even where the patient or some other person (who would require to be an applicant) is the person nominated by the trust instrument to appoint new trustees, see note (5).

(3) There are four conditions which must be fulfilled if a case is to come within s.54(2) of the Trustee Act 1925, namely:

1823

(i) the trust is not subject to an order for administration in the Chancery Division;

(ii) the new trustees are to be appointed *in place of the patient*;

(iii) a receiver is acting for the patient or an application for the appointment of a receiver is pending;

(iv) the patient is beneficially entitled to some interest in the trust property.

(4) If a vesting order is not required, new trustees should be appointed out of court by any of the persons so empowered by s.36 of the Trustee Act 1925, but where the patient has some beneficial interest *in possession*, and the appointment is being made by the continuing (or refusing or retiring) trustee, by virtue of subs.(1)(b) of that section, the prior leave of the Court of Protection is necessary under subs.(9).

(5) If the patient is the person nominated by the trust instrument to exercise the power of appointing new trustees and he is beneficially interested and there is a receiver, the appointment should be made in the Court of Protection (see *Re Blake* [1887] W.N. 173) under s.96(1)(k) of the Mental Health Act 1983, by exercising the power, and where the patient was the settlor, this course should be followed, even if he has no beneficial interest. If a vesting order is required it is preferable, where possible, to proceed under s.54(2) of the Trustee Act 1925 for an order appointing and vesting (see notes (2) and (3)).

(6) Where there is with the patient a capable trustee who wishes to retire, the matter does not fall within s.54(2) of the Trustee Act 1925, though there would be jurisdiction under s.96(1)(k) of the Mental Health Act 1983.

(7) Where it is desired that the patient shall retire from the trust under s.39 of the Trustee Act 1925, without a new trustee being appointed in his place, application can be made under s.96(1)(k) of the Mental Health Act 1983, for an order authorising the receiver to exercise the power with (if necessary) a vesting order under subs.(2) of that section.

—Generally, see Heywood and Massey, *Court of Protection Practice*, 2002 edition Chap. 16.

Vesting order, where necessary

6B–63 Usually no vesting provisions are required, unless the patient is a trustee. Where there stand in the name of the patient, either solely or jointly, mortgages or stocks or shares, etc. (see the Trustee Act 1925, s.40(4)) a vesting order is necessary, for, if the appointment of new trustees were made by deed either under s.96(1)(k) of the Mental Health Act 1983, or by the continuing trustee or other person empowered under s.36 of the Trustee Act 1925, such classes of property would not "follow the deed" under any express or implied vesting provisions under s.40 of the Trustee Act 1925.

Where, however, proceedings for appointment of new trustees are being taken under s.54 of the Trustee Act 1925 all property will be vested in the new trustees by or in pursuance of the order; there will be no deed of appointment.

Where new trustees are being appointed for the purposes of the Settled Land Act 1925, the order will not deal with the freehold and leasehold property (since—if vested in him—the legal estate remains in the tenant for life). Where land is vested in a patient as statutory owner (see the Settled Land Act 1925, s.23(1)(b)) the order will authorise the receiver to convey or join in conveying the land to the new statutory owners (see *ibid.*, s.7(4)).

Trustee Delegation Act 1999

6B–63.1 This Act came into effect on March 1, 2000 and all Enduring Powers of Attorney made on or after this date are subject to it.

An attorney of an EPA created on or after March 1, 2000 has acquired trustee functions under section 1(1) of the Trustee Delegation Act 1999 and can therefore exercise he Donor's trustee powers providing that:-

(i) the Donor has a beneficial interest in the trust at the time when the function is exercised

(ii) there is no indication that the Donor did not want the Attorney to exercise his/her trustee functions

(iii) the trust consisted of land, the proceeds of sale of land or income from land

This includes appointing a new trustee if there is no continuing trustee or the attorney is the continuing trustee.

A new Section 22(3) was added to the Law of Property Act whereby the incapacitated trustee does not need to be replaced if there is an Attorney acting under an EPA.

The Trustee Delegation Act also allows a Donor to make EPAs specifically to deal with any trustee functions whether or not the Donor has a beneficial interest, but these are only valid for one year.

(b) Application to Exercise Patient's Power of Appointment under Mental Health Act 1983, s.96(1)(k)

Mental Health Act 1983, s.96(1)(k)

Under this enactment an order may be made in the Court of Protection for the exercise of any power vested in the patient, whether beneficially, or as guardian or trustee, or otherwise, and a consequential order can be made under *ibid.*, subs.(2). See *Re Fuller* [1900] 2 Ch. 551; and *Re Shortridge* [1895] 1 Ch. 278. It is not the practice under this provision to authorise the exercise of functions of the patient in the administration of a trust, the proper course being to remove the patient from the trust.

6B–64

Mode of application and applicants

The application is made by way of formal application (r.7) in Form A the Schedule to the Rules. A transaction fee of £130 will be payable, see paras 6B–316 and 6B–337, and if the application is the first in the matter of the patient, a commencement fee of £240 will be payable.

By virtue of r.17, applicants are the same as for an application under s.54(2) of the Trustee Act 1925, and, accordingly, governed by r.15. Normally, however, the receiver is the sole applicant, but a joint donee of a power should be joined as applicant.

6B–65

Documents and evidence

The formal application should ask that the receiver be authorised in the name and on behalf of the patient to exercise (or concur with A.B. in exercising) the power of appointment vested in the patient (and A.B.) by appointing C.D. (*full name, address and description*) to be a new trustee of the trusts of the will dated   of   (*as the case may be*) and, if necessary, for the purposes of the Settled Land Act 1925; if a vesting order is required it should be asked that any necessary consequential vesting order be made; and costs be provided for.

The following are the main documents and evidence required:

  (i) Two copies of the formal application prepared on Form C.P. 9.

  (ii) Affidavit in support as for an application under s.54(2) of the Trustee Act 1925 (see para. 6B–76).

  (iii) Affidavit of fitness, except where the proposed new trustee is a trust corporation or is the receiver.

  (iv) Special Undertaking by trustees (Form C.P. 14) except where proposed new trustee is a trust corporation; a copy should be attached to the deed of appointment when executed.

  (v) Where the patient is not a trustee and no vesting directions are required, an undertaking by the present trustees to transfer the investments comprised in the trust funds into the names of the new trustees when appointed.

6B–66

The order

The order, if made, will authorise the receiver in the name and on behalf of the patient to exercise the power, and to execute the necessary deed but it is not necessary for the deed to be settled by the court, the court relying on the solicitors as to the accuracy and sufficiency of its contents. Any vesting provision will be dependent and consequent upon the execution of the deed. The order is drafted and settled as on a first application. See paras 6B–22 and 6B–25.

6B–67

Deed of appointment

A fair copy of the Deed of Appointment, and the Supplemental Deed if any required by s.35 of the Settled Land Act 1925, or the further deed (if any) required by s.35 of the Trustee Act 1925, to be executed by the receiver in pursuance of the order should be lodged for record purposes. For the form of the recitals as required by the court, see paras 6B–173 and 6B–179.

6B–68

Certificate of due execution

6B–69   Where a vesting provision is incorporated the order will read, "That upon the Certificate of the Court of the due execution of the said deed" (*i.e.* the deed appointing the new trustees) etc. (then follow the vesting provisions).

In order to procure this certificate an affidavit by the attesting witness of due execution of the deed by the appointor (exhibiting the deed) must be filed. Not until the issue of this certificate do the vesting provisions under the order actually take effect.

(c) Application to Exercise Patient's Power of Retirement under Mental Health Act 1983, s.96(1)(k)

Mental Health Act 1983, s.96(1)(k)

6B–70   Under this enactment an order may be made for the exercise of the power conferred upon a patient who is a trustee, by s.39 of the Trustee Act 1925, of retirement from a trust without any appointment of a new trustee in his place, with (if necessary) a consequential vesting order under s.96(2), thus eliminating the patient.

Generally, however, the court prefers that a new trustee should be appointed in place of the patient if he has a beneficial interest. Accordingly, unless the remaining trustee or trustees is or includes a trust corporation, or the trust is practically at an end, or the number of trustees exceeds four, the application is unlikely to be successful. See also *Re Harrison* [1965] 1 W.L.R. 1492.

Mode of application and applicants

6B–71   Generally, as for an application to exercise power of appointment of new trustees (see para. 6B–64); in particular, the co-trustees and such other person, if any, as is empowered to appoint trustees (see the Trustee Act 1925, s.39) must be applicants or otherwise notified of the application. A transaction fee of £130 will be payable (paras 6B–316 and 6B–337) and if the application is the first in the matter of the patient, a commencement fee of £240 will be payable.

Documents and evidence

6B–72   As for an application to exercise a power of appointment of new trustees (see para. 6B–66) save that no affidavit of fitness and consent to act will be required and, the special undertaking (where required) will be given by the remaining trustees.

The order, deed of retirement, certificate of due execution

6B–73   As for an application to exercise a power of appointment of new trustees (see para. 6B–66) save that instead of references to a "deed of appointment", there will be references to a "deed of retirement" and the affidavit of due execution will require to prove the execution by all necessary parties other than execution by corporations within s.74(1) of the Law of Property Act 1925.

(d) Application to Appoint New Trustee under Trustee Act 1925, s.54(2)

Trustee Act 1925, s.54

6B–74   This section, as amended by the Mental Health Act 1983, Sched.4, para. 4, provides as follows:

"**54.**—(1) Subject to the provisions of this section, the authority having jurisdiction under Part VII of the Mental Health Act 1983, shall not have power to make any order, or give any direction or authority, in relation to a patient who is a trustee if the High Court has power under this Act to make an order to the like effect.

(2) Where a patient is a trustee and a receiver appointed by the said authority is acting for him or an application for the appointment of a receiver has been made but not determined, then, except as respects a trust which is subject to an order for administration made by the High Court, the said authority shall have concurrent jurisdiction with the High Court in relation to—

    (a) mortgaged property of which the patient has become a trustee merely by reason of the mortgage having been paid off;

    (b) matters consequent on the making of provision by the said authority for the exercise of a power of appointing trustees or retiring from a trust;

(c) matters consequent on the making of provision by the said authority for the carrying out of any contract entered into by the patient;

(d) property to some interest in which the patient is beneficially entitled
but which, or some interest in which, is held by the patient under
an express, implied or constructive trust.

The Lord Chancellor may make rules with respect to the exercise
of the jurisdiction referred to in this subsection.

(3) In this section "patient" means a patient as defined by section 94(2) of the
Mental Health Act 1983, or a person as to whom powers are exercisable and have
been exercised under section 98 of that Act."

Part IV of the Trustee Act 1925, confers upon the High Court (or other court, see
ibid., s.67) extensive powers in regard to the appointment of new trustees and vesting
orders and by virtue of s.54(2) and subject to the provisions thereof, these powers are
exercisable in the Court of Protection where a patient is a trustee. As to the meaning
of the words "the authority having jurisdiction under Part VII of the Mental Health
Act 1983", see *ibid.*, s.111.

Settled Land Act trustees cannot be appointed under this section unless the patient
is such a trustee but, where he is such a trustee, a new trustee appointed in his place
thereunder is a trustee appointed by the court for the purposes of s.35(2) of the
Settled Land Act 1925 (*Re E. F. Jackson*, January 28, 1932, unrep., CA transcript 32/
401, *per* Romer L.J.).

Mode of application and applicants

The application is made by way of formal application in Form A (r.7) in the Sched-   **6B–75**
ule to the Rules.

Applicants are governed by r.15 and it should be noted that no person who is a
patient should be notified unless and until the court so directs. As regards persons to
be notified the practice is that all the trustees, if not applicants, should be notified, as
should also the principal beneficiaries in England and Wales, leaving it to the court to
direct who else should be notified. On an application for a vesting order only it is not
necessary to notify beneficiaries unless in any particular case the court so directs
(*Practice Note* [1908] W.N. 75). A donee of the power (other than the patient) should
preferably be an applicant.

Documents and evidence

The following are the main documents and evidence required: **6B–76**

(i) Two copies of the formal application prepared on Form C.P. 9.

(ii) Affidavit in support (see below).

(iii) Affidavit of fitness, except where the proposed new trustee is a trust corporation or is the receiver.

(iv) Special Undertaking by trustee (Form C.P. 14) except where the proposed
new trustee is a trust corporation. A copy should be attached to the working
copy of the order when completed.

The Master directed on October 1, 1959, that paras 1, 2, 3 and 7 of the Practice
Direction relating to title to proceedings in the Chancery Division and dated June 18,
1959, shall, so far as applicable, be followed in the Court of Protection (see *Practice
Notes* [1959] 2 All E.R. 629 and *Practice Note* [1959] 3 All E.R. 320).

The affidavit in support should:

(1) State the name, address and description of the applicant and the capacity in
which he applies.

(2) Describe the instrument (if any) creating the trust and set out the main trusts
and the investment clause and in the case of land showing whether it is settled
or is held upon trust for sale. The original trust instrument should be exhibited
and if the original instrument cannot be produced a certified copy should be
exhibited and an explanation why the original is not produced (see *Hansell v.
Spink* [1943] Ch. 396 as to lost settlement). There is no need to exhibit an original grant of representation.

(3) Show the devolution of the trust and, in the case of land, the legal estate, and
if the land is settled land whether or not there is a vesting instrument, and, if
so, identify it. In the case of a trust arising under a will or intestacy, where the
office has changed to that of trustee, show that administration has been

completed and that the property in respect of which a vesting order is required is vested in the capacity of trustee and no longer as personal representative (see *Re King* [1964] Ch. 542, and *Re Ponder* [1921] 2 Ch. 59; *Re Yerburgh* [1928] W.N. 208; *Re Pitt* (1928) 44 T.L.R. 371; *Re Cockburn* [1957] Ch. 438).

(4) Define the patient's beneficial interest.

(5) Give the names and addresses of the other beneficiaries, whether in possession or in reversion; if any are minors or patients it should be stated. If a beneficiary has settled or charged his interest particulars should be given and names of the trustees or encumbrancers stated. In showing the devolution of beneficial interests deaths need not be strictly proved.

(6) Set out, with full details, the trust property, showing in whose names the various securities stand, and whether fully paid, and whether registered or in bearer form.

(7) In the case of joint ownership of land being held on December 31, 1925, in undivided shares—whether or not there were at that date any encumbrances effecting undivided shares (see para. 1(2) Pt IV, First Schedule to the Law of Property Act 1925).

(8) State the present trustees.

(9) Show all previous changes in the trusteeship, exhibiting all previous deeds of appointment or retirement, which if produced from proper custody are sufficient evidence of their authenticity; the execution need not be proved strictly unless for any reason it is desirable that this should be done. The dates of death of any deceased trustees should be given; a certificate of death must be exhibited in proof unless the death was 20 years prior to the application.

(10) State the names, addresses, ages and descriptions of proposed new trustees.

(11) State the name of the person in whom, and the circumstances in which, the power of appointment of new trustees is vested by the instrument or statute.

(12) State that the trust is not subject to an order for administration in the Chancery Division.

On an application for a vesting order alone consequent upon an appointment of a new trustee out of court, due execution of the deed upon which the application is founded must be proved strictly (see *Re Rice* (1886) 32 Ch.D. 35; and the Evidence Act 1938, s.3) unless it is 20 years old (*ibid.*, s.4) but only if the appointor is not a party to the application or, if a party, does not admit due execution (see also Practice Note [1934] W.N. 334).

The order

6B–77   Where an order is made under s.54(2) of the Trustee Act 1925, appointing new trustees and vesting the property, no deed of appointment is necessary; when the order is finally completed any necessary transfers in respect of stocks or shares, etc., should be executed by the new trustees. The order is drafted and settled in the usual way.

A transaction fee of £130 will be payable—see para. 6B–337.

(e) Application for Leave to Appoint New Trustee under Trustee Act 1925, s.36(9)

Trustee Act 1925, s.36(9)

6B–78   This enactment, as amended by the Mental Health Act 1983, Sched.4, para. 4, provides that where a trustee is incapable by reason of mental disorder within the meaning of the Mental Health Act 1983, of exercising his functions as trustee and is also entitled *in possession* to some beneficial interest in the trust property, no appointment of a new trustee in his place shall be made by virtue of paragraph (b) of subs.(1) of that section unless leave to make the appointment has been given by the authority having jurisdiction under Pt VII of the Mental Health Act 1983. As to the meaning of "the authority," etc. see *ibid.*, s.111.

Mode of application and applicants

6B–79   Where the matter is free from complication the court is usually prepared to grant the certificate of leave under r.7 without the issue of a formal application unless the application is the first in the matter of the patient, where it is by way of formal application in Form A in the Schedule to the Rules.

As to applicants, see r.16. Subject to r.16 and the following notes the procedure is the same as for an application under s.54(2) of the Trustee Act 1925, para. 6B–74.

When the application is the first application in the matter the patient is served (Direction of the master, May 9, 1962) *i.e.* with a copy of the application—see rr.19(5)(a) and 23 (para. 6B–258).

Documents and evidence

Unless the court concerned otherwise directs, all evidence in support of the application will be by unsworn statements or certificates and relevant documents should be produced without being exhibited (Practice Direction (Court of Protection) February 29, 1968; (1968) 112 S.J. 200). **6B–80**

Otherwise the same documents and evidence are required as for an application under s.54(2) of the Trustee Act 1925 (see para. 6B–76). Where no receiver has been appointed (or applied for) the evidence should give such particulars and information as are known of the patient's property and circumstances and medical evidence as to the patient's incapacity to exercise his function as trustee is required.

Certificate of leave

The leave of the court is manifested by a certificate, a draft of which, if necessary, is sent to the solicitor. A transaction fee of £130 is payable and, if the application is the first in the matter of the patient, a commencement fee of £240. **6B–81**

Deed of appointment

The deed will no longer require to be settled by the court, the court relying on the Solicitors for the accuracy and sufficiency of the contents (see para. 6B–173). For recitals, see para. 6B–179. **6B–82**

MANAGEMENT AND ADMINISTRATION

Maintenance

The maintenance of the patient is the first consideration and will have priority over the creditors (*Re Plenderleith* [1893] 3 Ch. 332; and *Re Winkle* [1894] 2 Ch. 519); but the maintenance of his wife will not (*Re Winkle*). If the income is insufficient resort may be made to capital. The principle to be followed is that laid down in *Tye's Case* [1900] 1 Ch. 249, that the first object of the court and the PGO is to use the patient's property for his support. See also s.95 of the Mental Health Act 1983 (para. 6B–189) and r.66 (para. 6B–299). The extent to which this is done out of capital in addition to income will depend on the age of the patient, the cost of maintenance, and the amount of his property. When there is every probability that he can be maintained out of interest and capital for his whole life, this should be done instead of creating a charge on his property enforceable at his death. **6B–83**

The coming into force of the National Health Service Act 1946, on July 5, 1948, brought to an end chargeability to local authorities in respect of the maintenance of patients maintained in mental hospitals, and consequently the question will only require to be considered in regard to liability arising prior to that date and in regards to patients in residential accommodation provided under Pt III of the National Assistance Act 1948, and, possibly, under s.21 of the National Health Service Act 1977. In the case of a rate-aided patient, the authority to whom he was chargeable could claim six years' past maintenance (*Re Newbegin* (1887) 36 Ch.D. 477; *Re Watson, Stamford Union v. Bartlett* [1899] 1 Ch. 72; see also *Re T.R.M.* [1939] Ch. 260) and in such cases the court was usually prepared to direct payment of such arrears or give a charge therefore, as the case might require.

Directions in regard to the maintenance of the patient are given in the first order. Any capital required to supplement income is usually raised annually.

Voluntary allowances

Voluntary allowances are made out of the patient's estate in a proper case, especially if they have previously been made by the patient himself (see s.95(1)(c) of the Mental Health Act 1983). When applying for such an allowance a full disclosure should be made to the PGO of the applicant's means and circumstances. **6B–84**

As to bringing voluntary allowances into hotchpot see *Re Gist* [1906] 2 Ch. 280; and *Re Merrall* [1924] 1 Ch. 45.

Investments

6B–85   The provisions of the Trustee Investment Act 1961 do not apply to the investments of patients under the jurisdiction of the court. Nevertheless the court and the PGO bear in mind that they are dealing with the moneys of persons incapable of expressing their own wishes and consider a reasonably conservative policy should be adopted. The investments chosen by the patient prior to his incapacity are not disturbed without sufficient reason.

Advice on policy is given by a Strategic Investment Board (S.I.B.) appointed by the Lord Chancellor, which meets at regular intervals. The court also has the services of a panel of stockbrokers. Normally, the periodic review of a patient's investments is referred to the brokers unless the receiver prefers to consult his own brokers.

Each estate is considered on its merits; and an investment policy laid down taking into account the age of the patient, his income requirements, whether resort to capital will be necessary, and so on. The first duty is to the patient himself, but subject to this the objective is to preserve the real value of the estate for the benefit of all concerned. Where a patient's income is likely to exceed by a reasonable margin the foreseeable total annual expenditure, future investment or a portfolio review may well be on the basis of what will be most beneficial for those who will take on the patient's death.

The Committee has recommended that unless the particular circumstances of an estate otherwise require, the investments of a patient should consist partly of fixed interest securities and partly of equities. What is the proper proportion of one to the other will chiefly depend on the period during which the court can expect to exercise jurisdiction. If the period is likely to be a long one, say 10 years or more, it would be reasonable to have up to about two-thirds in equities and one-third in fixed interest securities. The shorter the period the smaller should be the proportion of equities. Generally where the funds are not sufficiently large to warrant an individual investment portfolio the court favours investment in the Equity Index Tracker Fund (para. 6B–86), unit trusts and investment trust, thus securing "spread" of investment and investment management.

The balance of a portfolio should not be changed merely because by lapse of time the expected duration of the court's jurisdiction has become short.

Equity Index Tracker Fund

6B–86   Funds lodged in court may, but not necessarily, be invested in accordance with the Common Investment Funds Scheme under Pt VI of the Administration of Justice Act 1982: there is now one type of trust unit, the Equity Index Tracker Funds units. The Fund is managed by Legal and General. The unit prices are published in *Financial Times* in the "F.T. Unit Trust Information Service".

The Fund is substantially an equity fund. It tracks the FTSE All Share Index (80 per cent) and the FTSE World index Ex UK (20 per cent).

The fund has certain advantages over other unit trusts. In particular, no initial charge is made on new purchases and the annual charge compares very favourably with the charges made by most commercial trusts.

In these circumstances the Committee had advised that where capital growth is required and income is not of primary importance, the whole of any cash requiring to be invested in equities can properly be invested in the Equity Index Tracker Fund. In a particular estate it may be possible to make out a case for investment in individual undertakings but in the normal course the court will expect the Equity Index Tracker Fund to be used.

When income is of importance the court's investments strategies will determine the proportion invested.

The units can be held by the Accountant General, in a client's name or in nominees names but they are not transferable. They must therefore be realized on the death of a client but can be retained in the event of recovery.

Sale and purchase of property

6B–87   The court or the PGO may direct the sale and purchase of any property on the patients' behalf (s.96(1)(b) and (c) of the Mental Health Act 1983).

A specific direction in the order appointing the receiver, or in a subsequent order or a separate direction under seal, is normally necessary in regard to a sale of any sort, and where the property to be sold is land (either freehold or leasehold) an order is invariably necessary. Before directing the sale of any property, the court desires to know whether the property has been specifically bequeathed or devised by the will of the patient. Section 101(1) and (3) of the Mental Health Act 1983, automatically prevents ademption on a sale under an order of the court, and where it is desirable to identify the proceeds, the proceeds may be lodged to a special credit or otherwise earmarked (see para. 6B–111).

Under s.96(1)(k) of the Act, an order may be made for the receiver to exercise on behalf of a patient mortgagee a power of sale under the mortgage (see para. 6B–108) or his power to sell as tenant for life under the Settled Land Act 1925 (see para. 6B–100).

Practice as to sale of land and house property

6B–88 Unless the receiver has already been authorised to sell the property in the First General Order, or an Interim Order for Sale has been issued, it will be necessary to apply by letter for an Order authorising the sale. The letter should be accompanied by a statement showing the reasons for the proposed sale and confirming that the title is in order (*i.e.* that the patient has a good and marketable title to the property, the same being vested in him as (beneficial owner) (tenant for life within the meaning of the Settled Land Act 1925) in which capacity he offers it for sale). This course is suitable either for a sale by private treaty or by auction. Where the solicitors are unfamiliar with the patient's affairs and the land to be dealt with is not registered land, a search in the Land Charges Register is advisable before confirming the position as to title.

6B–89 *Note* —It should be borne in mind, when asking for office copies of the order or direction authorising sale, that one will have to be handed to the purchaser on completion.

Once an order or direction for sale has been made the following points should be noted:

6B–90 *1. For a sale by private treaty* —The court does not require to approve the terms of the contract itself (other than the purchase price), it being the responsibility of the solicitors acting in the sale to ensure that the contract is adequate in all respects. Usually a certificate of value (see para. 6B–175) by the selling agent should be lodged as soon as it is decided to sell the property in question and the approval of the PGO of the proposed asking price sought unless there are exceptional circumstances (see *below*). It would be as well if the certificate were to state the lowest acceptable price that could reasonably be expected for the property because if that price is approved, then it follows that any higher offer may be accepted without further reference to the PGO. If the highest offer obtained is less than the figure given in the certificate the approval of the PGO must be sought for the sale to proceed at the lower figure. If the property has been put on the market prior to any application and approval is sought merely to a price already negotiated, then the certificate will state merely that the price is, in the agent's judgment and opinion, the full and fair value of the property, and fully as much as would probably be obtained therefore at a sale by public auction and recommending confirmation. The certificate is to be given by a *qualified valuer* whose qualifications must be stated or by *someone with at least five years' experience* with his present firm or another firm practising in the locality. The following professional qualifications of valuers are acceptable to the court: FRICS, ARICS, FSVA and ASVA.

In exceptional circumstances, *e.g.* the sale or purchase of business property, or where a receiver is buying from a patient or there is some similar inter-family transaction or other circumstances deemed to be exceptional by the court, *a sworn affidavit of value by a qualified valuer* will be required before approval to the price can be given.

A contract (which should not contain any reference to mental disorder) should be entered into by the vendor acting by the receiver (or other named person) pursuant to an order of the Court of Protection. Subject to any necessary adaptation, the following special conditions should be included:—

(1) The amount of the deposit shall be £10 per cent of the purchase money and shall be paid to Messrs. ...... [*the solicitors in the matter*] as stakeholders.

(2) The vendor as (beneficial owner) (tenant for life) is selling by his receiver pursuant to an order of the Court of Protection and an office-copy of the said order or of the relevant portion thereof will be handed over on completion and shall be deemed to be conclusive evidence of such authority to sell and the purchaser(s) shall not require the production of or make any requisition or objection in relation to any evidence matter or thing referred to in the said order or otherwise relating thereto.

(3) The purchase money shall be paid as directed or authorised by the relevant order or other direction of the court

Notes

(i) The court will rely entirely upon the solicitors for the accuracy and sufficiency of the contents of the contract and the draft particulars and conditions will not be settled or approved by the court.

(ii) The address of the vendor (if inserted) should be his home address or that of the receiver, never that of an institution.

(iii) As to preparation of the conveyance or transfer, see paras 6B–174 and 6B–183.

(iv) Restrictive or other covenants. If the property is subject to any such covenants, the conditions should provide that the property will be sold "and will be conveyed" subject thereto and (unless it is clear that the vendor will not remain liable after parting with the property) that the purchaser shall in the conveyance enter into a covenant for indemnity in respect thereof.

6B–91   *2. Special condition on sale of leasehold property* —In an assignment on sale of leasehold property by an assignor who is expressed to convey "as beneficial owner" there is implied a covenant (*inter alia*) that all the covenants of the lease have been observed up to the time of the assignment; see the Law of Property Act 1925, Sched.II, Pt II; the Land Registration Act 1925, s.24(1)(a). It is, of course, notorious that covenants for repair and decoration are seldom completely performed at any given moment, and the purchaser is probably well aware of the actual condition of the property; but liability under the implied convenants depends not on knowledge of the grantee but on what is actually expressed in the conveyance. It is therefore important that the implied covenants should be restricted when it is known or suspected that there has been a breach of covenant.

In ordinary cases, therefore, every contract for the sale of leasehold property on behalf of a patient should contain a clause to the following effect:

"The purchaser shall in the assurance of the property covenant to indemnify the vendor and the vendor's estate and effects from and against all subsisting and future liabilities arising out of the state of repair and condition of the property and the assurance shall contain a declaration negativing any implied covenant by the vendor that the covenants contained in the said lease (underlease) and relating to the repair decoration painting or condition of the property have been performed."

6B–92   *3. For a sale by public auction* —The sale may be advertised as being made "by order of the Court of Protection." The particulars and conditions of sale must not contain any reference to mental disorder or the name of the patient. Subject to any necessary adaptation the special conditions are set out in 1. above.

Not less than seven days before the date of the auction there should be lodged with the PGO for the purpose of fixing the reserves a certificate by an agent or deponent as to value and recommending reserves (and lotting, if necessary). The reserve biddings, as fixed by the PGO, will be forwarded to the auctioneer in a sealed envelope to be opened at the time of the sale and not before.

The result of the auction should be reported to the PGO as soon as possible by letter enclosing a certificate by the auctioneer showing the date of the sale, the purchaser's name and the purchase price.

Settlement and approval of the assurance

6B–93   It is no longer necessary for draft deeds to be settled and approved by the court, the court relying on the solicitors for the accuracy and sufficiency of the contents.

Entry to property prior to completion

6B–94   Upon exchange of contracts, no objection will be raised by the court to the purchaser being allowed:

(i) to enter into occupation of the property prior to completion, provided that the contract contains a relevant condition similar to that in the National Conditions of Sale or the Law Society's General Conditions, and the solicitors for the patient take all necessary steps to safeguard patient's interest.

(ii) access to the property to effect repairs or decorations prior to completion, provided the contract contains a provision or there is a subsequent agreement by the purchasers to the effect that if for any reason whether due to the default of the vendor or not the contract is not completed, the purchaser shall not have any claim against the vendor in respect of work done and the purchaser shall make good at his own expense any damage to the property.

Proceeds of sale

On completion, a statement should be forwarded to the PGO showing the approximate amount of the purchase money available for investment, after allowing for the payment off of any encumbrances and a reserve to cover costs and estate agents' charges. Solicitors will normally be asked to give an undertaking to receive the purchase money and deal with it as directed by the PGO. Pending the issue of directions by the PGO the proceeds of sale *must* be placed on deposit in the solicitor's name at the highest rate of interest available to him for deposits subject to the minimum period of notice for withdrawal.

6B–95

Fees

A Transaction Fee of £170 is payable when dealing with the sale of property standing in the sole name of a patient and in respect of the purchase of a property in the name of the patient. See para. 6B–305.

6B–96

Purchase of property for the patient

As in paras 6B–88 and 6B–89, unless authority has already been obtained for purchase of property it will be necessary to apply to the PGO by letter for a direction authorising the purchase. The letter should be accompanied by a statement showing the reasons for the purchase and the approximate amount of the intended expenditure. If approval is given, an order or direction will issue authorising the receiver to purchase such freehold or leasehold property as the PGO shall approve.

6B–97

Once an order or direction for purchase has been made, negotiations may proceed up to the exchange of contracts. However the PGO will need to approve the purchase price, and a certificate of value together with a surveyor's report should be lodged (see paras 6B–90 and 6B–91). The evidence of value should be to the effect that the price represents the fair market value of the property (see para. 6B–175).

Thereafter the procedure follows along similar lines as for a sale of property. If the patient is not an executing party, no reference should be made in the assurance to the fact that the purchaser is a patient, or that the purchase is proceeding pursuant to an order of the Court of Protection or that the purchaser is acting by a receiver.

Estate agent's charges

1. The charges of estate agents and auctioneers selling freehold or leasehold property pursuant to orders of the Chancery Division, Family Division, the Court of Protection, or divorce county courts will normally be considered reasonable by the court if they do not exceed the rate of commission which that agent would normally charge on a sole agency basis, and if they do not exceed 2½ per cent of the sale price, exclusive of value added tax.

6B–98

2. These charges are to include all commission, valuations, expenses and other disbursements, including making affidavits, the cost of advertising, and all other work except surveys. The allowance for a survey will be at the discretion of the PGO.

3. If:
   (a) an agent's charges do not fall within the limits set out in para. 1; or
   (b) there is a sale of any investment property, business property, or farm property; or
   (c) a property is sold in lots or by valuation,

an application must be made to the PGO to authorise the fee to be charged.

4. The limits set out in paras 1 and 2 above do not apply to sales of property for patients of the Court of Protection where an agreement has been concluded with the estate agent before the jurisdiction of the court has been invoked.

5. In matrimonial cases, either where the party who has been condemned in these costs has not agreed to the increased rate, or where the costs fall to be paid out of the legal aid fund, the higher charges will be subject to the discretion of the taxing officer.

6. This Practice Direction applies to all instructions for sale which are placed with estate agents and auctioneers after January 1, 1983.

Practice Direction (Estate Agents' and Auctioneers' Fees) (No. 2) [1972] 1 W.L.R. 1431 and Practice Direction (Family Division: Sale of Land) [1972] 1 W.L.R. 1471 are hereby revoked.

By direction of the Vice-Chancellor and the President of the Family Division and with the concurrence of the Lord Chancellor.

(Practice Direction, December 22, 1982 [1983] 1 W.L.R. 86; (1983) 127 S.J. 40.)

Joint tenant and tenant in common

6B–99 When a patient holds land with other co-owners upon trust for sale, a new trustee must be appointed in his place or he must be otherwise discharged from the trust before the legal estate is dealt with under the trust for sale or under the powers vested in the trustees for sale (s.22(2) of the Law of Property Act 1925). By s.36(9) of the Trustee Act 1925, the leave of the court is required before any such appointment is made in a case by virtue of s.36(1)(b) where the patient has a beneficial interest in possession. For procedure, see para. 6B–18.

In view of the undertaking required to be filed on the making of the application for leave to appoint a new trustee not to sell without first obtaining approval as to price and to deal with the patient's share of the proceeds as may be directed, directions must be obtained before any sale by the new trustees. The same evidence as to value will be required as on a sale of the patient's absolute property (see paras 6B–90 and 6B–91).

A sale of the patient's beneficial interest in property (either as joint tenant or tenant in common) to a third party can, of course, be ordered at any time, but a new trustee in place of the patient will sometimes be required if the legal estate is not to remain outstanding. If, however, the purchaser is the co-owner it may also be possible to assure the patient's interest in the legal estate, inasmuch as it would not appear that such a transaction would be invalidated by s.22(2) of the Law of Property Act 1925. Generally see Heywood and Massey, *Court of Protection Practice*, 2002 Edn., para. 12–019.

Tenant for life

6B–100 The jurisdiction to authorise the exercise of a patient's powers as tenant for life derives from s.96(1)(k) of the Mental Health Act 1983.

In view of s.13 of the Settled Land Act 1925, the principal powers of the tenant for life cannot be exercised until the requisite vesting instrument has been executed. An authority under seal to procure the execution of the necessary vesting instrument will be issued. If execution of such instrument on behalf of the patient is unnecessary no reference to incapacity is to be made. Where the land is leasehold or freehold subject to a rent or covenants, and if execution on behalf of the patient is required, the authority will authorise the receiver in the name and on behalf of the patient to execute. In either case the draft vesting instrument must be submitted to the court for approval.

The prior leave of the court is required before any notices under s.101 of the Settled Land Act 1925, can be given (*Re Ray's Settled Estates* (1884) 25 Ch.D. 464) where a sale of settled property is contemplated. The procedure to be followed is similar to that of a sale of the patient's absolute property under a general order (see paras 6B–88 and 6B–89). That order will authorise the receiver to give all necessary notices required by s.101 of the Settled Land Act 1925. The proceeds will be received by the trustees as capital moneys who will also be responsible for the payment of the taxed costs of the application and order and of the sale.

Generally, see Heywood and Massey, *Court of Protection Practice*, 2002 Edn., paras 12–014 to 12–015.

Business

6B–101 Under s.96(1)(f) of the Mental Health Act 1983, the court may direct the carrying on by a suitable person of any profession trade or business of the patient, and in such a case the following detailed directions to the receiver are usually incorporated in the order and should be strictly adhered to:

    (a) To procure forthwith a valuation of the (stock in trade) (and fixtures and fittings) (and live and dead stock) as on the date hereof or as near thereto as may be possible (such valuation to be made by a competent valuer at a fee to be agreed and sanctioned by the court beforehand) and to file the same with the court at the earliest possible moment and to report to the court at the expiration of three months from the date thereof as to the position and prospects of the business.

(b) To open a new banking account earmarked for the business and to use such account exclusively for transactions relating to such business.

(c) To open a second new banking account earmarked for the receivership generally and to use such account for all receipts and payments not relating to the said business.

(d) No overdraft is to be incurred nor any existing overdraft increased in respect of either of the said banking accounts except under an authority bearing the seal of the court.

(e) The business account is not to be drawn upon except for purposes wholly relating to the business (except when profits are sufficient to permit drawings therefrom to be made for the credit of the receivership account) and the receivership account is not to be drawn upon for purposes of the business.

(f) In the event of drawings being made from the business on account of profits a cheque is to be drawn upon the business account in favour of the receivership account.

(g) To keep proper books of account of the said business.

(h) In the event of the court authorising the carrying on of the business after the expiration of the said period of three months to cause a balance sheet and profit and loss account to be prepared annually (generally by accountants) and such balance sheet and profit and loss account together with a report upon the said business are to be submitted to the court (within one month after the close of the account)(with the annual receivership account).

A receiver carrying on the business of the patient, under an order of the court, cannot be made personally liable for trade debts unless it can be shown that he held himself out as principal (*Plumpton v. Burkinshaw* [1908] 2 K.B. 572).

Dissolution of partnership

The Court of Protection may order the dissolution of a partnership of which the **6B–102** patient is a member (s.96(1)(g) of the Mental Health Act 1983) but will only do so where there is a receiver and there are no partnership disputes; otherwise it may be necessary to apply in the Chancery Division. In any event the receiver may be authorised to give notice to dissolve, etc.

Limited companies

It is not the practice, save in exceptional circumstances, to authorise the exercise by **6B–103** a receiver of a patient's voting rights in respect of his shareholding in a public company, but where he is a substantial shareholder in a private company other considerations will apply, *e.g.* whether he holds a controlling interest, or his holding is sufficiently substantial to influence the running of the company.

If the patient is a director of the company it may be that his mental incapacity disqualifies him from continuing to act as a director in which case the court will consider whether he should be replaced as a director by his receiver or some other person nominated by the court. In any case, it is important that his directorship be relinquished if only to avoid the possibility of his incurring any personal liability for misfeasance or breach of trust committed by his fellow directors during his incapacity.

Following his removal from directorship the possibility of his being granted a pension by the company should be explored.

Where it is desired to replace the patient as a director by the receiver or some other person, *e.g.* his accountant or solicitor, to enable the court to exercise control on the more important aspects of the company's affairs, the receiver will be authorised to exercise the patient's voting rights to procure such election. When necessary the receiver will be authorised to transfer to himself sufficient shares to enable him to qualify as a director, upon his undertaking to credit the patient's account with the dividends thereon and to retransfer the shares to the patient and to resign from the directorship if and when directed by the court to do so. Any remuneration received by the receiver in respect of the directorship will belong to him in his own right.

The Court's Order will also provide for the exercise by the receiver of the patient's voting rights in respect of the remainder of the patient's shares in the company but, as to certain matters, only subject to the prior approval of the court. Such matters are (a) borrowing (b) increase or reduction of capital (c) alterations or amendments of or additions to the Memorandum and Articles of Association of the company (d) fixing director's fees (e) appointment or removal of directors (f) winding up (g) sale of assets or goodwill (h) entering into partnership with any person or company.

The above specific limitations as to voting will normally be included in any order where, the patient being a large shareholder in a private company, the receiver is authorised to exercise the patient's voting rights.

The basic information required to be supplied to enable the court to consider the patient's position is:

    (a) The total issued capital of the company.

    (b) The number of shares held by the patient.

    (c) The number of shares held by the other major shareholders.

    (d) The number of shares (if any) required to be held by a director.

    (e) The auditors' report and accounts of the company covering the three years previous to the application.

    (f) A copy of the Memorandum and Articles of Association.

    (g) A list of the present directors of the company.

Leases and surrenders

6B–104   The jurisdiction to authorise the granting of leases and accept surrenders derives from s.96(1)(b) and (c) of the Mental Health Act 1983.

A receiver by the order appointing him may sometimes be authorised to let property for periods not exceeding three years, but if there is a probability that sale may become desirable such authority will not be included. For longer periods an order may be required.

To obtain an order to grant a lease application should be made by letter setting out the facts. The order or direction will be an open order authorising the receiver, subject to the approval of the court or PGO, in the name and on behalf of the patient to grant a lease of the property in question and for that purpose to execute such documents as shall be necessary. When the proposed lease has been agreed the draft should be submitted to the court together with evidence of the sufficiency of the rent and the desirability of the terms by certificate of the estate agent. The draft should be exhibited to the evidence.

Performance of a contract

6B–105   The court may direct the carrying out of any contract entered into by the patient, either prior to incapacity or during incapacity (s.96(1)(h) of the Mental Health Act 1983). The adoption of a voidable contract for the purchase (and *semble*, sale) of freehold property entered into prior to the proceedings works conversion as from the date of the contract (*Baldwyn v. Smith* [1900] Ch. 588).

See also s.54(2)(c) of the Trustee Act 1925.

Exercise of power (including power to consent)

6B–106   Any such power may be exercised under s.96(1)(k) of the Mental Health Act 1983. It should be noted that powers of a patient as patron of a benefice are exercisable by the Lord Chancellor only and all inquiries in regard thereto should be made to The Lord Chancellor's Ecclesiastical Secretary, 10 Downing Street, London, SW1A 2AA.

Among the powers exercisable under this provision are the powers of a patient as tenant for life; the powers of a patient as mortgagee; power to bar an entail (see *Re Pares* (1879) 12 Ch.D. 333; *Re E. D. S.* [1914] 1 Ch. 618, and *Re R. H. C.* [1963] 1 W.L.R. 1095); power to appoint in favour of children (*Re A.* [1904] 2 Ch. 328); powers of guardianship of an infant child (*Re L. H. B.* [1935] 1 Ch. 643); the exercise of a power to appoint trustee (*Re Fuller* [1900] 2 Ch. 551).

The question whether the Court of Protection could authorise a receiver, on behalf of a patient, to give his consent under s.2(1)(d) of the Divorce Reform Act 1969 (now s.1(2)(d) of the Matrimonial Causes Act 1973) was raised in *Mason v. Mason* [1972] Fam. 302; [1972] 3 All E.R. 315. The President declined to say whether the Court of Protection could give such authority.

A transaction fee of £130 will be payable in most cases. See paras 6B–316 and 6B–337.

Grant of administration

6B–107   If a patient is entitled to apply for a grant of representation to the estate of a deceased person, authority may be given by the Court of Protection for the receiver to apply for a grant for the use and benefit of the patient during his incapacity. Generally, see Heywood and Massey, *Court of Protection Practice* 2002 edition and the Non-Contentious Probate Rules 1987, r.35.

Where a patient is entitled to a grant but, either because no receiver has been appointed or for some other reason, no person has been authorised by the Court of Protection to apply for a grant or there is no lawful attorney acting under a registered enduring power of attorney and an application is being made for a grant under r.35(2)(c) of the Non-Contentious Probate Rules 1987, notice of the intended application is required to be given to the Court of Protection under r.35(5). The notice should include the name and address of the proposed administrator, his relationship to the deceased and the patient and short particulars of the deceased's estate and the extent of the patient's interest therein, and any proposals for dealing therewith for the benefit of the patient. The formal sealed acknowledgment issued by the court should be produced to the Probate Registry.

Patient mortgagee

Powers of a patient as mortgagee are exercisable under ss.95(1) and 96(1)(k) of the **6B–108** Mental Health Act 1983. An order or direction for the execution of a statutory receipt or reconveyance where the patient is beneficially entitled as mortgagee is applied for by letter (unless the court otherwise directs). The following undertaking should be included in the letter of application: "We undertake to produce on the hearing of the application the mortgage referred to in the within written application and any transfer of the said mortgage." The application must be supported by an affidavit by a solicitor dealing with (i) the patient's title to the mortgage and who is entitled to give a receipt; (ii) the title to the immediate equity of redemption and in whom vested; (iii) who is entitled to receive the deeds bearing in mind any subsequent incumbrances; and (iv) the amount due under the mortgage (capital and arrears of interest) bearing in mind any further advances, etc., or any moneys applied to protect the security.

The mortgagor should not be served, and if served is not entitled to his costs out of the patient's estate (*Re Phillips* (1869) L.R. 4 Ch.App. 629; and *Re Wheeler* (1852) 1 De G.M. & G. 434). The order or direction directs the receiver in the name and on behalf of the patient to execute the statutory receipt or to reconvey or transfer.

If the patient is one of several co-mortgagees and all of such mortgagees are living and each mortgagee is entitled to a definite amount of the mortgage money application can be made in the Court of Protection for the patient by his receiver to concur in the statutory receipt or transfer as the case may be, otherwise the appropriate proceedings must be taken for the appointment of a new trustee in place of the patient.

For form of statutory receipt see para. 6B–177.

In a proper case an order will be made for the advance of the patient's money on mortgage. The application would have to be supported by evidence as to value and the proposed advance should not normally exceed two-thirds of such valuation.

An application for sale by the patient as mortgagee would proceed substantially in the same manner as an application for sale of property belonging to a patient absolutely (paras 6B–87 *et seq.*); it must be shown that the power of sale has arisen.

Patient mortgagor

When a patient is the mortgagor of any of his property the mortgagee should com- **6B–109** municate with the receiver or his solicitor if the question arises of enforcing the mortgage or any of the covenants arising thereunder. Under s.96(1)(b) of the Mental Health Act 1983, the court can authorise the charging or other disposition of or dealing with any property of the patient. Application is made by letter (unless otherwise directed).

Improvements

When the patient is tenant for life and it is desired to expend money on improve- **6B–110** ments upon the settled property application should be made for leave for the receiver in the name and on behalf of the patient tenant for life to execute the required improvement, to give a direction to the Settled Land Act trustees for payment pursuant to s.75 of the Settled Land Act 1925, and, if there are no capital moneys available in the hands of the Settled Land Act trustees, to raise the money required on the security of the settled land or of any part thereof by a legal mortgage (Settled Land Act 1925, s.71(1)); or the application could be made for the money required to be advanced out of the patient's capital and a mortgage given by the trustees to the patient to secure the amount advanced (Settled Land Act 1925, s.68).

Preservation of interests in patient's property

6B–111   This is now governed by s.101 of the Mental Health Act 1983, to which reference should be made (para. 6B–198). Section 123(1) of the Lunacy Act 1890 which was replaced in the main by the Mental Health Act 1959, s.107, only applied to transactions wherein the element of conversion into money was present and did not apply, *e.g.* to the investment of money (*Walker, Re* [1921] 2 Ch. 63) purchase of property (*Searle, Re* [1912] 2 Ch. 365) and lodgment in court of funds *in specie* (*Palmer, Re* [1945] Ch. 8). The definition of "disposal" in subs. (3) nullifies the effect of these decisions. See Sched.5, para. 45 as to retrospective effect of s.101(1).

The paramount consideration is the interest of the patient, and the court pays no regard to those who come after, but in matters outside the ordinary course of management it is the duty of the court, so far as possible, not to alter the character of the patient's property or to interfere with any rights of succession (*Att.-Gen. v. Ailesbury* (1887) 12 L.R. App. Cas. 672).

As to proceeds of sale of real estate descending as realty, see *Re Matson* [1897] 2 Ch. 509; *Re Tugwell* (1885) 27 Ch.D. 309; *Re Alston* [1917] 2 Ch. 226.

When it is desired to relieve a legatee from the incidence of duty upon freehold property which has been purchased out of personal property bequeathed to the legatee (his interest being automatically preserved under s.101(1)) the court can give a direction under subs. (2) *ibid.*, that the property purchased shall, as long as it remains the property of the patient or forms part of his estate, be treated as personal property. The converse case of sale of real property and the acquisition in its place of personal property requires no direction of the court, and under subs. (1)(b) the property purchased would automatically be treated as real property.

As to devolution to the heir of a pre-1926 patient's interest in realty on his death intestate, without having recovered his testamentary capacity, see Administration of Estates Act 1925, s.51(2).

Creditors

6B–112   See ss.95(2) and 96(1)(i) of the Mental Health Act 1983. During the receivership proceedings the creditors are without remedy. They cannot obtain any payment unless the court in the exercise of its discretion, makes an order in their favour (*Re Seager Hunt* [1906] 2 Ch. 299). The patient's interest comes first, and if necessary the creditors will be ignored (*Re Plenderleith* [1893] 3 Ch. 332) or they can obtain a charging order under s.96(1)(b) and (j) of Mental Health Act 1983. After the patient's death the High Court, in administering his estate, will not be bound by any order of the Court of Protection directing payment of a dividend to creditors (*Re Seager Hunt* [1906] 2 Ch. 295); see also *Re Wheater* [1928] 1 Ch. 223. A creditor who is entitled to interest is to have it at 4 per cent together with the costs of proving his claim (*Re Hunt* [1902] 2 Ch. 318).

Where the property of a patient has become subject to the control of the Court of Protection by the appointment of a receiver, it cannot be seized under a writ of *fi. fa.* by an execution creditor of the patient; and the court will make an order dealing with his property, and for the payment thereout of costs and of an allowance for the maintenance of the patient—though not of his wife—in priority to any claim of the execution creditor; but subject to such allowance and to the costs incurred in relation to the patient's property, the order will be made without prejudice to any charge or priority which the creditor may have acquired by lodging his writ of *fi. fa.* with the sheriff (*Re Winkle* [1894] 2 Ch. 519, CA). An interim order has been made for the express purpose of protecting the patient's property from execution (*Re Pountain* (1888) 37 Ch.D. 609). Nevertheless, the jurisdiction of the Court of Protection does not interfere with the common law or statutory rights of a judgment creditor over funds which have not been brought within the control of the Court of Protection (*Re Brown* [1900] 1 Ch. 489) or with the rights of creditors to seize and sell by legal process property of the patient which at the time of seizure is not in the custody of such court, and the issuing of an application in the Court of Protection does not withdraw the property of the patient from such legal process by a creditor until an order is made showing that the court has actually taken the property under its protection (*Re Charles Clarke* [1898] 1 Ch. 336, CA, distinguishing *Re Winkle*). Further, an order authorising a person therein specified, in the name and on behalf of the patient to receive and give a discharge for all sums of money due to him, does not affect rights against the patient's property at law or in equity (such as a vendor's lien for unpaid purchase money) previously acquired by third persons (*Davies v. Thomas* [1900] 2 Ch. 462, explaining and distinguishing *Re Winkle*).

The Court of Protection will not normally pay statute barred debts (*Re Kenrick* [1907] 1 Ir. Ch. 480) but will recognise an honourable obligation on the part of the patient, and will order payment by way of bounty (*Re Whitaker* (1889) 42 Ch.D. 119). As to the admission of claims for the maintenance of what were formerly rate-aided patients, see "Maintenance," para. 6B–83.

Debts properly incurred by a receiver under the direction of the court or PGO will be paid; such debts are the liability of the patient and not of the receiver, unless he expressly pledges his credit (*Plumpton v. Burkinshaw* [1908] 2 K.B. 572; *Re E. G.* [1914] 1 Ch. 927).

Charging order

A charging order of the High Court under O.50 may be obtained against property **6B–113** of a patient in respect of a judgment for debts incurred before incapacity, and may be enforced against the estate of the patient after his death; for the effect of a charging order does not depend upon the capacity of the judgment debtor to give a valid charge but upon the validity of the judgment (*Re Leavesley* [1891] 2 Ch. 1, CA). The High Court is not precluded from giving effect to a charging order made by it upon the interest of a patient in a fund in the High Court during his life without regard to his needs where that fund has not been brought within the control of the Court of Protection, and the balance only of the funds after satisfying the charge, will be transferred to Court of Protection administration (*Re Brown* [1900] 1 Ch. 489; see also *Horne v. Pountain* (1889) 23 QBD 264). On the other hand, where the fund in court is under the control of the Court of Protection that court will order a proper allowance for the maintenance of the patient to be made out of the capital and income of the fund, though the effect may be to make the capital insufficient for the payment of the creditors who have obtained charging orders on the fund, and such creditors are not entitled to have impounded an amount of capital sufficient to meet their demands (*Re Plenderleith* [1893] 3 Ch. 332). Whether the obtaining of a charging order is, under such circumstances, of any value, *quaere*. See remarks of Lindley L.J., in *Re Plenderleith* [1893] 3 Ch. 332; *cf. Re Winkle* [1894] 2 Ch. 519; *Re Seager Hunt* [1900] 2 Ch. 54; and *CL v.C FW* [1928] P. 223 at 225.

O.50, does not apply to Court of Protection charging orders made under s.96(1)(b) and (j) of the Mental Health Act 1983 (*Re Cathcart* [1893] 1 Ch. 466, CA).

It is now the normal practice, though discretionary, for charging orders of the Court of Protection to carry simple interest at the judgment rate (see current Judgment Debts (Rate of Interest) Order).

Bankruptcy

The county court may, *ex parte*, and without notice appoint any person to act for a **6B–114** patient. A person under mental disability, whether a receiver has been appointed or not, may be adjudicated bankrupt without the concurrence of the Court of Protection, but such adjudication and the appointment of a trustee in bankruptcy does not affect the direction and control of the debtor's property which may have already been assumed by the Court of Protection (*Re a Debtor (No. 1 of 1941)* [1941] Ch. 487).

Where it is for the patient's benefit the Court of Protection will authorise the necessary steps to be taken with a view to the patient's adjudication as a bankrupt (*Re Lee* (1883) 23 Ch.D. 216; and *Re Farnham* [1895] 2 Ch. 799) but the receiver, as such, should take no further steps than the Court of Protection may have authorised (*Re R.S.A.* [1901] 2 K.B. 32).

A person under the jurisdiction of the Court of Protection, discharged from the mental hospital as recovered, who does not apply to determine the proceedings, cannot set up the Court of Protection order as a defence against bankruptcy (*Re Belton* [1913] W.N. 63).

Litigation by or against a patient

Under s.96(1)(i) of the Mental Health Act 1983, the Court of Protection may make **6B–115** orders and give directions and authorities for the conduct of legal proceedings in the name of the patient or on his behalf. Proceedings in the High Court by or against a patient are regulated and governed by O.80, and the Matrimonial Causes Rules 1977, rr.112–114. See also "Matrimonial causes," para. 6B–134. County court proceedings are regulated and governed by the County Court Rules 1981. As to seeking directions of the Court of Protection in regard to contemplated legal proceedings, including divorce, involving a patient, see *Re W. (E. E. M.)* [1971] Ch. 123 at 143 as explained in *Re S, (F. G.)* [1973] 1 W.L.R. 178.

The general effect of all the above Rules of Court is that a receiver (or other person) duly authorised by the Court of Protection to conduct the proceedings in question on behalf of a patient is entitled to be next friend or guardian *ad litem*, as the case may be, save that in the county court the actual appointment of the guardian *ad litem* is made by the district judge.

The receiver should before bringing or defending an action have the sanction of the Court of Protection, otherwise he will act at his own risk as to costs (*Re Nottley* (1839) 3 Jur. (o.s.) 719). To obtain such authority a statement of facts should be filed with, where the patient is defendant or respondent, a copy of the writ or originating summons as the case may be. The facts should be set out sufficiently to enable the master to form an opinion of the merits of the action.

Unless it is plainly manifest that the receiver has no interest adverse to the patient, a certificate of no adverse interest should be filed. If the receiver has an adverse interest, either a new receiver should be appointed or, alternatively, the name and address, etc., of some other person should be submitted and the solicitor should file a certificate of no adverse interest and that the person proposed is a fit and proper person to act as next friend or guardian *ad litem* for the patient in the proceedings. In such a case the master may prefer that the Official Solicitor should conduct the proceedings and become next friend or guardian *ad litem*.

Legal aid does not apply to proceedings in the Court of Protection *per se*. Where, however, a patient as defined in reg. 3(3) of the Legal Aid (General) Regulations 1980 is to commence or to defend proceedings in a court to which the legal aid regulations apply, application should be made in accordance with reg. 15. Where the Court of Protection is already seised of the matter it will, where appropriate, issue any necessary authority for such application to be made on behalf of the patient.

Damages recovered on behalf of patient

6B–116
Damages recovered on behalf of a patient should be administered by the Court of Protection (*Leather v. Kirby* (HL) [1965] 1 W.L.R. 1489; and *M. v. Lester (Practice Note)* [1966] 1 W.L.R. 134). When applying to the Court of Protection for directions to deal with damages recovered under a High Court order, the Pt I order must be produced. The Pt II order should be lodged with the Court Funds Office as soon as possible (see below).

Where a plaintiff who is a patient within the meaning of the Mental Health Act 1983 has been awarded damages in an action in the Queen's Bench Division, the transfer of the damages will be facilitated if the judgment includes a provision to the following effect:

"... that the defendant do within [   ] days pay the said sum of £[   ] into court to be placed to and accumulated in a Special Account pending an application by the next friend to the Court of Protection for the appointment of a receiver for the plaintiff and that upon such appointment being made the said sum of £[   ] together with any interest thereon [subject to a first charge under the Legal Aid Act 1988] be transferred to the Court of Protection to the credit of the plaintiff to be dealt with as the Court of Protection in its discretion shall think fit."

Similar provisions should be included in an order approving a compromise on behalf of a patient.

Once an award has been made or approved, the next friend and the plaintiff's carers will naturally be anxious to have access to it to meet the plaintiff's needs. Three steps can be taken by solicitors in such a case to expedite matters:

(1) Application may be made for the appointment of a receiver in anticipation of an award. Forms for this purpose are available from the Public Guardianship Office, Archway Tower, 2 Junction Road, London N19 5SZ. The next friend is usually the person to make the application and may also be the most suitable person to act as receiver.

(2) If the plaintiff was legally aided in the action, the award will effectively be frozen, because of the statutory charge, unless and until a reserve for costs can be

agreed with the Legal Aid Board. The plaintiff's solicitors should therefore take urgent steps to obtain and complete the appropriate form of undertaking, which is available from the area office, by inserting a figure which is sufficient to cover the full extent of their claim upon the legal aid fund. This sum should take into account costs and disbursements already incurred or to be incurred, less any legal aid contribution which has been paid by the plaintiff and any *inter partes* costs which have been recovered from the defendant. The plaintiff's solicitor should then return the signed undertaking to the legal aid area office (who will inform the Court Funds Office by letter of the amount to be retained to cover the statutory charge) and should obtain an order from the court making the award directing the Court Funds Office to release to the area office the amount from the award to cover the statutory charge. The balance will then be released to the Court of Protection, once the Pt II Order has been lodged.

(3) The solicitors in the matter should then follow the procedure known as "Lodging the Part II Order." A payment schedule (Form 200) should at once be prepared. This can be purchased from law stationers or copied from the precedent at para. 1209 in this volume. In the column headed "Details of payments, transfers or other operations required," they should insert "Transfer to Court of Protection credit," in the second column they should give the full name and address of the patient and in the third column they should insert the figure which represents the award, less the figure to be reserved for costs. In the space below, they should insert in the first column "Reserve for costs" and in the third column they should give details of that figure, as shown in the undertaking to the legal aid area office mentioned in para. (2) above. The solicitors should then forward the Form 200 for authentication to the District Registry which made the award. If the award was made in London and the patient is not also a minor, the form should be lodged in the Action Department of the Central Office at the Royal Courts of Justice. If the patient is also a minor, it should go to the Masters' Secretary's Office at the Royal Courts of Justice.

The court which made the award should be requested to forward the payment schedule (Form 200) to the Court Funds Office, Queen's Bench Division, 22 Kingsway, London WC2B 6LE. As soon as it is received there, arrangements will be made to carry the bulk of the award over to the Court of Protection, leaving the amount reserved for costs in the Special Account at the Court Funds Office to gain interest until the area office confirms that it can be released to the Court of Protection or to itself, as the case may be.

Practice Note (Transfer of Damages to Court of Protection) September 7, 1990 by the Senior Master of the Queen's Bench Division and the Master of the Court of Protection.

It is necessary to lodge a schedule of damages in accordance with Practice Direction (Damages: Personal Injuries) [1984] 1 W.L.R. 1127; [1984] 3 All E.R. 165.

Structured settlements involving patients

Where damages are awarded in respect of injuries of a kind such as to make the **6B–117** appointment of a receiver by the court appropriate, the award should include an element for receivership management costs and Court of Protection fees (*Futej v. Lewandowski* (1980) 124 S.J. 777; and *Duller v. South East Lines Engineers* [1981] C.L.Y. 585). There have been a number of cases in which "structured settlements" involving plaintiffs who are patients have been approved. Under this arrangement, part of the plaintiff's award is provided in the form of an annuity under which payments are made which represent slices of the antecedent debt and which are treated as tax-free capital payments. The payments are index-linked, or increased at a fixed percentage each year and are guaranteed during the plaintiff's lifetime or for a minimum period of years, whichever is the longer (*Kelly v. Dawes*, *The Times*, September 27, 1990 is the first reported case of a structured settlement).

Settlement on behalf of patient

There is no power in the High Court to order a settlement on behalf of a patient **6B–118** and/or his family and dependants of damages awarded to him as a result of litigation there: this power is reserved to the Court of Protection under s.96(1)(d) of the Mental Health Act 1983, para. 6B–190. It follows that where such a settlement is contemplated, application should first be made to the Master of the Court of Protection.

Orders for Settlement of Personal Injury Awards to Patients

Practice Note (Procedure for the Settlement of Personal Injury: Awards to Patients) **6B–119**

November 15, 1996, made by the Master of the Court of Protection sets out as follows (this note supersedes the former Practice Note dated May 6, 1994):

1. Disregard of personal injury awards in assessing entitlement to benefits

6B–120   1.1 In certain circumstances, funds derived from personal injury awards may be disregarded for the purposes of assessment of entitlement to income support under the Income Support (General) Regulations or local authority funding under the National Assistance (Assessment of Resources) Regulations 1992. Similar exemptions apply for the purposes of Housing Benefit and Council Tax. Until recently, the establishment of a trust was believed to be the only way to take advantage of these exemptions, but it has recently become clear that, in the case of funds held subject to the jurisdiction of the Court of Protection, the creation of a formal trust may not always be necessary.

Minors' funds

6B–121   1.2 An additional disregard was introduced from October 1994 under paragraph 44 to Schedule 10 of the Income Support (General) Regulations 1987 (as amended by the Income-related Benefits Schemes (Miscellaneous Amendments) (No. 5) Regulations 1994). Accordingly, any sum of capital administered in the Court of Protection on behalf of a person under the age of 18 which is derived either (i) from an award of damages for personal injury to that child; or (ii) an award of compensation for the death of a parent will be disregarded for the purpose of the assessment of capital. Similar disregards were introduced in respect of eligibility for other benefits.

Adult patients' funds

6B–122   1.3 On August 31, 1995, Social Security Commissioner Heald gave a decision (CIS/368/94) in which he held that a patient's funds derived from an award of compensation for personal injuries held subject to the control of the Public Trust Office (now the Public Guardianship Office) and the Court of Protection should be treated for capital assessment purposes under the income support legislation as if they were held on trust and should accordingly be disregarded. This is now reported at [1996] 3 J.S.S.L. D136. Enquiries made of the DSS indicate that no appeal is contemplated and representations have been made seeking clarification, possibly by way of amendments to the regulations. It is understood that a review of the general policy in this area is likely. Whilst this decision is not binding upon local authorities, indications are that it will be strongly persuasive (see para. 10.003 of the Charging for Residential Accommodation Guide which expressly contemplates an exemption for funds in the Court of Protection) and that for funding as well as benefits purposes, any capital derived from a personal injury award which is under the control of the Court of Protection can be disregarded without the necessity of placing it in a formal trust.

2. Orders for settlement of personal injury awards

6B–123   2.1 In cases where a formal trust (often known as a "special needs" trust) for a patient is required, there are two different methods by which it may be created.

An Application to the Court of Protection under section 96(1)(d) of the Mental Health Act 1983

6B–124   2.2 Under section 96(1)(d) the Court of Protection has power to order the creation of a settlement (that is to say, a trust) for a patient.

2.3 Where the amount of the award exceeds £30,000, the jurisdiction of the Court of Protection should be invoked by an application for the appointment of a receiver (where there is no existing receivership) and a formal application should also be made under section 96(1)(d) for the creation of a trust. The Official Solicitor will be asked to represent the patient for the purposes of the application and, depending upon the complexity of the case, an attended hearing may be required. The procedure set out in Procedure Note PN9 (obtainable from the Registrar) should be followed.

2.4 Where the amount of the award is below £30,000, a simplified procedure is available. In suitable cases, the Court of Protection may be prepared to deal with the application without asking the Official Solicitor to represent the patient and without requiring an attended hearing.

Settlement as part of the terms of compromise of litigation

2.5 The High Court has no power to order the settlement of an award of damages **6B–125** which is the absolute property of a patient (see RSC O.80/12/5), this can only be done by the Court of Protection. However, there are procedures whereby an award of damages can be settled, by consent, in trust for the patient as part of the terms of compromise of the action between the plaintiff and the defendant, with the approval of the High Court, in circumstances where the award never becomes the absolute property of the patient. If the award is proposed to be settled as a term of the compromise of the litigation and not to become the plaintiff's absolute property, and the plaintiff is a patient (by reason of being incapable, through mental disorder, of managing his property and affairs), the Court of Protection should be asked to approve the terms of compromise, the form of the draft trust deed and the draft consent order before the final application for the approval of the High Court takes place. The Court of Protection will also need to consider what directions should be given as to other assets which may need administration, which may involve the appointment of a receiver.

3. When are "special needs" trusts appropriate?

Possible disadvantages

3.1 In approving a compromise or a settlement under section 96(1)(d), the Court of **6B–126** Protection will have to consider not only the possible financial advantages to the patient in terms of preserved eligibility for public funding, but also the various possible disadvantages. These disadvantages may include a loss of supervision by the court, inflexibility, the imposition of a second layer of administration of the patient's affairs (which may be expensive), the difficulty of finding suitable trustees and, in the case of discretionary trusts, restricted access to the funds, the difficulty of finding alternative beneficiaries and possible tax disadvantages. Bare trusts are generally more straightforward. There may be no financial advantage in terms of preserved eligibility for public funding in setting up a trust if the income or capital are intended and used for an item of food, ordinary clothing or footwear, household fuel, rent in respect of which housing benefit is payable, council tax or water rate, even if paid to a third party as the regulations exclude such payments from the disregard (Income Support (General) Regulations 1987, Sched.9, para. 15).

Suitable cases

3.2 Normally, the Court of Protection will only approve the creation of a trust if **6B–127** this will result in some immediate and substantial benefit to the patient which will not accrue if the funds simply remain under a receivership. Accordingly, it is not considered that all cases where a person is entitled to public funding prior to the receipt of an award of damages should give rise to an application for a trust; in some cases it may be more appropriate to continue to manage the funds under a receivership. Also, if monies have been specifically received by the patient which will pay for all future care, these monies should generally remain available for that purpose.

3.3 The most suitable cases for settlement will therefore be those where such benefit to the patient can be demonstrated, and which also include one of the following features (i) the award is only small or (ii) in the case of a larger award, difficulties on liability or contributory negligence have resulted in substantially reduced damages, or (iii) the award does not include the cost of future care as an element of damages.

Timing

3.4 It is not to be assumed that time is of the essence, so far as creating a trust is **6B–128** concerned. It is now clear that it is not necessary to set up a trust as soon as the award is received. Provided the funds attributable to the personal injury compensation have been kept separate from other assets and remain identifiable, a trust can be set up at any time that the advantages to the patient of doing so become apparent. In some cases, it may be appropriate for the award to be held under normal receivership arrangements for a period of time to enable arrangements for the care of the patient to be developed and settle down into a pattern.

3.5 Solicitors advising the next friend are often concerned to ensure that any trust is created as early as possible. This is usually because they are concerned that the patient will otherwise be treated as possessing capital of which he has deprived himself for the purpose of securing entitlement to income support, overlooking the exception provided in regulation 51(1) of the Income Support (General) Regulations 1987 (as amended by the Income Support (General) (Amendment No. 3) Regulations 1990). Also, requests for the Court of Protection to approve trusts informally prior to hearings in the High Court are often presented as urgent because a hearing date in the High Court is approaching. Whilst approval to the settlement of small awards can often be given very quickly where necessary, experience has shown that it is rarely satisfactory to rush the preparation of trusts involving substantial sums of money. These require careful consideration, even at the expense of some addition to the costs or an adjournment of the High Court application. Accordingly, even where an award is to be settled as a term of the compromise of the personal injury claim rather than by an application under section 96(1)(d), the Court of Protection may still direct the application to be dealt with by an attended hearing, and request the Official Solicitor to represent the patient for the purposes of the hearing of that application before the master.

4. Which method of setting up a trust should be chosen?

6B–129   4.1 The separate methods of creating a trust have certain different consequences, which may sometimes influence the choice.

The accumulation period

6B–130   4.2 Trusts set up following an order of the High Court can only be done in the form of a declaration of trusts by the trustees, whereas trusts set up by an order of the Court of Protection will take the form of a settlement, with the patient being the settlor. In the former case, the period over which income can be accumulated by the trustees is restricted to 21 years, whereas, in the case of trusts set up by an order of the Court of Protection, provision can be made for income to be accumulated, if appropriate, for the lifetime of the patient as section 164(1)(a) of the Law of Property Act 1925 applies.

Revocation

6B–131   4.3 Because of uncertainties about possible future changes in the benefits legislation, it is generally preferable for trusts to be revocable, to retain the flexibility to restore the capital to the patient absolutely, should this become desirable. There are, however, problems about including a power of revocation in trusts set up as part of the terms of compromise of a personal injury claim, as the award has never been the absolute property of the patient and it is accordingly arguable that exercising a power of revocation would restore the funds to the defendants.

Inheritance tax

6B–132   4.4 All applications are expected to address the inheritance tax implications of the proposed settlement, where the relevant funds exceed the levels at which inheritance tax is charged. The method chosen to establish the trust may have an effect upon this. Also, the tax implications of the form of trust should be considered. For example, there may in some cases be advantages in setting up a trust under the trusts for disabled persons regime, by virtue of which the trust will be treated for inheritance tax purposes as an income in possession trust and the patient as an income beneficiary even though there may be a power to accumulate income (Inheritance Tax Act 1984, section 89). Fully discretionary trusts will be liable to the ten-year charge and to the proportionate (or exit) charge on assets leaving the settlement at other times. When discretionary trusts are applied for, it will generally be necessary to demonstrate that, notwithstanding any tax disadvantages, such a trust is in the patient's best interests.

5. The terms of the trust

6B–133   5.1 A number of precedent clauses are issued by the Court of Protection with Procedure Note PN9. These are not prescriptive and are for guidance only. However, a number of general points arise.

5.2 Placing funds in trust may entail the Court of Protection giving up control, or partial control of the assets of a patient in derogation of the powers entrusted to it by the Mental Health Act 1983. Consequently, it is not to be assumed that the Court of Protection will automatically authorise a trust which gives complete discretion to the trustees as to the distribution of income and capital. In some cases, it may prefer to retain control of certain critical powers exercised by the trustees and of the trustees themselves, particularly in relation to the distribution of capital and the appointment of new trustees. It should be appreciated that if the involvement of the Court of Protection in a case is continuing on this account, then it is possible that a receivership will be necessary even if there are no assets apart from the assets in the trust to administer. In some cases, this may be regarded as an acceptable price to pay for the benefits obtained by placing the funds in trust. Sometimes a receiver may be needed to deal with income applied for the benefit of the patient or with assets in the patient's free estate and to deal with tax returns.

5.3 Further, it is not to be assumed that the Court of Protection will necessarily authorise discretionary trusts including beneficiaries other than the patient. It will be expected that the trust will be revocable, and that if the patient recovers his capacity, he will have the right to bring the trust to an end and call for the trust fund to be paid to him. In most cases, the trust should provide that on the death of the patient, the fund should be payable to his personal representatives for the benefit of his estate. Whilst it is possible for the Court of Protection to approve a trust which makes testamentary provision for the devolution of the fund after the patient's death for a patient who lacks testamentary capacity, it is nearly always more satisfactory to deal with this by way of a separate statutory will application which will also make provision for the devolution of any assets falling into the patient's free estate. If, exceptionally, the trust is to make testamentary provisions, it may also provide for a general or special power of appointment by will. The court will not, however, normally authorise the execution of a settlement which includes incidental testamentary provisions where the patient is still a minor.

5.4 As the principal beneficiary of the trust will be a patient, it is normally expected that the trust will include some method of regulating professional trustees' costs.

Matrimonial causes

Generally, see r.112 of the Matrimonial Causes Rules 1977 and Heywood and Massey, *Court of Protection Practice* (12th ed., 1991) pp.243 *et seq.*   **6B–134**

Under s.96(1)(i) of the Mental Health Act 1983, the master may authorise the receiver (or other person) to present a petition in the name or on behalf of a patient for matrimonial relief (see para. 10B–7 and *Baker v. Baker* (1860) 5 P.D. 152; affirmed (1860) 6 P.D. 12, and *Re W. (E. E. M.)* [1971] Ch. 123) nullity (see *Portsmouth v. Portsmouth* (1828) 1 Hagg. E.R. 355) presumption of death and dissolution of marriage, or judicial separation (see *Woodgate v. Taylor* (1861) L.J.P. 197).

The jurisdiction to authorise the bringing of a divorce suit on behalf of a patient was fully considered by Ungoed-Thomas J. in *Re W. (E. E. M.)* [1971] Ch.123.

Where a receiver (or other person) is authorised in the Court of Protection to bring a suit or defend a suit on behalf of a patient, he is entitled to be next friend or guardian *ad litem* without an order of the Divorce Court (Matrimonial Causes Rules 1977, r.112(4)).

Where a patient is a respondent in a suit and it is desired that the receiver should be authorised to conduct the proceedings on behalf of the patient, a statement of facts should be filed in the Court of Protection, accompanied by a copy of the petition and any other relevant documents. It may well be that the master may prefer that the Official Solicitor should act as guardian. The sealed authority of the master would be required before the receiver or the Official Solicitor could conduct the proceedings, and so become guardian under *ibid.* r.112(4) (*Re W. (E. E. M.)* as explained in *Re S. (F. G.)* [1973] 1 W.L.R. 178).

In cases where the petitioning spouse is the receiver and the Official Solicitor is to act as guardian, the Official Solicitor will, normally, in accordance with the usual practice, bring the matter to the attention of the court so that it may consider the appointment of an officer of the court or some other person as new receiver in place of such spouse.

As to the importance of the duties and functions of the guardian *ad litem*, see *Timins v. Timins* [1938] 4 All E.R. 180; *Randall v. Randall* [1939] P.131; *Bailey v. Bailey* [1942] 2 All E.R. 89.

As to consent by a patient to a decree being granted, see *Mason v. Mason* [1972] Fam. 302; [1972] 3 All E.R. 315.

Settlement or gift of patient's property

6B–135   Under s.96(1)(d) of the Mental Health Act 1983, the court may direct a settlement or gift to be made of any property of the patient with any consequential directions under subs. (2). There is power to vary a settlement so made on the grounds of non-disclosure of material facts or substantial change in circumstances but this power is only exercisable by the Lord Chancellor or a nominated judge (s.96(3)).

Application is by way of formal application supported by affidavit evidence. Applicants are governed by r.18 (para. 6B–252). Generally as to practice, see Heywood and Massey, *Court of Protection Practice* 2002 ed., ch.15. See also paras 6B–136 to 6B–142. A transaction fee will be payable. See para. 6B–305.

For reported cases, see *Re Freeman* [1927] 1 Ch. 479; *Re Greene* [1928] Ch. 528; *Re C. W. M.* [1951] 2 K.B. 714 and *Re C.* [1960] 1 W.L.R. 92. *Re C. E. F. D.* [1963] 1 W.L.R. 329 (costs); *Re R. H. C.* [1963] 1 W.L.R. 1095 (disentailing and resettlement). *Re D. M. L.* [1965] Ch. 1133 (meaning of "family" and "persons for whom patient might be expected to provide"); *Re L. (W. J. G.)* [1966] Ch. 135 (disentailing and meaning of "family," etc.); *Re T. B.* [1967] Ch. 247; [1966] 3 All E.R. 599 (settlement in favour of the illegitimate son of the patient).

Statutory wills

6B–136   Under s.96(1)(e) of the Mental Health Act 1983 the court has jurisdiction to provide for the making of a will, or a codicil, for a patient who does not possess testamentary capacity.

The court in drafting a will for a patient assumes that the patient is having a brief lucid interval at the time when the will is made. During that lucid interval, the patient is assumed to have a full knowledge of the past, and a full realisation that as soon as the will is executed he will relapse into the mental state that previously existed. The court considers not a hypothetical patient but the actual patient, with all the antipathies and affections he had while of full capacity, and seeks to make the will which he, acting reasonably, would have made. The patient is to be envisaged during the hypothetical lucid interval as being advised by a competent solicitor and, in normal cases, the patient is to be envisaged as taking a broad brush to the claims on his bounty rather than an accountant's pen (*Re D. (J.)* [1982] Ch. 237; [1982] 2 All E.R. 37).

A transaction fee of £540 will be payable. See para. 6B–305.

Procedure on application for settlement, gift or statutory will

6B–137   Generally as to settlements (or gifts) of patients' property, see Heywood and Massey, *Court of Protection Practice* 2002 ed., Ch.15; and as to statutory wills, see *ibid.*, at Chapter 14. See also para. 10E–11 as to applications by attorneys under registered enduring powers of attorney for orders to execute statutory wills and codicils.

In view of the affinity between applications for settlements and capital gifts and those for the execution of a will for the patient, the Master of the Court of Protection has issued the following *Practice Note* (1983) 133 L.J. 6124.

All applications

6B–138   This note refers to applications for the execution of wills and codicils under s.96(1)(e) of the Mental Health Act 1983 and for gifts and settlements under s.96(1)(d). The note is intended for the general guidance of solicitors as to the practice of the court.

These applications usually require the attendance of the solicitor having the conduct of the proceedings. Country solicitors may attend or instruct London agents if they so wish. Counsel may be instructed in appropriate cases. It is frequently helpful if the applicant attends as well. Applications will normally be heard by the master in chambers, subject to r.39 of the Court of Protection Rules 1984 (succeeded by r.40 of the Court of Protection Rules 2001).

Parties

6B–139   Applications may be made by one or more of the persons specified in r.17 of the

Court of Protection Rules 1984 (Rule 18 Court of Protection Rules 2001). The receiver, if not the applicant or one of the applicants, should be given notice of the hearing of the application. Otherwise, no person should be given notice until the court has so directed.

If the receiver is personally interested in the relief sought, or if there is any other reason for having the interests of the patient separately represented, it is likely that the court will direct that the patient be represented by the Official Solicitor, who must then be given notice by the applicant's solicitors.

The principles which guide the court in deciding who should be given notice of the hearing of an application are that, in general, all persons whose interests will be materially affected by the proposals should be notified, but the discretion is a wide one and will be exercised according to the particular facts of each case (see *Re B* [1987] 1 W.L.R. 552).

Service

Notice is drawn to r.20 of the Court of Protection Rules 1984 (r.21 Court of Protection (Enduring Powers of Attorney) Rules 2001) with regard to acceptance of service by solicitors (including the Official Solicitor). **6B–140**

Evidence

Evidence must be by way of affidavit or affirmation, with relevant exhibits. The facts directly relating to the application should be set out in full and the following further information should be included: **6B–141**

(1) Details of the patient's family, by way of a family tree showing the relationship between the patient and the other members of his family on both sides, naming the members of the family and giving their dates of birth or current ages.

(2) Particulars of the patient's current assets, with updated valuations. (If there is a fund in court, an up-to-date transcript may be obtained from the PGO by the receiver or the receiver's solicitors. The court will give any further help it can from the receivership papers, for example by confirming the correctness of information supplied by the receiver.)

(3) A statement of the patient's needs (at present and expected in future) and general circumstances.

(4) Full information as to the patient's general health at present and in the future.

(5) Where a patient is living in National Health Service accommodation, information as to the likelihood of discharge to Pt III local authority accommodation, to other fee-paying accommodation or to the patient's own home.

(6) Full particulars of the resources of any proposed beneficiary, with details of the likely changes if the application succeeds.

(7) A clear explanation of the incidence of capital and income tax liabilities as a result of the proposals.

(8) An illustration of the effect of the proposals on the patient's resources, preferably in the form of a "before" and "after" schedule of assets and income.

Affidavits must conform with the requirements of the Practice Directions issued by the Lord Chief Justice on July 21, 1983 as amended on March 23, 1995 [1983] 1 W.L.R. 922; [1983] 3 All E.R. 33, and the master on August 15, 1984 *Practice Direction* [1984] 1 W.L.R. 1171; [1984] 3 All E.R. 128.

The execution of statutory wills and codicils

As well as the matters common to all applications and mentioned above, attention is drawn to the following points: **6B–142**

(a) Section 96(4)(b) of the Mental Health Act 1983 requires that the master must have reason to believe that the patient is incapable of making a valid will for himself. It can be assumed that in most cases the court will require recent evidence as to lack of testamentary capacity in the form of a letter or certificate (which should be the original document, not a photocopy) from a doctor. If recent evidence is not available, the court may adjourn the application and possibly call for a report from one of the Lord Chancellor's Medical Visitors on this question.

(b) Section 97(1) of the Act directs how a statutory will is to be executed and attested. A suitable form is set out at the foot of this note (see para. 6B–181). Section 97(2) provides that s.9 of the Wills Act 1837, which relates to the execution and attestation of wills, shall not apply.

(c) Having regard to s.97(4) of the Act, the evidence on the application should state the patient's domicile, whether any immovable property will be affected by the proposed will and, if so, the situation of that property if already belonging to the patient.

(d) Where a will for the patient already exists, the evidence in support of the application must substantiate the need for the execution of a further will or codicil. The consents to act of the executors named in the proposed will should be filed with the supporting evidence.

(e) The Court of Protection has no jurisdiction to adjudicate upon the validity of an existing will; it can only authorise the execution of a further will in the light of evidence submitted.

(f) Every application should be accompanied by a draft of the proposed statutory will, with a spare copy in case amendment is required.

(g) Statutory wills will not be sealed by the court until they have been executed and attested in accordance with the provisions of s.97(1) of the Act.

(h) In cases of extreme urgency, the court will make every effort to assist; a telephone call to the Judicial Support Unit 020 7664 7178 is advisable. It may be sensible, for example, to provide for the will to be executed by someone more readily available in an emergency than the applicant; for example, the Official Solicitor.

(i) Full supporting information is needed even if the application seeks a codicil or new will addressed to a change of executors or other simple point because the court will need to review all the provisions of the existing will.

Gifts

6B–143   *Smaller gifts* —Gifts not exceeding £15,000 in any year that are insignificant in the context of a patient's assets, and gifts in consideration of marriage are usually considered on application to the PGO by letter only; no attendance, nor the issue of a formal application, is required.

6B–144   *Larger gifts* —If the proposed gifts do not fall within the above limits, a formal application must be issued. The notes on parties and evidence set out above will need to be followed.

Settlements, deeds of variation, deeds of family arrangement or the exercise of powers and similar dealings

6B–145   If a settlement, a deed of variation, a deed of family arrangement or the exercise of a power under section 96(1)(k) or any similar dealing is proposed, a draft of the deed that is proposed to be executed should be exhibited, with a spare copy in case amendment is required. Relevant settlements include those under insurance "Inheritance Trust" and similar schemes. The notes on parties and evidence set out above will need to be followed.

As to a proposed gift to the persons in charge of a private mental hospital, see *Re C. M. G.* [1970] Ch. 574.

A statutory will ordered by the master should be executed forthwith without delay notwithstanding the pendency of an appeal to the nominated judge (*Re D. (J.)* [1982] Ch. 237; [1982] 2 All E.R. 37).

Named charities may be "interested" persons (within the meaning of r.21(4) in proceedings for a new will where they have expectations under a previous will, as well as the Attorney-General, representing the interests of the public as beneficiaries of all charities. The court has a discretion whether to direct the joinder of the charities or the Attorney-General or both (*Re H. M. F.* [1976] Ch. 33; [1975] 2 All E.R. 795).

The giving of notice of an application to a husband or relatives is within the discretion of the court (*Re Davey (decd.)* [1981] 1 W.L.R. 164; [1980] 3 All E.R. 342). In that case, the court had dispensed with notice and ordered the execution of a statutory will and such had been properly executed. The patient died shortly afterwards and her husband appealed against the order. The will was held to be valid and, since the patient had died, irrevocable.

Testimony (perpetuation of)

6B–146   See O.39, r.15; and *Re Stoer* (1884) 9 P.D. 120.

The practice of the action to perpetuate testimony would appear to have fallen entirely into disuse. However, the jurisdiction remains and the law on this subject can be found as mentioned above. Section 96(1)(d) or (e) of the Mental Health Act 1983 enables any injustice in the vast majority of cases to be remedied.

Variation of Trusts Act 1958

6B–147

For the guidance of those who have reason to apply to the court under s.1(3) of the Act, the master directed, on December 9, 1959, that:

(1) As soon as an originating summons under the Act to which a patient is a respondent has been issued in the Chancery Division, the Court of Protection should be notified and an authority sought for leave to conduct the proceedings on behalf of the patient.

(2) No application should be issued in the Court of Protection for relief under s.1(3) of the Act until the originating summons has been issued in the Chancery Division and evidence filed in support thereof, but the master will in suitable cases authorise counsel to be instructed on behalf of the patient to look after the patient's interest during negotiations for an arrangement.

(3) The application should only be entitled in the matter of the patient. The master will direct whether the patient is to be served or service dispensed with, and where the master considers that the patient should be separately represented he may request the Official Solicitor to act as a solicitor for the patient on the application.

(4) A copy of the originating summons (or an office copy if the arrangement is to be found in the summons itself) and office copies of the evidence in support thereof, together with the exhibits, should be lodged with the application and an affidavit filed stating how the patient will be affected by the arrangement and whether it is considered to be for or against his benefit.

(5) The master's order will make provision for subsequent approval of amendments which may be made to the arrangement after the date of the order. See *Re Sanderson's Settlement Trusts* [1961] 1 W.L.R. 36; [1961] 1 All E.R. 25n.

If the only consent to the proposed variation requiring judicial approval is that of a patient for whom a receiver is acting (or about to be applied for) there is no need to proceed under the Variation of Trusts Act 1958, since consent and authority to join in any necessary deed of variation on behalf of the patient may be given by the Court of Protection alone under Pt VII of the Mental Health Act 1983, either under one or other of the particular provisions of s.96 or the general provisions of s.95.

Where, however, the court in Chancery is being asked to approve an arrangement under the Act and a patient for whom a receiver is acting has an interest, it would not be proper for the Court of Protection to authorise the receiver to consent to the scheme on his behalf; in such a case it is for the Chancery Court, if it thinks fit, to approve the scheme, subject to the Court of Protection having determined that the variation would be for the patient's benefit under s.1(3) as set out above (*Re C. L.* [1969] 1 Ch. 587; [1968] 1 All E.R. 1104).

The term "benefit" in this context is not confined to some element of financial advantage: it is for a patient's benefit to do what he would have done if of full capacity (*Re C. L.*).

A transaction fee will be payable. See para. 6B–305.

Wills

6B–148

Rule 70 empowers the court to call for production of testamentary dispositions executed by a patient. Normally the court directs that the patient's will is to be deposited at the receivership bank for safe custody. Since banks now charge for this service it is now the practice to allow the will to remain with the solicitors who prepared it to be held subject (during the lifetime of the patient) to the directions of the court, and the usual undertaking (Form C.P. 12) must be filed (see *Practice Note* [1935] W.N. 202).

When a patient whose affairs are under the jurisdiction of the court desires to make a will, the directions of the Cocurt should be obtained first, otherwise costs may be disallowed (see *Practice Note* [1935] W.N. 54). Medical evidence must be furnished to the effect that the patient is of testamentary capacity, *i.e.* capacity to understand the nature of the document proposed to be executed, the extent of the property to be disposed of, and the claims of those it is proposed to benefit or exclude (see *Banks v. Goodfellow* (1870) 5 Q.B. 549; and *Roe v. Nix* [1893] P.55). Evidence given by a hospital doctor should be given by one of consultant status. In some cases the court will request one of the Lord Chancellor's Medical Visitors to visit the patient and report as to testamentary capacity. The will should be witnessed by a solicitor and the hospital doctor, or the patient's medical attendant, as the case may require.

Where a patient does not possess testamentary capacity consideration should, where appropriate, be given to the execution of a statutory will on behalf of the patient. See paras 6B–136 to 6B–142.

Accounts

Duty to account

6B–149   Normally a receiver has to account annually to the anniversary of his appointment, although where special reasons exist the court or the PGO may direct that his accounts be taken to some other date (*e.g.* the close of a business year). In suitable cases accounts by the receiver are sometimes dispensed with. (Generally, see s.107 of the Mental Health Act 1983, and r.61.) Where the property of the patient is extensive and complicated the court or the PGO may direct the account to be certified by a chartered accountant or solicitor.

A final account of a receiver, where required to be passed, on the death of the patient (see *Re Walker* [1907] 2 Ch. 120) or receiver, will be made up to the date of death, but where the receiver has retired from office or for any other reason has been discharged, including the recovery of the patient, the account will require to be made up to the date of the order discharging the receiver. See r.65.

An account is required to be lodged within one month of the closing date thereof.

An account fee of £100 is payable on the twenty-eighth day after the last day of the period in respect of which an account is to be delivered under rule 61(1) or 65(2).

Form of account

6B–150   The receiver's account should be prepared on Form C.P. 28. This is sent by the PGO free of charge with the notice calling for the account. Endorsed on the form are full instructions as to how the account should be prepared, and as to what documents to accompany. It should be particularly noted that the account is essentially an account of actual receipts and payments within the accounting period. If any rents are collected, or outgoings on property paid, by the receiver (as distinct from agents) details should be shown in Form C.P. 28A, and the totals brought into the account.

The court is empowered to direct a receiver to render an account in a specific form and made up to a date of the court's choosing (*Re C. M. R.* (1982) 79 L.S.Gaz. 407).

In connection with the vouching of the account where the allowance for maintenance of the patient or any other person is for "so much as may be necessary not exceeding £. ... a year (or the net income)" the expenditure is required, so far as reasonably practicable, to be accounted for and vouched in detail but where the allowance is of a specified sum or net surplus income (unqualified) the allowance need not normally be accounted for in detail and only the amount charged pursuant to the allowance entered in the account; where, however, the court has reason to believe that such allowance has been misapplied the court can direct a proper account to be taken (see *Re French* (1868) 3 Ch. App. 317 at 318, *per* Lord Cairns L.J., and *Strangwayes v. Read* [1898] 2 Ch. 419).

Where the patient is living at home with his family, detailed accounts of expenditure on household expenses are not usually expected, provided the court is satisfied that the patient is enjoying proper care and attention. If the patient is the owner of the house, evidence of payment for rates, taxes, insurance premiums, repairs and any mortgage repayments may be required. In cases where a large establishment is maintained, more detailed information on household expenditure may be required, for example, books of account showing the wages and salaries paid to staff and the payments made in settlement of tradesmen's accounts. Vouchers for the entries in the account books should only be produced if requested.

Where there is a business the instructions for keeping accounts in connection with the business will be found in the directions given in the order. See para. 6B–101.

Lodging account

6B–151   The account should be lodged promptly. Such of the following documents as are applicable to the case should be lodged with the account:

    (a) Counterfoils of dividend warrants and any other vouchers for sums received, *if specifically requested.*

(b) Form C.P. 28A (see above) where any rents are collected by or outgoings on property paid by receiver.

(c) Rent accounts (and, *if specifically requested*, vouchers in support of payments included therein) where any rents are collected by an agent.

(d) A copy of the trustee's income account where income is collected and distributed by the trustees.

(e) A copy of the audited accounts and balance sheet of any business or partnership in which the patient has an interest.

(f) Receipts for amounts paid, *if specifically requested*.

(g) The receivership bank account pass book (sheets) covering the period of the account.

As regards the receivership bank account, the receiver should keep a separate receivership account opened in his own name "as Receiver for (*Patient*)" into which, as far as possible, all sums received should be paid and from which all payments should be made.

Passing account

The account will be examined and vouched by an officer of the Protection Division **6B–152** and, if necessary, a questionnaire will be sent. The matter as a whole will be reviewed and consideration will be given to the application or investment of the surplus balance of the account.

The PGO may disallow any excess of authorised allowances or other unauthorised payments. The circumstances will be considered and if disallowance is directed the offending items will be struck out of the account.

Upon the passing of the account directions will be given in respect of the costs thereof and any, if necessary, costs of general management. See para. 6B–171.

Annual administration fee

An annual fee is payable from the date of the issue of the first application until the **6B–153** termination of the proceedings. Generally as to the administration fee, see rr.76, 78 and 83 and the Appendix thereto.

The administration fee is payable on the first and on every subsequent anniversary of the date of the appointment of a receiver or short orderuntil the termination of the proceedings and is collected by a demand sent to the solicitor by post or by deduction from the fund in court.

Method of payment of the annual administration fee

The fee is levied: **6B–154**

(1) By a "demand" issued on the passing of the account (or on the settlement of a final order or order determining proceedings when the account is dispensed with). The demand form (certificate) gives full instructions as to payment which may be made either in cash accompanied by the certificate at the Protection Division, Archway Tower, 2 Junction Road, London, N19 5SZ, or by returning the certificate with a cheque (including a giro cheque) or postal order made payable to the Public Guardianship Office and crossed.

(2) By being carried over by the Accountant General of the Supreme Court from the fund in court to a special account entitled "Court of Protection Administration Fee Account". This is done on a "carry over" certificate issued by the PGO to the Accountant General.

Costs

General note

See the Court of Protection Rules, rr.87–92. Costs are in the discretion of the court **6B–155** (see *Re Cathcart* [1893] 1 Ch. 466 at 472 *per* Halsbury L.C.) and the court may order them to be paid by the patient or charged on or paid out of his estate or paid by any other party or any person attending the proceedings (r.84(1)). The order is enforceable in the same manner as an order as to costs made by the High Court (subs. (2)) but is appealable without leave and is not a charging order within the meaning of O.50, r.2 (*Re Cathcart* [1893] 1 Ch. 466).

Subject to the Court of Protection Rules and Civil Procedure Rules 1998, O.62 applies and the costs are assessed where required accordingly. They are awarded either on the indemnity basis (which is usually the case in receivership proceedings) or on the standard basis, but the court will not in either case allow costs which have been unreasonably incurred or are unreasonable in amount.

On assessment on the indemnity basis the court will resolve any doubts which it may have as to whether costs were unreasonably incurred or were unreasonable in amount in favour of the receiving party.

On assessment of costs on the standard basis the court will (a) only allow costs which are proportionate to the matters in issue, and (b) resolve any doubts which it may have as to whether costs were reasonably incurred or reasonable and proportionate in amount in favour of the paying party.

The rules against champerty (now obsolete) did not apply. A solicitor who fairly and properly conducts an objection to an application for the appointment of a receiver on a retainer from the patient ought to be allowed his costs in any event (see *Wentworth v. Tubb* (1842) 7 Jur.(o.s.) 738). A solicitor will not be deprived of his costs merely because he represents the patient and other parties as well, but where there is a conflict of interest, and the solicitor acts on behalf of the other parties rather than the patient, the costs may be disallowed (*Re Weston* (1903) 116 L.T.J. 34).

The receiver acts as agent for the patient, and solicitors instructed by the receiver are entitled to look to the patient's estate for payment; the relationship of "solicitor and client" does not exist between the solicitor and the receiver (*Re E. G.* [1914] 1 Ch. 927).

The costs of the notes of the judgment of the Lords Justices (in Lunacy) were allowed (*Re Cathcart*).

A surety is liable for costs directed to be paid by the receiver and which remain unsatisfied (*Re Graham* [1895] 1 Ch. 66).

6B–156   Practice Note (Taxation of Court of Protection Costs), August 11, 1995 made by the Master of the Court of Protection and the Chief Master, Supreme Court Costs Office, sets out as follows:

This Practice Note is issued in order to clear up any misunderstandings that may have arisen as to taxation procedures for Court of Protection costs. Solicitors are reminded that the court's jurisdiction extends to the management and administration of a patient's financial affairs only and it cannot be concerned with aspects of a patient's affairs which are not financial; and the costs of work beyond these limits will not be the subject of an order by the court or a direction by the Public Guardianship Office. Consequently no such costs will be allowed by the Supreme Court Taxing Office on assessment.

If solicitors believe that an item in their bill is properly chargeable as work relating to financial affairs, but that contention is not accepted by the Supreme Court Costs Office, they should bring in objections and, if that is unsuccessful, take the question to appeal. The Court of Protection itself cannot assist by reinstating any costs disallowed by the Supreme Court Costs Office, since the function of deciding the quantum of costs belongs to them, by reason of r.86 of the Court of Protection Rules 2001 and the Civil Procedure Rules 1998.

In cases where the receiver is not a professional person, he or she is nonetheless expected to be able to carry out the whole range of a receiver's duties, as outlined in the Receiver's Handbook issued by the PGO. The court may, however, in suitable cases authorise a receiver (under r.87 of the Court of Protection Rules 2001) to employ at the patient's expense a solicitor or other professional person to do any work not usually requiring professional assistance. This authority should always be sought in appropriate cases. However, the rule does not extend the limits of a receiver's authority beyond financial affairs. Out-of-pocket expenses are allowed to non-professional receivers.

If the receiver is a solicitor, costs are allowed for the whole range of receivership duties, subject to detailed assessment, and there is no need for him or her to seek authority under r.87. Accountant-receivers are allowed remuneration fixed by the court and their fees are not liable to detailed assessment. As regards visits by solicitor-receivers to patients, or attendances by solicitor-receivers at case conferences, it has become apparent that, with more patients living in the community, patients may need a visit or require the receiver's help in connection with case conferences or similar attendances, which may be necessary in order to safeguard the financial interests of the patient. In such cases the Supreme Court Costs Office will accept well-founded arguments that the costs should be allowed on detailed assessment.

Practice Note (Authority to Solicitors to act for patients or donors), August 9, 1995 **6B–157**
made by the Master of the Court of Protection sets out as follows:

In Court of Protection matters, problems may arise for solicitors in knowing for whom they act.

In the case of *Re EG* [1914] 1 Ch. 927, it is established that where a receiver has been appointed, the solicitor acting in the matter is acting for the patient and not for the receiver. The decision leaves undecided the question of who is the patient's solicitor in cases where more than one solicitor has been instructed to make an application for receivership or where a patient himself wishes to instruct another solicitor for a particular area of his affairs, for example, where he remains of testamentary capacity and wishes to instruct a different solicitor to draw up a will for him. Where more than one solicitor has been instructed, perhaps each by a different member of the patient's family, this places the solicitors in a position of uncertainty as to who is acting for the patient on the principle of *Re EG*.

A further difficulty may arise as a result of the case of *Yonge v. Toynbee* [1910] 1 K.B. 215, which decided that the retainer of a solicitor came to an end when the patient lost capacity (as an extension of the general rule that, except in the case of an enduring power of attorney, the mental incapacity of the principal revokes any agency). Nevertheless, incapacitated people may need solicitors to act for them and them alone.

Assuming that a patient or donor is within the jurisdiction of the Court of Protection, the solicitor's authority to act for him can be expressly confirmed by the Court of Protection. Solicitors are also entitled to look upon themselves as acting for a patient or donor and not for the person who has given them instructions (if that is not the patient or donor) from the time that an application which is in order is received by the Court of Protection or the Public Guardianship Office. This may, for example, be an application for the appointment of a receiver, for an order determining proceedings, for the appointment of a new receiver, for confirmation of the revocation of an enduring power of attorney or for some other relief or authorisation. Where two or more solicitors have been instructed (expressly or by implication) to act for the same patient or donor, preliminary directions should be sought from the court as to who will be deemed to be the solicitor in the matter.

A solicitor instructed by an applicant for receivership (or by an attorney) will be treated by the court as the patient's (or donor's) solicitor until an objection to the application, or a competing application, is received by the court. As soon as this happens, the solicitor instructed by the first applicant must elect whether to continue representing the patient or to represent the first applicant. If the solicitor elects to represent the first applicant, then it is for the court to decide whether the patient needs separate representation and if so, to instruct a different private solicitor or the Official Solicitor (if he agrees) to act for him. If the solicitor elects to remain as the patient's solicitor, then the first applicant will have to instruct another firm.

Solicitors will no doubt wish to make clear to the person from whom they take initial instructions relating to patients or donors that their client will be the patient or donor and that the solicitors will have a duty of confidentiality to the patient or donor, even if the instructions come from somebody else.

The court would like applicants and solicitors to be aware that if a reference which is received by the court in respect of an applicant is not satisfactory, no further enquiry will be made as to the applicant's suitability but the applicant will not be appointed as receiver. This may be considered unfair to the applicant but in the court's view, the best interests of the patient must come first.

Legal aid

The Legal Aid Act 1988 does not apply to proceedings in the Court of Protection, **6B–158** but as to its application to patients involved in proceedings in other courts, see paras 6B–115 *et seq.*

Lodgment of order to assess, etc.

The solicitors having the carriage of an order which directs detailed assessment of **6B–159** costs should send to or leave at the Supreme Court Costs Office, Court of Protection Branch, Room 1–18, Cliffords Inn, Fetter Lane, London EC4A 1DQ, a copy of the order a request for detailed assessment suitably amended and a statement showing the names and addresses of the parties (if any) appearing in person and of the solicitor of the parties (if any).

A statement of parties however is not required unless the costs clause directs the taxation of costs of a party separately represented or unless the costs are payable other than out of the estate of a patient.

The copy order may be typed or photographed and should be properly endorsed with the title of the matter, the date of entry, and the name and address of the solicitor. The following is the form of certificate which should be signed in the name of the firm:

"I/We hereby certify this to be a true copy of the Order dated as passed and entered."

(Signed)

The Bill will be assessed and returned by post. If desired an appointment for detailed assessment will be given.

Form of bill

6B–160   Every bill of costs should be headed with the full title of the matter, also the name of the party and date of the order directing the assessment as under:—

IN THE COURT OF PROTECTION   No ....

In the matter of ....

The costs of the .... to be

assessed pursuant to Order dated ....

Bills of costs should be prepared on A4 paper bookwise, in accordance with Civil Procedure Rules 1998, Practice Direction supplementing Pt 43.

As to the names of solicitors have to appear in all certificates of costs, it is essential that the full forenames of a single practitioner or the correct title of a firm should be endorsed on the bill. In agency matters, copies of orders and bills should show the name of the country solicitor.

Small bills of costs, for any type of business, are now accepted in summary form provided that the narrative is adequate for the work done and a summary of the number of personal attendances, telephone attendances and letters is provided. Care should be taken that in such bills all disbursements are included and summarised.

Documents to accompany bill

6B–161   To facilitate the checking of the bills, before provisional assessment, all drafts of affidavits, deeds, orders, cases to counsel (if authorised) correspondence file, notes of attendances and vouchers should be lodged. In the case of sales of land the original contracts for sale, requisitions and draft transfers or conveyances should be lodged.

As to payment of estate agents' fees, see para. 6B–166.

Prior costs

6B–162   (a) If such costs are due to the Solicitor acting in the proceedings, they may be included in his bill without special mention in the Order.

(b) Should the prior costs be due to another Solicitor, particulars thereof should be forwarded to the court. In either case a request must be obtained from the PGO referring such costs to a Costs Judge of the Supreme Court so that the amount due may be ascertained by him or under his direction (r.89 of the Court of Protection Rules 2001).

Receivership general management costs

6B–163   General management costs may be brought in for assessment at least every second year.

The bill and papers should be lodged with the Costs Office and the following request endorsed upon the front of the bill:

"I/We request that the within bill of costs of general management may be assessed whereupon we will apply to the court with a recommendation as to how payment should be effected."

(Signed)

(Dated)

Costs of passing accounts are dealt with on the passing of the receivership account. Costs for income tax returns, recovering overpaid tax and the lodgment in court of any part of the balance on the account must be included in a bill of costs of general management. See also para. 10A–176.

Short Form Bill of Costs

6B–163A   With effect from 1st June 2004 the Supreme Court Costs Office will accept a short form bill of costs where the amount of the bill does not exceed £3000, excluding VAT and disbursements. A model form for a short form bill is printed hereunder. When lodging the request for assessment, the following should be submitted:

1. Short Form Bill
2. Request for Assessment (Form N258B)
3. Fee of £100
4. The document giving the right to detailed assessment.
5. A statement giving the name and address for service of any person having a financial interest in the outcome of the assessment.
6. The relevant papers in support of the bill including the correspondence and attendance file for the period covered by the claim in the bill. No duplicates should be lodged.
7. Any fee notes of counsel and receipts or accounts for other disbursements relating to items claimed.

Model Short Form Bill

6B–163B

Model Short Form Bill

IN THE COURT OF PROTECTION

Case No: - ....

SCCO reference ....
(to be completed by the court)

IN THE MATTER OF

.... (A patient)

Short form bill of costs of the Receiver of *(e.g.)* General Management for the period ....
to be assessed pursuant to the First General Order dated .... and General Direction dated *19/11/82*

Summary of work carried out

Fee earner category .... Rate claimed ....

Work done:-   **Charge:-**

Time spent in personal attendances
e.g. 22/9/02   45mins   Upon patient   ....

Time spent in travel ....

Letters Sent ....

Telephone Calls ....

Time spent on documents ....

Other work *(give details)*
....
....

....

                                                                        Sub Total   ....
                                                                        V.A.T.   ....
Disbursements (list below)
....
....   Disbursements   ....
                                                                        V.A.T.   ....

                                                                        Grand Total   ....

I certify that this bill is both accurate and complete.

.... (name and position)

**Short form bill of costs for use in Court of Protection assessments
where the total costs claimed do not exceed £3000
excluding VAT and disbursements**

Name, address and reference of person filing bill

Unnecessary employment of solicitor

6B–164   Special attention is drawn to r.87, which provides that no receiver, other "than the Official Solicitor, shall, unless authorised by the court, be entitled at the expense of the patient's estate to employ a solicitor or other professional person to do work not usually requiring professional assistance."

Costs of preparing wills

6B–165   Costs in respect of drawing wills for patients during the course of the proceedings will normally only be allowed against the patient's estate where the leave of the court has previously been obtained for the preparation of such will.

Estate agents' fees

6B–166   These should not be included in bills of costs as a disbursement. The limit on estate agents' commission is advised to solicitors in the note which accompanies the order for sale (PN4). If the commission (and other expenses) proposed exceeds that limit solicitors are required to obtain prior approval from the PGO before committing the estate to such expenditure. When prior approval has been obtained, or if it is not necessary, solicitors will continue with the sale in the normal way and pay the estate agents' fees. Estate agents' fees will appear neither in the bill of costs nor, normally, in the receiver's account, but in the completion statement which is produced to the PGO when directions are being sought for investment of the net proceeds of sale.

The court will normally consider estate agents' charges reasonable if they do not exceed 2¹/₂ per cent of the sale price, to include all commission, expenses, etc. For full details of estate agents' charges solicitors should read the Practice Direction published jointly by the Chief Chancery Master, the Master of the Court of Protection, and the Senior Registrar of the Family Division, dated December 22, 1982 [1983] 1 All E.R. 160. See para. 6B–98.

Assessed bills of costs

A receipt will be issued when the assessed bill is lodged, stamped and completed in the Costs Office, and this receipt must be produced on any future enquiry: Direction dated November 1968 of Chief Taxing Master (*Practice Direction* (1968) 118 New L.J. 1097).

6B–167

Certificate of costs

If the costs are payable out of the fund in court the office copy certificate of costs will be sent by the Costs Office direct to the Accountant General of the Supreme Court. London Solicitors must lodge with the Accountant General, Court Funds Office, 22 Kingsway, London, WC2B 6LE a form of postal request, but in country cases the Accountant General will forward this form direct to the solicitors.

Where the costs are not payable out of the fund in court the office copy certificate will be sent by post to the solicitors concerned.

6B–168

Fees on assessment

As from October 1, 1999, there shall be payable on the filing of a request for a detailed assessment of costs a fee of £200.

On an appeal against a decision made in a detailed assessment of costs or on an application to set aside a default costs certificate there shall be payable a fee of £60.

6B–169

Costs not assessed

Where an Order is referred for assessment and for any reason it is desired subsequently not to assess the costs, notification must be given to the Supreme Court Costs Office that an assessment will not take place.

For precedents and Costs generally, see Heywood and Massey, *Court of Protection Practice* (12th ed., 1991), Chap. 20.

6B–170

Fixed costs

Some items of costs may be dealt with in accordance with a *Practice Note* issued by the master on September 1, 1983 (see *Practice Note* (1983) 133 New L.J. 6121) whereby fixed costs were introduced by agreement with the Law Society in respect of certain Court of Protection work.

It has been agreed with the Law Society that fixed costs will be allowed at amounts not exceeding the following:

6B–171

Category I	Work up to and including the date upon which the First General Order or Short Order is entered.	£695 (plus VAT)
	Note: The commencement fee, appointment fee and fees for medical evidence and evidence of notification of the patient may be added. Please produce receipts for fees paid.	
Category II	(a) Preparation and lodgment of a receivership account.	£200 (plus VAT)

	(b) Preparation and lodgment of a receivership account which has been certified by a solicitor under the provisions of the Practice Notes dated September 13, 1984 and March 5, 1985 reported at [1984] 3 All E.R. 320 and [1985] 1 All E.R. 884 respectively.	£215 (plus VAT)
Category III	General management costs in the first year:	
	(a) where there are lay receivers and the court has authorised the receiver to employ solicitors to carry out work not usually requiring professional assistance under Rule 87 of the Court of Protection Rules 2001.	£615 (plus VAT)
	(b) where there are professional receivers.	£1275 (plus VAT)

General management work in the second and subsequent years:

	(c) Where there are lay receivers and the Court has authorised the receiver to employ solicitors to carry out work not usually requiring professional assistance under rule 87 of the Court Protection Rules 2001.	£545 (plus VAT)
	(d) Where there are professional receivers.	£1025 (plus VAT)

(e) Where a professional is dealing with the affairs of an individual under an order of the court, and the assets of that individual are less than £16,000, then the professional may take a general management fee of 4% of the patient's assets on the anniversary of the date of the order appointing the professional to act (plus VAT).

Note 1: Categories II and III may be claimed together.

Note 2: Where te period for which general management costs are claimed is less than one year, the professional must take the proportion of the applicable fee as the period bears to one year.

Category IV	Applications under s.36(9)or 54 of the Trustee Act 1925 or section 20 of the Trusts of Land and Appointment of Trustees Act 1996 for the appointment of a new trustee in the place of the patient and applications under section 96(1)k of the Mental Health Act 1983 for authority to exercise any power vested in the patient, whether beneficially, or as guardian or trustee, or otherwise.	£330 (plus VAT)
Category V	In respect of conveyancing, two elements will be allowable as follows: (a) a sum of £130 in every case to cover correspondence with the Public Guardianship Office, the preparation of the Certificate or affidavit of value and all other work solely attributable to the Court of Protectionor the Public Guardianship Office, together with (b) a value element of ¼ per cent of the consideration with a minimum sum for this element of £385 and a maximum sum of £1,500. As well as a fee for both the above elements, VAT and disbursements will be allowed.	
Category VI	Work up to and including the date upon which an order appointing a replacement receiver is entered.	£460 (plus VAT)
Category VII	Preparation of an Inland Revenue income tax return on behalf of a patient.	£180 (plus VAT)

New rates of fixed costs will apply as follows:

In Category I, to all First General Orders and Short Orders made by the Court on or after January 1, 2006.

In Category II to all receivership accounts lodged on or after January 1, 2006.

In Category III to all general management costs in respect of years ended on or after January 1, 2006.

In Category IV and V, to all orders sent out on or after January 1, 2006.

In Category VI, to all orders appointing a replacement receiver made by the court on or after January 1, 2006.

In Category VII, to all Inland Revenue income tax returns completed in respect of the tax year ending on April 5, 2006 and thereafter.

In all categories, except for category III(e), professionals will have the option of the Costs Officer carrying out a detailed assessment of the costs rather than accepting fixed costs, if they wish. However, professionals must take fixed costs where it is appropriate to do so: in other words, where the amount of the bill is within the maximum allowed under the relevant category. The Supreme Court Costs Office may refuse to carry out a detailed assessment if, in its view, it is more appropriate for the professional to receive fixed costs. If professionals seek an order for detailed assessment of the costs under Category II as well as Category III, the relevant items for both categories should be included in the same bill.

[THE NEXT PARAGRAPH IS 6B–173.]

Deeds, Forms, Recitals, etc.

Following the coming into effect of the Court of Protection Rules 1994 draft deeds **6B–173** are not, as a general rule settled and approved by the court, the court relying on the solicitors for the accuracy and sufficiency of the contents.

Only the relevant part of the particular order or direction should be recited. The order appointing the receiver need only be recited where the deed is being executed under a sealed direction, as distinct from an order.

In deeds generally, such as conveyances, leases, etc., the patient is the "party" and is cited as "A. B. (*the patient, no address*) acting by C.D. (*the Receiver*) of etc., pursuant to the hereinafter recited Order (hereinafter called 'the Receiver') ...". The fact of mental disability should not appear in the description of the patient.

The actual wording of the direction contained in the order should wherever possible be strictly adhered to in the recital thereof, except that the recital is in the past tense.

Usual form of conveyance when an order for sale has been made

6B–174 Parties A.B. [no address required] (hereinafter called "the Vendor") acting by C.D. of .... pursuant to the hereinafter recited (Order) (Direction) (hereinafter called "the Receiver") of one part and E.F. of .... (hereinafter called "the Purchaser") of the other part.

Whereas (1) The Vendor is (seised in fee simple in possession [free from encumbrances]) (or as the case may be) of the property hereinafter described.

(2) By an (Order) (Direction) dated the .... day of .... 20 ...... and made (in the Court of Protection) (by the Public Trustee) in the matter of the Vendor the Receiver was authorised subject to the approval of the said Court in the name and on behalf of the Vendor to sell [the freehold/leasehold property belonging to the Vendor] [the said freehold/leasehold property] and for that purpose to receive and give a discharge for the purchase money and to execute such deeds as shall be necessary.

(3) (Pursuant to the said (Order) (Direction) and with such approval the Receiver on behalf of the Vendor has agreed to sell the said property hereinafter described to the Purchaser at the price of £......) or (Pursuant to the said (Order) (Direction) and with such approval the said property was on the .... day of .... 20 ...... put up for sale by public auction in [one] lot and at the said sale the Purchaser was the highest bidder for and was declared the Purchaser of the said property at the price of £......).

NOW THIS DEED WITNESSETH as follows:

In pursuance of the said (Order) (Direction) and agreement and in consideration of the sum of £...... now paid by the Purchaser to the Vendor acting by the Receiver as aforesaid (the receipt whereof is hereby acknowledged) the Vendor as Beneficial Owner acting by the Receiver as aforesaid hereby conveys unto the Purchaser (parcels) TO HOLD unto the Purchaser in fee simple [SUBJECT to etc.]

[If the property is subject to any restrictive or other covenants or conditions in respect of which the Vendor may remain liable after he has parted with the property, the usual covenant for indemnity by the purchaser should be inserted]. [Certificate of value in common form].

IN WITNESS whereof the parties hereto have hereunto set their hands the day and year first above written.

Signed and delivered as a deed by the said A.B.   (A.B.)
by the said C.D. acting as aforesaid in the   by
presence of   (C.D.)

NOTE No acknowledgment is required as regards production and delivery of copies of the recited Order of the Court of Protection. That is a document of record and the original is retained by the Court. The office copy thereof or of the relevant extracts therefrom handed over on completion is sufficient evidence of the contents of the original.

Certificate of Value

COURT OF PROTECTION   NO.   **6B–175**

In the matter of   (the Patient)
I, AB   of
                                       HEREBY CERTIFY as follows:

1. I have the following professional qualifications:
(or [I have at least five years' experience as a valuer with my present firm or another firm practising in the locality] and I believe myself well qualified to judge the value of the premises hereinafter mentioned and of the property in the vicinity thereof.

(sale by private treaty or auction) 2. I have carefully inspected the freehold/leasehold property known as which by (order) (direction) in this matter dated the 20 is to be sold in order to form an opinion as to the value thereof and as to the amount which should be realised on a sale of the said premises.

(sale by private treaty on instructions from Patient prior to proceedings or from the Receiver) 3. I was recently employed by to find a purchaser of the said freehold/leasehold property and was successful in negotiating the sale thereof to at a price of £

(sale by private treaty) 4. The negotiated price of £ for the said property is in my judgement and opinion fully as much as would probably be obtained at a sale by public auction and on that basis the lowest price I would advise to be accepted is £

(Sale by auction) 5. In my judgement the full and fair market value of the said premises is £ and on a sale by public auction I recommend that a reserve of £ should be placed on the said property.

Dated the   day of   20

(Signed) AB

Form of conveyance where an order for purchase has been made (necessary only where the Purchaser is an Executing Party)

Parties A.B. (hereinafter called "the Vendor") of the one part and C.D. (hereinafter called "the **6B–176** Purchaser") [acting by E.F. of .... pursuant to the hereinafter recited order (hereinafter called "the Receiver") of the other part.

(1) Recital of seisin.
(2) By an (Order) (Direction) dated the .... day of .... 20 ...... made (in the Court of Protection) in the matter of the Purchaser the Receiver was authorised in the name and on behalf of the Purchaser to purchase such property upon such terms as should be approved and to procure a conveyance/assignment/transfer of the said property to the Purchaser and for that purpose to execute such deeds as shall be necessary.
(3) (Pursuant to the said (Order) (Direction) and in consideration of the said sum of £...... now paid by [the Receiver out of moneys in his hands belonging to] the Purchaser to the Vendor (the receipt whereof is hereby acknowledged) the Vendor as (Beneficial Owner) hereby conveys unto the Purchaser (parcels) to hold unto the Purchaser in fee simple. (Any covenants by the Purchaser should be expressed to the "by the Purchaser acting by the Receiver as aforesaid-). [Certificate of Value in common form].

IN WITNESS   whereof the parties hereto have hereunto set their hands the day and year first above written.

Signed and delivered as a deed by the said C.D.   (C.D.)
by the said E.F. acting as aforesaid in the   by
presence of   (E.F.)

Statutory Receipt (on a Mortgage)

I A.B. of   acting by C.D. of   pursuant to an Order dated the   made in the **6B–177** Court of Protection hereby acknowledge that pursuant to the said Order on the   day of   I have received the sum of £   representing the principal money (*or balance remaining owing in respect of the principal money if such is the case*) secured by the written mortgage by lodgment thereof in Court to my credit and that I have received all interest and costs, such lodgment and payment having been made by E.F.
In witness whereof I have hereunto set my hand this   day of   .

Usual Form of Transfer of Registered Land

6B–178   (County or County Borough) ....
(District) ....
Title No. ....
Property ....
(Date .... In consideration of .... pounds (£.................... the receipt whereof
is hereby acknowledged (or paid to (names of Settled Land Act Trustees) I(P.) acting by R. of
.... pursuant to an (order) (direction) dated the .... 20...... and made (in the
Court of Protection) (by the Public Trustee) as Beneficial Owner (as Trustee) hereby transfer to
X.Y. of etc. the land comprised in the title above mentioned (for the residue of the term granted
by the registered Lease).

Add covenant for indemnity against restrictive covenants if required).

(Certificate of Value)

Signed and delivered as a deed	(P)
by the said (P) by the said	by
(R) acting as aforesaid in the	(R)
presence of:	

Leave to appoint new trustees under s.36(9) of the Trustee Act 1925

6B–179   And whereas the said A.B. has become incapable of acting in the trusts of the said (*trust*) and
the appointor is desirous of appointing the said E.F. to be a trustee of the said (*trust*) in place of
the said A.B.
And whereas pursuant to s.36(9) of the Trustee Act 1925, leave to make such appointment was
given on the   20   by the Court of Protection as appears by the seal of the Court
impressed in the margin hereof.

Certificate of Examination of Engrossment of Deed

6B–180   We Hereby Certify that this deed is an exact copy of the draft thereof as settled and approved by
the Court.

Signed (*Solicitor*)
by (*person certifying*)
Date

Statutory Will for Patient

6B–181   (This merely shows the manner in which the authorised person makes the will and executes the
same.)

THIS IS THE LAST WILL of me AB (the patient) of etc. acting by CD the person authorised in
that behalf by an Order dated the   day of   20   made under the Mental Health Act
1983.
I hereby revoke all former Wills and Codicils made by me and declare this to be my last Will.
    1. I appoint EF and GH to be Executors and Trustees of this my Will
    2. I Give and Bequeath etc.
In witness whereof this Will is signed by me AB acting by CD pursuant to the said Order
this   day of   20   .
Signed by the said AB (the patient) by the
said CD (authorised person) and by the AB (Patient)   said CD with his (her) own name
pursuant   CD (Authorised Person) to the said Order in our presence and attested by us in
the presence of the
said CD
(Names and addresses of witnesses)
Sealed with the official Seal of the
Court of Protection this   day of
  20

Certificate of Examination of Statutory Will
We Hereby Certify that this Will is an exact copy of the draft thereof as approved by the Court.
Signed (*Solicitor*)
by (*person certifying*)
Date

Affidavit proving Death

The court no longer requires such an affidavit to be filed as a matter of general **6B–182**
practice.

Certificate as to Recovery of Patient

Court of Protection..20   , No.   In the Matter of I [*Insert full* **6B–183**
name, address and medical qualification of deponent]
of
Hereby Certify as follows:
    1. I am the Medical Attendant of the above-named Patient and have so acted since
    2. I have to-day read a copy of [*Dele ` lines that do not apply*] my Certificate given in this matter on
the   Certificate of   given in this matter on the
    3. I have attended the Patient on the following dates   and I specially examined the Patient
on the   with the object of ascertaining the state of his/her mind.
    4. As a result of such special examination I am of the opinion that the Patient is now capable of
managing and administering his/her property and affairs and I base my conclusions on the
following grounds: [*Set out fully the grounds on which you base your conclusions*].
Dated this   day of   20 .
[Signed]

Mental Health Act 1983 (As amended by the Public Trustee and Administration of Funds Act 1986)

(1983 c.20)   **6B–184**

ARRANGEMENT OF SECTIONS

PART I

APPLICATION OF ACT

PART I

APPLICATION OF ACT

Application of Act: "mental disorder"

6B–185   **1.**—(1) The provisions of this Act shall have effect with respect to the reception, care and treatment of mentally disordered patients, the management of their property and other related matters.

(2) In this Act—

"mental disorder" means mental illness, arrested or incomplete development of mind, psychopathic disorder and any other disorder or disability of mind and "mentally disordered" shall be construed accordingly:

"severe mental impairment" means a state of arrested or incomplete development of mind which includes severe impairment of intelligence and social functioning and is associated with abnormally aggressive or seriously irresponsible conduct on the part of the person concerned and "severely mentally impaired" shall be construed accordingly;

"mental impairment" means a state of arrested or incomplete development of mind (not amounting to severe mental impairment) which includes significant impairment of intelligence and social functioning and is associated with abnormally aggressive or seriously irresponsible conduct on the part of the person concerned and "mentally impaired" shall be construed accordingly.

"psychopathic disorder" means a persistent disorder or disability of mind (whether or not including significant impairment of intelligence) which results in abnormally aggressive or seriously irresponsible conduct on the part of the person concerned;

and other expressions shall have the meanings assigned to them in section 145 below.

(3) Nothing in subsection (2) above shall be construed as implying that a person may be dealt with under this Act as suffering from mental disorder, or from any form of mental disorder described in this section, by reason only of promiscuity or other immoral conduct, sexual deviancy or dependence on alcohol or drugs.

* * * *

PART VII

Judicial authorities and Court of Protection

93.—(1) The Lord Chancellor shall from time to time nominate **6B–186** one or more judges of the Supreme Court (in this Act referred to as "nominated judges") to act for the purposes of this Part of this Act.

(2) There shall continue to be an office of the Supreme Court, called the Court of Protection, for the protection and management, as provided by this Part of this Act, of the property and affairs of persons under disability; and there shall continue to be a Master of the Court of Protection appointed by the Lord Chancellor under section 89 of the Supreme Court Act 1981.

(3) The Master of the Court of Protection shall take the oath of allegiance and judicial oath in the presence of the Lord Chancellor; and the Promissory Oaths Act 1868 shall have effect as if the officers named in the Second Part of the Schedule to that Act included the Master of the Court of Protection.

(4) The Lord Chancellor may nominate other officers of the Court of Protection (in this Part of this Act referred to as "nominated officers") to act for the purposes of this Part of this Act.

Exercise of the judge's functions: "the patient"

94.—(1) Subject to subsection (1A) below, the functions expressed **6B–187** to be conferred by this Part of this Act on the judge shall be exercisable by the Lord Chancellor or by any nominated judge, and shall also be exercisable by the Master of the Court of Protection, by the Public Trustee or by any nominated officer, but—

> (a) in the case of the Master, the Public Trustee or any nominated officer, subject to any express provision to the contrary in this Part of this Act or any rules made under this Part of this Act,
>
> (aa) in the case of the Public Trustee, subject to any directions of the Master and so far only as may be provided by any rules made under this Part of this Act or (subject to any such rules) by directions of the Master,
>
> (b) in the case of any nominated officer, subject to any directions of the Master and so far only as may be provided by the instrument by which he is nominated;

and references in this Part of this Act to the judge shall be construed accordingly.

(1A) In such cases or circumstances as may be prescribed by any rules under this part of this Act or (subject to any such rules) by directions of the Master, the functions of the judge under this part of this Act shall be exercised by the Public Trustee (but subject to any directions of the Master as to their exercise).

(2) The functions of the judge under this Part of this Act shall be exercisable where, after considering medical evidence, he is satisfied that a person is incapable, by reason of mental disorder, of managing

and administering his property and affairs; and a person as to whom the judge is so satisfied is referred to in this part of this Act as a patient.

Public Trustee's functions

6B–188   Section 94 was amended by the Public Trustee and Administration of Funds Act 1986 which came into operation on January 2, 1987.

This amended section enables the Public Trustee to carry out for the Court of Protection functions given to the court under enactments other than the Mental Health Act 1983. It is intended, for example, that the registration work given to the court under the Enduring Powers of Attorney Act 1985 should normally be undertaken within the Public Trust Office.

General functions of the judge with respect to property and affairs of patient

6B–189   **95.**—(1) The judge may, with respect to the property and affairs of a patient, do or secure the doing of all such things as appear necessary or expedient—

    (a) for the maintenance or other benefit of the patient,

    (b) for the maintenance or other benefit of members of the patient's family,

    (c) for making provision for other persons or purposes for whom or which the patient might be expected to provide if he were not mentally disordered, or

    (d) otherwise for administering the patient's affairs.

(2) In the exercise of the powers conferred by this section regard shall be had first of all to the requirements of the patient, and the rules of law which restricted the enforcement by a creditor of rights against property under the control of the judge in lunacy shall apply to property under the control of the judge; but, subject to the foregoing provisions of this subsection, the judge shall, in administering a patient's affairs, have regard to the interests of creditors and also to the desirability of making provision for obligations of the patient notwithstanding that they may not be legally enforceable.

Powers of the judge as to patient's property and affairs

6B–190   **96.**—(1) Without prejudice to the generality of section 95 above, the judge shall have the power to make such orders and give such directions and authorities as he thinks fit for the purposes of that section and in particular may for those purposes make orders or give directions or authorities for—

    (a) the control (with or without the transfer or vesting of property or the payment into or lodgment in the Supreme Court of money or securities) and management of any property of the patient;

    (b) the sale, exchange, charging or other disposition of or dealing with any property of the patient;

    (c) the acquisition of any property in the name or on behalf of the patient;

    (d) the settlement of any property of the patient, or the gift of any property of the patient to any such persons or for any such purposes as are mentioned in paragraphs (b) and (c) of section 95(1) above;

(e) the execution for the patient of a will making any provision (whether by way of disposing of property or exercising a power or otherwise) which could be made by a will executed by the patient if he were not mentally disordered;

(f) the carrying on by a suitable person of any profession, trade or business of the patient;

(g) the dissolution of a partnership of which the patient is a member;

(h) the carrying out of any contract entered into by the patient;

(i) the conduct of legal proceedings in the name of the patient or on his behalf;

(j) the reimbursement out of the property of the patient, with or without interest, of money applied by any person either in payment of the patient's debts (whether legally enforceable or not) or for the maintenance or other benefit of the patient or members of his family or in making provision for other persons or purposes for whom or which he might be expected to provide if he were not mentally disordered;

(k) the exercise of any power (including a power to consent) vested in the patient, whether beneficially, or as guardian or trustee, or otherwise.

(2) If under subsection (1) above provision is made for the settlement of any property of a patient, or the exercise of a power vested in a patient of appointing trustees or retiring from a trust, the judge may also make as respects the property settled or trust property such consequential vesting or other orders as the case may require, including (in the case of the exercise of such a power) any order which could have been made in such a case under Part IV of the Trustee Act 1925.

(3) Where under this section a settlement has been made of any property of a patient, and the Lord Chancellor or a nominated judge is satisfied, at any time before the death of the patient, that any material fact was not disclosed when the settlement was made, or that there has been any substantial change in circumstances, he may by order vary the settlement in such manner as he thinks fit, and give any consequential directions.

(4) The power of the judge to make or give an order, direction or authority for the execution of a will for a patient—

(a) shall not be exercisable at any time when the patient is a minor, and

(b) shall not be exercised unless the judge has reason to believe that the patient is incapable of making a valid will for himself.

(5) The powers of a patient as patron of a benefice shall be exercisable by the Lord Chancellor only.

Settlement of property

Notwithstanding subs.(3) of this section, if the court has directed a settlement of a **6B–191** patient's property for the benefit of, for example, his family, it is permissible to distribute any capital of the settled property during the lifetime of the patient. *Re C. W. H. T.* [1978] Ch. 67; [1978] 1 All E.R. 210.

Supplementary provisions as to wills executed under s.96

6B-192   **97.**—(1) Where under section 96(1) above the judge makes or gives an order, direction or authority requiring or authorising a person (in this section referred to as "the authorised person") to execute a will for a patient, any will executed in pursuance of that order, direction or authority shall be expressed to be signed by the patient acting by the authorised person, and shall be—

> (a) signed by the authorised person with the name of the patient, and with his own name, in the presence of two or more witnesses present at the same time, and
>
> (b) attested and subscribed by those witnesses in the presence of the authorised person, and
>
> (c) sealed with the official seal of the Court of Protection.

(2) The Wills Act 1837 shall have effect in relation to any such will as if it were signed by the patient by his own hand, except that in relation to any such will—

> (a) section 9 of that Act (which makes provision as to the signing and attestation of wills) shall not apply, and
>
> (b) in the subsequent provisions of that Act any reference to execution in the manner required by the previous provisions of that Act shall be construed as a reference to execution in the manner required by subsection (1) above.

(3) Subject to the following provisions of this section, any such will executed in accordance with subsection (1) above shall have the same effect for all purposes as if the patient were capable of making a valid will and the will had been executed by him in the manner required by the Wills Act 1837.

(4) So much of subsection (3) above as provides for such a will to have effect as if the patient were capable of making a valid will—

> (a) shall not have effect in relation to such a will in so far as it disposes of any immovable property, other than immovable property in England or Wales, and
>
> (b) where at the time when such a will is executed the patient is domiciled in Scotland or Northern Ireland or in a country or territory outside the United Kingdom, shall not have effect in relation to that will in so far as it relates to any other property or matter, except any property or matter in respect of which, under the law of his domicile, any question of his testamentary capacity would fall to be determined in accordance with the law of England and Wales.

6B-193   *Note* —As from January 1, 1983, the Wills Act 1837 must be read as amended by the Administration of Justice Act 1982.

Judge's powers in cases of emergency

6B-194   **98.** Where it is represented to the judge, and he has reason to believe, that a person may be incapable, by reason of mental disorder, of managing and administering his property and affairs, and the judge is of the opinion that it is necessary to make immediate provision for any of the matters referred to in section 95 above, then pending the determination of the question whether that person is so incapable the judge may exercise in relation to the property and affairs of that person any of the powers conferred on him in relation to the property and affairs of a patient by this Part of this Act so far as is requisite for enabling that provision to be made.

Power to appoint receiver

99.—(1) The judge may by order appoint as receiver for a patient a person specified in the order or the holder for the time being of an office so specified.

6B–195

(2) A person appointed as receiver for a patient shall do all such things in relation to the property and affairs of the patient as the judge, in the exercise of the powers conferred on him by sections 95 and 96 above, orders or directs him to do and may do any such thing in relation to the property and affairs of the patient as the judge, in the exercise of those powers, authorises him to do.

(3) A receiver appointed for any person shall be discharged by order of the judge on the judge being satisfied that person has become capable of managing and administering his property and affairs, and may be discharged by order of the judge at any time if the judge considers it expedient to do so; and a receiver shall be discharged (without any order) on the death of the patient.

Note—See *Re W. L. W.* [1972] Ch. 456; [1972] 1 All E.R. 433 and para. 6B–202.
"Expedient" in subs.(3) means, "expedient for the patient". (*Re N. (decd.)* [1977] 1 W.L.R. 676; [1977] 2 All E.R. 687, CA).

6B–196

Vesting of stock in curator appointed outside England and Wales

100.—(1) Where the judge is satisfied—

6B–197

   (a) that under the law prevailing in a place outside England and Wales a person has been appointed to exercise powers with respect to the property or affairs of any other person on the ground (however formulated) that that other person is incapable, by reason of mental disorder, of managing and administering his property and affairs, and

   (b) that having regard to the nature of the appointment and to the circumstances of the case it is expedient that the judge should exercise his powers under this section,

the judge may direct any stock standing in the name of the said other person or the right to receive the dividends from the stock to be transferred into the name of the person so appointed or otherwise dealt with as requested by that person, and may give such directions as the judge thinks fit for dealing with accrued dividends from the stock.

(2) In this section "stock" includes shares and also any fund, annuity or security transferable in the books kept by any body corporate

or unincorporated company or society, or by an instrument of transfer either alone or accompanied by other formalities, and "dividends"shall be construed accordingly.

Preservation of interests in patient's property

6B-198   **101.**—(1) Where any property of a person has been disposed of under this Part of this Act, and under his will or his intestacy, or by any gift perfected or nomination taking effect on his death, any other person would have taken an interest in the property but for the disposal—

(a) he shall take the same interest, if and so far as circumstances allow, in any property belonging to the estate of the deceased which represents the property disposed of; and

(b) if the property disposed of was real property any property representing it shall so long as it remains part of his estate be treated as if it were real property.

(2) The judge, in ordering, directing or authorising under this Part of this Act any disposal of property which apart from this section would result in the conversion of personal property into real property, may direct that the property representing the property disposed of shall, so long as it remains the property of the patient or forms part of his estate, be treated as if it were personal property.

(3) References in subsections (1) and (2) above to the disposal of property are references to—

(a) the sale, exchange, charging or other dealing (otherwise than by will) with property other than money,

(b) the removal of property from one place to another,

(c) the application of money in acquiring property, or

(d) the transfer of money from one account to another;

and references to property representing property disposed of shall be construed accordingly and as including the result of successive disposals.

(4) The judge may give such directions as appear to him necessary or expedient for the purpose of facilitating the operation of subsection (1) above, including the carrying of money to a separate account and the transfer of property other than money.

(5) Where the judge has ordered, directed or authorised the expenditure of money for the carrying out of permanent improvements on, or otherwise for the permanent benefit of, any property of the patient, he may order that the whole or any part of the money expended or to be expended shall be a charge upon the property, whether without interest or with interest at a specified rate; and an order under this subsection may provide for excluding or restricting the operation of subsection (1) above.

(6) A charge under subsection (5) above may be made in favour of such person as may be just, and in particular, where the money charged is paid out of the patient's general estate, may be made in favour of a person as trustee for the patient; but no charge under that subsection shall confer any right of sale or foreclosure during the lifetime of the patient.

Lord Chancellor's Visitors

102.—(1) There shall continue to be the following panels of Lord **6B–199** Chancellor's Visitors of patients constituted in accordance with this section, namely—

    (a) a panel of Medical Visitors;

    (b) a panel of Legal Visitors; and

    (c) a panel of General Visitors (being Visitors who are not required by this section to possess either a medical or legal qualification for appointment).

(2) Each panel shall consist of persons appointed to it by the Lord Chancellor, the appointment of each person being for such term and subject to such conditions as the Lord Chancellor may determine.

(3) A person shall not be qualified to be appointed—

    (a) to the panel of Medical Visitors unless he is a registered medical practitioner who appears to the Lord Chancellor to have special knowledge and experience of cases of mental disorder;

    (b) to the panel of Legal Visitors unless he has a 10 year general qualification, within the meaning of section 71 of the Courts and Legal Services Act 1990.

(4) If the Lord Chancellor so determines in the case of any Visitor appointed under this section, he shall be paid out of money provided by Parliament such remuneration and allowances as the Lord Chancellor may, with the concurrence of the Treasury, determine.

Note—Amended by the Courts and Legal Services Act 1990, Sched.10, para. 51. **6B–200**

Function of Visitors

103.—(1) Patients shall be visited by Lord Chancellor's Visitors in **6B–201** such circumstances, and in such manner, as may be prescribed by directions of a standing nature given by the Master of the Court of Protection with the concurrence of the Lord Chancellor.

(2) Where it appears to the judge in the case of any patient that a visit by a Lord Chancellor's Visitor is necessary for the purpose of investigating any particular matter or matters relating to the capacity of the patient to manage and administer his property and affairs, or otherwise relating to the exercise in relation to him of the functions of the judge under this Part of this Act, the judge may order that the patient shall be visited for that purpose.

(3) Every visit falling to be made under subsection (1) or (2) above shall be made by a General Visitor unless, in a case where it appears to the judge that it is in the circumstances essential for the visit to be made by a Visitor with medical or legal qualifications, the judge directs that the visit shall be made by a Medical or a Legal Visitor.

(4) A Visitor making a visit under this section shall make such report on the visit as the judge may direct.

(5) A Visitor making a visit under this section may interview the patient in private.

(6) A Medical Visitor making a visit under this section may carry

out in private a medical examination of the patient and may require the production of and inspect any medical records relating to the patient.

(7) The Master of the Court of Protection may visit any patient for the purpose mentioned in subsection (2) above and may interview the patient in private.

(8) A report made by a Visitor under this section, and information contained in such a report, shall not be disclosed except to the judge and any person authorised by the judge to receive the disclosure.

(9) If any person discloses any report or information in contravention of subsection (8) above, he shall be guilty of an offence and liable on summary conviction to imprisonment for a term not exceeding three months or to a fine not exceeding level 3 on the standard scale or both.

(10) In this section references to patients include references to persons alleged to be incapable, by reason of mental disorder, of managing and administering their property and affairs.

Reports, disclosure and liability of Medical Visitors

6B–202   The nature of reports of the Lord Chancellor's Medical Visitors under this section, the questions of their disclosure and the liability of a visitor to be summoned to be examined and cross-examined thereon were considered in *Re W. L. W.* [1972] Ch. 456; [1972] 2 All E.R. 433. Section 103(8) enables the court to withhold disclosure of a report of a visitor and in this connection a distinction is drawn between the court's paternalistic jurisdiction, concerned for the care of an undoubted patient and the management of his property and affairs, on the one hand, and the question of whether a person should become or remain subject to such jurisdiction, on the other. Such latter question was held to be outside the court's paternalistic jurisdiction under the Act and that the principles of natural justice apply and, accordingly, an alleged patient should be allowed to test any disclosed report of a visitor: in such a case although the court has power under s.103(8), to keep the report to itself it then has to resolve any conflict of fact or medical opinion as best it can and should only in exceptional cases, when it would be injurious to the (alleged) patient, refuse to allow the report to be disclosed and questions put to the visitor (see below).

Further, on the question of disclosure, Goff J. expressed the view, as *obiter*, that when the question is the initial one of whether a person is a "patient" within s.94(2) of the Act or whether proceedings should be determined, the court should lean towards allowing disclosure, at least to the patient's legal and medical advisers, and should refuse it only where the court feels that the interest of the particular alleged patient would be served thereby. In other cases, the court should only direct disclosure if it sees a positive advantage.

Where a visitor's report, or information contained in such a report has been disclosed to any person in pursuance of s.103(8), the court may, on the application of any person who appears to the court to be interested, give leave for written questions relevant to the issues before the court to be put to the visitor by whom the report was made (Court of Protection Rules 1984 (r.27(1)).

It should be noted that, with the leave of the court, a witness summons may issue against a Lord Chancellor's Medical Visitor under the Court of Protection Rules 1984, r.47.

General powers of the judge with respect to proceedings

6B–203   **104.**—(1) For the purposes of any proceedings before him with respect to persons suffering or alleged to be suffering from mental disorder, the judge shall have the same powers as are vested in the High Court in respect of securing the attendance of witnesses and the production of documents.

(2) Subject to the provisions of this section, any act or omission in the course of such proceedings which, if occurring in the course of proceedings in the High Court would have been a contempt of the court, shall be punishable by the judge in any manner in which it could have been punished by the High Court.

(3) Subsection (2) above shall not authorise the Master, or any other officer of the Court of Protection to exercise any power of attachment or committal, but the Master or officer may certify any such act or omission to the Lord Chancellor or a nominated judge, and the Lord Chancellor or judge may upon such certification inquire into the alleged act or omission and take any such action in relation to it as he could have taken if the proceedings had been before him.

(4) Subsections (1) to (4) of section 36 of the Supreme Court Act 1981 (which provides a special procedure for the issue of writs of subpoena ad testificandum and duces tecum so as to be enforceable throughout the United Kingdom) shall apply in relation to proceedings under this Part of this Act with the substitution for references to the High Court of references to the judge and for references to such writs of references to such document as may be prescribed by rules under this Part of this Act for issue by the judge for securing the attendance of witnesses or the production of documents.

Appeals

105.—(1) Subject to and in accordance with rules under this Part **6B–204** of this Act, an appeal shall lie to a nominated judge from any decision of the Master of the Court of Protection or any nominated officer.

(2) The Court of Appeal shall continue to have the same jurisdiction as to appeals from any decision of the Lord Chancellor or from any decision of a nominated judge, whether given in the exercise of his original jurisdiction or on the hearing of an appeal under subsection (1) above, as they had immediately before the coming into operation of Part VIII of the Mental Health Act 1959 as to appeals from orders in lunacy made by the Lord Chancellor or any other person having jurisdiction in lunacy.

Note—An appeal to the Court of Appeal under subs.(2) lies without leave. See para. **6B–205** 6B–9.

Rules of procedure

106.—(1) Proceedings before the judge with respect to persons suf- **6B–206** fering or alleged to be suffering from mental disorder (in this section referred to as "proceedings") shall be conducted in accordance with the provisions of rules made under this Part of this Act.

(2) Rules under this Part of this Act may make provision as to—
    (a) the carrying out of preliminary or incidental inquiries;
    (b) the persons by whom and manner in which proceedings may be instituted and carried on;
    (c) the persons who are to be entitled to be notified of, to attend, or to take part in proceedings;

(d) the evidence which may be authorised or required to be given in proceedings and the manner (whether on oath or otherwise and whether orally or in writing) in which it is to be given;

(e) the administration of oaths and taking of affidavits for the purposes of proceedings; and

(f) the enforcement of orders made and directions given in proceedings.

(3) Without prejudice to the provisions of section 104(1) above, rules under this Part of this Act may make provision for authorising or requiring the attendance and examination of persons suffering or alleged to be suffering from mental disorder, the furnishing of information and the production of documents.

(4) Rules under this Part of this Act may make provision as to the termination of proceedings, whether on the death or recovery of the person to whom the proceedings relate or otherwise, and for the exercise, pending the termination of the proceedings, of powers exercisable under this Part of this Act in relation to the property or affairs of a patient.

(5) Rules under this Part of this Act made with the consent of the Treasury may—

(a) make provision as to the scale of costs, fees and percentages payable in relation to proceedings, and as to the manner in which and funds out of which such costs, fees and percentages are to be paid;

(b) contain provision for charging any percentage upon the estate of the person to whom the proceedings relate and for the payment of costs, fees and percentages within such time after the death of the person to whom the proceedings relate or the termination of the proceedings as may be provided by the rules; and

(c) provide for the remission of fees and percentages.

(6) A charge upon the estate of a person created by virtue of subsection (5) above shall not cause any interest of that person in any property to fail or determine or to be prevented from recommencing.

(7) Rules under this Part of this Act may authorise the making of orders for the payment of costs to or by persons attending, as well as persons taking part in, proceedings.

Security and accounts

6B–207   **107.**—(1) Rules under this Part of this Act may make provision as to the giving of security by a receiver and as to the enforcement and discharge of the security.

(2) It shall be the duty of a receiver to render accounts in accordance with the requirements of rules under this Part of this Act, as well after his discharge as during his receivership; and rules under this Part of this Act may make provision for the rendering of accounts by persons other than receivers who are ordered, directed or authorised under this Part of this Act to carry out any transaction.

General provisions as to rules under Part VII

6B–208   **108.**—(1) Any power to make rules conferred by this Part of this Act shall be exercisable by the Lord Chancellor.

(2) Rules under this Part of this Act may contain such incidental and supplemental provisions as appear requisite for the purposes of the rules.

Effect and proof of orders, etc.

109.—(1) Section 204 of the Law of Property Act 1925 (by which orders of the High Court are made conclusive in favour of purchasers) shall apply in relation to orders made and directions and authorities given by the judge as it applies in relation to orders of the High Court. **6B–209**

(2) Office copies of orders made, directions or authorities given or other instruments issued by the judge and sealed with the official seal of the Court of Protection shall be admissible in all legal proceedings as evidence of the originals without any further proof.

Reciprocal arrangements in relation to Scotland and Northern Ireland as to exercise of powers

110.—(1) This Part of this Act shall apply in relation to the property and affairs in Scotland or Northern Ireland of a patient in relation to whom powers have been exercised under this Part of this Act, or a person as to whom powers are exercisable and have been exercised under section 98 above as it applies in relation to his property and affairs in England and Wales unless a curator bonis— **6B–210**

> (a) in Scotland, a judicial factor has been appointed for him; or
>
> (b) in Northern Ireland, he is a patient in relation to whom powers have been exercised under Part VIII of the Mental Health (Northern Ireland) Order 1986, or a person as to whom powers are exercisable and have been exercised under Article 97(2) of that Order.

(2) Where under the law in force in Scotland with respect to the property and affairs of persons suffering from mental disorder, a judicial factor has been appointed for any person, the provisions of that law shall apply in relation to that person's property and affairs in England and Wales unless he is a patient in relation to whom powers have been exercised under this Part of this Act, or a person as to whom powers are exercisable and have been exercised under section 98 above.

(2A) Part VIII of the Mental Health (Northern Ireland) Order 1986 shall apply in relation to the property and affairs in England and Wales of a patient in relation to whom powers have been exercised under that Part, or a person as to whom powers are exercisable and have been exercised under Article 97(2) of that Order as it applies in relation to his property and affairs in Northern Ireland unless he is a patient in relation to whom powers have been exercised under this Part of this Act, or a person as to whom powers are exercisable and have been exercised under section 98 above.

(3) Nothing in this section shall affect any power to execute a will under section 96(1)(e) above or Article 99(1)(e) of the Mental Health (Northern Ireland) Order 1986 or the effect of any will executed in the exercise of such a power.

(4) In this section references to property do not include references to land or interests in land but this subsection shall not prevent the receipt of rent or other income arising from land or interests in land.

Construction of references in other Acts to judge or authority having jurisdiction under Part VII

6B–211   **111.**—(1) The functions expressed to be conferred by any enactment not contained in this Part of this Act on the judge having jurisdiction under this Part of this Act shall be exercisable by the Lord Chancellor or by a nominated judge.

(2) Subject to subsections (3) and (3A) below, the functions expressed to be conferred by any such enactment on the authority having jurisdiction under this Part of this Act shall, subject to any express provision to the contrary, be exercisable by the Lord Chancellor, a nominated judge, the Master of the Court of Protection by the Public Trustee or a nominated officer.

(2A) The exercise of the functions referred to in subsection (2) above by the Public Trustee shall be subject to any directions of the Master and they shall be exercisable so far only as may be provided by any rules made under this Part of this Act or (subject to any such rules) by directions of the Master.

(3) The exercise of the functions referred to in subsection (2) above by a nominated officer shall be subject to any directions of the Master and they shall be exercisable so far only as may be provided by the instrument by which the officer is nominated.

(3A) In such cases or circumstances as may be prescribed by any rules under this Part of this Act or (subject to any such rules) by directions of the Master, the functions referred to in subsection (2) above shall be exercisable by the Public Trustee (but subject to any directions of the Master as to their exercise).

(4) Subject to the foregoing provisions of this section—

(a) references in any enactment not contained in this Part of this Act to the judge having jurisdiction under this Part of this Act shall be construed as references to the Lord Chancellor or a nominated judge, and

(b) references in any such enactment to the authority having jurisdiction under this Part of this Act shall be construed as references to the Lord Chancellor, a nominated judge, the Master of the Court of Protection or a nominated officer.

Public Trustee's functions

6B–212   Section 111 was amended by the Public Trustee and Administration of Funds Act 1986 which came into operation on January 2, 1987.

This amended section allows the Public Trustee to carry out work on behalf of the Court of Protection (which is a separately constituted entity outside the Public Trust Office structure). The Public Trustee undertakes the administrative tasks whereas matters requiring judicial decision are dealt with by the court. Whilst it enables the Public Trustee to carry out the functions given to the court under Pt VII of the Mental Health Act 1983 such authority is subject to the directions of the Master or so far as provided by rules. The Master is able to direct not only what functions under Pt VII of the Mental Health Act 1983 should be carried out by the Public Trustee but how this function should be exercised.

Interpretation of Part VII

112. In this Part of this Act, unless the context otherwise requires— **6B–213**

"nominated judge" means a judge nominated in pursuance of subsection (1) of section 93 above;

"nominated officer" means an officer nominated in pursuance of subsection (4) of that section;

"patient" has the meaning assigned to it by section 94 above;

"property" includes any thing in action, and any interest in real or personal property;

"the judge" shall be construed in accordance with section 94 above;

"will" includes a codicil.

Disapplication of certain enactments in relation to persons within the jurisdiction of the judge

113. The provisions of the Acts described in Schedule 3 to this Act **6B–214** which are specified in the third column of that Schedule, so far as they make special provision for persons suffering from mental disorder, shall not have effect in relation to patients and to persons as to whom powers are exercisable and have been exercised under section 98 above.

* * * * *

PART IX

OFFENCES

Forgery, false statements, etc.

126.—(1) Any person who without lawful authority or excuse has **6B–215** in his custody or under his control any document to which this subsection applies, which is, and which he knows or believes to be, false within the meaning of Part I of the Forgery and Counterfeiting Act 1981, shall be guilty of an offence.

(2) Any person who without lawful authority or excuse makes or has in his custody or under his control, any document so closely resembling a document to which subsection (1) above applies as to be calculated to deceive shall be guilty of an offence.

(3) The documents to which subsection (1) above applies are any documents purporting to be—

(a) an application under Part II of this Act;

(b) a medical or other recommendation or report under this Act; and

(c) any other document required or authorised to be made for any of the purposes of this Act.

(4) Any person who—

(a) wilfully makes a false entry or statement in any application, recommendation, report, record or other document required or authorised to be made for any of the purposes of this Act; or

(b) with intent to deceive, makes use of any such entry or statement which he knows to be false,

shall be guilty of an offence.

(5) Any person guilty of an offence under this section shall be liable—

(a) on summary conviction, to imprisonment for a term not exceeding six months or to a fine not exceeding the statutory maximum, or to both;

(b) on conviction on indictment, to imprisonment for a term not exceeding two years or to a fine of any amount, or to both.

6B–216   *Note* —Amended by the Mental Health (Patients in the Community) Act 1995, Sched.1, para. 17.

* * * * *

Obstruction
6B–217   **129.**—(1) Any person who without reasonable cause—

(a) refuses to allow the inspection of any premises; or

(b) refuses to allow the visiting, interviewing or examination of any person by a person authorised in that behalf by or under this Act or to give access to any person to a person so authorised;

(c) refuses to produce for the inspection of any person so authorised any document or record the production of which is duly required by him; or

(d) otherwise obstructs any such person in the exercise of his functions,

shall be guilty of an offence.

(2) Without prejudice to the generality of subsection (1) above, any person who insists on being present when required to withdraw by a person authorised by or under this Act to interview or examine a person in private shall be guilty of an offence.

(3) Any person guilty of an offence under this section shall be liable on summary conviction to imprisonment for a term not exceeding three months or to a fine not exceeding level 4 on the standard scale or to both.

* * * *

6B–217.1   *Note* —Amended by the Mental Health (Patients in the Community) Act 1995, Sched.1, para. 19.

PART X

MISCELLANEOUS AND SUPPLEMENTARY

MISCELLANEOUS PROVISIONS

Correspondence of patients
6B–218   **134.**—(1) A postal packet addressed to any person by a patient

detained in a hospital under this Act and delivered by the patient for dispatch may be withheld from the postal operator concerned—

> (a) if that person has requested that communications addressed to him by the patient should be withheld; or
>
> (b) subject to subsection (3) below, if the hospital is is one at which high security psychiatric services are provided and the managers of the hospital consider that the postal packet is likely—
>
>> (i) to cause distress to the person to whom it is addressed or to any other person (not being a person on the staff of the hospital); or
>>
>> (ii) to cause danger to any person;

and any request for the purposes of paragraph (a) above shall be made by a notice in writing given to the managers of the hospital, the registered medical practitioner in charge of the treatment of the patient or the Secretary of State.

(2) Subject to subsection (3) below, a postal packet addressed to a patient detained under this Act in a hospital at which high security psychiatric services are provided may be withheld from the patient if, in the opinion of the managers of the hospital, it is necessary to do so in the interests of the safety of the patient or for the protection of other persons.

(3) Subsections (1)(b) and (2) above do not apply to any postal packet addressed by a patient to, or sent to a patient by or on behalf of—

> (a) any Minister of the Crown or the Scottish Ministers or Member of either House of Parliament or member of the Scottish Parlaiment;
>
> (b) the Master or any other officer of the Court of Protection or any of the Lord Chancellor's Visitors;
>
> (c) the Parliamentary Commissioner for Administration, the Welsh Administration Ombudsman the Health Service Commissioner for England, the Health Service Commissioner for Wales or a Local Commissioner within the meaning of Part III of the Local Government Act 1974;
>
> (d) a Mental Health Review Tribunal;
>
> (e) a Strategic Health Authority, Health Authority, Special Health Authority, a local social services authority, a patients' Forum or a local probation board established under section 4 of the Criminal Justice and Court Services Act 2000;
>
> (ea) a provider of a patient advocacy and liaison service for the assistance of patients at the hospital and their families and carers;
>
> (eb) a provider of independent advocacy services for the patient;
>
> (f) the managers of the hospital in which the patient is detained;
>
> (g) any legally qualified person instructed by the patient to act as his legal adviser; or

    (h) the European Commission of Human Rights or the European Court of Human Rights.

(3A) In subsection (3) above—

    (a) "patient advocacy and liaison service" means a service of a description prescribed by regulations made by the Secretary of State, and

    (b) "independent advocacy services" means services provided under arrangements under section 19A of the National Health Service Act 1977.

(4) The managers of a hospital may inspect and open any postal packet for the purposes of determining—

    (a) whether it is one to which subsection (1) or (2) applies, and

    (b) in the case of a postal packet to which subsection (1) or (2) above applies, whether or not it should be withheld under that subsection;

and the power to withhold a postal packet under either of those subsections includes power to withhold anything contained in it.

(5) Where a postal packet or anything contained in it is withheld under subsection (1) or (2) above the managers of the hospital shall record that fact in writing.

(6) Where a postal packet or anything contained in it is withheld under subsection (1)(b) or (2) above the managers of the hospital shall within seven days give notice of that fact to the patient and, in the case of a packet withheld under subsection (2) above, to the person (if known) by whom the postal packet was sent; and any such notice shall be given in writing and shall contain a statement of the effect of section 121(7) and (8) above.

(7) The functions of the managers of a hospital under this section shall be discharged on their behalf by a person on the staff of the hospital appointed by them for that purpose and different persons may be appointed to discharge different functions.

(8) The Secretary of State may make regulations with respect to the exercise of the powers conferred by this section.

(9) In this section "hospital" has the same meaning as in Part II of this Act, "postal packet" and "postal operator" and "postal packet" have the same meaning as in the Postal Services Act 2000.

6B–219   *Note* —Amended by the Probation Service Act 1993, Sched.3, para. 7; and the Health Authorities Act 1995, Sched.1, para. 107(10). Subs. (3)(c) amended by the Government of Wales Act 1998 (c.38), s.125, Sched.12, para. 22. In subs.(3)(e) the words "a Patients' Forum" added by the National Health Service Reform and Health Care Professions Act 2002, s.19(6).

* * * *

Protection for acts done in pursuance of this Act

6B–220   **139.**—(1) No person shall be liable, whether on the ground of want of jurisdiction or on any other ground, to any civil or criminal proceedings to which he would have been liable apart from this section in respect of any act purporting to be done in pursuance of this

Act or any regulations or rules made under this Act, or in, or in pursuance of anything done in, the discharge of functions conferred by any other enactment on the authority having jurisdiction under Part VII of this Act, unless the act was done in bad faith or without reasonable care.

(2) No civil proceedings shall be brought against any person in any court in respect of any such act without the leave of the High Court; and no criminal proceedings shall be brought against any person in any court in respect of any such act except by or with the consent of the Director of Public Prosecutions.

(3) This section does not apply to proceedings for an offence under this Act, being proceedings which, under any other provision of this Act, can be instituted only by or with the consent of the Director of Public Prosecutions.

(4) This section does not apply to proceedings against the Secretary of State or against a Health Authority or Special Health Authority or against a National Health Service trust established under the National Health Service and Community Care Act 1990 or NHS foundation trust.

(5) In relation to Northern Ireland the reference in this section to the Director of Public Prosecutions shall be construed as a reference to the Director of Public Prosecutions for Northern Ireland.

Note —Amended by the National Health Service and Community Care Act 1990, **6B–221** Sched.9, para. 24(7); and the Health Authorities Act 1995, Sched.1, para. 107(11) and by the Health and Social Care (Community Health and Standards) Act 2003, Sched. 4, para. 56.

Application for leave under this section to bring proceedings against any person must be made to a judge in Chambers. See PD2B, para. 3.1(g).

An application under subs.(2) is an interlocutory matter coming within the Supreme Court Act 1981, s.18 and a decision thereon is accordingly not appealable without leave (*Moore v. Commissioner of Metropolitan Police* [1968] 1 Q.B. 26; [1967] 2 All E.R. 827 (decision under T.A. 1925)).

The nature of the acts covered by the section and the protection afforded to members of the nursing staff of hospitals in consequence were considered in *R. v. Bracknell Justices, ex p. Griffiths* [1975] 2 W.L.R. 291; [1975] 1 All E.R. 900. See also report of the appeal to the House of Lords [1975] 3 W.L.R. 140; [1975] 2 All E.R. 881.

The section does not apply to proceedings brought by informal patients (*R. v. Runighian* [1977] Crim.L.R. 361).

See articles in (1979) 129 New L.J. 213 and [1979] J.S.W.L. 337.

* * * *

SUPPLEMENTAL

General provisions as to regulations, orders and rules

143.—(1) Any power of the Secretary of State or the Lord Chancel- **6B–222** lor to make regulations, orders or rules under this Act shall be exercisable by statutory instrument.

(2) Any Order in Council under this Act and any statutory instrument containing regulations or rules made under this Act or any order made under section 54A or 65 above shall be subject to annulment in pursuance of a resolution of either House of Parliament.

(3) No order shall be made under section 45A(10), 68(4) or 71(3) above unless a draft of it has been approved by a resolution of each House of Parliament.

6B–223   *Note* —Amended by the Criminal Justice Act 1991, s.27; the Crime (Sentences) Act 1997, Sched.4, para. 12; and the Health Authorities Act 1995, Sched.1, para. 107(13).

* * * *

Application to Scotland

6B–224   **146.** Sections 42(6), 80, 88 (and so far as applied by that section sections 18, 22 and 138), 104(4), 110 (and so much of Part VII of this Act as is applied in relation to Scotland by that section), 116, 122, 128 (except so far as it relates to patients subject to guardianship), 137, 139(1), 141, 142, 143 (so far as applicable to any Order in Council extending to Scotland) and 144 above shall extend to Scotland together with any amendment or repeal by this Act of or any provision of Schedule 5 to this Act relating to any enactment which so extends; but, except as aforesaid and except so far as it relates to the interpretation or commencement of the said provisions, this Act shall not extend to Scotland.

Application to Northern Ireland

6B–225   **147.** Sections 81, 82, 86, 87, 88 (and so far as applied by that section sections 18, 22 and 138), 104(4), 110 (and so much of Part VII as is applied in relation to Northern Ireland by that section), section 128 (except so far as it relates to patients subject to guardianship), 137, 139, 141, 142, 143 (so far as applicable to any Order in Council extending to Northern Ireland) and 144 above shall extend to Northern Ireland together with any amendment or repeal by this Act of or any provision of Schedule 5 to this Act relating to any enactment which so extends; but except as aforesaid and except so far as it relates to the interpretation or commencement of the said provisions, this Act shall not extend to Northern Ireland.

* * * *

Court of Protection Rules 2001

6B–226   (S.I. 2001 No. 824)

ARRANGEMENT OF RULES

PART I

PRELIMINARY

PART II

EXERCISE OF JURISDICTION

PART III

APPLICATIONS

PART IV

SERVICE

PART V

EVIDENCE

PART VI

HEARING OF PROCEEDINGS

PART VII

RECEIVERS

PART VIII

ENTRY AND ENFORCEMENT OF ORDERS

PART XVIII

COSTS

PART XIX

APPROVAL OF DEEDS

PART XX

TRANSITIONAL PROVISIONS

PART XXI

REVOCATION

*as amended by the Court of Protection (Amendment) Rules 2004 (S.I. 2004
No. 1291) subject to transitional provisions specified in rule 11*

PART I

PRELIMINARY

Title and Commencement

1. These Rules may be cited as the Court of Protection Rules
2001[1] and shall come into force on 1st April 2001.

6B–227

Interpretation

2.—(1) In these Rules, unless the context otherwise requires—
expressions used in the Supreme Court Act 1981 shall have the same
meanings as they have for the purposes of that Act;

6B–228

"the Act" means the Mental Health Act 1983;

"attended hearing" means a hearing where one or more of the
parties to the proceedings have been invited to attend the
court for the determination of the application;

"court" means the Court of Protection;

"direction" means a direction or authority given under the seal
of the court;

"entered" means entered in the books of the court;

"filed" mean filed in the court office;

---

[1] 1981, c.5.

"function" means any power, discretion or function conferred by the Act;

"hearing" means an attended or unattended hearing;

"judge" means the Lord Chancellor or a nominated judge;

"Master" means the Master of the Court of Protection;

"medical certificate" means a certificate by a registered medical practitioner that a patient is incapable, by reason of mental disorder, of managing and administering his property and affairs;

"nominated officer" means an officer nominated by the Lord Chancellor under section 93(4) of the Act to act for the purposes of Part VII of the Act;

"order" includes a certificate, direction or authority of the court under seal;

"patient" includes a person who is alleged to be or who the court has reason to believe may be incapable by reason of mental disorder of managing and administering his property and affairs;

"receiver" means a receiver appointed under section 99(1) of the Act;

"seal" means an official seal of the Court and "sealed" shall be construed accordingly;

"stock" includes shares and also any fund, annuity or security transferable in the books kept by any body corporate or unincorporated company or society, or by an instrument of transfer either alone or accompanied by other formalities and includes any dividends paid in respect of them;

"Visitor" means one of the Lord Chancellor's Visitors.

(2) In these Rules—

(a) any reference to a numbered rule is a reference to the rule of these Rules so numbered in these Rules;

(b) any reference in a rule to a numbered paragraph is a reference to the paragraph so numbered in the rule in which the reference occurs;

(c) a form referred to by letter alone means the form so designated in the Schedule to these Rules or a form to the same effect with such variations as the circumstances may require or the court may approve and in all cases shall include a Welsh translation of the form.

Exercise of the court's functions

6B–229 3. Where any function (in whatever words) is expressed by these Rules to be exercisable by the court then, subject to the provisions of the Act, that functions may be exercised—

(a) by a judge;

(b) by the Master;

(c) to the extent to which he is authorised to exercise it under section 94 of the Act, by any nominated officer.

Computation of time

6B–230 4.—(1) Where a period of time fixed by these Rules or by any or-

1886

der or direction of the court for doing an act expires on a day on which the court office for doing that act is closed and for that reason the act cannot be done on that day, the act shall be done in time if done on the next day on which that office is open.

(2) Where the act is required to be done within a specified period after or from a specified date, the period begins immediately after that date.

(3) Where any period of time as mentioned in paragraph (1) is less than six days, any day on which the court office is closed shall not be included in that computation.

Power to vary time

5. The court may extend or abridge the time limited by these Rules or any order or direction of the court for doing any act or taking any proceedings upon such terms as the court thinks fit and notwithstanding, in the case of an extension, that the time so limited has expired.

6B–231

PART II

EXERCISE OF JURISDICTION

Exercise of jurisdiction

6. Except where these Rules otherwise provide, any function may be exercised—

6B–232

    (a) without fixing an appointment for a hearing;

    (b) by the court of its own motion or at the instance or on the application of any person interested;

    (c) whether or not any proceedings have been commenced in the court with respect to the patient.

PART III

APPLICATIONS

Forms of application

7.—(1) Subject to paragraph (3), a first application to the court for the appointment of a receiver shall state the name and address of the applicant and the proposed receiver and their relationship (if any) to the patient in such manner as the court shall direct and an application to the court respecting the exercise of any of its other jurisdiction in relation to a patient, may be made by letter unless the court otherwise directs that it should be formal, in which case it shall be made in Form A.

6B–233

(2) An application for the appointment of a receiver shall be treated as an application for the appointment as receiver of the person named in the application or some other suitable person.

(3) On grounds of urgency the court may dispense with the need for an application in writing.

(4) An application relating to the committal of a person for contempt of court shall be made to a judge but all other applications to the court shall be made in the first instance to the Master.

Procedure for short order or direction without appointment of a receiver

6B–234   8.—(1) Without prejudice to the generality of Rule 6, if it appears to the court that—

        (a) the property of the patient does not exceed £16,000 in value; or

        (b) it is otherwise appropriate to proceed under this rule,

and that it is not necessary to appoint a receiver for a patient, the court may make a short order or direction under this rule whether or not the application was made for the appointment of a receiver for the patient.

(3) A short order or direction under this rule is an order or direction directing an officer of the court or some other suitable person named in the order or direction to deal with the patient's property (or any part of it), or with his affairs, in any manner authorised by the Act and specified in the order or direction.

Date for hearing

6B–235   9.—(1) Upon receiving an application under rule 7 the court shall fix a date for the hearing of the application unless it considers that the application can properly be dealt with without a hearing, and on this ground the court may cancel any hearing fixed under this paragraph.

(2) Where a hearing is fixed under paragraph (1) an officer shall notify the applicant, by letter, of the date and time of the hearing.

(3) Where the court decides that the application can properly be dealt without a hearing and a hearing is cancelled, an officer shall so notify the applicant by letter.

Consolidation of Proceedings

6B–236   10. The court may allow one application to be made in respect of two or more patients or may consolidate an application relating to two or more patients, if in its opinion the proceedings relating to them can be more conveniently dealt with together.

Power to direct applications by officer of the court or Official Solicitor

6B–237   11. Where, in the opinion of the court, an application ought to be made for the appointment or discharge of a receiver or for a direction with regard to the exercise of any other function with respect to the property and affairs of a patient, and there appears to be no other suitable person able and willing to make the application, or the court for any other reason thinks fit, the court may direct that the application be made by an officer of the court or, if he consents, the Official Solicitor.

Representation of patient by receiver

12.—(1) Except as mentioned in rule 18(c), (d), (e) and (f), an ap- **6B–238**
plication on behalf of a patient for whom a receiver has been appointed shall, unless the court otherwise directs, be made by a
receiver in his own name.

(2) Subject to any directions given by the court, a patient for
whom a receiver has been appointed may be represented by the
receiver at any hearing relating to the patient or of which the patient
has been given notice.

Representation of patient by the Official Solicitor

13. Where, in any proceedings, the court considers that the **6B–239**
interests of the patient are not adequately represented, the court
may, with the consent of the Official Solicitor, direct that the Official
Solicitor shall act as a solicitor for the patient either generally in the
proceedings or for any particular purpose connected with the
proceedings, except that it shall not be necessary to appoint the Official Solicitor to be receiver or guardian ad litem for the patient.

Persons under a disability

14.—(1) In this rule, "person under a disability" means a minor **6B–240**
or a patient for whom no receiver has been appointed.

(2) A person under a disability shall not make an application in
proceedings relating to another person except by his next friend and
shall not resist an application in any such proceedings except by his
guardian ad litem.

(3) Where a person is to be appointed next friend or guardian ad
litem of a person under a disability in substitution for the person
previously acting as next friend or guardian ad litem, the appointment shall be made by the court but, except for this, an order of the
court appointing a next friend or guardian ad litem of a person
under a disability shall not be necessary.

(4) Before the name of any person is used in any proceedings as
next friend or guardian ad litem of a person under a disability there
shall be filed—

> (a) a written consent of the first-mentioned person to act as
> next friend or (as the case may be) guardian ad litem of
> the person under a disability in the proceedings, and
> (b) a certificate by the solicitor acting for the person under a
> disability certifying—
>> (i) that he knows or believes that the person to whom
>> the certificate relates is a minor or patient giving
>> (in the case of a patient) the grounds of his knowl-
>> edge or belief, and
>> (ii) except where the person named in the certificate
>> is the Official Solicitor, that the person so named
>> has no interest in the proceedings adverse to that
>> of the person under a disability.

Application under section 54 of the Trustee Act 1925

15. An application to the court with respect to the jurisdiction **6B–241**

referred to in section 54(2) of the Trustee Act 1925 may be made only by—

    (a) the receiver for the patient, or

    (b) any person who has made an application for the appointment of a receiver which has not yet been fully determined, or

    (c) a continuing trustee, or

    (d) any other person who, according to the practice of the Chancery Division, would have been entitled to make the application if it had been made in the High Court.

Application under section 36(9) of the Trustee Act 1925

6B–242   16. No person other than a co-trustee, or other person with power to appoint a new trustee, may make an application to the court under section 36(9) of the Trustee Act 1925 for leave to appoint a new trustee in place of a patient.

Application under section 96(1)(k) of the Act

6B–243   17. The provisions of rule 15 shall apply with such modifications as may be necessary to an application under section 96(1)(k) of the Act for an order for the exercise of any power vested in a patient of appointing trustees or retiring from a trust.

Application for settlement or gift of patient's property or for execution of will of patient

6B–244   18. An application under section 96(1)(d) of the Act for an order for the settlement or gift of any property of a patient, or an application under section 96(1)(e) of the Act for an order of execution for a patient of a will, may be made only by—

    (a) the receiver for the patient, or

    (b) any person who has made an application for the appointment of a receiver which has not yet been determined, or

    (c) any person who, under any known will of the patient or under his intestacy, may become entitled to any property of the patient or any interest in it, or

    (d) any person for whom the patient might be expected to provide if he were not mentally disordered, or

    (e) any attorney acting under a registered enduring power of attorney, or

    (f) any other person whom the court may authorise to make it.

Rule 19—Notice of hearing

PART IV

SERVICE

Notice of hearing

6B–245   19.—(1) Except where these rules provide otherwise or the court directs otherwise, the applicant shall give notice of the hearing of an application in accordance with the following provisions of this rule.

(2) Where a receiver has been appointed for a patient he shall, unless he is the applicant, be given notice of the hearing of any application relating to the patient.

(3) Where the application is one to which rules 15 or 17 relate, notice of the hearing of the application shall also be given to every person who would have been required to be served with the application notice if the application had been made to the High Court.

(4) Notice of the hearing of the application shall also be given to such other persons who appear to the court to be interested as the court may specify.

(5) Notice of a hearing shall be given—
    (a) in the case of a first application for the appointment of a receiver, or an application under rule 16, not less than ten clear days and
    (b) in the case of any other application, not less than two clear days before the date fixed for the hearing.

(6) For the purposes of this rule notice of a hearing shall be given to the person concerned in such manner as the court may direct.

Mode of service

20. Except where these rules otherwise provide, any document required by these Rules to be served on any person shall be served by—
    (a) delivering it to him personally;
    (b) sending it to him by first class post or through a document exchange at his last known address; or
    (c) by transmitting it to him at his last known address by fax or other electronic means.

6B–246

Rule 21—Service on solicitor

Service on solicitor

21. Where a solicitor acting for the person to be served with any document endorses on the document or a copy of it a statement that he accepts service on behalf of that person, the document shall be deemed to have been duly served on that person and to have been served on the date on which the endorsement was made.

6B–247

Substituted service

22. Where it appears to the court that it is impracticable for any reason to serve a document in accordance with rule 20, the court may make an order for substituted service of the document by taking such steps as the court may direct to bring it to the notice of the person to be served.

6B–248

Service on person under a disability

23.—(1) Unless the court otherwise directs, any document

6B–249

required by these Rules to be served on a person who is a minor or patient (in this rule referred to as a person under a disability) shall be served—

    (a) in the case of a minor who is not also a patient, on his parent or guardian or, if he has no parent or guardian, on the person with parental responsibility as defined in section 3 of the Children Act 1989[1];

    (b) in the case of a patient—

        (i) on his receiver or, if he has no receiver,

        (ii) on the person acting in pursuance of an order or direction under rule 8, or, if there is no such person,

        (iii) on an attorney acting under a registered power of attorney, or, if there is no such attorney,

        (iv) on the person with whom he resides or in whose care he is;

and must be served in a manner required by these Rules.

(2) Notwithstanding anything in paragraph (1), the court may order that any document which has been served on the person under a disability or on a person other than a person mentioned in that paragraph shall be deemed to be duly served on the person under a disability.

(3) Nothing in this rule shall apply to an order required by rule 42 to be served on a patient.

Notification of application for appointment of receiver, etc.

6B–250   24.—(1) In the following paragraphs of this rule, "relevant application" means an application for any order, direction or certificate exercising the court's jurisdiction in respect of a patient, including an application for the appointment of a receiver.

(1A) Subject to paragraph (1B), where a relevant application is made, the applicant, or such other person as the court may direct, shall give notice to the patient in accordance with paragraphs (1D) to (1F).

(1B) Subject to paragraph (1C), paragraph (1A) shall not apply where a relevant application ("the previous relevant application") has already been made in respect of the same patient, unless there has been any finding by the court since the previous relevant application was made that the patient is capable of managing and administering his property and affairs or, where an enduring power of attorney created by the patient has been registered, and the registration has not been cancelled.

(1BB) Subject to paragraph 1C, paragraph 1A shall not apply to a relevant application where the court is of the opinion that it is necessary to make an immediate order directing or authorising any person to do any action or carry out any transaction on behalf of a patient, and directs that notice to the patient may be disposed with.

---

[1] 1989, c.41.

(1C) Paragraph (1A) shall in any case apply where the relevant application referred to in that paragraph is a first application for the appointment of a receiver except where the court is of the opinion, on the application, that it is necessary to appoint an interim receiver for the patient under rule 42(1)(b).

(1D) Notice under paragraph (1A) shall consist of notice—

    (a) that an application has been made;

    (b) of the effect, if made, of—

        (i) the appointment of a receiver, in the case of a first application for appointment of a receiver; or

        (ii) such other order, direction or certificate as may have been applied for;

    (c) of the identity of the applicant and, if different, that of any proposed receiver;

    (d) of any hearing fixed by the court; and

    (e) of any such other information as the court may direct.

(1E) Notice under paragraph (1A) shall be given to the patient personally.

(1F) Where the court has fixed a hearing, the time limits set out in rule 19(5) shall apply to the giving of notice under paragraph (1A).

(2) Where the patient is a minor, notification under paragraph (1) shall be given to his parent or guardian or, if he has no parent or guardian, to the person with parental responsibility within the meaning of the Children Act 1989.

Notification to next of kin etc. of intention to make application for appointment of receiver

25.—(1) Where an applicant proposes to make an application for the appointment of a receiver or a new receiver, the applicant shall give notice of his intention to—   **6B–251**

    (a) all relatives of the patient who have the same or a nearer degree of relationship to the patient than the applicant or proposed receiver; and

    (b) such other persons who appear to the court to be interested as the court may specify;

unless the court directs that such notification shall be dispensed with.

(2) For the purposes of this rule, notice of the intention to make an application is given if the person concerned is notified, in such manner as the court may direct, of the identities of the patient, the applicant and the proposed receiver and supplied with such additional information as the court may direct.

Certificate of service or notification

26.—(1) A certificate of service shall be filed as soon as practicable after service of a document has been effected in accordance with these Rules—   **6B–252**

(a) in the case of notice given under rules 24(1A), unless the court directs otherwise;

(b) otherwise, if the court so directs.

(1A) A certificate of service under paragraph (1) shall show where, when, how and by whom service was effected and, in relation to a notice given under rules 24(1A), shall also contain a certificate as to whether or not the patient appeared, to the person giving it, to understand the notice.

(2) The provisions of paragraphs (1) and (1A) shall apply to the giving of notification under rules 24 and 25 as they apply to the service of documents and references in those paragraphs to service shall accordingly be construed as including references to notification and the giving of notification respectively.

(3) References in paragraphs (1) and (1A) to notice given under rules 24(1A) shall be taken not to include such notice when it is given to a parent, guardian or person with parental responsibility in accordance with rules 24(2).

PART V

EVIDENCE

Affidavit evidence

6B–253   27.—(1) Except where these Rules provide otherwise, evidence in proceedings governed by these Rules shall be given by affidavit.

(2) An affidavit for use in proceedings under these Rules may be sworn—

(a) in England or Wales, before any person authorised to take affidavits under the Commissioners for Oaths Acts 1889 and 1891[1], under the Solicitors Act 1974[2], or under the Courts and Legal Services Act 1990[3] or before any officer of the court so authorised by the Master;

(b) outside England and Wales, before any person before whom an affidavit may be sworn for use in the Supreme Court.

Rule 28—Unsworn Evidence

Unsworn evidence

6B–254   28.—(1) Notwithstanding rule 27(1), the court may accept and act upon a statement of facts or other such evidence, whether oral or written, as the court considers sufficient, although not given on oath and whether or not it would be admissible in a court of law apart from this rule.

(2) The court may give directions as to the manner in which a

---

[1] 1889 c.10; 1891 c.50.
[2] 1974, c.47.
[3] 1990, c.41.

statement of facts or other written evidence under paragraph (1) is to be given but subject to such directions any such statement or other evidence shall—

    (a) be drawn up in numbered paragraphs and dated; and

    (b) be signed by the person by whom it is given.

Rule 29—Written questions to Visitors

Written questions to Visitors

29.—(1) Where a Visitor's report, or information contained in such a report, has been disclosed to any person in pursuance of section 103(8) of the Act, the court may, on the application of any person who appears to the court to be interested, give leave for written questions relevant to the issues before the court to be put to the Visitor by whom the report was made.   **6B–255**

(2) The questions sought to be put to the Visitor shall be submitted to the court, which may put them to the Visitor with such amendments (if any) as it thinks fit and the Visitor shall give his replies in writing to the questions so put.

(3) The court may disclose the replies given by the Visitor under this rule to any person who appears to the court to be interested, or to his legal or medical adviser, on such conditions (if any) as it thinks fit.

(4) No Visitor shall be required to give written evidence for the purpose of any proceedings to which these rules relate, other than in accordance with this rule.

(5) In this rule, "Visitor" means a Medical or Legal Visitor.

Cross-examination of deponent

30. Any person who has made an affidavit or given a certificate or other written evidence for use in proceedings under these Rules may be ordered by the court to attend for cross-examination.   **6B–256**

Administration of oaths

31. The court may direct that an oath be administered to any witness or interpreter in any proceedings before the court.   **6B–257**

Filing of written evidence

32.—(1) Before an affidavit certificate or other evidence is used in any proceedings under these rules it shall be filed but the court may make an order on the basis of such evidence before it is filed if the person tendering it undertakes to file it before the order is drawn up.   **6B–258**

(2) There shall be endorsed on every affidavit, certificate or other written evidence the name and address of the solicitor, if any, acting for the person on whose behalf it is filed.

Use of evidence in subsequent proceedings

33.—(1) Except where the court otherwise directs, evidence which has been used in any proceedings relating to a patient may be used   **6B–259** at any subsequent stage of those proceedings or in any other proceedings relating to the same patient or to another member of the patient's family.

(2) Without prejudice to paragraph (1), the Master may, upon application being made for that purpose, authorise the use of such evidence in any legal proceedings that he may specify.

Evidence to be filed on a first application for receiver, etc

6B–260   34.—(1) Where a first application has been made for the appointment of a receiver for a patient or for a short order or direction under rule 8 authorising any person to do any act or carry out any transaction on behalf of a patient without appointing him receiver—

    (a) the applicant shall, unless the court otherwise directs, file a medical certificate and evidence of family and property; and

    (b) the court may—

        (i) require the applicant to produce to it such evidence as it shall direct of the suitability of the applicant to be appointed a receiver or to do any such act or carry out any such transaction without being appointed receiver; and

        (ii) make such enquiries as it shall think fit with regard to the suitability of the applicant for such appointment.

(2) In this rule, "evidence of family and property" means a certificate or, if the court so directs, in a particular case, an affidavit giving particulars of the patient's relatives and such other persons as the court may direct, property and affairs and of the circumstances giving rise to the application.

(3) Rule 28 applies to unsworn evidence of family and property as it applies to unsworn evidence generally.

Evidence of patient's recovery or death and inquiry by court as to whether patient has recovered

6B–261   35.—(1) Where at any stage of proceedings relating to a patient the court has reason to believe that the patient has recovered or has died, the court may require medical evidence of the recovery or evidence of the death (as the case may be) to be furnished to it by such person as it thinks appropriate.

(2) The court shall, from time to time, review a patient's case where a medical certificate provided to the court expressed an opinion that there is a possibility of mental recovery and make such inquiries and carry out such investigations as it thinks fit to establish whether or not the patient has recovered.

Proof of amount due to public authority

6B–262   36. The amount due to any public authority for the past maintenance of a patient may, unless the court otherwise directs, be proved by the filing of an account certified under the hand of the proper officer of the authority.

Rule 37—Privacy of applications

PART VI

HEARING OF PROCEEDINGS

Privacy of applications

37.—(1) Every application shall be heard in chambers unless, in the case of an application for a hearing by the judge, the judge otherwise directs.   **6B–263**

(2) The court shall give such directions as it thinks fit concerning the privacy of applications made to it.

Rule 38—Persons attending the hearing

Persons attending the hearing

38. Subject to rule 14 the court may determine what persons are to be entitled to attend at any stage of the proceedings relating to a patient.   **6B–264**

Rule 39—Representation at hearing

Representation at hearing

39. Where two or more persons appearing at a hearing are represented by the same legal representative, the court may, if it thinks fit, require any of them to be separately represented.   **6B–265**

Reference of proceedings to judge

40. Where a function of the court is not being exercised by a judge, the court, after giving such direction as it thinks fit, shall refer to the judge any proceedings or any question arising in any proceedings which ought, by virtue of any enactment or in its opinion, to be considered by the judge.   **6B–266**

Reference of proceedings to Master

41. The judge may refer any proceedings before him or any question arising in them to the Master for inquiry and report.   **6B–267**

Rule 42—Interim provision

PART VII

RECEIVERS

Interim provision

42.—(1) Where in the opinion of the court it is necessary to make immediate provision in relation to the property and affairs of a patient for any of the matters referred to in section 95(1) of the Act—   **6B–268**

COURT OF PROTECTION

    (a) the court may by certificate or direction direct or authorise any named person to do any act or carry out any transaction specified in the certificate or direction; or

    (b) the court may by order appoint an interim receiver for the patient and, subject to any direction given by the court, such appointment shall continue until further order.

(2) An order appointing an interim receiver shall, unless the court otherwise directs, be served upon the patient within such time as the order may specify and the patient may, within such further time as the order may specify, apply under rule 54 for the review of the order by the court or, if the order was made by a judge, apply to have the order set aside.

Remuneration of receiver

6B–269   43.—(1) Where a receiver is appointed for a patient, or where the Court orders directs or authorises any named person ("the named person") to deal with a patients property (or any of it) or affairs, including (but not limited to) by way of an order under rule 8, the court may during the receivership or (as the case may be) the period for which the order, direction or authority remains in force, allow the receiver or (as the case may be) named person remuneration for his services at such moment or at such rate as it considers reasonable and proper, and any renumeration so allowed shall constitute a debt due to the receiver or (as the case may be) named person from the patient and his estate.

(2) No request by a receiver or named person to have the sum payable for this remuneration fixed after the death or recovery of the patient shall be entertained unless the court has during the receivership or, as the case may be, the period for which the order, direction or authorisation remains in force directed that remuneration be allowed and the request is made within six years from the date of the receiver's discharge or, (as the case may be) the date on which the order, direction or authorisation ceases to have effect.

Appointment of receivers with survivorship

6B–270   44. Where in the opinion of the court two or more persons ought to be appointed receivers of the same patient and more than one of them ought to continue to act after the death or discharge of any of the others, the court may when appointing them receivers direct that the receivership shall continue in favour of the surviving or continuing receiver or receivers.

PART VIII

ENTRY AND ENFORCEMENT OF ORDERS

Sealing and filing of orders

6B–271   45. Every order, certificate, direction or authority of the court which is drawn up shall, when entered, be sealed and filed.

Entry of order after notification to a patient

46.—(1) Where—

    (a) an order is made on a first application appointing a receiver for a patient or directing or authorising any person to do any act or carry out any transaction on behalf of a patient without appointing him receiver; or

    (b) an order or direction with respect to a patient's property is made under rule 8, the order or direction shall not be entered until the expiration of ten clear days after the patient has been notified in accordance with rule 24(1) unless such notification is dispensed with.

6B–272

(2) Nothing in paragraph (1) shall prevent the entry of an interim order, certificate or direction under rule 42 for the protection of a patient's property or for the application of a patient's property for his benefit.

Enforcement of orders

47. Every writ of execution or other process for the enforcement of an order of the court shall be issued out of the Central Office of the Supreme Court.

6B–273

PART IX

SUMMONSES AND ORDERS FOR ATTENDANCE OF WITNESSES AND OTHER PERSONS

Summoning of witnesses

48.—(1) In any proceedings under these Rules the court may allow or direct any person to take out a witness summons in Form B requiring the person named in it to attend before the court and give oral evidence or produce any document.

6B–274

(2) An application by a person allowed to take out a witness summons shall be made by filing a statement giving—

    (a) the name and address of the person making the application and of his solicitor, if any;

    (b) the name, address and occupation of the proposed witness;

    (c) particulars of any document which the proposed witness is to be required to produce; and

    (d) the grounds on which the application is made.

(3) A witness summons shall be served on the witness personally a reasonable time before the day fixed for his attendance and he shall be entitled to the same conduct money and payment of expenses and loss of time as if he had been summoned to attend the trial of an action in the High Court.

Powers of court where undue delay, etc

49.—(1) If the court is dissatisfied with the conduct of any proceedings or the carrying out of an order whether by reason of

6B–275

undue delay or otherwise, the court may require the person having the conduct of the proceedings, or any other person appearing to be responsible, to explain the delay or any other cause of dissatisfaction, and may then make such order for expediting the proceedings or otherwise as may be appropriate.

(2) For the purposes of paragraph (1), the court may direct any person to make any application and to conduct any proceedings and carry out any directions which the court may specify; and the court may, if it thinks fit and he consents, appoint the Official Solicitor to act as solicitor for the patient in the proceedings in the place of any solicitor previously acting for him.

Order for examination of patient

6B–276   50. In any proceedings relating to a patient, a judge or Master may make an order for the patient's attendance at such time and place as he may direct for examination by the Master, a Visitor or any medical practitioner.

PART X

AMENDMENT

Amendment of application

6B–277   51.—(1) The court may allow or direct an applicant, at any stage of the proceedings, to amend his application in such manner and on such terms as to costs or otherwise as may be just.

(2) The amendment may be effected by making in writing the necessary alterations to the application, but if the amendments are so numerous or of such a nature or length that written alterations would make it difficult or inconvenient to read, a fresh application amended as authorised or directed may be issued.

Clerical mistakes and slips

6B–278   52. The court may at any time correct any clerical mistakes in an order or direction or any error arising in an order or direction from any accidental slip or omission.

Endorsement of amendment

6B–279   53. Where an application, order or direction has been amended under rule 51 or 52, a note shall be placed on it showing the date on which it was amended and the alteration shall be sealed.

PART XI

REVIEWS AND APPEALS

Review of decision not made on an attended hearing

6B–280   54.—(1) Any person who is aggrieved by a decision of the court that was made without an attended hearing may apply to the court within fourteen days of the date on which the decision was given to have the decision reviewed by the court.

(2) No review shall lie from any decision under rule 83 of these Rules.

(3) On considering an application for review the court may either confirm or revoke the previous decision or make any other order or decision which it thinks fit.

(4) Any person aggrieved by any order or decision of the court made on considering an application for review may, within fourteen days of the date on which the order was made or decision given, apply to the court for an attended hearing.

Appeal from a decision made on an attended hearing

55.—(1) Any person aggrieved by a decision of the court made on **6B-281** an attended hearing may, within fourteen days from the date of entry of the order or (as the case may be) from the date of the decision, appeal to a nominated judge.

(2) The applicant shall within the fourteen days—

    (a) serve a notice of appeal in Form C on—

        (i) every person who appeared, or was represented before, the court when the order or decision was made or given, and

        (ii) any other person whom the court may direct; and

    (b) lodge a copy of the notice at the court office.

(3) The time and place at which the appeal is to be heard shall be fixed by the court and it shall cause notice of the time and place so fixed to be sent to the appellant who shall immediately send notice of it to every person who has been served with notice of the appeal.

(4) No evidence further to that given at the hearing shall be filed in support of or in opposition to the appeal without leave of the court.

PART XII

SECURITY

Receiver to give security

56.—(1) Where an order is made appointing a person other than **6B-282** an officer of the court or the Official Solicitor as receiver for a patient—

    (a) the person appointed shall, unless the court otherwise directs, give such security for the due performance of his duties as the court may approve and shall give it before acting as receiver unless the court allows it to be given subsequently; and

    (b) the order shall not be entered until the person appointed has given to the satisfaction of the court any security required to be given by him before acting.

(2) The court may from time to time vary or dispense with any security required.

Manner of giving security

6B-283 57. Subject to any directions of the court, security may be given in any one of the following ways, or partly in one of those ways and partly in another—

(a) by a bond approved by the court and given by the person giving security and also by—

(i) an insurance company, a group of underwriters or a bank approved by the court; or

(ii) with the approval of the court, two personal sureties; or

(b) in such other manner as the court may approve.

6B-284 Rule 58 was omitted pursuant to The Court of Protection (Amendment) Rule 2005 (S.I. 2005 No. 667).

Discharge of security where new security given

6B-285 59. Where a receiver is authorised or directed to give new security, and—

(a) the new security has been completed; and

(b) he has paid or secured to the satisfaction of the court any balance due from him,

the former security shall, unless the court otherwise directs, be discharged.

Maintenance of security by bond

6B-286 60. Every person who has given security by a bond shall, whenever his accounts are passed, or the court so directs, satisfy the court—

(a) that any premiums payable in respect of the bond have been duly paid;

(b) if the bond was given by personal sureties, that each surety is living and within the jurisdiction and has neither been adjudicated bankrupt nor compounded with his creditors,

and, if the court is not so satisfied, it may require new security to be given or may give such other directions as it thinks fit.

PART XIII

ACCOUNTS

Passing of accounts

6B-287 61.—(1) Every receiver shall—

(a) annually;

(b) on the death or recovery of the patient for whom he has been appointed receiver; and

(c) at any other time that the court may direct

deliver his accounts to the court within such time and in such manner as the court shall direct.

(2) The receiver shall answer such requisitions on his accounts as the court shall raise and in such manner and in such time as the court shall direct.

(3) On the passing of any accounts the court shall make all proper allowances out of the patient's estate, including an allowance in respect of the reasonable and proper costs of the receiver in passing the accounts.

(4) The court may direct that a receiver need not account under this rule or may dispense with the passing of any accounts at any time at which they would otherwise require to be passed.

Application of balance due from receiver

62. The balance found due from a receiver on the passing of his accounts or so much of it as the court may direct, shall—   **6B–288**

    (a) be paid by the receiver into court to the credit of the proceedings and invested in such manner as the court may direct, or

    (b) be invested or otherwise dealt with by the receiver in such manner as the court may direct.

Default by receiver

63. Where a receiver fails to comply with rule 61 or 62 or fails to pay into court or invest or otherwise deal with any money in accordance with any direction of the court, the court may disallow any remuneration which would otherwise be due to the receiver and, if he has made default in paying into court or investing or otherwise dealing with any money, may charge him with interest on it at such rate as the court may reasonably fix, for the period of his default.   **6B–289**

Payment of maintenance and costs

64. Unless otherwise directed, any money ordered to be paid by a receiver for maintenance shall be paid out of income and any costs ordered to be paid by a receiver may, when agreed, assessed by way of detailed assessment or fixed, be paid out of any moneys coming into his hands, after providing for any maintenance and fees payable under these Rules.   **6B–290**

Final accounts

65.—(1) [Revoked]   **6B–291**

(2) On the discharge or death of a receiver, the receiver, or in the case of his death, his personal representatives, shall deliver a final account to the court within such time as the court shall direct.

(3) The court shall pass the final account of a receiver from the date of the receiver's last account or, if no account of his has previously been passed, from the date of his appointment, unless in the opinion of the court the passing of such accounts may properly be dispensed with.

(4) If a balance is found due from a receiver or his estate, he or his personal representatives (as the case may be) shall pay it into court or otherwise deal with it as the court may direct.

(5) If a balance is found due to the receiver or his estate, it shall be paid to him or his personal representatives (as the case may be) by the patient or out of the patient's estate.

(6) On payment of any balance found due from a receiver, or if no balance is found due from him or the passing of his accounts has been dispensed with under paragraph (3), the security of the receiver shall be discharged.

Accounting by other persons

6B–292 66. Rules 61 and 63 to 65 shall also apply, to the extent directed by the court, to any person who is—

  (a) directed to deal with the patient's property or affairs under rule 8;

  (b) directed or otherwise authorised to act under rule 42(1)(a); or

  (c) appointed an interim receiver under rule 42(1)(b),

as they apply to a receiver.

PART XIV

INQUIRIES

Inquiries as to desirability of appointment of receiver, etc

6B–293 67.—(1) Where the court has reason to believe that a receiver should be appointed for a patient or that any other function of the court should be exercised with respect to the property and affairs of a patient, the court may direct—

  (a) a Medical or Legal Visitor, or, if he consents, the Official Solicitor or any other appropriate person to visit the patient and report to the court whether it is desirable in the interests of the patient that an application should be made for that purpose, and, in the case of a report by a Medical or Legal Visitor, whether there is any other matter which the court should consider before exercising its functions in relation to a patient's property and affairs; or

  (b) a Medical Visitor to visit the patient and report to the court on the capacity of the patient to manage and administer his property and affairs.

(2) On receiving any report pursuant to paragraph (1), the court may—

  (a) direct an application to be made pursuant to rule 11; or

  (b) if the report is by a Medical Visitor and the court is satisfied that the patient is incapable, by reason of mental disorder, of managing and administering his property and affairs, make an order appointing a receiver or exercising any other function with respect to the patient's property and affairs.

(3) The court may direct a General Visitor or any other appropriate person to visit the patient and report whether it is desirable for any functions in relation to the patient's property and affairs to be exercised.

(4) On receiving any report pursuant to paragraph (3)—

    (a) the court may direct that an application be made pursuant to rule 11; or

    (b) the court may exercise any function conferred on it in relation to a patient's property and affairs.

Inspection of a patient's property

68. For the purpose of any proceedings relating to the property **6B–294** of a patient—

    (a) the court may inspect the property or direct an officer of the court, the Official Solicitor (if he consents) or any other appropriate person to inspect the property, make any necessary enquiries and report to the court; and

    (b) the court may, if it thinks fit and of its own motion, make such an inspection and inquiries or direct some other appropriate person to do so and report to it.

Inquiries as to prior dealing with the patient's property

69. In any proceedings relating to a patient the court may make **6B–295** or cause to be made such inquiries as it thinks fit as to any dealing with the patient's property before the commencement of the proceedings and as to the patient's mental capacity at the time of such dealing.

Inquiries as to testamentary documents executed by patient

70. The court may make or cause to be made inquiries whether **6B–296** any person has in his possession or under his control or has any knowledge of any testamentary document executed by a patient, and may direct that person to answer the inquiries on oath and to produce any such document which is in his possession or under his control and to deal with it in such manner as the court may direct.

Power to direct other inquiries

71. The court may make or cause to be made any other inquiries **6B–297** which it may consider necessary or expedient for the proper discharge of its functions under the Act or these Rules.

PART XV

CUSTODY AND DISPOSAL OF FUNDS AND OTHER PROPERTY

Statement of property retained or deposited

72. Where under a direction of the court any furniture or effects **6B–298** of a patient are allowed to remain in the possession of, or deposited

with, any person, that person shall, unless the court otherwise directs, sign and file an inventory of the furniture or effects and an undertaking not to part with them during the patient's lifetime except on a direction under seal.

Stock in name of patient or receiver

6B–299   73.—(1) Where any stock—

> (a) is standing in the name of a patient beneficially entitled to it; or
>
> (b) is standing in the name of a receiver in trust for a patient, or as part of his property, and the receiver dies intestate or himself becomes incapable by reason of mental disorder of acting as receiver, or is out of the court's jurisdiction, or it is uncertain whether he is still alive, or he neglects or refuses to transfer the stock or to receive and pay over the dividends as the court directs,

the court may order some proper person to transfer the stock into the name of the receiver or, as the case may be, a new receiver for the patient or into court or otherwise deal with it as the court may direct and also to receive and pay over the dividends as the court directs.

(2) Where an order is made under paragraph (1) or under section 100 of the Act directing stock to be transferred into court, the person required to effect the transfer shall be—

> (a) in the case of stock standing in the stock register kept by the Bank of England or any other bank or by the Crown Agents for Overseas Governments and Administrations, some proper officer of the bank or Crown Agents;
>
> (b) in any other case, some proper officer of the company or other body whose stock is to be transferred,

and that person shall, if so ordered, receive any sum accrued due before the transfer by way of dividend, bonus or periodical payment in respect of the stock and pay it into court to the general account of the patient or to a separate account or otherwise deal with it as the court may direct.

Disposal of property on patient's recovery or death

6B–300   74.—(1) On the recovery of a patient the court may order any money, securities or other property belonging to the patient, or forming part of his estate, or remaining under the control of, or held under the directions of the court, to be transferred to the person who appears to be entitled to it.

(2) On the death of a patient the court may direct any money, securities or other property belonging to the patient or forming part of his estate, remaining under the control of, or held under the direction of the court, to be transferred to the person who appears to be entitled to it.

(3) If no grant of representation has been taken out to the estate of a deceased patient and it appears to the court that the assets of the estate, after deduction of debts and funeral expenses, do not exceed

£5,000 in value, the court may, if it thinks fit, provide for payment of the funeral expenses out of any funds in court standing to the credit of the deceased and order that any such funds, or the balance of them, or any other property of the patient remaining under the control, or held under the directions, of the court be paid, transferred, delivered or released (as appropriate) to the personal representative of the deceased when constituted or to the person who appears to be entitled to apply for a grant of representation to his estate.

(4) The court may at any time, pending notification to it of the grant of representation to the estate of a patient, direct that any money or securities which belonged to the patient when he died and were not already in court shall be transferred to the court.

Copies of documents in court

75.—(1) Any person who has filed an affidavit or other document shall, unless the court otherwise directs, be entitled, on request, to be supplied with a copy of it. **6B–301**

(2) The person having the conduct of any proceedings shall, unless the court otherwise directs, be entitled, on request, to be supplied by the court with a copy of any order, certificate, authority, direction or other document made, given or prepared by the court in the proceedings.

(3) Any other person may, on request, be supplied with a copy of any such document as is mentioned in paragraph (1) or (2), if the court is satisfied that he has good reason for requiring it and that it is not reasonably practicable for him to obtain it form the person entitled to bespeak a copy from the court.

(4) Any copy of any document supplied under paragraphs (1), (2) or (3) shall, if so required, be marked as an office copy.

PART XVII

FEES

Appendix of fees

76.—(1) The Appendix to these Rules, in this Part of these Rules described as "the Appendix", shall apply so as to fix the fees payable pursuant to the following provisions of this Part of these Rules. **6B–302**

(2) Subject to paragraph (3), the fee specified in the Appendix shall be taken in respect of proceedings governed by these Rules.

(3) The fees prescribed by rules 77A, 78 and 78A and contained in the corresponding provisions of the Appendix shall not be payable where an officer of the court has been appointed and is acting as receiver for the patient.

(4) Subject to paragraph (5), the person by whom any fee (other than a fee payable under rule 82) is payable shall, unless the court otherwise directs make the payment out of the income of the patient or, if dead, out of his estate.

(5) Where the payment of a fee is made by the Accountant General then, unless the court directs that payment is to be made out of the income of the fund, the Accountant General shall meet the fee from any cash sums held in court to the account of the patient.

Commencement fee

6B–303   77. A commencement fee shall be payable on any first application for the appointment of a receiver or other originating process in respect of any patient.

77A—(1)Subject to paragraph (2), an appointment fee shall be payable, as set out in paragraph 1A of the Appendix, upon the appointment of a receiver for a patient

(2) Where the proceedings are terminated less than four weeks from the appointment of a receiver, the fee payable under paragraph (1) shall be refunded if it has been paid or, if it has not been paid, it shall cease to be payable.

Administration fee

6B–304   78.—(1) Subject to paragraph (1A), an administration fee shall be payable—

   (a) on the first and every subsequent anniversary of the date of the appointment of a receiver, until the termination of the proceedings;

   (b) on the court making an order or direction authorising an officer of the court or some other suitable person named in the order or direction to deal with a patient's property or affairs under rule 8 and on every subsequent anniversary of that date, until the termination of the proceedings; and

   (c) at such other times either during the proceedings or at their termination as the court may direct, and where the period for which the administration fee is payable is for less than one year, the fee payable shall be the proportion of the full fee as such period bears to one year.

(1A) Where the proceedings are terminated less than six months from the date of the order or direction referred to in paragraph 1(b) authorising an officer of the court or some other suitable person named in the order or direction to deal with a patient's property or affairs under rule 8, the fee payable under that paragraph shall be refunded if it has been paid or, if it has not been paid, it shall cease to be payable.

(2) The court shall annually, or at such other intervals as may be convenient, issue a certificate in respect of each patient stating—

   (a) the amount of the administration fee payable in respect of the patient at the date of the certificate;

   (b) the period in respect of which the administration fee is payable; and

   (c) the name of the person by whom the payment is to be made.

(3) Upon the issue of a certificate under this rule the amount of the fee shall be charged upon the patient's estate, and the payment shall be made within such time (not exceeding one month from the date of the certificate) as the court may allow.

(4) In any case in which it appears to the court that the amount of the fee certified under this rule has been wrongly assessed, the court may direct that the fee is to be adjusted as it appears to it to be convenient.

(5) [Revoked]

Note —Amended by S.I. 2002 No. 833; S.I. 2004 No. 1291; and S.I. 2005 No. 667.

Account fee

78A.—(1) Subject to paragraph (1A), an administration fee shall be payable— **6B–304A**

- (a) on the first and every subsequent anniversary of the date of the appointment of a receiver, until the termination of the proceedings;
- (b) on the court making an order or direction authorising an officer of the court or some other suitable person named in the order or direction to deal with a patient's property or affairs under rule 8 and on every subsequent anniversary of that date, until the termination of the proceedings; and
- (c) at such other times either during the proceedings or at their termination as the court may direct, and

where the period for which the administration fee is payable is for less than one year, the fee payable shall be the proportion of the full fee as such period bears to one year.

(1A) Where the proceedings are terminated less than six months from the date of the order or direction referred to in paragraph 1(b) authorising an officer of the court or some other suitable person named in the order or direction to deal with a patient's property or affairs under rule 8, the fee payable under that paragraph shall be refunded if it has been paid or, if it has not been paid, it shall cease to be payable.

(2) Where the court dispenses with the passing of an account under rule 61(4) or 65(3) the account fee—

- (a) if paid, shall be refunded; or
- (b) if not paid, shall cease to be payable.

Estate account fee

78B. An estate account fee as specified in paragraph 2B of the Appendix shall be payable upon the approval of an estate account by the court, when the patient has— **6B–304B**

- (a) an absolute interest; or
- (b) a life interest

in a residuary estate under the terms of a will, partial intestacy or intestacy.

Transaction fee

6B–305   79.—(1) A transaction fee shall be payable in respect of any order or direction or, as the case may be, any application for an order or direction to be made in exercise of the specific powers conferred by—

(a) paragraphs (d), (e), (h) or (k) of section 96(1) of the Act;

(b) section 100 of the Act;

(c) sections 36(9) and 54 of the Trustee Act 1925; and

(d) section 1(3) of the Variation of Trusts Act 1958.

(2) A transaction fee shall be payable in respect of an application for authorisation of a person under section 20 of the Trusts of Land and Appointment of Trustees Act 1996.

(3) In a special case, the standard fee payable in accordance with the Appendix shall be increased in accordance with the Appendix where there is readily ascertainable pecuniary consideration in the nature of capital arising to or provided by the patient (otherwise than by way of a loan to, or repayment of a loan by, the patient) in excess of £10,000, no account being taken of the possible capitalisation of the value of rents or interests or other income payments.

(3A) In a special case, the value of any readily ascertainable pecuniary consideration in the nature of capital arising to or provided by the donor (otherwise than by a loan to, or repayment of a loan by, the donor), no account being taken of the possible capitalisation of the value of rents or interests or other income payments, shall be set out in the application for the direction.

(3B) Where it appears to the court that any fee under paragraph 3(1)(i) or (ii) of the Appendix has been incorrectly assessed upon the making of the application, the court may direct that the fee is to be adjusted as it appears to it to be convenient.

(4) Where on any application for approval of a transaction mentioned in paragraph (1), or authorisation as mentioned in paragraph (2)—

(a) the fee, or in a special case the standard fee, shall be taken upon the making of the application for the order, direction or authorisation; and

(b) subject to paragraph (4A), in a special case, the additional fee shall be taken upon the court fixing a date for a hearing under rule 9.

(4A) In a special case, where a hearing is cancelled, the additional fee payable in accordance with the Appendix shall be refunded if it has been paid or, if it has not been paid, it shall cease to be payable (but the court may take a fee in accordance with paragraph (4)(b) if it subsequently fixes another date for the hearing).

(5) A transaction fee as specified in paragraph 3(4) of the Appendix shall be payable on application for the appointment of a new receiver.

(6) A transaction fee as specified in paragraph 3(5) of the Appendix shall be payable upon the making of the application for an order or direction to be made in exercise of the specific powers conferred by paragraph (b) or (c) of section 96(1) of the Act, order-

ing or authorising the sale or purchase of any land as defined in the Law of Property Act 1925[1].

(6A) Where the proceedings are terminated before an order or direction under paragraph (6) is entered, the fee payable under that paragraph—

    (a) if paid, shall be refunded; or

    (b) if not paid, shall cease to be payable.

(6B) A transaction fee as specified in paragraph 3(6) of the Appendix shall be payable upon the making of an application for an order or direction to be made in exercise of the powers conferred by paragraph (a) or (b) of section 96(1) of the Act, authorising a person to manage and let a patient's property.

(7) Except where the court otherwise directs, no fee shall be payable under this rule upon the sale or purchase of personal chattels or any investment for the time being authorised by law for the investment of trust property or in securities quoted on any stock exchange in the United Kingdom.

(8) In this rule—

    (a) "special case" means an order made by the court under paragraphs (d) or (h) of section 96(1) of the Act or under section 1(3) of the Variation of Trusts Act 1958; and

    (b) references to an application for an order or direction include (without limitation) an application for an order or direction made at the same time as a first application for the appointment of a receiver or other originating process.

Fee on detailed assessment of costs

80. A fee is payable in respect of the detailed assessment of costs and on an appeal against a decision made in a detailed assessment of costs.

6B–306

Fees where officer of the court appointed receiver

80A.—(1) Subject to paragraph (2), an appointment fee shall be payable, as set out in paragraph 4A of the Appendix, on the appointment of an officer of the court as receiver for a patient.

6B–306A

(2) Where proceedings are terminated within 4 weeks after the appointment, the fee referred to in paragraph (1) shall cease to be payable and any fee paid in accordance with that paragraph shall be refunded.

(3) Where an officer of the court has been appointed receiver for a patient—

    (a) a fee shall be payable, as set out in paragraph 4B of the Appendix, in respect of completing an Inland Revenue tax return on behalf of the patient;

    (b) a receivership administration fee shall be payable, as set out in paragraph 4C of the Appendix—

---

[1] The definition of "land" in section 205(1)(x) was amended by Schedule 4 to the Trusts of Land and Appointment of Trustees Act 1996.

> > (i) on the first and every subsequent anniversary of the date of the officer's appointment as receiver until the termination of the proceedings; and
> >
> > (ii) at such other times either during the proceedings or at their termination as the court may direct, and

where the period for which the receivership administration fee is payable is for less than one year, the fee payable shall be the proportion of the full fee as such period bears to one year; and

> (c) the court shall annually, or at such other intervals as it may direct, issue a certificate in respect of each patient stating—
>
> > (i) the amount of the receivership administration fee payable in respect of the patient at the date of the certificate;
> >
> > (ii) the period in respect of which that fee in payable; and
> >
> > (iii) the name of the person who must make the payment.

(4) Upon the issue of a certificate under paragraph (3)(c) the amount of the fee shall be charged upon the patient's estate, and the payment shall be made within such time (not exceeding one month from the date of the certificate) as the court may allow.

(5) In any case in which it appears to the court that the amount of the fee certified under paragraph (3)(c) has been wrongly assessed, the court may direct that the fee is to be adjusted as it appears to it to be convenient.

Receivership fees

6B–307   81. Note: This rule was omitted in its entirety in the Court of Protection (Amendment) Rules 2002.

Winding up fee

6B–308   82. In cases where a receiver has been appointed, a winding up fee shall be payable—

> (a) on the death of a patient; and
>
> (b) on every subsequent anniversary of that date,

until the court passes the final account of the receiver or directs that the final account may be dispensed with.

Remission and postponement

6B–309   83.—(1) The court may remit or postpone the payment of the whole or part of any fee where in its opinion hardship might otherwise be caused to the patient or his dependants or the circumstances are otherwise exceptional.

(2) The court may remit a payment of the whole or any part of any fee where the cost of calculation and collection would be disproportionate to the amount involved.

PART XVIII

COSTS

Costs generally

84.—(1) All costs incurred in relation to proceedings under these **6B–310**
Rules and not provided by way of remuneration under rule 43,
shall be in the discretion of the court and it may order or direct
them to be paid by the patient or charged on or paid out of his
estate or paid by any other person attending or taking part in the
proceedings.

(2) Every order made or direction given under paragraph (1)
shall be enforceable in the same manner as an order as to costs made
by the High Court.

(3) An order or direction that costs incurred during the lifetime
of a patient be paid out of or charged on his estate may be made
within six years after his death.

Applications under sections 36(9) and 54 of the Trustee Act 1925

85. The court may make any such order with respect of the costs **6B–311**
of an application under section 36(9) or 54 of the Trustee Act 1925
as the High Court could make under section 60 of that Act in relation to any matter referred to in that section.

Civil Procedure rules to apply

86.—(1) Subject to the provisions of these Rules, Parts 43, 44, 47 **6B–312**
and 48 of the Civil Procedure Rules 1998[1] ("the 1998 Rules") shall
apply, with the modifications in paragraph (2) and such other
modifications as may be necessary, to costs incurred in relation to
proceedings under these Rules as they apply to costs incurred in
relation to proceedings in the High Court.

(2) The modifications referred to in paragraph (1) are—
  (a) in rule 43.2(1)(c) of the 1998 Rules, costs officer shall
    include—
      (i) a judge;
      (ii) the Master;
  (b) in rule 43.2(1)(d) of the 1998 Rules, authorised court of-
    ficer shall include an officer of the court;
  (c) rule 44.3(2) of the 1998 Rules (costs follow the event)
    does not apply;
  (d) rules 44.9 to 44.12 of the 1998 Rules (costs on small
    claims and fast tracks and on track allocation or realloca-
    tion) do not apply;
  (e) rules 48.1 to 48.3 (costs payable by or to particular
    persons) and 48.7 to 48.10 (costs relating to solicitors

---

[1] As amended by S.I.s 1999 No. 1008, 2000 No. 221, 2000 No. 941, 2000 No. 1317
and 2000 No. 2092 and 2003 No. 1329.

and other legal representatives) of the 1998 Rules do not apply;

(f) rule 44.7(a) of the 1998 Rules (Summary assessment) does not apply where the patient is paying party;

(g) rules 47.9(4), 47.10 and 47.11 of the 1998 Rules (default costs certificate) do not apply where the patient is the paying party.

(3) Where the court orders costs to be assessed by way of detailed assessment, the detailed assessment proceedings shall take place in the High Court.

Costs of unnecessary employment of solicitor, etc not to be allowed

6B-313   87.—(1) No receiver for a patient, other than the Official Solicitor, shall, unless authorised by the court, be entitled at the expense of the patient's estate to employ a solicitor or other professional person to do any work not usually requiring professional assistance. Where two or more persons having the same interest in relation to the matter to be determined attend any hearing by separate legal representatives, they shall not be allowed more than one set of costs of that hearing unless the court certifies that the circumstances justify separate representation.

Costs of Official Solicitor

6B-314   88. Any costs incurred by the Official Solicitor in relation to proceedings under these Rules or in carrying out any directions given by the court, and not provided for by remuneration under rule 43, shall be paid by such person on or out of such funds as the court may direct.

Ascertainment of costs not relating to the proceedings

6B-315   89. Where in any proceedings relating to a patient a claim is made against his estate in respect of any costs alleged to have been incurred by him or on his behalf or otherwise than in relation to proceedings, the court may refer the claim to a costs judge of the Supreme Court so that the amount due to the claimant may be ascertained by him or under his direction.

PART XIX

APPROVAL OF DEEDS

Approval of deeds

6B-316   90. The seal of the court on any deed or other document shall be evidence that its terms have been approved by the court.

PART XX

TRANSITIONAL PROVISIONS

Transitional provisions

6B-317   91.—(1) Where any matter is pending before the Public Trustee before the coming into force of these Rules, which, by virtue of these Rules relates to a function exercised by the court, the court shall decide the matter in accordance with these Rules.

(2) Where any review or appeal is pending before the court or the Public Trustee before the coming into force of these Rules, it shall be dealt with in accordance with the provisions of these Rules.

PART XXI

REVOCATION

Revocation of previous rules

92. The Court of Protection Rules 1994[1], the Court of Protection (Amendment) Rules 1999[2] and the Court of Protection (Amendment) Rules 2000[3] are hereby revoked.

6B–318

APPENDIX COURT OF PROTECTION FEES

Column 1	Column 2	
Commencement fee (rule 77)		
1. On the first application for the appointment of a receiver or other originating process.	£240.00	
Receivership appointment fee (rule 77A)		
1A. Receivership appointment fee.	£315.00	
Administration fee (rule 78)		
2(1). Annually from the appointment of a receiver until the proceedings are concluded.	£240.00	
2. Annually from the making of a short order or direction under rule 8 until the proceedings are concluded.	£190.00	
Account fee (rule 78A)		
2A. On the twenty-eighth day after the last day of the period in respect of which an account is to be delivered under rule 61(1) or 65(2) .		£100.00
2B. On the approval of an estate account.		£100.00
Transaction fee (rule 79)		
3.—(1) On any order or, as the case may be, on any application for such an order or approval, made by the court in the exercise of powers conferred by:—		
(i) the following paragraphs of section 96(1) of the Act:—	(a) A standard fee of—	
(d) (settlement or gift of property)	(i) £100.00 or	
(h) (carrying out of contract) or	(ii) in a case to which rule 79(3) applies, £360.00; and	
(ii) section 1(3) of the Variation of Trusts Act 1958 (variation of trusts for the benefit of patient)	(b) an additional fee as referred to in rule 79(4)(b) of £500.00.	

---

[1] S.I. 1994 No. 3046
[2] S.I. 1999 No. 2504
[3] S.I. 2000 No. 2025

Column 1	Column 2
provided that no fee under sub-paragraph (i) or (ii) shall be taken if the property is worth less than £100.00	
(iii) section 100 of the Act vesting of stock in curator appointed outside England and Wales)	£60.00
(iv) section 96(1)(k) of the Act (exercise of powers)	£130.00
(v) section 54 of the Trustee Act 1925 (concurrent jurisdiction with High Court over trusts)	£130.00
(vi) section 20 of the Trusts of Land and Appointment of Trustees Act 1996 (authorisation of person to Act as trustee).	£130.00
(2) On an application for an order or direction to be made by the court in exercise of the powers conferred by section 36(9) of Trustee Act 1925 (appointment of trustees).	£130.00
(3) On an application for an order or authority to be made by the court under section 96(1)(e) of the Act (execution of will).	£540.00
(4) On the application for the appointment of a new receiver.	£200.00
(5) On an application for an order or direction under section 96(1)(b) or (c) of the Act ordering or authorising the sale or purchase of any land.	£170.00
(6) On an application for an order or direction under section 96(1)(a) or (b) authorising management and letting of property.	£170.00

Detailed assessment of costs (rule 80)

4.—(1) On the filing of a request for a detailed assessment of costs—	
(i) where the bill of costs does not exceed £3,000 excluding VAT and disbursements	£100.00
(ii) in all other cases.	£200.00
(2) On an appeal against a decision made in a detailed assessment of costs or on an application to set aside a default costs certificate.	£60.00

Fees where officer of the court appointed receiver (rule 80A)

4A. On the appointment of an officer of the court as receiver.	£1,000.00
4B. On the completion of an Inland Revenue tax return on behalf of the patient, where an officer of the court has been appointed receiver.	£520.00
4C. Receivership administration fee, where an officer of the court has been appointed receiver.	£4,500.00

Note – Paragraph 5 and 6 were omitted in their entirety in the Court of Protection (Amendment) Rules 2002 .

Winding up fee (rule 82)

7.—(1) On the death of a patient:	
(i) where an officer of the court has been appointed receiver	£885.00
(ii) otherwise	£290.00

Column 1	Column 2
(2) On each anniversary of the death of the patient until the court passes the final account of the receiver or directs that the final account may be dispensed with.	£150.00

TRANSITIONAL PROVISIONS

Transitional provisions

(1) Where an appointment fee is payable under rule 77A upon the appointment of a receiver but the application for his appointment was received by the court before 1st June 2004, the Court of Protection Rules 2001 ("the 2001 Rules ") shall have effect as if— **6B–318A**

    (a) rule 10(3) of these Rules had not been made; and

    (b) in column 2 of paragraph 1A of the Appendix to the 2001 Rules for "£515.00", there were substituted "£460.00".

(2) Where—

    (a) a transaction fee under rule 79(1) is payable which, by virtue of rule 79(4)(a), is to be taken upon the approval of the transaction; and

    (b) the application for approval was received by the court before 1st June 2004,

    the 2001 Rules shall have effect as if rules 10(6) and 10(7) of these Rules had not been made.

(3) No transaction fee under rule 79(1) shall be payable where—

    (a) an officer of the court is receiver for the patient;

    (b) but for this paragraph that fee would, by virtue of rule 79(4)(a), be taken upon the approval of the transaction; and

    (c) the application for such approval was received by the court before 1st June 2004.

(4) No appointment fee under rule 80A(1) shall be payable where the application for the appointment of a receiver was received by the court before 1st June 2004.

(5) Where a receivership administration fee is payable under rule 80A(3)(b) on an anniversary date falling before 31st May 2005, the fee payable shall be the proportion of the full fee as the period between 1st June 2004 and the anniversary bears to one year.

POWERS OF ATTORNEY

The Enduring Powers of Attorney Act 1985

The Enduring Powers of Attorney Act 1985 came into operation pursuant to Enduring Powers of Attorney Act 1985 (Commencement) Order 1986 (S.I. 1986 No. 125) on March 10, 1986, and enables powers of attorney to be created which will survive any subsequent mental incapacity of the donor and makes provision in connection with such powers. **6B–319**

The Act is set out at paras 6B–340 *et seq*. The rules are the Court of Protection (Enduring Powers of Attorney) Rules 2001. These are made pursuant to s.10(1)(d) of the Enduring Powers of Attorney Act 1985, and ss.106, 107 and 108 of the Mental Health Act 1983 and are referred to in this Section as "EPA Rules" for the purpose of distinguishing them from the Court of Protection Rules 2001, which apply equally to proceedings under the Enduring Powers of Attorney Act 1985 save that in case of inconsistency or ambiguity the EPA Rules prevail. There are also the Enduring Powers of Attorney (Prescribed Form) Regulations 1990 and these are made pursuant to s.2(2) of the Enduring Powers of Attorney Act 1985. They are set out at paras 6B–421 *et seq*.

Forms

See EPA Rules r.3(2) and Sched.1 to the EPA Rules. The following forms may be obtained (free of charge) from the Court of Protection: **6B–320**

COURT OF PROTECTION

Notice of intention to register EP1
Application for registration.............. EP2
General form of application EP3
Application for search EP4

The form of enduring power of attorney itself is not provided by the court but can be purchased from any law stationer. It may of course be prepared by the practitioner himself but in any event it must (subject to the transitional provisions set out in reg. 4) be in the prescribed form (see reg. 2 and the Schedule to the Regulations (paras 6B–423 and 6B–457)).

Fees

6B–321 See EPA Rules, r.26 and Sched.2 to the EPA Rules (paras and 6B–453). Payment of fees may be made as follows:

(i) In cash at Protection Division, Archway Tower, 2 Junction Road, London N19 5SZ; or

(ii) By cheque or postal order made payable to the Public Guardianship Office and crossed and sent by post.

ENDURING POWER OF ATTORNEY

Characteristics

6B–322 These are fully described in s.2 of the Act (see para. 6B–344) but basically such a power must (subject to the transitional provisions set out in reg. 5) be executed in the manner and form prescribed in reg. 3 of the Regulations and the schedule thereto (see paras 6B–424, 6B–456 and 6B–457). The donor at the time of execution must be mentally capable of understanding what the enduring power is and what it is intended to do (*Re K, Re F* [1988] Ch. 310) and have attained 18 years. An enduring power may confer a general authority, a specific authority or a general or specific authority subject to conditions and restrictions.

Action on incapacity of donor

6B–323 If the attorney has reason to believe that the donor is or is becoming mentally incapable he is obliged to make application to the court for the registration of the instrument creating the power. Before making such an application, the attorney is required pursuant to s.4(3) of the Act and the First Schedule thereto to give notice of the application in Form EP1 in Sched.1 to the EPA Rules (see paras 6B–408, 6B–404 and) to those relatives entitled to receive notice and any co-attorney (by first-class post) and to the donor himself (personally). (See EPA Rules, 15 rr.6(1) and 15, para. 6B–428.) An application to dispense with notice must be made before any application for registration is made. (See EPA Rules, r.6(2).)

Mode of application

6B–324 Application for registration in Form EP2 in Sched.1 to the EPA Rules must be lodged with the Public Guardianship Office not later than three days after the date on which notice was given or leave to dispense with notice was given. (See EPA Rules, r.7). The application must be accompanied by the original power of attorney and a remittance of £220 made payable to the PGO in respect of the fee. (See EPA Rules, r.26).

Objections to registration

6B–325 Any objection to registration under s.6(5) of the Act must, pursuant to EPA Rules r.9(1), set out:

(a) The name and address of the objector

(b) The name and address of the donor if he is not the donor

(c) Any relationship of the objector to the donor

(d) The name and address of the attorney and

(e) The grounds for objecting to registration of the enduring power of attorney

Any objection to registration received by the court on or after the date of registration shall be treated by the court as an application to cancel the registration. (See EPA Rules, r.9(2)).

On receipt of any objection the court will fix an appointment to hear the objection and will give such directions as are necessary and in particular whether any further information is required or whether any other persons are to be notified of the hearing.

Upon supervening incapacity and until the power is registered the attorney may not do anything under the authority of the power except:—

   (a) to maintain the donor or prevent loss to his estate; or

   (b) to maintain himself or other persons in so far as section 3(4) permits, or

   (c) as authorised or directed by the court.

Any objection to registration will be considered by the court and will be subject on application by any aggrieved person within fourteen days to review by the court. (See EPA Rules, r.23). An appeal from a decision made by the court on an attended hearing lies to a nominated judge in the usual way. (See EPA Rules, r.24).

Registration

Where there is no objection to registration or any objection has been withdrawn or dismissed the enduring power of attorney will be registered. The PGO will, after retaining a copy, return the original instrument duly sealed and stamped with the date of registration to the applicant attorney. **6B–326**

After registration

The effect of registration is that: **6B–327**

   (a) no revocation of the power by the donor shall be valid except as provided in section 8(3) (para. 6B–364);

   (b) no disclaimer of the power shall be valid until the attorney gives notice of it to the PGO;

   (c) the donor may not alter the scope of the power.

The court may pursuant to s.8(1):

   (a) determine any question as to the meaning or effect of the power;

   (b) give directions with respect to the management or disposal by the attorney of the property and affairs of the patient, the rendering of accounts by the attorney and his remuneration or expenses;

   (c) require the attorney to furnish information or produce documents;

   (d) give any consent or authorisation to act which the attorney would have to obtain from a mentally capable donor;

   (e) authorise the attorney to benefit himself or other persons;

   (f) relieve the attorney from any liability which he may incur on account of a breach of duty.

Leave to bring an application

Any person other than a person who has been served with a notice of intention to register an enduring power of attorney shall apply to the court for leave to make application for relief specified in the Act. (See EPA Rules, r.21). **6B–328**

Any other application (other than an application for registration)

The court is primarily concerned with applications for registration and consequently it is not intended to deal here, with the scope of an attorney's authority under and enduring power which is governed by s.3 of the EPA Act and of course any restrictions or conditions imposed by the instrument itself. In the ordinary course of events, following registration of an enduring power of attorney, the court does not expect to be further involved in any dealings with the donor's affairs. Apart from the registration process, the court's powers under the EPA Act are mainly directed to the proper supervision of the attorney and to giving necessary supplementary consents and authorisations which are not inconsistent with the restrictions imposed by the donor (*Re R.* [1990] 2 W.L.R. 1219, where the applicant was not the attorney). **6B–329**

Any person other than a person who has been served with notice of intention to register an enduring power of attorney must apply to the court, as mentioned in para. 6B–328, for leave to make any application for relief specified in the EPA Act. Such application may, pursuant to EPA Rules, r.8(1), be made by letter unless the court directs that the application should be formal, in which case it should be made on Form EP3.

It has been found in practice that situations arise which call for three particular applications.

First, it may be necessary for the attorney in the course of his stewardship to realise an asset which is specifically bequeathed or devised by the donor's will. If the donor was testamentary capacity, he is able to make a new will to cater for the changed circumstances. Otherwise, the devise or bequest will be adeemed. However, s.101 of the Mental Health Act 1983 provides that where any property of a person has been disposed of under Pt VII of that Act, and under his will or his intestacy or by any gift perfected or nomination taking effect on his death any other person would have taken an interest in the property but for the disposal, that person shall take the same interest in any property belonging to the estate of the deceased which represents the property disposed of. It is therefore open to the attorney or any other person entitled to make an application for the appointment of a Receiver and for an order for the sale of the asset in question under the provisions of Pt VII of the Act mentioned above to preserve the devise. Such an application would have to be made in form CP. 1 supported with the evidence usually required in connection with a receivership application (that is to say, evidence of the donor's incapacity to manage and administer his property and affairs by reason of mental disorder (Form CP. 3) and a certificate of family and property (Form (CP. 5). It may be possible for the court to deal with the application by issuing a Short Procedure Order under r.8 of the Court of Protection Rules 2001 and thereafter to direct (pursuant to s.2(11) of the EPA Act 1985) that the EPA shall not be revoked by the exercise by the court of its powers under the Mental Health Act 1983.

Secondly, the attorney may wish to re-organise the donor's affairs with a view to mitigating the incidence of inheritance tax. If such a scheme involves an element of gift which goes beyond the gifts permitted by s.3(5) of the EPA Act and the instrument itself, an application to the court for the necessary relief will most probably be necessary.

Thirdly, it may be considered that for any one of a variety of reasons the will of a donor who lacks testamentary capacity is no longer appropriate to his circumstances and does not reflect his current wishes. The procedure for making an application for a statutory will is dealt with below.

Cancellation of registration

6B–330 The court shall cancel the registration of any power:
- (a) on confirming the revocation of the power or receiving notice of disclaimer;
- (b) on giving a direction revoking the power or exercising any of its powers under the Mental Health Act 1983;
- (c) on being satisfied that the donor is and is likely to remain mentally capable;
- (d) on being satisfied that the power has expired or has otherwise been revoked;
- (e) on being satisfied that the power was not valid when registration was effected;
- (f) on being satisfied that fraud or undue pressure was used;
- (g) on being satisfied the attorney is unsuitable.

On the death of a donor or attorney the original instrument, any office copies thereof and evidence of death should be forwarded to the court.

Searches of the register

6B–331 Any person may upon payment of a fee of £20 request the court in Form EP4 to search the register and to say whether an enduring power has been registered. (See EPA Rules, r.13).

The Master of the Court of Protection issued the following Practice Direction on February 28, 1989.

Practice Direction: Enduring Powers of Attorney Act 1985

6B–332 The Enduring Powers of Attorney (Prescribed Form) Regulations 1987 (see paras 6B–421 et seq.)

Inclusion of Marginal Notes

The Enduring Powers of Attorney (Prescribed Form) Regulations 1987 came into force on November 1, 1987 and any enduring power of attorney executed on or after July 1, 1988 has to be in the form prescribed by those regulations in order to be a valid enduring power of attorney.

Regulation 2(1) of the regulations provides that a valid form must include the requisite explanatory information and all the relevant marginal notes. Regulation 2(2) refers to omissions or deletions of one of the various pairs of alternatives given in the form and allows omission or deletion of the corresponding marginal note.

Section 2(6) of the Enduring Powers of Attorney Act 1985 provides that an instrument differing in an immaterial respect in form or mode of expression from the prescribed form shall be treated as sufficient in point of form and expression.

Consequently, marginal notes may only be omitted if they are irrelevant (regulation 2(1)), correspond to the omitted or deleted one of a pair of alternatives (regulation 2(2)) or constitute an immaterial difference from the prescribed form (section 2(6)).

On several occasions recently, solicitors have submitted for registration enduring powers of attorney bearing no marginal notes at all, on the basis that the instrument had in each case been drawn up by the solicitors after the various choices had been explained to the donor and he had selected the options he wished to include and had decided the precise terms of the power.

There is no provision in the regulations for differences in form where donors prepare the form themselves and where solicitors prepare the form. Solicitors should therefore include in the forms to be completed by their client all marginal notes unless they come within one of the exceptions already mentioned.

Practice Direction (Court of Protection) (Power of Attorney: Form) [1989] 1 W.L.R. 311; [1989] 2 All E.R. 64.

Termination of enduring power of attorney

An enduring power of attorney may be revoked by the donor; by the court; or automatically. The donor may revoke the power in the same way as he is able to do at common law provided an application for registration has not been made. Revocation by the donor after registration of the power is not valid unless and until it is confirmed by the court. **6B–333**

It is open to the court to revoke the power on exercising of any of its powers under Pt VII of the Mental Health Act 1983 (EPA Act 1985, s.2(11)) and in practice it usually so directs. The court also directs revocation of the power if it finds that fraud or undue pressure was used to induce the donor to create the power or concludes that the attorney is not suitable.

An enduring power of attorney is automatically revoked by the bankruptcy of the attorney whatever the circumstances of the bankruptcy. The power may also be terminated by the attorney exercising his right to disclaim the power. However, he is required to give notice of disclaimer to the donor or, if he has reason to believe that the donor is or is becoming mentally incapable or if the power has been registered, to the PGO.

An enduring power of attorney will be terminated by the death of the donor or the death, mental incapacity or, as already mentioned, the bankruptcy of the attorney.

Protection of attorney and third parties

The main function of the court is to receive and consider applications for registration and following registration does not expect to be further involved in relation to the attorney's dealings with the donor's affairs unless anything untoward is reported or an application such as mentioned above is made. It is not thought necessary to deal here with the protection of the attorney and third parties for which provision is made in s.9 of the EPA Act. However, it is stressed that subss. (1) (2) (3) and (4) of s.9 which afford protection after the enduring power has been registered are wider than those given by the Powers of Attorney Act 1971. Further, subs. (5) enables the attorney and third parties to disregard any attempted revocation by the donor until it has been confirmed by the court. **6B–334**

Applications by attorneys under registered enduring powers of attorney for orders for execution of statutory wills and codicils

Generally —Guidance as to the practice and procedure of the court in connection with applications for statutory wills and codicils is given at paras 6B–137 to 6B–146. The following notes give additional information for use in cases where the application is made by an attorney under a registered enduring power of attorney, and should be read in conjunction with the notes at paras 6B–137 to 6B–146. **6B–335**

Although applications may be accepted from attorneys if the enduring power is registered, it will be appreciated that the court will have little knowledge in those cases of the donor's family or property and will probably have received no medical evidence at all concerning the donor's mental condition.

6B–336   *Medical evidence* —The jurisdiction to order the execution of a statutory will or codicil is conferred by s.96(1)(e) of the Mental Health Act 1983 and is only exercisable in respect of someone who is a "patient" (defined in the Act as a person who is incapable, by reason of mental disorder, of managing and administering his property and affairs). The court will need to see medical evidence of such incapacity (s.94(2) of the Act) and the best way in which that evidence can be supplied is on form CP. 3, the usual form of medical evidence in receivership matters, which gives a great deal of helpful information as well as giving a categorical statement of incapacity to satisfy the requirements of the Act. An enduring power of attorney is able to be registered at a stage where the donor is becoming, but has not yet necessarily become, mentally incapable and consequently the fact that the enduring power of attorney has been registered is not in itself sufficient evidence of mental incapacity.

Furthermore, medical evidence is also always required specifically stating that the donor is not of testamentary capacity—see paragraph 1(a) at para. 6B–142.

6B–337   *Parties* —Applications for statutory wills are governed by the Mental Health Act 1983 and not by the Enduring Powers of Attorney Act 1985. There is guidance at para. 6B–142 as to those who may apply and those who should be joined.

Additionally, in cases arising out of enduring powers of attorney, if the power appoints joint attorneys to act jointly, both or all must concur in making the application. If joint attorneys have been appointed to act jointly and severally, and not all are making the application, those who are not applicants should be given notice of the hearing of the application, together with such other persons as the court may direct. The Official Solicitor may be directed to represent the donor.

6B–338   *Evidence* —It is stressed that the information mentioned in notes 1(a) to (h) at para. 6B–143 will be required, with full details, since the court will have no other particulars of the donor's family or property.

Enduring Powers of Attorney Act 1985

6B–339   ### (1985 c.29)

ARRANGEMENT OF SECTIONS

ENDURING POWERS OF ATTORNEY

Enduring Powers of Attorney

Enduring power of attorney to survive mental incapacity of donor

1.—(1) Where an individual creates a power of attorney which is **6B–340** an enduring power within the meaning of this Act then—

(a) the power shall not be revoked by any subsequent mental incapacity of his; but

(b) upon such incapacity supervening the donee of the power may not do anything under the authority of the power except as provided by subsection (2) below or as directed or authorised by the court under section 5 unless or, as the case may be, until the instrument creating the power is registered by the court under section 6; and

(c) section 5 of the Powers of Attorney Act 1971(protection of donee and third persons) so far as applicable shall apply if and so long as paragraph (b) above operates to suspend the donee's authority to act under the power as if the power had been revoked by the donor's mental incapacity.

(2) Notwithstanding subsection (1)(b) above, where the attorney has made an application for registration of the instrument then, until the application has been initially determined, the attorney may take action under the power—

(a) to maintain the donor or prevent loss to his estate; or

(b) to maintain himself or other persons in so far as section 3(4) permits him to do so.

(3) Where the attorney purports to act as provided by subsection (2) above, then, in favour of a person who deals with him without knowledge that the attorney is acting otherwise than in accordance with paragraph (a) or (b) of that subsection, the transaction between them shall be as valid as if the attorney were acting in accordance with paragraph (a) or (b).

Definitions

"enduring power", "the court" (s.13(1)). **6B–341**

Subsection (1)

This subsection provides that an enduring power is not revoked by the mental **6B–342** incapacity of the donor and in that event, until the instrument is registered with the Court of Protection, makes it clear that the authority of the attorney is suspended except to the limited extent that the Act otherwise provides. Although suspension is removed on registration, it does not restore full authority retrospectively.

The effect of s.1(1)(c) is to confer upon attorneys and third parties the protection given by the Powers of Attorney Act 1971 when the donor of an enduring power has become mentally incapable.

Subsection (2)

6B–343 This subsection enables the attorney to act with limited authority pending registration, provided he has applied for registration. The attorney is able, pursuant to s.5, to apply to the court for any further powers he requires pending registration.

Characteristics of an enduring power

6B–344 **2.**—(1) Subject to subsections (7) to (9) below and section 11, a power of attorney is an enduring power within the meaning of this Act if the instrument which creates the power—

    (a) is in the prescribed form; and

    (b) was executed in the prescribed manner by the donor and the attorney; and

    (c) incorporated at the time of execution by the donor the prescribed explanatory information.

(2) The Lord Chancellor shall make regulations as to the form and execution of instruments creating enduring powers and the regulations shall contain such provisions as appear to him to be appropriate for securing—

    (a) that no document is used to create an enduring power which does not incorporate such information explaining the general effect of creating or accepting the power as may be prescribed; and

    (b) that such instruments include statements to the following effect—

        (i) by the donor, that he intends the power to continue in spite of any supervening mental incapacity of his;

        (ii) by the donor, that he read or had read to him the information explaining the effect of creating the power;

        (iii) by the attorney, that he understands the duty of registration imposed by this Act.

(3) Regulations under subsection (2) above—

    (a) may include different provision for cases where more than one attorney is to be appointed by the instrument than for cases where only one attorney is to be appointed; and

    (b) may, if they amend or revoke any regulations previously made under that subsection, include saving and transitional provisions.

(4) Regulations under subsection (2) above shall be made by statutory instrument which shall be subject to annulment in pursuance of a resolution of either House of Parliament.

(5) An instrument in the prescribed form purporting to have been executed in the prescribed manner shall be taken, in the absence of evidence to the contrary, to be a document which incorporated at the time of execution by the donor the prescribed explanatory information.

(6) Where an instrument differs in an immaterial respect in form or mode of expression from the prescribed form the instrument shall be treated as sufficient in point of form and expression.

(7) A power of attorney cannot be an enduring power unless, when he executes the instrument creating it, the attorney is—

    (a) an individual who has attained eighteen years and is not bankrupt; or

    (b) a trust corporation.

(8) [...]

(9) A power of attorney which gives the attorney a right to appoint a substitute or successor cannot be an enduring power.

(10) An enduring power shall be revoked by the bankruptcy of the attorney whatever the circumstances of the bankruptcy.

(11) An enduring power shall be revoked on the exercise by the court of any of its powers under Part VII of the Mental Health Act 1983 if, but only if, the court so directs.

(12) No disclaimer of an enduring power, whether by deed or otherwise, shall be valid unless and until the attorney gives notice of it to the donor or, where section 4(6) or 7(1) applies, to the court.

(13) In this section "prescribed" means prescribed under subsection (2) above.

Definitions

"enduring power", "trust corporation", "the court", and "notice" (s.13(1)). **6B–345** "prescribed" (s.2(13)).

General note

This section deals with the formal requirements and characteristics of an enduring **6B–346** power. A power which is not an enduring power within the meaning of the Act is at best an ordinary power of attorney which will be revoked by the mental incapacity of the donor. Joint attorneys must be appointed to act jointly or jointly and severally and there is no restriction on the appointment of a number of attorneys by separate instruments.

Subsection (8)

Subsection (8) was repealed by the Trustee Delegation Act 1999, Sched.1, para. 1. **6B–347**

Scope of authority, etc. of attorney under enduring power

3.—(1) An enduring power may confer general authority (as **6B–348** defined in subsection (2) below) on the attorney to act on the donor's behalf in relation to all or a specified part of the property and affairs of the donor or may confer on him authority to do specified things on the donor's behalf and the authority may, in either case, be conferred subject to conditions and restrictions.

(2) Where an instrument is expressed to confer general authority on the attorney it operates to confer, subject to the restriction imposed by subsection (5) below and to any conditions or restrictions contained in the instrument, authority to do on behalf of the donor anything which the donor can lawfully do by an attorney.

(3) [...]

(4) Subject to any conditions or restrictions contained in the instrument, an attorney under an enduring power, whether general or limited, may (without obtaining any consent) act under the power so as to benefit himself or other persons than the donor to the following extent but no further, that is to say—

> (a) he may so act in relation to himself or in relation to any other person if the donor might be expected to provide for his or that person's needs respectively; and
>
> (b) he may do whatever the donor might be expected to do to meet those needs.

(5) Without prejudice to subsection (4) above but subject to any conditions or restrictions contained in the instrument, an attorney under an enduring power, whether general or limited, may (without obtaining any consent) dispose of the property, of the donor by way of gift to the following extent but no further, that is to say—

> (a) he may make gifts of a seasonal nature or at a time, or on an anniversary, of a birth or marriage, to persons (including himself) who are related to or connected with the donor, and
>
> (b) he may make gifts to any charity to whom the donor made or might be expected to make gifts,

provided that the value of each such gift is not unreasonable having regard to all the circumstances and in particular the size of the donor's estate.

Definition

6B–349   "enduring power" (s.13(1)).

Subsection (3)

6B–350   Subsection (3) was repealed by the Trustee Delegation Act 1999, Sched.1, para. 1.

ACTION ON ACTUAL OR IMPENDING INCAPACITY OF DONOR

Duties of attorney in event of actual or impending incapacity of donor

6B–351   4.—(1) If the attorney under an enduring power has reason to believe that the donor is or is becoming mentally incapable subsections (2) to (6) below shall apply.

(2) The attorney shall, as soon as practicable, make an application to the court for the registration of the instrument creating the power.

(3) Before making an application for registration the attorney shall comply with the provisions as to notice set out in Schedule 1.

(4) An application for registration shall be made in the prescribed form and shall contain such statements as may be prescribed.

(5) The attorney may, before making an application for the registration of the instrument, refer to the court for its determination any question as to the validity of the power and he shall comply with any direction given to him by the court on that determination.

(6) No disclaimer of the power shall be valid unless and until the attorney gives notice of it to the court.

(7) Any person who, in an application for registration, makes a statement which he knows to be false in a material particular shall be liable—

> (a) on conviction on indictment, to imprisonment for a term not exceeding two years or to a fine, or both; and

(b) on summary conviction, to imprisonment for a term not exceeding six months or to a fine not exceeding the statutory maximum, or both.

(8) In this section and Schedule 1 "prescribed" means prescribed by rules of the court.

Definitions

"enduring power", "mentally incapable", "the court", "notice", "statutory maximum", "rules of the court" (s.13(1)). "prescribed" (s.4(8)). **6B–352**

General note

Registration is the cornerstone of the Act and besides safeguarding against abuse of the power it protects attorneys and third parties as provided in s.9 in cases where an instrument did not create a valid power of attorney. **6B–353**

Subsection (2)

An attorney must give notice of his application for registration to the donor, any co-attorney and certain relatives as provided in Sched.1. See r.14 of the EPA Rules as to the mode of service. If the attorney does not make application for registration when he has reason to believe that the donor is or is becoming mentally incapable he is at risk that the donor has in fact so become and his authority has been suspended. **6B–354**

Functions of court prior to registration

5. Where the court has reason to believe that the donor of an enduring power may be, or may be becoming, mentally incapable and the court is of the opinion that it is necessary, before the instrument creating the power is registered, to exercise any power with respect to the power of attorney or the attorney appointed to act under it which would become exercisable under section 8(2) on its registration, the court may exercise that power under this section and may do so whether the attorney has or has not made an application to the court for the registration of the instrument. **6B–355**

Definitions

"the court", "enduring power", "mentally incapable" (s.13(1)). **6B–356**

General note

This section enables the court, prior to registration, to take any necessary steps to protect the interests of a donor who may be or who may be becoming mentally incapable. **6B–357**

Functions of court on application for registration

6.—(1) In any case where— **6B–358**

    (a) an application for registration is made in accordance with section 4(3) and (4), and

    (b) neither subsection (2) nor subsection (4) below applies,

the court shall register the instrument to which the application relates.

(2) Where it appears to the court that there is in force under Part VII of the Mental Health Act 1983 an order appointing a receiver for the donor but the power has not also been revoked then, unless it directs otherwise, the court shall not exercise or further exercise its functions under this section but shall refuse the application for registration.

(3) Where it appears from an application for registration that no-

tice of it has not been given under Schedule 1 to some person entitled to receive it (other than a person in respect of whom the attorney has been dispensed or is otherwise exempt from the requirement to give notice) the court shall direct that the application be treated for the purposes of this Act as having been made in accordance with section 4(3), if the court is satisfied that, as regards each such person—

      (a) it was undesirable or impracticable for the attorney to give him notice; or

      (b) no useful purpose is likely to be served by giving him notice.

(4) If, in the case of an application for registration—

      (a) a valid notice of objection to the registration is received by the court before the expiry of the period of five weeks beginning with the date or, as the case may be, the latest date on which the attorney gave notice to any person under Schedule 1, or

      (b) it appears from the application that there is no one to whom notice has been given under paragraph 1 of that Schedule, or

      (c) the court has reason to believe that appropriate inquiries might bring to light evidence on which the court could be satisfied that one of the grounds of objection set out in subsection (5) below was established,

the court shall neither register the instrument nor refuse the application until it has made or caused to be made such inquiries (if any) as it thinks appropriate in the circumstances of the case.

(5) For the purposes of this Act a notice of objection to the registration of an instrument is valid if the objection is made on one or more of the following grounds, namely—

      (a) that the power purported to have been created by the instrument was not valid as an enduring power of attorney;

      (b) that the power created by the instrument no longer subsists;

      (c) that the application is premature because the donor is not yet becoming mentally incapable;

      (d) that fraud or undue pressure was used to induce the donor to create the power;

      (e) that, having regard to all the circumstances and in particular the attorney's relationship to or connection with the donor, the attorney is unsuitable to be the donor's attorney.

(6) If, in a case where subsection (4) above applies, any of the grounds of objection in subsection (5) above is established to the satisfaction of the court, the court shall refuse the application but if, in such a case, it is not so satisfied, the court shall register the instrument to which the application relates.

(7) Where the court refuses an application for registration on ground (d) or (e) in subsection (5) above it shall by order revoke the power created by the instrument.

(8) Where the court refuses an application for registration on any ground other than that specified in subsection (5)(c) above the instrument shall be delivered up to be cancelled, unless the court otherwise directs.

Definitions

"the court", "notice", "enduring power", "mentally incapable" (s.13(1)).　　6B–359

Subsection (3)

This subsection enables the court to proceed with an application where for the　6B–360 reasons mentioned an attorney has not given the required notices. The court may also dispense with the giving of notices as provided in Sched.1, paras 3(2) and 4(2), the former subsection applying also to any co-attorney.

LEGAL POSITION AFTER REGISTRATION

Effect and proof of registration, etc.

7.—(1) The effect of the registration of an instrument under sec-　6B–361 tion 6 is that—

(a) no revocation of the power by the donor shall be valid unless and until the court confirms the revocation under section 8(3);

(b) no disclaimer of the power shall be valid unless and until the attorney gives notice of it to the court;

(c) the donor may not extend or restrict the scope of the authority conferred by the instrument and no instruction or consent given by him after registration shall, in the case of a consent, confer any right and, in the case of an instruction, impose or confer any obligation or right on or create any liability of the attorney or other persons having notice of the instruction or consent.

(2) Subsection (1) above applies for so long as the instrument is registered under section 6 whether or not the donor is for the time being mentally incapable.

(3) A document purporting to be an office copy of an instrument registered under this Act or under the Enduring Powers of Attorney (Northern Ireland) Order 1987 shall, in any part of the United Kingdom, be evidence of the contents of the instrument and of the fact that it has been so registered.

(4) Subsection (3) above is without prejudice to section 3 of the Powers of Attorney Act 1971 (proof by certified copies) and to any other method of proof authorised by law.

Note—Amended by the Enduring Powers of Attorney (Northern Ireland　6B–362 Consequential Amendment) Order 1987 (S.I. 1987 No. 1628).

Definitions

"the court", "notice", "mentally incapable" (s.13(1)).　　6B–363

Functions of court with respect to registered power

8.—(1) Where an instrument has been registered under section 6,　6B–364 the court shall have the following functions with respect to the power and the donor of and the attorney appointed to act under the power.

(2) The court may—

 (a) determine any question as to the meaning or effect of the instrument;

 (b) give directions with respect to—

  (i) the management or disposal by the attorney of the property and affairs of the donor;

  (ii) the rendering of accounts by the attorney and the production of the records kept by him for the purpose;

  (iii) the remuneration or expenses of the attorney, whether or not in default of or in accordance with any provision made by the instrument, including directions for the repayment of excessive or the payment of additional remuneration;

 (c) require the attorney to furnish information or produce documents or things in his possession as attorney;

 (d) give any consent or authorisation to act which the attorney would have to obtain from a mentally capable donor;

 (e) authorise the attorney to act so as to benefit himself or other persons than the donor otherwise than in accordance with section 3(4) and (5) (but subject to any conditions or restrictions contained in the instrument);

 (f) relieve the attorney wholly or partly from any liability which he has or may have incurred on account of a breach of his duties as attorney.

(3) On application made for the purpose by or on behalf of the donor, the court shall confirm the revocation of the power if satisfied that the donor has done whatever is necessary in law to effect an express revocation of the power and was mentally capable of revoking a power of attorney when he did so (whether or not he is so when the court considers the application).

(4) The court shall cancel the registration of an instrument registered under section 6 in any of the following circumstances, that is to say—

 (a) on confirming the revocation of the power under subsection (3) above or receiving notice of disclaimer under section 7(1)(b);

 (b) on giving a direction revoking the power on exercising any of its powers under Part VII of the Mental Health Act 1983;

 (c) on being satisfied that the donor is and is likely to remain mentally capable;

 (d) on being satisfied that the power has expired or has been revoked by the death or bankruptcy of the donor or the death, mental incapacity or bankruptcy of the attorney or, if the attorney is a body corporate, its winding up or dissolution;

 (e) on being satisfied that the power was not a valid and subsisting enduring power when registration was effected;

(f) on being satisfied that fraud or undue pressure was used to induce the donor to create the power; or

(g) on being satisfied that, having regard to all the circumstances and in particular the attorney's relationship to or connection with the donor, the attorney is unsuitable to be the donor's attorney.

(5) Where the court cancels the registration of an instrument on being satisfied of the matters specified in paragraph (f) or (g) of subsection (4) above it shall by order revoke the power created by the instrument.

(6) On the cancellation of the registration of an instrument under subsection (4) above except paragraph (c) the instrument shall be delivered up to be cancelled, unless the court otherwise directs.

Definitions

"the court", "mentally capable", "notice", "mental incapacity", "enduring power" (s.13(1)). **6B–365**

General note

The court has the same powers under s.5 where prior to registration it has reason to believe that the donor may be or may be becoming mentally incapable. **6B–366**

Subsection (6)

If the court cancels registration because it is satisfied the donor is mentally capable and is likely to remain so, the enduring power will revert to being an unregistered enduring power. **6B–367**

PROTECTION OF ATTORNEY AND THIRD PARTIES

Protection of attorney and third persons where power invalid or revoked

9.—(1) Subsections (2) and (3) below apply where an instrument which did not create a valid power of attorney has been registered under section 6 (whether or not the registration has been cancelled at the time of the act or transaction in question). **6B–368**

(2) An attorney who acts in pursuance of the power shall not incur any liability (either to the donor or to any other person) by reason of the non-existence of the power unless at the time of acting he knows—

(a) that the instrument did not create a valid enduring power; or

(b) that an event has occurred which, if the instrument had created a valid enduring power, would have had the effect of revoking the power; or

(c) that, if the instrument had created a valid enduring power, the power would have expired before that time.

(3) Any transaction between the attorney and another person shall, in favour of that person, be as valid as if the power had then been in existence, unless at the time of the transaction that person has knowledge of any of the matters mentioned in subsection (2) above.

(4) Where the interest of a purchaser depends on whether a trans-

COURT OF PROTECTION

action between the attorney and another person was valid by virtue of subsection (3) above, it shall be conclusively presumed in favour of the purchaser that the transaction was valid if—

    (a) the transaction between that person and the attorney was completed within twelve months of the date on which the instrument was registered; or

    (b) that person makes a statutory declaration, before or within three months after the completion of the purchase, that he had no reason at the time of the transaction to doubt that the attorney had authority to dispose of the property which was the subject of the transaction.

(5) For the purposes of section 5 of the Powers of Attorney Act 1971 (protection of attorney and third persons where action is taken under the power of attorney in ignorance of its having been revoked) in its application to an enduring power the revocation of which by the donor is by virtue of section 7(1)(a) above invalid unless and until confirmed by the court under section 8(3) above, knowledge of the confirmation of the revocation is, but knowledge of the unconfirmed revocation is not, knowledge of the revocation of the power.

(6) Schedule 2 shall have effect to confer protection in cases where the instrument failed to create a valid enduring power and the power has been revoked by the donor's mental incapacity.

(7) In this section "purchaser" and "purchase" have the meanings specified in section 205(1) of the Law of Property Act 1925.

Definitions

6B–369   "enduring power" (s.13(1)). "purchaser", "purchase" (s.9(7)).

Subsections (1) (2) (3) and (4)

6B–370   The protection afforded by these subsections to the attorney and third parties, which are wider than those given by the Powers of Attorney Act 1971, apply after the enduring power has been registered.

Subsection (5)

6B–371   This subsection enables the attorney and third parties to disregard any attempted revocation by the donor until it has been confirmed by the court.

SUPPLEMENTARY

Application of Mental Health Act provisions relating to the court

6B–372   **10.**—(1) The provisions of Part VII of the Mental Health Act 1983(relating to the Court of Protection) specified below shall apply to persons within any proceedings under this Act in accordance with the following paragraphs of this subsection and subsection (2) below, that is to say—

    (a) section 103 (functions of Visitors) shall apply to persons within this Act as it applies to persons mentioned in that section;

    (b) section 104 (powers of judge) shall apply to proceedings under this Act with respect to persons within this Act as it applies to the proceedings mentioned in subsection (1) of that section;

(c) section 105(1) (appeals to nominated judge) shall apply to any decision of the Master of the Court of Protection or any nominated officer in proceedings under this Act as it applies to any decision to which that subsection applies and an appeal shall lie to the Court of Appeal from any decision of a nominated judge whether given in the exercise of his original jurisdiction or on the hearing of an appeal under section 105(1) as extended by this paragraph;

(d) section 106 except subsection (4) (rules of procedure) shall apply to proceedings under this Act and persons within this Act as it applies to the proceedings and persons mentioned in that section.

(2) Any functions conferred or imposed by the provisions of the said Part VII applied by subsection (1) above shall be exercisable also for the purposes of this Act and the persons who are "within this Act" are the donors of and attorneys under enduring powers of attorney whether or not they would be patients for the purposes of the said Part VII.

(3) In this section "nominated judge" and "nominated officer" have the same meanings as in Part VII of the Mental Health Act 1983.

Definitions

"nominated judge", "nominated officer" (s.10(3)). "enduring power" (s.13(1)).　　**6B–373**

General note

This section extends the powers given by the Mental Health Act 1983 to donors **6B–374** whether or not they are patients within the meaning of that Act and whether or not the instrument creating the enduring power has been registered.

Application to joint and joint and several attorneys

11.—(1) An instrument which appoints more than one person to **6B–375** be an attorney cannot create an enduring power unless the attorneys are appointed to act jointly or jointly and severally.

(2) This Act, in its application to joint attorneys, applies to them collectively as it applies to a single attorney but subject to the modifications specified in Part I of Schedule 3.

(3) This Act, in its application to joint and several attorneys, applies with the modifications specified in subsections (4) to (7) below and in Part II of Schedule 3.

(4) A failure, as respects any one attorney, to comply with the requirements for the creation of enduring powers, shall prevent the instrument from creating such a power in his case without however affecting its efficacy for that purpose as respects the other or others or its efficacy in his case for the purpose of creating a power of attorney which is not an enduring power.

(5) Where one or more but not both or all the attorneys makes or joins in making an application for registration of the instrument then—

(a) an attorney who is not an applicant as well as one who is may act pending the initial determination of the application as provided in section 1(2) (or under section 5);

(b) notice of the application shall also be given under Schedule 1 to the other attorney or attorneys; and

(c) objection may validly be taken to the registration on a ground relating to an attorney or to the power of an attorney who is not an applicant as well as to one or the power of one who is an applicant.

(6) The court shall not refuse under section 6(6) to register an instrument because a ground of objection to an attorney or power is established if an enduring power subsists as respects some attorney who is not affected thereby but shall give effect to it by the prescribed qualification of the registration.

(7) The court shall not cancel the registration of an instrument under section 8(4) for any of the causes vitiating registration specified in that subsection if an enduring power subsists as respects some attorney who is not affected thereby but shall give effect to it by the prescribed qualification of the registration.

(8) In this section—

"prescribed" means prescribed by rules of the court; and

"the requirements for the creation of enduring powers" means the provisions of section 2 other than subsections (10) to (12) and of regulations under subsection (2) of that section.

Definitions

6B–376   "enduring powers", "notice", "the court", "rules of the court" (s.13(1)). "prescribed", "the requirements for the creation of enduring powers" (s.11(8)).

Subsection (1)

6B–377   This subsection invalidates an EPA which purports to appoint a succession of attorneys or substitutes and if it does it will at best be an ordinary power of attorney which will be revoked on the donor becoming mentally incapacitated.

Power of Lord Chancellor to modify pre-registration requirements in certain cases

6B–378   12.—(1) The Lord Chancellor may by order exempt attorneys of such descriptions as he thinks fit from the requirements of this Act to give notice to relatives prior to registration.

(2) Subject to subsection (3) below, where an order is made under this section with respect to attorneys of a specified description then, during the currency of the order, this Act shall have effect in relation to any attorney of that description with the omission of so much of section 4(3) and Schedule 1 as requires notice of an application for registration to be given to relatives.

(3) Notwithstanding that an attorney under a joint or joint and several power is of a description specified in a current order under this section, subsection (2) above shall not apply in relation to him if any of the other attorneys under the power is not of a description specified in that or another current order under this section.

(4) The power to make an order under this section shall be exercisable by statutory instrument which shall be subject to annulment in pursuance of a resolution of either House of Parliament.

General note

6B–379   No order under this section has yet been made (February 2000).

Interpretation

6B–380

13.—(1) In this Act—

"the court", in relation to any functions under this Act, means the authority having jurisdiction under Part VII of the Mental Health Act 1983;

"enduring power" is to be construed in accordance with section 2;

"mentally incapable" or "mental incapacity", except where it refers to revocation at common law, means, in relation to any person, that he is incapable by reason of mental disorder of managing and administering his property and affairs and "mentally incapable" and "mental capacity" shall be construed accordingly;

"mental disorder" has the same meaning as it has in the Mental Health Act 1983;

"notice" means notice in writing;

"rules of the court" means rules under Part VII of the Mental Health Act 1983 as applied by section 10;

"trust corporation" means the Public Trustee or a corporation either appointed by the High Court or a county court (according to their respective jurisdictions) in any particular case to be a trustee or entitled by rules under section 4(3) of the Public Trustee Act 1906 to act as custodian trustee.

(2) Any question arising under or for the purposes of this Act as to what the donor of the power might at any time be expected to do shall be determined by assuming that he had full mental capacity at the time but otherwise by reference to the circumstances existing at that time.

Note — Section 13 repealed in part by the Statute Law (Repeals) Act 1993.

6B–381

Short title, commencement and extent

6B–382

14.—(1) This Act may be cited as the Enduring Powers of Attorney Act 1985.

(2) This Act shall come into force on such day as the Lord Chancellor appoints by order made by statutory instrument.

(3) This Act extends to England and Wales only except that section 7(3) and section 10(1)(b) so far as it applies section 104(4) of the Mental Health Act 1983 extend also to Scotland and Northern Ireland.

Note —The Act came into force on March 10, 1986 (S.I. 1986 No. 125).

6B–383

SCHEDULES

SECTION 4(3)

SCHEDULE 1

PART I

DUTY TO GIVE NOTICE TO RELATIVES AND DONOR

Duty to give notice to relatives

6B–384

1. Subject to paragraph 3 below, before making an application for registration the attorney shall give notice of his intention to do so to all those persons (if any) who are entitled to receive notice by virtue of paragraph 2 below.

2.—(1) Subject to the limitations contained in sub-paragraphs (2) to (4) below, persons of the following classes (referred to in this Act as "relatives") are entitled to receive notice under paragraph 1 above—

(a) the donor's husband or wife;

(b) the donor's children;

(c) the donor's parents;

(d) the donor's brothers and sisters, whether of the whole or half blood;

(e) the widow or widower of a child of the donor;

(f) the donor's grandchildren;

(g) the children of the donor's brothers and sisters of the whole blood;

(h) the children of the donor's brothers and sisters of the half blood;

(i) the donor's uncles and aunts of the whole blood; and

(j) the children of the donor's uncles and aunts of the whole blood.

(2) A person is not entitled to receive notice under paragraph 1 above if—

(a) his name or address is not known to the attorney and cannot be reasonably ascertained by him; or

(b) the attorney has reason to believe that he has not attained eighteen years or is mentally incapable.

(3) Except where sub-paragraph (4) below applies, no more than three persons are entitled to receive notice under paragraph 1 above and, in determining the persons who are so entitled, persons falling within class (a) of sub-paragraph (1) above are to be preferred to persons falling within class (b) of that sub-paragraph, persons falling within class (b) are to be preferred to persons falling within class (c) of that sub-paragraph; and so on.

(4) Notwithstanding the limit of three specified in sub-paragraph (3) above, where—

(a) there is more than one person falling within any of classes (a) to (j) of sub-paragraph (1) above, and

(b) at least one of those persons would be entitled to receive notice under paragraph 1 above,

then, subject to sub-paragraph (2) above, all the persons falling within that class are entitled to receive notice under paragraph 1 above.

3.—(1) An attorney shall not be required to give notice under paragraph 1 above to himself or to any other attorney under the power who is joining in making the application, notwithstanding that he or, as the case may be, the other attorney is entitled to receive notice by virtue of paragraph 2 above.

(2) In the case of any person who is entitled to receive notice under paragraph 1 above, the attorney, before applying for registration, may make an application to the court to be dispensed from the requirement to give him notice; and the court shall grant the application if it is satisfied—

(a) that it would be undesirable or impracticable for the attorney to give him notice; or

(b) that no useful purpose is likely to be served by giving him notice.

Duty to give notice to donor

6B–385   4.—(1) Subject to sub-paragraph (2) below, before making an application for registration the attorney shall give notice of his intention to do so to the donor.

(2) Paragraph 3(2) above shall apply in relation to the donor as it applies in relation to a person who is entitled to receive notice under paragraph 1 above.

PART II

CONTENTS OF NOTICES

6B–386   5. A notice to relatives under this Schedule—

(a) shall be in the prescribed form;

(b) shall state that the attorney proposes to make an application to the Court of Protection for the registration of the instrument creating the enduring power in question;

    (c) shall inform the person to whom it is given that he may object to the proposed registration by notice in writing to the Court of Protection before the expiry of the period of four weeks beginning with the day on which the notice under this Schedule was given to him;

    (d) shall specify, as the grounds on which an objection to registration may be made, the grounds set out in section 6(5).

6. A notice to the donor under this Schedule—

    (a) shall be in the prescribed form;

    (b) shall contain the statement mentioned in paragraph 5(b) above; and

    (c) shall inform the donor that, whilst the instrument remains registered, any revocation of the power by him will be ineffective unless and until the revocation is confirmed by the Court of Protection.

PART III

DUTY TO GIVE NOTICE TO OTHER ATTORNEYS

7.—(1) Subject to sub-paragraph (2) below, before making an application for registration an attorney under a joint and several power shall give notice of his intention to do so to any other attorney under the power who is not joining in making the application; and paragraphs 3(2) and 5 above shall apply in relation to attorneys entitled to receive notice by virtue of this paragraph as they apply in relation to persons entitled to receive notice by virtue of paragraph 2 above. **6B–387**

(2) An attorney is not entitled to receive notice by virtue of this paragraph if—

    (a) his address is not known to the applying attorney and cannot reasonably be ascertained by him; or

    (b) the applying attorney has reason to believe that he has not attained eighteen years or is mentally incapable.

PART IV

SUPPLEMENTARY

8.—(1) For the purposes of this Schedule an illegitimate child shall be treated as if he were the legitimate child of his mother and father. **6B–388**

(2) Notwithstanding anything in section 7 of the Interpretation Act 1978 (construction of references to service by post), for the purposes of this Schedule a notice given by post shall be regarded as given on the date on which it was posted.

SECTION 9(6)   # SCHEDULE 2

FURTHER PROTECTION OF ATTORNEY AND THIRD PERSONS

1. Where— **6B–389**

    (a) an instrument framed in a form prescribed under section 2(2) creates a power which is not a valid enduring power; and

    (b) the power is revoked by the mental incapacity of the donor, paragraphs 2 and 3 below shall apply, whether or not the instrument has been registered.

2. An attorney who acts in pursuance of the power shall not, by reason of the revocation, incur any liability (either to the donor or to any other person) unless at the time of acting he knows—

    (a) that the instrument did not create a valid enduring power; and

    (b) that the donor has become mentally incapable.

3. Any transaction between the attorney and another person shall, in favour of that person, be as valid as if the power had then been in existence, unless at the time of the transaction that person knows—

    (a) that the instrument did not create a valid enduring power; and

    (b) that the donor has become mentally incapable.

4. Section 9(4) shall apply for the purpose of determining whether a transaction was valid by virtue of paragraph 3 above as it applies for the purpose of determining whether a transaction was valid by virtue of section 9(3).

SCHEDULE 3

JOINT AND JOINT AND SEVERAL ATTORNEYS

PART I

JOINT ATTORNEYS

6B–390   1. In section 2(7), the reference to the time when the attorney executes the instrument shall be read as a reference to the time when the second or last attorney executes the instrument.

2. In section 2(9) and (10), the reference to the attorney shall be read as a reference to any attorney under the power.

3. In section 5, reference to the attorney shall be read as including references to any attorney under the power.

4. Section 6 shall have effect as if the ground of objection to the registration of the instrument specified in subsection (5)(e) applied to any attorney under the power.

5. In section 8(2), references to the attorney shall be read as including references to any attorney under the power.

6. In section 8(4), references to the attorney shall be read as including references to any attorney under the power.

PART II

JOINT AND SEVERAL ATTORNEYS

6B–391   7. In section 2(10), the reference to the bankruptcy of the attorney shall be construed as a reference to the bankruptcy of the last remaining attorney under the power; and the bankruptcy of any other attorney under the power shall cause that person to cease to be attorney, whatever the circumstances of the bankruptcy.

8. The restriction upon disclaimer imposed by section 4(6) applies only to those attorneys who have reason to believe that the donor is or is becoming mentally incapable.

Court of Protection (Enduring Powers of Attorney) Rules 2001

6B–392   (S.I. 2001 No. 825)

ARRANGEMENT OF RULES

PART I

PRELIMINARY

PART I

PRELIMINARY

Title and commencement

1. These Rules may be cited as the Court of Protection (Enduring **6B–392.1** Powers of Attorney) Rules 2001 and shall come into force on 1st April 2001.

Application

2. Subject to the provisions of these Rules, the Court of Protec- **6B–393** tion Rules 2001 shall apply to the proceedings under the Enduring Powers of Attorney Act 1985.

Interpretation

3.—(1) In these Rules, unless the context otherwise requires— **6B–394** expressions used in the Supreme Court Act 1981 shall have the same meanings as they have in that Act;

"the Act" means the Enduring Powers of Attorney Act 1985;

"the 1983 Act" means the Mental Health Act 1983;

"the 2001 Rules" means the Court of Protection Rules 2001;

"applicant" includes an objector;

"application" includes an objection;

"attended hearing" means a hearing where one or more of the parties to the proceedings have been invited to attend the court for the determination of the application;

"the court" means the Court of Protection;

"direction" means a direction or authority given under the seal of the court;

"enduring power of attorney" shall be construed in accordance with section 2 of the Act;

"entered" means entered in the register of enduring powers of attorney kept by the court;

"filed" means filed in the court office;

"hearing" means an attended or unattended hearing;

"judge" means the Lord Chancellor or a judge nominated under section 93(1) of the 1983 Act;

"Master" means the Master of the Court of Protection;

"nominated officer" means an officer of the court nominated under section 93(4) of the 1983 Act;

"order" means an order of the court under seal and includes a certificate, direction or authority of the court under seal;

"relative" means one of the persons referred to as relatives and entitled to receive notice under the provisions of paragraphs 1 and 2 of Schedule 1 to the Act;

"seal" means an official seal of the court and "sealed" shall be construed accordingly.

(2) In these Rules—

    (a) any reference to a numbered rule or to a numbered Schedule is a reference to the rule of, or the Schedule to, these Rules so numbered in these Rules;

    (b) any reference in a rule to a numbered paragraph is a reference to the paragraph so numbered in the rule in which the reference occurs; and

    (c) a form referred to by a letter alone means—

        (i) the form so designated in Schedule 1 ("the core form"); or

        (ii) a form published by the court which differs in immaterial respects, in wording or layout (or both), from the core form; or

        (iii) a form to the same effect as the core form or as a form satisfying sub-paragraph (ii) above with such variations as circumstances may require and the court may approve; or

        (iv) a Welsh translation of the core form or of a form satisfying sub-paragraph (ii) or (iii) above.

Exercise of court's functions

6B–395   4. Where any discretion, power or function is (in whatever words) expressed by these Rules to be exercisable by the court then, subject to the provisions of the Act, that discretion, power or other function may be exercised—

    (a) by a judge;

    (b) by the Master;

    (c) to the extent to which he is authorised to exercise it under section 94 of the 1983 Act, by a nominated officer.

Note—Amended by the Court of Protection (Enduring Powers of Attorney) (Amendment No. 2) Rules 2002 (S.I. 2002 No. 1944), r.2.   **6B–395.1**

Computation of time

5.—(1) Where a period of time fixed by the Act or by these Rules or by a judgment, order or direction for doing any act expires on a day on which the court office is closed and for that reason cannot be done on that day, the act shall be done in time if done on the next day on which the office is open.   **6B–396**

(2) Where the act is required to be done within a specified period after or from a specified date, the period begins immediately after that date.

(3) Where any period of time, fixed as mentioned in paragraph (1), is three days or less, any day on which the court office is closed shall not be included in the computation of that period.

PART II

APPLICATIONS

Notice of intention to register

6.—(1) Notice of the attorney's intention to apply to register an enduring power of attorney shall be given in Form EP1 to the donor and to those relatives entitled to receive such notice and to any co-attorney, all such notices to be served within fourteen days of each other.   **6B–397**

(2) An application to dispense with such notice shall be made in Form EP3 before any application for registration is made and shall be accompanied by the original power of attorney.

Time limits

7. An application to register an enduring power of attorney shall be made in Form EP2 and shall be lodged with the court office not later than 10 days after the date on which, in relation to the donor and every relative entitled to receive notice and every co-attorney, either—   **6B–398**

    (a) notice has been given; or

    (b) leave has been given to dispense with notice

Note—Amended by the Court of Protection (Enduring Powers of Attorney) (Amendment) Rules 2002 (S.I. 2002 No. 832), r.3.   **6B–398.1**

Form of application

8.—(1) Subject to the provisions of rules 6 and 7 and to the fol-   **6B–399** lowing provisions of this rule, an application may be made by letter unless the court directs that it should be formal, in which case it shall be made in Form EP3.

(2) Any application made by letter to the court, other than an objection to registration, shall include the name and address of the applicant, the name of the donor if he is not the applicant, the form of relief or determination required and the grounds for the application.

Objections to registration

6B–400   9.—(1) Any objection to registration shall be made in writing and shall set out—

    (a) the name and address of the objector;

    (b) the name and address of the donor if he is not the objector;

    (c) any relationship of the objector to the donor;

    (d) the name and address of the attorney; and

    (e) the grounds for objecting to registration of the enduring power of attorney.

(2) Any objection to registration received by the court on or after the date of registration shall be treated by the court as an application to cancel the registration.

Exercise of the court's powers and functions under the provisions of the 1985 Act

6B–401   10.—(1) This rule shall apply to applications made to the court—

    (a) for relief or for determination of any question under sections 1(1)(b), 4(5), 5, 6(3), 6(4), 8(2), 8(3), 8(4) or 11(5)(c) of the Act; or

    (b) under paragraphs 2(1), 3(2), 4(2) or 7(1) of Schedule 1 to the Act,

which are not made simultaneously with an application for registration of an enduring power of attorney.

(2) On receipt of an application, the court may decide either that no hearing shall be held, in which case the application shall be dealt with by written representations, or it may fix an appointment for directions or for the application to be heard.

(3) The court may at any time, on application or of its own motion, give such direction as it thinks proper with regard to any matter arising in the course of an application.

(4) Notification of an appointment for directions or a hearing shall be given by the applicant to the attorney (if he is not the applicant), to any objector and to any other person directed by the court to be notified.

(5) The applicant, the attorney (if he is not the applicant) and any person given notice of the hearing may attend or be represented.

(6) If it appears to the court that any order for relief should be made or any question determined, the court may make such order or give such directions as it thinks fit, of its own motion.

(7) Where an attorney seeks to disclaim an enduring power of attorney pursuant to sections 4(6) or 7(1)(b) of the Act, the disclaimer shall not take effect earlier than the day on which the notice of disclaimer is received at the court.

Consolidation of proceedings

11. The court may consolidate any application for registration or relief or any objection to registration if it considers that the proceedings may be dealt with more conveniently together.

6B–402

Registration of an enduring power of attorney

12.—(1) Where there is no objection to the registration of an enduring power of attorney or any objection has been withdrawn or dismissed, the enduring power of attorney shall be registered and sealed by the court.

6B–403

(2) The court shall retain a copy of the registered enduring power of attorney and shall return the original instrument to the applicant attorney.

(3) Any alterations which appear on the face of the instrument when an application for registration is made shall be sealed.

(4) Any qualification to registration imposed by reason of section 11(6) or (7) of the Act shall be noted on the register and on the instrument and sealed.

(5) The date of registration shall be the date stamped by the court on the instrument at the time of its registration.

Searches of the register and copies of registered enduring powers of attorney

13.—(1) On payment of the appropriate fee, any person shall be entitled to request the court in Form EP4 to search the register and to state whether an enduring power of attorney has been registered and the court shall so state in Form EP5.

6B–404

(2) The court may supply a person with an office copy of a registered enduring power of attorney if it is satisfied that he has a good reason for requesting a copy and that it is not reasonably practicable to obtain a copy from the attorney.

(3) For the purposes of this rule, an office copy is a photocopy or a facsimile copy of an enduring power of attorney, marked as an office copy and sealed.

(4) An office copy of an enduring power of attorney need not contain the explanatory information endorsed on the original power.

PART III

HEARINGS

Notice of hearing

14.—(1) Except where these rules otherwise provide or the court

6B–405

otherwise directs, the following minimum periods of notice of a hearing shall be given by the applicant—

    (a) ten clear days in the case of—

        (i) an application to dispense with notice to the donor;

        (ii) an application to dispose of the donor's property prior to registration; and

        (iii) an objection to registration of an enduring power of attorney; and

    (b) seven clear days in the case of any other application.

(2) Unless the court otherwise directs, notice of a hearing shall be given to the attorney, the donor, every relative, any co-attorney and to such other persons who appear to the court to be interested as the court may specify.

(3) The court may extend or abridge the time limited by these Rules or any order or direction for doing any act upon such terms and notwithstanding in the case of an extension that the time so limited has expired.

(4) For the purpose of this rule, notice of a hearing is given if the applicant sends a copy of the application, endorsed by the court with the hearing date, to the person concerned.

Mode of giving documents

6B–406   15.—(1) Any document required by these Rules to be given to the donor shall be given to him personally.

(2) Except where these Rules otherwise provide, any document required by these Rules to be given to any person shall be given to him by—

    (a) sending it to him by first class post or through a document exchange; or

    (b) transmitting it to him by fax or other electronic means.

Giving documents to a solicitor

6B–407   16. Where a solicitor acting for the person to be given any document, other than the donor, endorses on that document, or on a copy of it, a statement that he accepts the document on behalf of that person, the document shall be deemed to have been duly given to that person and to have been received on the date that the endorsement was made.

Alternative method of giving documents

6B–408   17. Where it appears to the court that it is impracticable for any document to be given to a person in accordance with rule 15(2), the court may give such directions for the purpose of bringing the document to the notice of the person to whom it is addressed as it thinks fit.

Use of evidence in subsequent proceedings

6B–409   18. Except where the court otherwise directs, evidence which has been used in any proceedings relating to a donor may be used at any subsequent stage of those proceedings or in any other proceedings before the court.

Copies of documents in court

19.—(1) Any person who has filed an affidavit or other document shall, unless the court otherwise directs, be entitled on request to be supplied with a copy of it.

(2) An attorney or his solicitor may have a search made for and may inspect and request a copy of any document filed in proceedings relating to the enduring power of attorney under which the attorney has been appointed.

(3) Subject to paragraphs (1) and (2), no documents filed in the court shall be open to inspection without the leave of the court and no copy of any such document or an extract from it shall be taken by or issued to any person without such leave.

6B–410

Summoning of witnesses

20. Any witness summons required to be issued in any proceedings under these Rules shall be in Form EP6.

6B–411

Leave to bring an application

21. Any person other than a person who has been served with a notice of intention to register an enduring power of attorney shall apply to the court for leave to make an application for relief specified in the Act.

6B–412

Notification of decision

22. All persons to whom notice is to be given under rule 10(4) shall be notified by the applicant of the court's decision and shall also be sent by the applicant a copy of any order made or direction given.

6B–413

PART IV

REVIEWS AND APPEALS

Review of decision not made on an attended hearing

23.—(1) Any person who is aggrieved by a decision of the court that was made without an attended hearing may apply to the court within fourteen days of the date on which the decision was given to have the decision reviewed by the court.

(1A) No application for review shall lie from any decision under rule 26A.

(2) On considering an application for review, the court may either confirm or revoke the previous decision or give any other order or decision which it thinks fit.

(3) Any person aggrieved by any order or decision of the court made on considering an application for review may within fourteen

6B–414

days of the date on which the order was made or decision given apply to the court for an attended hearing.

Appeal from decision made on an attended hearing

6B–415   24.—(1) Any person aggrieved by an order or decision of the court made on an attended hearing, may, within fourteen days from the date of entry of the order or as the case may be, from the date of the decision, appeal to a nominated judge.

(2) The appellant shall within fourteen days—

    (a) serve notice of appeal in form EP7 on every person who is directly affected by the decision and on any other person whom the court may direct; and

    (b) lodge a copy of the notice at the court.

(3) The court shall fix a time and place at which the appeal is to be heard and shall cause notice of the time and place to be sent to the appellant, who shall immediately send notice of it to every person who has been served with notice of the appeal.

(4) No evidence further to that given at the hearing shall be filed in support of, or in opposition to, the appeal without leave of the court.

PART V

CANCELLATION OF REGISTRATION

Cancellation of a registered power of attorney

6B–416   25.—(1) Where the court cancels a power of attorney in accordance with section 8(4) of the Act it shall, subject to paragraph (2), send a notice to the attorney requiring him to deliver the original instrument to the court.

(2) Where the court is satisfied that the power has been revoked by the death or bankruptcy of the attorney the reference to the attorney in paragraph (1) shall be read as a reference to the attorney's personal representative or (as the case may be) Trustee in bankrupcy and where the court is satisfied that the power has been revoked by the winding up or dissolution of the attorney, being a body corporate, that reference shall be read as a reference to the attorney's liquidator or (as the case may be) receiver

(3) Where the instrument creating an enduring power of attorney has been lost or destroyed, the attorney shall give to the court written details of that date of such loss or destruction and of the circumstances in which the loss or destruction occurred.

(4) Where registration has been cancelled for any reason other than that set out in section 8(4)(c) of the Act, the court shall mark the power of attorney as cancelled.

(4A) Where registration has been cancelled for the reason set out in section 8(4)(c) of the Act, the court shall mark on the power of attorney an endorsement that registration has been cancelled.

(5) Any notices issued by the court under this rule may contain a

warning that failure to comply with the notice may lead to punishment for contempt of court.

PART VA

ACCOUNTS

25A.—(1)Where the court directs, under section 8(2)(b)(ii) of the Act, that the attorney renders accounts, that direction shall include directions as to—   **6B–417**

> (a) whether the accounts are to be delivered annually or, if not, the intervals at which the accounts are to be delivered and
>
> (b) the time and manner in which accounts are to be delivered

(2) The attorney shall answer such requisitions on his accounts as the court shall raise and in such manner in such time as the court shall direct.

PART VI

FEES

Schedule of fees

26.—(1) Fees shall be payable in accordance with the provisions of Schedule 2.   **6B–418**

(2) The fees specified in column 2 of Schedule 2 shall apply in respect of the corresponding event referred to in column 1.

(3) The person liable to pay the fee for the registration of a power of attorney shall, unless the court otherwise directs, make the payment out of the assets of the donor.

(4) In a special case, the standard fee payable in accordance with item 4 of Schedule 2 shall be increased in accordance with that item where there is a readily ascertainable pecuniary consideration in the nature of capital arising to or provided by the donor (otherwise than by a loan to, or repayment of a loan by, the donor) in excess of £10,000, no account being taken of the possible capitalisation of the value of rents or interests or other income payments.

(4A) In a special case, the value of any readily ascertainable pecuniary consideration in the nature of capital arising to or provided by the donor (otherwise than by a loan to, or repayment of a loan by, the donor), no account being taken of the possible capitalisation of the value of rents or interests or other income payments, shall be set out in the application for the direction.

(4B) Where it appears to the court that any fee under item 4 of Schedule 2 has been incorrectly assessed upon the making of the application, the court may direct that the fee is to be adjusted as it appears to it to be convenient.

(5)

> (a) The fee payable in accordance with Item 4 of Schedule

2, or in a special case the standard fee, shall be taken upon the making of the application for the direction approving the transaction; and

(b) subject to paragraph (5A), in a special case, the additional fee shall be taken upon the court fixing a date for a hearing under rule 10.

(5A) In a special case, where a hearing is cancelled, the additional fee referred to in paragraph (5)(b) shall be refunded if it has been paid or, if it has not been paid, it shall cease to be payable (but the court may take a fee in accordance with paragraph (5)(b) if it subsequently fixes another date for the hearing).

(6) In this rule "special case" means a direction made by the court—

(a) authorising the settlement of any property of the donor, or the gift of any property of the donor; or

(b) approving any arrangement in accordance with section 1 of the Variation of Trust Act 1958.

Remission and postponement

6B–419   26A.—(1) The court may remit or postpone the payment of the whole or any part of any fee where in its opinion hardship might otherwise be caused to the donor, or such other person liable to pay the fee, or his dependants, or the circumstances are otherwise exceptional.

(2) The court may remit a payment of the whole or any part of any fee where the cost of calculation would be disproportionate to the amount involved.

PART VII

TRANSITIONAL PROVISIONS

6B–420   27.—(1)Where any matter is pending before the Public Trustee before the coming into force of these Rules which by virtue of these Rules relates to a function to be exercised by the court, the court shall deal with the matter in accordance with these Rules.

(2) Where any review or appeal is pending before the court or the Public Trustee before the coming into force of these Rules, it shall be dealt with in accordance with the provisions of these Rules.

PART VIII

REVOCATION

Revocation of previous Rules

6B–421   28. The Court of Protection (Enduring Powers of Attorney) Rules 1994 and the Court of Protection (Enduring Powers of Attorney) (Amendment) Rules 1999 are hereby revoked.

RULE 26

SCHEDULE 2
FEES

6B–422

Column 1	Column 2
Item	Fee
Registration Fee	
1. On lodging an application for registration of an enduring power of attorney.	£120.00
Search Fee	
2. On application for a search of the register.	£20.00
Fee on passing of accounts	
3. On the passing of an attorney's accounts by the court	£100.00
Fees for certain directions	
4. On making of an application for a direction under section 8(2)(d) or (e) of the Act, or for a direction under section 5 of the Act which, if the power were registered, would be a direction under section 8(2)(d) or (e).	£100.00, or, in a special case— (a) a standard fee of— (i) £100.00 or (ii) in a case to which rule 26(4) applies, £360.00; and (b) an additional fee of £500.00.provided that no fee under this item shall be taken if the property is worth less than £100.00.

Enduring Powers of Attorney (Prescribed Form) Regulations 1990

(S.I. 1990 No. 1376)

Introductory note —The Enduring Powers of Attorney (Prescribed Form) Regulations 1987 (S.I. 1987 No. 1612), which revoked the 1986 Regulations (S.I. 1986 No. 126), have themselves been revoked by the Enduring Powers of Attorney (Prescribed Form) Regulations 1990 (S.I. 1990 No. 1376). An EPA made in the form which was prescribed at the time may be registered at any time thereafter; but if it is made on a form which was out-of-date when the EPA was made, it will be invalid. There are transitional periods allowed by the 1987 and the 1990 Regulations and consequently there are some overlaps between the relevant periods.

6B–423

The 1986 prescribed form could be used for EPAs created between March 10, 1986 and June 30, 1988, the 1987 prescribed form for those created between November 1, 1987 and July 30, 1991 and the 1990 prescribed form for those from July 31, 1990 onwards. (See 1986 Regulations, regs 1 and 3; 1987 Regulations, regs 1, 2 and 4 and 1990 Regulations, regs 1, 2 and 5).

The form prescribed by the 1990 Regulations was necessary because of the coming into force (also on July 31, 1990) of s.1 of the Law of Property (Miscellaneous Provisions) Act 1989. This is the section which abolishes the need for deeds to be sealed by people who execute them, although signing is still required. The facility for signing by direction is extended to enduring powers of attorney by the new regulations, so that a donor, if incapable of signing or making a mark on the document, is able to instruct someone else to sign the EPA on his behalf. If an EPA is being signed by direction, two witnesses to the signing will be needed.

Citation and commencement

1. These Regulations may be cited as the Enduring Powers of At-

6B–424

COURT OF PROTECTION

torney (Prescribed Form) Regulations 1990 and shall come into force on 31st July 1990.

Prescribed form

6B–425 **2.**—(1) Subject to paragraphs (2) and (3) of this regulation and to regulation 4, an enduring power of attorney must be in the form set out in the Schedule to these Regulations and must include all the explanatory information headed "About using this form" in Part A of the Schedule and all the relevant marginal notes to Parts B and C. It may also include such additions (including paragraph numbers) or restrictions as the donor may decide.

(2) In completing the form of enduring power of attorney—
    (a) there shall be excluded (either by omission or deletion)—
        (i) where the donor appoints only one attorney, everything between the square brackets on the first page of Part B; and
        (ii) one and only one of any pair of alternatives;
    (b) there may also be so excluded—
        (i) the words on the second page of Part B "subject to the following restrictions and conditions", if those words do not apply;
        (ii) the attestation details for a second witness in Parts B and C if a second witness is not required; and
        (iii) any marginal notes which correspond with any words excluded under the provisions of this paragraph and the two notes numbered 1 and 2 which appear immediately under the heading to Part C.

(3) The form of execution by the donor or by an attorney may be adapted to provide—
    (a) for a case where the donor or an attorney signs by means of a mark; and
    (b) for the case (dealt with in regulation 3) where the enduring power of authority is executed at the direction of the donor or of an attorney; and the form of execution by an attorney may be adapted to provide for execution by a trust corporation.

(4) Subject to paragraphs (1) (2) and (3) of this regulation and to regulation 4, an enduring power of attorney which seeks to exclude any provision contained in these Regulations is not a valid enduring power of attorney.

Execution

6B–426 **3.**—(1) An enduring power of attorney in the form set out in the Schedule to these Regulations shall be executed by both the donor and the attorney, although not necessarily at the same time, in the presence of a witness, but not necessarily the same witness, who shall sign the form and give his full name and address.

(2) The donor and an attorney shall not witness the signature of each other nor one attorney the signature of another.

(3) Where an enduring power of attorney is executed at the direction of the donor—

    (a) it must be signed in the presence of two witnesses who shall each sign the form and give their full names and addresses; and

    (b) a statement that the enduring power of attorney has been executed at the direction of the donor must be inserted in Part B;

    (c) it must not be signed by either an attorney or any of the witnesses to the signature of either the donor or an attorney.

(4) Where an enduring power of attorney is executed at the direction of an attorney—

    (a) paragraph 3(a) above applies; and

    (b) a statement that the enduring power of attorney has been executed at the direction of the attorney must be inserted in Part C;

    (c) it must not be signed by either the donor, an attorney or any of the witnesses to the signature of either the donor or an attorney.

4. Where more than one attorney is appointed and they are to act **6B–427** jointly and severally, then at least one of the attorneys so appointed must execute the instrument for it to take effect as an enduring power of attorney, and only those attorneys who have executed the instrument shall have the functions of an attorney under an enduring power of attorney in the event of the donor's mental incapacity or on the registration of the power, whichever first occurs.

Revocation

5. The Enduring Powers of Attorney (Prescribed Form) Regula- **6B–428** tions 1987 are hereby revoked, except that—

    (a) a power executed in the form prescribed by those Regulations and executed by the donor before 31st July 1991 shall be capable (whether or not seals are affixed to it) of being a valid enduring power of attorney;

    (b) regulation 3(3) shall apply to a power executed by the donor before 31st July 1991 under the provisions of those Regulations and the form of enduring power of attorney prescribed by those Regulations may be modified accordingly.

SCHEDULE

6B–429

SCHEDULE   Regulation 2

ENDURING POWER OF ATTORNEY

Part A: About using this form

1. You may choose one attorney or more than one. If you choose one attorney then you must delete everything between the square brackets on the first page of the form. If you choose more than one, you must decide whether they are able to act:
• Jointly (that is, they must all act together and cannot act separately) or
• Jointly and severally (that is, they can all act together but they can also act separately if they wish).

On the first page of the form, show what you have decided by crossing out one of the alternatives.

2. If you give your attorney(s) general power in relation to all your property and affairs, it means that they will be able to deal with your money or property and may be able to sell your house.

3. If you don't want your attorney(s) to have such wide powers, you can include any restrictions you like. For example, you can include a restriction that your attorney(s) must not act on your behalf until they have reason to believe that you are becoming mentally incapable; or a restriction as to what your attorney(s) may do. Any restrictions you choose must be written or typed where indicated on the second page of the form.

4. If you are a trustee (and please remember that co-ownership of a home involves trusteeship), you should seek legal advice if you want your attorney(s) to act as a trustee on your behalf.

5. Unless you put in a restriction preventing it your attorney(s) will be able to use any of your money or property to make any provision which you yourself might expect to make for their own needs or the needs of other people. Your attorney(s) will also be able to use your money to make gifts, but only for reasonable amounts in relation to the value of your money and property.

6. Your attorney(s) can recover the out-of-pocket expenses of acting as your attorney(s). If your attorney(s) are professional people, for example solicitors or accountants, they may be able to charge for their professional services as well. You may wish to provide expressly for remuneration of your attorney(s) (although if they are trustees they may not be allowed to accept it).

7. If your attorney(s) have reason to believe that you have become or are becoming mentally incapable of managing your affairs, your attorney(s) will have to apply to the Court of Protection for registration of this power.

8. Before applying to the Court of Protection for registration of this power, your attorney(s) must give written notice, using a special form of notice, that that is what they are going to do, to you and your nearest relatives as defined in the Enduring Powers of Attorney Act 1985. You or your relatives will be able to object if you or they disagree with registration.

9. This is a simplified explanation of what the Enduring Powers of Attorney Act 1985 and the Rules and Regulations say. If you need more guidance, you or your advisers will need to look at the Act itself and the Rules and Regulations. You can obtain details of these from the Court of Protection.

10. Note to attorney(s)
After the power has been registered you should notify the Court of Protection if the donor dies or recovers.

11. Note to Donor
Some of these explanatory notes may not apply to the form you are using if it has been adapted to suit your particular requirements.

Please do not detach these notes. They are part of the Enduring Power of Attorney.
YOU CAN CANCEL THIS POWER AT ANY TIME BEFORE IT HAS TO BE REGISTERED

© Crown copyright 2005.

2

Part B: To be completed by the 'donor' (the person appointing the attorney(s))

Don't sign this form unless you understand what it means

Please read the notes in the margin which follow and which are part of the form itself.

Donor's full name and address.

I _____

of _____

Donor's date of birth.

born on _____

Attorney's full name and address.

appoint _____

of _____

See note 1 on the front of this form. If you are appointing only one attorney you should cross out everything between the square brackets. If appointing more than two attorneys please give the additional name(s) on an attached sheet.

• [and _____

of _____

Cross out the one which does not apply (see note 1 on the front of this form).

• jointly
• jointly and severally]

to be my attorney(s) for the purpose of the Enduring Power of Attorney Act 1985

Cross out the one which does not apply (see note 2 on the front of this form). Add any additional powers.

• with general authority to act on my behalf
• with authority to do the following on my behalf:

If you don't want the attorney(s) to have general power, you must give details here of what authority you are giving the attorney(s).

Cross out the one which does not apply.

in relation to
• all my property and affairs
• the following property and affairs:

3

Part B: continued

Please read the notes in the margin which follow and which are part of the form itself.	• Subject to the following restrictions and conditions:
If there are restrictions or conditions, insert them here, if not, cross out these words if you wish (see note 3 on the front of this form).	
If this form is being signed at your direction:- • The person signing must not be an attorney or any witness (to Parts B or C). • You must add a statement that this form has been signed at your direction. • A second witness is necessary (please see below).	I intend that this power shall continue even if I become mentally incapable. I have read or have had read to me the notes in Part A which are part of, and explain, this form. I understand the purpose and effect of this document and the nature and extent of the powers I am granting my attorney(s).
Your signature or mark.	Signed by me as a deed_____ and delivered
Date.	on_____
Someone must witness your signature.	
Signature of witness.	in the presence of_____ Full name of witness_____
Your attorney(s) cannot be your witness.	Address of witness_____ _____ _____ _____
A second witness is only necessary if this form is not being signed by you personally but at your direction (for example, if a physical disability prevents you from signing). Signature of second witness.	in the presence of_____ Full name of witness_____ Address of witness_____ _____ _____ _____

YOUR ATTORNEY MUST NOW COMPLETE PART C

4

Part C: To be completed by the attorney(s)

Note: 1. This form may be adapted to provide for execution by a corporation.

2. If there is more than one attorney additional sheets in the form as shown below must be added to this Part C.

Please read the notes in the margin which follow and which are part of the form itself. Don't sign this form before the donor has signed Part B or if, in your opinion, the donor was already mentally incapable at the time of signing Part B.	I understand that I have a duty to apply to the Court for the registration of this form under the Enduring Powers of Attorney Act 1985 when the donor is or is becoming mentally incapable.
If this form is being signed at your direction:- • The person signing must not be an attorney or any witness (to Parts B or C); • You must add a statement that this form has been signed at your direction; • A second witness is necessary (please see below).	I understand that I am able to use the donor's money to make gifts, but only on specified occasions and for reasonable amounts in relation to the donor's money and property. I also understand that I have a duty to keep proper accounts and records and produce them to the Court when requested. I am not a minor.
Signature (or mark) of attorney.	Signed by me as a deed _____ and delivered
Date.	on _____
Signature of witness.	In the presence of _____
The attorney must sign the form and his signature must be witnessed. The donor may not be the witness and one attorney may not witness the signature of another.	Full name of witness _____ Address of witness _____ _____ _____ _____
A second witness is only necessary if this form is not being signed by you personally but at your direction (for example, if a physical disability prevents you from signing).	
Signature of second witness.	In the presence of _____ Full name of witness _____ Address of witness _____ _____ _____

5

Note — Schedule substituted by the Enduring Powers of Attorney (Prescribed Form) (Amendment) Regulations 2005 (SI 2005 No.3116), subject to transitional provisions contained in reg.3 of those regulations.

6B–430

COURT OF PROTECTION

6C   NON-CONTENTIOUS PROBATE

Supreme Court Act 1981

ARRANGEMENT OF SECTIONS

PART II

JURISDICTION

OTHER PARTICULAR FIELDS OF JURISDICTION

PART IV

OFFICERS AND OFFICES

DISTRICT PROBATE REGISTRIES

PART V

PROBATE CAUSES AND MATTERS

PROCEDURE IN PROBATE REGISTRIES IN RELATION TO GRANTS OF REPRESENTATION

POWERS OF COURT IN RELATION TO PERSONAL REPRESENTATIVES

REVOCATION OF GRANTS AND CANCELLATION OF RESEALING AT INSTANCE OF COURT

ANCILLARY POWERS OF COURT

PROVISIONS AS TO DOCUMENTS

PROBATE RULES

INTERPRETATION OF PART V AND OTHER PROBATE PROVISIONS

NON-CONTENTIOUS PROBATE

* * * *

PART II

JURISDICTION

OTHER PARTICULAR FIELDS OF JURISDICTION

Probate jurisdiction of High Court

6C–2   **25.**—(1) Subject to the provisions of Part V, the High Court shall, in accordance with section 19(2), have the following probate jurisdiction, that is to say all such jurisdiction in relation to probates and letters of administration as it had immediately before the commencement of this Act, and in particular all such contentious and non-contentious jurisdiction as it then had in relation to—

(a) testamentary causes or matters;

(b) the grant, amendment or revocation of probates and letters of administration; and

(c) the real and personal estate of deceased persons.

(2) Subject to the provisions of Part V, the High Court shall, in the exercise of its probate jurisdiction, perform all such duties with respect to the estates of deceased persons as fell to be performed by it immediately before the commencement of this Act.

6C–3   *Note* —Derived from the J.A. 1925, s.20. For contentious probate proceedings see O.76.

* * * *

PART IV

OFFICERS AND OFFICES

DISTRICT PROBATE REGISTRIES

District probate registries

6C–4   **104.**—(1) The Lord Chancellor may [*after consulting the Lord Chief Justice*] by order direct that there shall be district probate registries of the High Court at such places and for such districts as are specified in the order.

(2) Any order under this section shall be made by statutory instrument, which shall be laid before Parliament after being made.

[(3) *The Lord Chief Justice may nominate a judicial office holder (as defined in section 109(4) of the Constitutional Reform Act 2005) to exercise his functions under this section.*]

6C–5   *Note* —Derived from the J.A. 1925, s.108. For list of district probate registries, see notes to r.2 of the Non-Contentious Probate Rules 1987, paras 6C–71 to 6C–73; words in square brackets and italics prospectively inserted and subs.(3) prospectively inserted by the Constitutional Reform Act 2005, s.15(1), Sch.4, Pt 1, para.135, with effect from a date to be appointed.

PART V

PROBATE CAUSES AND MATTERS

PROCEDURE IN PROBATE REGISTRIES IN RELATION TO GRANTS OF REPRESENTATION

Applications

105. Applications for grants of probate or administration and for the revocation of grants may be made to—   **6C–6**

    (a) the Principal Registry of the Family Division (in this Part referred to as "the Principal Registry"); or

    (b) a district probate registry.

Note —Derived from the J.A. 1925, s.150.   **6C–7**

Grants by district probate registrars

106.—(1) Any grant made by a district probate registrar shall be made in the name of the High Court under the seal used in the registry.   **6C–8**

    (2)–(4) [...].

Note —Derived from the J.A. 1925, s.151. Amended by the Administration of Justice Act 1985, Sched.8.   **6C–9**

No grant where conflicting applications

107. Subject to probate rules, no grant in respect of the estate, or part of the estate, of a deceased person shall be made out of the Principal Registry or any district probate registry on any application if, at any time before the making of a grant, it appears to the registrar concerned that some other application has been made in respect of that estate or, as the case may be, that part of it and has not been either refused or withdrawn.   **6C–10**

Note —Derived from the J.A. 1925, s.152.   **6C–11**

Caveats

108.—(1) A caveat against a grant of probate or administration may be entered in the Principal Registry or in any district probate registry.   **6C–12**

    (2) On a caveat being entered in a district probate registry, the district probate registrar shall immediately send a copy of it to the Principal Registry to be entered among the caveats in that Registry.

Note —Derived from the J.A. 1925, s.154.   **6C–13**

Practice

See the Non-Contentious Probate Rules 1987, r.44, para. 6C–157.   **6C–14**

Refusal of grant where capital transfer tax unpaid

109.—(1) No grant shall be made, and no grant made outside the United Kingdom shall be resealed, except—   **6C–15**

NON-CONTENTIOUS PROBATE

(a) on the production of information or documents under regulations under section 256(1)(aa) of the Inheritance Tax Act 1984 (excepted estates); or

(b) on the production of an account prepared in pursuance of that Act showing by means of such receipt or certification as may be prescribed by the Commissioners either—

(i) that the inheritance tax payable on the delivery of the account has been paid; or

(ii) that no such tax is so payable.

(2) Arrangements may be made between the President of the Family Division and the Commissioners providing for the purposes of subsection (1)(b) in such cases as may be specified in the arrangements that the receipt or certification of an account may be dispensed with or that some other document may be substituted for the account required by the Capital Transfer Tax Act 1984.

(3) [. . .]

6C–16 *Note* —Derived from the J.A. 1925, s.156A. Amended by the Capital Transfer Tax Act 1984, Sched.8; and by the Finance Act 2004, ss.294(1), 326, Sched.42, Pt 4(1).

Documents to be delivered to commissioners of Inland Revenue

6C–17 **110.** Subject to any arrangements which may from time to time be made between the President of the Family Division and the Commissioners, the Principal Registry and every district probate registry shall, within such a period after a grant as the President may direct, deliver to the Commissioners or their proper officer the following documents—

(a) in the case of a grant of probate or of administration with the will annexed, a copy of the will;

(b) in every case, such certificate or note of the grant as the Commissioners may require.

6C–18 *Note* —Derived from the J.A. 1925, s.157.

Records of grants

6C–19 **111.**—(1) There shall continue to be kept records of all grants which are made in the Principal Registry or in any district probate registry.

(2) Those records shall be in such form, and shall contain such particulars, as the President of the Family Division may direct.

6C–20 *Note* —Derived from the J.A. 1925, s.156.

Presidents Direction dated November 3, 1998

6C–21 As from November 9, 1998, records of all grants of representation made in the Principal Registry and in district probate registries, kept pursuant to s.111 of the Supreme Court Act 1981, shall be maintained in the form of a computer record. Annual calendar books will continue to be prepared and will incorporate the information held on computer.

The information held on computer and in the annual calendar books will comprise:

(a) a full name of the deceased and any alias names;

(b) the last address of the deceased;

(c) the date of death and domicil of the deceased;

(d) the name(s) and address(es) of the executor(s) or administrator(s);

(e) the type of grant;

(f) the gross and net values of the estate or in the case of an excepted estate the limits within which the estate falls;

(g) the name and address of the extracting solicitor (if any) or the fact that the grant was obtained by way of personal application;

(h) the date of the grant and the issuing registry.

The President's Direction, as published in the Registrar's circular dated December 22, 1969, is revoked.

POWERS OF COURT IN RELATION TO PERSONAL REPRESENTATIVES

Summons to executor to prove or renounce

112. The High Court may summon any person named as executor **6C–22** in a will to prove, or renounce probate of, the will, and to do such other things concerning the will as the court had power to order such a person to do immediately before the commencement of this Act.

Note —Derived from the J.A. 1925, s.159.   **6C–23**

Practice

The procedure is by way of citation. See the Non-Contentious Probate Rules 1987, **6C–24** rr.46, 47 and 48, paras 6C–162 to 6C–165.

Power of court to sever grant

113.—(1) Subject to subsection (2), the High Court may grant **6C–25** probate or administration in respect of any part of the estate of a deceased person, limited in any way the court thinks fit.

(2) Where the estate of a deceased person is known to be insolvent, the grant of representation to it shall not be severed under subsection (1) except as regards a trust estate in which he had no beneficial interest.

Note —Derived from the J.A. 1925, s.155.   **6C–26**

Practice

See the Non-Contentious Probate Rules 1987, r.51, para. 6C–170.   **6C–27**

Number of personal representatives

114.—(1) Probate or administration shall not be granted by the **6C–28** High Court to more than four persons in respect of the same part of the estate of a deceased person.

(2) Where under a will or intestacy any beneficiary is a minor or a life interest arises, any grant of administration by the High Court shall be made either to a trust corporation (with or without an individual) or to not less than two individuals, unless it appears to the court to be expedient in all the circumstances to appoint an individual as sole administrator.

(3) For the purpose of determining whether a minority or life interest arises in any particular case, the court may act on such evidence as may be prescribed.

(4) If at any time during the minority of a beneficiary or the sub-

sistence of a life interest under a will or intestacy there is only one personal representative (not being a trust corporation), the High Court may, on the application of any person interested or the guardian or receiver of any such person, and in accordance with probate rules, appoint one or more additional personal representatives to act while the minority or life interest subsists and until the estate is fully administered.

(5) An appointment of an additional personal representative under subsection (4) to act with an executor shall not have the effect of including him in any chain of representation.

6C–29 *Note* —Derived from the J.A. 1925, s.160.

Grants to trust corporations

6C–30   115.—(1) The High Court may—
>   (a) where a trust corporation is named in a will as executor, grant probate to the corporation either solely or jointly with any other person named in the will as executor, as the case may require; or
>   (b) grant administration to a trust corporation, either solely or jointly with another person;

and the corporation may act accordingly as executor or administrator, as the case may be.

(2) Probate or administration shall not be granted to any person as nominee of a trust corporation.

(3) Any officer authorised for the purpose by a trust corporation or its directors or governing body may, on behalf of the corporation, swear affidavits, give security and do any other act which the court may require with a view to the grant to the corporation of probate or administration; and the acts of an officer so authorised shall be binding on the corporation.

(4) Subsections (1) to (3) shall also apply in relation to any body which is exempt from the provisions of section 23(1) of the Solicitors Act 1974 (unqualified persons not to prepare papers for probate, etc.) by virtue of any of paragraphs (e) to (h) of subsection (2) of that section.

6C–31 *Note* —Derived from the J.A. 1925, s.161. Amended by the Courts and Legal Services Act 1990, s.54.

Power of court to pass over prior claims to grant

6C–32   116.—(1) If by reason of any special circumstances it appears to the High Court to be necessary or expedient to appoint as administrator some person other than the person who, but for this section, would in accordance with probate rules have been entitled to the grant, the court may in its discretion appoint as administrator such person as it thinks expedient.

(2) Any grant of administration under this section may be limited in any way the court thinks fit.

6C–33 *Note* —Derived from the J.A. 1925, s.162.

Practice
6C–34   See the Non-Contentious Probate Rules 1987, r.52, para. 6C–172.

Administration pending suit

117.—(1) Where any legal proceedings concerning the validity of 6C–35 the will of a deceased person, or for obtaining, recalling or revoking any grant, are pending, the High Court may grant administration of the estate of the deceased person in question to an administrator pending suit, who shall, subject to subsection (2), have all the rights, duties and powers of a general administrator.

(2) An administrator pending suit shall be subject to the immediate control of the court and act under its direction; and, except in such circumstances as may be prescribed, no distribution of the estate, or any part of the estate, of the deceased person in question shall be made by such an administrator without the leave of the court.

(3) The court may, out of the estate of the deceased, assign an administrator pending suit such reasonable remuneration as it thinks fit.

Note —Derived from the J.A. 1925, s.163.   **6C–36**

Application

By summons in the Chancery Division (O.76, r.15(1)). If an order is made appoint- **6C–37** ing an administrator pending suit, application for the grant is made at the Principal Registry of the Family Division.

Effect of appointment of minor as executor

118. Where a testator by his will appoints a minor to be an execu- 6C–38 tor, the appointment shall not operate to vest in the minor the estate, or any part of the estate, of the testator, or to constitute him a personal representative for any purpose, unless and until probate is granted to him in accordance with probate rules.

Note —Derived from the J.A. 1925, s.165.   **6C–39**

Administration with will annexed

119.—(1) Administration with the will annexed shall be granted, 6C–40 subject to and in accordance with probate rules, in every class of case in which the High Court had power to make such a grant immediately before the commencement of this Act.

(2) Where administration with the will annexed is granted, the will of the deceased shall be performed and observed in the same manner as if probate of it had been granted to an executor.

Note —Derived from the J.A. 1925, s.166.   **6C–41**

Probate Rules

The order of entitlement is in the Non-Contentious Probate Rules 1987, r.20, para. **6C–42** 6C–105.

Power to require administrators to produce sureties

120.—(1) As a condition of granting administration to any person 6C–43 the High Court may, subject to the following provisions of this section and subject to and in accordance with probate rules, require one or more sureties to guarantee that they will make good, within any limit imposed by the court on the total liability of the surety or sureties, any loss which any person interested in the administration of the estate of the deceased may suffer in consequence of a breach by the administrator of his duties as such.

(2) A guarantee given in pursuance of any such requirement shall enure for the benefit of every person interested in the administration of the estate of the deceased as if contained in a contract under seal made by the surety or sureties with which every such person and, where there are two or more sureties, as if they had bound themselves jointly and severally.

(3) No action shall be brought on any such guarantee without the leave of the High Court.

(4) Stamp duty shall not be chargeable on any such guarantee.

(5) This section does not apply where administration is granted to the Treasury Solicitor, the Official Solicitor, the Public Trustee, the Solicitor for the affairs of the Duchy of Lancaster or the Duchy of Cornwall or the Crown Solicitor for Northern Ireland, or to the consular officer of a foreign state to which section 1 of the Consular Conventions Act 1949 applies, or in such other cases as may be prescribed.

6C–44   *Note* —Derived from the J.A. 1925, s.167.

Practice

6C–45   Under the Non-Contentious Probate Rules 1987 there is no longer any requirement for sureties on an application for letters of administration.

REVOCATION OF GRANTS AND CANCELLATION OF RESEALING AT INSTANCE OF COURT

Revocation of grants and cancellation of resealing at instance of court

6C–46   **121.**—(1) Where it appears to the High Court that a grant either ought not to have been made or contains an error, the court may call in the grant and, if satisfied that it would be revoked at the instance of a party interested, may revoke it.

(2) A grant may be revoked under subsection (1) without being called in, if it cannot be called in.

(3) Where it appears to the High Court that a grant resealed under the Colonial Probates Acts 1892 and 1927 ought not to have been resealed, the court may call in the relevant document and, if satisfied that the resealing would be cancelled at the instance of a party interested, may cancel the resealing.

In this and the following subsection "the relevant document" means the original grant or, where some other document was sealed by the court under those Acts, that document.

(4) A resealing may be cancelled under subsection (3) without the relevant document being called in, if it cannot be called in.

6C–47   *Note* —Derived from Administration of Justice Act 1956, s.17.

Practice

6C–48   See the Non-Contentious Probate Rules 1987, r.39, para. 6C–149.

ANCILLARY POWERS OF COURT

Examination of person with knowledge of testamentary document

122.—(1) Where it appears that there are reasonable grounds for **6C–49** believing that any person has knowledge of any document which is or purports to be a testamentary document, the High Court may, whether or not any legal proceedings are pending, order him to attend for the purpose of being examined in open court.

(2) The court may—

> (a) require any person who is before it in compliance with an order under subsection (1) to answer any question relating to the document concerned; and
>
> (b) if appropriate, order him to bring in the document in such manner as the court may direct.

(3) Any person who, having been required by the court to do so under this section, fails to attend for examination, answer any question or bring in any document shall be guilty of contempt of court.

Note —Derived from the Court of Probate Act 1857, ss.24 and 26. **6C–50**

Practice
  See the Non-Contentious Probate Rules 1987, r.50, para. 6C–168. **6C–51**

Subpoena to bring in testamentary document

123. Where it appears that any person has in his possession, **6C–52** custody or power any document which is or purports to be a testamentary document, the High Court may, whether or not any legal proceedings are pending, issue a subpoena requiring him to bring in the document in such manner as the court may in the subpoena direct.

Note —Derived from the Court of Probate Act 1857, s.23. **6C–53**

Practice
  See the Non-Contentious Probate Rules 1987, r.50 at para. 6C–168 (where no ac- **6C–54** tion commenced); O.76, r.14 (where action commenced).

PROVISIONS AS TO DOCUMENTS

Place for deposit of original wills and other documents

124. All original wills and other documents which are under the **6C–55** control of the High Court in the Principal Registry or in any district probate registry shall be deposited and preserved in such places <u>as the Lord Chancellor may direct</u> [*as may be provided for in directions given in accordance with Part 1 of Schedule 2 to the Constitutional Reform Act 2005*]; and any wills or other documents so deposited shall, subject to the control of the High Court and to probate rules, be open to inspection.

Note —Derived from the J.A. 1925, s.170; words underlined prospectively repealed **6C–56** and words in square brackets and italics prospectively substituted by the Constitutional Reform Act 2005, s.13, Sched.2, Pt II, para.5, with effect from a date to be appointed.

Copies

6C–57   See the Non-Contentious Probate Rules 1987, r.58, para. 6C–181.

Copies of wills and grants

6C–58   **125.** An office copy, or a sealed and certified copy, of any will or part of a will open to inspection under section 124 or of any grant may, on payment of the fee prescribed by an order under section 92 of the Courts Act 2003 (fees), be obtained—

(a) from the registry in which in accordance with section 124 the will or documents relating to the grant are preserved; or

(b) where in accordance with that section the will or such documents are preserved in some place other than a registry, from the Principal Registry; or

(c) subject to the approval of the Senior Registrar of the Family Division, from the Principal Registry in any case where the will was proved in or the grant was issued from a district probate registry.

6C–59   *Note*—Derived from the J.A. 1925, s.171. Amended by the Courts Act 2003, s.109(1), Sched.8, para.262(a).

Practice

6C–60   See the Non-Contentious Probate Rules 1987, r.59, para. 6C–182.

As from December 3, 1990 requests for copies of wills and grants deposited in accordance with s.124 of the Supreme Court Act 1981, received through the post in the Principal Registry of the Family Division, will be forwarded to the York Probate Sub-Registry for the necessary search to be undertaken. The Probate Registry, identified by the search as that from which the grant has issued, will be requested to forward to the applicant the copies required. There may be some advantage in terms of saving time for an applicant who knows that the will was proved in, or that the grant issued from, a District Probate Registry to apply direct to that Registry or direct to York Probate Sub-Registry, Duncombe Place, York YO1 2EA, DX 61543 York, instead of to the Principal Registry. The Senior District Judge continues to give his approval in accordance with s.125(c) of the Supreme Court Act 1981 to the practice of allowing applicants who attend in person at the Principal Registry to obtain copies of wills and grants from the Principal Registry regardless of the fact that the will may have been proved in, or the grant issued from, a District Probate Registry. (Practice Direction (Supply of Copies of Wills and Grants), October 31, 1990).

Depositories for wills of living persons

6C–61   **126.**—(1) There shall be provided, under the control and direction of the High Court, safe and convenient depositories for the custody of the wills of living persons; and any person may deposit his will in such a depository on payment of the fee prescribed by an order under section 92 of the Courts Act 2003 (fees) and subject to such conditions as may be prescribed by regulations made by the President of the Family Division with the concurrence of the Lord Chancellor.

(2) Any regulations made under this section shall be made by statutory instrument which shall be laid before Parliament after being made; and the Statutory Instruments Act 1946 shall apply to a statutory instrument containing regulations under this section in like manner as if they had been made by a Minister of the Crown.

6C–62   *Note*—Derived from the J.A. 1925, s.172. Amended by the Courts Act 2003, s.109(1), Sch.8, para.262(b). Section 126 prospectively repealed by Administration of Justice Act

1982, s.75 and Sched.9, Pt I and replaced by *ibid.*, ss.23–26 from a date to be appointed.

PROBATE RULES

Probate rules

127.—(1) The President of the Family Division may, with the **6C–63** concurrence of the Lord Chancellor, make rules of court (in this Part referred to as "probate rules") for regulating [*Rules of court (in this Part referred to as "probate rules") may be made in accordance with Part 1 of Schedule 1 to the Constitutional Reform Act 2005 for regulating*] and prescribing the practice and procedure of the High Court with respect to non-contentious or common form probate business.

(2) Without prejudice to the generality of subsection (1), probate rules may make provision for regulating the classes of persons entitled to grants of probate or administration in particular circumstances and the relative priorities of their claims thereto.

(3) Probate rules shall be made by statutory instrument subject to annulment in pursuance of a resolution of either House of Parliament; and the Statutory Instruments Act 1946 shall apply to a statutory instrument containing probate rules in like manner as if they had been made by a Minister of the Crown.

Note —Derived from the J.A. 1925, s.100; words underlined prospectively repealed, **6C–64** words in square brackets and italics prospectively substituted and subs.(3) prospectively repealed by the Constitutional Reform Act 2005, ss. 12, 146, Sched.1, Pt II, para.12, Sched.18, Pt II, with effect from a date to be appointed.

Probate rules
See the Non-Contentious Probate Rules 1987, as amended, paras 6C–69 *et seq.* **6C–65**

INTERPRETATION OF PART V AND OTHER PROBATE PROVISIONS

Interpretation of Part V and other probate provisions

128. In this Part, and in other provisions of this Act relating to **6C–66** probate causes and matters, unless the context otherwise requires—

"administration" includes all letters of administration of the effects of deceased persons, whether with or without a will annexed, and whether granted for general, special or limited purposes;

"estate" means real and personal estate, and "real estate" includes—

(a) chattels real and land in possession, remainder or reversion and every interest in or over land to which the deceased person was entitled at the time of his death, and

(b) real estate held on trust or by way of mortgage or security, but not [...] money secured or charged on land;

"grant" means a grant of probate or administration;

"non-contentious or common form probate business" means the business of obtaining probate and administration where there is no contention as to the right thereto, including—

(a) the passing of probates and administrations through the High Court in contentious cases where the contest has been terminated,

(b) all business of a non-contentious nature in matters of testacy and intestacy not being proceedings in any action, and

(c) the business of lodging caveats against the grant of probate or administration;

"Principal Registry" means the Principal Registry of the Family Division;

"probate rules" means rules of court made under section 127;

"trust corporation" means the Public Trustee or a corporation either appointed by the court in any particular case to be a trustee or authorised by rules made under section 4(3) of the Public Trustee Act 1906 to act as a custodian trustee;

"will" includes a nuncupative will and any testamentary document of which probate may be granted.

6C–67   *Note* —Derived from the J.A. 1925, s.175. Amended by the Trusts of Land and Appointment of Trustees Act 1996, Sched.4.

Non-contentious Probate Rules 1987

(S.I. 1987 No. 2024)

6C–68   [As amended by the Non-Contentious Probate (Amendment) Rules 1991 (S.I. 1991 No. 1876); the Non-Contentious Probate (Amendment) Rules 1998 (S.I. 1998 No. 1903); the Non-Contentious Probate (Amendment) Rules 1999 (S.I. 1999 No. 1015); and the Non-Contentious Probate (Amendment) Rules 2003 (S.I. 2003 No. 185).]

ARRANGEMENT OF RULES

The President of the Family Division, in exercise of the powers conferred upon him by section 127 of the Supreme Court Act 1981, and section 2(5) of the Colonial Probates Act 1892, and with the concurrence of the Lord Chancellor, hereby makes the following Rules:

Citation and commencement

6C–69 1. These Rules may be cited as the Non-Contentious Probate Rules 1987 and shall come into force on 1st January 1988.

Interpretation

6C–70 2.—(1) In these Rules, unless the context otherwise requires—

"the Act" means the Supreme Court Act 1981;

"authorised officer" means any officer of a registry who is for the time being authorised by the President to administer any oath or to take any affidavit required for any purpose connected with his duties;

"The Crown" includes the Crown in right of the Duchy of Lancaster and the Duke of Cornwall for the time being;

"district judge" means a district judge of the Principal Registry;

"grant" means a grant of probate or administration and includes, where the context so admits, the resealing of such a grant under the Colonial Probates Act 1892and 1927;

"gross value" in relation to any estate means the value of the estate without deduction for debts, incumbrances, funeral expenses or inheritance tax (or other capital tax payable out of the estate);

"judge" means a judge of the High Court;

"oath" means the oath required by rule 8 to be sworn by every applicant for a grant;

"personal applicant" means a person other than a trust corporation who seeks to obtain a grant without employing a solicitor or probate practitioner, and "personal application" has a corresponding meaning;

"probate practitioner" means a person to whom s.23(1) of the Solicitors Act 1974 does not apply by virtue of s.23(2) of that Act or section 55 of the Courts and Legal Services Act 1990;

"registrar" means the district probate registrar of the district probate registry—

(a) to which an application for a grant is made or is proposed to be made,

(b) in rules 26, 40, 41 and 61(2), from which the grant issued, and

(c) in rules 46, 47 and 48, from which the citation has issued or is proposed to be issued;

"registry" means the Principal Registry or a district probate registry;

"the senior district judge" means the Senior District Judge of the Family Division or, in his absence, the senior of the district judges in attendance at the Principal Registry;

"the Treasury Solicitor" means the solicitor for the affairs of Her Majesty's Treasury and includes the solicitor for the affairs of the Duchy of Cornwall;

"trust corporation" means a corporation within the meaning of section 128 of the Act as extended by section 3 of the Law of Property (Amendment) Act 1926;

(2) A form referred to by number means the form so numbered in the First Schedule; and such forms shall be used wherever applicable, with such variations as a district judge or registrar may in any particular case direct or approve.

Note —Amended by the Administration of Justice Act 1985, s.7; and by S.I. 2004 No. 2985.

District probate registries

The district probate registries and their attached sub-registries are now as follows **6C–71** (S.I. 1982 No. 379); (S.I. 1994 No. 1103); (S.I. 1994 No. 3079):

District Probate Registries	Sub-registries	**6C–72**
Birmingham	Stoke-on-Trent	
Brighton	Maidstone	
Bristol	Bodmin, Exeter	
Cardiff (Probate Registry of Wales)	Bangor, Carmarthen	
Ipswich	Norwich, Peterborough	
Leeds	Lincoln, Sheffield	
Liverpool	Chester, Lancaster	
Manchester	Nottingham	
Newcastle upon Tyne	Carlisle, Middlesbrough, York	
Oxford	Leicester, Gloucester	
Winchester		

The Administration of Estates (Small Payments) (Increase of Limit) Order 1984 (S.I. 1984 No. 539)

This increases to an upper limit of £5,000 the amount of property which is allowed **6C–73** under specified statutory provisions to be disposed of on death without the necessity for probate or other proof of title or in pursuance of a nomination made by the deceased.

Application of other rules

3.—(1) Subject to the provisions of these rules and to any enact- **6C–74** ment, the Rules of the Supreme Court 1965 as they were in force immediately before 26th April 1999 shall apply, with any necessary modifications to non-contentious probate matters, and any reference in these rules to those rules shall be construed accordingly.

(2) Nothing in Order 3 of the Rules of the Supreme Court shall prevent time from running in the Long Vacation.

Note —Amended by the Non-Contentious Probate (Amendment) Rules 1999 (S.I. **6C–75** 1999 No. 1015).

Application for grants through solicitors or probate practitioner

4.—(1) A person applying for a grant through a solicitor or **6C–76** probate practitioner may apply at any registry or sub-registry.

(2) Every solicitor or probate practitioner through whom an application for a grant is made shall give the address of his place of business within England and Wales.

Application by post

Postal facilities are available at all district probate registries and sub-registries and at **6C–77** the Principal Registry.

Second or subsequent grants

There are now no restrictions as to the registries at which applications can be made **6C–78** for second or subsequent grants.

6C–78.1   *Note* —See Practice Direction, January 12, 1999.

Personal applications

6C–79   5.—(1) A personal applicant may apply for a grant at any registry or sub-registry.

(2) Save as provided for by rule 39 a personal applicant may not apply through an agent, whether paid or unpaid, and may not be attended by any person acting or appearing to act as his adviser.

(3) No personal application shall be proceeded with if—

   (a) it becomes necessary to bring the matter before the court by action or summons unless a judge, district judge or registrar permits;

   (b) an application has already been made by a solicitor or probate practitioner on behalf of the applicant and has not been withdrawn; or

   (c) the district judge or registrar so directs.

(4) After a will has been deposited in a registry by a personal applicant, it may not be delivered to the applicant or to any other person unless in special circumstances the district judge or registrar so directs.

(5) A personal applicant shall produce a certificate of the death of the deceased or such other evidence of the death as the district judge or registrar may approve.

(6) A personal applicant shall supply all information necessary to enable the papers leading to the grant to be prepared in the registry.

(7) Unless the district judge or registrar otherwise directs, every oath or affidavit required on a personal application shall be sworn or executed by all the deponents before an authorised officer.

(8) No legal advice shall be given to a personal applicant by an officer of a registry and every such officer shall be responsible only for embodying in proper form the applicant's instructions for the grant.

6C–80   *Note* —The personal application department of the Principal Registry is now situated within the Registry at First Avenue House, 42–49 High Holborn, London WC1V 6NP.

Duty of district judge or registrar on receiving application for grant

6C–81   6.—(1) A district judge or registrar shall not allow any grant to issue until all inquiries which he may see fit to make have been answered to his satisfaction.

(2) Except with the leave of a district judge or registrar, no grant of probate or of administration with the will annexed shall issue within seven days of the death of the deceased and no grant of administration shall issue within fourteen days thereof.

Grants by registrars

6C–82   7.—(1) No grant shall be made by a registrar—

   (a) in any case in which there is contention, until the contention is disposed of; or

(b) in any case in which it appears to him that a grant ought not to be made without the directions of a judge or a district judge.

(2) In any case in which paragraph (1)(b) applies, the registrar shall send a statement of the matter in question to the Principal Registry for directions.

(3) A district judge may either confirm that the matter be referred to a judge and give directions accordingly or may direct the registrar to proceed with the matter in accordance with such instructions as are deemed necessary, which may include a direction to take no further action in relation to the matter.

Oath in support of grant

8.—(1) Every application for a grant other than one to which rule **6C-83**
39 applies shall be supported by an oath by the applicant in the form applicable to the circumstances of the case, and by such other papers as the district judge or registrar may require.

(2) Unless otherwise directed by a district judge or registrar, the oath shall state where the deceased died domiciled.

(3) Where the deceased dies on or after 1st January 1926, the oath shall state whether or not, to the best of the applicant's knowledge, information and belief, there was land vested in the deceased which was settled previously to his death and not by his will and which remained settled land notwithstanding his death.

(4) On an application for a grant of administration the oath shall state in what manner all persons having a prior right to a grant have been cleared off and whether any minority or life interest arises under the will or intestacy.

Minority or life interest (para. (2))

If there is a minority or a life interest under a will or intestacy, administration must **6C-84**
be granted either to a trust corporation (with or without an individual) or to not less than two individuals unless it appears to the Court to be expedient in all the circumstances to appoint an individual as sole administrator. Representation will not however be granted to more than four persons in regard to the same property (Supreme Court Act 1981, s.114(1)).

If an oath swears to "a minority interest" but is silent as to "life interest" or conversely swears to "a life interest" making no mention of "minority interest" the omission may be rectified by a certificate from the applicants or their solicitor (*Registrar's Direction (Oath: Minority and Life Interests)*, July 9, 1951).

Domicile (para. (2))

A statement of the domicile of the deceased, as sworn to in the oath, appears in the **6C-85**
grant in order to indicate whether the grant covers the whole of the estate in the United Kingdom (where the deceased died domiciled in England and Wales) or only that in England and Wales (where the deceased died domiciled elsewhere); see the Administration of Estates Act 1971, ss.2–3.

Where a country has no uniform system of law, the statement of domicile should specify the state, province or other judicial division of the country (*Registrar's Direction (Notation of Domicile)*, January 24, 1961).

Grant in additional name

9. Where it is sought to describe the deceased in a grant by some **6C-86**

name in addition to his true name, the applicant shall depose to the true name of the deceased and shall specify some part of the estate which was held in the other name, or give any other reason for the inclusion of the other name in the grant.

Marking of wills

6C–87 10.—(1) Subject to paragraph (2) below, every will in respect of which an application for a grant is made—

    (a) shall be marked by the signatures of the applicant and the person before whom the oath is sworn; and

    (b) shall be exhibited to any affidavit which may be required under these rules as to the validity, terms, condition or date of execution of the will.

(2) The district judge or registrar may allow a facsimile copy of the will to be marked or exhibited in lieu of the original document.

Engrossments for purposes of record

6C–88 11.—(1) Where the district judge or registrar considers that in any particular case a facsimile copy of the original will would not be satisfactory for purposes of record, he may require an engrossment suitable for facsimile reproduction to be lodged.

(2) Where a will—

    (a) contains alterations which are not to be admitted to proof; or

    (b) has been ordered to be rectified by virtue of section 20(1) of the Administration of Justice Act 1982

there shall be lodged an engrossment of the will in the form in which it is to be proved.

(3) Any engrossment lodged under this rule shall reproduce the punctuation, spacing and division into paragraphs of the will and shall follow continuously from page to page on both sides of the paper.

Engrossment

6C–89 By *Registrar's Direction (Notation on Fiat)* March 1, 1950, it is directed that where, following a probate action, a will has been pronounced for, any engrossment of the will lodged on the subsequent application for a grant should reproduce the notation appearing on the will.

Evidence as to due execution of will

6C–90 12.—(1) Subject to paragraphs (2) and (3) below, where a will contains no attestation clause or the attestation clause is insufficient, or where it appears to the district judge or registrar that there is doubt about the due execution of the will, he shall before admitting it to proof require an affidavit as to due execution from one or more of the attesting witnesses or, if no attesting witness is conveniently available, from any other person who was present when the will was executed; and if the district judge or registrar, after considering the evidence, is satisfied that the will was not duly executed, he shall refuse probate and mark the will accordingly.

(2) If no affidavit can be obtained in accordance with paragraph (1) above, the district judge or registrar may accept evidence on affidavit from any person he may think fit to show that the signature on the will is in the handwriting of the deceased, or of any other matter which may raise a presumption in favour of due execution of the will, and may if he thinks fit require that notice of the application be given to any person who may be prejudiced by the will.

(3) A district judge or registrar may accept a will for proof without evidence as aforesaid if he is satisfied that the distribution of the estate is not thereby affected.

Note —An affidavit of due execution will not be required solely because in a printed **6C–91** will form the words "his/her" or "his or her" or the incompleted words "h" appear in the attestation clause. *Registrar's Direction (Will, Execution)*, May 31, 1951.

Rule 12 does not apply to a will which it is sought to establish otherwise than by reference to s.9 of the Wills Act 1837; see r.17.

Execution of will of blind or illiterate testator

13. Before admitting to proof a will which appears to have been **6C–92** signed by a blind or illiterate testator or by another person by direction of the testator, or which for any other reason raises doubt as to the testator having had knowledge of the contents of the will at the time of its execution, the district judge or registrar shall satisfy himself that the testator had such knowledge.

Note — Rule 13 does not apply to a will which it is sought to establish otherwise **6C–93** than by reference to s.9 of the Wills Act 1837; see r.17.

Evidence as to terms, condition and date of execution of will

14.—(1) Subject to paragraph (2) below, where there appears in a **6C–94** will any obliteration, interlineation, or other alteration which is not authenticated in the manner prescribed by section 21 of the Wills Act 1837, or by the re-execution of the will or by the execution of a codicil, the district judge or registrar shall require evidence to show whether the alteration was present at the time the will was executed and shall give directions as to the form in which the will is to be proved.

(2) The provisions of paragraph (1) above shall not apply to any alteration which appears to the district judge or registrar to be of no practical importance.

(3) If a will contains any reference to another document in such terms as to suggest that it ought to be incorporated in the will, the district judge or registrar shall require the document to be produced and may call for such evidence in regard to the incorporation of the document as he may think fit.

(4) Where there is a doubt as to the date on which a will was executed, the district judge or registrar may require such evidence as he thinks necessary to establish the date.

Note — Rule 14 does not apply to a will which it is sought to establish otherwise **6C–95** than by reference to s.9 of the Wills Act 1837; see r.17.

See Practice Direction (Fam.D.) (Incorporation of Standard Forms and Clauses in Wills) April 10, 1995.

Date of will

6C–96   Where a will bears on its face no date, or an imperfect date, but there is endorsed on the back of the will (and not part of it) a date which there is no reason to suppose is not the true date of the will, the latter is accepted as such and a notation made on the face of the will "Endorsement of will dated ...."

Attempted revocation of will

6C–97   15. Any appearance of attempted revocation of a will by burning, tearing, or otherwise destroying and every other circumstance leading to a presumption of revocation by the testator, shall be accounted for to the district judge or registrar's satisfaction.

6C–98   *Note* — Rule 15 does not apply to a will which it is sought to establish otherwise than by reference to s.9 of the Wills Act 1837; see r.17.

See *Re Adams (dec'd)* [1990] Ch. 601; [1990] 2 W.L.R. 924; [1990] 2 All E.R. 97— testatrix who, according to the evidence, had intended to revoke her will, scribbled on it with a ball-point pen to such an extent that her signature and the signatures of the witnesses were so obliterated that it was impossible to discern them with the naked eye: held that in deciding whether a will had been destroyed by obliteration the same test should be applied for the revocation of the entire will under s.20 of the Wills Act 1837 as was to be used for the revocation of part of a will under s.21, namely whether or not the words were "apparent" so that experts using magnifying glasses where necessary could decipher them; the signatures had been so obliterated that they were illegible, and that accordingly they were not apparent to the eye and a material part of the will had been destroyed; taken with the testatrix's evident intention to revoke, the result was that the will as a whole was revoked.

Affidavit as to due execution, terms, etc., of will

6C–99   16. A district judge or registrar may require an affidavit from any person he may think fit for the purpose of satisfying himself as to any of the matters referred to in rules 13, 14 and 15, and in any such affidavit sworn by an attesting witness or other persons present at the time of the execution of a will the deponent shall depose to the manner in which the will was executed.

Will proved otherwise than under section 9 of the Wills Act 1837

6C–100   17.—(1) Rules 12 to 15 shall apply only to a will that is to be established by reference to section 9 of the Wills Act 1837 (signing and attestation of wills).

(2) A will that is to be established otherwise than as described in paragraph (1) of this rule may be so established upon the district judge or registrar being satisfied as to its terms and validity, and includes (without prejudice to the generality of the foregoing)—

(a) any will to which rule 18 applies; and

(b) any will which, by virtue of the Wills Act 1963, is to be treated as properly executed if executed according to the internal law of the territory or state referred to in section 1 of that Act.

Will made abroad before Notary

6C–101   Where a will is shown by a properly authenticated copy issued by a notary practising out of England and Wales to have been executed in his presence, or that of his predecessor, and recorded in his archives at the time of execution, it may be assumed for the purpose of an uncontested application to prove the will in this country, provided that there are no unusual features, that the will is valid as to form by the internal law of the place where it was made.

Practice Note [1972] 1 W.L.R. 1539; [1972] 3 All E.R. 1019.

Wills of persons on military service and seamen

18. Where the deceased died domiciled in England and Wales and it appears to the district judge or registrar that there is prima facie evidence that a will is one to which section 11 of the Wills Act 1837 applies, the will may be admitted to proof if the district judge or registrar is satisfied that it was signed by the testator or, if unsigned, that it is in the testator's handwriting. **6C–102**

Unattested will

See *In the estate of Rapley (dec'd), Rapley v. Rapley* [1983] 1 W.L.R. 1069; [1983] 3 All E.R. 248, unattested will made at time testator, an apprentice seaman, had been discharged from one ship and not yet posted to another, held not to be privileged as, in the circumstances, the testator was not a "mariner or seaman being at sea". **6C–103**

Evidence of foreign law

19. Where evidence as to the law of any country or territory outside England and Wales is required on any application for a grant, the district judge or registrar may accept— **6C–104**

    (a) an affidavit from any person whom, having regard to the particulars of his knowledge or experience given in the affidavit, he regards as suitably qualified to give expert evidence of the law in question; or

    (b) a certificate by, or an act before, a notary practising in the country or territory concerned.

Order of priority for grant where deceased left a will

20. Where the deceased died on or after 1st January 1926 the person or persons entitled to a grant in respect of a will shall be determined in accordance with the following order of priority, namely— **6C–105**

    (a) the executor (but subject to rule 36(4)(d) below);

    (b) any residuary legatee or devisee holding in trust for any other person;

    (c) any other residuary legatee or devisee (including one for life) or where the residue is not wholly disposed of by the will, any person entitled to share in the undisposed of residue (including the Treasury Solicitor when claiming bona vacantia on behalf of the Crown), provided that—

        (i) unless a district judge or registrar otherwise directs, a residuary legatee or devisee whose legacy or devise is vested in interest shall be preferred to one entitled on the happening of a contingency, and

        (ii) where the residue is not in terms wholly disposed of, the district judge or registrar may, if he is satisfied that the testator has nevertheless disposed of the whole or substantially the whole of the known estate, allow a grant to be made to any legatee or devisee entitled to, or to share in, the estate so disposed of, without regard to the persons entitled to share in any residue not disposed of by the will;

(d) the personal representative of any residuary legatee or devisee (but not one for life, or one holding in trust for any other person), or of any person entitled to share in any residue not disposed of by the will;

(e) any other legatee or devisee (including one for life or one holding in trust for any other person) or any creditor of the deceased, provided that, unless a district judge or registrar otherwise directs, a legatee or devisee whose legacy or devise is vested in interest shall be preferred to one entitled on the happening of a contingency;

(f) the personal representative of any other legatee or devisee (but not one for life or one holding in trust for any other person) or of any creditor of the deceased.

Grant to legatee under proviso

6C–106   The proviso to r.20(c)(ii) in no way derogates from the right of the person entitled to the undisposed-of estate to take a grant if he applies for it, and such applications will be granted without enquiry. The proviso, however, allows discretion to make a grant instead to a legatee if he applies for it and if he satisfies the district judge or registrar that the interest of the person entitled to the undisposed-of estate is small enough to justify his being passed over.

For example, where the whole of the estate has been left by enumeration to one or more legatees, and a legatee having a substantial interest applies for the grant, it is sufficient for the oath, in addition to clearing executors, to contain a statement after the gross amount "all of which is disposed of by the said will". The applicant should describe himself merely as "a legatee named in the said will".

Where a legatee's application is on the ground that "substantially the whole" estate is disposed of, the wording should be "of which £   is disposed of by the said will". It will be for the district judge or registrar, having regard to the size of the estate and the amount disposed of, to decide whether the facts bring the case within the proviso, and, if so, whether the grant should be made to the applicant. In cases of doubt he may require notice to be given to the person entitled to the undisposed-of estate.

If it is clear from the papers that there are kin entitled to share in any undisposed-of estate, the Treasury Solicitor need not be regarded as interested. Unless this is clear, however, the applicant will be required either to provide evidence that there are such kin, or to give notice under Rule 38 (even though the whole of the ascertained estate is disposed of). Where such notice is to be given, the district judge or registrar will specify a reasonable period under Rule 38 in order to give the Treasury Solicitor the opportunity of opposing the grant if he wishes.

It should be noted that the proviso does not extend to the personal representatives of legatees or devisees, whose only title is under r.20(f) (*Registrar's Direction (Grant to Legatee)*, August 5, 1954).

Grants to attesting witnesses, etc.

6C–107   21. Where a gift to any person fails by reason of section 15 of the Wills Act 1837, such person shall not have any right to a grant as a beneficiary named in the will, without prejudice to his right to a grant in any other capacity.

Wills Act 1837, s.15

6C–108   The operation of this section is restricted by the Wills Act 1968.

Order of priority for grant in case of intestacy

22.—(1) Where the deceased died on or after 1st January 1926, **6C–109** wholly intestate, the person or persons having a beneficial interest in the estate shall be entitled to a grant of administration in the following classes in order of priority, namely—

    (a) the surviving husband or wife;

    (b) the children of the deceased and the issue of any deceased child who died before the deceased;

    (c) the father and mother of the deceased;

    (d) brothers and sisters of the whole blood and the issue of any deceased brother or sister of the whole blood who died before the deceased;

    (e) brothers and sisters of the half blood and the issue of any deceased brother or sister of the half blood who died before the deceased;

    (f) grandparents;

    (g) uncles and aunts of the whole blood and the issue of any deceased uncle or aunt of the whole blood who died before the deceased;

    (h) uncles and aunts of the half blood and the issue of any deceased uncle or aunt of the half blood who died before the deceased.

(2) In default of any person having a beneficial interest in the estate, the Treasury Solicitor shall be entitled to a grant if he claims bona vacantia on behalf of the Crown.

(3) If all persons entitled to a grant under the foregoing provisions of this rule have been cleared off, a grant may be made to a creditor of the deceased or to any person who, notwithstanding that he has no immediate beneficial interest in the estate, may have a beneficial interest in the event of an accretion thereto.

(4) Subject to paragraph (5) of rule 27, the personal representative of a person in any of the classes mentioned in paragraph (1) of this rule or the personal representative of a creditor of the deceased shall have the same right to a grant as the person whom he represents provided that the persons mentioned in sub-paragraphs (b) to (h) of paragraph (1) above shall be preferred to the personal representative of a spouse who had died without taking a beneficial interest in the whole estate of the deceased as ascertained at the time of the application for the grant.

Family Law Reform Act 1987: entitlement to grant

1. Parts I and III of the Family Law Reform Act 1987 came into force on April 4, **6C–110** 1988.

2. Where the deceased died—

    (a) intestate on or after April 4, 1988, *or*

    (b) died leaving a will or codicil dated on or after April 4, 1988 containing dispositions which refer to relationships between two persons,

then any question of entitlement to a grant of representation will be determined in accordance with the provisions of s.1 of the Act whereby references in the Act or any instrument made after the coming into force of s.1 to any relationship between two persons shall be construed without regard to whether or not the father or mother of either of them, or the father and mother of any person through whom the relationship is deduced, have or had been married to each other at any time, unless the contrary intention appears. Where the applicant is the spouse of the deceased the present terminology in use should continue to be adopted *i.e.* "the lawful widow/husband," but otherwise it will no longer be necessary to describe an applicant's relationship to the deceased as either "lawful" or "natural." When clearing off prior claims, there is no need to describe the same as either "lawful" or "natural."

By ss.18 and 21 of the Act presumptions are created whereby (i) a person whose father and mother were not married to each other at the time of his birth shall be presumed not to have been survived by his father or by any person related to him only through his father and (ii) a deceased person shall be presumed not to have been survived by any person related to him whose father and mother were not married to each other at the time of his birth or by any person whose relationship with him is deduced through such a person, unless the contrary is shown. The applicant's title, as sworn to in the oath, will be taken as sufficient to rebut any such presumption. Evidence of paternity will not be required except in exceptional circumstances.

The following tables set out the appropriate wording to be used in oaths:

Clearing of	Wording	
Spouse	Swear that deceased died: a bachelor a spinster a widower a widow a single man a single woman	
Children or other issue	without issue	
Parents	[or] parent	
Brother or sister and their issue	[or] brother or sister of the whole [or half] blood or their issue	or any other person entitled in priority to share in his [her] estate by virtue of any enactment
Grandparents	[or] grandparent	
Uncles and aunts and their issue	[or] uncle or aunt of the whole [or half] blood or their issue	

Applicant's relationship	Description	
Spouse	Lawful husband Lawful widow	and only person [now] entitled to the estate (if so)
Child*	son daughter	and only person [one of the persons] entitled to [share in] the estate
Grandchild* with stirpital interest	son/daughter of C.D. the son/daughter of the said deceased who died before the said deceased	and only person [one of the persons] (etc.)
Parent	mother/father	

* Adopted children or grandchildren should be described as "the lawful adopted son/daughter, etc." (*Practice Direction* (*Oath: Family Law Reform Act 1987: Entitlement to Grant*) [1988] 1 W.L.R. 610; [1988] 2 All E.R. 308).

"Persons having a beneficial interest in the estate" (para. (1))

6C-111   Section 46 of the Administration of Estates Act 1925 (as amended) indicates the order of classes having a beneficial interest in an intestate's estate. Where the date of death was on or after June 1, 1987 and the value of the net estate after permissible deductions (personal chattels, debts and incumbrances, Inheritance Tax, costs and fees) does not exceed £75,000 (£125,000 where the deceased left no issue) the whole is taken by the surviving spouse.

Where the date of death was on or after March 1, 1981, and the value of the net estate after permissible deductions does not exceed £40,000 (£85,000 where the deceased left no issue) the whole is taken by the surviving spouse. Lower figures are applicable in the case of earlier deaths.

The provisions as to distribution also apply to estate undisposed of by will. But in the case of death after 1952 a surviving spouse must set off against the fixed net sum any beneficial interest acquired under the will other than personal chattels specifically bequeathed.

Under the Family Law Reform Act 1969, s.14, illegitimate children of the deceased take the same interest on intestacy as his lawful children, and the parents of an illegitimate child take the same interest as if he had been born legitimate. These provisions apply where the death occurred on or after January 1, 1970.

"Personal representatives ... shall have the same right" (para. (4))

The effect is that where the size of the estate brings in the kin who share with a surviving spouse, the former are preferred to the personal representative of the latter. If in like circumstances kin and surviving spouse all die without extracting representation, the personal representative of the spouse has priority, unless the spouse's interest in the estate has been wholly satisfied.   **6C–112**

Order of priority for grant in pre-1926 cases

23. Where the deceased died before 1st January 1926, the person or persons entitled to a grant shall, subject to the provisions of any enactment, be determined in accordance with the principles and rules under which the court would have acted at the date of death.   **6C–113**

Right of assignee to a grant

24.—(1) Where all the persons entitled to the estate of the deceased (whether under a will or on intestacy) have assigned their whole interest in the estate to one or more persons, the assignee or assignees shall replace, in the order of priority for a grant of administration, the assignor or, if there are two or more assignors, the assignor with the highest priority.   **6C–114**

(2) Where there are two or more assignees, administration may be granted with the consent of the others to any one or more (not exceeding four) of them.

(3) In any case where administration is applied for by an assignee the original instrument of assignment shall be produced and a copy of the same lodged in the registry.

Assignment to minor: two grantees

Where a person has assigned his interest in the estate of a deceased to a person who is a minor, it is necessary for the grant to issue to two or more persons or to a trust corporation.   **6C–115**

Copy deed to be lodged

It is necessary to produce the original deed for inspection.   **6C–116**

Trustee as assignee

If the terms of a deed and the circumstances of the case permit, a trustee under a deed of arrangement may be able to establish title to a grant under this rule. Failing this he may apply for an order under the Supreme Court Act 1981, s.116, but in either event the grant—describing him as trustee under the deed—will be limited to such period as he shall remain the trustee of the property (*Registrar's Direction (Grant: Trustee in Bankruptcy)*, July 24, 1956).   **6C–117**

Note—For application for grant under s.116 of the S.C.A. 1981 see r.52, para. 6C–172.   **6C–118**

Joinder of administrator

25.—(1) A person entitled in priority to a grant of administration may, without leave, apply for a grant with a person entitled in a   **6C–119** lower degree, provided that there is no other person entitled in a higher degree to the person to be joined, unless every other such person has renounced.

(2) Subject to paragraph (3) below, an application for leave to join with a person entitled in priority to a grant of administration a person having no right or no immediate right thereto shall be made to a district judge or registrar, and shall be supported by an affidavit by the person entitled in priority, the consent of the person proposed to be joined as administrator and such other evidence as the district judge or registrar may direct.

(3) Unless a district judge or registrar otherwise directs, there may without any such application be joined with a person entitled in priority to administration—

      (a) any person who is nominated under paragraph (3) of rule 32 or paragraph (3) of rule 35;

      (b) a trust corporation.

Additional personal representatives

6C–120   26.—(1) An application under section 114(4) of the Act to add a personal representative shall be made to a district judge or registrar and shall be supported by an affidavit by the applicant, the consent of the person proposed to be added as personal representative and such other evidence as the district judge or registrar may require.

(2) On any such application the district judge or registrar may direct that a note shall be made on the original grant of the addition of a further personal representative, or he may impound or revoke the grant or make such other order as the circumstances of the case may require.

Grants where two or more persons entitled in same degree

6C–121   27.—(1) Subject to paragraphs (1A) (2) and (3) below, where, on an application for probate, power to apply for a like grant is to be reserved to such other of the executors as have not renounced probate, notice of the application shall be given to the executor or executors to whom power is to be reserved; and, unless the district judge or registrar otherwise directs, the oath shall state that such notice has been given.

(1A) Where power is to be reserved to executors who are partners in a firm, notice need not be given to them under paragraph (1) above if probate is applied for by another partner in that firm.

(2) Where power is to be reserved to partners of a firm, notice for the purposes of paragraph (1) above may be given to the partners by sending it to the firm at its principal or last known place of business.

(3) A district judge or registrar may dispense with the giving of notice under paragraph (1) above if he is satisfied that the giving of such a notice is impracticable or would result in unreasonable delay or expense.

(4) A grant of administration may be made to any person entitled thereto without notice to other persons entitled in the same degree.

(5) Unless a district judge or registrar otherwise directs, administration shall be granted to a person of full age entitled thereto in preference to a guardian of a minor, and to a living person entitled thereto in preference to the personal representative of a deceased person.

(6) A dispute between persons entitled to a grant in the same degree shall be brought by summons before a district judge or registrar.

(7) The issue of a summons under this rule in a registry shall be noted forthwith in the index of the pending grant applications.

(8) If the issue of a summons under this rule is known to the district judge or registrar, he shall not allow any grant to be sealed until such summons is finally disposed of.

Grants where two or more persons entitled in same degree

Where the appointment of executors of a will is that of the partners in a firm of **6C–122** solicitors without naming them and not all partners wish to apply for probate, it will be sufficient for the oath to recite that the applicant is/was a partner or that the applicants are/were partners (as the case may be) in the firm at the appropriate date.

Rule 27(1) of the Non-Contentious Probate Rules 1987 requires the oath to lead a grant of probate to recite that notice of the application has been given to executors to whom power is to be reserved. The oath must therefore contain a statement that notice of the application has been given to all the other partners at the relevant date but need not name them. The manner of giving such notice is a matter for the proving executors.

This direction applies only to those cases where partners in a firm of solicitors are appointed executors without naming them (Practice Direction (Executors) (Appointment of Firm of Solicitors), June 12, 1990).

Power reserved to non-proving executor

A new provision as contained in r.27 is that notice of an application for a grant of **6C–123** probate is to be given to any executor to whom power is reserved. The district judge or registrar may however dispense with the giving of such notice if he is satisfied that to do so is impracticable or would result in unreasonable delay or expense.

Accordingly, subject to the concession set out below, where application for probate is made on or after January 1 the oath should contain the following paragraph, completed as appropriate to the circumstances:—

"And I/we further make oath and say that notice of this application has been given to the executor(s) to whom power is to be reserved, save ... ."

Solicitors may wish to consult the district judge or registrar in advance of preparing their oaths to ascertain whether in the circumstances of the particular case the district judge or registrar would be prepared to dispense with notice. Such preliminary enquiry should be supported by a letter by the solicitors setting out the reasons why the district judge or registrar is being asked to dispense with the giving of notice. If no preliminary enquiry is made, and the case is one in which notice has not been given to any executor to whom power is to be reserved, the application for the grant must be accompanied by a similar letter.

The concession referred to above is that, subject to the discretion of the district judge or registrar to decide otherwise, applications may continue to be accepted for a period up to the end of March 1988 notwithstanding that the oath does not contain the above paragraph.

Practice Direction (Non-Contentious Probate Rules 1987) [1988] 1 W.L.R. 195; [1988] 1 All E.R. 192.

Exceptions to rules as to priority

28.—(1) Any person to whom a grant may or is required to be **6C–124** made under any enactment shall not be prevented from obtaining such a grant notwithstanding the operation of rules 20, 22, 25 or 27.

(2) Where the deceased died domiciled outside England and Wales rules20, 22, 25 or 27 shall not apply except in a case to which paragraph (3) of rule 30 applies.

"Grant made under any enactment"

6C–125   Grants of representation may, under certain statutory provisions, be made in favour of persons other than those set out in the normal rules as to priority. For example—

6C–126   *(a) Consular Conventions Act 1949* —Application by a consul for a grant of representation under a convention that has been concluded with his State in accordance with the provisions of the Consular Conventions Act 1949, and applied by an Order in Council, will be dealt with in common form, no order being required unless necessary to establish the right of the foreign national whom the consul desires to represent. It must be established, by the oath, that the applicant is consul of a country with which there is a convention which has been applied by an Order in Council; that the person on whose behalf the consul is applying is a national of the country in question, is not resident in England and Wales, is a person to whom a grant in respect of the estate in England and Wales may be made—showing the character in which he is entitled, and that no application has been made by the national or by a duly constituted attorney on his behalf. The grant will be to the consular officer by his official title, and to his successors in office, for the use and benefit of the national, and limited until further representation be granted. It must set out the national's title, in the same way as a grant to the attorney of a foreign national.

No guarantee by sureties is required. A minority or life interest does not necessitate a second grantee (*Registrar's Direction (Consular officer; Grant to)* January 31, 1952).

6C–127   *(b) Companies Act 1985* — Section 539 provides that in a winding-up by the Court the liquidator of a company is constituted a creditor of any deceased contributory and has the same priority as any other creditor.

Grants in respect of settled land

6C–128   29.—(1) In this rule "settled land" means land vested in the deceased which was settled prior to his death and not by his will, and which remained settled land notwithstanding his death.

(2) The person or persons entitled to a grant of administration limited to settled land shall be determined in accordance with the following order of priority—

    (i) the special executors in regard to settled land constituted by section 22 of the Administration of Estates Act 1925;

    (ii) the trustees of the settlement at the time of the application for the grant; and

    (iii) the personal representatives of the deceased.

(3) Where there is settled land and a grant is made in respect of the free estate only, the grant shall expressly exclude the settled land.

6C–129   *Note* —On application for a settled land grant before the will has been proved by the general executors or persons otherwise entitled, the applicants for the settled land grant must establish the validity of the documents offered for proof, identify them in the oath and "mark" them in the usual way.

Where the save and except grant is extracted first the will need not be marked by the applicants for the settled land grant.

Grants where deceased died domiciled outside England and Wales

6C–130   30.—(1) Subject to paragraph (3) below, where the deceased died domiciled outside England and Wales, a district judge or registrar may order that a grant, limited in such way as the district judge or registrar may direct, do issue to any of the following persons—

    (a) to the person entrusted with the administration of the estate by the court having jurisdiction at the place where the deceased died domiciled; or

    (b) where there is no person so entrusted, to the person beneficially entitled to the estate by the law of the place where the deceased died domiciled or, if there is more than one person so entitled, to such of them as the district judge or registrar may direct; or

    (c) if in the opinion of the district judge or registrar the circumstances so require, to such person as the district judge or registrar may direct.

(2) A grant made under paragraph (1)(a) or (b) above may be issued jointly with such person as the district judge or registrar may direct if the grant is required to be made to not less than two administrators.

(3) Without any order made under paragraph (1) above—

    (a) probate of any will which is admissible to proof may be granted—

        (i) if the will is in the English or Welsh language, to the executor named therein; or

        (ii) if the will describes the duties of a named person in terms sufficient to constitute him executor according to the tenor of the will, to that person; and

    (b) where the whole or substantially the whole of the estate in England and Wales consists of immovable property, a grant in respect of the whole estate may be made in accordance with the law which would have been applicable if the deceased had died domiciled in England and Wales.

6C–131

Note.—Applications in respect of a deceased person dying domiciled in a country in which to the district judge or registrar's knowledge a grant is required must be accompanied by an official copy of the grant, when an order will be made to the person entrusted. If there is no grant, a discretionary order may be made under r.29(c) if the circumstances justify it. Subject to the above, an affidavit of law stating that the person is "entitled to administer" will be accepted without further enquiry and an order made under r.29(b).

On application for an order for a grant under r.29, any affidavit of law should refer to the facts and state the law applicable, but this must be supported by adequate evidence (normally an affidavit, or statement in the oath, by the applicant) as to the facts themselves. (*Registrar's Direction (Foreign Law; Consolidation)* November 20, 1972).

Grants to attorneys

6C–132

31.—(1) Subject to paragraphs (2) and (3) below, the lawfully constituted attorney of a person entitled to a grant may apply for administration for the use and benefit of the donor, and such grant shall be limited until further representation be granted, or in such other way as the district judge or registrar may direct.

NON-CONTENTIOUS PROBATE

(2) Where the donor referred to in paragraph (1) above is an executor, notice of the application shall be given to any other executor unless such notice is dispensed with by the district judge or registrar.

(3) Where the donor referred to in paragraph (1) above is mentally incapable and the attorney is acting under an enduring power of attorney, the application shall be made in accordance with rule 35.

Enduring power of attorney

6C–133 1. The Enduring Powers of Attorney Act 1985 came into force on March 10, 1986. The Act provides that an enduring power of attorney, within the meaning of the Act, is not revoked by the subsequent mental incapacity of the donor, but once the donor has become incapable the rights of the attorney are limited until the power of attorney has been registered with the Court of Protection. Even a registered enduring power of attorney may confer only limited powers on the attorney, so that it will be necessary to ensure that the power covers an application for a grant.

2. Effect on grants made before March 10, 1986:—

  (a) If a sole, or sole surviving, grantee becomes mentally incapable his attorney under an enduring power of attorney is not able to continue the administration on behalf of the grantee in reliance on the power of attorney, whether or not it has been registered with the Court of Protection. Where the attorney subsequently applies for a grant in respect of any unadministered estate the grant to the donor should be lodged with the application for the grant and will be retained by the Court.

  (b) If one of two or more grantees becomes mentally incapable, the attorney under an enduring power of attorney of the incapable administrator similarly will not be able to continue the administration with the capable grantee(s). The grant in these circumstances should be revoked and a fresh grant will be needed to continue the administration.

  (c) Where a grant has issued to an attorney of a donor for the use and benefit of that donor and the donor becomes mentally incapable, the attorney will be able to continue with the administration, provided that the donor has also appointed the same attorney under a sufficient enduring power of attorney which has been registered with the Court of Protection, even if the power of attorney used on the grant application was a different power of attorney and it has been revoked by the donor's mental incapacity.

3. Applications for grants after March 10, 1986:—

  (a) Where the donor is mentally capable of managing his affairs, an application for a grant by an attorney may be made, as before, under r.31 of the Non-Contentious Probate Rules 1987 in reliance on a power of attorney which is not an enduring power of attorney. The existing practice and procedure will apply.

  (b) Where the donor is mentally capable of managing his affairs and the application for a grant is supported by a power of attorney which is in the form of an enduring power of attorney but which has not been registered with the Court of Protection the application may proceed under r.31 of the Non-Contentious Probate Rules 1987 and the existing practice and procedure will apply, save that the original power of attorney should normally be produced on the application. If a copy of the power of attorney certified in accordance with s.3 of the Powers of Attorney Act 1971 is lodged, instead of the original, the oath to lead to the grant should confirm that no application has been made to the Court of Protection for the registration of the enduring power of attorney.

  (c) Where the donor is mentally capable of managing his affairs and the application for the grant is supported by an enduring power of attorney which has been registered with the Court of Protection (the donor's incapacity being impending) it must be sworn in the oath to lead to the grant (and in the affidavit in support of any application for a direction under r.31(2) of the Non-Contentious Probate Rules 1987) that the donor is mentally capable of managing his affairs. The original power of attorney sealed by the Court of Protection should be produced on the application.

(d) Where the donor is mentally incapable of managing his affairs and the application for the grant is supported by an enduring power of attorney which has been registered with the Court of Protection it will not be apparent from the fact of registration whether the donor is mentally incapable or whether the incapacity is impending. It must be sworn in the oath to lead to the grant that the donor is mentally incapable of managing his affairs. No other evidence of mental incapacity will be called for. Notice of the application for the grant must be given to the Court of Protection as required by r.35(5) of the Non-Contentious Probate Rules 1987. The original power of attorney, sealed by the Court of Protection, should be produced on the application.

4. Unless there is a relevant restriction in the power of attorney, the limitation to be included in a grant issuing to an attorney under an enduring power of attorney should be "to AB the lawful attorney of CD for his use and benefit and until further representation be granted", whether the donor is capable and the application is made under r.31 of the Non-Contentious Probate Rules 1987 or whether the donor is mentally incapable and the application is made under r.35 of the Non-Contentious Probate Rules 1987.

(Practice Direction (Enduring Power of Attorney—Grants of Administration) [1986] 1 W.L.R. 419.)

Note —See also the Enduring Powers of Attorney (Prescribed Form) Regulations **6C–134** 1990 (S.I. 1990 No. 1376) set out in Section 6B at paras 6B–412 *et seq.*

Grants on behalf of minors

32.—(1) Where a person to whom a grant would otherwise be **6C–135** made is a minor, administration for his use and benefit, limited until he attains the age of eighteen years, shall, unless otherwise directed, and subject to paragraph (2) of this rule, be granted to;

    (a) a parent of the minor who has, or is deemed to have, parental responsibility for him in accordance with—

        (i) section 2(1), 2(2)or 4 of the Children Act 1989,

        (ii) paragraph 4 or 6 of Schedule 14 to that Act, or

        (iii) an adoption order within the meaning of section 12(1) of the Adoption Act 1976, or

    (aa) a person who has or is deemed to have parental responsibility for the minor by virtue of section 12(2) of the Children Act 1989 where the court has made a residence order under section 8 of that Act in respect to the minor in favour of that person; or

    (b) a guardian of the minor who is appointed, or deemed to have been appointed, in accordance with section 5 of the Children Act 1989 or in accordance with paragraph 12, 13 or 14 of Schedule 14 to that Act; or

    (c) a local authority which has, or is deemed to have, parental responsibility for the minor by virtue of section 33(3) of the Children Act 1989 where the court has made a care order under section 31(1)(a) of that Act in respect of the minor and the local authority is designated in that order.

provided that where the minor is sole executor and has no interest in the residuary estate of the deceased, administration for the use and benefit of the minor limited as aforesaid, shall, unless a district judge or registrar otherwise directs, be granted to the person entitled to the residuary estate.

(2) A district judge or registrar may by order appoint a person to obtain administration for the use and benefit of the minor, limited as aforesaid, in default of, or jointly with, or to the exclusion of, any person mentioned in paragraph (1) of this rule; and the person intended shall file an affidavit in support of his application to be appointed.

(3) Where there is only one person competent and willing to take a grant under the foregoing provisions of this rule, such person may, unless a district judge or registrar otherwise directs, nominate any fit and proper person to act jointly with him in taking the grant.

Practice Direction (Probate: Minor's Grants)

6C–136   The Non-Contentious Probate (Amendment) Rules 1991 (S.I. 1991 No. 1876) in force from October 14, 1991, amend r.32 of the Non-Contentious Probate Rules 1987 (S.I. 1987 No. 2024) which relates to grants on behalf of minors. The amendments are consequential upon the coming into effect of the Children Act 1989.

The evidence required in support of an application for such a grant in specified circumstances is as follows:

(1) Where the applicant is the mother of the child she must state in the oath that she is the mother of the minor.

(2) Where the applicant is the father of the child having parental responsibility under s.2(1) of the 1989 Act the oath must state that the applicant is the father of the minor and has parental responsibility under that provision.

(3) Where the applicant is the father of the child and has acquired parental responsibility as provided by s.4 of the 1989 Act the oath must state that he is the father of the minor and has parental responsibility "under an order" or "under a duly recorded parental responsibility agreement." A copy of the order or sealed copy of the agreement recorded in the principal registry of the Family Division under the Parental Responsibility Agreement (Amendment) Regulations 1994 (S.I. 1994 No. 3157) must be produced.

(4) Where the applicant is the father of the child and was not married to the mother at the time of the child's birth, but has parental responsibility in accordance with para. 4 or 6 of Sched.14 to the 1989 Act either (a) by virtue of an order under s.4(1) of the Family Law Reform Act 1987 or (b) by virtue of an order giving him custody or care and control of the child in force immediately before the commencement of Pts. I and II of the 1989 Act, the oath must state that he is the father of the minor and a parent having parental responsibility by virtue of such an order which was in force immediately before the commencement of the 1989 Act. A copy of the order must be produced in each instance.

(5) Where the applicant has parental responsibility by virtue of an adoption order the oath must state that he or she is the adopter or one of the adopters of the minor by an order made within the meaning of s.12 of the Adoption Act 1976. A copy of the order must be produced.

(6) Where the applicant is a guardian who has been appointed in accordance with s.5 of the 1989 Act the oath must state that he or she is a guardian of the minor having parental responsibility by virtue of (a) an order made under s.5 of the 1989 Act or (b) an appointment made by "AB, a parent having parental responsibility for the minor by will" (or "by deed" as appropriate) or (c) an appointment made by "CD, a duly appointed guardian having parental responsibility for the minor by will" (or "by deed" as appropriate). The order, will or deed must be produced (or, in the case of a proved will, an official copy), together with such further evidence as a district judge or registrar may require in the circumstances of a case. The date of death of the person making the appointment must be included in the oath as must the date of death of any other person upon whose death the appointment takes effect.

(7) An applicant who is a guardian of the child having parental responsibility by virtue of an appointment under the Guardianship of Minors Act 1971, the Sexual Offences Act 1956 or the High Court's inherent jurisdiction with respect to children which is deemed to be an appointment made and having effect under s.5 of the 1989 Act (by paras 12 and 13 of Sched.14 of the 1989 Act) must include such information in the oath. A copy of the order must be produced.

Practice Direction (Fam Div: Probate: Non-contentious Probate: Grant on Behalf of Minor)
[1991] 1 W.L.R. 1069; [1991] 4 All E.R. 562).

Child in care of local authority

Where the person to whom a grant would otherwise be granted is a minor who is **6C–137**
in the care of a local authority, that authority may apply for an order assigning it as
guardian of the minor for the purpose of taking the grant for the use and benefit of
the minor. The local authority will qualify as custodian trustee and hence as a trust
corporation where property devolves for the sole benefit of the minor (see the Public
Trustee (Custodian Trustee) Rules 1976 (S.I. 1976 No. 836) amending r.30 of the
Public Trustee Rules 1912 as substituted by the Public Trustee (Custodian Trustee)
Rules 1971 (S.I. 1971 No. 1894). Where the local authority does not so qualify as
custodian trustee and thereby as a trust corporation the application may be made for
the nominees of the local authority to be appointed guardian to take the grant for the
use and benefit of the minor. A copy of the resolution assuming parental rights under
s.5 of the Child Care Act 1980 or a copy of the care order should be lodged.

Ward of court

Where the minor is a ward of court the direction of the district judge or judge deal- **6C–138**
ing with the wardship is necessary before applying for the assignment of guardians for
the purpose of taking a grant for the use and benefit of the minor. This may involve a
formal application on notice to other parties to the wardship proceedings but if the
wardship proceedings are inactive the direction of the district judge to whom the case
is assigned should be sought informally.

Grants where a minor is a co-executor

33.—(1) Where a minor is appointed executor jointly with one or **6C–139**
more other executors, probate may be granted to the executor or
executors not under disability with power reserved to the minor
executor, and the minor executor shall be entitled to apply for
probate on attaining the age of 18 years.

(2) Administration for the use and benefit of a minor executor
until he attains the age of 18 years may be granted under rule 32 if,
and only if, the executors who are not under disability renounce or,
on being cited to accept or refuse a grant, fail to make an effective
application therefore.

Renunciation of the right of a minor to a grant

34.—(1) The right of a minor executor to probate on attaining the **6C–140**
age of 18 years may not be renounced by any person on his behalf.

(2) The right of a minor to administration may be renounced
only by a person appointed under paragraph (2) of rule 32, and authorised by the district judge or registrar to renounce on behalf of
the minor.

Grants in case of mental incapacity

35.—(1) Unless a district judge or registrar otherwise directs, no **6C–141**
grant shall be made under this rule unless all persons entitled in the
same degree as the incapable person referred to in paragraph (2)
below have been cleared off.

(2) Where a district judge or registrar is satisfied that a person
entitled to a grant is by reason of mental incapacity incapable of
managing his affairs, administration for his use and benefit, limited
until further representation be granted or in such other way as the

district judge or registrar may direct, may be granted in the following order of priority—

> (a) to the person authorised by the Court of Protection to apply for a grant;
>
> (b) where there is no person so authorised, to the lawful attorney of the incapable person acting under a registered enduring power of attorney;
>
> (c) where there is no such attorney entitled to act, or if the attorney shall renounce administration for the use and benefit of the incapable person, to the person entitled to the residuary estate of the deceased.

(3) Where a grant is required to be made to not less than two administrators, and there is only one person competent and willing to take a grant under the foregoing provisions of this rule, administration may, unless a district judge or registrar otherwise directs, be granted to such person jointly with any other person nominated by him.

(4) Notwithstanding the foregoing provisions of this rule, administration for the use and benefit of the incapable person may be granted to such other person as the district judge or registrar may by order direct.

(5) Unless the applicant is the person authorised in paragraph (2)(a) above, notice of an intended application under this rule shall be given to the Court of Protection.

Incapacity

6C–142   The effect of para. (1) is that it is not mandatory to clear off all persons entitled in the same degree as an incapable person before making a grant for his use and benefit because the district judge or registrar may in special circumstances prefer the person representing an incapable person to other persons entitled in the same degree who are not under disability.

Evidence of mental incapacity

6C–143   Where application is made for a grant of representation for the use and benefit of a person incapable of managing his own affairs, and the applicant is not a person authorised by the Court of Protection to apply, evidence of incapacity will be required.

When the incapable person is a patient who is resident in an institution, the district judge or registrar will normally accept a certificate from the Responsible Medical Officer in the following terms:—

[Name of institution]

[Name of patient]

I certify that:

1. The above-named patient, who is now resident in this institution, is in my opinion by reason of mental disorder incapable of managing and administering his property and affairs.

2. In my opinion the above named patient is unlikely to be fit to manage and administer his property and affairs within a period of three months

(Sgd.) ....

Date ....

Responsible Medical officer.

If the Responsible Medical Officer is unable to give such a certificate, the matter should be referred to the district judge or registrar for directions.

Evidence of the incapacity of a person not a resident patient may be given by a similar certificate by the patient's doctor certifying the period for which he has attended the patient and that, in his opinion the patient is incapable of managing his property and affairs and is unlikely to become capable within a period of three months. (*Practice Direction (PDAD: Representation: Mental Incapacity (No.2))* [1969] 1 W.L.R. 301; [1969] 1 All E.R. 494).

Grants to trust corporations and other corporate bodies

36.—(1) An application for a grant to a trust corporation shall be **6C–144** made through one of its officers, and such officer shall depose in the oath that the corporation is a trust corporation as defined by these Rules and that it has power to accept a grant.

(2) (a) Where the trust corporation is the holder of an official position, any officer whose name is included on a list filed with the senior district judge of persons authorised to make affidavits and sign documents on behalf of the office holder may act as the officer through whom the holder of that official position applies for the grant.

(b) In all other cases a certified copy of the resolution of the trust corporation authorising the officer to make the application shall be lodged, or it shall be deposed in the oath that such certified copy has been filed with the senior district judge, that the officer is therein identified by the position he holds, and that such resolution is still in force.

(3) A trust corporation may apply for administration otherwise than as a beneficiary or the attorney of some person, and on any such application there shall be lodged the consents of all persons entitled to a grant and of all persons interested in the residuary estate of the deceased save that the district judge or registrar may dispense with any such consents as aforesaid on such terms, if any, as he may think fit.

(4) (a) Subject to sub-paragraph (d) below, where a corporate body would, if an individual, be entitled to a grant but is not a trust corporation as defined by these Rules, administration for its use and benefit, limited until further representation be granted, may be made to its nominee or to its lawfully constituted attorney.

(b) A copy of the resolution appointing the nominee or the power of attorney (whichever is appropriate) shall be lodged, and such resolution or power of attorney shall be sealed by the corporate body, or be otherwise authenticated to the district judge's or registrar's satisfaction.

(c) The nominee or attorney shall depose in the oath that the corporate body is not a trust corporation as defined by these Rules.

(d) The provisions of paragraph (4)(a) above shall not apply where a corporate body is appointed executor jointly with an individual unless the right of the individual has been cleared off.

Note—A grant to a trust corporation acting as attorney for a foreign company will **6C–145** be limited "until further representations be granted". Where all persons entitled to administration are minors a grant may issue to a trust corporation on the consent of all persons qualified as statutory or testamentary guardians and of any other guardians already lawfully appointed of such minors. Where, of the persons entitled to an estate, some are minors, then on the renunciation and consent of those persons of full age a grant may issue to a trust corporation. In either case the grant is limited "until one of the minors applies for and obtains a grant".

Renunciation of probate and administration

6C–146 37.—(1) Renunciation of probate by an executor shall not operate as renunciation of any right which he may have to a grant of administration in some other capacity unless he expressly renounces such right.

(2) Unless a district judge or registrar otherwise directs, no person who has renounced administration in one capacity may obtain a grant thereof in some other capacity.

(2A) Renunciation of a probate or administration by members of a partnership—

    (a) may be affected, or

    (b) subject to paragraph (3) below, may be retracted by any two of them

with the authority of the others and any such renunciation or retraction shall recite such authority.

(3) A renunciation of probate or administration may be retracted at any time with the leave of a district judge or registrar; provided that only in exceptional circumstances may leave be given to an executor to retract a renunciation of probate after a grant has been made to some other person entitled in a lower degree.

(4) A direction or order giving leave under this rule may be made either by the registrar of a district probate registry where the renunciation is filed or by a district judge.

6C–147 *Note* —Where an executor is permitted to withdraw his renunciation and prove the will, the probate shall take effect without prejudice to the previous acts and dealings of any other personal representative who has previously taken a grant (Administration of Estates Act 1925, s.6).

Notice to Crown of intended application for grant

6C–148 38. In any case in which it appears that the Crown is or may be beneficially interested in the estate of a deceased person, notice of intended application for a grant shall be given by the applicant to the Treasury Solicitor, and the district judge or registrar may direct that no grant shall issue within 28 days after the notice has been given.

Resealing under Colonial Probates Acts 1892 and 1927

6C–149 39.—(1) An application under the Colonial Probates Acts 1892 and 1927 for the resealing of probate or administration granted by the court of a country to which those Acts apply may be made by the person to whom the grant was made or by any person authorised in writing to apply on his behalf.

(2) On any such application an Inland Revenue affidavit or account shall be lodged.

(3) Except by leave of a district judge or registrar, no grant shall be resealed unless it was made to such a person as is mentioned in sub-paragraph (a) or (b) of paragraph (1) of rule 30 or to a person to whom a grant could be made under sub-paragraph (a) of paragraph (3) of that rule.

(4) No limited or temporary grant shall be resealed except by leave of a district judge or registrar.

(5) Every grant lodged for resealing shall include a copy of any will to which the grant relates or shall be accompanied by a copy thereof certified as correct by or under the authority of the court by which the grant was made, and where the copy of the grant required to be deposited under subsection (1) of section 2 of the Colonial Probates Act 1892 does not include a copy of the will, a copy thereof shall be deposited in the registry before the grant is resealed.

(6) The district judge or registrar shall send notice of the resealing to the court which made the grant.

(7) Where notice is received in the Principal Registry of the resealing of a grant issued in England and Wales, notice of any amendment or revocation of the grant shall be sent to the court by which it was resealed.

Application

The countries and territories to which the Colonial Probates Act 1892, applies were **6C–150** specified in Sched.1 to the Colonial Probates Act Application Order 1965 (S.I. 1965 No. 1530). The Act now applies to the following:

Alberta, Antigua, Australian Capital Territory, Bahamas, Barbados, Belize (formerly British Honduras), Bermuda, Botswana (formerly Bechuanaland), British Antarctic Territory, British Columbia, British Solomon Islands Protectorate, British Sovereign Base Areas in Cyprus, Brunei, Cayman Islands, Christmas Island (Australian), Cocos (Keeling) Islands, Cyprus (Republic), Dominica, Falkland Islands Colony, Falkland Islands Dependencies, Fiji, Gambia, Ghana, Gibraltar, Gilbert Islands, Grenada, Guyana (formerly British Guiana), Hong Kong, Jamaica, Kenya, Lesotho (formerly Basutoland), Malawi, Malaysia, Manitoba, Montserrat, New Brunswick, New Guinea (Trust Territory), New South Wales, New Zealand, Newfoundland, Nigeria, Norfolk Island, Northern Territory of Australia, North-West Territories of Canada, Nova Scotia, Ontario, Papua, Prince Edward Island, Queensland, St. Christopher, Nevis and Anguilla, St. Helena, St. Lucia, St. Vincent, Saskatchewan, Seychelles, Sierra Leone, Singapore, South Africa, South Australia, Sri Lanka (formerly Ceylon), Swaziland, Tanzania, Tasmania, Tortola (formerly Virgin Islands), Trinidad and Tobago, Turks and Caicos Islands, Tuvalu (formerly Ellice Islands), Uganda, Victoria, Western Australia, Zambia, Zimbabwe.

Authorised in writing (para. (1))

If a power of attorney is not lodged with the application, anything in writing **6C–151** indicating that the grantee would wish to have the grant resealed will normally suffice.

Para. (4)

A colonial grant expressly limited to estate within the jurisdiction of the issuing **6C–152** Court will not be resealed (*Registrar's Direction (Resealing, Limited Colonial Grant)* July 16, 1951).

Application for leave to sue on guarantee

40. An application for leave under section 120(3) of the Act or **6C–153** under section 11(5) of the Administration of Estates Act 1971 to sue a surety on a guarantee given for the purposes of either of those sections shall, unless the district judge or registrar otherwise directs

under rule 61, be made by summons to a district judge or registrar and notice of the application shall be served on the administrator, the surety and any co-surety.

Amendment and revocation of grant

6C–154 41.—(1) Subject to paragraph (2) below, if a district judge or registrar is satisfied that a grant should be amended or revoked he may make an order accordingly.

(2) Except on the application or with the consent of the person to whom the grant was made, the power conferred in paragraph (1) above shall be exercised only in exceptional circumstances.

Certificate of delivery of Inland Revenue affidavit

6C–155 42. Where the deceased died before 13th March 1975 the certificate of delivery of an Inland Revenue affidavit required by section 30 of the Customs and Inland Revenue Act 1881 to be borne by every grant shall be in Form 1.

Standing searches

6C–156 43.—(1) Any person who wishes to be notified of the issue of a grant may enter a standing search for the grant by lodging at, or sending by post to, any registry or sub-registry, a notice in Form 2.

(2) A person who has entered a standing search will be sent an office copy of any grant which corresponds with the particulars given on the completed Form 2 and which—

    (a) issued not more than twelve months before the entry of the standing search; or

    (b) issues within a period of six months after the entry of the standing search.

    (3) (a) Where an applicant wishes to extend the said period of six months, he or his solicitor or probate practitioner may lodge at, or send by post to, the registry or sub-registry at which the standing search was entered written application for extension.

    (b) An application for extension as aforesaid must be lodged, or received by post, within the last month of the said period of six months, and the standing search shall thereupon be effective for an additional period of six months from the date on which it was due to expire.

    (c) A standing search which has been extended as above may be further extended by the filing of a further application for extension subject to the same conditions as set out in sub-paragraph (b) above.

6C–156.1 *Note* —See Practice Direction, January 1, 1999.

Caveats

6C–157 44.—(1) Any person who wishes to show cause against the sealing of a grant may enter a caveat in any registry or sub-registry, and the district judge or registrar shall not allow any grant to be sealed (other than a grant *ad colligenda bona* or a grant under section 117 of the Act) if he has knowledge of an effective caveat; provided that no caveat shall prevent the sealing of a grant on the day on which the caveat is entered.

(2) Any person wishing to enter a caveat (in these Rules called "the caveator"), or a solicitor or probate practitioner on his behalf, may effect entry of a caveat—

> (a) by completing Form 3 in the appropriate book at any registry or sub-registry; or
>
> (b) by sending by post at his own risk a notice in Form 3 to any registry or sub-registry and the proper officer shall provide an acknowledgement of the entry of the caveat.

(3) (a) Except as otherwise provided by this rule or by rules 45 or 46, a caveat shall be effective for a period of six months from the date of entry thereof, and where a caveator wishes to extend the said period of six months, he or his solicitor or probate practitioner may lodge at, or send by post to, the registry or sub-registry at which the caveat was entered a written application for extension.

> (b) An application for extension as aforesaid must be lodged, or received by post, within the last month of the said period of six months, and the caveat shall thereupon (save as otherwise provided by this rule) be effective for an additional period of six months from the date on which it was due to expire.
>
> (c) A caveat which has been extended as above may be further extended by the filing of a further application for extension subject to the same conditions as set out in sub-paragraph (b) above.

(4) An index of caveats entered in any registry or sub-registry shall be maintained and upon receipt of an application for a grant, the registry or sub-registry at which the application is made shall cause a search of the index to be made and the appropriate district judge or registrar shall be notified of the entry of a caveat against the sealing of a grant for which the application has been made.

(5) Any person claiming to have an interest in the estate may cause to be issued from the nominated registry a warning in Form 4 against the caveat, and the person warning shall state his interest in the estate of the deceased and shall require the caveator to give particulars of any contrary interest in the estate; and the warning or a copy thereof shall be served on a caveator forthwith.

(6) A caveator who has no interest contrary to that of the person warning, but who wishes to show cause against the sealing of a grant to that person, may within eight days of service of the warning upon him (inclusive of the day of such service), or at any time thereafter if no affidavit has been filed under paragraph (12) below, issue and serve a summons for directions.

(7) On the hearing of any summons for directions under paragraph (6) above the district judge or registrar may give a direction for the caveat to cease to have effect.

(8) Any caveat in force when a summons for directions is issued shall remain in force until the summons has been disposed of unless a direction has been given under paragraph (7) above or until it is withdrawn under paragraph (11) below.

(9) The issue of a summons under this rule shall be notified forthwith to the nominated registry.

(10) A caveator having an interest contrary to that of the person warning may within eight days of service of the warning upon him (inclusive of the day of such service) or at any time thereafter if no affidavit has been filed under paragraph (12) below, enter an appearance in the nominated registry by filing Form 5; and he shall serve forthwith on the person warning a copy of Form 5 sealed with the seal of the court.

(11) A caveator who has not entered an appearance to a warning may at any time withdraw his caveat by giving notice at the registry or sub-registry at which it was entered, and the caveat shall thereupon cease to have effect; and, where the caveat has been so withdrawn, the caveator shall forthwith give notice of withdrawal to the person warning.

(12) If no appearance has been entered by the caveator or no summons has been issued by him under paragraph (6) of this rule, the person warning may at any time after eight days of service of the warning upon the caveator (inclusive of the day of such service) file an affidavit in the nominated registry as to such service and the caveat shall thereupon cease to have effect provided that there is no pending summons under paragraph (6) of this rule.

(13) Unless a district judge or, where application to discontinue a caveat is made by consent, a registrar by order made on summons otherwise directs, any caveat in respect of which an appearance to a warning has been entered shall remain in force until the commencement of a probate action.

(14) Except with the leave of a district judge, no further caveat may be entered by or on behalf of a caveator whose caveat is either in force or has ceased to have effect under paragraphs (7) or (12) of this rule or under rule 45(4) or rule 46(3).

(15) In this rule "nominated registry" means the registry nominated for the purpose of this rule by the senior district judge or in the absence of any such nomination the Leeds District Probate Registry.

6C–157.1   *Note* —See Practice Direction, January 12, 1999.

Warnings and Appearances

6C–158   *1. Warnings* —As from August 1, 1988 the index of caveats will be moved from the Principal Registry to the Leeds District Probate Registry, 3rd Floor, Coronet House, Queen Street, Leeds LS1 2BA, DX 26451 Leeds Park Square, and as a consequence warnings to caveats under Rule 44(5) of the Non-Contentious Probate Rules 1987 will, from that date, be issued only on lodging Form 4 in the Appendix to the Rules either personally, through the post or through the document exchange at Leeds District Probate Registry.

6C–159   *2. Appearance to warning* —Appearances to warnings may, from August 1, 1988, be entered only at Leeds District Probate Registry at the address above. Rule 44(10) of the Non-Contentious Probate Rules 1987 requires the person entering an appearance to make an entry in the appropriate book and accordingly personal attendance is necessary.

3. Removal of Caveat —If no appearance is entered by the caveator and no sum- **6C–160** mons has been issued by him under r.44(6) of the Non-Contentious Probate Rules 1987 the caveat will cease to have effect if the person warning files an affidavit under r.44(12) in the Leeds District Probate Registry (*Registrar's Direction (Warnings and appearances)* July 12, 1988).

Probate actions

45.—(1) Upon being advised by the court concerned of the com- **6C–161** mencement of a probate action the senior district judge shall give notice of the action to every caveator other than the plaintiff in the action in respect of each caveat that is in force.

(2) In respect of any caveat entered subsequent to the commencement of a probate action the senior district judge shall give notice to that caveator of the existence of the action.

(3) Unless a district judge by order made on summons otherwise directs, the commencement of a probate action shall operate to prevent the sealing of a grant (other than a grant under section 117 of the Act) until application for a grant is made by the person shown to be entitled thereto by the decision of the court in such action.

(4) Upon such application for a grant, any caveat entered by the plaintiff in the action, and any caveat in respect of which notice of the action has been given, shall cease to have effect.

Citations

46.—(1) Any citation may issue from the Principal Registry or a **6C–162** district probate registry and shall be settled by a district judge or registrar before being used.

(2) Every averment in a citation, and such other information as the district judge or registrar may require, shall be verified by an affidavit sworn by the person issuing the citation (in these Rules called the "citor"), provided that the district judge or registrar may in special circumstances accept an affidavit sworn by the citor's solicitor or probate practitioner.

(3) The citor shall enter a caveat before issuing a citation and, unless a district judge by order made on summons otherwise directs, any caveat in force at the commencement of the citation proceedings shall, unless withdrawn pursuant to paragraph (11) of rule 44, remain in force until application for a grant is made by the person shown to be entitled thereto by the decision of the court in such proceedings, and upon such application any caveat entered by a party who had notice of the proceedings shall cease to have effect.

(4) Every citation shall be served personally on the person cited unless the district judge or registrar, on cause shown by affidavit, directs some other mode of service, which may include notice by advertisement.

(5) Every will referred to in a citation shall be lodged in a registry

before the citation is issued, except where the will is not in the citor's possession and the district judge or registrar is satisfied that it is impracticable to require it to be lodged.

(6) A person who has been cited to appear may, within eight days of service of the citation upon him (inclusive of the day of such service), or at any time thereafter if no application has been made by the citor under paragraph (5) of rule 47 or paragraph (2) of rule 48, enter an appearance in the registry from which the citation issued by filing Form 5 and shall forthwith thereafter serve on the citor a copy of Form 5 sealed with the seal of a registry.

Citations: acceptance by post

6C–163   The Principal Registry will accept applications for the issue of citations by post.

The procedure which should be adopted for the issue of probate citations by post is as follows:

1. Drafts of the citation and supporting affidavit should be sent for the citation to be settled to the Receiver of Papers, Principal Registry of the Family Division, First Avenue House, 42–49 High Holborn, London WC1V 6NP together with a photographic copy of any relevant will and codicil or the originals thereof. In the event of originals being sent registered post should be used and the Registry will retain them unless their return is requested or necessary by reason of the intention to exhibit them to the affidavit.

2. After the citation has been settled the papers (but not original wills and codicils except in the circumstances set out in (1)) will be returned to the solicitor who should then, if he has not already done so, enter a caveat (by post to any Probate Registry with fee £4 payable to "H.M. Paymaster General" (H.M.P.G. is acceptable) if entered in the Principal Registry or to the District Registrar if entered elsewhere). The solicitor should return to the Principal Registry the settled draft citation, an engrossment of the citation, the sworn affidavit, any relevant original wills and codicil in the solicitor's possession at this stage and the receipt for entry of caveat. A cheque for £5, made payable to "H.M.P.G." should also be sent.

3. The engrossed citation will be returned to the solicitor after signature by the District Judge and sealing. The receipt for caveat will be returned at the same time.

4. After the citation has been served the necessary procedure to be followed, which involves amongst other matters the entry of an appearance by the citee or, in default, search of the appearance book by the citor must be carried out by personal attendance of the solicitor (*Registrar's Practice Direction (Citation; Acceptance by Post)* July 25, 1969 with revised fees).

Citation to accept or refuse or to take a grant

6C–164   47.—(1) A citation to accept or refuse a grant may be issued at the instance of any person who would himself be entitled to a grant in the event of the person cited renouncing his right thereto.

(2) Where power to make a grant to an executor has been reserved, a citation calling on him to accept or refuse a grant may be issued at the instance of the executors who have proved the will or the survivor of them or of the executors of the last survivor of deceased executors who have proved.

(3) A citation calling on an executor who has intermeddled in the estate of the deceased to show cause why he should not be ordered to take a grant may be issued at the instance of any person interested in the estate at any time after the expiration of six months from the death of the deceased, provided that no citation to take a grant shall issue while proceedings as to the validity of the will are pending.

(4) A person cited who is willing to accept or take a grant may, af-

ter entering an appearance, apply ex parte by affidavit to a district judge or registrar for an order for a grant to himself.

(5) If the time limited for appearance has expired and the person cited has not entered an appearance, the citor may—

    (a) in the case of a citation under paragraph (1) of this rule, apply to a district judge or registrar for an order for a grant to himself;

    (b) in the case of a citation under paragraph (2) of this rule, apply to a district judge or registrar for an order that a note be made on the grant that the executor in respect of whom power was reserved has been duly cited and has not appeared and that all his rights in respect of the executorship have wholly ceased; or

    (c) in the case of a citation under paragraph (3) of this rule, apply to a district judge or registrar by summons (which shall be served on the person cited) for an order requiring such person to take a grant within a specified time or for a grant to himself or to some other person specified in the summons.

(6) An application under the last foregoing paragraph shall be supported by an affidavit showing that the citation was duly served.

(7) If the person cited has entered an appearance but has not applied for a grant under paragraph (4) of this rule, or has failed to prosecute his application with reasonable diligence, the citor may—

    (a) in the case of a citation under paragraph (1) of this rule, apply by summons to a district judge or registrar for an order for a grant to himself;

    (b) in the case of a citation under paragraph (2) of this rule, apply by summons to a district judge or registrar for an order striking out the appearance and for the endorsement on the grant of such a note as is mentioned in sub-paragraph (b) of paragraph (5) of this rule; or

    (c) in the case of a citation under paragraph (3) of this rule, apply by summons to a district judge or registrar for an order requiring the person cited to take a grant within a specified time or for a grant to himself or to some other person specified in the summons;

and the summons shall be served on the person cited.

Citation to propound a will

48.—(1) A citation to propound a will shall be directed to the **6C–165** executors named in the will and to all persons interested thereunder, and may be issued at the instance of any citor having an interest contrary to that of the executors or such other persons.

(2) If the time limited for appearance has expired, the citor may—

    (a) in the case where no person has entered an appearance, apply to a district judge or registrar for an order for a grant as if the will were invalid and such application shall be supported by an affidavit showing that the citation was duly served; or

(b) in the case where no person who has entered an appearance proceeds with reasonable diligence to propound the will, apply to a district judge or registrar by summons, which shall be served on every person cited who has entered an appearance, for such an order as is mentioned in paragraph (a) above.

6C–166   *Note* —This procedure is not appropriate after probate has been granted in common form (*Re Jolly (dec'd), Jolley v. Jarvis* [1964] P. 262).

Address for service
6C–167   49. All caveats, citations, warnings and appearances shall contain an address for service in England and Wales.

Application for order to attend for examination or for subpoena to bring in a will
6C–168   50.—(1) An application under section 122 of the Act for an order requiring a person to attend for examination may, unless a probate action has been commenced, be made to a district judge or registrar by summons which shall be served on every such person as aforesaid.

(2) An application under section 123 of the Act for the issue by a district judge or registrar of a subpoena to bring in a will shall be supported by an affidavit setting out the grounds of the application, and if any person served with the subpoena denies that the will is in his possession or control he may file an affidavit to that effect in the registry from which the subpoena issued.

Subpoena to bring in will and order to attend for examination
6C–169   It should be noted that by r.50(2) a person to whom a subpoena to bring in a will is directed *may*, if the will is not in his possession or control, file an affidavit to that effect. The filing of such an affidavit in the circumstances mentioned is not mandatory. Accordingly, if the will is not lodged and no affidavit has been filed, the applicant will remain uncertain whether the person to whom the subpoena was directed is in contempt of court. In these circumstances, rather than issue committal proceedings against the person, it is better to require his attendance for examination by order, under s.122 of the Supreme Court Act 1981.

Where a probate action is pending application under either section is made in the Chancery Division under RSC O.76, r.14.

Grants to part of an estate under section 113 of the Act
6C–170   51. An application for an order for a grant under section 113 of the Act to part of an estate may be made to a district judge or registrar, and shall be supported by an affidavit setting out the grounds of the application, and
(a) stating whether the estate of the deceased is known to be insolvent; and
(b) showing how any person entitled to a grant in respect of the whole estate in priority to the applicant has been cleared off.

Trust estate only (para. (a))
6C–171   Section 2 of the Administration of Justice Act 1932 permitted the issue of a grant where the deceased left no estate. That section was repealed by the Supreme Court

Act 1981 but by *ibid.*, s.25 the Court retains all such jurisdiction as it had prior thereto. Where there is no estate other than trust property the practice is to make a *nil* grant without limitation and no order is necessary unless to pass over persons with a prior right who will not renounce.

Grants of administration under discretionary powers of court, and grants ad colligenda bona

52. An application for an order for— 6C–172

 (a) a grant of administration under section 116 of the Act; or

 (b) a grant of administration ad colligenda bona,

may be made to a district judge or registrar and shall be supported by an affidavit setting out the grounds of the application.

Orders for ad colligenda grants to the Treasury Solicitor and to the Solicitor for the Duchy of Lancaster

In cases where it is not known whether there are kin of a deceased person entitled 6C–173
to take administration of his estate and the Treasury Solicitor or the Solicitor for the Duchy of Lancaster is of opinion that representation should be granted for the preservation of the estate or for other sufficient reason, he may apply for an order for a grant.

Applications for leave to swear to death

53. An application for leave to swear to the death of a person in 6C–174
whose estate a grant is sought may be made to a district judge or registrar, and shall be supported by an affidavit setting out the grounds of the application and containing particulars of any policies of insurance effected on the life of the presumed deceased together with such further evidence as the district judge or registrar may require.

Grants in respect of nuncupative wills and copies of wills

54.—(1) Subject to paragraph (2) below, an application for an or- 6C–175
der admitting to proof a nuncupative will, or a will contained in a copy or reconstruction thereof where the original is not available, shall be made to a district judge or registrar.

(2) In any case where a will is not available owing to its being retained in the custody of a foreign court or official, a duly authenticated copy of the will may be admitted to proof without the order referred to in paragraph (1) above.

(3) An application under paragraph (1) above shall be supported by an affidavit setting out the grounds of the application, and by such evidence on affidavit as the applicant can adduce as to—

 (a) the will's existence after the death of the testator or, where there is no such evidence, the facts on which the applicant relies to rebut the presumption that the will has been revoked by destruction;

 (b) in respect of a nuncupative will, the contents of that will; and

 (c) in respect of a reconstruction of a will; the accuracy of that reconstruction.

(4) The district judge or registrar may require additional evidence in the circumstances of a particular case as to due execution of the will or as to the accuracy of the copy will, and may direct that notice be given to persons who would be prejudiced by the application.

Applications for rectification of a will

6C–176 55.—(1) An application for an order that a will be rectified by virtue of section 20(1) of the Administration of Justice Act 1982 may be made to a district judge or registrar, unless a probate action has been commenced.

(2) The application shall be supported by an affidavit, setting out the grounds of the application, together with such evidence as can be adduced as to the testator's intentions and as to whichever of the following matters as are in issue:—

> (a) in what respects the testator's intentions were not understood; or
> (b) the nature of any alleged clerical error.

(3) Unless otherwise directed, notice of the application shall be given to every person having an interest under the will whose interest might be prejudiced or such other person who might be prejudiced by the rectification applied for and any comments in writing by any such person shall be exhibited to the affidavit in support of the application.

(4) If the district judge or registrar is satisfied that, subject to any direction to the contrary, notice has been given to every person mentioned in paragraph (3) above, and that the application is unopposed, he may order that the will be rectified accordingly.

Application for rectification of a will

6C–177 See (1985) 82 L.S.Gaz. 595, for an article by Chief Chancery Master and Senior Registrar of Family Division in the following terms:

> "By section 20 of the Administration of Justice Act 1982, if a court is satisfied that a will is so expressed that it fails to carry out the testator's intentions, in consequence (a) of a clerical error, or (b) of a failure to understand his instructions, it may order that the will be rectified so as to carry out his intentions.
>
> After the end of the period of six months from the date on which representation to the estate of the deceased is first taken out, an application for an order under this section cannot be made except with the permission of the court.
>
> Proceedings under the Act may be taken by writ, originating summons or by counterclaim in a probate action. RSC O.76, r.16 provides that where an application is made for rectification of a will and probate has already been granted, the grant of probate must be lodged at Room 157, Royal Courts of Justice, in accordance with O.76, r.4.
>
> There is also provision for rectification in the Non-Contentious Probate Rules 1987, r.55. An application may be made under these rules to a registrar of the Principal Registry, Family Division or to a district probate registrar unless a probate action has been commenced. The application must be supported by an affidavit setting out the grounds of the application together with such evidence as can be adduced as to the testator's intentions and whichever of the following matters are in issue:
>
> > (a) in what respects the testator's intentions were not understood; or
> > (b) the nature of any alleged clerical error.
>
> Unless otherwise directed, notice of the application must be given to every person having an interest under the will whose interest might be prejudiced by the rectification applied for. Any comments in writing by any such persons are to

be exhibited to the affidavit in support of the application. If the registrar is satisfied from the evidence that the application is unopposed he may order the will to be rectified but if it is opposed, proceedings must be commenced in the Chancery Division. Where a question of construction arises the application for rectification, whether opposed or not, should be made to the Chancery Division.

It appears that in many cases the need for rectification arises owing to a typing mistake or a clerical error made by the solicitors, and where the application is unopposed the best course is to apply to a registrar of the Principal Registry, the Family Division or a district probate registrar, for rectification. Applications under (a) and (b) above can be made either before or after probate has been granted."

E. R. Heward, Chief Chancery Master; B.P. Tickle, Senior Registrar, Family Division.

Rectification

The failure by the draftsman of a will to incorporate a clause exercising a power of appointment, as a result of inadvertence rather than a misunderstanding of his instructions, was a clerical error within the meaning of s.20(1)(a) of the Administration of Justice Act 1982 and was a ground for the rectification of the will (*Wordingham v. Royal Exchange Trust Co. Ltd, The Times*, December 11, 1991). **6C–178**

Notice of election by surviving spouse to redeem life interest

56.—(1) Where a surviving spouse who is the sole or sole surviving personal representative of the deceased is entitled to a life interest in part of the residuary estate and elects under section 47A of the Administration of Estates Act 1925 to have the life interest redeemed, he may give written notice of the election to the senior district judge in pursuance of subsection (7) of that section by filing a notice in Form 6 in the Principal Registry or in the district probate registry from which the grant issued. **6C–179**

(2) Where the grant issued from a district probate registry, the notice shall be filed in duplicate.

(3) A notice filed under this rule shall be noted on the grant and the record and shall be open to inspection.

Index of grant applications

57.—(1) The senior district judge shall maintain an index of every pending application for a grant made in any registry or sub-registry. **6C–180**

(2) Every registry or sub-registry in which application is made shall cause the index to be searched and shall record the result of the search.

Inspection of copies of original wills and other documents

58. An original will or other document referred to in section 124 of the Act shall not be open to inspection if, in the opinion of a district judge or registrar, such inspection would be undesirable or otherwise inappropriate. **6C–181**

Issue of copies of original wills and other documents

59. Where copies are required of original wills or other documents deposited under section 124 of the Act, such copies may be facsimile copies sealed with the seal of the court and issued either as **6C–182**

office copies or certified under the hand of a district judge or registrar to be true copies.

Costs

6C–183   60.—(1) Order 62 of the Rules of the Supreme Court 1965 (a) shall not apply to costs in non-contentious probate matters, and Parts 43, 44 (except rules 44.9 to 44.12), 47 and 48 of the Civil Procedure Rules 1998 (b) ("the 1998 Rules") shall apply to costs in those matters, with the modifications contained in paragraphs (3) to (7) of this rule.

(2) Where detailed assessment of a bill of costs is ordered, it shall be referred—

(a) where the order was made by a district judge, to a district judge, a costs judge or an authorised court officer within rule 43.2(1)(d)(iii) or (iv) of the 1998 Rules;

(b) where the order was made by a registrar, to that registrar or, where this is not possible, in accordance with sub-paragraph (a) above.

(3) Every reference in Parts 43, 44, 47 and 48 of the 1998 Rules to a district judge shall be construed as referring only to a district judge of the Principal Registry.

(4) The definition of "costs officer" in rule 43.2(1)(c) of the 1998 Rules shall have effect as if it included a paragraph reading—"(iv) a district probate registrar."

(5) The definition of "authorised court officer" in rule 43.2(1)(d) of the 1998 Rules shall have effect as if paragraphs (i) and (ii) were omitted.

(6) Rule 44.3(2) of the 1998 Rules (costs follow the event) shall not apply.

(7) Rule 47.4(2) of the 1998 Rules shall apply as if after the words "Supreme Court Costs Office" there were inserted ", the Principal Registry of the Family Division or such district probate registry as the court may specify".

(8) Except in the case of an appeal against a decision of an authorised court officer (to which rules 47.20 to 47.23 of the 1998 Rules apply), an appeal against a decision in assessment proceedings relating to costs in non-contentious probate matters shall be dealt with in accordance with the following paragraphs of this rule.

(9) An appeal within paragraph (8) above against a decision made by a district judge, a costs judge (as defined by rule 43.2(1)(b) of the 1998 Rules) or a registrar, shall lie to a judge of the High Court.

(10) Part 52 of the 1998 Rules applies to every appeal within paragraph (8) above, and any reference in Part 52 to a judge or a district judge shall be taken to include a district judge of the Principal Registry of the Family Division.

(11) The 1998 Rules shall apply to an appeal to which Part 52 or rules 47.20 to 47.23 of those Rules apply in accordance with paragraph (8) above in the same way as they apply to any other appeal within Part 52 or rules 47.20 to 47.23 of those Rules as the case

may be; accordingly the Rules of the Supreme Court 1965 and the County Court Rules 1981 shall not apply to any such appeal.".

Power to require applications to be made by summons

61.—(1) Subject to rule 7(2), a district judge or registrar may require any application to be made by summons to a district judge or registrar in chambers or a judge in chambers or open court. **6C–184**

(2) An application for an inventory and account shall be made by summons to a district judge or registrar.

(3) A summons for hearing by a district judge or registrar shall be issued out of the registry in which it is to be heard.

(4) A summons to be heard by a judge shall be issued out of the Principal Registry.

Will, omission of words from probate

Contested applications for omission of words from probate should be made by summons to a district judge of the Principal Registry. **6C–185**

Uncontested applications for the omission of words should be made to the registrar of the Probate Registry at which it is proposed to make application for the grant. Any such application should be made *ex parte* by lodging with the registrar affidavit evidence (exhibiting the will or codicil in question) together with any consents in writing of persons not under disability who might be prejudiced by the order. If the registrar is satisfied on the facts, and in the absence of consent, that there is no substantial interest unprotected, he will make the order.

A registrar may require an application for the omission of words from probate to be made by summons to a judge.

A copy of any order to omit words from probate should be lodged with the application for the grant and will be annexed to the original will and filed therewith. A typewritten copy of the will, omitting such part, should be lodged at the Registry for the *fiat* of the Principal or the District Registrar to be written in the margin before photography.

(President's Direction [1968] 1 W.L.R. 987; [1968] 2 All E.R. 592).

Transfer of applications

62. A district judge or registrar to whom any application is made under these Rules may order the transfer of the application to another district judge or registrar having jurisdiction. **6C–186**

Exercise of a registrar's jurisdiction

62A. A registrar may hear and dispose of an application under these Rules on behalf of any other registrar by whom the application would otherwise have been heard, if that other registrar so requests or an application in that behalf is made by a party making an application under these Rules; and where the circumstances require it, the registrar shall, without the need for any request or application, hear and dispose of the application. **6C–187**

Power to make orders for costs

63. On any application dealt with by him on summons, the registrar shall have full power to determine by whom and to what extent the costs are to be paid. **6C–188**

Exercise of powers of judge during Long Vacation

64. All powers exercisable under these Rules by a judge in **6C–189**

chambers may be exercised during the Long Vacation by a district judge.

Appeals from district judges or registrars

6C–190   65.—(1) An appeal against a decision or requirement of a district judge or registrar shall be made by summons to a judge.

(2) If, in the case of an appeal under the last foregoing paragraph, any person besides the appellant appeared or was represented before the district judge or registrar from whose decision or requirement the appeal is brought, the summons shall be issued within seven days thereof for hearing on the first available day and shall be served on every such person aforesaid.

(3) This Rule does not apply to an appeal against a decision in proceedings for the assessment of costs.

Service of summons

6C–191   66.—(1) A judge or district judge or, where the application is to be made to a district probate registrar, that registrar, may direct that a summons for the service of which no other provision is made by these Rules shall be served on such person or persons as the judge, district judge or registrar may direct.

(2) Where by these Rules or by any direction given under the last foregoing paragraph a summons is required to be served on any person, it shall be served not less than two clear days before the day appointed for the hearing, unless a judge, district judge or registrar at or before the hearing dispenses with service on such terms, if any, as he may think fit.

Notices, etc.

6C–192   67. Unless a district judge or registrar otherwise directs or these Rules otherwise provide, any notice or other document required to be given to or served on any person may be given or served in the manner prescribed by Order 65 Rule 5 of the Rules of the Supreme Court 1965.

Application to pending proceedings

6C–193   68. Subject in any particular case to any direction given by a judge, district judge or registrar, these Rules shall apply to any proceedings which are pending on the date on which they come into force as well as to any proceedings commenced on or after that date.

Revocation of previous rules

6C–194   69.—(1) Subject to paragraph (2) below, the rules set out in the Second Schedule are hereby revoked.

(2) The rules set out in the Second Schedule shall continue to apply to such extent as may be necessary for giving effect to a direction under rule 68.

FIRST SCHEDULE

FORMS

Form 1

6C–195

Rule 42   **Certificate of Delivery of Inland Revenue Affidavit**

And it is hereby certified that an Inland Revenue affidavit has been delivered wherein it is shown that the gross value of the said estate in the United Kingdom (exclusive of what the said deceased may have been possessed of or entitled to as a trustee and not beneficially) amount to £................and that the net value of the estate amounts to £...............
   And it is further certified that it appears by a receipt signed by an Inland Revenue officer on the said affidavit that £............... on account of estate duty and interest on such duty has been paid.

Form 2

6C–196

Rule 43(1)   **Standing Search**

In the High Court of Justice

Family Division

The Principal [or .... District probate] Registry

I/We apply for the entry of a standing search so that there shall be sent to me/us an office copy of every grant of representation in England and Wales in the estate of—

Full name of deceased: ....

Full address: ....

Alternative or alias names: ....

Exact date of death: ....

which either has issued not more than 12 months before the entry of this application or issues within 6 months thereafter.

Signed ....

Name in block letters ....

Full address ....

Reference No. (if any) ....

Form 3

6C–197

Rule 44(2)   **Caveat**

In the High Court of Justice

Family Division

The Principal [or .... District probate] Registry
   Let no grant be sealed in the estate of (*full name and address*) deceased, who died on the day of 19....... without notice to (*name of party by whom or on whose behalf the caveat is entered*).
Dated this .... day of .... 19 ....
(*Signed*)   (*to be signed by the caveator's solicitor or probate practitioner or by the caveator if acting in person*)

Form 4

6C–198

Rule 44(5)   **Warning to Caveator**

In the High Court of Justice

Family Division

[*The nominated registry as defined by rule 44(5)*]

To .... of .... a party who has entered a caveat in the estate of .... deceased.

You have eight days (starting with the day on which this warning was served on you):

(i) to enter an appearance either in person or by your solicitor or probate practitioner, at the [*name and address of the nominated registry*] set out what interest you have in the estate of the above-named   of   deceased contrary to that of the party at whose instance this warning is issued; or

(ii) if you have no contrary interest but wish to show cause against the sealing of a grant on such party, to issue and serve a summons for directions by a district judge of the Principal Registry or a registrar of a district probate registry.

If you fail to do either of these, the court may proceed to issue a grant to probate or administration in the said estate notwithstanding your caveat.

Dated the .... day of .... 19....

Issued at the instance of ....

[Here set out the name and interest (including the
date of the will, if any, under which the interest
arises) of the party warning, the name of his
solicitor or probate practitioner and the address for
service. If the party warning is acting in person,
this must be stated.]   Registrar

6C–199

Form 5

Rules 44(10), 46(6)   **Appearance to Warning or Citation**

In the High Court of Justice

Family Division

The Principal [*or* .... District probate] Registry

Caveat No. .... dated the .... day of .... 19....

[Citation dated the .... day of .... 19....]

Full name and address of deceased: ....

Full name and address of person warning [*or* citor]: ....

(Here set out the interest of the person warning, or citor, as shown in warning or citation.)

Full name and address of caveator [*or* person cited.]

(Here set out the interest of the caveator or person cited, stating the date of the will (if any) under which such interest arises.)

Enter an appearance for the above-named caveator [*or* person cited] in this matter.

Dated the .... day of .... 19....

(Signed)

whose address for service is:

Solicitor or probate practitioner (*or* 'In person').

Form 6

Rule 56　　　　　**Notice of Election to Redeem Life Interest**

In the High Court of Justice

Family Division

The Principal [*or* .... District probate] Registry

In the estate of .... deceased.

Whereas .... of .... died on the .... day of ....

19....

wholly/partially intestate leaving his/her/lawful wife/husband and ....

lawful issue of the said deceased;

And whereas Probate/Letters of Administration of the estate of the said ....

were granted to me, the said .... [and to .... of

....] at the Probate Registry on the .... day of .... 19....;

And whereas [the said .... has ceased to be a personal

representative because ....] and I am [now] the sole

personal representative;

Now I, the said .... hereby give notice in accordance with

section 47A of the Administration of Estates Act 1925 that I elect to redeem the life interest to

which I am entitled in the estate of the late ....

by retaining £........ its capital value, and £........ the costs of the transaction.

Dated the .... day of .... 19....

(Signed)

To the senior district judge of the Family Division.

SECOND SCHEDULE

REVOCATIONS

Rules revoked	References
The Non-Contentious Probate Rules 1954	S.I. 1954/796
The Non-Contentious Probate (Amendment) Rules 1961	S.I. 1961/72
The Non-Contentious Probate (Amendment) Rules 1962	S.I. 1962/2653
The Non-Contentious Probate (Amendment) Rules 1967	S.I. 1967/748
The Non-Contentious Probate (Amendment) Rules 1968	S.I. 1968/1675
The Non-Contentious Probate (Amendment) Rules 1969	S.I. 1969/1689
The Non-Contentious Probate (Amendment) Rules 1971	S.I. 1971/1977
The Non-Contentious Probate (Amendment) Rules 1974	S.I. 1974/597
The Non-Contentious Probate (Amendment) Rules 1976	S.I. 1976/1362
The Non-Contentious Probate (Amendment) Rules 1982	S.I. 1982/446
The Non-Contentious Probate (Amendment) Rules 1983	S.I. 1983/623
The Non-Contentious Probate (Amendment) Rules 1985	S.I. 1985/1232

Rules of the Supreme Court (Non-Contentious Probate Costs) 1956

(S.I. 1956 No. 552)

6C–202 [*This order is printed as amended by the Non—Contentious Probate Fees (Amendment) Order (S.I. 2000 No. 642)]*

[*The Rules of the Supreme Court (Non-Contentious Probate Costs) 1956 are revoked by S.I. 1994 No. 1975*].

Non-Contentious Probate Fees Order 1999

6C–202.1

(S.I. 1999 No. 688)

ARRANGEMENT OF RULES

The Lord Chancellor, in exercise of the powers conferred on him by section 130 of the Supreme Court Act 1981, with the concurrence of the Lord Chief Justice, the Master of the Rolls, the President of the Family Division, the Vice-Chancellor and the Treasury under section 130(2) of the Supreme Court Act 1981, makes the following Order:

Citation and commencement
6C–203   1. This Order may be cited as the Non-Contentious Probate Fees Order 1999 as amended and shall come into force on 25th April 2000.

Interpretation
6C–204   2. In this Order, unless the context otherwise requires—

(a) a fee referred to by number means the fee so numbered in Schedule 1to this Order;

(b) "assessed value" means the value of the net real and personal estate (excluding settled land if any) passing under the grant as shown—

(i) in the Inland Revenue affidavit (for a death occurring before 13th March 1975), or

(ii) in the Inland Revenue account (for a death occurring on or after 13th March 1975), or

(iii) in a case in which, in accordance with arrangements made between the President of the Family Division and the Commissioners of Inland Revenue, or regulations made under section 256(1)(a) of the Inheritance Tax Act 1984 and from time to time in force, no such affidavit or account is required to be delivered, in the oath which is sworn to lead to the grant,

and in the case of an application to reseal a grant means the value, as so shown, passing under the grant upon its being resealed;

(c) "authorised place of deposit" means any place in which, by virtue of a direction given under section 124 of the Supreme Court Act 1981 original wills and other documents under the control of the High Court (either in the principal registry or in any district registry) are deposited and preserved;

(d) "grant" means a grant of probate or letters of administration;

(e) "district registry" includes the probate registry of Wales, any district probate registry and any sub-registry attached to it;

(f) "the principal registry" means the Principal Registry of the Family Division and any sub-registry attached to it.

Fees to be taken

3. The fees set out in column 2 of Schedule 1 to this Order shall be **6C–205** taken in the principal registry and in each district registry in respect of the items described in column 1 in accordance with and subject to any directions specified in column 1.

Exclusion of certain death gratuities

4. In determining the value of any personal estate for the purposes **6C–206** of this Order there shall be excluded the value of a death gratuity payable under section 17(2) of the Judicial Pensions Act 1981 or section 4(3) of the Judicial Pensions and Retirement Act 1993, or payable to the personal representatives of a deceased civil servant by virtue of a scheme made under section 1 of the Superannuation Act 1972.

Exemptions, reductions and remissions

5.—(1) Where it appears to the Lord Chancellor that the payment **6C–207** of any fee prescribed by this Order would, owing to the exceptional circumstances of the particular case, involve undue hardship, he may reduce or remit the fee in that case.

(1A) Subject to paragraph (1B) where a fee has been paid at a time (a) where the Lord Chancellor, if he had been aware of all the circumstances, would have reduced the fee under article 5(1), the amount by which the fee would have been reduced shall be refunded; and (b) where the Lord Chancellor, if he had been aware of all the circumstances, would have remitted the fee under article 5(1), the fee shall be refunded.

(1B) No refund shall be made under paragraph (1A) unless the party who paid the fee applies within 6 months of paying the fee.

(1C) The Lord Chancellor may extend the period of 6 months referred to in paragraph (1B) if he considers that there is good reason for an application being made after the end of the period of 6 months.

(2) Where by any convention entered into by Her Majesty with any foreign power it is provided that no fee shall be required to be paid in respect of any proceedings, the fees specified in this Order shall not be taken in respect of those proceedings.

(3) Where any application for a grant is withdrawn before the issue of a grant, a registrar may reduce or remit a fee.

(4) Fee 7 shall not be taken where a search is made for research or similar purposes by permission of the President of the Family Division for a document over 100 years old filed in the principal registry or a district registry or another authorised place of deposit.

Revocations

6C–208   6. The Orders specified in Schedule 2 shall be revoked, except as to any fee or other sum due or payable under those Orders before the commencement of this Order.

SCHEDULE 1

Fees to be taken

6C–209

Number and description of fee	Amount of fee
1. Application for a grant On an application for a grant (or for resealing a grant) other than on an application to which fee 3 applies, where the [assessed value] of the estate exceeds £5,000	£50
2. Personal application fee Where the application under fee 1 is made by a personal applicant (not being an application to which fee 3 applies) fee 2 is payable in addition to fee 1, where the [assessed value] of the estate exceeds £5,000	£80
3. Special applications (1) For a duplicate or second or subsequent grant (including one following a revoked grant) in respect of the same deceased person, other than a grant preceded only by a grant limited to settled land, to trust property, or to part of the estate	£15
(2) On an application for a grant in respect of an estate exempt from inheritance tax by virtue of section 154 of the Inheritance Tax Act 1984(c) (exemption for members of the armed forces, *etc.*)	£8
4. Caveats For the entry or the extention of a caveat	£15
5. Search On an application for a standing search to be carried out in an estate, for each period of six months including the issue of a copy grant and will, if any (irrespective of the number of pages)	£5
6. Deposit of wills On depositing a will for safe custody in the principal registry or a district registry	£15
7. Inspection On inspection of any will or other document retained by the registry (in the presence of an officer of the registry)	£15

Number and description of fee	Amount of fee
8. Copy documents On a request for a copy of any document whether or not provided as a certified copy:	
(a) for the first copy	£5
(b) for every subsequent copy of the same document if supplied at the same time	£1
(c) where copies of any document are made available on a computer disk or in other electronic form, for each such copy	£3
(d) where a search of the index is required, in addition to fee 8(a), (b) or (c) as appropriate, for each period of 4 years searched after the first 4 years	£3
9. Oaths Except on a personal application for a grant for administering an oath,	
9.1 for each deponent to each affidavit	£5
9.2 for making each exhibit	£2
10. Determination of costs For determining costs	The same fees as are payable from time to time for determining costs under the Supreme Court Fees Order 1999 (the relevant fees are set out in fee 10 in Schedule 1 to that Order)
11. Settling documents For perusing and settling citations, advertisements, oaths, affidavits, or other documents, for each document settled	£10

NB. In Column 1, in fees 1 & 2 the words "assessed value" in square brackets are substituted by S.I. 2000 No. 642, Art. 4.

SCHEDULE 2

ORDERS REVOKED

6C–210

Title	S.I. number
The Non-Contentious Probate Fees Order 1981	S.I. 1981/861
The Non-Contentious Probate Fees (Amendment) Order 1981	S.I. 1981/1103
The Non-Contentious Probate Fees (Amendment) Order 1986	S.I. 1986/705
The Non-Contentious Probate Fees (Amendment) (No. 2) Order 1986	S.I. 1986/2185
The Non-Contentious Probate Fees (Amendment) Order 1987	S.I. 1987/1176
The Non-Contentious Probate Fees (Amendment) Order 1989	S.I. 1989/1140

6D TRUSTEES

Judicial Trustees Act 1896

(1896 59 & 60 VICT. C.35)

An Act to provide for the Appointment of Judicial Trustees and otherwise to amend the Law respecting the Administration of Trusts and the Liability of Trustees.

[14th August, 1896] **6D–1**

Power of Court on application to appoint judicial trustee

1.—(1) Where application is made to the Court by or on behalf of **6D–2** the person creating or intending to create a trust, or by or on behalf of a trustee or beneficiary, the Court may, in its discretion, appoint a person (in this Act called a judicial trustee) to be a trustee of that trust, either jointly with any other person or as sole trustee, and, if sufficient cause is shown, in place of all or any existing trustees.

(2) The administration of the property of a deceased person, whether a testator or intestate, shall be a trust, and the executor or administrator a trustee, within the meaning of this Act.

(3) Any fit and proper person nominated for the purpose in the application may be appointed a judicial trustee, and, in the absence of such nomination, or if the Court is not satisfied of the fitness of a person so nominated, an official of the Court may be appointed, and in any case a judicial trustee shall be subject to the control and supervision of the Court as an officer thereof.

(4) The Court may, either on request or without request, give to a judicial trustee any general or special directions in regard to the trust or the administration thereof.

(5) There may be paid to a judicial trustee out of the trust property such remuneration, not exceeding the prescribed limits, as the Court may assign in each case, subject to any Rules under this Act respecting the application of such remuneration where the judicial trustee is an official of the Court, and the remuneration so assigned to any judicial trustee shall, save as the Court may for special reasons otherwise order, cover all his work and personal outlay.

(6) In any case where the Court shall so direct, an inquiry into the administration by a judicial trustee of any trust, or into any dealing or transaction of a judicial trustee, shall be made in the prescribed manner.

(7) Where an application relating to the estate of a deceased person is made to the Court under this section, the Court may, if it thinks fit, proceed as if the application were, or included, an application under section 50 of the Administration of Justice Act 1985

(power of High Court to appoint substitute for, or to remove, personal representative).

6D–3 *Note* —Amended by A.J.A. 1982. Subs. (7) added by A.J.A. 1985, s.50(6) with effect from April 28, 1986.

Subs. (1) "The Court may, in its discretion"
6D–4   A person interested in an estate, therefore, is not entitled as of right to have a judicial trustee appointed (*Re Ratcliff* [1898] 2 Ch. 352). It was further held by that authority that under s.1(2) the Court can remove an executor and appoint a judicial trustee, and that under s.1(4) the Court can give to such a trustee directions for the administration of the trust.

See also *Re Marshall's Will Trusts* [1945] Ch. 217, as to Settled Land Act trustees being held to be trustees of a trust within the meaning of the Judicial Trustees Act.

Subs. (2)
6D–5   The Court cannot appoint a judicial trustee of part of an estate during the period of administration unless separate executors have been appointed (*Re Wells* [1968] 1 W.L.R. 44; [1967] 3 All E.R. 908.) Where the administration has been completed an appointment in respect of part of an estate is possible (*Re Cohen* [1918] W.N. 252).

Court to exercise jurisdiction
6D–6   **2.** The jurisdiction of the Court under this Act may be exercised by the High Court and (subject to the prescribed definition of the jurisdiction) by any county court Judge to whom such jurisdiction may be assigned under this Act.

6D–7   *Note* —Amended by the Courts Act 1971, Sched.11.

6D–8   **3.** [*Repealed and re-enacted*, T.A. 1925, s.61.]

Rules
6D–9   **4.**—(1) Rules may be made for carrying into effect this Act, and especially—

(1) for requiring judicial trustees, who are not officials of the Court, to give security for the due application of any trust property under their control:

(2) respecting the safety of the trust property, and the custody thereof:

(3) respecting the remuneration of judicial trustees and for fixing and regulating the fees to be taken under this Act so as to cover the expenses of the administration of this Act, and respecting the payment of such remuneration and fees out of the trust property, and, where the judicial trustee is an official of the Court, respecting the application of the remuneration and fees payable to him:

(4) for dispensing with formal proof of facts in proper cases:

(5) for facilitating the discharge by the Court of administrative duties under this Act without judicial proceedings, and otherwise regulating procedure under this Act and making it simple and inexpensive:

(6) for assigning jurisdiction under this Act to county court Judges and defining such jurisdiction:

(7) respecting the suspension or removal of any judicial trustee, and the succession of another person to the of-

fice of any judicial trustee who may cease to hold office, and the vesting in such person of any trust property:

(8) respecting the classes of trusts in which officials of the Court are not to be judicial trustees, or are to be so temporarily or conditionally:

(9) respecting the procedure to be followed where the judicial trustee is executor or administrator:

(10) for preventing the employment by judicial trustees of other persons at the expense of the trust, except in cases of strict necessity:

(11) for the preparation, auditing (by the Court or otherwise) and filing of the accounts of any trust of which a judicial trustee has been appointed;

(12) for the making of a report to the Court on the accounts of any such trust.

(1A) The Rules under this Act may make different provision for different classes of trust, trustees, beneficiaries or trust property.

(2) The Rules under this Act may be made by the Lord Chancellor, subject to the consent of the Treasury in matters relating to fees and to salaries and numbers of officers, and to the consent of the authority for making orders under the Solicitors Remuneration Act 1881, in matters relating to the remuneration of solicitors. The Rules shall be laid before Parliament and if, within thirty days after such Rules have been laid before either House of Parliament during which that House has sat, the House presents to Her Majesty an address against such Rules or any of them, such Rules or the Rule specified in the address shall henceforward be of no effect.

Note —Amended by the Administration of Justice Act 1982, s.57 (2), (3); and the **6D–10** Statute Law (Repeals) Act 1986.

Definitions
5. In this Act— The expression "official of the Court" means the **6D–11** holder of such paid office in or connected with the Court as may be prescribed. The expression "prescribed" means prescribed by Rules under this Act.

Short title, extent and commencement of Act
6.—(1) This Act may be cited as the Judicial Trustees Act, 1896. **6D–12**

(2) This Act shall not extend to any charity.

(3) This Act shall not extend to Scotland or Ireland.

(4) [...]

Note —Amended by the Charities Act 1960, Sched.7; and the Statute Law Revision **6D–13** Act 1908.

Judicial Trustee Rules 1983

(S.I. 1983 No. 370 (L.4)) **6D–14**

ARRANGEMENT OF RULES

RULE

6D–15 *Note* —These rules which came into force on April 1, 1983, revoke and replace the Judicial Trustee Rules 1972 (S.I. 1972 No. 1096) which in turn revoked and replaced the Judicial Trustee Rules 1897.

Citation and commencement

6D–16 1. These Rules may be cited as the Judicial Trustee Rules 1983 and shall come into operation on 1st April 1983.

Interpretation

6D–17 2.—(1) In these Rules, unless the context otherwise requires—

"the Act" means the Judicial Trustees Act 1896;

"the Court" has the same meaning as in the Rules of the Supreme Court;

"Corporate Trustee" means the Official Solicitor, the Public Trustee or a corporation either appointed by the Court in any particular case to be a trustee or entitled by rules made under section 4(3) of the Public Trustee Act 1906 to act as custodian trustee;

"judicial trustee" means a sole judicial trustee or two or more judicial trustees appointed to act together;

"master" means a master of the Supreme Court other than a master of the Supreme Court (Taxing Office) and includes a district registrar of a district registry of the High Court;

"official of the Court" means the holder of any paid office in or connected with the Supreme Court and includes the Official Solicitor to the Supreme Court;

"Official Solicitor" means the Official Solicitor to the Supreme Court;

"qualified accountant" means a person who is a member or a firm all the partners in which are members of the Institute of Chartered Accountants in England and Wales or of the Association of Certified and Corporate Accountants;

2018

" Rules of the Supreme Court" has the same meaning as in section 151(4) of the Supreme Court Act 1981.

(2) Subject to the provisions of these Rules and of any enactment, the Rules of the Supreme Court shall apply with the necessary modification to proceedings under the Act and these Rules.

Note —Further to the Courts and Legal Services Act 1990, s.74, the office of district registrar for each district registry of the High Court has become the office of district judge.   **6D–18**

Making of application

3.—(1) An application to the Court for the appointment of a judicial trustee must be made by originating summons or, if it is made in a pending cause or matter, by summons or motion in the cause or matter.   **6D–19**

(2) An application for an injunction ancillary or incidental to an order appointing a judicial trustee may be joined with the application for such order.

(3) The Court hearing an application under paragraph (2) may grant an injunction restraining any trustee or person entitled to any interest in the property of which a judicial trustee is sought from assigning, charging or otherwise dealing with that property until after the hearing of a summons for the appointment of the judicial trustee and may require such summons returnable on such date as the Court may direct, to be issued.

(4) The evidence in support of such an application must include an affidavit by the applicant containing the following particulars so far as the applicant can gain information with regard to them:—

   (a) a short description of the trust and instrument by which it is, or is to be, created;

   (b) short particulars of the trust property, with an approximate estimate of its income, and capital value;

   (c) short particulars of the incumbrances (if any) affecting the trust property;

   (d) particulars as to the persons who are in possession of the documents relating to the trust;

   (e) the names and addresses of the beneficiaries and short particulars of their respective interests; and

   (f) the name, address and description of the proposed judicial trustee (if any) together with any proposal the applicant may make for his remuneration.

(5) Where the applicant cannot gain the information required on any point he must mention his inability in the affidavit.

Note —Applications are now made by a claim form instead of by an originating summons.   **6D–20**

Service of summons and notice

4.—(1) Subject to any direction of the Court—   **6D–21**

   (a) the summons shall be served on every existing trustee

who is not an applicant and on such of the beneficiaries as the applicant thinks fit; but

    (b) a summons issued by or on behalf of a person creating or intending to create a trust need not be served on any person.

(2) The Court may give such directions as it thinks fit for the service of the summons or the dispensing with service of the summons on any person.

(3) Where an applicant has no nomination for a judicial trustee he may, if he thinks fit, give not less than four days' notice of the hearing of the application to any official of the Court who may be appointed judicial trustee.

(4) Where an official of the Court receives notice under paragraph (3) of this rule he shall not be a party to the proceedings but shall be entitled to attend the hearing.

Service of order

6D–22   5. A copy of the order appointing a judicial trustee shall be served by the party having conduct of the proceedings on the judicial trustee, such beneficiaries, former trustees and other persons as the Court may direct.

Security

6D–23   6.—(1) This rule shall apply where the judicial trustee is not an official of the Court.

(2) Subject to paragraph (3) below, an order appointing a judicial trustee may include such directions as the Court thinks fit for the giving of security by the person appointed.

(3) The Court shall not, except for special reasons, require security to be given when the application is made by a person creating or intending to create a trust.

(4) Where, by virtue of paragraph (2), a person is required to give security in accordance with this rule he must give security approved by the Court duly to account for what he receives as judicial trustee and to deal with it as the Court directs.

(5) Unless the Court otherwise directs, the security shall be by guarantee.

(6) Any guarantee or undertaking ordered to be filed as security shall be filed in Chancery Chambers or, if the cause or matter is proceeding in a district registry, that registry.

Custody of trust funds, property and documents

6D–24   7. The Court may give such directions as it thinks fit as to the manner in which and the conditions subject to which—

    (a) the trust fund is to be held;

    (b) any title deeds, certificates or other documents which are evidence of the trust property are to be held or disposed of;

(c) trust property may be vested in the judicial trustee; and

(d) any payments received or made on behalf of the trust are to be dealt with and accounts thereof are to be kept.

Applications for directions

8.—(1) A judicial trustee or any person interested in the trust may **6D–25** at any time request the Court to give directions as to the trust or its administration, including a direction that there shall cease to be a judicial trustee, and such request shall state in writing the matters with regard to which directions are required.

(2) The Court may require the trustee or any other person to attend at chambers (if it appears that such attendance is necessary or convenient) or may direct a summons to be issued in the proceedings, or direct an issue or issues to be tried.

Preparation of accounts

9. Unless the Court otherwise orders a judicial trustee shall make **6D–26** up his accounts (in such form as the Court shall require) in each year to the anniversary of his appointment and shall deliver them in accordance with rules 12 or 13, as the case may be, within one calendar month after such anniversary.

10. A judicial trustee shall endorse on his accounts a certificate of **6D–27** the approximate capital value of the trust property at the commencement of the year of account.

Remuneration and disbursements

11.—(1) A person appointed judicial trustee shall be allowed on **6D–28** the examination of his accounts—

(a) by way of remuneration, if any such reasonable amount in respect of work reasonably performed as may be authorised by the Court and the Court may direct that such remuneration shall be fixed by reference to such scales or rates of professional charges as it thinks fit provided that remuneration authorised under this rule shall not, in any year of account, exceed 15 per cent of the capital value of the trust property.

(b) such disbursements as have actually and properly been expended in his trusteeship.

(2) For the purpose of sub-paragraph (1)(a) of this rule:—

(a) the capital value shall be ascertained from the certificate under rule 10 in respect of the year of account, or, if the Court sees fit in the case of a final account, from the certificate in respect of the preceding year.

(b) The Court may, if it thinks fit, indicate to a judicial trustee upon his appointment the scale or rate of professional charges that it considers would be appropriate in relation to the appointment.

Note — See *Practice Note (Remuneration of Judicial Trustees)* [2003] 1 W.L.R. 1653 as to **6D–28.1** factors to be taken into account by court and common form of order when dealing with assignment of remuneration to a judicial trustee.

This recent *Practice Note* emphasises the court's determination to control the level of remuneration of judicial trustees and to ensure the court's involvement. It sets out best practice and, interestingly, para. 2 and the last draft paragraph emphasise that the judicial trustee should specifically have in mind proportionality when seeking authority for payment. In fact, the *Practice Note* reflects the position under CPR Pt 69, r.7 (Receivers).

PRACTICE NOTE (REMUNERATION OF JUDICIAL TRUSTEES)

6D–28.2 **1.** When dealing with the assignment of remuneration to a judicial trustee under section 1(5) of the Judicial Trustees Act 1896 and rule 11 of the Judicial Trustee Rules 1983 the court will consider directions as to remuneration based on the common form of order set out below, subject to such modifications as may be required in any particular case.

2. In general the court when considering reasonable remuneration for the purposes of rule 11(1)(a) will need to be satisfied as to the basis upon which the remuneration is claimed, that it is justified and that the amount is reasonable and proportionate and within the limit of 15% of the capital value of the trust property specifed in the rule.

3. The court may, before determining the amount of remuneration, require the judicial trustee to provide further information, alternatively refer the matter to a costs judge for him to assess remuneration.

4. When an application is made to the court for the appointment of a judicial trustee or when the court gives directions under rule 8 practitioners should produce to the court a draft order which should take account of the common form of order.

DRAFT PARAGRAPHS OF ORDER

[IT IS ORDERED]

...that the remuneration of the Judicial Trustee shall be in such amount as may be approved from time to time by this court upon application for payment on examination of his accounts

...that the Judicial Trustees accounts shall be endorsed by him with a certificate of the approximate capital value of the trust property at the commencement of the year of account

...that every application for payment by the Judicial Trustee shall be in the form of a letter to the court (with a copy to the beneficiaries) which shall (a) set out the basis of the claim to remuneration, the scales of rates of any professional charges, the work done and time spent, any information concerning the complexity of the trusteeship that may be relied on and any other matters which the court shall be invited by the Judicial Trustee to take into account and (b) certify that he considers that the claim for remuneration is reasonable and proportionate

J. Winegarten
Chief Chancery Master
With the authority of the Vice-Chancellor
July 1, 2003

Filing, examination and inspection of accounts

6D–29 **12.—(1)** This rule shall apply where the judicial trustee is not a corporate trustee.

(2) Unless the Court otherwise directs a judicial trustee must submit his accounts to the Court.

(3) The accounts shall be examined by the Court unless it considers that the accounts are likely to involve questions of difficulty and refers them to a qualified accountant for report, in which case the Court may order payment to him out of the trust of such reasonable amount in respect of his report as it thinks fit.

(4) Following examination by or on behalf of the Court, the result of such examination must be certified by a master and an order may thereupon be made as to the incidence of any costs or expenses incurred.

(5) The judicial trustee shall send a copy of the accounts, or if the Court thinks fit, a summary of the accounts, of the trust to such beneficiaries or other persons as the Court may direct.

(6) If an application is made by any person to inspect the filed accounts, the Court may, if it thinks fit, having regard to the nature of the relation of the applicant to the trust, allow them to be inspected on giving reasonable notice.

(7) Any person who is served with a copy of the accounts, or a summary of the accounts under paragraph (5), or, after inspection of the accounts under paragraph (6), remains dissatisfied with them, may apply to the Court for directions.

13.—(1)This rule shall apply where the judicial trustee is a **6D–30** corporate trustee.

(2) A judicial trustee shall submit for examination such accounts to such persons as the Court may direct.

(3) Any person to whom a judicial trustee is required to submit accounts may, on giving reasonable notice to the judicial trustee, inspect, either personally or by an agent, the books and other papers relating to such accounts.

(4) Any person to whom the judicial trustee is required to submit accounts, or any beneficiary, who is dissatisfied with them may give notice specifying the item or items as to which objection is taken and requiring the judicial trustee within not less than 14 days to lodge his accounts with the Court and a copy of such notice shall be lodged in Chancery Chambers or, if the cause or matter is proceeding in a district registry, that registry.

(5) Following an examination by or on behalf of the Court of an item or items in an account to which objection is taken the result of such examination must be certified by a master and an order may thereupon be made as to the incidence of any costs or expenses incurred.

Default by judicial trustee

14.—(1) Where a judicial trustee fails to submit his account in the **6D–31** prescribed manner or do any other thing which he is required to submit, provide or do, he and any or all of the beneficiaries and such other persons as the Court may direct may be required to attend in chambers to show cause for the failure and the Court may, either in chambers or after adjourning into Court, give such directions as it thinks proper, including if necessary, directions for the discharge of the judicial trustee and the appointment of another and the payment of costs.

(2) Without prejudice to paragraph (1) of this Rule, where the judicial trustee has failed to comply with the Act or with these Rules or with any direction of the Court made in accordance with these Rules or has otherwise misconducted himself in relation to the trust the Court may disallow any remuneration claimed in any subsequent account.

(3) If the Court is satisfied that the judicial trustee has failed to pay any sum into the trust account within a reasonable period of time it may charge him with interest at the rate currently payable in respect of judgment debts on that sum while in his possession.

Special Provisions Relating to Officials of the Court

6D–32   15. An official of the Court shall not be appointed or act as judicial trustee—

- (a) for any persons in their capacity as members or debenture holders of, or being in any other relation to, any corporation or unincorporated body, or any club, or
- (b) of a trust which involves the carrying on of any trade or business unless the Court, with or without special conditions to ensure the proper supervision of the trade or business, specifically directs.

6D–33   16.—(1) The appointment of an official of the Court as a judicial trustee shall be an appointment of the holder of that office for the time being, and no further order or appointment shall be necessary by reason only of the person appointed dying or ceasing to hold office.

(2) Any property vested in an official of the Court as a judicial trustee shall, on his dying or ceasing to hold office, vest in the person appointed to succeed him without any conveyance, assignment or transfer.

District Registries

6D–34   17.—(1) Notwithstanding any provisions contained in the Rules of the Supreme Court, an originating summons may be issued out of a district registry for the purpose of an application to appoint a judicial trustee.

(2) Where a judicial trustee is appointed on a summons or motion or in a cause or matter proceeding in a district registry all proceedings with respect to the trust and the administration thereof under the Act or these Rules shall, subject to paragraph (3) of this rule, be taken in the district registry.

(3) The Court may transfer any trust of which there is a judicial trustee from a district registry to Chancery Chambers or from Chancery Chambers to a district registry, or from one district registry to another, according as it appears convenient for the administration of the trust.

Fees

6D–35   18. Where in any matter proceeding under these Rules a fee would be payable under the Order for the time being in force relating to Supreme Court Fees, that fee shall be paid.

Revocations

19.—(1)The Judicial Trustee Rules 1972 are hereby revoked.   **6D–36**

(2) The provisions of the rules in force immediately before the commencement of the Judicial Trustee Rules 1972 shall continue to apply to proceedings taken before that date in a county court.

Public Trustee Act 1906

(1906 6 EDW. 7, C.55)   **6D–37**

ARRANGEMENT OF SECTIONS

ESTABLISHMENT OF PUBLIC TRUSTEE

ESTABLISHMENT OF PUBLIC TRUSTEE

Office of Public Trustee

1.—(1) There shall be established the office of public trustee.   **6D–38**

(2) The public trustee shall be a corporation sole under that name, with perpetual succession and an official seal, and may sue and be sued under the above name like any other corporation sole, but any instruments sealed by him shall not, by reason of his using a seal, be rendered liable to a higher stamp duty than if he were an individual.

Note —The Office of Public Trustee of England and Wales was established on   **6D–39**
November 29, 1907.

Powers and Duties of Public Trustee

General powers and duties of Public Trustee

6D–40   **2.**—(1) Subject to and in accordance with the provisions of this Act and Rules made thereunder, the public trustee may, if he thinks fit—

(a) act in the administration of estates of small value;

(b) act as custodian trustee;

(c) act as an ordinary trustee;

(d) be appointed to be a judicial trustee;

(e) [*Repealed by* Criminal Justice Act 1948, Sched.10, Pt I.]

(2) Subject to the provisions of this Act, and to the rules made thereunder, the public trustee may act either alone or jointly with any person or body of persons in any capacity to which he may be appointed in pursuance of this Act, and shall have all the same powers, duties, and liabilities, and be entitled to the same rights and immunities and be subject to the control and orders of the Court, as a private trustee acting in the same capacity.

(3) The public trustee may decline, either absolutely or except on the prescribed conditions, to accept any trust, but he shall not decline to accept any trust on the ground only of the small value of the trust property.

(4) The public trustee shall not accept any trust which involves the management or carrying on of any business, except in the cases in which he may be authorised to do so by rules made under this Act, nor any trust under a deed of arrangement for the benefit of creditors, nor the administration of any estate known or believed by him to be insolvent.

(5) The public trustee shall not accept any trust exclusively for religious or charitable purposes, and nothing in this Act contained, or in the rules to be made under the powers in this Act contained, shall abridge or affect the powers or duties of the official trustee of charity lands or official trustees of charitable funds.

"The Public Trustee may"

6D–41   As to further authorised trusts and duties, see the Public Trustee Rules 1912, rr.6 and 7; also L.P.A. 1925, Sched.1, Pts 3, 4 and 5; and the Friendly Societies Act 1974, s.55.

Administration

6D–42   In ordinary cases the Public Trustee has no power to take a grant of administration to the estates of persons domiciled abroad; the circumstances in *Re Grundt* [1915] P. 126, were quite exceptional; see *Re Woolf* [1918] W.N. 205, and cf. *Re Busche* [1922] P. 30, where there was a charge under the Treaty of Peace Order 1919.

Foreign settlement

6D–43   The Public Trustee can only accept trusteeship of an English settlement (*Re Hewitt's Settlement* [1915] 1 Ch. 228) but he can accept a settlement made by a person domiciled abroad if the forum of administration is England or Wales.

"Shall have all the same powers"

6D–44   Amongst these powers is the power to apply to the Court for advice and assistance (*e.g.* on questions of construction). The procedure to be followed is identical to that followed in the case of a private trustee.

Dual capacity

The Public Trustee has no more power than a private trustee, where he has conflict- **6D–45** ing interests, to make a bargain with himself, and must accordingly come to the Court for sanction to such a bargain (*The New Haw Estate Trust* (1912) 56 S.J. 538). He is subject to the same rules as ordinary litigants and cannot be claimant and defendant as trustee of different instruments (*Re Phillips* [1931] W.N. 271).

Costs

As to costs of the Public Trustee when a party to proceedings in two capacities, see **6D–46** *Re Abercrombie's Will Trusts* [1931] W.N. 109.

Charitable objects

The Public Trustee is precluded by subs. (5) from accepting a trust where the sole **6D–47** object thereof involves the selection of charitable objects for the testator's bounty (*Re Hampton* (1919) 88 L.J. Ch. 103). This restriction, however, is considered not to apply to executorship under a will, even when the whole estate is given to charity, nor to trusteeship under wills or settlements where the whole of the trust property is not to be devoted to charitable purposes.

See note to s.4(3).

(1) In the Administration of Small Estates

Administration of small estates

3.—(1) Any person who in the opinion of the public trustee would **6D–48** be entitled to apply to the Court for an order for the administration by the Court of an estate, the gross capital value whereof is proved to the satisfaction of the public trustee to be less than one thousand pounds, may apply to the public trustee to administer the estate, and, where any such application is made and it appears to the public trustee that the persons beneficially entitled are persons of small means, the public trustee shall administer the estate, unless he sees good reason for refusing to do so.

(2) On the public trustee undertaking, by declaration in writing signed and sealed by him, to administer the estate the trust property other than stock shall, by virtue of this Act, vest in him, and the right to transfer or call for the transfer of any stock forming part of the estate shall also vest in him, in like manner as if vesting orders had been made for the purpose by the High Court under the [Trustee Act 1893], and that Act shall apply accordingly. As from such vesting any trustee entitled under the trust to administer the estate shall be discharged from all liability attaching to the administration, except in respect of past acts:

Provided that—

(a) the public trustee shall not exercise the right of himself transferring the stock without the leave of the Court; and

(b) [*relating to copyholds*].

(3) For the purposes of the administration the public trustee may exercise such of the administrative powers and authorities of the High Court as may be conferred on him by rules under this Act, subject to such conditions as may be imposed by the rules.

(4) Rules shall be made under this Act for enabling the public trustee to take the opinion of the High Court on any question arising

in the course of any administration without judicial proceedings, and otherwise for making the procedure under this section simple and inexpensive.

(5) Where proceedings have been instituted in any Court for the administration of an estate, and by reason of the small value of the estate it appears to the Court that the estate can be more economically administered by the public trustee than by the Court, or that for any other reason it is expedient that the estate should be administered by the public trustee instead of the Court, the Court may order that the estate shall be administered by the public trustee, and thereupon (subject to any directions by the Court) this section shall apply as if the administration of the estate had been undertaken by the public trustee in pursuance of this section.

Trustee Act 1893

6D–49   The Trustee Act 1893 has been replaced by the Trustee Act 1925. All references in the text should therefore refer to the 1925 Act.

Scope of section

6D–50   Where three fifth parts of an intestate's estate amounting to £1,281 gross had been distributed and the Public Trustee, on application made to him on behalf of infants entitled to one of the two undistributed fifth parts, had undertaken to administer the intestate's estate, Eve J., held that the above section applied throughout to the estates of deceased persons and had no application to trusts, and that having regard to the wording above of subs. (2) which contemplates the Public Trustee intervening at any stage, and the words "is proved to be" (not "to have been") and the power in any particular estate given to him to refuse to administer in subs. (1) the estate came within this section (*Re Devereux* [1911] 2 Ch. 545).

(2) As CUSTODIAN TRUSTEE

Custodian trustee

6D–51   **4.**—(1) Subject to rules under this Act the public trustee may, if he consents to act as such, and whether or not the number of trustees has been reduced below the original number, be appointed to be custodian trustee of any trust—

    (a) by order of the Court made on the application of any person on whose application the Court may order the appointment of a new trustee; or

    (b) by the testator, settlor, or other creator of any trust; or

    (c) by the person having power to appoint new trustees.

(2) Where the public trustee is appointed to be custodian trustee of any trust—

    (a) The trust property shall be transferred to the custodian trustee as if he were sole trustee, and for that purpose vesting orders may, where necessary, be made under the [Trustee Act 1893]:

[(b)(c)(d)(e) *relate to the division of duties between the custodian trustees and the managing trustees*].

    (f) The power of appointing new trustees, when exercisable by the trustees, shall be exercisable by the managing trustees alone, but the custodian trustee shall have the same power of applying to the Court for the appointment of a new trustee as any other trustee:

TRUSTEES

(g) In determining the number of trustees for the purposes of the [Trustee Act 1893], the custodian trustee shall not be reckoned as a trustee:

(h) [*Relates to the liability of the custodian trustee*]:

(i) The Court may, on the application of either the custodian trustee, or any of the managing trustees, or of any beneficiary, and on proof to their satisfaction that it is the general wish of the beneficiaries, or that on other grounds it is expedient, to terminate the custodian trusteeship, make an order for that purpose, and the Court may thereupon make such vesting orders and give such directions as under the circumstances may seem to the Court to be necessary or expedient.

(3) The provisions of this section shall apply in like manner as to the public trustee to any banking or insurance company or other body corporate entitled by rules made under this Act to act as custodian trustee, with power for such company or body corporate to charge and retain or pay out of the trust property fees not exceeding the fees chargeable by the public trustee as custodian trustee.

Trustee Act 1893   6D–52

See para. 6D–49.

Subs. (1)—"Custodian trustee"   6D–53

The persons having power by statute or otherwise to appoint new trustees when a vacancy arises can properly appoint a custodian trustee under this section (*Re Cherry's Trusts* [1914] 1 Ch. 83).

Subs. (3)   6D–54

This subsection does not entitle a corporate trustee appointed as managing and custodian trustee to receive remuneration as managing trustee (*Forster v. Williams Deacon's Bank Ltd* [1935] Ch. 359, CA). Where a corporation was purported to be appointed joint managing trustee and custodian trustee, the whole appointment was held void (*Arning v. James* [1936] Ch. 158). The Public Trustee while acting as custodian trustee cannot be appointed to act also as managing or ordinary trustee and he must first be discharged by the Court from the custodian trusteeship (*Re Squire's Settlement* (1946) 62 T.L.R. 133).

The restriction imposed by s.2(5) forbidding the acceptance by the Public Trustee of trusts exclusively for charitable or religious purposes, is personal to him and is not imported into this section, and does not apply to a corporate body empowered to undertake trusts under r.30 (*Re Cherry's Trusts* [1914] 1 Ch. 83).

(3) AS AN ORDINARY TRUSTEE

Appointment of Public Trustee to be trustee, executor, etc.

5.—(1) The public trustee may by that name, or any other sufficient description, be appointed to be trustee of any will or settlement or other instrument creating a trust or to perform any trust or duty belonging to a class which he is authorised by the rules made under this Act to accept, and may be so appointed whether the will or settlement or instrument creating the trust or duty was made or came into operation before or after the passing of this Act, and either as an original or as a new trustee, or as an additional trustee, in the same cases, and in the same manner, and by the same persons or Court, as if he were a private trustee, with this addition, that, though   6D–55 the trustees originally appointed were two or more, the public trustee may be appointed sole trustee.

(2) Where the public trustee has been appointed a trustee of any trust, a co-trustee may retire from the trust under and in accordance with [section eleven of the Trustee Act 1893], notwithstanding that there are not more than two trustees, and without such consents as are required by that section.

(3) The public trustee shall not be so appointed either as a new or additional trustee where the will, settlement, or other instrument creating the trust or duty contains a direction to the contrary, unless the Court otherwise order.

(4) Notice of any proposed appointment of the public trustee either as a new or additional trustee shall where practicable be given in the prescribed manner to all persons beneficially interested who are resident in the United Kingdom and whose addresses are known to the persons proposing to make the appointment, or, if such beneficiaries are infants, to their guardians, and if any person to whom such notice has been given within twenty-one days from the receipt of the notice applies to the Court, the Court may, if having regard to the interests of all the beneficiaries it considers it expedient to do so, make an order prohibiting the appointment being made, provided that a failure to give any such notice shall not invalidate any appointment made under this section.

"As a new trustee"

6D–56   Neville J., appointed the Public Trustee in the place of the retiring trustee, upon the application of the retiring trustee and the beneficiaries having vested interests, notwithstanding the objection of the continuing trustee (*Re Kensit* [1908] W.N. 235).

"Sole trustee"

6D–57   The Public Trustee may be appointed and act as sole trustee despite any provision in the trust instrument that the number of trustees shall not be less than some larger number (*Re Leslie's Hassop Estates* [1911] 1 Ch. 611, and *Re Moxon* [1916] 2 Ch. 595); or that the trustees powers shall not be exercisable when there are less than some larger number of trustees (*Re Duxbury's Settlement Trusts* [1995] 1 W.L.R. 425). Where an appointment of the Public Trustee has been made, capital money may be paid and notices given to him as sole trustee, see S.L.A. 1925, s.94, and Sched.4, para. 12. This applies to land in N. Ireland (*Re Ardagh's Estate* [1914] I Ir. R. 5). The Public Trustee has all the attributes of an ordinary trustee; he can therefore hold all kinds of trust property; including land (*Re Leslie's Hassop Estates*). An undertaking to seal his consent to act is required from the Public Trustee before his appointment by the Court.

Foreign settlement

6D–58   See *Re Hewitt's Settlement*, cited n. to s.2(1).

"Section 11 of the Trustee Act 1893"

6D–59   See now TA 1925, s.39.

"Prohibiting the appointment"

6D–60   When the majority of the beneficiaries are in favour of the appointment of the Public Trustee the Court will not as a rule prohibit his appointment merely because of the expense (*Re Firth* [1912] 1 Ch. 806).

The settlor issued proceedings to restrain the trustees, who desired to be relieved of the trusts of the settlement, from appointing the Public Trustee to act in their place. The settlement was made for the protection of the settlor and contained wide discretionary trusts, and the circumstances were special. Parker J. remarked that in such a case the wishes of the settlor ought to be primarily considered, and that if he objected to the appointment of the Public Trustee, the Court ought, in deference to his wishes, to endeavour to get a member of his family to act. The trustees agreeing to the Judge's suggestion to continue to act, no order was made (*Re Hope Johnstone's Settlement* (1909) 53 S.J. 321).

Romer J. (commenting on *Re Hope Johnstone's Settlement*) declined to restrain the trustees of a settlement of heirlooms from appointing the Public Trustee in their place (*Re Drake's Settlement* (1926) 42 T.L.R. 467).

Power as to granting probate

6.—(1) If in pursuance of any rule under this Act, the Public Trustee is authorised to accept by that name probates of wills or letters of administration, the Court having jurisdiction to grant probate of a will or letters of administration may grant such probate or letters to the Public Trustee by that name, and for that purpose the Court shall consider the Public Trustee as in law entitled equally with any other person or class of persons to obtain the grant of letters of administration, save that the consent or citation of the public trustee shall not be required for the grant of letters of administration to any other person, and that, as between the public trustee and the widower widow or next-of-kin of the deceased, the widower widow or next-of-kin shall be preferred, unless for good cause shown to the contrary.

6D–61

(2) Any executor who has obtained probate or any administrator who has obtained letters of administration, and notwithstanding he has acted in the administration of the deceased's estate, may, with the sanction of the Court, and after such notice to the persons beneficially interested as the Court may direct, transfer such estate to the Public Trustee for administration either solely or jointly with the continuing executors or administrator, if any. And the order of the Court sanctioning such transfer shall, subject to the provisions of this Act, give to the Public Trustee all the powers of such executor and administrator, and such executor and administrator shall not be in any way liable in respect of any act or default in reference to such estate subsequent to the date of such order, other than the act or default of himself or of persons other than himself for whose conduct he is in law responsible.

Administration

The Court has power to make a grant of administration to the Public Trustee passing over the widow and other successors on intestacy (*Re Woolley* (1911) 55 S.J. 220).

6D–62

Effect of section

There is no power under the section to add the Public Trustee as executor or administrator. He can merely be substituted for an executor or administrator. The Court sanctions the transfer and the retiring executor or administrator actually carries it out.

6D–63

LIABILITY: OFFICERS AND OFFICES: FEES

7. [*Relates to the liability of the Consolidated Fund.*][*Repealed by Public Trustee (Liability and Fees) Act 2002.*]

6D–64

Officers and offices

8.—(1) The Lord Chancellor shall appoint such person as he thinks fit to the office of Public Trustee and the person so appointed shall

6D–65

hold and vacate office in accordance with the terms of his appointment.

(1A) The Public Trustee shall be paid such salary or fees as the Lord Chancellor determines with the consent of the Treasury.

(1B) If one person holds office both as the Public Trustee and as the Accountant General of the Supreme Court then, if he ceases to be the Accountant General, he shall also cease to be the Public Trustee unless the Lord Chancellor otherwise directs.

(1C) If a vacancy occurs in the office of Public Trustee or the person appointed to hold office is for any reason unable to act for any period such person as the Lord Chancellor appoints as deputy in that office shall, during the vacancy or that period, perform the functions of that office (and any property vested in the Public Trustee may accordingly be dealt with by the deputy in all respects as if it were vested in him instead).

(2) The Lord Chancellor shall appoint such persons to be officers of the Public Trustee as, subject to the sanction of the Treasury, he may consider necessary for the purposes of this Act, and those officers shall hold office upon such terms, and be remunerated at such rates and in such manner, as the Treasury may sanction.

(3) Any person appointed to be Public Trustee or an officer of the Public Trustee may, and shall, if the Treasury so require, be a person already in the public service.

[*(4) and (5) relate to offices and salaries.*]

6D–66   *Note* — subs. (1) amended and subss. (1A) (1B) and (1C) added from January 2, 1987 by the Public Trustee and Administration of Funds Act 1986.

Fees charged by Public Trustee

6D–67   **9.**—(1) There shall be charged in respect of the duties of the Public Trustee such fees, whether by way of percentage or otherwise, as the Lord Chancellor may fix.

(2) Any expenses which might be retained or paid out of the trust property if the Public Trustee were a private trustee shall be so retained or paid, and the fees shall be retained or paid in the like manner as and in addition to such expenses.

(3) Such fees shall be applied as an appropriation in aid of monies provided by Parliament for expenses under this Act, and so far as not so applied shall be paid into the Exchequer.

(4) [...]

(5) The incidence of any expenses retained or paid under this section as between capital and income shall be determined by the Public Trustee.

6D–67A   *Note* —Amended by the Public Trustee (Liability and Fees) Act 2002, s.2(1).

"Fees"

6D–68   See the Public Trustee (Fees) Act 1957, and Public Trustee (Fees) Order 1999 (S.I. 1999 No. 855) as amended by the Public Trustee (Fees) (Amendment) Order 2002 (S.I. 2002 No. 2232), the Public Trustee (Fees) (Amendment) Order 2003 (S.I. 2003 No. 690) , the Public Trustee (Fees) (Amendment) Order 2004 (S.I. 2004 No. 799) and the Public Trustee (Fees) (Amendment) Order 2005 (S.I. 2005 No. 351) . By s.2(2) of the Public Trustee (Fees) Act 1957, the Public Trustee has power in certain cases to direct that the fees in force immediately before April 1, 1957 shall continue to apply.

SUPPLEMENTAL PROVISIONS AS TO PUBLIC TRUSTEE

Appeal to the Court

10.—(1) A person aggrieved by any act or omission or decision of **6D–69** the Public Trustee in relation to any trust may apply to the Court, and the Court may make such order in the matter as the Court thinks just.

(2) Subject to Rules of Court, an application under this section to the High Court shall be made to a Judge of the Chancery Division of the High Court in Chambers.

Appeal from order of Public Trustee

An appeal lies under this section from an order made by the Public Trustee under **6D–70** s.13(5) ordering the costs of an investigation and audit of the trust accounts to be borne by the beneficiaries who applied for such investigation and audit. On such an appeal the Public Trustee, since he has exercised quasi-judicial functions, should not be made a party (*Re Oddy* [1911] 1 Ch. 532).

Mode of action of Public Trustee

11.—(1) The Public Trustee shall not, nor shall any of his officers, **6D–71** act under this Act for reward, except as provided by this Act.

(2) The Public Trustee may, subject to the rules made under this Act, employ for the purposes of any trust such solicitors, bankers, accountants, and brokers, or other persons as he may consider necessary, and in determining the persons to be so employed in relation to any trust the Public Trustee shall have regard to the interests of the trust, but subject to this shall, whenever practicable, take into consideration the wishes of the creator of the trust and of the other trustees (if any), and of the beneficiaries, either expressed or as implied by the practice of the creator of the trust, or in the previous management of the trust.

(3) On behalf of the Public Trustee such person as may be prescribed may take any oath, make any declaration, verify any account, give personal attendance at any Court or place, and do any act or thing whatsoever which the Public Trustee is required or authorised to take, make, verify, give, or do: Provided that nothing in this Act or in any rule made under this Act shall confer upon any person not otherwise entitled thereto any right to appear, or act, or be heard in or before any Court or Tribunal, on behalf or instead of the Public Trustee, or to do any act whatsoever on behalf or on the instructions of the Public Trustee, which could otherwise only be lawfully done by a barrister or a duly certified solicitor.

[(4) *relieves the Public Trustee from liability to give a bond on a grant of administration.*]

(5) The entry of the Public Trustee by that name in the books of a company shall not constitute notice of a trust, and a company shall not be entitled to object to enter the name of the Public Trustee on its books by reason only that the Public Trustee is a corporation, and,

in dealings with property, the fact that the person or one of the persons dealt with is the Public Trustee, shall not of itself constitute notice of a trust.

Application of Act to Palatine Courts

6D–72   **12.** [*The Palatine Courts were abolished by the* Courts Act 1971, s.41.]

INVESTIGATION AND AUDIT OF TRUST ACCOUNTS

Investigation and audit of trust accounts

6D–73   **13.**—(1) Subject to rules under this Act and unless the Court otherwise orders, the condition and accounts of any trust shall, on an application being made and notice thereof given in the prescribed manner by any trustee or beneficiary, be investigated and audited by such solicitor or public accountant as may be agreed on by the applicant and the trustees or, in default of agreement, by the Public Trustee or some person appointed by him: Provided that (except with the leave of the Court) such an investigation or audit shall not be required within twelve months after any such previous investigation or audit, and that a trustee or beneficiary shall not be appointed under this section to make an investigation or audit.

(2) The person making the investigation or audit (hereinafter called the auditor) shall have a right of access to the books, accounts, and vouchers of the trustees, and to any securities and documents of title held by them on account of the trust, and may require from them such information and explanation as may be necessary for the performance of his duties, and upon the completion of his investigation and audit shall forward to the applicant and to every trustee a copy of the accounts, together with a report thereon, and a certificate signed by him to the effect that the accounts exhibit a true view of the state of the affairs of the trust and that he has had the securities of the trust fund investments produced to and verified by him or (as the case may be) that such accounts are deficient in such respects as may be specified in such certificate.

(3) Every beneficiary under the trust shall, subject to rules under this Act, be entitled at all reasonable times to inspect and take copies of the accounts, report, and certificate, and, at his own expense, to be furnished with copies thereof or extracts therefrom.

(4) The auditor may be removed by order of the Court, and, if any auditor is removed, or resigns, or dies, or becomes bankrupt or incapable of acting before the investigation and audit is completed, a new auditor may be appointed in his place in like manner as the original auditor.

(5) The remuneration of the auditor and the other expenses of the investigation and audit shall be such as may be prescribed by rules under this Act, and shall, unless the Public Trustee otherwise directs, be borne by the estate; and, in the event of the Public Trustee so directing, he may order that such expenses be borne by the applicant or by the trustees personally or partly by them and partly by the applicant.

(6) If any person having the custody of any documents to which the auditor has a right of access under this section fails or refuses to allow him to have access thereto or in anywise obstructs the investigation or audit, the auditor may apply to the Court, and thereupon the Court shall make such order as it thinks just.

(7) Subject to Rules of Court, applications under or for the purposes of this section to the High Court shall be made to a Judge of the Chancery Division in Chambers.

(8) If any person in any statement of accounts, report, or certificate required for the purposes of this section wilfully makes a statement false in any material particular, he shall be liable on conviction on indictment to imprisonment for a term not exceeding two years, and on summary conviction to imprisonment for a term not exceeding six months, [...] and in either case to a fine in lieu of or in addition to such imprisonment.

Note —Amended by the Criminal Justice Act 1948, s.1(2). **6D–74**

Deposit on account of expenses
The Public Trustee has power to require an applicant for an audit to deposit with **6D–75** him a sum of money on account of the expenses of the audit, and to refuse to undertake an audit or appoint an auditor until the deposit has been made (Public Trustee Rules 1912, r.32(1) and (2)).

Application by auditor to the Court
A trustee cannot refuse the auditor access to the books of account of the trust (*Re* **6D–76** *James Williams* (1910) 26 T.L.R. 604).

Audit expenses
Rule 37(1) of the Public Trustee Rules 1912, provides that, before making any or- **6D–77** der under subs. (5) the Public Trustee shall, if any of the parties so desire, hear the said parties in such manner as he shall think fit.

In a proper case the costs of the investigation will come out of the estate, but if the application is considered unnecessary the Public Trustee has power to order the applicant to pay the costs (*Re Utley, Russell v. Cubitt* [1912] W.N. 147).

As to an appeal from an order by the Public Trustee directing parties to pay the expenses of an audit, see *Re Oddy* [1911] 1 Ch. 532.

Where the Public Trustee has made an order under s.13(5) charging the expenses against the trustees or the applicant, it is doubtful whether s.13(7) applies so as to provide a method of enforcing the order. That subsection appears to be directed to the procedure for carrying out subss. (4) and (6) and the proviso to subs. (1).

In *Gane v. Russell*, 1911, unreported a writ was issued by the auditor, the solicitor to the trustees, and the Public Trustee, against the party charged to recover the amount of the fees and expenses, and judgment obtained for the payment thereof, which was enforced by the appointment of a receiver of the defendant's income.

Audit Fee
Under the Public Trustee (Fees) Order (S.I. 1999 No. 855) a fee of £750 is payable **6D–78** to the Public Trustee in addition to the remuneration of the auditor. An additional fee may be charged for conducting a hearing in accordance with r.37 of the Public Trustee Rules 1912 and for duties of an unusual, complex or exacting nature.

RULES: DEFINITIONS: SHORT TITLE AND EXTENT

Rules
14.—(1) The Lord Chancellor shall, with the concurrence of the **6D–79** Treasury, make rules for carrying into effect the objects of this Act,

and in particular for all or any of the following purposes (that is to say):—

(a) establishing the office of Public Trustee and prescribing the trusts or duties he is authorised to accept or undertake, and the security, if any, to be given by the Public Trustee and his officers:

(b) the transfer to and from the Public Trustee of any property:

(c) the accounts to be kept and an audit thereof:

(d) the establishment and regulation of any branch office:

(e) excluding any trusts from the operation of this Act or any part thereof:

(f) the classes of corporate bodies entitled to act as custodian trustees:

(g) the form and manner in which notices under this Act shall be given.

(2) Every rule under this Act shall be laid before each House of Parliament forthwith, and, if an address is presented to His Majesty by either House of Parliament, within the next subsequent thirty days on which the House has sat next after any such rule is laid before it, praying that the rule may be annulled, His Majesty in Council may annul the rule, and it shall thenceforth be void, but without prejudice to the validity of anything previously done thereunder.

(3) If the rules require a declaration to be made for any purpose, a person who makes such declaration, knowing the same to be untrue in any material particular, shall be guilty of a misdemeanour.

Definitions

6D–80   **15.** In this Act, unless the context otherwise requires—

the expression "Court" means the High Court and, as respects trusts within its jurisdiction, the county court:

the expression "letters of administration" means letters of administration of the estate and effects of a deceased person, whether general or with a will annexed, or limited either in time or otherwise:

the expression "trust" includes an executorship or administratorship; and the expression "trustee" shall be construed accordingly; and the expression "trust property" shall include all property in the possession or under the control wholly or partly of the Public Trustee by virtue of any trust:

the expression "private trustee" means a trustee other than the Public Trustee

the expression "expenses" means costs and charges:

the expression "prescribed" means prescribed for the time being by rules under this Act:

other expressions have the same meaning as in the [Trustee Act 1893].

"Trustee Act 1893"

6D–81   See now T.A. 1925, s.68.

Commencement of Act

16. [*Repealed by* Statute Law Revision Act 1927.]   **6D–82**

Short title and extent

17.—(1) This Act may be cited as the Public Trustee Act, 1906.   **6D–83**

(2) This Act shall not extend to Ireland or Scotland.

"Foreign settlement"

The Public Trustee cannot be appointed trustee of a "foreign settlement," *i.e.* a   **6D–84**
settlement made according to the law of a foreign country or any part of the United
Kingdom to which the Act does not extend; notwithstanding the fact that the trustees,
the beneficiaries and property are in England. He may, however, be appointed trustee
to a settlement made according to English law, though the trust property is outside
the jurisdiction (*Re Hewitt's Settlement* [1915] 1 Ch. 228).

<h2 style="text-align:center">Public Trustee Rules 1912</h2>

(S. R. & O. 1912 No. 348)   6D–85

ARRANGEMENT OF RULES

INTERPRETATION

Interpretation

6D–86   **1.** In these Rules the expression "the Act" means the Public Trustee Act, 1906, and unless there is anything in the context or in the Act inconsistent therewith—

> The expression "trust" includes any trust duty or office which the Public Trustee is authorised by the Act or these Rules to accept; and the expression "trustee" shall be construed accordingly.

> The expression "trust instrument" includes any instrument, Act of Parliament, or Order of Court by which a trust is created or declared.

> The expression "trust property" includes all property subject to a trust, or comprised in an estate, which is proposed to be administered by the Public Trustee.

6D–87   **2.** The Interpretation Act, 1889, applies for the purpose of the interpretation of these rules as it applies for the purpose of the interpretation of an Act of Parliament.

Offices

6D–88   **3.**—(1) The Central Office of the Public Trustee shall be situate in London.

(2) Branch Offices may from time to time be established as may be prescribed by the Lord Chancellor by notice in the *London Gazette*. The Office of the Public Trustee is at 81 Chancery Lane London WC2A 1DD; DX 0012 London Chancery Lane WC2. Telephone 020 7911 7100; Fax 020 7911 7105; e-mail enquiries@offsol.gsi.gov.uk.

Deputy Public Trustees

6D–89   **4.** There shall be Deputy Public Trustees at any branch office so established who shall be officers of the Public Trustee, and shall have the powers and perform the duties assigned to them by or under these Rules. Their number shall be such as the Lord Chancellor, with the sanction of the Treasury, may from time to time prescribe, and every such appointment shall be notified in the *London Gazette*.

Security

5.Security shall be given by such persons employed under the Act **6D–90** as the Treasury may direct for the due performance of their duties, and for the due accounting for and payment of all moneys received by them in pursuance of the Act and these Rules. The security shall be for such sum and shall be given in such manner and form as the Treasury shall order in the case of each such person, and the Treasury may at any time require that the amount or nature of any such security be varied.

Authorised Trusts and Duties

6.Subject to the Act and these Rules the Public Trustee is autho- **6D–91** rised—

- (a) to accept any trust created or declared by any trust instrument or arising upon an intestacy;
- (b) to accept any duty incident to, and to act in, any of the following offices, *viz.*: (i) as incident to the office of trustee of any trust accepted by him the office of guardian of any infant beneficiary (ii) the office (where the execution of any trust is involved therein) of agent or attorney for any person.
- (c) to accept by the name of the Public Trustee probate or letters of administration of any kind and either as principal or as agent for any person;
- (d) to accept as custodian trustee any trust created or declared by any trust instrument;
- (e) to receive any money or damages paid to him in pursuance of the Rules of the Supreme Court, Order 22, Rule 15, or any rule which may be substituted therefor, and to apply the same in accordance with such rule or any directions of the Court or a Judge thereunder.

Provided that he shall not accept the trusts of any instrument made solely by way of security for money.

7.The Public Trustee may if he thinks fit— **6D–92**

- (1) act as custodian trustee of a trust which involves the management or carrying on of any business, but upon the conditions that (a) he shall not act in the management or carrying on of such business, and (b) he shall not hold any property of such a nature as will expose the holder thereof to any liability except under exceptional circumstances and when he is satisfied that he is fully indemnified or secured against loss; and
- (2) accept as ordinary trustee, under exceptional circumstances a trust which involves the management or carrying on of any business, but upon the conditions that, except with the consent of the Treasury, he shall only

carry on the same (a) for a short time not exceeding 18 months, and (b) with a view to sale disposition or winding-up, and (c) if satisfied that the same can be carried on without risk of loss.

Trusteeships

6D–93 8.—(1)A testator may appoint the Public Trustee to be trustee or custodian trustee under any testamentary instrument without previously applying to him for his consent to act as such.

(2) No such appointment by a testator shall have effect, and no appointment of the Public Trustee to be trustee or custodian trustee shall be made except by a testator, unless and until (in either case) the consent of the Public Trustee to act as such trustee shall have been obtained in accordance with these Rules. Provided that in the case of any such appointment by a testator the Public Trustee shall at any time after the fact of his appointment shall have come to his knowledge be at liberty to act as if an application for his consent had been received by him.

(3) It shall be the duty of any person appointed by a testator to be co-trustee with the Public Trustee, and not renouncing or disclaiming the trust, to give to the Public Trustee notice in writing of such appointment as soon as practicable after the same has come to his knowledge.

"Shall have effect"

6D–94   A deed appointing the Public Trustee to be a trustee does not become operative until the Public Trustee has given his formal consent to act under his official seal (*Re Shaw, Public Trustee v. Little* [1914] W.N. 141, CA).

6D–95 9.Upon receiving an application for his consent to act as trustee or as custodian trustee the Public Trustee may require to be produced to him the trust instrument (if any) and may require to be supplied to him a copy of that instrument, and of any other document affecting the trust, and such particulars as to the nature and value of any trust property, and the liabilities (if any) attaching to such property, or the holder thereof, and the names and places of abode of any beneficiaries and trustees under the trust, and such other information relating to the trust as he may consider it desirable to obtain in any particular case.

6D–96 10.As soon as may be after receiving any such application the Public Trustee shall take into consideration upon such evidence as may appear to him sufficient—

(a) the gross capital value of the trust property;

(b) the mode of investment and the condition of the trust property;

(c) the situation, tenure, and character of any land comprised in the trust property;

(d) any liabilities attaching to the trust property or the holder thereof;

(e) the duties incident to the office of trustee of the trust;

(f) the places of abode and circumstances of any beneficiaries; and

(g) all the circumstances of the case;

and shall decide whether the application ought to be accepted or refused, and shall give notice to the applicant of such acceptance or refusal, and in case of acceptance shall in writing under his official seal signify his consent to act in the trust.

Note —Amended by the Public Trustee Rules 1916 (S. R. & O. 1916, No. 489). **6D–97**

Appointment by the Court
An undertaking to seal his consent to act is required from the Public Trustee before **6D–98** his appointment as trustee by the Court. Where such a consent has been sealed prior to the application to the Court, its effect is merely an expression of willingness on the part of the Public Trustee to act if the Court thinks proper to appoint him.

The sealed consent is accepted without verification.

11. Upon the appointment of the Public Trustee being completed, **6D–99** the Public Trustee shall consider and determine whether the trust shall be administered from his central office or from a branch office, and shall give directions accordingly, and any such directions may at any time be rescinded or varied by the Public Trustee at his discretion.

Administration of Small Estates
12. Upon receiving an application under section 3(1) of the Act the **6D–100** Public Trustee shall require to be supplied to him such evidence as to the value of the estate, and the circumstances of the persons beneficially entitled, and such other information relating thereto as he may consider it desirable to obtain in any particular case.

13.—(1) If it is not proved to the satisfaction of the Public Trustee **6D–101** that the gross capital value of the estate is less than £1,000, or if it does not appear to him that the persons beneficially entitled are persons of small means, or if he sees any other good reason for refusing the application, he shall refuse the same, and shall forthwith give notice to the applicant of such refusal.

(2) In any other case the Public Trustee shall make in respect of the estate the declaration mentioned in section 3(2) of the Act, and shall give notice to the applicant that the application is accepted, and shall take such other steps as may be necessary or proper to enable him to administer the estate; and any person having the custody of the probate or letters of administration, or other document relating to the estate, shall, upon the request in writing of the Public Trustee, deliver the same to him, or as he shall direct.

(3) A refusal under this rule shall not prevent the Public Trustee from exercising, with respect to the estate, any powers (other than powers under section 3 of the Act) exercisable by him with respect thereto under the Act or these rules, if duly appointed to exercise the same.

(4) Upon the acceptance of any application the Public Trustee shall consider and determine whether the estate shall be administered from his central office or from a branch office, and shall give directions accordingly, and any such directions may at any time be rescinded or varied by the Public Trustee at his discretion.

6D–102   14.For the purposes of the administration the Public Trustee shall (subject as hereinafter provided) have all the administrative powers and authorities exercisable by a master of the Supreme Court acting in the administration of an estate.

Master

6D–103   *i.e.* of the Chancery Division.

6D–104   15.—(1)The Public Trustee may without judicial proceedings, take the opinion of the High Court upon any question arising in the course of an administration.

(2) Any such question shall be submitted—

    (a) to such Judge of the Chancery Division as the Vice-Chancellor may specify; and

    (b) in such manner as that judge may direct.

(3) [...]

(4) The Judge may, before giving his opinion, require the attendance of, or communicate with any person interested in the estate as trustee or beneficiary, but no such person shall have a right to be heard by the Judge unless he otherwise directs.

(5) The Judge shall give his opinion to the Public Trustee, and the Public Trustee shall act in accordance with such opinion, and shall, upon the request in writing of any such interested person, communicate to him the effect of such opinion.

6D–105   *Note* —Amended by the Public Trustee (Amendment) Rules 1983 (S.I. 1983 No. 1050).

Administration of Trusts and Estates

6D–106   16.There shall be kept at the Central Office in London of the Public Trustee such registers and other books as shall be required for recording or entering in a convenient form as to each trust or estate which the Public Trustee is administering the particulars following:—

    (a) the date of the acceptance of the trust or of the declaration made under section 3(2) of the Act;

    (b) particulars of the trust property from time to time;

    (c) the names and place of abode of the person in receipt of the income of the trust property;

    (d) a reference to any notice received of any dealing with any beneficial interest in the trust property, and of any exercise or release of any power relating to the trust or estate;

    (e) an entry of any decision or opinion of the High Court in respect of the trust or estate;

    (f) such entries of his decisions and such other particulars as the Public Trustee may think fit;

and such particulars shall be recorded or entered accordingly.

6D–107   17.The Public Trustee may—

    (a) invest or retain invested money belonging to any trust or estate and coming into his hands in any mode of investment

    (i) expressly or implicitly authorised by the trust
        instrument, or

    (ii) if there is no trust instrument, authorised by law
          for the investment of trust funds,

  (b) pay and deposit such money in court for investment in
      any manner authorised by rules made under section
      38(7) of the Administration of Justice Act 1982.

  (c) if authorised by the trust instrument or otherwise by
      law, retain any investment existing at the date of the
      commencement of the trust.

Provided that he shall not invest in or hold any investment in such manner as to expose him to liability as the holder thereof, unless he is satisfied that he is fully indemnified or secured against loss.

Note —Substituted by the Public Trustee (Amendment) Rules 1987 (S.I. 1987 No. **6D–108** 2249). With reference to the amended r.17(b) see the Court Funds Rules 1987 (S.I. 1987 No. 821) (as amended) paras 6A–18 *et seq.*

18.—(1)The securities and documents belonging or relating to a **6D–109** trust or estate which the Public Trustee is administering shall, if under his control, be kept at the bank to the trust or estate or at some other safe place of deposit allowed generally or specially by the Treasury, so far as the convenience of business will admit.

(2) All orders for the withdrawal of securities or documents from any such bank or other place of deposit shall be signed by not less than two persons, *viz.*: (a) by the Public Trustee and a co-trustee, or (b) by the Public Trustee and an officer of the Public Trustee authorised in writing by him to act in that behalf, either generally or in any particular case, or (c) by a co-trustee and one such duly authorised officer, or (d) by two such duly authorised officers.

19.—(1)Separate accounts shall be kept for every trust or estate. **6D–110**

(2) A separate account shall be kept of the capital of the trust property and of the mode in which it is from time to time invested, and all dealing with such capital shall be entered in such account.

(3) A separate account shall be kept of the income of the trust property (if received by the Public Trustee) and of the mode in which it is from time to time dealt with by the Public Trustee.

20. All payments of money to or from the capital of the trust prop- **6D–111** erty shall be made through the bank to the trust or estate.

21. In all cases where any deed or other instrument requires to be **6D–112** executed by the Public Trustee under his official seal, the affixing of the seal may be authenticated by the signature either of the Public Trustee or of some officer of the Public Trustee duly authorised by the Public Trustee in that behalf under his seal, and any deed or other instrument purporting to be a deed or instrument executed by the Public Trustee and to be sealed with his seal authenticated in manner provided by this Rule shall be received in evidence and be deemed to be a deed or instrument so executed without further proof unless the contrary is shown.

Note —Amended by r.3 of the Public Trustee Rules 1916 (S. R. & O., 1916, No. **6D–113** 489, dated February 25, 1916) which revoked the former r.21.

6D–114 22.All sums payable out of the income or capital of the trust property shall be made by a cheque on the Bank of England bearing a signature or a facsimile signature of an officer of the Public Trustee authorised in writing by him to act in that behalf or a cheque on a bank signed by not less than two persons, *viz.*: (a) by the Public Trustee and a co-trustee, or (b) by the Public Trustee and an officer of the Public Trustee authorised in writing by him to act in that behalf either generally or in any particular case, or (c) by a co-trustee and one such duly authorised officer, or (d) by two such duly authorised officers. Provided that in any particular case the Public Trustee may authorise the payment of income by the person liable to pay the same direct to the person entitled to receive the same, or to his bank.

6D–115 *Note* —Amended by the Public Trustee (Amendment) Rules 1983 (S.I. 1983 No. 1050).

6D–116 23.—(1)The income of the trust property may be paid to the person for the time being entitled to receive the same either through a bank or direct, and where such person is a married woman may be so paid notwithstanding any restraint on anticipation.

(2) Where authority is given to any corporation or bank to pay any income to any person, the books of that corporation or bank showing the payment of that income in accordance with the authority shall be a sufficient discharge to the Public Trustee.

(3) Where authority is given to any person to pay any income to the bank of the person entitled, the certificate of that bank stating the receipt of that income shall be a sufficient discharge to the Public Trustee.

(4) Where any person is solely entitled to receive any income, the Public Trustee may, on the request in writing of that person, and notwithstanding any restraint on anticipation, authorise that person for such period as the Public Trustee may think fit to collect or arrange for the collection of such income. During the continuance of any such authority such request in writing shall be a sufficient discharge to the Public Trustee in respect of such income.

6D–117 24.The Public Trustee may, if the special circumstances of the case appear to him to render it desirable, pay to any other trustee of the trust or allow him to receive, the income of the trust property or any part thereof, on such trustee undertaking to apply it in manner directed by the trust.

6D–118 25.The Public Trustee may make advances for the purposes of any trust or estate in course of administration, or about to be administered, by him, out of any moneys which may be placed at his disposal by the Treasury for that purpose, and upon such terms as he may think proper.

6D–119 26.Subject to the provisions of the Act and of these Rules and to the terms of any particular trust, the Public Trustee may, in the administration of any trust or estate, take and use professional advice and assistance in regard to legal and other matters, and may act on credible information (though less than legal evidence) as to matters of fact.

27. The Public Trustee may at any time require a statutory declara- **6D–120** tion or other sufficient evidence that a person is alive and is the person to whom any money or property is payable or transferable, and may refuse payment or transfer until such declaration or evidence is produced.

Onus of proof

See *Re Wilson (dec'd)* [1964] 1 W.L.R. 214; [1964] 1 All E.R. 196, wherein it was held **6D–121** that the onus of proving that a missing life tenant was alive rested on an applicant under s.10(1) of the Act who sought payment of income under an order for sequestration against the life tenant.

28. Where a person appearing to be beneficially entitled to any sum **6D–122** of money under the trust or to be interested in the trust property cannot be found, or it is not known whether he is living or dead, the Public Trustee may apply to the Court for directions as to the course to be taken with reference to such person, and until an Order of the Court is made shall keep any sum payable to such person, and if it is kept for more than six months shall invest the same or deposit the same at interest and shall accumulate the dividends or interest thereof.

Discretion of Public Trustee

The Public Trustee has a discretion as to whether or not to seek direction of the **6D–123** Court under r.28. See *Re Wilson (dec'd)* [1964] 1 W.L.R. 214; [1964] 1 All E.R. 196.

29.—(1) Upon an application in writing by or with the authority of **6D–124** any person interested in the trust property the Public Trustee—

> (a) shall permit the applicant or his solicitor or other authorised agent to inspect and take copies of any entry in any register or book relating to the trust or estate and (so far as the interest of the applicant in the trust property is or may be affected thereby) of any account, notice, or other document in the custody of the Public Trustee;
>
> (b) shall at the expense of the applicant supply him or his solicitor or other authorised agent with a copy of any such entry, account, notice, or document as aforesaid, or with any extract therefrom;
>
> (c) shall give to the applicant or his solicitor or other authorised agent such information respecting the trust or estate and the trust property as shall be reasonably requested in the application and shall be within the power of the Public Trustee.

(2) Subject as aforesaid the Public Trustee shall observe strict secrecy in respect of every trust or estate in course of administration by him.

Corporate Bodies as Custodian Trustees

30.—(1) The following corporations shall be entitled to act as **6D–125** custodian trustees:—

> (a) the Treasury Solicitor;
>
> (b) any corporation which:—

(i) is constituted under the law of the United Kingdom or of any part thereof, or under the law of any other Member State of the European Economic Community or of any part thereof;

(ii) is empowered by its constitution to undertake trust business (which for the purpose of this rule means the business of acting as trustee under wills and settlements and as executor and administrator) in England and Wales;

(iii) has one or more places of business in the United Kingdom; and

(iv) is—

a company incorporated by special Act of Parliament or Royal Charter, or

a company registered (with or without limited liability) in the United Kingdom under the Companies Act 1948 or under the Companies Act (Northern Ireland) 1960 or in another Member State of the European Economic Community and having a capital (in stock or shares) for the time being issued of not less than £250,000 (or its equivalent in the currency of the State where the company is registered), of which not less than £100,000 (or its equivalent) has been paid up in cash, or

a company which is registered without limited liability in the United Kingdom under the Companies Act 1948 or the Companies Act (Northern Ireland) 1960 or in another Member State of the European Economic Community and of which one of the members is a company within any of the classes defined in this sub-paragraph;

(c) any corporation which is incorporated by special Act or Royal Charter or under the Charitable Trustees Incorporation Act 1872 which is empowered by its constitution to act as a trustee for any charitable purposes, but only in relation to trusts in which its constitution empowers it to act;

(d) any corporation which is constituted under the law of the United Kingdom or of any part thereof and having its place of business there, and which is either:

(i) established for the purpose of undertaking trust business for the benefit of Her Majesty's Navy, Army, Air Force or Civil Service or of any unit, department, member or association of members thereof, and having among its directors or members any persons appointed or nominated by the Defence Council or any Department of State or any one or more of those Departments, or

     (ii) authorised by the Lord Chancellor to act in rela-
tion to any charitable, ecclesiastical or public trusts
as a trust corporation, but only in connection with
any such trust as is so authorised;

(e)

     (i) any Regional Health Authority, District Health
Authority or special health authority, but only in
relation to any trust which the authority is authorised to accept or hold by virtue of section 90 of
the National Health Service Act 1977;

     (ii) any preserved Board as defined by section 15(6)
of the National Health Service Reorganisation Act
1973, but only in relation to any trust which the
Board is authorised to accept or hold by virtue of
an order made under that section;

(f) the British Gas Corporation or any subsidiary of the
British Gas Corporation, but only in relation to a pension scheme or pension fund established or maintained
by the Corporation by virtue of section 36 of the Gas Act
1972;

(g) the London Transport Executive, but only in relation to
a pension scheme or pension fund—

     (i) which is established or administered by the Exec-
utive by virtue of section 6 of the Transport
(London) Act 1969, or

     (ii) in relation to which rights, liabilities and functions
have been transferred to the Executive by an or-
der under section 74 of the Transport Act 1962 as
applied by section 18 of the Transport (London)
Act 1969;

(h) any of the following, namely:—

     (i) the Greater London Council,

     (ii) the corporation of any London borough (acting
by the council),

     (iii) a county council, district council, parish council or
community council,

     (iv) the Council of the Isles of Scilly,

     (v) the Common Council of the City of London,

but only in relation to charitable or public trusts (and not trusts
for an ecclesiastical charity or for a charity for the relief of poverty)
for the benefit of the inhabitants of the area of the local authority
concerned and its neighbourhood, or any part of that area.

(i) any of the following, namely:—

     (i) a metropolitan district council or a non-
metropolitan county council,

     (ii) the corporation of any London borough (acting
by the council),

     (iii) the Common Council of the City of London,

     (iv) the Council of the Isles of Scilly,

but only in relation to any trust under which property devolves for the sole benefit of a person who occupies residential accommodation provided under section 21(1)(a) of the National Assistance Act 1948 by the local authority concerned or is in the care of that authority; and a corporation acting as a custodian trustee by virtue of this paragraph in relation to any trust shall be entitled to continue so to act in relation to that trust until a new custodian trustee is appointed, notwithstanding that the person concerned ceases to occupy such accommodation or to be in the care of that authority, as the case may be.

(j) The National Coal Board or any subsidiary of the National Coal Board, but only in relation to a scheme or arrangements established under regulations made under section 37 of the Coal Industry Nationalisation Act 1946.

(k) Any corporation acting as trustee of the trusts of any pension scheme or pension fund established or maintained by the British Broadcasting Corporation, but only in relation to those trusts.

(l) any corporation appointed by the Secretary of State as a trustee of any scheme having effect by virtue of regulations made under section 37 of the Coal Industry Nationalisation Act 1946 for purposes relating to pensions, gratuities or other like benefits and in relation to which provision is, or has been, made by regulations made under paragraph 2(1) of Schedule 5 to the Coal Industry Act 1994 for the scheme to continue in force notwithstanding the repeal by the Coal Industry Act 1994 of section 37 of the Coal Industry Nationalisation Act 1946 and of the enactments modifying that section, but only in relation to such a scheme.

(2) In this rule "subsidiary" has the same meaning as in section 154 of the Companies Act 1948.

6D–126   Note —Substituted by the Public Trustee (Custodian Trustee) Rules 1975 (S.I. 1975 No. 1189) as amended by the Public Trustee (Custodian Trustee) Rules 1976 (S.I. 1976 No. 836); the Public Trustee (Custodian Trustee) Rules 1981 (S.I. 1981 No. 358); the Public Trustee (Custodian Trustee) Rules 1984 (S.I. 1984 No. 109); the Public Trustee (Custodian Trustee) (Amendment) Rules 1985 (S.I. 1985 No. 132); the Public Trustee (Custodian Trustee) Rules 1987 (S.I. 1987 No. 1891); and the Public Trustee (Custodian Trustee) Rules 1994 (S.I. 1994 No. 2519). The Bank of Ireland is within the rule (*Re Bigger (dec'd)* [1977] Fam. 203).

Investigation and Audit of Trust Accounts

6D–127   **31.**Any application under section 13(1) of the Act shall be made to the Public Trustee, and notice thereof shall (unless the Public Trustee otherwise directs) be given by the applicant to every other person being a trustee or beneficiary under the trust.

6D–128   **32.**—(1)Upon receiving any such application the Public Trustee may in his absolute discretion by notice to the applicant require that before a day to be specified in the notice such security (by deposit of a sum of money) as he shall deem sufficient shall be given to him by the applicant for the payment of any expenses of the investigation and audit which may be ordered by the Public Trustee to be paid by the applicant personally.

(2) Where any such requirement is made no further proceedings shall be taken upon the application until the security has been given, and if the same is not given before the day specified in the notice the application shall be disallowed unless under special circumstances the Public Trustee thinks fit to extend the time for giving the security or to dispense therewith.

(3) Any sum so deposited shall be kept by the Public Trustee on deposit in his name and to a separate account at a bank until all proceedings in connection with the investigation and audit have been concluded, and thereupon the deposited sum and the interest (if any) allowed thereon by the bank shall be applied in or towards payment of any expenses of the investigation and audit which may be so ordered to be paid by the applicant personally and the balance (if any) shall be paid to the applicant.

33. The Public Trustee may in his absolute discretion upon the application of any trustee or beneficiary direct that the investigation and audit shall extend only to a specified period of time or to a specified part of the trust property or shall be otherwise restricted. **6D–129**

34. If within one month from the date of the application under section 13(1) of the Act no solicitor or public accountant shall have been appointed by the applicant and the trustees to conduct the investigation and audit, there shall be deemed to be a default of agreement within the meaning of the said section 13(1) and the applicant may apply to the Public Trustee accordingly. **6D–130**

35. The remuneration of the auditor and the other expenses of the investigation and audit shall be such as may be determined by the Public Trustee. Provided that the Public Trustee may refer the costs of any solicitor (being part of such expenses) for taxation to a Taxing Master of the Supreme Court, and in such case the amount of the said costs when taxed shall be included in such expenses. **6D–131**

Note —Taxation has been replaced by assessment. For this purpose a Taxing Master is referred to as a "Costs Judge". **6D–132**

36.—(1)Where any investigation or audit has been made, copies of the report and certificate of the auditor under section 13(2) of the Act and such copies of accounts and other documents as the Public Trustee may require shall be forwarded to him by the auditor, and shall be considered by the Public Trustee before giving any direction or making any order under section 13(5) of the Act. **6D–133**

(2) The expense of making and forwarding any such copies as aforesaid and the fee of the Public Trustee (within the limits prescribed by or in pursuance of any order relating to the fees of the Public Trustee for the time being in force) shall for the purpose of section 13(5) of the Act be part of the expenses of the investigation and audit.

37.—(1)Before making any order under section 13(5) of the Act the Public Trustee shall, if any of the parties interested so desire, hear the said parties in such manner as he shall think fit. **6D–134**

(2) Any such order shall specify the person by or to whom any sum is to be paid and the amount of such sum Provided that such an order may direct payment of the taxed costs of any solicitor employed

in connection with the investigation and audit, and such costs shall be taxed by a Taxing Master of the Supreme Court, and the amount of such costs when taxed shall be paid as if such amount had been specified in the order.

(3) Any such order may be enforced in the same manner as a judgment or order of the Court to the same effect.

Miscellaneous

6D–135 **38.**The accounts of the Public Trustee shall be audited and the securities held by him verified from time to time by such person or persons as the Treasury may appoint in accordance with regulations made by the Treasury.

6D–136 **39.**Any officer of the Public Trustee who shall be authorised by him in writing in that behalf may take any oath, make any declaration, verify any account and give personal attendance at any Court or place.

6D–137 **40.**—(1)Any notice or application required to be given or made for the purpose of the Act or these Rules to the Public Trustee may be addressed to the Public Trustee at his office in London, or if the same relates to a trust or estate in course of administration or proposed to be administered from a branch office then at that branch office.

(2) Any notice or application required to be given or made for the purpose of the Act or these Rules to any person other than the Public Trustee may be addressed to that person at his last known place of abode or place of business.

(3) Any such notice or application may be delivered at the place to which it is addressed or may be served by post.

6D–138 **41.**Where any person who (if not under disability) might have made an application, given any consent, done any act, or been party to any proceedings in pursuance of these Rules is an infant, idiot, or lunatic, the guardian or (as the case may require) the committee or receiver of the estate of such person may make such application, give such consent, do such act, and be party to such proceedings as such person if free from disability might have made, given, done or been party to, and shall otherwise represent such person for the purposes of these Rules. Where there is no guardian or committee or receiver of the estate of any such infant, idiot, or lunatic, or where any person is of unsound mind, or incapable of managing his affairs but has not been found lunatic under any inquisition, it shall be lawful for the Court to appoint a guardian of such a person for the purpose of any proceedings under these Rules and from time to time to change such guardian.

6D–139 **42.**—(1)The Public Trustee may in writing authorise any Deputy Public Trustee to exercise and perform (either generally or in relation to any particular case and subject to such conditions and restrictions (if any) as the Public Trustee may impose) all or any of the powers and duties of the Public Trustee under any of the foregoing Rules except—

(a) the power or duty of determining whether a trust or estate shall be administered from his Central Office or from a Branch Office; and

(b) the power of authorising officers of the Public Trustee to transfer securities or assure land or to sign cheques;

(c) the power of making advances for the purpose of any trust or estate.

(2) Any such authority conditions or restrictions may at any time in like manner be withdrawn or varied by the Public Trustee at his discretion.

43. No Deputy Public Trustee and no firm or member of a firm of **6D–140** Solicitors of which such Deputy is a member shall, except with the consent in writing of the Public Trustee and subject to such conditions as he may impose, act as Solicitor or Solicitors to a trust or estate which is in course of administration by such Deputy.

44. The Public Trustee may frame and cause to be printed and **6D–141** circulated or otherwise promulgated such forms and directions and regulations as he may deem requisite or expedient for facilitating proceedings under the Act and these Rules.

45. The Public Trustee Rules 1907, are hereby rescinded. **6D–142**

46. These Rules may be cited as "The Public Trustee Rules, 1912", **6D–143** and shall come into operation on the 15th day of April, 1912.

Variation of Trusts Act 1958

(1958 6 & 7 ELIZ. 2, C.53)

An Act to extend the jurisdiction of Courts of law to vary trusts in **6D–144** the interests of beneficiaries and sanction dealings with trust property.

[23rd July, 1958.]

Jurisdiction of Courts to vary trusts

1.—(1) Where property, whether real or personal, is held on trusts **6D–145** arising, whether before or after the passing of this Act, under any will, settlement or other disposition, the Court may if it thinks fit by order approve on behalf of—

(a) any person having, directly or indirectly, an interest, whether vested or contingent, under the trusts who by reason of infancy or other incapacity is incapable of assenting, or

(b) any person (whether ascertained or not) who may become entitled, directly or indirectly, to an interest under the trusts as being at a future date or on the happening of a future event a person of any specified description or a member of any specified class of persons, so however that this paragraph shall not include any person who would be of that description, or a member of that class, as the case may be, if the said date had fallen or the said event had happened at the date of the application to the Court, or

(c) any person unborn, or

(d) any person in respect of any discretionary interest of his under protective trusts where the interest of the principal beneficiary has not failed or determined, any arrangement (by whomsoever proposed, and whether or not there is any other person beneficially interested who is capable of assenting thereto) varying or revoking all or any of the trusts, or enlarging the powers of the trustees of managing or administering any of the property subject to the trusts:

Provided that except by virtue of paragraph (d) of this subsection the Court shall not approve an arrangement on behalf of any person unless the carrying out thereof would be for the benefit of that person.

(2) In the foregoing subsection "protective trusts" means the trusts specified in paragraphs (i) and (ii) of subsection (1) of section thirty-three of the Trustee Act, 1925, or any like trusts, "the principal beneficiary" has the same meaning as in the said subsection (1) and "discretionary interest" means an interest arising under the trust specified in paragraph (ii) of the said subsection (1) or any like trust.

(3) The jurisdiction conferred by subsection (1) of this section shall be exercisable by the High Court, except that the question whether the carrying out of any arrangement would be for the benefit of a person falling within paragraph (a) of the said subsection (1) shall be determined by order of the authority having jurisdiction under Part VII of the Mental Health Act 1983, if that person is a patient within the meaning of the said Part VII.

(4) [...]

(5) Nothing in the foregoing provisions of this section shall apply to trusts affecting property settled by Act of Parliament.

(6) Nothing in this section shall be taken to limit the powers conferred by section sixty-four of the Settled Land Act, 1925, section fifty-seven of the Trustee Act, 1925, or the powers of the authority having jurisdiction under Part VII of the Mental Health Act 1983.

6D–146   *Note* —Amended by the County Courts Act 1959, Sched.3; and the Mental Health Act 1959, Sched.7 and, M.H.A. 1983, Sched.4.

Extent and provisions as to Northern Ireland
6D–147   **2.**—(1) This Act shall not extend to Scotland.

(2) The foregoing section shall not extend to Northern Ireland.

6D–148   *Note* —Amended by the Northern Ireland Constitution Act 1973, Sched.6.

Short title
6D–149   **3.** This Act may be cited as the Variation of Trusts Act 1958.

Equity jurisdiction of county courts
6D–150   See Section 9A, paras, 9A–525 and 9A–527 and ss.23 to 24 of the County Courts Act 1984.

SECTION 7

LEGAL REPRESENTATIVES – COSTS AND LITIGATION FUNDING

7A GENERAL

GENERAL

INTRODUCTION

Conditional fees

The Access to Justice Act 1999 has amended the law relating to conditional fee **7A–1** agreements between lawyers and their clients, in particular to allow the uplift payable in successful cases to be recovered from the other side. It also enables insurance premiums to be recovered and allows for third parties to establish funds to support litigation on a conditional basis. (This provision is not yet in force). The Courts and Legal Services Act 1990 has been amended by the insertion of new ss.58 and 58A dealing with conditional fee agreements and Section 58B dealing with Litigation Funding Agreements. Sections 29 and 30 of the Access to Justice Act provide for recovery of insurance premiums by way of costs and recovery where a membership organisation undertakes to meet costs liabilities.

After the introduction of Conditional Fees in 1995 the government extended the availability of Conditional Fees to all civil cases excluding family cases (in July 1998) following the decision of the Court of Appeal in *Thai Trading Co v. Taylor* [1998] 3 All E.R. 65, CA that there were no longer public policy grounds to prevent lawyers agreeing to work for less than their normal fees in the event that they were unsuccessful, provided that they did not seek to recover more than their normal fees if they were successful. The Act and Regulations have been drafted in such a way as to permit such agreements. Similarly the decision in *Bevan Ashford v. Geoff Yeandle (Contractors) Limited* [1998] 3 All E.R. 238, Scott V.-C., confirmed that conditional fees could extend to a case which was to be resolved by arbitration, even though it was not court proceedings, provided that all the requirements specified by regulations as to the form and content of the conditional fee agreement were complied with.

It is now possible for an intending litigant to take out a policy of insurance to cover both the costs of the other party and his or her own legal costs (including the solicitors' fees if they are not subject to the conditional fee agreement). Premiums paid for such policies may be recovered as costs. The decision of the Court of Appeal in *Geraghty v. Awad Awwad* [1999] N.P.C. 148 confirmed that contingency fee agreements entered into before the January 7, 1999 where champertous and unlawful. Although the law has now been clarified by the Access to Justice Act 1999 the decision is still of relevance because of the large number of conditional fee agreements entered into following the decision of the Court of Appeal in *Thai Trading* (above). The judgement rejected the possibility that such an agreement could be made at common law, and effectively outlawed all contingency fee agreements other than those authorised by statute.

THE INDEMNITY PRINCIPLE

The Indemnity principle, as affirmed in *Gundry v. Sainsbury* [1910] 1 K.B. 645 and **7A–2** referred to in many cases since, has been amended as a result of Government policy. The policy was announced in the Government's response to the Collective Conditional Fee Agreements Consultation Paper in September 2000 following extensive consultation with the profession.

Section 31 of the Access to Justice Act 1999 amends s.51 of the Supreme Court Act 1981 by inserting at the end of subs. (2) the words:

"or for securing that the amount awarded to a party in respect of the costs to be paid by him to such representatives is not limited to what would have been payable by him to them if he had not been awarded costs".

The effect of this is to enable the court to disregard funding arrangements between solicitor and client when assessing the amount of costs to be recovered from a paying party.

Section 31 of the 1999 Act was brought into force on June 2, 2003 (Access to Justice Act 1999 (Commencement No.10) Order 2003 (S.I. 2003 No.1241)).

Supreme Court Act Sections 51(1)–(7)

The following paragraphs do not apply, as regards a party to any proceedings in **7A–3** relation to which the party entered into a conditional agreement before April 1, 2000; or any proceedings arising out of the same cause of action. Section 27 of the Access Justice Act 1999 (dealing with conditional fee agreements) does not affect the validity of any conditional fee agreement entered into before April 1, 2000 and any such agreement continues to have effect after that date as if s.27 had not come into force. See para. 9A–262.

Courts and Legal Services Act Sections 58 & 58A
7A–4   See paras 9B–110 to 9B–112. Subsections 58A(6) and (7) do not apply as regards a party to any proceedings in relation to which the party entered into a conditional fee agreement before April 1, 2000; or any proceedings arising out of the same cause of action.

Access to Justice Act 1999 sections 29 & 30

7A–5   *Section 29* —The provisions of this section do not apply, as regards a party, to any proceedings in relation to which that party took out an insurance policy of the sort referred to in section 29, before April 1, 2000; or any other proceedings arising out of the same cause of action. See para. 9A–867.

Section 30 —The provisions of this section do not apply, as regards a party, to any proceedings in relation to which that party gave an undertaking before April 1, 2000, which, if it had been given after that date, would have been an undertaking to which s.30(1) applied, or any proceedings arising out of the same cause of action. See para. 9A–869.

The Conditional Fee Agreements Order 2000

(S.I. 2000 No. 823)

The Lord Chancellor, in exercise of the powers conferred upon him by section 58(4)(a) and (c) of the Courts and Legal Services Act 1990[1], and all other powers enabling him in that behalf, having consulted in accordance with section 58A(5)[2] of that Act, makes the following Order, a draft of which has been laid before and approved by resolution of each House of
7A–6   *Parliament:*

Citation, commencement and interpretation
7A–7   **1.**—(1) This Order may be cited as the Conditional Fee Agreements Order 2000 and shall come into force on 1st April 2000.

(2) In this Order "the Act" means the Courts and Legal Services Act 1990.

Revocation of 1998 Order
7A–8   **2.** The Conditional Fee Agreements Order 1998 is revoked.

Agreements providing for success fees
7A–9   **3.** All proceedings which, under section 58 of the Act, can be the subject of an enforceable conditional fee agreement, except proceedings under section 82 of the Environmental Protection Act 1990, are proceedings specified for the purposes of section 58(4)(a) of the Act.

Amount of for success fees
7A–10   **4.** In relation to all proceedings specified in article 3, the percent-

---

[1] Section 58 was substituted by section 27(1) of the Access to Justice Act 1999 (c. 22).
[2] Section 58A was added by section 27(1) of the Access to Justice Act 1999 (c. 22).

age specified for the purposes of section 58(4)(c) of the Act shall be 100%.

Irvine of Lairg, C.

Dated 20th March 2000

The Conditional Fee Agreements Regulations 2000

(S.I. 2000 No. 692)

[The Conditional Fee Agreements Regulations 2000 have been revoked with effect from November 1, 2005 by the Conditional Fee Agreements (Revocation) Regulations 2005 S.I. 2005 No. 2305. The CFA Regulations 2000 continue to have effect for the purposes of a CFA agreement entered into before November 1, 2005.]

The Lord Chancellor, in exercise of the powers conferred on him by sections 58(3)(c), 58A(3) and 119 of the Courts and Legal Services Act 1990[1] and all other powers enabling him hereby makes the following Regulations:

7A–11

Citation, commencement and interpretation

1.—(1) *These Regulations may be cited as the Conditional Fee Agreements Regulations 2000.* **7A–12**

(2) *These Regulations come into force on 1st April 2000.*

(3) *In these Regulations–*

"*client*" *includes, except where the context otherwise requires, a person who–*

(a) *has instructed the legal representative to provide the advocacy or litigation services to which the conditional fee agreement relates, or*

(b) *is liable to pay the legal representative's fees in respect of those services; and*

"*legal representative*" *means the person providing the advocacy or litigation services to which the conditional fee agreement relates.*

Requirements for contents of conditional fee agreements: general

2.—(1) *A conditional fee agreement must specify–* **7A–13**

(a) *the particular proceedings or parts of them to which it relates (including whether it relates to any appeal, counterclaim or proceedings to enforce a judgement or order),*

(b) *the circumstances in which the legal representative's fees and expenses, or part of them, are payable,*

(c) *what payment, if any, is due–*

(i) *if those circumstances only partly occur,*

(ii) *irrespective of whether those circumstances occur, and*

(iii) *on the termination of the agreement for any reason, and*

---

[1] Sections 58 and 58A are substituted by section 27 of the Access to Justice Act 1999 (c. 22); section 119 is an interpretation provision and is cited because of the meaning given to the word "prescribed".

(d) *the amounts which are payable in all the circumstances and cases specified or the method to be used to calculate them and, in particular, whether the amounts are limited by reference to the damages which may be recovered on behalf of the client.*

(2) *A conditional fee agreement to which regulation 4 applies must contain a statement that the requirements of that regulation which apply in the case of that agreement have been complied with.*

Requirements for contents of conditional fee agreements providing for success fees

7A–14   **3.**—(1) *A conditional fee agreement which provides for a success fee–*

(a) *must briefly specify the reasons for setting the percentage increase at the level stated in the agreement, and*

(b) *must specify how much of the percentage increase, if any, relates to the cost to the legal representative of the postponement of the payment of his fees and expenses.*

(2) *If the agreement relates to court proceedings, it must provide that where the percentage increase becomes payable as a result of those proceedings, then–*

(a) *if–*

(i) *any fees subject to the increase are assessed, and*

(ii) *the legal representative or the client is required by the court to disclose to the court or any other person the reasons for setting the percentage increase at the level stated in the agreement,*

he may do so,

(b) *if–*

(i) *any such fees are assessed, and*

(ii) *any amount in respect of the percentage increase is disallowed on the assessment on the ground that the level at which the increase was set was unreasonable in view of facts which were or should have been known to the legal representative at the time it was set,*

that amount ceases to be payable under the agreement, unless the court is satisfied that it should continue to be so payable, and

(c) *if–*

(i) *sub-paragraph (b) does not apply, and*

(ii) *the legal representative agrees with any person liable as a result of the proceedings to pay fees subject to the percentage increase that a lower amount than the amount payable in accordance with the conditional fee agreement is to be paid instead,*

the amount payable under the conditional fee agreement in respect of those fees shall be reduced accordingly, unless the court is satisfied that the full amount should continue to be payable under it.

(3) *In this regulation "percentage increase" means the percentage by which the amount of the fees which would be payable if the agreement were not a conditional fee agreement is to be increased under the agreement.*

Requirements where the client's liability is limited to sums recovered

7A–14A   **3A.**—(1) *This regulation applies to a conditional fee agreement under* which, except in the circumstances set out in paragraphs (5) and (5A), the client is liable to pay his legal representative's fees and expenses only to the extent that sums are recovered in respect of the relevant proceedings, whether by way of costs or otherwise.

(2) In determining for the purposes of paragraph (1) the circumstance in which a client is liable to pay his legal representative's fees and expenses only to the extent that sums are recovered in respect of the relevant proceedings, whether by way of costs or otherwise.

(3) Regulations 2, 3 and 4 do not apply to a conditional fee agreement to which this regulation applies.

(4) A conditional fee agreement to which this regulation applies must
　　(a) specify—
　　　　(i) the particular proceedings or parts of them to which it relates (including whether it relates to any appeal, counterclaim or proceedings to enforce a judgment or order); and
　　　　(ii) the circumstances in which the legal representative's fees and expenses, or part of them, are payable; and
　　(b) if it provides for a success fee—
　　　　(i) briefly specify the reasons for setting the percentage increase at the level stated in the agreement; and
　　　　(ii) provide that if, in court proceedings, the percentage increase becomes payable as a result of those proceedings and the legal representative or the client is ordered to disclose to the court or any other person the reasons for setting the percentage increase at the level stated in the agreement, he may do so.

(5) A conditional fee agreement to which this regulation applies may specify that the client will be liable to pay the legal representative's fees and expenses whether or not sums are recovered in respect of the relevant proceedings, if the client—
　　(a) fails to co-operate with the legal representative;
　　(b) fails to attend any medical or expert examination or court hearing which the legal representative reasonably requests him to attend;
　　(c) fails to give necessary instructions to the legal representative;
　　(d) withdraws instructions from the legal representative.
　　(e) is an individual who is adjudged bankrupt or enters into an arrangement or a composition with his creditors, or against whom an administration order is made; or
　　(f) is a company for which a receiver, administrative receiver or liquidator is appointed.

(5A) A conditional fee agreement to which this regulation applies may specify that, in the event of the client dying in the course of the relevant proceedings, his estate will be liable for the legal representative's fees and expenses, whether or not sums are recovered in respect of those proceedings.

(6) Before a conditional fee agreement to which this regulation applies is made, the legal representative must inform the client as to the circumstances in which the client or his estate may be liable to pay the legal representative's

fees and expenses, and provide such further explanation, advice or other information as to those circumstances as the client may reasonably require.

Note —Amended by the Conditional Fee Agreements (Miscellaneous Amendments) (No. 2) Regulations 2003 (S.I. 2003 No. 3344).

Information to be given before conditional fee agreements made

7A–15   **4.**—(1) *Before a conditional fee agreement is made the legal representative must–*

    (a) *inform the client about the following matters, and*

    (b) *if the client requires any further explanation, advice or other information about any of those matters, provide such further explanation, advice or other information about them as the client may reasonably require.*

(2) *Those matters are–*

    (a) *the circumstances in which the client may be liable to pay the costs of the legal representative in accordance with the agreement,*

    (b) *the circumstances in which the client may seek assessment of the fees and expenses of the legal representative and the procedure for doing so,*

    (c) *whether the legal representative considers that the client's risk of incurring liability for costs in respect of the proceedings to which agreement relates is insured against under an existing contract of insurance,*

    (d) *whether other methods of financing those costs are available, and, if so, how they apply to the client and the proceedings in question,*

    (e) *whether the legal representative considers that any particular method or methods of financing any or all of those costs is appropriate and, if he considers that a contract of insurance is appropriate or recommends a particular such contract–*

        (i) *his reasons for doing so, and*

        (ii) *whether he has an interest in doing so.*

(3) *Before a conditional fee agreement is made the legal representative must explain its effect to the client.*

(4) *In the case of an agreement where–*

    (a) *the legal representative is a body to which section 30 of the Access to Justice Act 1999 (recovery where body undertakes to meet costs liabilities) applies, and*

    (b) *there are no circumstances in which the client may be liable to pay any costs in respect of the proceedings,*

paragraph (1) does not apply.

(5) *Information required to be given under paragraph (1) about the matters in paragraph (2)(a) to (d) must be given orally (whether or not it is also given in writing), but information required to be so given about the matters in paragraph (2)(e) and the explanation required by paragraph (3) must be given both orally and in writing.*

(6) *This regulation does not apply in the case of an agreement between a legal representative and an additional legal representative.*

Form of agreement

5.—(1) *A conditional fee agreement must be signed by the client and the* **7A–16**
legal representative.

(2) *This regulation does not apply in the case of an agreement between a legal representative and an additional legal representative.*

Amendment of agreement

6. *Where an agreement is amended to cover further proceedings or parts of* **7A–17**
them—

    (a) *regulations 2, 3 , 3A and 5 apply to the amended agreement as if it were a fresh agreement made at the time of the amendment, and*

    (b) *the obligations under regulation 4 apply in relation to the amendments in so far as they affect the matters mentioned in that regulation.*

Revocation of 1995 Regulations

7. *The Conditional Fee Agreements Regulations 1995 are revoked.* **7A–18**

Regulation 3(1)(b)

The Regulation requires that the CFA must specify how much of the percentage **7A–18.1**
increase relates to the cost of the legal representative of the postponement of the payment of his fees and expenses. This element of the success fee is not recoverable from a paying party. This continues the principle laid down by the Court of Appeal in a decision under the earlier rules, *Hunt v. R M Douglas (Roofing) Ltd*, *The Times*, November 23, 1987, CA.

The Collective Conditional Fee Agreements Regulations 2000

(S.I. 2000 No. 2988)

[The Collective Conditional Fee Agreements Regulations 2000 have been revoked with effect from November 1, 2005 by the Conditional Fee Agreements (Revocation) Regulations 2005 S.I. 2005 No. 2305. The CCFA Regulations 2000 continue to have effect for the purposes of a CFA agreement entered into before November 1, 2005.]

The Lord Chancellor, in exercise of the powers conferred upon him by sections 58(3)(c), 58A(3) and 119 of the Courts and Legal Services Act 1990[1] hereby makes the following Regulations: **7A–19**

Citation, commencement and interpretation

1.—(1) *These regulations may be cited as the Collective Conditional Fee* **7A–20**
Agreements Regulations 2000, and shall come into force on 30th November 2000.

(2) *In these Regulations, except where the context requires otherwise—*
    "client" means a person who will receive advocacy or litigation services to which the agreement relates;

---

[1] Sections 58 and 58A are substituted by section 27 of the Access to Justice Act 1999 (c.22); section 119 is an interpretation provision and is cited because of the meaning given to the word "prescribed".

"collective conditional fee agreement" has the meaning given in regulation 3;

"conditional fee agreement" has the same meaning as in section 58 of the Courts and Legal Services Act 1990;

"legal representative" means the person providing the advocacy or litigation services to which the agreement relates.

Transitional provisions

7A–21 **2.** *These Regulations shall apply to agreements entered into on or after 30th November 2000, and agreements entered into before that date shall be treated as if these Regulations had not come into force.*

Definition of "collective conditional fee agreement"

7A–22 **3.**—(1) *Subject to paragraph (2) of this regulation, a collective conditional fee agreement is an agreement which—*

(a) *disregarding section 58(3)(c) of the Courts and Legal Services Act 1990, would be a conditional fee agreement; and*

(b) *does not refer to specific proceedings, but provides for fees to be payable on a common basis in relation to a class of proceedings, or, if it refers to more than one class of proceedings, on a common basis in relation to each class.*

(2) *An agreement may be a collective conditional fee agreement whether or not—*

(a) *the funder is a client; or*

(b) *any clients are named in the agreement.*

Requirements for contents of collective conditional fee agreements: general

7A–23 **4.**—(1) *A collective conditional fee agreement must specify the circumstances in which the legal representative's fees and expenses, or part of them, are payable.*

(1A) *The circumstances referred to in paragraph (1) may include the fact that the legal representative's fees and expenses are payable only to the extent that sums are recovered in respect of the proceedings, whether by way of costs or otherwise.*

(2) *A collective conditional fee agreement must provide that, when accepting instructions in relation to any specific proceedings the legal representative must—*

(a) *inform the client as to the circumstances in which the client or his estate may be liable to pay the costs of the legal representative; and*

(b) *if the client requires any further explanation, advice or other information about the matter referred to in sub-paragraph (a), provide such further explanation, advice or other information about it as the client may reasonably require.*

(3) *Paragraph (2) does not apply in the case of an agreement between a legal representative and an additional legal representative.*

(4) *A collective conditional fee agreement must provide that, after accepting instructions in relation to any specific proceedings, the legal representative must confirm his acceptance of instructions in writing to the client.*

Requirements for contents of collective conditional fee agreements providing for success fees

5.—(1) *Where a collective conditional fee agreement provides for a success* **7A–24** *fee the agreement must provide that, when accepting instructions in relation to any specific proceedings the legal representative must prepare and retain a written statement containing—*

    (a) *his assessment of the probability of the circumstances arising in which the percentage increase will become payable in relation to those proceedings ("the risk assessment");*

    (b) *his assessment of the amount of the percentage increase in relation to those proceedings, having regard to the risk assessment; and*

    (c) *the reasons, by reference to the risk assessment, for setting the percentage increase at that level.*

(2) *If the agreement relates to court proceedings it must provide that where the success fee becomes payable as a result of those proceedings, then—*

    (a) *if—*

        (i) *any fees subject to the increase are assessed, and*

        (ii) *the legal representative or the client is required by the court to disclose to the court or any other person the reasons for setting the percentage increase at the level assessed by the legal representative,*

  he may do so,

    (b) *if—*

        (i) *any such fees are assessed by the court, and*

        (ii) *any amount in respect of the percentage increase is disallowed on the assessment on the ground that the level at which the increase was set was unreasonable in view of facts which were or should have been known to the legal representative at the time it was set*

  that amount ceases to be payable under the agreement, unless the court is satisfied that it should continue to be so payable, and

    (c) *if—*

        (i) *sub-paragraph (b) does not apply, and*

        (ii) *the legal representative agrees with any person liable as a result of the proceedings to pay fees subject to the percentage increase that a lower amount than the amount payable in accordance with the conditional fee agreement is to be paid instead,*

  the amount payable under the collective conditional fee agreement in respect of those fees shall be reduced accordingly, unless the court is satisfied that the full amount should continue to be payable under it.

(3) *In this regulation "percentage increase" means the percentage by which the amount of the fees which would have been payable if the agreement were not a conditional fee agreement is to be increased under the agreement.*

(4) *Sub-paragraphs (b) and (c) of paragraph (2) do not apply to a collective conditional fee agreement under which, except in the circumstances set out in paragraphs (6) and (7), the client is liable to pay his legal representative's fees and expenses only to the extent that sums are recovered in respect of the proceedings, whether by way of costs or otherwise.*

(5) *In determining for the purposes of paragraph (4) the circumstances in which a client is liable to pay his legal representative's fees and expenses, no account is to be taken of any obligation to pay costs in respect of the premium of a policy taken out to insure against the risk of incurring a liability in the relevant proceedings.*

(6) *A collective conditional fee agreement to which paragraph (4) applies may specify that the client will be liable to pay his legal representative's fees and expenses whether or not sums are recovered in respect of the relevant proceedings, if the client—*

    (a) *fails to co-operate with the legal representative;*

    (b) *fails to attend any medical or expert examination or court hearing which the legal representative reasonably requests him to attend;*

    (c) *fails to give necessary instructions to the legal representative;*

    (d) *withdraws instructions from the legal representative.*

    (e) *is an individual who is adjudged bankrupt or enters into an arrangement or a composition with his creditors, or against whom an administration order is made; or*

    (f) *is a company for which a receiver, administrative receiver or liquidator is appointed;*

(7) *A collective conditional fee agreement to which paragraph (4) applies may specify that, in the event of the client dying in the course of the relevant proceedings, his estate will be liable for the legal representative's fees and expenses, whether or not sums are recovered in respect of those proceedings.*

Note —Amended by the Conditional Fee Agreements (Miscellaneous Amendments) (No. 2) Regulations 2003 (S.I. 2003 No. 3344).

Form and amendment of collective conditional fee agreement

7A–25   **6.**—(1) *Subject to paragraph (2), a collective conditional fee agreement must be signed by the funder, and by the legal representative.*

(2) *Paragraph (1) does not apply in the case of an agreement between a legal representative and an additional legal representative.*

(3) *Where a collective conditional fee agreement is amended, regulations 4 and 5 apply to the amended agreement as if it were a fresh agreement made at the time of the amendment.*

Amendment to the Conditional Fee Agreements Regulations 2000

7A–26   **7.** *After regulation 7 of the Conditional Fee Agreements Regulations 2000 there shall be inserted the following new regulation:—*

Exclusion of collective conditional fee agreements

"**8.** *These Regulations shall not apply to collective conditional fee agreements within the meaning of regulation 3 of the Collective Conditional Fee Agreements Regulations 2000*".

<h2 style="text-align:center">The Access to Justice (Membership Organisations) Regulations 2000</h2>

(S.I. 2000 No. 693)

[The Access to Justice (Membership Organisation) Regulations 2000 have

been revoked with effect from November 1, 2005 by the Access to Justice (Membership Organisation) Regulations 2005 S.I. 2005 No. 2306. The 2000 Regulations continue to have effect for the purposes of arrangements entered into before November 1, 2005 as if the 2005 Regulations had not come into force. New simplified client care provisions are contained in the 2005 regulations for agreements entered into after 1 November 2005.]

The Lord Chancellor, in exercise of the powers conferred on him by section 30(1) and (3) to (5) of the Access to Justice Act 1999 and all other powers enabling him hereby makes the following Regulations: **7A–27**

Citation, commencement and interpretation
1.—(1) *These Regulations may be cited as the Access to Justice (Member-* **7A–28**
ship Organisations) Regulations 2000.

(2) *These Regulations come into force on 1st April 2000.*

Bodies of a prescribed description
2. *The bodies which are prescribed for the purpose of section 30 of the Ac-* **7A–29**
cess to Justice Act 1999 (recovery where body undertakes to meet costs liabilities) are those bodies which are for the time being approved by the Lord Chancellor for that purpose.

Requirements for arrangements to meet costs liabilities
3.—(1) *Section 30(1) of the Access to Justice Act 1999 applies to arrange-* **7A–30**
ments which satisfy the following conditions.

(2) *The arrangements must be in writing.*

(3) *The arrangements must contain a statement specifying–*
    (a) *the circumstances in which the member or other party may be liable to pay costs of the proceedings,*
    (b) *whether such a liability arises–*
        (i) *if those circumstances only partly occur,*
        (ii) *irrespective of whether those circumstances occur, and*
        (iii) *on the termination of the arrangements for any reason,*
    (c) *the basis on which the amount of the liability is calculated, and*
    (d) *the procedure for seeking assessment of costs.*

(4) *A copy of the part of the arrangements containing the statement must be given to the member or other party to the proceedings whose liabilities the body is undertaking to meet as soon as possible after the undertaking is given.*

Recovery of additional amount for insurance costs
4.—(1) *Where an additional amount is included in costs by virtue of sec-* **7A–31**
tion 30(2) of the Access to Justice Act 1999 (costs payable to a member of a body or other person party to the proceedings to include an additional amount in respect of provision made by the body against the risk of having to meet the member's or other person's liabilities to pay other parties' costs), that additional amount must not exceed the following sum.

(2) *That sum is the likely cost to the member of the body or, as the case may be, the other person who is a party to the proceedings in which the costs order is made of the premium of an insurance policy against the risk of incurring a liability to pay the costs of other parties to the proceedings.*

The Access to Justice (Membership Organisations) Regulations 2005

(S.I. 2000 No. 2306)

7A–32 *The Secretary of State, in exercise of the powers conferred upon the Lord Chancellor by sections 30(1) and (3) to (5) of the Access to Justice Act 1999 and now vested in him makes the following Regulations:*

Citation, commencement and interpretation

7A–33 **1.**—(1) These Regulations may be cited as the Access to Justice (Membership Organisation) Regulations 2005 and shall come into force on 1st November 2005.

(2) In these Regulations a reference to a section by number alone is a reference to the section so numbered in the Access to Justice Act 1999.

Revocation and transitional

7A–34 **2.**—(1) Subject to paragraph (2), the Access to Justice (Membership Organisation) Regulations 2000 (the "2000 Regulations") are revoked.

(2) The 2000 Regulations shall continue to have effect for the purposes of arrangements entered into before 1st November 2005 as if these Regulations had not come into force.

Bodies of a prescribed description

7A–35 **3.** The bodies which are prescribed for the purpose of section 30 (recovery where body undertakes to meet costs liabilities) are those bodies which are for the time being approved by the Secretary of State for that purpose.

Requirements of arrangements to meet costs liabilities

7A–36 **4.**—(1) Section 30(1) applies to arrangements which satisfy the following conditions.

(2) The arrangements must be in writing.

(3) The arrangements must contain a statement specifying the circumstances in which the member may be liable to pay costs of the proceedings.

Recovery of additional amount for insurance costs

7A–37 **5.**—(1) Where an additional amount is included in costs by virtue of section 30(2) (costs payable to a member of a body or other person party to the proceedings to include an additional amount in respect of provision made by the body against the risk of having to meet the member's or other person's liabilities to pay other parties' costs), that additional amount must not exceed the following sum.

(2) That sum is the likely cost to the member of the body or, as the case may be, the other person who is a party to the proceedings in which the costs order is made of the premium of an insurance policy against the risk of incurring a liability to pay the costs of other parties to the proceedings.

FUNDING ARRANGEMENTS

CONDITIONAL FEES

Conditional fee agreements (CFAs) cannot be used in respect of criminal and family proceedings. CFAs allow clients to agree with their lawyers that the lawyer will not receive all or part of their usual fees or expenses if the case is lost, but that if it is won the client will pay an uplift to the solicitor in addition to the usual fee. Prior to the coming into force of the Access to Justice Act 1999 CFAs had been allowed for a limited range of cases. The maximum uplift (which was not recoverable from an opposing party) was fixed at 100 per cent and the Law Society recommended that lawyers should voluntarily limit the uplift to a maximum of 25 per cent of the damages.

Following the decision of the Court of Appeal in *Thai Trading Co v. Taylor* [1983] 3 All E.R. 65 CA, the Government accepted that there were no longer public policy grounds to prevent lawyers agreeing to work for less than their normal fees if they were successful. In *Bevan Ashford v. Geoff Yeandle (Contractors) Ltd* [1998] 3 All E.R. 238 Scott V.-C., it was held that it was also lawful for a CFA to apply in a case which was to be resolved by arbitration even though they were not court proceedings, provided that all requirements specified by regulations were complied with. Section 58 of the Courts and Legal Services Act 1990 as substituted by the Access to Justice Act 1999 is sufficiently wide to include *Thai Trading* type agreements.

Paragraph 32.7 of the Costs Practice Direction requires the receiving party to serve on the paying party various documents including a statement of the reasons for the percentage increase (success fee) in relation to a CFA. In a case where the receiving party declined to serve this information and sought an order restricting disclosure to solicitors, counsel and costs draftsmen for the paying party, because of concerns that it could be used for the purpose of criminal proceedings against him in Kuwait, the court held that it had inherent jurisdiction to restrict disclosure in an appropriate case. In order to warrant the exercise of the jurisdiction it was necessary to show a tangible risk of misuse of the information. Relief from the sanction for non disclosure was granted on condition that disclosure was made within ten days. The Costs Judge was directed to take into account the refusal to disclose in determining any claim for interest on the success fee: *Grupo Torras v. Al-Sabah* [2003] EWHC 262 (QB); [2003] 2 Costs LR 294, decision of Tracey J.

The defendant in libel proceedings argued that it was an abuse of process that such proceedings should be brought with a maximum 100 per cent success fee since this pre-supposed that lawyers would only take on cases with a prospect of success of at least 50 per cent. It further argued that the availability of CFAs in defamation cases had a potentially chilling effect on the activities of journalists, contrary to the European Convention right of freedom of speech. The court held that there was nothing inconsistent with the intention of the legislature in lawyers agreeing to support a claim by means of a CFA, even where a dispassionate assessment of the likely outcome would lead them to the conclusion the claim was unlikely to succeed. The application that the claimant should be ordered to make a payment into court unless ATE insurance was in place was rejected: *King v. Telegraph* [2003] EWHC 1312 (QB) Eady J.

On appeal the court referred to *Olatawura v. Abiloye* [2002] EWCA Civ 998 at [26] as setting out the principles relating to security for costs, and declined to make any different type of order to the one the judge at first instance had been asked to make. The appeal was accordingly dismissed. The court went on to consider the power of the court to keep the balance fairly between the interests of a claimant seekng to vindicate his/her reputation with the help of a CFA who cannot afford appropriate ATE cover and the interests of the media as the eyes and ears of the public. [55]. Brooke L.J. stated:

> "[94] It would be helpful if the senior master were to assign a particular master to case management applications in this specialist field of law because they demand a degree of practical experience that will not become available if they distributed generally among the masters. If the master considers that a budget or cap is required, he should refer the issue of imposing a cap to the costs judge. The costs judge should determine what sum is reasonable and proportionate to fix as the recoverable costs of the action. Similar arrangements should be made, if and when necessary, in district registaries of the High Court outside London".

King v. Telegraph Group Ltd [2004] EWCA Civ 613; [2005] 1 W.L.R. 2282 CA.

The House of Lords has held that the scheme allowing success fees to be recovered from the losing party to an action for defamation is compatible with Art.10 ECHR and it was not open to a defendant to argue that the threat of liability to pay a large sum by way of costs infringed its right to freedom of expression. Parliament was entitled to lay down a general rule that CFAs were open to everybody taking into account the impracticality of requiring a means test and the small number of individuals who would have sufficient resources to fund their own litigation. The financial position of the claimant was therefore not relevant in deciding whether it was appropriate to proceed with a CFA. The controls imposed by the court through costs capping and assessment, applying the test of reasonableness and proportionality were palliatives, and any perceived difficulty could only be resolved by legislation: *Campbell v MGN Ltd* [2005] UKHL 61.

For an explanation of the transitional provisions contained in the Access to Justice Act 1999 (Transitional Provisions) Order 1999 see *C v. M* [2003] EWHC 250 (Fam) Sumner J. Where a claimant has entered into a CFA prior to April 1, 2000 no success fee is recoverable from the paying party.

Collective Conditional Fee Agreements

7A–39   The Regulations governing CFAs and those governing CCFAs establish two mutually exclusive sets of requirements. (The Regulations have been revoked with effect from November 1, 2005. See paras 7A–11, 7A–19 and 7A–27). An obvious reason why the Regulations governing CCFAs are less exacting than those governing CFAs is that CCFAs involve bulk users of legal services who are less vulnerable than lay clients. Often these users will be contracting to purchase, at their own expense, legal services to be provided to litigants. In those circumstances the litigants will not be exposed to significant risk of liability to pay for the legal services provided to them. Sections 58 and 58A of the Courts and Legal Services Act 1990 and the Regulations are intended to give effect to fundamental changes to the manner in which litigation is funded in this country. The requirements of the Regulations are designed to protect those who enter into CFAs, and are of no legitimate concern to defendants. Furthermore where legal services are provided to a litigant under a CCFA by a trade union or other body, there is normally little need for such protection. The manifest object of having a different regime for CCFAs from that applying to CFAs is to simplify the formalities of supplying legal services. In a case in which a union agreed with their solicitors that they should represent a claimant under a CCFA (which was accepted to be valid), the union had agreed with the authority of the claimant. Alternatively the claimant had ratified the agreement reached by the union on his behalf by availing himself of the services of the solicitors. On either footing the contract pursuant to which he came under a liability to pay the solicitors for their services was a CCFA. The court confirmed that the agreement was not subject to the CFA Regulations: *Thornley v. Lang* [2003] EWCA Civ 1484.

7A–40   The Court of Appeal has dealt with the question of success fees in RTA claims arising out of accidents which took place before October 5, 2003 and which were therefore not covered by Pt 45 Sect. III. The court held:

"49. ... In our judgment the guidance given by this court in *Callery v. Gray* can be applied by analogy to this case even though it was allocated to the multi track and settled for a sum exceeding £15,000. We consider that there are no factors here which could legitimately have taken the success fee over 20 per cent ... The only significant risk related to the possibility of the claimant accepting her solicitor's advice and then not beating a payment in. This is just one of the rare risks which justified a success fee set as high as 20 per cent in the simplest of claims."

The court continued:

"Because there seems to be some lingering uncertainty about the combined effect of *Callery v. Gray* and *Halloran v. Delaney* we feel we ought to restate, for the benefit of District Judges and Costs Judges, the principles in cases governed by the old regime ... The reasonableness of the success fee has to be assessed as at the time the CFA was agreed. It is permissible for any CFA to include a two stage success fee and this is to be encouraged. In other words the success fee may be a higher percentage (up to 100 per cent in an appropriate case) in the event that a claim does not settle within the protocol period and a lower success fee (down to 5 per cent in the very simplest of cases) in claims which do settle within that period. Further statistical evidence is now available ... to which it will be legitimate for parties to refer in relation to success fees agreed in an old regime case after the date of this judgment whether it is permissible on the assessment of costs for a Judge to have recourse to paragraph 11.8(2) of the [Costs] Practice Direction and to set a two stage success fee when no such fee was contained in the CFA is an issue that will be determined by this court [in due course].

52. It is not permissible simply to adopt the new CPR fixed rates for success fees when assessing the reasonableness of a success fee in an RTA case where the assessment of the CFA is not governed by the new rules. The reason for this is that the new CPR approach (informed by an industry wide agreement) does not take into account the individual effects of each particular case ...".

Atak v. Lee [2004] EWCA Civ. 1712.

The Court of Appeal, in carrying out a summary assessment of costs with a success fee, found it hard to understand how responsible counsel could have agreed with responsible solicitors a success fee of 100 per cent in respect of the appeal, or how responsible solicitors could have agreed with their client a success fee of 70 per cent. Success fees negotiated at that level discredited and devalued the whole of the arrangements for conditional fee agreements. In *Callery v. Gray* the House of Lords had expressed great concern about the new regime where success fees were in effect being negotiated between parties to the agreement and there was no direct financial incentive to drive the level of the success fee down. The court found that there was a small amount of risk in the litigation which would properly have been provided for by a success fee of 15 per cent: *Begum v. Klarit* [2005] EWCA Civ 210 .

The Court of Appeal has considered the extent to which, whether, in a case where the CFA does not provide for variable success fees, the court has power to direct that a success fee is recoverable at different rates for different periods of the proceedings, including detailed assessment of costs. The court found:

"47. ...Once it is clear...that a CFA may only carry one success fee and that the task of a Costs Judge is to determine whether that success fee was a reasonable one in the light of the matters that the legal representative knew or should have known when it was made, there is simply no room for a Costs Judge to substitute different percentage increases for different items of costs, or for different periods when costs were incurred. He could only do this with the benefit of hindsight which is prohibited, and the Rules and the Regulations give him no power to remake the parties' agreement. His powers of interference are limited to altering the success fee to a more reasonable one when he considers the size of the additional liability the paying party should bear. This is because there is nothing in the statute or the regulations to suggest that he is required to do anything other than carry out his usual function of deciding whether an item on a bill is reasonable, and if he decides it is not, of substituting a reasonable amount or deleting the item altogether."

...

"49. It follows...that the court has no power to direct that a success fee is recoverable at different rates for different periods of the proceedings. In so far as paragraph 11.8(2) of the Costs Practice Direction suggests otherwise, it is wrong."

U v. Liverpool City Council [2005] EWCA Civ 475.

INSURANCE PREMIUMS

7A-41 The development of CFAs has gone hand in hand with major developments in the insurance products being offered in respect of litigation. It is now possible for a person contemplating litigation to take out an insurance policy to cover, in the event that the case is lost, both the costs of the other party and his or own legal costs (including the solicitor's fees if they are not subject to a CFA). Some of these policies were developed to support the use of CFAs but others are used to meet lawyers' fees in the traditional way. Section 29 of the 1999 Act makes premiums paid for protective insurance recoverable in costs.

Recoverability of Insurance Premiums

7A-42 Whilst it is Government policy that damages awarded to a successful party are not "unreasonably eroded" (*Hansard*, December 12, 2000: David Lock, Parliamentary Secretary to the Lord Chancellor's Department), by unrecovered success fees or insurance premiums; putting that intention into effect depends on test cases dealing with the recoverability and level of insurance premiums and the interpretation of ss.29 and 30 of the Access to Justice Act 1999.

It was not the intention of Parliament when it enacted s.29 of the 1999 Act to overload the recoverable premium by adding to the costs customarily embraced by such a premium, the costs which a company providing personal injury claims handling services (including a costs indemnity in the event that a claimant's compensation clam was dismissed or discontinued), had to incur if insurers were to accept the risk at all. It was therefore permissible for the judge to consider what was actually being provided for the payment in order to identify what should truly be treated as premium: *Re Claims Direct Test Cases* [2003] EWCA Civ 136; [2003] 4 All E.R. 508, CA.

The Costs Judge had been correct to "deconstruct" the sum of money payable for legal costs insurance by claimant clients of The Accident Group to establish how much of that money was properly to be regarded as recoverable premium within the meaning of s.29 of the 1999 Act. The fee paid to AIL (an associate company) was a referral fee. It had not been properly payable by the panel solicitors and had not therefore been chargeable to their clients and was certainly not recoverable from the paying party. The arrangement viewed objectively was that the fee had been compulsory for any solicitor wishing to be sent cases by TAG: *Sharratt v. London Central Bus Co & Other Cases (No.2), The Accident Group Test Cases* [2004] EWCA Civ 575; [2004] 3 All E.R. 325, CA.

Recoverability of Success Fees and Insurance Premiums

7A–43   The Court of Appeal has considered four main questions:

(i) the time at which it is appropriate to enter into a CFA and take out an ATE policy;

(ii) the reasonableness of the success fee when a claim is quickly resolved without the need for court proceedings;

(iii) whether the claimants are entitled to recover an ATE premium where there has been no need to commence proceedings;

(iv) the reasonableness of ATE premiums.

After a hearing at which representatives of interested bodies were also allowed to make representations the court found:

(i) it is in principle permissible for a claimant to enter into a CFA with a success fee and to take out ATE insurance when he first consults his solicitor and before the solicitor writes a letter of claim and receives the prospective defendant's response;

(ii) in relation to modest and straightforward claims for compensation resulting from road traffic accidents where a CFA is agreed at the outset, 20 0s the maximum uplift that can reasonably be agreed in such a case;

(iii) ATE premiums are in principle recoverable as part of a claimant's costs even though his claim is quickly resolved without the need for proceedings;

(iv) The court requested a Costs Judge to investigate and report on the reasonableness of ATE premiums.

The court also considered that it is open to a solicitor and to a client to agree a two stage success fee at the outset of proceedings. It gave an example of an uplift agreed at 100 per cent subject to a reduction to a maximum of 5 per cent should the claim settle before the end of the period fixed by a pre-action protocol. Such an uplift would normally reflect the risks of the individual case. The court suggested that once the necessary data becomes available consideration will need to be given to the question whether the requirement to act reasonably mandates the agreement of a two stage success fee in a case where a CFA with a success fee is agreed at the outset: *Callery v. Gray* [2001] EWCA Civ. 1117; [2001] 3 All E.R. 833, CA. See now Pt 45, s.III with regard to success fees in RTA cases occurring after 2003.

The Court of Appeal subsequently held that the words "insurance against the risk of incurring a costs liability" in s.29 of the Access to Justice Act 1999 mean "insurance against the risk of incurring a costs liability that cannot be passed on to the opposite party". In the particular case the small element of cover for "own costs insurance" could be regarded as falling within the description of insurance against the risk of liability within s.29 and the premium of £350 was held to be reasonable.

The circumstances in which and the terms upon which "own costs" cover would be reasonable in relation to other policies so that the whole premium could be recovered as costs would have to be determined by the courts when dealing with individual cases. Other issues mentioned in the Costs Judge's Report would fall to be judicially determined as and when they arose in individual cases. A copy of the Report was annexed to the Court of Appeal judgment with the warning that the views expressed might be helpful but were not definitive: *Callery v. Gray (No.2)* [2001] EWCA Civ 1244; [2001] 4 All E.R. 1, CA.

The decision of the Court of Appeal in *Callery v. Gray* was upheld by the House of Lords: [2002] UKHL 28; [2002] 1 W.L.R. 2000; [2002] 3 All E.R. 417, HL. The Court of Appeal has again considered the question of success fees in simple claims which settle without the need for court proceedings. The court stated:

"...it is now time to reappraise the appropriate level of success fee which should be recoverable on these simple claims when they are settled without the need for court proceedings ... we consider that Judges concerned with questions relating to the recoverability of a success fee in claims as simple as this which are settled without the need to commence proceedings should now ordinarily decide to allow an uplift of 5% on the claimant's lawyers costs (including the costs of any costs only proceedings which are awarded to them) pursuant to their powers contained in CPD 11.8(2) unless persuaded that a higher uplift is appropriate in the particular circumstances of the case. This policy should be adopted in relation to all CFAs however they are structured which are entered into on and after 1 August 2001 when both Callery judgments had been published and the main uncertainties about costs recovery had been removed."

Halloran v. Delaney [2002] EWCA Civ 1258.

The Court of Appeal in *Callery v. Gray* (above) had been dealing with a case which involved success fees in simple claims. The court upheld the allowance of a success fee of 87 per cent in a claim by the widow of the original claimant in a mesothelioma case, in which the damages awarded were £185,000. The Court of Appeal held that advising on quantum was not straightforward, particularly in the instant case where there had been several factors affecting the final award. Whilst liability issues and quantum issues could be considered separately, ultimately a single success fee was to be arrived at on an assessment of the prospect of winning: *Smiths Dock Ltd v. Edwards* [2004] EWHC 1116, (QBD) Crane J.

The Court of Appeal subsequently (in *Claims Direct Test Cases* [2003] EWCA Civ 136; [2003] 4 All E.R. 508 CA) explained that *Halloran* had been an extremely simple road traffic accident claim which was swiftly settled with a minimum of fuss and bother. The type of case to which the court was referring in *Halloran v. Delaney* was a case similar to that in *Callery v. Gray* and *Halloran v. Delaney* in which the prospects of success are virtually 100 per cent. The two step fee advocated by the court in *Callery* is apt to allow a solicitor in such a case to cater for the wholly unexpected risk lurking below the limpid waters of the simplest of claims. It did not require any research evidence or submissions from other parties in the industry to persuade the court that in this type of extremely simple claim a success fee of over 5 per cent was no longer tenable in all the circumstances. The guidance given in the Halloran judgment was not intended to have any wider application. In the *Claims Direct Test Cases* (see above) the Court of Appeal held that, where a premium for litigation protection insurance includes sums other than for the underwriters' "risk for liability for the Claimant's" costs, those sums may not be recovered under a costs order. It was not the intention of Parliament, when enacting s.29, to overload the recoverable premium by adding to the costs customarily embraced by a premium, the costs which a company had to incur if underwriters were to accept the risk at all.

Before the Event Insurance

The Court of Appeal, dealing with a simple road traffic accident in which a passenger was injured stated: **7A–44**

"45. In our judgment proper modern practice dictates that a solicitor should normally invite a client to bring to the first interview any relevant motor insurance policy, any household insurance policy and any stand alone BTE insurance policy belonging to the client and/or any spouse or partner living in same household of the client ..."

The court went on to say that if the motor accident claim is likely to be less than about £5,000 and there are no features of the cover which make it inappropriate, the solicitor should refer the client to the BTE insurer without further ado. The solicitor is not obliged to embark on a treasure hunt in case by chance an insurance policy belonging to a member of the client's family contains relevant BTE cover. The availability of ATE cover at a modest premium will inevitably restrict the extent to which it will be reasonable for a solicitor's time to be used in investigating alternative sources of insurance. On the facts of the case the Court of Appeal allowed the claimant to recover the ATE premium on the ground that the BTE policy did not provide him with appropriate cover in the circumstances of the case. Representation arranged by the insurer of the defendant to which the claimant had never been a party, and of which he had no knowledge at the time it was entered into and where the opposing insurer through its chosen representative reserved to itself the full conduct and control of the claim was not a reasonable alternative to representation by a lawyer of the claimant's own choice backed by an ATE policy (paragraphs 52 to 58). The position might be different if BTE insurers finance some transparently independent organisation to handle such claims and made it clear in the policy that this was what they were doing. The overriding principle is that the claimant assisted by his/her solicitor should act in a manner which is reasonable (paragraph 50): *Sarwar v. Alam* [2000] EWCA Civ 1401; [2001] All E.R. 541.

Clinical Negligence

7A–45   In a straightforward case in which a dental patient swallowed a reamer but suffered no injury other than shock and upset and in which the claim settled quickly without proceedings having been commenced the success fee claimed at 50 per cent was allowed at 20 per cent: *Bensusan v. Freedman* September 20, 2001, Senior Costs Judge.

The Court of Appeal in *Halloran v. Delaney* [2002] EWCA Civ 1258 agreed with the comment of the Senior Costs Judge in relation to paragraphs 11.7 and 17.8(2) of the Costs Practice Direction: "The combined effect of these two paragraphs is to prevent the costs officer from using hindsight in arriving at the appropriate success fee and to prevent excessive claims for success fees in cases which settle without the need for proceedings when it was clear, or ought to have been clear from the outset, that the risk of having to commence proceedings was minimal."

How long does the ATE policy remain in force?

7A–46   17. In deciding that the policy remained in force until the conclusion of costs only proceedings Master Hurst was influenced by the language of the Law Society model CFA which was also used in that case. This agreement expressly covered the claim and it also covered any proceedings taken to enforce a judgment, order or agreement...in these circumstances Master Hurst accepted...an argument by counsel for the claimant in these terms:

> "[counsel for the claimant], in support of his argument that costs only proceedings precede the conclusion [of the case], relies upon the duration of the conditional fee agreement which he submits covers enforcement proceedings. The assessment of costs is not an enforcement proceeding but, until costs are assessed, the agreement to pay costs cannot be enforced. By commencing costs only proceedings the claimant will obtain a detailed assessment of her costs which will result in a final certificate and that certificate will be enforceable in the same way as any other judgment for a civil debt."

18. Master Hurst went on to say: "...that, taken together, the insurance policy and the CFA made it clear that the insurance cover extended to all necessary steps in relation to resolving the claimant's claim, including her claim to be paid her reasonable costs. He therefore found that the ATE insurance policy was still in force, the case not yet having concluded. The case would be concluded when the costs were finally assessed.

19. We accept Master Hurst's conclusion and the reasons he gave". *Halloran v. Delaney* [2002] EWCA Civ 1258 referring to *Tilby v. Perfect Pizza Ltd*, unrep. February 28, 2002.

Enforceability of CFAs

7A–47   The provision in Section 58 of the Courts and Legal Services Act 1990, that any conditional fee agreement which did not satisfy all of the conditions applicable to it should be unenforceable, led to paying parties taking every possible point on detailed assessment in an effort to demonstrate that the underlying CFA was unenforceable and that therefore by operation of the indemnity principle, no costs should be payable. Against this background six appeals came before the Court of Appeal (see *Hollins v. Russell* below), and at the same time the Lord Chancellor introduced amendments to the Conditional Fee Agreement Regulations, making it possible for legal representatives to enter into conditional fee agreements with their clients under which the client is liable to pay the legal representatives fees and expenses, only to the extent that sums are recovered in respect of the relevant proceedings, whether by way of costs or otherwise. In respect of such agreements Regulations 2, 3 and 4 of the CFA Regulations are disapplied. Corresponding amendments were made to CPR r.43.2, similar provisions were inserted into the Collective Conditional Fee Agreements Regulations 2000 and s.31 of the Access to Justice Act 1999 amending s.51 of the Supreme Court Act 1981 was brought into force.

In *Hollins v. Russell* (and five other appeals) [2003] EWCA Civ 718; [2003] 1 W.L.R. 2487 CA, *sub nom.Sharratt v. London Central Bus Co Ltd* [2003] 4 All E.R. 590, CA the Court of Appeal dealt with a number of issues:

(i) The circumstances in which the court should put a receiving party in detailed assessment proceedings to its election so that it must choose whether to disclose its CFA to the paying party or to prove its claim by other means.

(ii) The proper construction of the words "satisfies all of the conditions applicable to it" in Section 58(1) of the 1990 Act and whether any costs or disbursements are recoverable from a paying party in the event of non compliance with the CFA Regulations.

(iii) Whether on the particular facts the requirements contained in one or other of Regulations 2, 3 and 4 of the CFA Regulations were not complied with.

Disclosure —The court referred to the decision in *Bailey v. IBC Vehichles Ltd* [1998] 3 **7A–48** All E.R. 570, CA stating (at paragraph 68):

"In our judgment the solicitor's certificate as to accuracy, important though it is, may not be sufficient, where the quality and quantity of the information served on the paying party about the success fee is less than would be made available in respect of the other aspects of the bill in the case on an assessment where there is no additional liability claimed."

The court declined to extend the decision in Bailey beyond the facts with which it was dealing, continuing (at 71):

"... where there is a CFA a Costs Judge should normally exercise his discretion under the Costs Practice Direction and the Pamplin procedure [*Pamlin v. Express Newspapers Ltd* [1985] 1 W.L.R. 689] so as to require the receiving parties (subject to their right of election preserved by paragraph 40.14 of the Costs Practice Direction and the Goldman case [*Goldman v. Hesper* [1988] 1 W.L.R. 1238]) to produce a copy of their CFAs to the paying parties in order that they can see whether or not the Regulations were complied with and (where a CFA provides for a success fee) whether the liability of the receiving party to pay that success fee is indeed enforceable.

* * * * *

72. If the CFA contains confidential information which is not required to be disclosed for the purposes of fairly determining the receiving party's claim to costs ... the Costs Judge may permit that material to be redacted before service."

The court declined to decide whether or not a CFA is of itself privileged. The court approved Pumfrey J. in *South Coast Shipping Co Ltd v. Havant Borough Council* [2002] 3 All E.R. 779 when he found that there was no incompatibility of the European Convention on Human Rights.

Satisfying the conditions in Section 58

Under this head, having rehearsed the arguments, the court stated (paragraph **7A–49** 107):

"The key question therefore is whether the conditions applicable to the CFA by virtue of Section 58 of the 1990 Act have been sufficiently complied with in the light of their purposes. Costs Judges should accordingly ask themselves the following question: "Has the particular departure from a Regulation pursuant to Section 58(3)(c) of the 1990 Act or a requirement in Section 58, either on its own or in conjunction with any other such departure in this case, had a materially adverse effect either upon the protection afforded to the client or upon the proper administration of justice?" If the answer is "yes" the conditions have not been satisfied. If the answer is "no" then the departure is immaterial and (assuming that there is no other reason to conclude otherwise) the conditions have been satisfied.

108. We would not draw any formal distinction between the conditions contained in the section itself and those contained in the Regulations. The meaning of

"satisfies" must be the same in each case. However, it is more difficult to envisage questions of degree coming into the question whether the conditions in the section have been sufficiently met. Either the CFA relates to permissible proceedings or it does not. But one example might be that in Section 58(4)(b), which requires that a CFA providing for a success fee "must state the percentage by which the amount of the fees which would be payable if it were not a conditional fee agreement is to be increased". Was that condition sufficiently met by agreement ... which left blank the percentage in the clause where it should have been filled in but stated it clearly in the risk assessment ...? The answer to that question is obviously "yes".

109. ... Sufficiency or materiality will depend upon the circumstances of each case. This is not to encourage paying parties to trawl through the facts of each case in order to try to discover a material breach. Quite the reverse. At the stage when the agreement has been made, acted upon, and success for the client has been achieved, it is most unlikely that any minor shortcoming which the paying party might discover in the agreement or the procedures leading up to its making will amount to a material breach of the requirements or mean that the applicable conditions have not been sufficiently met." —The court dealt with two other points under the heading of compliance which they felt could be of considerable importance in practice. First the recoverability of the ATE premium:

"114. ...ATE insurance premiums are recoverable as costs in any proceedings, irrespective of whether or not there is a CFA between the receiving party and her legal representatives. The clients liability to pay the insurance premium arises from the contract of insurance, not from her contract with the legal representative. It arises whether or not there is a CFA and whether or not the CFA is enforceable. ... It would appear therefore that there is no bar to the recovery of the ATE insurance premium as costs whatever may be the bar to the recovery of the lawyers charges and success fee."

The second point which the court dealt with related to disbursements which the client has in fact paid to the solicitor either personally or by taking out a loan to do so:

"115. ... The solicitor is required to retain this money on client's account until it is expended in accordance with the client's instructions. If the CFA fails, and the money has not been paid out, the solicitor would be required to pay it back to the client. If the money has been paid out, then this is money actually paid by the client. ... This should be recoverable by the client as costs. The costs claim is that of the client not of the solicitor. If the client has actually paid a debt to a third party, properly incurred in the conduct of the litigation, there seems no reason why this should not be recoverable from the paying party, insofar as it is reasonable and proportionate ... This is irrespective of whether the solicitor can enforce the CFA for this charges and success fee."

7A–50   *Particular allegations of breach* —Dealing with reg.2(i)(d) the court stated (at para. 118):

"No difficulty will arise under regulation 2(i)(d) for solicitors who use the Law Society's model CFA which came into use in July 2000 ..."

On the facts of the particular appeals the court took the view that the effect of the CFA, read as a whole, was sufficiently clear and that the failure to specify the position accurately did not affect the protection given to the client or the administration of justice to any material degree. The result would have been different if the CFA was less clear as to its effect, that is, if it would not have been reasonably comprehensible to the lay person.

In respect of reg.3(1)(b), the point had been taken that the CFA did not specify how much of the percentage increase related to the cost to the legal representative of the postponement of the payment of fees and expenses. The court found this submission unattractive and unmeritorious. The court found that the language of Clause 32 of the CFA made the position clear. The reality being that despite what was said in the risk assessment calculation none of the recoverable success fee was attributable to the postponement in payment of the solicitor's fees. The court found that taken together Clause 32 and 33 prevailed over the risk assessment schedule and thus, on its true construction, the CFA complied with the regulations.

Under reg.4(2)(c), the paying parties argued that there was a breach because the client had not been informed that the risk of incurring a liability for costs in respect of proceedings to which the agreement related was insured against under an existing contract of insurance. The court found that attendance notes dealing with this issue should not ordinarily be disclosed. The court found that it was sufficient to satisfy s.58 that the solicitor had discussed the matter with the client and had formed a view on the funding options. The court pointed out that the recovery of the insurance premium is an entirely separate matter from the enforceability of the CFA.

The argument under reg.4(2)(e)(ii) was as to the meaning of "whether" and "whether or not". The court held (at 144):

"... In this context there is no reason to construe "whether" as meaning anything other than "if". The language of the regulation ... mirrored the language of the Government's February 2000 paper ... The mischief which this regulation was introduced to remedy was the risk that the client's legal representative might induce the client to enter into insurance arrangements in which he had an interest. If he had no interest, then there was no identified mischief ..."

regulation 4(5) requires the legal representative to explain the effect of the CFA in writing to the client before she enters into it and in addition to explain it orally. In the particular case the client had received an oral explanation and a copy of the CFA, which itself had attached to it an explanation of its clauses. The court stated:

"153. All these cases turn on their own facts. The regulatory intention is that the client should not be left in ... confusion ... If these documents had been in small print and as far removed from winning a prize for plain English as many documents of their type, then it is obvious that regulation 4(5) would have been breached ...

154. We therefore agree with the approach adopted by the Judge and also with his preference for a free standing explanatory letter, which may of course cross refer to any part of the Law Society conditions which sets out the effect of the CFA with clarity."

In the TAG Test Cases, the issue was whether the regulation 4 information was given to the claimants by someone who qualified as "the legal representative" for the purposes of that regulation. The court, having extensively reviewed the argument, felt that it was not driven to the conclusion that the person who actually gave the reg.4 advice must inevitably be someone who was himself qualified to conduct litigation services. Parliament had not made this requirement and, in the context of the liberalising effect of Part 2 of the 1990 Act, it would be wrong for the court to do so. The question therefore arose: if a wider degree of delegation is legally possible can a solicitor lawfully delegate his responsibility to an organisation like TAG, and can TAG sub-delegate it to one of their representatives? The court concluded (at 216):

"...For the purposes [of this appeal] it is sufficient if we make it clear that it will be in theory permissible for a solicitors firm to delegate the performance of his regulation 4 duties to an organisation like TAG, and for TAG to sub-delegate to it representatives, provided that in so doing the solicitor is not abandoning the supervisory responsibilities required of him by Practice Rule 3.07 and the Guide to Professional Conduct. Whether the TAG scheme can and does provide properly for this is a matter for the fact finding trial.

217. Part 2 of the 1990 Act is concerned with the search for new or better ways of providing litigation services. A national organisation like TAG may be able to achieve economies of scale and standards of client service which simply are not available to an ordinary solicitor's firm. Quality control, however, is all important, and if a solicitor abjurs his duty to maintain supervisory responsibility, through an established framework for reporting and accountability, over the TAG representatives when they visit his client's home on his behalf, it is likely that it would be found that it was not he who gave the information he was required by regulation 4 to give and that the regulation has therefore been broken."

The court concluded by saying:

"226. In future District Judges and Costs Judges must be equally astute to prevent satellite litigation about costs from being protracted by allegations about breaches of the CFA regulations where the breaches do not matter. They should remember that the law does not care about very little things, and that they should only declare a CFA unenforceable if the breach does matter and if the client could have relied on it successfully against his solicitor."

Hollins v. Russell and other appeals [2003] EWCA Civ 718[2003] 1 W.L.R. 2487 CA *sub nom.Sharratt v. London Central Bus Co Ltd* [2003] 4 All E.R. 590 CA.

See also *Myler & Mirror Group Newspapers v. Williams* [2003] EWHC 1387 (QB), Crane J.

Where a CFA made no mention of the fee deferral element in its schedule, although the body of the agreement stated that this was set out in the schedule, the solicitors argued that s.58(1) of the Courts and Legal Services Act 1990 should be interpreted by inserting words such as "to the extent that it does not satisfy all requirements" so that the court could assess the effect of a particular breach. If the consequences were comparatively trivial this would penalise the solicitor far less than rendering the whole agreement unenforceable. The Court of Appeal rejected that argument pointing out that in *Hollins v. Russell* the court had found: "there is no graduated response to different types of breach: it is all or nothing." The words "shall be unenforceable" mean what they say. The court held that Parliament had decided that unless a CFA satisfied all the conditions applicable to it, by virtue of s.58(1), it would not be exempt from the general rules as to the unenforceability of CFAs at common law: *Spencer v. Wood (t/a Gordon's Tyres)* [2004] EWCA Civ 352.

A CFA with a contingent uplift as a success fee was held to be enforceable as the fact that an agreement was a conditional fee agreement under the Courts and Legal Services Act 1990 was sufficient to render it enforceable regardless of how the success fee was calculated: *Benaim (UK) Ltd v. Davies Middleton & Davies Ltd* [2004] EWHC 737 (TCC) HHJ Rich QC

Maintenance and Champerty

7A–51   See note *Times Newspapers Ltd v. Burstein (Costs: Champertous Retainer)* [2002] EWCA Civ 1739 at 47.14.3. The court's concern is with the nature of the contract of retainer and not with the behaviour of the solicitor subsequently, save in so far as it might throw light upon the true nature of the original agreement. What the court is concerned with is establishing the true nature of the contract entered into between the client and the solicitor. The court referred to the dictum of Lloyd J. in *R v. Miller* and *R v. Glennie* [1983] 1 W.L.R. 1056:

> "... costs are incurred by a party if he is responsible or liable for those costs even though they are in fact paid by a third party, whether an employer insurance company, motoring organisation or trade union and even though the third party is also liable for those costs. It is only if it has been agreed that the client shall in no circumstances be liable for the costs that they cease to be costs incurred by him ..."

Whilst the client's impecuniosity may be relevant to determining what the true nature of the agreement was, the mere fact that the solicitor may have been conducting the action on credit or continuing an action in the knowledge of his client's lack of means does not justify a conclusion that he was unlawfully maintaining the action. The court went on to quote the judgment of Schiemann L.J. in *Awwad v. Geraghty & Co* [2001] QB 570, CA where he listed public policy arguments in favour of enforceability. At page 588F:

> "6. If the lawyer's client has no assets then a conditional normal fee agreement merely gives legal form to what is a practical reality – the lawyer only gets paid if the client wins. Yet it is accepted as laudable for lawyers to act in such circumstances.
>
> 7. There is nothing improper in the lawyer agreeing to act for the client for his normal fee whilst having it in his mind, for reasons of friendship or wishing to foster future work from that client, not to exact his fee if the client should lose. It seems odd that an open contractual statement of what is unobjectionable in a solicitor's mind should render unenforceable an agreement which would have been enforceable had the solicitor not shared his thoughts with his client and promised not to change his mind."

The court went on to hold that the Deputy Costs Judge had been correct to refuse the paying party's application requiring the receiving party's solicitors to give full particulars of their dealings with the client both in relation to their original retention as his solicitors and the conditional fee agreement: *Times Newspapers Ltd v. Burstein* [2002] EWCA Civ 1739.

MEMBERSHIP ORGANISATIONS

7A–52   Section 30 of the Access to Justice Act 1999 enables a membership organisation to recover, through a costs order made in favour of any of the members, an additional amount in respect of any provision made by or on behalf of the body in connection with the proceedings against the risk of having to meet the costs of the other parties to the proceedings. The additional amount recoverable must not exceed the likely cost of the premium of an insurance policy against the risk of incurring a liability to pay the costs of other parties to the proceedings.

The Lord Chancellor has the power to prescribe bodies as membership organisations for the purpose of s.30 of the 1999 Act. The organisations prescribed include most Trade Unions and Associations, as well as the Defence Police Federation, the Engineering Employers Federation, the Police Federation of England and Wales, the Automobile Association and RAC Motoring Services.

BARRISTERS

INTRODUCTION

A barrister may enter into a conditional fee agreement (CFA) with a solicitor as an **7B–1** "additional legal representative". The agreement is not with the lay client. A barrister in independent practice, whether or not acting for a fee, may supply legal services only if he or she is instructed by a professional client or by a BarDirect client or is appointed by the court. The barrister must not enter into a contract for the supply of legal services by him or her with any person other than a professional or a bar BarDirect client. A "professional client" means a solicitor or other professional person by whom a barrister in independent practice is instructed (See Code of Conduct of the Bar paragraphs 401 and 1001).

Although the solicitor will probably have a CFA (with a success fee) with the lay client, the agreements between counsel and solicitor and solicitor and client are entirely separate. The barrister and the solicitor will not necessarily seek the same level of success fee and the two success fees may be dealt with differently on assessment. When the solicitor bills the client there will be included in that bill an amount in respect of counsel's fees and any success fee due to counsel. Section 20 of the Costs Practice Direction deals with the procedure where the legal representative wishes to recover from the client an agreed percentage increase which has been disallowed or reduced on assessment (r.44.16).

Although counsel's fee and any success fee is separately recoverable by the solicitor from the client as a disbursement, counsel is unable to recover it separately. There is no direct relationship with the lay client, contractual or otherwise. Counsel is only able to recover fees from the solicitor who is personally liable for them. The Bar Council takes the view that barristers may enter into binding contracts for work under a CFA, but whether or not they do so depends upon the general law and the terms of the agreement used. APIL/PIBA have model forms of CFA which cover agreements which are non binding or binding contracts. The Chancery Bar Association's standard form of CFA contains an option for the agreement to be contractually binding. All BarDirect work has to be performed under contract.

[THE NEXT PARAGRAPH IS 7C–1.]

Solicitors Act 1974

1974 (c.47)

An Act to consolidate the Solicitors Acts 1957 to 1974 and certain other enactments relating to solicitors.

[31st July 1974] **7C–1**

Miscellaneous and General

Supplementary

* * * *

* * * *

[THE NEXT PARAGRAPH IS 7C–3.]

Part I

Rights and privileges of solicitors

Rights of practising and rights of audience

19.—(1) Subject to subsection (2) every person qualified in accor-   **7C–3**
dance with section 1 may practise as a solicitor—

(a) in the Supreme Court;

(b) in any county court;

(c) in all courts and before all persons having jurisdiction in
ecclesiastical matters; and

(d) in all matters relating to applications to obtain notarial
faculties,

and shall be entitled to all the rights and privileges, and may
exercise and perform all the powers and duties, formerly appertain-
ing to the office or profession of a proctor in the provincial, diocesan
or other jurisdictions in England and Wales.

(2) Nothing in subsection (1) shall affect the provisions of section
94 of the Supreme Court Act 1981, section 13 or 60 of the County
Courts Act 1984 or any other enactment in force at the commencement of this Act which restricts the right of any solicitor to practise as
such in any court.

(3) Nothing in subsection (1) or (2) shall prejudice or affect any
right of practising or being heard in, before or by any court, tribunal
or other body which immediately before the commencement of this
Act was enjoyed by virtue of any enactment, rule, order, or regulation or by custom or otherwise by persons qualified to act as solicitors.

Note—Amended by the SCA 1981, s.152, Sched.5; and the County Courts Act 1984,   **7C–4**
Sched.2.

Unqualified persons acting as solicitors

Unqualified person not to act as solicitor

20.—(1) No unqualified person shall—   **7C–5**

(a) act as a solicitor, or as such issue any writ or process, or
commence, prosecute or defend any action, suit or other

proceeding, in his own name or in the name of any other person, in any court of civil or criminal jurisdiction; or

(b) act as a solicitor in any cause or matter, civil or criminal, to be heard or determined before any justice or justices or any commissioners of Her Majesty's revenue.

(2) Any person who contravenes the provisions of subsection (1)—

(a) shall be guilty of an offence and liable on conviction on indictment to imprisonment for not more than two years or to a fine or to both; and

(b) shall be guilty of contempt of the court in which the action, suit, cause, matter or proceeding in relation to which he so acts is brought or taken and may be punished accordingly;

(c) [...]

(3) [...]

(4) [...]

7C–5.1   There is no breach and no contempt if the acts in question are carried out pursuant to a right of audience or a right to conduct litigation granted under the Courts and Legal Services Act 1990: *Noueiri v. Paragon Finance Plc (No. 1)* [2001] EWCA Civ 1114.

7C–6   *Note* —Amended by the Courts and Legal Services Act 1990, Scheds 18 and 20.

Unqualified person not to pretend to be a solicitor

7C–7   **21.** Any unqualified person who wilfully pretends to be, or takes or uses any name, title, addition or description implying that he is, qualified or recognised by law as qualified to act as a solicitor shall be guilty of an offence and liable on summary conviction to a fine not exceeding the fourth level on the standard scale.

7C–8   *Note* —Amended by the Criminal Justice Act 1982; and the AJA 1985, Sched.1.

Unqualified person not to prepare certain instruments

7C–9   **22.**—(1) Subject to subsections (2) and (2A) any unqualified person who directly or indirectly—

(a) draws or prepares any instrument of transfer or charge for the purposes of the Land Registration Act 2002, or makes any application or lodges any document for registration under that Act at the registry, or

(b) draws or prepares any other instrument relating to real or personal estate, or any legal proceeding,

shall, unless he proves that the act was not done for or in expectation of any fee, gain or reward, be guilty of an offence and liable on summary conviction to a fine not exceeding level 3 on the standard scale.

(2) Subsection (1) does not apply to—

(a) a barrister or duly certified notary public;

(aa) a registered trade mark agent drawing or preparing any instrument relating to any design, or trade mark;

(ab) a registered patent agent drawing or preparing any instrument relating to any invention, design, technical information, or trade mark;

    (ac) any accredited person drawing or preparing any instrument—

        (i) which creates, or which he believes on reasonable grounds will create, a farm business tenancy (within the meaning of the Agricultural Tenancies Act 1995), or

        (ii) which relates to an existing tenancy which is, or which he believes on reasonable grounds to be, such a tenancy;

    (b) any public officer drawing or preparing instruments or applications in the course of his duty;

    (c) any person employed merely to engross any instrument, application or proceeding;

and paragraph (b) of that subsection does not apply to a duly certificated solicitor in Scotland.

(2A)　Subsection (1) also does not apply to any act done by a person at the direction and under the supervision of another person if—

    (a) that other person was at the time his employer, a partner of his employer or a fellow employee; and

    (b) the act could have been done by that other person for or in expectation of any fee, gain or reward without committing an offence under this section.

(3) For the purposes of subsection (1)(b) "instrument" includes a contract for the sale or other disposition of land (except a contract to grant such a lease as is referred to in section 54(2) of the Law of Property Act 1925 (short leases)), but does not include—

    (a) a will or other testamentary instrument;

    (b) an agreement not intended to be executed as a deed other than a contract that is included by virtue of the preceding provisions of this subsection;

    (c) a letter or power of attorney; or

    (d) a transfer of stock containing no trust or limitation thereof.

(3A) In subsection (2)—

"accredited person" means any person who is—

        (a) a Full Member of the Central Association of Agricultural Valuers,

        (b) an Associate or Fellow of the Incorporated Society of Valuers and Auctioneers, or

        (c) an Associate or Fellow of the Royal Institution of Chartered Surveyors;

"registered trade mark agent" has the same meaning as in the Trade Marks Act 1994; and

"registered patent agent" has the same meaning as in section 275(1) of the Copyright, Designs and Patents Act 1988.

(4) A local weights and measures authority may institute proceedings for an offence under this section.

Note —Amended by the Criminal Justice Act 1982; the AJA 1985, s.6; the Law of **7C–10**

Property (Miscellaneous Provisions) Act 1989, Sched.1; the Courts and Legal Services Act 1990, s.68; the Trade Marks Act 1994, s.106(1), Sched.4, para. 5; the Agricultural Tenancies Act 1995, s.35 and by the Land Registration Act 2002, Sched.11, para.12. Disapplied for certain purposes by the Building Societies Act 1986.

Subs. (1)(b) "Fee, gain or reward."

7C–11   In *Reynolds v. Hoyle* [1976] 1 W.L.R. 207; [1975] 3 All E.R. 934 it was held that an offence was committed when an unqualified person draws or prepares the document regardless of the identity of the person to whom the fee is paid. But see the associated cases of *Ashford v. Hoyle* [1976] 1 W.L.R. 207 and *Green v. Hoyle* [1976] 1 W.L.R. 575; [1976] 2 All E.R. 633) where the appellants were held not to have "indirectly" drawn a transfer merely because they received the fee. See also *House Owners Co-operative Society Ltd. v. Hoyle* (1976) 120 S.J. 540.

Powers of entry, etc., of local weights and measures authorities

7C–12   **22A.**—(1) Any authorised officer who has reasonable cause to suspect that an offence may have been committed under section 22 may, at any reasonable time—

    (a) enter any premises which are not used solely as a dwelling;

    (b) require any officer, agent or other competent person on the premises who is, or may be, in possession of information relevant to an investigation under section 22, to provide such information;

    (c) require the production of any document which may be relevant to such an investigation;

    (d) take copies, or extracts, of any such documents;

    (e) seize and retain any document which he has reason to believe may be required as evidence in proceedings for an offence under section 22.

(2) Any person exercising any power given by subsection (1) shall, if asked to do so, produce evidence that he is an authorised officer.

(3) A justice of the peace may issue a warrant under this section if satisfied, on information on oath given by an authorised officer, that there is reasonable cause to believe that an offence may have been committed under section 22 and that—

    (a) entry to the premises concerned, or production of any documents which may be relevant to an investigation under section 22, has been or is likely to be refused to an authorised officer; or

    (b) there is reasonable cause to believe that, if production of any such document were to be required by the authorised officer without a warrant having been issued under this section, the document would not be produced but would be removed from the premises or hidden, tampered with or destroyed.

(4) A warrant issued under this section shall authorise the authorised officer accompanied, where he considers it appropriate, by a constable or any other person—

    (a) to enter the premises specified in the information, using such force as is reasonably necessary; and

(b) to exercise any of the powers given to the authorised officer by subsection (1).

(5) If a person—

(a) intentionally obstructs an authorised officer in the exercise of any power under this section;

(b) intentionally fails to comply with any requirement properly imposed on him by an authorised officer in the exercise of any such power;

(c) fails, without reasonable excuse, to give to an authorised officer any assistance or information which he may reasonably require of him for the purpose of exercising any such power; or

(d) in giving to an authorised officer any information which he has been required to give to an authorised officer exercising any such power, makes any statement which he knows to be false or misleading in a material particular,

he shall be guilty of an offence.

(6) A person guilty of an offence under this section shall be liable on summary conviction to a fine not exceeding level 3 on the standard scale.

(7) Nothing in this section shall be taken to require any person to answer any question put to him by an authorised officer, or to give any information to an authorised officer, if to do so might incriminate him.

(8) In this section—

"authorised officer" means any officer of a local weights and measures authority who is authorised by the authority to exercise the powers given by subsection (1); and

"document" includes information recorded in any form.

(9) In relation to information recorded otherwise than in legible form, references in this section to its production include references to producing a copy of the information in legible form.

Note —Added by the Courts and Legal Services Act 1990, s.96.   **7C–13**

Unqualified person not to prepare papers for probate, etc.

23.—(1) Subject to subsections (2) and (3), any unqualified person, **7C–14** who, directly or indirectly, draws or prepares any papers on which to found or oppose—

(a) a grant of probate, or

(b) a grant of letters of administration,

shall, unless he proves that the act was not done for or in expectation of any fee, gain or reward, be guilty of an offence and liable on summary conviction to a fine not exceeding the first level on the standard scale.

(2) Subsection (1) does not apply to a barrister or duly certificated notary public.

(3) Subsection (1) also does not apply to any act done by a person at the direction and under the supervision of another person if—

(a) that other person was at the time his employer, a partner of his employer or a fellow employee; and

(b) the act could have been done by that other person for or in expectation of any fee, gain or reward without committing an offence under this section.

7C–15   *Note* —Substituted by the Administration of Justice Act 1985, s.7; amended by the Courts and Legal Services Act 1990, s.54; and the Friendly Societies Act 1992, s.120, Sched.21, para. 5.

Courts and Legal Services Act 1990: s.54 is amended and repealed in part by the Bank of England Act, s.23, Sched.5, para. 41 and s.43, Sched.9, Pt I respectively. Schedule 10, para. 58 is repealed by the Data Protection Act 1998, Sched.16, Pt I, and Sched.11 is amended by Employment Rights (Dispute Resolution) Act 1998, Sched.1, para. 6.

Renewal of practising certificate

7C–16   In *Hudgell, Yeates & Co v. Watson* [1978] Q.B. 451; [1978] 2 All E.R. 363, the Court of Appeal held that a firm of solicitors were not prevented from recovering their costs merely because one of the partners, who took no part in the conduct of the case in question, had inadvertently failed to renew his practising certificate.

Application of penal provisions to body corporate

7C–17   **24.**—(1) If any act is done by a body corporate, or by any director, officer or servant of a body corporate, and is of such a nature or is done in such a manner as to be calculated to imply that the body corporate is qualified or recognised by law as qualified to act as a solicitor—

(a) the body corporate shall be guilty of an offence and liable on summary conviction to a fine not exceeding the fourth level on the standard scale, and

(b) in the case of an act done by a director, officer or servant of the body corporate, he also shall be guilty of an offence and liable on summary conviction to a fine not exceeding the fourth level on the standard scale.

(2) For the avoidance of doubt it is hereby declared that in sections 20, 22 and 23 references to unqualified persons and to persons include references to bodies corporate.

7C–18   *Note* —Amended by the Criminal Justice Act 1982; and the AJA 1985, Sched.1.

Costs where unqualified person acts as solicitor

7C–19   **25.**—(1) No costs in respect of anything done by any unqualified person acting as a solicitor shall be recoverable by him, or by any other person, in any action, suit or matter.

(2) Nothing in subsection (1) shall prevent the recovery of money paid or to be paid by a solicitor on behalf of a client in respect of anything done by the solicitor while acting for the client without holding a practising certificate in force if that money would have been recoverable if he had held such a certificate when so acting.

(3) [...]

7C–20   *Note* —Amended by the Courts and Legal Services Act 1990, Sched.18, para. 12.

Time limit for commencement of certain proceedings

7C–21   **26.** Notwithstanding anything in the Magistrates' Courts Act 1980, proceedings in respect of any offence under section 21, 22 or 23 may be brought at any time before the expiration of two years from the commission of the offence or six months from its first discovery by the prosecutor, whichever period expires first.

Note —Amended by the Magistrates' Courts Act 1980, Sched.7.　　　**7C–22**

Savings for persons authorised to conduct legal proceedings

27. Nothing in this Part shall affect any enactment empowering an **7C–23** unqualified person to conduct, defend, or otherwise act in relation to any legal proceedings.

Regulations

28.—(1) The Master of the Rolls may make regulations, with the **7C–24** concurrence of the Secretary of State and the Lord Chief Justice, about the following matters, namely—

    (a) admission as a solicitor;

    (b) the keeping of the roll;

    (c) practising certificates and applications for them;

    (d) the keeping of the register under section 9.

(2) The power conferred by subsection (1) includes power to specify—

    (a) one or more conditions (in this Act referred to as "training conditions") to be imposed on the issue of practising certificates to solicitors to whom training regulations apply; and

    (b) one or more conditions (in this Act referred to as "indemnity conditions") to be imposed on the issue of practising certificates to solicitors who are exempt from indemnity rules.

(3) Regulations about the keeping of the roll and of the register under section 9 may provide for the manner in which entries are to be made, altered and removed.

(3A) Regulations about the keeping of the roll may—

    (a) provide for the Society, at such intervals as may be specified in the regulations, to enquire of solicitors of any class so specified whether they wish to have their names retained on the roll;

    (b) require solicitors of any such class, at such intervals as aforesaid, to pay to the Society a fee in respect of the retention of their names on the roll of such amount as may be prescribed by the regulations; and

    (c) authorise the Society to remove from the roll the name of any solicitor who—

        (i) fails to reply to any enquiry made in pursuance of paragraph (a) or to pay any fee payable by virtue of paragraph (b), or

        (ii) replies to any such enquiry by indicating that he does not wish to have his name retained on the roll;

    (d) authorise the Society to remove from the roll the name of any solicitor who has died.

(4) Regulations about the keeping of the roll may also provide for rights of appeal to the Master of the Rolls in connection with the making and alteration of entries on the roll and the removal of entries from it.

(5) The Master of the Rolls may make regulations about the procedure for any appeals to him authorised by this Part or regulations under this section.

7C–25 *Note* —Amended by the AJA 1985, Sched.1 and by the Secretary of State for Constitutional Affairs Order 2003 (S.I. 2003 No. 1887), Sched. 2, para. 3.

Non-British subjects as solicitors

7C–26 **29.** Nothing in section 3 of the Act of Settlement (which provides among other things that aliens are incapable of enjoying certain offices or places of trust) shall be taken to disqualify a person from becoming or practising as a solicitor of the Supreme Court or of the Supreme Court of Northern Ireland.

Evidence as to solicitors in Scotland

7C–27 **30.** For the purposes of this Part, a letter purporting to be signed by or on behalf of the registrar of solicitors in Scotland—

(a) stating that a person specified in the letter is or is not a solicitor in Scotland shall be evidence that that person is or, as the case may be, is not a solicitor in Scotland;

(b) stating that a person specified in the letter did not at any time during a period so specified have in force a practising certificate as a solicitor in Scotland shall be evidence that that person was not during any part of that period a duly certified solicitor in Scotland.

PART II

PROFESSIONAL PRACTICE, CONDUCT AND DISCIPLINE OF SOLICITORS AND CLERKS

PRACTICE RULES

Rules as to professional practice, conduct and discipline

7C–28 **31.**—(1) Without prejudice to any other provision of this Part the Council may, if they think fit, make rules, with the concurrence of the Master of the Rolls, for regulating in respect of any matter the professional practice, conduct and discipline of solicitors and for empowering the Society to take such action as may be appropriate to enable the Society to ascertain whether or not the provisions of rules made; or if any code or guidance issued, by the Council are being complied with.

(2) If any solicitor fails to comply with rules made under this section, any person may make a complaint in respect of that failure to the Tribunal.

(3) Where, under Schedule 4 to the Courts and Legal Services Act 1990 (approval of certain rules in connection with the grant of

rights of audience or rights to conduct litigation), the Master of the Rolls approves any rule made under this section he shall be taken, for the purposes of this section, to have concurred in the making of that rule.

(4) Subsection (3) shall have effect whether or not the rule required to be approved under Schedule 4 to the Act of 1990.

Note —Amended by the Courts and Legal Services Act 1990, Sched.17, para. 10 and **7C–29** the Access to Justice Act 1999, Sched.7.

ACCOUNTS, ETC.

Accounts rules and trust accounts rules

32.—(1) The Council shall make rules, with the concurrence of the **7C–30** Master of the Rolls—

(a) as to the opening and keeping by solicitors of accounts at banks or with building societies for clients' money; and

(b) as to the keeping by solicitors of accounts containing particulars and information as to money received or held or paid by them for or on account of their clients; and

(c) empowering the Council to take such action as may be necessary to enable them to ascertain whether or not the rules are being complied with;

and the rules may specify the location of the banks' branches at which the accounts are to be kept.

(2) The Council shall also make rules, with the concurrence of the Master of the Rolls—

(a) as to the opening and keeping by solicitors of accounts at banks or with building societies for money comprised in controlled trusts; and

(b) as to the keeping by solicitors of accounts containing particulars and information as to money received or held or paid by them for or on account of any such trust; and

(c) empowering the Council to take such action as may be necessary to enable them to ascertain whether or not the rules are being complied with,

and the rules may specify the location of the banks' branches at which the accounts are to be kept.

(3) If any solicitor fails to comply with rules made under this section, any person may make a complaint in respect of that failure to the Tribunal.

(4) The Council shall be at liberty to disclose a report on or information about a solicitor's accounts obtained in the exercise of powers conferred by rules made under subsection (1) or (2) [...] for use in investigating the possible commission of an offence by the solicitor and [...] for use in connection with any prosecution of the solicitor consequent on the investigation.

(5) Rules under this section may specify circumstances in which solicitors or any class of solicitors are exempt from the rules by virtue of their office or employment.

(6) For the purposes of this section and section 33 references to clients' money and money of a kind mentioned in subsection (1)(b) of this section or (1)(a) of section 33 include references to money held by a solicitor as a stakeholder (whether or not paid by a client of his).

7C–31 *Note* —Amended by the Building Societies Act 1986, Scheds 18 and 19; and the Courts and Legal Services Act 1990, Sched.18 and the Access to Justice Act 1999, Sched.15, Pt II.

Interest on clients' money

7C–32 **33.**—(1) Rules made under section 32 shall make provision for requiring a solicitor, in such cases as may be prescribed by the rules, either—

(a) to keep on deposit in a separate account at a bank or with a building society for the benefit of the client money received for or on account of a client; or

(b) to make good to the client out of the solicitor's own money a sum equivalent to the interest which would have accrued if the money so received had been so kept on deposit.

(2) The cases in which a solicitor may be required by the rules to act as mentioned in subsection (1) may be defined, among other things, by reference to the amount of any sum received or the period for which it is or is likely to be retained or both; and the rules may include provision for enabling a client (without prejudice to any other remedy) to require that any question arising under the rules in relation to the client's money be referred to and determined by the Society.

(3) Except as provided by the rules, a solicitor shall not be liable by virtue of the relation between solicitor and client to account to any client for interest received by the solicitor on money deposited at a bank or with a building society being money received or held for or on account of his clients generally.

(4) Nothing in this section or in the rules shall—

(a) affect any arrangement in writing, whenever made, between a solicitor and his client as to the application of the client's money or interest on it;

(b) [...]

7C–33 *Note* —Amended by the Building Societies Act 1986, Sched.18. Subsection (4)(b) repealed by the Courts and Legal Services Act 1990, Sched.20.

Inspection of practice bank accounts, etc.

7C–33.1 **33A.**—(1) The Council may make rules, with the concurrence of the Master of the Rolls, empowering the Council to require a solicitor to produce documents relating to any account kept by him at a bank or with a building society—

(a) in connection with his practice; or

(b) in connection with any trust of which he is or formerly was a trustee,

for inspection by a person appointed by the Council pursuant to the rules.

(2) The Council shall be at liberty to disclose information obtained in exercise of the powers conferred by rules made under subsection (1) for use in investigating the possible commission of an offence by the solicitor and for use in connection with any prosecution of the solicitor consequent on the investigation.

Note —Inserted by the Access to Justice Act 1999, Sched.7, para. 3.   **7C–33.2**

Accountants' reports

34.—(1) Every solicitor shall once in each period of twelve months ending with 31st October, unless the Council are satisfied that it is unnecessary for him to do so, deliver to the Society, whether by post or otherwise, a report signed by an accountant (in this section referred to as an "accountant's report") and containing such information as may be prescribed by rules made by the Council under this section.   **7C–34**

(2) An accountant's report shall be delivered to the Society not more than six months (or such other period as may be prescribed by rules made under this section) after the end of the accounting period for the purposes of that report.

(3) Subject to any rules made under this section, the accounting period for the purposes of an accountant's report—

    (a) shall begin at the expiry of the last preceding accounting period for which an accountant's report has been delivered;

    (b) shall cover not less than twelve months; and

    (c) where possible, consistently with the preceding provision of this section, shall correspond to a period or consecutive periods for which the accounts of the solicitor or his firm are ordinarily made up.

(4) The Council shall make rules to give effect to the provisions of this section, and those rules shall prescribe—

    (a) the qualification to be held by an accountant by whom an accountant's report is given;

    (b) the information to be contained in an accountant's report;

    (c) the nature and extent of the examination to be made by an accountant of the books and accounts of a solicitor or his firm and of any other relevant documents with a view to the signing of an accountant's report;

    (d) the form of an accountant's report; and

    (e) the evidence, if any, which shall satisfy the Council that the delivery of an accountant's report is unnecessary and the cases in which such evidence is or is not required.

(5) Rules under this section may include provision—

    (a) permitting in such special circumstances as may be defined by the rules a different accounting period from that specified in subsection (3); and

    (b) regulating any matters of procedure or matters incidental, ancillary or supplemental to the provisions of this section.

REPRESENTATIVES

(5A) Without prejudice to the generality of subsection (5)(b), rules under this section may make provision requiring a solicitor in advance of delivering an accountant's report to notify the Society of the period which is to be the accounting period for the purposes of that report in accordance with the preceding provisions of this section.

(6) If any solicitor fails to comply with the provisions of this section or of any rules made under it, a complaint in respect of that failure may be made to the Tribunal by or on behalf of the Society.

(7) A certificate under the hand of the Secretary of the Society shall, until the contrary is proved, be evidence that a solicitor has or, as the case may be, has not delivered to the Society an accountant's report or supplied any evidence required under this section or any rules made under it.

(8) Where a solicitor is exempt from rules under section 32—
   (a) nothing in this section shall apply to him unless he takes out a practising certificate;
   (b) an accountant's report shall in no case deal with books, accounts or documents kept by him in the course of employment by virtue of which he is exempt from those rules; and
   (c) no examination shall be made of any such books, accounts and documents under any rules made under this section.

7C–35   *Note* —Amended by the AJA 1985, Sched.1.

* * * *

INADEQUATE PROFESSIONAL SERVICES

Redress for inadequate professional services
7C–36   **37A.** Schedule 1A shall have effect with respect to the provision by solicitors of services which are not of the quality which it is reasonable to expect of them.

7C–37   *Note* —Added by the Courts and Legal Services Act 1990, s.93(2).

* * * *

IMPOSITION BY COUNCIL OF DISCIPLINARY SANCTIONS FOR INADEQUATE PROFESSIONAL SERVICES

Power of Council to impose sanctions for inadequate professional services
7C–38   **44A.** [*Repealed by* Courts and Legal Services Act 1990, s.93(1) and (2).]

7C–39   *Note* —Any case in which the final bill of costs was delivered to the client concerned before the commencement of s.93 (April 1, 1991) is not affected (Courts and Legal Services Act 1990, Sched.19).

50.—(1) Any person duly admitted as a solicitor shall be an officer **7C–40**
of the Supreme Court.

(2) Subject to the provisions of this Act, the High Court, the
Crown Court and the Court of Appeal respectively, or any division
or judge of those courts, may exercise the same jurisdiction in respect of solicitors as any one of the superior courts of law or equity
from which the Supreme Court was constituted might have exercised
immediately before the passing of the Supreme Court of Judicature
Act 1873 in respect of any solicitor, attorney or proctor admitted to
practise there.

(3) An appeal shall lie to the Court of Appeal from any order
made against a solicitor by the High Court or the Crown Court in
the exercise of its jurisdiction in respect of solicitors under subsection
(2).

Note —Amended by the SCA 1981, ss.147, 152(4) and Sched.7. **7C–41**

Subs. (2)

The jurisdiction of the Court is frequently exercised, notwithstanding the existence **7C–42**
of the Office for the Supervision of Solicitors. For the circumstances in which it will be
exercised see *Gupta v. Comer* [1991] 2 W.L.R. 494; *Holden & Co (a firm) v. Crown Prosecution Service* [1990] 1 All E.R. 368, CA.

Procedure upon certain applications to High Court

51.—(1) Where an application to strike the name of a solicitor off **7C–43**
the roll or to require a solicitor to answer allegations contained in an
affidavit is made to the High Court, then, subject to section 54, the
following provisions of this section shall have effect in relation to that
application.

(2) The court shall not entertain the application except on production of an affidavit proving that the applicant has served on the
Society fourteen clear days' notice of his intention to make the application, together with copies of all affidavits intended to be used in
support of the application.

(3) The Society may appear by counsel on the hearing of the application and any other proceedings arising out of or in reference to
the application, and may apply to the court—

    (a) to make absolute any order nisi which the court may
        have made on the application;

    (b) to make an order that the name of the solicitor be struck
        off the roll; or

    (c) to make such other order as the court may think fit.

(4) The Court may order the costs of the Society of or relating to
any of the matters mentioned in subsections (2) and (3) to be paid by
the solicitor against whom, or by the person by whom, the application was made, or was intended to be made, or partly by one and
partly by the other of them.

Subs. (4)

On a client's application to have a solicitor struck off, where the Law Society was **7C–44**
not a party but appeared in the role of *amicus curiae*, it could not be made liable for
costs (*Re A Solicitor*, (1983) 80 L.S.G. 2998).

Power of Society to draw up order of court

7C–45   **52.** Where an order, whether nisi or absolute, is made by the High Court or the Court of Appeal on a motion to strike the name of a solicitor off the roll, or to require a solicitor to answer allegations contained in an affidavit, and that order is not drawn up by the applicant within one week of its being made, the Society may cause the order to be drawn up, and all future proceedings on the order shall be taken as if the motion had been made by the Society.

Production of order of court to Society

7C–46   **53.** Where an order is made by the High Court or the Court of Appeal that the name of a solicitor be struck off the roll, or that a solicitor be suspended from practice, the proper officer of the court shall forthwith send a copy of the order to the Society, and the Society shall enter a note of the order on the roll against the name of the solicitor and, where the order so directs, shall strike that name off the roll.

DISCIPLINARY PROCEEDINGS—GENERAL

Restrictions on powers to strike names off roll

7C–47   **54.**—(1) No solicitor shall be liable to have his name struck off the roll on account of any failure to comply with the requirements with respect to service under articles of any training regulations or on account of any defect in his admission and enrolment, unless—

(a) the application to strike his name off the roll is made within twelve months of the date of his enrolment; or

(b) fraud is proved to have been committed in connection with the failure or defect.

(2) No solicitor shall be liable to have his name struck off the roll by reason only—

(a) that a solicitor whom he has served for the whole or any part of the term or articled service required in his case by training regulations has neglected or omitted to take out a practising certificate; or

(b) that the name of a solicitor whom he has served for any period has after the termination of that period been removed from or struck off the roll.

Applications to require solicitor to answer allegations

7C–48   **55.** For the avoidance of doubt it is hereby declared that an application by any person to require a solicitor to answer allegations contained in an affidavit, whether that application is made to the Tribunal or to the High Court, may be treated as an application to strike the name of that solicitor off the roll on the grounds of the matters alleged.

PART III

REMUNERATION OF SOLICITORS

NON-CONTENTIOUS BUSINESS

Orders as to remuneration for non-contentious business

56.—(1) For the purposes of this section there shall be a committee **7C–49** consisting of the following persons—

(a) the Lord Chancellor;

(b) the Lord Chief Justice;

(c) the Master of the Rolls;

(d) the President of the Society;

(e) a solicitor, being the president of a local law society, nominated by the Lord Chancellor to serve on the committee during his tenure of office as president; and

(f) for the purpose only of prescribing and regulating the remuneration of solicitors in respect of business done under the Land Registration Act 2002, the Chief Land Registrar appointed under that Act.

(2) The committee, or any three members of the committee (the Lord Chancellor being one) may make general orders prescribing and regulating in such manner as they think fit the remuneration of solicitors in respect of non-contentious business.

(3) The Lord Chancellor, before any order under this section is made, shall cause a draft of the order to be sent to the Council: and the committee shall consider any observations of the Council submitted to them in writing within one month of the sending of the draft, and may then make the order, either in the form of the draft or with such alterations or additions as they may think fit.

(4) An order under this section may prescribe the mode of remuneration of solicitors in respect of non-contentious business by providing that they shall be remunerated—

(a) according to a scale of rates of commission or a scale of percentages, varying or not in different classes of business; or

(b) by a gross sum; or

(c) by a fixed sum for each document prepared or perused, without regard to length; or

(d) in any other mode; or

(e) partly in one mode and partly in another.

(5) An order under this section may regulate the amount of such remuneration with reference to all or any of the following, among other, considerations, that is to say—

(a) the position of the party for whom the solicitor is concerned in the business, that is, whether he is vendor or purchaser, lessor or lessee, mortgagor or mortgagee, or the like;

(b) the place where, and the circumstances in which, the business or any part of it is transacted;

2093

(c) the amount of the capital money or rent to which the business relates;

(d) the skill, labour and responsibility on the part of the solicitor which the business involves;

(e) the number and importance of the documents prepared or perused without regard to length.

(6) An order under this section may authorise and regulate—

(a) the taking by a solicitor from his client of security for payment of any remuneration, to be ascertained by taxation or otherwise, which may become due to him under any such order; and

(b) the allowance of interest.

(7) So long as an order made under this section is in operation the taxation of bills of costs of solicitors in respect of non-contentious business shall, subject to the provisions of section 57, be regulated by that order.

(8) Any order made under this section may be varied or revoked by a subsequent order so made.

(9) The power to make orders under this section shall be exercisable by statutory instrument which shall be subject to annulment in pursuance of a resolution of either House of Parliament; and the Statutory Instruments Act 1946 shall apply to a statutory instrument containing such an order in like manner as if the order had been made by a Minister of the Crown.

7C–50   *Note* —For the definition of "non-contentious business" see s.87, para. 7–137. Amended by the Land Registration Act 2002, Sched.11, para. 12.

Subs.(7)

7C–51   The order now in force is the Solicitors (Non-Contentious Business) Remuneration Order 1994 (S.I. 1994 No. 2616), paras 7–188 to 7–205.

Non-contentious business agreements

7C–52   **57.**—(1) Whether or not any order is in force under section 56, a solicitor and his client may, before or after or in the course of the transaction of any non-contentious business by the solicitor make an agreement as to his remuneration in respect of that business.

(2) The agreement may provide for the remuneration of the solicitor by a gross sum, or by reference to an hourly rate, or by a commission or percentage, or by a salary, or otherwise, and it may be made on the terms that the amount of the remuneration stipulated for shall or shall not include all or any disbursements made by the solicitor in respect of searches, plans, travelling, stamps, fees or other matters.

(3) The agreement shall be in writing and signed by the person to be bound by it or his agent in that behalf.

(4) Subject to subsections (5) and (7) the agreement may be sued and recovered on or set aside in the like manner and on the like grounds as an agreement not relating to the remuneration of a solicitor.

(5) If on any taxation of costs the agreement is relied on by the

solicitor and objected to by the client as unfair or unreasonable, the taxing officer may enquire into the facts and certify them to the court, and if from that certificate it appears just to the court that the agreement should be set aside, or the amount payable under it reduced, the court may so order and may give such consequential directions as it thinks fit.

(6) Subsection (7) applies where the agreement provides for the remuneration of the solicitors to be by reference to an hourly rate.

(7) If, on the taxation of any costs, the agreement is relied on by the solicitor and the client objects to the amount of the costs (but is not alleging that the agreement is unfair or unreasonable), the taxing officer may enquire into—

    (a) the number of hours worked by the solicitor; and

    (b) whether the number of hours worked by him was excessive.

Note —Amended by the Courts and Legal Services Act 1990, s.98.   **7C–53**

Subs.(1)—"Non-contentious business"

See s.87 for the meaning of the term.   **7C–54**

Subs.(3)—"Agreement"

The agreement need not be signed by both parties, but only by the party to be   **7C–55** charged (*Re Frape* [1893] 2 Ch. 284). As to what amounts to a signature, see *ibid*. All the terms of the agreement must be found in the document itself, which must sufficiently identify the costs (*Re Frape*). The solicitor cannot rely on an unwritten agreement (*Re West, King & Adams* [1892] 2 Q.B. 102 at 106) nor can the client (*Re A Solicitor (No.2)* [1956] 1 Q.B. 155) and a cash account signed by the client containing an item for "costs as agreed" pursuant to a verbal agreement only, is not a sufficient agreement in writing (*Re Baylis* [1896] 2 Ch. 107). An agreement to employ solicitors in work which might extend over a period of years and involve non-contentious business of various kinds, but for which it was contemplated that bills would be rendered and paid as matters proceeded, is not an entire contract, and the client can determine the retainer at any time on giving notice (*J. H. Milner and Son v. Percy Bilton Ltd* [1966] 1 W.L.R. 1582; [1966] 2 All E.R. 894).

Subs.(5)—"On any taxation of costs"

Although the Court has power to refer an agreement within the section to the Costs   **7C–56** Judge on the ground that it is unfair and unreasonable, yet such an order should not be made if unsupported by evidence leading to such conclusion. See *Re Palmer* (1890) 45 Ch D 291; *Re Frape* [1893] 2 Ch. 284. In *Re A & B* (1900) 44 S.J. 315, delivery of a bill was ordered after a delay of eight years, and the Costs Judge ordered to certify if the agreement was fair and reasonable, the agreed sum being prima facie unreasonable and no statute of limitations being applicable. In *Rutter v. Sheridan-Young* [1958] 1 W.L.R. 44; [1958] 2 All E.R. 13, the Court of Appeal ordered delivery of an itemised bill and detailed assessment, where the agreement for a gross sum followed an erroneous statement by the solicitor as to the basis on which he was permitted to charge. On the other hand, in *Re Gray* (1886) 30 S.J. 551, the Court thought the matter more fit to be decided in an action than by a reference to the costs judge.

The amount payable under an agreement cannot be included in a cash account on the detailed assessment of other bills under an order of course (*Re Templeton and Cox* (1909) 101 L.T. 144, CA).

"Taxation of costs" is now referred to as detailed assessment of costs.

Non-professional work

Where an agreement has been made for the remuneration of a solicitor, and the so-   **7C–57** licitor alleges the remuneration was for non-professional work, the person chargeable cannot obtain the common order for delivery and detailed assessment of a bill of costs: the question of fact must first be decided (*Re Inderwick* (1883) 25 Ch D 279; *Re Fanshawe* [1905] W.N. 64).

For instances of unreasonable agreements, see *Re Montague Scott* [1889] W.N. 40; *Mearns v. Knapp* (1889) 37 W.R. 585; and *cf. Re Haslam & Hier-Evans* [1902] 1 Ch. 705; and nn. to s.61, paras 7C–79 to 7C–83.

As to whether an agreement between a mortgagee or lessor and his solicitor is binding on the mortgagor or lessee, see *Hester v. Hester* (1887) 34 Ch D 607 at 617; *Re Gray* [1901] 1 Ch. 239 at 245. See further para. 7C–124.

An agreement by a mortgagor to pay a lump sum for mortgagor's and mortgagee's costs to a common solicitor is within the section (*Re Palmer* (1890) 45 Ch D 291).

Interest

7C–58   See *Walton v. Egan*, para. 7C–205.

Remuneration of a solicitor who is a mortgagee

7C–59   **58.**—(1) Where a mortgage is made to a solicitor, either alone or jointly with any other person, he or the firm of which he is a member shall be entitled to recover from the mortgagor in respect of all business transacted and acts done by him or them in negotiating the loan, deducing and investigating the title to the property, and preparing and completing the mortgage, such usual costs as he or they would have been entitled to receive if the mortgage had been made to a person who was not a solicitor and that person had retained and employed him or them to transact that business and do those acts.

(2) Where a mortgage has been made to, or has become vested by transfer or transmission in, a solicitor, either alone or jointly with any other person, and any business is transacted or acts are done by that solicitor or by the firm of which he is a member in relation to that mortgage or the security thereby created or the property thereby charged, he or they shall be entitled to recover from the person on whose behalf the business was transacted or the acts were done, and to charge against the security, such usual costs as he or they would have been entitled to receive if the mortgage had been made to and had remained vested in a person who was not a solicitor and that person had retained and employed him or them to transact that business and do those acts.

(3) In this section "mortgage" includes any charge on any property for securing money or money's worth.

CONTENTIOUS BUSINESS

Contentious business agreements

7C–60   **59.**—(1) Subject to subsection (2) a solicitor may make an agreement in writing with his client as to his remuneration in respect of any contentious business done, or to be done, by him (in this Act referred to as a "contentious business agreement") providing that he shall be remunerated by a gross sum, or by reference to an hourly rate, or by a salary, or otherwise, and whether at a higher or lower rate than that at which he would otherwise have been entitled to be remunerated.

(2) Nothing in this section or in section 60 to 63 shall give validity to—

(a) any purchase by a solicitor of the interest, or any part of

the interest, of his client in any action, suit or other
contentious proceeding; or

(b) any agreement by which a solicitor retained or employed
to prosecute any action, suit or other contentious
proceeding, stipulates for payment only in the event of
success in that action, suit or proceeding; or

(c) any disposition, contract, settlement, conveyance,
delivery, dealing or transfer which under the law relating to bankruptcy is invalid against a trustee or creditor
in any bankruptcy or composition.

Note —Amended by Courts and Legal Services Act 1990, s.98. **7C–61**

"Contentious business"
See s.87, para. 7C–137. **7C–62**

Subs.(1)

"Agreement in writing"
The section enables solicitors to make binding agreements in writing. In *Chamberlain* **7C–63**
v. Boodle & King (1980) 124 S.J. 186, Smith J. held it was essential for the agreement
to be in writing and must show all the terms of the bargain between the parties. This
decision was upheld by the Court of Appeal [1982] 1 W.L.R. 1443; [1982] 3 All E.R.
188.
In *Martin Boston & Co v. Levy* [1982] 1 W.L.R. 1434; [1982] 3 All E.R. 193, it was
held that the client's rights under the Solicitors Act would not be defeated where
solicitors sued on a dishonoured cheque received in payment of their account.

Cross claims and account stated
The solicitor cannot rely on a parol agreement (*Re Russell, Son & Scott* (1885) 30 Ch **7C–64**
D 114) yet where there is a claim for costs and a cross-claim, and an account stated,
but not in writing, showing a balance in favour of the solicitor, he can sue for it
without delivering a signed bill (*Turner v. Willis* [1905] 1 K.B. 468).

Agreement for security
The section has no application to an agreement by a client to give his solicitor secu- **7C–65**
rity for such costs as he may become entitled to, whether the security be by cash cover,
or charge upon or assignment of part of a fund to be received by the solicitor, and
such agreement may be oral (*Re Jackson* [1915] 1 K.B. 371; *Jonesco v. Evening Standard*
[1932] 2 K.B. 340, CA).

Bill of exchange
A solicitor cannot evade his obligations under the Act by taking a bill of exchange **7C–66**
(*Ray v. Newton* [1913] 1 K.B. 249, CA).

Signature by client
The agreement may be enforced by the solicitor though signed by the client alone **7C–67**
(*Re Thompson* [1894] 1 Q.B. 462; *Re Jones* [1895] 2 Ch. 719; *Beake v. French (No.2)*
[1907] 2 Ch. 215).

"Gross sum ... hourly rate ... or salary or otherwise"
Contingency fee agreements are not enforceable in English law, but s.58 of the **7C–68**
Courts and Legal Services Act 1990, introduced conditional fees subject to appropriate
orders being made by the Lord Chancellor. See the Conditional Fee Agreements Order 2000 para. 7A–6, and the Conditional Fee Agreements Regulations 2000 para.
7A–12. The 1974 Act is not intended to legalise champertous agreements (*Anon.*
(1875) 1 Ch D 573) as to the nature of which see *Simpson v. Lamb* (1857) 7 E. & B. 84;
Davis v. Freethy (1890) 24 QBD 519 at 523; *Pittman v. Prudential Deposit Bank* (1896) 13
T.L.R. 110; *Re a Solicitor* [1912] 1 K.B. 302. So, a solicitor who receives a proper
retainer subsequently varied so as to be champertous, cannot recover his fees (*Wild v.*

Simpson [1919] 2 K.B. 544; *Awwad v. Geraghty & Co* [2000] 1 All E.R. 608, CA). This includes disbursements as well as profit costs (*Re Trepca Mines Ltd* [1963] Ch. 199, CA). Similarly, an agreement for the collection of rents, interest, or debts, the remuneration for which is to be a percentage of the amount recovered, and which contemplates litigation, would be an infringement of the law against champerty and illegal; but such an agreement, if it excludes the taking of legal proceedings, is neither unprofessional nor objectionable. *Wallersteiner v. Moir (No. 2)* [1975] Q.B. 373; [1975] 1 All E.R. 849, CA and see *AXA Equity & Law Life Assurance Society Plc (No.2), Re; Axa Sun Life Plc, Re* [2001] 1 All E.R. (Comm) 1010.

Salaried solicitor

7C–69   A solicitor can be remunerated by salary for contentious as well as non-contentious business (see *Galloway v. Corporation of London* (1867) L.R. 4 Eq. 90) and the client can recover usual costs from his opponent in litigation unless the latter can show that such costs would exceed the appropriate amount of the salary (see s.60(2), para. 7C–72 and *Henderson v. Merthyr Urban DC* [1900] 1 Q.B. 434). See also *Re Eastwood (dec'd), Lloyds Bank Ltd v. Eastwood* [1975] Ch. 112; [1974] 3 All E.R. 607, CA and *Maes Finance Ltd v. W.G. Edwards & Partners*, February 11, 2000 (QBD unreported). Reaffirmed: *Cole v. British Telecommunications Plc* [2000] 2 Costs L.R. 310, CA.

Lump sum where no agreement

7C–70   See s.64.

Bankruptcy

7C–71   A solicitor may retain moneys paid under an agreement before notice of an act of bankruptcy, though the services are rendered later, *Re Charlwood* [1894] 1 Q.B. 643).

Subs.(2)

7C–72   This section merely provides that nothing in the Act shall give validity to arrangements of the kind specified. The Act does not legitimise any arrangements which would otherwise be unlawful but neither does it made them unlawful if they are otherwise lawful. The Court of Appeal found nothing in the 1974 Act which prohibits the charging of contingent fees. The fact that the Solicitors Practice Rules 1990 made it professional misconduct for a solicitor to enter into any agreement, even for his normal fee, where this was dependent on achieving a successful result in litigation, did not of itself make the practice contrary to law (following *Picton Jones & Co v. Arcadia Developments Ltd* [1989] 1 E.G.L.R. 42). The Court found that the rules were based on a perception of public policy derived from judicial decisions which were flawed, *Thai Trading Co v. Taylor* [1998] 2 W.L.R. 893, CA. In *Hughes v. Kingston Upon Hull City Council* [1999] 2 All E.R. 49, DC, the Divisional Court decided that *Thai Trading* (above) had been decided *per incuriam* because *Swain v. The Law Society* [1983] 1 A.C. 598, HL decided that the (Solicitors Practice Rules 1990, r.8) had the force of statute (see also *Leeds City Council v. Carr*; *Wells v. Barnsley MBC, The Times*, November 12, 1999, DC). Since that decision the Solicitors' Practice Rules 1990 have been altered (with effect from January 7, 1999, see para. 7C–159) to forbid contingency fee agreements save those permitted under statute or by the common law. In *Awwad v Geraghty & Co*, [2001] Q.B. 570, CA, the Court of Appeal held that all contingency fee agreements other than those permitted by statute are unlawful; *i.e.* there can be no lawful contingency fee agreement under the common law. The decision in *Thai Trading* has thus been reversed and the only valid contingency fee agreements are those which accord with statute (see Conditional Fee Agreements Order 2000, para. 7A–5, and Conditional Fee Agreements Regulations 2000, para. 7A–11). The Access to Justice Act 1999, ss.27–31 brings all types of fee agreements into one statutory framework backed up by statutory instrument.

Effect of contentious business agreements

7C–73   **60.**—(1) Subject to the provisions of this section and to sections 61 to 63, the costs of a solicitor in any case where a contentious business agreement has been made shall not be subject to taxation or (except in the case of an agreement which provides for the solicitor to be remunerated by reference to an hourly rate) to the provisions of section 69.

(2) Subject to subsection (3) a contentious business agreement shall not affect the amount of, or any rights or remedies for the recovery of, any costs payable by the client to, or to the client by, any person other than the solicitor, and that person may, unless he has otherwise agreed, require any such costs to be taxed according to the rules for their taxation for the time being in force.

(3) A client shall not be entitled to recover from any other person under an order for the payment of any costs to which a contentious business agreement relates more than the amount payable by him to his solicitor in respect of those costs under the agreement.

(4) A contentious business agreement shall be deemed to exclude any claim by the solicitor in respect of the business to which it relates other than—

    (a) a claim for the agreed costs; or

    (b) a claim for such costs as are expressly excepted from the agreement.

(5) A provision in a contentious business agreement that the solicitor shall not be liable for negligence, or that he shall be relieved from any responsibility to which he would otherwise be subject as a solicitor, shall be void.

Note —Amended by the Courts and Legal Services Act 1990, s.98.

"Contentious business"
See s.87, para. 7C–137.   **7C–74**

Subs.(2)
See *Henderson v. Merthyr Urban DC* [1900] 1 Q.B. 434.   **7C–75**

Subs.(3)
Subsection (3) does no more than express the common law doctrine under which **7C–76** costs are given to the successful party by way of indemnity only. A claimant therefore who has an oral agreement with his solicitor to pay no costs cannot recover any from the defendant (*Gundry v. Sainsbury* [1910] 1 K.B. 99 at 645, CA) *aliter* if he is merely indemnified by another (*Baillie v. Neville* (1920) 149 L.T.J. 300) or is a member of a trade union and he and the union are both liable for the costs (*Adams v. London, etc., Builders* [1921] 1 K.B. 495 or where an employer is indemnified by an insurance Company. (*Cornish v. Lynch* (1910) 3 B.W.C.C. 343, CA) and see *R. v. Miller and Glennie* [1983] 1 W.L.R. 1056; [1983] 3 All E.R. 186.

The words "any costs" in the phrase "an order for the payment of any costs" in s.60(3) relate not to costs at large or to the costs payable by the receiving party to his own solicitor but to the costs and items of costs to be identified on the detailed assessment between the parties as the proper and recoverable costs. The words "costs" clearly refer to the same costs.

The operation of the cap then becomes readily intelligible. Where applicable the figures in the contentious business agreement provide both a measure and a ceiling for each recoverable item of costs. *Per* Sir Brian Neill in *General of Berne Insurance Co, The v. Jardine Reinsurance Management Ltd* [1998] 2 All E.R. 301, CA.

Enforcement of contentious business agreements

61.—(1) No action shall be brought on any contentious business **7C–77** agreement, but on the application of any person who—

    (a) is a party to the agreement or the representative of such a party; or

    (b) is or is alleged to be liable to pay, or is or claims to be entitled to be paid, the costs due or alleged to be due in respect of the business to which the agreement relates,

the court may enforce or set aside the agreement and determine every question as to its validity or effect.

(2) On any application under subsection (1) the court—

(a) if it is of the opinion that the agreement is in all respects fair and reasonable, may enforce it;

(b) if it is of the opinion that the agreement is in any respect unfair or unreasonable, may set it aside and order the costs covered by it to be taxed as if it had never been made;

(c) in any case, may make such order as to the costs of the application as it thinks fit.

(3) If the business covered by a contentious business agreement (not being an agreement to which section 62 applies) is business done, or to be done, in any action, a client who is a party to the agreement may make application to a taxing officer of the court for the agreement to be examined.

(4) A taxing officer before whom an agreement is laid under subsection (3) shall examine it and may either allow it, or, if he is of the opinion that the agreement is unfair or unreasonable, require the opinion of the court to be taken on it, and the court may allow the agreement or reduce the amount payable under it, or set it aside and order the costs covered by it to be taxed as if it had never been made.

(4A) Subsection (4B) applies where a contentious business agreement provides for the remuneration of the solicitor to be by reference to an hourly rate.

(4B) If on the taxation of any costs the agreement is relied on by the solicitor and the client objects to the amount of the costs (but is not alleging that the agreement is unfair or unreasonable), the taxing officer may enquire into—

(a) the number of hours worked by the solicitor; and

(b) whether the number of hours worked by him was excessive.

(5) Where the amount agreed under any contentious business agreement is paid by or on behalf of the client or by any person entitled to do so, the person making the payment may at any time within twelve months from the date of payment, or within such further time as appears to the court to be reasonable, apply to the court, and, if it appears to the court that the special circumstances of the case require it to be re-opened, the court may, on such terms as may be just, re-open it and order the costs covered by the agreement to be taxed and the whole or any part of the amount received by the solicitor to be repaid by him.

(6) In this section and in sections 62 and 63 "the court" means—

(a) in relation to an agreement under which any business has been done in any court having jurisdiction to enforce and set aside agreements, any such court in which any of that business has been done;

    (b) in relation to an agreement under which no business has been done in any such court and under which not more than £50 is payable, the High Court;

    (c) in relation to an agreement under which no business has been done in any such court and under which not more than £50 is payable, any county court which would, but for the provisions of subsection (1) prohibiting the bringing of an action on the agreement, have had jurisdiction in any action on it;

and for the avoidance of doubt it is hereby declared that in paragraph (a) "court having jurisdiction to enforce and set aside agreements" includes a county court.

Note — Subsections (4A) and (4B) added by the Courts and Legal Services Act 1990, s.98. **7C–78**

Subs.(1)—"No action"

An action for damages for breach of such an agreement is not precluded by this section (*Rees v. Williams* (1875) L.R. 10 Ex. 200). **7C–79**

"Representative"

For the right of a trustee in bankruptcy to go behind an agreement made before bankruptcy, see *Re Van Laun* [1907] 1 K.B. 155, affirmed [1907] 2 K.B. 23 and see the Insolvency Act 1986, ss.283–291. **7C–80**

Subs.(2)—"Fair and reasonable"

For the meaning of the expression, see *Re Stuart, Ex p. Cathcart* [1893] 2 Q.B. 201, CA. An agreement to pay 5 per cent on all amounts deducted from a bill is not reasonable (*Re Stuart* [1893] 2 Q.B. 201). An agreement to pay a percentage on the amount recovered otherwise than by action is legitimate (*Re Hoggart's Settlement* (1912) 56 S.J. 415). A one-sided provision inserted by solicitors into the contract between them and the client justified the construction of ambiguous provisions in that contract *contra proferentem* (*Re A Debtor (No. 1594 of 1992), The Times*, December 8, 1992 Knox J.). **7C–81**

Subs.(3)—"Examined"

The allowance of the agreement by the costs officer under this section does not preclude an independent application under subs.(1) to set it aside, or under subs.(5) to reopen it (*Re Stuart* [1893] 2 Q.B. 201; *Re Simmons & Politzer* [1954] 2 Q.B. 296). **7C–82**

The costs officer cannot go into such an agreement and deal with the amount payable under it as an item in the solicitor's cash account in assessing other bills (*Re Templeton and Cox* (1909) 101 L.T. 144, CA).

In taking accounts in a foreclosure action which involved the validity of such an agreement, the Court referred the agreement to the Cost Judge (*Bake v. French (No.2)* [1907] 2 Ch. 215).

Subs.(5)—"Within 12 months after payment"

Payment within the meaning of this subsection "must be made under such circumstances as to show that the client understands that in making the payment he is carrying out the terms of the agreement and ratifying it" (*Re Jackson* [1915] 1 K.B. 371 at 381, 383). **7C–83**

Contentious business agreements by certain representatives

62.—(1) Where the client who makes a contentious business agreement makes it as a representative of a person whose property will be chargeable with the whole or part of the amount payable under the agreement, the agreement shall be laid before a taxing officer of the court before payment. **7C–84**

(2) A taxing officer before whom an agreement is laid under

subsection (1) shall examine it and may either allow it, or, if he is of the opinion that it is unfair or unreasonable, require the opinion of the court to be taken on it, and the court may allow the agreement or reduce the amount payable under it, or set it aside and order the costs covered by it to be taxed as if it had never been made.

(3) A client who makes a contentious business agreement as mentioned in subsection (1) and pays the whole or any part of the amount payable under the agreement without it being allowed by the officer or by the court shall be liable at any time to account to the person whose property is charged with the whole or any part of the amount so paid for the sum so charged, and the solicitor who accepts the payment may be ordered by the court to refund the amount received by him.

(4) A client makes a contentious business agreement as the representative of another person if he makes it—

    (a) as his guardian,

    (b) as a trustee for him under a deed or will,

    (c) as his receiver appointed under Part VII of the Mental Health Act 1983, or

    (d) as a person other than a receiver authorised under that Part of that Act to act on his behalf.

7C–85   *Note* —Amended by the Mental Health Act 1983, s.148, Sched.4.

Effect on contentious business agreement of death, incapability or change of solicitor

7C–86   **63.**—(1) If, after some business has been done under a contentious business agreement but before the solicitor has wholly performed it—

    (a) the solicitor dies, or becomes incapable of acting; or

    (b) the client changes his solicitor (as, notwithstanding the agreement, he shall be entitled to do)

any party to, or the representative of any party to, the agreement may apply to the court, and the court shall have the same jurisdiction as to enforcing the agreement so far as it has been performed, or setting it aside, as the court would have had if the solicitor had not died or become incapable of acting, or the client had not changed his solicitor.

(2) The court, notwithstanding that it is of the opinion that the agreement is in all respects fair and reasonable, may order the amount due in respect of business under the agreement to be ascertained by taxation, and in that case—

    (a) the taxing officer, in ascertaining that amount, shall have regard so far as may be to the terms of the agreement; and

    (b) payment of the amount found by him to be due may be enforced in the same manner as if the agreement had been completely performed.

(3) If in such a case as is mentioned in subsection (1)(b) an order is made for the taxation of the amount due to the solicitor in respect of the business done under the agreement, the court shall direct the

taxing officer to have regard to the circumstances under which the change of solicitor has taken place, and the taxing officer, unless he is of the opinion that there has been no default, negligence, improper delay or other conduct on the part of the solicitor affording the client reasonable ground for changing his solicitor, shall not allow to the solicitor the full amount of the remuneration agreed to be paid to him.

Form of bill of costs for contentious business

64.—(1) Where the remuneration of a solicitor in respect of conten-   **7C–87** tious business done by him is not the subject of a contentious business agreement, then, subject to subsections (2) to (4) the solicitor's bill of costs may at the option of the solicitor be either a bill containing detailed items or a gross sum bill.

(2) The party chargeable with a gross sum bill may at any time—
>   (a) before he is served with a writ or other originating process for the recovery of costs included in the bill, and
>   (b) before the expiration of three months from the date on which the bill was delivered to him,

require the solicitor to deliver, in lieu of that bill, a bill containing detailed items; and on such a requirement being made the gross sum bill shall be of no effect.

(3) Where an action is commenced on a gross sum bill, the court shall, if so requested by the party chargeable with the bill before the expiration of one month from the service on that party of the writ or other originating process, order that the bill be taxed.

(4) If a gross sum bill is taxed, whether under this section or otherwise, nothing in this section shall prejudice any rules of court with respect to taxation, and the solicitor shall furnish the taxing officer with such details of any of the costs covered by the bill as the taxing officer may require.

Note —Solicitors delivered a gross sum bill to their client in respect of wardship   **7C–88** proceedings. The client, after the expiration of three months, asked for a detailed bill, which was greater than the gross sum bill. In *Carlton v. Theodore Goddard & Co* [1973] 1 W.L.R. 623; [1973] 2 All E.R. 877, Megarry J. ordered the gross sum bill to be assessed and refused an application by the solicitors for leave to substitute the detailed bill for the gross sum bill. See also notes to s.69, paras 7C–101 *et seq*.

Where a bill has been delivered to a client, that bill may be withdrawn later and substituted by a second bill if the client consents or with the leave of the court. The first bill is not conclusive evidence of the reasonableness of the amounts charged in it although it may be relevant evidence. Detailed assessment of the second bill would be valid and not without jurisdiction. *Rezvi v. Brown Cooper* (1997) 1 Costs L.R. 109 (Newman J.).

Security for costs and termination of retainer

65.—(1) A solicitor may take security from his client for his costs,   **7C–89** to be ascertained by taxation or otherwise, in respect of any contentious business to be done by him.

(2) If a solicitor who has been retained by a client to conduct contentious business requests the client to make a payment of a sum of money, being a reasonable sum on account of the costs incurred or to be incurred in the conduct of that business and the client re-

fuses or fails within a reasonable time to make that payment, the refusal or failure shall be deemed to be a good cause whereby the solicitor may, upon giving reasonable notice to the client, withdraw from the retainer.

Taxation with respect to contentious business

7C–90   **66.** Subject to the provisions of any rules of court, on every taxation of costs in respect of any contentious business, the taxing officer may—

(a) allow interest at such rate and from such time as he thinks just on money disbursed by the solicitor for the client, and on money of the client in the hands of, and improperly retained by, the solicitor; and

(b) in determining the remuneration of the solicitor, have regard to the skill, labour and responsibility involved in the business done by him.

Interest
7C–91   The power to allow interest relates only to disbursements by the solicitor and, in respect of money belonging to the client, only if it is in the hands of and improperly retained by the solicitor. There is no power to allow interest on profit charges and the Act applies only as between the solicitor and his client and not to the detailed assessment of costs to be paid out of a fund in Court belonging wholly or partly to persons other than the client. The solicitor cannot appropriate payments to costs so as to leave disbursements unpaid and therefore bearing interest (*Hartland v. Murrell* (1873) L.R. 16 Eq. 285, 43 L.J. Ch. 94). Nor does the section apply to accounts between a London agent and his country solicitor client (*Ward v. Eyre* (1880) 15 Ch D 130, 49 L.J. Ch. 657; *Re Savery* (1851) 15 Beav. 58).

A contentious business agreement which includes a provision that the client should pay interest on costs would appear to be binding if it is valid in all other respects (*Re Fanshawe* (1905) 59 S.J. 404). A solicitor who sues on his bill of costs and recovers judgment is entitled to interest upon the amount recovered from the time of signing judgment. The rate of interest is fixed periodically. (Currently 8 per cent, Judgment Debts (Rates of Interest) Order 1993.)

The mere receipt of clients' money by his solicitor does not entitle the client to receive interest but as soon as the demand is made by the client for payment, which is not complied with within a reasonable time, interest becomes payable (*Barclay v. Harris & Cross* (1915) 85 L.J.K.B. 115, 112 L.T. 1134). A credit in favour of the client produced only by a reduction of the solicitors' bill on detailed assessment does not automatically carry interest (*Wright v. Southwood* (1827) 1 Y & J 527).

In detailed assessment proceedings of a solicitors' bill to their client, the client claimed interest on one of four alternative bases:

(a) Section 35(A) of the Supreme Court Act 1981;

(b) the general equitable jurisdiction of the courts;

(c) Section 66(a) of the Solicitors Act 1974; and

(d) Regulation 25 of the 1998 Solicitors Accounts Rules.

The court held that s.35(A) could not apply because the claim was not one for a debt or damages. So far as the equitable jurisdiction of the court was concerned following *Wright v. Southwood* (above) no such claim was permissible in the circumstances of the case. The court held that, so far as s.66(a) of the Solicitors Act 1974 was concerned, the money was not "improperly retained" by the solicitor since the money had been retained pending the decision of the Costs Judge as to whether or not the bills were payable in full or in part. Finally the court held that the Solicitors Accounts Rules applied only to money held in a client account, whereas in the particular case the money had been paid direct into the office account because it was paid in settlement of bills. In any event the solicitors' terms of business expressly excluded the right of the claimant to interest *Argonaut Property Development Ltd v. Collyer-Bristow* October 16, 2001 QB, Nelson J.

The House of Lords in *Hunt v. Douglas (R.M.) (Roofing)* [1988] 3 W.L.R. 975; [1988] 2 All E.R. 823, ruled that a litigant who has been awarded costs is entitled to interest from the date upon which judgment is pronounced rather than the date of the costs officer's certificate. The rate of interest will be the rate prescribed for judgment debts.

This judgment does not of itself make any difference to the interest position on a detailed assessment between solicitor and client, but if the solicitor sues the client for his fees, it would seem that the costs of reference could carry interest from the date of judgment in the solicitor's favour, notwithstanding that the amount of the judgment is to be ascertained on detailed assessment.

REMUNERATION—GENERAL

67. A solicitor's bill of costs may include costs payable in discharge **7C–92** of a liability properly incurred by him on behalf of the party to be charged with the bill (including counsel's fees) notwithstanding that those costs have not been paid before the delivery of the bill to that party; but those costs—

    (a) shall be described in the bill as not then paid; and

    (b) if the bill is taxed, shall not be allowed by the taxing officer unless they are paid before the taxation is completed.

"Costs payable in discharge of a liability properly incurred by the solicitor on behalf of the party to be charged with the bill"

These words define the "disbursements" which may be included as costs. They are **7C–93** those payments only which are made in pursuance of the professional duty undertaken by the solicitor, and which he is bound to perform whether kept in funds by his client or not, or payments which are sanctioned as professional payments by the established custom and practice of the profession (*Re Remnant* (1849) 11 Beav. 603) such as court fees (*Langridge v. Lynch* (1876) 34 L.T. 695)) counsel's fees, payments to witnesses (*Franklin v. Featherstonhaugh* (1834) 1 A. & E. 475) deposit on presentation of bankruptcy petition (*Re Grant Bulcraig & Co* [1906] 1 Ch. 124) stamp duties on deeds, printer's charges and fees for certificates of birth, etc. Payments for photographs are usually reckoned in this class even though the solicitor be not personally liable for them (*Wakefield v. Duckworth* [1915] 1 K.B. 218). Such disbursements are properly placed in the bill even though actually paid by the client (*Re Metcalf* (1862) 30 Beav. 406; *Re Seal* (1893) 37 S.J. 685 at 842; *Devereaux v. White* (1896) 41 S.J. 67) or though security has been taken for them (*Re Bedson (No.1)* (1845) 9 Beav. 5). Since these disbursements form part of the bill and the law implies authority to make them from the solicitor's character as solicitor, it follows that where that character is wanting (*e.g.* where the solicitor is uncertificated) the disbursements as well as the charges are disallowed (*Fowler v. Monmouthshire Ry.* (1879) 4 QBD 334; *Kent v. Ward* (1894) 70 L.T. 612; *Browne v. Barber* [1913] 2 K.B. 553).

But payments which neither law nor custom required the solicitor himself to make, such as purchase-money (*Re Remnant* (1849) 11 Beav. 603) deposit for security for costs (*Re Buckwell* [1902] 2 Ch. 596) payments to other parties' solicitors (except for copy documents, etc.) (*Re Fletcher & Dyson* [1903] 2 Ch. 688) debt and costs paid to opponents (*Prothero v. Thomas* (1815) 6 Taunt. 196; *Woollison v. Hodgson* (1834) 2 Dowl. 360) capital duty on registering a company (*Re Blair & Girling* [1906] 2 K.B. 131) are not properly charged in the bill, but should appear in the cash account. Agents' charges should not appear as a disbursement in either (*Re Pomeroy & Tanner* [1897] 1 Ch. 284) though the charges of other solicitors for service of process or answering inquiries are generally treated as professional disbursements.

"Shall be described as not then paid"

For a case in which there were defects in the original bill and leave was given for **7C–94** delivery of a fresh bill, see paras 7C–107 and 7C–108.

In *Tearle & Company (a firm) v. Sherring*, October 29, 1993, (unrep.), Wright J. in chambers, reviewed the law surrounding s.67 and concluded that he had the power to permit the solicitors to amend their original bill of costs to include the necessary words (*i.e.* "not paid"). Furthermore, relying on the judgment of Farwell J. in *Re Grant Bul-*

craig & Co [1906] 1 Ch. 124, stated *obiter* that it might have been within the power of a costs judge or district judge to do likewise if the application had been made during the course of a hearing.

Power of court to order solicitor to deliver bill, etc.

7C–95   **68.**—(1) The jurisdiction of the High Court to make orders for the delivery by a solicitor of a bill of costs, and for the delivery up of, or otherwise in relation to, any documents in his possession, custody or power, is hereby declared to extend to cases in which no business has been done by him in the High Court.

(2) A county court shall have the same jurisdiction as the High Court to make orders making such provision as is mentioned in subsection (1) in cases where the bill of costs or the documents relate wholly or partly to contentious business done by the solicitor in that county court.

(3) In this section and in sections 69 to 71 "solicitor" includes the executors, administrators and assignees of a solicitor.

Orders for the delivery of a bill of costs

7C–96   It is a matter for the discretion of the Court whether it will order the delivery of a bill in a given set of circumstances (*Re A Solicitor* [1953] Ch. 480; at 487 [1953] 2 All E.R. 23 at 26). For example, the delivery of a bill can be waived (*Re Van Laun* [1907] 1 K.B. 162, affirmed [1907] 2 K.B. 23, CA). A valid agreement dispenses with delivery (*Re Chapman* (1903) 20 T.L.R. 3, CA); and if a third party has paid a sum in settlement of costs, the client is not entitled to an order for delivery *ibid.* Nor will a solicitor who refuses to make a charge be ordered to deliver a bill (see *Re Griffith* (1891) 7 T.L.R. 268) though he may be ordered to deliver a cash account (*Re Landor* [1899] 1 Ch. 818). It is an answer to the application that the solicitor has already delivered his bill, but not if it was a mere constructive delivery (*Re Robertson* (1889) 42 Ch D 553) or if the delivery was to a third person not shown to be an authorised agent (*Re Layton Steele & Co* (1890) 38 W.R. 652).

Practice

7C–97   The application is under CPR Pt 8 (see Costs Practice Direction s.56).

Application for delivery of a cash account or securities or the payment of moneys

7C–98   If no costs are due to or from the solicitor, there is no jurisdiction under the Act to order an account of monetary transactions between him and his client (see *Re Landor* [1899] 1 Ch. 818).

Action to recover solicitor's costs

7C–99   **69.**—(1) Subject to the provisions of this Act, no action shall be brought to recover any costs due to a solicitor before the expiration of one month from the date on which a bill of those costs is delivered in accordance with the requirements mentioned in subsection (2); but if there is probable cause for believing that the party chargeable with the costs—

(a) is about to quit England and Wales, to become bankrupt or to compound with his creditors, or

(b) is about to do any other act which would tend to prevent or delay the solicitor obtaining payment,

the High Court may, notwithstanding that one month has not expired from the delivery of the bill, order that the solicitor be at liberty to commence an action to recover his costs and may order that those costs be taxed.

(2) The requirements referred to in subsection (1) are that the bill—

    (a) must be signed by the solicitor, or if the costs are due to a firm, by one of the partners of that firm, either in his own name or in the name of the firm, or be enclosed in, or accompanied by, a letter which is so signed and refers to the bill; and

    (b) must be delivered to the party to be charged with the bill, either personally or by being sent to him by post to, or left for him at, his place of business, dwelling-house, or last known place of abode;

and, where a bill is proved to have been delivered in compliance with those requirements, it shall not be necessary in the first instance for the solicitor to prove the contents of the bill and it shall be presumed, until the contrary is shown, to be a bill bona fide complying with this Act.

(3) Where a bill of costs relates wholly or partly to contentious business done in a county court and the amount of the bill does not exceed £5,000, the powers and duties of the High Court under this section and sections 70 and 71 in relation to that bill may be exercised and performed by any county court in which any part of the business was done.

(4) [...]

7C–100 Amended by the Administration of Justice Act 1982; the County Courts Jurisdiction Order 1981 (S.I. 1981 No. 1123); and the High Court and County Courts Jurisdiction Order 1991 (S.I. 1991 No.724).

Subs.(1)—"No action shall be brought"

7C–101 Therefore equally no counterclaim lies (see *Spencer v. Watts* [1889] W.N. 121). But even without delivering a signed bill the solicitor may sue on an account stated (*Turner v. Willis* [1905] 1 K.B. 468) or a promissory note given on account of costs (*Jeffreys v. Evans* (1845) 14 M. & W. 210) or to foreclose a mortgage given to secure them (*Thomas v. Cross* (1864) 11 L.T. 430); and they may be the subject of a set-off (*Harrison v. Turner* (1847) 10 Q.B. 482; *Ex p. Cooper* (1854) 14 C.B. 663; *Brown v. Tibbits* (1862) 11 C.B. (n.s.) 855) provided they are not statute-barred (*Smith v. Betty* [1903] 2 K.B. 317 at 323) or of a proof in bankruptcy (*Eicke v. Nokes* (1829) Moo. 8 M. 303; *Re Howell* (1812) 1 Rose 312; and see *Ex p. Peacock* (1873) L.R. 8 Ch. 682).

The service of a statutory demand for payment of solicitor's costs does not constitute the bringing of an action. Accordingly, a statutory demand may be served before the expiration of a month from the date of the delivery of the bill (*Re A Debtor (No. 88 of 1991)* [1992] 4 All E.R. 301).

A claim by a solicitor for his fees is a liquidated claim for the purposes of section 28(5) of the Limitation Act 1980: *Byatt v. Nash* [2002] All E.R.(D) 254, Mr J Crowley QC.

"To recover any costs"

7C–102 See definition of costs (s.87) as including "fees, charges, disbursements, expenses and remuneration", and for disbursements see s.67 n. This section only applies to an action for work done in a professional capacity (*Bush v. Martin* (1863) 2 H. & C. 311; *Re Inderwick* (1883) 25 Ch D 279). See, for example, as to a solicitor acting as election agent. *Re Osborne* (1858) 25 Beav. 353; *Re Oliver* (1866) 36 L.J.Ch. 261: as parliamentary agent. *Baker & Lees* [1903] 1 K.B. 189, CA: as rent collector. *Re Shilson & Co* [1904] 1 Ch. 837.

It is non performance of a contract to provide legal services by a solicitor, where a firm of solicitors is asked to provide a solicitor and, without telling the client that the adviser is not a solicitor, provides such an adviser. Accordingly, the firm of solicitors was not entitled to recover anything by way of costs (*Pilbrow v. Pearless de Rugemont & Co* [1999] 3 All E.R. 355, CA).

In *Pilbrow* (above) the client did not receive what he thought he was receiving because of a mistake within the solicitor's firm. The decision was followed where the client was fraudulently deceived into believing that he was being advised by a qualified solicitor: *Adrian Alan Ltd v. Fuglers* [2003] EWCA Civ 1655.

"One month from the date on which a bill is delivered"

7C–103

The following cases were decided on the somewhat different wording of s.68 of the Solicitors Act 1957 and its predecessors. This is a calendar month (Interpretation Act 1978, Sched.1) and excludes the day of delivery of the bill and the day of the commencement of the action (*Blunt v. Heslop* (1838) 4 A. & E. 577). If the bill is sent by post, delivery for this purpose is on the day on which in the ordinary course of post it would be delivered, and the month excludes that day (*Browne v. Black* [1912] 1 K.B. 316, CA).

Prima facie the right to deliver a bill arises on completion of the work for which the solicitor was retained (for example, the termination of the suit: *Harris v. Osbourn* (1834) 2 C. & M. 629; *Re Romer & Haslam* [1893] 2 Q.B. 286) and therefore the Limitation Act runs from that time, and not from the expiry of the month (*Coburn v. Colledge* [1897] 1 Q.B. 702). And if an appeal is brought and the same solicitor retained for it, there is a continuance of the contract so that it includes the appeal, and postpones the commencement of the period of limitation (*Harris v. Quine* (1869) L.R. 4 Q.B. 653). But the circumstances may give rise to a right to deliver a bill at stages in the work (*Re Romer & Haslam* [1893] 2 Q.B. 286; *Re Hall & Barker* (1878) 9 Ch D 538; *Harris v. Osbourn*, above) and a bill may be a final bill, though one of a series (*ibid.* and *Re Hudson* [1904] W.N. 32): and see *Davidsons v. Jones-Fenleigh* (1980) 124 S.J. 204, where the Court of Appeal held that as three of a series of four bills had been paid more than 12 months prior to the application each was complete and final in its own right and only the fourth fell to be assessed; but see *Chamberlain v. Boodle & King* [1982] 1 W.L.R. 1443; [1982] 3 All E.R. 188; where the Court of Appeal held that a series of bills were rendered as part of a current account in the same matter and should be treated as one bill. Before obtaining an acknowledgment of the debt so as to take it out of the operation of the Limitation Act, it may be the duty of the solicitor to advise his client as to his rights (*Lloyd v. Coote & Ball* [1915] 1 K.B. 242).

A Costs Judge held that certain bills sent by a solicitor to its client were interim bills not statute bills and that the client was entitled to detailed assessment. The Costs Judge further held that if the bills were not interim bills there were special circumstances, within the meaning of s.70(3) Solicitors Act 1974, that justified assessment of the bills including that the letter of retainer between the parties failed to deal with the calculation of legal costs, the disparity between the estimated legal costs and the costs as billed. Permission to appeal was refused by the single Judge and the application to rely on fresh evidence was refused since the evidence was available at the time of the hearing before the Costs Judge. *Nigel Adams & Co v. Al Malick Carpets Ltd* [2003] EWHC (QB) December 4, 2003 Fulford J.

Subs.(2)—The bill

7C–104

It must be a complete bill containing sufficient information to enable the client to obtain advice as to its detailed assessment (*Haigh v. Ousey* (1857) 7 E. & B. 578 at 582; *Eversheds v. Osman*, April 7, 1998, CA (unrep.)) and the costs judge to assess it (*Slingsby v. Att.-Gen.* [1918] P. 236; *Waller v. Lacey* (1840) 1 M. & Gr. 54). Otherwise there is no "bill" (*Duffet v. McEvoy* (1885) 10 App.Cas. 300 at 302; *Re Baylis* [1896] 2 Ch. 107; *Cobbett v. Wood* [1908] 2 K.B. 420; *Lomas v. Joseph* (1909) 53 S.J. 271). So, if costs between the parties have been assessed and paid by the opponent, or disbursements paid by the client, they must yet be included in the client's bill (*Cobbett v. Wood* [1908] 2 K.B. 420, CA; *Re Osborne and Osborne* [1913] 3 K.B. 862, CA); and the same applies to the items of charges of a London agent, if they form a substantial portion of the charges of a country solicitor (*Re Pomeroy & Tanner* [1897] 1 Ch. 284). If, by reason of the absence of details, there is no "bill", an itemised bill may be delivered (*cf. Re Russell* (1886) 55 L.T. 71). If the work is not ordinary professional work of a solicitor it must not be included in the bill (see notes to subs.(1)).

This note must be read in conjunction with the Solicitors' (Non-Contentious Business) Remuneration Order 1994.

For an extensive examination of the authorities relating to the information properly to be contained in a solicitor's bill see *Ralph Hulme Gary (A Firm) v. Gwillim* [2002] EWCA Civ 1500. Ward L.J. stated:

"63. I accept the principle ... that the defendant who undertakes to prove that the bill is not a bona fide compliance with the act cannot found an objection upon want of information in the bill if it appears that he is already in possession of that information.

...

64. Thus I would accept the proper principle to be that the there must be something in the written bill to indicate the ambit of the work but that inadequacies of description of that work may be redressed by accompanying documents ... or by other information already in possession of the client. That it seems to me would serve the purpose of the Act to give the client the knowledge he reasonably needs in order to decide whether to insist on taxation. If the solicitor satisfies that then the bill is one bona fide complying with the Act.

...

70. This review of the legislation and the case law leads me to conclude that the burden on the client under Section 69(2) to establish that a bill for a gross sum in contentious business will not be a bill 'bona fide complying with the Act' is satisfied if the client shows;– (i) that there is no sufficient narrative in the bill to identify what it is he is being charged for; and (ii) that he does not have sufficient knowledge from other documents in his possession or from what he has been told reasonably to take advice whether or not to apply for that bill to be taxed.

The sufficiency of the narrative and the sufficiency of his knowledge will vary from case to case, and the more he knows, the less the bill may need to spell it out for him. The interests of justice require that the balance be struck between protection of the client's right to seek taxation and the solicitor's right to recover not being defeated by opportunistic resort to technicality."

Ward L.J. went on to suggest that a copy of the solicitor's computer print-out containing a description of the fee earner, the rate of charging and some description of the work done, adjusted to remove items recorded for administrative purposes but not chargeable to the client, could easily be rendered to a client and thus avoid the problems which had arisen in the instant case "in these days where there seems to be a need for transparency in all things, is a print out not the least a client is entitled to expect?".

Signature of bill

7C–105

The bill may be signed by the solicitor, or one of the firm of solicitors, in his own name or in the name in which the practice is carried on (*Goodman v. Eban Ltd* [1954] 1 Q.B. 550). It may also be signed by the executors or administrators of the solicitor (s.67(3)), or by an assignee (*ibid.*) even if he is a layman (*Ingle v. McCutchan* (1884) 12 QBD 518; *Penley v. Anstruther* (1883) 52 L.J.Ch. 367; *M'Lean v. Weaver* (1924) 41 T.L.R. 47, CA; *Medlicott v. Emery* (1933) 49 T.L.R. 427). Signature by a clerk is not enough (cf. *Angell v. Tratt* (1883) 1 Cab. & El. 118). The signature may be by a facsimile representation by stamp affixed by the solicitor, though this is not desirable (*Goodman v. Eban Ltd*, above). But the client may preclude himself by his acts from objecting that the bill is unsigned (*Re Pender* (1846) 2 Ph. 69; *Re Gedge* (1851) 14 Beav. 56; *Young v. Walker* (1847) 16 M. & W. 446). See *Bartletts de Reya v. Byrne*, *The Times*, January 14, 1983; (1983) 127 S.J. 69; where the Court of Appeal considered a contraction of the firm's name was sufficient but thought it sensible if the full name was used. An unsigned bill, if delivered, may be assessed (*Ex p. D'Aragon* (1887) 3 T.L.R. 815) and may be a paid bill within s.69 (*Re Sutton* (1883) 11 QBD 377) and cannot be withdrawn without leave (*Re Jones* (1886) 54 L.T. 648).

Delivery of bill

7C–106

The bill may be delivered to an agent authorised for the purpose (*Re Bush* (1844) 8 Beav. 66; *Daubney v. Phipps* (1849) 18 L.J.Q.B. 337) or to a servant at his dwelling-house (*Macgregor v. Keily* (1849) 3 Ex. 794). If actually delivered, it does not matter that it was misdirected (*Welsh v. Sitwell* (1847) 11 Jur. 471). Delivery to the client's new solicitor is not enough (*Re Abbott* (1861) 4 L.T. (n.s.) 576; see *Re Kellock* (1887) 56 L.T. (n.s.) 887, p.890), unless in accordance with the clients' direction or authority (*Spier v. Barnard* (1863) 8 L.T. (n.s. 396) or an order of the Court (*Vincent v. Slaymaker* (1810) 12 East 372). Delivery to one of a number of persons jointly liable is delivery to each (*Crowder v. Shee* (1808) 1 Camp. 437; *Finchett v. Howe* (1809) 2 Camp. 275; *Mant v. Smith* (1859) 4 H. & N. 324; and cf. *Edwards v. Lawless* (1848) 6 C.B. 329; *Blandy v. De Burgh* (1848) 6 C.B. 623).

Delivery of a fresh bill

7C–107   The Court has a wide discretion to deal with the circumstances which arise in any particular case, *per* Newman J., *Rezvi v. Brown Cooper (a firm)*, January 12, 1996 (Open Court—unrep.). If a bill has been delivered it cannot be substituted by a new bill without the consent of the parties or an order of the Court, the grant of which is a matter of discretion (*Polak v. Marchioness of Winchester* [1956] 1 W.L.R. 819; [1956] 2 All E.R. 660, CA, and cases there cited; see also *Chappel v. Mehta* [1981] 1 All E.R. 349 where the Court of Appeal upheld an order allowing a detailed assessment to be set aside, for bills to be withdrawn and fresh ones submitted to include counsel's fees; and even where certain items in a bill have been struck out by consent, the Court has held that the bill to be assessed must be a bill as delivered (*Re Heather* (1870) L.R. 5 Ch. 694; *Sadd v. Griffin* [1908] 2 K.B. 512, *per* Farwell L.J. at 512). Where an action has been brought on the basis of a Bill of Costs which fails to comply with the statutory requirements or which contains erroneous items the Court is not bound to dismiss the action but can consider the merits of the case and if appropriate allow the solicitor to withdraw the bill and deliver another one *Zuliani v. Veira* [1994] 1 W.L.R. 1149, PC. The one-fifth rule in s.70(9) governing the incidence of the costs of detailed assessment, relates to the amount of the whole bill. But a bill may be delivered subject to a condition, if it is lawful and fair and the situation is clearly stated to the client (*Re Thompson* (1885) 30 Ch D 441, CA; *Re Jones* (1886) 54 L.T. 648). Arithmetical errors can be corrected on assessment (*Re Grant* [1906] 1 Ch. 124). The general rule stated above only applies to a detailed assessment under the Solicitors Act and not to an assessment between parties (*Davis v. Dysart (No. 2)* (1855) 21 Beav. 124) nor to a reference to a costs officer by order of a court to fix the reasonable charge for the work done (*Lumsden v. Shipcote Land Co* [1906] 2 K.B. 433; and *Rollinson v. Eversheds Hepworth and Chadwick*, May 11, 1993, CA (unrep.).

Subss.(3) and (4): county court

7C–108   Although references to "the county court limit" have been removed, the situation has not altered since 1981 when the limit was £5,000.

A county court has jurisdiction under ss.69, 70 and 71 of the Act where a bill of costs relates wholly or partly to contentious business done in a county court and the amount of the bill does not exceed £5,000 (High Court and County Court Jurisdiction Order 1991 (S.I. 1991 No.724)).

Taxation on application of party chargeable or solicitor

7C–109   **70.**—(1) Where before the expiration of one month from the delivery of a solicitor's bill an application is made by the party chargeable with the bill, the High Court shall, without requiring any sum to be paid into court, order that the bill be taxed and that no action be commenced on the bill until the taxation is completed.

(2) Where no such application is made before the expiration of the period mentioned in subsection (1) then, on an application being made by the solicitor or, subject to subsections (3) and (4) by the party chargeable with the bill, the court may on such terms, if any, as it thinks fit (not being terms as to the costs of the taxation) order—

(a) that the bill be taxed; and

(b) that no action be commenced on the bill, and that any action already commenced be stayed, until the taxation is completed.

(3) Where an application under subsection (2) is made by the party chargeable with the bill—

(a) after the expiration of 12 months from the delivery of the bill, or

(b) after a judgment has been obtained for the recovery of the costs covered by the bill, or

(c) after the bill has been paid, but before the expiration of 12 months from the payment of the bill, no order shall be made except in special circumstances and, if an order is made, it may contain such terms as regards the costs of the taxation as the court may think fit.

(4) The power to order taxation conferred by subsection (2) shall not be exercisable on an application made by the party chargeable with the bill after the expiration of 12 months from the payment of the bill.

(5) An order for the taxation of a bill made on an application under this section by the party chargeable with the bill shall, if he so requests, be an order for the taxation of the profit costs covered by the bill.

(6) Subject to subsection (5) the court may under this section order the taxation of all the costs, or of the profit costs, or of the costs other than profit costs and, where part of the costs is not to be taxed, may allow an action to be commenced or to be continued for that part of the costs.

(7) Every order for the taxation of a bill shall require the taxing officer to tax not only the bill but also the costs of the taxation and to certify what is due to or by the solicitor in respect of the bill and in respect of the costs of the taxation.

(8) If after due notice of any taxation either party to it fails to attend, the officer may proceed with the taxation ex parte.

(9) Unless—

    (a) the order for taxation was made on the application of the solicitor and the party chargeable does not attend the taxation, or

    (b) the order for taxation or an order under subsection (10) otherwise provides,

the costs of a taxation shall be paid according to the event of the taxation, that is to say, if one-fifth of the amount of the bill is taxed off, the solicitor shall pay the costs, but otherwise the party chargeable shall pay the costs.

(10) The taxing officer may certify to the court any special circumstances relating to a bill or to the taxation of a bill, and the court may make such order as respects the costs of the taxation as it may think fit.

(11) Subsection (9) shall have effect in any case where the application for an order for taxation was made before the passing of the Solicitors (Amendment) Act 1974 and—

    (a) the bill is a bill for contentious business, or

    (b) more than half of the amount of the bill before taxation consists of costs for which a scale charge is provided by an order for the time being in operation under section 56,

as if for the reference to one-fifth of the amount of the bill there were substituted a reference to one-sixth of that amount.

(12) In this section "profit costs" means costs other than counsel's fees or costs paid or payable in the discharge of a liability incurred by the solicitor on behalf of the party chargeable, and the reference in subsection (9) to the fraction of the amount of the bill taxed off

shall be taken, where the taxation concerns only part of the costs covered by the bill, as a reference to that fraction of the amount of those costs which is being taxed.

Subs.(1)—"One month"

7C–110 This is a calendar month (Interpretation Act 1978, Sched.1).

"The party chargeable therewith"

7C–111 Where the retainer is joint all the clients ought to concur in the application, but the bill may be ordered to be assessed on the application of one if the others refuse to join (*Lockhart v. Hardy* (1841) 4 Beav. 224; and see *Re Hair* (1847) 10 Beav. 187; *Re Lewin* (1853) 16 Beav. 608). If the retainer is not joint, each client may have the bill assessed, but the Court will, if possible, order one detailed assessment and the application should be served on all (*Re Salaman* [1894] 2 Ch. 201). The application may be made by a personal representative (*Jefferson v. Warrington* (1840) 7 M. & W. 137) or trustee in bankruptcy (*Re Allingham* (1886) 32 Ch D 36, CA); or liquidator (*Re Foss, Bilborough & Co* [1912] 2 Ch. 261; *Re Palace Restaurants* [1914] 1 Ch. 492); or a country solicitor in respect of his London agent's costs (*Re William Wilde* [1910] 1 Ch. 100). The co-trustee of a solicitor may assess the latter's bill for work done as a solicitor for the trust (*Re H. P. Davies & Son* [1917] 1 Ch. 216).

As to the power of a solicitor, on reasonable notice, to determine the retainer of a client who fails to pay a reasonable amount on account of costs incurred or to be incurred, see s.65(2).

A dispute arose as to whether a solicitor, whose practice had been intervened by the Law Society, was the "party chargeable" with the bill for the purposes of s.70(3) or a third party under s.71. The Costs Judge hearing the application ordered detailed assessment of all the bills delivered to the Law Society without deciding the status of the solicitor but ordering as a condition of assessment the payment of £50,000 on account. If the solicitor was found to be the party chargeable with the bill then time ran only from when the bills were served upon him, his application would have been within the one month prescribed by s.70(1) and the court would have no power to impose any condition. On appeal the court found that the "person chargeable with the bill" was the person to whom the solicitor was contractually entitled to look for payment and if necessary to sue for payment of the bill. On the facts of the case that could only be the Law Society. The intervened solicitor was therefore a third party with rights under s.71 of the Act. Permission to appeal was refused and the associated challenge under the Human Rights Act also failed: *MacPherson v. Bevan Ashford* [2003] EWHC 636 (Ch), Patten J.

The application

7C–112 Applications are made by CPR Part 8 claim form or, if the claim is made in existing proceedings, by application notice in accordance with Part 23. A claim in the High Court under Part III of the 1974 Act may be determined by a High Court Judge; a Master, a Costs Judge or a District Judge of the Principal Registry of the Family Division; or a District Judge if the costs are for:

(i) contentious business done in proceedings in the District Registry of which he is the District Judge;

(ii) contentious business done in proceedings in a County Court within the district of that District Registry; or

(iii) non contentious business (CPR Part 47, Rule 67.3(3)).

A claim for an order under Part III of the Act for the assessment of costs payable to a solicitor by his client, which relates to contentious business done in a County Court; and is within the financial limit of the County Court's jurisdiction specified in s.69(3) of the Act, may be made in that County Court. In every other case the application must be made in the High Court (r.67.3(1)).

Where an application was made by a client and the claim form contained a list of bills, a clear statement that the bills were disputed, the grounds upon which they were disputed, a proper identification of the parties and a duly signed statement of truth—the solicitors argued that the Part 8 claim form contained a number of discrepancies which meant that Section 70 of the 1974 Act had not been satisfied. The court held that although there were defects in the claim form they did not affect the proper interpretation of the document as a whole, the effect of which was to convey to the solicitors the message that the client wanted the bills to be assessed within the statutory period and that she had commenced proceedings to do so. Once it was established that the claim form sufficiently identified the claim for it to have been taken to have commenced the proceedings, there was no basis upon which the court could decline to make a formal order. the client's cause of action was an indefeasible statutory right to have bills assessed and there was no defence on the merits of the claim: *Szekeres v. Alan Smeath & Co* [2005] EWHC 1733, Ch, Pumfrey J .

If the order to assess is insufficient for the client's purpose—for example where the bill does not relate to any professional business (*Baker & Lees & Co* [1903] 1 K.B. 189, CA; *Re Landor* [1899] 1 Ch. 818) or where the retainer is wholly disputed (*Re Inderwick* (1883) 25 Ch D 279; *Re Ames* (1883) 25 Ch D 73; *Re Hulbert* (1894) 71 L.T. 748); or there is an agreement, the client must bring an action (*Re Lymn* (1910) 130 L.T.J. 9).

Disputed retainer

In the absence of special provision in the order for detailed assessment, if made at the instance of the client, he would be entitled to dispute particular items on the ground of want of retainer, but not the whole bill (*Re Herbert* (1887) 34 Ch D 504; *Re Frape* [1894] 2 Ch. 290. Where the order includes several bills, the same rule applies to each bill (*Re Frape*). If there is any dispute as to whether the solicitor was in fact retained, an *ex parte* order ought not to be obtained (*Re Inderwick* (1883) 25 Ch D 279). But where the solicitor obtains the order to assess, the client, having made no admission, can object to the whole bill for want of a retainer (*Re Jones* (1887) 36 Ch D 105; *Re Graham & Wigley* (1908) 52 S.J. 684; *Re Wingfield & Blew* (1904) 2 Ch. 665 at 675).

7C–113

In a case where retainer was disputed Mr Justice Butterfield quoted with approval the judgment of Denning L.J. in *Griffiths v. Evans* [1953] 2 All E.R. 1364 at 1369:

"On this question of retainer, I would observe that where there is difference between a solicitor and his client on it, the courts have said for the last 100 years or more that the word of the client is to be preferred to the word of the solicitor, or, at any rate, more weight is to be given to it: see *Crossley v. Crowther per* Sir George J. Turner V.-C.; *re Paine per* Warrington J. The reason is plain. It is because the client is ignorant and the solicitor is, or should be, learned. If the solicitor does not take the precaution of getting a written retainer, he has only himself to thank for being at variance with his client over it and must take the consequences." *Moy v. Pettman Smith (A Firm)* [2002] EWCA Civ 875.

The insertion by solicitors of a one-sided provision into a contract between them and a client justified the construction of ambiguous provisions in that contract *contra proferentem*, that is in the client's favour (*Re A Debtor (No. 1594 of 1992), The Times*, December 9, 1992).

Solicitor to give credit

For the meaning of the clause in the common order, directing the solicitor to give credit for all moneys received for or on account of his client, see *Re Le Brasseur & Oakley* [1896] 2 Ch. 487 at 493; *Re Templeton & Cox* (1909) 101 L.T. 144.

7C–114

Subs. (2)—Statutory Demand

It would place solicitors in an intolerable position if a debtor could apply to have a statutory demand set aside on the basis that it was intended to have the bill assessed under the 1974 Act. *Per* Vinelott J., *Re A Debtor (Nos. 833 and 834 of 1993)* 1994 N.P.C. 82.

7C–115

Where a solicitor was instructed to act in liquidation proceedings by the liquidator, bills were delivered but remained unpaid. The solicitor sued for non payment of fees and the liquidator counterclaimed seeking an account and inquiry in respect of the bills. The court held that this was sufficient to enable it to order assessment under s.70(2) even though no formal written application and been made. The order was made on the implicit application under s.70(2) and/or under the relevant jurisdiction of the court: *Connolly v. Harrington* May 17, 2002, QB, unreported, HHJ Chapman.

Subs. (3)—"Except in special circumstances"

There is no hard and fast rule as to what are special circumstances; each case must stand on its own circumstances, and the Court of Appeal will not lightly interfere with the exercise of the Judge's discretion (*Re Cheeseman* [1891] 2 Ch. 289, CA; *Re Ward, Bowie & Co* (1910) 102 L.T. 881, CA). "Special circumstances" are "those which appear to the Judge exercising such discretion so special and exceptional as to justify [detailed

7C–116

assessment]", and are not confined to misconduct or fraud, as laid down in some earlier cases *Re Hirst & Capes* [1908] 1 K.B. 982, CA, affirmed [1908] A.C. 416). The client should point to items of overcharge (*Boycott, Re* (1885) L.R. 29 Ch D 571; *Re A Solicitor* [1961] Ch. 491; [1961] 2 All E.R. 321). Charges may be unreasonably large (*Re Norman* (1886) 16 QBD 673) or such as to call for explanation (*Re Robinson* (1867) L.R. 3 Ex. 4) or there may be gross blunders in the bill (*Re Norman*). Payment of the bill with an express reservation of the right to assess has been held, in all the circumstances of the case, to be a "special circumstance" (*Re Tweedie* [1909] W.N. 110; *Re Solicitors* (1934) 50 T.L.R. 327) and so has the delivery of the bill with the reservation of the right to deliver a further bill (*Harris v. Yarm* [1960] Ch. 256 at 259); and so have overcharges by mistake under the then Solicitors' Remuneration Order 1883 (*Re G.* (1909) 53 S.J. 469; *Re N.* (1912) 56 S.J. 520). The fact that there was an agreement that the bill should be assessed was as powerful a special circumstances as it is possible to conceive for ordering detailed assessment. Although there had been unexplained delay there was no evidence of significant prejudice to the defendants as a result of that delay and detailed assessment was ordered accordingly: *Arrowfield Services Ltd v. BP Collins (A Firm)* [2003] EWHC 830 (Ch) (Michael Briggs QC). The fact that the solicitor has not paid disbursements before delivery of the bill was held not to be a "special circumstance" (*Re Massey* (1909) 101 L.T. 517; 26 T.L.R. 68). Whether or not payment with a reservation was alone sufficient to constitute special circumstances it was an important factor which, together with the exercise by the solicitors of their lien over the papers while asking to be relieved of their retainer and evidence pointing to substantial overcharging in the bills, were sufficient to justify the court in ordering detailed assessment (*Sanders v. Isaacs* [1971] 1 W.L.R. 240; [1971] 1 All E.R. 755).

A client queried the bill sent to her by her solicitors and requested that it be assessedpursuant to the Solicitors Act 1974. The solicitor wrote stating that it was for the client to apply for the assessment and that since over a month had passed since the bill had been delivered any order for assessment would be conditional upon her paying 40 per cent of the bill into court. Eleven months after delivery of the bill the solicitor served a statutory demand for payment. At first instance the Costs Judge found that there were no special circumstances within the meaning of s.70(3) of the 1974 Act justifying assessment more than 12 months after delivery of the bill. On appeal the court found that the purpose of the solicitor's letter was to induce payment, it was not merely inaccurate and a misrepresentation, but, given the inequality of the parties, exerted pressure that was capable of amounting to special circumstances. The appeal was allowed: *Kundrath v. Harry Kwatia & Gooding* [2004] EWHC 2852 (QB) Beatson J.

Solicitors acting for a limited company in litigation which went into creditors voluntary liquidation delivered fourteen bills in respect of work done, and the company applied for detailed assessment under s.70. The two most recent bills had not been paid and were ordered to be assessed. Six were delivered and paid after the company had gone into liquidation, and six were delivered and paid before the company went into liquidation. The court held that apart from the two most recent bills, all the statute bills had all been paid within 12 months of the application for assessment. The application could only succeed if special circumstances were shown. The level of fees was high but this was explicable by virtue of the particular expertise of the solicitors and each had been paid without any major complaint. The high level of fees did not amount to special circumstances (*Winchester Commodities Group Ltd v. R. D. Black & Co* [2000] B.C.C. 310, Mr John Martin QC.

If 12 months have expired from the delivery of the bill

7C–117   When a series of bills have been delivered, which the Court regards as one, the time runs from the delivery of the last bill. The distinction is between a retainer to perform an entire contract (*e.g.* to conduct an action) and a retainer to act for the client generally (*e.g.* to get him out of his difficulties, see *Warmingtons v. McMurray* [1937] 1 All E.R. 565). In regard to an application to assess by a company in liquidation, the 12 months are counted back from the date of the winding-up (*Re James* (1850) 4 De G. & Sm. 183; *Re Foss, Bilborough & Co* [1912] 2 Ch. 261). The 12 months run from the delivery of a complete bill (*Re Pomeroy & Tanner* [1897] 1 Ch. 284). After 12 months from payment detailed assessment can only be ordered under the inherent jurisdiction of the Court, and not under the Act, and the one-fifth rule as to costs does not apply (*Re Park* (1889) 41 Ch D 326.

Subsection (3)(c) applies also to an application for detailed assessment by a third party under subs.(1). Where payment had been made by deduction with the consent of a mortgagor company which since had a compulsory winding-up order made against it, no order for detailed assessment on the application of the liquidator more than 12 months after the deduction could be made (*Forsinard Estate Ltd v. Dykes* [1971] 1 W.L.R. 232; [1971] 1 All E.R. 1018). See also subs.(4).

Where a client applied for a remuneration certificate from the Law Society under the provisions of the Solicitors' (Non-Contentious Business) Remuneration Order 1994 it was held that the fact that the remuneration certificate procedure occupied more than twelve months from the delivery of the bill, was a special circumstance enabling the Court to order a detailed assessment under s.70(3) (*Riley v. Dibb Lupton Alsop* June 5, 1997, Sedley J. (unrep.)).

Where parties came before the court on an application for an order for detailed assessment under s.70(3), where there subsisted an agreement that there should be such an assessment (albeit that the client had delayed making any application), that was as powerful a special circumstance as it was possible to conceive for ordering the detailed assessment. The solicitors had not been caused any prejudice by the delay and accordingly the court exercised its discretion and ordered detailed assessment: *Arrowfield Services Ltd v. BP Collins (A Firm)* [2003] EWHC 830, Mr M. Briggs QC

Payment of the bill

As a general rule, there can be no "payment" before delivery of the bill *Re Foster* [1920] 3 K.B. 306). Mere retainer by the solicitor of the amount of the costs, coupled with an oral agreement as to the amount (*Re Frape* [1893] 2 Ch. 284) or a settled account (*Re Baylis* [1896] 2 Ch. 107, CA) is not payment if no bill has been delivered (*Re Foss, Bilborough & Co* [1912] 2 Ch. 261 contrast *Re Webb* [1894] 1 Ch. 73, CA, where there was a settled account in writing and the expiry of the period of limitation, the solicitors were also trustees, and no error in the account shown). If a bill has been delivered, the retention of moneys by the solicitors is no payment unless there has been a settlement of account (*ibid.*); mere acquiescence is not enough (*Re Ingle* (1855) 25 L.J.Ch. 169; *Re West, King & Adams* [1892] 2 Q.B. 102) but retention with the client's express assent may amount to payment (*Re David* (1861) 30 Bav. 278; *Hitchcock v. Stretton* [1892] 2 Ch. 343; *Re Thompson* [1894] 1 Q.B. 462; *Re Baylis*). Retention under an invalid agreement to charge a lump sum is not payment (*Re West, King & Adams*). Contrast *Re Thompson*, where there was a valid agreement in writing. There may be a good payment where the bill of costs is delivered subsequently to the payment or retention, if the payment or retention can be referred to the bill (*Re Thompson*, and cases there cited; *Re Baylis*; *Smith v. Betty* [1903] 2 K.B. 317, CA) but not if the business is "business done, or to be done, in any action" (see s.61(3) and *Re Simmons & Politzer* [1954] 2 Q.B. 296).

The giving of a negotiable instrument is *prima facie* only payment of a debt if it is honoured, and the same applies when it is given in payment of a bill of costs (*Sayer v. Wagstaff* (1844) 14 L.J.Ch. 116) and the date of payment is the date when the instrument is honoured (*Re Harries* (1844) 13 M. & W. 2; *Re Romer & Haslam* [1893] 2 Q.B. 286, CA; *Ray v. Newton* [1913] 1 K.B. 249, CA; but the facts may show that the instrument is given by way of unconditional payment (*Re Harries*; *Re Romer & Haslam*). If payment is made of less than the full amount, it is only a payment on account unless there is accord and satisfaction (*Re Woodard* (1869) 18 W.R. 37; *Re Callis* (1901) 49 W.R. 316).

The transfer of funds from an estate into the solicitor's account amounted to satisfaction of the bill with the consent of the payers. The solicitors, one of whom was executor, had completed the administration of the estate and presented a final bill to the principal beneficiary which was then paid by way of transfer with the knowledge and consent of the trustees. The beneficiary made no application for detailed assessment until more than 12 months had expired, the application for detailed assessment was therefore struck out. The fact that one of the executors was a partner in the firm of solicitors was of no relevance to the issue of payment (*Gough v. Chivers & Jordan, The Times*, July 15, 1996, CA).

A firm of solicitors consisting of three partners rendered a bill to their client relating to the administration of an estate. A number of charities who were residuary beneficiaries of the estate sought detailed assessment because sums equal to the full amount of the bill had already been paid to them to one of the partners before he joined the firm. They sought repayment of any amounts found on assessment to have been overpaid. The partner to whom the money was originally paid had since disappeared. The Costs Judge found that the remaining partners were bound by

2115

representations made by the partner who had disappeared, even though the representations were made before the partnership was formed. The court rejected the suggestion that there was a novation which had the effect of rendering the firm liable for matters arising in the course of the prior retainer. The court also rejected the argument that the partners were estopped from denying that there had been a novation, nor was it persuaded that there was any statutory liability to pay under ss.70 and 71 of the Solicitors Act 1974. The continuing partners were therefore held to be not liable to repay any sum by which the bill was reduced, the only person being so liable being the partner who had disappeared: *Marsden v. Guide Dogs for the Blind Association* [2004] EWHC 593 (Ch); [2004] 3 All E.R. 222 , also known as *Burton Marsden Douglas (A Firm), Re* , Lloyd J.

"After a judgment has been obtained"

7C–119   If the solicitor sues on the bill, and before verdict or judgment an order is made to assess it, it usually directs detailed assessment according to the Solicitors Act and applies the one-fifth rule as to costs (*Smith v. Edwardes* (1888) 22 QBD 103, and see *Smith v. Howes* [1922] 1 K.B. 590; *Lumley v. Brookes* (1889) 41 Ch D 323; *Hirst & Capes v. Fox* [1908] 1 K.B. 982). But a detailed assessment after verdict or judgment can only be ordered under the Act in "special circumstances". Yet the Court has inherent jurisdiction to refer the bill to a costs judge to fix the proper amount of remuneration, in which case the one-fifth rule would not apply (*Lumsden v. Shipcote* [1906] 2 K.B. 433; *Hirst & Capes v. Fox* [1908] 1 K.B. 982).

Inherent jurisdiction to order detailed assessment

7C–120   Even more than 12 months after payment of the bill, though there is no jurisdiction under the Act to order detailed assessment, the Court retains its inherent jurisdiction to do so (*Re A Solicitor* [1961] Ch. 591). In *Symbol Park Lane Ltd v. Steggles Palmer* [1985] 1 W.L.R. 668; [1985] 2 All E.R. 167, the Court of Appeal held that inherent jurisdiction should only be invoked to avoid a clear injustice and that the clearest descriptions of the three jurisdictions were set out in *Re Park*, para. 7C–117 above. But in *Harrison v. Tew* [1988] 2 W.L.R. 1; [1987] 3 All E.R. 865, the Court of Appeal by a majority overruled *Re A Solicitor* [1961] Ch. 591 and held that the preservation of the inherent powers over solicitors expressed in s.50 of the Solicitors Act 1974 was subject to the provisions of s.70(4) and therefore detailed assessment of a bill of costs could not be ordered on an application made after the expiration of 12 months from payment of the bill. The House of Lords held that the Courts' inherent jurisdiction was displaced by s.70(4) of the 1974 Act and upheld the Court of Appeal decision (*Harrison v. Tew* [1990] 2 W.L.R. 210).

Where solicitors sued for their costs and the defendant counterclaimed for negligence, all of which allegations failed, the court (the time for applying for detailed assessment having expired) nonetheless made an order that the solicitors' bill should be examined. "Where a quantum meruit is claimed for work done, the benefit of which has been obtained under a contract, but where the contract sum has not been agreed, there may be an order for judgment for the claimant with the quantum to be assessed. The judicial assessment should be carried out by a Costs Judge. It is the Costs Judges that have the requisite expertise for that purpose", *per* Sir Richard Scott, *Thomas Watts & Co v. Smith* (1998) 2 Costs L.R. 59, CA.

Where solicitors delivered five bills which the client paid, and the solicitors then issued proceedings claiming a further £67,000 said to be outstanding, the client sought detailed assessment of the bills on the basis that they were interim requests for payment. The application for detailed assessment was refused on the basis that 12 months had expired since the payment of the bills. The solicitors for their part applied for summary judgment. The Court of Appeal held on the facts that the bills were not statute bills and that the solicitors were not entitled to summary judgment because the client was entitled to defend the solicitors' claim on the ground that the fees claimed were unreasonably high, even though the time for assessment under s.70 of the 1974 Act had expired. The statutory right to claim detailed assessment in accordance with s.70 does not exclude any other common law right to challenge the bill. See *Re Park* (1889) 41 Ch D 326; *Jones v. Whitehouse* [1918] 2 K.B. 61; *Thomas Watts & Co v. Smith* (1998) 2 Costs L.R. 59; *Turner & Co v. O. Palomo SA* [1999] 4 All E.R. 353, CA.

Subs. (9)—"One-fifth of the amount of the bill"

7C–121   The rule is imperative that the solicitor shall pay the costs if one-fifth of the amount is disallowed; except that if the costs officer certifies "special circumstances" under proviso (ii) the Court has power to relax the rule (see *Re Richards* [1912] 1 Ch. 49). The amount, on which one-fifth is taken, includes disbursements (*Re Haigh* (1849) 12 Beav. 307) and costs already assessed and paid by the opposite party (*Re Osborne & Osborne* [1913] 3 K.B. 861, CA). It includes the total of the bills ordered to be assessed by one order, but not other bills delivered under the same retainer (*Devereaux v. White* (1896) 13 T.L.R. 52). It includes the full amount of the bill, and disregards the added expression "say £X" (*Re Carthew* (1884) 27 Ch D 485; *Re Mackenzie* (1894) 69 L.T. 751) or the fact that a lesser figure is alone claimed (*Re Paull* (1884) 27 Ch D 485). It includes in the lessor's solicitor's bill the costs of the concurring parties' solicitors, if he has included them (*Re Fletcher & Dyson* [1903] 2 Ch. 688). On the other hand the amount, on which one-fifth is taken, excludes items in the cash account (*Re Haigh*) and excludes items struck out of the bill for want of retainer (*Re Taxation of Costs*; *Re a Solicitor* [1936] 1 K.B. 523).

In calculating whether one-fifth of a bill is taxed off, VAT is ignored for the purpose of the calculation.

County courts

See note at para. 7C–108.

7C–122

Taxation on application of third parties

7C–123

71.—(1) Where a person other than the party chargeable with the bill for the purposes of section 70 has paid, or is or was liable to pay, a bill either to the solicitor or to the party chargeable with the bill, that person or his executors, administrators or assignees may apply to the High Court for an order for the taxation of the bill as if he were the party chargeable with it, and the court may make the same order (if any) as it might have made if the application had been made by the party chargeable with the bill.

(2) Where the court has no power to make an order by virtue of subsection (1) except in special circumstances it may, in considering whether there are special circumstances sufficient to justify the making of an order, take into account circumstances which affect the applicant but do not affect the party chargeable with the bill.

(3) Where a trustee, executor or administrator has become liable to pay a bill of a solicitor, then, on the application of any person interested in any property out of which the trustee, executor or administrator has paid, or is entitled to pay, the bill, the court may order—

(a) that the bill be taxed on such terms, if any, as it thinks fit; and

(b) that such payments, in respect of the amount found to be due to or by a solicitor and in respect of the costs of the taxation, be made to or by the applicant, to or by the solicitor, or to or by the executor, administrator or trustee, as it thinks fit.

(4) In considering any application under subsection (3) the court shall have regard—

(a) to the provisions of section 70 as to applications by the party chargeable for the taxation of a solicitor's bill so far as they are capable of being applied to an application made under that subsection;

(b) to the extent and nature of the interest of the applicant.

(5) If an applicant under subsection (3) pays any money to the so-

licitor, he shall have the same right to be paid that money by the trustee, executor or administrator chargeable with the bill as the solicitor had.

(6) Except in special circumstances, no order shall be made on an application under this section for the taxation of a bill which has already been taxed.

(7) If the court on an application under this section orders a bill to be taxed, it may order the solicitor to deliver to the applicant a copy of the bill on payment of the costs of that copy.

Subs.(1)—"Person other than ... the party chargeable with the bill"

7C–124   Examples are—a mortgagee, the trustee in bankruptcy of a mortgagor, the liquidator of a company, a subsequent encumbrancer, a lessee in respect of his lessor's costs, a *cestui que trust*, a party liable to pay the costs of the umpire's solicitor (*Re Collyer-Bristow & Co* [1901] 2 K.B. 839, CA) a third person who, as a term of an agreement of compromise, agrees to pay costs as between solicitor and client (*Re Grundy, Kershaw & Co* (1881) 17 Ch D 108; *Re Chapman* (1903) 20 T.L.R. 3). In the latter case, if there is a question as to the construction of the agreement, the Costs Judge has jurisdiction to determine it for the purposes of the detailed assessment (*Re Hirst & Capes* [1908] A.C. 416) though not exclusive jurisdiction (*Mosley v. Kitson* (1912) 57 S.J. 12). The following have been held not to be entitled to detailed assessment—a volunteer who pays the costs (*Re Becke & Flower* (1843) 5 Beav. 406; *Langford v. Nott* (1820) 1 Jac. & W. 291; *Re Cookson* (1886) 30 S.J. 305); ratepayers where the bill has been paid by a surveyor of highways (*Re Barber* (1845) 14 M. & W. 720); a party who agrees to pay the opposite party a fixed sum for costs on discontinuing proceedings (*Re Morris* (1872) 27 L.T. 554; *Ex p. Docker, Re Heritage* (1878) 3 QBD 726; *Re Grundy, Kershaw & Co*, above).

"As if he were the party chargeable"

7C–125   The detailed assessment at the instance of the third person is to proceed on the same principles of allowance as though it were at the instance of the party chargeable (see *Re Wells* (1845) 8 Beav. 416; *Re Holliday & Godlee* (1888) 58 L.T. 301; *Re Massey* (1865) 34 L.J.Ch. 492).

Where a third party's liability is dependent on a contract, express or implied, to pay costs the fact that he obtains an order for detailed assessment under this section does not alter the nature or enlarge or extend the scope of that liability which will be determined on a proper construction of that contract. Nor can he dispute the amount properly payable as between the solicitor and his client.

The Law Society instructed solicitors to intervene in another solicitor's practice. The intervening solicitor submitted five bills to the Law Society for their professional charges. The Society paid the bills and sought reimbursement from the solicitor whose practice had been intervened. That solicitor applied for detailed assessment of the bills under s.71. The Court of Appeal held that the bills clearly were solicitors bills within the meaning of s.70(1) of the 1974 Act and that para. 13 of Pt 2 of Sched.I to the Act did not override or exclude the right conferred by s.71. Section 71 was of general application, it recognised that the person chargeable with the bill might not be ultimately liable to pay the costs thereby claimed. Its evident purpose was to confer on one with a secondary liability for those costs a right comparable to that possessed by the person primarily liable: *Pine v. The Law Society* [2002] EWCA Civ 175; [2002] 2 All E.R. 658; [2002] 1 W.L.R. 2189, CA.

Subs.(3)—"Any person interested in any property"

7C–126   This includes a creditor who has obtained a judgment in an administration action, and he can assess a bill of costs paid by the deceased (*Re Jones & Everett* [1904] 2 Ch. 365). For the rights of a *cestui que trust* in respect of a bill delivered to his trustee, see *Re Downes* (1844) 5 Beav. 425; *Re Brown* (1867) L.R. 4 Eq. 464). A trustee in bankruptcy is not such a "trustee" as to enable the bankrupt to obtain detailed assessment (*Re Leadbitter* (1878) 10 Ch D 388).

Subs.(4)—"The provisions of section 70"

7C–127   So, if the bill has already been paid, no order will be made in the absence of "special circumstances" (*Re Wellborne* [1901] 1 Ch. 312); and see nn. to s.69, paras 7C–101 *et seq.*

The court allowed a beneficiary under a will to apply to have assessed solicitors' bills which had been discharged out of the estate even though some had been paid more than twelve months before the application, and in respect of others there were no special circumstances. The court held that the power under s.71(3) of the Act was a separate power and although s.70(3) had to be taken into account under s.71(4), it was not determinative of the application. It was for the applicant to persuade the court that it should, in all the circumstances, order assessment. *McIlwraith v. McIlwraith and Stevens & Bolton* [2002] EWHC Ch, July 24, 2002, HHJ, Rich QC.

The application
As to the application see para. 7C-112 .   **7C–128**

County courts
See note at para. 7C–108.   **7C–129**

Supplementary provisions as to taxations

72.—(1) Every application for an order for the taxation of a **7C–130** solicitor's bill or for the delivery of a solicitor's bill and for the delivery up by a solicitor of any documents in his possession, custody or power shall be made in the matter of that solicitor.

(2) Where a taxing officer is in the course of taxing a bill of costs, he may request the taxing officer of any other court to assist him in taxing any part of the bill, and the taxing officer so requested shall tax that part of the bill and shall return the bill with his opinion on it to the taxing officer making the request.

(3) Where a request is made as mentioned in subsection (2) the taxing officer who is requested to tax part of a bill shall have such powers, and may take such fees, in respect of that part of the bill, as he would have or be entitled to take if he were taxing that part of the bill in pursuance of an order of the court of which he is an officer; and the taxing officer who made the request shall not take any fee in respect of that part of the bill.

(4) The certificate of the taxing officer by whom any bill has been taxed shall, unless it is set aside or altered by the court, be final as to the amount of the costs covered by it, and the court may make such order in relation to the certificate as it thinks fit, including, in a case where the retainer is not disputed, an order that judgment be entered for the sum certified to be due with costs.

Subs.(1)—"Every application"
See nn. to ss.68–70.   **7C–131**

Non-compliance with order
For non-compliance by the solicitor with the common order for detailed assessment **7C–132** in failing to pay the amount certified to be due, the remedy is by attachment of the solicitor as an officer of the Court (*Re Wilde* [1910] W.N. 128, CA).

Charging orders

73.—(1) Subject to subsection (2) any court in which a solicitor has **7C–133** been employed to prosecute or defend any suit, matter or proceeding may at any time—

　　　　(a) declare the solicitor entitled to a charge on any property
　　　　　　 recovered or preserved through his instrumentality for

his taxed costs in relation to that suit, matter or proceeding; and

(b) make such orders for the taxation of those costs and for raising money to pay or for paying them out of the property recovered or preserved as the court thinks fit;

and all conveyances and acts done to defeat, or operating to defeat, that charge shall, except in the case of a conveyance to a bona fide purchaser for value without notice, be void as against the solicitor.

(2) No order shall be made under subsection (1) if the right to recover the costs is barred by any statute of limitations.

Where a District Judge of the County Court granted a charging order over land which had been the subject of litigation for costs to be assessed by the court it was held that the detailed assessment had to take place at the Supreme Court Costs Office since the bill fell outside the parameters laid down in Section 69(3): *Jones v. Twinsectra Ltd* [2002] EWCA, April 16, 2002.

"taxed costs"

7C–134   The court has jurisdiction to make a charging order over costs recoverable in an action by a client company where that company has become dormant and incapable of acting or unwilling to act further, even though the order for costs contains no direction that the costs be assessed and the costs have not been assessed.

The court is not bound to order that the costs in question be assessed as between solicitor and client (*Fairfold Properties Ltd v. Exmouth Docks Company Ltd (No. 2)* [1993] 2 W.L.R. 241).

"Taxed costs" in this context must refer to costs which have been assessed by detailed assessment.

The provisions of s.73(1) are plainly directed to cases in which the court has made an order for costs; where the question of costs was dealt with in a compromise agreement there was therefore no power to continue a freezing order or to make a declaration under s.73(1): *Al-Abbas v. Al-Dabbagh* [2002] EWCA Civ 1962.

The taking of a legal charge by a firm of solicitors over the property of former clients to secure legal costs does not necessarily waive the rights of the firm under the Solicitors Act 1974, s.73. Although it is well established that in certain circumstances the taking of security by a solicitor would be treated as a waiver of his right to a common law lien, the court had not been referred to any case indicting that the taking of a charge on an unrelated asset was inconsistent with a possessory lien or a solicitor's right to apply for a charge on different property. It was at least arguable that the grant of the legal charge was not inconsistent or incompatible with the exercise by the solicitors of its right to apply for a charge under s.73. *Clifford Harris & Co v. Solland International Ltd* [2004] EWHC 2488, (Ch),Richards J.

7C–134.1   In proceedings for infringement of a patent the claimant was unsuccessful in respect of part of the claim and a declaration of non infringement was made in favour of the defendant. The claimant paid £75,000 costs into a joint account of the parties' solicitors pending appeal. The defendant subsequently went into administrative receivership. The defendants' solicitors obtained a charging order over the £75,000 under s.73 of the Solicitors Act 1974 in order to protect their fees. The claimants' appeal was dismissed but the claimant then sought judgment in default and costs in respect of the defendant's non compliance with the court's directions in respect of the remaining part of the claim. The claimants sought to set off those costs against the £75,000 held in the joint account. Although the court gave judgment in default to the claimants it did not allow set off of the cost to be awarded so as to defeat the charging order. Whilst there was no direct prejudice to the defendant in allowing a set off, the existence of the charging order meant there would be prejudice to the defendant's solicitors. The protection afforded by the charging order should be upheld unless there were good reasons to come to a contrary decision: *Rhom & Hass Co v. Collag Ltd* [2001] EWHC (Ch) November 14, 2001, Pumfrey J.

Where solicitors took out a charge on the freehold property of their clients as secu- **7C–134.2**
rity for fees and disbursements, the question arose whether, in taking the charge, the
solicitors had waived their rights under s.73 of the Solicitors Act 1974 as the security
was inconsistent with the original lien. The court held that the taking of any alternative security by a solicitor would not necessarily waive his lien, the lien was only waived
if the security taken was inconsistent with it. The solicitor could not enforce a stipulation for interest markedly higher than would ever be allowed by the court under
s.35A of the Supreme Court Act 1981 unless he established that the client had been
informed that the law would not otherwise enable the solicitor to claim interest at that
rate. A solicitor who took security confirming a right to interest that he did not
otherwise possess, waived his right to a lien unless it was expressly reserved. The
same principle applied to the solicitors in the present case and their rights under s.73 which
they had waived by taking the charge. Once the rights were waived there had to be a
fresh agreement between solicitor and client that the rights were to be exercisable
thereafter. The solicitors could not revive their s.73 right simply by making it clear to
the client that they expected to look to any recoveries under the settlement. If,
however, the client was able to have the security avoided then the solicitors s.73 rights
would revive, as they would be entitled to be put back in the same position they would
have been in had the security never been granted. On the facts the court found that
there was an equitable charge over the settlement monies in favour of the solicitors:
Clifford Harris & Co v. Solland International Ltd & Ors [2005] EWHC 141; [2005] 2 All
E.R. 34, Christopher Nugee QC .

Special provisions as to contentious business done in county courts

74.—(1) The remuneration of a solicitor in respect of contentious **7C–135**
business done by him in a county court shall be regulated in accordance with sections 59 to 73, and for that purpose those sections
shall have effect subject to the following provisions of this section.

(2) The registrar of a county court shall be the taxing officer of
that court but any taxation of costs by him may be reviewed by a
judge assigned to the county court district, or by a judge acting as a
judge so assigned, on the application of any party to the taxation.

(3) The amount which may be allowed on the taxation of any
costs or bill of costs in respect of any item relating to proceedings in
a county court shall not, except in so far as rules of court may
otherwise provide, exceed the amount which could have been allowed in respect of that item as between party and party in those
proceedings, having regard to the nature of the proceedings and the
amount of the claim and of any counterclaim.

Saving for certain enactments

75. [*Repealed by the* Statute Law (Repeals) Act 1989; *and the* Legal **7C–136**
Aid Act 1988, Sched.6.]

PART IV

MISCELLANEOUS AND GENERAL

SUPPLEMENTARY

* * * * *

Interpretation

87.—(1) In this Act, except where the context otherwise requires,— **7C–137**

"articles" means written articles of clerkship binding a person to serve a solicitor as an articled clerk;

"authorised insurer" means a person who—

(a) is permitted under the Insurance Companies Act 1982 to carry on insurance business of class 13 in Schedule 2 to that Act or, being an insurance company the head office of which is in a member State, is permitted under the law of a member State other than the United Kingdom to carry on business of a corresponding class; or

(b) is permitted under the Insurance Companies Act 1982 to carry on insurance business of classes 1, 2, 14, 15, 16 and 17 in that Schedule or, being an insurance company the head office of which is in a member State, is permitted under the law of a member State other than the United Kingdom to carry on insurance business of corresponding classes.

"bank" means—

(a) the Bank of England, the Post Office, in the exercise of its power to provide banking services, or an institution authorised under the Banking Act 1987.

(b) [...]

(c) [...]

"building society" means a building society within the meaning of the Building Societies Act 1986; [...]

"the Charter" means the Royal Charter dated 26th February 1845, whereby the Society was incorporated, together with the Royal Charters supplemental to it dated respectively, 26th November 1872, 4th June 1903, 2nd June 1909 and 10th March 1954;

"client"— includes

(a) in relation to contentious business, any person who as principal or on behalf of another person retains or employs, or is about to retain or employ, a solicitor, and any person who is or may be liable to pay a solicitor's costs;

(b) in relation to non-contentious business, any person who, as a principal or on behalf of another, or as a trustee or executor, or in any other capacity, has power, express or implied, to retain or employ, and retains or employs or is about to retain or employ a solicitor, and any person for the time being liable to pay to a solicitor for his services any costs;

"client account" means an account in the title of which the word "client" is required by rules under section 32;

"contentious business" means business done, whether as solicitor or advocate, in or for the purposes of proceedings begun before a court or before an arbitrator, not being business which falls within the definition of non-contentious or common form probate business contained in section 128 of the Supreme Court Act 1981;

2122

"contentious business agreement" means an agreement made in pursuance of section 59;

"controlled trust", in relation to a solicitor, means a trust of which he is a sole trustee or co-trustee only with one or more of his partners or employees;

"costs" includes fees, charges, disbursements, expenses and remuneration;

"the Council" means the Council of the Society elected in accordance with the provisions of the Charter and this Act;

"duly certificated notary public" means a notary public who either—

(a) has in force a practising certificate as a solicitor issued under this Act, and duly entered in the court of faculties of the Archbishop of Canterbury in accordance with rules made by the master of the faculties; or

(b) has in force a practising certificate as a notary public issued by the said court of faculties in accordance with rules so made;

"employee" includes an articled clerk;

"indemnity conditions" has the meaning assigned to it by section 28(2)(b);

"indemnity rules" means rules under section 37;

"local law society" means a society which is for the time being recognised by the Council as representative of solicitors in some particular part of England and Wales;

"non-contentious business" means any business done as a solicitor which is not contentious business as defined by this subsection;

"practising certificate" has the meaning assigned to it by section 1;

"replacement date", in relation to a practising certificate, means the date prescribed under section 14(2)(a) or specified by the Society under any regulation made by virtue of section 14(4)(b);

"the roll" means the list of solicitors of the Supreme Court kept by the Society under section 6;

"Secretary" of the Society includes any deputy or person appointed temporarily to perform the duties of that office;

"the Society" means the Law Society, that is to say, the Society incorporated and regulated by the Charter;

"sole solicitor" means a solicitor who is the sole principal in a practice;

"solicitor" means solicitor of the Supreme Court;

"solicitor in Scotland" means a person enrolled or deemed to have been enrolled as a solicitor in pursuance of the Solicitors (Scotland) Act 1933;

"training conditions" has the meaning assigned to it by section 28(2)(a);

"training regulations" means regulations under section 2;

"the Tribunal" means the Solicitors Disciplinary Tribunal;

"trust" includes an implied or constructive trust and a trust where the trustee has a beneficial interest in the trust property, and also includes the duties incident to the office of a personal representative, and "trustee" shall be construed accordingly;

"unqualified person" means a person who is not qualified under section 1 to act as a solicitor.

In this Act "authorised insurer" means

(a) a person who has permission under Part 4 of the Financial Services and Markets Act 2000 to effect or carry out contracts of insurance of a relevant class;

(b) a person who carries on an insurance market activity, within the meaning of section 316(3) of that Act;

(c) an EEA firm of the kind mentioned in paragraph 5(d) of Schedule 3 to that Act, which has permission under paragraph 15 of that Schedule (as a result of qualifying for authorisation under paragraph 12 of that Schedule) to effect or carry out contracts of insurance of a relevant class; or

(d) a person who does not fall within paragraph (a), (b) or (c) and who may lawfully effect or carry out contracts of insurance of a relevant class in a member state other than the United Kingdom.

(1B) A contract of insurance is of a relevant class for the purposes of subsection (1A) if it insures against risks arising from

(a) accident;

(b) credit;

(c) legal expenses;

(d) general liability to third parties;

(e) sickness;

(f) suretyship;

(g) miscellaneous financial loss.

(1C) The definition of "bank" in subsection (1) and subsections (1A) and (1B) must be read with—

(a) section 22 of the Financial Services and Markets Act 2000;

(b) any relevant order under that section; and

(c) Schedule 2 to that Act.

(2) In this Act—

(a) references to the removal of a solicitor's name from the roll are references to its removal at his own request or in pursuance of regulations under section 28(3A);

(b) references to striking a solicitor's name off the roll are references to striking it off as a disciplinary sanction; and

(c) references to removal or striking off include references to deleting an entry made by means of a computer by whatever means are appropriate.

(3) In this Act, except where otherwise indicated—

(a) a reference to a numbered Part, section or Schedule is a reference to the Part or section of, or the Schedule to, this Act so numbered;

(b) a reference in a section to a numbered subsection is a reference to the subsection of that section so numbered;

(c) a reference in a section, subsection or Schedule to a numbered paragraph is a reference to the paragraph of that section, subsection or Schedule so numbered; and

(d) a reference in a paragraph to a numbered sub-paragraph is a reference to the sub-paragraph of that paragraph so numbered.

(4) Except where the context otherwise requires, references in this Act to any enactment shall be construed as references to that enactment as amended or applied by or under any other enactment, including this Act.

Note—Amended by the Finance (No. 2) Act 1975, s.74; Banking Act 1979, Sched.6; **7C–138** the Insurance Companies Act 1981, Sched.4; the Trustee Savings Banks Act 1981, Sched.6; the Insurance Companies Act 1982, Sched.5; the Trustee Savings Banks Act 1985, Sched.4; the Administration of Justice Act 1985, Sched.1; the Building Societies Act 1986; the Banking Act 1987, s.108 Sched.6, para. 5; the Courts and Legal Services Act 1990, Sched.18; the Insurance Companies (Amendment) Regulations 1992 (S.I. 1992 No. 2890); the Statute Law (Repeals) Act 1993; the Arbitration Act 1996, Sched.4; the Access to Justice Act 1999, Sched.15, Pt II and the Financial Services and Markets Act 2000 (Consequential Amendments and Repeals) Order 2001 (S.I. 2001 No. 3649), art.286(4).

Saving for solicitors to public departments and City of London

88.—(1) Nothing in this Act shall prejudice or affect any rights or **7C–139** privileges of the solicitor to the Treasury, any other public department, the Church Commissioners or the Duchy of Cornwall, or require any such officer or any clerk or officer appointed to act for him to be admitted or enrolled or to hold a practising certificate in any case where it would not have been necessary for him to be admitted or enrolled or to hold such a certificate if this Act had not been passed.

(1A) The exemption from the requirement to hold a practising certificate conferred by subsection (1) above shall not apply to solicitors who are Crown Prosecutors.

(2) Sections 31 and 32(1) shall not apply to, and nothing in this Act shall prejudice or affect any rights or privileges which immediately before the commencement of this Act attach to the office of, the Solicitor of the City of London.

Subs. (1A)
Added by the Prosecution of Offences Act 1985, s.4.   **7C–140**

Consequential amendments, repeals, savings, etc.

89.—(1) The enactments specified in Schedule 3 shall have effect **7C–141** subject to the amendments there specified, being amendments consequential upon the provisions of this Act.

(2) The enactments specified in Schedule 4 are hereby repealed to the extent specified in the third column of that Schedule.

(3) In so far as any instrument or other document made, issued, served or kept or treated as having been or having effect as if made, issued, served or kept, or other thing done or treated as having been or having effect as if done, under or for the purposes of any of the enactments repealed by this Act (in this section referred to as "the repealed enactments") could have been made, issued, served, kept or done under or for the purposes of a corresponding provision of this Act, it shall not be invalidated by the repeal but shall have effect as if made, issued, served, kept or done under or for the purposes of that corresponding provision; and anything begun under any of the repealed enactments may be continued under any corresponding provision of this Act as if begun under that provision.

(4) Any enactment or other document referring to any of the repealed enactments shall, so far as may be necessary for preserving its effect, be construed as referring to this Act or to the corresponding provision of this Act.

(5) References in any enactment or instrument to the disciplinary committee constituted under section 46 of the Solicitors Act 1957 shall be construed as references to the Tribunal.

(6) References in any enactment to solicitors, attorneys or proctors, or to the registrar of attorneys and solicitors or the registrar of solicitors, shall be construed as references to solicitors and to the Society respectively.

(7) References in any enactment to a duly certificated notary public shall be construed as references to a duly certificated notary public within the meaning of this Act.

(8) Nothing in this Act shall be taken as prejudicing the operation of [...] (which relates to the effect of repeals).

7C–141.1   *Note* —Amended by the Interpretation Act 1978, s.25(2).

Short title, commencement and extent

7C–142   **90.**—(1) This Act may be cited as the Solicitors Act 1974.

(2) This Act shall come into force on such day as the Lord Chancellor may by order made by statutory instrument appoint, not being earlier than the first day on which all the provisions of the Solicitors (Amendment) Act 1974 are in force.

(3) If any order made under section 19(7) of the Solicitors (Amendment) Act 1974 makes any savings from the effect of any provision of that Act which it brings into force, the order under subsection (2) may make corresponding savings from the effect of the corresponding provisions of this Act.

(4) The provisions of this Act extend to England and Wales only, with the exception of—

(a) section 4(4) and the repeal of section 5(3) of the Solicitors Act 1957, which extend to Scotland;

(b) section 29 and the repeal of section 1 of the Solicitors (Amendment) Act 1974, which extend to Northern Ireland;

(c) sections 5(3) and 86 [...] and the repeals of section 5(2) of the Solicitors Act 1957 and paragraphs 1 and 5 of Schedule 2to the Solicitors (Amendment) Act 1974, all of which extend both to Scotland and to Northern Ireland.

Note —Amended by the House of Commons Disqualification Act 1975, Sched.3.

7C–142.1

SCHEDULES
SCHEDULE 1A

INADEQUATE PROFESSIONAL SERVICES

* * * *

Circumstances in which Council's powers may be exercised

1.—(1) The Council may take any of the steps mentioned in paragraph 2 ("the **7C–143** steps") with respect to a solicitor where it appears to them that the professional services provided by him in connection with any matter in which he or his firm have been instructed by a client have, in any respect, not been of the quality which it is reasonable to expect of him as a solicitor.

(2) The Council shall not take any steps unless they are satisfied that in all the circumstances of the case it is appropriate to do so.

(3) In determining in any case whether it is appropriate to take any of the steps, the Council may—

  (a) have regard to the existence of any remedy which it is reasonable to expect to be available to the client in civil proceedings; and

  (b) where proceedings seeking any such remedy have not been begun by him, have regard to whether it is reasonable to expect him to begin them.

Directions which may be given

2.—(1) The steps are—

  (a) determining that the costs to which the solicitor is entitled in respect of his services ("the costs") are to be limited to such amount as may be specified in the determination and directing him to comply, or to secure compliance, with such one or more of the permitted requirements as appear to the Council to be necessary in order for effect to be given to their determination;

  (b) directing him to secure the rectification, at his expense or at that of his firm, of any such error, omission or other deficiency arising in connection with the matter in question as they may specify;

  (c) directing him to pay such compensation to the client as the Council sees fit to specify in the direction;

  (d) directing him to take, at his expense or at that of his firm, such other action in the interests of the client as they may specify.

(2) The "permitted requirements" are—

  (a) that the whole or part of any amount already paid by or on behalf of the client in respect of the costs be refunded;

  (b) that the whole part of the costs be remitted;

  (c) that the right to recover the costs be waived, whether wholly or to any specified extent.

(3) The power of the Council to take any such steps is not confined to cases where the client may have a cause of action against the solicitor for negligence.

Compensation

3.—(1) The amount specified in a direction by virtue of paragraph 2(1)(c) shall **7C–145** not exceed £15,000.

(2) The Secretary of State may by order made by statutory instrument amend sub-paragraph (1) by substituting for the sum of £1000 such other sum as he considers appropriate.

7C–144

(3) Before making any such order the Secretary of State shall consult the Law Society.

(4) Any statutory instrument made under this paragraph shall be subject to annulment in pursuance of a resolution of either House of Parliament.

7C–145.1   *Note* —Amended by Solicitors (Compensation for Inadequate Professional Services) Order 2005 (S.I. 2005 No. 2749).

Taxation of costs

7C–146   4.—(1) Where the Council have given a direction under paragraph 2(1)(a), then—

(a) for the purposes of any taxation of a bill covering the costs, the amount charged by the bill in respect of them shall be deemed to be limited to the amount specified in the determination; and

(b) where a bill covering the costs has not been taxed, the client shall, for the purposes of their recovery (by whatever means and notwithstanding any statutory provision or agreement) be deemed to be liable to pay in respect of them only the amount specified in the determination.

(2) Where a bill covering the costs has been taxed, the direction shall, so far as it relates to the costs, cease to have effect.

Failure to comply with direction

7C–147   5.—(1) If a solicitor fails to comply with a direction given under this Schedule, any person may make a complaint in respect of that failure to the Tribunal; but no other proceedings whatever shall be brought in respect of it.

(2) On the hearing of such a complaint the Tribunal may, if it thinks fit (and whether or not it makes any order under section 47(2)), direct that the direction be treated, for the purpose of enforcement, as if it were contained in an order made by the High Court.

Fees

7C–148   6.—(1) The Council may, by regulations made with the concurrence of the Secretary of State and the Master of the Rolls, make provision for the payment, by any client with respect to whom the Council are asked to consider whether to take any of the steps, of such fee as may be prescribed.

(2) The regulations may provide for the exemption of such classes of client as may be prescribed.

(3) Where a client pays the prescribed fee it shall be repaid to him if the Council take any of the steps in the matter with respect to which the fee was paid.

(4) In this paragraph "prescribed" means prescribed by the regulations.

Costs

7C–149   7. Where the Council take any of the steps with respect to a solicitor they may also direct him to pay to the Council—

(a) the amount of the fee repayable by the Council to the client under paragraph 6(3); and

(b) an amount which is calculated by the Council as the cost to them of dealing with the complaint, or which in their opinion represents a reasonable contribution towards that cost.

Duty of Tribunal

7C–150   8. Where the Tribunal—

(a) is considering, or has considered, an application or complaint with respect to a solicitor; and

(b) is of the opinion that the Council should consider whether to take any of the steps with respect to that solicitor,

it shall inform the Council.

Interpretation

7C–151   9. The Council's powers under this Schedule are exercisable in relation to a person even though his name has been removed from, or struck off, the roll and references to a solicitor in this Schedule, so far as they relate to the exercise of those powers, shall be construed accordingly.

Note —Added by Courts and Legal Services Act 1990, s.93(3), Sched.15. Amended **7C–152** by the Secretary of State for Constitutional Affairs Order 2003 (S.I. 2003 No. 1887), Sched. 2, para.3.

Where the Complaints Bureau makes a finding of failure to provide adequate professional services it is not necessary for prejudice to a client or the possibility of prejudice to have been established (*R. v. The Law Society, Ex p. Singh & Choudry (a firm)*, *The Times*, April 1, 1994, DC).

Solicitors' Practice Rules 1990

(1990 JULY 18)

Basic principles
1. A solicitor shall not do anything in the course of practising as a **7C–153** solicitor, or permit another person to do anything on his or her behalf, which compromises or impairs or is likely to compromise or impair any of the following:
   (a) the solicitors' independence or integrity;
   (b) a person's freedom to instruct a solicitor of his or her choice;
   (c) the solicitor's duty to act in the best interests of the client;
   (d) the good repute of the solicitor or of the solicitors' profession;
   (e) the solicitor's proper standard of work;
   (f) the solicitor's duty to the Court.

* * * *

Introductions and referrals
3. Solicitors may accept introductions and referrals of business **7C–154** from other persons and may make introductions and refer business to owner persons, provided there is no breach of these rules and provided there is compliances with a Solicitors' Introduction and Referral Code promulgated from time to time by the Council of the Law Society with the concurrence of the Master of the Rolls.

Employed solicitors
4.—(1) Solicitors who are employees of non-solicitors shall not: **7C–155**
   (a) choose an advocate; nor
   (b) exercise any extended right of audience under one of the Law Society's higher courts qualifications; nor
   (c) as part of their employment do for any person other than their employer work which is or could be done by a solicitor acting as such;
in any way which breaches the Employed Solicitor's Code promulgated from time to time by the Council of the Law Society with the concurrence of the Master of the Rolls.

REPRESENTATIVES

(2) Solicitors who are employees of multi-national partnerships shall not be regarded as "employees of non-solicitors" for the purpose of this rule.

Providing services other than as a solicitor

7C–156   5. Solicitors must comply with the Solicitors' Separate Business Code in controlling, actively participating in or operating (in each case alone, or by or with others) a business which:

(a) provides any service which may properly be provided by a solicitor's practice, and

(b) is not itself a solicitor's practice or a multi-national partnership.

* * * *

Fee sharing

7C–157   7.—(1) A solicitor shall not share or agree to share his or her professional fees with any person except:

(a) a practising solicitor;

(b) a practising foreign lawyer (other than a foreign lawyer whose registration in the register of foreign lawyers is suspended or whose name has been struck off the register);

(c) the solicitor's *bona fide* employee, which provision shall not permit under the cloak of employment a partnership prohibited by paragraph (6) of this rule; or

(d) a retired partner or predecessor of the solicitor or the dependants or personal representatives of a deceased partner or predecessor.

(2) Notwithstanding paragraph (1) of this rule a solicitor who instructs an estate agent as sub-agent for the sale of properties may remunerate the estate agent on the basis of a proportion of the solicitor's professional fee.

(3) The exceptions set out in paragraphs 2 to 9 of the Employed Solicitors Code shall where necessary also operate as exceptions to this rule but only to permit fee sharing with the solicitor's employer.

(4) A solicitor who works as a volunteer in a law centre or advice service operated by a charitable or similar non-commercial organisation may pay to the organisation any fees or costs that he or she receives under the legal aid scheme.

(5) For the purposes of sub-paragraph (1)(d) above, the references to a retired or deceased partner shall be construed, in relation to a recognised body, as meaning a retired or deceased director or member of that body, or a retired or deceased beneficial owner of any share in that body held by a member as nominee.

(6) (a) A solicitor shall not enter into partnership with any person other than a solicitor, a registered foreign lawyer or a recognised body.

(b) A recognised body shall not enter into partnership with any person other than a solicitor or a recognised body.

(c) In this paragraph, "solicitor" means a solicitor of the Supreme Court of England and Wales.

(7) A solicitor shall not practise through any body corporate except a recognised body, or save as permitted under rule 4 of these rules.

Note —A fee sharing agreement is unenforceable even if only one party was aware **7C–158** of the impropriety. *Mohamed v. Alaga & Co* [1999] 3 All E.R. 699, CA.

Contingency fees

8.—(1) A solicitor who is retained or employed to prosecute or **7C–159** defend any action, suit or other contentious proceeding shall not enter into any arrangement to receive a contingency fee in respect of that proceeding, save one permitted under statute or by the common law.

(2) Paragraph (1) of this rule shall not apply to an arrangement in respect of an action, suit or other contentious proceeding in any country other than England and Wales to the extent that a local lawyer would be permitted to receive a contingency fee in respect of that proceeding.

Claims assessors

9.—(1) A solicitor shall not, in respect of any claim or claims aris- **7C–160** ing as a result of death or personal injury, either enter into an arrangement for the introduction of clients with or act in association with any person (not being a solicitor) whose business or any part of whose business is to make, support or prosecute (whether by action or otherwise, and whether by a solicitor or agent or otherwise) claims arising as a result of death or personal injury and who in the course of such business solicits or receives contingency fees in respect of such claims.

(2) The prohibition in paragraph (1) of this rule shall not apply to an arrangement or association with a person who solicits or receives contingency fees only in respect of proceedings in a country outside England and Wales, to the extent that a local lawyer would be permitted to receive a contingency fee in respect of such proceedings.

Receipt of commissions from third parties

10.—(1) Solicitors shall account to their clients for any commission **7C–161** received of more than £20 unless, having disclosed to the client in writing the amount or basis of calculation of the commission or (if the precise amount or basis cannot be ascertained) an approximation thereof, they have the client's agreement to retain it.

(2) Where the commission actually received is materially in excess of the amount or basis or approximation disclosed to the client the solicitor shall account to the client for the excess.

(3) This rule does not apply where a member of the public deposits money with a solicitor who is acting as agent for a building society or other financial institution and the solicitor has not advised that person as a client as to the disposition of the money.

Supervision and management of an office

7C–162   13.—(1) Solicitors shall ensure that every office where they or their firms practice is and can reasonably be seen to be properly supervised in accordance with the following minimum standards:

    (a) Every such office shall be attended on each day when it is open to the public or open to telephone calls from the public by:

        (i) a solicitor who holds a practising certificate and has been admitted for at least three years; or

        (ii) in the case of an office from which no right of audience or right to conduct litigation is exercised and from which no exercise of any such right is supervised, a registered foreign lawyer who is a principal of the firm and who has been qualified in his or her own jurisdiction for at least three years;

who shall spend sufficient time at such office to ensure adequate control of the staff employed there and afford requisite facilities for consultation with clients. In the case of a firm in private practice such solicitor may be a principal, employee or consultant of the firm, provided that the firm must have at least one principal who is a solicitor who has been admitted for at least three years, or alternatively, in the case of a firm none of whose principals exercise any right of audience or right to conduct litigation or supervise or assume responsibility for the exercise of any such right, a foreign lawyer who has been qualified in his or her own jurisdiction for at least three years.

    (b) Every such office shall be managed by one of the persons listed below who shall normally be in attendance at that office during all the hours when it is open to the public or open to telephone calls from the public:

        (i) a solicitor holding a current practising certificate;

        (ii) a Fellow of the Institute of Legal Executives confirmed by the Institute as being of good standing and having been admitted as a Fellow for not less than three years;

        (iia) in the case of an office from which no right of audience or right to conduct litigation is exercised and from which no exercise of any such right is supervised, a registered foreign lawyer who is a principal of the firm;

        (iii) in the case of an office dealing solely with conveyancing, a licensed conveyancer; or

        (iv) in the case of an office dealing solely with property selling and surveying, a chartered surveyor or person holding another professional qualification approved by the Council under Rule 14 of these rules.

    (2) In determining whether or not there has been compliance with the requirement as to supervision in paragraph (1) of this rule,

account shall be taken of, *inter alia*, the arrangements for principals to see incoming mail.

(3) Where daily attendance or normal attendance in accordance with sub-paragraphs (1)(a) or (1)(b) of this rule is prevented by illness, accident or other sufficient or unforeseen cause for a prolonged period, suitable alternative arrangements shall be made without delay to ensure compliance.

(4) [Transitional provision now expired.]

(5) In this rule:

    (a) references to a principal shall be constructed, in relation to a recognised body, as references to a director of that body;

    (b) in paragraph (2) of this rule, "principals" shall be construed, except in relation to a firm none of whose principals exercise any right of audience or right to conduct litigation or supervise or assume responsibility for the exercise of any such right, as referring to principals who are solicitors; and

    (c) "right of audience" and "right to conduct litigation" shall be construed in accordance with Part II and section 119 of the Courts and Legal Services Act 1990.

Costs information and client care

15. Solicitors shall: 7C–163

    (a) give information about costs and other matters, and

    (b) operate a complaints handling procedure,

in accordance with a Solicitors' Costs Information and Client Care Code made from time to time by the Council of the Law Society with the concurrence of the Master of the Rolls, but subject to the notes.

Notes

  (i) *A serious breach of the code, or persistent breaches of a material nature, will be a breach of the rule, and may also be evidence of inadequate professional services under section 37A of the Solicitors Act 1974.*

 (ii) *Material breaches of the code which are not serious or persistent will not be a breach of the rule, but may be evidence of inadequate professional services under section 37A.*

(iii) *The powers of the Office for the Supervision of Solicitors on a finding of inadequate professional services include:*

 (a) *disallowing all or part of the solicitors costs; and*

 (b) *directing the solicitor to pay compensation to the client up to a limit of £1,000.*

 (iv) *Non-material breaches of the code will not be a breach of the rule, and will not be evidence of inadequate professional services under section 37A.*

  (v) *Registered foreign lawyers, although subject to rule 15 as a matter of professional conduct, are not subject to section 37A. However, solicitor partners in a multi-national partnership are subject to section 37A for professional services provided by the firm.*

Solicitors acting as advocates

7C–164   16A. Any solicitor acting as advocate shall at all times comply with the Law Society's Code for Advocacy.

Choice of advocate

7C–165   16B.—(1) A solicitor shall not make it a condition of providing litigation services that advocacy services shall also be provided by that solicitor or by the solicitor's firm or the solicitor's agent.

(2) A solicitor who provides both litigation and advocacy services shall as soon as practicable after receiving instructions and from time to time consider and advise the client whether having regard to the circumstances including:

　　　(i) the gravity, complexity and likely cost of the case;
　　　(ii) the nature of the solicitor's practice;
　　　(iii) the solicitor's ability and experience;
　　　(iv) the solicitor's relationship with the client;
　the best interests of the client would be served by the solicitor, another advocate from the solicitor's firm, or some other advocate providing the advocacy services.

Waivers

7C–166   17. In any particular case or cases the Council of the Law Society shall have power to waive in writing any of the provisions of these rules for a particular purpose or purposes expressed in such waiver, and to revoke such waiver.

Application and interpretation

7C–167   18.—(1) *Application to solicitors*

These rules shall have effect in relation to the practice of solicitors whether as a principal in private practice, or in the employment of a solicitor or of a non-solicitor employer, or in any other form of practice, and whether on a regular or on an occasional basis.

　　(1A) *Application to registered foreign lawyers*
　　　(a) For the avoidance of doubt, neither registration in the register of foreign lawyers, nor anything in these rules or in any other rules made under Part II of the Solicitors Act 1974 or section 9 of the Administration of Justice Act 1985, shall entitle any registered foreign lawyer to be granted any right of audience or any right to conduct litigation within the meaning of Part II and section 119of the Courts and Legal Services Act 1990 , or any right to supervise or assume responsibility for the exercise of any such right.
　　　(b) A registered foreign lawyer shall do nothing in the course of practising in partnership with a solicitor which, if done by a solicitor, would put the solicitor in breach of any of these rules, or any other rules, principles or requirements of conduct applicable to solicitors.
　　　(c) A registered foreign lawyer shall do nothing in the

course of practising as the director of a recognised body
which puts the recognised body in breach of any of these
rules, or any other rules, principles or requirements of
conduct applicable to recognised bodies.

(2) *Interpretation*

In these rules, except where the context otherwise requires:

(a) "arrangement" means any express or tacit agreement
between a solicitor and another person whether contractually binding or not;

(b) "contentious proceeding" is to be construed in accordance with the definition of "contentious business" in
section 87 of the Solicitors Act 1974;

(c) "contingency fee" means any sum (whether fixed, or
calculated either as a percentage of the proceeds or
otherwise howsoever) payable only in the event of success in the prosecution or defence of any action, suit or
other contentious proceeding;

(d) "firm" includes a sole practitioner or a recognised body;

(da) "foreign lawyer" means a person who is a member, and
entitled to practise as such, of a legal profession
regulated within a jurisdiction outside England and
Wales;

(db) "multi-national partnership" has the meaning given in
section 89 of the Courts and Legal Services Act 1990;

(e) "person" includes a body corporate or unincorporated
association or group of persons;

(ea) "principal in private practice" includes a recognised
body;

(f) "recognised body" means a body corporate for the time
being recognised by the Council under the Solicitors'
Incorporated Practice Rules from time to time in force;

(fa) "registered foreign lawyer" means a person registered in
accordance with section 89 of the Courts and Legal Services Act 1990; and "register" and "registration" are to
be construed accordingly.

(g) "solicitor" means a solicitor of the Supreme Court of
England and Wales and, except in rule 7(6) of these
rules, also includes a firm of solicitors or a recognised
body; and

(h) words in the singular include the plural, words in the
plural include the singular, and words importing the
masculine or feminine gender include the neuter.

Repeal and commencement

19.—(1) The Solicitors Practice Rules 1988 are hereby repealed.   **7C–168**

(2) These rules shall come into force on 1st September 1990.

Solicitors' Costs Information and Client Care Code 1999

1. Introduction

7C–169
    (a) This code replaces the written professional standards on costs information for clients (see paragraph 3–6) and the detail previously contained in Practice Rule 15 (client care) (see paragraph 7).

    (b) The main object of the code is to make sure that clients are given the information they need to understand what is happening generally and in particular on:

        (i) the cost of legal services both at the outset and as a matter progresses; and

        (ii) responsibility for clients' matters.

    (c) The code also requires firms to operate a complaints handling procedure.

    (d) It is good practice to record in writing:

        (i) all information required to be given by the code including all decisions relating to costs and the arrangements for updating costs information; and

        (ii) the reasons why the information required by the code has not been given in a particular case.

    (e) References to costs, where appropriate, include fees, VAT and disbursements.

2. Application

7C–170
    (a) The code is of general application, and it applies to registered foreign lawyers as well as to solicitors. However, as set out in paragraph 2(b), parts of the code may not be appropriate in every case, and solicitors should consider the interests of each client in deciding which parts not to apply in the particular circumstances.

    (b) The full information required by the code may be inappropriate, for example:

        (i) in every case, for a regular client for whom repetitive work is done, where the client has already been provided with the relevant information, although such a client should be informed of changes; and

        (ii) if compliance with the code may at the time be insensitive or impractical. In such a case relevant information should be given as soon as reasonably practicable.

    (c) Employed solicitors should have regard to paragraphs 3–6 of the code where appropriate, *e.g.* when acting for clients other than their employer. Paragraph 7 does not apply to employed solicitors.

    (d) Solicitors should comply with paragraphs 3–6 of the code even where a client is legally aided if the client may have a financial interest in the costs because contributions are payable or the statutory charge may apply or they may become liable for the costs of another party.

    (e) The code also applies to contingency fee and conditional fee arrangements and to arrangements with a client for the solicitor to retain commissions received from third parties.

3. Informing the client about costs

(a) Costs information must not be inaccurate or misleading.

(b) Any costs information required to be given by the code must be given clearly, in a way and at a level which is appropriate to the particular client. Any terms with which the client may be unfamiliar, for example "disbursement", should be explained.

(c) The information required by paragraphs 4 and 5 of the code should be given to a client at the outset of, and at appropriate stages throughout, the matter. All information given orally should be confirmed in writing to the client as soon as possible.

7C–171

4. Advance costs information – general

The overall costs

(a) The solicitor should give the client the best information possible about the likely overall costs, including a breakdown between fees, VAT and disbursements.

(b) The solicitor should explain clearly to the client the time likely to be spent in dealing with a matter, if time spent is a factor in the calculation of the fees.

(c) Giving "the best information possible" includes:

    (i) agreeing a fixed fee; or

    (ii) giving a realistic estimate; or

    (iii) giving a forecast within a possible range of costs; or

    (iv) explaining to the client the reasons why it is not possible to fix, or give a realistic estimate or forecast of, the overall costs, and giving instead the best information possible about the cost of the next stage of the matter.

(d) The solicitor should, in an appropriate case, explain to a privately paying client that the client may set an upper limit on the firms costs for which the client may be liable without further authority. Solicitors should not exceed an agreed limit without first obtaining the clients consent.

(e) The solicitor should make it clear at the outset if an estimate, quotation or other indication of cost is not intended to be fixed.

7C–172

Basis of firms charges

(f) The solicitor should also explain to the client how the firms fees are calculated except where the overall costs are fixed or clear. If the basis of charging is an hourly charging rate, that must be made clear.

(g) The client should be told if charging rates may be increased.

Further information

(h) The solicitor should explain what reasonably foreseeable payments a client may have to make either to the solicitor or to a third party and when those payments are likely to be needed.

(i) The solicitor should explain to the client the arrangements for updating the costs information as set out in paragraph 6.

Clients ability to pay

(j) The solicitor should discuss with the client how, when and by whom any costs are to be met, and consider:

    (i) whether the client may be eligible and should apply for legal aid (including advice and assistance);

    (ii) whether the clients liability for their own costs may be covered by insurance;

    (iii) whether the clients liability for another party's costs may be covered by pre-purchased insurance and, if not, whether it would be advisable for the client's liability for another party's costs to be covered by after the event insurance (including in every case where a conditional fee or contingency fee arrangement is proposed); and

    (iv) whether the clients liability for costs (including the costs of another party) may be paid by another person, *e.g.* an employer or trade union.

Cost-benefit and risk

(k) The solicitor should discuss with the client whether the likely outcome in a matter will justify the expense or risk involved including, if relevant, the risk of having to bear an opponent's costs.

5. Additional information for particular clients

Legally aided clients

7C–173
(a) The solicitor should explain to a legally aided client the client's potential liability for the client's own costs and those of any other party, including:

    (i) the effect of the statutory charge and its likely amount;

    (ii) the clients obligation to pay any contribution assessed and the consequences of failing to do so;

    (iii) the fact that the client may still be ordered by the court to contribute to the opponents costs if the case is lost even though the clients own costs are covered by legal aid; and

    (iv) the fact that even if the client wins, the opponent may not be ordered to pay or be capable of paying the full amount of the client's costs.

Privately paying clients in contentious matters (and potentially contentious matters)

(b) The solicitor should explain to the client the client's potential liability for the client's own costs and for those of any other party, including:

    (i) the fact that the client will be responsible for paying the firm's bill in full regardless of any order for costs made against an opponent;

    (ii) the probability that the client will have to pay the opponent's costs as well as the client's own costs if the case is lost;

    (iii) the fact that even if the client wins, the opponent may not be ordered to pay or be capable of paying the full amount of the client's costs; and

    (iv) the fact that if the opponent is legally aided the client may not recover costs, even if successful.

Liability for third party costs in non-contentious matters

(c) The solicitor should explain to the client any liability the client may have for the payment of the costs of a third party. When appropriate, solicitors are advised to obtain a firm figure for or agree a cap to a third party's costs.

"Clients represented under a conditional fee agreement (including a collective conditional fee agreement)

(d) Where a client is represented under a conditional fee agreement, the solicitor should explain:

    (i) the circumstances in which the client may be liable for their own costs and for the other party's costs;

    (ii) the client's right to assessment of costs, wherever the solicitor intends to seek payment of any or all of their costs from the client; and

    (iii) any interest the solicitor may have in recommending a particular policy or other funding.

Note — [The Solicitors' Practice (Client Care) Amendment Rule [2005]

7C–173.1
Rule dated [the date of notification of the Lord Chancellor's approval] made by the Council of the Law Society under part II of the Solicitors Act 1974 and section 9 of the Administration of Justice Act 1985, with the concurrence of the Master of the Rolls under that section and the approval of the Lord Chancellor under Schedule 4 to the Courts and Legal services Act 1990, regulating the conduct of solicitors, registered European lawyers, registered foreign lawyers and recognised bodies.

    (1) [Add] At the end of paragraph 5 of the Solicitors' Costs Information and Client Care Code 1999.

    (2) This rule will come into force on [the date of notification of the Lord Chancellor's approval or the date of repeal of the Conditional Fee Agreements Regulations (2000), whichever is the later].

6. Updating costs information

7C–174
The solicitor should keep the client properly informed about costs as a matter progresses. In particular, the solicitor should:

(a) tell the client, unless otherwise agreed, how much the costs are at regular intervals (at least every six months) and in appropriate cases deliver interim bills at agreed intervals;

(b) explain to the client (and confirm in writing) any changed circumstances which will, or which are likely to, affect the amount of costs, the degree of risk involved, or the cost-benefit to the client of continuing with the matter;

(c) inform the client in writing as soon as it appears that a costs estimate or agreed upper limit may or will be exceeded; and

(d) consider the clients eligibility for legal aid if a material change in the client's means comes to the solicitor's attention.

7. Client care and complaints handling

Information for clients

(a) Every solicitor in private practice must ensure that the client:　　　**7C–175**

    (i) is given a clear explanation of the issues raised in a matter and is kept properly informed about its progress (including the likely timescale);

    (ii) is given the name and status of the person dealing with the matter and the name of the principal responsible for its overall supervision;

    (iii) is told whom to contact about any problem with the services provided; and

    (iv) is given details of any changes in the information required to be given by this paragraph.

Complaints handling

(b) Every principal in private practice must:

    (i) ensure the client is told the name of the person in the firm to contact about any problem with the service provided;

    (ii) have a written complaints procedure and ensure that complaints are handled in accordance with it; and

    (iii) ensure that the client is given a copy of the complaints procedure on request.

Solicitors' Accounts Rules 1998

(1998 JULY 22)

Receipt and transfer of costs

19.—(1) A *solicitor* who receives money paid in full or part settle-　**7C–176**
ment of the *solicitor's* bill (or other notification of *costs*) **must follow
one of the following four options**:

    (a) **determine the composition of the payment** *without delay*, **and deal with the money accordingly:**

        (i) if the sum comprises *office money* only, it must be placed in an *office account*;

        (ii) if the sum comprises only *client money* (for example an unpaid *professional disbursement*—see rule 2(2)(s), and note (v) to rule 2), the entire sum must be placed in a *client account*;

        (iii) if the sum includes both *office money* and *client money* (such as unpaid *professional disbursements*; purchase money; or payments in advance for court fees, stamp duty land tax, Land Registry registration fees or telegraphic transfer fees), the *solicitor* must follow rule 20 (receipt of mixed payments); **or**

   (b) **ascertain that the payment comprises only** *office money*, **and/or** *client money* **in the form of** *professional disbursements* **incurred but not yet paid, and deal with the payment as follows:**

      (i) place the entire sum in an *office account* at a *bank* or *building society* branch (or head office) in England and Wales; and

      (ii) by the end of the second working day following receipt, either pay any unpaid *professional disbursement*, or transfer a sum for its settlement to a *client account*; **or**

   (c) **pay the entire sum into a** *client account* **(regardless of its composition), and transfer any** *office money* **out of the** *client account* **within 14 days of receipt; or**

   (d) **on receipt of** *costs* **from the Legal Aid Board, follow the option in rule 21(1)(b).**

(2) A *solicitor* who properly requires payment of his or her *fees* from money held for the *client* or *controlled trust* in a *client account* must first give or send a bill of *costs*, or other written notification of the *costs* incurred, to the *client* or the paying party.

(3) Once the *solicitor* has compiled with paragraph (2) above, the money earmarked for *costs* becomes *office money* and must be transferred out of the *client account* within 14 days.

(4) A payment on account of *costs* generally is *client money*, and must be held in a *client account* until the *solicitor* has complied with paragraph (2) above. (For an exception in the case of legal aid payments, see rule 21(1)(a)).

(5) A payment for an *agreed fee* must be paid into an *office account*. An "agreed fee" is one that is fixed—not a *fee* that can be varied upwards, nor a *fee* that is dependent on the transaction being completed. An *agreed fee* must be evidenced in writing.

Treatment of payments to legal aid practitioners

7C–177   21. Payments from the Legal Services Commission

(1) Two special dispensations apply to payments (other than regular payments) from the Legal Services Commission:

   (a) An advance payment in anticipation of work to be carried out, although *client money*, may be placed in an *office account*, provided the Commission instructs in writing that this may be done.

   (b) A payment for *costs* (interim and/or final) may be paid into an *office account* at a *bank* or *building society* branch (or head office) in England and Wales, regardless of whether it consists wholly of *office money*, or is mixed with *client money* in the form of:

      (i) advance payments for *fees* or *disbursements*; or

      (ii) money for unpaid *professional disbursements*;

provided all money for payment of *disbursements* is transferred to a *client account* (or the *disbursements* paid) within 14 days of receipt.

(2) The following provisions apply to *regular payments* from the Legal Services Commission:

- (a) "Regular payments" (which are office money) are:
    - (i) standard monthly payments paid by the Commission under the civil legal aid contracting arrangements;
    - (ii) monthly payments paid by the Commission under the criminal legal aid contracting arrangements; and
    - (iii) any other payments for work done or to be done received from the Commission under an arrangement for payments on a regular basis.
- (b) *Regular payments* must be paid into an *office account* at a *bank* or *building society* branch (or head office) in England and Wales.
- (c) A *solicitor* must within 28 days of submitting a report to the Commission, notifying completion of a matter, either:
    - (i) pay any unpaid *professional disbursement(s)*, or
    - (ii) transfer to a *client account* a sum equivalent to the amount of any unpaid *professional disbursement(s)*,

relating to that matter.

- (d) In cases where the Commission permits solicitors to submit reports at various stages during a matter rather than only at the end of a matter, the requirement in paragraph (c) above applies to any unpaid *professional disbursement(s)* included in each report so submitted.

Payments from a third party

(3) If the Legal Services Commission has paid any costs to a *solicitor* or a previously nominated *solicitor* in a matter (advice and assistance or legal help *costs*, advance payments or interim *costs*), or has paid *professional disbursements* direct, and costs are subsequently settled by a third party:

- (a) The entire third party payment must be paid into a *client account*.
- (b) A sum representing the payments made by the Commission must be retained in the *client account*.
- (c) Any balance belonging to the *solicitor* must be transferred to an *office account* within 14 days of the *solicitor* sending a report to the Commission containing details of the third party payment.
- (d) The sum retained in the client account as representing payments made by the Commission must be:
    - (i) **either** recorded in the individual *client's* ledger account, and identified as the Commission's money;
    - (ii) **or** recorded in a ledger account in the Commission's name, and identified by reference to the *client* or matter;

and kept in the *client account* until notification from the Commission that it has recouped an equivalent sum from subsequent payments due to the *solicitor*. The retained sum must be transferred to an *office account* within 14 days of notification.

Withdrawals from a client account

7C–178   **22.**—(1)   Client money may only be withdrawn from a *client account* when it is:

(a) properly required for a payment to or on behalf of the *client* (or other person on whose behalf the money is being held);

(b) properly required for payment of a *disbursement* on behalf of the *client*;

(c) properly required in full or partial reimbursement of money spent by the *solicitor* on behalf of the *client*;

(d) transferred to another *client account*;

(e) withdrawn on the *client's* instructions, provided the instructions are for the *client's* convenience and are given in writing, or are given by other means and confirmed by the *solicitor* to the *client* in writing;

(f) a refund to the *solicitor* of an advance no longer required to fund a payment on behalf of a *client* (see rule 15(2)(b));

(g) money which has been paid into the account in breach of the rules (for example, money paid into the wrong *separate designated client account*)—see paragraph (4) below; or

(h) money not covered by (a) to (g) above, withdrawn from the account on the written authorisation of the *Society*. The *Society* may impose a condition that the *solicitor* pay the money to a charity which gives an indemnity against any legitimate claim subsequently made for the sum received.

(2) *Controlled trust money* may only be withdrawn from a *client account* when it is:

(a) properly required for a payment in the execution of the particular *trust*, including the purchase of an investment (other than money) in accordance with the *trustee's* powers;

(b) properly required for payment of a *disbursement* for the particular *trust*;

(c) properly required in full or partial reimbursement of money spent by the *solicitor* on behalf of the particular *trust*;

(d) transferred to another *client account*;

(e) transferred to an account other than a *client account* (such as an account outside England and Wales), but only if the *trustee's* powers permit, or to be properly retained in cash in the performance of the *trustee's* duties;

(f) a refund to the *solicitor* of an advance no longer required to fund a payment on behalf of a *controlled trust* (see rule 15(2)(b));

(g) money which has been paid into the account in breach of the rules (for example, money paid into the wrong *separate designated client account*)—see paragraph (4) below; or

(h) money not covered by (a) to (g) above, withdrawn from the account on the written authorisation of the *Society*. The *Society* may impose a condition that the *solicitor* pay the money to a charity which gives an indemnity against any legitimate claim subsequently made for the sum received.

(3) *Office money* may only be withdrawn from a *client account* when it is:

(a) money properly paid into the account to open or maintain it under rule 15(2)(a);

(b) properly required for payment of the *solicitor's costs* under rule 19(2) and (3);

(c) the whole or part of a payment into a *client account* under rule 19(1)(c);

(d) part of a *mixed payment* placed in a *client account* under rule 20(2)(b); or

(e) money which has been paid into a *client account* in breach of the rules (for example, interest wrongly credited to a *general client account*)—see paragraph (4) below.

(4) Money which has been paid into a *client account* in breach of the rules must be withdrawn from the *client account* promptly upon discovery.

(5) Money withdrawn in relation to a particular *client* or *controlled trust* from a *general client account* must not exceed the money held on behalf of that *client* or *controlled trust* in all the *solicitor's general client accounts* (except as provided in paragraph (6) below).

(6) A *solicitor* may make a payment in respect of a particular *client* or *controlled trust* out of a *general client account*, even if no money (or insufficient money) is held for that *client* or *controlled trust* in the *solicitor's general client account(s)*, provided:

(a) sufficient money is held for that *client* or *controlled trust* in a *separate designated client account*; and

(b) the appropriate transfer from the *separate designated client account* to a *general client account* is made immediately.

(7) Money held for a *client* or *controlled trust* in a *separate designated client account* must not be used for payments for another *client* or *controlled trust*.

(8) A *client account* must not be overdrawn, except in the following circumstances:

(a) A *separate designated client account* for a *controlled trust* can be overdrawn if the *controlled trustee* makes payments on behalf of the *trust* (for example, inheritance tax) before realising sufficient assets to cover the payments.

(b) If a sole practitioner dies and his or her *client accounts* are frozen, the *solicitor*-manager can operate *client accounts* which are overdrawn to the extent of the money held in the frozen accounts.

Method of and authority for withdrawals from client account

7C–179 23.—(1) A withdrawal from a *client account* may be made only after a specific authority in respect of that withdrawal has been signed by at least one of the following:

(a) a *solicitor* who holds a current practising certificate or a *registered European lawyer*;

(b) a Fellow of the Institute of Legal Executives of at least three years standing who is employed by such a *solicitor*, a *registered European lawyer* or a *recognised body*;

(c) in the case of an office dealing solely with conveyancing, a licensed conveyancer who is employed by such a *solicitor*, a *registered European lawyer* or a *recognised body*; or

(d) a *registered foreign lawyer* who is a *partner* in the practice, or who is a director of the practice (if it is a company), or who is a member of the practice (if it is a limited liability partnership).

(2) There is no need to comply with paragraph (1) above when transferring money from one *general client account* to another *general client account* at the same *bank* or *building society*.

(3) A withdrawal from a *client account* in favour of the *solicitor* or the practice must be either by way of a cheque to the *solicitor* or practice, or by way of a transfer to the *office account* or to the *solicitor's* personal account. The withdrawal must not be made in cash.

PART C

INTEREST

When interest must be paid

7C–180 24.—(1) When a *solicitor* holds money in a *separate designated client account* for a *client*, or for a person funding all or part of the *solicitor's fees*, the *solicitor* must account to the *client* or that person for all interest earned on the account.

(2) When a *solicitor* holds money in a *general client account* for a *client*, or for a person funding all or part of the *solicitor's fees* (or if money should have been held for a *client* or such other person in a *client account* but was not), the *solicitor* must account to the *client* or that person for a sum in lieu of interest calculated in accordance with rule 25.

(3) A *solicitor* is not required to pay a sum in lieu of interest under paragraph (2) above:

(a) if the amount calculated is £20 or less;

(b)

    (i) if the solicitor holds a sum of money not exceeding the amount shown in the left hand column below for a time not exceeding the period indicated in the right hand column:

Amount	Time
£1,000	8 weeks

£2,000	4 weeks
£10,000	2 weeks
£20,000	1 week

      (ii) if the solicitor holds a sum of money exceeding £20,000 for one week or less, unless it is fair and reasonable to account for a sum in lieu of interest having regard to all the circumstances;

(c) on money held for the payment of counsel's fees, once counsel has requested a delay in settlement;

(d) on money held for the Legal Services Commission;

(e) on an advance from the *solicitor* under rule 15(2)(b) to fund a payment on behalf of the *client* in excess of funds held for that *client*; or

(f) if there is an agreement to contract out of the provisions of this rule under rule 27.

(4) If sums of money are held intermittently during the course of acting, and the sum in lieu of interest calculated under rule 25 for any period is £20 or less, a sum in lieu of interest should still be paid if it is fair and reasonable in the circumstances to aggregate the sums in respect of the individual periods.

(5) If money is held for a continuous period, and for part of that period it is held in a *separate designated client account*, the sum in lieu of interest for the rest of the period when the money was held in a *general client account* may as a result be £20 or less. A sum in lieu of interest should, however, be paid if it is fair and reasonable in the circumstances to do so.

(6)

(a) If a *solicitor* holds money for a *client* (or person funding all or part of the *solicitor's fees*) in an account opened on the instructions of the *client* (or that person) under rule 16(1)(a), the *solicitor* must account to the *client* (or that person) for all interest earned on the account.

(b) If a *solicitor* has failed to comply with instructions to open an account under rule 16(1)(a), the *solicitor* must account to the *client* (or the person funding all or part of the *solicitor's fees*) for a sum in lieu of any net loss of interest suffered by the *client* (or that person) as a result.

(7) This rule does not apply to *controlled trust money*.

Amount of interest

25.—(1) *Solicitors* must aim to obtain a reasonable rate of interest **7C–181** on money held in a *separate designated client account*, and must account for a fair sum in lieu of interest on money held in a *general client account* (or on money which should have been held in a *client account* but was not). The sum in lieu of interest need not necessarily reflect the highest rate of interest obtainable but it is not acceptable to look only at the lowest rate of interest obtainable.

(2) **The sum in lieu of interest** for money held in a *general client account* (or on money which should have been held in a *client account* but was not) **must be calculated**

- on the balance or balances held over the whole period for which cleared funds are held
- at a rate not less than (whichever is the higher of) the following

(i) the rate of interest payable on a *separate designated client account* for the amount or amounts held, or

(ii) the rate of interest payable on the relevant amount or amounts if placed on deposit on similar terms by a member of the business community

- at the *bank* or *building society* where the money is held.

(3) If the money, or part of it, is held successively or concurrently in accounts at different *banks* or *building societies*, the relevant *bank* or *building society* for the purpose of paragraph (2) will be whichever of those *banks* or *building societies* offered the best rate on the date when the money was first held.

(4) If, contrary to the rules, the money is not held in a *client account*, the relevant *bank* or *building society* for the purpose of paragraph (2) will be a clearing bank or *building society* nominated by the *client* (or other person on whose behalf *client money* is held).

Interest on stakeholder money

7C–182 26. When a *solicitor* holds money as stakeholder, the *solicitor* must pay interest, or a sum in lieu of interest, on the basis set out in rule 24 to the person to whom the stake is paid.

Contracting out

7C–183 27.—(1) In appropriate circumstances a *client* and his or her *solicitor* may by a written agreement come to a different arrangement as to the matters dealt with in rule 24 (payment of interest).

(2) A *solicitor* acting as stakeholder may, by a written agreement with his or her own *client* and the other party to the transaction, come to a different arrangement as to the matters dealt with in rule 24.

Interest certificates

7C–184 28. Without prejudice to any other remedy:

(a) any *client*, including one of joint *clients*, or a person funding all or part of a *solicitor's fees*, may apply to the *Society* for a certificate as to whether or not interest, or a sum in lieu of interest, should have been paid and, if so, the amount; and

(b) if the *Society* certifies that interest, or a sum in lieu of interest, should have been paid, the *solicitor* must pay the certified sum.

PART G

COMMENCEMENT

Commencement

7C–185 50.—(1) These rules must be implemented not later than May 1,

2000; until a practice implements these rules, it must continue to operate the Solicitors' Accounts Rules 1991.

(2) Practices opting to implement these rules before May 1, 2000 must implement them in their entirety, and not selectively.

(3) Part F of the rules (accountants' reports) will apply to:

    (a) reports covering any period of time after April 30, 2000; and also

    (b) reports covering any earlier period of time for which a practice has opted to operate these rules.

(4) The Accountant's Report Rules 1991 will continue to apply to:

    (a) reports covering any period of time before July 22, 1998; and also

    (b) reports covering any period of time after July 21, 1998 and before May 1, 2000 during which a practice continued to operate the Solicitors' Accounts Rules 1991.

(5) If a practice operated the Solicitors' Accounts Rules 1991 for part of an *accounting period*, and these rules for the rest of the *accounting period*, the practice may, in respect of that *accounting period* ("the transitional accounting period") either:

    (a) deliver a single accountant's report covering the whole of the transitional accounting period, made partly under the Accountant's Report Rules 1991 and partly under Part F of these rules, as appropriate; or

    (b) deliver a separate accountant's report for each part of the transitional accounting period, one under the Accountant's Report Rules 1991 and the other under Part F of these rules; or

    (c) deliver a report under the Accountant's Report Rules 1991 to cover that part of the transitional accounting period during which the practice operated the Solicitors' Accounts Rules 1991; and subsequently a report under Part F of these rules to cover the remaining part of the transitional accounting period plus the whole of the next *accounting period*; or

    (d) deliver a report under the Accountant's Report Rules 1991 to cover the last complete *accounting period* during which the practice operated the Solicitors' Accounts Rules 1991 plus that part of the transitional accounting period during which the practice continued to operate those rules; and subsequently a report under Part F of these rules to cover the remaining part of the transitional accounting period.

[THE NEXT PARAGRAPH IS 7C–188.]

Solicitors' (Non Contentious Business) Remuneration Order 1994

(S.I. 1994 No. 2616)

Citation, Commencement and Revocation

1.—(1) This Order may be cited as the Solicitors' (Non-Contentious   **7C–188** Business) Remuneration Order 1994.

(2) This Order shall come into force on November 1, 1994 and shall apply to all non-contentious business for which bills are delivered on or after that date.

(3) The Solicitors' Remuneration Order 1972 is hereby revoked except in its application to business for which bills are delivered before this Order comes into force.

Interpretation

7C–189   2. In this Order—

"client" means the client of a solicitor;

"costs" means the amount charged in a solicitor's bill, exclusive of disbursements and value added tax, in respect of non-contentious business or common form probate business;

"entitled person" means a client or an entitled third party;

"entitled third party" means a residuary beneficiary absolutely and immediately (and not contingently) entitled to an inheritance, where a solicitor has charged the estate for his professional costs for acting in the administration of the estate, and either

(a) the only personal representatives are solicitors (whether or not acting in a professional capacity); or

(b) the only personal representatives are solicitors acting jointly with partners or employees in a professional capacity;

"paid disbursements" means disbursements already paid by the solicitor;

"recognised body" means a body corporate recognised by the Council under section 9 of the Administration of Justice Act 1985;

"remuneration certificate" means a certificate issued by the Council pursuant to this Order;

"residuary beneficiary" includes a person entitled to all or part of the residue of an intestate estate;

"solicitor" includes a recognised body;

"the Council" means the Council of the Law Society.

Solicitors' costs

7C–190   3. A solicitor's costs shall be such sum as may be fair and reasonable to both solicitor and entitled person, having regard to all the circumstances of the case and in particular to—

(a) the complexity of the matter or the difficulty or novelty of the questions raised;

(b) the skill, labour, specialised knowledge and responsibility involved;

(c) the time spent on the business;

(d) the number and importance of the documents prepared or perused, without regard to length;

(e) the place where and the circumstances in which the business or any part thereof is transacted;

(f) the amount or value of any money or property involved;

   (g) whether any land involved is registered land;

   (h) the importance of the matter to the client; and

   (i) the approval (express or implied) of the entitled person or the express approval of the testator to—

      (i) the solicitor undertaking all or any part of the work giving rise to the costs or

      (ii) the amount of the costs.

Right to certification

4.—(1) Without prejudice to the provisions of sections 70, 71, and 72of the Solicitors Act 1974 (which relate to taxation of costs), an entitled person may, subject to the provisions of this Order, require a solicitor to obtain a remuneration certificate from the Council in respect of a bill which has been delivered where the costs are not more than £50,000.   **7C–191**

(2) The remuneration certificate must state what sum, in the opinion of the Council, would be a fair and reasonable charge for the business covered by the bill (whether it be the sum charged or a lesser sum). In the absence of taxation the sum payable in respect of such costs is the sum stated in the remuneration certificate.

Disciplinary and other measures

5.—(1) If on a taxation the taxing officer allows less than one half of the costs, he must bring the facts of the case to the attention of the Council.   **7C–192**

(2) The provisions of this Order are without prejudice to the general powers of the Council under the Solicitors Act 1974.

Commencement of proceedings against a client

6. Before a solicitor brings proceedings to recover costs against a client on a bill for non-contentious business he must inform the client in writing of the matters specified in article 8, except where the bill has been taxed.   **7C–193**

Costs paid by deduction

7.—(1) If a solicitor deducts his costs from monies held for or on behalf of a client or of an estate in satisfaction of a bill and an entitled person objects in writing to the amount of the bill within the prescribed time, the solicitor must immediately inform the entitled person in writing of the matters specified in article 8, unless he has already done so.   **7C–194**

(2) In this article and in article 10, "the prescribed time" means—

   (a) in respect of a client, three months after delivery of the relevant bill, or a lesser time (which may not be less than one month) specified in writing to the client at the time of delivery of the bill, or

   (b) in respect of an entitled third party, three months after delivery of notification to the entitled third party of the amount of the costs, or a lesser time (which may not be less than one month) specified in writing to the entitled third party at the time of such notification.

Information to be given in writing to entitled person

7C–195   8. When required by articles 6 or 7, a solicitor must inform an entitled person in writing of the following matters—

    (a) where article 4(1) applies—

        (i) that the entitled person may, within one month of receiving from the solicitor the information specified in this article or (if later) of delivery of the bill or notification of the amount of the costs, require the solicitor to obtain a remuneration certificate; and

        (ii) that (unless the solicitor has agreed to do so) the Council may waive the requirements of article 11(1), if satisfied from a client's written application that exceptional circumstances exist to justify granting a waiver;

    (b) that sections 70, 71 and 72 of the Solicitors Act 1974 set out the entitled person's rights in relation to taxation;

    (c) that (where the whole of the bill has not been paid, by deduction or otherwise) the solicitor may charge interest on the outstanding amount of the bill in accordance with article 14.

Loss by client of right to certification

7C–196   9. A client may not require a solicitor to obtain a remuneration certificate—

    (a) after a bill has been delivered and paid by the client, other than by deduction;

    (b) where a bill has been delivered, after the expiry of one month from the date on which the client was informed in writing of the matters specified in article 8 or from delivery of the bill if later;

    (c) after the solicitor and client have entered into a non-contentious business agreement in accordance with the provisions of section 57 of the Solicitors Act 1974;

    (d) after a court has ordered the bill to be taxed;

    (e) if article 11(2) applies.

Loss by entitled third party of right to certification

7C–197   10. An entitled third party may not require a solicitor to obtain a remuneration certificate—

    (a) after the prescribed time (within the meaning of article 7(2)(b)) has elapsed without any objection being received to the amount of the costs;

    (b) after the expiry of one month from the date on which the entitled third party was (in compliance with article 7) informed in writing of the matters specified in article 8 or from notification of the costs if later;

    (c) after a court has ordered the bill to be taxed.

Requirement to pay a sum towards the costs

7C–198   11.—(1) On requiring a solicitor to obtain a remuneration certificate a client must pay to the solicitor the paid disbursements and value added tax comprised in the bill together with 50% of the costs unless—

    (a) the client has already paid the amount required under this article, by deduction from monies held or otherwise; or

    (b) the solicitor or (if the solicitor refuses) the Council has agreed in writing to waive all or part of this requirement.

(2) The Council shall be under no obligation to provide a remuneration certificate, and the solicitor may take steps to obtain payment of his bill, if the client, having been informed of his right to seek a waiver of the requirements of paragraph (1), has not:

    (a) within one month of receipt of the information specified in article 8, either paid in accordance withparagraph (1) or applied to the Council in writing for a waiver of the requirements of paragraph (1); or

    (b) made payment in accordance with the requirements of paragraph (1) within one month of written notification that he has been refused a waiver of those requirements by the Council.

Miscellaneous provisions

12.—(1) After an application has been made by a solicitor for a re- **7C–199** muneration certificate the client may pay the bill in full without invalidating the application.

(2) A solicitor and entitled person may agree in writing to waive the provisions of sub-paragraphs (a) or (b) of articles 9 or 10.

(3) A solicitor may take from his client security for the payment of any costs, including the amount of any interest to which the solicitor may become entitled under article 14.

Refunds by solicitor

13.—(1) If a solicitor has received payment of all or part of his **7C–200** costs and a remuneration certificate is issued for less than the sum already paid, the solicitor must immediately pay to the entitled person any refund which may be due (after taking into account any other sums which may properly be payable to the solicitor whether for costs, paid disbursements, value added tax or otherwise) unless the solicitor has applied for an order for taxation within one month of receipt by him of the remuneration certificate.

(2) Where a solicitor applies for taxation, his liability to pay any refund under paragraph (1) shall be suspended for so long as the taxation is still pending.

(3) The obligation of the solicitor to repay costs under paragraph (1) is without prejudice to any liability of the solicitor to pay interest on the repayment by virtue of any enactment, rule of law or professional rule.

Interest

14.—(1) After the information specified in article 8 has been given **7C–201** to an entitled person in compliance with articles 6 or 7, a solicitor may charge interest on the unpaid amount of his costs plus any paid disbursements and value added tax, subject to paragraphs (2) and (3) below.

(2) Where an entitlement to interest arises under paragraph (1), and subject to any agreement made between a solicitor and client, the period for which interest may be charged may run from one month after the date of delivery of a bill, unless the solicitor fails to lodge an application within one month of receipt of a request for a remuneration certificate under article 4, in which case no interest is payable in respect of the period between one month after receiving the request and the actual date on which the application is lodged.

(3) Subject to any agreement made between a solicitor and client, the rate of interest must not exceed the rate for the time being payable on judgment debts.

(4) Interest charged under this article must be calculated, where applicable, by reference to the following—

- (a) if a solicitor is required to obtain a remuneration certificate, the total amount of the costs certified by the Council to be fair and reasonable plus paid disbursements and value added tax;
- (b) if an application is made for the bill to be taxed, the amount ascertained on taxation;
- (c) if an application is made for the bill to be taxed or a solicitor is required to obtain a remuneration certificate and for any reason the taxation or application for a remuneration certificate does not proceed, the unpaid amount of the costs shown in the bill or such lesser sum as may be agreed between the solicitor and the client, plus paid disbursements and value added tax.

Application by solicitor

7C-202   15. A solicitor, when making an application for a remuneration certificate in accordance with the provisions of this Order, must deliver to the Council the complete relevant file and working papers, and any other information or documentation which the Council may require for the purpose of providing a remuneration certificate.

7C-203   Note —In *Property and Reversionary Investment Corp Ltd v. Department of the Environment* [1975] 1 W.L.R. 1504; [1975] 2 All E.R. 436, guidance was given on the assessment of costs for commercial conveyancing. See also *Treasury Solicitor v. P. J. Dinsmore Regester* [1978] 1 W.L.R. 446; [1978] 2 All E.R. 920; and *Re D. J. Freeman & Co (a firm)*, *Maltby v. D. J. Freeman* [1978] 1 W.L.R. 431; [1978] 2 All E.R. 913, CA.

Guidance was given in respect of high value probate. The Court of Appeal considered whether solicitors, engaged in relation to the administration of an estate, are entitled, in the absence of agreement, to charge not only for the time they spend on the administration but also a fee based on the value of the estate. The court also considered how the value element should be calculated. The court saw no reason to say that it was no longer appropriate for solicitors to make a separate charge based on value provided that it was remembered that the solicitor was entitled only to what was fair and reasonable remuneration taking all relevant factors into account. It is not in any way decisive that, in an assessment of costs in contentious litigation, it is now usual to incorporate the value element of any money or property into the hourly rate. There are significant differences in the circumstances in which charges are made for contentious and non contentious business and the approach to such charges can properly differ, even though the same factors fall to be taken into account. The court was persuaded that it was right to make some increase in the bands to allow for inflation since 1978 when Maltby was decided. The court was of the view that the appropriate regressive scale should be 1.5 per cent up to £750,000, 0.5 per cent between £750,000 and £3 million, 0.1666 per cent £3 million to £6 million and 0.08333 per cent above £6 million. The court went on to emphasise the importance of looking at the final figure in the round in order to ensure that the appropriate factors were taken into account in every individual case to arrive at no more than fair and reasonable remuneration overall: *Jemma Trust Co Ltd v. Liptrott* [2003] EWCA Civ 1476; [2004] 1 W.L.R. 646, CA.

The court went on to give guidance suggesting that it would be appropriate for solicitors to adhere to the following principles:

"(1) Much the best practice is for a solicitor to obtain prior agreement as to the basis of his charges not only from the executors but also, where appropriate, from any residuary beneficiary who is an entitled third party under the 1994 Order. This is encouraged in the 1994 booklet and letter 8 of Appendix 2 to the 1999 booklet provides a good working draft of such agreement. We support that encouragement;

(2) in any complicated administration, it will be prudent for solicitors to provide in their terms of retainer for interim bills to be rendered for payment on account; this is, of course, subject to the solicitor's obligation to review the matter as a whole at the end of the business so as to ensure that he has claimed no more than is fair and reasonable, taking into account the factors set out in the 1994 Order;

(3) there should be no hard and fast rule that charges cannot be made separately by reference to the value of the estate; value can, by contrast, be taken into account as part of the hourly rate; value can also be taken into account partly in one way and partly in the other. What is important is that—

(a) it should be transparent on the face of the bill how value is being taken into account; and

(b) in no case, should it be taken into account more than once;

(4) in many cases, if a charge is separately made by reference to the value of the estate, it should usually be on a regressive scale. The bands and percentages will be for the costs judge in each case; the suggestions to the costs judge set out in paragraph 30 may be thought by him to be appropriate for this case but different bands and percentages will be appropriate for other cases and the figures set out in paragraph 30 cannot be any more than a guideline;

(5) it may be helpful at the end of the business for the solicitor or, if there is an assessment, for the costs judge, when a separate element of the bill is based on the value of the estate, to calculate the number of hours that would notionally be taken to achieve the amount of the separate charge. That may help to determine whether overall the remuneration claimed or assessed is fair and reasonable within the terms of the 1994 Order.

(6) it may also be helpful to consider the Law Society's Guidance in cases where there is no relevant and ascertainable value factor which is given in the 1994 booklet at paragraph 13.4. If the time spent on the matter is costed out at the solicitors' expense rate (which should be readily ascertainable from the Solicitors' Expense of Time calculations) the difference between that sum (the cost to the solicitor of the time spent on the matter) and the final figure claimed will represent the mark-up. The mark-up (which should take into account the factors specified in the 1994 Order including value) when added to the cost of the time spent must then be judged by reference to the requirement that this total figure must represent "such sum as may be fair and reasonable to both solicitor and entitled person".

Article 8

In *Clement-Davies v. Inter G.S.A.* (1979) 123 S.J. 505, the Court of Appeal held that **7C–204** to discharge his duty the client must be told of his rights under Art.3(1) (now Art.8) and his attention must also be directed to ss.70, 71 and 72 of the Solicitors Act 1974. See also *Re Laceward Ltd* [1981] 1 W.L.R. 133; [1981] 1 All E.R. 254.

Article 14

In *Walton v. Egan* [1982] 3 W.L.R. 352; [1982] 3 All E.R. 849; it was held that a **7C–205** special agreement under s.57 of the Solicitors Act 1974 providing for the payment of interest on unpaid fees may be enforced without compliance with the procedure prescribed by Art.5(1) (now Art.14), and was so even where the agreement was made after the solicitor's bill was first delivered.

[THE NEXT PARAGRAPH IS 7C–208.]

NOTES ON THE GENERAL LAW RELATING TO SOLICITORS

1. SUMMARY JURISDICTION OF THE COURT OVER SOLICITORS

The inherent jurisdiction

7C–208   Section 50(2) of the Solicitors Act 1974, reserves to the High Court, the Crown Court and Court of Appeal, and any division or judge thereof (subject to the provisions of the Act) the same jurisdiction in respect of solicitors as any one of the superior Courts of law or equity, from which the Supreme Court of Judicature was constituted, might have exercised immediately before the Judicature Act 1873, in respect of any solicitor, attorney or proctor. The inherent jurisdiction is ousted or curtailed by legislation—at least in so far as that legislation is negative in character (*Harrison v. Tew* [1990] 2 A.C. 523, HL; affirming [1989] Q.B. 307, CA). The jurisdiction is exercised over solicitors as officers of the Court, and may be instanced as follows:

Jurisdiction to strike a solicitor off the roll

7C–209   An applicant to the High Court must show that it was reasonable to take the exceptional and more expensive course of applying to the Court, or risk being ordered to pay the extra costs involved (*Parsons v. Davies*, November 18, 1982, McCowan J. (unrep.)). The jurisdiction of the Court was exercised either upon an application for a rule calling upon the solicitor to show cause why he should not be struck off the roll, or for a rule calling upon him to answer matters alleged in an affidavit supporting the application. Sections 51 *et seq.* of the 1974 Act set out the present procedure. The misconduct complained of need not be of a pecuniary nature and need not have direct relation to his character as a solicitor: any such offence as makes a person guilty of it unfit to remain a member of the profession is ground for striking him off the roll (*Re Blake* (1860) 3 E. & E. 34; *Re Weare* [1893] 2 Q.B. 439). A solicitor found guilty of a criminal offence will not as a matter of course be struck off: the nature of the offence will be inquired into (*Re Blake*; *Re Weare*; *Re Cooper* (1898) 67 L.J.Q.B. 176).

The Court can only entertain an application under ss.50 and 51of the Solicitors Act 1974, to strike solicitors off the roll when it is made by counsel. The Court undoubtedly had jurisdiction to entertain an application if supported by counsel, but it was not obliged to do so. It did not have jurisdiction to entertain an application made by an applicant in person, and even if it did, that discretion should not be exercised save in an exceptional case. *Per* Stuart-Smith L.J. in *Re Solicitors, Ex p. Peasegood* [1994] 1 All E.R. 298, DC.

Mortgage frauds committed by solicitors will not be tolerated by the profession. Such conduct is professional suicide, leading to striking off (*Re A Solicitor, The Times*, June 20, 1991).

A solicitor who lapsed from the standard of integrity, probity and complete trustworthiness required by his membership of the Profession had to expect that severe sanctions would be imposed on him. The fundamental purpose in making disciplinary orders was not primarily punitive or deterrent, but to maintain a well founded confidence among members of the public that any solicitor whom they might instruct would be of unquestionable integrity and trustworthiness (*Bolton v. The Law Society, The Times*, December 8, 1993, CA).

It is a matter of public policy that a collateral attack on a criminal conviction (for dishonesty) by way of civil proceedings amounts to an abuse of process unless fresh evidence, obtained after conviction, is of such probative value that it justifies an exception being made (*Re a Solicitor, The Times*, March 18, 1996, *per* Lord Taylor of Gosforth C.J.).

Jurisdiction to order the solicitor to compensate others for his neglect or misconduct in proceedings before the Court

7C–210   See notes as to Wasted Costs and the Court's inherent jurisdiction, CPR 48.7.

Solicitor acting in proceedings without authority

A solicitor warrants his authority to take any positive step which he takes in the **7C–211** action. He warrants his authority to issue the claim, to put in a defence or any other positive step. If he has no authority, even if he does not know that he has no authority, it is likely that he is personally liable. *Quaere* whether a solicitor is to be treated as continuing to warrant his authority whilst he is "inert" (*Geraldo Orchestras Ltd v. Sarl Dale*, October 16, 1991, CA (unrep.)). Solicitors may be ordered to pay personally the costs of proceedings taken by them without a client's authority. This principle applies where proceedings are instituted without authority or acknowledgment of service is served (*Re Gray* (1891) 65 L.T. 743; *The Neptune* [1919] P. 17) or the proceedings are defended without authority or an authority once given comes to an end. For example, the claimant may be non-existent (*Simmons v. Liberal Opinion Ltd* [1911] 1 K.B. 966) or may die (*Tetlow v. Orela Ltd* [1920] 2 Ch. 24) or may be a minor (*Geilinger v. Gibbs* [1897] 1 Ch. 479) or may be or become of unsound mind (*Yonge v. Toynbee* [1910] 1 K.B. 210, CA) or may be a limited company which has no directors properly appointed or other officers capable of giving instructions to institute proceedings (see *West End Hotels Syndicate v. Bayer* (1912) 29 T.L.R. 92) or the instructions may have come from minority directors (*Fergus Navigation Co. v. Kingdon* (1861) 4 L.T. 262) or directors not properly appointed (*John Morley Building Co v. Barras* [1891] 2 Ch. 386) or dissident directors acting *mala fide* (*Marshall's Valve Gear Co v. Manning Wardle & Co* [1909] 1 Ch. 267). The jurisdiction exists even where the solicitor bona fide believes he has authority and if there is a substantial dispute as to the facts, may in a proper case leave the party asking for costs to bring his action for damages for breach of warranty of authority (*Yonge v. Toynbee*). Usually it will, if necessary inquire or direct an inquiry into the facts—for example, whether a claimant, alleged to be of unsound mind, was capable of instructing a solicitor (see *Pomery v. Pomery* [1909] W.N. 158); for if the proceedings are unauthorised they should be stayed. There is even authority for the proposition that a solicitor wilfully bringing an action without authority may be attached or committed (2 Hawkins P.C. II, Chap. 22, s.6; *Re Stuckey* (1791) 2 Cox 283). In *Babury Ltd v. London Industrial plc* (1989), 189 New L.J. 1596, solicitors were ordered to pay costs where they had pursued in good faith an action on behalf of a company which had been dissolved. Similar principles apply in the case of a parent agent (*Bell Fruit Manufacturing Co v. Twin Falcon* [1995] F.S.R. 144, Ford J.).

The want of authority of the claimant's solicitor cannot be raised as a defence: it should be raised promptly to avoid the answer that it was ratified (*Reynolds v. Howell* (1873) L.R. 8 Q.B. 398 at 400; *Danish Mercantile Co v. Beaumont* [1951] 1 All E.R. 925) and should be made by application (*Russian, etc., Bank v. Comptoir de Mulhouse* [1925] A.C. 112) to a Master in the Chancery Division and a Master in the QBD Nevertheless if in the course of an action the Court becomes aware that the claimant is incapable of giving any retainer at all, it will not allow the action to proceed (*Daimler Co Ltd v. Continental Tyre & Rubber, etc., Ltd* [1916] 2 A.C. 307 at 337).

There are no conceivable circumstances in which it would be proper for a solicitor who has acted for a defendant in criminal proceedings, the retainer having been terminated, to then act for a co-defendant where there is a cut-throat defence between the two defendants. *Per* Lord Donaldson M.R. in *Saminadhen v. Khan* [1992] 1 All E.R. 963, CA.

The ordinary practice is to serve the application on the opposing party as well as the solicitor responsible, and, where the want of authority is that of the claimant's solicitor, asking that the action may be stayed or dismissed and that the solicitor do pay the costs of the claimant and of the defendant on the indemnity basis. If the want of authority only relates to one claimant that party's name should be struck out (see *Fricker v. Van Grutten* [1896] 2 Ch. 649, CA). But if the want of authority can and should be cured, the Court will, in a proper case, only stay the proceedings *Cooper v. Dummett* [1930] W.N. 248). If it is an acknowledgment of service which was served without authority, it will be vacated. The application may be made at any stage in the proceedings—for example, after the action has been discontinued (*Gold Reefs of Western Australia Ltd v. Dawson* [1897] 1 Ch. 115) or at the conclusion of the trial (*Simmons v. Liberal Opinion*, above) or to strike out the applicant's name from a final order (*Re Savage* (1880) 15 Ch D 557).

See *Waugh v. H. B. Clifford & Sons Ltd* [1982] Ch. 374; [1982] 1 All E.R. 1095, where the Court of Appeal held that solicitors, without express or implied authority to bind their client to the terms of a compromise of an action, had ostensible authority to do so.

Where a solicitor has apparent and ostensible authority to compromise a claim for compensation, a compromise achieved by the solicitor is binding on the client. If the solicitor has acted without instructions from the client to do so the client has a remedy against the solicitor (*Harford v. Birmingham City Council* (1993) 66 P. & C.R. 468, Land Tribunal).

Other improper proceedings

7C–212   Similarly a solicitor may be ordered to pay the costs where the proceedings are not genuinely brought in the client's interest, as for example where they are so frivolous and vexatious that they could not have been brought in expectation of a favourable result, or are controlled by the solicitor who has given his client an indemnity, or a commission on the proceeds, or are brought solely for the solicitor's purposes (see *Cockle v. Whiting* (1829) 1 R. & M. 43; *Re Jones* (1870) L.R. 6 Ch.App. 497; *Harbin v. Masterman* [1896] 1 Ch. 351; *Danzey v. Metropolitan Bank* (1912) 28 T.L.R. 327). A person who takes advantage of a right of appeal conferred by statute cannot be said to be behaving disgracefully or deserving of moral condemnation so as to justify an order for costs against him on the indemnity basis, merely because the appeal has no chance of success. In the case of such an appeal the respondent's remedy is to apply for an order to strike it out or to apply for an order for security for costs or both (*Burgess v. Stafford Hotel Ltd* [1990] 1 W.L.R. 1215, CA). Over vigorous conduct of breach of confidence actions is different in nature from overt or deliberate dishonesty in the prosecution of an action and does not attract assessment on a higher basis (*Berkeley Administration v. McClelland* [1990] 2 Q.B. 407). It is not to the point that the action is speculative: "if a solicitor heard of an injury to a client and honestly took pains to inform himself whether there was a *bona fide* cause of action, it was consistent with the honour of the profession that the solicitor should take up the action" per Lord Russell of Killowen in (*Ladd v. London Road Car Co, The Times*, March 24, 1900; *Rich v. Cook* (1900) 110 L.T.J. 94, CA; and see *Abraham v. Jutsun* [1963] 1 W.L.R. 658; [1963] 2 All E.R. 402, CA). In *Re Trepca Mines Ltd.* [1963] Ch. 199, CA, it was held that a solicitor retained to conduct litigation on the ordinary terms is not debarred from acting or claiming his remuneration if he knew that his client had made a champertous agreement to share the proceeds with another; but if he actively participated in the illegal transaction he cannot recover his remuneration, enforce a charging order on a fund recovered, nor claim his disbursements.

Where a lay client instructs solicitors to take no action in respect of an appeal and not to communicate with the Court, the solicitors, as officers of the Court, should either come off the record or inform the Court of that situation (*Grosvenor Mayfair Estates Ltd v. Raja, The Times*, November 2, 1990, CA).

Jurisdiction to enforce undertakings given by solicitors

7C–213   The Court has jurisdiction to enforce an undertaking given by a solicitor in his capacity as solicitor, even though it was not given directly or indirectly to a Court or in the presence of the Court or to a party to a suit, and was not embodied in any order, and was not given to the solicitor's own client, and even though the solicitor has ceased to act for his client, and whether or not the undertaking was gratuitous, and though no dishonourable conduct on the part of the solicitor is involved (*United Mining & Finance Corporation Ltd v. Becher* [1910] 2 K.B. 296, and cases there cited). The ground for the exercise of the jurisdiction is that the solicitor is an officer of the Court, and it is therefore no answer that an action could not be maintained against him by reason of the Statute of Frauds (*Evans v. Duncombe* (1831) 1 Cr. & J. 372; *Re Greaves* (1827) 374n.) though the Limitation Act may be a good answer (*Re Kerly, Son & Verden* [1901] 1 Ch. 467 at 472, and see *The Ring* [1931] P. 58). So, for example, the Court will enforce an undertaking to pay money (*Re Hilliard* (1891) 2 D. & L. 919) or to repay costs if an appeal succeeds or to stamp documents (*Re Coolgardie Goldfields* [1900] 1 Ch. 475). Even where the solicitor makes a mere statement to the other party in legal proceedings that he is holding money available to meet a certain claim, he has been held liable to pay it over (*Ex p. Hales* [1907] 2 K.B. 539).

But the Court may in its discretion relieve the solicitor from his undertaking and decline to enforce it (see *United Mining, etc., Ltd v. Becher* (1910)) as, for example, if it was given by mistake (*Mullins v. Howell* (1879) 11 Ch D 763) or in ignorance of facts known to the other side (see *Wade v. Simeon* (1843) 13 M. & W. 647); but it will not as a rule excuse a solicitor from an undertaking made in the mistaken belief that he had authority (see *The Gertrud* [1927] W.N. 265) especially if another party relied upon it.

The Court will not enforce an undertaking which has become impossible of performance so that the solicitor cannot realistically be expected to carry it out, but in such circumstance the Court may order the solicitor to compensate a person who has suffered loss in consequence of the failure to implement the undertaking (*Udall v. Capri Lighting Ltd* [1988] Q.B. 907, CA), see also *Bentley v. Gaisford* [1997] 2 W.L.R. 401, CA (solicitor holding documents to the order of another solicitor to preserve their lien—breach of undertaking to photocopy the documents for the client). There is no general principle under which a solicitor may rid himself of liability for an undertaking by notifying the recipient of a change in circumstances. It was for the solicitors to satisfy themselves that they could safely give the undertaking: *Hole & Pugsley v. Sumption, The Times,* January 29, 2002, Hart J.

Undertakings given by a solicitor in a transaction which was part of the normal business of a solicitor are enforceable against the firm of solicitors for whom he works (*United Bank of Kuwait v. Hammand; City Trust Ltd. v. Levy* (1988) 1 W.L.R. 1051, CA; [1988] 3 All E.R. 418).

Where a solicitor gives an undertaking, but not in the capacity as a solicitor, the court has no inherent jurisdiction to enforce the undertaking. In the particular case the solicitor had had no ostensible authority to bind the partnership and the undertaking could not therefore be enforced against a partner: *Ruparel v. Awan* [2001] Lloyds Rep. 258, David Donaldson QC.

A solicitor who gives an undertaking as a reply to a requisition on title that he will discharge all subsisting charges is bound by the undertaking to discharge a local land charge if his client fails to discharge it (*Bray v. Stuart A. West & Co* (1989) 139 New L.J. 753). An unconditional undertaking to be responsible for the costs of another solicitor could not be impugned on the sole ground of bad faith in that other solicitor's lay client; merely to act for a client could not give rise to an implied guarantee of the client's probity (*Rooks Rider (a firm) v. J. R. Steel* [1993] 4 All E.R. 716, Knox J.).

The application

This must be made by the person to whom the undertaking was given and, if the **7C–214** undertaking was given in proceedings, should be made to the Division in which the proceedings took place (see *Re Garland* (1818) 6 Dowl. 512) Breach of undertaking is enforceable by committal. Service of an order embodying an undertaking given in Court is not a necessary preliminary (*Re Launder* (1908) 98 L.T. 554). An undertaking given in a non-contentious matter may be enforced by a single judge (*Re A Solicitor* [1969] 1 W.L.R. 1068, DC).

In *Re A Solicitor* [1966] 1 W.L.R. 1604, Pennycuick J. stated: "No case has been cited in which the Court has made an order for committal upon a direct application to commit for breach of a solicitor's undertaking, without first having made an order to perform the undertaking, but that is not to say that there is no jurisdiction to make such an order." The summary procedure, by which the Court can in the exercise of its discretion control the conduct of solicitors as officers of the Court, should only be invoked in clear cases where there has been a breach of an undertaking by a solicitor in his capacity as a solicitor and if the case is not clear, *e.g.* where there are matters in dispute, the Court should leave the complainant to another mode of action in which there would be an opportunity for oral evidence and cross-examination (*Geoffrey Silver and Drake (a firm) v. Baines* [1971] 1 Q.B. 396, CA).

Jurisdiction to order payment of money and delivery up of papers

The Court has an inherent jurisdiction over a solicitor, as its officer, to order him **7C–215** summarily to deliver up money and documents received by him as a solicitor, if he has no lien thereon (*Ex p. Cobeldick* (1883) 12 QBD 149). But if there is a bona fide dispute as to the right to hold the papers, it has been said that the applicant should be left to his remedy by action (*Ex p. Cobeldick*, per Bowen L.J. (1883) 12 QBD 149 at 150). The usual practice, however, is to apply for the common order for detailed assessment of costs and delivery up of all papers upon payment by the client of what is due from him. There is also the express jurisdiction under RSC 106, to make a summary order against the solicitor for delivery of a cash account and the payment of moneys or delivery of securities. The Court may under that rule provide for detailed assessment of costs, and payment or security for the costs, and may provide for the protection of the solicitor's lien.

Note —An agreement between solicitors and a non-solicitor party to share the fees earned by the former in consideration for the introduction of clients by the latter, who would also provide associated services, is contrary to the Solicitors Practice Rules 1990, rr.3–7 made under the Solicitors Act 1974, s.31 and is illegal and unenforceable; however, although no claim in restitution can be made by the non-solicitor party for the recovery of the shared fees, he may bring a *quantum meruit* claim in respect of the services he had performed (*Mohamed v. Alaga & Co* [1999] 3 All E.R. 699, CA, *sub nom. Mohammed v. Alaga & Co, The Times,* July 29, 1999, CA).

Financial Services Act 1986

7C–216   Solicitors knowingly concerned in contraventions of certain sections of the 1986 Act can be ordered by the Court under ss.6(2) and 61(1) to repay sums lost by investors (*Securities and Instruments Board v. Pantell, The Times,* August 13, 1991).

2. RIGHTS, PRIVILEGES AND AGENCY OF SOLICITORS

Authority of solicitors

In litigation

7C–217   A clear authority is required to justify a solicitor in issuing a claim or acknowledging service of proceedings (*Wright v. Castle* (1817) 3 Mer. 12; *Re Gray* (1891) 65 L.T. (n.s.) 743) and see para. 7C–211. But once retained "the attorney is the general agent of the client in all matters which may reasonably be expected to arise for decision in the cause" (*Prestwich v. Poley* (1865) 18 C.B. (n.s.) 806 at 816). The solicitor has a general control and authority over the procedure in the action (*Prestwich v. Poley,* at 813, above) and a solicitor has a general authority to compromise an action, provided he acts bona fide and reasonably and not in defiance of the client's express instructions (*ibid., Re Newen* [1903] 1 Ch. 812 at 818; *Little v. Spreadbury* [1910] 2 K.B. 658). And see *Waugh v. H. B. Clifford & Sons Ltd* [1982] Ch. 374; [1984] 1 All E.R. 1095. But a solicitor, retained to bring an action, has no implied authority to compromise it before issue of a claim (*Macauley v. Polley* [1897] 2 Q.B. 122) and it is doubtful if he has authority to compromise a judgment which he has obtained for his client; certainly he has no authority to do so by entering into a deed of arrangement with the debtor, trustee and other creditors (*Re a Debtor* [1914] 2 K.B. 758).

Solicitor is agent for his client and owes no duty to anybody except his principals

7C–218   The relationship of solicitor and client includes that of agent and principal, where a solicitor receives clients' money it must be kept in a separate account, the solicitor may therefore also be considered to hold the money as trustee.

   A solicitor instructed by an insurance company to represent a party is bound to act in the common interest of the insurer and insured, and has no authority to admit the negligence of the client contrary to the fact (*Groom v. Crocker* [1939] 1 K.B. 194).

   The solicitor has a duty independent of counsel to protect the interest of a client and that duty may require the instruction of different counsel if it appears that the clients interests are not being fully protected because counsel is incompetent (*Re A. (A Minor)* (1988) 138 New L.J. 79, CA).

   In ordinary conveyancing transactions a vendor's solicitor does not owe a duty of care to a purchaser (*Gran Gelato v. Richcliff (Group)* [1992] Ch. 560).

   If a solicitor acts for both parties in a transaction, that does not alter his duty to each client, the proper course being to refuse to act for one client because his duty to the first might involve him in a breach of duty to the second by disclosing information he had received in confidence. If he does act for both he is under a duty to advise on the basis of all the knowledge he possesses (*Neushul v. Mellish and Harkavy* (1966) 111 S.J. 399). See *R. v. Gregson* (1980) 124 S.J. 497, where the Court of Appeal held it was doubted whether the judge had any right to inquire into the solicitor's behaviour. There is no general rule that solicitors who act for a client can never thereafter act for another client against the former client. But if it could be reasonably anticipated that there was a danger that information gained while acting for the former client could be used against him, solicitors would not be permitted to act (*Re A Firm of Solicitors* [1992] 1 All E.R. 353, CA).

   Solicitors cannot properly act for both sides in a property development transaction. They are under a duty to inform one client that they already acted for the other and could not act for him, and that he should seek legal advice from other solicitors. It is the solicitor's duty to act in his clients' best interests and not do anything likely to damage those interest as far as was consistent with the Solicitors Professional Duty. To disclosure discreditable facts about a client and to do so without the client's informed consent was likely to be a breach of duty, even if the facts were in the public domain. On the facts of the case disclosure by the solicitors of their original client's past would have been a breach of their duty to him. The House of Lords found that the Court of Appeal was wrong to hold that the solicitor's retainer by the second client contained an implied exclusion from the duty of disclosure. Such an implied term would not satisfy the test for implied terms and would have amounted to the client agreeing that, because its solicitors had failed in their duty to tell him to take separate advice, and had instead proceeded to act for him as well as for their original client in a matter in which they had a financial duty, their duty to the second client had to be curtailed in order to accommodate their first breach of duty. The notion that one breach of duty by the solicitor should exonerate them in respect of a subsequent more serious breach was contrary to common sense and justice: *Hilton v. Barker Booth and Eastwood* [2005] UKHL February 3, 2005 .

When a client in full command of his faculties and apparently aware of what he was doing sought assistance of a solicitor in the carrying out of a particular transaction, that solicitor was under no duty whether before or after accepting instructions to go beyond those instructions by proffering unsought advice on the wisdom of the transaction (*Clark Boyce v. Mouat* [1993] 4 All E.R. 268, PC).

A Solicitor acting for both lender and borrower in a conveyance owes a duty to both to protect their interests and must inform both of information which puts him on enquiry as to the accuracy of a valuation (*Mortgage Express v. Bowerman & Partners (a firm), The Times*, May 19, 1994, Arden J.). A solicitor acting on behalf of joint clients one of whom is not contractually bound to pay the solicitor is in serious breach of duty in withholding information from that client and acting on instruction from one to the detriment of the other (*Perry v. Edwin Coe (a firm), Independent*, April 1, 1994, Harman J.).

Where an agent entered into an unauthorised agreement in relation to legal fees on behalf of his principals, but had passed a copy of the solicitor's letter to the principals, the court held that, whilst it would be slow to conclude that an unauthorised act by an agent had been ratified by the principal when the only evidence of ratification was silence and/or inactivity of the principal, to any objective observer the principal's conduct could only be rationally explained by their acceptance of the unauthorised agreement made by the agent on their behalf. The solicitor's fees having been agreed by the agent, there was no obligation upon them to prove or justify the amount of their fees and they were entitled to sue for the balance on the basis of the agreement reached and without recourse to s.57 of the 1974 Act: *Lass Salt Garvin v. Pommeroy & Ors* [2003] EWHC 1007 (QB), Richard Fernyhough QC.

Client's privilege where fraud suspected

Where a solicitor suspects that client's assets have been obtained by fraudulent means he can apply to the High Court for administrative directions (*Finers (A firm) v. Miro* [1991] 1 W.L.R. 35).   **7C–219**

Solicitors' confidentiality—where partners act on his behalf

Where a consultant retains partners to act on his behalf, the duty to disclose information overrides the duty of confidentiality (*Moser v. Cotton* (1990) 140 New. L.J. 1313, CA).   **7C–220**

Authority to receive money

A solicitor has no general authority to receive money on behalf of his client. But it may be implied—for example, where the solicitor has applied for payment on his client's instructions, or is acting for the client in litigation (see *Powell v. Little* (1746–1779) 1 W. Bl. 8; *Mason v. Whitehouse* (1838) 4 Bing. N.C. 692; *Wilmot v. Smith* (1828) 3 C. & P. 453); and in the latter case he may receive it before or after judgment (*Bevins v. Hulme* (1846) 15 M. & W. 88 (1846) 95–6). But he has no general authority to receive it by cheque (*Blumberg v. Life, etc., Society* [1897] 1 Ch. 171; [1898] 1 Ch. 27) or where the client is a minor or a patient (see *Leather v. Kirby* [1965] 3 All E.R. 927n., HL).   **7C–221**

Right of audience of solicitors

The (Courts and Legal Services Act 1990, ss.27 and 28) makes provision with re-   **7C–222** spect to rights of audience and rights to conduct litigation. These provisions are also applicable to persons who are neither solicitors not barristers. The rights may be granted by the appropriate authorised body, *i.e.* the General Council of the Bar (in respect of rights of audience); the Law Society, and any professional or other body which has been designated as an authorised body (in respect of both rights).

The Lord Chancellor and the four Designated Judges (under s.119 of the Courts and Legal Services Act 1990) decided to extend rights of audience to solicitors in the higher courts. As a result of this the Law Society introduced new Practice Rules namely: r.16A (solicitors acting as advocates) and r.16B (choice of advocate) (see paras 7C–165 and 7C–166), also issued by the Law Society are the code for advocacy and guidance on choice of advocates.

The Higher Courts Qualifications Regulations 2000 are designed to extend solicitors' rights of audience to the higher courts. Solicitors may qualify for higher audience rights by completing various courses of training and assessment in procedure, evidence, ethics and advocacy skills and also acquire requisite experience. It is no longer necessary to have three year post qualification experience before attaining higher courts advocacy rights. Those solicitors who have at least three years post qualification experience will qualify if they can satisfy the Law Society that through their level of experience they have acquired the requisite understanding of the procedure, evidence and ethics applicable to the higher courts. They must also complete an assessment in advocacy skills (after November 1, 2005 this route will no longer be available). Those more senior solicitors with sufficient advocacy and judicial experience may obtain exemption from the Law Society from all training courses and assessment (this route will not be available after November 1, 2005).

7C–223   Under section 36 of the Access to Justice Act 1999 implemented on September 27, 1999, all solicitors have full rights of audience on admission to the Roll. Only those solicitors with higher courts qualification will have rights of audience in the higher courts.

The Chartered Institute of Patent Agents and the Institute of Legal Executives have both been designated authorised bodies to grant rights of audience to members. See Chartered Institute of Patent Agents Order 1999 (S.I. 1999 No. 3137), and Institute of Legal Executives Order 1999 (S.I. 1999 No. 1077).

As to rights of audience in Chambers under s.27(2)(e) of the Courts and Legal Services Act 1990 the Court has no discretion to exclude an individual without legal qualifications who falls within the ambit of the section: *Re H-S (Minors) (Chambers proceedings rights of audience)*, The Times, February 20, 1998, CA.

In relation to the immunity of advocates (both counsel and solicitors) the House of Lords has decided that none of the reasons formerly said to justify the immunity of of advocates had sufficient weight to sustain immunity in relation to civil proceedings. The House of Lords found that powers of the courts and the CPR were such as to restrict the ability of clients to bring unmeritorious and vexatious claims against advocates and accordingly public interest in the administration of justice no longer required that advocates should enjoy immunity from suit for alleged negligence in the conduct of civil proceedings. There was a similar finding in respect of criminal proceedings. *Arthur JS Hall & Co v. Simons ; Barrett v. Woolf; Harris v. Schofield, Roberts & Hill* [2002] 1 A.C. 615, HL.

The House of Lords has held that public interest does not require advocates to be held immune from suit for the consequences of their negligence, but that interest does require that the application of the principle should not stifle advocates' independence of mind and action in the manner in which they conduct litigation and advise their clients. In a case where it was alleged that counsel had been negligent in failing to give the claimant sufficiently detailed advice in deciding whether to accept a payment into court or proceed with the claim, it was held that the advice given fell within the range of that to be expected of reasonably competent counsel of that seniority and experience. It was possible in hindsight that the advice to the claimant to proceed was a wrong decision but it was not as mistaken a decision as had been represented: *Moy v. Petman Smith & Perry* [2005] UKHL February 3, 200 5.

The London agent
7C–224   The London agent looks to the country solicitor as his principal, and there is no privity of contract between the London agent and the client. He cannot sue the client for his costs (*Scrace v. Whittington* (1823) 2 B. & C. 11) though the client may invoke against him the inherent jurisdiction of the Court over its officers. As principal the

country solicitor is liable to the client for the acts of the London agent (*Collins v. Griffin* (1734) Barnes 37; *Re Ward* (1896) 31 Beav. 1) and in his bill to his client sets out in detail the agent's charges (*Pomeroy and Tanner* [1897] 1 Ch. 284). But in regard to other parties in an action the London agent is the solicitor of the client, with the general authority of a solicitor over the procedure, including authority to compromise (*Re Newen* [1903] 1 Ch. 812) to give consent (*Withers v. Parker* (1860) 5 H. & N. 725) and to grant indulgences—except that his authority is limited by the authority of his principal, the country solicitor, and the instructions of the client. In the absence of express agreement a London agent is not entitled to share in interest paid by the client on costs (*Ward v. Lawson (No. 2)* (1872) 43 Ch D 353, CA). The London agent presents his bill to the country solicitor, and the whole or part of it can be assessed by the Court under its inherent jurisdiction (*Storer v. Johnson* (1890) 15 App. Cas. 203).

Conflict of interests

Where a firm of solicitors obtained confidential information in the course of a work- **7C–225** ing relationship with a company independent of but closely associated with a former client, some of which was relevant to an action between the claimant and the defendant, the Court granted the company and claimant (neither of which were former clients) an injunction preventing the firm from acting for the defendant (*Re A Firm of Solicitors*, [1992] 1 Q.B. 959, CA).

Where a solicitor was a member of a firm acting for claimants in an intellectual property action and left to join another firm which, some years later, was instructed by one of the defendants in the intellectual property litigation, the Court refused an application for an injunction holding that a partner in such a position could not act unless he could prove not merely that he was not in possession of any relevant confidential information but that there was no real risk that he (unwittingly) had the information. The Court did not adopt the test applied in the USA whereby a former partner would be precluded from acting on the ground that it would give rise to a possible perception of impropriety (*Re A Firm of Solicitors* [1997] Ch. 1, Lightman J.).

It is not for the judge to take a point about conflict of interest of his own motion. The essential starting point was an objection taken by another party whose interests and confidentiality needed to be protected. See *Bolkiah v. KPMG* [1992] 2 W.L.R. 215; *Hood Sail Makers Ltd v. Berthon Boat Co Ltd* [1999] EWCA Civ 1079; (1999) 149 New L.J. 529, CA.

It is for the client to establish that the solicitor is in possession of potentially relevant information and for the solicitor to establish the heavy burden of showing that there is no risk of inadvertent disclosure. *Re: Firm of Solicitors* [2000] 1 Lloyd's Rep. 31, *per* Timothy Walker, J.

It is beyond doubt that communications by a client to her solicitor are of a confidential nature. Therefore conclusions reached by the solicitor from that information are also confidential. It is not open to a solicitor without the client's consent to communicate information passed by that client to a solicitor involved under another retainer. The mere fact that two solicitors were employed on different matters by the same client is insufficient to justify the passing of confidential information from one solicitor to the other. Where the client had limited intellectual capacity leading to her being unable to manage her affairs this would mean that she would be unable to relax the duty of confidence between her and her solicitor. The mere fact of low intellect cannot justify a breach of confidence. The solicitor's duty of confidence is absolute unless there has been some relaxation by law or by the client: *Marsh v. Sofaer (Application to Strike Out)* [2003] EWHC 3264 (Ch) Sir Andrew Morritt V.C.

Kinds of solicitors' liens

There are two common law rights of solicitors, known as liens. One is the "general" **7C–226** or "retaining lien"—the right of the solicitor to retain all papers or other chattels of his client, which come into his possession as the client's solicitor, until all his costs and charges as solicitors are paid. The other is a "lien" over any property, except real property, recovered or preserved, or any judgment obtained, for the client by his exertions in litigation. It is a *particular* lien, and does not extend to any of his costs except the costs of recovering or preserving that property or obtaining that judgment. It is not a mere right of retention: it extends to property which is not in the solicitor's possession, and includes a right to the intervention of the Court for its protection. And it is in effect extended by the power given to the Court by s.73 of the Solicitors Act 1974, to make an order charging property (including real property) for his asessed costs of the proceedings.

There is no reason in principle why the court is not able to interfere in the enforcement of the common law lien on equitable principles even where it is the client and not the solicitor who has terminated the retainer. The court must be satisfied that there are matters affecting the relationship between the solicitor and the client which, as a matter of conscience, make it inappropriate for the client to continue and be enforced in particular circumstances: *Slatter v. Ronaldsons* [2001] EWHC Ch; December 14, 2001, Patten, J.

General or retaining lien

7C–227　　This extends to all papers or other chattels of his client (with certain exceptions) which come into his possession as the client's solicitor, and it is available in respect of all costs of the solicitor whether statute-barred or not (*Re Broomhead* (1847) 5 Dow. & L. 52; *Curwen v. Milburn* (1889) 42 Ch D 424; *Re Margetts* [1896] 2 Ch. 263). It applies in divorce as well as other proceedings (*Hughes v. Hughes* [1958] P. 224, CA). It applies to money held in client accounts and the Court may order the release of money from the client account to enable the solicitors to recoup their costs (*Prekookeanska Plovidba v. L.N.T. Lines SrL.* [1988] 3 All E.R. 897). It avails only against the client and therefore gives the solicitor no greater rights against a third person than the client has. It is not destroyed by the bankruptcy or winding up of the client (*Re Meter Cabs Ltd* [1911] 2 Ch. 557) or the death of either party. Nor does it cease when the solicitor ceases to be the solicitor in the action, unless he is discharged by the client for misconduct. If he discharges himself he may be ordered to deliver up the papers to the new solicitor on the latter undertaking to hold them without prejudice to his lien and to return them intact after the action is over and allow the former solicitor access to them in the meantime (*Robins v. Goldingham* (1872) L.R. 13 Eq. 440), see also *Gamlen Chemical Co (U.K.) Ltd v. Rochem Ltd* [1980] 1 W.L.R. 614; [1980] 1 All E.R. 1049. The court does have the power to override a solicitor's lien where the client has terminated the retainer as opposed to where the solicitor has discharged himself. the court has discretion under CPR 25.1(1)(m). *Paragon Finance Plc v. Rosling King*, May 26, 2000, *per* Hart J. The claimants terminated their solicitors' retainer and sought delivery up of documents. The solicitors retained the documents under their lien pending payment of outstanding fees. The court refused to make an order for delivery up of the documents on payment of the balance of the fees into court on the basis that the only possible prejudice to the claimant was the possibility of not being able to recover any overpayment it was found to have made. The court found there was no reason to suppose that the solicitors would not be able to repay the amount of any overpayment and the balance came down in favour of not making the order. In the absence of convincing evidence of the solicitors' inability to repay any overpayment, the claimant in fact suffered no prejudice if the court made no order: *Paragon Finance Plc v. Rosling King* [2001] E.W. Ch. June 12, Hart J. The overriding principle is that the Court should make such order as is most conclusive to the interests of justice by weighing up (a) the fact that the litigant should not be deprived of material relevant to the conduct of his case and (b) that litigation should be conducted with due regard to the interests of the court's own officers who should not be left without payment for what was justly due to them (*Ismail v. Richards Butler*, [1996] 3 W.L.R. 129 , Moore-Bick J. The lien is discharged by payment of the costs, by the solicitor parting with the papers except for a limited purpose (*e.g.* to enable a conveyance to be executed) or by waiver (*e.g.* where he acts for his client in obtaining a loan on the documents, *Fitzgerald v. Bermingham* (1842) 1 Con. & Law. 405; or takes security for his costs (*Re Morris* [1908] 1 K.B. 473, CA). In *Caldwell v. Sumpters (a firm)* [1971] 3 W.L.R. 748; [1971] 3 All E.R. 780, it was held that where solicitors who claimed a lien on certain deeds sent them to their clients' new solicitors with a letter saying they were being sent on the understanding that "you will hold them to our order pending payment of our fees etc.", and the new solicitors replied that they were unable to accede to the request either to hold the deeds to the order of the former solicitors or to give undertakings mentioned, the solicitors had lost their lien, but this decision was reversed by the Court of Appeal (see [1972] Ch. 478); [1972] 1 All E.R. 567). An application pursuant to s.236 of the Insolvency Act 1986 by the clients receivers for papers was successful, and the lien did not extend to those papers as the receivers were third parties in the proceedings (*Re Aveling Barford Ltd* [1989] 1 W.L.R. 360). The arrest of the clients' vessel did not amount to waiver of a solicitor's lien by taking alternative security (*A. v. B.* [1984] 1 All E.R. 265 , Leggatt J.) and the general practice of ordering papers to be handed over when the solicitors discharge themselves from their retainer would not be followed by the Court automatically but regard should be had to the conduct of the parties and the interests of justice.

A solicitor's lien will be allowed over documents such as debentures and land charges which confer title to property despite the company from whom the documents have been received being in liquidation. Section 246 of the Insolvency Act 1986 connotes the manner or capacity in which the documents must be held so as to confer a lien, it does not require that the document should be held in a capacity which confers a propriety interest in the underlying property (*Brereton v. Nicholls* [1993] BCLC 593, Morritt J.).

Although the Court has power to grant relief in equity against retention of papers by solicitors, there is a discretion, where to do so would in reality diminish the value of the solicitors' lien, to require the client to provide some security for the solicitors' claim for costs (*Ismail v. Richards Butler* [1996] 3 W.L.R. 129).

Even where the client has terminated the retainer the court may interfere with the solicitor's lien on an equitable basis but must be satisfied that there are matters affecting the solicitor client relationship which make it inappropriate for the lien to be enforced. For matters to be relevant to the exercise of this jurisdiction they must either go to the state of the account between the solicitor and client or to the effect on the client of not having access to his papers. The court is precluded by authority from ordering delivery up simply because of the prejudice to the client in the conduct of litigation: *Slatter v. Ronaldsons* [2001] All E.R. (D) 251 (Dec), Patten J.

The lien on property recovered or preserved

A solicitor has at common law, and apart from any order of the Court or statute, a **7C–228** "lien" over property recovered or preserved or the proceeds of any judgment obtained (*Ex p. Morrison* (1868) L.R. 4 Q.B. 153 at 156, *per* Blackburn J.) for the client by his exertions in litigation (*Rhodes v. Sugden* (1886) 34 Ch D 155 at 157—not in mere negotiation, *Meguerditchian v. Lightbound* [1917] 1 K.B. 297; [1917] 2 K.B. 298). It is not a mere lien, but a claim to the equitable interference of the Court to protect the solicitor (*Barker v. St. Quintin* (1844) 12 M. & W. 441; *Ross v. Buxton* (1889) 42 Ch D 190 at 200). It is a *particular* lien, and is only available for the costs of recovering and preserving the property in question (*Bozon v. Bollard* (1839) 4 My. & Cr. 354; *Smith v. Betty* [1903] 2 K.B. 317, CA) and the costs of establishing and protecting the right to the lien (*Lucas v. Peacock* (1846) 9 Beav. 177; *Re Meter Cabs Ltd* [1911] 2 Ch. 557). It is available though the right to recover the costs may be statute-barred (*Higgins v. Scott* (1831) 2 B. & Ad. 413).

The reference to "property" in s.73 of the 1974 Act is to be interpreted as including property of every kind including a chose in action and as such, includes an order for costs where those costs have not been assessed. The Court has jurisdiction under s.73 of the 1974 Act to make a charging order in favour of a firm of solicitors over costs recoverable in an action by a client company notwithstanding that the order for costs itself incorporates no direction providing for the detailed assessment of the costs in the absence of agreement and the costs have not in any event been assessed (*Fairfold Properties Ltd v. Exmouth Docks Company Ltd (No. 2)* [1993] 2 W.L.R. 241).

Property to which it applies

The lien attaches to all property except real property (*Shaw v. Neale* (1858) 6 **7C–229** H.L.Cas. 581)— *e.g.* money payable under a judgment or award (*Jones v. Turnbull* (1837) 2 M. & W. 601; *Macfarlane v. Lister* (1887) 37 Ch D 88 at 95) including costs (*Aspinal v. Stamp* (1824) 3 B. & C. 108) the proceeds of an execution in the sheriff's hands (*Re Bank of Hindustan* (1867) L.R. 3 Ch. 125) money paid into Court (*Hall v. Hall* [1891] P. 302, CA; *Emden v. Carte* (1881) 19 Ch D 311) or money payable under a compromise (*Ross v. Buxton* (1889) 42 Ch D 190 at 195). The lien gives the solicitor no greater rights than his client has (*Re Harrald* (1884) 53 L.J.Ch. 505; *Re Union Cement, etc., Co* (1872) 26 L.T. 240) and is subject to all equities between his client and other parties interested in the property (*Taylor v. Popham* (1808) 15 Ves. 72). So, for example, a set-off for damages or costs between the parties may be allowed, notwithstanding the solicitor's lien (*Edwards v. Hope* (1885) 14 QBD 922; *Blakey v. Latham* (1889) 41 Ch D 518). As regards damages, the set-off may be allowed in respect of different actions (*Goodfellow v. Gray* [1899] 2 Q.B. 498; compare *Ward v. Haddrill* [1904] 1 K.B. 399); and as regards costs, although, as a general rule, the set-off is only available in respect of costs incurred in the same proceedings, the Court has a discretion to allow a set-off of costs of independent proceedings where it is just as between the parties themselves to allow it, and no fraud or collusion has been practised by them upon the solicitor (*Knight v. Knight* [1925] 1 Ch. 835; and see CPR 44.3(9)). In proceedings under s.17 of the M. W. P. Act 1882, a wife obtained a garnishee order absolute in respect of her costs of the proceedings against proceeds of sale of property in the husband's solicitors' hands. The latters' claim to a lien in respect of their own costs against the husband was upheld (*Walters v. D. Miles-Griffiths & Co.* (1964) 108 S.J. 561, CA). Funds held in a solicitors' client account could not be attached for enforcement purposes to the extent that the solicitors' lien for costs applied to them (*Prekookeanska Plovidba v. L.N.T. Lines SrL.* [1988] 3 All E.R. 897).

Effect of compromise of proceedings

7C–230   The solicitor's lien is normally subject to the compromise of the suit, and the Court will not interfere to preserve it if the compromise is bona fide (*M'Pherson v. Allsop* (1839) 8 L.J.Ex. 262; *Quested v. Callis* (1842) 1 Dowl. (n.s.) 888; *Ex p. Morrison* (1868) L.R. 4 Q.B. 153; *The Paris* [1896] P. 77; *Moxon v. Sheppard* (1890) 24 QBD 627). But if the compromise is collusive, entered into for the purpose of depriving the solicitor of his lien, the Court will interfere to protect it (*Chapman v. Haw* (1808) Taunt. 341; *Reynolds v. Reynolds* (1909) 26 T.L.R. 104, CA) and on summary application by the solicitor may order either of the parties to the collusive arrangement to pay his costs (*Re Williams v. Lloyd* (1864) 3 H. & C. 294; *Ex p. Morrison*; *Price v. Crouch* (1891) 60 L.J.Q.B. 767; *Re Margetson* [1897] 2 Ch. 314 at 321). And even if the compromise is bona fide, and involves payment to the claimant, and the defendant has previously received notice from the claimant's solicitor of his lien for costs, he must not pay the claimant in disregard of it (*Ross v. Buxton* (1889) 42 Ch D 190 at 202).

A solicitor may lose the lien if acting in bad faith (*Manley v. Law Society* [1981] 1 W.L.R. 335, CA; *Clark v. Clark* [1989] F.L.R. 174). Where money was held in a joint account "to abide the event", solicitors were entitled to ask the Court to grant equitable relief in the payment of money out in order to preserve their rights. Thus the solicitors had an equitable charge over the money in the joint account (*Halvanon Insurance Co Ltd v. Central Reinsurance Corp* [1988] 1 W.L.R. 1122).

Enforcement of lien

7C–231   As said above, the solicitor may give notice of his lien to the party liable to his client, who, if he nevertheless pays the client, becomes liable to the solicitor (*ibid.*; and *Ormerod v. Tate* (1801) 1 East 464; *ex p. Morrison*). If money due to the client is in the solicitor's hands, he may pay himself out of it (see *Watson v. Maskell* (1834) 1 Bing. N.C. 366. And in any case where there is a probability of his client depriving him of his costs the solicitor may apply to the Court to intervene to protect his lien (*Hough v. Edwards* (1857) 1 H. & N. 171; *Mercer v. Graves* (1872) L.R. 7 Q.B. 499) *e.g.* by granting him an injunction restraining the client from receiving payment without notice to him (*Lloyd v. Jones* (1879) 40 L.T. 514; *Hobson v. Shearwood* (1845) 8 Beav. 486) or, if there is a fund in Court, to which the client is entitled, by ordering payment of his costs out of it (*Moore v. Smith* (1851) 14 Beav. 393).

Charging order on property recovered or preserved

7C–232   In effect the solicitor's common law lien on property recovered through his exertions in litigation is extended by the power given to the Court by s.73 of the Solicitors Act 1974 to "declare the solicitor entitled to a charge on the property". Unlike the lien, it applies to real as well as personal property, but does not apply in any case where the right to recover the costs is statute-barred (see s.73).

Jurisdiction to make a charging order

7C–233   See Charging Orders Act 1979 CPR Part 73. In regard to arbitration proceedings the High Court is given jurisdiction to make the order (Arbitration Act 1950, s.18(5)). The Bankruptcy Court has power to make the order on moneys recovered or preserved in bankruptcy proceedings (*Re Wood* [1897] 1 Q.B. 314; *Re Deakin* [1900] 2 Q.B. 489; compare *Re Cook* [1899] 1 Q.B. 863) but rarely does so because of the provisions in the Insolvency Rules 1986 relating to the priority of costs and charges payable out of the bankrupt's estate (*Re Humphreys* [1898] 1 Q.B. 520, CA).

"Court ... may at any time"

7C–234   See s.73. The application for an order may be made at any time where the conditions set out in the section exist (*Harris v. Yarm* [1960] Ch. 256) and delay in applying is no ground for refusing an order unless other rights in respect of the property have arisen in the meantime (*Re Born* [1900] 2 Ch. 433). Costs judges have the powers of the Court under Pt III of the Solicitors Act 1974.

"Declare the solicitor entitled to a charge"
These words in s.73 enable the personal representative of the solicitor to obtain the order (*Baile v. Baile* (1872) L.R. 13 Eq. 497) or an assignee of the costs (*Briscoe v. Briscoe* [1892] 3 Ch. 543) but do not enable a London agent to obtain an order against the lay client (*Macfarlane v. Lister* (1887) 13 Ch D 88, CA) nor any other solicitor employed by the client's solicitor and unknown to him (*Re Beckett, Purnell v. Paine* [1918] 2 Ch. 72). And a solicitor who has ceased to act may obtain the order subject to the lien for costs of the solicitor for the time being (*Re Wadsworth* (1885) 29 Ch D 517; *Clover v. Adams* (1881) 6 QBD 622).

7C–235

"On the property recovered or preserved"
See para. 7C–229, "Property to which it applies". Property of any kind is embraced, including real property. It is a question of fact what property is "recovered or preserved" (*Rowland v. Williams* [1885] W.N. 194, CA) and the section "must be construed with reference to various classes of litigation" (*In the Estate of White* (1933) 49 T.L.R. 325 at 326). It includes an unpaid debt under a judgment or award (*Birchall v. Pugin* (1875) L.R. 10 C.P. 397; *Farrant v. Caley* [1924] W.N. 170, CA) and costs ordered to be paid by one party to the other (*Dallow v. Garrold* (1884) 14 QBD 54, and see *Re Deakin* [1900] 2 Q.B. 489) subject to the set-off provided by the rules (nowCPR 44.3(9)) and costs ordered to be repaid by the Court of Appeal as the result of an appeal (*Guy v. Churchill* (1887) 35 Ch D 489). It includes money payable on the compromise of an action (*The Paris* [1896] P. 77; *Ross v. Buxton* (1889) 42 Ch D 190; *Ratcliff v. Swift* (1888) 32 S.J. 787) including an action by an infant (*Re Wright's Trusts* [1901] 1 Ch. 317, CA). Though the amount is not ascertained it may still be a sum "recovered" (*Ross v. Buxton*; *The Paris*). The term "property recovered or preserved" includes even the interest of persons not employed by the solicitor and not parties to the suit, if they adopt the benefit obtained by the suit (*Green v. Young* (1883) 24 Ch D 545). It includes money recovered for the client by the appointment of a receiver by way of equitable execution (*Duff v. Tuite* [1914] 2 I.R. 31) when the order appointing the receiver has been completed (*Wingfield v. Wingfield* [1919] 1 Ch. 462); and also the produce of rents paid into Court by the receiver appointed in the action (*Re Knight* [1892] 2 Ch. 368 at 372) even if the proceedings are afterwards compromised (*Twynam v. Porter* (1870) L.R. 11 Eq. 181) but not if they are discontinued (see *Wingfield v. Wingfield*, above). It includes the client's interest in a fund in Court consisting of dividends payable to a company which has been wound up (*Re Born* [1900] 2 Ch. 433). Property may have been "recovered or preserved" by a judgment for foreclosure of a mortgage (*Wilson v. Round* (1863) 4 Giff. 416) and a one-third share recovered in a partition action may be charged (*Lloyd v. Jones* (1879) 27 W.R. 655). So may the amounts recovered by a receiver in a debenture-holder's action as the result of proceedings taken by his solicitors (*Re Horne & Sons Ltd.* [1906] 1 Ch. 271, and see *Re Drew* (1913) 135 L.T.J. 323). Property devised and bequeathed by a will established in a probate action (*Ex p. Tweed* [1899] 2 Q.B. 167) from the time the declaration has been made ((1933) 49 T.L.R. 460) or property recovered under a declaration of intestacy, under which the client takes a share (*In the Estate of White* (1933) 49 T.L.R. 325) may be charged under the section.

7C–236

Note —Money ordered to be paid into Court by a defendant, as a condition of leave to defend, is property "recovered or preserved" through the instrumentality of the claimant's solicitor, and he may obtain a charging order upon it (*Moxon v. Sheppard* (1890) 24 QBD 627). The same applies to money paid into Court by a defendant, for the claimant may take it out (*Emden v. Carte* (1881) 19 Ch D 311, CA); and the claimant's solicitor may obtain such an order even if he has discharged himself, provided that he has not done so wrongfully (*Clover v. Adams* (1881) 6 QBD 622). But if the claimant does not take the money out of Court and recovers a lesser sum at the trial, his solicitor could then only obtain a charging order on the sum recovered; and if there is a counterclaim by the defendant, which has succeeded, he may only obtain a charging order on the balance (*Westacott v. Bevan* [1891] 1 Q.B. 774)." Money ordered to be paid into Court by a party to abide the further order of the Court, and later ordered to be repaid to that party, is not money "recovered", or even "preserved"

7C–237

(*Pierson v. Knutsford Estates Co* (1884) 13 QBD 666; *Re Wadsworth* (1885) 29 Ch D 517). The same applies to money paid into Court as security for costs (*Re Wadsworth*). Where a fund was paid into Court by one party to abide the Court's decision, and it was not till later that the other party instructed his solicitor, who was successful in establishing his client's right to a share in the fund, that share was held to be "property recovered or preserved" and the solicitor was entitled to a charging order over it (*Wimborne v. Fine* [1952] Ch. 869).

Where an action is dismissed, and thereby the claimant's claim to property in the hands of the defendant is defeated, such property is "preserved" for the defendant (*Bulley v. Bulley* (1878) 8 Ch D 479; *Ex p. Tweed* [1899] 2 Q.B. 167, CA) and where a claim is resisted and a lesser claim established, the balance between the two may be "property preserved" (see *The Birnam Wood* [1907] P. 1, CA). Property "managed or retained" for the person entitled, has been "preserved" within the section, though yielding little or nothing (*Re Turner* [1907] 2 Ch. 126). The assets of a company "preserved" by a scheme approved by the Court have been charged for the company's solicitor's costs of the winding-up and reconstruction (*Re John Clayton Ltd.* (1905) 92 L.T. 223). Property may be "preserved" within the section by any proceedings for administration or relating to its ownership (*Foxon v. Gascoigne* (1874) L.R. 9 Ch. 654; *Scholefield v. Lockwood* (1868) L.R. 7 Eq. 83; *Pritchard v. Roberts* (1873) L.R. 17 Eq. 222). But property is not "preserved" by the mere successful resistance to an application for a mandatory injunction respecting light and air (*Foxon v. Gascoigne*). And property preserved from a solicitor's own attacks is not property preserved for the owner (*Wingfield v. Wingfield* [1919] 1 Ch. 462).

The amount paid by the defendant to the solicitor for a legally-aided claimant by way of compromise and in settlement of the claim for damages constitutes "property recovered". The legal advisers of a legally-aided person, should not try and manipulate the destination of the "property recovered or preserved" so as to avoid the statutory charge (*Manley v. Law Society* [1981] 1 All E.R. 401, CA).

But the Court will not, in the exercise of its discretion, make a charging order on property which, by statute or rule, is intended for the benefit of the client or is intended to be inalienable. So, although a gross or annual sum secured to the wife after dissolution or nullity of marriage under ss.16 and 19 of the (then) Matrimonial Causes Act 1965, was charged (*Harrison v. Harrison* (1888) 13 P.D. 180) monthly or weekly payments of maintenance under s.16 and alimony *pendente lite* under s.15 were not charged (*Watkins v. Watkins* [1896] P. 222; *Smith v. Smith* [1923] P. 191 at 200; *Leete v. Leete* (1879) 48 L.J.P. 61; *Cross v. Cross* (1880) 43 L.T. 533).

"For his taxed costs in reference to that suit"

7C–238   The Court has refused to extend the charge in a foreclosure action to the costs of a supplementary action of ejectment (*Wilson v. Round* (1863) 4 Giff. 416; *Macfarlane v. Lister* (1887) 37 Ch D 88) but has charged future costs (*Re Eden* [1920] 2 K.B. 333 at 341) the costs of proving the retainer (*Re Hill* (1886) 33 Ch D 266; *Re Meter Cabs* [1911] 2 Ch. 557 at 562) and the costs of applying for the order and the costs of an appeal (*Waterland v. Serle* [1897] W.N. 163). The charge may be for costs as between solicitor and client (*quare* on the indemnity basis) (*Re Hill* (1886); *Guy v. Churchill* (1887) 35 Ch D 489; *The Paris* (1896)) but the difference between costs as between solicitor and his client and costs between the parties will not be charged on a fund out of which it would not normally be allowed, where the client is able to pay (see *Re Horne & Sons Ltd* [1906] 1 Ch. 271 at 275f.).

In *In the Estate of Fuld (decd.) (No. 4)* [1968] P. 727, where there was a fund over which the solicitors' lien might prevail, and the Court had jurisdiction to intervene, it would not do so as the client's indebtedness to the solicitors had not been ascertained; but it ordered no payment to be made out of the fund to the client without 14 days' notice being given to the solicitor who should then have liberty to apply to the Court for directions.

Priorities

7C–239   The order gives the solicitor priority over all other creditors and all other claims except that of a purchaser for value without notice (see *Haymes v. Cooper* (1864) 33 L.J.Ch. 488; *Re Suffield and Watts, Ex p. Brown* (1888) 20 QBD 693 at 696, 698; *Hamer v. Giles* (1879) 11 Ch D 942 at 947; *Greer v. Young* (1883) 24 Ch D 552; *Mackenzie v. Macintosh* (1891) 64 L.T. 706; *The Paris* [1896] P. 77). A judgment creditor garnisheeing a debt is not a purchaser (*Dallow v. Garrold* (1884) 14 QBD 543). "Notice" means notice of the right to a charging order, not of the making of an order (*Cole v. Eley* [1894] 2 Q.B. 350; *Ridd v. Thorne* [1902] 2 Ch. 344; *The Paris* (1896); *Wimborne v. Fine* [1952] Ch. 869). So that where there is a fund in Court, the solicitor has priority for his lien, independently of the statute, and his charge is absolute and has priority over all other charges or assignments without actual notice, for a person who takes a charge on money in Court knows it is subject to the solicitor's lien for costs (*Haymes v. Cooper* (1864); *Faithfull v. Ewen* (1878) 7 Ch D 495; *Macfarlane v. Lister* (1887) 37 Ch D 88; *Rhodes v. Sugden* (1885) 29 Ch D 517 at 520); and similar considerations apply to the assignee of a judgment (*Cole v. Eley* (1894)). But where trust property is preserved the trustee's right to an indemnity for his proper expenses has priority over the solicitor's charge (*Re Turner* [1907] 2 Ch. 126 at 539). The section expressly provides that "all conveyances and acts done to defeat, or operating to defeat, that charge shall, except in the case of a conveyance to a *bona fide* purchaser without notice be void as against the solicitor" (see *Re Suffield and Watts, Ex p. Brown*, per Lord Esher at 692; *Hamer v. Giles* (1879) *per* Jessel M.R. at 947; *Baile v. Baile* (1872) L.R. 13 Eq. 497 at 509). These words apply to a voluntary conveyance made by the client before the charging order (*Baile v. Baile* (1872); and see *Watts v. Hetley* (1899) 44 S.J. 134).

The charge has priority over a mortgage (*Faithfull v. Ewen* (1878)) and also over a garnishee order (*Shippey v. Grey* (1880) 49 L.J.C.P. 524); *Re Suffield and Watts, ex p. Brown* (1888); *The Leader* (1868) L.R. 2 A. & E. 314; *Dallow v. Garrold* (1884); *Watts v. Hetley* (1899); *Campbell v. Campbell* [1941] 1 All E.R. 274; *Loescher v. Dean* [1950] Ch. 491; and *North v. Stewart* (1890) 15 App.Cas. 452). But as the making of a charging order is discretionary, the notice to the creditor and the neglect, delay or *mala fides* of the solicitor are relevant matters to be considered (see cases cited above). Where the client becomes bankrupt during the proceedings, the solicitor is entitled as against the trustee in bankruptcy to a charging order for his costs incurred before notice of an available act of bankruptcy (*Re Nicholas & Paine* (1889) 61 L.T. (n.s.) 87; *Re Graydon* [1896] 1 Q.B. 417) or intervention of the trustee (*Emden v. Carte*, 19 Ch D 311; see *Keeson v. Luxmoore* (1889) 61 L.T. (n.s.) 199). On a change of solicitors during the proceedings, the last solicitor has priority over the former (*Re Knight* [1892] 2 Ch. 368).

Practice

The application is made under CPR Part 8 to a master, Costs Judge or district judge. It should state that the application is made for the solicitor's protection and not to further any interest of the client (see *Harrison v. Cornwall Minerals Ry.* (1883) 53 L.J.Ch. 596; *Johnston v. McKenzie* [1911] 2 I.R. 118). **7C–240**

The order

See s.73 and *Kay v. Lovell* [1940] Ch. 650. The charge may be upon the whole fund whether it all belongs to the client or not (*Greer v. Young* (1883) 24 Ch D 545 at 557; *Scholey v. Peck* [1893] 1 Ch. 709; *Re Pelsall Coal Co.* (1892) 8 T.L.R. 629) that is to say, the net proceeds recovered, not the gross (*Ex p. Brown* (1888) 20 QBD 693). **7C–241**

Enforcing the order by sale

See s.73 and *Re Green* (1884) 26 Ch D 16; *Rowley v. Austin* (1882) 9 QBD 598 (for the procedure where the client has disappeared) and *Re Pelsall Coal Co* (order made against debenture holders). For the procedure where the judgment creditor declines to enforce a judgment debt upon which a charging order has been made, see *Farrant v. Caley* [1924] W.N. 170, CA. **7C–242**

LSC FUNDED PROCEEDINGS

GENERAL INTRODUCTION

The Access to Justice Act 1999 established the Legal Services Commission ("LSC"), which replaced the Legal Aid Board. The Commission itself has responsibility for two separate schemes for the provision of public funding for legal services, the Community Legal Service (the "CLS") and the Criminal Defence Service. Both the LSC and the CLS came into being on April 1, 2000. **7D–1**

The scheme for public funding and the establishment of the CLS under the 1999 Act mark a radical change from the funding of legal services under former legal aid schemes. The public funding of civil cases is no longer permitted by Parliament to be demand-led, but is subject to priorities which seek to balance competing needs and allocate money within a finite budget.

As to the commencement provisions which brought the relevant sections of Part I of the 1999 Act into force, these are contained in the Access to Justice Act 1999 (Commencement No.3 Transitional Provisions and Savings) Order 2000 (S.I. 2000 No. 774). This Order, read together with Part I of Sched. 15 of the 1999 Act, largely repealed and revoked the Legal Aid Act 1988.

A number of cases are still before the Courts (in particular on assessment proceedings) under the old legal aid regime governed by the 1988 Act. This is by reason of art.5 of the Transitional Provisions and Savings Order 2000, the most significant effect of which has been the preservation of the 1988 Act system in respect of cases where funding was applied for prior to April 1, 2000 and the application reached the Board before May 2, 2000. The 1988 Act scheme is also preserved for a residual category of other matters. For such cases the old regulations must be consulted and these are set out in the *Legal Aid Handbook 1998/99* (Sweet & Maxwell).

Since April 1, 2001 solicitors have only been able to provide services funded by the CLS if they have been licensed by contract. In respect of certificates granted before that date in non-contracted areas, art.4, the Community Legal Service (Funding) Order 2000 (S.I. 2000 No. 627) also provides that provisions under the Civil Legal Aid (General) Regulations (as amended) apply.

Save for the cases referred to in the previous two paragraphs, therefore, the provision of public funding in respect of civil cases and consequential costs rules are governed by the 1999 Act and regulations made thereunder.

This section of the *White Book Service* summarises the main parts of the current regime insofar as they concern civil (non-family) representation. In particular these include the following:

- the statutory charge and the right of set-off under a Lockley order (s.10(7), Access to Justice Act 1999 and Part III, the Community Legal Service (Financial) Regulations 2000 (S.I. 2000 No. 516))

- security for costs (reg.6, the Community Legal Service (Costs) Regulations 2000 (S.I. 2000 No. 441))

- costs protection and orders for costs against funded clients and the LSC (s.11, Access to Justice Act 1999 and Part II, the Community Legal Service (Costs) Regulations 2000 (S.I. 2000 No. 441) and the Community Legal Service (Cost Protection) Regulations 2000 (S.I. 2000 No. 824).

The commentary to the Act will detail the services which may be funded under the 1999 Act, (s.6), the financial eligibility requirements of funded clients (s.7) and the Funding Code (s.8). The Funding Code is at the heart of the new public funding scheme and seeks to set out the criteria by which decisions are to be made about which cases are to be funded by public money.

Contempt proceedings

7D–2   Contempt committed by an individual in the face of the court is covered by s.12(1)(f), Access to Justice Act 1999 and funded by the Criminal Defence Service. Any court, whether civil or criminal can grant a Representation Order so long as the interests of justice criteria contained in para.5 of the Sched. 3 to the Act are satisfied (see s.14). Any solicitor or barrister can provide representation where a Representation Order has been made (s.15). A judge, before dealing with a contempt in the face of the court has a duty to inform the alleged contemnor of the right to legal advice and public funding (see further, Part 11 of PD–Committal Applications at scpd 52.7).

Access to Justice Act 1999

(1999 c. 22)

PART I

LEGAL SERVICES COMMISSION

Community Legal Service

7D–3   **4.**—(1) The Commission shall establish, maintain and develop a service known as the Community Legal Service for the purpose of promoting the availability to individuals of services of the descriptions specified in subsection (2) and, in particular, for securing (within the resources made available, and priorities set, in accordance with this Part) that individuals have access to services that effectively meet their needs.

* * * *

Services which may be funded

6.— * * * *

7D–4

(2) Subject to that (and to subsection (6)), the services which the Commission may fund as part of the Community Legal Service are those which the Commission considers appropriate.

* * * *

(6) The Commission may not fund as part of the Community Legal Service any of the services specified in Schedule 2.

(7) Regulations may amend that Schedule by adding new services or omitting or varying any services.

(8) The Lord Chancellor—

  (a) may by direction require the Commission to fund the provision of any of the services specified in Schedule 2 in circumstances specified in the direction, and

  (b) may authorise the Commission to fund the provision of any of those services in specified circumstances or, if the Commission request him to do so, in an individual case.

* * * *

Note —Subsections 6(1) and 6(3) of the 1999 Act (which are not reproduced) require **7D–5** the LSC to set priorities for the funding of services and prescribe the means by which services may be funded. The remainder of s.6 must be read in conjunction with Sched.2, which specifies which services may not be funded. Some services, however, are brought back into the scope of the Act either by way of directions from the Secretary of State (formerly the Lord Chancellor) (see s.6(8)(a)), or where an express authorisation has been granted to the Commission (under s.6(8)(b)). See para. 7D–15below.

Individuals for whom services may be funded

7.—(1) The Commission may only fund services for an individual **7D–6** as part of the Community Legal Service if his financial resources are such that, under regulations, he is an individual for whom they may be so funded.

* * * *

Note —The eligibility criteria which must be satisfied before funding can be granted **7D–7** are set out in Part II, the Community Legal Service (Financial) Regulations 2000 (S.I. 2000 No. 516). Part D of the Funding Code (see para.7D–9 below) contains the LSC's Guide to Assessing Financial Eligibility.

Code about provision of funded services

8.—(1) The Commission shall prepare a code setting out the **7D–8** criteria according to which it is to decide whether to fund (or continue to fund) services as part of the Community Legal Service for an individual for whom they may be so funded and, if so, what services are to be funded for him.

* * * * *

7D–9   *Note* —The Funding Code (which runs to about 700 pages) is an attempt to ensure that decision-makers who are to determine whether an individual should obtain public funding for legal services make their decisions both consistently and with the ultimate objective of appropriately allocating the money which is made available to fund the CLS.

Part A of the Funding Code establishes levels of services which will be funded by the CLS, of which two are particularly relevant in civil proceedings. The first is "legal representation" which includes litigation and advocacy services in current and contemplated proceedings. The second is "support funding" which is a means for the partial funding of proceedings which are to be pursued under a CFA.

In order to obtain funding the individual concerned must be able to satisfy the specified criteria set out in Part A of the Code, which are likely to include an application of a costs-benefit matrix unless some wider public interest is at stake.

Specific criteria apply to High Cost Cases (handled by the Special Cases Unit), judicial review, claims against public authorities, clinical negligence, housing, family, mental health and immigration. Separate rules govern multi-party actions.

Part C of the Funding Code sets out detailed guidance on making decisions about the Funding Code criteria. As the Code says, it "is a flexible set of Rules which seeks to direct the resources available to areas of work where the need is greatest and the priority highest".

Terms of provision of funded services

7D–10   **10.**—(1) An individual for whom services are funded by the Commission as part of the Community Legal Service shall not be required to make any payment in respect of the services except where regulations otherwise provide.

* * * *

(7) Except so far as regulations otherwise provide, where services have been funded by the Commission for an individual as part of the Community Legal Service—

    (a) sums expended by the Commission in funding the services (except to the extent that they are recovered under section 11), and

    (b) other sums payable by the individual by virtue of regulations under this section,

shall constitute a first charge on any property recovered or preserved by him (whether for himself or any other person) in any proceedings or in any compromise or settlement of any dispute in connection with which the services were provided.

* * * *

7D–11   *The Statutory Charge—General Note* —Section 10(7) substantially reproduces s.16(6) of the Legal Aid Act 1988. Section 10(8) allows regulations to be made which "make provision about the charge" and these are contained in Part III, the Community Legal Service (Financial) Regulations 2000 and reg.21, the Community Legal Service (Costs) Regulations 2000, which are reproduced in full below.

These regulations substantially reproduce their equivalents in regs.93–99, Civil Legal Aid (General) Regulations 1999. The main differences are that the LSC may waive the statutory charge in cases which have a significant wider interest (reg.47 of the Costs Regulations 2000) and a funded client is not obliged to agree that interest shall accrue to the benefit of the LSC if the enforcement of the charge is to be postponed in respect of money recovered in family proceedings for the purpose of purchasing a home (reg.21 of the Costs Regulations).

"Recovered or preserved" (s.10(7)) —Whether property has been recovered or

preserved is a matter of fact (and not of theoretical risk) based on an examination of the pleadings and the evidence. It has been recovered by the claimant if it has been the subject of a successful claim, and preserved to the respondent if the claim fails. (See *Hanlon v. Law Society* [1981] A.C. 124 as applied in *Till v. Till* [1974] Q.B. 558, *Manley v. Law Society* [1981] 1 W.L.R. 335 and *Curling v. Law Society* [1985] 1 W.L.R. 470). The charge has been held to extend to the costs allowed in respect of all proceedings to which a certificate relates, and not just to the application in which the property was recovered or preserved (*Watkinson v. Legal Aid Board* [1991] 1 W.L.R. 419).

"Compromise or settlement" (s.10(7)) —In *Van Hoorn v. Law Society* [1985] Q.B. 106 it was held that any rights under a compromise arrived at to avoid the proceedings were encompassed by the statutory charge even though the property which was subject to the compromise had not been "recovered or preserved" in the proceedings within the meaning of the test set out in *Hanlon's* case (see above).

Set-Off —Section 16(8) of the Legal Aid Act 1988 expressly preserved the right of set-off notwithstanding the existence of the statutory charge. A "Lockley Order" was commonplace by which an unassisted party was entitled to set off against any sum it might be ordered to pay to an assisted party costs which it was to receive from the assisted party (*Lockley v. National Blood Transfusion Service* [1992] 1 W.L.R. 492). Section 16(8) has not been reproduced into s.10 of the 1999 Act. In *R. (on the application of Burkett) v. Hammersmith and Fulham LBC (Costs)* [2004] EWCA Civ 1342, s.16(8) was described as mere surplusage, and it was made clear that the discretionary power to make a Lockley Order (which exists by virtue of s.51, Supreme Court Act 1981) is not affected by the new statutory framework.

Costs in funded cases

11.—(1) Except in prescribed circumstances, costs ordered against **7D–12** an individual in relation to any proceedings or part of proceedings funded for him shall not exceed the amount (if any) which is a reasonable one for him to pay having regard to all the circumstances including—

(a) the financial resources of all the parties to the proceedings, and

(b) their conduct in connection with the dispute to which the proceedings relate;

and for this purpose proceedings, or a part of proceedings, are funded for an individual if services relating to the proceedings or part are funded for him by the Commission as part of the Community Legal Service.

(2) In assessing for the purposes of subsection (1) the financial resources of an individual for whom services are funded by the Commission as part of the Community Legal Service, his clothes and household furniture and the tools and implements of his trade shall not be taken into account, except so far as may be prescribed.

(3) Subject to subsections (1) and (2), regulations may make provision about costs in relation to proceedings in which services are funded by the Commission for any of the parties as part of the Community Legal Service.

* * * *

General Note

Costs Protection and the Funded Party —Section 11 contains costs protection provi- **7D–13** sions which were found previously in ss.12, 13, 17, 18 and 34(2)(b) of the Legal Aid Act 1988. The former position which existed in relation to the liability of an assisted party who enjoyed civil legal aid is preserved (see s.17 of the 1988 Act), namely that a funded client cannot be compelled to pay more than an amount which is reasonable given all the circumstances, including the financial resources of all of the parties and their conduct in connection with the dispute.

Notwithstanding the general rule as to costs protection set out in s.11(1), reg.3, the Community Legal Service (Costs Protection) Regulations 2000 prohibits the application of costs protection in most cases of Help at Court, Litigation Support and Legal Help (as defined by the Funding Code made under s.6). Regulation 3 also sets out additional prescribed circumstances in which costs protection does or does not apply.

Costs Orders against the Commission —This is a limited provision for a non-funded party to obtain an order for costs against the LSC. Where such an application is made the court must always be satisfied that it is just and equitable for costs to be paid out of public funds (reg.5(3)(d), the Costs Protection Regulations 2000). In cases in which applications for public funding were made prior to December 3, 2001, the court must also be satisfied in relation to costs incurred in a court of first instance that the non-funded party will suffer 'severe' financial hardship (reg.5(3)(c)). Since December 3, 2001 only an individual can recover costs against the LSC in respect of his costs incurred in a court of first instance.

Procedures for Ordering Costs against Funded Clients and the Commission —This topic is comprehensively dealt with in the Guidance notes on the Application of s.11 Access to Justice Act 1999 issued by the Senior Costs Judge and approved by the Master of the Rules ((see para. 48.14.9 *et seq.*).

The Costs Practice Direction ss.21 to 23 (44PD.15 – 44PD.17) sets out the Procedure to be followed.

"the amount ...which is a reasonable one...to pay having regard to all the circumstances" (s.11(1)) —What is a "reasonable amount" in all the circumstances has been considered for instance in *Nolan v. C & C Marshall Ltd* [1954] 2 Q.B. 42, *Crystall v. Crystall* [1963] 1 W.L.R. 574, *Godfrey v. Smith* [1955] 1 W.L.R. 692, *Mercantile Credit Co. Ltd v. Cross* [1965] 2 Q.B. 205, *Chaggar v Chaggar* [1997] 1 All E.R. 104. The basis of which an appeal court is likely to interfere is set out in *Gooday v. Gooday* [1969] P.1.

Guidance

7D–14   23.—(1) The Secretary of State may give guidance to the Commission as to the manner in which he considers it should discharge its functions.

(2) The Commission shall take into account any such guidance when considering the manner in which it is to discharge its functions.

(3) Guidance may not be given under this section in relation to individual cases.

* * * *

General Note on the scope of the Community Legal Service Fund and on Guidance and Directions which affect what can be funded

7D–15   Whilst Sched. 2 to the 1999 Act excludes certain categories of case from the scope of the CLS Fund, the effect of various Directions and Guidance is to enable some otherwise excluded matters to be funded.

Four directions have been made to date under s.6(8), Access to Justice Act 1988. These include Lord Chancellor's Direction—Exceptions to the Exclusions, reproduced below. All Directions must be read in conjunction with the various Guidances issued under s.23 of the 1999 Act and Guidance issued by the LSC itself.

LORD CHANCELLOR'S DIRECTION—EXCEPTIONS TO THE EXCLUSIONS

7D–16   —1. This is a direction by the Lord Chancellor under Section 6(8) of the Access to Justice Act 1999 authorising the Legal Services Commission to fund in specified circumstances services generally excluded from the scope of the Community Legal Service Fund by paragraph

1 of Schedule 2 to the Act. In this direction "excluded services" means services which would, but for this direction, be excluded under that paragraph.

2. In this direction descriptions of types of case and other terms should be interpreted in accordance with definitions contained in the Act and in the Funding Code. For convenience, separate rules are given below in relation to the main levels of service under the Code. For the avoidance of doubt, nothing in this direction authorises the Commission to fund conveyancing services or the making of wills save where the direction specifically authorises this. Applications for funding under this direction must still satisfy all relevant criteria in the Funding Code and regulations.

* * * * *

Legal Representation

Part 2 *Case Categories*

7. The Lord Chancellor authorises the Commission to fund Legal Representation, including excluded services, in any of the following types of case:

> (a) Proceedings under section 7 of the Code (Judicial Review), subject to the restrictions set out at paragraph 8 below.
>
> (b) Proceedings under section 8 of the Code (Proceedings against public authorities concerning serious wrongdoing, abuse of position or power, or significant breach of human rights).
>
> (c) Proceedings under section 10 of the Code (Housing) subject to the restrictions set out in paragraph 9 below.
>
> (d) Proceedings under section 11 of the Code (Family Proceedings).
>
> (e) Professional negligence proceedings, save where the alleged negligence relates to services provided to the client's business.
>
> (f) Personal insolvency proceedings.

8. Paragraph 7(a) above does not authorise the Commission to fund judicial review proceedings which arise out of the carrying on of the client's business unless those proceedings concern the serious wrongdoing, abuse of position or power or significant breach of human rights by a public authority.

9. Paragraph 7(c) above does not authorise the Commission to fund housing proceedings relating to business tenancies or otherwise arising out of the carrying on of the client's business, save where possession of the client's home is in issue in those proceedings.

Public Interest Cases

10. The Lord Chancellor authorises the Commission to fund excluded services in Legal Representation in proceedings which have a significant wider public interest, other than proceedings arising out of the carrying on of the client's business.

Liberty of the client

11. The Lord Chancellor authorises the Commission to fund excluded services in Legal Representation in relation to hearings at which the liberty of the client is in issue.

Scope of specific exclusions

12. The following paragraphs limit the scope specific subparagraphs of paragraph 1 of Schedule 2 of the Act. Cases which benefit from paragraphs 13 to 16 below may still be excluded under any other subparagraph of paragraph 1 of Schedule 2. For example, a case concerning a constructive trust would still be excluded if the case arose out of the carrying on of a business.

13. Paragraph 1(b) conveyancing. Where the Commission is funding Legal Representation in proceedings, the Lord Chancellor authorises the Commission to fund conveyancing services as part of Legal Representation where this is necessary to give effect to a court order made in those proceedings. Where the Commission is funding Legal Representation in family proceedings the Lord Chancellor authorises the Commission to fund conveyancing services as part of Legal Representation where this is necessary to give effect to an agreement reached, with the help of funded services, to settle or avoid those proceedings.

14. Paragraph 1(e) matters of trust law. The Lord Chancellor authorises the Commission to fund services relating to matters of trust law as part of Legal Representation where the matters of trust law concern implied, resulting or constructive trusts, trusts arising when a person dies intestate or where matters of trust law arise in cases under section 14 of the Trusts for Land and Appointment of Trustees Act 1996 concerning the ownership or possession of the client's home.

15. Paragraph (g) matters of company or partnership law. The Lord Chancellor authorises the Commission to fund services relating to matters of partnership law as part of Legal Representation where the Commission is satisfied that the client needs to rely on partnership law only in order to dispute whether a partnership existed, for example in order to contest liability on the grounds of undue influence.

16. Paragraph (h) other matters arising out of the carrying on of a business. The Lord Chancellor authorises the Commission to fund services in relation to matters arising out of the carrying on a business as part of Legal Representation where the Commission is satisfied that the client is reasonably disputing whether he or she was carrying on a business, for example where the client is contesting liability on the grounds of undue influence.

Mixed Cases

17. The Lord Chancellor authorises the Commission to fund excluded services in Legal Representation when the excluded services relate to issues which are only minor or incidental to the main purpose of the proceedings.

18. The Lord Chancellor authorises the Commission to fund Legal Representation in partially excluded proceedings where any of the following conditions apply:

(a) The client is a defendant or third party in proceedings brought against him or her by an opponent.

(b) The excluded issues were introduced into existing proceedings by an opponent.

(c) The client is bringing the proceedings but it is or would have been impracticable for the client to bring proceedings without also covering the excluded services.

19. In paragraph 18 above "partially excluded proceedings" means proceedings which (apart from this direction) are mostly within scope but which also include specific issues or causes of action which are excluded under paragraph 1 of Schedule 2 of the Act.

* * * * * * *

Support Funding

Part 4—21. The Lord Chancellor authorises the Commission to fund Investigative Support in relation to personal injury claims which satisfy the funding criteria for Investigative Support set out in the General Funding Code.

22. The Lord Chancellor authorises the Commission to fund Litigation Support in relation to personal injury claims which satisfy the funding criteria for Litigation Support set out in the General Funding Code.

23. The Lord Chancellor authorises the Commission to fund Investigative Support or Litigation Support in relation to personal injury claims which have a significant wider public interest.

Date: April 2, 2001

Signed: Irvine of Lairg

"Proceedings against public authorities concerning serious wrongdoing" (para.7(b))

In *R. (on the application of G) v. Legal Services Commission* [2004] EWHC 276 (an action for personal injuries) Pitchford J. gave the Court's guidance as to the meaning of "proceedings against public authorities concerning serious wrongdoing, abuse of position or power, or significant breach of Human Rights" (see 7D–16 paras 8 and 9). Criteria were set out by which "serious wrongdoing by a public authority" ought generally to be considered, including: "(1) the nature of the duty owed; (2) the purpose of that duty, [which] will involve a consideration to whom and to what class of person was the duty owed, and the protection the duty was designed to afford; (3) the quality of the acts and omissions which are alleged to constitute the serious wrongdoing, and the circumstances in which those acts or omissions occur; (4) the harm or risk of harm which the breach occasioned; and (5) the public dimension of the duty and the breach which informs the priority for funding Legal Representation".

7D–17

The Community Legal Service (Financial) Regulations 2000

(S.I. 2000 No. 516)

Interpretation

2.—(1) In these Regulations, unless the context requires otherwise: **7D–18**
    "the Act"means the Access to Justice Act 1999;
    * * * * *

    "certificate" means a certificate issued under the Funding Code
        certifying a decision to fund services for the client;

"client" means an individual who applies for or receives funded services and, in the case of actual or contemplated proceedings, is a party or prospective party to the proceedings;

* * * * *

"family proceedings" means proceedings which arise out of family relationships, including proceedings in which the welfare of children is determined. Family proceedings also include all proceedings under any one or more of the following:

    (a) the Matrimonial Causes Act 1973;

    (b) the Inheritance (Provision for Family and Dependants) Act 1975;

    (c) the Adoption Act 1976;

    (d) the Domestic Proceedings and Magistrates' Courts Act 1978;

    (e) art III of the Matrimonial and Family Proceedings Act 1984;

    (f) Parts I, II and IV of the Children Act 1989;

    (g) Part IV of the Family Law Act 1996; and

    (h) the inherent jurisdiction of the High Court in relation to children.

7D–19   **40.—**   * * * * * *

(2) The net cost of the funded services means the cost paid by the Commission less any costs recovered by the Commission from another party.

(3) Where funding is provided by the Commission under a contract which does not differentiate between the remuneration for the client's case and remuneration for other cases, or require the cost of individual cases to be assessed, the reference in paragraph (2) to the cost paid by the Commission shall be construed as a reference to such part of the remuneration payable under the contract as may be specified in writing by the Commission.

(4) For the purposes of this regulation and regulation 43, where a certificate is discharged the cost of any assessment proceedings under CPR Part 47 or of taxation in the House of Lords shall not be included as part of the cost of the funded services, and the cost of drawing up a bill is not part of the cost of assessment proceedings.

PART III

THE STATUTORY CHARGE

7D–20   **42.** In regulations 43 to 53:

"relevant dispute" means the dispute in connection with which funded services are provided;

"relevant proceedings" means proceedings in connection with which funded services are provided;

"recovered", in relation to property or money, means property or money recovered or preserved by a client, whether for himself or for any other person;

2176

"statutory charge" means the charge created by section 10(7) of the Act in respect of the amount defined in regulation 43; and

"success fee" is defined in accordance with section 58 of the Courts and Legal Services Act 1990.

43.—(1) Subject to paragraphs (3), (4) and (5), where any money   **7D–21**
or property is recovered for a client in a relevant dispute or proceedings, the amount of the statutory charge shall be the aggregate of the sums referred to in section 10(7)(a) and (b) of the Act.

(2) For the purposes of this regulation:

(a) the sum referred to in section 10(7)(a) shall be defined in accordance with regulation 40(2) to (4), less any contribution paid by the client;

(b) the sum referred to in section 10(7)(b) shall include:

(i) any interest payable under regulation 52; and

(ii) any sum which the client has agreed to pay only in specific circumstances under section 10(2)(c) of the Act.

(3) Subject to paragraph (4), the amount of the charge created by section 10(7) of the Act shall not include sums expended by the Commission in funding any of the following services:

(a) Legal Help;

(b) Help at Court;

(c) Family Mediation; or

(d) Help with Mediation.

(4) Paragraph (3)(a) and (b) does not apply where the funded services are given in relation to family, clinical negligence or personal injury proceedings or a dispute which may give rise to such proceedings.

(5) Where Legal Help is provided as part of the family advice and information networks pilot, the amount of the statutory charge shall not exceed the sum which would have been expended by the Commission, had the Legal Help been provided otherwise than as a part of that pilot.

44.—(1) The charge created by section 10(7) of the Act shall not   **7D–22**
apply to any of the following:

(a) any periodical payment of maintenance;

(b) other than in circumstances which are exceptional having regard in particular to the quantity or value of the items concerned, the client's clothes or household furniture or the tools or implements of his trade;

(c) any sum or sums ordered to be paid under section 5 of the Inheritance (Provision for Family and Dependants) Act 1975 or Part IV of the Family Law Act 1996;

(d) [. . .]

(e) one-half of any redundancy payment within the meaning of Part XI of the Employment Rights Act 1996 recovered by the client;

(f) any payment of money made in accordance with an order made by the Employment Appeal Tribunal (excluding an order for costs);

(g) where the statutory charge is in favour of the supplier, the client's main or only dwelling; or

(h) any sum, payment or benefit which, by virtue of any provision of or made under an Act of Parliament, cannot be assigned or charged.

(2) [. . .]

(4) In paragraph (1)(a), "maintenance" means money or money's worth paid towards the support of a former partner, child or any other person for whose support the payer has previously been responsible or has made payments.

Note —Amended by S.I. 2001 No. 3663; and S.I. 2005 No. 1793.

7D–23   **45.**—(1) Subject to paragraph (2), the statutory charge shall be in favour of the Commission.

(2) Subject to paragraph (3), where it relates to the cost of Legal Help or Help at Court, the statutory charge shall be in favour of the supplier.

(3) Where Legal Help or Help at Court has been provided, the statutory charge shall be in favour of the Commission if it attaches to money or property recovered after a certificate has been granted in relation to the same matter.

7D–24   **46.**—(1) This regulation applies only where the statutory charge is in favour of the supplier.

(2) The Commission may grant a supplier authority, either in respect of individual cases or generally, to waive either all or part of the amount of the statutory charge where its enforcement would cause grave hardship or distress to the client or would be unreasonably difficult because of the nature of the property.

7D–25   **47.**—(1) [. . .]

(2) Paragraph (3) applies where:

(a) [. . .]

(b) the Commission considers it cost-effective to fund those services for a specified claimant or claimants, but not for other claimants or potential claimants who might benefit from the litigation.

(3) Where this paragraph applies, the Commission may, if it considers it equitable to do so, waive some or all of the amount of the statutory charge.

Note —Amended by S.I. 2001 No. 3663; and S.I. 2005 No. 1793.

7D–26   **48.** Regulations 49 to 53 apply only in relation to a statutory charge in favour of the Commission.

7D–27   **49.**—(1) Where a certificate has been revoked or discharged, section 10 (7) of the Act shall apply to any money or property recovered as a result of the client continuing to pursue the relevant dispute or take, defend or be a party to the relevant proceedings.

(2) In paragraph (1), "client" means the person whose certificate

has been revoked or discharged, or, as the case may be, his personal representatives, trustee in bankruptcy or the Official Receiver.

50.—(1) Paragraph (2) applies where any money recovered by a client in any proceedings is ordered to be paid into or remain in court and invested for the benefit of the client.

7D–28

(2) Where this paragraph applies, the statutory charge shall attach only to such part of the money as, in the opinion of the Commission, will be sufficient to safeguard the interests of the Commission, and the Commission shall notify the court in writing of the amount so attached.

51. Subject to regulation 52, the Commission may enforce the statutory charge in any manner which would be available to a charge in respect of a charge given between parties.

7D–29

52.—(1) Where the condition in regulation 52A is satisfied the Commission may postpone the enforcement of the statutory charge where:

7D–30

    (a) by order of the court or agreement it relates to property to be used as a home by the client or his dependants, or, where the relevant proceedings were family proceedings, to money to pay for such a home;

    (b) the Commission is satisfied that the property in question will provide such security for the statutory charge as it considers appropriate; and

    (c) as soon as it is possible to do so, the Commission registers a charge under the Land Registration Act 2002 to secure the amount in regulation 43 or, as appropriate, takes equivalent steps (whether in England and Wales or in any other jurisdiction) to protect its interest in the property.

(2) Where the client wishes to purchase a property in substitution for the property over which a charge is registered under paragraph (1)(c), the Commission may release the charge if the conditions in paragraph (1)(b) and (c) are satisfied.

(3) Where the enforcement of the statutory charge is postponed, interest shall accrue for the benefit of the Commission in accordance with regulation 53.

(4) Without prejudice to the provisions of the Land Registration Act 2002 and the Land Charges Act 1972, all conveyances and acts done to defeat, or operating to defeat, any charge shall, except in the case of a bona fide purchaser for value without notice, be void as against the Commission.

52A The Commission may only postpone enforcement of the statutory charge if it appears to the Commission that it would be unreasonable for the client to repay the amount of the charge.

7D–30.1

52B—(1) The Commission may review any decision to postpone enforcement of the charge at any time and, unless it appears to the Commission that it would be unreasonable for the client to repay the amount of the charge which has been postponed, it shall either—

7D–30.2

    (i) proceed to enforce the charge; or

    (ii) where the conditions in regulation 52(1) (a) to (c) are satisfied continue to postpone enforcement of the charge, in which case the provisions of regulation 52(3) shall also continue to apply.

(2) If the Commission continues to postpone enforcement under paragraph (1) (ii) it may do so on such terms or conditions as to repayment of the amount of the charge by way of interim payments of either capital or interest or both, or otherwise, as appear to the Commission to be appropriate.

7D–31   **53.**—(1) Where interest is payable by the client under regulation 52, that interest shall continue to accrue until the amount of the statutory charge is paid.

(2) The client may make interim payments of interest or capital in respect of the outstanding amount of the statutory charge, but no interim payment shall be used to reduce the capital outstanding while any interest remains outstanding.

(3) Where interest is payable by the client under regulation 52:

    (a) it shall run from the date when the charge is first registered;

    (b) the applicable rate shall be:

        (i) 8% per annum until 31st March 2002;

        (ii) 5% per annum from 1st April 2002 until 30th September 2005;

        (iii) 8% per annum from 1st October 2005;

    (c) [. . .]

    (d) [. . .]

    (e) the capital on which it is calculated shall be the lesser of:

        (i) the amount of the statutory charge outstanding from time to time, less any interest accrued by virtue of regulation 52(3), or

        (ii) the value of the property recovered at the time of such recovery.

Note —Amended by S.I. 2001 No. 3663; and S.I. 2005 No. 589.

The Community Legal Service (Costs) Regulations 2000

(S.I. 2000 No. 441)

PART I

GENERAL

Citation and commencement
7D–32   **1.** These Regulations may be cited as the Community Legal Service (Costs) Regulations 2000 and shall come into force on 1st April 2000.

Interpretation
7D–33   **2.** In these Regulations:

"the Act" means the Access to Justice Act 1999;

"certificate" means a certificate issued under the Funding Code certifying a decision to fund services for the client;

"child" means a person under 18;

"client" means an individual who receives funded services;

"Commission" means the Legal Services Commission established under section 1 of the Act;

"costs judge" has the same meaning as in the CPR;

"costs order" means an order that a party pay all or part of the costs of proceedings;

"costs order against the Commission" means an order, made under regulation 5 of the Community Legal Service (Cost Protection) Regulations 2000 (but not one under regulation 6 of those Regulations), that the Commission pay all or part of the costs of a party to proceedings who has not received funded services in relation to those proceedings under a certificate, other than a certificate which has been revoked;

"cost protection" means the limit on costs awarded against a client set out in section 11(1) of the Act;

"court" includes any tribunal having the power to award costs in favour of, or against, a party;

"CPR" means the Civil Procedure Rules 1998, and a reference to a Part or rule, prefixed by "CPR", means the Part or rule so numbered in the CPR;

"Financial Regulations" means the Community Legal Service (Financial) Regulations 2000;

"Funding Code" means the code approved under section 9 of the Act;

"full costs" means , where a section 11(1) costs order is made against a client, the amount of costs which that client would, but for section 11(1) of the Act, have been ordered to pay;

"funded services" means services which are provided directly for a client and funded for that client by the Commission as part of the Community Legal Service under sections 4 to 11 of the Act;

"litigation friend" has the meaning given by CPR Part 21;

"partner", in relation to a party to proceedings, means a person with whom that party lives as a couple, and includes a person with whom the party is not currently living but from whom he is not living separate and apart;

"patient" means a person who by reason of mental disorder within the meaning of the Mental Health Act 1983 is incapable of managing and administering his own affairs;

"proceedings" include proceedings in any tribunal which is a court, as defined, in this paragraph;

"receiving party" means a party in favour of whom a costs order is made;

"Regional Director" means any Regional Director appointed by the Commission in accordance with the Funding Code and any other person authorised to act on his behalf, except a supplier;

"rules of court", in relation to a tribunal, means rules or regulations made by the authority having power to make rules or regulations regulating the practice and procedure of that tribunal and, in relation to any court, includes practice directions;

"section 11(1) costs order" means a costs order against a client where cost protection applies;

"solicitor" means solicitor or other person who is an authorised litigator within the meaning of section 119(1) of the Courts and Legal Services Act 1990;

"statement of resources" means :

(a) a statement, verified by a statement of truth, made by a party to proceedings setting out:

(i) his income and capital and financial commitments during the previous year and, if applicable, those of his partner;

(ii) his estimated future financial resources and expectations and, if applicable, those of his partner; and

(iii) a declaration stating whether he, and if applicable his partner, has deliberately foregone or deprived himself of any resources or expectations, together (if applicable and as far as is practical) with details of those resources or expectations and the manner in which they have been foregone or deprived;

(iv) particulars of any application for funding made by him in connection with the proceedings; and

(v) any other facts relevant to the determination of his resources; or

(b) a statement, verified by a statement of truth, made by a client receiving funded services, setting out the information provided by the client under regulation 6 of the Financial Regulations, and stating that there has been no significant change in the client's financial circumstances since the date on which the information was provided or, as the case may be, details of any such change;

"statement of truth" has the same meaning as in CPR Part 22;

"supplier" means any person or body providing funded services to the client, including any authorised advocate (within the meaning of section 119(1) of the Courts and Legal Services Act 1990) engaged by the client's solicitor to act in proceedings.

Effect of these Regulations

7D–34   **3.** Nothing in these Regulations shall be construed, in relation to proceedings where one or more parties are receiving, or have received, funded services, as:

(a) requiring a court to make a costs order where it would not otherwise have made a costs order; or

(b) affecting the court's power to make a wasted costs order against a legal representative.

Termination of retainer where funding is withdrawn

4.—(1) The following paragraphs of this regulation apply where funding is withdrawn by revoking or discharging the client's certificate. **7D–35**

(2) Subject to paragraphs (3) and (4), on the revocation or discharge of the client's certificate, the retainer of any supplier acting under that certificate shall terminate immediately.

(3) Termination of retainers under paragraph (2) shall not take effect unless and until any procedures under the Funding Code for review of the decision to withdraw the client's funding are concluded, and confirm the decision to withdraw funding.

(4) The solicitor's retainer shall not terminate until he has complied with any procedures under the Funding Code that require him to send or serve notices.

PART II

COSTS ORDERS AGAINST CLIENT AND AGAINST COMMISSION

Application of regulations 6 to 13

5. Regulations 6 to 13 apply only where cost protection applies. **7D–36**

Security for costs

6. Where in any proceedings a client is required to give security for costs, the amount of that security shall not exceed the amount (if any) which is a reasonable one having regard to all the circumstances, including the client's financial resources and his conduct in relation to the dispute to which the proceedings relate. **7D–37**

Note —In the absence of special circumstances an order for security for costs should not be made against a funded client (*Conway v. George Wimpey & Co Ltd (No.1)* [1951] 1 All E.R. 56). Special circumstances which may justify such an order were considered on *Wyld v. Silver (No.2)* [1962] 1 W.L.R. 863, *Jackson v. John Dickinson & Co. (Bolton)* [1952] 1 All E.R. 104, *Friedmann v. Austay (London), Ltd* [1954] 1 W.L.R. 466 and *Bampton v. Cook* [1954] 1 W.L.R. 450. **7D–38**

7.—(1) The first £100,000 of the value of the client's interest in the main or only dwelling in which he resides shall not be taken into account in having regard to the client's resources for the purposes of section 11(1) of the Act. **7D–39**

(2) Where, but only to the extent that, the court considers that the circumstances are exceptional, having regard in particular to the quantity or value of the items concerned, the court may take into account the value of the client's clothes and household furniture, or

the tools and implements of his trade, in having regard to the client's resources for the purposes of section 11(1) of the Act.

(3) Subject to paragraph (4), in having regard to the resources of a party for the purposes of section 11(1) of the Act, the resources of his partner shall be treated as his resources.

(4) The resources of a party's partner shall not be treated as that party's resources if the partner has a contrary interest in the dispute in respect of which the funded services are provided.

(5) Where a party is acting in a representative, fiduciary or official capacity, the court shall not take the personal resources of the party into account for the purposes of section 11(1) of the Act, but shall have regard to the value of any property or estate, or the amount of any fund out of which he is entitled to be indemnified, and may also have regard to the resources of the persons, if any, including that party where appropriate, who are beneficially interested in that property, estate or fund.

(6) For the purposes of section 11(1) of the Act, where a party is acting as a litigation friend to a client who is a child or a patient, the court shall not take the personal resources of the litigation friend into account in assessing the resources of the client.

Statements of resources

7D–40   8.—(1) Any person who is a party to proceedings in which another party is a client may make a statement of resources, and file it with the court.

(2) A person making and filing a statement of resources under paragraph (1) shall serve a copy of it on the client.

(3) Where a copy of a statement of resources has been served under paragraph (2) not less than seven days before the date fixed for a hearing at which the amount to be paid under a section 11(1) costs order falls, or may fall, to be decided, the client shall also make a statement of resources, and shall produce it at that hearing.

Procedures for ordering costs against client and Commission

7D–41   9.—(1) Where the court is considering whether to make a section 11(1) costs order, it shall consider whether, but for cost protection, it would have made a costs order against the client and, if so, whether it would, on making the costs order, have specified the amount to be paid under that order.

(2) If the court considers that it would have made a costs order against the client, but that it would not have specified the amount to be paid under it, the court shall, when making the section 11(1) costs order:

    (a) specify the amount (if any) that the client is to pay under that order if, but only if:

        (i) it considers that it has sufficient information before it to decide what amount is, in that case, a reasonable amount for the client to pay, in accordance with section 11(1) of the Act; and

        (ii) it is satisfied that, if it were to determine the full

costs at that time, they would exceed the amount referred to in sub-paragraph (i);

    (b) otherwise, it shall not specify the amount the client is to pay under the section 11(1) costs order.

(3) If the court considers that it would have made a costs order against the client, and that it would have specified the amount to be paid under it, the court shall, when making the section 11(1) costs order:

    (a) specify the amount (if any) that the client is to pay under that order if, but only if, it considers that it has sufficient information before it to decide what amount is, in that case, a reasonable amount for the client to pay, in accordance with section 11(1) of the Act;

    (b) otherwise, it shall not specify the amount the client is to pay under the section 11(1) costs order.

(4) Any order made under paragraph (3) shall state the amount of the full costs.

(5) The amount (if any) to be paid by the client under an order made under paragraph (2)(b) or paragraph (3)(b), and any application for a costs order against the Commission, shall be determined in accordance with regulation 10, and at any such determination following an order made under paragraph (2)(b), the amount of the full costs shall also be assessed.

(6) Where the court makes a section 11(1) costs order that does not specify the amount which the client is to pay under it, it may also make findings of fact, as to the parties' conduct in the proceedings or otherwise, relevant to the determination of that amount, and those findings shall be taken into consideration in that determination.

10.—(1) The following paragraphs of this regulation apply where   **7D–42** the amount to be paid under a section 11(1) costs order, or an application for a costs order against the Commission, is to be determined under this regulation, by virtue of regulation 9(5).

(2) The receiving party may, within three months after a section 11(1) costs order is made, request a hearing to determine the costs payable to him.

(3) A request under paragraph (2) shall be accompanied by:

    (a) if the section 11(1) costs order does not state the full costs, the receiving party's bill of costs, which shall comply with any requirements of relevant rules of court relating to the form and content of a bill of costs where the court is assessing a party's costs;

    (b) unless the conditions set out in paragraph (3A) are satisfied, a statement of resources; and

    (c) if the receiving party is seeking, or, subject to the determination of the amount to be paid under the section 11(1) costs order, may seek, a costs order against the Commission, written notice to that effect.

(3A) The conditions referred to in paragraph (3)(b) above are that—

    (a) the court is determining an application for a costs order against the Commission;

(b) the costs were not incurred in a court of first instance.

(4) The receiving party shall file the documents referred to in paragraph (3) with the court and at the same time serve copies of them:

(a) on the client, if a determination of costs payable under section 11(1) of the Act is sought; and

(b) on the Regional Director, if notice has been given under paragraph (3)(c).

(5) Where documents are served on the client under paragraph (4)(a), the client shall make a statement of resources.

(6) The client shall file the statement of resources made under paragraph (5) with the court, and serve copies of it on the receiving party and, if notice has been given under paragraph (3)(c), on the Regional Director, not more than 21 days after the client receives a copy of the receiving party's statement of resources.

(7) The client may, at the same time as filing and serving a statement of resources under paragraph (6), file, and serve on the same persons, a statement setting out any points of dispute in relation to the bill of costs referred to in paragraph (3)(a).

(8) If the client, without good reason, fails to file a statement of resources in accordance with paragraph (6), the court shall determine the amount which the client shall be required to pay under the section 11(1) costs order (and, if relevant, the full costs), having regard to the statement made by the receiving party, and the court need not hold an oral hearing for such determination.

(9) If the client files a statement of resources in accordance with paragraph (6), or the period for filing such notice expires, or if the costs payable by the client have already been determined, the court shall set a date for the hearing and, at least 14 days before that date, serve notice of it on:

(a) the receiving party;

(b) the client (unless the costs payable by the client have already been determined); and

(c) if a costs order against the Commission is or may be sought, the Regional Director.

(10) The court's functions under this regulation may be exercised:

(a) in relation to proceedings in the House of Lords, by the Clerk to the Parliaments;

(b) in relation to proceedings in the Court of Appeal, High Court or a county court, a costs judge or a district judge;

(c) in relation to proceedings in a magistrates' court, by a single justice or by the justices' clerk;

(d) in relation to proceedings in the Employment Appeal Tribunal, by the Registrar of that Tribunal.

(11) The amount of costs to be determined under this regulation may include the costs incurred in relation to a request made under this regulation.

7D–43   **10A.**—(1) Subject to paragraph (2), where the court makes a section 11(1) costs order but does not specify the amount which the client is to pay under it, the court may order the client to pay an amount on account of the costs which are the subject of the order.

(2) The court may order a client to make a payment on account of costs under this regulation only if it has sufficient information before it to decide the minimum amount which the client is likely to be ordered to pay on a determination under regulation 10.

(3) The amount of the payment on account of costs shall not exceed the minimum amount which the court decides that the client is likely to be ordered to pay on such a determination.

(4) Where the court orders a client to make a payment on account of costs—

    (a) it shall order the client to make the payment into court; and

    (b) the payment shall remain in court unless and until the court—

        (i) makes a determination under regulation 10 of the amount which the client should pay to the receiving party under the section 11(1) costs order, and orders the payment on account or part of it to be paid to the receiving party in satisfaction or part satisfaction of the client's liability under that order; or

        (ii) makes an order under paragraph (5)(b) or (5)(c) of this regulation that the payment on account or part of it be repaid to the client.

(5) Where a client has made a payment on account of costs pursuant to an order under paragraph (1) of this regulation—

    (a) the receiving party shall request a hearing under regulation 10 to determine the amount of costs payable to him;

    (b) if the receiving party fails to request such a hearing within the time permitted by regulation 10(2), the payment on account shall be repaid to the client;

    (c) if upon the hearing under regulation 10 the amount of costs which it is determined that the client should pay is less than the amount of the payment on account, the difference shall be repaid to the client.

Appeals, etc

11.—(1) Subject to the following paragraphs of this regulation, and to regulation 12, any determination made under regulation 9 or regulation 10 shall be final.

7D–44

(2) Any party with a financial interest in an assessment of the full costs may appeal against that assessment, if and to the extent that that party would, but for these Regulations, be entitled to appeal against an assessment of costs by the court in which the relevant proceedings are taking place.

(3) Where, under regulation 9(2)(a), the court has specified the amount which a client is required to pay under a section 11(1) costs order, the client may apply to the court for a determination of the full costs and if, on that determination, the amount of the full costs is

less than the amount which the court previously specified under regulation 9(2)(a), the client shall instead be required to pay the amount of the full costs.

(4) The receiving party or the Commission may appeal, on a point of law, against the making of a costs order against the Commission (including the amount of costs which the Commission is required to pay under the order), or against the court's refusal to make such an order.

Variation and late determination of amount of costs

7D–45 **12.**—(1) The following paragraphs of this regulation apply where the court makes a section 11(1) costs order.

(2) Where the amount (if any) which the client is required to pay under the section 11(1) costs order, together with the amount which the Commission is required to pay under any costs order against the Commission, is less than the full costs, the receiving party may, on the ground set out in paragraph (4)(a), apply to the court for an order varying the amount which the client is required to pay under the section 11(1) costs order.

(3) Where the court has not specified the amount to be paid under the section 11(1) costs order, and the receiving party has not, within the time limit in regulation 10(2), applied to have that amount determined in accordance with regulation 10, the receiving party may, on any of the grounds set out in paragraph (4), apply for a determination of the amount that the client is required to pay.

(4) The grounds referred to in paragraphs (2) and (3) are the grounds that:

    (a) there has been a significant change in the client's circumstances since the date of the order;

    (b) material additional information as to the client's financial resources is available, and that information could not with reasonable diligence have been obtained by the receiving party in time to make an application in accordance with regulation 10; or

    (c) there were other good reasons justifying the receiving party's failure to make an application within the time limit in regulation 10(2).

(5) Any application under paragraph (2) or (3) shall be made by the receiving party within six years from the date on which the section 11(1) costs order is first made.

(6) On any application under paragraph (2), the order may be varied as the court thinks fit, but the amount of costs ordered (excluding any costs ordered to be paid under paragraph (9)) shall not exceed the amount of the full costs as stated in any previous order of the court.

(7) When the amount which the client is required to pay under the section 11(1) costs order has been determined under regulation 9(2)(a), and the receiving party applies under paragraph (2) for an order varying that amount:

    (a) the receiving party shall file with the application under paragraph (2) his bill of costs, which shall comply with any requirements of relevant rules of court relating to the form and content of a bill of costs where the court is assessing a party's costs; and

(b) the court shall, when determining the application, assess the full costs.

(8) Where the receiving party has received funded services in relation to the proceedings, the Commission may make an application under paragraph (2) or paragraph (3), and:

(a) when making the application the Commission shall file with the court a statement of the receiving party's costs or, if those costs have not been assessed, the receiving party's bill of costs; and

(b) paragraphs (4) to (6) shall apply to that application as if "the Commission" were substituted for "the receiving party" in those paragraphs.

(9) The amount of costs to be determined under this regulation may include the costs incurred in relation to an application made under this regulation.

Rights to appear

13.—(1) The Regional Director may appear at: **7D–46**

(a) any hearing in relation to which notice has been given under regulation 10(3)(c);

(b) the hearing of any appeal under regulation 11(4); or

(c) the hearing of any application under regulation 12(8).

(2) The Regional Director may, instead of appearing under paragraph (1), give evidence in the form of a written statement to the court, verified by a statement of truth.

(3) The Regional Director shall file with the court any statement under paragraph (2), and serve a copy on the receiving party, not less than seven days before the hearing to which it relates.

The Community Legal Service (Cost Protection) Regulations 2000

(S.I. 2000 No. 824)

Citation and commencement

1. These Regulations may be cited as the Community Legal Service (Cost Protection) Regulations 2000 and shall come into force on 1st April 2000. **7D–47**

Interpretation

2.—(1) In these Regulations: **7D–48**

"the Act" means the Access to Justice Act 1999;

"certificate" means a certificate issued under the Funding Code certifying a decision to fund services for the client and "emergency certificate" means a certificate certifying a decision to fund Legal Representation for the client in a case of emergency;

"client" means an individual who receives funded services;

"Commission" means the Legal Services Commission established under section 1 of the Act;

"costs judge" has the same meaning as in the Civil Procedure Rules 1998;

"costs order" means an order that a party pay all or part of the costs of proceedings;

"cost protection" means the limit on costs awarded against a client set out in section 11(1) of the Act;

"court" includes any tribunal having the power to award costs in favour of, or against, a party;

'family proceedings' means –

(a) all proceedings under any one or more of the following—

(i) the Matrimonial Causes Act 1973;

(ii) the Domestic Proceedings and Magistrates' Courts Act 1978;

(iii) Part III of the Matrimonial and Family Proceedings Act 1984;

(iv) the Child Abduction and Custody Act 1985;

(v) Parts I and II of and Schedule 1 to the Children Act 1989;

(vi) section 53 of and Schedule 7 to the Family Law Act 1996; and

(b) proceedings which arise out of family relationships under either or both of the following—

(i) the Inheritance (Provision for Family and Dependants) Act 1975;

(ii) the Trusts of Land and Appointment of Trustees Act 1996;

'family relationships' has the same meaning as in the Funding Code which came into force on 1st April 2000 and the Funding Code Guidance published on 1st April 2000 by the Commission for the purpose of making decisions under the Funding Code;

"full costs" means , where a section 11(1) costs order is made against a client, the amount of costs which that client would, but for section 11(1) of the Act, have been ordered to pay;

"funded proceedings" means proceedings (including prospective proceedings) in relation to which the client receives funded services or, as the case may be, that part of proceedings during which the client receives funded services;

"funded services" means services which are provided directly for a client and funded for that client by the Commission as part of the Community Legal Service under sections 4 to 11 of the Act;

"Funding Code" means the code approved under section 9 of the Act;

"non-funded party" means a party to proceedings who has not received funded services in relation to those proceedings under a certificate, other than a certificate which has been revoked;

"partner" means a person with whom the person concerned lives as a couple, and includes a person with whom the person concerned is not currently living but from whom he is not living separate and apart;

"proceedings" include proceedings in any tribunal which is a court, as defined in this paragraph;

"receiving party" means a party in favour of whom a costs order is made;

"section 11(1) costs order" means a costs order against a client where cost protection applies;

"solicitor" means a solicitor or another person who is an authorised litigator within the meaning of section 119(1) of the Courts and Legal Services Act 1990.

(2) References to the levels of service listed in paragraph (3) shall be construed as references to the receipt or provision of those levels of service granted in accordance with the Funding Code.

(3) The levels of service referred to in paragraph (2) are:

    (a) Legal Help;

    (b) Help at Court;

    (c) Legal Representation;

    (d) General Family Help and Help with Mediation

    (e) [. . .]

    (f) [. . .]

Note —Amended by S.I. 2001 No. 823; and S.I. 2005 No. 2006.

Cost protection

3.—(1) Cost protection shall not apply in relation to such parts of proceedings, or prospective proceedings, as are funded for the client by way of:

    (a) Help at Court;

    (b) [. . .]

    (c) subject to paragraph (2), Legal Help.

    (d) General Family Help and Help with Mediation in family proceedings;

    (e) Legal Representation in family proceedings.

(2) Subject to paragraph (4), where the client receives Legal Help, but later receives Legal Representation or General Family Help or Help with Mediation in respect of the same dispute, other than Legal Representation in family proceedings or General Family Help or Help with Mediation in family proceedings, cost protection shall apply, both in respect of:

    (a) the costs incurred by the receiving party before the commencement of proceedings which, as regards the client, are funded proceedings by virtue of the client's receipt of Legal Help, and

> (b) the costs incurred by the receiving party in the course of proceedings which, as regards the client, are funded proceedings by virtue of the client's receipt of Legal Representation , General Family Help or Help with Mediation.

(3) Subject to paragraph (4), cost protection shall apply only to costs incurred by the receiving party in relation to proceedings which, as regards the client, are funded proceedings, and:

> (a) where work is done before the issue of a certificate, cost protection shall (subject to paragraphs (2) and (5)) apply only to costs incurred after the issue of the certificate;
>
> (b) where funding is withdrawn by discharging the client's certificate, cost protection shall apply only to costs incurred before the date when funded services under the certificate ceased to be provided.

(4) Where funding is withdrawn by revoking the client's certificate, cost protection shall not apply, either in respect of work done before or after the revocation.

(5) Cost protection shall apply to work done immediately before the grant of an emergency certificate, other than an emergency certificate granted in relation to family proceedings, if:

> (a) no application for such a certificate could be made because the Commission's office was closed; and
>
> (b) the client's solicitor applies for an emergency certificate at the first available opportunity, and the certificate is granted.

Note —Amended by S.I. 2005 No. 2006.

Enforcement of costs order against client

7D–50   **4.** Where, in a case where costs protection applies, for the purpose of enforcing a costs order against a client (alone or together with any other judgment or order), a charging order under section 1 of the Charging Orders Act 1979 is made in respect of the client's interest in the main or only dwelling in which he resides:

> (a) that charging order shall operate to secure the amount payable under the costs order (including, without limitation, any interest) only to the extent of the amount (if any) by which the proceeds of sale of the client's interest in the dwelling (having deducted any mortgage debts) exceed £100,000; and
>
> (b) an order for the sale of the dwelling shall not be made in favour of the person in whose favour the charging order is made.

Costs order against Commission

7D–51   **5.**—(1) The following paragraphs of this regulation apply where:

> (a) funded services are provided to a client in relation to proceedings;
>
> (b) those proceedings are finally decided in favour of a non-funded party; and

(c) cost protection applies.

(2) The court may, subject to the following paragraphs of this regulation, make an order for the payment by the Commission to the non-funded party of the whole or any part of the costs incurred by him in the proceedings (other than any costs that the client is required to pay under a section 11(1) costs order).

(3) An order under paragraph (2) may only be made if all the conditions set out in sub-paragraphs (a), (b), (c) and (d) are satisfied:

(a) a section 11(1) costs order is made against the client in the proceedings, and the amount (if any) which the client is required to pay under that costs order is less than the amount of the full costs;

(b) unless there is a good reason for the delay, the non-funded party makes a request under regulation 10(2) of the Community Legal Service (Costs) Regulations 2000 within three months of the making of the section 11(1) costs order;

(c) as regards costs incurred in a court of first instance, the proceedings were instituted by the client, the non-funded party is an individual, and the court is satisfied that the non-funded party will suffer financial hardship unless the order is made; and

(d) in any case, the court is satisfied that it is just and equitable in the circumstances that provision for the costs should be made out of public funds.

(3A) An order under paragraph (2) may be made—

(a) in relation to proceedings in the House of Lords, by the Clerk to the Parliaments;

(b) in relation to proceedings in the Court of Appeal, High Court or a county court, by a costs judge or a district judge;

(c) in relation to proceedings in a magistrates' court, by a single justice or by the justices' clerk;

(d) in relation to proceedings in the Employment Appeal Tribunal, by the Registrar of that tribunal.

(4) Where the client receives funded services in connection with part only of the proceedings, the reference in paragraph (2) to the costs incurred by the non-funded party in the relevant proceedings shall be construed as a reference to so much of those costs as is attributable to the part of the proceedings which are funded proceedings.

(5) Where a court decides any proceedings in favour of the non-funded party and an appeal lies (with or without permission) against that decision, any order made under this regulation shall not take effect:

(a) where permission to appeal is required, unless the time limit for applications for permission to appeal expires without permission being granted;

(b) where permission to appeal is granted or is not required, unless the time limit for appeal expires without an appeal being brought.

(6) Subject to paragraph (7), in determining whether the conditions in paragraph (3)(c) and (d) are satisfied, the court shall have regard to the resources of the non-funded party and of his partner.

(7) The court shall not have regard to the resources of the partner of the non-funded party if the partner has a contrary interest in the funded proceedings.

(8) Where the non-funded party is acting in a representative, fiduciary or official capacity and is entitled to be indemnified in respect of his costs from any property, estate or fund, the court shall, for the purposes of paragraph (3), have regard to the value of the property, estate or fund and the resources of the persons, if any, including that party where appropriate, who are beneficially interested in that property, estate or fund.

"Costs incurred by him in the proceedings" (reg.5(2))

7D–52   The costs "incurred...in the proceedings" include costs incurred before the successful party himself received a grant of public funding (see *H (Minors) (Abduction: Custody Rights) (No.2), Re* [1992] 2 A.C. 303).

"A court of first instance" (reg.5(3)(c))

7D–53   The Divisional Court has been held to be a court of first instance where a decision under review was that of a body other than a court or tribunal (*R. v. Greenwich LBC ex p. Lovelace (No.2)* [1992] Q.B. 155).

"Severe financial hardship" (reg.5(3)(c))

7D–54   Whether or not financial hardship is severe is a question of fact and degree in the particular circumstances of the case (see *Kelly v. London Transport Executive* [1982] 1 W.L.R. 1055; *Hanning v. Maitland (No.3)* [1970] 1 Q.B. 580 and *Stewart v. Stewart* [1974] 1 W.L.R. 877). A local authority or some other large body must be able to show by evidence that it would sustain "some real impairment of the ability to function normally" (*R. v. Greenwich LBC ex p. Lovelace (No.2)* [1992] Q.B. 155).

"Just and equitable in all the circumstances" (reg.5(3)(d))

7D–55   In *Gallie v. Lee* [1971] A.C. 1039 Lord Reid stated that this is one composite phrase which should not be separated and which is to be applied broadly (at p.1047G). This dictum has been approved by the House of Lords in *Davies v. Taylor (No.2)* [1974] A.C. 225 and *Din (Taj) v. Wandsworth LBC (No.2)* [1982] 1 W.L.R. 418, and has been followed, for instance in *Maynard v. Osmond (No.2)* [1979] 1 W.L.R. 31.

Orders for costs against Commission — Litigation Support

7D–56   **6.—**(1) [. . . .]

Note —Regulation 6 revoked by S.I. 2005 No. 2006.

Effect of these Regulations

7D–57   **7.—**(1) No order to pay costs in favour of a non-funded party shall be made against the Commission in respect of funded proceedings except in accordance with these Regulations, and any costs to be paid under such an order shall be paid out of the Community Legal Service Fund.

(2) Nothing in these Regulations shall be construed, in relation to proceedings where one or more parties are receiving, or have received, funded services, as:

(a) requiring a court to make a costs order where it would not otherwise have made a costs order; or

(b) affecting the court's power to make a wasted costs order against a legal representative.

SECTION 8

LIMITATION

8 LIMITATION ACT 1980

Limitation Act 1980

(1980 c.58)

An Act to consolidate the Limitation Acts 1939 to 1980

[13 November 1980]

Northern Ireland. With a minor exception this Act does not apply; **8–1** see s.41(4) post.

PART I

ORDINARY TIME LIMITS FOR DIFFERENT CLASSES OF ACTION

Time limits under Part I subject to extension or exclusion under Part II

1.—(1) This Part of this Act gives the ordinary time limits for bring- **8–2** ing actions of the various classes mentioned in the following provisions of this Part.

(2) The ordinary time limits given in this Part of this Act are subject to extension or exclusion in accordance with the provisions of Part II of this Act.

Scope and operation of the Act

The Act is a consolidating Act, not a codifying or reforming measure. It embodies **8–3** substantively without amendment the relevant provisions of the Limitation Acts of 1939, 1963 and 1975 and the Limitation Amendment Act 1980, and some other statutory provisions dealing with limitation periods (*e.g.* limitation periods for recovery of contribution).

The Limitation Act 1963 was designed to mitigate the injustice caused to a plaintiff who did not know that he had suffered injury until after the expiry of the current period of limitation and thus had his claim barred without knowing that he had a claim (see *Cartledge v. Jopling (E.) and Sons Ltd* [1963] A.C. 758).

There have been introduced, by amendment into the Act, further important provisions extending the time limit for bringing actions for negligence causing latent damage and not involving personal injuries: see s.14A, below which was added by the Latent Damage Act 1986, and s.14B which provides for finality after 15 years. Such new statutory provision for extension has reversed the effect of cases such as *Pirelli General Cable Works Ltd v. Faber (Oscar) and Partners* [1983] 2 A.C. 1, HL. Furthermore by s.3 of the Latent Damage Act, 1986, provision is now made, subject to the terms of that section, for accrual of a fresh cause of action to successive purchasers of property suffering from latent damage. By the transitional provisions of the Latent Damage Act 1986, some actions will continue to be governed by the law applicable before the introduction of the Act (see s.4). Thus, the new provisions will not enable any action to be brought which was already barred before the new Act came into force; or affect any action commenced before such time. The Act came into force on September 18, 1986 (see s.5(3)).

In applying the Limitation Act 1980, there are three points which need, subject to the above, to be borne in mind.

First, the Act is a consolidating statute. The previous case-law relating to the earlier statutory provisions replaced without amendment by the Act still remain binding and authoritative, subject of course to the overriding judicial power in applying earlier decisions to the instant case. Further, an accrued right to plead a six year time bar under s.2(1) of the Limitation Act 1939, prior to its amendment by the Law Reform (Limitation of Actions, etc.) Act 1954, is not overcome by the operation of the Limitation Act 1975: *Arnold v. Central Electricity Generating Board* [1988] A.C. 228, applied in *McDonnell v. Congregation of Christian Brothers Trustees* [2003] UKHL 63; [2004] 1 A.C. 1101; [2003] 3 W.L.R. 1627, HL.

Second, the requirement of the rules of pleading that any relevant statute of limitation must be specifically pleaded also remains binding and must be complied with (see, Practice Direction 16, para. 13.1, see Vol. 1, para. 16PD.13).

Third, following the introduction of the CPR , whilst the Court has a very wide power to strike out proceedings as being an abuse of process it may always wish to have regard to the fact that the limitation period is still on foot and that future proceedings might be brought on the same cause of action within the limitation period. It is submitted that a ready use of the power to impose conditions upon the bringing of a new claim, whether on the occasion of striking out the existing claim, or upon any new claim being made, and including an order that such new claim be not brought or pursued without permission of the Court, is to be expected: see, *e.g.* CPR 3.1(3) and 3.4(4) and (5).

It should be further observed that the 1980 Act applies to arbitrations as it applies to actions in the High Court (see s.34).

ACTIONS FOUNDED ON TORT

Time limit for actions founded on tort

8–4   **2.** An action founded on tort shall not be brought after the expiration of six years from the date on which the cause of action accrued.

Accrual of cause of action

8–4.1   A commentary on the principles relevant to the ascertainment of the date of accrual of a cause of action founded on tort is contained in McGee, *Limitation Periods*, (2002) 4th ed., Ch.5. In relation to the particular tort of negligence, the principles are summarised in the judgment of the Court of Appeal in *Polley v. Warner Goodman & Streat (a firm)* [2003] EWCA Civ 1013; [2003] P.N.L.R. 40, at paras 15 and 16 of the judgment.

Time limit in case of successive conversions and extinction of title of owner of converted goods

8–5   **3.**—(1) Where any cause of action in respect of the conversion of a chattel has accrued to any person and, before he recovers possession of the chattel, a further conversion takes place, no action shall be brought in respect of the further conversion after the expiration of six years from the accrual of the cause of action in respect of the original conversion.

(2) Where any such cause of action has accrued to any person and the period prescribed for bringing that action has expired and he has not during that period recovered possession of the chattel, the title of that person to the chattel shall be extinguished.

Special time limit in case of theft

8–6   **4.**—(1) The right of any person from whom a chattel is stolen to bring an action in respect of the theft shall not be subject to the time limits under sections 2 and 3(1) of this Act, but if his title to the chattel is extinguished under section 3(2) of this Act he may not bring an action in respect of a theft preceding the loss of his title, unless the theft in question preceded the conversion from which time began to run for the purposes of section 3(2).

(2) Subsection (1) above shall apply to any conversion related to the theft of a chattel as it applies to the theft of a chattel; and, except as provided below, every conversion following the theft of a chattel before the person from whom it is stolen recovers possession of it shall be regarded for the purposes of this section as related to the theft.

If anyone purchases the stolen chattel in good faith neither the purchase nor any conversion following it shall be regarded as related to the theft.

(3) Any cause of action accruing in respect of the theft or any conversion related to the theft of a chattel to any person from whom the chattel is stolen shall be disregarded for the purpose of applying section 3(1) or (2) of this Act to his case.

(4) Where in any action brought in respect of the conversion of a

chattel it is proved that the chattel was stolen from the plaintiff or anyone through whom he claims it shall be presumed that any conversion following the theft is related to the theft unless the contrary is shown.

(5) In this section "theft" includes—

(a) any conduct outside England and Wales which would be theft if committed in England and Wales; and

(b) obtaining any chattel (in England and Wales or elsewhere) in the circumstances described in section 15(1) of the Theft Act 1968 (obtaining by deception) or by blackmail within the meaning of section 21 of that Act;

and references in this section to a chattel being "stolen" shall be construed accordingly.

Time limit for actions for defamation or malicious falsehood

4A. The time limit under section 2 of this Act shall not apply to an **8–7** action for—

(a) libel or slander, or

(b) slander of title, slander of goods or other malicious falsehood,

but no such action shall be brought after the expiration of one year from the date on which the cause of action accrued.

Note —Added by the Administration of Justice Act 1985, s.57(2), 69(2), Sched.9, **8–8** para. 14. Substituted, in relation to causes of action arising after September 4, 1996, by the Defamation Act 1996, s.5(2).

ACTIONS FOUNDED ON SIMPLE CONTRACT

Time limit for actions founded on simple contract

5. An action founded on simple contract shall not be brought after **8–9** the expiration of six years from the date on which the cause of action accrued.

Special time limit for actions in respect of certain loans

6.—(1) Subject to subsection (3) below, section 5 of this Act shall **8–10** not bar the right of action on a contract of loan to which this section applies.

(2) This section applies to any contract of loan which—

(a) does not provide for repayment of the debt on or before a fixed or determinable date; and

(b) does not effectively (whether or not it purports to do so) make the obligation to repay the debt conditional on a demand for repayment made by or on behalf of the creditor or on any other matter;

except where in connection with taking the loan the debtor enters into any collateral obligation to pay the amount of the debt or any part of it (as, for example, by delivering a promissory note as security for the debt) on terms which would exclude the application of this section to the contract of loan if they applied directly to repayment of the debt.

(3) Where a demand in writing for repayment of the debt under a contract of loan to which this section applies is made by or on behalf of the creditor (or, where there are joint creditors, by or on behalf of any one of them) section 5 of this Act shall thereupon apply as if the cause of action to recover the debt had accrued on the date on which the demand was made.

(4) In this section "promissory note" has the same meaning as in the Bills of Exchange Act 1882.

Time limit for actions to enforce certain awards

8–11   **7.** An action to enforce an award, where the submission is not by an instrument under seal, shall not be brought after the expiration of six years from the date on which the cause of action accrued.

Application for leave to enforce award

8–11.1   It was common ground in *Good Challenger Navegante SA v. Metalexportimport SA (The "Good Challenger")* [2003] EWCA Civ. 1668; [2004] 1 Lloyd's Rep. 67, CA that when an *ex parte* application for leave to enforce award was made under s.26 of the Arbitration Act 1950, an action was brought for the purposes of s.7 above. This was because such an application was an alternative to proceeding by way of writ or originating summons.

Accrual of cause of action

8–11.2   It was also common ground in the above case that time runs, not from the date upon which the award is made or published, but from the date when the paying party is in breach of its implied obligation to pay the award.

GENERAL RULE FOR ACTIONS ON A SPECIALTY

Time limit for actions on a specialty

8–12   **8.**—(1) An action upon a specialty shall not be brought after the expiration of twelve years from the date on which the cause of action accrued.

(2) Subsection (1) above shall not affect any action for which a shorter period of limitation is prescribed by any other provision of this Act.

Claims to recover money

8–12.1   See the note to section 9 below.

ACTIONS FOR SUMS RECOVERABLE BY STATUTE

Time limit for actions for sums recoverable by statute

8–13   **9.**—(1) An action to recover any sum recoverable by virtue of any enactment shall not be brought after the expiration of six years from the date on which the cause of action accrued.

(2) Subsection (1) above shall not affect any action to which section 10 of this Act applies.

Claim to recover money

8–13.1   The reference in subsection (1) to any sum is not limited to claims for liquidated sums of money. The scheme of the Act is to impose a 6 year limitation period on claims for money under an enactment, thus constituting an exception to the general rule as regards specialties: *Rowan Companies Inc. v. Lambert Eggink Offshore Transport Consultants V.O.F.* [1999] 2 Lloyd's Rep 443.

Special time limit for claiming contribution

10.—(1) Where under section 1 of the Civil Liability (Contribution) **8–14**
Act 1978 any person becomes entitled to a right to recover contribution in respect of any damage from any other person, no action to recover contribution by virtue of that right shall be brought after the expiration of two years from the date on which that right accrued.

(2) For the purposes of this section the date on which a right to recover contribution in respect of any damage accrues to any person (referred to below in this section as "the relevant date") shall be ascertained as provided in subsections (3) and (4) below.

(3) If the person in question is held liable in respect of that damage—

      (a) by a judgment given in any civil proceedings; or

      (b) by an award made on any arbitration;

the relevant date shall be the date on which the judgment is given, or the date of the award (as the case may be).

For the purposes of this subsection no account shall be taken of any judgment or award given or made on appeal in so far as it varies the amount of damages awarded against the person in question.

(4) If, in any case not within subsection (3) above, the person in question makes or agrees to make any payment to one or more persons in compensation for that damage (whether he admits any liability in respect of the damage or not), the relevant date shall be the earliest date on which the amount to be paid by him is agreed between him (or his representative) and the person (or each of the persons, as the case may be) to whom the payment is to be made.

(5) An action to recover contribution shall be one to which sections 28, 32 and 35 of this Act apply, but otherwise Parts II and III of this Act (except sections 34, 37 and 38) shall not apply for the purposes of this section.

Operation of this section

This section is derived from para. 6 of Schedule I to the Civil Liability (Contribu- **8–15** tion) Act 1978. It prescribes the time limit within which a claim to recover contribution may be brought under s.1 of that Act against any other person as defined by s.6(1). Section 10 provides that the claim to recover contribution must not be brought more than two years from the date upon which that right accrued. That date is referred to in s.10 as "the relevant date."

If the right to recover contribution arises from a judgment or award then the relevant date is the date of judgment or award. If the amount of the judgment or award is varied on appeal the relevant date remains the date of the judgment at first instance or the original award. Presumably, if no right to contribution arose until the decision on appeal then the date of judgment of the higher Court would be the relevant date.

If the right to recover contribution arises from an agreement to settle (whether liability be admitted or not) then the relevant date is the date of agreement, *not* the date of payment. *Semble*, if payment into Court (now a Part 36 offer) is made and accepted, the relevant date would be the date of acceptance.

The two year period may be extended where the person claiming contribution is under a disability (s.28) or under s.32 where fraud, concealment or mistake are present.

And, by subs.(5), an action for contribution is one by definition to which s.35 applies; *i.e.* the same rules as to the date of bringing of third party proceedings, set-offs and counterclaims as are laid down by s.35 in the case of actions generally are also to apply to actions for contribution.

This section sets a time limit for the bringing of the contribution proceedings themselves. There remains the question of the effect on contribution proceedings of the expiry of the period of limitation applicable between the person who has suffered the damage and the person claiming contribution. The effect of s.1(2) of the Civil Liability (Contribution) Act 1978 appears to be that the running of time as between such person and the person claiming contribution does not affect the entitlement to recover contribution provided that immediately before the person claiming contribution made or was ordered or agreed to make the payment in respect of which contribution is sought, he (*i.e.* the person claiming) was liable in respect of the damage. Thus, he will not be entitled to recover where, for example, the claim against him by the person who has suffered the damage is settled at a time when an action brought upon that claim would be statute-barred. The drafting of s.1 of the 1978 Act is not without its difficulties and for a full commentary see Current Law Statutes Annotated 1978, Chap. 47.

ACTIONS IN RESPECT OF WRONGS CAUSING PERSONAL INJURIES OR DEATH

Special time limit for actions in respect of personal injuries

8–16   11.—(1) This section applies to any action for damages for negligence, nuisance or breach of duty (whether the duty exists by virtue of a contract or of provision made by or under a statute or independently of any contract or any such provision) where the damages claimed by the plaintiff for the negligence, nuisance or breach of duty consist of or include damages in respect of personal injuries to the plaintiff or any other person.

(1A) This section does not apply to any action brought for damages under section 3 of the Protection from Harassment Act 1997.

(2) None of the time limits given in the preceding provisions of this Act shall apply to an action to which this section applies.

(3) An action to which this section applies shall not be brought after the expiration of the period applicable in accordance with subsection (4) or (5) below.

(4) Except where subsection (5) below applies, the period applicable is three years from—

(a) the date on which the cause of action accrued; or

(b) the date of knowledge (if later) of the person injured.

(5) If the person injured dies before the expiration of the period mentioned in subsection (4) above, the period applicable as respects the cause of action surviving for the benefit of his estate by virtue of section 1 of the Law Reform (Miscellaneous Provisions) Act 1934 shall be three years from—

(a) the date of death, or

(b) the date of the personal representative's knowledge;

whichever is the later.

(6) For the purposes of this section "personal representative" includes any person who is or has been a personal representative of the deceased, including an executor who has not proved the will (whether or not he has renounced probate) but not anyone appointed only as a special personal representative in relation to settled land; and regard shall be had to any knowledge acquired by any such person while a personal representative or previously.

(7) If there is more than one personal representative, and their dates of knowledge are different, subsection (5)(b) above shall be read as referring to the earliest of those dates.

Note — Subs.(1A) was added by the Protection from Harassment Act 1997, s.6.
For notes on ss.11 to 14 of this Act see commentary which follows s.14, below.

Actions in respect of defective products

11A.—(1) This section shall apply to an action for damages by **8–18**
virtue of any provision of Part I of the Consumer Protection Act
1987.

(2) None of the time limits given in the preceding provisions of
this Act shall apply to an action to which this section applies.

(3) An action to which this section applies shall not be brought after the expiration of the period of ten years from the relevant time,
within the meaning of section 4 of the said Act of 1987; and this
subsection shall operate to extinguish a right of action and shall do
so whether or not that right of action had accrued, or time under the
following provisions of this Act had begun to run, at the end of the
said period of ten years.

(4) Subject to subsection (5) below, an action to which this section
applies in which the damages claimed by the plaintiff consist of or
include damages in respect of personal injuries to the plaintiff or any
other person or loss of or damage to any property, shall not be
brought after the expiration of the period of three years from whichever is the later of—

> (a) the date on which the cause of action accrued; and
> (b) the date of knowledge of the injured person or, in the
> case of loss of or damage to property, the date of knowl-
> edge of the plaintiff or (if earlier) of any person in whom
> his cause of action was previously vested.

(5) If in a case where the damages claimed by the plaintiff consist
of or include damages in respect of personal injuries to the plaintiff
or any other person the injured person died before the expiration of
the period mentioned in subsection (4) above, that subsection shall
have effect as respects the cause of action surviving for the benefit of
his estate by virtue of section 1 of the Law Reform (Miscellaneous
Provisions) Act 1934 as if for the reference to that period there were
substituted a reference to the period of three years from whichever is
the later of—

> (a) the date of death; and
> (b) the date of the personal representative's knowledge.

(6) For the purposes of this section "personal representative"
includes any person who is or has been a personal representative of
the deceased, including an executor who has not proved the will
(whether or not he has renounced probate) but not anyone appointed
only as a special personal representative in relation to settled land,
and regard shall be had to any knowledge acquired by any such
person while a personal representative or previously.

(7) If there is more than one personal representative and their
dates of knowledge are different, subsection (5)(b) above shall be
read as referring to the earliest of those dates.

(8) Expressions used in this section or section 14 of this Act and
in Part I of the Consumer Protection Act 1987 have the same mean-

ings in this section or that section as in that Part; and section 1(1) of that Act (Part I to be construed as enacted for the purpose of complying with the product liability Directive) shall apply for the purpose of construing this section and the following provisions of this Act so far as they relate to an action by virtue of any provision of that Part as it applies for the purpose of construing that Part.

8–19 *Note* —Added by the Consumer Protection Act 1987, s.6, s.50(2) and Sched.1, para. 1.

For notes on ss.11 to 14 of this Act see commentary which follows s.14, below.

For a case deciding that the 10-year long-stop provision under s.11A(3) is a period of limitation for the purposes of s.35(3) of the Act, and that the court had a discretion pusuant to s.35 and to CPR 19.5 to allow substitution of the defendant after the expiry of such time limit, see *Horne-Roberts v. Smithkline Beecham PLC* [2001] EWCA Civ 2006; [2002] 1 W.L.R. 1662; [2002] C.P. Rep. 20; (2002) 65 BMLR 79, CA.

Special time limit for actions under Fatal Accidents legislation

8–20 **12.**—(1) An action under the Fatal Accidents Act 1976 shall not be brought if the death occurred when the person injured could no longer maintain an action and recover damages in respect of the injury (whether because of a time limit in this Act or in any other Act, or for any other reason). Where any such action by the injured person would have been barred by the time limit in section 11 or 11A of this Act, no account shall be taken of the possibility of that time limit being overridden under section 33 of this Act.

(2) None of the time limits given in the preceding provisions of this Act shall apply to an action under the Fatal Accidents Act 1976, but no such action shall be brought after the expiration of three years from—

    (a) the date of death; or

    (b) the date of knowledge of the person for whose benefit the action is brought;

whichever is the later.

(3) An action under the Fatal Accidents Act 1976 shall be one to which sections 28, 33 and 35 of this Act apply, and the application to any such action of the time limit under subsection (2) above shall be subject to section 39; but otherwise Parts II and III of this Act shall not apply to any such action.

8–21 *Note* —Amended by the Consumer Protection Act 1987, s.6(6), 50(2) and Sched.1, para. 2.

For notes on ss.11 to 14 of this Act see commentary which follows s.14, below.

Operation of time limit under section 12 in relation to different dependants

8–22 **13.**—(1) Where there is more than one person for whose benefit an action under the Fatal Accidents Act 1976 is brought, section 12(2)(b) of this Act shall be applied separately to each of them.

(2) Subject to subsection (3) below, if by virtue of subsection (1) above the action would be outside the time limit given by section 12(2) as regards one or more, but not all, of the persons for whose benefit it is brought, the court shall direct that any person as regards

whom the action would be outside that limit shall be excluded from those for whom the action is brought.

(3) The court shall not give such a direction if it is shown that if the action were brought exclusively for the benefit of the person in question it would not be defeated by a defence of limitation (whether in consequence of section 28 of this Act or an agreement between the parties not to raise the defence, or otherwise).

Note —For notes on ss.11 to 14 of this Act see commentary which follows s.14, **8–23** below.

Definition of date of knowledge for purposes of sections 11 and 12

14.—(1) Subject to subsection (1A) below, in sections 11 and 12 of **8–24** this Act references to a person's date of knowledge are references to the date on which he first had knowledge of the following facts—

    (a) that the injury in question was significant; and

    (b) that the injury was attributable in whole or in part to the act or omission which is alleged to constitute negligence, nuisance or breach of duty; and

    (c) the identity of the defendant, and

    (d) if it is alleged that the act or omission was that of a person other than the defendant, the identity of that person and the additional facts supporting the bringing of an action against the defendant;

and knowledge that any acts or omissions did or did not, as a matter of law, involve negligence, nuisance or breach of duty is irrelevant.

(1A) In section 11A of this Act and in section 12 of this Act so far as that section applies to an action by virtue of section 6(1)(a) of the Consumer Protection Act 1987 (death caused by defective product) references to a person's date of knowledge are references to the date on which he first had knowledge of the following facts—

    (a) such facts about the damage caused by the defect as would lead a reasonable person who had suffered such damage to consider it sufficiently serious to justify his instituting proceedings for damages against a defendant who did not dispute liability and was able to satisfy a judgment; and

    (b) that the damage was wholly or partly attributable to the facts and circumstances alleged to constitute the defect; and

    (c) the identity of the defendant;

but, in determining the date on which a person first had such knowledge there shall be disregarded both the extent (if any) of that person's knowledge on any date of whether particular facts or circumstances would or would not, as a matter of law, constitute a defect and, in a case relating to loss of or damage to property, any knowledge which that person had on a date on which he had no right of action by virtue of Part I of that Act in respect of the loss or damage.

(2) For the purposes of this section an injury is significant if the person whose date of knowledge is in question would reasonably have considered it sufficiently serious to justify his instituting proceedings for damages against a defendant who did not dispute liability and was able to satisfy a judgment.

(3) For the purposes of this section a person's knowledge includes knowledge which he might reasonably have been expected to acquire—

> (a) from facts observable or ascertainable by him, or
>
> (b) from facts ascertainable by him with the help of medical or other appropriate expert advice which it is reasonable for him to seek;

but a person shall not be fixed under this subsection with knowledge of a fact ascertainable only with the help of expert advice so long as he has taken all reasonable steps to obtain (and, where appropriate, to act on) that advice.

8–25   *Note* — Subs. (1A) inserted by the Consumer Protection Act 1987, s.6(6), s.50(2) and Sched.1, para. 3.

Actions for damages for personal injuries or death

8–26   Sections 11–14 and 28 and 33 re-enact the provisions of the Limitation Act 1975.

The main changes introduced by the Act of 1975, and embodied in the provisions of the Act of 1980, may be summarised as follows:

> (1) the introduction of new time limits for commencing
>
> > (a) actions for personal injuries (s.11);
> >
> > (b) actions under the Law Reform (Miscellaneous Provisions) Act 1934 (see s.11(5)); and
> >
> > (c) actions under the Fatal Accidents Act 1976 (see ss.12, 13).
>
> (2) the introduction of a new time limit for commencing such actions, namely, "the date of knowledge" if later than the date of actual accrual of the cause of action. "Date of knowledge" is defined by s.14; and see paras 8–29, 8–30 and 8–31 below.
>
> (3) the introduction of a power conferred on the Court to "override" or "disapply" the time limits provided, in the sense that an action may be allowed to proceed notwithstanding the expiry of such time limits; see s.33, below (para. 8–67).
>
> (4) the abolition of the need for obtaining the leave of the Court for the purposes of the Limitation Act 1963.
>
> (5) the exclusion of the limitation period in case of disability (see s.28 of the 1980 Act).

These statutory provisions of the 1980 Act, embodying those of the 1975 Act, do not envisage the need for rules of court to govern their operation, and no such rules have been made; nevertheless, they will inevitably have a great influence on the conduct of actions for personal injuries or death. See for the practice in relation to the pleading of matters arising under ss.11–14, SCP 1999, Vol. 1, paras 18/8/23 to 18/8/26 *et seq.*

The statutory provisions do not affect periods of limitation prescribed by other enactments, *e.g.* Merchant Shipping Act 1995, Carriage by Air Act 1961, Nuclear Installations Act 1965, and the International Transport Conventions Act 1983 (see 1980 Act, s.39).

The defendant may, in a case where the cause of action arose sufficiently long ago, be entitled to rely on accrued limitation defences under the regime of the unamended Limitation Act 1939: see *Arnold v. Central Electricity Generating Board*, applied in *McDonnell v. Congregation of Christian Brothers Trustees*, both cited at para. 8–3 above.

Time limits for actions for personal injuries

8–26.1   For the purposes of s.11, an action for personal injuries includes any action for damages for negligence, nuisance or breach of duty (whether the duty exists by virtue of a contract or of a provision made by or under a statute or independently of any contract or any such provision) where the damages claimed by the plaintiff for the negligence, nuisance or breach of duty consist of or include damages in respect of personal injuries to the plaintiff or any other person (subs.(1)); and personal injuries include any disease and any impairment of a person's physical or mental condition; and "injury" and cognate expressions are to be construed accordingly (s.38(1)).

The definition of personal injuries (*cf.* O.1, r.4) is wide enough to cover all proceedings, whether in tort or contract or under statute, in which a claim is made for personal injuries, save that under the law as laid down in *Stubbings v. Webb* [1993] A.C. 498, HL (overruling *Letang v. Cooper* [1965] 1 Q.B. 232; and *Long v. Hepworth* [1968] 1 W.L.R. 1299; [1968] 3 All E.R. 248, CA), claims for trespass to the person and, it would appear, false imprisonment, malicious prosecution or defamation are excluded from the ambit of s.11(1). Thus the limitation period in such cases remains at six years as laid down by s.2. In *Stubbings v. Webb*, where the allegations were of rape and sexual abuse, the cause of action was barred six years after the plaintiff reached the age of majority and there was no provision for extending time.

It should be noted that the other ground on which *Letang v. Cooper* was decided, namely that no cause of action in trespass to the person lies for negligent driving, was held by *Stubbings v. Webb* to be correct.

A claim by a daughter against her mother for breach of her duty as a parent to protect her against the risk of foreseeable injury from sexual abuse by her father was not a claim for trespass to the person. Distinguishing *Stubbings v. Webb* it was held that the action fell within section 11. Subject to the primary limitation period, extensions were possible under both ss.14 and 33; *S. v. W.* [1995] 1 F.L.R. 862 [1995] P.I.Q.R. 470, CA.

It has been held at first instance that a claim under s.2(2) of the Animals Act 1971 is not a claim for "negligence, nuisance or breach of duty" within s.11: *Clarke v. Barber* [2002] 5 C.L. 70.

Although a failed sterilisation operation is not itself a personal injury within the meaning of s.38(1), the subsequent unwanted pregnancy is such an injury, in the sense of an "impairment". The whole claim for damages, including economic loss, was barred by the 3 year rule under s.11 (*Walkin v. S. Manchester HA* [1995] 1 W.L.R. 1543; [1995] 1 W.L.R. 1543, CA). *Walkin* was applied, subject to a ruling under s.33, in *Godfrey v. Gloucestershire Royal Infirmary NHS Trust* [2003] Lloyd's Rep. Med. 398 (a case of alleged negligent advice leading to failure to terminate a pregnancy in the case of an injured child).

A claim for damages in respect of a failure to address a dyslexic's difficulties in reading and writing so as to ameliorate the effects of that condition was a claim for personal injuries and thus subject to the provisions of sections 11 and 14: *Adams v. Bracknell Forest BC* [2004] UKHL 29; [2004] 3 W.L.R. 89, HL.

The question whether an action is for damages in respect of personal injuries is one of substance, not a matter of pleading (*Walkin's* case, applying *Howe v. David Brown Tractors (Retail) Ltd* [1991] 4 All E.R. 30, CA).

A claim containing claims for both damages for personal injuries and for damages for economic loss which is time-barred under section 11 may be amended by permission by deletion of the claim for personal injuries if the remaining claim would not have been barred if raised in new proceedings commenced at the time of the hearing of the application to amend. In a proper case, the amendment may be allowed under CPR r.17.4(2) where the new claim can be regarded as arising "out of the same facts or substantially the same facts": *Shade v. The Compton Partnership* [2000] Lloyd's Rep. P.N. 81, CA. The Court went further in *Pounds v. Eckford Rands* [2003] Lloyd's Rep. P.N. 195, holding that a claim for damages for personal injuries and financial loss as a result of negligence might be amended by excising the claim for personal injuries when each element of the claim would have been time-barred at the date of application for permission to amend. The remaining, narrowed, claim was not a new claim; even if it was, it fell squarely within CPR 17.4(2).

Section 11(1) does not apply to an action for breach of contract against insurance brokers to arrange cover for a passenger who suffers personal injuries (*Ackbar v. C.F. Green & Co. Ltd* [1975] Q.B. 582).

A claim for damages against a solicitor for negligence in permitting an action by the plaintiff for damages for personal injury to be struck out for want of prosecution is not itself a claim for damages in respect of personal injury. See *Hopkins v. MacKenzie* [1995] 6 Med.L.R. 26, CA. Nor is a claim by an employee against his employers for failing to advise him as to the benefits to which he was entitled on suffering personal injury in the course of his employment: *Gould v. Leeds H.A.*, *The Times*, May 14, 1999, CA. But a claim against solicitors for alleged mishandling of a case, causing clinical depression, is a claim which includes damages for personal injuries: *Bennett v. Greenland Houchen & Co.* [1998] P.N.L.R. 458, CA.

An action will include a claim "in respect of personal injuries to the plaintiff or any other person" where a firm claims damages for loss of profits by reason of injury to one of its partners (*Howe v. David Brown Tractors (Retail) Ltd* [1991] 4 All E.R. 30, CA).

On the other hand, s.11, which provides the time limit for actions for personal injuries, does not apply to actions under the Fatal Accidents Act, as to which a separate limitation period is provided (see s.12).

For actions for personal injuries (except for claims for the benefit of the estate of a deceased under the Law Reform (Misc. Prov.) Act 1934, s.1) the limitation period for commencing such actions runs from:

(a) the date on which the cause of action accrued; or

(b) the date (if later) of the plaintiff's knowledge (s.11(3) and (4)).

Thus, for such actions, s.11 of the 1980 Act has preserved unchanged the existing period of three years and it has also preserved the general rule that this limitation period will run from the date on which the cause of action accrued, including presumably the rule that in an action in tort the cause of action accrues at the date on which the injury was suffered, whether or not it was then apparent (see *Cartledge v. Jopling* [1963] A.C. 758). On the other hand if "the date of knowledge" of the plaintiff is later than the date on which the cause of action accrued, the limitation period will run from such date of knowledge. As to what is the "date of knowledge," see s.14(1)–(3).

The use of the expression in ss.11(3) and 12(1) that "an action ... shall not be brought" has not altered the law that an action may be brought without the leave of the Court after the expiry of the limitation periods, leaving the defendant, if he so wishes, to raise the defence of the limitation period (see *Dawkins v. Lord Penrhyn* (1878) 4App.Cas. 51, *per* Earl Cairns L.C. at 59; *Dismore v. Milton* [1938] 3 All E.R. 762, CA).

Time limits for actions under Law Reform (Misc. Prov.) Act 1934, s.1

8–27 In an action under the Law Reform (Misc. Prov.) Act 1934, s.1, by or on behalf of the estate of an injured person who dies, *e.g.* a claim for loss of expectation of life (so far as such an action may still survive: see ss.1 and 73 of the Administration of Justice Act 1982), the limitation period is three years from (a) the date of his death or (b) the date of knowledge of his personal representative, whichever is the later (s.11(5)) or if there is more than one personal representative and their dates of knowledge are different, from the earliest date of knowledge of any of them (s.11(7)). Such an action will lie where an action has been started by him in his lifetime and continued by his personal representatives or the action is started by his personal representatives within three years of his death or within three years of the earliest date of knowledge of any one of them whichever is the later (s.11(5) of the Act). On the other hand, such an action will be barred if the injured person dies *after* the expiration of the period in which he could have brought the action during his own lifetime (*ibid.*); but in such a case the Court has power to override the time-limits under s.33 (see subss.(4) and (5)). If however the deceased has brought an action in his own lifetime, a claim by his estate under the 1943 Act may be barred under the *Walkley* principle. The estate is in no better position in this respect than the deceased: *Young (Deceased) v. Western Power Distribution (South West) Plc* [2003] EWCA Civ 1034, CA.

Time limits under the Fatal Accidents Act

8–28 In an action under the Fatal Accidents Act 1976, the limitation period is three years from (a) the date of death or (b) the date of knowledge of the persons for whose benefit the action is brought, whichever is the later (s.12(2)). If, however, an action brought under the Fatal Accidents Acts is out of time by virtue of this provision, the Court may nevertheless allow the action to proceed in the exercise of its discretion under s.33 of the Act.

On the other hand, an action under the Fatal Accidents Act may not be brought if at the time of his death the injured person could no longer maintain an action and recover damages in respect of the injury, whether because of a time limit in the Act (see

Williams v. Mersey Docks and Harbour Board [1905] 1 K.B. 804) or in any other Act or for any other reason, *e.g.* because he had settled his claim, s.12(1). And if the action by the injured person would have been barred by the time limit in s.11 of the Act, no account may be taken of the possibility that such time limit may be overridden by the Court under s.33 of the Act, though the Court still has power to exercise its discretion under s.33 of the Act in an action under the Fatal Accidents Act in favour of the *dependants* of the deceased.

In the case of a dependant under disability in an action under the Fatal Accidents Act 1976, the period of limitation is extended to within three years of the disability ceasing (see ss.12(3) and 28).

Where, in an action under the Fatal Accidents Act, there are a number of dependants whose dates of knowledge differ, the date of knowledge from which the limitation period is to be calculated must be applied separately to each of them (see s.13(1) of the Act) and if one or more of them, but not all, are debarred, any person so debarred will be excluded from those for whom the action is brought unless it is shown that if the action were brought exclusively for the benefit of that person, it would not be defeated by a defence of limitation whether in consequence of section 28 of the Act or an agreement between the parties not to raise the defence or otherwise, *e.g.* where such dependant could rely on s.33 (s.13(3)).

Time limits for actions from date of knowledge

An essential feature of this Act re-enacting the Limitation Act 1975 is the extension **8–29** of the limitation period from the "date of knowledge" of the relevant person, if this is later than the date of the accrual of the cause of action. This fundamental development in the law relating to actions for personal injuries or death was designed to overcome the rule that in actions in tort the cause of action accrues when the damage first occurs and not when the plaintiff first discovers the same, by which time his action may already have become statute-barred (see *Cartledge v. E. Jopling & Sons Ltd* [1963] A.C. 758; *Higgins v. Arfon Borough Council* [1975] 1 W.L.R. 524; [1975] 2 All E.R. 589; see also *Pirelli General Cable Works Ltd v. Oscar Faber & Partners* [1983] 2 A.C. 1; [1983] 1 All E.R. 65).

The date of knowledge as the date from which, in a proper case, the limitation period runs applies both to actions for personal injuries (see s.11(4)(b)) including claims under the Law Reform (Misc. Prov.) Act 1934 (see s.11(5)(b)) and to actions under the Fatal Accidents Act 1976 (see s.12(2)(b)).

For the purposes of both ss.11 and 12 of the Act, a person's date of knowledge is defined (see s.14 of the 1980 Act) as a reference to the date on which he had knowledge of the four following facts, namely,

(a) that the injury in question was significant; and

(b) that the injury was attributable in whole or in part to the act or omission which is alleged to constitute negligence, nuisance or breach of duty; and

(c) the identity of the defendant; and

(d) if it is alleged that the act or omission was that of a person other than the defendant, the identity of that person and the additional facts supporting the bringing of an action against the defendant. These four facts are stated conjunctively. The plaintiff must have knowledge of them all. But they are exhaustive (*Dobbie v. Medway H.A.* [1994] 1 W.L.R. 1234, CA).

It has been held that, for the purposes of s.14(1)(b), "attributable" means capable of being attributed to rather than caused by: see *Wilkinson v. Ancliff (B.L.T.) Ltd* [1986] 1 W.L.R. 1352, CA, adopted in *Dobbie v. Medway HA* [1994] 1 W.L.R. 1234, *supra*, in which it was pointed out that the words of subs. (1)(b) are "that the injury *was* attributable ... to the act or omission which *is* alleged to constitute negligence ..." (emphasis added by the Court). Attributability does not mean legal responsibility. It can only refer to causation: *per* Steyn L.J. at 1247.

It is specifically provided that ignorance of matters of law as to whether any act or omission involved negligence, nuisance or breach of duty is not relevant in determining whether a person had knowledge (see s.14(1)).

A person's knowledge includes knowledge which he might reasonably have been expected to acquire:

(a) from facts observable or ascertainable by him; or

(b) from facts ascertainable by him with the help of medical or other appropriate expert advice which it is reasonable for him to seek (see s.14(3)).

Nevertheless a person is not fixed with knowledge of a fact ascertainable only with the help of expert advice so long as he has taken all reasonable steps to obtain (and where appropriate, to act on) that advice (*ibid.*).

8–30   The plaintiff will not be fixed with knowledge which he might reasonably have been expected to ascertain with the help of a solicitor if that knowledge would not itself have been ascertained by a solicitor acting reasonably on his behalf (*Nash v. Eli Lilly & Co* [1991] 2 Med.L.R. 169; *Hepworth v. Kerr* [1995] 6 Med.L.R. 135). However, the name of a party liable for a wrongdoing is not, save in exceptional circumstances, a fact ascertainable only with the help of expert advice, and accordingly a claimant may, under ss.14(1)(c) and 14(3)(a), be fixed with constructive knowledge of the identity of the defendant which his advisers, as reasonably competent legal representatives, ought to have acquired: *Henderson v. Temple Pier Co Ltd* [1998] 1 W.L.R. 1540; [1998] 3 All E.R. 324, CA.

The questions which the court may have to decide in any case involving the plaintiff's knowledge under s.14(1), (2) and (3) were fully considered by the Court of Appeal in *Nash v. Eli Lilly & Co* [1993] 1 W.L.R. 782, [1993] 4 All E.R. 383, CA. In particular, the court's judgment, delivered by Purchas L.J., is addressed to the questions of "significant injury" under s.14(1)(a) and (2), "attributability" for the purposes of s.14(1)(b), and "constructive knowledge" for the purposes of s.14(3). It was held at p.796 that:

(a) "Knowledge" in the meaning of s.14 is a state of mind experienced by the plaintiff actually existing or which might have existed had the plaintiff, acting reasonably, acquired knowledge from the facts observable or ascertainable by him or which he could have acquired with the help of medical or other appropriate expert advice which it was reasonable for him to obtain.

(b) The period of limitation begins to run when the plaintiff can first be said to have knowledge of the nature of his injury to justify the particular plaintiff taking the preliminary steps for the institution of proceedings against the person or persons whose act or omission has caused the significant injury concerned.

(c) By s.14(3) "knowledge" for the purposes of s.14(1) includes knowledge reasonably expected to be acquired. There will be cases in which a firmly held belief actually held by the plaintiff precluded consideration of any further steps which he might reasonably have taken to acquire from knowledge of further facts before initiating proceedings. In other cases the state of the plaintiff's belief would make it reasonable for him to make the further inquiries envisaged in s.14(3). The temporal and circumstantial span of reasonable inquiry will depend on the factual context of the case and the subjective characteristics of the individual plaintiff involved.

(d) It is to be noted that a firm belief held by the plaintiff that his injury was attributable to the act or omission of the defendant, but in respect of which he thought it necessary to obtain reassurance or confirmation from experts, medical or legal, or others, would not be regarded as knowledge until the result of his inquiries was known to him or, if he delayed in obtaining that confirmation, until the time at which it was reasonable for him to have got it. If negative expert advice is obtained, that fact must be considered in combination with all other relevant facts in deciding when, if ever, the plaintiff had knowledge. If no inquiries were made, then, if it were reasonable for such inquiries to have been made, and if the failure to make them is not explained, constructive knowledge within the terms of s.14(3) must be considered. If the plaintiff held a firm belief which was of sufficient certainty to justify the taking of the preliminary steps for proceedings by obtaining advice about making a claim for compensation, then such belief is knowledge and the limitation period would begin to run.

(e) Finally it is important to remember where the onus of proof lies. If the writ is not issued within three years of the date when the cause of action arose (s.11(4)(a)), the onus is on the plaintiff to plead and prove a date within the three years preceding the date of the issue of the writ (section 11(4)(b)). If the defendant wishes to rely on a date prior to the three year period immediately preceding the issue of the writ, the onus is on the defendant to prove that the plaintiff had or ought to have had knowledge by that date.

The passage cited above on the onus of proof has been subject to comment by Mance, J. (as he then was) in *Crocker v. British Coal Corporation* [1996] 29 B.M.L.R. 159 at 172 and 173. The judge held that there cannot be opposing legal onuses on opposite parties on the single issue whether there was or was not knowledge within the three year period. He held that the legal burden rests throughout on the claimant, whether the issue is when the cause of action accrued or when the claimant first had knowledge of the facts in the sense identified in s.14. An issue as to constructive knowledge arising under s.14(3) is however apt to involve an evidential burden on a defendant, at all events if there is nothing in the claimant's own case or evidence to raise the issue, although in some respects, for example in relation to the words "so long as he had taken all reasonable steps to obtain (and, where appropriate, to act on) that advice" in the proviso where they became material, it may be easy to envisage both the legal and an evidential burden on a claimant.

In relation to the question of "attributability" the court held, at p.799, "it was not, in our judgment, the intention of Parliament to require for the purposes of s.11 and s.14 of the Act proof of knowledge of the terms in which it will be alleged that the act or omission of the defendants constituted negligence or breach of duty. What is required is knowledge of the essence of the act or omission to which the injury is attributable".

This view has been reinforced by the Court of Appeal in *Broadley v. Guy Clapham & Co*. [1994] 4 All E.R. 439, CA, where it was held that there was nothing in s.14 of the Limitation Act 1980 to suggest that the plaintiff must have known that the defendant's act or omission was capable of being attributed to some fault on his part, and the words "which is alleged to constitute negligence, nuisance or breach of duty" were intended to identify the facts of which the plaintiff had knowledge, without implying that she needed to know that there was some breach of rule.

This decision was followed in *Fennan v. Anthony Hodari & Co* [2001] Lloyd's Rep. PN 183, CA (a case where the claimant did not know that the defendant's omission to tell her the nature and effect of a document amounted to a breach of duty of care). See further, as to the issue of attributability, the authorities cited in the note to s.14A, at para. 8-34 below.

Furthermore, the court has firmly rejected the argument that the plaintiff must know that he has a possible cause of action (*Dobbie v.Medway HA* [1994] 1 W.L.R. 1234, above at p.1248). Likewise, in *Whitfield v. North Durham H.A.* [1995] 6 Med L.R. 32, CA, it was held that the court must look at the essence of a complaint and enquire how far the plaintiff had knowledge in broad terms of the facts on which it was based. It was erroneous to seek to anticipate how the case might ultimately be put—in terms of positive act or negligent omission. The issue of an earlier writ claiming damages for the negligence alleged may itself not be determinative of the plaintiff's state of knowledge.

Significant injury. The test for the purpose of deciding knowledge of significant injury under s.14(2) was explained by Geoffrey Lane L.J. in *McCafferty v. Receiver for the Metropolitan Police District* [1977] 1 W.L.R. 1073, CA at 1081 as follows: "... it is clear that the test is partly a subjective test, namely: 'would this plaintiff have considered the injury sufficiently serious?' And partly an objective test, namely: 'would he have been reasonable if he did not regard it as sufficiently serious?' It seems to me that the subsection is directed at the nature of the injury as known to the plaintiff at that time. Taking that plaintiff, with that plaintiff's intelligence, would he have been reasonable in considering the injury not sufficiently serious to justify instituting proeedings for damages?" Such test was followed by the Court of Appeal in *Nash v. Eli Lilly & Co*, above, and in *KR v. Bryn Alyn Community (Holdings) Ltd* [2003] EWCA Civ 85; [2003] Q.B. 1441; [2003] 3 W.L.R. 107; [2004] 2 All E.R. 716, CA.

The requirement that the injury of which a plaintiff has knowledge should be "significant" is directed solely to the quantum of the injury and not to the plaintiff's evaluation of its cause, nature or usualness. Time does not run against a plaintiff if he would reasonably have considered it insufficiently serious to justify proceedings against a creditworthy defendant (*Dobbie v. Medway H.A.* [1994] 1 W.L.R. 1234, above at p.1241).

A claimant's contention that he did not have knowledge of a significant injury until he was aware that the physical side effects of the presribed drug were not justified by its therapeutic value was rejected. Knowledge of significant injury is not determined by such an equation: *Briggs v. Pitt-Payne* [1999] Lloyd's Rep. Med. 1, CA.

Each case must of course depend on its own facts, but it is thought that the follow- **8–31** ing two cases may provide useful examples of the court's approach when considering questions under s.14. In a case where the plaintiff had been told by a doctor what had happened in the first operation and that a second operation had put things right she was held to have the necessary knowledge even though the precise terms of what had gone wrong were not known to her (*Hendy v. Milton Keynes H.A.* [1992] 3 Med.L.R. 114). Compare *Driscoll-Varley v. Parkside H.A.* [1991] 2 Med.L.R. 346, in which it was held reasonable for the plaintiff not to initiate proceedings while she was still undergoing a long and complex course of treatment at the hands of those persons against whom any action would be directed. She had not known that her injury was attributable to the acts alleged to constitute negligence until she had sought the advice of another surgeon. The burden was on the defendants to establish the constructive knowledge required by s.14(3) and they had failed to do so.

Knowledge was shown where the plaintiff was sufficiently clear in her own mind to establish a causal link between the negligence and her injury. It was not necessary to ask what would have been the reasonable layman's state of mind without seeking expert confirmation (*Spargo v. N. Esse H.A.* [1997] 8 Med.L.R. 125, CA). Applying the third principle in *Spargo* it is necessary to distinguish between a claimant who has a firm belief that he has a significant injury, attributable to his working conditions, especially one which takes him to a solicitor for advice about a claim, a belief which he retains whatever contrary advice he receives, and a claimant who believes that he may have or even probably has, a significant injury which is attributable to his working conditions, but is not sure and feels it necessary to have expert advice on those questions: *Sniezek v. Bundy (Letchworth) Ltd.* [2000] P.I.Q.R. 213, CA.

In *Forbes v. Wandsworth HA* [1997] Q.B. 402; [1996] 3 W.L.R. 1108; [1996] 4 All E.R. 881, CA, the Court of Appeal expressed difficulty with the proposition in *Nash v. Eli Lilley & Co.*, *supra*at [1993] 1 W.L.R. p.799, that the standard of reasonableness for the purposes of s.14(3) must be qualified by the position, circumstances and character of a particular plaintiff. It was held, by a majority, that a reasonable man of moderate intelligence, such as the deceased in that case, if he thought about the matter, would say that the lack of success of the operation was:

> "Either just one of those things, a risk of the operation or something may have gone wrong and there may have been a want of care; I do not know which, but if I am ever to make a claim, I must find out."

Constructive knowledge was found and the action held statute-barred.

In *Smith v. Leicestershire H.A.* (1996) 36 B.M.L.R. 23 May J. (as he then was) held that the Court was bound by the majority decision in *Forbes v. Wandsworth HA* [1997] Q.B. 402 to adopt an objective test when applying section 14(3). His judgment contains a useful review of the leading decisions on the question of knowledge. The Court of Appeal in *Smith* at [1998] Lloyd's Rep. Med. 77, whilst overruling the Judge's decision on the facts, held that it was free to decide which of the two conflicting decisions in *Nash* and *Forbes v.Wandsworth HA* [1997] Q.B. 402 it should follow. It expressly approved the observations Evans L.J. in *Forbes v. Wandsworth H.A* [1997] Q.B. 402 that the test of objectivity and reasonableness should be applied. It posed this question "what would the reasonable person have done placed in the situation of the plaintiff?" Moreover, the reasoning in *Forbes* has received the support of the House of Lords. In determining under s.14(3) whether a claimant had knowledge which he might reasonably have been expected to acquire the Court was to consider how a reasonable person in the situation of the claimant would have acted, save that (per Lord Hoffmann, Lord Phillips of Worth Matravers and Lord Scott of Foscote) aspects of character or intelligence peculiar to the claimant were to be disregarded: *Adams v. Bracknell Forest BC* [2004] UKHL 29; [2004] 3 W.L.R. 89, HL.

Where a plaintiff knows that his injury is attributable to the defendant's act or omission and the injury is sufficiently serious in the eyes of a reasonable man to justify bringing an action, the time limit will not be extended simply because the injury subsequently becomes worse (*Miller v. London Electrical Manufacturing Co. Ltd* [1976] 2 Lloyd's Rep. 284, applying *Goodchild v. Greatness Timber Co. Ltd* [1968] 2 Q.B. 37, CA).

Different injuries. *KR v. Bryn Alyn Community (Holdings) Ltd* [2003] EWCA Civ 85; [2003] Q.B. 1441; [2003] 3 W.L.R. 107; [2004] 2 All E.R. 716, C.A., (where the claimants as minors had suffered immediate physical injury and long-term psychiatric injury by reason of sexual abuse) is authority on the impact of s.14 in cases where the claimant's knowledge of the injuries occurs at different times: see in particular paras 37 to 58 of the judgment.

Vicarious liability. In circumstances where a defendant is held vicariously liable for acts of deliberate abuse by his employee, but not liable by reason of his own negligence, the deliberate abuse does not fall within s.11, and is therefore governed by a non-extendable six years period of limitation rather than an extendable three years period: *KR v. Bryn Alyn Community (Holdings) Ltd*, above, at para. 108 of the judgment.

As regards the question of knowledge which may, in any particular case, be imputed to the plaintiff only with the help of medical or other appropriate expert advice (see s.14(3)), it should be noted that knowledge of facts which are capable of giving rise to a claim is not knowledge of facts ascertainable only with the help of expert advice (*Halford v. Brookes* [1991] 1 W.L.R. 428, CA, where the plaintiff, who realised that her daughter's death was capable of being attributed to the defendants or one or other of them, was held to have the necessary knowledge without recourse to legal advice). Further, only in exceptional circumstances would the name of a party liable for a wrongdoing be a fact ascertainable "only with the help of expert advice": *Henderson v. Temple Pier Co. Ltd* [1998] 1 W.L.R. 1540; [1998] 3 All E.R. 324, CA.

Where a severely disabled person, dependent on his parents, has brought proceedings after attaining his majority, the question has arisen at first instance whether the knowledge of the parents is attributable to the plaintiff for the purposes of ss.11 and 14. Compare, *e.g. Parry v. Clwyd HA* [1997] P.I.Q.R. 1 with *O'Driscoll v. Dudley HA* [1998] Lloyd's Rep. Med. 210. It is submitted that the decision in *Parry*, that the Court is to look exclusively to the knowledge of the plaintiff, is to be preferred on this point. The relevance of a parent's knowledge was treated in *Bates v. Leicester HA* [1998] Lloyd's Rep. Med. 93 as related to the information which the plaintiff would have acquired from his parents on the assumption that he ought reasonably to have pressed them for more information. The judge's decision in *O'Driscoll v. Dudley HA* [1998] Lloyd's Rep. Med. 210 on constructive knowledge was reversed by the Court of Appeal on the facts: see [1998] Lloyd's Rep. Med. 210, CA. See also *Appleby v. Walsall HA* [1999] Lloyd's Rep. 154 in which *Parry v. Clwyd HA* was followed.

While in any case a plaintiff may fail the objective test of his knowledge for the purposes of s.11(4)(b) he may nonetheless succeed in an application under s.33 (see para. 8–67) to disapply the relevant time limit applying the proper tests under that section (see, *e.g. Brookes v. J. & P. Coates (UK) Ltd* [1984] I.C.R. 158).

As regards the identity of the defendant where at the time of his injury the plaintiff did not know the exact identity of his employers (they were described in the statement given to him as "Norwest Holst Group" which did not identify any legal entity) and he learnt of their precise identity only at a later date, it was held that since the action for damages for personal injuries started within three years of such later date, the action was not barred (*Simpson v. Norwest Holst Southern Ltd* [1980] 1 W.L.R. 968; [1980] 2 All E.R. 471, CA; and if it were, it would be a case, having regard to all the circumstances, to make it equitable to allow the action to proceed under s.33 of the Act (*ibid.*). See also *Eidi v. Dowell Schlumberger SA* [1990] 3 C.L. 269. See further, in relation to cases where the identity of the employer is uncertain or even wrongly stated to the employee, *Cressey* v. E Timm & Son Ltd [2005] EWCA Civ 763, CA.

In relation to the pleading of any question of knowledge under s.14 of the Act, and of any right to relief under s.33 thereof, see SCP 1999, Vol. 1, para. 18.8.25.

ACTIONS IN RESPECT OF LATENT DAMAGE NOT INVOLVING PERSONAL INJURIES

Special time limit for negligence actions where facts relevant to cause of action are not known at date of accrual

14A.—(1) This section applies to any action for damages for **8–32** negligence, other than one to which section 11 of this Act applies, where the starting date for reckoning the period of limitation under subsection (4)(b) below falls after the date on which the cause of action accrued.

(2) Section 2 of this Act shall not apply to an action to which this section applies.

(3) An action to which this section applies shall not be brought after the expiration of the period applicable in accordance with subsection (4) below.

(4) That period is either—

    (a) six years from the date on which the cause of action accrued; or

    (b) three years from the starting date as defined by subsection (5) below, if that period expires later than the period mentioned in paragraph (a) above.

(5) For the purposes of this section, the starting date for reckoning the period of limitation under subsection (4)(b) above is the earliest date on which the plaintiff or any person in whom the cause of action was vested before him first had both the knowledge required for bringing an action for damages in respect of the relevant damage and a right to bring such an action.

(6) In subsection (5) above "the knowledge required for bringing an action for damages in respect of the relevant damage" means knowledge both—

    (a) of the material facts about the damage in respect of which damages are claimed; and

    (b) of the other facts relevant to the current action mentioned in subsection (8) below.

(7) For the purposes of subsection (6)(a) above, the material facts about the damage are such facts about the damage as would lead a reasonable person who had suffered such damage to consider it sufficiently serious to justify his instituting proceedings for damages against a defendant who did not dispute liability and was able to satisfy a judgment.

(8) The other facts referred to in subsection (6)(b) above are—

    (a) that the damage was attributable in whole or in part to the act or omission which is alleged to constitute negligence; and

    (b) the identity of the defendant; and

    (c) if it is alleged that the act or omission was that of a person other than the defendant, the identity of that person and the additional facts supporting the bringing of an action against the defendant.

(9) Knowledge that any acts or omissions did or did not, as a matter of law, involve negligence is irrelevant for the purposes of subsection (5) above.

(10) For the purposes of this section a person's knowledge includes knowledge which he might reasonably have been expected to acquire—

    (a) from facts observable or ascertainable by him; or

    (b) from facts ascertainable by him with the help of appropriate expert advice which it is reasonable for him to seek;

but a person shall not be taken by virtue of this subsection to have knowledge of a fact ascertainable only with the help of expert advice so long as he has taken all reasonable steps to obtain (and, where appropriate, to act on) that advice.

8–33   *Note*—Added by the Latent Damage Act 1986, s.1

Knowledge of plaintiff in negligence actions

8–34   This section was added by the Latent Damage Act 1986, s.1. See para. 8–3 above.

The plain purpose of the reform was to avoid the injustice which might occur where a cause of action accrued by reason of the existence of damage without the plaintiff being aware of it. In such a case, lapse of a period of six years from the actual occurrence of damage would, ordinarily, bar the right to bring an action. See *Pirelli General Cable Works Ltd v. Faber (Oscar) & Partners* [1983] 2 A.C. 1, HL. By the transitional provisions of the Latent Damage Act 1986, some actions will continue to be governed by the law applicable before the introduction of the Act (see s.4). Thus, the new provisions will not enable any action to be brought which was already barred before the new Act came into force; or affect any action commenced before such time. The Act came into force on September 18, 1986 (see s.5(3)). For a full commentary on the provisions of the Act, and on the law as it stood when the Act was passed, see *Current Law Statutes*, Latent Damage Act 1986.

The section applies only to actions for negligence. It has been held that the negligence referred to is negligence in tort only, and that the section does not apply to claims for breach of duty of care arising out of contract: see *Iron Trades Mutual Insurance Co Ltd v. J. K. Buckenham Ltd* [1990] 1 All E.R. 808, where the action, so far as it was framed in contract, was struck out as statute-barred. This decision was approved in *Société Commerciale de Réassurance v. ERAS (International) Ltd* [1992] 2 All E.R. 82; [1992] 1 Lloyd's Rep. 570, CA, deciding that s.14A is limited to actions for negligence where the duty of care, the breach of which constitutes the negligence relied on, arises solely in tort. In *West Bromwich Building Society v. Mander Hadley & Co, The Times*, March 9, 1998, CA (a case where the plaintiff wished to guard against future unascertained claims against it outside the limitation period by issuing protective writs claiming contribution) Millett L.J. observed that it was not clear why Parliament had confined the operation of section 14A so that it was not available for claims in negligence framed in contract; nor why Parliament had not provided that a contingent cause of action should not be treated for limitation purposes as accruing before the contingency occurred. But it was not for the courts to extend the limitation period in hard cases by permitting writs to be issued at a time when the plaintiff was unaware of any valid basis for the claim.

It has been held that the scope of the Latent Damage Act 1986 extends to cover negligent misstatements by professional advisers after the construction of a building; and that, for the purposes of the commencement of the three year period under s.14A, "damage" was the single cause of action suffered by the plaintiff when she bought the house: *Horbury v. Craig Hall and Rutley* [1991] E.G.C.S. 81. This decision has been approved in the Court of Appeal in *Hamlin v. Edwin Evans, The Times*, July 15, 1996, CA. Where the tort complained of was negligence by error or omission in a survey there could only be one cause of action which accrued when the damage was suffered. It made no difference that the damage was multiple or single or whether, if multiple, it came to light at varying times with varying degrees of gravity. Thus, where a claim for lesser defects had been settled but more serious defects were discovered later, it was held that time for the purposes of s.14A ran from the date of knowledge regarding the lesser defects and that a writ issued some two years after discovery of the serious defects was out of time. It has however been held that knowledge of facts relating to a cause of action not relied on by the plaintiff in his claim, being a cause of action truly separate from that on which he does rely, will not enable the defence of limitation to succeed: *Birmingham Midshires Building Society v. Wretham* [1999] 07 E.G. 138, a case where the differing nature of the various duties of a solicitor acting for a purchaser or mortgagee is discussed.

The section itself does not provide any definition of when the cause of action accrues: see subs.(4)(a). *Pirelli General Cable Works v. Faber (Oscar) & Partners* [1983] 2 A.C. 1, above, and cases decided subsequently thereto (see *Current Law Statutes*, Latent Damage Act 1986), will continue to govern the resolution of this question.

In addition, the extended period provided by subs.(4)(b) arises only where that period itself expires after the period of six years from accrual of the cause of action. In these circumstances, it will in many cases be necessary to determine when the cause of action accrued in order to ascertain whether or not the three year rule under subs.(4)(b) applies. For a full commentary on the question when, for the purposes of the Limitation Act 1980, a cause of action in tort is held to accrue, see McGee, *Limitation Periods* (2002) 4th edn., Chap. 5; and in particular, in relation to that question in the tort of negligence causing either physical damage or economic loss (where recoverable), see *Islander Trucking Ltd v. Hogg Robinson & Gardner Mountain (Marine) Ltd* [1990] 1 All E.R. 826.

In *Graham v. Entec Europe Ltd* [2003] EWCA Civ 1177; [2003] 4 All E.R. 1345, CA it was held that, in relation to a subrogated claim, the nominal claimant is fixed with the knowledge of the insurer for whose benefit the action was brought; it was appropriate to construe the words "the plantiff" in s.14A(5) as meaning/extending to a plaintiff whether suing in his own name or the name of another by way of subrogation. Further the knowledge of a loss adjuster acting on behalf of insurers for the purpose of pursuing a subrogated claim by the insurers was to be treated as the knowledge of the insurers for the purposes of s.14A(5). Subsection (10) was not engaged.

The provisions of subss.(6)–(10), which relate to ascertaining whether the plaintiff had the requisite knowledge are closely modelled on those of s.14, which relate to actions for personal injuries (see paras 8–29, 8–30 and 8–31 above).

In applying the test propounded in *Nash v. Eli Lilly & Co* [1993] 1 W.L.R. 782 (see paras 8–29, 8–30 and 8–31) it is necesssary to ask what a reasonable person placed in the situation of the plaintiff and having his character and intelligence would or would not have done. A reasonable man was one who obeyed the law. Thus a plaintiff seeking to rely upon an extended time-limit under s.14A could not rely on his fear of being exposed as an illegal immigrant as a reason for not seeking professional advice so as to acquire constructive knowledge under s.14A(10) (*Coban v. Allen, The Times,* October 14, 1996, CA).

Section 14A (8)(a) requires that the act or omission of which the claimant must have knowledge must be that which is causally relevant for the purposes of an allegation of negligence. Section 14A is based on ss.11 and 14, and the authorities decided under s.14(1)(b) were equally applicable to s.14A(8)(a). The claimant did not have to know that he had a cause of action or that the defendant's acts could be characterised as negligent. But the words "which is alleged to constitute negligence" served to identify the facts of which the claimant must have knowledge: *Hallan-Eames v. Merrett Syndicates Ltd* [2001] Lloyd's Rep. P.N. 178; [1996] 7 Med. L.R. 122, CA, applying *Broadley v. Guy Clapham & Co* [1994] 4 All E.R. 439; [1993] 4 Med. L.R. 328, CA. It was held in *HF Pension Trustees Ltd v. Ellison* [1999] Lloyd's Rep. P.N. 489 that the claimants had knowledge for the purposes of s.14A at the time when they made payments under a transfer even though they did not know, and could not have known at the time, that the transfer would subsequently be held unlawful. Mere ignorance that the known facts might give rise to a claim in law could not postpone the running of time. The above case was distinguished in *Haward v. Fawcwtts* [2004] EWCA Civ 240; [2004] P.N.L.R. 34, CA, in which Jonathan Parker LJ reviewed the authorities, under both s.14 and s.14A, on the issue of attributability.

It has been held at first instance that the burden of proving the necessary facts to establish the extended time limit under s.14A falls on the plaintiff (*Iron Trades Mutual Insurance Co Ltd v. J.K. Buckenham Ltd* [1990] 1 All E.R. 808 at 824). In a case under s.14, rather than s.14A, the Court of Appeal has held that if the writ is not issued within three years of the date when the cause of action arose (see s.11(4)(a)), the onus is on the plaintiff to plead and prove a date within the three years preceding the date of issue of the writ (see s.11(4)(b)). If the defendant wishes to rely on a date prior to the three year period immediately preceding the issue of the writ, the onus is on the defendant to prove that the plaintiff had or ought to have had knowledge by that date (*Nash v. Eli Lilly & Co.* [1993] 4 All E.R. 383 at 396, CA). See however *Crocker v. British Coal Corporation* [1996] BMLR 159 at 172 and 173 per Mance J.

Where the question whether the plaintiff did or did not have the requisite knowledge turns on disputed questions of fact it will be inappropriate to decide the matter on an application by the defendant to strike out the cause of action. The issue must be tried, either at trial or by way of preliminary issue (*Iron Trades Mutual Insurance Co Ltd, ibid.,* at 824).

Where the plaintiff seeks to amend to add a new defendant, and the date of the plaintiff's knowledge for the purposes of determining the starting date of the secondary period of limitation is in issue, the court does not lack jurisdiction to decide whether to allow the amendment. The issue may be tried as a preliminary issue in the action (*Busby v. Cooper, The Times,* April 15, 1996, CA, approving the note to this effect in the preceding paragraph.

Deliberate concealment

8–35   It is expressly provided that s.14A shall not apply to any action to which s.32(1)(b) of the Act applies, *i.e.* where any fact relevant to the plaintiff's right of action has been deliberately concealed from him by the defendant. To achieve that purpose Parliament, by s.2(2) of the Latent Damage Act 1986, introduced a new subs.(5) into s.32. This ensures that in cases of deliberate concealment the provisions of ss.14A and 14B, with their respective provisions for an extended period of three years from the date of knowledge, and a long stop of 15 years, do not apply. Thus the period of limitation is that laid down by s.2 of the Limitation Act, with the beginning of the period postponed by virtue of s.32 until the plaintiff has discovered the concealment, or could with reasonable diligence have discovered it. See paras 8–63 and 8–64. For a commentary on the provisions of s.32(1)–(4) relating to fraud, concealment or mistake, see *Current Law Statutes*, Limitation Act 1980.

Overriding time limit for negligence actions not involving personal injuries

14B.—(1) An action for damages for negligence, other than one to **8–36** which section 11 of this Act applies, shall not be brought after the expiration of fifteen years from the date (or, if more than one, from the last of the dates) on which there occurred any act or omission—

    (a) which is alleged to constitute negligence; and

    (b) to which the damage in respect of which damages are claimed is alleged to be attributable (in whole or in part).

(2) This section bars the right of action in a case to which subsection (1) above applies notwithstanding that—

    (a) the cause of action has not yet accrued; or

    (b) where section 14A of this Act applies to the action, the date which is for the purposes of that section the starting date for reckoning the period mentioned in subsection (4)(b) of that section has not yet occurred;

before the end of the period of limitation, prescribed by this section.

Note—Added by the Latent Damage Act 1986, s.1   **8–37**

Section 14B provides a long stop period of 15 years after the day of the negligence relied on; and this even though the cause of action has not yet accrued (*e.g.* by reason of the absence of any damage) or the starting date for the three year period under s.14A(5), if applicable, has not yet occurred.

Deliberate concealment

See commentary to s.14A above.   **8–38**

ACTIONS TO RECOVER LAND AND RENT

Time limit for actions to recover land

15.—(1) No action shall be brought by any person to recover any **8–39** land after the expiration of twelve years from the date on which the right of action accrued to him or, if it first accrued to some person through whom he claims, to that person.

(2) Subject to the following provisions of this section, where—

    (a) the estate or interest claimed was an estate or interest in reversion or remainder or any other future estate or interest and the right of action to recover the land accrued on the date on which the estate or interest fell into possession by the determination of the preceding estate or interest; and

    (b) the person entitled to the preceding estate or interest

2219

(not being a term of years absolute) was not in possession of the land on that date;

no action shall be brought by the person entitled to the succeeding estate or interest after the expiration of twelve years from the
date on which the right of action accrued to the person entitled to
the preceding estate or interest or six years from the date on which
the right of action accrued to the person entitled to the succeeding
estate or interest, whichever period last expires.

(3) Subsection (2) above shall not apply to any estate or interest
which falls into possession on the determination of an entailed interest and which might have been barred by the person entitled to the
entailed interest.

(4) No person shall bring an action to recover any estate or interest in land under an assurance taking effect after the right of action
to recover the land had accrued to the person by whom the assurance was made or some person through whom he claimed or some
person entitled to a preceding estate or interest, unless the action is
brought within the period during which the person by whom the assurance was made could have brought such an action.

(5) Where any person is entitled to any estate or interest in land
in possession and, while so entitled, is also entitled to any future
estate or interest in that land, and his right to recover the estate or
interest in possession is barred under this Act, no action shall be
brought by that person, or by any person claiming through him, in
respect of the future estate or interest, unless in the meantime possession of the land has been recovered by a person entitled to an intermediate estate or interest.

(6) Part I of Schedule 1 to this Act contains provisions for
determining the date of accrual of rights of action to recover land in
the cases there mentioned.

(7) Part II of that Schedule contains provisions modifying the
provisions of this section in their application to actions brought by,
or by a person claiming through, the Crown or any spiritual or eleemosynary corporation sole.

Time limit for redemption action

8–40   16. When a mortgagee of land has been in possession of any of the
mortgaged land for a period of twelve years, no action to redeem the
land of which the mortgagee has been so in possession shall be
brought after the end of that period by the mortgagor or any person
claiming through him.

Extinction of title to land after expiration of time limit

8–41   17. Subject to—
   (a) section 18 of this Act; and
   (b) [...]

8–41.1   *Note* —Amended by the Land Registration Act 2002, Sched.13, para.1.

Settled land and land held on trust

8–42   18.—(1) Subject to section 21(1) and (2) of this Act, the provisions
of this Act shall apply to equitable interests in land [...] as they apply

to legal estates. Accordingly a right of action to recover the land shall, for the purposes of this Act but not otherwise, be treated as accruing to a person entitled in possession to such an equitable interest in the like manner and circumstances, and on the same date, as it would accrue if his interest were a legal estate in the land (and any relevant provision of Part I of Schedule 1 to this Act shall apply in any such case accordingly).

(2) Where the period prescribed by this Act has expired for the bringing of an action to recover land by a tenant for life or a statutory owner of settled land—

> (a) his legal estate shall not be extinguished if and so long as the right of action to recover the land of any person entitled to a beneficial interest in the land either has not accrued or has not been barred by this Act; and
>
> (b) the legal estate shall accordingly remain vested in the tenant for life or statutory owner and shall devolve in accordance with the Settled Land Act 1925;

but if and when every such right of action has been barred by this Act, his legal estate shall be extinguished.

(3) Where any land is held upon trust [...] and the period prescribed by this Act has expired for the bringing of an action to recover the land by the trustees, the estate of the trustees shall not be extinguished if and so long as the right of action to recover the land of any person entitled to a beneficial interest in the land [...] either has not accrued or has not been barred by this Act; but if and when every such right of action has been so barred the estate of the trustees shall be extinguished.

(4) Where—

> (a) any settled land is vested in a statutory owner; or
>
> (b) any land is held upon trust [...];

an action to recover the land may be brought by the statutory owner or trustees on behalf of any person entitled to a beneficial interest in possession in the land [...] whose right of action has not been barred by this Act, notwithstanding that the right of action of the statutory owner or trustees would apart from this provision have been barred by this Act.

Note —Amended by the Trusts of Land and Appointment of Trustees Act 1996, **8–43** s.25(2) and Sched.4.

Time limit for actions to recover rent

19. No action shall be brought, or distress made, to recover arrears **8–44** of rent, or damages in respect of arrears of rent, after the expiration of six years from the date on which the arrears became due.

Actions for breach of commonhold duty

19A An action in respect of a right or duty of a kind referred to in **8–44A** section 37(1) of the Commonhold and Leasehold Reform Act 2002 (enforcement) shall not be brought after the expiration of six years from the date on which the cause of action accrued.

Note —This section was added by the Commonhold and Leasehold Reform Act **8–44B**

2002 (c.15) s.68 and Schedule. Regulations made under s.37(1) confer on the courts certain jurisdiction in relation to the enforcement of particular rights and duties arising under Part 1 (Commonhold) of the Act.

ACTIONS TO RECOVER MONEY SECURED BY A MORTGAGE OR CHARGE OR TO RECOVER PROCEEDS OF THE SALE OF LAND

Time limit for actions to recover money secured by a mortgage or charge or to recover proceeds of the sale of land

8–45   **20.**—(1) No action shall be brought to recover—

    (a) any principal sum of money secured by a mortgage or other charge on property (whether real or personal); or

    (b) proceeds of the sale of land;

after the expiration of twelve years from the date on which the right to receive the money accrued.

(2) No foreclosure action in respect of mortgaged personal property shall be brought after the expiration of twelve years from the date on which the right to foreclose accrued.

But if the mortgagee was in possession of the mortgaged property after that date, the right to foreclose on the property which was in his possession shall not be treated as having accrued for the purposes of this subsection until the date on which his possession discontinued.

(3) The right to receive any principal sum of money secured by a mortgage or other charge and the right to foreclose on the property subject to the mortgage or charge shall not be treated as accruing so long as that property comprises any future interest or any life insurance policy which has not matured or been determined.

(4) Nothing in this section shall apply to a foreclosure action in respect of mortgaged land, but the provisions of this Act relating to actions to recover land shall apply to such an action.

(5) Subject to subsections (6) and (7) below, no action to recover arrears of interest payable in respect of any sum of money secured by a mortgage or other charge or payable in respect of proceeds of the sale of land, or to recover damages in respect of such arrears shall be brought after the expiration of six years from the date on which the interest became due.

(6) Where—

    (a) a prior mortgagee or other incumbrancer has been in possession of the property charged; and

    (b) an action is brought within one year of the discontinuance of that possession by the subsequent incumbrancer;

the subsequent incumbrancer may recover by that action all the arrears of interest which fell due during the period of possession by the prior incumbrancer or damages in respect of those arrears, notwithstanding that the period exceeded six years.

(7) Where—

    (a) the property subject to the mortgage or charge comprises any future interest or life insurance policy, and

(b) it is a term of the mortgage or charge that arrears of interest shall be treated as part of the principal sum of money secured by the mortgage or charge;

interest shall not be treated as becoming due before the right to recover the principal sum of money has accrued or is treated as having accrued.

Note —In *West Bromwich Building Society v. Wilkinson* [2005] UKHL 44; [2005] 1 **8–45.1** W.L.R. 2303, the House of Lords held that the cause of action for a debt secured on a mortgage arose, on the construction of the deed, one month after default in payment of a monthly instalment. The subsequent exercise of the power of sale by the mortgagee did not stop time running. Nor did s.20 cease to apply when the security was subsequently realised.

ACTIONS IN RESPECT OF TRUST PROPERTY OR THE PERSONAL ESTATE OF DECEASED PERSONS

Time limit for actions in respect of trust property

21.—(1) No period of limitation prescribed by this Act shall apply **8–46** to an action by a beneficiary under a trust, being an action—

(a) in respect of any fraud or fraudulent breach of trust to which the trustee was a party or privy; or

(b) to recover from the trustee trust property or the proceeds of trust property in the possession of the trustee, or previously received by the trustee and converted to his use.

(2) Where a trustee who is also a beneficiary under the trust receives or retains trust property or its proceeds as his share on a distribution of trust property under the trust, his liability in any action brought by virtue of subsection (1)(b) above to recover that property or its proceeds after the expiration of the period of limitation prescribed by this Act for bringing an action to recover trust property shall be limited to the excess over his proper share.

This subsection only applies if the trustee acted honestly and reasonably in making the distribution.

(3) Subject to the preceding provisions of this section, an action by a beneficiary to recover trust property or in respect of any breach of trust, not being an action for which a period of limitation is prescribed by any other provision of this Act, shall not be brought after the expiration of six years from the date on which the right of action accrued.

For the purposes of this subsection, the right of action shall not be treated as having accrued to any beneficiary entitled to a future interest in the trust property until the interest fell into possession.

(4) No beneficiary as against whom there would be a good defence under this Act shall derive any greater or other benefit from a judgment or order obtained by any other beneficiary than he could have obtained if he had brought the action and this Act had been pleaded in defence.

Section 21—actions for breach of trust and actions for breach of fiduciary duty

Paragon Finance Plc v. Thakerar &Co [1999] 1 All E.R. 400; (1998) 95(35) L.S.G. 36, **8–47** CA elucidates the true nature of the distinction between two different classes of persons described as constructive trustees, namely (1) those holding on trust by virtue of taking possession of property on trust for or on behalf of others before the occurrence of the transaction impeached, and (2) those to whom the description applies only by reason of that transaction. It was held that, arguably, s.21 of the 1980 Act, and its predecessor s.19 of the Limitation Act 1939, have not abrogated that distinction and that s.21 is intended to apply only to trustees of the first description. The limitation period applicable to those of the second description, whether the case against them be put in damages for fraud at common law or by a corresponding claim in equity "for an account as constructive trustee", is six years, though the start of the period may be deferred in such latter cases. Likewise, a claim against an agent for an account in equity, absent any trust, was subject to the statutes of limitation. His liability to account for more than six years before the issue of the writ depended on whether he was, not merely a fiduciary (for every agent owes fiduciary duties to his principal), but a trustee, *i.e.* on whether he owed fiduciary duties *in relation to the money* (*Nelson v. Rye* [1996] 2 All E.R. 186 disapproved). See also *Coulthard v. Disco Mix Club Ltd* [1999] 2 All E.R. 457, following *Paragon*.

For a decision on the application of the statute by analogy to claims for equitable damages for breach of fiduciary duty, see *Companha de Seguros Imperio v. Heath (REBX) Ltd* [2000] 2 All E.R. (Comm) 787, CA.

On the question of the extent to which an *executor de son tort* is in the same position as a trustee for the purposes of s.21(1)(b), see *James v. Williams* [1999] 3 W.L.R. 451, CA.

Time limit for actions claiming personal estate of a deceased person

8–48   **22.** Subject to section 21(1) and (2) of this Act—

(a) no action in respect of any claim to the personal estate of a deceased person or to any share or interest in any such estate (whether under a will or on intestacy) shall be brought after the expiration of twelve years from the date on which the right to receive the share or interest accrued; and

(b) no action to recover arrears of interest in respect of any legacy, or damages in respect of such arrears, shall be brought after the expiration of six years from the date on which the interest became due.

ACTIONS FOR AN ACCOUNT

Time limit in respect of actions for an account

8–49   **23.** An action for an account shall not be brought after the expiration of any time limit under this Act which is applicable to the claim which is the basis of the duty to account.

MISCELLANEOUS AND SUPPLEMENTAL

Time limit for actions to enforce judgments

8–50   **24.**—(1) An action shall not be brought upon any judgment after the expiration of six years from the date on which the judgment became enforceable.

(2) No arrears of interest in respect of any judgment debt shall be recovered after the expiration of six years from the date on which the interest became due.

Time limit for actions to enforce judgments

8–51   The House of Lords has held that proceedings to execute a judgment debt (in that case by charging and garnishee orders) were not an action upon a judgment within the meaning of s.24(1) and were not barred after six years by that subsection. Action meant a fresh action. But, as to subsection (2), the ordinary meaning of the words barred recovery of arrears of interest in respect of *all* judgments after six years, whether recovery was sought by a fresh action or by execution on the original judgment. Nor did s.32 of the Act apply to extend such period, since the recovery of interest by way of execution was not a "right of action" within the meaning of s.32(1)(b): *Lowsley v. Forbes* [1998] 3 W.L.R. 501, HL. Further, an action upon any judgement within the meaning of s.24(1) does not include insolvency proceedings, whether by winding up petition or bankruptcy petition, brought by a judgement creditor: *Ridgeway Motors (Isleworth) Ltd v. ALTS Ltd* [2005] EWCA Civ 92; [2005] 2 All E.R. 304, CA , following *WT Lamb & Sons v. Rider* [1948] 2 K.B. 331 CA , in which the statutory predecessor of s.24(1) was construed as applying only to suing for a judgment upon a judgment.

Time limit for actions to enforce advowsons and extinction of title to advowsons

25. [*Repealed by the* Patronage (Benefices) Measure 1986, s.4(3).]   **8–52**

Administration to date back to death

26. For the purposes of the provisions of this Act relating to actions for the recovery of land and advowsons an administrator of the estate of a deceased person shall be treated as claiming as if there had been no interval of time between the death of the deceased person and the grant of the letters of administration.   **8–53**

Cure of defective disentailing assurance

27.—(1) This section applies where—   **8–54**

>   (a) a person entitled in remainder to an entailed interest in any land makes an assurance of his interest which fails to bar the issue in tail or the estates and interests taking effect on the determination of the entailed interest, or fails to bar those estates and interests only, and

>   (b) any person takes possession of the land by virtue of the assurance.

(2) If the person taking possession of the land by virtue of the assurance, or any other person whatsoever (other than a person entitled to possession by virtue of the settlement) is in possession of the land for a period of twelve years from the commencement of the time when the assurance could have operated as an effective bar, the assurance shall thereupon operate, and be treated as having always operated, to bar the issue in tail and the estates and interests taking effect on the determination of the entailed interest.

(3) The reference in subsection (2) above to the time when the assurance could have operated as an effective bar is a reference to the time at which the assurance, if it had then been executed by the person entitled to the entailed interest, would have operated, without the consent of any other person, to bar the issue in tail and the estates and interests taking effect on the determination of the entailed interest.

Actions for recovery of property obtained through unlawful conduct etc.

27A.—(1) None of the time limits given in the preceding provi-   **8–54.1**

sions of this Act applies to any proceedings under Chapter 2 of Part 5 of the Proceeds of Crime Act 2002 (civil recovery of proceeds of unlawful conduct).

    (2) Proceedings under that Chapter for a recovery order in respect of any recoverable property shall not be brought after the expiration of the period of twelve years from the date on which the Director's cause of action accrued.

    (3) Proceedings under that Chapter are brought when—

        (a) a claim form is issued, or

        (b) an application is made for an interim receiving order,

whichever is the earlier.

    (4) The Director's cause of action accrues in respect of any recoverable property—

        (a) in the case of proceedings for a recovery order in respect of property obtained through unlawful conduct, when the property is so obtained,

        (b) in the case of proceedings for a recovery order in respect of any other recoverable property, when the property obtained through unlawful conduct which it represents is so obtained.

    (5) If—

        (a) a person would (but for the preceding provisions of this Act) have a cause of action in respect of the conversion of a chattel, and

        (b) proceedings are started under that Chapter for a recovery order in respect of the chattel,

section 3(2) of this Act does not prevent his asserting on an application under section 281 of that Act that the property belongs to him, or the court making a declaration in his favour under that section.

    (6) If the court makes such a declaration, his title to the chattel is to be treated as not having been extinguished by section 3(2) of this Act.

    (7) Expressions used in this section and Part 5 of that Act have the same meaning in this section as in that Part.

8–54.2   *Note* —Added by the Proceeds of Crime Act 2002, s.288(1).

Part II

Extension or Exclusion of Ordinary Time Limits

Disability

Extension of limitation period in case of disability

8–55   **28.**—(1) Subject to the following provisions of this section, if on the date when any right of action accrued for which a period of limitation is prescribed by this Act, the person to whom it accrued was under a disability, the action may be brought at any time before the expiration of six years from the date when he ceased to be under a disability or died (whichever first occurred) notwithstanding that the period of limitation has expired.

(2) This section shall not affect any case where the right of action first accrued to some person (not under a disability) through whom the person under a disability claims.

(3) When a right of action which has accrued to a person under a disability accrues, on the death of that person while still under a disability, to another person under a disability, no further extension of time shall be allowed by reason of the disability of the second person.

(4) No action to recover land or money charged on land shall be brought by virtue of this section by any person after the expiration of thirty years from the date on which the right of action accrued to that person or some person through whom he claims.

(4A) If the action is one to which section 4A of this Act applies, subsection (1) above shall have effect—

    (a) in the case of an action for libel or slander, as if for the words from "at any time" to "occurred)" there were substituted the words "by him at any time before the expiration of one year from the date on which he ceased to be under a disability"; and

    (b) in the case of an action for slander of title, slander of goods or other malicious falsehood, as if for the words "six years" there were substituted the words "one year".

(5) If the action is one to which section 10 of this Act applies, subsection (1) above shall have effect as if for the words "six years" there were substituted the words "two years".

(6) If the action is one to which section 11 or 12(2) of this Act applies, subsection (1) above shall have effect as if for the words "six years" there were substituted the words "three years".

(7) If the action is one to which section 11A of this Act applies or one by virtue of section 6(1)(a) of the Consumer Protection Act 1987 (death caused by defective product), subsection (1) above—

    (a) shall not apply to the time limit prescribed by subsection (3) of the said section 11A or to that time limit as applied by virtue of section 12(1) of this Act; and

    (b) in relation to any other time limit prescribed by this Act shall have effect as if for the words "six years" there were substituted the words "three years".

8–56   *Note* — Subs.(4A) added by the Administration of Justice Act 1985, s.57; substituted by the Defamation Act 1996, s.5(3). Subs. (7) added by the Consumer Protection Act 1987, Sched.1.

Effect of this section

8–57   This section extends the limitation period in case of a person under disability, *i.e.* during the period he is a minor or of unsound mind (see s.38(2), (3) and (4)) and in this respect it follows s.2(1) of the Act of 1975. Thus if a young child of two-and-a-half years of age is injured and an action is brought to recover damages within the primary period of limitation, but there is prolonged and inexcusable delay in the conduct of the action causing serious prejudice to the defendant, nevertheless the Court will not, under the doctrine of *Birkett v. James* [1978] A.C. 297, dismiss the action for want of prosecution, since the limitation period for the plaintiff to bring his action for damages is still current and will not expire until three years from the date when he ceases to be a minor (*Tolley v. Morris* [1979] 1 W.L.R. 592; [1979] 2 All E.R. 561, HL). Likewise, an action by a plaintiff under permanent disability will not be struck out for want of prosecution since a fresh action might be issued at any time; nor, it was held, should a condition be imposed on the continued progress of such an action (*Turner v. W.H. Malcolm Ltd*, *The Times*, August 24, 1992, CA).

In *Headford v. Bristol and District HA* [1995] 6 Med. L.R. 1, CA, an appeal was allowed against an order striking out the claim of a person under disability, the action having been brought 28 years after the events complained of. It was held that, whilst there was an inherent jurisdiction to strike out an action as an abuse of process even though the plaintiff remained under disability (see *Hogg v. Hamilton* [1993] 4 Med. L.R. 369, CA), in this case the facts did not warrant such a course. Section 28 conferred a right in general to bring proceedings in negligence during the period of disability. Section 28 contained no provision comparable with that in s.33 for carrying out a balancing exercise as to prejudice. Section 28(1) contained no longstop, in contrast to s.28(4). And, in permitting an action to be started within six years of the end of the disability, Parliament had expressly contemplated that, in the case of one well-known and substantial group of persons under disability, namely minors, an action might not be started until 24 years after the conduct complained of.

It is of course clear that a person under a disability may bring his action for damages while he is still under disability; the section is intended to extend the period of limitation, not to compel proceedings to await the cessation of disability.

Subs.(4) provides a long stop period of 30 years from accrual of the cause of action for bringing an action to recover land or money charged on land seemingly notwithstanding that the person entitled is or has been for the whole or part of such period under disability. For the ordinary time limits applicable to such actions, see ss.15 and 20 of the Act.

Among the factors to be regarded when considering whether to override any time limit in respect of actions for personal injuries is the duration of any disability of the plaintiff *arising after* the date of accrual of the cause of action (see s.33(3)(d)). This suggests that while regard is to be had to disability subsequently arising, regard will not necessarily be had, under that section, to disability existing at or continuing after the accrual of the cause of action. In such a case the plaintiff should be prompt to exercise his rights within the extended period provided under s.28.

Subs.(4A) in its original terms was inserted by the Administration of Justice Act 1985, s.57. It was totally replaced, with respect to causes of action arising after September 4, 1996, by the Defamation Act 1996, s.5(3). By the new subsection, as set out above, the extension of the limitation period in libel or slander in cases of disability is now one year after the plaintiff ceases to be under a disability. In actions for malicious falsehood the limitation period (now one year by virtue of s.4A of this Act) is extended in cases of disability by one year from the date on which the plaintiff ceases to be under a disability or dies.

Extension for cases where the limitation period is the period under section 14A(4)(b)

8–58   **28A.**—(1) Subject to subsection (2) below, if in the case of any action for which a period of limitation is prescribed by section 14A of this Act—

> (a) the period applicable in accordance with subsection (4) of that section is the period mentioned in paragraph (b) of that subsection;
>
> (b) on the date which is for the purposes of that section the starting date for reckoning that period the person by reference to whose knowledge that date fell to be determined under subsection (5) of that section was under a disability; and
>
> (c) section 28 of this Act does not apply to the action;
>
> the action may be brought at any time before the expiration of

three years from the date when he ceased to be under a disability or died (whichever first occurred) notwithstanding that the period mentioned above has expired.

(2) An action may not be brought by virtue of subsection (1) above after the end of the period of limitation prescribed by section 14B of this Act.

Note —Section 28A added by Latent Damage Act 1986, s.2, see Current Law Statutes, **8–59** Latent Damage Act 1986. Subs.(1) had the effect, in cases where the person whose knowledge is relevant for determining the starting date under s.14A is under disability *on that date*, of extending the limitation period until three years after cessation of disability or three years after his death. The long stop period under s.14B still remains.

ACKNOWLEDGMENT AND PART PAYMENT

Fresh accrual of action on acknowledgment or part payment

29.—(1) Subsections (2) and (3) below apply where any right of ac- **8–60** tion (including a foreclosure action) to recover land or an advowson or any right of a mortgagee of personal property to bring a foreclosure action in respect of the property has accrued.

(2) If the person in possession of the land, benefice or personal property in question acknowledges the title of the person to whom the right of action has accrued—

    (a) the right shall be treated as having accrued on and not before the date of the acknowledgment; and

    (b) in the case of a right of action to recover land which has accrued to a person entitled to an estate or interest taking effect on the determination of an entailed interest against whom time is running under section 27 of this Act, section 27 shall thereupon cease to apply to the land.

(3) In the case of a foreclosure or other action by a mortgagee, if the person in possession of the land, benefice or personal property in question or the person liable for the mortgage debt makes any payment in respect of the debt (whether of principal or interest) the right shall be treated as having accrued on and not before the date of the payment.

(4) Where a mortgagee is by virtue of the mortgage in possession of any mortgaged land and either—

    (a) receives any sum in respect of the principal or interest of the mortgage debt; or

    (b) acknowledges the title of the mortgagor, or his equity of redemption;

an action to redeem the land in his possession may be brought at any time before the expiration of twelve years from the date of the payment or acknowledgment.

(5) Subject to subsection (6) below, where any right of action has accrued to recover—

    (a) any debt or other liquidated pecuniary claim; or

    (b) any claim to the personal estate of a deceased person or to any share or interest in any such estate;

and the person liable or accountable for the claim acknowledges the claim or makes any payment in respect of it the right shall be treated as having accrued on and not before the date of the acknowledgment or payment.

(6) A payment of a part of the rent or interest due at any time shall not extend the period for claiming the remainder then due, but any payment of interest shall be treated as a payment in respect of the principal debt.

(7) Subject to subsection (6) above, a current period of limitation may be repeatedly extended under this section by further acknowledgments or payments, but a right of action, once barred by this Act, shall not be revived by any subsequent acknowledgment or payment.

Formal provisions as to acknowledgments and part payments

8–61   **30.**—(1) To be effective for the purposes of section 29 of this Act, an acknowledgment must be in writing and signed by the person making it.

(2) For the purposes of section 29, any acknowledgment or payment—

(a) may be made by the agent of the person by whom it is required to be made under that section; and

(b) shall be made to the person, or to an agent of the person, whose title or claim is being acknowledged or, as the case may be, in respect of whose claim the payment is being made.

Without prejudice acknowledgment
8–61.1   For a case turning on the question of privilege attaching to a without prejudice acknowledgment of liability see *Cadle Co v. Hearley* [2002] 1 Lloyd's Rep. 143.

Signature
8–61.2   As a matter of general principle, a document is signed by the maker of it when his name or mark is attached to it in a manner which indicates, objectively, his approval of the contents. The typed name of the sender at the end of a telex not only identifies the maker but leads to the inference that he has approved the contents: the typed name therefore constitutes his signature: *Good Challenger Navegante SA v. Metalexportimport SA (The "Good Challenger")* [2003] EWCA Civ 1668; [2004] 1 Lloyd's Rep. 67, CA, approving the judgment of the Court below.

Effect of acknowledgment or part payment on persons other than the maker or recipient

8–62   **31.**—(1) An acknowledgment of the title to any land, benefice, or mortgaged personalty by any person in possession of it shall bind all other persons in possession during the ensuing period of limitation.

(2) A payment in respect of a mortgage debt by the mortgagor or any other person liable for the debt, or by any person in possession of the mortgaged property, shall, so far as any right of the mortgagee to foreclose or otherwise to recover the property is concerned, bind all other persons in possession of the mortgaged property during the ensuing period of limitation.

(3) Where two or more mortgagees are by virtue of the mortgage

in possession of the mortgaged land, an acknowledgment of the mortgagor's title or of his equity of redemption by one of the mortgagees shall only bind him and his successors and shall not bind any other mortgagee or his successors.

(4) Where in a case within subsection (3) above the mortgagee by whom the acknowledgment is given is entitled to a part of the mortgaged land and not to any ascertained part of the mortgage debt the mortgagor shall be entitled to redeem that part of the land on payment, with interest, of the part of the mortgage debt which bears the same proportion to the whole of the debt as the value of the part of the land bears to the whole of the mortgaged land.

(5) Where there are two or more mortgagors, and the title or equity of redemption of one of the mortgagors is acknowledged as mentioned above in this section, the acknowledgment shall be treated as having been made to all the mortgagors.

(6) An acknowledgment of any debt or other liquidated pecuniary claim shall bind the acknowledgor and his successors but not any other person.

(7) A payment made in respect of any debt or other liquidated pecuniary claim shall bind all persons liable in respect of the debt or claim.

(8) An acknowledgment by one of several personal representatives of any claim to the personal estate of a deceased person or to any share or interest in any such estate, or a payment by one of several personal representatives in respect of any such claim, shall bind the estate of the deceased person.

(9) In this section "successor", in relation to any mortgagee or person liable in respect of any debt or claim, means his personal representatives and any other person on whom the rights under the mortgage or, as the case may be, the liability in respect of the debt or claim devolve (whether on death or bankruptcy or the disposition of property or the determination of a limited estate or interest in settled property or otherwise).

FRAUD, CONCEALMENT AND MISTAKE

Postponement of limitation period in case of fraud, concealment or mistake

32.—(1) Subject to subsections (3) and (4A) below, where in the **8–63** case of any action for which a period of limitation is prescribed by this Act, either—

(a) the action is based upon the fraud of the defendant; or

(b) any fact relevant to the plaintiff's right of action has been deliberately concealed from him by the defendant; or

(c) the action is for relief from the consequences of a mistake;

the period of limitation shall not begin to run until the plaintiff has discovered the fraud, concealment or mistake (as the case may be) or could with reasonable diligence have discovered it.

References in this subsection to the defendant include references to the defendant's agent and to any person through whom the defendant claims and his agent.

(2) For the purposes of subsection (1) above, deliberate commission of a breach of duty in circumstances in which it is unlikely to be discovered for some time amounts to deliberate concealment of the facts involved in that breach of duty.

(3) Nothing in this section shall enable any action—

    (a) to recover, or recover the value of, any property; or

    (b) to enforce any charge against, or set aside any transaction affecting, any property;

to be brought against the purchaser of the property or any person claiming through him in any case where the property has been purchased for valuable consideration by an innocent third party since the fraud or concealment or (as the case may be) the transaction in which the mistake was made took place.

(4) A purchaser is an innocent third party for the purposes of this section—

    (a) in the case of fraud or concealment of any fact relevant to the plaintiff's right of action, if he was not a party to the fraud or (as the case may be) to the concealment of that fact and did not at the time of the purchase know or have reason to believe that the fraud or concealment had taken place; and

    (b) in the case of mistake, if he did not at the time of the purchase know or have reason to believe that the mistake had been made.

(4A) Subsection (1) above shall not apply in relation to the time limit prescribed by section 11A(3) of this Act or in relation to that time limit as applied by virtue of section 12(1) of this Act.

(5) Sections 14A and 14B of this Act shall not apply to any action to which subsection (1)(b) above applies (and accordingly the period of limitation referred to in that subsection, in any case to which either of those sections would otherwise apply, is the period applicable under section 2 of this Act).

8–64   *Note* — Section 11A of the Act, referred to in subs. (4A) above, imposes special time limits for actions for damages in respect of defective products, and was introduced by the Consumer Protection Act 1987.

Subsection (1) was amended by the Consumer Protection Act 1987, s.6(6), s.50(2) and Sched.1, para. 5(a). Subsection (4A) was added by the Consumer Protection Act 1987, s.6(6), s.50(2) and Sched.1, para. 5(b).

The new subs.(5) of s.32 above was added by s.2(2) of the Latent Damage Act 1986. It ensures, in cases of deliberate concealment by the defendant within the meaning of s.32(1)(b), that ss.14A and 14B, with their respective provisions for an extended period of three years from the date of knowledge and a long stop of 15 years, do not apply. Thus the period of limitation is that laid down by s.2 (six years), with the beginning of the period postponed by virtue of s.32 until the plaintiff has discovered the concealment, or could with reasonable diligence have discovered it. For a commentary on the provisions of s.32(1)–(4) relating to fraud, concealment or mistake, see *Current Law Statutes*, Limitation Act 1980.

The House of Lords has held that on its true construction s.32(1)(b) operated to postpone the running of time in every case where there was deliberate concealment by the defendant of facts relevant to the plaintiff's cause of action, regardless of whether such concealment was contemporaneous with or subsequent to the accrual of the cause of action. In the case of subsequent concealment time did not begin to run until the concealment was or should have been discovered (*Sheldon v. RHM Outhwaite (Underwriting Agencies) Ltd* [1996] 1 A.C. 102; [1995] 2 W.L.R. 570; [1995] 2 All E.R. 558, HL). Where, however, the claimant was aware of the relevant facts during a period preceding the alleged concealment, no subsequent act on the part of the defendent can have concelaed them from him: see at [1996] 1 A.C., p.144, applied in *Ezekiel v. Lehrer* [2002] Lloyd's Law Reports (Professional Negligence) 260 at pp. 268, 270.

Section 32(1)(b) is not to be construed as a statutory enactment of the equitable doctrine of concealed fraud: *Sheldon, supra*, at p.145.

It has been held that deliberate concealment for the purposes of s.32(1)(b) and s.32(2) does not include failure to disclose a negligent breach of duty that the actor was not aware of committing: see *Cave v. Robinson Jarvis & Rolf* [2002] 2 W.L.R. 1107, HL (overruling *Brocklesbury v. Armitage & Guest* [2002] 1 W.L.R. 598, CA and *Liverpool Roman Catholic Archdiocese Trustees Inc v. Goldberg* [2001] 1 All E.R. 182. On the other hand, deliberate concealment by the defendant of the fact that he had been negligent satisfies the test in s.32(1)(b): *Williams v. Fanshaw Porter & Hazelhurst* [2004] EWCA Civ. 157; [2004] 2 All E.R. 616, CA.

It was held in *Skerratt v. Linfax Ltd* [2003] EWCA Civ 695; [2004] P.I.Q.R. 124, CA, a case where the claimant had signed a disclaimer before the accident, that it was difficult to conceive of a case of concealment unless the concealment took place either at the very time that the cause of action was accruing, or it took place after the cause of action had accrued, *i.e.* unless the defendant took some steps to deliberately conceal a fact relevant to the cause of action. Further, without deciding the point, there was some doubt whether the existence or otherwise of a cause of action was a fact relevant to the claimant's right of action on any view.

The normal rule is that, where there is a dispute as to whether a claim is time-barred, the claimant has to commence a fresh action in which the viability of the limitation defence can be determined (*Welsh Development Agency v. Redpath Dorman Long Ltd* [1994] 1 W.L.R. 1409; [1999] 4 All E.R. 10, CA). It has been held at first instance that this rule does not apply where there is an issue under s.32(2) whether any fact relevant to the claimant's right of action has been deliberately concealed and the deliberateness of the breach is an essential element of the new cause of action: *Mortgage Corporation v. Alexander Johnson, The Times*, September 22, 1999.

DISCRETIONARY EXCLUSION OF TIME LIMIT FOR ACTIONS FOR DEFAMATION OR MALICIOUS FALSEHOOD

Discretionary exclusion of time limit for actions for defamation or malicious falsehood

32A.—(1) If it appears to the court that it would be equitable to al-   **8–65**
low an action to proceed having regard to the degree to which—

> (a) the operation of section 4A of this Act prejudices the plaintiff or any person whom he represents, and
>
> (b) any decision of the court under this subsection would prejudice the defendant or any person whom he represents,

the court may direct that that section shall not apply to the action or shall not apply to any specified cause of action to which the action relates.

(2) In acting under this section the court shall have regard to all the circumstances of the case and in particular to—

> (a) the length of, and the reasons for, the delay on the part of the plaintiff;
>
> (b) where the reason or one of the reasons for the delay was that all or any of the facts relevant to the cause of action did not become known to the plaintiff until after the end of the period mentioned in section 4A—

        (i) the date on which any such facts did become known to him, and

        (ii) the extent to which he acted promptly and reasonably once he knew whether or not the facts in question might be capable of giving rise to an action; and

    (c) the extent to which, having regard to the delay, relevant evidence is likely—

        (i) to be unavailable, or

        (ii) to be less cogent than if the action had been brought within the period mentioned in section 4A.

(3) In the case of an action for slander of title, slander of goods or other malicious falsehood brought by a personal representative—

    (a) the references in subsection (2) above to the plaintiff shall be construed as including the deceased person to whom the cause of action accrued and any previous personal representative of that person; and

    (b) nothing in section 28(3) of this Act shall be construed as affecting the court's discretion under this section.

(4) In this section "the court" means the court in which the action has been brought.

8–66   *Note* —Added by the Administration of Justice Act 1985, s.57. Substituted by the Defamation Act 1996, s.5.

    Essentially, the reforms brought about by s.5 include the reduction of the limitation period in libel and slander cases from three years to one year (see amended s.4A of the 1980 Act), but with a discretionary power of exclusion, rather than extension, of that time limit where the court considers that it would be equitable to make an order. The new section applies as well to actions in malicious falsehood.

    The limitation period is deliberately short in defamation cases because a Claimant is expected vigorously to pursue a claim. Where no explanation for a 15 month delay was given, the Judge was justified in refusing to exercise his discretion to make a direction under s.32A: *Steedman v. BBC* [2001] EWCA Civ 1534; *The Times*, 13 December 2001, CA.

    The phrase "facts relevant to that cause of action" in the old section, which corresponds with the similar phrase in subs(2)(b) of the new section, is to be construed narrowly and relates only to those facts which the plaintiff has to plead and prove to establish a prima facie case. It does not extend to facts which are capable of rebutting possible defences as, for example, facts relevant to privilege in a libel action (*C v. Mirror Group Newspapers* [1996] E.M.L.R. 518, CA, following *Johnson v. Chief Constable of Surrey* [1992] T.L.R. 551, CA, a decision under s.32(1)(b) of the Act).

DISCRETIONARY EXCLUSION OF TIME LIMIT FOR ACTIONS IN RESPECT OF

PERSONAL INJURIES OR DEATH

Discretionary exclusion of time limit for actions in respect of personal injuries or death

8–67   **33.**—(1) If it appears to the court that it would be equitable to allow an action to proceed having regard to the degree to which—

    (a) the provisions of section 11 or 11A or 12 of this Act prejudice the plaintiff or any person whom he represents; and

(b) any decision of the court under this subsection would prejudice the defendant or any person whom he represents;

the court may direct that those provisions shall not apply to the action, or shall not apply to any specified cause of action to which the action relates.

(1A) The court shall not under this section disapply—

(a) subsection (3) of section 11A; or

(b) where the damages claimed by the plaintiff are confined to damages for loss of or damage to any property, any other provision in its application to an action by virtue of Part I of the Consumer Protection Act 1987.

(2) The court shall not under this section disapply section 12(1) except where the reason why the person injured could no longer maintain an action was because of the time limit in section 11 or subsection (4) of section 11A.

If, for example, the person injured could at his death no longer maintain an action under the Fatal Accidents Act 1976 because of the time limit in Article 29 in Schedule 1 to the Carriage by Air Act 1961, the court has no power to direct that section 12(1) shall not apply.

(3) In acting under this section the court shall have regard to all the circumstances of the case and in particular to—

(a) the length of, and the reasons for, the delay on the part of the plaintiff;

(b) the extent to which, having regard to the delay, the evidence adduced or likely to be adduced by the plaintiff or the defendant is or is likely to be less cogent than if the action had been brought within the time allowed by section 11, by section 11A or (as the case may be) by section 12;

(c) the conduct of the defendant after the cause of action arose, including the extent (if any) to which he responded to requests reasonably made by the plaintiff for information or inspection for the purpose of ascertaining facts which were or might be relevant to the plaintiff's cause of action against the defendant;

(d) the duration of any disability of the plaintiff arising after the date of the accrual of the cause of action;

(e) the extent to which the plaintiff acted promptly and reasonably once he knew whether or not the act or omission of the defendant, to which the injury was attributable, might be capable at that time of giving rise to an action for damages;

(f) the steps, if any, taken by the plaintiff to obtain medical, legal or other expert advice and the nature of any such advice he may have received.

(4) In a case where the person injured died when, because of section 11, or subsection (4) of section 11A he could no longer maintain an action and recover damages in respect of the injury, the court shall have regard in particular to the length of, and the reasons for, the delay on the part of the deceased.

(5) In a case under subsection (4) above, or any other case where the time limit, or one of the time limits, depends on the date of knowledge of a person other than the plaintiff, subsection (3) above shall have effect with appropriate modifications, and shall have effect in particular as if references to the plaintiff included references to any person whose date of knowledge is or was relevant in determining a time limit.

(6) A direction by the court disapplying the provisions of section 12(1) shall operate to disapply the provisions to the same effect in section 1(1) of the Fatal Accidents Act 1976.

(7) In this section "the court" means the court in which the action has been brought.

(8) References in this section to section 11 or 11A include references to that section as extended by any of the preceding provisions of this Part of this Act or by any provision of Part III of this Act.

8–68   *Note*—Amended by the Consumer Protection Act 1987, Sched.1, para. 6.

Discretionary power to override time limits in actions for personal injuries or death

8–69   Section 33, which is derived verbatim from s.2D of the 1939 Act, provides a most important and substantial change in the law of limitation relating to actions for personal injuries or death. It does so by conferring on the Court a discretionary power to direct that the provisions of sections 11 or 12 shall not apply to the action or shall not apply to any specified cause of action to which the action relates (s.33(1)). The court may not however disapply s.12(1), *i.e.* that provision which prevents dependants from recovering, where at the date of his death the deceased could not have maintained an action, except where the only reason why the deceased could not have recovered was the time bar under s.11. Accordingly, the court may still, in that particular case, exercise its jurisdiction in favour of the dependants to disapply s.11 (see s.33(2) and (4)). Similar provisions have now been added in relation to s.11A (see the Consumer Protection Act 1987, Sched.1).

Action begun within primary limitation period

8–70   The new discretionary power under this section is limited and restricted in its operation, this was how the section was interpreted by the House of Lords. The House has held that if the plaintiff has started an action within the primary period of limitation as prescribed by section 11 of the Act but for any reason he has failed to proceed with it, whether by dilatoriness so that the action is dismissed for want of prosecution or by discontinuance, it is only in the most exceptional circumstances that he would be able to bring himself within s.33 in respect of a second action brought to enforce the same cause of action, and therefore any application by him under s.33 would fail *in limine*, since the dismissal of the first action for want of prosecution because of his inordinate and inexcusable delay or his discontinuance of that action would not constitute prejudice to the plaintiff since it would be his own act (*Walkley v. Precision Forgings Ltd* [1979] 1 W.L.R. 606; [1979] 2 All E.R. 548, HL, reversing [1978] 1 W.L.R. 1228; [1979] 1 All E.R. 102, CA, and followed in *Chappell v. Cooper* [1980] 1 W.L.R. 958; [1980] 2 All E.R. 483, CA, expressing the view that *Firman v. Ellis* [1978] Q.B. 886, CA is no longer good law). See also *Whitfield v. North Durham HA* [1995] 6 Med. L.R. 32, CA, in which it was held that, in an action which had become defunct for want of service of the writ or any application to renew its validity, the court was precluded from exercising jurisdiction under s.33 by the decision in *Walkley*.

On this interpretation of the section, the Court does not have to proceed beyond s.33(1) and does not reach the point of exercising its discretionary powers under s.33(3). If the plaintiff brings his first action within the primary period of limitation, and it goes on, there is no need to resort to the remedial provisions of s.33 of the Act; but if the plaintiff fails to proceed with his first action, whether by discontinuance, dismissal for want of prosecution or failure to comply with a requirement of the rules or an order of the Court or otherwise, he will suffer no prejudice by reason of the provisions of s.11 in commencing his second action, and therefore the provisions of s.33(3) of the Act cannot be invoked to assist him to enable the Court to direct that s.11 of the Act should not apply to the second action. Thus, where the plaintiff had issued a writ within the primary limitation period claiming damages for personal injuries but had allowed the time for service of the writ to expire without serving the writ, the fact that the defendants had made an interim payment to him in respect of his claim in that action is no ground for allowing him to issue a second writ in respect of the same cause of action and the court will not override the statutory time limits or allow the second action to proceed under its discretionary powers under s.33 (*Deerness v. John R. Keeble & Son (Brantham) Ltd* [1983] 2 Lloyd's Rep. 260, HL). It is a misconception to assume that the fact that the defendants make an interim payment constitutes an admission of liability, and still more so to assume that in a claim for unliquidated damages an admission of liability resets what is sometimes called "the limitation clock" (*ibid.*).

Walkley v. Precision Forgings Ltd [1979] 1 W.L.R. 606 and *Deerness* were applied in circumstances where the first action failed for want of service of the writ (*Forward v. Hendricks* [1997] 2 All E.R. 395, CA).

Under the former RSC, as contained in O.6, r.8(2), in the absence of special circumstances, the court would not exercise its discretion to renew a writ after the time for service had expired if there was a likelihood or substantial risk that this would deprive the defendant of the benefit of a defence of limitation which had already accrued (see *Heaven v. Pender* (1883) L.R. 11 QBD 503; and *Wilkinson v. Ancliff (B.L.T.) Ltd* [1986] 1 W.L.R. 1352, CA). The application of the *Heaven* principle was not inconsistent with, and remained unaffected by, the provisions of s.33 (see *Chappell v. Cooper* [1980] 1 W.L.R. 958, at 966; and *Wilkinson v. Ancliff (B.L.T.) Ltd*, above, at 1358).

In *Firman v. Ellis* [1978] Q.B. 886 Lord Denning M.R. said that the grant by Parliament of the wide discretion to the Courts under s.2D (now s.33), *i.e.* to override time limits, is a revolutionary and valuable change which will enable justice to be done even at the expense of some certainty; the relevant words of the statute are so clear that they cannot be construed restrictively as applying only to exceptional cases (*ibid.*); see especially the judgment of Geoffrey Lane L.J.

This view has to some extent been reiterated by the Court of Appeal in *Simpson v. Norwest Holst Southern Ltd* [1980] 1 W.L.R. 968; [1980] 2 All E.R. 471, CA. In delivering the judgment of the Court, Lawton L.J. drew attention to the fact that the opening words of s.33(1) contain no restrictive words, and to the further fact that none can be implied because subs.(3) provides that when acting under this section, "the Court shall have regard to all the circumstances of the case" and in particular to six specified matters, and he added "In our judgment, s.33 cannot, and should not, be read in any restrictive sense so as to apply only in exceptional cases" (action allowed to proceed under s.33).

The solution to this conflict of judicial opinion will have to be resolved in due course. There may, no doubt, be ways in which these views can be reconciled, or at any rate be applied in parallel. It would be an unhappy outcome if the first view were to become doctrinal, in the sense that it will be applied unreflectively and bar the road to the application of the second view, which is essentially discretionary.

Action begun after expiry of primary limitation period

8–71   An important development has taken place in the jurisdiction to apply s.33 to actions for personal injuries or death under the decision of the House of Lords in *Thompson v. Brown* [1981] 1 W.L.R. 747; *sub nom. Thompson v. Brown Construction (Ebbw Vale) Ltd* [1981] 2 All E.R. 296, HL(E). In that case the House of Lords held that where the action is begun by the plaintiff *after* the expiry of the primary periods of limitation under ss.11 or 12, the Court has jurisdiction to apply s.33 to the action and that its discretionary power to make or refuse a direction to disapply those provisions to the action or to any specified cause of action to which the action relates, if it considered it equitable to do so, is unfettered, approving in this respect *Firman v. Ellis* [1978] Q.B. 886 although emphasising that the actual decision in that case must be regarded as having been overruled by *Walkley v. Precision Forgings Ltd* [1979] 1 W.L.R. 606; [1979] 2 All E.R. 548, HL(E). The House stressed that subs.(3) requires the Court to have regard to "all the circumstances of the case" but singles out six matters for particular attention which present a curious mixture. The onus of showing that in the particular circumstances of the case it would be equitable for the Court to give a direction under s.33 to allow the action to proceed, lies upon the plaintiff and the conduct of the parties as well as the prejudice one or the other will suffer if the Court makes such a direction are all to be put into the balance in order to see which way it falls (*ibid.*). Even if the plaintiff has an unanswerable claim against his solicitor for negligence for failure to issue the writ within the primary 3-year limitation period, and the damages he would be likely to recover in such an action would not be less and might be more than he would be able to recover against the defendant if the action were allowed to proceed, which of course is a highly relevant consideration, he would suffer some prejudice, albeit only minor if the action were not allowed to proceed, since he would have to find new solicitors, there would inevitably be further delay, he would incur a personal liability for costs of the action if it were not allowed to proceed and he might prefer to sue the real tortfeasor rather than sue his former solicitors with the probable consequences on their insurance premiums (*ibid.*).

The possible synthesis of the apparently divergent decisions of the House of Lords in *Walkley's* case above, and in *Thompson's* case, may be expressed in the following propositions:

1. If the plaintiff brings his action for damages for personal injuries or death within the primary period of three years from the date on which the cause of action accrued (s.11(4)) or the date of death (s.12(2)(a)), and this is a mere matter of calculating the period by reference to the calendar, the Court has no jurisdiction to apply s.33 to a second action or to exercise any discretionary power to allow that action to proceed, if the first action has been brought to an end before trial, *e.g.* by the refusal to allow the writ to be renewed for service, or by dismissal for want of prosecution or by discontinuance (except in this case in exceptional circumstances); *Walkley's* case.

2. If the plaintiff brings such an action within the requisite period from his date of knowledge, if it be later than three years (s.11(4)(b)), or the date of knowledge of the person for whose benefit the action is brought, if it be later than three years (s.12(2)(b)), the Court will have to decide what was the date of knowledge of the relevant persons under s.14. If the action was brought within three years from that date it will be in the same position as if it had been brought within the primary three year limitation period, and s.33 cannot be invoked to obtain a direction of the Court that the action should be allowed to proceed; see *Walkley's* case. On the other hand if the Court should find that the action was brought later than three years after the relevant date of knowledge under s.14, it may well be that the action will fall outside *Walkley's* case and come within the principle of *Thompson's* case. In that event, the Court would have jurisdiction to apply s.33 to that action and to exercise its discretionary power, if it be equitable to do so, to allow the action to proceed under *Thompson's* case.

3. If the plaintiff brings such an action outside the primary period of limitation under ss.11 or 12, the Court has jurisdiction to apply s.33 to that action and to exercise an unfettered discretion whether to give a direction that the action should be allowed to proceed (*Thompson's* case). It may seem anomalous that a defendant should be better off where, unknown to him, a writ has been issued but not served than he would be if the writ had not been issued at all (*ibid.*, *per* Lord Diplock). Equally if the first action brought by the plaintiff after the primary period of limitation is for any reason a nullity, it will be disregarded, and the Court will have jurisdiction to apply section 33. In its discretion it may allow that action to be amended after the expiry of the primary limitation period and direct that the action, as amended, should be allowed to proceed or to allow the plaintiff to issue a second action outside the primary period of limitation, directing that the second action be allowed to proceed. Thus, a writ served without leave of the Court upon a defendant company in liquidation in respect of an injury sustained by the plaintiff is a nullity since the requisite leave of the Court under s.231 of the Companies Act 1948 (now Insolvency Act 1986, s.130) is absolute and unqualified; but an amended writ served upon the company with the leave of the Court, after the expiry of the primary limitation period, entitles the plaintiff to invoke the provisions of s.33, and the Court may in its discretion having regard to all the circumstances, particularly to the fact that the plaintiff and his advisers were entirely ignorant that the defendant company was in liquidation at the date of the original service of writ on them, disapply the time bar and allow the action to proceed (*Wilson v. Banner Scaffolding Ltd*, *The Times*, June 22, 1982). In a case where the earlier proceedings were invalidly constituted as being commenced against a name which was not a legal entity, it was held that *Walkley's* case was distinguishable and that s.33 could be applied to the second action (see *White v. Glass*, *The Times*, February 18, 1989, CA).

Where a writ against the original defendant was struck out in the reasonable belief that it was a nullity the case was to be regarded as an exception to the rule in *Walkley v. Precision Forgings Ltd* [1979] 1 W.L.R. 606, so that discretion could be exercised to permit fresh proceedings to be brought against a second defendant added after the expiry of the limitation period. The Court of Appeal also considered, without deciding, whether *White v. Glass* had added to the rule in *Walkley v. Precision Forgings Ltd* [1979] 1 W.L.R. 606 a requirement that the first action must have been properly constituted against the same defendants: *McEvoy v. A.A. Welding and Fabrication Ltd* [1998] P.I.Q.R. 266, CA. See also *Shapland v. Palmer* [1999] 1 W.L.R. 2068; [1999] 3 All E.R. 50, CA in which it was held that where an action against a driver for negligence followed an earlier dismissed action against the driver's employers, there was an exception to the principle in *Walkley v. Precision Forgings Ltd* [1979] 1 W.L.R. 606. The two actions were not indistinguishable. Further it has been held that where earlier proceedings had been brought against the estate of a deceased person, but not served, and no person had been appointed to represent the estate, such proceedings were never properly constituted. Accordingly, there was jurisdiction to make an order under s.33 in fresh proceedings brought against the estate represented by personal representatives: *Piggott v. Aulton (deceased)* [2003] EWCA Civ 24; *The Times*, February 19, 2003, CA.

In *Young v. Western Power Distribution (South West) Plc* [2003] EWCA Civ 1034; [2003] 1 W.L.R. 2868, the Court of Appeal had to consider the impact of s.33(2) in a claim for loss of dependency under the Fatal Accident Acts in circumstances where the deceased had brought a claim for personal injuries for mesethelioma but had discontinued the claim following a diagnosis of carcinoma. It was held that the reason why the deceased could no longer maintain an action in his own lifetime was the *Walkley* principle and not s.11. The claim was dismissed.

In *Philip Powis Ltd, Re, The Times*, March 6, 1998, CA the applicant, who had a pending action for personal injuries on the date of the defendant company's dissolution sought a declaration under section 651(1) of the Companies Act 1985 that the dissolution was void in order to commence a second action outside the primary limitation period. The Judge described the decision in *Walkley v. Precision Forgings Ltd* [1979] 1 W.L.R. 606 as a formidable obstacle for the applicant. But the Court of Appeal, holding that the termination of the first action was not brought about by any act of the applicant and that an application under section 33 would have reasonable prospects of success, held that the decision in *Walkley v. Precision Forgings Ltd* [1979] 1 W.L.R. 606 should not necessarily be regarded as an obstacle and that the Judge had failed to give proper weight to the conduct of the company under section 33(3)(c), namely the liquidation and dissolution of the company without making any provision for its liability, if any, to the applicant. The appeal against dismissal of the application under section 651 was allowed.

In relation to section 651 it has been held that a cause of action against a company restored to the register accrued on the date on which it would otherwise have accrued but for this dissolution. It followed in that case that in the absence of a limitation direction the action was statute-barred. On the hearing of an application for restoration under section 651 the Court should not normally make a direction that the period between dissolution and restoration be discounted for limitation purposed unless:

   (a) notice of the application has been given to all parties who might be expected to oppose including the Company's insurers and

   (b) the Court is satisfied

      (i) that it has before it all the evidence that the parties would wish to advise on an application under s.33 and

      (ii) that an application under s.33 is bound to succeed. If those conditions are not met, the applicant should seek relief under section 33: *Smith v. White Knight Laundry* [2002] 3 All. E.R 862, CA, approving *Workvale Ltd., Re* [1992] 2 All E.R. 627; [1992] 1 W.L.R. 416, CA.

Discretion to disapply relevant limitation period

The wording of the section is to empower the Court to direct that the provisions of s.11 or s.12 shall not apply to the action or to any specified cause of action to which the action relates, and this enabling power may be exercised if it appears to the Court that it would be equitable to allow the action to proceed having regard both (a) to the degree to which the provisions of these sections prejudice the plaintiff and (b) to the extent to which a decision to allow the action to proceed would prejudice the defendant (s.33(1)). It would seem that such a direction may be given at the trial of an action, but nevertheless it is right that this issue should be decided at a preliminary stage

8–72

and if the Court is satisfied that it has all the circumstances of the case before it, there is no reason why it should not determine the issue at any interlocutory stage (see *Firman v. Ellis* (1978)) or preliminary hearing or upon a preliminary issue whether before or at the trial. See *Buck v. English Electric Co. Ltd* [1977] 1 W.L.R. 806; [1978] 1 All E.R. 271; *Davies v. British Insulated Callender's Cables Ltd* (1977) 121 S.J. 203.

The Act of 1980 does not lay down any specific procedure whereby the statutory power under s.33 ("to override time limits") is to be invoked. In order to preclude any undue prolongation of an action which it may not be equitable to permit to proceed and in seeking to limit the burden of costs which may be imposed on the defendant, an application by him to stay the claim under CPR r.3.1(f) would, provided that the plaintiff has given due notice of his intention to rely on the section, serve to initiate the investigation contemplated by s.33. In a clear case, the defendant may apply for summary judgment under CPR r.24.2(a)(i), though in some situations the substantive issues may be so intimately and inextricably bound up with the questions arising under s.33 as to make any summary resolution of the question impracticable (see *per* Shaw L.J. in *Walkley v. Precision Forgings Ltd* [1979] 1 W.L.R. 606 at 1238; [1979] 1 All E.R. 102, CA). It has however been observed that there is a "danger in the section 33 exercise of putting the cart before the horse, that is, determining the claim and relying on that determination in undertaking the balance of prejudice as to whether the claim should have preceded at all": see *KR v. Bryn Alyn Community (Holdings) Ltd* [2003] EWCA Civ 85; [2003] Q.B. 1441; [2003] 3 W.L.R. 107; [2004] 2 All E.R. 7116, CA, at paras 74(viii) and 309. It was also held at para. 74(vi), that "Whenever the judge considers it feasible to do so, he should decide the limitation point by a preliminary hearing by reference to the pleading and written witness statements and, importantly, the extent and content of discovery ... It may not always be feasible or produce savings in time and cost for the parties to deal with the matter by way of preliminary hearing, but a judge should strain to do so whenever possible."

The discretion conferred on the Court by s.33 requires that the Court must have regard to all the circumstances of the case (s.33(3)). This entitles the Judge to take account of the ultimate prospects of success, and it has been emphasised in *Davis v. Jacobs* [1999] Lloyd's Rep. Med. 72, CA that it is incumbent on the Judge to take great care when deciding to do so; he must specifically take care that all matters which might be taken into account are in fact considered. The Court however must have regard to certain matters in particular which may provide guidelines when deciding whether to override a defence of limitation although in *Donovan v. Gwentoys Ltd* [1990] 1 W.L.R. 472; and [1990] 1 All E.R. 1018, HL. Lord Griffiths emphasised that these specific considerations are not intended to place any fetter on the Court's general discretion. These are

    (a) the length and reasons for delay on the part of the plaintiff;
    (b) the effect of any delay on the cogency of the evidence;
    (c) the conduct of the defendant;
    (d) the duration of any disability of the plaintiff arising after accrual of the cause of action;
    (e) the conduct of the plaintiff;
    (f) the diligence on the part of the plaintiff in obtaining medical, legal or other expert advice.

The outcome of the balancing exercise under s.33 is not to be determined on comparative scales of hardship (though hardship can never be irrelevant in a jurisdiction where all circumstances are to be taken into account). The overriding question is one of equity: would it be equitable for the action to be allowed to proceed on a balance of prejudice weighed with due regard to all the circumstances and to the specific factors mentioned in the section?

Again, in *Nash v. Eli Lilly & Co.* [1993] 1 W.L.R. 782, it was emphasised by the Court of Appeal that subs. (1) establishes the balancing exercise in considering, from an equitable point of view, the prejudice to the plaintiff if he is deprived of his right of action as against the prejudice to the defendant if the action is permitted to continue. Subs. (3) provides that the court in carrying out this exercise must have regard to "all the circumstances of the case" and particularly to the considerations set out in paras (a) to (f). Subject to acting judicially, the discretion of the court is entirely unfettered. The specific matters set out in subs.(3) are exemplary and not definitive (*Nash v. Eli Lilly & Co.* [1993] 4 All E.R. 383 at 402, CA).

The burden of showing that it is equitable to disapply the limitation period is on the claimant. The court must take account of all the circumstances including the ability to have a fair trial. Where the claimant failed to disclose all the relevant circumstances of his medical history the judge's exercise of discretion in his favour was set aside even though liability had been established: *Long v. Tolchard and Sons Ltd*, *The Times*, January 5, 2000, CA. The burden is a heavy one. Another way of putting it is that it is an exceptional indulgence to a claimant to be granted only where equity between the parties demands it: see *KR v. Bryn Alyn Community (Holdings) Ltd (In Liquidation)* [2003] EWCA Civ 85, at para. 74(ii), referring to the dicta of Lord Diplock in *Thompson v. Brown Construction Ltd (t/a George Albert Brown (Builders) & Co)* [1981] 1 W.L.R. 744, CA, at 750C and 752E–F; and at para. 92.

There are no grounds for limiting the exercise of the court's discretion in group actions for reasons of public policy (*ibid.*, p.409).

For the purposes of s.33(3)(b), cogency is directed to the degree to which either party is prejudiced in the presentation of the claim or defence because the evidence is either no longer available or has been adversely affected by the passage of time. Consideration of cogency in the context of the plaintiff's delay under s.33(3)(a) must not be confused with the overall discretion which is to be exercised under subs.(1) (*ibid.*, p.406).

The factors to be taken into account under s.33(3)(b) may include potential prejudice to the defendant in relation to contribution proceedings: see *Buckler v. Sheffield City Council* [2004] EWCA Civ. 920; [2005] P.I.Q.R. P3 at p.36, CA .

The test to be applied under s.33(3)(a) to the reasons for the plaintiff's delay is a subjective test and not an objective one (*Coad v. Cornwall and Isles of Scilly HA* [1997] 8 Med.L.R. 154, CA).

Section 33(3)(c) relates to the conduct of the defendant after the cause of action arose. A health authority with a policy of destroying patients' X-rays after three years, even those of patients known to be contemplating actions in negligence and whose solicitors had requested notes, would have any prejudice pleaded in a limitation defence significantly discounted: *Hammond v. West Lancashire HA*, [1998] Lloyd's Rep. Med. 146 CA.

Where the defendant is insured, the defendant and his insurers are to be treated as **8–73** one composite unit. Thus, if the delay has seriously prejudiced the ability to defend, and the action would have been discounted by the court if the defendant had not been insured, no regard should be paid to the fact that he is insured (*Kelly v. Bastible*, *The Times*, November 15, 1996, CA).

In *Yates v. Thakeham Tiles Ltd* [1995] P.I.Q.R. 135, CA, it was held that, for the purpose of s.33(3)(d), "disability" was limited to the context of a person under disability by reason of being an infant or a patient under the Mental Health Act 1983. The judge had erroneously taken physical disability into account under s.33(3)(d). He was however entitled to take it into account in the overall exercise of his discretion under s.33 (see also *Davis v. Jacobs*, above) and the fact that he had taken it into account under subs. (3)(d) did not detract from that. It was observed that the very breadth of the discretion afforded to the judge under the section made an attack on its exercise inherently difficult. Again, in *Thomas v. Plaistow*, *The Times*, May 19, 1997, CA, it was held that the word "disability" clearly had the same meaning in s.33(3)(d) as in section 28. The rationale was that while section 28 conferred mandatory extension of time in the case of existing disability, supervening disability should be dealt with as an exercise of the Court's discretion.

It was emphasised in a pre-CPR case that the exercise of discretion under s.33 differed in two vital respects from that in applications to strike out for want of prosecution. Firstly, in a striking out application the onus was on the defendant to prove not merely delay but that he had been prejudiced by it. In an application under s.33 the onus was on the plaintiff. Secondly, under s.33(3) there were six criteria to which the court must have regard. Whilst it was not essential for the judge to go through the criteria referring to each, *i.e.* to use the section as a checklist, nevertheless it was a useful exercise to do so (*Barrand v. British Cellophane Plc*, *The Times*, February 16, 1995, CA).

The Court held in *Nash v. Eli Lilly & Co.* [1993] 1 W.L.R. 782, *supra*, that if it is shown that the claim is a poor case lacking in merit, there may be significant and relevant prejudice to the defendant if the limitation provisions are disapplied: *ibid.*, at pp. 403–404, considering *Hartley v. Birmingham City D.C.* [1992] 1 W.L.R. 968; [1992] 2 All E.R. 213, CA, where the Court of Appeal, whose leading judgment was delivered by Parker L.J., expressed the view that "as the prejudice resulting from the loss of the limitation defence will always or almost always be balanced by the prejudice to the plaintiff from the operation of the limitation provision, the loss of the defence *as such* will be of little importance. What is of paramount importance is the effect of the delay on the defendant's ability to defend". In the later case (*Nash v. Eli Lilly & Co.*), the Court held that it could not accept that in every case where the ability of a defendant to defend on the issue of liability has not been affected by the delay, the benefit of the limitation defence must be regarded as a "windfall" (*ibid.*, p.403).

The court has refused to lay down a guideline that, in the absence of fault on the part of the defendant, the limitation period will be enforced unless the delay has been minimal, especially if the plaintiff has a good claim against his solicitors. Such a guideline would lead to litigation as to what constitutes minimal delay (*Ramsden v. Lee* [1992] 2 All E.R. 204, CA).

In considering whether the plaintiff had received legal advice and the nature of any such advice, the Court will have regard to the character of the advice in so far as it is relevant to the question whether the plaintiff had acted promptly and reasonably after he had knowledge of the information which might give rise to the cause of action; therefore, the Court should know whether the advice was favourable to the plaintiff's alleged cause of action (*Jones v. G. D. Searle & Co. Ltd* [1979] 1 W.L.R. 101; [1978] 3 All E.R. 654, CA).

The test to be applied under s.33(3)(e) in deciding whether the plaintiff has acted reasonably in bringing the case late is an objective one: what would a reasonable man in the position of the plaintiff have done? A trade union member could usually be said to act reasonably if he followed union advice (*Dale v. British Coal Corporation (No. 2)* (1992) 136 S.J.L.B. 199, CA). It was further held that where, as in this case, both notice of the existence of the claim and sufficient particulars were given so late that it was virtually impossible for a defendant to investigate, the defendant was gravely prejudiced, and it would take exceptional circumstances to disapply the limitation period. The test to be applied under s.33(3)(a), rather than (3)(e), is however a subjective one (*Coad v. Cornwall and Isles of Scilly HA* [1997] 8 Med.L.R. 154, CA, distinguishing *Dale's* case, *supra*. And, it has been held, the person whose conduct is relevant to consider under (3)(e) is the claimant himself, and not his advisers: *Davis v. Jacobs* above.

In *Smith v. Leicestershire H.A.* (1996) 36 B.M.L.R. 23 negligence and causation were found by the trial Judge in favour of the plaintiff. But the question arose how s.33(3)(b) should operate in light of the fact that the plaintiff had succeeded in 1996 but might not have done so had the trial taken place even 20 years earlier. The Court of Appeal, at [1998] Lloyd's Rep. Med. 77, CA, overruling the Judge's decision, held that causation does not change with the passage of time and allowed the action to proceed.

8–74 In terms of evidence required on an application under s.33, where it was necessary for the plaintiff's case to show that a prudent employer should have taken precautions to protect an employee at special risk, expert evidence should normally be advanced on the application (*Dale v. BCC (No. 2)* above).

The Court may permit an action to proceed under s.33 where the plaintiff, in ignorance of his legal rights has delayed in suing, and cannot be criticised for doing so, even though he knew facts on which a claim was available (*Halford v. Brookes* [1991] 1 W.L.R. 428, CA). See also *Das v. Ganju, The Times*, May 4, 1999, CA, in which the claimant was permitted to proceed where the delay was caused by the fault of her lawyers and where she herself could not be criticised.

Das v. Ganju has established that there is no rule of law that a solicitor's faults are to be visited on the claimant: *Corbin v. Penfold Metallising Co Ltd, The Times*, May 2, 2000, CA. See also *Steeds v. Peverel Management Services Ltd, The Times*, May 16, 2001, CA.

On an application for a direction to disapply the relevant limitation period, the length of and reasons for delay which are required to be considered by the Court under s.33(3)(a) are those which had occurred between the expiry of the limitation period and the issue of the writ, and *not* between the beginning of the limitation period and the issue of the writ (*Eastman v. London County Bus Services Ltd, The Times*, November 2, 1985, applying *Thompson v. Brown* [1981] 1 W.L.R. 751, *per* Lord Diplock). Lord Diplock's dictum was approved in *Donovan v. Gwentoys Ltd* (above), although in that case, the House of Lords held that the Court should look at all the circumstances including those arising within the limitation period. Thus it was specifically held that prejudice caused to a defendant by the plaintiff's delay in notifying him of the claim during the limitation period is relevant and that this was a significant factor in weighing the relative prejudice to the plaintiff and defendant as required by s.33(1)(a) and (b) (*per* Lord Griffiths, at [1990] 1 W.L.R. 478–479; and [1990] 1 All E.R. 1024).

In deciding whether to exercise its discretion under s.33 to disapply the time limit it would not be proper to apply different principles for the ordinary single case and for multi-party litigation: *Nash v. Eli Lilly* [1991] 2 Med.L.R. 169, *per* Hidden J).

The overriding discretion of the Court arises if the Court considers it "equitable" to allow an action to proceed. This is the widest term that the legislature could have used to confer this discretion on the Court (see *per* Lord Cowper L.C. in *Dudley (Lord) v. Dudley (Lady)* (1705) Prec.Ch. 241 at 244, cited in Vol. 2, "Words & Phrases", p.173) and such discretion may be exercised to override the technical defence of limitation and to enable the Court to sustain the action if it would be fair and just in all the circumstances of the case to do so as between the plaintiff and defendant. Moreover, where a person has been added as a defendant after the expiry of the primary period of limitation against him the Court will not exercise its discretion to extend such period under s.33 of the Act where the plaintiff is not prejudiced because he has a cast-iron case against the original defendant and the Motor Insurers' Bureau would be required to satisfy any judgment against that defendant. Their presence in the case is one of the circumstances to which the Court is required to have regard under s.33(3) of the Act of 1980 (*Liff v. Peasley* [1980] 1 W.L.R. 781; [1980] 1 All E.R. 623, CA). Furthermore, the court was entitled to have regard to the fact that a plaintiff was impecunious and legally aided and that the defendant would have little prospect of recovering his costs (*Lye v. Marks and Spencer Plc, The Times*, February 15, 1988, CA).

Opposition by a defendant to an application to extend time under s.33 will not be upheld solely on the ground that the cause of action itself is to be regarded as inequitable. The question posed by s.33 is not whether the claim is equitable, but whether it was equitable to allow it to proceed (*Ward v. Foss, The Times*, November 29, 1993, CA (claim for damages for loss of earnings during the "lost years" after death arising out of a fatal accident in 1982. The Administration of Justice Act 1982, s.4(2), which was not retrospective, abolished such claims where the cause of action accrued on or after January 1, 1983)).

The jurisdiction of the Court under s.33 of the 1980 Act to direct that the time limits in actions for personal injuries or death shall not apply to an action or to any specified cause of action, may be exercised by a Judge, Master or District Judge: CPR r.2.4.

Appeal

It has been held in *Dale v. British Coal Corporation (No. 1)* [1992] 1 W.L.R. 964, CA, **8–75** applying *White v. Brunton* [1984] Q.B. 570, CA, that, for the purpose of leave to appeal, a determination under s.33 disapplying the time limits under s.11 is final and not interlocutory; this being so by whatever procedure the application is brought on, *e.g.* by trial of preliminary issue or on application by the defendant to strike out the action. These cases were applied in *Hughes v. Jones, The Times*, July 18, 1996, CA, deciding that the Court hearing a section 33 application is exercising final, not interlocutory, jurisdiction. Reference was made to the incorporation of the decision in *White v. Brunton* in RSC O.59, r.1A(4).

Under the CPR the distinction between an interlocutory order and a final order is no longer relevant for the purposes of permission to appeal to the Court of Appeal (see the note at para. R.59.1.96), though it may be relevant for other purposes. Those purposes may include an appeal from a District Judge under CPR Schedule 2, CCR O.37, r.6. The Practice Direction for the Court of Appeal (Civil Division), para. 2.12.1 (see para. 4A–16) lays down a definition of an interlocutory order which does not accord with the test in *White v. Brunton* but which may be held to be confined to questions of appeal in the Court of Appeal. It has to be observed however that RSC O.59, r.1A has not been re-enacted under the CPR and it appears to be open to question to what extent the rationale of the decision in *Hughes v. Jones*, above, is thereby affected.

Alternative dispute resolution

It has been held that a waiver by a defendant of its right to rely in an ADR scheme **8–76** on limitation defences did not extend, after the termination of that scheme, to litigation (*Blytheway v. British Steel Corporation Plc* [1997] 9 C.L. 103, CA).

Scope of s.33 in relation to other Statutes

Section 33 has been held not to apply to cases where a time limit imposed by statute **8–77** under the Merchant Shipping Act 1979 arises (2 year limit under the Athens Convention). The terms of the Convention provided for "suspension or interruption" of limitation periods but, unlike s.32, s.33 was concerned not with suspension or interruption but with exclusion altogether of a time period which had already run its course. Further, it was not possible to construe s.33, which refers expressly to the provisions of ss.11 and 12 of this Act, as extending to the Convention (*Higham v. Stena Sealink Ltd* [1996] 1 W.L.R. 1107, CA).

Article 6 of the ECHR

8–77.1   The Court of Appeal did not accept that, whilst the *Walkley* principle continues to hold good under domestic law, the UK are to be regarded as violating the Article 6 rights of those affected by it: *Young (Deceased) v. Western Power Distribution (South West) Plc* [2003] EWCA Civ 1034 at para. 55.

PART III

MISCELLANEOUS AND GENERAL

Application of Act and other limitation enactments to arbitrations

8–78   **34.** [*Repealed by the* Arbitration Act 1996, Sched.4]

New claims in pending actions: rules of court

8–79   **35.**—(1) For the purposes of this Act, any new claim made in the course of any action shall be deemed to be a separate action and to have been commenced—

>   (a) in the case of a new claim made in or by way of third party proceedings, on the date on which those proceedings were commenced; and

>   (b) in the case of any other new claim, on the same date as the original action.

(2) In this section a new claim means any claim by way of set-off or counterclaim, and any claim involving either—

>   (a) the addition or substitution of a new cause of action; or

>   (b) the addition or substitution of a new party;

and "third party proceedings" means any proceedings brought in the course of any action by any party to the action against a person not previously a party to the action, other than proceedings brought by joining any such person as defendant to any claim already made in the original action by the party bringing the proceedings.

(3) Except as provided by section 33 of this Act or by rules of court, neither the High Court nor any county court shall allow a new claim within subsection (1)(b) above, other than an original set-off or counterclaim, to be made in the course of any action after the expiry of any time limit under this Act which would affect a new action to enforce that claim.

For the purposes of this subsection, a claim is an original set-off or an original counterclaim if it is a claim made by way of set-off or (as the case may be) by way of counterclaim by a party who has not previously made any claim in the action.

(4) Rules of court may provide for allowing a new claim to which subsection (3) above applies to be made as there mentioned, but only

if the conditions specified in subsection (5) below are satisfied, and subject to any further restrictions the rules may impose.

(5) The conditions referred to in subsection (4) above are the following—

(a) in the case of a claim involving a new cause of action, if the new cause of action arises out of the same facts or substantially the same facts as are already in issue on any claim previously made in the original action; and

(b) in the case of a claim involving a new party, if the addition or substitution of the new party is necessary for the determination of the original action.

(6) The addition or substitution of a new party shall not be regarded for the purposes of subsection (5)(b) above as necessary for the determination of the original action unless either—

(a) the new party is substituted for a party whose name was given in any claim made in the original action in mistake for the new party's name; or

(b) any claim already made in the original action cannot be maintained by or against an existing party unless the new party is joined or substituted as plaintiff or defendant in that action.

(7) Subject to subsection (4) above, rules of court may provide for allowing a party to any action to claim relief in a new capacity in respect of a new cause of action notwithstanding that he had no title to make that claim at the date of the commencement of the action.

This subsection shall not be taken as prejudicing the power of rules of court to provide for allowing a party to claim relief in a new capacity without adding or substituting a new cause of action.

(8) Subsections (3) to (7) above shall apply in relation to a new claim made in the course of third party proceedings as if those proceedings were the original action, and subject to such other modifications as may be prescribed by rules of court in any case or class of case.

(9) *[Repealed by the* Supreme Court Act 1981, Sched.7]

Scope and operation of this section

This section re-enacts s.8 of the Limitation Amendment Act 1980, which had not **8–80** been brought into force and which had replaced s.28 of the Limitation Act 1939, relating to set-off and counterclaims. It deals in the scope of one section with a number of disparate procedural problems and it is a mix of both substantive and procedural law, with the added complication that it authorises rules of Court to be made but only within the limits laid down by the section itself. The connecting thread which runs through the section and which may justify its form is that it is dealing with "new claims in pending actions."

The matters which are dealt with by this section may be summarised as follows:

(1) definition of "new claims" in pending actions;

(2) time limits for third party proceedings;

(3) time limits for a set-off or counterclaim;

(4) amendments in pending actions after the expiry of a current period of limitation:

(a) to add or substitute a new cause of action;

(b) to add or substitute a new party;

(c) to add a claim for relief in a new capacity;

(5) powers under rules of Court to make such amendments.

It should be noted that s.35, with its provisions which are intended to permit, or refuse, as the case may be, new claims in pending actions in the light of statutory limitation periods under this Act, has no application where a contractual or substantive time-limit, such as in the Hague Rules, has expired and the action has ceased to exist: *Payabi v. Armstel Shipping Corporation* [1992] Q.B. 907; [1992] 2 W.L.R. 898.

Nature of new claims in pending actions

8–81   For the purposes of the 1980 Act, s.35 provides that any new claim made in the course of any action, *i.e.* while the action is pending or in being, is deemed to be "a separate action" (subs.(1)).

For this purpose a "new claim" means or includes:

(a) a claim made in or by way of third party proceedings (see s.35(1)(a));

(b) any claim made by way of set-off or counterclaim (see s.35(2));

(c) any claim involving the addition or substitution of a new cause of action (see s.35(2)(a));

(d) any claim involving the addition or substitution of a new party (see s.35(2)(b)).

For the analysis of the meaning of a "new claim" within s.35(2)(a) or (b) see *Yorkshire Regional HA v. Fairclough Building Ltd* [1996] 1 All E.R. 519, CA. The two paragraphs of the subsection are to be regarded as mutually exclusive, para. (a) being confined to claims involving a new cause of action but not the addition or substitution of a new party, and para. (b) being applicable to the addition or substitution of a new party, whether or not that involved a new cause of action.

It is not clear whether a claim for relief in a new capacity under s.35(7) is a "new claim," though it probably is if the relief is sought in respect of a new cause of action, but not if it is sought without the addition or substitution of a new cause of action.

Time limits for third party proceedings

8–82   In the case of a new claim made in or by way of third party proceedings, the separate action, which such claim is deemed to be, is deemed to have commenced on the date on which those proceedings were commenced (see s.35(1)(a)).

For this purpose, "third party proceedings" are defined as meaning any proceedings brought in the course of any action by any party to the action against a party not previously a party to the action, other than proceedings brought by joining any such person as defendant to any claim already made in the action by the party bringing the proceedings. Accordingly, an amendment made, or sought to be made, in existing proceedings by the addition of a new defendant to an existing claim falls to be treated as a new claim under subs.(1)(b), (*i.e.* proceedings deemed to have been commenced on the same date as the original action) whereas the addition by a defendant of a new party in the form of a third party falls to be dealt with under subs.(1)(a) (proceedings deemed to have been commenced on date of commencement of third party proceedings): and see *Kennett v. Brown* [1988] 1 W.L.R. 582, CA. In that case the party making the new claim was in fact the first defendant who sought, out of time, to recover by contribution notice against the second defendant damages for his own injuries incurred in the accident. It was held that these were not third party proceedings within the meaning of s.35(1). Any claim or issue within the former O.16, r.1(1) was a third party proceeding, but claims and issues between co-defendants under the former O.16, r.8 were not "third party proceedings" for the purposes of this section.

Of course, third party proceedings for the purposes of this section include fourth and subsequent party proceedings.

The former Rule of Court (RSC O.16) providing procedural machinery for the bringing and conduct of third party proceedings has been repealed. Indeed, the description "third party proceedings" is not now used in the CPR, the description being "Part 20 claim" and the relevant Rule being CPR Pt 20. As under RSC O.16, Part 20 does not itself contain any provision dealing with limitation. The matter is left to s.35 of the Act.

The provision that third party proceedings are deemed to have been commenced on the date on which those proceedings are begun is a provision of great importance. It is to be contrasted with the provision in s.35(1)(b) whereby other new claims in an action are deemed to have been commenced on the same date as the original action. Accordingly, in third party proceedings there is no backdating. However, the question still arises when, for the purposes of third party proceedings, does the relevant cause of action as between the defendant and third party accrue? In many cases the question may be of little relevance, for the third party proceedings will be grounded on a right to recover contribution for damage for which the defendant is liable to the plaintiff. In procedural terms, such right is plainly granted by CPR Pt 20. In substantive terms, the right arises under s.1 of the Civil Liability (Contribution) Act 1978. The limitation period in such cases is that set by s.10 of the Limitation Act 1980, *i.e.* two years from the date when the right to recover contribution accrued, as defined by s.10(3) and (4). Accordingly, the defendant seeking contribution will have two years from the date when he is ordered, or agrees, to make payment. And, it appears, the running of time as between the plaintiff and the person claiming contribution does not affect the entitlement to recover contribution provided that immediately before the person claiming contribution made or was ordered or agreed to make the payment in respect of which contribution is sought he (*i.e.* the person claiming contribution) was liable in respect of the damage: see para. 8–15 above. In other cases, however, where, for example, the defendant relies on a right of indemnity under contract against a third party, or where the defendant seeks to recover against the third party damages for damage suffered by himself, and is entitled to bring third party proceedings in respect thereof (see CPR Pt 20), the primary limitation periods imposed by the Limitation Act 1980 will apply to the defendant's cause of action. In such cases, the defendant will need to be diligent, especially if the claimant's proceedings against him are commenced towards the end of the limitation period, to commence the third party proceedings in time. It appears that, in view of the fact that subs.(1) deems that the new claim is to be a separate action, a defendant in such a position is to be regarded as claimant for the purposes of the Limitation Act 1980 and that accordingly, in appropriate circumstances in a personal injury action, such a defendant could apply to the court to override the bar of limitation under s.33 of the Act.

The section does not define the date when third party proceedings will be treated as having been commenced. The better view under the former RSC was that such proceedings were commenced only when the third party notice itself was issued (pursuant to leave if such leave was required). The issue of a third party notice took effect from its being sealed by an Officer of the Court out of which it was issued (see *College Street Market Gardens v. Short*, October 5, 1989 (unrep.) *per* Saville J.).

The position under the Civil Procedure Rules is that a Part 20 claim is made when the court issues the Part 20 claim form: see CPR r.20.7(1)–(5).

Time limits for set-off or counterclaim

A claim by way of set-off or counterclaim is a separate action and is deemed to have **8–83** been commenced on the same date as the original action (see s.35(1)(b)). This provision repeats the former law as prescribed by s.28 of the Limitation Act 1939.

In *Westdeutsche Landesbank v. Islington B.C.* [1994] 4 All E.R. 890, the meaning of the term "set off" in s.35 of this Act, and s.28 of the Limitation Act 1939, was considered. It was held, applying Lord Denning's judgment in *Henriksens Rederi A/S v. PHZ Rolimpex* [1974] Q.B. 233; [1973] 3 All E.R. 589, CA, that the time bars arising out of s.28 and s.35 did not apply to equitable set-offs in the nature of a defence but only to legal set-offs, properly so called, by way of cross-claim (see *Westdeutsche, supra* at pp. 944–945.

A party may of course seek to make a claim by way of set-off or counterclaim in an existing action. If he is a party who has not previously made any claim in the action such set-off or counterclaim will be regarded as "original" for the purposes of s.35(3) and may be allowed to be made after the expiry of the current period of limitation which would affect a new action to enforce that claim (*ibid.*).

It has been held under the former RSC that while O.15 permits the bringing of a counterclaim by the defendant against one or more of the plaintiffs by whom he has been sued and section 35 permits such counterclaim to be treated as having been brought on the same date as the original action, the discretion of the Court might be exercised against the defendant to say that the counterclaim shall be brought as a separate action. In the instant case the counterclaim should be struck out with the result that a separate action would be statute barred. Mutuality of the subject-matter of the claim and counterclaim are not necessary, but want of mutuality may be a weighty factor in exercising discretion. In the ordinary case procedural convenience is the primary consideration and limitation consequences are at best only secondary (*Ernst & Young v. Butte Mining Plc* [1997] 2 All E.R. 471).

See also *JFS (UK) Ltd v. Dwr Cymru Cyf*, *The Times*, October 10, 1998, CA, in which the word "claim" for the purposes of s.35(3) was held to mean a claim for relief rather than an averment by way of defence.

8-83.1   *Amendments in pending actions after the expiry of a current period of limitation—power under Rules of Court to make such amendments* —Subsection (3) of s.35 is of cardinal importance in considering the power of the court. It is enacted that, except as provided by s.33 or by rules of court, the court shall not allow a new claim within subs.(1)(b) "other than an original set-off or counterclaim" to be made after the expiry of a time limit which would affect a new action to enforce such claim. A new claim within subs.(1)(b) is any new claim other than third party proceedings (which are themselves limited by the rule that they are deemed to have been commenced on the date of commencement of the third party proceedings).

The purpose of this subsection is, subject to the qualifications stated, to bar new and additional causes of action being litigated outside the period of limitation and to prevent new and additional parties being sued outside such period. But set-offs and counterclaims, if they are "original," may be relied on. The subsection defines an original set-off and an original counterclaim as a claim by way of set-off or by way of counterclaim made by a party who has not previously made any claim in the action. Thus, a defendant served with a writ which has been issued before the end of the limitation period may claim once by way of set-off or counterclaim even though his set-off or counterclaim is not pleaded until after the limitation period has expired. See *Lloyds Bank Plc v. Wojcik*; *The Independent*, January 19, 1998 (C.S.), CA. But he may not do so again in the action, for his set-off or counterclaim would not then be "original." A defendant should in such circumstances make sure that he includes all claims on which he may wish to rely in his original pleading. A claim by way of set-off is treated as a new claim even though a set-off operates by way of defence. Accordingly, it would not appear to be open to a defendant, who has pleaded a set-off only, to seek to add (outside the limitation period) a counterclaim; though, if he has previously made no claim at all, he may do so. If, however, the new counterclaim arises out of the same or substantially the same facts as those upon which the set-off was based, the defendant may bring himself within s.35(5), and accordingly add a counterclaim.

The word "claim" in s.35(3) should be construed as a claim for relief. Accordingly, where a defendant had previously pleaded a defence stating that the plaintiff had extended time for payment of a debt, that was not a claim in the legal sense. There was power under s.35(3) to grant leave to amend to plead a counterclaim even though it was founded on a cause of action which was statute-barred: *JFS (UK) Ltd v. Dwr Cymru Cyf*, *The Times*, October 10, 1998, CA.

In *Kennett v. Brown* [1988] 1 W.L.R. 582, CA, where a first defendant sought by contribution notice against a second defendant to recover damages for his own injuries incurred in the accident, it was held that this was not an original set-off or counterclaim within the meaning of subs.(3), Lord Donaldson M.R. construing these words, at p.585, as meaning "a set-off or counterclaim by an original defendant against an original plaintiff."

The further decision in *Kennett v. Brown* [1988] 1 W.L.R. 582 that s.35(3) does not automatically bar a new claim but presents a procedural bar for the defendant to raise if he wishes, has been expressly overruled in *Welsh Development Agency v. Redpath Dorman Long Ltd*, [1994] 1 W.L.R. 1409 below. The onus was on the plaintiff to show that the amendment came within s.35(5) and the former O.20, r.5(5).

Relationship of s.35 with the Civil Procedure Rules 1998

8-84   It is important when considering the various matters for which this section makes provision to refer to the particular Civil Procedure Rules which apply in relation to that provision. Indeed, s.35(4) provides that rules of court may provide for allowing a new claim to be made outside the limitation period but only if the conditions of s.35(5) are satisfied and subject to any further restrictions the rules may impose. Those rules may be enumerated under the following headings:

8-85   *(1) Addition of a new cause of action* —Section 35(5)(a) applies, together with CPR 17.4(1) and (2). These provisions are correspondingly restrictive, though the Act refers to the addition of a "new cause of action", while the Rule refers to the addition of a "new claim". In each case, the addition must arise out of the same facts or substantially the same facts. The Act qualifies these words with the words "as are already in issue on any claim previously made in the original action". The words of restriction in the Rule are "as a claim in respect of which the party applying for permission has already claimed a remedy in the proceedings". The Rule may thus be regarded as imposing an additional restriction, but this is expressly envisaged by s.35(4).

As the Court of Appeal emphasised in *Lloyds Bank plc v. Rogers* [1999] E.G. 83, *per* Auld L.J. at p.85, "It is important to note that what makes a 'new claim' as defined in s.35(2) is not the newness of the claim according to the type or quantum of remedy sought, but the newness of the cause of action that it involves. The formula employed in s.35(2)(a) and (5) is 'a claim involving ... the addition or substitution of a new cause of action'." Auld L.J.'s judgment was applied in *Aldi Stores Ltd v. Holmes Buildings plc* [2005] P.N.L.R. 9, CA. *Aldi*, and the cases cited therein of *Gordon v. JB Wheatley & Co.* [2000] Lloyd's Rep. P.N. 605 and *Stock v. London Underground Ltd*, *The Times*, August 13, 1999, CA are examples, on their facts, of what may or may not amount to a new cause of action.

Amendment of a case to add a new cause of action after the expiry of a limitation period was governed under the former rules of the Supreme Court by Order 20, rule 5. That rule may be compared with CPR r.17.4(2). In *Welsh Development Agency v. Redpath Dorman Long Ltd* [1994] 1 W.L.R. 1409 and [1994] 4 All E.R. 10, CA, the Court of Appeal made it clear that in cases where s.35(1) does, or may well, give the plaintiff an advantage the correct test to apply is that leave to amend by adding a new claim should not be given unless the claimant could show that the defendant did not have a reasonably arguable case on limitation which would be prejudiced by the new claim, or could bring himself within Order 20, rule 5. The court held that the onus was on the plaintiff to show that the amendment came within s.35(5), and that s.35(3) was a mandatory direction to a court dealing with an application to amend by adding a new claim: commenting on *Grimsby Cold Stores Ltd v. Jenkins & Potter* (1985) 1 Const. L.J. 362, CA, and on *Leicester Wholesale Fruit Market Ltd v. Grundy* [1990] 1 W.L.R. 107; [1990] 1 All E.R. 442, CA, and stating that the decision in *Holland v. Yates Building Co. Ltd*, *The Times*, December 5, 1989, CA was one which should not be followed.

The court in *Welsh Development Agency* [1994] 1 W.L.R. 1409 further held that on a true construction of s.35, unless a new claim came within one of the exceptions provided by the rules of court, leave to amend could not be given where the limitation period had expired at the time when the court was considering the matter, even if it had not expired at the time when application for leave was made, since the relevant date was the date on which the amendment was actually made, which by definition must be no earlier than the date on which leave was granted: p.1421.

The decision in *Welsh Development Agency* [1994] 1 W.L.R. 1409, by preventing an amendment being permitted where limitation is arguable, may make it incumbent on a claimant to issue fresh proceedings asserting the new cause of action, whilst preserving the defendant's right to argue (including by way of an application to strike out) limitation as a defence in those proceedings. In appropriate circumstances, an order for consolidation might be made of the fresh proceedings with the original claim.

Under s.35(5)(a) it will often be necessary to consider whether the amended claim involves a new cause of action. While it is not appropriate to construe the original pleading unduly literally or pedantically, a pleading is a formal document and cannot be held to include a cause of action which its language does not adequately express (*Balfour Beatty Construction v. Parsons Brown and Newton* (1991) 7 Const.L.J. 205, CA).

In a case where an allegation in the statement of claim had, in further and better particulars, not been pursued, it was permissible as a matter of discretion, by amendment of the particulars after the expiry of the limitation period, to resuscitate the allegation. Such did not constitute the pleading of a new cause of action (*Burton v. MBC (Builders–Ashingdon) Ltd* (1995) 69 P.&C.R. 496, CA). Further, a writ might be amended out of time to include a new case of action which had been pleaded within time in the statement of claim but had been inadvertently omitted from the writ (*Phelps v. Spon-Smith & Co.*, *The Times*, November 26, 1999).

An existing statement of claim pleading negligent acts may not enable a plaintiff wishing to amend by alleging negligent statements to say that the new factual material arises out of the same or substantially the same facts as are already in issue (*Hydrocarbons Great Britain v. Cammell Laird Shipbuilders* (1991) 25 Con.L.R. 131).

A statement of claim which originally disclosed no sustainable cause of action might in a proper case be amended with leave of the Court despite the expiry of the limitation period, so that a cause of action based on the same or substantially the same facts could be introduced (*Sion v. Hampstead HA* [1994] 5 Med. L.R. 170, June 10, CA). But where the Court has refused an amendment to plead a new cause of action on the ground that the same is arguably time-barred, it may similarly refuse an amendment to plead a yet further new cause of action arising out of the same facts: *Goose v. Wilson Sandford and Co., The Times*, May 10, 1994, *per* Harman J.

Section 35(5)(a) enables a new cause of action to be asserted if it arises out of the same or substantially the same facts as are already in issue. This exception may, contrary to the general rule, permit a cause of action to be pleaded which did not exist at the date of the writ, as where the original proceedings were brought by an injured plaintiff and amendment is sought after his death to introduce his widow's claim under the Fatal Accidents Act after the expiry of the limitation period under that Act (*Booker v. Associated British Ports* [1995] P.I.Q.R. 375, CA).

Section 35(5)(a) will also permit, subject to the exercise of the court's discretion, a new claim to be made by way of amendment to a counterclaim to plead a claim in libel after the expiry of the limitation period in relation to that claim if by the same application an amendment is permitted to plead a contractual claim within the limitation period and if the two claims are based on substantially the same facts. The court will treat the new claim within the limitation period as a claim previously made in the original action for the purposes of s.35(5)(a) (*Lloyd's Bank Plc v. Rogers The Times*, April 11, 1996; affirmed in the Court of Appeal , *The Times*, March 24, 1997, CA).

An amendment to allege intentional wrongdoing by pleading fraud where previously only negligence had been alleged amounts to the introduction of a new cause of action: *Paragon Finance plc v. D.B. Thakerar & Co.* [1999] 1 All E.R. 400, CA.

For amendment of a claim containing claims both for damages for personal injuries and for damages for economic loss by deletion of the claim for personal injuries, see *Shade v. The Compton Partnership* [2000] Lloyd's Rep. P.N. 81, CA, and *Pounds v. Eckford Rands* [2003] Lloyd's Rep. P.N. 195, cited also in the note to section 11, *ante*.

8–86   *(2) Addition or substitution of parties* —Here, s.35(5)(b) and s.35(6) apply, together with CPR 19. Amendment may be allowed after the expiry of the limitation period only in restricted circumstances. Thus, by s.35(5)(b) the amendment must be necessary for the determination of the action. And, by s.35(6)(b), apart from mistake, such amendment shall not be regarded as necessary unless a claim already made cannot be maintained by or against an existing party unless the new party is joined or substituted. Likewise, by CPR r.19.4(3)(b) the restriction is that the claim cannot be properly carried on by or against the original party unless the new party is added or substituted.

The rationale of the restriction is that, by s.35(1)(b), the new claim, if permitted, is deemed to have commenced on the same date as the original action. It is for this reason of relation back that, on an application to add a new party, unless the court is satisfied that the question of limitation is unarguable, permission should be refused: *c.f. Welsh Development Agency* [1994] 1 W.L.R. 1409, above, where the application to amend related to the addition of a new cause of action.

It should be noted however that the restriction does not apply where substitution is necessary by reason of the original party having died or having had a bankruptcy order made against him and of his interest or liability having passed to the new party: CPR r.19.4(3)(c). This reflects the former RSC Order 15, rule 7(1) which is preserved by CPR Schedule 1. In *Yorkshire Regional H.A. v. Fairclough Building Ltd* [1996] 1 W.L.R. 210, CA it was held that the restrictive effect of the former Order 15, rule 6(5) and (6) did not apply in cases falling under the former rule 7, which provided for substitution of a party by reason of assignment, transmission or devolution of interest or liability. It was held that the substitution of a new party unless Order 15, rule 7 did not involve the making of a new claim as defined in s.35(2) of the Limitation Act 1980. There were two entirely different kinds of substitution provided by the rules, one where the party substituted had succeeded to a claim or liability already represented in the action, and one where he had not. It would be outside the scope of the 1980 Act to alter the law relating to the former kind of substitution, which involved no question of limitation. It is to be observed, in relation to this decision, that the former Order 15, rule 7 has survived only in respect of rule 7(1) (death and bankruptcy): see CPR Schedule 1; and further that CPR r.19.1(4) permits a new party to be substituted if the existing party's interest or liability has passed and it is *desirable* to substitute the new party. It is not clear to what extent CPR r.19.4(3) will be held restrictive of the general power in CPR r.19.1(4) but it is to be hoped that the reasoning in *Yorkshire Regional H.A. v. Fairclough Building* [1996] 1 W.L.R. 210 will survive. A further respect in which the restrictions of s.35(5)(b) will not apply arises where a claim is made to add a defendant in a personal injuries claim and the claimant relies on s.33 of the Limitation Act 1980. This is recognised by the combined operation of s.35(3) and CPR r.19.5(4). The rule provides that the new party may be added either where the court directs that ss.11 or 12 of the Act shall not apply or where it directs that that issue shall be determined at trial: see *Howe v. David Brown Tractors (Retail) Ltd* [1991] 4 All E.R. 30, CA, where it was held that the party whom it is sought to add could be heard on the question, even before he had become a party. And see *Bridgeman v. Brown* [2000] 12 C.L. 48, CA, *per* Hale L.J., where it was held that arrangements should be made for the trial of issues of identity, limitation and joinder of an added defendant to be heard together.

(3) *Mistake in name of party* —Section 35(6)(a) of the Act applies so as to permit the **8–87** substitution of a new party for a party whose name was given in any claim made in the original action in mistake for the new party's name. Section 35(4) provides that rules of court may provide for allowing a new claim in such circumstances and subject to any further restrictions the rules may impose.CPR 19.5 is made under such power and the words of the rule, including CPR 19.5(3)(a), should be noted. Further, the distinction between CPR 17.4(3) (power to allow amendment to correct a mistake as to the name of a party) and CPR 19.5(3)(a) (power to allow a new party to be substituted for a party who was named in the claim form in mistake for the new party) should be noted. See the commentary on each of the two rules in Volume 1 above. And see *Horne-Roberts v. Smithkline Beecham PLC* [2001] EWCA Civ 2006; [2002] 1 W.L.R. 1662; [2002] C.P. Rep. 20; (2002) 65 BMLR 79, CA.

In *Evans Constructions Co. Ltd* v. Charrington & Co. Ltd [1983] QB 810; [1983] 2 W.L.R. 117; [1983] 1 All E.R. 310, CA, Griffiths LJ held at p.825 in relation to the former RSC Order 20, r.5(3),

"The wording of the rule makes it clear that it is not the identity of the person sued that is crucial, but the identity of the person intended to be sued, which is a very different matter."

The court permitted an amendment to be made to substitute as intended the name of the current landlord as defendant. This was applied in *The Sardinia Sulcis* [1991] 1 Lloyd's Rep. 201, CA, Lloyd L.J. holding, at p.207,

"In all these cases it was possible to identify the intending plaintiff or intended defendant by reference to a description which was more or less specific to the particular case;"

and Stocker L.J. holding, at p.209,

"can the intending plaintiff or defendant be identified by reference to a description which is specific to the particular case— *e.g.* landlord, employer, owners or shipowners?"

The view was also expressed at p.208, without argument, that the amendment related back to the date of the writ, and that the writ was accordingly not a nullity by reason of the non-existence of the plaintiff. However, s.35 of the Act has no application where a substantive or contractual time limit, such as that in the Hague Rules, has expired and the action has ceased to exist: *Payabi v. Armstel Shipping Corporation* [1992] Q.B. 907; [1992] 2 W.L.R. 898; [1992] 3 All E.R. 329; [1992] 2 Lloyd's Rep. 62, *per* Hobhouse J. The reasoning in the *Sardinia Sulcis*, above was applied in *International Bulk Shipping and Services Ltd v. Mineral and Metals Trading Corp of india* [1996] 1 All E.R. 1017, CA, in which orders made under the former RSC after the expiry of the limitation period to substitute as plaintiff the trustee in bankruptcy of the plaintiffs' assets were set aside, and applications to amend the names of the plaintiffs to the trustee's name were dismissed, where the actions were a nullity at their commencement in that the plaintiff companies had been dissolved and ceased to exist and where the amendments would be to correct the identity of the person intending to sue rather than a mistake in the name of such person.

The above cases were considered, after the introduction of the CPR, in *Horne-Roberts v. Smithkline Beecham Plc*, cited above, where the manufacture of a vaccine had been wrongly attributed to the person named as defendant. Substitution of the true manufacturer as defendant was permitted under s.35 of the Act and CPR 19.5. See also the commentary under s.11A of the Act, above.

It has also been held, in *Parsons v. George* [2004] EWCA Civ 912; [2004] 3 All E.R. 633, CA, that the conditions of CPR 19.5(3)(a) were satisfied where the tenants had always intended to sue the persons who answered the description of competent landlord.

8–88   *(4) Claim in a new capacity* —Subject to the restrictive provisions of s.35(4), Rules of Court may authorise a party to claim relief in a new capacity in respect of a new cause of action notwithstanding that he had no title to make that claim at the commencement of the action. Indeed he will be allowed in appropriate circumstances to claim relief in a new capacity without adding or substituting a new cause of action: see s.35(7) and CPR r.17.4(4).

Service on new party

8–89   Practice Direction 19, para. 3.3 provides that a new defendant does not become a party to the proceedings until the amended claim form has been served on him. Service of a writ which had been amended to add a new defendant was the subject, under the former Rules, of O.15, r.8(4). The new defendant did not become a party until the writ had been amended and served on him. And that must take place before the expiry of the limitation period (*Bank of America National Trust and Savings Association v. Christmas, The Kyriaki* [1993] 1 Lloyd's Rep. 137). Hirst J. rejected the argument that under s.35(3) all that was required was an order within the limitation period giving leave to amend. He held that O.15, r.8(4) was directly applicable, and that since s.35(3)–(5) enacted the principle that joinder of a new defendant related back to the date of issue of the writ, Lord Keith's statement in *Ketteman v. Hansel Properties Ltd* [1987] A.C. 189, HL, that, if that theory applied it would be unjust to join a new defendant at a time when limitation had run in his favour, because to do so would have the effect of depriving him of a valid defence, was fully applicable under s.35. Service on the new defendant out of time was set aside. It was also held that O.2, r.1, with its provisions for correcting an irregularity in failing to draw in time an order granting leave to amend, was subordinate to s.35 and to those provisions of O.15, rr.6 and 8 which implement that section, and that there was no jurisdiction to grant an extension of time for making the amendment so as to allow the action to be brought against the new defendant by service after the expiry of the limitation period. The decision in *The Kyriaki* has been expressly approved by the CA in *Welsh Development Agency v. Redpath Dorman Long Ltd* [1994] 1 W.L.R. 1409, *supra*.

Equitable jurisdiction and remedies

8–90   **36.**—(1) The following time limits under this Act, that is to say—

    (a) the time limit under section 2 for actions founded on tort;

    (aa) the time limit under section 4A for actions for libel or slander, or for slander of title, slander of goods or other malicious falsehood;

    (b) the time limit under section 5 for actions founded on simple contract;

    (c) the time limit under section 7 for actions to enforce awards where the submission is not by an instrument under seal;

    (d) the time limit under section 8 for actions on a specialty;

    (e) the time limit under section 9 for actions to recover a sum recoverable by virtue of any enactment; and

    (f) the time limit under section 24 for actions to enforce a judgment;

shall not apply to any claim for specific performance of a contract or for an injunction or for other equitable relief, except in so far as any such time limit may be applied by the court by analogy in like manner as the corresponding time limit under any enactment repealed by the Limitation Act 1939 was applied before 1st July 1940.

(2) Nothing in this Act shall affect any equitable jurisdiction to refuse relief on the ground of acquiescence or otherwise.

Note — Subs. (1), para. (aa) was added by the Administration of Justice Act 1985, **8–91**
s.57; substituted, in regard to causes of action arising after September 4, 1996, by the
Defamation Act 1996, s.5.

Time limits in breach of fiduciary duty —In cases where the claimant had a cause of **8–91.1**
action for intentional breach of fiduciary duty independently of causes of action in
contract or tort, the limitation periods in sections 2 and 5 of the Act are not directly
applicable. Whilst there is no reference in the 1980 Act to breach of fiduciary duty, a
claim for equitable damages for breach of such duty is a claim for equitable relief. Accordingly section 36 applies. In applying it, the court is not looking to see whether a
limitation period was actually applied to a dishonest breach of fiduciary duty by analogy before July 1, 1940, but looking to see whether it would have been applied.
Where the facts to support the claim for breach of fiduciary duty are the same as those
relied on to support breach of contract, the statute will be applied by analogy. Even
where equity was acting in its exclusive, as opposed to its concurrent, jurisdiction, the
statute might be applied by analogy: *Cia de Seguros Imperio v. Heath (REBX) Ltd (formerly
CE Heath &Co (America) Ltd)* [2001] 1 W.L.R. 112, CA

Application to the Crown and the Duke of Cornwall

37.—(1) Except as otherwise expressly provided in this Act, and **8–92**
without prejudice to section 39, this Act shall apply to proceedings by
or against the Crown in like manner as it applies to proceedings between subjects.

(2) Notwithstanding subsection (1) above, this Act shall not apply
to—

> (a) any proceedings by the Crown for the recovery of any
> tax or duty or interest on any tax or duty;
> (b) any forfeiture proceedings under the customs and excise
> Acts (within the meaning of the Customs and Excise
> Management Act 1979); or
> (c) any proceedings in respect of the forfeiture of a ship.

In this subsection "duty" includes any debt due to Her Majesty
under section 16 of the Tithe Act 1936, and "ship" includes every description of vessel used in navigation not propelled by oars.

(3) For the purposes of this section, proceedings by or against the
Crown include—

> (a) proceedings by or against Her Majesty in right of the
> Duchy of Lancaster;
> (b) proceedings by or against any Government department
> or any officer of the Crown as such or any person acting
> on behalf of the Crown; and
> (c) proceedings by or against the Duke of Cornwall.

(4) For the purpose of the provisions of this Act relating to actions for the recovery of land and advowsons, references to the
Crown shall include references to Her Majesty in right of the Duchy
of Lancaster; and those provisions shall apply to lands and advowsons forming part of the possessions of the Duchy of Cornwall as if
for the references to the Crown there were substituted references to
the Duke of Cornwall as defined in the Duchy of Cornwall Management Act 1863.

(5) For the purposes of this Act a proceeding by petition of right
(in any case where any such proceeding lies, by virtue of any saving
in section 40 of the Crown Proceedings Act 1947, notwithstanding
the general abolition by that Act of proceedings by way of petition of

right) shall be treated as being commenced on the date on which the petition is presented.

(6) Nothing in this Act shall affect the prerogative right of Her Majesty (whether in right of the Crown or of the Duchy of Lancaster) or of the Duke of Cornwall to any gold or silver mine.

Interpretation

8–93 **38.**—(1) In this Act, unless the context otherwise requires—

"action" includes any proceeding in a court of law, including an ecclesiastical court;

"land" includes corporeal hereditaments, tithes and rentcharges and any legal or equitable estate or interest therein [...] but except as provided above in this definition does not include any incorporeal hereditament;

"personal estate" and "personal property" do not include chattels real;

"personal injuries" includes any disease and any impairment of a person's physical or mental condition, and "injury" and cognate expressions shall be construed accordingly;

"rent" includes a rentcharge and a rentservice;

"rentcharge" means any annuity or periodical sum of money charged upon or payable out of land, except a rent service or interest on a mortgage on land;

"settled land", "statutory owner" and "tenant for life" have the same meanings respectively as in the Settled Land Act 1925;

"trust" and "trustee" have the same meanings respectively as in the Trustee Act 1925; and

[...]

(2) For the purposes of this Act a person shall be treated as under a disability while he is an infant, or of unsound mind.

(3) For the purposes of subsection (2) above a person is of unsound mind if he is a person who, by reason of mental disorder is incapable of managing and administering his property and affairs; and in this section "mental disorder" has the same meaning as in the Mental Health Act 1983.

(4) Without prejudice to the generality of subsection (3) above, a person shall be conclusively presumed for the purposes of subsection (2) above to be of unsound mind—

(a) while he is liable to be detained or subject to guardianship under the Mental Health Act 1983 (otherwise than by virtue of section 35 or 89); and

(b) while he is receiving treatment for mental disorder as an in-patient in any hospital within the meaning of the Mental Health Act 1983 or independent hospital or care home within the meaning of the Care Standards Act 2000 without being liable to be detained under the said Act of 1983 (otherwise than by virtue of section 35 or 89), being treatment which follows without any interval a period during which he was liable to be detained or subject to guardianship under the Mental Health Act 1959, or the said Act of 1983 (otherwise than by virtue of section 35 or 89) or by virtue of any enactment repealed or excluded by the Mental Health Act 1983.

(5) Subject to subsection (6) below, a person shall be treated as claiming through another person if he became entitled by, through, under, or by the act of that other person to the right claimed, and any person whose estate or interest might have been barred by a person entitled to an entailed interest in possession shall be treated as claiming through the person so entitled.

(6) A person becoming entitled to any estate or interest by virtue of a special power of appointment shall not be treated as claiming through the appointor.

(7) References in this Act to a right of action to recover land shall include references to a right to enter into possession of the land or, in the case of rentcharges and tithes, to distrain for arrears of rent or tithe, and references to the bringing of such an action shall include references to the making of such an entry or distress.

(8) References in this Act to the possession of land shall, in the case of tithes and rentcharges, be construed as references to the receipt of the tithe or rent, and references to the date of dispossession or discontinuance of possession of land shall, in the case of rentcharges, be construed as references to the date of the last receipt of rent.

(9) References in Part II of this Act to a right of action shall include references to—

(a) a cause of action;
(b) a right to receive money secured by a mortgage or charge on any property;
(c) a right to recover proceeds of the sale of land; and
(d) a right to receive a share or interest in the personal estate of a deceased person.

(10) References in Part II to the date of the accrual of a right of action shall be construed—

(a) in the case of an action upon a judgment, as references to the date on which the judgment became enforceable, and
(b) in the case of an action to recover arrears of rent or interest, or damages in respect of arrears of rent or interest, as references to the date on which the rent or interest became due.

Note —Amended by the Trusts of Land and Appointment of Trustees Act 1996, **8–94** Sched.4 and, with respect to references in subsections (3) and (4) to the Mental Health Act 1959, by the Mental Health Act 1983, Sched.4, para. 55.

Further amended, as to subss.(3) and (4)(b), by the Care Standards Act 2000, Sched.4, para.8.

Saving for other limitation enactments

39. This Act shall not apply to any action or arbitration for which a **8–95** period of limitation is prescribed by or under any other enactment (whether passed before or after the passing of this Act) or to any action or arbitration to which the Crown is a party and for which, if it were between subjects, a period of limitation would be prescribed by or under any such other enactment.

Transitional provisions, amendments and repeals

8–96   **40.**—(1) Schedule 2 to this Act, which contains transitional provisions, shall have effect.

(2) The enactments specified in Schedule 3 to this Act shall have effect subject to the amendments specified in that Schedule, being amendments consequential on the provisions of this Act; but the amendment of any enactment by that Schedule shall not be taken as prejudicing the operation of section 17(2) of the Interpretation Act 1978 (effect of repeals).

(3) The enactments specified in Schedule 4 to this Act are hereby repealed to the extent specified in column 3 of that Schedule.

Short title, commencement and extent

8–97   **41.** This Act may be cited as the Limitation Act 1980.

(2) This Act, except section 35, shall come into force on 1st May 1981.

(3) Section 35 of this Act shall come into force on 1st May 1981 to the extent (if any) that the section substituted for section 28 of the Limitation Act 1939 by section 8 of the Limitation Amendment Act 1980 is in force immediately before that date; but otherwise section 35 shall come into force on such day as the Lord Chancellor may by order made by statutory instrument appoint, and different days may be appointed for different purposes of that section (including its application in relation to different courts or proceedings).

(4) The repeal by this Act of section 14(1) of the Limitation Act 1963 and the corresponding saving in paragraph 2 of Schedule 2 to this Act shall extend to Northern Ireland, but otherwise this Act does not extend to Scotland or to Northern Ireland.

SCHEDULES

SECTION 15(6), (7)   **SCHEDULE 1**

PROVISIONS WITH RESPECT TO ACTIONS TO RECOVER LAND

PART I

Accrual of right of action in case of present interests in land

8–98   1. Where the person bringing an action to recover land, or some person through whom he claims, has been in possession of the land, and has while entitled to the land been dispossessed or discontinued his possession, the right of action shall be treated as having accrued on the date of the dispossession or discontinuance.

2. Where any person brings an action to recover any land of a deceased person (whether under a will or on intestacy) and the deceased person—

(a) was on the date of his death in possession of the land or, in the case of a rentcharge created by will or taking effect upon his death, in possession of the land charged; and

(b) was the last person entitled to the land to be in possession of it; the right of action shall be treated as having accrued on the date of his death.

3. Where any person brings an action to recover land, being an estate or interest in possession assured otherwise than by will to him, or to some person through whom he claims, and—

(a) the person making the assurance was on the date when the assurance took effect in possession of the land or, in the case of a rentcharge created by the assurance, in possession of the land charged; and

(b) no person has been in possession of the land by virtue of the assurance;the right of action shall be treated as having accrued on the date when the assurance took effect.

Accrual of right of action in case of future interests

4. The right of action to recover any land shall, in a case where—

(a) the estate or interest claimed was an estate or interest in reversion or remainder or any other future estate or interest; and

(b) no person has taken possession of the land by virtue of the estate or interest claimed;be treated as having accrued on the date on which the estate or interest fell into possession by the determination of the preceding estate or interest.

5.—(1) Subject to sub-paragraph (2) below, a tenancy from year to year or other period, without a lease in writing, shall for the purposes of this Act be treated as being determined at the expiration of the first year or other period; and accordingly the right of action of the person entitled to the land subject to the tenancy shall be treated as having accrued at the date on which in accordance with this sub-paragraph the tenancy is determined.

(2) Where any rent has subsequently been received in respect of the tenancy, the right of action shall be treated as having accrued on the date of the last receipt of rent.

6.—(1) Where—

(a) any person is in possession of land by virtue of a lease in writing by which a rent of not less than ten pounds a year is reserved; and

(b) the rent is received by some person wrongfully claiming to be entitled to the land in reversion immediately expectant on the determination of the lease; and

(c) no rent is subsequently received by the person rightfully so entitled;

the right of action to recover the land of the person rightfully so entitled shall be treated as having accrued on the date when the rent was first received by the person wrongfully claiming to be so entitled and not on the date of the determination of the lease.

(2) Sub-paragraph (1) above shall not apply to any lease granted by the Crown.

Accrual of right of action in case of forfeiture or breach of condition

7.—(1) Subject to sub-paragraph (2) below, a right of action to recover land by virtue of a forfeiture or breach of condition shall be treated as having accrued on the date on which the forfeiture was incurred or the condition broken.

(2) If any such right has accrued to a person entitled to an estate or interest in reversion or remainder and the land was not recovered by virtue of that right, the right of action to recover the land shall not be treated as having accrued to that person until his estate or interest fell into possession, as if no such forfeiture or breach of condition had occurred.

Right of action not to accrue or continue unless there is adverse possession

8.—(1) No right of action to recover land shall be treated as accruing unless the land is in the possession of some person in whose favour the period of limitation can run (referred to below in this paragraph as "adverse possession"); and where under the preceding provisions of this Schedule any such right of action is treated as accruing on a certain date and no person is in adverse possession on that date, the right of action shall not be treated as accruing unless and until adverse possession is taken of the land.

(2) Where a right of action to recover land has accrued and after its accrual, before the right is barred, the land ceases to be in adverse possession, the right of action shall no longer be treated as having accrued and no fresh right of action shall be treated as accruing unless and until the land is again taken into adverse possession.

(3) For the purposes of this paragraph—

(a) possession of any land subject to a rentcharge by a person (other than the person entitled to the rentcharge) who does not pay the rent shall be treated as adverse possession of the rentcharge; and

(b) receipt of rent under a lease by a person wrongfully claiming to be entitled to the land in reversion immediately expectant on the determination of the lease shall be treated as adverse possession of the land.

(4) For the purpose of determining whether a person occupying any land is in adverse possession of the land it shall not be assumed by implication of law that his occupation is by permission of the person entitled to the land merely by virtue of the fact that his occupation is not inconsistent with the latter's present or future enjoyment of the land.

This provision shall not be taken as prejudicing a finding to the effect that a person's occupation of any land is by implied permission of the person entitled to the land in any case where such a finding is justified on the actual facts of the case.

Possession of beneficiary not adverse to others interested in settled land or land held on trust for sale

9. Where any settled land or any land subject to a trust of land is in the possession of a person entitled to a beneficial interest in the land (not being a person solely or absolutely entitled to the land), no right of action to recover the land shall be treated for the purposes of this Act as accruing during that possession to any person in whom the land is vested as tenant for life, statutory owner or trustee, or to any other person entitled to a beneficial interest in the land.

8–99   *Note* —Amended by the Trusts of Land and Appointment of Trustees Act 1996, s.25 and Sched.3, para. 18 and Sched.4.

PART II

MODIFICATIONS OF SECTION 15 WHERE CROWN OR CERTAIN CORPORATIONS SOLE ARE INVOLVED

8–100   10. Subject to paragraph 11 below, section 15(1) of this Act shall apply to the bringing of an action to recover any land by the Crown or by any spiritual or eleemosynary corporation sole with the substitution for the reference to twelve years of a reference to thirty years.

11.—(1) An action to recover foreshore may be brought by the Crown at any time before the expiration of sixty years from the date mentioned in section 15(1) of this Act.

(2) Where any right of action to recover land which has ceased to be foreshore but remains in the ownership of the Crown accrued when the land was foreshore, the action may be brought at any time before the expiration of—

(a) sixty years from the date of accrual of the right of action; or

(b) thirty years from the date when the land ceased to be foreshore; whichever period first expires.

(3) In this paragraph "foreshore" means the shore and bed of the sea and of any tidal water, below the line of the medium high tide between the spring tides and the neap tides.

12. Notwithstanding section 15(1) of this Act, where in the case of any action brought by a person other than the Crown or a spiritual or eleemosynary corporation sole the right of action first accrued to the Crown or any such corporation sole through whom the person in question claims, the action may be brought at any time before the expiration of—

(a) the period during which the action could have been brought by the Crown or the corporation sole; or

(b) twelve years from the date on which the right of action accrued to some person other than the Crown or the corporation sole;

whichever period first expires.

13. Section 15(2) of this Act shall apply in any case where the Crown or a spiritual or eleemosynary corporation sole is entitled to the succeeding estate or interest with the substitution—

(a) for the reference to twelve years of a reference to thirty years; and

(b) for the reference to six years of a reference to twelve years.

SECTION 40(1)

SCHEDULE 2

TRANSITIONAL PROVISIONS

1. Nothing in this Act shall affect the operation of section 4 of the Limitation Act **8–101** 1963, as it had effect immediately before 1 January 1979 (being the date on which the Civil Liability (Contribution) Act 1978 came into force), in relation to any case where the damage in question occurred before that date.

2. The amendment made by section 14(1) of the Limitation Act 1963 in section 5 of the Limitation (Enemies and War Prisoners) Act 1945 (which provides that section 5 shall have effect as if for the words "in force in Northern Ireland at the date of the passing of this Act" there were substituted the words "for the time being in force in Northern Ireland") shall continue to have effect notwithstanding the repeal by this Act of section 14(1).

3. It is hereby declared that a decision taken at any time by a court to grant, or not to grant, leave under Part I of the Limitation Act 1963 (which, so far as it related to leave, was repealed by the Limitation Act 1975) does not affect the determination of any question in proceedings under any provision of this Act which corresponds to a provision of the Limitation Act 1975, but in such proceedings account may be taken of evidence admitted in proceedings under Part I of the Limitation Act 1963.

4.—(1) In section 33(6) of this Act the reference to section 1(1) of the Fatal Accidents Act 1976 shall be construed as including a reference to section 1 of the Fatal Accidents Act 1846.

(2) Any other reference in that section, or in section 12 or 13 of this Act, to the Fatal Accidents Act 1976 shall be construed as including a reference to the Fatal Accidents Act 1846.

5. Notwithstanding anything in section 29(7) of this Act or in the repeals made by this Act, the Limitation Act 1939 shall continue to have effect in relation to any acknowledgment or payment made before the coming into force of section 6 of the Limitation Amendment Act 1980 (which amended section 23 of the Limitation Act 1939 and made certain repeals in sections 23 and 25 of that Act so as to prevent the revival by acknowledgment or part payment of a right of action barred by that Act) as it had effect immediately before section 6 came into force.

6. Section 28 of the Limitation Act 1939 (provisions as to set-off or counterclaim) shall continue to apply (as originally enacted) to any claim by way of set-off or counterclaim made in an action to which section 35 of this Act does not apply, but as if the reference in section 28 to that Act were a reference to this Act; and, in relation to any such action, references in this Act to section 35 of this Act shall be construed as references to section 28 as it applies by virtue of this paragraph.

7. Section 37(2)(c) of this Act shall be treated for the purposes of the Hovercraft Act 1968 as if it were contained in an Act passed before that Act.

8. In relation to a lease granted before the coming into force of section 3(2) of the Limitation Amendment Act 1980 (which substituted "ten pounds a year" for "twenty shillings" in section 9(3) of the Limitation Act 1939), paragraph 6(1)(a) of Schedule 1 to this Act shall have effect as if for the words "ten pounds a year" there were substituted the words "twenty shillings".

9.—(1) Nothing in any provision of this Act shall—

(a) enable any action to be brought which was barred by this Act or (as the case may be) by the Limitation Act 1939 before the relevant date; or

(b) affect any action or arbitration commenced before that date or the title to any property which is the subject of any such action or arbitration.

(2) In sub-paragraph (1) above "the relevant date" means—

(a) in relation to section 35 of this Act, the date on which that section comes into force in relation to actions of the description in question or, if section 8 of the Limitation Amendment Act 1980 (which substituted the provisions reproduced in section 35 for section 28 of the Limitation Act 1939) is in force immediately before 1st May 1981 in relation to actions of that description, the date on which section 8 came into force in relation to actions of that description; and

(b) in relation to any other provision of this Act, 1st August 1980 (being the date of coming into force of the remaining provisions of the Limitation Amendment Act 1980, apart from section 8).

SECTION 40(2)   **SCHEDULE 3**

CONSEQUENTIAL AMENDMENTS

8–102   1. [*Repealed by the* Land Registration Act 1997, s.4, Sched.2, Pt II.]

2. In section 21A of the Administration of Estates Act 1925 (debtor who becomes creditor's executor by representation or administrator to account for debt to estate) the reference in subsection (2) to the Limitation Act 1939 shall be construed as including a reference to this Act.

3. In section 2(1) of the Limitation (Enemies and War Prisoners) Act 1945 (interpretation), for the words "the Limitation Act 1939" in the definition of "statute of limitation" there shall be substituted the words "the Limitation Act 1980".

4. In section 3(4) of the Charitable Trusts (Validation) Act 1954 (application of section 31(2) to (4) of the Limitation Act 1939 for purposes of that section), for the words " Subsections (2) to (4) of section thirty-one of the Limitation Act 1939" there shall be substituted the words "Subsections (2) to (6) of section thirty-eight of the Limitation Act 1980 ".

5. In section 5(3) of the Carriage by Air Act 1961 (application of time limit in that Act to arbitrations) for the words "section twenty-seven of the Limitation Act 1939" there shall be substituted the words "section thirty-four of the Limitation Act 1980".

6. In section 7(2)(a) of the Carriage of Goods by Road Act 1965 (application of time limit in that Act to arbitrations) for the words "section 27 of the Limitation Act 1939" there shall be substituted the words "section 34 of the Limitation Act 1980".

7. In paragraph 7(6) of Schedule 3 to the Agriculture Act 1967 (conditions applying to amalgamated agricultural units) for the words "the Limitation Act 1939" there shall be substituted the words "the Limitation Act 1980".

8. In paragraph 6(2) of Schedule 3 to the Mines and Quarries (Tips) Act 1969 (time limits for claims for compensation under that Act to be treated as if contained in Part I of the Limitation Act 1939), for the words "the Limitation Act 1939" there shall be substituted the words "the Limitation Act 1980".

9. In section 25(5) of the Law of Property Act 1969 (accrual of cause of action to recover compensation for loss due to undisclosed land charges), for the words "the Limitation Act 1939" there shall be substituted the words "the Limitation Act 1980".

10. In section 10 of the Animals Act 1971 (application of certain enactments to liability under sections 2 to 4 of that Act) for the words "the Limitation Acts 1939 to 1963" there shall be substituted the words "the Limitation Act 1980".

11. In section 2(4) of the Deposit of Poisonous Waste Act 1972 (civil liability under that Act) for the words from "the Limitation Act 1939" and 1963 to "1954" there shall be substituted the words "the Limitation Act 1980".

12. In section 88(4) of the Control of Pollution Act 1974 (civil liability under that Act) for paragraph (c) there shall be substituted the following paragraph—

"(c) the Limitation Act 1980".

SCHEDULE 4

ENACTMENTS REPEALED

8–103

Chapter	Short title	Extent of Repeal
2 & 3 Geo. 6 c.21	The Limitation Act 1939	The whole Act.
7 & 8 Eliz. 2 c.72	The Mental Health Act 1959	In Schedule 7, Part I, the entry relating to the Limitation Act 1939.
1963 c.47	The Limitation Act 1963	Sections 4 and 5. Section 7(7). Section 14(1). Sections 15 and 16.
1975 c.54	The Limitation Act 1975	The whole Act.
1976 c.30	The Fatal Accidents Act 1976	In Schedule 1, paragraph 3.
1978 c.47	The Civil Liability (Contribution) Act 1978	In Schedule 1, paragraph 6.
1980 c.24	The Limitation Amendment Act 1980	Sections 1 to 9. Sections 11 to 13. Sections 14(2) to (4). Schedules 1 and 2.

LIMITATION

SCHEDULE 4

ENACTMENTS REPEALED

8–103

Chapter	Short title	Extent of Repeal
8 & 9 Geo. 6 c.21	The Limitation Act 1939	The whole Act
7 & 8 Eliz. 2 c.VII	The Mental Health Act 1959	In Schedule 7, Part I, the entry relating to the Limitation Act 1939
1963 c.47	The Limitation Act 1963	Sections 1 and 5, Section 7(2), Section 14(1), Sections 15 and 16
1975 c.54	The Limitation Act 1975	The whole Act
1976 c.30	The Fatal Accidents Act 1976	In Schedule 1, paragraph 3
1978 c.47	The Civil Liability (Contribution) Act 1978	In Schedule 1, paragraph 6
1980 c.24	The Limitation Amendment Act 1980	Sections 1 to 9, Sections 11 to 13, Sections 14(2) to (6), Schedules 1 and 2

SECTION 9

JURISDICTIONAL AND PROCEDURAL LEGISLATION

9A   MAIN STATUTES

Supreme Court Act 1981

(1981 c.54)

An Act to consolidate with amendments the Supreme Court of
Judicature (Consolidation) Act 1925 and other enactments
relating to the Supreme Court in England and Wales and the
administration of justice therein; to repeal certain obsolete or
unnecessary enactments so relating; to amend Part VIII of the
Mental Health Act 1959, the Courts-Martial (Appeals) Act 1968,
the Arbitration Act 1979 and the law relating to county courts;
and for connected purposes.

[28th July 1981] **9A–1**

LEGISLATION

* * * *

* * * *

Introductory note

This Act repealed and replaced the Supreme Court of Judicature (Consolidation) **9A–2** Act 1925 as well as the whole or parts of several other statutes, some ancient, obsolete or unnecessary and others more recent, which had dealt with the administration of justice in the Supreme Court in England and Wales. It also made consequential amendments in many other similar enactments and introduced several amendments.

The Act came into force on January 1, 1982 (s.153(2)) (para. 20A–566) except for ss.72, 143 and 152(2) which came into force on the day the Act received Royal Assent, July 28, 1981).

Interpretation

Whereas the JA 1925 was a consolidating statute, the SCA 1981 is not a mere **9A–3** consolidating statute but is, as expressly stated in its preamble, an Act "to consolidate with amendments" the JA 1925 and other enactments. A major consequence of this fact is that, in interpreting the provisions of the 1981 Act the Court will not be bound to apply the presumption, applicable to the construction of a consolidating statute that Parliament did not intend to alter but simply to reproduce or repeat the existing law; nor will the Court be bound by the presumption that the words used in the 1981 Act should have the same meaning as they had at the time the Act was passed (see Bennion, *Statutory Interpretation* (3rd ed. 1997) Sect. 211, and authorities cited there). The Court will bear in mind that these presumptions are rebuttable, and will lean towards giving effect to the overriding intention of Parliament to provide an efficient and effective system for the administration of justice, both civil and criminal.

Continuity of procedure

Whereas the JA 1925 contained an express provision for the saving of the former **9A–4** practice and procedure (see s.103 which replaced s.73 of the JA 1873), the SCA 1981 omits this provision (note also the JA 1925, s.32 was repealed but not replaced by the 1981 Act). Nevertheless, there are to be found scattered through the Act provisions which recall and reimpose those as to jurisdiction, practice and procedure which prevailed before the passing of the Act and which may, in some instances, refer back to the jurisdiction, practice and procedure prevailing before J.A.s 1873–1875 (see, *e.g.* s.15(2)(b) (jurisdiction, civil and criminal of the Court of Appeal); s.19(2)(b) (jurisdiction, civil and criminal exercisable by the High Court); s.28(3)(b) (jurisdiction of the High Court to determine appeals from Crown Court and inferior courts); s.29(1) (orders of mandamus, prohibition and certiorari); s.44 (extraordinary functions of Judges of High Court); s.49(2) (jurisdiction as to the current administration of law and equity to be exercised "as hitherto"); s.84(2) (powers to make rules of court); s.96(2) (business of the Central Office).

Impact of Constitutional Reform Act 2005

The Constitutional Reform Act 2005 (c.4) modifies the office of Lord Chancellor **9A–4.1** and makes provision relating to the functions of that office. The Act also (1) establishes a Supreme Court of the United Kingdom and abolishes the appellate jurisdiction of the House of Lords, and (2) makes provision about the jurisdiction of the Judicial Committee of the Privy Council. In addition the Act makes provision about the judiciary (their appointment and discipline). The Act is being brought into force over a period of time. It alters in many respects the Supreme Court Act 1981 (and other legislation printed in Section 9 of the *White Book*). At the time of going to press, only a few of the provisions in the 2005 Act had been brought into force. Those provisions having an impact on the SCA 1981 are referred to in commentary where relevant and some (but not all) of the prospective amendments are also noted. Provisions in the Courts Act 2003 (c.39) also amended sections in the 1981 Act. Some of those provisions are not yet in force. When they are they will take effect as amended (if at all) by the 2005 Act.

PART I

CONSTITUTION OF THE SUPREME COURT

THE SUPREME COURT

The Supreme Court

9A–5   **1.**—(1) The Supreme Court of England and Wales shall consist of the Court of Appeal, the High Court of Justice and the Crown Court, each having such jurisdiction as is conferred on it by or under this or any other Act.

(2) The Lord Chancellor shall be president of the Supreme Court.

9A–6   *Note* —Derived from the JA 1925, s.1, and the Courts Act 1971, s.1. Note para. 9A–4.1 above.

Constitution of Supreme Court

9A–7   The Supreme Court was formerly called "the Supreme Court of Judicature" (see the JA 1873, s.1 and the JA 1925, s.1). The Supreme Court consists of (1) the Court of Appeal (see s.2), which itself is divided into two Divisions, the Criminal and the Civil Divisions (see s.3); (2) the High Court of Justice (see s.4), which itself is divided into three Divisions, the Chancery, the Queen's Bench and the Family Division (see s.5) and (3) the Crown Court (see s.8).

THE COURT OF APPEAL

The Court of Appeal

9A–8   **2.**—(1) The Court of Appeal shall consist of *ex-officio* judges and not more than thirty-five ordinary judges.

(2) The following shall be *ex-officio* judges of the Court of Appeal—

  (a) *[omitted]*;

  (b) any person who was Lord Chancellor before 12 June 2005;

  (c) any Lord of Appeal in Ordinary who at the date of his appointment was, or was qualified for appointment as, an ordinary judge of the Court of Appeal or held an office within paragraphs (d) to (g);

  (d) the Lord Chief Justice;

  (e) the Master of the Rolls;

  (f) the President of the Queen's Bench Division;

  (g) the President of the Family Division;

  (h) the Chancellor of the High Court;

but a person within paragraph (b) or (c) shall not be required to sit and act as a judge of the Court of Appeal unless at the Lord Chancellor's request he consents to do so.

(3) An ordinary judge of the Court of Appeal (including the vice-president, if any, of either division) shall be styled "Lord Justice of Appeal" or "Lady Justice of Appeal".

(4) Her Majesty may by Order in Council from time to time

amend subsection (1) so as to increase or further increase the maximum number of ordinary judges of the Court of Appeal.

(5) No recommendation shall be made to Her Majesty in Council to make an Order under subsection (4) unless a draft of the Order has been laid before Parliament and approved by resolution of each House of Parliament.

(6) The Court of Appeal shall be taken to be duly constituted notwithstanding any vacancy in the office of Lord Chancellor, Lord Chief-Justice, Master of the Rolls, President of the Queen's Bench Division, President of the Family Division or Chancellor of the High Court.

Note —Derived from the JA 1925, s.6; and the AJA 1968, s.1. Amended by the **9A–9** Maximum Number of Judges Order 1996 (S.I. 1996 No. 1142), art.2. Subs.(3) was substituted by the Courts Act 2003 s.63(1) and brought into effect on January 26, 2004. Subsections (2) and (6) were amended by the Constitutional Reform Act 2005, s.148(1) and Sched. 4, para. 115(2)(c) and (5)(b). Further amendments to s.2 will be made as other provisions in the 2005 Act are brought into effect (see para. 9A–4.1 above).

Court of Appeal

The Court of Appeal was created by the JA 1873, ss.4 and 6, replaced by the JA **9A–10** 1925, s.6. This section determines who are to be Judges of the Court of Appeal: they comprise a number of *ex-officio* judges and a number of ordinary Judges not exceeding the number fixed by subs.(1), who will be styled "Lords Justices of Appeal". The Lord Chancellor may appoint one of the ordinary judges as vice-president of the Queen's Bench Division (Access to Justice Act 1999, s.69(1)); see further s.4 below.

Under s.9 (Assistance for transaction of judicial business of Supreme Court) former Lords Justices, and certain other holders of judicial office and certain retired judges may sit in the Court of Appeal on request. As to the consequences which follow where a Lord Justice becomes, or ceases to be, the holder of a judicial office in an "international court" (*e.g.* any court established for any purpose of the European Communities) or in the European Court of Human Rights, see Access to Justice Act 1999, s.68 and the Human Rights Act 1998, s.18(4).

Head of Civil Justice

The Lord Chancellor must appoint a Head of Civil Justice. No person may be so **9A–10.1** appointed unless he is (a) the Master of the Rolls, (b) the Vice-Chancellor, or (c) an ordinary judge of the Court of Appeal (Courts Act 2003, s.62).

Divisions of Court of Appeal

3.—(1) There shall be two divisions of the Court of Appeal, namely **9A–11** the criminal division and the civil division.

(2) The Lord Chief Justice shall be president of the criminal division of the Court of Appeal, and the Master of the Rolls shall be president of the civil division of that court.

(3) The Lord Chancellor may appoint one of the ordinary judges of the Court of Appeal as vice-president of both divisions of that court, or one of those judges as vice-president of the criminal division and another of them as vice-president of the civil division.

(4) When sitting in a court of either division of the Court of Appeal in which no ex-officio judge of the Court of Appeal is sitting, the vice-president (if any) of that division shall preside.

(5) Any number of courts of either division of the Court of Appeal may sit at the same time.

LEGISLATION

9A-12   *Note* —Derived from the JA 1925, s.6; and the Criminal Appeal Act 1966, s.1. Note para. 9A-4.1 above.

Divisions of the Court of Appeal

9A-13   The Court of Appeal consists of two Divisions, the Criminal Division presided over by the Lord Chief Justice and the Civil Division presided over by the Master of the Rolls; and the Lord Chancellor has power to appoint from among the ordinary Judges of the Court of Appeal, a vice-president of one or other or both of their Divisions (s.3(3)).

Either Division of the Court of Appeal may sit in as many numbers of courts at the same time as may be necessary or convenient (s.3(4)).

As to the jurisdiction of the Court of Appeal, see ss.15 to 18.

As to the composition of the Court of Appeal Civil Division, see s.54, and Criminal Division, see s.55.

Civil Appeals Office

9A-13.1   The Civil Appeals Office and its head are not susceptible to judicial review because they act only on the explicit or implicit directions of the Court of Appeal which as a superior court is not itself amenable to judicial review (*Lawrence v. Civil Appeals Office* [2002] EWHC 1849 (Admin), July 16, 2002, unrep. (Harrison J.)).

THE HIGH COURT

The High Court

9A-14   4.—(1) The High Court shall consist of—

(a) the Lord Chancellor;

(b) the Lord Chief Justice;

(ba) the President of the Queen's Bench Division;

(c) the President of the Family Division;

(d) the Chancellor of the High Court;

(dd) the Senior Presiding Judge; and

(ddd) the vice-president of the Queen's Bench Division;

(e) not more than ninety-eight puisne judges of that court.

(2) The puisne judges of the High Court shall be styled "Justices of the High Court."

(3) All the judges of the High Court shall, except where this Act expressly provides otherwise, have in all respects equal power, authority and jurisdiction.

(4) Her Majesty may by Order in Council from time to time amend subsection (1) so as to increase or further increase the maximum number of puisne judges of the High Court.

(5) No recommendation shall be made to Her Majesty in Council to make an Order under subsection (4) unless a draft of the Order has been laid before Parliament and approved by resolution of each House of Parliament.

(6) The High Court shall be taken to be duly constituted notwithstanding any vacancy in the office of Lord Chancellor, Lord Chief Justice, President of the Queen's Bench Division, President of the Family Division, Chancellor of the High Court or Senior Presiding Judge and whether or not an appointment has been made to the office of the vice-president of the Queen's Bench Division.

9A-15   *Note* —Derived from the JA 1925, s.1; the AJA 1970, s.1; and the AJA 1973, s.19(2). Amended by the Courts and Legal Services Act 1990, s.72; the Access to Justice Act

1999, s.69(2) and the Constitutional Reform Act 2005, s.148(1) and Sched.4, para. 117(2)(b) & (4). Further amendments to s.4 will be made as other provisions in the 2005 Act are brought into effect (see para. 9A–4.1 above).

The High Court

This section determines who are to be Judges of the High Court: they comprise a number of *ex-officio* Judges and a number of puisne Judges, who will be styled "Justices of the High Court". Although they rank in precedence according to the priority of the dates on which they respectively became Judges of the High Court (see s.13(6)), they have in all respects equal power, authority and jurisdiction, except where this Act expressly provides otherwise (s.4(3)); and this provision, together with s.5(5), which provides that all jurisdiction vested in the High Court will belong to all the Divisions alike, is designed to ensure that the High Court shall be and if necessary shall act as a single integrated Court of Judicature. **9A–16**

The Lord Chancellor may appoint one of the ordinary judges as vice-president of the Queen's Bench Division (Access to Justice Act 1999, s.69(1)).

The appointment of Presiding Judges and of the Senior Presiding Judge is provided for by the Courts and Legal Services Act 1990, s.72 (see para. 9B–122). The Senior Presiding Judge is appointed from among the Lords Justices of Appeal.

On January 17, 1996, the Lord Chancellor announced that the office of Vice-Chancellor should include the responsibilities of the position of "Head of Civil Justice" recommended in the Access to Justice Reports.

As to consequences which follow where a judge of the High Court becomes, or ceases to be, the holder of a judicial office in an "international court" (*e.g.* any court established for the purpose of the European Communities) or in the European Court of Human Rights, see the Access to Justice Act 1999, s.68 and the Human Rights Act 1998, s.18(4).

Divisions of High Court

5.—(1) There shall be three divisions of the High Court namely— **9A–17**

    (a) the Chancery Division, consisting of the Lord Chancellor, who shall be president thereof, the Vice-Chancellor, who shall be vice-president thereof, and such of the puisne judges as are for the time being attached thereto in accordance with this section;

    (b) the Queen's Bench Division, consisting of the Lord Chief Justice, the President of the Queen's Bench Division, the vice-president of the Queen's Bench Division and such of the puisne judges as are for the time being so attached thereto; and

    (c) the Family Division, consisting of the President of the Family Division and such of the puisne judges as are for the time being so attached thereto.

(2) The puisne judges of the High Court shall be attached to the various Divisions by direction of the Lord Chancellor; and any such judge may with his consent be transferred from one Division to another by direction of the Lord Chancellor, but shall be so transferred only with the concurrence of the senior judge of the Division from which it is proposed to transfer him.

(3) Any judge attached to any Division may act as an additional judge of any other Division at the request of the Lord Chief Justice made with the concurrence of the President of the Family Division or the Vice-Chancellor, or both, as appropriate.

(4) Nothing in this section shall be taken to prevent a judge of any Division (whether nominated under section 6(2) or not) from sit-

ting, whenever required, in a divisional court of another Division or for any judge of another Division.

(5) Without prejudice to the provisions of this Act relating to the distribution of business in the High Court, all jurisdiction vested in the High Court under this Act shall belong to all the Divisions alike.

9A-18   *Note* —Derived from the JA 1925, s.4; and the AJA 1970, s.1. Amended by the Courts and Legal Services Act 1990, Sched.17, para. 12; the Access to Justice Act 1999, s.69(3); and the Constitutional Reform Act 2005, s.148(1) and Sched.4, para. 118(3). Further amendments to s.5 will be made as other provisions in the 2005 Act are brought into effect (see para. 9A–4.1 above). Until sub-paras (2) and (5) of para. 118 of Sched. 4 to the Act come into force, the references to the Vice-Chancellor in s.5(1)(a) and s.5(3) are to be read as references to the Chancellor of the High Court.

Divisions of High Court
9A-19   This section provides for the High Court to consist of three Divisions, namely: (1) Chancery Division, nominally presided over by the Lord Chancellor, though as a matter of practice the head of the Division is the Vice-Chancellor; (2) Queen's Bench Division, presided over by the Lord Chief Justice; and (3) Family Division, presided over by the President of the Family Division.

The puisne Judges are attached to the various Divisions by direction of the Lord Chancellor, and may be transferred by his direction with the concurrence of the senior Judge of the Division from which the transfer is to be made. But every Judge of every Division may sit, when required, in a Divisional Court of another Division, or for any Judge of another Division.

As to the definition of:

> "Division," see s.151(1)
> "divisional court," see s.151(4)
> "senior judge," see s.151(1).

Exercise of all jurisdiction
9A-20   Section 5(5) is derived from s.6 of the AJA 1928, and should be read with s.4(3), and Practice Direction (High Court: Divisions) [1973] 1 W.L.R. 627; [1973] 2 All E.R. 233. The subsection nullifies the decision in *The Sheaf Brook* [1926] P. 61, CA, and gives statutory effect to earlier decisions.

An order of any Division or court of the High Court is the order of the High Court and not an order of a particular Division or Court (see *Re Hastings (No. 3)* [1959] Ch. 368, DC, at 377 *per* Vaisey J.).

For distribution of business among several Divisions, see s.61 *et seq.* below.

As to transfer of proceedings from one Division to another, see s.65 below.

The Patents, Admiralty and Commercial Courts
9A-21   6.—(1) There shall be—

> (a) as part of the Chancery Division, a Patents Court; and
> (b) as parts of the Queen's Bench Division, an Admiralty Court and a Commercial Court.

(2) The judges of the Patents Court, of the Admiralty Court and of the Commercial Court shall be such of the puisne judges of the High Court as the Lord Chancellor may from time to time nominate to be judges of the Patents Court, Admiralty Judges and Commercial Judges respectively.

9A-22   *Note* —Derived from the AJA 1970, ss.2 and 3; and the Patents Act 1977, s.96.

Specialist Courts
9A-23   This section provides for the three main specialist courts to be part of two of the Divisions of the High Court; *viz.* the Commercial Court, the Admiralty Court and the Patents Court. The judges of these specialised courts are those nominated from time to time by the Lord Chancellor.

The Commercial Court was established as part of the Queen's Bench Division in 1970 (see the AJA 1970, s.3(1)). For the business of the Commercial Court, see s.62(3) below. An important feature of the Commercial Court is its predominant role in arbitration proceedings.

The Admiralty Court was constituted as part of the Queen's Bench Division in 1970 (see the AJA 1970, s.1(3)). For the Admiralty jurisdiction of the High Court, see ss.20–24, and 27; for the business of the Admiralty Court, see s.62(2) below.

The Patents Court was constituted as part of the Chancery Division in 1977 (see Patents Act 1977, s.96). For the jurisdiction of the Patents Court to hear patent actions at first instance and appeals from the Comptroller General, see Pt III of the Act of 1977; for the business of the Patents Court, see s.62(1) below.

Practice Direction (Administrative Court: Establishment) [2000] 1 W.L.R. 1654, established within the Queen's Bench Division the Administrative Court as successor to the Crown Office list, and provided that, henceforward the Crown Office is to be known as the Administrative Court Office.

Power to alter Divisions or transfer certain courts to different Divisions

7.—(1) Her Majesty may from time to time, on a recommendation **9A–24** of the judges mentioned in subsection (2), by Order in Council direct that—

(a) any increase or reduction in the number of Divisions of the High Court; or

(b) the transfer of any of the courts mentioned in section 6(1) to a different Division,

be carried into effect in pursuance of the recommendation.

(2) Those judges are the Lord Chancellor, the Lord Chief Justice, the Master of the Rolls, the President of the Queen's Bench Division, the President of the Family Division and the Chancellor of the High Court.

(3) An Order in Council under this section may include such incidental, supplementary or consequential provisions as appear to Her Majesty necessary or expedient, including amendments of provisions referring to particular Divisions contained in this Act or any other Statutory provision.

(4) Any Order in Council under this section shall be subject to annulment in pursuance of a resolution of either House of Parliament.

Note —Derived from the JA 1925, s.5, as amended; and the AJA 1970, s.1(5). This **9A–25** section was also amended by the Constitutional Reform Act 2005, s.148(1) and Sched. 4, para. 120(3)(b), and further amendments will be made as other provisions in the 2005 Act are brought into effect (see para. 9A–4.1 above).

THE CROWN COURT

The Crown Court

8.—(1) The jurisdiction of the Crown Court shall be exercisable **9A–26** by—

(a) any judge of the High Court; or

(b) any Circuit judge, Recorder or District Judge (Magistrates' Courts); or

(c) subject to and in accordance with the provisions of sections 74 and 75(2), a judge of the High Court, Circuit judge or Recorder sitting with not more than four justices of the peace,

and any such persons when exercising the jurisdiction of the Crown Court shall be judges of the Crown Court.

(2) A justice of the peace is not disqualified from acting as a judge of the Crown Court merely because the proceedings are not at a place within the local justice area to which he is assigned or because the proceedings are not related to that area in any other way.

(3) When the Crown Court sits in the City of London it shall be known as the Central Criminal Court; and the Lord Mayor of the City and any Alderman of the City shall be entitled to sit as judges of the Central Criminal Court with any judge of the High Court, Circuit judge, Recorder or District Judge (Magistrates' Courts).

9A–26.1   *Note* —Amended by the Courts Act 2003.

OTHER PROVISIONS

Assistance for transaction of judicial business of Supreme Court

9A–27   **9.**—(1) A person within any entry in column 1 of the following Table may subject to the proviso at the end of that Table at any time, at the request of the appropriate authority, act—

   (a) as a judge of a relevant court specified in the request; or

   (b) if the request relates to a particular division of a relevant court so specified, as a judge of that court in that division.

9A–28

	1 Judge or ex-judge	2 Where competent to act on request
1.	A judge of the Court of Appeal.	The High Court and the Crown Court.
2.	A person who has been a judge of the Court of Appeal.	The Court of Appeal, the High Court and the Crown Court.
3.	A puisne judge of the High Court.	The Court of Appeal.
4.	A person who has been a puisne judge of the High Court.	The Court of Appeal, the High Court and the Crown Court.
5.	A Circuit judge.	The High Court and the Court of Appeal.
6.	A Recorder.	The High Court.

The entry in column 2 specifying the Court of Appeal in relation to a Circuit judge only authorises such a judge to act as a judge of a court in the criminal division of the Court of Appeal.

(1A) A person shall not act as a judge by virtue of subsection (1) after the day on which he attains the age of 75.

(2) In subsection (1)—

"the appropriate authority"—

   (a) in the case of a request to a judge of the High Court or a Circuit judge to act in the criminal division of the Court of Appeal as a judge of that court, means the Lord Chief Justice or, at any time when the Lord Chief Justice is unable to make such a request himself or there is a

vacancy in the office of Lord Chief Justice, the Master of
the Rolls;

    (b) in any other case means the Lord Chancellor;

but no request shall be made to a Circuit Judge to act as a judge of a
court in the criminal division of the Court of Appeal unless he is approved for the time being by the Lord Chancellor for the purpose of
acting as a judge of that division;

"relevant court", in the case of a person within any entry in column 1
of the Table, means a court specified in relation to that entry in column 2 of the Table.

(3) In the case of—

    (a) a request under subsection (1) to a Lord Justice of Ap-
peal to act in the High Court; or

    (b) any request under that subsection to a puisne judge of
the High Court or a Circuit judge,

it shall be the duty of the person to whom the request is made to
comply with it.

(4) Without prejudice to section 24 of the Courts Act 1971
(temporary appointment of deputy Circuit judges and assistant
Recorders), if it appears to the Lord Chancellor that it is expedient
as a temporary measure to make an appointment under this subsection in order to facilitate the disposal of business in the High Court
or the Crown Court, he may appoint a person qualified for appointment as a puisne judge of the High Court to be a deputy of the High
Court during such period or on such occasions as the Lord Chancellor thinks fit; and during the period or on the occasions for which a
person is appointed as a deputy judge under this subsection, he may
act as a puisne judge of the High Court.

(4A) No appointment of a person as a deputy judge of the High
Court shall be such as to extend beyond the day on which he attains
the age of 70, but this subsection is subject to section 26(4) to (6) of
the Judicial Pensions and Retirement Act 1993 (Lord Chancellor's
power to authorise continuance in office up to the age of 75).

(5) Every person while acting under this section shall, subject to
subsections (6) and (6A), be treated for all purposes as, and accordingly may perform any of the functions of, a judge of the court in
which he is acting.

(6) A person shall not by virtue of subsection (5)—

    (a) be treated as a judge of the court in which he is acting
for the purposes of section 98(2) or of any statutory provision relating to—

        (i) the appointment, retirement, removal or disquali-
fication of judges of that court;

        (ii) the tenure of office and oaths to be taken by such
judges; or

        (iii) the remuneration, allowances or pensions of such
judges; or

    (b) subject to section 27 of the Judicial Pensions and Retire-
ment Act 1993, be treated as having been a judge of a
court in which he has acted only under this section.

(6A) A Circuit judge or Recorder shall not by virtue of subsection (5) exercise any of the powers conferred on a single judge by sections 31, 31B, 31C and 44 of the Criminal Appeal Act 1968 (powers of single judge in connection with appeals to the Court of Appeal and appeals from the Court of Appeal to the House of Lords).

(7) [...]

(8) Such remuneration and allowances as the Lord Chancellor may, with the concurrence of the Minister for the Civil Service, determine may be paid out of money provided by Parliament—

    (a) to any person who has been—

        (i) a Lord of Appeal in Ordinary; or

        (ii) a judge of the Court of Appeal; or

        (iii) a judge of the High Court,

        and is by virtue of subsection (1) acting as mentioned in that subsection;

    (b) to any deputy judge of the High Court appointed under subsection (4).

9A–29   *Note* —Amended by the Administration of Justice Act 1982, s.58; the Judicial Pensions and Retirement Act 1993, ss.26 and 31, Scheds 6 and 9; the Criminal Justice and Public Order Act 1994, s.52; the Courts Act 2003, s.109(1), Sch.8, para.260. Note para. 9A–4.1 above.

Judicial assistance

9A–30   The most interesting feature of this section is that it provides for circumstances in which puisne judges of the High Court may sit in the Court of Appeal and in which circuit judges may sit in the High Court or in the Court of Appeal. This facilitates the flexible deployment of judge power and has other advantages. This section gathers together in simplified language and with the use of a table, scattered provisions from several enactments enabling judicial assistance to be obtained for the business of the Supreme Court, see the JA 1925, ss.3, 7 and 8; the A.J. (M.P.) A. 1933, s.2(1); the Criminal Appeal Act 1966, s.1(3); and the Courts Act 1971, ss.4(3), 23 and 24.

Under the common law doctrine of *de facto* authority, the acts of a circuit judge in dealing with a High Court case, though not authorised to do so under s.9, may be upheld (*Fawdry & Co v. Murfitt* [2002] EWCA Civ 643; [2002] 3 W.L.R. 1354, CA; see also *Baldock v. Webster* [2006] 1 W.L.R. 1, CA; *Coppard v. Customs and Excise Commissioners* [2003] EWCA Civ 511; [2003] 2 W.L.R. 1618, CA). Note also s.68 (Exercise of High Court jurisdiction otherwise than by judges of that court). Where the necessary judicial authority of a judge is provided by the *de facto* authority doctrine, the judge constitutes a tribunal established by law within the meaning of art. 6 of the Convention, as the doctrine validates the judge's office as well as his acts (*Coppard v. Customs and Excise Commisioners* [2003] EWCA Civ 511; [2003] 2 W.L.R. 1618, CA).

Subs.(1)

9A–31   Item 6 in the table was added by the AJA 1982, s.58.

Appointment of judges of Supreme Court

9A–32   **10.**—(1) Whenever the office of Lord Chief Justice, Master of the Rolls, President of the Queen's Bench Division, President of the Family Division or Chancellor of the High Court is vacant, Her Majesty may by letters patent appoint a qualified person to that office.

(2) Subject to the limits on numbers for the time being imposed by sections 2(1) and 4(1), Her Majesty may from time to time by letters patent appoint qualified persons as Lords Justices of Appeal or as puisne judges of the High Court.

(3) No person shall be qualified for appointment—

    (a) as Lord Chief Justice, Master of the Rolls, President of the Queen's Bench Division, President of the Family Division or Chancellor of the High Court, unless he is qualified for appointment as a Lord Justice of Appeal or is a judge of the Court of Appeal;

    (b) as a Lord Justice of Appeal unless—

        (i) he has a 10 year High Court qualification within the meaning of section 71 of the Courts and Legal Services Act 1990; or

        (ii) he is a judge of the High Court;

    or

    (c) as a puisne judge of the High Court unless—

        (i) he has a 10 year High Court qualification, within the meaning of section 71 of the Courts and Legal Services Act 1990; or

        (ii) he is a Circuit judge who has held that office for at least two years.

(4) Every person appointed to an office mentioned in subsection (1) or as a Lord Justice of Appeal or puisne judge of the High Court shall, as soon as may be after his acceptance of office, take the oath of allegiance and the judicial oath, as set out in the Promissory Oaths Act 1868, in the presence of the Lord Chancellor.

Note —Derived from the JA 1925, ss.9, 11, 12. Amended by the Courts and Legal Services Act 1990, s.71. Subsections (1) and (3) of s.10 were also amended by the Constitutional Reform Act 2005, s.148(1) and Sched. 4, para. 122(2)(b), and further amendments will be made to this section as other provisions in the 2005 Act are brought into effect (see para. 9A–4.1 above). **9A–33**

Qualifications for appointment

The Courts and Legal Services Act 1990 amended s.10(3)(b) and (c) (appointment of Lords Justices of Appeal and Judges of the High Court) by replacing the requirements that appointees should be barristers of 15 years' and 10 years' standing with the requirements that in both instances they should have "a 10 year High Court qualification," that is to say, appointees should have had a right of audience in relation to all proceedings in the High Court for at least 10 years. **9A–34**

Tenure of office of judges of Supreme Court

11.—(1) This section applies to the office of any judge of the Supreme Court except the Lord Chancellor. **9A–35**

(2) A person appointed to an office to which this section applies shall vacate it on the day on which he attains the age of seventy years unless by virtue of this section he has ceased to hold it before then.

(3) A person appointed to an office to which this section applies shall hold that office during good behaviour, subject to a power of removal by Her Majesty on an address presented to Her by both Houses of Parliament.

(4) A person holding an office within section 2(2)(d) to (g) shall vacate that office on becoming Lord Chancellor or a Lord of Appeal in Ordinary.

(5) A Lord Justice of Appeal shall vacate that office on becoming an *ex-officio* judge of the Court of Appeal.

(6) A puisne judge of the High Court shall vacate that office on becoming a judge of the Court of Appeal.

(7) A person who holds an office to which this section applies may at any time resign it by giving the Lord Chancellor notice in writing to that effect.

(8) The Lord Chancellor, if satisfied by means of a medical certificate that a person holding an office to which this section applies—

    (a) is disabled by permanent infirmity from the performance of the duties of his office; and

    (b) is for the time being incapacitated from resigning his office,

may, subject to subsection (9), by instrument under his hand declare that person's office to have been vacated; and the instrument shall have the like effect for all purposes as if that person had on the date of the instrument resigned his office.

(9) A declaration under subsection (8) with respect to a person shall be of no effect unless it is made—

    (a) in the case of any of the Lord Chief Justice, the Master of the Rolls, the President of the Queen's Bench Division, the President of the Family Division and the Chancellor of the High Court, with the concurrence of two others of them;

    (b) in the case of a Lord Justice of Appeal, with the concurrence of the Master of the Rolls;

    (c) in the case of a puisne judge of any Division of the High Court, with the concurrence of the senior judge of that Division.

(10) [...]

9A–36   *Note* —Derived from the JA 1925, ss.10, 12; the Judicial Pensions Act 1959, ss.2, 3; and the AJA 1973, s.12. Subss. (4) and (5) are new. Amended by the Statute Law (Repeals) Act 1989, Sched.1. Subsection (9) of s.11 was also amended by the Constitutional Reform Act 2005, s.148(1) and Sched.4, para. 123(4), and further amendments will be made to this section as other provisions in the 2005 Act are brought into effect (see para. 9A–4.1 above).

Removal

9A–37   Good behaviour means good behaviour in respect of the office (9 Co. Rep. 50a; *R. v. Richardson* (1758) 1 Burr. 517). A forfeiture is enforced by writ of *scire facias* (Com. Dig. tit. Officer, K. 11).

Liability to proceedings

9A–38   No action lies against any Judge of the Supreme Court in respect of any act done by him in his judicial capacity, even though he acted oppressively and maliciously *Sirros v. Moore* [1975] Q.B. 118; [1974] 3 All E.R. 776, CA, and the principle applies to all judges in the land, from the highest to the lowest, without any distinction being drawn between judges of different status or between judges and magistrates. The sole exception is in a case of denial of a writ of habeas corpus under the Habeas Corpus Act 1679, 31 Car. 2, c.2, s.9, or possibly where a judge does an act outside his jurisdiction (see *per* Buckley L.J. in *Sirros v. Moore*, above).

Salaries etc. of judges of Supreme Court

9A–39   **12.**—(1) Subject to subsections (2) and (3), there shall be paid to judges of the Supreme Court, other than the Lord Chancellor, such salaries as may be determined by the Lord Chancellor with the concurrence of the Minister for the Civil Service.

(2) Unless otherwise determined under this section, there shall be paid to the judges mentioned in subsection (1) the same salaries as at the commencement of this Act.

(3) Any salary payable under this section may, be increased, but not reduced, by a determination or further determination under this section.

(4) [...]

(5) Salaries payable under this section shall be charged on and paid out of the Consolidated Fund.

(6) There shall be paid out of money provided by Parliament to any judge of the Court of Appeal or of the High Court, in addition to his salary, such allowances as may be determined by the Lord Chancellor with the concurrence of the Minister for the Civil Service.

(7) Pensions shall be payable to or in respect of the judges mentioned in subsection (1) in accordance with section 2 of the Judicial Pensions Act 1981 or in the case of a judge who is a person to whom Part I of the Judicial Pensions and Retirement Act 1993 applies, in accordance with that Act.

9A–40

Note —Derived from the AJA 1973, s.9. The law relating to judicial pensions has been consolidated with amendments by the Judicial Pensions Act 1981. Amended by the Courts and Legal Services Act 1990, s.84, Sched.20; and the Judicial Pensions and Retirement Act 1993, Sched.8.

As to the consequences as to salary, etc. which may follow where a judge of the Supreme Court becomes, or ceases to be, the holder of a judicial office in an "international court" (*e.g.* any court established for any purpose of the European Communities) or in the European Court of Human Rights, see Access to Justice Act 1999, s.68(3) and (5) and the Human Rights Act 1998, s.18(4). Note para. 9A–4.1

Precedence of judges of Supreme Court

13.—(1) When sitting in the Court of Appeal—   **9A–41**

(a) the Lord Chief Justice and the Master of the Rolls shall rank in that order; and

(b) Lords of Appeal in Ordinary and persons who have been Lord Chancellor shall rank next after the Master of the Rolls and, among themselves, according to the priority of the dates on which they respectively became Lords of Appeal in Ordinary, as the case may be.

(2) Subject to subsection (1)(b), the President of the Queen's Bench Division shall rank next after the Master of the Rolls.

(2A) The President of the Family Division shall rank next after the President of the Queen's Bench Division.

(3) The Chancellor of the High Court shall rank next after the President of the Family Division.

(4) The vice-president or vice-presidents of the divisions of the Court of Appeal shall rank next after the Chancellor of the High Court; and if there are two vice-presidents of those divisions, they shall rank, among themselves, according to the priority of the dates on which they respectively became vice-presidents.

LEGISLATION

(5) The Lords Justices of Appeal (other than the vice-president or vice-presidents of the divisions of the Court of Appeal) shall rank after the ex-officio judges of the Court of Appeal and, among themselves, according to the priority of the dates on which they respectively became judges of that court.

(6) The puisne judges of the High Court shall rank next after the judges of the Court of Appeal and, among themselves, according to the priority of the dates on which they respectively became judges of the High Court.

9A–42 *Note* —Derived from the JA 1925, s.16. Subsections (2) and (3) of s.13 were also amended by the Constitutional Reform Act 2005, s.148(1) and Sched.4, para. 125, and further amendments will be made to this section as other provisions in the 2005 Act are brought into effect (see para. 9A–4.1 above).

Power of judge of Supreme or Crown Court to act in cases relating to rates and taxes

9A–43 **14.**—(1) A judge of the Supreme Court or of the Crown Court shall not be incapable of acting as such in any proceedings by reason of being, as one of a class of ratepayers, taxpayers or persons of any other description, liable in common with others to pay, or contribute to, or benefit from, any rate or tax which may be increased, reduced or in any way affected by those proceedings.

(2) In this section "rate or tax" means any rate, tax, duty or liability, whether public, general or local, and includes—

(a) any fund formed from the proceeds of any such rate, tax, duty or liability; and

(b) any fund applicable for purposes the same as, or similar to, those, for which the proceeds of any such rate, tax, duty or liability are or might be applied.

9A–44 *Note* —Derived from the JA 1925, s.17.

Judicial bias – judge "incapable of acting"

9A–44.1 This section provides for circumstances in which, otherwise, a judge might be regarded as incapable of dealing with a case on the ground of partiality or prejudice (judicial bias). The context of the section is explained below.

Under the Human Rights Act 1998, Sched.1, Pt 1, art.6.1 (right to a fair trial), in the determination of his civil rights and obligations, everyone is entitled to a fair hearing by an independent and impartial tribunal (see para. 3D–34 above). The requirement that the tribunal should be independent and impartial is one that has long been recognised by English common law. An appellate or reviewing court will set aside a decision affected by bias.

On the matter of impartiality, the decided cases draw a distinction between "actual bias" and "apparent bias" (*Director General of Fair Trading v. Proprietary Association of Great Britain* [2001] 1 W.L.R. 700, CA, para. 38). The phrase "actual bias" has been applied to the situation (1) where a judge has been influenced by partiality or prejudice in reaching his decision and (2) where it has been demonstrated that a judge is actually prejudiced in favour of or against a party. Findings of actual bias on the part of a judge are rare.

The phrase "apparent bias" describes the situation where circumstances exist which give rise to a reasonable apprehension that the judge may have been, or may be, biased. After *R. v. Bow Street Metropolitan Stipendiary Magistrate, ex p. Pinochet Ugarte (No. 2)* [1999] 2 W.L.R. 272, HL, allegations of apparent bias in the court became increasingly prevalent (in particular, allegations against part-time professional judges and against full-time judges recruited from the solicitors' branch of the legal profession).

In *Locabail (UK) Ltd v. Bayfield Properties Ltd* [2000] QB 451, CA, after hearing a number of appeals at the same time, the Court of Appeal sought to give guidance as to the principles which should be applied. Subsequently, in *Porter v. Magill* [2001] UKHL 67; [2002] 2 W.L.R. 37, HL, the House of Lords approved the following test formulated in the *Medicaments, Re* case: "The court must first ascertain all the circumstances which have a bearing on the suggestion that the judge was biased. It must then ask whether those circumstances would lead a fair-minded and informed observer to conclude that there was a real possibility or a real danger, the two being the same, that the tribunal was biased". Actual or apparent bias against a witness is as serious as bias against or in favour of a party (*Phillips v. Symes* [2003] EWCA Civ 1769; December 5, 2003, CA, unrep.).

On application or on his own motion a judge may recuse himself on the ground of bias. As an impartial judge is a fundamental prerequisite of a fair trial a judicial officer should not hesitate to recuse himself if there are reasonable grounds on the part of a litigant for apprehending that the judicial officer, for whatever reason, was not or will not be impartial (*Locabail (UK) Ltd v. Bayfield Properties Ltd, op. cit.*, at p.479). The reasonableness of the apprehension must be assessed in the light of the oath of office taken by the judges to administer justice without fear or favour; and their ability to carry out that oath by reason of their training and experience. It must be assumed that they can disabuse their minds of any irrelevant personal beliefs or predispositions. They must take into account the fact that they have a duty to sit in any case in which they are not obliged to recuse themselves (*ibid.*). The circumstances in which an application to a trial judge under CPR r.48.2 for a costs order against a non-party arise may be such as to cause the judge to consider whether he should recuse himself on the grounds of apparent bias (*Bahai v. Rashidian* [1985] 1 W.L.R. 1337, CA, *Symphony Group Plc. v. Hodgson* [1994] QB 179; [1993] 3 W.L.R. 830, CA, *Phillips v. Symes (No. 2)* [2004] EWHC 2330; 154 New L.J. 1615, (Ch) (Peter Smith J.)).

Other English cases on apparent bias coming to attention since the Locabail case include: *Hampshire County Council v. Gillingham* April 5, 2000, CA, unrep.; *Taylor v. Lawrence* [2001] EWCA Civ 119; January 25, 2001, CA, unrep.; *Re Bank of Credit and Commerce International (SA)* (2001) 151 New L.J. 1852, (Lawrence Collins J.); *Taylor v. Lawrence* [2002] EWCA Civ 90; [2002] 2 All E.R. 353, CA; *Taylor v. Williamsons* [2002] EWCA Civ 1380, *The Times*, August 9, 2002, CA; *Sengupta v. Holmes* [2002] EWCA Civ 1104; *The Times*, August 19, 2002, CA; *Berg v. I.M.L. London Ltd* [2002] 1 W.L.R. 3271; [2002] 4 All E.R. 87 (Stanley Burnton J.) (Master dealing with application for summary judgment seeing "without prejudice" correspondence); *Hart v. Relentless Records Ltd* (2002) 152 New L.J. 1562 (Jacobs J.) (corridor meeting between judge and counsel in which judge indicated case was weak and parties should reconsider settlement). See also *Geveran Trading Co. Ltd v. Skjevesland* [2002] EWCA Civ 1567; [2003] 1 W.L.R. 912, CA (test of apparent bias not relevant to application to prevent an advocate from acting) *Garratt v. Saxby (Practice Note)* [2004] EWCA Civ 341; [2004] 1 W.L.R. 2152, CA (offer to settle inadvertently disclosed to judge; *Foenander v. Foenander* [2004] EWCA Civ 1675, December 12, 2004, unrep., (judges formerly in same chambers as counsel); *Birmingham City Council v. Yardley*, *The Times* December 13, 2004, CA (part-time judge and counsel belonging to same chambers). In the Scottish case of *Davidson v. Scottish Ministers (No.2)* [2004] UKHL 34; *The Times* July 16, 2004, HL, it was held that a risk of apparent bias is liable to arise where a judge who had participated in the drafting or promotion of legislation during the parliamentary process is called upon to rule judicially on the effect of the legislation.

As to bias in arbitrators, see *Save and Prosper Pensions Ltd v. Homebase Ltd*, March 2, 2000, unrep.; *AT&T Corporation v. Saudi Cable Co* [2000] 2 Lloyd's Rep. 127, CA.

As to bias in tribunal, see *Harada Ltd v. Turner* [2001] EWCA Civ 599; April 6, 2001, CA unrep.; *Bennett v. London of Southwark* [2002] EWCA Civ 223; February 21, 2002, CA, unrep.; *Lawal v. Northern Spirit Limited* [2003] UKHL 35 (part-time tribunal member acting as advocate); *Bennett v. London Borough of Southwark* [2002] EWCA Civ 223; February 21, 2002, CA, unrep. (whether industrial tribunal should have recused itself when claimant's lay representative accused it of racism); *Jones v. DAS Legal Expenses Insurance Co Ltd* [2003] EWCA Civ 1071 (chairman of tribunal related to barrister in chambers routinely receiving cases from defendants).

Circumstances may arise where it would be improper for a judge to sit (1) to hear an application in, or (2) to try a particular issue arising for determination in, particular proceedings because of his earlier involvement in those proceedings or in related proceedings. An obvious example would be where, in the course of managing a case, a judge who was to try the case necessarily had communicated to him the fact that Pt 36 payment had been made (see r.36.19(2)). There are less obvious examples not specifically dealt with by extant legal provisions (such as r.36.19(2)). Under the CPR case management system, the risks of a judge sitting for certain purposes knowing of matters that in fairness he should not are increased. Such difficulties have arisen in a number of post-CPR cases. Examples are: *Thomson Directories Ltd v. Planet Telecom Plc* [2003] EWHC 1882 (Ch); July 4, 2003, unrep. (Laddie J.) (inquiry as to damages after trial of preliminary issue); *ALM Manufacturing v. Black & Decker* [2003] EWHC 1646 (Ch); May 21, 2003, unrep. (Pumfrey J.)(without prejudice communication between defendant and third party); *GE Capital Commercial Finance Ltd v. Sutton* [2003] EWHC 1648 (QB); July 4, 2003, unrep. (McCombe J.) (evidence ruling on material obtained by improper means); *Smithkline Beecham Plc v. Generics (UK) Ltd* [2003] EWCA Civ 1109, *The Times*, August 25, 2003, CA (confidential documents where clams tried together).

PART II

JURISDICTION

THE COURT OF APPEAL

General jurisdiction of Court of Appeal

9A–45   **15.**—(1) The Court of Appeal shall be a superior court of record.

(2) Subject to the provisions of this Act, there shall be exercisable by the Court of Appeal—

    (a) all such jurisdiction (whether civil or criminal) as is conferred on it by this or any other Act; and

    (b) all such other jurisdiction (whether civil or criminal) as was exercisable by it immediately before the commencement of this Act.

(3) For all purposes of or incidental to—

    (a) the hearing and determination of any appeal to the civil division of the Court of Appeal; and

    (b) the amendment, execution and enforcement of any judgment or order made on such an appeal,

the Court of Appeal shall have all the authority and jurisdiction of the court or tribunal from which the appeal was brought.

(4) It is hereby declared that any provision in this or any other Act which authorises or requires the taking of any steps for the execution or enforcement of a judgment or order of the High Court applies in relation to a judgment or order of the civil division of the Court of Appeal as it applies in relation to a judgment or order of the High Court.

Criminal and Civil Divisions of the Court of Appeal

9A–46   The Court of Appeal is divided into the Criminal Division and the Civil Division. For the provisions governing distribution of business between the Divisions see s.53 below.

Appeals in civil matters

9A–47   For procedure regulating appeals to the Court of Appeal (Civil Division), see CPR Pt 52 and the practice direction supplementing that Part. The courts and tribunals from which the Court of Appeal hears appeals in civil matters include:

    (1) *High Court*—Subject to exceptions, appeal lies to the Court of Appeal from all

Divisions of the High Court (s.16); see para. 9A–50A below and note (5) below (bankruptcy appeals).

(2) *County courts*—Subject to exceptions, appeal lies to the Court of Appeal from decisions of the county courts in civil matters, including matrimonial proceedings (County Courts Act 1984, s.77); see para. 9A–657.1.

(3) *Employment Appeal Tribunal*—Appeal lies to the Court of Appeal from the EAT, but only with the leave of the EAT or the Court of Appeal (Employment Protection (Consolidation) Act 1978, s.136(4)).

(4) *Patents Court*—Appeal lies to the Court of Appeal from decisions of the Patents Court (see the SCA 1981, s.6 (which provides that the Patents Court is part of the Chancery Division of the High Court) and the Patents Act 1977, s.97(3) (which sets out the requirements concerning leave to appeal)).

(5) *Bankruptcy*—An appeal lies from a decision made by a county court or by a registrar in bankruptcy of the High Court to a single judge of the High Court and an appeal lies from a decision of that judge with his leave or the leave of the Court of Appeal (Insolvency Act 1986, s.375(2)).

(6) *Lands Tribunal*—Appeal lies to the Court of Appeal from decisions of the Lands Tribunal Act 1949, s.3(4)). Section 4(1) of the 1949 Act was amended by the Civil Procedure (Modification of Enactments) Order 2000 (S.I. 2000 No. 941), with the result that the requirement that appeals from the Lands Tribunal on points of law should be by case stated was removed. Such appeals are now governed by CPR Pt 52, with permission to appeal being required in every case (*Practice Direction (Lands Tribunal: Appeals: Applications)* [2000] R.V.R. 223).

(7) *Social Security Commissioners*—Appeal lies to the Court of Appeal from decisions of the Social Security Commissioners, with the leave of the Commissioner or the Court of Appeal (Social Security Act 1980, s.14). Although s.55(1) of the Access to Justice Act 1999, s.55(1) (Second appeals) does not apply to these appeals, a robust attitude to the "prospect of success" criterion (CPR, r.52.3(6)) should be adopted in these cases (*Cooke v. Secretary of State for Social Security* [2001] EWCA Civ 734, April 25, 2001, CA, unrep.).

(8) *Restrictive Practices Court*— Restrictive Practices Court Act 1976, s.10.

For appeals to the Court of Appeal from the Pathogens Access Appeal Commission, and from the Proscribed Organisations Appeal Commission established, respectively, by the Anti-terrorism, Crime and Security Act 2001, and the Terrorism Act 2000, see respectively, Court of Appeal (Appeals from Pathogens Access Appeal Tribunal) Rules 2002 (S.I. 2002 No. 1844) and the Court of Appeal (Appeals from Proscribed Organisations Appeal Commission) Rules 2002 (S.I. 2002 No. 1843).

The Court of Appeal has no jurisdiction to hear an appeal from Immigration Appeal Tribunal decision on appeal from a special adjudicator sitting in Scotland; in these circumstances, appeal lies to the Court of Session (*Gardi v. Secretary of State for the Home Department (No. 2)* , [2002] EWCA Civ 1560; [2002] 1 W.L.R. 3282, CA.).

"all purposes of or incidental to"

In judicial review proceedings, the High Court has an inherent jurisdiction to make ancillary orders temporarily releasing an applicant from detention, and by virtue of s.15(3), on appeal in those proceedings, the Court of Appeal could make like order (*R. (Sezek) v. Secretary of State for the Home Department, The Times*, June 20, 2001, CA).

9A–47.1

Application of High Court enforcement provisions to Court of Appeal judgments

The purpose of the declaration in s.15(4) to the effect that provisions for the enforcement of High Court judgment or orders (which are legion) apply to the enforcement by the High Court of judgments and orders of the Court of Appeal (Civil Division) is obvious. The County Courts Act 1984 contains no similar provision. However, in *Ager v. Ager* [1998] 1 W.L.R. 1074, CA, it was held that the jurisdiction conferred on the High Court by s.15(4) constituted a "general principle of practice" within the meaning of s.76 of the 1984 Act which could be adopted and applied in proceedings in a county court.

9A–48

Jurisdiction where appeal raising "academic" or "hypothetical" point of law

See para. 9A–68 below.

9A–48.1

Appeals from High Court

16.—(1) Subject as otherwise provided by this or any other Act **9A–49**

LEGISLATION

(and in particular to the provision in section 13(2)(a) of the Administration of Justice Act 1969 excluding appeals to the Court of Appeal in cases where leave to appeal from the High Court directly to the House of Lords is granted under Part II of that Act) or as provided by any order made by the Lord Chancellor under section 56(1) of the Access to Justice Act 1999, the Court of Appeal shall have jurisdiction to hear and determine appeals from any judgment or order of the High Court.

(2) An appeal from a judgment or order of the High Court when acting as a prize court shall not be to the Court of Appeal, but shall be to Her Majesty in Council in accordance with the Prize Acts 1864 to 1944.

Appeals directly from the High Court to the House of Lords— "leap–frog" petitions

9A–50   See the AJA 1969, s.13 (para. 9B–41 below) and Practice Directions and Standing Orders Applicable to Civil Appeals, Direction 6 and see paras 4A–25 and 4A–115 (above).

Jurisdiction to hear appeals from High Court

9A–50.1   The general rule is that the Court of Appeal shall have jurisdiction "to hear and determine appeals from any judgment or order of the High Court" (s.16(1)). Two exceptions (provided for in s.16) are "leap-frog" appeals to the House of Lords and Prize Court appeals. The general rule is further qualified by the Access to Justice Act 1999. Section 56(1) of that Act states that the Lord Chancellor may by order provide that appeals "which would otherwise lie to the Court of Appeal", for example, appeals falling within the general rule stated above, shall lie instead to the High Court (see para. 9A–866 below). Accordingly, the power of the Lord Chancellor by order to affect the jurisdiction of the Court of Appeal in relation to appeals from the High Court was added to s.16(1) by the Access to Justice Act 1999 (Destination of Appeals) Order 2000 (S.I. 2000 No. 1071), art.7. Provisions exercising this power in relation to appeals to the Court of Appeal from the High Court are found in arts 2, 4 and 5 of that statutory instrument. Article 2 states that, where the decision to be appealed is a decision made by (*inter alia*) a Master or a district judge, then, subject to two exceptions, the appeal shall not go according to the general rule (*i.e.* from the High Court to the Court of Appeal) but shall go to a judge of the High Court. In this context, "decision" includes any judgment, order or direction. The two exceptions are: (1) where the decision is a final decision in a claim allocated to the multi-track under CPR, rr.12.7, 14.8 or 26.5, or is made in "specialist proceedings" provided for by CPR, Part 49 (*e.g.* proceedings in the Commercial Court, the Patents Court, or the Technology and Construction Court) (see art.4); and (2) where the decision appealed was itself a decision made on appeal (other than from the decision of an officer of the court authorised to assess costs) (so-called "second appeals") (see art.5). In this context, "final decision" means any decision that would finally determine (subject to any possible appeal or detailed assessment of costs) the entire proceedings whichever way the court decided the issues before it (*ibid.*, art.1(2)(c)). Certain decisions, though not strictly falling within this definition, are to be treated as final decisions (*ibid.*, art.1(3)) (see further *Roerig v. Valiant Trawlers Ltd* [2002] EWCA Civ 21; [2002] 1 W.L.R. 2304, CA, and authorities referred to therein).

The Access to Justice Act 1999, s.57 (see para. 9A–867 below) states that, where in any proceedings in a county court or the High Court a person seeks permission to make an appeal which, but for the operation of the alternative destination of appeals provisions explained above, would go to the Court of Appeal, the Master of the Rolls or the court from which or to which the appeal is made, or from which permission to appeal is sought, may direct that the appeal shall be heard instead by the Court of Appeal. Where this power is exercised, in effect the alternative destination provisions are overridden. In the case of *Re Claims Direct Test Cases* [2002] EWCA Civ 428; *The Times*, April 4, 2002, CA, it was held that this procedure could not be used to "leapfrog" the requirement that an application for permission to appeal should be made.

No appeal shall lie to the Court of Appeal: (1) from any order, judgment or decision of the High Court which is final, or (2) from any order of the High Court allowing an extension of time for appealing from a judgment or order (paras (b) & (c) of s.18(1); see para. 9A–53 below).

No appeal shall lie from a decision of the High Court refusing leave required by s.42 (Restriction of vexatious legal proceedings) (see para. 9A–132 below).

As to appeals from the Court of Appeal against an order of the High Court refusing permission to appeal, see *Foenander v. Bond Lewis & Co* [2001] EWCA Civ 759; [2001] 2 All E.R. 1019, CA.

For rules of court affecting appeals from the High Court to the Court of Appeal, see CPR Pt 52, and for further information as to the jurisdiction of the Court of Appeal in relation to appeals from the High Court, see notes on the rules in Pt 52 (Vol. 1, paras 52.0.1 *et seq*).

Section 13(2)(a) of the Administration of Justice Act 1969 provides that where a trial judge grants a certificate unders.12 of that Act and permission is given for an appeal from the High Court directly to the House of Lords, no appeal from "the decision of the judge" as to which the certificate relates shall lie to the Court of Appeal (see paras. 9B–41 & 9B–42 below). As to the meaning of "decision" in this context, see *R. (Jones) v. Ceredigion County Council* [2005] EWCA Civ 986; [2005] 1 W.L.R. 3626, CA (whether permission to appeal to Court of Appeal could be made contingent upon failure of application for permission to appeal directly to House of Lords).

Applications for new trial

17.—(1) Where any cause or matter, or any issue in any cause or **9A–51** matter, has been tried in the High Court, any application for a new trial thereof, or to set aside a verdict, finding or judgment therein, shall be heard and determined by the Court of Appeal except where rules of court made in pursuance of subsection (2) provide otherwise.

(2) As regards cases where the trial was by a judge alone and no error of the court at the trial is alleged, or any prescribed class of such cases, rules of court may provide that any such application as is mentioned in subsection (1) shall be heard and determined by the High Court.

(3) Nothing in this section shall alter the practice in bankruptcy.

Effect of the section
See CPR Pt 52 and notes thereto (see para. 52.1). **9A–52**

Restrictions on appeals to Court of Appeal

18.—(1) No appeal shall lie to the Court of Appeal— **9A–53**

(a) except as provided by the Administration of Justice Act 1960, from any judgment of the High Court in any criminal cause or matter;

(b) from any order of the High Court or any other court or tribunal allowing an extension of time for appealing from a judgment or order;

(c) from any order, judgment or decision of the High Court or any other court or tribunal which, by virtue of any provision (however expressed) of this or any other Act, is final;

(d) from a decree absolute or [...] nullity of marriage, by a party who, having had time and opportunity to appeal from the decree nisi on which that decree was founded, has not appealed from the decree nisi;

(dd) from a divorce order;

(e) [...]

(f) [...]

(g) except as provided by Part I of the Arbitration Act 1996, from any decision of the High Court under that Part;

(h) [...]

(1A) [...]

(1B) [...]

(2) [...]

9A–54 *Note* —Amended by the Children Act 1989, Sched.13; the Courts and Legal Services Act 1990, s.7(2) and s.125(7); the Arbitration Act 1996, Sched.3; the Family Law Act 1996, Sched.8, para. 30 and Sched.10; the Civil Procedure Act 1997, Sched.2 and the Access to Justice Act 1999, s.106, Sched.15, Pt III.

Restrictions on appeals

9A–55 Section 18(1) indicates that, in certain circumstances, no appeal shall lie to the Court of Appeal. The legislative basis for the requirement that an appeal may not be made to the Court of Appeal without permission (*i.e.* without leave) was removed from s.18 and is now found in the Access to Justice Act 1999, s.54; note also ss.55 to 58 of that Act (see para. 9A–861). The effect of other statutory provisions (either in this Act or elsewhere) may be to restrict appeals to the Court of Appeal. For example, s.28A of this Act (para. 9A–78 below) provides that certain decisions of the High Court are final. For powers of High Court in relation to arbitrations, see Arbitration Act 1996, ss. 66 to 71 (para. 2E–235); for appeals to Court of Appeal, see section 69 and notes thereto and note *Inco Europe Ltd v. First Choice Distribution* [2000] 1 W.L.R. 586, HL; *Henry Boot Construction (UK) Ltd v. Malmaison Hotel (Manchester) Ltd* [2001] 1 All E.R. 193, CA; [2000] 2 Lloyd's Rep. 625, CA.

The leading House of Lords authority on the phrase "in any criminal cause or matter" is *Amand v. Home Secretary and Minister of Defence of Royal Netherlands Government* [1943] A.C. 147, HL, see *United States Government v. Montgomery* [2001] UKHL 3; [2001] 1 W.L.R. 196, HL, where the Amand case and other authorities are examined. In *R. (South West Yorkshire Mental Health NHS Trust) v. Crown Court at Bradford* [2003] EWCA Civ 1857; [2004] 1 W.L.R. 1664, CA, it was held that, although an order made by the Crown Court upon a verdict being entered was made under a statute empowering the court to make a custodial order in the absence of conviction (in this instance, the Criminal Procedure (Insanity) Act 1964, s.5(2)(a)), the order did not for that reason cease to be an order in a criminal cause or matter. In determining whether an appeal is in a criminal cause or matter it is appropriate for the court to take an overall view and not to enter into a detailed order by order analysis.

The Magistrates' Courts Act 1981, s.111 is an important example of a statutory provision, other than one found in the 1981 Act, providing that a decision of the High Court in a non-criminal cause or matter will be final and ousting the jurisdiction of the Court of Appeal (*Westminster City Council v. O'Reilly* [2003] EWCA Civ 1007; *The Times*, August 21, 2003, CA (decision of High Court on appeal by way of cased stated from magistrates' court in licensing matter final)).

The effect of the various restrictions on appeals contained in this section is discussed in detail in notes to CPR Pt 52 (see Vol. 1, para. 52.1).

THE HIGH COURT

GENERAL JURISDICTION

General jurisdiction of High Court

9A–56 **19.**—(1) The High Court shall be a superior court of record.

(2) Subject to the provisions of this Act, there shall be exercisable by the High Court—

(a) all such jurisdiction (whether civil or criminal) as is conferred on it by this or any other Act; and

(b) all such other jurisdiction (whether civil or criminal) as was exercisable by it immediately before the commencement of this Act (including jurisdiction conferred on a judge of the High Court by any statutory provision).

(3) Any jurisdiction of the High Court shall be exercised only by a single judge of that court, except in so far as it is—

(a) by or by virtue of rules of court or any other statutory provision required to be exercised by a divisional court; or

(b) by rules of court made exercisable by a master, registrar or other officer of the court, or by any other person.

(4) The specific mention elsewhere in this Act of any jurisdiction covered by subsection (2) shall not derogate from the generality of that subsection.

Note —Derived from the JA 1925, s.18. **9A–57**

Jurisdiction exercisable by the High Court

By s.16 of the Judicature Act 1873, the High Court of Justice was created as a **9A–58** superior court of record and the jurisdiction which, at the commencement of that Act, was vested in or capable of being exercised by, certain courts of common law and equity, and certain other courts, was transferred to and vested in the High Court. The courts so merged in the High Court included, for example, the High Court of Chancery and the Court of Queen's Bench. Thus the jurisdiction of the High Court was co-extensive with the aggregate of the jurisdictions of the courts from whom jurisdiction was transferred, subject to legislative changes made by the 1873 Act itself (and by subsequent legislation) (see *Re Mill's Estate* (1886) 34 Ch D 24, at 33 *per* Cotton L.J.; *Bow, McLachlan and Co v. Ship Camosun* (1909) 101 L.T. 167, PC, at 170, *per* Lord Gorell).

In the main, questions as to the extent of the jurisdiction of the High Court had to be answered by investigating the extent of the jurisdictions of the courts from whom jurisdiction was transferred and, as is indicated by s.19(1)(b), to an important degree, this remains the position to the present day. Obviously, the jurisdiction of the High Court has been affected by legislation coming into force after 1873 (see s.19(1)(a)) and by case law. Section 19(1)(b) states that the High Court shall have all such jurisdiction "as was exercisable by it immediately before the commencement of this Act". Comparable provisions were found in the predecessors to the 1981 Act, the successive Judicature Acts (*e.g.* s.18(2) of the JA 1925). In effect, the cumulative effect of these provisions has been to keep alive s.16 of the 1873 Act referred to above.

Section 19 confers jurisdiction on the High Court in general terms. It is expressed as "subject to the provisions of this Act". Provisions following s.19 deal with particular fields of jurisdiction, *e.g.* ss.20 to 24 (Admiralty), s.25 (probate), etc.

The general jurisdiction defined in s.19 is vested in all the Judges of the High Court, irrespective of the Division to which they are attached (see subs.(4), ss.4(3) and 5(5)).

Inherent jurisdiction of the Court

The provision in s.19(2)(b), that there shall be exercisable by the High Court "all **9A–59** such other jurisdiction (whether civil or criminal) as was exercisable by it immediately before the commencement of the Act" of 1981, subsumes and incorporates "the inherent jurisdiction of the court". Such jurisdiction has been exercisable by the superior courts from the earliest days of the common law (see *e.g. Metropolitan Bank v. Pooley* (1885) 10 App.Cas. 210, HL, at 220–221 *per* Lord Blackburn).

The court may execute its inherent jurisdiction even in respect of matters which are regulated by statute or by rules of court (see *Willis v. Earl Beauchamp* (1886) 11 P.D. 59, at 63 *per* Bowen L.J., *Davey v. Bentick* [1893] 1 Q.B. 185, CA, at 187 *per* Lord Esher M.R., *Stewart Charting v. C. & O. Managements SA, The Venus Destiny* [1980] 1 W.L.R. 460, [1980] 1 All E.R. 718 (Goff J.)).

An important practical illustration of the Court's inherent jurisdiction is the Court's

LEGISLATION

power to stay proceedings. The power may be exercised in various contexts (*e.g.* on abuse of process grounds); see s.49(3) below and notes thereto.

The powers which may said to be "inherent" in the High Court's jurisdiction cannot be stated succinctly. It has been said by the highest authority that there can be no doubt that a court which is endowed with a particular jurisdiction has powers "which are necessary to enable it to act effectively within such jurisdiction" and that a court must enjoy such powers "in order to enforce its rules of practice and to suppress any abuse of its process and to defeat any attempted thwarting of its processes" (*Connelly v. Director of Public Prosecutions* [1964] A.C. 1254, HL, at 1301 *per* Lord Morris). It has also been said that it would be "conducive to legal clarity" if the use of the expressions "inherent power" and "inherent jurisdiction" were confined "to the doing by the court of acts which it needs must have power to do in order to maintain its character as a court of justice" (*Bremer Vulkan Schiffbau und Maschinenfabrik v. South India Shipping Corp Ltd* [1981] A.C. 909, HL, at 971 *per* Lord Diplock). See, further, Jacob, "The Inherent Jurisdiction of the Court" (1970) 23 *Current Legal Problems* 27, and authorities cited there.

The overriding features of the inherent jurisdiction of the court are that it is a part of procedural law, both civil and criminal and not part of substantive law: it is exercisable by summary process, without a plenary or full trial; it may be invoked not only in relation to parties in pending proceedings, but in relation to anyone, whether a party or not, and in relation to matters not raised in the litigation between the parties; it must be distinguished from the exercise of judicial discretion; and it may be exercised even in circumstances governed by rules of court (see *Jacob, ibid.*).

The Court of Appeal exercises its own inherent jurisdiction, *e.g.* the power to strike out a notice of appeal where the appeal is frivolous, vexatious or an abuse of the process of the court (*Burgess v. Stafford Hotel Ltd* [1990] 1 W.L.R. 1215; [1990] 3 All E.R. 222, CA; *Aviagents Ltd v. Balstravest Investments Ltd* [1966] 1 W.L.R. 150; [1966] 1 All E.R. 450, CA).

A county court has inherent jurisdiction to regulate its own procedures (*Langley v. North West Water Authority* [1991] 1 W.L.R. 697; [1991] 3 All E.R. 610, CA); but note County Courts Act 1984, s.74A (see para. 9A–656 below).

For modern illustrations of reliance by court on its inherent jurisdiction, see the following Court of Appeal cases: *Rocksteady Services Ltd, Re* [2001] C.P. Rep. 1 (court can decline to proceed with a trial which it feels it can no longer conduct fairly because of delay caused by the court); *Woodford & Ackroyd v. Burgess*, [2000] C.P. Rep. 79, CA (admissibility of an alleged expert's evidence); *C.J. Hurst (Lickfold) Ltd v. Belchamber*, November 20, 1998, CA, unrep. (county court's power to restrain a litigant from making further applications without leave, a "*Grepe v. Loam*" order); *DowlesManor Properties Ltd v. Bank of Namibia* [1999] C.P.L.R. 259, January 19, 1999, CA, unrep. (dismissing action for claimant's failure adequately to comply with an "unless" order requiring exchange of witness statements within particular period); *Riniker v. University College London, The Times* April 17, 1999, CA (backdating issue of writ from date when actually issued to date when received by the court for purpose of ensuring that action brought within relevant limitation period, see now CPR, r.7.2(2) and Practice Direction (How to Start Proceedings — The Claim Form), para. 5.1); *Reichhold Norway A.S.A. v. Goldman Sachs International* [2000] 1 W.L.R. 173; [2000] 2 All E.R. 679, CA (stay of English proceedings in favour of foreign arbitration); *Mainwaring v. Encyclopedia Britannica International Ltd*, June 21, 1999, CA, unrep. (jurisdiction (acknowledged in CPR, r.3.1) to strike out appeal, even though no "unless" order has been made); *Al-Naimi v. Islamic Press Agency Inc* [2000] 1 Lloyd's Rep. 522, CA (jurisdiction to stay in addition to power under Arbitration Act 1996, s.9); *Walsh v. Misseldine*, February 29, 2000, CA, unrep. (residual inherent abuse of process jurisdiction and power to strike out under CPR, r.3.4(2)); *R. (on the application of Sezek) v. Secretary of State for the Home Department (Bail Application)*, [2001] EWCA Civ 795, CA (ancillary order in judicial review proceedings temporarily releasing an applicant from detention). Note also, *Harley v. McDonald* [2001] UKPC 18; [2001] 2 W.L.R. 1749, PC (jusisdiction to award costs personally against practitioner where serious dereliction of duty) and *Grupo Torras SA v. Al-Sabah* February 25, 2003, unrep. (Treacy J.) (jurisdiction to restrict disclosure to paying party of reasons for success fee in receiving party's conditional fee agreement).

The court has inherent power to control its own process and it is entitled to bring argument to a close when it concludes that its process is being abused and that nothing of value will be lost by ending it (*Attorney General v. Scriven*, February 4, 2000, CA, unrep., courts are "not required to listen to litigants, whether represented or not, for as long as they like", *per* Simon Brown L.J.).

See also authorities referred to in notes following s.42 (Restriction on vexatious legal proceedings) (paras 9A–133 et seq. below).

The court has no power under the Family Law Reform Act 1969, s.21 or the inherent jurisdiction to enforce compliance with an order requiring samples to be taken of a child's blood for the purposes of determining paternity (In re O. (Minor) (Blood Tests: Constraint) [2000] 2 W.L.R. 1284; [2000] 2 All E.R. 29).

Jurisdiction to be exercised by single judge

Subsection (3)(a) requires that the jurisdiction of the High Court should be **9A–60** exercised only by a single Judge of the Court except where such jurisdiction is required by virtue of rules of court or other statutory provision to be exercised by a Divisional Court, constituted under s.66 (see s.151(1)) i.e. consisting of not less than two Judges. A Divisional Court consisting of two judges has no jurisdiction to deal with a matter or proceeding which the Act confers on the High Court (see, e.g. In Re Fletcher, The Times, June 12, 1984, where held that a Divisional Court had no jurisdiction to make a civil proceedings order under s.42).

Subsection (3)(b) requires that the jurisdiction of the High Court should be exercised only by a single Judge of the Court except where such jurisdiction "by or by virtue of rules of court" is made exercisable by a master, district judge or other officer of the Court or by any other person. CPR, r.2.4 provides that where the Civil Procedure Rules provide for the Court "to perform any act" masters and district judges may exercise any function of the High Court except where an enactment, rule or practice direction provides otherwise. Practice Direction (Allocation of Cases to Levels of Judiciary) sets out the matters over which masters and district judges do not have jurisdiction or which they may deal with only on certain conditions, but does not affect jurisdiction conferred by other enactments.

Ouster of jurisdiction

The general principle is that parties cannot by agreement between themselves oust **9A–61** the jurisdiction of the High Court. Such an agreement is void, as contrary to public policy (Czarnikow v. Roth & Co [1922] 2 K.B. 478, CA; Re Davstone Estates Ltd's Leases, Manprop Ltd v. O'Dell [1969] 2 Ch. 378). There are important exceptions. An agreement to refer to arbitration, or that the ascertainment of facts by the arbitrator is to be a condition precedent to the exercise of jurisdiction does not oust the jurisdiction of the court, and is valid (Scott v. Avery (1856) 5 H.L.C. 811; Atlantic Co v. Dreyfus [1922] 2 A.C. 250; Cipriani v. Burnett [1933] A.C. 83). An agreement that disputes shall be referred to a foreign tribunal equally does not oust the jurisdiction of the English Courts and is valid, and prima facie the English Courts will stay proceedings instituted in this country in breach of such agreement (The Fehmarn [1958] 1 W.L.R. 159; [1958] 1 All E.R. 333, CA). As to agreement to seek to settle a dispute by mediation, see Halifax Financial Services Ltd v. Intuitive Systems Ltd, December 21, 1998 (unrep.) (McKinnon J.).

The parties to an agreement may validly provide, expressly or impliedly, that it shall be an agreement of honour only and not enforceable at law (Balfour v. Balfour [1919] 2 K.B. 571; Rose & Frank Co v. Crompton [1923] 2 K.B. 261; Jones v. Vernon's Pools Ltd [1938] 2 All E.R. 626; Appleson v. Littlewood Ltd [1939] 1 All E.R. 464, CA).

A settlor is not entitled to make any power or discretion exercisable with consent of the Ch.D. or a Judge thereof except in the event of trustees failing or refusing to exercise such discretion (Re H.'s Settlement [1939] W.N. 318).

Ouster of jurisdiction by statute

Many statutes depute to other tribunals, or to officials, or other bodies, the right to **9A–62** determine questions of various kinds, and often give finality to such determination; e.g. Joseph Crosfield & Sons Ltd v. Manchester Ship Canal Co (1904) 90 L.J. 557. Unless the statute in clear terms deprives the claimant of his remedy at law, the jurisdiction of the Court is not ousted (Lowther v. Clifford [1927] 1 K.B. 130, CA, cf. R. & W. Paul v. Wheat Commission [1937] A.C. 139). In such cases, subject to exceptions that need not be canvassed here, the High Court has no jurisdiction to interfere by way of appeal, judicial review or otherwise.

Want of jurisdiction—waiver

It is sometimes a question of difficulty whether a proceeding is void for want of ju- **9A–63** risdiction or whether there has been merely an irregularity in procedure which has

LEGISLATION

been waived; see *Smythe v. Wiles* [1921] 2 K.B. 66; *Shrager v. Dighton* [1924] 1 K.B. 274; *Pringle v. Hales* [1925] 1 K.B. 573; *Key v. Bastin* [1925] 1 K.B. 650; *Wyndham v. Jackson* [1937] W.N. 291. See also CPR, r.3.10 (General power of the court to rectify matters where there has been an error of procedure). Want of jurisdiction cannot be cured by consent, see *Papadopoulos v. Papadopoulos* [1930] P. 44; *Simons v. Simons* [1939] 1 K.B. 490; *Rothman of Pall Mall (Overseas) Ltd v. Saudi Arabia Airlines Corporation* [1981] Q.B. 368; [1980] 3 All E.R. 359, CA.

Bail

9A–64   The High Court has an inherent jurisdiction to grant bail. This jurisdiction extends to the grant of bail to persons under remand but does not extend to the grant of bail to persons who have been tried and convicted (*In Re L.* (1944) 61 T.L.R. 180, *Ex p. Speculand* [1946] K.B. 48). The jurisdiction has been affected by, and is exercised in accordance with, legislative provisions. See, further, Archbold, Criminal Pleading, Evidence and Practice (2001), paras 3–186 to 3–194. For relevant rules of court, see CPR Sched.1, RSC O.79 (Criminal Proceedings), r.9 (Bail) (see Vol. 1, para. sc79.9).

Benefice

9A–65   Order to admit against bishop (*Notley v. Bp. of Birmingham* [1930] W.N. 110; [1931] 1 Ch. 529).

Domestic forum

9A–66   The Court cannot interfere with the decision of a "domestic tribunal" if made bona fide, in accordance with its rules, and not contrary to the elementary principles of justice (*Catt v. Wood* [1910] A.C. 404; *Leeson v. General Council of Medical Education* (1890) 43 Ch D 366; *Maclean v. Workers' Union* [1929] 1 Ch. 602; *Cotter v. N.U.S.* [1929] 2 Ch. 58).

Foreign state or sovereign

9A–67   See "Parties generally," s.17B.

Jurisdiction where proceedings raising "academic" or "hypothetical" point of law

9A–68   In *Ainsbury v. Millington (Note)* [1987] 1 W.L.R. 379, HL, Lord Bridge said (at 381) that it has always been a fundamental feature of the English judicial system that the courts, whether first instance or appellate, "decide disputes betwen the parties before them" and that they do not "pronounce on abstract questions of law where there is no dispute to be resolved". In a number of reported cases it has been argued that the court either lacked jurisdiction on the ground that the proceedings raised an "academic" or "hypothetical" point of law, or should decline to exercise its jurisdiction on that ground. Generally, the issue has arisen in courts exercising appellate or review jurisdiction (see, *e.g. Sun Life Assurance Co of Canada v. Jervis* [1944] A.C. 111, HL, at 113 *per* Viscount Simon L.C., and *R. v. Secretary of State for the Home Department, Ex p. Wynne* [1993] 1 W.L.R. 115, HL, at 120 *per* Lord Goff). In some cases, the outcome of this question of jurisdiction has turned on the question whether the point of law raised was truly "academic" or "hypothetical" (*e.g. R. v. Canons Park Mental Health Tribunal, ex p. A* [1995] Q.B. 60, CA).

A live issue between parties may become "academic" or "hypothetical" for various reasons. Generally, it is inappropriate for parties seeking to resolve a dispute between them as to costs to seek to do so by litigating to a conclusion a substantive issue that has become "academic" (*R. v. Holderness Borough Council, ex p. James Robert Developments Ltd* [1993] L.G.R. 643, *R. v. Hackney London Borough Council, ex p. Jarram*, June 14, 1999 (unrep.)), *R. (Tshikangu) v. Newham LBC, The Times*, April 27, 2001 (Stanley Burnton J).

In *Ainsbury v. Millington* [1987] 1 W.L.R. 379, *op. cit.* Lord Bridge conceded that the court may entertain proceedings where, although there was no lis to be determined directly affecting the parties' rights and obligations *inter se*, the proceedings could be described as a "friendly action" and, conceivably, where the proceedings were instituted specifically as a "test" case (*ibid.*, 381).

In modern times, the appellate courts have indicated a greater willingness to entertain proceedings which raise points of law which, although "academic" or "hypothetical", are points of general public interest (see cases cited arguendo in *R. v. Canons Park Mental Health Tribunal, ex p. A, op. cit.* at 63) but no general principle to this effect has emerged (see also *Don Pasquale v. Customs & Excise* [1990] 1 W.L.R. 1108, CA;

Watford Borough Council v. Simpson, February 10, 2000, CA, unrep.; *Prudential Assurance Co. Ltd v. McBains Cooper* [2000] 1 W.L.R. 2000, CA; *Callery v. Gray (No. 2)* [2001] EWCA Civ 1246; [2001] 1 W.L.R. 2142, CA (Court deciding not to resolve hypothetical questions as to recovery of insurance premiums as costs)). The law is not settled. In *R. v. Secretary of State for the Home Department, ex p. Salem* [1999] 2 W.L.R. 483, HL, it was held that the House of Lords has a discretion, to be exercised sparingly, to hear an appeal on an "academic" issue of public law involving a public authority where there was good reason in the public interest for doing so. Note also *R. v. Secretary of State for Health, Exe p. Imperial Tobacco Ltd* [2001] 1 W.L.R. 127, HL; *R. v. Secretary of State for Employment, ex p. Equal Opportunities Commission* [1995] 1 A.C. 1, HL; *R. (Barron) v. Surrey County Council* [2002] EWCA Civ 713; May 7, 2002, CA, unrep. (and cases cited therein); *Pridding v. Secretary of State for Work and Pensions* [2002] EWCA Civ 306; March 4, 2002, CA, unrep.; *R. (Commissioners of Customs and Excise) v. Canterbury Crown Court, The Times*, December 6, 2002, DC (court declaring that Crown Court judge had no jurisdiction to make order even though matter had become academic).

In *Bowman v. Fels* [2005] EWCA Civ 226; [2005] 1 W.L.R. 3083, CA, a county court judge made an order in a private law claim (involving a dispute as to the beneficial interest in property) requiring the claimant to make certain disclosures to the defendant. The claimant appealed. The appeal raised important issues as to the application to the legal profession of certain provisions in the Proceeds of Crime Act 2002. The Bar Council, The Law Society and the National Criminal Intelligence Service appeared as intervening parties in the appeal. By the time the appeal came on the substantive litigation between the parties had been settled. The Court held that, nevertheless, the Court had jurisdiction to hear the appeal. The Court said that, had this been a public law claim, the Court would readily have found that it had jurisdiction on the basis of *R. v. Secretary of State for the Home Department, ex p. Salem, op. cit.* The difficulty was that the underlying proceedings sounded in private law and not in public law. However, the question at the heart of this appeal was an issue of public law of very great importance and all of the parties involved in the appeal wished the appeal to proceed. The Court said (para. 10): "To send them away empty-handed on an issue of such importance seemed to be not only churlish but also in breach of the overriding objective which illuminates all civil practice today".

In public law cases, a declaration on a point which, though moot, may have public interest benefits. In *R. v. Oxfordshire County Council, Exe p. Pittick* [1996] E.L.R. 153, Laws J. said (at p.157): "A decision to refuse [a remedy] as a matter of discretion on the footing that the claim is academic ought not in my view to be made without some appreciation of the force of those arguments. In a public law case, [a claimant] may have an important point to bring to the court's attention whose resolution might be required in the public interest, even if [the claimant] himself has suffered no perceptible prejudice as a result of the decision in question". See also *Levy v. The Environment Agency* [2002] EWHC 1663 (Admin), July 30, 2002, unrep., *per* Silber J. (at para.127).

See further s.31(2) (declarations in judicial review proceedings), Human Rights Act 1998, s.4 (declarations of incompatibility), and CPR, r.40.20 (Binding declarations) and commentary following that rule. For other authorities on question whether court should make a declaration on a question that it or has become academic, see The Supreme Court Practice 1999, Vol. 1, paras 15/16/2 and 15/16/3.

In *A. v. B. (A Company)* [2002] EWCA Civ 337; [2002] 2 All E.R. 545, CA, the Court of Appeal, having apparently come to the conclusion that the defendant's appeal should be allowed on the merits, but reserving judgment, declined to hear oral argument on another ground of appeal. That other ground was not related to the merits, but raised the procedural issue whether the judge acted properly in acceding to an application to re-consider his judgment. In the light of the court's conclusions on the merits that issue had become academic. Nevertheless, in its reserved judgment the court gave a decision on the procedural appeal, having been urged to do so by the parties on the bases that the points involved raised issues of principle and could be relevant on the question of costs.

In *Fawdry & Co v. Murfitt* [2002] EWCA Civ 643; [2003] Q.B. 104, CA, the Court of Appeal, having held that a case had been validly transferred from the Queen's Bench Division for trial in the Technology and Construction Court, gave an extended judgment on the question (though it had become academic) whether, had the transfer not been valid, the circuit judge would have had de facto authority at common law. The point was of jurisdictional significance and the Court had heard full argument, including submissions from counsel for the Lord Chancellor intervening.

LEGISLATION

In *Williams v. Devon County Council* [2003] EWCA Civ 365; [2003] CP Rep. 47, CA, a two-judge court of the Court of Appeal, having disposed an appeal in a personal injuries case on the ground that the trial judge erred in finding that the claimant was guilty of contributory negligence, gave an extended judgment on a point (though it had become academic) concerning the costs implications of Pt 36 payments where social security benefits were recoverable. The point was of practical significance and the Court had heard full argument, including submissions from the Secretary of State.

In *Ebert v. Official Receiver (No.2)* [2001] EWCA Civ 340, [2002] 1 W.L.R. 320, CA, the Court of Appeal gave a considered judgment on the question whether a High Court judge's refusal to grant a vexatious litigant leave to apply to the Court of Appeal for permission to appeal infringed his rights under art. 6 of the Convention even though the point was moot as the judge had in fact granted such leave.

As to appropriate order for costs where the subject-matter of proceedings becomes academic during the course of proceedings, leaving costs as the only issue, see Vol. 1, para. 44.3.5.1.

For authorities concerning the issue of justiciability in the Court of Appeal, see notes to CPR Pt 52, Vol. 1, para. 52.1.

Rent for foreign property

9A–69 See *St. Pierre v. S. American Stoves Ltd* [1936] 1 K.B. 382, CA.

ADMIRALTY JURISDICTION

9A–70 **20–24.** [*Sections 20–24 are set out with notes in Section 2A, paras 2A–140 to 2A–190.*]

OTHER PARTICULAR FIELDS OF JURISDICTION

Probate jurisdiction of High Court

9A–71 **25.** [*Section 25 is set out in Section 11A, para. 11A–2.*]

Matrimonial jurisdiction of High Court

9A–72 **26.** The High Court shall, in accordance with section 19(2), have all such jurisdiction in relation to matrimonial causes and matters as was immediately before the commencement of the Matrimonial Causes Act 1857 vested in or exercisable by any ecclesiastical court or person in England and Wales in respect of—

(a) divorce a mensa et thoro (renamed judicial separation by that Act);

(b) [...]

(c) any matrimonial cause or matter except marriage licences.

9A–73 *Note* —Derived from the JA 1925, s.21. Amended by the Family Law Act 1986, s.68, Sched.1, para. 25, and Sched.2.

Prize jurisdiction of High Court

9A–74 **27.** [*Section 27 is set out in Section 2A, para. 2D–210.*]

Appeals from Crown Court and inferior courts

9A–75 **28.**—(1) Subject to subsection (2), any order, judgment or other decision of the Crown Court may be questioned by any party to the proceedings, on the ground that it is wrong in law or is in excess of jurisdiction, by applying to the Crown Court to have a case stated by that court for the opinion of the High Court.

(2) Subsection (1) shall not apply to—

    (a) a judgment or other decision of the Crown Court relating to trial on indictment; or

    (b) any decision of that court under the Betting, Gaming and Lotteries Act 1963, or the Gaming Act 1968, or by the Local Government (Miscellaneous Provisions) Act 1982 which, by any provision of any of those Acts, is to be final.

(3) Subject to the provisions of this Act and to rules of court, the High Court shall, in accordance with section 19(2), have jurisdiction to hear and determine—

    (a) any application, or any appeal (whether by way of case stated or otherwise), which it has power to hear and determine under or by virtue of this or any other Act; and

    (b) all such other appeals as it had jurisdiction to hear and determine immediately before the commencement of this Act.

(4) In subsection (2)(a) the reference to a decision of the Crown Court relating to trial on indictment does not include a decision relating to an order under section 17 of the Access to Justice Act 1999.

Note—Derived from the JA 1925, s.24; and the Courts Act 1971, s.10. Amended by **9A–76** the Local Government (Miscellaneous Provisions) Act 1982, s.3, Sched.3, para. 27(6) and the Access to Justice Act 1999, s.24 and Sched.4, para. 22. Further amended by the Licensing Act 2003, s.99 and Sched.7.

"rules of court"—For the procedure, see CPR Pt 52.   **9A–77**

Proceedings on case stated by magistrates' court or Crown Court

28A.—(1) This section applies where a case is stated for the opinion **9A–78** of the High Court—

    (a) by a magistrates' court under section 111 of the Magistrates' Courts Act 1980; or

    (b) by the Crown Court under section 28(1) of this Act.

(2) The High Court may, if it thinks fit, cause the case to be sent back for amendment and, where it does so, the case shall be amended accordingly.

(3) The High Court shall hear and determine the question arising on the case (or the case as amended) and shall—

    (a) reverse, affirm or amend the determination in respect of which the case has been stated; or

    (b) remit the matter to the magistrates' court, or the Crown Court, with the opinion of the High Court,

and may make such other order in relation to the matter (including as to costs) as it thinks fit.

(4) Except as provided by the Administration of Justice Act 1960 (right of appeal to House of Lords in criminal cases), a decision of the High Court under this section is final."

Note—Added by the Statute Law (Repeals) Act 1993 and substituted by the Access **9A–79** to Justice Act 1999, s.61.

"decision of the High Court...is final"

9A–79.1   In *Westminster City Council v. O'Reilly* [2003] EWCA Civ 1007; [2004] 1 W.L.R. 195, CA, the Court of Appeal held that a decision of the High Court on an appeal by way of case stated is indeed a decision that is final, and therefore, whatever may have been the position under the statutory antecedents of s.28A, its effect (at least when read with s.18) is to provide that no appeal from such a decision lies to the Court of Appeal.

In *Farley v. Secretary of State for Work and Pensions (No. 2)* [2005] EWCA Civ 869; *The Times*, June 30, 2005, CA, this point was overlooked and the Court of Appeal entertained and allowed the defendant's appeal from the decision of a High Court judge on case stated. The claimants petitioned the House of Lords for leave to appeal. Subsequently, when the Court's lack of jurisdiction was drawn to the attention of the Court by the parties the Court exercised its exceptional jurisdiction to re-open the appeal and set aside the decision (see r.52.17). However, by adopting considerable procedural ingenuity, the Court was able to retrieve the position for the parties (both of whom were anxious to have the important point upon which the case turned authoritatively determined). The Court noted that, had the judge's decision been made on an application for judicial review, the Court would have had jurisdiction to entertain an appeal. Accordingly, the Court ruled that, on the defendant's undertaking to make an application to the Court for permission to apply for judicial review the Court (a) first sitting as a court of first instance, would dismiss the application, but (b) then sitting as an appellate court, would allow the defendant's appeal against that refusal (issuing a declaration in the terms of the Court's previous decision made without jurisdiction). The claimants could then pursue their petition for leave to appeal to the House of Lords. The Court was satisfied that it had jurisdiction to proceed in this manner but stressed that, in doing so, it was exercising a wholly exceptional jurisdiction. In any usual circumstances the procedure would amount to an abuse of process.

Mandatory, prohibiting and quashing orders

9A–80   **29.**—(1) The orders of mandamus, prohibition and certiorari shall be known instead as mandatory, prohibiting and quashing orders respectively.

(1A) The High Court shall have jurisdiction to make mandatory, prohibiting and quashing orders in those classes of case in which, immediately before 1st May 2004, it had jurisdiction to make orders of mandamus, prohibition and certiorari.

(2) Every such order shall be final, subject to any right of appeal therefrom.

(3) In relation to the jurisdiction of the Crown Court, other than its jurisdiction in matters relating to trial on indictment, the High Court shall have all such jurisdiction to make mandatory, prohibiting and quashing orders as the High Court possesses in relation to the jurisdiction of an inferior court.

(3A) The High Court shall have no jurisdiction to make mandatory, prohibiting and quashing orders in relation to jurisdiction of a court-martial in matters relating to—

(a) trial by court martial for an offence, or

(b) appeals from a Standing Civilian Court;

and in this subsection "court-martial" means a court martial under the Army Act 1955, the Air Force Act 1955 or the Naval Discipline Act 1957.

(4) The power of the High Court under any enactment to require justices of the peace or a judge or officer of a county court to do any act relating to the duties of their respective offices, or to require a

magistrates' court to state a case for the opinion of the High Court, in any case where the High Court formerly had by virtue of any enactment jurisdiction to make a rule absolute, or an order, for any of those purposes, shall be exercisable by mandatory order.

(5) In any statutory provision —

(a) references to mandamus or to a writ or order of mandamus shall be read as reference to a mandatory order;

(b) references to prohibition or to a writ or order of prohibition shall be read as reference to a prohibiting order;

(c) references to certiorari or to a writ or order of certiorari shall be read as reference to a quashing order; and

(d) references to the issue or award of a writ of mandamus, prohibition and certiorari shall be read as references to the making of the corresponding mandatory, prohibiting or quashing order.

(6) In subsection (3) the reference to Crown Court's jurisdiction in matters relating to trial on indictment does not include if jurisdiction relating to orders under section 17 of the Access to Justice Act 1999.

Note —Derived from the A.J. (M.P.) A. 1938, ss.7, 8; and the Courts Act 1971, s.10. **9A–81** Amended by the Access to Justice Act 1999, s.24 and Sched.4, para. 23. Amended by the Armed Forces Act 2001, (c.19), s.23. With effect from May 1, 2004, amended by the Civil Procedure (Modification of Supreme Court Act 1981) Order 2004 (S.I. 2004 No. 1033), so as to provide that orders of mandamus, prohibition and certiorari should be known instead as mandatory, prohibiting and quashing orders respectively.

Matters relating to trial on indictment

The Crown Court is a superior court. Nevertheless, the High Court may make **9A–81.1** orders of mandamus, prohibition or certiorari in relation to the jurisdiction of the Crown Court "other than its jurisdiction in matters relating to trial on indictment" (subs.(3)) (see also s.28(1)). This provision first appeared as s.10(5) of the Courts Act 1971 and was designed to ensure that such jurisdiction as the High Court had over the jurisdiction of the courts of quarter sessions (whether civil or criminal) absorbed by the Crown Court, when the latter superior court was created and the former inferior courts were abolished by the 1971 Act, was preserved. In the years since, the meaning of the phrase "relating to trial on indictment" has fallen for determination on a number of occasions and the provision has been extended beyond the circumstances for which it was originally intended. The many authorities were referred to, in argument if not in speeches, in *R. v. Director of Public Prosecutions, ex p. Kebilene* [1999] 3 W.L.R. 972, HL; see also *R. v. Maidstone Crown Court, ex p. Harrow LBC* [1999] 3 All E.R. 542; *The Times*, May 14, 1999, DC (whether order under Criminal Procedure (Insanity) Act 1964, s.5, a matter relating to trial on indictment); see also *R. v. Canterbury Crown Court, ex p. Regentford Ltd*, *The Times*, February 6, 2001, DC, and *R. v. Leicester Crown Court, ex p. Commissioners for Customs and Excise*, *The Times*, February 23, 2001, DC; *R. (Kenneally) v. Crown Court at Snaresbrook* [2002] EWHC 968 (Admin); [2002] 2 W.L.R. 1430; *R. (Sullivan) v. Maidstone Crown Court* [2002] EWHC 967 (Admin); [2002] 4 All E.R. 427, DC.

Injunctions to restrain persons from acting in offices in which they are not entitled to act

30.—(1) Where a person not entitled to do so acts in an office to **9A–82** which this section applies, the High Court may—

(a) grant an injunction restraining him from so acting; and

(b) if the case so requires, declare the office to be vacant.

(2) This section applies to any substantive office of a public nature and permanent character which is held under the Crown or which has been created by any statutory provision or royal charter.

9A–83   *Note* —Derived from the A.J. (M.P.) A. 1938, s.9, which had abolished informations in the nature of *quo warranto*.

Application for judicial review

9A–84   31.—(1) An application to the High Court for one or more of the following forms of relief, namely—

(a) a mandatory, prohibiting or quashing order,

(b) a declaration or injunction under subsection (2); or

(c) an injunction under section 30 restraining a person not entitled to do so from acting in an office to which that section applies,

shall be made in accordance with rules of court by a procedure to be known as an application for judicial review.

(2) A declaration may be made or an injunction granted under this subsection in any case where an application for judicial review, seeking that relief, has been made and the High Court considers that, having regard to—

(a) the nature of the matters in respect of which relief may be granted by mandatory, prohibiting and quashing orders;

(b) the nature of the persons and bodies against whom relief may be granted by such orders; and

(c) all the circumstances of the case,

it would be just and convenient for the declaration to be made or the injunction to be granted, as the case may be.

(3) No application for judicial review shall be made unless the leave of the High Court has been obtained in accordance with rules of court; and the court shall not grant leave to make such an application unless it considers that the applicant has a sufficient interest in the matter to which the application relates.

(4) On an application for judicial review the High Court may award to the applicant damages, restitution or the recovery of a sum due if—

(a) the application includes a claim for such an award arising from any matter to which the application relates; and

(b) the court is satisfied that such an award would have been made if the claim had been made in an action begun by the applicant at the time of making the application.

(5) If, on an application for judicial review seeking a quashing order, the High Court quashes the decision to which the application relates, the High Court may remit the matter to the court, tribunal or authority concerned, with a direction to reconsider it and reach a decision in accordance with the findings of the High Court.

(6) Where the High Court considers that there has been undue delay in making an application for judicial review, the court may refuse to grant—

(a) leave for the making of the application; or

(b) any relief sought on the application,

if it considers that the granting of the relief sought would be likely to cause substantial hardship to, or substantially prejudice the rights of, any person or would be detrimental to good administration.

(7) Subsection (6) is without prejudice to any enactment or rule of court which has the effect of limiting the time within which an application for judicial review may be made.

Note—For relevant rules of court, see CPR Pt 54 (Judicial Review); see Vol. 1, paras **9A–85** 54.0.1 *et seq.* With effect from May 1, 2004, subss (1), (2) and (5) amended, and subs.(4) substituted, by the Civil Procedure (Modification of Supreme Court Act 1981) Order 2004 (S.I. 2004 No. 1033), as a consequence of amendments to s.31, see para. 9A–81 above. Subsection (4) provided that, on an application for judicial review, in certain circumstances the High Court should have power to award damages. As substituted, the subs.(4) provides that the Court has, in addition to the power to award damages, power to award restitution or the recovery of a sum due.

POWERS

Orders for interim payment

32.—(1) As regards proceedings pending in the High Court, provi- **9A–86** sion may be made by rules of court for enabling the court, in such circumstances as may be prescribed, to make an order requiring a party to the proceedings to make an interim payment of such amount as may be specified in the order, with provision for the payment to be made to such other party to the proceedings as may be so specified or, if the order so provides, by paying it into court.

(2) Any rules of court which make provision in accordance with subsection (1) may include provision for enabling a party to any proceedings who, in pursuance of such an order, has made an interim payment to recover the whole or part of the amount of the payment in such circumstances, and from such other party to the proceedings, as may be determined in accordance with the rules.

(3) Any rules made by virtue of this section may include such incidental, supplementary and consequential provisions as the rule-making authority may consider necessary or expedient.

(4) Nothing in this section shall be construed as affecting the exercise of any power relating to costs, including any power to make rules of court relating to costs.

(5) In this section "interim payment", in relation to a party to any proceedings, means a payment on account of any damages, debt or other sum (excluding any costs) which that party may be held liable to pay to or for the benefit of another party to the proceedings if a final judgment or order of the court in the proceedings is given or made in favour of that other party.

Note—Derived from the AJA 1969, s.20. See also County Courts Act 1984, s.50. **9A–87**

Rules of court

Rules of court are found in CPR, rr.25.6 to 25.9, and note Practice Direction **9A–88** (Interim Payments) (see Vol. 1, para. 25BPD.1).

Exclusion of costs

Subs.(5) expressly excludes "costs" from the definition of "interim payment", so that **9A–89** rules of court cannot be made to authorise a payment on account of costs which one party had been held liable to pay another.

Orders for provisional damages for personal injuries

9A–90 **32A.**—(1) This section applies to an action for damages for personal injuries in which there is proved or admitted to be a chance that at some definite or indefinite time in the future the injured person will, as a result of the act or omission which gave rise to the cause of action, develop some serious disease or suffer some serious deterioration in his physical or mental condition.

(2) Subject to subsection (4) below, as regards any action for damages to which this section applies in which a judgment is given in the High Court, provision may be made by rules of court for enabling the court, in such circumstances as may be prescribed, to award the injured person—

> (a) damages assessed on the assumption that the injured person will not develop the disease or suffer the deterioration in his condition; and
>
> (b) further damages at a future date if he develops the disease or suffers the deterioration.

(3) Any rules made by virtue of this section may include such incidental, supplementary and consequential provisions as the rule-making authority may consider necessary or expedient.

(4) Nothing in this section shall be construed—

> (a) as affecting the exercise of any power relating to costs, including any power to make rules of court relating to costs; or
>
> (b) as prejudicing any duty of the court under any enactment or rule of law to reduce or limit the total damages which would have been recoverable apart from any such duty.

9A–91 *Note*—Added by the AJA 1982, s.6(1). Referred to in the Social Security (Recovery of Benefits) Act 1997, s.11(4), and in the Damages Act 1996, s.3. See also County Courts Act 1984, s.51 (para. 9A–579 below).

"rules of court"
9A–92 For rules of court under this section, see CPR Pt 41.

Powers of High Court exercisable before commencement of action

9A–93 **33.**—(1) On the application of any person in accordance with rules of court, the High Court shall, in such circumstances as may be specified in the rules, have power to make an order providing for any one or more of the following matters, that is to say—

> (a) the inspection, photographing, preservation, custody and detention of property which appears to the court to be property which may become the subject-matter of subsequent proceedings in the High Court, or as to which any question may arise in any such proceedings; and
>
> (b) the taking of samples of any such property as is men-

tioned in paragraph (a), and the carrying out of any experiment on or with any such property.

(2) On the application, in accordance with rules of court, of a person who appears to the High Court to be likely to be a party to subsequent proceedings in that court [...], the High Court shall, in such circumstances as may be specified in the rules, have power to order a person who appears to the court to be likely to be a party to the proceedings and to be likely to have or to have had in his possession, custody or power any documents which are relevant to an issue arising or likely to arise out of that claim—

(a) to disclose whether those documents are in his possession, custody or power; and

(b) to produce such of those documents as are in his possession, custody or power to the applicant or, on such conditions as may be specified in the order—

(i) to the applicant's legal advisers; or

(ii) to the applicant's legal advisers and any medical or other professional adviser of the applicant; or

(iii) if the applicant has no legal adviser, to any medical or other professional adviser of the applicant.

9A–94
Note —Derived from the AJA 1969, s.21(1); and the AJA 1970, s.31. Subsection (2) amended by Civil Procedure Act 1997, s.8 and the Civil Procedure (Modification of Enactments) Order 1998 (S.I. 1998 No. 2940), art.5(a). See also County Courts Act 1984, s.52.

"rules of court"
9A–95
For rules of court under this section, see CPR Pt 25 and commentary in Vol. 1, paras 25.1.26 and 25.1.27; CPR, rr.31.16 and 48.1. For provisions supplementing s.33, see s.35 below.

Powers exercisable before action commenced
9A–96
The powers referred to in subs.(1) and subs.(2) may be exercised by the High Court after proceedings have been commenced (*Arsenal Football Club Plc v. Elite Sports Distribution Ltd (No.1)*, [2002] EWHC 3057 (Mr Geoffrey Vos QC)). The significance of this section is that it provides that, in accordance with rules of court, application may be made to the Court for those powers to be exercised before proceedings have been commenced. Initially, subs.(2) was confined to proceedings in which a claim in respect of personal injuries to a person, or in respect of a person's death, was likely to be made. That restriction was removed by an amendment coming into effect on April 25, 1999. (For discussion of changed arrangements, see *Black v. Sumito Corporation* [2001] EWCA Civ 1819; [2002] 1 W.L.R. 1562, CA.) Subsection (2), in its amended form, binds the Crown. However, in its application to the Crown subs.(1) is limited to property which may be the subject-matter of proceedings involving a claim for personal injuries or death (see s.35(4), para. 9A–100 below).

Section 35 (below) contains provisions supplementary to this section.

Persons to whom documents to be produced
9A–97
Under subs.(2) the Court may order that relevant documents should be produced to the applicant. Alternatively, the Court may order, on such conditions as may be specified in the order, that they should be produced to the applicant's legal adviser and any medical or other professional adviser of the applicant. In the latter event, the Court may impose a condition that the contents of a document should not be disclosed by the legal, medical or other adviser to the applicant (see *Dunning v. United Liverpool Hospitals' Board of Governors* [1973] 1 W.L.R. 586; [1973] 2 All E.R. 454, CA; *cf. McIvor v. Southern Health and Social Services Board* [1978] 1 W.L.R. 757; [1978] 2 All E.R. 625, HL).

Power of High Court to order disclosure of documents, inspection of property etc. in proceedings for personal injuries or death

9A–98 **34.**—(1) [...]

(2) On the application, in accordance with rules of court, of a party to any proceedings [...], the High Court shall, in such circumstances as may be specified in the rules, have power to order a person who is not a party to the proceedings and who appears to the court to be likely to have in his possession, custody or power any documents which are relevant to an issue arising out of the said claim—

    (a) to disclose whether those documents are in his possession, custody or power; and

    (b) to produce such of those documents as are in his possession, custody or power to the applicant or, on such conditions as may be specified in the order—

        (i) to the applicant's legal advisers; or

        (ii) to the applicant's legal advisers and any medical or other professional adviser of the applicant; or

        (iii) if the applicant has no legal adviser, to any medical or other professional adviser of the applicant.

(3) On the application, in accordance with rules of court, of a party to any proceedings [...], the High Court shall, in such circumstances as may be specified in the rules, have power to make an order providing for any one or more of the following matters, that is to say—

    (a) the inspection, photographing, preservation, custody and detention of property which is not the property of, or in the possession of, any party to the proceedings but which is the subject-matter of the proceedings or as to which any question arises in the proceedings;

    (b) the taking of samples of any such property as is mentioned in paragraph (a) and the carrying out of any experiment on or with any such property.

(4) The preceding provisions of this section are without prejudice to the exercise by the High Court of any power to make orders which is exercisable apart from those provisions.

9A–99 *Note*—Derived from the AJA 1970, s.32. Subsection (1) omitted and subss. (2) and (3) amended by the Civil Procedure (Modification of Enactments) Order 1998 (S.I. 1998 No. 2940), art.5(b) made by the Lord Chancellor in exercised of powers conferred by Civil Procedure Act 1997, s.4. The section is referred to in CPR, rr.25.1, 25.5, 31.17, 48.1.

"rules of court"

9A–99.1 See CPR Pt 25 and commentary in Vol. 1, paras 25.1.28 and 25.1.29. For provision supplementing s.34, see s.35 below.

Provisions supplementary to ss.33 and 34

9A–100 **35.**—(1) The High Court shall not make an order under section 33 or 34 if it consider that compliance with the order, if made, would be likely to be injurious to the public interest.

(2) Rules of court may make provision as to the circumstances in

which an order under section 33 or 34 can be made; and any rules making such provision may include such incidental, supplementary and consequential provisions as the rule-making authority may consider necessary or expedient.

(3) Without prejudice to the generality of subsection (2), rules of court shall be made for the purpose of ensuring that the costs of and incidental to proceedings for an order under section 33(2) or 34 incurred by the person against whom the order is sought shall be awarded to that person unless the court otherwise directs.

(4) Sections 33(2) and 34 and this section bind the Crown; and section 33(1) binds the Crown so far as it relates to property as to which it appears to the court that it may become the subject-matter of subsequent proceedings involving a claim in respect of personal injuries to a person or in respect of a person's death.

In this subsection references to the Crown do not include references to Her Majesty in Her private capacity or to Her Majesty in right of Her Duchy of Lancaster or to the Duke of Cornwall.

(5) In sections 32A, 33 and 34 and this section—

> "property" includes any land, chattel or other corporeal property of any description;
>
> "personal injuries" includes any disease and any impairment of a person's physical or mental condition.

Note —Derived from the AJA 1969, s.21; and the AJA 1970, ss.32, 33, 35; amended **9A–101** by AJA 1982, s.6(2).

"rules of court"
See CPR Pt 25 and paras 9A–95 and 9A–99.1 above. **9A–102**

"personal injuries"
See further commentary on meaning of "claim for personal injuries" in CPR, **9A–102.1** r.2.3(1) (Vol. 1, para. 2.3.6).

Power of High Court to award interest on debts and damages

35A.—(1) Subject to rules of court, in proceedings (whenever **9A–103** instituted) before the High Court for the recovery of a debt or damages there may be included in any sum for which judgment is given simple interest, at such rate as the court thinks fit or as rules of court may provide, on all or any part of the debt or damages in respect of which judgment is given, or payment is made before judgment, for all or any part of the period between the date when the cause of action arose and—

(a) in the case of any sum paid before judgment, the date of the payment; and

(b) in the case of the sum for which judgment is given, the date of the judgment.

(2) In relation to a judgment given for damages for personal injuries or death which exceed £200 subsection (1) shall have effect—

(a) with the substitution of "shall be included" for "may be included"; and

(b) with the addition of "unless the court is satisfied that there are special reasons to the contrary" after "given," where first occurring.

(3) Subject to rules of court, where—

(a) there are proceedings (whenever instituted) before the High Court for the recovery of a debt; and

(b) the defendant pays the whole debt to the plaintiff (otherwise than in pursuance of a judgment in the proceedings),

the defendant shall be liable to pay the plaintiff simple interest at such rate as the court thinks fit or as rules of court may provide on all or any part of the debt for all or any part of the period between the date when the cause of action arose and the date of the payment.

(4) Interest in respect of a debt shall not be awarded under this section for a period during which, for whatever reason, interest on the debt already runs.

(5) Without prejudice to the generality of section 84, rules of court may provide for a rate of interest by reference to the rate specified in section 17 of the Judgments Act 1838 as that section has effect from time to time or by reference to a rate for which any other enactment provides.

(6) Interest under this section may be calculated at different rates in respect of different periods.

(7) In this section "plaintiff" means the person seeking the debt or damages and "defendant" means the person from whom the plaintiff seeks the debt or damages and "personal injuries" includes any disease and any impairment of a person's physical or mental condition.

(8) Nothing in this section affects the damages recoverable for the dishonour of a bill of exchange.

9A–104   *Note*—Inserted by the AJA 1982, s.15(1), Sched.1, Pt I.

Award of interest on debts and damages

9A–105   Section 35A together with s.69 of the County Courts Act 1984 superseded ss.3 and 22 of the L.R.(M.P.) A. 1934 and the words from "and section 22" onwards in s.34(3) of the AJA 1969, so far as the provisions of those sections apply to the High Court and county courts (see the AJA 1982, s.15(4)(5)). The result is that s.3 of the Act of 1934 (see para. 9B–442 below) remains in force so far as courts of record, other than the High Court and county courts are concerned, *e.g.* the Court of Appeal (Civil Division) when it gives a judgment on appeal for debt or damages.

Various important amendments to provisions in the RSC were made after s.35A came into force. Where necessary, these provisions were carried forward into the Civil Procedure Rules. Rules in the CPR relating to the award of interest include r.12.6 (Interest on default judgment), r.14.14 (Interest where admission), r.16.4 (Contents of particulars of claim), and r.40.8 (Time from which interest begins to run). For detailed notes on the award of interest, see Vol. 1, paras 7.0.8 to 7.0.22. As to (1) reducing the period for which interest is payable on an award, or (2) altering the rate at which interest is calculated, or both, as a procedural sanction, see Vol. 1, para. 3.1.6.

It has been held at first instance that CPR, r.36.21(2), which grants the court power to award interest on damages awarded to a claimant in case where he recovers more than he proposed in his Pt 36 offer, is not *ultra vires* the rule-making power and that "interest" within r.36.21 is not the same as "interest" within s.35A (*All-in-One Design & Build Ltd v. Motcomb Estates Ltd* (2000) 144 S.J.L.B. 219).

There are some significant points of difference between s.35A of the 1981 Act and s.3 of the 1934 Act. Under s.35A interest is to be included in any judgment for debt or damages whether or not the proceedings have been "tried" (as required by s.3). Thus, the court may award interest on default judgments, summary judgments and judgments given in admissions (see, generally, CPR Pts 12, 14 and 24). Section 35A provides for interest to be included in the judgment, not only in respect of the debt or damages for which judgment is given but also in respect of any sum paid before the judgment up to the date of payment (see subs.(1)) thereby negativing the effect of *The Medina Princess* [1962] 2 Lloyd's Rep. 17. Section 35A provides that the defendant will be liable to pay simple interest in respect of the debt paid in full after proceedings are instituted, at such rate as the Court thinks fit or rules of court provide on all or part of the debt for the whole or part of the period from the date the cause of action arose and up to the date of payment. Section 35A provides for rates of interest to be fixed by rules of court by reference to the rate specified in s.17 of the Judgments Act 1838 as that section has effect from time to time. Section 35A makes awards of interest under that section "subject to rules of court".

Other significant points in the provisions of s.35A which should be emphasised are as follows.

(a) The award of interest in actions for personal injuries is mandatory unless the Court is satisfied that there are special reasons to the contrary.

(b) Except in the case of claims for damages for personal injuries or death, the award of interest under s.35A as it is under s.3 of the Act of 1934 is in the discretion of the Court which may award interest at such rate as it thinks fit on all or any part of the debt or damages in respect of which judgment is given or payment is made before judgment for all or any part of the period between the date when the cause of action arose and the date of payment or the date of judgment whichever is the earlier (see s.35A(1) (6)). The interest may be awarded at different rates in respect of different periods (see s.35A(6)), but interest will not be awarded under s.35A for a period during which, for whatever reason, interest on the debt already runs, *e.g.* under a contract (see s.35A(4), *cf.* proviso (b) of s.3 of the Act of 1934).

(c) The award of interest under s.35A must be for "simple interest" which is perhaps similar to the prohibition contained in proviso (a) to s.3 of the Act of 1934 against "the giving of interest upon interest" (see *Bushwall Properties Ltd v. Vortex Properties Ltd* [1975] 1 W.L.R. 1659; [1975] 2 All E.R. 214).

(d) As in the case of s.3 of the Act of 1934 under proviso (c), s.35A does not affect the damages recoverable for the dishonour of a bill of exchange (see s.35A(8)).

As to calculation of section 35A interest and of judgment interest where (1) defendant making installment payments under interim payment order, and (2) before all installments paid, claimant granted unopposed final judgment for same sum, see *Kuwait Airways Corporation v. Kuwait Insurance Co*, April 19, 2000, unrep. (where held by Langley J. that judgment interest on s.35A interest should not be backdated). Where interest is entered under the Arbitration Act 1996, s.66 in terms of an arbitration award, the court has no power to grant interest under s.35A on the sum awarded but remaining unpaid after the award (*Walker v. Rowe* [2000] 1 Lloyd's Rep. 116, (Aikens J.)

Subpoena issued by High Court to run throughout United Kingdom

9A–106   **36.**—(1) If in any cause or matter in the High Court it appears to the court that it is proper to compel the personal attendance at any trial of a witness who may not be within the jurisdiction of the court, it shall be lawful for the court, if in the discretion of the court it seems fit so to do, to order that a writ of subpoena ad testificandum or writ of subpoena duces tecum shall issue in special form commanding the witness to attend the trial wherever he shall be within the United Kingdom; and the service of any such writ in any part of the United Kingdom shall be as valid and effectual for all purposes as if it had been served within the jurisdiction of the High Court.

(2) Every such writ shall have at its foot a statement to the effect that it is issued by the special order of the High Court, and no such writ shall issue without such a special order.

(3) If any person served with a writ issued under this section does not appear as required by the writ, the High Court, on proof to the satisfaction of the court of the service of the writ and of the default, may transmit a certificate of the default under the seal of the court or under the hand of a judge of the court—

    (a) if the service was in Scotland, to the Court of Session at Edinburgh; or

    (b) if the service was in Northern Ireland, to the High Court of Justice in Northern Ireland at Belfast;

and the court to which the certificate is sent shall thereupon proceed against and punish the person in default in like manner as if that person had neglected or refused to appear in obedience to process issued out of that court.

(4) No court shall in any case proceed against or punish any person for having made such default as aforesaid unless it is shown to the court that a reasonable and sufficient sum of money to defray—

    (a) the expenses of coming and attending to give evidence and of returning from giving evidence; and

    (b) any other reasonable expenses which he has asked to be defrayed in connection with his evidence,

was tendered to him at the time when the writ was served upon him.

(5) Nothing in this section shall affect—

    (a) the power of the High Court to issue a commission for the examination of witnesses out of the jurisdiction of the court in any case in which, notwithstanding this section, the court thinks fit to issue such a commission; or

    (b) the admissibility at any trial of any evidence which, if this section had not been enacted, would have been admissible on the ground of a witness being outside the jurisdiction of the court.

(6) In this section references to attendance at a trial include references to attendance before an examiner or commissioner appointed by the High Court in any cause or matter in that court, including an examiner or commissioner appointed to take evidence outside the jurisdiction of the court.

9A–107   *Note* —Derived from the JA 1925, s.49, which replaced the Attendance of Witnesses Act 1854 as amended by the JA 1884, s.16; and the Arbitration Act 1889, s.18 as regards references by oath.

    Subsection (4) amended by the Courts and Legal Services Act 1990, Sched.17. Subsection (6) is derived from s.4 of the Evidence (Proceedings in Other Jurisdictions) Act 1975.

Channel Islands and the Isle of Man

9A–108   The Interpretation Act 1978, s.5, Sched.1 provides that in every Act the expression "British Islands" shall mean the United Kingdom, the Channel Islands, and the Isle of Man. By inference, these islands are not part of the United Kingdom. A High Court subpoena cannot be issued in the Islands as they are outside the jurisdiction. The Court has power under this section to give leave to issue a subpoena to Scotland or Northern Ireland, but it has no power to give such leave in respect of the Channel Islands or the Isle of Man. As to the Isle of Man, see also *Davison v. Farmer* (1851) 6 Exch. 242; *Re Brown* (1864) 33 L.J.Q.B. 193.

Powers of High Court with respect to injunctions and receivers

37.—(1) The High Court may by order (whether interlocutory or **9A–109** final) grant an injunction or appoint a receiver in all cases in which it appears to the court to be just and convenient to do so.

(2) Any such order may be made either unconditionally or on such terms and conditions as the court thinks just.

(3) The power of the High Court under subsection (1) to grant an interlocutory injunction restraining a party to any proceedings from removing from the jurisdiction of the High Court, or otherwise dealing with, assets located within that jurisdiction shall be exercisable in cases where that party is, as well as in cases where he is not, domiciled, resident or present within that jurisdiction.

(4) The power of the High Court to appoint a receiver by way of equitable execution shall operate in relation to all legal estate and interests in land, and that power—

(a) may be exercised in relation to an estate or interest in land whether or not a charge has been imposed on that land under section 1 of the Charging Orders Act 1979 for the purpose of enforcing the judgment, order or award in question; and

(b) shall be in addition to, and not in derogation of, any power of any court to appoint a receiver in proceedings for enforcing such a charge.

(5) Where an order under the said section 1 imposing a charge for the purpose of enforcing a judgment, order or award has been, or has effect as if, registered under section 6 of the Land Charges Act 1972, subsection (4) of the said section 6 (effect of non-registration of writs and orders registrable under that section) shall not apply to an order appointing a receiver made either—

(a) in proceedings for enforcing the charge; or

(b) by way of equitable execution of the judgment, order or award or, as the case may be, of so much of it as requires payment of moneys secured by the charge.

Note —Derived from the JA 1925, s.45; and the AJA 1956, s.36. Amended by the **9A–110** Charging Orders Act 1979, s.7.

Effect of this section

This section restates the law and practice governing the power of the Court with re- **9A–111** spect to injunctions and receivers. The section does not, in terms, fetter the court's power in any way (*Motorola Credit Corporation v. Uzan (No. 2)* [2003] EWCA Civ 752; [2004] 1 W.L.R. 113, CA), and neither does Civil Jurisdiction and Judgments Act 1982, s.25 (interim relief in absence of substantive proceedings) (*ibid*). Section 37(3) makes it clear (if it was a matter for doubt) that a Mareva injunction, described in the CPR as a "freezing" injunction (see CPR, r.25.1(1)), may be granted against a party domiciled, resident or present within the jurisdiction. The phrase "or otherwise dealing with" in s.37(3) confirms that a freezing injunction may be granted where there is a danger that assets of the defendant or judgment debtor within the jurisdiction may be dissipated by disposal sale or charge or otherwise "salted away" or placed out of the reach of the plaintiff or judgment creditor (see *Z Ltd v. A-Z and AA-LL* [1982] Q.B. 558; [1982] 1 All E.R. 796, CA; *C.B.S. United Kingdom v. Lambert* [1983] Ch. 37; [1982] 3 All E.R. 237, CA).

Application for injunctions

See CPR, r.25.1 and commentary thereto. The words in brackets in s.37(1) "whether **9A–112** interlocutory or final" are thought to be mere words of description of the practice prevailing before the passing of the Act and are not apt to create a new or extended jurisdiction to grant an injunction. It should, however, be explained that the power to grant an injunction may be exercised not only before judgment but also after judgment in order to assist the process of the enforcement of the judgment. This is specially important in relation to a freezing injunction (see *Stewart-Chartering Ltd v. C. & O. Managements SA* [1982] 1 W.L.R. 460; [1980] 1 All E.R. 718; *Faith Panton Property Plan v. Hodgetts* [1981] 1 W.L.R. 927; [1981] 2 All E.R. 877, CA). The words "whether interlocutory or final" do not have the effect of removing or diminishing this power.

The Human Rights Act 1998, s.3 and Art.6 of the ECHR do not require that insofar as section 37 confers jurisdiction to grant an anti-suit injunction it should be read more narrowly than heretofore (*O.T. Africa Line Ltd v. Hijazy (The Kribi)*, [2001] 1 Lloyd's Rep. 76, Aikens J.). The 1998 Act requires that a marginally higher threshold test than that which applied previously should apply in all applications for interlocutory injunctions likely to affect freedom of expression (*Imutran Ltd v. Uncaged Campaigns Ltd* [2001] 2 All E.R. 385, Sir Andrew Morritt V.-C.).

[THE NEXT PARAGRAPH IS 9A–114.]

Appointment of receiver

9A–114   See CPR Sched.1, RSC O.30 (Receivers); and RSC O.51 (Receivers; equitable execution).

Relief against forfeiture for non-payment of rent

9A–115   **38.**—(1) In any action in the High Court for the forfeiture of a lease for non-payment of rent, the court shall have power to grant relief against forfeiture in a summary manner, and may do so subject to the same terms and conditions as to the payment of rent, costs or otherwise as could have been imposed by it in such an action immediately before the commencement of this Act.

(2) Where the lessee or a person deriving title under him is granted relief under this section, he shall hold the demised premises in accordance with the terms of the lease without the necessity for a new lease.

9A–116   *Note* —See 3A–301.

Relief against forfeiture for non-payment of rent

9A–117   See 3A–301.

Execution of instrument by person nominated by High Court

9A–118   **39.**—(1) Where the High Court has given or made a judgment or order directing a person to execute any conveyance, contract or other document, or to indorse any negotiable instrument, then, if that person—

(a) neglects or refuses to comply with the judgment or order; or

(b) cannot after reasonable inquiry be found,

the High Court may, on such terms and conditions, if any, as may be just, order that the conveyance, contract or other document shall be executed, or that the negotiable instrument shall be indorsed, by such person as the court may nominate for that purpose.

(2) A conveyance, contract, document or instrument executed or indorsed in pursuance of an order under this section shall operate, and be for all purposes available, as if it had been executed or indorsed by the person originally directed to execute or indorse it.

Note —Derived from the JA 1925, s.47, replacing the JA 1884, s.14.   **9A–119**

Powers of the Court

An order under this section should not be made in anticipation of a failure to exe-   **9A–120**
cute unless the defendant has already shown by his conduct that he refuses and will
refuse to execute (*Savage v. Norton* [1908] 1 Ch. 290).

Once an order has been made under this section the document executed by the appointed person has the same effect as if it had been executed by the person originally
directed to execute it (see subs.(2), and *Savage v. Norton* [1908] 1 Ch. 290).

There is no limitation on the class of document in relation to which the powers accorded by this section might be invoked nor on the purpose for which a document executed in accordance with those powers might be used, and accordingly the Court has
jurisdiction to order a party to execute an essential document by a specified time on a
specified date, failing which to order a Master of the Queen's Bench Division to sign
such document even though the execution of such document would be to fulfil the
requirement of a contract other than the parties immediately before the Court (*Astro
Exito Navegacion SA v. Soutland Enterprise Co Ltd (No. 2)* [1983] 2 A.C. 787; [1983] 2 All
E.R. 725, HL).

The section applies where an order has been made for payment of costs to compel
obedience (*Re Cathcart* [1893] 1 Ch. 466; and see *Re Lumley* [1893] W.N. 13).

Where a wife was granted a writ of sequestration over the matrimonial home and
the court had ordered the husband to transfer the title to the sequestrators, the court
had the power under s.39(1) to order that, if such transfer was refused, the necessary
conveyance be executed (*Mir v. Mir* [1992] Fam. 79; [1992] 2 W.L.R. 225; [1992] 1 All
E.R. 765).

Person nominated by the Court

Cases have arisen in which masters and district judges have been nominated by the   **9A–121**
court to execute instruments (see *Re Edwards* (1885) 33 W.R. 578) or in the Family
Division the District Judge of the Principal Registry (*Howarth v. Howarth* (1886) 11 P.D.
68) and in which court officers have been nominated in vacations (see *Hoare v. Gray*
(1887) 31 S.J. 744). In protection cases the Official Solicitor has been appointed (*Re
Cathcart* [1893] 1 Ch. 466). In *Hood-Barrs v. Cathcart* (1895) 39 S.J. 639, the Bank of
England was ordered to execute, the Bank being given leave to move to discharge the
order.

Practice

Application is normally made by application notice. The Court has made an order   **9A–122**
under the section on an application for attachment for refusal to execute pursuant to
an order to do so.

For form of order, see *Savage v. Norton* [1908] 1 Ch. 290, at 301.

Alternative procedure

Before applying for an order under this section, consideration should be given to   **9A–123**
the advantages of an application for a vesting order (see *Jones v. Davies* [1940] W.N.
174) or for an order appointing a person to convey pursuant to the TA 1925, s.50, or
the AEA 1925, s.43(2), which give to a third person the protection of the TA 1925,
s.66.

Attachment of debts

40.—(1) Subject to any order for the time being in force under   **9A–124**
subsection (4), this section applies to any deposit account, and any
withdrawable share account, with a deposit-taker.

(2) In determining whether, for the purposes of the jurisdiction
of the High Court to attach debts for the purpose of satisfying judgments or orders for the payment of money, a sum standing to the
credit of a person in an account to which this section applies is a sum
due or accruing to that person and, as such, attachable in accordance
with rules of court, any condition mentioned in subsection (3) which
applies to the account shall be disregarded.

    (3) Those conditions are—
- (a) any condition that notice is required for any money or share is withdrawn;
- (b) any condition that a personal application must be made before any money or share is withdrawn;
- (c) any condition that a deposit book or share-account book must be produced before any money or share is withdrawn; or
- (d) any other prescribed condition.

    (4) The Lord Chancellor may by order make such provision as he thinks fit, by way of amendment of this section or otherwise, for all or any of the following purposes, namely—
- (a) including in, or excluding from, the accounts to which this section applies accounts of any description specified in the order;
- (b) excluding from the accounts to which this section applies all accounts with any particular deposit-taker so specified or with any deposit-taker of a description so specified.

    (5) Any order under subsection (4) shall be made by statutory instrument subject to annulment in pursuance of a resolution of either House of Parliament.

    (6) "Deposit-taker" means a person who may, in the course of his business, lawfully accept deposits in the United Kingdom.

    (7) Subsection (6) must be read with—
- (a) section 22 of the Financial Services and Markets Act 2000;
- (b) any relevant order under that section; and
- (c) Schedule 2 to that Act.

9A–125   *Note* —Derived from the AJA 1956, s.38. Amended by the Banking Act 1987, s.108(1), Sched.6. Subsections (1), (4)(b) and (6) were amended by, subs.(7) added by, the Financial Services and Markets Act 2000 (Consequential Amendments and Repeals) Order 2001 (S.I. 2001 No. 3649) art.290. As to garnishee proceedings, see CPR Sched.1, RSC O.49.

[THE NEXT PARAGRAPH IS 9A–127.]

Administrative and clerical expenses of garnishees

9A–127   **40A.**—(1) Where an interim third party debt order made in the exercise of the jurisdiction mentioned in subsection (2) of the preceding section is served on a deposit-taker, it may, subject to the provisions of this section, deduct from the relevant debt or debts an amount not exceeding the prescribed sum towards its administrative and clerical expenses in complying with the order; and the right to make a deduction under this subsection shall be exercisable as from the time the interim third party debt order is served on it.

    (1A) In subsection (1) "the relevant debt or debts," in relation to an interim third party debt order served on a deposit taker, means the amount, as at the time the order is served on it, of the debt or debts of which the whole or a part is expressed to be attached by the order.

(1B) A deduction may be made under subsection (1) in a case where the amount referred to in subsection (1A) is insufficient to cover both the amount of the deduction and the amount of the judgment debt and costs in respect of which the attachment was made, notwithstanding that the benefit of the attachment to the creditor is reduced as a result of the deduction.

(2) An amount may not in pursuance of subsection (1) be deducted or, as the case may be, retained in a case where, by virtue of section 346 of the Insolvency Act 1986 or section 183 of the Insolvency Act 1986 or otherwise, the creditor is not entitled to retain the benefit of the attachment.

(3) In this section—

"deposit-taker" has the meaning assigned to it by section 40(6); and

"prescribed" means prescribed by an order made by the Lord Chancellor.

(4) An order under this section—

    (a) may make different provision for different cases;

    (b) without prejudice to the generality of paragraph (a) of this subsection, may prescribe sums differing according to the amount due under the judgment or order to be satisfied.

    (c) may provide for this section not to apply to deposit-takers of any prescribed description.

(5) Any such order shall be made by statutory instrument subject to annulment in pursuance of a resolution of either House of Parliament.

9A–128

Note —Added by the AJA 1982, s.55, Sched. 4, Pt 1. Amended by the Companies Consolidation (Consequential Provisions) Act 1985, s.32, Sched.2; the Insolvency Act 1985, s.235, Sched.8, para. 35; the Insolvency Act 1986, s.439(2), Sched.14. The AJA 1985, s.52, replaced subs.(1) and added sub-ss.(1A) and (1B). Subsections (1), (1A), (3) and (4)(c) were amended by the Financial Services and Markets Act 2000 (Consequential Amendments and Repeals) Order 2001 (S.I. 2001 No. 3649), art.291. Referred to in the Attachment of Debts (Expenses) Order 1996 (S.I. 1996 No. 3098), art.2. In subss.(1) and (1A), with effect from March 23, 2002, "interim third party debt order" was substituted for "order nisi" by the Civil Procedure (Modification of Enactments) Order 2002 (S.I. 2002 No. 439); see further CPR Pt 72 (Third Party Debt Orders).

Wards of court

9A–129

41.—(1) Subject to the provisions of this section, no minor shall be made a ward of court except by virtue of an order to that effect made by the High Court.

(2) Where an application is made for such an order in respect of a minor, the minor shall become a ward of court on the making of the application, but shall cease to be a ward of court at the end of such period as may be prescribed unless within that period an order has been made in accordance with the application.

(2A) Subsection (2) does not apply with respect to a child who is the subject of a care order (as defined by section 105 of the Children Act 1989).

(3) The High Court may, either upon an application in that behalf

or without such an application, order that any minor who is for the time being a ward of court shall cease to be a ward of court.

9A–130   *Note* —Derived from the LR (M.P.) A 1949, s.9. Amended by the Children Act 1989, Sched.13.

[THE NEXT PARAGRAPH IS 9A–132.]

Restriction of vexatious legal proceedings

9A–132   *42.*—(1) If, on an application made by the Attorney General under this section, the High Court is satisfied that any person has habitually and persistently and without any reasonable ground—

    (a) instituted vexatious civil proceedings, whether in the High Court or any inferior court, and whether against the same person or against different persons; or

    (b) made vexatious applications in any civil proceedings, whether in the High Court or any inferior court, and whether instituted by him or another; or

    (c) instituted vexatious prosecutions (whether against the same person or different persons),

the court may, after hearing that person or giving him an opportunity of being heard, make a civil proceedings order, a criminal proceedings order or an all proceedings order.

(1A) In this section—

"civil proceedings order" means an order that—

    (a) no civil proceedings shall without the leave of the High Court be instituted in any court by the person against whom the order is made;

    (b) any civil proceedings instituted by him in any court before the making of the order shall not be continued by him without the leave of the High Court; and

    (c) no application (other than one for leave under this section) shall be made by him, in any civil proceedings instituted in any court by any person, without the leave of the High Court;

"criminal proceedings order" means an order that—

    (a) no information shall be laid before a justice of the peace by the person against whom the order is made without the leave of the High Court; and

    (b) no application for leave to prefer a bill of indictment shall be made by him without the leave of the High Court; and

"all proceedings order" means an order which has the combined effect of the two other orders.

(2) An order under subsection (1) may provide that it is to cease to have effect at the end of a specified period, but shall otherwise remain in force indefinitely.

(3) Leave for the institution or continuance of, or for the making of an application in, any Civil proceedings by a person who is the subject of an order for the time being in force under subsection (1)

shall not be given unless the High Court is satisfied that the proceedings or application are not an abuse of the process of the court in question and that there are reasonable grounds for the proceedings or application.

(3A) Leave for the laying of an information or for an application for leave to prefer a bill of indictment by a person who is the subject of an order for the time being in force under subsection (1) shall not be given unless the High Court is satisfied that the institution of the prosecution is not an abuse of the criminal process and that there are reasonable grounds for the institution of the prosecution by the applicant.

(4) No appeal shall lie from a decision of the High Court refusing leave required by virtue of this section.

(5) A copy of any order made under subsection (1) shall be published in the London Gazette.

Note—Amended by the Prosecution of Offences Act 1985, s.24. Derived from the JA **9A–133** 1925, s.51, as amended by the J(A)A 1959 s.1, replacing the Vexatious Actions Act 1896. The power to make a civil proceedings order under s.42 should be distinguished from the court's power under its inherent jurisdiction to make civil restraint orders as provided for in CPR r. 3.11 and elsewhere (see Vol. 1 para. 3.11.1). Exceptional circumstances may arise where the court is persuaded that neither a civil proceedings order nor a civil restraint order, or both types of order in combination, is sufficient to restrain an erstwhile litigant, and in the exercise of its inherent jurisdiction, the court may impose additional restraints by injunction (*e.g. Attorney General v. Ebert*, [2005] EWHC 1254 (Admin), May 24, 2005, unrep. (injunction restraining party from making any application at all under s. 42 in relation to particular proceedings, and from corresponding with any judge or officer of the Court service in an insulting or abusive manner)).

Applications for order

CPR Sched.1, O.94, r.15(I) states that every application to the High Court by the **9A–134** Attorney General under s.42 shall be heard and determined by a Divisional Court. For practice and procedure, see CPR Sched.1, O.94, r.15 and commentary thereon (Vol. 1, paras sc94.15 *et seq.*). For further guidance, see *Vexatious Litigants: A Guide* (Court Service Civil and Family Support Group, April 2002). A civil proceedings order should be distinguished from a civil restraint order. For power of court to make civil restraint orders, see CPR r.3.11.

Applications for leave

Applications for leave by persons subject to an order are made to a judge. Such an **9A–135** application may not be dealt with by a Master or a district judge (Practice Direction (Allocation of Cases to Level of Judiciary), para. 3.1(f), see Vol. 1, para. 2BPD.3). There is no appeal from a refusal of leave (subs.(4)). A High Court judge is not inhibited in any way by the provisions of the Convention or the Human Rights Act 1998 in his decision as to whether to grant leave (*Ebert v. Official Receiver* [2001] EWCA Civ 340; [2002] 1 W.L.R. 320, CA).

No appeal from decision refusing leave

The restriction on appeal in s.42(4) does not infringe Convention rights or any pro- **9A–135A** vision of the Human Rights Act 1998 (*Ebert v. Official Receiver* [2001] EWCA Civ 340; [2002] 1 W.L.R. 320, CA). In the circumstances where a judge (1) gives a person subject to a civil proceedings order leave to make an application, but (2) refuses that substantive application, and (3) also refuses that person's application to him for permission to appeal to the Court of Appeal, then (3) by virtue of s.42(4) there is no appeal against that decision (*ibid*).

Power of High Court to vary sentence on application for quashing order

43.—(1) Where a person has been sentenced for an offence— **9A–136**

LEGISLATION

    (a) by a magistrates' court; or

    (b) by the Crown Court after being convicted of the offence by a magistrates' court and committed to the Crown Court for sentence; or

    (c) by the Crown Court on appeal against conviction or sentence,

applies to the High Court in accordance with section 31 for a quashing order to remove the proceedings of the magistrates' court or the Crown Court into the High Court, then, if the High Court determines that the magistrates' court or the Crown Court had no power to pass the sentence, the High Court may, instead of quashing the conviction, amend it by substituting for the sentence passed any sentence which the magistrates' court or, in a case within paragraph (b), the Crown Court, has power to impose.

(2) Any sentence passed by the High Court by virtue of this section in substitution for the sentence passed in the proceedings of the magistrates' court or the Crown Court shall, unless the High Court otherwise directs, begin to run from the time when it would have begun to run if passed in those proceedings; but in computing the term of the sentence, any time during which the offender was released on bail in pursuance of section 37(1)(d) of the Criminal Justice Act 1948 shall be disregarded.

(3) Subsections (1) and (2) shall, with the necessary modifications, apply in relation to any order of a magistrates' court or the Crown Court which is made on, but does not form part of, the conviction of an offender as they apply in relation to a conviction and sentence.

9A–137   *Note* —Derived from the AJA 1960, s.16. Amended by the Courts Act 1971, Sched.8, para. 40; and the Bail Act 1976, Sched.2. With effect from May 1, 2004, amended by the Civil Procedure (Modification of Supreme Court Act 1981) Order 2004 (S.I. 2004 No. 1033), as a consequence of amendments to s.31, see para. 9A–81 above.

Effect of this section

9A–138   This section extends the powers of the High Court when an application for an order of certiorari is made in an application for judicial review under CPR Pt 54 (Judicial Review) to remove proceedings from a magistrates' court or the Crown Court on the ground that Court has no power to pass the sentence it imposed. In such case, the High Court is empowered, instead of quashing the conviction, to amend by substituting for the sentence passed any sentence which the magistrates' court or the Crown Court, as the case may be, has power to impose.

Power of High Court to vary committal in default

9A–139   **43ZA.**—(1) Where the High Court quashes the committal of a person to prison or detention by a magistrates' court or the Crown Court for—

    (a) a default in paying a sum adjudged to be paid by a conviction; or

    (b) want of sufficient distress to satisfy such a sum,

the High Court may deal with the person for the default or want of sufficient distress in any way in which the magistrates' court or Crown Court would have power to deal with him if it were dealing with him at the time when the committal is quashed.

(2) If the High Court commits him to prison or detention, the

period of imprisonment or detention shall, unless the High Court otherwise directs, be treated as having begun when the person was committed by the magistrates' court or the Crown Court (except that any time during which he was released on bail shall not be counted as part of the period).

Note —This section was inserted after s.43 by the Access to Justice Act 1999, s.62. **9A–140**
The section extends the powers of the High Court in the circumstances referred to in the section in a manner which avoids the necessity of proceedings being remitted to the Crown Court or a magistrates' court.

Specific powers of arbitrator exercisable by High Court

43A. In any cause or matter proceeding in the High Court in con- **9A–141** nection with any contract incorporating an arbitration agreement which confers specific powers upon the arbitrator, the High Court may, if all parties to the agreement agree, exercise any such powers.

Note —Added by the Courts and Legal Services Act 1990, s.100. **9A–142**
The addition of s.43A restores the law to the position existing before the decision of the Court of Appeal in *Northern Regional Health Authority v. Crouch (Derek) Construction Co* [1984] 1 Q.B. 644, CA, in so far as that case decided that the powers referred to in the new section were only exercisable under the contract by the arbitrator.

OTHER PROVISIONS

Extraordinary functions of judges of High Court

44.—(1) Subject to the provisions of this Act, every judge of the **9A–143** High Court shall be—

    (a) liable to perform any duty not incident to the administration of justice in any court of law which a judge of the High Court was, as the successor of any judge formerly subject to that duty, liable to perform immediately before the commencement of this Act by virtue of any statute, law or custom; and

    (b) empowered to exercise any authority or power not so incident which a judge of the High Court was, as the successor of any judge formerly possessing that authority of power, empowered to exercise immediately before that commencement by virtue of any statute, law or custom.

(2) Any such duty, authority or power which immediately before the commencement of this Act was imposed or conferred by any statute, law or custom on the Lord Chancellor, the Lord Chief Justice or the Master of the Rolls shall continue to be performed and exercised by them respectively.

Note —Derived from the JA 1925, s.34. **9A–144**

THE CROWN COURT

General jurisdiction of Crown Court

45.—(1) The Crown Court shall be a superior court of record. **9A–145**

(2) Subject to the provisions of this Act, there shall be exercisable by the Crown Court—

    (a) all such appellate and other jurisdiction as is conferred on it by or under this or any other Act; and

    (b) all such other jurisdiction as was exercisable by it immediately before the commencement of this Act.

(3) Without prejudice to subsection (2), the jurisdiction of the Crown Court shall include all such powers and duties as were exercisable or fell to be performed by it immediately before the commencement of this Act.

(4) Subject to section 8 of the Criminal Procedure (Attendance of Witnesses) Act 1965 (substitution in criminal cases of procedure in that Act for procedure by way of subpoena) and to any provision contained in or having effect under this Act, the Crown Court shall, in relation to the attendance and examination of witnesses, any contempt of court, the enforcement of its orders and all other matters incidental to its jurisdiction, have the like powers, rights, privileges and authority as the High Court.

(5) The specific mention elsewhere in this Act of any jurisdiction covered by subsections (2) and (3) shall not derogate from the generality of those subsections.

Exclusive jurisdiction of Crown Court in trial on indictment

9A–146   **46.**—(1) All proceedings on indictment shall be brought before the Crown Court.

(2) The jurisdiction of the Crown Court with respect to proceedings on indictment shall include jurisdiction in proceedings on indictment for offences wherever committed, and in particular proceedings on indictment for offences within the jurisdiction of the Admiralty of England.

Offences committed on ships and abroad

9A–147   **46A.**—(1) Sections 280, 281 and 282 of the Merchant Shipping Act 1995 (offences on ships and abroad by British citizens and others) apply in relation to other offences under the law of England and Wales as they apply in relation to offences under that Act or instruments under that Act.

9A–148   *Note* —Added by the Merchant Shipping Act 1995, Sched.13, para. 59.

Sentences and other orders of Crown Court when dealing with offenders

9A–149   **47.** [*Repealed by the Powers of Criminal Courts (Sentencing) Act 2000, s.165, Sched.9, para. 87 and Sched.12, Pt 1.*]

[THE NEXT PARAGRAPH IS 9A–151.]

Appeals to Crown Court

9A–151   **48.**—(1) The Crown Court may, in the course of hearing any appeal, correct any error or mistake in the order or judgment incorporating the decision which is the subject of the appeal.

(2) On the termination of the hearing of an appeal the Crown Court—

(a) may confirm, reverse or vary any part of the decision appealed against, including a determination not to impose a separate penalty in respect of an offence; or

(b) may remit the matter with its opinion thereon to the authority whose decision is appealed against; or

(c) may make such other order in the matter as the court thinks just, and by such order exercise any power which the said authority might have exercised.

(3) Subsection (2) has effect subject to any enactment relating to any such appeal which expressly limits or restricts the powers of the court on the appeal.

(4) Subject to section 11(6) of the Criminal Appeal Act 1995, if the appeal is against a conviction or a sentence, the preceding provisions of this section shall be construed as including power to award any punishment, whether more or less severe than that awarded by the magistrates' court whose decision is appealed against, if that is a punishment which that magistrates' court might have awarded.

(5) This section applies whether or not the appeal is against the whole of the decision.

(6) In this section "sentence" includes any order made by a court when dealing with an offender, including—

(a) a hospital order under Part III of the Mental Health Act 1983, with or without a restriction order, and an interim hospital order under that Act; and

(b) a recommendation for deportation made when dealing with an offender.

(7) The fact that an appeal is pending against an interim hospital order under the said Act of 1983 shall not affect the power of the magistrates' court that made it to renew or terminate the order or to deal with the appellant on its termination; and where the Crown Court quashes such an order but does not pass any sentence or make any other order in its place the Court may direct the appellant to be kept in custody or released on bail pending his being dealt with by that magistrates' court.

(8) Where the Crown Court makes an interim hospital order by virtue of subsection (2)—

(a) the power of renewing or terminating the order and of dealing with the appellant on its termination shall be exercisable by the magistrates' court whose decision is appealed against and not by the Crown Court; and

(b) that magistrates' court shall be treated for the purposes of section 38(7) of the said Act of 1983 (absconding offenders) as the court that made the order.

Note —Derived from the Courts Act 1971, s.9. Amended by the Mental Health **9A–152** (Amendment) Act 1982, Sched.3; and the Mental Health Act 1983, Sched.4. The section deals with two matters relating to the appeal jurisdiction of the Crown Court. First, there are the powers of the Court to amend defective orders and judgments referred to in subs.(1). This provision may be traced to the Quarter Sessions Act 1849, s.7. Secondly, there are the powers of the Court at the termination of an appeal referred to in subs.(2). This provision may be traced to the Summary Jurisdiction Act

1879, s.31(1)(vii). For fuller explanation, see Sweet & Maxwell's *Current Law Statutes Annotated* 1971.

GENERAL PROVISIONS

LAW AND EQUITY

Concurrent administration of law and equity

9A–153   **49.**—(1) Subject to the provisions of this or any other Act every court exercising jurisdiction in England and Wales in any civil cause or matter shall continue to administer law and equity on the basis that, wherever there is any conflict or variance between the rules of equity and the rules of the common law with reference to the same matter, the rules of equity shall prevail.

(2) Every court shall give the same effect as hitherto—

(a) to all equitable estates, titles, rights, reliefs, defences and counterclaims, and to all equitable duties and liabilities; and

(b) subject thereto, to all legal claims and demands and all estates, titles, rights, duties, obligations and liabilities existing by the common law or by any custom or created by any statute,

and, subject to the provisions of this or any other Act, shall so exercise its jurisdiction in every cause or matter before it as to secure that, as far as possible, all matters in dispute between the parties are completely and finally determined, and all multiplicity of legal proceedings with respect to any of those matters is avoided.

(3) Nothing in this Act shall affect the power of the Court of Appeal or the High Court to stay any proceedings before it, where it thinks fit to do so, either of its own motion or on the application of any person, whether or not a party to the proceedings.

9A–154   *Note* —Derived from the JA 1925, ss. 36–44.

Effect of section

9A–155   This section is derived from the JA 1925, ss.36–44. It lies at the heart of the administration of civil justice in England and Wales, since it embodies, in a concentrated form, the fundamental objectives of the Judicature Acts 1873–1875 (see *C.E. Heath Plc v. Ceram Holding Co* [1988] 1 W.L.R. 1219, CA, at 1229, *per* Neill L.J.), namely:

(a) to bring about the concurrent jurisdiction of law and equity in all civil causes and matters in all civil courts on the basis that in any matter where there is a conflict or variance between the rules of equity and the rules of the common law, the rules of equity shall prevail; and at the same time;

(b) to secure that the Court will be empowered to determine finally all matters in dispute between the parties and to avoid all multiplicity of proceedings.

The three subsections of this section deal with three different aspects of the concurrent administration of law and equity:

(a) rules of equity to prevail where conflict or variance (subs.(1)) (see paras 9A–157 to 9A–159 below).

(b) final determination and avoidance of multiplicity of proceedings (subs.(2)) (see paras 9A–160).

(c) stay of proceedings (subs.(3)) (paras 9A–161 to 9A–178).

Notes on these aspects of the three subsections, taken in turn, are set out below (see paras 9A–157 *et seq.*).

CPR Pt 20 claims (counterclaims and third party proceedings)

Section 49(2) is derived, in part, from the Judicature Act 1925, s.39, which in turn **9A–156** was derived from the Judicature Act 1873, s.24(3). Those earlier provisions had the effect of empowering the court to hear, in the same action (1) a counterclaim of any kind by the defendant against the plaintiff; (2) a counterclaim by the defendant against the plaintiff along with any other persons, claiming relief relating to or connected with the original subject-matter; (3) third party proceedings; (4) a counterclaim by the third party, brought in by third party proceedings, against the party bringing him in; (5) a counterclaim by the plaintiff to the defendant's counterclaim, in so far as it is merely intended as a protection against it. The legislative basis for these proceedings is now found in s.49(2). The significance of s.49(2) in this respect for the jurisdiction of the courts goes without notice. Very occasionally, cases arise in which the effect of the subsection, in the light of its history, falls for consideration; a recent example is *Coca Cola Financial Corporation v. Finsat International Ltd* [1998] Q.B. 43; [1996] 2 Lloyd's Rep. 274, CA.

Rules of court relating to counterclaims and third party proceedings are now found in Pt 20 of the CPR and are compendiously described as "Part 20 claims".

A. Section 49(1)

Rules of equity to prevail where conflict or variance

The Judicature Acts of 1873 and 1875 did not in any way alter the nature of legal **9A–157** and equitable rights. These Acts did not "fuse" law and equity. They did not abolish the distinctions between law and equity, nor between legal and equitable principles nor between legal and equitable interests or estates (see *per* Cotton L.J. in *Joseph v. Lyons* (1884) 15 QBD 280 at 286, and see *Manchester Brewery Co. v. Coombs* [1901] 2 Ch. 608 at 617). The distinct identity of the two systems of law was preserved and this has remained the case. However, the legislation did achieve the union of the administration of the two systems of law.

Section 49(1) states that, subject to the provisions of the 1981 Act itself or any other Act, every court exercising jurisdiction "in any civil cause or matter" shall administer law and equity on the basis that, wherever there is any conflict or variance between the rules of equity and the rules of the common law "with reference to the same matter", the rules of equity shall prevail. If there is no "conflict or variance" the subsection does not apply (*The Bernina* (1887) 12 P.D. 58 at 95; *Manners v. Mew* (1885) 29 Ch D 725 at 735; *Re Terry* (1886) 32 Ch D 14 at 23).

Section 49(1) may be traced to the Judicature Act 1873, s.25. That section endeavoured to remove a number of cases of conflict between law and equity which had occasioned difficulty beforehand. Subsections (1) to (10) dealt with ten particular matters of difficulty and then came subs.(11) which stated: "Generally in all matters not hereinbefore particularly mentioned in which there is any conflict or variance between the rules of equity and the rules of common law with reference to the same matter, the rules of equity shall prevail". Section 25(11) was re-enacted as s.44 of the Judicature Act 1925, and again as s.49(1) of the 1981 Act.

It may be noted that s.49(1) and its statutory ancestors, refers to "rules" of equity and "rules" of common law and it may be concluded from this that its effect is confined to matters of substantive law and does not extend to rules of practice, though equitable practice should be followed when it results from the adoption of equitable doctrines (*La Grange v. McAndrew* (1879) 4 QBD 210; *Poyser v. Minors* (1881) 7 QBD 329, at 335 *per* Lush J.; *Dalrymple v. Leslie* (1881) 8 QBD 5; *Harrison v. Rutland* [1893] 1 Q.B. 142 at 149). At an early date the Court of Appeal said that, in cases where no rule of practice was laid down by the rules of court enacted with the Judicature Acts, and there was a variance in the old practice of the Chancery and Common Law courts, "that practice is to prevail which is considered by the Court most convenient" (*Newbiggin-by-the-Sea Gas Co v. Armstrong* (1879) 13 Ch D 310, CA).

Particular illustrations of conflict or variance

Editions of the Supreme Court Practice and the Annual Practice made reference to **9A–158** many of the late nineteenth century and early twentieth century cases in which issues concerning conflict or variance between particular rules of equity and rules of common law were determined. Virtually all of these cases were concerned with matters of substantive law. A few of them had implications for procedural law. For example, some of them established the rule of equity that children and patients cannot make binding admissions (at common law it seems to have been otherwise as to children). One consequence of this was the practice of not allowing interrogatories to be administered to a minor (*Mayor v. Collins* (1890) 24 QBD 361; *Curtis v. Mundy* [1892] 2 Q.B. 178). In the light of the rule derived from equity, admissions, discovery and interrogatories by minors and patients came to be regulated by rules of court, and that remains the case. The rule of equity that children and patients cannot make binding admissions is now reflected in CPR, r.14.1(3).

Other illustrations of the consequences for practice and procedure of rules of equity prevailing over rules of common law which were in conflict or at variance could be given.

Giving effect to all equitable and legal rights and duties etc.

9A–159   Section 49(2) of the Act provides (in part) that every court shall give the same effect as hitherto to each of the matters specified in sub-paragraphs (a) and (b). In this respect, the subsection replaced, in shortened and simplified form, the following provisions of the Judicature Act 1925:

>   s.37 (Equities of plaintiff)
>   s.38 (Equitable defences)
>   s.39 (Counterclaims and third parties)
>   s.40 (Equities appearing incidentally)
>   s.42 (Common law and statutory rights and duties).

In the process of shortening and simplifying these provisions of the 1925 Act, much that throws light on what those provisions (and their predecessors in the 1873 legislation) were designed to effect was lost. However, it would seem that no change in the law was intended.

B. Section 49(2)

Final determination and avoidance of multiplicity of proceedings

9A–160   Section 49(2) of Act provides (in part) that, subject to the provisions of the 1981 Act itself or any other Act, every court shall so exercise its jurisdiction in every cause or matter before it as to secure that:

>   (a) as far as possible, all matters in dispute between the parties are completely and finally determined, and
>   (b) as far as possible, all multiplicity of legal proceedings with respect to any of those matters is avoided.

In this respect, the subsection replaced s.43 of the 1925 Act. However, it may be noted that s.43 was primarily concerned with remedies. The section said that the court, in exercising its jurisdiction in every cause or matter pending before it, shall grant, whether absolutely or on such terms and conditions as it thinks just, "all such remedies whatsoever as any the parties thereto may appear to be entitled in respect of any legal or equitable claim properly brought forward by them in the cause or matter". The section went on to state that the court shall grant all remedies (legal or equitable) to which the parties were entitled so that, as far as possible, all matters in controversy between the parties "may be completely and finally determined, and all multiplicity of legal proceedings concerning any of those matters is avoided". The section was to be read as subject to any other Act (see s.36 of the 1925 Act).

Before the concurrent administration of law and equity was fully achieved by the Judicature Acts of 1873 and 1875, there was a risk that parties bringing proceedings before a superior court might find that, in the event, the court was restricted in the remedies it could grant, and, therefore, could not grant remedies in relation to all of the matters in dispute between the parties. Consequently, in order to obtain full relief parties faced the prospect of having to bring separate proceedings in separate courts. The Judicature Acts solved this problem. The statutory provision under discussion here reinforced the solution by enjoining courts to exercise their power to grant all remedies whether legal or equitable to which parties appeared to be entitled and to do so for the purpose of ensuring that, as far as possible, all matters in dispute between the parties are completely and finally determined, and all multiplicity of legal proceedings with respect to any of those matters is avoided. In early cases it was said of this provision that "every remedy necessary for doing complete justice in an action in any division of the High Court" is provided for by it (*Serrao v. Noel* (1885) 15 QBD 549,

CA, *per* Baggallay L.J.) and that it was in the spirit of the "whole tenor of the Judicature Acts" which was "to require all proceedings as far as possible to be taken in one action" (*Searle v. Choat* (1884) 25 Ch D 723 at 727 *per* Cotton L.J.; see also *Harmer v. Armstrong* [1934] Ch. 65).

The principles (1) that all matters in dispute should be completely and finally determined, and (2) that multiplicity of legal proceedings should be avoided are deeply embedded in the law and s.49(2) is but one manifestation of them. In most instances, finality and avoidance of multiplicity will be compatible goals. However, they can be in conflict; for example, where case management rules require swift movement to finality at the expense of the uncovering of, and further development of, matters in dispute between the parties. It may be noted that the principle that all matters in dispute should be completely and finally determined is not the same as the principle that there should be finality in litigation. In some instances, the application of the latter principle will involve a violation of the former (*e.g.* where proceedings are brought to an end in the knowledge that some matters remain in dispute, at least in the opinion of one party). It may also be noted that there is a relationship between the principles stated in s.49(2) and the rule in *Henderson v. Henderson* (1843) 3 Hare 100 which holds that a party may be estopped from pursuing in subsequent proceedings issues that ought to have been pursued and determined in former proceedings; the link is illustrated by *Beoco Ltd v. Alfa Laval Co Ltd* [1995] Q.B. 137; [1994] 4 All E.R. 464, CA. The relationship between the rule in *Henderson v. Henderson* and the court's inherent jurisdiction to protect its processes from abuse was examined in *Johnson v. Gore Wood & Co (No.1)* [2002] 2 A.C. 1, HL.

The application of the principles, stated in s.49(2), (1) that all matters in dispute should be completely and finally determined, and (2) that multiplicity of legal proceedings should be avoided, may be seen at work in various parts of the law of procedure. A good example is provided by the rules relating to the amendment of statements of case (formerly pleadings). Traditionally, these rules have been generously applied for the purpose of ensuring that the real matters in dispute between the parties are reached and dealt with completely and finally, thereby avoiding further proceedings (assuming they are not statute barred). In some amendment cases, express reference has been made to s.49(2); see *e.g. Easton v. Ford Motor Co Ltd* [1993] 1 W.L.R. 1511, CA; [1993] 4 All E.R. 257, CA; in *Re Therm-a-Stor Ltd* [1996] 3 All E.R. 228. Under the case management principles implemented by the CPR this generosity is unlikely to extend to the granting of amendments where the consequence will be that a trial date will have to be abandoned.

Other aspects of practice and procedure in which the principles stated in s.49(2) may be seen at work include: the transfer of proceedings from one court to another, the consolidation of proceedings, the trial or two or more claims on the same occasion, the addition and substitution of parties, the joinder of claims, and counterclaims and other additional claims (see CPR seriatim and note, in particular, r.19.3 (provisions applicable where two or more persons are jointly entitled to a remedy), and r.20.9 (whether a Pt 20 claim should be separate from main claim). In *Knauf UK GmbH v. British Gypsum Ltd* [2001] EWCA Civ 1570, *The Times*, November 15, 2001, CA, the claimants were granted permission to serve their claim form out of the jurisdiction on a second defendant under CPR, r.6.8, partly for the purpose of ensuring that all disputes between all parties were determined in the same set of proceedings. The Court of Appeal found that the claimant's main objective was to render their claim immune from jurisdictional attack under the Brussels Convention and set aside service on the second defendants.

The terms of s.49(2) indicate that the court is to exercise its jurisdiction in a manner designed to secure the two principles discussed above "in every cause or matter". In former versions of the subsection the court was enjoined to secure the application of the principles "in every pending cause or matter". In the early cases the question of the point at which a cause or matter ceased to be "pending" and the court's duty to ensure that all matters in dispute between the parties were completely and finally determined no longer obtained. The question remains important (*Charlesworth v. Relay Roads Ltd (No.2)* [2000] 1 W.L.R. 230).

C. Section 49(3)

Stay of proceedings

Section 49(3) states that nothing in the 1981 Act shall affect the power of either the **9A–161**

Court of Appeal or the High Court "to stay any proceedings before it". The subsection suggests that provisions may be found in the 1981 Act which give the Court of Appeal and the High Court power to restrain pending proceedings and that it is necessary for it to be made clear that any such provisions do not affect the power of those courts to exercise their inherent jurisdiction to stay proceedings. The need for such a saving was apparent in 1873, when conflicts between common law and equity powers to restrain proceedings had to be ameliorated, and was found in s.24(5) of the Judicature Act 1873. The saving was re-enacted in the Judicature Act 1925, s.41. In its original form the section forbad the pre-1873 practice of restraint of actions by prohibition or injunction subject to the saving that any person who would formerly have been entitled to apply to any court to restrain the prosecution of any action could apply to the High Court for a stay of proceedings in the action (*Gore v. Van Der Lann* [1967] 2 Q.B. 31, CA, at 43 *per* Harman L.J.). The manner in which the saving is preserved in s.49(3) of the 1981 Act is confusing and may be regarded as an excess of caution.

In terms, s.49(3) takes the form, not of conferring a power on the Court of Appeal and High Court to order a stay of proceedings, but of statutorily recognising an inherent power which the courts already possess and exercise, and which it is said they exercised from "the earlier times" (*Metropolitan Bank v. Pooley* (1885) 10 App.Cas. 210 at 220–221 *per* Lord Blackburn). It has been said that the subsection applies to county court proceedings by virtue of the County Courts Act 1984, s.76 (*Gore v. Van Der Lann* [1967] 2 Q.B. 31, CA).

This subsection needs to be read in parallel with s.49 of the Civil Jurisdiction and Judgments Act 1982, which also provides for the saving of the powers of the Court to stay, strike out or dismiss any proceedings before it on the ground of forum non conveniens or otherwise, where to do so is not inconsistent with the 1968 Convention, *i.e.* the EEC Convention on Jurisdiction and the Enforcement of Judgments.

The extent of the court's inherent jurisdiction to stay proceedings cannot be stated exactly, certainly not in a short compass. Perhaps the best known manifestation of the jurisdiction is the court's power stay proceedings to prevent its procedures being abused. This jurisdiction is said to be extensive (*Ebert v. Venvil* [1999] 3 W.L.R. 670, CA). As there is a public interest in the finality of litigation, proceedings may be stayed on the grounds that they are an abuse of process to prevent a defendant from being vexed twice in the same matter (*Johnson v. Gore Wood & Co (No.1)* [2002] 2 A.C. 1, HL); but whether an action should be stayed on this basis should be judged broadly on the merits, taking account of all public and private interests involved and all the facts of the case, the crucial question being whether the claimant was in all the circumstances misusing or abusing the process of the court (*ibid.*). See also, *Stevens v. School of Oriental and African Studies, The Times,* February 2, 2001 (Pumphrey J.) (a stay to prevent, what was in substance, a re-litigation of earlier proceedings, was, in the circumstances, a reasonable exercise of the court's inherent jurisdiction and did not infringe the Human Rights Act 1998 Sched.1, art.6). Another common circumstance in which a stay of proceedings may be ordered is where a party has not complied with an order for security for costs (*e.g. CIBC Mellon Trust Co v. Mora Hotel Corp NV* [2002] EWCA Civ 1688, CA; *Aoun v. Bahri* [2002] EWCA Civ 1141, July 31, 2002, CA). See further para. 9A–163 below.

As to court's power under its inherent jurisdiction or statute to stay proceedings where parties have agreed to arbitrate their dispute, see para. 9A–162 below.

As to whether court has inherent jurisdiction, and if so whether it should exercise it, to stay legal proceedings where there is an agreement between the parties to negotiate or mediate (albeit an agreement that is lacking in the certainty traditionally regarded as necessary for enforceability and perhaps even non-binding), see *Cable & Wireless Plc v. IBM United Kingdom Ltd* [2002] EWHC 2059 (Colman J.) and authorities referred to there; *cf.*, *Halifax Financial Services Ltd v. Intuitive Systems Ltd* [1999] 1 All E.R. (Comm) 303 (McKinnon J.). See also Vol. 1, para. 1.4.11 above.

Where a civil proceedings order is made against a person under the Supreme Court Act 1981, s.42, or where a civil restraint order is made against a person (see CPR, r.3.11), depending on the circumstances the effects may include imposing a stay on proceedings.

A distinction is to be drawn between the situation (a) where no progress is made in proceedings because they have been stayed, and (b) where no progress is made because the court has made an order absolving the parties from the duty to take further steps in the proceedings (being steps that they would otherwise be required to take in accordance with rules, directions or orders) (*Simms v. The Law Society* [2005] EWCA Civ 849, July 12, 2005, CA, unrep.).

Stay under particular statutes

Further powers to stay proceedings or execution are conferred by particular **9A–162** statutes, *e.g.* to stay an action brought contrary to agreement to arbitrate (Arbitration Act 1950, s.4, Arbitration Act 1996, s.9); to stay proceedings against a debtor after presentation of bankruptcy petition (Insolvency Act 1986, s.285); to stay actions or proceedings against a company after the presentation of winding-up petition or in a voluntary winding up (Insolvency Act 1986, s.126); to prevent institution or continuance of proceedings by vexatious litigant (SCA 1981, s.42); to stay execution of judgment for delivery of possession of mortgaged property (Administration of Justice Act 1970, s.36(2)(b); to stay execution of possession orders in certain proceedings (Housing Act 1985, s.85(2)). Sometimes a clause in a statute conferring jurisdiction to grant a stay of proceedings in particular circumstances is intended to be, and takes effect as, a complete bar to proceedings (*e.g.* the Lunacy Act section considered in *Shackleton v. Swift* [1913] 2 K.B. 304, CA). In effect, such provisions are substantive and not procedural and, where applied, should lead to the dismissal of the claim.

For the stay of proceedings to which the Convention on Jurisdiction and Enforcement of Judgments in Civil and Commercial Matters applies, see para. 9A–171 below.

The question whether an action should be stayed under some special Act "is a very different thing ... to the case of a question under the Judicature Act and the Rules whether an action ought to be stayed or not" (*per* Vaughan Williams L.J. in *Shackleton v. Swift* [1913] 2 K.B. 304 at 312, a case decided under the Lunacy Act 1890, s.330, and see the Mental Health Act 1983, s.139).

The court has, in addition to the power granted under the Arbitration Act 1996, s.9 (see para. 2E–114 above), an inherent jurisdiction to stay proceedings, and this jurisdiction may be exercised if good sense and litigation management make it desirable for the matter to be referred to arbitration (*Al-Naimi v. Islamic Press Agency Inc* [2000] 1 Lloyd's Rep. 522, CA).

Domestic insolvency law does not apply to foreign insolvency proceedings and accordingly does not give the court power to stay English proceedings against a company on the ground that it is subject to insolvency proceedings in Germany (*Mazur Media Ltd. v. Mazur Media GmbH* [2004] EWHC 1566 (Ch); [2004] 1 W.L.R. 2966 (Lawrence Collins J.).

Stay under the CPR

The rules of court found in the CPR apply to proceedings in the Court of Appeal, **9A–163** in the High Court, and also to proceedings in the county courts.

In r.3.1(2)(f) the power to "stay the whole of part of any proceedings either generally or until a specified event or date" is listed among the court's "general powers of case management" which may be exercised except where the CPR provide otherwise. The several powers listed in r.3.1(2) are in addition to any powers (including powers to stay proceedings) given to the court by any other rule or practice direction or by any other enactment or any power it may otherwise have (*e.g.* the inherent power to stay proceedings). The discretion to stay granted by r.3.1(2)(f) is only available for a procedural reason and should not be exercised where (1) a stay under a particular statutory provision (*e.g.* Administration of Justice Act 1970, s.36(2)(a)) is refused and (2) such reason does not exist (*State Bank of New South Wales v. Harrison* [2002] EWCA Civ 363; March 8, 2002, CA, unrep.)).

In the Glossary attached to the CPR it is stated as follows: "A stay imposes a halt on proceedings, apart from taking any steps allowed by the Rules or the terms of the stay. Proceedings can be continued if the stay is lifted."

Specific provisions found in the "core" provisions in the CPR to stay orders, claims or proceedings include:

- r.3.3(5) (Application by party to stay order made by court of its own initiative without hearing parties or giving opportunity for representations)
- r.3.4(4) (Staying second claim until costs of first claim paid)
- r.11(6)(d) (Staying proceedings where court declaring it has no jurisdiction)
- r.14.5(5) (Where admission of part of claim for a specified amount money, claim stayed if claimant does not file notice)
- r.15.10(3)(4) (Where defence is that money claim has been paid, claim stayed if claimant does not file notice) [specific reference to application to lift in r.15.10(4)]
- r.15.11(1) (Claim stayed where claimant has not applied for default judgment

LEGISLATION

or summary judgment after specified time) [specific reference to application to lift in r.15.11(2)]

- r.26.4 (Stay to allow for settlement of the case) (see also r.26.5(1)(b))
- r.36.15(1) (Stay where Pt 36 offer or Pt 36 payment accepted) (see also r.36.19(3))
- r.38.8 (Stay of remainder of partly discontinued proceedings where costs not paid)
- r.40.6 (Consent judgments to stay proceedings or enforcement of a judgment)
- r.52.7 (Appeals to Court of Appeal - stay of order of lower court)
- r.52.9 (Stay pending discharge of conditions imposed on appeal to Court of Appeal)
- r.54.10 (Stay of judicial review claim)
- r.68.4 (Stay where reference to European Court for preliminary ruling)
- r.74.33 (Stay under art.23 of EEO Regulation)

Existing proceedings that did not come before a judge between April 26, 1999, and April 25, 2000, were stayed by operation of CPR, r.51.1 and Practice Direction (Transitional Arrangements), para.19(1). Any party to those proceedings may apply for the stay to be lifted (para. 19(2) (see Vol. 1, paras 51.1.2 and 51PD.19).

Practice Direction (Case Management-Preliminary Stage: Allocation and Reallocation), para.12.2 states that where the court, in certain circumstances, has given a judgment or made an order requiring an amount of money, to be decided by the court, to be paid by one party to another, the court will give directions. The circumstances include such judgment or order obtained, for example, by default or on a summary judgment application. It is expressly provided that the directions which the court may give include a direction staying the claim while the parties try to settle the case by alternative dispute resolution or other means (para.12.2(1)(d)).

In the former RSC and CCR rules now re-enacted in, respectively, Scheds 1 and 2 of the CPR, references to the stay of proceedings (by order or by rule) are found in a number of places (especially in provisions concerned with enforcement of judgments and execution). Such references include (the list is not exhaustive):

RSC O.17 (Interpleader), r.5 (Power to stay proceedings)

RSC O.47, r.1 (Power to stay execution by writ of *fieri facias*)

RSC O.45 (Enforcement of judgments and orders: general), r.11 (Matters occurring after judgment: stay of execution, etc.)

The court has power to stay an action where a party is funded by a non-party who would not or could not satisfactorily accept liability to pay a successful opponent's costs (*Abraham v. Thompson* [1997] 4 All E.R. 362, CA; *Stocznia S.A. v. Latvian Shipping Co (No. 2)* [1999] 3 All E.R. 822).

A defendant may be entitled to a stay of proceedings against him until the claimant satisfies an order for costs made against him and in favour of the defendant in previous proceedings (*Hines v. Birbeck College (No. 2)* [1991] 3 W.L.R. 557; [1991] 4 All E.R. 450, CA).

Modern examples of instances in which proceedings have been stayed until the claimant complied with procedural rules or orders include the following cases: *Dunn v. British Coal Corporation, The Times*, March 5, 1993, CA (disclosure of medical records), *Jackson v. Mirror Group Newspapers Ltd, The Times*, March 29, 1994, CA (submission to medical examination), *Jackson v. Pinchbeck* [1998] 3 All E.R. 97, CA ("unless" order requiring filing of statement of special damages). See also *Westminster City Council v. Porter* [2002] EWHC 1589 (Ch), July 16, 2002, unrep. (Hart J.) (judgment debtor's application for stay of execution of judgment pending application to European Court of Human Rights refused). See further para.9A–161 above.

As to stay of judicial review claim, see CPR, r.54.10 and Vol. 1, paras 54.10.2 *et seq.*

As to stay where parties have agreed to arbitrate or mediate dispute, see para. 9A–163 above.

Court staying proceedings of its own motion

9A–164   Section 49(3) recognises that the court's power to stay proceedings is exercisable, either (a) of its own motion or (b) on the application of any person, whether (i) a party to the proceedings or (ii) not a party to the proceedings. In CPR, r.3.3 it is expressly provided that, subject to conditions, the court may exercise its power to stay the whole or part of any proceedings (see r.3.1(2)(f)) on an application or of its own initiative.

Where the court stays proceedings by an order made of its own initiative, without hearing the parties or giving them an opportunity to make representations, a party affected by the order may apply to have it set aside, varied or stayed (r.3.3(5)).

Nature or effect of a stay of proceedings

In *Cohens v. Virginia* (1871) 6 Wheat. 264, Marshall C.J. said (at p.404, speaking for **9A–165** the United States Supreme Court): "We have no more right to decline the exercise of jurisdiction which is given, than to usurp that which is not given". When, for whatever reason, proceedings are stayed, in effect the court is declining to exercise its jurisdiction. That is a strong thing (*Shackleton v. Swift* [1913] 2 K.B. 304, CA, at 312 *per* Vaughan Williams L.J.). Obviously, jurisdiction should not be declined except for very good reason. In *Abraham v. Thompson* [1997] 4 All E.R. 363, CA, Potter L.J. said (at p.374) that, where a stay is sought in circumstances which are not provided for by statute or rules of court, the starting point is the fundamental rule that an individual who is not under a disability, a bankrupt or a vexatious litigant, is entitled to untrammelled access to a court of first instance in respect of a bona fide claim based on a properly pleaded cause of action".

With the emergence of modern case management practices (exemplified by many of the provisions of the CPR), the jurisdiction to stay proceedings has become a useful procedural sanction, available to ensure compliance by parties with rules of court, practice directions, and procedural orders. Nowadays, more than ever before, "good reason" justifying the exercise of the jurisdiction to stay proceedings includes the achievement of case management goals in individual cases (see, further, "Stay under the CPR", para. 9A–163 above).

For considerations relevant to the question whether a stay should take effect forthwith or at a later stage in the development of the proceedings (*e.g.* after the disclosure of documents and exchange of witness statements had been completed), see *Synstar Computer Service (UK Ltd v. I.C.L. (Sorbus) Ltd*, *The Times*, May 1, 2001 (Lightman J.).

In giving the opinion of the Judicial Committee in *Minister of Foreign Affairs, Trade & Industry v. Vehicles and Supplies Ltd* [1991] 1 W.L.R. 550, PC, [1991] 4 All E.R. 65, PC, Lord Oliver said (at p.556 & p.71): "A stay of proceedings is an order which puts a stop to the further conduct of proceedings in court or before an tribunal at the stage which they have reached, the object being to avoid the hearing or trial taking place". Whilst the stay endures, "the relevant court or tribunal cannot ... effectively entertain any further proceedings except for the purpose of lifting the stay". In general, "anything done prior to the lifting of the stay will be ineffective, although such an order would not, if imposed to enforce the performance of a condition by a plaintiff (*e.g.* to provide security for costs), prevent a defendant from applying to dismiss the action if the condition is not fulfilled". His lordship further explained that a stay order is not an order enforceable by proceedings for contempt because it is not, in its nature, capable of being "breached" by a party to the proceedings or anyone else.

By definition, a stay takes effect on proceedings which are on foot; that is to say, on claims (or other proceedings) within which some proceedings may still be taken. Section 49(3) speaks of the jurisdiction of the court to stay proceedings "before it", and earlier legislation spoke of "pending" proceedings. Thus, a stay may be imposed after judgment as well as before, and execution proceedings may be stayed.

The early authorities as to the nature and effect of a stay of proceedings were reviewed by Neill L.J. in *Rofa Sport Management A.G. v. D.H.L. International (UK) Ltd* [1989] 1 W.L.R. 902; [1989] 2 All E.R. 743, CA. His lordship noted that, historically speaking, it was possible to draw a distinction between an "absolute" order to stay, which was equivalent to a discontinuance or dismissal, and a "conditional" order to stay, which by its terms contemplated the continuance of the action if the condition was fulfilled. However, his lordship concluded that, nowadays, it would not be satisfactory to seek to draw a line between the two and to equate "absolute" stays with orders for dismissal or discontinuance. In his lordship's judgment, for the sake of clarity and certainty the word "stay" in an order should not be treated as a possible equivalent of a dismissal or a discontinuance, no matter how unlikely it is that the stay will be lifted by an order of the court enabling the case to "resume its active life"; *e.g.* where the proceedings are stayed by consent following a compromise (*Cooper v. Williams* [1963] 2 Q.B. 567; [1963] 2 All E.R. 282, CA; *Green v. Rozen* [1955] 1 W.L.R. 741; [1955] 2 All E.R. 797). It is submitted that the same result should follow (unless expressly provided otherwise) where proceedings are stayed, not by court order, but by operation of legislation (including rules of court).

Where proceedings are settled by agreement and stayed by a Tomlin order, the stay does not operate to deny the court jurisdiction to determine an application by the claimant for a wasted costs order against he defendant's solicitors (such an application being wholly tangential to the stayed proceedings and not affecting the defendant's rights in any way) (*Wagstaff v. Colls* [2003] EWCA Civ 469; *The Times*, April 17, 2003, CA).

The question whether costs incurred during a stay are allowable depends upon whether the work in respect of which they are charged was premature (*Pêcheries Ostendaises v. Merchant's Marine Insurance Co* [1928] 1 K.B. 750).

Costs, stay pending payment or security for

9A-166   The court has jurisdiction to stay proceedings until payment of costs in an interlocutory matter which have been ordered to be paid. In the early cases, such a stay was ordered where the party in default was acting vexatiously in withholding payment (*Re Wickham* (1887) 35 Ch D 272; *Graham v. Sutton, Carden & Co* [1897] 2 Ch. 367). A second application for the same relief as in a previous application which had been dismissed with costs will be stayed unless and until those costs are paid or a reasonable sum to cover those costs is paid into court, if the costs are unquantified (*Thames Investment and Securities v. Benjamin* [1984] 1 W.L.R. 1381; [1984] 3 All E.R. 393). Where an order is made requiring a party to provide security for costs, it may be further ordered that proceedings be stayed pending the provision of security (*e.g. Clive Brooks & Co Ltd v. Baynard*, *The Times*, April 30, 1998, CA). As to stay of second claim where order for costs of first claim not paid, see CPR, r.3.4(4)).

Stay pending changes in law

9A-167   It is conceivable that, after proceedings have been commenced, but before they are tried, legislative changes in the law affecting the respective positions of the parties to the proceedings may come into effect. Judges trying cases apply the law as it stands at the time of trial. It is also conceivable that, before proceedings are tried, it will become apparent that legislative changes in the law are to be anticipated. In those circumstances it may be argued that the proceedings should be stayed so as to ensure that they are not tried before the changes come into effect. In *Willow Wren Canal Carrying Co Ltd v. British Transport Commission* [1956] 1 W.L.R. 213; [1956] 1 All E.R. 567, legislation which would have given the defendants immunity from the plaintiff's claim was going through Parliament. The defendants applied to stay the proceedings long enough to gain the benefit of the legislation. If granted, the stay would have had the effect of preventing the case from going to trial. The application was refused. (See also *Wilson v. Dagnall* [1972] 1 Q.B. 509, CA.) In *Sparks v. Harland* [1997] 1 W.L.R. 143, the plaintiff's action was brought outside the limitation period and the defendant applied to have them dismissed on that ground. There was a prospect (depending on the likely response of the legislature to the outcome of other proceedings pending in the European Court of Human Rights) of retrospective legislation being enacted which would have the effect of removing the time bar from the plaintiff's claim. It was held that, in the circumstances, the plaintiff's action should not be struck out, but should be stayed.

It is conceivable that, in the course of the hearing of a case, it may become apparent that issues of law arising in the proceedings have arisen in other cases and are presently subject to appellate proceedings or references to the E.C.J. in those cases in which it is expected that the issues of law will be authoritatively determined. In those circumstances it may be argued that the hearing should be adjourned pending the outcome of the appeal or the reference (see *Re Yates' Settlement Trusts* [1954] 1 All E.R. 619, CA, and *Sprote v. Commissioner of Police of the Metropolis*, *The Times*, August 6, 1991, EAT). An adjournment of a hearing is not the same as a stay of proceedings. The question whether proceedings which have not reached the point of trial should be stayed (whether by consent or otherwise) where it has become apparent that issues of law arising in the proceedings have arisen in other cases which are presently subject to appellate proceedings or references to the E.C.J. raises different considerations.

Concurrent civil proceedings

9A-168   When civil proceedings are commenced, they proceed according to rules of practice and procedure, including case management rules designed to ensure that cases proceed with despatch.

Circumstances can arise in which it becomes apparent that two (or possibly more) separate sets of proceedings (perhaps in the same court, perhaps in different courts) are related in some material way and that it is just and convenient that one (or some) should be stayed pending the final determination of the other (or others). One set of proceedings may be "the senior of the two" in the sense that it was commenced before, or had reached a later stage of pre-trial development than, the other (*J. Bollinger S.A. v. Goldwell Ltd* [1971] R.P.C. 412 at 423 *per* Megarry J.). All of the parties involved may agree that one set of proceedings (not necessarily "the senior") should be stayed by consent pending the outcome of the other. The court may readily agree to the stay. However, despite the agreement amongst the parties, in the interests of effective case management the court may refuse to order a stay by consent and, instead, order (for example) that the claims should be consolidated, tried together, or one tried immediately after the other.

In the absence of agreement amongst the parties to the effect that one set of proceedings should be stayed whilst another proceeds, the question may arise whether, on the application of a party (or parties) or of its own initiative, the court should order such a stay. The question may arise in many different circumstances and procedural settings. Consequently, it is not possible to state general principles as to the exercise of the discretionary jurisdiction to stay proceedings in this context. Further, special considerations may arise in particular jurisdictions (especially in arbitration, bankruptcy, insolvency, and patents).

Perhaps the clearest example of a situation in which the court might be persuaded to order a stay would be where the several sets of proceedings involve the same parties and raise the same issues (*Slough Estates Ltd v. Slough Borough Council* [1968] Ch. 299; [1967] 2 All E.R. 270). The advantages to be gained in avoiding a duplication of proceedings are obvious; they include the avoidance of unnecessary costs and delays and of a party being vexed more than once with, in effect, the same claim. (It may be noted that the need to avoid "all multiplicity of legal proceedings" with respect to all matters in dispute between the same parties is referred to in s.49(2); see para. 9A–160 above.) The case for a stay is less strong where there is merely a considerable degree of common ground between the two claims (*J. Bollinger S.A. v. Goldwell Ltd op. cit.*).

Some of the early authorities suggest a stay will not be granted if the issues in the several proceedings are not the same (*Adamson v. Tuff* (1881) 44 L.T. 420; *Higgins v. Woodhall* (1890) 6 T.L.R. 1; *Perry v. Croydon Borough Council* [1938] 3 All E.R. 670) but this cannot be stated as a strict rule. If there are two courts faced with substantially the same question or issue, it is desirable that the question or issue should be determined in only one of those two courts if by that means justice can be done, and the court will if necessary stay one of the actions (*Royal Bank of Scotland Ltd v. Citrusdal Investments Ltd* [1971] 1 W.L.R. 1469; [1971] 3 All E.R. 558, applying *Thames Launches Ltd v. Trinity House Corporation (Deptford Strond)* [1961] Ch. 197; [1961] 1 All E.R. 26). A second action dealing with the same events as in the first action but alleging a different contract with different terms will not be stayed (*Hardy v. Elphick* [1974] Ch. 65; [1973] 2 All E.R. 914, CA).

Where there are multiple sets of proceedings against the same defendant raising the same issues one may be selected as a "test" case and the other proceedings stayed pending the outcome of that case (*Ashmore v. British Coal Corporation* [1990] 2 W.L.R. 1437; [1990] 2 All E.R. 981, CA).

Where an action founded on a certain cause of action is in existence, albeit stayed, it is an abuse of process to bring new proceedings founded upon that same cause of action; the second action will be struck out and the proper course would be to apply for the stay to be removed in respect of the first action (*Buckland v. Palmer* [1984] 1 W.L.R. 1109; [1984] 3 All E.R. 554, CA). See further CPR, rr.19.11(ii) and 19.15.

Where one set of proceedings has been stayed but another set has proceeded to final determination, the question may then arise as to whether the stay on the former proceedings should be lifted. The considerations relevant to this question need not be considered here. However, it may be noted that, depending on the circumstances, as a result of the determination of the latter proceedings, pleas of *res judicata* or issue estoppel may become relevant in the former proceedings and affect the question whether the stay should be lifted. Further, the rule stated in *Henderson v. Henderson* (1843) 3 Hare 100 (which holds that a party may be estopped from pursuing in subsequent proceedings issues that ought to have been pursued and determined in former proceedings) may also become relevant.

Many of the earlier authorities were referred to in editions of the Supreme Court Practice; see SCP 1991, Vol. 2, paras 20A–357 (Concurrent actions), 20A–363 (Cross actions in respect of same subject-matter), 20A–389 (Test actions), and 20A–394 (Two actions or proceedings for same matter).

Recent authorities on the matters referred to above include: *Re B (Minors: Abduction), The Times*, November 6, 1992; *Chorion Plc v. Lane, The Times*, April 7, 1999; *Steans Fashions Ltd v. Legal and General Assurance Society Ltd, The Times*, December 31, 1994, CA. See further authorities referred to in para. 9A–161 above.

Where several proceedings "give rise to common or related issues of fact or law", for purposes of case management they may be made subject to a Group Litigation Order (GLO) under the rules of court found in CPR Pt 19, Sect. III and the practice direction supplementing those rules. The authorities referred to above are relevant to the exercise of the court's jurisdiction to stay cases subject to a GLO, but as the CPR provisions are to be applied in accordance with the overriding objective (stated in r.1.1) they perhaps cannot be regarded as binding.

Concurrent civil and criminal proceedings

9A–169   Where there are concurrent civil and criminal proceedings against the same defendant arising out of the same subject-matter, there is no principle of law that the claimant in the civil proceedings is to be debarred from pursuing the action in accordance with the normal rules merely because so to do would or might result in the defendant, if he wished to defend the action, having to disclose his defence by taking some necessary procedural step, and so give an indication of what his defence was likely to be in contemporaneous criminal proceedings, but the civil court has a discretion to stay the proceedings if it appeared to the Court that justice between the parties so required having regard to concurrent criminal proceedings arising out of the same subject matter and taking into account the defendant's "right of silence" in the criminal proceedings (*Jefferson Ltd v. Bhetcha* [1979] 1 W.L.R. 898; [1979] 2 All E.R. 1108, CA). In *Barnet London Borough Council v. Hurst* [2002] EWCA Civ 1009; [2002] 4 All E.R. 457, CA, upon the defendant giving undertakings, the judge adjourned the hearing of a local authority's application to commit the defendant for breach of anti-social behaviour injunction pending the completion of criminal proceedings against the defendant.

There is no overriding right based on the privilege against self incrimination, to have a civil action stayed pending the conclusion of criminal proceedings. It is for a defendant to seek to avail himself of the privilege to take specific objection on an application at some point in the interlocutory stages of a civil action (*Guinness plc v. Saunders, The Times*, October 18, 1988, CA). See also the comments of Millett J. in *Re D.P.R. Futures Ltd* [1989] 1 W.L.R. 778, CA.

Where civil proceedings in the form of an application under the Directors Disqualification Act 1986 were stayed pending the outcome of a related criminal proceedings, and, after the completion of the criminal proceedings, the Secretary of State applied to restore the application, the civil proceedings were not barred by the doctrine of double recovery, and the continuation of the civil proceedings was not an abuse of process (*Re Cedarwood Productions Ltd, The Times*, July 12, 2001, CA). See also *Secretary of State for Trade and Industry v. Crane, The Times* June 4, 2001 (Ferris J.), and note *R. v. Panel on Takeovers and Mergers, ex p. Fayed* [1992] B.C.C. 524.

Lis alibi pendens, forum non conveniens and foreign jurisdiction clauses

9A–170   The court has an inherent jurisdiction to stay proceedings in England, or to restrain by injunction the institution or continuation of proceedings in a foreign court, whenever it is necessary to do so in order to prevent injustice.

Thus, where simultaneous proceedings are pending in England and in a foreign country between the same parties and involving the same or similar issues (*lis alibi pendens*), the English proceedings may be stayed. Further, in certain circumstances, although there is no *lis alibi pendens* English proceedings may be stayed on forum *non conveniens* grounds where there is a foreign forum to whose jurisdiction the defendant is amenable.

Also, pending English proceedings may be stayed where the parties have agreed by contract that all disputes between them shall be referred to the jurisdiction of a foreign tribunal (foreign jurisdiction clause).

The jurisdiction to grant stays of English proceedings in the circumstances mentioned above is highly discretionary and is exercised with extreme caution. The relevant law is complicated and extensive and need not be explained here.

The jurisdiction to stay proceedings on forum *non conveniens* grounds or otherwise is recognised by the Civil Jurisdiction and Judgments Act 1982, s.49).

For the stay of proceedings to which the Convention on Jurisdiction and Enforcement of Judgments in Civil and Commercial Matters applies, see para. 9A–171 below.

EC Convention actions

An action brought in an English court which is within the scope of the EC Conventions on Jurisdiction and the Enforcement of Judgments, which have been given the force of law by s.2 of the Civil Jurisdiction and Judgments Act 1982 set out in s.7 may be stayed and in some instances must be stayed or dismissed in the following classes or cases: **9A–171**

(i) Exclusive jurisdiction —(a) where the claim is principally concerned with a matter **9A–172** over which the courts of another Member State of the EC have exclusive jurisdiction under art.16, the English Court must declare of its own motion that it has no jurisdiction (see art.19), and presumably for this purpose the Court will make an order staying or dismissing the action; (b) where the English Court is not the court first seised of an action which comes within the exclusive jurisdiction of several Courts, it must decline jurisdiction in favour of the Court first seised (art.23).

(ii) Agreement conferring jurisdiction —(a) where an agreement is concluded between **9A–173** parties one or more of whom is domiciled in a Member State of the EC, that a Court or the Courts of a specified Member State are to have jurisdiction to settle disputes between them, that Court will have exclusive jurisdiction and presumably the Courts of another Member State must decline jurisdiction; (b) where such agreement is concluded between parties, one of whom is domiciled in a Member State of the EEC, the Courts of the contracting states will have no jurisdiction over their disputes, unless the Courts chosen have declined jurisdiction; (c) if a trust instrument has conferred jurisdiction on the Court or Courts of a Member State, that Court or Courts will have exclusive jurisdiction in proceedings brought against a settlor, trustee or beneficiary (see Art.17).

(iii) Default of acknowledgment of service —where a defendant is domiciled in an- **9A–174** other Member State of the EC but is sued in England and does not acknowledge service of process, the English Court must declare of its own motion that it has no jurisdiction, unless its jurisdiction is derived from other provisions of the EC Conventions (Art.20) and in any event, in such case, the Court must stay the proceedings so long as it is not shown that the defendant had been able to receive the originating document or its equivalent in sufficient time to arrange for his defence or that all necessary steps have been taken to this end (Art.20).

(iv) Lis pendens —where the English Court is not the Court first seised of proceed- **9A–175** ings involving the same cause of action between the same parties which are brought in the Courts of different Member States of the EC, it must of its own motion declare jurisdiction in favour of the Court first seised (Art.21), although if the jurisdiction of that Court is contested, it may stay the proceedings pending the outcome of that contest (Art.21).

(v) Related actions —where the English Court is not the Court first seised of related **9A–176** actions which are brought in the Courts of different Member States of the EC, it may stay the proceedings while the actions are pending at first instance (Art.22). It may also, on the application of one of the parties decline jurisdiction if the law of the court first seised permits the consolidation of related actions and that Court has jurisdiction over both actions (Art.22). For this purpose, actions are deemed to be related where they are so closely connected that it is expedient to hear and determine them together to avoid the risk of irreconcilable judgments resulting from separate proceedings (Art.22).

EC Jurisdiction Regulation

Council Regulation (EC) No. 44/2001 was implemented by the Civil Jurisdiction **9A–176.1** Order 2001 (S.I. 2001 No. 3929) (see para. 5–195 above). In this Regulation, Arts 23 to 29 correspond, respectively, with Arts 17 to 23 of the Brussels Convention. Under the Regulation, where (a) proceedings involving the same cause of action and between the same parties are brought in the courts of different Member States (lis pendens), or (b) where related actions are pending in the courts of different Member States (related actions), or (b) where actions come within the exclusive jurisdiction of several courts, and the English court has to determine whether it should stay proceedings because another court was first seised of the proceedings, reference has to be made to art. 30 (see para. 5–243 above). That Article has no counterpart on the Brussels Convention and is designed to overcome certain difficulties that have arisen under the Convention (*e.g. Dresser U.K. Ltd. v. Falcongate Freight Management Ltd* [1992] 1 Q.B. 502, CA.)

European Commission investigation

9A–177   Where a defendant alleges that he has a defence by reason of a breach of the Rome Treaty and makes a complaint to the EC Commission the Court may order a stay pending investigation by the Commission of the plaintiff's action upon terms providing some protection as to costs and damages (*British Leyland Motor Corporation Ltd v. Wyatt Interpart Co Ltd* [1979] F.S.R. 583; [1979] 3 C.M.L.R. 77 and further hearing [1980] F.S.R. 18). Paragraph 5.3 of Practice Direction (Competition Law, Etc) provides that, where the court is seised of competition claim and is aware that the Commission is contemplating adopting a decision in relation to proceedings that it has initiated, the court shall consider whether to stay the claim pending the Commission's decision (see Vol. 1, para. B12–005).

Cases illustrating exercise of jurisdiction to stay proceedings

9A–178   In successive editions of the Supreme Court Practice, many cases illustrating the exercise of jurisdiction to stay proceedings in particular contexts were given; see SCP 1999, Vol. 2, paras 20A–337 *et seq*. In the above paragraphs, no effort is made to reproduce all of the information formerly found in the Supreme Court Practice. Significant omissions include the information found in the following paragraphs of Vol. 2 of the 1999 edition: para. 20A–251 (Bankruptcy), paras 20A–353 and 20A–354 (Company winding-up), para. 20A–355 (Company—stay of petition and order).

[THE NEXT PARAGRAPH IS 9A–259.]

Power to award damages as well as, or in substitution for, injunction or specific performance

9A–259   **50.** Where the Court of Appeal or the High Court has jurisdiction to entertain an application for an injunction or specific performance, it may award damages in addition to, or in substitution for, an injunction or specific performance.

9A–260   *Note* —Derived from the Chancery Amendment Act 1858, s.2; and the JA 1925, ss.18, 26.

Effect of this section

9A–261   The purpose of this section was to make it possible for a claimant to claim both damages and an injunction in the same proceedings, whether those proceedings were brought in the Queen's Bench Division or the Chancery Division. In cases decided shortly after the Judicature Acts 1873–75 came into force it was said that, as a rule, the claimant should claim both in the same proceedings, if at all (*Serrao v. Noel* (1885) 15 QBD 549; *Gent v. Harrison* (1894) 69 L.T. 307; *Caton v. Hancock* (1890) 88 L.T.J. 138). See CPR, r.16.2(1)(b). Note also *Chiron Corporation v. Organon Teknika* [1995] F.S.R. 355.

The jurisdiction of the court to refuse to grant an injunction sought to restrain continuing trespass and breach of covenant and to award damages in lieu under s.50 was authoritatively reviewed in *Jaggard v. Sawyer* [1995] 1 W.L.R. 269, CA. It has been held at first instance that, since the coming into effect of the Human Rights Act 1998 Sched.1 Pt 1, damages for future infringements of a claimant's rights may be awarded under s.50 in lieu of an injunction (*Marcic v. Thames Water Utilities Ltd* [2000] 3 All E.R. 698 (Judge Richard Havery QC)).

COSTS

Costs in civil division of Court of Appeal, High Court and county courts

9A–262   **51.**—(1) Subject to the provisions of this or any other enactment and to rules of court, the costs of and incidental to all proceedings in—

    (a) the civil division of the Court of Appeal;

    (b) the High Court, and

    (c) any county court,

shall be in the discretion of the court.

(2) Without prejudice to any general power to make rules of court, such rules may make provision for regulating matters relating to the costs of those proceedings including, in particular, prescribing scales of costs to be paid to legal or other representatives or for securing that the amount awarded to a party in respect of the costs to be paid by him to such representatives is not limited to what would have been payable by him to them if he had not been awarded costs.

(3) The court shall have full power to determine by whom and to what extent the costs are to be paid.

(4) In subsections (1) and (2) "proceedings" includes the administration of estates and trusts.

(5) Nothing in subsection (1) shall alter the practice in any criminal cause, or in bankruptcy.

(6) In any proceedings mentioned in subsection (1), the court may disallow, or (as the case may be) order the legal or other representative concerned to meet, the whole of any wasted costs or such part of them as may be determined in accordance with rules of court.

(7) In subsection (6), "wasted costs" means any costs incurred by a party—

    (a) as a result of any improper, unreasonable or negligent act or omission on the part of any legal or other representative or any employee of such a representative; or

    (b) which, in the light of any such act or omission occurring after they were incurred, the court considers it is unreasonable to expect that party to pay.

(8) Where—

    (a) a person has commenced proceedings in the High Court; but

    (b) those proceedings should, in the opinion of the court, have been commenced in a county court in accordance with any provision made under section 1 of the Courts and Legal Services Act 1990 or by or under any other enactment,

the person responsible for determining the amount which is to be awarded to that person by way of costs shall have regard to those circumstances.

(9) Where, in complying with subsection (8), the responsible person reduces the amount which would otherwise be awarded to the person in question—

    (a) the amount of that reduction shall not exceed 25 per cent; and

    (b) on any taxation of the costs payable by that person to his legal representative, regard shall be had to the amount of the reduction.

(10) The Lord Chancellor may by order amend subsection (9)(a) by substituting, for the percentage for the time being mentioned there, a different percentage.

(11) Any such order shall be made by statutory instrument and may make such transitional or incidental provision as the Lord Chancellor considers expedient.

(12) No such statutory instrument shall be made unless a draft of the instrument has been approved by both Houses of Parliament.

(13) In this section "legal or other representative", in relation to a party to proceedings, means any person exercising a right of audience or right to conduct litigation on his behalf.

9A–263 *Note*—Substituted by the Courts and Legal Services Act 1990, s.4. Amended by the Access to Justice Act 1999, s.31.

Effect of this section

9A–264 This section came into its present form as a result of the Courts and Legal Services Act 1990, s.4(1). In its amended form the section implemented recommendations made in the Report of the Review Body on Civil Justice (Cm. 394, 1988), including the recommendation that there should be a single costs regime for the High Court and the county courts, subject to an exception for county court cases below £3,000. As amended, the section provides statutory bases for awarding costs, not only for proceedings in the Court of Appeal (Civil Division) and the High Court, but for the county courts also. Rules of court relating to costs are found in the CPR made by the rule committee established under the Civil Procedure Act 1997, s.2. Section 51 is referred to specifically in CPR, rr.48.2 and 48.7. In s.51(2), the words "or for securing" onwards were added by the Access to Justice Act 1999. This addition makes it possible for rules of court to provide that a successful party may recover by way of *inter partes* costs a sum in excess of his liability to his own legal representative (*cf. Gundry v. Sainsbury* [1910] 1 K.B. 645). This addition was brought into effect on June 2, 2003, by the Access to Justice Act 1999 (Commencement No. 10) Order 2002 (S.I. 2003 No. 1241), making possible amendments to CPR, r.43.2 brought about by the Civil Procedure (Amendment No. 2) Rules 2003 (S.I. 2003 No. 1242) and coming into effect on the same date. Note also, Access to Justice Act 1999, s.29 (recovery of insurance premium by way of costs) (see para. 9A–862).

"costs ... shall be in the discretion of the court"

9A–265 Subject to the provisions of the 1981 Act or any other enactment and to rules of court, the costs of and incidental to all proceedings shall be in the discretion of the court and the court shall have full power to determine by whom and to what extent the costs are to be paid (subss.(1) & (3)). This general principle applies in all forums. It is re-stated in CPR, r.44.3 and the exercise of the discretion is regulated by the many detailed provisions found in Pts 44 to 48 of the CPR and supplementing practice directions.

The breadth of the discretion was emphasised by the House of Lords in *Aiden Shipping Co. Ltd. v. Interbulk Ltd.* [1986] A.C. 965, HL, where it was held that it includes a power to award costs against a person who is not a party to the proceedings. In modern times, the jurisdiction to order that costs should be paid by a person who, though not actually a party to the proceedings, is sufficiently involved in them in support of a losing party for it to be appropriate for the court to order that they should bear at least some or a proportion of the winning party's costs (see further para. 9A–265A below), has been explained and developed in a number of cases. Significant authorities include the following: *Symphony Group Plc v. Hodgson* [1994] Q.B. 179, CA; *Tharros Shipping Co Ltd v. Bias Shipping Ltd (The Griparion) (No. 3)* [1995] 1 Lloyd's Rep. 541; *Murphy v. Young & Co's Brewery Plc* [1997] 1 W.L.R. 1591, CA; *Faryab v. Smyth* [1998] C.L.Y. 411; *Pendennis Shipyard Ltd v. Magrathea (Pendennis) Ltd* [1998] 1 Lloyd's Rep. 315; *TGA Chapman Ltd v. Christopher* [1998] 1 W.L.R. 12, CA; *Gloucestershire HA v. MA*

Torpy & Partners Ltd (t/a Torpy & Partners) (No. 2) [1999] Lloyd's Rep. I.R. 303; *Globe Equities Ltd v. Globe Legal Services Ltd, The Times,* April 14, 1999, CA, unrep.; *Fulton Motors Ltd v. Toyota (G.B.) Ltd* July 23, 1999, CA, unrep.; *Stocznia Gdanska SA v. Latreefers Inc,* [1999] 1 B.C.L.C. 271, CA; *Cormack v. Washbourne (formerly t/a Washbourne & Co),* [1999] Lloyd's Rep. P.N. 389, CA; *Secretary of State for Trade and Industry v. Aurum Marketing Ltd,* [1999] 2 B.C.L.C. 498, CA; *Secretary of State for Trade and Industry v. Backhouse, The Times,* February 23, 2001, CA; *Hamilton v. Al Fayed (No. 2)* [2002] EWCA Civ 665; [2002] 3 All E.R. 641, CA, *Gulf Azov Shipping Co Ltd v. Idisi (Costs)* [2004] EWCA Civ 292; March 15, 2004, CA.

The approach of the courts to the making of an award of costs against a non-party has had to accommodate the change in public policy which has recognised that access to justice can properly be procured by giving those who provide legal services an interest in the outcome of litigation through conditional fee agreements (*Gulf Azov Shipping Co Ltd v. Idisi (Costs)*).

The courts' general discretion as to costs referred to in s.51 includes a power to order that one order for costs should be set-off against another. In *R. (Burkett) v. London Borough of Hammersmith and Fulham* [2004] EWCA Civ 1342; *The Times* October 20, 2004, CA, where the Court of Appeal was concerned with the set-off of costs against costs (and not against damages) in the same proceedings (and not in different proceedings) the law as to set-off in this context and its history were explained in detailed (see para. 38 *et seq*).

Normally, orders made by the court in the exercise of the discretion to award costs referred to in s.51(1) are made at the end of the proceedings to which they relate (whether interlocutory, final or appeal). However the discretion is wide enough to enable the court to make an order for costs in advance, based on assumptions as to the possible outcomes (and, therefore, the possible costs liabilities) of the proceedings. Depending on the circumstances, such orders may be aptly described as "prospective", "pre-emptive" or "protective" costs orders. The clearest example is where the court makes an order that a party involved in legal proceedings in the capacity of trustee should be entitled to his own costs out of the fund and should be indemnified by the fund against any award for costs which may be made against him (*Re Beddoe, Downes v. Cottam* [1893] 1 Ch. 547, CA) (CPR r. 64.2 and Practice Direction (Estates, Trusts and Charities) para. 6.1; see Vol. 1 paras 48.1.5 and 64PD.6). In certain circumstances the costs protection enjoyed by trustees may be extended to beneficiaries (*Re Buckton, Buckton v. Buckton* [1907] 2 Ch. 406; *D'Abo v. Paget (No.1),* [2002] B.C.C. 31). The protection has also been extended to minority shareholders (*Wallersteiner v. Moir (No. 2)* [1975] Q.B. 373), to beneficiaries under pension funds (*McDonald v. Horn* [1995] 1 All E.R. 961, CA; *Machin v. National Power Plc.,* July 31, 1998, unrep. (Carnwath J.)), and to insurance policy-holders (*AXA Equity & Law Life Assurance Society Plc (No.1), Re,* [2001] 2 B.C.L.C. 447 (Evans-Lombe J.)). In modern times, pre-emptive costs orders have been sought in circumstances quite different to the trust and trust-related circumstances noted above, in particular in judicial review applications where organisations acting in the public interest are involved. It has been held that, in exceptional circumstances, pre-emptive costs orders may be granted in such "public interest challenge" cases; see *R. v. Lord Chancellor, ex p. Child Poverty Action Group,* [1999] 1 W.L.R. 347 (Dyson J.); *R. v. Hammersmith and Fulham LBC, ex p. CPRE London Branch,* October 26, 1999, unrep. (Richards J.); *R. v. Secretary of State for the Environment, Transport and the Regions ex p. O'Byrne (Application for Jo,* [2000] C.P. Rep. 9 (Hooper J.); *cf. Hodgson v. Imperial Tobacco Ltd* [1998] 1 W.L.R. 1056, CA. In giving the judgment of the Court of Appeal in *Gulf Azov Shipping Co Ltd v. Idisi (Costs)* [2004] EWCA Civ 292, CA March 15, 2004, unrep., Lord Phillips M.R. said (at para. 34) it was unfortunate that the application for costs against a non-party funder was heard, not by the judge who had dealt with the principal proceedings giving rise to the application, or by any other judge of the Commercial Court who had been involved with the litigation, but by a deputy High Court judge who had had no previous connection with the proceedings.

Costs order in favour of or against non–parties

The procedure to be followed where the court is considering whether to exercise its discretion under s.51 to make a costs order in favour or against a person who is not a party to the proceedings is stated in CPR, r.48.2. For information on the exercise of the discretion in this manner, see commentary following that rule (Vol 1, para. 48.2.1).

9A–265A

"court may disallow, or ... order ... wasted costs"

Subsections (6) and (7) deal with liability for "wasted costs". The court may disallow

9A–266

such costs, or it may make the the the legal or other representatives (see subs.(11)) concerned personally liable for such costs. Subsection (6) applies, not only in the Court of Appeal (Civil Division), the High Court and county courts, but also in relation to any civil proceedings in the Crown Court (s.52(1A)). The definition of "wasted costs" given in subs.(7) does not require a showing of misconduct or gross neglect, but is, at its lowest, a negligence test. The provisions and the rules of court elaborating on them were designed to deal with doubts which had arisen under former legislation and rules of court (for background, see White Paper on Legal Services Cm 740, 1989). The inherent jurisdiction to penalise in costs remains. Relevant rules of court are found in CPR, r.44.14 (Court's powers in relation to misconduct) (see Vol. 1, para. 44.14) and r.48.7 (Personal liability of legal representative for costs) (see Vol. 1, para. 48.7). For explanation, see commentaries following those rules.

Costs sanction for bringing proceedings in High Court

9A–267   In its amended form, the section introduced a modified costs sanction to discourage litigants from bringing in the High Court proceedings that could have been brought in a county court (subss.(8) to (12)). The statutory provisions which formerly provided the basis for this costs sanction were repealed. The power to impose such sanction is reflected in provisions found in the CPR and supplementing practice directions.

Costs in Crown Court

9A–268   **52.**—(1) Rules of court may authorise the Crown Court to award costs and may regulate any matters relating to costs of proceedings in that court, and in particular may make provision as to—

(a) any discretion to award costs;

(b) the taxation of costs, or the fixing of a sum instead of directing a taxation, and as to the officer of the court or other person by whom costs are to be taxed;

(c) a right of appeal from any decision on the taxation of costs, whether to a Taxing Master of the Supreme Court or to any other officer or authority;

(d) a right of appeal to the High Court, subject to any conditions specified in the rules, from any decision on an appeal brought by virtue of paragraph (c);

(e) the enforcement of an order for costs; and

(f) the charges or expenses or other disbursements which are to be treated as costs for the purposes of the rules.

(2) The costs to be dealt with by rules made in pursuance of this section may, where an appeal is brought to the Crown Court from the decision of a magistrates' court, or from the decision of any other court or tribunal, include costs in the proceedings in that court or tribunal.

(2A) Subsection (6) of section 51 applies in relation to any civil proceedings in the Crown Court as it applies in relation to any civil proceedings mentioned in subsection (1) of that section.

(3) Nothing in this section authorises the making of rules about the payment of costs out of central funds, whether under the Part II of the Prosecution of Offences Act 1985 or otherwise, but rules made in pursuance of this section may make any such provision as in relation to costs of proceedings in the Crown Court, is contained in section 18 of that Act or in regulations made under section 19 of that Act (awards of part and party costs in criminal proceedings).

(4) Rules made in pursuance of this section may amend or repeal all or any of the provisions of any enactment about costs between

party and party in criminal or other proceedings in the Crown Court, being an enactment passed before, or contained in, the Part II of the Prosecution of Offences Act 1985.

(5) Rules made in pursuance of this section shall have effect subject to the provisions of section 41 of, and Schedule 9 to, the Administration of Justice Act 1970 (method of enforcing orders for costs).

Note —Amended by the Prosecution of Offences Act 1985, Sched.1; the Courts and **9A-269** Legal Services Act 1990, s.4(2) and subject to transitional provisions specified in art.2 by the Courts Act 2003 (Consequential Amendments) Order 2004 (S.I. 2004 No. 2035), Sched.1, para. 12(a).

PART III

PRACTICE AND PROCEDURE

THE COURT OF APPEAL

DISTRIBUTION OF BUSINESS

Distribution of business between civil and criminal divisions

53.—(1) Rules of court may provide for the distribution of business **9A-270** in the Court of Appeal between the civil and criminal divisions, but subject to any such rules business shall be distributed in accordance with the following provisions of this section.

(2) The criminal division of the Court of Appeal shall exercise—

    (a) all jurisdiction of the Court of Appeal under Parts I and II of the Criminal Appeal Act 1968;

    (b) the jurisdiction of the Court of Appeal under section 13 of the Administration of Justice Act 1960 (appeals in cases of contempt of court) in relation to appeals from orders and decisions of the Crown Court;

    (c) all other jurisdiction expressly conferred on that division by this or any other Act; and

    (d) the jurisdiction to order the issue of writs of venire de novo.

(3) The civil division of the Court of Appeal shall exercise the whole of the jurisdiction of that court not exercisable by the criminal division.

(4) Where any class of proceedings in the Court of Appeal is by any statutory provision assigned to the criminal division of that court, rules of court may provide for any enactment relating to—

    (a) appeals to the Court of Appeal under Part I of the Criminal Appeal Act 1968; or

    (b) any matter connected with or arising out of such appeals,

to apply in relation to proceedings of that class or, as the case may be, to any corresponding matter connected with or arising out of such proceedings, as it applies in relation to such appeals or, as the case may be, to the relevant matter within paragraph (b), with or without prescribed modifications in either case.

9A–271 *Note* —The effect of ss.18 and 53 is that the Civil Division of the Court of Appeal has no jurisdiction to hear appeals in any criminal cause or matter.

COMPOSITION OF COURT

Court of civil division

9A–272 **54.**—(1) This section relates to the civil division of the Court of Appeal; and in this section "court", except where the context otherwise requires, means a court of that division.

(2) Subject as follows, a court shall be duly constituted for the purpose of exercising any of its jurisdiction if it consists of one or more judges.

(3) The Master of the Rolls may, with the concurrence of the Lord Chancellor, give (or vary or revoke) directions about the minimum number of judges of which a court must consist if it is to be duly constituted for the purpose of any description of proceedings.

(4) The Master of the Rolls, or any Lord Justice designated by him, may (subject to any directions under subsection (3)) determine the number of judges of which a court is to consist for the purpose of any particular proceedings.

(4A) The Master of the Rolls may give directions as to what is to happen in any particular case where one or more members of a court which has partly heard proceedings are unable to continue.

(5) Where—

(a) an appeal has been heard by a court consisting of an even number of judges; and

(b) the members of the court are equally divided,

the case shall, on the application of any party to the appeal, be reargued before and determined by an uneven number of judges not less than three, before any appeal to the House of Lords .

(6) *[Repealed]*

(7) *[Repealed]*

(8) Subsections (1) and (2) of section 70 (assessors in the High Court) shall apply in relation to causes and matters before the civil division of the Court of Appeal as they apply in relation to causes and matters before the High Court.

(9) Subsections (3) and (4) of section 60 (scientific advisers to assist the Patents Court in proceedings under the Patents Act 1949 and the Patents Act 1977) shall apply in relation to the civil division of the Court of Appeal and proceedings on appeal from any decision of the Patents Court in proceedings under those Acts as they apply in relation to the Patents Court and proceedings under those Acts.

(10) *[Repealed]*

9A–273 *Note* —Amended by the Courts and Legal Services Act 1990, s.7 and the Access to Justice Act 1999, ss.59, 106, Sched.15, Pt III. See para. 9A–4.1 above.

Composition of the Court of Appeal

9A–274 By operation of the Access to Justice 1999, s.59, subss.(2) to (4A) were substituted for subs.(2) to (4) and subss.(6), (7) and (10) were repealed. Previously, the basic rule was that, in order to be properly constituted, a court of the Division had to consist of "an uneven number of judges not less than three".

In exceptional cases, provided for in s.54 and regulations, a court of the Division was duly constituted for certain purposes if it consisted of two judges. In its amended form, subs.(2) states the basic rule that a court shall be duly constituted "for the purpose of exercising any of its jurisdiction if it consists of one or more judges". The circumstances in which a court of the Division should consist of two or more judges is provided for by directions given under subs.(3) and (4). Subsections (4A) states that the Master of the Rolls may give directions as to what is to happen in any particular case where one or more members of a court which has partly heard proceedings are unable to continue. This replaces former subs.(3) which stated that a court would remain duly constituted so long as the number of judges was not reduced to less than three. Where an appeal has been heard by a court consisting of an even number of judges, and the members of the court are eqully divided, subs.(5) applies. As a consequence of the amendments made by the 1999 Act, the Court of Appeal (Civil Division) Order 1982 (S.I. 1982 No. 543) will be repealed.

Assessors and scientific advisers

9A–275 Subss.(8) and (9) extend to the Court of Appeal the provisions of s.70 concerning assessors and scientific advisers (see para. 9A–328 below).

[THE NEXT PARAGRAPH IS 9A–280.]

Court of criminal division

9A–280 **55.**—(1) This section relates to the criminal division of the Court of Appeal; and in this section "court" means a court of that division.

(2) Subject to subsection (6), a court shall be duly constituted for the purpose of exercising any of its jurisdiction if it consists of an uneven number of judges not less than three.

(3) Where—

(a) part of any proceedings before a court has been heard by an uneven number of judges greater than three; and

(b) one or more members of the court are unable to continue,

the court shall remain duly constituted for the purpose of those proceedings so long as the number of members (whether even or uneven) is not reduced to less than three.

(4) Subject to subsection (6), a court shall, if it consists of two judges, be duly constituted for every purpose except—

(a) determining an appeal against—

(i) conviction; or

(ii) a verdict of not guilty by reason of insanity; or

(iii) a finding of a jury under section 4 of the Criminal Procedure (Insanity) Act 1964 (unfitness to plead) that a person is under a disability;

(aa) reviewing sentencing under Part IV of the Criminal Justice Act 1988;

(b) determining an application for leave to appeal to the House of Lords ; and

(c) refusing an application for leave to appeal to the criminal division against conviction or any such verdict or finding as is mentioned in paragraph (a)(ii) or (iii), other than an application which has been refused by a single judge.

(5) Where an appeal has been heard by a court consisting of an even number of judges and the members of the court are equally divided, the case shall be re-argued before and determined by an uneven number of judges not less than three.

(6) A court shall not be duly constituted if it includes more than one Circuit judge acting as a judge of the court under section 9.

9A–281   *Note* —Amended by the Criminal Justice Act 1988, s.170(1), Sched.15, para. 80; and the Criminal Justice and Public Order Act 1994, s.52. See para. 9A–4.1 above.

Judges not to sit on appeal from their own judgments, etc.

9A–282   **56.**—(1) No judge shall sit as a member of the civil division of the Court of Appeal on the hearing of, or shall determine any application in proceedings incidental or preliminary to, an appeal for a judgment or order made in any case by himself or by any court of which he was a member.

(2) No judge shall sit as a member of the criminal division of the Court of Appeal on the hearing of, or shall determine any application in proceedings incidental or preliminary to, an appeal against—

(a) a conviction before himself or a court of which he was a member; or

(b) a sentence passed by himself or such a court.

9A–283   *Note* —The fact that a judge in the Court of Appeal is a judge of the Division of the High Court in which the proceedings under appeal were brought does not preclude him from being a member of the Court of Appeal hearing the appeal, provided of course that he has himself taken no part in the making of the order appealed against (*Fisher v. Val de Travers Asphalte Co.* (1875) 1 C.P.D. 259).

Circuit judges not to sit on certain appeals

9A–284   **56A.** [*Repealed by the Courts Act 2003, Sched.10, para.1*]

Allocation of cases in criminal division

9A–285   **56B.**—(1) The appeals or classes of appeals suitable for allocation to a court of the criminal division of the Court of Appeal in which a Circuit judge is acting under section 9 shall be determined in accordance with directions given by or on behalf of the Lord Chief Justice with the concurrence of the Lord Chancellor.

(2) In subsection (1) "appeal" includes the hearing of, or any application in proceedings incidental or preliminary to, an appeal.

9A–286   *Note* — Sections 56A and 56B added by the Criminal Justice and Public Order Act 1994, s.52. See para. 9A–4.1 above.

SITTINGS AND VACATIONS

Sittings and vacations

9A–287   **57.**—(1) Sittings of the Court of Appeal may be held, and any other business of the Court of Appeal may be conducted, at any place in England or Wales.

(2) Subject to rules of court—

(a) the places at which the Court of Appeal sits outside the Royal Courts of Justice; and

(b) the days and times at which the Court of Appeal sits at any place outside the Royal Courts of Justice,

shall be determined in accordance with directions given by the Lord Chancellor.

(3) Rules of court may make provision for regulating the vacations to be observed by the Court of Appeal and in the offices of that court.

(4) Rules of Court—

(a) may provide for securing such sittings of the civil division of the Court of Appeal during vacation as the Master of the Rolls may with the concurrence of the Lord Chancellor determine;

(b) without prejudice to paragraph (a), shall provide for the transaction during vacation by judges of the Court of Appeal of all such business in the civil division of that court as may require to be immediately or promptly transacted; and

(c) shall providing for securing sittings of the criminal division of that court during vacation if necessary.

subs.(1)

See further, Practice Direction (Court Sittings), supplementing CPR Pt 39.　　**9A–288**

subs.(2)

Para. 10.8 of *Practice Direction (Court of Appeal (Civil Division))*, [1999] 1 W.L.R. 1027, **9A–289** CA (*sub nom Practice Note (Court of Appeal: Procedure)* [1999] 1 W.L.R. 1027; 2 All E.R. 490, CA) states that the Court of Appeal will sit in vacation on such days as the Master of the Rolls may direct and may hear such appeals and applications as the Court may direct. Details of the number of courts sitting in August and September will be published each year, normally before Easter.

OTHER PROVISIONS

Calling into question of incidental decisions in civil division

58.—(1) Rules of court may provide that decisions of the Court of **9A–290** Appeal which—

(a) are taken by a single judge or any officer or member of staff of that court in proceedings incidental to any cause or matter pending before the civil division of that court; and

(b) do not involve the determination of an appeal or of an application for permission to appeal,

may be called into question in such manner as may be prescribed.

(2) No appeal shall lie to the House of Lords from a decision which may be called into question pursuant to rules under subsection (1).

Note —Amended by the Access to Justice Act 1999, s.60. See para. 9A–4.1 above.　　**9A–291**

Jurisdiction of a single judge or any officer or member of court staff to hear incidental applications

Subsection (1) makes provision for any application incidental to any cause or matter **9A–292** pending before the Civil Division of the Court of Appeal to be heard by a single judge, or of any officer or member of court staff, so far as provided in rules of court. (The office of Registrar of Civil Appeals, formerly referred to in s.58, was abolished by the Access to Justice 1999, s.70.)

See CPR Pt 52, section II. In *Perotti v. Watson*, February 2, 2000, CA, unrep., it was held that by operation of s.58 and former RSC O.59, r.2B (see now CPR, r.52.16) a single Lord Justice may vary a procedural order for the conduct and management of a substantive appeal previously made by the Court constituted by two Lord Justices.

Form of judgment of court of criminal division

9A–293   **59.** Any judgment of a court of the criminal division of the Court of Appeal on any question shall, except where the judge presiding over the court states that in his opinion the question is one of law on which it is convenient that separate judgments should be pronounced by the members of the court, be pronounced by the judge presiding over the court or by such other member of the court as he directs and, except as aforesaid, no judgment shall be separately pronounced on any question by any member of the court.

Rules of court, and decisions of Court of Appeal, as to whether judgment or order is final or interlocutory

9A–294   **60.**—(1) Rules of court may provide for orders or judgments of any prescribed description to be treated for any prescribed purpose connected with appeals to the Court of Appeal as final or as interlocutory.

(2) No appeal shall lie from a decision of the Court of Appeal as to whether a judgment or order is, for any purpose connected with an appeal to that court, final or interlocutory.

9A–295   *Note* —The significance of the distinction between final and interlocutory orders in relation to the jurisdiction and procedure of the Court of Appeal (Civil Division) is not as important as it was. Former RSC O.59, r.1A elaborated on the distinction, principally for the purpose of distinguishing between those cases where leave to appeal was required under O.59, r.1B and where not. See now CPR Pt 52, section II.

THE HIGH COURT

DISTRIBUTION OF BUSINESS

Distribution of business among Divisions

9A–296   **61.**—(1) Subject to any provision made by or under this or any other Act (and in particular to any rules of court made in pursuance of subsection (2) and any order under subsection (3)), business in the High Court of any description mentioned in Schedule 1, as for the time being in force, shall be distributed among the Divisions in accordance with that Schedule.

(2) Rules of court may provide for the distribution of business in the High Court among the Divisions; but any rules made in pursuance of this subsection shall have effect subject to any orders for the time being in force under subsection (3).

(3) Subject to subsection (5), the Lord Chancellor may by order—

    (a) direct that any business in the High Court which is not for the time being assigned by or under this or any other Act to any Division be assigned to such Division as may be specified in the order;

(b) if at any time it appears to him desirable to do so with a view to the more convenient administration of justice, direct that any business for the time being assigned by or under this or any other Act to any Division be assigned to such other Division as may be specified in the order; and

(c) amend Schedule 1 so far as may be necessary in consequence of provision made by order under paragraph (a) or (b).

(4) The powers conferred by subsection (2) and subsection (3) include power to assign business of any description to two or more Divisions concurrently.

(5) No order under subsection (3)(b) relating to any business shall be made without the concurrence of the senior judge of—

(a) the Division or each of the Divisions to which the business is for the time being assigned; and

(b) the Division or each of the Divisions to which the business is to be assigned by the order.

(6) Subject to rules of court, the fact that a cause or matter commenced in the High Court falls within a class of business assigned by or under this Act to a particular Division does not make it obligatory for it to be allocated or transferred to that Division.

(7) Without prejudice to subsections (1) to (5) and section 63, rules of court may provide for the distribution of the business (other than business required to be heard by a divisional court) in any Division of the High Court among the judges of that Division.

(8) Any order under subsection (3) shall be made by statutory instrument, which shall be laid before Parliament after being made.

9A–297 *Note* —Derived from the JA 1925, ss.55–57, and the AJA 1970, s.1, Sched.1. See para. 9A–4.1 above.

Effect of section

9A–298 This section should be read closely with s.5, which provides for the constitution of three Divisions of the High Court, and with Sched.1 which provides for the distribution of the business of the High Court among the three Divisions. Such distribution of the business is intended to achieve a more convenient system of the administration of civil justice and a more effective machinery for the despatch of business. It reflects the high degree of specialisation which exists among the members of the legal profession, as well as to some extent of the judiciary. It is not intended to create, and does not have the effect of creating separate or self-contained Courts nor of distributing among the Divisions the jurisdiction and power of the High Court, which in spite of appearing to be fragmented into Divisions still remains a single, integrated Court. This section should also be read in conjunction with s.19(2)(b) which empowers the High Court to exercise all such other jurisdiction as was exercisable by it before the commencement of the Act.

The Admiralty, Commercial, and Administrative Courts are not separate Divisions within the High Court but are designated as courts within the Queen's Bench Division of the High Court, in the case of the first two mentioned, by s.6 of this Act (see para. 9A–21 above), and in the case of the last-mentioned, by *Practice Direction (Administrative Court: Establishment)* [2000] 1 W.L.R. 1654. The Patents Court is designated as a court within the Chancery Division of the High Court by s.6. See further s.62 below.

For considerations relevant to the proper distribution of business between the Administrative Court, on the one hand, and the Family Division of the High Court on the other, see *C. v. Bury Metropolitan Borough Council* [2002] EWHC 1438 (Fam), *The*

Times, July 25, 2002 (Butler-Sloss P.); *R.(P) v. Secretary of State for the Home Department*, *The Times*, July 20, 2001, and *A v. A Health Authority* [2002] EWHC 866 (Admin); [2002] 3 W.L.R. 24 (Munby J.).

Jurisdiction exercisable by all Divisions

9A–299
"There is but one High Court" (*Re Hastings (No. 3)* [1959] Ch. 368, at 379, *per* Vaisey J.). Section 5(5) expressly provides that all jurisdiction vested in the High Court under the Act belongs to all Divisions alike. This principle is further underscored by the direction issued by the Lord Chancellor that any Division of the High Court to which a cause or matter is assigned has jurisdiction to grant any remedy or relief arising out of or related to or connected with any claim made in that cause or matter notwithstanding that proceedings for such remedy or relief are assigned to another Division of the Court (*Practice Direction (High Court: Division)* [1973] 1 W.L.R. 627; [1973] 2 All E.R. 233.

A judge of one Division may decline to exercise his jurisdiction over a matter which is properly assignable to another Division, to which he may transfer the matter (see s.65 below). Equally, however, the judge may, in his discretion, decide to retain a matter which is properly assignable to another Division (*Russian Commercial and Industrial Bank v. British Bank for Foreign Trade Ltd* [1921] 2 A.C. 438; *Midland Bank Ltd v. Stamps* [1978] 1 W.L.R. 635; [1978] 3 All E.R. 1).

As to transfer of proceedings from one Division to another, see s.65 below.

Various CPR provisions stipulate that certain proceedings should be commenced, or applications made, in particular Divisions of the High Court. See *e.g.* r.7.1 and Practice Direction How to Start Proceedings – The Claim Form), paras 2.1 *et seq.* (see Vol. 1, para. 7PD.2), and Practice Direction (Interim Injunctions), para. 8.5 (all applications in intellectual property cases to be made in Chancery Division).

Re-distribution of business

9A–300
The distribution of business among the Divisions of the High Court in accordance with Sched.1 to the Act is not fixed or unalterable but is capable of addition, amendment or variation by orders made by the Lord Chancellor under s.61(3) and (5), under which he may direct that any business in the High Court not already assigned by the Act of 1981 or any other Act to any Division be assigned to a specified Division, and that any business already assigned by the Act of 1981 or any other Act to any Division be assigned to another specified Division, and for these purposes, he may amend Sched.1 to the Act under s.61(3)(c); and the Lord Chancellor has power to assign any business to two or more Divisions concurrently (s.61(4)). Such orders must be made with the concurrence of the senior Judge of the Division or Divisions concerned, and they must be made by statutory instrument (see s.61(8)). Amendments were made to Sched.1 of the Act concerning the distribution of business to the Family Division by the High Court (Distribution of Business) Order 1991 (S.I. 1991 No. 1210) and High Court (Distribution of Business) Order 1993 (S.I. 1993 No. 622).

Business of Patents, Admiralty and Commercial Courts

9A–301
62.—(1) The Patents Court shall take such proceedings relating to patents as are within the jurisdiction conferred on it by the Patents Act 1977, and such other proceedings relating to patents or other matters as may be prescribed.

(2) The Admiralty Court shall take Admiralty business, that is to say causes and matters assigned to the Queen's Bench Division and involving the exercise of the High Court's Admiralty jurisdiction or its jurisdiction as a prize court.

(3) The Commercial Court shall take such causes and matters as may in accordance with rules of court be entered in the commercial list.

9A–302
Note —Derived from the AJA 1970, ss.2, 3; and the Patents Act 1977, s.96. See also s.6.

Procedure

9A–303
Procedure before these specialised courts within the High Court is governed by the

CPR. However, the procedures for each of the courts mentioned in s.62 is subject to considerable elaboration and variation in Parts of the CPR specially dedicated to them; see Pt 58 (Commercial Court), Pt 61 (Admiralty Claims), Pt 63 (Patents and Other Intellectual Property Claims) and the practice directions supplementing those Parts.

Business assigned to specially nominated judges

63.—(1) Any business assigned, in accordance with this or any **9A–304** other Act or rules of court, to one or more specially nominated judges of the High Court may—

    (a) during vacation; or

    (b) during the illness or absence of that judge or any of those judges; or

    (c) for any other reasonable cause,

be dealt with by any judge of the High Court named for that purpose by the Lord Chancellor .

(2) If at any time it appears to the Lord Chancellor desirable to do so with a view to the more convenient administration of justice, he may by order direct that business of any description which is for the time being assigned, in accordance with this or any other Act or rules of court, to one or more specially nominated judges of the High Court shall cease to be so assigned and may be dealt with by any one or more judges of the High Court.

(3) An order under subsection (2) shall not be made in respect of any business without the concurrence of the senior judge of the Division to which the business is for the time being assigned.

Note —Derived from the JA 1925, s.60A. See also s.61(7). See para. 9A–4.1 above.   **9A–305**

Choice of Division by plaintiff

64.—(1) Without prejudice to the power of transfer under section **9A–306** 65, the person by whom any cause or matter is commenced in the High Court shall in the prescribed manner allocate it to whichever Division he thinks fit.

(2) Where a cause or matter is commenced in the High Court, all subsequent interlocutory or other steps or proceedings in the High Court in that cause or matter shall be taken in the Division to which the cause or matter is for the time being allocated (whether under subsection (1) or in consequence of its transfer under section 65).

Note —Derived from the JA 1925, s.58.   **9A–307**

Choice of Division

This section confers on the plaintiff the initiative to choose the Division in which he **9A–308** thinks fit to commence his proceedings. However, this is subject to the power of the Court to order the transfer of proceedings from one Division to another, or to or from a specialist list (see s.65 and CPR, r.30.5). The choice of the Division in which an action is commenced has the consequence that all subsequent interlocutory or other steps or proceedings must be taken in that Division. If the action is subsequently transferred to another Division, all further interlocutory or other steps or proceedings must be taken in the Division to which it has been transferred (s.64(2)), but the validity of the interlocutory or other steps or proceedings taken in the Division originally chosen will not be affected by the transfer (s.65(2)).

Power of transfer

65.—(1) Any cause or matter may at any time and at any stage **9A–309** thereof, and either with or without application from any of the parties, be transferred, by such authority and in such manner as rules of court may direct, from one Division or judge of the High Court to another Division or judge thereof.

(2) The transfer of a cause or matter under subsection (1) to a different Division or judge of the High Court shall not affect the validity of any steps or proceedings taken or order made in that cause or matter before the transfer.

9A–310   *Note* —Derived from the JA 1925, s.59.

Transfer to another Division

9A–311   This section should be read with s.64. For rules of court as to transfer, see CPR, r.30.5. The power of transfer from one Division or Judge of the High Court to another Division or Judge may be exercised either on the application of a party or by the Court of its own motion, s.65(1). A party bringing his action in the wrong Division may be ordered to pay all costs incurred thereby (see *Re Pollard* (1888) 20 QBD 656, CA).

The Judge has an absolute discretion whether to transfer to the appropriate Division a matter assigned to his Division or to deal with it. In *DBS Management Plc v. Excess Insurance Co Ltd* April 25, 1994, CA, (unrep.), it was said that the test for transfer from one Division to another is whether it is inappropriate for the case to be tried in the Division in which it was begun because that Division lacked a special expertise needed for the just and expeditious disposal of the case; the same test applies for transfers from the Q.B. general list and the commercial list. Other modern authorities include: *Boobyer v. David Holman & Co Ltd* [1992] 2 Lloyd's Rep. 436; *Deeny v. Littlejohn & Co (A Firm), The Times,* January 19, 1995; *O'Brien v. Hughes-Gibb & Co Ltd, The Times,* October 20, 1993.

See further, CPR, r.30.5 and notes following (see Vol. 1, para. 30.5).

DIVISIONAL COURTS

Divisional courts of the High Court

9A–312   **66.**—(1) Divisional courts may be held for the transaction of any business in the High Court which is, by or by virtue of rules of court or any other statutory provisions, required to be heard by a divisional court.

(2) Any number of divisional courts may sit at the same time.

(3) A divisional court shall be constituted of not less than two judges.

(4) Every judge of the High Court shall be qualified to sit in any divisional court.

(5) The judge who is, according to the order of precedence under this Act, the senior of the judges constituting a divisional court shall be the president of the court.

9A–313   *Note* —Derived from the JA 1925, s.63; and the AJA 1977, s.9.

Disagreement between two Judges

9A–314   There is authority for the proposition that whenever there is an appeal to two judges in a Divisional Court who differ, the judgment appealed from should stand (*Metropolitan Water Board v. Johnson & Co* [1913] 3 K.B. 900 at 904 *per* Channel J.; see also *Bradford Corporation v. Myers* [1916] 1 A.C. 242; *Barron v. Potter* [1915] 3 K.B. 593; *Cheater v. Cater* [1918] 1 K.B. 247). As to disagreement between equal numbers of the members of the Court of Appeal, see s.54(5) and notes following s.54 above (para. 9A–274). It is thought that, wherever possible, the provisions relating to disagreement between members of the Court of Appeal will be applied, by analogy, to disagreement between two judges in a Divisional Court.

MODE OF CONDUCTING BUSINESS

Proceedings in court and in chambers

67. Business in the High Court shall be heard and disposed of in **9A–315** court except in so far as it may, under this or any other Act, under rules of court or in accordance with the practice of the court, be dealt with in chambers.

Note —Derived from the JA 1925, s.61.   **9A–316**

Business to be conducted "in court" and "in public"

In this section, the expression "in court" means in open court, in open view, in **9A–317** public, in a court to which the public and the press are entitled to be admitted (see as to the meaning of "open court" *R. v. Lewes Prison (Governore), ex p. Doyle* [1917] 2 K.B. 254 at 271 *per* Lord Reading C.J.).

Art.6 of the European Convention on Human Rights, incorporated in the Human Rights Act 1998, Sched.1, states that in the determining of his civil rights "everyone is entitled to a fair and public hearing". Art.6 further states that, in certain circumstances, the press and public may be excluded "from all or part of the trial", for example, where publicity would prejudice the interests of justice.

CPR, r.39.2(1) states that the general rule is that "a hearing must be in public". Further, r.32.2(1) states that, where any facts needs to be proved by the evidence of witnesses at trial, it is to be proved "by their oral evidence given in public".

In early cases it was said that the obligation of the Court to hear and determine any proceeding in public is a mere matter of procedure, the departure from which is a mere irregularity and does not render the proceedings or the decision null and void (see *McPherson v. McPherson* [1936] A.C. 177, PC, applying *Dimes v. Proprietors of the Grand Junction Canal* (1852) 3 H.L.C. 750).

Business may be dealt with "in chambers" and "in private"

The expression "in chambers"used in this section in contrast to "in court", means in **9A–318** private, for example, in the judge's private room. The parties and their advisers are entitled to be present. Formerly, it was the practice that the public or the press were automatically excluded, unless invited to be present with the consent of the parties or the court. However, in *Hodgson v. Imperial Tobacco Ltd* [1998] 1 W.L.R. 1056, CA; [1998] 2 All E.R. 673, CA, the Master of the Rolls said, generally, the public has no right to attend hearings in chambers because of the nature of the work transacted and because of the physical restrictions on the room available, but if requested permission to attend may be granted if this is practical. Disclosure of proceedings in chambers is not a breach of confidence or amount to contempt so long as comment thereon does not substantially prejudice the administration of justice (for circumstances in which publication of information relating to proceedings before any court sitting in private may be contempt, see Administration of Justice Act 1960, s.12, see para. 9B–22). Proceedings in chambers are not confidential and any judgment or order will be made available on request (*ibid.*, see also *Forbes v. Smith* [1998] 1 All E.R. 973).

Section 67 states that business in the High Court may be dealt with in chambers, to the extent that this is permitted by the 1981 Act, any other Act, or rules of court. Whereas the expression "in chambers" was used throughout the RSC, in the CPR it is not used. After stating the general rule that a hearing is to be in public, r.39.2 goes on to state that, in certain circumstances, a hearing, or any part of it, may be "in private". Numerous provisions in the CPR state that particular proceedings shall be "in private". The result is that, nowadays, hearings "in chambers" (in so far as that expression is still apt) are not ipso facto hearings in private. See further, commentary on r.39.2 (Vol 1, paras 39.2.1 *et seq.*).

Business conducted in camera

Section 67 does not have the effect of derogating from the inherent jurisdiction of **9A–319** the Court to order that the hearing of the proceedings should be in camera, that is, in private, so that the court, when sitting in circumstances in which normally the press and public ought to be admitted, may be closed or cleared and the public and the press excluded (see *Scott v. Scott* [1913] A.C. 417, HL). The underlying principle that the public should be excluded is "that the administration of justice would be rendered impracticable by their presence" (*ibid*. at 446 *per* Earl Loreburn; see also *R. v. Lewes Prison (Governor), ex p. Doyle* [1917] 2 K.B. 254, at 271 *per* Lord Reading C.J., and *R. v. Chief Registrar of Friendly Building Societies, ex p. New Cross Building Society* [1984] Q.B. 227; [1984] 2 All E.R. 27, CA). (See also authorities referred to in S.C.P. 1999, Vol. 1, para. 33.4.6.) This power may be exercised in relation to the whole or only part of the proceedings, or to the whole or part of the evidence (*e.g. Hallam-Eames v. Merrett Syndicates Ltd, The Times*, June 16, 1995), even perhaps the evidence of one witness. The limits of this power, perhaps wisely have not been precisely defined. Most, if not all, of the circumstances justifying the Court's sitting in camera are covered by CPR, r.39.2. The exercise of the inherent jurisdiction is subject to art.6 of the Convention (see above).

Hearings in camera may be authorised by statute, see *e.g.* Matrimonial Causes Act 1973, s.48(2)).

[THE NEXT PARAGRAPH IS 9A–322.]

Exercise of High Court jurisdiction otherwise than by judges of that court

9A–322   **68.**—(1) Provision may be made by rules of court as to the cases in which jurisdiction of the High Court may be exercised by—

> (a) such Circuit judges, deputy Circuit judges or Recorders as the Lord Chancellor may from time to time nominate to deal with official referees' business; or
>
> (b) special referees.

(2) Without prejudice to the generality of subsection (1), rules of court may in particular—

> (a) [...]
>
> (b) authorise any question arising in any cause or matter to be referred to a special referee for inquiry and report.

(3) Rules of court shall not authorise the exercise of power of attachment and committal by a special referee or any officer or other staff of the court.

(4) Subject to subsection (5), the decision of—

> (a) any such person as is mentioned in subsection (1); or
>
> (b) any officer or other staff of the court,

may be called in question in such manner as may be prescribed by rules of court, whether by appeal to the Court of Appeal, or by an appeal or application to a divisional court or a judge in court or a judge in chambers, or by an adjournment to a judge in court or a judge in chambers.

(5) Rules of court may provide either generally or to a limited extent for decisions of persons nominated under subsection (1)(a) being called in question only by appeal on a question of law.

(6) The cases in which jurisdiction of the High Court may be exercised by person nominated under subsection (1)(a) shall be known as "official referees' business"; and, subject to rules of court, the distribution of official referees' business among persons so nominated shall be determined in accordance with directions given by the Lord Chancellor.

(7) Any reference to an official referee in any enactment, whenever passed, or in rules of court of any other instrument or document, whenever made, shall, unless the context otherwise requires,

be construed as, or (where the context requires) as including, a reference to a person nominated under subsection (1)(a).

Note—Derived from the AJA 1956, s.15, and the Courts Act 1971, s.25. Amended **9A–323** by the AJA 1982, s.59; the Civil Procedure Act 1997, Sched.2. See para. 9A–4.1 above.

Effect of section

Paragraph 2 of Sched.1 to the Civil Procedure Act 1997 states that Civil Procedure **9A–324** Rules may provide for the exercise of the jurisdiction of the High Court by officers of the Court or other staff of the Court. CPR, r.2.4 states that, where those Rules provide for the court "to perform any act" provided for by the CPR (an important qualification) then, except where an enactment, rule or practice direction provides otherwise, the act may be performed, in relation to proceedings in the High Court, by any judge, Master or district judge of that Court. The circumstances in which jurisdiction may be exercised only by a judge need not be listed here. However, it may be noted that s.68(3) states that rules of court shall not authorise the exercise of power of attachment and committal by any officer of the court or other staff of the court. Further, s.68(4) provides that the decision of any officer or other staff of the court may be called in question (*e.g.* by appeal) in such manner as may be prescribed by rules of court. The rules so prescribing need not be listed here.

Section 68 is principally concerned with the nomination of judges to deal with official referees' business and the handling of such business. Under the CPR, this business is described as Technology and Construction Court business; see CPR Pt 60 (Technology and Construction Court Claims) (see CPR Pt 60 para. 2C–1 above).

The section also preserves the exercise of High Court jurisdiction, in accordance with rules of court, by "special referees". Trial by a special referee was provided for by former RSC O.36, r.10 but no comparable provision appears in the CPR. The former rules made no provision for the appointment of special referees; nor do the CPR.

Under s.9 of this Act (see para. 9A–27 above) certain persons who are not judges of the High Court may act as judges of the Court on request.

Trial by jury

69.—(1) Where, on the application of any party to an action to be **9A–325** tried in the Queen's Bench Division, the court is satisfied that there is in issue—

    (a) a charge of fraud against that party; or

    (b) a claim in respect of libel, slander, malicious prosecution or false imprisonment; or

    (c) any question or issue of a kind prescribed for the purposes of this paragraph,

the action shall be tried with a jury, unless the court is of opinion that the trial requires any prolonged examination of documents or accounts or any scientific or local investigation which cannot conveniently be made with a jury.

(2) An application under subsection (1) must be made not later than such time before the trial as may be prescribed.

(3) An action to be tried in the Queen's Bench Division which does not by virtue of subsection (1) fall to be tried with a jury shall be tried without a jury unless the court in its discretion orders it to be tried with a jury.

(4) Nothing in subsections (1) to (3) shall affect the power of the court to order, in accordance with rules of court, that different questions of fact arising in any action be tried by different modes of trial; and where any such order is made, subsection (1) shall have effect only as respects questions relating to any such charge, claim, question or issue as is mentioned in that subsection.

LEGISLATION

(5) Where for the purpose of disposing of any action or other matter which is being tried in the High Court by a judge with a jury it is necessary to ascertain the law of any other country which is applicable to the facts of the case, any question as to the effect of the evidence given with respect to that law shall, instead of being submitted to the jury, be decided by the judge alone.

9A–326 *Note*—Derived from the A.J.(M.P.) A. 1938, s.6; and the and JA 1925, s.102.

"application... not later than such time before trial as may be prescribed"

9A–326.1 CPR, r.26.11 states that an application for a claim to be tried with a jury must be made within 28 days of the defence. In *Oliver v. Calderdale MBC*, *The Times*, July 7, 1999, CA, a case decided under the old rules, it was held that an application made wholly out of time could be rejected on the grounds that it was unreasonable.

Subject to the terms of s.69(l), either party to a defamation action has a right to trial by jury, and the power to make procedural rules under Civil Procedure Act 1997, s.4 does not permit the restriction of that fundamental right; consequently, although in terms CPR, r.24.2 makes no exception for defamation cases, summary judgment should not be granted where one party was entitled to exercise his right to jury trial and wished to do so (*Safeway Stores Plc v. Tate* [2001] 2 W.L.R. 1377, CA; see also *Elite Model Management Corporation v. British Broadcasting Corporation*, March 14, 2001, (unrep.), Eady J.).

If there is a material issue of fact in a libel case, s.69(l) entities a party to have that issue determined by a jury; however it is for the judge to decide whether there really is such an issue (*Alexander v. Arts Council of Wales*, *The Times*, April 27, 2001, CA). Where the judge comes to the conclusion that the evidence, taken at its highest, is such that a jury properly directed could not properly reach a necessary factual conclusion, it is his duty, upon a submission being made, to withdraw that issue from the jury; but where there is a risk that the judge's view on a particular issue might be overturned on appeal it is desirable that it should be left to the jury (*ibid.*).

Where appropriate, in the same proceedings the court may in the exercise of powers listed in CPR, r.3.1(2) order that certain issued be tried by judge alone and others by judge and jury (s.69(4)). However, where it is clear that some issues could not conveniently be tried with a jury it may be more appropriate for the whole case to be tried by judge alone (*e.g.* where questions of credibility are universally relevant) (*Phillips v. Commissioner of Police of the Metropolis* [2003] EWCA Civ 382; *The Times*, April 2, 2003, CA).

In defamation proceedings it may be appropriate for certain issues to be tried by the judge sitting with a jury and others by the judge sitting alone (*Gregson v. Channel Four Television Corp* [2002] EWCA Civ 941).

Questions of foreign law to be decided by Judge

9A–327 As to evidence of foreign law, see Civil Evidence Act 1972, s.4 (see para. 9B–255 below).

The trial judge is entitled to construe a statutory provision of foreign law put in evidence by an expert in that law (*Sharif v. Azad* [1967] 1 Q.B. 605; [1966] 3 All E.R. 785, CA). This is especially so where there is a conflict in the evidence between the expert witnesses as to the foreign law (*Parkasho v. Singh* [1968] P. 233; [1967] 1 All E.R. 737, DC).

Discharge of jury or of juror

9A–327A The trial judge has a discretion to continue the trial where a juror has to be discharged (*e.g.* by reason of ill health), thereby reducing the number of jurors to eleven (*Hamilton v Al-Fayed (Costs)*, *The Times*, July 25, 2001). Where the interests of justice make it appropriate for him to do so, a judge in civil proceedings may allow a discharged jury to make alterations to its verdict (*Igwemma v. Chief Constable of Greater Manchester Police* [2001] EWCA Civ 953; [2001] 4 All E.R. 751, CA.

Assessors and scientific advisers

9A–328 70.—(1) In any cause or matter before the High Court the court may, if it thinks it expedient to do so, call in the aid of one or more assessors specially qualified, and hear and dispose of the cause or matter wholly or partially with their assistance.

(2) The remuneration, if any, to be paid to an assessor for his services under subsection (1) in connection with any proceedings shall be determined by the court, and shall form part of the costs of the proceedings.

(3) Rules of court shall make provision for the appointment of scientific advisers to assist the Patents Court in proceedings under the Patents Act 1949 and Patents Act 1977 and for regulating the functions of such advisers.

(4) The remuneration of any such adviser shall be determined by the Lord Chancellor with the concurrence of the Minister for the Civil Service and shall be defrayed out of money provided by Parliament.

Note —Derived from the JA 1925, s.98; and the Patents Act 1977, s.96(4).   **9A–329**

Assessors and scientific advisers

Where assessors are called in aid to assist the court in hearing and disposing of any **9A–330** cause or matter, the provisions of CPR, r.35.15 apply.

As to nautical assessors in Admiralty proceedings, see CPR r.61.13 (para. 2D–80 above).

As to appointment of scientific advisers in patent actions, see CPR, r.35.15 (replacing former O.114, r.15).

As to assessors in the Court of Appeal, see s.54(8) above.

In *Esso Petroleum Co Ltd v. Southport Corporation* [1956] A.C. 218, Devlin J. said that he had appointed assessors to advise him after the hearing and stated that, in future, especially having regard to his earlier experience in *Waddle v. Wallsend Shipping Co Ltd* [1925] 2 Lloyd's Rep. 105, he would, if necessary, adjourn the court so that an assessor might be present during the hearing.

In *Ahmed v. University of Oxford* [2002] EWCA Civ 1907; [2003] 1 All E.R. 915, CA, unrep., the Court of Appeal examined the role of assessors appointed in various contexts, including under s.70 of this Act and the County Courts Act 1984, s.63 (see para. 9A–617 below), but particularly under the Race Relations Act 1976, s.67(4). Note also *Sutton v. Tesco Stores Plc*, July 30, 2002, unrep. (Mr Michael Yelton QC) (at directions hearing the judge making order under s.70 appointing an assessor to assist the court on the psychiatric evidence in the case). In *Bow Spring (Owners) v. Manzanillo II (Owners) (Note)* [2004] EWCA Civ 1007; [2004] 4 All E.R. 899, CA, the Court of Appeal held (partly on Art.6 grounds) that the practice of the Admiralty judge putting questions to assessors after discussion with counsel should be complemented by a practice of disclosing their answers to counsel in order that any appropriate submission could be made as to whether the judge should accept their advice. See further CPR, r.35.15, and commentary following that rule.

On appointing assessors to assist court under s.70 as alternative to practice of referring of fixing of remuneration of provisional liquidators to costs judge, see *Re Independent Insurance Company Limited* [2002] EWHC 1577 (Ch), July 25, 2002, unrep. (Ferris J.).

SITTINGS AND VACATIONS

Sittings and vacations

71.—(1) Sittings of the High Court may be held, and any other **9A–331** business of the High Court may be conducted, at any place in England or Wales.

(2) Subject to rules of court—

LEGISLATION

    (a) the places at which the High Court sits outside the Royal
        Courts of Justice; and

    (b) the days and times when the High Court sits at any place
        outside the Royal Courts of Justice,

shall be determined in accordance with directions given by the
Lord Chancellor.

(3) Rules of court may make provision for regulating the vacations to be observed by the High Court and in the offices of that court.

(4) Rules of court—

    (a) may provide for securing such sittings of any Division of
        the High Court during vacation as the senior judge of
        that Division may with the concurrence of the Lord
        Chancellor determine; and

    (b) without prejudice to paragraph (a), shall provide for the
        transaction during vacation by judges of the High Court
        of all such business in the High Court as may require to
        be immediately or promptly transacted.

(5) Different provision may be made in pursuance of subsection (3) for different parts of the country.

9A-332   *Note*—Derived as to subs.(1) and (2) from the Courts Act 1971, s.2 and as to subs.(3) and (4) from the JA 1925, ss.53–54. See para. 9A–4.1 above.

Sittings of High Court

9A-333   Directions as to the location of sittings of the High Court under the power now found in s.71(2) were first given by the Lord Chancellor in 1971 when the "court centres" system recommended by the Beeching Commission was implemented within a revised system of court circuits. Within each of the six circuits, court centres were classified as first-, second- or third-tier centres, and High Court business was taken at first-tier centres. These directions, indicating the places outside the Royal Courts of Justice at which the Lord Chancellor has directed sittings of the High Court shall be held, have been modified from time to time. There are four sittings in every year (see para. 1.1 of Practice Direction (Court Sittings), supplementing CPR Pt 39).

For sitting outside London of Chancery Division, see Chancery Guide para. 12.1 and practice direction referred to there (see Vol. 2, para. 1–91).

For power of Lord Chancellor to direct places at which district registries of the High Court shall be located, see s.99 below.

Vacations of High Court

9A-334   Provisions as to sittings of the High Court in vacations are found in paras 3.1 to 3.3 of Practice Direction (Court Sittings), the practice direction supplementing CPR Pt 39 (see Vol. 1, para. 39BPD.1).

"at any place in England and Wales"

9A-334.1   The taking of evidence abroad under procedures that enable that to be done in cases proceeding in the High Court does not constitute a sitting of the High Court outside England and Wales. Accordingly, s.71(1) does not prevent a High Court judge from appointing himself to be a special examiner under CPR, r.34.13(4) for the purpose of taking a deposition from a person out of the jurisdiction (*Peer International Corporation v. Termidor Music Publishers Ltd* [2005] EWHC 1048 (Ch), May 25, 2005, unrep. (Lindsay J.)).

OTHER PROVISIONS

Withdrawal of privilege against incrimination of self or spouse in certain proceedings

9A-335   **72.**—(1) In any proceedings to which this subsection applies a person shall not be excused, by reason that to do so would tend to expose that person, or his or her spouse, to proceedings for a related offence for the recovery of a related penalty—

    (a) from answering any question put to that person in the first-mentioned proceedings; or

    (b) from complying with any order made in those proceedings.

(2) Subsection (1) applies to the following civil proceedings in High Court, namely—

    (a) proceedings for infringement of rights pertaining to any intellectual property or for passing off;

    (b) proceedings brought to obtain disclosure of information relating to any infringement of such rights or to any passing off; and

    (c) proceedings brought to prevent any apprehended infringement of such rights or any apprehended passing off.

(3) Subject to subsection (4), no statement or admission made by a person—

    (a) in answering a question put to him in any proceedings to which subsection (1) applies; or

    (b) in complying with any order made in any such proceedings,

shall, in proceedings for any related offence or for the recovery of any related penalty, be admissible in evidence against that person (unless they married after the making of the statement or admission) against the spouse of that person.

(4) Nothing in subsection (3) shall render any statement or admission made by a person as there mentioned inadmissible in evidence against that person in proceedings for perjury or contempt of court.

(5) In this section—

    "intellectual property" means any patent, trade mark, copyright, design rights, registered design, technical or commercial information or other intellectual property;

    "related offence", in relation to any proceedings to which subsection (1) applies, means—

        (a) in the case of proceedings within subsection (2)(a) or (b)—

            (i) any offence committed by or in the course of the infringement or passing off to which those proceedings relate; or

            (ii) any offence not within sub-paragraph (i) committed in connection with that infringement or passing off, being an offence involving fraud or dishonesty;

        (b) in the case of proceedings within subsection (2)(c), any offence revealed by the facts on which the plaintiff relies in those proceedings;

    "related penalty", in relation to any proceedings to which subsection (1) applies means—

        (a) in the case of proceedings within subsection (2)(a)

LEGISLATION

or (b), any penalty incurred in respect of anything done or omitted in connection with the infringement or passing off to which those proceedings relate;

(b) in the case of proceedings within subsection (2)(c), any penalty incurred in respect of any act or omission revealed by the facts on which the plaintiff relies in those proceedings.

(6) Any reference in this section to civil proceedings in the High Court of any description includes a reference to proceedings on appeal arising in the High Court of that description.

9A-336 *Note* —Amended by the Copyright, Designs and Patents Act 1988, Sched.7, para. 28.

Effect of section

9A-337 In legal proceedings, a person (or that person's spouse) may refuse to answer any question or produce any document or thing if to do so would tend to expose that person to proceedings for an offence or for the recovery of a penalty (*Rank Film Distributors Ltd v. Video Information Centre* [1982] A.C. 380, HL). By operation of the Civil Evidence Act 1968, s.14, in legal proceedings other than criminal proceedings, that privilege is confined to the risk of exposure to proceedings and penalties under the law of any part of the UK (see para. 9B–240). The privilege may be withdrawn by statute (*ibid.*, s.14(3)).

This section withdraws the privilege in proceedings relating to the infringement of industrial property rights. It provides that it does not excuse a person (or that person's spouse) (a) from answering any question in such proceedings, or (b) from complying with any order made in those proceedings, for example, an order to disclose documents, a freezing injunction (formerly a Mareva injunction) or a search order (formerly Anton Piller order). The section is not limited to a case where criminal procedings have not yet been commenced (*Charles of the Ritz Group Ltd v. Jory* [1986] F.S.R. 14).

THE CROWN COURT

COMPOSITION OF COURT

General provisions

9A-338 **73.**—(1) Subject to the provisions of section 8(1)(c), 74 and 75(2) as respects courts comprising justices of the peace, all proceedings in the Crown Court shall be heard and disposed of before a single judge of that court.

(2) Rules of court may authorise or require a judge of the High Court, Circuit judge or Recorder, in such circumstances as are specified by the rules, at any stage to continue with any proceedings with a court from which any one or more of the justices initially constituting the court has withdrawn, or is absent for any reason.

(3) Where a judge of the High Court, Circuit judge or Recorder sits with justices of the peace he shall preside, and—

(a) the decision of the Crown Court may be a majority decision; and

(b) if the members of the court are equally divided, the judge of the High Court, Circuit judge or Recorder shall have a second and casting vote.

9A-338.1 *Note* —Amended subject to transitional provisions specified in art.2 by the Courts

Act 2003 (Consequential Amendments) Order (S.I. 2004 No. 2035), Sched.1, para.12(b).

Appeals and committals for sentence

74.—(1) On any hearing by the Crown Court—   **9A–339**

    (a) of any appeal;

    (b) [...]

the Crown Court shall consist of a judge of the High Court or a Circuit judge or a Recorder who, subject to the following provisions of this section, shall sit with not less than two nor more than four justices of the peace.

(2) Rules of Court may, with respect to hearings falling within subsection (1)—

    (a) prescribe the number of justices of the peace constituting the court (within the limits mentioned in that subsection); and

    (b) prescribe the qualifications to be possessed by any such justices of the peace;

and the rules may make different provisions for different descriptions of cases, different places of sitting or other different circumstances.

(3) Rules of Court may authorise or require a judge of the High Court, Circuit judge or Recorder, in such circumstances as are specified by the rules, to enter on, or at any stage to continue with, any proceedings with a court not comprising the justices required by subsections (1) and (2).

(4) The Lord Chancellor may from time to time, having regard to the number of justices, or the number of justices with any prescribed qualifications, available for service in the Crown Court, give directions providing that, in such descriptions of proceedings as may be specified by the Lord Chancellor, the provisions of subsections (1) and (2) shall not apply.

(5) Directions under subsection (4) may frame descriptions of proceedings by reference to the place of trial, or by reference to the time of trial, or in any other way.

(6) No decision of the Crown Court shall be questioned on the ground that the court was not constituted as required by or under subsections (1) and (2) unless objection was taken by or on behalf of a party to the proceedings not later than the time when the proceedings were entered on, or when the alleged irregularity began.

(7) Rules of the court may make provision as to the circumstances in which—

    (a) a person concerned with a decision appealed against is to be disqualified from hearing the appeal;

    (b) [...]; and

    (c) proceedings on the hearing of an appeal [...] are to be valid notwithstanding that any person taking part in them is disqualified.

Note—Paragraph (b) of subs.(1) and para. (b) of subs.(7) repealed by, and para. (c)   **9A–340** of subs.(7) amended by, the Access to Justice Act 1999, s.79, s.106 and Sched.15.

Subsection (7) amended subject to transitional provisions specified in art.2 by the Courts Act 2003 (Consequential Amendments) Order (S.I. 2004 No. 2035), Sched.10, para.1. See para. 9A–4.1 above.

DISTRIBUTION OF BUSINESS

Allocation of cases according to composition of court, etc.

9A–341   **75.**—(1) The cases or classes of cases in the Crown Court suitable for allocation respectively to a judge of the High Court and to a Circuit Judge or Recorder, and all other matters relating to the distribution of Crown Court business, shall be determined in accordance with directions given by or on behalf of the Lord Chief with the concurrence of the Lord Chancellor.

(2) Subject to section 74(1), the cases or classes of cases in the Crown Court suitable for allocation to a court comprising justices of the peace (including those by way of trial on indictment which are suitable for allocation to such a court) shall be determined in accordance with directions given by or on behalf of the Lord Chief Justice with the concurrence of the Lord Chancellor.

Committal for trial: alteration of place of trial

9A–342   **76.**—(1) Without prejudice to the provisions of this Act about the distribution of Crown Court business, the Crown Court may give directions, or further directions, altering the place of any trial on indictment, whether by varying the decision of a magistrates' court under section 7 of the Magistrates' Courts Act 1980 or by substituting some other place for the place specified in a notice under a relevant transfer position (notices of transfer from magistrates' court to Crown Court) or by varying a previous decision of the Crown Court.

(2) Directions under subsection (1) may be given on behalf of the Crown Court by an officer of the court.

(2A) Where a preparatory hearing has been ordered under section 7 of the Criminal Justice Act 1987, directions altering the place of trial may be given under subsection (1) at any time before the jury are sworn.

(3) The defendant or the prosecutor, if dissatisfied with the place of trial as fixed by the magistrates' court, as specified in a notice under a relevant transfer position or as fixed by the Crown Court, may apply to the Crown Court for a direction, or further direction, varying the place of trial; and the court shall take the matter into consideration and may comply with or refuse the application, or give a direction not in compliance with the application, as the court thinks fit.

(4) [...]

(5) In this section "relevant transfer provision" means—

    (a) section 4 of the Criminal Justice Act 1987, or

    (b) section 53 of the Criminal Justice Act 1991.

9A–343   *Note*—Amended by the Criminal Justice Act 1987, Sched.2, para. 10; and the Criminal Justice and Public Order Act 1994, Sched.9, para. 17. With the coming into effect on May 1, 2004, of s.86 of the Courts Act 2003, an application under s.76(3) is no longer required to be heard in open court by a judge of the High Court and accordingly subsection (4) was repealed by s.109(3) and Sched.10 of the 2003 Act.

Committal for trial: date of trial

77.—(1) Crminal Procedure Rules shall prescribe the minimum **9A-344** and the maximum period which may elapse between a person's committal for trial or the giving of a notice of transfer under a relevant transfer provision and the beginning of the trial; and such rules may make different provision for different places of trial and for other different circumstances.

(2) The trial of a person committed by a magistrates' court or in respect of whom a notice of transfer under a relevant transfer provision has been given—

> (a) shall not begin until the prescribed minimum period has expired except with his consent and the consent of the prosecutor; and
>
> (b) shall not begin later than the expiry of the prescribed maximum period unless a judge of the Crown Court otherwise orders.

(3) For the purposes of this section the prescribed minimum and maximum periods shall begin with the date of committal for trial or of a notice of transfer and the trial shall be taken to begin when the defendant is arraigned.

(4) In this section "relevant transfer provision" means—

> (a) section 4 of the Criminal Justice Act 1987, or
>
> (b) section 53 of the Criminal Justice Act 1991.

Note —Amended by the Criminal Justice Act 1987, Sched.2, para. 11; the Criminal **9A-345** Justice and Public Order Act 1994, Sched.9, para. 18; and subject to transitional provisions specified in art.2 by the Courts Act 2003 (Consequential Amendments) Order (S.I. 2004 No. 2035), Sched.1, para.13.

SITTINGS

Sittings

78.—(1) Any Crown Court business may be conducted at any place **9A-346** in England or Wales, and the sittings of the Crown Court at any place may be continuous or intermittent or occasional.

(2) Judges of the Crown Court may sit simultaneously to take any number of different cases in the same or different places, and may adjourn cases from place to place at any time.

(3) The places at which the Crown Court sits, and the days and times at which the Crown Court sits at any place, shall be determined in accordance with directions given by the Lord Chancellor.

OTHER PROVISIONS

Practice and procedure in connection with indictable offences and appeals

79.—(1) All enactments and rules of law relating to procedure in **9A-347**

LEGISLATION

connection with indictable offences shall continue to have effect in relation to proceedings in the Crown Court.

(2) Without prejudice to the generality of subsection (1), that subsection applies in particular to—

    (a) the practice by which, on any one indictment, the taking of pleas, the trial by jury and the pronouncement of judgment may respectively be by or before different judges;

    (b) the release, after respite of judgment, of a convicted person on recognizance to come up for judgment if called on, but meanwhile to be of good behaviour;

    (c) the manner of trying any question relating to the breach of a recognizance;

    (d) the manner of execution of any sentence on conviction, or the manner in which any other judgment or order given in connection with trial on indictment may be enforced.

(3) The customary practice and procedure with respect to appeals to the Crown Court, and in particular any practice as to the extent to which an appeal is by way of rehearing of the case, shall continue to be observed.

Process to compel appearance

9A-348   **80.**—(1) Any direction to appear and any condition of a recognizance to appear before the Crown Court, and any summons or order to appear before that court, may be so framed as to require appearance at such time and place as may be directed by the Crown Court, and if a time or place is specified in the direction, condition, summons or order, it may be varied by any subsequent direction of the Crown Court.

(2) Where an indictment has been signed although the person charged has not been committed for trial, the Crown Court may issue a summons requiring that person to appear before the Crown Court, or may issue a warrant for his arrest.

(3) Section 4 of the Summary Jurisdiction (Process) Act 1881 (execution of process of English courts in Scotland) shall apply to process issued under this section as it applies to process issued under the Magistrates' Courts Act 1980 by a magistrates' court.

Bail

9A-349   **81.**—(1) The Crown Court may, subject to section 25 of the Criminal Justice and Public Order Act 1994, grant bail to any person—

    (a) who has been committed in custody for appearance before the Crown Court or in relation to whose case a notice of transfer has been given under a relevant transfer provision; or

    (b) who is in custody pursuant to a sentence imposed by a magistrates' court, and who has appealed to the Crown Court against his conviction or sentence; or

    (c) who is in the custody of the Crown Court pending the disposal of his case by that court; or

(d) who, after the decision of his case by the Crown Court, has applied to that court for the statement of a case for the High Court on that decision; or

(e) who has applied to the High Court for a quashing order to remove proceedings in the Crown Court in his case into the High Court, or has applied to the High Court for leave to make such an application; or

(f) to whom the Crown Court has granted a certificate under section 1(2) or 11(1A) of the Criminal Appeal Act 1968 or under subsection (1B) below; or

(g) who has been remanded in custody by a magistrates' court on adjourning a case under—

    (i) section 5 (adjournment of inquiry into offence);

    (ii) section 10 (adjournment of trial);

    (iii) section 18 (initial procedure on information against adult for offence triable either way); or

    (iv) section 30 (remand for medical examination),

of the Magistrates' Courts Act 1980;

and the time during which a person is released on bail under any provision of this subsection shall not count as part of any term of imprisonment or detention or detention under his sentence.

(1A) The power conferred by subsection (1)(f) does not extend to a case to which section 12 or 15 of the Criminal Appeal Act 1968 (appeal against verdict of not guilty by reason of insanity or against findings that the accused is under a disability and that he did the act or made the omission charged against him) applies.

(1B) A certificate under this subsection is a certificate that a case is fit for appeal on a ground which involves a question of law alone.

(1C) The power conferred by subsection (1)(f) is to be exercised—

(a) where the appeal is under section 1 or 9 of the Criminal Appeal Act 1968, by the judge who tried the case; and

(b) where it is under section 10 of that Act, by the judge who passed the sentence.

(1D) The power may only be exercised within twenty-eight days from the date of the conviction appealed against, or in the case of appeal against sentence, from the date on which sentence was passed or, in the case of an order made or treated as made on conviction, from the date of the making of the order.

(1E) The power may not be exercised if the appellant has made an application to the Court of Appeal for bail in respect of the offence or offences to which the appeal relates.

(1F) It shall be a condition of bail granted in the exercise of the power that, unless a notice of appeal has previously been lodged in accordance with subsection (1) of section 18 of the Criminal Appeal Act 1968—

(a) such a notice shall be so lodged within the period specified in subsection (2) of that section; and

(b) not later than 14 days from the end of that period, the appellant shall lodge with the Crown Court a certificate from the registrar of criminal appeals that a notice of appeal was given within that period.

(1G) If the Crown Court grants bail to a person in the exercise of the power, it may direct him to appear—

(a) if a notice of appeal is lodged within the period specified in section 18(2) of the Criminal Appeal Act 1968 at such time and place as the Court of Appeal may require and

(b) if no such notice is lodged within that period at such time and place as the Crown Court may require.

(1H) Where the Crown Court grants a person bail under subsection (1)(g) it may direct him to appear at a time and place which the magistrates' court could have directed and the recognizance of any surety shall be conditioned accordingly.

(1J) The Crown Court may only grant bail to a person under subsection (1)(g) if the magistrates' court which remanded him in custody has certified under section 5(6A) of the Bail Act 1976 that it heard full argument on his application for bail before it refused the application.

(2) Provision may be made by Rules of Court as respects the powers of the Crown Court relating to bail, including any provision—

(a) except in the case of bail in criminal proceedings (within the meaning of the Bail Act 1976), allowing the court instead of requiring a person to enter into a recognizance, to consent to his giving other security;

(b) allowing the court to direct that a recognizance shall be entered into or other security given before a magistrates' court or a justice of the peace, or, if the rules so provide, a person of such other description as is specified in the rules;

(c) prescribing the manner in which a recognizance is to be entered into or other security given, and the persons by whom and the manner in which the recognizance or security may be enforced;

(d) authorising the recommittal, in such cases and by such courts or justices as may be prescribed by the rules, of persons released from custody in pursuance of the powers;

(e) making provision corresponding to sections 118 and 119 of the Magistrates' Courts Act 1980 (varying or dispensing with requirements as to sureties, and postponement of taking recognizances).

(3) Any reference in any enactment to a recognizance shall include, unless the context otherwise requires, a reference to any other description of security given instead of a recognizance, whether in pursuance of subsection (2)(a) or otherwise.

(4) The Crown Court, on issuing a warrant for the arrest of any person, may endorse the warrant for bail, and in any such case—

(a) the person arrested under the warrant shall, unless the Crown Court otherwise directs, be taken to a police station; and

    (b) the officer in charge of the station shall release him from custody if he, and any sureties required by the endorsement and approved by the officer, enter into recognizances of such amount as may be fixed by the endorsement.

Provided that in the case of bail in criminal proceedings (within the meaning of the Bail Act 1976) the person arrested shall not be required to enter into a recognizance.

(5) A person in custody in pursuance of a warrant issued by the Crown Court with a view to his appearance before that court shall be brought forthwith before either the Crown Court or a magistrates' court.

(6) A magistrates' court shall have jurisdiction, and a justice of the peace may act, under or in pursuance of rules under subsection (2) whether or not the offence was committed, or the arrest was made, within the court's area, or the area for which he was appointed.

(7) In subsection (1) above "relevant transfer provision" means—

    (a) section 4 of the Criminal Justice Act 1987 or who has been sent in custody to the Crown Court for trial under section 51 of the Crime and Disorder Act, 1998, or

    (b) section 53 of the Criminal Justice Act 1991.

9A–350 *Note* —Amended by the Criminal Justice Act 1982, ss.29 and 60; the Criminal Justice Act 1987, Sched.2, para. 12; the Criminal Procedure (Insanity and Unfitness to Plead) Act 1991, Sched.3, para. 6; the Criminal Justice and Public Order Act 1994, Sched.9, para. 19 and Sched.10, para. 48, and the Crime and Disorder Act 1998, s.119 and Sched.8, para. 48. Para. (e) of subsection (1) amended by the Civil Procedure (Modification of Supreme Court Act 1981) Order 2004 (S.I. 2004 No. 1033), as a consequence of amendments to s.31, see para. 9A–81 above. The Criminal Justice Act 2003, s.17(3) (brought into effect on April 5, 2004) states that the inherent power of the High Court to entertain an application in relation to bail where the Crown Court has determined an application under paras (a), (b), (c) or (g) of s.81 is abolished. Further, the High Court is to have no power to entertain an application in relation to bail where the Crown Court has determined an appeal under s.16 of the 2003 Act (s.17(4)).

Duties of officers of Crown Court

9A–351 **82.**—(1) The officers of the Crown Court shall be responsible for the keeping of the records of the proceedings of the court, the signing of indictments, the notification to the parties or their legal advisers of the place and time appointed for any proceedings, and such other formal or administrative matters as may be specified by directions given by the Lord Chancellor.

(2) Officers of the Crown Court shall in particular give effect to any orders or directions of the court for taking into custody, and detaining, any person committing contempt of court, and shall execute any order or warrant duly issued by the court for the committal of any person to prison for contempt of court.

Right of audience for solicitors in certain Crown Court centres

9A–352 **83.** [*Repealed by the Access to Justice Act 1999, Sched.15.*]

9A–353 *Note* —This section dealt with the right of audience of solicitors in certain Crown

Court centres. It was substituted by the Courts and Legal Services Act 1990, s.67, and repealed by the Access to Justice Act 1999, s.106 and Sched.15, Pt II.

RULES OF COURT

Power to make rules of court

9A–354 84.—(1) Rules of court may be made for the purpose of regulating and prescribing, except in relation to any criminal cause or matter, the practice and procedure to be followed in the Crown Court and the criminal division of the Court of Appeal.

(2) Without prejudice to the generality of subsection (1), the matters about which rules of court may be made under this section include all matters of practice and procedure in the Supreme Court which were regulated or prescribed by rules of court immediately before the commencement of this Act.

(3) No provision of this or any other Act, or contained in any instrument made under any Act, which—

(a) authorises or requires the making of rules of court about any particular matter or for any particular purpose; or

(b) provides (in whatever words) that the power to make rules of court under this section is to include power to make rules about any particular matter or for any particular purpose,

shall be taken as derogating from the generality of subsection (1).

(4) [...]

(5) Special rules may apply—

(a) any rules made under this section,

(b) Civil Procedure Rules,

(c) Criminal Procedure Rules, or

(d) Family Procedure Rules.

(5A) Rules made under this section may apply—

(a) any special rules,

(b) Civil Procedure Rules,

(c) Criminal Procedure Rules, or

(d) Family Procedure Rules.

(6) Where rules may be applied under subsection (5) or (5A), they may be applied—

(a) to any extent,

(b) with or without modification, and

(c) as amended from time to time.

(7) No rules which may involve an increase of expenditure out of public funds may be made under this section except with the concurrence of the Treasury, but the validity of any rule made under this section shall not be called in question in any proceedings in any court either by the court or by any party to the proceedings on the ground only that it was a rule as to the making of which the concurrence of the Treasury was necessary and that the Treasury did not concur or are not expressed to have concurred.

(8) Rules of court under this section shall be made by statutory instrument subject to annulment in pursuance of a resolution of ei-

ther House of Parliament; and the Statutory Instruments Act 1946 shall apply to a statutory instrument containing such rules in like manner as if the rules had been made by a Minister of the Crown.

(9) In this section "special rules" means rules applying to proceedings of any particular kind in the Supreme Court, being rules made by an authority other than the Civil Procedure Rule Committee, the Family Procedure Rule Committee, the Criminal Procedure Rule Committee or the Crown Court Rule Committee under any provision of this or any other Act which (in whatever words) confers on that authority power to make rules in relation to proceedings of that kind in the Supreme Court.

Note —Derived from the JA 1925, s.99. Amended by the Civil Procedure Act 1997, **9A–355** Sched.2; referred to in Criminal Procedure and Investigations Act 1996, s.19 and Sched.2, para. 4. Amended by the Courts Act 2003 (Consequential Amendments) Order 2004 (S.I. 2004 No. 2035), art.3, Sched., para. 15.

Effect of section

This section was substantially amended by the Civil Procedure Act 1997, Sched.2. **9A–356** That Act established the Civil Procedure Rule Committee (s.2), the body responsible for making rules of court (known as Civil Procedure Rules (CPR)) governing the practice and procedure to be followed in the Court of Appeal (Civil Division), the High Court and the county courts. Before the 1997 Act came into force, s.84 applied to the making of rules of court for the Supreme Court. In relation to the Court of Appeal (Civil Division) and the High Court, those rules were the Rules of the Supreme Court, and the rule making body was the Supreme Court Rule Committee, established under s.85 (below). Section 85 was repealed by the 1997 Act.

After the 1997 Act came into effect, the function of s.84 was to provide authority for the making of rules of court in relation to the Crown Court (which became a component part of the Supreme Court in 1971) and the Court of Appeal (Criminal Division). Such rules were made by the Crown Court Rule Committee set up under s.86 of this Act. The Courts Act 2003 completely restructured the arrangements for the making of rules of court for those courts. Provisions granting power to make rules for proceedings in the Court of Appeal (Criminal Division) and, when dealing with any criminal cause or matter, in the Crown Court and in magistrates' courts, and establishing the Criminal Procedure Rule Committee with authority to make such rules, are now found in Pt 7 of that Act. In order to give full effect to those provisions, the scope of s.84 was further restricted by the Courts Act 2003 (Consequential Amendments) Order 2004 (S.I. 2004 No. 2035) so as to provide authority for the making of rules of court regulating and prescribing the practice and procedure to be followed in the Court of Appeal (Criminal Division) and the Crown Court other than "in relation to criminal causes or matters"; that is to say, in relation to proceedings that might be described as civil proceedings. The Crown Court Rule Committee established under s.86 of this Act continues to make rules for the small number of civil matters that are dealt with by those courts.

[THE NEXT PARAGRAPH IS 9A–362.]

The Supreme Court Rule Committee

85. [*Repealed by the Civil Procedure Act 1997, Sched.2.*]   **9A–362**

Note —See notes following s.84, above.   **9A–363**

[THE NEXT PARAGRAPH IS 9A–365.]

The Crown Court Rule Committee

86.—(1) The power to make rules of court under section 84 shall **9A–365** be exercisable by the Lord Chancellor together with any four or more of the following persons, namely—

(a) the Lord Chief Justice,

(b) two other judges of the Supreme Court,

(c) two Circuit judges,

(d) *[revoked]*

(e) a justice of the peace,

(f) two persons who have a Supreme Court qualification (within the meaning of section 71 of the Courts and Legal Services Act 1990); and

(g) two persons who have been granted by an authorised body, under Part II of that Act, the right to conduct litigation in relation to all proceedings in the Supreme Court.

(2) The persons mentioned in subsection (1), acting in pursuance of that subsection, shall be known as "the Crown Court Rule Committee".

(3) The persons to act in pursuance of subsection (1) with the Lord Chancellor, other than those eligible to act by virtue of their office, shall be appointed by the Lord Chancellor for such time as he may think fit.

(4) Before appointing a person under paragraph (f) or (g) of subsection (1), the Lord Chancellor shall consult any authorised body with members who are eligible for appointment under that paragraph.

9A–366   *Note* —Amended by the Courts and Legal Services Act 1990, Sched.18, para. 36(2). See notes following s.84, above. Amended by the Courts Act 2003 (Consequential Amendments) Order 2004 (S.I. 2004 No. 2035), art.3, Sched., para. 16. See further commentary in para. 9A–356 above. This section will be further amended by the Constitutional Reform Act 2005; see para. 9A–4.1 above.

Particular matters for which rules of court may provide

9A–367   87.—(1) [...]

(2) [...]

(3) Rules of court made under section 84 may amend or repeal any statutory provision relating to the practice and procedure of the Crown Court (except so far as relating to criminal causes or matters) so far as may be necessary in consequence of provision made by the rules.

(4) Criminal Procedure Rules may require courts from which an appeal lies to the criminal division of the Court of Appeal to furnish that division with any assistance or information which it may request for the purpose of exercising its jurisdiction.

(5) Rules of Court made under section 84 may amend or repeal any statutory provision about appeals to the Crown Court so far as it relates to the practice and procedure with respect to such appeals (except so far as relating to criminal causes or matters).

9A–368   *Note* —Derived from the JA 1925, s.99; the Proceedings against Estates Act 1970, s.2; the AJA 1977, s.27; the Criminal Appeal Act 1968, s.46; and the Courts Act 1971, s.14. Amended by the Civil Procedure Act 1997, Sched.2; and by theCourts Act 2003 (Consequential Amendments) Order 2004 (S.I. 2004 No. 2035), art.3, Sched., para. 17.

[THE NEXT PARAGRAPH IS 9A–370.]

Part IV

Officers and Offices

Appointment of certain officers of Supreme Court

Qualification for office

88. A person shall not be qualified for appointment to any office in 9A–370
the Supreme Court listed in column 1 of any Part of Schedule 2 unless he is a person of any description specified in relation to that office in column 2 of that Part.

Note —Derived from the JA 1925, ss.110, 116, 122, 126. See further s.89, below **9A–371**

Masters and registrars

89.—(1) The power to make appointments to the offices in the 9A–372
Supreme Court listed in column 1 of Parts II and III of Schedule 2
shall be exercisable by the Lord Chancellor, with the concurrence of
the Minister for the Civil Service as to numbers and salaries.

(2) The person appointed to the office of Queen's coroner and attorney and master of the Crown Office and Registrar of Criminal Appeals shall, by virtue of his appointment, be a master of the Queen's
Bench Division.

(3) The Lord Chancellor shall appoint—

    (a) one of the masters of the Queen's Bench Division as
        Senior Master of that Division;

    (b) one of the masters of the Chancery Division as Chief
        Chancery Master;

    (c) one of the taxing masters of the Supreme Court as Chief
        Taxing Master;

    (d) one of the registrars in bankruptcy of the High Court as
        Chief Bankruptcy Registrar; and

    (e) one of the district judges of the Principal Registry of the
        Family Division as Senior District Judge of that Division;

    (f) [...]

with, in each case, such additional salary in respect of that appointment as the Lord Chancellor may, with the concurrence of the
Minister for the Civil Service, determine.

(4) The person appointed Senior Master under subsection (3)(a)
shall hold and perform the duties of the offices of the Queen's Remembrancer and registrar of judgments.

(5) [...]

(6) [...]

(7) [...]

(8) Salaries payable under or by virtue of this section shall be
paid out of money provided by Parliament.

Note —Derived from the JA 1925, ss.110, 122, 126 as amended by the AJA 1982, **9A–373**
s.60 and S.I. 1982 No. 1188. Amended by the Statute Law (Repeals) Act 1989, Sched.1;
and the Courts and Legal Services Act 1990, Sched.18. See para. 9A–4.1 above.

Power to make appointments to offices in the Supreme Court

9A–374   This section provides that the Lord Chancellor may appoint to the offices referred to in Pts II and III of Sched.2 to this Act (see paras 9A–575 and 9A–576 below). These Parts include, amongst other offices, the offices of Master and district judges. The sole office referred to in Pt III is that of district probate registrar. The only office now included in Pt I of that Schedule (as amended by the Supreme Court (Offices) Act 1997, s.1) is that of Official Solicitor. Section 90(1) states that the Lord Chancellor may appoint the Official Solicitor.

When the Head of the Civil Appeals Office exercises the jurisdiction of the Court of Appeal (Civil Division) pursuant to the CPR, r.52.16 he is known a Master (Practice Direction (Appeals)), para. 15.2, see Vol. 1, para. 52PD.51).

The Office of the Queen's Remembrancer

9A–375   By the Queen's Remembrancer Act 1859, the then Senior Master of the Court of Exchequer was appointed to be the Queen's Remembrancer: and under the J.A. 1873–1875 (replaced by JA 1925, s.122) the Senior Master of the Supreme Court was appointed to the office of Queen's Remembrancer and now the Lord Chancellor appoints the Senior Master of the Queen's Bench Division and by virtue of such appointment, the Senior Master holds the office of Queen's Remembrancer (see s.89(4)). On his appointment, the Queen's Remembrancer takes his oath of office before the Lord Chief Justice. His responsibilities and duties are many.

Estreats of Fines

9A–376   Under the 1859 Act, it was the responsibility of the Queen's Remembrancer to estreat any fines imposed by the Courts, particularly in matters relating to contempt of Court. The duty is now laid by s.140(2) of the SCA 1981, to proceed to enforce the payment of a fine imposed or any sum due under a recognisance forfeited, and he must do so as if that sum were due to him as a judgment debt. It may indeed be that the special Queen's Remembrancer's Warrant or Writ of Execution is still extant, since it is a common law writ and has not been expressly abolished, and the Writ requires the Sheriff to arrest the contemnor and to keep him in prison until the fine is actually paid.

Additional duties of Senior Master

9A–377   On his appointment the Senior Master ceases to do the ordinary judicial work of the Masters in Chambers or act as the Practice Master on a rota basis with his colleagues. Nevertheless, he remains available to do and ordinarily does a great deal of such work, *e.g.* to hear urgent matters or those that require prompt attention or speedy hearings at early special appointments or to relieve pressure on other Masters.

The Senior Master is responsible for the smooth running of the Central Office. He is daily consulted by the Chief Clerks of the Central Office, the Q.B. Masters' Secretary and other Chief or Head Clerks on matters of practice and procedure as well as matters pertaining to the staff, inter-departmental changes, standard of work, consideration of new appointments and of promotions and so forth.

The Senior Master is frequently consulted by the Lord Chancellor's Department on the formulation of new rules of court, and on proposed legislation that may have a hearing on practice and procedure.

[THE NEXT PARAGRAPH IS 9A–389.]

Official Solicitor

9A–389   **90.**—(1) There shall continue to be an Official Solicitor to the Supreme Court, who shall be appointed by the Lord Chancellor.

(2) There shall be paid to the Official Solicitor out of money provided by Parliament such salary as the Lord Chancellor may, with the concurrence of the Minister for the Civil Service determine.

(3) The Official Solicitor shall have such powers and perform such duties as may for the time being be conferred or imposed on the holder of that office—

(a) by or under this or any other Act; or

(b) by or in accordance with any direction given (before or after the commencement of this Act) by the Lord Chancellor.

(3A) The holder for the time being of the office of Official Solicitor shall have the right to conduct litigation in relation to any proceedings.

(3B) When acting as Official Solicitor a person who would otherwise have the right to conduct litigation by virtue of section 28(2)(a) of the Courts and Legal Services Act 1990 shall be treated as having acquired that right solely by virtue of subsection (3A).

(4) If—

(a) the Official Solicitor is not available because of his absence or for some other reason; or

(b) his office is vacant,

then, during such unavailability or vacancy, any powers or duties of the Official Solicitor shall be exercisable or fall to be performed by any person for the time being appointed by the Lord Chancellor as deputy to the Official Solicitor (and any property vested in the Official Solicitor may accordingly be dealt with by any such person in all respects as if it were vested in him instead).

Note —Derived from the JA 1925, s.129. Amended by the Courts and Legal Services **9A–390**
Act 1990, Sched.18.

Office of the Official Solicitor

The Official Solicitor is confidential adviser and assistant to the Judges of the High **9A–391**
Court and Court of Appeal on legal and other matters. His essential function is to ensure, by his intervention in proceedings or otherwise, that the ends of justice are achieved and that the legal rights and duties of those under disability or at disadvantage before the law are recognised and enforced.

He may be appointed so that proceedings are properly constituted, or otherwise to ensure that there is no denial or miscarriage of justice. However, he has a discretion whether or not to act, and even his appointment by the court is usually expressed to be subject to his consent. He may make his consent to act conditional upon his costs being secured (see below), but whenever a judge thinks it right to ask for the assistance of the Official Solicitor, he should be free to do so without being constrained by anxiety about the possible effect in relation to costs upon the parties.

The holder of the office is deemed to be a Trust Corporation for the purposes of the 1925 property legislation (Law of Property (Amendment) Act 1926, s.3(1)).

Functions and duties

The Official Solicitor's functions and duties are wide and various; some have been **9A–392**
imposed upon him by Lord Chancellors, some by the judges of the High Court and some by statute.

The principal categories of work which he undertakes are as follows:

A. *Assisting the Court*

(i) Confidential Adviser to the Judges. **9A–393**

(ii) *Amicus Curiae.*

(iii) Investigation and Report (*Harbin v. Masterman* [1896] 1 Ch. 351).

—The Official Solicitor may be called upon to give confidential advice to the Judges, to instruct counsel to appear to assist the court as *amicus curiae* or to investigate and report so that "the Judge may be informed as to where the real truth of the case lies." It is probably a contempt to interfere with an investigation by the Official Solicitor.

B. *Liberty of the Subject*

LEGISLATION

9A–394   (i) Bails.

(ii) Contempts.

(iii) *Habeas corpus.*

—Prisoners who have been refused bail may ask the Official Solicitor to make an application on their behalf to a Judge in chambers. By a direction made by Lord Dilhorne L.C. on May 29, 1963 the Official Solicitor is required to review the cases of those committed to prison for contempt of court. He will seek the release of those improperly committed and encourage those properly committed to purge their Contempt Applications for leave to issue a writ of habeas corpus are referred to him for investigation by the court if it thinks necessary.

C. Representing Persons under Disability in Civil Proceedings, e.g.:

9A–395   (i) Children's cases:

> Wardship and Inherent Jurisdiction
>
> Adoption
>
> Guardianship
>
> Proceedings under the Children Act 1989 (see below)

(ii) Civil Litigation: Personal Injury

> Proceedings against estates
>
> Medical Negligence
>
> Injunctions
>
> Landlord and Tenant
>
> Matrimonial Causes

(iii) Proceedings before the Court of Protection

(iv) Declaratory Proceedings in the High Court

—The Official Solicitor will act on behalf of those under disability, minors or mental patients (see O.80), in all kinds of civil litigation if there is no-one else able and willing to do so.

He will also represent the interests of patients whose affairs are subject to the Court of Protection in, for example, applications for a statutory will or a gift from the patient's estate. He will represent a minor or patient in wardship or declaratory proceedings relating to medical treatment (see *Practice Note (Sterilisation)* [1990] 2 F.L.R. 530). His involvement in family proceedings is dealt with below.

By a direction made by Lord Mackay L.C. on January 12, 1989 (Practice Direction (Mental Health: Appeal) [1989] 1 W.L.R. 133), the Official Solicitor is empowered to appeal to the Court of Appeal with the leave of that court in any case involving a mental patient which has been heard and determined in the High Court or a county court where he deems it to be in the patient's interest and the case may not otherwise be considered by the Court of Appeal.

D. Estates

9A–396   (i) Administrator of Estates

(ii) Trustee

(iii) Judicial Trustee of Estates and Trusts

(iv) Guardianship of Estates of minors

(v) Conveyancing

—The Official Solicitor may apply to the court for an order authorising him to extract a grant of letters of administration (with or without will) if there is no-one willing to administer an estate; he may represent the estate of a deceased tortfeasor so as to enable proceedings to be pursued against the estate; he may take out a grant for the use and benefit of minor beneficiaries. He may be authorised by the court to act as trustee of a trust for the benefit of a minor or patient and can be appointed to act as judicial trustee of an estate or trust under the Judicial Trustees Act 1896. He will act as guardian of the estates of minors, *inter alia*, to administer awards by the Criminal Injuries Compensation Board and he may also make claims to the Criminal Injuries Compensation Board on behalf of minors.

9A–397   *The Official Solicitor in Family Proceedings* —Following the implementation of the Children Act 1989 on October 14, 1991, the Official Solicitor will act in family proceedings, but not in Family Proceedings Courts, as follows:

A. Guardian ad litem of the child who is the subject of the proceedings:

"Public law" proceedings under the Children Act 1989 in the High Court and Court of Appeal, pursuant to a direction made by Lord Mackay L.C. on October 7, 1991 (reported at 1991 2 F.L.R. 471).

Pursuant to rule 9.5 of the Family Proceedings Rules 1991, in all other family proceedings (see the Matrimonial and Family Proceedings Act 1984, s.32), including proceedings under the wardship [inherent] jurisdiction.

High Court adoption and freeing proceedings (see The Adoption Rules 1984, rr.6(4) and 18(4)).

B. Guardian ad litem or next friend of a person under disability who is NOT the subject of the proceedings, pursuant to r.9.5 of the Family Proceedings Rules 1991.

C. Next Friend of a child seeking leave to make an application under the Children Act 1989, *or making an application in other family proceedings*.

Costs of the Official Solicitor

The Official Solicitor may make his involvement in proceedings conditional upon an undertaking to meet his costs, except in cases involving wardship or declaratory proceedings in respect of medical treatment, where his involvement is a matter of necessity (see *Re F. (Mental Patient: Sterilisation)* [1990] 2 A.C. 1) or where the other party is legally aided.

In proceedings relating to the welfare of minors, the Official Solicitor will seek an order for his costs in those cases in which he considers it appropriate, but in such cases he will always endeavour to negotiate his costs with the other public authority parties (see *Re G (Minors)* [1982] 1 W.L.R. 438 at 443H (wardship) and *Re H (A Minor)*, October 30, 1986, Sheldon J.).

Where the person on whose behalf the Official Solicitor is invited to act is eligible to apply for financial assistance by a scheme funded by the Legal Services Commission the Official Solicitor will apply on his behalf if it is in the interests of that person to do so.

There is nothing to prevent the Official Solicitor seeking his costs in the same way as any other successful litigant.

The costs of the Official Solicitor in proceedings before the Court of Protection are paid by such person or out of such funds as the court may direct pursuant to r.88 of the Court of Protection Rules 1984 (see Section 6, para. 6B–324).

9A–398

Deputies and temporary appointments

91.—(1) If it appears to the Lord Chancellor that it is expedient to do so in order to facilitate the disposal of business in the Supreme Court, he may appoint a person—

9A–399

> (a) to act as a deputy for any person holding an office listed in column 1 of Part II or III of Schedule 2; or
>
> (b) to act as a temporary additional officer in any such office,

during such period or on such occasions as the Lord Chancellor thinks fit .

(2) Subject to subsection (3), a person shall not be qualified for appointment under this section if the office in which he would act by virtue of the appointment is one to which he is not qualified for permanent appointment.

(3) A person may be appointed under this section if he would, but for his age, be qualified for permanent appointment to the office in question and he has previously held a permanent appointment to that office or—

> (a) where the office in question is listed in column 1 of Part II of Schedule 2, to any other office so listed; or—
>
> (b) where the office in question is listed in column 1 of Part III of that Schedule, to any other office listed in column 1 of either Part II or Part III; or

(c) (whatever the office in question) to the office of county court registrar

but no appointment by virtue of this subsection shall be such as to extend beyond the day on which the person in question attains the age of seventy-five years.

(4) Every person, while acting under this section, shall have all the jurisdiction of a person permanently appointed to the office in which he is acting.

(5) [...]

(6) The Lord Chancellor may, out of money provided by Parliament, pay to any person appointed under this section such remuneration and allowances as he may, with the concurrence of the Minister for the Civil Service, determine.

9A–400 *Note* —Derived from the JA 1925, s.116, as substituted by the AJA 1977, s.10(1). Amended by the Judicial Pensions and Retirement Act 1993, Scheds 6 and 9. See para. 9A–4.1 above.

OTHER PROVISIONS RELATING TO OFFICERS OF SUPREME COURT

Tenure of office

9A–401 **92.**—(1) Subject to the following provisions of this section and to subsections (4) to (6) of section 26 of the Judicial Pensions and Retirement Act 1993 (Lord Chancellor's power to authorise continuance in office up to the age of 75), a person who holds an office to which this subsection applies shall vacate it on the day on which he attains the age of seventy years.

(2) Subsection (1) applies to the offices listed in column 1 of Part II of Schedule 2 except the office of Queen's Coroner and Attorney and Master of the Crown Office and Registrar of Criminal Appeals.

(2A) Subject to the following provisions of this section, a person who holds an office to which this subsection applies shall vacate it at the end of the completed year of service in the course of which he attains the age of sixty-two years.

(2B) Subsection (2A) applies to the offices listed in column 1 of Part I of Schedule 2 [...].

(2C) For the purposes of subsections (1) and (2A) a person who has successively held two or more offices listed in column 1 of Part I or II of Schedule 2 shall be treated as completing a year of service on the anniversary of his appointment to the first of them.

(2D) Subject to the following provisions of this section, a person who holds an office to which this subsection applies shall vacate it on the day on which he attains the age of sixty-two years.

(2E) Subsection (2D) applies to the office of Queen's Coroner and Attorney and Master of the Crown Office and Registrar of Criminal Appeals.

(3) Where the Lord Chancellor considers it desirable in the public interest to retain in office a person who holds an office to which subsection (1) applies after the time when he would otherwise retire in accordance with that subsection, the Lord Chancellor may from

time to time authorise the continuance in office of that person until such date, not being later than the date on which that person attains the age of seventy-five years, as he thinks fit.

(3A) Where the Lord Chancellor considers it desirable in the public interest to retain in office a person who holds an office to which subsection (2A) applies after the time when he would otherwise retire in accordance with that subsection, the Lord Chancellor may from time to time authorise the continuance in office of that person until such date, not being later than the date on which he attains the age of sixty-five years, as he thinks fit.

(4) A person appointed to an office listed in column 1 of Part 1 or 2 of Schedule 2 shall hold that office during good behaviour.

(5) The power to remove such a person from his office on account of misbehaviour shall be exercisable by the Lord Chancellor.

(6) The Lord Chancellor may also remove such a person from his office on account of inability to perform the duties of his office.

(7) A person appointed to an office listed in column 1 of Part III of Schedule 2 shall hold that office during Her Majesty's pleasure.

Note —Derived from the JA 1925, ss.115, 127. Amended by the Courts and Legal **9A–402** Services Act 1990, s.77; the Judicial Pensions and Retirement Act 1993, Scheds 6 and 9; the Courts Act 2003, ss. 89(1)(a)–(c), 109(3), Sch.10. See para. 9A–4.1 above.

Status of officers for purposes of salary and pension

93.—(1) Subject to subsection (2), any person who holds an office **9A–403** listed in column 1 of any Part of Schedule 2 or the office of Accountant General of the Supreme Court and is not employed in the civil service of the State shall be deemed to be so employed for the purposes of salary and pension.

(2) Subsection (1), so far as it relates to pension, shall not apply to a person holding qualifying judicial office, within the meaning of the Judicial Pensions and Retirement Act 1993.

Note —Derived from the JA 1925, s.118. Amended by the AJA 1928; the Courts Act **9A–404** 1971; the Superannuation Act 1972; the Public Trustee and Administration of Funds Act 1986, s.1, Sched.; and the Judicial Pensions and Retirement Act 1993, Sched.8.

Officers not to practise as barristers or solicitors

94. [*Repealed by Courts and Legal Services Act 1990, Sched.20.*] **9A–405**

Property held by officers

95. Any property held in his official capacity by a person holding **9A–406** an office listed in column 1 of Part II of Schedule 2 or by the Official Solicitor shall, on his dying or ceasing to hold office, vest in the person appointed to succeed him without any conveyance, assignment or transfer.

CENTRAL OFFICE AND ACCOUNTANT GENERAL

Central Office

96.—(1) The Central Office of the Supreme Court shall perform **9A–407** such business as the Lord Chancellor may direct.

(2) Subject to any direction of the Lord Chancellor under this section, the Central Office shall perform such business as it performed immediately before the commencement of this Act.

9A–408 *Note* —Derived from the JA 1925, ss.104, 105, replacing the Supreme Court of Judicature (Officers) Act 1879, ss.4, 5, 6, and 12. See para. 9A–4.1 above.

Business of Central Office

9A–409 For the Central Office and its business, see Practice Direction (Court Offices), supplementing CPR Pt 2 (Vol. 1, para. 2PD.1). For enrolment of deeds and other documents in the Central Office, see notes following s.133 below.

Accountant General

9A–410 **97.** [*Section 97 is set out in Section 6A, para. 6A–1.*]

JUDGES' CLERKS AND SECRETARIES

Judges' clerks and secretaries

9A–411 **98.**—(1) A clerk and a secretary shall be attached to each of the following judges of the Supreme Court, namely the Lord Chief Justice, the Master of the Rolls, the President of the Queen's Bench Division, the President of the Family Division and the Chancellor of the High Court.

(2) A clerk shall be attached to each of the following judges of the Supreme Court, namely the Lords Justices of Appeal and the puisne judges of the High Court.

(3) Any clerk or secretary attached as mentioned in subsection (1) or (2)—

(a) shall be appointed by the Lord Chancellor; and

(b) if not already employed in the civil service of the State shall be deemed for all purposes to be so employed.

(4) If at any time it appears to any of the judges mentioned in subsection (1) desirable that there should be attached to him a legal secretary (that is to say a secretary with legal qualifications) in addition to the secretary provided for by that subsection, he may, with the concurrence of the Lord Chancellor, appoint a person who has a general qualification (within the meaning of s.71 of the Courts and Legal Services Act 1990) as his legal secretary.

(5) An appointment under subsection (4) may be on either a full-time or a part-time basis; and a person appointed by a judge as his legal secretary shall, except as regards remuneration, hold and vacate that office in accordance with such terms as the judge may, with the concurrence of the Lord Chancellor, determine when making the appointment.

(6) A person appointed under subsection (4)—

(a) shall not be treated as employed in the civil service of the State by reason only of that appointment; and

(b) if the Lord Chancellor so determines in his case, shall be paid out of money provided by Parliament such remuneration as the Lord Chancellor may, with the concurrence of the Minister for the Civil Service, determine.

Note —Derived from the Supreme Court Officers (Pensions) Act 1954, s.2. Amended **9A–412**
by the Courts and Legal Services Act 1990, Sched.10. Subsection (1) of s.98 was also
amended by the Constitutional Reform Act 2005, s.148(1) and Sched. 4, para. 142. See
para. 9A–4.1 above.

DISTRICT REGISTRIES AND DISTRICT JUDGES

District registries

99.—(1) The Lord Chancellor may by order direct that there will **9A–413**
be district registries of the High Court at such places and for such
districts as are specified in the order.

(2) Any order under this section shall be made by statutory instrument, which shall be laid before Parliament after being made.

Note —Derived from the JA 1925, s.84 itself derived from the JA 1873, s.60; and the **9A–414**
JA 1875, s.13. See para. 9A–4.1 above.

District registries

The district registries are as listed in the Civil Courts Order 1983, as amended from **9A–415**
time to time. For list, see para. 11–5, below. Former RSC O.63, r.11 expressly provided
that the practice of the Central Office should be followed in the district registries. No
such provision appears in the CPR.

District judges

100.—(1) Subject to subsection (2), for each district registry the **9A–416**
Lord Chancellor shall appoint a person who is a district judge for a
county court district, appointed under section 6 of the County Courts
Act 1984, as a district judge of the High Court.

(2) The Lord Chancellor may, if he thinks fit, appoint two or
more persons who are county court registrars to execute jointly the
office of district judge in any district registry.

(3) Where joint district registrars are appointed under subsection
(2) the Lord Chancellor may—

- (a) give directions with respect to the division between them
of the duties of the office of district judge; and
- (b) as he thinks fit, on the death, resignation or removal of
one of them, either appoint in place of that person another person to be joint district judge, or give directions
that the continuing district judge shall act as sole district
judge or (as the case may be) that the continuing
registrars shall execute jointly the office of district judge.

(4) Subsections (4) to (6) of section 92 shall apply in relation to a
person appointed as a district judge as they apply in relation to a
person appointed to an office to which subsection (1) of that section
applies, except that he shall vacate his office as district judge at such
time as, for any cause whatever, he vacates his office as district judge
for a county court district.

(5) [...]

Note —Derived from the JA 1925, s.84. Amended by the County Courts Act 1984, **9A–417**
s.148(1) and Sched.2; and by the Courts and Legal Services Act 1990, s.54, Scheds 18
and 20. See para. 9A–4.1 above.

Note — CPR, r.2.4 provides that district judges may exercise any function of the **9A–418** court (whether High Court or a county court) except where an enactment, rule or practice direction provides otherwise. See further Practice Direction (Allocation of Cases to Levels of Judiciary), supplementing CPR Pt 2 (Vol. 1, para. 2BPD.1).

"County court registrars ... district registrars ... registrars"

9A–419   By virtue of the Courts and Legal Services Act 1990, s.74(3) "district judges" should be substituted for these officers.

Power of one district judge to act for another

9A–420   **101.**—(1) A district judge of any registry shall be capable of acting in any other district registry for a district judge of that registry; and, where a district judge is so acting, the district judge of the other registry may divide the duties of his office as he thinks fit between himself and the district judge acting for him.

(2) [...]

9A–421   *Note* —Derived from the AJA 1956, s.13. Amended by the County Courts Act 1984, s.148(1) and Sched.2; and by the Courts and Legal Services Act 1990, s.74, Scheds 18 and 20.

Deputy district judges

9A–422   **102.**—(1) If it appears to the Lord Chancellor that it is expedient to do so in order to facilitate the disposal of business in the High Court, he may appoint a person to be a deputy district judge in any district registry during such period or on such occasions as the Lord Chancellor thinks fit.

(2) Subject to subsection (3), a person shall not be qualified for appointment as a deputy district judge unless he is, or is qualified for appointment as, a district judge for a county court district.

(3) A person may be appointed as a deputy district judge if he would, but for his age, be qualified for appointment as a district judge for a county court district and he has previously held the office of district judge for a county court district but no appointment by virtue of this subsection shall be such as to extend beyond the day on which the person in question attains the age of seventy-five years.

(4) A deputy district judge, while acting under this section, shall have the same jurisdiction as the district judge.

(5) Subsection (6) of section 91 applies in relation to a deputy district judge appointed under this section as it applies in relation to a person appointed under that section.

(6) [...]

9A–423   *Note* —Derived from the JA 1925, s.116. Amended by the Judicial Pensions and Retirement Act 1993, ss.26 and 31, Scheds 6 and 8; and the Courts and Legal Services Act 1990, Scheds 18 and 20. See para. 9A–4.1 above.

Assistant district judges

9A–424   **103.** [*Repealed by the Judicial Pensions and Retirement Act 1993, s.31, Sched.9.*]

DISTRICT PROBATE REGISTRIES

9A–425   **104.** [*Section 104 is set out with notes in Section 6C, para. 6C–4.*]

Part V

Probate Causes and Matters

105–128. [*Sections 105–128 are set out with notes in Section 6C, paras* **9A–426**
6C–5 to 6C–66.]

Part VI

Miscellaneous and Supplementary

Miscellaneous provisions

Lords Commissioners to represent Lord Chancellor when Great Seal in commission

129. When the Great Seal is in commission, the Lords Commis- **9A–427**
sioners shall represent the Lord Chancellor for the purposes of this
Act; but the powers vested in him by this Act in relation to—

(a) the appointment of officers, and

(b) any act for which the concurrence or presence of the
Lord Chancellor is required by this Act,

may be exercised by the senior Lord Commissioner for the time
being.

Note—Derived from the JA 1925, s.211. **9A–428**

Fees to be taken in Supreme Court

130. [Repealed by the Courts Act 2003 with effect from January 1, **9A–429**
2005, and replaced by s.92 of that Act. In so far as they were made
under s.130, the repeal of that section did not revoke the Fees Orders
referred to in the Courts Act 2003 (Commencement No. 8, Savings
and Consequential Provisions) Order 2004 (S.I. 2004 No. 3123)
Sched. Pt 2].

Conveyancing Counsel of Supreme Court

131.—(1) The conveyancing counsel of the Supreme Court shall be **9A–430**
persons who have a 10 year High Court qualification, within the
meaning of section 71 of the Courts and Legal Services Act 1990.

(2) The conveyancing counsel of the court shall be not more than
six, nor less than three, in number, and shall be appointed by the
Lord Chancellor.

Note—Derived from the JA 1925, s.217; and the AJA 1956, s.14. Amended by the **9A–431**
Courts and Legal Services Act 1990, Sched.10. See para. 9A–4.1 above.

Proof of documents bearing seal or stamp of Supreme Court or any office thereof

132. Every document purporting to be sealed or stamped with the **9A–432**
seal or stamp of the Supreme Court or of any office of the Supreme
Court shall be received in evidence in all parts of the United
Kingdom without further proof.

LEGISLATION

9A–433   *Note* —See also CPR, r.2.6(3).

Enrolment or engrossment of instruments

9A–434   **133.**—(1) The Master of the Rolls may make regulations for authorising and regulating the enrolment or filing of instruments in the Supreme Court, and for prescribing the form in which certificates of enrolment or filing are to be issued.

(2) Regulations under subsection (1) shall not affect the operation of any enactment requiring or authorising the enrolment of any instrument in the Supreme Court or prescribing the manner in which any instrument is to be enrolled there.

(3) Any instrument which is required or authorised by or under this or any other Act to be enrolled or engrossed in the Supreme Court shall be deemed to have been duly enrolled or engrossed if it is written on material authorised or required by regulations under subsection (1) and has been filed or otherwise preserved in accordance with regulations under that subsection.

(4) The Lord Chancellor may, with the concurrence of the Master of the Rolls and of the Treasury, make regulations prescribing the fees to be paid on the enrolment or filing of any instrument in the Supreme Court, including any additional fees payable on the enrolment or filing of any instrument out of time.

(5) Any regulations under this section shall be made by statutory instrument, which shall be laid before Parliament after being made; and the Statutory Instruments Act 1946 shall apply to a statutory instrument containing regulations under subsection (1) in like manner as if the regulations had been made by a Minister of the Crown.

9A–435   *Note* —Derived from JA, s.218. Paragraph 6.1 of Practice Direction (Court Documents) (supplementing CPR Pt 5) (see Vol. 1, para. 5PD.6) replaced former RSC O.63, r.10 and states that any deed or document which by virtue of any enactment is required or authorised to be enrolled in the Supreme Court may be enrolled in the Central Office of the High Court. The Enrolment of Deeds (Change of Name) Regulations 1994 (S.I. 1994 No. 604) were made by the Master of the Rolls under s.133(1). These Regulations are set out in the Appendix to this Practice Direction and the relevant practice is explained in paras 6.2 *et seq.* See para. 9A–4.1 above.

Power of attorney deposited before October 1971

9A–436   **134.**—(1) This section applies to any instrument creating, or verifying the execution of, a power of attorney which was deposited in the Central Office before 1st October 1971.

(2) A separate file of such instruments shall continue to be kept and, subject to payment of the fee prescribed by an order under section 92 of the Courts Act 2003 (fees)—

(a) any person may search that file, and may inspect any such instrument; and

(b) an office copy of any such instrument shall be issued to any person on request.

(3) A document purporting to be an office copy of any such instrument shall, in any part of the United Kingdom, without further proof be sufficient evidence of the contents of the instrument and of its having been deposited as mentioned in subsection (1).

Note —Derived from the JA 1925, s.219. Amended by the Courts Act 2003, s.109(1), **9A–437** Sched.8, para.262(c). This section relates only to powers of attorney prior to October 1, 1971. See also the Powers of Attorney Act 1971.

Bonds given under order of court

135.—(1) A bond to be given by any person under or for the **9A–438** purposes of any order of the High Court or the civil division of the Court of Appeal shall be given in such form and to such officer of the court as may be prescribed and, if the court so requires, with one or more sureties.

(2) An officer of the court to whom a bond is given in accordance with subsection (1) shall as such have power to enforce it or to assign it, pursuant to an order of the court under subsection (4), to some other person.

(3) Where by rules of court made for the purposes of this section another officer is at any time substituted for the officer previously prescribed as the officer to whom bonds of any class are to be given, the rules may provide that bonds of that class given before the rules come into operation shall have effect as if references in the bonds to the officer previously prescribed were references to the substituted officer.

(4) Where it appears to the court that the condition of a bond given in accordance with subsection (1) has been broken, the court may, on an application in that behalf, order the bond to be assigned to such person as may be specified in the order.

(5) A person to whom a bond is ordered to be assigned under subsection (4) shall be entitled by virtue of the order to sue on the bond in his own name as if it had been originally given to him, and to recover on it as trustee for all persons interested the full amount recoverable in respect of the breach of condition.

Note —Derived from the JA 1925, s.219A. Added by the AJA 1928, s.12. **9A–439**

Production of documents filed in, or in custody of, Supreme Court

136.—(1) The Lord Chancellor may, with the concurrence of the **9A–440** Lord Chief Justice, the Master of the Rolls, the President of the Family Division and the Vice-Chancellor, or of any three of them, make rules for providing that, in any case where a document filed in, or in the custody of, any office of the Supreme Court is required to be produced to any court or tribunal (including an umpire or arbitrator) sitting elsewhere than at the Royal Courts of Justice—

    (a) it shall not be necessary for any officer, whether served with a subpoena in that behalf or not, to attend for the purpose of producing the document; but

    (b) the document may be produced to the court or tribunal by sending it to the court or tribunal, in the manner prescribed in the rules, together with a certificate, in the form so prescribed, to the effect that the document has been filed in, or is in the custody of, the office;

and any such certificate shall be prima facie evidence of the facts stated in it.

(2) Rules under this section may contain—

(a) provisions for securing the safe custody and return to the proper office of the Supreme Court of any document sent to a court or tribunal in pursuance of the rules; and

(b) such incidental and supplementary provisions as appear to the Lord Chancellor to be necessary or expedient.

(3) Rules under this section shall be made by statutory instrument, which shall be laid before Parliament after being made.

9A–441 *Note* —Derived from the JA 1925, s.220 as amended by the A.J.(M.P.) A. 1938. Until para. 13 of Sched. 1 to the Constitutional Reform Act 2005 comes into force, the reference to the Vice-Chancellor in s.136(1) is to be read as a reference to the Chancellor of the High Court. See para. 9A–4.1 above.

"sending ... in the manner prescribed"

9A–442 The principal purpose behind the granting to the Lord Chancellor of power to make rules prescribing the manner in which court documents are to be produced to any court or tribunal is to facilitate production by post. The rule-making power as contained in JA 1925 s.220, the predecessor of s.136, insofar as it applied to production by post was confined to the making of rules permitting production by registered post. Rules to this effect were found in the Supreme Court Documents (Production) Rules 1926 (S.R. & 0) 1926 No. 461). After the coming into force of the Recorded Delivery Service Act 1962 those Rules, insofar as they permitted production by registered post, were to be read as also permitting production by recorded delivery service. The 1926 Rules were superseded by Practice Direction (Court Documents), para. 5.6 (see Vol. 1, para. 5PD.5). In terms, sub-para. (4) of para. 5.6 follows the 1926 Rules and permits production by the court by registered post. However, by virtue of the 1962 Act (referred to above) production by recorded delivery service is permitted. See further, Vol. 1, para. 5.1.4.

Money paid into court under enactment subsequently repealed

9A–443 **137.** Where in pursuance of any enactment, whenever passed, any money has (before or after the commencement of this Act) been paid—

(a) into the Bank of England in the name of the Accountant General of the Supreme Court; or

(b) into the Supreme Court,

then, if that enactment has been or is subsequently repealed—

(i) the Accountant General may continue to deal with the money; and

(ii) any powers of the High Court with respect to the money shall continue to be exercisable,

in all respects as if that enactment had not been repealed.

9A–444 *Note* —Derived from the Court Funds Act 1829, s.1.

Funds under repeated statutes

9A–445 This section is intended to provide continuing statutory authority to enable the Accountant General and the High Court to deal with money or exercise powers with respect thereto which was paid into court under enactments subsequently repealed.

Effect of writs of execution against goods

9A–446 **138.** [*Repealed by the Courts Act 2003, s.99 and Sched. 7*].

Sales under executions

9A–447 **138A.** [*Repealed by the Courts Act 2003, s.99 and Sched. 7*].

Protection of officer selling goods under execution

138B. [*Repealed by the Courts Act 2003, s.99 and Sched. 7*]. **9A–448**

Attachment of National Savings Bank deposits

139.—(1) In section 27 of the Crown Proceedings Act 1947 (attach- **9A–449**
ment of moneys payable by the Crown)—

> (a) in subsection (1), paragraph (c) of the proviso (which
> precludes the making of orders under that subsection by
> the High Court or a county court in respect of money
> payable on account of a deposit in the National Savings
> Bank) shall cease to have effect; and
>
> (b) after subsection (2) there shall be added—
>
>> "(3) In their application to England and Wales the pre-
>> ceding provisions of this section shall have effect
>> subject to any order for the time being in force
>> under section 139(2) of the Supreme Court Act
>> 1981."

(2) The Lord Chancellor may by order direct that section 27(1)
and (2) of the Crown Proceedings Act 1947 (attachment of moneys
payable by the Crown) shall not apply in relation to any money payable by the Crown to any person on account of—

> (a) any deposit in the National Savings Bank; or
>
> (b) a deposit in that Bank of any description specified in the
> order.

(3) Any order under subsection (2) shall be made by statutory
instrument subject to annulment in pursuance of a resolution of either House of Parliament.

(4) Without prejudice to section 153(4), this section extends to
England and Wales only.

Enforcement of fines and forfeited recognizances

140.—(1) Payment of a fine imposed, or sum due under a **9A–450**
recognizance forfeited, by the High Court or the civil division of the
Court of Appeal may be enforced upon the order of the court—

> (a) in like manner as a judgment of the High Court for the
> payment of money; or
>
> (b) in like manner as a fine imposed by the Crown Court.

(2) Where payment of a fine or other sum falls to be enforced as
mentioned in paragraph (a) of subsection (1) upon an order of the
High Court or the civil division of the Court of Appeal under that
subsection—

> (a) the court shall, if the fine or other sum is not paid in full
> forthwith or within such time as the court may allow,
> certify to Her Majesty's Remembrancer the sum payable;
> and
>
> (b) Her Majesty's Remembrancer shall thereupon proceed
> to enforce payment of that sum as if it were due to him
> as a judgment debt.

(3) Where payment of a fine or other sum falls to be enforced as
mentioned in paragraph (b) of subsection (1) upon an order of the

High Court or the civil division of the Court of Appeal under that subsection, the provisions of sections 139 and 140 of the Powers of Criminal (Sentencing) Act 2000 shall apply to that fine or other sum as they apply to a fine imposed by the Crown Court.

(4) Where payment of a fine or other sum has become enforceable by Her Majesty's Remembrancer by virtue of this section or section 16 of the Contempt of Court Act 1981, any payment received by him in respect of that fine or other sum shall be dealt with by him in such manner as the Lord Chancellor may direct.

(5) In this section, and in sections 139 and 140 of the Powers of Criminal Courts (Sentencing) Act 2000 as extended by this section, "fine" includes a penalty imposed in civil proceedings.

9A–451   *Note* —Amended by the Powers of Criminal Courts (Sentencing) Act 2000 (c.6), s.165, Sched.9, para. 88. See para. 9A–4.1 above.

Abolition of certain writs

9A–452   **141.** [*Repealed by the Statute Law (Repeals) Act 2004, Sched.1, Pt 1, Group 4*].

Writs of elegit

9A–453   These were writs of execution by which a judgment creditor could seize possession of the land of the judgment debtor and hold it until the debt was satisfied out of the rents and profits issuing from the land.

Writs of capias ad satisfaciendum

9A–454   These were writs for the arrest of a judgment debtor after judgment had been duly obtained but not satisfied. It would seem that this section has the effect of negativing (*Att.-Gen. v. Randall* [1944] 2 All E.R. 179).

Selection of judges for trial of election petitions

9A–455   **142.**—(1) The judges to be placed on the rota for the trial of parliamentary election petitions in England and Wales under Part II of the Representation of the People Act 1983 in each year shall be selected, in such manner as may be provided by rules of court, from the judges of the Queen's Bench Division of the High Court exclusive of any who are members of the House of Lords.

(2) Notwithstanding the expiry of the year for which a judge has been placed on the rota he may act as if that year had not expired for the purpose of continuing to deal with, giving judgment in, or dealing with any ancillary matter relating to, any case with which he may have been concerned during that year.

(3) Any judge placed on the rota shall be eligible to be placed on the rota again in the succeeding or any subsequent year.

9A–456   *Note* —Derived from the JA 1925, s.67. Amended by the Representation of the People Act 1983, Sched.8.

* * * *

Amendment of law relating to county courts

9A–457   **149.** [*Repealed by the County Courts Act 1984, s.148(3) and Sched.4*].

Admiralty jurisdiction: provisions as to Channel Islands, Isle of Man, Colonies etc.

9A–458   **150.** [*Section 150 is set out in Section 2A, para. 2D–212.*]

Interpretation of this Act, and rules of construction for other Acts and documents

151.—(1) In this Act, unless the context otherwise requires—   **9A–459**

"action" means any civil proceedings commenced by writ or in any other manner prescribed by rules of court;

"appeal", in the context of appeals to the civil division of the Court of Appeal, includes—

    (a) an application for a new trial, and

    (b) an application to set aside a verdict, finding or judgment in any cause or matter in the High Court which has been tried, or in which any issue has been tried, by a jury;

"arbitration agreement" has the same meaning as it has in Part I of the Arbitration Act 1996.

"cause" means any action or any criminal proceedings;

"Division", where it appears with a capital letter, means as division of the High Court;

"judgment" includes a decree;

"jurisdiction" includes powers;

"matter" means any proceedings in court not in a cause;

"party", in relation to any proceedings, includes any person who pursuant to or by virtue of rules of court or any other statutory provision has been served with notice of, or has intervened in, those proceedings;

"prescribed" means—

    (a) except in relation to fees, prescribed by rules of court;

    (b) [. . . .]

"senior judge" , where the reference is to the senior judge of a Division, means—

    (a) in the case of the Chancery Division, the Vice-Chancellor;

    (b) in any other case, the president of the Division in question;

"solicitor" means a solicitor of the Supreme Court;

"statutory provision" means any enactment, whenever passed, or any provision contained in subordinate legislation (as defined in section 21(1) of the Interpretation Act 1978), whenever made;

"this or any other Act" includes an Act passed after this Act.

(2) Section 128 contains definitions of expressions used in Part V and in the other provisions of this Act relating to probate causes and matters.

(3) Any reference in this Act to rules of court under section 84 includes a reference to rules of court in relation to the Supreme Court under any provision of this or any other Act which confers on the Civil Procedure Rule Committee or the Crown Court Rule Committee power to make rules of court.

(4) Except where the context otherwise requires, in this or any other Act—

[...];

[...];

"divisional court" (with or without capital letters) means a divisional court constituted under section 66;

"judge of the Supreme Court" means—

    (a) a judge of the Court of Appeal other than an ex-officio judge within paragraph (b) or (c) of section 2(2), or

    (b) a judge of the High Court, and accordingly does not include, as such, a judge of the Crown Court;

"official referees' business" has the meaning given by section 68(6);

(5) The provisions of Schedule 4 (construction of references to superseded courts and officers) shall have effect.

9A–460   *Note* —Derived from the JA 1925, s.225. Amended by the Courts and Legal Services Act 1990, Sched.18; the Arbitration Act 1996, Sched.3; the Civil Procedure Act 1997, Sched.2 and definitions in subs.(4) repealed subject to transitional provisions specified in art.2 by the Courts Act 2003 (Consequential Amendments) Order 2004 (S.I. 2004 No. 2035), Sched.1, para.18. Until para. 146 of Sched. 4 to the Constitutional Reform Act 2005 comes into force, the reference to the Vice-Chancellor in the definition of "senior judge" in s.151(1) is to be read as a reference to the Chancellor of the High Court. See para. 9A–4.1 above.

"Action" "Cause" "Matter"
9A–461   These words are terms of art. They were used throughout the Rules of the Supreme Court in their technical senses. Their meanings and the differences between them were important and, in some respects, of practical significance. However, in the Civil Procedure Rules they are not used. The result is that there is now a lack of consistency between the language of the primary legislation governing the jurisdiction, practice and procedure of the High Court and the Court of Appeal and the language of the rules of court applicable in those Courts and some distinctions which had a practical usefulness have been lost.

Judgment
9A–462   The definition of "judgment" as including a "decree" is not a general definition, but one for the purposes of the SCA 1981 only, *per* Chitty J. *Burrows v. Holley* (1887) 35 Ch D 124; *per* M.R., *Re Binstead* [1893] 1 Q.B. 199 at 203, in which case it was held that a decree made in a suit for divorce was not a final judgment within s.4(1)(g) of the B.A. 1883.

Judgments and orders are kept distinct by the SCA 1981 (as they were under the JA 1925), although they may be enforced in the same manner (*ex p.* Chinery (1884) 12 QBD 342 at 345; see Vol. 1, para. 40.2.3, "Orders Enforceable like Judgments"). In *Joyne v. MacCabe*, [1899] 1 Ir.R. 104, it was held that a consent order staying proceedings could not be registered as a "judgment"; and *cf. Shaw v. Hertford County Council* [1899] 2 Q.B. 282.

For the purposes of an appeal a judgment means a decision obtained in an action, and every other decision is an order (*Onslow v. Commissioners etc.* (1890) 25 QBD 465 at 466, adopting judgment in *ex p. Chinery; Austin Friars, etc. Co v. Strack* [1906] 2 K.B. 499, CA). And see *Tata Co v. Bombay C.R.A.* (1923) 39 T.L.R. 268.

Amendments of other Acts, transitional provisions, savings and repeals
9A–463   **152.**—(1) [*Consequential Amendments*]

   (2) [...]

   (3) This Act shall have effect subject to the transitional provisions and savings contained in Schedule 6.

(4) [*Repeals*]

(5) [...]

9A–464

Note —Words in subss. (2) and (5) are omitted were repealed by the Statute Law (Repeals) Act 2004, Sched.1, Pt 1, Group 4.

Citation, commencement and extent

153.—(1) This Act may be cited as the Supreme Court Act 1981.   9A–465

(2) This Act, except the provisions mentioned in subsection (3), shall come into force on January 1, 1982; and references to the commencement of this Act shall be construed as references to the beginning of that day.

(3) Sections 72, 143 and 152(2) and this section shall come into force on the passing of this Act.

(4) [*Extension of provisions of Act to Scotland, Northern Ireland, and other specified places.*] ... but, save as aforesaid, the provisions of this Act, other than those mentioned in subsection (5), extend to England and Wales only.

(5) The provisions of this Act whose extent is not restricted by subsection (4) are—

- (a) section 27;
- (b) section 150;
- (c) section 151(1);
- (d) section 152(4) and Schedule 7 as far as they relate to the Naval Prize Act 1864, the Prize Courts Act 1915 and section 56 of the Administration of Justice Act 1956;
- (e) this section;
- (f) paragraph 1 of Schedule 4.

SCHEDULE 1

DISTRIBUTION OF BUSINESS IN HIGH COURT

Chancery Division

1. To the Chancery Division are assigned all causes and matters relating to—   9A–466
- (a) the sale, exchange or partition of land, or the raising of charges on land;
- (b) the redemption of foreclosure of mortgages;
- (c) the execution of trusts;
- (d) the administration of the estates of deceased persons;
- (e) bankruptcy;
- (f) the dissolution of partnership or the taking of partnership or other accounts;
- (g) the rectification, setting aside or cancellation of deeds or other instruments in writing;
- (h) probate business, other than non-contentious or common form business;
- (i) patents, trade marks, registered designs, copyright or design right;
- (j) the appointment of a guardian of a minor's estate,and all causes and matters involving the exercise of the High Court's jurisdiction under the enactments relating to companies.

Queen's Bench Division

2. To the Queen's Bench Division are assigned—   9A–467
- (a) applications for writs of habeas corpus, except applications made by a parent or guardian of a minor for such a writ concerning the custody of the minor;
- (b) applications for judicial review;

(ba) all control order proceedings (within the meaning of the Prevention of Terrorism Act 2005);

(c) all causes and matters involving the exercise of the High Court's Admiralty jurisdiction or its jurisdiction as a prize court; and

(d) all causes and matters entered in the commercial list.

Family Division

9A–468 3. To the Family Division are assigned—

(a) all matrimonial causes and matters (whether at first instance or on appeal);

(b) all causes and matters (whether at first instance or on appeal) relating to—
   (i) legitimacy;
   (ii) the exercise of the inherent jurisdiction of the High Court with respect to minors, the maintenance of minors and any proceedings under the Children Act 1989, except proceedings solely for the appointment of a guardian of a minor's estate;
   (iii) adoption;
   (iv) non-contentious or common form probate business;

(c) applications for consent to the marriage of a minor or for a declaration under section 27B(5) of the Marriage Act 1949;

(d) proceedings on appeal under section 13 of the Administration of Justice Act 1960 from an order or decision made under section 63(3) of the Magistrates' Courts Act 1980 to enforce an order of a magistrates' court made in matrimonial proceedings or proceedings under Part IV of the Family Law Act 1996 or with respect to guardianship of a minor.

(e) proceedings under the Children Act 1989;

(f) all proceedings under:—
   (i) Part IV of the Family Law Act 1996;
   (ii) the Child Abduction and Custody Act 1985;
   (iii) the Family Law Act 1986;
   (iv) section 30 of the Human Fertilisation and Embryology Act 1990;
   (v) Council Regulation (EC) No 2201/2003 of 27th November 2003 concerning jurisdiction and the recognition and enforcement of judgments in matrimonial matters and matters of parental responsibility, so far as that Regulation relates to jurisdiction, recognition and enforcement in parental responsibility matters;

(g) all proceedings for the purpose of enforcing an order made in any proceedings of a type described in this paragraph.

(h) all proceedings under the Child Support Act 1991.

(i) all proceedings under section 6 and 8 of the Gender Recognition Act 2004.

(i) all civil partnership causes and matters (whether at first instance or on appeal);

(j) applications for consent to the formation of a civil partnership by a minor or for a declaration under paragraph 7 of Schedule 1 to the Civil Partnership Act 2004;

(k) applications under section 58 of that Act (declarations relating to civil partnerships).

9A–469 *Note* —Amended by the Marriage (Prohibited Degrees of Relationship) Act 1986, s.5; the Family Law Reform Act 1987, Sched.4; the Children Act 1989, Scheds 11 and 13; the High Court (Distribution of Business) Order 1991 (S.I. 1991 No. 1210); the High Court (Distribution of Business) Order 1993 (S.I. 1993 No. 622); the Family Law Act 1986, s.68(1), Sched.1; the Copyright, Designs and Patents Act 1988, s.303(1), Sched.7; the Family Law Act 1996, Sched.8, para. 51 and the High Court (Distribution of Business) Order 2004 (S.I. 2004 No. 3418); S.I. 2005 No. 265; the Civil Partnership Act 2004, s.261(1), Sched.27, para.70 (for certain purposes only: see S.I. 2005 No. 1112); and the Prevention of Terrorism Act 2005, s.11, Sched.1, para.10.

SCHEDULE 2

List of Offices in Supreme Court for Purposes of Part IV

9A–470 References in this Schedule to a person having a general qualification shall be construed in accordance with section 71 of the Courts and Legal Services Act 1990.

PART I

1. *Office*	2. *Persons qualified*
1. [...].	1. [...].
2. Official Solicitor.	2. A person who has a 10 year general qualification.

9A–471

PART II

1. *Office*	2. *Persons qualified*
3. Master, Queen's Bench Division.	3. A person who has a 7 year general qualification.
4. Queen's Coroner and Attorney and Master of the Crown Office and Registrar of Criminal Appeals.	4. A person who has a 10 year general qualification.
5. Admiralty Registrar.	5. A person who has a 7 year general qualification.
6. Master, Chancery Division.	6. A person who has a 7 year general qualification.
7. Registrar in Bankruptcy of the High Court.	7. A person who has a 7 year general qualification.
8. Taxing Master of the Supreme Court.	8. A person who has a 7 year general qualification.
9. District judge of the principal registry of the Family Division.	9. —(1) A person who has a 7 year general qualification. (2) A district probate registrar who either— (a) is of at least 5 years' standing; or (b) has, during so much of the 10 years immediately preceding his appointment as he has not been a district probate registrar, served as a civil servant in the principal registry or a district probate registry. (3) A civil servant who has served at least 10 years in the principal registry or a district registry.
10. [...].	10. [...].
11. Master of the Court of Protection.	11. A person who has a 7 year general qualification.

9A–472

PART III

1. *Office*	2. *Persons qualified*
12. District probate registrar.	12. —(1) A person who has a 5 year general qualification. (2) A civil servant who has served at least 5 years in the principal registry of the Family Division or a district probate registry.

9A–473

Note —Substituted by the Courts and Legal Services Act 1990, s.71(2), Sched.10, para. 49. Amended by Supreme Court (Offices) Act 1997, s.1 and Access to Justice Act, s.70 and Sched.15, Pt III.

9A–474

SCHEDULE 3

[*Repealed by the County Courts Act 1984, s.148(3) and Sched.4.*]

9A–475

LEGISLATION

SCHEDULE 4

[CONSTRUCTION OF REFERENCES TO SUPERSEDED COURTS AND OFFICERS]

9A–476   *   *   *   *

Principal registrar of Family Division

9A–477   4. In any enactment or document passed or made before the commencement of this Act any reference to the principal registrar of the Family Division shall be read as a reference to the Senior Registrar of that Division.

     *   *   *   *

(SEE S.152(3))   # SCHEDULE 6

TRANSITIONAL PROVISIONS AND SAVINGS

Continuance in office of Vice-Chancellor

9A–478   1. On and after the date of commencement of this Act the person who immediately before that date is Vice-Chancellor by nomination under section 5 of the Administration of Justice Act 1970 shall be deemed to have been appointed as from that date to the office of Vice-Chancellor under section 10(1) and to have duly taken the oaths required by section 10(4).

Continuity of appointments of officers

9A–479   2.—(1) Any person holding an office immediately before the commencement of this Act in the case of which provision for appointment is made by Part IV shall continue to hold that office as if he had been appointed under that Part (whether or not he is qualified to be so appointed).

     (2) Any person holding the office of Assistant Master, Queen's Bench Division immediately before the commencement of this Act shall, notwithstanding the repeals made by this Act, continue to hold that office.

County Courts Act 1984

(1984 c.28)

9A–480 An Act to consolidate certain enactments relating to county courts.

ARRANGEMENT OF SECTIONS

PART I

CONSTITUTION AND ADMINISTRATION

COUNTY COURTS AND DISTRICTS

LEGISLATION

LEGISLATION

Introductory note

9A–481   The County Courts Act 1984 replaced the County Courts Act 1959 and a number of other provisions set out in Sched.4 to the Act. By operation of the Civil Procedure Act 1997, s.10 and Sched.2, para. 2(2) throughout this Act, for "county court rules", wherever occurring, there is substituted "rules of court" and for "rule committee" there is substituted " Civil Procedure Rule Committee".

Jurisdiction of county courts

Formerly, in many sections in Pt II of this Act the jurisdiction of the county courts **9A–482** was determined by reference to "the county court limit" as defined in s.147(1). Since the coming into effect of Courts and Legal Services Act 1990 and the High Court and County Courts Jurisdiction Order 1991 the significance of this limit is very much reduced. Where it remains relevant in the sections printed below, *e.g.* s.23 (equity jurisdiction), the applicable "county court limit" has been inserted in brackets in the printed text. The effect of the 1990 Act and 1991 Order was to increase greatly the jurisdiction of the county courts. In relation to some proceedings, the Order places financial restrictions on the county court jurisdiction.

A county court has no jurisdiction to hear any action in which the title to any toll, fair, market or franchise is in question or any action for libel or slander (s.15(2)) and no action shall be brought in a county court on any judgment of the High Court (s.36). Further, a county court has no jurisdiction to hear any application for judicial review (Courts and Legal Services Act 1990, s.1(10)) (see para. 9B–6 below), or to grant relief prescribed by the County Court Remedies Regulations 1991, reg.2 (see para. 9B–82 below). In relation to certain proceedings, the county court jurisdiction is restricted by, for example, provisions in High Court and County Courts Jurisdiction Order 1991 and by "the county court limit" where it remains operative. In some instances exclusions and restrictions on jurisdiction may be overridden by agreement of the parties under s.18. Note also s.17 (Abandonment of part of claim to give court jurisdiction).

A county court claim commenced by a single plaint is a single action, irrespective of the number of plaintiffs to the claim, and the total amount to be recovered by all the plaintiffs in such action cannot exceed the relevant county court limit; a failure expressly to limit a county court claim to such limit is an irregularity, but does not deprive the county court of jurisdiction to hear and determine the claim and to award judgment up to such limit (*Doyle v. Talbot Motor Co Ltd* [1988] 1 W.L.R. 980, CA).

PART I

CONSTITUTION AND ADMINISTRATION

COUNTY COURTS AND DISTRICTS

County courts to be held for districts

1.—(1) For the purposes of this Act, England and Wales shall be **9A–483** divided into districts, and a court shall be held under this Act for each district at one or more places in it; and each court shall have such jurisdiction and powers as are conferred by this Act and any other enactment for the time being in force.

(2) Every court so held shall be called a county court and shall be a court of record and shall have a seal.

(3) Nothing in this section affects the operation of section 42 of the Courts Act 1971 (City of London).

Note—Amended by the Civil Procedure Act 1997, Sched.2. **9A–484**

County court districts, etc.

2.—(1) The Lord Chancellor may by order specify places at which **9A–485** county courts are to be held and the name by which the court held at any place so specified is to be known.

(2) Any order under this section shall be made by statutory instrument, which shall be laid before Parliament after being made.

(3) The districts for which county courts are to be held shall be

determined in accordance with directions given by or on behalf of the Lord Chancellor.

(4) Subject to any alterations made by virtue of this section, county courts shall continue to be held for the districts and at the places and by the names appointed at the commencement of this Act.

Civil Courts Order

9A–486   The Order made by the Lord Chancellor under this section is the Civil Courts Order 1983 (S.I. 1983 No. 713). This Order has been amended from time to time since 1983 (see para. 11–7 below). For meaning of "registrar", see para. 9A–493 below.

PLACES AND TIMES OF SITTINGS OF COURTS

Places and times of sittings

9A–487   **3.**—(1) In any district the places at which the court sits, and the days and times when the court sits at any place, shall be determined in accordance with directions given by or on behalf of the Lord Chancellor.

(2) A judge may from time to time adjourn any court held by him, and a registrar may from time to time adjourn—

(a) any court held by him, or

(b) in the absence of the judge, any court to be held by the judge.

(3) [*Omitted.*]

(4) References in this Act to sittings of the court shall include references to sittings by any registrar in pursuance of any provision contained in, or made under, this Act.

9A–488   *Note* — Subsection (3) omitted by the Civil Procedure Act 1997, Sched.2.

Use of public buildings for courts

9A–489   **4.**—(1) Where, in any place in which a county court is held, there is a building, being a town hall, court-house or other public building belonging to any local or other public authority, that building shall, with all necessary rooms, furniture and fittings in it, be used for the purpose of holding the court, without any charge for rent or other payment, except the reasonable and necessary charges for lighting, heating and cleaning the building when used for that purpose.

(2) Where any such building is used for the purpose of holding any court, the sittings of the court shall be so arranged as not to interfere with the business of the local or other public authority usually transacted in the building or with any purpose for which the building may be used by virtue of any local Act.

(3) This section shall not apply to any place in which a building was erected before 1st January 1889 for the purpose of holding and carrying on the business of a county court.

JUDGES

Judges of county courts

9A–490   **5.**—(1) Every Circuit judge shall, by virtue of his office, be capable of sitting as a judge for any county court district in England and Wales, and the Lord Chancellor shall assign one or more Circuit judges to each district and may from time to time vary the assignment of Circuit judges among the districts.

(2) Subject to any directions given by or on behalf of the Lord Chancellor, in any case where more than one Circuit judge is assigned to a district under subsection (1), any function conferred by or under this Act on the judge for a district may be exercised by any of the Circuit judges for the time being assigned to that district.

(3) The following, that is—

> every judge of the Court of Appeal,
> every judge of the High Court,
> every Recorder,

shall, by virtue of his office, be capable of sitting as a judge for any county court district in England and Wales and, if he consents to do so, shall sit as such a judge at such times and on such occasions as the Lord Chancellor considers desirable.

(4) Notwithstanding that he is not for the time being assigned to a particular district, a Circuit judge—

(a) shall sit as a judge of that district at such times and on such occasions as the Lord Chancellor may direct; and

(b) may sit as a judge of that district in any case where it appears to him that the judge of that district is not, or none of the judges of that district is, available to deal with the case.

DISTRICT JUDGES, ASSISTANT DISTRICT JUDGES AND DEPUTY DISTRICT JUDGES

District judges

6.—(1) Subject to the provisions of this section, there shall be a **9A–491** district judge for each district, who shall be appointed by the Lord Chancellor and paid such salary as the Lord Chancellor may, with the concurrence of the Treasury, direct.

(2) The Lord Chancellor may, if he thinks fit, appoint a person to be district judge for two or more districts.

(3) The Lord Chancellor may, if he thinks fit, appoint two or more persons to execute jointly the office of district judge for a district and may, in any case where joint district judges are appointed, give directions with respect to the division between them of the duties of the office.

(4) The Lord Chancellor may, as he thinks fit, on the death, resignation or removal of a joint district judge, either appoint another person to be joint district judge in his place or give directions that the continuing district judge shall act as sole district judge or, as the case may be, that the continuing district judges shall execute jointly the office of district judge.

(5) The district judge for any district shall be capable of acting in any other district for the district judge of that other district.

9A–492   *Note* —Amended by the Courts and Legal Services Act 1990, s.125(3), Sched.18, para. 42.

Office of district judge and deputy district judge

9A–493   By the Courts and Legal Services Act 1990, s.74(1), the offices of registrar, assistant registrar and deputy registrar became the offices of district judge. Section 74(2) of the Act states that any reference in any enactment to the offices of registrar, etc., shall be construed as a reference to that office by its new name.

Assistant district judges

9A–494   **7.** [*Repealed by the Judicial Pensions and Retirement Act 1993, s.31, Scheds 8 and 9*].

Deputy district judge

9A–495   **8.**—(1) If it appears to the Lord Chancellor that it is expedient as a temporary measure to make an appointment under this subsection in order to facilitate the disposal of business in county courts, he may appoint a person to be deputy district judge for any county court district during such period or on such occasions as the Lord Chancellor thinks fit; and a deputy district judge, while acting under his appointment, shall have the same powers and be subject to the same liabilities as if he were the district judge.

(1A) Any appointment of a person as a deputy district judge—

(a) if he has previously held office as a district judge, shall not be such as to extend beyond the day on which he attains the age of 75 years; and

(b) in any other case, shall not be such as to extend beyond the day on which he attains the age of 70 years, but subject to section 26(4) to (6) of the Judicial Pensions and Retirement Act 1993 (power to authorise continuance in office up to the age of 75).

(2) [...]

(3) The Lord Chancellor may pay to any person appointed under this section as deputy district judge such remuneration and allowances as he may, with the approval of the Treasury, determine.

9A–496   *Note* —Amended by the Courts and Legal Services Act 1990, s.125(3), Sched.18, para. 42; and the Judicial Pensions and Retirement Act 1993, ss.26 and 31; Scheds 6 and 9.

Qualifications

9A–497   **9.** No person shall be appointed a registrar, or deputy district judge unless he has a 7 year general qualification, within the meaning of section 71 of the Courts and Legal Services Act 1990.

9A–498   *Note* —Amended by the Courts and Legal Services Act 1990, ss.71(2) and 125(3), Sched.10, para. 57, Sched.18, para. 42; and the Judicial Pensions and Retirement Act 1993, s.31, Scheds 8 and 9.

Restrictions on practice as solicitor of district judges and assistant district judges

9A–499   **10.** [*Repealed by the Courts and Legal Services Act 1990, s.125(7), Sched.20*].

Tenure of office

11.—(1) This subsection applies to the office of district judge.　　**9A–500**

(2) Subject to the following provisions of this section and to subsections (4) to (6) of section 26 of the Judicial Pensions and Retirement Act 1993 (Lord Chancellor's power to authorise continuance in office up to the age of 75), a person who holds an office to which subsection (1) applies shall vacate his office on the day on which he attains the age of 70 years.

(3) [...]

(4) A person appointed to an office to which subsection (1) applies shall hold that office during good behaviour.

(5) The power to remove such a person from his office on account of misbehaviour shall be exercisable by the Lord Chancellor.

(6) The Lord Chancellor may also remove such a person from his office on account of inability to perform the duties of his office.

Note —Amended by the Judicial Pensions and Retirement Act 1993, ss.26 and 31, **9A–501**
Sched.6, para. 17, Sched.9.

Records of proceedings to be kept by district judges

12.—(1) The district judge for every district shall keep or cause to **9A–502** be kept such records of and in relation to proceedings in the court for that district as the Lord Chancellor may by regulations made by statutory instrument prescribe.

(2) Any entry in a book or other document required by the said regulations to be kept for the purposes of this section, or a copy of any such entry or document purporting to be signed and certified as a true copy by the district judge, shall at all times without further proof be admitted in any court or place whatsoever as evidence of the entry and of the proceeding referred to by it and of the regularity of that proceeding.

Note —Amended by the Courts and Legal Services Act 1990, s.125(3), Sched.18, **9A–503** paras 42 and 49.

MISCELLANEOUS PROVISIONS AS TO OFFICERS

Officers of court not to act as solicitors in that court

13.—(1) Subject to the provisions of this section, no officer of a **9A–504** court shall, either by himself or his partner, be directly or indirectly engaged as legal representative or agent for any party in any proceedings in that court.

(2) Every person who contravenes this section shall for each offence be liable on summary conviction to a fine of an amount not exceeding level 3 on the standard scale.

(3) Subsection (1) does not apply to a person acting as district judge by virtue of section 6(5).

(4) Subsection (1) does not apply to a deputy district judge; but a deputy district judge shall not act as such in relation to any proceedings in which he is, either by himself or his partner, directly or indirectly engaged as legal representative or agent for any party.

9A–505   *Note* —Amended by the Courts and Legal Services Act 1990, s.125(3), Sched.18, para. 42.

Penalty for assaulting officers

9A–506   **14.**—(1) If any person assaults an officer of a court while in the execution of his duty, he shall be liable—

>   (a) on summary conviction, to imprisonment for a term not exceeding 3 months or to a fine of an amount not exceeding level 5 on the standard scale, or both; or
>
>   (b) on an order made by the judge in that behalf, to be committed for a specified period not exceeding 3 months to prison or to such a fine as aforesaid, or to be so committed and to such a fine,

and a bailiff of the court may take the offender into custody, with or without warrant, and bring him before the judge.

(2) The judge may at any time revoke an order committing a person to prison under this section and, if he is already in custody, order his discharge.

(3) A district judge, assistant district judge or deputy district judge shall have the same powers under this section as a judge.

9A–507   *Note* —Amended by the Statute Law (Repeals) Act 1986; and the Courts and Legal Services Act 1990, s.74.

PART II

JURISDICTION AND TRANSFER OF PROCEEDINGS

ACTIONS OF CONTRACT AND TORT

General jurisdiction in actions of contract and tort

9A–508   **15.**—(1) Subject to subsection (2), a county court shall have jurisdiction to hear and determine any action founded on contract or tort.

(2) A county court shall not, except as in this Act provided, have jurisdiction to hear and determine—

>   (a) [...]
>
>   (b) any action in which the title to any toll, fair, market or franchise is in question; or
>
>   (c) any action for libel or slander.

9A–509   *Note* —Amended by the High Court and County Courts Jurisdiction Order (S.I. 1991 No. 724), art.2(8) and Sched., Pt I.

"any action founded on contract or tort"

9A–510   Before the High Court and County Courts Jurisdiction Order 1991 came into force on July 1, 1991, this general jurisdiction was limited to £5,000. Now the jurisdiction of county courts in claims for money is governed by the 1991 Order (para. 9B–138 below). As to whether a particular claim is an action "founded on contract", see *Hutchings v. Islington LBC* [1998] 3 All E.R. 445, CA.

Money recoverable by statute

9A–511   **16.** A county court shall have jurisdiction to hear and determine an action for the recovery of a sum recoverable by virtue of any enactment for the time being in force, if—

(a) it is not provided by that or any other enactment that such sums shall only be recoverable in the High Court or shall only be recoverable summarily;

(b) [...]

Note—Amended by the High Court and County Courts Jurisdiction Order (S.I. 1991 No. 724), art.2(8) and Sched., Pt I. **9A–512**

Abandonment of part of claim to give court jurisdiction

17.—(1) Where a plaintiff has a cause of action for more than a **9A–513** county court limit in which, if it were not for more than the county court limit, a county court would have jurisdiction, the plaintiff may abandon the excess, and thereupon a county court shall have jurisdiction to hear and determine the action, but the plaintiff shall not recover in the action an amount exceeding the county court limit.

(2) Where the court has jurisdiction to hear and determine an action by virtue of this section, the judgment of the court in the action shall be in full discharge of all demands in respect of the cause of action, and entry of the judgment shall be made accordingly.

Jurisdiction by agreement in certain actions

18. If the parties to any action, other than an action which, if com- **9A–514** menced in the High Court, would have been assigned to the Chancery Division or to the Family Division or have involved the exercise of the High Court's Admiralty jurisdiction, agree, by a memorandum signed by them or by their respective legal representatives, that a county court specified in the memorandum shall have jurisdiction in the action, that court shall have jurisdiction to hear and determine the action accordingly.

Note—Amended by the Courts and Legal Services Act 1990, Sched.18, para. 49(3). **9A–515**
The exclusions mentioned in s.15(2) may be overridden by an agreement under this section. This section applies only to actions which could be brought in the QBD. See s.24, para. 9A–527 for a similar provision relating to certain equity proceedings.

Limitation of recoverable costs of action of contract or tort commenced in High Court which could have been commenced in county court

19. [*Repealed by the Courts and Legal Services Act 1990, Sched.20*]. **9A–516**

Rules for limitation of recoverable costs

20. [*Repealed by the Courts and Legal Services Act 1990, Sched.20*]. **9A–517**

RECOVERY OF LAND AND CASES WHERE TITLE IN QUESTION

Actions for recovery of land and actions where title is in question

21.—(1) A county court shall have jurisdiction to hear and **9A–518** determine any action for the recovery of land.

LEGISLATION

(2) A county court shall have jurisdiction to hear and determine any action in which the title to any hereditament comes into question.

(3) Where a mortgage of land consists of or includes a dwelling-house and no part of the land is situated in Greater London then, subject to subsection (4), if a county court has jurisdiction by virtue of this section to hear and determine an action in which the mortgagee under that mortgage claims possession of the mortgaged property, no court other than a county court shall have jurisdiction to hear and determine that action.

(4) Subsection (3) shall not apply to an action for foreclosure or sale in which a claim for possession of the mortgaged property is also made.

(5) [...]

(6) [...]

(7) In this section—

"dwelling-house" includes any building or part of a building which is used as a dwelling;

"mortgage" includes a charge and "mortgagor" and "mortgagee" shall be construed accordingly;

"mortgagor" and "mortgagee" includes any person deriving title under the original mortgagor or mortgagee.

(8) The fact that part of the premises comprised in a dwelling-house is used as a shop or office for business, trade or professional purposes shall not prevent the dwelling-house from being a dwelling-house for the purposes of this section.

(9) This section does not apply to a mortgage securing an agreement which is a regulated agreement within the meaning of the Consumer Credit Act 1974.

9A–519 *Note* —Amended by the High Court and County Courts Jurisdiction Order (S.I. 1991 No. 724), art.2(8) and Sched., Pt I.

"title to any hereditament"

9A–520 Section 147 (Interpretation) states that "hereditament" includes both a corporeal and an incorporeal hereditament.

Injunctions and declarations relating to land

9A–521 **22.** [*Repealed by the Courts and Legal Services Act 1990, Sched.20*].

EQUITY PROCEEDINGS

Equity jurisdiction

9A–522 **23.** A county court shall have all jurisdiction of the High Court to hear and determine—

(a) proceedings for the administration of the estate of a deceased person, where the estate does not exceed in amount or value the county court limit [£30,000],

(b) proceedings—

(i) for the execution of any trust, or

(ii) for a declaration that a trust subsists, or

> (iii) under section 1 of the Variation of Trusts Act 1958,

where the estate or fund subject, or alleged to be subject, to the trust does not exceed in amount or value the county court limit [£30,000];

> (c) proceedings for foreclosure or redemption of any mortgage or for enforcing any charge or lien, where the amount owing in respect of the mortgage charge or lien does not exceed the county court limit [£30,000];
>
> (d) proceedings for the specific performance, or for the rectification, delivery up or cancellation, of any agreement for the sale, purchase or lease of any property, where, in the case of a sale or purchase, the purchase money, or in the case of a lease, the value of the property, does not exceed the county court limit [£30,000];
>
> (e) proceedings relating to the maintenance or advancement of a minor, where the property of the minor does not exceed in amount or value the county court limit [£30,000];
>
> (f) proceedings for the dissolution or winding-up of any partnership (whether or not the existence of the partnerships is in dispute), where the whole assets of the partnership do not exceed in amount or value the county court limit [£30,000];
>
> (g) proceedings for relief against fraud or mistake, where the damage sustained or the estate or fund in respect of which relief is sought does not exceed in amount or value the county court limit [£30,000].

9A–523

Note —The text of this section has been amended so as to indicate that, for the purposes of the equity jurisdiction, the County Court limit is £30,000 (see County Courts Jurisdiction Order 1981).

Jurisdiction by agreement in certain equity proceedings

9A–524

24.—(1) If, as respects any proceedings to which this section applies, the parties agree, by a memorandum signed by them or by their respective legal representatives or agents, that a county court specified in the memorandum shall have jurisdiction in the proceedings, that court shall, notwithstanding anything in any enactment, have jurisdiction to hear and determine the proceedings accordingly.

(2) Subject to subsection (3), this section applies to any proceedings in which a county court would have jurisdiction by virtue of—

> (a) section 113(3) of the Settled Land Act 1925,
>
> (b) section 63A of the Trustee Act 1925,
>
> (c) sections 3(7), 49(4), 66(4), 89(7), 90(3), 91(8), 92(2), 136(3), 181(2), 188(2) of, and paragraph 3A of Part III and paragraph 1(3A) and (4A) of Part IV of Schedule 1 to, the Law of Property Act 1925,
>
> (d) sections 17(2), 38(4), 41(1A) and 43(4) of the Administration of Estates Act 1925,
>
> (e) section 6(1) of the Leasehold Property (Repairs) Act 1938,

LEGISLATION

(f) sections 1(6A) and 5(11) of the Land Charges Act 1972, and

(g) section 23 of this Act,

but for the limits of the jurisdiction of the court provided in those enactments.

(3) This section does not apply to proceedings under section 1 of the Variation of Trusts Act 1958.

9A–525   Note —Amended by the Courts and Legal Services Act 1990, Sched.18, para. 49(3); the High Court and County Courts Jurisdiction Order (S.I. 1991 No. 724), art.2(8) and Sched., Pt I and the Statute Law (Repeals) Act 2004, Sched.1, Pt 1, Group 4.

FAMILY PROVISION PROCEEDINGS

Jurisdiction under Inheritance (Provisions for Family and Dependants) Act 1975

9A–526   **25.** A county court shall have jurisdiction to hear and determine any application for an order under section 2 of the Inheritance (Provision for Family and Dependants) Act 1975 (including any application for permission to apply for such an order and any application made, in the proceedings on an application for such an order under any other provision of that Act).

9A–527   Note —Amended by the High Court and County Courts Jurisdiction Order (S.I. 1991 No. 724), art.2(8) and Sched., Pt I.

ADMIRALTY PROCEEDINGS

Districts for Admiralty purposes

9A–528   **26.**—(1) If at any time it appears expedient to the Lord Chancellor that any county court should have Admiralty jurisdiction, it shall be lawful for him, by order—

(a) to appoint that court to have, as from such date as may be specified in the order, such Admiralty jurisdiction as is provided in this Act; and

(b) to assign to that court as its district for Admiralty purposes any part or parts of any county court district or of two or more county court districts.

(2) Where a district has been so assigned to a court as its district for Admiralty purposes, the parts of the sea (if any) adjacent to that district to a distance of 3 miles from the shore thereof shall be deemed to be included in that district, and the judge and all officers of the court shall have jurisdiction and authority for those purposes throughout that district as if it were the district for the court for all purposes.

(3) Where an order is made under this section for the discontinuance of the Admiralty jurisdiction of any county court, whether wholly or within a part of the district assigned to it for Admiralty purposes, provision may be made in the order with respect to any Admiralty proceedings commenced in that court before the order comes into operation.

(4) The power to make orders under this section shall be exercisable by statutory instrument.

Admiralty jurisdiction

27.—(1) Subject to the limitations of amount specified in subsection (2), an Admiralty county court shall have the following Admiralty jurisdiction, that is to say, jurisdiction to hear and determine— **9A–529**

- (a) any claim for damage received by ship;
- (b) any claim for damage done by a ship;
- (c) any claim for loss of life or personal injury sustained in consequence of any defect in a ship or in her apparel or equipment, or in consequence of the wrongful act, neglect and default of—
  - (i) the owners, charterers or persons in possession or control of a ship; or
  - (ii) the master or crew of a ship, or any other person for whose wrongful acts, neglects or defaults the owners, charterers or person in possession or control of a ship are responsible,

being an act, neglect or default in the navigation or management of the ship, in the loading, carriage or discharge of goods on, in or from the ship, or in the embarkation, carriage or disembarkation of persons on, in or from the ship;

- (d) any claim for loss or damage to goods carried in a ship;
- (e) any claim arising out of any agreement relating to the carriage of goods in a ship or to the use or hire of a ship;
- (f) any claim in the nature of salvage (including any claim arising by virtue of the application, by or under section 87 of the Civil Aviation Act 1982, of the law relating to salvage of aircraft and their apparel and cargo);
- (g) any claim in the nature of towage in respect of a ship or an aircraft;
- (h) any claim in the nature of pilotage in respect of a ship or an aircraft;
- (j) any claim in respect of goods or materials supplied to a ship for her operation or maintenance;
- (k) any claim in respect of the construction, repair or equipment of a ship or dock charges or dues;
- (l) any claim by a master or member of the crew of a ship for wages (including any sum allotted out of wages or adjudged by a superintendent to be due by way of wages);
- (m) any claim by a master, shipper, charterer or agent in respect of disbursements made on account of a ship.

(2) The limitations of amount referred to in subsection (1) are that the court shall not have jurisdiction to hear and determine—

- (a) a claim in the nature of salvage where the value of the property saved exceeds £15,000; or
- (b) any other claim mentioned in that subsection for an amount exceeding £5,000.

(3) References in this section to claims in the nature of salvage include references to such claims for services rendered in saving life from a ship or an aircraft or in preserving cargo, apparel or wreck as, under sections 544 to 546 of the Merchant Shipping Act 1894, or any Order in Council made under section 87 of the Civil Aviation Act 1982, are authorised to be made in connection with a ship or an aircraft.

(4) Subject to subsection (5), subsections (1) to (3) apply—

    (a) in relation to all ships or aircraft whether British or not and whether registered or not and wherever the residence or domicile of their owners may be, and

    (b) in relation to all claims, wheresoever arising (including in the case of cargo or wreck salvage, claims in respect of cargo or wreck found on land).

(5) Nothing in subsection (4) shall be construed as extending the cases in which money or property is recoverable under any of the provisions of the Merchant Shipping Acts 1894 to 1983.

(6) If, as regards any proceedings as to any such claim as is mentioned in subsection (1), the parties agree, by a memorandum signed by them or by their respective legal representatives or agents, that a particular county court specified in the memorandum shall have jurisdiction in the proceedings, that court shall, notwithstanding anything in subsection (2) or in rules of court for prescribing the courts in which proceedings shall be brought, have jurisdiction to hear and determine the proceedings accordingly.

(7) Nothing in this section shall be taken to affect the jurisdiction of any county court to hear and determine any proceedings in which it has jurisdiction by virtue of section 15 or 17.

(8) Nothing in this section, or in section 26 or in any order made under that section, shall be taken to confer on a county court the jurisdiction of a prize court within the meaning of the Naval Prize Acts 1864 to 1916.

(9) No county court shall have jurisdiction to determine any claim or question certified by the Secretary of State to be a claim or question which, under the Rhine Navigation Convention, falls to be determined in accordance with the provisions of that Convention; and any proceedings to enforce such a claim which are commenced in a county court shall be set aside.

(10) In subsection (9) "the Rhine Navigation Convention" means the Convention of 7th October 1868 as revised by any subsequent Convention.

(11) Section 555 of the Merchant Shipping Act 1894 shall have effect as if there were inserted after the word "agreement" the words "or by a county court in England or Wales."

9A–530   *Note* — Subsection (6) amended by the Courts and Legal Services Act 1990, Sched.18, para. 49(3). The High Court and County Courts Jurisdiction Order (S.I. 1991 No. 724) does not apply to proceedings to which s.27(1) applies, see art.12(b) of the Order.

Mode of exercise of Admiralty jurisdiction

9A–531   **28.**—(1) The following provisions of this section shall apply to cases within the Admiralty jurisdiction of a county court.

(2) Subject to the following provisions of this Part of this Act, an action in personam may be brought in all such cases.

(3) In any case in which there is a maritime lien or other charge on any ship, aircraft or other property for the amount claimed, an action in rem may be brought in a county court against the ship, aircraft or property.

(4) In the case of any such claim as is mentioned in paragraph (b) to (m) of section 27(1), where—

    (a) the claim arises in connection with a ship; and

    (b) the person who would be liable on the claim in an action in personam ("the relevant person") was, when the cause of action arose, the owner or charterer of, or in possession of or in control of the ship, an action in rem may (whether or not the claim gives rise to a maritime lien on that ship) be brought in a county court against—

        (i) that ship if at the time when the action is brought the relevant person is either the beneficial owner of that ship as respects all the shares in it or the charterer of it under a charter by demise; or

        (ii) any other ship of which, at the time when the action is brought, the relevant person is the beneficial owner as respects all the shares in it.

(5) In the case of a claim in the nature of towage or pilotage in respect of an aircraft, an action in rem may be brought in a county court against that aircraft if, at the time when the action is brought, it is beneficially owned by the person who would be liable on the claim in an action in personam.

(6) Where, in an exercise of its Admiralty jurisdiction, a county court orders any ship, aircraft or other property to be sold, the court shall have jurisdiction to hear and determine any question arising as to the title to the proceeds of sale.

(7) In determining for the purposes of subsections (4) and (5) whether a person would be liable on a claim in an action in personam it shall be assumed that he has his habitual residence or a place of business within England or Wales.

(8) Where as regards any such claim as is mentioned in section 27(1)(b) to (m), a ship has been served with a summons or arrested in an action in rem brought to enforce that claim, no other ship may be served with summons or arrested in that or any other action in rem brought to enforce that claim; but this subsection does not prevent the issue, in respect of any one such claim, of a summons naming more than one ship or of two or more summonses each naming a different ship.

(9) A county court may issue a warrant for the arrest and detention of any vessel, aircraft or property to which an action in rem brought in the courts relates unless or until bail to the amount of the claim made in the action and the reasonable costs of the plaintiff in the action be entered into and perfected by or on behalf of the defendant.

(10) Except as provided by subsection (9), no vessel, aircraft or

property shall be arrested or detained in Admiralty proceedings in a county court otherwise than in execution.

(11) Where—

(a) a vessel, aircraft or other property would or might be sold under an execution to enforce a judgment or order given or made by a county court in Admiralty proceedings; and

(b) the owner of the vessel, aircraft or property desires that the sale should be conducted in the High Court instead of in the county court,

he shall be entitled, on giving security for costs, and subject to such other provisions as may be prescribed, to obtain an order of the county court for transfer of the proceedings for sale, with or without (as the judge of the county court thinks fit) the transfer of any subsequent proceedings to the High Court.

(12) On an appeal by a party to any Admiralty proceedings, the Court of Appeal, if it appears to it expedient that any sale ordered to be made of the vessel, aircraft or other property to which the proceedings relate should be conducted in the High Court instead of in the county court, may direct the transfer of the proceedings for sale, with or without the transfer of the subsequent proceedings, to the High Court.

(13) Where an action is transferred to a county court under section 40, any vessel, aircraft or other property which has been arrested in the action before the transfer shall, notwithstanding the transfer, remain in the custody of the Admiralty Marshal who shall, subject to any directions of the High Court, comply with any orders made by the county court with respect to that vessel, aircraft or property.

Costs of certain Admiralty proceedings commenced in High Court which could have been commenced in county court

9A–532 29. [*Repealed by the Courts and Legal Services Act 1990, Sched.20*].

Restrictions on entertainment of actions in personam in collision and other similar cases

9A–533 30.—(1) The claims to which this section applies are claims for damage, loss of life or personal injury arising—

(a) out of a collision between ships;

(b) out of the carrying out of or omission to carry out a manoeuvre in the case of one or more of two or more ships; or

(c) out of the non-compliance, on the part of one or more of two or more ships,—

(i) with regulations for the prevention of collisions made under section 21 of the Merchant Shipping Act 1979; or

(ii) with any such rules as are mentioned in subsection (1) of section 421 of the Merchant Shipping Act 1894 or any rules made under subsection (2) of that section.

(2) No county court shall entertain an action in personam to enforce a claim to which this section applies unless—

    (a) the defendant has his habitual residence or a place of business within England and Wales; or

    (b) the cause of action arose within inland waters of England and Wales or within the limits of a port of England and Wales; or

    (c) an action arising out of the same incident or series of incidents is proceeding in the court or has been heard and determined in the court.

(3) In subsection (2)—

"inland waters" includes any part of the sea adjacent to the coast of the United Kingdom certified by the Secretary of State to be waters falling by international law to be treated as within the territorial sovereignty of Her Majesty apart from the operation of that law in relation to territorial waters; and

"port" means any port, harbour, river, estuary, haven, dock, canal or other place so long as a person or body of persons is empowered by or under an Act to make charges in respect of ships entering it or using the facilities in it, and "limits of a port" means the limits thereof as fixed by or under the Act in question or, as the case may be, by the relevant charter or custom;

"charges" means any charges with the exception of light dues, local light dues and any other charges in respect of lighthouses, buoys or beacons and of charges in respect of pilotage.

(4) No county court shall entertain an action in personam to enforce a claim to which this section applies until any proceedings previously brought by the plaintiff in any court outside England and Wales against the same defendant in respect of the same incident or series of incidents have been discontinued or otherwise come to an end.

(5) Subsections (1) to (4) shall apply to counterclaims (except counterclaims in proceedings arising out of the same incident or series of incidents) as they apply to actions in personam, but as if the references to the plaintiff and the defendant were respectively references to the plaintiff on the counterclaim and the defendant to the counterclaim.

(6) Subsections (1) to (5) shall not apply to any action or counterclaim if the defendant submits or has agreed to submit to the jurisdiction of the court.

(7) Nothing in this section shall prevent an action or counterclaim which is brought in accordance with the provisions of this section in a county court being transferred, in accordance with the enactments in that behalf, to some other court (whether a county court or not).

(8) This section applies in relation to the jurisdiction of any county court not being Admiralty jurisdiction, as well as in relation to its Admiralty jurisdiction, if any.

Admiralty—interpretation

9A-534   **31.**—(1) In the provisions of this Part of this Act relating to Admiralty proceedings, unless the context otherwise requires,—

    "goods" include baggage;

    "master" has the same meaning as in the Merchant Shipping Act 1894, and accordingly includes every person (except a pilot) having command or charge of a ship;

    "towage" and "pilotage", in relation to an aircraft, means towage and pilotage while the aircraft is waterborne.

(2) Nothing in those provisions shall—

    (a) be construed as limiting the jurisdiction of a county court to refuse to entertain an action for wages by the master or a member of the crew of a ship, not being a British ship;

    (b) affect section 552 of the Merchant Shipping Act 1894 (power of receiver of wreck to detain a ship in respect of a salvage claim);

    (c) authorise proceedings in rem in respect of any claim against the Crown, or the arrest, detention or sale of any of Her Majesty's ships or Her Majesty's aircraft, or of any cargo or other property belonging to the Crown.

(3) In subsection (2) "Her Majesty's ships" and "Her Majesty's aircraft" have the meanings given by section 38(2) of the Crown Proceedings Act 1947.

PROBATE PROCEEDINGS

Contentious probate jurisdiction

9A-535   **32.**—(1) Where—

    (a) an application for the grant or revocation of probate or administration has been made through the principal registry of the Family Division or a district probate registry under section 105 of the Supreme Court Act 1981; and

    (b) it is shown to the satisfaction of a county court that the value at the date of the death of the deceased of his net estate does not exceed the county court limit [£30,000],

the county court shall have the jurisdiction of the High Court in respect of any contentious matter arising in connection with the grant or revocation.

(2) In subsection (1) "net estate", in relation to a deceased person, means the estate of that person exclusive of any property he was possessed of or entitled to as a trustee and not beneficially, and after making allowances for funeral expenses and for debts and liabilities.

(3) In section 106 of the Supreme Court Act 1981 (grants by district probate registrars), subsections (2) to (4) shall be omitted.

9A-536   *Note* —Substituted by the AA 1985, s.51.

Effect of order of judge in probate proceedings

9A-537   **33.** Where an order is made by a county court for the grant or revocation of probate or administration, in pursuance of any jurisdiction conferred upon the court by section 32—

    (a) the registrar of the county court shall transmit to the principal registry of the Family Division or a district probate registry, as he thinks convenient, a certificate under the seal of the court certifying that the order has been made; and

    (b) on the application of a party in favour of whom the order has been made, probate or administration in compliance with the order shall be issued from the registry to which the certificate was sent or, as the case may require, the probate or letters of administration previously granted shall be recalled or varied by, as the case may be, a registrar of the principal registry of the Family Division or the district probate registrar according to the effect of the order.

Note —Amended by the AJA 1985, Scheds 7 and 8.   **9A–538**

MISCELLANEOUS PROVISIONS AS TO JURISDICTION

Proceedings beyond jurisdiction
    34. [*Repealed by the Courts and Legal Services Act 1990, Sched.20*].   **9A–539**

Division of causes of action
    35. It shall not be lawful for any plaintiff to divide any cause of ac- **9A–540**
tion for the purpose of bringing two or more actions in one or more of the county courts.

No action on judgment of High Court
    36. No action shall be brought in a county court on any judgment **9A–541**
of the High Court.

EXERCISE OF JURISDICTION AND ANCILLARY JURISDICTION

Persons who may exercise jurisdiction of court
    37.—(1) Any jurisdiction and powers conferred by this or any **9A–542**
other Act—

    (a) on a county court; or

    (b) on the judge of a county court,
may be exercised by any judge of the court.

    (2) Subsection (1) applies to jurisdiction and powers conferred on all county courts or judges of county courts or on any particular county court or the judge of any particular county court.

Remedies available in county courts
    38.—(1) Subject to what follows, in any proceedings in a county **9A–543**
court the court may make any order which could be made by the High Court if the proceedings were in the High Court.

    (2) Any order made by a county court may be—

    (a) absolute or conditional;

LEGISLATION

      (b) final or interlocutory.

  (3) A county court shall not have power—

      (a) to order mandamus, certiorari or prohibition; or

      (b) to make any order of a prescribed kind.

  (4) Regulations under subsection (3)—

      (a) may provide for any of their provisions not to apply in such circumstances or descriptions of case as may be specified in the regulations;

      (b) may provide for the transfer of the proceedings to the High Court for the purpose of enabling an order of a kind prescribed under subsection (3) to be made;

      (c) may make such provision with respect to matters of procedure as the Lord Chancellor considers expedient; and

      (d) may make provision amending or repealing any provision made by or under any enactment, so far as may be necessary or expedient in consequence of the regulations.

  (5) In this section "prescribed" means prescribed by regulations made by the Lord Chancellor under this section.

  (6) The power to make regulations under this section shall be exercised by statutory instrument.

  (7) No such statutory instrument shall be made unless a draft of the instrument has been approved by both Houses of Parliament.

9A–544   *Note* —Substituted by the Courts and Legal Services Act 1990, s.3, for old ss.38 and 39 of the County Court Act 1984.

"Regulations"

9A–545   See County Court Remedies Regulations 1991 (S.I. 1991 No. 1222) as amended by the County Court Remedies (Amendment) Regulations 1995 (S.I. 1995 No. 206) printed below at para. 9B–81.

"any order which could be made by the High Court"

9A–546   The County Court Remedies Regulations 1991 (S.I. 1991 No. 1222) restrict the grant of seizing orders and freezing injunctions by county courts, but otherwise the power of the county court to grant an interlocutory injunction is the same as that of the High Court (see SCA 1981, s.37 *supra*, paras 9A–109 and 9A–111). Further, art.3 of the High Court and County Courts Jurisdiction Order 1991 provides that the High Court shall have jurisdiction to hear an application for an injunction made in the course of, or in anticipation of, proceedings in a county court where a county court may not, by virtue of s.38(3)(b) or otherwise, grant such an injunction (see para. 9B–143 below). It is not necessary for a party seeking to invoke this jurisdiction to arrange for the county court proceedings to be transferred to the High Court or to initiate originating proceedings in that Court (*Schmidt v. Wong* [2005] EWCA Civ 1506, *The Times*, December 13, 2005, CA). In *Burris v. Azadani* [1995] 1 W.L.R. 1372, CA, [1995] 4 All E.R. 802, CA, it was held that a county court had power to grant an interlocutory injunction restraining A from molesting B containing a term excluding him from vicinity of B's home where such term was reasonably regarded as necessary for the protection of B's legitimate interest; it could not be objected that the conduct to be restrained by the term was not in itself tortious or otherwise unlawful. See also *C v. K (Ouster Order: Non-Parent)* [1996] 2 F.L.R. 506 (Wall J.) (molestation and ouster injunctions as injunctive relief). Article 3 of the High Court and County Courts Jurisdiction Order 1991 provides that the High Court shall have jurisdiction to hear an application for an injunction (including a freezing injunction) made in the course of or in anticipation of proceedings in a county court where a county court may not, by virtue of regulations under s.38(3)(b) or otherwise, grant an injunction. See further Vol. 1, para. 25.1.27.

Ancillary powers of judge

39. [*Repealed by the Courts and Legal Services Act 1990, s.3*]. 9A–547

TRANSFER OF PROCEEDINGS

Transfer of proceedings to county court

40.—(1) Where the High Court is satisfied that any proceedings 9A–548
before it are required by any provision of a kind mentioned in subsection (8) to be in a county court it shall—

    (a) order the transfer of the proceedings to a county court; or

    (b) if the court is satisfied that the person bringing the proceedings knew, or ought to have known, of that requirement, order that they be struck out.

(2) Subject to any such provision, the High Court may order the transfer of any proceedings before it to a county court.

(3) An order under this section may be made either on the motion of the High Court itself or on the application of any party to the proceedings.

(4) Proceedings transferred under this section shall be transferred to such county court as the High Court considers appropriate, having taken into account the convenience of the parties and that of any other persons likely to be affected and the state of business in the courts concerned.

(5) The transfer of any proceedings under this section shall not affect any right of appeal from the order directing the transfer.

(6) Where proceedings for the enforcement of any judgment or order of the High Court are transferred under this section—

    (a) the judgment or order may be enforced as if it were a judgment or order of a county court; and

    (b) subject to subsection (7), it shall be treated as a judgment or order of that court for all purposes.

(7) Where proceedings for the enforcement of any judgment or order of the High Court are transferred under this section—

    (a) the powers of any court to set aside, correct, vary or quash a judgment or order of the High Court, and the enactments relating to appeals from such a judgment or order, shall continue to apply; and

    (b) the powers of any court to set aside, correct, vary or quash a judgment or order of a county court, and the enactments relating to appeals from such a judgment or order, shall not apply.

(8) The provisions referred to in subsection (1) are any made—

    (a) under section 1 of the Courts and Legal Services Act 1990; or

    (b) by or under any other enactment.

(9) This section does not apply to family proceedings within the meaning of Part V of the Matrimonial and Family Proceedings Act 1984.

LEGISLATION

9A–549 *Note* —Substituted by the Courts and Legal Services Act 1990, s.2(1).

"Transfer of the proceedings"

9A–550 For the practice in relation to transfer, see CPR Pt 30, Vol. 1, para. 30.0.1. For procedure for appeal against order of transfer, see Practice Direction (Transfer), para. 5.1, Vol. 1, para. 30PD.5. For transfer of Chancery work from the High Court to a county court and patents county court, see Chancery Guide Chps. 13 and 23 (paras 1–108 and 1–140 above). For observations on time when transfer takes effect, see *Kings Quality Homes Ltd v. AJ Paints Ltd* [1998] 1 W.L.R. 124, CA (jurisdiction of county court judge to hear appeal from order made by district judge before proceedings transferred from High Court to a county court).

"order that they be struck out"

9A–551 Where, under s.40(1), the Court is satisfied that any proceedings before it are required to be in a county court the Court is not required to strike out the proceedings but may, and should normally, order their transfer to a county court (*Restick v. Crickmore* [1994] 1 W.L.R. 420; [1994] 2 All E.R. 112, CA. Presumably the same construction should be applied to s.42(1).

"provisions ... made"

9A–552 The provision made under s.1 of the 1990 Act is the High Court and County Courts Jurisdiction Order 1991 (see para. 9B–138 below).

Second application for transfer

9A–553 An order refusing the transfer of an action can never be final because circumstances can change. Nevertheless, if a party attempts but fails to obtain a transfer, and does not appeal against the refusal to transfer, but thereafter makes a second application, he will ordinarily be held to be guilty of an abuse of process unless there has been a material change of circumstances, or new grounds have arisen or new evidence has come to light; for to do otherwise would be oppressive or unjust to the party opposing the first application (*Habib Bank AG Zurich v. Mindi Investment Ltd* (1987) 131 S.J. 1455; *The Times*, October 9, 1987, CA). See further Vol. 1, para. 23.0.14 "Successive applications for same relief". See Vol. 1, paras 23.0.14 and 23.0.15

subs.(8), Courts and Legal Services Act 1990, s.1

9A–554 Provisions made under this section are found in the High Court and County Courts Jurisdiction Order 1991 (S.I. 1991 No. 724) (see para. 9B–138 below).

For transfer of proceedings under the Arbitration Act 1996, see the High Court and County Courts (Allocation of Arbitration Proceedings) Order 1996, art.5, see para. 2E–357.

Transfer to High Court by order of High Court

9A–555 **41.**—(1) If at any stage in proceedings commenced in a county court or transferred to a county court under section 40, the High Court thinks it desirable that the proceedings, or any part of them, should be heard and determined in the High Court, it may order the transfer to the High Court of the proceedings or, as the case may be, of that part of them.

(2) The power conferred by subsection (1) is without prejudice to section 29 of the Supreme Court Act 1981 (power of High Court to issue prerogative orders) but shall be exercised in relation to family proceedings (within the meaning of Part V of the Matrimonial and Family Proceedings Act 1984) in accordance with any direction given under section 37 of that Act (directions as to distribution and transfer of family business and proceedings).

(3) The power conferred by subsection (1) shall be exercised subject to any provision made—

(a) under section 1 of the Courts and Legal Services Act 1990; or

(b) by or under any other enactment.

Note — Subsection (2) was amended by the Matrimonial and Family Proceedings **9A–556**
Act 1984, Sched.1, para. 31; subs.(3) was added by the Courts and Legal Services Act
1990, s.2(2).

subs.(3), Courts and Legal Services Act 1990, s.1
Provisions made under this section are found in the High Court and County Courts **9A–557**
Jurisdiction Order 1991 (S.I. 1991 No. 724) (see para. 9B–138). In *McLaughlin v. British Coal Corporation, The Times,* December 16, 1992, CA, the defendants applied to a
county court judge to have proceedings transferred to the High Court where other
proceedings raising similar issues were pending. It was held the plaintiffs were entitled
to have their action treated separately and that the judge applied art.7 of the 1991 Order correctly in refusing to transfer the proceedings.

For transfer of proceedings under the Arbitration Act 1996, see the High Court
and County Courts (Allocation of Arbitration Proceedings) Order 1996, art.5, see
para. 2E–357 above.

For rules of court, see CPR Pt 30, Vol. 1, para. 30.0.1.

For transfer of proceedings from a county court to the High Court in insolvency
proceedings, see *Bullard & Taplin Ltd, Re* [1996] B.C.C. 973 (Knox J.), *Licence Holder,
Re* [1997] B.C.C. 666 (Carnwath J.), *Re Debtors (No. 13-Misc-2000 and No. 14-Misc-2000), The Times,* April 10, 2000 (Neuberger J.).

Transfer to High Court by order of a county court

42.—(1) Where a county court is satisfied that any proceedings **9A–558**
before it are required by any provision of a kind mentioned in subsection (7) to be in the High Court, it shall—

   (a) order the transfer of the proceedings to the High Court;
       or
   (b) if the court is satisfied that the person bringing the
       proceedings knew, or ought to have known, of that
       requirement, order that they be struck out.

(2) Subject to any such provision, a county court may order the
transfer of any proceedings before it to the High Court.

(3) An order under this section may be made either on the motion of the court itself or on the application of any party to the
proceedings.

(4) The transfer of any proceedings under this section shall not
affect any right of appeal from the order directing the transfer.

(5) Where the proceedings for the enforcement of any judgment
or order of a county court are transferred under this section—

   (a) the judgment or order may be enforced as if it were a
       judgment or order of the High Court; and
   (b) subject to subsection (6), it shall be treated as a judgment or order of that court for all purposes.

(6) Where proceedings for the enforcement of any judgment or
order of a county court are transferred under this section—

   (a) the powers of any court to set aside, correct, vary or
       quash a judgment or order of a county court, and the
       enactments relating to appeals from a judgment or order, shall continue to apply; and
   (b) the powers of any court to set aside, correct, vary or
       quash a judgment or order of the High Court, and the

enactments relating to appeals from such a judgment or order, shall not apply.

(7) The provisions referred to in subsection (1) are any made—

    (a) under section 1 of the Courts and Legal Services Act 1990; or

    (b) by or under any other enactment.

(8) This section does not apply to family proceedings within the meaning of Part V of the Matrimonial and Family Proceedings Act 1984.

9A–559   *Note* —Substituted by the Courts and Legal Services Act 1990, s.2(3).

subs.(7), Courts and Legal Services Act 1990, s.1
9A–560   The provision made under s.1 of the 1990 Act is the High Court and County Courts Jurisdiction Order 1991 (see para. 9B–138). An example of "any other enactment" concerning transfer to the High Court by order of a county court is the Copyright, Designs and Patents Act 1988, s.289, discussed in *Chaplin Patents Holdings Company Plc. v. Group Lotus Plc.*, The Times, January 12, 1994, CA.

For transfer of proceedings under the Arbitration Act 1996, see the High Court and County Courts (Allocation of Arbitration Proceedings) Order 1996, art.5, see para. 2E–357 above.

For rules of court, see CPR Pt 30.

Jurisdiction to deal with counterclaim or set-off and counterclaim

9A–561   **43.** [*Repealed by the Courts and Legal Services Act 1990, Sched.20*].

Transfer of interpleader proceedings from High Court to county court

9A–562   **44.** [*Repealed by the Courts and Legal Services Act 1990 , Sched.20.*]

Costs in transferred cases

9A–563   **45.**—(1) Where an action, counterclaim or matter is ordered to be transferred—

    (a) from the High Court to a county court; or

    (b) from a county court to the High Court; or

    (c) from one county court to another county court,

the costs of the whole proceedings both before and after the transfer shall, subject to any order of the court which ordered the transfer, be in the discretion of the court to which the proceedings are transferred; and that court shall have power to make orders with respect to the costs, and the costs of the whole proceedings shall be taxed in that court.

(2) [...]

9A–564   *Note* —Amended by the Courts and Legal Services Act 1990, Sched.20.

PART III

PROCEDURE

PARTIES

Proceedings by the Crown

9A–565   **46.**—(1) Subject to the provisions of any enactment limiting the jurisdiction of a county court, whether by reference to the subject matter of the proceedings to be brought or the amount sought to be recovered in the proceedings or otherwise, proceedings by the Crown may be instituted in a county court.

(2) Subject to section 40(5), all rules of law and enactments regulating the removal or transfer of proceedings from a county court to the High Court and the transfer of proceedings in the High Court to a county court shall apply respectively to the removal or transfer of proceedings in the High Court to a county court shall apply respectively to the removal or transfer of proceedings by the Crown in a county court and to the transfer of proceedings by the Crown in the High Court.

(3) Nothing in this section shall apply to proceedings affecting Her Majesty in Her private capacity.

Proceedings by the Crown

Subsection (1) states that proceedings may be instituted *by the Crown* in a county court. For statutory basis for proceedings *against the Crown* in a county court, see the Crown Proceedings Act 1947, s.15 (para. 9B–299). Rules of court for proceedings by and against the Crown whether in a county court of High Court are found in CPR, Pt 66 (Crown proceedings).

Subsection (2) is expressed as being "subject to section 40(5)". Section 40 (Transfer of proceedings to county court) was substituted by the Courts and Legal Services Act 1990, s.2(1). Before the substitution, s.40(5) stated that an order for the transfer to a county court of any proceedings by or against the Crown in the High Court "shall not be made without the consent of the Crown". No such provision appears in s.40 as substituted by the 1990 Act (see paras 9A–551 above). However, the High Court and County Courts Jurisdiction Order 1991, art.11 stated (see para. 9B–138) that, for a period of two years from the date upon which the Order came into force (*i.e.* until July 1, 1993), no order should be made transferring proceedings in the High Court to which the Crown is a party to a county court except (a) when the proceedings are set down to be tried or heard, or (b) with the consent of the Crown. Section 20(1) of the Crown Proceedings Act 1947, which gave the Attorney General power to require that proceedings against the Crown instituted in a county court be transferred to the High Court, was revoked when Pt 66 was inserted in the CPR by the Civil Procedure (Amendment No. 3) Rules 2005 (S.I. 2005 No. 2292). (At the same time, s.19 of the 1947 Act (Venue and related matters) was also revoked.) For provisions as to transfer of proceedings involving the Crown, whether from a county to the High Court or vice versa, insofar as they differ from provisions applying to proceedings where the Crown is not involved, see Pt 66 and the practice direction supplementing that Part.

9A–566

Minors

47. [*Omitted*]

9A–567

Note —Omitted by Civil Procedure (Modification of Enactments) Order 1998 (S.I. 1998 No. 2940), art.6(a). See now CPR, r.21.2.

9A–568

Persons jointly liable

48.—(1) Where a plaintiff has a demand recoverable under this Act against two or more persons jointly liable, it shall be sufficient to serve any of those persons with process, and judgment may be obtained and execution issued against any person so served, notwithstanding that others jointly liable may not have been served or sued or may not be within the jurisdiction of the court.

(2) Where judgment is so obtained against any person by virtue of subsection (1) and is satisfied by that person, he shall be entitled to

9A–569

recover in the court contribution from any other person jointly liable with him.

Persons jointly liable

9A–570   Two or more persons may be joined together in one action as defendants see CPR, r.7.3 (see Vol. 1, para. 7.3). Formerly, it was expressly provided by rules of court that no action or matter shall be defeated by reason of the non-joinder of any party as defendant (see CCR O.5, r.4 and note RSC O.15, r.6(1)); but no comparable provision is included in the CPR. At common law, where two (or more) persons were jointly liable for the payment of a debt or damages and the plaintiff proceeded to judgment against one only, the other was released from his obligations ("release by judgment"), even if the judgment remained unsatisfied. The result was that the plaintiff could not proceed against the other person. Further, the judgment debtor could not bring proceedings against him for a contribution. The "release by judgment" rule was removed by the Law Reform (Married Women and Tortfeasors) Act 1935 and the Civil Liability (Contribution) Act 1978. Section 48 also alters the effect of the rule but this provision has a much earlier provenance as it first appeared as the County Courts Act 1846, s.68. The section makes it clear that a defendant with a right to contribution from another person is not entitled, for the purpose of protecting that right, to a stay of proceedings until that other is joined as a defendant by the plaintiff. The plaintiff may proceed to judgment and the defendant's right to recover contribution against the other person is preserved. Whilst "demands recoverable under this Act" were limited to cases involving small sums, the impact on the release by judgment rule of the legislation now found in s.48 was slight. By the time those limits were significantly altered the rule had been abolished by the legislation referred to above.

Bankruptcy of plaintiff

9A–571   **49.**—(1) The bankruptcy of the plaintiff in any action in a county court which the trustee might maintain for the benefit of the creditors shall not cause the action to abate if, within such reasonable time as the court orders, the trustee elects to continue the action and to give security for the costs of the action.

(2) The hearing of the action may be adjourned until such an election is made.

(3) Where the trustee does not elect to continue the action and to give such security as is mentioned in subsection (1) within the time limited by the order, the defendant may avail himself of the bankruptcy as a defence to the action.

Bankruptcy of plaintiff

9A–572   In proceedings in the High Court, the implications of the bankruptcy of a plaintiff are dealt with by CPR, r.19.2. The most significant feature of s.49 is that it states that, upon the bankruptcy of the plaintiff, his cause of action shall not abate provided, within such reasonable time as the court orders, the trustee elects to continue the action "and to give security for the costs thereof". Generally, a plaintiff, whether bringing proceedings as a trustee or not, and whether bankrupt or not, cannot be required to give security for costs (CPR, r.25.13). Section 49 creates an exception in county court proceedings. It would seem that where proceedings are transferred from the High Court to a county court and, before the transfer takes effect, by order made in the High Court under CPR, r.19.2 a trustee becomes plaintiff, the county court has no jurisdiction under this section to require the trustee to give security for costs (*Hemming v. Davies* [1898] 1 Q.B. 660).

INTERIM PAYMENTS IN PENDING PROCEEDINGS

Orders for interim payment

9A–573   **50.**—(1) Provision may be made by rules of court for enabling the court, in such circumstances as may be prescribed, to make an order requiring a party to the proceedings to make an interim payment of such amount as may be specified in the order, with provision for the payment to be made to such other party to the proceedings as may be so specified or, if the order so provides, by paying it into court.

(2) Any rules of court which make provision in accordance with subsection (1) may include provision for enabling a party to any proceedings who, in pursuance of such an order, has made an interim payment to recover the whole or part of the amount of the payment in such circumstances, and from such other party to the proceedings, as may be determined in accordance with the rules.

(3) Any rules made by virtue of this section may include such incidental, supplementary and consequential provisions as the rule committee may consider necessary or expedient.

(4) Nothing in this section shall be construed as affecting the exercise of any power relating to costs, including any power to make rules of court relating to costs.

(5) In this section "interim payment", in relation to a party to any proceedings, means a payment on account of any damages, debt or other sum (excluding any costs) which that party may be held liable to pay to or for the benefit of another party to the proceedings if a final judgment or order of the court in the proceedings is given or made in favour of that other party; and any reference to a party to any proceedings includes a reference to any person who for the purposes of the proceedings acts as next friend or guardian of a party to the proceedings.

Note—Amended by the Civil Procedure Act 1997, Sched.2, para. 2(2). **9A–574**

Orders for interim payment

The jurisdictions of the High Court and the county courts to order interim payments may be traced to the Administration of Justice Act 1969, s.20. The Supreme Court Act 1981, s.32 is in similar terms to s.50. **9A–575**

For rules of court, see CPR, rr.25.6 *et seq.*

PROVISIONAL DAMAGES FOR PERSONAL INJURIES

Orders for provisional damages for personal injuries

51.—(1) This section applies to an action for damages for personal injuries in which there is proved or admitted to be a chance that at some definite or indefinite time in the future the injured person will, as a result of the act or omission which gave rise to the cause of action, develop some serious disease or suffer some serious deterioration in his physical or mental condition. **9A–576**

(2) Subject to subsection (4), as regards any action for damages to which this section applies in which a judgment is given in the county court, provision may be made by rules of court for enabling the court, in such circumstances as may be prescribed, to award the injured person—

(a) damages assessed on the assumption that the injured person will not develop the disease or suffer the deterioration in his condition; and

    (b) further damages at a future date if he develops the disease or suffers the deterioration.

(3) Any rules made by virtue of this section may include such incidental, supplementary and consequential provisions as the rule committee may consider necessary or expedient.

    (4) Nothing in this section shall be construed—

        (a) as affecting the exercise of any power relating to costs, including any power to make rules of court relating to costs; or

        (b) as prejudicing any duty of the court under any enactment or rule of law to reduce or limit the total damages which would have been recoverable apart from any such duty.

    (5) In this section "personal injuries" includes any disease and any impairment of a person's physical or mental condition.

9A–577   *Note* —Amended by the Civil Procedure Act 1997, Sched.2, para. 2(2). See also Supreme Court Act 1981, s.32A (para. 9A–90 above).

Orders for provisional damages for personal injuries

9A–578   The jurisdictions of the High Court and the county courts to order provisional damages may be traced to the Administration of Justice Act 1968. The Supreme Court Act 1981, s.32A (para. 9A–90) is in similar terms to s.51.

For rules of court, see CPR Pt 41.

As to appeal against a "certificate of total benefit" given by the Secretary of State in accordance with the Social Security Administration Act 1992, Pt IV, where an award of provisional damages has been made under s.51(2)(a) (or under the Supreme Court Act 1981, s.32A(2)), see s.98(3) of the 1992 Act. See also the Damages Act 1996, s.3; the Social Security (Recovery of Benefits) Act 1997; and *Willson v. Ministry of Defence* [1991] 1 All E.R. 638; [1991] I.C.R. 595; and *Curi v. Colina, The Times*, October 14, 1998, CA.

DISCOVERY AND RELATED PROCEDURES

Powers of court exercisable before commencement of action

9A–579   **52.**—(1) On the application of any person in accordance with rules of court, a county court shall, in such circumstances as may be prescribed, have power to make an order providing for any one or more of the following matters, that is to say—

        (a) the inspection, photographing, preservation, custody and detention of property which appears to the court to be property which may become the subject-matter of subsequent proceedings in the court, or as to which any question may arise in any such proceedings; and

        (b) the taking of samples of any such property as is mentioned in paragraph (a) and the carrying out of any experiment on or with any such property.

    (2) On the application, in accordance with rules of court, of a person who appears to a county court to be likely to be a party to subsequent proceedings in that court, the county court shall in such circumstances as may be prescribed, have power to order a person who appears to the court to be likely to be a party to the proceedings

and to be likely to have or to have had in his possession, custody or power any documents which are relevant to an issue arising or likely to arise out of that claim—

    (a) to disclose whether those documents are in his possession, custody or power; and

    (b) to produce such of those documents as are in his possession, custody or power to the applicant or, on such conditions as may be specified in the order—

        (i) to the applicant's legal advisers; or

        (ii) to the applicant's legal advisers and any medical or other professional adviser of the applicant; or

        (iii) if the applicant has no legal adviser, to any medical or other professional adviser of the applicant.

(3) This section is subject to any provision made under section 38.

Note — Subsection (3) added by the Courts and Legal Services Act 1990, s.125(3), Sched.18, para. 43. Amended by the Civil Procedure (Modification of Enactments) Order 1998 (S.I. 1998 No. 2940), art.6(b) and by the Civil Procedure Act 1997, Sched.2, para. 2(2).

9A–580

Powers of court exercisable before commencement of action

By order made under the Civil Procedure Act 1997, s.8, the Lord Chancellor may amend subs.(2) of this section for the purposes mentioned there (see para. 9A–846). By the Civil Procedure (Modification of Enactments) Order 1998 (S.I. 1998 No. 2940) para. 6(b), subs.(2) was amended with the effect that the court's power to make an order under this section is no longer restricted to proceedings in which a claim in respect of personal injuries to a person, or in respect of a person's death, is likely to be made. It may be noted that the 1998 Order was made, not under s.8 of the 1997 Act, but under s.4(2) of that Act.

The comparable provision to s.52(2) in the Supreme Court Act 1981 is s.33(3), which was also amended by the 1998 Order (see para. 9A–93).

9A–581

subs.(1) —The powers of the High Court and the county courts to order inspection, etc., and taking of samples, etc., before commencement of action may be traced to the Administration of Justice Act 1969, s.21. The Supreme Court Act 1981, s.33(1) (para. 9A–93) is in similar terms to s.52(1).

subs.(2) —The powers of the High Court and the county courts to order disclosure and inspection of documents before commencement of action may be traced to the Administration of Justice Act 1970, s.31. The Supreme Court Act 1981, s.33(2) (para. 9A–93) is in similar, terms to s.52(2).

9A–582

subs.(3) —Generally, s.52 gives the county court the same powers as those enjoyed by the High Court in relation to the matters dealt with in subss. (1) and (2). Section 38 states that, subject to that section and regulations made under it, in any in a county court the court may make any order which could be made in the High Court if the proceedings were in the High Court. Any restrictions so imposed apply to the powers granted by this section.

9A–583

Rules of court

The orders that a court may make under s.52 are listed among the interim remedies referred to in CPR, r.25.1; see further Vol. 1, paras 25.1.26 and 25.1.27.

9A–584

Power of court to order disclosure of documents, inspection of property, etc., in proceedings for personal injuries or death

53.—(1) [*Omitted*]

9A–585

(2) On the application, in accordance with county court rules, of a party to any proceedings, a county court shall, in such circumstances as may be prescribed, have power to order a person who is not a party to the proceedings and who appears to the court to be likely to have in his possession, custody or power any documents which are relevant to an issue arising out of the said claim—

> (a) to disclose whether those documents are in his possession, custody or power; and
>
> (b) to produce such of those documents as are in his possession, custody or power to the applicant or, on such conditions as may be specified in the order—
>
>> (i) to the applicant's legal advisers; or
>>
>> (ii) to the applicant's legal advisers and any medical or other professional adviser of the applicant; or
>>
>> (iii) if the applicant has no legal adviser, to any medical or other professional adviser of the applicant.

(3) On the application, in accordance with county court rules, of a party to any proceedings, a county court shall, in such instances as may be prescribed, have power to make an order providing for any one or more of the following matters, that is to say—

> (a) the inspection, photographing, preservation, custody and detention of property which is not the property of, or in the possession of, any party to the proceedings but which is the subject-matter of the proceedings or as to which any question arises in the proceedings;
>
> (b) the taking of samples of any such property as is mentioned in paragraph (a) and the carrying out of any experiment on or with any such property.

(4) The preceding provisions of this section are without prejudice to the exercise by a county court of any power to make orders which is exercisable apart from those provisions.

(5) This section is subject to any provision made under section 38.

9A–586 *Note* — Subsection (5) added by the Courts and Legal Services Act 1990, s.125(3), Sched.18, para. 44. Subsection (1) and subss. (2) and (3) amended by the Civil Procedure (Modification of Enactments) Order 1998 (S.I. 1998 No. 2940), art.6(b).

Power of court to order disclosure of documents, inspection of property, etc., in proceedings for personal injuries or death

9A–587 The powers of the High Court and the county courts to order, what could be called, "third party discovery" may be traced to the Administration of Justice Act 1970, s.32.

This section was amended by the Civil Procedure (Modification of Enactments) Order 1998 (S.I. 1998 No. 2940) para. 6(c), made under the Civil Procedure Act 1997, s.4(2), with the effect that the court's power to make an order under this section is no longer restricted to proceedings in which a claim in respect of personal injuries to a person, or in respect of a person's death, is likely to be made. In terms, the 1998 Order did not amend the title to s.53 which reads "Power of court to order disclosure of documents, inspection of property, etc., *in proceedings for personal injuries or death*". Obviously, the words in italics are no longer apposite.

The comparable provision to s.53 in the Supreme Court Act 1981 is s.34, which was also amended by the 1998 Order (see para. 9A–98).

This section is subject to s.38 (see commentary to s.52(3), above).

Rules of Court

The orders that a court may make under section 53 are listed among the interim **9A–588** remedies referred to in CPR, r.25.1; see further Vol. 1, paras 25.1.28 and 25.1.29. Note also CPR, rr.25.5, 31.17 and 48.1.

Provisions supplementary to sections 52 and 53

54.—(1) A county court shall not make an order under section 52 **9A–589** or 53 if it considers that compliance with the order, if made, would be likely to be injurious to the public interest.

(2) Rules of court may make provision as to the circumstances in which an order under section 52 or 53 can be made; and any rules making such provision may include such incidental, supplementary and consequential provisions as the Civil Procedure Rule Committee may consider necessary or expedient.

(3) Without prejudice to the generality of subsection (2), rules of court shall be made for the purpose of ensuring that the costs of and incidental to proceedings for an order under section 52(2) or 53 incurred by the person against whom the order is sought shall be awarded to that person unless the court otherwise directs.

(4) Sections 52(2) and 53 and this section bind the Crown; and section 52(1) binds the Crown so far as it relates to property as to which it appears to the court that it may become the subject-matter of subsequent proceedings involving a claim in respect of personal injuries to a person or in respect of a person's death.

In this subsection references to the Crown do not include references to Her Majesty in Her private capacity or to Her Majesty in right of Her Duchy of Lancaster or to the Duke of Cornwall.

(5) In sections 52 and 53 and this section—

"property" includes any land, chattel or other corporeal property of any description;

"personal injuries" includes any disease and any impairment of a person's physical or mental condition.

(6) This section is subject to any provision made under section 38.

Note — Subsection (6) added by the Courts and Legal Services Act 1990, s.125(3), **9A–590** Sched.18, para. 45. Amended by the Civil Procedure Act 1997, Sched.2, para. 2(2).

Provisions supplementary to sections 52 and 53

This section is in similar terms to the Supreme Court Act 1981, s.35 (para. 9A–100). **9A–591** This section is subject to s.38 (see commentary to s.52(3), above).

WITNESSES AND EVIDENCE

Penalty for neglecting or refusing to give evidence

55.—(1) Subject to subsections (2) and (3), any person who— **9A–592**

    (a) having been summoned in pursuance of rules of court as a witness in a county court refuses or neglects, without sufficient cause, to appear or to produce any documents required by the summons to be produced; or

    (b) having been so summoned or being present in court and

being required to give evidence, refuses to be sworn or give evidence,

shall forfeit such fine as the judge may direct.

(2) A judge shall not have power under subsection (1) to direct that a person shall forfeit a fine of an amount exceeding £1000.

(3) No person summoned in pursuance of rules of court as a witness in a county court shall forfeit a fine under this section unless there has been paid or tendered to him at the time of the service of the summons such sum in respect of his expenses (including, in such cases as may be prescribed, compensation for loss of time) as may be prescribed for the purposes of this section.

(4) The judge may at his discretion direct that the whole or any part of any such fine, after deducting the costs, shall be applicable towards indemnifying the party injured by the refusal or neglect.

(4A) A district judge, assistant district judge or deputy district judge shall have the same powers under this section as a judge.

(5) This section does not apply to a debtor summoned to attend by a judgment summons.

9A–593 *Note*—Amended by the Courts and Legal Services Act 1990, s.74; and the Criminal Justice Act 1991, s.17(3), Sched.4. Amended by the Civil Procedure Act 1997, Sched.2, para. 2(2).

Penalty for neglecting or refusing to give evidence

9A–594 For procedure for summoning witnesses, see CPR Pt 34. Notice to show cause why a fine should not be imposed (or should not have been imposed) under this section may be served on the witness (CPR Sched.2; CCR O.34, r.2). The limit of £1,000 in subs.(2) was set by the Criminal Justice Act 1991, s.17(3)(a), Sched.4, Pt I, and this figure may be altered by order made under the Magistrates' Courts Act 1980, s.143(1).

Examination of witnesses abroad

9A–595 **56.** The High Court shall have the same power to issue a commission, request or order to examine witnesses abroad for the purpose of proceedings in a county court as it has for the purpose of an action or matter in the High Court.

Examination of witnesses abroad

9A–596 For powers of High Court, see CPR, r.34.13. The power conferred on the High Court by this section is exercised by the Senior Master of the Queen's Bench Division (Practice Direction Depositions and Attendance by Witnesses), para. 5.5 (see Vol. 1, para. 34PD.6).

Evidence of prisoners

9A–597 **57.**—(1) Subject to subsection (2), in any proceedings pending before a county court, the judge may, if he thinks fit, upon application on affidavit by any party, issue an order under his hand for bringing up before the court any person (in this section referred to as a "prisoner") confined in any place under any sentence or following the transfer of proceedings against him for trial or otherwise, to be examined as a witness in the proceedings.

(2) No such order shall be made with respect to a person confined under process in any civil action or matter.

(3) Subject to subsection (4), the prisoner mentioned in any such

order shall be brought before the court under the same custody, and shall be dealt with in the same manner in all respects, as a prisoner required by a writ of habeas corpus to be brought before the High Court and examined there as a witness.

(4) The person having the custody of the prisoner shall not be bound to obey the order unless there is tendered to him a reasonable sum for the conveyance and maintenance of a proper officer or officers and of the prisoner in going to, remaining at, and returning from, the court.

Note —Amended by the Criminal Justice and Public Order Act 1994, s.44, Sched.4. **9A–598**

Evidence of prisoners
For procedure for application for habeas corpus to bring up a prisoner to give evidence in the High Court, see CPR Sched.1; RSC O.54, r.9. Provisions in the Criminal Justice and Public Order Act 1994 amending this section (see s.44(3) Sched.4, Pt II, para. 57) were never brought into force and those provisions were omitted from the 1994 Act by the Criminal Procedure and Investigations Act 1996, s.44. **9A–599**

Persons who may take affidavits for use in county courts

58.—(1) An affidavit to be used in a county court may be sworn before— **9A–600**

    (a) the judge or registrar of any court; or
    (b) any justice of the peace; or
    (c) an officer of any court appointed by the judge of that court for the purpose,

as well as before a commissioner for oaths or any other person authorised to take affidavits under the Commissioners for Oaths Acts 1889 and 1891 or a solicitor exercising the powers of a commissioner for oaths under section 81 of the Solicitors Act 1974.

(2) An affidavit sworn before a judge or registrar or before any such officer may be sworn without the payment of any fee.

Note —Amended by the Administration of Justice Act 1985, s.67, Scheds 7 and 8. **9A–601**

Persons who may take affidavits for use in county courts
The Family Proceedings Rules 1991, r.10.13 provides that in relation to family proceedings pending or treated as pending in a divorce county court an affidavit may be sworn before certain other persons in addition to those listed in s.58(1). **9A–602**

Evidence in Admiralty proceedings

59.—(1) In any Admiralty proceedings, evidence taken before a registrar of an Admiralty county court, in accordance with the directions of a judge or pursuant to rules of court, may be received as evidence in any other Admiralty county court. **9A–603**

(2) The registrar of any Admiralty county court shall, for the purpose of the examination of any witness within the district assigned to that court for Admiralty purposes, have all the power of an examiner of the High Court, and evidence taken by him in that capacity may be received as evidence in the High Court.

Note —Amended by the Civil Procedure Act 1997, Sched.2, para. 2(2). **9A–604**

Evidence in Admiralty proceedings
CPR, r.34.8 states that in High Court and county court proceedings a party may **9A–605**

LEGISLATION

apply for an order for a person to be examined before the hearing (which, in this context, includes a trial) takes place. The powers of the examiner (whether appointed by the High Court or a county court) are as stated in rr.34.8 *et seq.* (see also Practice Direction (Depositions and Court Attendance by Witnesses), supplementing Pt 34, Vol. 1, para. 34PD.1). The provisions of the CPR and supplementing Practice Directions apply to Admiralty proceedings, subject to the provisions of Practice Direction (Admiralty), para. 15 (see para. 2D–1 above). Para. 15 of that Practice Direction contains special provisions for the appointment of examiners in Admiralty proceedings (see para. 2D–126 above).

RIGHT OF AUDIENCE

Right of audience

9A–606   60.—(1) [...]

(2) Where an action is brought in a county court by a local authority for either or both of the following—

    (a) the recovery of possession of a house belonging to the authority;

    (b) the recovery of any rent, mesne profits, damages or other sum claimed by the authority in respect of the occupation by any person of such a house,

then, in so far as the proceedings in the action are heard by the registrar, any officer of the authority authorised by the authority in that behalf, not being a person entitled to address the court by virtue of subsection (1), may address the registrar as if he were a person so entitled.

(3) In this section—

    "local authority" means a county council, a district council, the Broads Authority, any National Park Authority, a London borough council, a Police authority established under section 3 of the Police Act 1996, the Metropolitan Police Authority, a joint authority established by Part IV of the Local Government Act 1985 the London Fire and Emergency Planning Authority, or the Common Council of the City of London; and

    "house" includes a part of a house, a flat or any other dwelling and also includes any yard, garden, outhouse or appurtenance occupied with a house or part of a house or with a flat or other dwelling

    and any reference to the occupation of a house by a person includes a reference to anything done by that person, or caused or permitted by him to be done, in relation to the house as occupier of the house, whether under a tenancy or licence or otherwise.

9A–607   *Note*—Amended by the Local Government Act 1985, ss.82 and 102, Scheds 14 and 17; the Norfolk and Suffolk Broads Act 1988, s.21, Sched.6; the Education Reform Act 1988, s.237, Sched.13; the Courts and Legal Services Act 1990, s.125(7), Sched.20; the Police and Magistrates' Courts Act 1994, s.43, Sched.4; the Environment Act 1995, s.78, Sched.10, the Police Act 1996, s.103 and Sched.7, Pt I, para. 1, the Police Act 1997, s.134 and Sched.9, para. 45. The definition of "local authority" in subs.(3) was amended by the Criminal Justice and Police Act 2001 (c.16), s.128 and Sched.6, para. 66, and s.137 and Sched.7, Pt 5. The references in this section to "registrar" should be construed as references to "district judge": Courts and Legal Services Act 1990, s.74.

Right of audience
   See commentary to s.61, below.   **9A–608**

Right of audience by direction of Lord Chancellor

61.—(1) The Lord Chancellor may at any time direct that such cat- **9A–609** egories of persons in relevant legal employment as may be specified in the direction may address the court in any proceedings in a county court, or in proceedings in a county court of such description as may be so specified.

   (2) In subsection (1), "relevant legal employment" means employment which consists of or includes giving assistance in the conduct of litigation to a legal representative whether in private practice or not.

   (3) A direction under this section may be given subject to such conditions and restrictions as appear to the Lord Chancellor to be necessary or expedient, and may be expressed to have effect as respects every county court or as respects a specified county court or as respects one or more specified places where a county court sits.

   (4) The power to give directions conferred by this section includes a power to vary or rescind any direciton given under this section.

Note —Amended by the Courts and Legal Services Act 1990, s.125(3), Sched.18, **9A–610** para. 49.

Right of audience by direction of Lord Chancellor
   The question whether a person has a right of audience before a county court, or **9A–611** any other court, is determined in accordance with the provisions of the Access to Justice Act 1999, Pt III and the Courts and Legal Services Act 1990, Pt II as amended by the 1999 Act. Section 27 of the 1990 Act (as amended) contains a statutory framework for defining and regulating rights of audience before any court. The 1990 Act preserved all existing rights of audience and, therefore, did not restrict the rights given in relation to county court proceedings by ss.60 and 61. Formerly, rights of audience for barristers and solicitors in any proceedings in a county court were granted by subs.(1) of s.60. This subsection was repealed by the 1990 Act but such rights are now granted under the statutory scheme. Nowadays, s.60 is restricted to proceedings before district judges in proceedings brought by local (and some other) authorities for the recovery of possession or recovery of rent, etc., in accordance with subs.(2). Section 61, originally introduced in 1977, survived the 1990 legal services reforms. The County Courts (Right of Audience) Direction 1978 was made under this section. It gives limited rights of audience to Fellows of the Institute of Legal Executives engaged in particular forms of legal work.

   In a county court, and also in the High Court, a corporation may be represented at a trial by an employee as provided by CPR, r.36.2.

   Section 11 of the 1990 Act gives the Lord Chancellor power to grant rights of audience in certain county court proceedings to lay representatives. (For an explanation of the purpose of this section, see Sweet & Maxwell *Statutes Annotated 1990*, p.41–19.) The Lay Representatives (Rights of Audience) Order 1999, made in exercise of this power, enables lay persons to exercise rights of audience in proceedings dealt with as a small claim in accordance with rules of court. See further para. 9B–598 below.

   Under s.27(2)(c) of the 1990 Act, in exceptional circumstances, the court may grant a lay person a right of audience for particular proceedings; see *e.g. Clarkson v. Gilbert (Rights of Audience)*, [2000] C.P. Rep. 58, CA (husband representing claimant wife who was sick and impecunious) *Paragon Finance Plc v. Noueiri (Practice Note)* [2001] EWCA Civ 1402; [2001] 1 W.L.R. 2357, CA (permission for lay person to address court as claimant's representative withdrawn); *Official Receiver v. Broad* [2003] EWCA Civ 404, CA, March 7, 2003, unrep. (Jonathan Parker L.J.) (forensic accountant representing applicant for permission to appeal); *cf. Milne v. Kennedy, The Times*, February 11, 1999, CA; *Zappia Middle East Construction Co Ltd v. Clifford Chance* [2001] EWCA Civ 1383, August 30, 2001, CA, unrep. (Court refusing party permission to enable his solicitor to act as advocate on application). Under s.27(2)(d) a person employed by or engaged to assist a qualified litigator may have a right of audience in certain chamber proceedings. Where a person satisfies the s.27(2)(e) criteria the court retains no discretion to refuse right of audience (*HS (Minors) (Chambers Proceedings: Right of Audience), Re*, [1998] 1 F.L.R. 868, CA). In *Zappia Middle East Construction Co Ltd v. Clifford Chance* [2001] EWCA Civ 1383; August 30, 2001, CA, on the ground that no good reason had been shown, the Court of Appeal refused an applicant's request for permission to enable his solicitor to act as advocate on an application to the Court for an extension of time for complying with an order for security for costs. See further, para. 9B–456.

Section 27(2)(d) of the 1990 Act confers a right of audience on "a party" to the proceedings if he would have that right "in his capacity as such a party" if the Act had not been passed. This provision preserves the position before the 1990 Act which allowed an individual to appear in his own case in any court, regardless of his qualifications. A "party" in this context does not include a party's agent (*Gregory v. Turner* [2003] EWCA Civ 183,CA (a party may not by power of attorney confer on another the right to appear in court as his lay advocate)).

In any proceedings in a county court any party to the proceedings may address the court. The court may permit any person to attend an unrepresented party before the court as a friend and to assist him by taking notes, by quietly making suggestions and giving advice (*McKenzie v. McKenzie* [1971] P. 33, CA; *R. v. Bow County Court, ex p. Pelling* [1999] 1 W.L.R. 1807, CA. As is explained in para. 15.11 of the Chancery Guide (para. 1-122 above), a litigant in person may be allowed to have the assistance of such a person (a "McKenzie friend") in the higher courts. Art. 6 of the Convention is engaged in any request for such assistance (*In re O. (Children) (Hearing in Private: Assistance)* [2005] EWCA Civ 759; [2005] 3 W.L.R. 1191, CA). In family proceedings, there is a strong presumption in favour of allowing assistance (*ibid.*). A court can permit the assistant to address the court on behalf of the litigant by making an order to that effect under s. 27(2)(c) of the 1990 Act.

For provisions permitting a company to be represented at trial by an employee, see CPR, r.39.6, and Practice Direction (Miscellaneous Provisions Relating to Hearings), para. 5.1 *et seq* (Vol. 1, paras 39.6.1 and 39PD.5).

For rights of audience of official receivers in proceedings under the Company Directors Disqualification Act 1986, see Practice Direction (Directors Disqualification Proceedings) para. 3.1 (see Vol. 1, para. B1–003).

MODE OF TRIAL

General power of judge to determine questions of law and fact

9A–612   **62.** Subject to the provisions of this Act and of county court rules, the judge of a county court shall be the sole judge in all proceedings brought in the court, and shall determine all questions of fact as well as of law.

Judge to determine all questions of law and fact

9A–613   Other "provisions of the Act" includes the sections immediately following. Where the rules found in the CPR provide for a county court to "perform any act", that act may be performed, not only by any judge, but also by any district judge. In terms, r.3.4 is subject to any enactment, rule or practice direction that provides otherwise. What is meant in this context by "perform any act" provided for by the CPR is not free from doubt. Practice Direction (Allocation of Cases to Levels of Judiciary) sets out the matters over which district judges do not have jurisdiction or which they may deal with only on certain conditions (see Vol. 1, 2BPD.1). Circuit judges and district judges have concurrent jurisdiction to hear trials of cases allocated to the fast track. For the jurisdiction of district judges to deal with trials and assessments of damages in multi-track cases, see Practice Direction (Allocation of Cases to Levels of Judiciary), para. 4.1.

Assessors

9A–614   **63.**—(1) In any proceedings the judge may, if he thinks fit, summon to his assistance, in such manner as may be prescribed, one or more persons of skill and experience in the matter to which the proceedings relate who may be willing to sit with the judge and act as assessors.

(2) *[Omitted]*

(3) Subject to subsection (4), the remuneration of assessors for sitting under this section shall be determined by the judge and shall be costs in the proceedings unless otherwise ordered by the judge.

(4) Where one or more assessors are summoned for the purposes of assisting the judge in reviewing the taxation by the district judge of the costs of any proceedings the remuneration of any such assessor—

    (a) shall be at such rate as may be determined by the Lord Chancellor with the approval of the Treasury; and

    (b) shall be payable out of moneys provided by Parliament.

(5) Where any person is proposed to be summoned as an assessor, objection to him, either personally or in respect of his qualification, may be taken by any party in the prescribed manner.

9A–615

Note — Subsections (1), (3) and (4) were amended by, and subs.(2) omitted by, the Civil Procedure (Modification of Enactments) Order 1998 (S.I. 1998 No. 2940), art.6(d). Amendments previously made to s.63 by the Courts and Legal Services Act 1990, s.14 were never brought into force.

Assessors summoned to assist judge

9A–616

The comparable provision in the Supreme Court Act 1981 is s.70 (see para. 9A–328). For rules of court relevant to the use of assessors generally see CPR, r.35.15 (this rule does not apply to proceedings allocated to the small claims track, see r.27.2(1)(e)); see also Practice Direction (Experts and Assessors), para. 6 (see Vol. 1, para. 35PD.6). For provisions as to the use of assessors in certain landlord and tenant proceedings, see Landlord and Tenant Act 1954, s.63, and CPR Sched.2, CCR O.43, r.13 (see Vol. 1, para. cc43.13).

In *Ahmed v. University of Oxford* [2002] EWCA Civ 1907; [2003] 1 W.L.R. 995; [2003] 1 All E.R. 915, CA, unrep., the Court of Appeal examined the role of assessors appointed in various contexts, including under s.63 of this Act and the Supreme Court Act 1981, s.70 (see para. 9A–330 above), but particularly under the Race Relations Act 1976, s.67(4). See further CPR, r.35.15, and commentary following that rule.

Reference to arbitration

9A–617

64.—(1) Rules of court—

    (a) may prescribe cases in which proceedings are (without any order of the court) to be referred to arbitration, and

    (b) may prescribe the manner in which and the terms on which cases are to be so referred, and

    (c) may, where cases are so referred, require other matters within the jurisdiction of the court in dispute between the parties also to be referred to arbitration.

(2) Rules of court—

    (a) may prescribe cases in which proceedings may be referred to arbitration by order of the court, and

    (b) may authorise the court also to order other matters in dispute between the parties and within the jurisdiction of the court to be so referred.

(2A) Rules of court may prescribe the procedures and rules of evidence to be followed on any reference under subsection (1) or (2).

(2B) Rules made under subsection (2A) may, in particular, make provision with respect to the manner of taking and questioning evidence.

(3) On a reference under subsection (1) or (2) the award of the arbitrator, arbitrators or umpire shall be entered as the judgment in the proceedings and shall be as binding and effectual to all intents, subject to subsection (4), as if it had been given by the judge.

(4) The judge may, if he thinks fit, on application made to him within such time as may be prescribed, set aside the award, or may, with the consent of the parties, revoke the reference or order another reference to be made in the manner specified in this section.

(5) In this section "award" includes an interim award.

9A–618   *Note* — Subsections (2A) and (2B) added by the Courts and Legal Services Act 1990, s.6. Amended by the Civil Procedure Act 1997, Sched.2, para. 2(2).

Rules of court prescribing reference to arbitration

9A–619   Before the CPR came into force, rules of court found in CCR O.19, Pt I and made under s.64 provided for two forms of reference to arbitration by the court. They were (1) reference on application by a party to proceedings, and (2) automatic reference by rule of proceedings falling within the "small claims" jurisdiction of the court. Under the CPR, the second form of reference has been replaced by the procedure for the allocation to the small claims track of minor claims. The relevant rules of court are found in CPR Pts 26 and 27. In these provisions, no use is made of the word "arbitration" for the purpose of describing the summary procedures used by the court for the handling and trial of small claims. It would seem that it would not be appropriate to describe the allocation of a claim to the small claims track as a reference to a form of statutory arbitration. Consequently, the significance of the Arbitration Act 1996, s.92, which states that nothing in Pt I of that Act applies to arbitrations under s.64 is diminished.

There are no express provisions in the CPR comparable to those formerly found in CCR O.19, Pt I for the first form of reference of county court proceedings to arbitration mentioned above, that is to say, a reference on the application of a party. However, r.1.4(2)(e) states that the court's duty to manage cases includes encouraging the parties "to use an alternative dispute resolution procedure if the court considers that appropriate and facilitating the use of such procedure". (In the Glossary attached to the CPR, "alternative dispute resolution" is described in terms sufficiently wide to include arbitration.) Further, r.26.4 states that, in certain circumstances, the court may stay proceedings whilst parties try to settle the case "by alternative dispute resolution or other means". It would seem, therefore, that the court has power under the CPR to refer proceedings to arbitration on the application of a party. However, it is doubtful whether the rules from which such power may be derived are rules of court of the express type envisaged by s.64. Further, it is doubtful whether a reference to arbitration on the application of a party (if it is permissible) could be described as a reference under s.64 (see above observations on the Arbitration Act 1996, s.92).

Power of judge to refer to district judge or referee

9A–620   **65.**—(1) Subject to rules of court, the judge may refer to the registrar or a referee for inquiry and report—

> (a) any proceedings which require any prolonged examination of documents or any scientific or local investigation which cannot, in the opinion of the judge, conveniently be made before him;
>
> (b) any proceedings where the question in dispute consists wholly or in part of matters of account;

(c) with the consent of the parties, any other proceedings;

(d) subject to any right to have particular cases tried with a jury, any question arising in any proceedings.

(2) In such cases as may be prescribed by, and subject to, rules of court the registrar may refer to a referee for inquiry and report any question arising in any proceedings.

(3) Where any proceedings or question are referred under subsection (1) or (2), the judge or, as the case may be, the registrar may direct how the reference shall be conducted, and may remit any report for further inquiry and report, and on consideration of any report or further report may give such judgment or make such order in the proceedings as may be just.

(4) The judge may, after deciding or reserving any question of liability, refer to the registrar any mere matter of account which is in dispute between the parties and, after deciding the question of liability, may give judgment on the registrar's report.

Note —Amended by Civil Procedure Act 1997, Sched.2, para. 2(2). The Courts and Legal Services Act 1990, s.74 states that any reference in any enactment to the offices of registrar, etc., shall be construed as a reference to the office of district judge. **9A–621**

Reference for inquiry and report
This section is comparable to the Supreme Court Act 1981, s.68, the provision upon which what was once called "official referees' business" was based. Before the CPR came into force, rules of court made in pursuance of s.65 were found in CCR O.19, Pt II (reference for inquiry and report). Initially, no comparable rules were found in the CPR, but official referees' business, now known as "Technology and Construction Court Business" was treated as a form of "specialist proceedings" under CPR, Pt 49. This ceased to be the case when, subsequently, provisions dealing with such Business (whether arising in the High Court or in a county court) were inserted in the CPR as Pt 60 (Proceedings in the Technology and Construction Court) (see para. 2C–1 above). **9A–622**

JURIES

Trial by jury
66.—(1) In the following proceedings in a county court the trial shall be without a jury— **9A–623**

(a) Admiralty proceedings;

(b) proceedings arising—

    (i) under Part I of the Rent (Agriculture) Act 1976, or

    (ii) under any provision of the Rent Act 1977 other than a provision contained in Part V, sections 103 to 106 or Part IX, or

    (iii) under Part I of the Protection from Eviction Act 1977; or

    (iv) under Part I of the Housing Act 1988.

(c) any appeal to the county court under the Housing Act 1985;

(2) In all other proceedings in a county court the trial shall be without a jury unless the court otherwise orders on an application

made in that behalf by any party to the proceedings in such manner and within such time before the trial as may be prescribed.

(3) Where, on any such application, the court is satisfied that there is in issue—

(a) a charge of fraud against the party making the application; or

(b) a claim in respect of libel, slander, malicious prosecution or false imprisonment; or

(c) any question or issue of a kind prescribed for the purposes of this paragraph,

the action shall be tried with a jury, unless the court is of the opinion that the trial requires any prolonged examination of documents or accounts of any scientific or local investigation which cannot conveniently be made with a jury.

(4) There shall be payable, in respect of the trial with a jury of proceedings in a county court, such fees as may be prescribed by an order under section 92 of the Courts Act 2003 (fees).

9A–624 *Note* —Amended by the Housing (Consequential Provisions) Act 1985, Sched.2, para. 57; and the Housing Act 1988, Sched.17, para. 35; subs. (4) amended by the Courts Act 2003, s.109(1), Sch.8, para. 271(a).

Trial by jury

9A–625 The general rule is that the judge shall determine all questions of fact as well as of law (s.62). The circumstances in which proceedings may be tried with a jury are stated in this section. (The section may be contrasted with the Supreme Court Act 1981, s.69). As to impanelling of jury, see s.67.

The structure of this section may be stated as follows. (1) The proceedings listed in subs.(1) may not be tried with a jury. (2) All other proceedings shall be without a jury unless the court, in the exercise of discretion, otherwise orders on application (subs.(2)). However, (3) on such application the court shall order jury trial if it is satisfied that an issue of the type listed in subs.(3) exists, unless (4) such trial would be inconvenient for any of the reasons stated in that subsection.

The discretion to grant jury trial is rarely exercised; the circumstances must be wholly exceptional (*H. v. Ministry of Defence* [1991] 2 W.L.R. 1192, CA).

Where a "charge of fraud" is an issue in the proceedings the party against whom it is made (but no other party) has a right to jury trial (subject to any inconvenience). A mere allegation of fraud does not raise a "charge of fraud" as an issue; such an issue must involve an allegation of actionable deceit (*Grant v. Travellers Cheque Associates Ltd, The Times*, April 19, 1995, CA, applying *Barclays Bank Ltd v. Cole* [1967] 2 Q.B. 738, CA; see also *Parsons v. Provincial Insurance Plc*, February 20, 1988, (unrep.), CA).

Where a claim in respect of libel, slander, malicious prosecution or false imprisonment is an issue in the proceedings a right to jury trial arises (subject to any inconvenience). In these circumstances, any application for jury trial is likely to be made by the party making the claim. An action against police for damages for assault and battery does not raise an issue of a claim for false imprisonment although the facts pleaded might bear the inference that the plaintiff was briefly falsely imprisoned (*Hendry v. Chief Constable of Lancashire Constabulary*, December 7, 1993, CA, unrep.).

Where an issue of the type listed in subs.(3) exists, nevertheless, jury trial may be refused where the court is of opinion that the trial requires "prolonged examination of documents, etc." which cannot conveniently be made with a jury. For principles to be applied and relevant considerations in these circumstances, see *Aitken v. Preston, The Times*, May 21, 1997, CA, and *Taylor v. Anderton* [1995] 1 W.L.R. 447, CA. See further notes following Supreme Courts Act 1981, s.69 (para. 9A–325 above).

Application made in such manner and within such time "as may be prescribed"

9A–626 Section 66(2) states that the trial of certain proceedings shall be without jury and that in all other proceedings trial should be without a jury unless the court otherwise orders "on an application made in that behalf by any party to the proceedings in such manner and within such time before the trial *as may be prescribed*", which means, as prescribed by rules of court (see County Courts Act 1984, s.147(1)) (see also Supreme Court Act 1981, s.69(2)). CPR, r.26.11 states that an application for a claim to be tried by a jury must be made within 28 days of service of the defence. This rule was inserted in the CPR by the Civil Procedure (Amendment No. 4) Rules 2000 (S.I. 2000 No. 2092). In *Oliver v. Calderdale Metropolitan Borough Council, The Times,* July 7, 1999, CA, a case decided under the old rules, it was held that an application made wholly out of time could be rejected on the ground that it was unreasonable.

Impanelling and swearing of jury

67. At any county court where proceedings are to be tried with a jury, eight jurymen shall be impanelled and sworn as occasion requires to give their verdicts in the proceedings brought before them, and being once sworn need not be re-sworn in each trial.

9A–627

Impanelling and swearing of jury

By tradition, a jury consists of twelve persons, but the number may be reduced by statute. By virtue of this provision juries in county court proceedings consist of eight persons. Any party to county court proceedings to be tried by jury has the same right of challenge to all or some of the jurors as he would in the High Court (Juries Act 1974, s.12(2)). Challenge in the High Court is governed by the common law as modified statute (see *ibid.*, s.12). A jury's verdict need not be unanimous if seven agree on it. However, a court should only accept a majority verdict if it is satisfied that the jury had such period of time for deliberation as the court thinks reasonable having regard to the nature and complexity of the case (*ibid.*, s.17(2), (4)). As to majority verdict in High Court cases, see *ibid.*, s.17(1).

9A–628

Duty of judge to determine foreign law in jury trials

68. Where, for the purpose of disposing of any proceedings which are being tried in a county court by the judge with a jury, it is necessary to ascertain the law of any other country which is applicable to the facts of the case, any question as to the effect of the evidence given with respect to that law shall, instead of being submitted to the jury, be decided by the judge alone.

9A–629

Duty of judge to determine foreign law in jury trials

This section is in same terms of the Supreme Court Act 1981, s.69(5) (para. 9A–327). As to evidence of foreign law, see the Civil Evidence Act 1972, s.4 (para. 9B–263).

9A–630

INTEREST ON DEBTS AND DAMAGES

Power to award interest on debts and damages

69.—(1) Subject to rules of court, in proceedings (whenever instituted) before a county court for the recovery of a debt or damages there may be included in any sum for which judgment is given simple interest, at such rate as the court thinks fit or as may be prescribed, on all or any part of the debt or damages in respect of which judgment is given, or payment is made before judgment, for all or any part of the period between the date when the cause of action arose and—

9A–631

    (a) in the case of any sum paid before judgment, the date of the payment; and

    (b) in the case of the sum for which judgment is given, the date of the judgment.

(2) In relation to a judgment given for damages for personal injuries or death which exceed £200 subsection (1) shall have effect—

    (a) with the substitution of "shall be included" for "may be included"; and

    (b) with the addition of "unless the court is satisfied that there are special reasons to the contrary" after "given", where first occurring.

(3) Subject to rules of court, where—

    (a) there are proceedings (whenever instituted) before a county court for the recovery of a debt; and

    (b) the defendant pays the whole debt to the plaintiff (otherwise than in pursuance of a judgment in the proceedings),

the defendant shall be liable to pay the plaintiff simple interest, at such rate as the court thinks fit or as may be prescribed, on all or any part of the debt for all or any part of the period between the date when the cause of action arose and the date of the payment.

(4) Interest in respect of a debt shall not be awarded under this section for a period during which, for whatever reason, interest on the debt already runs.

(5) Interest under this section may be calculated at different rates in respect of different periods.

(6) In this section "plaintiff" means the person seeking the debt or damages and "defendant" means the person from whom the plaintiff seeks the debt or damages and "personal injuries" includes any disease and any impairment of a person's physical or mental condition.

(7) Nothing in this section affects the damages recoverable for the dishonour of a bill of exchange.

(8) In determining whether the amount of any debt or damages exceeds that prescribed by or under any enactment, no account shall be taken of any interest payable by virtue of this section except where express provision to the contrary is made by or under that or any other enactment.

9A–632   *Note* — Subsection (8) substituted by the Courts and Legal Services Act 1990, s.125(3), Sched.18, para. 46.

Power to award interest on debts and damages

9A–633   With the exception of subs.(8), this section is in similar terms to the Supreme Court Act 1981, s.35A (para. 9A–103 and commentary thereto). A claim for interest under this section should be included in the particulars of claim (CPR, r.16.4(2)). Judgment by default in a claim for a specified amount of money may include interest claimed under this section in the circumstances provided by CPR, r.12.6. For interest on judgment under CPR, r.14.4 (admission of whole of claim for specified amount of money) where interest claimed under s.69, see CPR, r.14.14. Subsection (8) was substituted by the Courts and Legal Services Act 1990, Sched.18, para. 46. Some of the provisions for the allocation of business for commencement and trial between the High Court and the county courts found in the High Court and County Court Jurisdiction Order 1991 and in Practice Direction (How to Start Proceedings—The Claim Form), paras 2.1 *et seq.* turn on the "value" of the action. Art.9 of the Order states that in determining the value of an action for these purposes claims for interest shall be disregarded (see para. 9B–147 below). In the exercise of its discretion, the court may reduce the rate at which interest on an award of damages is payable or reduce the period for which interest is payable. Since the coming into effect of the CPR, this power has been increasingly used by the courts as a sanction where parties fail to comply with procedural rules, practice directions and case management orders. The Court of Appeal has encouraged the use of this sanction as an alternative to more serious sanctions (*e.g.* striking out); see, *e.g. Biguzzi v. Rank Leisure Plc* [1999] 1 W.L.R. 1926, CA; *Baron v. Lovell*, *The Times*, September 14, 1999, CA; *Abbahall Ltd v. Smee* [2002] EWCA Civ 1831; January 24, 2000, CA, unrep.; *Walsh v. Misseldine*, February 29, 2000, CA, unrep., *UYB Ltd v. British Railways Board*, *The Times*, November 15, 2000, CA; *Adcock v. Cooperative Insurance Society Ltd* [2000] Lloyd's Rep. I.R. 657, CA; note also Practice Direction (Protocols), para. 2.3 (see Vol. 1, para. C1–002).

JUDGMENTS AND ORDERS

Finality of judgments and orders

70. Every judgment and order of a county court shall, except as **9A–634** provided by this or any other Act or as may be prescribed, be final and conclusive between the parties.

Finality of judgments and orders

Originally, this section formed the first part of the County Courts Act 1846, s.93. A **9A–635** later part of the old provision went on to state that the judge should have a discretionary power to order a new trial in every case. The relationship between the two parts created difficulties and was subject to a considerable amount of case law. Subsequently, the power to order a new trial was removed from primary legislation, put into rules of court and substantially altered. Until it was revoked by the Civil Procedure (Amendment No. 4) Rules 2002 (S.I. 2002 No. 2058) the relevant rule was CPR, Sched.2, RSC O.37, r.1. Consequently, since 1934 this section has stated the simple general proposition that, except as provided by legislation or as may be prescribed, "every judgment and order of a county court shall be final and conclusive between the parties". The general proposition is unimpeachable. When considering s.93 of the 1846 Act, Willes J. said: "The very object of instituting courts of justice is that litigation should be decided, and decided finally" (*Great Northern Railway Co. v. Mossop* (1855) 17 C.B. 130 at 1022).

The exceptions to the general proposition are important and inherently difficult; the power to order a rehearing is but one. Another example is the power to set aside a judgment given in a party's absence (CPR, r.39.3(3)). Obviously, the various provisions as to appeals from particular judgments and orders must also be regarded as exceptions.

Under some statutes it is expressly provided that the decision of a court shall be "final" in the sense that no appeal shall lie. This is recognised by the County Courts Act 1984, s.79(1) (and by the Supreme Court Act 1981, s.18(1)(c)). Before CPR Pt 52 (Appeals) came into effect, the distinction between "final" and "interlocutory" appeals was important in appeal procedure (see Supreme Court Act 1981, s.60 and notes following, para. 9A–292 above). In s.70, the word "final" is used in a different sense. A judgment or order takes effect from the day when it is given or made, or such later date as the court may specify (CPR, r.40.7). In any system of adjudication there must come a point when a judgment or order rendered (particularly at the end of a trial) is final in the sense that it will not be re-considered by the court or other tribunal pronouncing it. The authorities show that a judgment becomes final in this sense, not when it is pronounced, but when the order giving it effect has been drawn up, registered or perfected (*R. v. Cripps, ex p. Muldoon* [1984] Q.B. 686, CA, at p.695 Sir John Donaldson M.R.; see also *Preston Banking Co v. William Allsupp & Sons* [1895] 1 Ch. 141, CA, at p.145 *per* A.L. Smith L.J.). After this point, a party's remedy lies, not in attempting to persuade the court which rendered the judgment to change its mind, but in challenging the judgment on appeal. Before this point, the court has jurisdiction in limited circumstances to recall the judgment for further consideration. Authority for this is provided by *Re Barrell Enterprises* [1973] 1 W.L.R. 19, CA, where it was said that the jurisdiction should not be exercised "save in the most exceptional circumstances" (see also *Pittalis v. Sherefettin* [1986] 1 Q.B. 868, CA, at p.882 Dillon L.J. and authorities referred to there). In modern times, pressures to reduce costs and delays in civil proceedings, coupled with the desire to discourage parties from mounting ap-

peals and the new restrictions on access to appellate courts, have focussed attention on
the circumstances in which the Barrell jurisdiction may and should be exercised (see
further Vol. 1, para. 40.2.2 and cases referred to there). Since the coming into effect
of the CPR, the extent of the jurisdiction has been considered at first instance in the
High Court (see *Charlesworth v. Relay Road Ltd*, [2000] 1 W.L.R. 230, [1999] 4 All E.R.
397, Neuberger J.; *Spice Girls Ltd v. Aprillia World Service B.V. (No. 3)*, *The Times*,
September 12, 2000, Arden J.; *Mamidoil-Jetoil Greek Petroleum SA v. Okta Crude Oil
Refinery AD (No. 2)* [2001] 1 Lloyd's Rep. 591, Thomas J.; *Compagnie Noga d'Importation
et d'Exportation SA v. Abacha* [2001] 3 All E.R. 513, Rix L.J.) and by the Court of Appeal
in *Stewart v. Engel* [2000] 1 W.L.R. 2268; [2000] 3 All E.R. 518, CA, where their lordships were agreed that the Barrell jurisdiction has survived the CPR, but were not
agreed on the question whether the jurisdiction remains subject to the "exceptional
circumstances" requirement as understood before the CPR came into effect; see also
Royal Brompton Hospital NHS Trust v. Hammond [2001] EWCA Civ 778.

Under rules of court which, on occasion, have been rather generously applied,
clerical mistakes in judgments or orders or errors arising therein from any accidental
slip or omission may at any time be corrected by the court (CPR r.40.12 and Practice
Direction (Judgments and Orders), paras 4.1 *et seq.*, Vol. 1, para. 40BPD.4).

Satisfaction of judgments and orders for payment of money

9A–636   **71.**—(1) Where a judgment is given or an order is made by a
county court under which a sum of money of any amount is payable,
whether by way of satisfaction of the claim or counterclaim in the
proceedings or by way of costs or otherwise, the court may, as it
thinks fit, order the money to be paid either—

    (a) in one sum, whether forthwith or within such period as
the court may fix; or

    (b) by such instalments payable at such times as the court
may fix.

(2) If at any time it appears to the satisfaction of the court that
any party to any proceedings is unable from any cause to pay any
sum recovered against him (whether by way of satisfaction of the
claim or counterclaim in the proceedings or by way of costs or
otherwise) or any instalment of such a sum, the court may, in its
discretion, suspend or stay any judgment or order given or made in
the proceedings for such time and on such terms as the court thinks
fit, and so from time to time until it appears that the cause of inability has ceased.

Satisfaction of judgments and orders for payment of money
9A–637   The general rule is that where judgment is given or an order is made for the payment of money, including costs, the money shall be payable at the expiration of 14
days from the date of the judgment or order (CPR, r.40.11). Obviously, if a day for
payment is specified in the judgment or order, then the money shall be payable on
that date. The significance of subs.(1) is that it makes it clear that the court has power
to order that a money judgment or order should be paid, not in a lump sum in 14
days or on a particular date, but by instalments. Subsection (2) gives the court power
to suspend or stay a money judgment or order against a party, whether requiring payment in a lump sum or by instalments, where the court is satisfied that the party is unable to pay. For practice where payment by instalments is ordered, see Practice Direction (Judgments and Orders), para. 12.

Set-off in cases of cross judgments in county courts and
High Court

9A–638   **72.**—(1) Where one person has obtained a judgment or order in a
county court against another person, and that other person has
obtained a judgment or order against the first-mentioned person in

the same or in another county court or in the High Court, either such person may, in accordance with rules of court, give notice in writing to the court or the several courts as the case may be, and may apply to the court or any of the said courts in accordance with rules of court for leave to set off any sums, including costs, payable under several judgments or orders.

(2) Upon any such application, the set-off may be allowed in accordance with the practice for the time being in force in the High Court as to the allowance of set-off and in particular in relation to any solicitor's lien for costs.

(3) Where the cross judgments or orders have not been obtained in the same court, a copy of the order made on any such application shall be sent by the proper officer of the court to which the application is made to the proper officer of the other court.

Set-off in cases of cross judgments in county courts and High Court

A set-off is a monetary cross-claim which is also a defence to the claim made in the **9A–639** action. The right of a party to plead a set-off avoids the need to commence a separate action for the purpose of asserting the claim. A party may plead a previous judgment as a set-off. (In these circumstances, unless the previous judgment is a foreign judgment, the alternative course of commencing a separate action does not exist). This section is concerned, not with the setting off of a previous judgment as a defence to a claim (see CPR, r.16.6), but with such set-off against a judgment debt.

The section states that where, in the High Court or a county court, X has obtained judgment against Y and Y has obtained judgment against X in other proceedings, either in the same or a different county court or in the High Court, for a lesser sum, Y may apply for permission to set-off his judgment against X's judgment. The section requires Y to make application "to the court or any of the said courts in accordance with rules of court". It is necessary to be clear as to what these rules of court might be.

Where the several judgments have been obtained in a county court, or several county courts, CPR Sched 2, O.22, r.11 applies and Y should make application to one of the relevant county courts in accordance with the provisions of that rule. That rule states that where X's judgment was obtained in one county court and Y's in another, Y may make application to either county court on notice (with notice also being given to the proper officer of the other county court) (r.11(3)). Where the several judgments were obtained in the same county court application should be made on notice to that court; however, if the application is made "on the day when the last judgment or order is obtained" notice is not required provided both parties are present (r.11(2)).

Where the several judgments have been obtained in the High Court it would seem that application must be made to the High Court but rules of court expressly dedicated to such applications are contained in the CPR. Accordingly, it seems that an application on notice pursuant to CPR Pt 23 is required (though by analogy with CPR Sched.2, CCR O.22, r.11(2), perhaps an application could be made without notice to the court "on the day when the last judgment or order is obtained" if both parties are present).

An anomaly still remains. Where X has obtained judgment against Y in a county court and Y has obtained judgment against X in the High Court for a lesser sum and Y wishes to apply for permission to set-off his High Court judgment against X's county court judgment, the provisions of CPR Sched.2, CCR O.22, r.11 do not apply. Prior to the CPR such applications were made to the High Court and were governed by RSC O.107, r.4. Order 107 is not replicated in the CPR. Consequently, the proper procedure is now a matter for doubt. As CPR Sched.2, CCR O.22, r.11 clearly does not apply it is submitted that application should be made to the High Court on notice pursuant to CPR Pt 23. CPR Sched.2, CCR O.22, r.11(8) clearly envisages such order being made in the High Court and directs the county court officer as to how he should proceed.

The section does not give a right to set-off (the application is for "leave" to do so). Section 72(2) expressly requires a county court to approach the application in accordance with the practice for the time being in force in the High Court and "in particular in relation to any solicitor's lien for costs".

Register of judgments and orders

9A–640 73.—(1) A register of every—

    (a) judgment entered in a county court;

    (b) administration order made under section 112; and

    (c) order restricting enforcement made under section 112A,

shall be kept in such manner and in such place as may be prescribed.

(2) The Lord Chancellor may, by statutory instrument, make regulations as to the keeping of the register, and in this section "prescribed" means prescribed by those regulations.

(3) Regulations under this section may—

    (a) prescribe circumstances in which judgments or orders are to be exempt from registration or in which the registration of any judgment or order is to be cancelled;

    (b) provide for any specified class of judgments or orders to be exempt from registration.

(4) Regulations under this section shall be subject to annulment in pursuance of a resolution of either House of Parliament.

(5) The Lord Chancellor may, with the concurrence of the Treasury, fix the fees to be paid in respect of—

    (a) the making of any information contained in an entry in the register available for inspection in visible and legible form;

    (b) the carrying out of any official search of the register;

    (c) the supply of a certified copy of any information contained in an entry in the register.

(6) The proceeds of the fees shall be applied in such manner as the Treasury may direct in paying the expenses incurred in maintaining the register, and any surplus, after providing for the payment of those expenses, shall be paid to the credit of the Consolidated Fund.

9A–641 *Note* —Amended by the Administration of Justice Act 1985, s.54; and the Courts and Legal Services Act 1990, s.125(2), Sched.17, para. 14.

Register of judgments and orders

9A–642 The regulations made under this section are the Register of County Court Judgments Regulations 1985 (S.I. 1985 No. 1807), as amended. For an analysis of the question whether a claim may be brought for negligence or breach of statutory duty where the register is inaccurate, see *Du Bey v. Lord Chancellor's Department and Registry Trust*, June 9, 2000, unrep. (Gray J.).

Provision for register under section 73 to be kept by body under contract to Lord Chancellor

9A–643 73A.—(1) If—

    (a) there is in force an agreement between the Lord Chancellor and a body corporate relating to the keeping by that body corporate of the register under section 73 ("the register"); and

    (b) provision is made by regulations under that section for the register to be kept in accordance with such an agreement,

the register shall be kept by that body corporate.

(2) Where the register is kept by a body corporate in pursuance of subsection (1)—

    (a) the Lord Chancellor may recover from that body any expenses incurred by the Lord Chancellor in connection with the supply of information to that body for the purposes of the register;

    (b) subsection (5) of section 73 shall have effect as if the words "maximum amounts in relation to" were inserted after the word "fix"; and

    (c) subsection (6) of that section shall not apply.

(3) Where subsection (1) of this section ceases to apply to a body corporate as a result of the termination (for any reason) of the agreement in question, the Lord Chancellor may require the information for the time being contained in the entries in the register to be transferred to such person as he may direct.

Note—Added by the Administration of Justice Act 1985, s.54.   **9A–644**

Provision of register under s.73 to be kept by body under contract to Lord Chancellor

  In the exercise of powers conferred by this section, the operation of the register of   **9A–645**
county court judgments and orders required to be kept under s.73 has been contracted
out to Registry Trust Limited, 173/5 Cleveland Street, London W1.

Interest on judgment debts, etc.

74.—(1) The Lord Chancellor may by order made with the concur- **9A–646**
rence of the Treasury provide that any sums to which this subsection
applies shall carry interest at such rate and between such times as
may be prescribed by the order.

(2) The sums to which subsection (1) applies are—

    (a) sums payable under judgments or orders given or made in a county court, including sums payable by instalments; and

    (b) sums which by virtue of any enactment are, if the county court so orders, recoverable as if payable under an order of that court, and in respect of which the county court has so ordered.

(3) The payment of interest due under subsection (1) shall be enforceable as a sum payable under the judgment or order.

(4) The power conferred by subsection (1) includes power—

    (a) to specify the descriptions of judgment or order in respect of which interest shall be payable;

    (b) to provide that interest shall be payable only on sums exceeding a specified amount;

    (c) to make provision for the manner in which and the periods by reference to which the interest is to be calculated and paid;

    (d) to provide that any enactment shall or shall not apply in relation to interest payable under subsection (1) or shall apply to it with such modifications as may be specified in the order; and

(e) to make such incidental or supplementary provisions as the Lord Chancellor considers appropriate.

(5) Without prejudice to the generality of subsection (4), an order under subsection (1) may provide that the rate of interest shall be the rate specified in section 17 of the Judgments Act 1838 as that enactment has effect from time to time.

(5A) The power conferred by subsection (1) includes power to make provision enabling a county court to order that the rate of interest applicable to a sum expressed in a currency other than sterling shall be such rate as the court thinks fit (instead of the rate otherwise applicable).

(6) The power to make an order under subsection (1) shall be exerciseable by statutory instrument subject to annulment in pursuance of a resolution of either House of Parliament.

9A–647   *Note* — Subsection (5A) added by the Private International Law (Miscellaneous Provisions) Act 1995, s.2.

Interest on judgment debts, etc.
9A–648   The County Court (Interest on Judgment Debts) Order 1991 (S.I. 1991 No. 1184) (as amended) was made by the Lord Chancellor in exercise of powers conferred by this section. For rate of interest specified from time to time under the Judgments Act 1838, s.17. See further Vol. 1, para. 40.8.1, and note CPR, rr.40.8, 44.12, 47.8 and 47.14.

Subsection (5A) was added by the Private International Law (Miscellaneous Provisions) Act 1995, s.2 and the additional powers granted by it were exercised in the 1996 amendment to the 1991 Order. For comparable provision to subs.(5A) applicable to High Court judgments, see the Administration of Justice Act 1970, s.44A (inserted by s.1 of the 1974 Act) (see para. 9B–54).

Practice directions
9A–649   **74A.**—(1) Directions as to the practice and procedure of county courts may be made by the Lord Chancellor.

(2) Directions as to the practice and procedure of county courts may not be made by any other person without the approval of the Lord Chancellor.

(3) The power of the Lord Chancellor to make directions under subsection (1) includes power—

(a) to vary or revoke directions made by him or any other person, and

(b) to make different provision for different cases or different areas, including different provision—

(i) for a specific court, or

(ii) for specific proceedings, or a specific jurisdiction,

specified in the directions.

(4) References in this section to the Lord Chancellor include any person authorised by him to act on his behalf.

9A–650   *Note* —Added by the Civil Procedure Act 1997, s.5.

Practice Directions
9A–651   This section was introduced by the Civil Procedure Act 1997, s.5 and brought into force on April 27, 1997 (see para. 9A–839 below). Former CCR O.50, r.1 stated that the Lord Chancellor may issue practice directions for the purpose of securing

uniformity of practice in the county courts. Before this section came into force, some county courts, acting on their own initiative, issued "local" practice directions, particularly for the purpose of dealing with case management problems. In *Langley v. North West Water Authority* [1991] 1 W.L.R. 697, Lord Donaldson M.R. said that there was no statutory authority for such directions but none was needed because every court had an inherent jurisdiction to regulate its own proceedings, save in so far as any such practice direction was inconsistent with statute law or rules of court (see also *Boyle v. Ford Motor Co Ltd* [1992] 1 W.L.R. 476). By this section, control over the issuing of directions as to the practice and procedure of county courts, whether of local or national application, is vested in the Lord Chancellor. Whereas CCR O.50, r.1 spoke of the issuing of practice directions for the purpose of securing uniformity of practice, s.74A(3) clearly foreshadows a need for diversity of practice. Section 74 is confined to practice and procedure of county courts (but see s.5(1) and s.9(2) of the 1997 Act).

County court rules

75. [*Omitted by Civil Procedure Act 1997 Sched.2, para. 2*].   **9A–652**

Application of practice of High Court

76. In any case not expressly provided for by or in pursuance of **9A–653** this Act, the general principles of practice in the High Court may be adopted and applied to proceedings in a county court.

Application of practice of High Court

This section says that the general principles of High Court practice may be adopted **9A–654** and applied to proceedings in a county court where there is, as it were, a "gap" in county court practice and procedure because the matter is "not expressly provided for by or in pursuance of this Act", that is to say, provided for by sections in the Act or in delegated legislation made under the Act, including, principally, rules of court. Before the CPR came into force, the CCR were made under s.75 of the Act (now omitted) and the rules found therein were significantly different in many respects to those found in the RSC and, generally, much simpler. In these circumstances, s.76 was occasionally brought into play to deal with "gaps" apparent in the CCR. CCR O.1, r.6 said that where by virtue of s.76 provisions of the RSC were applied in relation to proceedings in a county court, that provision "shall have effect with the necessary modifications". The CPR govern county court and High Court proceedings and, in the main, the procedures for both levels of court are the same. Nevertheless, some differences do remain and this leaves open the possibility that "gaps" in county court practice will continue to emerge and that s.76 may still have a role to play (*e.g. Ager v. Ager* [1998] 1 W.L.R. 1074, CA, where it was held that the jurisdiction conferred on the High Court by the Supreme Court Act 1981, s.15(4) could be conferred on county courts by operation of s.76). Further, there remains the possibility that, in county court proceedings to which rules in Sched.2 of the CPR apply (*viz.*, former CCR rules), rules in Sched.1 (*viz.*, former RSC rules) may be applied by operation of s.76. This prospect is specifically acknowledged by CCR O.1, r.6 (referred to above) which has survived in the CPR as one of the "schedule rules" (see Vol. 1, para. cc1.6) (see *Jephson Homes Housing Association Ltd v. Moisejevs* [2001] 2 All E.R. 901, CA, application to set aside warrant for possession).

PART IV

APPEALS ETC.

APPEALS

Appeals: general provisions

77.—(1) Subject to the provisions of this section and the following **9A–655** provisions of this Part of this Act, and to any order made by the Lord

Chancellor under section 56(1) of the Access to Justice Act 1999, if any party to any proceedings in a county court is dissatisfied with the determination of the judge or jury, he may appeal from it to the Court of Appeal in such manner and subject to such conditions as may be provided by Civil Procedure Rules.

(1A) Without prejudice to the generality of the power to make rules of court under section 75, such rules may make provision for any appeal from the exercise by a district judge, assistant district judge or deputy district judge of any power given to him by virtue of any enactment to be to a judge of a county court.

(2) [...]

(3) [...]

(4) [...]

(5) Subject to the provision of this section and the following provisions of this Part of this Act, where an appeal is brought under subsection (1) in any action, an appeal may be brought under that subsection in respect of any claim or counterclaim in the action notwithstanding that there could have been no such appeal if that claim had been the subject of a separate action.

(6) In proceedings in which either the plaintiff or the defendant is claiming possession of any premises this section shall not confer any right of appeal on any question of fact if by virtue of—

    (a) section 13(4) of the Landlord and Tenant Act 1954; or

    (b) Cases III to IX in Schedule 4 to the Rent (Agriculture) Act 1976; or

    (c) section 98 of the Rent Act 1977, as it applies to Cases 1 to 6 and 8 and 9 and Schedule 15 to that Act, or that section as extended or applied by any other enactment; or

    (d) section 69 of the Rent Act 1977, as it applies to Cases 1 to 6 and 9 in Schedule 15 to that Act; or

    (e) section 84(2)(a) of the Housing Act 1985; or

    (ee) section 7 of the Housing Act 1988, as it applies to the grounds in Part II of Schedule 2 to that Act; or

    (f) any other enactment,

the court can only grant possession on being satisfied that it is reasonable to do so.

(7) This section shall not—

    (a) confer any right of appeal from any judgment or order where a right of appeal is conferred by some other enactment; or

    (b) take away any right of appeal from any judgment or order where a right of appeal is so conferred,

and shall have effect subject to any enactment other than this Act.

(8) In this section—

"enactment" means an enactment whenever passed; [...]

9A–656   *Note*—Amended the by Housing (Consequential Provisions) Act 1985, Sched.2, para. 57(2); the Housing Act 1988, Sched.17, para. 35(2); the Civil Procedure Act 1997, Sched.2.; the Access to Justice (Destination of Appeals) Order 2000 (S.I. 2000 No. 1071). Subsection (1A) added by the Courts and Legal Services Act 1990, Sched.17, para. 15. Subsections (2) to (4) repealed by, and subs.(8) amended by, the Access to Justice Act 1999, Sched.15, Pt III. Section 75, referred to in subs.(1A) of this section, was repealed by the Civil Procedure Act 1997, Sched.2, para. 2(6).

Appeal from county court determination to Court of Appeal

The procedural rules relating to the proper routes for appeals from decisions made **9A–657** in proceedings in a county court, whether to the Court of Appeal or to some other forum, are complicated. In Sect. I of Practice Direction (Appeals), upplementing CPR, Pt 52, an effort is made to summarise the position in tabular form.

The Court of Appeal has all such jurisdiction as is conferred on it by the Supreme Court Act 1981 or any other Act, including the County Courts Act 1984 (Supreme Court Act 1981 s.15(2), see para. 9A–45 above). Section 77(1) of the 1984 Act states that the general rule is that any party to any proceedings in a county court who is "dissatisfied with the determination of the judge or jury" may appeal from it to the Court of Appeal (see para. 9A–655 below). This general rule is subject to the provisions of paras (1A) *et seq.* of s.77 (which, amongst other things, provide for appeals from a district judge to a judge of a county court) and other provisions in Pt IV of the 1984 Act. The general rule is further qualified by the Access to Justice Act 1999. Section 56(1) of that Act states that the Lord Chancellor may by order provide that appeals "which would otherwise lie to the Court of Appeal", for example, appeals falling within the general rule stated above, shall lie instead to the High Court or to a county court (see para. 9A–866 below). Accordingly, the power of the Lord Chancellor by order to affect the jurisdiction of the Court of Appeal in relation to appeals from the High Court was added to s.77(1) by the Access to Justice Act 1999 (Destination of Appeals) Order 2000 (S.I. 2000 No. 1071), art.7. Provisions exercising this power in relation to appeals to the Court of Appeal from a county court are found in arts 3, 4 and 5 of that statutory instrument. art.3(1) states that, subject to two exceptions, an appeal from a decision of a county court shall not go according to the general rule (*i.e.* from a county court to the Court of Appeal) but shall go to the High Court. And art.3(2) states that, subject to the same exceptions, where the decision to be appealed is a decision made by a district judge, the appeal shall go to a judge of a county court. In this context, "decision" includes any judgment, order or direction. The two exceptions are (1) where the decision is a final decision made in a mercantile claim dealt with in a county court (art.4(b), note also the exception provided for by 4(a)); and (2) where the decision appealed was itself a decision made on appeal (other than from the decision of an officer of the court authorised to assess costs) (so-called "second appeals") (see art.5). In this context, "final decision" means any decision that would finally determine (subject to any possible appeal or detailed assessment of costs) the entire proceedings whichever way the court decided the issues before it (*ibid.* art.(2)(c)).

No appeal shall lie to the Court of Appeal: (1) from any order, judgment or decision of a county court which is final, or (2) from any order of a county court allowing an extension of time for appealing from a judgment or order (paras (b) and (c) of s.18(1); see para. 9A–53 below).

For rules of court affecting appeals from a county court to the Court of Appeal, see CPR Pt 52, and for further information as to the jurisdiction of the Court of Appeal in relation to appeals from a county court, see notes on the rules in Pt 52 (Vol. 1, paras 52.0.1 *et seq.*).

Assistance of Trinity masters for Court of Appeal in Admiralty proceedings

78. Where, on an appeal by a party to any Admiralty proceedings **9A–658** which have been heard in a county court with the assistance of assessors, any party makes application to the Court of Appeal in that behalf, the court shall summon Trinity masters to assist on the hearing of the appeal if the court is of opinion that such assistance is necessary or desirable.

Agreement not to appeal

79.—(1) No appeal shall lie from any judgment, direction, decision **9A–659** or order of a judge of county courts if, before the judgment, direc-

LEGISLATION

tion, decision or order is given or made, the parties agree, in writing signed by themselves or their legal representatives or agents, that it shall be final.

(2) [...]

9A-660   *Note* —Amended by the Courts and Legal Services Act 1990, s.125(3) and Sched.18, para. 49(3); and the Statute Law (Repeals) Act 1986, Sched.1.

Judge's note on appeal

9A-661   **80.**—(1) At the hearing of any proceedings in a county court in which there is a right of appeal or from which an appeal may be brought with leave, the judge shall, at the request of any party, make a note—

    (a) of any question of law raised at the hearing; and

    (b) of the facts in evidence in relation to any such question; and

    (c) of his decision on any such question and of his determination of the proceedings.

(2) Where such a note has been taken, the judge shall (whether notice of appeal has been served or not), on the application of any party to the proceedings, and on payment by that party of such fee as may be prescribed by an order under section 92 of the Courts Act 2003 (fees), furnish him with a copy of the note, and shall sign the copy, and the copy so signed shall be used at the hearing of the appeal.

9A-661.1   *Note* —Subs (2) amended by the Courts Act 2003, s.109(1), Sched.8, para. 271(b).

Judge's note in small claim

9A-662   Practice Direction (Small Claims Track), para. 5.1 *et seq.* provides for the recording of evidence and the giving of reasons. Nothing in that direction affects the duty of the judge under s.80 (*ibid.* para. 5.8, see Vol. 1, para. 27PD.5).

Powers of Court of Appeal on appeal from county court

9A-663   **81.**—(1) On the hearing of an appeal, the Court of Appeal may draw any inference of fact and either—

    (a) order a new trial on such terms as the court thinks just; or

    (b) order judgment to be entered for any party; or

    (c) make a final or other order on such terms as the court thinks proper to ensure the determination on the merits of the real question in controversy between the parties.

(2) Subject to Civil Procedure Rules on any appeal from a county court the Court of Appeal may reverse or vary, in favour of a party seeking to support the judgment or order of the county court in whole or in part, any determinations made in the county court on questions of fact, notwithstanding that the appeal is an appeal on a point of law only, or any such determinations on points of law, notwithstanding that the appeal is an appeal on a question of fact only.

(3) Subsection (2) shall not enable the Court of Appeal to reverse or vary any determination, unless the party dissatisfied with the de-

termination would have been entitled to appeal in respect of it if aggrieved by the judgment or order.

Note —Amended by the Civil Procedure Act 1997, Sched.2.   **9A–664**

Decision of Court of Appeal on probate appeals to be final

82. No appeal shall lie from the decision of the Court of Appeal on **9A–665** any appeal from a county court in any probate proceedings.

CERTIORARI AND PROHIBITION

Stay of proceedings in case of certiorari or prohibition

83.—(1) The grant by the High Court of leave to make an applica- **9A–666** tion for an order of certiorari or prohibition to a county court shall, if the High Court so directs, operate as a stay of the proceedings in question until the determination of the application, or until the High Court otherwise orders.

(2) Where any proceedings are so stayed, the judge of the county court shall from time to time adjourn the hearing of the proceedings to such day as he thinks fit.

Prohibition

84.—(1) Where an application is made to the High Court for an **9A–667** order or prohibition addressed to any county court, the matter shall be finally disposed of by order.

(2) Upon any such application, the judge of the county court shall not be served with notice of it, and shall not, except by the order of a judge of the High Court—

    (a) be required to appear or be heard; or

    (b) be liable to any order for the payment of the costs of the application;

but the application shall be proceeded with and hear in the same manner in all respects as an appeal duly brought from a decision of the judge, and notice of the application shall be given to or served upon the same parties as in the case of an order made or refused by a judge in a matter within his jurisdiction.

PART V

ENFORCEMENT OF JUDGMENTS AND ORDERS

EXECUTION AGAINST GOODS

Execution of judgments or orders for payment of money

85.—(1) Subject to Article 8 of the High Court and County Courts **9A–668** Jurisdiction Order 1991, any sum of money payable under a judgment or order of a county court may be recovered, in case of default or failure of payment, forthwith or at the time or times and in the manner thereby directed, by execution against the goods of the party against whom the judgment or order was obtained.

(2) The district judge, on the application of the party prosecuting any such judgment or order, shall issue a warrant of execution in the nature of a writ of *fieri facias* whereby the district judge shall be empowered to levy or cause to be levied by distress and sale of the goods, wherever they may be found within the district of the court, the money payable under the judgment or order and the costs of the execution.

(3) The precise time of the making of the application to the district judge to issue such a warrant shall be entered by him in the record prescribed for the purpose under section 12 and on the warrant.

(4) It shall be the duty of every constable within his jurisdiction to assist in the execution of every such warrant.

Execution of judgments or orders for payment of money

9A–669   Execution by means of a warrant of execution is one of the principal means of enforcing a judgment. Important procedural rules are contained in CPR Sched.2, CCR O.25 and O.26. Broadly speaking, a warrant of execution in a county court is the equivalent of a writ of *fieri facias* in the High Court. Warrants in the county court are executed by county court bailiffs.

Section 85 imposes certain functions on the "registrar", an office now abolished by s.74 of the Courts and Legal Services Act 1990 and replaced by the district judge. By CPR Sched.2, CCR O.26, r.1(1A) these functions are now discharged by the "court officer".

The "precise time" referred to in s.85(3) is important for establishing priority of warrants (see also s.99, below).

Execution of orders for payment by instalments

9A–670   **86.**—(1) Where the court has made an order for payment of any sum of money by instalments, execution on the order shall not be issued until after default in payment of some instalment according to the order.

(2) Rules of court may prescribe the cases in which execution is to issue if there is any such default and limit the amounts for which and the times at which execution may issue.

(3) Except so far as may be otherwise provided by county court rules made for those purposes, execution or successive executions may issue if there is any such default for the whole of the said sum of money and costs then remaining unpaid or for such part as the court may order either at the time of the original order or at any subsequent time; but except so far as may be otherwise provided by such rules, no execution shall issue unless at the time when it issues the whole or some part of an instalment which has already become due remains unpaid.

9A–671   *Note*—Amended by the Civil Procedure Act 1997, Sched.2, para. 2(2).

Execution of orders for payment by instalments

9A–672   A county court has power under s.71 to order a sum of money payable under a judgment to be paid by instalments. In such cases warrants of execution may only be granted on default of the instalment order. The judgment creditor can issue a warrant for the whole or part of the debt (CPR Sched.2, CCR O.26, r.1(2)). The minimum sum for which a warrant may be issued is £50, or the amount of one monthly instalment or four weekly instalments, whichever is greater. See generally, CPR Sched.2, CCR O.26 and commentary to CPR Sched.2, CCR O.26, r.11 on suspension of part warrants.

In *Ropaigealach v. Allied Irish Bank Plc* [2001] EWCA Civ 1790; November 12, 2001, CA, unrep., an instalment order had been made and the Court held that, for the purposes of s.86, "execution" by charging order is "issued" when it is issued nisi. As, in this case, the order nisi had been obtained before the instalment order was made, the court had jurisdiction to make the charging order absolute. The Court explained that the existence of an instalment order is one of the circumstances to be considered by the court in exercising its discretion. In many circumstances it may be entirely sensible and satisfactory from both parties' points of view for an instalment order and an order absolute to co-exist, particularly where a long-running instalment order is made.

Execution to be superseded on payment

87.—(1) In or upon every warrant of execution issued from a **9A–673** county court against the goods of any person, the district judge shall cause to be inserted or indorsed the total amount to be levied, inclusive of the fee for issuing the warrant but exclusive of the fees for its execution.

(2) If the person against whom the execution is issued, before the actual sale of the goods, pays or causes to be paid or tendered to the district judge of the court from which the warrant is issued, or to the bailiff holding the warrant, the amount inserted in, or indorsed upon, the warrant under subsection (1), or such part as the person entitled agrees to accept in full satisfaction, together with the amount stated by the officer of the court to whom the payment or tender is made to be the amount of the fees for the execution of the warrant, the execution shall be superseded, and the goods shall be discharged and set at liberty.

Execution to be superseded on payment

This section states the obvious rule that the warrant of execution is to be superseded **9A–674** on payment of the amount for which the warrant is issued or such other sum as the judgment creditor accepts in full satisfaction of the warrant. Indeed sales under warrants of execution (see ss.93–98) follow only a small proportion of warrants issued.

Power to stay execution

88. If at any time it appears to the satisfaction of the court that any **9A–675** party to any proceedings is unable from any cause to pay any sum recovered against him (whether by way of satisfaction of the claim or counterclaim in the proceedings or by way of costs or otherwise), or any instalment of such a sum, the court may, in its discretion, stay any execution issued in the proceedings for such time and on such terms as the court thinks fit and so from time to time it appears that the cause of inability has ceased.

Power to stay execution

The district judge exercises the jurisdiction to stay execution of warrants (CPR **9A–676** Sched.2, CCR O.25, r.8). See also s.71(2) for a similar provision on suspension and stay of judgments.

SEIZURE AND CUSTODY OF GOODS, ETC.

Goods which may be seized

89.—(1) Every bailiff or officer executing any warrant of execution **9A–677** issued from a county court against the goods of any person may by virtue of it seize—

LEGISLATION

(a) any of that person's goods except—

    (i) such tools, books, vehicles and other items of equipment as are necessary to that person for use personally by him in his employment, business or vocation;

    (ii) such clothing, bedding, furniture, household equipment and provisions as are necessary for satisfying the basic domestic needs of that person and his family;

(b) any money, banknotes, bills of exchange, promissory notes, bonds, specialties or securities for money belonging to that person.

(2) Any reference to the goods of an execution debtor in this Part of this Act includes a reference to anything else of his that may lawfully be seized in execution.

(3) [...]

9A–678   *Note* —Amended by the Courts and Legal Services Act 1990, ss.15 and 125(7), Sched.20.

Goods which may be seized
9A–679   This section permits execution against the judgment debtor's "goods" and money, etc., but exempts certain goods from subjection to execution. See the detailed commentary to CPR Sched.1, RSC O.45.

For the device of "walking possession" see commentary to s.90, below.

Custody of goods seized

9A–680   **90.** Goods seized in execution under process of a county court shall, until sale—

(a) be deposited by the bailiff in some fit place; or

(b) remain in the custody of a fit person approved by the district judge to be put in possession by the bailiff; or

(c) be safeguarded in such other manner as the district judge directs.

Custody of goods seized
9A–681   If goods are actually removed they must be deposited in a "fit place" such as a warehouse or compound. An inventory must be made and notice of the time and place of the sale served on the judgment debtor (CPR Sched.2, CCR O.26, r.12).

To avoid some of the administrative inconvenience of actual removal, the device of "walking possession" is frequently used whereby the judgment debtor signs an agreement that in consideration of the bailiff not removing the goods, the judgment debtor undertakes not to remove the goods and agrees that the bailiff may re-enter, using force if necessary, at any time to seize the goods.

Disposal of bills of exchange, etc., seized

9A–682   **91.** The district judge shall hold any bills of exchange, promissory notes, bonds, specialties or other securities for money seized in execution under process of a county court as security for the amount directed to be levied by the execution, or for so much of that amount as has not been otherwise levied or raised, for the benefit of the plaintiff, and the plaintiff may sue in the name of the defendant, or in the name of any person in whose name the defendant might have sued, for the recovery of the sum secured or made payable thereby, when the time of payment arrives.

Disposal of bills of exchange, etc., seized

A "bill of exchange" includes a cheque (see the Bills of Exchange Act 1882, s.73).   **9A–683**

Penalty for rescuing goods seized

92.—(1) If any person rescues or attempts to rescue any goods **9A–684** seized in execution under process of a county court, he shall be liable—

    (a) on summary conviction, to imprisonment for a term not exceeding one month or to a fine of an amount not exceeding level 4 on the standard scale, or both; or

    (b) on an order made by the judge in that behalf, to be committed for a specified period not exceeding one month to prison or to a fine of an amount not exceeding level 4 on the standard scale or to be so committed and to such a fine,

and a bailiff of the court may take the offender into custody, with or without warrant, and bring him before the judge.

(2) The judge may at any time revoke an order committing a person to prison under this section and, if he is already in custody, order his discharge.

Note—Amended by the Statute Law (Repeals) Act 1986.   **9A–685**

Penalty for rescuing goods seized

This section enables the county court to punish any person who rescues or attempts **9A–686** to rescue goods seized in execution. Compare s.14. The procedure is the same under ss.14 and 92 (see CPR Sched.2, CCR O.34, r.1).

The "standard scale" is provided for by s.37 of the Criminal Justice Act 1982. Level 4 is currently £2,500.

SALE OF GOODS SEIZED

Period to elapse before sale

93. No goods seized in execution under process of a county court **9A–687** shall be sold for the purpose of satisfying the warrant of execution until the expiration of a period of at least 5 days next following the day on which the goods have been so seized unless—

    (a) the goods are of a perishable nature; or

    (b) the person whose goods have been seized so requests in writing.

Goods not to be sold except by brokers or appraisers

94. No goods seized in execution under process of a county court **9A–688** shall be sold for the purpose of satisfying the warrant of execution except by one of the brokers or appraisers appointed under this Part of this Act.

Appointment of brokers, appraisers, etc.

95.—(1) The registrar may from time to time as he thinks fit appoint such number of persons for keeping possession, and such **9A–689**

number of brokers and appraisers for the purpose of selling or valuing any goods seized in execution under process of the court, as appears to him to be necessary.

(2) The registrar may direct security to be taken from any broker, appraiser or other person so appointed for such sum and in such manner as he thinks fit for the faithful performance of his duties without injury or oppression.

(3) The judge or registrar may dismiss any broker, appraiser or other person so appointed.

(4) There shall be payable to brokers and appraisers so appointed in respect of their duties, out of the produce of goods distrained or sold, such fees as may be prescribed by an order under section 92 of the Courts Act 2003 (fees).

Note —Subs.(4) amended by the Courts Act 2003, s.109(1), Sched.8, para.271(c).

Registrar

9A–690   By the Courts and Legal Services Act 1990, s.74, the office of registrar became that of district judge and references in any enactment to "registrar" are to be construed as a reference to that office in its new name.

Power to appoint bailiffs to act as brokers and appraisers

9A–691   **96.**—(1) The judge may appoint in writing any bailiff of the court to act as a broker or appraiser for the purpose of selling or valuing any goods seized in execution under process of the court.

(2) A bailiff so appointed may, without other licence in that behalf, perform all the duties which brokers or appraisers appointed under section 95 may perform under this Act.

Sales under executions to be public unless otherwise ordered

9A–692   **97.**—(1) Where any goods are to be sold under execution for a sum exceeding £20 (including legal incidental expenses), the sale shall, unless the court from which the warrant of execution issued otherwise orders, be made by public auction and not by bill of sale or private contract, and shall be publicly advertised by the registrar on, and during 3 days next preceding, the day of sale.

(2) Where any goods are seized in execution and the registrar has notice of another execution or other executions, the court shall not consider an application for leave to sell privately until the prescribed notice has been given to the other execution creditor or creditors, who may appear before the court and be heard upon the application.

Sales under executions to be public unless otherwise ordered

9A–693   See generally CPR Sched.2, CCR O.26, and in particular, rr.12, 13 and 15. Where goods are sold under an execution, the proper officer shall furnish the debtor with a detailed account in writing of the sale and of the application of the proceeds (see CPR Sched.2, CCR O.26, r.13).

A sale not in conformity with s.97 will be voidable rather than void (*Crawshaw v. Harrison* [1894] 1 Q.B. 79; (1893) L.J.Q.B. 94).

Protection of district judge selling goods under execution without notice of claim by third party

9A–694   **98.**—(1) Where any goods in the possession of an execution debtor at the time of seizure by a district judge or other officer charged with the enforcement of a warrant or other process of execution issued from a county court are sold by that district judge or other officer without any claims having been made to them—

(a) the purchaser of the goods so sold shall acquire a good title to those goods; and

(b) no person shall be entitled to recover against the district judge or other officer, or anyone lawfully acting under his authority—

(i) for any sale of the goods, or

(ii) for paying over the proceeds prior to the receipt of a claim to the goods,

unless it is proved that the person from whom recovery is sought had notice, or might by making reasonable inquiry have ascertained, that the goods were not the property of the execution debtor.

(2) Nothing in this section shall affect the right of any claimant, who may prove that at the time of sale he had a title to any goods so seized and sold, to any remedy to which he may be entitled against any person other than the district judge or other officer.

(3) The provisions of this section have effect subject to those of sections 183, 184 and 346 of the Insolvency Act 1986.

Note — Subsection (3) substituted by the Insolvency Act 1986, s.439(2), Sched.14; subs.(1)(b) substituted by the Courts Act 2003, s.109(1), Sched.8, para.273. **9A–695**

Protection of district judge selling goods under execution without notice of claim by third party

For the anomalous position of the district judge in relation to execution, see the commentary to s.123, below. In the county court the "high bailiff" (*i.e.* nowadays, the district judge) has the same liabilities as the sheriff in the High Court. **9A–696**

Section 98 protects the district judge in the same way as s.138B of the SCA 1981 protects the sheriff (see Vol. 1, para. 9A–452 above).

CLAIMS IN RESPECT OF GOODS SEIZED

Effects of warrants of execution

99.—(1) Subject **9A–697**

(a) to subsection (2); and

(b) to section 103(2),

a warrant of execution against goods issued from a county court shall bind the property in the goods of the execution debtor as from the time at which application for the warrant was made to the district judge of the county court.

(2) Such a warrant shall not prejudice the title to any goods of the execution debtor acquired by a person in good faith and for valuable consideration unless he had at the time when he acquired his title—

(a) notice that an application for the issue of a warrant of execution against the goods of the execution debtor had been made to the district judge or a county court and that the warrant issued on the application either—

(i) remained unexecuted in the hands of the district judge of the court from which it was issued; or

          (ii) had been sent for execution to, and received by, the district judge of another county court, and remained unexecuted in the hands of the district judge of that court; or

(b) notice that a writ of fieri facias or other writ of execution by virtue of which the goods of the execution debtor might be seized or attached had been delivered to an enforcement officer or other officer charged with the execution of the writ and remained unexecuted in the hands of that person.

(3) It shall be the duty of the district judge (without fee) on application for a warrant of execution being made to him to endorse on its back the hour, day, month and year when he received the application.

(4) For the purposes of this section—

    (za) "enforcement officer" means an individual who is authorised to act as an enforcement officer under the Courts Act 2003;

(a) "property" means the general property in goods, and not merely a special property;

(b) [Omitted]

(c) a thing shall be treated as done in good faith if it is in fact done honestly whether it is done negligently or not.

Effects of warrants of execution

9A–698   This section corresponds with s.138 of the SCA 1981 (see commentary thereto) which replaced the only section in the Sale of Goods Act 1893 not consolidated into the Sale of Goods Act 1979 because it belonged in a statute concerned with the administration of justice.

    In *Woodland v. Fuller* (1840) 11 Ad. & El. 859; [1835–42] All E.R. Rep. 343, it was held that where goods are sold, the phrase "binds the property in goods" does not prevent the property from passing but constitutes the execution of a charge on the goods.

    See also s.103(2) which deals with execution of warrants outside the jurisdiction of the issuing court.

    With effect from March 15, 2004, subsections (2)(b) and (4) were amended by the Courts Act 2003, s.109(1) and Sched.8, para. 274(3)(a).

Sale of goods to which claim is made

9A–699   **100.**—(1) Where a claim is made to or in respect of any goods seized in execution under process of a county court, the claimant may—

(a) deposit with the bailiff either—

    (i) the amount of the value of the goods claimed; or

    (ii) the sum which the bailiff is allowed to charge as costs for keeping possession of the goods until the decision of the judge can be obtained on the claim; or

(b) give the bailiff in the prescribed manner security for the value of the goods claimed.

(2) For the purpose of this section, the amount of the value of the goods claimed shall, in the case of dispute, be fixed by appraisement,

and where that amount is deposited it shall be paid by the bailiff into court to abide the decision of the judge upon the claim.

(3) Subject to subsection (4), in default of the claimant's complying with this section, the bailiff shall sell the goods as if no such claim had been made, and shall pay into court the proceeds of the sale to abide the decision of the judge.

(4) The goods shall not be sold if the district judge decides that, in all the circumstances, the decision of the judge on the claim made to or in respect of them ought to be awaited.

Sale of goods to which claim is made

9A–700

This section is concerned with situations where there is a dispute as to title to the goods and spells out the action required of the person claiming the goods. Disputes will usually be resolved by interpleader proceedings. See generally CPR Sched.2, CCR O.33 and commentary thereto and s.101, below.

Interpleader by district judge

9A–701

101.—(1) If a claim is made to or in respect of any goods seized in execution under process of a county court, or in respect of the proceeds or value of any such goods, the district judge may, as well before as after any action brought against him, issue a summons calling before the court the party at whose instance the process issued and the party making the claim.

(2) Upon the issue of the summons, any action brought in any county court or other court in respect of the claim or of any damage arising out of the execution of the warrant shall be stayed.

(3) On the hearing of the summons, the judge shall adjudicate upon the claim, and shall also adjudicate between the parties or either of them and the district judge upon any claim to damages arising or capable of arising out of the execution of the warrant by the district judge, and shall make such order in respect of any such claim and the costs of the proceedings as he thinks fit.

Interpleader by district judge

9A–702

Interpleader is a process for determining rival claims to goods. This section enables the circuit judge (not the district judge) to adjudicate upon the rival claims where the goods have been seized in execution. The procedure is governed by CPR Sched.2, CCR O.33 (see commentary thereto). The district judge cannot determine an interpleader relating to execution in the county court (*cf.* the High Court; see CPR Sched.1, RSC O.17) because of his anomalous position as "high bailiff" (see commentary to s.123, below).

Claims for rent where goods seized in execution

9A–703

102.—(1) Section 1 of the Landlord and Tenant Act 1709 shall not apply to goods seized in execution under process of a county court, but the following provisions of this section shall apply in substitution.

(2) The landlord of any tenement in which any goods are seized may claim the rent of the tenement in arrear at the date of the seizure, at any time within the 5 days next following that date, or before the removal of the goods, by delivering to the bailiff or officer making the levy a claim in writing, signed by himself or his agent, stating—

(a) the amount of rent claimed to be in arrear; and

(b) the period in respect of which the rent is due.

(3) Where such a claim is made, the bailiff or officer making the levy shall in addition distrain for the rent so claimed and the cost of the distress, and shall not, within 5 days next after the distress, sell any part of the goods seized, unless—

(a) the goods are of a perishable nature; or

(b) the person whose goods have been seized so requests in writing.

(4) The bailiff shall afterwards sell under the execution and distress such of the goods as will satisfy—

(a) first, the costs of and incidental to the sale;

(b) next, the claim of the landlord not exceeding—

(i) in a case where the tenement is let by the week, 4 weeks' rent;

(ii) in a case where the tenement is let for any other term less than a year, the rent of two terms of payment;

(iii) in any other case, one year's rent; and

(5) If any replevin is made of the goods seized, the bailiff shall nevertheless sell such portion of them as will satisfy the costs of and incidental to the sale under the execution and the amount for which the warrant of execution issued.

(6) In any event the surplus of the sale, if any, and the residue of the goods shall be returned to the execution debtor.

(7) The fees of the district judge and broker for keeping possession, appraisement and sale under any such distress shall be the same as would have been payable if the distress had been an execution of the court, and no other fees shall be demanded or taken in respect thereof.

(8) Nothing in this section affects section 346 of the Insolvency Act 1986.

9A–704   *Note* — Subsection (8) substituted by the Insolvency Act 1986, s.439(2), Sched.14.

Claims for rent where goods seized in execution

9A–705   Subsection (8) of this section refers to s.346 of the Insolvency Act 1986 but this is clearly an error and should be a reference to s.347 which is titled "Distress, etc.".

Sections 6 and 7 of the Landlord and Tenant Act 1709 should be distinguished from s.1 of that Act. The former apply only to cases *between* landlord and tenant, whereas s.1 applies in other cases. Section 102(2) to (8) of the County Courts Act 1984 applies only in substitution for s.1 of the 1709 Act.

On replevin see s.144 and Sched.1, below.

EXECUTION OUT OF JURISDICTION OF COURT

Execution out of jurisdiction of court

9A–706   **103.**—(1) Where a warrant of execution has been issued from a county court (hereafter in this section referred to as a "home court") against the goods of any person and the goods are out of the jurisdiction of that court, the district judge of that court may send the warrant of execution to the district judge of any other county court

2448

within the jurisdiction of which the goods are or are believed to be, with a warrant endorsed on it or annexed to it requiring execution of the original warrant.

(2) The original warrant shall bind the property in goods of the execution debtor which are within the jurisdiction of the court to which it is sent as from the time when it is received by the district judge of that court.

(3) It shall be the duty of the district judge of the court to which the warrant is sent (without fee) on receipt of the warrant to endorse on its back the hour, day, month and year when he received it.

(4) On the receipt of the warrant, the district judge of the other county court shall act in all respects as if the original warrant of execution had been issued by the court of which he is district judge and shall within the prescribed time—

    (a) report to the district judge of the home court what he has done in the execution of the warrant; and

    (b) pay over all moneys received in pursuance of the warrant.

(5) Where a warrant of execution is sent by the district judge of a home court to the district judge of another court for execution under this section, that other court shall have the same power as the home court of staying the execution under section 88 as respects any goods within the jurisdiction of that other court.

(6) Rules of court may make provision for the suspension of any judgment or order, on terms, in connection with any warrant issued with respect to any instalment payable under the judgment or order.

Note — Subsection (6) added by the Courts and Legal Services Act 1990, s.125(2), Sched.17, para. 16. Amended by the Civil Procedure Act 1997, Sched.2, para. 2(2).   **9A–707**

Execution out of jurisdiction of court

The judge of one county court has no authority to order execution in the area of **9A–708** another county court because the jurisdiction of county courts is limited geographically. This section overcomes the difficulties this presents by adopting a procedure of reciprocal enforcement between county courts.

The functions of the district judge under s.103 are discharged by the "court officer" pursuant to CPR Sched.2, CCR O.26, r.1(1A).

Information as to writs and warrants of execution

104.—(1) Where a writ against the goods of any person issued **9A–709** from the High Court is delivered to an enforcement officer who is under a duty to execute the writ or to a sheriff, then on demand from the district judge of a county court that person shall—

    (a) in the case of an enforcement officer, by writing signed by that officer or a person acting under his authority, and

    (b) in the case of a sheriff, by writing signed by any clerk in the officer of the under-sheriff,

inform the district judge of the precise time the writ was delivered to him.

(2) A bailiff of a county court shall on demand show his warrant to any enforcement officer, any person acting under the authority of an enforcement officer and any sheriff's officer.

(3) Any writing purporting to be signed as mentioned in subsection (1) and the endorsement on any warrant issued from a county court shall respectively be sufficient justification to any district judge, or enforcement officer or sheriff, acting on it.

(4) In this section "enforcement officer" means an individual who is authorised to act as an enforcement officer under the Courts Act 2003.

Information as to writs and warrants of execution

9A–710   The purpose of this section is to facilitate the exchange of information concerning the enforcement of judgments between county courts and the High Court. This section was substituted by the Courts Act 2003, s.109(1) and Sched.8, para. 275, with effect from March 15, 2004.

Execution in county court of judgments and orders of High Court

9A–711   **105.** [*Repealed by the Courts and Legal Services Act 1990, Sched.20*].

ENFORCEMENT IN HIGH COURT OF JUDGMENTS AND ORDERS OF COUNTY COURTS

Transfer of judgments and orders to High Court

9A–712   **106.** [*Repealed by the Courts and Legal Services Act 1990, Sched.20*].

RECEIVERS AND ATTACHMENT OF DEBTS

Receivers

9A–713   **107.**—(1) The power of the county court to appoint a receiver by way of equitable execution shall operate in relation to all legal estates and interests in land.

(2) The said power may be exercised in relation to an estate or interest in land whether or not a charge has been imposed on that land under section 1 of the Charging Orders Act 1979 for the purpose of enforcing the judgment, decree, order or award in question, and the said power shall be in addition to and not in derogation of any power of any court to appoint a receiver in proceedings for enforcing such a charge.

(3) Where an order under section 1 of the Charging Orders Act 1979 imposing a charge for the purpose of enforcing a judgment, decree, order or award has been registered under section 6 of the Land Charges Act 1972, subsection (4) of that section (which provides that, amongst other things, an order appointing a receiver and any proceedings pursuant to the order or in obedience to it, shall be void against a purchaser unless the order is for the time being registered under that section) shall not apply to an order appointing a receiver made either in proceedings for enforcing the charge or by way of equitable execution of the judgment, decree, order or award or, as the case may be, of so much of it as requires payment of moneys secured by the charge.

Receivers

9A–714   The procedure for the appointment of a receiver is governed by CPR, Pt 69 (Court's Power to Appoint Receiver).

Attachment of debts

108.—(1) Subject to any order for the time being in force under **9A–715** subsection (4), this section applies to any deposit account, and any withdrawable share account, with a deposit-taker.

(2) In determining whether, for the purposes of the jurisdiction of the county court to attach debts for the purpose of satisfying judgments or orders for the payment of money, a sum standing to the credit of a person in an account to which this section applies is a sum due or accruing to that person and, as such, attachable in accordance with rules of court, any condition mentioned in subsection (3) which applies to the account shall be disregarded.

(3) Those conditions are—

(a) any condition that notice is required before any money or share is withdrawn;

(b) any condition that a personal application must be made before any money or share is withdrawn;

(c) any condition that a deposit book or share-account book must be produced before any money or share is withdrawn; or

(d) any other prescribed condition.

(4) The Lord Chancellor may by order make such provision as he thinks fit, by way of amendment of this section or otherwise, for all or any of the following purposes, namely—

(a) including in, or excluding from, the accounts to which this section applies accounts of any description specified in the order;

(b) excluding from the accounts to which this section applies all accounts with any particular deposit-taker so specified or with any deposit-taker of a description so specified.

(5) An order under subsection (4) shall be made by statutory instrument subject to annulment in pursuance of a resolution of either House of Parliament.

Note —Amended by the Civil Procedure Act 1997, Sched.2, para. 2(2). Subsections **9A–716** (1) and (4)(b) amended by the Financial Services and Markets Act 2000 (Consequential Amendments and Repeals) Order 2001 (S.I. 2001 No. 3649) art.294.

Attachment of debts

This section re-enacts amendments made to the CCA. 1959 by the SCA. 1981. The **9A–717** purpose of the section is to enable attachment of any deposit account or withdrawable share account of any deposit-taking institution. Deposit-taking institutions include banks, the National Savings Bank, building societies, trustee savings banks, and even credit unions. Proceedings for orders for the attachment of debts, formerly known as "garnishee orders" but now known as "third party debt orders", are governed by CPR, Pt 72.

Note the provisions for amendment in subss. (4) and (5). The section can be compared with s.40 of the SCA 1981.

It is not possible under this section to attach wages or salary but see instead the Attachment of Earnings Act 1971 and CPR Sched.2, CCR O.27.

Administrative and clerical expenses of garnishees

109.—(1) Where an interim third party debt order made in the **9A–718**

exercise of the jurisdiction mentioned in subsection (2) of the preceding section is served on a deposit-taker, it may, subject to the provisions of this section, deduct from the relevant debt or debts an amount not exceeding the prescribed sum towards its administrative and clerical expenses in complying with the order; and the right to make a deduction under this subsection shall be exercisable as from the time the interim third party debt order is served on it.

(1A) In subsection (1) "the relevant debt or debts", in relation to an interim third party debt order served on a deposit-taker, means the amount, as at the time the order is served on it, of the debt or debts of which the whole or a part is expressed to be attached by the order.

(1B) A deduction may be made under subsection (1) in a case where the amount referred to in subsection (1A) is insufficient to cover both the amount of the deduction and the amount of the judgment debt and costs in respect of which the attachment was made, notwithstanding that the benefit of the attachment to the creditor is reduced as a result of the deduction.

(2) An amount may not in pursuance of subsection (1) be deducted or, as the case may be, retained in a case where by virtue of section 346 of the Insolvency Act 1986 or section 325 of the Companies Act 1948 or otherwise, the creditor is not entitled to retain the benefit of the attachment.

(3) In this section "prescribed" means prescribed by an order made by the Lord Chancellor.

(4) An order under this section—

    (a) may make different provision for different cases;

    (b) without prejudice to the generality of paragraph (a) may prescribe sums differing according to the amount due under the judgment or order to be satisfied;

    (c) may provide for this section not to apply to deposit-taker of any prescribed description.

(5) Any such order shall be made by statutory instrument subject to annulment in pursuance of a resolution of either House of Parliament.

9A–719   *Note*—Amended by the Administration of Justice Act 1985, ss.52 and 67(2), Sched.8; and the Insolvency Act 1986, s.439(2), Sched.14. Subsections (1), (1A) and (4)(c) were amended by the Financial Services and Markets Act 2000 (Consequential Amendments and Repeals) Order 2001 (S.I. 2001 No. 3649), art.295. In subss.(1) and (1A), with effect from March 23, 2002, "interim third party debt order" was substituted for "order nisi" by the Civil Procedure (Modification of Enactments) Order 2002 (S.I. 2002 No. 439); see further CPR Pt 72 (Third Party Debt Orders).

Administrative and clerical expenses of garnishees

9A–720   The purpose of this section is to enable the "deposit-taking institution" (see s.108) to recover, from the judgment debtor's account, a "prescribed sum" towards its expenses of complying with the garnishee order. The "prescribed sum" is varied from time to time by statutory instrument and is currently £55 (see Attachment of Debts (Expenses) Order (S.I. 1996 No. 3098)).

MISCELLANEOUS PROVISIONS AS TO ENFORCEMENT OF JUDGMENTS AND

ORDERS

Penalty for non-attendance on judgment summons

9A–721   **110.**—(1) If a debtor summoned to attend a county court by a judgment summons fails to attend on the day and at the time fixed for any hearing of the summons, the judge may adjourn or further adjourn the summons to a specified time on a specified day and order the debtor to attend at that time on that day.

(2) If—

    (a) a debtor, having been ordered under subsection (1) to attend at a specified time on a specified day, fails to do so;

    (b) [omitted]

the judge may make an order committing him to prison for a period not exceeding 14 days in respect of the failure or refusal.

(3) In any case where the judge has power to make an order of committal under subsection (2) for failure to attend, he may in lieu of or in addition to making that order, order the debtor to be arrested and brought before the court either forthwith or at such time as the judge may direct.

(4) A debtor shall not be committed to prison under subsection (2) for having failed to attend as required by an order under subsection (1) unless there was paid to him at the time of the service of the judgment summons, or paid or tendered to him at the time of the service of the order, such sum in respect of his expenses as may be prescribed for the purposes of this section.

(5) The judge may at any time revoke an order committing a person to prison under this section and, if he is already in custody, order his discharge.

Penalty for non-attendance on judgment summons

"Judgment summons" is defined in s.147. Under s.5 of the Debtors Act 1869, a judge, sitting in open court, can commit to prison, for a term not exceeding six weeks, where it is proved that the judgment debtor has, or has had since the date of the judgment, the means to pay and has refused or neglected to do so. The procedure is governed by CPR Sched.2, CCR O.28 (see generally the commentary thereto). The judgment summons was once a very common method of enforcement but its availability was restricted by s.11 of the AJA 1970.

This section deals not with committal for failure to pay the judgment debt but with committal for failure to attend the hearing of the judgment summons. As to securing the debtor's attendance, see CPR Sched.2, CCR O.28, r.4.

On travelling expenses (see s.110(4)) the sum prescribed is "a sum reasonably sufficient to cover [the judgment debtor's] expenses" (see CPR Sched.2, CCR O.28, r.2(4) on tendering such expenses on service of the judgment summons, and CPR Sched.2, CCR O.28, r.10(2) on recovery of the sum).

Paragraph (b) was omitted from subs.(2) by the Civil Procedure (Modification of Enactments) Order 2002 (S.I. 2002 No. 439) with effect from March 23, 2002.

9A–722

Provisions as to warrants of possession

111.—(1) For the purpose of executing a warrant to give possession of any premises, it shall not be necessary to remove any goods from those premises.

(2) The duration of any warrant of possession issued by a county court to enforce a judgment or order for the recovery of land or for the delivery of possession of land shall be such as may be fixed by or in accordance with rules of court.

9A–723

Note —Amended by the Civil Procedure Act 1997, Sched.2, para. 2(2).

9A–724

9A–725   The procedure on warrants of possession is prescribed by CPR Sched.2, CCR O.26, r.17.

PART VI

ADMINISTRATION ORDERS

Power to make administration order
9A–726   112.—(1) Where a debtor—

(a) is unable to pay forthwith the amount of a judgment obtained against him, and

(b) alleges that his whole indebtedness amounts to a sum not exceeding the county court limit, inclusive of the debt for which the judgment was obtained;

a county court may make an order providing for the administration of his estate.

(2) In this Part of this Act

"administration order" means an order under this section; and

"the appropriate court", in relation to an administration order, means the court which has the power to make the order.

(3) Before an administration order is made, the appropriate court shall, in accordance with rules of court, send to every person whose name the debtor has notified to the appropriate court as being a creditor of his, a notice that that person's name has been so notified.

(4) So long as an administration order is in force, a creditor whose name is included in the schedule to the order shall not, without the leave of the appropriate court, be entitled to present, or join in, a bankruptcy petition against the debtor unless—

(a) his name was so notified; and

(b) the debt by virtue of which he presents, or joins in, the petition, exceeds £1,500; and

(c) the notice given under subsection (3) was received by the creditor within 28 days immediately preceding the day on which the petition is presented.

(5) An administration order shall not be invalid by reason only that the total amount of the debts is found at any time to exceed the county court limit, but in that case the court may, if it thinks fit, set aside the order.

(6) An administration order may provide for the payment of the debts of the debtor by instalments or otherwise, and either in full or to such extent as appears practicable to the court under the circumstances of the case, and subject to any conditions as to his future earnings or income which the court may think just.

(7) The Secretary of State may by regulations increase or reduce the sum for the time being specified in subsection (4)(b); but no such increase in the sum so specified shall affect any case in which the bankruptcy petition was presented before the coming into force of the increase.

(8) The power to make regulations under subsection (7) shall be exercisable by statutory instrument; and no such regulations shall be made unless a draft of them has been approved by resolution of each House of Parliament.

Note —Amended by the Insolvency Act 1985, s.220 and by the Civil Procedure Act **9A–727** 1997, Sched.2, para. 2(2).

Power to make administration order

Substantial amendments were made to s.112 by s.13 of the Courts and Legal Ser- **9A–728** vices Act 1990. In addition to amending s.112, new ss.112A and 112B were inserted into the CCA 1984. However, these amendments have not yet been brought into force and it is now uncertain whether they ever will be. Accordingly, the text is reproduced here in its unamended form as currently in force.

Detailed rules on administration orders are in CPR Sched.2, CCR O.39.

Administration orders are a means of consolidating debts where there are multiple debt problems. The effect of an order is to release the debtor from the burden of dealing with the debts (and arrangements with creditors) on an individual basis. The debtor under an administration order makes regular payments to the court which are then distributed among the scheduled creditors. The total debts must not exceed £5,000.

Notice of order and proof of debts

113. Where an administration order has been made— **9A–729**
    (a) notice of the order—
        (i) [...]
        (ii) shall be posted in the office of the county court for the district in which the debtor resides, and
        (iii) shall be sent to every person whose name the debtor has notified to the appropriate court as being a creditor of his or who has proved;
    (b) any creditor of the debtor, on proof of his debt before the district judge, shall be entitled to be scheduled as a creditor of the debtor for the amount of his proof;
    (c) any creditor may object in the prescribed manner to any debt scheduled, or to the manner in which payment is directed to be made by instalments;
    (d) any person who, after the date of the order, becomes a creditor of the debtor shall, on proof of his debt before the district judge, be scheduled as a creditor of the debtor for the amount of his proof, but shall not be entitled to any dividend under the order until the creditors who are scheduled as having been creditors before the date of the order have been paid to the extent provided by the order.

Note —Amended by the Administration of Justice Act 1985, s.67(2), Sched.8. **9A–730**

Notice of order and proof of debts

"Dividend" is the term used for the sums distributed to scheduled creditors. The **9A–731** practice is to wait until a sufficient sum has been paid into court to justify payment of dividends (see CPR Sched.2, CCR O.39, r.17).

Objection by a creditor before the order is made is governed by CPR Sched.2, CCR O.39, r.6, and objection after the order by CPR Sched.2, CCR O.39, r.10.

Effect of administration order

114.—(1) Subject to sections 115 and 116, when an administration **9A–732**

order is made, no creditor shall have any remedy against the person or property of the debtor in respect of any debt—

      (a) of which the debtor notified the appropriate court before the administration order was made; or

      (b) which has been scheduled to the order,

except with the leave of the appropriate court, and on such terms as that court may impose.

(2) Subject to subsection (3), any county court in which proceedings are pending against the debtor in respect of any debt so notified or scheduled shall, on receiving notice of the administration order, stay the proceedings, but may allow costs already incurred by the creditor, and such costs may, on application, be added to the debt.

(3) The requirement to stay proceedings shall not operate as a requirement that a county court in which proceedings in bankruptcy against the debtor are pending shall stay those proceedings.

9A–733   *Note* —Amended by the Civil Procedure Act 1997, Sched.2, para. 2(2).

Effect of administration order
9A–734   See commentary to s.116, below.

Execution by district judge

9A–735   **115.**—(1) Where it appears to the district judge of the appropriate court at any time while an administration order is in force that property of the debtor exceeds in value the minimum amount, he shall, at the request of any creditor, and without fee, issue execution against the debtor's goods.

(1A) In subsection (1) above "the minimum amount" means £50 or such other amount as the Lord Chancellor may by order specify instead of that amount or the amount for the time being specified in such an order; and an order under this subsection shall be made by statutory instrument subject to annulment in pursuance of a resolution of either House of Parliament.

(2) Section 89 applies on an execution under this section as it applies on an execution under Part V.

9A–736   *Note* —Amended by the Insolvency Act 1985, s.22.

Execution by district judge
9A–737   See commentary to s.116, below.

Right of landlord to distrain notwithstanding order

9A–738   **116.** A landlord or other person to whom any rent is due from a debtor in respect of whom an administration order is made, may at any time, either before or after the date of the order, distrain upon the goods or effects of the debtor for the rent due to him from the debtor, with this limitation, that if the distress for rent is levied after the date of the order, it shall be available only for six months' rent accrued due prior to the date of the order and shall not be available for rent payable in respect of any period subsequent to the date when the distress was levied, but the landlord or other person to whom the rent be due from the debtor may prove under the order for the surplus due for which the distress may not have been available.

Right of landlord to distrain notwithstanding order

An important protection afforded to the judgment debtor by an administration order is that no creditor may, without leave of the court and on conditions imposed by the court, take any enforcement action against the debtor. Unless the administration order is revoked under CPR Sched.2, O.39, r.14, a creditor will not get leave to issue execution for the purpose of the order is to secure equal treatment of creditors and proportionate distribution among them (*Re Frank* [1894] 1 Q.B. 9).

9A–739

Two important exceptions to the non-execution rule are:

(1) that a district judge, who considers that the judgment debtor has goods exceeding £50 in value (after discounting protected goods—see s.89) must, at the request of a creditor and without fee, levy execution and distribute the proceeds among all the scheduled creditors, and

(2) a landlord may distrain for rent in accordance with s.116.

Appropriation of money paid under order and discharge of order

117.—(1) Money paid into court under an administration order shall be appropriated—

9A–740

    (a) first in satisfaction of the costs of administration (which shall not exceed 10 pence in the pound on the total amount of the debts); and

    (b) then in liquidation of debts in accordance with the order.

(2) Where the amount received is sufficient to pay—

    (a) each creditor scheduled to the order to the extent provided by the order;

    (b) the costs of the plaintiff in the action in respect of which the order was made; and

    (c) the costs of the administration,

the order shall be superseded, and the debtor shall be discharged from his debts to the scheduled creditors.

PART VII

COMMITTALS

Power to commit for contempt

118.—(1) If any person—

9A–741

    (a) wilfully insults the judge of a county court, or any juror or witness, or any officer of the court during his sitting or attendance in court, or in going to or returning from the court; or

    (b) wilfully interrupts the proceedings of a county court or otherwise misbehaves in court;

any officer of the court, with or without the assistance of any other person, may, by order of the judge, take the offender into custody and detain him until the rising of the court, and the judge may, if he thinks fit,—

    (i) make an order committing the offender for a specified period not exceeding one month to prison; or

>   (ii) impose upon the offender, for every offence, a fine of an amount not exceeding £2,500, or may both make such an order and impose such a fine.

(2) The judge may at any time revoke an order committing a person to prison under this section, and if he is already in custody, order his discharge.

(3) A district judge, assistant district judge or deputy district judge shall have the same powers under this section in relation to proceedings before him as a judge.

9A–742   *Note* —Amended by the Statute Law (Repeals) Act 1986; the Courts and Legal Services Act 1990, s.74; and the Criminal Justice Act 1991, s.17(3), Sched.4.

Power to commit for contempt

9A–743   Section 118 is concerned with contempt "in the face of the court" and does not apply, for example, to committal for breach of an order or undertaking (as to which see CCR O.29). However, the time-honoured expression "in the face of the court" is not literally construed and includes contempt "in going to or returning from the court". See *Manchester City Council v. McCann* [1999] 2 W.L.R. 590, CA.

Generally, a county court can commit for a fixed term not exceeding two years (Contempt of Court Act 1981; County Courts (Penalties for Contempt) Act 1983) but specific statutory provisions (such as s.118) often provide a lesser maximum.

Contempt of court in connection with county court proceedings which was neither contempt in the face of the court nor disobedience of an order of a county court is punishable only by an order of committal made in the Queen's Bench Division (In *Re G (A Child) (Contempt: Committal)*, *The Times*, May 5, 2003, CA).

The procedure for dealing with a contempt in the face of the court is set out in Part II of Practice Direction—Committal Applications which can be found in Vol. 1 at scpd52.7. This PD is clearly distilled from a series of Court of Appeal decisions and should be regarded as authoritative.It is not a breach of Art 6 ECHR for a judge to deal with a contempt of his own court (*Wilkinson v. S & anor* [2003] 1 W.L.R. 1254) provided it is dealt with pursuant to the PD.

Issue and execution of orders of committal

9A–744   **119.**—(1) Whenever any order or warrant for the committal of any person to prison is made or issued by a county court (whether in pursuance of this or any other Act or of rules of court), the order or warrant shall be directed to the district judge of the court, who shall thereby be empowered to take the body of the person against whom the order is made or warrant issued.

(2) It shall be the duty of every constable within his jurisdiction to assist in the execution of every such order or warrant.

(3) The governor of the prison mentioned in any such order or warrant shall be bound to receive and keep the person mentioned in it until he is lawfully discharged.

9A–745   *Note* —Amended by the Civil Procedure Act 1997, Sched.2, para. 2(2).

Issue and execution of orders of committal

9A–746   This section is of general application and covers all situations in which committal to prison is a remedy available in the county court (see further CPR Sched.2, CCR O.29).

Prisons to which committals may be made

9A–747   **120.** Any person committed to prison by the judge of any county court, in pursuance of this or any other Act or of rules of court, shall be committed to such prison as may from time to time be directed in the case of that court by order of the Secretary of State.

Note —Amended by the Civil Procedure Act 1997, Sched.2, para. 2(2). **9A–748**

Power of judge to order discharge

121. If at any time it appears to the satisfaction of a judge of a **9A–749** county court that any debtor arrested or confined in prison by order of the court is unable from any cause to pay any sum recovered against him (whether by way of satisfaction of a claim or counterclaim or by way of costs or otherwise), or any instalments thereof, and ought to be discharged, the judge may order his discharge upon such terms (including liability to re-arrest if the terms are not complied with) as the judge thinks fit.

Execution of committal orders out of jurisdiction of court

122.—(1) Where any order or warrant for the committal of any **9A–750** person to prison has been made or issued (whether in pursuance of this or any other Act or of county court rules) by a county court (hereafter in this section referred to as a "home court") and that person is out of the jurisdiction of that court, the district judge may send the order or warrant to the district judge of any other county court within the jurisdiction of which that person is or is believed to be, with a warrant endorsed on it or annexed to it requiring execution of the original order or warrant.

(2) On receipt of the warrant, the district judge of the other county court shall act in all respects as if the original order or warrant had been issued by the court of which he is district judge and shall within the prescribed time—

    (a) report to the district judge of the home court what he has done in the execution of the order or warrant; and

    (b) pay over all moneys received in pursuance of the order or warrant.

(3) Where a person is apprehended under the order or warrant, he shall be forthwith conveyed, in custody of the officer apprehending him, to the prison of the court within the jurisdiction of which he was apprehended and kept there, unless sooner discharged by law, until the expiration of the period mentioned in the order or warrant.

(4) It shall be the duty of every constable within his jurisdiction to assist in the execution of every such order or warrant.

(5) Where an order of committal—

    (a) under the Debtors Act 1869; or

    (b) under section 110,

is sent by the district judge of a home court to the district judge of another court for execution under this section, the judge of that other court shall have the same powers to order the debtor's discharge as the judge of the home court would have under section 110 or 121.

Execution of committal orders out of jurisdiction of court

The jurisdiction of a county court is limited geographically. This section overcomes **9A–751** the difficulties this presents by adopting a procedure of reciprocal execution of committal orders between county courts. This section parallels the power of execution out of the jurisdiction of a county court contained in s.103.

PART VIII

RESPONSIBILITY AND PROTECTION OF OFFICERS

District judge to have same responsibilities as sheriff

9A-752   **123.** Every district judge shall be responsible for the acts and defaults of himself and of the bailiffs appointed to assist him in like manner as the sheriff of any county in England or Wales is responsible for the acts and defaults of himself and his officers.

District judge to have same responsibilities as sheriff

9A-753   Section 123 in its present form (March 1998) is an historical anomaly and is due for repeal. Under the County Courts Act 1846 the "high bailiff" was responsible for the acts and defaults of bailiffs in the same way as, in the High Court, the sheriff is responsible for the acts and defaults of sheriff's officers. Subsequently, the office of high bailiff was merged with that of the county court registrar. The office of "registrar" was abolished by s.74 of the Courts and Legal Services Act 1990 and replaced by the "district judge". Hence the anomaly that the district judge is now liable for the acts and defaults of county court bailiffs (see also s.124). For the duties of the sheriff, see Vol. 1, para. sc45.1.10.

For discussion of the liabilities of the "high bailiff" (see above) see *Smith v. Pritchard* (1849) 8 K.B. 565; (1849) L.J.C.P. 53; and *Burton v. Le Gros* (1864) 34 L.J.Q.B. 91.

Liability of bailiff for neglect to levy execution

9A-754   **124.**—(1) Where a bailiff of a county court, being employed to levy any execution against goods, loses the opportunity of levying the execution by reason of neglect, connivance or omission, any party aggrieved thereby may complain to the judge of that court.

(2) On any such complaint the judge, if the neglect, connivance or omission is proved to his satisfaction, shall order the bailiff to pay such damages as it appears that the complainant has sustained by reason of it, not exceeding in any case the sum for which the execution issued.

Liability of bailiff for neglect to levy execution

9A-755   The purpose and terms of this section are self-explanatory. For the procedure see CPR Sched.2, CCR O.34, r.1.

Irregularity in executing warrants

9A-756   **125.**—(1) No officer of a county court in executing any warrant of a court, and no person at whose instance any such warrant is executed, shall be deemed a trespasser by reason of any irregularity or informality—

(a) in any proceeding on the validity of which the warrant depends; or

(b) in the form of the warrant or in the mode of executing it;

but any person aggrieved may bring an action for any special damage sustained by him by reason of the irregularity or informality against the person guilty of it.

(2) No costs shall be recovered in such an action unless the damages awarded exceed £2.

Actions against bailiffs acting under warrants

9A-757   **126.**—(1) No action shall be commenced against any bailiff for anything done in obedience to a warrant issued by the district judge, unless—

- (a) a demand for inspection of the warrant and for a copy of it is made or left at the office of the bailiff by the party intending to bring the action, or his legal representative or agent; and
- (b) the bailiff refuses or neglects to comply with the demand within six days after it is made.

(2) The demand must be in writing and signed by the person making it.

(3) If an action is commenced against a bailiff in a case where such a demand has been made and not complied with, judgment shall be given for the bailiff if the warrant is produced or proved at the trial, notwithstanding any defect of jurisdiction or other irregularity in the warrant; but the district judge who issued the warrant may be joined as a defendant in the action, and if the district judge is so joined and judgment is given against him, the costs to be recovered by the plaintiff against the district judge shall include such costs as the plaintiff is liable to pay to the bailiff.

(4) In this section (except in paragraph (a) of subsection (1)) "bailiff" includes any person acting by the order and in aid of a bailiff.

Note —Amended by the Courts and Legal Services Act 1990, s.125(3), Sched.18. **9A–758**

Actions against bailiffs acting under warrants
See commentary to s.123 for an explanation of how the district judge became **9A–759**
included in this provision. Section 147 defines "bailiff" to include "registrar" (now to be construed as "district judge" (Courts and Legal Services Act 1990, s.74)). It follows that the district judge is protected by s.126.

Warrants evidence of authority

127. In any action commenced against a person for anything done **9A–760**
in pursuance of this Act, the production of the warrant of the county court shall be deemed sufficient proof of the authority of the court previous to the issue of the warrant.

Part IX

Miscellaneous and General

Financial provisions

Fees

128. [*Repealed by the Courts Act 2003 with effect from January 1, 2005,* **9A–761**
and replaced by s.92 of that Act.]

Enforcement of fines

129. Payment of any fine imposed by any court under this Act may **9A–762**
be enforced upon the order of the judge in like manner—

- (a) as payment of a debt adjudged by the court to be paid may be enforced under this Act; or

(b) as payment of a sum adjudged to be paid by a conviction of a magistrates' court may be enforced under the Magistrates' Courts Act 1980 (disregarding section 81(1) of that Act).

Payment and application of fees, fines, etc.

9A–763   130.—(1) Subject to subsection (2), all fees, forfeitures and fines payable under this Act and any penalty payable to an officer of a county court under any other Act shall be paid to officers designated by the Lord Chancellor and dealt with by them in such manner as the Lord Chancellor, after consultation with the Treasury, may direct.

(2) Subsection (1) does not apply to fines imposed on summary conviction or to so much of a fine as is applicable under section 55(4) to indemnify a party injured.

(3) The Lord Chancellor, with the concurrence of the Treasury, shall from time to time make such rules as he thinks fit for securing the balances and other sums of money in the hands of any officers of a county court, and for the due accounting for and application of those balances and sums.

Appointment of auditors and other officers

9A–764   131. The Lord Chancellor may, subject to the consent of the Treasury as to numbers and salaries, appoint as officers in his department such auditors and other officers as he may consider necessary for the purpose of controlling the accounts of county courts.

Payment of salaries and expenses

9A–765   132. There shall be paid out of money provided by Parliament—

(a) all salaries, remuneration and other sums payable under Part I of this Act or under section 131;

(b) the expenses of supplying the courts and offices with law and office books and stationery and postage stamps;

(c) expenses incurred in conveying to prison persons committed by the courts; and

(d) all other expenses arising out of any jurisdiction for the time being conferred on the courts of any officer of the courts.

SUMMONSES AND OTHER DOCUMENTS

Proof of service of summonses, etc.

9A–766   133.—(1) Where any summons or other process issued from a county court is served by an officer of a court, the service may be proved by a certificate in a prescribed form showing the fact and mode of the service.

(2) Any officer of a court wilfully and corruptly giving a false certificate under subsection (1) in respect of the service of a summons or other process shall be guilty of an offence and on conviction thereof, shall be removed from office and shall be liable—

(a) on conviction on indictment, to imprisonment for any term not exceeding 2 years; or

(b) on summary conviction, to imprisonment for any term not exceeding 6 months or to a fine not exceeding the statutory maximum or to both such imprisonment and fine.

Note — Subsection (1) amended by the Civil Procedure (Modification of Enact- **9A–767** ments) Order 1998 (S.I. 1998 No. 2940), art.6(e).

Proof of service of summonses, etc.
  On service of documents generally, CPR Pt 6. As to certification of service, see CPR, **9A–768** r.6.10.

Summonses and other process to be under seal
  134. [*Omitted*]   **9A–769**

Note —Omitted from the Civil Procedure (Modification of Enactments) Order 1998 **9A–770** (S.I. 1998 No. 2940), art.6(f).

Penalty for falsely pretending to act under authority of court
  135. Any person who—   **9A–771**
  (a) delivers or causes to be delivered to any other person any paper falsely purporting to be a copy of any summons or other process or a county court, knowing it to be false; or
  (b) acts or professes to act under any false colour or pretence of the process or authority of a county court;
shall be guilty of an offence and shall for each offence be liable on conviction on indictment to imprisonment for a term not exceeding 7 years.

Penalty for falsely representing document to have been issued from county court
  136.—(1) It shall not be lawful to deliver or cause to be delivered **9A–772** to any person any document which was not issued under the authority of a county court but which, by reason of its form or contents or both, has the appearance of having been issued under such authority.

  (2) If any person contravenes this section, he shall for each offence be liable on summary conviction to a fine of an amount not exceeding level 3 on the standard scale.

  (3) Nothing in this section shall be taken to prejudice section 135.

Lessee to give notice of summons for recovery of land
  137.—(1) Every lessee to whom there is delivered any summons is- **9A–773** sued from a county court for the recovery of land demised to or held by him, or to whose knowledge any such summons comes, shall forthwith give notice of the summons to his lessor or his bailiff or receiver.

  (2) If a lessee fails to give notice as required by subsection (1), he shall be liable to forfeit to the person of whom he holds the land an amount equal to the value of 3 years' improved or rack rent of the land to be recovered by action in any county court or other court having jurisdiction in respect of claims for such an amount.

LEGISLATION

Provisions as to forfeiture for non-payment of rent

9A–774   138.—(1) This section has effect where a lessor is proceeding by action in a county court (being an action in which the county court has jurisdiction) to enforce against a lessee a right of re-entry or forfeiture in respect of any land for non-payment of rent.

(2) If the lessee pays into court or to the lessor not less than 5 clear days before the return day all the rent in arrear and the costs of the action, the action shall cease, and the lessee shall hold the land according to the lease without any new lease.

(3) If—

    (a) the action does not cease under subsection (2); and

    (b) the court at the trial is satisfied that the lessor is entitled to enforce the right of re-entry or forfeiture,

the court shall order possession of the land to be given to the lessor at the expiration of such period, not being less than 4 weeks from the date of the order, as the court thinks fit, unless within that period the lessee pays into court or to the lessor all the rent in arrear and costs of the action.

(4) The court may extend the period specified under subsection (3) at any time before possession of the land is recovered in pursuance of the order under that subsection.

(5) [...] if—

    (a) within the period specified in the order; or

    (b) within that period as extended under subsection (4),

the lessee pays into court or to the lessor—

    (i) all the rent in arrear; and

    (ii) the costs of the action,

he shall hold the land according to the lease without any new lease.

(6) Subsection (2) shall not apply where the lessor is proceeding in the same action to enforce a right of re-entry or forfeiture on any other ground as well as for non-payment of rent, or to enforce any other claim as well as the right of re-entry or forfeiture and the claim for arrears of rent.

(7) If the lessee does not—

    (a) within the period specified in the order; or

    (b) within that period as extended under subsection (4),

pay into court or to the lessor—

    (i) all the rent in arrear; and

    (ii) the costs of the action,

the order shall be enforceable in the prescribed manner and so long as the order remains unreversed the lessee shall subject to subsections (8) and (9A) be barred from all relief.

(8) The extension under subsection (4) of a period fixed by a court shall not be treated as relief from which the lessee is barred by subsection (7) if he fails to pay into court or to the lessor all the rent in arrear and the costs of the action within that period.

(9) Where the court extends a period under subsection (4) at a time when—

(a) that period has expired; and

(b) a warrant has been issued for the possession of the land, the court shall suspend the warrant for the extended period; and, if, before the expiration of the extended period, the lessee pays into court or to the lessor all the rent in arrear and all the costs of the action, the court shall cancel the warrant.

(9A) Where the lessor recovers possession of the land at any time after the making of the order under subsection (3) (whether as a result of the enforcement of the order or otherwise) the lessee may, at any time within six months from the date on which the lessor recovers possession, apply to the court for relief; and on any such application the court may, if it thinks fit, grant to the lessee such relief, subject to such terms and conditions, as it thinks fit.

(9B) Where the lessee is granted relief on an application under subsection (9A) he shall hold the land according to the lease without any new lease.

(9C) An application under subsection (9A) may be made by a person with an interest under a lease of the land derived (whether immediately or otherwise) from the lessee's interest therein in like manner as if he were the lessee; and on any such application the court may make an order which (subject to such terms and conditions as the court thinks fit) vests the land in such a person, as lessee of the lessor, for the remainder of the term of the lease under which he has any such interest as aforesaid, or for any lesser term.

In this subsection any reference to the land includes a reference to a part of the land.

(10) Nothing in this section or section 139 shall be taken to affect—

(a) the power of the court to make any order which it would otherwise have power to make as respects a right of re-entry or forfeiture on any ground other than non-payment of rent; or

(b) section 146(4) of the Law of Property Act 1925 (relief against forfeiture).

Note—See 3A–304 to 3A–308.7.	**9A–775**
General note See 3A–304 to 3A–308.7.	**9A–776**
Parties in forfeiture proceedings See 3A–304 to 3A–308.7.	**9A–777**
"lessor" "lessee" "lease" See 3A–304 to 3A–308.7.	**9A–778**
Service of summons See 3A–304 to 3A–308.7.	**9A–779**
"not less than 5 clear days before the return day" (subs.(2)) See 3A–304 to 3A–308.7.	**9A–780**

Lessee paying into court or to lessor (subss. (2), (3), (5), (7), (8) & (9))

9A–781   See 3A–304 to 3A–308.7.

"the court shall order possession" (subs.(3))

9A–782   See 3A–304 to 3A–308.7.

Possession to be given at expiration of specified period

9A–783   See 3A–304 to 3A–308.7.

"lessee pays ... all the rent in arrear" (subss. (2), (3), (5), (7) & (9))

9A–784   See 3A–304 to 3A–308.7.

Lessee's application for relief under subs.(9A)

9A–785   See 3A–304 to 3A–308.7.

Application "by a person with an interest ... derived ... from the lessee's interest" (subs.(9C))

9A–786   See 3A–304 to 3A–308.7.

Law of Property Act 1925, s.146(4)

9A–787   See 3A–304 to 3A–308.7.

Service of summons and re-entry

9A–788   **139.**—(1) In a case where section 138 has effect, if—

> (a) one-half-year's rent is in arrear at the time of the commencement of the action; and
>
> (b) the lessor has a right to re-enter for non-payment of that rent; and
>
> (c) no sufficient distress is to be found on the premises countervailing the arrears then due,

the service of the summons in the action in the prescribed manner shall stand in lieu of a demand and re-entry.

(2) Where a lessor has enforced against a lessee, by re-entry without action, a right of re-entry or forfeiture as respects any land for non-payment of rent, the lessee may, at any time within six months from the date on which the lessor re-entered apply to the county court for relief, and on any such application the court may, if it thinks fit, grant to the lessee such relief as the High Court could have granted.

(3) Subsections (9B) and (9C) of section 138 shall have effect in relation to an application under subsection (2) of this section as they have effect in relation to an application under subsection (9A) of that section.

9A–789   *Note* —See 3A–310 and 3A–311.

Effect of section

9A–790   See 3A–310 and 3A–311.

Service of summons standing in lieu of a demand and re-entry (subs.(1))

9A–791   See 3A–310 and 3A–311.

Relief from forfeiture where re-entry without action (subss. (2) & (3))

9A–792   See 3A–310 and 3A–311.

Interpretation of sections 138 and 139

9A–793   **140.** For the purposes of sections 138 and 139—

"lease" includes—

(a) an original or derivative under-lease;

(b) an agreement for a lease where the lessee has become entitled to have his lease granted; and

(c) a grant at a fee farm rent, or under a grant securing a rent by condition;

"lessee" includes—

(a) an original or derivative under-lessee;

(b) the persons deriving title under a lessee;

(c) a grantee under a grant at a fee farm rent, or under a grant securing a rent by condition; and

(d) the persons deriving title under such a grantee;

"lessor" includes—

(a) an original or derivative under-lessor;

(b) the persons deriving title under a lessor;

(c) a person making a grant at a fee farm rent, or a grant securing a rent by condition; and

(d) the persons deriving title under such a grantor;

"under-lease" includes an agreement for an under-lease where the under-lessee has become entitled to have his under-lease granted; and

"under-lessee" includes any person deriving title under an under-lease.

SOLICITORS

No privilege allowed to solicitors

141. [*Repealed by the Statute Law (Repeals) Act 1986*].　　9A–794

Power to enforce undertakings of solicitors

142. A county court shall have the same power to enforce an undertaking given by a solicitor in relation to any proceedings in that court as the High Court has to enforce an undertaking so given in relation to any proceedings in the High Court.　　9A–795

Power to enforce undertakings of solicitors

An undertaking is a promise. In the old books "undertaker" means a promisor (1 Salk. 27). "Undertaking" is today usually used in the sense of a promise given in the course of proceedings by a party or his solicitor or counsel.　　9A–796

Where a solicitor gives an undertaking he is bound as a matter of professional etiquette to implement it. Furthermore, a solicitor is, of course, a "solicitor of the Supreme Court" and consequently the High Court may exercise jurisdiction over solicitors (see also s.50 of the Solicitors Act 1974 see para. 7–40).

Section 142 of the CCA. 1984 enables the county court to enforce an undertaking given by a solicitor in that court in the same way as could the High Court. For the powers of the High Court see "*Summary Jurisdiction of the Court over solicitors*" at SCP 1999, Vol. 2, para 15G–1, and in particular "Jurisdiction to enforce undertakings given by solicitors" at SCP 1999, Vol. 2, para. 15G–6.

Prohibition on persons other than solicitors receiving remuneration for business done in county courts

143.—(1) No person other than—　　9A–797

(a) a legal representative; or

(b) a person exercising a right of audience or a right to conduct litigation by virtue of an order made under section 11 of the Courts and Legal Services Act 1990 (representation in county courts),

shall be entitled to have or recover any fee or reward for acting on behalf of a party in proceedings in a county court.

(2) [...]

9A–798   *Note* —Amended by the Courts and Legal Services Act 1990, s.125(3), (7), Scheds 8 and 20.

REPLEVIN

Replevin

9A–799   **144.** Schedule 1 to this Act shall have effect.

POWER TO RAISE MONETARY LIMITS

Power to raise monetary limits

9A–800   **145.**—(1) If it appears to Her Majesty in Council—

(a) that the county court limit for the purposes of any enactment referring to that limit, or

(b) that the higher limit or the lower limit referred to in section 20 of this Act,

should be increased, Her Majesty may by Order in Council direct that the limit in question shall be such amount as may be specified in the Order.

(2) An Order under subsection (1) may contain such incidental or transitional provisions as Her Majesty considers appropriate.

(3) No recommendation shall be made to Her Majesty in Council to make an Order under this section unless a draft of the Order has been laid before Parliament and approved by resolution of each House of Parliament.

9A–801   *Note* —No Order has been made under this section. See further, commentary to s.147(1).

GENERAL

Lord Commissioners to represent Lord Chancellor when Great Seal in commission

9A–802   **146.** When the Great Seal is in commission, the Lords Commissioners shall represent the Lord Chancellor for the purposes of this Act; but the powers vested in him by this Act in relation to the appointment of officers may be exercised by the senior Lord Commissioner for the time being.

Interpretation

9A–803   **147.**—(1) In this Act, unless the context otherwise requires—

"action" means any proceedings in a county court which may be commenced as prescribed by plaint;

"Admiralty county court" means a county court appointed to have Admiralty jurisdiction by order under this Act;

"Admiralty proceedings" means proceedings in which the claim would not be within the jurisdiction of a county court but for sections 26 and 27;

"bailiff" includes a registrar;

"the county court limit" means—

  (a) in relation to any enactment contained in this Act for which a limit for the time being specified by an Order under section 145, that limit,

  (b) [...]

  (c) in relation to any enactment contained in this Act and not within paragraph (a) [...], the county court limit for the time being specified by any other Order in Council or order defining the limit of county court jurisdiction for the purposes of that enactment; [...]

[...]

"court" and "county court" mean a court held for a district under this Act;

"deposit-taking institution" means a person who may, in the course of his business, lawfully accept deposits in the United Kingdom;

"district" and "county court district" mean a district for which a court is to be held under section 2;

[...]

"hearing" includes trial, and "hear" and "heard" shall be construed accordingly;

"hereditament" includes both a corporeal and incorporeal hereditament;

"judge", in relation to a county court, means a judge assigned to the district of that court under subsection (1) of section 5 and any person sitting as a judge for that district under subsection (3) or (4) of that section;

"judgment summons" means a summons issued on the application of a person entitled to enforce a judgment or order under section 5 of the Debtors Act 1869 requiring a person, or where two or more persons are liable under the judgment or order, requiring any one or more of them, to attend court;

"landlord", in relation to any land, means the person entitled to the immediate reversion or, if the property therein is held in joint tenancy, any of the persons entitled to the immediate reversion;

"legal representative" means an authorised advocate or authorised litigator, as defined by section 119(1) of the Courts and Legal Services Act 1990; [...]

"matter" means every proceeding in a county court which may be commenced as prescribed otherwise than by plaint;

"officer", in relation to a court, means any registrar, deputy registrar or assistant registrar of that court, and any clerk, bailiff, usher or messenger in the service of that court;

"part-time registrar" and "part-time assistant registrar" have the meaning assigned to them by section 10(3);

"party" includes every person served with notice of, or attending, any proceeding, whether named as a party to that proceeding or not;

"prescribed" means prescribed by rules of court;

"probate proceedings" means proceedings brought in a county court by virtue of section 32 or transferred to that court under section 40;

"proceedings" includes both actions and matters;

"registrar" and "registrar of a county court" mean a registrar appointed for a district under this Act, or in a case where two or more registrars are appointed jointly, either or any of those registrars;

"return day" means the day appointed in any summons or proceeding for the appearance of the defendant or any other day fixed for the hearing of any proceedings;

[...]

"ship" includes any description of vessel used in navigation;

"solicitor" means solicitor of the Supreme Court.

(1A) The definition of "deposit-taking institution" in subsection (1) must be read with—

(a) section 22 of the Financial Services and Markets Act 2000;

(b) any relevant order under that section; and

(c) Schedule 2 to that Act.

(2) [...]

(3) [...]

9A–804   *Note* — Subsection (1) amended by the Courts and Legal Services Act 1990, s.125(3), Sched.18, para. 49; the Matrimonial and Family Proceedings Act 1984, s.46(3), Sched.3; the High Court and County Courts Jurisdiction Order 1991 (S.I. 1991 No. 724); the Statute Law (Repeals) Act 1993; and the Civil Procedure Act 1997, Sched.2, paras 2(2) and 2(9).

Subsections (2) and (3) of this section were repealed by the Local Government Finance (Repeals, Savings and Consequential Amendments) Order 1990 (S.I. 1990 No. 776).

The definition of "judgment summons" in s.147(1) was amended by the Civil Procedure (Modification of Enactments) Order 2002 (S.I. 2002 No. 439) with effect from March 23, 2002.

The definition "deposit-taking institution" in s.147(1) was added by, and subs.(1A) were inserted by, the Financial Services and Markets Act 2000 (Consequential Amendments and Repeals) Order 2001 (S.I. 2001 No. 3649), art.296.

"The county court limit"

9A–805   No order has been made under s.145. See further "Jurisdiction of county courts" para. 9A–485 above.

Registrar, etc.

9A–806   By the Courts and Legal Services Act 1990, s.74, the office of registrar became that of district judge and references in any enactment to registrar are to be construed as a reference to that office by its new name.

Amendments of other Acts, transitory provisions, transitional provisions, savings and repeals

148.—(1) The enactments specified in Schedule 2 shall have effect subject to the amendments there specified. **9A–807**

(2) This Act shall have effect subject to the transitory provisions and transitional provisions and savings contained in Schedule 3.

(3) The enactments specified in Schedule 4 are hereby repealed to the extent specified in the third column of that Schedule.

Extent

149.—(1) Section 148(1) and Schedule 2 extend to Scotland so far as they amend enactments extending to Scotland. **9A–808**

(2) Section 148(1) and Schedule 2 extend to Northern Ireland so far as they amend enactments extending to Northern Ireland.

(3) Subject to subsections (1) and (2), this Act extends to England and Wales only.

Commencement

150. This Act shall come into force on 1st August 1984. **9A–809**

Short title

151. This Act may be cited as the County Courts Act 1984. **9A–810**

SECTION 144   SCHEDULE 1

1.—(1) The sheriff shall have no power or responsibility with respect to replevin **9A–811** bonds or replevins.

(2) The registrar for the district in which any goods subject to replevin are taken shall have power, subject to the provisions of this Schedule, to approve of replevin bonds and to grant replevins and to issue all necessary process in relation to them, and any such process shall be executed by a bailiff of the court.

(3) The registrar shall, at the instance of the party whose goods have been seized, cause the goods to be replevied to that party on his giving such security as is provided in this Schedule.

2.—(1) It shall be a condition of any security given under paragraph 1 that the replevisor will—

(a) commence an action of replevin against the seizor in the High Court within one week from the date when the security is given; or

(b) commence such an action in a county court within one month from that date.

(2) In either case—

(a) the replevisor shall give security, to be approved by the registrar having power in the matter, for such an amount as the registrar thinks sufficient to cover both the probable costs of the action and either—

(i) the alleged rent or damage in respect of which the distress has been made; or

(ii) in a case where the goods replevied have been seized otherwise than under colour of distress, the value of the goods; and

(b) it shall be a further condition of the security that the replevisor will—

(i) prosecute the action with effect and without delay; and

(ii) make a return of the goods, if a return of them is ordered in the action.

(3) [...]

3.—(1) [...]

(2) [...]

(3) [...]

(4) Section 45(1) applies to an action removed to the High Court under this paragraph as it applies to an action ordered to be transferred to that court.

9A–812 *Note* —Repealed in part by the Courts and Legal Services Act 1990, s.125, Scheds 17 and 20.

For meaning of "registrar" in this Schedule, see note following s.147 above.

SECTION 148(1) ## SCHEDULE 2

AMENDMENTS OF OTHER ENACTMENTS

9A–813 [The text of Schedule 2 is not reproduced here]

SECTION 148(2) ## SCHEDULE 3

TRANSITORY AND TRANSITIONAL PROVISIONS AND SAVINGS

Section 21 of this Act

9A–814 1. [...]

Section 51 of this Act

9A–815 2. [...]

Sections 105(1) and 106 of this Act

9A–816 3.—(1) [...]

(2) [...]

Administration Orders

9A–817 4.—(1) Any reference in Part VI of this Act to an administration order includes a reference to an administration order made under an enactment repealed by this Act.

2. [...]

County Court

9A–818 5. References in any enactment or document to a county court constituted under the County Courts Act 1888 or the County Courts Act 1934 or the County Courts Act 1959 shall be construed as references to a county court constituted under this Act and anything done or proceedings taken in respect of any action or matter whatsoever before the commencement of this Act in a county court under any of the enactments mentioned above shall be deemed to have been done or taken in a county court constituted under this Act.

Former enactments

9A–819 6. Any document referring to any former enactment relating to county courts shall be construed as referring to the corresponding enactment in this Act. In this paragraph "former enactment relating to county courts" means any enactment repealed by the County Courts Act 1959, by the County Courts Act 1934 or by the County Courts Act 1888.

High bailiffs

9A–820 7. References to a high bailiff in any enactment, Order in Council, order, rule, regulation or any document whatsoever shall be construed as a reference to a registrar.

Periods of time

9A–821 8. Where a period of time specified in an enactment repealed by this Act is current at the coming into force of this Act shall have effect as if the corresponding provision of it had been in force when that period began to run.

Offences

9. Nothing in this Act renders a person liable to punishment by way of fine or imprisonment for an offence committed before the coming into force of this Act which differs from the punishment to which he would have been liable if this Act had not been passed.

9A–822

Saving for certain provisions of the County Courts Act 1959

10. [...]

9A–823

General

11. Without prejudice to any express amendment made by this Act, a reference in an enactment or other document, whether express or implied, to an enactment repealed by this Act shall, unless the context otherwise requires, be construed as, or as including, a reference to this Act or to the corresponding provisions of this Act.

12. Nothing in this Schedule shall be taken as prejudicing the operation of the provisions of the Interpretation Act 1978 as respects the effects of repeals.

9A–824

Note — Schedule 3 repealed in part by the Statute Law (Repeals) Act 1989.

9A–825

SECTION 148(3)   SCHEDULE 4

REPEALS

[The text of Schedule 4 is not reproduced here]

9A–826

Civil Procedure Act 1997

(1997 c.12)

9A–827

ARRANGEMENT OF SECTIONS

RULES AND DIRECTIONS

Introductory note

The provisions in this Act, with the exception of s.7 (which has a different provenance), paved the way for the implementation of the recommendations contained in the Report by Lord Woolf to the Lord Chancellor on the civil justice system in England and Wales: "Access to Justice Final Report" (July 1996).

9A–828

Section 11 came into effect on February 27, 1997. Sections 1 to 9 and Sched.1 were brought into force on April 27, 1997, by the Civil Procedure Act 1997 (Commencement No. 1) Order 1997 (S.I. 1997 No. 841). That statutory instrument also brought into force on that date some of the minor and consequential amendments contained in Sched.2. The remaining provisions of the Act were brought into force by the Civil Procedure Act 1997 (Commencement No. 2) Order 1999 (S.I. 1999 No. 1009).

For further notes on this Act, see Sweet & Maxwell's *Current Law Statutes Annotated* 1997, Vol. 1.

The Constitutional Reform Act 2005 (c. 4) modifies the office of Lord Chancellor and makes provision relating to the functions of that office. That Act also amends many statutes, including this Act. Provisions in the 2005 Act amending the 1997 Act are not yet in force. Thos provisions will amend ss.1, 2, 2A, 3, 4 and 6, and will insert a new s.3A.

RULES AND DIRECTIONS

Civil Procedure Rules

9A-829   **1.**—(1) There are to be rules of court (to be called "Civil Procedure Rules") governing the practice and procedure to be followed in—

    (a) the civil division of the Court of Appeal,

    (b) the High Court, and

    (c) county courts.

(2) Schedule 1 (which makes further provision about the extent of the power to make Civil Procedure Rules) is to have effect.

(3) Any power to make or alter Civil Procedure Rules is to be exercised with a view to securing that—

    (a) the system of civil justice is accessible, fair and efficient, and

    (b) the rules are both simple and simply expressed.

Civil Procedure Rules

9A-830   This section and Sched.1 indicate the extent of the Civil Procedure Rules. The Civil Procedure Rules 1998 were made in 1998 (see (S.I. 1998 No. 3132) and came into force on April 24, 1999. Before coming into force, the CPR were amended by the Civil Procedure (Amendment) Rules 1999 (S.I. 1999 No. 1008). Subsection (3) was substituted by the Courts Act 2003 s.82(1) and brought into effect on January 26, 2004.

CPR, Pt 76 was inserted in the CPR by the Civil Procedure (Amendment No. 2) Rules 2005 (S.I. 2005 No. 656) and contains provisions relating to proceedings arising under the jurisdiction given to the High Court by the Prevention of Terrorism Act 2005. Those additional rules (which also amended CPR, r.1.2 and disapplied or modified other CPR provisions in certain circumstances) were not made by the Civil Procedure Committee (see s.2 below), but by the Lord Chancellor exercising special powers granted to him by paras 4 and 5 of the Schedule to that Act.

9A-831   *Subs.(1)*—This subsection states that rules of court to be known as "Civil Procedure Rules" (CPR), made by statutory instrument (see s.3), will govern the practice and procedure of the civil division of the Court of Appeal, the High Court and county courts. Previously, ss.84 and 85 of the Supreme Court Act 1981 stated that the making of rules of court for the purpose of regulating and prescribing the practice and procedure to be followed in the High Court and the civil division of the Court of Appeal, should be delegated to "the Supreme Court Rule Committee" as constituted under s.85. The Rules of the Supreme Court (Revision) 1965 were brought into being under comparable statutory provisions found in the Supreme Court of Judicature Act 1925, and from time to time were amended subsequently. Section 75 of the County Courts Act 1984 stated that rules of court for regulating the practice and procedure in county courts were to be made by a rule committee as provided for by that section. The County Court Rules 1981 were brought into being under a comparable provision in the County Courts Act 1959, and from time to time were amended subsequently. Henceforth, instead of two rule-making regimes, one for the civil division of the Court of Appeal and the High Court, and the other for the county courts, there is to be one. Accordingly, s.84 of the 1981 Act is amended and s.85 of that Act and s.75 of the 1984 Act are omitted (see s.10 and Sched.2). Whereas previously there were two rule committees, now there is to be one (for the constitution of this body, see s.2). Section 1 and Sched.1 are not the sole legislative source of the rule-making power. Examples of other statutory provisions are: Supreme Court Act 1981, s.32 (interim payments) and s.58 (rules of court affecting Court of Appeal), Access to Justice Act 1999, s.54 (permission to appeal), Limitation Act 1980, s.35 (new claims in pending actions). Such statutory provisions may impose conditions as to how the rule-making power is to be exercised in certain contexts. See further 9A–832 below.

9A–832 *Subss. (2) and (3) "the extent of the power to make Civil Procedure Rules"* —The power to make Civil Procedure Rules (CPR) is to be exercised "with a view to securing that the civil justice system is accessible, fair and efficient". The rules are to be made by a rule committee (see s.2) and the committee should "try to make rules which are both simple and simply expressed" (s.2(7)). The Lord Chancellor may by order amend, repeal or revoke any enactment to the extent he considers it necessary or desirable to facilitate the making of Civil Procedure Rules (s.4(2)) or in consequence of such rules or of s.1 or s.2 of this (Act, s.4(1)) (*cf.*, s.87(3) of the 1981 Act which said that rules of court may amend or repeal any statutory provision relating to the practice and procedure of the Supreme Court "so far as may be necessary in consequence of provision made by the rules"; see further notes to s.4, below).

9A–833 *Sched.1* —Provisions stating the extent of the rule-making power are found in Sched.1.

Para. 1 of Sched.1 states that the CPR may deal with matters which were governed by the former RSC and CCR. Section 84 of the 1981 Act stated that the former Supreme Court Rule Committee was empowered to make rules of court "for the purpose of regulating and prescribing ... practice and procedure" including all such matters regulated by rules of court before the 1981 Act came into force (see also the County Courts Act 1984, s.75(4)) and certain particular matters for which rules of court might provide were listed in subss.(1) and (2) of s.87. It should be noted that neither the RSC nor the CCR covered all proceedings which, conceivably, could come within the jurisdiction of, on the one hand, the High Court, and on the other, the county courts (*e.g.* proceedings covered by the Family Proceedings Rules (made under the Matrimonial and Family Proceedings Act 1984, s.40) and by the Insolvency Rules (made under the Insolvency Act 1986, s.411)).

Paragraph 2 of Sched.1 states that the CPR may provide for the exercise of the jurisdiction of any court within the scope of the rules (that is to say, the civil division of the Court of Appeal, the High Court, and county courts) by officers or other court staff. In modern times, increasingly the discharge of certain judicial tasks has been devolved to court staff, particularly in the county courts. Usually, this was accomplished by expanding the definition of "proper officer" in CCR O.1, r.3 to include the court manager (or an officer acting on his behalf in accordance with directions given by the Lord Chancellor), and by further rule amendments increasing the range of matters that could be dealt with by the proper officer. (See now CPR, r.2.5.) Paragraph 2 makes it clear (as did the County Courts Act 1984, s.75(3)) that rules devolving judicial responsibilities in this way are not *ultra vires*.

Paragraph 3 of Sched.1 states that the CPR may provide for the transfer of proceedings (or any part of proceedings) within the High Court, for example, between different divisions or different district registries. Similar rules may be made for the transfer of proceedings (or part) from one county court to another (as permitted by s.75(3)(b) and rules in the CCR made thereunder). In addition, rules may provide for any jurisdiction in any proceedings (or in any part of proceedings) to be exercised (whether concurrently or not) elsewhere within the High Court without the proceedings being transferred. Similar rules may provide for any jurisdiction in any proceedings (or part) to be exercised (whether concurrently or not) by another county court without the proceedings being transferred (*cf.*, Courts and Legal Services Act 1990, s.1(6)). The allocation of business between the High Court and the county courts is not a matter to be dealt with by the CPR Legislation regulating the allocation of business is found in the Courts and Legal Services Act 1990, s.1 and in Orders made by the Lord

LEGISLATION

Chancellor under that section (see the High Court and County Courts Jurisdiction Order 1991, as amended, para. 9B–138). The power to make rules of court contained in s.1(6) of the 1990 Act may be exercised in the CPR.

Paragraph 4 of Sched.1 states that the CPR may modify "the rules of evidence" as they apply to proceedings in the civil division of the Court of Appeal, the High Court, and county courts. The scope of this paragraph is not immediately apparent. The RSC and the CCR contain provisions dealing with the taking of evidence. In some instances the authority for such rules comes from the general power to make rules as to practice and procedure, in other instances they are derived from particular statutory provisions, for example, the Civil Evidence Act 1968, s.8 (hearsay) and the Courts and Legal Services Act 1990, s.5 (service of witness statements). The County Courts Act 1984, s.64 states that in relation to proceedings referred to arbitration rules of court may prescribe "the rules of evidence" to be followed and may make provision with respect to the taking and questioning of evidence. Generally, in the past it has been accepted that what could be called the substantive law of evidence, in particular the exclusionary rules rendering inadmissible relevant and material evidence, lay outside the rule-making power. The reform of the exclusionary hearsay rule was accomplished by primary legislation in the form of the Civil Evidence Act 1995. In terms, para. 4 seems to make the whole of the law of evidence susceptible to changes wrought by rules of court but, presumably, it does not extend to matters that cannot be regarded as mere rules of evidence (*e.g.* rules of law relating to claims of privilege).

Paragraph 5 of Sched.1 states that the CPR may apply any rules of court which relate to courts "outside the scope of" the CPR, that is to say, courts other than the civil division of the Court of Appeal, the High Court and, the county courts (see s.9(1)). Consequently, for example, rules made for the criminal division of the Court of Appeal or the Crown Court, could be applied by the CPR to the civil division of the Court of Appeal, the High Court and, the county courts (just as, in the past, the CCR could apply rules relating to the practice and procedure of courts other than county courts, see s.75(6A)(a) of the 1984 Act). Paragraph 5 further states that any rules of court not made by the Civil Procedure Rules Committee (see s.2), but which apply to particular proceedings in the civil division of the Court of Appeal, the High Court and, the county courts, for example, the Family Proceedings Rules and the Insolvency Rules, may be applied by the CPR to other proceedings in those courts.

Paragraph 6 states that the CPR may, instead of providing for any matter, refer to provision made or to be made about that matter by directions. Under s.74A of the 1984 Act, as inserted by s.5 of this Act (see below), directions as to the practice and procedure of county courts may be made by the Lord Chancellor.

Paragraph 7 of Sched.1 states that the power to make CPR includes the power to make different provision for different cases "including different provision ... for specific proceedings, or a specific jurisdiction" (*e.g.* mercantile courts sitting at district registries). To that extent para. 7 is unremarkable. However, the paragraph also states that different provision may be made for different areas, "including different provision ... for a specific court or specific division of a court" (see also s.74A of the 1984 Act as substituted by s.5 of this Act). This aspect of the rule making power opens up the possibility that, in relation to proceedings which are indistinguishable, rules of practice and procedure may vary from court centre to court centre, perhaps for the purpose of taking account of the state of business at particular centres (*cf.*, s.40(4) of the 1984 Act). It may be noted that the Matrimonial and Family Proceedings Act 1984, s.40, the section containing the rule making power for the Family Proceedings Rules, is amended (see Sched.2, para. 3) so that different provision may be made for different cases, etc., in those rules also.

Under various provisions in the Supreme Court Act 1981, the Lord Chancellor is given power to make orders affecting specific matters of practice and procedure (see para. 9A–356); these are not affected by the 1997 Act.

In a number of cases it has been argued at first instance that particular provisions in the CPR are outside the rule-making power as stated in s.1 and Sched.1 of the 1997 Act. In *All-in-One Design & Build Ltd v. Motcomb Estates Ltd* (2000) 144 S.J.L.B. 219, r.36.21(2) (power of court to award interest on damages awarded to a claimant in case where he recovers more that he proposed in his Pt 36 offer) was held to be *intra vires*. In *General Mediterranean Holdings S.A. v. Patel* [2000] 1 W.L.R. 272, [1999] 3 All E.R. 673, r.48.7(3) (power of court to order disclosure of privileged documents on wasted costs application) was held to be ultra vires (subsequently the paragraph in Practice Direction (Pt 48 - Costs - Special Cases) Sect. II drawing attention to r.48.7(3) was revoked). In *Safeway Stores Plc v. Tate* [2001] 2 W.L.R. 1377, CA, it was said that the power to make procedural rules under s.4 does not permit the restriction of a party's right to trial by jury in a defamation claim (*cf. Alexander v. Arts Council of Wales, The Times*, April 27, 2001, CA).

Rule Committee

2.—(1) Civil Procedure Rules are to be made by a committee **9A–834** known as the Civil Procedure Rule Committee, which is to consist of—

- (aa) the Head of Civil Justice,
- (ab) the Deputy Head of Civil Justice (if there is one),
- (a) the Master of the Rolls (unless he holds an office mentioned in paragraph (aa) or (ab)), and
- (c) the persons currently appointed by the Lord Chancellor under subsection (2).

(2) The Lord Chancellor must appoint—

- (a) either two or three judges of the Supreme Court,
- (b) one Circuit judge,
- (c) one district judge,
- (d) one person who is a Master referred to in Part II of Schedule 2 to the Supreme Court Act 1981,
- (e) three persons who have a Supreme Court qualification (within the meaning of section 71 of the Courts and Legal Services Act 1990), including at least one with particular experience of practice in county courts,
- (f) three persons who have been granted by an authorised body, under Part II of that Act, the right to conduct litigation in relation to all proceedings in the Supreme Court, including at least one with particular experience of practice in county courts,
- (g) two persons with experience in and knowledge of the lay advice sector and consumer affairs.

(3) Before appointing a judge of the Supreme Court under subsection (2)(a), the Lord Chancellor must consult the Lord Chief Justice.

(4) Before appointing a person under paragraph (e) or (f) of subsection (2), the Lord Chancellor must consult any body which—

- (a) has members who are eligible for appointment under that paragraph, and
- (b) is an authorised body for the purposes of section 27 or 28 of the Courts and Legal Services Act 1990.

(5) The Lord Chancellor may reimburse the members of the Civil Procedure Rule Committee their travelling and out-of-pocket expenses.

Civil Procedure Rule Committee

The CPR are to be made by a committee of fourteen members known as the Civil **9A–835** Procedure Committee, constituted in accordance with this section. (Provisions in the Supreme Court Act 1981 and the County Courts Act 1984 governing the composition and powers of the Supreme Court Rule Committee and County Court Rule Committee are repealed.) The committee includes *ex officio* members and members appointed by the Lord Chancellor. The Lord Chancellor is not a member of the committee. The committee is obliged to consult "such persons as they consider appropriate". Rules made by the committee should be submitted to the Lord Chancellor. The committee does not have to be unanimous; rules submitted to the Lord Chancellor must be signed by eight members. Former s.85 of the 1981 Act stated that the power to make Rules of the Supreme Court was "exercisable by the Lord Chancellor together with any four or more" members of the Supreme Court Rule Committee. Thus, the power was exercisable only if the Lord Chancellor was himself a party to their exercise. On the other hand, under former s.75(9) any County Court Rules certified by any three or more members of the County Court Rule Committee could be allowed, disallowed or altered by the Lord Chancellor. This section states that the Lord Chancellor "may allow or disallow" rules submitted to him by the Civil Procedure Committee but gives him no power to alter such rules. Paras. (a) and (b) of s.2(1), paras. (a), (g) and (h) of s.2(2) were substituted by, and paras. (6) to (8) of s.2 were omitted by, the Courts Act 2003 s.83(2) & (3) and s.85(1) and brought into effect on January 26, 2004.

Power to change certain requirements relating to Committee

9A–836   **2A.**—(1) The Lord Chancellor may by order—

    (a) amend section 2(2) (persons to be appointed to Committee by Lord Chancellor), and

    (b) make consequential amendments in any other provision of section 2.

(2) Before making an order under this section the Lord Chancellor must consult —

    (a) the Head of Civil Justice,

    (b) the Deputy Head of Civil Justice (if there is one),

    (c) the Master of the Rolls (unless he holds an office mentioned in paragraph (a) or (b)).

(3) The power to make an order under this section is exercisable by statutory instrument.

(4) A statutory instrument containing such an order is subject to annulment in pursuance of a resolution of either House of Parliament.

Note

9A–837   Section 2A was inserted by the Courts Act 2003 s.84, with effect from January 24, 2004.

Process for making Civil Procedure Rules

9A–838   **3.**—(1) The Civil Procedure Rule Committee must, before making Civil Procedure Rules—

    (a) consult such persons as they consider appropriate, and

    (b) meet (unless it is inexpedient to do so).

(2) Rules made by the Civil Procedure Rule Committee must be—

    (a) signed by a majority of the members of the Committee, and

    (b) submitted to the Lord Chancellor.

(3) The Lord Chancellor may allow, disallow or alter rules so made.

(4) Before altering rules so made the Lord Chancellor must consult the Committee.

(5) Rules so made, as allowed or altered by the Lord Chancellor—

(a) come into force on such day as the Lord Chancellor directs, and

(b) are to be contained in a statutory instrument to which the Statutory Instruments Act 1946 applies as if the instrument contained rules made by a Minister of the Crown.

(6) Subject to subsection (7), a statutory instrument containing Civil Procedure Rules is subject to annulment in pursuance of a resolution of either House of Parliament.

(7) A statutory instrument containing rules altered by the Lord Chancellor is of no effect unless approved by a resolution of each House of Parliament before the day referred to in subsection (5)(a).

CPR to be in statutory instrument

With effect from January 26, 2004, s.3 was substituted by the Courts Act 2003 **9A–839** s.85(2) with the result that the arrangements for the enactment of Civil Procedure Rules were changed significantly. This section will be further amended by the Constitutional Reform Act 2005. Also, a new section, s.3A (Rules to be made if required by the Lord Chancellor), will be added by that Act.

Power to make consequential amendments

4.—(1) The Lord Chancellor may by order amend, repeal or **9A–840** revoke any enactment to the extent he considers necessary or desirable in consequence of—

(a) section 1 or 2, or

(b) Civil Procedure Rules.

(2) The Lord Chancellor may by order amend, repeal or revoke any enactment passed or made before the commencement of this section to the extent he considers necessary or desirable in order to facilitate the making of Civil Procedure Rules.

(3) Any power to make an order under this section is exercisable by statutory instrument.

(4) A statutory instrument containing an order under subsection (1) shall be subject to annulment in pursuance of a resolution of either House of Parliament.

(5) No order may be made under subsection (2) unless a draft of it has been laid before and approved by resolution of each House of Parliament.

Power to make consequential and other amendments to enactments

This section enables the Lord Chancellor to make changes to other enactments by **9A–841** order. For exercise of this power, see Civil Procedure (Modification of Enactments) Order 1998 (S.I. 1998 No. 2940), Civil Procedure (Modification of Enactments) Order 1999 (S.I. 1999 No. 1217), Civil Procedure (Modification of Enactments) Order 2000 (S.I. 2000 No. 941), Civil Procedure (Modification of Enactments) Order 2001 (S.I. 2001 No. 2717), Civil Procedure (Modification of Enactments) Order 2002 (S.I. 2002 No. 439), Civil Procedure (Modification of Supreme Court Act 1981) Order 2004 (S.I. 2004 No. 1033), Civil Procedure (Modification of Crown Proceedings Act 1947) Order 2005 (S.I. 2005 No. 2712). Note also (amending CPR) Postal Services Act 2000 (Consequential Modifications No. 1) Order 2001 (S.I. 2001 No. 1149).

Subsection (1) states that the Lord Chancellor may by order (subject to the negative resolution procedure) amend, repeal or revoke any enactment (whenever passed or made) to the extent he considers it necessary or desirable (a) in consequence of Civil Procedure Rules or (b) in consequence of s.1 or s.2 of this Act.

Subsection (2) states that the Lord Chancellor may by order (subject to the positive resolution procedure) amend, repeal or revoke any enactment (passed or made before this section was brought into force on April 27, 1997) to the extent he considers it necessary or desirable to facilitate the making of Civil Procedure Rules. This subsection is not confined to amendments, etc., which are merely consequential. Thus, where a particular rule is proposed which is inconsistent with an enactment in force at commencement, the Lord Chancellor may amend, etc., the enactment by order. Where a particular rule is proposed which is inconsistent with an enactment in force subsequently, necessary or desirable amendments, etc., cannot be made to the enactment under this subsection as it stands.

It was explained above (see notes to s.1(2) and (3)) that this section may be contrasted with s.87(3) of the 1981 Act and s.75(6A)(b) of the 1984 Act. Those sections provided that rules in the RSC and CCR could amend or repeal any statutory provision relating to the practice or procedure of the courts concerned "so far as may be necessary in consequence of any provision made by the rules". Such consequential amendments cannot be accomplished by provisions in the CPR but the same result may be achieved by the exercise by the Lord Chancellor of powers given by this section.

Practice directions

9A–842   5.—(1) Practice directions may provide for any matter which, by virtue of paragraph 3 of Schedule 1, may be provided for by Civil Procedure Rules.

(2) After section 74 of the County Courts Act 1984 there is inserted—

"PRACTICE DIRECTIONS

Practice directions

74A.—(1) Directions as to the practice and procedure of county courts may be made by the Lord Chancellor.

(2) Directions as to the practice and procedure of county courts may not be made by any other person without the approval of the Lord Chancellor.

(3) The power of the Lord Chancellor to make directions under subsection (1) includes power—

   (a) to vary or revoke directions made by him or any other person, and

   (b) to make different provision for different cases or different areas, including different provision—

      (i) for a specific court, or

      (ii) for specific proceedings, or a specific jurisdiction,

specified in the directions.

(4) References in this section to the Lord Chancellor include any person authorised by him to act on his behalf."

High Court practice directions

9A–843   In the High Court, practice directions are issued by the heads of division in the exercise of inherent power. Rules in the CPR may, instead of providing for any matter which may be provided for in the CPR, refer to provision made about that matter by directions (see Sched.1, para. 6). Among the matters which may be dealt with in the CPR is the removal of proceedings from one court to another as permitted by para. 3 of Sched.1 s.5(1) makes it clear that that matter can be dealt with by practice directions. In C (Legal Aid: Preparation of Bill of Costs), Re [2001] 1 F.L.R. 602, CA, the Court of

Appeal noted that para. 6 of Sched.1 "tells us nothing about who may make such practice directions". An attempt to rectify this was made by the "Note of Practice Directions" issued in May 2001, and referred to in para. 9A–841.1 below.

County court practice directions

Former CCR O.50, r.1 gave the Lord Chancellor power to issue directions for the **9A–844** purpose of security uniformity of practice in the county courts. Before the CPR came into force, some county courts developed the practice of making practice directions of local application only. subs.(2) inserts a new section in the 1984 Act giving the Lord Chancellor overall control (see further the County Courts Act 1984, s.74A, paras 9A–652 *et seq.*). Practice directions made in exercise of this power may deal with the removal of proceedings from one court to another as permitted by para. 3 of Sched.1 (see subs.(1)).

Definition of "practice directions"

In Stationery Office Civil Procedure Rules Update 23, May 2001, what is described **9A–845** as a "Note on Practice Directions" was published. By whom the Notes was drafted and with whose authority it was issued is not clear. The Note explains that "practice directions to the Civil Procedure Rules" (presumably this means practice directions supplementing CPR Parts) apply to civil litigation in the Queen's Bench Division and the Chancery Division of the High Court and to litigation in the county courts other than family proceedings, and where relevant they also apply to the Court of Appeal. The Note further explains that such practice directions are made (1) for the Queen's Bench Division by the Lord Chief Justice as president of that Division, (2) for the Civil Division of the Court of Appeal by the Master of the Rolls as president of that Division, (3) for the Chancery Division by the Vice-Chancellor as vice-president of that Division, and (4) for the county courts by the Lord Chancellor or a person authorised to act on his behalf under section 74A of the 1984 Act. In *Godwin v. Swindon Borough Council* [2001] EWCA Civ 1478; [2001] 4 All E.R. 641, May L.J. expressed the opinion that practice directions supplementing the CPR are "at best a weak aid to the interpretation of the rules themselves" (*ibid.* at para. [11]).

Within this Act, and therefore within s.5(1), "practice directions" means "directions as to the practice and procedure of any court within the scope of Civil Procedure Rules" (s.9(2)). See further Vol. 1, para. 2.3.4 (Practice directions as aids to interpretation).

For authoritative discussions of the power to make CPR practice directions, see *C. (Legal Aid: Preparation of Bill of Costs), Re* [2001] 1 F.L.R. 602, CA, and *Leigh v. Michelin Tyre Plc*, [2003] EWCA Civ 1766, December 8, 2003, CA, unrep., *R. (Mount Cook Land Limited) v. Westminster City Council* [2003] EWCA Civ 1346, October 14, 2003, CA, unrep.

Practice directions are not made by statutory instrument. They are not laid before Parliament or subject to either the negative or positive resolution procedures in Parliament. They go through no democratic process at all, although if approved by the Lord Chancellor he will bear ministerial responsibility for them to Parliament. There is no ministerial responsibility for practice directions made for the Supreme Court by the Heads of Division (In *Re C (Legal Aid: Preparation of Bill of Costs)* [2001] 1 F.L.R. 602, CA, at para. 21 *per* Hale L.J.). The practice directions supplementing CPR provisions differ from rules in the CPR in that (a) in general they provide guidance that should be followed, but do not have binding effect, and (b) they should yield to rules in the CPR where there is a clear conflict between them (*Mount Cook* case (*op. cit.*) *per* Auld L.J. at para. 68. See further vol. 1, para. 2.3.4.

LEGISLATION

CIVIL JUSTICE COUNCIL

Civil Justice Council

6.—(1) The Lord Chancellor is to establish and maintain an advi- **9A–846** sory body, to be known as the Civil Justice Council.

(2) The Council must include—

    (a) members of the judiciary,

    (b) members of the legal professions,

(c) civil servants concerned with the administration of the courts,

(d) persons with experience in and knowledge of consumer affairs,

(e) persons with experience in and knowledge of the lay advice sector, and

(f) persons able to represent the interests of particular kinds of litigants (for example, businesses or employees).

(3) The functions of the Council are to include—

(a) keeping the civil justice system under review,

(b) considering how to make the civil justice system more accessible, fair and efficient,

(c) advising the Lord Chancellor and the judiciary on the development of the civil justice system,

(d) referring proposals for changes in the civil justice system to the Lord Chancellor and the Civil Procedure Rule Committee, and

(e) making proposals for research.

(4) The Lord Chancellor may reimburse the members of the Council their travelling and out-of-pocket expenses.

Civil Justice Council

9A–847 In the report by Lord Woolf to the Lord Chancellor on the civil justice system in England and Wales: "Access to Justice Final Report" (July 1996), it was recommended that a Civil Justice Council should be established as an advisory body to keep the civil justice system under review. This section carries that recommendation into effect. The Council is to include judges, lawyers, Lord Chancellor's Department staff and others including those representing consumer, advice sector, business and other interests.

Court orders

Power of courts to make orders for preserving evidence, etc.

9A–848 7.—(1) The court may make an order under this section for the purpose of securing, in the case of any existing or proposed proceedings in the court—

(a) the preservation of evidence which is or may be relevant, or

(b) the preservation of property which is or may be the subject-matter of the proceedings or as to which any question arises or may arise in the proceedings.

(2) A person who is, or appears to the court likely to be, a party to proceedings in the court may make an application for such an order.

(3) Such an order may direct any person to permit any person described in the order, or secure that any person so described is permitted—

(a) to enter premises in England and Wales, and

(b) while on the premises, to take in accordance with the terms of the order any of the following steps.

(4) Those steps are—

(a) to carry out a search for or inspection of anything described in the order, and

(b) to make or obtain a copy, photograph, sample or other record of anything so described.

(5) The order may also direct the person concerned—

(a) to provide any person described in the order, or secure that any person so described is provided, with any information or article described in the order, and

(b) to allow any person described in the order, or secure that any person so described is allowed, to retain for safe keeping anything described in the order.

(6) An order under this section is to have effect subject to such conditions as are specified in the order.

(7) This section does not affect any right of a person to refuse to do anything on the ground that to do so might tend to expose him or his spouse to proceedings for an offence or for the recovery of a penalty.

(8) In this section—

"court" means the High Court, and

"premises" includes any vehicle;

and an order under this section may describe anything generally, whether by reference to a class or otherwise.

Effect of section

This section puts on a statutory footing the High Court's powers to grant orders **9A–849** aimed at securing the preservation of evidence for the purposes of civil proceedings. It does not implement recommendations made in "Access to Justice Final Report" (July 1996), but has a different provenance.

In a report prepared by a committee of judges appointed by the Judges' Council and published in 1992, the uncertainty of the basis of the Court's jurisdiction to grant Anton Piller orders was noted. Some judges had suggested that the jurisdiction may be based on the general power to grant injunctions found in the Supreme Court Act 1981, s.37(1); others preferred to say that it is based on the Court's inherent jurisdiction to make interlocutory orders for a securing a just and proper trial of the issues joined between the parties. The committee recommended that the legal basis for the making of these orders should be laid down in primary legislation which should also make provision for covering the principal features of the remedy (see "Anton Piller Orders: A Consultation Paper" (LCD 1992), para. 3.2).

Such legislation is now found in this section. The person against whom the order is made is required to comply with the order so as to permit entry to premises, to facilitate inspection of matters specified in the court order and to permit the removal of items for safe keeping. It may be noted that this provision preserves the privilege against self-incrimination. In the 1992 report it was recommended that s.72 of the 1981 Act should be extended so that the privilege should no longer apply to civil proceedings generally. This recommendation raised wider issues which still await official attention.

For limits on jurisdiction of county courts in relation to grant relief of the type referred to in s.7, see County Court Remedies Regulation 1991, reg.2(a) (para. 9B–82).

Disclosure etc. of documents before action begun

8.—(1) The Lord Chancellor may by order amend the provisions **9A–850** of section 33(2) of the Supreme Court Act 1981, or section 52(2) of the County Courts Act 1984 (power of court to order disclosure etc. of documents where claim may be made in respect of personal injury or death), so as to extend the provisions—

  (a) to circumstances where other claims may be made, or

  (b) generally.

 (2) The power to make an order under this section is exercisable by statutory instrument which shall be subject to annulment in pursuance of a resolution of either House of Parliament.

Supreme Court Act 1981, s.33(2) and the County Courts Act 1984, s.52(2)

9A–851 This section provides an order-making power to extend the circumstances in which courts have power to order disclosure of documents before legal proceedings commence. Before 1970, where proceedings had been commenced an order for discovery of documents could be made under rules of court against a party to those proceedings but an order could not be made (1) before proceedings had been commenced, or (2) if they had been commenced, against a person, who was not a party. These two restrictions on, respectively, "pre-action" discovery and "third party" discovery were modified by statute. Nowadays, the power to order "pre-action" discovery is derived from the Supreme Court Act 1981, s.33(2) and the County Courts Act 1984, s.52(2) (see paras 9A–93 and 9A–582). The power to order "third party" discovery is derived from the Supreme Court Act 1981, s.34(2) and the County Courts Act 1984, s.53(2) (see paras 9A–98 and 9A–587).

 In the report by Lord Woolf to the Lord Chancellor on the civil justice system in England and Wales: "Access to Justice Final Report" (July 1996), no recommendation was made concerning "third party" discovery, but it was recommended that "pre-action" discovery under s.33(2) of the 1981 Act and s.52(2) of the 1984 Act should be altered in two respects. It was recommended, first, that "pre-action" discovery should no longer be limited to situations in which personal injury and wrongful death proceedings are in prospect (*ibid.*, paras 47 *et seq.*), and secondly, that it should be possible where a personal injury or wrongful death action is in prospect for an application to be made against a person who is not likely to be a party (*ibid.*, paras 51 *et seq.*).

Effect of section

9A–852 This section provides legislation necessary for carrying those two recommendations into effect. The Lord Chancellor is given power to amend s.33(2) and s.52(2) by statutory instrument (subject to negative resolution) so as to extend the provisions of those subsections (a) to circumstances where other claims may be made, or (b) generally. Amendments to s.33(2) and s.52(2), sufficient to carry into effect the first (but not the second) of these recommendations, were made by the Civil Procedure (Modification of Enactments) Order 1998 (S.I. 1998 No. 2940), paras 5(a) and 6(b). (It may be noted that this Order was made, not under s.8, but under s.4(2) of this Act.) In the "Access to Justice Final Report" it was not specifically recommended that s.33(2) and s.52(2) should be amended so as to enable that courts to grant "pre-action" orders for discovery against third parties where claims for other than personal injury and wrongful death are likely to be made in subsequent proceedings. It may be noted, however, that the powers given to the Lord Chancellor by this section are wide enough to enable him to amend s.33(2) and s.52(2) to accomplish such a change in the law.

 As explained above, once proceedings are commenced, the court has power under s.34 of the 1981 Act and s.53 of the 1984 Act, in accordance with rules of court, to make an order requiring a person who is not a party to the proceedings to give disclosure of documents (and to permit inspection of property and the taking of samples). It is convenient to note here that, as a result of amendments to these sections made by the Civil Procedure (Modification of Enactments) Order 1998 (S.I. 1998 No. 2940), paras 5(b) and 6(c), that power is not restricted to proceedings in respect of personal injuries or wrongful death.

GENERAL

Interpretation

9A–853 **9.**—(1) A court the practice and procedure of which is governed by Civil Procedure Rules is referred to in this Act as being "within the scope" of the rules; and references to a court outside the scope of the rules are to be read accordingly.

(2) In this Act—

"enactment" includes an enactment contained in subordinate legislation (within the meaning of the Interpretation Act 1978), and

"practice directions" means directions as to the practice and procedure of any court within the scope of Civil Procedure Rules.

Minor and consequential amendments

10. Schedule 2 (which makes minor and consequential amendments) is to have effect.   **9A–854**

Short title, commencement and extent

11.—(1) This Act may be cited as the Civil Procedure Act 1997.   **9A–855**

(2) Sections 1 to 10 are to come into force on such day as the Lord Chancellor may by order made by statutory instrument appoint, and different days may be appointed for different purposes.

(3) This Act extends to England and Wales only.

SECTION 1   SCHEDULE 1

CIVIL PROCEDURE RULES

Matters dealt with by the former rules

1. Among the matters which Civil Procedure Rules may be made about are any matters which were governed by the former Rules of the Supreme Court or the former county court rules (that is, the Rules of the Supreme Court (Revision) 1965 and the County Court Rules 1981).   **9A–856**

Exercise of jurisdiction

2. Civil Procedure Rules may provide for the exercise of the jurisdiction of any court within the scope of the rules by officers or other staff of the court.   **9A–857**

Removal of proceedings

3.—(1) Civil Procedure Rules may provide for the removal of proceedings at any stage—   **9A–858**

(a) within the High Court (for example, between different divisions or different district registries), or

(b) between county courts.

(2) In sub-paragraph (1)—

(a) "provide for the removal of proceedings" means—

(i) provide for transfer of proceedings, or

(ii) provide for any jurisdiction in any proceedings to be exercised (whether concurrently or not) elsewhere within the High Court or, as the case may be, by another county court without the proceedings being transferred, and

(b) "proceedings" includes any part of proceedings.

Evidence

4. Civil Procedure Rules may modify the rules of evidence as they apply to proceedings in any court within the scope of the rules.   **9A–859**

Application of other rules

5.—(1) Civil Procedure Rules may apply any rules of court which relate to a court which is outside the scope of Civil Procedure Rules.   **9A–860**

(2) Any rules of court, not made by the Civil Procedure Rule Committee, which apply to proceedings of a particular kind in a court within the scope of Civil Procedure Rules may be applied by Civil Procedure Rules to other proceedings in such a court.

(3) In this paragraph "rules of court" includes any provision governing the practice and procedure of a court which is made by or under an enactment.

(4) Where Civil Procedure Rules may be made by applying other rules, the other rules may be applied—

    (a) to any extent,

    (b) with or without modification, and

    (c) as amended from time to time.

Practice directions

9A–861   6. Civil Procedure Rules may, instead of providing for any matter, refer to provision made or to be made about that matter by directions.

Different provision for different cases etc.

9A–862   7. The power to make Civil Procedure Rules includes power to make different provision for different cases or different areas, including different provision—

    (a) for a specific court or specific division of a court, or

    (b) for specific proceedings, or a specific jurisdiction, specified in the rules.

9A–863   *Note* —For explanation of paragraphs in this Schedule, see notes to s.1 above.

SECTION 10

SCHEDULE 2

Minor and Consequential Amendments

9A–864   *Note* —By this Schedule, minor and consequential amendments were made to the Supreme Court Act 1981, the County Courts Act 1984, the Courts and Legal Services Act 1990, and the Matrimonial and Family Proceedings Act 1984. The first three of these Acts are printed elsewhere in this volume and, where necessary, the amendments made by this Schedule have been incorporated.

Access to Justice Act 1999

9A–865

(1999 c.22)

Arrangement of Sections

Part II

Other Funding of Legal Services

Costs

Note

9A–866   The functions of the Secretary of State for Constitutional Affairs under Pts 1 to 3 and Pt 7 of this Act, so far as relating to any provisions of those Parts, were transferred to the Lord Chancellor by The Transfer of Functions (Lord Chancellor and Secrtary of State) Order 2005 (S.I. 2005 No. 3429) with effect from January 12, 2006.

* * * *

PART II

OTHER FUNDING OF LEGAL SERVICES

COSTS

Recovery of insurance premiums by way of costs

29. Where in any proceedings a costs order is made in favour of **9A–867** any party who has taken out an insurance policy against the risk of incurring a liability in those proceedings, the costs payable to him may, subject in the case of court proceedings to rules of court, include costs in respect of the premium of the policy.

Note — For commentary on the recovery of insurance premiums as costs, see para. **9A–868** 7A–33.1 above, and Vol. 1, para. 44.3A.3.

Recovery where body undertakes to meet costs liabilities

30.—(1) This section applies where a body of a prescribed descrip- **9A–869** tion undertakes to meet (in accordance with arrangements satisfying prescribed conditions) liabilities which members of the body or other persons who are parties to proceedings may incur to pay the costs of other parties to the proceedings.

(2) If in any of the proceedings a costs order is made in favour of any of the members or other persons, the costs payable to him may, subject to subsection (3) and (in the case of court proceedings) to rules of court, include an additional amount in respect of any provision made by or on behalf of the body in connection with the proceedings against the risk of having to meet such liabilities.

(3) But the additional amount shall not exceed a sum determined in a prescribed manner; and there may, in particular, be prescribed as a manner of determination one which takes into account the likely cost to the member or other person of the premium of an insurance policy against the risk of incurring a liability to pay the costs of other parties to the proceedings.

(4) In this section "prescribed" means prescribed by regulations made by the Lord Chancellor by statutory instrument; and a statutory instrument containing such regulations shall be subject to annulment in pursuance of a resolution of either House of Parliament.

(5) Regulations under subsection (1) may, in particular, prescribe as a description of body one which is for the time being approved by the Lord Chancellor by a prescribed person.

* * * *

Note —Words in subss.(4) and (5) substituted by The Transfer of Functions (Lord **9A–870** Chancellor and Secretary of State) Order 2005 (S.I. 2005 No. 3429).

PART IV

APPEALS, COURTS, JUDGES AND COURT PROCEEDINGS

APPEALS

Permission to appeal

9A–871   54.—(1) Rules of court may provide that any right of appeal to—

(a) a county court,

(b) the High Court, or

(c) the Court of Appeal,

may be exercised only with permission.

(2) This section does not apply to a right of appeal in a criminal cause or matter.

(3) For the purposes of subsection (1) rules of court may make provision as to—

(a) the classes of case in which a right of appeal may be exercised only with permission,

(b) the court or courts which may give permission for the purposes of this section,

(c) any considerations to be taken into account in deciding whether permission should be given, and

(d) any requirements to be satisfied before permission may be given,

and may make different provision for different circumstances.

(4) No appeal may be made against a decision of a court under this section to give or refuse permission (but this subsection does not affect any right under rules of court to make a further application for permission to the same or another court).

(5) For the purposes of this section a right to make an application to have a case stated for the opinion of the High Court constitutes a right of appeal.

(6) For the purposes of this section a right of appeal to the Court of Appeal includes—

(a) the right to make an application for a new trial, and

(b) the right to make an application to set aside a verdict, finding or judgment in any cause or matter in the High Court which has been tried, or in which any issue has been tried, by a jury.

9A–872   *Note*—Section 54 paved the way for substantial alterations for the circumstances in which permission (formerly "leave") is required for the purpose of making appeals in civil proceedings. For relevant rules of court, see CPR Pt 52, especially r.52.3 and r.52.13. The effect of the rule stated in s.54(4) that, generally, no appeal may be made against a decision of a court to give or refuse permission to appeal has been explained by the Court of Appeal; see *Riniker v. University College London (Practice Note)* [2001] 1 W.L.R. 13, CA; *Foenander v. Bond Lewis & Co* [2001] EWCA Civ 759; [2002] 1 W.L.R. 525, CA; *State Bank of New South Wales v. Harrison* [2002] EWCA Civ 363; March 8, 2002, CA, unrep.; *Seray-Wurie v. Hackney London Borough Council* [2002] EWCA Civ 909; [2003] 1 W.L.R. 257, CA; *Gregory v. Turner* [2003] EWCA Civ 183, [2003] 1 W.L.R. 1149, CA, and authorities referred to therein; see also Vol. 1, para. 52.3.6. Under s.54 and CPR, r.52.3 permission to appeal is only required where the appeal is from a judge sitting in the High Court or in a county court. Consequently, there is no need to obtain permission where (for example) the appeal is from the decision of a judge nominated to hear appeals relating to the management of property and affairs of patients under the Mental Health Act 1983 (*In re B. (A Patient) (Court of Protection: Appeal)* [2005] EWCA Civ 1293, November 11, 2005, CA, unrep.).

Second appeals

55.—(1) Where an appeal is made to a county court or the High **9A–873** Court in relation to any matter, and on hearing the appeal the court makes a decision in relation to that matter, no appeal may be made to the Court of Appeal from that decision unless the Court of Appeal considers that—

> (a) the appeal would raise an important point of principle or practice, or
>
> (b) there is some other compelling reason for the Court of Appeal to hear it.

(2) This section does not apply in relation to an appeal in a criminal cause or matter.

Note —Section 55 implemented the recommendation of the Bowman Report that, **9A–874** generally, an unsuccessful appellant should not be able to make a further (second) appeal to the Court of Appeal. CPR, r.52.13 states that a second appeal as provided for by s.55(1) shall not be made without permission of the Court of Appeal itself. The appeal court, from whose decision permission to make a second appeal is sought, may give an indication of its opinion as to whether permission should be given by the Court of Appeal for a second appeal (Practice Direction (Appeals), para. 4.3; *R.. (Westminster City Council) v. Secretary of State for the Environment Transport and the Regions*, April 2, 2001, unrep. (Jackson J.)). Although s.55 is in wide terms, it has not impliedly repealed or amended the Patents Act 1977, s.97(3) or otherwise limited its scope. Consequently, the second appeal provisions in s.55 and CPR, r.52.13 do not apply to appeals under s.97(3) (*Smith International Inc. v. Specialised Petroleum Services Group Limited* [2005] EWCA Civ 1357, November 17, 2005, CA, unrep.)

Power to prescribe alternative destination of appeals

56.—(1) The Lord Chancellor may by order provide that appeals **9A–875** which would otherwise lie to—

> (a) a county court,
>
> (b) the High Court, or
>
> (c) the Court of Appeal,

shall lie instead to another of those courts, as specified in the order.

(2) This section does not apply to an appeal in a criminal cause or matter.

(3) An order under subsection (1)—

> (a) may make different provision for different classes of proceedings or appeals, and
>
> (b) may contain consequential amendments or repeals of enactments.

(4) Before making an order under subsection (1) the Lord Chancellor shall consult

> (a) the Lord Chief Justice,
>
> (b) the Master of the Rolls,
>
> (c) the President of the Queen's Bench Division;
>
> (d) the President of the Family Division; and

(e) the Chancellor of the High Court;

(5) An order under subsection (1) shall be made by statutory instrument.

(6) No such order may be made unless a draft of it has been laid before and approved by resolution of each House of Parliament.

(7) For the purposes of this section an application to have a case stated for the opinion of the High Court constitutes an appeal.

9A–876   Note —Section 56 gives the Lord Chancellor power by Order in Council to direct that appeals of a certain type that would normally go to one court, for example, the Court of Appeal, shall go instead to another court, for example, the High Court. The principal objective of this device is to relieve the Court of Appeal (Civil Division) of work. The Lord Chancellor exercised the powers granted by this provision in the Access to Justice (Destination of Appeals) Order 2000 (S.I. 2000 No. 1071); see para. 9A–884 below. Subsection (4) of s.56 was amended by the Constitutional Reform Act 2005, s.148(1) and Sched.4, para. 280(2), and further amendments will be made to this section as other provisions in the 2005 Act are brought into effect.

Assignment of appeals to Court of Appeal

9A–877   **57.**—(1) Where in any proceedings in a county court or the High Court a person appeals, or seeks permission to appeal, to a court other than the Court of Appeal or the House of Lords

      (a) the Master of the Rolls, or

      (b) the court from which or to which the appeal is made, or from which permission to appeal is sought,

may direct that the appeal shall be heard instead by the Court of Appeal.

(2) The power conferred by subsection (1)(b) shall be subject to rules of court.

*   *   *   *

JUDGES ETC.

Judges holding office in European or international courts

9A–878   **68.**—(1) A holder of a United Kingdom judicial office may hold office in a relevant international court without being required to relinquish the United Kingdom judicial office.

(2) In this section—

"United Kingdom judicial office" means the office of—

      (a) Lord Justice of Appeal, Justice of the High Court or Circuit Judge, in England and Wales,

      (b) judge of the Court of Session or sheriff, in Scotland, or

      (c) Lord Justice of Appeal, judge of the High Court or county court judge, in Northern Ireland, and

"relevant international court" means—

      (a) any court established for any purposes of the European Communities, or

      (b) any international court (apart from the European Court of Human Rights) which is designated for the purposes of this section by the Lord Chancellor or the Secretary of State.

(3) A holder of a United Kingdom judicial office who also holds office in a relevant international court is not required to perform any duties as the holder of the United Kingdom judicial office but does not count as holding the United Kingdom judicial office—

(a) for the purposes of section 12(1) to (6) of the Supreme Court Act 1981, section 9(1)(c) or (d) of the Administration of Justice Act 1973, section 18 of the Courts Act 1971, section 14 of the Sheriff Courts (Scotland) Act 1907 or section 106 of the County Courts Act (Northern Ireland) 1959 (judicial salaries),

(b) for the purposes of, or of any scheme established by and in accordance with, the Judicial Pensions and Retirement Act 1993, the Judicial Pensions Act 1981, the Sheriffs' Pensions (Scotland) Act 1961 or the County Courts Act (Northern Ireland) 1959 (judicial pensions), or

(c) for the purposes of section 2(1) or 4(1) of the Supreme Court Act 1981, section 1(1) of the Court of Session Act 1988 or section 2(1) or 3(1) of the Judicature (Northern Ireland) Act 1978 (judicial numbers).

(4) If the sheriff principal of any sheriffdom also holds office in a relevant international court, section 11(1) of the Sheriff Courts (Scotland) Act 1971 (temporary appointment of sheriff principal) applies as if the office of sheriff principal of that sheriffdom were vacant.

(5) The appropriate Minister may be order made by statutory instrument make in relation to a holder of a United Kingdom judicial office who has ceased to hold office in a relevant international court such transitional provision (including, in particular, provision for a temporary increase in the maximum number of judges) as he considers appropriate.

(6) In subsection (5) "the appropriate Minister" means—

(a) in relation to any United Kingdom judicial office specified in paragraph (a) or (c) of the definition in subsection (2), the Lord Chancellor, and

(b) in relation to any United Kingdom judicial office specified in paragraph (b) of that definition, the Secretary of State.

(7) A statutory instrument containing an order made under subsection (5) shall be subject to annulment in pursuance of a resolution of either House of Parliament.

* * * *

Access to Justice Act 1999 (Destination of Appeals) Order 2000

(S.I. 2000 No. 1071) (L.10)   9A–879

Introductory note

See also CPR Pt 52.   9A–880

This Order was made under the Access to Justice Act 1999, s.56, and came into effect on May 2, 2000. That section gives the Lord Chancellor power to provide by Order that appeals which would lie to (a) a county court, (b) the High Court, or (c) the Court of Appeal, shall lie instead to another of those courts, as specified in the Order.

The references to CPR Pts 57 to 62 were added to para. (b) of art.4 of this Order by the Civil Procedure (Modification of Enactments) Order 2002 (S.I. 2002 No. 439) with effect from March 23, 2002. The heading to art.2 is misleading, as it is concerned, not with appeals from, but with appeals to, the High Court.

Art.4 was amended by the Civil Procedure (Modification of Enactments) Order 2003 (S.I. 2003 No. 490) with effect from April 1, 2003.

Citation, commencement and interpretation

9A–881 **1.**—(1) This Order may be cited as the Access to Justice Act 1999 (Destination of Appeals) Order 2000 and shall come into force on 2nd May 2000.

(2) In this Order—

> (a) "decision" includes any judgment, order or direction of the High Court or a county court;
>
> (b) "family proceedings" means proceedings which are business of any description which in the High Court is for the time being assigned to the Family Division and to no other Division by or under section 61 of (and Schedule 1 to) the Supreme Court Act 1981; and
>
> (c) "final decision" means a decision of a court that would finally determine (subject to any possible appeal or detailed assessment of costs) the entire proceedings whichever way the court decided the issues before it.

(3) A decision of a court shall be treated as a final decision where it—

> (a) is made at the conclusion of part of a hearing or trial which has been split into parts; and
>
> (b) would, if made at the conclusion of that hearing or trial, be a final decision under paragraph (2)(c).

(4) Articles 2 to 6—

> (a) do not apply to an appeal in family proceedings; and
>
> (b) are subject to—
>
> > (i) any enactment that provides a different route of appeal (other than section 16(1) of the Supreme Court Act 1981 or section 77(1) of the County Courts Act 1984); and
> >
> > (ii) any requirement to obtain permission to appeal.

Appeals from the High Court

9A–882 **2.** Subject to articles 4 and 5, an appeal shall lie to a judge of the High Court where the decision to be appealed is made by—

(a) a person holding an office referred to in Part II of Schedule 2 to the Supreme Court Act 1981;

(b) a district judge of the High Court; or

(c) a person appointed to act as a deputy for any person holding such an office as is referred to in sub-paragraphs (a) and (b) or to act as a temporary additional officer in any such office.

Appeals from a county court

3.—(1) Subject to articles 4 and 5 and to paragraph (2), an appeal shall lie from a decision of a county court to the High Court.

(2) Subject to articles 4 and 5, where the decision to be appealed is made by a district judge or deputy district judge of a county court, an appeal shall lie to a judge of a county court.

Appeals in a claim allocated to the multi-track or in specialist proceedings

4. An appeal shall lie to the Court of Appeal where the decision to be appealed is a final decision—

(a) in a claim made under Part 7 of the Civil Procedure Rules 1998 and allocated to the multi-track under those Rules, or

(b) made in proceedings under the Companies Act 1985 or the Companies Act 1989 or to which Sections I, II or III of Part 57 or any of Parts 58 to 63 of the Civil Procedure Rules 1998 apply.

Appeals where decision was itself made on appeal

5. Where —

(a) an appeal is made to a county court or the High Court (other than from the decision of an officer of the court authorised to assess costs by the Lord Chancellor); and

(b) on hearing the appeal the court makes a decision,

an appeal shall lie from that decision to the Court of Appeal and not to any other court.

Transitional provisions

6. Where a person has filed a notice of appeal or applied for permission to appeal before 2nd May 2000—

(a) this Order shall not apply to the appeal to which that notice or application relates; and

(b) that appeal shall lie to the court to which it would have lain before 2nd May 2000.

Consequential amendments

7. In section 16(1) of the Supreme Court Act 1981, before "the Court of Appeal" the second time it appears, insert "or as provided by any order made by the Lord Chancellor under section 56(1) of the Access to Justice Act 1999".

8. In section 77(1) of the County Courts Act 1984, after "Act" insert "and to any order made by the Lord Chancellor under section 56(1) of the Access to Justice Act 1999".

9B   OTHER STATUTES AND REGULATIONS

Administration of Justice (Appeals) Act 1934

(1934 24 & 25 GEO. 5 C.40)

Restriction on appeals from Court of Appeal to House of Lords

1.—(1) No appeal shall lie to the House of Lords from any order **9B-1**
or judgment made or given by the Court of Appeal after the first day
of October 1934, except with the leave of that Court or of the House
of Lords.

(2) The House of Lords may by order provide for the hearing
and determination by a Committee of that House of petitions for
leave to appeal from the Court of Appeal:

Provided that section five of the Appellate Jurisdiction Act 1876,
shall apply to the hearing and determination of any such petition by
a Committee of the House as it applies to the hearing and determination of an appeal by the House.

(3) Nothing in this section shall affect any restriction existing,
apart from this section, on the bringing of appeals from the Court of
Appeal to the House of Lords.

Appeals from county courts

2.—(1) Every appeal from a judgment, direction, decision, decree **9B-2**
or order of a Judge of a county court given or made after such date
as the Lord Chancellor may by order appoint, being an appeal under
any of the enactments set out in the first column of the Schedule to
this Act, shall lie to the Court of Appeal instead of to the High Court;
and accordingly those enactments shall have effect in relation to any
such appeal subject to the modifications respectively specified in the
second column of that Schedule.

Note —Amended by the County Courts Act 1934.   **9B-3**

Operation of section
By an order of the L.C., dated July 26, 1934, January 1, 1935 was fixed as the ap- **9B-4**
pointed day, and all appeals from judgments, etc., of a Judge of a county court made
after that day lie to CA direct. See CPR Sched.1, O.59, r.19, and nn. as to practice.

Short title and extent

3.—(1) This Act may be cited as the Administration of Justice (Ap- **9B-5**
peals) Act 1934.

(2) This Act shall not extend to Scotland or Northern Ireland.

* * * *

SCHEDULE

ENACTMENTS AS TO APPEALS FROM COUNTY COURTS

PART III

ENACTMENTS UNAFFECTED BY COUNTY COURTS ACT 1888
s.36, Building Societies Act 1874.   **9B-6**

s.4, Telegraph Act 1878.
s.10, Guardianship of Infants Act 1886.
s.1, Parliamentary Election (Ret. Officers) Act 1875 (Am) Act 1886.

9B–7 *Note*—Amended by the Control of Pollution Act 1974, Sched.4. Statutes replaced by the Building Societies Act 1986, Telecommunications Act 1984. Parliamentary, etc. Act 1886 repealed by S L (R) Act 1978.

Administration of Justice (Miscellaneous Provisions) Act 1933

(1933 23 & 24 GEO. 5 C.36)

Costs in Crown proceedings

9B–8 7.—(1) In any civil proceedings to which the Crown is a party in any Court having power to award costs in cases between subjects, and in any arbitration to which the Crown is a party, the costs of and incidental to the proceedings shall be in the discretion of the Court or arbitrator to be exercised in the same manner and on the same principles as in cases between subjects, and the Court or arbitrator shall have power to make an order for the payment of costs by or to the Crown accordingly: Provided that—

(a) in the case of proceedings to which by reason of any enactment or otherwise the Attorney-General, a Government department of any officer of the Crown as such is required to be made a party, the Court or arbitrator shall have regard to the nature of the proceedings and the character and circumstances in which the Attorney-General, the department or officer of the Crown appears, and may in the exercise of its or his discretion order any other party to the proceedings to pay the costs of the Attorney-General, department or officer, whatever may be the result of the proceedings; and

(b) nothing in this section shall affect the power of the Court or arbitrator to order, or any enactment providing for, the payment of costs out of any particular fund or property, or any enactment expressly relieving any department or officer of the Crown of the liability to pay costs.

(2) In this section the expression "civil proceedings" includes proceedings by petition of right and proceedings by the Crown in the High Court or a county court for the recovery of fines or penalties, and references to proceedings to which the Crown is a party include references to proceedings to which the Attorney-General or any Government department or any officer of the Crown as such is a party, so, however, that the Crown shall not be deemed to be a party to any proceedings by reason only that the proceedings are proceedings by the Attorney-General on the relation of some other person.

(3) [...]

9B–9 *Note* — Subsection (3) repealed by the Statute Law (Repeals) Act 1993.

Costs
9B–10 See, generally, notes to CPR Pts 43 and 49. The definition of civil proceedings in subs. (2) is not exhaustive, and presumably proceedings under s.3 are included. As to

proceedings by and against the Crown, see the Crown Proceedings Act 1947, para. 9B–299 and CPR Sched.1, O.77. Proceedings by way of petition of right have been abolished by that Act. Interest is payable on costs awarded to or against the Crown unless the Court otherwise orders (*ibid.*, s.24(2)).

Saving for proceedings affecting Her Majesty in Her private capacity

9. Nothing in this Act shall apply to proceedings affecting Her Majesty in Her private capacity.   9B–11

Short title, extent, repeal

10.—(1) This Act may be cited as the Administration of Justice (Miscellaneous Provisions) Act 1933.   9B–12

(2) This Act shall not extend to Scotland or to Northern Ireland.

(3) [...]

(4) [...]

Note — Subsections (3) and (4) repealed by the Statute Law Revision Act 1950.   9B–13

Administration of Justice Act 1925

(1925 15 & 16 GEO. 5 c.28)

MISCELLANEOUS

* * * *

Registration of deeds of arrangement

22.—(1) The office for the registration of deeds of arrangement under the Deeds of Arrangement Act 1914 (in this section referred to as "the Act of 1914") shall be transferred to the Board of Trade, and the Registrar for the purposes of the Act of 1914 shall be appointed by the Board of Trade, and references in that Act to the Registrar of bills of sale or to the Registrar for the purposes of that Act shall be construed as references to the Registrar so appointed.   9B–14

(2) Subsection (1) of section five of the Act of 1914 (which provides that a copy of every deed to be registered shall be presented to the Registrar) shall have effect as if it provided that there shall be presented to the Registrar such number of copies of the deed and of every schedule or inventory annexed thereto or referred to therein as he may deem to be necessary for the purpose of carrying out the requirements of the Act of 1914 as amended by this section.

(3) [...]

(4) All fees whatsoever to be taken under the Act of 1914 shall be prescribed by order made by the Lord Chancellor with the concurrence of the Treasury and not otherwise, and all such fees shall be paid into such account as the Treasury may direct.

(5) Subject to the provisions of subsection (4) of this section, rules for carrying into effect the provisions of the Act of 1914, as amended by this section, other than the provisions of section seven thereof,

may be made by the Lord Chancellor with the concurrence of the President of the Board of Trade, and, subject as aforesaid, the expression "prescribed" in the Act of 1914 shall mean prescribed by rules made under this subsection.

(6) This section shall be construed as one with the Act of 1914.

9B–15 *Note* — Subsection (3) repealed and subs. (4) amended by the Statute Law (Repeals) Act 1989, Sched.1.

Local registration of bills of sale under Bills of Sale Acts 1878 and 1882

9B–16 **23.**—(1) Section eleven of the Bills of Sale Act (1878) Amendment Act 1882 (which makes provision for the local registration of the contents of bills of sale) shall have effect as if it required the Registrar of bills of sale to transmit to county court registrars copies of the bills instead of abstracts of the contents of the bills, and references in this section to the abstract transmitted and the abstract registered shall be construed accordingly.

(2) Section ten of the Bills of Sale Act 1878 shall have effect as though it required the presentation to the registrar on the registration of a bill of sale, in addition to the copy of the bill of sale mentioned in paragraph (2) of that section, of such number of copies of the bill and every schedule and inventory annexed thereto as the Registrar may deem to be necessary for the purpose of carrying out the requirements of the said section eleven as amended by this section.

* * * *

Power to revoke and vary orders

9B–17 **28.** Any order made under this Act by the Lord Chancellor may at any time be revoked, varied or amended by a subsequent order made under this Act by the Lord Chancellor.

9B–18 *Note* —Amended by the Statute Law (Repeals) Act 1973, Sched.1.

Short title, interpretation, extent, repeal and commencement

9B–19 **29.**—(1) This Act may be cited as the Administration of Justice Act, 1925.

(2) [...]

(3) This Act shall not extend to Scotland or Northern Ireland.

(4) [...]

(5) [...]

9B–20 *Note* —Amended by the Statute Law Revision Act 1950; and the Statute Law (Repeals) Act 1973.

Administration of Justice Act 1960

9B–21 (1960 8 & 9 ELIZ. 2 C.65)

ARRANGEMENT OF SECTIONS

CONTEMPT OF COURT, HABEAS CORPUS AND CERTIORARI

CONTEMPT OF COURT, HABEAS CORPUS AND CERTIORARI

Publication of information relating to proceedings in private

12.—(1) The publication of information relating to proceedings **9B–22** before any court sitting in private shall not of itself be contempt of court except in the following cases, that is to say—

(a) where the proceedings—

    (i) relate to the exercise of the inherent jurisdiction of the High Court with respect to minors;

    (ii) are brought under the Children Act 1989; or

    (iii) otherwise relate wholly or mainly to the maintenance or upbringing of a minor;

(b) where the proceedings are brought under Part VIII of the Mental Health Act 1959, or under any provision of that Act authorising an application or reference to be made to a Mental Health Review Tribunal or to a county court;

(c) where the court sits in private for reasons of national security during that part of the proceedings about which the information in question is published;

(d) where the information relates to a secret process, discovery or invention which is in issue in the proceedings;

(e) where the court (having power to do so) expressly prohibits the publication of all information relating to the proceedings or of information of the description which is published.

(2) Without prejudice to the foregoing subsection, the publication of the text or a summary of the whole or part of an order made by a court sitting in private shall not of itself be contempt of court except where the court (having power to do so) expressly prohibits the publication.

(3) In this section references to a court include references to a judge and to a tribunal and to any person exercising the functions of a court, a judge or tribunal; and references to a court sitting in private include references to a court sitting in camera or in chambers.

(4) Nothing in this section shall be construed as implying that any publication is punishable as contempt of court which would not be so punishable apart from this section (and in particular where the publication is not so punishable by reason of being authorised by rules of court).

9B–23   *Note* — Part VIII of the Mental Health Act 1959 was replaced by Pt VII of the Mental Health Act 1983. Amended by the Children Act 1989, Sched.13; the Children Act 2004, s.62(2).

"court sitting in private"

9B–24   Traditionally, legal proceedings have been conducted either "in court" or "in chambers" (see Supreme Court Act 1981, s.67). Nowadays, it is common to draw a distinction between courts sitting "in public" or "in private" (see CPR, r.39.2). It is expressly provided that, in s.12 references to a court "sitting in private" include a court sitting "in court" but in camera, or a court sitting "in chambers" (s.12(3)). This would suggest that the section was drafted on the assumption that, contrary to the modern position, a court sitting "in chambers" was *ipso facto* a court sitting "in private". These pairings are not co-terminous; at least, a court sitting "in chambers" is not necessarily a court sitting "in private". See further paras 9A–315 to 9A–319 above, and Vol. 1, para. 39.2.1.

When enacted, s.12 was remedial in the sense that it had the effect of making it clear that the publication of information relating to proceedings "in private" is not necessarily contempt. The section sets out the circumstances in which, subject to exceptions, it shall be a contempt of court to publish information given in private proceedings. The stated exceptions are not exhaustive. For a recent review of the relevant law, see *Clibbery v. Allan* [2002] EWCA Civ 45; [2002] 2 W.L.R. 1511, CA, a case involving specifically the confidentiality of documents disclosed in, and the publication of information relating to, proceedings in the Family Division conducted in private.

Appeal in cases of contempt of court

9B–25   **13.**—(1) Subject to the provisions of this section, an appeal shall lie under this section from any order or decision of a court in the exercise of jurisdiction to punish for contempt of court (including criminal contempt); and in relation to any such order or decision the provisions of this section shall have effect in substitution for any other enactment relating to appeals in civil or criminal proceedings.

(2) An appeal under this section shall lie in any case at the instance of the defendant and, in the case of an application for committal or attachment, at the instance of the applicant; and the appeal shall lie—

   (a) from an order or decision of any inferior court not referred to in the next following paragraph, to the High Court;

   (b) from an order or decision of a county court or any other inferior court from which appeals generally lie to the civil division of the Court of Appeal, and from an order or decision (other than a decision on an appeal under this section) of a single judge of the High Court, or of any court having the powers of the High Court or of a judge of that court, to the civil division of the Court of Appeal;

   (bb) from an order or decision of the Crown Court to the Court of Appeal;

   (c) from a decision of a single judge of the High Court on an appeal under this section, from an order or decision of a Divisional Court or the civil division of the Court of Appeal (including a decision of either of those courts on an appeal under this section) and from an order or decision of the criminal division of the Court of Appeal or the Courts-Martial Appeal Court, to the House of Lords.

(3) The court to which an appeal is brought under this section may reverse or vary the order or decision of the court below, and make such other order as may be just; and without prejudice to the inherent powers of any court referred to in subsection (2) of this section, provision may be made by rules of court for authorising the release on bail of an appellant under this section.

(4) Subsections (2) to (4) of section one and section two of this Act shall apply to an appeal to the House of Lords under this section as they apply to an appeal to that House under the said section one, except that so much of the said subsection (2) as restricts the grant of leave to appeal shall apply only where the decision of the court below is a decision on appeal to that court under this section.

(5) In this section "court" includes any tribunal or person having power to punish for contempt; and references in this section to an order or decision of a court in the exercise of jurisdiction to punish for contempt of court include references—

    (a) to an order or decision of the High Court, the Crown Court or a county court under any enactment enabling that court to deal with an offence as if it were contempt of court;

    (b) to an order or decision of a county court, under section 14, 92 or 118 of the County Courts Act 1984;

    (c) to an order or decision of a magistrates' court under subsection (3) of section 63 of the Magistrates' Courts Act 1980,

    but do not include references to order under section five of the Debtors Act 1869, or under any provision of the Magistrates' Courts Act 1980, or the County Courts Act 1984, except those referred to in paragraphs (b) and (c) of this subsection and except sections 38 and 142 of the last mentioned Act so far as those sections confer jurisdiction in respect of contempt of court.

(6) This section does not apply to a conviction or sentence in respect of which an appeal lies under Part I of the Criminal Appeal Act 1968, or to a decision of the criminal division of the Court of Appeal under that Part of that Act.

9B–25.1   *Note* —Amended by the Courts Act 1971, Sched.8, para. 40(1) and Sched.11; and the Criminal Appeal Act 1968, Sched.5; the SCA 1981, s.152(4) and Sched.7; the County Courts Act 1984, Sched.2 and the Access to Justice Act 1999, s.64 and Sched.15, Pt III.

Destination of appeals against orders punishing for contempt

9B–25.2   In *Barnett LBC v. Hurst* [2002] EWCA Civ 1009; 152 New L.J. 1275 (2002), CA, the Court of Appeal explained the appropriate routes for appeals from decisions made in committal proceedings by judges exercising county court jurisdiction. See further CPR Pt 52.

Procedure on application for habeas corpus

9B–26   **14.**—(1) [...]

(2) Notwithstanding anything in any enactment or rule of law, where a criminal or civil application for habeas corpus has been

made by or in respect of any person, no such application shall again be made by or in respect of that person on the same grounds, whether to the same court or judge or to any other court or judge, unless fresh evidence is adduced in support of the application; and no such application shall in any case be made to the Lord Chancellor.

(3) In every case where the person by or in respect of whom an application for habeas corpus is made is restrained as a person liable, or treated by virtue of any enactment as liable, to be detained in pursuance of an order or direction under Part V of the Mental Health Act 1959 (otherwise than by virtue of paragraph (e) or paragraph (f) of subsection (2) of section seventy-three of that Act) the application shall be deemed for the purposes of his section and of any appeal in the proceedings to constitute a criminal cause or matter.

9B–27   *Note* —In subs.(3) see now the Mental Health Act 1983, s.48. Subs. (1) repealed by the Access to Justice Act 1999, Sched.15, Pt III.

Further application for habeas corpus
9B–28   The applicant for habeas corpus must put forward on his initial application the whole of the case then fairly available to him, and the doctrine of *res judicata*, whereby it is an abuse of the process to raise in subsequent proceedings matters which could have been litigated in earlier proceedings, applies to subsequent proceedings for habeas corpus; and moreover, to constitute "fresh evidence" in support of a subsequent application within the meaning of s.14(2) the evidence must not be merely additional to or different from that which was adduced before the Court on the first application but evidence which the applicant could not have, or could not reasonably have been expected to, put forward on the first application (*Re Tarling* [1979] 1 W.L.R. 1417; [1979] 1 All E.R. 981, DC).

Appeal in habeas corpus proceedings
9B–29   **15.**—(1) Subject to the provisions of this section, an appeal shall lie, in any proceedings upon application for habeas corpus, whether civil or criminal, against an order for the release of the person restrained as well as against the refusal of such an order.

(2) [...]

(3) In relation to a decision of the High Court on a criminal application for habeas corpus, section one of this Act shall have effect as if so much of subsection (2) as restricts the grant of leave to appeal were omitted.

(4) Except as provided by section five of this Act in the case of an appeal against an order of the High Court on a criminal application, an appeal brought by virtue of this section shall not affect the right of the person restrained to be discharged in pursuance of the order under appeal and (unless an order under subsection (1) of that section is in force at the determination of the appeal) to remain at large regardless of the decision on appeal.

9B–29.1   *Note* —Subsection (2) repealed by the Access to Justice Act 1999, Sched.15, Pt III.

Release on bail pending appeal
9B–30   In proceedings on application for habeas corpus in criminal matters, where the prosecutor is granted, or gives notice that he intends to apply for, leave to appeal to the House of Lords from the Divisional Court, the fugitive should not be released unconditionally, but only on bail pending the appeal to the House of Lords (*Govern-*

ment of USA v. McCaffery [1984] 1 W.L.R. 867; [1984] 2 All E.R. 570, HL, applying *DPP v. Merriman* [1974] 3 All E.R. 42).

Power of High Court to vary sentence on certiorari

16. [*Repealed by the SCA 1981 , s.15(4) and Sched.7. See now the SCA 1981 , s.43, para. 9A–136.*]

9B–31

SUPPLEMENTARY

Interpretation

17.—(1) In this Act any reference to the defendant shall be construed—

9B–32

    (a) in relation to proceedings for an offence, and in relation to an application for an order of mandamus, prohibition or certiorari in connection with such proceedings, as a reference to the person who was or would have been the defendant in those proceedings;

    (b) in relation to any proceedings or order for or in respect of contempt of court, as a reference to the person against whom the proceedings were brought or the order was made;

    (c) in relation to a criminal application for habeas corpus, as a reference to the person by or in respect of whom that application was made,

and any reference to the prosecutor shall be construed accordingly.

(2) In this Act "application for habeas corpus" means an application for a writ of habeas corpus *ad subjiciendum* and references to a criminal application or civil application shall be construed according as the application does or does not constitute a criminal cause or matter.

(3) In this Act any reference to the court below shall, in relation to any function of a Divisional Court, be construed as a reference to the Divisional Court or to a judge according as the function is by virtue of rules of court exercisable by the Divisional Court or a judge.

(4) An appeal under section one of this Act shall be treated for the purposes of this Act as pending until any application for leave to appeal is disposed of and, if leave to appeal is granted, until the appeal is disposed of; and for the purposes of this Act an application for leave to appeal shall be treated as disposed of at the expiration of the time within which it may be made, if it is not made within that time.

(5) [...]

(6) Any reference in this Act to any other enactment is a reference thereto as amended by or under any other enactment, including this Act.

Note — Subsection (5) repealed by the Criminal Appeal Act 1995, Sched.3.

9B–33

* * * * *

Minor and consequential amendments and repeals

19.—(1) [...]

9B–34

2503

(2) [...]

(3) The repeals effected by subsection (2) of this section in section four of the Geneva Conventions Act 1957, shall not affect the power of Her Majesty under subsection (2) of section eight of that Act to extend the provisions of that Act outside the United Kingdom.

9B–35   *Note* — Subsection (1) repealed by the Statute Law (Repeals) Act 1993; subs. (2) repealed by the Statute Law (Repeals) Act 1974.

Short title and extent

9B–36   **20.**—(1) This Act may be cited as the Administration of Justice Act 1960.

(2) This Act shall not extend to Scotland.

Administration of Justice Act 1969

(1969 c.58)

9B–37   *[22nd October 1969]*

ARRANGEMENT OF SECTIONS

PART II

APPEAL FROM HIGH COURT TO HOUSE OF LORDS

* * * *

PART II

APPEAL FROM HIGH COURT TO HOUSE OF LORDS

Grant of certificate by trial Judge

9B–38   **12.**—(1) Where on the application of any of the parties to any proceedings to which this section applies the judge is satisfied—

        (a) that the relevant conditions are fulfilled in relation to his decision in those proceedings, and

        (b) that a sufficient case for an appeal to the House of Lords under this Part of this Act has been made out to justify an application for leave to bring such an appeal, and

        (c) that all the parties to the proceedings consent to the grant of a certificate under this section,

the judge, subject to the following provisions of this Part of this Act, may grant a certificate to that effect.

(2) This section applies to any civil proceedings in the High Court which are either—

        (a) proceedings before a single judge of the High Court, or

        (b) [Repealed by the Courts Act 1971, Sched.11.]

        (c) proceedings before a Divisional Court.

(3) Subject to any Order in Council made under the following provisions of this section, for the purposes of this section the relevant

conditions, in relation to a decision of the judge in any proceedings, are that a point of law of general public importance is involved in that decision and that that point of law either—

(a) relates wholly or mainly to the construction of an enactment or of a statutory instrument, and has been fully argued in the proceedings and fully considered in the judgment of the judge in the proceedings, or

(b) is one in respect of which the judge is bound by a decision of the Court of Appeal or of the House of Lords in previous proceedings, and was fully considered in the judgments given by the Court of Appeal or the House of Lords (as the case may be) in those previous proceedings.

(4) Any application for a certificate under this section shall be made to the judge immediately after he gives judgment in the proceedings:

Provided that the judge may in any particular case entertain any such application made at any later time before the end of the period of fourteen days beginning with the date on which that judgment is given or such other period as may be prescribed by rules of court.

(5) No appeal shall lie against the grant or refusal of a certificate under this section.

(6) Her Majesty may by Order in Council amend subsection (3) of this section by altering, deleting, or substituting one or more new paragraphs for, either or both of paragraphs (a) and (b) of that subsection, or by adding one or more further paragraphs.

(7) Any Order in Council made under this section shall be subject to annulment in pursuance of a resolution of either House of Parliament.

(8) In this Part of this Act "civil proceedings" means any proceedings other than proceedings in a criminal cause or matter, and "the judge," in relation to any proceedings to which this section applies, means the judge or commissioner referred to in paragraph (a) of subsection (2) of this section, or the Divisional Court referred to in paragraph (c) of that subsection, as the case may be.

Note—Amended by the SCA 1981, s.152(4), Sched.7; and the Courts Act 1971, s.56, Sched.11. **9B–39**

Certificate for appeal from High Court to House of Lords   **9B–40**

For a case where a certificate under this section has been granted, see *Ealing London Borough Council v. Race Relations Board* [1970] 1 W.L.R. 1599.

For a review of the general operation of this section, see *Inland Revenue Commissioners v. Church Commissioners for England* [1975] 1 W.L.R. 251; [1974] 3 All E.R. 529). Even where the requirements of the section are satisfied, the Judge has a discretion whether or not to grant the certificate, as where he considers that the case does not fall within the spirit, as distinct from the letter, of the section (*ibid.*).

Leave to appeal to House of Lords

13.—(1) Where in any proceedings the judge grants a certificate **9B–41** under section 12 of this Act, then, at any time within one month from the date on which that certificate is granted or such extended time as in any particular case the House of Lords may allow, any of the parties to the proceedings may make an application to the House of Lords under this section.

(2) Subject to the following provisions of this section, if on such an application it appears to the House of Lords to be expedient to do so, the House may grant leave for an appeal to be brought directly to the House ; and where leave is granted under this section—

(a) no appeal from the decision of the judge to which the certificate relates shall lie to the Court of Appeal, but

(b) an appeal shall lie from that decision to the House of Lords.

(3) Applications under this section shall be determined without a hearing.

(4) Any order of the House of Lords which provides for applications under this section to be determined by a committee of the House—

(a) shall direct that the committee shall consist of or include not less than three of the persons designated as Lords of Appeal in accordance with section 5 of the Appellate Jurisdiction Act 1876, and

(b) may direct that the decision of the committee on any such application shall be taken on behalf of the House.

(5) Without prejudice to subsection (2) of this section, no appeal shall lie to the Court of Appeal from a decision of the judge in respect of which a certificate is granted under section 12 of this Act until—

(a) the time within which an application can be made under this section has expired, and

(b) where such an application is made, that application has been determined in accordance with the preceding provisions of this section.

No appeal to Court of Appeal

9B–41.1   In *R. (Jones) v. Ceredigion County Council* [2005] EWCA Civ 986; [2005] 1 W.L.R. 3626, CA, a High Court judge determined an application for judicial review in favour of the claimant and quashed a decision made by the defendant local authority, The judge granted the defendants a certificate under s. 12(1) to apply for permission to appeal to the House of Lords and, in addition, granted the defendants permission to appeal to the Court of Appeal if, in the event, the Lords did not grant permission. The House of Lords granted the defendants permission to appeal to them in relation to one of three issues on which the defendants sought to appeal. Subsequently, the defendants withdrew that appeal (in effect, abandoning the point), and applied for permission to appeal to the Court of Appeal on one of the two issues on which the House of Lords had refused permission. The claimant contended that, by virtue of s. 13(2)(a), the defendants were precluded from bringing an appeal to the Court of Appeal. The Court held (by majority) that it did have jurisdiction to entertain the appeal, rejecting the argument that "decision" in s. 13(2) could, in the circumstances of this case, refer only to the quashing order made by the judge.

Appeal where leave granted

9B–42   **14.** In relation to any appeal which lies to the House of Lords by virtue of subsection (2) of section 13 of this Act—

(a) section 4 of the Appellate Jurisdiction Act 1876 (which provides for the bringing of appeals to the House of Lords by way of petition)

    (b) section 5 of that Act (which regulates the composition of the House for the hearing and determination of appeals) and

    (c) except in so far as those orders otherwise provide, any orders of the House of Lords made with respect to the matters specified in section 11 of that Act (which relates to the procedure on appeals)

shall have effect as they have effect in relation to appeals under that Act.

Cases excluded from section 12

15.—(1) No certificate shall be granted under section 12 of this Act **9B–43** in respect of a decision of the judge in any proceedings where by virtue of any enactment, apart from the provisions of this Part of this Act, no appeal would lie from that decision to the Court of Appeal, with or without the leave of the judge or of the Court of Appeal.

(2) No certificate shall be granted under section 12 of this Act in respect of a decision of the judge where—

    (a) [...]

    (b) by virtue of any enactment, apart from the provisions of this Part of this Act, no appeal would (with or without the leave of the Court of Appeal or of the House of Lords) lie from any decision of the Court of Appeal on an appeal from the decision of the judge.

(3) Where by virtue of any enactment, apart from the provisions of this Part of this Act, no appeal would lie to the Court of Appeal from the decision of the judge except with the leave of the judge or of the Court of Appeal, no certificate shall be granted under section 12 of this Act in respect of that decision unless it appears to the judge that apart from the provisions of this Part of this Act it would be a proper case for granting such leave.

(4) No certificate shall be granted under section 12 of this Act where the decision of the judge, or any order made by him in pursuance of that decision, is made in the exercise of jurisdiction to punish for contempt of court.

Note — Subsection (2)(a) repealed by the Administration of Justice Act 1977, s.32(4), **9B–44** Sched.5.

Administration of Justice Act 1970

(1970 c.31)

[29th May 1970] **9B–45**

LEGISLATION

Part I

Courts and Judges

High Court

Redistribution of business among divisions of the High Court

9B–46   **1.**—(1)–(5) [...]

(6) In accordance with the foregoing subsections—

(a) the enactments specified in Schedule 2 to this Act (that is to say, the said Act 1925 and other enactments relative to the High Court, its jurisdiction, judges, divisions and business) shall be amended as shown in that Schedule; and

(b) references in any other enactment or document to the Probate, Divorce and Admiralty Division, the President of that division, the principal probate registry, the principal (or senior) probate registrar and a probate registrar shall, so far as may be necessary to preserve the effect of the enactment or document, be construed respectively as references to the Family Division and to the President, principal registry, principal registrar and a registrar of that division.

(7) [...]

9B–47   *Note* —Amended by the SCA 1981, s.152(4) and Sched.7.

* * * *

Patents and Registered Designs Appeal Tribunals

Temporary additional judges

9B–48   **10.**—(1) If it appears to the Lord Chancellor expedient, having regard to the state of business pending before the Registered Designs Appeal Tribunal, he may appoint—

    (a) a judge of the Court of Appeal; or

    (b) a person who has held office as a judge of the Court of Appeal or of the High Court; or

    (c) one of Her Majesty's counsel,

to sit and act as an additional judge of the Tribunal (either alone or with a judge of the High Court who is a judge of the Tribunal) for such period, or for the purpose of hearing such appeals, as the Lord Chancellor may specify.

(2) A person appointed to the Tribunal under this section shall, while sitting and acting as aforesaid, have all the jurisdiction of, but shall not otherwise be deemed to be, a judge of the Tribunal.

(3) The Lord Chancellor may pay to a person appointed to the Tribunal under this section (other than a judge of the Court of Appeal) such remuneration as he may determine with the approval of the Minister for the Civil Service; and any such remuneration shall be included in the expenses of the Tribunal.

(4) In this section "the Registered Designs Appeal Tribunal" means the Appeal Tribunal constituted under section 28 of the Registered Designs Act 1949 (as amended by section 24 of the Administration of Justice Act 1969).

(5) In subsection (8) of the said section 28 (which confers power on the Tribunal to make rules about procedure etc.) there shall be inserted at the end of the subsection the words "including right of audience."

Note—Amended by the Patents Act 1977, s.132, Scheds 5 and 6.   **9B–49**

PART II

ENFORCEMENT OF DEBT

PROVISIONS RESTRICTING SANCTION OF IMPRISONMENT

Restriction on power of committal under Debtors Act 1869

11. The jurisdiction given by section 5 of the Debtors Act 1869 to **9B–50** commit to prison a person who makes default in payment of a debt, or instalment of a debt, due from him in pursuance of an order or judgment shall be exercisable only—

    (a) by the High Court in respect of a High Court maintenance order; and

    (b) by a county court in respect of—

        (i) a High Court or a county court maintenance order; or

        (ii) a judgment or order which is enforceable by a court in England and Wales and is for the payment of any of the taxes, contributions premiums or liabilities specified in Schedule 4 to this Act.

LEGISLATION

9B–50   *Note* —Amended by Social Security Act 1973, Sched.27.

* * * *

ENFORCEMENT BY ATTACHMENT OF EARNINGS

Other provisions for interpretation of Part II

9B–51   **28.**—(1) In this Part of this Act, except where the context otherwise requires—

"High Court maintenance order" and "county court maintenance order" mean respectively a maintenance order enforceable by the High Court and a county court.

"maintenance order" means any order specified in Schedule 8
to this Act and includes such an order which has been
discharged, if any arrears are recoverable thereunder.

9B–52   *Note* —Repealed in part by the Attachment of Earnings Act 1971, s.29 and Sched.6;
and the Magistrates' Courts Act 1980, s.154 and Sched.9.

* * * *

ADDITIONAL POWERS OF COURT IN ACTION BY MORTGAGEE FOR

POSSESSION OF DWELLING-HOUSE

9B–53   **36.** [Section 36 is set out with notes in Section 3A, para. 3A–30.]

INTERPRETATION OF PART IV

39. [Section 39 is set out with notes in Section 3A, para. 3A–37.]

PART V

MISCELLANEOUS PROVISIONS

Interest on judgment debts

44.—(1) The Lord Chancellor may by order made with the concurrence of the Treasury direct that section 17 of the Judgments Act
1838 (as that enactment has effect for the time being whether by
virtue of this subsection or otherwise) shall be amended so as to
substitute for the rate specified in that section as the rate at which
judgment debts shall carry interest at such rate as may be specified in
the order.

(2) An order under this section shall be made by statutory instrument which shall be laid before Parliament after being made.

Interest on judgment debts expressed in currencies other than sterling

9B–54   **44A.**—(1) Where a judgment is given for a sum expressed in a currency other than sterling and the judgment debt is one to which section 17 of the Judgments Act 1838 applies, the court may order that
the interest rate applicable to the debt shall be such rate as the court
thinks fit.

(2) Where the court makes such an order, section 17 of the Judgments Act 1838 shall have effect in relation to the judgment debt as if the rate specified in the order were substituted for the rate specified in that section.

(3) Subsection (1) above does not apply in relation to a judgment given before the commencement of this section.

Note —Added by the Private International Law (Miscellaneous Provisions) Act 1995, **9B–55**
s.1.

Note — For commentary see Vol. 1, para. 40.8.1. Note also CPR, r.74.4(2)(e) (evidence of interest recoverable on foreign judgment). **9B–56**

* * * *

PART VI

GENERAL

Citation, interpretation, repeals, commencement and extent

54.—(1) This Act may be cited as the Administration of Justice Act **9B–57**
1970.

(2) References in this Act to any enactment include references to that enactment as amended or extended by or under any other enactment, including this Act.

(3) The enactments specified in Schedule 11 to this Act are hereby repealed to the extent specified in the third column of that Schedule.

(4) [. . .]

(5) [Application to Scotland.]

(6) [Application to Northern Ireland.]

* * * *

Note —Subs.(4) repealed by the Statute Law (Repeals) Act 2004, s.1(1), Sch.1, Pt 1.

SCHEDULE 3

APPLICATION OF ARBITRATION ACT 1950 TO JUDGE-ARBITRATORS

[*Schedule 3 repealed by the Arbitration Act 1996 , Sched.4.*] **9B–58**
* * * *

SCHEDULE 8

MAINTENANCE ORDERS FOR PURPOSES OF 1958 ACT AND PART II OF THIS ACT

1. An order for alimony, maintenance or other payments made, or having effect as if **9B–59**
made, under Part II of the Matrimonial Causes Act 1965 (ancillary relief in actions for divorce etc.).

2. An order for payments to or in respect of a child being an order made, or having effect as if made, under Part III of the said Act of 1965 (maintenance of children following divorce, etc.).

2A. An order for periodical or other payments made, or having effect as if made, under Part II of the Matrimonial Causes Act 1973.

3. An order for maintenance or other payments to or in respect of a spouse or child being an order made under Part I of the Domestic Proceedings and Magistrates' Courts Act 1978.

4. An order for periodical or other payments made or having effect as if made under Schedule 1 to the Children Act 1989.

5. [...]

6. An order under section 47 or 51 of the Child Care Act 1980

(a) made or having effect as if made under paragraph 23 of Schedule 2 to the Children Act 1989; or

(b) made under section 23 of the Ministry of Social Security Act 1966, section 18 of the Supplementary Benefits Act 1976 or section 24 of the Social Security Act 1986 or section 106 of the Social Security Administration Act 1992 (various provisions for obtaining contributions from a person whose dependants are assisted or maintained out of public funds).

7. An order under section 43 of the National Assistance Act 1948 (recovery of costs of maintaining assisted person).

8. An order to which section 16 of the Maintenance Orders Act 1950 applies by virtue of subsection (2)(b) or (c) of that section (that is to say an order made by a court in Scotland or Northern Ireland and corresponding to one of those specified in the foregoing paragraphs) and which has been registered in a court in England and Wales under Part II of that Act.

9. A maintenance order within the meaning of the Maintenance Orders (Facilities for Enforcement) Act 1920 (Commonwealth orders enforceable in the United Kingdom) registered in, or confirmed by, a court in England and Wales under that Act.

10. [...]

11. A maintenance order within the meaning of Part I of the Maintenance Orders (Reciprocal Enforcement) Act 1972 registered in a magistrates' court under the said Part I.

12. [Repealed.]

13. A maintenance order within the meaning of Part I of the Civil Jurisdiction and Judgments Act 1982 which is registered in a magistrates' court under that Part.

13A. A maintenance judgment within the meaning of Council Regulation (EC) No. 44/2001 of 22nd December 2000 on jurisdiction and the recognition and enforcement of judgments in civil and commercial matters, which is registered in a magistrates' court under that Regulation.

14. An order for periodical or other payments made under Part III of the Matrimonial and Family Proceedings Act 1984.

9B–60 *Note* —For definition of "maintenance" order, see s.28(1) above. This section has been amended by the following: the Guardianship of Minors Act 1971, ss.11B–D, Sched.1, the Matrimonial Causes Act 1973, Scheds 2 and 3, the Guardianship Act 1973, s.9(3)(b), the Children Act 1975, Sched.3, para. 73, the Supplementary Benefits Act 1976, Sched.7, para. 17, the Domestic Proceedings and Magistrates' Courts Act 1978, Sched.2, para. 26, Civil Jurisdiction and Judgments Act 1982, s.15, Sched.12, Matrimonial and Family Proceedings Act 1984, Sched.1, Child Care Act 1980, Sched.5, para. 28, Children Act 1989, Sched.13; the Courts and Legal Services Act 1990, Scheds. 16 and 20; the Maintenance Orders (Reciprocal Enforcement) Act 1972, s.22, Sched.; the Social Security Act 1986, s.86, Sched.10, the Family Law Reform Act 1987, s.33(1), Scheds 2 and 3; the Social Security (Consequential Provisions) Act 1992, Sched.2 and by the Civil Jurisdiction and Judgments Order 2001 (S.I. 2001 No. 3929), Sched.3, para.8.

Administration of Justice Act 1985

(1985 c.61)

[30th October 1985]

* * * *

PART IV

THE SUPREME COURT AND COUNTY COURTS

PROCEEDINGS RELATING TO ESTATES OF DECEASED PERSONS AND TRUSTS

Power of High Court to make judgments binding on persons who are not parties

47.—(1) This section applies to actions in the High Court relating **9B–61**
to the estates of deceased persons or to trusts and falling within any
description specified in rules of court.

(2) Rules of court may make provision for enabling any judgment
given in an action to which this section applies to be made binding
on persons who—

- (a) are or may be affected by the judgment and would not
  otherwise be bound by it; but
- (b) have in accordance with the rules been given notice of
  the action and of such matters connected with it as the
  rules may require.

(3) Different provision may be made under this section in relation
to actions of different descriptions.

Note

The functions of the Lord Chancellor under this Act were transferred to the Secre- **9B–61.1**
tary of State for Constitutional Affairs by the Secretary of State for Constitutional Affairs Order 2003 (S.I. 2003 No. 1887) with effect from August 19, 2003.

Rules of court

See, CPR, r.19.7A and r.19.8A. **9B–62**

Power of High Court to authorise action to be taken in reliance on counsel's opinion

48.—(1) Where— **9B–63**

- (a) any question of construction has arisen out of the terms
  of a will or a trust; and
- (b) an opinion in writing given by a person who has a 10
  year High Court qualification, within the meaning of
  section 71 of the Courts and Legal Services Act 1990 has
  been obtained on that question by the personal representatives or trustees under the will or trust,

the High Court may, on the application of the personal representatives or trustees and without hearing argument, make an order authorising those persons to take such steps in reliance on the said
opinion as are specified in the order.

(2) The High Court shall not make an order under subsection (1) if it appears to the court that a dispute exists which would make it inappropriate for the court to make the order without hearing argument.

9B–64   *Note* —Amended by the Courts and Legal Services Act 1990, Sched.10.

Rules of court
9B–65   See CPR 64PD.5.

Powers of High Court on compromise of probate action

9B–66   **49.**—(1) Where on a compromise of a probate action in the High Court—

> (a) the court is invited to pronounce for the validity of one or more wills, or against the validity of one or more wills, or for the validity of one or more wills and against the validity of one or more other wills; and
>
> (b) the court is satisfied that consent to the making of the pronouncement or, as the case may be, each of the pronouncements in question has been given by or on behalf of every relevant beneficiary,

the court may without more pronounce accordingly.

(2) In this section—

> "probate action" means an action for the grant of probate of the will, or letters of administration of the estate, of a deceased person or for the revocation of such a grant or for a decree pronouncing for or against the validity of an alleged will, not being an action which is non-contentious or common form probate business; and

"relevant beneficiary", in relation to a pronouncement relating to any will or wills of a deceased person, means—

>> (a) a person who under any such will is beneficially interested in the deceased's estate; and
>>
>> (b) where the effect of the pronouncement would be to cause the estate to devolve as on an intestacy (or partial intestacy), or to prevent it from so devolving, a person who under the law relating to intestacy is beneficially interested in the estate.

Power of High Court to appoint substitute for, or to remove, personal representative

9B–67   **50.**—(1) Where an application relating to the estate of a deceased person is made to the High Court under this subsection by or on behalf of a personal representative of the deceased or a beneficiary of the estate, the court may in its discretion—

> (a) appoint a person (in this section called a substituted personal representative) to act as personal representative of the deceased in place of the existing personal representative or representatives of the deceased or any of them; or
>
> (b) if there are two or more existing personal representa-

tives of the deceased, terminate the appointment of one or more, but not all, of those persons.

(2) Where the court appoints a person to act as a substituted personal representative of a deceased person, then—

(a) if that person is appointed to act with an executor or executors the appointment shall (except for the purpose of including him in any chain of representation) constitute him executor of the deceased as from the date of the appointment; and

(b) in any other case the appointment shall constitute that person administrator of the deceased's estate as from the date of the appointment.

(3) The court may authorise a person appointed as a substituted personal representative to charge remuneration for his services as such, on such terms (whether or not involving the submission of bills of charges for taxation by the court) as the court may think fit.

(4) Where an application relating to the estate of a deceased person is made to the court under subsection (1), the court may, if it thinks fit, proceed as if the application were, or included, an application for the appointment under the Judicial Trustees Act 1896 of a judicial trustee in relation to that estate.

(5) In this section "beneficiary", in relation to the estate of a deceased person, means a person who under the will of the deceased or under the law relating to intestacy is beneficially interested in the estate.

(6) [Adding subs. (7) to s.1 of the Judicial Trustees Act 1896, see Section 6D, para. 6D–2.]

51. [Amendments relating to ... district probate registrars in **9B–68** probate proceedings, see Section 11A, para. 11A–6.]

52. [Amendments to s.40A of the Supreme Court Act 1981, see **9B–69** para. 9A–127.]

Reimbursement of additional costs resulting from death or incapacity of presiding judge, etc.

53.—(1) Where—

(a) the judge, or (as the case may be) any of the judges, presiding at any proceedings to which this section applies becomes temporarily or permanently incapacitated from presiding at the proceedings, or dies, at any time prior to the conclusion of the proceedings; and

(b) any party represented at the proceedings incurs any additional costs in consequence of the judge's incapacity or death,

the Secretary of State may, if he thinks fit, reimburse that party in respect of any such additional costs, or in respect of such part thereof as he may determine; but the amount of any such reimbursement shall not exceed such sum as the Secretary of State may by order prescribe for the purposes of this section.

(2) Subject to subsection (3), this section applies to—

(a) proceedings in the civil division of the Court of Appeal;

9B–70

(b) civil proceedings in the High Court; and

(c) proceedings in a county court;

and, in the case of any interlocutory proceedings falling within paragraphs (a) to (c), applies separately to any such proceedings and to any other proceedings in the cause or matter in question.

(3) [...]

(4) For the purposes of this section the amount of any additional costs incurred by any person as mentioned in subsection (1)(b) shall be such amount as may be agreed between the Secretary of State and that person or, in default of agreement, as may be ascertained by taxation.

(5) Where any proceedings to which this section applies—

(a) are due to be begun before a judge at a particular time; but

(b) are not begun at that time by reason of the judge becoming temporarily or permanently incapacitated from presiding at the proceedings or by reason of his death,

subsection (1) shall have effect in relation to the incapacity or death of the judge as it has effect in relation to any such incapacity or death of a presiding judge as is mentioned in paragraph (a) of that subsection, but as if any reference to any party represented at the proceedings were a reference to any party who would have been so represented but for the judge's incapacity or death.

(6) In this section [...] "judge" in relation to any proceedings, includes—

(a) a master, registrar or other person acting in a judicial capacity in the proceedings; or

(b) a person assisting at the proceedings as an assessor or as an adviser appointed by virtue of section 70(3) of the Supreme Court Act 1981;

and, in relation to any such person as is mentioned in paragraph (b), any reference to presiding at any proceedings shall be construed as including a reference to assisting at the proceedings.

(7) Any order made by the Secretary of State under this section shall be made with the concurrence of the Treasury, and shall be so made by statutory instrument subject to annulment in pursuance of a resolution of either House of Parliament.

(8) Any sums required by the Secretary of State for making payments under this section shall be paid out of money provided by Parliament.

9B–71 Note — Section 53 came into force on October 1, 1988 (S.I. 1988 No. 1341). Amended by the Access to Justice Act 1999, Sched.15, Pt III and by the Secretary of State for Constitutional Affairs Order 2003 (S.I. 2003 No. 1887), Sched.2, para.6(a).

9B–72 **54.** [Register of county court judgments.]

9B–73 **55.** [Relief from forfeiture in county court.]

INTERPRETATION

Interpretation of Part IV

9B–74 **56.** In this Part—

"action" means any civil proceedings commenced by writ or in any other manner prescribed by rules of court;

"judgment" includes an order;

"will" includes a nuncupative will and any testamentary document of which probate may be granted.

* * * *

County Courts Act 1959

(1959 7 & 8 Eliz. 2 c.22)

[25th March 1959]

Introductory note

This Act, except for ss.99(3), 168 to 174, 174A and 176, has been repealed by the consolidating County Courts Act 1984 (c. 28) which came into force on August 1, 1984. Only ss.174 and 174A are printed here.   **9B–75**

PART VIII

FUNDS IN COURT

Transfer to county court of money recovered in High Court by infants, etc.

174.—(1) Where in any cause or matter in the High Court money **9B–76** is in any manner recovered by or on behalf of, or adjudged or ordered to be paid to or for the benefit of, a person who is an infant or a patient, the High Court may order the money or any part thereof to be paid into or transferred to the county court of the district in which that person resides or such other county court as the High Court may order.

(2) On the making of any such order, the money or the part thereof to which the order relates shall be paid or transferred according to the order, and shall, subject to any special order or direction of the High Court, and to rules of court and to the County Court Funds Rules, be invested, applied or otherwise dealt with for the benefit of the person to whom the order relates in such manner as the county court in its discretion thinks fit.

(2A) In this section "patient" has the meaning assigned to it by the Mental Health Act 1959.

(3) [...]

Note —Amended by the Courts Act 1971; and the SCA 1981, s.149(1) and Sched.3 **9B–77** and s.152(4) and Sched.7. Subsection (3) repealed by the Administration of Justice Act 1965. Subsection (2) amended by the Civil Procedure Act 1997, Sched.2, para. 2(2). The Mental Health Act 1959 was consolidated by the Mental Health Act 1983.

See CPR, rr. 21.11 and 21.12.

Effect — Section 174 is, at present, inoperative, since county courts do not now deal **9B–78** with the funds of minors and patients. If local control of investment and application is desirable, the fund remains in the High Court but all proceedings relating to its investment and applications are transferred to the appropriate district registry of the High Court.

Transfer to High Court of money held in a county court

174A.—(1) Where money is held in a county court in relation to **9B–79**

any cause or matter in that court, the court may order the money or any part of it to be paid into or transferred to the High Court.

(2) On the making of such an order, the sum to which the order relates shall be paid or transferred according to the order.

9B–79.1   *Note* —Added by the SCA 1981, s.149(1) and Sched.3.

The County Courts (Interest on Judgment Debts) Order 1991

1991 1184 (L.12)

The Lord Chancellor, in exercise of the powers conferred on him by section 74 of the County Courts Act 1984 and with the concurrence of the **9B–80**   *Treasury, hereby makes the following Order:*

Citation, commencement, interpretation and savings
9B–80.1   **1.**—(1) This Order may be cited as the County Courts (Interest on Judgment Debts) Order 1991 and shall come into force on 1st July 1991.

(2) In this Order, unless the context otherwise requires,—
"administration order" means an order under section 112 of the 1984 Act;
"given", in relation to a relevant judgment, means "given or made";
"judgment creditor" means the person who has obtained or is entitled to enforce the relevant judgment and "debtor" means the person against whom it was given;
"judgment debt" means a debt under a relevant judgment;
"relevant judgment" means a judgment or order of a county court for the payment of a sum of money (a) of not less than £5,000 or (b) in respect of a debt which is a qualifying debt for the purposes of the Late Payment of Commercial Debts (Interest) Act 1998 and, in relation to a judgment debt, means the judgment or order which gives rise to the judgment debt.
"the 1984 Act" means the County Courts Act 1984.

(3) Where in accordance with the provisions of this Order interest ceases to accrue on a specified day, interest shall cease to accrue at the end of that day.

(4) Nothing in this Order shall apply where the relevant judgment is given before 1st July 1991.

The general rule
9B–80.2   **2.**—(1) Subject to the following provisions of this Order, every judgment debt under a relevant judgment shall, to the extent that it remains unsatisfied, carry interest under this Order from the date on which the relevant judgment was given.

(2) In the case of a judgment or order for the payment of a judgment debt, other than costs, the amount of which has to be determined at a later date, the judgment debt shall carry interest from that later date.

(3) Interest shall not be payable under this Order where the relevant judgment—

    (a) is given in proceedings to recover money due under an agreement regulated by the Consumer Credit Act 1974;

    (b) grants—

        (i) the landlord of a dwelling house, or

        (ii) the mortgagee under a mortgage of land which consists of or includes a dwelling house,

a suspended order for possession.

(4) Where the relevant judgment makes financial provision for a spouse or a child, interest shall only be payable on an order for the payment of not less than £5,000 as a lump sum (whether or not the sum is payable by instalments).

For the purposes of this paragraph, no regard shall be had to any interest payable under section 23(6) of the Matrimonial Causes Act 1973.

Interest where payment deferred

3. Where under the terms of the relevant judgment payment of a judgment debt—   **9B-80.3**

    (a) is not required to be made until a specified date, or

    (b) is to be made by instalments,

interest shall not accrue under this Order—

      (i) until that date, or

      (ii) on the amount of any instalment, until it falls due,

as the case may be.

Interest and enforcement or other proceedings

4.—(1) Where a judgment creditor takes proceedings in a county court to enforce payment under a relevant judgment, the judgment debt shall cease to carry interest thereafter, except where those proceedings fail to produce any payment from the debtor in which case interest shall accrue as if those proceedings had never been taken.   **9B-80.4**

(2) For the purposes of this article "proceedings to enforce payment under a relevant judgment"include any proceeding for examining or summoning a judgment debtor or attaching a debt owed to him, but do not include proceedings under the Charging Orders Act 1979;

(3) Where an administration order or an attachment of earnings order is made, interest shall not accrue during the time the order is in force.

Rate of interest

5.—(1) Subject to paragraph (2), where a judgment debt carries interest the rate of interest shall be the rate for the time being specified in section 17 of the Judgments Act 1838.   **9B-80.5**

(2) Where a judgment debt carries interest and has been given for a sum expressed in a currency other than sterling, a county court may order that the rate of interest shall be such rate as the court

thinks fit (instead of the rate otherwise applicable under paragraph (1)) and, where the court makes such an order, section 17 of the Judgments Act 1838 shall have effect in relation to the judgment debt as if the rate specified in the order were substituted for the rate specified in that section.

Appropriation of interest

9B-80.6   6.—(1) Where the debtor is indebted to the same judgment creditor under two or more judgments or orders, money paid by him shall be applied to satisfy such of the judgments as the debtor may stipulate or, where no such stipulation is made, according to their priority in time.

(2) Money paid by the debtor in respect of any judgment debt shall be appropriated first to discharge or reduce the principal debt and then towards the interest.

Mackay of Clashfern, C.

13th May 1991

We concur,

Sydney Chapman
Gregory Knight
Two of the Lords Commissioners of Her Majesty's Treasury
20th May 1991

County Court Remedies Regulations 1991

(S.I. 1991 No. 1222)

9B–81   (As amended by S.I. 1995 No. 206)

Introductory note

See also CPR Pt 25.

The effect of the amendments to these Regulations brought about by the County Court Remedies (Amendment) Regulations 1995 (S.I. 1995 No. 206) is to give the nominated judge jurisdiction to grant freezing injunctions restraining parties from removing assets from the jurisdiction of the High Court or dealing with assets in proceedings which are to be handled by, or are being handled by, a Mercantile Court (see CPR Pt 59 (Mercantile Courts)).

9B–82   **1.** These Regulations may be cited as the County Court Remedies Regulations 1991 and shall come into force on 1st July 1991.

2. In these Regulations, "prescribed relief" means relief of any of the following kinds—

(a) an order requiring a party to admit any other party to premises for the purpose of inspecting or removing documents or articles which may provide evidence in any proceedings, whether or not the proceedings have been commenced;

(b) an interlocutory injunction—

(i) restraining a party from removing from the jurisdiction of the High Court assets located within that jurisdiction; or

      (ii) restraining a party from dealing with assets whether located within the jurisdiction of the High Court or not.

3.—(1) Subject to the following provisions of this regulation, a county court shall not grant prescribed relief or vary or revoke an order made by the High Court granting such relief.

(2) Paragraph (1) shall not apply to—

    (a) any county court held by a judge of the Court of Appeal or judge of the High Court sitting as a judge for any county court district;

    (b) a patents county court held by a person nominated under section 291 of the Copyright, Designs and Patents Act 1988 to sit as a judge of that court.

(3) A county court may grant relief of a kind referred to in regulation 2(b)—

    (a) when exercising jurisdiction in family proceedings within the meaning of Part V of the Matrimonial and Family Proceedings Act 1984;

    (b) for the purpose of making an order for the preservation, custody or detention of property which forms or may form the subject matter of proceedings,

    (c) in aid of execution of a judgment or order made in proceedings in a county court to preserve assets until execution can be levied upon them, or

    (d) where proceedings are to be or are included in the Central London County Court Mercantile List and the application is made to a Circuit judge nominated by the Senior Presiding Judge.

(3A) In paragraph (3)(d)—

"the Central London County Court Mercantile List" means the Mercantile Court established at the Central London County Court pursuant to Part 59 of the Civil Procedure Rules 1998; and

"the Senior Presiding Judge" means the judge appointed as such under section 72(2) of the Courts and Legal Services Act 1990.

(4) Paragraph (1) shall not—

    (a) affect or modify powers expressly conferred on a county court by or under any enactment other than section 38 of the County Courts Act 1984; or

    (b) prevent a county court from varying an order granting prescribed relief where all the parties are agreed on the terms of the variation.

4. An application to the High Court for relief of a kind referred to in regulation 2(a) in county court proceedings shall be deemed to include an application for transfer of the proceedings to the High Court.

5.—(1) After an application for prescribed relief has been disposed of by the High Court, the proceedings shall, unless the High Court orders otherwise, be transferred to a county court if—

    (a) they were transferred to the High Court; or

    (b) apart from these Regulations, they should have been commenced in a county court.

(2) Where an order is made on an ex parte application, the application shall not be treated as disposed of for the purposes of paragraph (1) until any application to set aside or vary the order has been heard, or until the expiry of 28 days (or such other period as the Court may specify) during which no such application has been made.

Courts Act 1971

(1971 c.23)

9B–83
                                       [12th May 1971]

ARRANGEMENT OF SECTIONS

PART III

JUDGES

PART III

JUDGES

Deputy Circuit judges and assistant Recorders

9B–84
    24.—(1) If it appears to the Lord Chancellor that it is expedient as a temporary measure to make an appointment under this section in order to facilitate the disposal of business in the Crown Court or a county court or official referees' business in the High Court, he may—

    (a) appoint to be a deputy Circuit judge, during such period or on such occasions as he thinks fit, any person who has held office as a judge of the Court of Appeal or of the High Court or as a Circuit judge; or

    (b) appoint to be an assistant Recorder, during such period or on such occasions as he thinks fit, any person who has a 10 year Crown Court or 10 year county court qualification, within the meaning of section 71 of the Courts and Legal Services Act 1990.

(1A) No appointment of a person under subsection (1) above shall be such as to extend—

(a) in the case of appointment as a deputy Circuit judge, beyond the day on which he attains the age of seventy-five; or

(b) in the case of appointment as an assistant Recorder, beyond the day on which he attains the age of seventy;

but paragraph (b) above is subject to section 26(4) to (6) of the Judicial Pensions and Retirement Act 1993 (Lord Chancellor's power to authorise continuance in office up to the age of 75).

(2) Except as provided by subsection (3) below, during the period or on the occasions for which a deputy Circuit judge or assistant Recorder is appointed under this section he shall be treated for all purposes as, and accordingly may perform any of the functions of, a Circuit judge or a Recorder, as the case may be.

(3) A deputy Circuit judge appointed under this section shall not be treated as a Circuit judge for the purpose of any provision made by or under any enactment and relating to the appointment, retirement, removal or disqualification of Circuit judges, the tenure of office and oaths to be taken by such judges or the remuneration, allowances or pensions of such judges; and section 21 of this Act shall not apply to an assistant Recorder appointed under this section.

(4) Notwithstanding the expiry of any period for which a person is appointed under this section, a deputy Circuit judge or an assistant Recorder may attend at the Crown Court or a county court or, in the case of a deputy circuit judge as regards official referees' business, at the High Court for the purpose of continuing to deal with, giving judgment in, or dealing with any ancillary matter relating to, any case which may have been begun before him when sitting as a deputy Circuit judge or an assistant Recorder, and for that purpose and for the purpose of any proceedings subsequent thereon he shall be treated as a Circuit judge or a Recorder, as the case may be.

(5) There shall be paid out of money provided by Parliament to deputy Circuit judges and assistant Recorders appointed under this section such remuneration and allowances as the Minister for the Civil Service determines.

Note —Substituted by the SCA 1981, s.146. Amended by the Administration of Justice Act 1982, s.59(3); the Courts and Legal Services Act 1990, Sched.10; and the Judicial Pensions and Retirement Act 1993, s.26, Sched.6, para. 9.   **9B–85**

* * * *

Administrative and other court staff

27.—(1) The Secretary of State may, with the concurrence of the **9B–86** Treasury as to numbers and salaries, appoint such officers and other staff for the Supreme Court and county courts as appear to him appropriate for the following purposes, namely—

(a) maintaining an administrative court service;

(b) discharging any functions in those courts conferred by or under this or any other Act on officers so appointed, and

(c) generally carrying out the administrative work of those courts.

(2) The principal civil service pension scheme within the meaning of section 2 of the Superannuation Act 1972 and for the time being in force shall, with the necessary adaptations, apply to officers and staff appointed under subsection (1) above as it applies to other persons employed in the civil service of the State.

(3) If and to the extent that an order made by the Secretary of State so provides, the Secretary of State may enter into contracts with other persons for the provision for the purposes mentioned in subsection (1) above, whether by those persons or by sub-contractors of theirs, of officers and staff for the Supreme Court and county courts.

(4) No order under subsection (3) above shall authorise the contracting out of any functions the discharge of which would constitute—

(a) making judicial decisions or advising persons making such decisions;

(b) exercising any judicial discretion or advising persons exercising any such discretion; or

(c) exercising any power of arrest.

(5) An order under subsection (3) above may authorise the contracting out of any functions—

(a) either wholly or to such extent as may be specified in the order;

(b) either generally or in such cases or areas as may be so specified; and

(c) either unconditionally or subject to the fulfilment of such conditions as may be so specified.

(6) Before making an order under subsection (3) above, the Secretary of State shall consult with the senior judges as to what effect (if any) the order might have on the proper and efficient administration of justice.

(7) An order under subsection (3) above shall be made by statutory instrument which shall be subject to annulment in pursuance of a resolution of either House of Parliament.

(8) References in this section to the contracting out of any functions are references to the Secretary of State entering into contracts for the provision of officers and staff for the purpose of discharging those functions.

(9) In this section—

"the senior judges" means the Lord Chief Justice, the Master of the Rolls, the Vice-Chancellor and the President of the Family Division;

"the Supreme Court" includes the district probate registries."

9B–87   *Note* —Substituted by the Deregulation and Contracting Out Act 1994, Sched.16. Amended by the Secretary of State for Constitutional Affairs Order (S.I. 2003 No. 1887), Sched.2, para.2(1).

* * * *

PART V

JURIES

[Repealed by the Juries Act 1974 , s.22(4) and Sched.3.]   **9B–88**

PART VI

MISCELLANEOUS AND SUPPLEMENTAL

MERGER OR ABOLITION OF CERTAIN COURTS AND OFFICES

Merger of Palatine Courts with High Court

41. *[Repealed by the Statute Law (Repeals) Act 2004, Sched.1, Pt 1,* **9B–89**
Group 3.]

Note —The Lancaster Palatine Court and the Durham Palatine Court have been **9B–90**
abolished on their merger with the High Court; see s.57(3)(b).

* * * *

Abolition of certain other local courts

43. *[Repealed by the Statute Law (Repeals) Act 2004, Sched.1, Pt 1,* **9B–91**
Group 3.]

MATRIMONIAL JURISDICTION AND PATENT APPEALS

Matrimonial jurisdiction

45. *[Repealed by the Matrimonial and Family Proceedings Act 1984 ,* **9B–92**
s.46(3), Sched.3.]

* * * *

Interpretation of this Act and rules of construction of other Acts

57.—(1) In this Act, unless the context otherwise requires—the **9B–93**
"appointed day" means the commencement of this Act which, as
provided by this Act, may be a different date for different purposes.

(2) [...]

(3) Except where the context otherwise requires, in this or any
other Act—

    (a) [...]

    (b) any reference to the courts abolished by this Act shall
        include a reference to the Lancaster Palatine Court and
        the Durham Palatine Court (which are abolished on
        merger with the High Court).

(4) Except where the context otherwise requires, in any Act passed
after this Act the expression "recorder" shall not include the Recorder of London or an honorary recorder of a borough.

(5) Any power of making orders contained in any provision of this Act shall include power to vary or revoke an order made under that provision.

(6) It is hereby declared that any power conferred by this Act on the Lord Chancellor or any other authority to give directions includes a power to vary or rescind any direction so given.

(7) Any reference in this Act to any other enactment is a reference thereto as amended, and includes a reference thereto as extended or applied, by or under any other enactment, including this Act.

Courts and Legal Services Act 1990

9B–94

(1990 c.41)

ARRANGEMENT OF SECTIONS

PART I

PROCEDURE ETC. IN CIVIL COURTS

ALLOCATION AND TRANSFER OF BUSINESS

Introductory note

For detailed commentary on this Act, see Courts and Legal Services Act 1990, Current Law Statutes Annotated 1991.   **9B–95**

The functions of the Lord Chancellor under Parts 2 and 4 and ss.113 and 125, and s.124 (Commencement) so far as relating to any of the provisions, were transferred to the Secretary of State for Constitutional Affairs by the Secretary of State for Constitutional Affairs Order 2003 (S.I. 2003 No. 1887) with effect from August 19, 2003.

PART I

PROCEDURE ETC. IN CIVIL COURTS

ALLOCATION AND TRANSFER OF BUSINESS

Allocation of business between High Court and county courts

1.—(1) The Lord Chancellor may by order make provision—   **9B–96**
   (a) conferring jurisdiction on the High Court in relation to proceedings in which county courts have jurisdiction;
   (b) conferring jurisdiction on county courts in relation to proceedings in which the High Court has jurisdiction;
   (c) allocating proceedings to the High Court or to county courts;
   (d) specifying proceedings which may be commenced only in the High Court;
   (e) specifying proceedings which may be commenced only in a county court;
   (f) specifying proceedings which may be taken only in the High Court;
   (g) specifying proceedings which may be taken only in a county court.

(2) Without prejudice to the generality of section 120(2), any such order may differentiate between categories of proceedings by reference to such criteria as the Lord Chancellor sees fit to specify in the order.

(3) The criteria so specified may, in particular, relate to—
   (a) the value of an action (as defined by the order);
   (b) the nature of the proceedings;

    (c) the parties to the proceedings;

    (d) the degree of complexity likely to be involved in any aspect of the proceedings; and

    (e) the importance of any question likely to be raised by, or in the course of, the proceedings.

(4) An order under subsection (1)(b) (e) or (g) may specify one or more particular county courts in relation to the proceedings so specified.

(5) Any jurisdiction exercisable by a county court, under any provision made by virtue of subsection (4), shall be exercisable throughout England and Wales.

(6) Rules of court may provide for a matter—

    (a) which is pending in one county court; and

    (b) over which that court has jurisdiction under any provision made by virtue of subsection (4),

to be heard and determined wholly or partly in another county court which also has jurisdiction in that matter under any such provision.

(7) Any such order may—

    (a) amend or repeal any provision falling within subsection (8) and relating to—

        (i) the jurisdiction, practice or procedure of the Supreme Court; or

        (ii) the jurisdiction, practice or procedure of any county court,

so far as the Lord Chancellor considers it to be necessary, or expedient, in consequence of any provision made by the order; or

    (b) make such incidental or transitional provision as the Lord Chancellor considers necessary, or expedient, in consequence of any provision made by the order.

(8) A provision falls within this subsection if it is made by any enactment other than this Act or made under any enactment.

(9) Before making any such order the Lord Chancellor shall consult the Lord Chief Justice, the Master of the Rolls, the President of the Queen's Division, the President of the Family Division, the Chancellor of the High Court and the Senior Presiding Judge (appointed under section 72).

(10) No such order shall be made so as to confer jurisdiction on any county court to hear any application for judicial review.

(11) For the purposes of this section the commencement of proceedings may include the making of any application in anticipation of any proceedings or in the course of any proceedings.

    (12) [. . .]

9B–97   *Note*—Subsection (9) amended by the Constitutional Reform Act 2005, s.15, Sch.4, para.212(3). subss (1A) and (13). This section empowers the Lord Chancellor, after consulting senior judges (see subs. (9)), by order to make provision for the allocation of business between the High Court and the county courts (subs. (1)). The powers given by this section are very wide. An order made under this section may amend or repeal existing provisions, including primary legislation and delegated legislation such as rules of court, on the jurisdiction, practice or procedure of the Supreme Court or of the county courts but may not amend or repeal any provision of this Act (subss. (7) (8)). By order, jurisdiction may be conferred on the High Court in relation to proceedings in which county courts have jurisdiction and vice versa; further, it may be specified that proceedings falling within the jurisdiction of the High Court should be commenced in a county court and vice versa (as to "commencement of proceedings," see subs. (11)); furthermore it may be specified that proceedings may be taken only in the High Court or only in a county court. The power is broad enough to enable provision to be made for the transfer of particular proceedings from one court to another at different stages of case progress, for example, for trial or enforcement. The exclusive jurisdiction of the High Court to hear applications for judicial review is preserved (subs. (10)). In conferring jurisdiction in relation to a particular type of proceeding on the county courts the Lord Chancellor may choose one or more county courts to exercise that jurisdiction rather than to confer such jurisdiction on all county courts (subss. (4) (5) (6)). (Such an arrangement would parallel the Copyright, Designs and Patents Act 1988, Pt VI which empowers the Lord Chancellor to confer patent jurisdiction on one or more particular county courts.)

The first exercise of the powers given by this section was the High Court and County Courts Jurisdiction Order 1991 (S.I. 1991 No. 724), see below, paras 9B–137 *et seq.*

As a result of the amendment of s.120(4) of this Act by the Civil Procedure Act 1997, s.10 and Sched.2, para. 4, instruments made by the Lord Chancellor under s.1(1) are now subject, not to approval by both Houses of Parliament, but merely to annulment in pursuance of a petition of both Houses (s.120(6)).

* * * * *

EVIDENCE

Witness statements

5.—(1) Rules of court may make provision—   **9B–98**

    (a) requiring, in specified circumstances, any party to civil proceedings to serve on the other parties a written statement of the oral evidence which he intends to adduce on any issue of fact to be decided at the trial;

    (b) enabling the court to direct any party to civil proceedings to serve such a statement on the other party; and

    (c) prohibiting a party who fails to comply with such a requirement or direction from adducing oral evidence on the issue of fact to which it relates.

(2) Where a party to proceedings has refused to comply with such a requirement or direction, the fact that his refusal was on the ground that the required statement would have been a document which was privileged from disclosure shall not affect any prohibition imposed by virtue of subsection (1)(c).

(3) This section is not to be read as prejudicing in any way any other power to make rules of court.

Note —This section provides the power for Rules of Court to require pre-trial   **9B–99** exchange of non-expert witness statements throughout the High Court and the county courts. (Henceforth, the bases of such rule-making power will not have to be found in the Supreme Court Act 1981, ss.85 and 87 or in the County Courts Act 1984, s.75). This provision makes it clear that rules of court may override the legal professional privilege attaching to witness statements prepared with a view to proceedings (subs. (2)) (*cf.*, the Civil Evidence Act 1972, s.2(3)) dealing with privilege and the disclosure of experts' evidence).

This section clarifies the rule-making authority underpinning CPR, r.32.4 (Requirement to serve witness statements for use at trial).

* * * *

APPEALS

Powers of Court of Appeal to award damages

9B–100 8.—(1) In this section "case" means any case where the Court of Appeal has power to order a new trial on the ground that damages awarded by a jury are excessive or inadequate.

(2) Rules of court may provide for the Court of Appeal, in such classes of case as may be specified in the rules, to have power, in place of ordering a new trial, to substitute for the sum awarded by the jury such sum as appears to the court to be proper.

(3) This section is not to be read as prejudicing in any way any other power to make rules of court.

9B–101 Note —This section was designed to meet concerns about excessively high jury awards in defamation cases. It enables Rules of Court to confer on the Court of Appeal the power to substitute its own award of damages for the sum awarded by a jury in the court of first instance instead of ordering a new trial and to do so in classes of cases as may be specified in the rules (subs. (2)). This rule-making power was first exercised by RSC (Amendment No. 3) 1990 (S.I. 1990 No. 2599), reg. 13, amending CPR Sched.1, RSC O.59, r.11.

Proper award

9B–102 In *Rantzen v. Mirror Group Newspapers Ltd* [1993] 3 W.L.R. 953, CA, in reducing a jury's award in a defamation case, the Court considered the operation of s.8(2) and O.52.10(3). See also *Clark v. Chief Constable of Cleveland*, [2000] C.P. Rep. 22; *Thompson v. Commissioner of Police of the Metropolis* [1998] Q.B. 498, CA; *Bennett v. Chief Constable of West Yorkshire* April 24, 1998, unrep. CA; *John v. MGN Ltd* [1997] Q.B. 586 CA; *Kiam v. M.G.N Ltd.* [2002] EWCA Civ 43; [2002] 2 All E.R. 219, CA.

FAMILY PROCEEDINGS

Allocation of family proceedings which are within the jurisdiction of county courts

9B–103 9.—(1) The Lord Chancellor may, with the concurrence of the President of the Family Division give directions that, in such circumstances as may be specified—

(a) any family proceedings which are within the jurisdiction of county courts; or

(b) any specified description of such proceedings,

shall be allocated to specified judges or to specified descriptions of judge.

(2) Any such direction shall have effect regardless of any rules of court.

(3) Where any directions have been given under this section allocating any proceedings to specified judges, the validity of anything done by a judge in, or in relation to, the proceedings shall not be called into question by reason only of the fact that he was not a specified judge.

(4) For the purposes of subsection (1) "county court" includes the principal registry of the Family Division of the High Court in so far as it is treated as a county court.

(5) In this section—

"family proceedings" has the same meaning as in the Matrimonial and Family Proceedings Act 1984 and also includes any other proceedings which are family proceedings for the purposes of the Children Act 1989;

"judge" means any person who—

    (a) is capable of sitting as a judge for a county court district;

    (b) is a district judge, an assistant district judge or a deputy district judge; or

    (c) is a district judge of the principal registry of the Family Division of the High Court; and

"specified" means specified in the directions.

Note —This section arose from the Children Act 1989 and the need for different arrangements for the handling of family proceedings. This section is concerned with the allocation of family proceedings which are within the jurisdiction of county courts. **9B–104**

"Family proceedings"

Under the Children Act 1989, s.8(3) "family proceedings," for the purposes of that Act, is defined as meaning proceedings "under the inherent jurisdiction of the High Court in relation to children" or under the enactments listed in s.8(4). The listed enactments include the Matrimonial and Family Proceedings Act 1984, Pt III. **9B–105**

"The Lord Chancellor may ... give directions"

See Practice Direction (Family Proceedings) [1993] Gazette No. 36, p.37 (replacing Practice Direction (Family Proceedings) [1991] 1 W.L.R. 1178). **9B–106**

*   *   *   *

MISCELLANEOUS

Penalty for failure to warn that hearing will not be attended

12. [*Repealed, never in force, by the Statute Law (Repeals) Act 2004, Sched.1, Pt 1, Group 4.*] **9B–107**

Note —This section enables courts to fine parties who fail to attend a hearing in the High Court or a county court without giving the court due notice of their inability to attend. **9B–108**

"The standard scale"

This is not defined in the Act (*cf.*, County Courts Act 1984, s.147(1) and the Solicitors Act 1974, s.87(1)). It has the meaning given by the Criminal Justice Act 1982, s.75 and therefore refers to the standard scale of fines for summary offences provided for in s.37 of that Act. By the Criminal Penalties etc. (Increase) Order 1984 (S.I. 1984 No. 447), Art. 2(4), the amount for level 3 was set at £400. **9B–109**

*   *   *   *

PART II

LEGAL SERVICES

MISCELLANEOUS

Conditional fee agreements

58.—(1) A conditional fee agreement which satisfies all of the condi- **9B–110**

tions applicable to it by virtue of this section shall not be unenforceable by reason only of its being a conditional fee agreement; but (subject to subsection (5)) any other conditional fee agreement shall be unenforceable.

(2) For the purposes of this section and section 58A—

(a) a conditional fee agreement is an agreement with a person providing advocacy or litigation services which provides for his fees and expenses, or any part of them, to be payable only in specified circumstances; and

(b) a conditional fee agreement provides for a success fee if it provides for the amount of any fees to which it applies to be increased, in specified circumstances, above the amount which would be payable if it were not payable only in specified circumstances.

(3) The following conditions are applicable to every conditional fee agreement—

(a) it must be in writing;

(b) it must not relate to proceedings which cannot be the subject of an enforceable conditional fee agreement; and

(c) it must comply with such requirements (if any) as may be prescribed by the Lord Chancellor.

(4) The following further conditions are applicable to a conditional fee agreement which provides for a success fee—

(a) it must relate to proceedings of a description specified by order made by the Lord Chancellor;

(b) it must state the percentage by which the amount of the fees which would be payable if it were not a conditional fee agreement is to be increased; and

(c) that percentage must not exceed the percentage specified in relation to the description of proceedings to which the agreement relates by order made by the Lord Chancellor.

(5) If a conditional fee agreement is an agreement to which section 57 of the Solicitors Act 1974 (non-contentious business agreements between solicitor and client) applies, subsection (1) shall not make it unenforceable.

9B–111   *Note* —Substituted by the Access to Justice Act 1999, s.27. Amended by the Secretary of State for Constitutional Affairs Order 2003 (S.I. 2003 No. 1887), Sched. 2, para. 8(1)(c); and by The Transfer of Functions (Lord Chancellor and Secretary of State) Order 2005 (S.I. 2005 No. 3429).

Conditional fee agreements: supplementary

9B–112   58A.—(1) The proceedings which cannot be the subject of an enforceable conditional fee agreement are—

(a) criminal proceedings; and

(b) family proceedings, apart from proceedings under section 82 of the Environmental Protection Act 1990.

(2) In subsection (1) "family proceedings" means proceedings under any one or more of the following—

(a) the Matrimonial Causes Act 1973;

(b) the Adoption Act 1976;

(c) the Domestic Proceedings and Magistrates' Courts Act 1978;

(d) Part III of the Matrimonial and Family Proceedings Act 1984;

(e) Parts I, II and IV of the Children Act 1989;

(f) Part IV of the Family Law Act 1996; and

(g) the inherent jurisdiction of the High Court in relation to children.

(3) The requirements which the Lord Chancellor may prescribe under section 58(3)(c)—

(a) include requirements for the person providing advocacy or litigation services to have provided prescribed information before the agreement is made; and

(b) may be different for different descriptions of conditional fee agreements (and, in particular, may be different for those which provide for a success fee and those which do not).

(4) In section 58 and this section (and in the definitions of "advocacy services" and "litigation services" as they apply for their purposes) "proceedings" includes any sort of proceedings for resolving disputes (and not just proceedings in a court), whether commenced or contemplated.

(5) Before making an order under section 58(4), the Lord Chancellor shall consult—

(a) the designated judges;

(b) the General Council of the Bar;

(c) the Law Society; and

(d) such other bodies as he considers appropriate.

(6) A costs order made in any proceedings may, subject in the case of court proceedings to rules of court, include provision requiring the payment of any fees payable under a conditional fee agreement which provides for a success fee.

(7) Rules of court may make provision with respect to the assessment of any costs which include fees payable under a conditional fee agreement (including one which provides for a success fee).

Note —Amended by the Secretary of State for Constitutional Affairs Order 2003 **9B–112.1** (S.I. 2003 No. 1887), Sched. 2, para. 8(1)(c); and by The Transfer of Functions (Lord Chancellor and Secretary of State) Order 2005 (S.I. 2005 No. 3429)

Litigation funding agreements

58B.—(1) A litigation funding agreement which satisfies all of the **9B–113** conditions applicable to it by virtue of this section shall not be unenforceable by reason only of its being a litigation funding agreement.

(2) For the purposes of this section a litigation funding agreement is an agreement under which—

(a) a person ("the funder") agrees to fund (in whole or in part) the provision of advocacy or litigation services (by someone other than the funder) to another person ("the litigant"); and

(b) the litigant agrees to pay a sum to the funder in specified circumstances.

(3) The following conditions are applicable to a litigation funding agreement—

(a) the funder must be a person, or person of a description, prescribed by the Lord Chancellor;

(b) the agreement must be in writing;

(c) the agreement must not relate to proceedings which by virtue of section 58A(1) and (2) cannot be the subject of an enforceable conditional fee agreement or to proceedings of any such description as may be prescribed by the Lord Chancellor;

(d) the agreement must comply with such requirements (if any) as may be so prescribed;

(e) the sum to be paid by the litigant must consist of any costs payable to him in respect of the proceedings to which the agreement relates together with an amount calculated by reference to the funder's anticipated expenditure in funding the provision of the services; and

(f) that amount must not exceed such percentage of that anticipated expenditure as may be prescribed by the Lord Chancellor in relation to proceedings of the description to which the agreement relates.

(4) Regulations under subsection (3)(a) may require a person to be approved by the Lord Chancellor or by a prescribed person.

(5) The requirements which the Lord Chancellor may prescribe under subsection (3)(d)—

(a) include requirements for the funder to have provided prescribed information to the litigant before the agreement is made; and

(b) may be different for different descriptions of litigation funding agreements.

(6) In this section (and in the definitions of "advocacy services" and "litigation services" as they apply for its purposes) "proceedings" includes any sort of proceedings for resolving disputes (and not just proceedings in a court), whether commenced or contemplated.

(7) Before making regulations under this section, the Lord Chancellor shall consult—

(a) the designated judges;

(b) the General Council of the Bar;

(c) the Law Society; and

(d) such other bodies as he considers appropriate.

(8) A costs order made in any proceedings may, subject in the case of court proceedings to rules of court, include provision requiring the payment of any amount payable under a litigation funding agreement.

(9) Rules of court may make provision with respect to the assess-

ment of any costs which include fees payable under a litigation funding agreement.

Note — Sections 58A and 58B were inserted by the Access to Justice Act 1999, ss.28. **9B–114** Amended by The Transfer of Functions (Lord Chancellor and Secretary of State) Order 2005 (S.I. 2005 No. 3429).

* * * *

Right of barrister to enter into contract for the provision of his services

61.—(1) Any rule of law which prevents a barrister from entering **9B–115** into a contract for the provision of his services as a barrister is hereby abolished.

(2) Nothing in subsection (1) prevents the General Council of the Bar from making rules (however described) which prohibit barristers from entering into contracts or restrict their right to do so.

Note —This section abolishes the rule of law which prevents a barrister from enter- **9B–116** ing into a contract for the provision of his services as a barrister (subs.(1)) but further states that the Bar Council shall remain free to make rules placing restrictions on such contracts (subs.(2)).

Immunity of advocates from actions in negligence and for breach of contract

62. [*Repealed, never in force, by the Statute Law (Repeals) Act 2004,* **9B–117** *Sched.1, Pt 1, Group 4.*]

Note —As to advocate's immunity from suit, see *Arthur JS Hall & Co v. Simons* [2002] **9B–117.1** 1 A.C. 615; [2000] 3 W.L.R. 543, HL.

Legal professional privilege

63.—(1) This section applies to any communication made to or by **9B–118** a person who is not a barrister or solicitor at any time when that person is—

(a) providing advocacy or litigation services as an authorised advocate or authorised litigator;

(b) providing conveyancing services as an authorised practitioner; or

(c) providing probate services as a probate practitioner.

(2) Any such communication shall in any legal proceedings be privileged from disclosure in like manner as if the person in question had at all material times been acting as his client's solicitor.

(3) In subsection (1), "probate practitioner" means a person to whom section 23(1) of the Solicitors Act 1974 (unqualified person not to prepare probate papers etc.) does not apply.

Note —This section extends legal professional privilege to the new classes of legal **9B–119** practitioner established by Pt II of this Act; that is to say, to authorised advocates, authorised litigators, authorised conveyancing practitioners and probate practitioners.

For definitions of "authorised advocate", "authorised litigator", "authorised practitioner", see s.119(1).

PART III

JUDICIAL AND OTHER OFFICES AND JUDICIAL PENSIONS

JUDICIAL APPOINTMENTS

Qualification for judicial and certain other appointments

9B–120   **71.**—(1) In section 10(3) of the Supreme Court Act 1981—

(a) in paragraph (b) (qualification for appointment as Lord Justice of Appeal) for the words "unless he is a barrister of at least fifteen years' standing or a judge of the High Court" there shall be substituted—

"unless—

(i) he has a 10 year High Court qualification within the meaning of section 71 of the Courts and Legal Services Act 1990; or

(ii) he is a judge of the High Court";

(b) in paragraph (c) (qualification for appointment as puisne judge of the High Court) for the words "unless he is a barrister of at least ten years' standing" there shall be substituted—

"unless—

(i) he has a 10 year High Court qualification, within the meaning of section 71 of the Courts and Legal Services Act 1990; or

(ii) he is a Circuit judge who has held that office for at least 2 years."

(2) Schedule 10 shall have effect for the purpose of making amendments to other enactments, measures and statutory instruments which relate to qualification for judicial and certain other appointments.

(3) For the purposes of this section, a person has—

(a) a "Supreme Court qualification" if he has a right of audience in relation to all proceedings in the Supreme Court;

(b) a "High Court qualification" if he has a right of audience in relation to all proceedings in the High Court;

(c) a "general qualification" if he has a right of audience in relation to any class of proceedings in any part of the Supreme Court, or all proceedings in county courts or magistrates' courts;

(d) a "Crown Court qualification" if he has a right of audience in relation to all proceedings in the Crown Court;

(e) a "county court qualification" if he has a right of audience in relation to all proceedings in county courts;

(f) a "magistrates' court qualification" if he has a right of audience in relation to all proceedings in magistrates' courts.

(4) References in subsection (3) to a right of audience are references to a right of audience granted by an authorised body.

(5) Any reference in any enactment, measure or statutory instrument to a person having such a qualification of a particular number of years' length shall be construed as a reference to a person who—

(a) for the time being has that qualification, and

(b) has had it for a period (which need not be continuous) of at least that number of years.

(6) Any period during which a person had a right of audience but was, as a result of disciplinary proceedings, prevented by the authorised body concerned from exercising it shall not count towards the period mentioned in subsection (5)(b).

(7) [...]

(8) [...]

Note — Subsections (7) and (8) repealed by the Access to Justice Act 1999, Sched.15, **9B–121** Pt II.

JUDGES

Presiding Judges

72.—(1) For each of the Circuits there shall be at least two Presiding Judges, appointed from among the puisne judges of the High Court. **9B–122**

(2) There shall be a Senior Presiding Judge for England and Wales, appointed from among the Lords Justices of Appeal.

(3) Any appointment under subsection (1) or (2) shall be made by the Lord Chief Justice with the agreement of the Lord Chancellor.

(4) In this section "the Circuits" means—

(a) the Midland and Oxford Circuit;

(b) the North Eastern Circuit;

(c) the Northern Circuit;

(d) the South Eastern Circuit;

(e) the Western Circuit; and

(f) the Wales and Chester Circuit,

or such other areas of England and Wales as the Lord Chancellor may from time to time, after consulting the Lord Chief Justice, direct.

(5) A person appointed as a Presiding Judge or as the Senior Presiding Judge shall hold that office in accordance with the terms of his appointment.

(6) In section 4 of the Supreme Court Act 1981 (composition of High Court)—

(a) in subsection (1), after the words "Vice-Chancellor" there shall be inserted—

"(dd) the Senior Presiding Judge"; and

(b) in subsection (6) for the words "or Vice-Chancellor" there shall be substituted "Vice-Chancellor or Senior Presiding Judge."

"Composition of High Court"

The Supreme Court Act 1981, s.4(1) provides that the High Court shall consist of **9B–123** puisne judges and holders of particular judicial offices. The Lords Justices of Appeal are not members of this Court but the Senior Presiding Judge, who is to be selected from among the Lords Justices, was added to the list of judicial office holders in s.4(1) by s.72(6).

Delegation of certain administrative functions of Master of the Rolls

9B–124　**73.**—(1) Where the Master of the Rolls expects to be absent at a time when it may be appropriate for any relevant functions of his to be exercised, he may appoint a judge of the Supreme Court to exercise those functions on his behalf.

(2) Where the Master of the Rolls considers that it would be inappropriate for him to exercise any such functions in connection with a particular matter (because of a possible conflict of interests or for any other reason), he may appoint a judge of the Supreme Court to exercise those functions on his behalf in connection with that matter.

(3) Where the Master of the Rolls is incapable of exercising his relevant functions, the Lord Chancellor may appoint a judge of the Supreme Court to exercise, on behalf of the Master of the Rolls, such of those functions as the Lord Chancellor considers appropriate.

(4) Any appointment under this section shall be in writing and shall specify—

    (a) the functions which may be exercised by the appointed judge; and

    (b) the period for which the appointment is to have effect.

(5) In this section "relevant functions" means any functions of the Master of the Rolls under—

    (a) section 144A of the Law of Property Act 1922 (functions in relation to manorial documents);

    (b) section 7(1) of the Public Records Act 1958 (power to determine where records of the Chancery of England are to be deposited);

    (c) the Solicitors Act 1974 (which gives the Master of the Rolls various functions in relation to solicitors);

    (d) section 9 of, and Schedule 2 to, the Administration of Justice Act 1985 (functions in relation to incorporated practices).

District Judges

9B–125　**74.**—(1) The offices of—

    (a) registrar, assistant registrar and deputy registrar for each county court district; and

    (b) district registrar, assistant district registrar and deputy district registrar for each district registry of the High Court,

shall become the offices of district judge, assistant district judge and deputy district judge respectively.

(2) The office of registrar of the principal registry of the Family Division of the High Court shall become the office of district judge of the principal registry of the Family Division.

(3) Any reference in any enactment, instrument or other document to an office which is, or includes, one to which this section applies shall be construed as a reference to, or (as the case may be) as including a reference to, that office by its new name.

(4) In section 14 of the County Courts Act 1984 (power of judge to impose penalty for an assault on an officer of the court) after subsection (2) there shall be inserted—

"(3) A district judge, assistant district judge or deputy district judge shall have the same powers under this section as a judge."

(5) In section 55 of that Act (power of judge to impose penalty for refusal to give evidence) after subsection (4) there shall be inserted—

"(4A) A district judge, assistant district judge or deputy district judge shall have the same powers under this section as a judge."

(6) In section 118 of that Act (power of judge to commit for contempt) after subsection (2) there shall be inserted—

"(3) A district judge, assistant district judge or deputy district judge shall have the same powers under this section in relation to proceedings before him as a judge."

(7) In section 42 of the Matrimonial and Family Proceedings Act 1984 (which allows certain county court proceedings to be taken in the principal registry of the Family Division) the following subsection shall be inserted after subsection (4)—

"(4A) Where a district judge of the principal registry is exercising jurisdiction in any matrimonial cause or matter which could be exercised by a district judge of a county court, he shall have the same powers in relation to those proceedings as if he were a district judge of a county court and the proceedings were in a county court."

Judges, etc., barred from legal practice

75. No person holding as a full-time appointment any of the offices **9B–126** listed in Schedule 11 shall—

    (a) provide any advocacy or litigation services (in any jurisdiction);

    (b) provide any conveyancing or probate services;

    (c) practise as a barrister, solicitor, public notary or licensed conveyancer, or be indirectly concerned in any such practice;

    (d) practise as an advocate or solicitor in Scotland, or be indirectly concerned in any such practice; or

    (e) act for any remuneration to himself as an arbitrator or umpire.

Note —This section prohibits a person who holds a full-time appointment of the **9B–127** type referred to in Sched.11 from practising, or offering the legal services, or acting for remuneration, in the manner described in paras (a) to (e). This standardises the prohibitions applicable to legal practitioners which depend on a combination of statutory provisions and the Bar's rules. The section supersedes such provisions as the SCA 1981, ss.100(5), 101(2) and 102(6) and the County Courts Act 1984, ss.10 and 13.

For definitions of "advocacy services", "litigation services", "conveyancing services", "probate services", see s.119(1).

Judicial oaths

9B–128 76.—(1) A person holding any of the following offices—

(a) district judge, including district judge of the principal registry of the Family Division;

(b) Master of the Queen's Bench Division;

(c) Master of the Chancery Division;

(d) Registrar in Bankruptcy of the High Court;

(e) Taxing Master of the Supreme Court;

(f) Admiralty Registrar,

shall take the oath of allegiance and the judicial oath before a judge of the High Court or a Circuit judge.

(2) The Promissory Oaths Act 1868 shall have effect as if the offices listed in the Second Part of the Schedule to that Act includes those offices.

SUPREME COURT OFFICERS

* * * *

Registrar of Criminal Appeals

9B–129 78.—(1) The office of Registrar of Criminal Appeals shall be combined with the office of Queen's Coroner and Attorney and Master of the Crown Office.

(2) [...]

(4) [...]

9B–130 Note — Subsection (2), which amends the Judicial Pensions Act 1981, is omitted. Subsections (3) and (4) are repealed by the Statute Law (Repeals) Act 2004, Sched.1, Pt 1, Group 4.

PART VI

MISCELLANEOUS AND SUPPLEMENTAL

MISCELLANEOUS

* * * *

Administration of oaths and taking of affidavits

9B–131 113.—(1) In this section—

"authorised person" means—

(a) any authorised advocate or authorised litigator, other than one who is a solicitor (in relation to whom provision similar to that made by this section is made by section 81 of the Solicitors Act 1974); or

(b) any person who is a member of a professional or other body prescribed by the Lord Chancellor for the purposes of this section; and

"general notary" means any public notary other than—

(a) an ecclesiastical notary;

(b) [...]

(2) Section 1(1) of the Commissioners for Oaths Act 1889 (appointment of commissioners by Lord Chancellor) shall cease to have effect.

(3) Subject to the provisions of this section, every authorised person shall have the powers conferred on a commissioner for oaths by the Commissioners for Oaths Acts 1889 and 1891 and section 24 of the Stamp Duties Management Act 1891; and any reference to such a commissioner in an enactment or instrument (including an enactment passed or instrument made after the commencement of this Act) shall include a reference to an authorised person unless the context otherwise requires.

(4) Subject to the provisions of this section, every general notary shall have the powers conferred on a commissioner for oaths by the Commissioners for Oaths Acts 1889 and 1891; and any reference to such a commissioner in an enactment or instrument (including an enactment passed or instrument made after the commencement of this Act) shall include a reference to a general notary unless the context otherwise requires.

(5) No person shall exercise the powers conferred by this section in any proceedings in which he is interested.

(6) A person exercising such powers and before whom any oath or affidavit is taken or made shall state in the jurat or attestation at which place and on what date the oath or affidavit is taken or made.

(7) A document containing such a statement and purporting to be sealed or signed by an authorised person or general notary shall be admitted in evidence without proof of the seal or signature, and without proof that he is an authorised person or general notary.

(8) The Secretary of State may, with the concurrence of the Lord Chief Justice and the Master of the Rolls, by order prescribe the fees to be charged by authorised persons exercising the powers of commissioners for oaths by virtue of this section in respect of the administration of an oath or the taking of an affidavit.

(9) In this section "affidavit" has the same meaning as in the Commissioners for Oaths Act 1889.

(10) Every—

    (a) solicitor who holds a practising certificate which is in force;

    (b) authorised person;

    (c) general notary;

    (d) [...]

shall have the right to use the title "Commissioner for Oaths".

Note —For definitions of "authorised advocate" and "authorised litigator," see **9B–132** s.119(1). Amended by the Access to Justice Act 1999, Sched.2, Pt II and by the Secretary of State for Constitutional Affairs Order 2003 (S.I. 2003 No. 1887), Sched.2, para.8(1)(c).

* * * * *

Law reports

115. A report of a case made by a person who is not a barrister but **9B–133**

who is a solicitor or has a Supreme Court qualification (within the meaning of section 71) shall have the same authority as if it had been made by a barrister.

SUPPLEMENTAL

Interpretation

9B–134   119.—(1) In this Act— [...]

"advocacy services" means any services which it would be reasonable to expect a person who is exercising, or contemplating exercising, a right of audience in relation to any proceedings, or contemplated proceedings, to provide;

"authorised advocate" means any person (including a barrister or solicitor) who has a right of audience granted by an authorised body in accordance with the provisions of this Act;

"authorised body" and "appropriate authorised body"—

   (a) in relation to any right of audience or proposed right of audience, have the meanings given in section 27; and

   (b) in relation to any right to conduct litigation or proposed right to conduct litigation, have the meanings given in section 28;

"authorised litigator" means any person (including a solicitor) who has a right to conduct litigation granted by an authorised body in accordance with the provisions of this Act;

"authorised practitioner" has the same meaning as in section 37;

"conveyancing services" means the preparation of transfers, conveyances, contracts and other documents in connection with, and other services ancillary to, the disposition or acquisition of estates or interests in land; [...]

"designated judge" means the Lord Chief Justice, the Master of the Rolls, the President of the Queen's Division, the President of the Family Division or the Chancellor of the High Court; [...]

"litigation services" means any services which it would be reasonable to expect a person who is exercising, or contemplating exercising, a right to conduct litigation in relation to any proceedings, or contemplated proceedings, to provide; [...]

"the OFT" means the Office of Fair Trading;

"probate services" means the drawing or preparation of any papers on which to found or oppose a grant of probate or a grant of letters of administration and the administration of the estate of a deceased person;

"prescribed" means prescribed by regulations under this Act;

"proceedings" means proceedings in any court; [...]

"right of audience" means the right to appear before and address a court including the the right to call and examine witnesses;

"right to conduct litigation" means the right—
      (a) [...] issue proceedings before any court; and
      (b) to perform any ancillary functions in relation to proceedings (such as entering appearances to actions); [...]
(2) and (3) [...]

Note —This interpretation section has been reduced so as to exclude definitions not relevant to the selected sections of the Act printed above. Amended by the Access to Justice Act 1999, Sched.6, para. 10(3) and the Enterprise Act 2002, Sched.25, para. 23(9)(b); definition of "designated judge" amended by the Constitutional Reform Act 2005, s.15, Sched.4, para.216.

9B–135

Regulations and orders

120.—(1) Any power to make orders or regulations conferred by this Act shall be exercisable by statutory instrument.

9B–136

(2) Any such regulations or order may make different provision for different cases or classes of case.

(3) Any such regulations or order may contain such incidental, supplemental or transitional provisions or savings as the person making the regulations or order considers expedient.

(4) No instrument shall be made under 26(1), 37(10), 40(1), 58(4), 60, 89(5) or (7), 125(4), paragraph 24 of Schedule 4, paragraph 4 or 6 of Schedule 9 or paragraph 9(c) of Schedule 14 unless a draft of the instrument has been approved by both Houses of Parliament.

(5) An Order in Council shall not be made in pursuance of a recommendation made under Part I or Part IV of Schedule 4 unless a draft of the Order has been approved by both Houses of Parliament.

(6) Any other statutory instrument made under this Act other than one under section 124(3) shall be subject to annulment in pursuance of a resolution of either House of Parliament.

Note —Amended by the Civil Procedure Act 1997, s.10, Sched.2, para. 4; and with savings by the Access to Justice Act 1999, s.27(2), and Sch.6, para.11.

9B–137

High Court and County Courts Jurisdiction Order 1991

(S.I. 1991 No. 724)

Introductory note

The Order was made by the Lord Chancellor in exercise of powers granted by the Courts and Legal Services Act 1990, s.1 (see para. 9B–96, above).

9B–138

The Lord Chancellor may by order make provision (a) allocating proceedings under the Arbitration Act 1996 to the High Court or to county courts, or (b) specifying proceedings under that Act which may be commenced or taken only in the High Court or in a county court (s.105(2)). The High Court and County Courts (Allocation of Arbitration Proceedings) Order 1996 (S.I. 1996 No. 3215) (see para. 2E–357) was made in exercise of this power.

This Order has been amended by the following statutory instruments: High Court and County Courts Jurisdiction (Amendment) Order 1993 (S.I. 1993 No. 1407), High Court and County Courts Jurisdiction (Amendment) Order 19954 (S.I. 1995 No. 205), High Court and County Courts Jurisdiction (Amendment) Order 1996 (S.I. 1996 No. 3141), High Court and County Courts Jurisdiction (Amendment) Order 1999 (S.I. 1999 No. 1014), High Court and County Courts Jurisdiction (Amendment) Order

LEGISLATION

2001 (S.I. 2001 No. 1387), High Court and County Courts Jurisdiction (Amendment No. 2) Order 2001 (S.I. 2001 No. 2685), High Court and County Courts Jurisdiction (Amendment) Order 2005 (S.I. 2005 No. 587). The 1999 Order provides, amongst other things, that for the word "plaintiff", wherever it appears in the 1991 Order, there should be substituted the word "claimant".

Title and commencement
9B–139   **1.** This Order may be cited as the High Court and County Courts Jurisdiction Order 1991 and shall come into force on 1st July 1991.

Jurisdiction
9B–140   **2.**—(1) A county court shall have jurisdiction under—

    (a) sections 146 and 147 of the Law of Property Act 1925,

    (b) [omitted]

    (c) section 26 of the Arbitration Act 1950,

    (d) section 63(2) of the Landlord and Tenant Act 1954,

    (e) section 28(3) of the Mines and Quarries (Tips) Act 1969,

    (f) section 66 of the Taxes Management Act 1970,

    (g) section 41 of the Administration of Justice Act 1970,

    (h) section 139(5)(b) of the Consumer Credit Act 1974,

    (i) section 13 of the Torts (Interference with Goods) Act 1977,

    (j) section 87 of the Magistrates' Courts Act 1980,

    (k) sections 19 and 20 of the Local Government Finance Act 1982,

    (l) sections 15, 16, 21, 25 and 139 of the County Courts Act 1984,

    (m) section 39(4) of, and paragraph 3(1) of Schedule 3 to, the Legal Aid Act 1988,

    (n) sections 99, 102(5), 114, 195, 204, 230, 231 and 235(5) of the Copyright, Designs and Patents Act 1988,

    (o) section 40 of the Housing Act 1988, and

    (p) sections 13 and 14 of the Trusts of Land and Appointment of Trustees Act 1996.

whatever the amount involved in the proceedings and whatever the value of any fund or asset connected with the proceedings.

(2) A county court shall have jurisdiction under—

    (a) section 10 of the Local Land Charges Act 1975, and

    (b) section 10(4) of the Rentcharges Act 1977,

where the sum concerned or amount claimed does not exceed £5,000.

(3) A county court shall have jurisdiction under the following provisions of the Law of Property Act 1925 where the capital value of the land or interest in land which is to be dealt with does not exceed £30,000:

    (a) sections 3, 49, 66, 181, and 188;

    (b) proviso (iii) to paragraph 3 of Part III of Schedule 1;

    (c) proviso (v) to paragraph 1(3) of Part IV of Schedule 1;

    (d) provisos (iii) and (iv) to paragraph 1(4) of Part IV of Schedule 1.

(4) A county court shall have jurisdiction under sections 89, 90, 91 and 92 of the Law of Property Act 1925 where the amount owing

in respect of the mortgage or charge at the commencement of the proceedings does not exceed £30,000.

(5) A county court shall have jurisdiction under the proviso to section 136(1) of the Law of Property Act 1925 where the amount or value of the debt or thing in action does not exceed £30,000.

(6) A county court shall have jurisdiction under section 1(6) of the Land Charges Act 1972—

    (a) in the case of a land charge of Class C(i), C(ii) or D(i), if the amount does not exceed £30,000;

    (b) in the case of a land charge of Class C(iii), if it is for a specified capital sum of money not exceeding £30,000 or, where it is not for a specified capital sum, if the capital value of the land affected does not exceed £30,000;

    (c) in the case of a land charge of Class A, Class B, Class C(iv), Class D(ii), Class D(iii) or Class E, if the capital value of the land affected does not exceed £30,000;

    (d) in the case of a land charge of Class F, if the land affected by it is the subject of an order made by the court under section 1 of the Matrimonial Homes Act 1983 or an application for an order under that section relating to that land has been made to the court;

    (e) in a case where an application under section 23 of the Deeds of Arrangement Act 1914 could be entertained by the court.

(7) A county court shall have jurisdiction under sections 69, 70 and 71 of the Solicitors Act 1974 where a bill of costs relates wholly or partly to contentious business done in a county court and the amount of the bill does not exceed £5,000.

(7A) A patents county court and the county courts listed in paragraph (7B) shall have jurisdiction under the following provisions of the Trade Marks Act 1994—

    (a) sections 15, 16, 19, 23(5), 25(4)(b), 30, 31, 46, 47, 64, 73 and 74;

    (b) paragraph 12 of Schedule 1;

    (c) paragraph 14 of Schedule 2,

to include jurisdiction to hear and determine any claims or matters ancillary to, or arising from proceedings brought under such provisions.

(7B) For the purposes of paragraph (7A), the county courts at—

    (a) Birmingham;

    (b) Bristol;

    (c) Cardiff;

    (d) Leeds;

    (e) Liverpool

    (f) Manchester; and

    (g) Newcastle upon Tyne,

shall have jurisdiction.

(8) The enactments and statutory instruments listed in the Sched-

ule to this Order are amended as specified therein, being amendments which are consequential on the provisions of this article.

9B–141   *Note* —Amended by the High Court and County Courts Jurisdiction (Amendment) Order 1996 (S.I. 1996 No. 3141) and by the High Court and County Courts Jurisdiction (Amendment) Order 2005 (S.I. 2005 No. 587).

Effect

9B–142   The amendments made by S.I. 1996 No. 3141 to the 1991 Order grant county courts jurisdiction in proceedings under the Trusts of Land and Appointment of Trustees Act 1996, ss.13 and 14 (Art. 2(1)), reduce to £1,000 (from £2,000) the value-limit for enforcement by execution against goods, above which judgment debts may be transferred from a county court to the High Court (Art. 8(1)), and make consequential amendments to take account of extension to areas outside London of statutory scheme for enforcement through county courts of certain road traffic debts. The amendments made by S.I. 2005 No. 587 altered the jurisdictions of a patents county court and certain county courts in relation to proceedings under the Trade Marks Act 1994 (see paras (7A) and (7B) of art.2).

Injunctions

9B–143   **3.** The High Court shall have jurisdiction to hear an application for an injunction made in the course of or in anticipation of proceedings in a county court where a county court may not, by virtue of regulations under section 38(3)(b) of the County Courts Act 1984 or otherwise, grant such an injunction.

"Regulations under s.38(3)(b)"

9B–144   See the County Court Remedies Regulations 1991 (S.I. 1991 No. 1222), para. 9B–81, above.

Allocation—Commencement of proceedings

9B–145   **4.** Subject to articles 5, 6 and 6A, proceedings in which both the county courts and the High Court have jurisdiction may be commenced either in a county court or in the High Court.

4A. Except for proceedings to which article 5 applies, a claim for money in which county courts have jurisdiction may only be commenced in the High Court if the financial value of the claim is more than £15,000.

5.—(1) Proceedings which include a claim for damages in respect of personal injuries may only be commenced in the High Court if the financial value of the claim is £50,000 or more.

(2) In this article "personal injuries" means personal injuries to the plaintiff or any other person, and includes disease, impairment of physical or mental condition, and death.

(3) This article does not apply to proceedings which include a claim for damages in respect of an alleged breach of duty of care committed in the course of the provision of clinical or medical services (including dental or nursing services).

6. Applications and appeals under section 19 of the Local Government Finance Act 1982 and appeals under section 20 of that Act shall be commenced in the High Court.

6A. Applications under section 1 of the Access to Neighbouring Land Act 1992 shall be commenced in a county court.

9B–146   *Note* —Amended by the High Court and County Courts Jurisdiction (Amendment)

Order 1993 (S.I. 1993 No. 1407); and the Access to Neighbouring Land Act 1992, s.7(2).

Allocation—Trial

7. [Repealed.]

9B–147

Enforcement

8.—(1) Subject to paragraph (1A) a judgment or order of a county court for the payment of a sum of money which it is sought to enforce wholly or partially by execution against goods—

9B–148

    (a) shall be enforced only in the High Court where the sum which it is sought to enforce is £5,000 or more;

    (b) shall be enforced only in a county court where the sum which it is sought to enforce is less than £600.

(1A) A judgment of order of a county court for the payment of a sum of money in proceedings arising out of an agreement regulated by the Consumer Credit Act 1974 shall be enforced only in a county court.

(2) Section 85(1) of the County Courts Act 1984 is amended by the insertion, at the beginning of the subsection, of the words "Subject to article 8 of the High Court and County Courts Jurisdiction Order 1991,".

Note —Amended by S.I. 1993 No. 1407; S.I. 1995 No. 205, Art. 5, and S.I. 1996 No. 3141.

9B–149

Transfer to the High Court for execution

The amendments made by S.I. 1996 No. 3141 to the 1991 Order reduce to £1,000 (from £2,000) the value-limit for enforcement by execution against goods, above which judgment debts may be transferred from a county court to the High Court (Art. 8(1)).

9B–150

"enforced … in the High Court"

For procedure and practice where transfer of county court judgment or order to High Court for enforcement, see CPR Pt 30.

9B–151

Where county court judgments between £2,000 and £5,000 are transferred to the High Court for enforcement interest is earned from the date of transfer.

The amendments brought about by S.I. 1995 No. 205 make clear that judgments given in proceedings arising out of the Consumer Credit Act 1974 may only be enforced in a county court, whatever the enforcement chosen (whether execution against grounds or some other method).

Enforcement of traffic penalties

8A.—(1) Proceedings for the recovery of—

9B–152

    (a) increased penalty charges provided for in charge certificates issued under–

        (i) paragraph 6 of Schedule 6 to the 1991 Act[1]; and

        (ii) paragraph 8 of Schedule 1 to the London Local Authorities Act 1996[2]

    (b) amounts payable by a person other than a local author-

---

[1] The Road Traffic Act 1991 c.40

[2] 1996 c.ix ; paragraph 8 of Schedule 1 was amended by paragraph 7 of Schedule 2 to the London Local Authorities Act 2000 (c. vii) and Schedule 1 is repealed by Schedule 31 to the Transport Act 2000 (c.38) on such day as the Secretary of State may by order provide.

ity under an adjudication of a parking adjudicator pursuant to section 73 of the 1991 Act

(c) fixed penalties are payable under notices issued under regulation 5 of the Road Traffic (Vehicle Emissions) (Fixed Penalty) Regulations 1997[1]

shall be taken in Northampton County Court

(2) In this article, "the 1991 Act" means the Road Traffic Act 1991 and expressions which are used in the 1991 Act have the same meaning in this article as they have in that Act

(3) In this article, "a local authority" means—

(a) in England, a London authority, a county or district council or the Council of the Isles of Scilly; and

(b) in Wales, a county or county borough council.

9B–153 *Note* —Amended by the High Court and County Courts Jurisdiction (Amendment) Order 1993 (S.I. 1993 No. 1407), the High Court and County Courts Jurisdiction (Amendment) Order 1995 (S.I. 1995 No. 205) and the High Court and County Courts Jurisdiction (Amendment) Order 2001 (S.I. 2001 No. 1387).

Road traffic debts

9B–154 The Road Traffic Act 1991 introduced a new regime for the enforcement of parking charges in London removing the enforcement proceedings from the jurisdiction of magistrates' courts. CPR Sched.2, CCR O.48B, introduced into the CCR in 1993, enables local authorities to issue county court orders to recover certain parking charges and to enforce such orders. This article gives Cardiff County Court exclusive jurisdiction to deal with the initial processing of orders.

Enforcement of possession orders against trespassers

9B–155 **8B.**—(1) A judgment or order of a county court for possession of land made in a possession claim against trespassers may be enforced in the High Court or a county court.

(2) In this article "a possession claim against trespassers" has the same meaning as in Part 55 of the Civil Procedure Rules 1998.

9B–155.1 *Note* —Paragraph 8B was added to the Order by the High Court and County Courts Jurisdiction (Amendment No. 2) Order 2001 (S.I. 2001 No. 2685). CPR Pt 55 (Possession Claims) came into force on October 15, 2001. For transitional provisions relating to Pt 55, see Vol. 1, para. 51.1.4.

Financial value of claim

9B–156 **9.** For the purposes of Articles 4A, and 5, the financial value of the claim shall be calculated in accordance with rule 16.3(6) of the Civil Procedure Rules 1998.

CPR r.16.3(6)

9B–157 This provision states that, in calculating how much he expects to recover, certain sums that the claimant might possibly recover in addition to the basic claim should be disregarded (*e.g.* interest and costs). Further, the possibility that the amount claimed may in the event be reduced by certain factors (*e.g.* a set-off included in the defence) should also be disregarded. In addition to CPR, r.16.3(6), note also Practice Direction (How to Start Proceedings – The Claim Form) para. 2.2 (Vol. 1, para. 7PD.2).

9B–158 **10.** [Repealed.]

---

[1] S.I. 1997 No. 3058

Crown proceedings—transitional provisions

11. For a period of two years from the date upon which this Order **9B–159** comes into force no order shall be made transferring proceedings in the High Court to which the Crown is a party to a county court, except—

      (a) when the proceedings are set down to be tried or heard; or

      (b) with the consent of the Crown.

Savings

12. This Order shall not apply to: **9B–160**

      (a) family proceedings within the meaning of Part V of the Matrimonial and Family Proceedings Act 1984;

      (b) [Repealed.]

Attachment of Earnings Act 1971

(1971 c.32)

An Act to consolidate the enactments relating to the attachment of earnings as a means of enforcing the discharge of monetary obligations

[May 12, 1971] **9B–161**

ARRANGEMENT OF SECTIONS

CASES IN WHICH ATTACHMENT IS AVAILABLE

LEGISLATION

CASES IN WHICH ATTACHMENT IS AVAILABLE

Courts with power to attach earnings

9B–162   1.—(1) The High Court may make an attachment of earnings order to secure payments under a High Court maintenance order.

(2) A county court may make an attachment of earnings order to secure—

(a) payments under a High Court or a county court maintenance order;

(b) the payment of a judgment debt, other than a debt of less than £5 or such other sum as may be prescribed by county court rules; or

(c) payments under an administration order.

(3) A magistrates' court may make an attachment of earnings order to secure—

(a) payments under a magistrates' court maintenance order;

(b) the payment of any sum adjudged to be paid by a conviction or treated (by any enactment relating to the collection and enforcement of fines, costs, compensation or forfeited recognisances) as so adjudged to be paid; or

(c) the payment of any sum required to be paid by an order under section 17(2) of the Access to Justice Act 1999.

(4) The following provisions of this Act apply, except where otherwise stated, to attachment of earnings orders made, or to be made, by any court.

(5) Any power conferred by this Act to make an attachment of earnings order includes a power to make such an order to secure the discharge of liabilities arising before the coming into force of this Act.

Note —Amended by the Access to Justice Act 1999, Sched.4, para. 8. **9B–162.1**

Principal definitions

2. In this Act— **9B–163**

(a) "maintenance order" means any order specified in Schedule 1 to this Act and includes such an order which has been discharged if any arrears are recoverable thereunder;

(b) "High Court maintenance order", "county court maintenance order" and "magistrates' court maintenance order" mean respectively a maintenance order enforceable by the High Court, a county court and a magistrates' court;

(c) "judgment debt" means a sum payable under—

(i) a judgment or order enforceable by a court in England and Wales (not being a magistrates' court);

(ii) an order of a magistrates' court for the payment of money recoverable summarily as a civil debt; or

(iii) an order of any court which is enforceable as if it were for the payment of money so recoverable,

but does not include any sum payable under a maintenance order or an administration order;

(d) "the relevant adjudication", in relation to any payment secured or to be secured by an attachment of earnings order, means the conviction, judgment, order or other adjudication from which there arises the liability to make the payment; and

(e) "the debtor", in relation to an attachment of earnings order, or to proceedings in which a court has power to make an attachment of earnings order, or to proceedings arising out of such an order, means the person by whom payment is required by the relevant adjudication to be made.

Application for order and conditions of court's power to make it

3.—(1) The following persons may apply for an attachment of **9B–164** earnings order:—

(a) the person to whom payment under the relevant adjudication is required to be made (whether directly or through an officer of any court);

(b) where the relevant adjudication is an administration order, any one of the creditors scheduled to the order;

(c) without prejudice to paragraph (a) above, where the application is to a magistrates' court for an order to secure maintenance payments, and there is in force an order under section 59 of the Magistrates' Courts Act 1980 or section 19(2) of the Maintenance Orders Act 1950, that those payments be made to the designated officer for a magistrates' court, that officer;

(d) in the following cases the debtor—

(i) where the application is to a magistrates' court; or

(ii) where the application is to the High Court or a

county court for an order to secure maintenance payments.

(2) [...]

(3) Subject to subsection (3A) below, for an attachment of earnings order to be made on the application of any person other than the debtor it must appear to the court that the debtor has failed to make one or more payments required by the relevant adjudication.

(3A) Subsection (3) above shall not apply where the relevant adjudication is a maintenance order.

(3B) [...]

(3C) Where—

(a) a magistrates' court makes in the case of a person convicted of an offence an order under section 130 of the Powers of Criminal Courts (Sentencing) Act 2000 (a compensation order) requiring him to pay compensation or to make other payments, and

(b) that person consents to an order being made under this subsection,

the court may at the time it makes the compensation order, and without the need for an application, make an attachment of earnings order to secure the payment of the compensation or other payments.

(4) Where proceedings are brought—

(a) in the High Court or a country court for the enforcement of a maintenance order by committal under section 5 of the Debtors Act 1869; or

(b) in a magistrates' court for the enforcement of a maintenance order under section 76 of the Magistrates' Courts Act 1980 (distress or committal),

then [...], the court may make an attachment of earnings order to secure payments under the maintenance order, instead of dealing with the case under section 5 of the said Act of 1869 or, as the case may be, section 76 of the said Act of 1980.

(5) [...]

(6) Where proceedings are brought in a county court for an order of committal under section 5 of the Debtors Act 1869 in respect of a judgment debt for any of the taxes, contributions premiums or liabilities specified in Schedule 2 to this Act, the court may, in any circumstances in which it has power to make such an order, make instead an attachment of earnings order to secure the payment of the judgment debt.

(7) A county court shall not make an attachment of earnings order to secure the payment of a judgment debt if there is in force an order or warrant for the debtor's committal, under section 5 of the Debtors Act 1869, in respect of that debt; but in any such case the court may discharge the order or warrant with a view to making an attachment of earnings order instead.

9B–165   Note —Amended by the Social Security Act 1973, Sched.27; the Magistrates' Courts Act 1980, Sched.7; and the Maintenance Enforcement Act 1991, Sched.2. Subs. (3B) and (3C) were added by the Criminal Procedure and Investigations Act 1996, s.53.

Subsection (3B) was repealed by the Fines Collection Regulations (S.I. 2004 No. 176), reg.4(c) and subs. (3C) amended by the Powers of Criminal Courts (Sentencing) Act 2000, Sched.9, para. 44.

Subs.(1)(c) amended by the Courts Act 2003, s.109(1), Sched.8, para.141.

ADMINISTRATION ORDERS IN THE COUNTY COURT

Extension of power to make administration order

4.—(1) Where, on an application to a county court for an attach- **9B–166** ment of earnings order to secure the payment of a judgment debt, it appears to the court that the debtor also has other debts, the court—

(a) shall consider whether the case may be one in which all the debtor's liabilities should be dealt with together and that for that purpose an administration order should be made; and

(b) if of opinion that it may be such a case, shall have power (whether or not it makes the attachment of earnings order applied for), with a view to making an administration order, to order the debtor to furnish to the court a list of all his creditors and the amounts which he owes to them respectively.

(2) If, on receipt of the list referred to in subsection (1)(b) above, it appears to the court that the debtor's whole indebtedness amounts to not more than the amount which for the time being is the county court limit for the purposes of section 112 of the County Courts Act 1984 (limit of total indebtedness governing county court's power to make administration order on application of debtor), the court may make such an order in respect of the debtor's estate.

(2A) Subsection (2) above is subject to section 112(3) and (4) of the County Courts Act 1984 (which require that, before an administration order is made, notice is to be given to all the creditors and thereafter restricts the right of any creditor to institute bankruptcy proceedings).

(3) [...]

(4) Nothing in this section is to be taken as prejudicing any right of a debtor to apply, under section 112 of the County Courts Act 1984, for an administration order.

Note —Amended by the Insolvency Act 1976, s.13, Sched.3; and the County Court **9B–167** Act 1984, s.148, Sched.2.

Attachment of earnings to secure payments under administration order

5.—(1) Where a county court makes an administration order in re- **9B–168** spect of a debtor's estate, it may also make an attachment of earnings order to secure the payments required by the administration order.

(2) At any time when an administration order is in force a county court may (with or without an application) make an attachment of earnings order to secure the payments required by the administration order, if it appears to the court that the debtor has failed to make any such payment.

(3) The power of a county court under this section to make an attachment of earnings order to secure the payments required by an administration order shall, where the debtor is already subject to an attachment of earnings order to secure the payment of a judgment debt, include power to direct that the last-mentioned order shall take effect (with or without variation under section 9 of this Act) as an order to secure the payments required by the administration order.

CONSEQUENCES OF ATTACHMENT ORDER

Effect and contents of order

9B–169 **6.**—(1) An attachment of earnings order shall be an order directed to a person who appears to the court to have the debtor in his employment and shall operate as an instruction to that person—

  (a) to make periodical deductions from the debtor's earnings in accordance with Part I of Schedule 3 to this Act; and

  (b) at such times as the order may require, or as the court may allow, to pay the amounts deducted to the collected officer of the court, as specified in the order.

(2) For the purposes of this Act, the relationship of employer and employee shall be treated as subsisting between two persons if one of them, as a principal and not as a servant or agent, pays to the other any sums defined as earnings by section 24 of this Act.

(3) An attachment of earnings order shall contain prescribed particulars enabling the debtor to be identified by the employer.

(4) Except where it is made to secure maintenance payments, the order shall specify the whole amount payable under the relevant adjudication (or so much of that amount as remains unpaid), including any relevant costs.

(5) The order shall specify—

  (a) the normal deduction rate, that is to say, the rate (expressed as a sum of money per week, month or other period) at which the court thinks it reasonable for the debtor's earnings to be applied to meeting his liability under the relevant adjudication; and

  (b) the protected earnings rate, that is to say the rate (so expressed) below which, having regard to the debtor's resources and needs, the court thinks it reasonable that the earnings actually paid to him should not be reduced.

(6) In the case of an order made to secure payments under a maintenance order (not being an order for the payment of a lump sum), the normal deduction rate—

  (a) shall be determined after taking account of any right or liability of the debtor to deduct income tax when making the payments; and

  (b) shall not exceed the rate which appears to the court necessary for the purpose of—

    (i) securing payment of the sums falling due from time to time under the maintenance order, and

(ii) securing payment within a reasonable period of any sums already due and unpaid under the maintenance order.

(7) For the purposes of an attachment of earnings order, the collecting officer of the court shall be (subject to later variation of the order under section 9 of this Act)—

(a) in the case of an order made by the High Court, either—

(i) the proper officer of the High Court, or

(ii) the appropriate officer of such county court as the order may specify;

(b) in the case of an order made by a county court, the appropriate officer of that court; and

(c) in the case of an order made by a magistrates' court, the clerk either of that court of of another magistrates' court specified in the order.

(8) In subsection (7) above "appropriate officer" means an officer designated by the Lord Chancellor.

(9) The Lord Chancellor may by order make such provision as he considers expedient (including transitional provisions) with a view to providing for the payment of amounts deducted under attachment of earnings orders to be made to such officers as may be designated by the order rather than to collecting officers of the court.

(10) Any such order may make such amendments in this Act, in relation to functions exercised by or in relation to collecting officers of the court as he considers expedient in consequence of the provision made by virtue of subsection (9) above.

(11) The power to make such an order shall be exercisable by statutory instrument.

(12) Any such statutory instrument shall be subject to annulment in pursuance of a resolution of either House of Parliament.

Note—Amended by the Administration of Justice Act 1977, s.19.　　**9B–170**

Compliance with order by employer

7.—(1) Where an attachment of earnings order has been made, **9B–171** the employer shall, if he has been served with the order, comply with it; but he shall be under no liability for non-compliance before seven days have elapsed since the service.

(2) Where a person is served with an attachment of earnings order directed to him and he has not the debtor in his employment, or the debtor subsequently ceases to be in his employment, he shall (in either case), within ten days from the date of service or, as the case may be, the cesser, give notice of that fact to the court.

(3) Part II of Schedule 3 to this Act shall have effect with respect to the priority to be accorded as between two or more attachment of earnings orders directed to a person in respect of the same debtor.

(4) On any occasion when the employer makes, in compliance with the order, a deduction from the debtor's earnings—

LEGISLATION

    (a) he shall be entitled to deduct, in addition, £1.00, or such other sum as may be prescribed by order made by the Lord Chancellor, towards his clerical and administrative costs; and

    (b) he shall give to the debtor a statement in writing of the total amount of the deduction.

(5) An order of the Lord Chancellor under subsection (4)(a) above—

    (a) may prescribe different sums in relation to different classes of cases;

    (b) may be varied or revoked by a subsequent order made under that paragraph; and

    (c) shall be made by statutory instrument subject to annulment by resolution of either House of Parliament.

9B–172   *Note*—Amended by the Attachment of Earnings (Employer's Deduction) Order 1991 (S.I. 1991 No. 356).

Interrelation with alternative remedies open to creditors

9B–173   **8.**—(1) Where an attachment of earnings order has been made to secure maintenance payments, no order or warrant of commitment shall be issued in consequence of any proceedings for the enforcement of the related maintenance order begun before the making of the attachment of earnings order.

(2) Where a county court has made an attachment of earnings order to secure the payment of a judgment debt—

    (a) no order or warrant of commitment shall be issued in consequence of any proceedings for the enforcement of the debt begun before the making of the attachment of earnings order; and

    (b) so long as the order is in force, no execution for the recovery of the debt shall issue against any property of the debtor without the leave of the county court.

(3) An attachment of earnings order made to secure maintenance payments shall cease to have effect upon the making of an order of commitment or the issue of a warrant of commitment for the enforcement of the related maintenance order, or upon the exercise for that purpose of the power conferred on a magistrates' court by section 77(2) of the Magistrates' Courts Act 1980 to postpone the issue of such a warrant.

(4) An attachment of earnings order made to secure the payment of a judgment debt shall cease to have effect on the making of an order of commitment or the issue of a warrant of commitment for the enforcement of the debt.

(5) An attachment of earnings order made to secure any payment specified in section 1(3)(b) or (c) of this Act shall cease to have effect on the issue of a warrant committing the debtor to prison for default in making that payment.

9B–174   *Note*—Amended by the Magistrates' Courts Act 1980, s.154, Sched.7.

Variation, lapse and discharge of orders

9.—(1) The court may make an order discharging or varying an **9B–175** attachment of earnings order.

(2) Where an order is varied, the employer shall, if he has been served with notice of the variation, comply with the order as varied; but he shall be under no liability for non-compliance before seven days have elapsed since the service.

(3) Rules of court may make provision—

    (a) as to the circumstances in which an attachment of earnings order may be varied or discharged by the court of its own motion;

    (b) in the case of an attachment of earnings order made by a magistrates' court, for enabling a single justice, on an application made by the debtor on the ground of a material change in his resources and needs since the order was made or last varied, to vary the order for a period of not more than four weeks by an increase of the protected earnings rate.

(4) Where an attachment of earnings order has been made and the person to whom it is directed ceases to have the debtor in his employment, the order shall lapse (except as respects deduction from earnings paid after the cesser and payment to the collecting officer of amounts deducted at any time) and be of no effect unless and until the court again directs it to a person (whether the same as before or another) who appears to the court to have the debtor in his employment.

(5) The lapse of an order under subsection (4) above shall not prevent its being treated as remaining in force for other purposes.

Normal deduction rate to be reduced in certain cases

10.—(1) The following provisions shall have effect, in the case of **9B–176** an attachment of earnings order made to secure maintenance payments, where it appears to the collecting officer of the court that—

    (a) the aggregate of the payments made for the purposes of the related maintenance order by the debtor (whether under the attachment of earnings order or otherwise) exceeds the aggregate of the payments required up to that time by the maintenance order; and

    (b) the normal deduction rate specified by the attachment of earnings order (or, where two or more such orders are in force in relation to the maintenance order, the aggregate of the normal deduction rates specified by those orders) exceeds the rate of payments required by the maintenance order; and

    (c) no proceedings for the variation or discharge of the attachment of earnings order are pending.

(2) In the case of an order made by the High Court or a county court, the collecting officer shall give the prescribed notice to the

person to whom he is required to pay sums received under the attachment of earnings order, and to the debtor; and the court shall make the appropriate variation order, unless the debtor requests it to discharge the attachment of earnings order, or to vary it in some other way, and the court thinks fit to comply with the request.

(3) In the case of an order made by a magistrates' court, the collecting officer shall apply to the court for the appropriate variation order; and the court shall grant the application unless the debtor appears at the hearing and requests the court to discharge the attachment of earnings order, or to vary it in some other way, and the court thinks fit to comply with the request.

(4) In this section, "the appropriate variation order" means an order varying the attachment of earnings order in question by reducing the normal deduction rate specified thereby so as to secure that that rate (or, in the case mentioned in subsection (1)(b) above, the aggregate of the rates therein mentioned)—

> (a) is the same as the rate of payments required by the maintenance order; or
>
> (b) is such lower rate as the court thinks fit having regard to the amount of the excess mentioned in subsection (1)(a).

Attachment order in respect of maintenance payments to cease to have effect on the occurrence of certain events

9B–177   11.—(1) An attachment of earnings order made to secure maintenance payments shall cease to have effect—

> (a) upon the grant of an application for registration of the related maintenance order under section 2 of the Maintenance Orders Act 1958 (which provides for the registration in a magistrates' court of a High Court or county court maintenance order, and for registration in the High Court of a magistrates' court maintenance order);
>
> (b) where the related maintenance order is registered under Part I of the said Act of 1958, upon the giving of notice with respect thereto under section 5 of that Act (notice with view to cancellation of registration);
>
> (c) subject to subsection (3) below, upon the discharge of the related maintenance order while it is not registered under Part I of the said Act of 1958;
>
> (d) upon the related maintenance order ceasing to be registered in a court in England or Wales, or becoming registered in a court in Scotland or Northern Ireland, under Part II of the Maintenance Orders Act 1950.

(2) Subsection (1)(a) above shall have effect, in the case of an application for registration under section 2(1) of the said Act of 1958, notwithstanding that the grant of the application may subsequently become void under subsection (2) of that section.

(3) Where the related maintenance order is discharged as mentioned in subsection (1)(c) above and it appears to the court discharging the order that arrears thereunder will remain to be

recovered after the discharge, that court may, if it thinks fit, direct that subsection (1) shall not apply.

Termination of employer's liability to make deductions

12.—(1) Where an attachment of earnings order ceases to have effect under section 8 or 11 of this Act, the proper officer of the prescribed court shall give notice of the cesser to the person to whom the order was directed.

(2) Where, in the case of an attachment of earnings order made otherwise than to secure maintenance payments, the whole amount payable under the relevant adjudication has been paid, and also any relevant costs, the court shall give notice to the employer that no further compliance with the order is required.

(3) Where an attachment of earnings order—

    (a) ceases to have effect under section 8 or 11 of this Act; or

    (b) is discharged under section 9,

the person to whom the order has been directed shall be under no liability in consequence of his treating the order as still in force at any time before the expiration of seven days from the date on which the notice required by subsection (1) above or, as the case may be, a copy of the discharging order is served on him.

ADMINISTRATIVE PROVISIONS

Application of sums received by collecting officer

13.—(1) Subject to subsection (3) below, the collecting officer to whom a person makes payments in compliance with an attachment of earnings order shall, after deducting such court fees, if any, in respect of proceedings for or arising out of the order, as are deductible from those payments, deal with the sums paid in the same way as he would if they had been paid by the debtor to satisfy the relevant adjudication.

(2) Any sums paid to the collecting officer under an attachment of earnings order made to secure maintenance payments shall, when paid to the person entitled to receive those payments, be deemed to be payments made by the debtor (with such deductions, if any, in respect of income tax as the debtor is entitled or required to make) so as to discharge—

    (a) first, any sums for the time being due and unpaid under the related maintenance order (a sum due at an earlier date being discharged before a sum due at a later date); and

    (b) secondly, any costs incurred in proceedings relating to the related maintenance order which were payable by the debtor when the attachment of earnings order was made or last varied.

(3) Where a county court makes an attachment of earnings order to secure the payment of a judgment debt and also, under section 4(1) of this Act, orders the debtor to furnish to the court a list of all his creditors, sums paid to the collecting officer in compliance with

9B–178

9B–179

LEGISLATION

the attachment of earnings order shall not be dealt with by him as mentioned in subsection (1) above, but shall be retained by him pending the decision of the court whether or not to make an administration order and shall then be dealt with by him as the court may direct.

Power of court to obtain statement of earnings, etc.

9B–180 **14.**—(1) Where in any proceedings a court has power to make an attachment of earnings order, it may—

    (a) order the debtor to give to the court, within a specified period, a statement signed by him of—

        (i) the name and address of any person by whom earnings are paid to him;

        (ii) specified particulars as to his earnings and anticipated earnings, and as to his resources and needs; and

        (iii) specified particulars for the purpose of enabling the debtor to be identified by any employer of his;

    (b) order any person appearing to the court to have the debtor in his employment to give to the court, within a specified period, a statement signed by him or on his behalf of specified particulars of the debtor's earnings and anticipated earnings.

(2) Where an attachment of earnings order has been made, the court may at any time thereafter while the order is in force

    (a) make such an order as is described in subsection 1(a) or (b) above; and

    (b) order the debtor to attend before it on a day and at a time specified in the order to give the information described in subsection 1(a) above.

(3) In the case of an application to a magistrates' court for an attachment of earnings order, or for the variation or discharge of such an order, the power to make an order under subsection (1) or (2) above shall be exercisable also, before the hearing of the application, by a single justice.

(4) Without prejudice to subsections (1) to (3) above, rules of court may provide that where notice of an application for an attachment of earnings order is served on the debtor, it shall include a requirement that he shall give to the court, within such period and in such manner as may be prescribed, a statement in writing of the matters specified in subsection (1)(a) above and of any other prescribed matters which are, or may be, relevant under section 6 of this Act to the determination of the normal deduction rate and the protected earnings rate to be specified in any order made on the application.

(5) In any proceedings in which a court has power to make an attachment of earnings order, and in any proceedings for the making, variation or discharge of such an order, a document purporting to be a statement given to the court in compliance with an order under subsection (1)(a) or (b) above, or with any such requirement of a no-

tice of application for an attachment of earnings order as is mentioned in subsection (4) above, shall, in the absence of proof to the contrary, be deemed to be a statement so given and shall be evidence of the facts stated therein.

Note —Amended by the Administration of Justice Act 1982, s.53.   **9B–181**

Obligation of debtor and his employers to notify changes of employment and earnings

15. While an attachment of earnings order is in force—   **9B–182**

    (a) the debtor shall from time to time notify the court in writing of every occasion on which he leaves any employment, or becomes employed or re-employed, not later (in each case) than seven days from the date on which he did so;

    (b) the debtor shall, on any occasion when he becomes employed or re-employed, include in his notification under paragraph (a) above particulars of his earnings and anticipated earnings from the relevant employment; and

    (c) any person who becomes the debtor's employer and knows that the order is in force and by what court it was made shall, within seven days of his becoming the debtor's employer or of acquiring that knowledge (whichever is the later) notify that court in writing that he is the debtor's employer, and include in his notification a statement of the debtor's earnings and anticipated earnings.

Power of court to determine whether particular payments are earnings

16.—(1) Where an attachment of earnings order is in force, the **9B–183** court shall, on the application of a person specified in subsection (2) below, determine whether payments to the debtor of a particular class or description specified by the application are earnings for the purposes of the order; and the employer shall be entitled to give effect to any determination for the time being in force under this section.

    (2) The persons referred to in subsection (1) above are—

    (a) the employer;

    (b) the debtor.

    (c) the person to whom payment under the relevant adjudication is required to be made (whether directly or through an officer of any court); and

    (d) without prejudice to paragraph (c) above, where the application is in respect of an attachment of earnings order made to secure payments under a magistrates' court maintenance order, the collecting officer.

    (3) Where an application under this section is made by the employer, he shall not incur any liability for non-compliance with the order as respects any payments of the class or description specified

by the application which are made by him to the debtor while the application, or any appeal in consequence thereof, is pending; but this subsection shall not, unless the court otherwise orders, apply as respects such payments if the employer subsequently withdraws the application or, as the case may be, abandons the appeal.

Consolidated attachment orders

9B–184 17.—(1) The powers of a county court under sections 1 and 3 of this Act shall include power to make an attachment of earnings order to secure the payment of any number of judgment debts; and the powers of a magistrates' court under those sections shall include power to make an attachment of earnings order to secure the discharge of any number of such liabilities as are specified in section 1(3).

(2) An attachment of earnings order made by virtue of this section shall be known as a consolidated attachment order.

(3) The power to make a consolidated attachment order shall be exercised subject to and in accordance with rules of court; and rules made for the purposes of this section may provide—

    (a) for the transfer from one court to another—

        (i) of an attachment of earnings order, or any proceedings for or arising out of such an order; and

        (ii) of functions relating to the enforcement of any liability capable of being secured by attachment of earnings;

    (b) for enabling a court to which any order, proceedings or functions have been transferred under the rules to vary or discharge an attachment of earnings order made by another court and to replace it (if the court thinks fit) with a consolidated attachment order;

    (c) for the cases in which any power exercisable under this section or the rules may be exercised by a court of its own motion or on the application of a prescribed person;

    (d) for requiring the clerk or registrar of a court who receives payments made to him in compliance with an attachment of earnings order, instead of complying with section 13 of this Act, to deal with them as directed by the court or the rules; and

    (e) for modifying or excluding provisions of this Act of Part III of the Magistrates' Courts Act 1980, but only so far as may be necessary or expedient for securing conformity with the operation of rules made by virtue of paragraphs (a) to (d) of this subsection

9B–185 *Note* —Amended by the Magistrates' Courts Act 1980, s.154, Sched.7

SPECIAL PROVISIONS WITH RESPECT TO MAGISTRATES' COURTS

Certain action not to be taken by collecting officer except on request

9B–186 18.—(1) A designated officer for a magistrates' court who is entitled to receive payments under a maintenance order for transmission to another person shall not—

> (a) apply for an attachment of earnings order to secure payments under the maintenance order; or
>
> (b) except as provided by section 10(3) of this Act, apply for an order discharging or varying such an attachment of earnings order; or
>
> (c) apply for a determination under section 16 of this Act,

unless he is requested in writing to do so by a person entitled to receive the payments through him.

(2) Where the designated officer for a magistrates' court is so requested—

> (a) he shall comply with the request unless it appears to him unreasonable in the circumstances to do so; and
>
> (b) the person by whom the request was made shall have the same liabilities for all the costs properly incurred in or about any proceedings taken in pursuance of the request as if the proceedings has been taken by that person.

(3) For the purposes of subsection (2)(b) above, any application made by the designated officer for a magistrates' court as required by section 10(3) of this Act shall be deemed to be made on the request of the person in whose favour the attachment of earnings order in question was made.

Note —Amended by the Courts Act 2003, s.109(1), Sched.8, para.143.

Procedure on applications

19.—(1) Subject to rules of court made by virtue of the following **9B–187** subsection, an application to a magistrates' court for an attachment of earnings order, or an order discharging or varying an attachment of earnings order, shall be made by complaint.

(2) Rules of court may make provision excluding subsection (1) in the case of such an application as is referred to in section 9(3)(b) of this Act.

(3) An application to a magistrates' court for a determination under section 16 of this Act shall be made by complaint.

(4) For the purposes of section 51 of the Magistrates' Courts Act 1980 (which provides for the issue of a summons directed to the person against whom an order may be made in pursuance of a complaint)—

> (a) the power to make an order in pursuance of a complaint by the debtor for an attachment of earnings order, or the discharge or variation of such an order, shall be deemed to be a power to make an order against the person to whom payment under the relevant adjudication is required to be made (whether directly or through an officer of any court); and
>
> (b) the power to make an attachment of earnings order, or an order discharging or varying an attachment of earnings order, in pursuance of a complaint by any other

person (including a complaint in proceedings to which section 3(4)(b) of this Act applies) shall be deemed to be a power to make an order against the debtor.

(5) A complaint for an attachment of earnings order may be heard notwithstanding that it was made within the six months allowed by section 127(1) of the Magistrates' Courts Act 1980.

9B–188 *Note* —Amended by the Magistrates' Court Act 1980, s.154, Sched.7.

Jurisdiction in respect of persons residing outside England and Wales

9B–189 **20.**—(1) It is hereby declared that a magistrates' court has jurisdiction to hear a complaint by or against a person residing outside England and Wales for the discharge or variation of an attachment of earnings order made by a magistrates' court to secure maintenance payments; and where such a complaint is made, the following provisions shall have effect.

(2) If the person resides in Scotland or Northern Ireland, section 15 of the Maintenance Orders Act 1950 (which relates to the service of process on persons residing in those countries) shall have effect in relation to the complaint as it has effect in relation to the proceedings therein mentioned.

(3) Subject to the following subsection, if the person resides outside the United Kingdom and does not appear at the time and place appointed for the hearing of the complaint, the court may, if it thinks it reasonable in all the circumstances to do so, proceed to hear and determine the complaint at the time and place appointed for the hearing, or for any adjourned hearing, in like manner as if the person had then appeared.

(4) Subsection (3) above shall apply only if it is proved to the satisfaction of the court, on oath or in such other manner as may be prescribed, that the complainant has taken such steps as may be prescribed to give to the said person notice of the complaint and of the time and place appointed for the hearing of it.

Costs on application under s.16

9B–190 **21.**—(1) On making a determination under section 16 of this Act, a magistrates' court may in its discretion make such order as it thinks just and reasonable for payment by any of the persons mentioned in subsection (2) of that section of the whole or any part of the costs of the determination (but subject to section 18(2)(b) of this Act).

(2) Costs ordered to be paid under this section shall—

    (a) in the case of costs to be paid by the debtor to the person in whose favour the attachment of earnings order in question was made, be deemed—

        (i) if the attachment of earnings order was made to secure maintenance payments, to be a sum due under the related maintenance order, and

        (ii) otherwise, to be a sum due to the designated officer for the magistrates' court; and

(b) in any other case, be enforceable as a civil debt.

Note —Amended by the Courts Act 2003, s.109(1), Sched.8, para.144.

MISCELLANEOUS PROVISIONS

Persons employed under the Crown

22.—(1) The fact that an attachment of earnings order is made at **9B–191** the suit of the Crown shall not prevent its operation at any time when the debtor is in the employment of the Crown.

(2) Where a debtor is in the employment of the Crown and an attachment of earnings order is made in respect of him, then for the purposes of this Act—

   (a) the chief officer for the time being of the department, office or other body in which the debtor is employed shall be treated as having the debtor in his employment (any transfer of the debtor from one department, office or body to another being treated as a change of employment); and

   (b) any earnings paid by the Crown or a Minister of the Crown, or out of the public revenue of the United Kingdom, shall be treated as paid by the said chief officer.

(3) If any question arises, in proceedings for or arising out of an attachment of earnings order, as to what department, office or other body is concerned for the purposes of this section, or as to who for those purposes is the chief officer thereof, the question shall be referred to and determined by the Minister for the Civil Service; but that Minister shall not be under any obligation to consider a reference under this subsection unless it is made by the court.

(4) A document purporting to set out a determination of the said Minister under subsection (3) above and to be signed by an official of the Office of Public Service shall, in any such proceedings as are mentioned in that subsection, be admissible in evidence and be deemed to contain an accurate statement of such a determination unless the contrary is shown.

(5) This Act shall have effect notwithstanding any enactment passed before 29th May 1970 and preventing or avoiding the attachment or diversion of sums due to a person in respect of service under the Crown, whether by way of remuneration, pension or otherwise.

Note —Amended by the Transfer of Functions (Minister for the Civil Service and **9B–192** Treasury) Order 1981 (S.I. 1981 No. 1670); the Transfer of Functions (Minister for the Civil Service and Treasury) Order 1987 (S.I. 1987 No. 2039); the Transfer of Functions (Science) Order 1992 (S.I. 1992 No. 1296); and the Transfer of Functions (Science) Order 1995 (S.I.1995 No. 2985).

Enforcement provisions

23.—(1) If, after being served with notice of an application to a **9B–193** county court for an attachment of earnings order or for the variation of such an order or with an order made under section 14(2)(b) above, the debtor fails to attend on the day and at the time specified for any hearing of the application or specified in the order, the court may adjourn the hearing and order him to attend at a specified time on another day; and if the debtor—

    (a) fails to attend at that time on that day; or

    (b) attends, but refuses to be sworn or give evidence,

he may be ordered by the judge to be imprisoned for not more than fourteen days.

(1A) In any case where the judge has power to make an order of imprisonment under subsection (1) for failure to attend, he may, in lieu of or in addition to making that order, order the debtor to be arrested and brought before the court either forthwith or at such time as the judge may direct.

(2) Subject to this section, a person commits an offence if—

    (a) being required by section 7(1) or 9(2) of this Act to comply with an attachment of earnings order, he fails to do so; or

    (b) being required by section 7(2) of this Act to give a notice for the purposes of that subsection, he fails to give it, or fails to give it within the time required by that subsection; or

    (c) he fails to comply with an order under section 14(1) of this Act or with any such requirement of a notice of application for an attachment of earnings order as is mentioned in section 14(4), or fails (in either case) to comply within the time required by the order or notice; or

    (d) he fails to comply with section 15 of this Act; or

    (e) he gives a notice for the purposes of section 7(2) of this Act, or a notification for the purposes of section 15, which he knows to be false in a material particular, or recklessly gives such a notice or notification which is false in a material particular; or

    (f) in purported compliance with section 7(2) or 15 of this Act, or with an order under section 14(1), or with any such requirement of a notice of application for an attachment of earnings order as is mentioned in section 14(4), he makes any statement which he knows to be false in a material particular, or recklessly makes any statement which is false in a material particular.

(3) Where a person commits an offence under subsection (2) above in relation to proceedings in, or to an attachment of earnings order made by, the High Court or a county court, he shall be liable on summary conviction to a fine of not more than level 2 on the standard scale or he may be ordered by a judge of the High Court or the county court judge (as the case may be) to pay a fine of not more than £250 or, in the case of an offence specified in subsection (4) below, to be imprisoned for not more than fourteen days; and where a person commits an offence under subsection (2) otherwise than as mentioned above in this subsection, he shall be liable on summary conviction to a fine of not more than level 2 on the standard scale.

(4) The offences referred to above in the case of which a judge may impose imprisonment are—

    (a) an offence under subsection (2)(c) or (d), if committed by the debtor; and

    (b) an offence under subsection (2)(e) or (f), whether committed by the debtor or any other person.

(5) It shall be a defence—

    (a) for a person charged with an offence under subsection (2)(a) above to prove that he took all reasonable steps to comply with the attachment of earnings order in question;

    (b) for a person charged with an offence under subsection (2)(b) to prove that he did not know, and could not reasonably be expected to know, that the debtor was not in his employment, or (as the case may be) had ceased to be so, and that he gave the required notice as soon as reasonably practicable after the fact came to his knowledge.

(6) Where a person is convicted or dealt with for an offence under subsection (2)(a), the court may order him to pay, to whoever is the collecting officer of the court for the purposes of the attachment of earnings order in question, any sums deducted by that person from the debtor's earnings and not already paid to the collecting officer.

(7) Where under this section a person is ordered by a judge of the High Court or a county court judge to be imprisoned, the judge may at any time revoke the order and, if the person is already in custody, order his discharge.

(8) Any fine imposed by a judge of the High Court under subsection (3) above and any sums ordered by the High Court to be paid under subsection (6) above shall be recoverable in the same way as a fine imposed by that court in the exercise of its jurisdiction to punish for contempt of court; section 129 of the County Courts Act 1984 (enforcement of fines) shall apply to payment of a fine imposed by a county court judge under subsection (3) and of any sums ordered by a county court judge to be paid under subsection (6); and any sum ordered by a magistrates' court to be paid under subsection (6) shall be recoverable as a sum adjudged to be paid on a conviction by that court.

(9) For the purposes of section 13 of the Administration of Justice Act 1960 (appeal in cases of contempt of court), subsection (3) above shall be treated as an enactment enabling the High Court or a county court to deal with an offence under subsection (2) above as if it were contempt of court.

(10) In this section references to proceedings in a court are to proceedings in which that court has power to make an attachment of earnings order or has made such an order.

(11) A district judge, assistant district judge or deputy district judge shall have the same powers under this section as a judge of a county court.

Note —Amended by the Contempt of Court Act 1981, Sched.2; the Criminal Justice **9B–194**

Act 1982, Sched.4; the Administration of Justice Act 1982, s.53; the County Courts Act 1984, Sched.2; the Court and Legal Services Act 1990, Sched.17; and the Criminal Justice Act 1991, Sched.4.

Meaning of "earnings"

9B–195   24.—(1) For the purposes of this Act, but subject to the following subsection, "earnings" are any sums payable to a person—

  (a) by way of wages or salary (including any fees, bonus, commission, overtime pay or other emoluments payable in addition to wages or salary or payable under a contract of service);

  (b) by way of pension (including an annuity in respect of past services, whether or not rendered to the person paying the annuity, and including periodical payments by way of compensation for the loss, abolition or relinquishment, or diminution in the emoluments, of any office or employment);

  (c) by way of statutory sick pay.

  (2) The following shall not be treated as earnings:—

  (a) sums payable by any public department of the Government of Northern Ireland or of a territory outside the United Kingdom;

  (b) pay or allowances payable to the debtor as a member of Her Majesty's forces other than pay or allowances payable by his employer to him as a special member of a reserve force (within the meaning of the Reserve Forces Act 1996);

  (ba) a tax credit (within the meaning of the Tax Credits Act 2002);

  (c) pension, allowances or benefit payable under any enactment relating to social security;

  (d) pension or allowances payable in respect of disablement or disability;

  (e) except in relation to a maintenance order wages payable to a person as a seaman, other than wages payable to him as a seaman of a fishing boat;

  (f) guaranteed minimum pension within the meaning of the Pension Schemes Act 1993.

  (3) In subsection (2)(e) above:

"fishing boat" means a vessel of whatever size, and in whatever way propelled, which is for the time being employed in sea fishing or in the sea-fishing service;

"seaman" includes every person (except masters and pilots) employed or engaged in any capacity on board any ship; and

"wages" includes emoluments.

9B–196   *Note* —Amended by the Social Security Pensions Act 1975, Sched.4; the Merchant Shipping Act 1979, s.39; the Social Security Act 1985, Sched.4; the Social Security Act 1986, Sched.10; the Pension Schemes Act 1993, Sched.8; the Merchant Shipping Act 1995, Sched.13, para.46; the Reserve Forces Act 1996 (Consequential Provisions, etc.)

Regulations 1998 (S.I. 1998 No. 3086), reg. 6; and by the Tax Credits Act 2002, Sched.3, para. 1.

General interpretation

25.—(1) In this Act, except where the context otherwise requires— **9B–197**

"administration order" means an order made under, and so referred to in, Part VI of the County Courts Act 1984;

"the court", in relation to an attachment of earnings order, means the court which made the order, subject to rules of court as to the venue for, and the transfer of, proceedings in county courts and magistrates' courts;

"debtor" and "relevant adjudication" have the meanings given by section 2 of this Act;

"the employer", in relation to an attachment of earnings order, means the person who is required by the order to make deductions from earnings paid by him to the debtor;

"judgment debt" has the meaning given by section 2 of this Act; [...];

"maintenance order" has the meaning given by section 2 of this Act;

"maintenance payments" means payments required under a maintenance order;

"prescribed" means prescribed by rules of court; [.] [...];

and, in relation to a magistrates' court, references to a single justice are to a justice of the peace acting for the same petty sessions area as the court.

(2) Any reference in this Act to sums payable under a judgment or order, or to the payment of such sums, includes a reference to costs and the payment of them; and the references in sections 6(4) and 12(2) to relevant costs are to any costs of the proceedings in which the attachment of earnings order in question was made, being costs which the debtor is liable to pay.

(3) References in sections 6(5)(b), 9(3)(b) and 14(1)(a) of this Act to the debtor's needs include references to the need of any person for whom he must, or reasonably may, provide.

(4) [...]

(5) Any power to make rules which is conferred by this Act is without prejudice to any other power to make rules of court.

(6) This Act, so far as it relates to magistrates' courts, and Part III of the Magistrates' Courts Act 1980 shall be construed as if this Act were contained in that Part.

(7) References in this Act to any enactment include references to that enactment as amended by or under any other enactment, including this Act.

Note —Amended by the Legal Aid Act 1974, Sched.4; the Magistrates' Courts Act, **9B–198** ss.144, 154, Sched.7; the County Courts Act 1984, s.148, Sched.2; the Legal Aid Act 1988, s.45, Sched.5; the Dock Work Act 1989, Sched.1; the Access to Justice Act 1999, Sched.15 and the definition repealed subject to saving specified in S.I. 2004 No. 2066, art.3 by the Courts Act 2003, Sched.10, para.1.

LEGISLATION

Transitional provision

9B-199   26.—(1) As from the appointed day, an attachment of earnings order made before that day under Part II of the Maintenance Orders Act 1958 (including an order made under that Part of that Act as applied by section 46 or 79 of the Criminal Justice Act 1967) shall take effect as an attachment of earnings order made under the corresponding power in this Act, and the provisions of this Act shall apply to it accordingly, so far as they are capable of doing so.

(2) Rules of court may make such provision as the rule-making authority considers requisite—

>   (a) for enabling an attachment of earnings order to which subsection (1) above applies to be varied so as to bring it into conformity, as from the appointed day, with the provisions of this Act, or to be replaced by an attachment of earnings order having effect as if made under the corresponding power in this Act;

>   (b) to secure that anything required or authorised by this Act to be done in relation to an attachment of earnings order made thereunder is required or, as the case may be, authorised to be done in relation to an attachment of earnings order to which the said subsection (1) applies.

(3) In this section "the appointed day" means the day appointed under section 54 of the Administration of Justice Act 1970 for the coming into force of Part II of that Act.

Consequential amendment of enactments

9B-200   27.—(1) In consequence of the repeals effected by this Act, section 20 of the Maintenance Orders Act 1958 (which contains certain provisions about magistrates' courts and their procedure), except subsection (6) of that section (which amends section 52(3) of the Magistrates' Courts Act 1952), shall have effect as set out in Schedule 5 to this Act.

(2), (3) [...]

9B-201   *Note*—Amended by the Insolvency Act 1976, Sched.3.

9B-202   28. [*Repealed with savings by the Northern Ireland Constitution Act 1973 , s.42 , Sched.6.*]

Citation, repeal, extent and commencement

9B-203   29.—(1) This Act may be cited as the Attachment of Earnings Act 1971.

(2) The Enactments specified in Schedule 6 to this Act are hereby repealed to the extent specified in the third column of that Schedule.

(3) This Act, except section 20(2), does not extend to Scotland and, except sections 20(2) ... does not extend to Northern Ireland.

(4) This Act shall come into force on the day appointed under section 54 of the Administration of Justice Act 1970 for the coming into force of Part II of that Act.

Note —Amended by the Northern Ireland Constitution Act 1973, s.42, Sched.6.   **9B–204**

SCHEDULE 1

MAINTENANCE ORDERS TO WHICH THIS ACT APPLIES

1. An order for alimony, maintenance or other payments made, or having effect as if **9B–205** made, under Part II of the Matrimonial Causes Act 1965 (ancillary relief in actions for divorce etc.).

2. An order for payments to or in respect of a child, being an order made, or having effect as if made, under Part III of the said Act of 1965 (maintenance of children following divorce, etc.).

3. An order for periodical or other payments made, or having effect as if made, under Part II of the Matrimonial Causes Act 1973.

4. An order for maintenance or other payments to or in respect of a spouse or child, being an order made under Part I of the Domestic Proceedings and Magistrates' Court Act 1978.

5. An order for periodical or other payments made or having effect as if made under Schedule 1 to the Children Act 1989.

6. [...]

7. An order under paragraph 23 of Schedule 2 to the Children Act 1989... section 23 of the Ministry of Social Security Act 1966 ... section 18 of the Supplementary Benefits Act 1976 ... or section 106 of the Social Security Administration Act 1992 (various provisions for obtaining contributions from a person whose dependants are assisted or maintained out of public funds).

8. An order under section 43 of the National Assistance Act 1948 (recovery of costs of maintaining assisted person).

9. An order to which section 16 of the Maintenance Orders Act 1950 applies by virtue of subsection (2)(b) or (c) of that section (that is to say an order made by a court in Scotland or Northern Ireland and corresponding to one of those specified in the foregoing paragraphs) and which has been registered in a court in England and Wales under Part II of that Act.

10. A maintenance order within the meaning of the Maintenance Orders (Facilities for Enforcement) Act 1920 (Commonwealth orders enforceable in the United Kingdom) registered in, or confirmed by, a court of England and Wales under that Act.

11. A maintenance order within the meaning of Part I of the Maintenance Orders (Reciprocal Enforcement) Act 1972 registered in a magistrates' court under the said Part I.

12. An order under section 34(1)(b) of the Children Act 1975 (payments of maintenance in respect of a child to his custodian).

13. A maintenance order within the meaning of Part I of the Civil Jurisdiction and Judgments Act 1982 which is registered in a magistrates' court under that Part.

14. A maintenance judgment within the meaning of Council Regulation (EC) No. 44/2001 of 22nd December 2000 on jurisdiction and the recognition and enforcement of judgments in civil and commercial matters, which is registered in a magistrates' court under that Regulation.

Note —Amended by the Maintenance Orders (Reciprocal Enforcement) Act 1972; **9B–206** Sched.; the Matrimonial Causes Act 1973, Sched.2; Guardianship Act 1973, s.9; the Children Act 1975, Sched.3; the Supplementary Benefits Act 1976, Sched.7; the Domestic Proceedings and Magistrates' Courts Act 1978, s.89, Sched.2; the Child Care Act 1980, Sched.5; the Civil Jurisdiction and Judgments Act 1982, s.15, Sched.12; the Social Security Act 1986, Sched.10; the Family Law Reform Act 1987, s.33, Scheds. 2 and 4; the Children Act 1989, s.108, Sched.3; the Courts and Legal Services Act 1990, Sched.16; the Social Security (Consequential Provisions) Act 1992, Sched.2; and by the Civil Jurisdiction and Judgments Order (S.I. 2001 No. 3929), Sched.3, para. 9.

SECTION 3   # SCHEDULE 2

TAXES, SOCIAL SECURITY CONTRIBUTIONS ETC RELEVANT FOR PURPOSES OF SECTION 3(6)

1. Income tax or any other tax or liability recoverable under section 65, 66 or 68 of **9B–207** the Taxes Management Act 1970.

2. [...]

3. Contributions equivalent premiums under Part III of the Pension Schemes Act 1993.

3A. Class 1, 2 and 4 contributions under Part I of the Social Security Contributions and Benefits Act 1992.

4. [...]

9B–208 *Note* —Amended by the Social Security Act 1973, Sched.28; the Social Security (Consequential Provisions) Act 1975, Sched.2; the Social Security Pensions Act 1975, Sched.4; the Statute Law (Repeals) Act 1989, s.1, Sched.1; the Social Security (Consequential Provision) Act 1992, Sched.2; the Pension Schemes Act 1993, Sched.8; and the Pensions Act 1995, Sched.5.

SECTIONS 6 AND 7   **SCHEDULE 3**

DEDUCTIONS BY EMPLOYER UNDER ATTACHMENT OF EARNINGS ORDER

PART I

SCHEME OF DEDUCTIONS

Preliminary definitions

9B–209 1. The following three paragraphs have effect for defining and explaining, for purposes of this Schedule, expressions used therein.

2. "Pay-day", in relation to earnings paid to a debtor, means an occasion on which they are paid.

3. "Attachable earnings", in relation to a pay-day, are the earnings which remain payable to the debtor on that day after deduction by the employer of—

(a) income tax;

(b) ...

(bb) primary Class 1 contributions under Part I of the Social Security Act 1975.

(c) amounts deductible under any enactment, or in pursuance of a request in writing by the debtor, for the purposes of a superannuation scheme, namely any enactment, rules, deed or other instrument providing for the payment of annuities or lump sums—

(i) to the persons with respect to whom the instrument has effect on their retirement at a specified age or on becoming incapacitated at some earlier age, or

(ii) to the personal representatives or the widows, relatives or dependants of such persons on their death or otherwise, whether with or without any further or other benefits.

4.—(1) On any pay-day—

(a) "the normal deduction" is arrived at by applying the normal deduction rate (as specified in the relevant attachment of earnings order) with respect to the relevant period; and

(b) "the protected earnings" are arrived at by applying the protected earnings rate (as so specified) with respect to the relevant period.

(2) For the purposes of this paragraph the relevant period in relation to any pay-day is the period beginning—

(a) if it is the first pay-day of the debtor's employment with the employer, with the first pay-day of the employment; or

(b) if on the last pay-day earnings were paid in respect of a period falling wholly or partly after that pay-day, with the first day after the end of that period; or

(c) in any other case, with the first day after the last pay-day, and ending—

(i) where earnings are paid in respect of a period falling wholly or partly after the pay-day, with the last day of that period; or

(ii) in any other case, with the pay-day.

Employer's deduction (judgment debts and administration orders)

9B–210 5. In the case of an attachment of earnings order made to secure the payment of a judgment debt or payments under an administration order, the employer shall on any pay-day—

(a) if the attachable earnings exceed the protected earnings, deduct from the attachable earnings the amount of the excess or the normal deduction, whichever is the less;

(b) make no deduction if the attachable earnings are equal to, or less than, the protected earnings.

Employer's deduction (other cases)

6.—(1) The following provision shall have effect in the case of an attachment of **9B–211** earnings order to which paragraph 5 above does not apply.

(2) If on a pay-day the attachable earnings exceed the sum of—

    (a) the protected earnings; and

    (b) so much of any amount by which the attachable earnings on any previous pay-day fell short of the protected earnings as has not been made good by virtue of this sub-paragraph on another previous pay-day,

    then, in so far as the excess allows, the employer shall deduct from the attachable earnings the amount specified in the following sub-paragraph.

(3) The said amount is the sum of—

    (a) the normal deduction; and

    (b) so much of the normal deduction on any previous pay-day as was not deducted on that day and has not been paid by virtue of this sub-paragraph on any other previous pay-day.

(4) No deduction shall be made on any pay-day when the attachable earnings are equal to, or less than, the protected earnings.

PART II

PRIORITY AS BETWEEN ORDERS

7. Where the employer is required to comply with two or more attachment of earn- **9B–212** ings orders in respect of the same debtor, all or none of which orders are made to secure either the payment of judgment debts or payments under an administration order, then on any pay-day the employer shall, for the purpose of complying with Part I of this Schedule,—

(a) deal with the orders according to the respective dates on which they were made, disregarding any later order until an earlier one has been dealt with;

(b) deal with any later order as if the earnings to which it relates were the residue of the debtor's earnings after the making of any deduction to comply with any earlier order.

8. Where the employer is required to comply with two or more attachment of earnings orders, and one or more (but not all) of those orders are made to secure either the payment of judgment debts or payments under an administration order, then on any pay-day the employer shall, for the purpose of complying with Part I of this Schedule—

(a) deal first with any order which is not made to secure the payment of a judgment debt or payments under an administration order (complying with paragraph 7 above if there are two or more such orders); and

(b) deal thereafter with any order which is made to secure the payment of a judgment debt or payments under an administration order as if the earnings to which it relates were the residue of the debtor's earnings after the making of any deduction to comply with an order having priority by virtue of sub-paragraph (a) above; and

(c) if there are two or more orders to which sub-paragraph (b) above applies, comply with paragraph 7 above in respect of those orders.

Note —Amended by the Social Security (Consequential Provisions) Act 1975, **9B–213** Sched.2; the Wages Councils Act 1979, Sched.6; the Administration of Justice Act 1982, s.54; the Wages Act 1986, Sched.4; and the Employment Rights Act 1996, Sched.1, para. 3

SECTION 24   SCHEDULE 4

ENACTMENTS PROVIDING BENEFITS WHICH ARE NOT TO BE TREATED AS DEBTOR'S
EARNINGS

9B–214 [*Repealed by the Social Security Act 1986 , s.86 , Sched.11.*]

SECTION 27   SCHEDULE 5

SECTION 20 OF MAINTENANCE ORDERS ACT 1958 AS HAVING EFFECT IN CON-
SEQUENCE OF THIS ACT

Special provisions as to magistrates' courts

9B–215   20.—(1) Notwithstanding anything in this Act, the clerk of a magistrates' court who
is entitled to receive payments under a maintenance order for transmission to another
person shall not apply for the registration of the maintenance order under Part I of
this Act or give notice in relation to the order in pursuance of subsection (1) of section
five thereof unless he is requested in writing to do so by a person entitled to receive
the payments through him; and where the clerk is requested as aforesaid—

   (i) he shall comply with the request unless it appears to him unreasonable in the
       circumstances to do so;
   (ii) the person by whom the request was made shall have the same liabilities for all
        the costs properly incurred in or about any proceedings taken in pursuance of
        the request as if the proceedings had been taken by that person.

   (2) An application to a magistrates' court by virtue of subsection (2) of section four
of this Act for the variation of a maintenance order shall be made by complaint.

   (3)–(7) [*Not reproduced here*]

   (8) For the avoidance of doubt it is hereby declared that a complaint may be made
to enforce payment of a sum due and unpaid under a maintenance order notwithstanding that a previous complaint has been made in respect of that sum or a part thereof
and whether or not an order was made in pursuance of the previous complaint.

CHARGING ORDERS

9B–217   1.—(1) Where, under a judgment or order of the High Court or a
county court, a person (the "debtor") is required to pay a sum of
money to another person (the "creditor") then, for the purpose of
enforcing that judgment or order, the appropriate court may make
an order in accordance with the provisions of this Act imposing on
any such property of the debtor as may be specified in the order a
charge for securing the payment of any money due or to become
due under the judgment or order.

   (2) The appropriate court is—
      (a) in a case where the property to be charged is a fund in
          court, the court in which that fund is lodged;
      (b) in a case where paragraph (a) above does not apply and
          the order to be enforced is a maintenance order of the
          High Court, the High Court or a county court;
      (c) in a case where neither paragraph (a) nor paragraph (b)
          above applies and the judgment or order to be enforced
          is a judgment or order of the High Court for a sum
          exceeding the county court limit, the High Court or a
          county court; and
      (d) in any other case, a county court.
   In this section "county court limit" means the county court limit
for the time being specified in an Order in Council under section

145 of the County Courts Act 1984, as the county court limit for the purposes of this section and "maintenance order" has the same meaning as in section 2(a) of the Attachment of Earnings Act 1971.

(3) An order under subsection (1) above is referred to in this Act as a "charging order".

(4) Where a person applies to the High Court for a charging order to enforce more than one judgment or order, that court shall be the appropriate court in relation to the application if it would be the appropriate court, apart from this subsection, on an application relating to one or more of the judgments or orders concerned.

(5) In deciding whether to make a charging order the court shall consider all the circumstance of the case and, in particular, any evidence before it as to—

    (a) the personal circumstances of the debtor, and

    (b) whether any other creditor of the debtor would be likely to be unduly prejudiced by the making of the order.

Note—Amended by the County Courts Jurisdiction Order 1981 (S.I. 1981 No. 1123); the Administration of Justice Act 1982, ss.34, 37, Sched.3; and the County Courts Act 1984, Sched.2.   **9B–218**

"the county court limit"
The limit is £5,000. See para. 9B–218.2 below   **9B–218.1**

"appropriate court may make an order"
In a case where a High Court judgment or order is to be enforced and neither paras (a) nor (b) of s.1(2) applies, generally the appropriate court to make a charging order will be a county court. Where the amount required to be paid exceeds a statutory sum, the appropriate court will be the High Court or a county court. Originally, the statutory sum was fixed at £2,000. Subsequently it was set at the same level as "the county court limit" (s.1(2)(c)). By operation of the County Court Jurisdiction Order 1981 (S.I. 1981 No. 1123) that limit currently stands at £5,000.   **9B–218.2**

Property which may be charged

2.—(1) Subject to subsection (3) below, a charge may be imposed by a charging order only on—   **9B–219**

    (a) any interest held by the debtor beneficially—

        (i) in any asset of a kind mentioned in subsection (2) below, or

        (ii) under any trust; or

    (b) any interest held by a person as trustee of a trust ("the trust"), if the interest is in such an asset or is an interest under another trust and—

        (i) the judgment or order in respect of which a charge is to be imposed was made against that person as trustee of the trust, or

        (ii) the whole beneficial interest under the trust is held by the debtor unencumbered and for his own benefit, or

        (iii) in a case where there are two or more debtors all of whom are liable to the creditor for the same debt, they together hold the whole beneficial interest under the trust unencumbered and for their own benefit.

(2) The assets referred to in subsection (1) above are—
  (a) land,
  (b) securities of any of the following kinds—
      (i) government stock,
      (ii) stock of any body (other than a building society) incorporated within England and Wales,
      (iii) stock of any body incorporated outside England and Wales or of any state or territory outside the United Kingdom, being stock registered in a register kept at any place within England and Wales,
      (iv) units of any unit trust in respect of which a register of the unit holders is kept at any place within England and Wales, or
  (c) funds in court.

(3) In any case where a charge is imposed by a charging order on any interest in an asset of a kind mentioned in paragraph (b) or (c) of subsection (2) above, the court making the order may provide for the charge to extend to any interest or dividend payable in respect of the asset.

Provisions supplementing sections 1 and 2

9B–220   **3.**—(1) A charging order may be made either absolutely or subject to conditions as to notifying the debtor or as to the time when the charge is to become enforceable, or as to other matters.

(2) The Land Charges Act 1972 and the Land Registration Act 2002 shall apply in relation to charging orders as they apply in relation to other orders or writs issued or made for the purpose of enforcing judgments.

(3) [...]

(4) Subject to the provisions of this Act, a charge imposed by a charging order shall have the like effect and shall be enforceable in the same courts and in the same manner as an equitable charge created by the debtor by writing under his hand.

(5) The court by which a charging order was made may at any time, on the application of the debtor or of any person interested in any property to which the order relates, make an order discharging or varying the charging order.

(6) Where a charging order has been protected by an entry registered under the Land Charges Act 1972 or the Land Registration Act 2002, an order under subsection (5) above discharging the charging order may direct that the entry be cancelled.

(7) The Lord Chancellor may be order made by statutory instrument amend section 2(2) of this Act by adding to, or removing from, the kinds of asset for the time being referred to there, any asset of a kind which in his opinion ought to be so added or removed.

(8) Any order under subsection (7) above shall be subject to annulment in pursuance of a resolution of either House of Parliament.

9B–220.1   *Note* —Amended by the Land Registration Act 2002, Sched.11, para. 15.

4. [*Repealed by the Insolvency Act 1985 , s.235 , Sched.10.*] **9B–221**

Stop orders and notices

5.—(1) In this section— **9B–222**

"stop order" means an order of the court prohibiting the taking, in respect of any of the securities specified in the order, of any of the steps mentioned in subsection (5) below;

"stop notice" means a notice requiring any person or body on whom it is duly served to refrain from taking, in respect of any of the securities specified in the notice, any of those steps without first notifying the person by whom, or on whose behalf, the notice was served; and

"prescribed securities" means securities (including funds in court) of a kind prescribed by rules of court made under this section.

(2) The power to make rules of court under section 1 of, and Schedule 1 to, the Civil Procedure Act 1997 shall include power by any such rules to make provision—

(a) for the High Court to make a stop order on the application of any person claiming to be entitled to an interest in prescribed securities; and

(b) for the service of a stop notice by any person claiming to be entitled to an interest in prescribed securities.

(3) [Deleted]

(4) Rules of court made by virtue of subsection (2) above shall prescribe the person or body on whom a copy of any stop order or a stop notice is to be served.

(5) The steps mentioned in subsection (1) above are—

(a) the registration of any transfer of the securities;

(b) in the case of funds in court, the transfer, sale, delivery out, payment or other dealing with the funds, or of the income thereon;

(c) the making of any payment by way of dividend, interest or otherwise in respect of the securities; and

(d) in the case of a unit trust, any acquisition of or other dealing with the units by any person or body exercising functions under the trust.

(6) Any rules of court made by virtue of this section may include such incidental, supplemental and consequential provisions as the authority making them consider necessary or expedient, and may make different provision in relation to different cases or classes of case.

Note —Amended by the Supreme Court Act 1981, s.153, Sched.5; and the County **9B–223**
Courts Act 1984, s.148, Sched.2. Section 75 of the County Courts Act 1984 (referred
to in subs. (3)) was omitted by, and s.84 of the Supreme Court Act 1981 (referred to in
subs. (2)) was amended by, the Civil Procedure Act 1997, Sched.2, paras 1(4) and 2(6).

Interpretation

9B–224   6.—(1) In this Act—

"building society" has the same meaning as in the Building Societies Act 1986;

"charging order" means an order made under section 1(1) of this Act;

"debtor" and "creditor" have the meanings given by section 1(1) of this Act;

"dividend" includes any distribution in respect of any unit of a unit trust;

"government stock" means any stock issued by her Majesty's government in the United Kingdom or any funds of, or annuity granted by, that government;

"stock" includes shares, debentures and any securities of the body concerned, whether or not constituting a charge on the assets of that body;

"unit trust" means any trust established for the purpose, or having the effect, of providing, for persons having funds available for investment, facilities for the participation by them, as beneficiaries under the trust, in any profits or income arising from the acquisition, holding management or disposal of any property whatsoever.

(2) For the purposes of section 1 of this Act references to a judgment or order of the High Court or a county court shall be taken to include references to a judgment, order, decree or award (however called) of any court or arbitrator (including any foreign court or arbitrator) which is or has become enforceable (whether wholly or to a limited extent) as if it were a judgment or order of the High Court or a county court.

(3) References in section 2 of this Act to any securities include references to any such securities standing in the name of the Accountant General.

9B–225   *Note* —Amended by the Building Societies Act 1986, ss.54, 120, Sched.18.

Consequential amendment, repeals and transitional provisions

9B–226   7.—(1) [...]

(2) [...]

(3) Any order made or notice given under any enactment repealed by this Act or under any rules of court revoked by rules of court made under this Act (the "new rules") shall, if still in force when the provisions of this Act or, as the case may be, the new rules come into force, continue to have effect as if made under this Act or, as the case may be, under the new rules.

(4) [...]

9B–227   *Note* —Amended by the Supreme Court Act 1981, Sched.7; the County Courts Act 1984, s.148, Sched.4; and by the Land Registration Act 2002, Sched.13, para.1.

Short title, commencement and extent

8.—(1) This Act may be cited as the Charging Orders Act 1979. **9B–228**

(2) This Act comes into force on such day as the Lord Chancellor may appoint by order made by statutory instrument.

(3) This Act does not extend to Scotland or Northern Ireland.

Civil Evidence Act 1968

(1968 c.64) **9B–229**

ARRANGEMENT OF SECTIONS

PART II

MISCELLANEOUS AND GENERAL

CONVICTIONS, ETC. AS EVIDENCE IN CIVIL PROCEEDINGS

PART II

MISCELLANEOUS AND GENERAL

CONVICTIONS, ETC. AS EVIDENCE IN CIVIL PROCEEDINGS

Convictions as evidence in civil proceedings

11.—(1) In any civil proceedings the fact that a person has been **9B–230** convicted of an offence by or before any court in the United Kingdom or by a court-martial there or elsewhere shall (subject to subsection (3) below) be admissible in evidence for the purpose of proving, where to do so is relevant to any issue in those proceedings, that he committed that offence, whether he was so convicted upon a plea of guilty or otherwise and whether or not he is a party to the civil proceedings; but no conviction other than a subsisting one shall be admissible in evidence by virtue of this section.

(2) In any civil proceedings in which by virtue of this section a person is proved to have been convicted of an offence by or before any court in the United Kingdom or by a court-martial there or elsewhere—

(a) he shall be taken to have committed that offence unless the contrary is proved; and

(b) without prejudice to the reception of any other admissible evidence for the purpose of identifying the facts on which the conviction was based, the contents of any document which is admissible as evidence of the conviction, and the contents of the information, complaint, indictment or charge-sheet on which the person in question was convicted, shall be admissible in evidence for that purpose.

(3) Nothing in this section shall prejudice the operation of section 13 of this Act or any other enactment whereby a conviction or a finding of fact in any criminal proceedings is for the purposes of any other proceedings made conclusive evidence of any fact.

(4) Where in any civil proceedings the contents of any document are admissible in evidence by virtue of subsection (2) above, a copy of that document, or of the material part thereof, purporting to be certified or otherwise authenticated by or on behalf of the court or authority having custody of that document shall be admissible in evidence and shall be taken to be a true copy of that document or part unless the contrary is shown.

(5) Nothing in any of the following enactments, that is to say—

(a) section 1C of the Powers of Criminal Courts Act 1973 (under which a conviction leading to discharge is to be disregarded except as therein mentioned);

(b) section 191 of the Criminal Procedure (Scotland) Act 1975 (which makes similar provision in respect of convictions on indictment in Scotland); and

(c) section 8 of the Probation Act (Northern Ireland) 1950 (which corresponds to the said section 12) or any corresponding enactment of the Parliament of Northern Ireland for the time being in force,

shall affect the operation of this section; and for the purposes of this section any order made by a court of summary jurisdiction in Scotland under section 383 or section 384 of the said Act of 1975 shall be treated as a conviction.

(6) In this section "court-martial" means a court-martial constituted under the Army Act 1955, the Air Force Act 1955 or the Naval Discipline Act 1957 and in relation to a court-martial "conviction" means a finding of guilty which is, or falls to be treated as, the finding of the court, and "conviction" shall be construed accordingly.

9B–231 *Note*—This section came into force on December 2, 1968 (Civil Evidence Act 1968 (Commencement No. 1) Order 1968 (S.I. 1968 No. 1734)). Amended by the Powers of Criminal Courts Act 1973, s.56(1); Sched.5; the Criminal Justice Act 1991, Sched.11; the Armed Forces Act 1996, Sched.1, para. 100, Sched.7, Pt II; and by the Armed Forces Act 2001, Sched.7, para.1.

Subs. (1): "Admissible in evidence"

9B–232 The effect of admitting the conviction in evidence is in civil proceedings to shift on to the convicted person the burden of proving that he is innocent. This should be contrasted with the effect of s.13, below.

"A subsisting one"

9B–233 A conviction which has been quashed on appeal cannot be "subsisting"; nor, it is thought, can it be "subsisting" if a free pardon has been granted. Moreover, although a conviction as to which an appeal is pending is "subsisting", a court cannot enter judgment in reliance upon it in a civil action, since the conviction may be quashed on appeal (*Re Raphael Dec'd, Raphael v. D'antin* [1973] 1 W.L.R. 998).

Findings of adultery and paternity as evidence in civil proceedings

9B–234

12.—(1) In any civil proceedings—

    (a) the fact that a person has been found guilty of adultery in any matrimonial proceedings; and

    (b) the fact that a person has been found to be the father of a child in relevant proceedings before any court in England and Wales or Northern Ireland or has been adjudged to be the father of a child in affiliation proceedings before any court in the United Kingdom,

shall (subject to subsection (3) below) be admissible in evidence for the purpose of proving, where to do so is relevant to any issue in those civil proceedings, that he committed the adultery to which the finding relates or, as the case may be, is (or was) the father of that child, whether or not he offered any defence to the allegation of adultery or paternity and whether or not he is a party to the civil proceedings; but no finding or adjudication other than a subsisting one shall be admissible in evidence by virtue of this section.

(2) In any civil proceedings in which by virtue of this section a person is proved to have been found guilty of adultery as mentioned in subsection (1)(a) above or to have been found or adjudged to be the father of a child as mentioned in subsection (1)(b) above—

    (a) he shall be taken to have committed the adultery to which the finding relates or, as the case may be, to be (or have been) the father of that child, unless the contrary is proved; and

    (b) without prejudice to the reception of any other admissible evidence for the purpose of identifying the facts on which the finding or adjudication was based, the contents of any document which was before the court, or which contains any pronouncement of the court, in the other proceedings in question shall be admissible in evidence for that purpose.

(3) Nothing in this section shall prejudice the operation of any enactment whereby a finding of fact in any matrimonial or affiliation proceedings is for the purposes of any other proceedings made conclusive evidence of any fact.

(4) Subsection (4) of section 11 of this Act shall apply for the purposes of this section as if the reference to subsection (2) were a reference to subsection (2) of this section.

(5) In this section—

    "matrimonial proceedings" means any matrimonial cause in the High Court or a county court in England and Wales or in the High Court in Northern Ireland, any consistorial action in Scotland, or any appeal arising out of any such cause or action;

"relevant proceedings" means—

(a) proceedings on a complaint under section 42 of the National Assistance Act 1948 or section 26 of the Social Security Act 1986;

(b) proceedings under the Children Act 1989;

(c) proceedings which would have been relevant proceedings for the purposes of this section in the form in which it was in force before the passing of the Children Act 1989;

"affiliation proceedings" means, in relation to Scotland, any action of affiliation and aliment;

and in this subsection "consistorial action" does not include an action of aliment only between husband and wife raised in the Court of Session or an action of interim aliment raised in the sheriff court.

9B–235   *Note* —This section came into force on December 2, 1968 (Civil Evidence Act 1968 (Commencement No. 1) Order 1968 (S.I. 1968 No. 1734)). It has been amended by the Family Law Reform Act 1987, s.29; the Children Act 1989, Sched.13; the Courts and Legal Services Act 1990, Sched.16; and the Children (Northern Ireland Consequential Amendments) Order 1995 (S.I. 1995 No. 756).

Subs.(1): "Found guilty of adultery"
9B–236   See Practice Direction [1969] 1 W.L.R. 1192.

Conclusiveness of convictions for purposes of defamation actions

9B–237   **13.**—(1) In an action for libel or slander in which the question whether the plaintiff did or did not commit a criminal offence is relevant to an issue arising in the action, proof that, at the time when that issue falls to be determined, he stands convicted of that offence shall be conclusive evidence that he committed that offence; and his conviction thereof shall be admissible in evidence accordingly.

(2) In any such action as aforesaid in which by virtue of this section the plaintiff is proved to have been convicted of an offence, the contents of any document which is admissible as evidence of the conviction, and the contents of the information, complaint, indictment or charge-sheet on which he was convicted, shall, without prejudice to the reception of any other admissible evidence for the purpose of identifying the facts on which the conviction was based, be admissible in evidence for the purpose of identifying those facts.

(2A) In the case of an action for libel or slander in which there is more than one plaintiff—

(a) the references in subsections (1) and (2) above to the plaintiff shall be construed as references to any of the plaintiffs, and

(b) proof that any of the plaintiffs stands convicted of an offence shall be conclusive evidence that he committed that offence so far as that fact is relevant to any issue arising in relation to his cause of action or that of any other plaintiff.

(3) For the purposes of this section a person shall be taken to

stand convicted of an offence if but only if there subsists against him a conviction of that offence by or before a court in the United Kingdom or by a court-martial there or elsewhere.

(4) Subsections (4) to (6) of section 11 of this Actshall apply for the purposes of this section as they apply for the purposes of that section, but as if in the said subsection (4) the reference to subsection (2) were a reference to subsection (2) of this section.

(5) The foregoing provisions of this section shall apply for the purposes of any action begun after the passing of this Act, whenever the cause of action arose, but shall not apply for the purposes of any action begun before the passing of this Act or any appeal or other proceedings arising out of any such action.

Note —Amended by the Defamation Act 1996, s.12. **9B–238**

Subs.(1): "Shall be conclusive"
This should be contrasted with the effect of s.11 above. It is of course elementary **9B–239** that an *acquittal* in a criminal trial of the plaintiff is no bar to a plea of justification by a defendant in defamation proceedings.

PRIVILEGE

Privilege against incrimination of self or spouse

14.—(1) The right of a person in any legal proceedings other than **9B–240** criminal proceedings to refuse to answer any question or produce any document or thing if to do so would tend to expose that person to proceedings for an offence or for the recovery of a penalty—

(a) shall apply only as regards criminal offences under the law of any part of the United Kingdom and penalties provided for by such law; and

(b) shall include a like right to refuse to answer any question or produce any document or thing if to do so would tend to expose the husband or wife of that person to proceedings for any such criminal offence or for the recovery of any such penalty.

(2) In so far as any existing enactment conferring (in whatever words) powers of inspection or investigation confers on a person (in whatever words) any right otherwise than in criminal proceedings to refuse to answer any question or give any evidence tending to incriminate that person, subsection (1) above shall apply to that right as it applies to the right described in that subsection; and every such existing enactment shall be construed accordingly.

(3) In so far as any existing enactment provides (in whatever words) that in any proceedings other than criminal proceedings a person shall not be excused from answering any question or giving any evidence on the ground that to do so may incriminate that person, that enactment shall be construed as providing also that in such proceedings a person shall not be excused from answering any question or giving any evidence on the ground that to do so may incriminate the husband or wife of that person.

(4) Where any existing enactment (however worded) that—

(a) confers powers of inspection or investigation; or

(b) provides as mentioned in subsection (3) above,

further provides (in whatever words) that any answer or evidence given by a person shall not be admissible in evidence against that person in any proceedings or class of proceedings (however described, and whether criminal or not) that enactment shall be construed as providing also that any answer or evidence given by that person shall not be admissible in evidence against the husband or wife of that person in the proceedings or class of proceedings in question.

(5) In this section "existing enactment" means any enactment passed before this Act; and the references to giving evidence are references to giving evidence in any manner, whether by furnishing information, making discovery, producing documents or otherwise.

Subs. (1): "Recovery of a penalty"

9B–241   "Penalty" is apt to include a fine imposed under the EEC Treaty (*Rio Tinto Zinc Corp'n v. Westinghouse Electrical Corp'n* [1978] A.C. 547), or a fine imposed by a civil court as a penalty for contempt (*Bhimji v. Chatwani (No. 2)* [1992] 4 All E.R. 912).

Subs. (1)(a): "Proceedings for an offence"

9B–242   The phrase does not include proceedings in respect of a contempt of court (*Garvin v. Domus Publishing* [1989] Ch. 335).

"Under the law of any part of the United Kingdom"

9B–243   For an example of a case in which consideration was given to the risk of incrimination by reference to foreign law, see *Arab Monetary Fund v. Hashim* [1989] 1 W.L.R. 565.

Privilege for certain communications relating to patent proceedings

9B–244   **15.** [*Repealed by the Patents Act 1977 , s.132 and Sched.6. See ibid., ss.103–105.*]

9B–245   *Note* —It has been held that s.105 applies to protect the disclosure of communications made for the purpose of patent proceedings in connection with a patent which was in existence on the appointed day, notwithstanding that the communications and relevant proceedings were completed prior to that date (*Santa Fe International Corp. v. Napier Shipping SA* [1986] R.P.C. 72).

Patent proceedings include an application for a patent whose contemplation requires only the contemplation of the applicant; but in all contentious proceedings in which there are two parties the party *in a position to bring proceedings* must in some way or other indicated that there might in certain circumstances be each proceedings brought, before they can be said to be contemplated. The mere seeking of advice by a potential infringer as to some proposed construction does not amount to contemplation (*Rockwell International Corp. v. Serck Industries Ltd* [1987] R.P.C. 89 affirmed CA [1988] F.S.R. 187). *Semble* however that even an infringer could bring proceedings for a declaration of non-infringement, and the advice he obtains might well be in contemplation thereof.

Abolition of certain privileges

9B–246   **16.**—(1) The following rules of law are hereby abrogated except in relation to criminal proceedings, that is to say—

(a) the rule whereby, in any legal proceedings, a person cannot be compelled to answer any question or produce any document or thing if to do so would tend to expose him to a forfeiture; and

(b) the rule whereby, in any legal proceedings, a person other than a party to the proceedings cannot be compelled to produce any deed or other document relating to his title to any land.

(2) The rule of law whereby, in any civil proceedings, a party to the proceedings cannot be compelled to produce any document relating solely to his own case and in no way tending to impeach that case or support the case of any opposing party is hereby abrogated.

(3) Section 3 of the Evidence (Amendment) Act 1853 (which provides that a husband or wife shall not be compellable to disclose any communication made to him or her by his or her spouse during the marriage) shall cease to have effect except in relation to criminal proceedings.

(4) In section 43(1) of the Matrimonial Causes Act 1965 (under which the evidence of a husband or wife is admissible in any proceedings to prove that marital intercourse did or did not take place between them during any period, but a husband or wife is not compellable in any proceedings to give evidence of the matters aforesaid) the words from "but a husband or wife" to the end of the subsection shall cease to have effect except in relation to criminal proceedings.

(5) A witness in any proceedings instituted in consequence of adultery, whether a party to the proceedings or not, shall not be excused from answering any question by reason that it tends to show that he or she has been guilty of adultery; and accordingly the proviso to section 3 of the Evidence (Further Amendment) Act 1869 and, in section 43(2) of the Matrimonial Causes Act 1965, the words from "but" to the end of the subsection shall cease to have effect.

Consequential amendments relating to privilege

17.—(1) In relation to England and Wales—   9B–247

(a) [.   .   .]

(b) section 8(5) of the Parliamentary Commissioner Act 1967 (which provides that, subject as there mentioned, no person shall be compelled for the purposes of an investigation under that Act to give any evidence or produce any document which he could not be compelled to give or produce in proceedings before the High Court) shall have effect as if before the word "proceedings" there were inserted the word "civil";

and, so far as it applies to England and Wales, any other existing enactment, however framed or worded, which in relation to any tribunal, investigation or inquiry (however described) confers on persons required to answer questions or give evidence any privilege described by reference to the privileges of witnesses in proceedings before any court shall, unless the contrary intention appears, be construed as referring to the privileges of witnesses in civil proceedings before that court.

(2) [...]

(3) Without prejudice to the generality of subsection (2) to (4) of section 14 of this Act, the enactments mentioned in the Schedule to

this Act shall have effect subject to the amendments provided for by that Schedule (being verbal amendments to bring those enactments into conformity with the provisions of that section).

(4) Subsection (5) of section 14 of this Act shall apply for the purposes of this section as it applies for the purposes of that section.

9B–248   *Note* — Subsection (2) repealed by the Evidence (Proceedings in Other Jurisdictions) Act 1975, s.8(2), Sched.2; subs.(1)(a) repealed by the Inquiries Act 2005, s.49(2), Sch.3.

GENERAL

General interpretation, and savings

9B–249   **18.**—(1) In this Act "civil proceedings" includes, in addition to civil proceedings in any of the ordinary courts of law—

    (a) civil proceedings before any other tribunal, being proceedings in relation to which the strict rules of evidence apply; and

    (b) an arbitration or reference, whether under an enactment or not,

    but does not include civil proceedings in relation to which the strict rules of evidence do not apply.

(2) In this Act—

"court" does not include a court-martial, and, in relation to an arbitration or reference, means the arbitrator or umpire and, in relation to proceedings before a tribunal (not being one of the ordinary courts of law) means the tribunal;

"legal proceedings" includes an arbitration or reference, whether under an enactment or not;

and for the avoidance of doubt it is hereby declared that in this Act, and in any amendment made by this Act in any other enactment, references to a person's husband or wife do not include references to a person who is no longer married to that person.

(3) Any reference in this Act to any other enactment is a reference thereto as amended, and includes a reference thereto as applied, by or under any other enactment.

(4) Nothing in this Act shall prejudice the operation of any enactment which provides (in whatever words) that any answer or evidence given by a person in specified circumstances shall not be admissible in evidence against him or some other person in any proceedings or class of proceedings (however described).

In this subsection the reference to giving evidence is a reference to giving evidence in any manner, whether by furnishing information, making discovery, producing documents or otherwise.

(5) Nothing in this Act shall prejudice—

    (a) any power of a court, in any legal proceedings, to exclude evidence (whether by preventing questions from being put or otherwise) at its discretion; or

    (b) the operation of any agreement (whenever made) between the parties to any legal proceedings as to the evidence which is to be admissible (whether generally or for any particular purpose) in those proceedings.

(6) It is hereby declared that where, by reason of any defect of speech or hearing from which he is suffering, a person called as a witness in any legal proceedings gives his evidence in writing or by signs, that evidence is to be treated for the purposes of this Act as being given orally.

Note—Committal proceedings for contempt of court in the course of civil litigation **9B–250**
are not criminal but remain civil proceedings for the purposes of s.18, and although
they were unreasoned or extraordinary because of possible penal consequences and
thus the proof required was the criminal standard of proof that did not convert such
proceedings (*Savings and Investment Bank Ltd v. Gasco Investments (Netherlands) BV (No.
2)* [1988] Ch. 422, CA).

Subs. (1): "Proceedings in relation to which the strict rules of evidence apply"
Some courts and tribunals, notably coroners', election and prize courts, are not **9B–251**
bound by the rules of evidence (*R. v. Deputy Industrial Injuries Commissioner, Ex p. Moore*
[1965] 1 Q.B. 456; and *Wednesbury Corporation v. Ministry of Housing and Local Government (No. 2)* [1966] 2 Q.B. 275).

Northern Ireland
19. [*Repealed by the Northern Ireland Constitution Act 1973 , s.41(1)* **9B–252**
and Sched.6.]

Short title, repeals, extent and commencement
20.—(1) This Act may be cited as the Civil Evidence Act 1968. **9B–253**

(2) Sections 1, 2, 6(1)(except the words from "Proceedings" to "references") and 6(2)(b) of the Evidence Act 1938 are hereby repealed.

(3) This Act shall not extend to Scotland or to Northern Ireland.

(4) The following provisions of this Act, namely sections 13 to 19, this section (except subsection (2)) and the Schedule, shall come into force on the day this Act is passed, and the other provisions of this Act shall come into force on such day as the Lord Chancellor may by order made by statutory instrument appoint; and different days may be so appointed for different purposes of this Act or for the same purposes in relation to different courts or proceedings or otherwise in relation to different circumstances.

Note—Amended by the Northern Ireland Constitution Act 1973, Sched.6. **9B–254**

Civil Evidence Act 1972

(1972 c.30)

An Act to make, for civil proceedings in England and Wales, provision as to the admissibility in evidence of statements of opinion and the reception of expert evidence; and to facilitate proof in such proceedings of any law other than that of England and Wales.

[12th June 1972] **9B–255**

ARRANGEMENT OF SECTIONS

Note

9B–256   This Act is concerned with (1) evidence of opinion, and (2) foreign evidence. Initially, s.5 (Interpretation, application to arbitration, etc.) stated that the provisions of the Act applied to "civil proceedings" and in "courts" as defined in the Civil Evidence Act 1968, s.18 (see para. 9B–249 above). This provision, in combination with Commencement Orders issued in 1973 and 1974, restricted the application of the Act to certain civil proceedings in certain courts. However, s.5(1) was amended by the Civil Evidence Act 1995 and now states (see para. 9B–264 below) that "civil proceedings" means civil proceedings "before any tribunal in relation to which the strict rules of evidence apply, whether as a matter of law or by agreement between the parties" (*e.g.* an arbitration agreement); references to "court" should be construed accordingly (note also s.5(2)).

Application of Part I of Civil Evidence Act 1968 to statements of opinion

9B–257   1. [*Repealed by the Civil Evidence Act 1995 , s.15(2) , Sched.2.*]

Rules of court with respect to expert reports and oral expert evidence

9B–258   **2.—(1)** [...]

(2) [...]

(3) Notwithstanding any enactment or rule of law by virtue of which documents prepared for the purpose of pending or contemplated civil proceedings or in connection with the obtaining or giving of legal advice are in certain circumstances privileged from disclosure, provision may be made by rules of court—

> (a) for enabling the court in any civil proceedings to direct, with respect to medical matters or matters of any other class which may be specified in the direction, that the parties or some of them shall each by such date as may be so specified (or such later date as may be permitted or agreed in accordance with the rules) disclose to the other or others in the form of one or more expert reports the expert evidence on matters of that class which he proposes to adduce as part of his case at the trial; and
>
> (b) for prohibiting a party who fails to comply with a direction given in any such proceedings under rules of court made by virtue of paragraph (a) above from adducing in evidence except with the leave of the court, any statement (whether of fact or opinion) contained in any expert report whatsoever in so far as that statement deals with matters of any class specified in the direction.

(4) Provision may be made by rules of court as to the conditions

subject to which oral expert evidence may be given in civil proceedings.

(5) Without prejudice to the generality of subsection (4) above, rules of court made in pursuance of that subsection may make provision for prohibiting a party who fails to comply with a direction given as mentioned in subsection (3)(b) above from adducing, except with the leave of the court, any oral expert evidence whatsoever with respect to matters of any class specified in the direction.

(6) Any rules of court made in pursuance of this section may make different provisions for different classes of cases, for expert reports dealing with matters of different classes, and for other different circumstances.

(7) References in this section to an expert report are references to a written report by a person dealing wholly or mainly with matters on which he is (or would if living be) qualified to give expert evidence.

(8) [. . .]

Note—Amended by the MCA 1980, s.154, Sched.7; the SCA 1981, s.152(4), Sched.7; **9B–259** the County Courts Act 1984, s.148(1), Sched.2; the Civil Evidence Act 1995, s.15(2), Sched.2; the Courts Act 2003, s.109(1), (3), Sch.8, para.165, Sch.10.

Subs. (2): "Documents"
This word is apt to include a letter (*Carlish v. East Ham Corporation and Edwards* **9B–260** [1948] 3 K.B. 380; a tape-recording: *Grant v. South-Western and County Properties* [1975] Ch. 185; or a film: *Senior v. Holdsworth, ex parte Independent Television* [1976] Q.B. 23).

Admissibility of expert opinion and certain expressions of non-expert opinion

3.—(1) Subject to any rules of court made in pursuance of this Act, **9B–261** where a person is called as a witness in any civil proceedings, his opinion on any relevant matter on which he is qualified to give expert evidence shall be admissible in evidence.

(2) It is hereby declared that where a person is called as a witness in any civil proceedings, a statement of opinion by him on any relevant matter on which he is not qualified to give expert evidence, if made as a way of conveying relevant facts personally perceived by him, is admissible as evidence of what he perceived.

(3) In this section "relevant matter" includes an issue in the proceedings in question.

Note—Amended by the Civil Evidence Act 1995, s.15(2), Sched.2. **9B–262**

"shall be automatically given in evidence"
An expert' report is not automatically admissible solely by virtue of its coming **9B–262.1** within s.3; it must also be helpful to the court in arriving at its conclusions where the court accepted that there existed a recognised expertise (*Barings Plc (In Liquidation) v. Coopers & Lybrand (No.2)* [2001] Lloyd's Rep. Bank. 85; [2001] Lloyd's Rep. P.N. 379; [2001] P.N.L.R. 22; (2001) 98(13) L.S.G. 40 (Evans-Lombe J.)).

Evidence of foreign law

4.—(1) It is hereby declared that in civil proceedings a person who **9B–263** is suitably qualified to do so on account of his knowledge or experience is competent to give expert evidence as to the law of any country or territory outside the United Kingdom, or of any part of the United Kingdom other than England and Wales, irrespective of whether he has acted or is entitled to act as a legal practitioner there.

(2) Where any question as to the law of any country or territory outside the United Kingdom, or of any part of the United Kingdom other than England and Wales, with respect to any matter has been determined (whether before or after the passing of this Act) in any such proceedings as are mentioned in subsection (4) below, then in any civil proceedings (not being proceedings before a court which can take judicial notice of the law of that country, territory or part with respect to that matter)—

(a) any finding made or decision given on that question in the first-mentioned proceedings shall, if reported or recorded in citable form, be admissible in evidence for the purpose of proving the law of that country, territory or part with respect to that matter; and

(b) if that finding or decision, as so reported or recorded, is adduced for that purpose, the law of that country, territory or part with respect to that matter shall be taken to be in accordance with that finding or decision unless the contrary is proved:

Provided that paragraph (b) above shall not apply in the case of a finding or decision which conflicts with another finding or decision on the same question adduced by virtue of this subsection in the same proceedings.

(3) Except with the leave of the court, a party to any civil proceedings shall not be permitted to adduce any such finding or decision as is mentioned in subsection (2) above by virtue of that subsection unless he has in accordance with rules of court given to every other party to the proceedings notice that he intends to do so.

(4) The proceedings referred to in subsection (2) above are the following, whether civil or criminal, namely—

(a) proceedings at first instance in any of the following courts, namely the High Court, the Crown Court, a court of quarter sessions, the Court of Chancery of the county palatine of Lancaster and the Court of Chancery of the county palatine of Durham;

(b) appeals arising out of any such proceedings as are mentioned in paragraph (a) above;

(c) proceedings before the Judicial Committee of the Privy Council on appeal (whether to Her Majesty in Council or to the Judicial Committee as such) from any decision of any court outside the United Kingdom.

(5) For the purposes of this section a finding or decision on any such question as is mentioned in subsection (2) above shall be taken to be reported or recorded in citable form if, but only if, it is reported or recorded in writing in a report, transcript or other document which, if that question had been a question as to the law of England and Wales, could be cited as an authority in legal proceedings in England and Wales.

Interpretation, application to arbitrations, etc., and savings

5.—(1) In this Act "civil proceedings" means civil proceedings, **9B–264** before any tribunal, in relation to which the strict rules of evidence apply, whether as a matter of law or by agreement of the parties; and references to "the court" shall be construed accordingly.

(2) The rules of court made for the purposes of the application of sections 2 and 4 of this Act to proceedings in the High Court apply, except in so far as their application is excluded by agreement, to proceedings before tribunals other than the ordinary courts of law, subject to such modifications as may be appropriate.

Any question arising as to what modifications are appropriate shall be determined, in default of agreement, by the tribunal.

(3) Nothing in this Act shall prejudice—

    (a) any power of a court, in any civil proceedings, to exclude evidence (whether by preventing questions from being put or otherwise) at its discretion; or

    (b) the operation of any agreement (whenever made) between the parties to any civil proceedings as to the evidence which is to be admissible (whether generally or for any particular purpose) in those proceedings.

Note — Subss. (1) and (2) substituted by the Civil Evidence Act 1995, s.15(1), **9B–265** Sched.1, para. 7.

Short title, extent and commencement

6.—(1) This Act may be cited as the Civil Evidence Act 1972. **9B–266**

(2) This Act shall not extend to Scotland or Northern Ireland.

(3) This Act, except sections 4(2) to (5) shall come into force on 1st January 1973, and sections 4(2) to (5) shall come into force on such day as the Lord Chancellor may by order made by statutory instrument appoint; and different days may be so appointed for different purposes or for the same purposes in relation to different courts or proceedings or otherwise in relation to different circumstances.

Note —Amended by the Civil Evidence Act 1995, s.15(2), Sched.2. **9B–267**

Civil Evidence Act 1995

(1995 c.38)

An Act to provide for the admissibility of hearsay evidence, the proof of certain documentary evidence and the admissibility and proof of official actuarial tables in civil proceedings; and for connected purposes.

[8th November 1995] **9B–268**

ARRANGEMENT OF SECTIONS

ADMISSIBILITY OF HEARSAY EVIDENCE

LEGISLATION

Introduction

9B–269   The Civil Evidence Act 1995 received the Royal Assent on November 8, 1995, and, with the single exception of s.10 (Ogden Tables), came into force on January 31, 1997 (S.I. 1996 No. 3217). Essentially, it:

(1) Abolishes the principle excluding evidence on the ground that it is hearsay.

(2) Creates provisions governing the receiving of such evidence.

(3) Preserves certain Common Law rules relating to hearsay.

(4) Provides for the manner of proving documents and records.

(5) Applies to any proceedings in England and Wales to which the strict rules of evidence apply.

(6) Does not apply to cases started before January 31, 1996 (but see below, "Important note").

(7) Repeals the Civil Evidence Act 1968, Pt I.

Editorial comment

9B–270   For rules of court, see CPR Pt 33. In 1998, the Lord Chancellor decided not to bring s.10 into force, pending further consideration.

ADMISSIBILITY OF HEARSAY EVIDENCE

Admissibility of hearsay evidence

9B–271   **1.**—(1) In civil proceedings evidence shall not be excluded on the ground that it is hearsay.

(2) In this Act—

(a) "hearsay" means a statement made otherwise than by a person while giving oral evidence in the proceedings which is tendered as evidence of the matters stated; and

(b) references to hearsay include hearsay of whatever degree.

(3) Nothing in this Act affects the admissibility of evidence admissible apart from this section.

(4) The provisions of sections 2 to 6 (safeguards and supplementary provisions relating to hearsay evidence) do not apply in relation to hearsay evidence admissible apart from this section, notwithstanding that it may also be admissible by virtue of this section.

SAFEGUARDS IN RELATION TO HEARSAY EVIDENCE

Notice of proposal to adduce hearsay evidence

9B–272   **2.**—(1) A party proposing to adduce hearsay evidence in civil proceedings shall, subject to the following provisions of this section, give to the other party or parties to the proceedings—

    (a) such notice (if any) of that fact, and

    (b) on request, such particulars of or relating to the evidence,

as is reasonable and practicable in the circumstances for the purpose of enabling him or them to deal with any matters arising from its being hearsay.

  (2) Provision may be made by rules of court—

    (a) specifying classes of proceedings or evidence in relation to which subsection (1) does not apply, and

    (b) as to the manner in which (including the time within which) the duties imposed by that subsection are to be complied with in the cases where it does apply.

  (3) Subsection (1) may also be excluded by agreement of the parties; and compliance with the duty to give notice may in any case be waived by the person to whom notice is required to be given.

  (4) A failure to comply with subsection (1), or with rules under subsection (2)(b), does not affect the admissibility of the evidence but may be taken into account by the court—

    (a) in considering the exercise of its powers with respect to the course of proceedings and costs, and

    (b) as a matter adversely affecting the weight to be given to the evidence in accordance with section 4.

Power to call witness for cross-examination on hearsay statement

3. Rules of court may provide that where a party to civil proceed- **9B–273** ings adduces hearsay evidence of a statement made by a person and does not call that person as a witness, any other party to the proceedings may, with the leave of the court, call that person as a witness and cross-examine him on the statement as if he had been called by the first-mentioned party and as if the hearsay statement were his evidence in chief.

Considerations relevant to weighing of hearsay evidence

4.—(1) In estimating the weight (if any) to be given to hearsay evi- **9B–274** dence in civil proceedings the court shall have regard to any circumstances from which any inference can reasonably be drawn as to the reliability or otherwise of the evidence.

  (2) Regard may be had, in particular, to the following—

    (a) whether it would have been reasonable and practicable for the party by whom the evidence was adduced to have produced the maker of the original statement as a witness;

    (b) whether the original statement was made contemporaneously with the occurrence or existence of the matters stated;

    (c) whether the evidence involves multiple hearsay;

(d) whether any person involved has any motive to conceal or misrepresent matters;

(e) whether the original statement was an edited account, or was made in collaboration with another or for a particular purpose;

(f) whether the circumstances in which the evidence is adduced as hearsay are such as to suggest an attempt to prevent proper evaluation of its weight.

SUPPLEMENTARY PROVISIONS AS TO HEARSAY EVIDENCE

Competence and credibility

9B–275   **5.**—(1) Hearsay evidence shall not be admitted in civil proceedings if or to the extent that it is shown to consist of, or to be proved by means of, a statement made by a person who at the time he made the statement was not competent as a witness. For this purpose "not competent as a witness" means suffering from such mental or physical infirmity, or lack of understanding, as would render a person incompetent as a witness in civil proceedings; but a child shall be treated as competent as a witness if he satisfies the requirements of section 96(2)(a) and (b)of the Children Act 1989 (conditions for reception of unsworn evidence of child).

(2) Where in civil proceedings hearsay evidence is adduced and the maker of the original statement, or of any statement relied upon to prove another statement, is not called as a witness—

(a) evidence which if he had been so called would be admissible for the purpose of attacking or supporting his credibility as a witness is admissible for that purpose in the proceedings; and

(b) evidence tending to prove that, whether before or after he made the statement, he made any other statement inconsistent with it is admissible for the purpose of showing that he had contradicted himself.

Provided that evidence may not be given of any matter of which, if he had been called as a witness and had denied that matter in cross-examination, evidence could not have been adduced by the cross-examining party.

Previous statements of witnesses

9B–276   **6.**—(1) Subject as follows, the provisions of this Act as to hearsay evidence in civil proceedings apply equally (but with any necessary modifications) in relation to a previous statement made by a person called as a witness in the proceedings.

(2) A party who has called or intends to call a person as a witness in civil proceedings may not in those proceedings adduce evidence of a previous statement made by that person, except—

(a) with the leave of the court, or

(b) for the purpose of rebutting a suggestion that his evidence has been fabricated.

This shall not be construed as preventing a witness statement (that is, a written statement of oral evidence which a party to the proceedings intends to lead) from being adopted by a witness in giving evidence or treated as his evidence.

(3) Where in the case of civil proceedings section 3, 4 or 5of the Criminal Procedure Act 1865applies, which make provision as to—

    (a) how far a witness may be discredited by the party producing him,

    (b) the proof of contradictory statements made by a witness, and

    (c) cross-examination as to previous statements in writing,

this Act does not authorise the adducing of evidence of a previous inconsistent or contradictory statement otherwise than in accordance with those sections.

This is without prejudice to any provision made by rules of court under section 3 above (power to call witness for cross-examination on hearsay statement).

(4) Nothing in this Act affects any of the rules of law as to the circumstances in which, where a person called as a witness in civil proceedings is cross-examined on a document used by him to refresh his memory, that document may be made evidence in the proceedings.

(5) Nothing in this section shall be construed as preventing a statement of any description referred to above from being admissible by virtue of section 1 as evidence of the matters stated.

Evidence formerly admissible at common law

7.—(1) The common law rule effectively preserved by section 9(1) **9B–277** and (2)(a) of the Civil Evidence Act 1968 (admissibility of admissions adverse to a party) is superseded by the provisions of this Act.

(2) The common law rules effectively preserved by section 9(1) and (2)(b) to (d) of the Civil Evidence Act 1968, that is, any rule of law whereby in civil proceedings—

    (a) published works dealing with matters of a public nature (for example, histories, scientific works, dictionaries and maps) are admissible as evidence of facts of a public nature stated in them,

    (b) public documents (for example, public registers, and returns made under public authority with respect to matters of public interest) are admissible as evidence of facts stated in them, or

    (c) records (for example, the records of certain courts, treaties, Crown grants, pardons and commissions) are admissible as evidence of facts stated in them.

shall continue to have effect.

(3) The common law rules effectively preserved by section 9(3) and (4) of the Civil Evidence Act 1968, that is, any rule of law whereby in civil proceedings—

    (a) evidence of a person's reputation is admissible for the purpose of proving his good or bad character, or

    (b) evidence of reputation or family tradition is admissible—

        (i) for the purpose of proving or disproving pedigree or the existence of a marriage, or

> > (ii) for the purpose of proving or disproving the existence of any public or general right or of identifying any person or thing,

shall continue to have effect in so far as they authorise the court to treat such evidence as proving or disproving that matter.

Where any such rule applies, reputation or family tradition shall be treated for the purposes of this Act as a fact and not as a statement or multiplicity of statements about the matter in question.

(4) The words in which a rule of law mentioned in this section is described are intended only to identify the rule and shall not be construed as altering it in any way.

OTHER MATTERS

Proof of statements contained in documents

9B–278   8.—(1) Where a statement contained in a document is admissible as evidence in civil proceedings, it may be proved—

> (a) by the production of that document, or
> (b) whether or not that document is still in existence, by the production of a copy of that document or of the material part of it,

authenticated in such manner as the court may approve.

(2) It is immaterial for this purpose how many removes there are between a copy and the original.

Proof of records of business or public authority

9B–279   9.—(1) A document which is shown to form part of the records of a business or public authority may be received in evidence in civil proceedings without further proof.

(2) A document shall be taken to form part of the records of a business or public authority if there is produced to the court a certificate to that effect signed by an officer of the business or authority to which the records belong.

For this purpose—

> (a) a document purporting to be a certificate signed by an officer of a business or public authority shall be deemed to have been duly given by such an officer and signed by him; and
> (b) a certificate shall be treated as signed by a person if it purports to bear a facsimile of his signature.

(3) The absence of an entry in the records of a business or public authority may be proved in civil proceedings by affidavit of an officer of the business or authority to which the records belong.

(4) In this section—

"records" means records in whatever form;

"business" includes any activity regularly carried on over a period of time, whether for profit or not, by any body (whether corporate or not) or by an individual;

"officer" includes any person occupying a responsible position in relation to the relevant activities of the business or public authority or in relation to its records; and

"public authority" includes any public or statutory undertaking, any government department and any person holding office under Her Majesty.

(5) The court may, having regard to the circumstances of the case, direct that all or any of the above provisions of this section do not apply in relation to a particular document or record, or description of documents or records.

Admissibility and proof of Ogden Tables

10.—(1) The actuarial tables (together with explanatory notes) for use in personal injury and fatal accident cases issued from time to time by the Government Actuary's Department are admissible in evidence for the purpose of assessing, in an action for personal injury, the sum to be awarded as general damages for future pecuniary loss. **9B–280**

(2) They may be proved by the production of a copy published by Her Majesty's Stationery Office.

(3) For the purposes of this section—

    (a) "personal injury" includes any disease and any impairment of a person's physical or mental condition; and

    (b) "action for personal injury" includes an action brought by virtue of the Law Reform (Miscellaneous Provisions) Act 1934 or the Fatal Accidents Act 1976.

GENERAL

Meaning of "civil proceedings"

11. In this Act "civil proceedings" means civil proceedings, before any tribunal, in relation to which the strict rules of evidence apply, whether as a matter of law or by agreement of the parties. References to "the court" and "rules of court" shall be construed accordingly. **9B–281**

Provisions as to rules of court

12.—(1) Any power to make rules of court regulating the practice or procedure of the court in relation to civil proceedings includes power to make such provision as may be necessary or expedient for carrying into effect the provisions of this Act. **9B–282**

(2) Any rules of court made for the purposes of this Act as it applies in relation to proceedings in the High Court apply, except in so far as their operation is excluded by agreement, to arbitration proceedings to which this Act applies, subject to such modifications as may be appropriate.

Any question arising as to what modifications are appropriate shall be determined, in default of agreement, by the arbitrator or umpire, as the case may be.

Interpretation

13. In this Act— **9B–283**

LEGISLATION

"civil proceedings" has the meaning given by section 11 and "court" and "rules of court" shall be construed in accordance with that section;

"document" means anything in which information of any description is recorded, and "copy", in relation to a document, means anything onto which information recorded in the document has been copied, by whatever means and whether directly or indirectly;

"hearsay" shall be construed in accordance with section 1(2);

"oral evidence" includes evidence which, by reason of a defect of speech or hearing, a person called as a witness gives in writing or by signs;

"the original statement", in relation to hearsay evidence, means the underlying statement (if any) by—

(a) in the case of evidence of fact, a person having personal knowledge of that fact, or

(b) in the case of evidence of opinion, the person whose opinion it is; and

"statement" means any representation of fact or opinion, however made.

Savings

9B–284   **14.**—(1) Nothing in this Act affects the exclusion of evidence on grounds other than that it is hearsay. This applies whether the evidence falls to be excluded in pursuance of any enactment or rule of law, for failure to comply with rules of court or an order of the court, or otherwise.

(2) Nothing in this Act affects the proof of documents by means other than those specified in section 8 or 9.

(3) Nothing in this Act affects the operation of the following enactments—

(a) section 2 of the Documentary Evidence Act 1868 (mode of proving certain official documents);

(b) section 2 of the Documentary Evidence Act 1882 (documents printed under the superintendence of Stationery Office);

(c) section 1 of the Evidence (Colonial Statutes) Act 1907 (proof of statutes of certain legislatures);

(d) section 1 of the Evidence (Foreign, Dominion and Colonial Documents) Act 1933 (proof and effect of registers and official certificates of certain countries);

(e) section 5 of the Oaths and Evidence (Overseas Authorities and Countries) Act 1963 (provision in respect of public registers of other countries).

Consequential amendments and repeals

9B–285   **15.**—(1) The enactments specified in Schedule 1 are amended in accordance with that Schedule, the amendments being consequential on the provisions of this Act.

(2) The enactments specified in Schedule 2 are repealed to the extent specified.

Short title, commencement and extent

16.—(1) This Act may be cited as the Civil Evidence Act 1995.　　**9B–286**

(2) The provisions of this Act come into force on such day as the Lord Chancellor may appoint by order made by statutory instrument, and different days may be appointed for different provisions and for different purposes.

(3) Subject to subsection (3A), the provisions of this Act shall not apply in relation to proceedings begun before commencement.

(3A) Transitional provisions for the application of the provisions of this Act to proceedings begun before commencement may be made by rules of court or practice directions.

(4) This Act extends to England and Wales.

(5) Section 10 (admissibility and proof of Ogden Tables) also extends to Northern Ireland.

As it extends to Northern Ireland, the following shall be substituted for subsection (3)(b)—

> "(b) "action for personal injury" includes an action brought by virtue of the Law Reform (Miscellaneous Provisions) (Northern Ireland) Act 1937 or the Fatal Accidents (Northern Ireland) Order 1977."

(6) The provisions of Schedules 1 and 2(consequential amendments and repeals) have the same extent as the enactments respectively amended or repealed.

Note — Subsection (3) was replaced by, and subs. (3A) was added by, the Civil Pro-　**9B–287** cedure (Modification of Enactments) Order 1999 (S.I. 1999 No. 1217), art. 4. These modifications enabled the 1995 Act and the CPR provisions related to it to be applied to cases begun before the original commencement date of the Act (*i.e.* before January 31, 1997) (see further Vol. 1, para. 33.0.2).

* * * * *

Civil Liability (Contribution) Act 1978

(1978 c.47)

An Act to make new provision for contribution between persons who are jointly or severally, or both jointly and severally, liable for the same damage and in certain other similar cases where two or more persons have paid or may be required to pay compensation for the same damage; and to amend the law relating to proceedings against persons jointly liable for the same debt or jointly or severally, or both jointly and severally, liable for the same damage.

[31st July 1978]　**9B–288**

ARRANGEMENT OF SECTIONS

PROCEEDINGS FOR CONTRIBUTION

PROCEEDINGS FOR CONTRIBUTION

Entitlement to contribution

9B–289   **1.**—(1) Subject to the following provisions of this section, any person liable in respect of any damage suffered by another person may recover contribution from any other person liable in respect of the same damage (whether jointly with him or otherwise).

(2) A person shall be entitled to recover contribution by virtue of subsection (1) above notwithstanding that he has ceased to be liable in respect of the damage in question since the time when the damage occurred, provided that he was so liable immediately before he made or was ordered or agreed to make the payment in respect of which the contribution is sought.

(3) A person shall be liable to make contribution by virtue of subsection (1) above notwithstanding that he has ceased to be liable in respect of the damage in question since the time when the damage occurred, unless he ceased to be liable by virtue of the expiry of a period of limitation or prescription which extinguished the right on which the claim against him in respect of the damage was based.

(4) A person who has made or agreed to make any payment in bona fide settlement or compromise of any claim made against him in respect of any damage (including a payment into court which has been accepted) shall be entitled to recover contribution in accordance with this section without regard to whether or not he himself is or ever was liable in respect of the damage, provided, however, that he would have been liable assuming that the factual basis of the claim against him could be established.

(5) A judgment given in any action brought in any part of the United Kingdom by or on behalf of the person who suffered the damage in question against any person from whom contribution is sought under this section shall be conclusive in the proceedings for contribution as to any issue determined by that judgment in favour of the person from whom the contribution is sought.

(6) References in this section to a person's liability in respect of any damage are references to any such liability which has been or could be established in an action brought against him in England and Wales by or on behalf of the person who suffered the damage; but it is immaterial whether any issue arising in any such action was or would be determined (in accordance with the rules of private international law) by reference to the law of a country outside England and Wales.

9B–290   *Note* —The words "any person liable in respect of any damage suffered by another person ... *in respect of the same damage*" means the damage suffered by the same person (*Birse Construction Ltd v. Haiste Ltd* [1996] 1 W.L.R. 675; [1996] 2 All E.R. 1, CA). See also *Howkins & Harrison v. Taylor* [2001] Lloyd's Rep. PN 1, and *Eastgate Group Ltd v. Lindsey Morden Group Inc* (2001) 151 New L.J. 458. In *Royal Brompton Hospital NHS Trust v. Hammond* [2002] UKHL 14; [2002] 1 W.L.R. 1397, HL, it was said that, although the purpose of the 1978 Act was to enlarge the category of causes of action capable of giving rise to claims for contribution, the requirement of a shared, or common, liability among contributors remains the root of the contribution principle. The word "payment" in s. 1(4) includes a payment in kind, at any rate where the payment in kind is capable of valuation in monetary terms. There is no suggestion in s. 1(1) of a limit or restriction on the right of a person to claim contribution from another person liable in respect of the same damage. Sub-ss. (2) to (4) of s. 1 were designed, not to restrict such right, but to remove restrictions or defences that might otherwise be raised (*Baker & Davies plc. v. Leslie Wilks* [2005] EWHC 1179 (TCC); [2005] 3 All E.R. 603).

Claims for contribution are subject to a special time limit for limitation purposes (Limitation Act 1980 s. 10, see para. 8–14 above).

Assessment of contribution

2.—(1) Subject to subsection (3) below, in any proceedings for contribution under section 1 above the amount of the contribution recoverable from any person shall be such as may be found by the court to be just and equitable having regard to the extent of that person's responsibility for the damage in question.

9B–291

(2) Subject to subsection (3) below, the court shall have power in any such proceedings to exempt any person from liability to make contribution, or to direct that the contribution to be recovered from any person shall amount to a complete indemnity.

(3) Where the amount of the damages which have or might have been awarded in respect of the damage in question in any action brought in England and Wales by or on behalf of the person who suffered it against the person from whom the contribution is sought was or would have been subject to—

(a) any limit imposed by or under any enactment or by any agreement made before the damage occurred;

(b) any reduction by virtue of section 1 of the Law Reform (Contributory Negligence) Act 1945 or section 5 of the Fatal Accidents Act 1976; or

(c) any corresponding limit or reduction under the law of a country outside England and Wales;

the person from whom the contribution is sought shall not by virtue of any contribution awarded under section 1 above be required to pay in respect of the damage a greater amount than the amount of those damages as so limited or reduced.

Note—The similarity in the language used in s.2(1) and in the Law Reform (Contributory Negligence) Act 1945 s.1(1) (see para. 9B–432 below) is striking and there is no reason why the principles applicable under the two provisions should be different in cases where the facts are themselves similar (*J (A Child) v. Wilkins* [2001] R.T.R. 19). An apportionment made under s.2(1) by a trial judge will only be interfered with on appeal where it is clearly wrong or there has been an error of principle or mistake of fact (*ibid.*). As the discretion as to costs granted by the Supreme Court Act, s.51 is not limited so as to exclude an order in contribution proceedings in respect of a sum paid to the original claimants in respect of their costs, the court is entitled to order a contribution in respect of the full sum paid by the person applying for contribution inclusive of any part referable to costs (*B.I.C.C. Ltd. v. Cumbrian Industrials Ltd* [2001] EWCA Civ 1621; October 30, 2001, CA, unrep.).

9B–291.1

LEGISLATION

For an illustration of circumstances where, because the defendant had assigned his contribution claim against his co-defendant to the claimant on terms that did not extinguish the defendant's liability entirely, the court held that it was not possible in the proceedings on the assigned claim to identify the just and equitable proportion of the claim for which the defendant was liable, see *Abbey National Bank Plc v. Matthews & Son* [2003] EWHC 925 (Mr Simon Berry Q.C.).

Section 2(1) requires the court to have regard to the parties' responsibility for the damage. The personal innocence of a person vicariously liable for the wrongful act of his employee or partner is not relevant for the purposes of determining contribution proceedings between that person and another wrongdoer, even in cases of dishonesty (*Dubai Aluminium Co Ltd v. Salaam*, [2002] UKHL 48 [2003] 1 All E.R. 97, H.L.).

PROCEEDINGS FOR THE SAME DEBT OR DAMAGE

Proceedings against persons jointly liable for the same debt or damage

9B–292 **3.** Judgment recovered against any person liable in respect of any debt or damage shall not be a bar to an action, or to the continuance of an action, against any other person who is (apart from any such bar) jointly liable with him in respect of the same debt or damage.

Successive actions against persons liable (jointly or otherwise) for the same damage

9B–293 **4.** If more than one action is brought in respect of any damage by or on behalf of the person by whom it was suffered against persons liable in respect of the damage (whether jointly or otherwise) the plaintiff shall not be entitled to costs in any of those actions, other than that in which judgment is first given, unless the court is of the opinion that there was reasonable ground for bringing the action.

SUPPLEMENTAL

Application to the Crown

9B–294 **5.** Without prejudice to section 4(1) of the Crown Proceedings Act 1947 (indemnity and contribution) this Act shall bind the Crown, but nothing in this Act shall be construed as in any way affecting Her Majesty in Her private capacity (including in right of Her Duchy of Lancaster) or the Duchy of Cornwall.

Interpretation

9B–295 **6.**—(1) A person is liable in respect of any damage for the purposes of this Act if the person who suffered it (or anyone representing his estate or dependants) is entitled to recover compensation from him in respect of that damage (whatever the legal basis of his liability whether tort, breach of contract, breach of trust or otherwise).

(2) References in this Act to an action brought by or on behalf of the person who suffered any damage include references to an action brought for the benefit of his estate or dependants.

(3) In this Act "dependants" has the same meaning as in the Fatal Accidents Act 1976.

(4) In this Act, except in section 1(5) above, "action" means an action brought in England and Wales.

Savings

7.—(1) Nothing in this Act shall affect any case where the debt in **9B–296** question became due or (as the case may be) the damage in question occurred before the date on which it comes into force.

(2) A person shall not be entitled to recover contribution or liable to make contribution in accordance with section 1 above by reference to any liability based on breach of any obligation assumed by him before the date on which this Act comes into force.

(3) The right to recover contribution in accordance with section 1 above supersedes any right, other than an express contractual right, to recover contribution (as distinct from indemnity) otherwise than under this Act in corresponding circumstances; but nothing in this Act shall affect—

    (a) any express or implied contractual or other right to indemnity; or

    (b) any express contractual provision regulating or excluding contribution;

which would be enforceable apart from this Act (or render enforceable any agreement for indemnity or contribution which would not be enforceable apart from this Act).

* * * *

Consequential amendments and repeals

9.—(1) The enactments specified in Schedule 1 to this Act shall **9B–297** have effect subject to the amendments set out in that Schedule, being amendments consequential on the preceding provisions of this Act.

(2) The enactments specified in Schedule 2 to this Act are hereby repealed to the extent specified in column 3 of that Schedule.

Short title, commencement and extent

10.—(1) This Act may be cited as the Civil Liability (Contribution) **9B–298** Act 1978.

(2) This Act shall come into force on January 1 next following the date on which it is passed.

(3) This Act, with the exception of paragraph 1 of Schedule 1 thereto, does not extend to Scotland.

Crown Proceedings Act 1947

(1947 10 & 11 GEO. 6 C.44)   **9B–299**

ARRANGEMENT OF SECTIONS

PART I

SUBSTANTIVE LAW

LEGISLATION

Introduction

9B–300   Part I of this Act contains provisions broadening the liability of the Crown. Provisions in other Parts of the Act concern matters relating to the jurisdiction of the High Court and the county courts in civil proceedings brought by or against the Crown and to the procedures to be adopted in such cases.

The broad intention of the 1947 Act is that proceedings by and against the Crown should be taken in the same circumstances and in the same way as proceedings between subjects. However, procedurally speaking, in a significant number of ways (and usually for obvious reasons) the Crown as a party is in a special position and enjoys advantages not extended to the ordinary party in civil proceedings. Some of these advantages are granted expressly by particular provisions in the 1947 Act (supplemented by rules of court). Others are granted indirectly by s.35(1) of the Act. That sub-section states that any power to make rules of court may contain provisions to have effect in Crown proceedings "in substitution for or by way of addition to any of the provisions of the Rules applying to proceedings between subjects". In relation to the procedural matters listed in s.35(2), rules conferring on the Crown procedural advantages not available to ordinary parties must be made (*e.g.* as to default judgment, summary judgment, and interrogatories).

Before the CPR came into effect, rule making powers granted by the 1947 Act were exercised principally through the provisions of RSC O.77 and CCR O.42. Both of these Orders were carried forward into the CPR. They were revoked by the Civil Procedure (Amendment No. 3) Rules 2005 (S.I. 2005 No. 2292) and, with effect from October 1, 2005, replaced by CPR, Pt 66 (Crown Proceedings). In the new provisions, the effects of some of the rules formerly found in RSC O.77 and CCR O.42 were retained. But to an extent the new provisions altered the effects of former provisions by removing or limiting some of the advantages enjoyed by the Crown as a party. Inevitably, certain of the new rule provisions conflicted with statutory provisions in the 1947 Act. Accordingly, by the Civil Procedure (Modification of Crown Proceedings Act 1947) Order 2005 (S.I. 2005 No. 2712), the Lord Chancellor has exercised his powers under the Civil Procedure Act 1997, s.4(2) (see vol. 2, para. 9A–840), for the purpose of making necessary changes to sections in the 1947 Act that placed the Crown in a special position. The principal modifications were: the repeal of s.19 (Venue and related matters) and s.20(1) (Removal and transfer of proceedings), and the substantial amendment of s.35(2) (removing statutory requirements placing the Crown in a special position as to default judgment, summary judgment, and interrogatories).

"The Crown"

An agency or person carrying out functions of executive government on behalf of the Crown, such as a health board established under legislation relating to the National Health Service, is not itself or himself "the Crown"; the general purpose of the Act is to make it easier rather than more difficult for a subject to sue the Crown, and to hold that the Act had clothed with immunity from proceedings a body which prior to its passing would have enjoyed no such immunity would be to run wholly counter to its spirit (*British Medical Association v. Greater Glasgow Health Board* [1989] A.C. 1211; [1989] 1 All E.R. 984, HL). **9B–301**

PART I

SUBSTANTIVE LAW

Right to sue the Crown

1. Where any person has a claim against the Crown after the commencement of this Act, and, if this Act had not been passed, the claim might have been enforced, subject to the grant of His Majesty's fiat, by petition of right, or might have been enforced by a proceeding provided by any statutory provision repealed by this Act, then, subject to the provisions of this Act, the claim may be enforced as of right, and without the fiat of His Majesty, by proceedings taken against the Crown for that purpose in accordance with the provisions of this Act. **9B–302**

"Might have been enforced"

A claim which would have been statute-barred against a defendant other than the Crown is not within this phrase (*Benson v. Home Office* [1949] 1 All E.R. 48). **9B–303**

"By petition of right"

This proceeding was abolished by the First Schedule to the Act. **9B–304**

Until 1948, the petition of right was the process by which property of any kind (including money and damages) was recovered from the Crown whether the basis of the claimants' title was legal or equitable.

Liability of the Crown in tort

9B–305   2.—(1) Subject to the provisions of this Act, the Crown shall be subject to all those liabilities in tort to which, if it were a private person of full age and capacity, it would be subject:—

    (a) in respect of torts committed by its servants or agents;

    (b) in respect of any breach of those duties which a person owes to his servants or agents at common law by reason of being their employer; and

    (c) in respect of any breach of the duties attaching at common law to the ownership, occupation, possession or control of property:

Provided that no proceedings shall lie against the Crown by virtue of paragraph (a) of this subsection in respect of any act or omission of a servant or agent of the Crown unless the act or omission would apart from the provisions of this Act have given rise to a cause of action in tort against that servant or agent or his estate.

(2) Where the Crown is bound by a statutory duty which is binding also upon persons other than the Crown and its officers, then, subject to the provisions of this Act, the Crown shall, in respect of a failure to comply with that duty, be subject to all those liabilities in tort (if any) to which it would be so subject if it were a private person of full age and capacity.

(3) Where any functions are conferred or imposed upon an officer of the Crown as such either by any rule of the common law or by statute, and that officer commits a tort while performing or purporting to perform those functions, the liabilities of the Crown in respect of the tort shall be such as they would have been if those functions had been conferred or imposed solely by virtue of instructions lawfully given by the Crown.

(4) Any enactment which negatives or limits the amount of the liability of any Government department or officer of the Crown in respect of any tort committed by that department or officer shall, in the case of proceedings against the Crown under this section in respect of a tort committed by that department or officer, apply in relation to the Crown as it would have applied in relation to that department or officer if the proceedings against the Crown had been proceedings against that department or officer.

(5) No proceedings shall lie against the Crown by virtue of this section in respect of anything done or omitted to be done by any person while discharging or purporting to discharge any responsibilities of a judicial nature vested in him, or any responsibilities which he has in connection with the execution of judicial process.

(6) No proceedings shall lie against the Crown by virtue of this section in respect of any act, neglect or default of any officer of the Crown, unless that officer has been directly or indirectly appointed by the Crown and was at the material time paid in respect of his duties as an officer of the Crown wholly out of the Consolidated

Fund of the United Kingdom, moneys provided by Parliament, the Road Fund, or any other Fund certified by the Treasury for the purpose of this subsection or was at the material time holding an office in respect of which the Treasury certify that the holder thereof would normally be so paid.

Note — Subsection (6) amended by the Statute Law (Repeals) Act 1981, Sched.1. **9B–306**

Liability of the Crown in tort—general
The liability of the Crown in tort is under this Act only; it is not possible to **9B–307** circumvent the limitation imposed by the Act by suing the Attorney-General for a declaration that proposed acts of the Crown that would not be justiciable under the Act would be wrongful (*Trawnik v. Lennox* [1985] 1 W.L.R. 532; [1985] 2 All E.R. 368).

Subs. (1) "Subject to the provisions of this Act"
There are certain provisions of the Act which materially diminish the liability of the **9B–308** Crown. See, *e.g.* s.40.

"Provided that"
It appears that, as a result of the proviso, proceedings will not lie under subs. (1)(a) **9B–309** unless in proceedings before the commencement of the Act the tortfeasor could have been sued in his own, as distinct from his representative, capacity (*Mackenzie-Kennedy v. Air Council* [1927] 2 K.B. 517, CA, *per* Atkin, L.J.).

Subs. (5) "Responsibilities of a judicial nature"
Since a Judge is not liable in an action by a party for anything that he does as a **9B–310** Judge (*Groenwelt v. Barwill* (1699) 12 Mod. 386), it is difficult to see how those who appoint him could run any risk of action.

Subs. (6) "And was at the material time paid"
The Crown apparently escapes responsibility for any act or omission of a gratuitous **9B–311** agent.

Infringement of intellectual property rights
3.—(1) Civil proceedings lie against the Crown for an infringement **9B–312** committed by a servant or agent of the Crown, with the authority of the Crown, or—
    (a) a patent,
    (b) a registered trade mark,
    (c) the right in a registered design,
    (d) design right, or
    (e) copyright:
but save as provided by this subsection no proceedings lie against the Crown by virtue of this Act in respect of an infringement of any of those rights.

(2) Nothing in this section, or any other provision of this Act, shall be construed as affecting—
    (a) the rights of a government department under section 55 of the Patents Act 1977, Schedule 1 to the Registered Designs Act 1949 or section 240 of the Copyright, Designs and Patents Act 1988 (Crown use of patents and designs), or
    (b) the rights of the Secretary of State under section 22 of the Patents Act 1977 or section 5 of the Registered Designs Act 1949 (security of information prejudicial to defence or public safety).

9B–313   *Note* —Substituted by the Copyright, Designs and Patents Act 1988, Sched.7, para. 4(1). Amended by the Trade Marks Act 1994, s.106(2), Sched.5.

Application of law as to indemnity, contribution, joint and several tortfeasors, and contributory negligence

9B–314   **4.**—(1) Where the Crown is subject to any liability by virtue of this Part of this Act, the law relating to indemnity and contribution shall be enforceable by or against the Crown in respect of the liability to which it is so subject as if the Crown were a private person of full age and capacity.

(2) [...]

(3) Without prejudice to the general effect of section one of this Act, the Law Reform (Contributory Negligence) Act 1945 (which amends the law relating to contributory negligence) shall bind the Crown.

9B–315   *Note* — Subs. (2) repealed by the Civil Liability (Contribution) Act 1978, s.9(2), Sched.2.

[THE NEXT PARAGRAPH IS 9B–317.]

*   *   *   *   *

Liability in connection with postal packets

9B–317   **9.** [*Repealed by the Post Office Act 1969 , s.141 and Sched.11.*]

Provisions relating to the Armed Forces

9B–318   **10.** [...]

9B–319   *Note* — Section 10 was repealed by the Crown Proceedings (Armed Forces) Act 1987 except in relation to anything suffered by a person in consequence of an act or omission committed before May 15, 1987. By virtue of s.2 of the 1987 Act, however, the Secretary of State for Defence may revive s.10 of the 1947 Act by statutory order in wartime or by reason of imminent national danger or great emergency. Section 10 is substantive not procedural and is not incompatible with the right to a fair hearing in determination of "civil rights" provided for by the Human Rights Act 1998, Sched.1, Pt I, art.6, (*Matthews v. Ministry of Defence* [2002] UKHL 4; [2003] 2 W.L.R. 435, HL).

Saving in respect of acts done under prerogative and statutory powers

9B–320   **11.**—(1) Nothing in Part I of this Act shall extinguish or abridge any powers or authorities which, if this Act had not been passed, would have been exercisable by virtue of the prerogative of the Crown, or any powers or authorities conferred on the Crown by any statute, and, in particular, nothing in the said Part I shall extinguish or abridge any powers or authorities exercisable by the Crown, whether in time of peace or of war, for the purpose of the defence of the realm or of training, or maintaining the efficiency of, any of the armed forces of the Crown.

(2) Where in any proceedings under this Act it is material to determine whether anything was properly done or omitted to be done in the exercise of the prerogative of the Crown, a Secretary of State may, if satisfied that the act or omission was necessary for any

such purpose as is mentioned in the last preceding subsection, issue a certificate to the effect that the act or omission was necessary for that purpose; and the certificate shall, in those proceedings, be conclusive as to the matter so certified.

Note —Amended by S.I. 1964 No. 488.　　　　　　　　　　　　**9B–321**

* * * *

PART II

JURISDICTION AND PROCEDURE

THE HIGH COURT

Civil proceedings in the High Court

13. Subject to the provisions of this Act, all such civil proceedings **9B–322** by or against the Crown as are mentioned in the First Schedule to this Act are hereby abolished, and all civil proceedings by or against the Crown in the High Court shall be instituted and proceeded with in accordance with Rules of Court and not otherwise. In this section the expression "Rules of Court" means, in relation to any claim against the Crown in the High Court which falls within the jurisdiction of that Court as a Prize Court, Rules of Court made under section three of the Prize Courts Act 1894.

"Civil proceedings"
See ss.23 and 38.　　　　　　　　　　　　　　　　　　　　**9B–323**

"Rules of Court"
See CPR, Pt 66.　　　　　　　　　　　　　　　　　　　　　**9B–324**

Summary applications to High Court in certain revenue matters

14.—(1) Subject to and in accordance with Rules of Court, the **9B–325** Crown may apply in a summary manner to the High Court:—

    (a) for the furnishing of information required to be furnished by any person under the enactments relating to capital transfer tax;

    (b) for the delivery of accounts and payment of inheritance tax under the Inheritance Tax Act 1984;

    (c) for the delivery of an account under section two of the Stamp Duties Management Act 1891, or under that section as amended or applied by any subsequent enactment;

    (d) for the payment of sums improperly withheld or retained within the meaning of the said section two.

(2) Subject to and in accordance with Rules of Court, the Crown may apply in a summary manner to the High Court:—

    (a) for the payment of duty under the enactments relating to excise duties;

(b) for the delivery of any accounts required to be delivered, or the furnishing of any information required to be furnished, by the enactments relating to excise duties or by any regulations relating to such duties;

(c) for the payment of tax under the enactments relating to value added tax;

(d) for the delivery of any accounts, the production of any books, or the furnishing of any information, required to be delivered, produced or furnished under the enactments relating to value added tax.

9B-326   *Note* —Amended by the Finance Act 1972, s.55; the Finance Act 1975, Sched.12; the Capital Transfer Tax Act 1984, Sched.8, para. 22; and the Finance Act 1986, s.100(1).

"Rules of Court"

9B-327   See CPR, r.66.5.

"In a summary manner"

9B-328   The procedure provided by this Section is appropriate only where a straightforward issue of law or fact is involved (*Re Park, I.R.C. v. Park* [1970] 1 W.L.R. 626).

Civil proceedings in the county court

9B-329   **15.**—(1) Subject to the provisions of this Act, and to any enactment limiting the jurisdiction of a county court (whether by reference to the subject matter of the proceedings to be brought or the amount sought to be recovered in the proceedings or otherwise) any civil proceedings against the Crown may be instituted in a county court.

(2) Any proceedings by or against the Crown in a county court shall be instituted and proceeded with in accordance with rules of court and not otherwise.

Note —Amended by S.I. 2005 No. 2712.

"Civil proceedings; proceedings by or against the Crown"

9B-330   See ss.23 and 38.

GENERAL

Interpleader

9B-331   **16.** The Crown may obtain relief by way of interpleader proceedings, and may be made a party to such proceedings, in the same manner in which a subject may obtain relief by way of such proceedings or be made a party thereto, and may be made a party to such proceedings notwithstanding that the application for relief is made by a sheriff or other like officer; and all Rules of Court relating to interpleader proceedings shall, subject to the provisions of this Act, have effect accordingly.

9B-332   *Note* —Amended by S.I. 2005 No. 2712. As to interpleader proceedings, see CPR Sched.1, RSC O.17.

Parties in proceedings

9B-333   **17.**—(1) The Minister for the Civil Service shall publish a list specifying the several Government departments which are authorised departments for the purposes of this Act, and the name and address for service of the person who is, or is acting for the purposes of this Act as, the solicitor for each such department, and may from time to time amend or vary the said list. Any document purporting to be a copy of a list published under this section and purporting to be printed under the superintendence or the authority of His Majesty's Stationery Office shall in any legal proceedings be received as evidence for the purpose of establishing what departments are authorised departments for the purposes of this Act, and what person is, or is acting for the purposes of this Act as, the solicitor for any such department.

(2) Civil proceedings by the Crown may be instituted either by an authorised Government department in its own name, whether that department was or was not at the commencement of this Act authorised to sue, or by the Attorney-General.

(3) Civil proceedings against the Crown shall be instituted against the appropriate authorised Government department, or, if none of the authorised Government departments is appropriate or the person instituting the proceedings has any reasonable doubt whether any and if so which of those departments is appropriate, against the Attorney-General.

(4) Where any civil proceedings against the Crown are instituted against the Attorney-General, an application may at any stage of the proceedings be made to the Court by or on behalf of the Attorney-General to have such of the authorised Government departments as may be specified in the application substituted for him as defendant to the proceedings; and where any such proceedings are brought against an authorised Government department, an application may at any stage of the proceedings be made to the Court on behalf of that department to have the Attorney-General or such of the authorised Government departments as may be specified in the application substituted for the applicant as the defendant to the proceedings.

Upon any such application the Court may if it thinks fit make an order granting the application on such terms as the Court thinks just, and on such an order being made the proceedings shall continue as if they had been commenced against the department specified in that behalf in the order, or, as the case may require, against the Attorney-General.

(5) No proceedings instituted in accordance with this Part of this Act by or against the Attorney-General or an authorised Government department shall abate or be affected by any change in the person holding the office of Attorney-General or in the person or body of persons constituting the department.

Note —The words in square brackets were added by the Minister for the Civil Service Order 1968 (S.I. 1968 No. 1656). **9B–334**

Subs.(1) "A list"

A list of authorised government departments and the solicitors designated for service of documents, under the Crown Proceedings Act 1947 is annexed to Practice Direction (Addition and Substitution of Parties), see Vol. 1, para. 19PD.7. **9B–335**

"Trial at bar"

9B-336   This phrase appears to mean trial before a Divisional Court (*Anderson v. Gorrie* [1895] 1 Q.B. 668; *Dixon v. Farrer* [1886] 18 Q.B.D. 43).

[THE NEXT PARAGRAPH IS 9B-340.]

Service of documents

9B-340   **18.** All documents required to be served on the Crown for the purpose of or in connection with any civil proceedings by or against the Crown shall, if those proceedings are by or against an authorised Government department, be served on the solicitor, if any, for that department, or the person, if any, acting for the purposes of this Act as solicitor for that department, or if there is no such solicitor and no person so acting, or if the proceedings are brought by or against the Attorney-General, on the Solicitor for the affairs of His Majesty's Treasury.

Service

9B-341   As to service of documents, see CPR, r.6.4(2A) and r.6.5(8). For list of authorised Government Departments, see commentary following s.17 above.

Venue and related matters

9B-342   **19.**—(1) [. . .]

(2) [. . .]

(3) [. . .]

[THE NEXT PARAGRAPH IS 9B-344.]

9B-344   *Note* —Section 19 was repealed by S.I. 2005 No. 2712.
See CPR Sched.1, RSC O.77, r.2 and r.13.

Removal and transfer of proceedings

9B-345   **20.**—(1) [. . .]

(2) All rules of law and enactments relating to the removal or transfer of proceedings from a county court to the High Court, or the transfer of proceedings from the High Court to a county court, shall apply in relation to proceedings against the Crown.

9B-346   *Note* —Amended by the SCA 1981, s.139 and Sched.7. The proviso, repealed in 1981, has been re-introduced as County Courts Act 1984, s.40(5). Subs.(1) repealed and subs.(2) amended by S.I. 2005 No. 2712.

Transfer of proceedings

9B-347   See CPR, Pt 30, and in particular r.30.3(2).

[THE NEXT PARAGRAPH IS 9B-349.]

Nature of relief

9B-349   **21.**—(1) In any civil proceedings by or against the Crown the Court shall, subject to the provisions of this Act, have power to make all such orders as it has power to make in proceedings between subjects, and otherwise to give such appropriate relief as the case may require: Provided that:—

    (a) where in any proceedings against the Crown any such relief is sought as might in proceedings between subjects be granted by way of injunction or specific performance, the Court shall not grant an injunction or make an order for specific performance, but may in lieu thereof make an order declaratory of the rights of the parties; and

    (b) in any proceedings against the Crown for the recovery of land or other property the Court shall not make an order for the recovery of the land or the delivery of the property, but may in lieu thereof make an order declaring that the plaintiff is entitled as against the Crown to the land or property or to the possession thereof.

  (2) The Court shall not in any civil proceedings grant any injunction or make any order against an officer of the Crown if the effect of granting the injunction or making the order would be to give any relief against the Crown which could not have been obtained in proceedings against the Crown.

Note —For authority on the operation of this provision in the context of a breach of fundamental rights by the Crown see *Gairy v. Attorney-General of Grenada*, June 19, 2001, unrep., PC.

9B–349.1

[THE NEXT PARAGRAPH IS 9B–350.]

"Proceedings by the Crown"
  See ss.5–8, 11, 14 and 16.

9B–350

"Appropriate relief"
  The Court has no power under this section "to make something in the nature of an interim declaration of right which would have no legal effect and which ... might be the very opposite of the final declaration of right which would be made at the trial" (*Underhill and Waywell v. Min. of Food* (1950) 66 T.L.R. 730, *per* Romer J. at 733; followed by the CA in *International General Electric Co of New York v. Commissioners of Customs & Excise* [1962] Ch. 784; [1962] 2 All E.R. 398).

9B–351

  A stay of proceedings of a warrant issued by the Secretary of State ordering the applicant to be surrendered to the United States authorities pursuant to their request for his extradition pending the hearing of the application for judicial review under O.53, r.3(10), will be discharged, since such a stay is equivalent to an injunction restraining the Secretary of State from exercising his executive functions which the Court is prohibited from granting by virtue of s.21 of the 1947 Act (*R. v. Secretary of State for the Home Department, Ex p. Kirkwood* [1984] 1 W.L.R. 913; [1984] 2 All E.R. 390).

Injunction
  In general there is no jurisdiction to grant an interim injunction against the Crown in proceedings begun by writ or in proceedings for judicial review (*R. v. Secretary of State for Transport, Ex p. Factortame Ltd* [1990] 2 A.C. 85; [1989] 2 W.L.R. 997, *sub nom.* *Factortame Ltd v. Secretary of State for Transport* [1989] 2 All E.R. 692, HL). Pending a decision on a reference to the European Court of Justice, however, for a ruling on European Community law, where the rights claimed under Community law are at issue, a national court is required to grant interim relief to protect the rights claimed under Community law; accordingly, in such a case the normal rule that an interim injunction may not be granted against the Crown must be set aside if it is the sole obstacle to the grant of interim relief (*Factortame Ltd v. Secretary of State for Transport (No. 2)* [1991] 1 All E.R. 70, European Court of Justice).

9B–352

  Matters of considerable weight, however, have to be put into the balance to outweigh the desirability of enforcing, in the public interest, what is on its face the law of England, so as to justify the refusal of an interim injunction in favour of the Crown or other public authority, or to restrain the Crown or other public authority for the time being from enforcing such law. This is not to say that a party challenging the validity of a national law must go to the extent of showing a strong prima facie case that such law is invalid, but the court should not restrain the Crown or other public authority by interim injunction from enforcing an apparently authentic national law unless it is satisfied that the challenge to the validity of such law is, *prima facie*, so firmly based as to justify so exceptional a course being taken (*Factortame Ltd v. Secretary of State for Transport (No. 2)* [1991] 1 All E.R. 70, HL).

"Proceedings against the Crown"

9B–353   See ss.1–3, 8, 16 and 27.

Appeals and stay of execution

9B–354   **22.** Subject to the provisions of this Act, all enactments and rules of court relating to appeals and stay of execution shall, with any necessary modification, apply to civil proceedings by or against the Crown as they apply to proceedings between subjects.

Note —Amended by S.I. 2005 No. 2712.

Scope of Part II

9B–355   **23.**—(1) Subject to the provisions of this section, any reference in this Part of this Act to civil proceedings by the Crown shall be construed as a reference to the following proceedings only:—

(a) proceedings for the enforcement or vindication of any right or the obtaining of any relief which, if this Act had not been passed, might have been enforced or vindicated or obtained by any such proceedings as are mentioned in paragraph 1 of the First Schedule to this Act;

(b) proceedings for the enforcement or vindication of any right or the obtaining of any relief which, if this Act had not been passed, might have been enforced or vindicated or obtained by an action at the suit of any Government department or any officer of the Crown as such;

(c) all such proceedings as the Crown is entitled to bring by virtue of this Act;

and the expression "civil proceedings by or against the Crown" shall be construed accordingly.

(2) Subject to the provisions of this section, any reference in this Part of this Act to civil proceedings against the Crown shall be construed as a reference to the following proceedings only:—

(a) proceedings for the enforcement or vindication of any right or the obtaining of any relief which, if this Act had not been passed, might have been enforced or vindicated or obtained by any of such proceedings as are mentioned in paragraph 2 of the First Schedule to this Act;

(b) proceedings for the enforcement or vindication of any right or the obtaining of any relief which, if this Act had not been passed, might have been enforced or vindicated or obtained by an action against the Attorney-General, and Government department, or any officer of the Crown as such; and

(c) all such proceedings as any person is entitled to bring against the Crown by virtue of this Act;

and the expression "civil proceedings by or against the Crown" shall be construed accordingly.

(3) Notwithstanding anything in the preceding provisions of this section, the provisions of this Part of this Act shall not have effect with respect to any of the following proceedings, that is to say:—

    (a) proceedings brought by the Attorney-General on the relation of some other person;

    (b) proceedings by or against the Public Trustee;

    (c) proceedings by or against the Charity Commissioners;

    (e) [Repealed by the Education Act 1973, Sched.2.]

    (f) proceedings by or against the Registrar of the Land Registry or any officers of that Registry.

(4) Subject to the provisions of any Order in Council made under the provisions hereinafter contained, this part of this Act shall not affect proceedings initiated in any Court other than the High Court or a county court.

Note —Amended by the Charities Act 1960, Sched.7.   **9B–356**

PART III

JUDGMENTS AND EXECUTION

Interest on debts, damages and costs

24.—(1) Section seventeen of the Judgments Act 1838 (which **9B–357** provides that a judgment debt shall carry interest) and section 44A of the Administration of Justice Act 1970 (which enables the court to order an appropriate rate for a judgment debt expressed in a currency other than sterling) shall apply to judgment debts due from or to the Crown.

(2) Where any costs are awarded to or against the Crown in the High Court, interest shall be payable upon those costs unless the Court otherwise orders, and any interest so payable shall be at the same rate as that at which interest is payable upon judgment debts due from or to the Crown.

(3) Section 35A of the Supreme Court Act 1981 and section 69 of the County Courts Act 1984 (which respectively empower the High Court and county courts to award interest on debts and damages) see section 3 of the Law Reform (Miscellaneous Provisions) Act 1934 (which empowers other courts of record to do so) shall apply to judgments given in proceedings by and against the Crown.

(4) [...]

Note —Amended by the Administration of Justice Act 1982, s.15, Sched.1, Pt III; **9B–358** the County Courts Act 1984, Sched.2; the Statute Law (Repeals) Act 1993; and the Private International Law (Miscellaneous Provisions) Act 1995, s.4.

Satisfaction of orders against the Crown

25.—(1) Where in any civil proceedings by or against the Crown, **9B–359** or in any proceedings on the Crown side of the King's Bench Division, or in connection with any arbitration to which the Crown is a party, any order (including an order for costs) is made by any Court in favour of any person against the Crown or against a Government department or against an officer of the Crown as such, the proper officer of the Court shall, on an application in that behalf made by or on behalf of that person at any time after the expiration of twenty-one days from the date of the order or, in case the order provides for the payment of costs and the costs require to be taxed, at any time after the costs have been taxed, whichever is the later, issue to that person a certificate in the prescribed form containing particulars of the order: Provided that, if the Court so directs, a separate certificate shall be issued with respect to the costs (if any) ordered to be paid to the applicant.

(2) A copy of any certificate issued under this section may be served by the person in whose favour the order is made upon the person for the time being named in the record as the solicitor, or as the person acting as solicitor, for the Crown or for the Government department or officer concerned.

(3) If the order provides for the payment of any money by way of damages or otherwise, or of any costs, the certificate shall state the amount so payable, and the appropriate Government department shall, subject as hereinafter provided, pay to the person entitled or to his solicitor the amount appearing by the certificate to be due to him together with the interest, if any, lawfully due thereon:

Provided that the Court by which any such order as aforesaid is made or any Court to which an appeal against the order lies may direct that, pending an appeal or otherwise, payment of the whole of any amount so payable, or any part thereof, shall be suspended, and if the certificate has not been issued may order any such directions to be inserted therein.

(4) Save as aforesaid no execution or attachment or process in the nature thereof shall be issued out of any Court for enforcing payment by the Crown of any such money or costs as aforesaid, and no person shall be individually liable under any order for the payment by the Crown, or any Government department, or any officer of the Crown as such of any such money or costs.

(5) [...]

9B–360   *Note*—Amended by the Statute (Repeals) Act 1993.

Orders, etc., against the Crown
9B–361   See CPR, r.66.6(1), .

Execution by the Crown

9B–362   **26.**—(1) Subject to the provisions of this Act, any order made in favour of the Crown against any person in any civil proceedings to which the Crown is a party may be enforced in the same manner as an order made in an action between subjects, and not otherwise.

(2) Sections four and fiveof the Debtors Act 1869 (which provide respectively for the abolition of imprisonment for debt, and for saving the power of committal in case of small debts) shall apply to sums of money payable and debts due to the Crown:

Provided that for the purpose of the application of the said section four to any sum of money payable or debt due to the Crown, the section shall have effect as if there were included among the exceptions therein mentioned default in payment of any sum payable in respect of death duties.

(3) Nothing in this section shall affect any procedure which immediately before the commencement of this Act was available for enforcing an order made in favour of the Crown in proceedings brought by the Crown for the recovery of any fine or penalty, or the forfeiture or condemnation of any goods, or the forfeiture of any ship or any share in a ship.

Note —Amended by the Statute (Repeals) Act 1993; and the Finance Act 1972, s.134, Sched.28.

9B–363

Section 5
Since the abolition by the SCA 1981, s.141 of the writ of *capias ad satisfaciendum*, the only special method of enforcing Crown debts which remains is the very limited power of committal under s.5 preserved to the county court by the AJA 1970, s.11; it extends only to income tax and certain other social security and tax payments (see AJA 1970, Sched.4).

9B–364

Attachment of moneys payable by the Crown

27.—(1) Where any money is payable by the Crown to some person who, under any order of any Court, is liable to pay any money to any other person, and that other person would, if the money so payable by the Crown were money payable by a subject, be entitled under Rules of Court to obtain an order for the attachment thereof as a debt due or accruing due, or an order for the appointment of a sequestrator or receiver to receive the money on his behalf, the High Court may, subject to the provisions of this Act and in accordance with Rules for receiving that money, and directing payment thereof to that other Court, make an order restraining the first-mentioned person from receiving that money and directing payment thereof to that other person, or to the sequestrator or receiver: Provided that no such order shall be made in respect of:—

9B–365

    (a) any wages or salary payable to any officer of the Crown as such;

    (b) any money which is subject to the provisions of any enactment prohibiting or restricting assignment or charging or taking in execution.

(2) The provisions of the preceding subsection shall, so far as they relate to forms of relief falling within the jurisdiction of a county court, have effect in relation to county courts as they have effect in relation to the High Court.

(3) In their application to England and Wales the preceding provisions of this section shall have effect subject to any order for the time being in force under section 139(2) of the Supreme Court Act 1981.

Note —Amended by the Post Office Act 1969, Sched.6; and the SCA 1981, ss.139(1), 152(4) and Sched.7.

9B–366

Orders, etc., against the Crown
See CPR, r.66.7.

9B–367

2617

LEGISLATION

Part IV

Miscellaneous and Supplemental

Miscellaneous

Discovery

9B–368   28.—(1) Subject to and in accordance with Rules of Court:—

    (a) in any civil proceedings in the High Court or a county court to which the Crown is a party, the Crown may be required by the Court to make discovery of documents and produce documents for inspection; and

    (b) in any such proceedings as aforesaid, the Crown may be required by the Court to answer interrogatories:

Provided that this section shall be without prejudice to any rule of law which authorises or requires the withholding of any document or the refusal to answer any question on the ground that the disclosure of the document or the answering of the question would be injurious to the public interest.

Any order of the Court made under the powers conferred by paragraph (b) of this subsection shall direct by what officer of the Crown the interrogatories are to be answered.

(2) Without prejudice to the proviso to the preceding subsection, any Rules made for the purposes of this section shall be such as to secure that the existence of a document will not be disclosed if, in the opinion of a Minister of the Crown, it would be injurious to the public interest to disclose the existence thereof.

Note —Amended by S.I. 2005 No. 2712.

Discovery in proceeding by or against the Crown

9B–369   See CPR, r.66.3. See also CPR, r.31.19(1), as to Crown privilege and n. "Documents ... injurious to the public interest," Vol. 1, para. 31.3.33.

Exclusion of proceedings in rem against the Crown

9B–370   29.—(1) Nothing in this Act shall authorise proceedings *in rem* in respect of any claim against the Crown, or the arrest, detention or sale of any of His Majesty's ships or aircraft, or of any cargo or other property belonging to the Crown, or give to any person any lien on any such ship, aircraft, cargo or other property.

(2) Where proceedings *in rem* have been instituted in the High Court or in a county court against any such ship, aircraft, cargo or other property, the Court may, if satisfied, either on an application by the plaintiff for an order under this subsection or an application by the Crown to set aside the proceedings, that the proceedings were so instituted by the plaintiff in the reasonable belief that the ship, aircraft, cargo or other property did not belong to the Crown, order that the proceedings shall be treated as if they were *in personam* duly instituted against the Crown in accordance with the provisions of this Act, or duly instituted against any other person whom the Court regards as the proper person to be sued in the circumstances, and that the proceedings shall continue accordingly.

Any such order may be made upon such terms, if any, as the Court thinks just; and where the Court makes any such order it may make such consequential orders as the Court thinks expedient.

Mode of application

Although no such expression provision as appeared in former CPR, Sched. 1, RSC **9B–371** O.77, r.18(2) appears CPR, Pt 66, it remains the case that an application such as is referred to in s.29(2) may be made to the court at any time before trial in accordance with CPR, Pt 23 or may be made at the trial of the proceedings.

Limitation of actions

30. [*Repealed: see now Merchant Shipping Act 1995, s.314 and Sched.12,* **9B–372** *in force January 1, 1996.*]

Application to the Crown of certain statutory provisions

31.—(1) This Act shall not prejudice the right of the Crown to take **9B–373** advantage of the provisions of an Act of Parliament although not named therein; and it is hereby declared that in any civil proceedings against the Crown the provisions of any Act of Parliament which could, if the proceedings were between subjects, be relied upon by the defendant as a defence to the proceedings, whether in whole or in part, or otherwise, may, subject to any express provision to the contrary, be so relied upon by the Crown.

(2) Section six of the Debtors Act 1869 (which empowers the Court in certain circumstances to order the arrest of a defendant about to quit England) shall, with any necessary modifications, apply to civil proceedings in the High Court by the Crown.

No abatement on demise of Crown

32. No claim by or against the Crown, and no proceedings for the **9B–374** enforcement of any such claim, shall abate or be affected by the demise of the Crown.

Abolition of certain writs

33. No writ of extent or of *diem clausit extremum* shall issue after the **9B–375** commencement of this Act.

Proceedings in courts other than High Court and county courts

34. [*Repealed by the A. J. A. 1977, s.32(4), Sched.5(v).*] **9B–376**

SUPPLEMENTAL

Rules of Court

35.—(1) Any power to make Rules of Court shall include power to **9B–377** make Rules for the purpose of giving effect to the provisions of this Act, and any such Rules may contain provisions to have effect in relation to any proceedings by or against the Crown in substitution for or by way of addition to any of the provisions of the Rules applying to proceedings between subjects.

(2) Provision shall be made by Rules of Court with respect to the following matters:—

(a) for providing for service of process, or notice thereof, in the case of proceedings by the Crown against persons, whether British subjects or not, who are not resident in the United Kingdom;

(b) for securing that where any civil proceedings are brought against the Crown in accordance with the provisions of this Act the claimant shall provide the Crown with information as to the circumstances in which it is alleged that the liability of the Crown has arisen and as to the departments and officers of the Crown concerned;

(c) [Repealed]

(d) [Repealed]

(e) [Repealed]

(f) for enabling evidence to be taken on commission in proceedings by or against the Crown;

(g) for providing:—

(i) that a person shall not be entitled to avail himself of any set-off or counterclaim in any proceedings by the Crown for the recovery of taxes, duties or penalties, or to avail himself in proceedings of any other nature by the Crown of any set-off or counterclaim arising out of a right or claim to repayment in respect of any taxes, duties or penalties;

(ii) that a person shall not be entitled without the leave of the Court to avail himself of any set-off or counterclaim in any proceedings by the Crown if either the subject matter of the set-off or counterclaim does not relate to the Government department in the name of which the proceedings are brought or the proceedings are brought in the name of the Attorney-General;

(iii) that the Crown, when sued in the name of a Government department, shall not, without the leave of the Court, be entitled to avail itself of any set-off or counterclaim if the subject matter thereof does not relate to that department; and

(iv) that the Crown, when sued in the name of the Attorney-General, shall not be entitled to avail itself of any set-off or counterclaim without the leave of the Court.

Provision may be made by Rules of Court for regulating any appeals to the High Court, whether by way of case stated or otherwise, under enactments relating to the revenue, and any rules made under this subsection may revoke any enactments or Rules in force immediately before the commencement of this Act as far as they regulate any such appeals, and may make provision for any matters for which provision was made by any enactments or Rules so in force.

9B–379 Note —Para. (b) of sub-s. (2) was amended by, and paras. (c), (d) and (e) were repealed by, the Civil Procedure (Modification of Crown Proceedings Act 1947) Order

2005 (S.I. 2005 No. 2712). The rules of court referred to in this section are found principally in CPR, Pt 66 (Crown Proceedings) but also in other CPR provisions introduced or amended when Pt 66 came into effect on October 1, 2005 (*e.g.* provisions as to default judgments in Pt 12, and as to summary judgment in Pt 24).

36. [*Repealed by the Statute Law (Repeals) Act 1993.*]   **9B–385**

37. [Financial provisions.]

Interpretation

38.—(1) Any reference in this Act to the provisions of this Act shall,   **9B–386** unless the context otherwise requires, include a reference to Rules of Court made for the purposes of this Act.

(2) In this Act, except in so far as the context otherwise requires or it is otherwise expressly provided, the following expressions have the meanings hereby respectively assigned to them, that is to say:—

"Agent", when used in relation to the Crown, includes an independent contractor employed by the Crown;

"Civil proceedings" includes proceedings in the High Court or the county court for the recovery of fines or penalties, but does not include proceedings on the Crown side of the King's Bench Division;

"His Majesty's aircraft" does not include aircraft belonging to His Majesty otherwise than in right of His Government in the United Kingdom;

"His Majesty's ships" means ships of which the beneficial interest is vested in His Majesty or which are registered as Government ships for the purposes of the Merchant Shipping Acts, 1894 to 1940, or which are for the time being demised or subdemised to or in the exclusive possession of the Crown, except that the said expression does not include any ship in which His Majesty is interested otherwise than in right of His Government in the United Kingdom unless that ship is for the time being demised or subdemised to His Majesty in right of His said Government or in the exclusive possession of His Majesty in that right;

"Officer", in relation to the Crown, includes any servant of His Majesty, and accordingly (but without prejudice to the generality of the foregoing provision) includes a Minister of the Crown;

"Order" includes a judgment, decree, rule, award or declaration;

"Prescribed" means prescribed by Rules of Court;

"Proceedings against the Crown" includes a claim by way of set-off or counterclaim in proceedings by the Crown;

"Ship" has the meaning assigned to it by section seven hundred and forty-two of the Merchant Shipping Act 1894;

"Statutory duty" means any duty imposed by or under any Act of Parliament.

(3) Any reference in this Act to His Majesty in His private capacity shall be construed as including a reference to His Majesty in right of His Duchy of Lancaster and to the Duke of Cornwall.

(4) Any reference in Part III or IV of this Act to civil proceedings by or against the Crown, or to civil proceedings to which the Crown is a party, shall be construed as including a reference to civil proceedings to which the Attorney-General, or any Government department, or any officer of the Crown as such is a party:

Provided that the crown shall not for the purposes of Parts III and IV of this Act be deemed to be a party to any proceedings by reason only that they are brought by the Attorney-General upon the relation of some other person.

(5) [...]

(6) References in this Act to any enactment shall be construed as references to that enactment as amended by or under any other enactment, including this Act.

9B–387   *Note* — Subs. (5) repealed by the Armed Forces Act 1981, s.28, Sched.5; subss (1), (2) amended by S.I. 2005 No. 2712.

"Against His Majesty in His private capacity"

9B–388   See s.38(3) above. The general rule continues to be that, so far as concerns Her Majesty in Her private capacity, the Sovereign can do no wrong.

Repeals, etc.

9B–389   **39.** [*This section and Schedule 2 have been repealed.*]

Savings

9B–390   **40.**—(1) Nothing in this Act shall apply to proceedings by or against, or authorise proceedings in tort to be brought against, His Majesty in His private capacity.

(2) Except as therein otherwise expressly provided, nothing in this Act shall:—

    (a) affect the law relating to prize salvage, or apply to proceedings in causes or matters within the jurisdiction of the High Court as a Prize Court or to any criminal proceedings; or

    (b) authorise proceedings to be taken against the Crown under or in accordance with this Act in respect of any alleged liability of the Crown arising otherwise than in respect of His Majesty's Government in the United Kingdom or the Scottish Administration, or affect proceedings against the Crown in respect of any such alleged liability as aforesaid; or

    (c) affect any proceedings by the Crown otherwise than in right of His Majesty's Government in the United Kingdom or the Scottish Administration; or

    (d) subject the Crown to any greater liabilities in respect of the acts or omissions of any independent contractor employed by the Crown than those to which the Crown would be subject in respect of such acts or omissions if it were a private person; or

    (e) [...]

    (f) affect any rules of evidence or any presumption relating to the extent to which the Crown is bound by any Act of Parliament; or

(g) affect any right of the Crown to demand a trial at bar or to control or otherwise intervene in proceedings affecting his rights, property or profits; or

(h) affect any liability imposed on the public trustee or on the Consolidated Fund of the United Kingdom [...] or the Scottish Administration by the Public Trustee Act 1906;

and, without prejudice to the general effect of the foregoing provisions, Part III of this Act shall not apply to the Crown except in right of His Majesty's Government in the United Kingdom or the Scottish Administration.

(3) A certificate of a Secretary of State:—

(a) to the effect that any alleged liability of the Crown arises otherwise than in respect of His Majesty's Government in the United Kingdom;

(b) to the effect that any proceedings by the Crown are proceedings otherwise than in right of His Majesty's Government in the United Kingdom;

shall, for the purposes of this Act, be conclusive as to the matter so certified.

(3A) A certificate of the Scottish Ministers to the effect that—

(a) any alleged liability of the Crown arises otherwise than in respect of teh Scottish Administration,

(b) any proceedings by the Crown are proceedings otherwise than in right of the Scottish Administration,

shall, for the purposes of this Act, be conclusive as to that matter.

(4) Where any property vests in the Crown by virtue of any rule of law which operates independently of the acts or the intentions of the Crown, the Crown shall not by virtue of this Act be subject to any liabilities in tort by reason only of the property being so vested; but the provisions of this subsection shall be without prejudice to the liabilities of the Crown under this Act in respect of any period after the Crown or any person acting for the Crown has in fact taken possession or control of any such property, or entered into occupation thereof.

(5) This Act shall not operate to limit the discretion of the Court to grant relief by way of mandamus in cases in which such relief might have been granted before the commencement of this Act, notwithstanding that by reason of the provisions of this Act some other and further remedy is available.

9B–391

Note — Subs.(2)(e) repealed by the Highways (Miscellaneous Provisions) Act 1961, s.1(6).

Amended by the Public Trustee (Liability and Fees) Act 2002, s.1(2).

Savings

9B–392

A plaintiff claiming to be entitled to trustee stock to which the Colonial Stock Acts 1877 to 1948 apply is entitled to proceed by way of petition of right as provided by the Colonial Stock Act 1877, s.20 to recover unpaid interest, since this is a liability of the Crown arising otherwise than in respect of Her Majesty's Government in the

United Kingdom within the terms of s.40(2)(b) of the Crown Proceedings Act 1947, and the appropriate form of procedure is that which was in force prior to the Petitions of Right Act 1860 (*Franklin v. Att.-Gen.* [1974] Q.B. 185; [1973] 1 All E.R. 879). Such a petition can only be presented by the registered holder of such stock at the date it is presented, since otherwise he would not have a sufficient interest to do so, but since there is no procedure for the joinder of parties to a petition of right, a joint stockholder can present a petition on his own, without the jointer of other joint holders of the stock with him (*Barclays Bank Ltd v. The Queen* [1974] Q.B. 823; [1974] 1 All E.R. 305).

Subs. (3) Certificate of Secretary of State

9B–393 A genuine certificate issued within the terms of the Act cannot be questioned by judicial review but is conclusive as to the facts stated in it (*R. v. Secretary of State for Foreign and Commonwealth Affairs, ex p. Trawnik, The Times*, April 18, 1985).

* * * *

PART VI

EXTENT, COMMENCEMENT, SHORT TITLE, ETC.

Extent of Act

9B–394 52. Subject to the provisions hereinafter contained with respect to Northern Ireland, this Act shall not affect the law enforced in Courts elsewhere than in England and Scotland, or the procedure in any such Courts.

* * * *

Short title

9B–395 54.—(1) This Act may be cited as the Crown Proceedings Act 1947.

(2) [...]

9B–396 *Note* — Subs.(2) repealed by the Statute Law Revision Act 1950.

FIRST SCHEDULE

PROCEEDINGS ABOLISHED BY THIS ACT

9B–397 1.—(1) Latin informations and English informations.

(2) Writs of *capias ad respondendum*, writs of *subpoena ad respondendum*, and writs of appraisement.

(3) Writs of *scire facias*.

(4) Proceedings for the determination of any issue upon a writ of extent or of *diem clausit extremum*.

(5) Writs of summons under Part V of the Crown Suits Act 1865.

2.—(1) Proceedings against His Majesty by way of petition of right, including proceedings by way of petition of right intituled in the Admiralty Division under section fifty-two of the Naval Prize Act, 1864.

(2) Proceedings against His Majesty by way of *monstrans de droit*.

Evidence (Proceedings in Other Jurisdictions) Act 1975

(1975 c.34)

An Act to make new provisions for enabling the High Court, the Court of Session and the High Court of Justice in Northern Ireland to assist in obtaining evidence required for the purposes of proceedings in other jurisdictions; to extend the powers of those courts to issue process effective throughout the United Kingdom for securing the attendance of witnesses; and for purposes connected with those matters.

[22nd May 1975] **9B–398**

"General"

The Act enables a foreign or international court to obtain an order from specified **9B–399** courts of the United Kingdom requiring evidence to be given in the United Kingdom for purposes of proceedings before the requesting court. See, generally, O.70 and notes thereto.

EVIDENCE FOR CIVIL PROCEEDINGS

Application to United Kingdom court for assistance in obtaining evidence for civil proceedings in other court

1. Where an application is made to the High Court, the Court of **9B–400** Session or the High Court of Justice in Northern Ireland for an order for evidence to be obtained in the part of the United Kingdom in which it exercises jurisdiction, and the court is satisfied—

(a) that the application is made in pursuance of a request issued by or on behalf of a court or tribunal ("the requesting court") exercising jurisdiction in any other part of the United Kingdom or in a country or territory outside the United Kingdom; and

(b) that the evidence to which the application relates is to be obtained for the purposes of civil proceedings which either have been instituted before the requesting court or whose institution before that court is contemplated,

the High Court, Court of Session or the High Court of Justice in Northern Ireland, as the case may be, shall have the powers conferred on it by the following provisions of this Act.

9B–401 *Note* — For relevant rules of court, see Section II of CPR Pt 34, replacing CPR Sched.1, RSC O.70 with effect from December 2, 2002.

Power of United Kingdom court to give effect to application for assistance

9B–402   **2.**—(1) Subject to the provisions of this section, the High Court, the Court of Session and the High Court of Justice in Northern Ireland shall each have power, on any such application as is mentioned in section 1 above, by order to make such provision for obtaining evidence in the part of the United Kingdom in which it exercises jurisdiction as may appear to the court to be appropriate for the purpose of giving effect to the request in pursuance of which the application is made; and any such order may require a person specified therein to take such steps as the court may consider appropriate for that purpose.

(2) Without prejudice to the generality of subsection (1) above but subject to the provisions of this section, an order under this section may, in particular, make provision—

(a) for the examination of witnesses, either orally or in writing;

(b) for the production of documents;

(c) for the inspection, photographing, preservation, custody or detention of any property;

(d) for the taking of samples of any property and the carrying out of any experiments on or with any property;

(e) for the medical examination of any person;

(f) without prejudice to paragraph (e) above, for the taking and testing of samples of blood from any person.

(3) An order under this section shall not require any particular steps to be taken unless they are steps which can be required to be taken by way of obtaining evidence for the purposes of civil proceedings in the court making the order (whether or not proceedings of the same description as those to which the application for the order relates); but this subsection shall not preclude the making of an order requiring a person to give testimony (either orally or in writing) otherwise than on oath where this is asked for by the requesting court.

(4) An order under this section shall not require a person—

(a) to state what documents relevant to the proceedings to which the application for the order relates are or have been in his possession, custody or power; or

(b) to produce any documents other than particular documents specified in the order as being documents appearing to the court making the order to be, or to be likely to be, in his possession, custody or power.

(5) A person who, by virtue of an order under this section, is required to attend at any place shall be entitled to the like conduct money and payment for expenses and loss of time as on attendance as a witness in civil proceedings before the court making the order.

9B–403   *Note* —See notes to CPR Sched.1, RSC O.70, Vol. 1, para. sc70.6.1. For discussion of this section, see *Refco Capital Markets Ltd v. Credit Suisse (First Boston) Ltd* [2001] EWCA Civ 1733; *The Times*, December 7, 2001 CA, and *Commerce and Industry Insurance Co of Canada v. Certain Underwriters at Lloyd's of London* [2002] 1 W.L.R. 1323 (Moore-Bick J.). For relevant rules of court, see Section II of CPR Pt 34, replacing CPR Sched.1, RSC O.70 with effect from December 2, 2002.

Privilege of witnesses

3.—(1) A person shall not be compelled by virtue of an order under **9B–404** section 2 above to give any evidence which he could not be compelled to give—

> (a) in civil proceedings in the part of the United Kingdom in which the court that made the order exercises jurisdiction; or
>
> (b) subject to subsection (2) below, in civil proceedings in the country or territory in which the requesting court exercises jurisdiction.

(2) Subsection (1)(b) above shall not apply unless the claim of the person in question to be exempt from giving the evidence is either—

> (a) supported by a statement contained in the request (whether it is so supported unconditionally or subject to conditions that are fulfilled); or
>
> (b) conceded by the applicant for the order;

and where such a claim made by any person is not supported or conceded as aforesaid he may (subject to the other provisions of this section) be required to give the evidence to which the claim relates but that evidence shall not be transmitted to the requesting court if that court, on the matter being referred to it, upholds the claim.

(3) Without prejudice to subsection (1) above, a person shall not be compelled by virtue of an order under section 2 above to give any evidence if his doing so would be prejudicial to the security of the United Kingdom; and a certificate signed by or on behalf of the Secretary of State to the effect that it would be so prejudicial for that person to do so shall be conclusive evidence of that fact.

(4) In this section references to giving evidence include references to answering any question and to producing any document and the reference in subsection (2) above to the transmission of evidence given by a person shall be construed accordingly.

Note — See CPR, r.34.20, replacing CPR Sched.1, RSC O.70, r. 6 (with effect from **9B–404.1** December 2, 2002).

Extension of powers of High Court, etc., in relation to obtaining evidence for proceedings in that court

4. The Attendance of Witnesses Act 1854 (which enables the Court **9B–405** of Session to order the issue of a warrant of citation in special form throughout the United Kingdom, for the attendance of a witness at trial) shall have effect as if references to attendance at a trial included references to attendance before an examiner or commissioner appointed by the court or a judge thereof in any cause or matter in that court, including an examiner or commissioner appointed to take evidence outside the jurisdiction of the court.

Note —Amended by the Judicature (Northern Ireland) Act 1978, s.122(2) and **9B–406** Sched.7; and the SCA 1981, s.152(4) and Sched.7.

EVIDENCE FOR CRIMINAL PROCEEDINGS

Power of United Kingdom court to assist in obtaining evidence for criminal proceedings in overseas court

9B–407   **5.** [*Repealed by the Criminal Justice (International Co-operation) Act 1990 , Sched.5.*]

EVIDENCE FOR INTERNATIONAL PROCEEDINGS

Power of United Kingdom court to assist in obtaining evidence for international proceedings

9B–408   **6.**—(1) Her Majesty may by Order in Council direct that, subject to such exceptions, adaptations or modifications as may be specified in the Order, the provisions of sections 1 to 3 above shall have effect in relation to international proceedings of any description specified in the order.

(2) An Order in Council under this section may direct that section 1(4) of the Perjury Act 1911 or Article 3(4) of the Perjury (Northern Ireland) Order 1979 shall have effect in relation to international proceedings to which the Order applies as it has effect in relation to a judicial proceeding in a tribunal of a foreign state.

(3) In this section "international proceedings" means proceedings before the International Court of Justice or any other court, tribunal, commission, body or authority (whether consisting of one or more persons) which in pursuance of any international agreement or any resolution of the General Assembly of the United Nations, exercises any jurisdiction or performs any functions of a judicial nature or by way of arbitration, conciliation or inquiry or is appointed (whether permanently or temporarily) for the purpose of exercising any jurisdiction or performing any such functions.

9B–409   *Note* —Amended by S.I. 1979 No. 1714.

SUPPLEMENTARY

Rules of court

9B–410   **7.** Civil Procedure Rules or rules of court under section 7 of the Northern Ireland Act 1962 shall include power to make rules of court—

> (a) as to the manner in which any such application as is mentioned in section 1 above is to be made;
>
> (b) subject to the provisions of this Act, as to the circumstances in which an order can be made under section 2 above; and
>
> (c) as to the manner in which any such reference as is mentioned in section 3(2) above is to be made;

and any such rules may include such incidental, supplementary and consequential provision as the authority making the rules may consider necessary or expedient.

9B–411   *Note* —Amended by the SCA 1981, s.152(4) and Sched.7; and by the Courts Act 2003, s.109(1), Sched.8, para.177(a).

With effect from December 2, 2002, the provisions in Sect.II of CPR, Pt 34 replaced RSC O.70 (Obtaining Evidence for Foreign Courts, Etc.) as the rules of court authorised by this section.

Consequential amendments and repeals

8.—(1) The enactments mentioned in Schedule 1 to this Act shall have effect subject to the amendments there specified, being amendments consequential on the provisions of this Act.   **9B–412**

(2) The enactments mentioned in Schedule 2 to this Act are hereby repealed to the extent specified in the third column of that Schedule.

(3) Nothing in this section shall affect—

    (a) any application to any court or judge which is pending at the commencement of this Act;

    (b) any certificate given for the purposes of any such application;

    (c) any power to make an order on such an application; or

    (d) the operation or enforcement of any order made on such an application.

(4) Subsection (3) above is without prejudice to section 38(2) of the Interpretation Act 1889 (effect of repeals).

Interpretation

9.—(1) In this Act—   **9B–413**

    "civil proceedings", in relation to the requesting court, means proceedings in any civil or commercial matter;

    "requesting court" has the meaning given in section 1 above;

    "property" includes any land, chattel or other corporeal property of any description;

    "request" includes any commission, order or other process issued by or on behalf of the requesting court.

(2) In relation to any application made in pursuance of a request issued by the High Court under section 56 of the County Courts Act 1984 or the High Court of Justice in Northern Ireland under Article 43 of the County Courts (Northern Ireland) Order 1980, the reference in section 1(b) above to proceedings instituted before the requesting court shall be construed as a reference to the relevant proceedings in the county court.

(3) Any power conferred by this Act to make an Order in Council includes power to revoke or vary any such Order by a subsequent Order in Council.

(4) Nothing in this Act shall be construed as enabling any court to make an order that is binding on the Crown or on any person in his capacity as an officer or servant of the Crown.

(5) Except so far as the context otherwise requires, any reference in this Act to any enactment is a reference to that enactment as amended or extended by or under any other enactment.

Note —Amended by the County Courts Act 1984, s.148(1) and Sched.2.   **9B–414**

"Civil or commercial matters"

The words "civil or commercial matters" in the Act of 1975 cannot be construed   **9B–415**

LEGISLATION

with reference to any internationally acceptable meaning but equally they are not to be given a restricted construction derived from the distinction between public and private law in civil law systems and accordingly the definition extends to relevant proceedings in a civil or commercial matter in both the United Kingdom and the requesting state, *e.g.* proceedings in the foreign court challenging a tax assessment made by a foreign tax authority (*Re State of Norway's Application (Nos. 1 and 2)* [1990] 1 A.C. 723; [1989] 2 W.L.R. 458, HL(E), affirming [1987] Q.B. 433).

Short title, commencement and extent

9B–416   **10.**—(1) This Act may be cited as the Evidence (Proceedings in Other Jurisdictions) Act 1975.

(2) This Act shall come into operation on such day as Her Majesty may by Order in Council appoint.

(3) Her Majesty may by Order in Council make provision for extending any of the provisions of this Act (including section 6 or any Order in Council made thereunder) with such exceptions, adaptations or modifications as may be specified in the Order, to any of the Channel Islands, the Isle of Man, any colony (other than a colony for whose external relations a country other than the United Kingdom is responsible) or any country or territory outside Her Majesty's dominions in which Her Majesty has jurisdiction in right of Her Majesty's Government in the United Kingdom.

Commencement

9B–417   The Act was brought into force on May 4, 1976, by S.I. 1976 No. 429.

* * * *

SECTION 8(12)   SCHEDULE 2

REPEALS

9B–418

Chapter	Short Title	Extent
19 & 20 Vict. c. 133.	The Foreign Tribunals Evidence Act 1856.	The whole Act.
22 Vict. c. 20.	The Evidence by Commission Act 1859.	The whole Act.
33 & 34 Vict. c. 52	The Extradition Act 1870.	Section 24.
48 & 49 Vict. c. 74.	The Evidence by Commission Act 1885.	The whole Act.
53 & 54 Vict. c. 37.	The Foreign Jurisdiction Act 1890.	In Schedule 1 the entries relating to the Foreign Tribunals Evidence Act 1856, the Evidence by Commission Act 1859 and the Evidence by Commission Act 1885 but without prejudice to any Order in Council made in respect of any of those Acts before the commencement of this Act.
4 & 5 Eliz. 2. c. 2.	The German Conventions Act 1955.	Section 1(3).

Chapter	Short Title	Extent
10 & 11 Eliz. 2. c. 30.	The Northern Ireland Act 1962.	In Schedule 1 the entry relating to the Evidence by Commission Act 1859.
1963 c. 27.	The Oaths and Evidence (Overseas Authorities and Countries) Act 1963.	Section 4.
1966 c. 41	The Arbitration (International Investment Disputes) Act 1966.	In section 3(1), paragraph (b) together with the word "and" immediately preceding that paragraph. In section 7(e), subsection (2) of the section 3 there set out.
1968 c. 64.	The Civil Evidence Act 1968.	Section 17(2).
1971 c. 36. (N.I.)	The Civil Evidence Act (Northern Ireland) 1971.	Section 13(2).

Law Reform (Contributory Negligence) Act 1945

(1945 8 & 9 GEO. 6 C.28)

Apportionment of liability in case of contributory negligence

1.—(1) Where any person suffers damage as the result partly of his **9B–419** own fault and partly of the fault of any other person or persons, a claim in respect of that damage shall not be defeated by reason of the fault of the person suffering the damage, but the damages recoverable in respect thereof shall be reduced to such extent as the Court thinks just and equitable having regard to the claimant's share in the responsibility for the damage: Provided that—

    (a) this subsection shall not operate to defeat any defence arising under a contract;

    (b) where any contract or enactment providing for the limitation of liability is applicable to the claim, the amount of damages recoverable by the claimant by virtue of this subsection shall not exceed the maximum limit so applicable.

(2) Where damages are recoverable by any person by virtue of the foregoing subsection subject to such reduction as is therein mentioned, the Court shall find and record the total damages which would have been recoverable if the claimant had not been at fault.

(3) [*Repealed by the Civil Liability (Contribution) Act 1978 , s.9(2) and Sched.2.*]

(4) [*Repealed by the Fatal Accidents Act 1976 , s.6 and Sched.6.*]

(5) Where, in any case to which subsection (1) of this section applies, one of the persons at fault avoids liability to any other such person or his personal representative by pleading the Limitation Act 1939, or any other enactment limiting the time within which proceedings may be taken, he shall not be entitled to recover any damages from that other person or representative by virtue of the said subsection.

(6) [Repealed by the Carriage by Air Act 1961, Sched.2.]

(7) [Repealed by the Carriage by Air Act 1961, s.14 and Sched.2.]

9B–420   *Note* — Subsection 5 amended by the Civil Liability (Contribution) Act 1978, s.9(2) and Sched.2; see now Limitation Act 1980, Vol. 2, Section 8.

9B–421   *Note* —Where the plaintiff brings a claim in tort and the defendant makes a counterclaim in contract, both claims being attributable to two concurrent causes contemporaneously, the apportionment of liability cannot be solved by applying the Act of 1945 but can only be resolved by assessing the recoverable damages per each claim on the basis of causation (*Tenant Radiant Heat Ltd v. Warrington Development Corp* (1988) 11 E.G. 71, CA, distinguishing *Forsikringsaktielskapet Vesta v. Butcher* [1988] 3 W.L.R. 565, CA, apportionment of liability between two claims in contract).

In the case of a claimant "fault" in this context means "negligence, breach of statutory duty or other act or omission" (see s.4) which gives rise, at common law, to a defence of contributory negligence (*Standard Chartered Bank v. Pakistan National Shipping Corporation (No. 2)* [2002] UKHL; [2003] 1 All E.R. 173, HL (there is no common law defence of contributory negligence in the case of fraudulent misrepresentation)).

* * * *

Saving for Maritime Conventions Act 1911, and past cases

9B–422   **3.**—(1) This Act shall not apply to any claim to which section one of the Maritime Conventions Act, 1911, applies and that Act shall have effect as if this Act had not passed.

(2) This Act shall not apply to any case where the acts or omissions giving rise to the claim occurred before the passing of this Act.

Interpretation

9B–423   **4.** The following expressions have the meanings hereby respectively assigned to them, that is to say—

"Court" means, in relation to any claim, the Court or arbitrator by or before whom the claim falls to be determined;

"damage" includes loss of life and personal injury;

[*Meaning of "dependant" repealed by the* Fatal Accidents Act 1976 .]

[*Meaning of "employer" and "workman" repealed by the* National Insurance (Industrial Injuries) Act 1946 .]

"fault" means negligence, breach of statutory duty or other act or omission which gives rise to a liability in tort or would, apart from this Act, give rise to the defence of contributory negligence;

* * * *

Short title and extent

9B–424   **7.** This Act may be cited as the Law Reform (Contributory Negligence) Act 1945.

9B–425   *Crown* —This Act applies to the Crown (Crown Proceedings Act 1947, s.4(3)).

Law Reform (Miscellaneous Provisions) Act 1934

(1934 24 & 25 GEO. 5 C.41)

Effect of death on certain causes of action

9B–426   **1.**—(1) Subject to the provisions of this section, on the death of any person after the commencement of this Act all causes of action subsisting against or vested in him shall survive against, or, as the case may be, for the benefit of his estate: Provided that this subsection shall not apply to causes of action for defamation.

(1A) The right of a person to claim under section 1A of the Fatal Accidents Act 1976 (bereavement) shall not survive for the benefit of his estate on his death.

(2) Where a cause of action survives as aforesaid for the benefit of the estate of a deceased person, the damages recoverable for the benefit of the estate of that person:—

 (a) shall not include—

  (i) any exemplary damages;

  (ii) any damages for loss of income in respect of any period after that person's death;

 (b) [...]

 (c) where the death of that person has been caused by the act or omission which gives rise to the cause of action, shall be calculated without reference to any loss or gain to his estate consequent on his death, except that a sum in respect of funeral expenses may be included.

(3) [...]

(4) Where damage has been suffered by reason of any act or omission in respect of which a cause of action would have subsisted against any person if that person had not died before or at the same time as the damage was suffered, there shall be deemed, for the purposes of this Act, to have been subsisting against him before his death such cause of action in respect of that act or omission as would have subsisted if he had died after the damage was suffered.

(5) The rights conferred by this Act for the benefit of the estates of deceased persons shall be in addition to and not in derogation of any rights conferred on the dependants of deceased persons by the Fatal Accidents Acts 1846 to 1908, and so much of this Act as relates to causes of action against the estates of deceased persons shall apply in relation to causes of action under the said Acts as it applies in relation to other causes of action not expressly excepted from the operation of subsection (1) of this section.

(6) In the event of the insolvency of an estate against which proceedings are maintainable by virtue of this section, any liability in respect of the cause of action in respect of which the proceedings are maintainable shall be deemed to be a debt provable in the administration of the estate, notwithstanding that it is a demand in the nature of unliquidated damages arising otherwise than by a contract, promise or breach of trust.

(7) [...]

Note —Amended by the Statute Law Revision Act 1950; the Law Reform (Miscellaneous Provisions) Act 1970, Sched.; the Proceedings Against Estates Act 1970; and the Administration of Justice Act 1982, ss.4, 41 and 75, Sched.9. Subs.(5) extended by the Fatal Accidents Act 1976, s.6(1), Sched.1. **9B–427**

2. [*Repealed by the Fatal Accidents Act 1976 , Sched.2.*] **9B–428**

Power of Courts of Record to award interest on debts and damages

3.—(1) In any proceedings tried in any Court of Record for the **9B–429**

recovery of any debt or damages, the Court may, if it thinks fit, order that there shall be included in the sum for which judgment is given interest at such rate as it thinks fit on the whole or any part of the debt or damages for the whole or any part of the period between the date when the cause of action arose and the date of the judgment: Provided that nothing in this section—

    (a) shall authorise the giving of interest upon interest; or

    (b) shall apply in relation to any debt upon which interest is payable as of right whether by virtue of any agreement or otherwise; or

    (c) shall affect the damages recoverable for the dishonour of a bill of exchange.

(1A) Where in any such proceedings as are mentioned in subsection (1) of this section judgment is given for a sum which (apart from interest on damages) exceeds £200 and represents or includes damages in respect of personal injuries to the plaintiff or any other person, or in respect of a person's death, then (without prejudice to the exercise of the power conferred by that subsection in relation to any part of that sum which does not represent such damages) the court shall exercise that power so as to include in that sum interest on those damages or on such part of them as the court considers appropriate, unless the court is satisfied that there are special reasons why no interest should be given in respect of those damages.

(1B) Any order under this section may provide for interest to be calculated at different rates in respect of different parts of the period for which interest is given, whether that period is the whole or part of the period mentioned in subsection (1) of this section.

(1C) For the avoidance of doubt it is hereby declared that in determining, for the purposes of any enactment contained in the County Courts Act 1959, whether an amount exceeds, or is less than, a sum specified in that enactment, no account shall be taken of any power exercisable by virtue of this section or of any order made in the exercise of such a power.

(1D) In this section "personal injuries" includes any disease and any impairment of a person's physical or mental condition [...].

(2) [...]

9B–430   *Note* —Amended by the Statute Law Revision Act 1950; and the Administration of Justice Act 1969, s.22.

By the A.J.A 1982, s.15(4) and (5), the provisions of this section have ceased to have effect in relation to the High Court and the county courts, but they remain in force and operation in relation to other Courts of Record, *e.g.* the Court of Appeal (Civil Division), so that on the hearing of an appeal, where that Court gives judgment for any debt or damages, it may also award interest under this section. It would seem that the hearing of an appeal will be regarded as coming within the word "tried", since the Court will have made a judicial decision (see *per* Lord Denning M.R. in *Wallersteiner v. Moir (No. 2)* [1975] Q.B. 373 at 387).

For the power to award interest on any debt or damages in the High Court, see SCA 1981, s.35A; in the county courts see C.C.A. 1984, s.69; in arbitration proceedings, see Arb. A. 1950, s.19A. See also AJA 1982, s.15; and by the Statute Law (Repeals) Act 2004, Sched.1, Part 1, Group 4.

Short title and extent

9B–431   4.—(1) This Act may be cited as the Law Reform (Miscellaneous Provisions) Act 1934.

(2) This Act shall not extend to Scotland or Northern Ireland.

Litigants in Person (Costs and Expenses) Act 1975

(1975 c.47)

An Act to make further provisions as to the costs or expenses recoverable by litigants in person in civil proceedings.

[1st August 1975] **9B–432**

Costs or expenses recoverable

1.—(1) Where, in any proceedings to which this subsection applies, **9B–433** any costs of a litigant in person are ordered to be paid by any other party to the proceedings or in any other way, there may, subject to rules of court, be allowed on the taxation or other determination of those costs sums in respect of any work done, and any expenses and losses incurred, by the litigants in or in connection with the proceedings to which the order relates. This subsection applies to civil proceedings—

> (a) in a county court, in the Supreme Court or in the House of Lords on appeal from the High Court or the Court of Appeal,
>
> (b) before the Lands Tribunal or the Lands Tribunal for Northern Ireland, or
>
> (c) in or before any other court or tribunal specified in an order made under this subsection by the Lord Chancellor.

(2) Where, in any proceedings to which this subsection applies, any costs or expenses of a party litigant are ordered to be paid by any other party to the proceedings or in any other way, there may, subject to rules of court, be allowed on the taxation or other determination of those costs or expenses sums in respect of any work done, and any outlays and losses incurred, by the litigant or in connection with the proceedings to which the order relates.

This subsection applies to civil proceedings—

> (a) in the sheriff court, the Scottish Land Court, the Court of Session or the House of Lords on appeal from the Court of Session.
>
> (b) before the Lands Tribunal for Scotland, or
>
> (c) in or before any other court or tribunal specified in an order made under this subsection by the Lord Advocate.

(3) An order under subsection (1) or (2) above shall be made by statutory instrument and shall be subject to annulment in pursuance of the resolution of either House of Parliament.

(4) In this section "rules of court"—

> (a) in relation to the Lands Tribunal or the Lands Tribunal for Scotland, means rules made under section 3 of the Lands Tribunal Act 1949,

(b) in relation to the Lands Tribunal for Northern Ireland means rules made under section 9 of the Lands Tribunal and Compensation Act (Northern Ireland) 1964, and

(c) in relation to any other tribunal specified in an order made under subsection (1) or (2) above, shall have the meaning given by the order as respects that tribunal.

(5) In the application of subsection (1) above to Northern Ireland, the expression "county court," "the Supreme Court," "the High Court" and "the Court of Appeal" shall have the meanings respectively assigned to them by section 29(1) of the Northern Ireland Act 1962.

Short title, commencement and extent

9B–434 **2.**—(1) This Act may be cited as the Litigants in Person (Costs and Expenses) Act 1975.

(2) [...]

(3) [...]

9B–435 *Note*—See also CPR, r.48.6.

This Act applies to all costs incurred after April 1, 1976, and was partially brought into force on that day by the Litigants in Person (Costs and Expenses) Act 1975 Commencement Order 1976 (S.I. 1976 No. 364) and the residue by (Commencement No. 2) Order 1980 (S.I. 1980 No. 1158). The scope of the Act was extended to the Employment AppealTribunal by the Litigants in Person (Costs and Expenses) Order 1980 (S.I. 1980 No. 1159) and to civil proceedings in magistrates' courts by the Litigants in Person (Costs and Expenses) (Magistrates' Courts) Order 2001 (S.I. 2001 No. 3438).

There is no provision for the costs of litigants in person in criminal proceedings.

For notes on costs and expenses which are recoverable see Vol. 1, para. 48.6.1.

Subss (2) and (3) repealed by the Statute Law (Repeals) Act 2004, Sched.1, Pt 1, Group 4.

Litigants in person—rights of audience

9B–436 Where a non legally qualified but experienced advocate sought leave to appear on behalf of a litigant in person and where the applicant was in need of skilled assistance but did not wish to apply for legal aid which could be provided by the proposed representative, the Court found that the Courts and Legal Services Act 1990 gave the Court a discretion that made it clear by its terms that the discretion was to be exercised only in exceptional circumstances. The assistance in the litigation process which was proposed was out of accord with the spirit of the Act, the application was refused (*D v. S (Rights of Audience)*, *The Times*, January 1, 1997; *Chauhan v. Chauhan*, October 26, 1994, CA, unrep., considered). See also *Izzo v. PhilipRoss & Co* [2002] B.P.I.R. 310.

See further, para. 9A–612 above, and sources referred to there.

Oaths Act 1978

9B–437 (1978 c.19)

ARRANGEMENT OF SECTIONS

PART I

ENGLAND, WALES AND NORTHERN IRELAND

* * * *

9B–438

Note —This Act repealed and replaced the Oaths Acts of 1838, 1888, 1909 and 1961 and ss.8 and 32(2) of the AJA 1977. It came into force on August 1, 1978.

PART I

ENGLAND, WALES AND NORTHERN IRELAND

Manner of administration of oaths

9B–439

1.—(1) Any oath may be administered and taken in England, Wales or Northern Ireland in the following form and manner— "The person taking the oath shall hold the New Testament, or, in the case of a Jew, the Old Testament, in his uplifted hand, and shall say or repeat after the officer administering the oath the words "I swear by Almighty God that ...", followed by the words of the oath prescribed by law".

(2) The officer shall (unless the person about to take the oath voluntarily objects thereto, or is physically incapable of so taking the oath) administer the oath in the form and manner aforesaid without question.

(3) In the case of a person who is neither a Christian nor a Jew, the oath shall be administered in any lawful manner.

(4) In this section "officer" means any person duly authorised to administer oaths.

Form and manner of taking oath

9B–440

The Act provides for the form in which a Christian and a Jew should take an oath and although s.1(3) provides for persons of other religious beliefs, no guidance is given as to the form of oath and the manner of administrating the same to such persons. The Judicial Studies Board have issued notes of guidance which include the form of the most common oaths taken by witnesses other than those taking the oath on the New Testament:

Hindu (Taken on the Gita)
"I swear by the Gita that ..."
Jew (Taken on the Old Testament)
"I swear by Almighty God that ..."
Muslim/follower of Islam (Taken on the Koran)
"I swear by Allah that ..."
Sikh (Taken on the Adi Granth)
"I swear by Guru Nanak that ..."
Quaker or Moravian Witness (affirmation)
"I, being of the people called Quakers/United Brethren called Moravians do solemnly ..."

If the appropriate holy book is not available the witness should be invited to affirm.

The Koran, Gita and Adi Granth should be kept wrapped or in a suitable container and only removed therefrom by the witness.

The usual practice is for the testament to be held in the right hand though the Act only requires that the testament be held in the "uplifted" hand.

LEGISLATION

Solicitors and commissioners for oaths practising in a locality with a particular ethnic minority may wish to seek further guidance from the Judicial Studies Board.

Consequential amendments

9B–441   2. In the following provisions, namely—

(a) section 28(1) of the Children and Young Persons Act 1963; and

(b) section 56(1) of the Children and Young Persons Act (Northern Ireland) 1968

(each of which prescribes the form of oath for use in juvenile courts and by children and young persons in other courts) for the words "section 2 of the Oaths Act 1909" there shall be substituted the words " section 1 of the Oaths Act 1978".

PART II

UNITED KINGDOM

OATHS

Swearing with uplifted hand

9B–442   3. If any person to whom an oath is administered desires to swear with uplifted hand, in the form and manner in which an oath is usually administered in Scotland, he shall be permitted so to do, and the oath shall be administered to him in such form and manner without further question.

Validity of oaths

9B–443   4.—(1) In any case in which an oath may lawfully be and has been administered to any person, if it has been administered in a form and manner other than that prescribed by law, he is bound by it if it has been administered in such form and with such ceremonies as he may have declared to be binding.

(2) Where an oath has been duly administered and taken, the fact that the person to whom it was administered had, at the time of taking it, no religious belief, shall not for any purpose affect the validity of the oath.

Validity of oaths

9B–444   The validity of an oath depended not on the particular tenets of the religion adhered to by the witness as to the form and manner of taking oaths, but whether it was an oath which appeared to the court to be binding on the conscience of the witness and if so, whether it was an oath which the witness himself considered binding on his conscience. The Court of Appeal so held in a case where a witness of the Muslim faith took the oath on the New Testament but when questioned in the Court of Appeal said "whether I had taken the oath on the Koran or on the Bible or on the Torah, I would have considered that [oath] to be binding on my conscience" (*R. v. Kemble* [1990] 1 W.L.R. 1111, CA).

SOLEMN AFFIRMATIONS

Making of solemn affirmations

9B–445   5.—(1) Any person who objects to being shown shall be permitted to make his solemn affirmation instead of taking an oath.

(2) Subsection (1) above shall apply in relation to a person to whom it is not reasonably practicable without inconvenience or delay to administer an oath in the manner appropriate to his religious belief as it applies in relation to a person objecting to be sworn.

(3) A person who may be permitted under subsection (2) above to make his solemn affirmation may also be required to do so.

(4) A solemn affirmation shall be of the same force and effect as an oath.

Form of affirmation

6.—(1) Subject to subsection (2) below, every affirmation shall be as follows:— "I,   do solemnly, sincerely and truly declare   and   affirm,"   and then proceed with the words of the oath prescribed by law, omitting any words of impreciation or calling to witness.

9B–446

(2) Every affirmation in writing shall commence:—

"I,   of   , do solemnly and sincerely affirm,"   and the form in lieu of jurat shall be "Affirmed at   this   day of   19 , Before me."

SUPPLEMENTARY

* * * *

Short title, extent and commencement

8.—(1) This Act may be cited as the Oaths Act 1978.

9B–447

* * * *

The High Court Enforcement Officers Regulations 2004

S.I. 2004 No. 400

PART 1

INTRODUCTION

Citation and commencement

1. These Regulations may be cited as the High Court Enforcement Officers Regulations 2004 and shall come into force on 15th March 2004.

9B–448

Interpretation

2.—(1) In these Regulations—

9B–449

    (a) "application" means an application by an individual for authorisation to act as an enforcement officer;

    (b) "district" means a district set out in Schedule 1 to these Regulations;

(c) "enforcement officer" means an individual authorised by the Lord Chancellor under Schedule 7 to act as such;

(d) "Schedule 7" means Schedule 7 to the Courts Act 2003.

(2) References in these Regulations to—

(a) the Lord Chancellor shall include a person acting on his behalf under Schedule 7;

(b) a writ of execution shall not include—

(i) a writ of sequestration; or

(ii) a writ relating to ecclesiastical property.

Districts for enforcement of writs of execution by enforcement officers

9B–450   **3.**—(1) For the purposes of Schedule 7 and these Regulations, England and Wales is to be divided into 105 districts.

(2) Such districts correspond with the postal areas for England and Wales and are listed in Schedule 1 to these Regulations.

Note —Amended by S.I. 2004 No. 673.

PART 2

AUTHORISATION OF ENFORCEMENT OFFICERS

Conditions to be satisfied

9B–451   **4.**—(1) An individual will not be authorised to act as an enforcement officer unless the conditions in paragraph (2) are satisfied.

(2) The individual must not —

(a) have been convicted of any criminal offence—

(i) for which he received a custodial sentence; or

(ii) involving dishonesty or violence;

(b) be liable for any unpaid fines;

(c) be liable for any court judgment granted within the last 6 years which remains unsatisfied;

(d) be an undischarged bankrupt;

(e) have been disqualifed from acting as a director of a company within the last 6 years;

(f) carry on or be involved in any business relating to or including the purchase or sale of debts.

Application procedure

9B–452   **5.**—(1) An application for authorisation to act as an enforcement officer may only be made by an individual and must—

(a) be made in writing; and

(b) contain a statement signed and dated by the individual certifying that the contents of the application are true.

(2) The application must contain the following information about the individual—

(a) his name, address and date of birth;

(b) whether he has been convicted of any criminal offence,

whether or not punishable by imprisonment, and if so details of each offence and conviction;

(c) whether he is liable for any unpaid fines and if so appropriate details;

(d) whether he is or has been liable for any court judgment and if so appropriate details including whether any judgment remains unsatisfied;

(e) whether he is or has ever been subject to any of the following proceedings and if so with what result—

(i) bankruptcy proceedings;

(ii) an administration order under section 112 of the County Courts Act 1984;

(iii) a deed of arrangement under the Deeds of Arrangement Act 1914 or an individual voluntary arrangement under Part VIII of the Insolvency Act 1986;

(iv) proceedings under the Company Directors Disqualification Act 1986;

(v) insolvency proceedings in relation to any partnership in which he was a partner or any company of which he was a director; or

(vi) any other proceedings under the Insolvency Act 1986.

(3) The application shall also—

(a) specify to which district or districts the applicant is requesting assignment; and

(b) include details and documentation giving evidence of—

(i) any relevant insurance policies held by the applicant;

(ii) any licence held by the applicant under the Consumer Credit Act 1974;

(iii) any notification given by the applicant to the Information Commissioner under section 18 of the Data Protection Act 1998;

(iv) any current membership held by the applicant of a professional body which is listed in Schedule 2 to these Regulations as a professional body recognised by the Lord Chancellor;

(v) the bank account or accounts held by the applicant through which it is proposed that monies recovered on behalf of judgment debtors are to be collected and paid;

(vi) the applicant's relevant experience;

(vii) the applicant's knowledge of the laws and the practice and procedure of the High Court in relation to enforcement of debts;

(viii) the applicant's business plan including any person whom the applicant is proposing to engage to act on his behalf to assist with his work as an enforcement officer;

2641

(ix) the applicant's policies in relation to the selection and employment of staff; and

(x) any existing or previous businesses of the applicant.

(4) Where the applicant has an existing business, the application shall be accompanied by audited or certified accounts of the applicant and of any company associated with the applicant for the preceding 3 years, or for the period of trading if this is shorter.

(5) In the case of any application, the Lord Chancellor may require further details of information already given or any additional information or documentation which seems to him to be necessary.

(6) For the purposes of this regulation and regulation 8, "relevant insurance policies" means—

(a) professional indemnity insurance;

(b) public liability insurance;

(c) employers liability insurance, where the individual is an employer; and

(d) goods in transit insurance, where the individual will be conducting his own removals.

Authorisation and assignment

9B–453 **6.**—(1) The Lord Chancellor may take account, in deciding whether to authorise an individual to act as an enforcement officer, of—

(a) the information contained in or provided with the individual's application; and

(b) any other relevant information available to him.

(2) Upon being authorised to act as an enforcement officer, an individual may be assigned to—

(a) any or all of the districts to which he has requested assignment; and

(b) any other district or districts, if the Lord Chancellor considers it necessary or expedient in order to ensure that sufficient enforcement officers are assigned to each district.

PART 3

POST AUTHORISATION

Duty to execute writs

9B–454 **7.** Once assigned to a district or a number of districts, the enforcement officer must undertake enforcement action for all writs of execution received which are to be executed at addresses which fall within his assigned district.

Conditions to be satisfied following authorisation

9B–455 **8.** Every enforcement officer is under a continuing duty to—

(a) successfully complete any required training;

(b) comply with any requirements set by the Lord Chancellor for his continuous professional development;
(c) hold current relevant insurance policies;
(d) hold a bank account through which monies recovered on behalf of judgment debtors are to be collected and paid;
(e) produce to the Lord Chancellor—
  (i) annual audited or certified accounts;
  (ii) performance statistics when requested; and
  (iii) such other information or documentation relevant to his work as an enforcement officer as may be required.

Change of details

9. An enforcement officer must immediately give the Lord Chancellor written notification of any change in— **9B–456**
(a) his name;
(b) his address;
(c) the bank account or accounts held by him through which monies recovered on behalf of judgment debtors are collected and paid; or
(d) the information or documentation contained in his application for authorisation to act as an enforcement officer.

Changes to assignment

10.—(1) An enforcement officer may at any time apply to the Lord **9B–457** Chancellor to change the districts to which he is assigned.

(2) An application under paragraph (1) must be made in writing and must include a declaration of any changes in the information and documentation contained in the individual's application for authorisation to act as an enforcement officer.

(3) An enforcement officer may at any time be assigned to an additional district or districts without having applied for such assignment, if the Lord Chancellor considers it necessary or expedient in order to ensure that sufficient enforcement officers are assigned to each district.

Resignation

11. If an enforcement officer wishes to resign from his appointment he must provide the Lord Chancellor with at least 28 days' **9B–458** written notice of his intended resignation.

Termination of authorisation or assignment

12.—(1) The Lord Chancellor may at any time terminate— **9B–459**
(a) the authorisation of an individual to act as an enforcement officer; or
(b) the assignment of an enforcement officer to any one or more of the districts to which he is assigned,
on any of the grounds in paragraph (2).

LEGISLATION

(2) The grounds are that—

(a) it would be in the public interest to do so;

(b) any of the—

(i) information provided in the application for authorisation; or

(ii) documentation supplied,

under regulation 5 is found to be incomplete or untrue;

(c) the enforcement officer or any person acting on his behalf who assists with his work as an enforcement officer has behaved in a manner which the Lord Chancellor reasonably considers to be unprofessional or unacceptable; or

(d) the enforcement officer has failed to satisfy one or more of the conditions of regulation 8.

(3) Where practicable, the Lord Chancellor when considering whether to terminate the authorisation or assignment of an enforcement officer shall firstly notify the enforcement officer of the reasons and provide the enforcement officer with a reasonable opportunity to—

(a) make representations about the Lord Chancellor's reasons for proposing to terminate his authorisation or assignment; and

(b) remedy the circumstances giving rise to the Lord Chancellor's proposal to terminate his authorisation or assignment.

PART 4

MISCELLANEOUS

Fees

9B–460   **13.**—(1) Schedule 3 to these Regulations sets out the fees that may be charged by enforcement officers.

(2) Where the execution of a writ of fieri facias is completed by sale, fees 1, 2, 3, 4, 5, 6 (1) and 7 under Schedule 3 may be levied by deducting them from the proceeds of sale.

(3) Where a writ is withdrawn or satisfied or its execution is stopped, the fees set out under Schedule 3 must be paid by—

(a) the person upon whose application the writ was issued; or

(b) the person at whose instance the execution is stopped, as the case may be.

(4) An enforcement officer or a party liable to pay any fees under Schedule 3 may apply to a costs judge or a district judge of the High Court for an assessment of the amount payable, by the detailed assessment procedure in accordance with the Civil Procedure Rules 1998 .

Directories

9B–461   **14.** Directories containing details of all current enforcement officers, the districts to which they have been assigned and the addresses to which writs of execution issued from the High Court to enforcement officers are to be sent shall be published and available for inspection at—

        (a) the Royal Courts of Justice;

        (b) district registries of the High Court; and

        (c) county courts,

during the hours when the offices of such courts are open.

Walking possession agreement

15. Schedule 4 to these Regulations sets out the form of an agree- **9B–462** ment under which an enforcement officer may take walking possession of goods.

REGULATION 3   **SCHEDULE 1**

DISTRICTS FOR WRITS OF EXECUTION ENFORCED BY ENFORCEMENT OFFICERS

9B–463

District	Postal Area
Bath	BA
Birmingham	B
Blackburn	BB
Bolton	BL
Bournemouth	BH
Bradford	BD
Brighton	BN
Bristol	BS
Bromley	BR
Cambridge	CB
Canterbury	CT
Cardiff	CF
Carlisle	CA
Chelmsford	CM
Chester	CH
Cleveland (Teesside)	TS
Colchester	CO
Coventry	CV
Crewe	CW
Croydon	CR
Darlington	DL
Dartford	DA
Derby	DE
Doncaster	DN
Dorchester	DT
Dudley	DY
Durham	DH
Enfield	EN
Exeter	EX
Fylde (Blackpool)	FY
Gloucester	GL

District	Postal Area
Guildford	GU
Halifax	HX
Harrogate	HG
Harrow	HA
Hemel Hempstead	HP
Hereford	HR
Huddersfield	HD
Hull	HU
Ilford	IG
Ipswich	IP
Kingston upon Thames	KT
Lancaster	LA
Leeds	LS
Leicester	LE
Lincoln	LN
Liverpool	L
Llandrindod Wells	LD
Llandudno	LL
London East	E
London East Central	EC
London North	N
London North West	NW
London South East	SE
London South West	SW
London West	W
London West Central	WC
Luton	LU
Manchester	M
Medway	ME
Milton Keynes	MK
Newcastle	NE
Newport	NP
Northampton	NN
Norwich	NR
Nottingham	NG
Oldham	OL
Oxford	OX
Peterborough	PE
Plymouth	PL
Portsmouth	PO
Preston	PR
Reading	RG
Redhill	RH
Romford	RM
Salisbury	SP
Sheffield	S
Shrewsbury	SY
Slough	SL

District	Postal Area
Southall (Uxbridge)	UB
Southampton	SO
Southend on Sea	SS
St. Albans	AL
Stevenage	SG
Stockport	SK
Stoke on Trent	ST
Sunderland	SR
Sutton	SM
Swansea	SA
Swindon	SN
Taunton	TA
Telford	TF
Tonbridge	TN
Torquay	TQ
Truro	TR
Tweeddale (Berwick upon Tweed)	TD
Twickenham	TW
Wakefield	WF
Walsall	WS
Warrington	WA
Watford	WD
Wigan	WN
Wolverhampton	WV
Worcester	WR
York	YO

Note —Amended by S.I. 2004 No. 673.

REGULATION 5   **SCHEDULE 2**

PROFESSIONAL BODIES RECOGNISED BY THE LORD CHANCELLOR

The Lord Chancellor recognises the following as professional bodies: **9B–464**

- High Court Enforcement Officers Association

REGULATION 13   **SCHEDULE 3**

FEES CHARGEABLE BY ENFORCEMENT OFFICERS

The fees chargeable by enforcement officers on execution of writs are as follows. Value   **9B–465**
Added Tax, if payable, may be added to the fees specified.

A. Fees chargeable on execution of writs of fieri facias	
1. Percentage of amount recovered	
For executing a writ of fieri facias, the following percentages of the amount recovered:	
(a) on the first £100	5 per cent
(b) above £100	2.5 per cent
2. Mileage	

Mileage from the enforcement officer's business address to the place of execution and return, in respect of one journey to seize goods and, if appropriate, one journey to remove the goods	
	29.2 pence per mile, up to a maximum of £50.00 in total
3. Seizure of goods	
For each building or place at which goods are seized	£2.00
4. Making enquiries or dealing with claims for rent or to the goods	
(1) For making enquiries as to claims for rent or to goods, including giving notice to parties of any such claims	a sum not exceeding £2.00
(2) For all expenses actually and reasonably incurred in relation to such work including any postage, telephone, fax and e-mail charges	a further sum not exceeding £2.00
5. Taking possession, removal and storage of goods	
(1) Where a person is left in physical possession of goods seized	£3.00 per person per day
(2) Where an enforcement officer takes walking possession under a walking possession agreement in the form set out in Schedule 4 to these Regulations	£0.25 per day
(Fees 5(1) and 5(2) are payable in respect of the day on which execution is levied, but fee 5(1) may not be charged where a walking possession agreement is signed at the time of levy. Fees 5(1) and 5(2) may not be charged after the goods have been removed.)	

(3) For—
 	
     (a) the removal of goods;
 	
     (b) the storage of goods which have been removed; and
 	
     (c) where animals have been seized, their upkeep while in the custody of the enforcement officer, whether before or after removal	

	the sums actually and reasonably paid
6. Sale of goods by auction	
(1) To cover the auctioneer's commission and expenses, where goods are sold by auction or work has been done with a view to sale by auction: (a) when goods are sold by auction on the auctioneer's premises, the following percentages of the sum realised—	
(i) on the first £100	15 per cent
(ii) on the next £900	12.5 per cent
(iii) above £1,000	10 per cent
(b) when goods are sold by auction on the debtor's premises, 7.5 per cent of the sum realised plus expenses actually and reasonably incurred.	

(2) When no sale takes place either by auction or private contract, but work has been done by the auctioneer or enforcement officer in preparing for a sale by auction, including the preparation of a detailed inventory of the goods seized—
 	
     (a) if the goods have been removed to the auctioneer's premises, 10 per cent of the value of the goods;
 	
     (b) if the goods have not been removed from the debtor's premises, 5 per cent of the value of the goods plus expenses actually and reasonably incurred.	

7. Sale of goods by private contract	
Where an enforcement officer sells goods by private contract—	

(a) the following percentages of the proceeds of sale—	
(i) on the first £100	7.5 per cent
(ii) on the next £900	6.25 per cent
(iii) above £1,000	5 per cent; and
(b) when work has been done in preparing for a sale by auction, including the preparation of a detailed inventory of the goods seized, an additional sum not exceeding 2.5 per cent of the value of the goods plus expenses actually and reasonably incurred.	
B. Fees chargeable on executing writs of possession or delivery	
8. Mileage	
Mileage from the enforcement officer's business address to the place of execution and return, in respect of one journey	29.2 pence per mile, up to a maximum of £25.00 in total
9. Writs of possession	
(1) Where an enforcement officer executes a writ of possession of domestic property within the meaning of section 66 of the Local Government Finance Act 1988, 3 per cent of the net annual value for rating shown in the valuation list in force immediately before 1st April 1990 in respect of the property seized, subject to paragraph (3).	
(2) Where an enforcement officer executes a writ of possession to which paragraph (1) does not apply, 0.4 per cent of the net annual value for rating of the property seized, subject to paragraph (4).	
(3) For the purposes of paragraph (1), where the property does not consist of one or more hereditament which, immediately before 1st April 1990—	
(a) had a separate net annual value for rating shown on the valuation list then in force; and	
(b) was domestic property within the meaning of section 66 of the Local Government Finance Act 1988,	
the property or such part of it as does not so consist shall be taken to have had such a value for rating equal to two-fifteenths of its value by the year when seized.	
(4) For the purposes of paragraph (2), where the property does not consist of one or more hereditaments having a separate net annual value for rating, the property or such part of it as does not so consist shall be taken to have such a value equal to its value by the year when seized.	
10. Writs of delivery	
For executing a writ of delivery, 4 per cent of the value of the goods as stated in the writ or judgment.	
C. General fees	
11. Copies of returns	
For a copy of any return indorsed by the enforcement officer on a writ of execution	£5.00
12. Miscellaneous	
For any matter not otherwise provided for, such sum as a Master, district judge or costs judge may allow upon application.	

REGULATION 15   **SCHEDULE 4**

WALKING POSSESSION AGREEMENT

In the High Court of Justice

..........Division

..........District Registry

High Court Claim number ....

[County Court Claim number ....]

9B–466

[Sent from the .... County Court by Certificate dated ....]

Claimant ....

Defendant ....

To .... an enforcement officer authorised to execute writs of execution issued from the High Court

I request that you will not leave a possession man on my premises in close possession of the goods which you have seized under the writ of execution issued in this claim.

If this request is allowed to me, I undertake, pending withdrawal or satisfaction of the writ—

(a) not to remove the goods or any part of them nor to permit their removal by any person not authorised by you;

(b) to inform any person who may visit my premises for the purpose of levying any other execution or distress that you are already in possession of my goods under the writ;

(c) to notify you immediately of any such visit.

AND I authorise you or a person acting on your behalf, pending the withdrawal or satisfaction of the writ, to re-enter my premises at any time and as often as you may consider necessary for the purpose of inspecting the goods or completing the execution of the writ.

Dated this .... day of .... 20 ....

Signed .... Judgment Debtor

THE PROCEEDS OF CRIME ACT 2002 (LEGAL EXPENSES IN CIVIL RECOVERY PROCEEDINGS) REGULATIONS 2005

The Proceeds of Crime Act 2002 (Legal Expenses in Civil Recovery Proceedings) Regulations 2005

S.I. 2005 No. 3382

PART 1

INTRODUCTION

Citation and commencement

9B–467   **1.** These Regulations may be cited as the Proceeds of Crime Act 2002 (Legal Expenses in Civil Recovery Proceedings) Regulations 2005 and shall come into force on 1st January 2006.

Interpretation

9B–468   **2.**—(1) In these Regulations—

"the 1990 Act" means the Courts and Legal Services Act 1990;

"the 2002 Act" means the Proceeds of Crime Act 2002;

"CPR" means the Civil Procedure Rules 1998;

"the Order in Council" means the Proceeds of Crime Act 2002 (External Requests and Orders) Order 2005;

"RSC (NI)" means the Rules of the Supreme Court (Northern Ireland) 1980;

"civil recovery proceedings" means proceedings under Part 5 of the 2002 Act or Part 5 of the Order in Council;

"notice" means notice in writing;

"solicitor" means a solicitor of the Supreme Court and, in relation to England and Wales, includes any other person who is an authorised litigator within the meaning of section 119(1) of the 1990 Act.

(2) Any reference in these Regulations to the assessment of legal expenses by the court shall, in relation to Northern Ireland, be interpreted as referring to the taxation of those expenses by the Master (Taxing Office).

PART 2

REQUIRED CONDITIONS: GENERAL

Effect of this part

3. This Part specifies the required conditions for the purposes of sections 245C(5) and 252(4) of the 2002 Act and articles 149(5) and 157(4) of the Order in Council.

9B–469

Condition relating to work covered by exclusion

4. An exclusion from a property freezing order or interim receiving order must specify—

9B–470

    (a) the stage or stages in civil recovery proceedings to which it relates; and

    (b) the maximum amount which may be released in respect of legal expenses for each stage to which it relates.

Condition relating to notification

5. If the solicitor acting for the person to whose legal expenses the exclusion relates becomes aware that—

9B–471

    (a) that person's legal expenses in respect of any stage in civil recovery proceedings have exceeded or will exceed the maximum amount specified in the exclusion for that stage; or

    (b) that person's total legal expenses in respect of all the stages to which the exclusion relates have exceeded or will exceed the total amount that may be released pursuant to the exclusion,

the solicitor must give notice to the Director and the court as soon as reasonably practicable.

Condition relating to payment of expenses

6. Where a person has incurred legal expenses in relation to a stage in civil recovery proceedings specified in an exclusion—

9B–472

    (a) during any period when the property freezing order or interim receiving order has effect, a sum may only be released in respect of those expenses in accordance with Part 3;

    (b) where the court makes a recovery order which provides for the payment of that person's reasonable legal expenses in respect of civil recovery proceedings, the sum payable in respect of his legal expenses shall be determined in accordance with Part 4, regardless of whether a sum has been released in respect of any of those expenses under Part 3.

PART 3

REQUIRED CONDITIONS: RELEASE OF INTERIM PAYMENTS

Effect of this Part

9B–473   **7.** This Part applies where, during a period when a property freezing order or interim receiving order has effect, a person to whose property the order applies seeks the release of a sum in respect of his legal expenses pursuant to an exclusion from the order.

Request for Director's agreement to release of interim payment

9B–474   **8.**—(1) A request for the Director's agreement to the release of a sum in respect of legal expenses pursuant to an exclusion must be made in writing to the Director by the person to whose expenses the exclusion relates.

(2) The request must—

    (a) describe the stage or stages in the civil recovery proceedings in relation to which the legal expenses were incurred;

    (b) summarise the work done in connection with each stage;

    (c) be accompanied by any invoices, receipts or other documents which are necessary to show that the expenses have been incurred; and

    (d) identify any item or description of property from which the person making the request wishes the sum to be released.

(3) A person may not make a request under this regulation—

    (a) in respect of legal expenses which he has not yet incurred; or

    (b) more than once in any 2 month period.

Director's response to request

9B–475   **9.**—(1) Not later than 21 days after he receives the request, the Director must give notice to the person who made the request stating—

    (a) whether he agrees to the release of the requested sum; and

    (b) if he does not agree to the release of the requested sum—

        (i) the amount (if any) which he agrees may be released; and

        (ii) the reasons for his decision.

(2) Where an interim receiving order applies to the property from which it is proposed that the requested sum should be released, the Director must at the same time send copies of the request and the notice referred to in paragraph (1) to the interim receiver.

(3) In determining the amount which may be released in respect of legal expenses with his agreement, the Director must have regard

2652

to the provisions of Part 5 which would apply on the assessment of those expenses by the court.

Release of interim payment

10.—(1) The sum which may be released pursuant to the exclusion is the greater of—

    (a) the amount which the Director agrees may be released; and

    (b) 65% of the requested sum.

(2) The sum may only be released to—

    (a) the solicitor who is instructed to act in the civil recovery proceedings for the person to whose legal expenses the exclusion relates; or

    (b) where appropriate, to the solicitor who was so instructed when the legal expenses to which the sum relates were incurred.

9B–476

PART 4

AGREEMENT OR ASSESSMENT OF EXPENSES AT CONCLUSION OF CIVIL RECOVERY PROCEEDINGS

Effect of this Part

11. This Part specifies the procedure for determining the amount payable in respect of a person's reasonable legal expenses in civil recovery proceedings, where the court has made a recovery order which provides for the payment of those expenses.

9B–477

Agreement of expenses by the Director

12.—(1) This regulation applies where a person seeks the Director's agreement to the payment of a sum in respect of his legal expenses pursuant to section 266(8B)(a) of the 2002 Act or article 177(11)(a) of the Order in Council.

(2) In determining the amount which may be paid in respect of legal expenses with his agreement, the Director must have regard to the provisions of Part 5 which would apply on the assessment of those expenses by the court.

(3) Where the Director agrees to the payment of the sum which a person seeks in respect of his legal expenses—

    (a) he shall give that person and the trustee for civil recovery notice of the agreed sum; and

    (b) the sum payable in respect of those expenses shall be the agreed sum.

9B–478

Expenses to be assessed if not agreed

13.—(1) Unless the Director agrees to the payment of the sum which a person seeks in respect of his legal expenses pursuant to provision made in a recovery order, that person must commence proceedings for the assessment of those expenses in accordance with paragraph (2).

9B–479

(2) Where paragraph (1) requires a person to commence proceedings for the assessment of his legal expenses—

    (a) in relation to civil recovery proceedings in England and Wales, he must commence proceedings for the detailed assessment of those expenses in accordance with CPR Part 47, subject to the modifications that—

        (i) rule 47.7 shall have effect as if it provided that he must commence those proceedings not later than 2 months after the date of the recovery order; and

        (ii) rule 47.14(2) shall have effect as if it provided that he must file a request for a detailed assessment hearing not later than 2 months after the expiry of the period for commencing the detailed assessment proceedings;

    (b) in relation to civil recovery proceedings in Northern Ireland, he must begin proceedings for the taxation of those expenses in accordance with RSC (NI) Order 62, subject to the modification that rule 29(1) shall have effect as if it provided that he must begin those proceedings not later than 4 months after the date of the recovery order.

(3) The court will assess the person's legal expenses in accordance with the provisions of Part 5 and the relevant rules of court, and the sum payable in respect of those expenses shall be the assessed amount.

Payment of expenses

9B–480   **14.**—(1) Where the sum payable in respect of a person's legal expenses—

    (a) exceeds the total amount which has been released in respect of those expenses in accordance with Part 3, the trustee for civil recovery must pay the balance out of the sums referred to in section 280(1) of the 2002 Act or article 191(1) of the Order in Council;

    (b) is less than the total amount which has been released in respect of those expenses in accordance with Part 3, the person to whose expenses the sum relates must repay the balance to the trustee.

(2) The trustee for civil recovery may only make a payment in respect of a person's legal expenses to—

    (a) the solicitor who is instructed to act for that person; or

    (b) where appropriate, the solicitor who was so instructed when the legal expenses to which the sum relates were incurred.

PART 5

BASIS OF ASSESSMENT OF LEGAL EXPENSES

Effect of this Part

9B–481   **15.** This Part sets out the basis on which the court must assess the amount payable in respect of a person's reasonable legal expenses of civil recovery proceedings pursuant to provision made in a recovery order.

General principles

16.—(1) Subject to regulation 17, the court will assess a person's legal expenses on the standard basis.

9B–482

(2) The court must give effect to—

(a) any provision made in the recovery order for the purpose of enabling the person to meet his reasonable legal expenses of civil recovery proceedings; and

(b) subject to sub-paragraph (a), the terms of any exclusion made for the purpose of enabling that person to meet those legal expenses (including the required conditions).

(3) In paragraph (1), "the standard basis" has the meaning given in—

(a) CPR rule 44.4 in relation to proceedings in England and Wales;

(b) RSC (NI) Order 62 rule 12 in relation to proceedings in Northern Ireland.

Rates of remuneration

17.—(1) Subject to the following paragraphs of this regulation, remuneration for work done by a legal representative may only be allowed at the appropriate hourly rate shown in the Table below.

9B–483

(2) The higher hourly rates specified in the third column of the Table may only be allowed where the case involves substantial novel or complex issues of law or fact.

(3) The rates specified in the Table will be increased by—

(a) 20% for legal representatives whose offices are situated in Central London; and

(b) 10% for legal representatives whose offices are situated in Outer London.

(4) In paragraph (3)—

(a) "Central London" means postcode districts EC1–4, SW1, W1 and WC1–2;

(b) "Outer London" means all other postcode districts in postcode areas BR, CR, DA, E, N, NW, SE, SW, UB and W.

and "postcode area" and "postcode district" shall be construed in accordance with the Postcode Address File within the meaning given in section 116 of the Postal Services Act 2000.

LEGISLATION

TABLE:

TABLE: RATES OF REMUNERATION FOR LEGAL REPRESENTATIVES

Category of fee earner[1]	Standard hourly rate (excluding VAT)	Higher hourly rate (excluding VAT)
Solicitors and their employees		
Senior solicitor (of at least 8 years' standing)	£187.50	£225.00
Solicitor (of at least 4 years' and less than 8 years' standing)	£150.00	£187.50
Junior solicitor (of less than 4 years' standing)	£107.50	£131.25
Trainee solicitor, paralegal or other fee earner	£75.00	£93.75
Counsel		
Queen's Counsel	—	£275.00
Senior junior counsel (of at least 10 years' standing)	£150.00	£225.00
Junior counsel (of less than 10 years' standing)	£100.00	£150.00

[1] In relation to England and Wales, a reference to a number of years' standing as a solicitor or counsel to be interpreted as referring to that number of years' general qualification (within the meaning of section 71 of the 1990 Act).

SECTION 10

COURT FEES

COURT FEES

10 COURT FEES

The Civil Proceedings Fees Order 2004

(S.I. 2004 No. 3121)(L. 23)

The Lord Chancellor, in exercise of the powers conferred upon him by **10–1**
*sections 92 and 108(6) of the Courts Act 2003, sections 414 and 415 of
the Insolvency Act 1986, and section 128 of the Finance Act 1990, with
the consent of the Treasury under section 92(1) of the Courts Act 2003
and after consultation with the Lord Chief Justice, the Master of the Rolls,
the President of the Family Division, the Vice-Chancellor, the Head of
Civil Justice and the Deputy Head of Civil Justice and the Civil Justice
Council under section 92(5) and (6) of the Courts Act 2003 and with the
sanction of the Treasury under sections 414(1) and 415(1) of the
Insolvency Act 1986, hereby makes the following Order:*

Citation, commencement and interpretation

1.—(1) This Order may be cited as the Civil Proceedings Fees Or- **10–2**
der 2004 and shall come into force on the 4th January 2005.

(2) In this Order–

(a) a fee referred to by number means the fee so numbered
in Schedule 1 to this Order;

(b) "CCBC" means County Court Bulk Centre;

(c) "CPC" means Claim Production Centre;

(d) "the CPR" means the Civil Procedure Rules 1998;

(e) expressions also used in the CPR have the same meaning as in those Rules;

(f) "family proceedings" means family proceedings in the
High Court or in a county court as appropriate;

(g) "LSC" means the Legal Services Commission established
under section 1 of the Access to Justice Act 1999[1];

(h) "Funding Code" means the code approved under section 9 of the Access to Justice Act 1999[2];

(i) "GLO" means a Group Litigation Order.

Fees to be taken

2. The fees set out in column 2 of Schedule 1 to this Order shall **10–3**
be taken in the Supreme Court and in county courts respectively in
respect of the items described in column 1 in accordance with and
subject to the directions specified in column 1.

3. The provisions of this Order shall not apply to– **10–4**

(a) non-contentious probate business;

(b) proceedings in the Court of Protection, except in so far
as fees 1, 2, 3, 6, 9 and 10 in Schedule 1 (High Court
only) are applicable;

(c) the enrolment of documents;

---

[1] Section 1 was amended by article 9 of and Schedule 2, paragraph 11(1)(a) to the
Secretary of State for Constitutional Affairs Order 2003 (S.I. 2003 No. 1887).
[2] Section 9 was amended by article 9 of and Schedule 2, paragraph 11(1)(a) to the
Secretary of State for Constitutional Affairs Order 2003 (S.I. 2003 No. 1887).

      (d) criminal proceedings (except proceedings on the Crown side of the Queen's Bench Division to which the fees contained in Schedule 1 are applicable);

      (e) proceedings by sheriffs, under-sheriffs, deputy-sheriffs or other officers of the sheriff; and

      (f) family proceedings.

Exemptions, reductions, remissions and refunds

10–5   **4.**—(1) No fee shall be payable under this Order by a party who, at the time when a fee would otherwise become payable–

      (a) is in receipt of any qualifying benefit, and

      (b) is not in receipt of, as appropriate, either–

          (i) representation under Part IV of the Legal Aid Act 1988[1] for the purposes of the proceedings; or

          (ii) funding provided by the LSC for the purposes of the proceedings and for which a certificate has been issued under the Funding Code certifying a decision to fund services for that party.

  (2) The following are qualifying benefits for the purposes of paragraph (1)(a) above–

      (a) income support under the Social Security Contributions and Benefits Act 1992;

      (b) working tax credit, provided that–

          (i) child tax credit is being paid to the party, or otherwise following a claim for child tax credit made jointly by the members of a couple (as defined in section 3(5A) of the Tax Credits Act 2002(d)) which includes the party; or

          (ii) there is a disability element or severe disability element (or both) to the tax credit received by the party;

   and that the gross annual income taken into account for the calculation of the working tax credit is £14,600 or less;

      (c) income-based jobseeker's allowance under the Jobseekers Act 1995; and

      (d) guarantee credit under the State Pension Credit Act 2002.

  (3) In the county courts paragraph (1) shall not apply to fee 7.8 (fee payable on a consolidated attachment of earnings order or an administration order).

10–6   **5.** Where it appears to the Lord Chancellor that the payment of any fee prescribed by this Order would, owing to the exceptional circumstances of the particular case, involve undue financial hardship, he may reduce or remit the fee in that case.

---

[1] Part IV was repealed by section 106 of and Part 1 of Schedule 15 to the Access to Justice Act 1999 (c. 22), from April 1, 2000 subject to the transitional and savings provisions in article 5 of the Access to Justice Act 1999 (Commencement No. 3, Transitional Provisions and Savings) Order 2000 (S.I. 2000 No. 774), in respect of an application for legal aid signed before April 1, 2000 and received by the Legal Aid Board by the May 2, 2000.

6.—(1) Subject to paragraph (2), where a fee has been paid at a time–   **10–7**

    (a) when, under article 4, it was not payable, the fee shall be refunded;

    (b) where the Lord Chancellor, if he had been aware of all the circumstances, would have reduced the fee under article 5, the amount by which the fee would have been reduced shall be refunded; and

    (c) where the Lord Chancellor, if he had been aware of all the circumstances, would have remitted the fee under article 5, the fee shall be refunded.

(2) No refund shall be made under paragraph (1) unless the party who paid the fee applies within 6 months of paying the fee.

(3) The Lord Chancellor may extend the period of 6 months referred to in paragraph (2) if he considers that there is good reason for an application being made after the end of the period of 6 months.

7. Where by any convention entered into by Her Majesty with any   **10–8** foreign power it is provided that no fee shall be required to be paid in respect of any proceedings, the fees specified in this Order shall not be taken in respect of those proceedings.

Revocations
8. The Orders specified in Schedule 2, in so far as they were   **10–9** made under sections 414 and 415 of the Insolvency Act 1986 and section 128 of the Finance Act 1990, shall be revoked.

The Civil Proceedings Fees (Amendment) Order 2005

(S.I. 2005 No. 3445) (L.31)

The Lord Chancellor, in exercise of the powers conferred upon him by sections 92   **10–9.1** and 108(6) of the Courts Act 2003(a) and sections 414 and 415 of the Insolvency Act 1986(b), makes the following Order.

The Lord Chancellor has obtained the consent of the Treasury in accordance with section 92(1) of the Courts Act 2003, and the sanction of the Treasury in accordance with sections 414(1) and 415(1) of the Insolvency Act 1986, to the making of this Order.

The Lord Chancellor has consulted the Lord Chief Justice, the Master of the Rolls, the President of the Queen's Bench Division, the President of the Family Division, the Chancellor of the High Court, the Head of Civil Justice and Deputy Head of Civil Justice in accordance with section 92(5) of the Courts Act 2003, and the Civil Justice Council in accordance with section 92(6) of that Act.

Citation, commencement and interpretation
1.—(1) This Order may be cited as the Civil Proceedings Fees   **10–9.2** (Amendment) Order 2005 and shall come into force on 10th January 2006.

(2) In this Order "the Order" means the Civil Proceedings Fees Order 2004(c).

Amendments to the Civil Proceedings Fees Order 2004
2. In article 4(2)(b)(i) of the Order, for the words from "married   **10–9.3** couple" to "includes the party" substitute "couple (as defined in section 3(5A) of the Tax Credits Act 2002(d)) which includes the party".

10–9.4 **3.** For Schedule 1 to the Order substitute the Schedule to this Order.

10–10

SCHEDULE 1

FEES TO BE TAKEN

Column 1 Number and description of fee	Column 2 Amount of fee
1. Commencement of proceedings (High Court and county court)	
1.1 On the commencement of originating proceedings in the High Court (including originating proceedings issued after permission to issue is granted) to recover a sum of money where the sum claimed:	
(a) does not exceed £50,000	£400
(b) exceeds £50,000 but does not exceed £100,000 .	£700
(c) exceeds £100,000 but does not exceed £150,000...................................	£900
(d) exceeds £150,000 but does not exceed £200,000....................................	£1,100
(e) exceeds £200,000 but does not exceed £250,000....................................	£1,300
(f) exceeds £250,000 but does not exceed £300,000.	£1,500
(g) exceeds £300,000 or is not limited.............	£1,700
1.2 On the commencement of originating proceedings in the county court (including originating proceedings issued after permission to issue is granted) to recover a sum of money, except in CPC cases brought by Centre users:	
(a) does not exceed £300	£30
(b) exceeds £300 but does not exceed £500........	£50
(c) exceeds £500 but does not exceed £1,000	£80
(d) exceeds £1,000 but does not exceed £5,000	£120
(e) exceeds £5,000 but does not exceed £15,000....	£250
(f) exceeds £15,000 but does not exceed £50,000...	£400
(g) exceeds £50,000 but does not exceed £100,000 .	£700
(h) exceeds £100,000 but does not exceed £150,000....................................	£900
(i) exceeds £150,000 but does not exceed £200,000.	£1,100
(j) exceeds £200,000 but does not exceed £250,000.	£1,300
(k) exceeds £250,000 but does not exceed £300,000....................................	£1,500
(l) exceeds £300,000 or is not limited	£1,700
1.3 On the commencement of originating proceedings in the county court to recover a sum of money in Claim Production Centre cases brought by Centre users, where the sum claimed:	
(a) does not exceed £300	£20
(b) exceeds £300 but does not exceed £500........	£40
(c) exceeds £500 but does not exceed £1,000	£70
(d) exceeds £1,000 but does not exceed £5,000	£110
(e) exceeds £5,000 but does not exceed £15,000....	£240

Column 1 *Number and description of fee*	Column 2 *Amount of fee*
(f) exceeds £15,000 but does not exceed £50,000...	£390
(g) exceeds £50,000 but does not exceed £100,000 .	£690
Fee 1.3 Claims above £99,999.99 cannot be issued through the Claim Production Centre. Parties should issue the claim in the relevant court.	
Fee 1.3 Claims above £99,999.99 cannot be issued through the Claim Production Centre. Parties should issue the claim in the relevant court.	
Fee 1.1, 1.2 and 1.3 Where the claimant is making a claim for interest on a specified sum of money, the sum claimed for the purposes of calculating fees 1.1, 1.2 and 1.3 shall be taken to include the interest in addition to that specified sum.	
1.4 On the commencement of originating proceedings for any other remedy or relief (including originating proceedings issued after leave to issue is granted): — in the High Court — in the county court	 £400 £150
Fees 1.1, 1.2 and 1.4 Recovery of land or goods Where a claim for money is additional or alternative to a claim for recovery of land or goods, only fee 1.4 shall be payable.	
Fees 1.1, 1.2 and 1.4 Claims other than recovery of land or goods Where a claim for money is additional to a non money claim (other than a claim for recovery of land or goods), then fee 1.1 or fee 1.2 as appropriate shall be payable in addition to fee 1.4.	
Where a claim for money is alternative to a non money claim (other than a claim for recovery of land or goods), only fee 1.1 shall be payable in the High Court, and, in the county court, fee 1.2 or fee 1.4 shall be payable, whichever is the greater.	
Fees 1.1 or 1.2 as appropriate and 1.4 — Generally Where more than one non money claim is made in the same proceedings, fee 1.4 shall be payable once only, in addition to any fee which may be payable under fee 1.1 or fee 1.2 as appropriate.	
Fees 1.1 or fee 1.2 as appropriate and fee 1.4 shall not be payable where fee 1.7(b), fee 1.8(a) (in the High Court only), fee 9.1 (in the High Court only) or fee 3 apply.	
Fees 1.1 or 1.2 as appropriate and 1.4 — Amendment of claim or counterclaim Where the claim or counterclaim is amended, and the fee paid before amendment is less than that which would have been payable if the document, as amended, had been so drawn in the first instance, the party amending the document shall pay the difference.	

Column 1 Number and description of fee	Column 2 Amount of fee
1.5 On the filing of proceedings against a party or parties not named in the originating proceedings:	
— in the High Court	£50
— in the county court	£35
Fee 1.5 Fee 1.5 shall be payable by a defendant who adds or substitutes a party or parties to the proceedings or by a claimant who adds or substitutes a defendant or defendants.	
1.6 On the filing of a counterclaim	The same fee as if the relief or remedy sought were the subject of separate proceedings
Fee 1.6 No fee is payable on a counterclaim which a defendant is required to make under the CPR because he contends that he has any claim or is entitled to any remedy relating to a grant of probate of a will, or letters of administration of an estate, of a deceased person.	
1.7 (a) On an application for permission to issue originating proceedings:	
— in the High Court	£50
— in the county court	£35
(b) On an application for an order under Part III of the Solicitors Act 1974 [1] **for the assessment of costs payable to a solicitor by his client or on the commencement of costs-only proceedings**	
— in the High Court	£50
— in the county court	£35
1.8(a) On the commencement of the judicial review procedure (High Court only) Where the court has made an order giving permission to proceed with a claim for judicial review, there shall be payable by the claimant within 7 days of service on the claimant of that order:	£50
1.8(b) if the judicial review procedure has been commenced	£180
1.8(c) if the claim for judicial review was commenced otherwise than by using the judicial review procedure	£50
2. General Fees (High Court and county court)	
2.1 On the claimant filing an allocation questionnaire; or — where the court dispenses with the need for an allocation questionnaire, within 14 days of the date of despatch of the notice of allocation to track; or	

[1] 1974 c.47

Column 1 *Number and description of fee*	Column 2 *Amount of fee*
— where the CPR or a Practice Direction provide for automatic allocation or provide that the rules on allocation shall not apply, within 28 days of the filing of the defence (or the filing of the last defence if there is more than one defendant), or within 28 days of the expiry of the time permitted for filing all defences if sooner:	
— in the High Court	£200
— in the county court	£100
Fee 2.1 Fee 2.1 shall be payable by the claimant except where the action is proceeding on the counterclaim alone, when it shall be payable by the defendant— — on the defendant filing an allocation questionnaire; or — where the court dispenses with the need for an allocation questionnaire, within 14 days of the date of despatch of the notice of allocation to track; or — where the CPR or a Practice Direction provide for automatic allocation or provide that the rules on allocation shall not apply, within 28 days of the filing of the defence to the counterclaim (or the filing of the last defence to the counterclaim if there is more than one party entitled to file a defence to a counterclaim), or within 28 days of the expiry of the time permitted for filing all defences to the counterclaim if sooner	
2.2 On the claimant filing a listing questionnaire; or where the court fixes the trial date or trial week without the need for a listing questionnaire, within 14 days of the date of despatch of the notice (or the date when oral notice is given if no written notice is given) of the trial week or the trial date if no trial week is fixed	
— in the High Court	£600
— in the county court if the case is on the multi-track	£500
— in the county court in any other case	£275
Fee 2.2 Fee 2.2 shall be payable by the claimant except where the action is proceeding on the counterclaim alone, when it shall be payable by the defendant— — on the defendant filing a listing questionnaire; or — where the court fixes the trial date or trial week without the need for a listing questionnaire, within 14 days of the date of despatch of the notice (or the date when oral notice is given if no written notice is given) of the trial week or the trial date if no trial week is fixed. Where the court receives notice in writing– — before the trial date has been fixed or, — where a trial date has been fixed, at least 14 days before the trial date from the party who paid fee 2.2 that the case is settled or discontinued, fee 2.2 shall be refunded.	

Column 1 *Number and description of fee*	Column 2 *Amount of fee*
Fees 2.1 and 2.2 in the High Court and the county court Fees 2.1 and 2.2 shall be payable as appropriate where the court allocates a case to track for a trial of the assessment of damages. Fees 2.1 and 2.2 shall not be payable in relation to claims managed under a GLO after that GLO is made.	
Fees 2.1 and 2.2 shall be payable once only in the same proceedings. Fee 2.1 shall not be payable where the procedure in Part 8 of the CPR is used.	
Fees 2.1 and 2.2 in the county court Fee 2.1 shall not be payable in proceedings where the only claim is a claim to recover a sum of money and the sum claimed does not exceed £1,500. Fee 2.2 shall not be payable in respect of a small claims hearing.	
2.3 In the High Court on filing: — an appellant's notice, or — a respondent's notice where the respondent is appealing or wishes to ask the appeal court to uphold the order of the lower court for reasons different from or additional to those given by the lower court	£200
2.4 In the county court on filing— — an appellant's notice, or —a respondent's notice where the respondent is appealing or wishes to ask the appeal court to uphold the order of the lower court for reasons different from or additional to those given by the lower court	
(a) in a claim allocated to the small claims track	£100
(b) in all other claims	£120
Fee 2.3 and 2.4 Fee 2.3 and 2.4 do not apply on appeals against a decision made in detailed assessment proceedings.	
2.5 On an application on notice where no other fee is specified	
— in the High Court	£100
— in the county court	£65
2.6 **On an application by consent or without notice for a judgment or order** where no other fee is specified	
— in the High Court	£50
— in the county court	£35
For the purpose of fee 2.6 a request for a judgment or order on admission or in default shall not constitute an application and no fee shall be payable.	

Column 1	Column 2
Number and description of fee	Amount of fee
Fee 2.6 shall not be payable in relation to an application by consent for an adjournment of a hearing where the application is received by the court at least 14 days before the date set for that hearing.	
Fees 2.5 and 2.6 Fees 2.5 and 2.6 shall not be payable when an application is made in an appeal notice or is filed at the same time as an appeal notice.	
2.7 On an application for a summons or order for a witness to attend court to be examined on oath or an order for evidence to be taken by deposition, other than an application for which fee 6.2 or 7.3 is payable	
— in the High Court	£50
— in the county court	£35
2.8 On an application to vary a judgment or suspend enforcement (where more than one remedy is sought in the same application only one fee shall be payable)	
— in the High Court	£50
— in the county court	£35
3. Companies Act 1985 [1] and Insolvency Act 1986 [2] (High Court and county court)	
3.1 On entering a bankruptcy petition:	
(a) if presented by a debtor or the personal representative of a deceased debtor	£150
(b) if presented by a creditor or other person	£190
3.2 On entering a petition for an administration order	£150
3.3 On entering any other petition One fee only is payable where more than one petition is presented in relation to a partnership.	£190
3.4(a) On a request for a certificate of discharge from bankruptcy	£60
(b) and after the first certificate for each copy	£1
3.5 On an application under the Companies Act 1985 or the Insolvency Act 1986 other than one brought by petition and where no other fee is specified.	£130
Fee 3.5 Fee 3.5 is not payable where the application is made in existing proceedings.	
3.6 On an application for the conversion of a voluntary arrangement into a winding up or bankruptcy under Article 37 of Council Regulation (EC) No 1346/2000.	£130

[1] 1985 c.6
[2] 1986 c.45

Column 1 Number and description of fee	Column 2 Amount of fee
3.7 On an application, for the purposes of Council Regulation (EC) No 1346/2000, for an order confirming creditors' voluntary winding up (where the company has passed a resolution for voluntary winding up, and no declaration under section 89 of the Insolvency Act 1986 has been made).	£30
3.8 On filing — a notice of intention to appoint an administrator under paragraph 14 of Schedule B1 to the Insolvency Act 1986 or in accordance with paragraph 27 of that Schedule; or — a notice of appointment of an administrator in accordance with paragraphs 18 or 29 of that Schedule.	£30
Fee 3.8 Where a person pays fee 3.8 on filing a notice of intention to appoint an administrator, no fee shall be payable on that same person filing a notice of appointment of that administrator.	
3.9 On submitting a nominee's report under section 2(2) of the Insolvency Act 1986	£30
3.10 On filing documents in accordance with paragraph 7 (1) of Schedule A1 to the Insolvency Act 1986	£30
3.11 On an application by consent or without notice within existing proceedings where no other fee is specified	£30
3.12 On an application with notice within existing proceedings where no other fee is specified	£60
Requests and applications with no fee: No fee is payable on a request or on an application to the Court by the Official Receiver when applying only in the capacity of Official Receiver to the case (and not as trustee or liquidator), or on an application to set aside a statutory demand.	
4. Copy Documents (Court of Appeal, High Court and county court)	
4.1 On a request for a copy of any document (other than where fee 4.2 applies): (a) for the first page (except the first page of a subsequent copy of the same document supplied at the same time)	£1
(b) per page in any other case	20p
Fee 4.1 Fee 4.1 shall be payable for a faxed copy or for examining a plain copy and marking it as an examined copy. Fee 4.1 shall be payable whether or not the copy is issued as an office copy.	
4.2 On a request for a copy of a document required in connection with proceedings and supplied by the party making the request at the time of copying, for each page.	20p

Column 1	Column 2
Number and description of fee	Amount of fee
4.3 On a request for a copy of a document on a computer disk or in other electronic form, for each such copy.	£3
5 Determination of costs (Supreme Court and county court)	
5.1 On the filing of a request for detailed assessment where the party filing the request is legally aided or is funded by the LSC and no other party is ordered to pay the costs of the proceedings	
— in the Supreme Court	£120
— in the county court	£105
5.2 On the filing of a request for a detailed assessment hearing in any case where fee 5.1 does not apply; or on the filing of a request for a hearing date for the assessment of costs payable to a solicitor by his client pursuant to an order under Part III of the Solicitors Act 1974	
— in the Supreme Court	£600
— in the county court	£300
Where there is a combined party and party and legal aid, or a combined party and party and LSC, or a combined party and party, legal aid and LSC determination of costs, fee 5.2 shall be attributed proportionately to the party and party, legal aid, or LSC (as the case may be) portions of the bill on the basis of the amount allowed.	
5.3 On a request for the issue of a default costs certificate	
— in the Supreme Court	£50
— in the county court	£45
5.4 On an appeal against a decision made in detailed assessment proceedings	
— in the Supreme Court	£200
— in the county court	£105
5.5 On applying for the court's approval of a certificate of costs payable from the Community Legal Service Fund.	
— in the Supreme Court	£50
— in the county court	£35
Fee 5.5	
Fee 5.5 is payable at the time of applying for the court's approval and is recoverable only against the Community Legal Service Fund.	
5.6 On a request or application to set aside a default costs certificate	
— in the Supreme Court	£100
— in the county court	£65
6. Enforcement in the High Court	
6.1 On sealing a writ of execution/possession/ delivery	£50
Where the recovery of a sum of money is sought in addition to a writ of possession and delivery, no further fee is payable.	

Column 1 Number and description of fee	Column 2 Amount of fee
6.2 On an application for an order requiring a judgment debtor or other person to attend court to provide information in connection with enforcement of a judgment or order.	£50
6.3(a) On an application for a third party debt order or the appointment of a receiver by way of equitable execution	£100
6.3(b) On an application for a charging order	£100
Fee 6.3(a) and (b) Fee 6.3(a) shall be payable in respect of each third party against whom the order is sought. Fee 6.3(b) shall be payable in respect of each application issued.	
6.4 On an application for a judgment summons	£100
6.5 On a request or application to register a judgment or order, or for permission to enforce an arbitration award, or for a certificate or a certified copy of a judgment or order for use abroad	£50
7. Enforcement in the county court **7.1 On an application for or in relation to enforcement of a judgment or order of a county court or through a county court:** In cases other than CCBC cases brought by Centre users, by the issue of a warrant of execution against goods except a warrant to enforce payment of a fine;	
(a) Where the amount for which the warrant issues does not exceed £125	£35
(b) Where the amount for which the warrant issues exceeds £125 In CCBC cases brought by Centre users, by the issue of a warrant of execution against goods except a warrant to enforce payment of a fine	£55
(c) Where the amount for which the warrant issues does not exceed £125	£25
(d) Where the amount for which the warrant issues exceeds £125	£45
7.2 On a request for a further attempt at execution of a warrant at a new address following a notice of the reason for non-execution (except a further attempt following suspension and CCBC cases brought by Centre users)	£25
7.3 On an application for an order requiring a judgment debtor or other person to attend court to provide information in connection with enforcement of a judgment or order	£45
7.4(a) On an application for a third party debt order or the appointment of a receiver by way of equitable execution	£55
(b) On an application for a charging order	£55
Fee 7.4(a) and (b) Fee 7.4(a) shall be payable in respect of each third party against whom the order is sought.	

Column 1	Column 2
Number and description of fee	*Amount of fee*
Fee 7.4(b) shall be payable in respect of each application issued.	
7.5 On an application for a judgment summons	£95
7.6 On the issue of a warrant of possession or a warrant of delivery	£95
Where the recovery of a sum of money is sought in addition, no further fee is payable.	
7.7 On an application for an attachment of earnings order (other than a consolidated attachment of earnings order) to secure payment of a judgment debt	£65
Fee 7.7 Fee 7.7 is payable for each defendant against whom an order is sought. Fee 7.7 is not payable where the attachment of earnings order is made on the hearing of a judgment summons.	
7.8 On a consolidated attachment of earnings order or on an administration order	For every £1 or part of a £1 of the money paid into court in respect of debts due to creditors........10p
Fee 7.8 Fee 7.8 shall be calculated on any money paid into court under any order at the rate in force at the time when the order was made (or, where the order has been amended, at the time of the last amendment before the date of payment).	
7.9 On the application for the recovery of a tribunal award	£35
7.10 On a request for an order to recover a sum that is: — a specified debt within the meaning of the Enforcement of Road Traffic Debts Order 1993 [1] as amended from time to time; or — pursuant to an enactment, treated as a specified debt for the purposes of that Order No fee is payable on: — an application for an extension of time to serve a statutory declaration in connection with any such order; or — a request to issue a warrant of execution to enforce any such order	£5
8 Sale (county court only)	
8.1 For removing or taking steps to remove goods to a place of deposit	The reasonable expenses incurred
Fee 8.1 is to include the reasonable expenses of feeding and caring for any animals.	
8.2 For advertising a sale by public auction pursuant to section 97 of the County Courts Act 1984 [2]	The reasonable expenses incurred
8.3 For the appraisement of goods	5p in the £1 or part of a £1 of the appraised value

[1] S.I. 1993/2073
[2] 1984 c.28

Column 1 *Number and description of fee*	Column 2 *Amount of fee*
8.4 For the sale of goods (including advertisements, catalogues, sale and commission and delivery of goods)	15p in the £1 or part of a £1 on the amount realised by the sale or such other sum as the district judge may consider to be justified in the circumstances
8.5 Where no sale takes place by reason of an execution being withdrawn, satisfied or stopped	(a) 10p in the £1 or part of a £1 on the value of the goods seized, the value to be the appraised value where the goods have been appraised or such other sum as the district judge may consider to be justified in the circumstances; and in addition (b) any sum payable under fee 8.1, 8.2 or 8.3
FEES PAYABLE IN HIGH COURT ONLY	
9. Miscellaneous proceedings or matters (High Court only)	
Bills of Sale **On filing any document under the Bills of Sale Acts 1878** [1] **and the Bills of Sale Act (1878) Amendment Act 1882** [2] **or on an application under section 15 of the Bills of Sale Act 1878 for an order that a memorandum of satisfaction be written on a registered copy of the bill**	£10
Searches **9.2 For an official certificate** of the result of a search for each name, in any register or index held by the court; or in the Court Funds Office, for an official certificate of the result of a search of unclaimed balances for a specified period of up to 50 years	£5
9.3 On a search in person of the bankruptcy and companies records, including inspection, for each 15 minutes or part of 15 minutes	£5
Judge sitting as arbitrator **9.4 On the appointment of—**	
(a) a judge of the Commercial Court as an arbitrator or umpire under section 93 of the Arbitration Act 1996 [2]; or	£1,800
(b) a judge of the Technology and Construction Court as an arbitrator or umpire under section 93 of the Arbitration Act 1996	£1,400
9.5 For every day or part of a day (after the first day) of the hearing before—	

[1] 1878 c. 31, section 15 was repealed, in relation to bills of sale given as security for payment of money in so far as inconsistent with the Bills of Sale Act (1978) Amendment Act 1882, by sections 3 and 15 of that Act.

[2] 1882 c.43

[2] 1996 c.23

Column 1 Number and description of fee	Column 2 Amount of fee
(a) a judge of the Commercial Court; or	£1,800
(b) a judge of the Technology and Construction Court, so appointed as arbitrator or umpire	£1,400
Where fee 9.4 has been paid on the appointment of a judge of the Commercial Court or a judge of the Technology and Construction Court as an arbitrator or umpire but the arbitration does not proceed to a hearing or an award, the fee shall be refunded.	
10. Fees payable in Admiralty Matters (High Court only) **In the Admiralty Registrar and Marshal's Office—**	
10.1 On the issue of a warrant for the arrest of a ship or goods	£100
10.2 On the sale of a ship or goods— Subject to a minimum fee of £200,	
(a) for every £100 or fraction of £100 of the price up to £100,000	£1
(b) for every £100 or fraction of £100 of the price exceeding £100,000	50p
Where there is sufficient proceeds of sale in court, fee 10.2 shall be taken by transfer from the proceeds of sale in court.	
10.3 On entering a reference for hearing by the Registrar	£50
FEES PAYBLE IN HIGH COURT AND COURT OF APPEAL ONLY **11. Affidavits** **11.1 On taking an affidavit or an affirmation or attestation** upon honour in lieu of an affidavit or a declaration except for the purpose of receipt of dividends from the Accountant General and for a declaration by a shorthand writer appointed in insolvency proceedings — for each person making any of the above	£5
11.2 For each exhibit referred to in an affidavit, affirmation, attestation or declaration for which fee 11.1 is payable	£2
FEES PAYABLE IN COURT OF APPEAL ONLY **12 Fees payable in appeals to the Court of Appeal** **12.1(a) Where in an appeal notice** permission to appeal or an extension of time for appealing is applied for (or both are applied for)— – on filing an appellant's notice, or – where the respondent is appealing, on filing a respondent's notice	£200
12.1(b) Where permission to appeal is not required or has been granted by the lower court— on filing an appellant's notice, or	£400

Column 1	Column 2
Number and description of fee	Amount of fee
on filing a respondent's notice where the respondent is appealing	
12.1(c) On the appellant filing an appeal questionnaire (unless the appellant has paid fee 12.1(b), or on the respondent filing an appeal questionnaire (unless the respondent has paid fee 12.1(b))	£400
12.2 On filing a respondent's notice where the respondent wishes to ask the appeal court to uphold the order of the lower court for reasons different from or additional to those given by the lower court	£200
12.3 On filing an application notice	£200
Fee 12.3 Fee 12.3 shall not be payable for an application made in an appeal notice.	
FEES PAYABLE IN COUNTY COURT ONLY **13 Registry of County Court Judgments** **13.1 On a request for the issue of a certificate of satisfaction**	£15

ARTICLE 8   **SCHEDULE 2**

ORDERS REVOKED

10–11

Title	Reference
The Supreme Court Fees Order 1999	S.I. 1999/687
The Supreme Court Fees (Amendment) Order 1999	S.I. 1999/2569
The Supreme Court Fees (Amendment) Order 2000	S.I. 2000/641
The Supreme Court Fees (Amendment) Order 2003	S.I. 2003/646
The Supreme Court Fees (Amendment) Order 2004	S.I. 2004/2100
The Supreme Court Fees (Amendment No. 2) Order 2000	S.I. 2000/937
The Supreme Court Fees (Amendment No. 2) Order 2003	S.I. 2003/717
The County Court Fees Order 1999	S.I. 1999/689
The County Court Fees (Amendment) Order 1999	S.I. 1999/2548
The County Court Fees (Amendment) Order 2000	S.I. 2000/639
The County Court Fees (Amendment) Order 2003	S.I. 2003/648
The County Court Fees (Amendment) Order 2004	S.I. 2004/2098
The County Court Fees (Amendment No. 2) Order 2000	S.I. 2000/939
The County Court Fees (Amendment No. 2) Order 2003	S.I. 2003/718
The County Court Fees (Amendment No. 4) Order 2000	S.I. 2000/2310

The Non-Contentious Probate Fees Order 2004

(S.I. 2004 No. 3120)(L. 22)

Note —This Order replaces the Non–Contentious Probate Fees (Amendment) Order **10–12**
2000 (S.I. 2000 No. 642) insofar as it was made under s.128 of the Finance Act 1990.

Citation, commencement and interpretation

1.—(1) This Order may be cited as the Non-Contentious Probate **10–13**
Fees Order 2004 and shall come into force on the 4th January
2005.

(2) In this Order–

    (a) a fee referred to by number means the fee so numbered
in Schedule 1 to this Order;

    (b) "assessed value" means the value of the net real and
personal estate (excluding settled land if any) passing
under the grant as shown–

      (i) in the Inland Revenue affidavit (for a death occurring
before 13th March 1975), or

      (ii) in the Inland Revenue account (for a death occurring
on or after 13th March 1975), or

      (iii) in the case in which, in accordance with arrangements
made between the President of the Family Division and
the Commissioners of the Inland Revenue, or regulations
made under section 256(1)(a) of the Inheritance Tax Act
1984 and from time to time in force, no such affidavit or
account is required to be delivered, in the oath which is
sworn to lead to the grant, and in the case of an application to reseal means the value, as shown, passing under
the grant upon its being resealed;

    (c) "authorised place of deposit" means any place in which,
by virtue of a direction given under section 124 of the
Supreme Court Act 1981 original wills and other documents under the control of the High Court (either in the
principal registry or in any district registry) are deposited
and preserved;

    (d) "grant" means a grant of probate or letters of administra-
tion;

    (e) "district registry" includes the probate registry of Wales,
any district probate registry and any sub-registry attached to it;

    (f) "the principal registry" means the Principal Registry of
the Family Division and any sub-registry attached to it.

Fees to be taken

2. The fees set out in column 2 of Schedule 1 to this Order shall **10–14**
be taken in the principal registry and in each district registry in respect of the items described in column 1 in accordance with and
subject to any directions specified in column 1.

COURT FEES

10–15   **3.** In determining the value of any personal estate for the purposes of this Order there shall be excluded the value of a death gratuity payable under section 17(2) of the Judicial Pensions Act 1981 or section 4(3) of the Judicial Pensions and Retirement Act 1993, or payable to the personal representatives of a deceased civil servant by virtue of a scheme made under section 1 of the Superannuation Act 1972.

Exemptions, reductions, remissions and refunds
10–16   **4.** Where it appears to the Lord Chancellor that the payment of any fee prescribed by this Order would, owing to the exceptional circumstances of the particular case, involve undue financial hardship, he may reduce or remit the fee in that case.

10–17   **5.**—(1) Subject to paragraph (2) where a fee has been paid at a time–

(a) where the Lord Chancellor, if he had been aware of all the circumstances, would have reduced the fee under article 4, the amount by which the fee would have been reduced shall be refunded; and

(b) where the Lord Chancellor, if he had been aware of all the circumstances, would have remitted the fee under article 4, the fee shall be refunded.

(2) No refund shall be made under paragraph (1) unless the party who paid the fee applies within 6 months of paying the fee.

(3) The Lord Chancellor may extend the period of 6 months referred to in paragraph (2) if he considers that there is good reason for an application being made after the end of the period of 6 months.

10–18   **6.**—(1) Where by any convention entered into by Her Majesty with any foreign power it is provided that no fee shall be required to be paid in respect of any proceedings, the fees specified in this Order shall not be taken in respect of those proceedings.

(2) Where any application for a grant is withdrawn before the issue of a grant, a registrar may reduce or remit a fee.

(3) Fee 7 shall not be taken where a search is made for research or similar purposes by permission of the President of the Family Division for a document over 100 years old filed in the principal registry or a district registry or another authorised place of deposit.

Special exemption–Armed Forces
10–19   **7.** Where a fee has been paid or fees have been paid for the application of a grant (other than fee 3.2) and at the time of payment of that fee or those fees–

(a) the application for the grant was in respect of an estate exempt from Inheritance Tax by virtue of section 154 of the Inheritance Tax Act 1984 (exemption for members of the armed forces etc); and

(b) was in respect of a death occurring before 20th March 2003;

the Lord Chancellor shall upon receiving a written application refund the difference between any fee or fees paid and fee 3.2.

8. The Order specified in Schedule 2 in so far as it was made under section 128 of the Finance Act 1990 shall be revoked.

10–20

ARTICLE 2   SCHEDULE 1

FEES TO BE TAKEN

10–21

Column 1 Number and description of fee	Column 2 Amount of fee
1. Application for a grant On an application for a grant (or for resealing a grant) other than on an application to which fee 3 applies, where the assessed value of the estate exceeds £5,000	£40
2. Personal application fee Where the application under fee 1 is made by a personal applicant (not being an application to which fee 3 applies) fee 2 is payable in addition to fee 1, where the assessed value of the estate exceeds £5,000	£50
3. Special applications **3.1** For a duplicate or second or subsequent grant (including one following a revoked grant) in respect of the same deceased person, other than a grant preceded only by a grant limited to settled land, to trust property, or to part of the estate	£15
3.2 On an application for a grant relating to a death occurring on or after 20th March 2003 and in respect of an estate exempt from inheritance tax by virtue of section 154 of the Inheritance Tax Act 1984 (exemption for members of the armed forces etc)	£8
4. Caveats For the entry or the extension of a caveat	£15
5. Search On an application for a standing search to be carried out in an estate, for each period of six months including the issue of a copy grant and will, if any (irrespective of the number of pages)	£5
6. Deposit of wills On depositing a will for safe custody in the principal registry or a district registry	£15
7. Inspection On inspection of any will or other document retained by the registry (in the presence of an officer of the registry)	£15

10-21

Column 1 Number and description of fee	Column 2 Amount of fee
8. Copy documents On a request for a copy of any document whether or not provided as a certified copy:	
(a) for the first copy	£5
(b) for every subsequent copy of the same document if supplied at the same time	£1
(c) where copies of any document are made available on a computer disk or in other electronic form, for each such copy	£3
(d) where a search of the index is required, in addition to fee 8(a), (b) or (c) as appropriate, for each period of 4 years searched after the first 4 years	£3
9. Oaths Except on a personal application for a grant, for administering an oath,	
9.1 for each deponent to each affidavit	£5
9.2 for marking each exhibit	£2
10. Determination of costs For determining costs	The same fees as are payable from time to time for determining costs under the Civil Proceedings Fees Order 2004, (the relevant fees are set out in fee 5 in Schedule 1 to that Order)
11. Settling documents For perusing and settling citations, advertisements, oaths, affidavits, or other documents, for each document settled	£10

ARTICLE 8   SCHEDULE 2

ORDER REVOKED

10-22

Title	Reference
The Non-Contentious Probate Fees (Amendment) Order 2000	S.I. 2000/642

The Enrolment Of Deeds (Fees) Regulations 1994

(S.I. 1994 No. 601)(L.2)

The Lord Chancellor, in exercise of the powers conferred on him by section 133(4) of the Supreme Court Act 1981, with the concurrence of the Master of the Rolls and the Treasury, hereby makes the following Regulations:

10-23   **1.** These Regulations may be cited as the Enrolment of Deeds (Fees) Regulations 1994 and shall come into force on 1st April 1994.

2. These Regulations provide for the fees to be taken on or in connection with the enrolment of any deed in the Central Office (Enrolment Department) of the Supreme Court.

3. The fees set out in column 2 of the Schedule to these Regulations shall be taken in the circumstances described in column 1 of that Schedule.

4. These Regulations do not apply to deeds filed in the Queen's Remembrancer's Department.

5. In these Regulations the expression "deed" includes an assurance or other instrument or document.

6. Where the enrolment of a deed poll (within the meaning of the Enrolment of Deeds (Change of Name) Regulations 1994) is to be advertised in the London Gazette in accordance with those Regulations, the cost of the advertisement shall be borne by the person seeking to enrol the deed poll and shall be paid by him at the time when the deed poll is enrolled to the clerk in charge of the Filing and Record Department of the Central Office of the Supreme Court.

7. The Enrolment of Deeds (Fees) Regulations 1992 and the Enrolment of Deeds (Fees) (Amendment) Regulations 1951 are hereby revoked except in respect of any fee due before the Regulations come into force.

REGULATION 3   SCHEDULE

10–24

Column 1	Column 2
	£ p
1. For enrolling any deed.	10.00
2. For making and examining a photographic or other copy of any enrolled deed whether or not issued as an office copy.	0.25
3. Searches by applicant in person.	1.00
Searches by staff on behalf of applicant.	5.00

The Insolvency Fees Order 1986

(S.I. 1986 No. 2030)

[Repealed with savings by S.I. 2004 No.593—Sch.1 of that Order states:—   10–25

The whole Order is revoked except in relation to any case where a winding-up or bankruptcy order is made under the Act before the commencement date but in such a case the Order shall continue to have effect with the deletion of all the entries in the Schedule to the Order except, in relation to a winding up by the court, that relating to Fee 10 in Part 1 of the Schedule and, in relation to a bankruptcy, that relating to Fee 13 in Part 2 of the Schedule.]

[As amended by the Insolvency Fees (Amendment) Orders 1988, 1990, 1991, 1992 and 1994 (S.I. 1988 No. 95; S.I. 1990 No. 560; S.I. 1991 No. 496; S.I. 1992 No. 34; and S.I. 1994 No. 2541)].

The Lord Chancellor, in exercise of the powers conferred on him by s.133 of the Bankruptcy   10–26 *Act 1914, ss.414 and 415 of the Insolvency Act 1986 and s.2 of the Public Offices Fees Act 1879, and with the sanction of the Treasury, hereby makes the following Order:*

Citation, Commencement and Application

1.—(1) *This Order may be cited as the Insolvency Fees Order 1986 and*   10–27 *shall come into force on 29th December 1986.*

(2) *This Order applies to proceedings under the Insolvency Act 1986 and the Insolvency Rules 1986 where—*

      (a) *in the case of bankruptcy proceedings, the petition was presented on or after the day on which this Order comes into force, and*

(b) *in the case of any other proceedings, those proceedings commenced on or after that day.*

(3) *This Order extends to England and Wales only.*

Interpretation

10-28   2. *In this Order, unless the context otherwise requires—*

(a) *"the Act" means the Insolvency Act 1986 (any reference to a numbered section being to a section of that Act);*

(b) *"the Rules" means the Insolvency Rules 1986 (any reference to a numbered rule being to a rule so numbered in the Rules);*

(c) *"the Regulations" means the Insolvency Regulations 1994 (any reference to a numbered regulation being to a regulation so numbered in the Regulations).*

Fees payable in company and individual insolvency proceedings

10-29   3. *The fees to be charged in respect of proceedings under Parts I to VII of the Act (Company Insolvency; Companies Winding Up), and the performance by the official receiver or Secretary of State of functions under those Parts, shall be those set out in Part I of the Schedule to this Order.*

4. *Subject to article 4A below, the fees to be charged in respect of proceedings under Parts VIII to XI of the Act (Insolvency of Individuals; Bankruptcy) and the performance by the official receiver or Secretary of State of functions under those Parts, shall be those set out in Part II of the Schedule to this Order.*

Limits on certain fees

10-30   **4A.**—(1) *Fee No. 5 listed in Part II of the Schedule to this Order shall not exceed the sum which is arrived at by applying the scale by which that fee is calculated to such part of the payments made by the official receiver into the Insolvency Services Account as a result of the performance of his functions as receiver and manager under section 287 as is required to pay the maximum amount.*

(2) *Fee No. 13 listed in Part II of the Schedule to this Order shall not exceed the sum which is arrived at by applying the scale by which that fee is calculated to such part of the amounts paid into the Insolvency Services Account by trustees under regulation 20 and by the official receiver as receiver and manager under section 287 as is required to pay the maximum amount.*

(3) *In paragraphs (1) and (2) above, "the maximum amount" means the total sum of—*

(a) *the bankruptcy debts to the extent required to be paid by the Rules (ignoring those debts paid otherwise than out of the proceeds of the realisation of the bankrupt's assets or which have been secured to the satisfaction of the court);*

(b) *the expenses of the bankruptcy other than:*

(i) *fees or the remuneration of the official receiver;*

(ii) *for the purposes of paragraph (1) above, any sums spent in carrying on the business of the debtor;*

(iii) *for the purposes of paragraph (2) above, any sums spent out of money received in carrying on the business of the debtor;*

(c) *fees payable under this Order other than Fee No. 5 and Fee No. 13 in Part II of the Schedule to this Order; and*

      (d) *the remuneration of the official receiver, other than remuneration calculated pursuant to regulation 33 by reference to the realisation scale in Table 1 of Schedule 2 to the Regulations.*

    (4) *For the purposes of this article—*

      (a) *the expression "bankruptcy debts" shall include any interest payable by virtue of section 328(4); and*

      (b) *the expression "the expenses of the bankruptcy" shall have the meaning which it bears in the Rules.*

  5.—(1) *All fees shall be taken in cash.*

    (2) *When a fee is paid to an officer of a court the person paying the fee shall inform the officer whether the fee relates to a company insolvency proceeding or an individual insolvency proceeding.*

  6. *Where Value Added Tax is chargeable in respect of the provision of a service for which a fee is prescribed in the Schedule, there shall be payable in addition to that fee the amount of the Value Added Tax.*

Deposits on presentation of bankruptcy or winding-up petition

  7. *The following 5 Articles apply where it is intended to present to the court* **10–31** *a winding-up or bankruptcy petition under the Act.*

  8.—(1) *Before a winding-up or bankruptcy petition can be presented the appropriate deposit (as specified in Article 9 below) must be paid to the court in which the petition is to be presented.*

    (2) *That deposit is security—*

      (a) *for Fee No. 1 listed in Part I of the Schedule to this Order or Fee No. 2 listed in Part II of that Schedule, as the case may be (each such fee being referred to in this Order as "the administration fee"), or*

      (b) *where an insolvency practitioner is appointed under section 273, for the payment of his fee under Article 12 below.*

  9. *The appropriate deposit referred to in Article 8 is—*

      (a) *in relation to a winding-up petition to be presented under the Act, £500;*

      (b) *in relation to a bankruptcy petition to be presented under section 264(1)(b), £250;*

      (c) *in relation to a bankruptcy petition to be presented under section 264(1)(a), (c) or (d), £300.*

  10. *The court shall (except in a case falling within Article 12 below) transmit the deposit paid to the official receiver attached to the court.*

  11.—(1) *In the circumstances specified in this Article a deposit made under Article 8 above is to be repaid to the person who made it.*

    (2) *Where a winding-up or bankruptcy petition under the Act is dismissed or withdrawn the deposit shall be repaid in full, unless—*

      (a) *a winding-up or bankruptcy order has been made, or*

      (b) *a fee has become payable to an insolvency practitioner under Article 12 below.*

    (3) *If the assets of the company being would up are, or (as the case may be) the bankrupt's estate is, sufficient to pay the whole or part of the relevant administration fee, then the deposit shall be repaid to the extent that it is not required for payment of that fee.*

(4) *Where a winding-up or bankruptcy order is annulled, rescinded or recalled, the deposit shall be repaid to the extent that it is not required for payment of the relevant administration fee, unless a fee has become payable to an insolvency practitioner under Article 12 below.*

Fees payable to insolvency practitioner appointed under section 273

10–32   **12.** *Where the court appoints an insolvency practitioner under section 273(2) to prepare and submit a report under section 274 the court shall, on submission of that report, pay to the practitioner a fee of £250 (that sum being inclusive of Value Added Tax).*

Revocation

10–33   **13.** *Fee No. 6 in Table B in the Schedule to the Bankruptcy Fees Order 1984 (fee payable on application to the Department of Trade and Industry to search public records) is hereby revoked.*

SCHEDULE

FEES PAYABLE UNDER INSOLVENCY ACT 1986

PART I

COMPANY INSOLVENCY, COMPANIES WINDING-UP

10–34

No. of Fee	Description of Proceeding	Amount £
1	For the performance by the official receiver of his general duties as official receiver on the making of a winding-up order...	640.00
2	For all official stationery, printing, postage and telephone charges, including notices to creditors and contributors in respect of the first meetings of creditors and contributories and of sittings of the court—	
	(i) for a number of creditors and contributories not exceeding 25...	175.00
	(ii) for every additional 10 creditors and contributories or part thereof...	40.00
3	(a) Where the official receiver decides to summon meetings of creditors and contributories under section 136(4), for the holding of those meetings...	65.00
	(b) Where any other meetings of creditors and contributories are held by the official receiver, for summoning and holding the meetings—	
	(i) for a number of creditors and contributories not exceeding 25...	155.00
	(ii) for every additional 10 creditors and contributories or part thereof...	20.00
4	On any application to the court for the recission or recall of a winding-up order or a stay of the winding-up order or a stay of the winding-up proceedings under section 147 where the official receiver attends or makes a report to the court...	90.00
	for each further attendance or report...	45.00

No. of Fee	Description of Proceeding	Amount £
5	Where the official receiver supervises a special manager or the carrying on of a company's business—for each week or part thereof...	90.00
6	For taking an affidavit, affirmation or declaration, except affidavits or debt—	
	(i) for each person making the same...	4.00
	(ii) for each exhibit or schedule to be marked...	1.00
7	[...]	[...]
	On each application by a liquidator to the Secretary of State or to the official receiver to exercise the powers of a liquidation committee by virtue of section 141(4) or rule 4.172...	27.00
9	On an application to the Secretary of State under regulations 7 and 8 for a payment from the Insolvency Services Account or for the re-issue of a cheque, money order or payable order in respect of moneys standing to the credit of the Insolvency Services Account, for each cheque, money order or payable order issued or re-issued...	0.65
10	For the performance by the Secretary of State of his general duties under the Act, the Rules and the Regulations in relation to the administration of the affairs of companies which are being wound-up by the court, a fee in accordance with the following scale, calculated on the amount paid into the Insolvency Services Account by liquidators under regulations 5(1) and 18 (after deducting any sums paid to secured creditors in respect of their securities and any sums spent out of money received in carrying on the business of the company):—	
	(i) on the first £50,000 or fraction thereof...	per cent 15.00
	(ii) on the next £50,000 or fraction thereof...	per cent 11.25
	(iii) on the next £400,000 or fraction thereof...	per cent 9.75
	(iv) on the next £500,000 or fraction thereof...	per cent 5.625
	(v) on the next £4,000,000 or fraction thereof...	per cent 3.00
	(vi) on the next £15,000,000 or fraction thereof...	per cent 1.50
	(vii) on the next £30,000,000 or fraction thereof...	per cent 0.25
	(viii) on all further amounts...	per cent 0.10
11	For the performance by the Secretary of State of his general duties under the Act, the Rules and the Regulations in relation to the administration of the affairs of companies which are being wound-up voluntarily, the following fees calculated on payments into the Insolvency Services Account by liquidators under regulations 5(2) and 18:	
	(1) Where the money consists of unclaimed dividends...	per cent 1.75
	(2) Where the money consists of undistributed funds or balances:—	
	(i) on the first £50,000 or fraction thereof...	per cent 1.75
	(ii) on all further amounts...	per cent 1.25
	but so that the total fee payable under this subparagraph (2) shall not exceed £12,500.	
12	On the amount expended on any purchase of Government securities (including the renewal of Treasury Bills) pursuant to a request made under regulation 9...	per cent 0.625

COURT FEES

PART II

INSOLVENCY OF INDIVIDUALS; BANKRUPTCY

10–35

No. of Fee	Description of Proceeding	Amount £
1	On registration with the Secretary of State of an individual voluntary arrangement under Part VIII of the Act...	35.00
2	For the performance by the official receiver of his general duties as official receiver on the making of a bankruptcy order...	320.00
3	For all official stationery, printing, postage and telephone charges, including notices to creditors in respect of the first meeting of creditors and of sittings of the court—	
	(i) for a number of creditors not exceeding 25...	175.00
	(ii) for every additional 10 creditors or part thereof...	40.00
	(a) Where the official receiver decides to summon a meeting of creditors under section 293(1), for the holding of that meeting...	65.00
	(b) Where any other meeting of creditors is held by the official receiver, for summoning and holding the meeting—	
	(i) for a number of creditors not exceeding 25...	155.00
	(ii) for every additional 10 creditors or part thereof...	20.00
5	On the payments made by the official receiver into the Insolvency Services Account as a result of the performance of his functions as receiver and manager under section 287 (after deducting any sums paid to secured creditors in respect of their securities and any sums spent in carrying on the business of the debtor) a fee in accordance with the following scale—	
	(i) on the first £5,000 or fraction thereof...	per cent 20.00
	(ii) on the next £5,000 or fraction thereof...	per cent 15.00
	(iii) on the next £90,000 or fraction thereof...	per cent 10.00
	(iv) on all further sums...	per cent 5.00
6	Where the official receiver, acting as receiver and manager under section 287, makes any payment to creditors, a fee of one-half the scale fee calculated under Fee No. 5 on the amount of the payment.	
7	On any application to the court for the recission or annulment of a bankruptcy order or relating to the discharge of a bankrupt, where the official receiver attends or makes a report to the court...	90.00
	for each further attendance or report...	45.00
8	Where the official receiver supervises a special manager or the carrying on of a debtor's business—for each week or part thereof...	90.00
9	For taking an affidavit, affirmation or declaration, except affidavits of debt—	
	(i) for each person making the same...	4.00
	(ii) for each exhibit or schedule to be marked...	1.00
10	On the insertion in the Gazette by the Secretary of State or the official receiver of any notice authorised by the Act or the Rules...	17.33

No. of Fee	Description of Proceeding	Amount £
11	On each application by a trustee to the Secretary of State or to the official receiver to exercise the powers of a creditors' committee by virtue of section 302 or rule 6.166...	27.00
12	On an application to the Secretary of State under regulations 22 and 23 for a payment from the Insolvency Services Account or for the re-issue of a cheque, money order or payable order in respect of moneys standing to the credit of the Insolvency Services Account, for each cheque, money order or payable order issued or re-issued...	0.65
13	For the performance by the Secretary of State of his general duties under the Act, the Rules and the Regulations in relation to the administration of the estates of individuals, a fee in accordance with the following scale, calculated on the amount paid into the Insolvency Service Account by trustees under regulation 20 and by the official receiver as receiver and manager under section 287 (after deducting any sums paid to secured creditors in respect of their securities and any sums spent out of money received in carrying on the business of the debtor):—	
	(a) on the first £50,000 or fraction thereof...	per cent 15.00
	(b) on the next £50,000 or fraction thereof...	per cent 11.25
	(c) on the next £400,000 or fraction thereof...	per cent 9.75
	(d) on the next £500,000 or fraction thereof...	per cent 5.625
	(e) on the next £4,000,000 or fraction thereof...	per cent 3.00
	(f) on the next £15,000,000 or fraction thereof...	per cent 1.50
	(g) on the next £30,000,000 or fraction thereof...	per cent 0.25
	(h) on all further amounts...	per cent 0.10

Poundage and Fees

Introductory note

Listed below are the fees fixed under the Sheriffs Act 1887 which are the fees to be demanded taken and received by any sheriff or officer of a sheriff concerned in the execution of process directed to the sheriff in the proceedings set out below (S.I. 1920 No. 1250).   **10–36**

"To be demanded"

Overcharge—An overcharge made from an innocent mistake does not render a sheriff liable to penalties under Sheriffs Act 1887, s.29(2)(b) (*Lee v. Dangar* [1892] 1 Q.B. 231; 2 Q.B. 337).   **10–37**

The High Court Enforcement Officers Regulations 2004

(S.I. 2004 No. 400)

REGULATION 3   **SCHEDULE 1**

DISTRICTS FOR WRITS OF EXECUTION ENFORCED BY ENFORCEMENT OFFICERS

10–38

District	Postal Area
Bath	BA
Birmingham	B
Blackburn	BB

COURT FEES

District	Postal Area
Bolton	BL
Bournemouth	BH
Bradford	BD
Brighton	BN
Bristol	BS
Bromley	BR
Cambridge	CB
Canterbury	CT
Cardiff	CF
Carlisle	CA
Chelmsford	CM
Chester	CH
Cleveland (Teesside)	TS
Colchester	CO
Coventry	CV
Crewe	CW
Croydon	CR
Darlington	DL
Dartford	DA
Derby	DE
Doncaster	DN
Dorchester	DT
Dudley	DY
Durham	DH
Enfield	EN
Exeter	EX
Fylde (Blackpool)	FY
Gloucester	GL
Guildford	GU
Halifax	HX
Harrogate	HG
Harrow	HA
Hemel Hempstead	HP
Hereford	HR
Huddersfield	HD
Hull	HU
Ilford	IG
Ipswich	IP
Kingston upon Thames	KT
Lancaster	LA
Leeds	LS
Leicester	LE
Lincoln	LN
Liverpool	L
Llandrindod Wells	LD
Llandudno	LL
London East	E
London East Central	EC

District	Postal Area
London North	N
London North West	NW
London South East	SE
London South West	SW
London West	W
London West Central	WC
Luton	LU
Manchester	M
Medway	ME
Milton Keynes	MK
Newcastle	NE
Newport	NP
Northampton	NN
Norwich	NR
Nottingham	NG
Oldham	OL
Oxford	OX
Peterborough	PE
Plymouth	PL
Portsmouth	PO
Preston	PR
Reading	RG
Redhill	RH
Romford	RM
Salisbury	SP
Sheffield	S
Shrewsbury	SY
Slough	SL
Southall (Uxbridge)	UB
Southampton	SO
Southend on Sea	SS
St. Albans	AL
Stevenage	SG
Stockport	SK
Stoke on Trent	ST
Sunderland	SR
Sutton	SM
Swansea	SA
Swindon	SN
Taunton	TA
Telford	TF
Tonbridge	TN
Torquay	TQ
Truro	TR
Tweeddale (Berwick upon Tweed)	TD
Twickenham	TW
Wakefield	WF
Walsall	WS

District	Postal Area
Warrington	WA
Watford	WD
Wigan	WN
Wolverhampton	WV
Worcester	WR
York	YO

10–39   *Note* —Amended by the High Court Enforcement Officers (Amendment) Regulations 2004 (S.I. 2004 No. 673), regulation 4.

REGULATION 5   SCHEDULE 2

PROFESSIONAL BODIES RECOGNISED BY THE LORD CHANCELLOR

10–40   The Lord Chancellor recognises the following as professional bodies:
* High Court Enforcement Officers Association

REGULATION 13   SCHEDULE 3

FEES CHARGEABLE BY ENFORCEMENT OFFICERS

10–41   The fees chargeable by enforcement officers on execution of writs are as follows. Value Added Tax, if payable, may be added to the fees specified.

A. Fees chargeable on execution of writs of fieri facias	
1. Percentage of amount recovered	
For executing a writ of fieri facias, the following percentages of the amount recovered:	
(a) on the first £100	5 per cent
(b) above £100	2.5 per cent
2. Mileage	
Mileage from the enforcement officer's business address to the place of execution and return, in respect of one journey to seize goods and, if appropriate, one journey to remove the goods	
	29.2 pence per mile, up to a maximum of £50.00 in total
3. Seizure of goods	
For each building or place at which goods are seized	£2.00
4. Making enquiries or dealing with claims for rent or to the goods	
(1) For making enquiries as to claims for rent or to goods, including giving notice to parties of any such claims	a sum not exceeding £2.00
(2) For all expenses actually and reasonably incurred in relation to such work including any postage, telephone, fax and e-mail charges	a further sum not exceeding £2.00
5. Taking possession, removal and storage of goods	
(1) Where a person is left in physical possession of goods seized	£3.00 per person per day
(2) Where an enforcement officer takes walking possession under a walking possession agreement in the form set out in Schedule 4 to these Regulations	£0.25 per day

(Fees 5(1) and 5(2) are payable in respect of the day on which execution is levied, but fee 5(1) may not be charged where a walking possession agreement is signed at the time of levy. Fees 5(1) and 5(2) may not be charged after the goods have been removed.)

(3) For–
     (a) the removal of goods;
     (b) the storage of goods which have been removed; and
     (c) where animals have been seized, their upkeep while in the custody of the enforcement officer, whether before or after removal	

	the sums actually and reasonably paid

6. Sale of goods by auction

(1) To cover the auctioneer's commission and expenses, where goods are sold by auction or work has been done with a view to sale by auction: (a) when goods are sold by auction on the auctioneer's premises, the following percentages of the sum realised–	
(i) on the first £100	15 per cent
(ii) on the next £900	12.5 per cent
(iii) above £1,000	10 per cent

(b) when goods are sold by auction on the debtor's premises, 7.5 per cent of the sum realised plus expenses actually and reasonably incurred.

(2) When no sale takes place either by auction or private contract, but work has been done by the auctioneer or enforcement officer in preparing for a sale by auction, including the preparation of a detailed inventory of the goods seized–

    (a) if the goods have been removed to the auctioneer's premises, 10 per cent of the value of the goods;

    (b) if the goods have not been removed from the debtor's premises, 5 per cent of the value of the goods plus expenses actually and reasonably incurred.

7. Sale of goods by private contract

Where an enforcement officer sells goods by private contract– (a) the following percentages of the proceeds of sale–	
(i) on the first £100	7.5 per cent
(ii) on the next £900	6.25 per cent
(iii) above £1,000	5 per cent; and

(b) when work has been done in preparing for a sale by auction, including the preparation of a detailed inventory of the goods seized, an additional sum not exceeding 2.5 per cent of the value of the goods plus expenses actually and reasonably incurred.

B. Fees chargeable on executing writs of possession or delivery

8. Mileage

Mileage from the enforcement officer's business address to the place of execution and return, in respect of one journey	29.2 pence per mile, up to a maximum of £25.00 in total

9. Writs of possession

(1) Where an enforcement officer executes a writ of possession of domestic property within the meaning of section 66 of the Local Government Finance Act 1988,3 per cent of the net annual value for rating shown in the valuation list in force immediately before 1st April 1990 in respect of the property seized, subject to paragraph (3).

COURT FEES

(2) Where an enforcement officer executes a writ of possession to which paragraph (1) does not apply, 0.4 per cent of the net annual value for rating of the property seized, subject to paragraph (4).

(3) For the purposes of paragraph (1), where the property does not consist of one or more hereditament which, immediately before 1st April 1990–

> (a) had a separate net annual value for rating shown on the valuation list then in force; and

> (b) was domestic property within the meaning of section 66 of the Local Government Finance Act 1988 ,

the property or such part of it as does not so consist shall be taken to have had such a value for rating equal to two-fifteenths of its value by the year when seized.

(4) For the purposes of paragraph (2), where the property does not consist of one or more hereditaments having a separate net annual value for rating, the property or such part of it as does not so consist shall be taken to have such a value equal to its value by the year when seized.

10. Writs of delivery	
For executing a writ of delivery, 4 per cent of the value of the goods as stated in the writ or judgment.	
C. General fees	
11. Copies of returns	
For a copy of any return indorsed by the enforcement officer on a writ of execution	£5.00
12. Miscellaneous	
For any matter not otherwise provided for, such sum as a Master, district judge or costs judge may allow upon application.	

REGULATION 15

SCHEDULE 4

WALKING POSSESSION AGREEMENT

10–42

WALKING POSSESSION AGREEMENT

In the High Court of Justice

......................Division

......................District Registry

High Court Claim number ....

[County Court Claim number...................................]

[Sent from the ....County Court by Certificate dated.....................]

Claimant ....

Defendant ....

To .... an enforcement officer authorised to execute writs of execution issued from the High Court

I request that you will not leave a possession man on my premises in close possession of the goods which you have seized under the writ of execution issued in this claim.

If this request is allowed to me, I undertake, pending withdrawal or satisfaction of the writ—

    (a) not to remove the goods or any part of them nor to permit their removal by any person not authorised by you;

    (b) to inform any person who may visit my premises for the purpose of levying any other execution or distress that you are already in possession of my goods under the writ;

    (c) to notify you immediately of any such visit.

AND I authorise you or a person acting on your behalf, pending the withdrawal or satisfaction of the writ, to re-enter my premises at any time and as often as you may consider necessary for the purpose of inspecting the goods or completing the execution of the writ.

Dated this ....day of .... 20...

Signed................................ Judgment Debtor

COURT FEES

SECTION 11

COURTS DIRECTORY

11 COURTS DIRECTORY

The Daily Cause List

1. Copies of the Daily Cause List will be available in Room EO1, Royal Courts of Justice, at 4 p.m. on each sitting day during Term. The Daily Cause List is also available from the Court Service website: www.courtservice.gov.uk/cms/8039.htm

2. If an alteration has to be made in any list after 2.45 p.m. on any day the solicitors affected by the alteration will be notified by telephone by the appropriate official at the Royal Courts of Justice. Except in rare instances such alterations will be by way of deletion of cases appearing in the printed List published at 4 p.m., as opposed to the insertion of cases not so appearing.

Circuit Arrangements

The unified administrative court service set up under the provisions of the Courts Act 1971 (see particularly, Pt IV, ss.27–29) is under the control of the Lord Chancellor and its headquarters are at the Department for Constitutional Affairs, Selbourne House, 54–60 Victoria Street, London SW1E 6QW.

For the purposes of administration, the country is divided into six Circuits, namely, Midland, North-Eastern, Northern, South-Eastern (including London) Wales and Chester, and Western.

Each Circuit is under the administrative control of a Circuit Administrator who, subject to the overriding judicial control of the Presiding Judges assigned to each Circuit, is responsible to the Lord Chancellor for the efficient conduct of court business in the High Court, the Crown Court, and the county courts in his Circuit.

Each Circuit is further divided into a number of areas containing county courts and a centre or centres of the High Court and the Crown Court for which a Group Manager is responsible to the Circuit Administrator for the efficient conduct of business in all courts in his area. He will in practice act as a point of contact for all concerned, including judges, the legal profession and others to ensure the flexible arrangements for the disposal of court business, including the planning of court sittings, the allocation of judge-power and court accommodation.

The following is the list of Circuits and trial centres for the High Court, together with the addresses and telephone numbers of the Circuit and Group Managers.

Amendments to Circuit Arrangements

Circuit Administrator	Trial Centres	Group Manager
MIDLAND CIRCUIT Circuit Administrator's Office The Priory Courts, 33 Bull Street, Birmingham, B4 6DW Tel: 0121 681 3246 Fax: 0121 681 3210 DX: 701987 Birmingham-7	Birmingham	West Midlands and Warwickshire Group Manager's Office 5th Floor, The Priory Courts, 33 Bull Street, Birmingham, B4 6DW Tel: 0121 681 3226 Fax: 0121 681 3060
	Stafford	West Mercia and Staffordshire Group Manager's Office 1st Floor, Combined Court Centre, Victoria Square, Stafford, ST16 2QQ Tel: 01785 610 800 Fax: 01785 241 643

11-4	Circuit Administrator	Trial Centres	Group Manager
		Coventry	The Priory Courts, 33 Bull Street, Birmingham, B4 6DN Tel: 0121 681 3221 Fax: 0121 681 3060 DX: 701987
		Northampton	St Katherines House, 21–27 St Katherines Street, Northampton, NN1 2TD Tel: 01604 633 776 Fax: 01604 633 995 DX: 702887 Northampton-7
		Lincoln	4th Floor, 11–15 Brayford Wharf East, Lincoln, LN5 7BQ Tel: 01522 544 164 Fax: 01522 544 167 DX: 28027 LINCOLN 3
		Nottingham	East Midlands Group Manager's Office 11th Floor, Market Square House, St James's Street, Nottingham, NG1 6JH Tel: 0115 911 1666 Fax: 0115 911 1667
	NORTHERN CIRCUIT ADMINISTRATOR'S OFFICE The Court Service 15 Quay Street, Manchester, M60 9FD Tel: 0161 833 1005 Fax: 0161 839 9611	Liverpool	Merseyside Group Manager's Office 1st Floor, The Queen Elizabeth II Law Courts, Derby Square, Liverpool, L2 1XA Tel: 0151 330 9605 Fax: 0151 236 5180 DX: 702600 Liverpool 5
		Central Manchester and Outer Manchester	Greater Manchester Group Manager's Office 3rd Floor, 15 Quay Street, Manchester, M60 9ED Tel: 0161 833 1005 Fax: 0161 835 1725
		Preston	Lancashire and Cumbria Group Manager's Office Sessions House, Lancaster Road, Preston, PR1 2PD Tel: 01772 821451 Fax: 01772 884767 DX: 724880 Preston 21
	NORTH-EASTERN CIRCUIT 17th Floor, West Riding House, Albion Street, Leeds, LS1 5AA Tel: 0113 251 1200 Fax: 0113 251 1247/8	Leeds	North and West Yorkshire Group Manager's Office 1st Floor Symons House, Belgrave Street, Leeds, LS2 8DD Tel: 0113 245 9611 Fax: 0113 242 3631

Circuit Administrator	Trial Centres	Group Manager	**11–4**
	Newcastle	Tyne-Tees Group Manager's Office 3rd Floor, Merchant House, 30 Cloth Market, Newcastle upon Tyne, NE1 1EE Tel: 0191 230 8260 Fax: 0191 232 6784	
	Sheffield	Humberside and South Yorkshire Group Manager's Office Sovereign House, Queen's Street, Sheffield, S1 2DW Tel: 0114 275 5866 Fax: 0114 275 5284	
	Teeside	The Law Courts, Russell Street, Middlesbrough, TS1 2AE Tel: 01642 340 000 Fax: 01642 340 002 DX: 65152 Middlesborough-2	
	Bradford	Bradford Combined Court, The Law Courts, Exchange Square, Drake Street, Bradford, BD1 1JA Tel: 01274 843 553 Fax: 01274 843 568	
SOUTH-EASTERN CIRCUIT ADMINISTRATOR'S OFFICE New Cavendish House, 18 Maltravers Street, London, WC2R 3EV Tel: 020 7947 7473 Fax: 020 7947 7230	Chelmsford	East Anglia, Bedfordshire and Hertfordshire Group Manager's Office 1st Floor, Steeple House, Church Lane, Chelmsford, Essex, CM1 1NH Tel: 01245 287974 Fax: 01245 491676 DX: 97375 Chelmsford-3	
	Greater London (Royal Courts of Justice)	The Group Manager Royal Courts of Justice, Strand, London, WC2A 2LL Tel: 020 7947 6000	
	Kingston	6–8 Penrhyn Road, Kingston upon Thames, Surrey, KT1 2BB Tel: 020 8240 2599 Fax: 020 8240 2600 DX: 97430 Kingston-upon-Thames	
	Lewes	The Law Courts, 182 High Street, Lewes, East Sussex, BN7 1YB Tel: 01273 485292 Fax: 01273 485282 DX: 97395 LEWES 4	

COURTS DIRECTORY

11–4

Circuit Administrator	Trial Centres	Group Manager
	London County Courts	London County Court Group Manager's Office 11th floor, Thomas More Building Royal Courts of Justice, Strand, London, WC2A 2LL Tel: 020 7947 7840 Fax: 020 7947 7841 DX: 114 LDE
	London Crown Courts	London County Court Group Manager's Office Central Criminal Court, Old Bailey, London, EC4M 7EH Tel: 020 7248 3277 Fax: 020 7489 1812 DX: 46700 Old Bailey
	Luton	Thames Valley, Surrey and Oxford Group Manager's Office 2nd Floor, 7 George Street, Luton, LU1 2AA Tel: 01582 522 086 Fax: 01582 522 081 DX: 120504 Luton-b
	Maidstone	Kent and Sussex Group Manager's Office Upper Ground Floor Concorde House, 10–12 London Road, Maidstone, Kent, ME16 8QA Tel: 01622 200 120 Fax: 01622 685 428 DX: 141481 Maidstone-12
WALES AND CHESTER CIRCUIT ADMINISTRATOR'S OFFICE 2nd Floor, Churchill House, Churchill Way, Cardiff, CF10 2HH Tel: 029 20415500 Fax: 029 20415511	Cardiff	South Wales Group Manager's Office 2nd Floor, Churchill House, Churchill Way, Cardiff, CF10 2HH Tel: 02920 415512 Fax: 02920 415511 DX: 121723 Cardiff-9
	Swansea	First Floor, Caravella House, Quay West, Quay Parade, Swansea, SA1 1SP Tel: 01792 510350 Fax: 01792 510352 DX: 99740 Swansea-5
	Mold	North Wales and Cheshire Group Manager's Offices The Law Courts Civil Centre, Mold, Flintshire, CH7 1AE Tel: 01352 707 400 Fax: 01352 707 409 DX: 702521 Mold-2

Circuit Administrator	Trial Centres	Group Manager	**11–4**
WESTERN CIRCUIT SECRETARIAT 5th Floor, Greyfriars, Lewins Mead, Bristol, BS1 2NR Tel: 0117 910 3600 Fax: 0117 910 3650	Bristol	1st Floor, White Friars, Southgate, Lewins Mead, Bristol, BS1 2NT Tel: 0117 925 0296 Fax: 0117 925 0300	
	Exeter	West Group Manager's Office Ground Floor Pembroke House Southernhay Gardens Exeter, EX1 1UN Tel: 01392 455900 Fax: 01392 455909	
	Winchester	East Group Manager's Office Swindon Combined Courts The Law Courts Islington Street Wiltshire, SN1 2HG Tel: 01793 690570 Fax: 0196 2851093 DX: 98430 Swindon-5	

List of District Registries

[Civil Courts Order 1983 (S.I. 1983 No. 713), as amended]   **11–5**

District Registry	Districts defined by reference to County Court Districts	Designated Trial Centre
ABERYSTWYTH	Aberystwyth	Swansea
BARNSLEY	Barnsley	Sheffield
BARNSTAPLE	Barnstaple	Exeter
BARROW IN FURNESS	Barrow in Furness	Preston
BASINGSTOKE	Basingstoke	London
BATH	Bath Trowbridge	Bristol
BEDFORD	Bedford	London
BIRKENHEAD	Birkenhead	Liverpool
BIRMINGHAM (CHANCERY)	Birmingham Redditch	Birmingham
BLACKBURN	Blackburn	Preston
BLACKPOOL	Blackpool	Preston
BLACKWOOD	Blackwood	Cardiff
BOLTON	Bolton	Manchester
BOSTON	Boston Skegness	Lincoln
BOURNEMOUTH	Bournemouth Poole	Winchester
BRADFORD	Bradford	Leeds
BRECKNOCK	Brecknock	Cardiff
BRIDGEND	Bridgend Neath and Port Talbot	Cardiff

District Registry	Districts defined by reference to County Court Districts	Designated Trial Centre
BRIGHTON	Brighton Haywards Heath Lewes	Lewes
BRISTOL (CHANCERY)	Bristol Weston super Mare	Bristol
BURNLEY	Accrington Burnley Nelson Rawtenstall	Preston
BURY	Bury	Manchester
BURY ST. EDMUNDS	Bury St. Edmunds	Norwich
CAERNARFON	Caernarfon Conwy and Colwyn	Caernarfon
CAMBRIDGE	Cambridge	London
CANTERBURY	Ashford Canterbury	London
CARDIFF (CHANCERY)	Cardiff	Cardiff
CARLISLE	Carlisle Penrith	Carlisle
CARMARTHEN	Carmarthen Llanelli	Swansea
CHELMSFORD	Chelmsford	Chelmsford
CHELTENHAM	Cheltenham	Bristol
CHESTER	Chester Runcorn	Chester/Mold
CHESTERFIELD	Chesterfield Worksop	Nottingham
CHICHESTER	Chichester	Lewes
COLCHESTER	Braintree Colchester	Chelmsford
COVENTRY	Banbury Coventry Nuneaton Stratford on Avon Warwick	Birmingham
CREWE	Crewe Northwich	Chester/Mold
CROYDON	Bromley Croydon	London
DARLINGTON	Darlington	Teesside
DERBY	Burton upon Trent Buxton Derby	Nottingham
DEWSBURY	Dewsbury	Leeds
DONCASTER	Doncaster Goole Rotherham	Sheffield
DUDLEY	Dudley Kidderminster Stourbridge	Birmingham
DURHAM	Bishop Auckland Durham	Newcastle

District Registry	Districts defined by reference to County Court Districts	Designated Trial Centre
EASTBOURNE	Eastbourne	Lewes
EXETER	Exeter	Exeter
GLOUCESTER	Gloucester	Bristol
GREAT GRIMSBY	Great Grimsby	Lincoln
GUILDFORD	Aldershot and Farnham Epsom Guildford Reigate	London
HALIFAX	Halifax	Leeds
HARLOW	Bishop's Stortford Harlow Hertford	Chelmsford
HARROGATE	Harrogate	Leeds
HARTLEPOOL	Hartlepool	Teesside
HASTINGS	Hastings	Lewes
HAVERFORDWEST	Haverfordwest	Swansea
HEREFORD	Hereford Ludlow	Birmingham
HUDDERSFIELD	Huddersfield	Leeds
IPSWICH	Ipswich	Norwich
KEIGHLEY	Keighley Skipton	Leeds
KENDAL	Kendal	Preston
KING'S LYNN	King's Lynn	Norwich
KINGSTON UPON HULL	Kingston upon Hull	Leeds
LANCASTER	Lancaster	Preston
LEEDS (CHANCERY)	Leeds	Leeds
LEICESTER	Leicester Loughborough Melton Mowbray	Nottingham
LINCOLN	Grantham Lincoln Newark	Lincoln
LIVERPOOL (CHANCERY)	Liverpool	Liverpool
LLANGEFNI	Llangefni	Caernarfon
LOWESTOFT	Lowestoft Great Yarmouth	Norwich
LUTON	Hitchin Luton	London
MACCLESFIELD	Macclesfield	Chester/Mold
MAIDSTONE	Maidstone	London
MANCHESTER (CHANCERY)	Altrincham Manchester	Manchester
MANSFIELD	Mansfield	Nottingham
MEDWAY	Dartford Gravesend Medway	London
MERTHYR TYDFIL	Merthyr Tydfil	Cardiff
MIDDLESBROUGH	Middlesbrough	Teesside

COURTS DIRECTORY

District Registry	Districts defined by reference to County Court Districts	Designated Trial Centre
MILTON KEYNES	Aylesbury Milton Keynes	London
NEWCASTLE UPON TYNE (CHANCERY)	Alnwick Berwick upon Tweed Blyth Morpeth Newcastle upon Tyne	Newcastle
NEWPORT (SOUTH WALES)	Chepstow Monmouth Newport (Gwent) Pontypool	Cardiff
NEWPORT (ISLE OF WIGHT)	Newport (Isle of Wight)	Winchester
NORTHAMPTON	Kettering Northampton Rugby Wellingborough	London
NORWICH	Norwich	Norwich
NOTTINGHAM	Nottingham	Nottingham
OLDHAM	Oldham Tameside	Manchester
OXFORD	Oxford	Oxford
PETERBOROUGH	Huntingdon Peterborough	Nottingham
PLYMOUTH	Plymouth	Exeter
PONTEFRACT	Pontefract	Leeds
PONTYPRIDD	Aberdare Caerphilly Pontypridd	Cardiff
PORTSMOUTH	Portsmouth	Winchester
PRESTON (CHANCERY)	Chorley Preston	Preston
READING	Newbury Reading Slough	London
RHYL	Rhyl	Chester/Mold
ROMFORD	Basildon Grays Thurrock Ilford Romford	Chelmsford
ST. HELENS	St. Helens	Liverpool
SALFORD	Salford	Manchester
SALISBURY	Salisbury	Winchester
SCARBOROUGH	Bridlington Scarborough	Leeds
SCUNTHORPE	Scunthorpe	Lincoln
SHEFFIELD	Sheffield	Sheffield
SHREWSBURY	Shrewsbury Telford	Stafford
SOUTHAMPTON	Southampton	Winchester
SOUTHEND-ON-SEA	Southend-on-Sea	Chelmsford
SOUTHPORT	Southport	Liverpool

District Registry	Districts defined by reference to County Court Districts	Designated Trial Centre
SOUTH SHIELDS	North Shields South Shields	Newcastle
STAFFORD	Stafford	Stafford
STOCKPORT	Stockport	Manchester
STOKE ON TRENT	Stoke on Trent	Stafford
SUNDERLAND	Consett Gateshead Sunderland	Newcastle
SWANSEA	Swansea	Swansea
SWINDON	Swindon	Bristol
TAUNTON	Taunton Bridgewater	Bristol
THANET	Thanet	London
TORQUAY AND NEWTON AB-BOT	Torquay and Newton Ab-bot	Exeter
TRURO	Bodmin Penzance Truro	Truro
TUNBRIDGE WELLS	Tunbridge Wells	Lewes
WAKEFIELD	Wakefield	Leeds
WALSALL	Lichfield Tamworth Walsall	Birmingham
WARRINGTON	Warrington	Chester/Mold
WELSHPOOL	Welshpool and Newtown	Chester/Mold
WEYMOUTH	Weymouth	Winchester
WHITEHAVEN		
WIGAN	Leigh Wigan	Liverpool
WINCHESTER	Winchester	Winchester
WOLVERHAMPTON	Wolverhampton	Stafford
WORCESTER	Evesham Worcester	Birmingham
WORTHING	Horsham Worthing	Lewes
WREXHAM	Mold Oswestry Wrexham	Chester/Mold
YEOVIL	Yeovil	Exeter
YORK	York	Leeds

Note—Printed as amended by Civil Courts (Amendment No. 2) Order 1993 (S.I. **11–6** 1993 No. 3120) and 1994 (S.I. 1994 No. 1536); the Civil Courts (Amendment No. 3) Order 1994 (S.I. 1994 No. 2626); the Civil Courts (Amendment No. 4) Order 1994 (S.I. 1994 No. 2893); the Civil Courts (Amendment) Order 1995 (S.I. 1995 No. 1897); the Civil Courts (Amendment No. 2) Order 1995 (S.I. 1995 No. 3173); the Civil Courts (Amendment) Order 1996 (S.I. 1996 No. 68); the Civil Courts (Amendment) (No. 2) Order 1995 (S.I. 1995 No. 3173); the Civil Courts (Amendment) (No. 2) Order 1996 (S.I. 1996 No. 588); the Civil Courts (Amendment) (No. 3) Order 1996 (S.I. 1996 No. 2579); the Civil Courts (Amendment) Order 1997 (S.I. 1997 No. 361) and the Civil Courts (Amendment) (No. 2) Order 1997 (S.I. 1997 No. 1085); the Civil

COURTS DIRECTORY

Courts (Amendment) (No. 2) Order 1998 (S.I. 1998 No. 2910); the Civil Courts (Amendment) Order 1998 (S.I. 1998 No. 1880); the Civil Courts (Amendment) Order 1999 (S.I. No. 216).

County Court Directory

[Civil Courts Order 1983 (S.I. 1983 No. 713), as amended, up to and including the **11–7** Civil Courts (Amendment No. 2) Order 1998 (S.I. 1998 No. 2910).]

Court (Courts with Bankruptcy jurisdiction in bold)	Address	Contact Nos
ABERDARE AA	The Court House Cwmbach Road Aberdare Wales CF44 OJE	Tel: 01685 888575 Fax: 01685 883412 DX: 99600 Aberdare-2
ABERYSTWYTH AB	Edlestone House Queens Road Aberystwyth Ceredigion SY23 2HP	Tel: 01970 636370 Fax: 01970 625985 DX: 99560 Aberystwyth-2
ACCRINGTON AC	Bradshawgate House 1 Oak Street Accrington Lancs BB5 1EQ	Tel: 01254 237490 Fax: 01254 393869 DX: 702645 Accrington-2
ALDERSHOT & FARNHAM AF	Court House 84–86 Victoria Rd Aldershot Hants GU11 1SS *Postal Address:* 78/82 Victoria Road Aldershot Hants GU11 1SS	Tel: 01252 796800 Fax: 01252 345705 DX: 98530 Aldershot-2
ALTRINCHAM AL	Trafford Courthouse PO Box 240 Ashton Lane Sale Cheshire M33 7WX *Postal address:* Altrincham County Court PO Box 240 Trafford Courthouse Ashton Lane Sale Cheshire M33 7WX	Tel: 0161 975 4760 Fax: 0161 975 4761 DX: 708292 Sale-6
ASHFORD AS	The Court House Tufton Street Ashford Kent TN23 1QQ	Tel: 01233 632464 Fax: 01233 612786 DX: 98060 Ashford-3 (Kent)
AYLESBURY AY	2nd Floor Heron House 49 Buckingham Street Aylesbury Bucks HP20 2NQ	Tel: 01296 393498 Fax: 01296 397363 DX: 97820 Aylesbury-3

Court (Courts with Bank-ruptcy jurisdiction in bold)	Address	Contact Nos
BANBURY ZA	35 Parsons Street Banbury Oxon OX16 8BW	Tel: 01295 265799 Fax: 01295 277025 DX: 701967 Banbury-2
BARNET BT	St Mary's Court Regents Park Road Finchley London N3 1BQ	Tel: (020) 8343 4272 Fax: (020) 8343 1324 DX: 122570 Finchley (Church End)
BARNSLEY BY	12 Regent Street Barnsley South Yorkshire S70 2EW	Tel: 01226 203471 Fax: 01226 779126 DX: 702080 Barnsley-3
BARNSTAPLE BP	The Law Courts 7th Floor Civic Centre North Walk Barnstaple Devon EX31 1DY	Tel: 01271 372252 Fax: 01271 322968 DX: 98560 Barnstaple-2
BARROW-IN-FURNESS BW	Government Buildings Michaelson Road Barrow in Furness Cumbria LA14 2EZ	Tel: 01229 820046 Fax: 01229 430039 DX: 65210 Barrow-in-Furness-2
BASILDON BQ	The Gore Basildon Essex SS14 2BU	Tel: 01268 458000 Fax: 01268 458149 DX: 97633 Basildon–5 Email: e-filing@basildon.county court.gsi.gov.uk Email: bailiffs@basildon.county court.gsi.gov.uk Email: hearings@basildon.county court.gsi.gov.uk Email: enquiries@basildon.county court.gsi.gov.uk Email: family@basildon.county court.gsi.gov.uk
BASINGSTOKE BK	3rd Floor Grosvenor House Basing View Basingstoke Hants RG21 4HG	Tel: 01256 318200 Fax: 01256 318225 DX: 98570 Basingstoke-3
BATH BA	Cambridge House Henry Street Bath Somerset BA1 1DJ	Tel: 01225 310282 Fax: 01225 480915 DX: 98580 Bath-2
BEDFORD BE	May House 29 Goldington Road Bedford MK40 3NN	Tel: 01234 760400 Fax: 01234 327431 DX: 97590 Bedford-3

2706

Court (Courts with Bank-ruptcy jurisdiction in bold)	Address	Contact Nos
BIRKENHEAD BI	76 Hamilton Street Birkenhead Merseyside L41 5EN	Tel: 0151 666 5800 Fax: 0151 666 5873 DX: 725000 Birken-head–10
BIRMINGHAM BM, ZB	Birmingham Civil Justice Centre The Priory Courts 33 Bull Street Birmingham B4 6DS	Tel: 0121 681 4441 Fax: 0121 681 3001/2 DX: 701987 Birmingham-7 Email: e-filing@birmingham.county court.gsi.gov.uk Email: bailiffs@birmingham.county court.gsi.gov.uk Email: hearings@birmingham.county court.gsi.gov.uk Email: enquiries@birmingham.county court.gsi.gov.uk Email: family@birmingham.county court. gsi.gov.uk
BISHOP AUCKLAND ZH	Saddler House Saddler Street Bishop Auckland Co Durham DL14 7HF	Tel: 01388 602423 Fax: 01388 606651 DX: 65100 Bishop Auckland-2
BLACKBURN BB	64 Victoria Street Blackburn Lancs BB1 6DJ	Tel: 01254 680640 Fax: 01254 692712 DX: 702650 Blackburn-4
BLACKPOOL BC	The Law Courts Chapel Street Blackpool Lancs FY1 5RJ	Tel: 01253 754020 Fax: 01253 295255 DX: 724900 Blackpool-10
BLACKWOOD ZJ	County Court Office Blackwood Road Blackwood South Wales NP2 2XB	Tel: 01495 223197 Fax: 01495 220289 DX: 99470 Blackwood-2
BODMIN BJ	Cockswell House Market Street Bodmin Cornwall PL31 2HJ	Tel: 01208 74224 Fax: 01208 77255
BOLTON BL	Bolton Combined Court The Law Courts Blackhorse Street Bolton Lancs BL1 1SU	Tel: 01204 392881 Fax: 01204 363204 DX: 702611 Bolton-3
BOSTON	55 Norfolk St. Boston Lincs PE21 6PE	Tel: 01205 366080 Fax: 01205 311692 DX: 701922 Boston-2

Court (Courts with Bank-ruptcy jurisdiction in bold)	Address	Contact Nos
BOURNEMOUTH BH	The Bournemouth Crown and County Courts The Courts of Justice Deansleigh Road Bournemouth BH7 7DS	Tel: 01202 502800 Fax: 01202 502801 DX: 98420 Bournemouth-4 Email: e-filing@bournemouth. countycourt.gsi.gov.uk Email: bailiffs@bournemouth. countycourt.gsi.gov.uk Email: hearings@bournemouth. countycourt.gsi.gov.uk Email: enquiries@bournemouth. countycourt.gsi.gov.uk Email: family@bournemouth. countycourt.gsi.gov.uk
BOW BO	96 Romford Road Stratford London E15 4EG	Tel: (020) 8536 5200 Fax: (020) 8503 1152 DX: 97490 Stratford (London)-2
BRADFORD BD	The Bradford Combined Court Centre Exchange Square Drake Street Bradford BD1 1JA	Tel: 01274 840274 Fax: 01274 840275 DX: 702083 Bradford-3
BRECKNOCK ZM	Cambrian Way Brecon Powys LD3 7HR	Tel: 01874 622671 Fax: 01874 611607 DX:124340 Brecon 2
BRENTFORD BF	Alexandra Road High Street Brentford Middx TW8 0JJ	Tel: (020) 8231 8940 Fax: (020) 8568 2401 DX: 97840 Brentford-2
BRIDGEND BG	Crown Buildings Angel Street Bridgend CF31 4AS	Tel: 01656 768881 Fax: 01656 647124 DX: 99750 Bridgend-2
BRIGHTON BN	William Street Brighton E. Sussex BN2 2RF	Tel: 01273 674421 Fax: 01273 602138 DX: 98070 Brighton-3
Brighton County Court–Family Centre	1 Edward Street Brighton BN2 0JD	Tel: 01273 811333 Fax: 01273 607638 DX: 142600 Brighton-12
BRISTOL BS	Greyfriars Lewins Mead Bristol BS1 2NR	Tel: 0117 9106700 Fax: (General) 0117 9106729 (Bailiffs)–0117 9106730; (Family)–0117 910 6728 DX: 95903 Bristol-3

Court (Courts with Bank-ruptcy jurisdiction in bold)	Address	Contact Nos
BROMLEY BR	Court House College Road Bromley Kent BR1 2RD	Tel: (020) 8290 9620 Fax: (020) 8313 9624 DX: 98080 Bromley-2
BULK CENTRE	County Court Bulk Cen-tre St Katharines House 21–27 St Katherines Street Northampton NN1 2LH	Tel: 0845 408 5302 Fax: 0845 408 5304 DX: 702885 Northampton-7 Centralised Attachment of Earning Payments (CAPs) Tel: 0845 408 5312 Fax: 0845 408 5314 Traffic Enforcement Centre Tel: 0845 704 5007 Fax: 0845 707 8607 Money Claim Online (MCOL) Tel: 0845 601 5935 Fax: 0845 601 5889
BURNLEY	The Law Courts Hammerton Street Burnley Lancs BB11 1XD	Tel: 01282 416899 Fax: 01282 414911 DX: 724940 Burnley-4
BURTON-UPON-TRENT BX	165 Station Street Burton-upon-Trent Staffs DE14 1BP	Tel: 01283 568241 Fax: 01283 517245 DX: 702044 Burton-upon-Trent-3
BURY BU	Tenterden Street Bury Lancs BL9 0HJ	Tel: 0161 764 1344 Fax: 0161 763 4995 DX: 702615 Bury-2
BURY ST. EDMUNDS BV	Triton House Entrance B St. Andrews Street North Bury St. Edmunds Suffolk IP33 1TR	Tel: 01284 753254 Fax: 01284 702687 DX: 97640 Bury St. Edmunds-3
BUXTON ZQ	1–3 Hardwick Street Buxton Derbyshire SK17 6DH	Tel: 01298 23734 Fax: 01298 73281 DX: 701970 Buxton-2
CAERNARFON CJ	Llanberis Road Caernarfon Gwynedd LL55 2DF	Tel: 01286 678911 Fax: 01286 678965 DX: 702483 Caernarfon-2
CAMBRIDGE CB	197 East Road Cambridge CB1 1BA	Tel: 01223 224500 Fax: 01223 224590 DX: 97650 Cambridge-3

Court (Courts with Bankruptcy jurisdiction in bold)	Address	Contact Nos
CANTERBURY CT	The Law Courts Chaucer Road Canterbury Kent CT1 1ZA	Tel: 01227 819200 Fax: 01227 819329 DX: 99710 Canterbury-3
CARDIFF CF	Cardiff Civil Justice Centre 2 Park Street Cardiff Wales CF1 1ET	Tel: (029) 20 376400 Fax: (029) 20 376475 DX: 99500 Cardiff-6
CARLISLE CA	Courts of Justice Earl Street Carlisle Cumbria CA1 1DJ	Tel: 01228 520619 Fax: 01228 590588 DX: 65331 Carlisle-2
CARMARTHEN CX	The Old Vicarage Picton Terrace Carmarthen Wales SA31 1BJ	Tel: 01267 228010 Fax: 01267 221844 DX: 99570 Carmarthen-2
CENTRAL LONDON CL Patents County Court	13–14 Park Crescent London W1B 1HT	Tel: (020) 7917 5000 Fax: (020) 7917 5014
Business List	Court House 26–29 Park Crescent London W1N 4HT	Business List Fax: (020) 7917 7935/7940 DX: 97325 Regents Park-2
CHELMSFORD CM	London House New London Road Chelmsford Essex CM2 0QR	Tel: 01245 264670 Fax: 01245 496216 DX: 97660 Chelmsford-4
CHELTENHAM CN	The Court House County Court Road Cheltenham Glos GL50 1HB	Tel: 01242 519983 Fax: 01242 252741 DX: 98630 Cheltenham-4
CHESTER CH	Chester Civil Justice Centre Trident House Little St John Street Chester CH1 1SN	Tel: 01244 404200 Fax: 01244 404300 DX: 702460 Chester-4
CHESTERFIELD CD	St Mary's Gate Chesterfield Derbyshire S41 7ED	Tel: 01246 501200 Fax: 01246 501205 DX: 703160 Chesterfield 3
CHICHESTER CI	The Law Courts Southgate Chichester West Sussex PO19 1SX	Tel: 01243 520700 Fax: 01243 533756 DX: 97460 Chichester-2
CHORLEY CY	59 St Thomas's Road Chorley Lancashire PR7 1JE	Tel: 01257 262778 Fax: 01257 232843 DX: 702655 Chorley-3

Court (Courts with Bank-ruptcy jurisdiction in bold)	Address	Contact Nos
CLERKENWELL CK	33 Duncan Terrace Islington London N1 8AN	Tel: (020) 7359 8458 Fax: (020) 7354 1166 DX: 146640 Islington-4
COLCHESTER CO	Falkland House 25 Southway Colchester Essex CO3 3EG	Tel: 01206 717200 Fax: 01206 717250 DX: 97670 Colchester-3
CONSETT CZ	Victoria Road Consett Co Durham DH8 5AU	Tel: 01207 502854 Fax: 01207 582626 DX: 65106 Consett-2
CONWY AND COL-WYN CC	36 Princes Drive Colwyn Bay Conwy LL29 8LA	Tel: 01492 530807 Fax: 01492 533591 DX: 702492 Colwyn Bay-2
COVENTRY CV	Coventry Combined Court Centre 140 Much Park Street Coventry West Midlands CV1 2SN	Tel: (024) 76 536166 Fax: (024) 76 520443 DX: 701580 Coventry-5
CREWE CW	The Law Courts Civic Centre Crewe Cheshire CW1 2DP	Tel: 01270 212255 Fax: 01270 216344 DX: 702504 Crewe-2
CROYDON CR	Croydon Combined Court Centre The Law Courts Altyre Road Croydon Surrey CR9 5AB	Tel: (020) 8410 4797 Fax: (020) 8760 0432 DX: 97470 Croydon-6
DARLINGTON DL	4 Coniscliffe Road Darlington Co. Durham DL3 7RL	Tel: 01325 463224 Fax: 01325 362829 DX: 65109 Darlington-3
DARTFORD DA	Court House Home Gardens Dartford Kent DA1 1DX	Tel: 01322 223396 Fax: 01322 270902 DX: 98080 Dartford-2
DERBY DE	Derby Combined Court Centre The Morledge Derby DE1 2XE	Tel: 01332 622600 Fax: 01332 622543 DX: 11526 Derby 2
DEWSBURY DW	County Court House Eightlands Road Dewsbury West Yorkshire WF13 2PE	Tel: 01924 466135 Fax: 01924 456419 DX: 702086 Dewsbury-2
DONCASTER DN	74 Waterdale Doncaster South Yorkshire DN1 3BT	Tel: 01302 381730 Fax: 01302 768090 DX: 702089 Doncaster-4

Court (Courts with Bankruptcy jurisdiction in bold)	Address	Contact Nos
DUDLEY DD	Harbour Buildings Waterfront West Dudley Road Brierley Hill Dudley West Midlands DY5 1LN	Tel: 01384 480799 Fax: 01384 482799 DX: 701494 Dudley-2
DURHAM DH	Hallgarth Street Durham DH1 3RG	Tel: 0191 386 5941 Fax: 0191 386 1328 DX: 65115 Durham-5
EASTBOURNE EA	4 The Avenue Eastbourne East Sussex BN21 3SZ	Tel: 01323 735195 Fax: 01323 638829 DX: 98110 Eastbourne-2
EDMONTON ED	Court House 59 Fore Street Edmonton London N18 2TN	Tel: (020) 8884 6500 Fax: (020) 8803 0564 DX: 136686 Edmonton-3
EPSOM EP	The Parade Epsom Surrey KT18 5DN	Tel: 01372 721801 Fax: 01372 726588 DX: 97850 Epsom-3
EVESHAM EV	1st Floor 87 High Street Evesham Worcs WR11 4EE	Tel: 01386 442287 Fax: 01386 49203 DX: 701910 Evesham-3
EXETER EX	Exeter Combined Courts Southernhay Gardens Exeter Devon EX1 1UH	Tel: 01392 415300 Fax: 01392 415642 DX: 98440 Exeter
GATESHEAD GH	5th Floor Chad House Tynegate Precinct Gateshead Tyne and Wear NE8 3HZ	Tel: 0191 477 2445 Fax: 0191 477 8562 DX: 65118 Gateshead-2
GLOUCESTER GL	Combined Court Building Kimbrose Way Gloucester GL1 2DE	Tel: 01452 834900 Fax: 01452 386309 DX: 98660 Gloucester-5
GRANTHAM GR	10 Guildhall Street Grantham Lincs NG31 6NJ	Tel: 01476 563638 Fax: 01476 570181 DX: 701931 Grantham-2
GRAVESEND GV	26 King Street Gravesend Kent DA12 2DU	Tel: 01474 321771 Fax: 01474 534811 DX: 98140 Gravesend-2
GREAT GRIMSBY GG	Great Grimsby Combined Court Centre Town Hall Square Great Grimsby N.E. Lincs DN31 1HX	Tel: 01472 311811 Fax (Crown Court): 01472 312038 Fax (County Court): 01472 312039 DX: 702007 Grimsby-3

Court (Courts with Bank-ruptcy jurisdiction in bold)	Address	Contact Nos
GUILDFORD GU	The Law Courts Mary Road Guildford Surrey GU1 4PS	Tel: 01483 595200 Fax: 01483 300031 DX: 97860 Guildford-5
HALIFAX HX	Prescott Street Halifax West Yorkshire HX1 2JJ	Tel: 01422 344700 Fax: 01422 360132 DX: 702095 Halifax-2
HARLOW HA	Gate House The High Harlow Essex CM20 1UW	Tel: 01279 443291 Fax: 01279 451110 DX: 97700 Harlow-2
HARROGATE HG	2 Victoria Avenue Harrogate North Yorkshire HG1 1EL	Tel: 01423 503921 Fax: 01423 528679 DX: 702098 Harrogate-3
HARTLEPOOL HL	Law Courts Victoria Road Hartlepool TS24 8BS	Tel: 01429 268198 Fax: 01429 862550 DX: 65121 Hartlepool-2
HASTINGS HS	The Law Courts Bohemia Road Hastings East Sussex TN34 1QX	Tel: 01424 435128 Fax: 01424 421585 DX: 98150 Hastings-2
HAVERFORDWEST HV	Penffynnon Hawthorn Rise Haverfordwest Pembs SA61 2AZ	Tel: 01437 772060 Fax: 01437 769222 DX: 99610 Haverfordwest-2
HAYWARDS HEATH HH	Milton House Milton Road Haywards Heath West Sussex RH16 1YZ	Tel: 01444 447970 Fax: 01444 415282 DX: 98160 Haywards Heath-3
HEREFORD HR	First Floor Barclays Bank Chambers 1/3 Broad Street Hereford HR4 9BA	Tel: 01432 357233 Fax: 01432 352593 DX: 701904 Hereford-2
HERTFORD HF	4th Floor Sovereign House Hale Road Hertford SG13 8DY	Tel: 01992 503954 Fax: 01992 501274 DX: 97710 Hertford-2
HIGH WYCOMBE HW	The Law Courts Easton Street High Wycombe Bucks HP11 1LR	Tel: 01494 436374 Fax: 01494 459430 DX: 97880 High Wycombe-3
HITCHIN HI	Park House 1–12 Old Park Road Hitchin Herts SG5 1LX	Tel: 01462 443750 Fax: 01462 432161/ 01462 443795 (Bailiff) DX: 97720 Hitchin

Court (Courts with Bank-ruptcy jurisdiction in bold)	Address	Contact Nos
HORSHAM HM	The Law Courts Hurst Road Horsham West Sussex RH12 2EU	Tel: 01403 252474 Fax: 01403 258844 DX: 98170 Horsham-2
HOVE	Hove Court Centre The Courthouse Lansdowne Road Hove BN3 3BN	Tel: 01273 770643 Fax: 01273 738523
HUDDERSFIELD HD	Queensgate House Queensgate Huddersfield HD1 2RR	Tel: 01484 421043 Fax: 01484 426366 DX: 703013 Huddersfield-2
HUNTINGDON HN	Ground Floor Godwin House George Street Huntingdon Cambs PE29 3BD	Tel: 01480 450932 Fax: 01480 435397 DX: 96650 Huntingdon-2
ILFORD IG	Buckingham Road Ilford Essex IG1 1BR	Tel: (020) 8478 1132 Fax: (020) 8553 2824 DX: 97510 Ilford-3
IPSWICH IP	8 Arcade Street Ipswich Suffolk IP1 1EJ	Tel: 01473 214256 Fax: 01473 251 797 DX: 97730 Ipswich-3
KEIGHLEY KE	Yorkshire Bank Chambers North Street Keighley West Yorkshire BD21 3SH	Tel: 01536 602803 Fax: 01536 610549 DX: 703007 Keighley-2
KENDAL KN	Kendal Courthouse Burneside Road Kendal Cumbria LA9 4NF	Tel: 01539 721218 Fax: 01539 733840 DX: 63450 Kendal-2
KETTERING KG	Dryland Street Kettering Northants NN16 0BE	Tel: 01536 512471 Fax: 01536 416857 DX: 701886 Kettering-2
KIDDERMINSTER KI	10 Comberton Place Kidderminster Worcs DY10 1QR	Tel: 01562 822480 Fax: 01562 827809 DX: 701946 Kidderminster-2
KING'S LYNN KL	Chequer House 12 King Street King's Lynn Norfolk PE30 1ES	Tel: 01553 772067 Fax: 01553 769824 DX: 97740 King's Lynn-2
KINGSTON-UPON-HULL KH	Lowgate Kingston-upon-Hull HU1 2EZ	Tel: 01482 586161 Fax: 01482 588527 DX: 703010 Hull-5

Court (Courts with Bank-ruptcy jurisdiction in bold)	Address	Contact Nos
KINGSTON-UPON-THAMES KT	St James Road Kingston-upon-Thames KT1 2AD	Tel: (020) 8546 8843 Fax: (020) 8547 1426 DX: 97890 Kingston-u-Thames-3
LAMBETH LB	Court House Cleaver Street Kennington Road London SE11 4DZ	Tel: (020) 7091 4420 Fax: (020) 7735 8147 DX: 33254 Kennington
LANCASTER LA	2nd Floor Mitre House Church Street Lancaster LA1 1UZ	Tel: 01524 68112 Fax: 01524 846478
LEEDS LS	The Courthouse 1 Oxford Row Leeds LS1 3BG	Tel: 0113 2830040 Fax: Issue–0113 2429050 Listings–0113 2426846 Enforcement–0113 2439991 Family–0113 2429151 Order production–0113 2426380 Crown Court Listing–0113 2451512 Crown Court general Office–0113 2452305 Civil Hearing Centre–0113 2423733 DX: 703016 Leeds-6
LEICESTER LE	90 Wellington Street Leicester LE1 6ZZ	Tel: 0116 2225700 Fax: 0116 2223450 DX: 17401 Leicester
LEIGH LG	22 Walmseley Road Leigh Greater Manchester WN7 1YF	Tel: 01942 673639 Fax: 01942 681216 DX: 702555 Leigh-2
LEWES LW	Lewes Combined Court The Law Courts 182 High Street Lewes East Sussex BN7 1YB	Tel: 01273 480400 Fax: 01273 485269 DX: 97395 Lewes-4
LINCOLN LN	The Court House 360 High Street Lincoln LN5 7RL	Tel: 01522 883000 Fax: 01522 883003 DX: 703231 Lincoln-6
LIVERPOOL LV	Queen Elizabeth II Law Courts Derby Square Liverpool L2 1XA	Tel: 0151 473 7373 Fax: 0151 227 2806 DX: 702600 Liverpool-5
LLANELLI LI	2nd Floor Court Buildings Town Hall Square Llanelli Carmarthenshire SA15 3AL	Tel: 01554 757171 Fax: 01554 758079 DX: 99510 Llanelli-2

Court (Courts with Bankruptcy jurisdiction in bold)	Address	Contact Nos
LLANGEFNI LL	County Court Buildings Glanhwfa Road Llangefni Anglesey LL77 7EN	Tel: 01248 750225 Fax: 01248 750778 DX: 702480 Llangefni-2
LONDON	*See* BARNET BOW CENTRAL LONDON CLERKENWELL EDMONTON LAMBETH MAYOR'S AND CITY OF LONDON SHOREDITCH WANDSWORTH WEST LONDON WILLESDEN WOOLWICH	
LOWESTOFT LO	"Lyndhurst" 28 Gordon Road Lowestoft Suffolk NR32 1NL	Tel: 01502 573701 Fax: 01502 569319 DX: 97750 Lowestoft-2
LUDLOW LD	9–10 King Street Ludlow Shropshire SY8 1QW	Tel: 01584 872091 Fax: 01584 877606 DX: 702013 Ludlow-2
LUTON LU	5th Floor Cresta House Alma Street Luton Beds LU1 2PU	Tel: 01582 506700 Fax: 01582 506701 DX: 97760 Luton-4
MACCLESFIELD MC	2nd Floor Silk House Park Green Macclesfield Cheshire SK11 7NA	Tel: 01625 412800 Fax: 01625 501262 DX: 702498 Macclesfield-3
MAIDSTONE MS	The Law Courts Barker Road Maidstone Kent ME16 8EQ	Tel: 01622 202000 Fax: 01622 202002 (County) Fax: 01622 202001 (Crown) DX: 130065 Maidstone-7
MANCHESTER MA	The Courts of Justice Crown Square Manchester M60 9DF	Tel: 0161 954 1800 Fax: 0161 954 1661 (General Office)/ 0161 954 1662 (Family)/ 0161 954 1667 (Chancery/ Mercantile Listing)/ 0161 954 1669 (Bailiffs)/ 0161 954 1803 (Administration) DX: 702541 Manchester-11

Court (Courts with Bankruptcy jurisdiction in bold)	Address	Contact Nos
MANSFIELD MF	Beech House 58 Commercial Gate Mansfield Notts NG18 1EU	Tel: 01623 656406 Fax: 01623 626561 DX: 702180 Mansfield-3
MAYOR'S AND CITY OF LONDON MY	Guildhall Buildings Basinghall Street London EC2V 5AR	Tel: (020) 77965400 Fax: (020) 77965424 DX: 97520 Moorgate-2
MEDWAY ME	Anchorage House 47–67 High Street Chatham Kent ME4 4DW	Tel: 01634 810720 Fax: 01634 811332 DX: 98180 Chatham-4
MELTON MOWBRAY MM	Crown House 50–52 Scalford Road Melton Mowbray Leics LE13 1JY	Tel: 01664 568336 Fax: 01664 480241 DX: 701937 Melton Mowbray-2
MERTHYR TYDFIL MT	The Law Courts Glebeland Place Merthyr Tydfil Mid Glamorgan CF47 8BH	Tel: 01685 358200 Fax: 01685 359727 DX: 99582 Merthyr Tydfil-2
MIDDLESBROUGH MB	Teeside Combined Court Centre The Law Courts Russell Street Middlesbrough TS1 2AE	Tel: 01642 340000 Fax: 01642 340002 DX: 65152 Middlesbrough-2
MILTON KEYNES MK	351 Silbury Boulevard (Rear) Witan Gate East Central Milton Keynes MK9 2DT	Tel: 01908 302800 Fax: 01908 230063 DX: 136266 Milton Keynes 6
MOLD ML	Law Courts Civic Centre Mold Flintshire CH7 1AE	Tel: 01352 707330 Fax: 01352 707333/ 01352 707334 (Bailiff) DX: 702521 Mold-2
MORPETH and BERWICK MP	Fountain House New Market Morpeth Northumberland NE6 1LA	Tel: 01670 512221 Fax: 01670 504188 DX: 65124 Morpeth-2
NEATH & PORT TALBOT NT	Forster Road Neath Port Talbot SA11 3BN	Tel: 01639 642267 Fax: 01639 633505 DX: 99550 Neath-2
NELSON NL	Phoenix Chambers 9/13 Holme Street Nelson Lancs BB9 9SU	Tel: 01282 601177 Fax: 01282 619557 DX: 702560 Nelson-2

Court (Courts with Bank-ruptcy jurisdiction in bold)	Address	Contact Nos
NEWARK NK	The County Court Crown Building 41 Lombard Street Newark Notts NG24 1XN	Tel: 01636 703607 Fax: 01636 613726 DX: 701928 Newark-2
NEWBURY NB	Kings Road West Newbury Berks RG14 5AH	Tel: 01635 40928 Fax: 01635 37704 DX: 30816 Newbury-1
NEWCASTLE UPON TYNE NE	Newcastle Combined Court The Law Courts Quayside Newcastle upon Tyne NE1 3LA	Tel: 0191 201 2000 Fax: 0191 201 2001 DX: 65128 Newcastle-u-Tyne-2
NEWPORT (I.O.W.) NI	1 Quay Street Newport I.o.W. PO30 5YT	Tel: 01983 526821 Fax: 01983 821039 DX: 98460 Newport-2 (I.O.W.)
NEWPORT (SOUTH WALES) NP	Olympia House 3rd Floor Upper Dock Street Newport South Wales NP9 1PQ Court House The Concourse Clarence House Clarence Place Newport	Tel: 01633 227150 Fax: 01633 263820 DX: 99480 Newport (South Wales)-4
NORTHAMPTON NN	Northampton Combined Court 85–87 Lady's Lane Northampton NN1 3HQ N.B. See Bulk Centre for bulk issue	Tel: 01604 470400 Fax: 01604 232398 DX: 725380 Northampton-21
NORTH SHIELDS NS	2nd Floor Kings Court Earl Grey Way Royal Quays North Shields NE29 6AR	Tel: 0191 298 2339 Fax: 0191 298 2337 DX: 65137 North Shields-2
NORTHWICH HN	25/27 High Street Northwich Cheshire CW9 5DB	Tel: 01606 42554 Fax: 01606 331490 DX: 702515 Northwich-3
NORWICH NR	Norwich Combined Court The Law Courts Bishopgate Norwich NR3 1UR	Tel: 01603 728200 Fax: 01603 760863 DX: 97385 Norwich-5
NOTTINGHAM NG	60 Canal Street Nottingham NG1 7EJ	Tel: 0115 9103500 Fax: 0115 9103524 DX: 702380 Nottingham-7

Court (Courts with Bank-ruptcy jurisdiction in bold)	Address	Contact Nos
NUNEATON NU	Heron House Newdegate Street Nuneaton Warwickshire CV11 4EL	Tel: 0247 6386134 Fax: 0247 6352769 DX: 701940 Nuneaton-2
OLDHAM OL	New Radcliffe Street Oldham Greater Manchester OL1 1NL	Tel: 0161 290 4200 Fax: 0161 290 4222 DX: 702595 Oldham-2
OSWESTRY OS	2nd Floor The Guidhall Bailey Head Oswestry Shropshire SY11 2EW	Tel: 01691 652127 Fax: 01691 671239 DX: 701958 Oswestry-2
OXFORD OX	Oxford Combined Court Centre St Aldates Oxford OX1 1TL	Tel: 01865 264200 Fax: 01865 790773 DX: 96450 Oxford-4
PENRITH PN	The Court House Lowther Terrace Penrith CA11 7QL	Tel: 01768 862535 Fax: 01768 899700 DX: 65207 Penrith
PENZANCE PZ	Trevear Alverton Penzance Cornwall TR18 4JH	Tel: 01736 362987 Fax: 01736 330595
PETERBOROUGH PE	Crown Buildings Rivergate Peterborough PE1 1EJ	Tel: 01733 355400 Fax: 01733 557348 DX: 702302 Peterborough-8
PLYMOUTH PL	Plymouth Combined Court The Law Courts 10 Armada Way Plymouth Devon PL1 2ER	Tel: 01752 677400 Fax: 01752 208286 (Civil)/ 01752 677 455 (Family) DX: 98470 Plymouth-7
PONTEFRACT PF	Horsefair House Horsefair Pontefract West Yorkshire WF8 1RJ	Tel: 01977 702357 Fax: 01977 600204 DX: 703022 Pontefract-2
PONTYPOOL PP	Park Road Riverside Pontypool Torfaen NP4 6NZ	Tel: 01495 762248 Fax: 01495 762467 DX: 117500 Pontypool 2
PONTYPRIDD PD	The Court House Courthouse Street Pontypridd Wales CF37 1JR	Tel: 01443 490800 Fax: 01443 480305 DX: 99620 Pontypridd-2

Court (Courts with Bank-ruptcy jurisdiction in bold)	Address	Contact Nos
POOLE PH	The Law Courts Civic Centre Park Road Poole BH15 2NS	Tel: 01202 741150 Fax: 01202 747245 DX: 98700 Poole-4
PORTSMOUTH PO	Portsmouth Combined Court The Courts of Justice Winston Churchill Ave- nue Portsmouth PO1 2EB	Tel: (023) 92 893000 Fax: (023) 92 826385 DX: 98490 Portsmouth 5
PRESTON PR	The Law Courts Openshaw Place Ring Way Preston Lancs PR1 2LL	Tel (General): 01772 844700 Tel (Bailiffs): 01772 844881 Fax (County Court): 01772 844710 Fax (Crown Court): 01772 844767 DX: 702660 Preston-5
RAWTENSTALL RA	1 Grange Street Rawtenstall Lancs BB4 7RT	Tel: 01706 214614 Fax: 01706 219814 DX: 702565 Rawtenstall
READING RG	161–163 Friar Street Reading Berks RG1 1HE	Tel: 01189 870500 Fax: 01189 870555 DX: 98010 Reading-6
REDDITCH RD	Court Office 13 Church Road Redditch Worcs B97 4AB	Tel: 01527 67822 Fax: 01527 65791 DX: 701880 Redditch-2
REIGATE RH	Law Courts Hatchlands Rd Redhill Surrey RH1 6BL	Tel: 01737 763637 Fax: 01737 766917 DX: 98020 Redhill West
RHYL RI	The Court House Clwyd Street Rhyl Denbighshire LL18 3LA	Tel: 01745 330216 Fax: 01745 336726 DX: 702489 Rhyl-2
ROMFORD RM	2a Oaklands Avenue Romford Essex RM1 4DP	Tel: 01708 775353 Fax: 01708 756653 DX: 97530 Romford-2
ROTHERHAM RT	Portland House Mansfield Road Rotherham South Yorkshire S60 2BX	Tel: 01709 364786 Fax: 01709 838044 DX: 703025 Rotherham-4
RUGBY RU	5 Newbold Road Rugby Warwickshire CV21 2RN	Tel: 01788 542543 Fax: 01788 550212 DX: 701934 Rugby-2

Court (Courts with Bank-ruptcy jurisdiction in bold)	Address	Contact Nos
RUNCORN RC	The Law Courts Halton Lea Runcorn Cheshire WA7 2HA	Tel: 01928 716533 Fax: 01928 701692 DX: 702466 Runcorn-3
St ALBANS SI	Victoria House 117 Victoria Street St. Albans Herts AL1 3TJ	Tel: 017278 56925 Fax: 017278 52484 DX: 97770 St Albans-2
St HELENS HW	1st Floor Rexmore House Cotham Street St Helens Merseyside WA10 1SE	Tel: 01744 27544 Fax: 01744 20484 DX: 702570 St Helens-2
SALFORD SF DB	Prince William House Peel Cross Road Salford M5 2RR	Tel: 0161 745 7511 Fax: 0161 745 7202 DX: 702630 Salford-5
SALISBURY SB	Courts of Justice Alexandra House St. John's Street Salisbury Wilts SP1 2PN	Tel: 01722 325444 Fax: 01722 412991 DX: 98500 Salisbury-2
SCARBOROUGH SZ	Pavilion House Valley Bridge Rd Scarborough North Yorkshire YO11 2JS	Tel: 01723 366361 Fax: 01723 501992 DX: 65140 Scarborough-2
SCUNTHORPE SC	Crown Buildings Comforts Avenue Scunthorpe N. Lincs DN15 6PR	Tel: 01724 289111 Fax: 01724 291119 DX: 702010 Scunthorpe-3
SHEFFIELD SE	The Law Courts 50 West Bar Sheffield South Yorkshire S3 8PH	Tel: 0114 281 2400 Fax: 0114 281 2425 DX: 703028 Sheffield-6
SHOREDITCH SD	19 Leonard Street London EC2A 4AL	Tel: (020) 7253 0956 Fax: (020) 7490 5613 DX: 121000 Shoreditch-2
SHREWSBURY SY	4th Floor Cambrian Business Centre Chester Street Shrewsbury Shropshire SY1 1NA	Tel: 01743 289069 Fax: 01743 237954 DX: 702047 Shrewsbury-3

Court (Courts with Bankruptcy jurisdiction in bold)	Address	Contact Nos
SKEGNESS AND SPILSBY ZV Hearings and counter service available at: The Court House Park Avenue Skegness Lincs PE25 1BH	Town Hall Annex North Parade Skegness PE25 1DA	Tel: 01754 762429 Fax: 01754 761165 DX: 701919 Skegness-2
SKIPTON SP	The Old Courthouse Otley Street Skipton North Yorkshire BD23 1EH	Tel: 01756 793315 Fax: 01756 799989 DX: 703031 Skipton-2
SLOUGH	The Law Courts Windsor Road Slough Berks SL1 2HE	Tel: 01753 690300 Fax: 01753 575990 DX: 98030 Slough-3
SOUTHAMPTON SO	Southampton Combined Court The Courts of Justice London Road Southampton Hants SO9 1DR	Tel: (023) 8021 3200 Fax: (023) 8021 3222 (County)/ 023 8021 3234 (Crown)/ 023 8021 3232 (Listing)/ 023 8021 3227 (Bailiffs) DX: 111000 Southampton-11
SOUTHEND SS	Tylers House Tylers Avenue Southend-on-Sea Essex SS1 2AW	Tel: 01702 601991 Fax: 01702 603090 DX: 97780 Southend-on-sea-2
SOUTHPORT DC	Duke's House 34 Hoghton Street Southport Sefton Merseyside PR9 0PU	Tel: 01704 531541 Fax: 01704 542487 DX: 702580 Southport-2
SOUTH SHIELDS SH	Millbank Secretan Way South Shields Tyne & Wear NE33 1AG	Tel: 0191 456 3343 Fax: 0191 427 9503 DX: 65143 South Shields-3
STAFFORD ST	Victoria Square Stafford ST16 2QQ	Tel: 01785 610730 Fax: 01785 213250 DX: 703190 Stafford-4
STAINES SM	The Law Courts Knowle Green Staines Middlesex TW18 1XH	Tel: 01784 459175 Fax: 01784 460176 DX: 98040 Staines-2
STOCKPORT SK	5th Floor Heron House Wellington Street Stockport Greater Manchester SK1 3OJ	Tel: 0161 474 7707 Fax: 0161 476 3129 DX: 702621 Stockport-4

Court (Courts with Bankruptcy jurisdiction in bold)	Address	Contact Nos
STOKE-ON-TRENT SQ	Bethesda Street Hanley Stoke-on-Trent Staffs ST1 3BP	Tel: 01782 854000 Fax: 01782 854046 DX: 703360 Hanley-3
STOURBRIDGE SX	7 Hagley Road Stourbridge West Midlands DY8 1QL	Tel: 01384 394232 Fax: 01384 441736 DX: 701889 Stourbridge-2
STRATFORD-UPON-AVON SV	5 Elm Court Arden Street Stratford-upon-Avon Warwickshire CV37 6PA	Tel: 01789 293056 Fax: 01789 293056 DX: 701998 Stratford-u-Avon-3
SUNDERLAND SR	The Court House 44 John Street Sunderland Tyne and Wear SR1 1RB	Tel: 0191 5680750 Fax: 0191 514 3028 DX: 65149 Sunderland-2
SWANSEA SA	Swansea Civil Justice Centre Caravella House Quay West Quay Parade Swansea West Glamorgan SA1 1SP	Tel: 01792 510350 Fax: 01792 473520 DX: 99740 Swansea-5
SWINDON SN	The Law Courts Islington Street Swindon Wilts SN1 2HG	Tel: 01793 690500 (Switchboard) Fax: 01793 690555 (County)/ 01793 690511 (Listing)/ 01793 690514 (Family)/ 01793 690521 (Bailiffs) DX: 98430 Swindon-5
TAMESIDE TS	PO Box 166 Henry Square Ashton-under-Lyne Lancs OL6 7TP	Tel: 0161 331 5614 (General)/ 0161 331 5626 (Bailiffs) Fax: 0161 331 5649 DX: 702625 Ashton-under-Lyne 2
TAMWORTH TM	The Precinct Lower Gungate Tamworth Staffs B79 7AJ	Tel: 01827 62664 Fax: 01827 65289 DX: 702016 Tamworth-2
TAUNTON TA	Shire Hall Taunton Somerset TA1 4EU	Tel: 01823 335972 Fax: 01823 351337 DX: 98410 Taunton-2
TEESSIDE	*See* MIDDLESBROUGH	
TELFORD TF	Telford Square Malinsgate Town Centre Telford Shropshire TF3 4JP	Tel: 01952 291045 Fax: 01952 291601 DX: 701976 Telford-3

Court (Courts with Bankruptcy jurisdiction in bold)	Address	Contact Nos
THANET TT	2nd Floor Cecil Square Margate Kent CT9 1RL	Tel: 01843 221722/ 228771 Fax: 01843 224313 DX: 98210 Cliftonville-2
TORQUAY TQ	Torquay & Newton Abbott County Court The Willows Nicholson Road Torquay TQ2 7AZ	Tel: 01803 616791 Fax: 01803 616795 DX: 98740 Torquay-4
TROWBRIDGE TW	Ground Floor Clarke's Mill Stallard Street Trowbridge Wilts BA14 8DB	Tel: 01225 752101 Fax: 01225 776638 DX: 98750 Trowbridge-2
TRURO TR	The Courts of Justice Edward Street Truro Cornwall TR1 2PB	Tel: 01872 222340 Fax: 01872 222348 DX: 98800 Truro-2
TUNBRIDGE WELLS TN	Merevale House 42/46 London Road Tunbridge Wells Kent TN1 1DP	Tel: 01892 515515 Fax: 01892 513676 DX: 98220 Tunbridge Wells-3
UXBRIDGE UB	501 Uxbridge Road Hayes Middx UB4 8HL	Tel: 020 85618562 Fax: 020 85612020 DX: 44658 HAYES (MIDDX)
WAKEFIELD WF	Crown House 127 Kirkgate Wakefield West Yorkshire WF1 1JW	Tel: 01924 370268 Fax: 01924 200818 DX: 703040 Wakefield-3

Court (Courts with Bankruptcy jurisdiction in bold)	Address	Contact Nos
WALSALL WJ	Bridge House Bridge Street Walsall West Mids WS1 1JQ	General enquiries: Tel: 01922 728855 Fax: 01922 728891 DX: 701943 Walsall-2 Email: enquiries@walsallcounty court.gsi.gov.uk Family enquiries: Tel: 01922 728855 Fax: 01922 728891 Email: family@walsallcounty court.gsi.gov.uk Bailiffs enquiries: Tel: 01922 728855 Fax: 01922 728891 Email: bailiffs@walsallcounty court.gsi.gov.uk Listing enquiries: Tel: 01922 728855 Fax: 01922 728891 Email: hearings@walsallcounty court.gsi.gov.uk
WANDSWORTH WT	76/78 Upper Richmond Road Putney London SW15 2SU	Tel: (020) 8333 4351/2 Fax: (020) 8877 9854 DX: 97540 Putney-2
WARRINGTON WA	Leigh Street Warrington Cheshire WA1 1UR	Tel: 01925 256700 Fax: 01925 413335 DX: 702501 Warrington-3
WARWICK WW	Warwick Combined Court Centre Northgate South Side Warwick CV34 4RB	Tel: 01926 492276 Fax: 01926 474227 DX: 701964 Warwick-2
WATFORD WD	Cassiobury House 11/19 Station Road Watford Herts WD17 1EZ	Tel: 01923 699400/ 699401 Fax: 01923 251317 DX: 122740 Watford-5
WELLINGBOROUGH WE	Lothersdale House West Villa Road Wellingborough Northants NN8 4NF	Tel: 01933 226168 Fax: 01933 272977 DX: 701883 Wellingborough-2
WELSHPOOL AND NEWTOWN WP	The Mansion House 24 Severn Street Welshpool Powys SY21 7UX	Tel: 01938 552004 Fax: 01938 555395 DX: 702524 Welshpool-2

Court (Courts with Bank-ruptcy jurisdiction in bold)	Address	Contact Nos
WEST LONDON WL	West London Courthouse 181 Talgarth Road Hammersmith London W6 8DN	Tel: (020) 8600 6868 Fax: (020) 8600 6860 DX: 97550 Hammer-smith 8
WESTON-SUPER-MARE WM	Second Floor Regent House High Street Weston-super-Mare Somerset BS23 1JF	Tel: 01934 626967 Fax: 01934 643028 DX: 98810 Weston-s-Mare-2
WEYMOUTH AND DORCHESTER WY	Weymouth and Dorches-ter Combined Court Cen-tre 2nd Floor Westwey House Westwey Road Weymouth Dorset DT4 8TE	Tel: 01305 752510 Fax: 01305 788293 DX: 98820 Weymouth-3
WHITEHAVEN WH	Old Town Hall Duke Street Whitehaven Cumbria CA28 7NU	Tel: 01946 67788 Fax: 01946 691219 DX: 63990 Whitehaven-2
WIGAN WN	The Court House Crawford Street Wigan Greater Manchester WN1 1NG	Tel: 01942 246481 Fax: 01942 829164 DX: 724820 Wigan-9
WILLESDEN WI	9 Acton Lane Harlesden London NW10 8SB	Tel: (020) 8963 8200 Fax: (020) 8453 0946 DX: 97560 Harlesden-2
WINCHESTER WC	The Law Courts Winchester Hants SO23 9EL	Tel: 01962 841212 Fax: 01962 853821 DX: 98830 Winchester-3
WOLVERHAMPTON WV	Wolverhampton Combined Court Pipers Row Wolverhampton West Midlands WV1 3LQ	Tel: 01902 481000 Fax: 01902 481076 DX: 702019 Wolverhampton-4
WOOLWICH WO	The Court House 165 Powis Street Woolwich London SE18 6JW	Tel: (020) 8854 2127 Fax: (020) 8316 4842 DX: 123450 Woolwich-8
WORCESTER WR	Worcester Combined Court The Shirehall Foregate Street Worcester WR1 1EQ	Tel: 01905 730800 Fax: 01905 730801 DX: 716262 Worcester-1
WORKSOP WS	8 Slack Walk Worksop Notts S80 1LN	Tel: 01909 472358 Fax: 01909 530181 DX: 702190 Worksop-2

Court (Courts with Bank-ruptcy jurisdiction in bold)	Address	Contact Nos
WORTHING WG	The Law Courts Christchurch Road Worthing Sussex BN11 1JD	Tel: 01903 221920 Fax: 01903 235559 DX: 98230 Worthing-4
WREXHAM WX	2nd Floor Crown Build-ings 31 Chester Street Wrexham LL13 8XN	Tel: 01978 351738 Fax: 01978 290677 DX: 721921 Wrexham-2
YEOVIL YE	22 Hendford Yeovil Somerset BA20 2QD	Tel: 01935 474133 Fax: 01935 410004 DX: 98520 Yeovil-2
YORK YO	The Courthouse Piccadilly House 55 Piccadilly York YO1 5PL	Tel: 01904 629935 Fax: 01904 679963 DX: 65165 York-4

Directory of High Court Enforcement Officers – Listed Alphabetically by Postal District

11–8

District	Code	Name
Bath	BA	ANDERSON, Michael
		ASKER, David
		BARNETT, Simon
		BASTIN, Simon
		BULLOCK, Richard
		DUNCAN, Andrew
		EGMORE, Angela
		EVANS, Philip
		FARRINGTON, Patrick
		GATER, Jonathan
		GRIFFITHS, Richard
		HARGROVE, John
		HATHAWAY, John
		HORNER, Nigel
		JAMES, John
		KIMBER, Michael
		LEYSHON, Martin
		PEPPER, Nigel
		SANDBROOK, Claire
		SMITH, Alan
		TRICKEY, David
Birmingham	B	ANDERSON, Michael
		ASKER, David
		BULLOCK, Richard
		BUTLER, Malcolm
		DEAN, Paul
		DUNCAN, Andrew
		EVANS, Philip
		FARRINGTON, Patrick
		GATER, Jonathan
		GRIFFITHS, Richard
		HARGROVE, John
		HARRISON, Karl
		HATHAWAY, John
		HORNER, Nigel
		JACKSON, Michael
		JAMES, John
		KIMBER, Michael
		LEYSHON, Martin
		MARSTON, John
		MORGAN, Ian
		PEPPER, Nigel
		SANDBROOK, Claire
		SMITH, Alan
		THOMPSON, Patricia
		WILSON, Andrew
Blackburn	BB	ASKER, David
		BOVAN, Gary
		DEAN, Derek
		DEAN, Gordon
		DEAN, Paul
		HARGROVE, John
		HARRISON, Karl
		LAING, John
		SANDBROOK, Claire
		SMITH, Alan
		THOMPSON, Patricia
		WILSON, Andrew

District	Code	Name
Bolton	BL	ASKER, David
		DEAN, Derek
		DEAN, Gordon
		DEAN, Paul
		HARGROVE, John
		HARRISON, Karl
		SANDBROOK, Claire
		SMITH, Alan
		THOMPSON, Patricia
		VANN, Edward
		WILSON, Andrew
Bournemouth	BH	ASKER, David
		BARNETT, Simon
		BASTIN, Simon
		COOMBE, Geoffrey
		EGMORE, Angela
		GATER, Jonathan
		GRIFFITHS, Richard
		HARGROVE, John
		SANDBROOK, Claire
		SMITH, Alan
		TRICKEY, David
Bradford	BD	ASKER, David
		BOVAN, Gary
		HARGROVE, John
		HARRISON, Dion
		HARRISON, Karl
		LAING, John
		SANDBROOK, Claire
		SMITH, Alan
		THOMPSON, Patricia
		TOWERS, Jonathan
		WHITWORTH, Frank
		WILSON, Andrew
Brighton	BN	ASKER, David
		GATER, Jonathan
		GRIFFITHS, Richard
		HARGROVE, John
		SANDBROOK, Claire
		SMITH, Alan
Bristol	BS	ALEXANDER, Nicholas
		ANDERSON, Michael
		ASKER, David
		BULLOCK, Richard
		DUNCAN, Andrew
		EVANS, Philip
		EWART-JAMES, Andrew
		FARRINGTON, Patrick
		GATER, Jonathan
		GRIFFITHS, Richard
		HARGROVE, John
		HATHAWAY, John
		HORNER, Nigel
		JAMES, John
		KIMBER, Michael
		LEYSHON, Martin
		PEPPER, Nigel
		SANDBROOK, Claire
		SMITH, Alan
Bromley	BR	ASKER, David
		BUTLER, Malcolm
		GATER, Jonathan
		GRIFFITHS, Richard
		JACKSON, Michael
		HARGROVE, John
		MARSTON, John
		MORGAN, Ian
		SANDBROOK, Claire
		SMITH, Alan

District	Code	Name
Cambridge	CB	ASKER, David
		CONSTANT, Bryan
		HALL, Brian
		HARGROVE, John
		SANDBROOK, Claire
		SILLS, Tim
		SMITH, Alan
		STEPHENS, Martin
		WATT, Peter
Canterbury	CT	ASKER, David
		GATER, Jonathan
		GRIFFITHS, Richard
		HARGROVE, John
		SANDBROOK, Claire
		SMITH, Alan
Cardiff	CF	ANDERSON, Michael
		ASKER, David
		BOWEN, David
		BULLOCK, Richard
		DUNCAN, Andrew
		EVANS, Philip
		FARRINGTON, Patrick
		GATER, Jonathan
		GRIFFITHS, Richard
		HARGROVE, John
		HATHAWAY, John
		HORNER, Nigel
		JAMES, John
		KIMBER, Michael
		LEYSHON, Martin
		PEPPER, Nigel
		SANDBROOK, Claire
		SMITH, Alan
Carlisle	CA	ASKER, David
		DEAN, Derek
		DEAN, Gordon
		DEAN, Paul
		FITZGERALD, Hugh
		HARGROVE, John
		HARRISON, Karl
		SANDBROOK, Claire
		SMITH, Alan
		THOMPSON, Patricia
		WILSON, Andrew
Chelmsford	CM	ASKER, David
		BUTLER, Malcolm
		HARGROVE, John
		JACKSON, Michael
		MARSTON, John
		MORGAN, Ian
		SANDBROOK, Claire
		SMITH, Alan
		TUNSTILL, Peter
		WILLIAMS, James

District	Code	Name
Chester	CH	ANDERSON, Michael
		ARNOLD, John
		ASKER, David
		BOVAN, Gary
		BULLOCK, Richard
		DEAN, Derek
		DEAN, Gordon
		DEAN, Paul
		DUNCAN, Andrew
		EVANS, Philip
		FARRINGTON, Patrick
		GATER, Jonathan
		GREGORY, John
		GRIFFITHS, Richard
		GUEST, Robin
		HARGROVE, John
		HARRISON, Karl
		HATHAWAY, John
		HORNER, Nigel
		JAMES, John
		KIMBER, Michael
		LEYSHON, Martin
		MASON, David
		MORRIS-JONES, Gareth
		PARRY, Anthony
		PEPPER, Nigel
		SANDBROOK, Claire
		SMITH, Alan
		SOUTHERN, Norman
		THOMPSON, Patricia
		WILSON, Andrew
Cleveland (Teeside)	TS	ASKER, David
		DAVIES, Malcolm
		ELLIOTT, Chris
		FELLOWS, Kathleen
		HARGROVE, John
		HARRISON, Karl
		SANDBROOK, Claire
		SMITH, Alan
		STOREY, Roy
		THOMPSON, Patricia
		WILSON, Andrew
Colchester	CO	ASKER, David
		HARGROVE, John
		SANDBROOK, Claire
		SMITH, Alan
		STEPHENS, Martin
Coventry	CV	ANDERSON, Michael
		ASKER, David
		BULLOCK, Richard
		BUTLER, Malcolm
		DUNCAN, Andrew
		EVANS, Philip
		FARRINGTON, Patrick
		GATER, Jonathan
		GRIFFITHS, Richard
		HARGROVE, John
		HARRISON, Karl
		HATHAWAY, John
		HORNER, Nigel
		JACKSON, Michael
		JAMES, John
		KIMBER, Michael
		LEYSHON, Martin
		MARSTON, John
		MORGAN, Ian
		PEPPER, Nigel
		SANDBROOK, Claire
		SMITH, Alan
		THOMPSON, Patricia
		WILSON, Andrew

District	Code	Name
Crewe	CW	ANDERSON, Michael
		ARNOLD, John
		ASKER, David
		BOVAN, Gary
		BULLOCK, Richard
		DEAN, Gordon
		DEAN, Paul
		DUNCAN, Andrew
		EVANS, Philip
		FARRINGTON, Patrick
		GATER, Jonathan
		GRIFFITHS, Richard
		HARGROVE, John
		HARRISON, Karl
		HATHAWAY, John
		HORNER, Nigel
		JAMES, John
		KIMBER, Michael
		LEYSHON, Martin
		MASON, David
		PEPPER, Nigel
		SANDBROOK, Claire
		SMITH, Alan
		SOUTHERN, Norman
		THOMPSON, Patricia
		WILSON, Andrew
Croydon	CR	ASKER, David
		BUTLER, Malcolm
		GATER, Jonathan
		HARGROVE, John
		GRIFFITHS, Richard
		JACKSON, Michael
		MARSTON, John
		MORGAN, Ian
		SANDBROOK, Claire
		SMITH, Alan
Darlington	DL	ASKER, David
		DAVIES, Malcolm
		ELLIOTT, Chris
		FELLOWS, Kathleen
		HARGROVE, John
		HARRISON, Karl
		SANDBROOK, Claire
		SMITH, Alan
		STOREY, Roy
		THOMPSON, Patricia
		WILSON, Andrew
Dartford	DA	ASKER, David
		BUTLER, Malcolm
		GATER, Jonathan
		GRIFFITHS, Richard
		HARGROVE, John
		JACKSON, Michael
		MARSTON, John
		MORGAN, Ian
		SANDBROOK, Claire
		SMITH, Alan

District	Code	Name
Derby	DE	ANDERSON, Michael
		ASKER, David
		BULLOCK, Richard
		BUTLER, Malcolm
		DEAN, Paul
		DUNCAN, Andrew
		EVANS, Philip
		FARRINGTON, Patrick
		GATER, Jonathan
		GRIFFITHS, Richard
		HARGROVE, John
		HARRISON, Karl
		HATHAWAY, John
		HORNER, Nigel
		JACKSON, Michael
		JAMES, John
		KIMBER, Michael
		LEYSHON, Martin
		MARSTON, John
		MORGAN, Ian
		PEPPER, Nigel
		SANDBROOK, Claire
		SMITH, Alan
		THOMPSON, Patricia
		WILSON, Andrew
Doncaster	DN	ASKER, David
		BAITSON, Helen
		BAITSON, Michael
		BUTLER, Malcolm
		DEAN, Paul
		HARGROVE, John
		HARRISON, Dion
		HARRISON, Karl
		JACKSON, Michael
		MARSTON, John
		McGARRAGH, Robert
		MORGAN, Ian
		SANDBROOK, Claire
		SMITH, Alan
		THOMPSON, Patricia
		WILSON, Andrew
Dorchester	DT	ASKER, David
		BARNETT, Simon
		BASTIN, Simon
		EGMORE, Angela
		HARGROVE, John
		SANDBROOK, Claire
		SMITH, Alan
		TRICKEY, David

District	Code	Name
Dudley	DY	ANDERSON, Michael
		ASKER, David
		BULLOCK, Richard
		BUTLER, Malcolm
		DUNCAN, Andrew
		EVANS, Philip
		FARRINGTON, Patrick
		GATER, Jonathan
		GRIFFITHS, Richard
		HARGROVE, John
		HARRISON, Karl
		HATHAWAY, John
		HORNER, Nigel
		JACKSON, Michael
		JAMES, John
		KIMBER, Michael
		LEYSHON, Martin
		MARSTON, John
		MORGAN, Ian
		PEPPER, Nigel
		SANDBROOK, Claire
		SMITH, Alan
		THOMPSON, Patricia
		WILSON, Andrew
Durham	DH	ASKER, David
		DAVIES, Malcolm
		ELLIOTT, Chris
		FELLOWS, Kathleen
		HARGROVE, John
		HARRISON, Karl
		SANDBROOK, Claire
		SMITH, Alan
		STOREY, Roy
		THOMPSON, Patricia
		WILSON, Andrew
Enfield	EN	ASKER, David
		BUTLER, Malcolm
		HARGROVE, John
		JACKSON, Michael
		MARSTON, John
		MORGAN, Ian
		SANDBROOK, Claire
		SMITH, Alan
		TUNSTILL, Peter
		WILLIAMS, James
Exeter	EX	ASKER, David
		BARNETT, Simon
		BASTIN, Simon
		EGMORE, Angela
		HARGROVE, John
		SANDBROOK, Claire
		SMITH, Alan
		TRICKEY, David
Fylde (Blackpool)	FY	ASKER, David
		DEAN, Derek
		DEAN, Gordon
		DEAN, Paul
		HARGROVE, John
		HARRISON, Karl
		SANDBROOK, Claire
		SMITH, Alan
		THOMPSON, Patricia
		WILSON, Andrew

District	Code	Name
Gloucester	GL	ALEXANDER, Nicholas
		ANDERSON, Michael
		ASKER, David
		BOWEN, David
		BULLOCK, Richard
		DUNCAN, Andrew
		EVANS, Philip
		EWART-JAMES, Andrew
		FARRINGTON, Patrick
		GATER, Jonathan
		GRIFFITHS, Richard
		HARGROVE, John
		HATHAWAY, John
		HORNER, Nigel
		JAMES, John
		KIMBER, Michael
		LEYSHON, Martin
		PEPPER, Nigel
		SANDBROOK, Claire
		SMITH, Alan
Guildford	GU	ANDERSON, Michael
		ASKER, David
		BUTLER, Malcolm
		DUNCAN, Andrew
		EVANS, Philip
		FARRINGTON, Patrick
		GATER, Jonathan
		GRIFFITHS, Richard
		HARGROVE, John
		HATHAWAY, John
		HORNER, Nigel
		JACKSON, Michael
		JAMES, John
		KIMBER, Michael
		LEYSHON, Martin
		MARSTON, John
		MORGAN, Ian
		PEPPER, Nigel
		SANDBROOK, Claire
		SMITH, Alan
Halifax	HX	ASKER, David
		BOVAN, Gary
		HARGROVE, John
		HARRISON, Dion
		HARRISON, Karl
		LAING, John
		SANDBROOK, Claire
		SMITH, Alan
		THOMPSON, Patricia
		WHITWORTH, Frank
		WILSON, Andrew
Harrogate	HG	ASKER, David
		BOVAN, Gary
		HARGROVE, John
		HARRISON, Dion
		HARRISON, Karl
		LAING, John
		SANDBROOK, Claire
		SMITH, Alan
		THOMPSON, Patricia
		WHITWORTH, Frank
		WILSON, Andrew

District	Code	Name
Harrow	HA	ASKER, David
		BUTLER, Malcolm
		GATER, Jonathan
		GRIFFITHS, Richard
		HARGROVE, John
		JACKSON, Michael
		KIMBER, Michael
		MARSTON, John
		MORGAN, Ian
		SANDBROOK, Claire
		SMITH, Alan
Hemel Hempstead	HP	ANDERSON, Michael
		ASKER, David
		BULLOCK, Richard
		BUTLER, Malcolm
		DUNCAN, Andrew
		EVANS, Philip
		FARRINGTON, Patrick
		GATER, Jonathan
		GRIFFITHS, Richard
		HARGROVE, John
		HATHAWAY, John
		HORNER, Nigel
		JACKSON, Michael
		JAMES, John
		KIMBER, Michael
		LEYSHON, Martin
		MARSTON, John
		MORGAN, Ian
		PEPPER, Nigel
		SANDBROOK, Claire
		SMITH, Alan
		TUNSTILL, Peter
		WILLIAMS, James
Hereford	HR	ALEXANDER, Nicholas
		ANDERSON, Michael
		ASKER, David
		BOWEN, David
		BULLOCK, Richard
		BUTLER, Malcolm
		DUNCAN, Andrew
		EVANS, Philip
		EWART-JAMES, Andrew
		FARRINGTON, Patrick
		GATER, Jonathan
		GRIFFITHS, Richard
		HARGROVE, John
		HATHAWAY, John
		HORNER, Nigel
		JACKSON, Michael
		JAMES, John
		KIMBER, Michael
		LEYSHON, Martin
		MARSTON, John
		MORGAN, Ian
		PEPPER, Nigel
		SANDBROOK, Claire
		SMITH, Alan
Huddersfield	HD	ASKER, David
		BOVAN, Gary
		DEAN, Paul
		HARGROVE, John
		HARRISON, Dion
		HARRISON, Karl
		LAING, John
		SANDBROOK, Claire
		SMITH, Alan
		THOMPSON, Patricia
		WHITWORTH, Frank
		WILSON, Andrew

District	Code	Name
Hull	HU	ASKER, David
		BAITSON, Helen
		BAITSON, Michael
		HARGROVE, John
		HARRISON, Dion
		HARRISON, Karl
		McGARRAGH, Robert
		SANDBROOK, Claire
		SMITH, Alan
		THOMPSON, Patricia
		WILSON, Andrew
Ilford	IG	ASKER, David
		BUTLER, Malcolm
		GATOR, Jonathan
		GRIFFITHS, Richard
		HARGROVE, John
		JACKSON, Michael
		MARSTON, John
		MORGAN, Ian
		SANDBROOK, Claire
		SMITH, Alan
Ipswich	IP	ASKER, David
		CONSTANT, Bryan
		HALL, Brian
		HARGROVE, John
		SANDBROOK, Claire
		SILLS, Tim
		SMITH, Alan
		STEPHENS, Martin
		WATT, Peter
Kingston upon Thames	KT	ASKER, David
		BUTLER, Malcolm
		GATER, Jonathan
		GRIFFITHS, Richard
		HARGROVE, John
		JACKSON, Michael
		KIMBER, Michael
		MARSTON, John
		MORGAN, Ian
		SANDBROOK, Claire
		SMITH, Alan
Lancaster	LA	ASKER, David
		DEAN, Derek
		DEAN, Gordon
		DEAN, Paul
		FITZGERALD, Hugh
		HARGROVE, John
		HARRISON, Karl
		SANDBROOK, Claire
		SMITH, Alan
		THOMPSON, Patricia
		WILSON, Andrew
Leeds	LS	ASKER, David
		BOVAN, Gary
		HARGROVE, John
		HARRISON, Dion
		LAING, John
		SANDBROOK, Claire
		SMITH, Alan
		THOMPSON, Patricia
		WHITWORTH, Frank
		WILSON, Andrew

District	Code	Name
Leicester	LE	ANDERSON, Michael
		ASKER, David
		BULLOCK, Richard
		BUTLER, Malcolm
		DUNCAN, Andrew
		EVANS, Philip
		FARRINGTON, Patrick
		GATER, Jonathan
		GRIFFITHS, Richard
		HARGROVE, John
		HARRISON, Karl
		HATHAWAY, John
		HORNER, Nigel
		JACKSON, Michael
		JAMES, John
		KIMBER, Michael
		LEYSHON, Martin
		MARSTON, John
		MORGAN, Ian
		PEPPER, Nigel
		SANDBROOK, Claire
		SMITH, Alan
		STEPHENS, Martin
		WATT, Peter
Lincoln	LN	ASKER, David
		BAITSON, Helen
		BAITSON, Michael
		BULLOCK, Richard
		BUTLER, Malcolm
		HARGROVE, John
		HARRISON, Karl
		JACKSON, Michael
		MARSTON, John
		McGARRAGH, Robert
		MORGAN, Ian
		SANDBROOK, Claire
		SMITH, Alan
		THOMPSON, Patricia
		WILSON, Andrew
Liverpool	L	ARNOLD, John
		ASKER, David
		BOVAN, Gary
		DEAN, Derek
		DEAN, Gordon
		DEAN, Paul
		HARGROVE, John
		HARRISON, Karl
		MASON, David
		SANDBROOK, Claire
		SMITH, Alan
		THOMPSON, Patricia
		WILSON, Andrew
Llandridnod Wells	LD	ANDERSON, Michael
		ASKER, David
		BOWEN, David
		BULLOCK, Richard
		DUNCAN, Andrew
		EVANS, Philip
		FARRINGTON, Patrick
		GATER, Jonathan
		GRIFFITHS, Richard
		HARGROVE, John
		HATHAWAY, John
		HORNER, Nigel
		JAMES, John
		KIMBER, Michael
		LEYSHON, Martin
		PEPPER, Nigel
		SANDBROOK, Claire
		SMITH, Alan

District	Code	Name
Llandudno	LL	ANDERSON, Michael
		ASKER, David
		BULLOCK, Richard
		DEAN, Derek
		DEAN, Gordon
		DEAN, Paul
		DUNCAN, Andrew
		EVANS, Philip
		FARRINGTON, Patrick
		GATER, Jonathan
		GREGORY, John
		GRIFFITHS, Richard
		GUEST, Robin
		HARGROVE, John
		HARRISON, Karl
		HATHAWAY, John
		HORNER, Nigel
		JAMES, John
		KIMBER, Michael
		LEYSHON, Martin
		MORRIS-JONES, Gareth
		OWEN, William
		PARRY, Anthony
		PEPPER, Nigel
		SANDBROOK, Claire
		SMITH, Alan
		THOMPSON, Patricia
		WILSON, Andrew
London East	E	ASKER, David
		BUTLER, Malcolm
		GATER, Jonathan
		GRIFFITHS, Richard
		HARGROVE, John
		JACKSON, Michael
		MARSTON, John
		MORGAN, Ian
		SANDBROOK, Claire
		SMITH, Alan
London East Central	EC	ASKER, David
		BUTLER, Malcolm
		GATER, Jonathan
		GRIFFITHS, Richard
		HARGROVE, John
		HENTY, Charles
		JACKSON, Michael
		MARSTON, John
		MORGAN, Ian
		SANDBROOK, Claire
		SMITH, Alan
London North	N	ASKER, David
		BUTLER, Malcolm
		GATER, Jonathan
		GRIFFITHS, Richard
		HARGROVE, John
		JACKSON, Michael
		MARSTON, John
		MORGAN, Ian
		SANDBROOK, Claire
		SMITH, Alan
London North West	NW	ASKER, David
		BUTLER, Malcolm
		GATER, Jonathan
		GRIFFITHS, Richard
		HARGROVE, John
		JACKSON, Michael
		KIMBER, Michael
		MARSTON, John
		MORGAN, Ian
		SANDBROOK, Claire
		SMITH, Alan

District	Code	Name
London South East	SE	ASKER, David
		BUTLER, Malcolm
		GATER, Jonathan
		GRIFFITHS, Richard
		HARGROVE, John
		JACKSON, Michael
		MARSTON, John
		MORGAN, Ian
		SANDBROOK, Claire
		SMITH, Alan
London South West	SW	ASKER, David
		BUTLER, Malcolm
		GATER, Jonathan
		GRIFFITHS, Richard
		HARGROVE, John
		JACKSON, Michael
		MARSTON, John
		MORGAN, Ian
		SANDBROOK, Claire
		SMITH, Alan
London West	W	ASKER, David
		BUTLER, Malcolm
		GATER, Jonathan
		GRIFFITHS, Richard
		HARGROVE, John
		JACKSON, Michael
		KIMBER, Michael
		MARSTON, John
		MORGAN, Ian
		SANDBROOK, Claire
		SMITH, Alan
London West Central	WC	ASKER, David
		BUTLER, Malcolm
		GATER, Jonathan
		GRIFFITHS, Richard
		HARGROVE, John
		JACKSON, Michael
		KIMBER, Michael
		MARSTON, John
		MORGAN, Ian
		SANDBROOK, Claire
		SMITH, Alan
Luton	LU	ASKER, David
		CONSTANT, Bryan
		HALL, Brian
		HARGROVE, John
		HATHAWAY, John
		SANDBROOK, Claire
		SILLS, Tim
		SMITH, Alan
		STEPHENS, Martin
		WATT, Peter
Manchester	M	ARNOLD, John
		ASKER, David
		DEAN, Derek
		DEAN, Gordon
		DEAN, Paul
		HARGROVE, John
		HARRISON, Karl
		MASON, David
		SANDBROOK, Claire
		SMITH, Alan
		THOMPSON, Patricia
		VANN, Edward
		WILSON, Andrew

District	Code	Name
Medway	ME	ASKER, David
		BUTLER, Malcolm
		GATER, Jonathan
		GRIFFITHS, Richard
		HARGROVE, John
		JACKSON, Michael
		MARSTON, John
		MORGAN, Ian
		SANDBROOK, Claire
		SMITH, Alan
Milton Keynes	MK	ASKER, David
		CONSTANT, Bryan
		HALL, Brian
		HARGROVE, John
		SANDBROOK, Claire
		SILLS, Tim
		SMITH, Alan
		STEPHENS, Martin
		WATT, Peter
Newcastle	NE	ASKER, David
		DAVIES, Malcolm
		ELLIOTT, Chris
		FELLOWS, Kathleen
		HARGROVE, John
		HARRISON, Karl
		SANDBROOK, Claire
		SMITH, Alan
		STOREY, Roy
		THOMPSON, Patricia
		WILSON, Andrew
Newport	NP	ALEXANDER, Nicholas
		ANDERSON, Michael
		ASKER, David
		BOWEN, David
		BULLOCK, Richard
		DUNCAN, Andrew
		EVANS, Philip
		EWART-JAMES, Andrew
		FARRINGTON, Patrick
		GATER, Jonathan
		GRIFFITHS, Richard
		HARGROVE, John
		HATHAWAY, John
		HORNER, Nigel
		JAMES, John
		KIMBER, Michael
		LEYSHON, Martin
		PEPPER, Nigel
		SANDBROOK, Claire
		SMITH, Alan
Northampton	NN	ASKER, David
		CONSTANT, Bryan
		HALL, Brian
		HARGROVE, John
		SANDBROOK, Claire
		SILLS, Tim
		SMITH, Alan
		STEPHENS, Martin
		WATT, Peter
Norwich	NR	ASKER, David
		CONSTANT, Bryan
		HALL, Brian
		HARGROVE, John
		SANDBROOK, Claire
		SILLS, Tim
		SMITH, Alan
		STEPHENS, Martin
		WATT, Peter

District	Code	Name
Nottingham	NG	ANDERSON, Michael
		ASKER, David
		BULLOCK, Richard
		BUTLER, Malcolm
		DEAN, Paul
		DUNCAN, Andrew
		EVANS, Philip
		FARRINGTON, Patrick
		GATER, Jonathan
		GRIFFITHS, Richard
		HARGROVE, John
		HARRISON, Karl
		HATHAWAY, John
		HORNER, Nigel
		JACKSON, Michael
		JAMES, John
		KIMBER, Michael
		LEYSHON, Martin
		MARSTON, John
		MORGAN, Ian
		PEPPER, Nigel
		SANDBROOK, Claire
		SMITH, Alan
		THOMPSON, Patricia
		WILSON, Andrew
Oldham	OL	ASKER, David
		BOVAN, Gary
		DEAN, Gordon
		DEAN, Paul
		HARGROVE, John
		HARRISON, Karl
		LAING, John
		SANDBROOK, Claire
		SMITH, Alan
		THOMPSON, Patricia
		VANN, Edward
		WHITWORTH, Frank
		WILSON, Andrew
Oxford	OX	ALEXANDER, Nicholas
		ANDERSON, Michael
		ASKER, David
		BULLOCK, Richard
		DUNCAN, Andrew
		EVANS, Philip
		EWART-JAMES, Andrew
		FARRINGTON, Patrick
		GATER, Jonathan
		GRIFFITHS, Richard
		HARGROVE, John
		HATHAWAY, John
		HORNER, Nigel
		JAMES, John
		KIMBER, Michael
		LEYSHON, Martin
		PEPPER, Nigel
		SANDBROOK, Claire
		SMITH, Alan
Peterborough	PE	ASKER, David
		CONSTANT, Bryan
		HALL, Brian
		HARGROVE, John
		SANDBROOK, Claire
		SILLS, Tim
		SMITH, Alan
		STEPHENS, Martin
		WATT, Peter

District	Code	Name
Plymouth	PL	ASKER, David
		BARNETT, Simon
		BASTIN, Simon
		EGMORE, Angela
		HARGROVE, John
		HUGHES, David
		POTE, David
		REED, Philip
		SANDBROOK, Claire
		SMITH, Alan
		TRICKEY, David
Portsmouth	PO	ANDERSON, Michael
		ASKER, David
		DUNCAN, Andrew
		EVANS, Philip
		FARRINGTON, Patrick
		GATER, Jonathan
		GRIFFITHS, Richard
		HARGROVE, John
		HORNER, Nigel
		JAMES, John
		KIMBER, Michael
		LEYSHON, Martin
		PEPPER, Nigel
		SANDBROOK, Claire
		SMITH, Alan
Preston	PR	ASKER, David
		BOVAN, Gary
		DEAN, Derek
		DEAN, Gordon
		DEAN, Paul
		HARGROVE, John
		HARRISON, Karl
		LAING, John
		SANDBROOK, Claire
		SMITH, Alan
		THOMPSON, Patricia
		WILSON, Andrew
Reading	RG	ANDERSON, Michael
		ASKER, David
		BULLOCK, Richard
		DUNCAN, Andrew
		EVANS, Philip
		FARRINGTON, Patrick
		GATER, Jonathan
		GRIFFITHS, Richard
		HARGROVE, John
		HATHAWAY, John
		HORNER, Nigel
		JAMES, John
		KIMBER, Michael
		LEYSHON, Martin
		PEPPER, Nigel
		SANDBROOK, Claire
		SMITH, Alan
Redhill	RH	ASKER, David
		BUTLER, Malcolm
		GATER, Jonathan
		GRIFFITHS, Richard
		HARGROVE, John
		JACKSON, Michael
		MARSTON, John
		MORGAN, Ian
		SANDBROOK, Claire
		SMITH, Alan

District	Code	Name
Romford	RM	ASKER, David
		BUTLER, Malcolm
		GATER, Jonathan
		GRIFFITHS, Richard
		HARGROVE, John
		JACKSON, Michael
		MARSTON, John
		MORGAN, Ian
		SANDBROOK, Claire
		SMITH, Alan
Salisbury	SP	ASKER, David
		BARNETT, Simon
		BASTIN, Simon
		EGMORE, Angela
		GATER, Jonathan
		GRIFFITHS, Richard
		HARGROVE, John
		HATHAWAY, John
		SANDBROOK, Claire
		SMITH, Alan
		TRICKEY, David
Sheffield	S	ASKER, David
		BOVAN, Gary
		BULLOCK, Richard
		BUTLER, Malcolm
		DEAN, Paul
		HARGROVE, John
		HARRISON, Dion
		HARRISON, Karl
		JACKSON, Michael
		LAING, John
		MARSTON, John
		MORGAN, Ian
		SANDBROOK, Claire
		SMITH, Alan
		THOMPSON, Patricia
		TODD, Nicholas
		WILSON, Andrew
Shrewsbury	SY	ANDERSON, Michael
		ARNOLD, John
		ASKER, David
		BULLOCK, Richard
		DUNCAN, Andrew
		EVANS, Philip
		FARRINGTON, Patrick
		GATER, Jonathan
		GRIFFITHS, Richard
		HARGROVE, John
		HARRISON, Karl
		HATHAWAY, John
		HORNER, Nigel
		JAMES, John
		KIMBER, Michael
		LEYSHON, Martin
		MASON, David
		PEPPER, Nigel
		SANDBROOK, Claire
		SMITH, Alan
		THOMPSON, Patricia
		WILSON, Andrew

District	Code	Name
Slough	SL	ANDERSON, Michael
		ASKER, David
		BULLOCK, Richard
		DUNCAN, Andrew
		EVANS, Philip
		FARRINGTON, Patrick
		GATER, Jonathan
		GRIFFITHS, Richard
		HARGROVE, John
		HATHAWAY, John
		HORNER, Nigel
		JAMES, John
		KIMBER, Michael
		LEYSHON, Martin
		PEPPER, Nigel
		SANDBROOK, Claire
		SMITH, Alan
Southall (Uxbridge)	UB	ASKER, David
		BUTLER, Malcolm
		GATER, Jonathan
		GRIFFITHS, Richard
		HARGROVE, John
		JACKSON, Michael
		KIMBER, Michael
		MARSTON, John
		MORGAN, Ian
		SANDBROOK, Claire
		SMITH, Alan
Southampton	SO	ANDERSON, Michael
		ASKER, David
		DUNCAN, Andrew
		EVANS, Philip
		FARRINGTON, Patrick
		GATER, Jonathan
		GRIFFITHS, Richard
		HARGROVE, John
		HATHAWAY, John
		HORNER, Nigel
		JAMES, John
		KIMBER, Michael
		LEYSHON, Martin
		PEPPER, Nigel
		SANDBROOK, Claire
		SMITH, Alan
Southend on Sea	SS	ASKER, David
		BUTLER, Malcolm
		HARGROVE, John
		JACKSON, Michael
		MARSTON, John
		MORGAN, Ian
		SANDBROOK, Claire
		SMITH, Alan
St. Albans	AL	ASKER, David
		BUTLER, Malcolm
		HARGROVE, John
		JACKSON, Michael
		MARSTON, John
		MORGAN, Ian
		SANDBROOK, Claire
		SMITH, Alan
		TUNSTILL, Peter
		WILLIAMS, James

District	Code	Name
Stevenage	SG	ASKER, David
		BUTLER, Malcolm
		CONSTANT, Bryan
		HALL, Brian
		HARGROVE, John
		JACKSON, Michael
		MARSTON, John
		MORGAN, Ian
		SANDBROOK, Claire
		SILLS, Tim
		SMITH, Alan
		STEPHENS, Martin
		TUNSTILL, Peter
		WATT, Peter
		WILLIAMS, James
Stockport	SK	ARNOLD, John
		ASKER, David
		BUTLER, Malcolm
		DEAN, Derek
		DEAN, Gordon
		DEAN, Paul
		HARGROVE, John
		HARRISON, Dion
		HARRISON, Karl
		JACKSON, Michael
		MARSTON, John
		MASON, David
		MORGAN, Ian
		SANDBROOK, Claire
		SMITH, Alan
		THOMPSON, Patricia
		VANN, Edward
		WILSON, Andrew
Stoke on Trent	ST	ANDERSON, Michael
		ASKER, David
		BULLOCK, Richard
		BUTLER, Malcolm
		DEAN, Paul
		DUNCAN, Andrew
		EVANS, Philip
		FARRINGTON, Patrick
		GATER, Jonathan
		GRIFFITHS, Richard
		HARGROVE, John
		HARRISON, Karl
		HATHAWAY, John
		HORNER, Nigel
		JACKSON, Michael
		JAMES, John
		KIMBER, Michael
		LEYSHON, Martin
		MARSTON, John
		MORGAN, Ian
		PEPPER, Nigel
		SANDBROOK, Claire
		SMITH, Alan
		THOMPSON, Patricia
		WILSON, Andrew
Sunderland	SR	ASKER, David
		DAVIES, Malcolm
		ELLIOTT, Chris
		FELLOWS, Kathleen
		HARGROVE, John
		HARRISON, Karl
		SANDBROOK, Claire
		SMITH, Alan
		STOREY, Roy
		THOMPSON, Patricia
		WILSON, Andrew

District	Code	Name
Sutton	SM	ASKER, David
		BUTLER, Malcolm
		GATER, Jonathan
		GRIFFITHS, Richard
		HARGROVE, John
		JACKSON, Michael
		MARSTON, John
		MORGAN, Ian
		SANDBROOK, Claire
		SMITH, Alan
Swansea	SA	ANDERSON, Michael
		ASKER, David
		BULLOCK, Richard
		DUNCAN, Andrew
		EVANS, Philip
		FARRINGTON, Patrick
		GATER, Jonathan
		GRIFFITHS, Richard
		HARGROVE, John
		HATHAWAY, John
		HORNER, Nigel
		JAMES, John
		JENKINS, Anthony
		KIMBER, Michael
		LEYSHON, Martin
		PEPPER, Nigel
		SANDBROOK, Claire
		SMITH, Alan
Swindon	SN	ALEXANDER, Nicholas
		ANDERSON, Michael
		ASKER, David
		BULLOCK, Richard
		DUNCAN, Andrew
		EVANS, Philip
		EWART-JAMES, Andrew
		FARRINGTON, Patrick
		GATER, Jonathan
		GRIFFITHS, Richard
		HARGROVE, John
		HATHAWAY, John
		HORNER, Nigel
		JAMES, John
		KIMBER, Michael
		LEYSHON, Martin
		PEPPER, Nigel
		SANDBROOK, Claire
		SMITH, Alan
Taunton	TA	ASKER, David
		BARNETT, Simon
		BASTIN, Simon
		EGMORE, Angela
		HARGROVE, John
		HATHAWAY, John
		SANDBROOK, Claire
		SMITH, Alan
		TRICKEY, David

District	Code	Name
Telford	TF	ANDERSON, Michael
		ASKER, David
		BULLOCK, Richard
		DUNCAN, Andrew
		EVANS, Philip
		FARRINGTON, Patrick
		GATER, Jonathan
		GRIFFITHS, Richard
		HARGROVE, John
		HARRISON, Karl
		HATHAWAY, John
		HORNER, Nigel
		JAMES, John
		KIMBER, Michael
		LEYSHON, Martin
		PEPPER, Nigel
		SANDBROOK, Claire
		SMITH, Alan
		THOMPSON, Patricia
		WILSON, Andrew
Tonbridge	TN	ASKER, David
		BUTLER, Malcolm
		GATER, Jonathan
		GRIFFITHS, Richard
		HARGROVE, John
		JACKSON, Michael
		MARSTON, John
		MORGAN, Ian
		SANDBROOK, Claire
		SMITH, Alan
Torquay	TQ	ASKER, David
		BARNETT, Simon
		BASTIN, Simon
		EGMORE, Angela
		HARGROVE, John
		SANDBROOK, Claire
		SMITH, Alan
		TRICKEY, David
Truro	TR	ASKER, David
		BARNETT, Simon
		BASTIN, Simon
		EGMORE, Angela
		HARGROVE, John
		HUGHES, David
		POTE, David
		REED, Philip
		SANDBROOK, Claire
		SMITH, Alan
		TRICKEY, David
Tweeddale (Berwick upon Tweed)	TD	ASKER, David
		DAVIES, Malcolm
		ELLIOTT, Chris
		HARGROVE, John
		HARRISON, Karl
		SANDBROOK, Claire
		SMITH, Alan
		THOMPSON, Patricia
		WILSON, Andrew
Twickenham	TW	ASKER, David
		BUTLER, Malcolm
		GATER, Jonathan
		GRIFFITHS, Richard
		HARGROVE, John
		JACKSON, Michael
		KIMBER, Michael
		MARSTON, John
		MORGAN, Ian
		SANDBROOK, Claire
		SMITH, Alan

District	Code	Name
Wakefield	WF	ASKER, David
		BOVAN, Gary
		DEAN, Paul
		HARGROVE, John
		HARRISON, Dion
		HARRISON, Karl
		LAING, John
		SANDBROOK, Claire
		SMITH, Alan
		THOMPSON, Patricia
		WHITWORTH, Frank
		WILSON, Andrew
Walsall	WS	ANDERSON, Michael
		ASKER, David
		BULLOCK, Richard
		BUTLER, Malcolm
		DUNCAN, Andrew
		EVANS, Philip
		FARRINGTON, Patrick
		GATER, Jonathan
		GRIFFITHS, Richard
		HARGROVE, John
		HARRISON, Karl
		HATHAWAY, John
		HORNER, Nigel
		JACKSON, Michael
		JAMES, John
		KIMBER, Michael
		LEYSHON, Martin
		MARSTON, John
		MORGAN, Ian
		PEPPER, Nigel
		SANDBROOK, Claire
		SMITH, Alan
		THOMPSON, Patricia
		WILSON, Andrew
Warrington	WA	ARNOLD, John
		ASKER, David
		DEAN, Derek
		DEAN, Gordon
		DEAN, Paul
		HARGROVE, John
		HARRISON, Karl
		MASON, David
		SANDBROOK, Claire
		SMITH, Alan
		SOUTHERN, Norman
		THOMPSON, Patricia
		WILSON, Andrew
Watford	WD	ASKER, David
		BUTLER, Malcolm
		HARGROVE, John
		JACKSON, Michael
		MARSTON, John
		MORGAN, Ian
		SANDBROOK, Claire
		SMITH, Alan
		TUNSTILL, Peter
		WILLIAMS, James
Wigan	WN	ARNOLD, John
		ASKER, David
		DEAN, Derek
		DEAN, Gordon
		DEAN, Paul
		HARGROVE, John
		HARRISON, Karl
		MASON, David
		SANDBROOK, Claire
		SMITH, Alan
		THOMPSON, Patricia
		WILSON, Andrew

District	Code	Name
Wolverhampton	WV	ANDERSON, Michael
		ASKER, David
		BULLOCK, Richard
		BUTLER, Malcolm
		DUNCAN, Andrew
		EVANS, Philip
		FARRINGTON, Patrick
		GATER, Jonathan
		GRIFFITHS, Richard
		HARGROVE, John
		HATHAWAY, John
		HORNER, Nigel
		JACKSON, Michael
		JAMES, John
		KIMBER, Michael
		LEYSHON, Martin
		MARSTON, John
		MORGAN, Ian
		PEPPER, Nigel
		SANDBROOK, Claire
		SMITH, Alan
Worcester	WR	ALEXANDER, Nicholas
		ANDERSON, Michael
		ASKER, David
		BULLOCK, Richard
		BUTLER, Malcolm
		DUNCAN, Andrew
		EVANS, Philip
		EWART-JAMES, Andrew
		FARRINGTON, Patrick
		GATER, Jonathan
		GRIFFITHS, Richard
		HARGROVE, John
		HARRISON, Karl
		HATHAWAY, John
		HORNER, Nigel
		JACKSON, Michael
		JAMES, John
		KIMBER, Michael
		LEYSHON, Martin
		MARSTON, John
		MORGAN, Ian
		PEPPER, Nigel
		SANDBROOK, Claire
		SMITH, Alan
		THOMPSON, Patricia
		WILSON, Andrew
York	YO	ASKER, David
		BAITSON, Helen
		BAITSON, Michael
		BOVAN, Gary
		FELLOWS, Kathleen
		HARGROVE, John
		HARRISON, Dion
		HARRISON, Karl
		LAING, John
		SANDBROOK, Claire
		SMITH, Alan
		STOREY, Roy
		THOMPSON, Patricia
		WILSON, Andrew

*Directory of High Court Enforcement Officers – Addresses and Contact
Details for Appointed Enforcement Officers*

Name	Postal Address	Telephone and Fax Numbers	Email address	**11–9**
	(DX Address in italics)	*(Mobile or out of hours numbers in italics)*	*(Web address in italics)*	
ALEXANDER, Nicholas	2nd Floor 65 London Road Gloucester Gloucestershire GL1 3HF *DX 7514 Gloucester*	Tel: 01452 429883 *01531 636108* Fax: 01452 300922	nalexander @whitemans.com	
ANDERSON, Michael	141 Walter Road Swansea SA1 5RW *DX 52966 Swansea*	Tel: 01792 466771 Fax: 01792 455755	mike@mleyshon. co.uk *www.mleyshon.co.uk*	
ARNOLD, John	Birch Cullimore, Solicitors Friars White Friars Chester CH1 1XS *DX 19985 Chester*	Tel: 01244 321066 Fax: 01244 312582	john.arnold@bclaw. co.uk	
ASKER, David	20-21 Tooks Court London EC4A 1LB *DX 70 London/ Chancery Lane WC2*	Tel: 020 7025 2550 *07775 590469* Fax: 020 7025 2556	sysman@sheriffs. co.uk *www.sherforce.co.uk*	
BAITSON, Helen	The Edwardian Auction Galleries Wiltshire Road Hull HU4 6PG	Tel: 01482 500500 *07860 649230* Fax: 01482 500501	Info@gilbert-baitson.co.uk *www.gilbert-baitson.co.uk*	
BAITSON, Michael	The Edwardian Auction Galleries Wiltshire Road Hull HU4 6PG	Tel: 01482 500500 *07860 674714* Fax: 01482 500501	info@gilbert-baitson.co.uk *www.gilbert-baitson.co.uk*	

11–9

Name	Postal Address *(DX Address in italics)*	Telephone and Fax Numbers *(Mobile or out of hours numbers in italics)*	Email address *(Web address in italics)*
BARNETT, Simon	High Court Enforcement Group Limited 2nd Floor Lloyds Bank Chambers 30 High Street Crediton Devon EX17 3AH *DX 54207 Crediton*	Tel: 01363 775118 Fax: 01363 773009	shb@hceo. fsbusiness.co.uk
BASTIN, Simon	High Court Enforcement Group Limited 2nd Floor Lloyds Bank Chambers Crediton Devon EX17 3AH *DX 54207 Crediton*	Tel: 01363 775118 Fax: 01363 773009	scb@hceo. fsbusiness.co.uk
BOVAN, David	CN Gaunt & Son 12 New John Street Bradford West Yorkshire BD1 2QZ *DX11701 Bradford*	Tel: 01274 391929 01274 721711 Fax: 01274 734773	post@cngaunt.co.uk
BOWEN, David	Victoria Chambers 11 Clythia Park Road Newport South Wales NP20 4PB *DX 33204 Newport (South Wales)*	Tel: 01633 264194 01633 266595 Fax: 01633 841146	bowen@colbornes. demon.co.uk
BULLOCK, Richard	Freethhcartwright LLP Cumberland Court 80 Mount Street Nottingham NG1 6HH	Tel: 0115 9369396 Fax: 0115 8599617	richard.bullock @freethcartwright. co.uk

Name	Postal Address *(DX Address in italics)*	Telephone and Fax Numbers *(Mobile or out of hours numbers in italics)*	Email address *(Web address in italics)*	11–9
	DX 10039 Nottingham			
BUTLER, Malcolm	John Marston & Co 24/26 Broadway North Walsall West Midlands WS1 2AJ *DX 12143 Walsall*	Tel: 01922 720 777 Fax: 01922 647 222	post@johnmarston.co.uk *www.hceo.co.uk*	
CONSTANT, Bryan	Invicta House 71 High Street Riseley Bedford MK44 1DD *DX 5641 Bedford*	Tel: 01234 708044 01234 708688 Fax: 01234 708177	sheriffsofficer@kbnet.net	
DAVIES, Malcolm	32 Front Street Whickenham Tyne & Wear NE16 4DT *DX 60414 Whickham*	Tel: 0191 4888800 Fax: 0191 4888811	info@elliottdavies.com	
DEAN, Derek	A & D Dean Trident House 31/33 Dale Street Liverpool L2 2DA *DX 14104 Liverpool*	Tel: 0151 236 4751 0151 236 6406 Fax: 0151 236 8071	sheriff@a-d-dean.co.uk	
DEAN, Gordon	A & D Dean Trident House 31/33 Dale Street Liverpool L2 2DA *DX 14104 Liverpool*	Tel: 0151 236 4751 0151 236 6406 Fax: 0151 236 8071	sheriff@a-d-dean.co.uk	
DEAN, Paul	A & D Dean Trident House 31/33 Dale Street Liverpool L2 2DA *DX 14104 Liverpool*	Tel: 0151 236 4751 0151 236 6406 Fax: 0151 236 8071	sheriff@a-d-dean.co.uk	

COURTS DIRECTORY

11–9

Name	Postal Address *(DX Address in italics)*	Telephone and Fax Numbers *(Mobile or out of hours numbers in italics)*	Email address *(Web address in italics)*
DUNCAN, Andrew	16 The Tything Worcester WR1 1HD *DX 716264 Worcester*	Tel: 01905 732881 Fax: 01905 22347	a.duncan@wwf.co.uk
EGMORE, Angela	High Force Enforcement Group Limited 2nd Floor Lloyds Bank Chambers 30 High Street Crediton Devon EX17 3AH *DX 54207 Crediton*	Tel: 01363 775118 Fax: 01363 773009	are@hceo. fsbusiness.co.uk
ELLIOTT, Chris	32 Front Street Whickenham Tyne & Wear NE16 4DT *DX 60414 Whickham*	Tel: 0191 4888800 Fax: 0191 4888811	info@elliottdavies. com
EVANS, Philip	22 St Andrews Crescent Cardiff CF10 3DD *DX 50752 Cardiff 2*	Tel: 029 20229716 Fax: 029 20377761	pevans@cardiff-law.co.uk
EWART-JAMES, Andrew	2nd Floor 65 London Road Gloucester Gloucestershire GL1 3HF *DX 7514 Gloucester*	Tel: 01452 429883 *01453 872470* Fax: 01452 300922	aewartjames @whitemans.com
FAR-RINGTON, Patrick	17 Martin Street Stafford ST16 2LF *DX 14554 Stafford 1*	Tel: 01785 211411 Fax: 01785 248573	pfarrington@hmo. co.uk

Name	Postal Address (DX Address in italics)	Telephone and Fax Numbers (Mobile or out of hours numbers in italics)	Email address (Web address in italics)	11–9
FELLOWS, Kathleen	Storey & Fellows Albert Chambers 50 Albert Road Middlesbrough TS1 1QD DX 60534 Middlesbrough	Tel: 01642 218819 Fax: 01642 246456	k.fellows@virgin.net	
FITZGERALD, Hugh	39 High Street Wigton Cumbria CA7 9PE DX 714666 Wigton	Tel: 016973 43241 Fax: 016973 44820	hugh_f @atkinsonoritson. co.uk	
GATER, Jonathan	Blandy & Blandy 1 Friar Street Reading Berkshire RG1 1DA DX 4008 Reading	Tel: 0118 951 6947 Fax: 0118 958 3032	hceo@blandy.co.uk	
GREGORY, John	95 High Street Mold CH7 1BJ DX 26556 Mold	Tel: 01352 753882 Fax: 01352 758927	office @keeneandkelly. fsnet.co.uk	
GRIFFITHS, Richard	Blandy & Blandy 1 Friar Street Reading Berkshire RG1 1DA DX 4008 Reading	Tel: 0118 951 6947 Fax: 0118 958 3032	hceo@blandy.co.uk	
GUEST, Robin	95 High Street Mold CH7 1BJ DX 26556 Mold	Tel: 01352 753882 Fax: 01352 758927	office @keeneandkelly. fsnet.co.uk	
HALL, Brian	6 Bedford Road Sandy Bedfordshire SG19 1EN DX 47801 Sandy	Tel: 01767 680251 Fax: 01767 691775	brian.hall @leedssmith.co.uk www.leedssmith. co.uk	

	Name	Postal Address *(DX Address in italics)*	Telephone and Fax Numbers *(Mobile or out of hours numbers in italics)*	Email address *(Web address in italics)*
11–9	HARGROVE, John	20-21 Tooks Court London EC4A 1LB *DX 70 London/ Chancery Lane WC2*	Tel: 020 7025 2551 *07775 590475* Fax: 020 7025 2556	j-hargrove@sheriffs. co.uk *www.sherforce.co.uk*
	HARRISON, Dion	Ashfield House Illingworth Street Ossett West Yorkshire WF5 8AL *DX 707162, Ossett 2*	Tel: 01924 279005 Fax: 01924 280114	sheriffs @cwharrison.net
	HARRISON, Karl	The Sheriffs Office 26 Missouri Avenue Salford Manchester M50 2NP *DX 710252 Manchester 3*	Tel: 0161 925 1800 Fax: 0161 925 1801	karl.harrison @northernsheriffs. com *www.northernsheriffs. com*
	HATHAWAY, John	42 Brook Street Warwick Warwickshire CV34 4BL *DX 18109 Warwick*	Tel: 01926 492407 Fax: 01926 401424	heath.blenkinson @btopenworld.com
	HENTY, Charles	Office of the Secondary Central Criminal Court Old Bailey London EC4M 7EH	Tel: 020 7248 3277 ext: 2326/ 2323/2338 Fax: 020 7192 2444	charles.henty @corpoflondon .gov.uk
	HORNER, Nigel	16 The Tything Worcester WR1 1HD *DX 716264 Worcester*	Tel: 01905 732881 Fax: 01905 22347	n.horner@wwf.co.uk

Name	Postal Address *(DX Address in italics)*	Telephone and Fax Numbers *(Mobile or out of hours numbers in italics)*	Email address *(Web address in italics)*	11–9
HUGHES, David	Cornwall High Court Recovery Graham & Graham Solicitors High Cross House St Austell PL25 4AE *DX 81253 St Austell*	Tel: 01726 75565 Fax: 01726 61484	sheriff@graham-graham.co.uk	
JACKSON, Michael	John Marston & Co. 24/26 Broadway North Walsall West Midlands WS1 2AJ DX 12143 Walsall	Tel: 01922 720771 Fax: 01922 647222	post@johnmarston.co.uk	
JAMES, John	17 Martin Street Stafford ST16 2LF *DX 14554 Stafford 1*	Tel: 01785 211411 Fax: 01785 248573	info@hmo.co.uk *www.hmo.co.uk*	
JENKINS, Anthony	Messrs Ungoes Thomas and King Gwynne House Quay Street Carmarthen SA33 3JX	Tel: 01267 237441 (Switchboard) 01267 239192 (Direct Line) *07974 071739* Fax: 01267 238317	ajenkins@utk.co.uk	
KIMBER, Michael	6 Bellman Court Great Knollys Street Reading RG1 7HU *DX 40135 Castle Street Reading*	Tel: 0118 939 1816 *07831 436112* Fax: 0118 958 8258	sheriff @berksandoxon. co.uk michael.kimber @thimbleby-shorland.co.uk	

11–9

Name	Postal Address (DX Address in italics)	Telephone and Fax Numbers (Mobile or out of hours numbers in italics)	Email address (Web address in italics)
LAING, John	C N Gaunt & Son 12 New John Street Bradford West Yorkshire BD1 2QZ *DX 11701 Bradford*	Tel: 01274 391929/ 01274 721711 Fax: 01274 734773	post@cngaunt.co.uk
LEYSHON, Martin	141 Walter Road Swansea SA1 5RW *DX 52966 Swansea*	Tel: 01792 466771 Fax: 01792 455755	martin@mleyshon. co.uk *www.mleyshon.co.uk*
McGAR-RAGH, Robert	PO Box 654 Lincoln LN2 2XP	Tel: 01673 862899 *07785 902352* Fax: 01673 862899	r.mcgarrach @tiscali.coluk
MARSTON, John	John Marston & Co 24/26 Broadway North Walsall West Midlands WS1 2AJ *DX 12143 Walsall*	Tel: 01922 720 777 Fax: 01922 647 222	post@hceo.co.uk *www.hceo.co.uk*
MASON, David	Birch Cullimore, Solicitors Friars White Friars Chester CH1 1XS *DX 19985 Chester*	Tel: 01244 321066 Fax: 01244 312582	david.mason @bclaw.co.uk
MORGAN, Ian	John Marston & Co 24/26 Broadway North Walsall West Midlands WS1 2AJ *DX 12143 Walsall*	Tel: 01922 720 777 Fax: 01922 647 222	post@johnmarston. co.uk *www.hceo.co.uk*

Name	Postal Address *(DX Address in italics)*	Telephone and Fax Numbers *(Mobile or out of hours numbers in italics)*	Email address *(Web address in italics)*	11–9
MORRIS-JONES, Gareth	95 High Street Mold CH7 1BJ *DX 26556 Mold*	Tel: 01352 753882 Fax: 01352 758927	office @keeneandkelly. fsnet.co.uk	
OWEN, William	314 High Street Bangor Gwynedd LL57 1YA	Tel: 01248 353357 Fax: 01248 372272	wowenestate @yahoo.co.uk	
PARRY, Anthony	9 Chester Street Mold CH7 1EG *DX 26556 Mold*	Tel: 01352 752552 Fax: 01352 752542	auctions.dodds @tesco.net dodds @door__key.com	
PEPPER, Nigel	17 Martin Street Stafford ST16 2LF *DX 14554 Stafford 1*	Tel: 01785 211411 Fax: 01785 248573	npepper@hmo.co.uk	
POTE, David	Cornwall High Court Recovery Graham & Graham Solicitors High Cross House St Austell PL25 4AE *DX 81253 St Austell*	Tel: 01726 75565 Fax: 01726 61484	sheriff@graham-graham.co.uk	
REED, Philip	Cornwall High Court Recovery Graham & Graham Solicitors High Cross House St Austell PL25 4AE *DX 81253 St Austell*	Tel: 01726 75565 Fax: 01726 61484	sheriff@graham-graham.co.uk	
SANDBROOK, Claire	Shergroup Westwood Park London Road Little Horkesley Colchester Essex CO6 4BS	Tel: 01206 274255 *07775 590454* Fax: 01206 274176	c-sandbrook @sheriffs.co.uk *www.sherforce.co.uk*	

11–9	Name	Postal Address (DX Address in italics)	Telephone and Fax Numbers (Mobile or out of hours numbers in italics)	Email address (Web address in italics)
		DX 3654 COLCHESTER		
	SILLS, Tim	6 Bedford Road Sandy Bedfordshire SG19 1EN DX 47801 Sandy	Tel: 01767 680251 Fax: 01767 691775	tim.sills @leedssmith.co.uk www.leedssmith. co.uk
	SMITH, Alan	12 Greek Street Leeds LS1 5RU DX 26416 LEEDS PARK SQUARE	Tel: 0113 2855979 07717 508105 Fax: 0113 2855977	asmith@sheriffs. co.uk www.sherforce. co.uk
	SOUTHERN, Norman	A & D Dean Trident House 31/33 Dale Street Liverpool L2 2DA DX 14104 Liverpool	Tel: 0151 236 4751 0151 236 6406 Fax: 0151 236 8071	sheriff@a-d- dean.co.uk
	STEPHENS, Martin	Beattie Son & Leslie 35 Palmerston Road Northampton NN1 5EU	Tel: 01604 605400 07860 762736 Fax: 01604 605069	sheriffs @supanet.com
	STOREY, Roy	Storey & Fellows Albert Chambers 50 Albert Road Middlesbrough TS1 1QD DX 60534 Middlesbrough	Tel: 01642 218819 Fax: 01642 246456	k.fellows@virgin.net
	THOMPSON, Patricia	The Sheriffs Office 26 Missouri Avenue Salford Manchester M50 2NP DX 710252 Manchester 3	Tel: 0161 925 1800 Fax: 0161 925 1801	tricia.thomson @northernsheriffs .com www. northernsheriffs.com

Name	Postal Address (DX Address in italics)	Telephone and Fax Numbers (Mobile or out of hours numbers in italics)	Email address (Web address in italics)	11–9
TODD, Nicholas	The Old Bull's Head Dun Street Sheffield S3 8SL DX 10531 Sheffield	Tel: 0114 2729667 07764 559748 Fax: 0114 276160	info@ewbauctions.co.uk	
TRICKEY, David	High Court Enforcement Group Limited 2nd Floor Lloyds Bank Chambers 30 High Street Crediton Devon EX17 3AH DX 54207 Crediton	Tel: 01363 775118 Fax: 01363 773009	dt@hceo.fsbusiness.co.uk	
TUNSTILL, Peter	Breeze & Wyles 114 Fore Street Hertford Hertfordshire SG14 1AG DX 57901 Hertford	Tel: 01992 558411 Fax: 01992 503889	peter.tunstill @breezeandwyles.co.uk	
VANN, Edward	Rahleigh House 48 Park Road Ellesmere Park Eccles Manchester M6 8JR DX 14331 Manchester 1	Tel: 0161 449 7766 07979 774422 Fax: 0161 449 7755	edward.vann @enforcement.uk.com	
WATT, Peter	Beattie Son & Leslie 35 Palmerston Road Northampton NN1 5EU	Tel: 01604 605400 Fax: 01604 605069	sheriffs@supanet.com	
WHITWORTH, Frank	17 Cloth Hall Street Huddersfield HD1 2DX DX 713001 Huddersfield	Tel: 01484 427467 07767 385223 Fax: 01484 484313	frank@whitworthsestateagents.co.uk	

11–9	Name	Postal Address *(DX Address in italics)*	Telephone and Fax Numbers *(Mobile or out of hours numbers in italics)*	Email address *(Web address in italics)*
	WILLIAMS, James	Breeze & Wyles 114 Fore Street Hertford Hertfordshire SG14 1AG *DX 57901 Hertford*	Tel: 01992 558411 Fax: 01992 503889	james.williams @breezeand wyles.co.uk
	WILSON, Andrew	The Sheriffs Office 26 Missouri Avenue Salford Manchester M50 2NP *DX 710252 Manchester 3*	Tel: 0161 925 1800 Fax: 0161 925 1801	andrew.wilson @northern sheriffs.com *www.northern sheriffs.com*

INDEX

This index has been prepared using Sweet and Maxwell's Legal Taxonomy. Main index entries conform to keyworks provided by the Legal Taxonomy except where references to specific documents or non-standard terms (denoted by quotation marks) have been included. These keywords provide a means of identifying similar concepts in other Sweet & Maxwell publications and online services to which keywords from the Legal Taxonomy have been applied. Readers may find some minor differences between terms used in the text and those which appear in the index. Suggestions to *taxonomy@sweetandmaxwell.co.uk*

(All references are to paragraph number)

All references to material in Volume 2 are enclosed within square parentheses.

All references to material in Volume 2 are enclosed within square parentheses.

All references to material in Volume 2 are enclosed within square parentheses.

All references to material in Volume 2 are enclosed within square parentheses.

Administration claims—*cont.*
  administration orders, 64PD.3
  AJA 1985, applications under, 64PD.5
  application for directions, 64PD.2
  prospective costs orders, 64PD.6
  relevant claims, 64PD.1
  Variation of Trusts Act, applications
    under, 64PD.4
  prospective costs orders
    form, 64PD.11
    generally, 64PD.6
  scope of Part, 64.2 — 64.2.1
  time limits, [8–46] — [8–47]
  variation of trusts
    applications under s.48 AJA 1985, [1A–
      196]
    disability of trustee, [1A–198]
    generally, [1A–194]
    Practice directions, 64PD.4
    stamp duty, [1A–195]
    vesting orders, [1A–197]

Administration of estates
  claims
    And see Administration claims
    claim forms, 64.3
    editorial introduction, 64.0.2
    general, 64.1
    parties, 64.4
    Practice directions, 64PD.1 — 64PD.8
  Rules, [6D–100] — [6D–105]
  statutory basis, [6D–49] — [6D–51]

Administration of Justice Act 1920
    (enforcement)
  English judgments in foreign court
    application to District Registry, 74.13.4
    expiry of time to appeal, 74.13.2
    foreign policy documents, 74.13.3
    general provisions, 74.12 — 74.13
    introduction, 74.13.1
  foreign judgments
    costs, 74.11.10
    different matters, judgment in respect of,
      74.11.11
    effect of registration, 74.11.16
    entitlement to enforce, 74.11.12
    forms, 74.11.8
    general provisions, 74.2 — 74.11
    introduction, 74.11.7
    rate of exchange, 74.11.9
    security for costs, 74.11.14 — 74.11.15
    setting aside registration, 74.11.17 —
      74.11.19.1
    stay of execution, 74.11.20
    submission by appearance, 74.11.13
  generally, 74.11.2 — 74.11.3
  introduction, 74.11.1
  Queens Bench Guide, [1B–82]

Administration of Justice Act 1925
  general provisions, [9B–14] — [9B–18]

Administration of Justice Act 1960
  appeals
    generally, sc109.2 — sc109.2.1
    Part 8 claims, 8BPD.6
    procedure, 52PD.102
    Queens Bench Guide, [1B–70]

Administration of Justice Act 1960—*cont.*
    release of appellant on bail, sc109.3 —
      sc109.4.1
    statutory basis, [9B–25] — [9B–25.2]
  applications
    generally, sc109.1
    Part 8 claims, 8BPD.5
  certiorari, [9B–31]
  contempt, [9B–22] — [9B–25.1]
  definitions, [9B–32] — [9B–33]
  habeas corpus, [9B–26] — [9B–30]
  release of appellant on bail
    Court of Appeal, by, sc109.4 — sc109.4.1
    generally, sc109.3

Administration of Justice Act 1969
  appeal from High Court, [9B–38] — [9B–
    44]

Administration of Justice Act 1970
  definitions, [3A–49]
  general provisions
    enforcement, [9B–50] — [9B–52]
    generally, [9B–45] — [9B–60]
    High Court, [9B–46] — [9B–49]
    housing, [3A–40] — [3A–49]
    interest, [9B–53] — [9B–56]
    mortgage actions, [3A–41] — [3A–48]
  schedules, [9B–58] — [9B–60]

Administration of Justice Act 1973
  mortgage actions, [3A–60] — [3A–61]

Administration of Justice Act 1982
  Court Funds Office, [6A–5] — [6A–17]

Administration of Justice Act 1985
  claims
    claim forms, 64.3
    editorial introduction, 64.0.2
    general, 64.1
    parties, 64.4
    Practice directions, 64PD.5
    scope of Part, 64.2 — 64.2.1
  definitions, [9B–74] — [9B–73]
  estate of deceased persons, [9B–61] — [9B–
    69]
  reimbursement of costs due to incapacitated
    judge, [9B–70] — [9B–73]

Administration of Justice (Appeals) Act 1934
  general provisions, [9B–1] — [9B–4]
  schedules, [9B–6] — [9B–7]

Administration of Justice (Miscellaneous
    Provisions) Act 1933
  general provisions, [9B–8] — [9B–11]

Administration of oaths
  statutory basis, [9B–131] — [9B–132]

Administration of small estates
  Rules, [6D–100] — [6D–105]
  statutory basis, [6D–49] — [6D–51]

Administration orders (execution)
  See also Administration orders (insolvency)

All references to material in Volume 2 are enclosed within square parentheses.

All references to material in Volume 2 are enclosed within square parentheses.

All references to material in Volume 2 are enclosed within square parentheses.

All references to material in Volume 2 are enclosed within square parentheses.

All references to material in Volume 2 are enclosed within square parentheses.

All references to material in Volume 2 are enclosed within square parentheses.

All references to material in Volume 2 are enclosed within square parentheses.

All references to material in Volume 2 are enclosed within square parentheses.

All references to material in Volume 2 are enclosed within square parentheses.

Alternative dispute resolution—*cont.*
non-co-operation, [2C–81]
procedure, [2C–80]
timing, [2C–79]

Alternative method of service
See Service by alternative permitted method

Alternative percentage increases
employers liability claim, 45.22
road traffic accidents
application, 45.18
assessment, 45.19
generally, 45.19.1 — 45.19.2

Alternative procedure
See Part 8 claims

Amendments
affidavits, 32.16.3
appellants notices
generally, 52.8
point not raised below, 5.8.2
point raised below, 5.8.1
Practice directions, 52PD.34
Commercial Court
Guide, [2A–60]
Practice directions, [2A–29]
Court of Protection Rules
clerical errors, [6B–278]
endorsement, [6B–279]
generally, [6B–277]
judgments
Court of Protection Rules, [6B–278]
generally, 40.12 — 40.12.1
Practice directions, 40BPD.4
prior to entry, 40.2.1
procedure, 3.10 — 3.10.3
Supreme Court Costs Office Guide,
48.141 — 48.142
winding up, [3E–4]
Patents Court
infringement claims, [2F–14] — [2F–15]
invalidity claims, [2F–60]
respondents notices
generally, 52.8
point not raised below, 5.8.2
point raised below, 5.8.1
Practice directions, 52PD.34
specifications (patents)
discretion to refuse, [2F–66]
generally, [2F–63] — [2F–64]
Practice directions, [2F–94]
terms, [2F–65]
statements of case
And see Amendments (statements of case)
after expiry of limitation periods, 17.4 —
17.4.6
generally, 17.1 — 17.1.3
Practice directions, 17PD.1 — 17PD.2
with permission of court, 17.3 — 17.3.9
without permission of court, 17.2 —
17.2.2
statements of truth, 22.1.8
stop notices, 73.19
winding up, [3E–4]
witness statements
generally, 32.4.13
objections to content, 32.4.20

Amendments—*cont.*
Practice directions, 32PD.22

Amendments (statements of case)
application to disallow
generally, 17.2 — 17.2.1
time limits, 17.2.2
disallowance of
generally, 17.2 — 17.2.1
time limits, 17.2.2
editorial introduction, 17.0.2
expiry of limitation periods, after
addition of new cause of action, 17.4.4
addition of new party, 19.5 — 19.5.10
alteration of capacity of party, 17.4.6
correction of name of party, 17.4.5
generally, 17.4 — 17.4.2
new claims, 17.4.3
substitution of new cause of action, 17.4.4
substitution of new party, 19.5 — 19.5.10
generally, 17.1 — 17.1.3
late amendments
after evidence, 17.3.8
prior to trial, 17.3.7
permission
effect, 17.3.4
generally, 17.3 — 17.3.1
late amendments after evidence, 17.3.8
late amendments prior to trial, 17.3.7
Practice directions, 17PD.1
principles for grant, 17.3.5
procedure, 17.3.2 — 17.3.3
prospects of success, 17.3.6
statute-barred counterclaims, 17.3.9
Practice directions
generally, 17PD.2
permission, 17PD.1
procedure
generally, 17.1.3
Practice directions, 17PD.2
prospects of success, 17.3.6
related sources, 17.0.3
statute-barred counterclaims, 17.3.9
time limits, E1–045
with permission of court
effect, 17.3.4
generally, 17.3 — 17.3.1
late amendments after evidence, 17.3.8
late amendments prior to trial, 17.3.7
Practice directions, 17PD.1
principles for grant, 17.3.5
procedure, 17.3.2 — 17.3.3
prospects of success, 17.3.6
statute-barred counterclaims, 17.3.9
without permission of court
application to disallow, 17.2 — 17.2.2
generally, 17.1 — 17.1.2
practice, 17.1.3

Ancillary credit businesses
meaning, [3H–48]
unlicensed trader, by, [3H–278] — [3H–
283]

Annulment
bankruptcy, [3E–108]

Anonymity
control orders, 76.19

All references to material in Volume 2 are enclosed within square parentheses.

All references to material in Volume 2 are enclosed within square parentheses.

All references to material in Volume 2 are enclosed within square parentheses.

All references to material in Volume 2 are enclosed within square parentheses.

All references to material in Volume 2 are enclosed within square parentheses.

All references to material in Volume 2 are enclosed within square parentheses.

All references to material in Volume 2 are enclosed within square parentheses.

All references to material in Volume 2 are enclosed within square parentheses.

All references to material in Volume 2 are enclosed within square parentheses.

All references to material in Volume 2 are enclosed within square parentheses.

All references to material in Volume 2 are enclosed within square parentheses.

All references to material in Volume 2 are enclosed within square parentheses.

All references to material in Volume 2 are enclosed within square parentheses.

All references to material in Volume 2 are enclosed within square parentheses.

All references to material in Volume 2 are enclosed within square parentheses.

All references to material in Volume 2 are enclosed within square parentheses.

All references to material in Volume 2 are enclosed within square parentheses.

All references to material in Volume 2 are enclosed within square parentheses.

All references to material in Volume 2 are enclosed within square parentheses.

All references to material in Volume 2 are enclosed within square parentheses.

All references to material in Volume 2 are enclosed within square parentheses.

All references to material in Volume 2 are enclosed within square parentheses.

All references to material in Volume 2 are enclosed within square parentheses.

All references to material in Volume 2 are enclosed within square parentheses.

All references to material in Volume 2 are enclosed within square parentheses.

All references to material in Volume 2 are enclosed within square parentheses.

All references to material in Volume 2 are enclosed within square parentheses.

All references to material in Volume 2 are enclosed within square parentheses.

All references to material in Volume 2 are enclosed within square parentheses.

All references to material in Volume 2 are enclosed within square parentheses.

All references to material in Volume 2 are enclosed within square parentheses.

All references to material in Volume 2 are enclosed within square parentheses.

All references to material in Volume 2 are enclosed within square parentheses.

All references to material in Volume 2 are enclosed within square parentheses.

All references to material in Volume 2 are enclosed within square parentheses.

All references to material in Volume 2 are enclosed within square parentheses.

All references to material in Volume 2 are enclosed within square parentheses.

All references to material in Volume 2 are enclosed within square parentheses.

All references to material in Volume 2 are enclosed within square parentheses.

All references to material in Volume 2 are enclosed within square parentheses.

All references to material in Volume 2 are enclosed within square parentheses.

All references to material in Volume 2 are enclosed within square parentheses.

All references to material in Volume 2 are enclosed within square parentheses.

All references to material in Volume 2 are enclosed within square parentheses.

All references to material in Volume 2 are enclosed within square parentheses.

All references to material in Volume 2 are enclosed within square parentheses.

All references to material in Volume 2 are enclosed within square parentheses.

All references to material in Volume 2 are enclosed within square parentheses.

All references to material in Volume 2 are enclosed within square parentheses.

All references to material in Volume 2 are enclosed within square parentheses.

All references to material in Volume 2 are enclosed within square parentheses.

All references to material in Volume 2 are enclosed within square parentheses.

All references to material in Volume 2 are enclosed within square parentheses.

All references to material in Volume 2 are enclosed within square parentheses.

All references to material in Volume 2 are enclosed within square parentheses.

All references to material in Volume 2 are enclosed within square parentheses.

All references to material in Volume 2 are enclosed within square parentheses.

All references to material in Volume 2 are enclosed within square parentheses.

All references to material in Volume 2 are enclosed within square parentheses.

All references to material in Volume 2 are enclosed within square parentheses.

All references to material in Volume 2 are enclosed within square parentheses.

All references to material in Volume 2 are enclosed within square parentheses.

All references to material in Volume 2 are enclosed within square parentheses.

All references to material in Volume 2 are enclosed within square parentheses.

All references to material in Volume 2 are enclosed within square parentheses.

All references to material in Volume 2 are enclosed within square parentheses.

All references to material in Volume 2 are enclosed within square parentheses.

County courts (jurisdiction)—*cont.*

monetary limits
generally, [9A–499]
raising, [9A–800] — [9A–801]
probate
effect of order, [9A–537] — [9A–538]
generally, [9A–535] — [9A–536]
proceedings beyond, [9A–539]
recovery of land
declarations, [9A–521]
generally, [3A–220] — [3A–227], [9A–518]
— [9A–520]
injunctions, [9A–521]
remedies, [9A–543] — [9A–546]
repair covenants, [3A–557]
secure tenancies, [3A–434] — [3A–434]
statutory basis
generally, [9A–508] — [9A–547]
introductory note, [9A–482]
tort, actions in
abandonment of part of claim, [9A–513]
agreement, by, [9A–514] — [9A–515]
costs limit, [9A–516] — [9A–517]
generally, [9A–508] — [9A–510]

County courts (procedure)

discovery
personal injury actions, [9A–585] — [9A–588]
pre-action, [9A–579] — [9A–584]
supplementary provisions, [9A–589] —
[9A–591]
evidence
Admiralty claims, [9A–603] — [9A–605]
failure to give, [9A–592] — [9A–594]
foreign witness, [9A–595] — [9A–596]
oaths, taking of, [9A–600] — [9A–602]
prisoners, [9A–597] — [9A–599]
interest
generally, [9A–631] — [9A–633]
judgment debt, [9A–646] — [9A–648]
interim payments, [9A–573] — [9A–575]
judgments and orders
enforcement, [9A–668] — [9A–725]
finality, [9A–634] — [9A–635]
interest, [9A–646] — [9A–648]
payment of money, [9A–636] — [9A–637]
register, [9A–640] — [9A–645]
set off, [9A–638] — [9A–639]
jury trial
foreign law, determination of, [9A–629]
— [9A–630]
generally, [9A–623] — [9A–626]
impanellment, [9A–627] — [9A–628]
mode of trial
arbitration, reference to, [9A–617] — [9A–619]
assessors, [9A–614] — [9A–616]
district judges, to, [9A–620] — [9A–622]
generally, [9A–612] — [9A–613]
referee, to, [9A–620] — [9A–622]
Registrars, to, [9A–620] — [9A–622]
officers
responsibilities, [9A–752] — [9A–753]
order
enforcement, [9A–668] — [9A–725]
finality, [9A–634] — [9A–635]
payment of money, [9A–636] — [9A–637]
register, [9A–640] — [9A–645]
set off, [9A–638] — [9A–639]

County courts (procedure)—*cont.*

Part 8 claims
commencement, 8BPD.3
parties
bankrupt, [9A–571] — [9A–572]
Crown, [9A–565] — [9A–566]
jointly liable persons, [9A–569] — [9A–570]
minors, [9A–567] — [9A–568]
personal injury actions (discovery)
generally, [9A–585] — [9A–588]
supplementary provisions, [9A–589] —
[9A–591]
Practice directions, [9A–649] — [9A–651]
pre-action discovery
generally, [9A–579] — [9A–584]
supplementary provisions, [9A–589] —
[9A–591]
provisional damages, [9A–576] — [9A–578]
rights of audience
direction of Lord Chancellor, [9A–609] —
[9A–611]
generally, [9A–606] — [9A–608]
Rules, [9A–653] — [9A–654]
transfer of proceedings
costs, [9A–563]
counterclaims, [9A–561]
county courts, to, [9A–548] — [9A–554]
High Court, to, [9A–555] — [9A–560]
interpleader proceedings, [9A–562]
second application, [9A–553]
set off, [9A–561]
transfer of proceedings from
order of county courts, by, [9A–558] —
[9A–560]
order of High Court, by, [9A–555] —
[9A–557]
transfer of proceedings to
generally, [9A–548] — [9A–554]
interpleader proceedings, [9A–562]
second application, [9A–553]

County Courts Remedies Regulations 1991

introductory note, [9B–81]
Mareva injunctions, [9B–82]

Court appointed assessors

Admiralty claims
generally, [2D–80] — [2D–81]
Guide, [2A–141]
reference to Registrars, [2D–118]
remuneration, [2D–134]
appointment
Court of Appeal, [9A–275]
generally, 35.15.2
High Court, [9A–329] — [9A–330]
Chancery Guide, [1A–26]
generally, 35.15 — 35.15.1
Practice directions, 35PD.6
Queens Bench Guide, [1B–50]
references to Admiralty Registrar, [2D–118]
role
advising court at trial, 35.15.3
preparing report for court, 35.15.4
small claims, 27.2 — 27.2.1

Court committees

Admiralty Court, [2A–129]
Commercial Court, [2A–42]

All references to material in Volume 2 are enclosed within square parentheses.

All references to material in Volume 2 are enclosed within square parentheses.

All references to material in Volume 2 are enclosed within square parentheses.

All references to material in Volume 2 are enclosed within square parentheses.

All references to material in Volume 2 are enclosed within square parentheses.

All references to material in Volume 2 are enclosed within square parentheses.

All references to material in Volume 2 are enclosed within square parentheses.

All references to material in Volume 2 are enclosed within square parentheses.

All references to material in Volume 2 are enclosed within square parentheses.

All references to material in Volume 2 are enclosed within square parentheses.

Death—*cont.*
patients, [6B–182]
representation, 19.8
substitution of parties, 19.2.7

De bonis ecclesiasticis
See Writs of fieri facias de bonis ecclesiasticis

Debentures
writs of *fieri facias*, sc46.1.22

Debt already paid
See States paid defence

Debtor creditor agreements
exempt agreements, and, [3H–36]
generally, [3H–26] — [3H–27]

Debtor creditor supplier agreements
exempt agreements, and, [3H–36]
generally, [3H–24] — [3H–25]

Debtors Act 1869
And see Committal for debt
generally, sc46.1.26 — sc46.1.47

Debts
And see Admissions (debt)
imprisonment
And see Committal for debt
generally, sc46.1.26 — sc46.1.47
interest
county courts, [9A–631] — [9A–633]
Court of Record, [9B–429] — [9B–430]
Crown proceedings, [9B–357] — [9B–358]
generally, 7.0.11
High Court, [9A–103] — [9A–105]

Deceased persons
court powers
acting on counsel's opinion, [9B–63] — [9B–65]
binding on third parties, [9B–61] — [9B–62]
compromise of probate claims, [9B–66]
replacement personal representative, [9B–67] — [9B–69]
Lloyds Names
Chancery Guide, [1A–200]
witness statement, [1A–240] — [1A–241]
Part 8 claims, 8.2A.2
notice to non-parties
generally, 19.8A — 19.8A.1
Motor Insurers Bureau, 19.8A.2
time limits, [8–48]

Declarations
accounts fail to comply with requirements, that
claim forms, [2G–85]
evidence, [2G–86]
generally, [2G–84]
order, [2G–87]
affairs of company ought to be investigated, that, [2G–114]
county courts

Declarations—*cont.*
prohibition, [9A–667]
stay of proceedings, [9A–666]
dissolution of company is void, that
claim forms, [2G–121]
evidence, [2G–122]
generally, [2G–120]
hearings, [2G–123]
order, [2G–124]
jurisdiction, [9A–80] — [9A–81.1]

Declarations of incompatibility
addition of parties
generally, 19.4A — 19.4A.1
notice to the Crown, 19.4A.2
Practice directions, 19PD.6
generally, [3D–17] — [3D–19]

Declarations of invalidity
amendments of particulars, [2F–60]
commercial success, [2F–62]
counterclaims, [2F–56]
estoppel, [2F–61]
generally, [2F–54] — [2F–55]
grounds, [2F–57]
particulars of objection, [2F–58] — [2F–59]
Practice directions, [2F–93]

Declaratory judgments
default judgments, 40.20.3
editorial introduction, 40.0.7
generally, 40.20 — 40.20.1
incapacitated adults, 21.0.6
jurisdiction, 40.20.2
medical and welfare decisions, 21.0.6
summary judgments, 40.20.3

Decorative repairs notices
generally, [3A–22] — [3A–23]

Deductions (benefits)
interim payments
generally, 25.7.17
Practice directions, 25BPD.4, 40BPD.6
Part 36 offers
generally, 36.23 — 36.23.2
Practice directions, 36PD.10

Deeds of arrangement
And see Enrolment of deeds
registration
Queens Bench Guide, [1B–84]
statutory basis, [9B–14] — [9B–15]

Deeds of Arrangement Act 1914
applications, sc94.4 — sc94.4.1

Deeds
enrolment
fees, [10–23] — [10–24]
Queens Bench Guide, [1B–87]

Deemed orders (costs)
discontinuance, 44.12.3
generally, 44.12 — 44.12.2
interest, 44.12.4

Deemed service
calculation, 6.7.6

All references to material in Volume 2 are enclosed within square parentheses.

All references to material in Volume 2 are enclosed within square parentheses.

All references to material in Volume 2 are enclosed within square parentheses.

All references to material in Volume 2 are enclosed within square parentheses.

All references to material in Volume 2 are enclosed within square parentheses.

All references to material in Volume 2 are enclosed within square parentheses.

All references to material in Volume 2 are enclosed within square parentheses.

All references to material in Volume 2 are enclosed within square parentheses.

All references to material in Volume 2 are enclosed within square parentheses.

All references to material in Volume 2 are enclosed within square parentheses.

All references to material in Volume 2 are enclosed within square parentheses.

All references to material in Volume 2 are enclosed within square parentheses.

All references to material in Volume 2 are enclosed within square parentheses.

All references to material in Volume 2 are enclosed within square parentheses.

All references to material in Volume 2 are enclosed within square parentheses.

All references to material in Volume 2 are enclosed within square parentheses.

All references to material in Volume 2 are enclosed within square parentheses.

All references to material in Volume 2 are enclosed within square parentheses.

All references to material in Volume 2 are enclosed within square parentheses.

All references to material in Volume 2 are enclosed within square parentheses.

All references to material in Volume 2 are enclosed within square parentheses.

All references to material in Volume 2 are enclosed within square parentheses.

All references to material in Volume 2 are enclosed within square parentheses.

Expert evidence—*cont.*
  nomination, C2–015
  Practice directions
    assessors, 35PD.7
    contents, 35PD.2
    general requirements, 35PD.1
    instructions, 35PD.4
    provision of information, 35PD.3
    questions to experts, 35PD.5
    service of orders, 35PD.6A
    single expert, 35PD.6
  pre-action protocols
    Clinical Disputes, C3–017
    Personal Injury Claims, C2–009
  privilege, 35.10.5
  Protocol for Instruction of Experts to give
    Evidence
    acceptance of instructions, 35.23
    advice only, 35.20
    aims, 35.17
    amendment of reports, 35.31
    application, 35.18
    appointment, 35.22
    attendance at trial, 35.38
    contents of reports, 35.28 — 35.29
    direction by court to party to provide in-
      formation, 35.27
    discussions between experts, 35.36 —
      35.37
    duties of experts, 35.19
    generally, 35.10.4
    introduction, 35.16
    limitation periods, 35.18
    need, 35.21
    payment, 35.22
    procedure after receipt of report, 35.30
    request for directions, 35.26
    single joint experts, 35.33 — 35.35
    withdrawal, 35.25
    written questions for experts, 35.32
  provision of information
    generally, 35.9 — 35.9.1
    Practice directions, 35PD.3
  Queens Bench Guide, [1B–50]
  related sources, 35.0.3
  restrictions
    court powers, 35.4 — 35.4.5
    duty of experts, 35.1 — 35.1.1
  service of orders, 35PD.6A
  single joint experts
    Chancery Guide, [1A–21]
    Code of Guidance, 35.31
    conferences, 35.8.5
    directions, 35.8.4
    examination, 35.7.2
    experiments, 35.7.2
    fees, 35.8.3
    generally, 35.7 — 35.7.1
    inspection, 35.7.2
    instructions, 35.8 — 35.8.2
    obtaining further evidence, 35.7.3
    Practice directions, 35PD.5
    weight to be given to report, 35.8.6
  small claims
    fees, 27.14.2
    generally, 27.5 — 27.5.1
    introduction, 27.2.1, 35.0.2
  statements of truth, 22.1.15
  TCC claims, [2C–108] — [2C–114]
  use of, 35.11 — 35.11.1
  written questions

Expert evidence—*cont.*
  Chancery Guide, [1A–24]
  generally, 35.6 — 35.6.1
  Practice directions, 35PD.4
  written report
    Code of Guidance, 35.10.4
    contents, 35.10 — 35.10.5
    fast track claims, 35.5.2
    generally, 35.5 — 35.5.1
    inspection of, 35.5.6
    models, 35.5.3
    photographs, 35.5.3
    plans, 35.5.3
    Practice directions, 35PD.2
    privilege, 35.10.5

Expert reports
And see Expert evidence
  Chancery Guide, [1A–222]
  statements of truth, 22.1.15

Expert witnesses
And see Expert evidence
  Admiralty claims, [2D–31]
  Commercial Court
    general requirements, [2A–168]
    generally, [2A–104]
  costs, 48.15.3
  discussions between, 35.12 — 35.12.3
  duties, 35.3 — 35.3.1
  fees
    generally, 35.4.4
    introduction, 48.14.30
    small claims, 27.14.2
  generally, 35.2.2
  immunity, 35.12.3
  pre-action protocols, 35.4.3
  professional negligence protocol
    generally, C7–011
    guidance notes, C7–018
  Queens Bench Guide, [1B–50]
  service of orders on, 35PD.6A
  small claims
    fees, 27.14.2
    generally, 27.5 — 27.5.1
    introduction, 27.2.1, 35.0.2
  witness summonses, 35.5.5

Extended civil restraint orders
  form, 3CPD.7
  generally, 3.1.14
  introduction, 3.1.12
  Practice Direction, 3CPD.3

Extended warranties
  unfair contract terms, [3H–554]

Extensions of time
  acknowledgment
    effect, [8–62]
    formal provisions, [8–61] — [8–61.1]
    generally, [8–60]
    signature, [8–61.2]
    without prejudice, [8–61.1]
  allocation questionnaires, 26.3.9
  appeals
    consequences of refusal, 52.6.1
    criteria, 52.6.2
    generally, 52.6 — 52.6.2

All references to material in Volume 2 are enclosed within square parentheses.

Extensions of time—*cont.*
Practice directions, 52PD.17
arbitration claims
award, [2E–198] — [2E–199]
court powers, [2E–266]
proceedings, [2E–113] — [2E–116]
case management, 3.1.2
consumer credit
generally, [3H–239] — [3H–242]
supplemental provisions, [3H–243] —
[3H–244]
disability
generally, [8–55] — [8–57]
latent damage, [8–58] — [8–59]
fraud, [8–63] — [8–64]
House of Lords (civil appeals)
appendix, [4A–67] — [4A–68]
permission to appeal, [4A–15]
petitions of appeal, [4A–44]
standing orders, [4A–132]
statement of facts, [4A–67] — [4A–68]
House of Lords (criminal appeals), [4B–10]
receivership, [3E–50]
registering company charges
generally, [2G–106]
Re Charles order, [2G–107]
registering company documents
claim forms, [2G–65]
evidence, [2G–66]
generally, [2G–64]

Extensions of time (service)
claim forms
evidence, 7.6.2
generally, 7.6 — 7.6.1
Practice directions, 7PD.8
defence
agreement, by, 15.5.1
court, by, 15.5.2
generally, 15.5
notification, 15.5.5
generally, 3.1.2
made without notice, 7.6.3
particulars of claim, 7.6.4

Extent, writs of
See Writs of extent

External confiscation orders
And see Confiscation orders
application, sc115.13 — sc115.13.4
Criminal Justice Act 1988, under
generally, sc115.22 — sc115.22.1
procedure, sc115.23 — sc115.23.2
enforcement, sc115.19 — sc115.19.1
evidence, sc115.14 — sc115.14.1
generally, sc115.12 — sc115.12.3
notice, sc115.17 — sc115.17.1
Orders in Council, sc115.21
Register of orders, sc115.16
setting aside, sc115.18 — sc115.18.1
variation
registered order, sc115.20
registration, sc115.18 — sc115.18.1

External forfeiture orders
generally, sc115.21A — sc115.21A.3

Extortionate credit bargains
alternative challenges, [3H–263]

Extortionate credit bargains—*cont.*
burden of proof, [3H–260] — [3H–261]
definition, [3H–268]
generally, [3H–256] — [3H–258]
interest rates, [3H–262]
reopening
generally, [3H–264] — [3H–265]
procedure, [3H–267]
restrictions, [3H–266]

Extortionate credit transacations
liquidation, [3E–82]

Extradition Act 2003
appeals, 52PD.120

Extradition (appeals)
filing, 52PD.85
generally, 52PD.84
procedure, 52PD.120
service, 52PD.87
supporting evidence, 52PD.86

Facsimile
See Fax

Facts
admissions
And see Admissions (fact)
application for judgment, 14.3 — 14.3.6
form, 14.1.2 — 14.1.8
generally, 14.1 — 14.1.1
time limits, 14.2 — 14.2.4
particulars of claim, 16.4.1

Failure to act
And see Committal (failure to act)
committal, sc45.5 — sc45.7.8

Failure to attend
And see Failure to attend (trials)
application notices, 23.11 — 23.11.3
depositions, 34.10 — 34.10.1
summary judgments, 39.3.8

Failure to attend (trials)
application to restore, 39.3.6 — 39.3.7
claimants, by, 39.3.4
defendants, by, 39.3.5
generally, 39.3 — 39.3.3
Practice directions, 39PD.2
striking out, 39.3.2
summary judgments, 39.3.8

Failure to disclose
effect
generally, 31.21
introduction, 31.10.7
expert reports, 35.13 — 35.13.1

Fair comment
pleading, 53PD.6 — 53PD.6.2
reply, 53PD.8 — 53PD.8.1

Fair Trading Act 1973
appeals
generally, sc93.19 — sc93.19.1

All references to material in Volume 2 are enclosed within square parentheses.

All references to material in Volume 2 are enclosed within square parentheses.

All references to material in Volume 2 are enclosed within square parentheses.

All references to material in Volume 2 are enclosed within square parentheses.

All references to material in Volume 2 are enclosed within square parentheses.

All references to material in Volume 2 are enclosed within square parentheses.

All references to material in Volume 2 are enclosed within square parentheses.

All references to material in Volume 2 are enclosed within square parentheses.

All references to material in Volume 2 are enclosed within square parentheses.

All references to material in Volume 2 are enclosed within square parentheses.

All references to material in Volume 2 are enclosed within square parentheses.

All references to material in Volume 2 are enclosed within square parentheses.

All references to material in Volume 2 are enclosed within square parentheses.

All references to material in Volume 2 are enclosed within square parentheses.

All references to material in Volume 2 are enclosed within square parentheses.

All references to material in Volume 2 are enclosed within square parentheses.

All references to material in Volume 2 are enclosed within square parentheses.

All references to material in Volume 2 are enclosed within square parentheses.

All references to material in Volume 2 are enclosed within square parentheses.

All references to material in Volume 2 are enclosed within square parentheses.

All references to material in Volume 2 are enclosed within square parentheses.

All references to material in Volume 2 are enclosed within square parentheses.

All references to material in Volume 2 are enclosed within square parentheses.

All references to material in Volume 2 are enclosed within square parentheses.

All references to material in Volume 2 are enclosed within square parentheses.

All references to material in Volume 2 are enclosed within square parentheses.

All references to material in Volume 2 are enclosed within square parentheses.

All references to material in Volume 2 are enclosed within square parentheses.

All references to material in Volume 2 are enclosed within square parentheses.

All references to material in Volume 2 are enclosed within square parentheses.

All references to material in Volume 2 are enclosed within square parentheses.

All references to material in Volume 2 are enclosed within square parentheses.

Injunctions—*cont.*
    County Courts Remedies Regulations
      1991, [9B–81] — [9B–82]
    Supreme Court Act 1981, [9A–82] — [9A–
      83]
  meaning, G1.1
  restraint of foreign proceedings
    generally, 25.1.12
    jurisdiction clause, 6.21.23
  restraint of presentation of winding up peti-
    tions
    introduction, [3E–60]
    Practice directions, [3E–8]
  restraint of publication of confidential infor-
    mation, 25.1.13
  search orders
    And see Search orders
    form, 25PD.14
    generally, 25.1.29
    Practice directions, 25PD.7
  sequestration
    injunctions in aid, sc46.5.10
    injunctions in lieu, sc46.5.11
  service out of jurisdiction, 6.21.26 —
    6.21.27
  small claims track, 27.3 — 27.3.1
  statutory basis
    generally, [9A–109] — [9A–111]
    procedure, [9A–112]
  supply of supporting material, 5.4.17
  time limits, [8–90] — [8–91.1]
  trade marks, [2F–75]
  unlawful use of premises
    And see Unlawful use of premises
    exclusion orders, [3A–1143] — [3A–1147]
    generally, [3A–1137] — [3A–1142]
    powers of arrest, [3A–1156] — [3A–1167]
    relevant accommodation, [3A–1141]
    relevant landlord, [3A–1139]
    supplementary, [3A–1153] — [3A–1155]
    unlawful purpose, [3A–1142]

Inland Revenue
  See Revenue and Customs

Innocent publication
  contempt of court, [3C–7]

Innuendos
  extraneous facts, 53PD.3.3
  generally, 53PD.3 — 53PD.3.2

Inquiries
  See Accounts and inquiries
  Court of Protection Rules
    appointment of receivers, [6B–293]
    execution of documents, [6B–296]
    further inquiries, [6B–297]
    inspection of property, [6B–294]
    prior dealing of property, [6B–295]
  damages, as to, 25.1.16.1

Insolvency
  charging orders, 73.8.5
  package holidays, [3H–529]

Insolvency Act 1986 (applications)
  editorial introduction, sc95.0.2

Insolvency Act 1986 (applications)—*cont.*
  generally, sc95.6 — sc95.6.2
  related sources, sc95.0.3

Insolvency practitioners
  remuneration
    generally, [3E–113]
    Practice Note, [3E–119]
    Practice Statement, [3E–114] — [3E–118]

Insolvency proceedings
  administration orders
    And see Administration orders (insolvency)
    generally, [3E–35] — [3E–48]
  Admiralty claims, [2D–21]
  appeals, 52.3.1
  application of Civil Procedure Rules, 2.1.4
  applications, [3E–21]
  bankruptcy, [3E–95] — [3E–112]
  Chancery Guide
    appeals, [1A–101]
    generally, [1A–151] — [1A–152]
    stay of proceedings, [1A–99]
  charging orders, 73.8.5
  companies
    generally, [3E–26]
    voluntary arrangements, [3E–30] — [3E–
      33]
  company voluntary arrangements
    challenges, [3E–33]
    filing, [3E–31]
    partnerships, [3E–32]
    with moratorium, [3E–30]
    without moratorium, [3E–29]
  costs
    generally, 43.2.5
    liquidation, 48.15.4
  Court Users Committees, [1A–144]
  EC Regulation, [3E–25]
  editorial notes
    administration orders, [3E–34] — [3E–48]
    bankruptcy, [3E–95] — [3E–112]
    company voluntary arrangements, [3E–
      29] — [3E–33]
    individual voluntary arrangements, [3E–
      87] — [3E–94]
    insolvency practitioners remuneration,
      [3E–113] — [3E–119]
    introduction, [3E–19] — [3E–28]
    liquidation, [3E–81] — [3E–86]
    receivership, [3E–49] — [3E–52]
    winding up petions, [3E–53] — [3E–80]
  evidence, [3E–22]
  fees, [10–25] — [10–37]
  individual voluntary arrangements, [3E–87]
    — [3E–94]
  insolvency practitioners remuneration
    generally, [3E–113]
    Practice Note, [3E–119]
    Practice Statement, [3E–114] — [3E–118]
  introduction, 2.1.4
  jurisdiction
    bankruptcy, [3E–24]
    Companies Court, [3E–23]
    EC Regulation, [3E–25]
  liquidation, [3E–81] — [3E–86]
  partnership voluntary arrangements, [3E–
    32]
  partnerships
    generally, [3E–27]

All references to material in Volume 2 are enclosed within square parentheses.

Insolvency proceedings—*cont.*
limited liability, [3E–28]
Practice directions
bankruptcy, [3E–9] — [3E–18]
generally, [3E–1]
winding up, [3E–2] — [3E–8]
procedure, [3E–20]
receivership, [3E–49] — [3E–52]
winding up petitions, [3E–53] — [3E–80]

Inspection
definitions
copy, 31.4
document, 31.4 — 31.4.1
disclosed document
generally, 31.3
withholding, 31.3.1 — 31.3.40
expert evidence
single joint experts, by, 35.8.4
written report, of, 35.5.6
foreign language document, 31.15.1
forms, 31.0.8
generally, 31.15 — 31.15.3
meaning, 31.15.2
minutes of company general meeting, [2G–105]
non-parties
And see Non-parties (inspection)
application notices, 25.4 — 25.4.3
evidence, 25.5 — 25.5.1
generally, 25.1.30 — 25.1.31
grounds, 25.2.4
time limits, 25.2.2 — 25.2.3
Patents Court
generally, [2F–41]
Practice directions, [2F–87]
secret process, [2F–50]
validity of patent, [2F–52]
place of inspection, 31.15.3
pre-action
And see Pre-action inspection
application notices, 25.4 — 25.4.3
evidence, 25.5 — 25.5.1
generally, 25.1.30 — 25.1.31
grounds, 25.2.4
time limits, 25.2.2 — 25.2.3
Procedural Guide
generally, D1–024
procedure, D1–025
property
generally, 25.1.20
non-parties, 25.1.32
pre-action, 25.1.30 — 25.1.31, 25.2.2
Queens Bench Guide, [1B–12]
related sources, 31.0.7
relevant documents, 31.4 — 31.4.1
scope of Part, 31.1
service charges, [3A–606] — [3A–607]
small claims, 27.2 — 27.2.1
specific inspection
generally, 31.12
procedure, 31.12.1 — 31.12.2
staged inspection, 31.13 — 31.13.1
time limits, E1–020
withholding inspection
And see Withholding inspection
grounds, 31.3.5 — 31.3.40
Practice directions, 31PD.6
Procedural Guide, D1–024
procedure, 31.3.3, 31.19 — 31.19.3

Inspection—*cont.*
proportionality, 31.3.4
reasons, 31.3.1 — 31.3.2
witness statements
generally, 32.13 — 32.13.1
Practice directions, 32PD.24

Inspection of property orders
And see Interim remedies
generally, 25.1.20
non-parties, against, 25.1.32
pre-action, 25.1.30 — 25.1.31, 25.2.2

Instalments
charging orders, 73.4.4
interim payments
generally, 25.6.6
Practice directions, 25BPD.3
judgments, 40BPD.12

Insurance
arrested property
generally, [2D–94]
Guide, [2A–140]

Insurance companies
Part 36 payments, and, 37PD.7 — 37PD.8

Insurance Companies Act 1982 (applications)
allocation of business, [2G–3]
case management, [2G–11]
commencement, [2G–2]
drawing up orders, [2G–14]
filing, [2G–13]
generally, [2G–1]
introduction, 23.0.5
petitions, [2G–5] — [2G–6]
reduction of capital, [2G–7] — [2G–10]
schemes of arrangement, [2G–7] — [2G–10]
service, [2G–12]

Insurance contracts
European jurisdiction
allocation within EC, [5–60] — [5–68]
allocation within UK, [5–150]
domicile, [5–39] — [5–40]

Insurance premiums
compensation for improvements, [3B–55] — [3B–59]
funding arrangements
generally, 44.3A.3
introduction, [7A–41] — [7A–46]
Supreme Court Costs Office Guide, 48.80, 48.168, 48.170
statutory provisions, [9A–867] — [9A–869]
summary assessment, 48.26
Supreme Court Costs Office Guide
entitlement, 48.80
generally, 48.168
relevant details, 48.170
summary assessment, 48.26

Intellectual property claims
And see Patents Court (claims)
allocation
generally, [2F–69] — [2F–70]
Practice directions, [2F–100]

All references to material in Volume 2 are enclosed within square parentheses.

All references to material in Volume 2 are enclosed within square parentheses.

All references to material in Volume 2 are enclosed within square parentheses.

All references to material in Volume 2 are enclosed within square parentheses.

All references to material in Volume 2 are enclosed within square parentheses.

All references to material in Volume 2 are enclosed within square parentheses.

All references to material in Volume 2 are enclosed within square parentheses.

All references to material in Volume 2 are enclosed within square parentheses.

Judgments and orders—*cont.*
  summary judgments, 40.20.3
  default
    And see Default judgments
    generally, 12.0.1 — 12.11.2
    Practice directions, 12PD.1 — 12PD.5
    Procedural Guide, D1–011 — D1–012
  definition, [9A–462]
  detention of goods, 40.14 — 40.14.1
  drawing up
    generally, 40.3 — 40.3.1
    Practice directions, 40BPD.1
  editorial introduction, 40.0.2 — 40.0.3
  effective date
    ante-dating, 40.7.1
    default judgments against foreign states,
      40.10 — 40.10.2
    generally, 40.7 — 40.7.1
    introduction, 40.2.1
  enforcement
    And see Enforcement
    County Court Rules, cc25.1 — cc25.13.2
    generally, 50.1.2
    Rules of the Supreme Court, sc45.1 —
      sc45.12
  enforcement of foreign
    And see Reciprocal enforcement of judgments
    Brussels Convention, [5–11] — [5–15],
      [5–95] — [5–115]
    domicile, [5–32] — [5–44]
    generally, [5–3] — [5–4]
    Lugano Convention, [5–16] — [5–20],
      [5–162] — [5–188]
    Northern Ireland, [5–144] — [5–159]
    Scotland, [5–144] — [5–159]
    stay of proceedings, [5–45] — [5–47]
  entry
    generally, 40.2 — 40.2.1
    nunc pro tunc, 40.4.2
  errors
    generally, 40.12 — 40.12.1
    Practice directions, 40BPD.4
    procedure, 3.10 — 3.10.3
  filing
    generally, 40.3 — 40.3.1
    Practice directions, 40BPD.1
  foreign currencies
    charging orders, 73.10.7
    Court Funds Office, [6A–90] — [6A–92]
    generally, 40.2.2
    interest, 40.8.2 — 40.8.5
    Practice directions, 40BPD.10
    statutory basis, [9B–54] — [9B–56]
    writs of *fieri facias*, sc46.1.3
  foreign states, 40.10 — 40.10.2
  form, B8–001
  handing down judgments
    further statement, B6–001
    generally, 40.2.5
    initial statement, B5–001
  House of Lords (civil appeals)
    attendance of counsel, [4A–90]
    conditions for release in advance, [4A–91]
    place, [4A–89]
    time, [4A–89]
  House of Lords (criminal appeals)
    attendance of counsel, [4B–74]
    conditions for relase in advance, [4B–75]
    place, [4B–73]
    time, [4B–73]
  instalments, 40BPD.12

Judgments and orders—*cont.*
  interest
    damages, 40.8.6
    foreign currency judgments, 40.8.2 —
      40.8.5
    generally, 40.8 — 40.8.1
    rate, 40.8.7
    statutory authority, [9B–53] — [9B–56],
      [9A–646] — [9A–648]
  meaning, 40.1.1
  Mercantile Courts
    generally, [2B–13]
    Practice directions, [2B–14]
  non-compliance
    generally, 40.11 — 40.11.1
    Practice directions, 40BPD.9
  post dating, 40.7.1
  Practice directions
    act to be done, requiring, 40BPD.8
    adjustment of final figures, 40BPD.5-
      40BPD.6
    consent, by, 40BPD.3
    correction of errors, 40BPD.4
    costs, 40BPD.11
    drawing up, 40BPD.1
    filing, 40BPD.1
    foreign currency, 40BPD.10
    form, B8–001
    generally, 40.0.10
    House of Lords order, conversion of,
      40BPD.13
    instalments, payment by, 40BPD.12
    non-compliance, 40BPD.9
    preparation of documents, 40BPD.2
    statement of service of claim forms,
      40BPD.7
  Queens Bench Guide
    generally, [1B–66]
    payment on behalf of child or patients,
      [1B–66]
    provisional damages, [1B–66]
  related sources, 40.0.9
  reopening final determination of appeal,
    40.2.1.1
  reserved judgments
    editorial introduction, 40.0.7
    generally, 40EPD.1
  route of appeal, 40.2.7
  scope of Part, 40.1 — 40.1.1
  sealing, 40.2.7
  service
    experts, on, 35PD.6A
    Chancery Guide, [1A–87]
    generally, 40.4 — 40.4.1
    party and solicitor, on, 40.5 — 40.5.1
  service out of jurisdiction, 6.21.41
  setting aside
    And see Setting aside (judgments)
    applicants, 40.9 — 40.9.5
    small claims, 27.11 — 27.11.6
    striking out, after, 3.6 — 3.6.1
  slip rule
    generally, 40.12 — 40.12.1
    Practice directions, 40BPD.4
    procedure, 3.10 — 3.10.3
  summary
    And see Summary judgments
    generally, 24.0.1 — 24.6.9
    Practice directions, 24PD.1 — 24PD.10
    Procedural Guide, D1–013 — D1–014
  TCC claims, [2C–8.1]

All references to material in Volume 2 are enclosed within square parentheses.

All references to material in Volume 2 are enclosed within square parentheses.

All references to material in Volume 2 are enclosed within square parentheses.

All references to material in Volume 2 are enclosed within square parentheses.

All references to material in Volume 2 are enclosed within square parentheses.

All references to material in Volume 2 are enclosed within square parentheses.

All references to material in Volume 2 are enclosed within square parentheses.

All references to material in Volume 2 are enclosed within square parentheses.

All references to material in Volume 2 are enclosed within square parentheses.

All references to material in Volume 2 are enclosed within square parentheses.

All references to material in Volume 2 are enclosed within square parentheses.

Litigation privilege—*cont.*
  confidential documents, 31.3.15 — 31.3.16
  medical advisers, 31.3.19
  other advisers, 31.3.19
  pre-existing documents or copies, 31.3.14
  solicitors and non professional agents,
    31.3.12
  spiritual advisers, 31.3.19

Live link evidence
  Chancery Guide, [1A–136]
  Commercial Court
    generally, [2A–104]
    protocol, [2A–171] — [2A–173]
  depositions, 34.8.6
  generally, 32.3 — 32.3.1
  Guidance, 32PD.33
  introduction, 34.0.4
  Practice directions
    generally, 32PD.29
    guidance, 32PD.33
  TCC claims, [2C–107]

Lloyds names
  Chancery Guide
    form of order, [1A–242]
    generally, [1A–200]
    witness statement, [1A–240] — [1A–241]
  Part 8 claims, 8.2A.2

Loans
  time limits, [8–10]

Local authorities
  assured tenancies, [3A–890]
  statutory tenancies, [3A–142] — [3A–148]

Local connection
  asylum seekers, [3A–1522] — [3A–1524]

Local Government Act 1972
  costs, 48.13.4

**Local Government (Miscellaneous Provisions)
  Act 1976**
  appeals, 52PD.135

**Local Government, Planning and Land Act
  1980 (applications)**
  claim forms, sc94.2 — sc94.2.2
  evidence, sc94.3 — sc94.3.2
  generally, sc94.1 — sc94.1.3
  Part 8 claims, 8BPD.6

Local housing authorities
  duties
    discharge, [3A–18]
    generally, [3A–29] — [3A–30]
    introduction, [3A–31] — [3A–37]
    relevant authorities, [3A–39]
    meaning, [3A–312] — [3A–313]

Locus standi
  judicial review, 54.1.11

Lodgment of documents
  See Filing

Lodgment of funds
  And see Funds Office
  And see Investment of funds
  Admiralty claims, [6A–57]
  county courts, in, [6A–66]
  court, in, [6A–59] — [6A–62]
  generally, [6A–43]
  schedules, on receipt of
    generally, [6A–44] — [6A–50]
    security for costs of appeal, [6A–46]
  securities, of, [6A–64]
  security for costs
    appeals, [6A–46]
    election petitions, [6A–56]
  written request, on receipt of
    Admiralty claims, [6A–57]
    generally, [6A–52] — [6A–57]
    security for costs of election petitions,
      [6A–56]

Lodgment schedules
  amendments, [6A–33] — [6A–34]
  generally, [6A–29] — [6A–30]
  preparation, [6A–33] — [6A–34]

London agents
  House of Lords (civil appeals), [4A–46]
  House of Lords (criminal appeals), [4B–34]

"Long tenancies"
  secure tenancies, [3A–449] — [3A–450]

Lord Chancellor
  CLS funding (Directions)
    introduction, [7D–15]
    text, [7D–16] — [7D–17]
  enduring powers of attorney, [6B–378] —
    [6B–379]
  rights of audience
    Directions, [9A–609] — [9A–611]
  Supreme Court Costs Office Guide, 48.230
    — 48.239

Lord Chancellors Visitors
  functions, [6B–201] — [6B–202]
  generally, [6B–199] — [6B–200]

Lords Commissioners
  role, [9A–427] — [9A–428]

Loss of earnings
  small claims, 27.14.2

Loss of expectation of life
  date of knowledge, [8–27]

Low rent tenancies
  See Tenancies at low rent

LSC funded client
  And see CLS funding
  And see Legal Services Commission
  costs
    generally, 44.17 — 44.17.2
    Guidance Notes, 48.14.9 — 48.14.21
    Practice directions, 44PD.15 — 44PD.17
    Procedural Guide, D1–038

All references to material in Volume 2 are enclosed within square parentheses.

All references to material in Volume 2 are enclosed within square parentheses.

All references to material in Volume 2 are enclosed within square parentheses.

All references to material in Volume 2 are enclosed within square parentheses.

All references to material in Volume 2 are enclosed within square parentheses.

All references to material in Volume 2 are enclosed within square parentheses.

All references to material in Volume 2 are enclosed within square parentheses.

All references to material in Volume 2 are enclosed within square parentheses.

All references to material in Volume 2 are enclosed within square parentheses.

All references to material in Volume 2 are enclosed within square parentheses.

"Official copy"
meaning, G1.1

Official Receiver
arbitrator, as, [2E–303] — [2E–304], [2E–345]
costs, 48.6.5

Official Referees
And see TCC claims
definition, [9A–459]
statutory basis, [9A–322] — [9A–324]

Official Solicitor
Advocate to the Court, and, 39.8.5
costs, [9A–398]
functions
acting in family proceedings, [9A–397]
administration of estates, [9A–396]
assisting the Court, [9A–393]
generally, [9A–392]
liberty of subject, [9A–394]
representing persons under disability, [9A–395]
generally, [9A–389] — [9A–390]
property held by, [9A–406]
qualifications
details, [9A–469]
generally, [9A–370] — [9A–371]
role, [9A–391]
salary, [9A–403] — [9A–404]
tenure, [9A–401] — [9A–402]

Ogden tables
commencement, [9B–269] — [9B–270]
generally, [9B–280]
introduction, [3F–40]

Oil pollution
Admiralty claims, [2D–112] — [2D–112A]

Olympic Symbol, etc., Protection Act 1995
And see Patents Court
application of Civil Procedure Rules, 2.1.2
applications, 23.0.5
Practice directions, [2F–22] — [2F–27]
statements of case, 16.1.3

Online money claims
See Money Claim Online

Open court
See Hearings in open court

Opening speeches
Chancery Guide, [1A–80]
Commercial Court, [2A–113]
TCC claims, [2C–121]

Opinion evidence
expert, [9B–258] — [9B–260]
non-expert opinion, [9B–261] — [9B–262.1]

Oral evidence
generally, 32.2.1
Part 8 claims, 8.6 — 8.6.1

Oral evidence—*cont.*
summary judgments, 24.5.2
TCC claims
preliminary issues, [2C–84]
trial, [2C–124]

Oral examination
See Information from judgment debtor

Oral submissions
See Closing speeches
See Opening speeches

Orders
ante dating
generally, 40.7.1
House of Lords judgment, 40.2.4
clerical errors
generally, 40.12 — 40.12.1
Practice directions, 40BPD.4
procedure, 3.10 — 3.10.3
County Court Rules
appellate court orders, cc22.13
certificate of judgment, cc22.8 — cc22.8.2
enforcement, cc25.1 — cc25.13.2
set off of cross-judgments, cc22.11 — cc22.11.1
variation of payment, cc22.10 — cc22.10.1
Chancery Guide
consent order, [1A–90] — [1A–92]
copies, [1A–89]
drafting, [1A–87]
forms, [1A–88]
generally, [1A–86]
service, [1A–87]
Tomlin orders, [1A–93]
Commercial Court
generally, [2A–21]
Guide, [2A–79]
Practice directions, [2A–35]
compliance, 2.9 — 2.9.1
consent orders
Chancery Guide, [1A–90] — [1A–92]
generally, 40.6 — 40.6.1
Patents Court, [2F–46]
Practice directions, 23PD.10, 40BPD.3, 41PD.4
provisional damages, 41.2.3
setting aside, 40.6.3
Tomlin orders, 40.6.2
contents
date, 40.2.1
foreign currency judgment, 40.2.2
generally, 40.2
re-opening final determination of appeal, 40.2.1.1
correction of errors
generally, 40.12 — 40.12.1
Practice directions, 40BPD.4
procedure, 3.10 — 3.10.3
date of order
default judgments against foreign states, 40.10 — 40.10.2
generally, 40.7 — 40.7.1
House of Lords judgment, 40.2.4
dating of order, 40.2.6
detention of goods, 40.14 — 40.14.1
drawing up

All references to material in Volume 2 are enclosed within square parentheses.

All references to material in Volume 2 are enclosed within square parentheses.

All references to material in Volume 2 are enclosed within square parentheses.

All references to material in Volume 2 are enclosed within square parentheses.

All references to material in Volume 2 are enclosed within square parentheses.

All references to material in Volume 2 are enclosed within square parentheses.

All references to material in Volume 2 are enclosed within square parentheses.

All references to material in Volume 2 are enclosed within square parentheses.

All references to material in Volume 2 are enclosed within square parentheses.

All references to material in Volume 2 are enclosed within square parentheses.

All references to material in Volume 2 are enclosed within square parentheses.

All references to material in Volume 2 are enclosed within square parentheses.

Permission to appeal—*cont.*
  Procedural Guide, D1–035
  real prospect of success, 52.3.6
  some other compelling reason, 52.3.6
  hearings
    generally, 52.3.5
    legal representation, 52.3.14
    Practice directions, 52PD.9
  High Court, from
    generally, [9B–41] — [9B–41.1]
    House of Lords (civil appeals), to, [4A–7],
      [4A–134]
    House of Lords (criminal appeals), to,
      [4B–7], [4B–114]
  House of Lords (civil appeals), to
    And see House of Lords (civil appeals)
    Court of Appeal in England, Wales & NI,
      from, [4A–5]
    Court of Session in Scotland, from, [4A–6]
    High Court, from, [4A–7]
    petitions, [4A–8] — [4A–42]
    standing orders, [4A–133] — [4A–134]
  House of Lords (criminal appeals)
    And see House of Lords (criminal appeals)
    Court of Appeal, from, [4B–113]
    England & Wales, in, [4B–5]
    High Court, from, [4B–114]
    Northern Ireland, in, [4B–5]
    petitions, [4B–7] — [4B–30]
    Scotland, in, [4B–6]
    standing orders, [4B–113] — [4B–114]
  imposition of conditions
    court powers, 52.9.1
    generally, 52.9
    introduction, 52.9.4
  judge initially refusing permission, position
    of, 52.3.16
  LSC funded clients, 52PD.12
  limited permission
    generally, 52.3.12
    Practice directions, 52PD.13
  Practice directions
    case management decisions, 52PD.7
    determination, 52PD.10
    generally, 52PD.6
    relevant court, 52PD.8 — 52PD.9
  Procedural Guide, D1–034
  Queens Bench Guide, [1B–68]
  refusal, 52.3.7
  respondents costs, 52PD.14
  respondents role, 52.3.15
  second appeals
    generally, 52.3.9
    Practice directions, 52PD.9
    statutory basis, [9A–873] — [9A–874]
  setting aside
    court powers, 52.9.1
    generally, 52.9
  specialist tribunals, from, 52.3.10
  statutory appeals, 52.3.3
  statutory basis, [9A–871] — [9A–872]
  subsequent procedure
    generally, 52.3.17
    Practice directions, 52PD.35 — 52PD.37
  TCC claims, 52.3.11
  time estimates, 52.3.19

Permission to issue
  charity proceedings
    generally, 64.6 — 64.6.1

Permission to issue—*cont.*
  Practice directions, 64PD.9
  committal, sc52.2 — sc52.2.1
  discontinuance
    generally, 38.2 — 38.2.2
    subsequent proceedings, 38.7 — 38.7.1
  judicial review
    criteria, 54.4.2
    decision without hearings, 54.12 —
      54.12.5
    delay, 54.4.3
    directions, 54.10 — 54.10.4
    discretion, 54.4.4
    generally, 54.4
    limited, 54.4.5
    procedure, 54.4.1
    service of order, 54.11 — 54.11.1
  sequestration
    application for, sc46.4 — sc46.5.2
    duration, sc46.2.13
    generally, sc46.2 — sc46.2.1
    grounds, sc46.2.3 — sc46.2.11
    procedure, sc46.4 — sc46.4.1
    time limits, sc46.2.12
  writs of delivery
    application for, sc46.4 — sc46.4.1
    duration, sc46.2.13
    generally, sc46.2 — sc46.2.1
    grounds, sc46.2.3 — sc46.2.11
    procedure, sc46.4 — sc46.4.1
    time limits, sc46.2.12
  writs of execution
    application for, sc46.4 — sc46.4.1
    duration, sc46.2.13
    generally, sc46.2 — sc46.2.1
    grounds, sc46.2.3 — sc46.2.11
    in aid of other writ, sc46.3
    procedure, sc46.4 — sc46.4.1
    sequestration, writs of, sc46.5 — sc46.5.2
    time limits, sc46.2.12
  writs of *fieri facias*
    application for, sc46.4 — sc46.4.1
    duration, sc46.2.13
    generally, sc46.2 — sc46.2.1
    grounds, sc46.2.3 — sc46.2.11
    procedure, sc46.4 — sc46.4.1
    time limits, sc46.2.12
  writs of possession
    application for, sc46.4 — sc46.4.1
    duration, sc46.2.13
    generally, sc46.2 — sc46.2.1
    grounds, sc46.2.3 — sc46.2.11
    procedure, sc46.4 — sc46.4.1
    time limits, sc46.2.12

Perpetuation of testimony
  patients, [6B–146]

Person under mental disorder
  See Patients

Personal injury claims
  Admiralty jurisdiction
    contribution, [2D–235] — [2D–243]
    costs, [2D–240]
    Crown ships, [2D–229], [2D–237]
    joint and several liability, [2D–227] —
      [2D–234]
    jurisdiction, [2D–151]

All references to material in Volume 2 are enclosed within square parentheses.

All references to material in Volume 2 are enclosed within square parentheses.

All references to material in Volume 2 are enclosed within square parentheses.

All references to material in Volume 2 are enclosed within square parentheses.

All references to material in Volume 2 are enclosed within square parentheses.

All references to material in Volume 2 are enclosed within square parentheses.

Postal service—*cont.*
generally, 6.2 — 6.2.1.1

Postal Services Act 2000
See Postal packets

Postponement
accelerated possession claims
generally, 55.18 — 55.18.1
Practice directions, 55PD.12
fast track, 28.4.1
recognisances, [3A–1415]

Poverty
security for costs, 25.13.12 — 25.13.14

Powers of arrest (anti-social behaviour)
duration, [3A–1167]
ex parte applications, [3A–1156] — [3A–1157]
medical examination and report, [3A–1162]
— [3A–1164]
postponement of recognisances, [3A–1415]
remand
generally, [3A–1158] — [3A–1161]
medical examination and report, [3A–
1162] — [3A–1164]
miscellaneous, [3A–1412] — [3A–1414]
statutory provisions
s.152 HA 1996, [3A–1112]
s.153 HA 1996, [3A–1118] — [3A–1119]
ss.153A and 153B, [3A–1143] —
[3A–1147]
s.153D, under, [3A–1148] — [3A–1152]
supplementary, [3A–1165] — [3A–1167]

Powers of attorney
And see Enduring powers of attorney
fees, [6B–321]
filing, 63.6
forms
Court of Protection direction, [6B–332]
generally, [6B–320]
Regulations, [6B–423] — [6B–429]
generally, [6B–322] — [6B–338]
inspection, 63.8 — 63.8.1
introduction, [6B–319]
Rules, [6B–392] — [6B–422]
statutory basis, [6B–339] — [6B–391]

Powers of entry
compensation for improvements, [3B–35] —
[3B–37]
Competition Act 1998
forms, B3–011
general provisions, B3–001 — B3–010
data protection, [3G–35] — [3G–51]
interim remedies, 25.1.25

Practice directions
And see under individual headings
county courts, [9A–649] — [9A–651]
interpretation of CPR, 2.3.4
statutory basis, [9A–842] — [9A–845], [9A–
861]

Practice forms
generally, 4PD.4
meaning, G1.1

Practice notes
handed down reserved judgments, B7–001
remuneration of judicial trustees, [6D–28B]
restoration of name of company to register,
[2G–130]

Practice statements
handing down written judgments
further statement, B6–001
initial statement, B5–001

Pre-action admissions
personal injury protocol, C2A–005

Pre-action applications
Commercial Court, [2A–24]
evidence for foreign courts, 34.21.5
interim receiving orders, B11–005A
Mercantile Courts, [2B–14]
pre-action protocols, C1A–013
interim receiving orders, B11–005A
TCC claims, [2C–14]

Pre-action costs
personal injury protocol, C2A–006
protocols, C1A–015

Pre-action disclosure
And see Interim remedies
application notices, 31.16.2
costs
generally, 48.1 — 48.1.2
Supreme Court Costs Office guide, 48.81
county courts
generally, [9A–579] — [9A–584]
supplementary provisions, [9A–589] —
[9A–591]
evidence, 31.16.2
evidence for foreign courts, 34.21.5
generally, 31.16 — 31.16.3
place of making application, 23.2.3
Practice directions, 23PD.5
pre-action protocols, C1A–012
procedure, 31.16 — 31.16.3
Queens Bench Guide, [1B–18]
statutory basis
CPA 1997, [9A–850] — [9A–852]
SCA 1981, [9A–93] — [9A–102.1]

Pre-action inspection
And see Interim remedies
costs, 48.1 — 48.1.2
generally, 25.1.30 — 25.1.31
grounds, 25.2.4
procedure
application notices, 25.4 — 25.4.3
evidence, 25.5 — 25.5.1
generally, 25.2.2
grounds, 25.2.4
place of making application, 23.2.3
time limits, 25.2.2 — 25.2.3

Pre-action offers
generally, 36.10 — 36.10.3

Pre-action orders
See Pre-action applications

All references to material in Volume 2 are enclosed within square parentheses.

All references to material in Volume 2 are enclosed within square parentheses.

All references to material in Volume 2 are enclosed within square parentheses.

All references to material in Volume 2 are enclosed within square parentheses.

All references to material in Volume 2 are enclosed within square parentheses.

All references to material in Volume 2 are enclosed within square parentheses.

All references to material in Volume 2 are enclosed within square parentheses.

Provisional damages—*cont.*

case file
   generally, 41.2.2
   Practice directions, 41PD.3
consent orders
   generally, 41.2.3
   Practice directions, 41PD.4
county courts, [9A–576] — [9A–578]
default judgments
   generally, 41.2.4
   Practice directions, 41PD.5
definitions, 41.1 — 41.1.2
editorial introduction, 41.0.2
fatal accident claims, [3F–55] — [3F–56]
forms
   generally, 41.2.1
   introduction, 41.0.4
further applications
   causation, 41.3.3
   generally, 41.3 — 41.3.2
generally, 41.2 — 41.2.1
particulars of claim, 16.4.3
Practice directions
   case file, 41PD.3
   default judgments, 41PD.5
   generally, 41PD.1
   judgment, 41PD.2
   order, 41PD.6 — 41PD.7
Queens Bench Guide
   generally, [1B–37]
   orders, [1B–66]
related sources, 41.0.3
statutory basis, [9A–90] — [9A–92]

Public authorities

proof of records
   generally, 33.6.2
   statutory provision, [9B–279]
service charges, [3A–618] — [3A–623]

Public funding

And see Community Legal Service
contempt of court, [3C–35]
discharge of certificate
   change of solicitor, 42.2.4
House of Lords (civil appeals)
   costs, [4A–87]
   generally, [4A–121]
   standing orders, [4A–143]
House of Lords (criminal appeals)
   costs, [4B–71]
   generally, [4B–101]
   standing order, [4B–123]
revocation of certificate
   change of solicitor, 42.2.4
Supreme Court Costs Office Guide, 48.193
   — 48.202
VAT, 43PD.5
wasted costs orders, 48.7.6

Public hearings

See Hearings in open court

Public holidays

service, 6.7.3

Public inquiries

costs, 48.14.22 — 48.14.29

Public interest

production of documents, 31.3.33

Public interest—*cont.*

winding up, [3E–76]

Public law

See Administrative law

Public Order Act 1936 (applications)

generally, sc93.5 — sc93.5.1
Part 8 claims, 8BPD.5

Public Trustee

And see Public Trustee Act 1906
And see Public Trustee Rules 1912
address, [6D–88]
administration of small estates
   Rules, [6D–100] — [6D–105]
   statutory basis, [6D–49] — [6D–51]
administration of trusts
   accounts, [6D–110] — [6D–111]
   advances, [6D–118]
   execution of documents, [6D–112] —
      [6D–115]
   income, payment of, [6D–116] — [6D–
      117]
   investment, [6D–107] — [6D–109]
   professional advice, [6D–119]
   proof of life, [6D–120] — [6D–124]
   registration, [6D–106
appeals, [6D–69] — [6D–70]
appointment, [6D–65] — [6D–66]
audit of trust accounts
   Rules, [6D–127] — [6D–134]
   statutory basis, [6D–74] — [6D–79]
authority, [6D–94] — [6D–95]
conduct of business, [6D–71]
contact details, [6D–88]
costs, [6D–46]
Custodian trusteess
   Rules, [6D–125] — [6D–126]
   statutory basis, [6D–51] — [6D–54]
deputies, [6D–89]
directions, [6D–122] — [6D–123]
duties
   Custodian trustees, as, [6D–51] — [6D–
      54]
   dual capacity, [6D–45] — [6D–46]
   foreign settlement, [6D–43], [6D–58],
      [6D–84]
   generally, [6D–40] — [6D–47], [6D–91] —
      [6D–92]
   grant of probate, [6D–62] — [6D–64]
   ordinary trustee, as, [6D–55] — [6D–60]
   receivers, as, [6D–48], [6D–86]
   small estates, administration of, [6D–48]
      — [6D–50]
   trust accounts, audit of, [6D–73] — [6D–
      78]
establishment, [6D–38] — 6D–39]
fees
   audit, [6D–78]
   generally, [6D–67] — [6D–68]
foreign settlement, [6D–43], [6D–58], [6D–
   84]
offices, [6D–88]
ordinary trustee, as, [6D–55] — [6D–60]
powers
   Custodian trustees, as, [6D–51] — [6D–
      54]
   dual capacity, [6D–45] — [6D–46]

All references to material in Volume 2 are enclosed within square parentheses.

Public Trustee—*cont.*

foreign settlement, [6D–43], [6D–58], [6D–84]

generally, [6D–40] — [6D–47], [6D–91] — [6D–92]

grant of probate, [6D–62] — [6D–64]

ordinary trustee, as, [6D–55] — [6D–60]

receivers, as, [6D–48], [6D–86]

small estates, administration of, [6D–48] — [6D–50]

trust accounts, audit of, [6D–73] — [6D–78]

receivers, as, [6D–48], [6D–86]

Rules
And see Public Trustee Rules 1912
generally, [6D–85] — [6D–143]

security, [6D–90]

small estates, administration of
Rules, [6D–100] — [6D–105]
statutory basis, [6D–49] — [6D–51]

statutory basis
And see Public Trustee Act 1906
generally, [6D–37] — [6D–84]

trust accounts
Rules, [6D–127] — [6D–134]
statutory basis, [6D–73] — [6D–78]

trusts
accounts, [6D–110] — [6D–111]
advances, [6D–118]
execution of documents, [6D–112] — [6D–115]
income, payment of, [6D–116] — [6D–117]
investment, [6D–107] — [6D–109]
professional advice, [6D–119]
proof of life, [6D–120] — [6D–124]
registration, [6D–106]

trusteeship
application, [6D–93] — [6D–94]
considerations, [6D–96] — [6D–99]
supporting documents, [6D–95]

Public Trustee Act 1906

And see Public Trustee
applications, sc93.2 — sc93.2.1
definitions, [6D–80] — [6D–81]
general provisions
appeals, [6D–69] — [6D–70]
conduct of business, [6D–71]
duties, [6D–40] — [6D–66], [6D–85] — [6D–86]
fees, [6D–67] — [6D–68]
office of Public Trustee, [6D–38] — [6D–39]
Palatine Courts, [6D–72]
powers, [6D–40] — [6D–64], [6D–85] — [6D–86]
trust accounts, audit of, [6D–73] — [6D–78]
Rules, [6D–79]

Public Trustee Rules 1912

And see Public Trustee
definitions, [6D–86] — [6D–87]
general provisions
Custodian trusteess, [6D–125] — [6D–126]
deputies, [6D–89]
office, [6D–88]
powers, [6D–91] — [6D–92]

Public Trustee Rules 1912—*cont.*

security, [6D–90]
small estates, administration of, [6D–100] — [6D–105]
trust accounts, audit of, [6D–127] — [6D–134]
trusts, administration of, [6D–106] — [6D–124]
trusteeship, [6D–93] — [6D–99]
miscellaneous provisions, [6D–135] — [6D–143]
statutory basis, [6D–79]

Publication

contempt of court, [3C–3] — [3C–6]
group litigation orders, 19BPD.19 — 19BPD.19.1

Publication (contempt of court)

active actions
appellate, [3C–56]
criminal, [3C–54]
first instance, at, [3C–55]
generally, [3C–6], [3C–53]
generally, [3C–3] — [3C–4]
substantial risk, [3C–5]

"Qualified accountant"

meaning, [3A–631] — [3A–632]

Qualified duty to consent

application, [3B–298] — [3B–301]
approval, [3B–302] — [3B–305]
breach of, [3B–306] — [3B–307]
generally, [3B–295] — [3B–297]

Qualified privilege

defamation claims, 53PD.7 — 53PD.7.1

Quashing orders

And see Judicial review
generally, 54.1.12

Queens Bench Division

appeals to
And see Appeals to High Court
generally, sc94.1 — sc94.15
Part 8 claims, 8BPD.6
allocation of business, [9A–466]
generally, [9A–17] — [9A–20]
Guide
And see Queens Bench Guide
generally, [1B–1] — [1B–93]

Queens Bench Guide

abbreviations, [1B–93]
acknowledgment of service, [1B–25]
additional claims, [1B–39]
admissions, [1B–26]
allocation of business, [1B–34]
alternative dispute resolution, [1B–35]
appeal notices, [1B–69]
appeals
contempt of court, [1B–70]
generally, [1B–67]
notices, [1B–69]
permission to appeal, [1B–68]
applications

All references to material in Volume 2 are enclosed within square parentheses.

All references to material in Volume 2 are enclosed within square parentheses.

All references to material in Volume 2 are enclosed within square parentheses.

All references to material in Volume 2 are enclosed within square parentheses.

All references to material in Volume 2 are enclosed within square parentheses.

All references to material in Volume 2 are enclosed within square parentheses.

All references to material in Volume 2 are enclosed within square parentheses.

All references to material in Volume 2 are enclosed within square parentheses.

All references to material in Volume 2 are enclosed within square parentheses.

All references to material in Volume 2 are enclosed within square parentheses.

All references to material in Volume 2 are enclosed within square parentheses.

All references to material in Volume 2 are enclosed within square parentheses.

All references to material in Volume 2 are enclosed within square parentheses.

All references to material in Volume 2 are enclosed within square parentheses.

All references to material in Volume 2 are enclosed within square parentheses.

All references to material in Volume 2 are enclosed within square parentheses.

All references to material in Volume 2 are enclosed within square parentheses.

All references to material in Volume 2 are enclosed within square parentheses.

All references to material in Volume 2 are enclosed within square parentheses.

All references to material in Volume 2 are enclosed within square parentheses.

All references to material in Volume 2 are enclosed within square parentheses.

All references to material in Volume 2 are enclosed within square parentheses.

All references to material in Volume 2 are enclosed within square parentheses.

All references to material in Volume 2 are enclosed within square parentheses.

All references to material in Volume 2 are enclosed within square parentheses.

All references to material in Volume 2 are enclosed within square parentheses.

All references to material in Volume 2 are enclosed within square parentheses.

All references to material in Volume 2 are enclosed within square parentheses.

All references to material in Volume 2 are enclosed within square parentheses.

All references to material in Volume 2 are enclosed within square parentheses.

All references to material in Volume 2 are enclosed within square parentheses.

All references to material in Volume 2 are enclosed within square parentheses.

All references to material in Volume 2 are enclosed within square parentheses.

All references to material in Volume 2 are enclosed within square parentheses.

All references to material in Volume 2 are enclosed within square parentheses.

All references to material in Volume 2 are enclosed within square parentheses.

All references to material in Volume 2 are enclosed within square parentheses.

All references to material in Volume 2 are enclosed within square parentheses.

All references to material in Volume 2 are enclosed within square parentheses.

All references to material in Volume 2 are enclosed within square parentheses.

Supply of goods—*cont.*

quality, [3H–390] — [3H–391]
samples, [3H–392] — [3H–393]
title to goods, [3H–384] — [3H–387]
remedies
  generally, [3H–383]
  modification, [3H–394] — [3H–395]

Supply of Goods and Services Act 1982

editorial introduction, [3H–485] — [3H–486]
implied terms, [3H–489] — [3H–495]
relevant contracts, [3H–487] — [3H–488]

Supply of Goods (Implied Terms) Act 1973

conditional sale agreements, [3H–396] — [3H–397]
editorial introduction, [3H–381]
exclusion of liability, [3H–382]
implied terms, [3H–384] — [3H–393]
remedies, [3H–383], [3H–394] — [3H–395]
supplementary provisions, [3H–398] — [3H–399]

Supply of services

guarantees, [3H–551] — [3H–553]
implied terms
  care and skill, [3H–489] — [3H–490]
  consideration, [3H–493]
  exclusion of, [3H–494] — [3H–495]
  time for performance, [3H–491] — [3H–492]
relevant contracts, [3H–487] — [3H–488]

Supreme Court

generally, [9A–4.1]

Supreme Court Act 1981

abolition of writs, [9A–452] — [9A–454]
Accountant General, [9A–410]
Admiralty Court
  See Admiralty Court
Admiralty jurisdiction
  Channel Islands, [2D–191] — [2D–192]
  claims, [2D–142] — [2D–168]
  definitions, [2D–186] — [2D–188]
  generally, [2D–139] — [2D–141], [9A–70], [9A–458]
  introductory note, [2D–138]
  Isle of Man, [2D–191] — [2D–192]
  mode of exercise, [2D–169] — [2D–181]
amendments of other Acts, [9A–463] — [9A–464]
amendments to
  CLSA 1990, by, [9B–120] — [9B–121]
applications
  generally, sc94.15 — sc94.15.4
  Part 8 claims, 8BPD.6
assistance with business, [9A–27] — [9A–31]
bonds, [9A–438] — [9A–439]
Central Office, [9A–407] — [9A–409]
citation, [9A–465]
commencement, [9A–465]
Commercial Court, [9A–21] — [9A–23]
constitution
  Admiralty Court, [9A–21] — [9A–23]
  Commercial Court, [9A–21] — [9A–23]
  Court of Appeal, [9A–8] — [9A–10.1]
  Crown Courts, [9A–26] — [9A–26.1]

Supreme Court Act 1981—*cont.*

High Court, [9A–14] — [9A–16]
Patents Court, [9A–21] — [9A–23]
Supreme Court, [9A–5] — [9A–7]
continuity of procedure, [9A–4] — [9A–4.1]
Conveyancing Counsel, [9A–430] — [9A–431]
costs
  Crown Courts, [9A–268] — [9A–269]
  generally, [9A–262] — [9A–267]
Court Funds Office, [6A–1] — [6A–1]
Court of Appeal
  And see Court of Appeal
  constitution, [9A–8] — [9A–10.1]
  divisions, [9A–11] — [9A–13.1]
  jurisdiction, [9A–45] — [9A–55]
  practice, [9A–270] — [9A–295]
Crown Courts
  And see Crown Courts
  appeals, [9A–75] — [9A–77]
  constitution, [9A–26] — [9A–26.1]
  costs, [9A–268] — [9A–269]
  jurisdiction, [9A–145] — [9A–152]
  practice, [9A–338] — [9A–353]
damages, [9A–259] — [9A–261]
declaratory relief, [9A–80] — [9A–81.1]
definitions
  action, [9A–461]
  Admiralty Court, [2D–186] — [2D–188]
  cause, [9A–461]
  generally, [9A–459] — [9A–460]
  judgment, [9A–462]
  matter, [9A–461]
  official referee's business, [9A–459]
district judges
  assistants, [9A–424]
  deputies, [9A–422] — [9A–423]
  generally, [9A–416] — [9A–419]
  power to act, [9A–420] — [9A–421]
district registries
  generally, [9A–413] — [9A–415]
  probate, [6C–4] — [6C–5], [9A–425], [11–4] — [11–5]
divisions
  alteration, [9A–24] — [9A–25]
  Court of Appeal, [9A–11] — [9A–13.1]
  High Court, [9A–17] — [9A–20]
documents, production of, [9A–440] — [9A–442]
election petitions, [9A–455] — [9A–456]
enforcement of fines, [9A–450] — [9A–451]
equity
  And see Equitable jurisdiction
  generally, [9A–153] — [9A–178]
fees, [9A–429]
forfeiture for non-payment of rent, [3A–291] — [3A–292]
High Court
  And see High Court
  constitution, [9A–14] — [9A–16]
  divisions, [9A–17] — [9A–20]
  jurisdiction, [9A–56] — [9A–85]
  powers, [9A–86] — [9A–152]
  practice, [9A–296] — [9A–336]
injunctive relief, [9A–82] — [9A–83]
instruments
  engrossment, [9A–434] — [9A–435]
  seal, [9A–432] — [9A–433]
interpretation, [9A–3]
introductory note, [9A–2]
judges

All references to material in Volume 2 are enclosed within square parentheses.

All references to material in Volume 2 are enclosed within square parentheses.

All references to material in Volume 2 are enclosed within square parentheses.

All references to material in Volume 2 are enclosed within square parentheses.

All references to material in Volume 2 are enclosed within square parentheses.

All references to material in Volume 2 are enclosed within square parentheses.

All references to material in Volume 2 are enclosed within square parentheses.

All references to material in Volume 2 are enclosed within square parentheses.

All references to material in Volume 2 are enclosed within square parentheses.

All references to material in Volume 2 are enclosed within square parentheses.

All references to material in Volume 2 are enclosed within square parentheses.

All references to material in Volume 2 are enclosed within square parentheses.

All references to material in Volume 2 are enclosed within square parentheses.

All references to material in Volume 2 are enclosed within square parentheses.

All references to material in Volume 2 are enclosed within square parentheses.

All references to material in Volume 2 are enclosed within square parentheses.

All references to material in Volume 2 are enclosed within square parentheses.

All references to material in Volume 2 are enclosed within square parentheses.

All references to material in Volume 2 are enclosed within square parentheses.

All references to material in Volume 2 are enclosed within square parentheses.

All references to material in Volume 2 are enclosed within square parentheses.

All references to material in Volume 2 are enclosed within square parentheses.

All references to material in Volume 2 are enclosed within square parentheses.

All references to material in Volume 2 are enclosed within square parentheses.

All references to material in Volume 2 are enclosed within square parentheses.

All references to material in Volume 2 are enclosed within square parentheses.

All references to material in Volume 2 are enclosed within square parentheses.

All references to material in Volume 2 are enclosed within square parentheses.